1908 Sears, Roebuck & Co. Catalogue

1908 SEARS, ROEBUCK & Co. CATALOGUE

Skyhorse Publishing

Skyhorse Publishing books may be purchased in bulk at special discounts for sales promotion, corporate gifts, fund-raising, or educational purposes. Special editions can also be created to specifications. For details, contact the Special Sales Department, Skyhorse Publishing, 307 West 36th Street, 11th Floor, New York, NY 10018 or info@skyhorsepublishing.com.

Skyhorse® and Skyhorse Publishing® are registered trademarks of Skyhorse Publishing, Inc.®, a Delaware corporation.

Visit our website at www.skyhorsepublishing.com.

10 9 8 7 6 5 4

Library of Congress Cataloging-in-Publication Data is available on file.

ISBN: 978-1-63220-686-2

Cover design by Owen Corrigan

Printed in the United States of America

Contents

Introduction 1

Ordering Instructions 2

Sewing Machines 30

Wallpaper and Paint 42

Books 56

Vehicles, Harnesses, and Saddles 61

Bicycles 106

Stereoscopes and Optical Goods 116

Phonographs 130

Telephones and Electric Goods 136

Musical Instruments 143

Watches, Diamonds, and Jewelry 175

Tableware 205

Clocks 210

Crockery and Glassware 213

Furniture 223

Baby Carriages and Go-Carts 274

Enameled Ware and Kitchen Items 27

Tools and Hardware ....

Agricultural Implements 326

Washing Machines 364

Building Plans, Materials, and Appliances 371

Safes 408

Photography & Printing 410

Guns, Outdoors, and Sporting Goods 438

Cutlery and Razors 502

Toilet Preparations 518

Boots & Shoes 530

Carpets, Rugs & Curtains 543

Dress Goods 565

Hosiery and Underwear 580

Men's and Boys' Clothing 591

Women's Accessories 608

Men's and Boys' Suits 648

Women's and Girls' Gowns & Dresses 675

INTRODUCTION

By Nick Lyons

The prices have gone up a bit since I last looked at the 1897 Sears Roebuck Catalog, but the good news is that the company's commitment to a tremendous variety of really good stuff, for cheap, is better than ever. Like its predecessor catalogs, the 1908 edition is one of the most revealing portraits of an era and what hundreds of thousands of people wanted and used. And it is also a tremendous amount of fun, swimming in the nostalgia, exploring the spectacular range of offerings.

Along with the newly introduced items, like "The New Economy Chief Cream Separator—Marvel of 1908" for $28.80 and "sure to save $15 yearly on each cow," a reader is simply breathless with the diversity and the prices. From a "comfortable Nursing Corset" (77 cents) to "Kenwood Four-Cycle Marine Gasoline Engines" ($93.25), an "A. J. Aubrey Automatic Engraved Revolver, Improved Model" (only $4.25), men's suits for $10.43, steel walking plows ($8.62), farm bells (their Crystalline Composition Metal Bell—$1.04 to $2.63), China cabinets, "Imported Geneva Watches, "Colored Views of 'Geisha Girls'" (and a hundred other subjects), their "New Williams Special Style Strap Buggy Harness," and a "Phaeton" model buggy for $61.95, horse not included, and small road carts for simpler use, with "Sarven's Patent Wheels," with 7/8th-inch rims, for as low as $11.95.

Even though this edition, for economy, by the publishers, has cut the voluminous 1908 version of the Sears catalog from more than a thousand to only about 720, there is something for everyone. Need a "Whitewashing Machine, Fire Extinguisher, Spraying Machine All in One?" There's one here and it's only $7.65. There are sewing machines for under ten bucks, rugs, suits, shoes, skirts, washing machines, musical instruments, cameras, phonographs, stuff for plumbers and farmers and housewives and sportsfolk, medicines, diamonds, stoves, safes, a "New 1908 Model 'Motiograph' Motion Picture Machine," and, for the fly fisherman, which surely includes the addicted writer of this introduction, a "Walton Hand Split Bamboo Fly Rod, 9-1/2 to 10 feet for $3.49—with 20 cents extra for postage."

What a delicious trip back a hundred years, when the world was simpler . . . and a fly rod cost under four bucks. You'll enjoy the trip!

2

=== DEPARTMENT INDEX ===

IF YOU WISH TO REFER TO ANY PARTICULAR CLASS OF MERCHANDISE, SEE THE DEPARTMENT INDEX BELOW. FOR COMPLETE ITEMIZED INDEX, TURN TO THE PINK PAGES IN THE MIDDLE OF THE BOOK.

	PAGES		PAGES		PAGES		PAGES
AGRICULTURAL IMPLE-		DOMESTICS	921-943	JEWELRY	257-331	RUGS	869-878
MENTS	536-552	DRAWING INSTRUMENTS		LADIES' WEARING		SAFES	664-665
BABY CARRIAGES	456-460	AND MATERIALS	695-696	APPAREL	1133-1174	SCALES	470, 563-567
BELLS	479 and 552	DRESS GOODS	905-920	LAMPS	363-366	SEWING MACHINES	36-63
BICYCLES	162-173	DRUGS	782-807	MACKINTOSHES	1102, 1143-1144	SHOES	812-850
BLACKSMITHS' TOOLS	506-519	DRY GOODS	921-943	MAGIC LANTERNS	697	SILVERWARE	332-348
BOOKS	86-90	ELECTRICAL GOODS	202-208	MANTELS	159	SPORTING GOODS	702-765
BOOTS AND SHOES	812-850	ENGINES	559-562	MECHANICS' TOOLS	482-524	STEREOSCOPIC VIEWS	178-185
BUILDERS' HARDWARE	472-480	FENCING	568-573	MILLINERY	1027-1043	STOCK FOOD	531
BUTCHERS' TOOLS AND		FUR COATS	1093-1098	MILL WORK	589-599	STOVES	626-665
SUPPLIES	768	FURNACE DEPARTMENT	159	MOVING PICTURES	535	TINWARE	461-467
CARPETS	851-904	FURNISHING GOODS	963-991	MUSICAL GOODS	228-256	TOMBSTONES	160-161
CARRIAGE HARDWARE	516-519	FURNITURE	367-460	MUSLIN WEAR	1103-1132	TOYS	1046-1049
CEMENT BLOCK MACHINES	574-581	GAS FIXTURES	366	NOTIONS	996-1026	TRUNKS	989-991
CLOAKS	1133-1166	GLOVES AND MITTENS	977-983	OPTICAL GOODS	186-193	UNDERWEAR	948-962, 1103-1111
CLOCKS	344-348	GRAPHOPHONES	194-201	PAINTS AND OILS	67-85	VEHICLES	91-112
CLOTHING	1051-1102	GROCERIES	532-534	PHOTOGRAPHIC GOODS	670-697	VETERINARY GOODS	803-807
CREAM SEPARATORS	19-35	GUNS AND REVOLVERS	702-765	PIANOS AND ORGANS	209-227	WAGON MAKERS' SUP-	
CROCKERY and GLASSWARE	349-366	HARDWARE	461-524	PLUMBERS' SUPPLIES	604-621	PLIES	506-519
CURTAINS	883	HARNESS AND SADDLERY	113-158	POULTRY FOOD	531	WALL PAPER	64-67
CUT GLASS	362	HATS AND CAPS	984-988	PUMPS	614-619	WASH GOODS	921-943
CUTLERY	766-777	HEATING PLANTS (STEAM		REFRIGERATORS	379-382	WASHING MACHINES	582-587
DAIRY SUPPLIES	471	AND HOT WATER)	613	ROOFING	589-599	WATCHES	257-331
DIAMONDS	314-317	INCUBATORS AND BROOD-				WINDMILLS	556-558
		ERS	554-555			WRINGERS	588

FOR COMPLETE ITEMIZED INDEX REFER TO PINK PAGES 525 TO 530 IN MIDDLE OF BOOK

No. 1—YOUR MONEY BACK IF YOU ARE NOT SATISFIED

EVERY ORDER SENT US IS ACCEPTED with the understanding and agreement that if the goods we send you are not found perfectly satisfactory they can be returned to us at our expense and the money sent us, together with any freight or express charges paid, will be immediately refunded. Accompanying every shipment are these plainly printed conditions:

IF THESE GOODS PLEASE YOU, you cannot do us a greater favor than to tell your neighbors and allow them to use your catalogue to send us orders.

IF THEY DON'T PLEASE YOU, you cannot do us a greater favor than to return the goods at our expense and get your money back, together with any transportation charges you may have paid.

No. 2—ABOUT OUR RELIABILITY. YOU ARE PERFECTLY SAFE IN SENDING US YOUR ORDERS AND YOUR MONEY.

We are one of the largest commercial institutions in the world and we occupy by far the largest mercantile plant in the world. We own this entire plant, free of indebtedness of any kind, comprising forty acres of ground in one of the best districts in Chicago; our ground and buildings alone are valued at more than six million dollars. We have nearly nine thousand employes and our customers now number nearly five millions. If you have any doubt, you are at liberty to refer to any bank, business house or resident of Chicago, and we especially refer to our millions of satisfied customers. Ask your neighbor about **Sears, Roebuck & Co.** We have customers in every neighborhood in the United States and we gladly refer you to any customer.

BE SURE to read the bank letter of the First National Bank of Chicago, capital and surplus $14,000,000.00, signed by its cashier, C. N. Gillett, also the Corn Exchange National Bank letter, capital and surplus $6,000,000.00, signed by Frank W. Smith, its cashier; see page 18. Consider our standing everywhere and be convinced it is perfectly safe to send your money to us, we agreeing to return it if the goods do not please you.

No. 3—LOW PRICE AND HIGH QUALITY GUARANTEE.

Every order sent us is accepted with the understanding and agreement that if you do not find our prices lower, quality considered, and the quality of our merchandise higher than the average, you are at liberty to return the goods to us at our expense of transportation charges both ways, and we will promptly return all your money.

DON'T BUY ANYTHING ANYWHERE until after you refer to this catalogue and see how much money we can save you.

No. 4—VERY SIMPLE RULES FOR ORDERING, printed in three languages. See page 1.

No. 5—WHY OUR NAME NEVER APPEARS ON ANY BOX, package, wrapper, tag, envelope or article of merchandise, thus making every transaction strictly confidential. See page 8.

No. 6—WHY WE WILL ACCEPT no order for less than 50 cents. See page 8.

No. 7—FREIGHT AND EXPRESS RATES TO ANY POINT. See pages 13 to 17 for full information. You pay the freight or express charges when you get the goods; but remember, freight or express amounts to nothing compared with what we save you in cost. Don't be afraid of the freight charges.

No. 8—YOU CANNOT do us a greater favor than to show this catalogue to your friends and allow them to use it for sending us orders.

No. 9—WE HAVE NO AGENTS. Anyone claiming to represent us and soliciting orders for us is a swindler.

No. 10—QUICK SHIPMENT. With a stock of merchandise larger than all other mail order houses combined, we are prepared to make very prompt shipment. If you send us your order, you will get your goods much quicker than if you ordered from any other house.

ORDERING INSTRUCTIONS

WRITE A LETTER OR A POSTAL CARD AND SAY "SEND ME YOUR BIG CATALOGUE" AND IT WILL BE SENT TO YOU IMMEDIATELY FREE BY MAIL, POSTPAID.

IF YOU LIVE IN A CITY OF 25,000 OR MORE POPULATION, don't fail to give your street address when you ask for the book, as without street address the postal authorities will refuse to deliver the book to you. If you live on a Rural Route, don't forget to put down your route number.

SIMPLE RULES FOR ORDERING.

USE OUR ORDER BLANK, IF YOU HAVE ONE. If you haven't one, use any plain paper.

TELL US IN YOUR OWN WAY WHAT YOU WANT, always giving the CATALOGUE NUMBER of each article, and be sure to state size and color where required. Enclose in the letter the amount of money, either a postoffice money order, which you get at the postoffice, an express money order, which you get at the express office, or a draft, which you get at any bank; or put the money in the letter, take it to the postoffice and tell the postmaster you want it registered.

IF YOU LIVE ON A RURAL MAIL ROUTE, just give the letter and the money to the mail carrier and he will get the money order at the postoffice and mail it in the letter for you.

DON'T BE AFRAID YOU WILL MAKE A MISTAKE. We receive hundreds of orders every day from young and old who never before sent away for goods. We are accustomed to handling all kinds of orders.

TELL US WHAT YOU WANT IN YOUR OWN WAY, written in any language, no matter whether good or poor writing, and the goods will be promptly sent to you.

WE HAVE TRANSLATORS TO READ ALL LANGUAGES.

DON'T BE AFRAID OF THE FREIGHT OR EXPRESS CHARGES. You must pay them when you get the goods at the station, but they never amount to much compared with what we save you in cost.

IF YOU FIND IT NECESSARY TO HAVE SOME SPECIAL INFORMATION you can undoubtedly obtain it by referring to the matter contained within the first twelve pages of this catalogue.

Einfache Regeln für Bestellungen.

Gebrauchen Sie unser Bestellungsformular, wenn Sie eins haben. Haben Sie keins, so gebrauchen Sie irgendwelches Papier.

Sagen Sie uns auf Ihre eigene Weise was Sie wünschen, geben Sie immer die Katalognummer jedes Artikels an, sowie Größe und Farbe, wo es nöthig ist. Fügen Sie dem Briefe den Geldbetrag bei, entweder eine Post-Geldanweisung, in der Post zu erlangen, eine Expreß-Geldanweisung, in der Expreß-Office zu erlangen, oder eine Tratte, die Sie in jeder Bank bekommen können; oder legen Sie das Geld in den Brief, bringen Sie ihn zur Post und beauftragen Sie den Postmeister ihn zu registriren.

Wohnen Sie an einer Landpost-Route, so geben Sie den Brief und das Geld dem Briefträger, und er wird für Sie die Geldanweisung besorgen und sie in dem Briefe wegschicken.

Fürchten Sie nicht einen Fehler zu machen. Wir erhalten täglich hunderte von Bestellungen von jungen und alten Leuten, die noch nie zuvor eine Bestellung einsandten. Wir sind gewöhnt Bestellungen jeder Art auszuführen.

Sagen Sie uns auf Ihre eigene Weise was Sie wünschen, schreiben Sie in irgend einer Sprache, ob gute oder schlechte Handschrift, und die Waaren werden Ihnen prompt zugeschickt werden.

Wir haben Uebersetzer um alle Sprachen zu lesen.

Scheuen Sie sich nicht vor den Fracht- oder Expreßkosten. Sie müssen sie bei Empfang der Waaren auf der Station bezahlen, aber sie sind niemals bedeutend, im Verhältniß zu dem was wir Ihnen am Preise sparen.

Wenn Sie weitere spezielle Auskunft benöthigen, können Sie dieselbe ohne Zweifel erhalten indem Sie die ersten zwölf Seiten dieses Kataloges durchlesen.

ENKLA REGLER ATT IAKTTAGA VID BESTÄLLNING.

Begagna vår beställningsblankett om ni har en sådan. Om icke, begagna vanligt rent papper.

Säg oss på edert eget sätt hvad ni önskar, alltid uppgifvande katalognumret på hvarje sak och glöm inte att nämna kulör och storlek, om så fordras. Inneslut beloppet i brefvet, antingen en postoffice money order, hvilken köpes å postkontoret, express money order, hvilken köpes å expresskontoret, vexel hvilken kan köpas å hvilken bank som helst; eller också inneslut kontanta penningar i brefvet, tag det till postkontoret och säg till postmästaren att ni önskar få det registreradt.

Om ni bor på en Rural Mail Route, gif brefvet och penningarne till brefbäraren och han vill köpa money ordern å postkontoret, innesluta den i brefvet och sända det för er.

Var inte rädd för att ni gör ett misstag. Vi erhålla hundratals beställningar dagligen, från unga och gamla, hvilka aldrig förr sändt efter varor. Vi äro vana vid att expediera alla slags beställningar.

Säg oss på edert eget sätt hvad ni önskar. Skrif på hvilket språk som helst, god eller dålig stafning, god eller dålig handstil, och varorna skola blifva eder prompt tillsända.

Vi ha öfversättare som läsa alla språk.

Var inte rädd för frakt- och expressomkostnaderna. Ni får betala dem när ni mottager varorna vid stationen, men beloppet är aldrig stort, jämfördt med hvad vi spara er i priset.

Om ni önskar någon särskild upplysning, kan ni otvifvelaktigt finna den genom att hänvisa till de första tolf sidorna af denna katalog.

DO NOT FAIL TO GIVE SIZE, COLOR, WEIGHT, ETC., IF REQUIRED, WHEN WRITING YOUR ORDER.

DOES THE BIG MAIL ORDER HOUSE HELP USERS AND COUNTRY DEALERS ALIKE TO LOWER PRICES AND BETTER CONDITIONS ?

DOES THE BIG MAIL ORDER HOUSE DO THE GREATEST GOOD TO THE GREATEST NUMBER, BRINGING LUXURIES TO THOUSANDS WHO FORMERLY ENJOYED ONLY THE NECESSITIES? DOES THE BIG MAIL ORDER HOUSE TEND TO PROMOTE PROSPERITY TO ALL?

A GREAT DEAL HAS BEEN SAID **against the mail order house by retail dealers and wholesale dealers and manufacturers,** and a great deal has been said for and in behalf of mail order houses by the millions of customers who have patronized mail order houses.

IN A SINGLE YEAR WE HAVE SOLD OVER FIFTY MILLION DOLLARS' WORTH OF GOODS TO ACTUAL USERS AND HAVE SAVED THESE USERS OF FIFTY MILLION DOLLARS' WORTH OF GOODS FROM TEN TO FIFTEEN MILLION DOLLARS.

THIS TEN TO FIFTEEN MILLION DOLLARS ACTUALLY SAVED represents the difference between our prices and the prices at which the same goods are sold by dealers generally, and tremendous though this saving seems, it is in reality a mere fraction of the savings that we have indirectly accomplished and the benefits we have indirectly effected to dealers as well as users of merchandise all over this country.

IN EVERY CASE the lowering of our own prices has accomplished the lowering of the prices charged by other dealers and in helping other dealers to sell goods at much lower prices we have indirectly helped them to do a vastly larger business. Our own tremendous buying advantages and manufacturing facilities have caused radical reductions not only in our own selling prices, but indirectly have been the cause of reducing the selling prices of almost everyone on almost everything. Our wonderfully low prices have caused certain lines of goods formerly used by only the favored few to be used by the multitudes all over the country. Our low prices have increased the demand for merchandise of every kind, have increased the volume of business done not only by ourselves but have increased the volume of business done everywhere by everyone, by manufacturers, by jobbers and retail dealers. Indirectly our business methods are responsible for the fact that all makers and jobbers and all retailers of merchandise are doing more business and making more money than ever before, and at the same time doing all this at a tremendous saving in cost to the actual user of the goods. Indirectly we have converted articles of restricted use into articles of everyday use; we have converted luxuries into necessities and some day these facts will be realized. Some day those dealers throughout the country who are at present disposed to say anything but nice things about us will recognize the fact that we have helped, are helping and shall continue to help the dealer and the consumer alike; will realize that we originated a revolution in merchandising methods whose benefits will never cease.

DIDN'T YOU AT ONE TIME PAY $150.00 AND UPWARD for a good top buggy? You must have paid that much if you bought one, but very few people felt they could own a buggy at the prevailing high prices and because of the limited demand comparatively few buggies were sold and comparatively few people had the use of a top buggy; therefore, comparatively few people were employed in the manufacture of buggies and very little money was made in the buggy industry.

WHO HAS DONE MORE THAN WE HAVE DONE to bring about this tremendous change in the vehicle industry? True we only sell about 60,000 out of the 800,000 vehicles annually sold in this country, but we sell these 60,000 buggies at prices that vitally affect the entire 800,000, whether sold by ourselves or other people. We sell our vehicles at such prices that compel every manufacturer to fit himself to compete in some measure with our prices and our methods, and the result is that we today not only make astonishingly low prices on the 60,000 vehicles we sell annually, but we directly affect, to the advantage of the purchaser, the prices of all vehicles sold through retail dealers. When the price of a top buggy comes down in a few years from $150.00 to $50.00 it means a tremendous increase in the demand, a tremendous increase in the number of top buggies annually sold; it means that the same retailers who formerly ordered an occasional buggy from the manufacturer now orders them in carload lots, and today the same retailer makes $10.00 profit in the buggy business where formerly he made but $1.00, and this increased profit is the result of the increase in the volume of his business, not the result of a large profit on a single buggy. We believe we have done more than any other institution in the world toward effecting this beneficial result.

TAKE THE ITEM OF SHOTGUNS.

A few years ago no dealer could buy a double barrel hammerless breech loading shotgun from any factory or jobber at a price that would permit him to sell it and get any profit at less than $30.00 to $40.00. Today the retail dealer can sell such a gun at about one-half the price, a price that enables him to sell five to ten times as many, brings the gun of luxury that formerly could be owned only by a man of means, at a price within the reach of anyone who has use for a shotgun. **Do you think this condition would ever be brought about if someone didn't set the pace, make a price that the manufacturer was compelled to recognize and attempt in some measure to meet?**

TAKE THE ITEM OF PLUMBING.

Ten years ago how many people, in building an ordinary house, to cost from $600.00 to $1,200.00, thought they could afford to put in a bath room and equip the house with plumbing throughout or with an up to date heating system? When they would come to get the figures on the plumbing or heating system they would find the prices prohibitively high, and we don't claim that they were prohibitively high because the retail dealer necessarily asked too much profit. He could not buy the goods at the right price. **Today you can buy plumbing at a mere fraction of the price charged ten years ago.** Today anyone building a new house can equip it with all the plumbing conveniences of a city home. Today, by reason of the low prices of plumbing, the luxury of 10 years ago has become the necessity of today. Today there is an enormous business done in plumbing by retail dealers in small towns all over the United States, done because it is sold at a price within the reach of the people. **Who has brought about this condition? Who has helped to make this business for the retail plumber** of the country?

TAKE THE ITEM OF CREAM SEPARATORS.

Until within two or three years cream separators have been generally sold at about $75.00 each. There was five times as much profit above the cost of manufacture at the price the retail dealer sold them at as there should be, although the retailer may have gotten only a fair profit for himself. The result has been, at this high price, where one farmer bought a separator twenty farmers went without one. We have gotten well started in the manufacture of cream separators; we have already gotten our prices down to from $26.30 upward, and we hope some day to see our manufacturing facilities enlarged to where we can materially reduce these prices. We believe that within less than five years any dealer in cream separators will be able to and will sell as good a machine as there is on the market, direct to the farmer, for $40.00 or less. Today he can buy and sell a cream separator much cheaper than he could a few years ago, and when the time comes, as it surely will in the near future, when the retail dealer can sell you as good a machine as there is on the market for $40.00 or less, he will be selling five to ten times as many cream separators annually as when he had to get $75.00 to $100.00. He will make a great deal more money out of the cream separator business than he did at the high price, by reason of the increased volume, and the cream separator, at a price that makes it a luxury, will be sold at a price that makes it a common necessity, everybody benefited, and we claim that we are more responsible for this revolution than any other concern in the world.

TAKE THE ITEM OF STOVES.

A good many retail dealers, selling stoves in a short sighted way, will point the finger of criticism at us because we sell stoves for so little money. What did that dealer have to get, what did he have to pay for a high grade steel range or a high grade hard coal base burner five years ago? How much does he pay today for a base burner or a steel range of the same grade that he bought five years ago?

FOR YEARS WE HAVE BEEN MAKING PRICES on stoves because we make them in our own foundry, stoves on which the selling price is consistent with the cost of material and labor, and we have been forcing every manufacturer in the United States to materially reduce his prices. We have forced the stove manufacturers of this country to adjust their expenses and methods so as to make much lower prices. The result is, we have multiplied the number of stoves manufactured and the number sold through retail dealers. The retail dealer, not by increasing his profit or lessening his profit, but by increasing the volume of business done on stoves by reason of the lower prices at which he has been able to buy, has greatly increased his selling power and the earnings of his business and has helped his customers beyond measure, and we claim we are more responsible for this condition than any other house in the world.

GO BACK TEN YEARS.

MR. DEALER AND MR. CUSTOMER, reflect just that far back and recall the prices you paid for sewing machines, organs, pianos, vehicles, stoves, watches, jewelry, hardware, furniture, agricultural implements, bicycles, plumbing goods, guns, cameras, dishes, clothing, dry goods and the other necessities of life, and compare the prices you paid for these goods ten years ago with the prices you are paying today. Mr. Dealer, reflect, if you will, how much business you were doing ten years ago, how much are you doing today? How many goods were sold in your town ten years ago, how many goods are sold in your town today?

IN SPITE OF THE PAST TEN YEARS of wonderful prosperity, when the highest prices ever known have been paid to labor, when the raw materials of all kinds, over the ten years, have been constantly advancing, in spite of all this, compare your buying cost today with the buying cost of ten years ago, compare your sales, your volume of business today with the volume of ten years ago, figure out as an estimate, if you will, the volume of sales, goods distributed from your town today with ten years ago, compare, if you will, the number of buggies, up to date agricultural implements, bicycles, sewing machines, pianos, organs and plumbing that are being used in your community within a radius of five or ten miles of your town today with what was being used ten years ago. Ten years ago they were luxuries by reason of the high prices; today they are the necessities by reason of the low prices.

WHO HAS BEEN RESPONSIBLE FOR THIS GREAT CHANGE, for the multiplied consumption, the multiplied sales? Who has been responsible for making it possible for you, Mr. Dealer, to sell goods, many of them at only half the price you were compelled to get ten years ago? Who has been responsible for making it possible for you to sell a carload of buggies now where ten years ago you sold one, two or three? Make the same apply in a great measure to all the goods you handle.

WE CLAIM WE ARE MORE RESPONSIBLE FOR THIS THAN ANY OTHER ONE INSTITUTION IN THE WORLD.

TO SAVE YOU FIFTEEN MILLION DOLLARS on the goods you buy from us direct in one year is in itself a great item for consideration, but if the process of saving you Fifteen Million Dollars on the goods you buy from us in a year compels competition to so regulate and reduce the prices at which goods are sold, if we alone are responsible for a saving of at least 5 per cent average on the Billions of Dollars' worth that are bought and sold through dealers of all kinds, increasing and in many instances multiplying their sales, either by increasing their volume and their earnings, converting luxuries, by the process of reduction in price, into necessities, by helping to eliminate for everybody what is known to all manufacturers as overhead expenses or waste; if we are doing this, and we claim we are, then there is some credit due us for everything that is sold, by everyone who sells to everyone who buys, and if the manufacturer, the jobber, the retail dealer and the consumer (the one who buys the goods for his own use) will carefully analyze the workings and effects of the great mail order house, he will find it is a friend to everyone on earth and an enemy to no living being.

BUILDINGS AND GROUNDS IN CHICAGO WHICH WE OWN FREE OF ENCUMBRANCE

FACTORIES IN VARIOUS STATES WHICH WE OWN IN THEIR ENTIRETY, IN PART OR CONTROL THE PRODUCT OF.

IN our various catalogues most of our customers, no doubt more than one-half of all the families in the United States, have, by the pictures we have shown them in the past, had their attention called to the grounds and to the big buildings in our Chicago plant as well as pictures of many of the big manufacturing plants which we own or are interested in. To those who have not as yet had their attention called we take pleasure, on these pages, in showing, but, unfortunately, for the want of room, in small illustrations that in no way do these buildings, grounds and plants justice, pictures of some of our buildings and grounds in Chicago and some of the more important factories in different states in the Union which we own in their entirety, in part or control the output of.

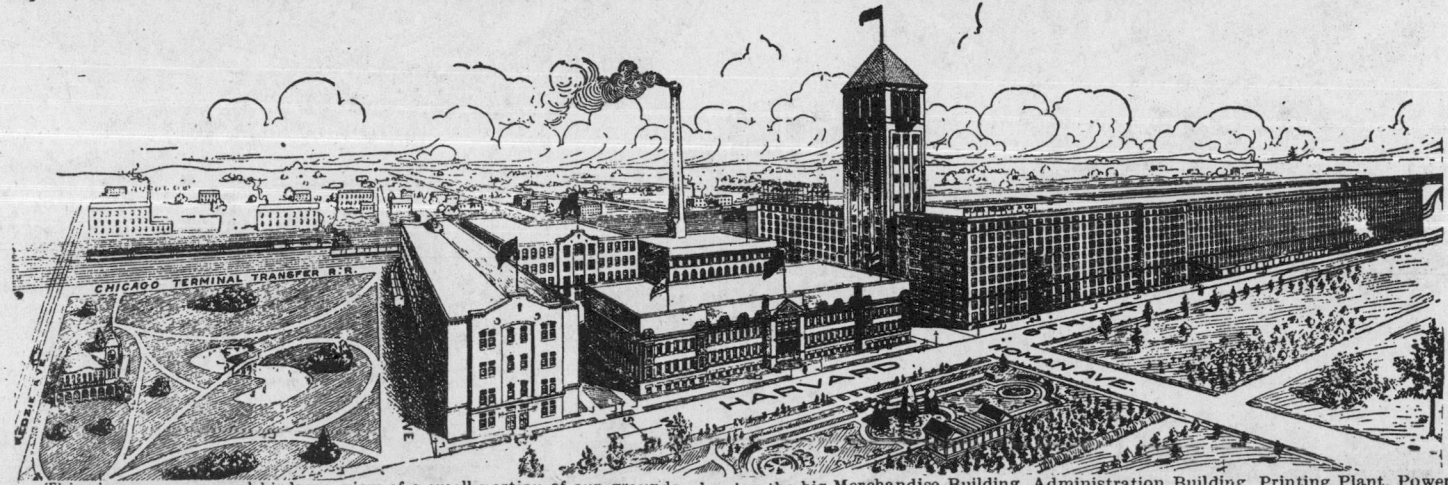

This gives you a general birdseye view of a small portion of our grounds, showing the big Merchandise Building, Administration Building, Printing Plant, Power House, etc., but you must consider that these grounds are nearly one-half a mile long or, to be exact, twenty-four hundred feet in length, and this in an important part of Chicago, to appreciate the size of these grounds.

This picture shows our Administration or Office Building in Chicago, in which all the clerical work is done. Architecturally it is one of the most beautiful and one of the largest buildings for its purpose in this country.

This building is used for printing and for the manufacture of this Great Catalogue. It is the most modernly equipped printing plant for the purpose in this country, and one of the largest, if not the largest, of its kind in the world.

This picture shows our Merchandise Building in Chicago, undoubtedly the largest building of its kind and purpose in the world.

This shows a picture of the Power Plant, one of the most modern, largest and handsomest power plants in the country.

View No. 1. This gives you a small sectional view of a corner of our Merchandise Building in Chicago, giving you an idea of our railroad track facilities for incoming merchandise, but to get an idea of these facilities you must remember that these tracks extend 2,400 feet or nearly one-half a mile, the entire length of our property.

View No. 2. This shows you a small view of our train shed under cover. Four railroad tracks running directly into the building. Here is where our outgoing freight is loaded directly into the cars.

View No. 3. This small view will give you just a little idea of what we have done to decorate our grounds, to make them attractive, pleasant for our employes as well as to generally beautify this portion of the city.

View No. 4. Another small sectional view of our private park and grounds, showing fountains and beautiful flower beds, to give you an idea of what we are doing for our people, ourselves and the city.

View No. 5. Small sectional view showing our new Fire Department in action, a department we maintain at all times for the protection of life and property in an immense plant.

Some of these are small pen drawings, as taken from the big set of fifty stereoscopic views, offered on another page of this catalogue for 35 cents. We could fill many pages with interesting views of the many activities in this great institution. A better idea can be had, however, from the set of stereoscopic views offered on another page in this catalogue for 35 cents.

FACTORIES IN VARIOUS STATES WHICH WE OWN IN THEIR ENTIRETY, IN PART, OR OF WHICH WE CONTROL THE PRODUCT.

The Safe Plant at Newark, Ohio.

The Great Stove Foundry at Newark, Ohio.

The Plumbing Goods Factory in Wisconsin.

The Modern Wall Paper Mill in Chicago.

The Agricultural Implement Factory in Wisconsin.

The Upholstered Furniture Factory in Chicago.

The Wire Fence Mill at Knightstown, Indiana.

The Big Furniture Factory at Binghamton, New York.

The Great Organ Factory at Louisville, Kentucky.

The Big Paint Factory in Chicago.

The Saw Factory in Michigan.

The Enormous Vehicle Factory at Evansville, Indiana.

The Camera Factory at Rochester, Minnesota.

The Great Gun Factory at Meriden, Connecticut.

The Cream Separator Plant in Iowa.

The Modern Shoe Factory at Littleton, New Hampshire.

THESE very small illustrations will give you but a very faint idea of the combined strength and capital represented in these enormous factories. Among them are factories that cover acres and acres of ground. For example, the stove plant is the largest stove foundry in the world. Many of the other factories are among the largest in the world.

IN addition to these factories we own in their entirety, in a large part, or control the output of many other factories, included in which might be mentioned another cream separator factory in New York, furniture factories, factories for the manufacture of clothing, wearing apparel, millinery, hardware, etc. The factories we illustrate are but a few of the vast number in which we wield a controlling influence.

FOR example, in the manufacture of wall paper which we make in our own mill, from the raw paper stock to the finished wall paper in all shades, grades and colorings, in order to make absolutely certain that we own our wall paper at the lowest possible cost, we go to the very bottom of the source of supply. We contract with the manufacturer of raw hanging paper stock who owns thousands of acres of standing timber, who can make our paper stock with the smallest loss of time or expense, who can deliver this raw wall paper stock to our mill under positively ideal conditions, thus forging the last link in the chain of conditions necessary to produce high grade wall paper at our marvelously low prices, all of which is plainly shown in our free Wall Paper Sample Book illustrated on another page of this catalogue.

IN addition to the factory connections which we have mentioned, and illustrated, we might go on and tell you of many other connections, arrangements and advantages by means of which we have effected wonderful economy for our customers on such items as Sewing Machines, Harness, Saddles, Horse Clippers, Sheep Shearing Machines, Watches, Jewelry, Silverware, Clocks, Musical Instruments, Hardware, Washing Machines, Cement Block Machines, Doors, Sash, Blinds, Mill Work, Bicycles, Electrical Goods, Photographic Goods, Cutlery, Sporting Goods, Graphophones, Crockery, Carpets, Rugs, Curtains, Blankets, Furnishing Goods, Notions and thousands of other items mentioned in this Big Catalogue. To get the right quality and the right cost on these thousands of items, we have gone to the very bottom of the sources of supply, of manufacture, of raw materials; we have investigated every point in connection with the manufacture and marketing of merchandise that possibly could be of benefit to our customers; and every advantage that could be gained by the investment of capital or the employment of experts has been secured for only one purpose, for only one reason—to give you a better quality in any given article than you could get elsewhere, to give you a much lower price than you could secure from any other product.

OUR CAPITAL AND FINANCIAL STANDING

THIS IS A SUBJECT SO THOROUGHLY ESTABLISHED in the minds and to the knowledge, not only of all our millions of customers, but also to every other citizen of the United States, that it is perhaps altogether unnecessary to refer at all to our financial strength and standing; but since our present position, our accumulative capital and standing financially reflect the soundness of our policy of high quality standards and low price making, and are after all, with the good will of our millions of customers, the reward for our policy of merchandising, it may be interesting to refer to the question of our position in finance and strength, to show you what has been the measure of success up to date, as a result of making prices such as were never made before, giving values such as no other house is giving, has given, or can give, treating our customers certainly as well as any other house could possibly treat them, applying the Golden Rule, which says among other things that we must have the highest quality at the lowest price, treating our customers as we would like to be treated.

FROM A COMPARATIVELY SMALL BEGINNING we have grown in point of capital, accumulated and employed, in the volume of business done, in the size and money value of our stocks of merchandise, in the ground area, in the size of buildings and factories which we own, to where we stand out apart and alone, among all the mercantile institutions of the land, as by far the largest institution of the kind in the world, and one that sells more goods to users than all other mail order houses in the United States combined. Today we have a capital and surplus of Forty Million Dollars, fully paid; we own the grounds here in one of the best portions of Chicago (nearly 40 acres in area) on which our buildings are erected; these grounds we own free of any encumbrance; the mammoth buildings on these grounds, in which are located our headquarters and where the larger part of our stocks of merchandise is carried, are among the largest buildings of their kind in the world. The big merchandise building is undoubtedly the largest of its kind in the world; the office building, a mammoth architectural beauty; the power plant, perhaps one of the largest and finest in the city; the printing plant, the largest of its kind in this country—all these enormous buildings with vast grounds and real estate holdings we own free of any encumbrance. They are part of our reward for honest effort, bigger values, better qualities, lower prices than were ever offered before, a policy that has guided and shall continue to guide us.

IN ADDITION TO THESE VAST HOLDINGS REFERRED TO, we own other very large and valuable real estate in Chicago, included in which are the enormous buildings that we occupied prior to our moving out, two years ago, to this present enormous plant. We own in their entirety, free of any encumbrance, a large number of big manufacturing plants in different states in the Union. In other very large manufacturing plants scattered throughout the land we are large stockholders or we own or control the output. Among these many factories that we own in their entirety, are large stockholders, or we own and control the output, some of these factories being the largest of their kind in the world, are factories manufacturing stoves, shoes, wearing apparel, furniture, cream separators, organs, musical instruments, mill work (doors, sash, blinds, etc.), agricultural implements, plumbing goods, guns, revolvers, wire fencing, safes, cameras, saws, hardware, vehicles, paint, wall paper, etc.

ONE NOT FULLY ACQUAINTED WITH OUR VAST REAL ESTATE and factory and merchandise holdings in Chicago, and scattered throughout the various states of the Union, can form no idea of the enormous capital that is required to place us in a position to own and offer you the big variety of goods we offer and the high standard of qualities that we demand and the low prices we make.

WE HAVE A CAPITAL STOCK OF FORTY MILLION DOLLARS, fully paid, enormous real estate, factory and merchandise holdings in Chicago and elsewhere all over the United States. The various commercial agencies give us the highest capital and credit rating given to any concern. We are known by every resident of Chicago, who could tell any interested person almost anything they might want to know about Sears, Roebuck & Co. We enjoy the highest credit at the various banking and financial institutions, and this latter point is especially important because we buy from all the markets of the entire world, and with this end in view our financial credit standing and strength is fully established in all the large banking and financial centers of all the leading foreign countries, and we refer, by special permission, to the First National Bank and Corn Exchange National Bank of Chicago, the Chase National Bank of New York, the National Shawmut Bank of Boston, with the special request that should you write to any of these banks for information, you will be sure to enclose a stamped envelope for reply. We produce on page 18 facsimile copies of bank letters furnished us by the First National Bank and the Corn Exchange National Bank of Chicago and could, of course, furnish you with similar letters of many other banks with which we have corresponding accounts or with whom we do business, and we name some of the banks in foreign lands to which we are especially permitted to refer and invite anyone to make inquiry, only requesting that should inquiry be made of any of these banks that sufficient postage be enclosed to cover the return postage. Referring fearlessly as we do to everyone and anyone who knows us, whether the big commercial agencies or great banking institutions, leaders of business in the great financial and money centers, **it affords us pleasure to specially refer to our millions of customers in every state and territory, in every city, every town and every hamlet, every little community in every corner and quarter of the whole United States.**

NEARLY ONE-HALF OF ALL THE FAMILIES IN THE UNITED STATES, especially those residing outside of the larger cities, have sent to us for goods, they have tried us out, they have had the opportunity of measuring our standard of quality, the goods we furnish, how they compare with our illustrations and descriptions, the values we give, the money we save, they know how we treat our customers, and therefore we especially refer any interested parties to our customers in their own immediate neighborhood. If you are not a customer of ours, most likely your next door neighbor is. You will surely find at least one-half of all the families in your immediate neighborhood able to tell you all about us. They can tell you from their own experience, which is the best proof we have to offer. If one-half of all your neighbors have sent to us for goods, then we refer you to these, to every one of them, one-half of all the people in your neighborhood, and if every one of these tells you that our goods are of the highest standard of quality, much lower in price than they can buy elsewhere, that they have saved money on everything they have bought from us, and we have done everything that we could do to satisfy them, and if they advise you to send your orders to us, that you may be sure of the highest standard of quality at the lowest possible price, that you may be sure of saving money by dealing with us, then we may hope to receive your order; if they don't so advise you, we cannot expect to receive an order from you. Therefore, on the advice of our customers, one-half of all your neighbors, we rest our case.

WE SOLICIT HONEST CRITICISM MORE THAN ORDERS

FROM THE MILLIONS OF CATALOGUES we send out annually our customers might be led to believe that we ask for nothing but orders. But when you once send us an order you will find we solicit something else, we solicit criticism, for when you send us an order and the goods reach you, you will find conspicuously placed in the top of the box in which the goods are packed or on a tag attached to the goods, just as you will find on the inside cover of every one of our Big Catalogues, the very first printing that you find in the book, and it reads as follows: **"YOUR MONEY BACK IF YOU ARE NOT SATISFIED."**

EVERY ORDER SENT US is accepted with the understanding and agreement that if the goods we send you are not found perfectly satisfactory, they can be returned to us at our expense, and the money sent us together with any freight or express charges paid, will be immediately returned. And then these words, "If these goods do not please you, you cannot do us a greater favor than to return the goods at our expense and get your money back, together with any transportation charges you may have paid."

WHILE WE STRIVE WITH EVERY MEASURE of resource we can command to leave no room for honest criticism, still, occasionally errors will creep in and again misunderstandings for which we may not be to blame, occasional unavoidable delays on the part of railroad or express companies, or other causes beyond our control, will give reason for honest criticism.

AND WE DO MOST EARNESTLY SOLICIT HONEST CRITICISM. WE SOLICIT CRITICISM MORE THAN ORDERS.

IF YOU HAVE REASON TO CRITICISE and you don't criticise us, we therefore never learn that you are not entirely satisfied with a transaction with us, it means an awful loss to us. It may mean the loss of your good will, your trade and your influence for us. A mistake on one order on our part left uncorrected may cost us dozens, yes hundreds of orders; therefore we tell you honestly, anxious as we are for orders, if you have an honest criticism to make and an order to send, and we can't have both, we beg of you to send us the criticism and don't send the order. Your criticism may involve money. It may be ten cents or one hundred dollars. It doesn't matter, we want to treat it as a principle, regardless of its importance as measured by dollars. Our policy says, it's got to be made right. In fairness you must be satisfied.

This gives a glimpse of the tower of the great Merchandise Building, in which the main entrance to the various merchandise departments is located. Through this entrance more than six thousand people pass in and out every working day of the year.

This shows a part of our Clothing Manufacturing Plant on the ninth floor of the great Merchandise Building, flooded with daylight from windows and skylights, the cleanest and most sanitary plant in existence.

This little sketch gives you just a faint idea of the army of men engaged in packing merchandise for shipment by freight to our customers. Nearly two million wooden boxes of various sizes were used in this room last year.

Here we show just one corner of a room in which about 200 young women are engaged in writing the letters dictated by correspondents throughout our institution. More than 10,000 letters are written every day.

Here is the Boiler Room of our Power House, having an ultimate capacity of 12,000 horse power. The coal carrying machinery in this boiler room has a capacity of 100 tons per hour. Sufficient to run a dozen good sized factories.

COMPARED WITH THE VAST VOLUME OF BUSINESS handled by us, the thousands of orders filled daily, we receive surprisingly few complaints, and the complaints we get are, as a rule, of trivial importance in a way, yet measured as we measure them, they are of vast importance. A pair of shoes, a suit of clothes or some other garment may not fit satisfactorily, a customer may have erred in the measurements; perchance something has been broken by the railroad company in transit, which occasionally, but not frequently, happens. You may receive something from us in the way of a machine or other article that you do not fully understand how to operate, and then again, there is that very small percentage of errors that will creep in and which, guard as closely as we will, we cannot altogether overcome. Sometimes there is a delay on the part of one of our factories for a few days in making shipment, sometimes the express company or railroad company will cause a shipment to be delayed, giving rise to inquiry or complaint. Fortunately for us, our customers are very charitably inclined, and when they send goods back for exchange or for any other reason have occasion to point out any shortcomings or any dissatisfaction, their letters, while carrying the words of complaint, also carry with them the manifestation of a spirit of the fullest confidence in our desire to apply the Golden Rule and do by them as we would like to be done by, and which we always try to do.

WE WANT TO SO CONDUCT OUR BUSINESS as to make it impossible for any customer anywhere to have any sort of a transaction with us, and when the transaction is completed, not to be able to find himself better off by reason of having had this transaction. By this we mean, if you have but a dollar in money, and you wish a certain article which we have to sell, and you would prefer to have this article as we have pictured and described it rather than the dollar which you have, then we would like to exchange that article which we have and which you desire for your dollar, provided only that after the trade has been made and we have exchanged the article for the dollar, we may know that you are perfectly satisfied, that you have received from us the exact thing that you wanted, that the article when received measures in the fullest measure to our illustration (picture) and description, that it is at least as good as described, if not better, and, compared with similar articles sold by others, it is at least as good if not better in quality and much lower in price, at least enough lower in price to make it a most interesting inducement for you to have sent your order and your money to us.

NOW, IF YOU HAVE THIS TRANSACTION WITH US and it is finally completed and the exchange is made, and we have the money and you have the goods, and you do not accept our invitation and request that goes with these goods to return them to us at our expense and get your money back if you are not satisfied, and you do not send us any word of criticism or complaint, we have only to assume that you are perfectly satisfied; but if it should so happen (and no doubt occasionally it does) that after the exchange is made you are not altogether satisfied, you may have misunderstood the color, the shape, the style, or there may have been some other reason, big or little, to cause you to feel just a little dissatisfied with this transaction, to feel that finally when the transaction is completed that perhaps you should have bought this article or goods at home or elsewhere rather than to have sent to us; now if there is any such feeling, then we feel it is due us, as it certainly is due you, that you write us and tell us of your dissatisfaction, for a word from you is the only opportunity we have to show you our great anxiety to satisfy you; besides, as a matter of policy, it is so very expensive to let any transaction be finished except in the most satisfactory way to both parties. It is likely to prevent either one of us from again doing business together, prevent us from making a profit, prevent you from saving money, prevent us both from making money, whereas it's so easy to settle any misunderstanding if you will but give us the chance.

WE HAVE A LARGE BUSINESS, the largest business of the kind in the world. We undoubtedly sell more goods direct to the users (the consumers) than all other mail order houses in the United States combined, more than any other institution in the world. We have sold to nearly one-half of all the families in the United States. We are very well known, and, we are quite sure, very favorably known. We haven't a dissatisfied customer in the world that we know of, for we have always tried to give the people just what we advertised, just what they wanted, and at a much lower price than they could buy elsewhere. Where any complaint or criticism has been sent us we have tried to settle it in the most liberal way. We have tried invariably to apply the Golden Rule, to serve our customers as we would like to be served, and yet we have no doubt, in fact we know, there must be some who have felt there was ground here or there to criticise and yet they have not criticised. These are the ones we most earnestly make our appeal to, for we feel that our business has been a great success only so far as we have been successful in fully satisfying every customer in every transaction, and if there be those, and we hope there are very, very few, who feel that they have not been fully satisfied but have not so manifested, and therefore have not given us the opportunity of finally making them satisfied, to this extent our business has not reached the highest point of efficiency and success for which we are so earnestly and diligently striving, and to these, and we hope there are few, we hope in the future, if possible, there may be even less, but from these we earnestly solicit your honest criticism.

BECAUSE OUR BUSINESS IS BIG, we, as individuals, are not big, nor do we feel big. We do not permit ourselves; we do not permit any of our people to allow themselves to feel above their real position, which is in truth, the servants of our customers. We volunteer and agree to serve you, and we are here for that purpose.

BIG AS OUR BUSINESS IS, great as our volume of sales has grown, we are sure if every family in the United States knew as well as the writer knows the full measure of advantage, safety, the measure of high quality and low price, the measure of desire and ability to serve you and satisfy you, then every family in the United States would send to us for nearly everything they buy, and our business, now bigger than any other, would soon be many times larger than it now is. You cannot know the advantages we offer without being in and breathing the very atmosphere of privilege that is placed at your disposal. Such selections of merchandise, such offers, such high standard of quality, such incomparably low prices, an organization so able to do and so willing to do, a policy so broad, so liberal, so fair, an underlying guarantee, the foundation of our growth, the guarantee for our future that says, you must be satisfied, you must have everything your own way, you must get what you want, it must at least be as good if not better in quality than you can get from the other dealer, and we must show you a big saving in cost. These are the things that are here. They have cost a world of time, a world of effort, a vast amount of capital and a determination to do and do right and to accomplish.

WHAT IS OUR STANDARD OF QUALITY, HOW WE MEASURE IT AND HOW WE MAKE COMPARISONS

TO AID OUR BUYERS, and to keep them constantly in touch with everything that is being made and sold, with what is generally being sold by retail dealers throughout the country, we employ and place at the disposal of our various buyers what we term missionary men, the men on the road, traveling all over the United States, visiting retail stores of all kinds, big and small, in large, medium and small cities, in live country towns, large and small, watching their stocks of merchandise, seeing what they sell, how they sell it, and what they charge for it, learning the wants of the people by going to and visiting with the people in all parts of the country. By the people we mean the consuming families. These missionaries, directed by our various buyers, are constantly buying goods of all kinds and descriptions. They send them to us here in Chicago where they are brought together and analyzed, criticised and used for comparison by our various buyers, and these missionaries are especially instructed to look out for new and better things, for improvements, for betterments in styles, qualities, weights, measurements and general satisfaction, and especially are they requested to buy and send these goods to us from all parts of the country, all over the United States, that they may be analyzed, dissected, brought together and used for comparison, and only for the purpose of getting our goods even better than the best. From all the things that are sold by all the dealers that sell, from all parts of all the states in the United States, there is all the time a stream of merchandise flowing into our institution, samples which our missionaries have purchased. They tag each article, saying where they bought it, the name of town, the name of the retail dealer, his relative size in the town and all about it, and these various goods coming to us from all quarters, brought to one place, make a great museum, a museum of information, useful to our buyers. For example, it may be stoves, steel ranges, if you please. We may get together the very best from dozens of different localities, ranges made by almost as many different makers as the number of places from whence they come to us, and when they get into our museum they are taken apart and the manager of our Steel Range Department and the various superintendents and managers of the stove foundry at Newark, Ohio, will go over these various ranges to pick their good and weak points, to see if there is anything new, any betterment, any place where we are lacking, if anyone has produced anything that we can afford to use or, if possible, use and better, and so this work goes constantly on and on and we are ever and all the time in touch with the market conditions from the retailer's point of view, the one who distributes to the users. We keep thoroughly in touch with what the retailer is selling, and in a general way from whom he buys, in a general way what he pays for his goods, and very accurately do we record the price at which he sells these goods, what the consumer pays for them. We keep an accurate gauge at all times as to the prevailing standards of quality, checking them up, that we may do as we must do if we live, see that our goods are always at least as good, never poorer, and wherever possible better than those sold in the country and, of course, invariably offered by us at much lower prices, prices that will mean a big saving to the buyer, our customer.

IN ADDITION TO THE INFORMATION WE GATHER THROUGH OUR VARIOUS MISSIONARIES, our buyers are more or less constantly on the road, visiting almost every exhibition, every fair, every center where merchandise is gathered together for the purpose of exhibition and comparison. Our buyers are continually going through the various factories of the country, learning of and studying new methods and improvements, learning wherever a new way, a better quality or lowering of cost has been devised. Our buyers are constantly in touch with the wholesale distributors of the particular merchandise in which they are interested. They are watchful all the time of the selections and methods of discerning buyers in the largest retail department stores in Chicago, New York and other cities; in short, if they buy for us they must keep alive to every condition, from a point of protection, a point of wholesale distribution and, lastly, from the retailer's point of delivery, for they must all the time know, they must get the benefit of every possible improvement, they must know always that their goods are right in quality, as good if not better than any other dealer furnishes and always offered at prices lower than can be had elsewhere.

Here is a corner of the Composing Room in our Printing Building, where we employ more than 100 skilled printers to set the type used in the printing of all our catalogues and all the blank forms and stationery used in our business.

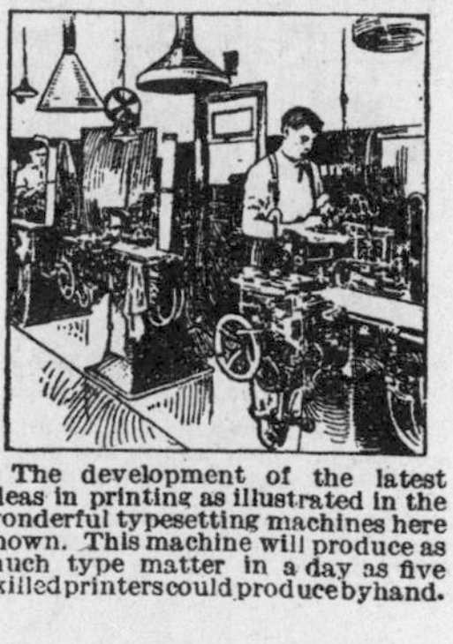

The development of the latest ideas in printing as illustrated in the wonderful typesetting machines here shown. This machine will produce as much type matter in a day as five skilled printers could produce by hand.

A glimpse of the center aisle of the Press Room in our Printing Building, the largest private press room in the world. Each of our twenty great presses deliver five thousand 32-page sections of our big catalogue every hour.

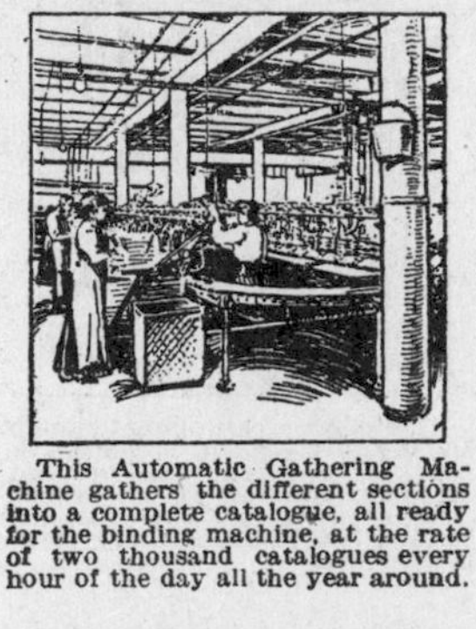

This Automatic Gathering Machine gathers the different sections into a complete catalogue, all ready for the binding machine, at the rate of two thousand catalogues every hour of the day all the year around.

One of our several Automatic Book Covering Machines, which bind together the various sections of the catalogue and automatically glue on the covers of 24,000 of our big 1,200-page catalogues every day.

HOW FAR WE HAVE GONE, ARE GOING and WILL CONTINUE TO GO, TO HELP OUR BUYERS GET SATISFACTORILY HIGH QUALITIES AT SATISFACTORILY LOW PRICES

IN MANY VARIETIES OF MERCHANDISE, such as furniture, shoes, guns, stoves, wearing apparel, plumbing, hardware, cameras, wall paper, paint, agricultural implements, buggies, leather goods, cream separators, clothing, musical goods, etc., etc., our buyers in these several lines have, in times gone by, reported to us that conditions governing many of these goods in their manufacture and sale were such that they could not, under any kind of a contract or contracts always get the satisfactorily high qualities at satisfactorily low prices, and as a result, and for the purpose of assisting ourselves to these needed goods of an acceptable high standard of quality at the lowest possible cost, we have bought, built and created many factories for the manufacture of these various wares, where we might with our own facilities and own control get just exactly what was wanted at the first cost of manufacture.

FOR EXAMPLE, a professional buyer unable to buy the particular wares which he is authorized to buy and of a satisfactorily high quality, at what he considers will be a satisfactorily low price, reaches his conclusions in this way: Necessarily knowing as much about the goods he is about to buy, how they should be made and what they should cost to make as the manufacturer could possibly know, he takes up an article, for example, clothing, a man's suit. We will assume the quality is fairly satisfactory, although, unfortunately, the manufacturer may have a reputation for varying quality, which would mean that out of a thousand suits they would not run absolutely uniform, a serious fault and one which the buyer could not accept. The manufacturer may offer our buyer this suit for say $7.00 in lots of 1,000, and our buyer will analyze this suit in the following manner: He will say, this suit of clothes contains so many yards of cloth made by such and such a mill, the value of which is so much. He will measure up the linings, buttons, trimmings, etc., etc., and he must have an accurate knowledge of their quality and market worth. He will then say the manufacturer paid or should have paid so much for making the coat, so much for making the vest, so much for making the trousers, and he will perhaps figure it that this suit of clothes should be produced at an actual cost of say $5.65, but being unable to buy these suits in any quantity from any maker anywhere at less than $7.00, he comes to us and tells us the only way this clothing can be produced with uniformly high quality controlled and guaranteed, and at the lowest possible price is that we manufacture them ourselves, and straightway we proceed to equip to manufacture our clothing, and which, by the way, we have been doing for a long time.

THE BUYER IN CHARGE OF CREAM SEPARATORS, who has been buying cream separators at about $45.00 each, the lowest price he could possibly get from any maker in any quantity, comes to us and says, at the price we are buying the manufacturer makes too much money. He tells us this machine is composed of so many pounds of cast iron, so many pounds of steel, so many parts of brass, worth a certain price; there is in this machine so much labor, such and such value in the various parts, bought or made, and therefore if we were to manufacture or control the manufacture of this machine in large quantities we should be able, at our one small percentage of profit, to sell a better machine at much less than the price we ourselves are now paying another manufacturer, and straightway we proceed to buy into and get control of factories and the output of factories for the manufacture of cream separators. This same process of calculation has driven us into the manufacture of a vast variety of merchandise, among which several of the more important lines have been referred to.

OUR BUYERS WILL SOMETIMES REPORT OTHER CONDITIONS which deprive them of getting the highest standard of quality at a satisfactorily low cost. For example, the buyer will come to us and tell us we are paying too much for certain furniture from a certain factory, and this furniture is costing this certain factory too much to manufacture. He will explain to us that this certain factory is, in his opinion, run with too much overhead expense or waste. They are making, perhaps, too great a variety of merchandise, too many styles, running very busy, perhaps, six months in the year and very light the other six months, while the period in which they are running very light, perhaps at half capacity, their management, superintendency, investment and other similar expenses are exactly the same as when they are running full capacity, and all these expenses tend to increase their cost, and to prevent this particular furniture factory from making us as low a price as we ought to have.

OUR BUYERS MEET THESE CONDITIONS CONSTANTLY, and we prevent this useless waste in such instances and we get the right quality at the right cost by pursuing this policy. We will, for example, go to this manufacturer who perhaps has a capacity of one million dollars' worth of goods in a year in his manufacturing plant, but is making say five hundred thousand dollars' worth, and we say to him that we will absorb and utilize all his excess capacity, so that instead of running part of the time with a small force, part of the time light and part full, he must run at his utmost capacity every day in the year, and for any surplus capacity he may have at any time he may make for us a certain few prescribed styles in furniture, which styles we will specify, and he will make a few in variety of a special high standard of quality. This sort of a position not only enables the manufacturer to make the few styles for us in enormous quantities at a very low cost, but also reduces the cost on the goods that he makes for himself. His power plant, his machinery, his buildings, his managerial force, superintendency and all is active, going at full capacity all the time. In this way we reduce to the very minimum what is known by manufacturers as overhead expense, we own these goods at the lowest possible cost, and we in turn, of course, give our customers the benefit of these savings charging, as we do on everything, our one small percentage of profit above the actual cost to us. You, our customers, who sit down to peruse our catalogue to make up an order for needed goods, cannot possibly have any idea of how far reaching are our efforts to make possible the prices we print in this catalogue, the values we give.

ALMOST EVERY LITTLE ITEM IN THIS ENTIRE BOOK has in it a history. A history could be written of almost every little item that would fill quite a volume, picturing in words all the effort, the research, the condition, the obligation that has gone to make possible the price and quality offering shown in more than one hundred thousand items in this Big Catalogue. Our buying organization is enormous. It's divided into a great many units. It reaches out into every part or resource in the United States and, in fact, over the civilized world. It begins with the most thorough research into the proper time, place and way of buying such staple raw materials as pig iron, steel, cotton, hides, lumber, wool and all those things which go to make up the endless variety of goods we sell. Our buying organization is a great college of commercial economics. Through this organization we study the methods of nearly all the manufacturers, wholesalers and retailers of the world. We bring together for comparison, selection and for study those things that are made in shops, big and small, all over the world. We devise ways and means of bettering, improving and perfecting styles. The history of a little ten-cent item, small, insignificant in itself, if you please, when you see it in this catalogue, it may mean, however, that to produce this article at the selling price we have had to find the one man with that peculiar experience and knowledge that fits him to make this one article and make it cheap. We have had to grub-stake him, as it were; that is, supply him with the necessary capital and then we have had to nurse him along by seeing that he bought his raw material right. We have had to send our statistician, or cost accountant, to his place of business from time to time, to see that it was economically and properly run, one of our master mechanics probably visits him, our inspectors inspect his work in process as well as finished, and so we nurse this little unit of activity along in our effort to finally produce this one little article in order that it may be at least a little better than any similar article you can buy elsewhere and at the same time much lower in cost, much lower in price to you. We must do all these things all the time, for we cannot possibly live as a business institution if our quality is not of a standard that satisfies, that is at least as good and, if possible, better than you can buy at home, nor can we live if our prices are not much lower than you can possibly buy elsewhere. If when you receive goods from us you do not find by comparison that you have gotten more for your money than you could have possibly gotten elsewhere, and are thus so pleased that you will be inclined to favor us with orders in the future; otherwise we know too well that you will do even as we ask you to do, a request that goes with every shipment, that is, you will return the goods to us at our expense and get your money back, and you will not be likely to send us another order.

WHAT A BUYER MUST KNOW TO QUALIFY HIM TO BUY FOR US, AND THE ONLY POSITION HE IS ALLOWED TO TAKE ON THE GREAT QUESTION OF

QUALITY AND PRICE

WE HAVE ABOUT ONE HUNDRED PROFESSIONAL BUYERS, and each buyer buys one kind of goods. For example, one man may buy ladies' shoes, one buyer will buy sewing machines, another harness, another buyer buys watches and jewelry, another clocks; one buyer may buy large goods, another small goods. Hardwares are divided into several divisions, with one professional buyer for each division. Pumps may be bought by one buyer; furniture is divided into several divisions and one professional buyer in charge of each division, buying only those particular goods consigned to him. And so it goes on through the entire line of all kinds of Wearing Apparel, Notions, Carpets, Curtains, Rugs, Dress Goods, Silks, Furnishing Goods, Trunks, Crockery, Books, Photographic Goods, Cutlery, Sporting Goods, etc., etc.

COMPARATIVELY FEW THINGS and on one class of merchandise in a limited variety, do we entrust to the care of one buyer, but this buyer must be a professional expert in the particular few things which we entrust him to purchase for us. For example, a buyer of ladies' shoes, he must have a thorough knowledge of ladies' shoes, the same as a buyer of any other article must have a thorough knowledge of the article or articles he is expected to buy. One man cannot possibly buy a great variety of merchandise, for it would be impossible for him to inform himself sufficiently on all the things essential to make him a good buyer. He must needs be a specialist in his limited line, and in this limited line he is not permitted to make any mistakes.

FOR EXAMPLE, the buyer of ladies' shoes, he must first know the best styles in ladies' shoes for all parts of the country, and they differ in different parts of the United States. He must know the styles suitable to all classes and all ages. He must through his own knowledge, gained from years of experience, and kept up to date through the assistance of our missionaries throughout the country; he must know what the retail dealers are selling, know their standards of quality, and he must know the average prices the retail dealers of the country are getting for ladies' shoes. He must know in a general way from where they are being supplied, from whom they buy and, in turn, he must know the factories that supply the wholesaler, who in turn supplies the retailer in the various sections of the country. This buyer of ladies' shoes when he goes into the market, among the different manufacturers, must know just what kind of shoes he must have to fill to the letter the demands of the people as to styles, he must know what standard of quality he must have in every number to be sure that his quality is up to and a little better than the corresponding numbers or kinds sold by dealers generally, and when he goes to a manufacturer in the shoe district, which for ladies' shoes is principally located around Boston, and looking to a contract, he asks one or more manufacturers to make up certain samples to submit to him, following the specifications laid down by our shoe buyer; our shoe buyer must be competent to take any one of these samples, cut it up, check it up and see that the manufacturer has fulfilled every requirement as specified for by our buyer. It's a long story. He must know the cost of producing shoes, the relation that the market price of green hides bears to the price of the particular leather furnished in the shoe, the vamps, the uppers, the sole, the counters, even to the eyelets, the lining and shoe strings; he must know the market, know the value of the materials as well as the manufacturer himself can possibly know. He must know, and almost to a cent, what it should cost in labor and other manufacturing expense to produce this shoe; this he must know in order to know that he gets the prescribed measure of quality, the high standard we must have, and then he must also know this to know that, once the question of quality is settled, the price is right.

WHEN IN THE MARKET, and before going to the several manufacturers for bids on certain shoes to be made according to our buyer's specifications, he must have a sufficient knowledge of the different facilities of the various manufacturers of ladies' shoes to select those particular factories that are best adapted, best equipped to make the particular style of shoe, best in quality, style and at the lowest cost, which our buyer is about to buy. Having completed his contract, his specifications as to quality having been specified, the price having been agreed upon, the contract closed, one or more pairs of these shoes are usually taken as exhibits in the contract and become a part of the contract in order that our Inspection Department, that must inspect these shoes when they come from the factory, can use the samples for the purpose of measuring the quality of the goods as they come from the factory, and thus knowing that every pair of shoes that comes in under the contract is exactly in accordance with the contract and has the full measure of quality.

AS THE ONE MAN IS AN EXPERT IN LADIES' SHOES and capable of buying for us, capable of getting all we demand in high quality and buying them at the right price, a price that enables us to give you the highest standard of quality, at a cost to you much lower than you can possibly buy elsewhere, this same sort of talent is used by us in the purchase of all the different goods shown in this catalogue.

THE BUYER OF DRESS GOODS will, with his magnifying glass that accurately measures the weave, and by chemical analysis that will accurately measure the materials, from his long experience find exactly the measure of quality, and will know if the goods delivered are exactly in accordance with the contract, from his knowledge of the relation of the cost of materials (wool, cotton or silk) and labor to the proper price of the finished article, whether or not we own these goods right, and with this knowledge will procure for us dress goods that we can sell you lower in price and better in quality than you can buy elsewhere.

FOR EXAMPLE, the man who buys our sewing machines has on his staff several expert sewing machine mechanics, especially two who have devoted their entire lives to the mechanical study of sewing machines, and after every conceivable point has been covered, every specification has been fulfilled, after the calculation of cost, which begins with the raw material (cast iron and steel) has been gone over and figured through its different processes to the finished machine, then samples of every little piece and part in the sewing machine are nailed on to boards and numbered, and these parts together with several sewing machines as samples are kept by us, representing a part of our contract, and the product of the factory is being constantly checked up against these two sets held by us to know that they are up to the standard of quality.

THE BUYER WHO BUYS OUR HARNESS, and, by the way, it is no small job for one man to buy all the harness we use, and he has quite enough responsibility to know everything necessary to know about harness in order to make sure that we get a satisfactorily high quality at a price so low that we can sell you any kind of a harness and give you a much better harness than you could get elsewhere, and yet show you a big saving in cost. This man who buys our harness keeps in as close touch with the market on green hides as if he were in the hide business. He keeps in as close touch with the conditions at the tannery, where the leather that goes into our harness is tanned, as if he were the owner of the tannery. He watches continually the leather as it comes out of the tannery. He is close in touch with every operation and every change in the factory; in fact, he is a practical harness man, he began his education at the bench and at the horse in a small country harness shop. He is an expert harness maker and can make any kind of harness. He is an expert judge of hides and he is equally expert as a judge of leather. He is only called upon by us to know everything about a harness. That is all we ask of him but we ask all of that in the fullest measure. He must know everything about quality, everything about cost, everything that enters into the cost of manufacture in a harness. He must know this in order that he may know that we get a satisfactory standard of quality. He must know what harness makers, sellers of harness everywhere get for harness, because he is expected to make ours better and yet permit us to sell them cheaper.

WE COULD GO ON AND FILL PAGES OF SPACE by telling you of the separate buying organizations, the peculiar experience and knowledge of the several buyers in their respective lines. All this is necessary to giving the goods we give, the high standard of quality we offer at the low prices we name, and anyone less equipped than this cannot possibly give you so much. This great ability to measure with accuracy, and the buying power that is without a parallel in the world, with a vast network of manufacturing plants of our own, and a disposition to give you all there is in it, and in no case save for ourselves anything other than our one small percentage of profit above the actual cost to us, is what makes possible the most extraordinary values shown in the upwards of one hundred thousand low price offerings shown in this big 1908 Catalogue.

ABOUT OUR RELIABILITY.

YOU ARE PERFECTLY SAFE IN SENDING US YOUR ORDERS AND YOUR MONEY. We are one of the largest commercial institutions in the world, and we occupy by far the largest mercantile plant in the world. We own this entire plant, free of indebtedness of any kind, comprising forty acres of ground, in one of the best districts in Chicago; our ground and buildings alone are valued at more than Six Million Dollars. We have nearly nine thousand employes, and our customers now number nearly five million. If you have any doubt, you are at liberty to refer to any bank, business house or resident of Chicago, and we especially refer to our millions of satisfied customers. Ask your neighbor about **Sears, Roebuck & Co.** We have customers in every neighborhood in the United States, and we gladly refer you to any customer.

BE SURE TO READ THE BANK LETTER OF THE FIRST NATIONAL BANK OF CHICAGO, capital and surplus $14,000,000.00, signed by its cashier. Charles N. Gillett; also the Corn Exchange National Bank letter, capital and surplus $6,000,000.00, signed by Frank W. Smith, its cashier; see page 18. Consider our standing everywhere and be convinced it is perfectly safe to send your money to us, we agreeing to return it and pay all transportation charges if the goods do not please you.

HOW WE MAKE EVERY TRANSACTION WITH US STRICTLY CONFIDENTIAL.

Why our name and address do not appear on any box, package, wrapper, tag, envelope or article of merchandise.

As many people, especially merchants, business houses, townspeople and others, do not care to have others know where or from whom they buy their goods, as many people object to having the name of the shipper spread across every box or package, so that when it is unloaded at the station or express office everyone can see what they are getting and where they buy it, to protect all those who care for this protection and make it possible for you to order your goods from us with no fear of anyone learning at the railroad station, express office or elsewhere what you bought or where you bought it, our name and address will not appear on any box, package, tag, envelope or article of merchandise.

For example: If you are a merchant and wish to buy goods to sell again, your customers will be unable to learn from any marks inside or outside where you bought the goods or what you paid for them.

If you are a professional man, or even in the employ of some merchant, who for personal reasons might object to your sending to us for goods, you need have no fear, our name will not appear on any goods or packages you get.

While we would be glad to have our name appear on every article of merchandise and on every box and package, as a valuable means of advertising, we have learned that thousands of our customers need the protection that the omitting of our name affords. This applies especially to townspeople.

NO ORDER WILL BE ACCEPTED FOR LESS THAN 50 CENTS.

PLEASE DO NOT SEND US ANY ORDER AMOUNTING TO LESS THAN 50 CENTS. If you want some article, the price of which is less than 50 cents, please include one or more other needed articles and make your order amount to 50 cents or more.

AS A MATTER OF ECONOMY, BOTH TO OUR CUSTOMERS AND OURSELVES, we do not fill orders for less than 50 cents. The postage or express charges especially make small orders under 50 cents unprofitable to the purchaser, or at least much more expensive than the orders amounting to 50 cents or more.

WE MAKE THIS EXCEPTION: In the case of needed repairs, attachments and supplies, such as needles for our sewing machines, parts of guns, etc., which can be secured only from us, we will fill the order no matter how small it may be.

TO MAKE ORDERING BY MAIL VERY PROFITABLE TO OUR CUSTOMERS we especially urge that you make your order as large as possible. Orders of from $2.00 to $5.00 or more are always very much more profitable to the purchaser than smaller orders, for the express or freight charges are in this way very greatly reduced. It always pays, even if you have to get some friend or neighbor to join with you, to make up an order of from $2.00 to $5.00 or more, and include enough heavy goods to make a profitable freight shipment of fifty to one hundred pounds. In this way you reduce the transportation charges on each item to next to nothing. You then pay the exact same freight charges that your storekeeper must pay on the goods he sells.

ON THE BASIS OF FAR GREATER VALUE FOR YOUR MONEY THAN YOU CAN POSSIBLY GET ELSEWHERE, lower prices than any other house does or can name, the best possible service, every item ordered guaranteed to reach you in perfect condition and give perfect satisfaction or your money to be immediately refunded to you; on our binding guarantee to please you in every way on every dollar sent us, wholly in your own interest we ask you to kindly conform to these terms.

OUR COMPLIMENTS TO THE RETAIL MERCHANT.

IT IS NOT OUR DESIRE TO ANTAGONIZE THE RETAIL MERCHANT (the storekeeper of the country). This is a big, growing country, and there is ample room for us all. Our prices are alike to all. Whether to the largest or the smallest merchant, farmer, mechanic or laborer, our price is exactly the same. Our goods are for sale at the prices plainly printed in this book, and occupation or position restricts no one from buying goods from us at our printed prices.

However, we number thousands of the best merchants of the United States among our valued customers. The prejudice which for a time existed because we would not sell to the dealer and refuse to sell to his customers, is dying out; for the shrewd, careful buying, up to date merchant of today has broader business views.

He buys his goods where he can get the best value for his money, and on the basis of more value for the money than is furnished by any other house we especially invite all classes of merchants to carefully compare our prices as printed in this book with the prices you have been in the habit of paying.

As explained on this page, we ship all our goods in plain boxes or packages, and our name appears on no package or article of merchandise. You can buy your goods from us at our selling prices, which are much lower than you can buy elsewhere, you can fix your profit to suit yourself and your customers will not know where you bought the goods or what you paid for them.

We want to correct the impression that may be in the minds of some merchants, that we sell exclusively to the consumer, the party who buys the goods to use. If you have this impression we are anxious to correct it. A goodly percentage of the goods we ship in all lines go direct to merchants, business houses who buy to sell again, and in some lines, especially materials and supplies, a large percentage of our goods go to manufacturers, which they use in the manufacture of their wares, which in turn they sell to dealers. Among our valued customers are the U. S. Government, state and city institutions, railroads and other large corporations, and also jobbers, brokers, retailers and consumers in all parts of the country.

WE ESPECIALLY SOLICIT THE TRADE OF THE SUCCESSFUL, SHREWD BUYING MERCHANT, who wishes to buy his wares where he can get the highest standard of quality at lower prices than he can get elsewhere.

TO THE SHREWD MERCHANT buying for cash to sell again at a profit, to the one who buys where he can get the most for his money.

TO THE PURCHASING AGENT OF RAILROAD COMPANIES and other large corporations, to contractors and builders and to manufacturers of all classes of goods, to all of these who are now dealing with us, we want to thank you for your liberal patronage in the past and again invite you to a careful comparison of our prices in this, our latest, large merchandise catalogue, with the very lowest prices the same goods can be had elsewhere, and on the basis of quality and price we earnestly solicit your future business.

To all this class who have not as yet dealt with us we earnestly solicit a careful study of our catalogue prices, which will point in many directions to a great saving for you.

TO RAILROAD PURCHASING AGENTS we especially direct attention to our incomparably low prices on safes and stoves for station use, also to furniture, hardware, etc., for other uses. We are doing a large business with a number of the large express and railroad companies; therefore, to the purchasing agents of these corporations especially do we direct your attention to the prices quoted in this catalogue and our ability to save you money on the goods we offer.

TO CONTRACTORS, BUILDERS, MANUFACTURERS, ETC., we can save you money on goods you consume and goods that go into your manufactured wares. If you are a builder we can save you money on a large part of all your building material. If you are a manufacturer using any kind of finished parts of iron, wood, leather or cloth, we can save you money on many items that go into your manufactured articles. If you are a contractor, mill operator or the like, you are consuming machinery, tools and supplies of all kinds, and we can save you money on these, and this in competition with any market in the world.

MANY MANUFACTURERS WORKING IN IRON buy all their files, emery wheels and various similar supplies, as well as tools and machinery from us.

MANY MANUFACTURERS WORKING IN WOOD buy their saws and other tools and supplies from us.

MANY MANUFACTURERS WORKING IN LEATHER, such as harness, etc., buy their buckles, trimmings and leather from us.

MANY MANUFACTURERS OF BUGGIES, HARNESS, ETC., buy their wheels, woodwork, leather, cloth, iron, trimmings, etc., from us.

MANY MANUFACTURERS OF FURNITURE buy their hardware, such as locks, hinges, knobs, casters, trimmings, etc., from us.

MANY MANUFACTURERS OF AGRICULTURAL IMPLEMENTS, ETC., buy their paint, various hardware and tools from us.

CONTRACTORS AND BUILDERS OF HOUSES buy their builders' hardware, such as doors, locks, nails, paint, paper, roofing, doors, sash, blinds, millwork, etc., from us.

LUMBERMEN, OPERATORS OF SAW MILLS, LOGGERS, ETC., in all sections of the country, north, south, east and west, buy their general supplies from us, such as saws, files, mechanical tools and supplies, including axes, chains, hooks and all kinds of provisions and supplies.

ALMOST EVERY DEALER IN MERCHANDISE, general store or special store in the United States, sells goods purchased from us, either directly or indirectly, for in the goods you buy from others to sell again, among some of them surely will be found goods that were bought from us, supplies of some kind that entered into the manufacture of the goods you bought. As we are operators, owners or controllers of a great many factories manufacturing finished materials in parts, goods made of iron, wood, leather, cloth, etc., it would be hardly possible for any dealer in hardware, groceries, dry goods, clothing, agricultural implements or other goods to buy the finished goods to sell, from any wholesale dealer anywhere without there would enter into some of the goods which he offers for sale, parts that have come either direct from our store or from one of the many factories in which we are interested.

WE OWN OR CONTROL THE OUTPUT OF FACTORIES MAKING VARIOUS KINDS OF HARDWARE AND HARDWARE SUPPLIES, carriage and wagon material, blacksmiths' materials, materials that enter into clothing, harness, furniture, etc. We also own or control many factories making shoes, stoves, cream separators, organs, musical instruments, plumbing goods of all kinds, paint, wall paper, guns, revolvers, furniture, safes, saws, mechanics' tools, photographic goods, washing machines, household supplies, cameras, clothing, ladies' wearing apparel, electrical goods, tents, canvas goods, gun implements, books, jewelry, stereoscopic goods, hardware, special mill work, radiators, agricultural implements, etc. We are either sole owners or controllers of a vast number of these factories. From some we sell the entire output; others, we allow the factory, under our direction, to sell to either wholesale or retail dealers, usually to wholesale dealers, and the wholesale dealers in turn sell to the retail dealer, and the retail dealer to his local trade. So if you could trace the original source of supply of every article in your store or on your shelves, you could trace a liberal percentage of all the goods you are now selling either directly to our store or indirectly to one of our many factories.

Therefore we urge you, if you are a live, up to date merchant, that you buy from first hands.

DO NOT FAIL TO GIVE SIZE, COLOR, WEIGHT, ETC., IF REQUIRED, WHEN WRITING YOUR ORDER.

IF YOU ARE A MERCHANT who buys to sell again you will find thousands of articles in this catalogue on which we can save you money. Remember, every transaction with us is treated in the strictest of confidence. No article you buy from us will bear our name; no box, package or shipment of any kind will bear our name. Our name will not appear on any tag, envelope or any piece of paper that is exposed that will go to you from us. If you buy goods from us no one will know from whom you buy your goods or what you pay for them. You can send your order to us for anything in this catalogue, the goods will go to you with the understanding that they will please you, you will find them lower in price and better in quality than you can buy elsewhere, and you are always at liberty to return any goods you get from us if you are not perfectly satisfied and always at our expense, and we will immediately return your money together with any express or freight charges paid by you.

OUR LIBERAL TERMS OF SHIPMENT.

WE HAVE NO DISCOUNTS, we sell for cash only, and the prices quoted in this catalogue are absolutely net, from which there is no discount whatever. Our prices are alike to one and all, regardless of the amount of the order; the same to the merchant, the manufacturer, contractor or corporation as to the farmer, mechanic or laborer. We especially recommend that you send cash in full with your order. Send us either a postoffice money order, express money order, bank draft, your own check or send the money in a registered letter.

If you are a farmer and live on a R. F. D. Route, make up your order, go to the R. F. D. carrier, give him the money you wish to send to us and he will give you a receipt for the money and either issue to you or get for you a postoffice money order for the amount you wish to send.

If you reside in a town, then either go to the postoffice and buy a postoffice money order, to the express office and buy an express money order, or to the bank and buy a draft, or enclose your own check.

WE ESPECIALLY REQUEST THAT YOU SEND THE FULL AMOUNT OF CASH WITH YOUR ORDER, for this is always much more satisfactory than to send part of the money with your order, the balance to be paid C. O. D., and understand, when you send us your order and money we accept your money and your order and ship the goods to you with the understanding and agreement that if they are not perfectly satisfactory in every way, you are at liberty to return any part or all of them to us, at our expense, and we will immediately return your money, together with any freight or express charges paid by you.

ABOUT C. O. D. SHIPMENTS.

WHILE FOR YEARS WE SHIPPED A GREAT MANY GOODS BY FREIGHT AND EXPRESS C. O. D., subject to examination, on receipt of a comparatively small cash deposit, usually about twenty-five per cent or one-fourth of the total amount of an order, or enough to fully cover the freight or express charges both ways on the goods ordered, and sent the goods by freight or express, C. O. D., subject to examination, allowing the purchaser to examine the goods at his nearest railroad station or express office, and if found to be perfectly satisfactory the customer would then pay the railroad agent or express agent our price and freight or express charges, less the amount of money sent with order, otherwise he would refuse the goods, the railroad or express agent would return the goods to us at our expense and we would return all the money sent us; of late years, and especially the past two or three years, we have sent comparatively few goods either by freight or express C. O. D., subject to examination, but rather have, in the interest of our customers and the interest of the greatest economy and lowest possible price making, urged our customers to send cash in full with their orders in every instance. We have advised our customers to invariably send cash in full with their orders, first because there is an extra charge for any goods shipped by freight or express C. O. D., subject to examination. By express there is an extra charge for collecting the money and returning it to us, which the customer must pay, and by freight there is a still higher charge for collecting the amount of the draft and returning the money to us, and also customers are frequently put to inconvenience in paying the draft at one office and getting the goods from the railroad station at another office. Then too, for some time past, many railroad companies have declined to allow their agents to permit customers to examine goods shipped by freight before paying for the same, so in the interest of our customers, with a view of saving them the extra charge for collecting money on C. O. D. shipments and returning the same to us, with a view of saving them the least possible trouble in receiving the goods promptly, with a view of effecting the greatest economy in handling and getting the goods to our customers in the shortest possible time, we advise our customers always to send cash in full with their orders.

WE FEEL NOW THAT WE ARE SO WELL KNOWN that we can afford to be perfectly frank with every customer in regard to C. O. D. shipments, for nearly everyone in the United States knows us, has dealt with us, knows our reputation for fair and honorable dealing, and to the comparatively few who may as yet be unacquainted with us, they can easily learn all about our financial and commercial standing and manner of treating our customers by asking their neighbors who have dealt with us, and when we say to you in your own interest that we advise you to always send cash in full with your order, remember, we bargain and agree with you that if the goods we send you are not perfectly satisfactory, do not reach you promptly and in perfect condition, free from any damage or flaw of any kind, you are always at liberty to return the goods to us at our expense, and we will immediately return your money, together with freight or express charges paid by you.

WHILE WE HAVE PRACTICALLY DISCONTINUED ALL C. O. D. SHIPMENTS, and nearly all our customers who at one time ordered their goods shipped C. O. D., sending a deposit with the order, now send cash in full, and we advise you to do likewise, if, for any reason you would prefer to see and examine any goods you might select from our catalogue before paying for them in full, and you wish us to ship them by freight or express C. O. D., subject to examination, you can send your order for such goods as you want, but be sure to enclose a sufficient cash deposit (at least one-fourth of the total amount of your order), and immediately your order is received, if it be for such goods as we can afford to ship C. O. D., subject to examination, on the amount of cash deposit you send us, the goods will go to you at once C. O. D., subject to examination, balance payable after the goods are received; otherwise we will immediately return your money and your order with a full explanation as to why we cannot ship the particular order by freight C. O. D., subject to examination; and please understand, on any order for goods to be sent by freight C. O. D., subject to examination, where goods are so shipped we will especially request the agent at your station to allow examination, but we cannot guarantee that examination will be so allowed, for, as before explained, many railroad companies have instructed their agents not to allow goods to be examined before they are paid for. Under any circumstances, however, whether goods ordered from us are shipped C. O. D., subject to examination, on receipt of a cash deposit, or whether shipped as a full paid order, the goods go to you with the understanding and agreement that if they are not perfectly satisfactory, they can be returned to us at our expense and we will immediately return your money, together with any freight or express charges you may have paid.

Paragraph A.

ABOUT OUR PRICES.

LOW PRICE AND HIGH QUALITY GUARANTEE.

Our prices on everything shown in this catalogue (market conditions of raw material and labor considered), are lower than you can buy elsewhere. Every order sent us is accepted with the understanding and agreement that if you do not find our prices lower, quality considered, and the quality of our merchandise higher than the average, you are at liberty to return the goods to us at our expense of transportation charges both ways, and we will promptly return all your money.

WE BUY AND SELL FOR CASH, and having no bad debts, no traveling men's expenses, no expenses for collecting, asking but one small profit, and by manufacturing the goods ourselves or by securing the manufacturers' lowest spot cash prices, we can sell goods at a smaller margin of profit than any other business house could do and still exist.

WE MAKE NO REDUCTION IN OUR PRICES. To those who are inclined to write us for a reduction from the prices quoted in this catalogue, we wish to state that we cannot make any reduction or concession, whether you order in large or small quantities. The price quoted on each and every article in this catalogue is as low as we can possibly make it, and it is out of the question to reduce these prices still further; and we earnestly believe a careful comparison of our prices with those of any other concern will convince you that we can furnish you better goods for less money than you can obtain from any other house in the United States.

ALL PRICES ARE SUBJECT TO THE FLUCTUATIONS OF THE MARKET. The prices quoted in this book are correct, according to market conditions at the date the catalogue is printed, and our wants have been anticipated as far as possible by contract, goods in stock, etc., but when our stock on hand is sold or when a contract expires and the market conditions at the time are such that we are compelled to pay more money for the goods, we reserve the right to advance our prices without notice, charging you the difference the advance represents, only the difference in cost to us. The necessity for advancing prices very rarely happens, but as a protection to us, at the extremely low prices we are making, we must reserve this right, and this space is used to inform everyone of the right so reserved. If prices decline so that we are able to buy any goods to fill orders at lower prices than those printed in this catalogue, you will always get the benefit of such prices and the difference will be returned to you in cash.

AS THE TENDENCY IS FOR LARGER CONTRACTS, larger purchases, closer buying, the history of our house and our records show that **we reduce prices and return the difference in cash ten times** where we make an advance and ask more money once; but for our protection the right to recognize advances and declines must be and is reserved.

IN THIS CATALOGUE you will find only such goods listed as we can save you money on, goods that can be delivered anywhere in the United States for less money than they can be bought at your local dealer's. The amount of money that we can save you over the prices you pay at home varies from 15 to 50 per cent, according to the nature of the goods, but there is not an item quoted in this entire catalogue on which the saving is not worth taking into consideration, to say nothing of the fact that our goods are, as a rule, of a higher grade than those carried by the average storekeeper or catalogue house.

THE ILLUSTRATIONS AND DESCRIPTIONS IN THIS CATALOGUE can be depended upon. We aim to illustrate and describe every article with the strictest accuracy. Most all of the illustrations are made from photographs taken direct from the article. They are such as enable you to order intelligently; in fact, with our assortment, correct illustrations and accurate descriptions, you can order from this catalogue with the same ease, confidence and security as though you were personally in our store selecting the goods yourself.

OUR CUSTOMERS MAY REST ASSURED that we will exert every effort to bring the best merchandise to them at still lower prices in the future and as the volume of our business increases on lines which are not at the present time manufactured by us in factories owned or controlled by us we shall build and equip or control factories which will produce these lines for us at a lower cost. Gradually our interests in manufacturing establishments have been extended until now we manufacture an enormous percentage of the goods we offer in this catalogue and as it has been our practice to sell at manufacturing cost, plus one small profit, we have been enabled to bring the best merchandise to our customers at lower prices than are quoted by any firm or individual engaged in general merchandising lines. We shall exert every effort to increase the opportunities offered our customers to still further reduce their living expenses and we are sure that a comparison of our prices with those quoted by others will influence you to send us an increasing share of your patronage.

Paragraph C.
HOW TO ORDER.

Use our regular order blank, if you have one; if not, use any plain paper.

Always keep well supplied with our order blanks, as it is more convenient for you to make out your order on our regular order blanks than in any other way. If out of them at any time, drop us a postal card and we will send you some.

Whether you write your order on our regular order blank or letter paper instead, be sure to observe the following instructions:

Always sign your full name (Christian name and surname).

Please write your name and address very plainly and in INK.

Write your name in full clearly and distinctly. Make it as plain as possible so that we cannot make a mistake.

Give your postoffice, county and state, rural route or street and number and your shipping point, if different from the postoffice.

Always give catalogue number in full (write every figure and letter in the catalogue number), description and price of each article ordered.

Always try to mention the number or name of the catalogue or circular from which your order is taken and be sure to give the size, color, weight and measurements when required.

Be sure to enclose your money with your order and state plainly in your order how much money you enclose and in what form. Sending us money in one envelope and your order in another causes delay and confusion in our office, as they become separated in the mails. For instructions on how to send money see paragraph F.

Be sure you have followed our rules carefully about enclosing the proper amount of money with the order, including enough to pay postage if the goods are to be sent by mail, and insurance fee if to be sent by insured mail.

Be sure your name and address is written plainly and in full, that your shipping directions are plainly stated, that the exact amount of money enclosed is plainly stated, that you have given us catalogue number, price, description, correct size and measurements and you will seldom, if ever, have any delay or inconvenience. By carefully observing these rules you will avoid errors and loss of time by our having to write you for further information.

AFTER WRITING AN ORDER, please compare it with these rules, check it over closely and see if you have written your order correctly.

IF YOU WISH TO REFER TO ANY MATTER not concerning the order, be sure to write it on a separate sheet. Do not write it on your order sheet, though you may enclose it in the same envelope with your order. Our orders and letters are handled in separate and distinct departments, and we ask you, therefore, please do not fail to observe this rule.

ALWAYS TRY TO WRITE REMARKS CONCERNING YOUR ORDER on the same sheet with the order. This will prevent the possibility of such remarks or instructions being separated from the order. Should you have occasion to write us concerning an order which you have already sent us, do not fail to mention the date on which your letter was mailed, also state the nature and value of your remittance and the name and address as given in your order. This information will enable us to promptly locate the matter you refer to.

Every time you send us an order sign your name in the exact same way you signed it the first time you ordered. For instance, if you signed your first order "Thomas J. Brown," sign every other order you send "Thomas J. Brown," and not "T. J. Brown," "T. Brown" nor "Tom Brown." This is very important, as it enables us to promptly adjust complaints which may arise in connection with your order.

SHOULD YOU CHANGE YOUR ADDRESS, please notify us, being sure to give old as well as new address in full.

Paragraph D.
ABOUT OMISSIONS.

ALL ORDERS FOR MERCHANDISE are accepted by us with the understanding that we will use every reasonable effort to promptly ship every item exactly as ordered, and in order to make this possible we carry in stock, constantly, merchandise to the value of more than seven million dollars, and if we do not have the goods in stock we invariably buy them in Chicago if we can, even if we are compelled to pay more than we get for them, rather than delay an order or withhold shipment of any part of an order. But it sometimes happens that on an order including several items of merchandise there may be one or two items that are not in stock and cannot be had in Chicago, usually for the reason that the manufacturers are behind with their orders, have met with some accident, or there has been some unusual delay in transportation.

THEREFORE, WE ACCEPT ALL ORDERS with the understanding that we reserve the right, when unable to ship every item, to cancel that portion of the order which we cannot ship promptly, filling the balance of the order, and returning to the customer in cash the amount for the item or items canceled. We make this explanation so that anyone ordering merchandise from us, and receiving the goods with one or more items missing, and receiving by mail his money returned for the omitted items, will understand that the reason for omitting is that the goods are not in stock and cannot be had in Chicago at that time. Where an omission for the above reason is necessary we usually send a letter telling when we expect to have a stock of the missing goods, so that the customer may renew his order if he so desires.

UNDERSTAND, it seldom happens that we are unable to fill an order complete and exactly as given, but out of the many thousands of orders we receive every day, there are always a few (a very small number) on which items must be cancelled, and we make this explanation in our catalogue so that none of our customers need misunderstand our position.

Paragraph E.
ABOUT SUBSTITUTION.

WE ARE BITTERLY OPPOSED TO SUBSTITUTING one article for another unless instructed to do so by the customer. We believe, except in rare cases, it is very presuming on the part of any house receiving an order for one kind of goods to send another, without first having the written consent of the customer to do so. There are, however, exceptions where we take upon ourselves the responsibility of substituting, and with reference to this we make the following explanation:

IF A PARTY SENDS US AN ORDER and there is some article in that order which we have not in stock and cannot get in Chicago, but we have the same kind of an article in a higher grade, we then take the liberty of sending the higher grade at the price of the lower grade, sacrificing our profit rather than to disappoint the customer. A customer ordering a watch may call for a 7-jeweled Elgin or Waltham movement and we may not have one in stock, and there may not be one in the Chicago market, in which case we would consider ourselves justified in taking the liberty of substituting a higher grade in an 11 or 15-jeweled Elgin or Waltham movement, but always at the price of the cheaper

one ordered, taking the loss ourselves for the difference in price. This is an example. The same would apply on hundreds of items in our stock, but only in cases where in our judgment the customer can only be the better pleased by reason of such action on our part. However, even this kind of substitution we admit is presuming on our part, and when such substitution is made it must be understood it is done entirely at our risk, and with the understanding that if our action is not entirely satisfactory to the customer, he is at liberty to return the goods at our expense of transportation charges both ways and his money is to be immediately returned to him.

Paragraph F.
HOW TO SEND MONEY.

SEND US A POSTOFFICE MONEY ORDER, express money order, bank draft, cash or stamps. Should you send stamps, fold them in waxed paper. We receive many orders with stamps stuck together and worthless. We do not accept revenue stamps, foreign stamps and due stamps, as they are of no value to us. Do not send them.

IF YOU LIVE ON A RURAL ROUTE you can just give the letter and the money to the mail carrier and he will get the money order at the postoffice and mail it in the letter for you.

IF YOU HAVE A CHECKING ACCOUNT AT A BANK, you may send us your personal check if it is more convenient for you to do this, although we prefer to receive a postoffice money order, an express money order or a bank draft. Personal checks of course, are accepted subject to payment immediately upon presentation to the bank on which they are drawn.

POSTAGE STAMPS in amounts exceeding $1.00 will be accepted only at a discount of five per cent (5%), or ninety-five cents on the dollar. If you order an article priced at $2.00 and send stamps you should send $2.10. If a $3.00 article you should send $3.15, in stamps. We are compelled to dispose of all surplus stamps at a discount of from 2 per cent to 5 per cent and besides there is an extra expense in handling stamps, and our very small profit will not admit of this expense. We advise remitting by postoffice or express money order, but will accept postage stamps in any amount at 95 cents on the dollar. As an accommodation to our customers we will accept postage stamps at the face value in amounts less than $1.00.

WE RECOMMEND THE POSTOFFICE AND EXPRESS MONEY ORDER SYSTEMS, because they are inexpensive, of less trouble and safe. Besides this, if the money order should get lost or miscarry, your loss will be made good.

DO NOT, UNDER ANY CIRCUMSTANCES, send money or stamps in a letter except by registered mail. If sent by open mail (not registered) the letter may never reach us, and in such a case a great amount of trouble and inconvenience is caused, as well as the loss you sustain. If you prefer to remit by registered mail, we advise the use of two envelopes, one inside the other, and the outer one carefully and securely sealed. Do not send coin unless absolutely necessary, but if you do, be sure to wrap up the coin in paper and use two envelopes, one inside the other, so there is no danger of the coin wearing through and getting lost; and be sure to register the letter. Do not send gold or silver coin that is defaced, as light weight coins are worth no more than bullion, and bullion is less than the face value of the coin.

TO INSURE SAFETY always register a letter containing money. Be sure to state in your order plainly how much cash you enclose and in what form. You need not be afraid of sending too much, as we always refund when too much money is sent.

Paragraph G.
METHODS OF SHIPMENT.

We can ship goods by mail (see paragraph H about mail shipments), by express (see paragraph I about express shipments), by freight (see paragraph K about freight shipments). If left to our judgment we will ship goods in the manner which will be the least expensive to our customers. In all cases transportation charges are to be paid by the customer.

Paragraph H.
MAIL SHIPMENTS.

The mail service affords a convenient method for the transportation of merchandise of small weight and considerable value to points that are distant from express or railroad offices. On all orders to be shipped by mail we require the full amount of cash with the order, together with sufficient money extra to pay postage and insurance or registration, when same is desired. There are three methods of shipping goods by mail.

SECTION 1. OPEN MAIL, which is so called because only the regular amount of postage, according to the classification of goods, is paid and the customer must assume all risk. We do not recommend sending goods by open mail, for if the package is lost or stolen, neither we nor the customer have any recourse. In sending goods by open mail the customer must assume all risk.

SECTION 2. INSURED MAIL. This we consider the best, safest and cheapest method of shipping by mail. The following is the rate, in addition to the regular postage: For orders valued at $5.00 or under, 5 cents each. For orders valued at $10.00 or under, 10 cents each. For each additional $5.00 in value, 5 cents extra. In case of loss, we refill the order on receipt of statement certified to by your local postmaster that goods were not received. We advise insuring everything of value. Insurance is less than the cost of registering, because no matter how many packages the order consists of, our insurance charge would be only on the value of the order and not on the number of packages, as is the case when sent by registered mail. We guarantee for our charge the safe arrival of the entire order. If you want your mail package insured be sure to write "Insure" in your order, and in addition to your remittance for the order be sure to add enough money to pay postage and insurance fee. To secure adjustment it is necessary to make prompt notification of the failure to receive package.

SECTION 3. REGISTERED MAIL, so called because in such cases the postoffice authorities keep a record of the transaction and are thus enabled to trace your shipment. Registry fee per package is 8 cents in addition to the regular postage. We are not responsible for loss of registered mail.

A PACKAGE SHIPPED BY MAIL CANNOT EXCEED 4 POUNDS, but any number of packages may be sent at one time, each weighing four pounds or less. If you live at a great distance from the express office, it might be more convenient to send an order by mail in two or more packages, each weighing four pounds. One book can be sent by mail, no matter what its weight. The rate is ½ cent per ounce.

THE RATE ON MERCHANDISE BY MAIL IS 1 CENT PER OUNCE, on books and printed matter, ½ cent per ounce, and you should allow, in addition to the weight of an article, from one to five ounces for packing material, according to size of package shipped.

IF YOU ARE NOT SURE as to the weight of the article, be sure to enclose enough money for postage; if you send too much, we will refund balance.

EXPLOSIVES, POISONOUS OR INFLAMMABLE ARTICLES cannot be mailed under any circumstances whatever.

LIQUIDS OVER 4 OUNCES CANNOT BE SENT BY MAIL, but liquids weighing four ounces and under can be safely shipped by mail when packed in special mailing cases. Always allow five cents extra for this special case.

SECTION 4. PROFITABLE MAIL SHIPMENTS. ARTICLES SUCH AS WATCHES, JEWELRY and other valuable merchandise of light weight make profitable

mail shipments. In all cases where other goods are not ordered at the same time, we advise that such articles can be sent by mail economically.

CERTAIN MEDIUM PRICED GOODS, which, being weighty, cost considerable postage for transportation, should, if possible, be ordered in connection with other needed articles, sufficient to make up express or freight shipment, thus reducing the transportation charges to one-quarter or one-eighth of the postage rate and effecting a far greater saving for you.

WITH THE EXCEPTION OF ARTICLES OF SMALL WEIGHT and of some value, sending goods by mail is by far the most expensive means of transportation, but even in cases where the postage may seem out of proportion to the value of the goods, the cost of the goods with the postage added is usually less than if purchased at the local dealer's and frequently the article wanted is not handled by them at all, while our immense stock of merchandise will supply your demands.

Paragraph I.

EXPRESS SHIPMENTS.

HOW TO FIGURE EXPRESS CHARGES. See pages 13 to 17.

SHIPPING GOODS BY EXPRESS is an absolutely safe method of transportation and offers the advantages of quick service. It is the most profitable method of shipping goods when the weight is less than 20 pounds. Frequently a customer is in a hurry for certain goods and is willing to pay the extra cost of express charges over freight, the money we save him making it profitable on such shipments instead of buying the goods at home.

WHERE LIGHT AND EXPENSIVE ARTICLES, such as watches, jewelry and high priced revolvers are ordered shipped with a miscellaneous freight or express order, we make separate shipment of the expensive goods, sending them by sealed express for greater safety.

IF YOU HAVE NO AGENT at your station, all express shipments will be carried to the nearest town where there is an agent. If there is no agent at your station, always state in your order at what station you prefer to receive your goods.

A RECOMMENDATION THAT WILL SAVE YOU MONEY: If you live at a far distant point and wish to order some article of merchandise which would weigh about 20 pounds and amount to $6.00 or less, on which the express charges would be from $1.25 to $2.75, and you require nothing further from our catalogue at the time, show the book to your friends, let them add articles they may be in need of and the shipment can go by freight at about the same cost per 100 pounds as by express for 20 pounds, your proportion of the transportation charges being then about 60 cents. We frequently find it greatly to a customer's advantage to ship by freight instead of by express, and when we can save them money by changing the shipping directions we will often do so, unless the goods are wanted in great haste.

ALWAYS RESPOND PROMPTLY TO THE NOTIFICATION OF THE EXPRESS AGENT AS TO THE ARRIVAL OF MERCHANDISE. We are constantly in receipt of requests from them for disposition of packages by reason of the fact that consignee does not call promptly for his goods when notified by the agent that they have arrived.

WHEN YOU WRITE US CONCERNING AN EXPRESS SHIPMENT, please write your name and address very plainly and in INK.

Paragraph K.

FREIGHT SHIPMENTS.

FOR FREIGHT CLASSIFICATION and freight rates, see pages 13 to 17. Heavy, bulky merchandise, such as agricultural implements, household goods, furniture, groceries, hardware, etc., can be shipped most profitably by freight. When a shipment weighs 100 pounds or more, the railroad companies will charge only for the actual number of pounds.

WHERE LIGHT AND EXPENSIVE ARTICLES, such as watches, jewelry and high priced revolvers are ordered shipped with a miscellaneous freight or express order, we make separate shipment of the expensive goods, sending them by sealed express for greater safety.

HOW TO SAVE MONEY ON FREIGHT SHIPMENTS. Railroad companies usually charge no more for 100 pounds than they do for 20 pounds. While the extremely low prices at which we sell our merchandise would make even a small order by freight profitable, as you would certainly be getting the goods cheaper than you could possibly buy them through a dealer, at the same time it would be a considerable saving of money if you could make up a larger order, either of your own wants or club together with your neighbors, as the freight charges will amount to comparatively very little more. The saving that may be effected by anticipating your wants and sending one large order instead of five or six smaller orders at different times is quite an item, and therefore should be taken into consideration by our customers.

YOU MUST PAY THE FREIGHT OR EXPRESS CHARGES, but it will amount to very little as compared with what you will save in the price.

IF YOU HAVE NO AGENT AT YOUR SHIPPING POINT, freight charges must be prepaid. If you do not know what the freight charges will amount to, be sure and allow liberally for same. If you send more than actual amount required, we will immediately refund the difference. If you have an agent at your station, it is not necessary to prepay charges, as they are the same whether paid by you or by us, as our system of checking rates insures for our customers almost absolute correctness in transportation charges.

WHEN WE MAKE A SHIPMENT to a railroad station where there is no agent, we guarantee safe delivery to the station. From the fact that there is no agent at the station to receive the goods the railroad company will not assume any responsibility if, after they are put on the platform, they are lost or damaged, and we consequently cannot hold them for such loss or damage.

CUSTOMERS WHO ORDER GOODS shipped to a station where there is no agent must make careful arrangements for the care of the goods after they are put on the platform; otherwise, they are liable to be damaged or stolen. We would recommend that you have the goods shipped, if possible, to your nearest open station where there is an agent, thus making the railroad company entirely responsible for the goods until they are delivered to you.

OVERCHARGES IN TRANSPORTATION. Whenever a customer suspects an overcharge on the part of the transportation company, we will be pleased to give same our most prompt and careful attention in his behalf, if he will send us the expense bill received from the agent, after he has paid the charges. Complaints for overcharges are very few, as our system of checking the rates on freight and express shipments insures for our customers almost absolute correctness in transportation charges.

IF YOU HAVE REASON TO BELIEVE THAT AN ERROR HAS OCCURRED IN THE WEIGHTS, as shown in the freight expense bill, ask the agent to weigh the goods, and if it is found that the shipment is billed overweight he will correct the error and ask you to pay only for the correct weight.

WHEN YOU WRITE US CONCERNING A FREIGHT SHIPMENT, please write your name and address very plainly and in INK.

Paragraph L.

INFORMATION ABOUT GOODS SHIPPED DIRECT FROM THE FACTORY.

IN ORDER TO GIVE OUR CUSTOMERS THE VERY LOW PRICES WE DO, prices based on the actual cost to manufacture, cost of material and labor only, with but our one small percentage of profit added, prices much lower than they could possibly get elsewhere, we find it necessary to ship many heavy goods direct from the factory where they are made, and in doing this we save the freight on the goods into our warehouse in Chicago, the cartage, handling and other expenses incident to merchandise passing through the store in Chicago, and we give our customers every particle of the benefit of this saving in our extremely low prices. Wherever the catalogue states the goods are shipped from the factory, the prices quoted are for these goods delivered on board the cars at the factory and the customer pays the transportation charges from the factory. In many cases, the freight from the factory will be less than from Chicago, the factory being nearer to the purchaser. In some cases the factory will be at a greater distance than Chicago, in which case there will be an additional freight beyond the Chicago rate, but even in such cases the saving to you is very great, for if we were to ship the goods to you ourselves we would be compelled to add the freight to Chicago to all the goods, and to this add the expense of handling to and from the railroad, in and out of our store and other expenses incident to general handling of merchandise in the city.

IT SOMETIMES HAPPENS that a customer orders several articles in one order that are shipped from different factories. For instance, he may order a buggy, to be shipped from our factory in Southern Indiana; a stove, to be shipped from our foundry in Central Ohio; a windmill, that will be shipped from our factory in Northeastern Indiana. In this case we would be compelled to make three different shipments. The goods would go direct to our customer from the three different factories, but there would be no extra freight charge by reason of the three shipments, as each shipment would weigh more than 100 pounds and would therefore entitle the customer to the same freight per 100 pounds as if the shipments were all made together.

WHILE THE GREATER PART OF OUR GOODS ARE CARRIED IN STOCK IN OUR STORE AND WAREHOUSES IN CHICAGO, and this factory shipment information does not apply to small or general merchandise, we have found it necessary to make factory shipments on many heavy and bulky articles, purely in the interest of our customers, in order to give our customers the greatest possible value for their money, to enable us to deliver the goods to them at our one small percentage of profit direct from the manufacturer to the consumer, and your attention is called to the explanation that is always made in the catalogue regarding any article that is to be shipped from the factory, that you may understand that the freight is to be paid by the purchasers from the factory direct, and also that you may understand our reason for this method of handling certain merchandise.

WE FREQUENTLY RECEIVE ORDERS which include merchandise, a part of which is to be shipped direct from the factory and part direct from our store. For example: A man may order a buggy and a harness. The buggy will be shipped from the factory, the harness from the store. He may order a stove and some stove furniture, cooking utensils, etc. The stove will be shipped direct from the foundry and the cooking utensils from the store.

WHEN AN ORDER INCLUDES SUCH HEAVY GOODS as we ship direct from the factory (in order to make the low price), and other goods which we ship direct from our store, if that portion of the order which is to be shipped direct from our store is a profitable shipment (see paragraph M about unprofitable shipments), we make two shipments; the stove, buggy or other heavy shipment going direct from the factory, the balance from our store. But it sometimes happens that that portion of the order to be shipped from our store would not be a profitable shipment. It may be for a few a cooking utensils, amounting to $1.00 or $2.00, or a very low priced harness of $5.00 or $6.00, or $1.00 or $2.00 worth of miscellaneous merchandise, on which the freight charges would amount to more than the saving, or difference between our price and the price at which the customer could buy in his own town. In such cases of unprofitable shipment we use our very best judgment, and where we deem that portion of the order that is to go from our house an unprofitable shipment, we cancel that portion of the order and return the amount to our customer in cash for the goods cancelled.

AS A FURTHER EXAMPLE: The customer may order a parlor suite for $15.00 to $20.00, which we ship from the factory, and may include with his order one chair for 90 cents, which we ship from the house. This one chair (except to nearby points), would be considered an unprofitable shipment. On such an order we would take the liberty of cancelling the order for the chair, returning the 90 cents to the customer at once, and we would ship the parlor suite to him direct from the factory by freight, with a letter of full explanation for our action. This article is intended to explain our methods of treating special orders only in the interest of the customers.

Paragraph M.

ABOUT UNPROFITABLE SHIPMENTS.

WE FREQUENTLY RECEIVE ORDERS which we term "unprofitable" shipments, which means that the shipment would not be profitable to the customer. For example: A party living far distant may order a dollar's worth of heavy goods to go by express. The express charges would equal the cost of the goods. We occasionally get an order for heavy hardware, the order amounting to perhaps less than $5.00. The goods weigh 100 pounds. We are asked to ship them by express. This is usually an "unprofitable" shipment. An order for a single pair of heavy cheap boots to go a great distance by express, or for very bulky woodenware or heavy and low priced merchandise, such as molasses, nails or cornmeal, might be what we term an "unprofitable" shipment for far distant points.

WE WOULD ADVISE OUR CUSTOMERS to study the freight and express rates, as given on the following pages, for we do not wish you to send us a dollar for anything unless we can save you money on the purchase.

ORDERS THAT WOULD BE UNPROFITABLE to ship by mail or express may be very profitable when sent by freight, but as 100 pounds is usually carried by freight for the same charge as ten pounds, by adding other merchandise to your order, either for yourself or by getting your neighbors to join you in making up a large order, **you can make the shipment very profitable. Read paragraph K before making up your order.**

Paragraph N.

CLUB ORDERS.

TO EQUALIZE OR REDUCE THE COST OF TRANSPORTATION, we advise the sending of club orders. Anyone can get up a club. Simply have your neighbors or friends send their orders in with yours and advise us to ship all to one person by freight. If each customer writes his order under his own name, it will be a very easy matter for us to keep each one's goods separate, and the freight charges will be next to nothing when shared by several persons.

IF YOU LIVE AT A FAR DISTANT POINT and wish to order some article or articles of merchandise which, together, would weigh about twenty pounds, the value of which may be $5.00 or less, and you find that the express charges will be from $1.25 to $2.75, and there is nothing further in our catalogue that you require at the time, show this catalogue to your friends. Let your friends add twenty, thirty or forty pounds, even fifty or seventy-five pounds of goods, then the goods can go by freight and the one hundred pounds by freight will cost no more than twenty pounds by express.

Paragraph O.

HOW TO RETURN GOODS.

BEFORE RETURNING THE GOODS to us in any manner, we would ask that you communicate with us in regard to them, as we are frequently able to adjust matters in a manner that will avoid the delay occasioned by return of goods.

EVERY ARTICLE IS SOLD BY US with the understanding and agreement that if you are not perfectly satisfied with the goods, if there is the slightest dissatisfaction by reason of quality, size, style, color or any other reason, and you wish to return the goods to us and have us return your money, or you wish to make an exchange for different size, style, color or different goods, you are at liberty to return the goods to us at our expense, and we will return your money or make such exchange as you may direct; but in returning goods to us for any reason the following rules must be observed:

INVOICE NUMBER. Be sure to mention the invoice number under which the goods were shipped to you.

BE SURE TO ENCLOSE WITH YOUR LETTER, all the sheets of our bill as well as any other papers you receive from us relating to the transaction.

ADDRESSING. When returning any goods to us, either by mail, express or freight, you must write **your name and address** on the outside of the box, package or tag, as plainly as you write ours, and use **ink.** Write the invoice number also.

DO NOT UNDER ANY CIRCUMSTANCES fail to write your name and address and invoice number plainly and distinctly on the outside of the package or wrapping of the goods that you are returning. This is absolutely necessary in order that we may know by whom the goods are returned.

WHEN YOU RETURN GOODS BY EXPRESS OR FREIGHT.

NEVER RETURN GOODS BY EXPRESS, if the package weighs more than 25 pounds, as it is cheaper to ship by freight.

WHEN RETURNING GOODS BY EXPRESS OR FREIGHT, BE SURE TO WRITE A LETTER telling us whether you want to **exchange** for other goods, or whether you want us to **refund your money,** and pack this letter together with the bill of your goods in the box. **Be sure** that your letter of instructions is complete, and that you mention **invoice number, catalogue number of the goods, color, size, etc.** Enclose your letter, bill and all other communications that you may have received from us in an envelope, and when the goods are packed, place this envelope containing these communications on top of the goods before enclosing them in the wrapper.

DO NOT SEND THEM SEPARATELY BY MAIL.

IF YOU SEND ADDITIONAL MONEY, send it by mail in a letter by itself and say in the letter which you pack in your goods, that you have sent another letter by mail, containing the necessary amount of money to complete payment for the goods you wish.

WHEN YOU RETURN GOODS BY MAIL, write **your** name and address as well as ours **plainly** and in **ink,** on the outside of the package, also the **invoice number,** but do not enclose your letter in the package. Send your letter of instructions, with the bill and any other papers referring to the transaction, separately by mail.

DO NOT SEAL A MAIL PACKAGE, but wrap it up in such a manner that the postmaster can open it and examine it without destroying the wrapper.

DO NOT FAIL TO REGISTER MAIL PACKAGES WORTH $2.00 or more. A package can be registered for 8 cents, and if it does not reach us on time it can be traced.

ABOUT FACTORY SHIPMENTS—SPECIAL NOTICE.

BEFORE YOU RETURN ANY ARTICLE shipped from one of our factories, **PLEASE WRITE US BEFORE YOU RETURN IT** so we can advise you how and where to ship it.

THINGS TO REMEMBER.

In order that your wishes may always have **prompt attention,** remember the following things:

YOUR NAME AND ADDRESS AND INVOICE NUMBER MUST ALWAYS BE ON OUTSIDE OF THE PACKAGE.

DO NOT ENCLOSE MONEY WITH GOODS.

IF YOU RETURN GOODS BY FREIGHT OR EXPRESS, PACK YOUR LETTER WITH THE GOODS.

IF YOU RETURN GOODS BY MAIL, SEND YOUR LETTER SEPARATELY.

ALWAYS INCLUDE WITH YOUR LETTER THE BILL FOR THE GOODS.

Paragraph P.

ABOUT DELAYED SHIPMENTS.

IF YOU HAVE SENT US AN ORDER FOR GOODS and you think it is time they should have arrived, before writing us concerning the delay, please consider the following:

WHILE WE ARE WILLING AND GLAD to answer all kinds of inquiries, to make every possible kind of research, to quickly look up and trace any shipment said to have been delayed, we are daily in receipt of hundreds of letters claiming that goods have been delayed when the orders have been filled by us with all possible promptness and have been handled by the railroad or express companies with their usual dispatch. The investigation simply shows the customer is impatient and has not allowed sufficient time for the order to reach us, for us to fill the order and the railroad or express company to deliver the goods.

WE FILL ALL ORDERS with the greatest possible dispatch consistent with proper care and safety. It requires from two to six days after your order is received for us to ship goods. Where goods are ordered that have to be made to order or finished after received, such as tailoring, upholstered furniture, vehicles, etc., additional time must be allowed. Goods shipped direct from our factory, such as stoves, sewing machines, furniture and a few other heavy items, require from five to ten days to make shipment; add to this the necessary time for the express company or railroad company to carry the goods to you and you will seldom, if ever, be disappointed in the arrival of your goods.

BEFORE WRITING US concerning goods ordered or before calling for them at your railroad station, first consider if you have allowed ample time for your order to reach Chicago, the required time for us to fill same, as above stated, and for the railroad or express company to carry it to you. If you will always do this, allowing liberal time, bearing in mind that express and railroad companies sometimes delay goods a few days after they receive them, you will seldom, if ever, have occasion to write us concerning a delay. If there is more than one freight or express agent in your town, always make inquiries at each office before writing us concerning non-arrival of goods, as it often happens that a shipment is at one office and the notification card has miscarried, while the customer has been making inquiries at another office.

IN CASE, HOWEVER, an order should be delayed beyond the time above referred to, and you write us, do not fail to mention the date on which you mailed your order, the name and address as given in the original order, the value and nature of the cash you sent, and, if possible, give us your invoice number, for if you received from us a postal card acknowledging the receipt of the order, you will find the invoice number on the card mailed you.

ABOUT MISTAKES. If we make a mistake in filling your order, kindly give us a chance to correct it. We try to fill every order absolutely correct, but errors sometimes creep in. They do in all business houses. You will always find us willing to correct ours. Do not fail to write us in case of an error; otherwise we may never know of it.

CHANGE OF ADDRESS. We would kindly request our customers to **immediately advise** us concerning any **change of address,** as we keep our records according to states and towns, and should you order from one town and then write from another, we would be compelled to send for further information before we could adjust the matter in question.

Paragraph Q.

ABOUT UNNECESSARY CORRESPONDENCE.

WHILE WE EMPLOY OVER ONE HUNDRED STENOGRAPHERS for the accommodation of our customers, and are willing and glad to answer all letters and furnish any special information that may be desired, we daily receive hundreds of letters of inquiry about things that are plainly answered in this catalogue, hundreds of letters which might be avoided, saving loss of time and unnecessary expense.

IT IS VERY SELDOM NECESSARY TO WRITE US, asking what the freight or express charge will be on any article to any point, for, from the weights given under each description and from the express and freight rates shown on pages 13 to 17, you can calculate very closely what the freight or express will amount to and save the time and trouble of writing for this information.

OUR OLD CUSTOMERS rarely ever have occasion to write us, asking what the freight or express will be on any article, and new customers will hardly ever have occasion to if they will refer to pages 13 to 17.

LETTERS CONCERNING SHIPMENTS CAN OFTEN BE AVOIDED. We receive hundreds of letters every day from parties who have ordered and have not allowed sufficient time for the order to reach us, the goods to be packed and shipped and for the goods to reach them. **(See paragraph P.) Never write about a shipment until ample time has been allowed for the goods to reach you.** We receive hundreds of letters asking for prices or special prices on articles on which the price is plainly printed in this catalogue. All such letters are unnecessary, for it only means an answer again, referring you to the catalogue.

WE RECEIVE HUNDREDS OF LETTERS DAILY from people who ask us if we can't make changes in the goods as advertised, that they want the same thing or things with slight changes. This is all irregular and could not be furnished excepting at an advanced price, and we have often found it impracticable to make any such changes, and to all such inquiries we can save you the time and trouble by saying that no changes can be made from those made plain in this catalogue. Since we answer as many as ten thousand letters a day, you will help us where a reply is necessary by answering on the back of our letter.

Paragraph R.

INSTALLMENT PLAN OR PARTIAL PAYMENT.

WE RECEIVE HUNDREDS OF LETTERS asking for prices on certain goods, especially on organs, pianos and other goods that run into money, from parties who wish to buy on the installment plan and to make settlement in notes. All these inquiries can be avoided for the reason that our only terms are cash, we never extend time, we open no accounts nor allow goods to be sold on the installment plan.

THE INSTALLMENT PLAN OR PARTIAL PAYMENT METHOD OF PURCHASING MERCHANDISE is the most costly any purchaser can adopt. The price you pay when you buy goods on time is always from 25 to 50 per cent **higher than it would be if you paid cash,** and whether you buy from us at our low prices for cash, or from some other house, our advice to you is: Do not buy on the partial payment or installment plan under any circumstances. Every dealer who sells on time, who accepts partial payments, must suffer large losses and every customer of his who does meet his payments promptly must make up for these large losses. It will pay you to borrow the money from your bank or from some other source and then pay cash, as the saving, especially if you purchase from us at our astonishingly low prices, will pay several times the interest on the borrowed money. When you buy merchandise from us for cash, you pay only the mere cost of materials and labor, with one small percentage of profit added; not one penny do you pay for bad debts; not one cent for bookkeeping and not one cent of extra profit to jobbers, wholesalers or other middlemen. You cannot afford to buy on time, at high prices, when we can sell you better merchandise at prices about one-half the prices asked by dealers who sell goods on the installment plan.

Paragraph S.

ABOUT CLAIMS FOR DAMAGE AND OVERCHARGE ON TRANSPORTATION.

WE CAREFULLY PACK AND DELIVER ALL OUR GOODS in good condition on board the cars, either in Chicago or at the factory, as made plain in this catalogue. We accept a receipt from the railroad company for the goods in good order, and it very rarely happens that any goods that we pack and ship reach their destination in bad order.

IF IT SHOULD EVER HAPPEN that any article reaches you marred, scratched, broken or in any way defective, be sure to have the railroad agent make a notation of such defect on the freight receipt (expense bill) he gives you. You can then present your claim for damage to the railroad agent from whom you received the goods, it being his duty at that end to take the matter up with the officials of that road and collect for you any damages that may have occurred.

WHILE THE PROPER PLACE FOR TAKING UP ANY CLAIMS FOR DAMAGE OR OVERCHARGE ON TRANSPORTATION on goods in transit, either by freight or express, is through the agent who delivers the goods, the trouble, delay and expense of writing us to do this can also be avoided. We, however, guarantee the goods we ship to reach you in the same perfect condition they leave us, and to be satisfactory to you in every way, and if you find them damaged in transit and you accept them and the agent hesitates to take and collect your claim for damage, you can write us, enclosing your receipt (expense bill) for the freight charges paid the agent, with the agent's written notation on the expense bill, stating what the damage is, and we will take the matter up at this end, collect the damage and send the money to you. **If you can discover at the station before taking the goods that there is any damage or anything missing you must be sure to have the agent write the facts across the expense bill, which he gives you when you pay the freight. Unless we have these facts written across the expense bill, we cannot make claim against the railroad company for the damage or shortage; so be sure to have him write the facts on the expense bill.**

WHILE WE HAVE A LARGE CORPS OF STENOGRAPHERS and corresponding clerks in our employ, whose duty it is to promptly and courteously answer all inquiries and give all desired information, in order to maintain our extremely low prices the cost of conducting our business must be cut down to the very mimimum, and to do this our customers are especially requested before writing us concerning freight rates, claims, delays, or before asking us for information of any kind to carefully consult this catalogue, and if they will do this they will find in nine cases out of ten the information can be had or the adjustment of damage made without going to the trouble of writing us or putting us to the expense of corresponding on the subject.

ON THE BASIS OF BETTER VALUE THAN YOU CAN POSSIBLY GET ELSEWHERE, the best possible service, every item you order guaranteed to reach you in perfect condition and to prove perfectly satisfactory or your money to be immediately returned to you; under our binding guarantee to please you in every way in your dealings with us, we respectfully solicit your orders.

FREIGHT AND EXPRESS RATES.

THE FOLLOWING TABLE IS TO VARIOUS POINTS IN EVERY STATE AND TERRITORY . . . . .

IT IS NOT NECESSARY to write us for freight and express rates, as the following tables and the instructions we herewith give will show just what the freight and express rates are to different points in the United States. Take the nearest town to your own in the table below, and the freight rate to your town will be almost, if not exactly, the same for 100 pounds.

YOU MUST PAY THE FREIGHT OR EXPRESS CHARGES AT THE TIME YOU GET THE GOODS FROM THE STATION.

Don't be afraid of the freight or express charges; they never amount to much compared with what we can save you in cost. In fact, we guarantee that you will save money on every purchase after you pay the freight or express charges and if you do not find it so, YOU CAN RETURN THE GOODS AND WE WILL REFUND ALL YOUR MONEY AND YOU WILL NOT BE OUT ONE CENT.

NO MATTER HOW FAR AWAY you may live, we can still save you money on your purchases. **DISTANCE IS NO DRAWBACK.** Remember, your local dealer must pay the exact same rate of freight that you pay on the goods, and this cost of freight he must add to the cost of the goods when he figures his selling price. But our prices on practically everything are so very much lower than the same quality of goods can be had from smaller concerns that, after you pay all transportation charges, even to very distant points, we can save you money.

HOW TO FIGURE FREIGHT CHARGES.

SEE PAGE 17 for list of articles and their class, then find the weight of the desired article (which we aim to give underneath its description in this catalogue), and if not given you can estimate the weight very closely. Find the rate in following table under its class, and multiply the rate by the weight, and you have the freight charges sufficiently correct for your information.

THE RAILROADS have what is called a **MINIMUM FREIGHT CHARGE,** meaning the least amount of money they will haul a freight shipment for, no matter how little it weighs. **In the first column we quote the minimum freight charge or explain how it is made up.**

Rule 1. THE MINIMUM CHARGE is for 100 pounds at the class to which the article belongs, but not less than 50 cents.

Rule 2. THE MINIMUM CHARGE is for 100 pounds at the class to which the article belongs.

Rule 3. THE MINIMUM CHARGE is for 100 pounds at the class to which the article belongs, but not less than 75 cents.

Rule 4. THE MINIMUM CHARGE is the class rate to El Paso, Texas, plus 50 cents.

EXPRESS CHARGES.

In the following table are given the express rates for 100 pounds, but for shipments weighing less than that see page 16. Freight is the cheapest way to ship orders weighing 20 pounds or more. Make your order for 100 pounds, if possible, and get the benefit of the minimum charge, as shipments weighing from 20 to 100 pounds usually cost no more than 20 pounds. Where two express rates are shown, add them together to figure the charges on packages weighing 7 pounds or under. For packages weighing more than 7 pounds, figure the charges at each rate separately, and then add these amounts for the total.

	Min. freight charge	1st class freight per 100 lbs	2d class freight per 100 lbs	3rd class freight per 100 lbs	4th class freight per 100 lbs	5th class freight per 100 lbs	6th class freight per 100 lbs	Express per 100 lbs
ALABAMA—								
Birmingham	Rule 1	$1 14	$0 99	$0 80	$0 62	$0 53	$0 40	$ 3 75
Brewton	Rule 2	1 48	1 22	1 00	82	75		4 00
Dadeville	Rule 3	1 73	1 48	1 20	97	82	63	4 50
Decatur	Rule 1	1 14	99	80	62	53	40	3 25
Gadsden	Rule 2	1 33	1 17	1 00	78	65	51	3 75
Mobile	$1 10	1 10	90	75	58	47	41	4 00
Montgomery	Rule 2	1 33	1 17	1 00	78	65	51	3 75
Ozark	Rule 2	1 71	1 46	1 24	1 02	86		4 75
Randolph, Bibb Co	Rule 3	1 27	1 11	98	83	73	52	4 00
Tuscaloosa	Rule 2	1 43	1 24	1 01	79	68	52	3 75
ARIZONA—								
Benson	Rule 4	3 51	3 09	2 70	2 10	......	......	10 75
Flagstaff	$1 97	3 90	3 40	2 70	2 10	......	......	10 50
Holbrook	1 97	3 74	3 39	2 70	2 10	......	......	10 25
Phœnix	Rule 4	3 79	3 33	2 90	2 30	......	......	12 25
Prescott	Rule 4	3 79	3 33	2 90	2 30	......	......	11 50
Seligman	$1 97	3 90	3 40	2 70	2 10	......	......	10 75
Solomonsville	Rule 4	3 39	3 13	2 82	2 33	......	......	10 25
Tucson	Rule 4	3 59	3 13	2 70	2 10	......	......	11 00
Yucca	$1 97	3 90	3 40	2 70	2 10	......	......	11 00
ARKANSAS—								
Daleville	Rule 2	1 12	1 01	80	60	......	......	3 75
Fort Smith	Rule 2	1 30	1 11	87	65	......	......	3 75
Fayetteville	Rule 2	1 40	1 19	98	72	......	......	3 75
Knobel	Rule 2	95	84	68	53	......	......	2 75
Little Rock	Rule 2	1 20	1 01	77	55	......	......	3 50
Morrillton	Rule 2	1 12	1 01	79	60	......	......	3 75
Newport, Jackson Co	Rule 2	1 00	83	67	55	......	......	3 00
Pine Bluff	Rule 2	1 20	1 01	77	55	......	......	3 50
Texarkana	Rule 2	1 37	1 23	1 08	94	......	......	4 00
Van Buren	Rule 2	1 30	1 11	87	65	......	......	4 00
CALIFORNIA—								
Bakerfield	......	3 71	3 28	2 84	2 51	......	......	11 50
Fresno	......	3 50	3 08	2 65	2 32	......	......	11 50
Los Angeles	$2 60	3 00	2 60	2 20	1 90	......	......	11 50
Needles	......	3 90	3 40	2 70	2 10	......	......	11 50
Redding	......	3 61	3 16	2 70	2 32	......	......	12 50
Sacramento	2 60	3 00	2 60	2 20	1 90	......	......	11 50
San Bernardino	......	3 34	2 90	2 46	2 13	......	......	11 50
San Diego	2 60	3 00	2 60	2 20	1 90	......	......	11 50
San Francisco	2 60	3 00	2 60	2 20	1 90	......	......	11 50
Santa Cruz	......	3 21	2 79	2 37	2 05	......	......	12 25
Termo	......	5 20	4 57	3 74	3 01	......	......	13 25
COLORADO—								
Alamosa	1 48	2 89	2 38	1 88	1 49	......	......	$6 00- 2 00
Cripple Creek	1 36	2 70	2 26	1 83	1 52	......	......	7 50
Denver	75	2 05	1 65	1 25	97	......	......	6 00
Eagle	1 95	3 35	2 85	2 19	1 67	......	......	6 00- 2 75
Grand Junction	2 05	3 50	2 95	2 35	1 72	......	......	8 00
Greeley	75	2 05	1 65	1 25	97	......	......	6 00
Gunnison	1 70	3 15	2 60	2 08	1 67	......	......	8 00
Kit Carson	75	1 99	1 65	1 25	97	......	......	5 50
La Junta	75	2 05	1 65	1 25	97	......	......	6 00
Mancos	2 45	3 95	3 35	2 70	2 05	......	......	6 00- 4 00
Montrose	2 60	3 45	2 90	2 30	1 72	......	......	6 00- 3 00
Pagosa Springs	2 15	3 65	3 15	2 40	1 87	......	......	6 00- 3 50
Pueblo	75	2 05	1 65	1 25	97	......	......	6 00
Sterling	75	1 81	1 58	1 25	97	......	......	5 50
Thatcher	75	2 05	1 65	1 25	97	......	......	6 00
CONNECTICUT—								
Bridgeport	82	82	71	55	39	33	......	3 00
Canaan	82	82	71	55	39	33	......	3 00
Hartford	82	82	71	55	39	33	......	3 00
New Haven	82	82	71	55	39	33	......	3 00
New London	82	82	71	55	39	33	......	3 00
New Milford	82	82	71	55	39	33	......	3 00
Putnam	82	82	71	55	39	33	......	3 00
DELAWARE—								
Dover	75	75	65	50	35	30	......	2 75
Farmington	75	75	65	50	35	30	......	2 75
Middletown	75	75	65	50	35	30	......	2 54
Newark	73	73	63	48	33	28	......	2 25
DIST. OF COLUMBIA—								
Langdon	72	72	62	47	32	27	......	2 25
Washington	72	72	62	47	32	27	......	2 25
FLORIDA—								
Carrabelle	Rule 3	1 93	1 62	1 33	1 08	91	76	5 75
Caryville	Rule 2	1 60	1 32	1 01	89	82	75	4 50
Gainesville	Rule 2	1 78	1 56	1 38	1 19	1 01	80	5 50
Jacksonville	Rule 2	1 30	1 10	97	85	71	56	5 00
Key West	Rule 2	1 38	1 63	1 45	1 21	1 01	84	6 00- 1 00
Pensacola	$1 10	1 10	90	75	58	47	41	4 25
Punta Gorda	Rule 2	2 19	1 89	1 69	1 50	1 26	1 07	6 50
Sebastian	Rule 2	2 24	1 94	1 65	1 47	1 26	1 06	6 50
Tallahassee	Rule 2	1 82	1 56	1 32	1 08	91	74	5 25
Tampa (all rail)	Rule 2	1 80	1 53	1 31	1 17	99	83	6 00
Tampa (rail and water; via Mobile)	$1 35	1 47	1 34	1 03	93	78	63	....
GEORGIA—								
Albany	Rule 2	1 58	1 37	1 18	98	78	62	4 75
Atlanta	Rule 2	1 33	1 17	1 00	78	65	51	3 75
Brunswick	Rule 2	1 30	1 10	97	85	71	56	4 50
Cairo	Rule 2	1 86	1 54	1 19	1 07	96	86	5 25

	Min. freight charge	1st class freight per 100 lbs	2d class freight per 100 lbs	3d class freight per 100 lbs	4th class freight per 100 lbs	5th class freight per 100 lbs	6th class freight per 100 lbs	Express per 100 lbs.
GEORGIA—Continued.								
Columbus	Rule 2	$1 38	$1 20	$1 03	$0 80	$0 67	$0 53	$4 50
Doerun	Rule 2	1 91	1 67	1 45	1 17	98	79	5 25
Folkston	Rule 2	1 69	1 45	1 29	1 14	94	74	5 25
Macon	Rule 2	1 38	1 20	1 03	80	67	53	4 25
Quitman	Rule 3	1 78	1 54	1 32	1 05	87	69	5 25
Rome	Rule 2	1 33	1 17	1 00	78	65	51	3 75
Savannah	Rule 2	1 30	1 10	97	85	71	56	5 00
Stillmore	Rule 2	1 85	1 59	1 40	1 20	98	78	5 00
Thomasville	Rule 3	1 78	1 54	1 32	1 05	87	69	5 00
Valdosta	Rule 3	1 78	1 54	1 32	1 05	87	69	5 50
Warrenton	Rule 2	1 68	1 47	1 28	1 01	83	66	4 50
IDAHO—								
American Falls	$2 15	3 05	2 55	2 10	1 72	......	......	8 75
Boise City	2 40	3 30	2 80	2 45	2 02	......	......	10 00
Gem	......	3 60	3 10	2 60	2 10	......	......	10 00
Idaho Falls	2 08	2 85	2 40	1 98	1 60	......	......	8 00
Ketchum	2 40	3 30	2 80	2 45	2 02	......	......	10 00
Moscow	......	3 60	3 10	2 60	2 10	......	......	10 00
Mountain Home	2 40	3 30	2 80	2 45	2 02	......	......	10 00
Pocatello	2 08	2 85	2 40	1 98	1 60	......	......	8 00
Spencer	2 15	2 85	2 40	1 98	1 60	......	......	8 00
ILLINOIS—								
Baldwin	50	70	54	40	32	26	......	2 00
Belvidere	25	28	23	17	11	11	......	75
Cairo	25	47	38	31	24	19	......	1 75
Danville	25	30	25	20	14	13	......	1 00
Freeport	25	31	25	20	15	12	......	1 00
Joliet	25	21	17	14	11	8	......	50
Litchfield	25	41	33	26	21	17	......	1 25
Milan, Rock Island Co	25	38	30	23	19	15	......	1 25
Mt. Vernon	25	50	40	30	25	20	......	1 50
Peoria	25	37	29	22	18	15	......	1 00
Quincy	25	42	35	27	22	17	......	1 25
Springfield	25	38	31	24	19	15	......	1 00
INDIANA—								
Bedford	37	37	32	24	16	14	......	1 25
Connersville	39	39	33	25	17	14	......	1 50
Elkhart	25	25	22	20	13	09	......	75
Evansville	40	40	34	25	17	15	......	1 75
Ft. Wayne	29	29	25	20	14	11	......	75
Goshen	25	25	22	20	13	09	......	75
Indianapolis	32	32	27	22	14	12	......	1 25
Lafayette	30	30	25	20	13	10	......	90
New Albany	40	40	34	25	17	15	......	1 50
Terre Haute	32	32	27	22	14	12	......	1 25
IOWA—								
Alta	......	80	65	45	32	......	......	2 00
Audubon	......	80	65	45	32	......	......	2 00
Bedford	......	80	65	45	32	......	......	2 00
Bode	......	74	56	43	31	......	......	1 75
Burlington	......	40	32	25	20	......	......	1 25
Carroll	......	79	64	44	31	......	......	2 00
Cedar Rapids	......	58	47	35	24	......	......	1 50
Centerville	......	68	53	40	29	......	......	1 75
Council Bluffs	......	80	65	45	32	......	......	2 00
Davenport	......	38	30	23	19	......	......	1 25
Des Moines	......	68	57	40	29	......	......	1 75
Hamburg	......	80	65	45	32	......	......	2 00
Ireton	......	83	67	46	33	......	......	2 40
Keokuk	......	42	34	26	21	......	......	1 25
Mason City	......	63	53	42	26	......	......	1 75
Muscatine	......	39	31	24	19	......	......	1 25
Ottumwa	......	61	50	36	26	......	......	1 75
Waterloo	......	60	50	40	25	......	......	1 75
Waukon	......	60	50	40	25	......	......	1 50
KANSAS—								
Atchison	......	80	65	45	32	......	......	2 00
Council Grove	......	1 29	1 05	80	59	......	......	3 25
Dodge City	......	1 67	1 43	1 16	92	......	......	4 50
Ft. Scott	......	94	81	55	37	......	......	2 75
Garnett	......	1 05	86	65	45	......	......	3 00
Great Bend	......	1 52	1 27	99	80	......	......	4 00
Hartland	......	1 74	1 49	1 20	97	......	......	5 00
Leavenworth	......	80	65	45	32	......	......	2 00
Leoti	......	1 71	1 48	1 19	97	......	......	4 75
Mankato	......	1 34	1 13	86	65	......	......	3 50
Meade	......	1 60	1 38	1 15	93	......	......	4 25
Norton	......	1 52	1 34	1 07	85	......	......	4 00
Sawyer	......	1 57	1 34	1 05	85	......	......	4 25
Topeka	......	1 09	89	64	47	......	......	2 75
Vesper	......	1 41	1 19	91	73	......	......	3 75
Wichita	......	1 40	1 18	91	69	......	......	3 75
KENTUCKY—								
Alexander, Fulton Co.	Rule 1	80	66	53	43	34	29	2 10
Ashland	$0 45	45	39	30	21	18	15	2 00
Burnside	Rule 1	90	76	65	47	42	36	2 75
Campbellsville	Rule 1	97	83	69	56	49	44	2 25
Frankfort	Rule 1	66	57	45	34	31	27	2 00
Henderson (Eastern Class.)	$0 48	48	41	30	22	18	......	2 00
Hickman	60	60	50	40	33	27	24	2 75
Louisville (East'n Class.)	41	41	35	26	18	16	......	1 50

	Min. freight charge	1st class freight per 100 lbs	2d class freight per 100 lbs	3d class freight per 100 lbs	4th class freight per 100 lbs	5th class freight per 100 lbs	6th class freight per 100 lbs	Express per 100 lbs.
KENTUCKY—Continued.								
Maysville (East'n Class.)	$0 44	$0 44	$0 37	$0 29	$0 20	$0 17	....	$2 00
Owensboro (East'n Class.)	48	48	41	30	22	18	....	2 00
Paducah	50	50	42	35	27	22	$0 20	1 75
Paris	Rule 1	63	55	43	30	27	23	2 00
***LOUISIANA—**								
Alexandria	Rule 2	1 37	1 17	99	84	....	....	4 75
Baton Rouge	$1 10	1 10	90	75	58	47	41	3 75
Crowley	Rule 2	1 43	1 22	98	82	....	....	5 00
Kentwood	Rule 2	1 39	1 13	95	78	65	57	3 75
Lake Charles	Rule 2	1 50	1 25	1 02	85	....	....	4 75
Many	Rule 2	1 50	1 29	1 09	1 00	....	....	5 00
Monroe	Rule 2	1 37	1 17	99	84	....	....	4 00
Morgan City	Rule 2	1 29	1 11	•89	75	....	....	4 50
Moreauville	Rule 2	1 57	1 37	1 16	1 06	....	....	5 25
New Orleans	$1 10	1 10	90	75	58	47	41	3 75
Ponchatoula	Rule 2	1 40	1 13	95	78	65	57	3 75
Shreveport	Rule 2	1 37	1 17	99	84	....	....	4 25
MAINE—								
Augusta	$1 07	94	91	64	45	33	....	3 00
Alfred	82	82	71	55	39	33	....	2 90
Bangor	1 07	98	85	65	47	40	....	3 25
Brownville Junction	82	82	71	55	39	33	....	3 75
Caribou	1 58	1 58	1 27	99	82	55	....	4 35
Eastport	1 07	1 07	91	72	51	43	....	4 00
Kennebunk	82	82	71	55	39	33	....	2 75
Lowelltown	82	82	71	55	39	33	....	$3 15- 60
Ludlow	1 32	1 32	1 10	86	69	50	....	4 00
Portland and Lewiston	82	82	71	55	39	33	....	3 00
Rockland	82	82	71	55	39	33	....	3 25
MARYLAND—								
Annapolis	80	80	70	53	38	32	....	2 50
Baltimore	72	72	62	47	32	27	....	2 25
Brandywine	75	75	65	49	34	29	....	2 50
Elkton	73	73	63	48	33	28	....	2 25
Finksburg	72	72	62	47	32	27	....	2 25
Frederick	72	72	62	47	32	27	....	2 25
Germantown	72	72	62	47	32	27	....	2 25
Hagerstown	72	72	62	47	32	27	....	2 25
Port Tobacco	75	75	65	49	34	29	....	2 25
MASSACHUSETTS—								
Ashley Falls	82	82	71	55	39	33	....	3 00
Barnstable	82	82	71	55	39	33	....	2 50- 75
Bellingham Jct	82	82	71	55	39	33	....	2 90
Boston	82	82	71	55	39	33	....	2 50
Graniteville	82	82	71	55	39	33	....	2 50
Hinsdale	82	82	71	55	39	33	....	2 50
Jefferson	82	82	71	55	39	33	....	2 75
Lakeville	82	82	71	55	39	33	....	2 30- 60
New Bedford	82	82	71	55	39	33	....	3 00
Provincetown	82	82	71	55	39	33	....	2 50- 75
Springfield	82	82	71	55	39	33	....	2 50
Templeton	82	82	71	55	39	33	....	2 75
***MICHIGAN—**								
Adrian	35	35	30	23	15	13	....	1 25
Alba	53	53	45	34	26	20	....	2 00
Alpena	53	53	45	34	26	20	....	2 40
Bay City	37	37	32	24	16	13	....	1 75
Boyne Falls	53	53	45	34	26	20	....	2 00
Cheboygan	55	55	45	35	26	20	....	2 50
Detroit	37	37	32	24	16	13	....	1 25
Emmett	37	37	32	24	16	13	....	1 50
Grand Rapids	33	33	29	22	15	12	....	1 25
Kalamazoo	30	30	26	21	14	11	....	75
Lansing	36	36	31	23	16	13	....	1 25
Lake Linden	....	85	71	57	37	....	....	2 25
Manistee	47	47	41	31	23	18	....	1 75
Munising	....	75	65	48	38	....	....	2 00
Ishpeming	....	60	50	40	28	....	....	1 75
Paris	42	42	36	27	19	16	....	1 50
Petoskey	53	53	45	34	26	20	....	2 00
MINNESOTA—								
Albert Lea	....	60	50	40	25	....	....	2 00
Audubon	....	1 10	92	74	50	....	....	3 75
Crookston	....	1 19	99	79	55	....	....	4 25
Duluth	....	65	55	44	28	....	....	2 25
Edgerton	....	77	63	43	31	....	....	2 50
Farris	....	1 16	97	77	53	....	....	2 00- 1 75
Hallock	....	1 27	1 06	85	58	....	....	2 00- 2 50
Mankato	....	65	55	43	27	....	....	2 00
Marshall	....	1 01	85	68	46	....	....	3 00
Menahga	....	1 08	90	72	49	....	....	2 00- 1 75
Milan	....	85	72	60	40	....	....	2 75
Minneapolis	....	60	50	40	25	....	....	2 00
Moorhead	....	1 06	79	70	48	....	....	3 50
Redwood Falls	....	65	55	43	27	....	....	2 75
St. Vincent	....	1 27	1 06	85	59	....	....	2 00- 2 50
Tower	....	96	81	65	44	....	....	2 75
MISSISSIPPI—								
Ackerman	Rule 2	1 25	1 02	82	70	57	51	3 50
Hazlehurst	Rule 2	1 36	1 10	92	76	63	55	3 50
Holly Springs	Rule 1	1 09	93	77	64	51	44	2 85
Jackson	$1 18	1 18	99	80	67	56	49	3 50
Meridian	1 18	1 18	99	80	67	56	49	3 75
Mississippi City	Rule 1	1 39	1 15	97	77	65	58	4 25
Natchez	$1 10	1 10	90	75	58	47	41	3 75
Ocean Springs	Rule 2	1 39	1 15	97	77	65	58	4 25
Pocahontas	Rule 2	1 35	1 09	92	76	62	54	3 50
Port Gibson	$1 47	1 49	1 24	1 03	82	68	59	3 50
Roxie	Rule 2	1 57	1 26	1 06	84	71	62	3 75
State Line, Wayne Co	Rule 2	1 49	1 29	1 06	86	72	61	4 00
Vicksburg	$1 10	1 10	90	75	58	47	41	3 50
MISSOURI—								
Charleston	....	65	55	42	33	....	....	2 40
Chicopee	....	87	77	56	45	....	....	3 25
Chillicothe	....	80	65	45	32	....	....	2 00
Clinton	....	82	72	50	37	....	....	2 50
Hannibal	....	42	35	27	22	....	....	1 25
Independence	....	80	65	45	32	....	....	2 00
Jefferson City	....	71	58	42	29	....	....	2 00
Kahoka	....	52	43	32	23	....	....	1 50
Kansas City	....	80	65	45	32	....	....	2 00
Kirkwood	....	58	48	38	32	....	....	1 90
Lincoln	....	96	79	57	43	....	....	2 50
Noel	....	1 12	91	68	49	....	....	3 50
Osceola	....	82	72	56	37	....	....	2 75
MISSOURI—Continued.								
Paris	....	$0 63	$0 49	$0 37	$0 26	....	....	$1 75
Poplar Bluff	....	77	66	55	45	....	....	2 50
Richards	....	94	81	55	37	....	....	2 75
Rolla	....	79	66	49	37	....	....	2 50
Springfield	....	82	72	50	37	....	....	3 00
St. Joseph	....	80	65	45	32	....	....	2 00
MONTANA—								
Big Timber	....	2 70	2 29	1 87	1 51	....	....	7 75
Billings	....	2 55	2 15	1 75	1 42	....	....	7 00
Butte	....	2 85	2 40	1 98	1 60	....	....	8 00
Chinook	....	2 50	2 12	1 73	1 39	....	....	$2 00- 5 25
Dillon	....	2 85	2 40	1 98	1 60	....	....	8 00
Glasgow	....	2 24	1 86	1 56	1 26	....	....	5 00- 2 00
Glendive	....	2 09	1 77	1 44	1 14	....	....	5 50
Great Falls	....	2 70	2 29	1 87	1 51	....	....	8 00
Helena	....	2 85	2 40	1 98	1 60	....	....	8 00
Iron Mountain	....	3 24	2 74	2 25	1 83	....	....	8 00
Kalispell	....	2 96	2 51	2 05	1 67	....	....	2 00- 7 00
Livingston	....	2 75	2 33	1 91	1 54	....	....	8 00
Missoula	....	2 96	2 51	2 05	1 67	....	....	9 00
NEBRASKA—								
Ainsworth	....	1 57	1 33	1 06	82	....	....	3 75
Alliance	....	1 81	1 58	1 25	97	....	....	4 75
Battle Creek	....	1 15	95	72	53	....	....	3 00
Beaver City	....	1 53	1 32	1 06	83	....	....	4 00
Chadron	....	1 90	1 64	1 34	1 03	....	....	4 75
Chappell	....	1 81	1 58	1 25	97	....	....	4 75
Cody	....	1 68	1 45	1 15	91	....	....	4 25
Crawford	....	2 02	1 76	1 43	1 17	....	....	4 75
Duncan	....	1 17	99	73	53	....	....	3 00
Grant	....	1 63	1 41	1 16	94	....	....	4 50
Hastings	....	1 31	1 11	83	62	....	....	3 50
Hemingford	....	1 85	1 62	1 31	1 01	....	....	5 00
Imperial	....	1 63	1 41	1 16	91	....	....	4 25
Lincoln	....	85	70	49	36	....	....	2 75
Loup City	....	1 45	1 23	96	75	....	....	3 75
McCook	....	1 55	1 35	1 09	85	....	....	4 00
Morrill	....	2 17	1 85	1 43	1 15	....	....	4 25
Nelson	....	1 31	1 11	83	62	....	....	3 50
Ogallala	....	1 63	1 41	1 16	91	....	....	4 50
Omaha	....	80	65	45	32	....	....	2 00
O'Neill	....	1 30	1 08	88	66	....	....	3 25
Pawnee, Pawnee Co	....	89	74	53	40	....	....	2 75
Sidney	....	1 81	1 58	1 25	97	....	....	5 00
Thedford	....	1 58	1 36	1 10	86	....	....	4 25
NEVADA—								
Austin	....	4 65	4 15	3 45	2 85	....	....	13 00
Carson	....	4 15	3 65	2 95	2 35	....	....	12 25
Elko	....	3 90	3 40	2 70	2 10	....	....	11 50
Eureka, Ormsby Co	....	4 20	3 70	3 00	2 40	....	....	13 00
Hawthorne	....	4 90	4 40	3 70	3 10	....	....	13 50
Reno	....	3 90	3 40	2 70	2 10	....	....	11 50
Toana	....	3 90	3 40	2 70	2 10	....	....	11 50
NEW HAMPSHIRE—								
Berlin	$0 82	82	71	55	39	$0 33	....	3 50
Colebrook	82	82	71	55	39	33	....	3 60
Conway	82	82	71	55	39	32	....	3 00
Dover	82	82	71	55	39	33	....	2 50
Enfield	82	82	71	55	39	33	....	3 00
Keene	82	82	71	55	39	33	....	2 75
Laconia	82	82	71	55	39	33	....	2 90
Manchester	82	82	71	55	39	33	....	2 50
Plymouth	82	82	71	55	39	33	....	3 25
Portsmouth	82	82	71	55	39	33	....	2 50
Suncook	82	82	71	55	39	33	....	2 75
NEW JERSEY—								
Bridgeton	80	80	70	55	40	35	....	2 50
Chatsworth	80	80	70	55	40	35	....	2 50
Lafayette	75	75	65	50	35	30	....	2 50
Middletown	80	80	70	55	40	35	....	2 75
Morristown	75	75	65	50	35	30	....	2 50
Mullica Hill	78	78	68	53	38	33	....	2 50
Newark	75	75	65	50	35	30	....	2 50
Oxford Furnace	75	75	65	50	35	30	....	2 50
Pleasantville	80	80	70	55	40	30	....	2 75
Pompton	75	75	65	50	35	30	....	2 75
NEW MEXICO—								
Albuquerque	Rule 2	2 32	2 10	1 80	1 52	....	....	7 25
Carlsbad	....	2 29	1 99	1 67	1 48	....	....	6 75
Clayton	$0 75	2 05	1 65	1 25	97	....	....	6 50
Las Vegas	Rule 2	2 32	2 10	1 80	1 52	....	....	7 25
Lordsburg	....	2 79	2 54	2 34	2 10	....	....	8 75
Raton	Rule 2	2 25	1 85	1 45	1 17	....	....	6 50
Roswell	....	2 29	1 99	1 67	1 48	....	....	6 75
Santa Fe	Rule 2	2 32	2 10	1 80	1 52	....	....	7 25
Socorro	Rule 2	2 32	2 10	1 80	1 52	....	....	7 25
NEW YORK—								
Albany	$0 72	72	63	48	34	29	....	2 25
Big Moose	82	82	71	55	39	33	....	3 00
Boston Corners	82	82	71	55	39	33	....	2 75
Buffalo	45	45	39	30	21	18	....	1 75
Canton, St. Lawrence Co.	82	82	71	55	39	33	....	3 00
Cortland	60	60	52	40	28	24	....	2 25
Delhi	86	86	73	56	30	33	....	2 75
Elmira	60	60	52	40	28	24	....	2 25
Fort Edward	82	82	71	55	39	33	....	2 75
Hastings, Oswego Co	68	68	59	45	32	27	....	2 50
Lake Placid	1 07	94	82	65	47	40	....	3 50
Lyons, Wayne Co	60	60	52	40	28	24	....	2 00
Malone	82	82	71	55	39	33	....	3 10
New York	75	75	65	50	35	30	....	2 50
North Creek	1 10	1 10	95	75	57	50	....	3 75
Nunda	56	56	48	37	26	22	....	2 25
Plattsburg	1 08	1 08	92	72	52	43	....	3 25
Poughkeepsie	75	75	65	50	35	30	....	2 50
Rochester	56	56	48	37	26	22	....	2 00
Saranac Lake	82	82	71	55	39	33	....	3 10
Warsaw	56	56	48	37	26	22	....	2 00
Watertown	75	75	65	50	35	30	....	2 75
NORTH CAROLINA—								
Belhaven	97	1 17	1 00	80	57	47	39	3 50
Charlotte	Rule 3	1 35	1 16	92	68	58	45	3 75
Clinton	Rule 3	1 35	1 16	92	68	58	45	4 00
Culberson	Rule 3	1 39	1 16	89	77	70	63	4 50
Elk Park	Rule 3	1 44	1 28	1 12	93	80	68	4 00—50
Fayetteville	Rule 3	1 35	1 16	92	68	56	40	4 00
Goldsboro	Rule 3	1 28	1 09	86	62	53	41	3 50
Goldston	Rule 3	1 35	1 16	97	68	58	45	4 00

*LOUISIANA—Towns with four class rates are governed by Western classification.
Towns with six class rates are governed by Southern classification.

*MICHIGAN—Towns with four class rates are governed by Western classification.
Towns with five class rates are governed by Eastern classification.

	Min. freight charge	1st class freight per 100 lbs	2nd class freight per 100 lbs	3d class freight per 100 lbs	4th class freight per 100 lbs	5th class freight per 100 lbs	6th class freight per 100 lbs	Express per 100 lbs.
NORTH CAROLINA—Con.								
Greensboro	Rule 3	$1 28	$1 09	$0 86	$0 62	$0 53	$0 41	$3 75
Halifax	Rule 3	1 27	1 08	86	62	53	41	3 50
Hertford	$0 97	1 10	95	75	54	44	36	3 25
Mount Airy	Rule 3	1 38	1 18	94	69	59	46	4 00
Newbern	Rule 3	1 13	94	74	56	46	37	4 00
Newport	Rule 3	1 30	1 11	87	63	54	42	4 00
Raleigh	Rule 3	1 28	1 09	86	62	53	41	3 50
Salisbury	Rule 3	1 35	1 16	92	68	58	45	3 75
Shelby	Rule 3	1 51	1 32	1 08	81	68	54	4 25
Wadesboro	Rule 3	1 35	1 16	92	68	58	45	4 25
Washington	Rule 3	1 12	93	74	55	45	35	3 50
Wilkesboro	Rule 3	1 39	1 20	96	75	62	50	4 00
NORTH DAKOTA—								
Aneta	......	1 35	1 13	91	66	......	......	$2 00- 2 40
Bismarck	......	1 58	1 32	1 05	74	......	......	4 75
Bottineau	......	1 69	1 43	1 16	85	......	......	2 00- 3 00
Carrington	......	1 45	1 21	97	68	......	......	4 50
Cooperstown	......	1 34	1 11	89	62	......	......	4 50
Dickinson	......	1 87	1 58	1 28	98	......	......	5 25
Ellendale	......	1 15	99	74	54	......	......	3 25
Fargo	......	1 06	79	70	48	......	......	3 50
Grand Forks	......	1 21	1 01	81	56	......	......	4 25
Hannah	......	1 57	1 32	1 06	77	......	......	2 00- 3 00
Jamestown	......	1 37	1 14	91	63	......	......	4 25
Lakota	......	1 40	1 18	94	67	......	......	2 00- 2 75
Maddock	......	1 56	1 30	1 04	73	......	......	5 09
Medora	......	1 94	1 64	1 34	1 05	......	......	5 50
Minot	......	1 70	1 44	1 17	86	......	......	5 00
Pembina	......	1 27	1 06	85	59	......	......	4 50
Stanley	......	1 79	1 51	1 23	90	......	......	2 00- 4 00
St. John	......	1 65	1 39	1 13	82	......	......	2 00- 3 00
OHIO—								
Bellefontaine	$0 37	37	32	24	16	13	......	1 50
Bucyrus	39	39	33	25	17	14	......	1 50
Caldwell	45	45	39	30	21	18	......	2 00
Canton	41	41	35	26	18	15	......	1 50
Chillicothe	44	44	38	29	19	17	......	1 75
Cincinnati	40	40	34	25	17	15	......	1 50
Cleveland	41	41	35	26	18	15	......	1 50
Columbus	41	41	35	26	18	15	......	1 50
Coshocton	44	44	38	29	19	17	......	1 75
Dayton	40	40	34	25	17	15	......	1 50
Defiance	33	33	29	22	15	12	......	1 00
Georgetown, Brown Co.	65	60	54	41	32	26	......	1 90
Greenville	39	39	33	25	17	14	......	1 25
Hillsboro	44	44	38	29	19	17	......	1 75
Jobs	45	45	39	29	21	18	......	2 00
Laura	39	39	33	25	17	14	......	1 50
Lima	37	37	32	24	16	13	......	1 25
Logan, Hocking Co	45	45	39	29	21	18	......	1 75
Marion	39	39	33	25	17	14	......	1 25
Ottawa, Putnam Co	37	37	32	24	16	13	......	1 25
Portsmouth	45	45	39	30	21	18	......	2 00
Steubenville	45	45	39	30	21	18	......	1 75
Toledo	37	37	32	24	16	13	......	1 25
Xenia	40	40	34	25	17	15	......	1 50
OKLAHOMA—								
Alva	Rule 2	1 50	1 29	1 07	88	......	......	4 25
Atoka	Rule 2	1 50	1 29	1 07	93	......	......	3 75
Calumet	Rule 2	1 50	1 29	1 07	95	......	......	4 25
Checotah	Rule 2	1 36	1 20	90	71	......	......	3 25
El Reno	Rule 2	1 50	1 29	1 07	89	......	......	4 25
Eufaula	Rule 2	1 37	1 20	92	74	......	......	3 50
Guthrie	Rule 2	1 50	1 29	1 07	89	......	......	3 75
Kingfisher	Rule 2	1 50	1 29	1 07	89	......	......	4 25
Kiowa	Rule 2	1 48	1 28	1 04	85	......	......	3 75
Newkirk	Rule 2	1 46	1 24	98	77	......	......	3 75
Oklahoma	Rule 2	1 50	1 29	1 07	89	......	......	4 00
Red Fork	Rule 2	1 35	1 20	90	70	......	......	3 75
South McAlester	Rule 2	1 40	1 20	95	74	......	......	3 75
Tecumseh	Rule 2	1 50	1 29	1 07	89	......	......	4 00
Vinita	Rule 2	1 25	1 03	83	60	......	......	3 25
Wagoner	Rule 2	1 35	1 20	90	69	......	......	3 25
Wewoka	Rule 2	1 50	1 29	1 07	89	......	......	4 00
OREGON—								
Arlington	......	3 60	3 10	2 60	2 15	......	......	11 00
Baker City	......	3 60	3 10	2 60	2 15	......	......	10 00
Elgin	......	3 60	3 10	2 60	2 15	......	......	10 00
Eugene	......	3 46	3 02	2 59	2 26	......	......	12 25
Heppner	......	3 60	3 10	2 60	2 15	......	......	11 50
Huntington	......	3 60	3 10	2 60	2 15	......	......	10 00
La Grande	......	3 60	3 10	2 60	2 15	......	......	10 00
Lebanon	......	3 32	2 89	2 46	2 15	......	......	12 00
Leland	......	3 90	3 40	2 70	2 10	......	......	13 00
Medford	......	3 90	3 40	2 70	2 10	......	......	13 00
Monmouth	......	3 10	2 70	2 30	2 00	......	......	12 00
Natron	......	3 48	3 03	2 60	2 27	......	......	12 25
Pendleton	......	3 60	3 10	2 60	2 10	......	......	10 00
Portland	......	3 00	2 60	2 20	1 90	......	......	11 50
Roseburg	......	3 72	3 24	2 79	2 40	......	......	13 00
Salem	......	3 10	2 70	2 30	2 00	......	......	12 00
Sheridan, Yamhill Co	......	3 10	2 70	2 30	2 00	......	......	12 00
Troutdale	......	3 15	2 73	2 32	2 00	......	......	11 50
PENNSYLVANIA—								
Allentown, Lehigh Co.	$0 73	73	63	48	33	28	......	2 50
Bedford	72	72	62	47	32	27	......	2 25
Blairsville	53	53	45	34	24	21	......	2 00
Driftwood	72	72	62	47	32	27	......	2 25
Erie	45	45	39	30	21	18	......	1 75
Gettysburg	72	72	62	47	32	27	......	25
Harrisburg	72	72	62	47	32	27	......	2 25
Huntingdon	72	72	62	47	32	27	......	2 25
Jackson Center	45	45	39	30	21	18	......	00
Larabee	56	56	48	37	26	22	......	25
Lewisburg	72	72	62	47	32	27	......	2 25
Nanticoke	73	73	63	48	33	28	......	2 50
New Castle	44	44	38	29	19	17	......	1 75
Philadelphia	73	73	63	48	33	28	......	2 25
Pittsburg	45	45	39	30	21	18	......	1 75
Pottsville	73	73	63	48	33	28	......	2 50
Reading, Berks Co	73	73	63	48	33	28	......	2 25
Scranton	73	73	63	48	33	28	......	2 50
Sharpsville	44	44	38	29	19	17	......	1 75
Tionesta	45	45	39	30	21	18	......	2 00
Towanda	73	73	63	48	33	28	......	2 25
Uniontown	50	50	43	33	23	20	......	2 00
RHODE ISLAND—								
Bristol	82	82	71	55	39	33	......	2 50- 40
Greene	82	82	71	55	39	33	......	3 00
RHODE ISLAND—Con.								
Pascoag	$0 82	$0 82	$0 71	$0 55	$0 39	$0 33	......	$3 00
Providence	82	82	71	55	39	33	......	2 50
Slocum	82	82	71	55	39	33	......	3 00
Westerly	82	82	71	55	39	33	......	3 00
SOUTH CAROLINA—								
Abbeville	Rule 3	1 51	1 37	1 08	82	68	$0 60	4 50
Aiken	Rule 3	1 51	1 33	1 06	80	65	52	5 00
Beaufort	Rule 3	1 30	1 12	87	64	55	43	5 25
Charleston	Rule 3	1 30	1 11	97	85	71	56	4 75
Columbia	Rule 3	1 39	1 21	1 03	80	66	54	4 50
Ehrhardt	Rule 3	1 83	1 58	1 36	1 18	1 00	79	5 50
Florence	Rule 3	1 47	1 28	1 04	80	65	52	4 50
Georgetown	Rule 3	1 45	1 24	1 07	90	77	58	5 25
Greenville	Rule 3	1 51	1 37	1 08	82	68	60	4 50
Greenwood	Rule 3	1 57	1 37	1 08	82	68	60	4 50
Hampton	Rule 3	1 70	1 46	1 26	1 12	92	74	5 25
Lancaster	Rule 3	1 47	1 28	1 04	80	65	52	4 50
Ridgeway	Rule 3	1 51	1 30	1 08	81	68	53⅓	4 25
Spartanburg	Rule 3	1 51	1 37	1 08	82	68	60	4 50
SOUTH DAKOTA—								
Aberdeen	......	1 10	91	64	48	......	......	3 25
Armour	......	1 10	95	74	50	......	......	2 75
Belle Fourche	......	2 35	2 05	1 63	1 32	......	......	5 75
Canton	......	80	65	44	32	......	......	2 25
Chamberlain	......	1 22	1 04	80	55	......	......	3 00
Deadwood	......	2 25	1 95	1 60	1 32	......	......	5 75
Edgemont	......	2 04	1 78	1 43	1 19	......	......	5 50
Eureka	......	1 26	1 01	84	62	......	......	3 50
Gettysburg	......	1 27	1 04	85	65	......	......	3 25
Huron	......	1 10	91	64	47	......	......	3 25
Milbank Junction	......	94	79	65	43	......	......	3 00
Mitchell	......	1 05	91	64	47	......	......	2 75
Pierre	......	1 22	1 04	80	60	......	......	3 25
Rapid City	......	2 16	1 90	1 55	1 28	......	......	5 50
Redfield	......	1 10	91	64	48	......	......	3 25
Sisseton	......	1 01	82	65	46	......	......	3 00
Spearfish	......	2 35	2 05	1 63	1 32	......	......	6 25
Vermilion	......	85	68	47	34	......	......	2 00
Watertown	......	88	75	58	40	......	......	3 25
Wolsey	......	1 10	91	64	47	......	......	3 25
TENNESSEE—								
Antioch	Rule 1	1 47	1 28	1 04	80	68	50	2 90
Allens Creek	Rule 2	1 18	1 03	85	69	58	52	3 25
Bristol (Eastern Class)	$0 84	84	72	55	39	33	......	3 50
Charleston	Rule 3	1 45	1 25	1 05	84	71	45	3 50
Chattanooga	Rule 1	1 11	95	79	62	53	40	3 00
Clarksville	Rule 1	81	70	56	43	36	30	2 65
Clinton	Rule 1	1 19	1 02	82	70	61	47	3 25
Greenfield	Rule 1	91	75	60	49	37	34	2 50
Knoxville	Rule 1	1 11	95	79	72	53	40	3 00
Jackson	Rule 1	1 03	85	70	57	42	39	2 60
Manchester	Rule 2	1 18	1 03	86	69	60	51	3 25
Memphis	$0 85	85	65	55	43	37	31	2 75
Monteagle	Rule 3	1 38	1 20	1 00	83	73	65	3 25
Parson	Rule 1	1 00	83	68	56	44	38	2 75
TEXAS—								
Abilene	Rule 2	1 57	1 37	1 16	1 06	......	......	5 50
Amarillo	Rule 2	1 67	1 46	1 24	1 13	......	......	5 50
Austin	Rule 2	1 57	1 37	1 16	1 06	......	......	5 25
Beaumont	Rule 2	1 57	1 37	1 16	1 06	......	......	5 25
Canadian	Rule 2	1 62	1 41	1 20	1 09	......	......	5 25
Corpus Christi	Rule 2	1 57	1 37	1 16	1 06	......	......	6 50
Dallas	Rule 2	1 57	1 37	1 16	1 06	......	......	4 25
Denison	Rule 2	1 57	1 37	1 16	1 06	......	......	3 75
El Paso	Rule 2	1 69	1 50	1 34	1 26	......	......	7 00
Henrietta	Rule 2	1 57	1 37	1 16	1 06	......	......	4 50
Houston	Rule 2	1 57	1 37	1 16	1 06	......	......	5 25
Kerrville	Rule 2	1 64	1 44	1 22	1 09	......	......	6 50
Laredo	Rule 2	1 69	1 50	1 34	1 26	......	......	6 75
Llano	Rule 2	1 57	1 37	1 16	1 06	......	......	5 75
Lufkin	Rule 2	1 57	1 37	1 16	1 06	......	......	5 25
Palestine	Rule 2	1 57	1 37	1 16	1 06	......	......	5 00
Pecos	Rule 2	1 93	1 66	1 47	1 36	......	......	6 75
Port Lavaca	Rule 2	1 57	1 37	1 16	1 06	......	......	5 75
San Angelo	Rule 2	1 57	1 37	1 16	1 06	......	......	5 75
San Antonio	Rule 2	1 57	1 37	1 16	1 06	......	......	5 75
Sanderson	Rule 2	1 94	1 67	1 48	1 37	......	......	7 00
Seymour	Rule 2	1 57	1 37	1 16	1 06	......	......	5 25
Sierra Blanca	Rule 2	1 94	1 67	1 48	1 37	......	......	6 75
Spofford	Rule 2	1 69	1 49	1 30	1 21	......	......	6 75
Waco	Rule 2	1 57	1 37	1 16	1 06	......	......	4 75
UTAH—								
Belknap	......	3 35	2 88	2 44	2 04	......	......	9 00
Bingham Jct	......	2 85	2 40	1 98	1 60	......	......	8 00
Cache Jct.	......	2 85	2 40	1 98	1 60	......	......	8 00
Colton	......	2 85	2 40	1 98	1 60	......	......	8 00
Dewey	......	2 85	2 40	1 98	1 60	......	......	8 00
Echo	......	2 85	2 40	1 98	1 60	......	......	8 00
Ephraim	......	3 05	2 58	2 14	1 74	......	......	8 25
Fairfield	......	3 10	2 61	2 16	1 75	......	......	8 50
Frisco	......	3 77	3 23	2 62	2 15	......	......	10 50
Heber	......	2 85	2 40	1 98	1 60	......	......	8 50
Kelton	......	3 55	3 01	2 48	2 03	......	......	9 25
Manti	......	3 05	2 58	2 14	1 74	......	......	8 25
Milford	......	3 69	3 14	2 57	2 10	......	......	10 25
Nephi	......	3 10	2 61	2 16	1 75	......	......	8 75
Ogden	......	2 85	2 40	1 98	1 60	......	......	8 00
Salt Lake City	......	2 85	2 40	1 98	1 60	......	......	8 00
VERMONT—								
Bradford	$0 82	82	71	55	39	33	......	3 25
Brattleboro	82	82	71	55	39	33	......	2 75
Burlington	82	82	71	55	39	33	......	3 25
Cavendish	82	82	71	55	39	33	......	3 00
Essex Jct.	82	82	71	55	39	33	......	3 25
Greensboro	82	82	71	55	39	33	......	3 25
Hartford	82	82	71	55	39	33	......	3 10
Leicester Jct.	82	82	71	55	39	33	......	3 25
Montpelier	82	82	71	55	39	33	......	3 25
North Bennington	82	82	71	55	39	33	......	2 75
Rutland	82	82	71	55	39	33	......	3 00
St. Albans	82	82	71	55	39	33	......	3 25
St. Johnsbury	82	82	71	55	39	33	......	3 25
***VIRGINIA—**								
Abingdon	84	84	72	55	39	33	......	3 75
Alexandria	72	72	62	47	32	27	......	2 25
Basic	72	72	62	47	32	27	......	2 75

*See note on page 16.

	Min. freight charge	1st class freight per 100 lbs	2d class freight per 100 lbs	3d class freight per 100 lbs	4th class freight per 100 lbs	5th class freight per 100 lbs	6th class freight per 100 lbs	Express per 100 lbs.
*** VIRGINIA—Continued.**								
Big Stone Gap	$1 09	$0 99	$0 85	$0 67	$0 50	$0 43	.....	$3 00
Clarksville	Rule 3	1 27	1 08	83	56	48	$0 39	3 50
Emporia	Rule 3	1 22	1 04	82	55	47	38	3 25
Farmville	$0 72	72	62	47	32	27	.....	3 25
Fredericksburg	72	72	62	47	32	27	.....	2 75
Harrisonburg	72	72	62	47	32	27	.....	2 50
Lexington	72	72	62	47	32	27	.....	2 75
Lynchburg	72	72	62	47	32	27	.....	2 75
Martinsville	Rule 3	1 03	86	67	48	41	31	3 50
Morley	$0 75	75	65	50	35	30	.....	3 00
New Castle	84	84	72	55	38	31	.....	2 75
Old Point Comfort	72	72	62	47	32	27	.....	2 75
Orange	72	72	62	47	32	27	.....	2 75
Pulaski City	84	84	72	55	39	33	.....	3 25
Richmond	72	72	62	47	32	27	.....	2 75
Riverton	72	72	62	47	32	27	.....	2 65
Salem	72	72	62	47	32	27	.....	3 25
Suffolk	72	72	62	47	32	27	.....	3 00
Swordscreek	84	84	72	55	39	33	.....	3 25
Virginia City	84	84	72	55	39	33	.....	3 25
West Point	72	72	62	47	32	27	.....	3 00
WASHINGTON—								
Anacortes	2 60	3 00	2 60	2 20	1 90	.....	.....	$2 00- 9 50
Chehalis	2 60	3 00	2 60	2 20	1 90	.....	.....	11 50
Colfax		3 60	3 10	2 60	2 15	.....	.....	10 00
Connell		3 60	3 10	2 60	2 10	.....	.....	10 00
Coulee City		3 60	3 10	2 60	2 10	.....	.....	10 50
Dayton		3 60	3 10	2 60	2 10	.....	.....	10 00
Easton		3 60	3 10	2 60	2 10	.....	.....	11 00
Hoquiam	2 60	3 00	2 60	2 20	1 90	.....	.....	11 50
Kalama	2 60	3 00	2 60	2 20	1 90	.....	.....	11 50
Meyers Falls		3 80	3 32	2 79	2 32	.....	.....	2 00- 9 50
Monroe		3 25	2 80	2 37	2 05	.....	.....	2 00- 9 00
New Whatcom	2 60	3 00	2 60	2 20	1 90	.....	.....	11 50
Northport		3 80	3 32	2 79	2 32	.....	.....	2 00- 9 50
North Yakima		3 60	3 10	2 60	2 10	.....	.....	11 00
Olympia	2 60	3 00	2 60	2 20	1 90	.....	.....	11 50
Pasco		3 60	3 10	2 60	2 10	.....	.....	10 00
Snohomish	2 60	3 00	2 60	2 20	1 90	.....	.....	11 50
South Bend	2 60	3 00	2 60	2 20	1 90	.....	.....	11 50
Spokane		3 60	3 10	2 60	2 10	.....	.....	10 00
Tacoma	2 60	3 00	2 60	2 20	1 90	.....	.....	11 50
Walla Walla		3 60	3 10	2 60	2 10	.....	.....	10 00
Wallula		3 60	3 10	2 60	2 10	.....	.....	10 00
Wenatchee		3 60	3 10	2 60	2 10	.....	.....	2 00- 9 00
WEST VIRGINIA—								
Acme	78	78	67	51	35	29	.....	2 50
Beverly	72	72	62	47	32	27	.....	2 25
Charleston	45	45	39	30	21	18	.....	2 50
Clarksburg	50	50	43	33	23	20	.....	2 00
Dingess	84	84	72	55	39	33	.....	2 50
Grafton	50	50	43	33	23	20	.....	2 00

*VIRGINIA—Towns with five class rates are governed by Eastern classification.
Towns with six class rates are governed by Southern classification.

	Min. freight charge	1st class freight per 100 lbs	2d class freight per 100 lbs	3d class freight per 100 lbs	4th class freight per 100 lbs	5th class freight per 100 lbs	6th class freight per 100 lbs	Express per 100 lbs.
WEST VIRGINIA—Con'd.								
Harpers Ferry	$0 72	$0 72	$0 62	$0 47	$0 32	$0 27	.....	$2 25
Hinton	72	72	62	47	32	27	.....	2 75
Martinsburg	72	72	62	47	32	27	.....	2 25
Parkersburg	45	45	39	30	21	18	.....	2 00
Parsons	72	72	62	47	32	27	.....	2 25
Ripley Landing	45	45	39	30	21	18	.....	2 25
Romney	77	77	66	50	34	29	.....	2 25
Spencer	63	63	55	46	34	27	.....	2 25
Wheeling	45	45	39	30	21	18	.....	1 75
WISCONSIN—								
Ashland		65	55	44	28	.....	.....	2 00
Athens		55	46	36	24	.....	.....	2 00
Beloit		37	30	24	18	.....	.....	75
Cameron		65	55	44	28	.....	.....	1 75
Chelsea		60	50	40	25	.....	.....	2 00
Chippewa Falls		60	50	40	25	.....	.....	1 75
Fond du Lac		40	33	28	20	.....	.....	1 00
Grand Rapids		50	42	33	23	.....	.....	1 50
Green Bay		43	36	29	20	.....	.....	1 25
Hudson		60	50	40	25	.....	.....	1 75
Hurley		65	55	44	28	.....	.....	2 00
Lancaster		50	42	33	23	.....	.....	1 50
Madison		39	34	26	18	.....	.....	1 00
Manitowoc		30	25	21	16	.....	.....	1 10
Milwaukee		25	20	15	12	.....	.....	60
Mineral Pt		46	38	30	21	.....	.....	1 10
Mondovi		60	50	40	25	.....	.....	1 75
Oconto		43	36	29	23	.....	.....	1 50
Pembine		60	50	40	25	.....	.....	1 50
Prairie du Chien		50	42	33	23	.....	.....	1 50
Prentice		60	50	40	25	.....	.....	2 00
Richland Center		50	42	33	23	.....	.....	1 25
Rhinelander		60	50	40	25	.....	.....	1 75
Sparta		50	42	33	23	.....	.....	1 50
Spooner		65	55	44	28	.....	.....	2 00
Sturgeon Bay		43	36	29	23	.....	.....	1 50
Wabeno		60	50	40	25	.....	.....	1 75
Wausau		50	42	33	23	.....	.....	1 75
WYOMING—								
Casper	75	2 62	2 19	1 75	1 42	.....	.....	6 00
Cheyenne	75	2 05	1 65	1 25	97	.....	.....	6 00
Cokeville	2 08	2 85	2 40	1 98	1 60	.....	.....	8 00
Dana	1 50	2 95	2 43	1 87	1 49	.....	.....	7 75
Evanston	2 00	3 10	2 65	2 15	1 75	.....	.....	8 00
Gillette	75	2 52	2 13	1 74	1 40	.....	.....	6 75
Green River	1 75	3 10	2 65	2 15	1 75	.....	.....	8 00
Hanna	1 50	2 91	2 40	1 85	1 47	.....	.....	7 50
Lander	1 00	3 38	2 85	2 30	1 89	.....	.....	.....
Laramie	1 25	2 56	2 10	1 64	1 29	.....	.....	6 75
Lusk	75	2 45	2 01	1 55	1 22	.....	.....	5 25
Medicine Bow	1 50	2 84	2 34	1 81	1 43	.....	.....	7 50
Rawlins	1 50	3 06	2 53	1 94	1 56	.....	.....	8 00
Sheridan	75	2 52	2 13	1 74	1 40	.....	.....	7 00
Wamsutter	1 75	3 10	2 65	2 06	1 68	.....	.....	8 00
Wheatland	1 16	2 45	2 01	1 55	1 22	.....	.....	6 50

HOW TO FIGURE EXPRESS CHARGES.

When rate per 100 pounds is ☞	$0.40	$0.50	$0.60	$0.75	$1.00	$1.25	$1.50	$1.75	$2.00	$2.50	$3.00	$3.50	$4.00	$4.50
Packages not over	1 lb $0 25	1 lb $0 25	1 lb $0 25	1 lb $0 25	1 lb $0 25	1 lb $0 25	1 lb $0 25	1 lb $0 25	1 lb $0 25	1 lb $0 25	1 lb $0 25	1 lb $0 25	1 lb $0 25	1 lb $0 30
Over 1 pound to	2 lb 25	2 lb 25	2 lb 25	2 lb 30	2 lb 30	2 lb 30	2 lb 30	2 lb 30	2 lb 35	2 lb 35	2 lb 35	2 lb 35	2 lb 35	2 lb 35
Over 2 pounds to	3 lb 25	3 lb 25	3 lb 25	3 lb 30	3 lb 30	3 lb 35	3 lb 35	3 lb 40	3 lb 45	3 lb 45	3 lb 45	3 lb 45	3 lb 45	3 lb 45
Over 3 pounds to	4 lb 25	4 lb 25	4 lb 30	4 lb 30	4 lb 35	4 lb 35	4 lb 40	4 lb 45	4 lb 50	4 lb 55	4 lb 60	4 lb 60	4 lb 60	4 lb 60
Over 4 pounds to	5 lb 25	5 lb 25	5 lb 30	5 lb 35	5 lb 40	5 lb 40	5 lb 45	5 lb 50	5 lb 55	5 lb 60	5 lb 65	5 lb 70	5 lb 70	5 lb 75
Over 5 pounds to	7 lb 30	7 lb 30	7 lb 35	7 lb 35	7 lb 40	7 lb 45	7 lb 50	7 lb 55	7 lb 60	7 lb 70	7 lb 75	7 lb 80	7 lb 85	7 lb 90
Over 7 pounds to	10 30	10 30	10 35	10 40	10 45	10 50	10 55	10 60	10 70	10 75	10 80	10 90	10 1 00	10 1 00
Over 10 pounds to	15 30	15 30	15 35	15 40	15 45	15 55	15 60	15 65	15 75	15 85	15 90	15 1 00	15 1 10	15 1 15
Over 15 pounds to	20 30	20 30	20 35	20 40	20 50	20 60	20 70	20 75	20 85	20 1 00	20 1 10	20 1 20	20 1 25	20 1 30
Over 20 pounds to	25 35	25 35	25 40	25 45	25 55	25 65	25 75	25 85	25 1 00	25 1 10	25 1 20	25 1 30	25 1 40	25 1 50
Over 25 pounds to	30 35	30 40	30 45	30 50	30 60	30 70	30 80	30 90	30 1 00	30 1 15	30 1 30	30 1 50	30 1 60	30 1 70
Over 30 pounds to	35 40	35 40	35 45	35 50	35 65	35 75	35 85	35 1 00	35 1 00	35 1 25	35 1 40	35 1 60	35 1 70	35 1 90
Over 35 pounds to	40 40	40 40	40 50	40 55	40 70	40 80	40 90	40 1 00	40 1 00	40 1 25	40 1 50	40 1 75	40 1 85	40 2 00
Over 40 pounds to	45 40	45 40	45 50	45 60	45 75	45 90	45 1 00	45 1 00	45 1 00	45 1 25	45 1 50	45 1 75	45 2 00	45 2 25
Over 45 pounds to	50 40	50 45	50 55	50 60	50 80	50 1 00	50 1 00	50 1 00	50 1 00	50 1 25	50 1 50	50 1 75	50 2 00	50 2 25
Over 50 pounds to	55 40	55 50	55 60	55 65	55 85	55 1 00	55 1 10	55 1 10						
Over 55 pounds to	60 40	60 50	60 60	60 70	60 90	60 1 10	60 1 20	60 1 20						
Over 60 pounds to	65 40	65 50	65 60	65 75	65 90	65 1 15	65 1 30	65 1 30						
Over 65 pounds to	70 40	70 50	70 60	70 75	70 1 00	70 1 25	70 1 40	70 1 40						
Over 70 pounds to	75 40	75 50	75 60	75 75	75 1 00	75 1 25	75 1 50	75 1 50						
Over 75 pounds to	80 40	80 50	80 60	80 75	80 1 00	80 1 25	80 1 50	80 1 60						
Over 80 pounds to	85 40	85 50	85 60	85 75	85 1 00	85 1 25	85 1 50	85 1 70						
Over 85 pounds to	100 40	100 50	100 60	100 75	100 1 00	100 1 25	100 1 50	100 1 75						

This scale is the same as used by all express companies and shows how they arrive at the charges on shipments at the rates given.

Where two rates are shown in the rate tables, charges on packages weighing over 7 pounds are arrived at by adding the rates of the two different amounts given.

Where weight is 7 pounds or less, add the two amounts together and take the rate shown under the sum of the two amounts.

When the rate per 100 pounds is $2.00 or more, and the weight of the shipment is greater than 50 pounds, the express companies charge at pound rates. For example: Rate per 100 pounds, $3.00; weight of shipment, 60 pounds; charges would be $1.80.

When rate per 100 pounds is ☞	$5.00	$6.00	$7.00	$8.00	$9.00	$10.00	$11.00	$12.00	$13.00	$14.00	$15.00	$16.00	$17.00	$18.00	$20.00
Packages not over	1 lb $0 30	1 lb $0 30	1 lb $0 30	1 lb $0 30	1 lb $0 30	1 lb $0 30	1 lb $0 30	1 lb $0 30	1 lb $0 30	1 lb $0 30	1 lb $0 35	1 lb $0 35	1 lb $0 35	1 lb $0 35	1 lb $0 40
Over 1 pound to	2 lb 35	2 lb 35	2 lb 35	2 lb 35	2 lb 35	2 lb 35	2 lb 35	2 lb 35	2 lb 35	2 lb 35	2 lb 40	2 lb 40	2 lb 45	2 lb 45	2 lb 50
Over 2 pounds to	3 lb 45	3 lb 45	3 lb 45	3 lb 45	3 lb 45	3 lb 45	3 lb 45	3 lb 45	3 lb 45	3 lb 45	3 lb 50	3 lb 50	3 lb 55	3 lb 60	3 lb 60
Over 3 pounds to	4 lb 60	4 lb 60	4 lb 60	4 lb 60	4 lb 60	4 lb 60	4 lb 60	4 lb 60	4 lb 60	4 lb 60	4 lb 65	4 lb 65	4 lb 75	4 lb 75	4 lb 80
Over 4 pounds to	5 lb 75	5 lb 75	5 lb 80	5 lb 80	5 lb 80	5 lb 80	5 lb 80	5 lb 80	5 lb 80	5 lb 80	5 lb 85	5 lb 85	5 lb 90	5 lb 95	5 lb 1 00
Over 5 pounds to	7 lb 1 00	7 lb 1 00	7 lb 1 00	7 lb 1 00	7 lb 1 00	7 lb 1 00	7 lb 1 00	7 lb 1 00	7 lb 1 00	7 lb 1 10	7 lb 1 15	7 lb 1 15	7 lb 1 25	7 lb 1 40	7 lb 1 50
Over 7 pounds to	10 1 10	10 1 15	10 1 20	10 1 25	10 1 35	10 1 50	10 1 50	10 1 50	10 1 50	10 1 50	10 1 65	10 1 65	10 1 75	10 1 80	10 2 00
Over 10 pounds to	15 1 25	15 1 35	15 1 50	15 1 60	15 1 75	15 2 00	15 2 00	15 2 15	15 2 15	15 2 15	15 2 35	15 2 50	15 2 60	15 2 75	15 3 00
Over 15 pounds to	20 1 40	20 1 65	20 1 75	20 2 00	20 2 00	20 2 50	20 2 50	20 2 75	20 2 75	20 2 85	20 3 00	20 3 20	20 3 40	20 3 60	20 4 00
Over 20 pounds to	25 1 60	25 1 85	25 2 00	25 2 25	25 2 50	25 3 00	25 3 25	25 3 50	25 3 50	25 3 50	25 3 75	25 4 00	25 4 25	25 4 50	25 5 00
Over 25 pounds to	30 1 75	30 2 10	30 2 50	30 2 75	30 3 00	30 3 25	30 3 75	30 4 00	30 4 00	30 4 20	30 4 50	30 4 80	30 5 10	30 5 40	30 6 00
Over 30 pounds to	35 2 00	35 2 50	35 2 75	35 3 25	35 3 50	35 3 75	35 4 25	35 4 75	35 4 75	35 4 90	35 5 25	35 5 60	35 5 95	35 6 30	35 7 00
Over 35 pounds to	40 2 25	40 2 75	40 3 25	40 3 50	40 4 00	40 4 25	40 4 75	40 5 25	40 5 25	40 5 60	40 6 00	40 6 40	40 6 80	40 7 20	40 8 00
Over 40 pounds to	45 2 50	45 3 00	45 3 50	45 4 00	45 4 50	45 4 75	45 5 25	45 5 75	45 5 85	45 6 30	45 6 75	45 7 20	45 7 65	45 8 10	45 9 00
Over 45 pounds to	50 2 50	50 3 00	50 3 50	50 4 00	50 4 50	50 5 00	50 5 50	50 6 00	50 6 50	50 7 00	50 7 50	50 8 00	50 8 50	50 9 00	50 10 00

FREIGHT CLASSIFICATION.

1 stands for First Class.
2 stands for Second Class.
3 stands for Third Class.
4 stands for Fourth Class.
5 stands for Fifth Class.
6 stands for Sixth Class.
1¼ stands for 1¼ times First Class.
1½ stands for 1½ times First Class.
D1 stands for 2 times First Class.
2½ stands for 2½ times First Class.
3T1 stands for 3 times First Class.
4T1 stands for 4 times First Class.

THE RAILROADS CHARGE FOR FREIGHT according to its classification. For example: Stoves take 3d class rate. By referring to pages 13 to 16 you will find the 3rd class rate to the nearest town in your state. Multiply the weight of the article (which you can get from our catalogue or estimate pretty closely) by the rate, and you will be able to figure the freight charges almost to a cent. If the following list does not contain the article you want, you can, as a rule, use the rate on some article of a similar nature.

THE CLASSIFICATION ON SOME ARTICLES is different to different sections of the country. For example: Hardware takes 2nd class rate to the western and southern states, and 3rd class rate to the eastern states. Hay presses take 3rd class rate to the western states, 2nd class to the eastern states and 4th class to the southern states.

REMEMBER, We always pack and ship our goods in a manner that secures for you the LOWEST FREIGHT CHARGES.

WEST. The railroads running west, northwest and southwest from Chicago, use the western classification. Use the classification in column marked "WEST" if you live in any of the following states: Arizona, Arkansas, California, Colorado, Idaho, Illinois, Indian Territory, Iowa, Kansas, Louisiana, Minnesota, Missouri, Montana, Nebraska, Nevada, New Mexico, North Dakota, Oklahoma, Oregon, South Dakota, Texas, Utah, Washington, Wisconsin, Wyoming.

EAST. The railroads running east and northeast from Chicago, use the eastern classification. Use the classification in column marked "EAST" if you live in any of the following states: Connecticut, Delaware, District of Columbia, Indiana, Maryland, Maine, Massachusetts, Michigan, New Hampshire, New Jersey, New York, Ohio, Pennsylvania, Rhode Island, Vermont, Virginia, West Virginia.

SOUTH. The railroads running south and southeast from Chicago, use the southern classification. Use the classification in column marked "SOUTH" if you live in any of the following states: Alabama, Florida, Georgia, Kentucky, Mississippi, North Carolina, South Carolina, Tennessee.

ARTICLES	CLASS West	CLASS East	CLASS South
Advertising Matter	1	1	2
Ammunition	1	2	1
Anvils	4	4	5
Asbestos Building Felt	3	3	3
Axes	2	3	3
Axles, Steel	3	4	5
Baby Carriages	2½	D.1	1
Bamboo Book Racks	3T1	3T1	1½
Barb Wire	4	4	6
Bar Iron	4	4	5
Barn Door Rail	3	3	4
Baskets, Nested	D-1	D-1	1
Bath Tubs	1	1	1
Beans, Dried	3	4	2
Bed Lounges	1½	1½	1
Beds, Folding	1½	1½	1
Beds, Iron or Wood	2	2	2
Bed Slats	3	3	4
Bed Springs, Spiral	D-1	D-1	D-1
Bed Springs, Woven Wire	1	1½	1
Bedsteads, Iron or Wood	2	2	2
Bells, Iron	3	3	3
Bellows	1	1	1
Belting, Rubber, Leather or Canvas	1	2	2
Bicycles	D-1	1½	1½
Binding Twine	3	3	3
Bird Cages	3T1	3T1	D-1
Blankets	1	1	1
Blinds	3	1	4
Blowers, Rotary	1	2	2
Boards, Shoveling	3	1	
Boats, Row	4T1	4T1	4T1
Boats, Stone	2	3	
Bob Sleds	2	1	
Boilers, Steam	3	2	3
Bone, Ground	4	4	6
Bookcases	1½	1½	1½
Books	1	1	1
Boots and Shoes	1	1	1
Buggies (See Vehicles)			
Buggy Bodies, Finished	1½	2½	1½
Buggy Bodies, Unfinished	1½	1½	2
Buggy Tops	1½	1½	1½
Buggy Wheels, Finished	1½	1	2
Buggy Wheels, Unfinished	1	1	2
Building Felt	3	3	3
Building Paper	3	3	5
Bureaus	1	1	2
Cameras	D-1	1	1½
Candles	3	3	4
Candy in Pails	2	2	4
Canned Goods	4	2	2
Cans, Milk	1	1½	1
Cant Hooks	3	2	2
Carpets	1	1	1
Carriages (See Vehicles)			
Carts, Hand, K. D	1	1	1
Carts, Road	1½	D-1	
Cement, Building	4	4	5
Cereals	3	4	4
Chains	2	3	5
Chairs, Bamboo, Rattan, Reed or Willow	3T1	3T1	D-1
Chairs, Cane Seat	1½	1½	1
Chairs, Invalid's Rolling	D-1	D-1	D-1
Chairs, Upholstered	D-1	1½	1½
Chairs, Wood or Leather Seat	1½	1½	1
Cheese	2	3	3
Chiffoniers	1	1	2
China Closets	D-1	1½	1½
Churns, Hand	2	1	2
Cigars and Cigarettes	1	1	1
Cloaks	1	1	1
Clocks	1	1	1
Clothes Bars	1	2	3
Clothing	1	1	1
Cobbler's Outfit	2	3	2
Cod Fish	4	5	5
Coffee	4	3	5
Coffee Mills	2	2	2
Commodes	1	1	2
Condensed Milk	4	3	3
Conductors, Pipe, Iron, not nested	D-1	1	1
Corn Cribs	4	3	5
Corn Huskers	1	1	1
Corn Planters	2	2	2
Corn Shellers, Hand, K. D.	3	2	2
Corrugated Iron	4	4	6
Cots, Folding, Wood	3	1	2
Couches	1	1	1
Crackers	2	2	4
Cream Separators	1	1	2

ARTICLES	CLASS West	CLASS East	CLASS South
Cribs, Iron or Wood	2	2	2
Crockery	2	2	4
Crowbars	4	4	6
Cultivators, Disc, Riding, K. D.	2	2	4
Cultivators, Hand, K. D., in bundles	1	2	4
Cultivators, Walking, K. D.	3	2	4
Cupboards	1½	1½	1½
Cutters, Bone, K. D.	2	2	2
Cutters, Feed and Ensilage, K. D.	3	2	3
Cutters, Food and Vegetable, K. D.	3	2	1
Cutters (Sleighs)	2½	3T1	
Decoy Ducks	2	1	1
Desks	1	1½	1
Disc Sharpeners	2	3	2
Dishes	2	2	4
Dog Powers	1	1	1
Door Hangers	3	3	4
Door Screens	1	1	2
Doors, Common	4	3	4
Doors, Common, Glazed	4	1	3
Doubletrees, Unfinished	3	3	4
Dressers	1	1	2
Dried Fruits	3	3	2
Drills, Blacksmiths' Post	2	2	2
Drills, Corn, S. U	1	1	1
Drugs	1	1	1
Drums	4T1	3T1	3T1
Dry Goods	1	1	1
Dynamite	D-1	D-1	D-1
Earthenware	2	2	4
Eave Troughs, nested	2	2	2
Egg Carrier Cases	1	1	1
Electric Batteries	1	1	1
Electrical Goods	1	1	1
Emery Wheels	3	3	3
Engines, Steam or Gasoline	1	2	3
Evaporators, Fruit, S. U	1½	1½	1
Evaporators, Sugar, K. D	2	1	2
Explosives	D-1	D-1	D-1
Fanning Mills, K. D	1	1	1
Feed Grinders, S. U	2	2	4
Feed Mills, Sweep, K. D	2	2	4
Felt, Building	3	3	5
Fence Wire, Barb and Smooth	4	4	6
Fencing	3	3	5
Fencing Machines, K. D	1	2	2
Fertilizers	4	4	6
Firearms	1	1	1
Fish, Canned	4	3	3
Fish, Pickled or Salted	4	5	5
Flax Meal	4	5	3
Flour	4	5	6
Flower Stands, Wire	3T1	3T1	D-1
Food, Animal or Poultry	4	4	3
Food Cookers, viz.:			
Acme	3	1	1
Economy	3	1	1
Farmers' Friend	3	3	4
Handy	3	1	1
Hercules	3	2	3
Kenwood	3	1	1
Forges, Portable	2	1	2
Forks, Horse Hay	2	2	3
Freezers	1	1	2
Fruit, Canned	4	3	3
Fruit, Dried	3	3	2
Fruit Jars	3	2	3
Galvanized Iron	4	4	6
Game Traps	2	3	2
Gas Fixtures	1	2	2
Gas for Calcium Lights	1	3	1
Gas Machines	1	1½	2
Gasoline Stoves	1	1	1
Gears, Running	1½	1	
Generators, Gas	1	1½	2
Glassware	2	2	2
Grain Drills, K. D.	3	2	2
Granite & Enameled Ware	2	2	2
Graphophones	1	1	1
Grease, Axle	4	3	5
Grindstone Frames	3	3	3
Grindstones	4	3	4
Grist Mills, Hand, boxed	2	2	4
Grits	4	5	5
Gunpowder	D-1	D-1	D-1
Guns, Revolvers, etc	1	1	1
Hall Trees	D-1	D-1	1½
Hammocks	1	1	1
Hardware	2	3	2
Harness and Saddles	1	1	2

ARTICLES	CLASS West	CLASS East	CLASS South
Harrows, N. O. S., K. D	3	2	4
Harrows, Disc, K. D	3	2	3
Hay Carriers	2	2	3
Hay Carrier Tracks	3	4	4
Hay Presses, Hand	3	2	4
Hay Presses, Power, loaded in box cars, actual weight	3	2	4
Hay Presses, S. U	1	1	1
Heaters, Tank	3	1	
High Explosives	D-1	D-1	D-1
Hinges, Iron	3	3	3
Hoes	2	2	3
Hollow Ware	3	3	3
Hominy	4	5	5
Horse and Mule Shoes	4	4	6
Horse Power Jacks	3	3	2
Horse Powers	3	2	2
Hullers, Pea, Hand	1	D-1	2
Ice Cream Freezers	1	1	2
Ice Plows	1	1	
Incubators	1	1	1
Iron Beds	2	2	2
Ironing Boards	1	3	3
Iron Pipe	4	4	6
Iron Tires	3	4	6
Iron Tuyeres	3	4	2
Iron Wagon Wheels	3	2	4
Kettles	3	3	3
Kitchen Sinks, Iron	2	3	3
Ladders	1	3	1
Lamps	1	1	1
Land Rollers, K. D.	3	2	3
Lard	4	3	5
Lasts, Iron	3	3	3
Lasts, Wood	2	3	2
Laundry Tubs, Galvanized Iron	3	1	1
Lawn Mowers	1	2	2
Lead Pipe	4	3	4
Lime	4	3	6
Linseed Meal	4	5	3
Lounges, K. D	1	1	1
Lye	4	3	5
Magic Lanterns	D-1	1	1
Mandrels	4	3	5
Matting	1	1	2
Mattresses, Woven Wire	1	1½	1
Meats, Cured	4	3	6
Milk Cans	1	1½	1
Mills, Cane	3	2	4
Mills, Cider and Wine Presses	2	2	4
Mills, Cob	2	2	4
Millwork (See Sash, Doors and Blinds).			
Mirrors	1	1	1
Molasses in Barrels or Kegs	4	4	5
Molasses in Cans or Kits	4	2	5
Mowers, Lawn	1	2	2
Musical Instruments	D-1	1½	1
Music Cabinets	D-1	D-1	1½
Nails	4	4	6
Notions	1	1	1
Nuts, Edible	2	2	2
Oars	1	3	3
Oat Meal	4	4	4
Oil in Barrels	3	3	3
Oil Cake Meal	4	5	3
Oil Cloth, under 13 ft. long	2	2	2
Oil Stoves	1	1	2
Organs	1	1	1
Ovens, Sheet Iron	1	1	1
Oyster Shells	4	4	6
Pails	2	1	3
Paint, in Barrel	4	3	4
Paint, in Cans or Pails	4	3	4
Paper Hangings	2	2	2
Pea Hullers, Hand	1	1	2
Phonographs	1½	1	1
Pianos	1	1	1
Pictures	1	1	1
Pipe, Lead	4	3	4
Planters, Corn, K. D.	3	2	2
Planters, Hand Corn, Bean and Potato	1	1	3
Planters, Potato, K. D	1	2	2
Plows, Gang or Sulky, K. D	3	2	4
Plows, Ice	3	2	4
Plow Points and Shares	3	3	4
Plows, Walking, K. D	3	2	4
Plumbing Material	2	2	2
Poles, Buggy, Carriage or Wagon. Finished	1½	1	3
Unfinished	2	3	4
Potato Diggers, K. D	3	2	4
Poultry Netting	3	3	5
Press Screws	3	3	3
Pulleys, Iron or Wood	2	3	4
Pumps	3	2	3
Queensware	2	3	2
Racks, Grain, Hay or Stalk, K. D.	2	2	3
Rakes, Revolving, K. D., Teeth in	1	1	3
Rakes, Sulky, K. D.	3	2	3
Range, Boilers, Iron	3	3	3
Refrigerators	2	2	2
Rice	4	4	6
Road Carts	1½	D-1	
Road Scrapers, Drag	3	2	3
Road Scrapers, Wheeled, K. D.	3	1	3
Rolled Oats	4	5	4
Roofing Paper	3	3	5
Rope	3	3	3
Rope, Wire	4	3	4

ARTICLES	CLASS West	CLASS East	CLASS South
Rubber Goods	1	1	1
Rugs, Woolen	1	1	1
Saddlery	1	1	2
Sad Irons	3	3	4
Safes, Iron	3	3	3
Salt	4	4	6
Sash, Unglazed, Common Pine	2	1	4
Sash Weights, Iron	4	4	6
Saw Frames, Circular, K. D	2	2	2
Saws, on Board	1	1	1
Sawing Machines, Drag, K. D	2	1	3
Scales, Wagon	2	2	3
Scientific Instruments	D-1	1	D-1
Screens, Door or Window	1	1	2
Seats, Carriage and Buggy	1½	1	2
Seeders, Broadcast, K. D.	3	2	2
Seeders, Endgate	3	2	2
Seeders, Hand, Crated	1	2	1
Separators, Cream	1	1	2
Settees, Lawn	D-1	D-1	1
Sewing Machines	1	1	1
Sewing Machines, Drop Head	1	1	2
Shafts, Carriage and Buggy, Finished	1½	D-1	1
Shot, in Boxes or Kegs	3	3	5
Shovels	2	2	3
Sideboards	1	1	2
Singletrees	3	3	
Skeins	3	4	5
Sleds, Bob	2	1	
Sleighs	2½	3T1	
Soap	4	3	6
Soap Powder	4	3	6
Sofas or Sofa Beds	D-1	D-1	1½
Sporting Goods	1	1	1
Spring Wagons (See Vehicles)			
Stalk Cutters, K. D	3	2	3
Stanchions, Cattle	2	3	4
Staples	4	4	6
Starch	3	3	3
Stationery	1	1	1
Stereopticons	D-1	1	1½
Stove Furniture	3	3	3
Stove Pipe, Crated	1½	1½	1½
Stove Pipe, Iron	3	4	4
Stoves and Ranges	3	3	3
Stump Pullers, K. D	3	2	4
Sugar	4	3	5
Sulkies	3T1	D-1	
Surreys (See Vehicles)			
Swage Blocks	3	3	5
Syrup in Barrels or Kegs	4	4	5
Tables, Extension	3	2	2
Tables, Parlor	D-1	1½	1½
Tackle Blocks	3	3	5
Tanks, Galvanized Iron (Set Up)	D-1	D-1	D-1
Tanks, Galvanized Iron (Knocked Down) Sides in Rolls	1	2	2
Tank Heaters	3	1	
Tea	1	1	1
Tents	1	1	1
Tent Poles	3	3	3
Tinware	2	2	2
Tire Benders	3	2	2
Tire Shrinkers	3	2	3
Tire Upsetters	3	2	3
Tobacco	1	1	1
Tombstones	3	3	4
Tools	2	3	2
Tools in Chest	1	3	2
Tops, Buggy	1½	1½	1½
Toys	1	1	1
Traps, Animal or Bird	2	2	2
Troughs, Galvanized Steel	1	2	3
Troughs, Pig, Cast Iron	2	2	3
Trunks	1	1½	1
Tubs, Wooden	1	1	3
Twine	2	3	3
Varnish in Cans	1	2	2
Varnish in Wood	2	3	3
Vehicles (such as Buggies, Carriages, Spring Wagons, Surreys), crated under 30 inches in height and 94 inches long	1½	1½	1
Vehicles, crated under 50 inches in height and 94 inches long	1½	D 1	1½
Vehicles, crated under 30 inches in height and over 94 inches long	1½	D-1	1
Vinegar, in Wood	4	3	6
Vises	2	3	4
Wagon Jacks	2	2	3
Wagons, Farm	1	1	4
Wall Paper	2	2	2
Wardrobes, set up	D-1	D-1	1½
Wardrobes, taken apart	2	2	3
Washing Machines	1	1	2
Washstands	1	1	2
Water Closets	1	2	3
Water Heaters	3	2	3
Weeders, K. D., in bundles	1	1	3
Wheelbarrows, K. D	2	2	2
Wheels, Buggy, Finished	1½	1	2
Wheels, Buggy, Unfinished	1	1	2
Wheels, Wagon, Iron	3	2	4
Wheels, Wagon, Wooden	1	1	4
White Lead, in kegs or barrels	4	4	4
Windmills and Towers	3	2	3
Window Screens	1	1	2
Wine	1	1	1
Wire, Barb or Smooth	4	4	6
Wire Fencing	3	3	5
Wire Rope	3	3	4
Woodenware	2	1	3
Wringers	2	2	3

CAPITAL $8,000,000
SURPLUS $6,000,000

JAMES B. FORGAN,
President.
CHARLES N. GILLETT,
Cashier.
WM. H. MONROE,
Assistant Cashier

Chicago, October 23, 1907.

TO WHOM IT MAY CONCERN:

It is with pleasure that we testify to our own good opinion of the integrity, responsibility and business ability of Sears, Roebuck & Company. They are one of the largest mercantile institutions in the United States.

Anyone can, in our judgment, feel perfectly secure in sending money to them with their orders, as we understand they ship their goods agreeing that anything not proving entirely satisfactory when received can be returned to them, and the money paid will immediately be returned to the purchaser.

The officers of the company are well and favorably known to us, command our full confidence, and we believe can be relied upon to do exactly as they agree.   Yours very truly,

In writing to the above bank as to our reliability, be sure to enclose a 2-cent stamp for reply.

ERNEST A. HAMILL, PRESIDENT
CHARLES L. HUTCHINSON, VICE PRESIDENT
CHAUNCEY J. BLAIR, VICE PRESIDENT
D. A. MOULTON, VICE PRESIDENT

JOHN C. NEELY, SECRETARY
FRANK W. SMITH, CASHIER
B. G. SAMMONS, ASS'T CASHIER
J. EDWARD MAASS, ASS'T CASHIER

No. 5196

THE CORN EXCHANGE NATIONAL BANK
OF CHICAGO

CAPITAL $3,000,000
SURPLUS $3,000,000

CHICAGO, October 22, 1907.

TO WHOM IT MAY CONCERN:

We are pleased to testify to the responsibility of Sears, Roebuck & Company. The company enjoys the highest credit with their Chicago banks, of which this bank is one.

We believe anyone who has dealings with this company will be treated in the fairest manner possible. We confidently assure anyone who is thinking of placing an order with them, that, in our judgment, there is absolutely no risk in sending the money with the order.

Yours very truly,

Cashier.

In writing to the above bank as to our reliability, be sure to enclose a 2-cent stamp for reply.

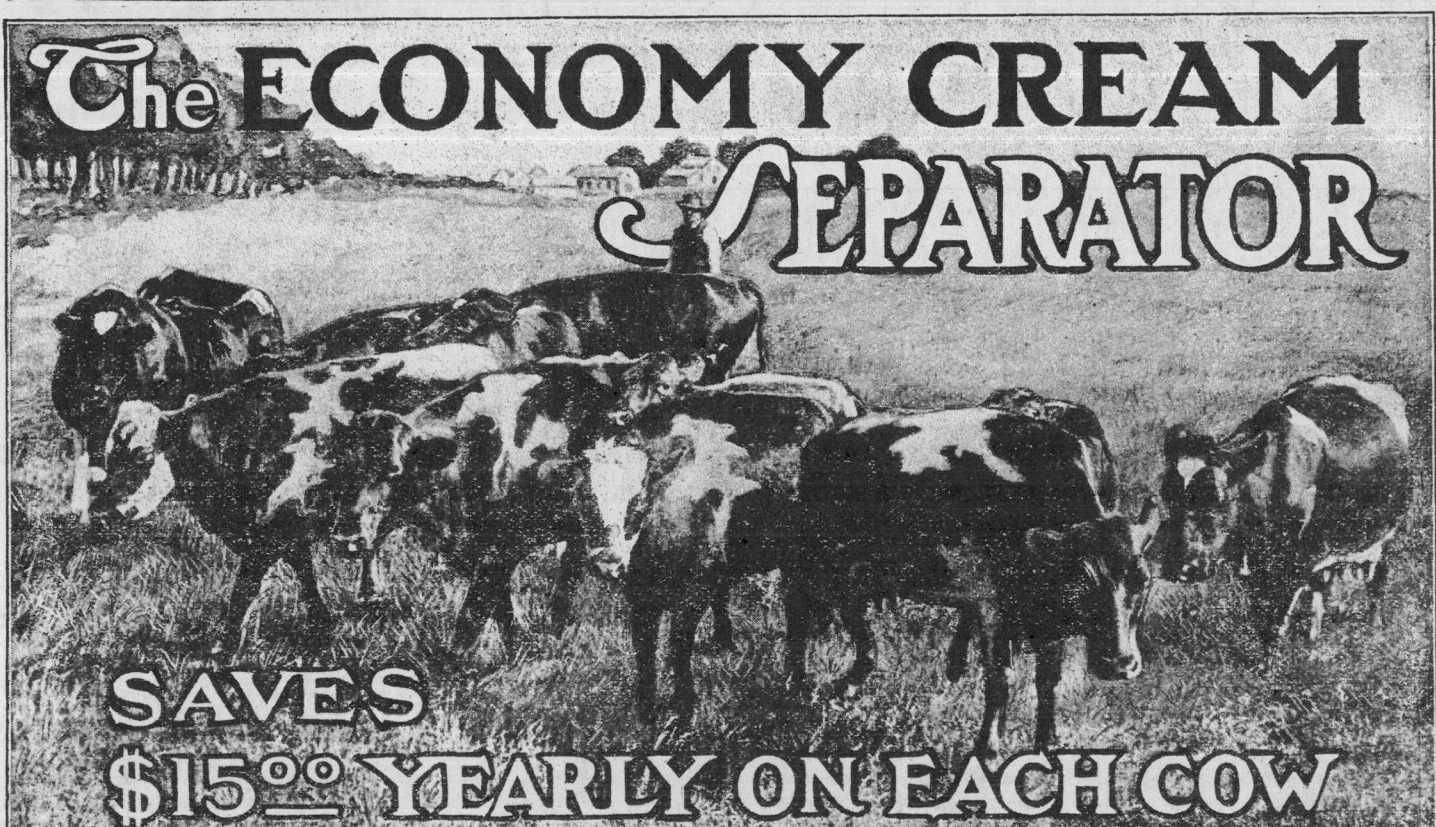

THE NEW ECONOMY CHIEF
CREAM SEPARATOR MARVEL of 1908 $28.80

OUR LATEST AND BEST. THE ENVY OF ALL OTHER SEPARATOR MANUFACTURERS. MORE SIMPLE THAN OTHERS, MORE EFFICIENT THAN OTHERS. THE REAL WONDER OF THE CREAM SEPARATOR WORLD.

MONEY CANNOT BUY A SEPARATOR that will compare with the new Economy Chief for 1908. It is built in by far the biggest separator factory in the world by our own mechanical experts, picked men, the cream of the country, whose reputation is established wherever high grade machinery is made. It far surpasses any other machine offered by any other maker. No other maker has the facilities we have. No other maker has the same amount of money invested in specially designed machinery built for the sole purpose of constructing perfect cream separators.

FIRST OF ALL the new Economy Chief is a skimming wonder of wonders. It skims to the last small drop of cream under the hardest conditions. It skims every particle of cream where all others fail, clog up and become useless. Nothing affects its wonderful skimming. It skims milk that is icy cold or milk that is steaming hot. Old milk or new milk. Mixed milk, milk from stripper cows and cows on dry feed. It skims everything in the milk line that can be skimmed and always skims from three to five times closer than the very best separators offered by the Trust or anyone else.

THE NEW ECONOMY CHIEF FOR 1908, we now offer to our customers for the first time at only $28.80 to $43.65, prices below the actual cost to produce separators in other factories and only possible by combining the facilities of the biggest and most complete cream separator factory on the globe with our great and unapproachable selling power, the power to reach and put our goods before the eyes of practically every farmer in the United States at a cost so small it is only nominal on each sale; our enormous factory with its perfect facilities and organization, splendid facilities for disposing of goods at a small selling expense, and our single small, very small factory profit, all three combined enable us to furnish our customers with the new Economy Chief Cream Separator at less than one-half the price charged by the Separator Trust for their inferior machines, none of which are comparable with the $1,000.00 challenge Economy Separator, to say nothing of our latest and best, the new Economy Chief.

WE FULLY GUARANTEE TO YOU that the new Economy Chief, when run by yourself or anyone else competent to run a cream separator, will outskim any $125.00 separator on the market two to one on your own farm. We expect it to outskim all other separators at least two to one at all temperatures or you can send it back and get all your money back, including the freight charges both ways.

IT HAS A DOZEN NEW AND VALUABLE IMPROVEMENTS.

The new low down supply tank, just the right height and low enough that anyone, even a child, can fill it easily. High enough to be out of the way. At a convenient height to use for washing the tinware after you have finished skimming. The whole inside is visible from top to bottom. You can clean it without removing it from the machine if you want to. It is pressed from a single piece of heavy steel, with rounding corners, not a seam or joint anywhere, and is tinned and retinned so that there is no wear out to it. It has our improved flush key faucet and can be set on the table or anywhere when filled without the faucet key being driven up and leaking as the tanks of other makers all do.

THE CRANK IS JUST THE RIGHT HEIGHT, in the position recommended by medical authorities as the most natural and healthy. A position that makes the operation of a light running separator like the Economy Chief delightful and healthy exercise for man, woman, boy or girl. It is neither too high nor too low; at just the height where you would have it if you were to build a cream separator to suit yourself.

IT RUNS SURPRISINGLY EASY. The new Economy Chief is easily brought up to speed and after that almost runs itself. The simplest possible gearing, the fewest possible bearings or points of friction, perfect adjustment throughout, small, compact bowl and moderate speed all combine to make it an easy running wonder, just the separator for women and boys to operate.

MANY OTHER IMPROVEMENTS aid in making the new Economy Chief the most perfect separator ever produced. Our newly improved oil feed. The wonderful new self adjusting, easily removable upper bearing. The improved supply tank holder which prevents all noise and vibration. The new clean-easy tinware with rounding corners and no crevices where milk can collect and sour. The handy little drip cup which catches all the oil and dirt and keeps the inside of the separator clean and sanitary and prevents dripping on the floor. The new rigid frame, solid as a rock. No weaving or vibration as in four-legged machines. Improvements here and there and everywhere suggested by our own experience and that of hundreds of thousands of Economy Separator users put the new and perfect Economy Chief in a class by itself.

THE MOST SIMPLE SEPARATOR ever devised. With a screwdriver and wrench a boy can take the entire machine apart in ten minutes and put it together ready to run in ten minutes more. No chance to get out of adjustment, no tinkering, no places hard to get at. No special tools required. Every part true to pattern and interchangeable. No possibility of putting together wrong. Only one way and that is the right way. To take out and replace the upper bearing takes but a minute in the new Economy Chief. In all other machines it takes from one hour to a day. Every other part is just as simple.

IT WILL LAST LONGER, from three to ten times as long as other separators. Every bearing runs in extra long anti-friction Harding formula phosphor bronze bushings. The shafting is turned from the finest of steel that money can buy and there is no wear out to it. The bowl is of solid, tough wrought steel; from top to bottom nothing but steel. The supply tank will outlast a dozen ordinary tanks. It is built of solid steel, without a seam or a joint. The tinware is extra heavy, tinned and retinned, and will last almost forever.

OUR PRICES AS GIVEN BELOW ARE FACTORY COST with our one small profit added and nothing more. Don't forget that when you buy a separator from the Trust or from an agent you pay a long string of profits over the cost to build, which are something like this: Your local agent's profit is $15.00 on each machine; the county agent or state agent gets $15.00 more; the general agent or jobber takes $20.00 of your money for his share and the factory must have a lot of your money in addition to the cost, for they have an army of salesmen, promoters and exhibitors running around the country from one end to the other, stirring their long line of agents into activity and traveling in palace cars, all at your expense. And, of course, selling most of their separators on time, the factory loses considerable money which you help to pay for when you buy a separator from them. In buying the Economy Chief all your money goes into the machine and none of it into the pockets of the hungry agents.

FACTORY TO YOU PRICES FOR THE NEW 1908 ECONOMY CHIEF CREAM SEPARATOR.

No. 23K61 The New Economy Chief Cream Separator for 1908, with all the latest improvements, capacity 250 to 300 pounds per hour. Shipping weight, 185 pounds. Special price to introduce on sixty days' trial...................................... **$28.80**

No. 23K62 The New Economy Chief Cream Separator for 1908, with all the latest improvements, capacity 350 to 400 pounds per hour. Shipping weight, 195 pounds. Special price to introduce on sixty days' trial....................................... **34.95**

No. 23K64 The New Economy Chief Cream Separator for 1908, with all the latest improvements, capacity 600 pounds per hour. Shipping weight, 205 pounds. Special price to introduce on sixty days' trial **43.65**

For Quick Delivery and Low Freight Offer on Our Large Economy Chief Separator, see page 34.

TWO MONTHS' FREE TRIAL

ALL YOUR MONEY BACK IF NOT SATISFIED AND YOUR TRIAL DOESN'T COST YOU A CENT

WE ARE DIFFERENT from other houses and especially different from separator houses, because we sell almost everything under the sun; we sell goods needed by everyone at all seasons of the year. Our greatest object and desire is to make every customer a permanent customer and with this end in view, the great principle upon which our business is conducted is that each customer must be satisfied with every article he buys, and if not, we will never rest until he is satisfied.

NO CUSTOMER CAN LOSE MONEY by buying from us if we know anything about it. Our customers' interests are our interests and we will do anything within the limits of reason to not only satisfy our customers but please them so well that they will consider it a pleasure and a privilege to order everything they need from us.

HOW DIFFERENT IS THE AGENT! He is interested only in selling you one separator. He never expects to sell you another. His sole object is to cover the weak points of his machine and point out the strong ones. Having made the sale he pockets his portion of your money and turns the rest over to his superior and then loses interest in you at once. He has nothing else to sell you. He doesn't want to ever see or hear from you again.

BUT IT IS NOT THIS WAY WITH US. We must satisfy you at first and must keep you satisfied to hold your trade on other goods. That's why it is we give you two months' trial while some makers give ten days, others five days and most of them give no trial at all. On this page we explain in detail the three different ways in which you can order. One is as good as another and we can only advise you to order by whichever way is the easiest and best for you; but no matter how you order, no matter whether you specify it in your order or not, you get sixty days' trial on every Improved Economy or Economy Chief Separator. Two full months in which to test it out most thoroughly. Run it morning and night. Week days and Sundays, 120 times. Skim hot milk and cold milk. Have your skim milk and your cream tested at the local creamery or test it with a Babcock tester and if at the end of the two months you say you are satisfied with the machine and would not want to do without it, we are satisfied also.

IF, ON THE OTHER HAND, you are not satisfied with it we are not satisfied until you have sent it back to us and we have returned all your money and paid all the freight charges both ways, so that your two months' trial has not cost you a cent. It pays us to be fair and liberal and we want to be. We don't know a fairer way to sell cream separators than this or we would adopt it.

YOU MIGHT NOT BE ABLE to learn all the details of running and skimming with the Economy Chief or the Improved Economy Separator in five or ten days, although either of them is remarkably simple, so we do not expect you to. You have two full months to put any separator you buy from us to every test right on your own farm, running it yourself or having it run by any member of your family or by power, before you finally decide to keep it.

IF YOU HAVE TWO COWS OR MORE don't delay but order a cream separator from us at once because we want you to find out that you are losing money every day you do without it. The free trial which we give costs you nothing, not a cent under any circumstances, and it will surely be the means of a gain to you, a gain large in proportion to the number of cows you keep.

THE KIND OF A GUARANTEE WE GIVE

OUR GUARANTEE makes us very careful in the quality of the machines we send out. We have a big inspection department entirely separate from our manufacturing department, where trained observers do nothing else but inspect, test and gauge every part that enters into the building of each of our separators.

THE CASTINGS from the foundry are carefully tested for flaws, blow holes and sand holes before any work is done on them, as were any flaw discovered after the work was started the labor and time which we had put on this casting will have been wasted. Every finished part before going to the assembling room is measured with fine gauges and micrometers, by which the slightest variance from the true standard, a variation too small to be detected by the keenest eye, is instantly noted. All parts varying from the standard even a trifle are destroyed, and those which are perfect are sent to various departments for assembling.

AFTER THE MACHINES ARE ASSEMBLED they get the hardest and most important test of all—our finishing test. They are first run by power for a long period and carefully watched, a delicate registering apparatus shows any undue friction in the bearings, any binding or lack of adjustment which would cause the machine to run hard, and after any trifling defect thus shown has been remedied, all machines pass into the hands of our final hand inspectors, who give every machine the actual test of use. Run liquid through the bowl. Carefully inspect every bushing, bearing, screw and nut, and by long practice detect any trifling irregularity which even our delicate registering apparatus does not show.

AFTER PASSING THROUGH THE INSPECTOR'S HANDS every machine is boxed before his eyes, so that it should reach you in absolutely perfect condition.

THIS IS THE REASON WHY we can and do give you a twenty-year written ironclad guarantee against defects of material and workmanship. No other separator maker attempts to do this. Ask any separator agent to give you a twenty-year guarantee with his machine and he may tell you one thing or he may tell you another, but you may be sure that he will not and cannot give you the guarantee as we do.

CERTIFICATE No......

CERTIFICATE OF GUARANTEE.

This is to Certify, that the Catalogue No.________ CREAM SEPARATOR, sold________ Town of________ State of________ is warranted to be perfect in material and workmanship, and perfect in operation, if properly set up and managed. We agree to replace, free of charge, any piece or part giving out by reason of defect in material or workmanship, for a period of 20 years from date.

When referring to this guarantee, please do not fail to mention Certificate Number, and also bowl number, which will be found stamped on bottom of bowl of machine.

Dated at Chicago, this________day of________A.D., 190____

SEARS, ROEBUCK & CO.

THIS IS AN EXACT COPY, excepting the name and address, of THE GREAT TWENTY-YEAR IRONCLAD SIGNED GUARANTEE which goes with every Improved Economy or Economy Chief Cream Separator. By its terms, as you will see by reading it over, we bind ourselves to replace, free of all charge, any piece or part which gives out through defect in material or workmanship for a period of twenty years from the date on which the machine was bought.

THREE EASY WAYS OF ORDERING

THERE ARE THREE WAYS IN WHICH YOU CAN ORDER EITHER THE IMPROVED ECONOMY OR ECONOMY CHIEF CREAM SEPARATOR. ALL OF THEM ARE EASY AND ALL OF THEM ARE GOOD. IT MAKES NO DIFFERENCE TO US WHICH WAY YOU ORDER. YOU CAN SUIT YOURSELF AND ORDER BY WHICHEVER METHOD YOU THINK IS THE BEST.

NO MATTER HOW YOU ORDER you get the same twenty-year ironclad signed guarantee with your separator, the same sixty days' free trial which we always give on separators. You are carefully protected and cannot lose a penny, no matter which method of ordering you follow.

YOU CAN SEND US $1.00 DEPOSIT if you wish if you live east of the Rocky Mountains or $5.00 deposit if you live west of the Rocky Mountains, and we will ship the separator which you order to you C. O. D. for the balance. When the machine arrives at your station the railroad agent will notify you and you can then go to the express agent and by paying him the balance of the purchase price due he will turn over to you the bill of lading and upon presenting this to the railroad agent he will deliver the separator to you upon payment of the freight charges, which, of course, are very small.

THE DISADVANTAGE OF THIS WAY is that the express companies make a charge of from 50 to 75 cents usually for the collection and return of the money to us. This is not a large amount, still by sending us cash in full with your order you can save it and it is, of course, well worth saving.

WE HAVE ANOTHER WAY by which you send us no money. Just drop us a line asking us to send you a copy of our Separator Certificate of Deposit and we will send you a certificate that reads just like this:

CERTIFICATE OF DEPOSIT.

Town________ State________ Date________

RECEIVED FROM Mr.________

________Dollars in payment of Sears, Roebuck & Co.'s Cream Separator No.________

We agree to hold this money until the Cream Separator has been received by Mr.________ residing in________ and has had 30 days' trial, when we shall forward the amount to Sears, Roebuck & Co., Chicago, Ill.

If Mr.________ is not perfectly satisfied with the machine, we will return his money to him on surrender to us of a bill of lading showing the machine has been reconsigned to Sears, Roebuck & Co.

____

Take this certificate to your local bank, the bank where you do business or any other bank in your town and deposit the purchase price of the cream separator with your banker and he will fill out and sign the certificate which we send you and you can then enclose this certficate with your order and we will ship the separator which you select to you just as soon as we receive the order.

IN A FEW DAYS the separator will arrive at your railroad station. The railroad agent will notify you when it comes and will deliver it to you when you call for it upon payment of the freight charges, which are always small. You can take it home and use it every day for thirty days separating your morning and evening milk. Give it a good trial and if at the end of thirty days the banker does not hear from you or if you let him know that you are satisfied with the machine he will send the money which you have deposited with him to us.

IF, ON THE OTHER HAND, you change your mind and conclude that you do not want the separator or if you are not well satisfied with it in every way, simply pack it up and deliver it to the railroad station and the railroad agent will give you a bill of lading. By presenting this bill of lading to your banker he will at once give you back all the money you have deposited and then when he sends the bill of lading to us showing that you have returned the separator we will pay back to you all the freight charges which you paid when the separator was received, so that your trial has cost you nothing, not a cent.

YOU UNDERSTAND that after the banker has held the money for thirty days after you have received the machine and has then sent it to us you still have an additional thirty days' trial in which to decide finally to keep the separator, or sixty days' trial in all, and should you send the machine back to us during the second thirty days we will promptly refund all the money you have paid and pay the freight charges both ways, so that your sixty days' trial will be free of all cost. This is a very good way to order as your money remains right in your own town in your home bank while you are testing the separator.

THE BEST AND EASIEST WAY OF ALL, however, and the plan which is followed by almost all of our customers is to simply send us the full price of the machine selected with their order, either in the form of an express order, bank draft or postoffice money order. As soon as we receive it we make prompt shipment of the separator. In a few days it arrives at your railroad station, you merely call for it, pay the agent the small amount of freight charges due, take it home, set up and use it for sixty days before finally deciding to keep it, and then if you don't want it, send it back to us and we promptly, without quibble or question, send back all your money and pay freight charges both ways. This is the simplest way to order. No bother, no extra expense, no running to the bank, no collection charges to pay to the express companies and we feel sure that if you adopt this method of ordering, as nearly all of our customers have, you will find it to be by far the easiest, cheapest and quickest for you.

FOR FREIGHT RATES ON CREAM SEPARATORS TO ALL STATES SEE PAGE 35.

WHAT DO YOU KEEP COWS FOR?

On the road to the creamery. A single can carries all the cream from a wagon load of milk if you separate it at home with the Economy.

NEARLY ALL FARMERS KEEP COWS TO MAKE MONEY

DAIRYING IS ONE OF THE MOST IMPORTANT FARM INDUSTRIES AND IS BECOMING MORE IMPORTANT EVERY DAY. A LARGE PART OF THE AVERAGE FARMER'S ENERGY AND TIME IS GIVEN TO THE CARE AND FEEDING OF HIS COWS, AND IF HE HAS GIVEN THE MATTER ANY THOUGHT HE KNOWS THAT HE DOES IT IN ORDER THAT HE MAY MAKE MONEY FROM THE PRODUCT OF THE COWS.

IF YOU KEEP COWS a considerable portion of your land is no doubt reserved for the purpose of feeding the cows, either to raise forage crops or for pasture. You get up early in the morning to milk and feed them and in the evening you milk them again. If you were to make a careful record of how you spent your working hours you would find that during the year a quarter, a third or perhaps one-half of your time and labor has been given to the dairying end of your business.

YOU KEEP COWS PRINCIPALLY FOR THEIR MILK. The most valuable part of the milk and, in fact, the most valuable of all farm products is the butter fat. Butter fat is worth from $20.00 to $30.00 per hundred pounds and there is nothing else raised upon the farm which will compare with it in value. Corn is worth from 80 cents to $1.20 per hundred pounds. Oats are worth from $1.25 to $1.80 per hundred pounds. Even wheat is worth but $1.50 to $1.80 per hundred pounds. Skim milk after the butter fat has been extracted is worth from 6 cents to 40 cents per hundred pounds, according to its condition and what it is used for, being only about one-hundredth part as valuable as the butter fat. Before you get an ounce of butter fat or cream in marketable condition you have put in all your time and labor, and your profit or loss depends, first, upon the amount of butter fat that you get and, second, upon its quality.

BUTTER FAT IS SO VERY VALUABLE, so much higher in price than any other farm product that if any considerable part of it is wasted the farmer not only makes no profit but actually is a loser. He cannot sell what remains of the butter fat for enough money to pay for the cost of feeding and caring for his cows. Dairying has never paid for the farmer who has wasted one-third or more of the butter fat, and as land becomes more valuable from year to year it cannot but lose money for him. One-third of the butter fat lost means all the profit lost. Two-thirds of the butter fat usually is required to pay for the cost of keeping up the herd and the other one-third is the dairyman's profit. It is the last third that pays the profit, so that is the most important of all. The first two-thirds pays no profit. It simply goes to pay for the expense and labor of keeping the cows and according to the greater or less proportion of the remaining one-third that you get your prosperity will depend.

IF YOUR COWS ARE GOOD and intelligently selected for their milk giving and butter fat producing qualities, properly fed and cared for and you get all the butter fat, the two-thirds that goes to pay the expense of keeping up the herd and the other third, which is your profit, you will surely prosper. You cannot help doing so. There is no business in the world in which returns are so certain as in dairying if it is properly and intelligently handled. No merchant in business, no manufacturer can be certain of a surer and safer margin of profit than the dairyman who gets all of the last one-third of the butter fat in his milk.

THE EXTRA COST OF A FINE DAIRY COW, even if it be two or three times as much as an ordinary cow, is nothing compared to the profit. A poor cow but little more than pays her board in butter fat. If your cows are poor and you get but two-thirds of the butter fat, you must lose money. If you get all the butter fat you will make some money. If your cows are good and you get two-thirds of the butter fat you will make a little money, but all the butter fat from good cows must give you a handsome return for your time and labor.

THERE ARE A NUMBER OF WAYS of taking all or part of the butter fat from the whole milk in general use. The oldest one, as everybody knows, is the old fashioned way of setting the milk in crocks or tin pans in a cool place and waiting for the cream to rise to the surface. Another and later way is to set the milk in tall, narrow cans submerged in cool running water or ice water. The third way and one which has had some considerable popularity of late is to separate the cream, or a portion of it, by diluting the whole milk with a large quantity of cold water. A fourth way, and better than any of these, is to ha the milk to the creamery and have it skimmed by power separators, selling the butter fat to the creamery and hauling the skim milk back to the farm.

THE BEST WAY OF ALL and the one which is now being very generally adopted is to separate the cream containing the butter fat from the whole milk by means of the hand separator. This method is so far ahead of all others that it makes any dairy a sure money making investment while the other methods are all more or less uncertain.

RAISING CREAM IN PANS AND CROCKS DOESN'T PAY

IF YOU HAVE BEEN RAISING CREAM IN CROCKS AND PANS in the old fashioned way we feel safe in saying that your dairy does not pay for the time and trouble that it takes, and it would be to your advantage to either change your method of gathering cream or sell your cows and go out of the dairy business altogether. The first cost of a pan or crock when you buy it from the dealer is not very much, perhaps 25 cents, but if it is a good one and lasts you a long time it may cost you $25.00 before you get through with it in the valuable butter fat which you lose through its use.

THERE IS VERY LITTLE DIFFERENCE in specific gravity between butter fat and skim milk. The skim milk is only about one-seventh heavier than the butter fat, and when you set your whole milk away in pans for the butter fat to rise, or rather for the skim milk to settle down and force the globules of butter fat to the surface, the difference in weight between the skim milk and the fat globules is so small that the fat comes to the surface very, very slowly and much of it being in very small globules does not rise at all. In time the milk thickens and sours and the raising of the cream ceases. You skim off what has come to the surface, which is about two-thirds of the butter fat usually, and the remaining one-third, which represents all or nearly all of your dairy profit, remains in the sour skim milk where it cannot do you nor anybody else any good; so to start with you have lost the greatest part of your profit in the valuable butter fat, the most costly of any farm product, which is lost in the skim milk.

THE CREAM THAT HAS RISEN to the surface has stood for hours exposed to the dust and dirt (which is always floating in the air), the action of germs, and has perhaps absorbed musty odors which are always present in the cellar or spring house, no matter how careful you are, and all this affects the flavor of the butter and reduces its values. Ask any dealer in butter and he will tell you that practically all the low grade butter on the market, or butter that sells for 10 or 12 cents a pound, is made from cream raised by gravity in pans and cans, and that all the fine high priced butter, the 25-cent or 30-cent per pound kind, is made from separator cream properly cared for.

THE LOSS IN THE PAN RAISING SYSTEM is not always one-third. It varies. At times three-fourths of the butter fat will rise to the surface. At other times, owing to weather conditions, great heat and humidity, or perhaps thunder storms, very little if any of the cream will rise before the milk thickens, so that the average loss of cream by the pan raising system is easily one-third.

The one-third that is lost is what should be your profit over the cost of feeding and caring for your cows.

THE HARD WORK AND SLAVERY of the pan raising way of gathering cream is one of its worst features. The cold sour milk must be heated before feeding it to the calves. Pans without number must be washed and scalded; large quantities of water heated; you are continually building fires and burning fuel. In fact, in the pan raising system continuous work and continuous waste go hand in hand.

THE RESULT OF IT ALL is that one-third of your butter fat, which is all your profit, goes to waste in the sour skim milk. The animals to which sour milk is fed are done more harm than good because it is neither natural nor healthy food for any living animal.

THE DILUTION SYSTEM, by which a large quantity of cold water is mixed with the whole milk to assist in raising the cream, is no better than the pan raising. The loss in the cream which never rises to the top is just as great and the skim milk has been thinned down by the dilution to such an extent that it hardly pays to heat it up for feeding purposes, as animals refuse to touch it.

THE DEEP SETTING SYSTEM of raising the cream in deep round or oval cans plunged in ice water is better than raising it in open pans. You get more cream and the quality is better. Still the waste is very great; fully 20 per cent of the butter fat is lost. That is, one pound wasted to every four pounds gathered, and the work is just as hard and perhaps harder because of the quantity of cold water or ice which is necessary to get good results.

A DISADVANTAGE OF ALL GRAVITY RAISED CREAM is that it will not churn completely. The fibrous matter which forms in the cream while it is standing prevents the gathering of butter particles, so that the butter is not only not of a uniform quality, but there is a greater loss of the butter fat in the buttermilk than there is when churning separator cream. This amounts to a considerable item in the course of the year.

THIS IS THE HARD, OLD FASHIONED, MONEY LOSING WAY of dairying. All the cream or butter that you can sell by this method at the best price that you can get for it will not pay for the cost of keeping up the dairy, and if you are still using it, it would be better for you to sell your cows than to continue.

THE WHOLE MILK CREAMERY

THE DOUBLE HAULING SYSTEM by which the whole milk is hauled to the creamery to be skimmed and the skim milk hauled back to the farm has been very extensively used during the past ten or fifteen years, but is rapidly being superseded by the hand separator system, which does away with practically all of the hauling.

IF YOU ARE NOW HAULING or have ever hauled a wagon load of whole milk to your creamery every day over good roads and bad, up hill and down dale, at all seasons of the year and in all kinds of weather, and then hauled back your share of the sour milk, we need say nothing about it. You know the time it takes, especially during the busy season when every minute of daylight is doubly valuable, the long wait at the creamery, the double hauling, wearing alike on man, team and rig. The everlasting cleaning and scalding of milk cans, the work of building fires to heat the sour skim milk so that it will be half way fit for animal food, the heavy lifting and the endless hard work.

ALL THIS FOR THE PURPOSE of having three or four pounds of butter fat taken from each one hundred pounds of milk. Or perhaps you have been paying to have your whole milk hauled. The average haul is six miles and the average cost of hauling is 15 cents per hundred pounds and as the whole milk usually contains about 3¾ per cent of butter fat it will make about four pounds of butter to each 100 pounds, so that the average cost of hauling the milk for each four pounds of butter is 15 cents, or 3¾ cents a pound. This is a great tax and absorbs a large part of the dairy profits.

THERE ARE OTHER DISADVANTAGES to the whole milk creamery system which are just as important. The skim milk which you get in return is always ice cold in winter by the time you get back home and must be heated before feeding it. In summer it is thick and sour and is not fit for food, frequently causing sickness and death to young animals. The expense of keeping your milk cans in repair and replacing them with new ones as they become rusted amounts to quite an item in the course of a year.

THEN THERE IS THE WEAR AND TEAR on the harness and wagon, which will require constant repairs and attention. The whole milk creamery system means an endless amount of work and comparatively small profit, while, on the other hand, the hand separator system makes the work easy and the profits generously large.

THE SURE WAY AND EASY WAY TO MAKE YOUR DAIRY PAY

TO GET EVERY BIT OF THE CREAM from the milk, not only the two-thirds of it which is necessary to pay expenses, but also the one-third which you should have for your dairy profit, to get all the cream in its sweetest and best condition, you must use a centrifugal hand cream separator.

IT SEPARATES ALL THE CREAM from the milk immediately after milking. It cleanses and purifies it and makes butter of the highest quality certain if ordinary care is used in butter making. It gives you warm sweet skim milk for feeding, which is practically as good as whole milk, and enables you to raise strong, healthy calves and pigs at a very low cost.

IT MAKES YOU INDEPENDENT of the local market, as the sweet cream can be shipped for hundreds of miles profitably if you can get a better price for it elsewhere. The difference in the work and time required where a hand separator is used is wonderful. Within half an hour from the time the milking is finished the cream has been separated and put to cool, the separator cleaned and the work is finished. It reduces a task which under the old gravity raising system is almost unending, to half an hour's work in the morning and evening.

NO FARM MACHINE commences to pay as well as a hand cream separator. It harvests its crop twice a day at all seasons of the year, the most valuable crop, weight for weight, that is produced on the farm. The farm, with a good herd of dairy cows and a hand cream separator is proof against all ordinary bad seasons or poor crops. From the sale of butter or cream there is a continual stream of money flowing into such a farm, the soil is continually becoming richer and more fertile and the harvest is not confined to one season, but is continuous.

PERHAPS YOU ARE HAULING your whole milk to the creamery for separation. If so, whether you haul it yourself or pay to have it hauled, the hand separator will save you on an average of $6.00 to $8.00 in the cost of hauling the milk on each cow. If you are raising cream by any gravity system, your loss on each cow per year is not less than forty to sixty pounds of butter fat lost in the skim milk; at 20 cents per pound this amounts to $8.00 to $12.00 yearly on each cow.

THE FRESH WARM SKIM MILK from the separator, with a little oil meal or oatmeal added to it, at a cost of only about a cent a pound, has been estimated by eminent dairy experts to be worth from 25 cents to 40 cents per hundred pounds for stock food, depending upon the age of the stock and the market prices. The sweet skim milk from each cow, figured at only 30 cents per hundred pounds, is worth from $12.00 to $15.00.

IF YOU MAKE YOUR OWN BUTTER you will find that your hand separator butter, because of its superior flavor and keeping qualities, will bring from 3 to 10 cents per pound more than butter made from gravity raised cream. This is a big item in itself. A hand cream separator will save $15.00 a year on the product of every single cow you have, to say nothing of the saving in time and labor. No one has ever been known to go back to the old fashioned way after having used a hand separator, it pays for itself so quickly and brings such big returns.

WHILE OTHER FARM MACHINES may save you money for a few days, or at the most for a week or two each season, the hand cream separator is the only one which will save time, labor and money twice every day in the year.

SEPARATOR CREAM IS THE CREAM OF ALL CREAM

A HIGHEST GRADE CREAM SEPARATOR such as the Improved Economy or Economy Chief, not only delivers the cream in the smoothest and most velvety condition with any desired percentage of butter fat but also purifies it, removes the dirt and hair, germs and bacteria which are present and which have a tendency to spoil the flavor of the butter and cause the cream to sour quickly, so that after being cooled, separator cream will keep in good condition fully three or four times as long as gravity raised cream which has been spread out over the top of more or less sour milk for hours gathering dust and rapidly fermenting.

SEPARATOR CREAM CHURNS MUCH MORE COMPLETELY than gravity raised cream. The butter granules separate more quickly and there is less fat left in the buttermilk. The reason for this is that a stringy, weblike substance forms in the milk as it becomes old. A part of this is carried to the top of the cream and prevents the butter granules from separating readily in churning, so that it usually takes twice the time to churn gravity raised cream that is required for separator cream.

SEPARATOR CREAM CHURNING more completely, there is naturally an increase in the quantity of butter you can get from cream of equal weight and richness. This will run at least 10 per cent of the butter made, or from fifteen to twenty pounds extra a year from the milk of each cow.

THIS IS ONLY ONE OF THE MANY SAVINGS, small and large, made by the dairyman who uses a separator, yet this saving alone will almost pay for an Economy in the course of a year if ten cows are milked. If you have read the market reports you know that it pays to make separator butter. The best separator or creamery butter is always quoted at from three to ten cents per pound more than ordinary dairy butter. In shipping cream a very important point is to ship as heavy a cream as possible, as the railroads charge so much per can for carrying, and by skimming a heavy cream you get a much larger percentage of butter fat in each can. For instance: A can containing eighty pounds of cream which is 25 per cent butter fat costs just as much to ship as a can containing the same quantity of cream which is 50 per cent butter fat and the value of the contents of the can of 50 per cent cream is twice as much, so that the carrying charges are proportionately one-half of what they are where the thinner cream is shipped.

THE IMPROVED ECONOMY OR ECONOMY CHIEF CREAM SEPARATORS are noted for their wide range of skimming. They will skim any cream from the thinnest to a cream so rich that it will scarcely flow. It is a big advantage to be able to skim a 30, 40, 50 or even a 60 per cent cream, such as can easily be done with our new Economy Chief Cream Separator.

SWEET, WARM SKIM MILK THE BEST OF FOODS

SEPARATOR SKIM MILK, FRESH, SWEET AND PURE, still warm from the cow, is one of the most valuable foods in the world for young animals, and they thrive on it. It contains the rich and nutritious sugar of milk, the casein, everything necessary to build muscle and bone quickly and economically.

THE ONLY THING that is lacking is the butter fat which supplies the heat and fat producing elements. Just a little oil meal, which costs only 1 cent a pound, or oatmeal if oil meal is not at hand, takes the place of the valuable butter fat and makes the skim milk just as good as sweet whole milk fresh from the cow. Calves and pigs brought up on a sweet skim milk diet thrive and at the end of their first year are as large and healthy and in much more marketable condition than they would be at the age of two or three years if brought up on old sour milk.

SEPARATOR SKIM MILK MAKES SPLENDID FOOD for chickens if mixed with cornmeal. It is also very valuable as human food and is in great demand by bakeries. Another great advantage of keeping and feeding the separator skim milk on the farm is its fertilizing value. It loses practically none of this in passing through the body of the animal and when you sell only the butter fat, keeping and feeding the skim milk, your farm will grow richer and more fertile year by year and will constantly increase in value.

MANY INTERESTING EXPERIMENTS have been made by the state agricultural colleges in the dairy states, all of which agree in proving that the value of warm sweet separator skim milk for feeding purposes is practically equal to whole milk, and that it is worth for feeding from 20 to 40 cents per hundred pounds according to the age of the stock to which it is fed and their market value. Consider what a big item this is. A good average cow gives 5,000 pounds of milk yearly; 4,500 pounds of this is skim milk. Figuring its average value at 30 cents per hundred pounds your clear yearly gain on this one single item alone by using a cream separator is $13.50 on every cow you have.

A CENTRIFUGAL CREAM SEPARATOR is such a big advantage in every way that no farmer who has ever used one has been known to go back to the old fashioned way. It insures prosperity and not only makes big profits certain, but by reducing the labor of caring for a herd makes it possible to handle double the number of cows. It is as easy to care for the product of twenty cows with a cream separator as for ten cows with any old fashioned method, and the increased product will bring not less than $15.00 extra yearly from each cow.

SOUR SKIM MILK, on the other hand, is almost useless as animal food, whether it has been soured in pans or crocks at home or has been hauled for miles over rough country roads to the creameries. After being separated and mixed with the skim milk from hundreds of other cows in all conditions of filth or cleanliness and then hauled home again, it is very poor food at best.

THE SUGAR OF MILK, which is so healthful and nutritious in the warm sweet milk, has turned to lactic acid, which is nothing more or less than a form of vinegar, and, as every one knows, vinegar is not good food. In fact, it is not fit for any living animal in large quantities. Sickly and stunted pigs, small scrubby calves afflicted with scours and a large death rate are some of the results of feeding the sour skim milk.

BY FEEDING THE SWEET, NUTRITIOUS, FRESH SKIM MILK you will produce stock that you will be proud to show to your neighbors and which will sell readily on the market at a good big price. On the other hand, if you stick to feeding the old sour swill your stock will be a drug on the market and will hardly pay for the trouble of bringing them up.

HEATING THE COLD SOUR MILK for feeding is another hard and irksome task with its accompanying fire building, heavy lifting and everlasting cleaning.

ANOTHER VERY SERIOUS DISADVANTAGE of creamery skim milk is that the milk from cows from the entire neighborhood is mixed in one vat and disease germs are spread from one herd to another. It is well known that the cattle in whole communities have become infected with tuberculosis, lumpy jaw or arthrax from feeding the creamery skim milk which has been mixed with that of infected cows.

SEPARATOR BUTTER ALWAYS TAKES THE PRIZES

EVERYONE WHO WATCHES THE MARKET REPORTS knows that separator or creamery butter brings from 3 to 10 cents per pound more on the market than dairy butter at all times, and even in the spring when butter is the most plentiful, there is always a greater demand for high grade butter that can possibly be supplied. At fairs, exhibitions and dairy shows separator butter has always taken the prize in competition with dairy butter because of its superior grain and flavor, and always will for many reasons.

CREAM after passing through the separator has been purified. All dirt, germs and harmful bacteria have been removed and remain in the bowl of the machine. It is smooth, velvety and heavy, in just the best condition to be properly ripened for butter making. It ripens more evenly, churns more completely and with proper care the grain of the butter is perfect, the flavor unsurpassed, and in keeping qualities it has no equal. It will keep fully two or three times as long under the same conditions as dairy butter which is loaded with harmful ferment germs, bad odors and is sure to be more or less off in flavor.

IT WOULD PAY TO USE A CREAM SEPARATOR because of the higher price which can be obtained for the butter made from separator cream, if for no other reason. If you use the Economy Chief there will be a bigger demand for your butter than you can supply and it will sell for high prices all the year around. Hundreds of our customers have told us that they are now getting from 8 to 10 cents a pound more for their butter than they did before buying a cream separator.

NOTHING BUT WASTE AND WORK IN THE OLD WAY

ALL THE OLD METHODS OF DAIRYING are wasteful from start to finish. Wasteful of time and money, labor, butter fat, skim milk and everything in connection with the dairy. Not one dairy in twenty can stand the waste and still make money. The waste of butter fat, the richest product of the farm, in the sour skim milk of the gravity raising process would make a dairy pay a handsome profit if it were saved. The waste of the sour skim milk, which is almost useless for feeding, amounts to $10.00 or $12.00 a year on each cow.

THE WASTE IN THE POOR QUALITY of the butter produced under gravity raising conditions is from 3 to 10 cents on every pound butter. The waste of time and of money in hauling whole milk to the creamery and hauling the skim milk back again averages 4 cents for every pound of butter.

IT IS ONLY under the most favorable conditions, with the present high prices for land and feed, that a farmer can make his dairy pay any profit at all under any of the old fashioned systems. Every cent taken in goes to pay the expense of keeping up the dairy and there is nothing left for profit, because the profit which should be large has all been wasted—wasted in the butter fat left in the skim milk, in the useless sour, fermented milk, the poor quality and uneven butter and the sickly, stunted young stock, all of which go with the old gravity raising or whole milk creamery systems.

CHANGE TODAY. Send in your order for one of our new Economy Chief Separators and start on the road to sure prosperity and big profits by simply saving what you have wasted heretofore. If you use the hand separator you cannot lose. Your harvest is continuous. You are making money, not during one short season of a month or two, but all the time, 365 days in the year, money is flowing into your pocket. Bad seasons and poor crops will affect you but little, for the dairy crop is continuous, and though the feed costs a little more during the bad seasons, the increased price which the products bring will more than make it up.

THERE IS NO SUCH THING as a crop failure in the dairy where a hand separator is used. Start right and start at once by ordering one of our new Economy Chief Separators, the latest production of our big factory and fully guaranteed to you as the best cream separator ever sold, with two months' free trial on your own farm to prove to your own satisfaction that every claim we make is true and justified.

THE CREAM SEPARATOR LEADS TO SURE PROSPERITY

ORDER A NEW ECONOMY CHIEF at once and we will guarantee that the returns will surprise you. Don't delay. Order today. Your result will be better cream and more of it, cream of any density from the richest to the thinnest, a wonderful reduction in dairy work, better butter with less churning, sweet, pure skim milk in the finest condition for feeding, larger and better calves and pigs, bigger prices for everything, for butter or cream and for stock.

ORDER AN ECONOMY CHIEF NOW and do away with the springhouse, the creamery, the cellar and the ice house, the handling and hauling, the endless drudgery and labor of building fires and washing cans, the heavy lifting, the wear and tear on man and beast in the long hauls to the creamery.

THERE IS A SURE PROFIT for you in the new Economy Chief, a profit in every turn of the crank weekdays and Sundays, all the year around. It will make your dairy returns so large that you will be surprised. It will reduce your work in caring for the milk to almost nothing, a half hour in the morning and evening instead of a continuous task morning, noon and night. Get big returns and make big money with one-quarter the labor and time that you have spent heretofore in getting small returns or no returns.

PLEASE ORDER TODAY. Order an Improved Economy or, better still, our latest and best model, the new Economy Chief Cream Separator, which so far surpasses all others in closeness of skimming, ease of running, easy cleaning qualities and in every other way, that there is really no chance for comparison.

WE OFFER THIS SEASON TWO MODELS, our Improved Economy, on which we have reduced the prices, already low, still lower, and which we offer at a lower price than a high grade cream separator has ever before been offered heretofore, and our latest and best the new Economy Chief, at a price which only covers the actual cost of production in the largest and most complete cream separator factory in the world, with our one single small profit added.

WE BY ALL MEANS RECOMMEND the purchase of the new Economy Chief, which is not only the closest approach to mechanical perfection which has ever been attained in the art of cream separator manufacturing, but is so strong and durable that there is practically no wear out to it. So simple that a child can understand it and it runs so easy that a woman or half grown boy can operate it as well as a man. The new Economy Chief is the separator to buy. We recommend it and guarantee it.

ORDER IT subject to the sixty days' trial which we give on every cream separator we sell and if at the end of that time you are not more than satisfied and do not feel that we have done you a favor in putting into your hands the most perfect cream separator ever built, we want you to send it back at our expense and get all your money back.

WE COULD NOT MAKE a fairer or more liberal proposition than this. We want everybody who has any use for a cream separator to order one of our latest Economy Chief Separators on these terms.

$26.30 IMPROVED ECONOMY CREAM SEPARATOR

THIS IS THE ORIGINAL $1,000.00 challenge Economy Cream Separator which has time and again outskimmed all other makes, and up to the time that we put our new Economy Chief on the market it was undoubtedly by far the closest skimmer of any, skimming from two to ten times as close as any competing machine.

IT IS A REMARKABLY EASY RUNNING MACHINE yet does not run as easy as the new Economy Chief, which, because of its fewer parts and points of friction, runs still easier. Easier, in fact, than any separator ever offered for sale heretofore. At our prices, ranging from $26.30 for the small size to $37.65 for the big 600 pounds per hour capacity size, our Improved Economy Separator is a wonderful bargain as these prices are less than one-half the prices charged by others for machines that do not compare with it, yet purely in your own interest we believe that it will be greatly to your advantage to order the new Economy Chief Cream Separator, our latest and best, which we have just put on the market.

THE ECONOMY CHIEF not only runs easier but because of the genuine extra length Harding phosphor bronze bushings used on every bearing it is much more durable, and at the very small difference in price, which only represents the actual difference in cost to us, it will be greatly to your advantage to order the Economy Chief. Either machine will do splendid work and if you never knew about our new machine, the Economy Chief, you would be more than satisfied with the Improved Economy, because it outclasses all competition.

THE DIFFERENCE IN PRICE is small, and the new Economy Chief machine has so many improvements and advantages, the one piece drawn steel supply tank, the simple frictionless gearing, our improved upper bearing and a dozen other improvements at vital points which make it by far the most convenient as well as the most durable separator made, that we strongly recommend its purchase.

PRICES FOR THE IMPROVED ECONOMY CREAM SEPARATOR.

No. 23K9173 Capacity, 250 to 300 pounds per hour. Suitable for a dairy of two to eight cows. Price.......... **$26.30**

No. 23K9174 Capacity, 350 to 400 pounds per hour. Suitable for a dairy of three to ten or twelve cows. Price.......... **$31.60**

No. 23K9176 Capacity, 600 pounds per hour. Suitable for a dairy of from three to thirty-five cows. Price.......... **$37.65**

$28.80 THE NEW ECONOMY CHIEF SEPARATOR

60 Days' Free Trial

20-YEAR GUARANTEE

ONLY $28.80 and up for the genuine Economy Chief Separator, the latest production of our big separator factory, largest in the world. Fully guaranteed by us to be without exception the closest skimming cream separator in the world. (See our $1,000.00 in gold challenge.)

THE EASIEST RUNNING OF ANY, the strongest and most durable. So well and strongly made that there is almost no wear out to it. So simple that a mere boy can take it apart and put together in no time. Anyone, man, woman or child, can run it. Capacity for capacity, we guarantee it to be the easiest running separator ever manufactured. Wonderfully strong and lasting. Built to be used twice a day year in and year out under the hardest dairy conditions and require practically no repairs.

EVERY ONE accompanied by our great ironclad twenty-year signed guarantee against any defect of material or workmanship. Separators sold at from $100.00 to $125.00 by other concerns cannot compare with our new wonder, the Economy Chief, under every and all dairy conditions. Skims hot milk or cold milk, milk of any temperature from freezing to boiling point closer than milk has ever been skimmed before.

NOTICE OUR GREAT ANTI-TRUST PRICES. Just a narrow margin over the cost to build in the largest and most complete cream separator factory in the world. Remember, you have sixty days' free trial on every Economy Chief Cream Separator during which you can put it to any test, comparing it in skimming qualities, ease of running and in every other way with any cream separator sold by any other concern at $125.00 or less, and if the new Economy Chief does not outdo the competitive machine on every point you can return it to us and get all your money back, including freight charges.

PRICES FOR THE NEW ECONOMY CHIEF SEPARATOR.

No. 23K61 Capacity, 250 to 300 pounds per hour. Suitable for a dairy of two to eight cows. Price.......... **$28.80**

No. 23K62 Capacity, 350 to 400 pounds per hour. Suitable for a dairy of three to ten or twelve cows. Price.......... **$34.95**

No. 23K64 Capacity, 600 pounds per hour. Suitable for a dairy of from three to thirty-five cows. Price.......... **$43.65**

THE BEST SIZE TO BUY

WE BY ALL MEANS RECOMMEND the purchase of the largest size machine, the big 600-pound capacity size. This size runs practically as easy as the smaller sizes and does the skimming in less than one-half the time of the 250 to 300-pound size. It reduced the work of skimming to one-half and saves time every day in the year; and because of the fact that it is used about one-half as much each day it will last twice as long.

THE BIG 600-POUND CAPACITY MACHINE with ordinary care will not only last almost a lifetime but it will, because of its excess capacity, take care of the extra large quantity of milk which you may have at certain seasons of the year and will provide for an increase in the size of your herd in the future. You will surely want to increase the number of your cows, because after you receive the new Economy Chief Cream Separator you will find that you can take care of twice the number of cows you have now in less time and with less work than is now taken up by the old method, and by buying the big 600-pound capacity machine, which costs you very little more, you have a machine which will handle the extra quantity of milk nicely.

FOR SPECIAL QUICK DELIVERY AND LOW FREIGHT RATE OFFER, SEE PAGE 34.

READ THIS BEFORE ORDERING

MOST IMPORTANT INFORMATION FOR THE CREAM SEPARATOR BUYER

IN PURCHASING A CREAM SEPARATOR it is very greatly to your advantage to buy the largest size. The only reason for buying a small size is that it will run a trifle easier on account of the small difference in the weight of the bowl. There is so little difference in the running, however, that it can only be detected by a delicate registering apparatus and to the person running it there is apparently almost no difference.

THE LARGEST SIZE MACHINE, the big 600-pound capacity size, is just as easy to clean and to care for as the smaller machine and it does its work in just one-half the time of the smaller size. If it takes you half an hour to skim your milk in the morning and evening with the 250 to 300-pound capacity machine you can do the same work in fifteen minutes with the big 600-pound size. By saving one-half the time spent in skimming the milk twice every day in the year you will be surprised at the enormous amount of time and work which you will save in the course of the year.

ANOTHER REASON for buying the big size is that it will provide for an increase in the size of your herd in the future. You will find that a cream separator will reduce your dairy work so much that you can care for twenty-five cows with a separator easier than you could care for ten cows before you had one and naturally you will want to increase the size of your herd and hence your profits. The big size will take care of this and you will not be obliged to buy another separator.

IT WILL ALSO TAKE CARE of the extra large quantity of milk which you will have at certain seasons of the year and do it easily. By buying the large size you save time and work every day in the year. At some seasons of the year every hour and every minute is worth big money. Your time is so valuable that you cannot afford to waste it or use it uselessly.

WHEN YOU THINK that with the big machine you can do the work in one-half the time and that it provides for increasing your herd in the future and for the excess milk which you will have at some seasons, you will realize the advantage of buying the big size and paying the small difference in price.

THE MOST IMPORTANT REASON OF ALL, the biggest reason and best reason for buying the big capacity, 600-pound machine is that it will last twice as long. Just twice as many years as the smaller size. There is a plain, simple reason for this which perhaps you might not think of. A cream separator is only worn as it is used and can be used for a certain length of time before it is worn out or requires repairs. As the big capacity machine does twice the work in the same amount of time and the same work in one-half the time of the smaller size it is naturally used one-half as much each day or each year and hence will last twice as many days and twice as many years.

IF THE SMALLER MACHINE will last you ten years, the big machine will do the same work and last you twenty years, so that even if it cost you twice as much as the smaller machine it would still be the cheapest machine for you to buy without considering your big saving in time and labor by using it and it does not cost you anything like twice as much. The difference in price between the largest and smallest machine is only $14.85, so that when you consider the big advantages of the large machine it is by far the most wonderful bargain we have to offer, because it is worth much more than twice the price of the smaller machine, as you can readily see.

IT ONLY REQUIRES ONE-HALF as much oil, as it is only run one-half as much each day. Best of all, these big advantages which you get the benefit of every day in the year really cost you nothing because as the big capacity separator will last twice as long, it actually costs you less per year than the smaller machine.

IN YOUR OWN INTEREST, therefore, please order the big 600-pound capacity new Economy Chief Separator, the Jumbo size, fully described on the preceding page. You will never regret it. You will find it to be the biggest bargain and greatest value you ever saw or heard of. A machine which has so many advantages over all other separators that there is no room for comparison.

QUICK DELIVERY AND LOW FREIGHT RATE

GREAT SPECIAL OFFER ON OUR BIG CAPACITY ECONOMY CHIEF

WE SELL SO MANY of our big capacity Economy Chief Separators, the large 600 pounds per hour, the Jumbo size machine, illustrated and described on the preceding page, that we have been able to make a special arrangement which is very greatly to the benefit of those who purchase this size. A special arrangement for you which saves a world of time and reduces the freight rate to almost nothing, from one-fourth to one-half the regular rate, and insures the quickest, safest and surest possible delivery.

TO GET YOUR MACHINE with the least delay and the least possible expense for freight, order our new Economy Chief Separator in the large size, which we describe fully on the preceding page and now offer at the unheard of price for a machine of this size and capacity of $43.65.

OUR SALES on this big capacity separator, our No. 23K64, are so great that we have made arrangements for the benefit of the customers who purchase this size to store these machines at a number of convenient warehouses throughout the land close to the homes of nearly all of our customers, so that the delivery is only a matter of a day or two.

INSTEAD OF WAITING for the big machine to be shipped from our factory at Waterloo, Iowa, from which we ship all our Improved Economy Separators and the two smaller sizes of the Economy Chief, we, the moment we get your order for the large size Economy Chief Separator, forward it to the warehouse at which we have these machines stored that is the nearest to you.

THE VERY DAY THEY GET THE ORDER they ship the machine, for they have them all ready for delivery to the railroad company the minute the order is received. It only takes one or two days for the separator to reach you. The distance is short, there is no transferring at terminal points, so there is not only little, if any, delay in your receiving the separator, but it will reach you in splendid condition, as goods, if damaged at all, are damaged in transferring from one car to another and not while they are in transit in the cars.

BEST OF ALL, you save a large part of the freight charges. Owing to the great sale of the big capacity Economy Chief we are continually shipping them to our various warehouses scattered throughout the country in carloads, and as the rate of freight in carloads is very much less per 100 pounds, than the local rate which is charged for a single cream separator, in fact, only about one-half as much, you get the benefit of this because we have made arrangements with the railroad companies by which we collect from them only the carload rate of freight from our factory at Waterloo, Iowa, to the warehouse located near you and you pay your proportion of this carload rate on the separator which we ship you plus the local rate from the warehouse to your railroad station, and these two rates added together are usually less than one-half and rarely more than two-thirds of what you would be obliged to pay were the separator which you ordered shipped from our factory at Waterloo, Iowa, by local freight all the way.

HERE IS A LIST OF TOWNS at which we will warehouse our largest size 600 pounds per hour capacity Economy Chief Separator, our catalogue No. 23K64, which we list on the preceding page at $43.65, all ready for instant shipment. The towns are as follows:

ALBANY, N. Y.	KANSAS CITY, MO.	OMAHA, NEB.
MILWAUKEE, WIS.	PITTSBURG, PA.	FARGO, NO. DAK.

JUST AS SOON AS YOUR ORDER for the large capacity Economy Chief Separator is received, we will make shipment from the warehouse which is nearest to you. The machine will reach you in just a day or two and you will only be charged the carload rate of freight from our factory to the warehouse plus the local rate from the warehouse to your town.

A BIG SAVING FOR YOU IN EVERY WAY. Delivery is sure and quick. The chances of damage in transit are practically nothing. You make a saving in freight charges that is well worth considering.

PLEASE REMEMBER, however, that in no case are the freight charges large or is there likely to be any great delay in transit. No matter which size separator you order, whether an Improved Economy or the Economy Chief in the two smaller sizes, we will ship promptly from our big stock in our warehouse at Waterloo, Iowa, and the freight charges, as you will see by looking at the table below, will be small, and as we use the greatest care in routing there should not be any big delay in transit; but to get our very best machine, the greatest value we have to offer, in the quickest and safest way and at the lowest possible rate of freight, to get the benefit of the carload rate for the largest part of the distance, by all means place your order for our No. 23K64 Economy Chief Cream Separator offered at $43.65 on the preceding page, which is the greatest value and the finest separator ever offered at any price by ourselves or any other concern.

THREE BIG IMPORTANT ADVANTAGES FOR YOU. Quickest possible delivery, lowest possible freight rate and the biggest capacity, quickest working and most durable separator if you take advantage of this offer. Remember, we can make this offer only on our No. 23K64 Economy Chief Cream Separator in our largest size, which we sell at $43.65.

ORDER THE NEW ECONOMY CHIEF in the large size and get all the advantages that our big sales on this particular size have enabled us to secure for our customers. Quick delivery, lowest freight rate and, best of all, our very best cream separator, the $1,000.00 challenge machine in the big capacity which has outskimmed and outclassed every other separator made and will be such a wonderful money maker for you that it will pay for itself several times over every year. It is the one we recommend purely in your own interest as the best in every way for you if you have more than three or four cows.

FREIGHT CHARGES ARE LOW ON SEPARATORS

SO THAT YOU WILL KNOW ALMOST EXACTLY what the freight charges will be and can see for yourself how little they amount to, we print below a table giving you the total amount of freight charges on our biggest and heaviest cream separator from our factory at Waterloo, Iowa, to several points in each state. The freight charges to your town will be almost exactly the same as they are to the town which is nearest to you.

REMEMBER THAT THESE FIGURES are the total freight charges on our biggest and heaviest separator, the 600-pound capacity machine, and not the rate per 100 pounds as is often given. See how small these charges are. To almost any point in Iowa they amount to 45 cents to 95 cents for our largest separator. To points in Illinois from $1.20 to $1.60, and to points in Kansas and Nebraska from $1.44 to $3.64 for the big machine, and to all other states they are proportionately small. Really such a small item that it is hardly worth considering. The total freight charges, in fact, are usually about one-tenth to one-fortieth of your big saving in buying a cream separator from us.

THE TOTAL FREIGHT CHARGES ON OUR LARGEST ECONOMY SEPARATOR FROM OUR FACTORY TO POINTS IN EVERY STATE.

CHARGES ON 200-POUND SEPARATOR FROM WATERLOO, IOWA.

ALABAMA.	
Birmingham	$2.98
ARIZONA.	
Phoenix	7.58
ARKANSAS.	
Fayetteville	2.10
Little Rock	2.40
CALIFORNIA.	
Redding	7.22
San Bernardino	6.68
Stockton	6.00
COLORADO.	
Colorado Springs	3.70
La Junta	3.70
CONNECTICUT.	
New Haven	2.84
DELAWARE.	
Dover	2.70
DISTRICT OF COLUMBIA	
Washington	2.64
FLORIDA.	
Jacksonville	3.20
Pensacola	2.14
GEORGIA.	
Macon	3.60
Rome	3.34
Savannah	3.20
IDAHO.	
Boise	$6.20
Montpelier	6.20
Wallace	7.10
ILLINOIS.	
Bloomington	1.20
Freeport	1.20
Peoria	1.20
Mt. Carmel	1.60
Murphysboro	1.44
INDIANA.	
Auburn	1.56
Evansville	1.82
Frankfort	1.58
North Judson	1.56
North Vernon	1.82
IOWA.	
Marshalltown	.45
Mount Pleasant	.80
New Hampton	.45
Red Oak	.95
Sheldon	.95
KANSAS.	
Colby	2.92
Great Bend	2.64
Manhattan	2.00
Parsons	1.70
Syracuse	3.10
KENTUCKY.	
Greenup	$1.90
Junction City	1.25
Princeton	2.14
LOUISIANA.	
New Orleans	2.14
MAINE.	
Lewiston	2.84
MARYLAND.	
Baltimore	2.64
Hagerstown	2.64
MASSACHUSETTS.	
Boston	2.84
Pittsfield	2.84
MICHIGAN.	
Au Sable	1.56
Detroit	1.66
Lansing	1.56
Manistee	1.30
Marquette	2.40
Niles	1.56
MINNESOTA.	
Crookston	2.44
Duluth	1.30
Faribault	1.10
Redwood Falls	1.94
St. Cloud	1.78
MISSISSIPPI.	
Durant	$2.30
Tupelo	2.14
MISSOURI.	
Albany	1.20
Edina	1.20
Jefferson City	1.75
Poplar Bluff	2.18
Springfield	1.24
MONTANA.	
Lewiston	6.60
Miles City	4.40
NEBRASKA.	
Beatrice	1.44
Crawford	3.64
Norfolk	1.90
Sidney	3.22
Thedford	2.76
NEVADA.	
Elko	7.40
Reno	7.40
NEW MEXICO.	
Albuquerque	4.24
NEW HAMPSHIRE.	
Berlin	2.84
Nashua	2.84
NEW JERSEY.	
Paterson	$2.70
NEW YORK.	
Little Falls	2.64
Oswego	2.40
Plattsburg	2.84
Poughkeepsie	2.70
Watertown	2.70
NORTH CAROLINA.	
Raleigh	3.18
NORTH DAKOTA.	
Carrington	2.96
Dickinson	3.64
Ellendale	2.64
Grafton	2.68
Minot	3.40
OHIO.	
Dayton	1.82
Defiance	1.66
Gallipolis	1.90
Warren	1.86
OKLAHOMA.	
El Reno	2.60
Enid	2.60
Lawton	2.60
Tishomingo	2.60
South McAlester	2.40
Vinita	2.10
OREGON.	
Pendleton	$7.10
Portland	6.00
Roseburg	7.44
PENNSYLVANIA.	
Emporium	2.32
Franklin	1.90
Harrisburg	2.64
Reading	2.66
Pittsburg	1.90
RHODE ISLAND.	
Providence	2.84
SOUTH CAROLINA.	
Columbia	3.42
SOUTH DAKOTA.	
Aberdeen	2.32
Pierre	2.32
Rapid City	3.92
Sioux Falls	1.16
TENNESSEE.	
Jackson	1.98
McMinnville	3.00
Morristown	3.44
TEXAS.	
Amarillo	3.34
Beaumont	3.14
Kerrville	3.28
Marfa	3.88
Paris	3.14
UTAH.	
Ogden	$5.30
Provo City	5.30
Richfield	6.14
VERMONT.	
Bennington	2.84
VIRGINIA.	
Charlottesville	2.64
Suffolk	2.64
WASHINGTON.	
Mount Vernon	6.00
Walla Walla	7.10
Wenatche	7.10
WEST VIRGINIA.	
Elkins	2.64
Wayne	2.88
WISCONSIN.	
Grand Rapids	1.00
LaCrosse	1.20
Marinette	1.40
Milwaukee	1.20
Superior	1.40
WYOMING.	
Casper	4.84
Laramie	4.72
Minturn	5.00

Two Big Complete Cream Separator Catalogues FREE

THE **ECONOMY CHIEF CREAM SEPARATOR**

OUR $1000.00 CHALLENGE OFFER

WE WILL GIVE $1,000.00 IN GOLD to the separator manufacturer who can produce a machine that will outskim the Economy Chief at temperatures of 50, 60, 70, 80 and 90 degrees. We make this offer to the makers of the DeLaval, Sharples, Empire, United States and every other machine sold in the United States. We have tested them all and we know what we are talking about. The Economy Chief ranks first. The best of the others is a poor second.

Sears, Roebuck & Co.
CHICAGO

IF YOU HAVE TWO COWS OR MORE YOU NEED A CREAM SEPARATOR BADLY

FOR YOU ARE LOSING MONEY EVERY DAY YOU ARE WITHOUT ONE. You can make no mistake in sending us your order at once for an Improved Economy, or better still, one of our latest and best machines, the NEW ECONOMY CHIEF for 1908, direct from the pages of this catalogue, because, as we have told you here, our sole aim is to satisfy our customers so well that they would not think of buying their goods elsewhere, and for this reason we give a free trial of sixty days on every cream separator we sell, and during these sixty days you have the time and the opportunity to give the separator which you buy a most thorough try out.

YOU CAN RUN IT IN COMPETITION with other machines of other makes. You have an opportunity to test your cream and skim milk or have it tested at your local creamery. You will become thoroughly familiar with the easy running qualities, convenience and strong, durable construction of our cream separator during this time and, of course, if for any reason you decide you would rather have your money than the cream separator, you can send the machine back to us and we will immediately return all your money, including any freight charges which you have paid out, so you run no risk in placing your order direct from this catalogue.

FOR THE BENEFIT OF THOSE who desire more complete information than we can give in the limited space allowed cream separators in our large catalogue, we issue two special Cream Separator Catalogues, the finest and most complete ever printed.

IN ONE WE FULLY DESCRIBE our Improved Economy Cream Separator, which has been such a big success everywhere, and in the other we tell all about our new 1908 Model ECONOMY CHIEF, which we claim and are prepared to prove is so far ahead of all other cream separators that comparison is impossible.

THESE TWO CREAM SEPARATOR CATALOGUES ARE FREE

They are the most comprehensive and cover the subject more fully than any catalogues issued heretofore. They give the history of the cream separator business from the time of the first invention of centrifugal separators down to the present day. They trace the various improvements that have been made. They fully explain the advantages and disadvantages of the different styles of gearing and various skimming devices now in use.

THEY EXPLAIN WHY some separators run so much easier than others. They give a series of expert tests in which the comparative merit of the separators of all the principal makers are plainly shown. They take up all the subjects of interest to the dairymen and go into them in detail, show the results of experiments conducted by the agricultural experiment stations in the various states to ascertain the feeding value of skim milk in various stages.

THEY EXPLAIN THE CHEMICAL CHANGES which take place in milk as it sours. Give valuable hints on the care and feeding of cattle so as to get the best

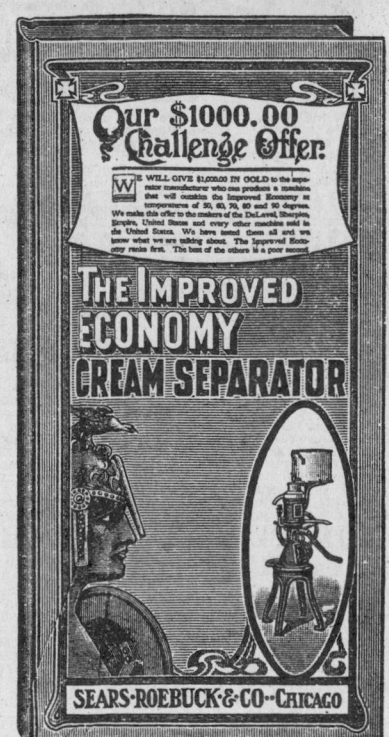

results. Tell you how to cool and care for the cream so as to get the biggest price for it. Give valuable hints to buttermakers. Explain the advantages and disadvantages of the whole milk creamery system in comparison with the hand separator system.

THESE CATALOGUES make a careful comparison of the selling methods of the high priced separator manufacturers with our own. They show you plainly that while we sell our separators at about one-third the prices charged by the separator trust, their machine costs no more to build than ours and that the difference in price which is paid by you is made up entirely of profits and selling expenses of which you get no benefit.

THEY PROVE CLEARLY that it is impossible for any other separator manufacturer to compete with us in price because of our wonderful manufacturing facilities and economical selling system. They show a great many interior views of our cream separator factory, the largest and finest in the world. They show pictures of many special machines built to our order and used by us exclusively for the purpose of turning out cream separators finer than other makers can possibly furnish.

THEY SHOW THE VARIOUS OPERATIONS and processes of construction by which the raw material is converted into the finished part. Views of our testing and assembling rooms. In fact, these catalogues give you almost as good an idea of our vast cream separator factory as if you were to visit it in person.

PLEASE DO NOT THINK OF ORDERING a cream separator from any other concern at any price without first sending for our Cream Separator Catalogues. They are free. Simply send us a letter or a postal card saying, "Send me both of your Cream Separator Catalogues," and the two books with all the information, the instruction and tests and thousands of letters of testimony from our customers, in fact, everything in regard to the subject will be sent to you immediately by return mail, postpaid.

SEWING MACHINES

LOWER PRICES, NEW MODELS, MORE IMPROVEMENTS, MORE WONDERFUL VALUES THAN EVER BEFORE.

WE ARE THE LARGEST DEALERS IN SEWING MACHINES

IN THE WORLD, SELLING BY FAR MORE machines than any wholesalers, jobbers and retailers, about three times as many sewing machines as all other mail order dealers. You will find our sewing machines in every neighborhood, in every village, town and city in the United States, and if you have any idea of buying a sewing machine, please make a little inquiry in your own neighborhood, for you will surely find one or more sewing machines that were furnished by Sears, Roebuck & Company. Just ask the owners of these machines what they think of our sewing machines, and whether they would advise you to send us your order.

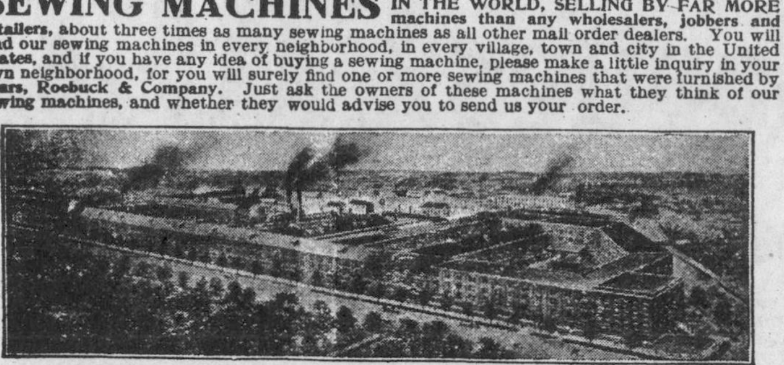

BIRDSEYE VIEW OF MINNESOTA SEWING MACHINE FACTORY.

One of the largest sewing machine factories in the world. Now making 1,000 sewing machines per day.

THE ABOVE ILLUSTRATION

IS A BIRDSEYE VIEW of the Minnesota Sewing Machine Factory. Every sewing machine which we sell is made for us under contract in this immense sewing machine factory, one of the largest in the world. It is one of the pioneer sewing machine factories of this country. Every Minnesota Sewing Machine turned out of this factory, from the cheapest to the best, is built under the same careful supervision, with the same high standard of quality always in mind, thus giving even our cheapest machines the mechanical construction, appearance, finish, wearing qualities, simplicity and ease of operation which you will not find in any machine you may get from any other house even at two or three times our price.

WE GUARANTEE OUR SEWING MACHINES

THE HIGHEST GRADE MADE IN THE WORLD, REGARDLESS OF NAME, MAKE OR price, and we positively guarantee our prices lower than those asked by any other house. We guarantee safe delivery, we guarantee the freight charges will be very low, a few cents, nothing compared to the enormous saving in price; we guarantee the machine itself for full twenty years, we guarantee to give you a full three months' trial on the machine, we guarantee if you consider our sewing machine proposition thoroughly you will realize that you cannot afford to place your order elsewhere. We guarantee everything. We know that with our experience as the largest dealers in the world in sewing machines, with our surprisingly liberal terms of shipment, our liberal guarantees, our Minnesota Sewing Machine representing the greatest advance and the highest type in sewing machine building that we can furnish you, such a sewing machine as you could not get anywhere else for quality, and at a wonderful saving to you in price.

OUR 20 YEARS' WRITTEN BINDING GUARANTEE.

WE GUARANTEE THE MINNESOTA SEWING MACHINE for 20 years. With every sewing machine, we issue a written binding twenty-year guarantee, by the terms and conditions of which if any piece or part gives out at any time within twenty years by reason of defect in material or workmanship, we will replace or repair it free of charge. This is the longest, strongest and most binding guarantee issued by any sewing machine maker or seller, and in this way we make you absolutely secure against any possible defect of any kind.

OUR BINDING GUARANTEE.

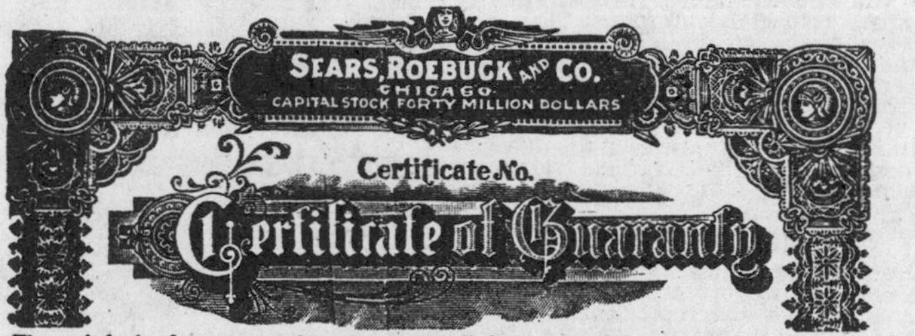

Through lack of space we show only a small facsimile of the heading of the beautiful engraved guarantee which goes with every sewing machine which we ship, except the Homan which we guarantee for five years only. This guarantee protects you in every way and reads as follows:

"This is to certify that this sewing machine is warranted to be perfect in material and manufacture and to be perfect in operation if properly managed. This machine has been carefully inspected and adjusted and there are no defects in material or workmanship. It has been delivered to the transportation company in perfect condition, carefully packed, and we guarantee it to reach your station in good order. This means that if it is damaged in transit it may be returned to us and we will pay all expenses connected with the transaction and send a new machine without extra charge.

With fair usage we hereby agree to make good any defect in material or workmanship for a period of twenty years. Natural wear and tear on any of the parts is not considered a defect in material or workmanship.

When referring to this Guarantee, please do not fail to state certificate number.

Dated at Chicago, this........day of.................A. D., 19...

SEARS, ROEBUCK & CO., Chicago, Ill."

OUR LIBERAL TERMS OF SHIPMENT.

WE SELL THE MINNESOTA SEWING MACHINES ON THE BROADEST AND MOST liberal terms offered by any sewing machine manufacturer or dealer. Send us your order for the style sewing machine that you want, selected from the pages of this catalogue, enclose our price and we will make immediate shipment of the machine of your selection, carefully crated, safe delivery guaranteed, and in just a few days' time it will reach you at your nearest railway station. We bargain and agree with you that you are to have three months' trial, as explained elsewhere on this page, and if in that time you are in any way dissatisfied, if you do not find that the machine you order from us is wonderful value and the very best sewing machine made as compared with any other sewing machine offered by other dealers, we will gladly refund your money and pay all the transportation charges when you return the machine to us. Surely, under these very liberal conditions, you cannot afford to order a sewing machine from any agent or dealer until you have first tried the Minnesota.

OUR THREE MONTHS' FREE TRIAL PROPOSITION.

WHEN YOU SEND US YOUR ORDER FOR A Minnesota Sewing Machine we fill your order and ship the machine to you with the understanding that we give you the privilege of returning the sewing machine to us any time within three months after you receive it if for any reason you are dissatisfied with the machine. The Homan's excepted. The money paid for the machine, including the freight paid by you, will be returned to you without question. This gives you the opportunity for testing and trying the machine in every way without its costing you one penny. If you are not satisfied any time within three months we agree to return not only the price of the machine but the freight charges as well.

SAFE DELIVERY GUARANTEED.

WE GUARANTEE every sewing machine to reach the purchaser in the exact same perfect condition it leaves us, and if any piece or part is broken by reason of rough handling in transit, or for any other reason, we will either replace or repair it or send you a new machine, all at our own expense.

OUR SPECIAL SEWING MACHINE CATALOGUE IS FREE.

ALTHOUGH OUR COMPLETE LINE OF SEWING machines is thoroughly illustrated and described on the following pages and our very lowest prices and best offers are shown in this our General Catalogue, we issue a Special Sewing Machine Catalogue, a very handsome book that we will gladly mail free on application. This Special Sewing Machine Catalogue, as illustrated hereon, shows the same line of Minnesota Sewing Machines, but shows them with larger pictures, and in this special book we are able to show the sewing machines beautifully illustrated in colors, exactly as they appear. We are also able, in the Special Sewing Machine Catalogue, to go into the subject of sewing machines more thoroughly, and if you would like to see finer illustrations of these machines and a more extended description, you can write and ask for our free Sewing Machine Catalogue and it will be sent to you immediately by mail, postpaid, FREE.

UNDERSTAND,

YOU CAN ORDER A SEWING MACHINE WITH EVERY assurance of perfect satisfaction, direct from the following pages, and you need not delay to first write for the free Sewing Machine Catalogue, for our entire line of sewing machines is shown on the following pages; all are thoroughly described and our lowest prices printed, and you cannot take any risk in ordering immediately without waiting to write for a free Sewing Machine Catalogue, because if the machine is not all and more than you expected, or if you have any reason to feel dissatisfied at any time during three months, you can return the machine to us at our expense, and all your money, including the freight charges you paid, will be immediately returned to you. But if you hesitate to order immediately and there is a little further information on the sewing machine subject that you would like, don't fail to write and ask for our free Sewing Machine Catalogue.

IN THIS SPECIAL FREE SEWING MACHINE CATALOGUE

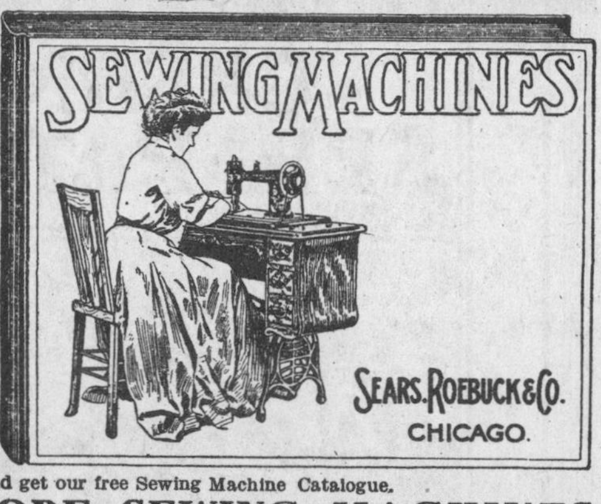

WE NOT ONLY SHOW beautiful colored illustrations of the machines, but we give a history of the sewing machine business. We explain how our low prices are possible; we explain how the sewing machine agent operates his expensive selling methods; we show facsimiles of our Three Months' Trial Contract; our Twenty-Year Binding Guarantee; our Prompt Shipment and Safe Delivery Guarantee; freight rates on a sewing machine to different towns in every state, and, in fact, this is the most complete book on sewing machines ever published. It contains 88 pages, 11½x8½ inches in size, has 165 illustrations, 42 of which are full page and in colors, and if you cannot make an immediate selection from the following pages, don't under any circumstance place your order elsewhere before you first write and get our free Sewing Machine Catalogue.

WE SELL MORE SEWING MACHINES

THAN ANY OTHER FIRM OR INDIVIDUAL IN THE WORLD. OUR MINNESOTA machines are better made, of more durable materials, they are made under the direct supervision of the most expert sewing machine men in the world, and with our tremendous output of sewing machines, with our modern selling methods through which we place these unapproachable machines direct from the factory into the hands of the customer without the intervention of a single middleman, we are able to name such low prices that no such sewing machine values can possibly be offered under any other name, make or price. Every modern factory facility is at our command, special machines developed by our factory experts have largely contributed to reduce manufacturing cost, we manufacture in such enormous quantities that our employes are in almost every case specialists in their line, and it is a well known fact that a mechanic who makes one thing only is able to make it better than a mechanic who gives a portion of his time to one part and a portion to some other part or parts. All these manifold advantages, all the reasons why we are able to undersell all other firms or individuals, all the reasons why we have been able to make the very best sewing machine in all the world at such astonishingly low prices, are fully explained in our free Sewing Machine Catalogue, which we will be glad to send you if you will just write us a letter or a postal card and say, "Please send me your free Sewing Machine Catalogue."

OUR FREE TRIAL

GIVES YOU THE OPPORTUNITY FOR THOROUGHLY testing and trying the sewing machine in your own home. You can compare it with machines of any other make and if you are not perfectly satisfied with your purchase, if you are not convinced that you have received a better sewing machine at a much lower price than you can get from any other dealer, agent or catalogue house; if you are not perfectly satisfied in every way you may return the machine to us at our expense and we will immediately return all your money paid for the machine, together with the freight charges paid by you.

REMEMBER,

WHEN YOU SEND US AN ORDER FOR A SEWING MACHINE and enclose our price we guarantee that the machine we send you will be wonderful value, such value as no other sewing machine manufacturer or dealer can possibly offer you, and remember, too, that you have three months' free trial and every machine carries our twenty-year written binding guarantee with the exception the Homan.

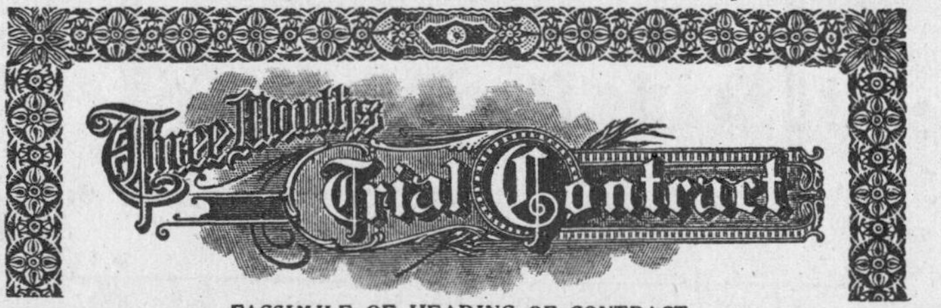

FACSIMILE OF HEADING OF CONTRACT.

THE MINNESOTA SEWING MACHINE

REPRESENTS A HIGH STANDARD OF QUALITY THROUGHOUT. IT IS OUR OLD established name for our very finest machine, and in order to give our customers a variety to select from, so that we could offer a range of prices to appeal to everyone, we have the Minnesota Sewing Machine made in four models, namely: "A," "B," "C," and "D," illustrated and described on the following pages. In addition to the Minnesota Machines we have the Homan and the Belmont.

WHETHER YOU BUY

THE HIGHEST GRADE SEWING MACHINE made in the world, the Minnesota Model "A," or one of the cheaper grades, the Minnesota Model "B," "C," or "D" (any one of the Minnesota models is far superior to a machine you may get elsewhere). It goes to you direct from the factory and embodies all of the Minnesota standard for quality.

THE FREIGHT CHARGES

ON A SEWING MACHINE from the factory at Dayton, Ohio, to any point in the United States will be next to nothing as compared with what you save in price. For example, the average sewing machine, crated ready for shipment, weighs about 120 pounds. Sewing machines are accepted by the railroad companies as first class freight, and the freight on a sewing machine from the factory at Dayton, Ohio, would average about as follows: 200 miles or less, 35 to 50 cents; 200 to 500 miles, 50 to 75 cents; 500 to 1,000 miles, 75 cents to $1.00. Greater or less distances in proportion.

REPAIRS AND SUPPLIES.

WE WILL ALWAYS CARRY, AT the factory, a full supply of all the different pieces and parts in which our various styles of sewing machines are made, and if you should meet with an accident of any kind and should want any part or parts of any sewing machine purchased from us, you can get these parts promptly and at actual factory cost.

WHAT WE ARE DOING TO MAKE QUICK DELIVERY

ON OUR HIGHEST GRADE TWENTY-YEAR GUARANTEED, BALL BEARING, MINNESOTA MODEL "A" FIVE-DRAWER DROP HEAD STYLE, AUTOMATIC LIFT SEWING MACHINE WITH ACCESSORIES AND A COMPLETE SET OF STEEL FOOT ATTACHMENTS

TO GET THIS OUR VERY BEST AND HIGHEST GRADE MINNESOTA MODEL "A" SEWING MACHINE IN the five-drawer drop head style with the complete set of extra attachments in just a day or two at the farthest, a few days from the date we receive your order, to make sure that the sewing machine reaches you in perfect order, to remove any chance for breakage or damage, and to insure your having very little freight charges, we have arranged to ship this highest grade five-drawer, drop head style Minnesota Model "A" Sewing Machine complete with the extra attachments as fully described and illustrated on pages 51 to 62.

THIS HIGH GRADE SEWING MACHINE, COMPLETE WITH THE EXTRA SET OF STEEL FOOT ATTACHMENTS, IN THE POPULAR five-drawer drop head style with automatic lift, we carry in stock in warehouses in various parts of the United States, securely crated and well packed, ready for immediate shipment, so no matter where you live we can ship one of these five-drawer Minnesota Model "A" Sewing Machines complete with the extra set of attachments from the point nearest to you and thus get it to you in a very short time, with very little freight charges for you. We carry a stock of these machines in warehouses and can ship to you immediately from the following points: Kansas City, Mo., Omaha, Neb., Minneapolis, Minn. and Dayton, Ohio.

TO MAKE FREIGHT CHARGES VERY LOW, WE KEEP A STOCK OF THE MINNESOTA MODEL "A" FIVE-DRAWER Drop Head Sewing Machines in the warehouse right near you, well packed and securely crated, ready for immediate shipment and in perfect condition. We first ship these machines to the various points named in solid carload lots, receiving from the railroad company the very lowest carload freight rate, so when we receive your order here in Chicago and order the sewing machine shipped to you from our sewing machine warehouse, the one nearest you, and order the sewing machine shipped to your railroad station, on your order at once. We know it leaves the warehouse near you in perfect condition. We know it will reach you from a very few hours to a day or two at the most from the time it leaves the warehouse and when you do get it, you will only have the carload rate to pay from Dayton, Ohio, factory to the warehouse nearest you, which is

usually one-half the freight charges that one has to pay when shipping one sewing machine by freight. In addition to this very low carload rate from the factory at Dayton, Ohio, to the warehouse near you, you will also have to pay a very small freight charge for the short haul from this warehouse to your nearest railroad station, but the total freight you will have to pay when you receive the machine will not, as a rule, amount to more than one-half or two-thirds the freight charges you would have to pay if the sewing machine was shipped to you singly as one shipment from the factory at Dayton, Ohio, to your railroad station.

THE FIVE-DRAWER DROP HEAD STYLE MINNESOTA MODEL "A" SEWING MACHINE WHICH WE carry in stock in these different warehouses and which we can get to almost any station east of the Rocky Mountains in just a day or two, is the highest grade, lightest running sewing machine made, regardless of name, make or price, and by this warehouse method you will be surprised to find how quickly we can get this sewing machine to you. Besides quick delivery, under this system there is practically no chance for the machine to reach you in any way damaged, no chance for any delay, and no chance for any disappointment; therefore if you want to get the greatest value we can possibly give you in a sewing machine, the best sewing machine made, if you want to get it in the shortest possible time and take advantage of the very low carload freight rate that this system allows, then by all means go to your Postmaster, R. F. D. Carrier, Express Agent, or the Bank and get a money order drawn in our favor, select this five-drawer drop head style Minnesota Model "A" Ball Bearing Sewing Machine complete with the extra set of steel foot attachments, enclose the amount of $16.50 in a letter addressed direct to Sears, Roebuck & Co., Chicago, Ill., and tell us to send you this high grade five-drawer drop head style Minnesota Model "A" Ball Bearing Sewing Machine complete with the extra set of steel foot attachments and we will surprise you in the promptness of delivery, low freight charges and most extraordinary value.

PLEASE REMEMBER THAT THE ONLY SEWING MACHINE WE have stored in the different warehouses named above is our Minnesota Model "A" Five-Drawer Drop Head Style Ball Bearing Machine complete with the extra set of steel foot attachments, the price of which complete with attachments is $16.50. Please remember furthermore that we only carry this machine with the attachments in our warehouse nearest you. All of the other sewing machines illustrated and described in this catalogue are well packed, securely crated and shipped from the factory at Dayton, Ohio.

$7.58 HOMAN FIVE-DRAWER DROP HEAD SEWING MACHINE

Lower in price than ever before offered. The lowest price ever quoted on a Sewing Machine of this grade.

IN THIS, OUR $7.58 HOMAN SEWING MACHINE, we are offering an example of the wonderful value to be found in our entire selection of sewing machines illustrated and described on the following pages.

OUR ABILITY to furnish this five-drawer drop head oak cabinet sewing machine for $7.58, a price never before attempted by any manufacturer or dealer in high grade sewing machines, is only a further proof of our ability to furnish the highest grade sewing machines at prices far below all competition.

WE ARE LEADERS in the sewing machine business in this country, selling direct to the consumer, and by our progressive methods of furnishing sewing machines that will stand the test of time at extremely low prices, have succeeded in establishing a reputation that sells more machines for us than are sold by all other dealers combined selling direct to the consumer.

FOR ANYONE desiring a sewing machine that will do an average amount of work, we recommend our Homan Five-Drawer Drop Head Machine at $7.58. But if you are desirous of procuring a machine that will compare favorably with the highest grade sewing machines on the market, regardless of name, make or price, then we recommend that you select one of our Minnesota machines, preferably the Model "A," which represents the highest grade of sewing machine construction throughout, as fully illustrated and described on pages 51 to 62. We conscientiously place this machine in competition with the highest grade machines in the market, constructed especially for family use, and have thousands of testimonials to bear out our representations.

OUR HOMAN FIVE-DRAWER Drop Head Machine is the only machine on which we place our name and address, as a necessary protection to our customers to prevent dealers from buying these machines from us and offering them again as high grade machines.

With each machine we furnish a complete set of the usual accessories, but not the special attachments.

We require cash in full on all orders for the Homan Sewing Machine. ORDER BY NUMBER.

No. 26K201 Homan Five-Drawer Drop Head Sewing Machine. Guaranteed for five years. Price........$7.58
Delivered on board cars at Dayton, Ohio.

$9.85 FOR THE BELMONT FIVE-DRAWER DROP HEAD, OAK CABINET Sewing Machine

THIS $9.85 MACHINE is furnished in this one style only. A high grade, nicely finished sewing machine, which is guaranteed for twenty years. At $9.85 for the Belmont Five-Drawer Drop Head Sewing Machine we offer a better value, a better finished and lighter running and higher grade sewing machine than can be purchased elsewhere, a better machine than you can buy from your dealers and agents for from $15.00 to $18.00. Our prices are figured as low as we could possibly make them, every unnecessary expense common to other sellers of sewing machines is eliminated and the price you pay us, every penny of it is represented in material and skillful labor with just the one small margin of profit added. Understand, our Belmont Sewing Machine at $9.85 is offered to you to meet a certain class of competition and is not offered by us as a strictly high grade machine. If you want the best that your money can buy, a machine that will give life long satisfaction, then we recommend our Ball Bearing Minnesota Model "A" Automatic Lift Sewing Machine to all our customers. There is only a few dollars' difference between the cost of our Belmont and the highest grade sewing machine we sell, the Ball Bearing Minnesota Model "A," which is put out under our guarantee as the highest grade sewing machine made in the world. We always feel like urging our customers to select one of our highest grade sewing machines because the difference in price represents only the actual difference in cost, and by buying a Ball Bearing Minnesota Model "A" Automatic Lift you get the highest grade sewing machine construction it is possible to produce, a machine capable of doing any and all classes of family sewing, a machine which will sew the thinnest and finest fabrics, as well as the heaviest and coarsest cloth, without necessitating a change in the tension. You get the lightest and easiest running sewing machine, the only family sewing machine on the market today constructed with ball bearings in the operating parts of the head. The stand is the lightest running because all the bearing parts have ball bearing adjustment. In fact, you get the very best of everything, and you get it on the basis of the actual cost of material and labor and with but our one small margin of profit added.

DESCRIPTION OF OUR FIVE-DRAWER DROP HEAD BELMONT SEWING MACHINE.

THE BELMONT HEAD is of the double thread lock stitch vibrating shuttle type. It has a round needle bar, self setting needle and self threading cylinder shuttle. The feed is positive and of the four-motion type. It extends on both sides of the needle. The shuttle is the most perfect self threading cylindrical shuttle, made of the finest steel, hardened and ground, absolutely self threading, being open at one end for inserting the bobbin, after which the thread is instantly drawn into place by two motions of the hand. There are no holes to thread through and the shuttle can be threaded with the eyes shut. The bobbin carries a large amount of thread. The needle is self setting, both as to height and position in the needle bar, making it impossible to set a needle improperly. The bobbin winder is automatic and of the latest pattern, being operated by direct contact with the belt. THE WOODWORK is solid oak throughout and finished in golden oak. THE DRAWERS are large and roomy and are all fitted with locks. THE STAND is neat and graceful and is very strong. THE WHEEL and TREADLE are perfectly adjusted and operate with the least possible friction and resistance.

No. 26K202 Belmont Five-Drawer Drop Head Sewing Machine. Guaranteed for twenty years. Price....**$9.85**

$9.85

The above price does not include attachments. A full set of attachments, 75 cents extra.

No. 26K202

DESCRIPTION OF THE

MINNESOTA MODEL "C" HEAD

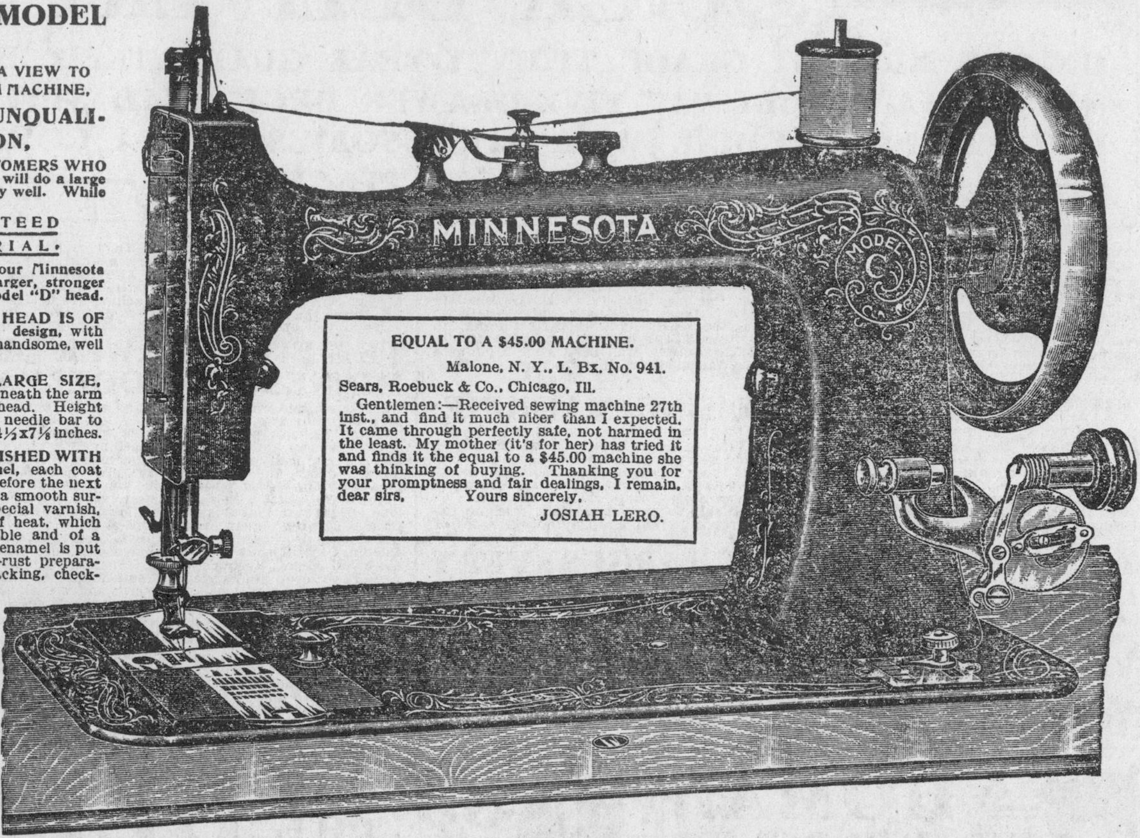

EQUAL TO A $45.00 MACHINE.

Malone, N. Y., L. Bx. No. 941.

Sears, Roebuck & Co., Chicago, Ill.

Gentlemen:—Received sewing machine 27th inst., and find it much nicer than I expected. It came through perfectly safe, not harmed in the least. My mother (it's for her) has tried it and finds it the equal to a $45.00 machine she was thinking of buying. Thanking you for your promptness and fair dealings, I remain, dear sirs, Yours sincerely,

JOSIAH LERO.

THE MINNESOTA MODEL "C" HEAD

HAS BEEN CONSTRUCTED WITH A VIEW TO FURNISHING AN EXTRA HIGH ARM MACHINE,

ONE THAT WILL GIVE UNQUALIFIED SATISFACTION,

TO MEET THE NEEDS OF OUR CUSTOMERS WHO desire a medium priced machine which will do a large range of work, heavy and light, equally well. While the parts are all

ABSOLUTELY GUARANTEED FIRST CLASS MATERIAL,

they are not of as fine construction as our Minnesota Models "A," and "B" heads, but larger, stronger and better finished than our Minnesota Model "D" head.

DESIGN. OUR MODEL "C" HEAD IS OF the very latest design, with gracefully rounded lines which give it a handsome, well proportioned and strong appearance.

SIZE. THE HEAD IS EXTRA LARGE SIZE, having as much room underneath the arm as the largest family sewing machine head. Height of arm from bed plate, 5⅜ inches; from needle bar to base of arm, 8¾ inches; size of bed plate, 14½x7⅛ inches.

FINISH. THE HEAD IS FINISHED WITH three coats of enamel, each coat being thoroughly baked and hardened before the next is put on and carefully rubbed down to a smooth surface, and finally treated to a coat of special varnish, which is also baked at a high degree of heat, which makes the finish practically indestructible and of a beautiful, rich black luster. Before the enamel is put on the head is treated to a coat of anti-rust preparation, which prevents the finish from cracking, checking or peeling, which so frequently occurs with other makes of machines.

DECORATION. THE ARM AND BED PLATE ARE decorated with handsome floral figures in a combination of silver and gold, especially designed for this machine.

NICKEL PLATING. THE RIM OF THE BALance wheel, face plate, shuttle slides, tension plates, needle bar, presser bar, stitch regulating plate, presser bar lifter and screw heads are all heavily nickel plated and form a handsome contrast to the black enamel finish.

IN THE CONSTRUCTION OF THE MINNESOTA MODEL "C" head no effort or expense has been spared to make this one of the highest grade sewing machine heads in the world, combining all the best known features in sewing machine head construction, in order to produce a sewing machine head which for simplicity, ease of operation and ability to perform a large variety of work would not be excelled by any sewing machine used by any other manufacturer, regardless of the price of sewing machine it is used on. Our Minnesota sewing machine heads throughout are built along the lines of the most advanced ideas in sewing machine construction. We have in our factory a corps of the most expert mechanics, who are continually experimenting and trying out new features, new ideas, always working for the betterment of the machine, and wherever we can improve the machine in the slightest degree, such idea is immediately adopted, even if it increases the manufacturing expense. We aim to give our customers, not only a sewing machine as good as they can obtain elsewhere at any price, but even a little better. We feel that our customers are entitled to the best it is possible to produce, and entirely different from the policy of many dealers, particularly among catalogue concerns, it is our constant effort to improve the quality of our merchandise, to make it a little better than is necessary, perhaps, so that the machine or other item of merchandise cannot fail to give satisfaction to the customer. This is the policy we have followed in the construction of our line of Minnesota sewing machines, and if at any time within a month or a year after this catalogue is issued we are able to make a still further improvement on this Minnesota machine head, you can feel sure that you will get the benefit of such improvement, and a machine embodying our very best ideas and latest improvements will be furnished you. In our line of Minnesota sewing machine heads we can state without fear of contradiction that we produce the highest grade sewing machine head made, of highest grade materials, and put together by more skilled mechanics and with better care than is used by other makers. We use a better grade of iron and steel, we use heavier nickeling, heavier enamel, more time and effort is put on every single operation, such as the drawing, shaping, punching and bending of the steel parts, the length of time the nickel plated parts stay in the battery, the amount of work put into the enameling, finishing and polishing. All this enters into the result of producing a sewing machine head, the most important part of the machine, such as cannot be compared with the sewing machine heads found on the general run of machines.

ALL BEARINGS ARE MADE OF THE BEST STEEL THAT CAN BE procured, especially selected for its durable qualities, properly tempered and case hardened so as to minimize the friction and prevent wear. All bearings are fitted with adjusting devices whereby any lost motion caused by the slight wear through years of constant use can be taken up.

RUNNING SPEED. EVERY MACHINE BEFORE BEING SHIPPED from the factory is put to the severest possible test, being set up and attached to a power pulley and run at a speed five times greater than it is possible to run any machine by foot power, and by this severe test we first learn that every machine is perfectly true in every particular and capable of the highest possible speed.

OPERATING PARTS. OUR MINNESOTA MACHINES ARE CONstructed with less running or operating parts than any other machine on the market, rendering them easy to understand and operate, light running and free from vibration and noise. To do away with the liability to get out of order, common to many machines, the mechanism is so constructed that the few running parts in the Minnesota head operate entirely independent of one another and all driving power is supplied direct from the main shaft without the agency of the numerous connections, cogs and many unnecessary devices used in some machines to propel the feed, shuttle and needle bar. The operator does not have to tamper with or adjust these parts, regardless of the weight of goods being sewed. The construction has made the Minnesota head famous as the most durable head ever produced.

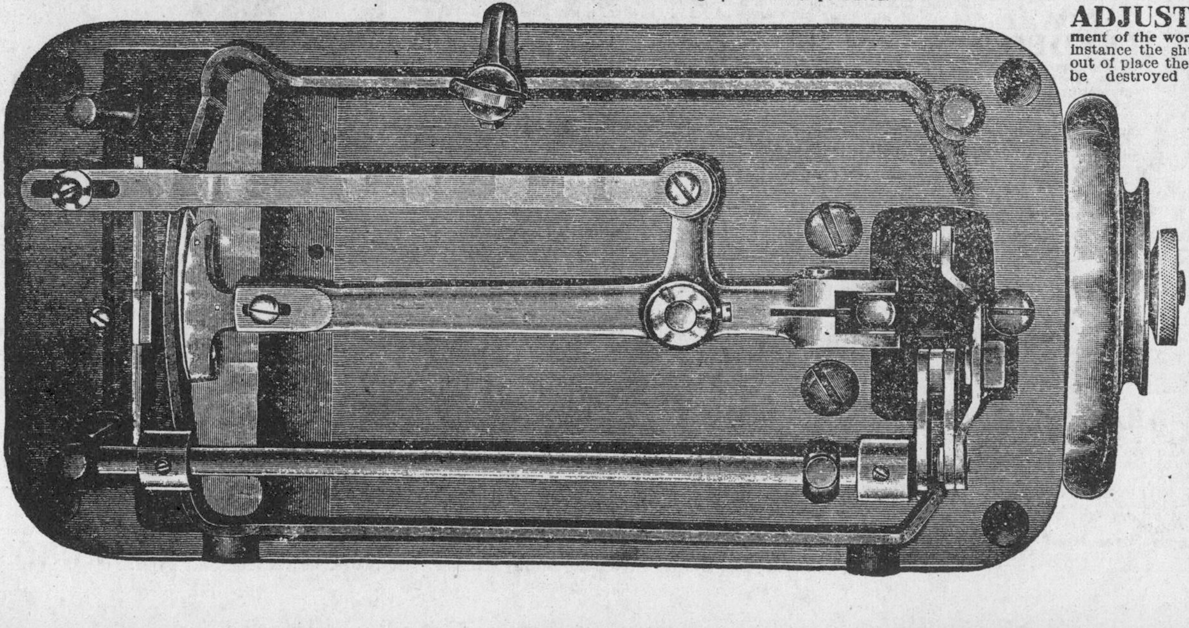

ADJUSTMENT. MUCH DEPENDS upon the adjustment of the working parts, for should any part, for instance the shuttle, be adjusted 1-32 of an inch out of place the harmony between the parts will be destroyed and imperfect work will result. The operating parts of our Minnesota machines receive the finest and most accurate adjustment and are tested on all grades of materials and pass through numerous inspections, so that it is practically impossible for a Minnesota machine to leave our factory unless perfect in construction and adjustment.

THE NEEDLE BAR IS ROUND AND MADE of the very best quality tool steel, highly tempered. It is absolutely positive in its action, insuring even and automatic operation on materials of any weight and thickness.

THE SELF SETTING NEEDLES FOR THIS MACHINE ARE THE very best grade of needle it is possible to procure. Every needle is inspected and tested as to size, temper, position of the eye, etc. The needle bar is constructed with a groove so that the needle can only be placed in the proper position. It is not necessary to guess at the height or position of the needle, as is the case with many other makes of machines.

DESCRIPTION OF MODEL "C" HEAD—(Continued.)

THE SHUTTLE IS CYLINDRICAL IN SHAPE, made of the finest hardened tool steel and ground. It is absolutely self threading, being open at one end for inserting the bobbin, after which the thread is instantly drawn into place by two motions of the hand.

THE SHUTTLE CARRIER IS MADE of steel and is fitted with a spring lining which holds the shuttle firmly in place and prevents it from rattling when the machine is in operation. It is adjustable so that when the shuttle shows signs of wear it can be moved closer to the race, thus enabling the operator to use the same shuttle for many years with the same satisfaction as when new.

THREAD SCALE. THE FRONT SHUTTLE slide is stamped with a scale indicating the proper size needles to be used with the different numbers of sewing thread.

THE DOUBLE FOUR-MOTION FEED IS MADE OF THE VERY BEST CASE HARDened steel, constructed with four sets of teeth, two sets on each side of the needle, which carry the goods forward firmly and evenly; as the action of the feed is entirely controlled and operated by the main shaft it is strong and certain in its movements. When you get the machine the feed will be regulated for light and medium weight materials generally used in the household, but when desiring to sew extra light goods, such as silks, dimities, lawns, etc., or extra heavy weight materials, such as skirtings, cheviots, kerseys, etc., the feed can be raised or lowered, as necessary, by means of a small screw attaching the feed to the feed rod below the bed plate. The feed can be adjusted in an instant's time, which will be highly appreciated by some of our customers who have used machines of such construction as to make it almost impossible for the operator to adjust the feed.

THE PRESSER FOOT HAS A VERY large under surface, which extends on both sides of the needle and holds any weight goods firmly in place over the feed. The forward part of the presser foot nearest the operator is curved upward so that foot will not catch in seams of fleecy materials.

THE PRESSER BAR IS ROUND AND fitted with a presser bar adjuster by which the pressure on the goods is regulated. At the factory, before shipping the machine, this bar is regulated to give the proper pressure for most household materials and it is only necessary for you to adjust this bar when sewing on extra light or extra heavy materials. The presser bar lifter can be turned to the right and to the left, producing both the high lift and the low lift. When putting on attachments or sewing bulky materials the high lift is used.

THE TAKE-UP. BOTH THE NEEDLE BAR and take-up are driven by the shaft head at the left end of the main shaft, and therefore act simultaneously and in perfect harmony, insuring perfect stitching.

THE TENSION OF OUR MODEL "C" IS placed on top of the arm and consists of two flexible nickel plated steel plates, through which the thread passes. The pressure on the thread is regulated by a small thumbscrew. By pressing a small projection on the lower tension plate, called the tension release, the goods being sewed can be taken away from under the presser foot without bending the needle or breaking the thread.

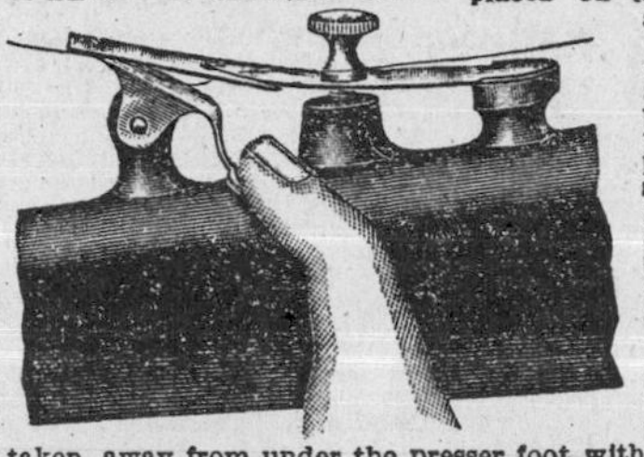

STITCH REGULATOR. THE STITCH can be regulated to run from 7 to 24 stitches to the inch by means of a regulator which is located on the bed plate just below the bobbin winder in easy reach of the operator. The stitch regulator shortens or lengthens the movement of the feed, which in turn controls the size of the stitch.

THREAD CUTTER. TO DO AWAY WITH the necessity of using scissors and to prevent the possibility of breaking or cutting the thread too short, our Model "C" head is provided with a sharp steel thread cutter placed on the presser bar in such a position that the thread can instantly be cut and sufficient thread remains drawn from the needle and also from the shuttle so that the machine remains threaded and ready to sew the next piece of goods.

BOBBIN WINDER. THE BOBBIN WINDER is very neatly finished in black enamel and nickel plate. It is so simple a child can operate it. The thread is wound on the bobbin automatically and so evenly and smoothly as to make the bobbin work perfectly in the shuttle, producing an even tension and greatly improving the perfection of the stitch.

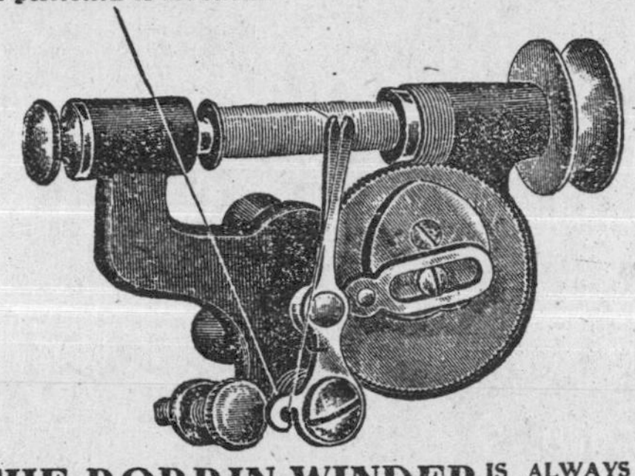

THE BOBBIN WINDER IS ALWAYS IN position and ready to operate. It is operated by means of the belt which is placed in contact with the small pulley wheel of the bobbin winder.

MODEL "C" ATTACHMENTS.

IT HAS BEEN CUSTOMARY FOR DEALERS IN SEWING MACHINES TO FURNISH A SET OF ATTACHMENTS WITH every machine, including their price of the attachments in the selling price of the machine, and also adding a margin of profit on the attachments. The purchaser is, therefore, forced to receive and pay for them whether they are required or not. From our many years' experience in selling sewing machines and carefully studying the wants of our customers we have found that about 33⅓ per cent of sewing machine users do not need the attachments, using the machine for plain sewing only, for which are necessary only the needles, bobbin, quilter, cloth guide, foot hemmer, screwdriver and wrench, which we furnish with each machine at no additional charge. We have, therefore, deducted the cost of the attachments from our selling price and quote prices which represent only the actual cost of material and labor used in the construction of the machine alone, with our one small percentage of profit added.

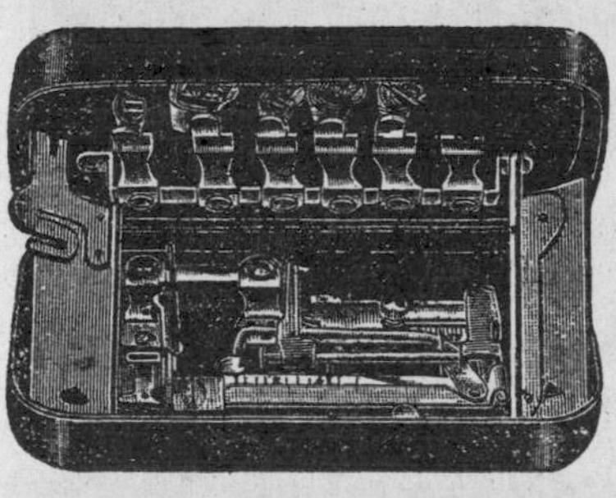

THE ATTACHMENTS WILL BE FURNISHED AT 75 CENTS PER SET.

THE ATTACHMENTS ARE FITTED ON THE PRESSer bar after the sewing foot has been removed, each attachment being provided with a grooved foot, which fits tightly on the presser bar and holds the attachment firmly in place and is put on and removed by hand without the aid of any tool. The set of attachments, as illustrated on the left, consists of one ruffler, one shirring plate, one tucker, one short foot, one underbraider, one binder and one set of four hemmers of different widths up to ⅝ of an inch. Price, per set..........75c

For description of Model "C" Woodwork, see following page.
For our Liberal Terms of Shipment, see page 36.
For our Three Months' Free Trial, see page 36.
For our 20-Year Written Binding Guarantee, see page 36.
For freight rates, see column first class freight rates, pages 13 to 17.

ACCESSORIES FURNISHED FREE.

WE FURNISH with every machine a complete set of accessories, consisting of one quilter, six bobbins, one cloth guide, one large screwdriver, one oil can filled with oil, one shuttle screwdriver, one wrench, one foot hemmer, one package of needles and one instruction book.

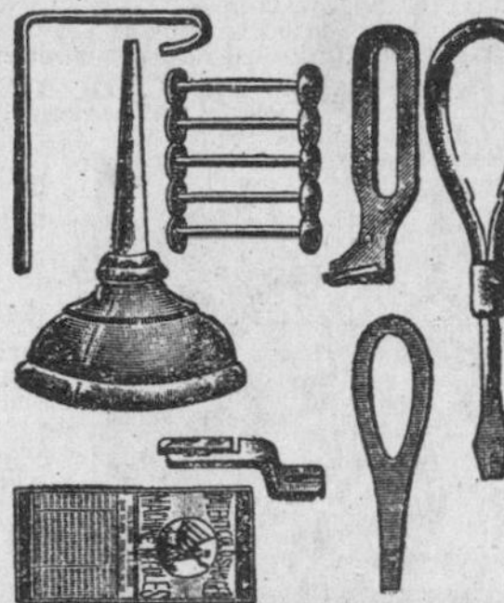

WE FURNISH, FREE OF CHARGE, WITH EVERY MINNESOTA MODEL "C" SEWING MACHINE, a Book of Instructions telling how to operate the sewing machine. The book covers every point, makes everything so plain and simple that anyone without previous experience can learn to run the machine at once and do perfect work; tells you how to get the best results, how to take care of your machine; tells you where to oil and when. It tells you how to use the different attachments, the ruffler, tucker, hemmers and binders, and contains illustrations of these attachments in use.

HOW WE MAKE QUICK DELIVERY

THE WAY WE CAN DELIVER A MACHINE AND HAVE IT IN YOUR HOME IN A DAY OR TWO IS FULLY EXPLAINED ON PAGE 37.

READ WHAT OUR CUSTOMERS HAVE TO SAY ABOUT THE MINNESOTA SEWING MACHINES.

WOULD NOT EXCHANGE OUR MODEL "A" MINNESOTA FOR A $65.00 SINGER.

Sears, Roebuck & Co., Chicago, Ill. Rosedale, Miss.

Gentlemen:—The Model "A" Sewing Machine bought of you about eight months ago is very satisfactory. Mrs. McBroom was very much opposed to buying one of your machines. She wanted to buy a Singer from an agent here, at $65.00, on the installment plan. She never knew when I ordered the machine from you, so when it came I had it hauled home while she was visiting. When she came home and found the new sewing machine she thought the agent had left it for her to examine, until she noticed the "A." She at once began sewing and was so pleased she sent out for a neighbor to examine it. While they were discussing the different machines, I came in and informed them that I had paid Sears, Roebuck & Co. $17.20 for it. They all seemed surprised and declared it equal if not better than the $65.00 machines sold by the agents, and now Mrs. McBroom would not exchange it for any machine on the market. We truly recommend this machine to those wishing to buy a truly reliable, high class, light running sewing machine.

Yours very truly, J. M. McBROOM.

THE MINNESOTA EQUAL TO A $70.00 MACHINE.

Sears, Roebuck & Co., Chicago, Ill. Basalt, Idaho.

Gentlemen:—I purchased a Minnesota Sewing Machine April 23. I have thoroughly tested this machine on all kinds of work and do not think it can be equaled for the price and I would not part with it at any price if I could not get another. We have changed our residence from Spanish Fork, Utah, to Basalt, Idaho, and the people here are simply astonished to find that such a high grade machine could be purchased for so little. My Minnesota machine cost me (freight included) $20.20 and I consider it equal to a sewing machine of my neighbor that cost $70.00. I am,

Very respectfully yours, MRS. H. L. STERLING.

MR. PIERCE WILLIAMS CONSIDERS THE MINNESOTA BY FAR THE BEST MACHINE ON THE MARKET. IT RUNS MUCH EASIER AND WITH MUCH LESS NOISE THAN THE SINGER, WHEELER & WILSON, OR NEW HOME, AND HE HAS TRIED THEM ALL. THE MINNESOTA SIMPLY COULD NOT BE IMPROVED.

Sears, Roebuck & Co., Chicago, Ill. Dingus, Ky.

Gentlemen:—Having received my machine (Minnesota) can say that I consider it the best we ever tried. In workmanship, finest finish, working qualities, durability, ease of running, the best by far; less noise by two-thirds than the Singer, Wheeler & Wilson, New Home or any other we ever tried, and proves satisfactory in every way and in general is the one I consider best on the market and it would retail in my neighborhood for at least $40.00. I can heartily recommend it to anyone who wants to purchase a machine. I am quite sure there cannot be any improvement put on this machine and, as for my part, don't want any improvement. The freight was 75 cents.

Very truly, PIERCE WILLIAMS.

MRS. HOLLOWAY SAYS: YOUR LIBRARY TABLE SEWING MACHINE IS EQUAL TO ANY MACHINE I HAVE EVER USED THAT COST DOUBLE WHAT THAT DID. I HAVE USED IT AS A LIBRARY TABLE FOR SOME TIME AND IT TAKES THE PLACE OF ONE PERFECTLY.

Sears, Roebuck & Co., Chicago, Ill. Delhi, N. Y.

Dear Sirs:—In regard to the sewing machine you sent me, would say that it is certainly a well finished machine and equal to any machine I have ever used that cost double what that did. I have not used it so very much as yet, but like it very much so far. I have asked several what they would expect to pay if they bought it around here or from agents and they said from forty to fifty dollars at least. I have not found one that could tell the difference between it and a common library table until I opened it. They also admire the high polish and finish of it. I have used it as a library table for some time and it takes the place of one perfectly. If you wish to sew you only have to remove the top board and do not have to remove any of the things that may be on it as you do any other machine. It is very easily put in running order. I can recommend this machine to anyone.

Yours respectfully, MRS. ROBT. N. HOLLOWAY.

MRS. HODGE SAYS:—I AM WELL PLEASED WITH THE MACHINE AND I THINK THERE IS NO BETTER MACHINE SOLD AT ANY PRICE THAN THE MINNESOTA MODEL "A." ALSO THAT SHE CONSIDERS IT AS GOOD A MACHINE IN EVERY WAY AS ANY MACHINE EVER USED BY HER AND SOLD AT PRICES RANGING FROM FORTY TO FIFTY DOLLARS.

Sears, Roebuck & Co., Chicago, Ill. Brogado, Texas.

Dear Sirs:—Concerning the Minnesota Model "A" sewing machine which I purchased from you some five or six months ago, I am pleased with the machine and do not think there is a better machine sold at any price than my Minnesota Model "A." I consider it as good a machine in every way as any machine I ever used at prices ranging from forty dollars to sixty dollars as sold by agents. It does the work in a perfect manner, is almost noiseless and runs very light. The workmanship and finish are equal to any machine sold at double the price of yours. I never miss an opportunity to speak a word of praise of the machine, and at the price you sell it I advise everyone in need of a first class machine to buy your machine. I have already induced one lady, Mrs. Pinkerton, to order one from you. She was a neighbor of mine who used my machine and after using it and hearing my praise of it she took my advice and ordered one like it from you. Will speak a good word for your Model "A" whenever an opportunity affords. You may use this letter in any way you see fit.

Respectfully, MRS. HODGE.

IN WRITING TO ANY OF THESE PEOPLE, PLEASE ENCLOSE A 2-CENT STAMP FOR REPLY.

Our Minnesota Model "C" Sewing Machine $14⁴⁵

IN THE FULL CABINET STYLE.   NEW AND IMPROVED CABINET.

SEE THE ILLUSTRATIONS, ONE ILLUSTRATION showing the machine fully closed so that it appears to be only a handsome desk cabinet; a second illustration showing the machine open, ready for work, and a third illustration showing the machine partly closed with the head lowered and extension leaf folded over. The desk cabinet is perhaps the most beautiful style of sewing machine cabinet construction and in Model "C" cabinet style, at $14.45, we offer the lowest priced cabinet machine on the market. This style of machine must really be seen to be appreciated. It is very rich and handsome in appearance. We furnish a beautiful high grade cabinet, an extra handsome piece of woodwork, a cabinet that compares favorably with the cabinet machines sold elsewhere at double our price.

THIS HANDSOME, FULL OAK DESK
CABINET IS MADE OF THE VERY BEST SOLID OAK, THOROUGHLY AIR AND KILN DRIED. THE DOOR is made of specially selected quarter sawed oak with panel front, ornamented with handsome design drop carvings and massive mouldings and caps. Please note the rich and tasteful decorations on this woodwork. The sides are solid full oak panels. The lid is made of built up stock with special selected quarter sawed oak top. This construction prevents warping and cracking. The inside of the door is fitted with wooden pockets to hold the oil can, bobbins, screwdriver and other accessories so they will be convenient for use when the machine is being operated. The cabinet is the product of the finest cabinet makers. It is finished throughout in a strictly first class manner, every piece and part is thoroughly sandpapered before it is put together, insuring perfect cabinet work. The varnish used on this cabinet is exceptionally high grade. It brings out the rich golden oak finish which is so popular. It is worked over and hand rubbed, giving a rich, glossy appearance, the same as the hand polished effect shown in the highest grade furniture. The cabinet rests on four rollers so it can be easily moved about. In this, our Minnesota Model "C" cabinet, we believe we have the handsomest desk cabinet offered by anyone, such a grade of woodwork as is only found in the highest class of furniture. The workmanship of the cabinet is most thorough and it is not to be compared with the cheap woodwork offered by many other sewing machine dealers which enables them to make a low price, and we will guarantee that our full desk cabinet will never warp, check, or split.

SAFE DELIVERY GUARANTEED ATTACHMENTS 75c EXTRA

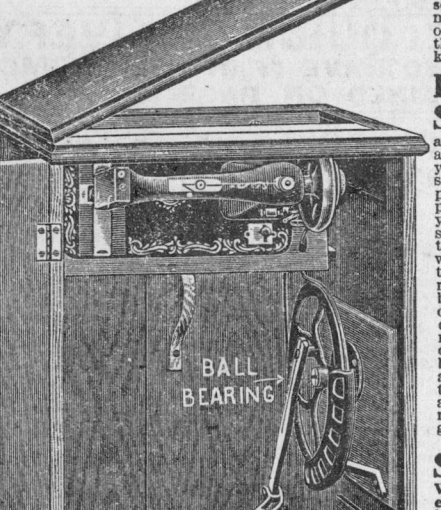

BALL BEARING

OUR MODEL "C" FULL CABINET MACHINE IS BALL bearing. It is fitted with our celebrated bicycle ball bearing hanger, which gives the same rapidity of action and ease of operation as the ball bearing arrangement on a bicycle. All wearing parts are made of case hardened ground out steel and the steel balls in the bearing are the best in the market. The bearing is simple in construction, no getting out of order, all parts easily accessible so that the balls or cups can be replaced at any time in the future, if in the years to come there is reason to replace anything. By means of this ball bearing, practically all friction is eliminated and the running of the machine made a real pleasure.

UNLESS WE CAN INDUCE YOU TO ORDER A MINNESOTA MODEL "B" or Model "A" we certainly want you to order this, our next best machine, the full desk cabinet, Model "C." It will please you so well, look so beautiful in your home, represent to you such a great saving in price that we can anticipate how delighted you will be and how much good it will do us as an advertisement. Our only advantage in urging you to order the best machine we offer is for the additional satisfaction you yourself will get from such a purchase. It is not because we make any more profit, for we really do not. Our margin of profit is exactly the same and the additional money asked by us for a higher grade machine, the highest grade we make, buys so much in the way of superior construction, finer cabinet work, better mechanical construction, a closer approach to perfection in every feature that we feel we can conscientiously make such a recommendation. Be sure that you do not make the mistake of buying a sewing machine from anyone else before you have the opportunity of seeing and trying a Minnesota. Order any Minnesota Sewing Machine, put it side by side with the sewing machine you get from anyone else, give them both a thorough test, and if our machine is not far superior to the machine offered by anyone else at the same price, or if our sewing machine is not much lower in price than any sewing machine you can get from anyone else to equal ours in quality, then we won't expect you to keep our machine; you are perfectly welcome to return it to us at once, and we will promptly return your money, including any freight charges you may have paid.

═══ THREE MONTHS' ═══
FREE TRIAL

BALL BEARING

WE INVITE COMPARISON. WE URGE A TRIAL. WE know positively that no sewing machine will excel in quality our Models "A" and "B." We know that no sewing machines offered by others at our prices will compare in all the essential features with our other models, for we have made such side by side, piece by piece and part by part comparison that we are sure of our ground, and if we can only induce you to make a comparison we know that it will amount to a sale.

IF YOU ARE THINKING OF BUYING A
SEWING MACHINE THAT IS OFFERED TO YOU BY A SEWING machine agent we know that we are placed at a great disadvantage. The agent is right there on the ground with his machine, can point out all the good features of his machine, can show you its many advantages, and all we can offer you, unless you will take advantage of our liberal terms of shipment, is an illustration and description. However, we have this advantage, and that is, the agent must also tell you the price, and when he tells you the price and you compare it with our price the difference will compel you to pause and give us a fair trial before you finally place your order. We know that if you could be in the factory where our sewing machines are made for just one hour and could see the kind of material that we use, the care that is given to every detail of the manufacture, the class of skilled mechanics we employ, the tests we make; if you could see how thoroughly well made the Minnesota machines are, if you could watch our method of drying the oak, the matching and fitting, our cabinet making, the varnishing, polishing and rubbing, the drawing and shaping of the parts of the head, the plating and polishing of the bright parts, the grinding and tempering of the bearings, you would be convinced that no other manufacturer goes to such lengths to produce a perfect sewing machine. You can quickly see where every penny over and above our small margin of profit goes into the machine itself, into the cost of material and labor. You would understand why we claim that our Minnesota Sewing Machines are not at all to be compared with the sewing machines you buy from other mail order houses. There is no other mail order house whose sewing machines are made in the one factory, under the same conditions as prevail in our sewing machine factory. No other mail order house really knows anything about how their sewing machines are actually made nor could they guarantee that their sewing machines are produced from the best material, the most skilled labor and under such careful supervision which is such a great safeguard for quality in the Minnesota factory.

SEND US YOUR ORDER FOR THE MINNESOTA MODEL "C" full desk cabinet at $14.45. We guarantee you will receive from us a perfect machine, nothing better to be had from anyone else. We guarantee the machine to reach you in perfect condition, the same as it left our hands. We guarantee that you will make a big saving in the price after paying the freight charges. We guarantee to return your money and pay all the expenses of the transaction if at any time during the three months' trial you have any reason to feel dissatisfied. We take all the risk. You take none.

READ OUR LIBERAL TERMS OF SHIP-
MENT. REMEMBER, YOU HAVE ALL THE PRIVILEGES WE OFFER. THE three months' trial agreement is in force the moment you send us your order. If there is any question in your mind, if you are inclined to buy a sewing machine from any agent or dealer, let us ship you a machine on three months' trial, and if you are not satisfied in every way you may return the machine and the money paid for the machine as well as freight charges will be cheerfully returned to you without any delay.

OUR PRICE OF $14.45 FOR THE FULL DESK CABINET Minnesota Model "C" does not include attachments. We do include a full set of accessories as shown on page 41, but we do not charge you a price to include attachments, as you may not need them if you expect to do plain sewing only. For 75 cents additional we will send you a full set of highest grade attachments described on page 41. We guarantee this machine for twenty years.

IN ORDERING ALWAYS WRITE CATALOGUE NUMBER PLAINLY AND IN FULL—WRITE EVERY FIGURE AND LETTER IN THE CATALOGUE NUMBER.

No. 26K229 Model "C" Full Cabinet, finished in golden oak only...... $14.45

ILLUSTRATED FEATURES OF THE MECHANICAL CONSTRUCTION OF OUR

Minnesota Model "B" Head

IT WILL DO ANY WORK, LIGHT OR HEAVY, FANCY OR PLAIN SEWING, THAT CAN BE DONE ON ANY FAMILY SEWING MACHINE.

It is impossible to devise a more perfect or more suitable sewing machine for household or domestic purposes than our MINNESOTA MODEL "B." In the matter of improvements, labor and time saving conveniences, it is second only to our Minnesota Model "A," and is built on the latest up to date principles of construction.

DESIGN. BY REFERENCE TO THE ILLUStration it will be seen that the Minnesota Model "B" Head is extremely handsome and pleasing in appearance, the general design being worked out in easy curves and rounded corners so as to avoid any suggestion of harshness or angularity.

SIZE. OUR MODEL "B" HEAD IS THE regular standard, high arm, family style, and measures 5 inches in height under the arm, 8½ inches from needle to upright part of arm and 9¾ inches from bed plate to top of the needle bar. The bed plate is 6¾ inches wide by 13½ inches long. These measurements provide sufficient space for practically any family sewing.

FINISH. THE FINISH OF THE HEAD is as fine as can be put on a sewing machine. Three coats of the highest grade of enamel are used, each coat being separately baked at a high temperature, rubbed down to a smooth surface by hand and finally beautifully decorated in an elaborate design worked out in gold and bright colors, after which it is given a coat of special varnish, also baked in a high degree of heat, which gives the machine a durable, rich and lustrous finish. Before the enamel is put on, the head is treated to a coat of anti-rust preparation which prevents the finish from cracking, checking or peeling which so frequently occurs with other makes of machines.

NICKEL PLATING. ALL OF THE bright parts, including the face plate, are first copper plated, then nickel plated and finally highly polished. This applies to the working parts underneath the bed of the machine as well as to those that are exposed to view.

LOCK STITCH. OUR MODEL "B" IS a regular lock stitch machine, which is the popular type adopted by all manufacturers of high grade machines.

OPERATING PARTS

THE OPERATING PARTS OF THE MODEL "B" Head are practically the same as those of our Model "A," with the exception of the round needle bar and the shuttle and feed mechanism, which is of a slightly different construction, as will be noted by referring to the illustration of the under view of the head. All operating and working parts in this machine are made of the finest tool steel that can be obtained, and after being thoroughly hardened by the latest and most improved process, are accurately ground to a perfect fit and so constructed that any lost motion due to the slight wear that may result after many years of usage can be easily and quickly taken up. This renders it practically indestructible and one of the most durable machines ever produced.

SPECIAL FEATURES

HIGH ARM. INDEPENDENT, POSITIVE CAM TAKE-UP. DISC TENSION. AUTOMATIC TENSION RELEASE. ROLLER BEARING ANTI-FRICTION FEED BAR. LIGHT RUNNING. NOISELESS.

THE INDEPENDENT TAKE-UP.
THE TAKE-UP IS OPERATED by a cam on the main shaft, thereby becoming absolutely positive in its action and insuring uniformity of stitch in all classes of work. In many machines, even some of the most expensive, springs are used to partly control the movement of the take-up, and the instant the spring is weakened the harmony between the take-up and other important running parts is destroyed, consequently resulting in imperfect stitches or the breaking of needles.

DOUBLE ECCENTRIC.
THE DOUBLE ECCENTRIC ON THE main shaft through the arm of the head operates the shuttle, feed and needle bar mechanism. The double eccentric is made of one piece, accurately balanced so as to prevent any vibration when the machine is being operated and which also contributes greatly to its light and noiseless running qualities. This construction does away with all irregular movements and produces a shuttle and feed movement which is absolutely positive in every sense of the term. A glance at the working parts of this machine shows how remarkably simple it is. There are no springs, cushions, pads or other appliances required which necessarily add to the number of parts and the liability of the machine to get out of order.

EASY TO OIL.
BY MEANS OF CONVENIENT OIL HOLES AND A movable metal plate on the back of the head, all bearings are easily gotten at to oil. This is a most important feature, as thorough lubrication prevents friction and wear.

THE NEEDLE CLAMP
HOLDS THE NEEDLE FIRMLY IN place and permits the needle to be removed in an instant when required, even though it should break accidently in the bar where it cannot be reached by the fingers. The needles can be had from us at factory cost. For prices, see page 63.

RUNNING SPEED.
EVERY MACHINE BEfore being shipped from the factory is put to the severest possible test, being set up and attached to a power pulley and run at a speed five times greater than it is possible to run any machine by foot power, and by this severe test we first learn that every machine is perfectly true in every particular and capable of the highest possible speed.

THE NEEDLE BAR
IS ROUND AND MADE OF THE best quality of tool steel, properly hardened and tempered. It is accurately fitted, insuring absolutely uniform wear at all points.

SELF SETTING NEEDLES
FOR THIS MACHINE are the very best grade of flat shank needle it is possible to procure. Every needle is inspected and tested as to size, temper and position of eye. The needle bar is constructed with a groove so that the needle can only be placed in the proper position. It is not necessary to guess at the height or position when setting the needle as is the case with many other makes of machines.

THE MINNESOTA HEAD
IS CONSTRUCTED WITH less running or operating parts than any other machine on the market, rendering it easy to understand and operate, light running and free from vibration and noise, doing away with the liability to get out of order, common to many machines. The mechanism is so constructed that the full line of parts in the Minnesota head operate entirely independent of one another and all driving power is supplied direct from the main shaft, without the agency of the numerous connections, cogs and many unnecessary devices used in some machines to operate the feed, shuttle and needle power. The operator does not need to tamper with or adjust these parts, regardless of the weight of goods being sewed. This construction has made the Minnesota head famous as the most durable and simplest head ever produced.

ADJUSTMENT.
MUCH DEpends upon the adjustment of the working parts, for should any part, for instance the shuttle, be adjusted 1-32 of an inch out of place, the harmony between the parts would be destroyed and imperfect work will result. The operating parts in our Minnesota machines receive the finest and most accurate adjustment and are tested on all kinds of materials, and pass other numerous inspections, so that it is practically impossible for a Minnesota machine to leave our factory, unless perfect in construction and adjustment.

OUR FACTORY,
WHERE the Minnesota sewing machines are manufactured, is equipped with every labor saving device as well as every possible machine or device, to improve the quality of the product. We have many expensive machines that are designed solely to do one little operation, which does this little operation faster and more accurately than could be done by hand. Unless we had an immense output of machines we could not afford this kind of machinery. This is only one of our advantages over the smaller dealer in sewing machines. With us, the cost of an expensive machine to perfect just one little operation is soon absorbed by the immense number of sewing machines we make and really figures only a few cents, practically nothing, as an expense to be charged against each machine.

DESCRIPTION OF OUR MODEL "B" HEAD—Continued.

EVERY SINGLE MACHINE WE PUT OUT IS COVERED by our written, binding twenty-year guarantee. In order that we can guarantee our sewing machines for 20 years, it is necessary that only the very finest material be used, and put together by the most skilful workmanship. You can feel assured that our sewing machines are the finest it is possible to manufacture, that we spare no effort or expense in our endeavor to produce an almost everlasting machine, since we are able to guarantee every machine for the full term of 20 years. We aim to protect you in every way and if the machine you get from us gives out in any way, by reason of any defect in material or workmanship, at any time, in 20 years, we will replace it or repair it free of charge.

PRESSER FOOT. THE PRESSER foot is very large so that it will hold any weight and thickness of goods firmly in place. The edge of the foot nearest the operator is bent upward slightly so that it will not catch in fleecy material. The presser foot can be removed from the machine in an instant without the aid of a screwdriver. The illustration shows the foot being removed after the thumbscrew has been loosened.

PRESSER BAR LIFTER THE PRESSER BAR IS fitted with a steel, case hardened, nickel plated lifter, so constructed that it can be turned to the right or to the left, raising the bar to the desired height for heavy or light material.

NEEDLE AND THREAD SCALE. A SCALE INDICATING THE proper needle to be used with the different sizes of thread is stamped on the forward shuttle slide. Breaking of the thread and needles often occurs if incorrect sizes of needles or thread are used.

A SHARP STEEL THREAD CUTTER IS PLACED ON THE presser bar, convenient to the operator, by the aid of which the thread can be easily cut, obviating the use of scissors and the danger of breaking or cutting the thread too short.

DOUBLE FEED. THE FEED is made of the best quality tool steel; has four sets of teeth, two on each side of the needle, and so constructed that when in operation the goods must be carried forward with absolute accuracy.

FEED MOVEMENT. (FOUR-MOTION.) THE FEED IN THIS machine is operated by four movements. The feed comes up, takes a firm hold on the goods, carries them foward the full length of the stitch, then it falls, releasing the goods, and comes back again toward the operator ready for the next stitch. These four movements are provided entirely by the main shaft, insuring positive action on either heavy or light work.

THE SHUTTLE. THE SHUTtle is the most perfect, self-threading, cylindrical shuttle ever produced. It is extra large in size, made of the finest tool steel, hardened, ground and finished. It is absolutely self threading, being open at one end for inserting the bobbin, after which the thread is instantly drawn into place by two movements of the hand. There are no holes to pass through, and the shuttle can be threaded with the eyes shut. It has a perfect tension, which is practically automatic. It does not require regulating for any ordinary work. The bobbin carries a large amount of thread. The illustration shows the shuttle being held between the thumb and forefinger while threading.

THE SHUTTLE CARRIER. THE BODY IN which the shuttle rests is fitted with a spring which holds the bobbin firmly in place and prevents it from rattling while the machine is in operation. The carrier is adjustable, so that when the shuttle shows signs of wear, after many years of use, the carrier can be moved closer to the shuttle race, thus enabling the operator to use the same shuttle for many years, with the same satisfaction as when new.

FOR DESCRIPTION OF MODEL "B" WOODWORK See page 47.

FOR DESCRIPTION OF MODEL "B" STAND See page 49.

FOR DESCRIPTION OF MODEL "B" CABINET See page 50.

FOR OUR LIBERAL TERMS OFFER See page 36.

FOR OUR THREE MONTHS' FREE TRIAL OFFER See page 36.

FOR OUR TWENTY YEARS' GUARANTEE See page 36.

DISC TENSION. THE UPper tension of this machine is of the modern disc type and practically automatic on all classes of work. The tension is located on the side face plate toward the operator. This location of the tension is not only far more convenient, but brings the point at which the tension is applied to the thread much nearer to the eye of the needle, thus reducing the amount of thread under tension and doing away, in a large measure, with the stretch in the thread, which on the old style machines frequently caused bad stitching or skipping of stitches.

SEE PAGE 62 FOR ILLUSTRATION AND DESCRIPTION OF THE NEW LIBRARY TABLE SEWING MACHINE.

AUTOMATIC TENSION RELEASE MAKES IT POSSIBLE to remove the work from the machine as soon as you raise the presser foot, so that the work can be drawn from underneath the presser foot with ease.

THE AUTOMATIC BOBBIN WINDER ON THIS MACHINE is nickel plated throughout and is the most perfect bobbin winder ever produced. It is so simple that any child can operate it, and the thread is wound on the bobbin automatically and so evenly and smoothly as to make the bobbin work perfectly in the shuttle, producing an even tension and greatly improving the perfection of the stitch. This also prevents the breaking of the lower thread, which is liable to occur with an unevenly wound bobbin.

THE BOBBIN WINDER IS ALWAYS IN POSITION AND READY TO operate. It is operated by means of the belt which is placed in contact with the small pulley wheel of the bobbin winder.

STITCH REGULATOR. THE illustration shows the stitch regulator, which is fastened to the bed plate just in front of the arm in plain sight and within easy reach of the operator. The length of the stitch can be adjusted instantly by loosening the thumb nut and moving the pointer to the desired figure on the scale stamped on the stitch regulator plate. The stitch can be varied from six to thirty-two stitches to the inch, thereby affording a range from the very smallest to the largest stitch.

LOCK NUT. THE LOCK NUT, which is located at the end of the main shaft and used to release and tighten the hand wheel, is turned out of one piece of case hardened steel, has milled edge and is heavily nickel plated and polished. The lock nut is plainly marked with arrows, showing which way it must be turned to loosen or tighten the hand wheel.

Attachments for Our Model "B" Machines

WE USE THE CELEBRATED GREIST FOOT ATTACHMENTS.

OUR CUSTOMERS HAVE THE ADVANTAGE AND PRIVILEGE OF BEING ABLE TO PURCHASE A MACHINE WITHOUT attachments, and are not obliged to receive and pay for attachments which are not required. From our many years of experience in selling sewing machines we have found that about one-third of the sewing machine users do not need the attachments, using the machine for plain sewing only; the only necessary attachments being the shuttle, needle, bobbin, quilter, screwdriver, wrench and foot hemmer, which are always furnished with our machines at no additional charge. We have, therefore, deducted the cost of the attachments from the selling price and quote each machine without any extra attachments.

THE ATTACHMENTS FOR OUR MINNESOTA MODEL "B" SEWing Machine, furnished at 75 cents extra, are made by the Greist Mfg. Co., the largest manufacturing plant devoted exclusively to the manufacture of sewing machine attachments. This illustration shows the Model "B" attachments arranged in a velvet lined metal box. Each attachment may be kept in its particular place as provided for by the construction of the box. The complete set includes one ruffler, one shirring blade, one tucker, one under braider, one binder, one short foot and one set of four hemmers up to 5/8 of an inch wide. The attachments are made of steel, heavily nickel plated and polished.

ATTACHMENTS WILL BE FURNISHED AT 75 CENTS EXTRA. IF YOU, THE READER OF THIS CATalogue, intend to use your machine for plain sewing only, and do not wish to buy extra attachments, you will appreciate our departure from the old custom of including, at the purchaser's expense, a set of attachments with every machine. If you wish to purchase a machine without attachments, and later on wish to secure attachments, we can always supply you at our lowest price.

ACCESSORIES FURNISHED FREE. WE FURNISH WITH EVERY MINNEsota Model "B" Machine a complete set of accessories, such as are usually furnished with every high grade machine, consisting of one quilter, five bobbins (and one in the machine), one cloth guide, a large screwdriver, one oil can filled with oil, one screwdriver and wrench, one foot hemmer, one package of needles and one instruction book.

WE CARRY IN STOCK A FULL supply of needles, bobbins, shuttles, attachments, etc., which are used in the operation of our machines. We can, therefore, fill orders for repairs promptly. An order for repairs for the Minnesota Model "B" Machines, placed with us fifteen or twenty years from date, would be filled as promptly as a repair order sent us today.

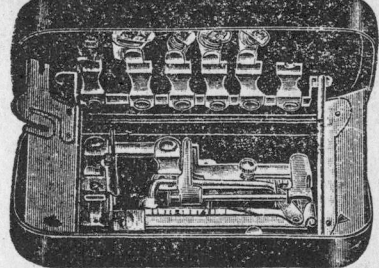

WE FURNISH, FREE OF CHARGE, WITH EVERY MINNESOTA MODEL "B" SEWING MACHINE A BOOK OF INSTRUCTIONS telling how to operate the sewing machine. This book covers every point, makes everything so plain and simple that anyone without previous experience can learn to run the machine at once and do perfect work; tells you how to get the best results, how to take care of your machine, tells you where to oil and when. It tells you how to use the different attachments, the ruffler, tucker, hemmers and binders, and contains illustrations of these attachments in use.

OUR 7-DRAWER DROP LEAF AND BOX COVER MINNESOTA MODEL "B" SEWING MACHINE

$13.85

DO NOT BE MISLED

BY SEWING MACHINE ADVERTISEMENTS. There are any number of sewing machine advertisers in the field, any number of very attractive sewing machine catalogues published, with beautiful illustrations, and even prices that are very attractive. Do not believe for a minute that anyone else can furnish you with a sewing machine of the same quality as our Minnesota at our price. No other dealer or manufacturer can do it. If you doubt our ability to furnish you a very much finer sewing machine in every way than you can get for the money from anyone else, just let us send you a sewing machine to examine and try. We are very anxious to have you give the Minnesota a trial in your own home. Take our machine home, try it, do any kind of work on it, put the agent's sewing machine next to it for comparison, get the sewing machine offered in any other catalogue, try them all, and if the Minnesota does not lead them all and come out of the test with flying colors, then we won't expect to make a sale; you may return our machine, and any money you have paid us will be promptly returned to you, and we will return the amount you paid for freight charges. It is true that you can find seven-drawer sewing machines in other catalogues priced at $15.00 to $16.00, a very near approach to our wonderful $13.85 price, but the difference is not alone in the $1.15 or $2.15; it is a far greater difference than this in the quality. You will find by comparison that the Minnesota Model "B" seven-drawer machine as illustrated on

this page is worth $10.00 to $15.00 more than the machine that would be furnished for $15.00 to $16.00 by anyone else. We know all this from comparison; there is no doubt about it, and we do not want you to be deceived by attractive pictures and catchy prices that may be offered in other catalogues. IN THIS, OUR SEVEN-DRAWER DROP LEAF and box cover Minnesota Model "B" Sewing Machine you will find all of the high grade features that have made the Minnesota Sewing Machines famous for years. You will find the head of this machine the best sewing machine head on the market, the least complicated, the least liable to get out of order, the simplest, the easiest running, a sewing machine that will do the greatest variety of work. You will find the cabinet itself almost a work of art. The illustration will give you only a little idea of the beautiful rich carving and heavy embossing. It is impossible to bring out the rich grain effect of the oak, nor can we show the same effect in the box cover, which you see behind the machine. The drop leaf is large and ample for the handling of any kind of material. In the illustration the leaf is extended. While most of our customers prefer the drop head cabinet style of sewing machine, this upright style of sewing machine with the drop

BALL BEARING

Mrs. Mixon says, "I Have Used All the Attachments and they Worked All Right. I Saved $15.00 to $20.00 by Ordering a Minnesota."

Sears, Roebuck & Co., Chicago, Ill.

Gentlemen:—I received the Minnesota machine which I bought of you about four months ago, in good condition, and I am well pleased with it. I think it is as good as the machines which sell here for $30.00 to $40.00. I have used all the attachments and they work all right, and I am well pleased with my machine. I think that I saved $15.00 to $20.00 by ordering my machine from you.

Yours truly,
MRS. MAY MIXON.

For full description of Model "B" Head, Attachments and Accessories, see pages 45 and 46. Stand, see page 49.

leaf and separate box cover is still very popular, is preferred by quite a few people, and so far as a work doer is concerned, this style machine will turn out as much work and as good work as any other. The Model "B" head is exactly the same, a very high grade head on the upright as well as the drop head style; the stand is the same, an extra high grade, thoroughly well made, strongly braced, very durable and rigid stand. The treadle and dress guard are exactly the same. The only difference is in the style of woodwork of the cabinet. Each and every machine is a leader in its class, and we guarantee you cannot duplicate it, style for style, quality for quality, for much less than double the price we ask, and no matter whether you order the Model "B" sewing machine in this seven-drawer upright style with box cover, or the drop head cabinet style described on the next page, or the Model "A" in any of the various styles we furnish it, you will be getting a wonderful bargain in a sewing machine. You will be saving a great deal of money, getting a very fine sewing machine, much better than the sewing machine offered by any other catalogue house, even very much better than the sewing machines offered by dealers and agents at $40.00.

Before placing your order for any machine, be sure to read the descriptions of our improved Ball Bearing Minnesota Model "A" Sewing Machine, Ball Bearing Head, Ball Bearing Stand, Double Ball Bearing Steel Pitman.

AT OUR SPECIAL PRICE OF $13.15

FOR THE MODEL "B" THREE-DRAWER BOX COVER, $13.45 FOR THE MODEL "B" five-drawer box cover, $13.85 for the Model "B" seven-drawer box cover, just as illustrated, we furnish a sewing machine on board the cars at our factory in Dayton, Ohio, from which point the customer pays the freight. However, the freight charges are small compared with your saving in price. The sewing machine weighs, strongly crated for shipment, 120 pounds, and no matter where you live, we guarantee that you will make a big saving at our price after you have paid the freight charges. With each Minnesota Sewing Machine we furnish a complete set of accessories, as shown on page 46. We do not include the case of attachments in making our selling prices, as there are many people who do not want the attachments. If you want attachments, we can furnish them for 75 cents additional, a complete set of the highest grade attachments, as explained on page 46.

DESCRIPTION OF WOODWORK ON OUR MINNESOTA MODEL "B" SEWING MACHINES.

THE WOODWORK ON OUR MODEL "B" SEWING Machines is of a very much higher grade than is usually used in sewing machines. It is made especially for our machines, under contract, by the largest manufacturers of sewing machine woodwork in the world, who supply cabinets only for the highest grade sewing machines, and it cannot be in any way classed with the woodwork commonly used on machines that sell generally at $25.00 or less.

MATERIALS. ONLY THE MOST SELECT GRADE OF solid oak is used in the construction of our Model "B" woodwork. It is carefully selected with reference to grain and color and is thoroughly aired and kiln dried to insure against warping, splitting or cracking.

DESIGN. THE MINNESOTA MODEL "B" CABINET IS A model of beauty and artistic design, second only to our Model "A." It is made on the lines of the high grade, up to date furniture, especially designed for us and not made for nor used on any other machines.

TABLE. THE TABLE IS MADE OF BUILT UP STOCK AND faced with highly figured quartered oak. This construction has proven the most durable, being practically indestructible. The front edge of the table is handsomely shaped. All tables on the upright box cover Model "B" machines, as illustrated, have a drop leaf, which, when raised into place, is supported by an iron brace and produces a table of ample length for any and all requirements.

DRAWER FRAMES. THE DRAWER FRAMES IN which the side drawers are fitted are of the latest skeleton type, much handsomer in appearance and far preferable to the old fashioned solid cases.

DRAWERS. THE DRAWERS ARE VERY LARGE AND roomy, made with rounded corners to harmonize with the table. The fronts are handsomely decorated with drop carvings of floral design and fitted with brass, nickel plated and polished ring pulls. The center drawer is made of built up stock, with swell front; the interior is partitioned off for bobbins, needles and other accessories, which are in constant demand when the machine is being used. Every drawer is fitted with a lock and one key fits them all.

FINISH. IN POINT OF FINISH OUR MODEL "B" MACHINE is strictly first class and of the very latest golden color, the popular finish put on high grade oak furniture. Before the finish is put on, the woodwork is most carefully sandpapered so that the varnish, which is of the very best quality, produces a hard glossy surface. The table is hand rubbed and polished.

COVER. ALL UPRIGHT MACHINES ARE PROVIDED with box cover, made of built up stock, surfaced with quartered oak and strengthened with mouldings. The front is ornamented with carved, raised panel. The cover is fitted with socket hinges and lock, so that when placed on the machine it can be locked, thereby affording full protection to the head.

No. 26K231

No. 26K230	Model "B" Three-Drawer Box Cover.	Price	$13.15
No. 26K231	Model "B" Five-Drawer Box Cover.	Price	13.45
No. 26K232	Model "B" Seven-Drawer Box Cover.	Price	13.85

The above prices do not include attachments. We furnish a complete set at 75 cents extra, as fully explained on page 46
The small illustration shows the Model "B" upright machine with five drawers at $13.45. Attachments, 75 cents extra.

Detailed Construction of the Minnesota Model "A" Head

AN X-RAY PICTURE OF THE WONDERFUL MODEL "A" HEAD. NOTE THE GREAT FEATURES.

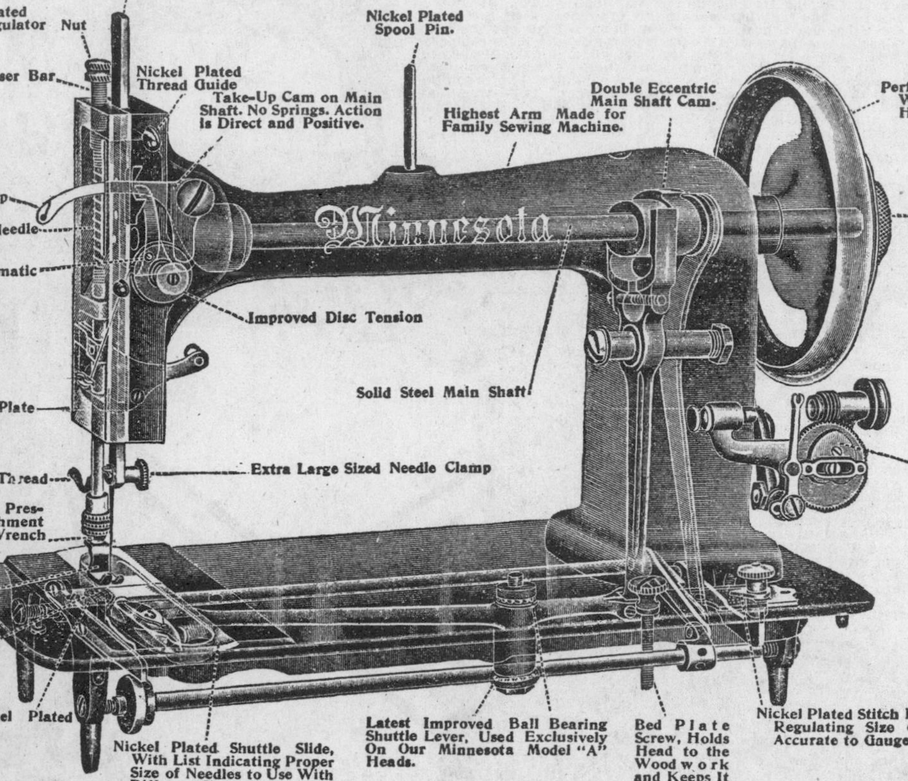

Highest Grade Improved Tool Steel Frictionless Flat Needle Bar.

Nickel Plated Presser Bar Regulator Nut

Presser Bar.

Nickel Plated Thread Guide

Nickel Plated Spool Pin.

Take-Up Cam on Main Shaft. No Springs. Action is Direct and Positive.

Double Eccentric Main Shaft Cam.

Highest Arm Made for Family Sewing Machine.

Perfectly Balanced Hand Wheel, Nickel Plated and Highly Polished.

Independent, Direct and Positive Take-Up.

Tempered Tool Steel Needle Bar Cam.

New Improved Automatic Tension Release.

Improved Disc Tension

Extra Large Sized Milled Friction Nut, With Arrows Indicating Which Way to Turn.

Nickel Plated Face Plate

Solid Steel Main Shaft

Extra Sharp Steel Thread Cutter.

Improved Nickel Plated Presser Foot and Attachment Nut. Requires No Wrench.

Extra Large Sized Needle Clamp

Automatic Bobbin Winder. All Bobbins Evenly Wound.

Extra Large Nickel Plated Presser Foot. Extends On Both Sides of Needle.

Positive, Four-Motion Tool Steel Feed, Having Four Rows of Teeth, Extending On Both Sides of Needle.

Extra Large Nickel Plated Needle Plate.

Nickel Plated Shuttle Slide, With List Indicating Proper Size of Needles to Use With Different Sizes of Thread.

Latest Improved Ball Bearing Shuttle Lever, Used Exclusively On Our Minnesota Model "A" Heads.

Bed Plate Screw, Holds Head to the Wood work and Keeps It Securely in Place.

Nickel Plated Stitch Indicator Regulating Size of Stitch Accurate to Gauge.

TO TRY TO CONVEY TO YOU SOME IDEA OF THE STRENGTH, simplicity and correctness of the mechanical principles embodied in the Minnesota Model "A" Head, our artist has succeeded in producing these X-Ray pictures shown on this page and also on the succeeding page. This X-Ray picture shows the mechanical construction of the Model "A" Head, and if you follow it closely and read the detailed description on the next page, we are sure you will understand why the Minnesota Model "A" is so far ahead of all other sewing machines in mechanical construction, and why we so strongly recommend the selection of our Model "A." Even in these illustrations we have called attention by means of dotted lines only to the most improved features. There are many other mechanical details which go to prove the superiority of the Minnesota Model "A" which we are unable to present satisfactorily on a catalogue page, and we are also unable to show you the wonderful workmanship in this machine, the manner in which every piece and part is so carefully made and finished, everything fitting and operating perfectly, a class of finest skilled workmanship that is not excelled by any fine watch or any complicated high grade mechanical device of any kind costing 100 times as much.

THE TOP ILLUSTRATION IS WHAT WE CALL AN X-RAY PICture or shadowgraph of the head, and the bottom illustration is made from a regular photograph showing the under side of the bed plate, giving you a better view of many of the improved mechanical features.

ANY MECHANIC CAN SEE FROM THESE ILLUSTRATIONS THAT OUR Minnesota Model "A" embodies all of the very latest, up to date improvements in mechanical construction. Many sewing machines, even some of the well known makes and practically all of the stenciled machines handled by other mail order houses retain the old time complicated construction, using many rods and bars to connect the operating parts with the main shaft, also employing springs, cushions, pads, cogs and other unnecessary devices to partly control the movements of the needle, feed and take-up. When new from the factory, such machines work satisfactorily, but there is no positive assurance that the mechanism will remain in working order without frequent repair. Our constant aim has been to simplify the principle of construction by decreasing as far as possible, the number of working parts and making each part independent of the others and thereby positive in its action.

Hardened Tool Steel Feed Lift Cam. This Gives the Positive Feed.

Hardened Tool Steel Feed Bar.

This Shaft Raises the Feed.

Special Bed Plate Reinforcements.

Needle Guide, Used Only On Minnesota Heads, Prevents Breaking of Needle.

Extra Strong Nickel Plated Shuttle Carrier.

Best Made and Largest Size Self Threading Cylinder Shuttle Manufactured.

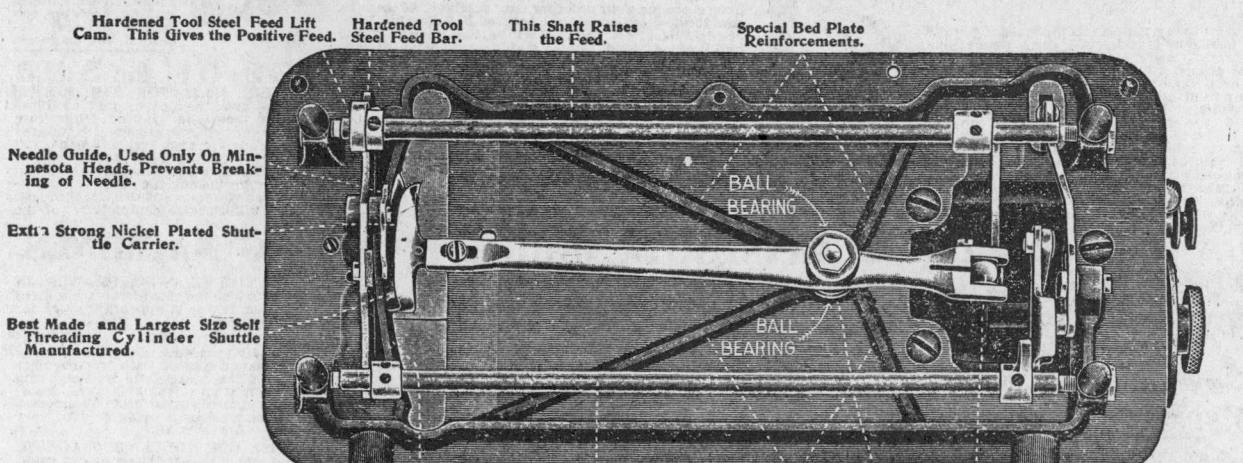

Remember, this is the only family sewing machine that is made with ball bearings in the working parts of the head. Our Model "A" is therefore the easiest running sewing machine in the world.

Automatic Self Oiling Shuttle Race.

This Shaft Operates In Connection With the Stitch Regulator and Causes the Machine to Make the Number of Stitches to the Inch As is Indicated By the Stitch Regulator

Special Bed Plate Reinforcements.

Ball Bearing Shuttle Lever.

Frictionless Ball and Socket Joint.

OUR MINNESOTA MODEL "A" IS BUILT ON THE ECCENtric system, and all clumsy, hard working, sticky cog wheels are done away with. Less working parts are used in its make up than in any other shuttle machine, and its transmitting power construction is exceedingly simple. All running parts, even to the bobbin winder, are supplied with operating power direct from the main shaft and act absolutely independent of one another. The eccentric at the right end of the main shaft operates both the feed and shuttle, while the shaft head at the left end of the arm drives the needle bar and take-up simultaneously. By the use of this eccentric action much less power is required to run the machine, and insures a light running, easy operating movement, harmonious action and unfailing certainty of absolute evenness in the action of the different parts, and makes it impossible for one part to be slower or quicker in movement than another. It runs smoothly, nearly noiseless and will never wear loose or shaky.

OUR NEW SELF OILING SHUTTLE RACE FOUND ON ALL MINNESOTA MODEL "A" SEWING MACHINES.

THIS NEW IMPROVEMENT, THIS SELF oiling device for the shuttle race, solves the problem of keeping the race properly oiled without danger of getting too much oil on the race and soiling the upper and lower threads. It keeps the shuttle race always properly oiled and thereby reduces the friction of the shuttle against the race and prevents wear of the shuttle.

BALL BEARING SHUTTLE LEVER

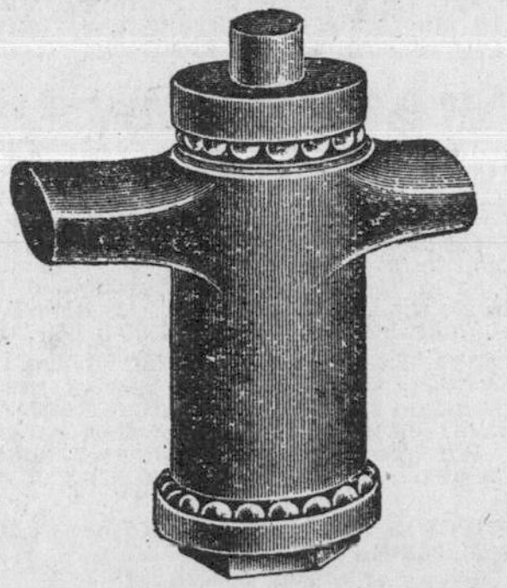

(See illustration) which makes our Minnesota Model "A" the lightest running sewing machine on the market. The adjustment is perfect and positively will not get out of order. The cups and cones used in this construction are turned out of the best tool steel, they are ground out until the surface is as smooth as glass, after which all are case hardened in oil, making them IMPERVIOUS TO WEAR.

THE ARRANGEMENT OF the two sets of ball bearings on the shuttle lever does away with practically all the friction at this important point. Instead of friction on a 2-inch axle surface of the lever we have, by application of the ball bearings, reduced the contact surface to about one-sixteenth of an inch, the result being a machine that runs lighter, makes less noise and requires less than one-half the power to operate than any other sewing machine on the market.

BEARINGS. THE BEARINGS OF this machine are of the highest mechanical type. They are either roller or ball joint bearing, or full ball bearing, according to requirement. They are automatic in their workings, have special take-up devices, doing away with all unnecessary friction, insuring an easy running and nearly noiseless machine.

ADJUSTMENT. ALL BEARings and working parts of this machine which require adjustment are made of the finest tool steel that can be obtained, and after being thoroughly hardened by the latest and most improved process, are accurately ground to a perfect fit and so constructed that any lost motion, due to the slightest wear that may result after many years of use, can be easily and quickly taken up. This renders it practically indestructible and one of the most durable machines ever produced.

EASY TO OIL. BY MEANS of convenient oil holes and a movable metal plate on the back of the head, all bearings are easily gotten at to oil. This is a most important feature, as thorough lubrication prevents friction and wear.

RUNNING SPEED. EVERY machine, before being shipped from the factory, is put to the severest possible test, being set up and attached to a power pulley and run at a speed five times greater than it is possible to run any machine by foot power, and by this severe test we first learn that every machine is perfectly true in every particular and capable of the highest possible speed.

WE FURNISH, FREE OF CHARGE, WITH EVERY MINNEsota Model "A" Sewing Machine, a book of instructions telling how to operate the sewing machine. This book covers every point, makes everything so plain and simple that anyone without previous experience can learn to run the machine at once and do perfect work; tells you how to get the best results, how to take care of your machine, tells you where to oil and when. It tells you how to use the different attachments, the ruffler, tucker, hemmers and binders, and contains illustrations of these attachments in use.

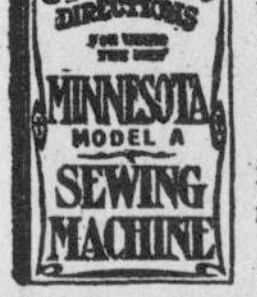
DIRECTIONS
MINNESOTA
MODEL A
SEWING
MACHINE

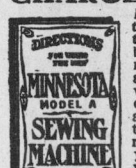

The letters published on pages 41, 46 and 54 tell the story of the Minnesota Sewing Machines.

THE SHUTTLE.

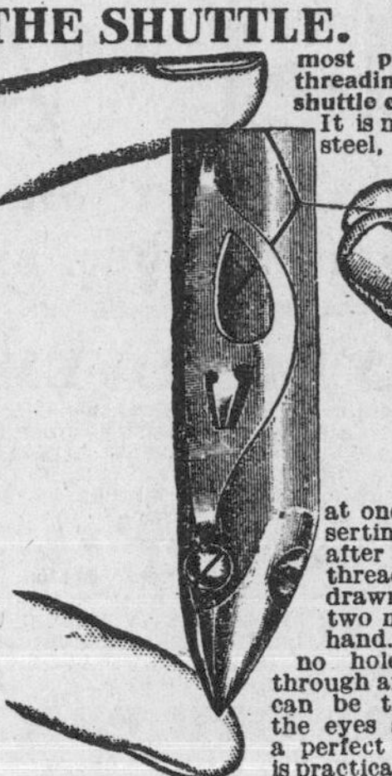

THE SHUTTLE is the most perfect, self threading, cylindrical shuttle ever produced. It is made of finest steel, hardened and ground. It is absolutely self threading, being open at one end for inserting the bobbin, after which the thread is instantly drawn into place by two motions of the hand. There are no holes to thread through and the shuttle can be threaded with the eyes shut. It has a perfect tension which is practically automatic and does not require regulating for any ordinary range of work. The bobbin carries a large amount of thread. The illustration shows shuttle being held between the thumb and forefinger while threading.

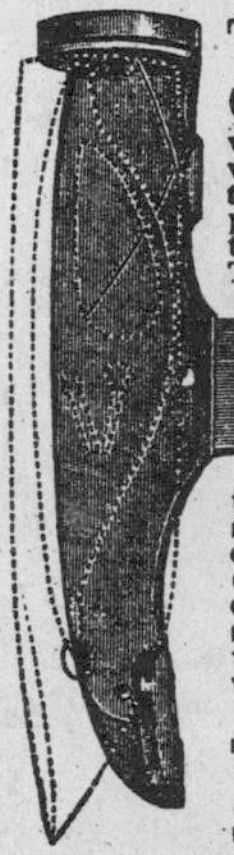

THE SHUTTLE CARRIER. THE body in which the shuttle rests is fitted with a spring lining which holds the shuttle firmly in place and prevents it from rattling while the machine is in operation. The carrier is adjustable, so that when the shuttle shows signs of wear, after many years of use, the carrier can be moved closer to the shuttle race, thus enabling the operator to use the same shuttle for many years with the same satisfaction as when new.

THE TWO SHUTTLE SLIDES ARE MADE OF STEEL, BEVeled, nickel plated and highly polished and enable the operator to get at the shuttle from the front or back.

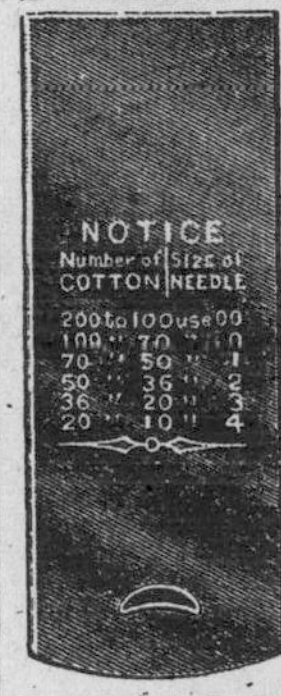
NOTICE
Number of COTTON | Size of NEEDLE
200 to 100 use 00
100 " 70 " 0
70 " 50 " 1
50 " 36 " 2
36 " 20 " 3
20 " 10 " 4

THE SCALE, INDICATING THE PROPer needles to be used with the different sizes of thread, is stamped on the forward shuttle slide.

DOUBLE FEED. THE FEED in this machine is made of the best quality of steel properly tempered and equipped with four sets of teeth, two sets on each side of the needle hole. It is so constructed that when in motion the goods must be carried forward with absolute accuracy.

POSITIVE FOUR-MOTION FEED.

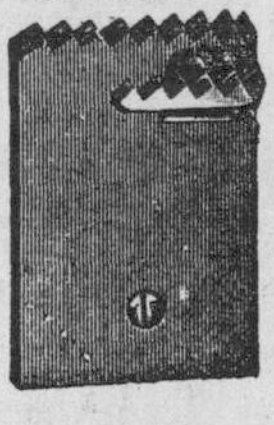

THE FEED IS OPERATED with four movements. The feed comes up, takes a firm hold on the goods, carries the goods forward the length of the stitch, then it falls, releasing the goods and comes back again toward the operator, ready for the next stitch. These four movements are provided entirely by the main shaft, insuring positive action on either heavy or light goods.

PRESSER BAR LIFTER.

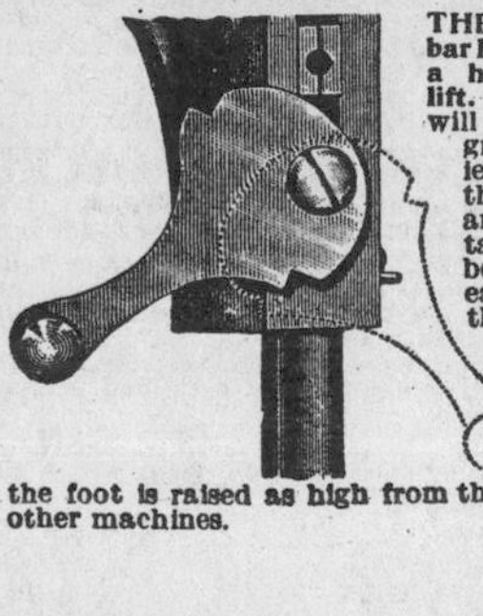

THE PRESSER bar lifter has both a high and low lift. The low lift will be found a great convenience in using the hemmers and other attachments, it being much easier to start the goods into the attachment properly than when the foot is raised as high from the plate as on other machines.

PRESSER FOOT. THIS presser foot has a large surface and the forward part, nearest the operator, is curved upward so that the foot will not catch in the seams of fleecy materials and insures for the operator thorough control at all times.

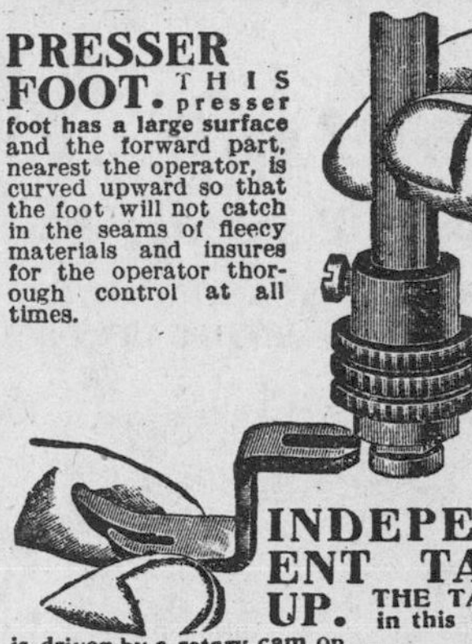

INDEPENDENT TAKE-UP. THE TAKE-UP in this machine is driven by a rotary cam on the end of the main shaft, making it positive in its action, insuring a perfect stitch and with no springs to get out of order or break. The positive action of this take-up makes it unnecessary to alter the tensions when the length of stitch or weight of material is changed.

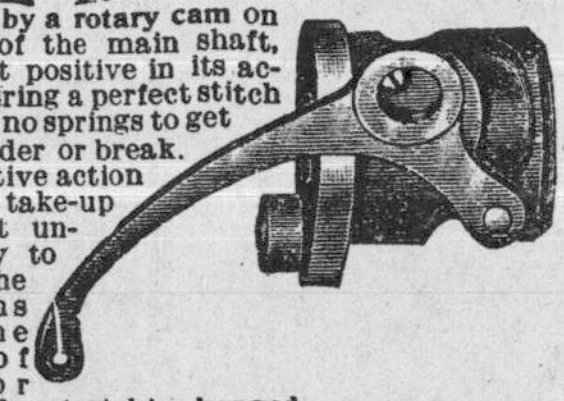

DISC TENSION. THE UPper tension of this machine is of the modern disc type, and adjusts itself on all classes of work. The tension is located on the side of the cam house toward the operator. This location of the tension is not only far more convenient, but brings the point at which the tension is applied to the thread much nearer to the eye of the needle, thus reducing the amount of thread under tension and doing away, in a large measure, with the stretch in the thread, which, on old style machines, frequently causes bad stitching or skipping of stitches.

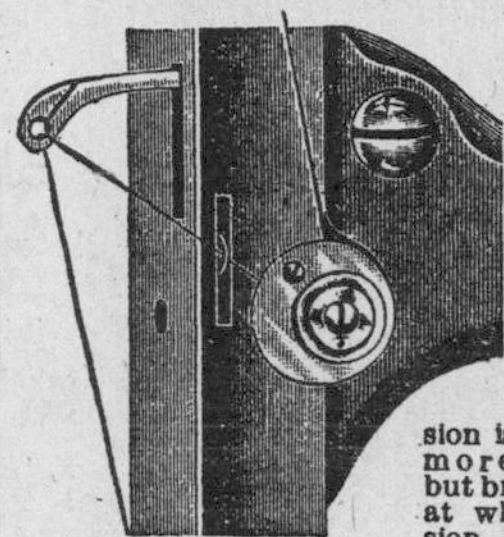

TENSION RELEASE. THIS MACHINE IS PROVIDED WITH AN automatic tension release, which makes it possible to remove the work from the machine by merely raising the presser bar so that the work can be drawn from underneath the presser foot with ease.

THE STITCH REGULATOR IS FASTENED TO THE BED plate just in front of the arm in plain sight and within easy reach of the operator. The length of the stitch can be adjusted instantly by loosening the thumbnut and moving the point to the desired figure on the scale stamped on the stitch regulator plate.

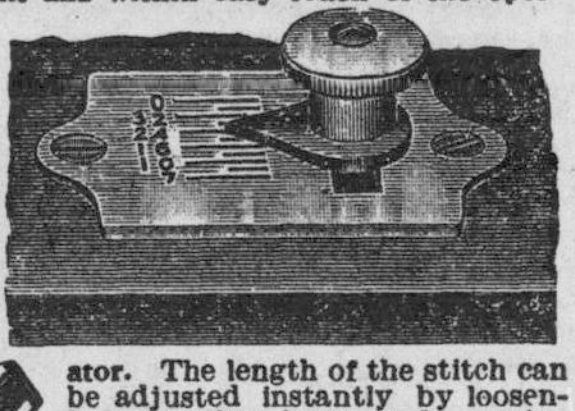

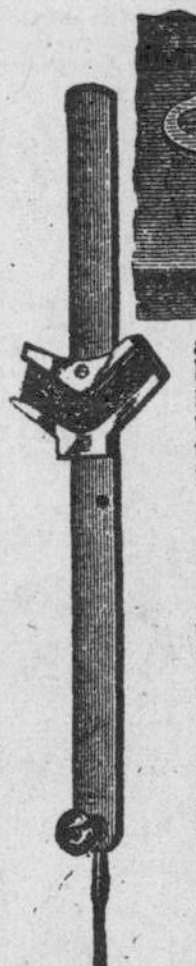

FLAT NEEDLE BAR. WHILE FAR MORE expensive to manufacture, we use in this head a flat needle bar, made of finest steel, hardened, milled to exact size, making its bearings absolutely perfect, thus securing noiseless movement without friction. With this construction, lost motion and rattling of the needle bar is an impossibility, even after years of usage. The illustration shows the flat needle bar of our Model "A" machine, fitted with needle bar cam which connects the bar directly with the main shaft, from which it derives its operating power.

AUTOMATIC BOBBIN WINDER. THE BOBBIN Winder on this machine is nickel plated throughout, and is the most perfect bobbin winder ever produced. It is so simple that a child can operate it, and the thread is wound on the bobbin automatically and so even and smoothly as to make the bobbin work perfectly in the shuttle, producing an even tension and greatly improving the perfection of the stitch. This also prevents the breaking of the lower thread, which is liable to occur with an unevenly wound bobbin.

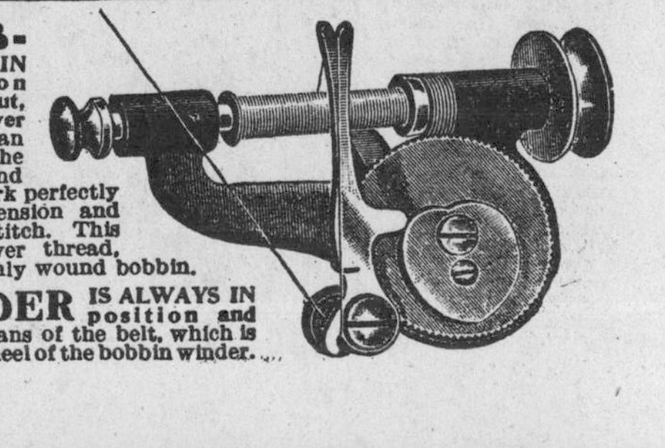

THE BOBBIN WINDER IS ALWAYS IN position and ready to operate. It is operated by means of the belt, which is placed in contact with the small pulley wheel of the bobbin winder.

SELF SETTING NEEDLE.

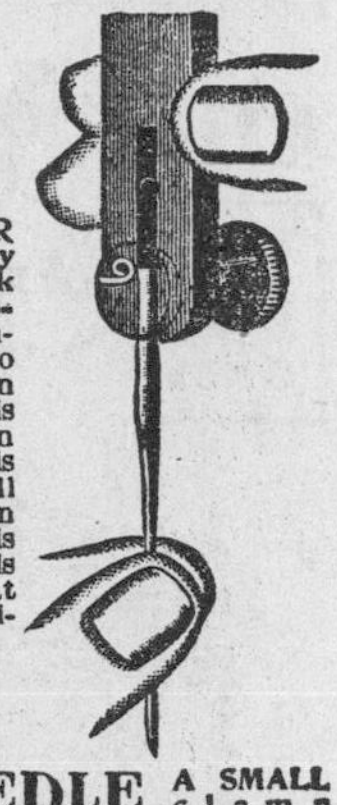

THE NEEDLES FOR this machine are the very best grade of flat shank needle it is possible to procure. Every needle is inspected and tested as to size, temper and position of eye. The needle bar is provided with a groove in which the needle shank is inserted as far as it will go, so that the operation of setting the needle is absolutely positive. It is not necessary to guess at the proper height or position of the needle.

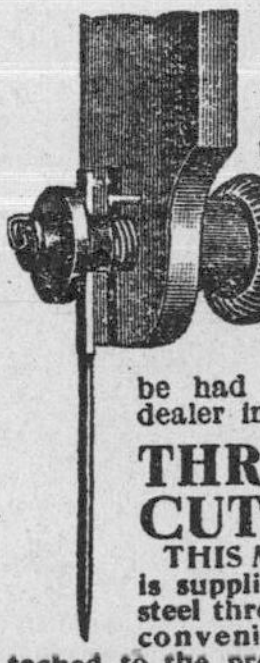

NEEDLE CLAMP. A SMALL clamp holds the needle firmly in place and permits the needle to be removed in an instant when required, even though it should break accidentally in the bar where it cannot be reached with the fingers. The needles can be had from us at any time at factory cost, or they can be had from any sewing machine dealer in your town.

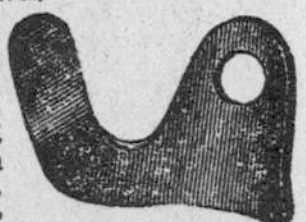

THREAD CUTTER. THIS MACHINE is supplied with a steel thread cutter, conveniently attached to the presser bar, by the aid of which the thread can be easily cut, obviating the use of scissors and the danger of breaking or cutting the thread too short.

THE HAND WHEEL. THE HAND WHEEL IS OF THE VERY latest pattern, with handsome nickel plated and polished rim, and is so constructed that it can be easily released and made to run free in either direction for the purpose of winding the bobbin without the necessity of removing the work from the machine and without causing the working parts to operate.

LOCK NUT. THE LOCK NUT, which is located at the end of the shaft and used to release and tighten the hand wheel, is turned out of one piece of case hardened steel, has milled edge and is heavily nickel plated and polished. The lock nut is plainly marked with arrows showing which way it must be turned to loosen or tighten the hand wheel.

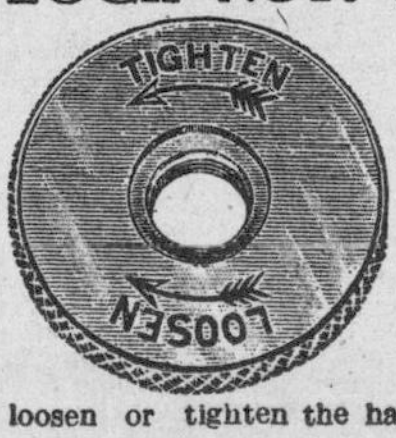
TIGHTEN
LOOSEN

PRESSER BAR. THE PRESSER BAR IS MADE of the best quality tool steel, properly tempered and accurately fitted.

PRESSER BAR REGULATOR. A PRESSER BAR NUT, MADE of the best grade of steel, nickel plated and polished, is provided at the top of the presser bar to regulate the pressure of the foot, more or less, as required for different weights of material.

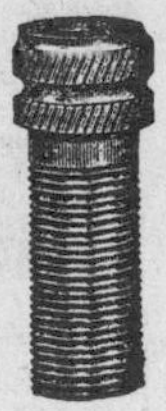

OUR MINNESOTA MODEL "A"

IS THE ONLY FAMILY SEWING MAchine manufactured with ball bearings in the working parts of the head. The ball bearing adjustment is attached to the shuttle lever under the bed plate. The shuttle lever moves twice every time a stitch is made. Our ball bearing adjustment on the shuttle lever reduces the friction, almost does away with it entirely, and makes our Minnesota Model "A" the lightest running sewing machine made.

Our Minnesota Model "A" $18.95

Automatic Lift, Ball Bearing, Full Desk Cabinet Machine,

GREATLY IMPROVED FOR THIS SEASON, MANY NEW FEATURES ADDED, BROUGHT RIGHT UP TO DATE.

A GREAT IMPROVEMENT IN QUALITY. WE HAVE FORTU-nately been able through our enormous sales of this particular style of cabinet work to effect a material reduction in the manufacturing cost. We have been able to make better contracts for the woodwork, have secured other advantages, have been able to save a few cents here and there by increasing the quantity of machines put through daily, and all these advantages, no matter how slight, we give our customers the benefit of by offering a sewing machine cabinet at $18.95 which will compare with cabinets sold by agents and others at $40.00 and more.

WE GUARANTEE TO YOU THAT THE QUALITY OF THIS, OUR CELE-brated Minnesota Model "A," Automatic Lift, Ball Bear-ing Drop Desk Cabinet Machine has been maintained in every way, in fact, if you buy a Minnesota Drop Desk Cabinet Machine from us today, you will get a better machine than you would if you had bought from our last catalogue. It now embodies all our latest improve-ments, strengthened, improved in many small details, a better machine and handsomer woodwork than we have ever offered under this catalogue number.

COMPARE OUR PRICE OF $18.95 WITH THE PRICE asked by any retail dealer, agent, or by any other catalogue house for their highest grade sewing machines in a beautiful carved and decorated, all quarter sawed oak, drop desk cabinet. See if you can find anything in any catalogue or in any store in the line of a fine sewing machine at anything like our price, that will compare with this special Minnesota Model "A." You will not find a machine at within a good many dollars of our price. If you find it at three times the price you would not find a better sewing machine. Money cannot build a better sewing machine than the Minnesota Model "A." In all the essential points, all the features that make a fine machine in range of work of plain and fancy sewing, ease of operation, noiselessness, light running quality, the Minnesota Model "A" is really in a class by itself, not surpassed in quality by even such sewing machines that sell at $50.00 to $60.00.

WE ASK YOU TO REMEMBER THAT THE MINNESOTA MACHINE is not the kind of a sewing machine that is handled by catalogue houses generally. It is a standard sewing machine, our standard for quality, the kind of article we want you to get from us and then judge us by its quality, something to use every day and serve as a reminder of our house. We guarantee every Minnesota machine for 20 years, let you take it for a full 90 days' trial in your own home, and we stand back of every machine in every way.

SEE ILLUSTRATIONS AND DESCRIPTION on page 62 of our Library Table Sewing Machine.

AS MANY OF OUR CUSTOMERS HAVE expressed a desire to purchase our Minnesota Model "A" Sewing Machine with a plainer and lighter weight cabinet than our No. 26K270, shown on page 61, we present the style shown in these illustrations, which we are confident will meet the approval of our friends who wish a tasty appearing, light weight, cabinet sewing machine. The cabinet is made of the same high grade care-fully selected quarter sawed oak as our No. 26K270, the bottom and back being of solid oak while the top or cover, sides and door are made of beautifully figured quarter sawed oak. The sides, back and door are paneled, which prevents the oak from cracking or splitting.

THE DE-SIGN OF THE

CABINET WHILE PLAIN, IS VERY ATTRACTIVE, AND IS STRONGLY BUILT; CARVED AND ornamented mouldings. The quarter sawed oak panels on the door and sides of the cabinet are arched. The door is decorated with hand made artistic wood carvings, which gives the cabinet a very rich and elegant appearance. A compartment securely fastened to the door is arranged to contain the attachments and accessories and such other supplies as are in constant demand when sewing. This compart-ment, as may be seen by reference to the illustrations, is most conveniently arranged, so that it will not be necessary for the person using the machine to move her chair or even change her position when wishing to use any of the attachments or accessories contained in this compartment. The cabinet is fitted with four large wooden casters, which make it very easy to move the cabinet from one part of the room to another.

THE HEAD USED IN THIS MACHINE IS THE SAME AS IS USED ON ALL OF OUR "A" GRADE Minnesota machines. For complete description of mechanical construction, attach-ments, etc., see pages 51 to 54.

WE FIND THE BEST ADVERTISEMENT WE CAN POSSIBLY GET IS A well satisfied customer, and we have hundreds of these in every community, and among them are quite a number in every town who have bought and are now using our sewing machines, and if you will ask anyone in your neighborhood who is using one of our machines whether they have ever seen a sewing machine furnished by any other house that will compare with the machine we sold them, either in quality or price, on their answer we are sure we will receive your order.

WE FURNISH, FREE OF CHARGE, WITH EVERY MINNESOTA MODEL "A" SEWING MACHINE, a book of instructions, telling how to operate the sewing machine. This book covers every point, makes everything so plain and simple that any-one without previous experience can learn to run the machine

> THE BEAUTIFUL CABINET WORK ON THIS MACHINE WILL ORNA-MENT ANY HOME.

at once and do perfect work, tells you how to get the best results, how to take care of your machine, tells you where to oil and when. It tells how to use the dif-ferent attachments, the ruffler, tucker, hemmers and binders and contains illustrations of these attachments in use.

ONE ADVANTAGE IN ORDERING A SEW-ing machine from us is that you can be sure of getting all kinds of sewing machine repairs and supplies in the years to come and always at the very lowest cost.

This beautiful sewing machine will prove a real ornament in any home.

THIS MACHINE IS EQUIPPED WITH OUR special ball bearing hanger, which by actual use and experiment has been demonstrated to be twenty per cent lighter running than the ball bearing arrangement used in any other sewing machine. We can therefore recommend our Minnesota Model "A" cabinet sewing machine as very light running, exceedingly easy in operation and rapid in action, making it possible to do the work of a household in one-third less time than is required with machines fitted with ordinary non-ball bearing hanger.

THE EQUAL OF MACHINES SOLD by other dealers and agents at $40.00 to $50.00.

In ordering the machine use the following description:

No. 26K269 Minnesota Model "A" Machine, one-door cabinet (without attachments, but with accessories). Price **$18.95**
This price does not include attachments. We can furnish a complete set, as fully described on page 54, for 75 cents additional.

The machine is delivered free on board the cars at our factory in Dayton, Ohio, from which point customers pay the freight.

OUR BINDING GUARANTEE.

We send with every machine Our Binding 20 Years' Guarantee. Should any piece or part be found defect-ive we will replace it free of charge, and our liberal terms of ship-ment, allowing you the privilege of trying and examining the machine, and if not found satisfactory, re-turning it to us and we will pay the freight and refund your money, will at once convince you that you run no risk in send-ing your order to us.

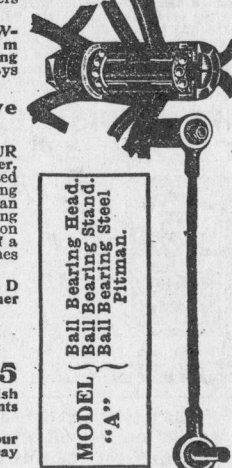

MODEL "A" { Ball Bearing Head. Ball Bearing Stand. Ball Bearing Steel Pitman.

$20^{85} FOR THE MINNESOTA MODEL "A"

BALL BEARING, AUTOMATIC, DROP DESK, OAK CABINET

WITH NEW FEATURES

$1.00 EXTRA FOR THIS CABINET IF FURNISHED IN SOLID BLACK WALNUT.

A REDUCTION IN PRICE AND AN IMPROVEMENT IN QUALITY.

THIS IS THE VERY HIGHEST GRADE FULL CABINET Style Sewing Machine we are able to produce. It is our very best effort, nothing finer made in the world, the genuine Minnesota Model "A," high grade, ball bearing sewing machine in the very finest kind of an automatic lift, two-door drop desk cabinet, beautifully designed, richly carved and decorated, such woodwork as has never before been used on sewing machines. Your choice of the beautiful quarter sawed oak, golden finish, or for $1.00 extra a very attractive and massive black walnut cabinet.

THE FINEST DESK CABINET WE MAKE, THE FINEST DESK CABINET OFFERED IN THE WORLD. THE OAK STYLE is made of extra special selected quarter sawed oak, beautifully grained and polished, hand rubbed to a piano finish. The walnut style is made of carefully selected and the best seasoned solid black walnut, the same grade of walnut that is used in the finest pieces of walnut furniture. In either the oak or the walnut the design of the cabinet is exactly the same, the highly polished panels are faced with Italian veneering, the cabinet is ornamented with heavy, deep scroll carving.

NOTE THE ILLUSTRATIONS. THE FIRST illustration shows the cabinet open with the leaf extended and ready for work, you can see what ample space this gives for the handling of all kinds of material. The next illustration shows the machine partly closed, and shows the automatic lift feature by which the head is raised and brought into place as soon as the top leaf is lifted. The lower illustration shows the cabinet closed, in appearance representing a beautiful stand or writing desk; a piece of furniture that will certainly ornament any home. It can take the machine from place to place.

GUARANTEED FOR 20 YEARS.

Illustration Showing How Cabinet Opens.

Illustration Showing Cabinet Open.

The cabinet is mounted on easy running rollers so that a child can take the machine from place to place. The top of the cabinet is selected quarter sawed oak, highly polished and hand rubbed. We call especial attention to the practical and patented automatic feature whereby the sewing machine head rises to the surface of the table, ready for sewing when you lift the top and turn it over. The machine head moves up and down, and, as it is counterbalanced it requires little or no exertion to put it into place. In this beautiful, two-door, automatic full desk cabinet, in which we can furnish the Minnesota Model "A," we have endeavored to eclipse all other makes of sewing machine cabinets, to provide for our customers something far better than even the cabinets that are furnished on machines that retail at $60.00; in fact, we have practically exhausted every means of improving the quality and appearance of this woodwork. While it is without question the finest sewing machine cabinet ever produced, yet our price for this cabinet is far below the prices asked by others.

IN THIS MINNESOTA CABINET STYLE WE FURNISH the same high grade improved sewing machine head, our Model "A," as is furnished in the other Model "A" styles. The Minnesota Model "A" head and the working parts are fully described on pages 51 to 54. We invite your careful reading of the description of the Model "A" head, for the head is really the vital part of the sewing machine, and we firmly believe that the Minnesota Model "A" head is a better sewing machine head than is used on any other sewing machine made in the world, regardless of its name or price.

ORDER THIS OUR VERY FINEST MODEL "A" MACHINE IN OUR BEST DESK CABINET STYLE, AND WE KNOW YOU WILL surely be delighted with your purchase. It will be an everlasting pleasure to you and the more you use the machine, the longer you have it the better you will like it. Our customers in sending us orders for various goods from our catalogue, very often tell us that they have one of our Minnesota Sewing Machines bought four or five years ago and that it is still the best sewing machine they have ever seen and that they would not trade it for any other. We have constantly improved our machines. Every season has seen some new feature added that makes our sewing machines better than ever before. For this season we have been able to add several small improvements, all thoroughly tested out before we have adopted them, so that you can feel when you buy a sewing machine from us you get the very latest ideas, the highest type of construction throughout. Our new features of the ball bearing head, ball bearing stand and the ball bearing steel pitman are wonderful improvements, the greatest advance in sewing machine construction that has been made in the last three years and make our sewing machines easier to operate than ever before, less energy required and almost noiseless in action.

Illustration Showing Cabinet Closed.

IF YOU ARE DESIROUS OF OWNING THE HIGHEST GRADE, VERY BEST sewing machine made, you must send us your order for a Model "A." If we asked $10.00 more on each Model "A" machine, it would still pay you well to place your order with us." $10.00 does not begin to represent the difference in quality between the Model "A" and the sewing machines offered by dealers and agents, and particularly those shown by other catalogue houses. When considering quality alone, we could certainly ask $10.00 more for a machine than the prices of other catalogue houses, but fortunately for our customers our policy is to ask just a narrow margin of profit on every article, and we figure our prices on the actual cost of the material and labor. When you consider that our sewing machines are so far superior to those offered by others, and the fact that our prices are very much lower, you really cannot afford to place your order elsewhere.

DON'T FORGET THAT IT IS IMPOSSIBLE FOR YOU TO LOSE ANYTHING WHEN YOU PLACE your order with us. You have three months in which to give the machine a thorough trial and test. If at any time during the three months you have any reason to feel dissatisfied with your purchase, you can return the machine to us at our expense and we will promptly return your money, including all freight charges you paid. Freight charges, by the way, amount to only a few cents compared with what you save in price. This machine weighs, crated for shipment, about 140 pounds and can be shipped to any part of the United States at an expense for freight charges varying from 25 cents to $1.50. The machine is shipped direct from the factory at Dayton, Ohio. It is thoroughly and carefully packed and crated and is guaranteed to reach you in the same perfect condition that it leaves the factory. This machine is covered by our written, binding 20-year guarantee, by which you are protected against defect in material or workmanship for 20 years. This is the longest and strongest guarantee issued by any concern. The two-door Model "A" cabinet is made of solid oak or black walnut throughout, as desired. Only the highest grade of material, thoroughly air seasoned and kiln dried, is used in the construction of this cabinet. The rigid inspection of the material before entering into the construction of the cabinet insures it against swelling and cracking.

THE TWO-DOOR AUTOMATIC MODEL "A" DESK CABINET WHEN CLOSED IS 30 INCHES HIGH, 21 INCHES DEEP AND 25 INCHES WIDE. (See lower illustration.) When open and ready for work the table space measures 21 inches by 50 inches, more than twice the table space afforded by other machines. There is no cabinet so strongly made as our Model "A." The top or lid is made up of five layers of wood, the grain of each layer running at right angles with the layer above it, by having nothing but tops made of built-up stock, we do away with all possibility of warping, checking or splitting. The entire front of the cabinet as well as the two side panels, are made of specially selected quarter sawed oak. The heavy rope moulding on the doors and the handsome hand carvings on the panels give the cabinet a massive appearance. There are two large drawers securely fastened to the lower left hand side and fitted with strong locks and handsome nickel plated drawer pulls.

These prices do not include attachments. We furnish a complete set at 75 cents, as fully explained on page 54.

BALL BEARINGS. OUR MINNESOTA MODEL "A" DROP DESK CABINET Machine is as light running as either the upright or drop head styles. It is fitted with our celebrated "bicycle" ball bearing hanger, found only on our cabinet machines, which give the same rapidity of action and ease of operation to the machine as the ball bearing arrangement to a bicycle.

No. 26K270 Minnesota Model "A" Full Automatic Lift, Oak Cabinet Machine. Price $20.85
No. 26K271 Minnesota Model "A" Full Automatic Lift, Walnut Cabinet Machine. Price 21.85

WALLPAPER AND PAINT

FROM OUR OWN MILL

READ HOW LOWEST MANUFACTURING COST WITH ONLY ONE SMALL PROFIT ADDED MAKES LOWEST SELLING PRICES

3 CENTS A DOUBLE ROLL OF 16 YARDS,

which is equal to 1½ cents per single roll, is what we ask for wall papers usually sold at 5 to 8 cents per single roll or 10 to 15 cents for one of our double rolls. In other words, our prices on our 3-cent papers are just 70 per cent lower than what most dealers ask. With these wall papers at 3 cents per double roll of 16 yards you can **paper a room 11 x 11 feet with ceiling 9 feet** high for the wonderfully low price of **26 cents,** and less than one dollar will be required (if you order from us) to paper an ordinary room with a quality of paper that any paper hanger in the country would charge three dollars for without his labor. The same wonderfully low scale of prices will be found throughout our line.

OUR FREE WALL PAPER SAMPLE BOOK

and our Free Illustrated Wall Paper Book, both splendid books, fully described on opposite page, are free for the asking. **SEND FOR THEM TODAY.**

THE MANUFACTURE OF WALL PAPER HAS ALWAYS BEEN ONE OF THE MOST PROFITABLE LINES OF BUSINESS IN EXISTENCE. We doubt if there could be a manufacturing industry in which we could operate with greater advantage to our customers than in the wall paper line. Restricted to a few manufacturers, overloaded with unnecessary selling expenses and exorbitant profits, the wall paper business offered one of the greatest opportunities of our entire business career for the application of our well known principles of merchandising—our policy of eliminating all middlemen's profits and selling directly to the user of the goods with only one small profit added to the lowest manufacturing costs.

THE percentage of profit you pay varies greatly in the different lines of goods you purchase. Some lines yield the maker a very small profit because of free and wide spread competition, because many different concerns are making similar goods and all want a share of the business and each maker finds that he can get his share of business only by voluntarily reducing his profits. Other lines of goods are entirely monopolized by one or only a few manufacturers. Either the raw materials are exclusively controlled by a few, or the facilities for manufacturing and marketing are restricted in such a way that just competition is impossible and the result is that the public must pay exorbitant profits. In these lines where competition does not exist, where prices are controlled by trusts, by manufacturers' agreements made to increase profits, the interests of the buying public are entirely ignored, the maker's sole aim being to realize great profits quickly and without regard for the future.

RIGHT FROM OUR OWN MODERN WALL PAPER MILL

THE MOST UP TO DATE WALL PAPER OF HIGHEST QUALITY GOES DIRECTLY TO YOU AT THE LOWEST PRICES EVER KNOWN.

Our customers know what we have accomplished in lowering the prices of wall paper; our customers know that we have brought wall paper of highest quality and most modern design within the reach of every family in the country. We have weeded out the unnecessary selling expenses and the exorbitant profits. In our own wall paper mill in Chicago where eight of the most improved multi-color wall paper machines ever built are running night and day turning out the enormous total of fifty thousand rolls of wall paper every 24 hours in the year, we have solved the problem of high grade wall paper at low prices. We have solved the problem in the simplest way possible—by going out into the markets independently for our raw materials and by **paying no profits to jobbers or middlemen of any sort.**

OUR PAPER STOCK especially manufactured according to specifications furnished by our own experts comes directly to our wall paper mill from the world's largest paper producers. It is carefully examined and tested for fiber, for quality and for thickness. The grinding of colors, an art in itself, is carried on under the eyes of our own superintendent, to insure not only the most perfect effects in the pattern but to secure permanence and durability in the paper. We keep our styles and patterns up to date by securing the latest designs and newest ideas from the country's leading authorities on interior decoration. **Our machinery and entire factory equipment is of the very latest pattern;** nothing that could improve the quality of our wall paper or reduce the labor and expense of manufacturing it has been omitted. Our wall paper

is loaded into cars on our own private switch track directly at the doors of our wall paper mill, giving us wonderful economy and speed in shipping. When you consider why our prices are lower than the prices charged by your local dealer all of these points must be taken into consideration; all of these advantages of manufacture and advantages of marketing combine to give us the pre-eminent position we hold in the wall paper field. Our prices are different because our business methods are different. When you buy wall paper from us your saving is the difference between our one small percentage of profit and the five or six profits that you, the user of the wall paper, must pay when you purchase from your local dealer, and furthermore, don't forget that in purchasing from us you get brand new up to date wall paper shipped direct from our factory, which is in constant operation—not an old style wall paper that has been stored with the jobber or wholesaler until it is out of fashion.

ON THE FOLLOWING TWO PAGES WE DESCRIBE AND TELL YOU HOW YOU CAN GET ABSOLUTELY FREE OF CHARGE

the two most valuable books on Wall Paper ever published—our Illustrated Wall Paper Book and our Wall Paper Sample Book. Read every word of these two pages carefully for they point the way to unparalleled economy in the finest and most up to date wall paper manufactured.

WE MANUFACTURE ALL OUR OWN PAINT

39 CENTS A GALLON
BUYS A GOOD BARN PAINT
50 CENTS A GALLON BUYS THE BEST BARN PAINT MADE

WE SELL IT FOR HALF THE PRICE OF OTHER BRANDS AND GUARANTEE IT FOR TEN YEARS

SEROCO PAINT REPRESENTS THE RESULT OF TWENTY-SIX YEARS' EXPERIENCE IN PRACTICAL PAINT MAKING

BY MR. V. MICHAELSEN, PRESIDENT OF THE ILLINOIS PAINT MANUFACTURING COMPANY, ONE OF THE LARGEST PAINT FACTORIES IN THE WORLD, WHICH IS CONTROLLED ENTIRELY BY US AND WHOSE FULL OUTPUT WE TAKE. SEROCO PAINT COVERS MORE SURFACE, SPREADS EASIER AND MAKES A BETTER FINISH THAN ANY OTHER PAINT MADE AT ANY PRICE, AND IS GUARANTEED NOT TO PEEL, BLISTER OR RUB OFF WITHIN TEN YEARS. THERE IS NO OTHER PAINT TO COMPARE WITH IT FOR QUALITY.

AT 59 CENTS PER GALLON in 50-gallon barrels, to 98 cents per gallon in gallon cans for house paint, at 39-cents to 65 cents per gallon for barn or fence paint, at correspondingly low prices for carriage or wagon paint, etc., we will furnish you all the paint you need and send you our book of instructions on "How to Paint" FREE, showing you exactly how to paint any surface, house, barn, fence or vehicle, or do any interior finishing. Not only can you save almost half the money you will pay out for the paint alone, but you can save all the cost of labor by painting your buildings yourself in your spare time; or, if you wish to hire a practical painter, the labor will cost you much less than with the use of any other paint because we guarantee that our paint spreads easier and covers more surface and can be put on quicker than any other paint known. If you have any doubt at all on this proposition, just buy a small quantity of any of our paints and test it alongside of other paint you may think of and prove our statements to your own satisfaction before you buy enough for the entire job.

ARE YOU GOING TO PAINT YOUR HOUSE, BARN OR FENCE?
Are you going to do any interior finishing or varnishing? Then don't buy a dollar's worth of paint, varnish or supplies of any kind at any price or any other brand until you have first given the Seroco Brand a trial, with the understanding that it will cover more surface, spread easier and give you longer service than any other brand of paint, and that we guarantee it for ten years. By manufacturing our own dry colors we can offer you a paint of a richer, deeper color and colors that last longer than those in any other brand. When you use Seroco Paint you can see at once for yourself exactly what it will do and that it bears us out in every statement or claim we make for it in regard to spreading easy, covering larger surface and making a superior finish, and as for its wearing qualities we give you our guarantee that it will not peel, blister or rub off within ten years, a guarantee backed by our immense capital of Forty Million Dollars. Furthermore, we will save you about half the money that you would pay out for any other brand of paint of anywhere near as good quality. Won't you give Seroco Paint a trial under this broad and liberal guarantee? Remember, it represents the result of years of experience on the part of Mr. V. Michaelsen, President of our big paint factory and a corps of experts working under his orders. There is no other paint made that has been given so much study as Seroco Paint and we guarantee it to represent perfection in paint quality. Don't be deceived by the claims of other manufacturers who ask you to pay about twice our price. Don't imagine that they can possibly give you finer paint because they ask you nearly twice the price. The difference between our prices and theirs represents merely expenses and profits that they add to the original cost. They won't give you a single cent's worth of better paint quality for the difference in price. They can't do it. Seroco Paint represents the height of paint quality in materials and the best methods of paint manufacturing known, offered to you at the mere cost of the material and the making of the paint with but our one very small margin of profit added. Therefore, why pay a cent more for paint anywhere?

MR. V. MICHAELSEN, President Illinois Paint Manufacturing Company.

HIS PICTURE and name go on every can, every kit and every barrel of paint we sell and in itself is a guarantee of the perfection of paint quality represented by Seroco Paint.

WE, TOGETHER WITH MR. MICHAELSEN, CHALLENGE ANY PAINT MAKER IN THE COUNTRY to produce a paint that they can guarantee for ten years, or to produce one case where our Seroco Paint has not been found to do all we claim for it and where we have not stood back of our claims. Other manufacturers do not guarantee their paint for the very good reason that they don't believe in it themselves. Ours is not a hollow claim, but a binding ten-year guarantee. We guarantee to furnish you additional paint if the paint you get is not found to be as good as we advertise it to be in every way.

WE MAKE OUR OWN DRY COLORS
AND GUARANTEE OUR PAINT COLORS TO LAST LONGER and LOOK BETTER THAN THOSE USED IN ANY OTHER BRAND of PAINT

WE HAVE GONE FURTHER IN THE MANUFACTURING OF PAINT to make paint better than any other paint manufacturer. All other paint factories are more or less dependent on dry color manufacturers; but, as we have had much difficulty in forcing dry color companies to at all times furnish us with perfect color, and as we have had to time and time again reject shipments of dry colors after subjecting them to chemical tests, we have therefore decided to manufacture our own dry colors. We have built a dry color manufacturing plant adjacent to our paint factory and have secured the services of one of the ablest and best chemical experts in the country to prepare and superintend the manufacturing of dry colors. We can therefore guarantee that our paint colors will remain permanent and not fade or affect the quality of the paint in any way except to improve its appearance and lasting qualities.

THE COLORS IN OTHER BRANDS OF PAINT usually fade rapidly, as they are dependent on dry color manufacturers who, wishing to make the greatest possible profits out of their industry, fail at times to exercise as much care as is necessary in order to insure a perfect and fadeless color, or who cheapen their products deliberately in order to increase their profits. We have no other purpose in our dry color factory, built in connection with our paint factory, than to make our Seroco Paint better and more lasting than any other paint. This fact shows you how far we are willing to go in the interests of our customers in insuring that they get the best paint it is possible to make. Our salesmen are our catalogues and paint color sample books and our prices, with the recommendation of our customers who have used our paints, and it is a certainty that we could not afford, depending upon these means to sell our goods, to do otherwise than make the best paint that it is possible to make. Seroco Paint represents the highest standard in paint quality (guaranteed for ten years, as shown on this page) and you can't afford to consider any other brand in the painting of any of your property.

GUARANTEE
THE ILLINOIS PAINT MANUFACTURING CO. AND SEARS, ROEBUCK & CO.

Hereby guarantee that this Seroco Paint is composed of the highest grade ingredients, is a perfect preservative, contains nothing injurious, will cover 300 square feet and over, two coats to each gallon, will not peel, blister or rub off, and to wear well on buildings for at least 10 years. We agree to furnish new paint free, should our Seroco Paint fail to come up to our guarantee.

SEARS, ROEBUCK & CO.

Richard W Sears PRESIDENT

ILLINOIS PAINT MANUFACTURING CO.

V Michaelsen PRESIDENT

THIS IS A COPY of our ten-year guarantee which goes on every can, kit or barrel of Seroco Paint we sell and is the only guarantee of its kind in existence. No other paint manufacturer dares to make such a liberal, binding and long term guarantee, simply because no other manufacturer has the confidence in his paints. We have secured the services of Mr. Michaelsen, one of the greatest paint experts known, and with him a number of others who, like himself, have the largest possible experience in the paint business, and we know we can guarantee our paint for ten years with the perfect assurance that it will do exactly as we claim. Why pay double our price for any other paint?

59 CENTS A GALLON
BUYS A GOOD HOUSE PAINT
85 CENTS A GALLON BUYS THE BEST HOUSE PAINT MADE.

Sig. 5—1st Ed.

85¢ SEROCO READY MIXED GUARANTEED

PER GALLON

THE VERY BEST READY MIXED PAINT that has ever been offered is manufactured and sold by us as our Seroco Brand. No paint offered by any other firm or individual at any price begins to equal this, our Seroco Brand, in any of the qualities which go to make a high class, satisfactory paint for houses, barns, fences, wood and iron, for exterior or interior work, where a paint of extra quality and wonderful durability is required. Seroco Ready Mixed Paint, is manufactured by us in our own paint factory under the supervision of the most expert paint chemist in the country and it is because this paint is made by us from tested materials of our own selection that we are able to give a binding ten-year guarantee on every gallon of paint sold by us. It is ground and mixed in the finest appointed paint factory in this country. There is just the right proportion of each ingredient necessary to give an extra high grade, free working paint and it will last longer and look better than any other brand offered for a similar purpose at double the price we ask even under the most adverse conditions.

WHEN YOU PAY US 85 cents to 98 cents per gallon for Seroco Ready Mixed Paint, according to the quantity ordered, remember that you get absolutely full weight and full measure and at these remarkably low prices, which are based on the cost of materials and labor in our own factory with but our one small percentage of profit added, we give you a paint guaranteed to last ten years, guaranteed to be equal to any ready mixed house paint sold, a paint which will cover greater surface and which wears better, with greater strength of color than you can possibly get from any local dealer. Remember, when you buy from him, you pay the profits of the manufacturer, the jobber and the retailer, and though you pay him a great deal more money than our prices you do not get paint of equal quality and not nearly so great value as we will give you.

SEROCO READY MIXED HOUSE PAINT
THE BEST WEARING PAINT IT IS POSSIBLE TO MAKE
GUARANTEED FOR 10 YEARS

$9.10 PAINTS THIS HOUSE

YOU CAN ORDER DIRECT from this catalogue, selecting the color wanted from the colors on page 71, with our guarantee that the color and quality will please you, or we will immediately return your money; but if you prefer to see the exact colors before ordering, write us and we will mail you our special Paint Color Sample Booklet free with our compliments. This booklet shows samples of the actual colors of all the different paints we handle.

DIRECTIONS FOR USE OF SEROCO READY MIXED HOUSE PAINT.
For first coat, thin the paint with boiled linseed oil, in the proportion of one-half gallon of oil to one gallon ready mixed paint. For second coat, use the paint as received, unless it should be very thick, when a little linseed oil may be added.

OUR GUARANTEE: We guarantee our Seroco Ready Mixed House Paint to wear for ten years, if the directions are carefully followed. Seroco Ready Mixed House Paint will not peel, scale, blister or chalk; our guarantee covers this.

YOU WILL READILY SEE FROM THE TWO PICTURES SHOWN HERE FOR HOW LITTLE MONEY YOU CAN BEAUTIFY AND PROTECT YOUR HOME AND INCREASE ITS VALUE.

IF YOU ARE UNABLE TO FIGURE THE QUANTITY required for the building you intend to paint, or fear that you might make a mistake, send us the dimensions of the building and we will gladly figure it for you and tell you exactly how much paint would be required and the total cost of the paint. Give the width, length and height of the building. The height is measured at one of the corners, not necessary to measure up to the point of the gable.

A Large Two-Story House Like This, Painted With Seroco Ready Mixed House Paint, Two Coats, for $9.10.

This house, measuring 20 feet wide by 30 feet long by 22 feet in height with annex measuring 11 by 12 feet, will require

8 gallons for body, 5 gallons at 93 cents per gallon	$4.65
3 gallons at 98 cents per gallon	2.94
1½ gallons for trimmings, 1 gallon at 98 cents per gallon	.98
½ gallon for	.53
	$9.10

$4.90 PAINTS THIS COTTAGE

Cottage Like This, Painted With Seroco Ready Mixed House Paint, Two Coats, for $4.90.

This cottage, measuring 18 feet wide by 32 feet long and 12 feet in height, will require

4 gallons for body, at 98 cents per gallon	$3.92
1 gallon for trimmings, at 98 cents per gallon	.98
	$4.90

YOU CAN DO THE WORK YOURSELF EVEN IF YOU NEVER DID ANY PAINTING BEFORE.

OUR instruction book "HOW TO PAINT" will tell you exactly how to do the work and do it well. This book with our "COLOR SAMPLE BOOK" will be sent to you absolutely **FREE** on request, as explained on page 68.

SEND FOR THESE BOOKS TODAY

YOUR MONEY WILL BE IMMEDIATELY RETURNED TO YOU FOR ANY GOODS NOT PERFECTLY SATISFACTORY.

45

HOUSE PAINT 85¢
FOR 10 YEARS
PER GALLON

WE FURNISH OUR SEROCO READY MIXED HOUSE PAINT, the highest grade house paint on the market, at prices ranging from 85 to 98 cents per gallon, according to package, as follows:

| 1 GALLON SEROCO HOUSE PAINT, 98c. | 5 GALLONS SEROCO HOUSE PAINT, 93 CENTS PER GALLON. | 88 CENTS PER GALLON FOR SEROCO MIXED PAINT IN 25-GALLON HALF BARRELS. |

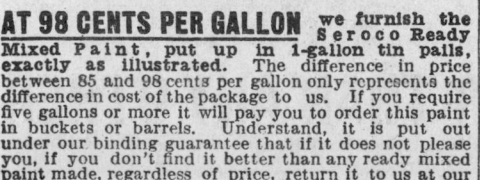

AT 98 CENTS PER GALLON we furnish the Seroco Ready Mixed Paint, put up in 1-gallon tin pails, exactly as illustrated. The difference in price between 85 and 98 cents per gallon only represents the difference in cost of the package to us. If you require five gallons or more it will pay you to order this paint in buckets or barrels. Understand, it is put out under our binding guarantee that if it does not please you, if you don't find it better than any ready mixed paint made, regardless of price, return it to us at our expense, and we will immediately return your money.

AT 93 CENTS PER GALLON we furnish our Seroco, the highest grade ready mixed paint made, in 5-gallon buckets, exactly as illustrated. In this package, in a 5-gallon wooden baled bucket, we can furnish our Seroco paint at 93 cents per gallon. 93 cents barely covers the actual cost of material and labor; made, ground and put up in our own factory, with but our one small percentage of profit added. If you buy this paint from us you would get such value as you could not get from any other house.

88 CENTS PER GALLON buys our highest grade Seroco Ready Mixed House Paint, put up in 25-gallon half barrels, exactly as illustrated. This shows the style in which we put up Seroco Paint in half barrel lots and are able to offer it at 88 cents per gallon, just enough to cover the cost of manufacture, with but our one small percentage of profit added.

85 CENTS PER GALLON FOR SEROCO MIXED PAINT IN 50-GALLON BARRELS.

LIST OF COLORS OF SEROCO READY MIXED HOUSE PAINT.
ALWAYS MENTION NAME OF COLOR AS WELL AS CATALOGUE NUMBER.

No.		No.		No.	
30K0201	French Gray	30K0217	Pure Blue	30K0237	Dark Gray
30K0202	Lavender	30K0218	Buff	30K0239	Black
30K0203	Straw	30K0219	Terra Cotta	30K0240	Yellow Stone
30K0204	Pea Green	30K0220	Apple Green	30K0241	Green Tint
30K0205	Light Drab	30K0221	Leather Brown	30K0242	Light Slate
30K0206	Canary	30K0223	Light Blue	30K0243	Outside White
30K0207	Lemont Stone	30K0224	Maroon	30K0244	Sky Blue
30K0208	Pearl	30K0225	Bronze Green	30K0246	Colonial Yellow
30K0209	Beaver	30K0226	Willow Green	30K0250	Azure Blue
30K0210	Pink	30K0227	Drab	30K0251	Orange
30K0211	Milwaukee Brick	30K0229	Red	30K0252	Oakwood
30K0214	Nile Green	30K0230	Brown	30K0254	Cream Tint
30K0214	Olive Drab	30K0231	French Yellow	30K0255	Flesh Color
30K0215	Cream	30K0233	Slate	30K0256	Tinted White
30K0216	Fawn	30K0235	Light Stone	30K0257	Inside White

PRICES FOR ABOVE COLORS:

Per 1-quart can	28c
Per ½-gallon can	53c
1-gallon can, per gallon	98c
5-gallon bucket, per gallon	93c
25-gallon half-barrel, per gallon	88c
50-gallon barrel, per gallon	85c

Be sure to mention name of color and catalogue number.

SPECIAL COLORS.

No.		5-gallon bucket, per gallon	1 gal	2 qts.	1 qt.
30K0232	Myrtle Green	$1.25	$1.30	70c	40c
30K0234	Vermilion	1.75	1.80	95c	50c
30K0236	Emerald Green	1.25	1.30	70c	40c
30K0247	Carmine	1.75	1.80	95c	50c
30K0253	Golden Green	1.25	1.30	70c	40c

BRUSHES TO USE WITH SEROCO READY MIXED HOUSE PAINT.

For inside wall painting use a No. 30K3084 or No. 30K3086 wall brush, any size, 3½ or 4-inch recommended. For interior woodwork use a round paint brush, No. 30K3076 or 30K3078, any size, 3-0 or 4-0 recommended. For windows use a sash tool, No. 30K3072 or No. 30K3074; sizes 4 to 8 are best adapted for this work.

For outside house painting the following brushes are required: Wall brush, round paint brush, two or three sash tools; No. 30K3084 or No. 30K3086 wall brush, sizes 3½, 4 or 4½ inches in width are recommended for the walls. No. 30K3076 or No. 30K3078 round paint brush, sizes 3-0 to 5-0 for applying the trimming colors. No. 30K3072 and No. 30K3074 sash tools, one each, sizes 4 and 8, for general trimming and used where the round paint brush will be found too large.

85 CENTS PER GALLON buys our guaranteed Seroco Ready Mixed House Paint, put up in 50-gallon barrels. Seroco Ready Mixed House Paint comes to you fresh from our big paint factory and the price of 85 cents per gallon in 50-gallon barrels is the actual manufacturing cost with a small percentage of profit added.

SAVED 52 CENTS A GALLON.
Boyden, Iowa.

Sears, Roebuck & Co., Chicago, Ill.

Gentlemen:—Seroco Ready Mixed is as good a paint as I ever used; I am well pleased with it. The same paint I would have to pay $1.50 per gallon for here, I got of you for 98 cents; so you see I have saved 52 cents per gallon.

Yours truly,
ALBERT DEAN.

THIS PAINTER HAS HAD TWENTY-SIX YEARS' EXPERIENCE.
Sears, Roebuck & Co., Chicago, Ill.   Fort Wayne, Ind.

Dear Sirs:—Having had twenty-six years' experience, I think I am well qualified to speak of your Seroco Ready Mixed House Paint after the test I have given it. I find that it has great covering capacity and that the colors are very clear and very well adapted to all classes of work where a good, clear, handsome finish is desired. Your price of 85 cents per gallon is very cheap, considering the covering capacity when compared to other mixed paints. Yours truly, J. W. FLICKINGER.

50¢ PER GALLON

SEROCO WEATHERPROOF MINERAL BARN, ROOF AND FENCE PAINT

GUARANTEED FOR TEN YEARS

IN OUR SEROCO WEATHERPROOF MINERAL BARN, ROOF AND FENCE PAINT we offer our customers the most durable mineral paint manufactured. It is ground to unusual fineness by the most modern and up to date paint grinding machinery with highest grade linseed oil, both minerals and oils thoroughly ground and reground together, more thoroughly mixed than they could possibly be mixed by hand and giving us the very best barn, roof and fence paint that it is possible to manufacture and one that we especially recommend for all purposes where the paint is to be exposed to the weather.

SEROCO WEATHERPROOF MINERAL PAINT IS A PRESERVATIVE.

OUR 10-YEAR GUARANTEE.

WE GUARANTEE OUR SEROCO WEATHERPROOF MINERAL BARN, ROOF AND FENCE PAINT TO WEAR FOR TEN YEARS IF THE DIRECTIONS ARE CAREFULLY FOLLOWED. OUR GUARANTEE COVERS ANY AND ALL DEFECTS DUE TO THE QUALITY OF THE PAINT.

OUR SEROCO WEATHERPROOF MINERAL PAINT is compounded by one of the most expert paint chemists in the country, now in charge of our paint factory, and it possesses peculiar properties not common to the ordinary barn, roof and fence paints. It is a high class preservative that cannot be excelled and we recommend it especially for shingled, tin or iron roofs, structural iron work, barns, elevators, and posts and timbers which are to be put underground. Our Seroco Mineral Paint is absolutely waterproof. It has been tested out under the most trying conditions and it is universally acknowledged to be the best and the most durable preservative of wood. It will stop leaks, it prevents corrosion and it is absolutely free from acids. You may therefore use it in the confident belief that you are getting the very best possible mineral paint now offered in the market, no matter what the name, make or price, and when you are asked to pay one cent more than the prices we charge, as quoted below, remember that the additional price asked by any dealer at home or elsewhere cannot possibly secure for you any better mineral paint than our Seroco, and if you pay more than the price we ask you are simply wasting money, and in nine cases out of ten you do not secure an article which begins to compare with this in all the qualities which make the highest grade mineral paint.

$8.60 PAINTS THIS LARGE BARN

A large modern barn like this, painted with our Seroco Weatherproof Mineral Barn, Roof and Fence Paint, two coats, for $8.60.

This large barn measuring 30 feet wide by 50 feet long and 22 feet in height will require

12 gallons for body, 10 gallons at 60 cents per gallon.	**$6.00**
2 gallons at 65 cents per gallon.	1.30
2 gallons for trimming, at 65 cents per gallon......	1.30
	$8.60

SEROCO MINERAL PAINT GOES FURTHER THAN ANY OTHER

ONE GALLON OF SEROCO WEATHERPROOF MINERAL BARN, ROOF AND FENCE PAINT covers about three hundred square feet of surface with two good coats. We know that Seroco Mineral Paint will cover more surface than any other. Its spreading qualities are unequaled. It will last longer than any other. It will give better satisfaction and is in every way the most desirable and the most durable paint for these purposes ever manufactured, and when you consider its wonderful covering properties and its unequaled wearing qualities, it is indeed worth double the price of any ordinary roof, fence or barn paint.

WHY IT PAYS TO USE SEROCO MINERAL PAINT

IF YOU HAVE A BARN, A DAIRY, A CORN CRIB, A GRANARY, in short any farm building on your premises in need of paint, you can well afford to order this Seroco Mineral Paint, because every time you treat any of your farm buildings to two good coats of this high grade mineral paint, you add immensely to the appearance of your premises, besides giving your buildings a coat of wood preservative which will make them last longer and look better than any other paint you might use and therefore save you repair bills which come sooner or later when farm buildings are neglected. Our paints are so thoroughly well made, so carefully mixed that it is no trouble at all for you to use them yourself without employing a skilled painter. Remember, we issue a book entitled, "How to Paint," which we will send you free, and in this book we tell you all about our paints, how to apply them, explain the brushes and tools necessary, give you the fullest information, in fact, giving such a comprehensive knowledge of painting that you can do this work in your odd moments just as well as if you were to hire it done. Well painted buildings add hundreds of dollars to the value of any farm and inasmuch as we sell this high grade mineral paint at such astonishingly low prices, the investment in the raw materials necessary to give your buildings proper attention is almost insignificant. Paint your buildings. Keep them painted—first as an investment, second for appearance sake; and then remember our guarantee covers this paint, that we warrant it to wear for ten years if directions are carefully followed.

WHILE OUR FREE COLOR SAMPLE BOOKLET shows the six different colors in which we manufacture this special weatherproof mineral barn, roof and fence paint, and we will send it to any person free on application, we would advise you to send your order direct from this catalogue, stating which of the six colors you desire. We will send the paint to you guaranteeing the color to please you and the paint to prove satisfactory or you can return it to us at our expense and we will immediately refund your money. It is put up in one-gallon cans, five-gallon buckets, one-half barrels containing 25 gallons, and barrels containing fifty gallons.

This illustration shows the 1-gallon can.

PRICES AND LIST OF COLORS OF SEROCO WEATHERPROOF MINERAL BARN, ROOF AND FENCE PAINT.

Mention name of color as well as the catalogue number when ordering.

No. 30K800	Oxide Red	No. 30K830	Yellow
No. 30K810	Lead Color	No. 30K850	Maroon
No. 30K820	Dark Gray	No. 30K860	Natural Green

1-gallon can......................................	65c
5-gallon bucket, per gallon....................	60c
25-gallon barrel, per gallon...................	55c
50-gallon barrel, per gallon...................	50c

THE KIND OF BRUSHES TO USE WITH SEROCO BARN, ROOF AND FENCE PAINT.

For painting roofs and the walls of barns, sheds, etc., use a No. 30K3084 or No. 30K3086 wall brush, 4 or 4½ inches in width, see page 82. For fences use the same brush but narrower, 3 or 3½ inches in width, or No. 30K3076 or No. 30K3078 round paint brush, size 3-0. For trimming use a round paint brush, No. 30K3076 or No. 30K3078, size 3-0.

Illustration shows the 5-gallon bucket.

39c PER GALLON COMPETITION BRAND MINERAL BARN PAINT

AT 39 CENTS PER GALLON IN 50-GALLON BARRELS to 54 cents per gallon in one-gallon cans, we offer our Competition Brand Mineral Barn Paint, a paint that is being made by us simply to meet the many cheap mineral paints on the market sold at from 50 to 70 cents per gallon according to quantity. While this, our Competition Brand, is a better paint, in fact, very much better than the cheap mineral paints put out by other paint manufacturers, still, we do not recommend it, because it does not contain the best wearing minerals such as are used in our Guaranteed Weatherproof Mineral Barn, Roof and Fence Paint, described on page 72 of this catalogue. It has always been our policy to sell our customers a class of merchandise that would give the best of satisfaction but we are sometimes forced into making a cheaper article because other manufacturers have seen fit to put a cheaper grade of goods on the market in order to meet our low prices on high grade goods. They cannot meet our prices and give you as good a quality on account of the big profits you are compelled to pay, the manufacturer must add a big profit to cover the heavy expense he is under, for instance, he is compelled to employ a force of salesmen with heavy traveling expenses, he also suffers a big loss from bad accounts, now the dealer wants a fair profit, and before you can get the paint you are compelled to pay two big fat profits.

IF YOU FEEL THAT YOU CANNOT AFFORD TO PURCHASE OUR BEST PAINT, namely, our Seroco Weatherproof Mineral Barn, Roof and Fence Paint, although there is only a difference of a few cents per gallon, then send us your order for this, our Competition Brand Mineral Paint and we will send you a better paint in quality and covering capacity than you can secure elsewhere at from 50 cents to 70 cents per gallon, according to quantity, but we urge you, for real economy, to purchase our Guaranteed Weatherproof Mineral Barn, Roof and Fence Paint described on page 72 of this catalogue because it is the highest grade mineral paint made, in fact, a better paint could not be made even if you were willing to pay $1.00 per gallon for it, it gives a better finish, covers more surface and works better under the brush, besides, you are protected by our binding ten-year guarantee, such as no other manufacturer dare put out on the quality of paint he makes.

AS EXPLAINED ABOVE, this paint is made and sold by us solely for the purpose of meeting the cheap paints put into the dealers' hands to compete with our highest grade Weatherproof Mineral Barn, Roof and Fence Paint, and while our profit remains the same, whether you buy our Competition Brand or our Weatherproof Mineral Barn, Roof and Fence Paint, we prefer that you purchase our highest grade paint, costing only a few cents per gallon more than the cheaper grade, because it will look so much better and wear longer than any other paint, that it will astonish you how it is possible for us to furnish so high a grade of paint for so low a price. Remember, we operate or own paint factory, we purchase the raw materials direct from first hands because we use such large quantities; we have equipped our factory with the latest labor saving machinery, in fact, everything has been done to lower the manufacturing cost.

PRICES AND LISTS OF COLORS OF COMPETITION BRAND MINERAL BARN PAINT
MENTION NAME OF COLOR AS WELL AS CATALOGUE NUMBER.

No. 30K880 Red Mineral	No. 30K883 Yellow	No. 30K884 Brown Mineral	No. 30K885 Maroon

1-gallon can	54c
5-gallon can, per gallon	49c
25-gallon barrel, per gallon	44c
50-gallon barrel, per gallon	39c

SEROCO SHINGLE STAIN AND PRESERVATIVE

While our mineral paint is highly recommended for shingled roofs, still some prefer a shingle stain. Our shingle stains are the best it is possible to make. They are made in our own paint factory and every package leaving our factory contains full measure and is guaranteed as to quality. Strong in color with the highest preserving qualities. Water will not penetrate shingles coated with our stains, rendering them practically immune from decay. Our prices quoted below are based on the actual manufacturing cost with but our one small percentage of profit added, therefore do not be deceived by paying a higher price, as a better shingle stain cannot be made. Send us your order; we guarantee satisfaction or money refunded. The shingles can be dipped in the stain or it may be applied with a brush. A shingled roof coated with these stains will last twice as long. When applied with a brush, one gallon will cover about 150 square feet of surface, one coat, or 100 square feet, two coats. When dipped, 2½ to 3 gallons will cover 1,000 of the regulation 4x16 shingles. Two-thirds the length of the shingle only need be dipped. Furnished in the following shades:

No. 30K1181	Moss Green	No. 30K1185	Red
No. 30K1182	Dark Green	No. 30K1186	Brown
No. 30K1183	Dark Slate	No. 30K1187	Black
No. 30K1184	Light Slate		

IT IS JUST AS IMPORTANT to preserve the roof as it is to preserve any other portion of the house. No one thinks of building a home, a barn or any other building without painting it to preserve the woods from the elements, yet 90 per cent or more of those who build never think of giving the roof a coat of preservative for the same purpose. It is a real economy to use Seroco Shingle Stain and Preservative as it will preserve the roof for many years longer than it would be of service if left exposed to the weather. Seroco Shingle Stains are easily applied and it requires no skill whatsoever to use this splendid preservative and our little free book "How to Paint" explains it all to you so that you may do this work yourself. It is cheaper to paint your shingles than it is to reshingle the house and we advise all our customers to make the trifling investment necessary to give every roof on the premises a good coat of this splendid preservative.

PRICES FOR ABOVE COLORS.

1-gallon can	60c
5-gallon jacket can, per gallon	55c
25-gallon half barrel, per gallon	50c
50-gallon barrel, per gallon	45c

Apply above Seroco Shingle Stain with a No. 30K3084 or No. 30K3086 wall brush, the larger size recommended, see page 82.
BE SURE TO MENTION NAME OF COLOR AND CATALOGUE NUMBER.

$1.00 PAINTS YOUR BUGGY WITH SEROCO BUGGY AND CARRIAGE PAINT

A strictly high grade paint for buggies, carriages, wagons or any kind of vehicle. It is made from the best pigments ground in the finest carriage varnish, and for durability and finish our buggy paints are unexcelled. One coat makes a beautiful and durable finish and no varnish required. Two quarts costing $1.00, with very little labor will make an old buggy look like new. No experience necessary; anyone can apply it, as it comes to you ready for use. While this paint is made expressly for buggies, etc., it can be used with excellent results on settees, benches, lawn swings, chairs or any article exposed to the weather. Our buggy paints are made from the finest materials it is possible to obtain; for instance, the colors are non-fading and the costliest the market affords. We cannot afford to use cheap materials because we want your future orders, also the orders from your friends and neighbors. Manufacturing the paint ourselves enables us to use the very best materials and still be able to quote a price others ask for inferior goods.

No. 30K1600	Yellow	No. 30K1640	Dark Green
No. 30K1610	Vermilion	No. 30K1650	Blue
No. 30K1620	Light Wine	No. 30K1660	Dark Wine
No. 30K1630	Coach Green	No. 30K1670	Black

MAKE THE OLD BUGGY LOOK LIKE NEW. Perhaps you have a rig that one that is in every way in first class condition, except that it has been run over muddy, rough roads and has become scratched and disfigured and all it needs to make it look like new is a fresh coat of paint. You will be surprised how easy it will be for you to paint this rig yourself if you order Seroco Buggy Paint and it can be done at a trifling cost. Our little booklet "How to Paint," which we send you free, will explain to you just how to handle this buggy paint, and every other kind of paint, varnish and enamel manufactured and sold by us. It explains the tools necessary, and this book so simplifies the painting proposition that any man with average intelligence can do just as good work with our superior, high grade, ready mixed paint as an experienced painter will do. You cannot only make your buggy look like new, but your wagon or any other vehicle around the farm. Not only will a new coat of paint make it look like new, but it will also preserve an otherwise sound and well built vehicle by giving all wood and iron parts a coat of preservative, thus preventing decay, etc. Just a few cents invested in Seroco Buggy Paint and a brush will save you many dollars, and will make your vehicle almost as good as new.

PRICES FOR ABOVE COLORS.

Per ½-pint can	$0.20
Per 1-pint can	.30
Per 1-quart can	.50
Per 1-gallon can	1.85

Apply Seroco Buggy Paint with a varnish brush. We recommend No. 30K3028 or No. 30K3036 for fine work. A 2-inch brush is the best size.
Be sure to mention name of color and catalogue number.

SEROCO GLOSS ENAMEL
A HIGH GLOSS INTERIOR PAINT.

The highest grade interior enamel for all purposes. Anyone can apply this enamel and produce that high gloss finish on woodwork, plastered or board walls, furniture, etc. It is the only sanitary finish for walls and woodwork because all dirt and grease is readily removed with soap and hot water without affecting the high gloss finish. Seroco Gloss Enamel is ready mixed and comes to you prepared ready for use and the directions are so simple that the most inexperienced can secure that smooth glossy porcelain finish on woodwork, walls, etc., the equal of the most costly enamel work produced by expert painters.

Seroco Gloss Enamel is not an ordinary enamel paint but is a scientifically prepared mixture and should not be compared with the cheap, worthless enamels on the market. We are anxious that our customers give this enamel a trial. Send us an order and finish the walls and woodwork of one of your bedrooms—we guarantee that you will be so well pleased with the porcelain like finish that you will immediately treat other rooms likewise. The finest material on earth for finishing the walls and woodwork of bathrooms and kitchens. Since Seroco Gloss Enamel is made in a variety of beautiful shades, harmonious color combinations are possible; for instance, use a certain color for the walls and a harmonizing color for the woodwork. Remember, we are offering here the highest grade enamel it is possible to make and so prepared that the most inexperienced can produce with it the most perfect enamel finish. Apply with a varnish brush, No. 30K3036, size, 2½ or 3.

No. 30K2150	Pearl	No. 30K2158	Lavender
No. 30K2151	Light Slate	No. 30K2159	Pink
No. 30K2152	Cream	No. 30K2160	Lilac
No. 30K2153	Apple Green	No. 30K2161	Carmine
No. 30K2154	Pea Green	No. 30K2162	Ivory
No. 30K2155	Nile Green	No. 30K2163	Black
No. 30K2156	Light Blue	No. 30K2164	White
No. 30K2157	Dark Blue		

PRICES FOR ABOVE COLORS.

Per 1-quart can	$0.45
Per ½-gallon can	.78
Per 1-gallon can	1.48

Be sure to mention name of color and catalogue number.

80c PAINTS YOUR WAGON WITH SEROCO WAGON AND IMPLEMENT PAINT

½-gallon will paint any ordinary wagon and make it look like new.

A paint made expressly for wagons and farm implements, has wonderful wearing qualities and covering power. Made of the very best materials with non-fading colors. Being extremely tough, it will not crack nor peel off. It is cheaper to use paint than to allow your wagon or farm implements to go to decay. One gallon will in many instances refinish every implement on the farm. It is an ideal implement paint because it can be used on iron as well as wood with equal results. Saves many times its cost in preventing rust and decay. Anyone can apply it and do perfect work as it is ready mixed and ready to be applied when you receive it. Dries hard with a high gloss. Apply with a No. 30K3028, No. 30K3034 or No. 30K3036 varnish brush, 1, 2 or 2½ inches in width.

No. 30K1854	Red	
No. 30K1855	Blue	
No. 30K1856	Green	No. 30K1858 Vermilion
No. 30K1857	Yellow	No. 30K1859 Black

PRICES FOR ABOVE COLORS.

Per 1-quart can	$0.45
Per 1-½-gallon can	.80
Per 1-gallon can	1.50

Be sure to mention name of color and catalogue number.

ONE GALLON of this Seroco Wagon and Implement Paint, and a brush, used on a rainy day, will serve to put probably every implement on your place in first class condition again. Just a few cents invested in paint, just a little time in applying it to your sulky plow, your hay rake, your binder, your mowing machine and other machinery, will preserve them from rust and make them look as good as new.

Liquid Weatherproof Canvas Coating.

No. 30K2117 The greatest waterproof preparation for cotton duck. A coat of this material applied on cotton duck or canvas of the lightest weight will make it absolutely waterproof. The canvas can be folded without the danger of cracking; it acts like rubber. Especially adapted for hay stack covers, tents, wagon covers, tarpaulins, awnings; in fact, it can be applied to anything made of cotton or canvas duck and make it absolutely waterproof. Five gallons will cover an ordinary hay stack cover.

1-gallon can	60c
5-gallon can, per gallon	50c
10-gallon can, per gallon	48c

GOLD AND SILVER PAINTS, BRONZES, ETC.

15c PER BOX Japanese Gold Paint.

No. 30K2120 For gilding everything and anything, fancy baskets, picture frames, toys, chandeliers, iron beds, mantels, cistern pumps, gas pipes, mouldings, iron shelf brackets, metal ornaments, stationery and all kinds of paper work. Put up in neat wooden box, brush included.

Small size. Price, each........15c

Large size, three times the quantity. Price, each........29c
Weight, small size, 8 ounces; large size, 16 ounces.

25c PER BOX Lustre Bronze PowderOutfit.

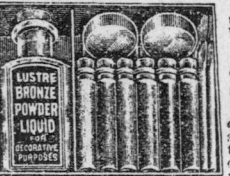

No. 30K2121 Assorted colors Gold Paint. This outfit contains six assorted colors of bronze powder in small vials, two brushes, two mixing cups and a 1-ounce bottle of mixing liquid. Just the thing for fancy bronze work. Weight, 12 ounces.
Price for complete outfit........25c

Sapolin Aluminum and Cold Radiator Enamel.

For radiators or other steam or hot water heated surfaces. The brightest silver or gold finish may be obtained with this material. The powder and liquid come separately in cans, a mixing cup and brush are included. The entire outfit is packed in a neat pasteboard box. This material dries very hard with a smooth finish and will not discolor.

No. 30K2124 Aluminum.
No. 30K2125 Gold.
No. 2 can, containing one-half pint, aluminum or gold. Price........43c
No. 4 can, containing one pint, aluminum or gold. Price........82c
Be sure to state kind wanted.

Seroco Aluminum Enamel or Silver Paint.

No. 30K2145 The brightest and most brilliant AluminumEnamel made. The dry powder and liquid come separately in a neat, compact can and are mixed when ready to use. It is unlike the ready mixed article in that the finish is bright and smooth, almost like nickel plate. Old scratched picture frames can be reclaimed and made to look like new with one coat of this material. It produces a rich aluminum or silver finish on picture frames, room moulding, chairs, iron beds, tables, baskets, bicycles, statues, sewing machines, curtain poles and trimmings, baby carriages, trays, mail boxes, umbrella holders, chandeliers and gas fixtures, kitchen and bathroom fixtures, iron fences, water and gas pipes.

Medium can	13c	½-pint can	31c
Large can	21c	Pint can	49c

We include a brush free with each can.

Seroco Indestructible Aluminum Paint for Heated Surfaces.

No. 30K2146 This Aluminum Paint will withstand tremendous heat and is especially prepared for stoves, boilers, engines, motors, mantels, furnace fronts, interior of ovens, smokestacks or any metal surface likely to be subjected to intense heat.

Medium can	14c	½-pint can	36c
Large can	23c	Pint can	59c

We include a brush free with each can.

Seroco Gold Leaf Enamel.

No. 30K2147 The best Gold Paint on the market. It dries with a bright, smooth finish, almost like gold leaf. Ordinary gold paint dries out very dull and sandy, but this article will leave a smooth finish as though it were burnished. The gold powder and liquid are put up separately in a patented double can and are mixed when ready to use. If you do not find this the best gold paint you have ever used, brighter than any other, also that it will cover more surface than any other, write to us and we will promptly refund your money. For picture frames, lamps, chandeliers, statuary, bird cages, hinges, baby carriages, iron beds, chairs, baskets, wickerware, toys, curtain poles, room moulding, bric-a-brac, etc.

Small can	15c
Medium can	25c
Large can	37c
½-pint can	57c

We include a brush free with each can.

Bronze Powders.

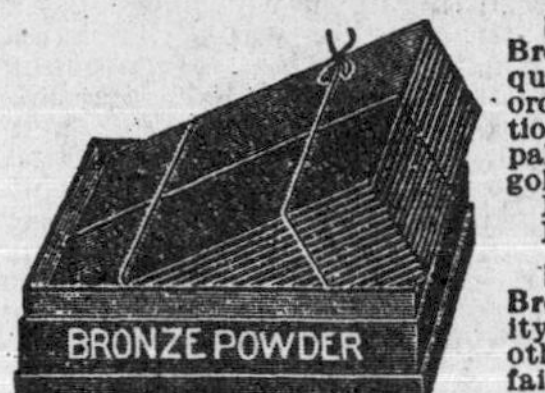

No. 30K2190 Gold Bronze Powder. A good quality for general use. When ordering do not fail to mention shade desired; light or pale gold; medium or rich gold; deep gold.
Price, per pound 75c
Per 2-ounce package, 12c

No. 30K2192 Gold Bronze Powder. Finest quality. Will go further than any other. When ordering do not fail to mention shade desired; light or pale gold; medium or rich gold; deep gold.
Price, per pound, 95c; per 2-ounce package 16c

No. 30K2194 Aluminum or Silver Powder. Fine quality for general use. Nothing better on the market.
Price, per pound, $1.05; per 2-ounce package 18c

No. 30K2196 Diamond Dust. For decorating cards, fancy work, etc. Make your own birthday and New Year cards. Price, per 4-ounce package 15c

Banana Liquid for Mixing Gold, Aluminum and Other Bronzes.

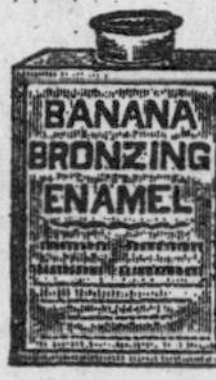

No. 30K2166 Best Banana Liquid for mixing with bronze powders. Weatherproof and durable.

Price, per 4-ounce can	10c
Price, per 8-ounce can	18c
Price, per pint can	30c
Price, per quart can	48c

20c PER ½ PINT. Seroco Decorative Enamel.

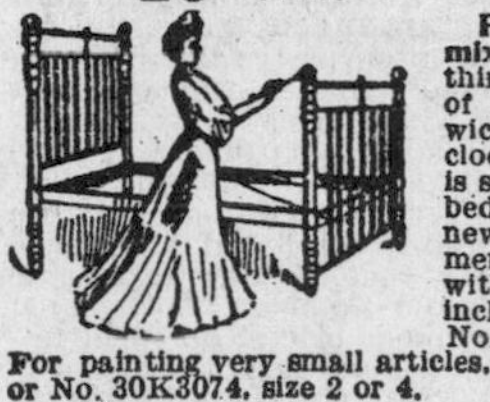

For all decorative work; is ready mixed, can be applied on anything and everything, any kind of furniture, iron beds, shelves, wickerwork, baby carriages, clocks, etc. One-half pint can is sufficient for an ordinary iron bed and will make it look like new. When ordering, be sure to mention color wanted. Apply with a varnish brush, 1 or 1½ inches in width. No. 30K3034 or No. 30K3036 will do good work. For painting very small articles, use a sash tool, No. 30K3072 or No. 30K3074, size 2 or 4.

No.		No.	
30K2130	White	30K2138	Maroon
30K2131	Pink	30K2139	Dark Green
30K2132	Light Blue	30K2140	Gloss Black
30K2133	Light Green	30K2141	Dull Black
30K2134	Lemon Yellow	30K2142	Rose
30K2136	Cardinal Red	30K2143	Violet
30K2137	Brown		

Price, 1-pint can, 35c; ½-pint can 20c

Bath Tub Enamel.

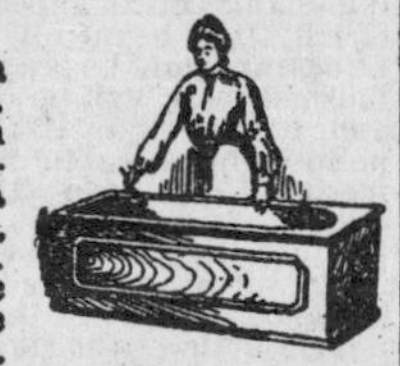

No. 30K2170 White Bath Tub Enamel, Liquid Porcelain. A common iron tub coated with this preparation will have a beautiful appearance. Apply with a good varnish brush. No. 30K3036, 1½ in. in width, is recommended.
Per ½-pint can 25c
Per 1-pint can 45c
Cannot be sent by mail.

14c PER ½ PINT. Wire Screen Enamel.

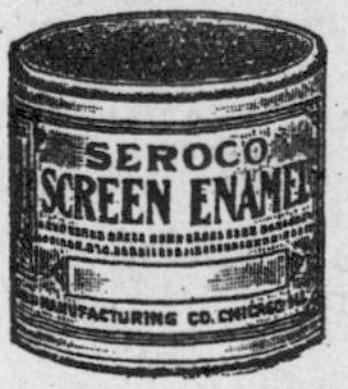

Green or Black Wire Screen Enamel. Ready for use and easily applied; does not clog meshes or screens, and one coat gives to old, rusty screens a rich, brilliant and lasting finish. Apply with a varnish brush, 1 or 1½ inches wide. **Be sure to mention name of color and catalogue number.**
No. 30K2175 Green
No. 30K2176 Black
Per 1-pint can, 24c; ½ pint can 14c
Cannot be sent by mail.

Sapolin Stove Pipe Enamel.

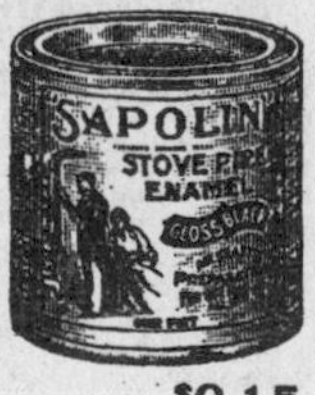

No. 30K2180 Sapolin Stove Pipe Enamel. Especially prepared for use on stove pipes, stoves, furnaces, grates, steam and water pipes, boilers, smokestacks, garden tools, iron fences, brackets, etc. **One coat produces a brilliant black finish; very elastic.** Will not crack, chip, peel or burn off. Ready for instant use. Brush included.

Per ½-pint can, weight, ⅝ pound	$0.15
Per 1-pint can, weight, 1⅛ pounds	.26
Per 1-gallon can	1.60

Cannot be sent by mail.

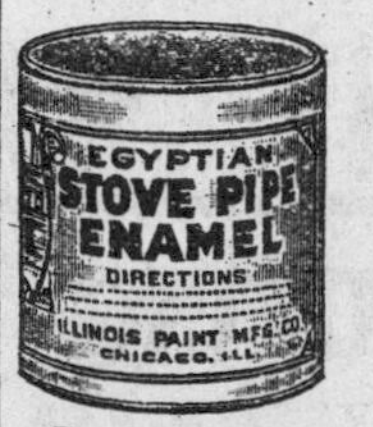

12c PER ½ PINT. Egyptian Stove Pipe Enamel.

No. 30K2181 The most satisfactory stove pipe and iron enamel ever put on the market. It is not so extensively advertised as some brands, but it will wear longer and produce a better finish than anything you can possibly obtain in stove pipe enamels. We include a brush, **free with each can.**

Per ½-pint can, including brush	$0.12
Per 1-pint can, including brush	.20
Per ½-gallon can, including brush	.70
Per 1-gallon can, including brush	1.25

Cannot be sent by mail.

Putty.

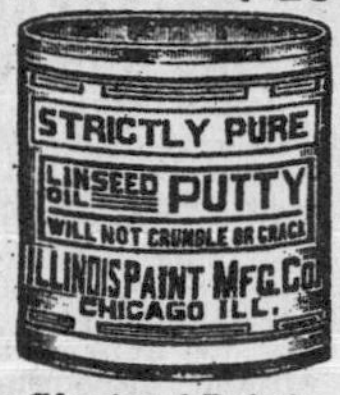

No. 30K2205 Guaranteed strictly pure. Will not crumble or crack.
4-pound sealed can, per lb. 3½c
10-pound sealed can, per lb. 3c
20-pound sealed can, per lb. 2¾c

Glaziers' Points.

No. 30K2208 Zinc Glaziers' Points, for fastening glass in sash. We can furnish sizes 1, 2 and 3. The illustration herewith is the actual size of No. 3. Nos. 1 and 2 are larger. Price, per ¼-pound paper 3c

White Lead.

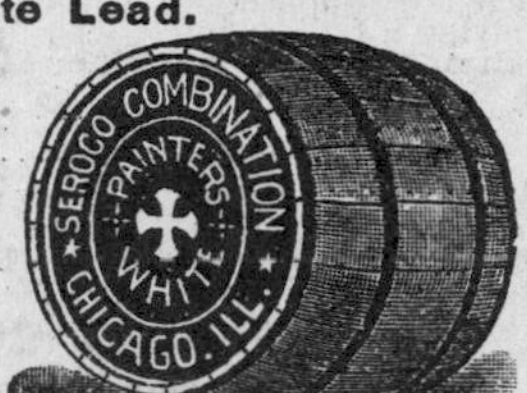

No. 30K2210 Fulton Lead Co.'s Painters' Lead in Oil; a special grade. Kegs of 12½, 25, 50 or 100 pounds.
Price, per pound 4½c

Seroco Brand Painters' Lead.

No. 30K2214 A combination of Painters' Lead ground in refined linseed oil. The ingredients used in the manufacture of our Seroco Brand are the purest it is possible to obtain and we guarantee that our Seroco Brand will cover almost twice the surface and outwear any white lead on the market, regardless of its purity and price.
Kegs of 12½, 25, 50 and 100 pounds. Per pound. 5½c
5-pound can, per pound 8c
1-pound can, per pound 9c

The Seroco Colors in Oil.

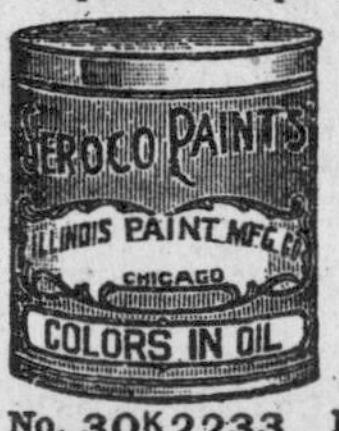

For tinting paints. Ground in pure linseed oil, strong and permanent.

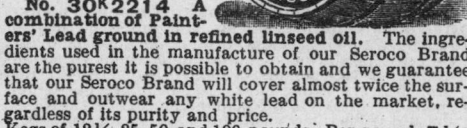

Put up in 1 and 5-pound cans. Per lb.

No.	Color	Per lb.
No. 30K2230	Lamp Black	14c
No. 30K2231	Coach Black	13c
No. 30K2232	Ivory Black	12c
No. 30K2233	Drop Black	10c
No. 30K2235	Prussian Blue	34c
No. 30K2236	Ultramarine Blue	15c
No. 30K2237	Cobalt Blue	25c
No. 30K2240	Raw Umber	11c
No. 30K2241	Burnt Umber	11c
No. 30K2242	Raw Sienna	9c
No. 30K2243	Burnt Sienna	9c
No. 30K2244	Vandyke Brown	11c
No. 30K2248	Blind Green	16c
No. 30K2249	Chrome Green	12c
No. 30K2253	English Venetian Red	7c
No. 30K2254	Indian Red	13c
No. 30K2255	Tuscan Red	14c
No. 30K2256	Unfading Red	28c
No. 30K2257	English Rose Pink	17c
No. 30K2258	English Rose Lake	26c
No. 30K2259	Scarlet Vermilion	17c
No. 30K2262	Chrome Yellow, Light	15c
No. 30K2263	Chrome Yellow, Medium	15c
No. 30K2264	Chrome Yellow, Orange	15c
No. 30K2265	Yellow Ochre	7c
No. 30K2268	Light Oak Graining	10c
No. 30K2269	Dark Oak Graining	10c
No. 30K2270	Antique Oak Graining	10c
No. 30K2271	Walnut Graining	10c
No. 30K2272	Cherry Graining	10c
No. 30K2273	Mahogany Graining	10c

All of the above colors furnished in 25-pound cans at 2 cents per pound less. Don't forget to state color wanted. Cannot be sent by mail.

Pure French Ochre in Oil.

No. 30K2280 Pure French Ochre in Oil. 12½ and 25-pound cans. Price, per pound 4c

English Venetian Red in Oil.

No. 30K2282 English Venetian Red, especially adapted for painting brick buildings. 12½ and 25-pound cans. Price, per pound 4c

White Ochre in Oil.

No. 30K2284 White Ochre Ground in Oil. Ground in pure linseed oil. 12½ and 25-pound cans.
Price, per pound 4c

Zinc in Oil.

No. 30K2286 Pure French Zinc in Oil. 12½ and 25-pound cans. Price, per pound 10c
No. 30K2287 Pure French Zinc in Oil. 1 to 5-pound cans. Price, per pound 12c
No. 30K2288 Zinc in Oil, American snow white. 12½ and 25-pound pails.
Price, per pound 7c

Pure Graphite Paint Paste.

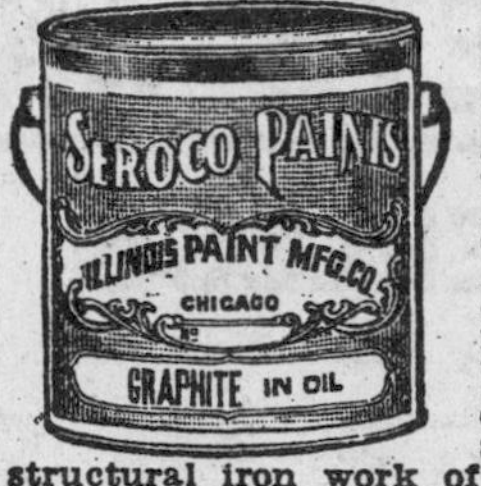

No. 30K2292 To 12½ pounds (1 gallon) paste add 3 gallons boiled oil, making 4 gallons of **Pure Graphite Paint, ready for use.** Will cover 500 square feet smooth metal per gallon. Will not crack, blister or peel off; is not affected by heat or cold, smoke, steam, moisture, acids, alkali or brine, or by climatic changes. **For use on roofs, stacks, boilers, bridges, structural iron work of any kind.** This paint is manufactured from pure graphite and absolutely pure linseed oil. Is a dark slate color.

Per 5-pound can	$0.40
Per 12½-pound can	.85
Per 25-pound can	1.60

Oil Stain.

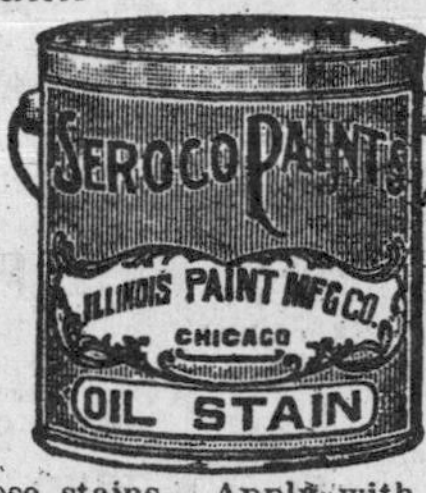

Perfect imitation of natural wood, cherry, rosewood, mahogany, walnut, light oak, dark oak, antique oak. For staining interior woodwork or any work not finished. This stain cannot be applied over varnish or painted surfaces. One or two coats of varnish applied over it will produce a fine finish. Nos. 30K2714, 30K2718 and 30K2710 or 30K2711 varnishes can be used in connection with these stains. Apply with a varnish brush. Don't forget to state color wanted.

No. 30K2300	Light Oak	Cannot be sent by mail.
No. 30K2301	Dark Oak	
No. 30K2302	Antique Oak	
No. 30K2303	Cherry	
No. 30K2304	Walnut	
No. 30K2305	Mahogany	
No. 30K2306	Rosewood	

Per ½-pint can	$0.13
Per 1-pint can	.19
Per 1-quart can	.34
Per ½-gallon can	.66
Per 1-gallon can	1.24

Varnish Stain.

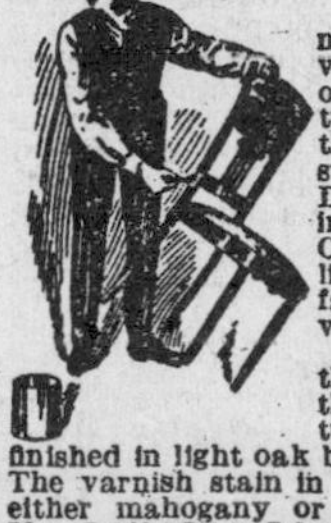

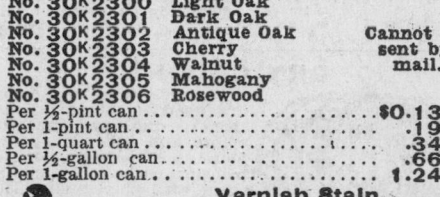

Stain and varnish used separately, on new work, produce a better finish than varnish stain, but for refinishing painted or varnished surfaces, such as old furniture or painted or varnished woodwork, this varnish stain is recommended. It stains and varnishes in one operation. Dries hard with a fine luster. Furnished in the following natural wood colors: Cherry, rosewood, mahogany, walnut, light oak, dark oak, antique oak. Do not fail to mention color wanted. Apply with a varnish brush; 2-inch brush recommended.

In selecting a color it is necessary that the color selected be of a similar shade as the old finish; for instance, a piece of furniture finished in mahogany cannot be refinished in light oak by applying the light oak varnish stain. The varnish stain in this case will have to be of a dark color, either mahogany or walnut.

No. 30K2310	Light Oak	Per ¼-pt. can	$0.15
No. 30K2311	Dark Oak	Per 1-pt. can	.21
No. 30K2312	Antique Oak	Per 1-qt. can	.38
No. 30K2313	Cherry	Per ½-gal. can	.72
No. 30K2314	Walnut	Per 1-gal. can	1.30
No. 30K2315	Mahogany	Cannot be sent by mail.	
No. 30K2316	Rosewood		

Seroco Mission Finishes.

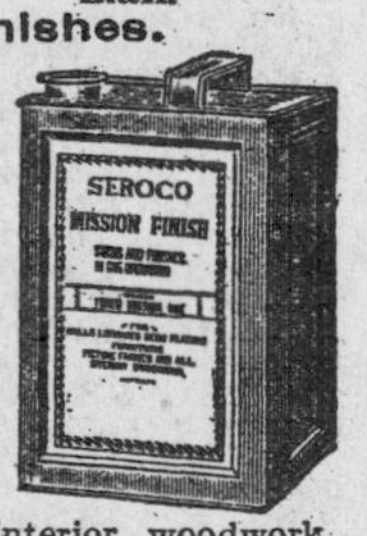

It stains and finishes with one operation. All the modern finishes can be had with these stains. It will produce that soft velvety effect with one coat and no rubbing down or waxing necessary. These finishes cannot be applied over painted or varnished surfaces. The paint or varnish must first be removed with our Seroco Paint and Varnish Remover and then finished with the stain. The latest mission effects in weathered and flemish oak are produced with this material and the finest finish is obtained with the least labor. Used for finishing interior woodwork, furniture, picture frames, halls, doors, mantels, plate rails, mouldings, etc. Adapted for all hardwood, also cypress and Georgia pine.

No. 30K2319	Dutch Mission Oak
No. 30K2320	Fumed Mission Oak
No. 30K2321	Dull Black Mission Oak
No. 30K2322	Dark Weathered Oak
No. 30K2323	Medium Weathered Oak
No. 30K2324	Light Weathered Oak

Per ½-pint can	$0.22
Per 1-pint can	.35
Per 1-quart can	.60
Per ½-gallon can	1.15
Per 1-gallon can	2.10

The Black Flemish is an alcohol production and dries out a very dull black, therefore, if an egg shell gloss is desired, apply a thin coat of our Seroco Prepared Floor Wax and rub briskly with a soft cloth. All other shades require no waxing. Color card showing natural pieces of oak wood finished with the above stains, mailed free on application.

CONCRETE AND CEMENT WATERPROOFING

PEERLESS WATERPROOFING COMPOUND

CEMENT BLOCK AND BRICK BUILDINGS POSITIVELY WATERPROOFED WITH OUR PEERLESS WATERPROOFING COMPOUND.

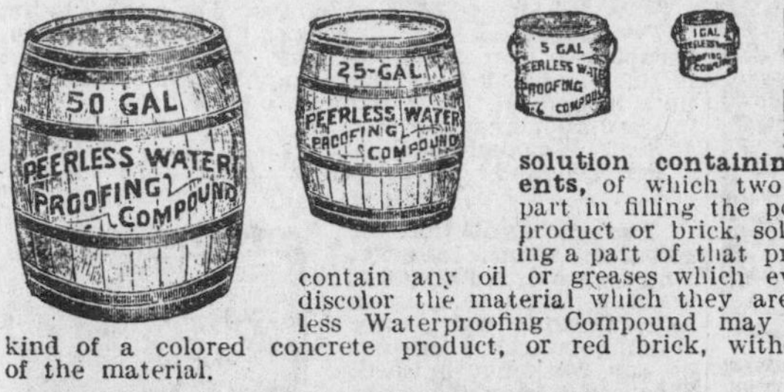

PEERLESS WATERPROOFING COMPOUND is a mineral liquid solution containing eight ingredients, of which two play an important part in filling the pores in the concrete product or brick, solidifying and becoming a part of that product. It does not contain any oil or greases which evaporate easily and discolor the material which they are applied to. Peerless Waterproofing Compound may be applied to any kind of a colored concrete product, or red brick, without discoloring any of the material.

PEERLESS WATERPROOFING COMPOUND is the only perfect waterproofing on the market, there is no other that can compare with it, and if it does not thoroughly waterproof any brick, cement, concrete or plaster to which it is applied, we will refund you your money and pay you for the labor in applying it.

PLASTERED WALLS can be made absolutely water and dampproof with one coat of Peerless Waterproofing Compound. If the walls of your home or any building are damp, resulting in the wall paper, paint or calcimine coming off the walls, then waterproof the exterior walls, if a brick or cement block building. If a frame building, then apply the waterproofing directly on the plaster, and we guarantee dry walls or money refunded. Peerless Waterproofing Compound applied to cement, concrete or brick walls, keeps them looking new, because every rain, instead of soaking in, washes the dirt and dust off the walls. That whitish bloom you so often see on brick and concrete is simply the sulphates, carbonates, salts and acids that are brought to the surface by water penetrating the wall and then evaporating. This can be overcome by preventing any water from penetrating the wall and Peerless Waterproofing Compound is the only material that will prevent that whitish bloom from appearing on the surface.

PLASTERING DIRECTLY upon the cement block met with dissatisfaction previous to the application of Peerless Waterproofing Compound, but today we can recommend to any of the users of concrete products, that they would be absolutely safe in plastering directly upon the concrete block should they treat the block with our Peerless Waterproofing Compound. Consider the great saving that is effected through the use of Peerless Waterproofing Compound, for should you build a concrete home and not use a guaranteed waterproofing compound, it would be absolutely necessary for you to ferr and lath the walls before you would be safe in plastering.

Applied with a calcimine brush, paint brush or spraying machine. One gallon will waterproof 100 to 125 square feet of concrete, cement, brick or plaster.

No. 30K2550	**1 gallon cans,** per gallon	$1.10
	5 gallon cans, per gallon	1.05
	10 gallon cans, per gallon	1.00
	50 gallon barrels, per gallon	.90

GUARANTEED TO DO THE WORK OR MONEY REFUNDED.

DRY COLORS.

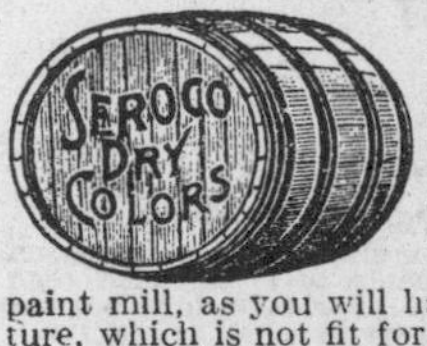

The following dry colors are used for tinting calcimines, making graining colors and other purposes. Some use these dry colors for painting purposes by mixing them with linseed oil. This we do not recommend unless the mixture is put through a paint mill, as you will have nothing but a coarse mixture, which is not fit for anything. If a mineral paint is desired at a low price you will profit by purchasing the Seroco Weatherproof Mineral Barn, Roof and Fence Paint, as then you will have a substantial paint, a paint that will wear three times as long, therefore cheapest in the end.

We handle only best qualities.	Bbl., per lb.	Per lb.
No. 30K2335 Yellow Rochelle Ochre, 450 pounds in barrel	1c	2c
No. 30K2336 Imported Marseilles Yellow Ochre, strong in color, 400-pound barrels	3½c	4c
No. 30K2338 American Venetian Red, 365 pounds in barrel	¾c	1½c
No. 30K2339 Imperial English Venetian Red, 336 pounds in barrel	1½c	2c
No. 30K2340 Snow White Wood Filler, 550 pounds in barrel	1½c	2c
No. 30K2341 Prince's Brown Mineral, 350 pounds in barrel	1c	2c
No. 30K2342 White Ochre, 550 pounds in barrel	1½c	2c
No. 30K2343 Lampblack, Germantown, 80 pounds in barrel	9c	10c
No. 30K2344 Burnt Turkey Umber, 350 pounds in barrel	3½c	6c
No. 30K2345 Raw Turkey Umber, 350 pounds in barrel	3½c	6c
No. 30K2346 Burnt Italian Sienna, 350 pounds in barrel	4½c	7c
No. 30K2347 Red Lead, 100 pounds	7½c	8c
No. 30K2348 Raw Italian Sienna, 350 pounds in barrel	4½c	7c
No. 30K2349 Chrome Green, best	....	8c
No. 30K2350 Chrome Yellow Lemon	....	10c
No. 30K2358 Ultramarine Blue	....	7c

Plaster Paris.

No. 30K2359 Price, per barrel of about 200 pounds $2.25
Less quantity, per pound .... .02

Whiting.

No. 30K2360 Extra Gilders' Whiting, fine quality bolted. Barrels, about 400 pounds, per pound 1c
Less quantity, per pound 2c

Limeproof Colors for Tinting Calcimines and Whitewash.

A small quantity will tint a large bucket of calcimine or whitewash.

No. 30K2362	**Limeproof Green,** per pound	9c
No. 30K2363	**Limeproof Blue,** per pound	9c
No. 30K2364	**Limeproof Red,** per pound	9c
No. 30K2365	**Limeproof Yellow,** per lb	9c

Soluble Blue for Manufacturing Bluing.

No. 30K2366 This soluble blue is used by the large bluing manufacturers. Guaranteed the best on the market. If interested in manufacturing liquid bluing, we will be pleased to furnish the formula.

Price, per pound 40c
25-pound drums, per pound 38c

CEMENT COLORS.

Pure mineral colors for coloring cement blocks, brick and concrete work. Guaranteed permanent and the strongest colors made. No. 30K2390 Red Oxide will produce a medium shade, about 15 pounds required to 100 pounds cement. No. 30K2391 Red Oxide is a very strong red of very brilliant color, about 12 pounds required to 100 pounds cement. No. 30K2392 Extra Red Oxide is the brightest and lightest red made, about 10 pounds required to 100 pounds cement. No. 30K2393 Brown Mineral will produce a deep rich brown color, about 20 pounds required to 100 pounds cement. No. 30K2394 Yellow Oxide is a good strong domestic yellow, about 15 pounds required to 100 pounds cement. No. 30K2395 Extra Yellow Oxide is used for making light and dark color cement brick, can be varied and deepened by the addition of red, about 15 pounds required to 100 pounds cement. No. 30K2396 Black is the strongest black known and absolutely permanent, about 2¼ pounds required to 100 pounds cement.

	Bbl. per lb.	100 lbs.	Less per lb.
No. 30K2390 Red Oxide, 400-pound barrels	2c	2½c	3c
No. 30K2391 Red Oxide, 400-pound barrels	3¼c	3¾c	4c
No. 30K2392 Extra Red, 600-pound barrels	9c	9½c	10c
No. 30K2393 Brown Mineral, 350-pound barrels	2c	2½c	3c
No. 30K2394 Yellow Oxide, 350-pound barrels	1½c	2c	2½c
No. 30K2395 Extra Yellow, 400-pound barrels	2½c	3c	3½c
No. 30K2396 Black, 30-lb. barrels	14c		16c

26-Cent Package Seroco Sanitary Kalsomine.

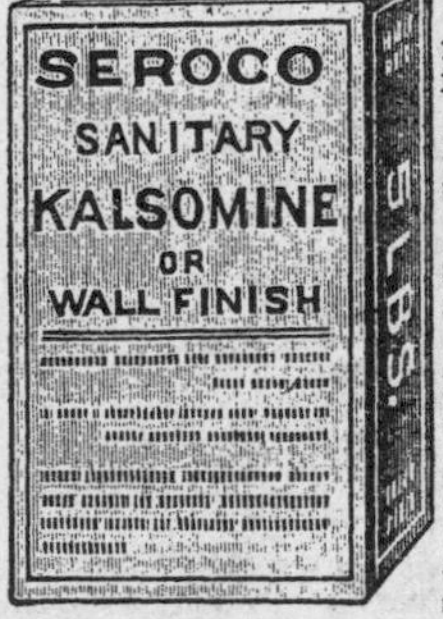

Durable wall finish; absolutely healthful; mixed with water only; will not rub off; cannot fade. Made in 16 colors and white.

The Sanitary Wall Finish is ready for use when it is mixed with water, and is unequaled for plain or high class decorative work on walls and ceilings. It covers well and one coat will generally be found sufficient. It can be recoated at any time when necessary, it forms a durable coating which will not decay, peel away or rub off if applied to a solid surface. **One pound properly mixed** and applied covers from 60 to 100 square feet, according to the surface. To obtain good results, all surfaces that have been calcimined should be thoroughly cleaned, and all lime and whitewashed walls should be well scraped and sized before applying.

No. 30K2601	Ivory
No. 30K2602	Lavender
No. 30K2603	Salmon Pink
No. 30K2604	Light Green
No. 30K2605	Yellow
No. 30K2606	Cream
No. 30K2607	Olive Gray
No. 30K2608	Buff
No. 30K2609	Light Pink
No. 30K2610	Medium Green
No. 30K2611	Pink
No. 30K2612	Blue
No. 30K2613	Pea Green
No. 30K2614	Slate
No. 30K2615	Green
No. 30K2616	Drab

Above tints, any shade, per 5-pound package .. 26c
No. 30K2617 **White,** per 5-pound package . 24c

CHINESE GLOSS LACQUER.

WE WANT EVERY CUSTOMER OF OURS TO KNOW ALL ABOUT CHINESE GLOSS LACQUER, THE NEW WOOD FINISH THAT WILL MAKE OLD FURNITURE LOOK JUST LIKE NEW.

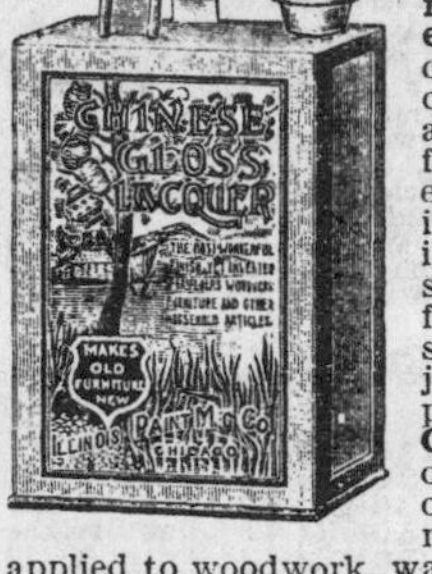

This is without doubt the most wonderful wood finish ever produced, wonderful because it surpasses in brilliancy of colors and lasting qualities any wood finish heretofore sold for a similar purpose. It is so easily applied that the most inexperienced woman can use it, and it is offered at a price so low that it makes it possible for you to make old and scratched pieces of furniture just as good as new at an expense of a few cents. **Chinese Gloss Lacquer** applied to an old table, chair, dresser, or any other article of furniture, will make it look like new; when applied to woodwork, wainscoting, doors and windows, it gives them renewed life and beauty, and when applied to an old stained floor, will work such a pleasing change in its appearance as will astonish you. Best of all, this beautiful new finish, our **Chinese Gloss Lacquer,** can be applied by any housewife, and the finished work will be just as satisfactory, just as rich and beautiful as if it had been done by an expert painter or a cabinet finisher. Indeed, the greatest merit of **Chinese Gloss Lacquer** lies in this one quality—that it does not require expert handling to produce the very finest results. It is put up by us ready for use just as it comes from the can, nothing is to be added by the purchaser, just open the can, pour a little of the liquid in a saucer or cup and brush it on the piece of furniture, the floor or the woodwork you wish to decorate, following the very simple directions we send with the can, and in twenty-four hours' time the newly finished piece of furniture, floor or woodwork will be ready for use.

Apply Chinese Gloss Lacquer with a flat varnish brush. Any of the following brushes may be used: Nos. 30K3028, 30K3034, 30K3036. 1½ and 2½ inches in width. (See page 81.)

Chinese Gloss Lacquer is made in the following colors:

Always order by number and name color wanted.

No. 30K2690	Light Oak.
No. 30K2691	Dark Oak.
No. 30K2692	Mahogany.
No. 30K2693	Cherry.
No. 30K2694	Walnut.
No. 30K2695	Green.
No. 30K2696	Natural or Clear.
No. 30K2697	Ground Color.

IF YOU WANT TO SEE COLOR SAMPLES of Chinese Gloss Lacquer send for our Paint Sample Book and we will send it to you by return mail, free and postpaid. In its pages we show actual color samples of our **Chinese Gloss Lacquer** in all the colors that we make it, so that you can see just how this high grade wood finish will look on any piece of furniture or woodwork in your home.

Prices for Chinese Gloss Lacquer.

Always order by number and name color wanted.

5 Gallons	$9.00
1 Gallon	1.90
Quart	.57
Pint	.32
½ Pint	.20

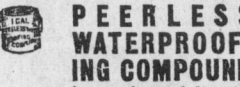

VARNISH DEPARTMENT

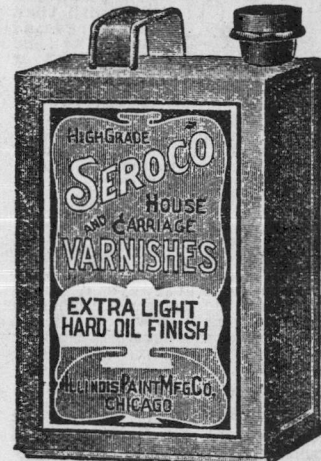

SEROCO HOUSE VARNISHES.

THE FOLLOWING VARNISHES ARE MADE BY ONE OF THE LARGEST AND BEST VARNISH MANUFACTURERS IN THE COUNTRY.

The very same varnishes are sold under the manufacturers' brands at from 50 cents to $1.50 per gallon higher than the prices we are quoting. We guarantee every ounce of our varnishes and no matter how costly the job, we guarantee satisfaction or money refunded.

Let us have a trial order; it will cost you nothing should it fail to give satisfaction.

Seroco Extra Light Hard Oil Finish.
No. 30K2710 An exceptionally light hard oil finish designed for finishing all kinds of interior woodwork; preserves the natural grain and color of the wood; works freely and dries in about 24 hours with an elegant gloss.

5 Gallons	1 Gallon	½ Gallon	Quart	Pint
$5.75	$1.25	73c	40c	23c

Seroco No. 1 Hard Oil Finish.
No. 30K2711 Splendidly adapted for general interior woodwork. Is pale, free flowing and durable and possesses a full and substantial body. Dries free from dust in 2 to 3 hours.

5 Gallons	1 Gallon	½ Gallon	Quart	Pint
$4.75	$1.05	63c	35c	20c

Seroco Furniture Varnish.
No. 30K2714 This varnish may be used to brighten up worn and lusterless furniture of every description. It dries over night and imparts a fine gloss finish. For general repair work in the household, on articles in daily use that must be finished hurriedly, this material is recommended.

5 Gallons	1 Gallon	½ Gallon	Quart	Pint
$3.50	75c	48c	25c	15c

Seroco Extra Furniture Varnish.
No. 30K2715 An extra fine varnish which is used by high grade furniture manufacturers; very tough and dries hard with a high gloss which can be rubbed and polished. Recommended for first class furniture finishing.

5 Gallons	1 Gallon	½ Gallon	Quart	Pint
$5.50	$1.20	70c	40c	22c

Seroco Cabinet Finish.
No. 30K2716 This varnish is designed for highest grade interior woodwork that is to be rubbed and polished; also gives a beautiful finish when left in the gloss. Is exceptionally rich and lustrous and on account of its elasticity is extremely durable. Dries free from dust in 3 to 4 hours and sufficiently hard for rubbing in 48 hours.

5 Gallons	1 Gallon	½ Gallon	Quart	Pint
$6.00	$1.30	75c	43c	23c

Seroco Interior Varnish.
No. 30K2718 An excellent varnish for use on all ordinary woodwork, furniture or over graining. Produces a fine gloss and gives a lasting finish. Dries in about 24 hours.

5 Gallons	1 Gallon	½ Gallon	Quart	Pint
$5.00	$1.10	65c	37c	20c

Seroco Interior Spar Finish.
No. 30K2719 Specially adapted for finishing highest class interior woodwork that is to be left in the gloss; may, however, be rubbed if desired. Exceedingly pale, free working and durable. Dries hard in 2 to 3 days.

5 Gallons	1 Gallon	½ Gallon	Quart	Pint
$8.00	$1.70	95c	52c	28c

Seroco Durable Floor Varnish.
No. 30K2720 Unequaled for finishing floors of all kinds, natural wood, painted or oil cloth. Will not turn white under repeated washing or foot friction, and dries to walk on over night. It is easily applied and gives an elegant and durable finish. This is undoubtedly the best floor varnish on the market.

5 Gallons	1 Gallon	½ Gallon	Quart	Pint
$8.00	$1.70	95c	53c	29c

Seroco Church and School Seat Varnish.
No. 30K2721 An extremely hard drying and durable article prepared especially for use on church and school seats. It will not soften up under heat of the body. Dries dust free in 5 to 6 hours and hardens in 48 hours.

5 Gallons	1 Gallon	½ Gallon	Quart	Pint
$8.25	$1.75	98c	54c	30c

Seroco Outside Spar Varnish.
No. 30K2722 For finishing all kinds of exposed surfaces, such as outside doors, vestibules and store fronts. It is also especially recommended for finishing inside blinds and the woodwork in bath rooms and on sinks, where a very elastic and durable varnish should be employed.

5 Gallons	1 Gallon	½ Gallon	Quart	Pint
$10.75	$2.25	$1.25	65c	35c

Seroco White Damar Varnish.
No. 30K2724 Made from imported Batavia gum. For finishing over any enameled surfaces, white or ivory, without producing discoloration. It may also be used with excellent satisfaction on fine wall paper hangings or on delicately tinted painted walls. Is of good body and dries well.

5 Gallons	1 Gallon	½ Gallon	Quart	Pint
$7.00	$1.50	85c	47c	25c

Seroco Black Asphaltum.
No. 30K2726 For finishing all kinds of castings, smokestacks, stovepipes, fenders, coal hods, iron work of agricultural implements, etc. It produces a jet black, brilliant finish and absolutely prevents rust or corrosion. It is heavy in body and quick drying.

5 Gallons	1 Gallon	½ Gallon	Quart	Pint
$2.50	60c	40c	22c	13c

Seroco Turpentine Japan Dryer.
No. 30K2728 A first class house painters' japan, dependable in all kinds of weather. A good binder and a sure and quick dryer. It contains no acids and will not cause the paint with which it is mixed to burn, blister, crack, chalk or peel. It mixes readily with oil and does not detract from the elasticity of the paint.

5 Gallons	1 Gallon	½ Gallon	Quart	Pint
$3.50	80c	50c	30c	18c

Seroco Oil Shellac.
No. 30K2730 This is a clear first coater or filler for new woods that have not been previously finished. It has a good body and produces a substantial and safe surface or base coat. It dries to sandpaper in 6 to 8 hours.

5 Gallons	1 Gallon	½ Gallon	Quart	Pint
$5.40	$1.15	65c	35c	20c

FINE CARRIAGE VARNISHES.

Seroco Wearing Body Varnish.

No. 30K2740 A brilliant, durable and elastic varnish for finishing carriage and buggy bodies. It works and flows with surprising freedom and may be used on the largest surfaces, such as carriage bodies, with the greatest safety and satisfaction. It is very pale and will not darken or injure the lightest shades of body color. It dries free from dust in 12 to 16 hours and hardens properly in from 2 to 3 days.

1 Gallon	½ Gallon	Quart	Pint
$3.00	$1.60	85c	45c

Seroco Elastic Gear Varnish.
No. 30K2744 Used for finishing gear parts and wheels. It is free working, brilliant and durable. It sets in 6 to 8 hours and dries hard in 36 to 48 hours. This varnish may also be used for body finishing when drying, despatch being an important consideration. This is a superior all around varnish for carriage finishing.

1 Gallon	½ Gallon	Quart	Pint
2.85	$1.55	80c	43c

Seroco One Coat Coach.
No. 30K2752 A splendid varnish for general repair work. On carriages, when work is simply dull or lusterless, otherwise in good condition, one coat of this varnish on the entire vehicle will produce a finish practically equal to a new job. It is light in color, elastic, brilliant and durable. Dries free from dust in about 12 hours and hardens to admit the use of the vehicle in about 3 days.

1 Gallon	½ Gallon	Quart	Pint
$2.50	$1.35	72c	38c

Seroco Wagon and Implement Varnish.
No. 30K2754 For agricultural implements, wagons, etc. A good varnish for general outside work; has a good body, a fine luster and is light in color and wears well. Dries in about 10 to 14 hours.

1 Gallon	½ Gallon	Quart	Pint
$1.45	83c	46c	25c

Seroco Coach Japan.
No. 30K2758 A reliable japan for binding and drying colors and rough stuff.

1 Gallon	½ Gallon	Quart	Pint
$1.35	78c	44c	25c

Grain Alcohol Orange Shellac.
No. 30K2760 Orange Shellac.

1 Gallon	½ Gallon	Quart	Pint
$1.90	$1.00	55c	30c

Grain Alcohol White Shellac.
No. 30K2762 White Shellac.

1 Gallon	½ Gallon	Quart	Pint
$2.00	$1.10	58c	31c

Seroco Knot Killer.
No. 30K2764 Especially prepared for coating knots and sappy streaks before painting. It will do the work as well as the pure shellac, although very much lower in price.

1 Gallon	½ Gallon	Quart	Pint
$1.50	85c	48c	27c

Seroco Floor Oil.
No. 30K2635 Seroco Floor Oil. A special preparation for floors of residences and stores. A very small quantity applied with a cloth will bring out a rich color; also, it will do away with scrubbing, as floors oiled with Seroco Floor Oil are easily cleaned by simply washing them with soap and water.

Per 1-pint can	$0.20
Per 1-quart can	.30
Per ½-gallon can	.52
Per 1-gallon can	.90
Per 5-gallon jacket can	4.00

Seroco Floor Wax. 25c PER POUND.
No. 30K2636 Seroco Floor Wax. A lasting, brilliant polish can be obtained on floors when using our prepared floor wax. It is perfectly transparent and will not change the color of wood. Dirt and dust will not stick to floors waxed with the Seroco Floor Wax. One pound will cover about 300 square feet. Directions are simple and plainly printed on every can. Put up in 1-pound cans.
Price, per can 25c

30c PER POUND. Dancing Floor Wax.
No. 30K2637 Dancing Floor Wax (powdered). This is the best preparation for dancing floors, easily applied and can be used on new, old or canvas covered floors. Guaranteed not to soil the most delicate fabric. Sprinkle it on the floors and the dancers will do the rest. Put up in 1-pound cans.
Price, per can 30c

25c PER PINT. 15-Minute Floor Finish.
No. 30K2640 A most wonderful finish for floors, interior stairs, etc. It is a compound consisting of wax and other ingredients and applied to the floor in liquid form with a cloth. Floors may be finished in fifteen minutes and immediately used after applied. The most durable wax finish ever manufactured, superior to floor oil. Brings out the grain of the wood and imparts a rich color. Floors finished with this material can be kept thoroughly clean without scrubbing, as all dust and dirt is readily removed with an ordinary broom or floor brush. Highly recommended for schools, colleges, stores, public halls, churches, as well as residences. The scrubbing expense of large schools, colleges, etc., is enormous. We guarantee that this expense can be reduced 75 per cent by using our 15-Minute Floor Finish. Please send us a trial order. Money refunded if not as represented. One quart will finish 150 square feet of surface.

Per pint can	$0.25
Per 1-quart can	.40
Per 1-gallon can	1.30
Per 5-gallon can	6.00
Per 10-gallon can	11.00

WHITEWASHING MACHINE, FIRE EXTINGUISHER, SPRAYING MACHINE ALL IN ONE

CAN YOU AFFORD TO BE WITHOUT ONE OF THESE MACHINES? DO YOU KNOW THE DIFFERENT USES THIS MACHINE CAN BE PUT TO?

$7.65

THIS MACHINE was originally made for whitewashing only, where it has derived its name, "Whitewashing Machine," but we have found that it can be put to a dozen different uses. First, it may be used for whitewashing chicken houses, barns, sheds, warehouses, basements, factories, etc., and do the work better and more thorough than with brushes, simply because it forces the whitewash into crevices and corners, where the disease germs lodge, that cannot be reached with brushes; also when whitewashing chicken houses infected with chicken lice the work can be done from a door or window, doing away with the inconvenience of allowing yourself to be covered from head to foot with chicken lice and dirt. Second, as a fire extinguisher it cannot be excelled because the machine without any exertion will throw a fine stream thirty feet; also used for washing buggies, outside windows, porches, sidewalks, outside walls of buildings, etc., sprinkling flowers, spraying fruit trees and plants, washing the feet of horses and cattle. Occupies but very little space as legs can be removed instantly and machine conveniently carried on cars, buggies, etc. Always ready, nothing to take apart nor attach, a bucket of water and you are ready to throw a thirty-foot stream.

AFTER YOU HAVE GIVEN THIS MACHINE A TRIAL
you would not take a hundred dollars for it if another could not be secured. Send us your order now for one of these machines, use it for several days or a week, if after that time you are not satisfied with your purchase and find that you can get along without the machine, pack it up and return to us and we will cheerfully refund your money including freight charges. Equipment consists of spray pipe with ⅛-inch shut-off cock and spray nozzle, extra nozzle for straight-stream work, follower wrench and 5 feet of ⅜-inch discharge hose.

No. 30K2382 Whitewashing and Spraying Machine, complete. Price...............**$7.65**

Shipping weight, 40 pounds; net weight, 30 pounds.

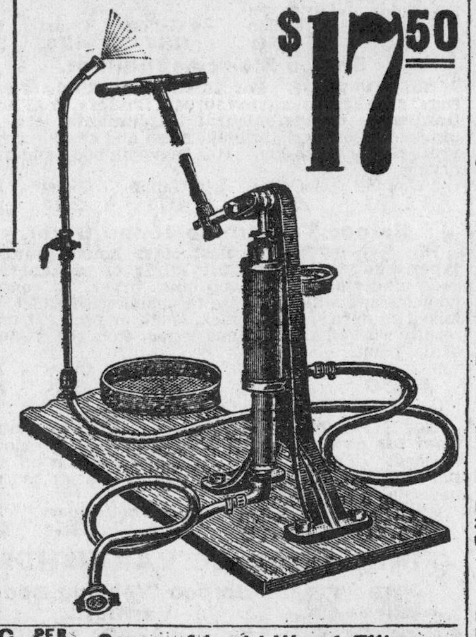

OUR JUMBO WHITEWASHING AND SPRAYING MACHINE

$17.50

THIS MACHINE is especially suitable for large factories, fruit farms, nurserymen and large stock farms. For whitewashing, its capacity is equal to work of fifteen men with brushes. It is the most powerful sprayer made, constructed of the very best material and guaranteed to do better and more work than any $25.00 or $30.00 machine on the market. Equipment consists of spray pipe complete with ¼-inch cock and spray nozzle, one extra spray tip, 200-pound pressure gauge, special galvanized sieve, follower wrench, one length of 1-inch suction hose and ten feet of ½-inch special high pressure discharge hose.

No. 30K2384 Jumbo Whitewashing and Spraying Machine, complete. Price.........**$17.50**

12c PER POUND. Seroco Crevice Filler.

No. 30K2660 Seroco Filler for cracks in floors. A specially prepared, elastic, non-shrinkable compound for filling cracks in floors or furniture before applying paint or varnish; also adapted for smoothing rough surfaces.

Per 1-pound can.........12c
Per 5-pound can.........55c

8c PER POUND. Seroco Paste Wood Filler.

All open grained hardwood, such as oak, ash, etc., must be filled in order to produce a perfect varnish finish. This filler is the best made, easily applied and dries very hard. Made in two shades, light oak and dark oak.

No. 30K2661 Light Oak
No. 30K2662 Dark Oak
Per 1-pound can.......$0.08
Per 5-pound can........ .35
Per 25-pound can....... 1.50

18c PER PINT. Seroco Liquid Wood Filler.

No. 30K2664 For filling or first coating all kinds of close grained, natural woods, such as pine, poplar, etc., that have not been previously finished. It thoroughly seals up the wood pores and effectually prevents suction or the absorption of moisture. This material is transparent and does not need to be rubbed off or sandpapered before applying the varnish coats. It does not sink away like varnish, but dries on the surface, thus equaling, for work of this nature, two coats of varnish. A coat or two of varnish applied over this material produces a really remarkable finish.

5 Gallons	1 Gallon	½ Gallon	Quart	Pint
$5.15	$1.10	62c	33c	18c

NO SUCH PRICE REDUCTIONS have ever been made by any firm or individual as we have made in the pages of this Big Catalogue on the HIGHEST GRADE MERCHANDISE.

Success Linoleum and Floor Oilcloth Finish.

No. 30K2642 Why allow your linoleum or floor oilcloth to wear away when it can be preserved for a few cents and give you a better finish than the original finish of the linoleum or floor oilcloth. This material puts a coating on the linoleum and dries hard but remains elastic like the linoleum or oilcloth itself, therefore it will not crack or check. Linoleum is today one of the most popular of all floor coverings, it's most objectionable feature has been the continual unevenness of wear, causing color to become dull and pattern to be lost, leaving a decidedly spotted effect in the linoleum. By using Success Linoleum Finish the linoleum or oilcloth will retain all its original brightness and luster, thus making the life of linoleum much longer. Hot or cold water does not affect it. A quart can costing 68 cents and a few minutes of your time will save you ten times this amount. One coat will do the work, applied in the evening it will be dry, ready to walk on, in the morning. One quart will cover a square 12x15 feet.

Per 1 pint can.....................36c
Per 1 quart can...................68c

Steel Wool and Shavings.

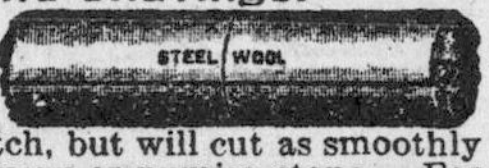

No. 30K2670 Steel Wool is a mass of fine fibers of steel, resembling curled hair, which, while sharp, does not scratch, but will cut as smoothly as the finest sandpaper, emery or pumice stone. For many purposes it is superior to sandpaper, etc. Used for rubbing down fillers and varnishes; in fact, it takes the place of sandpaper or pumice stone and will be found a much better article to use. Steel shavings is a coarse grade and is used for removing rust from iron preparatory to painting; also for cleaning floors or any surface of old varnish.

No. 0.   Very fine, per pound................45c
No. 1.   Fine, per pound...................35c
No. 3.   Fine, per pound...................30c
Steel Shavings.   Per pound..............25c

Steel Wool for Household Use.

No. 30K2671 For housekeepers and amateur wood finishers. Better than sandpaper for rubbing down varnish, removing old paint, cleaning hardwood floors and a hundred other uses. For the housekeeper it is unexcelled for cleaning pots and pans, removes burnt matter from pans instantly; also used for removing rust, cleaning sinks, bath tubs, stoves, removing paint or varnish from windows, etc.

No. 1 For rubbing down varnish and fine work. Per package......................10c
No. 3 For household and general use. Per package.......................10c
Fine Shavings for removing old paint and other coarse work. Per package..........10c
Package contains about 3 ounces.

15c Pumice Stone Bricks.

No. 30K2672 Pumice Stone Bricks are used by the painter and varnisher for rubbing down varnished surfaces. These bricks are now used by the thousands for scouring stone window sills, steps and sidewalks. Weight, about 1¾ pounds.
Price, per dozen $1.70; each..........15c

Powdered Pumice Stone.

No. 30K2673 Finest Imported Powdered Pumice Stone. Price, per pound.........4c
100-pound drums, per pound..........2¾c

English Rotten Stone.

No. 30K2676 Used for polishing varnished surfaces, after rubbing down with pumice stone and water or oil. The powdered is most generally used. Powdered, per pound..............6c
Selected Lump, per pound...........12c

Rubbing Oil.

No. 30K2678 Used with powdered pumice stone and rotten stone for rubbing down varnished surfaces. Rubbing felt is recommended, but many furniture finishers use the common burlap.

Per 1-pint can...........................8c
Per 1-quart can........................13c
Per 1-gallon can.......................35c
50-gallon barrel, per gallon..........19c

Varnish and Paint Remover.

No. 30K2770 Guaranteed to remove paints, varnish or oil from wood, iron or bath tubs without damage to the wood, veneer, glue or filler. Does not injure the hands of the operator in any way

1 Gallon	Quart	Pint
$1.88	53c	30c

What a Customer Says After 5 Years.

Monson, Mass.
Sears, Roebuck & Co., Chicago.
Gentlemen:—I painted my house with your paint (Seroco) five years ago, and that is why you get this new order. Seroco is good enough for me.
Respectfully,
C. A. SWEET.

22c PER PINT. Seroco Furniture Polish.

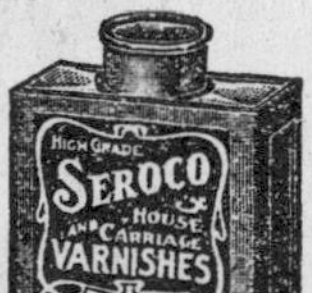

No. 30K2772 Adapted for use on old as well as on new furniture. It has the advantage over other polishes of not gumming up in the corners, and therefore will not collect dust or dirt. It is perfectly harmless and will not affect the varnish in any way. It can be used as well on ordinary furniture as on the finest piano, organ, and other highly finished work. This is, without question, the finest and safest polish on the market.

Per 1-pint can $0.22
Per 1-quart can .... .40
Per 1-gallon can 1.50

Preserver for Leather Furniture and Cushions.

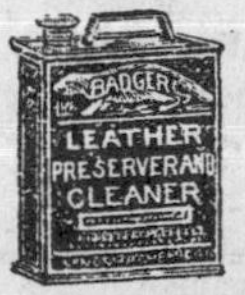

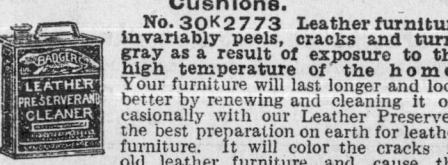

No. 30K2773 Leather furniture invariably peels, cracks and turns gray as a result of exposure to the high temperature of the home. Your furniture will last longer and look better by renewing and cleaning it occasionally with our Leather Preserver, the best preparation on earth for leather furniture. It will color the cracks in old leather furniture and cause the leather to assume its natural color. Automobile cushions are soon ruined as a result of exposure to the rain and weather and then the hot rays of sun, which draws all life out of the leather. Our Leather Preserver is guaranteed to produce new life in leather, clean and soften it, color the cracks and make it look like new. Dark olive for black and olive colors. Maroon for all red leathers. State color wanted.

Per ½-pint can $0.35
Per 1-pint can .... .48
Per 1-quart can .... .82

9c Seroco Liquid Metal Polish.

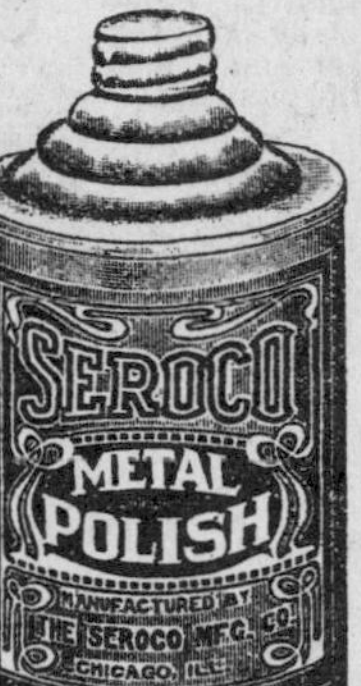

No. 30K2776 For polishing brass, zinc, tin, nickel, copper or silver. Can be used on anything made of metal, and is especially recommended for outdoor metal work, such as brass and zinc signs, show cases, railings, metal parts of harness, etc. Warranted not to injure the finest metals. No other polish will give the brilliant and lasting luster obtained when using Seroco Liquid Metal Polish.

Per ½-pint can 9c
Per 1-pint can 17c
Per 1-quart can 28c

12c Electric Wall Paper Cleaner.

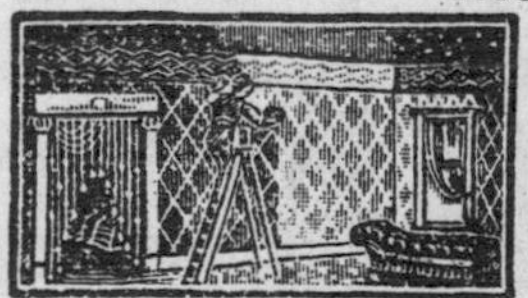

No. 30K2780 This wall paper cleaner is in dry powder form and can instantly be prepared for use by mixing the powder with cold water. One pound of the powder will make two pounds of prepared cleaner. The easiest working and best wall paper cleaner made. It will do the work better than any other. Used by the best paperhangers throughout the country.

Per 1-pound package 12c

9c Seroco Wall Paper Cleaner.

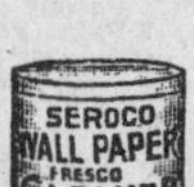

No. 30K2782 Put up in a tin box, prepared ready for use; no mixing required. No experience necessary; anyone can clean wall paper with the Seroco Wall Paper Cleaner. It will remove smoke and dust from wall paper, window shades and fresco and bring out the original color. One pound can is sufficient for one room.

Price, per 1-pound can 9c

Seroco Patent Prepared Paste Flour.

Only Boiling Necessary.

No. 30K2786 Warranted never to sour and to make the strongest and most adhesive paste. One pound will make three gallons of ready to use paste or one gallon of solid paste. No chemicals or preservatives required.

Per 1-pound package $0.07
Per 25-pound drum 1.40
Per 50-pound drum 2.50

20c PER PACKAGE. Seroco Perfect Cold Water Dry Paste.

NO SMELL. NO VERMIN. NO WASTE.

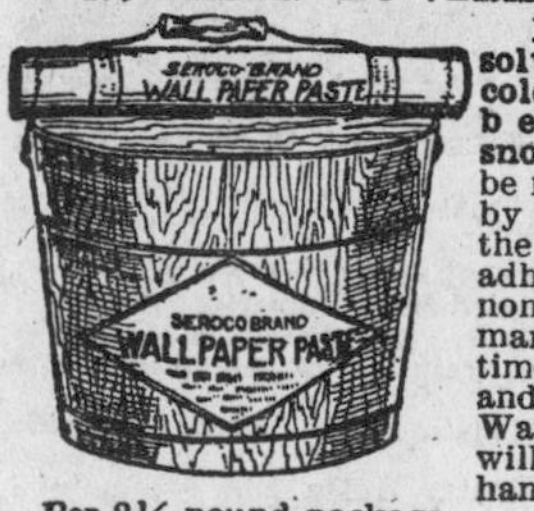

No. 30K2788 Dissolves immediately in cold water. Makes the best transparent and snow white paste. Can be made to any consistency by adding more or less of the dry paste. It is very adhesive and the most economical dry paste on the market. Convenient, saves time, is mixed at the job and ready for immediate use. Warranted chemically pure, will never sour, and will hang any kind of wall paper.

Per 2½-pound package $0.20
Per 25-pound pail 1.75
Per 100-pound drum 6.00

One 2½-pound package will make a large pail of ready to use paste.

11c PER PACKAGE. Dry Paste for Household Use.

No. 30K2789 Dissolves instantly in cold water. Makes a beautiful milk white paste; mends and sticks anything made of paper. One pound package will make 1 gallon of ready to use paste, but any quantity can be made as wanted.

Per 1 pound package $0.11
Per dozen packages 1.30

Seroco Prepared Paperhangers' Sizing.

DISSOLVES INSTANTLY IN COLD WATER.

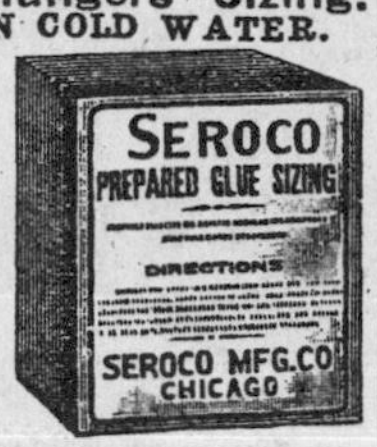

No. 30K2790 Unequaled for sizing walls which have been painted or varnished, or on new or rough walls. Painted walls will not take paste before being sized, new walls are very porous and absorb the paste, resulting in the wall paper becoming loose. With this preparation anyone can hang wall paper on new or painted or varnished walls with the assurance that the wall paper will stick. One pound will make 1 gallon of size ready for use.

Per 2-pound package $0.20
Per 5-pound package .... .45
Per 50-pound drum 4.00

PAPERHANGERS' TOOLS.

Paperhangers' Seam and Smoothing Rollers.

Our Seam Rollers are guaranteed the very best and with ordinary care will last a lifetime. A seam roller is necessary to do good work, and as our prices are very low, it will pay you to include a roller with your order for wall paper.

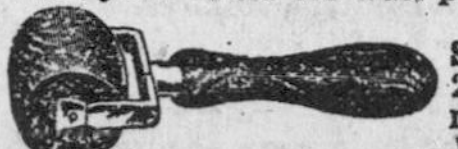

No. 30K2800 Large Seam Roller, 1¾ inches wide, 2 inches in diameter. Maple roller, polished handle. Wt., 4 ounces. Price... 13c

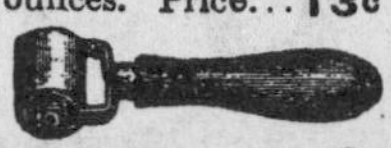

No. 30K2802 Seam Roller, 1¼ inches wide, flat face, rubber covered. Shipping weight, 5 ounces.
Price 9c

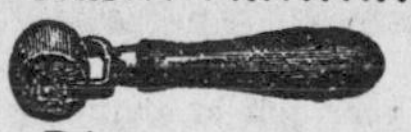

No. 30K2804 Seam Roller, 1 inch wide, oval face, maple roller, as illustrated. Shipping weight, 4 ounces.
Price 9c

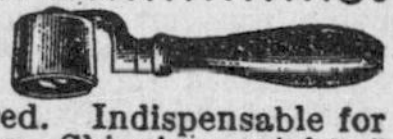

No. 30K2806 Side Arm Seam Roller, bevel face, celluloid covered, 1 inch wide. The handiest roller manufactured. Indispensable for ceilings, door casings and frames. Shipping weight, 5 ounces. Price 26c

Smoothing Roller.

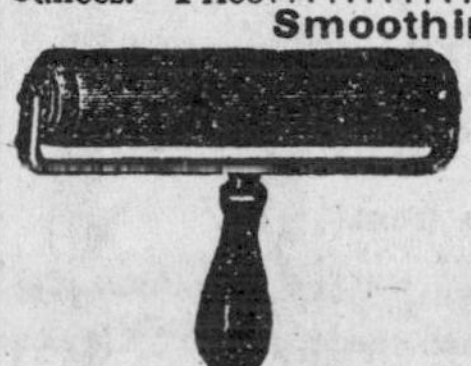

No. 30K2808 Smoothing Roller, 8 inches wide, felt covered. The most satisfactory smoothing roller made. Shipping weight, 12 oz. Price... 48c

No. 30K2810 Smoothing Roller, same as above, but without covering; maple roller. Shipping weight, 12 oz. Price... 32c

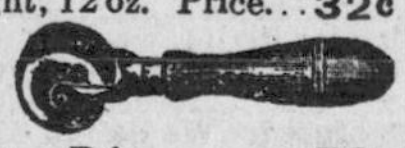

No. 30K2812 The Zylonite Ivory Seam Roller, oval face. For the professional paperhanger; will never wear out. Shipping weight, 7 ounces. Price 50c

Wheel Knives, Base Trimmers, Etc.

We deal direct with the manufacturer of paperhangers' tools. Should a blade or other parts break, caused by any defect, we will cheerfully replace the tool absolutely free of charge.

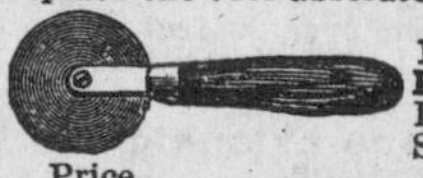

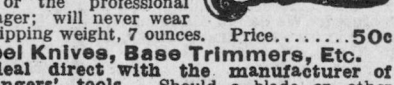

No. 30K2820 Wheel Knife for Trimming Wall Paper. Shoulder on both sides. Blade 2 inches in diameter. Shipping weight, 3 ounces.
Price 20c

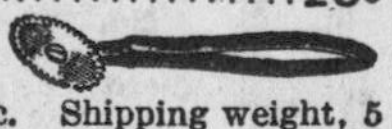

No. 30K2822 Base Trimmer. Serrated edge, iron handle. A handy tool for trimming around casings, frames, etc. Shipping weight, 5 ounces. Price 22c

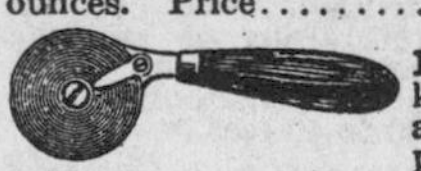

No. 30K2824 Wheel Knife, with patent device for keeping the paste off the blade; always clean and sharp. Shipping weight, 5 ounces.
Price 40c

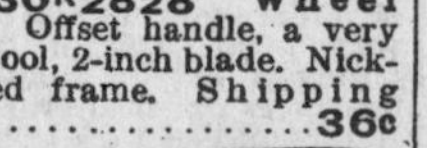

No. 30K2826 Combination Base Trimmer and Paper Knife. No paperhanger should be without this handy tool. Shipping weight, 5 ounces.
Price 35c

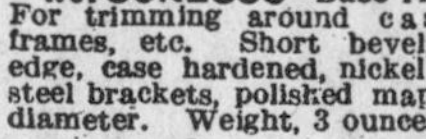

No. 30K2828 Wheel Knife. Offset handle, a very handy tool, 2-inch blade. Nickel plated frame. Shipping weight, 6 ounces. Price 36c

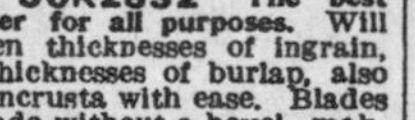

No. 30K2830 Base Trimmer. For trimming around casings, frames, etc. Short bevel, plaid edge, case hardened, nickel plated steel brackets, polished maple handles. Blade, 1⅜ inches in diameter. Weight, 3 ounces. Price 25c

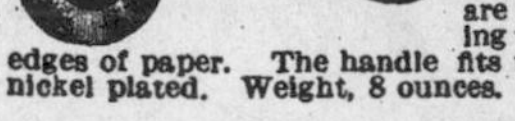

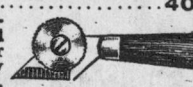

No. 30K2832 The best trimmer for all purposes. Will cut ten thicknesses of ingrain, four thicknesses of burlap, also cuts lincrusta with ease. Blades are made without a bevel, making a clean cut without crushing edges of paper. The handle fits the hand perfectly. Highly nickel plated. Weight, 8 ounces. Price 63c

Paperhangers' Shears.

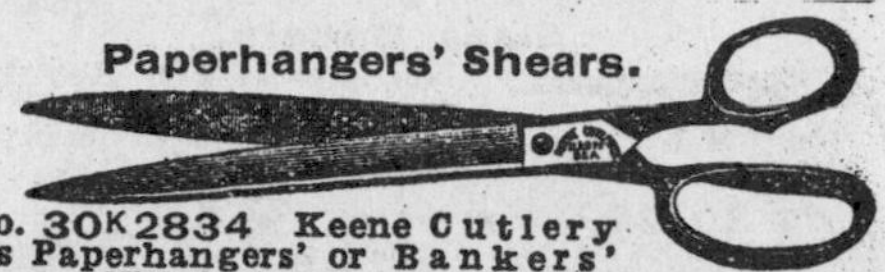

No. 30K2834 Keene Cutlery Co.'s Paperhangers' or Bankers' Shears. Nickel plated steel laid blades and enameled handles. Fully warranted. Shipping weight, 10 to 14 ounces.

Size, inches	10	12	14	16
Length of cut, inches	5¾	7	8⅛	10
Price	65c	80c	$1.05	$1.35

Folding Paste Table.

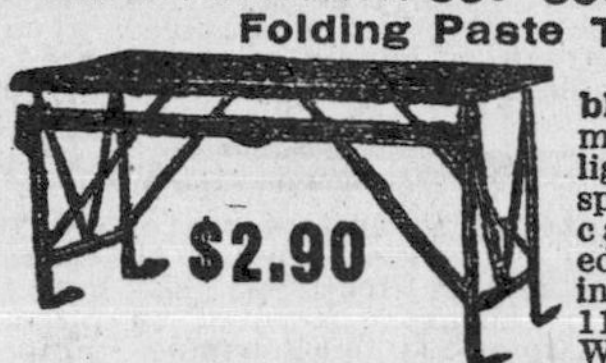

Folding Paste Table. The best on the market. Strong and light in weight, with space and hooks for carrying straight edge and tools. 22 inches wide, open; 11 inches, closed. Weight, 20 to 23 lbs.

No. 30K2840 Price, 7 feet long $2.90
No. 30K2841 Price, 8 feet long 3.10

Improved Paste Boards.

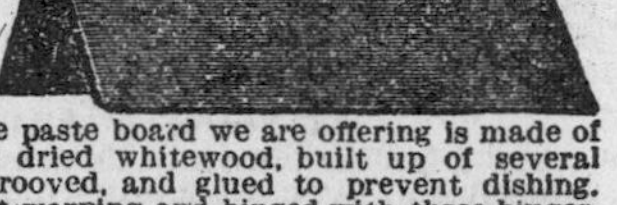

We have been compelled in the past to handle the cheap ⅜-inch lumber paste board, owing to competition, but we have come to the conclusion that it is a dear board at any price. The paste board we are offering is made of ½-inch thick, clear, air dried whitewood, built up of several boards, tongued and grooved, and glued to prevent dishing. Four battens to prevent warping and hinged with three hinges. A better board cannot be made. 23 inches wide, open; 11½ inches wide, closed. Weight, about 14 pounds.

No. 30K2844 Price, 7 feet long, plain $1.20
No. 30K2845 Price, 7 feet long, with 4-inch strip. Weight, about 16 pounds $1.43

$1.60 Folding Box Paste Board.

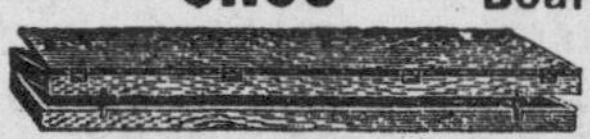

No. 30K2846 The handiest paste board made. Folds into space 8 inches wide by 2 inches deep and will hold straight edge, trestles and tools, so that the entire outfit can be easily carried. Notches hold boards rigid on trestles. 24 inches wide when opened. Weight about 15 pounds.
Price, 7 feet long $1.60

98c Paperhangers' Folding Trestle.

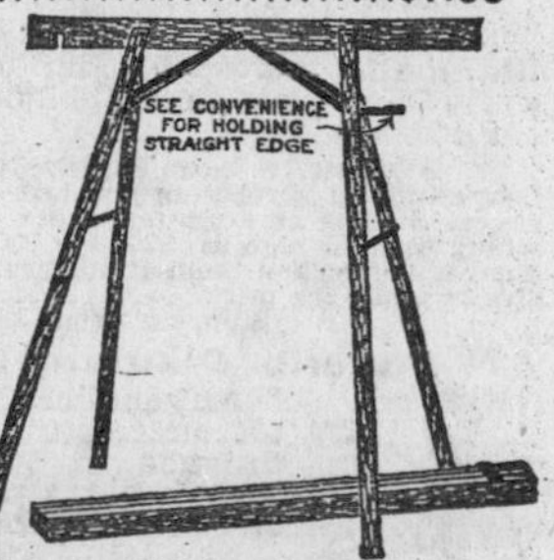

No. 30K2849 This trestle is an improvement over the old style, being very much stronger. Made of select material and will stand more rough usage than any other. Quickly set up, also folded. Weight, 4 pounds. Price, per pair 98c

Ridgely's Newest Trimmer.

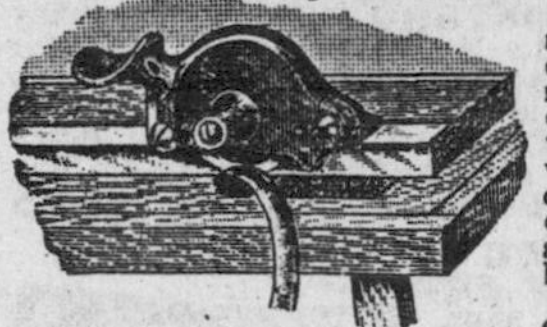

Model "B" Ideal Trimmer. This new trimmer is designed for a whole hand rest, therefore the leverage obtained is enormous and will cut anything in the way of paper or burlap for decorations. The straight edge furnished with the above trimmer is five-piece, brass bound edge.

No. 30K2850 6-foot outfit complete.
Price $4.00
No. 30K2851 7-foot outfit complete. Price 4.25
No. 30K2852 8-foot outfit complete. Price 4.50

The Simplex Trimmer.

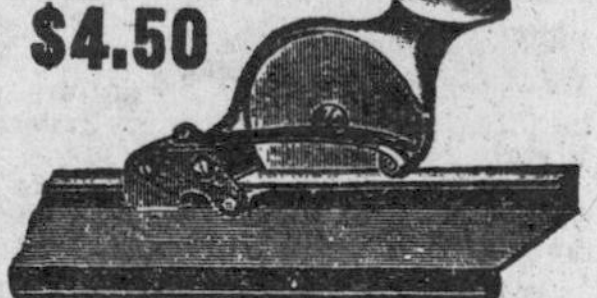

The Simplex All Steel Roller Bearing Trimmer, as shown in the accompanying illustration, is the latest achievement in wall paper trimmers. The Simplex is the simplest and most serviceable trimmer on the market; being an all roller bearing tool, reduces the friction to the minimum, enabling the operator to manipulate it back and forth on the straight edge without effort. The most important feature is the all steel straight edge. It is not affected by climatic conditions, therefore, will always be true and straight. Finished in white nickel on copper plating. Will not rust. The trimmer adheres closely to the straight edge under all conditions, and will not drop off, slide or shake off, remaining always where it is left or set, regardless of the position of the straight edge, and yet can be instantly removed when desired. Trimmers are highly polished and nickel plated. Weight of straight edge, about 6 pounds.

No. 30K2854 Simplex Outfit, consists of trimmer, zinc and steel straight edge, 7-foot. Price $4.50

Ridgely's Five-Piece Straight Edge.

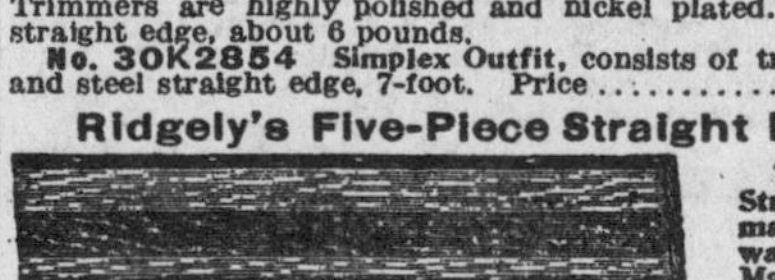

The best Straight Edge made, cannot warp or twist. Made of the best seasoned wood and with proper care will remain true and last a lifetime. Bound on both sides with angle and channel brass. This is the regular Ridgely Model "B" Trimmer Straight Edge, but can be used for knife work. The best all around straight edge.

No. 30K2860 Price, 7 ft. long. Weight, 3½ lbs. $2.00
No. 30K2861 Price, 8 ft. long. Weight, 4 lbs. 2.25

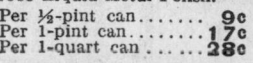

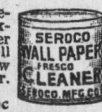

Glass Cutters.

No. 30K2870 Revolving Steel Wheel Glass Cutter, metal handle, polished and bronzed, extra quality cutting wheel. Shipping weight, 3 ounces. Price....3c

No. 30K2872 Revolving Steel Wheel Glass Cutter, bronzed, with knife sharpener, corkscrew and can opener combined. Shipping weight, 4 ounces. Price....4c

No. 30K2874 Glass Cutter. Damascus Coal Carbon Disc Wheel Glass Cutter. The best revolving wheel glass cutter made. A smooth cut guaranteed when using this cutter. Rosewood handle, solid steel head. Shipping weight, 3 ounces. Price....12c

No. 30K2876 Goodell's Improved Glass Cutter with turret head. The cutters are carefully hardened and ground by special process. Polished and nickel plated frame; turret head, six cutter wheels, which can be instantly revolved to place. Nickel plated ferrule, rosewood finish handle. Shipping weight, 3 ounces. Price....18c

No. 30K2878 Magazine Glass Cutters. Six extra wheels are stored in the upper end of handles, absolutely secure and always ready when needed. You get the equal of seven individual glass cutters for the price of one. The wheels are the best coal carbon. Each wheel guaranteed to cut 500 feet glass. Weight, 3 ounces. Price....20c

Glaziers' Diamonds.

Our Glaziers' Diamonds are made of the best quality genuine diamonds. The mountings are made in the very best possible manner, highly finished and heavily nickel plated. We guarantee our diamonds to reset not less than four times and give good satisfaction, provided they are sent to us to reset. NEVER CUT TWICE IN THE SAME PLACE.

No. 30K2880 The Standard Keyed Diamond, for single thick glass. A good diamond for ordinary use. Shipping weight, 4 ounces. Price....$2.95

No. 30K2882 Superior Keyed Diamond. A very fine diamond for general use. Will cut double strength glass. Shipping weight, 4 ounces. Price....$4.35

No. 30K2884 Superior Keyed Plate Glass Diamond. A very superior cutter for general use, and will cut plate glass. Shipping weight, 5 ounces. Price....$9.00

No. 30K2886 Extra Superior Keyed Plate Glass Diamond. Cuts any kind of rough or polished plate glass. Dealers have always charged an exorbitant profit on this class of diamond, selling them as high as $20.00. By contracting for a large number and selling them at our usual one small profit we are able to make the price....$10.95
Shipping weight, 5 ounces.

Superior Diamond Glass Cutter.

Anyone can cut glass with this tool successfully. Genuine diamond, finished in the best manner and metal parts nickel plated. Never cut twice in the same place.

No. 30K2888 Sure cut. Will cut single strength glass. Price....$2.80

No. 30K2890 Sure cut, superior diamond. A very fine diamond for general use. Will cut double strength glass. Price....$3.75

No. 30K2892 Sure cut, extra superior diamond. Will cut anything excepting plate glass. Price....$4.85

Hacking Knives.

No. 30K2900 For digging old putty from sash. Made of the best material, with heavy steel blade. Weight, 5 ounces. Price....30c

Putty Knives.

No. 30K2904 Putty Knife, with stiff blade, square point. Weight, 3 ounces. Price....5c

No. 30K2908 Putty Knife, with stiff blade, square point, with cocobolo handle, lap bolster, strongly riveted. A superior tool. Weight, 4 ounces. Price....12c

No. 30K2910 Putty Knife, with spring blade, square point, cocobolo handle, lap bolster. Strongly riveted. Weight, 4 ounces. Price....12c

No. 30K2915 Glaziers' Putty Knife. Extra heavy crucible steel blade, solid redwood handle, brass ferrule. Width of blade, 1⅛ inches; length, 3¾ inches. None better made in this country. Weight, 4 ounces. Price....18c

Special Putty Knives.

The following line of putty knives are the best in the world and will last a lifetime. They are made in Sheffield, England. Blades, bolsters and tangs are hand forged from one piece of highest grade steel. Brass ferrules, solid ebony handles.

No. 30K2916 Stiff; length of blade, 4¼ inches. Weight, 5 ounces. Price....25c

No. 30K2918 Elastic; length of blade, 4¼ inches. Weight, 5 ounces. Price....25c

No. 30K2920 Special Glaziers' Putty Knife, stiff, blade, 3¾ inches. Weight, 5 ounces. Price....25c

Scraping Knives.

No. 30K2924 Scraping Knife. Best steel blade, cocobolo handle, lap bolster. Weight, 5 to 7 ounces each.

| Width of blade, inches | 2½ | 3 | 3½ | 4 |
| Price | 30c | 35c | 43c | 50c |

No. 30K2926 Wall Scraping Knife, stiff blade, 3-inch square point, beechwood handle. Shipping weight, 7 ounces. Price....8c

16c Socket or Pole Scraper.

No. 30K2927 Socket or Pole Scraper. Polished steel spring blade, 4 inches wide, beveled edges, malleable iron screw sockets. Without pole. Price....16c

Spatula or Painters' Palette Knife.

No. 30K2928 Spatula or Painters' Palette Knife, lap bolster, cocoa handle.

| Length of blade, inches | 4 | 6 | 8 | 10 |
| Price, each | 16c | 22c | 35c | 58c |

Paperhangers' Knives.

No. 30K2934 Paperhangers' Square Point Knife, extra quality steel, wood handle. Shipping weight, 3 ounces. Price....12c

No. 30K2936 Paperhangers' Round Point Butting Knife, best of steel; blade, 3 inches long. Weight, 3 ounces. Price....12c

Paint Pot Hooks.

No. 30K2940 A very convenient article when painting from ladders. Price, per dozen, 32c; each....3c

Iron Paint Paddle.

PAINT PADDLE

No. 30K2942 Many a poor job of painting can be traced directly to the paint pot, in that the paint was not properly stirred. This paint paddle will mix the paint thoroughly in less time than can be done with a wood paddle; furthermore, a wood paddle will float and be always in the way of the brush. Made of malleable iron, strong and durable. Price, each....10c

13c PER FOOT. Extension Ladders.

Extension Ladders are always shipped direct from our Chicago factory. Weight, about 2½ pounds per foot.

No. 30K2944 Made from selected and seasoned Norway pine and hickory rungs. Our new double roller, single piece top iron is much stronger than the angle rollers and strengthens the ladder in its weakest place. Our hooks are also the best. This is the best extension ladder manufactured. We do not allow for lap. Made in two sections. Length, 20 to 40 feet.
Price, per foot....13c
If made in three sections, per foot....14c

Owing to the prohibitive freight rates, orders for ladders over 20 feet in one section will not be accepted. Ladders over 40 feet in length must be ordered in three sections.

17c PER FOOT. Rope Extension Ladder.

No. 30K2946 Top section raised and lowered by rope and pulley attachment, easily handled. Has new roller iron, automatic locking hooks, and made same as our regular extension. We put our crank attachment for raising or lowering section on all these ladders and crank and rope are furnished. Made only in two sections. Length, 20 to 40 feet.
Price, per foot....17c

75c Improved Stepladders.

No. 30K2948 Made of clear genuine Norway pine. One of the strongest ladders made; has bolts under alternate steps and steel leg spreaders. Every ladder is fitted with a handy pail shelf which can be folded up out of the way when not in use. Weight, 2½ pounds per foot.

Height	Price
5 feet	$0.75
6 feet	.88
8 feet	1.16

90c Painters' Trestles or Stepladders.

No. 30K2949 Made of clear selected Norway pine, very light in weight, yet strong. Braces so arranged that plank can be put on either step. Steps are braced with irons in front and back. Weight, 2½ pounds per foot.

	Price
5 feet	$0.90
6 feet	1.08
8 feet	1.44
10 feet	1.80

SPECIAL OUTFITS FOR PAINTING.

For the convenience of our customers who may be unable to make a proper selection of paint brushes for outside house or barn painting, we have made up several outfits consisting of the necessary brushes required and other accessories. These outfits have been carefully selected and we suggest that you include one of these outfits with your order for paint.

Paint Brush Outfit No. 30K2950. This assortment consists of good, serviceable brushes and is especially adapted for small jobs of painting. This outfit includes the following:
1 Fine White Bristle Sash Tool No. 4.
1 Fine White Bristle Sash Tool No. 6.
1 Round Paint Brush, size, 4-0.
1 Flat Chinese Bristle Paint Brush, 4 inches wide.
1 Steel Blade Putty Knife.
4 Pounds Strictly Pure Putty.
No. 30K2950 Price, for complete outfit....70c

$1.45 Paint Brush Outfit No. 30K2952.

This assortment consists of extra good quality brushes and first class work can be done with these tools. This outfit includes the following:
1 Chinese Bristle Chiseled Sash Tool No. 4.
1 Chinese Bristle Chiseled Sash Tool No. 6.
1 Pure Russian Bristle Round Point Brush, size 3-0.
1 Flat Extra Chinese Bristle Paint Brush, 4 inches wide.
1 High Grade Polished Steel Blade Putty Knife.
1 Patent Paint Paddle.
1 Paint Pot Hook.
4 Pounds Strictly Pure Putty.
No. 30K2952 Price, for complete outfit....$1.45

$3.15 Paint Brush Outfit No. 30K2954.

This assortment has been especially selected for the professional painter and for large jobs where strictly high grade brushes are necessary. These brushes are made from the best stock and were you to purchase them singly from a dealer the outfit would cost at least double our price. This outfit includes the following:
1 Chinese Bristle Chiseled Sash Tool No. 6.
1 Chinese Bristle Chiseled Sash Tool No. 8.
1 Round Russian Bristle Paint Brush, size, 4-0.
1 Flat Russian Bristle Paint Brush, extra long bristles, No. 7.
1 Flat Extra Chinese Bristle Paint Brush, 4 in. wide.
1 Painters' Duster.
1 Extra High Grade Putty Knife.
1 Patent Paint Paddle.
2 Paint Pot Hooks.
10 Pounds Strictly Pure Putty.
No. 30K2954 Price, for complete outfit, $3.15

Transfer Graining Paper.

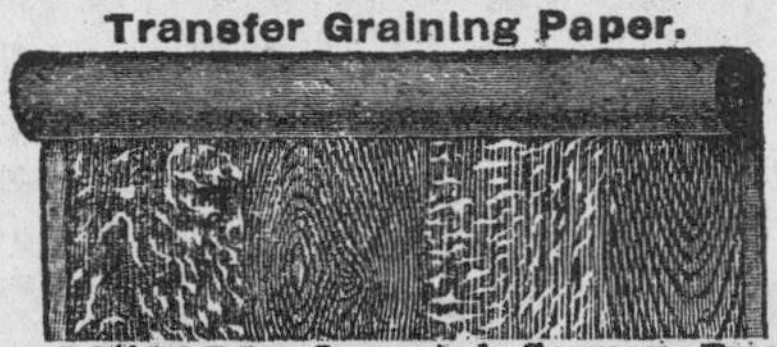

No. 30K2958 Imported German Transfer Graining Paper, will give you a better grained surface than is possible to produce by hand or with any device. It gives you a perfect grain in one-tenth the time it would take when done by hand or with tools. The directions are so simple that the most inexperienced can do perfect graining, the equal of the best handwork of professional grainers. Professional grainers are using the Transfer Graining Paper in preference to handwork because it gives them a finer and more perfect grain in less time. No graining colors to bother with, all that you require are ground color, if necessary a small quantity of boiled linseed oil and your finishing varnish. Ground color is only necessary when it is desired to grain over painted or grained surfaces, or very knotty wood. A single roll contains 9 yards, 26 inches wide. Two single rolls or one double roll is sufficient to grain the doors and casings of a 6-room house, as several impressions may be taken from one strip. Furnished in light, medium and dark oak. State color wanted.

No. 3 Quarter sawed and heart oak, like illustration.
No. 9 Straight oak, heavy heart grain and lines.
No. 20 Straight oak, small heart grain and lines.
Price, per single roll of 9 yards **35c**
When ordering, mention catalogue number and number of pattern.

No. 30K2697 Ground color.

Gallon	Quart	Pint	½ Pint
$1.90	57c	32c	20c

Handy Household Grainer.

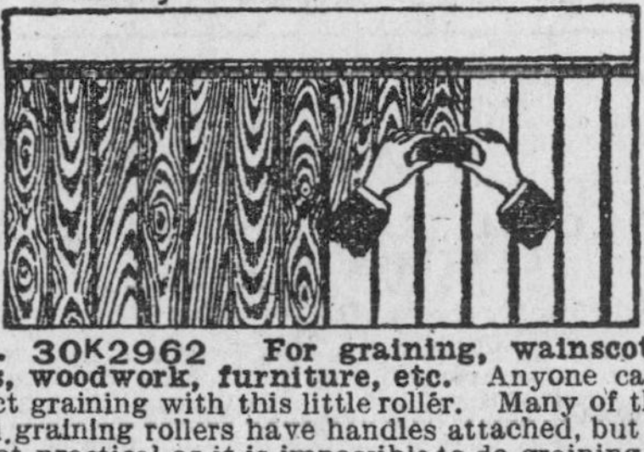

No. 30K2962 For graining, wainscoting, floors, woodwork, furniture, etc. Anyone can do perfect graining with this little roller. Many of the so called graining rollers have handles attached, but they are not practical as it is impossible to do graining with them since you cannot control the roller with one hand and adapt it to uneven surfaces. Include one of these rollers in your order, if you do not find it the most practical graining tool on the market, return it and we will promptly refund your money. Weight, 4 ounces.
Price **38c**

Extra Oak Graining Rollers.

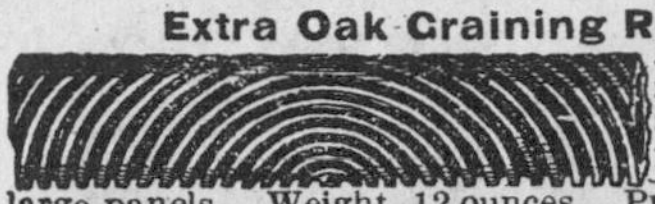

No. 30K2960 Extra Graining Roller, 8 inches wide, for graining large panels. Weight, 12 ounces. Price **75c**

Improved Davis Wood Grainers.

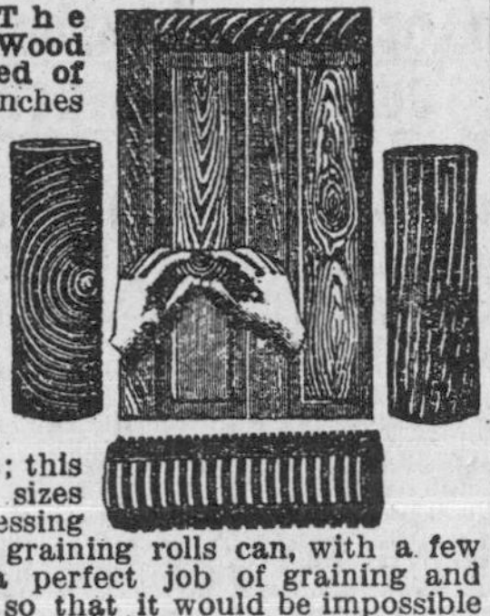

No. 30K2964 The Improved Davis Wood Grainers are composed of three rubber rolls, 5 inches in length. With the corrugated roll any known growth of wood can be imitated. Quarter sawed oak grain is produced with roll No. 2, the one with the irregular grooves. Roll No. 3 is used in place of combs for straight line work in connection with the other two rolls; this roll is made with three sizes of combs. Anyone possessing a set of our improved graining rolls can, with a few minutes' practice, do a perfect job of graining and natural wood imitated so that it would be impossible to distinguish the natural grain of any wood from the grain made by our improved wood grainers. Complete instructions packed with every set. Weight, 14 ounces.
Price, per set of three rolls .. **$1.20**

Steel Grainers.

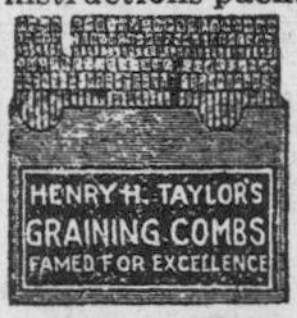

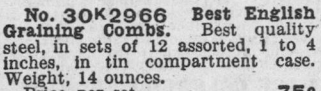

No. 30K2966 Best English Graining Combs. Best quality steel, in sets of 12 assorted, 1 to 4 inches, in tin compartment case. Weight, 14 ounces.
Price, per set **75c**

Check Graining Rollers.

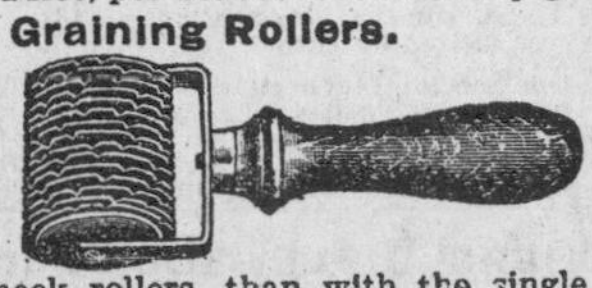

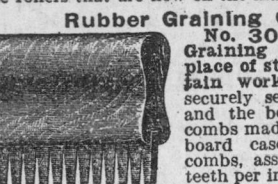

No. 30K2968 Double Line Check Graining Rollers. For producing the oak overgrain. A truer representation is obtained with these double line check rollers than with the single line rollers that are now on the market. Price... **55c**

Rubber Graining Combs.

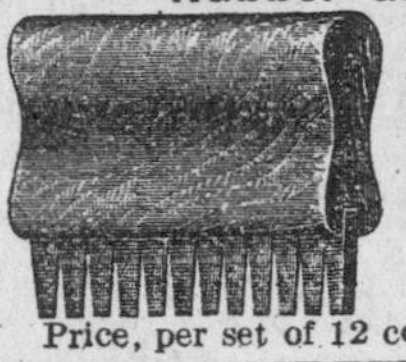

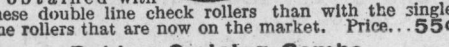

No. 30K2975 Rubber Graining Combs, used in place of steel combs for certain work. The rubber is securely set in wood handles, and the best rubber graining combs made. Packed in cardboard cases, in sets of 12 combs, assorted 6, 9, and 12 teeth per inch.
Price, per set of 12 combs **75c**

Varnish Brushes.

For fine carriage and piano work, No. 30K3026 is recommended, but for varnishing woodwork, wagons and implements any of the other brushes will give excellent satisfaction. Where a little varnishing is to be done a cheap brush will answer, but No. 30K3028 or No. 30K3036 are recommended where particular work is required.

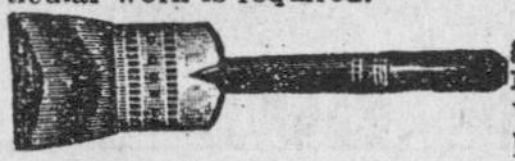

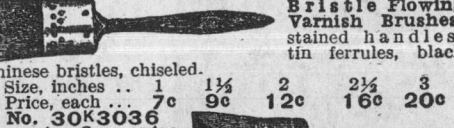

No. 30K3026 Badger Hair Flowing Varnish Brushes, for fine varnishing, carriages, pianos, etc. Single thick, chiseled, tin ferrules.

Size, inches	1	1½	2	2½	3
Price, each	20c	30c	40c	55c	60c

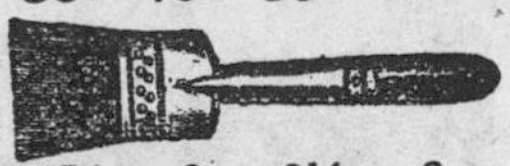

No. 30K3028 Fitch Flowing Varnish Brushes, superfine quality, single thick. Tin ferrules.

Size, inches	1	1½	2	2½	3
Price, each	15c	21c	27c	33c	40c

No. 30K3030 Double Thick Fitch Flowing Varnish Brushes, chiseled, superfine quality. For fine varnishing.

Width, inches	1	1½	2	2½	3
Price, each	19c	26c	36c	45c	51c

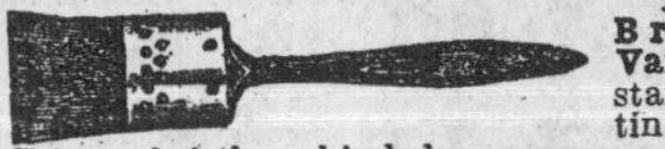

No. 30K3034 Bristle Flowing Varnish Brushes, stained handles, tin ferrules, black Chinese bristles, chiseled.

Size, inches	1	1½	2	2½	3
Price, each	7c	9c	12c	16c	20c

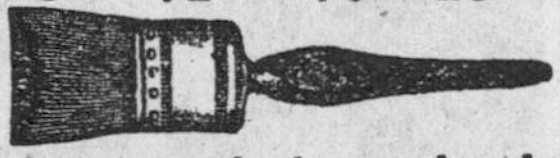

No. 30K3036 An extra fine, extra thick, soft elastic Chinese Bristle Flowing Varnish Brush. Something for the painter who does good work.

Size, inches	1	1½	2	2½	3
Price each	12c	20c	25c	34c	39c

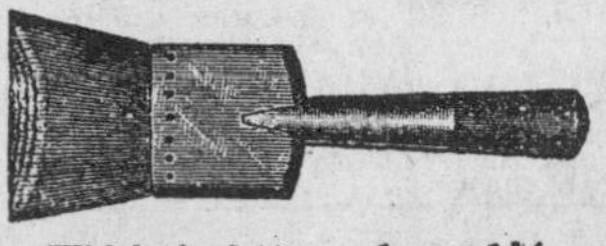

No. 30K3038 Extra English White French Bristle Double Thick Varnish Brushes, chiseled; used for varnishing and enameling.

Width, inches	1	1½	2	2½	3
Price, each	20c	27c	33c	40c	52c

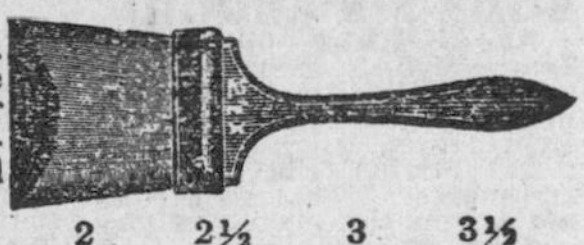

No. 30K3040 Rubberset Varnish Brush. best white French bristles. For varnishing and enameling. Bristles will never come out.

Width, inches	1½	2	2½	3	3½
Price, each	27c	35c	44c	53c	73c

No. 30K3042 Rubberset Varnish Brushes. Best black Chinese bristles. Will not shed.

Width, inches	1½	2	2½	3	3½
Price, each	24c	31c	42c	51c	67c

Wall Stippler.

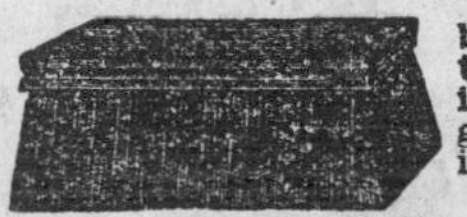

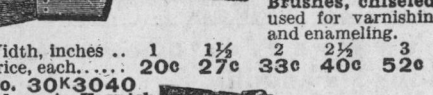

No. 30K3046 This brush is used to produce the rough effect on painted interior walls. Made of best gray Russian bristles, 3½ inches long.
Price **$1.80**

Walnut Stippler or Grainer.

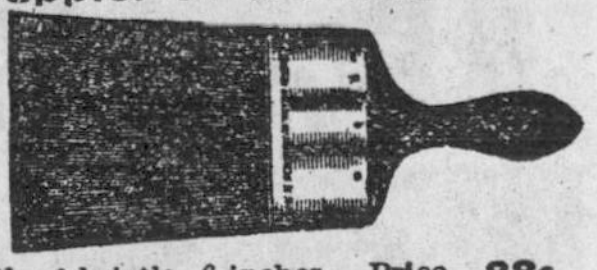

No. 30K3048 Used the same as No. 30K3046 but produces an entirely different grain. This is a well made brush and the best work can be done with it. Width, 3½ inches; length of bristles, 5¼ in. Price, **75c**
Width, 4 inches, length of bristle, 6 inches. Price.. **88c**

BRUSHES.

In our line of brushes listed below, we aim to quote such as are more commonly used. These goods are all of durable quality.

Camel's Hair Brushes.

The following brushes are used by carriage painters for striping, lettering and other carriage work.

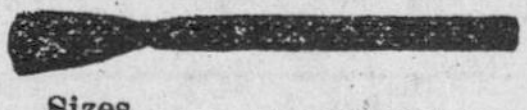

No. 30K3000 Camel's Hair Lettering Pencils, silk bound, superfine quality. Hair, 1 inch long.

Sizes	1	2	3	4
Price, each	2c	2c	3c	3c
Per dozen	20c	22c	29c	32c
Sizes	5	6	7	8
Price, each	4c	4c	5c	5c
Per dozen	35c	38c	48c	50c

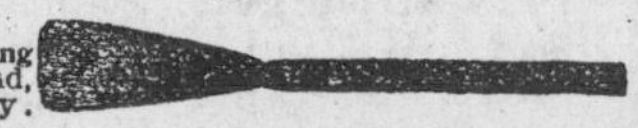

No. 30K3002 Camel's Hair Striping Pencils. Silk bound, superfine quality. Hair, 2 inches long.

Sizes	1	2	3	4
Price, each	2c	3c	3c	3c
Per dozen	22c	24c	32c	34c
Sizes	5	6	7	8
Price, each	4c	5c	6c	6c
Per dozen	45c	49c	64c	68c

No. 30K3004 Camel's Hair Swan quill Pencils, for lettering and striping.

Sizes, inches	½	¾	1	1¼
Price, each	6c	6c	7c	8c
Sizes, inches	1½	1¾	2	2¼
Price, each	9c	10c	11c	12c

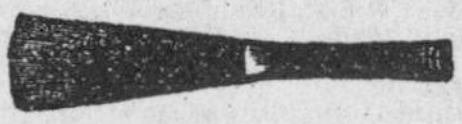

No. 30K3006 Camel's Hair Flat or Sword Stripers. Square ends, tin ferrules, without handles, for carriage work. Hair, 1½ to 2¼ inches long.

Sizes	1	2	3	4
Price, each	6c	7c	8c	9

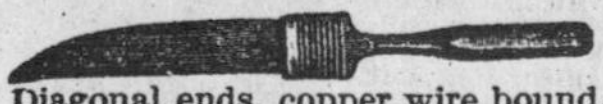

No. 30K3008 Camel's Hair Dagger Stripers. Diagonal ends, copper wire bound, small cedar handle; for carriage work. Hair, 1½ to 2¼ inches long.

Sizes	1	2	3	4
Price, each	9c	10c	11c	12c

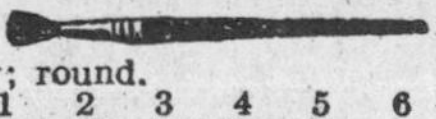

No. 30K3010 Camel's Hair Lacquering Brushes. Polished handles; fine quality; round.

Sizes	1	2	3	4	5	6
Price, each	4c	4c	5c	6c	7c	9c

No. 30K3012 Camel's Hair Lacquering Brushes. Polished handles; fine quality; flat.

Sizes	⅜	½	⅝	¾	⅞	1
Price, each	5c	6c	7c	8c	10c	13c

Flat Camel's Hair Brushes.

Flat Camel's Hair Brushes are used for high class carriage work in putting on color and should not be used as a varnish brush. Very thin paints such as gold, silver or aluminum should be put on with this brush.

Mottling Brushes.

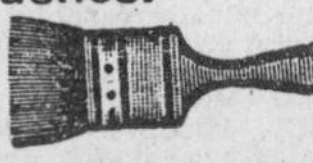

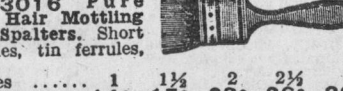

No. 30K3016 Pure Camel's Hair Mottling Brushes or Spalters. Short cedar handles, tin ferrules, fine quality.

Size, inches	1	1½	2	2½	3
Price, each	14c	17c	23c	36c	39c

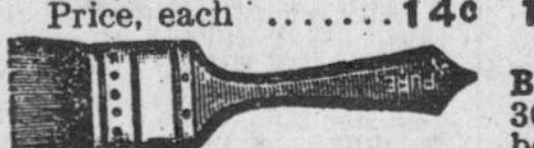

No. 30K3018 Color Brush, same as No. 30K3016, but brass bound, a thicker brush.

Size, inches	1	1½	2	2½	3
Price, each	22c	31c	41c	59c	72c

Blenders.

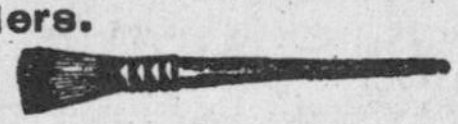

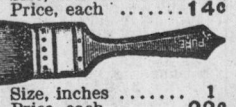

No. 30K3020 Round Badger Hair Blenders or Softeners, for graining and oil painting; polished handles.

Sizes	1	2	3	4	5	6
Price, each	13c	17c	20c	27c	35c	43c

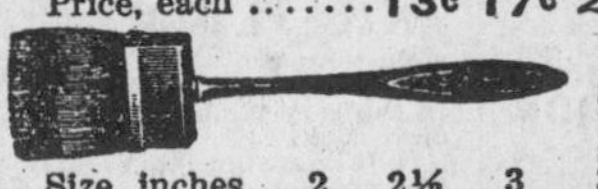

No. 30K3022 Flat Knotted Badger Hair Blenders, polished handles, set in bone.

Size, inches	2	2½	3	3½	4	4½
Price, each	55c	65c	83c	$1.05	$1.27	$1.53

Special Household Brush.

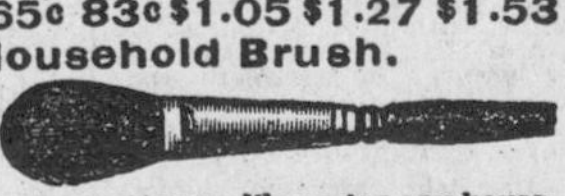

No. 30K3024 Soft Hair Brush specially made for household use. For enameling, varnishing, lacquering and bronzing any household article, picture frames, bric-a-brac, small articles of furniture, iron beds, chandeliers, etc. Exceptionally fine for gold and silver paints. Green enameled handle, nickel plated ferrule.
Price **10c**

Sign Writers' Brushes.

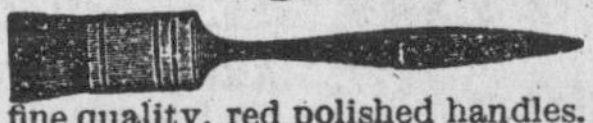

No. 30K3050 Ox Hair Sign Writers' Brushes; fine quality, red polished handles. State width wanted.

Width, inches	⅜	½	¾	1
Price, each	15c	18c	26c	32c

No. 30K3052 Fitch Hair Sign Writers' Brushes, chiseled; fine quality, red polished handles.

Width, inches	⅜	½	¾	1
Price, each	25c	28c	32c	38c

Ox Hair Riggers.

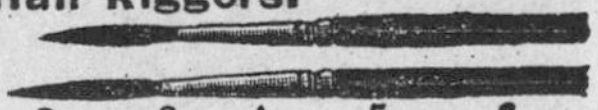

No. 30K3053 Ox Hair Riggers, for sign writers.

Size, No.	1	2	3	4	5	6
Price, each	4c	4c	5c	6c	7c	7c
Per dozen	42c	46c	55c	65c	77c	80c

Marking Brushes.

No. 30K3054 Camels' Hair Marking Brushes; polished handles.

Sizes	1	2	3	4
Price, each	3c	3c	4c	5c
Per dozen	32c	35c	40c	50c

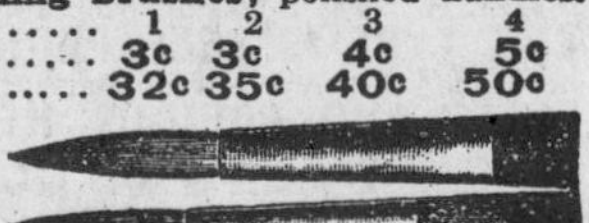

No. 30K3056 Ox Hair Marking Brushes, round polished handles. This brush is used in the large mercantile houses for marking cases, bales, etc.

Sizes	1	2	3	4
Price, each	5c	6c	7c	8c

No. 30K3058 Bristle Marking Brushes, round polished handles.

Sizes	1	2	3	4	5	6
Price, each	2c	2c	3c	3c	3c	4c
Per dozen	18c	20c	25c	26c	28c	31c

BOOKS

$1.43

TWO BIBLES IN ONE. MAGNIFICENTLY ILLUSTRATED. LARGE BOURGEOIS TYPE. BOLD FACE CLEAR PRINT. SUPERB BINDINGS, LINEN LINED COVERS. 60,000 REFERENCES. FULL TEACHERS' AND STUDENTS' HELPS.

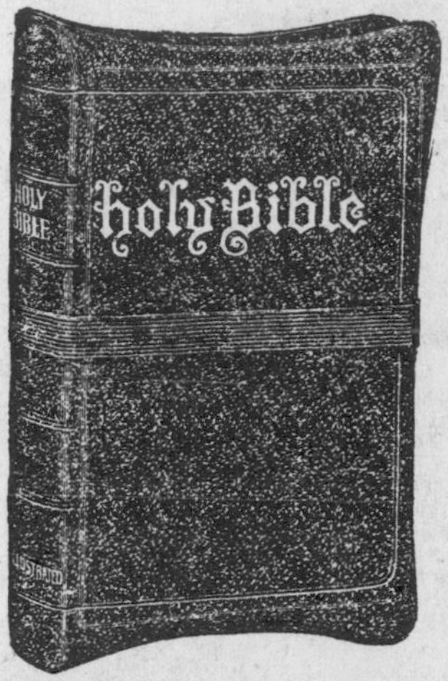

TWO BIBLES IN ONE—THE COMBINATION FEATURE. The King James and revised version on the same page, without increasing the size or weight. The text is the authorized King James version unchanged, while all the changes are given in the footnotes. When purchasing our **Combination Self Pronouncing Teachers' Bible**, you really purchase two Bibles in one. This **Combination Feature** is indispensable to Bible teachers, students and readers. It shows at a glance, in simple form, what changes, additions and omissions were made by the revisers, where they considered such change, addition or omission in the original text necessary to the more perfect understanding of the Scriptures. 1,800 pages, size 6x8 inches.

SUPERB BINDINGS. Our bindings are a marvel of attractiveness and combine serviceability with strength and flexibility. We bind our **Combination Self Pronouncing Teachers' Bible** in two grades. These two styles of bindings are made full divinity circuit and are **interlined with linen crash** in addition to the linen or leather linings. We do not use paper lining in any of our Bibles, because it has not the wearing qualities of either linen or leather. The two styles of bindings are: ANGORA—We use this style of binding on our lowest price Bible. It is a strong, durable binding with a handsome grain. It is far superior to other publishers' French morocco binding. GENUINE ALASKA SEAL—**the best and most durable binding known for Bibles.** The leather with which we bind this Bible is an extra quality of genuine Alaska seal, most carefully selected, **a leather that will not peel off nor get rough from rubbing.**

SELF PRONOUNCING TEXT. Our Teachers' Bible is printed from new, clear, large Bourgeois type (really a Long Primer type), and the text is self pronouncing, in which all proper names are accented and divided into syllables for clear and easy pronunciation. The self pronouncing markings are exceptionally accurate.

60,000 CENTER MARGINAL REFERENCES. There are over 60,000 center column references, enabling the reader, teacher or student to find quickly all the passages of the Bible relating to any subject or theme.

THE ILLUSTRATIONS. Our Teachers' Bible is profusely illustrated, including a beautiful halftone frontispiece and sixty-four (64) full page illustrations (photogravures) of the important places and events of Bible times. Each of these illustrations is accompanied by full descriptions. Also thirty-one (31) full page plates, illustrating ancient monuments, money, inscriptions, etc., and writings of the Bible.

SIXTEEN FULL PAGE COLORED MAPS of the Bible, both ancient and modern Palestine and the Holy Land, showing Christ's journeyings, the geography of that country and the places visited by Him.

RONICLES, 22. *building of the temple.*

B. C. 1017.
ᵍ Deut. 12. 5.
2 Sam. 24. 18.
ch. 21. 18, 19, 26, 28.
2 Chr. 3. 1.
² Heb. *Give.*
ᵉ 1 Kin. 9. 21.

THEN Dā'-vĭd said, ᵍThis *is* the house of the LORD God, and this *is* the altar of the burnt offering for Ĭs'-rā-ēl.

2 And Dā'-vĭd commanded to gather together ᵉthe strangers that *were* in the land of Ĭs'-rā-ēl; and he set masons to hew wrought stones to

This shows the exact size and style of type in our Teachers' Bible

FULL TEACHERS' AND STUDENTS' HELPS. Our Special Teachers' Bible has over 400 pages of helps to the study of the Bible, prepared by the world's greatest and most eminent Biblical scholars, including Chronological and other valuable tables. Life and Teachings of Our Lord, Miracles and Parables, etc. Lives of the Apostles, Missionary Journeys of St. Paul, Tables of Scripture Measures, Weights and Coins, Geology of Bible Lands, Animals, Birds, table showing the principal events in Jewish history, etc. In addition our Teachers' Bible (with the exception of No. 3K8000, the Bible bound in angora) contains the **4,000 Questions and Answers** on both the Old and New Testaments, and the **Fully Illustrated Dictionary of the Bible**, by William Smith, LL.D.

OUR SPECIAL TEACHERS' BIBLE—BOUND IN ANGORA.

No. 3K8000 Our Special Teachers' Bible, bound in angora, full divinity circuit, linen lined to edge and linen crash interlining, red under gold edges, round corners, silk headband and marker. This style does not contain the 4,000 Questions and Answers and Smith's Illustrated Bible Dictionary. A regular $3.00 Bible.
Our price............$1.43

No. 3K8005 Our Special Teachers' Bible. Same as No. 3K8000, but indexed.
Price...............$1.65

If by mail, postage extra, either style, 28 cents.

OUR SPECIAL TEACHERS' BIBLE—BOUND IN GENUINE ALASKA SEAL.

No. 3K8025 Our Special Teachers' Bible. **Bound in genuine Alaska seal,** with a very heavy grain to the leather (a very superior Bible leather that is rich in effect, strong and lasting). Full divinity circuit, lined to the edge with watered silk finish linen lining, and a linen crash interlining, making the Bible absolutely non-tearable. Silk headband and silk marker. Round edges on cover and full silk sewed. Red under burnished gold edges. Gold side and back titles. Self pronouncing text. This style contains the full helps, and in addition the **4,000 Questions and Answers** and the **Illustrated Bible Dictionary,** which are indispensable to either the teacher or the student. We recommend this Bible to everyone as being the best and handsomest and the most durable Bible that can be bought, and the cheapest because it will last the longest. A regular $4.00 Bible. Our special price..............$1.92

No. 3K8026 Same as No. 3K8025, but indexed. Price.............. 2.15

No. 3K8030 Same as No. 3K8025, but with full leather lining to edge and linen crash interlining. A regular $5.00 Bible. Price..............$2.33

No. 3K8031 Same as No. 3K8030, but indexed. Price.............. 2.55

If by mail, postage extra, for any of the above styles, 30 cents.

OUR SPECIAL TEACHERS' BIBLE—RED LETTER EDITION.

No. 3K8060 Our Special Teachers' Bible Red Letter Edition. This superb edition is exactly the same as No. 3K8025, except that all the words spoken by Christ are printed in red. It contains the same full and copious helps as No. 3K8025, including the 4,000 Questions and Answers and the Illustrated Dictionary of the Bible. The binding of this Bible is genuine Alaska seal, lined to the edge with watered silk finished linen lining, and linen crash interlining. A regular $4.50 Bible. Our special price.......$2.22

No. 3K8061 Same as No. 3K8060, but indexed.
Price.............. 2.45

No. 3K8065 Same as No. 3K8060, but with full leather lining and linen crash interlining to edge. A regular $5.50 Bible.
Our price..............$2.62

No. 3K8066 Same as No. 3K8065, but indexed.
Price.............. 2.95

If by mail, postage extra, for any of the above styles, 30 cents.

$3.89 FOR THIS $12.00 SELF PRONOUNCING FAMILY BIBLE

SUPERBLY BOUND IN GENUINE ARABIAN MOROCCO, HAND TOOLED WITH GOLD, MAGNIFICENTLY ILLUSTRATED, GENUINE STEEL ENGRAVINGS.

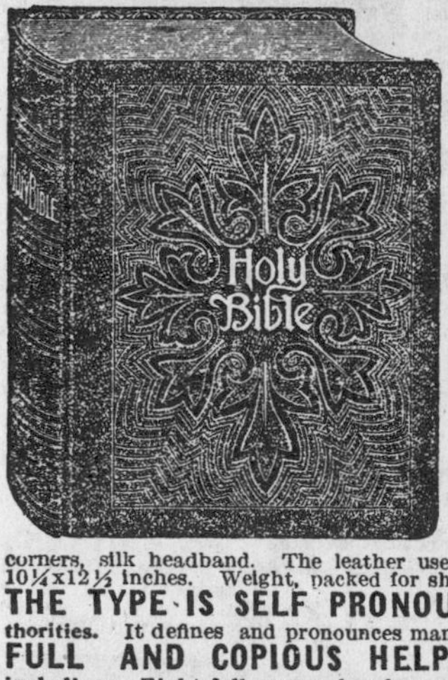

STRONG, HANDSOME AND DURABLE. Acknowledged by ministers, Bible students, able critics and all those who have seen this book, to be superior to any other Bible ever published at double the price we ask. This Bible is printed on the best quality of paper, from new clear plates with extra heavy type, so that it is equally readable by old and young. **Over 60,000 marginal references.**

MAGNIFICENTLY EXECUTED FULL PAGE STEEL ENGRAVINGS, DORE ILLUSTRATIONS AND COLOR PLATES. Contains two genuine steel frontispiece engravings by famous engravers (worth $1.00 apiece) before the New and Old Testaments, respectively. Thirty-two full page Biblical illustrations by Gustave Dore. Six full page colored plates, including a full page colored plate of the Ten Commandments and a full page colored plate containing the Lord's Prayer. Presentation page in colors. Title page in brilliant colors. An elegant marriage certificate artistically engraved in colors, together with marriage, birth and death record and family temperance pledge.

SUPERB BINDINGS. Richly padded sides, handsomely embossed, with words HOLY BIBLE stamped on back and sides in pure gold leaf. The inside edge being hand tooled with pure gold leaf in elaborate design. Red under burnished gold edges, round corners, silk headband. The leather used is the finest quality of **Arabian morocco.** Size, 10¼x12½ inches. Weight, packed for shipment, 15 pounds.

THE TYPE IS SELF PRONOUNCING. All proper names are divided and accented according to the standard authorities. It defines and pronounces many difficult words which occur throughout the Bible.

FULL AND COPIOUS HELPS AND PRACTICAL INFORMATION including: **Eight full page colored maps. Comprehensive history of all the books of the Bible, illustrated with 46 three-quarter page engravings.** A gallery of Scripture illustrations, showing the cities, countries, manners, religious rites, animals, etc., with 215 beautiful halftone illustrations. Complete household dictionary of the Bible, with over 500 illustrations. 77 halftone illustrations of famous Old Testament scenes, also 150 pictures of Biblical antiquities. A self pronouncing dictionary of Scripture proper names. A complete and practical concordance; the Apocrypha. **History of Religious Denominations,** which contains a short story of every known religious denomination. **4,500 Questions and Answers** on the Sacred Scriptures. **The Psalms of David in Meter,** by Charles Wesley, etc.,

No. 3K8500 **Our Self Pronouncing Family Bible.** Just as described above. Retail price, $12.00. Our special price..............$3.89

No. 3K8510 **Red Letter Edition of our Self Pronouncing Family Bible.** Exactly the same as our No. 3K8500, except that all the words spoken by Christ are printed in red. Retail price, $15.00. Our special price..............$4.39

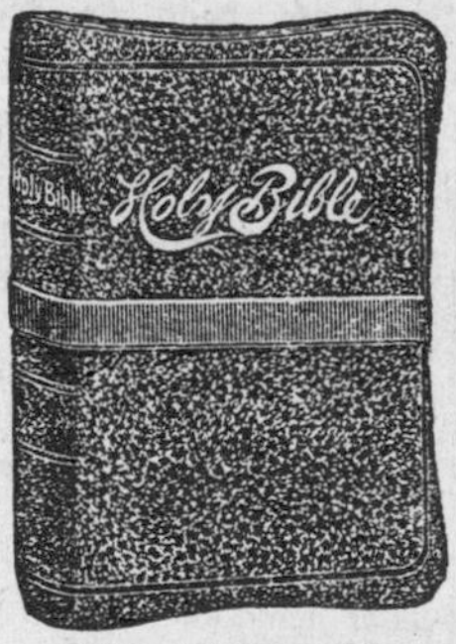

OLD FOLKS' BIBLES

EXTRA LARGE TYPE BIBLE FOR THE HOME

Self pronouncing Small Pica type reference Bible with 60,000 references. This Bible contains extra large type so as to be perfectly readable for those even with the weakest eyes. All proper names are accented and divided into syllables for quick and easy pronunciation.

16 And Jā'cob begat Jō'seph the husband of Mā'ry̆, of whom was born Jē'sus, who is called Christ.

17 So all the generations from Ā'brăhăm to Dā'vid *are* fourteen genera-

Sample of Small Pica type showing actual size and style.

It has all the good features that made the old fashioned family Bibles so popular, without their great weight and bulk. Printed on extra quality of paper, with maps printed in colors. Family record and marriage certificate printed in gold and colors. Gold side and back title. Size, 6⅛x9 inches.

No. 3K8580 Morocco Grained Cloth. Red edges. Price..............$1.23
No. 3K8582 French Morocco, Limp. Red under gold edges. Price..... 1.82
No. 3K8584 French Morocco. Full divinity circuit, red under gold edges, silk headband and marker, extra grained lining with linen interlining. Price,..............$2.22
No. 3K8586 French Morocco. Full leather lining. Price.............. 2.63
No. 3K8588 French Morocco. Same as No. 3K8584, but in addition it contains **32 beautiful colored plates,** illustrating famous Biblical scenes. Price..............$2.95

If by mail, postage extra, any style, 28 cents.

SUNDAY SCHOOL SCHOLARS' BIBLE.

WITH FULL SCHOLARS' HELPS TO THE STUDY OF THE BIBLE.

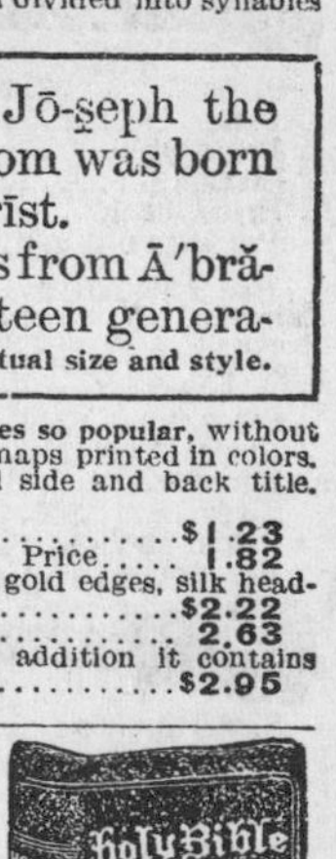

Prepared by the Most Eminent Biblical Scholars. Large Nonpareil Type, Elegant Paper, Substantially Made. Full Divinity Circuit.

AN IDEAL BIBLE. It is clearly printed on fine white paper, and has the largest type in the smallest possible compass. This edition of the Holy Bible is especially adapted to the Sunday School scholar, and, in fact, to the general reader, inasmuch as the very plain print meets the great demand for a hand Bible with clear type.

It contains full Sunday School Scholars' Helps, with instructions how to study and learn the Sunday School lessons. Designed especially for the Home, the Sunday School and Young People's Societies, and to Promote a Greater Love for the Holy Scriptures. **Illustrated with 32 superb phototype engravings. The most valuable art collection ever introduced in any hand Bible.** Bound with silk headband and marker. Red under gold edges.

No. 3K8625 Bound in Angora. Linen lining. Price..............$0.94
No. 3K8626 Same as No. 3K8625, but indexed. Price.............. 1.12
No. 3K8630 Bound in Genuine Venetian Morocco, linen lined. Price.... 1.15
No. 3K8631 Same as No. 3K8630, but indexed. Price.............. 1.33
No. 3K8635 Bound in Venetian Morocco. Full leather lining. Price...... 1.38
No. 3K8636 Same as No. 3K8635, but indexed. Price.............. 1 55

If by mail, postage extra, any style, 15 cents.

WEBSTER'S MONARCH DICTIONARY $4.84

2,500 ILLUSTRATIONS. NEW COLOR PLATES AND TABLES. 2,173 PAGES.

BEAUTIFUL CLEAR TYPE. THOUSANDS OF NEW WORDS. PRINTED FROM NEW PLATES.

PATENT THUMB INDEX CUT IN ON EDGE.

WEBSTER DEFINES MONARCH AS FOLLOWS: "MONARCH: ONE SUPERIOR TO ALL OTHERS OF THE SAME KIND." That definition fully describes WEBSTER'S MONARCH DICTIONARY and explains why we have named our special dictionary "MONARCH."

WE OFFER TWO EDITIONS: SPLENDID EDITION: Bound in full sheep, leather labels on back, title stamped in gold, blind side stamp. SUPERB EDITION: Bound in full turkey morocco, side and back elaborately stamped in pure gold.

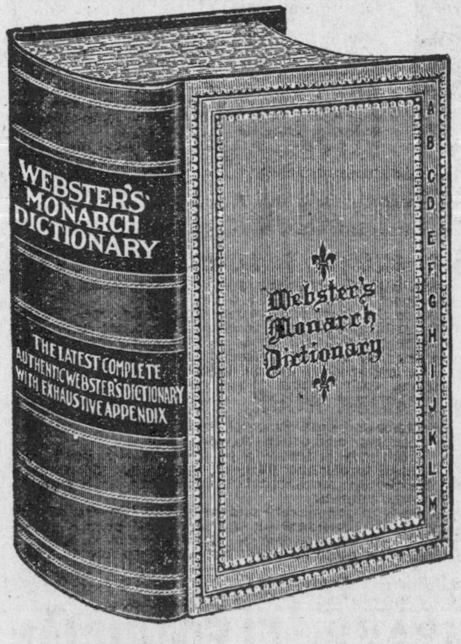

WEBSTER'S MONARCH DICTIONARY SPLENDID EDITION.

IF YOU WANT THE LATEST AND BEST DICTIONARY; if you want a good dictionary at practically half what is asked for dictionaries of a similar character, then buy Webster's Monarch Dictionary. Webster's Monarch Dictionary contains 2,173 pages. It is new from A to Z, and has enlisted the co-operation of a host of scholars and college professors, scientists and specialists. It defines 25,000 more words than are contained in any other Webster's Dictionary. Its system of capitalization, of indicating pronunciation and many minor details in dictionary making, represents the most practical and admirable methods. No good dictionary features have been omitted.

SPECIAL FEATURES OF WEBSTER'S MONARCH DICTIONARY. It contains among other special features the following: A modern gazetteer of the world. A dictionary of authors with the titles of their principal works. A dictionary of noted names in standard fiction, mythology, legend, etc. A dictionary of foreign words, phrases, noteworthy sayings and colloquial expressions from the Latin, Greek and modern languages used in current literature. A pronouncing dictionary of scriptural proper names and foreign words, with their meaning. A dictionary of abbreviations and contractions commonly used in writing and printing. A pronouncing dictionary of biography. Signs and symbols used in writing and printing. Values of standard foreign coins. A list of amended spelling. A department devoted to faulty diction (which no other Webster ever contained), treating over 1,000 subjects, etc.

THOUSANDS OF ILLUSTRATIONS are scattered in great profusion throughout the text. There are also full page color plates of the arms of the states and territories and the American Union, arms of various nations, flags of various nations, and United States naval flags.

HANDSOMELY AND SUBSTANTIALLY BOUND with the best materials that can be selected for durability, with flexible back which opens perfectly flat, thus making the book easy to consult. Webster's Monarch Dictionary, Splendid Edition, is bound in full law sheep, of the very best quality, with cover design stamped on side, and leather labels on back, with titles stamped in gold on side and back. It has a patent thumb index cut in on edge. Contains 2,173 pages. Full marbled edges. Size of dictionary, 9½x11½ inches, 4¾ inches thick.

No. 3K6950 Webster's Monarch Dictionary, Splendid Edition, bound in full law sheep, with patent index cut in on edge. Price $4.84

Shipping weight, 15 pounds. If by mail, postage extra, $1.20.

THE NEW NOYES DICTIONARY AND BOOK HOLDER.

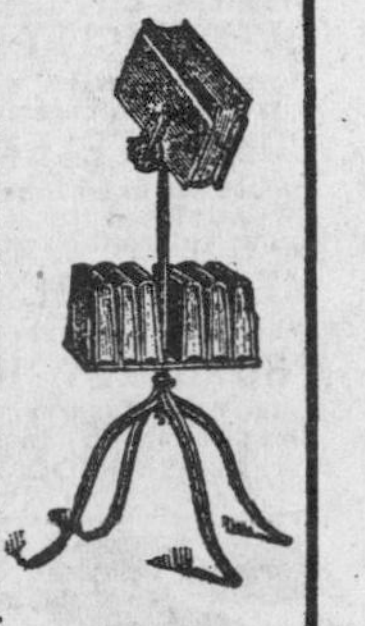

A perfect book holder. Combines strength, beauty and convenience. The entire base is made from cold rolled steel; consequently is non-destructible. Can be easily set up. This holder is adjustable to any height or angle and pivoted to turn to any position. With revolving shelf, finished in bronze, nickel trimmings.

No. 3K6895 Single Adjustable Book Holder. Price $1.98

No. 3K6896 Double Adjustable Book Holder. Otherwise same as No. 3K6895. Price $2.98

Weight, packed, 18 pounds.

WEBSTER'S MONARCH DICTIONARY SUPERB EDITION

BOUND IN GENUINE TURKEY MOROCCO, ELABORATELY STAMPED WITH PURE GOLD. The most superb dictionary ever offered to the public. Exactly the same dictionary as far as contents, number of pages and illustrations are concerned, as No. 3K6950 described above, but it is bound in full turkey morocco, with the back and sides elaborately stamped with pure gold.

No. 3K6951 Webster's Monarch Dictionary, Superb Edition, bound in genuine turkey morocco, stamped with gold, with patent thumb index cut in on edge. Price $6.95

Shipping weight, 15 pounds. If by mail, postage extra, $1.20.

HARPER'S COOK BOOK ENCYCLOPAEDIA $1.12

NEARLY 4,000 WHOLESOME, PALATABLE, INEXPENSIVE RECIPES. ARRANGED LIKE A DICTIONARY, AND COMPILED UNDER THE DIRECTION OF THE EDITOR OF "HARPER'S BAZAAR," with the assistance of such famous authorities on cooking as Marion Harland, Margaret Sangster, Maria Blay, Margaret J. Lincoln, Christine T. Herreck, etc. On the inside of the front and back covers are complete tables of weights and measures and a time table for cooking, both of which are invaluable in any kitchen. There is also a table of proportions showing the proper quantities to use in mixing materials.

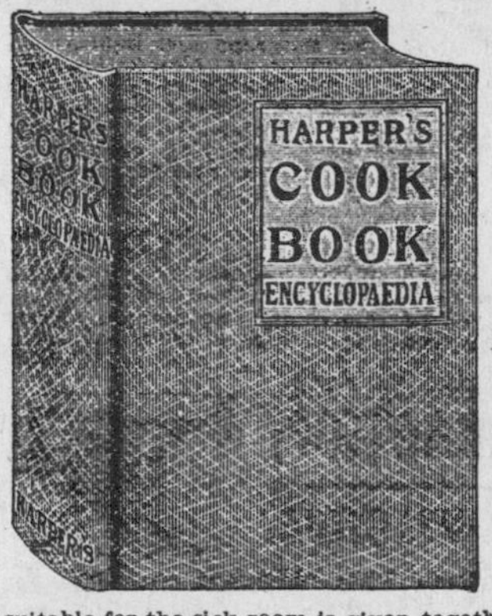

INEXPENSIVE PRACTICAL TESTED RECIPES. Do not think because this is a high grade cook book that the recipes given in it are expensive. In this book are recipes for all times and all tastes, but the majority of these recipes are capable of being carried out at very low cost. They are chiefly medium priced, inexpensive recipes of good, wholesome, tasty dishes such as the majority of the people want.

ARRANGEMENT OF RECIPES. The first effort in preparing this work has been to arrange every recipe on each subject so that any housekeeper can find exactly what is wanted at once, simply by opening the book, as you would find a word in a dictionary. This has been done by arranging the whole work, every subject, alphabetically.

INVALID COOKERY. Cooking for invalids and the sick is also described, and the list of dishes suitable for the sick room is given together with suggestions to the nurse or cook, how to prepare something that will be both appetizing and healthful for the invalid.

REQUISITE KITCHEN UTENSILS. A full list of the usual necessary utensils is given. This is a subject on which the housewife can go very easily astray, and without practical experience this item may prove a very expensive one. The kind of material best suited for the various utensils is stated, so that the housewife will have no trouble in making an intelligent as well as economical selection.

ECONOMY AND WASTEFULNESS. Economy in cooking does not consist primarily in buying cheap foods. It does consist in the intelligent saving and combination of things left over, which can be made, with a little attention, into attractive, desirable dishes. The various uses to which the remnants may be put and the methods by which they may be turned into appetizing, wholesome and attractive dishes are given.

ILLUSTRATIONS. It contains full page engravings, showing tables set for breakfast, luncheon, dinner and informal Sunday evening supper. There are additional engravings illustrating fancy dishes and methods of serving them.

LEATHER CLOTH BINDING. It is bound in washable pigskin color specially prepared leather cloth, 450 double column pages. Each page has a heading and key to the recipes on that page. Size of book is 6⅛x8 inches, 2 inches thick.

No. 3K7505 Price $1.12

If by mail, postage extra, 28 cents.

THE PRACTICAL FAMILY DOCTOR $1.45

20TH CENTURY HOUSEHOLD MEDICAL GUIDE.

THE LARGEST, MOST COMPLETE AND AUTHENTIC MEDICAL ADVISER EVER PUBLISHED, STRICTLY UP TO DATE. 1,157 PAGES, 20 COLOR PLATES.

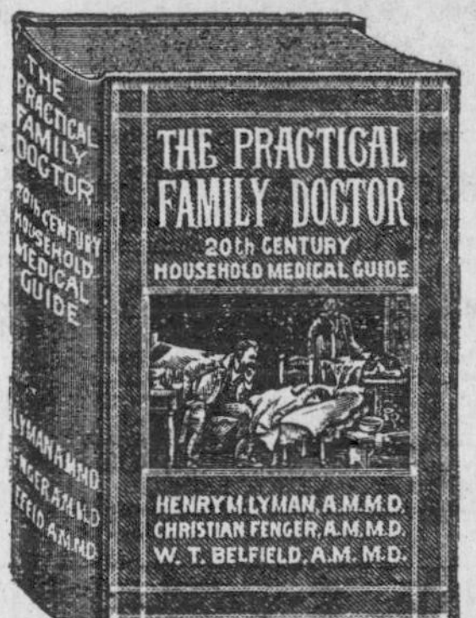

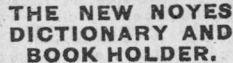

NO HOME SHOULD BE WITHOUT ITS PRICELESS ADVICE. It explains everything in plain home talk fashion, yet in most delicate terms, inoffensive to the most sensitive person. The secret science of medicine and surgery is bared to the reader of this grand volume. In its medical department this work treats in a sensible way the Household Management of Disease. This work gives the history, cause, means of prevention and symptoms of all diseases, and the most approved methods of treatment; with plain instructions for the care of the sick; full and accurate directions for treating wounds, injuries, poisoning, etc.

COMPLETE LIST OF MEDICINES, telling what each is good for, and how much of each to take for a dose. The prescriptions are all written in plain English, so they can be copied and filled without the aid of a doctor.

SPECIAL CHAPTERS are given over to the consideration of constitutional diseases, which include scarlet fever, typhoid fever and other fevers, small pox, chicken pox, diphtheria, measles, rheumatism, etc. There are also special chapters on Private or Venereal Diseases. A full account of the symptoms, treatment, etc.

DISEASES OF WOMEN. More than 200 pages are devoted to this important subject alone. Both the cause and the cure of diseases are taken up, together with their symptoms. Among the subjects treated are: Diseases of the vulva, diseases of the womb, inflammation and enlargement of the womb, displacement and falling of the womb, tumors and cancers of the uterus, etc., diseases of the ovaries, special diseases of the organs of generation, sterility and its causes.

DISEASES OF CHILDREN have been gone into very thoroughly. The subjects covered include indigestion, disorders of the bowels, diarrhea, summer complaints, constipation, croup, influenza, convulsions. A careful study of this chapter will enable the mother to ward off many of the diseases common to children.

THE DELICATE AND WONDERFUL MATTERS pertaining to the nature and relations of the sexes are fully discussed. Exhaustive treatment of all sexual considerations, distinctive traits of the sexes, development of the sexual organs, determining the sex of offspring in advance. Here are answered in plain language a thousand questions that occur in the minds of both young and old, but about which they feel a delicacy in consulting their physician.

MARRIAGE. Factors to be considered in entering the marriage relation, physical basis of marriage, time to marry, the wedding tour, etc. The Practical Family Doctor will prevent invalid wives, weak children, deformities, etc.

PREGNANCY. Rules of conduct during pregnancy, diseases of pregnancy, hygiene of pregnancy, accidents of pregnancy—causes, symptoms and treatment, prevention of pregnancy, to calculate the time of confinement. Care of the mother after labor. Lactation, its relation to the sexual functions, weaning, diseases of child bed, milk leg, etc.

BEAUTIFULLY ILLUSTRATED WITH COLOR PLATES, containing two lithograph manikins, one of the body and one of the head, in layers to dissect, showing all the organs of the body and the head in their proper positions and colors. Regular retail price of each one is $1.00. Also a chart showing all the blood vessels and a skeleton chart. Colored plates of 64 medical plants, together with descriptions and directions for use. Bound in full sheep with blind side stamp and gold back title, or buff colored buckram with title and cover design stamped in white and sepia with sepia colored photographic inlay of the world famous picture, "The Doctor." Contains 1,157 pages. Size of book, 7x9½ inches, 2½ inches thick, with colored edges. Contains a complete index, making it an easy matter to locate any particular subject. Weight, packed for shipment, 5 pounds.

No. 3K7550 Bound in cloth. Regular subscription price, $4.50. Our price $1.45

No. 3K7555 Bound in full sheep. Regular subscription price, $6.00. Our price 2.18

STANDARD AMERICAN CYCLOPEDIA OF STEAM ENGINEERING, $2 78

Including Care and Management of Steam Engines, Boilers, Steam Turbines, Refrigeration, Lubrication, Pumps, Valve Setting, Marine Engines, Electricity for Engineers, Examination Questions and Answers for Stationary and Marine Engineers, Mechanical Drawing and Machine Design.

By CALVIN F. SWINGLE and Others. Four Volumes in One. Bound in Full Persian Morocco. Pocketbook Style with Flap. Stamped in Gold, Full Gold Edges. 1,200 Pages, Fully Illustrated.

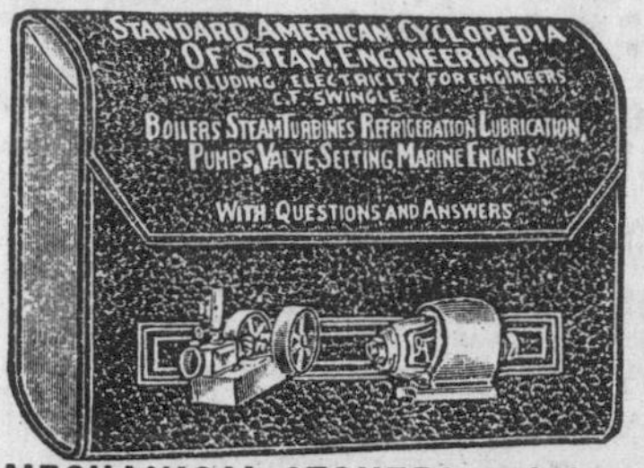

CARE AND MANAGEMENT OF STEAM ENGINES, BOILERS AND DYNAMOS, including detail instructions for an efficient management of all classes of steam engines; boiler settings and appurtenances; boiler operation, care of the boiler, including washing out, scraping the flues, fire cracks, how to fire a boiler, etc.

VALVES AND VALVE SETTING. Full particulars of valves and valve setting, including correct adjustment, single valve engines, setting valves, description of Corliss valves and valve gear, and directions for adjusting same. It also covers the subject of indicators, with diagram analysis.

MECHANICAL STOKERS and the principles involved in the action of automatic stokers are explained.

THE STEAM TURBINE ENGINE of various makes, their construction and operation. Points out difference between the turbine and reciprocating engine; fundamental principles of the steam turbine; types of steam turbine; speed regulation; efficiency of steam turbine.

REFRIGERATION, PUMPS, AIR COMPRESSORS, LUBRICATION, are all subjects that are treated of very fully, accompanied by numerous diagrams, tables, etc.

ELECTRICITY FOR ENGINEERS. A treatise on the principles, construction and operation of dynamos, motors, lamps, storage batteries, etc., including indicators, measuring instruments, circulation of wires, wiring tables, commutators, the construction of electrical parts, etc.

COMPLETE ENGINEERS' CATECHISM, embodying questions and answers upon everything necessary to pass successful examinations for licenses for either stationary or marine engineering. It gives the latest and most approved answers to all leading questions which will be asked by all municipalities and government boards of examining engineers.

MECHANICAL AND MACHINE DRAWING. Beginning with mechanical drawing, it leads by easy graduations to practical machine drawing, in which plain and simple instructions are given.

PROFUSELY ILLUSTRATED. This work is more elaborately illustrated than any other similar work on these lines. It contains over 1,000 engravings, illustrations, drawings, diagrams, figures, folding plates, etc. Size of book, 5x7 inches.

No. 3K9200 Standard American Cyclopedia of Steam Engineering. Price....$2.78
If by mail, postage extra, 22 cents.

STANDARD AMERICAN LOCOMOTIVE ENGINEERING COMPLETE IN ALL ITS BRANCHES. $2 85

Including Breakdowns, Valves, Boilers, Air Brakes, Railroad Signaling Block System, with Complete Questions and Answers. Fully Illustrated.

By C. F. SWINGLE and W. G. WALLACE. Over Four Volumes in One. Bound in Full Persian Morocco, with Flap, Pocketbook Style Stamped in Gold. Full Gold Edges. 1,150 pages

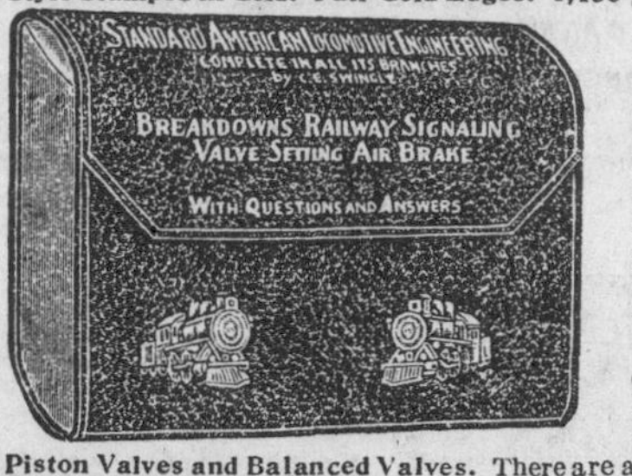

A VERITABLE ENCYCLOPEDIA OF LOCOMOTIVE ENGINEERING. Some special subjects to which one or more chapters are given are: Locomotive Firemen's Duties, including firing locomotives and how to do it economically and successfully; Combustion; Black Smoke, How to Avoid It; Steam and its Properties; the Indicator; Locomotive Appliances; Locomotive Equipments; Link Motion; Firing Locomotives with Oil as Fuel, etc. Special chapters are also given to the following subjects:

BOILERS, including their construction, care and operation are fully described, with illustrations, as is also done with the Throttle and Dry Pipe.

VALVES, including valve gear and valve setting, in all its details. Also Piston Valves and Balanced Valves. There are also special chapters on the Indicator, Injectors, Stem Gauges, Pop Valves and other fittings.

AUTOMATIC AIR BRAKE PRACTICE. Both the New York and the Westinghouse systems. Profusely illustrated and explained in detail, including the various parts of air brake equipment and every device now in use, together with their duties, etc.

WALSCHAERT VALVE GEAR AND E. T. LOCOMOTIVE BRAKE EQUIPMENT. Special chapters with full illustrations and a complete and accurate description of the two most important systems.

LOCOMOTIVE BREAKDOWNS in the form of Questions and Answers. Engine failures and what to do in case of an emergency, including the disarrangement of valve gear, broken cylinder heads, broken piston rods, broken driving axle, hole in the boiler, failure of injector to work, failure of lubricator to work, etc.

COMPOUND LOCOMOTIVES. The important various types of compound locomotives, their various parts, operation, repairs, etc.

RAILWAY SIGNALING AND STATION WORK, including Freight, Passenger and Baggage Departments, Block systems, with trainmen's questions and answers on all kinds of signals. This portion of the book illustrated with full page diagrams and other drawings.

QUESTIONS AND ANSWERS. Not only is there to be found in this book, after each important subject, questions and answers, but there are complete first, second and third year mechanical examinations, with standard questions and answers on locomotive firing and running.

FULLY ILLUSTRATED. This work is completely and profusely illustrated with nearly 1,000 illustrations, diagrams and charts. Many full page folding plates. Two extra large plates showing every part of the Prairie type and Balance Compound Locomotive, numbered with marginal side references to the numbers. Size of book, 5x7 inches.

No. 3K9210 Standard American Locomotive Engineering. Price............$2.85
If by mail, postage extra, 22 cents.

$2 19 —STANDARD AMERICAN— GAS AND OIL ENGINE, AUTOMOBILE AND FARM ENGINE GUIDE.

A Complete Encyclopedia of the Construction, Operation and Management of Gas Engines, Gasoline Engines, Automobiles, Farm Engines and Traction Engines, Together with Complete Questions and Answers.

By STEVENSON and BROOKES. Three Volumes in One, Over 600 Pages, Fully Illustrated. Bound in Full Persian Morocco, with Flap, Pocketbook Style.

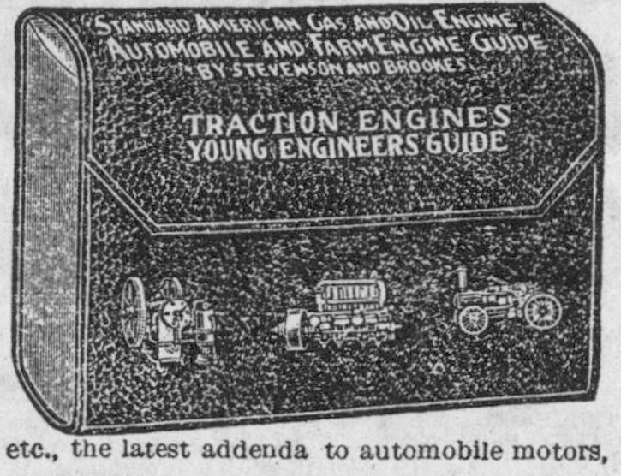

GAS AND OIL ENGINES. Their construction, operation, connecting rods, crank shafts, pistons, valves, speed regulating governors. Troubles, Breakdowns, Marine Motors, Steam Fire Engines, Tables, etc.

AUTOMOBILES. Full and concise information on all questions relating to the care, construction and operation of gasoline and electrical automobiles, including road, motor, carbureter, ignition, battery, clutch and starting troubles, etc., the latest addenda to automobile motors, from Brookes' "Automobile Hand Book."

FARM ENGINES, TRACTION ENGINES AND HOW TO RUN THEM. Different makes fully described. Valuable advice relative to buying a farm engine. How to start up a boiler, when to let engine alone, economical firing, firing with wood or straw and its results, starting fire, smoke, sparks, lubrication, hot boxes, etc.

HOW TO RUN A THRESHING MACHINE, including a full description of its various parts and their uses. How to set up a threshing machine, how to take it apart, repairing breakdowns, etc.

QUESTIONS AND ANSWERS are scattered throughout the text, including questions and answers for examination when applying for engineer's license. This is the only work that contains questions and answers on the subject of the farm or traction engine.

THIS WORK IS PROFUSELY ILLUSTRATED with over 250 engravings, diagrams, plans and halftones, showing in detail the different parts of the engine, etc. Size of book, 5x7 inches.

No. 3K9220 Standard American Gas and Oil Engine, Automobile and Farm Engine Guide. Price..........$2.19
If by mail, postage extra, 22 cents.

$2 68 STANDARD AMERICAN ELECTRICIAN A COMPLETE CYCLOPEDIA OF ELECTRICITY. By SWINGLE, HORSTMANN and TOUSLEY.

Four Volumes in One Bound in Full Persian Morocco. Pocketbook Style, with Flap. Stamped in Gold, Full Gold Edges, 600 Pages, Fully Illustrated. By SWINGLE, HORSTMANN and TOUSLEY.

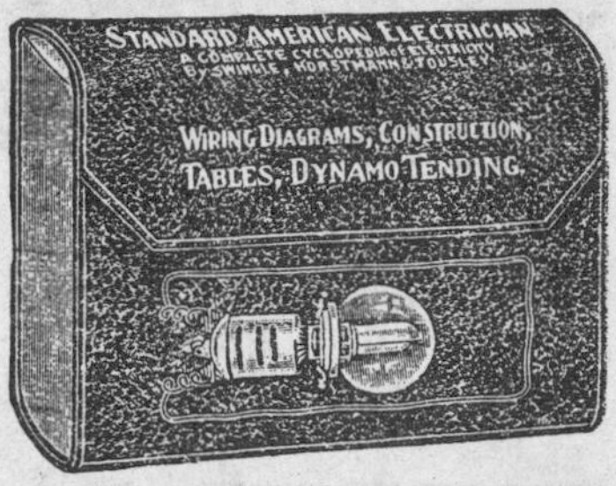

THIS COMPLETE AND AUTHORITATIVE WORK shows the latest approved methods of installing work of all kinds according to the safety rules of the National Board of Underwriters. From it may be obtained a good knowledge of the fundamental principles of electricity and magnetism, of dynamos and motors, methods of electric lighting, the latest methods of wiring all classes of buildings for light and power, including fittings, materials and details of contruction.

WIRING DIAGRAMS AND DESCRIPTIONS. It explains how to wire for call and alarm bells, for burglar and fire alarms, how to run bells from dynamo's current, how to install and manage batteries, how to test batteries, how to wire for annunciators, for telegraph and lighting. It tells how to locate trouble, ring out circuits, about meters and transformers, electrical lighting, including arc lights, Neurnst lamps, Cooper Hewett lamps, etc. Explains alternating and direct current, alternators, transformers, armatures, etc., electric signs, flashes, display lighting, etc.

ELECTRICAL WIRING CONSTRUCTION TABLES, showing combined carrying capacity of different wires and pole line data dimensions, various kinds of wires and fittings, calculation of materials, capacity of conduits for various kinds of wiring, light and motor wiring tables. Tables for 1 per cent and up loss, rating of motors, etc.

DYNAMO TENDING FOR ENGINEERS. A treatise on the principles, construction and operation of dynamos, motors, lamps, storage batteries, etc., together with explanation of the fundamental principles of the generation of currents. Teaches the engineers how to operate a plant successfully.

PROFUSELY ILLUSTRATED with hundreds of diagrams, engravings, charts, plates and line drawings. Size of book, 5x7 inches.

No. 3K9230 Standard American Electrician. Price..............$2.68
If by mail, postage extra, 20 cents.

AMERICAN BLACKSMITHING, —TOOLSMITHS'— AND STEELWORKERS' MANUAL $1 62

By Holmstrom and Holford. Two volumes in one. 600 pages. Size, 5¾x8 inches. Fully illustrated. Bound in silk cloth.

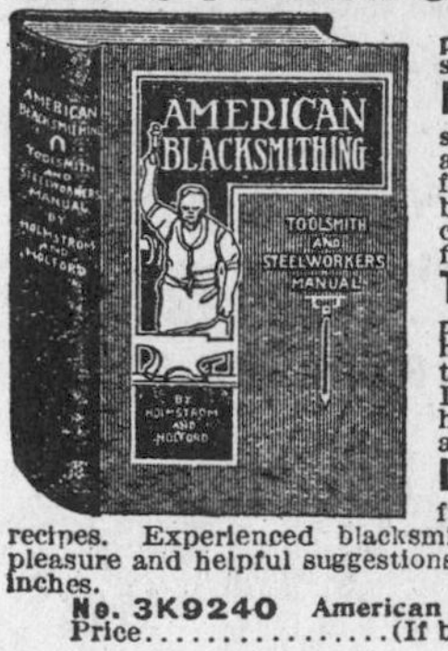

BLACKSMITHING. It comprises particulars and details regarding the anvil, tool table, sledge, tongs, hammers, how to use them, correct position at anvil, welding, tube expanding, the horse, anatomy of the foot, horseshoes, horseshoeing, hardening a plowshare, babbitting, etc. The subject of farm blacksmithing is fully covered in this volume, together with many useful tables and figures.

TOOLSMITHING AND STEELWORKING covers composition of cast tool steel, heating, forging, hammering, hardening, etc. Tempering, welding, annealing, cause of tools cracking when hardening. To tell good from poor steel. Instructions in tool making. Punching holes, etc. Heavy, hot, cold and railroad chisels; drills and drilling; how to make a gun, revolver, trap and all fine springs. Colors of temper, etc.

LINE ENGRAVINGS AND DIAGRAMS. The book is very fully illustrated and contains numerous working rules and recipes. Experienced blacksmiths, steel and tool workers, as well as beginners will get pleasure and helpful suggestions from this book. Bound in silk cloth. Size of book, 5½x7¾ inches.

No. 3K9240 American Blacksmithing, Toolsmiths' and Steelworkers' Manual. Price...........(If by mail, postage extra, 22 cents)...............$1.62

MODERN MACHINE SHOP PRACTICE, —INCLUDING— PATTERN MAKING AND FOUNDRY PRACTICE. $1 78

By Brookes and Hand. Two volumes in one. 800 pages, size, 5¾x8 inches, fully illustrated. Bound in cloth.

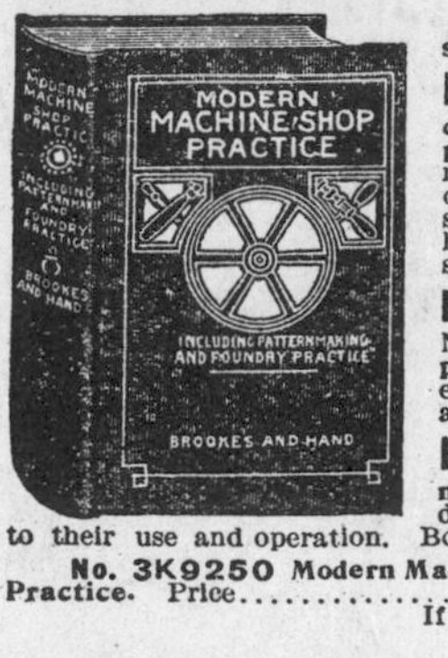

MODERN MACHINE SHOP PRACTICE. It clearly, but concisely describes the properties of steam, the indicator, horse power, electricity, measuring devices, machinists' tools, lathes of many different styles, boring machines, grinding machines, gear cutting machines, drill presses, planers and shapers of various styles, portable, also auxiliary machine tools, slotting machines, how to use them and methods of working, notes on working steel, gas furnaces, and fifty-seven valuable reference tables.

PATTERN MAKING AND FOUNDRY PRACTICE. Nearly every problem explained is taken from an actual pattern. It will enable any good wood mechanic, in an emergency, to make patterns which are likely to be required around an ordinary railroad or machine shop.

HUNDREDS OF ILLUSTRATIONS showing views of the latest machines, the most up to date and improved belt and motor driven machine tools and patterns, with full information as to their use and operation. Bound in silk cloth. Size of book, 5x7 inches. Over 800 pages.

No. 3K9250 Modern Machine Shop Practice, including Pattern Making and Foundry Practice. Price..............................$1.78
If by mail, postage extra, 24 cents.

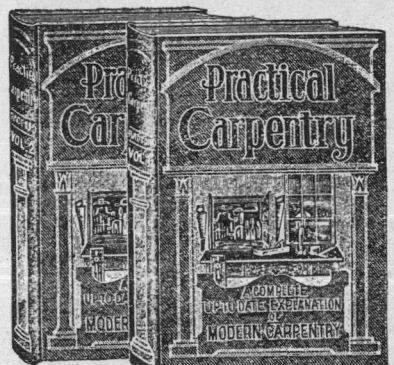

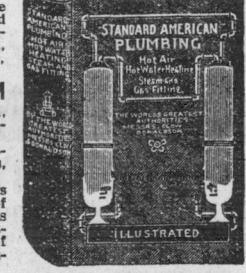
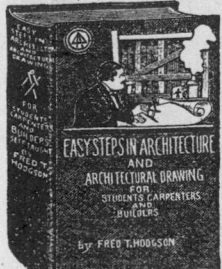
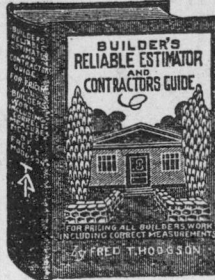

SIX MONTHS' COURSE IN BOOKKEEPING

A $50.00 BUSINESS COURSE FOR $4.89

A Regular Six Months' Business Course in Double Entry Bookkeeping, by Samuel B. Willey, LL. B., Former Superintendent of Bryant & Stratton Business College, Chicago.

WHY PAY $50.00 TO $100.00 FOR A COURSE IN BOOK-KEEPING THAT IS NOT EVEN AS GOOD AS THE ONE WE OFFER TO YOU FOR $4.89?

WHY LEAVE HOME or give up your present position in order to attend a business college when you can learn bookkeeping from this course in your own home, at your own convenience, without interfering with either your work or your pleasure? The course is adapted to the young man or young woman, to the business man, lawyer, physician, teacher, to everybody. It reads like a story book. The model books are gems of neatness and artistic display. Anybody can keep books, check books, or teach bookkeeping by this wonderful system, endorsed by business men and educators.

THIS REMARKABLE COURSE tells you how and then shows you how to keep books. The statements in the 238-page text book are made clear to you by referring to the model books, where you will find the entry made just as you should make it in the student books and just as it would appear in the office or counting room. You read the way to do it and then see how it is done.

The first month the pupil is taught the use of the two columnar journal, cash book, ledger, and trial balance and balance sheet book.

The second month teaches the two columnar journal, cash book, ledger, and trial balance and balance sheet book, as applied to partnership business.

The third month teaches wholesale bookkeeping with three partners. Books used are our two columnar journal, cash book, invoice book, sales book, ledger and trial balance book.

The fourth month teaches special columnar bookkeeping as applied to wholesale business. Books used are the special columnar journal, ledger, and trial balance and balance sheet book.

The fifth month teaches corporation bookkeeping. Books used are special columnar corporation journal, ledger, and trial balance and balance sheet book. Tells how to change partnership books to corporation books, and how to keep corporation books.

The sixth month teaches farmers how to keep books. The farmers' journal, ledger, and trial balance and balance sheet book.

Single entry is but a part of double entry. We teach double entry bookkeeping in this course because after you have learned double entry you will understand single entry.

THE SIX MONTHS' COURSE IN BOOKKEEPING, consisting of complete detailed instruction in retail, wholesale, special columnar, corporation and farmers' double entry bookkeeping, is made up of:

1 Book of Transactions and Instructions. That tells how. 238 pages. Size, 6½x10 in.
1 Set of 11 Model Blank Books, each measuring 8½x13½ inches. That shows how. Containing:
1 Model Journal
1 Model Cash Book.
1 Model Ledger. First part.
1 Model Ledger. Second part, Stockholders' Ledger.
1 Model Ledger. Third part, Farmers' Ledger.
1 Model Trial Balance and Balance Sheet Book.
1 Model Sales Book.
1 Model Invoice Book.
1 Model Special Columnar Journal. First part, General.
1 Model Special Columnar Journal. Second part, Corporations.
1 Model Special Columnar Journal. Third part, Farmers'.

1 Set of 11 Students' Blank Books, each measuring 8½x13½ inches; containing:
1 Students' Journal.
1 Students' Cash Book.
1 Students' Ledger. First part.
1 Students' Ledger. Second part, Stockholders.
1 Students' Ledger. Third part, Farmers'.
1 Students' Trial Balance and Balance Sheet Book.
1 Students' Sales Book.
1 Students' Invoice Book.
1 Students' Special Columnar Journal. First part, General.
1 Students' Special Columnar Journal. Second part, Special Columnar Corporation Journal.
1 Students' Special Columnar Journal. Third part, Special Columnar Farmers' Journal.

EVERYTHING YOU WILL NEED in this six months' course is provided for you. There are no other expenses. No extras, as there are in all business colleges. Your only outlay is $4.89. For that we put in your hands not only this wonderful system, but we give you free the materials and supplies necessary for a complete six months' course in bookkeeping. We also give you free a course in penmanship and a book of everyday business forms.

FREE We will give, absolutely free, to anyone ordering "Six Months' Course in Bookkeeping":

A Six Months' Course in Sensible Business Penmanship, with complete detailed instructions and copies (60 penmanship lessons and copies). A course such as would cost at colleges $45.00 to $60.00. This course is prepared by Samuel B. Willey, LL. B., and used by him in college instructions.

1 Book of Everyday Business Forms.
Will assist you every day to handle intelligently business affairs and correspondence.
Six Months' Supply of Materials to be used in the Bookkeeping Course, consisting of:

36 sheets, 72 pages, writing paper, 8x12 ins.	125 sheets, 250 pages, figuring paper, 6x9 ins.
1 black ink penholder.	1 red ink penholder.
1 C. B. T. S. leadpencil.	1 ruler, brass edge.	1 dozen business pens.
1 dozen blotters.	1 bottle red ink.	12 pages everyday business forms.

No. 3K7310 One Complete Six Months' Course in Bookkeeping, with free course in penmanship, book of business forms and materials, just as described above, neatly boxed. Weight, packed for shipment, 7 pounds. Not mailable on account of weight. Price **$4.89**

ONE YEARS SUPPLY of STATIONERY $1.95

OUR NEW MAMMOTH STATIONERY OUTFIT

BETTER, BIGGER, HANDSOMER THAN EVER. **$1.95** BUYS $6.40 WORTH OF STATIONERY.

WHY WE CAN GIVE YOU GREATER VALUE IN OUR STATIONERY OUTFIT than we have ever been able to offer before in our stationery line. Do you know why we can give you so much stationery for $1.95? Because we can afford to sell cheaper when we sell in large quantities. We can afford to give you better quality, and a larger quantity of stationery for the same money when we sell you $1.95 worth at a time, than when we sell you this $1.95 worth, split up into many small orders, which causes us additional shipping and handling expense.

JUST THE STATIONERY NEEDED IN EVERY HOME. Send us an order for this big outfit, and be sure of a good, big, generous supply of everything you will need in the way of writing paper, envelopes, pencils, pens, box paper, etc., for the next year, and so make a big saving by getting about three times as much for your money as you would get if the various items were purchased separately. From the picture shown hereon and from the list of the many articles given, you can get just some little idea of the wonderful values we are giving in this enormous outfit, this great aggregation of useful stationery and supplies for only $1.95.

EVERY HOME, every grown person has use for writing paper, envelopes, pencils, stationery and the various articles shown in this illustration and in this list, a list of goods that would cost you in any retail store in the country at least $6.40 and which we offer you for only $1.95. If you are about to buy anything in the line of stationery, paper, pads, envelopes, tablets, pens, pencils or other stationery, take advantage of this most extraordinary offer.

The outfit contains the following items:	Regular retail price.
500 White Envelopes, XXX Stock	$2.50
1 Box of Persian Silk (White Wove Writing Paper, ruled, tied with baby blue silk ribbon and bow)	.15
1 Box of Sole De Paon (Laid Writing Paper, tied with silk cord and tassel)	.20
1 Box of Criterion (Ivory White Writing Paper, ruled, tied with silk cord and tassel)	.25
1 Box of Brookside (Wedding Plate Finish Writing Paper, banded and tied with silk cord and tassel)	.25

1 Box of Royal Holland (Superfine White Wove Writing Paper, ruled, double, tied with red silk ribbon and banded)	$0.25
1 Box of Sweet Sixteen (Cream Writing Paper, ruled, banded and tied with silk cord and tassel)	.25
¼ Ream Superfine White Wove Ruled Writing Paper, 480 pages, (120 double sheets)	.50
1 Dozen Blotters	.10
1 London Bond Tablet (Royal Bond Paper, letter size, 8x10 inches, ruled)	.15

1 Idle Thoughts Tablet (Superfine Cream Wove Paper, letter size, 8x10 inches)	$0.15
1 Birchbark Linen Tablet (Embossed Cover, Irish Linen Paper, ruled)	.15
1 Post Card Tablet (each cover is composed of two post cards, lithographed in colors, which can be torn off and mailed. Each post card is worth 5 cents. Wedding Plate Paper Ruled)	.15
1 Pencil Sharpener	.05
1 Bottle Red Ink	.05
1 Bottle Black Ink	.05
1 Bottle Mucilage	.05
1 Ink Well (pressed glass, fancy design)	.25

1 Eraser, Pen and Pencil	$0.05
1 Dozen Pens (Falcon Medium Point)	.10
1 Dozen Pens (Judge's Stub)	.10
1 Dozen Pens (Fine Point Elastic)	.10
1 Automatic Nickel Pencil	.15
2 Pencils (No. 2 "Beats All")	.05
2 Pencils (Traffic No. 2)	.05
2 Pencils (Self Sharpening, Paper Pencils)	.05
1 Penholder (Cedar, Metal Tip)	.05
1 Penholder (Ebony Handle, Nickel Tip)	.05
1 Penholder (Patent Ventilated Spring Tip)	.10
Would cost you at retail	$6.40

No. 3K9525 Special Stationery Outfit, just as illustrated and described above, all complete. Our price............(Weight, packed for shipment, 15 pounds)............**$1.95**

VEHICLES, HARNESSES, AND SADDLES

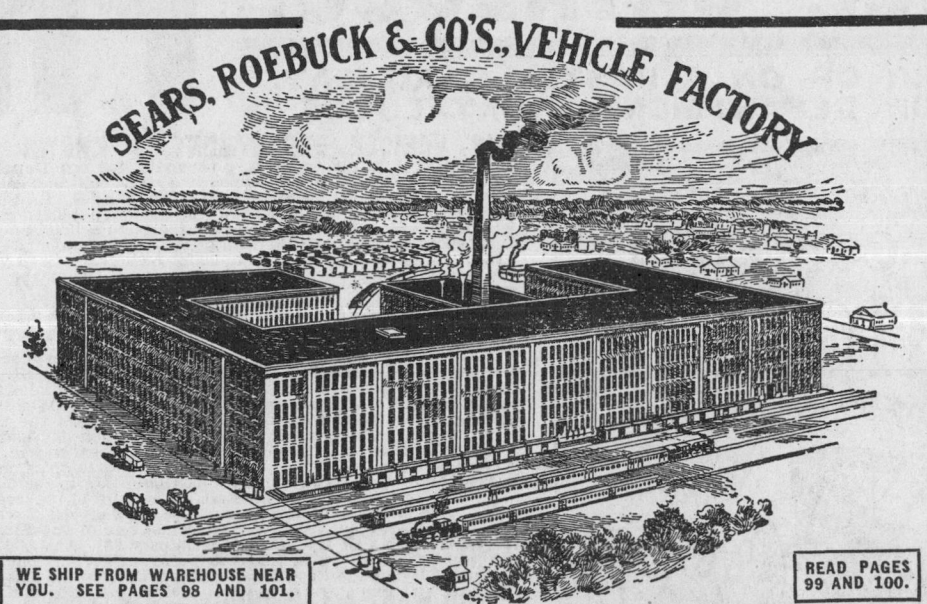

SEARS, ROEBUCK & CO'S., VEHICLE FACTORY

THREE SEPARATE AND DISTINCT CLASSES OF MATERIAL USED IN OUR LARGE VEHICLE FACTORY.

EASIEST RIDING, STRONGEST AND MOST COMFORTABLE VEHICLES BUILT.

We use in the construction of our vehicles three separate and distinct classes of material, we build three separate and distinct classes of top buggies, our Big Value Line shown on page 96, the world renowned American Beauty Line, and the highest grade buggies built in any factory, no matter what make, name or price, our Solid Comfort Vehicles. We give the greatest possible value, no matter what priced buggy ordered, we make the same small margin of profit on our cheapest top buggy that we do on the higher grades, therefore, to get the greatest possible value in return for the money invested, we always advise our customers to order either one of our American Beauties or one of our Solid Comfort Vehicles.

WE SHIP FROM WAREHOUSE NEAR YOU. SEE PAGES 98 AND 101.

OUR LIBERAL TERMS OF SHIPMENT

Select the vehicle you want, as shown on the following pages, enclose our price as quoted, state the catalogue number and whether you want wide or narrow track, and we will ship direct to you any kind of a vehicle shown on the following pages that you may select. The vehicle will go forward in a very few days after you send us your order, as we carry on hand at all times a very large stock of complete finished vehicles, you can give it a FREE TEN DAYS' TRIAL, during which time you can compare it with other vehicles, if you are not satisfied that you have the easiest riding, easiest running and most comfortable vehicle that was ever built, if you are not satisfied that you saved anywhere from $20.00 to $35.00, you can ship the vehicle back to us and we will refund your money and pay you back the freight charges.

READ PAGES 99 AND 100.

$20.00 TO $35.00 WILL BE SAVED IF YOU ORDER A VEHICLE FROM US

HERE IS THE STORY IN A NUTSHELL.

WHEN YOU ORDER FROM US YOU PAY:

Our actual factory cost of material and labor (much lower than others)	$0.00
Our exceedingly small profit	1.00
Freight charges from our factory to your railroad station	.00
Total profit over and above actual cost of material, labor and freight charges	$1.00

WHEN YOU ORDER FROM A LOCAL DEALER YOU PAY:

Actual factory cost of material and labor	$00.00
Manufacturer's profit, never less than	3.00
Jobber's profit, never less than	5.00
Dealer's profit, never less than	15.00
Freight charges always figured in the dealer's price	00.00
Total profits over and above actual cost of material, labor and freight charges	$23.00

$22.00 INVESTED IN EXTRA PROFITS THAT DO NOT ADD ONE CENT OF VALUE TO THE VEHICLE.

WHY SHOULD YOU BE ASKED TO PAY from $20.00 to $35.00 in extra profits that do not add one cent of value to the vehicle, when we can ship direct to your railroad station from our large factory, a vehicle priced at actual factory cost to produce, with our one small margin of profit added? The comparison made opposite allows other factories the same factory cost as ours, which is rarely the case, as we have one of the largest vehicle factories in the United States, we procure our raw material at the lowest possible cost, and the actual factory cost of material and labor in any finished vehicle at our factory, is from $2.00 to $3.00 lower than the same vehicle can be produced in other factories. We have allowed only $3.00 for the manufacturer's profit, most manufacturers' profits run nearer $5.00. We have allowed only $5.00 profit for the jobber, most jobbers make from $7.00 to $10.00. We have allowed only $15.00 for the dealer's profit, but the dealer usually makes from $20.00 to $25.00, but giving everybody the lowest possible margin of manufacturing cost and profits, it is easy to be seen that by ordering a vehicle direct from us you can save at least $22.00 in extra profits. You can avoid paying $22.00 to the manufacturer, jobber and dealer, and can secure a much better vehicle by sending your order to us than you can possibly secure elsewhere.

HOW TO ORDER

IT IS EASY TO ORDER A BUGGY FROM THIS CATALOGUE. In a letter or on one of our order blanks if you have it, state the catalogue number of the vehicle you desire, say whether you want wide or narrow track, enclose the price plainly quoted, and we will ship the vehicle selected just as illustrated and described in the catalogue. It is not necessary for you to mention anything but the catalogue number and width of track unless you desire some changes, which, of course, it will be necessary for you to state. Remember, unless you want some changes it will only be necessary to give us the catalogue number and width of track.

WE SHIP BUGGIES FROM OUR WAREHOUSE NEAREST YOU

READ ON PAGE 98 ABOUT OUR WONDERFUL WAREHOUSE ARRANGEMENT TO SAVE OUR CUSTOMERS TIME AND FREIGHT CHARGES

OUR THREE-YEAR BINDING GUARANTEE.

WE REPRODUCE BELOW A COPY of our three-year written binding guarantee furnished with our best vehicles, as stated throughout the following pages. The most binding guarantee furnished by any vehicle manufacturer. Every one of our vehicles is so constructed that it will with proper care, outwear three ordinary factory grade vehicles, and as a guarantee that everything is first class, exactly as described and free from the slightest defect in material or workmanship, we send with each vehicle purchased, this handsome registered guarantee. We guarantee to furnish you a much better job of painting and finishing than is turned out of any other factory, as we grind and mix our own colors in our own paint factory.

SEARS, ROEBUCK AND CO.
CHICAGO
CAPITAL STOCK FORTY MILLION DOLLARS

Certificate No.

Certificate of Guaranty

This Certifies that the vehicle (registered under above certificate number), is made of carefully selected material by skilled mechanics, and for ordinary use should last for years. Any piece or part of this vehicle breaking on account of defective material or poor workmanship, will be repaired or replaced without charge to the customer. This certificate is good for three years from date of shipment, subject to conditions on the other side. SEARS, ROEBUCK & CO.
Per R. W. Sears, President.

REPAIRS

WE CAN ALWAYS FURNISH REPAIRS AT FACTORY COST.
We have a complete record of each vehicle we build and ship, and we keep this record for years in order to serve our customers in case of accidents.

ABOUT THE FREIGHT CHARGES.

ON PAGE 112 we tell you all about the freight charges on vehicles. It will surprise you how small the freight charges on a vehicle are as compared with the amount you will save by sending your order to us. Be sure to read all about the freight charges on page 112.

BE SURE TO STATE WIDTH OF TRACK.

With the exception of a few special track vehicles, as noted in this catalogue, all vehicles are furnished either in the 4 feet 8 inches, narrow, or 5 feet 2 inches, wide track, as desired.

NOTICE—Not all but most all street car tracks are narrow tracks, 4 feet 8 inches.

FARM WAGONS ARE MEASURED FROM CENTER TO CENTER OF TIRE.

NARROW TRACK 4 FT. 8 IN.
WIDE TRACK 5 FT. 2 IN.

The opposite illustration shows the method of measuring track, same being distance from outside to outside of rear wheels on the ground.

INSPECTION AND SAFE DELIVERY GUARANTEED. Thoroughly experienced and competent inspectors, men who are expert vehicle builders, men who have had years of experience in shipping vehicles, are employed in our factory to carefully inspect each vehicle before it is shipped to our customers; every detail of the construction and finish is rigidly examined before the vehicle is crated for shipment; each vehicle, after being thoroughly inspected as to workmanship, material, construction and finish, is covered with a dustproof bag so that it will not gather dirt or dust while in transit. We aim to so wrap, cover, pack and crate our work that it can travel any distance, and be sure to open up at destination in the same perfect condition in which it leaves our factory. We load all our vehicles direct from the shipping room floor into the car; no carting, hauling or handling; we crate in the best possible manner, in fact, we guarantee safe delivery.

IF YOU WANT OUR SPECIAL VEHICLE CATALOGUE FREE

IN A LETTER OR ON A POSTAL CARD SAY, "SEND YOUR DEPARTMENT 11 CATALOGUE"

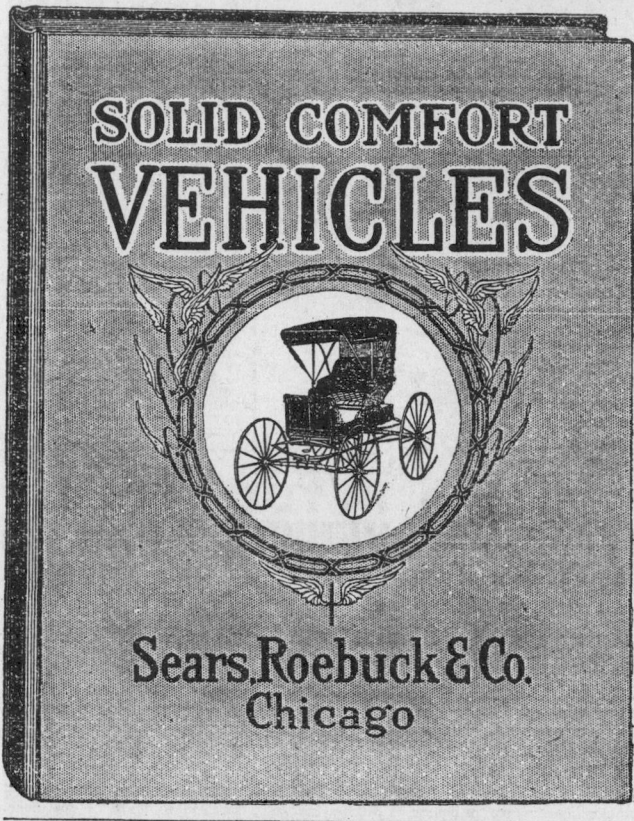

SOLID COMFORT VEHICLES

Sears, Roebuck & Co.
Chicago

OUR VEHICLE DEPARTMENT IS KNOWN AS DEPARTMENT 11, and while it is not necessary to write for our Department 11 Catalogue, as we show in this large General Catalogue a very full and complete line of all the popular latest style runabouts, driving wagons, top buggies, phaetons, surreys, spring wagons and farm wagons, at the same time, if you, before purchasing, would like to see all of these jobs illustrated and described on good paper, in a handsomely bound catalogue with large illustrations, complete detail descriptions, send for our Department 11 Catalogue. In a letter, on a postal, or even in an order for goods, say, "Send your Department 11 Catalogue," and we will send you by return mail, postpaid, one of the handsomest vehicle catalogues ever published.

OUR ADVICE IN ORDERING A VEHICLE

ON THE FOLLOWING PAGES we show a very complete line of all kinds of vehicles. Naturally, on account of our large sales making for economy in our factory, there are certain vehicles we always advise our customers to order when they ask us, so that they will get not only the latest style and the most popular vehicle of its kind, but will also obtain the most durable, strongest, easiest riding, easiest running, most comfortable and best finished vehicle on the market. Our profit is the same on each vehicle we sell. It is, therefore, always to the interest of our customers, from a purely economical standpoint, to order one of our higher grade rigs, and as there are certain styles which we mention below in the different classes of vehicles that sell much better than others, we are, on account of the large number built in our factory, able to give far greater value than on the other styles; therefore,

IF YOU WANT A RUNABOUT select one of the Blue Ribbon Runabouts shown on page 95. Any one of these runabouts represents the greatest possible value that can be secured. Any one of these runabouts gives you more actual value returned for every cent invested than any other runabouts we sell.

IF YOU WANT A TOP BUGGY select our No. 11K525, illustrated and fully described on page 100. This is the most popular buggy in the world. It is carried in warehouse so as to serve our customers promptly. Our profit is the same on this top buggy as on our cheaper top buggies; therefore, we advise our customers in their own interest, from a purely economical standpoint, to order our No. 11K525, which will be shipped from a nearby warehouse; very quick service, small freight charges.

IF YOU WANT A SURREY OR FAMILY CARRIAGE refer to page 106, our Solid Comfort Surreys, built in four different styles; the most stylish, strongest, easiest riding, easiest running, most durable and most comfortable surreys ever built.

IF YOU WANT A SPRING WAGON order our No. 11K1105 Two-Seated Half Platform Spring Wagon, illustrated and described on page 108, the most serviceable and the handiest wagon, which can be used either for pleasure or for business, that was ever built, more actual value, more returns for the money invested than any other wagon we manufacture.

IF YOU WANT A FARM WAGON refer to page 110, either our No. 11K1509, 3,500 pounds capacity, or our No. 11K1510, 4,500 pounds capacity. Either one of these wagons represents great value for the money, either one is the popular size used on the different farms in the United States. However, if you do not find on page 110 just the kind of farm wagon you want, if you require something special, send for our Special Farm Wagon Catalogue; in a letter or on a postal card say, "Send me your Special Farm Wagon Catalogue," and we will send you a handsome catalogue showing the most complete line of farm wagons ever manufactured and ever assembled in one catalogue, our prices representing the actual factory cost of materials and labor with our one small margin of profit added.

IT IS NOT NECESSARY TO DELAY YOUR ORDER, as practically our complete line of vehicles, with the same prices, are shown on the pages of this Big General Catalogue.

KELLY SPRINGFIELD RUBBER TIRES

GUARANTEED WE FURNISH THE BEST

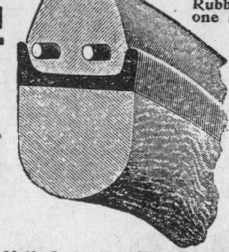

We furnish the well known Kelly Springfield Buckeye Brand Solid Rubber Tires, recognized by everyone as the best rubber tire that is made for vehicles. Any vehicle quoted on the following pages can be fitted with these rubber tires at our factory for the prices quoted below. We recommend and guarantee these tires. We also furnish guaranteed cushion rubber tires. Do not buy a cheap rubber tire. Get the best.

KELLY SPRINGFIELD BUCKEYE BRAND

Guaranteed Tires. Look for this brand on every tire. "The Kelly Springfield Tire, Pat. Feb. 18, 1896. Made in America."

¾-inch solid rubber tires in place of steel tires.	Price	$13.10
⅞-inch solid rubber tires in place of steel tires.	Price	14.95
1-inch solid rubber tires in place of steel tires.	Price	17.85

GUARANTEED CUSHION RUBBER TIRES.

1-inch cushion rubber tires in place of steel tires.	Price	$15.70
1⅛-inch cushion rubber tires in place of steel tires.	Price	18.95

UNGUARANTEED SOLID RUBBER TIRES.

Some few of our customers desire to use a cheap tire, and for this reason we furnish a cheap, unguaranteed rubber tire at the prices quoted below. Our guaranteed Kelly Springfield Buckeye Brand Tires will outwear three sets of these tires.

⅞-inch.	Price.	$10.75
1-inch.	Price.	13.25

CATELY & ETTLING'S TOP ADJUSTER.

THIS ILLUSTRATION shows the celebrated Cately & Ettling Top Adjuster. The top can be raised or lowered from the seat when the side curtains are on, by pulling the levers at the side of the top, as shown in the illustration. This adjuster has been used extensively and found satisfactory. This top adjuster is furnished regularly on No. 11K517 buggy, page 97. If you want a buggy fitted with this top adjuster order No. 11K517, page 97.

TOUCH THIS LEVER
SELF ACTING SPRING

THE COLUMBUS WHEEL WITH DODGED OR STAGGERED SPOKES

$1.50 EXTRA

The accompanying illustration shows the well known Columbus wheel. This wheel is made with the dodged or staggered spokes, as shown in the illustration, that is, the spokes are not in a straight line at the hub, but are set out at either side from the center, considered by many the correct principle on which to build a strong, substantial wheel. We positively guarantee that the spokes in this wheel will not become loose from any ordinary wear or tear and we will replace, without charge, any wheel that may fail for this reason. This wheel must not be compared with a cheap compressed band wood hub wheel. It is strictly a high class wheel, made as near perfect as human ingenuity and mechanical skill can make it. The hub consists of a solid piece of tough hardwood, with the spokes compressed and then driven in after being dipped in hot glue; the entire hub is then completely covered with a pressed steel shell. The point band is part of the front shell, and is pressed on the rear of the shell under twenty-five tons hydraulic pressure. The spokes are pressed in a corrugated form, dipped in hot glue, then immediately driven into the hub. The glue causes them to swell to their original shape, thus making it impossible for a spoke to ever become loose. Where any job to be shipped from our factory is described with a Sarven's patent wheel and this guaranteed Columbus wheel is wanted, we will be pleased to furnish it if you will so specify in your order and allow $1.50 extra. Please remember, if the Columbus wheel is ordered, the vehicle will be shipped from our factory at Evansville, Indiana, as none of the warehouse jobs are fitted with this wheel.

W. S. SHULER'S PATENT ROLLER BEARING SPRINGS

This spring can be furnished on any of our open or top buggies in place of the elliptic end spring. While we do not show any style buggy in this catalogue built with this spring, we have some calls for the Shuler spring and are in a position to furnish it, as stated above, without extra charge, if you will so specify in your order.

ROAD WAGONS AND ROAD CARTS

THIS ROAD WAGON AT $25.95 IS A WONDER OF VALUE

while it is built in our own factory, covered by our one year binding guarantee and is much better value than you could possibly secure elsewhere, and is a grade of rig that is sold by other concerns at from $5.00 to $10.00 in advance of our price, we advise ordering one of our higher grade runabouts, one of the 1908 models shown on the following pages. Our profit is the same on this runabout as on our higher grades; therefore, to secure the greatest possible return for the money invested, we always urge our customers to select one of our higher grade runabouts, where you will get better wheels, better axles, better springs, stronger and better made body, better upholstering, a better finish and a more serviceable runabout.

$25.95

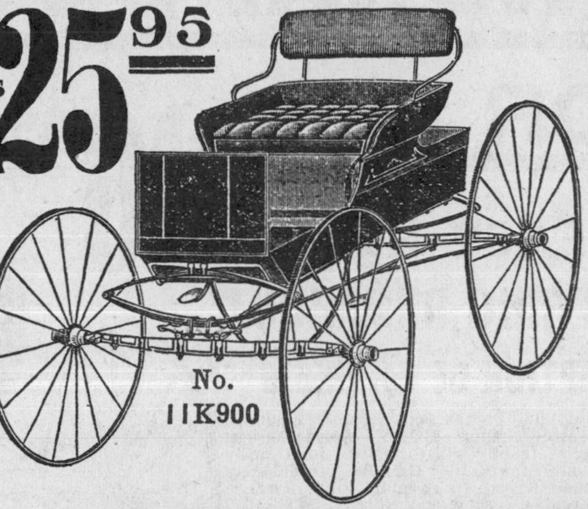

No. 11K900

DESCRIPTION OF No. 11K900

SEAT—29½ inches; skeleton back; tufted and padded cushion and back; lined seat ends; imitation leather upholstering. **BODY**—23 inches wide by 55 inches long; Corning style, well made, fitted with short carpet and Evans' enameled black duck dash. **GEAR**—Drop axles, 15-16 inch, double collar; full length axle caps; double reach, ironed and braced full bearing fifth wheel; three and four-plate elliptic springs; center bearing body loops. **WHEELS**—Sarven's patent style; 38 inches front and 42 inches rear; ⅞-inch rims, fitted with ¼-inch oval edge steel tires. **SHAFTS**—Hickory shafts, double braced, neatly trimmed. **PAINTING**—Body and seat black, neatly striped; gear, wheels and shafts a dark Brewester green, neatly striped. **TRACK**—4 feet 8 inches narrow or 5 feet 2 inches wide. Shipped from Evansville Indiana. Crated under 30 inches, weight 420 pounds.

No. 11K900 Price complete with shafts and steel tires...... **$25.95**

$32.15

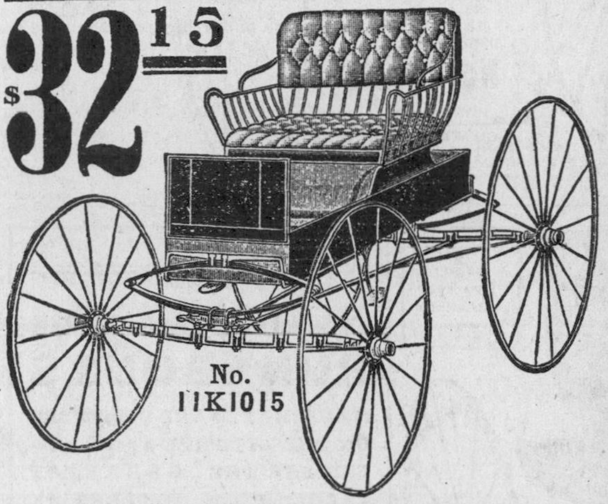

No. 11K1015

TAKE YOUR CHOICE OF THESE TWO ROAD WAGONS

COVERED BY OUR ONE YEAR BINDING GUARANTEE

THESE ROAD WAGONS are better value than can be secured elsewhere at within $5.00 to $10.00 of our price, but our Blue Ribbon Runabouts for 1908 shown on page 95 are much better runabouts and are guaranteed for three years.

$34.15

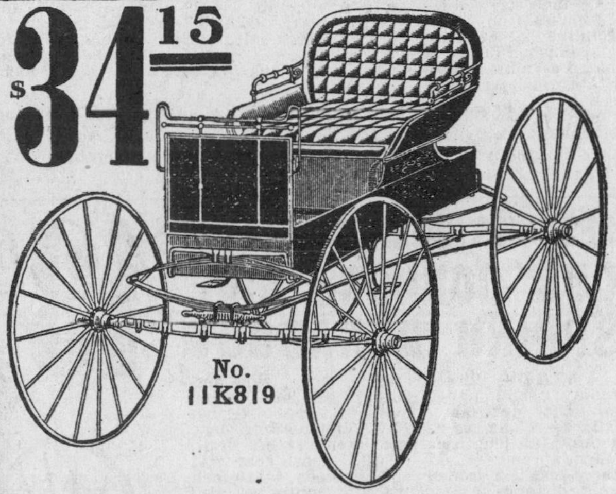

No. 11K819

DESCRIPTION OF No. 11K1015

SEAT—Stick seat, made with bent sticks; seat handles; measures 29½ inches; 10-inch curved panel back; spring cushion; whipcord upholstering. **BODY**—23 inches wide by 55 inches long; piano box style; body is glued, screwed and plugged; short carpet; end panel lined with carpet; drill fiber boot on rear of body; leather dash; storm apron. **GEAR**—15-16-inch axles, dust and mudproof bell collars, long distance spindles; three and four-plate elliptic springs; new style center bearing body loops; double reach, ironed full length. **WHEELS**—38 inches front and 42 inches rear; Sarven's patent style; ⅞-inch screwed rims, fitted with full ¼-inch oval edge steel tires. **SHAFTS**—Double braced hickory shafts, trimmed with leather 22 inches back from the point, flat straps; quick shifting shaft couplers. **PAINTING**—Body and seat painted plain black; gear, wheels and shafts painted blood carmine. **TRACK**—4 feet 8 inches narrow or 5 feet 2 inches wide. Shipped from Evansville, Ind. Weight, crated, under 30 inches, 440 pounds.

No. 11K1015 Price, complete with double braced shafts and steel tires.............................. **$32.15**

DESCRIPTION OF No. 11K819

SEAT—29½ inches; Georgia drop back; spring cushion, well padded and tufted; seat ends padded and lined; double bar nickel arm rails; upholstered in keratol leather. **BODY**—Piano box style, 23 inches wide by 55 inches long; swell body panels and convex seat panels; boot on rear of body; carpet; end panel lined with carpet; side panels finished inside; leather dash with nickel plated dash rail; storm apron. **GEAR**—15-16-inch axles; dust and mudproof bell collar long distance spindles; hickory wood caps; double reach, ironed and braced; three and four-plate elliptic springs; new style center bearing body loops; full bearing fifth wheel. **WHEELS**—⅞-inch screwed rims, fitted with ¼-inch oval edge steel tires; Sarven's patent style; 38 inches front and 42 inches rear. **SHAFTS**—Hickory shafts, trimmed with leather 22 inches from the tip, flat straps; double braced; quick shifting shaft couplers. **PAINTING**—Body and seat painted plain black, with neat design on seat riser; gear, wheels and shafts blood carmine, striped with black. **TRACK**—4 feet 8 inches or 5 feet 2 inches. Shipped from Evansville, Indiana. Weight crated under 30 inches, 435 pounds.

No. 11K819 Price, complete with double braced shafts and steel tires.............................. **$34.15**

EXTRAS ON ANY OF THE ABOVE ROAD WAGONS

Pole in place of shafts	$2.00
Both pole and shafts	4.65
Extra grade genuine leather upholstering in place of regular	2.00

$11.95

COVERED BY OUR ONE YEAR BINDING GUARANTEE.

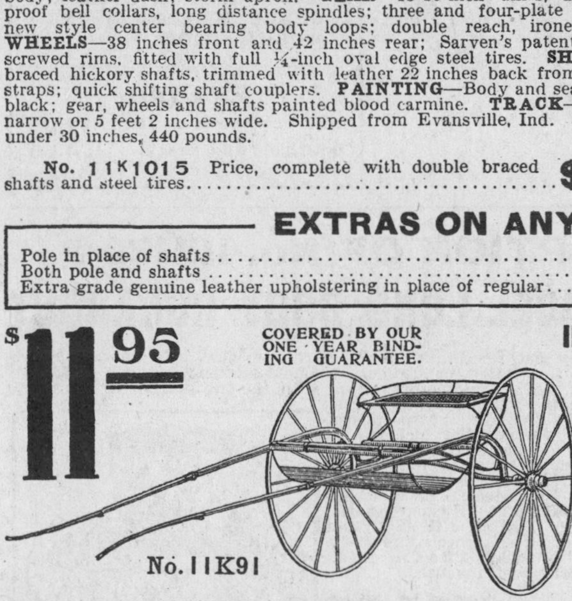

No. 11K91

IN BUILDING THESE CARTS

we use Sarven's patent wheels, with ⅞-inch rims; rims are fitted with oval edge steel tires; heavy hardwood spring block; seat frame, foot rack, etc., made of hardwood; hickory shafts; 1-inch double collar steel axle, square at the shoulders and round in the center with a high arch; easy riding oil tempered springs, hung so as to balance the seat perfectly. On our No. 11K91 we furnish a skeleton seat, with a seat rail, as shown in illustration. On the phaeton body cart, No. 11K101, we furnish a seat and lazy back, as shown in illustration. The seat is upholstered on the phaeton body cart in imitation leather. The body of the No. 11K101 is so constructed that the seat can be raised on hinges and small articles carried in the box under the seat. Both carts are built to carry two passengers, although the adjustment of the springs is so that they ride very easy with only one passenger. We use the same care in painting and finishing these road carts as we do our regular buggies. We paint the No. 11K91 road cart a rich carmine color. The body of the No. 11K101 road cart is painted black, with a rich blood carmine gear, neatly striped. We can furnish either one of these carts in the 4 feet 8 inches narrow or the 5 feet 2 inches wide track. Shipped from factory in Northern Illinois. Shipping weight, No. 11K91, 150 pounds; No. 11K101, 180 pounds.

COVERED BY OUR ONE YEAR BINDING GUARANTEE.

$14.65

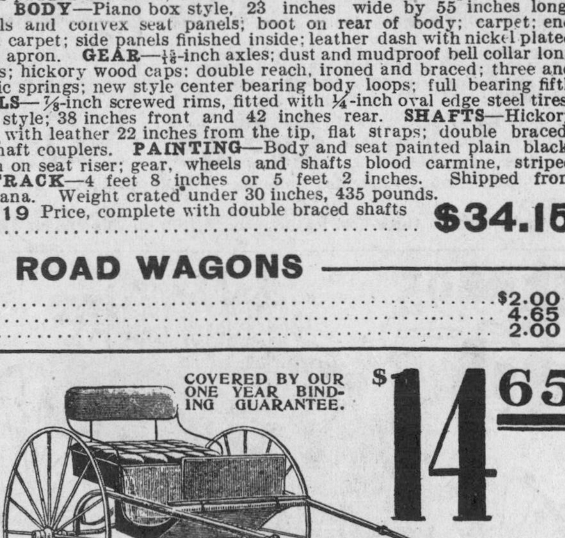

No. 11K101

No. 11K91 Skeleton Cart, as shown in the illustration. Price, complete.............................. **$11.95**

No. 11K101 Phaeton Body Cart, as shown in the illustration. Price, complete.............................. **14.65**

LEADING RUNABOUT STYLES

FOR 1908

$36.95

OUR EASY RIDING SIDE SPRING RUNABOUT

DESCRIPTION OF No. 11K616

This illustration shows the Shuler Roller Bearing Spring which has become very popular with vehicle users, can be furnished on No. 11K616, if ordered, without extra charge.

SEAT—Special design panel stick seat, measuring 29½ inches across top of cushion; spring cushion, upholstered with good serviceable keratol leather. BODY—Special design spindle body, 23 inches wide by 55 inches long; bracket front (will furnish 20-inch body if ordered); carpet; handsome patent leather dash; storm apron. GEAR—Special easy riding side spring gear as shown in illustration; arched axles, 15-16-inch, long distance dust and mudproof bell collar; hickory axle caps; no reaches, very easy riding. WHEELS—⅞-inch screwed rims; Sarven's patent wheels, fitted with full ¼-inch oval edge steel tires; 38 inches front and 42 inches rear. SHAFTS—Second growth hickory, trimmed with genuine leather; double braced; quick shifting shaft couplers. PAINTING—Body painted and finished in the best possible manner, black panels; gear, wheels and shafts a rich red blood carmine, neatly striped with black. TRACK—4 feet 8 inches or 5 feet 2 inches. State width wanted.

No. 11K616 Price, complete with double braced shafts and steel tires.........**$36.95**

Shipped from Evansville, Indiana. Shipping weight, crated under 30 inches, 410 pounds.

No. 11K616

COVERED BY OUR TWO-YEAR BINDING GUARANTEE.

DESCRIPTION OF No. 11K715
OUR CONCORD SIDE SPRING RUNABOUT

$43.65

Covered by our Two-Year Binding Guarantee.

SEAT—Phaeton style, very wide and roomy; solid panel spring back and spring cushion; genuine leather upholstering. BODY—27 inches wide by 56 inches long, very roomy; full length carpet; patent leather dash; storm apron. GEAR—Full Concord gear with three reaches; ironed and braced; 15-16-inch long distance axles; dust and mudproof bell collars; hickory axle caps; four-plate springs, hung on equalizers, front and rear. WHEELS—⅞-inch screwed rims, fitted with ¼-inch oval edge steel tires; Sarven's patent style; 38 inches front and 42 inches rear. SHAFTS—Second growth hickory, trimmed with genuine leather; double braced; quick shifting shaft couplers. PAINTING—Body and panels black, striped, shutter work on seat risers painted dark red; gear, wheels and shafts painted rich blood carmine, neatly striped. TRACK—4 feet 8 inches or 5 feet 2 inches. State width wanted.

No. 11K715 Price, complete with double braced shafts and steel tires.........**$43.65**

Shipped from Evansville, Indiana. Shipping weight, crated under 30 inches, 450 pounds.

Can furnish a three-bow leather quarter top on this job for **$9.75**.

No. 11K715

OUR
BLUE RIBBON RUNABOUTS

ILLUSTRATED AND DESCRIBED ON THE OPPOSITE PAGE, REPRESENT THE GREATEST VALUE EVER OFFERED IN HIGH CLASS, STYLISH RUNABOUTS. FOUR STYLES OF WINNERS.

GUARANTEED 3 YEARS.

MADE OF OUR HIGHEST GRADE MATERIALS AND WORKMANSHIP.

EXTRAS.

Pole in place of shafts....$2.00
Both pole and shafts..... 4.65

$35.95

DESCRIPTION OF No. 11K1304
OUR NEW MODEL LONG BODY RUNABOUT

SEAT—Very large, roomy seat, small take out seat in rear, so that it is well adapted for either business or pleasure; button tufted, padded cushion back; seat ends padded and lined; imitation leather upholstering. Prices quoted are for job with the two seats or with just one seat, or with one seat and a top. BODY—27x74 inches; hardwood frame; side panels finished inside; carpet; dash. GEAR—15-16-inch drop axles, double collar; hickory axle caps; full circle fifth wheel; double reach, ironed full length; 1¼-inch four-plate elliptic spring in front, Hayes triple spring in rear. WHEELS—Sarven's patent; ⅞-inch rim, fitted with ¼-inch oval edge steel tires; 38 inches front and 42 inches rear. SHAFTS—Hickory shafts; double braced; neatly trimmed. PAINTING—Body and seats dark green, neatly striped; gear, wheels and shafts rich blood carmine, striped with black. TRACK—4 feet 8 inches or 5 feet 2 inches. State width wanted.

No. 11K1306

No. 11K1304 Price, complete with two seats, as shown in illustration, and double braced shafts.........**$35.95**

No. 11K1305 Price, complete with one seat and double braced shafts..................**$34.25**

No. 11K1306 Price, complete with one seat, four-bow buggy top and double braced shafts.....................**$43.85**

Shipped from Evansville, Indiana. Shipping weight, crated under 30 inches, 550 pounds.

COVERED BY OUR TWO-YEAR BINDING GUARANTEE.

No. 11K1304

AMERICAN BEAUTIES

GUARANTEED TWO YEARS.

THE QUEEN OF OUR AMERICAN BEAUTIES, THE GREATEST SELLING BUGGY OF OUR AMERICAN BEAUTY LINE, IS CARRIED IN WAREHOUSES AT DIFFERENT POINTS FOR IMMEDIATE SHIPMENT, AS FULLY EXPLAINED ON PAGE 98 AND 99. DON'T FAIL TO READ ABOUT OUR WONDERFUL AMERICAN QUEEN, ILLUSTRATED AND DESCRIBED ON PAGE 99, THE MOST POPULAR BUGGY OF OUR AMERICAN BEAUTY LINE, THE GREATEST SELLER OF THEM ALL.

This line of American Beauties represents great value, and the leader of them all, the largest seller, the greatest buggy ever built outside of our highest grade Solid Comfort Buggies, is fully illustrated and described on page 99; we carry it in warehouses, as fully explained on pages 98 and 99; we sell such a large number of this one American Queen Top Buggy, the one illustrated and described on page 99, that we carry it on hand at different warehouses, so as to serve our customers promptly and save them freight charges.

$44⁹⁵

$46⁷⁵

47⁸⁵

$45⁷⁵

$43⁹⁵

DESCRIPTION OF No. 11K610

SEAT—29½ inches; panel spring back and box spring cushion; seat ends padded and lined; upholstered in heavy dark green body cloth or extra grade moroccoline leather. BODY—Piano box style; 23 inches wide by 55 inches long; hardwood frame; boot on rear of body; carpet; toe carpet on front panel; leather dash, fitted with nickel dash rail. TOP—Three-bow genuine leather quarter top; padded and lined back stays; rubber roof and lined rubber back curtain; wool faced head lining; patent curtain fasteners; heavy side curtains; roll-up straps; nickel top propnuts; storm apron. GEAR—15-16-inch drop axles; long distance dust and mudproof spindles; hickory axle caps; double reach, ironed and braced; full bearing fifth wheel; three and four-plate elliptic oil tempered springs; new style center bearing body loops. WHEELS—Sarven's patent style; ⅞-inch screwed rims; full ¼-inch oval edge steel tires; 38 inches front and 42 inches rear. SHAFTS—Hickory shafts, trimmed with leather 22 inches back from tip, flat straps; double braced; quick shifting shaft couplers. PAINTING—Body, rosewood, striped, fancy design on seat risers; gear, wheels and shafts, rich blood carmine, striped. TRACK—4 feet 8 inches or 5 feet 2 inches. State width desired.
No. 11K610 Price, complete with double braced shafts and steel tires............$44.95
Shipped from Evansville, Indiana.

DESCRIPTION OF No. 11K517

SEAT—New style auto seat; 29½ inches; fancy back and cushion, fitted with plenty of springs; upholstered with heavy dark green cloth or extra grade moroccoline leather. BODY—Piano box style; 23x55 inches; hardwood frame; boot on rear of body; carpet; toe carpet on front panel; leather dash, fitted with nickel dash rail. TOP—Genuine leather quarters and back stays; rubber roof and back curtain; back stays padded and lined; wool faced head lining; lined back curtain; two roll-up straps; heavy side curtains; patent curtain fasteners; storm apron; nickel top propnuts; three bows. GEAR—15-16-inch steel axles; long distance, dust and mudproof bell collar; hickory axle caps; special fifth wheel; elliptic and springs; center bearing body loops; double reaches, ironed full length. WHEELS—Sarven's patent; ⅞-inch screwed rim; full ¼-inch oval edge steel tires; 38 inches front and 42 inches rear. SHAFTS—Hickory shafts; double braced; trimmed with leather 22 inches back from the tip, flat straps; quick shifting shaft couplers. PAINTING—Body, black, striped and decorated; fancy seat risers; gear, wheels and shafts, blood carmine, striped with black. TRACK—4 feet 8 inches narrow or 5 feet 2 inches wide. State width desired.
No. 11K517 Price, complete with double braced shafts and steel tires,...................$47.85
Shipped from Evansville, Indiana.

DESCRIPTION OF No. 11K612

BODY—Deep side panel phaeton seat; 29½ inches; solid spring overstuffed panel back and spring cushion; seat ends padded and lined; handsome seat handles; upholstered with dark green body cloth or extra grade moroccoline leather. BODY—23 inches wide by 55 inches long; piano box style; 8-inch panels; hardwood frame; drill fiber boot on rear of body; carpet; leather dash. TOP—Three-bow leather quarters and leather back stays; wool faced head lining; back stays padded and lined; lined back curtain; heavy side curtains; stitched valance; two roll-up straps; patent curtain fasteners; storm apron. GEAR—Arched axles, 15-16-inch; hickory axle caps; long distance dust and mudproof bell collar spindles; double reach, ironed; oil tempered, easy riding, three and four-plate springs; new style center bearing body loops. WHEELS—⅞-inch screwed rims, fitted with ¼-inch oval edge steel tires; full bolted; Sarven's patent style; 38 inches front and 42 inches rear. SHAFTS—Double braced hickory shafts; trimmed with leather 22 inches back from the point, flat straps; quick shifting shaft couplers. PAINTING—Body, plain black; gear, wheels and shafts, dark Brewster green, striped. TRACK—4 feet 8 inches or 5 feet 2 inches. State width desired.
No. 11K612 Price, complete with double braced shafts and steel tires.................$46.75
Shipped from Evansville, Indiana.

DESCRIPTION OF No. 11K514

SEAT—29½ inches; solid panel overstuffed spring back and box frame spring cushion; padded and lined seat ends; upholstered in heavy dark green body cloth or extra grade moroccoline leather. BODY—23x55 inches; piano box style; hardwood frame; 8-inch panels; boot on rear of body; carpet; leather dash. TOP—Leather quarter top and back stays; back stays padded and lined, fancy stitched; heavy waterproof side curtains and lined back curtain, wool faced head lining; raised, stitched valance; two roll-up straps; patent curtain fasteners; three bows; waterproof storm apron. GEAR—15-16-inch arched axles; dust and mudproof bell collars; long distance spindles; hickory axle caps; double reach, ironed; three and four-plate oil tempered elliptic springs; new style center bearing body loops. WHEELS—Sarven's patent; ⅞-inch screwed rims, fitted with ¼-inch oval edge steel tires; 38 inches front and 42 inches rear. SHAFTS—Double braced hickory shafts; trimmed with leather 22 inches from the tip, flat straps; quick shifting shaft couplers. PAINTING—Body plain black; gear wheels and shafts blood carmine, striped. TRACK—4 feet 8 inches or 5 feet 2 inches. State width desired.
No. 11K514 Price, complete with double braced shafts and steel tires.................$45.75
Shipped from Evansville, Indiana.

DESCRIPTION OF No. 11K619

SEAT—Georgia drop back; spring cushion, 25½ inches; padded and lined seat ends; double bar nickel arm rails; upholstered in heavy dark green body cloth or extra grade moroccoline leather. BODY—20 inches wide by 55 inches long; hardwood frame; piano box style; boot on rear of body; carpet; toe carpet on front panel; patent leather dash. TOP—Two and one-half-bow; leather quarters and back stays; wool faced head lining; patent curtain fasteners; two roll-up straps; storm apron. GEARS—15-16-inch axles; long distance dust and mudproof bell collar; hickory axle caps; long easy riding side springs; no reaches. WHEELS—38 inches front and 42 inches rear; Sarven's patent style; ⅞-inch screwed rims; ¼-inch oval edge steel tires, full bolted. SHAFTS—Hickory shafts, trimmed with leather 22 inches back from tip, flat straps; double braced; quick shifting shaft couplers. PAINTING—Body, plain black; gear, wheels and shafts, Brewster gear green, striped. TRACK—4 feet 8 inches or 5 feet inches. State width desired.
No. 11K619 Price, complete with double braced shafts and steel tires.................$43.95
Shipped from Evansville, Indiana.

SOLID COMFORT TOP BUGGIES

OVER 100,000 SOLID COMFORT TOP BUGGIES IN USE.

Since starting to build in our own factory a few years ago our Solid Comfort Top Buggies, we have shipped over 100,000 Solid Comfort Top Buggies to satisfied customers. The first season we introduced our Solid Comfort line of top buggies we sold 10,000, these 10,000 were a standing advertisement for us and brought more orders; the next season we sold over 25,000. Each buggy it seems, brought us more orders, with a result that we now have in daily use over 100,000 of these Solid Comfort Top Buggies. There are more Solid Comfort Top Buggies in use today than any other one line of top buggies manufactured.

THREE-YEAR GUARANTEE WITH EACH BUGGY.

THE EASIEST RIDING, easiest running, strongest, most durable and most comfortable top buggies built. Built in our own factory out of high grade material, positively the best material that can be secured for the money. Better wheels, better shafts, stronger gears, better bodies, higher grade seats and tops, higher grade dashes, carpets, upholstering, cloth and leather and the best possible finish on both the body and gear that can be produced.

$52.95

YOUNG MAN'S BUGGY

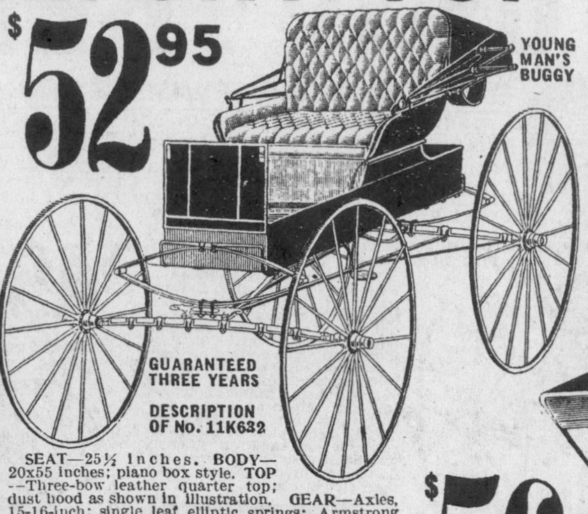

GUARANTEED THREE YEARS

DESCRIPTION OF No. 11K632

SEAT—25½ inches. BODY—20x55 inches; piano box style. TOP—Three-bow leather quarter top; dust hood as shown in illustration. GEAR—Axles, 15-16-inch; single leaf elliptic springs; Armstrong pattern; new style center bearing body loops; longitudinal spring running from front to rear axle. WHEELS—38 inches front and 42 inches rear; ¾-inch screwed rims. SHAFTS—XXX hickory shafts; double braced; Bradley shaft couplers. PAINTING—Body, plain black, no striping; gear, blood carmine, striped. TRACK—4 feet 8 inches or 5 feet 2 inches. State width wanted. Shipped from Evansville, Indiana.

No. 11K632 Price, complete with double braced shafts and steel tires..........$52.95

HIGH GRADE FANCY BUGGY

$54.75

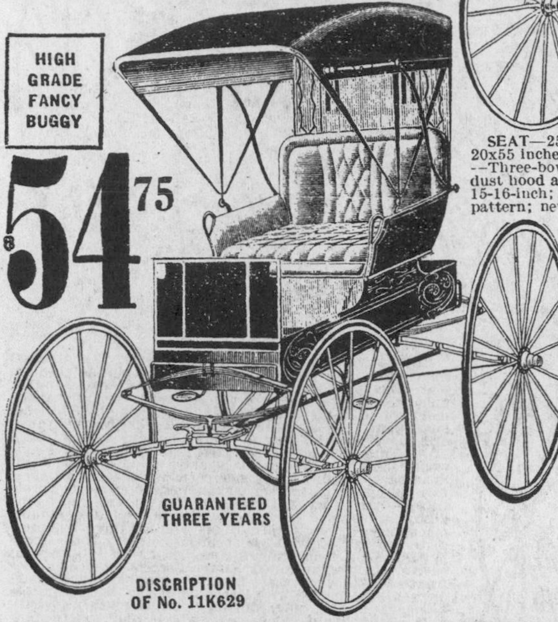

GUARANTEED THREE YEARS

DISCRIPTION OF No. 11K629

SEAT—Fancy pattern; springs in back; deep side panels. BODY—Piano box style; 23 inches wide by 55 inches long. TOP—Three-bow leather quarters. GEAR—15-16-inch steel axles. WHEELS—Sarven's patent; ⅞-inch rims; 38 inches front and 42 inches rear. SHAFTS—XXX hickory shafts; double braced; Bradley shaft couplers. PAINTING—Body, ebony black, fancy striped, design on seat riser; gear, wheels and shafts, rich blood carmine, striped. TRACK—4 feet 8 inches or 5 feet 2 inches. State width wanted. Shipped from Evansville, Indiana.

No. 11K629 Price, complete with double braced shafts and steel tires..........$54.75

STANDARD HIGH GRADE BUGGY

$56.45

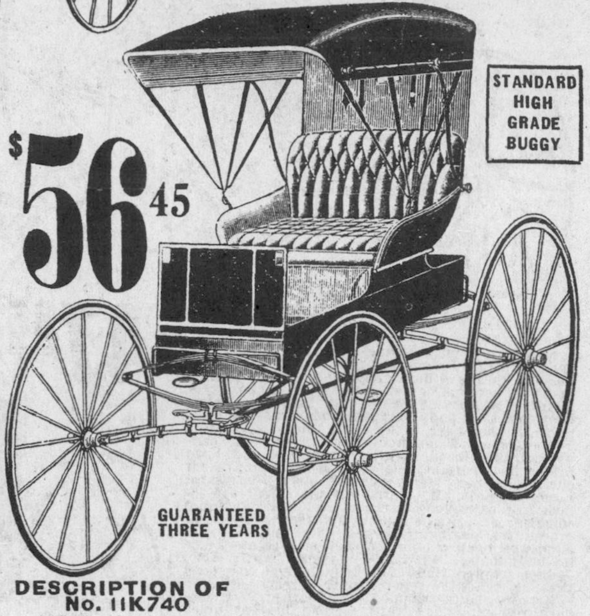

GUARANTEED THREE YEARS

DESCRIPTION OF No. 11K740

SEAT—32½ inches; high panel overstuffed back. BODY—Piano box style, 25x55 inches. TOP—Leather quarter, four-bow top. GEAR—15-16-inch long distance arched axles; 36-inch open head springs. WHEELS—38 inches front and 42 inches rear; ⅞-inch screwed rims. Sarven's patent style. SHAFTS—Extra XXX hickory shafts; double braced; Bradley shaft couplers. PAINTING—Body, jet black; gear, rich blood carmine, neatly striped. TRACK—4 feet 8 inches or 5 feet 2 inches. State width wanted. Shipped from Evansville, Indiana.

No. 11K740 Price, complete with double braced shafts and steel tires..........$56.45

THESE TOP BUGGIES

are upholstered in either 16-ounce all wool dark green (nearly black) body cloth or high grade upholstering leather, according to the section of the country to which they are shipped. If you have any preference, please state when ordering. The buggies are built of the same high grade material as our leader No. 11K525 (see page 100 for detailed description). These buggies all shipped from our factory, Evansville, Indiana. Weight, crated under 30 inches, about 500 pounds.

OPTIONS

You can have, if wanted, without extra charge three-bow in place of four-bow top, four-bow in place of three-bow top, drop axles in place of arched.

EACH SOLID COMFORT TOP BUGGY IS IN A CLASS BY ITSELF

Each Solid Comfort Top Buggy, no matter what style you may select from the different styles shown on these two pages, you will find when it is received, has an individuality, a snappy appearance, a style of its own that puts it in a class by itself. Each and every Solid Comfort Top Buggy is put through our factory with the care and attention it would receive were it the only top buggy we built, each part is made to fit accurately with the other part, every adjustment is carefully trued up and gauged, every part is carefully inspected, the complete buggy is set up in our factory, each wheel is turned to see that it runs true, measurements are taken of the front and rear wheels to see that they track perfectly, our gauge is put on each wheel to see that it has the proper dish to correspond with the other wheels; in fact, every part of the buggy is carefully inspected before it is packed and crated for shipment.

EXTRAS

Pole in place of shafts..	$ 2.00
Both pole and shafts ...	4.90
¾-inch Kelly Springfield guaranteed rubber tires	13.10
⅞-inch Kelly Springfield guaranteed rubber tires	14.95
1-inch Kelly Springfield guaranteed rubber tires	17.85

For cushion rubber tires, see page 92.

CONCORD SPRING TOP BUGGY.

$58.95

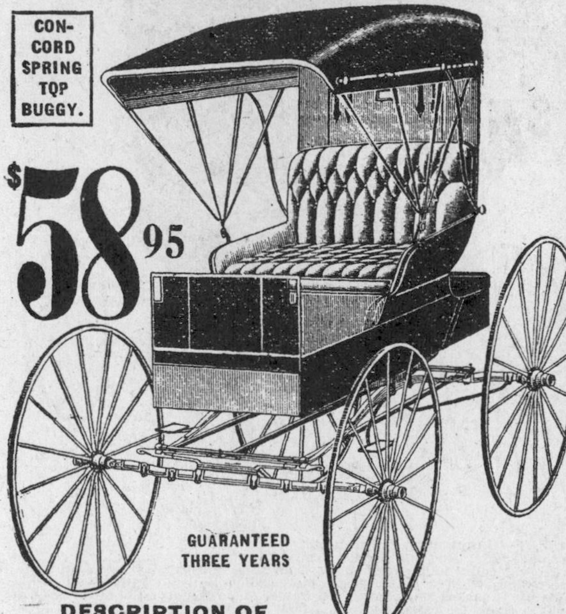

GUARANTEED THREE YEARS

DESCRIPTION OF No. 11K726

SEAT—Phaeton style, 32½ inches. BODY—25 inches wide by 55 inches long, piano box style. TOP—Four-bow leather quarter top. GEAR—Full Concord gear; three reaches, fully ironed and braced; 15-16-inch long distance axles, ⅝-inch Concord four-plate springs, the ends of which are attached to equalizers. WHEELS—Sarven's patent style, ⅞-inch screwed rims; wheels 38 inches front and 42 inches rear. SHAFTS—Extra XXX hickory shafts, double braced; Bradley shaft couplers. PAINTING—Body, plain black; gear, wheels and shafts, dark Brewster green, striped. TRACK—4 feet 8 inches or 5 feet 2 inches. Shipped from Evansville, Ind.

No. 11K726 Price, complete with double braced shafts and steel tires..........(State width wanted.)..........$58.95

AUTO SEAT BUGGY ON BIKE GEAR.

$61.85

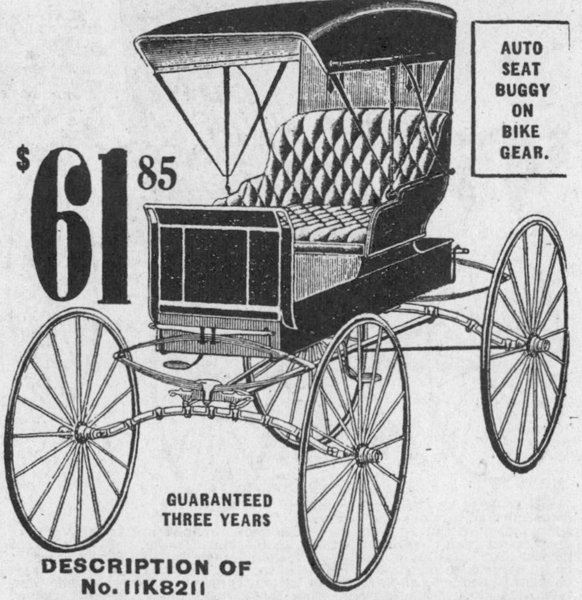

GUARANTEED THREE YEARS

DESCRIPTION OF No. 11K8211

SEAT—Automobile seat, 29½ inches. BODY—23x55 inches; piano box style; padded wing dash. TOP—Leather quarters, three bows; top is removable, and is fastened on a full shifting rail with a patent fastener making an open or a top job. GEAR—High arch full wood cap bike axles; long distance axles, 15-16-inch; 36-inch oil tempered elliptic open head springs, wood spring bars. WHEELS—37 inches front and 41 inches rear, ⅞-inch screwed rims; Sarven's patent style. SHAFTS—Second growth XXX hickory; double braced. Bradley shaft couplers. PAINTING—Body, plain black; gear, rich blood carmine, striped with black. TRACK—4 feet 6 inches only, not built in wide track. Shipped from Evansville, Indiana.

No. 11K8211 Price, complete with double braced shafts and steel tires..........$61.85

YOUR MONEY WILL BE IMMEDIATELY RETURNED TO YOU FOR ANY GOODS NOT PERFECTLY SATISFACTORY.

67

AUTOMOBILE SEAT TOP BUGGY == WITH == WING DASH $59.95

MADE THROUGHOUT OF HIGH GRADE MATERIAL, A VERY POPULAR STYLE OF OUR SOLID COMFORT LINE; REMOVABLE TOP FITTED ON A SHIFTING RAIL WITH PATENT FASTENERS; TOP CAN BE REMOVED SO THE JOB CAN BE USED AS A RUNABOUT; A HIGH CLASS STYLISH UP TO DATE AUTOMOBILE SEAT TOP BUGGY WITH THE LATEST STYLE WING DASH.

DESCRIPTION

No. 11K628

$59.95

SEAT. A very handsome design of automobile seat, roomy, comfortable, with a high bent back fitted with plenty of soft resilient coil springs, upholstered and tufted as shown in the illustration, including the seat ends; cushion is of the box frame pattern, neatly tufted and upholstered and fitted with plenty of soft wool springs; the seat measures 29½ inches across top of cushion. We use either an all wool dark green (nearly black) imported body cloth or a soft high grade leather in upholstering this seat. If any choice, be sure to state in order, otherwise we will use our best judgment, according to the section of country to which the job is to be shipped.

BODY. Well made, strong substantial body, 23 inches wide by 55 inches long; swell panels, made of the best seasoned material; hardwood frame, sills, corner posts and seat frame; well made in every particular, will outwear two ordinary bodies. Boot covering body rear of seat; full length velvet carpet; special design automobile bent front wing dash, made of high grade patent leather, padded.

TOP. Full sweep graceful three-bow genuine leather quarter top, with the quarters cut deep, of extra high grade enameled top leather; wide genuine leather back stays; heavy rubber roof and back curtain; heavy raised valance, stitched front and rear. The top throughout, including back curtain, is lined with a very substantial heavy dark green wool head lining to match the upholstering in the seat; four roll up straps; heavy waterproof rubber side curtains and storm apron. If wanted, we will furnish a four-bow top instead of a three-bow top, without extra charge.

GEAR. Special design graceful arch axle, fitted full length with a hickory wood axle cap, cemented, sanded and clipped to the axle; spindles are of the long distance dust and mudproof pattern, 15-16-inch bell collar; double reach, ironed full length, stayed and braced with wrought iron stays; large 11-inch full circle easy turned fifth wheel; 36-inch open head, elliptic, oil tempered easy riding springs, attached to body with our celebrated center bearing wrought iron body loops; steel plates running full length on body from one body loop to the other; a strong, substantial gear throughout, one that will outlast two ordinary factory grade gears.

Shipping weight, crated under 30 inches, about 475 pounds. Shipped from Evansville, Indiana.

WHEELS. Extra high grade Sarven's patent wheel with selected second growth hickory spokes, sixteen to each wheel; bent hickory rims, ⅞ inch wide, fitted with a full ¼-inch oval edge steel tire, bolted between each spoke. Each wheel is carefully tested and tried, guaranteed to run true, have the proper set, proper gather and the proper dish; front wheels 38 inches high, rear wheels 42 inches high. Can furnish the Columbus staggered spoke wheel if ordered at $1.50 extra. (See page 92). Can furnish wheels 40 inches front and 44 inches rear, if desired, without extra charge.

SHAFTS. Selected grade XXX shafts, neatly trimmed with 30-inch shaft leathers, round straps and double braced, also fitted with a celebrated Bradley quick shifting shaft coupler.

PAINTING. This Automobile Seat Top Buggy is given a first class job of painting and finishing, the body and seat are given a mirror finish and a jet black color, no striping; gear is painted a rich dark blood carmine, mirror finish, neatly striped with black. The whole appearance of the job with a plain black body and a rich blood carmine gear, neatly striped, makes a handsome appearance; it has just enough life without being at all flashy or loud. Can furnish dark Brewster green gear instead of blood carmine if ordered.

TRACK. 4 feet 8 inches or 5 feet 2 inches. State width wanted.

No. 11K628 Price, complete with double braced shafts and steel tires $59.95
Price, complete with ¾-inch Kelly Springfield guaranteed rubber tires .. 73.05
Price, complete with ⅞-inch Kelly Springfield guaranteed rubber tires. 74.90
Price, complete with 1-inch Kelly Springfield guaranteed rubber tires. 77.80
(⅞-inch rubber tires are the best suited for this top buggy.)

Covered by our regular binding three-year guarantee to be free from defect in either material or workmanship.

EXTRAS.
Pole in place of shafts with Bradley couplings $2.00
Both pole and shafts with Bradley couplings 4.90

HEAVY CONCORD TOP BUGGY
TWO-YEAR GUARANTEE.

$61.45

DESCRIPTION OF No. 11K263

No. 11K263

SEAT—Special style seat, large and roomy; solid panel spring back and spring cushion; upholstered in genuine leather.
BODY—28 inches wide by 58 inches long; panels, 8½ inches; hardwood frame; lifted panels; strap leather boot on rear of body; leather dash.
TOP—Leather quarters and leather back stays; back stays padded and lined; lined back curtain; rubber side curtains; wool head lining; rubber roof; full corded top; storm apron; four bows. **GEAR**—1 1-16-inch axles; dust and mudproof long distance spindles; hickory axle caps; full Concord side springs, hung on equalizers, attached to body with hickory spring bar; three perch gear; full bearing fifth wheel. **WHEELS**—1-inch oval edge steel tires, bolted between each spoke; Sarven's patent style; 38 inches front and 42 inches rear. **SHAFTS**—Double braced hickory shafts, neatly trimmed with leather; quick shifting couplers. **PAINTING**—Body, plain black; gear, wheels and shafts a dark Brewster green, neatly striped. **TRACK**—4 feet 8 inches or 5 feet 2 inches. State width wanted. Shipped from factory. Weight, crated under 30 inches, 600 pounds.
No. 11K263 Price, complete with double braced shafts and steel tires $61.45
No. 11K2635 Same job, only hung on drop axle and elliptic springs instead of Concord 60.15

EXTRAS.
Pole in place of shafts $2.25
Both pole and shafts 5.00
Full leather top with rubber side curtains in place of leather quarter top 4.00
Brake 5.00
1¼-inch wheels 2.30

1908 MODEL PHAETON
GUARANTEED TWO YEARS.

$61.95

DESCRIPTION OF No. 11K409

No. 11K409

SEAT—Special style; panel spring back and box spring cushion; seat panels lined; seat measures 32 inches across top of cushion and 19 inches deep; upholstered in either a heavy dark green body cloth or extra grade upholstering leather. **BODY**—Phaeton style, very roomy; hardwood frame; oil burning lamps; fenders; carpet; leather dash.
TOP—Leather quarter top; rubber roof and back curtain; lined raised valance, stitched front and rear full corded top; rubber side curtains; patent curtain fasteners; leather back stays, padded and lined, storm apron; three-bow top. **GEAR**—1⅛-inch axles, double collar; hickory axle caps; double reaches, ironed full length; full bearing fifth wheel; three and four-plate oil tempered elliptic springs. **WHEELS**—Sarven's patent style; 36 inches front and 44 inches rear; ⅞-inch screwed rims, fitted with full ¼-inch oval edge steel tires, full bolted. **SHAFTS**—Hickory shafts, nicely trimmed with leather 34 inches from the point; double braced; quick shifting shaft couplers. **PAINTING**—Body panels black, neatly decorated, Brewster green belt around edge; gear, Brewster green, neatly striped. **TRACK**—4 feet 8 inches or 5 feet 2 inches. State width wanted. Shipped from factory. Weight, crated under 30 inches, 500 pounds.
No. 11K409 Price, complete with double braced shafts and steel tires $61.95

EXTRAS.
Pole in place of shafts $2.25
Both pole and shafts 5.00
⅞-inch Kelly Springfield guaranteed rubber tires 14.95

— SURREYS—1908 MODELS —

$51⁹⁵

Covered by our one-year binding guarantee against defective material or workmanship.

DESCRIPTION OF No. 11K1300

SEATS—Phaeton style, O. G. shape, solid panel spring backs and box spring cushion seat ends padded and lined, upholstered with a heavy dark green imitation leather. **BODY**—5 feet 10 inches long by 26 inches wide, large and roomy; full length carpet; leather dash. **TOP**—Full size canopy top; good head lining; heavy fringe; attached with four standards, easily removed; full length side and back curtains. **GEAR**—1 1-16-inch double collar axles; heavy axle caps; double reach; ironed full length and braced; full bearing fifth wheel; four and five-plate elliptic oil tempered springs, hung on wood spring bars. **WHEELS**—Sarven's patent style; 38 inches front and 44 inches rear; 1-inch rims, fitted with full ¼-inch oval edge steel tires, bolted between each spoke. **SHAFTS**—Double braced hickory shafts, neatly trimmed, anti-rattlers. **PAINTING**—Body, black, neatly striped; seat panels striped; gear, wheels and shafts Brewster green, striped. **TRACK**—4 feet 8 inches or 5 feet 2 inches. State width of track wanted. Shipping weight, crated under 30 inches, 625 pounds.
No. 11K1300 Price, complete with double braced shafts and steel tires...**$51.95**

EXTRAS.

Pole in place of shafts	$2.00
Both pole and shafts	4.65
Cloth upholstering in place of regular	2.00
Genuine leather upholstering in place of regular	4.90

Shipped from Evansville, Indiana.

$58⁹⁵

Covered by our one-year binding guarantee against defective material or workmanship.

DESCRIPTION OF No. 11K1400

SEATS—Phaeton style seats O. G. shape solid panel spring backs and box spring cushions; seat ends padded and lined; upholstered with a heavy dark green imitation leather. **BODY**—5 feet 10 inches long by 26 inches wide, large and roomy; full length carpet; leather dash. **TOP**—Leather quarter extension top and leather back stays; back stays padded and lined; heavy dark green head lining; raised valance; rubber roof and back curtain; long curved top joint; enameled bow sockets; rubber drill side curtains; storm apron. **GEAR**—1 1-16-inch double collar axles; heavy axle caps; double reach, ironed full length and braced; full bearing fifth wheel; four and five-plate elliptic oil tempered springs, hung on wood spring bars. **WHEELS**—Sarven's patent style; 38 inches front and 44 inches rear; 1-inch rims; full 1-4-inch oval edge steel tires bolted between each spoke. **SHAFTS**—Hickory shafts, neatly trimmed; double braced; anti-rattlers. **PAINTING**—Body, black, neatly striped; seat panels striped; gear, wheels and shafts Brewster green, striped to match. **TRACK**—4 feet 8 inches or 5 feet 2 inches. State width of track wanted. Shipping weight, crated under 50 inches, 600 pounds.
No. 11K1400 Price, complete with double braced shafts and steel tires...**$58.95**

EXTRAS.

Pole in place of shafts	$2.00
Both pole and shafts	4.65
Cloth upholstering in place of regular	2.00
Genuine leather upholstering in place of regular	4.90

Shipped from Evansville, Indiana.

$57⁹⁵

GUARAN-TEED ONE YEAR

DESCRIPTION OF No. 11K266

SEATS—Roomy and comfortable; fastened with bolts and screws; front seat folds down flat on bottom of body, back seat moves forward making it the same as a one-seated buggy; full pad drop back on rear seat, pad lazy back on front seat; both seats upholstered in imitation leather. **BODY**—28x52 inches; hardwood frame; full length velvet carpet; patent leather dash. **TOP**—Four-bow full rubber top; inside of top and back stays lined with dark green cloth; top is fastened stationary to rear seat, can be raised or lowered; rubber side and back curtains; storm apron. **GEAR**—1 1-16-inch double collar axles; hickory axle caps; full circle fifth wheel; double reach, bolted and braced with wrought iron stay braces; four-plate front and five-plate rear elliptic end springs. **WHEELS**—38 inches front and 42 inches rear; 1-inch rims, fitted with oval edge steel tires; Sarven's patent style. **SHAFTS**—Hickory shafts, nicely trimmed and well ironed; anti-rattlers. **PAINTING**—Body black, neatly striped; gear, wheels and shafts a dark Brewster green, striped to match body. **TRACK**—4 feet 8 inches or 5 feet 2 inches. State width of track wanted. Shipping weight, crated under 30 inches, 600 pounds.
No. 11K266 Price, complete with two elliptic spring gear and shafts....**$57.95**
No. 11K267 Price, complete with Brewster side bar spring gear and shafts. 58.25
No. 11K268 Price, complete hung on three elliptic springs, one in front and two in rear and shafts 59.25
No. 11K2685 Price, complete hung on Concord springs, like shown on No. 11K263, and shafts 61.95

Shipped from factory.

EXTRAS.

Pole in place of shafts	$2.25
Both pole and shafts	5.00
Leather quarter top in place of rubber	3.90
Cloth cushions and backs in place of imitation leather	1.50
Genuine leather cushions and backs in place of imitation leather	3.85
1⅛-inch wheels with 1⅛x5-16-inch tires	2.30

$59⁹⁵

GUAR-AN-TEED ONE YEAR

DESCRIPTION OF No. 11K1118

SEATS—Double bend stick seats, 28 inches wide by 16 inches deep; 8-inch panel backs; spring cushions; upholstered in dark green body cloth or extra grade moroccoline leather. **BODY**—24 inches wide by 66 inches long; hardwood frame; full length velvet carpet; leather dash. **TOP**—Canopy top; hardwood frame, mortised and screwed; covered with heavy rubber drill; good head lining; fringe to match upholstering; full length side and back curtains; storm apron. **GEAR**—Long distance dust and mudproof bell collar 1 1-16-inch axles; hickory axle caps; single reach, ironed full length; full bearing fifth wheel; elliptic oil tempered springs, hung on wood spring bar. **WHEELS**—Sarven's patent style; 36 inches front and 44 inches rear; ⅞-inch screwed rims; ¼-inch oval edge steel tires, full bolted. **SHAFTS**—Double braced hickory shafts, trimmed with leather 22 inches back from tip, flat straps; quick shifting shaft couplers. **PAINTING**—Body black, neatly striped, and shaded belt; gear, wheels and shafts a rich blood carmine, neatly striped with black. **TRACK**—4 feet 8 inches or 5 feet 2 inches. State width of track wanted. Shipping weight, crated under 50 inches, 650 pounds.
No. 11K1118 Price, complete with double braced shafts and steel tires...**$59.95**

EXTRAS.

Pole in place of shafts	$2.00
Both pole and shafts	4.65

Shipped from Evansville, Indiana.

AUTOMOBILE SEAT SURREYS

1908 STYLES

HANDSOME DESIGNS, COMFORTABLE AND EASY RIDING. THESE AUTOMOBILE STYLE SEATS ARE VERY POPULAR AND VERY STYLISH

$77 45

$71.95

No. 11K1322
Surrey with Canopy Top.

$81.95

No. 11K1424
Cut Under Surrey with Extension Top.

No. 11K1422

Covered by our two year guarantee against defective material and workmanship.

DESCRIPTION No. 11K1422

SEAT. Auto seats; high phaeton spring backs; seat cushions are fitted with plenty of springs, making the job easy riding; seat ends padded and lined; upholstered in either a heavy 16-ounce all wool imported dark green body cloth or extra grade upholstering leather; according to the section of country to which it is shipped. If you have any preference be sure and specify in your order, otherwise we will upholster in the material best suited for the section of the country to which it is shipped.

BODY. 72 inches long by 27 inches wide, very comfortable and roomy; frame is made of well seasoned hardwood; the seat frames and corner posts are made of hardwood; body panels are made of seasoned poplar, thoroughly glued, screwed and plugged; full length ash sills; the whole body is reinforced by steel rocker plates, round corners on body and seats; full length carpet in bottom of body; handsome double fenders; oil burning lamps.

DASH. Our own original design of body, very strong.

TOP. Full sweep large leather quarter extension top, with very wide and deep genuine leather quarters and leather back stays; the back stays are padded and lined with heavy cloth; we use a dark green heavy head lining; raised valance; back curtain is lined with the same material as used in the

back stays and inside of top; the roof of this job is made of a heavy quality of rubber, with a heavy rubber back curtain; long curved top joint; enameled bow sockets; heavy waterproof side curtains, fastened at the top with loop straps; storm apron. A first class extension top, one that will give long and satisfactory service.

GEAR. We furnish a very strong and substantial gear on this surrey; the axles are 1 1-16 inches, best refined steel, fitted with dust and mudproof long distance spindles; the axles are fantailed, fitted with selected hickory axle caps, which are cemented, sanded and clipped to the axles; a heavy fifth wheel is used; two heavy selected second growth hickory reaches, ironed full length on the bottom, extending from the fifth wheel to the rear axle; the fifth wheel has the king bolt in rear of axle, heavy stay braces are used, together with wrought iron clips in connecting the reaches to the rear axle; four and five-plate 36-inch oil tempered elliptic springs, clipped to wood spring bar in rear.

WHEELS. Sarven's patent style; sixteen spokes to the wheel; 1-inch rims with screws on each side of the spokes; the rim is fitted with an oval edge steel tire, bolted between each spoke, a very strong and substantial wheel; the hubs are bored true

to the rim, so as to make them run perfectly true; the boxings are set in white lead by hydraulic press under a twenty-five ton pressure, which makes them almost everlasting, no loose boxings, no hubs that will rattle on these wheels, we guarantee them fully. they will track perfectly and run easily We furnish the wheels regularly, 38 inches front and 42 inches rear. Can furnish wheels 40 inches front and 44 inches rear if ordered.

SHAFTS. XXX selected second growth hickory shafts, trimmed with leather 22 inches back from the point; flat straps; double braced; quick shifting shaft couplers.

PAINTING. When painting this job we finish the body, seats and gear in the best possible manner, to correspond with balance of the makeup of the job; the body is painted plain black; the seat panels are black; the pillars on the seat and the moulding on the body are painted a rich dark carmine, making a very handsome effect. The gear, wheels and shafts are painted a rich dark Brewster green, neatly striped with carmine, making this a very handsome job of painting. Can furnish blood carmine gear if ordered.

TRACK. 4 feet 8 inches or 5 feet 2 inches. State width wanted. Net weight, about 550 pounds.

No. 11K1422	Price, complete as shown in large illustration	**$77.45**
No. 11K1322	Price, complete with canopy top (see small illustration)	$71.95
No. 11K1424	Price, complete with cut under body and extension top (see small illustration)	81.95

EXTRAS
Pole in place of shafts	2.00
Both pole and shafts	4.90
1-inch Kelly Springfield guaranteed rubber tires	17.85

Shipping weight, about 750 pounds, crated under 50 inches. Shipped from factory.

SOLID COMFORT SURREYS
1908 STYLES HIGH GRADE SURREYS

93^{95}

No. 11K1442

Covered by our three-year guarantee against defect in material or workmanship.

87^{95}

No. 11K1342
Conopy Top Surrey.

97^{75}

No. 11K1444
Extension Top and Cut Under Body.

92^{45}

No. 11K1344
Canopy Top and Cut Under Body.

DESCRIPTION OF No. 11K1442

SEATS. Latest style auto seats, very roomy and comfortable; high polished solid panel over-stuffed spring backs; seat cushions are of the box frame pattern, fitted with plenty of Staple & Hanford soft coil springs, making the job very easy riding; upholstered seat ends; seats are braced and reinforced throughout; upholstered in either a heavy 16-ounce all wool imported dark green body cloth or extra grade upholstering leather, according to the section of the country to which it is shipped. If you have any preference be sure to specify in your order, otherwise we will upholster in the material best suited for the section of the country to which it is shipped.

BODY. Large, roomy and comfortable body, made of the best material obtainable for the purpose; 6 feet 1 inch long by 28 inches wide; hardwood frame; seasoned ash sills; hardwood corner posts, uprights and seat frame; sills reinforced the entire length with a heavy steel rocker plate; hardwood skirting back and front seats; the step boards are put in in the most substantial manner, carefully fitted; body has a very nice belt or moulding, as shown in the illustration; body and seat panels are seasoned poplar with rounded corners; seat rods are bolted through sills; full length velvet carpet in bottom of body; large steps; patent leather double fenders; handsome oil burning lamps; padded leather dash.

TOP. Large, handsome, removable leather quarter extension top of the most improved pattern; quarters are very wide, running the full length from front to back, made of the best grade of black enameled top leather; back stays carefully padded and lined with a good heavy wool lining; the roof and back curtain of this top are made of an extra heavy quality

of rubber; a very handsome raised valance is used, front and rear; long curved top joints; large black prop nuts; top throughout is lined with an all wool very heavy dark green head lining; the back curtain is lined with the same material; the top has full length side and back curtains; auto curtain fasteners; enameled bow sockets; in fact, the top throughout is made of the best class material, to correspond with the balance of the job; waterproof storm apron. Top is fitted so it can be removed instantly without the use of tools.

GEAR. 1¼-inch axles, made of refined steel, the axles are of the drop pattern, tested in our micrometer gauge, so that they all have the same pitch, so that they will all set perfectly, so that our job will run easy and track true. The spindles are of the long distance dust and mudproof bell collar pattern; the axles are fitted with a heavy hickory axle cap, which is cemented, sanded and clipped to the axle with wrought iron clips; large full bearing fifth wheel is used, to which is connected two heavy reaches, which run to the rear axle, where they are connected with wrought iron stay braces; these reaches are ironed full length; the springs are four-plate front and five-plate rear, made of the best oil tempered spring steel, 36 inches in length, fully guaranteed, of the open head elliptic pattern; to the front spring is clipped a wood spring bar, which is attached to the body; to the rear spring is clipped wood spring bar; there is a steel strip running the full length of the body, connecting the front spring bar and the rear body loop.

WHEELS. We use a good substantial 1-inch surrey wheel on this job, of the Sarven's patent style; spokes are made of selected second growth hickory, fully guaranteed. To keep the rims from splitting we put a screw on each side of the spokes in the rim. When furnished with steel tires the wheels are fitted with an oval edge steel tire, and a bolt runs clear through the rim and tire between each spoke; the tires are heated before being put on the wheel, making the strongest kind of a wheel made. We furnish regular, wheels 38 inches front and 42 inches rear. Can furnish wheels 40 inches front and 44 inches rear if ordered. Can also furnish the Columbus staggered spoke wheel for $1.50 extra. (See page 92).

SHAFTS. Extra grade XXX second growth hickory shafts, trimmed with genuine leather 30 inches back from the point, four leather squares and oval straps; double braced; Bradley shaft couplers.

PAINTING. Every attention is paid to each little detail to make this one of the handsomest, most attractive and stylish jobs of painting that ever went out of any factory; we use more care to get a smooth finish on the body and gear; use more coats of painting, rubbing them in and out, use more rubbing varnish and finishing varnish than is put on any other surrey manufactured. The body panels are jet black; the seat panels and seat backs are finished with a rich Brewster green, which harmonizes beautifully with the black body; the pillars are painted a dark blood carmine. The gear, wheels and shafts are painted a rich Brewster green, neatly striped with a double line of glazed carmine. The entire effect of the painting on this job makes it very attractive. We furnish blood carmine gear if ordered.

TRACK. 4 feet 8 inches or 5 feet 2 inches. State width wanted. Net weight, about 575 pounds.

$93.95

No. 11K1442	Price, complete with extension top, double braced shafts and steel tires	$93.95
No. 11K1444	Price, complete with extension top, double braced shafts and cut under body	$97.75
No. 11K1342	Price, complete with canopy top in place of extension top	87.95
No. 11K1344	Price, complete with canopy top in place of extension top and cut under style body	92.45

EXTRAS
Pole in place of shafts 2.00
Both pole and shafts 4.90
1-inch Kelly Springfield guaranteed rubber tires 17.85

Shipping weight, crated under 50 inches, about 770 pounds. Shipped from factory.

SOLID COMFORT CABRIOLET

1908 MODEL—A HANDSOME DESIGN—HIGH GRADE

THE EASIEST RIDING, EASIEST RUNNING, HANDSOMEST AND MOST COMFORTABLE FAMILY CARRIAGE EVER BUILT. SOLD AT ACTUAL FACTORY COST WITH OUR ONE SMALL MARGIN OF PROFIT

FURNISHED WITH SHAFTS REGULARLY, BUT WILL FURNISH POLE IF WANTED AT SAME PRICE

$104.95

ITS EQUAL CANNOT BE PROCURED THROUGH THE REGULAR CHANNELS OF TRADE AT LESS THAN $175.00 TO $185.00

TWO FULL SWEEP EASY RIDING SCROLL SPRINGS IN THE REAR

No. 11K1447

COVERED BY OUR THREE-YEAR GUARANTEE AGAINST DEFECT IN MATERIAL OR WORKMANSHIP

DESCRIPTION OF No. 11K1447

SEATS. Latest design auto seats, very roomy, comfortable and easy riding; solid panel over stuffed spring backs; seat cushions are of the box frame pattern, fitted with Staple and Hanford soft coil springs; seat cushions and backs tufted in a very neat design; upholstered seat ends; seats are braced and reinforced throughout, one of the strongest seats built; upholstered in either a heavy 16-ounce all wool imported dark green body cloth or extra grade upholstering leather, according to the section of the country to which it is shipped. If you have any preference be sure and specify in your order, otherwise we will upholster in the material best suited for the section of the country to which it is shipped.

BODY. Cut-under style; 28 inches wide by 73 inches long; hardwood frame; hardwood corner posts and seat frame; sills reinforced the entire length with a heavy steel rocker plate, and over the cut-under part, adding extra strength to the body; the step strips are of hardwood, gained into the body frame; body has a very nice belt or moulding, as shown in the illustration; seasoned poplar panels, glued, clamped, screwed and plugged; rounded corners on body and seats; panel seat backs, reinforced with hardwood corner posts; graceful patent leather double fenders; large steps; large, handsome oil burning lamps; velvet carpet; padded leather dash. This is the best body that we can build, roomy and comfortable, at the same time of the right proportion to make it handsome in appearance.

TOP. Large handsome, removable leather quarter extension top; quarters are very wide, running the full length, from front to back, made of the best grade black enameled top leather; back stays are carefully padded and lined with a good heavy wool lining; the roof and back curtain of this top

are made of extra heavy quality of rubber; top is lined throughout with an all wool heavy dark green head lining; the back curtain is lined with the same material; heavy raised valance, stitched front and rear; top has full length rubber side curtains; auto curtain fasteners; large black propnuts; waterproof storm apron. Top is made of first class material, and is fitted so it can be removed instantly without the use of tools.

GEAR. We build under this job, a very substantial, strong and durable gear, one that we know will give perfect satisfaction and last twice as long as the ordinary gear found on surreys of this kind. We use a 1 1-16-inch axle, made of refined steel; the axles are tested in our micrometer gauge, so that they all have the same pitch, so that they will all set perfectly, so that our job will run easy and track true. These axles are fitted with a heavy second growth hickory axle cap, which is cemented to the axle, it is then sanded off so as to get a smooth finish and smooth joint with the axle, it is primed and then clipped with wrought iron clips; the spindles on the axles are of the long distance dust and mudproof bell collar pattern; large full bearing fifth wheel is used, to which is connected a strong single reach, ironed full length and braced, with wrought iron stays and braces; 36-inch open head, oil tempered four-plate elliptic spring in front, two special scroll springs in rear, as illustrated.

WHEELS. Sarven's patent style; 1-inch screwed rims, fitted with full 1/4-inch oval edge steel tires, full bolted between each spoke; spokes made of selected second growth hickory, fully guaranteed. The tires are heated before being put on the wheel, making the strongest kind of a wheel made, one that has the exact dish and the right strength for a surrey of this kind. We furnish regular, wheels

36 inches front and 44 inches rear. Can furnish wheels 34 inches front and 42 inches rear if ordered. Can also furnish the Columbus staggered spoke wheel for $1.50 extra. (See page 92.) We use a very strong and substantial wheel on this surrey.

SHAFTS. Extra grade selected second growth XXX hickory shafts, trimmed with genuine leather 30 inches back from the point, four leather squares and oval straps; double braced; Bradley shaft couplers.

PAINTING. We use more care in painting this surrey than any other job shown in our catalogue. The design of painting was taken from the highest class work that is built, jobs that were exhibited at the best vehicle shows in the country; we use more care to get a smooth finish on the body and gear; use more coats of painting, rubbing them in and out, use more rubbing varnish and finishing varnish than is put on any other surrey manufactured. The body panels are finished in a plain black; the seat panels are finished in a rich Brewster green, which harmonizes beautifully with the black body; the pillars and moulding on the body and seats, as shown in the illustration, are painted a very rich blood carmine. The entire effect makes one of the prettiest painted bodies that we can turn out. The gear, wheels and shafts of this job are painted a very rich Brewster green, striped to match body. The entire effect of the painting on this job makes it very attractive, and at the same time the colors blend in such a manner that it is not in any way gaudy, and it is painted after the same manner as the high priced rigs found in the best repositories in large cities. Can furnish blood carmine gear if ordered.

TRACK. 4 feet 8 inches or 5 feet 2 inches. State width desired. Net weight, about 575 pounds.

$104.95

No. 11K1447   Price, complete with double braced shafts and steel tires.. .... **$104.95**
EXTRAS Price, complete with pole in place of shafts **$104.95**
Both pole and shafts 5.00
1-inch Kelly Springfield guaranteed rubber tires.....................................17.85
Shipping weight, crated under 50 inches, about 790 pounds. Shipped from Evansville, Indiana.

SPRING WAGONS LATEST DESIGNS

$38.45

No. 11K1208

DESCRIPTION OF No. 11K1208

SEATS—Roomy and comfortable; skeleton backs, padded; padded cushions; seat ends padded and lined; solid wood seat risers; upholstered in imitation leather.
BODY—27 inches wide by 74 inches long, hardwood frame; leather dash.
GEAR—1 1-16-inch rear coached axle; 15-16-inch front axle, both fitted with double collar; hickory axle cap on front axle; single reach, 1⅜-inch four-plate springs in front; two 1⅜-inch four-plate springs in rear; wood spring bars.
WHEELS—Sarven's patent wheels; 38 inches front and 42 inches rear; 1-inch rims; oval edge steel tires, bolted between each spoke.
SHAFTS—Double braced hickory shafts.
PAINTING—Moulding on body painted a jet black, dark brown panels in between; seats black; gear wheels and shafts blood carmine, nicely striped.
TRACK—4 feet 8 inches or 5 feet 2 inches. State width wanted.
No. 11K1208 Price, complete with double braced shafts and steel tires **$38.45**
No. 11K1209 Price, complete with double braced shafts and canopy top **46.85**
Shipped from Evansville, Indiana.

DESCRIPTION OF No. 11K1203

$55.35

SEATS—Removable seats; solid panel backs, padded; padded cushions; padded and lined seat ends; upholstered with imitation leather.
BODY—7 feet 4 inches long by 34 inches wide; hardwood frame; panels 8 inches deep; drop endgate with corner irons and patent fasteners; braces on side of body; leather dash; edge irons around top of side panels.
TOP—Canopy top; ash frame; covered with heavy rubber drill; dark green head lining; heavy fringe; four steel standards connected to body so seats can be removed easily; full length side and back curtains.
GEAR—Front axle, 1⅛ inches, double collar, with axle bed; 1⅛-inch rear axle, coached; four-plate elliptic oil tempered springs, one in front and two in rear; 1⅜-inch leaf; double reach, ironed and braced; full length body loops.
WHEELS—1-inch riveted rims; oval edge steel tires, full bolted; 40 inches front and 44 inches rear; Sarven's patent style.
SHAFTS—Extra grade hickory shafts; double braced.
PAINTING—Body black, striped and neatly decorated; gear, wheels and shafts Brewster gear green, striped.
CAPACITY—About 900 pounds.
TRACK—4 feet 8 inches or 5 feet 2 inches. State width desired.
No. 11K1203 Price complete with double braced shafts and steel tires **$55.35**
Shipped from Evansville, Indiana.

No. 11K1203

EXTRAS   Brake $4.75
Genuine leather cushions and backs in place of imitation leather... 5.00
1⅛-inch wheels 2.25

No. 11K1104 has 1⅛-inch wheels and body 90 inches long.

$43.95

No. 11K1104

DESCRIPTION OF No. 11K1105

SEATS. Removable seats; high solid panel backs, button tufted and padded; seat cushions are of the box frame pattern, button tufted and padded; padded and lined seat ends; seat cushions and backs upholstered with imitation leather. Our No. 11K1104 is furnished with one seat, trimmed in imitation leather.
BODY. The strongest kind of a body made for a spring wagon, 34 inches wide by 7 feet long; hardwood frame, made of thoroughly seasoned bone dry material; well seasoned panels, 8 inches deep; reinforced corners with outside corner irons; edge irons on top of side panels; drop endgate with corner irons and patent fasteners; bottom boards are crossed, adding strength to the body; special braces on the side of body; leather dash. The No. 11K1104 is furnished with flare boards on the body, as shown in illustration.
GEAR. A very strong spring wagon gear; front axle 1⅛ inches; double collar with axle beds cemented, sanded and clipped to the axle with wrought iron clips; 1⅛-inch rear axle, coached; double reaches, ironed and braced; large full circle fifth wheel; elliptic spring in front, 1⅜-inch platform spring in rear; four-plate sides and five-plate ends. This is one of the strongest and most substantial wagon gears on the market today, will give satisfactory service, fully guaranteed by us; capacity, 1,000 pounds. The No. 11K1104 has Hayes spring in front.
WHEELS. Sarven's patent wheels, with iron flange; carefully selected hickory spokes; 1-inch rims with rivets on either side of the spoke; oval edge steel tires, bolted between each spoke; the best possible kind of a wheel for a wagon of this kind, a wheel that will stand the wear and tear and give the service that is desired in a wagon of this kind. We furnish wheels 40 inches front and 44 inches rear, but if desired and so specified in the order, we can furnish wheels 38 inches front and 42 inches rear.

$46.95

No. 11K1105

WE CAN FURNISH THIS WAGON AS FOLLOWS:
Body—34 inches by 7 feet 6 inches; bottom boards lengthwise; Hayes spring in front and 1⅛-inch wheels if wanted.
No. 11K1102 Price....$50.95

SHAFTS. Extra grade hickory shafts; double braced.
PAINTING. We paint this wagon so that it can be used by our customers as a combination pleasure and business wagon. The body is painted black, very handsomely striped and decorated with a very neat design on the seat riser, as shown in the illustration. The gear, wheels and shafts are painted a rich Brewster gear green, nicely striped to correspond with the body. Can furnish blood carmine gear in place of Brewster green if ordered.
TRACK. 4 feet 8 inches or 5 feet 2 inches. State width desired. Net weight, about 475 pounds.

No. 11K1105 Price, complete with double braced shafts and steel tires **$46.95**
No. 11K1104 Price, complete with double braced shafts and steel tires (see small illustration) **$43.95**

EXTRAS   Pole or shafts of shafts...........................$2.00
Both pole and shafts.................................. 4.65
Canopy top with full length side and back curtains... 7.75
Shipping weight, 670 pounds, crated under 30 inches.
Leather quarter extension top, full length, covering both seats.. 15.00
Genuine leather cushions and backs in place of imitation leather (two seats).......................... 5.00
Shipped from Evansville, Indiana.

$34.45 BUSINESS WAGONS $58.95

Send for our Special Catalogue of Business Wagons if none of these styles suit.

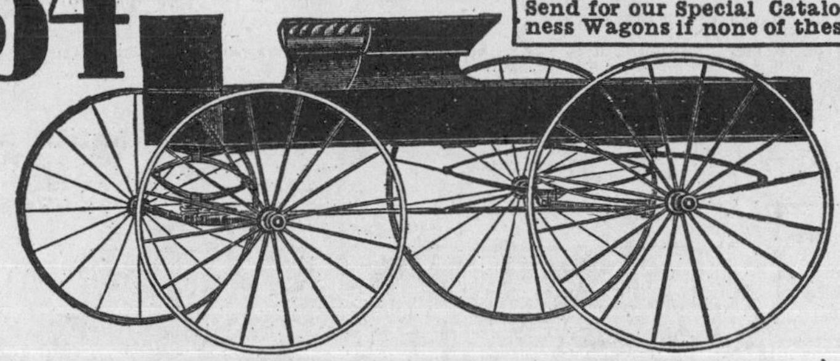

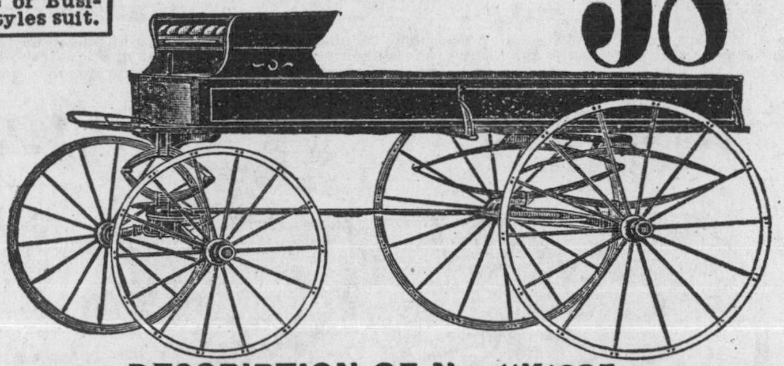

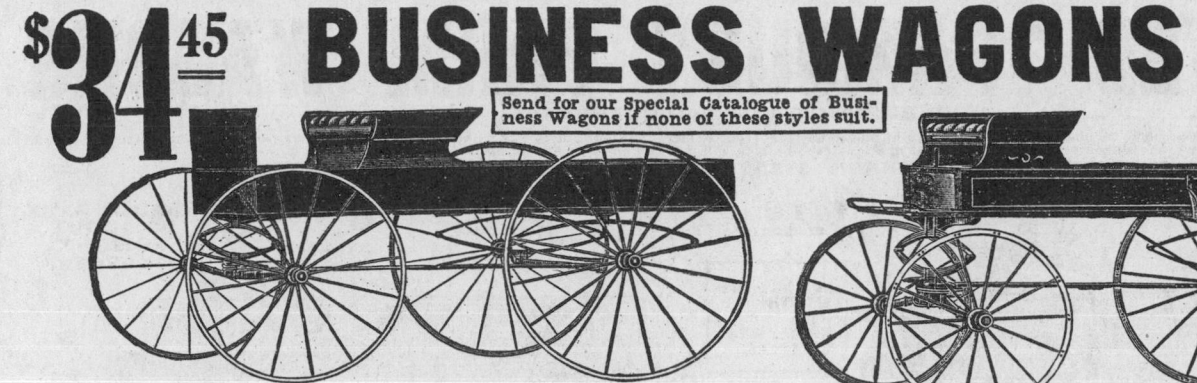

DESCRIPTION OF No. 11K1684

BODY—7 feet long by 34 inches wide; solid strap body, made of hardwood; boards in bottom run lengthwise; drop endgate; patent fasteners; removable seat with imitation leather cushion; wood dash, braced by two pieces of tire iron, each 1x¼ inches, from bottom of body to top of dash. GEAR—1-inch double collar steel axles; drop axle in front, fitted with a wood axle cap; coach axle in rear; single reach; rear king bolt fifth wheel; step on body; three elliptic springs, one four-plate, 1⅜ inches, in front and two three-plate, 1¼ inches, in rear. Sarven's patent wheels; 1-inch rims; oval edge steel tires; 40 inches front and 44 inches rear; shafts. PAINTING—Body black; gear, wheels and shafts, dark Brewster green. TRACK—4 feet 8 inches or 5 feet 2 inches. State width wanted.

No. 11K1684 Price, complete with shafts $34.45

EXTRAS.

Can furnish an extra seat trimmed in 28-oz. rubber with a lazy back.	4.25
Can furnish wagon with foot board in front without dash, so that seat can be moved forward, making a regular light spring delivery wagon.	1.00
Flare boards on the sides	1.75
1⅛-inch axle and wheels with body 7 feet 6 inches long and 34 inches wide	4.00

Shipped from factory, crated under 30 inches; weight, 600 pounds.

DESCRIPTION OF No. 11K1685

BODY—9 feet long by 40 inches wide; 10-inch panels; ironed on top and bottom of bed; drop endgate; 5-inch seat risers; seat cushion of imitation leather. GEAR—Axles, 1⅛ inches, double collar, steel; single reach, ironed and braced, 15-inch short turn fifth wheel; three elliptic springs, one in front and two in rear. Sarven's patent style wheels; 34 inches front and 44 inches rear; 1⅛-inch riveted rims, fitted with 1⅛-inch by 5-16-inch round edge steel tires; braced shafts. PAINTING—Body and seat dark green; black mouldings, neatly striped; gear blood carmine. If ordered we can furnish canary yellow gear. CAPACITY—1,500 pounds. TRACK—4 feet 8 inches or 5 feet 2 inches. State width wanted.

No. 11K1685 Price, complete with shafts $58.95

EXTRAS.

Flaring sideboards	2.75
Lettering, per letter	.10
Hand ratchet brake	4.90

Shipped from factory, crated 30x114 inches; weight, 825 pounds.

$46.95

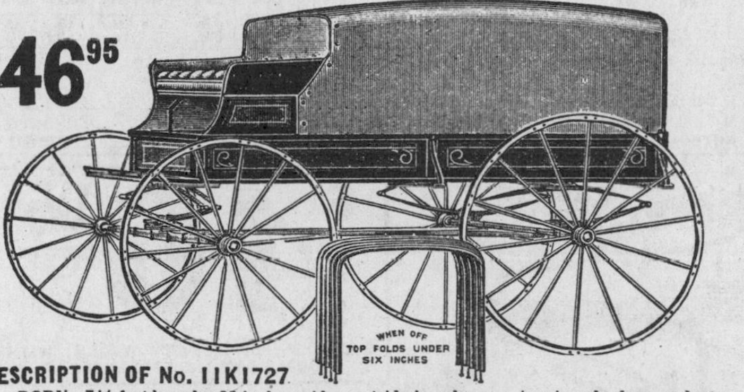
WHEN OFF
TOP FOLDS UNDER
SIX INCHES

DESCRIPTION OF No. 11K1727

BODY—7½ feet long by 36 inches wide; outside iron braces; toe board; drop endgate. Top is a folding canvas pattern, as shown in the illustration; imitation leather cushion. GEAR—1⅛-inch axles, double collar; easy riding oil tempered springs; Swan spring in front, two elliptic springs in rear, best kind of steel. Wheels 40 inches front and 44 inches rear; 5-16-inch tires; riveted rims; Sarven's patent, No. 7 flange. Double bend shafts, strongly ironed, well finished; steps attached. PAINTING—Body green, neatly striped; black mouldings; gear, New York red. If desired can paint the gear yellow or Brewster green. CAPACITY—1,500 pounds. TRACK—4 feet 8 inches or 5 feet 2 inches. State width wanted.

EXTRAS.

No. 11K1727 Price, as illustrated, with shafts	$46.95
If wanted without folding top deduct	4.00
Hand ratchet brake	4.90
Lettering, per letter	.10

Shipped from factory, crated under 30x94 inches; weight, 650 pounds.

$69.95

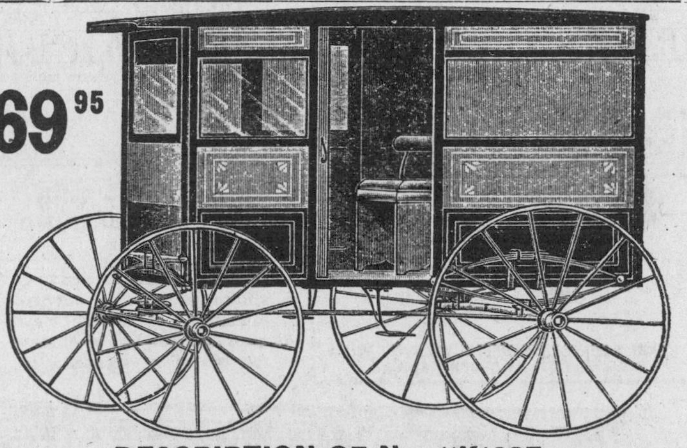

DESCRIPTION OF No. 11K1687

BODY—7 feet long by 34 inches wide; swinging glass transom 22x30 inches in front, lower part solid wood; front side panels are solid wood, fitted with glass, as illustrated; roller sliding door with glass; rear side panels solid wood; end panels solid wood with sliding window; portable seat, with hinge lazy back; bottom of body is 27 inches from the ground, body built in knock down construction to secure low freight rates. GEAR—Axles 1-inch, long distance spindles; large heavy iron fifth wheel; three-spring gear; heavy 1-inch Sarven's patent screwed rimmed wheels; 40 inches front and 44 inches rear; heavy braced shafts. PAINTING—Body rich dark green, handsomely striped in colors; gear blood carmine, neatly striped. CAPACITY—800 pounds. TRACK—4 feet 8 inches or 5 feet 2 inches. State width.

No. 11K1687 Price, complete with shafts $69.95

EXTRAS.

1⅛-inch axles and heavier gear throughout	3.25
Foot lever brake	4.50
Lettering, per letter	.10

Shipped from factory, crated 30x114 inches; weight, 850 pounds.

$89.95

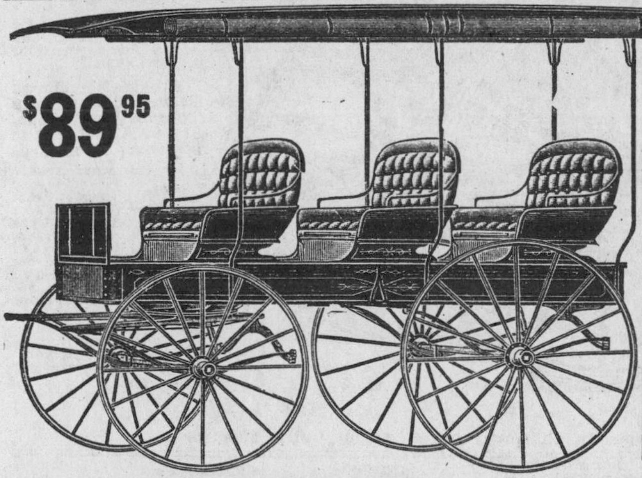

IF WANTED WITHOUT TOP DEDUCT $15.00

DESCRIPTION OF No. 11K1707

BODY—8 feet 6 inches long by 3 feet 2 inches wide; solid ash sills; seat cushions and backs upholstered with imitation leather; seat cushions have full length falls to bottom of wagon. TOP—Canopy style, hood shape in front; six standards; full length rubber roll up side and back curtains. GEAR—1¼-inch double bearing steel axle; full circle fifth wheel; clips are all wrought Norway iron; full platform springs, coupled together with equalizing shackles. Sarven's patent wheels; 40 inches front and 44 inches rear; 1¼-inch by 5-16-inch oval edge steel tires, strong pole. PAINTING—Body black; gear dark Brewster green. If desired can paint the gear blood carmine. CAPACITY—1,500 pounds. TRACK—4 feet 8 inches or 5 feet 2 inches. State width wanted.

No. 11K1707 Price, complete with pole, whiffletrees and neckyoke $89.95

No. 11K1708 Same wagon as No. 11K1707, except has 1⅜-inch axles and wheels with heavier springs, making capacity 2,000 pounds. Price.......... 99.95

No. 11K1709 Same wagon as No. 11K1708 except has body 9 feet 6 inches long by 42 inches wide. Built in 5 feet 2-inch track only. 2,000 pounds capacity. 103.75

If wanted without top, deduct $15.00.

EXTRAS.

Genuine machine buffed leather cushions and backs	8.50
Hand ratchet brake	5.00

Shipped from factory, crated under 30 inches high and over 94 inches long; weight, 950 pounds.

$64.25

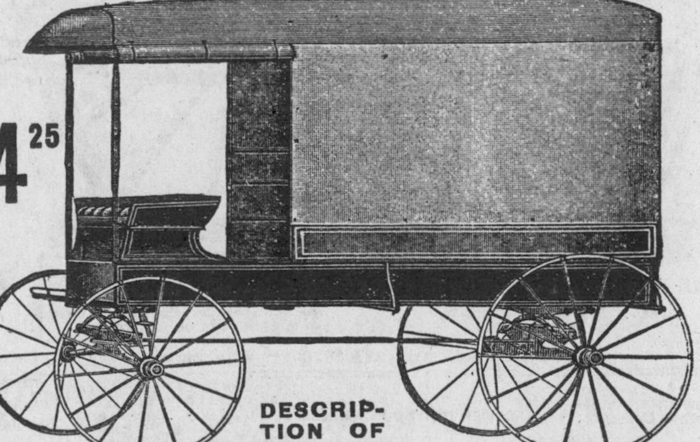

DESCRIPTION OF No. 11K1688

BODY—9 feet long by 3 feet 2 inches wide, heavily ironed and braced; drop endgate furnished with seat as shown in illustration when ordered with a top. When ordered without a top we build the seat higher. Seat has imitation leather cushion. TOP—Portable top, strongly constructed; white ash bows, standards and sides; poplar slats on the roof, oil finished, covered with heavy rubber duck, colored black. GEAR—1⅛-inch axles; double gear; 15-inch short turn full malleable circle; 38-inch duplex springs, ironed, bolted and clipped; Sarven's patent wheels, 36 inches front and 40 inches rear; 1¼ by 5-16-inch steel tires riveted rims; strong shafts. PAINTING—Body blue green, striped in colors; gear, dark wine, striped with black. CAPACITY—1,500 pounds. TRACK—4 feet 8 inches or 5 feet 2 inches. State width wanted.

No. 11K1688 Price, complete with shafts, as illustrated, with top $64.25

No. 11K1689 Price, without top 49.95

EXTRAS.

1⅛-inch axles, wheels and heavier springs, making 2,000 lbs. capacity.	3.50
Hand ratchet brake	4.90

Shipped from factory, crated 50x114 inches; weight, 900 pounds, with top.

IMPROVED "FAMOUS" FARM WAGONS

OUR BINDING TWO-YEAR GUARANTEE.

We guarantee our "Famous" Wagon to be made of the best material and to be free from defect. We guarantee our "Famous" Wagons to carry heavier loads, size for size, to run easier and last longer than any other wagon made no matter what make, name or price. If you can show us how to make it better we will do it.

HIGHEST GRADE, EASIEST RUNNING, STRONGEST AND BEST FINISHED WAGONS MADE.

READ ON PAGE 112 ABOUT FREIGHT CHARGES.

$31.15

NOTICE THE LENGTH OF OUR ONE-HORSE WAGON BOXES.

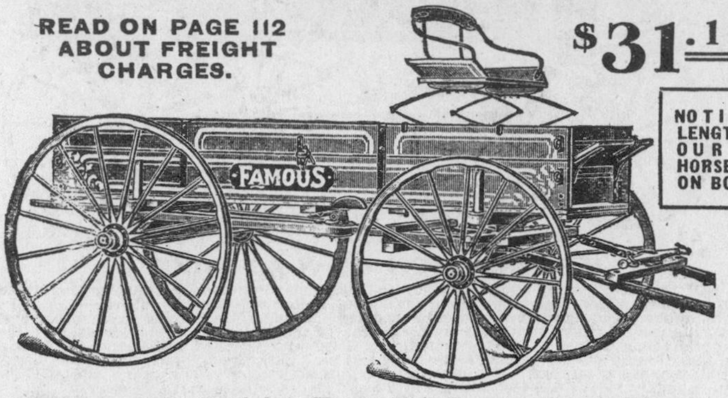

One-Horse Solid Steel Axle Wagon With Sarven's Patent Wheels.

Specify Number Wanted	Size of Axles	Capacity	Size of Tires	Length of Box	Depth of Sides		Weight of Complete Wagon	Complete Wagon with Shafts
					Bot.	Top		
No.	Inches	Pounds	Inches	Feet	In.	In.	Pounds	Price
11K1501	1¼x7	1,500	1¼x5/16	9	9	6	525	$31.15
11K1502	1⅜x7	2,000	1⅜x⅜	10	10	6	825	35.95

$34.45 WITHOUT BRAKE.

READ ON PAGE 112 ABOUT FREIGHT CHARGES.

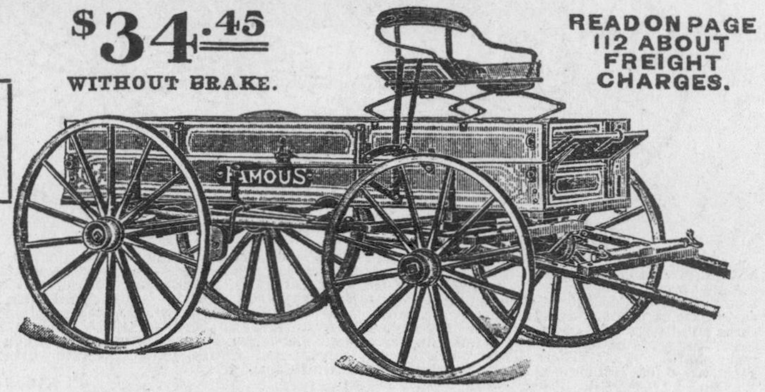

One-Horse Cast Skein Wagon with Wood Hub Wheels.

Specify Number Wanted	Size of Cast Skeins	Capacity, pounds	Size of Tires, inches	Length of Box	Depth of Sides		Weight of Complete Wagon	Price of Complete Wagon with Shafts, without Brake
No.					Bot.	Top		
11K1505	2¼ in.	1,500	1¼x5-16	9 ft.	9 in.	6 in.	525 lbs.	$34.45
11K1506	2½ in.	2,000	1⅜x⅜	10 ft.	10 in.	6 in.	825 lbs.	39.65

NOTE—Wheels are 3 feet 6 inches front and 4 feet rear. Boxes are all 3 feet 2 inches wide. When ordering state whether wide or narrow track is wanted.

EXTRAS.

If box brake is wanted, add $3.25
If gear brake is wanted, add 4.25
If pole in place of shafts is wanted, add 2.50
If pole in addition to shafts is wanted, add 5.00
If 2-inch tires in place of regular tires, add $1.75
If 2½-inch tires in place of regular tires, add 3.25
NOTE—If box and seat are not wanted, deduct 6.00

$41.45

2,000 POUNDS CAPACITY WAGON, WITH DOUBLE BOX AND SPRING SEAT.

COVERED BY OUR TWO-YEAR BINDING GUARANTEE.

NOTE—This illustration shows gear brake not included in the prices quoted. See list of extras, for brake if wanted.

READ ON PAGE 112 ABOUT FREIGHT CHARGES.

$46.95

3,500 POUNDS CAPACITY WAGON, WITH DOUBLE BOX AND SPRING SEAT.

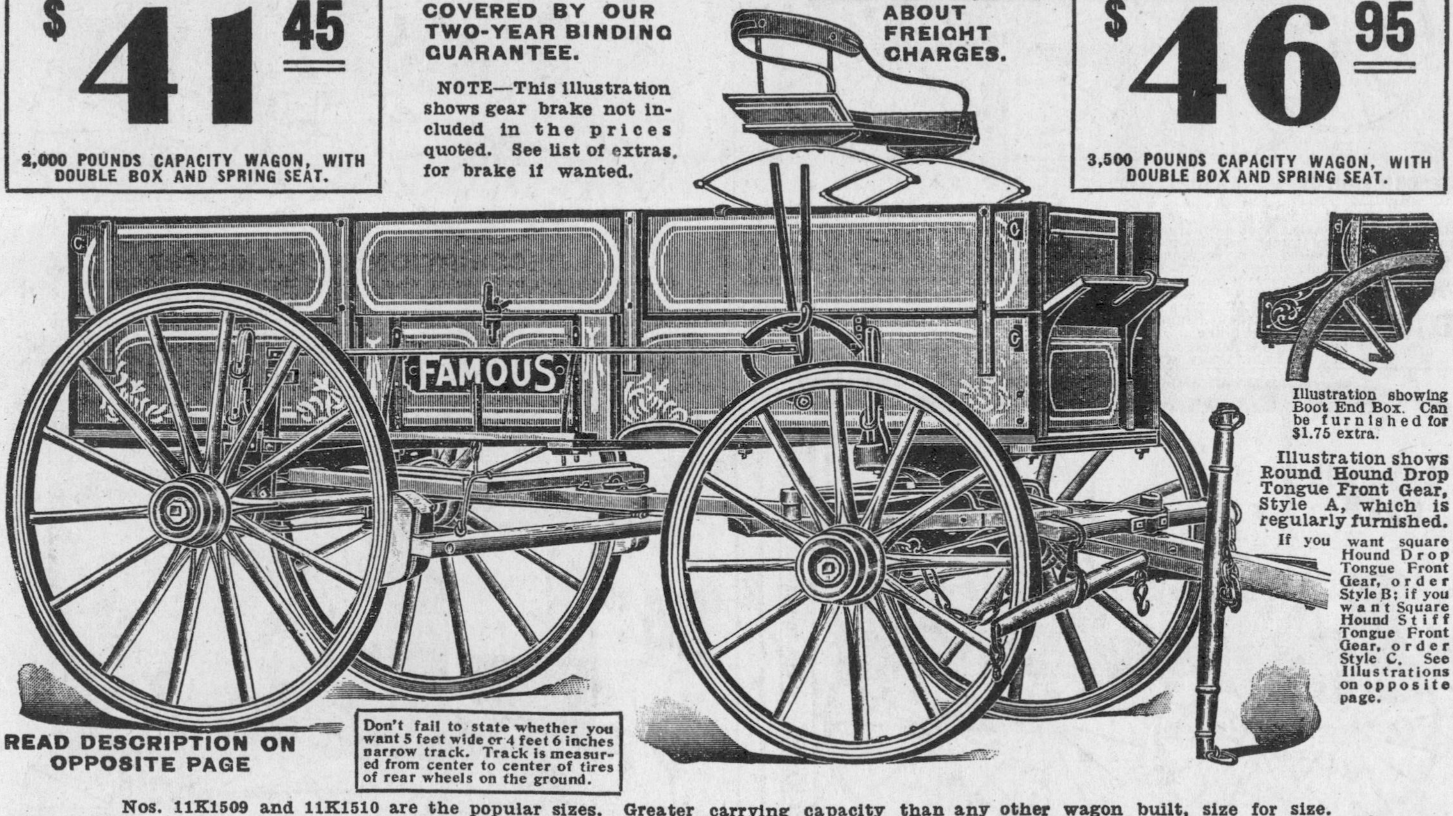

Illustration showing Boot End Box. Can be furnished for $1.75 extra.

Illustration shows Round Hound Drop Tongue Front Gear, Style A, which is regularly furnished.

If you want square Hound Drop Tongue Front Gear, order Style B; if you want Square Hound Stiff Tongue Front Gear, order Style C. See Illustrations on opposite page.

READ DESCRIPTION ON OPPOSITE PAGE

Don't fail to state whether you want 5 feet wide or 4 feet 6 inches narrow track. Track is measured from center to center of tires of rear wheels on the ground.

Nos. 11K1509 and 11K1510 are the popular sizes. Greater carrying capacity than any other wagon built, size for size.

Specify Number when Ordering	Capacity	Size of Skeins	Price of Wagon with Double Box and Seat. No Brake.	Price of Gear with Whiffletrees and Neckyoke. No Brake.	Size Regular Tires	Dimensions of Boxes (Outside Measurement)				Weight	EXTRAS			
						Length		Depth of Sides			Add extra for Gear Brake	Add extra for Steel Skeins	Add extra for 2-inch Tires	Add extra for 3-inch Tires
								Bottom	Top					
No.	Pounds	Inches	Cast Skein	Cast Skein	Inches	Feet	Inches	Inches	Inches	Pounds				
11K1507	2,000	2½x 8	$41.45	$32.95	1⅜x⅜	10	0	10	6	795	$3.25	$1.60	$1.20	$3.50
11K1508	2,500	2¾x 8	44.85	34.75	1½x½	10	0	12	8	875	4.00	1.95	1.50	4.40
11K1509	3,500	3 x 9	46.95	36.15	1½x9-16	10	6	13	9	1,015	4.75	2.35	1.60	4.50
11K1510	4,500	3¼x10	49.15	37.65	1½x⅝	10	6	14	10	1,080	5.00	2.75	1.75	5.25
11K1511	5,500	3½x11	51.65	39.95	1½x¾	10	6	16	12	1,220	5.75	3.20	2.05	6.10

NOTE — Wheels are regular 3 feet 8 inches front and 4 feet 4 inches rear, but we can furnish low wheels, 3 feet 4 inches front and 3 feet 8 inches rear if ordered. Boxes on narrow track wagons are 38 inches wide and on wide track wagons are 42 inches wide. We can furnish 38-inch boxes on wide track wagons if ordered. When steel skeins are furnished no truss rod can be used. All skeins are level bearing.

EXTRAS.

If deeper sides are wanted, add per inch $0.40
Third or tip top boxes, 6 inches to 10 inches deep 2.50
If boot end box is wanted, add 1.75
If grain cleats are wanted, add .... .60
If bow staples are wanted, add .... .50
If bows and bow staples are wanted, add $1.30
If feed box is wanted, add .... .80
If box brake is wanted, add 2.50
If riveted rims are wanted, add .... .50

HIGH GRADE "FAMOUS" FARM WAGONS

SHOW US HOW TO MAKE IT BETTER AND WE WILL DO IT. SHOW US WHERE TO GET BETTER MATERIAL AND WE WILL GET IT.

TEN DAYS' FREE TRIAL.

You may order any one of our "Famous" Farm Wagons, enclose our price, we will ship it to you; you may take it home, try it for ten days, during which time you may compare it with any other make of wagon, you may test its easy running qualities, compare it in every way with wagons that would sell in your section of the country at from $20.00 to $25.00 more than our price, and if for any reason you are not satisfied, if you do not feel after giving this wagon a thorough ten days' trial that you have made a big saving and have secured the best farm wagon built, return it to us at our expense of freight charges and we will refund your money, together with any freight charges you may have paid.

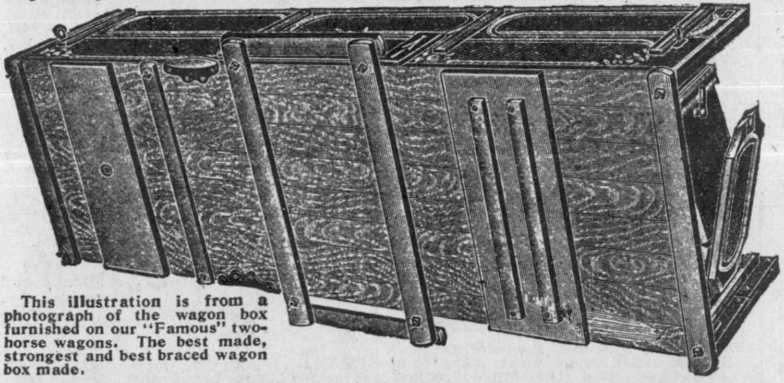

This illustration is from a photograph of the wagon box furnished on our "Famous" two-horse wagons. The best made, strongest and best braced wagon box made.

MATERIAL FOUND IN "FAMOUS" WAGONS.

Four of the strongest wheels made. Size for size, wheels on "Famous" Wagons have larger hubs, larger spokes and heavier rims, our gears have heavier axles, larger hounds, larger reaches and heavier irons than any farm wagon made. For instance, you will find that our standard 3x9-inch cast skein wagon, No. 11K1509, quoted on the opposite page at $46.95, is heavier throughout than any 3¼x10-inch skein wagon made by another manufacturer. You will find the hubs, the spokes, the rims, the reaches, the hounds and the ironing on our 3x9-inch standard wagon is as heavy and as large as found on ordinary standard 3¼x10-inch wagons. We use nothing but selected, bone dry, air seasoned material in the construction of our "Famous" Wagon. The wheels are made of air seasoned, bone dry stock; the spokes are second growth oak in the two-horse wagons and second growth hickory in the one-horse wagons; the rims are bent seasoned oak; the hubs are bored true to the rim; the boxings are set in red lead under a hydraulic press, the tires are put on in the best possible manner; the rims are clipped and bolted to the tires. The axles in our Two-Horse "Famous" Wagons are made of selected second growth hickory, hewn from a log, which insures their running with the grain, and they are far superior to axles that are sawed. Every wood part is dipped in boiling linseed oil before being ironed. We use a special strong truss rod on the axles. Our cast skeins are made from the very best iron that we can obtain, they are level bearing, so that the weight of the load rests the entire length of the skein, making the wagon exceedingly easy running. All of the gear wood, such as reaches, bolsters, hounds, etc., are made of thoroughly air seasoned, bone dry second growth oak and rock elm, each and every piece dipped in boiling linseed oil before being ironed. Our wagon boxes have pine flooring on the bottom, which is grooved and matched; the sides are made of poplar, the best material that can be obtained for the purpose; the stake and strap plates are on the outside of the box. We use heavy sills and cleats and heavy side braces; Comstock patent endgate is furnished regular. Our "Famous" Wagons are painted in the best possible manner, the work all being done by hand. The box is handsomely finished in green, neatly decorated and striped, with the word "Famous" on each side, as shown in the illustration on opposite page. The gear is painted a very handsome shade of red, neatly striped. We do not know of any farm wagons that are painted and finished better than the "Famous" Wagons. **Our name or trade mark does not appear anywhere on the wagon.**

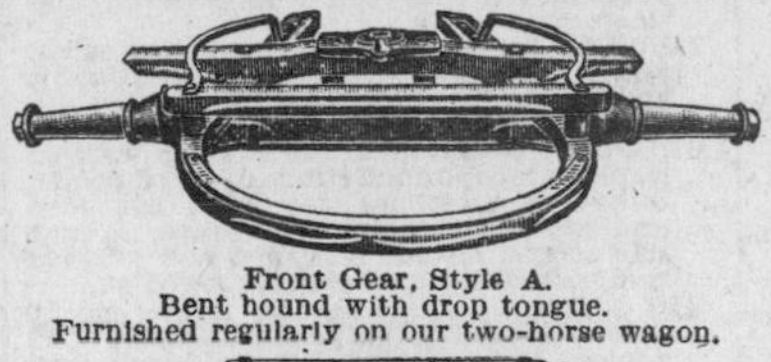

Front Gear, Style A.
Bent hound with drop tongue.
Furnished regularly on our two-horse wagon.

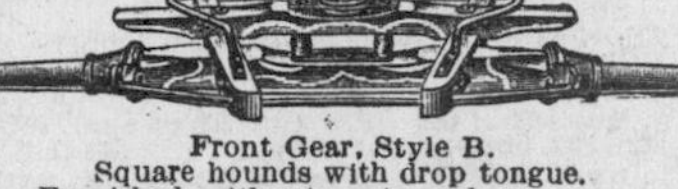

Front Gear, Style B.
Square hounds with drop tongue.
Furnished without extra charge on our two-horse wagon when ordered.

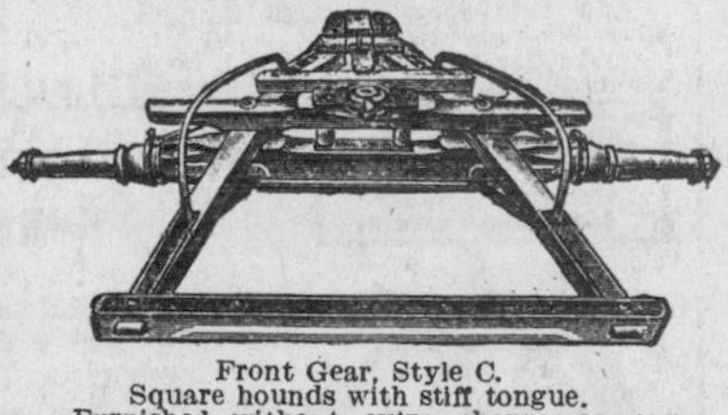

Front Gear, Style C.
Square hounds with stiff tongue.
Furnished without extra charge on our two-horse wagon when ordered.

OUR BINDING TWO-YEAR REGISTERED GUARANTEE WITH EACH WAGON.

With each wagon ordered we send our customer our special registered binding wagon guarantee, by the terms and conditions of which we agree to replace, for a period of two years, any part that may prove defective in either material or workmanship. While the "Famous" Wagons are built of air seasoned, carefully selected, bone dry material, while with ordinary use, wear and tear any of our "Famous" Wagons will last a lifetime, in order to protect our customers against any defect in either material or workmanship, we issue our registered binding guarantee, the strongest guarantee issued by any farm wagon manufacturer.

WHY WE CAN NAME SUCH LOW PRICES ON THESE HIGH GRADE FARM WAGONS.

If you could visit our large wagon factory, if you could see the improved machinery we use, the class of mechanics we employ, if you could see how we run through our factory hundreds of wheels at one time, hundreds of axles, all of one size and one shape, if you could see all of our improved facilities for manufacturing wagons at the lowest possible cost, if you could see the number of wagons we ship daily direct from our factory to the American farmer, you would readily understand why we are able to name such low prices on high grade farm wagons. When you purchase a farm wagon from us you pay actual factory cost of material and labor with but one small margin of profit added, a margin of profit which is exceedingly small on each wagon, in view of the fact that we sell thousands of wagons each year, and we feel that if we can make $1.00 net on each farm wagon, the profits from the farm wagon business will be more than satisfactory. On the other hand, when you purchase a farm wagon from a local dealer you are paying the manufacturer's profit, the jobber's profit, the dealer's profit and the freight; in other words you are paying three profits and the freight charges, as against one profit and the freight charges when you purchase from us.

WHY PAY OVER $20.00 TO $25.00 MORE THAN NECESSARY?

Why should you pay three profits and freight charges on a farm wagon? Why should you be asked to buy your farm wagon from the manufacturer to the jobber, from the jobber to the dealer, with their accumulated profits, amounting to from $20.00 to $25.00, when you can purchase direct from the manufacturer a high grade "Famous" Standard Farm Wagon, which represents better value than you could possibly secure elsewhere? When you purchase a farm wagon from a dealer you pay unnecessary profits, amounting to from $20.00 to $25.00, which do not add one cent of value to the wagon. It surely does not make a wagon wear longer, carry heavier loads or run easier just because it cost from $20.00 to $25.00 more, especially when this extra money does not mean an investment in material and labor, but means a price that you pay to keep up an expensive method of doing business. Why not order direct from us, and we, as manufacturers, will furnish you a wagon that we will guarantee to be better than any wagon you can purchase elsewhere, a wagon that we will agree to take back and refund your money if it is not satisfactory, a wagon that will represent more value for every cent invested than you could possibly secure elsewhere?

HOW TO ORDER A "FAMOUS" FARM WAGON.

On the opposite page, under each illustration, you will notice we quote our wagons in the different sizes. We give a catalogue number to each size. It is, therefore, only necessary to select the size you want, give us the catalogue number, state whether you want wide or narrow track, enclose our price, and the wagon will go forward to you within a few days after we receive your order. For instance, if you wanted a 3x9-inch skein, 3,000-pound capacity two-horse wagon, you would state in your letter or on an order blank, if you have one, No. 11K1509 wagon, enclose our price, $46.95 if you wanted the complete wagon, or $36.15 if you wanted the wagon without a box or seat; state whether you wanted wide or narrow track, and in a very short time after you send us your order the wagon will arrive at your railroad station.

PROMPT SHIPMENT.

We have such a large demand for our "Famous" One-Horse and Two-Horse Wagons that we always carry in stock a large number of finished wagons of various sizes at our wagon factory and can usually ship within a few days after your order is received. There is no other factory in the United States which can make as prompt shipment as our wagon factory, and remember, after the wagon is shipped to you, you can take it home, try it ten days, and if you are not satisfied that you have made a big saving, if you are not convinced that you have secured a much better wagon than you could possibly secure elsewhere, you can return it to us and we will refund every cent you paid and the freight charges.

FREIGHT CHARGES. (See page 112.)

On page 112 we tell you the freight charges on farm wagons. Remember that you always pay the freight charges, either directly or indirectly. When you purchase a wagon from the dealer you pay the freight charges. For instance, take our 3x9-inch standard cast skein wagon, No. 11K1509, shown on the opposite page, which we sell for $46.95. If this wagon were sold to the jobber he would add his profit, amounting to from $5.00 to $10.00 and the freight charges he paid from the factory to his warehouse; he would then sell the wagon to the dealer at a price which included his profit and freight charges; the dealer would then pay the freight charges from the jobber's warehouse to his town, and name a price to you which would include his profit and freight charges. When you purchase this wagon from us you pay our price of $46.95, which represents the actual factory cost of material and labor with our one small margin of profit added, a margin of profit that is about one-tenth of that the jobber or dealer would expect, you pay our price and the freight charges from our factory, you are cutting out the jobber's profit and the dealer's profit, which amount, combined, to anywhere from $20.00 to $25.00.

$22.86 OUR GIANT HANDY WAGON.

OUR GIANT HANDY WAGON is furnished on different heights of wheels, as shown in the table below. When on wheels 26 inches front and 32 inches rear, the top of bolsters are only 26 inches from the ground, making it a very handy wagon for loading. Axles are made of the best hickory; bolsters, coupling pole and tongue are made of the best oak; stakes are oak, bound with flat iron. Coupling pole is 9 feet 4 inches long and, if wanted, can be furnished 12 feet long at the same price. Front and rear hounds are of angle steel, almost indestructible, and the wheels are the best metal wheels made. Spokes and tires are made of the best wrought steel, guaranteed not to break on the rockiest roads. Hubs are made of superior cast iron, cast onto the spokes, making an almost one-piece construction, and we guarantee the spokes never to become loose in the hub. This wagon with its broad tires is handy in the field and over soft roads, and is guaranteed fully by us. Comes with either 4 feet 8 inches, narrow, or 5 feet, wide track. Do not fail to state track desired.

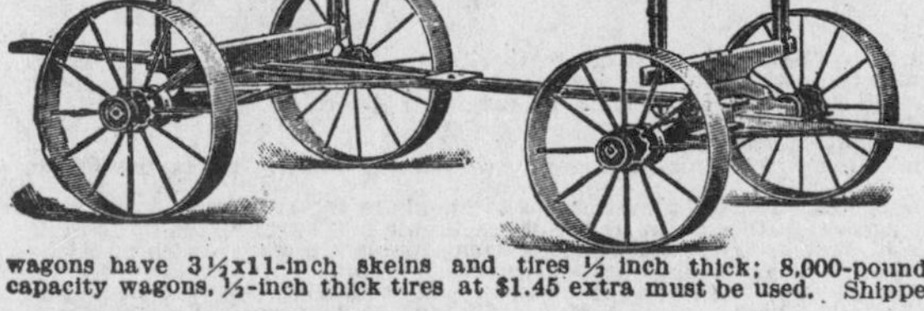

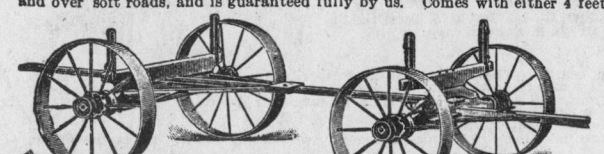

No. 11K1627 IS THE MOST POPULAR SIZE FOR ALL AROUND USE.

Catalogue Number	Diameter of Wheels	Tires	Carrying Capacity, 4,000 lbs.		Carrying Capacity, 6,000 lbs.		Carrying Capacity, 8,000 lbs.	
			Price	Weight	Price	Weight	Price	Weight
11K1626	24x30 in.	4 in.	$22.86	550 lbs.	$28.14	650 lbs.	$33.42	750 lbs.
11K1627	26x32 in.	4 in.	23.20	590 lbs.	28.80	700 lbs.	35.20	800 lbs.
11K1629	30x36 in.	4 in.	24.64	630 lbs.	29.92	780 lbs.	38.72	940 lbs.
11K1631	34x40 in.	4 in.	26.40	694 lbs.	31.68	850 lbs.	42.24	970 lbs.

NOTE—4,000-pound capacity wagons have 3¼x10-inch skeins and tires ⅜ inch thick; 6,000-pound capacity wagons have 3½x11-inch skeins and tires ½ inch thick; 8,000-pound capacity wagons have 4x12-inch skeins and tires ⅝ inch thick. Where brake is furnished on 4,000-pound capacity wagons, ½-inch thick tires at $1.45 extra must be used. Shipped from Northern Illinois factory.

EXTRAS.

If tires ½ inch thick are wanted on 4,000-pound capacity wagon, add $1.45
If tires 5 inches wide are wanted, add............1.40
If tires 6 inches wide are wanted, add............2.80
If tires 8 inches wide are wanted, add............5.60
Gear Brake, 4,000-pound capacity wagon. Price............3.20
Gear Brake, for 6,000 or 8,000-pound capacity wagon. Price............4.00
Neckyoke, Single and Doubletrees. Price............$1.90
Stay Chains. Price............40
Shafts instead of tongue, add............65
Skeleton Platform, 7 feet x 16 feet. Price............4.00
Skeleton Platform, 6 feet x 12 feet. Price............3.60

All sizes obtainable are quoted in above table. In ordering be particular to give the catalogue number and width of track, 4 feet 6 inches or 5 feet.
This wagon comes with pole complete, as shown in illustration, without whiffletrees or neckyoke.
Prices for extras apply only when furnished in connection with a regular order for wagon, as extras are not sold separately at the prices quoted.

SINGLE STRAP BUGGY HARNESS.

A Regular $25.00 Harness for only $12.96.

See our Hook and Terrets, Solid Nickel German Silver. Always the best. Will not wear yellow.

$12.96 German Silver Hook and Terrets.

$15.08 Genuine Rubber.

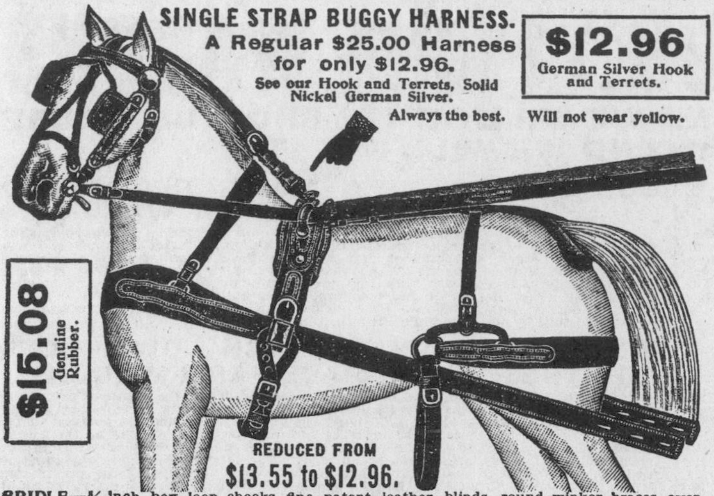

REDUCED FROM $13.55 to $12.96.

BRIDLE—⅝-inch, box loop cheeks, fine patent leather blinds, round winker braces, overcheck with nose band or side reins if desired, layer on the crown piece.
LINES—A very important part of the harness. Heavy ⅞-inch front with spring billets, 1⅛-inch hand parts.
BREAST COLLAR—Extra wide, V shaped, heavy solid leather single strap.
TRACES—1¼-inch, single strap, double and stitched at the back end with three holes, attached to breast collar with scalloped point, with neck strap.
BREECHING—1¾-inch single strap extra heavy harness leather, three-ring breeching stay with scalloped and stitched point, box loop lead up, ¾-inch hip straps, ⅞-inch side straps, ⅞-inch scalloped and stitched turnback with round crupper sewed on.
GIG SADDLE—Extra heavy single strap harness leather skirts, patent leather bottom pad, patent leather jockey, double and stitched swinging bearer, double and stitched shaft tugs with box loop, Griffith style bellyband to wrap around shafts.
TRIMMINGS—Nickel buckles, with German silver solid nickel hook and terrets, imitation rubber, genuine rubber and brass.
Weight, boxed for shipment, about 25 pounds.
No. 10K75 Price, nickel with solid nickel German silver hook and terrets $12.96
No. 10K79 Price, imitation rubber trimmed with genuine rubber hook and terrets 13.59
No. 10K83 Price, genuine rubber trimmed throughout..... 15.08
No. 10K87 Price, solid brass trimmed throughout..... 13.45
No. 10K90 Our Special Stallion Harness, made in nickel trimming only, all parts being made extra large for horses weighing from 1,450 to 1,800 pounds. Only large stallion harness we carry in stock. Made extra heavy and extra strong.
Price, nickel trimmed $15.36
Same style harness as described in No. 10K75, only a strictly hand made harness. All the stitching on this harness is done by hand, all laps sewed by hand; the balance of the trimming, the leather and the style of the harness is the same as described above.
No. 10K92 Price, hand made harness, nickel trimmed, with solid nickel German silver hook and terrets $15.77
No. 10K93 Price, hand made harness, imitation rubber buckles with genuine rubber hook and terrets 16.40
No. 10K96 Price, hand made, genuine rubber trimmed harness 17.91
Add extra for buckle cruppers..... .15
Add extra for russet hand parts on the lines..... .25
Add extra for ⅝-inch tie strap ..... .22
We recommend neck halter No. 10K2049, price, 88 cents, with this harness. It will prevent your horse from breaking the bridle.

REDUCED FROM $13.95 TO

$13.29 EASTERN HARNESS.

HEAVY SINGLE BUGGY HARNESS. Solid Nickel German Silver Hook and Terrets on this Harness.

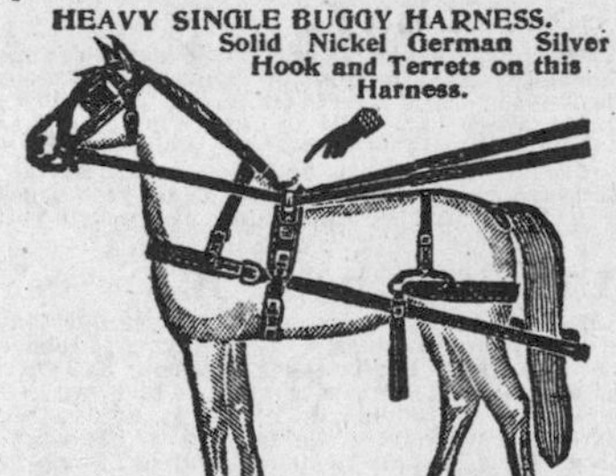

BRIDLE—¾-inch, box loop cheeks, heavy patent leather blinds, round winker braces, heavy overcheck or round side reins.
LINES—1⅛-inch throughout, with buckle and billets at the bit.
BREAST COLLAR—Heavy folded body with raised layer, buckle and box loop, folded neck strap with layer.
TRACES—1¼-inch, double and stitched, raised center, to buckle to breast collar.
BREECHING—Heavy folded body, double and stitched layer and breeching brace, ¾-inch hip straps, 1-inch side straps, ⅞-inch turnback with round crupper to buckle on.
GIG SADDLE—3-inch patent leather lace saddle, heavy folded bellyband, pollywog shaft tugs, old style with double bellyband.
TRIMMINGS—Nickel buckles, with German silver, solid nickel hook and terrets.
Weight of harness boxed for shipment, about 26 pounds.
No. 10K61 Price, nickel buckles with German silver hook and terrets.....$13.29
No. 10K64 Price, imitation rubber buckles with genuine rubber hook and terrets.....$14.24
Add extra for ⅝-inch tie strap..... .22

REDUCED FROM $13.59 TO

$12.97 BREAST COLLAR HARNESS.

Solid Nickel German Silver Hook and Terrets. Always the best. Solid throughout.

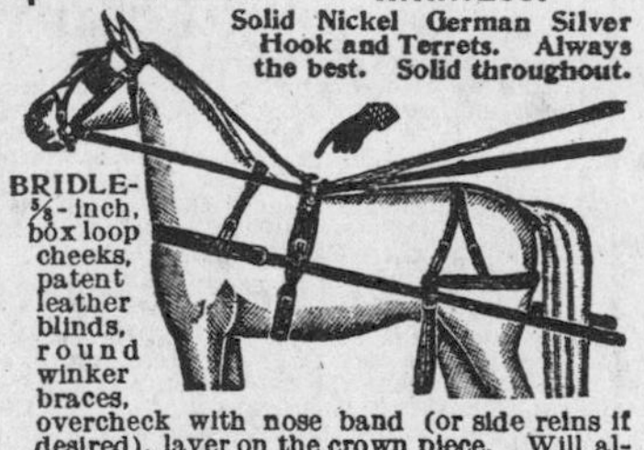

BRIDLE—⅝-inch, box loop cheeks, patent leather blinds, round winker braces, overcheck with nose band (or side reins if desired), layer on the crown piece. Will always send overcheck unless ordered side rein.
LINES—⅞-inch front with spring billets, 1⅛-inch russet or black hand parts. We always send the full black lines unless the russet hand parts are ordered.
BREAST COLLAR—Heavy leather, folded with raised layer, buckle, box loop, and neck strap with layer.
TRACES—1⅛-inch, double and stitched, raised center, round finish, to buckle to breast collar.
BREECHING—Folded leather body with raised layer, ¾-inch double hip straps, ⅞-inch side straps, ¾-inch scalloped and stitched turnback with crupper to buckle.
GIG SADDLE—3-inch full laced patent leather saddle with old style pollywog shaft tugs and double bellyband.
TRIMMINGS—Nickel buckles, with German silver solid nickel hook and terrets, or imitation rubber buckles with genuine rubber hook and terrets.
Weight of harness, boxed for shipment, about 25 pounds.
No. 10K69 Price, nickel buckles with German silver hook and terrets.....$12.97
No. 10K70 Price, imitation rubber buckles with genuine rubber hook and terrets.....$13.79
Add extra for russet hand parts on lines..... .25
Add extra for buckle crupper..... .15
Add extra for ⅝-inch tie strap..... .22
Add extra for 1¼-inch traces..... .90
Add extra for good neck halter ..... .88

OUR SPECIAL TRIMMING ON HARNESS.

Our Nickel Harness are trimmed with solid nickel German silver hooks and terrets. The lines will not wear these terrets yellow as they do the cheap composition nickel plated terrets. **Our Imitation Rubber Harness are trimmed with genuine rubber hooks and terrets.** The lines will not wear the rubber through to the iron in the first two or three weeks that you use the harness as is the case with the iron composition plated cheap hooks and terrets. **Our solid nickel German silver and genuine rubber hooks and terrets cost a little more,** but they add so much to the value and the wearing qualities of your harness that the small difference in price absolutely amounts to nothing. **Do not buy a nickel or imitation rubber trimmed harness without the genuine rubber and German silver hooks and terrets,** if you want something that will please you and give you perfect satisfaction.

$18.97 GERMAN SILVER TRIMMED HARNESS.

Solid Nickel German Silver Hook and Terrets on this Harness.

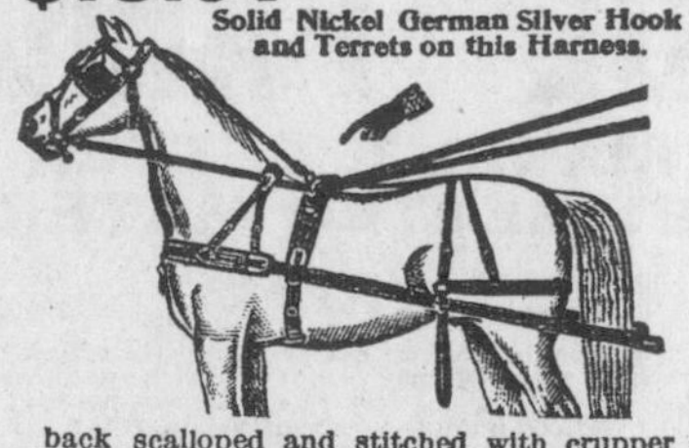

BRIDLE—⅝-inch, box loop cheeks, square patent leather fancy stitched blinds, overcheck with nose band, round winker braces, heavy crown piece, fronts and rosettes.
LINES—1-inch fronts with spring billets to buckle in the bit, 1⅛-inch hand parts, about 13½ feet long.
BREAST COLLAR — Folded glove finish leather with layer double and stitched the full length, trace buckle and box loop, double neck strap with line ring.
TRACES — 1⅛-inch, double and stitched, raised center, to buckle in the breast collar.
BREECHING—Folded glove finished leather body, layer double and stitched the full length, ⅞-inch side straps to wrap around the shafts, ⅝-inch double hip strap, turnback scalloped and stitched with crupper sewed on.
GIG SADDLE—Full patent leather, enamel lined, double and stitched shaft bearer, double and stitched shaft tugs, old style pollywog shaft tug and double bellyband.
TRIMMINGS—Nickel buckles with German silver solid nickel hook and terrets or imitation rubber buckles with genuine rubber hook and terrets. A high grade single harness made with folded breast collar and breeching and patent leather gig saddle. Weight of harness, boxed for shipment, about 27 pounds.
No. 10K66 Price of harness with solid nickel German silver hook and terrets, $18.97
No. 10K72 Price of harness with genuine rubber hook and terrets........... 21.33
Add extra for good neck halter to tie your horse........ .88

THE BEST $10.57 HARNESS

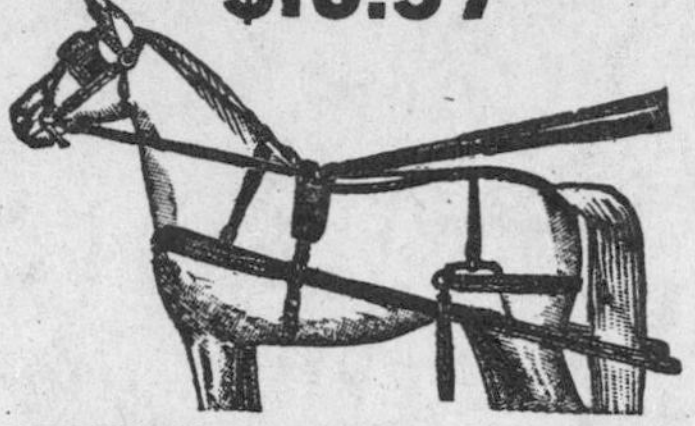

BRIDLE—⅝ inch, box loop cheeks, patent leather blinds, round wicker stays, overcheck or side reins. Open bridle if wanted.
LINES—⅞-inch front to loop in bit, with 1-inch hand parts.
BREAST COLLAR—1¾-inch single strap harness leather, with box loop lead up and single neck strap.
TRACES—1⅛-inch, stitched to breast collar, single strap heavy harness leather, double and stitched at the back end, with three holes to adjust hitch.
BREECHING—1⅝-inch single strap harness leather, scalloped and stitched, raised points, three-ring breeching stay with box loop lead up, ⅝-inch single hip straps, ⅞-inch side straps, ¾-inch scalloped and stitched turnback with round crupper sewed on.
GIG SADDLE—Single harness leather skirts, patent leather jockey, soft leather pad double and stitched bearer, double and stitched shaft tugs with box loop and Griffith style bellyband.
TRIMMINGS—Nickel or imitation rubber.
Weight of harness, packed for shipment, about 23 pounds.
No. 10K101 Price of harness, with straight breast collar..............$10.57
No. 10K107 Price of harness, with V-shaped breast collar............$10.93
Add extra for ⅝-inch tie strap... .22
Add extra for solid nickel German silver hook and terrets............. .75
Add extra for genuine rubber hook and terrets on imitation rubber harness, 1.50

$9.39 SINGLE HARNESS.

GERMAN SILVER OR GENUINE RUBBER HOOK AND TERRETS.

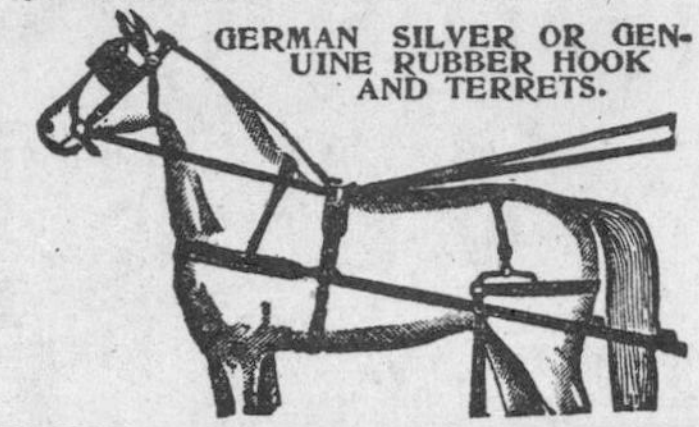

BRIDLE—⅝-inch box loop cheeks, patent leather blinds, round winker braces, overcheck or side reins if desired.
LINES—⅞-inch throughout, to loop in bit.
BREAST COLLAR—Single strap harness leather, 1⅞ inches wide.
TRACES—1⅛-inch, single strap, sewed to breast collar, double and stitched at the back end with three holes to adjust the hitch.
BREECHING—Single strap harness leather, 1½ inches wide, layer stitched on, three-ring breeching stay, ⅝-inch single hip straps, ¾-inch side straps, ¾-inch double and stitched turnback with round crupper sewed on.
GIG SADDLE—Harness leather skirts, patent leather jockey, enameled leather pad, double and stitched bearer, double and stitched shaft tugs and Griffith style bellyband.
TRIMMINGS—Nickel buckles with solid nickel German silver hook and terrets or imitation rubber buckles with genuine rubber hook and terrets.
Weight of harness, packed for shipment, about 21 pounds.
No. 10K116 Price, with German silver hook and terrets.................$9.39
No. 10K117 Price, with genuine rubber hook and terrets.................$10.17
Add extra for ⅝-inch tie strap... .22

THE BARGAIN SINGLE HARNESS.

$14.98 Genuine Rubber Hook and Terrets.

$13.99 Solid Nickel German Silver Hook and Terrets.

We use the best Solid Nickel German Silver Hook and Terrets on Gig Saddle and Genuine Rubber Hook and Terrets on Imitation Rubber Harness.

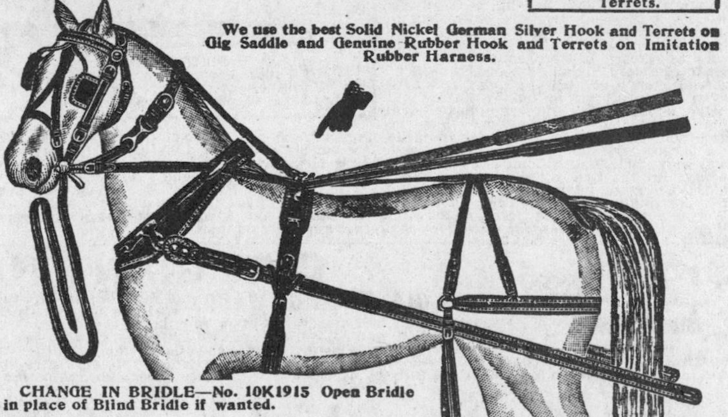

CHANGE IN BRIDLE—No. 10K1915 Open Bridle in place of Blind Bridle if wanted.

BRIDLE—⅝-inch, box loop cheeks, square patent leather blinds, fancy stitched heavy crown piece, front and rosettes, overcheck with nose band, heavy neck halter with the harness.
LINES—⅞-inch front with spring billet to buckle in the bit, 1⅛-inch hand parts sewed on, about 13½ feet long.
COLLAR—Kip, buggy weight, buckle top.
HAMES—3½-pound iron hame with nickel terrets, two hame straps, box loop hame tug riveted on.
TRACES—1⅛-inch double and stitched, raised center to buckle in the hame tug, 6 feet long.
BREECHING—Folded harness leather body, raised layer double and stitched the full length, ⅞-inch side straps to wrap around the shafts, ⅝-inch double hip straps with box loop lead up, scalloped and stitched turnback with crupper sewed on.
GIG SADDLE—Heavy single strap harness leather skirts, enamel leather pad, patent leather jockey, double and stitched bearer, Griffith style bellyband to wrap around the shafts.
TRIMMINGS—Nickel buckles with solid nickel German silver hook and terrets or imitation rubber buckles with genuine rubber hook and terrets.
Weight of harness, boxed for shipment, about 33 pounds. Be sure to state size collar wanted.
No. 10K94 Price, with solid nickel German silver hooks and terrets......$13.99
No. 10K97 Price, imitation rubber buckles, with genuine rubber hook and terrets 14.98
Add extra for buckle crupper ..... .15
Add extra for 1¼-inch traces ..... .75
Add extra for russet hand parts on lines..... .25
Add extra for old style dee shaft tug and double belly band ..... .85
Add extra for full padded patent leather saddle..... 1.00

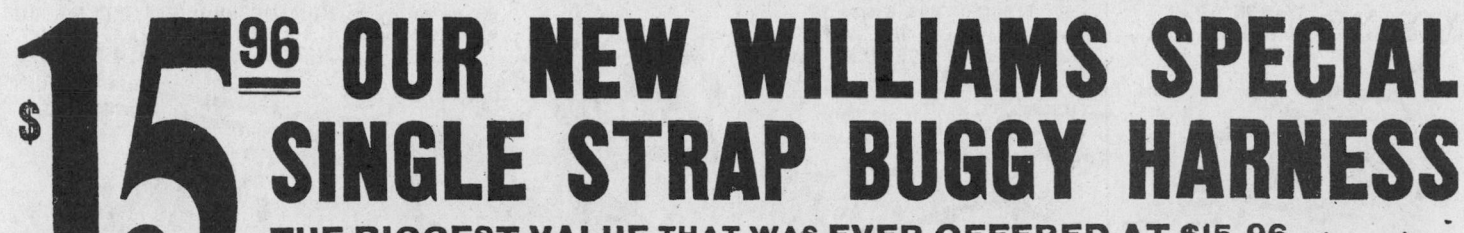

$15.96 OUR NEW WILLIAMS SPECIAL SINGLE STRAP BUGGY HARNESS

THE BIGGEST VALUE THAT WAS EVER OFFERED AT $15.96

IF DEALERS THROUGHOUT THE COUNTRY would sell you as good a harness, made out of as good leather, and as heavy leather and finished up as well, they could not afford to sell it to you for less than $25.00 to $35.00, and give you the same value and the same quality we are giving you in this harness for $15.96.

FOR EASTERN HARNESS order with the Berlin Saddle (Figure 3) and the pollywog shaft tug and double bellyband (Figure 4). For Western style order with Dresden Saddle (Figure 2) and Griffith style bellyband and shaft tugs as shown in the large illustration on the horse.

GUARANTEE. **We guarantee this harness to be all we claim for it, style, trimming and quality of leather.** We will replace any part that gives out because of a poor piece of leather or poor workmanship. If you do not find it a better harness than we claim it is, if you are not perfectly satisfied with the harness, if it is not the best value you ever saw, do not use it but return to us at our expense and we will refund your money with price and any transportation charges you paid.

A GREAT MANY OF OUR EASTERN CUSTOMERS want the crupper to buckle on, while others want the crupper sewed on. Some prefer full russet lines, and others full black lines, while others want the fancy boulevard beaded lines for which they are willing to pay $2.00 extra.

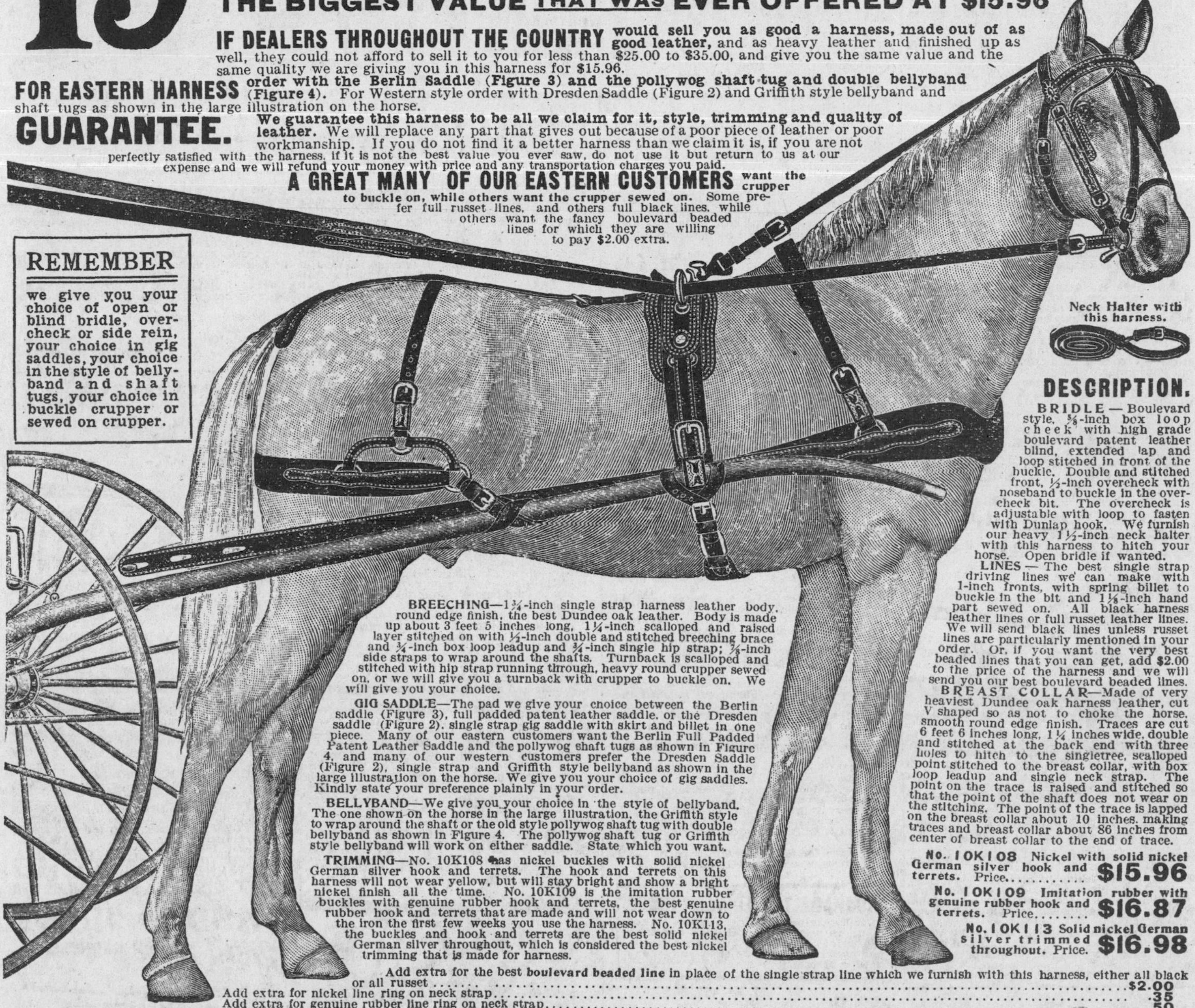

REMEMBER

we give you your choice of open or blind bridle, overcheck or side rein, your choice in gig saddles, your choice in the style of bellyband and shaft tugs, your choice in buckle crupper or sewed on crupper.

Neck Halter with this harness.

DESCRIPTION.

BRIDLE—Boulevard style, ⅝-inch box loop cheek with high grade boulevard patent leather blind, extended lap and loop stitched in front of the buckle. Double and stitched front, ½-inch overcheck with noseband to buckle in the overcheck bit. The overcheck is adjustable with loop to fasten with Dunlap hook. We furnish our heavy 1½-inch neck halter with this harness to hitch your horse. Open bridle if wanted.

LINES—The best single strap driving lines we can make with 1-inch fronts, with spring billet to buckle in the bit and 1⅛-inch hand part sewed on. All black harness leather lines or full russet leather lines. We will send black lines unless russet lines are particularly mentioned in your order. Or, if you want the very best beaded lines that you can get, add $2.00 to the price of the harness and we will send you our best boulevard beaded lines.

BREAST COLLAR—Made of very heaviest Dundee oak harness leather, cut V shaped so as not to choke the horse, smooth round edge finish. Traces are cut 6 feet 6 inches long, 1¼ inches wide, double and stitched at the back end with three holes to hitch to the singletree, scalloped point stitched to the breast collar, with box loop leadup and single neck strap. The point on the trace is raised and stitched so that the point of the shaft does not wear on the stitching. The point of the trace is lapped on the breast collar about 10 inches, making traces and breast collar about 86 inches from center of breast collar to the end of trace.

BREECHING—1¾-inch single strap harness leather body, round edge finish, the best Dundee oak leather. Body is made up about 3 feet 5 inches long, 1¼-inch scalloped and raised layer stitched on with ½-inch double and stitched breeching brace and ¾-inch box loop leadup and ¾-inch single hip strap; ⅝-inch side straps to wrap around the shafts. Turnback is scalloped and stitched with hip strap running through, heavy round crupper sewed on, or we will give you a turnback with crupper to buckle on. We will give you your choice.

GIG SADDLE—The pad we give your choice between the Berlin saddle (Figure 3), full padded patent leather saddle, or the Dresden saddle (Figure 2), single strap gig saddle with skirt and billet in one piece. Many of our eastern customers want the Berlin Full Padded Patent Leather Saddle and the pollywog shaft tugs as shown in Figure 4, and many of our western customers prefer the Dresden Saddle (Figure 2), single strap and Griffith style bellyband as shown in the large illustration on the horse. We give you your choice of gig saddles. Kindly state your preference plainly in your order.

BELLYBAND—We give you your choice in the style of bellyband. The one shown on the horse in the large illustration, the Griffith style to wrap around the shaft or the old style pollywog shaft tug with double bellyband as shown in Figure 4. The pollywog shaft tug or Griffith style bellyband will work on either saddle. State which you want.

TRIMMING—No. 10K108 has nickel buckles with solid nickel German silver hook and terrets. The hook and terrets on this harness will not wear yellow, but will stay bright and show a bright nickel finish all the time. No. 10K109 is the imitation rubber buckles with genuine rubber hook and terrets, the best genuine rubber hook and terrets that are made and will not wear down to the iron the first few weeks you use the harness. No. 10K113, the buckles and hook and terrets are the best solid nickel German silver throughout, which is considered the best nickel trimming that is made for harness.

No. 10K108 Nickel with solid nickel German silver hook and terrets. Price........ **$15.96**

No. 10K109 Imitation rubber with genuine rubber hook and terrets. Price........ **$16.87**

No. 10K113 Solid nickel German silver trimmed throughout. Price. **$16.98**

Add extra for the best **boulevard beaded line** in place of the single strap line which we furnish with this harness, either all black or all russet $2.00
Add extra for nickel line ring on neck strap........ .35
Add extra for genuine rubber line ring on neck strap........ .50

Dresden Single Strap Saddle.

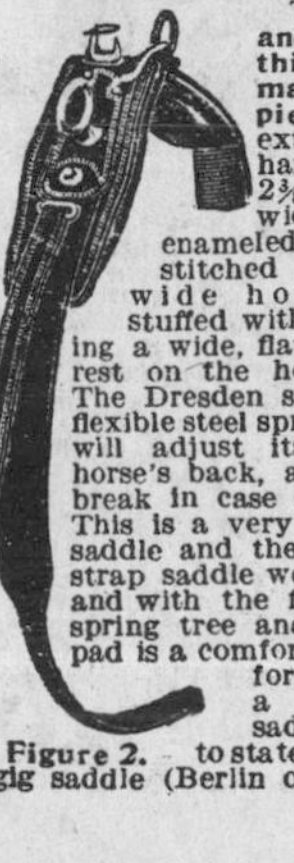

Figure 2.

The skirt and billet on this saddle are made in one piece, cut from extra heavy harness leather 2⅜ inches wide; pad is enameled leather stitched to an extra wide housing and stuffed with hair, making a wide, flat bottom to rest on the horse's back. The Dresden saddle has a flexible steel spring tree and will adjust itself to the horse's back, and will not break in case of accident. This is a very high grade saddle and the best single strap saddle we can make, and with the flexible steel spring tree and wide, soft pad is a comfortable saddle for a horse and a very strong saddle. Be sure to state your choice of gig saddle (Berlin or Dresden).

Berlin Full Padded Saddle.

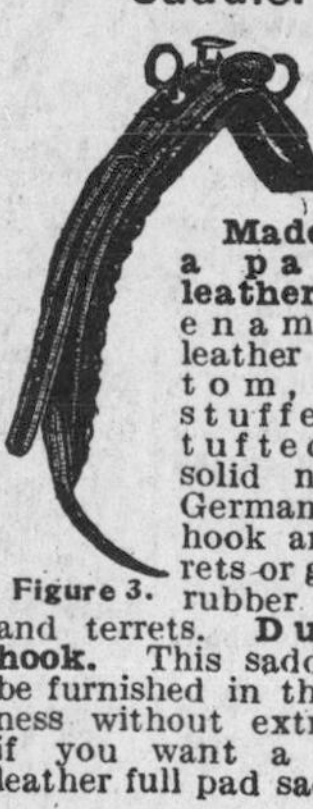

Figure 3.

Made with a patent leather skirt, enameled leather bottom, hair stuffed and tufted, with solid nickel German silver hook and terrets or genuine rubber hook and terrets. **Dunlap hook.** This saddle will be furnished in this harness without extra cost if you want a patent leather full pad saddle.

Pollywog Shaft Tug.

Old Style Shaft Tug or Griffith Style.

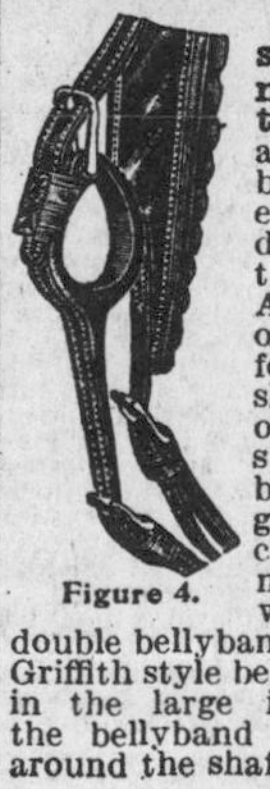

Figure 4.

This style of shaft tug is made with shaft tug and billet, and double bellyband; can be used either on the Dresden saddle or on the Berlin saddle. A great many of our customers prefer this Pollywog shaft tug in place of the Griffith style shaft tug and bellyband. We give you your choice on this harness of the Pollywog shaft tug and double bellyband Figure 4, or the Griffith style bellyband, as shown in the large illustration, with the bellyband straps to wrap around the shafts.

Turnback and Crupper.

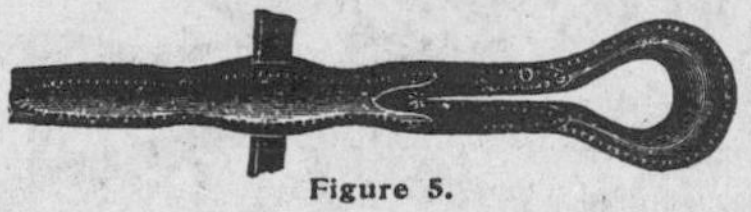

Figure 5.

This illustration represents the scalloped and stitched turnback with the round crupper sewed on. You will note the hip strap runs through the wide scallop on the turnback. A great many of our customers want the crupper to buckle on, and we will make no extra charge on this harness for buckled cruppers. Will send the crupper sewed on turnback, unless your order plainly states crupper to buckle.

End of Breeching.

This illustration represents the points of the breeching on this harness showing the raised scalloped layer, a double and stitched breeching brace, and the box loop leadup for the hip straps to buckle in. This illustration gives you a better idea of the way this breeching brace and layer is made at the points of this breeching on this harness.

Figure 6.

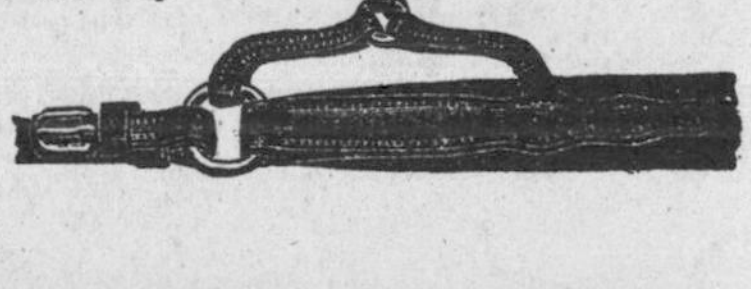

$18.26 WAGON HARNESS.

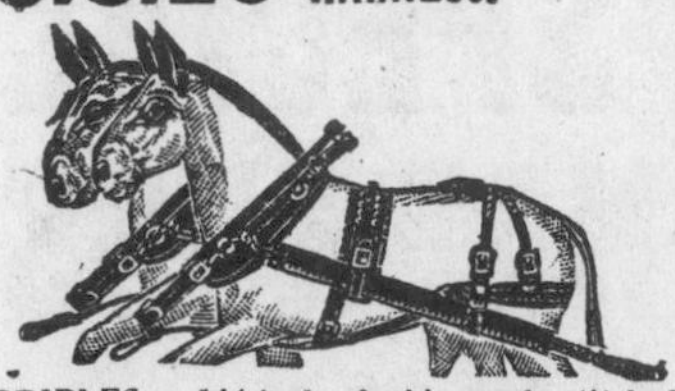

BRIDLES—1¼-inch, double and stitched cheeks, heavy Concord blinds, round winker braces, heavy bridle front, heavy crown piece and throat latch, flat rein.
LINES—1⅛ inches wide, 18 feet long, with snaps.
HAMES—Steel bound, XC ball top, hook hame, four hame straps, two spread straps.
BREAST STRAPS—1½-inch, with snaps and slides.
MARTINGALES—1½-inch (without collar strap), ring in the loop.
TRACES—Heavy twisted link trace chain, No. 0 wire and 7½ feet long.
PIPING—42-inch solid leather piping, 1½-inch flat bellyband.
PADS—Wide flat harness leather body, felt lined, with nickel spots.
BREECHING—Heavy folded harness leather body, with layer double and stitched the full length, 1¼-inch double hip straps, nickel spotted, and 1¼-inch back strap, 1¼-inch side straps to snap in the martingale.

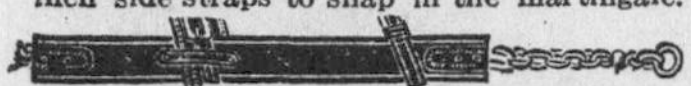

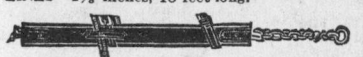

This harness is also furnished with 3½-inch single strap trace, 4 feet 6 inches long, with stage chain in place of trace chain and chain piping. Order this harness by catalogue number, as we furnish body parts only without bridles and lines, also furnish with chain trace and with 3½-inch single strap leather trace. Read the catalogue numbers when making out your order. Weight of harness, boxed for shipment, about 80 pounds.
No. 10K716 Price of bodies without lines, bridles or collars **$18.26**
No. 10K720 Price of complete harness, without collars **$24.49**
No. 10K723 Price of double harness, without collars, with bridles and lines and 3½-inch single strap traces **$26.79**
No. 10K724 Price of body parts only, with the 3½-inch single strap trace, without lines, bridles or collars **$20.68**
For prices on collars see collar page.

REDUCED FROM $19.99 TO

$16.99 WAGON HARNESS.

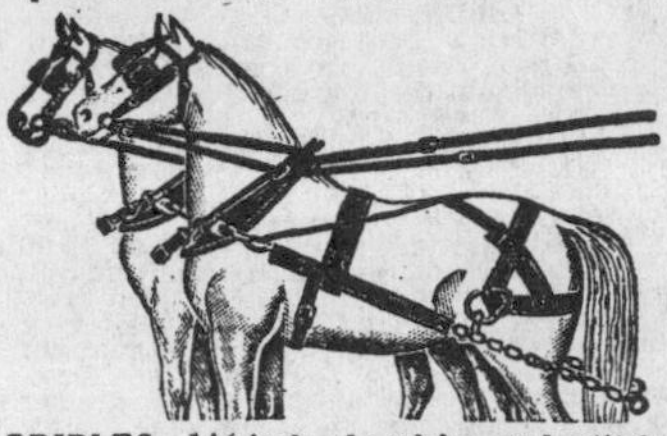

BRIDLES—1¼-inch, double and stitched cheeks, flat square harness leather blinds, double and stitched heavy crown piece and front, flat rein.
LINES—1 inch x 15 feet.
HAMES—Common hook hame, iron bound, four hame straps, two spread straps, 1½-inch breast straps with snap and slide.
TRACES—7-foot straight link trace chain, No. 2 wire with swivel and ring; 30-inch chain piping.
BACK BANDS—3½-inch leather with leather loops.
BREECHING—Pennsylvania style, 3½ inches, with 1-inch cross back straps to cross over the horse's back and tie in the trace chain.
Weight of harness, boxed for shipment, about 80 pounds.
No. 10K725 Price of harness, without collars **$16.99**
Add extra for ¾-inch tie straps, each .... **.26**
For prices on collars see collar page.

REDUCED FROM $26.50 TO

$24.99 OUR WHEEL SCRAPER CHAIN OR TRUCK HARNESS.

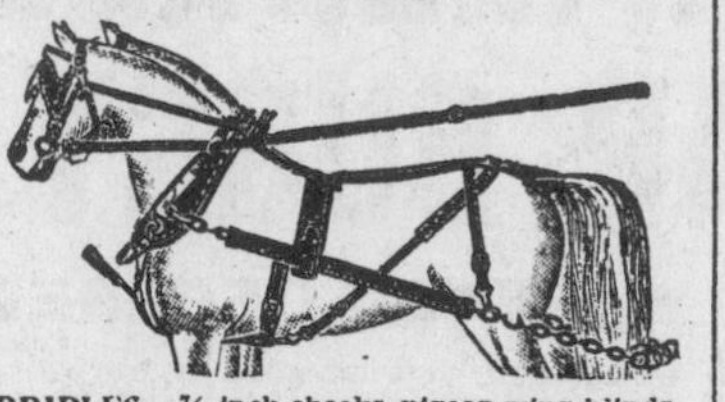

BRIDLES—⅞-inch cheeks, pigeon wing blinds, round winker stays and short flat bridle reins to hames. No tie strap.
LINES—1⅛ inches wide by 22 feet long with snaps, extra heavy.
HAMES—Concord hook, hame straps and spread straps.
TRACES—7-foot chain, No. 0 wire, with 42-inch leather piping, 4-inch backband, solid harness leather with leather loops, 2-inch bellybands, single strap.
BREECHING—2-inch body, Yankee style, 1¼-inch side straps to snap under the horse in martingale ring, 36-inch breast chains, with snaps, 1¾-inch martingales, with 1-inch collar straps, 1¾-inch back straps, from hame to ring on the hip, 1½-inch hip straps, to snap in the chain, with crupper to buckle on.
Weight of harness, boxed for shipment, about 80 pounds.
No. 10K733 Price of harness, without collars **$24.99**
Extra for 60-inch chain piping **1.25**

REDUCED FROM $30.36.

$28.99 CHAIN HARNESS.

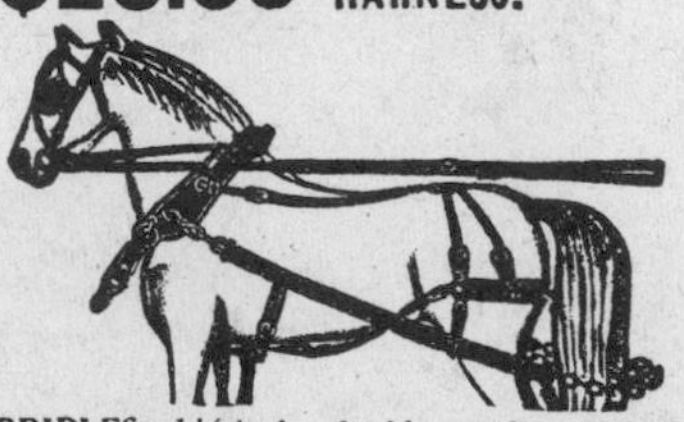

BRIDLES—1¼-inch, double and stitched cheeks, harness leather Concord blinds, round winker braces, brass spotted face piece, leather front, heavy leather crown piece, throat latch, flat rein.
HAMES—Concord style hook hame, heavy ironed with back strap ring, four hame straps, two spreaders.
BREAST STRAPS—2 inches, extra long to buckle with roller snap.
MARTINGALES—Extra heavy, 2 inches wide, with ring in the loop, no collar strap.
TRACES—Heavy 7½-foot twisted chain trace, No. 0 wire; very heavy chain.
PIPING—60-inch leather piping, 2-inch flat bellyband.
BREECHING—Heavy folded harness leather body with layer doubled and stitched the full length; 1¼-inch double hip straps sewed in the ring on the rump; 1¼-inch double back straps running to the hame; 1¼-inch double side straps to snap in the martingale, lazy strap to hold the trace chain up.
TRIMMINGS—Japan with brass spotted face piece.
LINES—1⅛ inches wide, 22 feet long, buckle and billet and snap in the bit.
Our heavy railroad chain harness. Weight, boxed for shipment, about 85 pounds.
No. 10K743 Price of harness, without collars **$28.99**
Add extra for ⅞-inch tie straps, each, **.32**
For prices on collars see collar page.

COMPARE THE LOWER PRICES
in this catalogue with the prices quoted by us in previous catalogues and with the prices quoted by any other house, and note how much we save you on any needed article.

$14.47 CHAIN HARNESS.

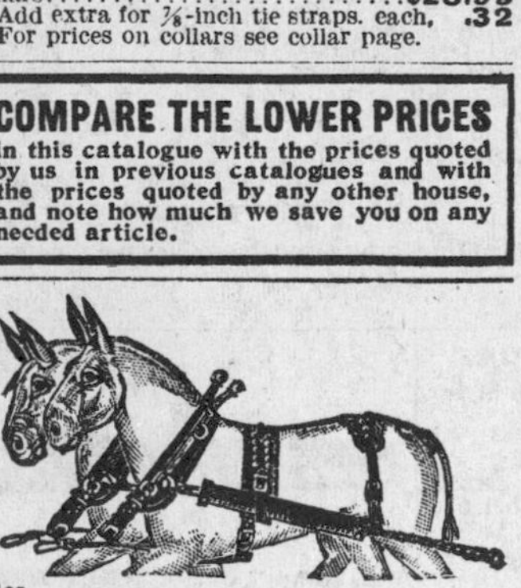

BRIDLES—1¼-inch, double and stitched cheeks, heavy Concord harness leather blinds, flat winker braces, spotted front, heavy crown piece and flat rein.
HAMES—Steel bound, iron clad, ball top, hook; four hame straps, two spread straps.
BREAST STRAPS—1½ inches with snaps and slides.
MARTINGALES—1½ inches with ring in the back end, no collar straps.
TRACES—7½-foot twisted chain, No. 0 wire, with ring and swivel; 36-inch leather piping for the trace chain, flat bellyband.
PADS—Felt lined leather pad with nickel spots with buckle and billet.
BACK STRAPS—1½ inches running from hame to the crupper with 1⅛-inch heavy hip straps with nickel spots to snap in the chain.
LINES—1⅛ inches, 18 feet long.

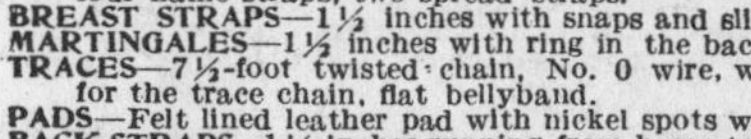

We furnish this harness with 3½-inch by 4-foot 6-inch solid leather trace with 3½-foot stage chain, in place of the chain trace and piping. Read description carefully and order harness you want by catalogue number.
Weight of harness, boxed for shipment, about 80 pounds.
No. 10K735 Price of bodies with chain trace, without lines, bridles or collars ... **$14.47**
No. 10K738 Price complete, harness with chain traces, with bridle and with lines, without collars **$20.57**
No. 10K741 Price, complete harness, with 3½-inch solid leather traces, 4 feet 6 inches long, with the bridles and with the lines, without collars **$22.99**
No. 10K744 Price of body parts only, with 3½-inch traces, 4 feet 6 inches long, without bridles, lines or collars **$16.89**
For prices on collars see collar page.

$23.99 OUR IMPROVED EASTERN WAGON HARNESS. EXTRA STRONG, WELL MADE.

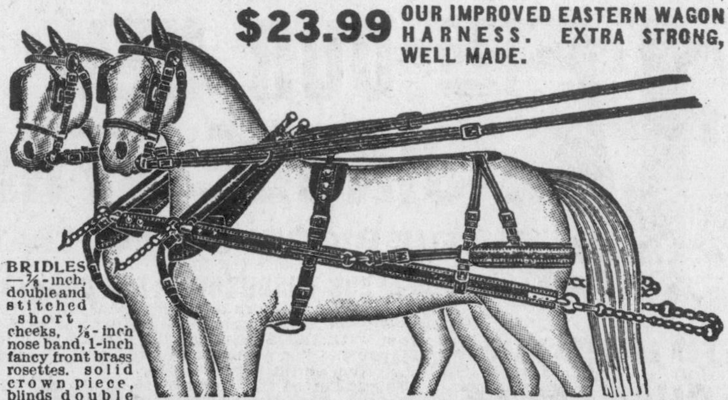

BRIDLES—⅞-inch, double and stitched short cheeks, ⅞-inch nose band, 1-inch fancy front brass rosettes, solid crown piece, blinds double thickness of harness leather with two rows of stitching without irons, flat winker braces, flat reins, bit straps with heavy bits.
LINES—1 inch, 15 feet long with buckle and billet and snaps.
HAMES—Brass ball top wood hame, clip and staple and hold back ring, four heavy hame straps and two spread straps.
TRACES—1¾ inches wide, double and stitched, 4 feet 6 inches long with 3½-foot stage chain.
PADS—Folded harness leather body, 1¼-inch layer, double and stitched, 1¼-inch billet to buckle in the trace loops, 1¼-inch bellyband billet, 1½-inch single strap bellyband.
MARTINGALES—1¼-inch from collar to bellyband with 1¼-inch billet to buckle around the collar, extra heavy.
BREAST STRAPS—Heavy twisted chains with snap on each end.
BREECHING—Heavy folded harness leather body, 1¼-inch layer, double and stitched the full length, 1⅛-inch back strap running to the hames, ⅞-inch double hip straps, 1⅛-inch side straps to snap in the ring on the trace.
MATERIAL—This harness is made out of extra heavy Dundee oak leather, strong hames, chain breast straps and with 1¾-inch traces, with heavy heel chains, making it a very strong harness.
TRIMMINGS—All buckles japan, brass ball hames, brass spots on the pads.
Weight of harness, boxed for shipment, about 68 pounds.
No. 10K795 Price, per set for two horses, without collars **$23.99**
Add extra for good ¾-inch tie straps, each .... **.26**
For price on collars, see collar page.

$11.25 SINGLE HARNESS.

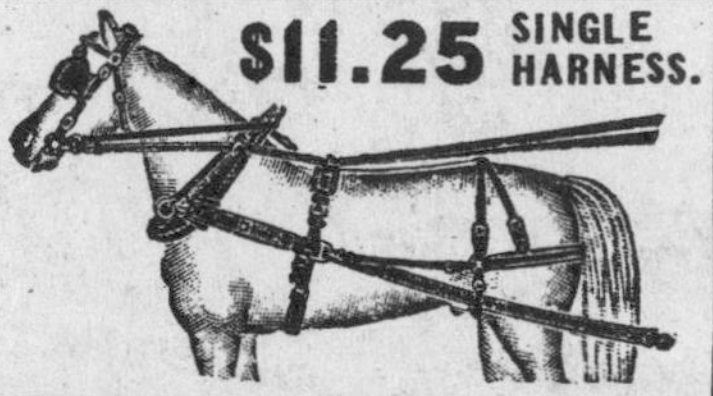

BRIDLE—¾-inch, sensible blinds, flat reins and round winker stays, flat rein check up over the hames.
LINES—1 inch by 13 feet long.
HAMES—Iron over top, or low top wood, iron bound hames, hame tugs folded with loops and trace buckle.
TRACES—1½ inches wide by 6 feet long, double and stitched, with clip cockeyes, to buckle in the hame tug.
BREECHING—Folded with layer, ⅞-inch side straps, double hip straps.
PADS—Flexible harness leather pad with loop and terrets, 1¼-inch bellyband, 1¼-inch double and stitched shaft tugs attached to the traces with buckle.
TRIMMINGS—XC trimmings.
Weight of harness, packed for shipment, about 40 pounds. Always state the kind of hame you want, low top or high hame.
No. 10K747 Price, with 1½-inch traces, without collar **$11.25**
No. 10K751 Price, with 1¼-inch traces, with collar **$12.79**
Add extra for ¾-inch tie strap, each ... **.26**
For prices on collars see collar page.

$23.99 FOLDED TRACE PENNSYLVANIA FARM HARNESS.

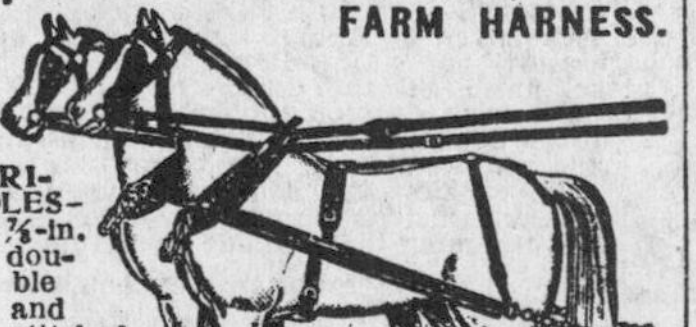

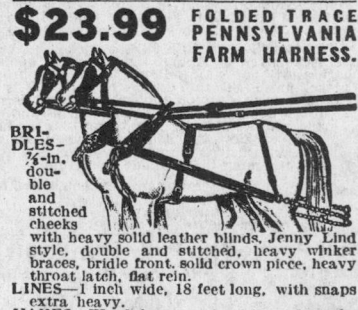

BRIDLES—⅞-in. double and stitched cheeks with heavy solid leather blinds, Jenny Lind style, double and stitched, heavy winker braces, bridle front, solid crown piece, heavy throat latch, flat rein.
LINES—1 inch wide, 18 feet long, with snaps extra heavy.
HAMES—Wood, iron over top, clip and staple, four heavy hame straps, two spread straps, heavy twisted breast chains with snap on each end.
MARTINGALES—1½ inches from bellyband to collar.
TRACES—Folded trace cut out of extra heavy Dundee leather, 6 inches wide and folded twice, making a solid three-ply trace, 4 feet 6 inches long with 3½-foot chain clipped to the trace and the trace fastened to the hame by a clip, 1½-inch bellyband billets and 1½-inch heavy folded bellyband.
PADS—Heavy folded harness leather body, 1½-inch layer, double and stitched the full length, 1½-inch billets to buckle around the trace, loop on top of the pad.
BACK STRAPS—1½ inches running through to the hames with 1-inch hip straps with crupper to buckle on.
TRIMMINGS—All buckles and rings japan black finish trimmed.
Weight of harness, boxed for shipment, about 65 pounds. We do not make any changes in this harness.
Sold in sets for two horses only.
No. 10K800 Price of harness without collars **$23.99**
Add extra for ¾-inch tie straps, each .. **.26**

$15.89 AND $16.97 FARM HARNESS.

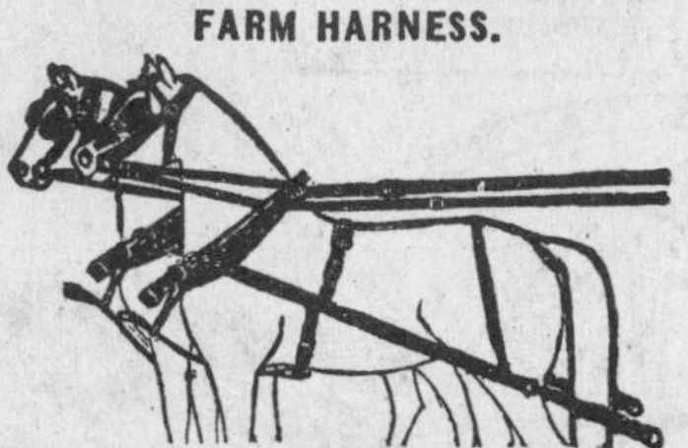

BRIDLES—⅞ inch, Jenny Lind blind or Concord blinds. No tie strap furnished with this harness.
LINES—⅞ inch by 18 feet long, with snaps.
HAMES—Clip iron over top hames, hame straps.
TRACES—1½ inches and 1¾ inches wide by 4 feet 6 inches long, 42-inch chain riveted to the trace and riveted to hames.
PADS—Leather housing, layer of harness leather, 1¼-inch billets and flat bellyband, 1¼-inch back straps, 1 inch hip straps with folded crupper to buckle on, 1½-inch breast strap with snaps and slide riveted.
MARTINGALES—1¼ inches, with collar straps.
TRIMMINGS—XC white metal.
Weight of harness, packed for shipment, about 60 pounds.
No. 10K765 Price, with 1½-inch traces, without collars **$15.89**
No. 10K775 Price, with 1¾-inch traces, without collars **$16.97**
Add extra for ¾-inch tie strap, each, **.26**

THIS HARNESS REDUCED IN PRICE FROM $19.50 AND $20.50 TO

$17.99 AND $18.99 FARM HARNESS.

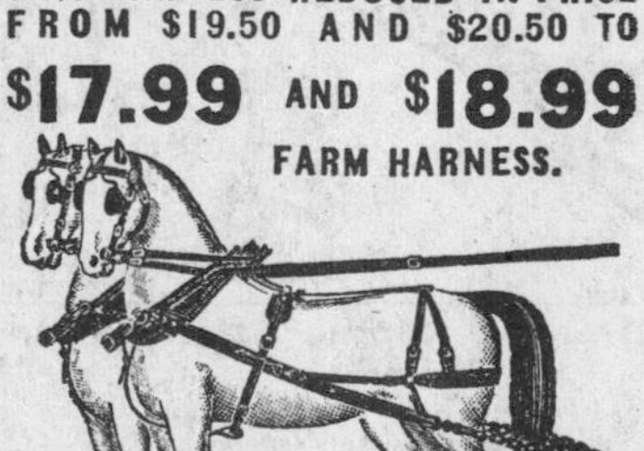

BRIDLES—¾-inch cheeks, flat reins, sensible blinds, round winker braces.
LINES—1 inch by 15 feet long.
HAMES—Iron oval top hames, clip and staple, four hame straps, two spread straps.
TRACES—1½ inches and 1¾ inches, double and stitched, 4½ feet long with 3½-foot stage chain riveted on, traces riveted to the hames.
PADS—Flat, with leather housings, 1¼-inch billets, single bellyband.
BREECHING—Harness leather fold, 1-inch double and stitched layer, 1⅛-inch back straps, ⅞-inch double hip straps, ⅞-inch side straps to snap in the ring on the traces, 1½-inch breast straps with snaps and slides, riveted.
MARTINGALES—1¼ inches.
TRIMMINGS—XC white metal finish.
Weight of harness, packed for shipment, about 45 pounds.
No. 10K785 Price, with 1½-inch traces, without collars **$17.99**
No. 10K793 Price, with 1¾-inch traces, without collars **$18.99**
Add extra for ¾-inch tie strap, each, **.26**

BRASS HARNESS. $30.49 AND $37.29

FINE BRASS TRIMMED FARM HARNESS

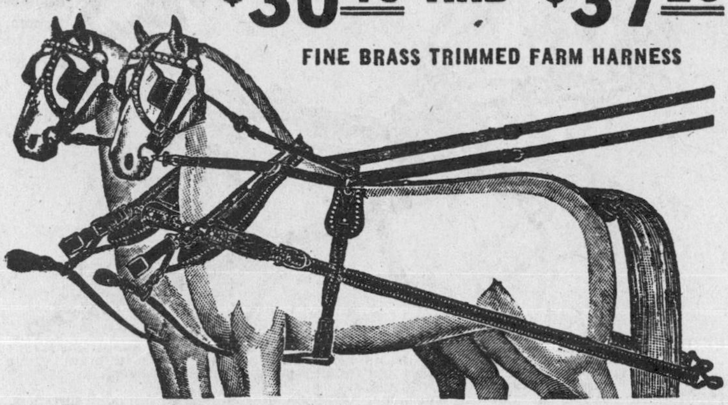

BRIDLES—¾ inch, box loop cheeks, patent leather blinds, round side reins, round winker stays, brass spotted face piece.
LINES—1 inch, 20 feet long, with buckle and billet with snap.
HAMES—Low top wood hames, brass long spot, Hayden holdback ring, four hame straps and two spread straps, box loop, scalloped, hame tug and Champion trace buckle.
TRACES—1½ inches wide by 6 feet 6 inches long, raised center, round edge finish, cockeye sewed in, to buckle in hame tug.
PADS—Harness leather sewed bottom, and stuffed with hai., brass spots all around pad. Flexible tree pad, single strap harness leather skirts, double and stitched raised bearer, bellyband folded, 1-inch back straps, scalloped and stitched with crupper to buckle on.
BREAST STRAPS—1½ inches, with snaps and slides, adjustable.
MARTINGALES—1½ inches, with collar straps, adjustable.
TRIMMINGS—Brass swage trimmings.
MATERIAL used in this harness is the very best grade, the best tanned, the best selected Dundee oak leather. All the straps of this harness are carefully cut and selected for weight of strap. The straps are carefully edged and blacked and the harness is smooth finished, using the best brass hardware. The workmanship is first class and together with the excellent quality of leather and trimming, makes it one of the best harness we have to offer for $30.49. Harness similar to this in description, but not as good in quality, are sold for $8.00 to $12.00 more than our price.
Weight of harness, packed for shipment, about 80 pounds.
No. 10K825 Price, brass trimmed, 1½-inch traces, without collars........$30.49
No. 10K826 Price, brass trimmed, 1½-inch traces, with double hip strap breeching, without collars........$37.29
Add extra for full brass iron hames in place of wood hames........2.50
Add extra for good ¾-inch tie straps, each.........26
Traces without cockeye will be furnished at same price if wanted.
For prices on collars see collar page.

REDUCED IN PRICE FROM $18.38 TO $17.39 AND REDUCED IN PRICE FROM $19.38 TO $18.29

FARM HARNESS.

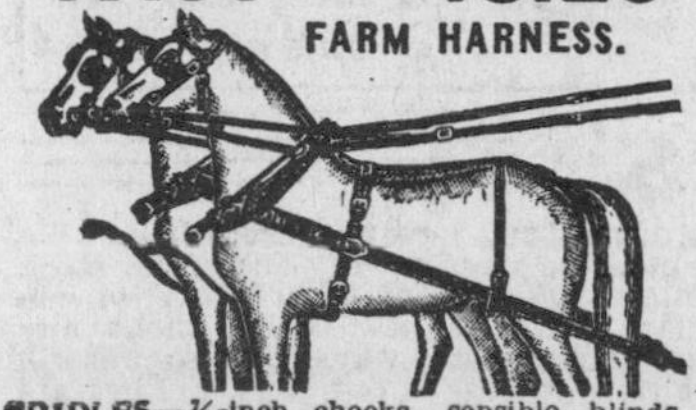

BRIDLES—⅝-inch cheeks, sensible blinds, flat winker stays, short reins to run over the hames.
LINES—⅞ inch wide by 15 feet long, with snaps.
HAMES—Common wooden hames, oval iron pattern with holdback ring, hame tugs folded with 1½-inch layer and Champion trace buckle, hame strap and spread strap.
TRACES—1½ inches and 1¾ inches, double and stitched, 6 feet long with clip cockeyes riveted on to buckle in the hame tug.
PADS—Folded body, flat layer, 1½-inch billets, folded and stitched bellyband, 1⅛-inch back straps, 1-inch hip straps, 1½-inch breast straps, with snaps and slides riveted.
MARTINGALES—1½ inches, no collar straps.
TRIMMINGS—XC white metal.
Weight of harness, packed for shipment, about 58 pounds.
No. 10K804 Price, with 1½-inch traces, without collars........$17.39
No. 10K808 Price, with 1¾-inch traces, without collars........$18.29
Add extra for team breeching........3.20
Add extra for ¾-inch tie strap, each,.26
For prices on collars, see collar page.

THE LOWER PRICES
QUOTED IN THIS CATALOGUE will be more interesting to you than the prices quoted by any other firm or individual.

$38.97 EASTERN HARNESS.

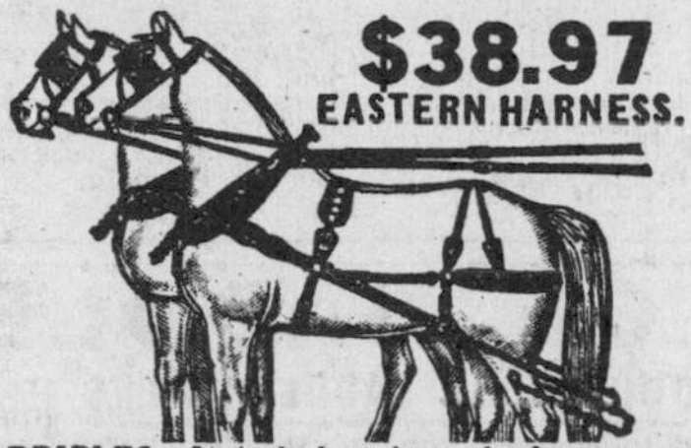

BRIDLES—⅞ inch, box loop cheeks, square patent leather blinds, spotted face pieces, fancy front, round winker stays, brass rosettes, solid crown piece, heavy throat latch and flat rein.
LINES—1 inch wide, 15 feet long, buckle and billet with snaps, extra heavy and well made.
HAMES—Brass long spot, ball top, iron clad, painted red, clip and staple, four hame straps and two spread straps.
BREAST CHAINS—Heavy twisted link chain with T bar and snap on one end.
MARTINGALES—1½-inch from collar to bellyband, heavy buckle and billet to buckle around the collar and loop for bellyband.
BREAST STRAPS—1½ inches, double and stitched, with snaps and slides.
TRACES—2 inches wide, 4 feet 6 inches long with three rows stitching and dee loop in center, making a sectional trace, 3½-foot trace chain to snap in the ring.
PADS—Swell housing, 1½-inch layer double and stitched the full length, brass spots, 1½-inch billet to buckle in the lead up from dee in trace, heavy folded bellybands.
BREECHING—Heavy folded harness leather body, 1½-inch layer, double and stitched the full length, heavy rings, 1¼-inch double hip straps, 1½-inch back straps running to the hame, 1¼-inch side straps from dee in trace to ring in the breeching, large padded safe under the ring on the hips.
TRIMMINGS—Brass.
Weight of harness, boxed for shipment, about 90 pounds. We do not make any changes in this harness.
Furnished in complete set for two horses.
No. 10K816 Price, of harness without collars........$38.97

$21.99 SHORT TUG FARM HARNESS.

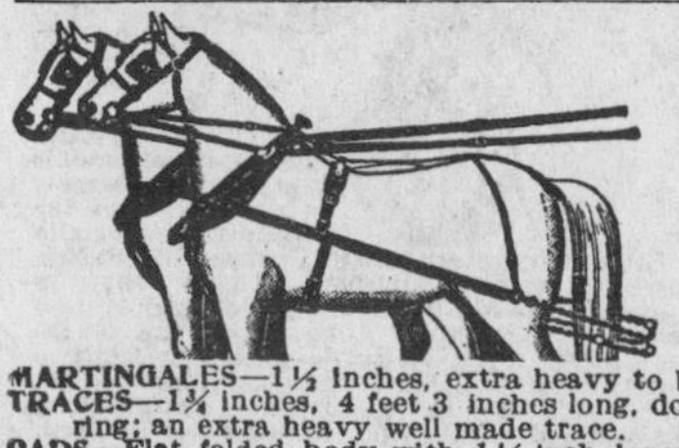

BRIDLES—⅞ inch, double and stitched short cheeks with noseband, heavy double harness leather blinds stitched together, flat winker braces, leather front, solid crown piece and heavy throat latch, flat rein.
LINES—1 inch wide, 18 feet long, with buckle and billets with snap at the bit.
HAMES—Red ball top clip and staple, four heavy hame straps and two spread straps.
BREAST CHAINS—Heavy twisted link chain with T bar and snap.
MARTINGALES—1½ inches, extra heavy to buckle around the collar and loop for bellyband.
TRACES—1¾ inches, 4 feet 3 inches long, double and stitched, 3½-foot chain to snap in the ring; an extra heavy well made trace.
PADS—Flat folded body with 1½-inch layer, 1½-inch billets to buckle around the trace, 1¼-inch bellyband billets, heavy folded bellyband.
BACK STRAPS—1½ inches running to the hame, 1-inch hip straps to buckle in the ring on the trace, folded crupper to buckle on.
TRIMMINGS—All trimming black japan finish with ball top hames.
Weight of harness boxed for shipment, about 50 pounds. We do not make any changes in this harness.
Furnished in sets for two horses.
No. 10K814 Price of harness without collars........$21.99
Add extra for 1¾-inch traces........1.00

WILLIAMS' SPECIAL HOOK AND TERRET FARM HARNESS

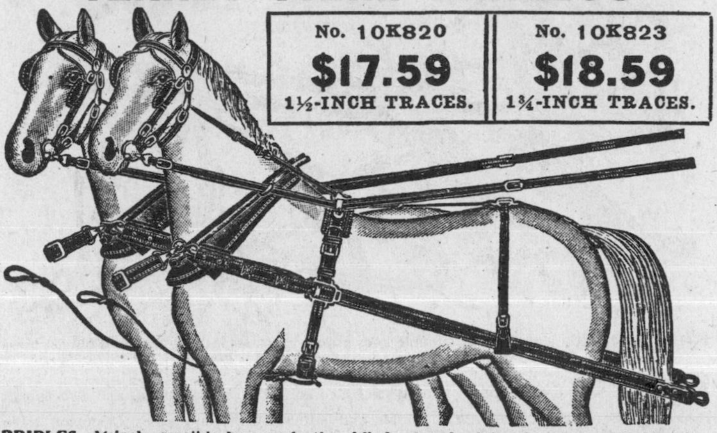
No. 10K820
$17.59
1½-INCH TRACES.
No. 10K823
$18.59
1¾-INCH TRACES.

BRIDLES—¾ inch, sensible harness leather blinds, round winker braces, round side reins, heavy crown piece.
LINES—⅞ inch by 18 feet long, with snap.
HAMES—Wood hames, iron bound over top, XC plated with Hayden holdback ring; hame tugs, folded harness leather, two leather loops, 1½-inch layer double and stitched with Champion trace buckle sewed in. Four hame straps, two spread straps.
BREAST STRAPS—1½ inches, double with snaps and slides.
TRACES—1½ inches and 1¾ inches wide by 6 feet long, double and stitched with clip cockeyes riveted on.
PADS—All harness leather flexible pads, with hooks and terrets, 1¼-inch double market strap skirts, to buckle in the hame tugs; 1-inch back straps and hip straps sewed in. Cooper trace carrier, folded crupper to buckle on, bellybands folded.
MARTINGALES—1½ inches.
TRIMMINGS—Full XC white metal.
Weight of harness, packed for shipment, about 65 pounds.
No. 10K820 Price, with 1½-inch traces, without collars........$17.59
No. 10K823 Price, with 1¾-inch traces, without collars........18.59
Add extra for team breeching........$3.25 Add extra for collar strap........30
Add extra for 1 inch by 18 feet lines........50 Add extra for ¾-inch tie strap, each........26
Add extra for extra large harness for 1,400 to 1,700-pound horses........3.25
For prices on collars see collar page.

HERCULES FARM HARNESS

REDUCED FROM PREVIOUS CATALOGUE. $20.99 AND $21.99

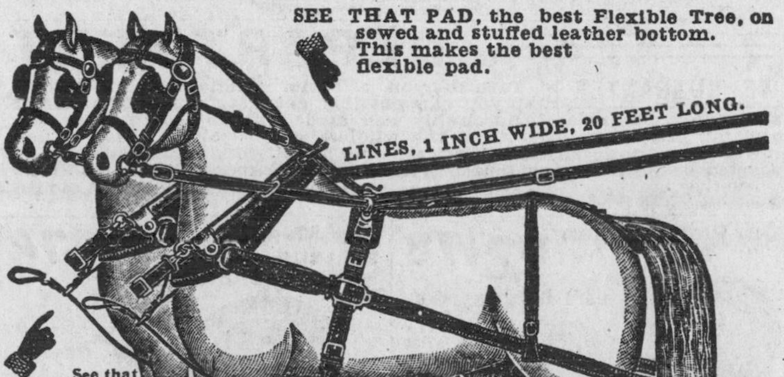
SEE THAT PAD, the best Flexible Tree, on sewed and stuffed leather bottom. This makes the best flexible pad.
LINES, 1 INCH WIDE, 20 FEET LONG.
See that Hame Attachment. The hame tug will not break at the hame.

Remember you can have either style breeching, the one to buckle on single hip strap at $3.18, or the one with double hip strap at $5.50 added extra to price of harness.
BRIDLES—¾ inch, double and stitched cheek, two leather loops, leather nose band, harness leather blinds, round winker braces, leather front, solid crown piece, heavy throat latch, round side reins.
LINES—1 inch wide, 20 feet long, good heavy, well selected line leather, well made.
HAMES—Wood hames iron bound, square staple, Concord clip attachment for hame tug, four hame straps, two spread straps.
BREAST STRAPS—1½ inches with snaps and slides.
MARTINGALES—1½ inches with collar strap, ring in the loop.
HAME TUGS—Folded body, 1½-inch double and stitched layer, double loop attached to the hame with Concord clip hame attachment, making a jointed bolt hame tug, will not break at the clip, Champion trace buckle, 1¼-inch bellyband billet, heavy folded bellyband.
PADS—Improved Moline tree, flexible joint, harness leather bottom, double and stitched, hair stuffed, single strap skirts with 1¼-inch layer doubled and stitched, to buckle in the trace buckle.
HIP AND BACK STRAPS—1 inch to buckle in the pad and 1-inch hip strap sewed in a Cooper brace carrier with trace lugs to buckle on. Folded crupper to buckle.
TRACES—1½ or 1¾-inch double and stitched trace, 6 feet long, with clip cockeye riveted on; a very strong, well made trace.
TRIMMINGS—Full XC white metal trimmed.
Weight of harness, boxed for shipment, about 70 pounds.

BREECHING $5.50 EXTRA

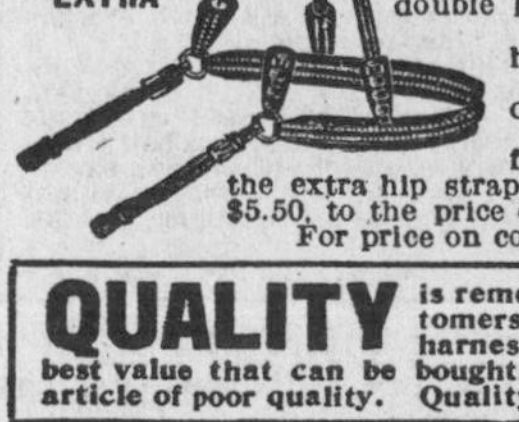

No. 10K849 Price of harness, 1½-inch traces, without collar........$20.99
No. 10K853 Price of harness, 1¾-inch traces, without collars........$21.99
Add extra for breeching to buckle on the hip strap with extra strap on the breeching to snap in the trace carrier, making a double hip strap breeching. Price, per set, extra........$5.50
Add extra for two ¾-inch tie straps with the harness........52
Add extra for single hip breeching to buckle on hip strap........3.18
This illustration shows the double hip strap breeching furnished with this harness to buckle on the hip strap, and the extra hip strap to snap in the trace carrier, for $5.50. Add this price, $5.50, to the price of the harness if you want the breeching with the harness.
For price on collars see collar page.

QUALITY is remembered a long time after the price is forgotten. Our customers would rather pay $1.00 or $2.00 more for a good set of harness or saddle, strap work, collars, or fly nets, and get the best value that can be bought, than to pay $1.00 or $2.00 less and get an inferior article of poor quality. Quality considered, our prices are the lowest in the world.

THIS HARNESS REDUCED FROM $38.71 TO

FARM HARNESS. $36.96

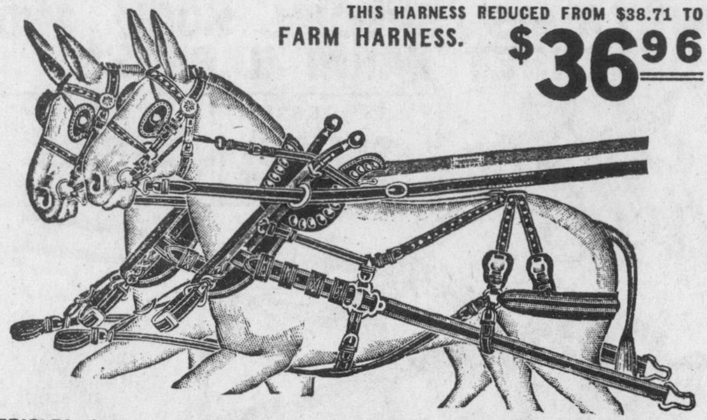

BRIDLES—⅞-inch, short cheeks, double and stitched harness leather, Concord blinds, brass spotted nose band and brass spotted front, round winker braces, round side reins, heavy crown piece and throat latch.
LINES—Extra heavy, 1 inch wide, 20 feet long.
HAMES—Brass trimmed ball top hames, steel clad bolt, four hame straps, and two spread straps.
HAME TUGS—Concord bolt style, double and stitched with four loops, Champion trace buckles, 1¼-inch billets and heavy folded bellybands, attached to hames with a bolt.
TRACES—1½ inches and 1¾ inches double and stitched, 6 feet long, with triangular cockeye sewed in, or single strap harness leather trace 3½ inches wide, 6 feet long, with heel chain.
BREAST STRAPS—1½ inches wide, extra heavy, with breast strap slide and snap, adjustable.
MARTINGALES—1½ inches wide, extra heavy, with collar strap and ring in the loop.
BREECHING—Heavy folded harness leather body, heavy layer double and stitched the full length, 1-inch double hip straps, 1-inch double back straps with brass spots and buckle shields, 1-inch side straps to snap in the martingale ring, short strap running from trace buckle to the hames.
HOUSING—Harness leather housing, double and stitched, Scotch shape with brass spots all around.
TRIMMINGS—Japan buckles all around with brass spots and brass buckle shields on the breeching, brass trimmed hames with brass balls, brass spotted housing, and brass spotted front and noseband.
LEATHER—The best Dundee oak harness leather is used in this harness.

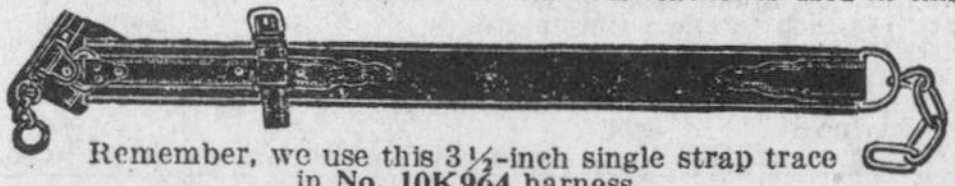

This 3½-inch solid harness leather trace, 6 feet long, is used in No. 10K964 harness.

Remember, we use this 3½-inch single strap trace in No. 10K964 harness.

Weight of harness, boxed for shipment, about 85 pounds.

No. 10K956 Price, 1½-inch traces, without collars, brass spotted hame housing, brass spots on the hip and back straps, brass buckle shields, and brass spots on the nose band, bridle front and blinds....................**$36.96**

No. 10K957 Price, 1¾-inch traces, without collars, brass spots on the hame housing, brass spots on hip and back straps, brass buckle shields, brass spots on nose band, bridle front and blinds....................**$38.47**

No. 10K964 Price of harness with 3½-inch single strap harness leather trace, balance of harness as described above, without collars....................**$36.95**

Add extra for heavy breeching, with 1¼-inch double hip strap, 1¼-inch back strap, 1¼ side strap with brass spots and buckle shields....................**$1.29**

For price of collars see page 138.

BRASS TRUCK HARNESS $43.29

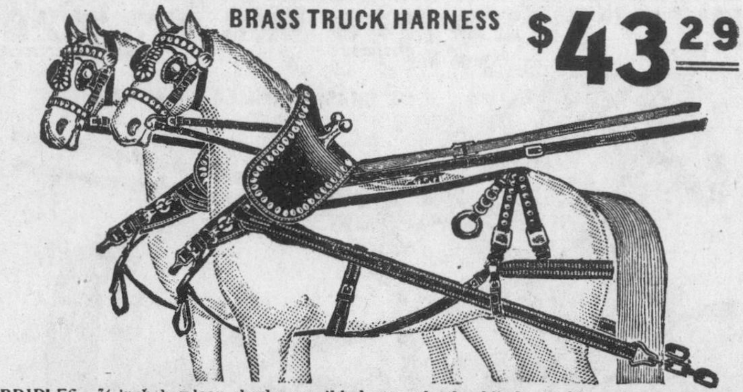

BRIDLES—⅞-inch, box loop cheeks, sensible harness leather blinds, double and stitched front and nose band with brass peanut spots, double and stitched face drop with brass peanut spots, brass spots on the blinds, brass rosettes, heavy crown piece, flat reins.
LINES—1¼ inches wide, 18 feet long with snaps.
HAMES—Brass trimmed, brass ball bolt hame, four hame straps and two celluloid spreaders, one ring, four small celluloid dees, four loops and snaps to the hame.
BREAST STRAPS—1½-inch, extra heavy with roller snap, adjustable with roller breast strap snap.
MARTINGALE—1½-inch, Chicago style with ring in the loop.
TRACES—1½ or 1¾-inch, double and stitched with heel chain attached to the hames by bolt.
BREECHING—Heavy folded harness leather body, double and stitched layer the full length, 1-inch double hip straps and 1-inch double back straps running to the hame with buckle shields and brass spots on the hip and back straps; 1-inch side straps to snap in the martingales and two celluloid spreaders to snap in the ring in the breeching.
HOUSING—Double and stitched harness leather housing, 16 inches long and 12¾ inches wide at the bottom, harness leather double and stitched with brass peanut spots on the outside of each horse.
TRIMMINGS—All buckles japanned, with brass spotted bridles, brass spotted housings, brass spotted hip and back straps, and brass buckle shields on the hip straps.
LEATHER—Highest grade pure Dundee oak.

Weight of harness, boxed for shipment, about 95 pounds.
No. 10K996 Price of harness with 1½-inch traces, without collars.......**$43.29**
No. 10K998 Price of harness with 1¾-inch traces, without collars....... **44.33**
If harness is wanted without housing deduct $5.50 from price of harness.
Changes we will make for you in this harness.
Add extra to price of harness, for 1¾-inch breast strap, 1¾-inch martingale, 1¼x20 feet lines, heavy breeching 1¼-inch double hip strap, 1¼-inch back strap, 1¼-inch side strap....................**$2.30**
Add extra for 2-inch trace on 10K998 harness.................... **1.75**
Add extra for pads with double brass loop, and brass spotted to match housing and bridle....................**$4.80**
Add extra for 2-inch trace on 10K996 harness.................... **3.11**

For prices of collars see page 138.

Sears, Roebuck & Co., Chicago, Ill. Moorcroft, Wyo.
Gentlemen:—The harness I ordered from you some time ago has reached me in perfect condition and I had the opportunity of using it and am well satisfied with it. I found the quality far better than I expected. It would have cost me from $10.00 to $15.00 more if I had bought it anywhere else, for it only cost me $32.75 with the freight. If I had bought it here it would have cost me between $45.00 and $50.00. I will recommend its purchase to others. I remain, Yours very truly,
JOHN BERGER.

DEPARTMENT OF SADDLES

WE GUARANTEE to furnish you a better saddle for less money than you can possibly get elsewhere. Our saddles are strictly high class, thoroughly well made, guaranteed in every way and our prices are lower than the wholesaler's or jobber's, very much lower than the retail dealer's prices. Our line of stock saddles is especially adapted for western and southwestern trade and all parts of the United States where they use heavy stock saddles; they are the strongest and handsomest saddles it is possible to produce.

OUR STOCK SADDLE TREES are guaranteed against breaking. We guarantee the tree in every one of our stock saddles and if the tree should break in roping cattle or doing other work, you can send the saddle back to us and we will replace it with a new tree without any expense to you and pay the transportation charges both ways, or else we will send you a new saddle. We know that the trees we use in our stock saddles are built to last and stand any amount of hard usage and we therefore positively guarantee them against breaking.

Our Plain English Saddle, $2.78

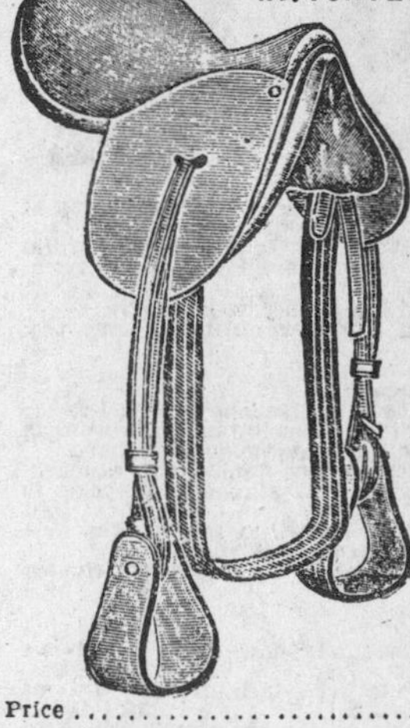

No. 10K1205 Made in russet leather only. Has 15½-inch tree, full leather covered seat, pigskin impression skirts, full pad, sheepskin face, drill lined. **Stirrup leathers,** ⅞ inch wide, with 3-inch wood stirrups and woven web girth. At this exceptionally low price we offer a good easy riding saddle. Wt., 6 pounds. Packed for shipment, about 12 pounds.
Price....................**$2.78**

WE GUARANTEE OUR SADDLES TO FIT COMFORTABLY ON THE HORSE'S BACK, TO BE EASY RIDING AND TO BE MADE OF THE BEST MATERIALS THROUGHOUT.

Our Men's Russet and Black Morgan Saddle, $4.74

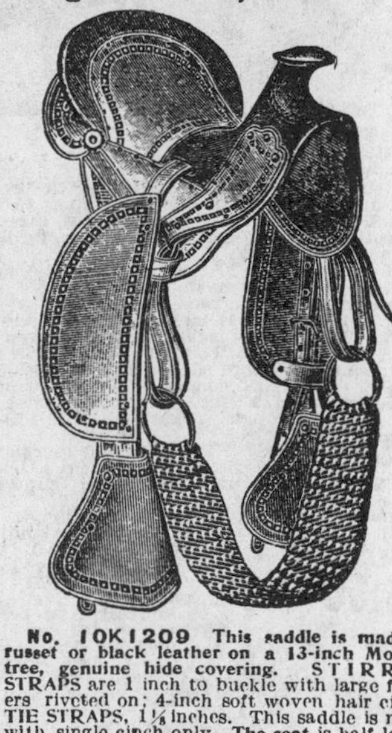

No. 10K1209 This saddle is made in russet or black leather on a 13-inch Morgan tree, genuine hide covering. STIRRUP STRAPS are 1 inch to buckle with large fenders riveted on; 4-inch soft woven hair cinch. TIE STRAPS, 1¼ inches. This saddle is made with single cinch only. **The seat** is half leather covered and we consider it to be an exceptionally good value for the money. Weight of saddle, about 9 pounds. Shipping weight, 15 pounds.
Price....................**$4.74**

Special Roll Cantle, Smooth Seat Saddle, $6.67

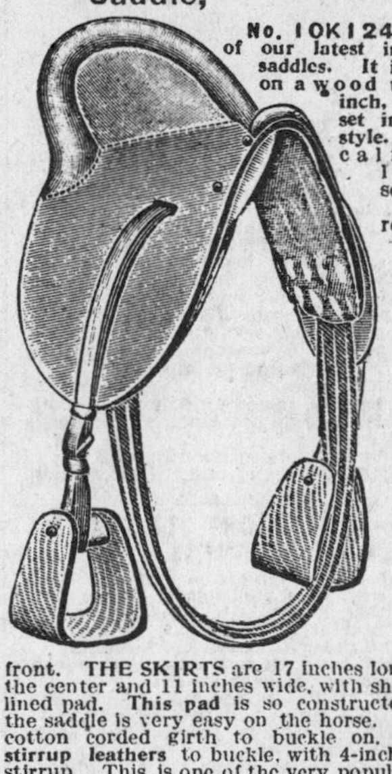

No. 10K1242 One of our latest improved saddles. It is made on a wood tree, 16-inch, Somerset improved style. Plain calfskin leather seat and calfskin roll plain front. THE SKIRTS are 17 inches long from the center and 11 inches wide, with sheepskin lined pad. **This pad** is so constructed that the saddle is very easy on the horse. Heavy cotton corded girth to buckle on. **1-inch stirrup leathers** to buckle, with 4-inch Texas stirrup. This is one of the very popular style saddles and one of our big sellers. It is one of the best values for the money in this line. The quality of leather used in this saddle is the very best russet tanned saddle skirting. Weight of saddle, packed for shipment, about 20 pounds. Price....................**$6.67**

Our Southwest Style Saddle, $11.67

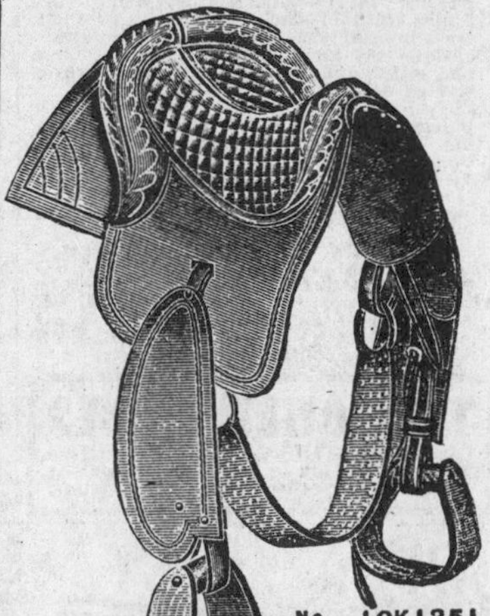

No. 10K1251 This style of saddle is used very largely in all sections of the country, especially in the southwestern states, Kansas, Nebraska, Missouri and Oklahoma. It is what is known as the Mosby tree saddle and is used also very extensively throughout the southern states. THE TREE is higher in front so that the saddle will not rub the horse's withers. Made with fancy skirt and apron. **Roll and stitched cantle** and handsomely quilted, well stitched calfskin seat, **14-inch Mosby tree, 1¼-inch stirrup straps,** with heavy Texas bolt STIRRUPS to buckle and with heavy fenders attached. Cotton woven cinch with rings and 1¼-inch tie strap. Made of a fine grade of russet leather; skirt has hogskin impression and fancy creased edge. A strictly up to date Mosby saddle. Weight of saddles packed for shipment, about 24 pounds.
Price....................**$11.67**

The GREAT REDUCTIONS in the prices shown in the pages of this catalogue we feel sure will be very pleasing to our millions of customers.

Our Special Spring Bar Kentucky Style Saddle, $14.50.

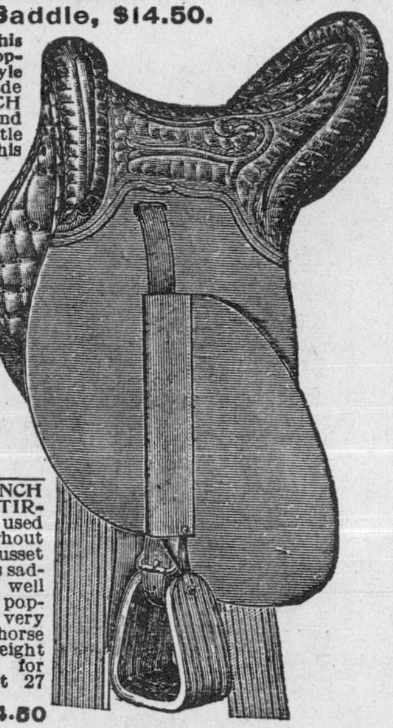

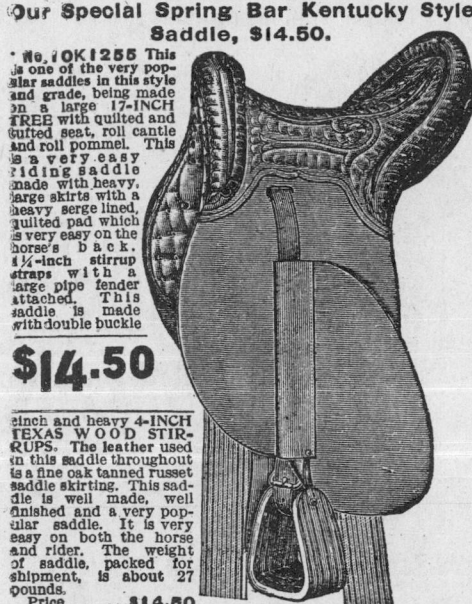

No. 10K1255 This is one of the very popular saddles in this style and grade, being made on a large 17-INCH TREE with quilted and tufted seat, roll cantle and roll pommel. This is a very easy riding saddle made with heavy, large skirts with a heavy serge lined, quilted pad which is very easy on the horse's back. 1¼-inch stirrup straps with a large pipe fender attached. This saddle is made with double buckle

$14.50

cinch and heavy 4-INCH TEXAS WOOD STIRRUPS. The leather used in this saddle throughout is a fine oak tanned russet saddle skirting. This saddle is well made, well finished and a very popular saddle. It is very easy on both the horse and rider. The weight of saddle, packed for shipment, is about 27 pounds.

Price........$14.50

Our Improved Somerset Saddle, Kentucky Style, $8.99.

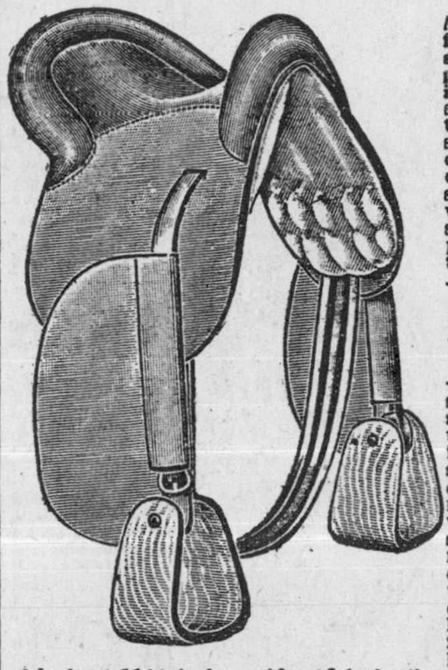

No. 10K1275 Made with pipe fenders, calfskin seat, roll cantle and pommel. The skirting used in this saddle is the russet tanned saddle skirting with a plain calfskin seat, roll cantle and pommel, so that the rider will sit easy in the saddle. Serge lined pad, quilted to protect the horse. This

$8.99

saddle is made on a 15-inch Somerset tree with the skirting pigskin impression. The pipe fenders are easily removed in case you want to use the saddle without fenders. The fenders always protect the rider's clothing from the horse. It has a large SKIRT 17 inches long from center and about 11½ inches wide. 1-inch stirrup straps to buckle; heavy large pipe fenders attached and large WOOD STIRRUPS. Heavy cotton cord girth with 1½-inch billets to buckle. Weight of saddle, packed for shipment, about 18 to 20 pounds.

Price..............................$8.99

Our Special Morgan Saddle, $8.20.

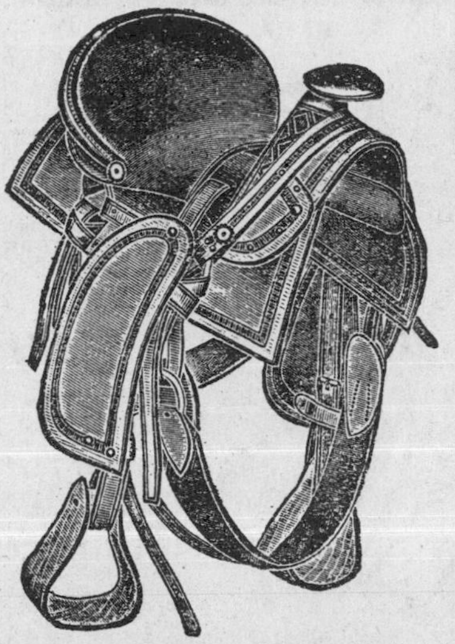

No. 10K1293 Made on a good heavy 13-inch solid covered Morgan tree with solid leather skirts 21 inches long. Half leather seat with leather roll cantle, double cinch rigging. 1⅛-inch tie straps. COTTON WEB CINCHES

$8.20

with leather chafes and connecting straps. Cinches to tie. Heavy 1⅛-inch STIRRUP STRAPS to buckle with 14-inch fender attached. 3-inch WOOD STIRRUPS. This saddle is made of russet saddle skirting fancy embossed edges. Just the style of a saddle that is used on a farm for light riding. It is light and quick to handle, easily adjusted and suitable for man or boy. Weight of saddle, packed for shipment, about 21 pounds. Price............$8.20

Our Special Black McClellan Saddle, $9.20.

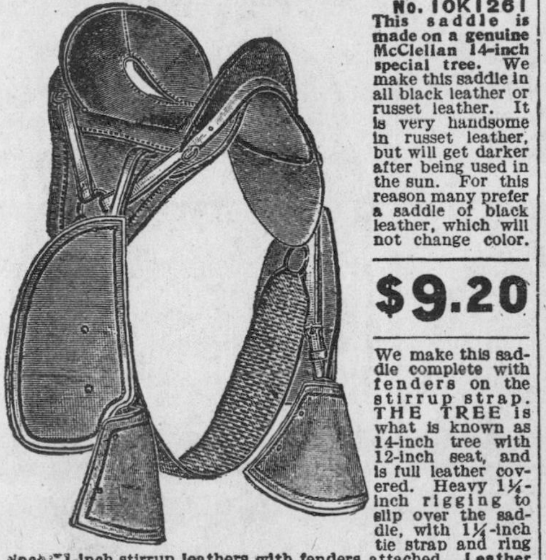

No. 10K1261 This saddle is made on a genuine McClellan 14-inch special tree. We make this saddle in all black leather or russet leather. It is very handsome in russet leather, but will get darker after being used in the sun. For this reason many prefer a saddle of black leather, which will not change color.

$9.20

We make this saddle complete with fenders on the stirrup strap. THE TREE is what is known as 14-inch tree with 12-inch seat, and is full leather covered. Heavy 1¼-inch rigging to slip over the saddle, with 1¼-inch tie strap and ring cinch. 1-inch stirrup leathers with fenders attached. Leather covered hooded stirrup. This is a very popular saddle for farm or livery stable use. Weight of saddle, packed for shipment, about 20 pounds.

Price..............................$9.20

Our Extra Large Special Leather Tree Kansas Style Saddle, $12.13.

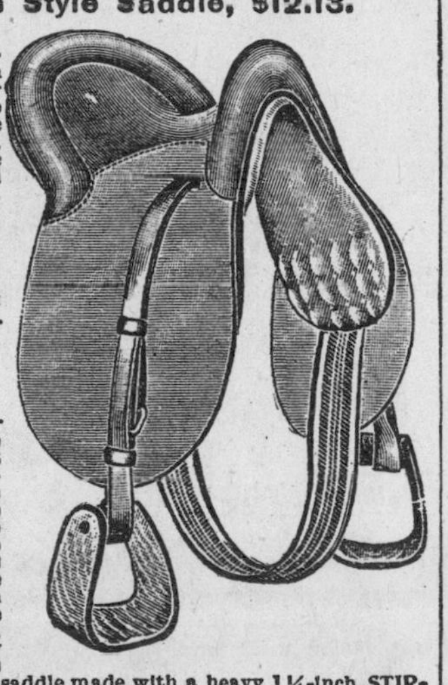

No. 10K1281 It would be impossible for us to make a more substantial or better high grade saddle than we have made in this our No. 10K1281 as it is made on our special solid LEATHER TREE, which is specially constructed for wear and easily shapes itself to the horse's back and to the rider. THE SKIRTING

$12.13

used in this saddle is a high grade russet tanned saddle skirting with buckle cinches and serge lined pad, quilted so as to make the tree easy on the horse's back. Saddle is made with a plain calfskin seat with roll cantle and roll pommel, which makes it easy for the rider. It is a very popular style saddle made with a heavy 1¼-inch STIRRUP STRAP on this our special solid leather tree with double gullet heavy ironed. LARGE SKIRTS, 23 inches long from center and 12 inches wide. Heavy cotton cord girth to buckle on. Heavy 1¼ billet and large wood stirrup. Weight, packed for shipment, about 25 pounds.

Price..............................$12.13

Our Special Short Skirt Morgan Saddle, $6.54.

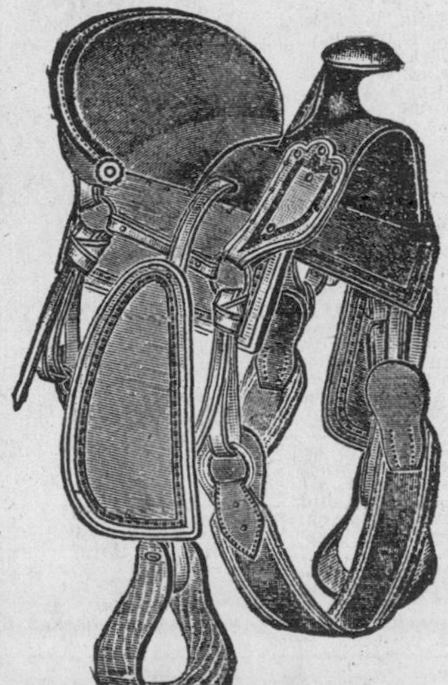

No. 10K1295 Made with three-fourth solid leather seat with heavy leather roll cantle. Short skirts on the side of the saddle to protect the horse from the cinch rings. 1-inch tie strap. Double WEB CINCHES with leather chafes and connecting strap with rings for ties on the saddle. STIRRUP STRAPS are 1 inch to buckle.

$6.54

with 13-inch fender attached, and 3-inch wood stirrups. This is a very popular style saddle, and one that will give excellent service. Russet saddle skirting used in this saddle with handsomely embossed edges. A high grade and very popular style Morgan saddle. Weight of saddle, packed for shipment, about 18 pounds. Price......$6.54

Our Kentucky Style Saddle, $8.51.

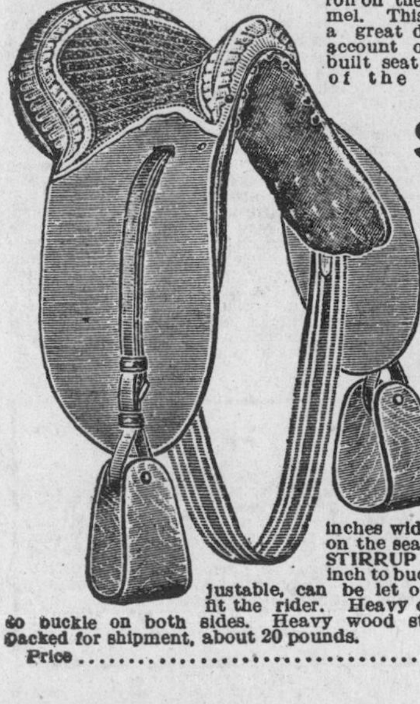

No. 10K1270 This is one of our improved Kentucky style saddles. It is made with a fine calfskin quilted seat without a roll on the cantle or pommel. This saddle is used a great deal by ladies on account of the peculiarly built seat and the shape of the saddle. It is

$8.51

easy riding and one of the best saddles for ladies who ride astride. Made with a heavy German linen serge lined pad, sheepskin top, quilted and tufted so it is easy on the horse. Handsomely pop stitched quilted seat. Heavy long wide SKIRTS, hogskin impression 25 inches from center and 12 inches wide. The stitching on the seat is of fine silk. STIRRUP LEATHERS, 1 inch to buckle. They are adjustable, can be let out or taken up to fit the rider. Heavy cotton cord cinch to buckle on both sides. Heavy wood stirrups Weight, packed for shipment, about 20 pounds.

Price..............................$8.51

Our Full Leather Covered Quilted McClellan Saddle, $8.15.

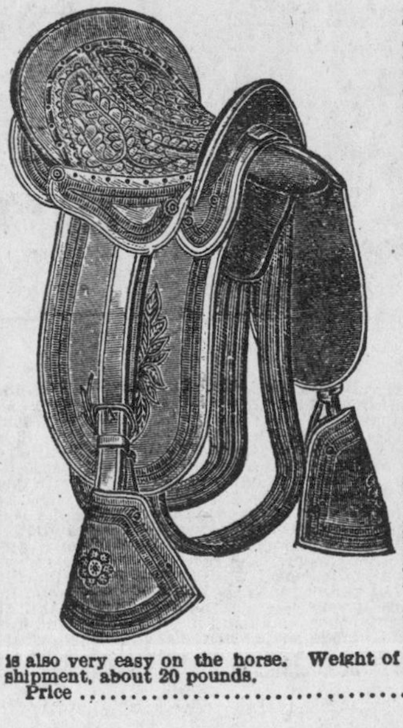

No. 10K1289 This saddle is made on a 14-inch genuine McClellan tree. All leather covered and quilted and stitched 12-inch seat, leather jockey. Heavy 1-inch stirrup straps to buckle with covered hooded stirrups. Double cotton web cinch to buckle on each side. Large fancy

$8.15

impression skirt to protect the rider's clothes. The SKIRTS are 20 inches long from center. This saddle is made out of fine russet saddle skirting fancy embossed. All around makes an attractive, handsome and durable saddle. This saddle is also used by ladies for riding astride. It is narrow and an easy sitting saddle. It is also very easy on the horse. Weight of saddle, packed for shipment, about 20 pounds.

Price..............................$8.15

Our Fancy Stamped Light Stock or Farm Saddle, $11.47.

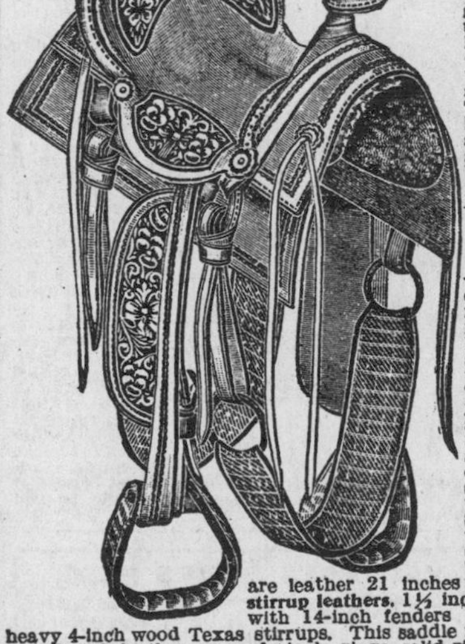

No. 10K1296 This is a very popular style saddle and one that is used a great deal on the farm for light riding. It is full size and will fit the average man or boy. The STIRRUP STRAPS are adjustable and can be buckled up for the boy and let

$11.47

out for a man to ride. Made of russet tanned Dundee oak saddle skirting, well finished. The fenders, jockey and seat are of fancy impression stamped leather. Full length stirrup leathers to buckle. Steel fork tree with wool sheep skin lined bars. The SKIRTS are leather 21 inches long. Heavy stirrup leathers, 1½ inches to buckle, with 14-inch fenders attached and heavy 4-inch wood Texas stirrups. This saddle is made double rigged with leather covered cinch rings, solid rigging over the front and around the horn. TIE STRAPS, 1¼ inches to tie in the cinch rings, 4-inch soft woven HAIR CINCHES. This saddle is made with solid seat and jockey in one piece and roll cantle; a very popular style runabout saddle. Weight of saddle, packed for shipment, about 25 pounds. Price...$11.47

Our Full Leather Covered Morgan Saddle, $6.87.

No. 10K1297 Made on a 13-inch Morgan tree. Full leather covered seat. Solid leather skirts 21 inches long. Heavy 1-inch STIRRUP STRAPS to buckle with fender 13 inches long attached; 3-inch wood stirrups. Woven-hair cinches; 1-inch tie straps to tie as

$6.87

shown in the illustration. The saddle is made with roll cantle. This is one of our very popular style Morgan saddles. The rigging in front is attached by a solid piece over the saddle, which gives it strength and durability. Weight of saddle, packed for shipment, about 19 pounds. Price...$6.87

One of Our Special Sheepskin Lined Bars Saddle, $7.99.

No. 10K1298 Made with steel fork, full leather covered tree. Solid leather seat with roll cantle. Heavy double ring CINCH with rigging going over the saddle and around the horn. Heavy 1½-inch

$7.99

STIRRUP STRAPS to buckle, with 14-inch fender attached. Woven HAIR CINCHES with rings and 1-inch heavy tie straps. Leather SKIRTS, 21 inches, and good, heavy, well made russet leather skirting saddle. Just the style of a steel fork saddle for common farm use. Suitable for man or boy. Weight of saddle, packed for shipment, about 22 pounds. Price...$7.99

Our Steel Fork Saddle, $10.25.

No. 10K1299 This saddle is made with steel fork tree, hide covered wool

$10.25

sheepskin lined bars. Double rigged saddle with rigging going over the front of the saddle and around the horn making it very strong. 1-inch tie straps to tie in the rings, with woven HAIR CINCHES to tie on both sides. 1½-inch stirrup leathers with 14-inch fender attached and Texas wood bolt stirrups. 21-inch leather skirt. Roll cantle. Saddle suitable for man or boy and just the saddle that is needed around the farm for light riding. Weight of saddle, packed for shipment, about 25 pounds. Price...$10.25

One of Our Runabout Steel Fork Saddles, $11.74.

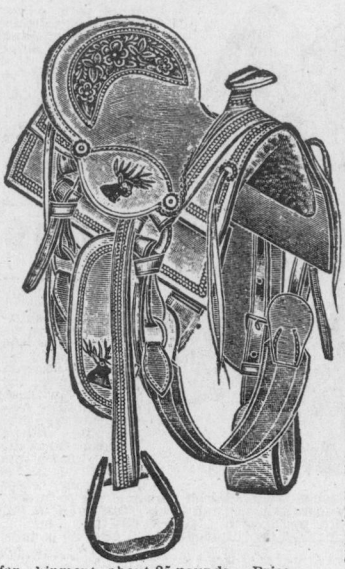

No. 10K1301 Made of good russet leather saddle skirting. 21-inch skirts. Wool sheepskin covered bars so that the saddle is easy on the horse. Solid full leather seat and jockey with roll cantle. Heavy double rigging with strap running

$11.74

over the front of the saddle and around the horn. Heavy 1½-inch stirrup straps to buckle, with 14-inch FENDERS attached. Large 4-inch Texas stirrups. WEB CINCHES with ring on each end with leather chafes and connecting straps. 1½-inch TIE STRAPS to tie on each side. This is a first class saddle for farm use. Weight of saddle, packed for shipment, about 25 pounds. Price...$11.74

Our Arapahoe Stock Saddle, $21.32.

$21³²

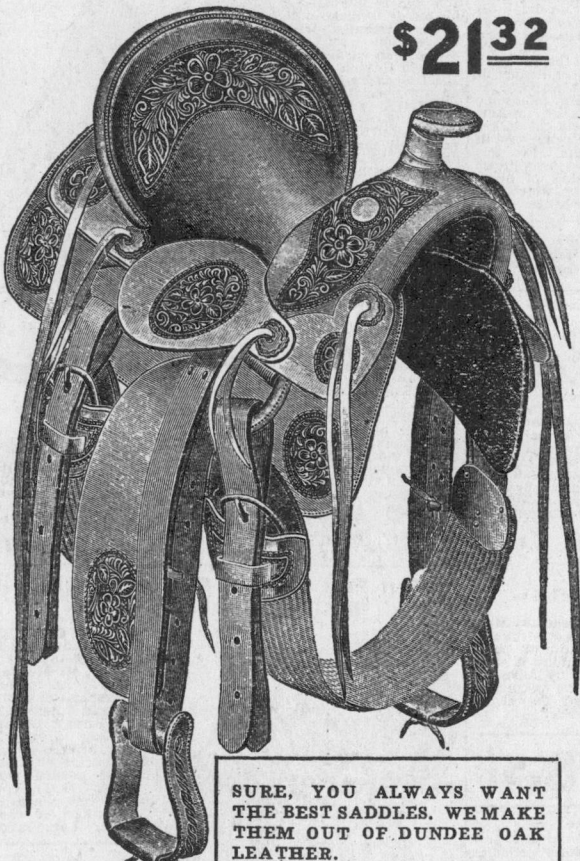

SURE, YOU ALWAYS WANT THE BEST SADDLES. WE MAKE THEM OUT OF DUNDEE OAK LEATHER.

NO. 10K1306 Made on 15-inch swell fork tree, 25-inch round cornered skirts, sheepskin wool lined, solid seat and jockey in one piece. Steel fork, bound or roll cantle; TIE STRAPS, 1½ inches extra long on the near side to buckle and 1½ inches, to buckle on the off side; 2-inch STIRRUP LEATHERS to lace with 15-inch fender attached; steel leather covered STIRRUPS. This is a medium weight stock saddle. Remember, this saddle is made on a strictly new, up to date swell fork tree, with good heavy steel horn, leather covered and low cantle. We use the very best quality of Dundee oak saddle skirting in this saddle. The leather is especially tanned and prepared for strictly high grade stock saddles. The parts of this saddle where the most wear and strain is expected are extra heavy and strengthened so as to give the very best service. Every part of this saddle is made good and strong. The saddle as constructed is easy on the horse's back, will not gall or pinch the shoulders. The solid seat and jockey in one piece makes it very easy on the rider. Compare this saddle with similar saddles of any other make and if you do not find it a better bargain, a better saddle, made out of better saddle skirting, than any other saddle at a higher price, you can return this saddle and we will cheerfully refund your money. Weight of saddle, packed for shipment, about 32 pounds.

Price...$21.32

Our Special Saddle, $10.78.

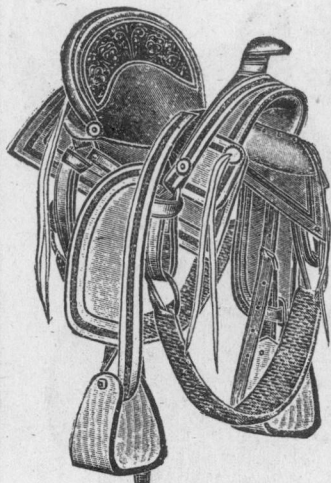

No. 10K1303 Made of Dundee oak tanned saddle skirting. Heavy solid 1½-inch STIRRUP LEATHERS to buckle and long enough for the average man, with extra heavy wood STIRRUPS. Saddle is double rigged with front rigging running around the horn. The TREE used in this saddle

$10.78

is a good heavy hide covered tree with steel fork. LEATHER SEAT with a heavy roll cantle. The SKIRTS on this saddle are about 22½ inches long, unlined. This saddle is made especially strong in all parts. Heavy woven HAIR CINCHES with ring on each end and 1½-inch tie straps to tie on each side. Good heavy fenders attached to the 1½-inch stirrup strap. A strictly first class light weight stock saddle. Weight, packed for shipment, about 25 pounds. Price...$10.78

Our Light Weight Stock Saddle, $12.29.

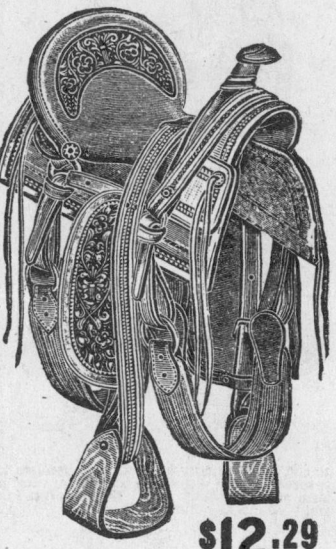

$12.29

NO. 10K1307 This is one of our new patterns and new style light weight double cinch stock saddle for light riding and general farm work. A saddle for man or boy. STIRRUP STRAPS are adjustable, can be buckled up to fit young men or good size boys, or let out for the average size man. This saddle is made out of Dundee oak saddle skirting on a good, solid, substantial, well made tree, with a steel horn and fork. The saddle is made in roll cantle only. Full length STIRRUP STRAP, 1½ inches wide to buckle, with 15-inch fender attached. Fancy flowered stamped and fancy impression stamped seat. Large 4-inch wood Texas stirrup which is easy on the rider. The saddle is made double rigged with a solid rigging over the front and around the horn which makes it very substantial; 1½-inch tie straps to tie on each side; cotton web back band CINCHES with leather chafes and connecting straps, which makes a very strong cinch and is easy on the horse; the skirts are 22½ inches long, sheepskin wool lined. This is a very good saddle in every way, substantially made, well finished and good looking. Weight of saddle, packed for shipment, about 25 pounds. Price...$12.29

Our Improved "Lincoln" Double Cinch Saddle.

LEATHER—We use in this saddle our high grade Dundee oak saddle skirting, velvet finish.

WORKMANSHIP—This saddle is made by experienced saddle makers who have had years of experience in making high grade stock saddles. The double rigging is so adjusted that the saddle fits easy on the horse's back. The seat is built up so it is round and nice for the rider. One of the best light weight stock saddles on the market.

TREE—14½-inch, hide covered, steel fork, leather covered, bucking roll bulge, medium flat cantle, the proper shape.

SEAT—Full seat and jockey in one piece, fancy stamped jockey, hood, fenders and seat.

SKIRTS—22½ inches long, sheepskin wool lined, stitched around the edge with heavy row of stitching, laced to the tree with heavy lace strings and fancy scalloped leather rosettes.

RIGGING—Double cinch rigged, iron rings, leather covered, 1¼-inch long tie straps on the near side to tie and buckle, and 1½-inch on the off side to buckle.

CINCHES—Fifteen-strand soft hair with buckle tongue.

$14.67

JUST THE KIND OF SADDLE FOR FARMER USE

STIRRUP LEATHERS—1½-inch, to buckle with fenders 7 inches wide and 14 inches long attached; 3-inch Texas wood stirrup, leather bottom.

If you want a popular light weight stock saddle, order a "Lincoln." Weight of saddle, about 20 pounds; packed for shipment, about 30 pounds.
No. 10K1309   Price.....................$14.67
Add extra for two Tackaberry Cinch Buckles.....................25

Our Red Cloud Special Light Weight Stock Saddle, $13.99.

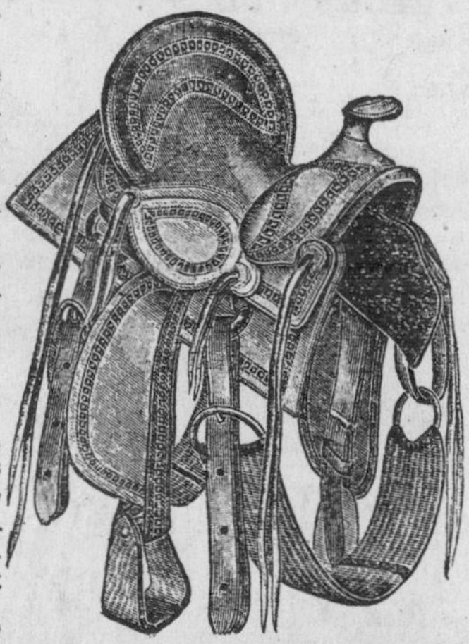

TREE—14½-inch, hide covered, steel fork, leather covered, bucking roll bulge, medium flat cantle.

SEAT—Full seat and jocky in one piece. The tree is built up so the seat pulls down over the tree and makes a smooth riding surface for the rider; bound or roll cantle.

SKIRTS—22 inches long, sheepskin wool lined, stitched around the edge with heavy row of stitching laced to the tree with heavy lace strings and leather rosettes.

RIGGING—Made double cinch rigged, heavy rigging front and rear, iron rings, leather covered; 1¼-inch tie straps on the near side to tie and 1½-inch on the off side to buckle.

CINCHES—Fifteen-strand soft hair with buckle tongue on one side.

$13.99

STIRRUP STRAPS—1½-inch, to buckle with fenders 7 inches wide and 14 inches long attached; 3-inch Texas wood stirrup, leather bottom.

LEATHER—We use in this saddle our Dundee oak saddle skirting, fancy edge stamped. A good well made light weight stock saddle. Weight of saddle, about 20 pounds; packed for shipment, about 30 pounds.
No. 10K1311   Price.......$13.99

Our Idaho Special Light Weight Medium Priced Stock Saddle, $19.97

TREE—15-inch, hide covered, steel fork, leather covered, bucking roll bulge, medium flat cantle, the proper shape.

SEAT—Full seat and jockey in one piece, bound or roll cantle.

STAMPING—Fancy waffle corner stamped.

SKIRTS—12½ inches wide, 25 inches long, sheepskin wool lined, heavy row machine stitching around the edge of the skirts. Laced to the tree with heavy large strings and fancy scalloped leather rosettes.

RIGGING—Double rigged front and rear, heavy iron rings leather covered, 1½-inch long leather tie straps on the near side to tie and buckle and 1¾-inch on the off side to buckle. Twenty-strand Angora hair cinches with leather chafes, connecting straps and buckle tongues.

$19.97

STIRRUP STRAPS—2-inch, to lace with fenders 8 inches wide and 15 inches long attached; steel stirrup, leather covered.

LEATHER—Best grade Dundee oak saddle skirting used in this saddle.
Weight of saddle, about 25 pounds; packed for shipment, about 32 pounds.
No. 10K1315   Price........$19.97
Add extra for two Tackaberry Cinch Buckles with saddle.....................25c

One of Our Extra Heavy Well Made Stock Saddles, Reduced in Price from $34.79 to $32.90.

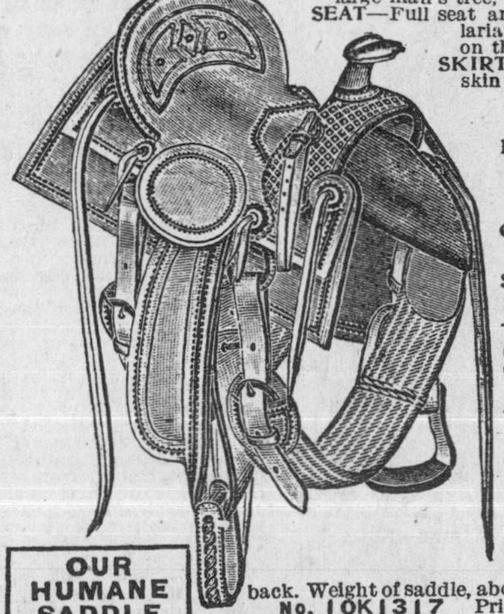

TREE—17-inch, beef hide covered, steel fork, wide pommel, a large man's tree, our Improved Nelson.

SEAT—Full seat and jocky in one piece, bound or roll cantle, lariat strap on the off side and long lace string on the near side.

SKIRTS—15½ inches wide, 30 inches long, sheepskin wool lined, heavy row stitching around the edge of the skirts, laced to the saddle with heavy lace strings and leather scalloped rosettes.

RIGGING—Double cinch rigging, front and rear, heavy iron rings, leather covered, 1¾-inch leather tie strap on the near side extra long to tie and buckle and 2-inch on the off side to buckle.

CINCHES—Twenty-strand hard hair, wool lined chafes and connecting straps and buckle tongues.

STIRRUP STRAPS—3 inches wide, extra long to lace, with fender 9 inches wide and 17 inches long attached, with heavy steel leather covered stirrups.

$32.90

OUR HUMANE SADDLE

LEATHER—The best grade specially selected Dundee oak saddle skirting, russet color, soft velvet finish.

WORKMANSHIP—The very best class of workmen employed on this saddle. They have had years of experience making high grade, well made stock saddles, they know just how to build up the seat to fit the rider and how the double rigging must be adjusted to make the saddle fit the horse's back. Weight of saddle, about 34 lbs.; packed for shipment, about 50 lbs.
No. 10K1317   Price $32.90
Add extra for two Tackaberry Cinch Buckles with the saddle.....25

Our Special Improved Kit Carson Saddle.

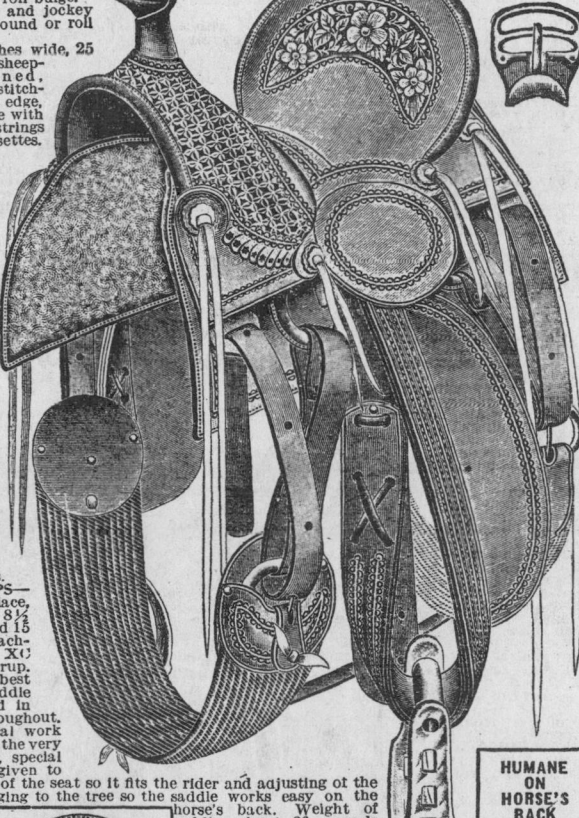

TREE—15-inch, hide covered, steel fork, leather covered, heavy bucking roll bulge.

SEAT—Full seat and jockey in one piece, bound or roll cantle.

SKIRTS—13 inches wide, 25 inches long, sheepskin wool lined, heavy row of stitching around the edge, laced to the tree with heavy lace strings and leather rosettes.

RIGGING—Heavy double cinch under rigging, front and rear; heavy iron rings, leather covered.

TIE STRAPS—1½-inch leather, extra long on the near side to tie and buckle and 1¾-inch on the off side to buckle.

$22.67

CINCHES—6-inch cotton cord front cinch and 3½-inch belting web rear cinch with leather chafes and connecting straps and buckle tongues.

STIRRUP STRAPS—2½-inch, to lace, with fenders 8½ inches wide and 15 inches long attached, with the XC plain iron stirrup.

LEATHER—The best Dundee oak saddle skirting is used in this saddle throughout. The mechanical work on this saddle is the very best we can get, special attention being given to the building up of the seat so it fits the rider and adjusting of the double cinch rigging to the tree so the saddle works easy on the horse's back. Weight of saddle, about 26 pounds packed for shipment, about 35 pounds.

HUMANE ON HORSE'S BACK

No. 10K1319   Price $22.67
Add extra for two Tackaberry cinch buckles with saddle..............25c

The Eugene Single Cinch Saddle, $13.47.

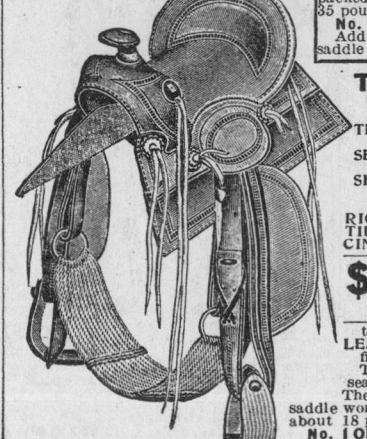

TREE—14½-inch, nickel plated steel horn, bucking roll bulge, medium flat cantle.

SEAT—Full seat and jockey in one piece, bound or roll cantle.

SKIRTS—13 inches wide, 23 inches long, sheepskin wool lined, laced to the tree with heavy lace springs and scalloped heavy leather rosettes.

RIGGING—Single cinch rigging.

TIE STRAPS—1½-inch heavy latigo tie straps to tie.

CINCH—Twenty-strand Angora hair with heavy iron rings.

$13.47

STIRRUP STRAPS—2 inches wide, to lace, with fenders 7 inches wide and 14 inches long attached; 3-inch Texas wood stirrup, leather bottom. Long head string on the near side.

LEATHER—The leather used in this saddle is our fine Dundee oak saddle skirting. This saddle is made plain finish, creased edge. The seat is built up round and nice to fit the rider. The cinch rigging is adjusted so as to make this saddle work easy on the horse's back. Weight of saddle, about 18 pounds; packed for shipment, about 28 pounds.
No. 10K1337   Price..............$13.47
Add extra for Tackaberry Cinch Buckle....13

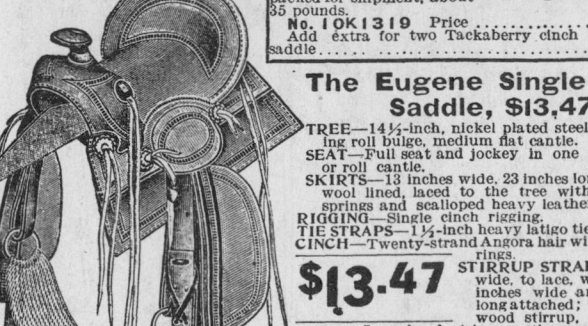

Wallawalla Stock Saddle Improved and Reduced in Price from $28.33 to $27.50.

TREE—14½-inch, beef hide covered, steel fork, and large bulge bucking roll style. One of the best beef hide covered trees made. The cantle is the proper shape and fits the rider.

SEAT—The seat and jockey are in one piece, bound or roll cantle, lariat strap on the off side and long lace string on the near side.

SKIRTS—27 inches long, about 13

$27.50

inches wide, sheepskin wool lined, laced to the saddle with heavy lace strings and scalloped leather rosettes.

CINCH RIGGING—Strong well made rear and front rigging, heavy iron cinch rings, leather covered, hand riveted.

TIE STRAPS—On the near side 1⅜ inches wide extra long to tie and buckle and 1⅞ inches on the off side to buckle.

CINCHES—Hard twisted cotton front cinch with extra stay strap from cap to cap, and 4-inch belting web rear cinch with connecting strap; leather chafes.

STIRRUP STRAPS—3 inches wide, extra long to lace with large fender 9 inches wide and 17 inches long attached. X.C. Turner stirrup, leather looped and lined.

LEATHER—High grade selected Dundee oak saddle skirting.

WORKMANSHIP—The very highest class. It is necessary for the best mechanics to work on this saddle. Experience in making high grade saddles is necessary to adjust the rigging to the proper place and to make the saddle set easy on the horse's back and be comfortable to the rider. The seat must be built up in the center so it is easy for the rider.

Weight of saddle, about 32 pounds; packed for shipment, about 42 pounds. Made single and double rigged.

No. 10K1403   Double Cinch Saddle.   Price..$27.50
No. 10K1404   Single Cinch Saddle.   Price.. 27.45

OUR "WASHINGTON" HIGH GRADE UP TO DATE SPECIALLY CONSTRUCTED HEAVY STOCK SADDLE.

A man that rides many hours a day, wants an easy riding saddle, it pays to get the best.

TREE—16-inch hide covered, steel fork, large bulge bucking roll style. The cantle is made with the correct slant, and the horn has the correct slant. The tree will stand all kind of roping.

SEAT—Full seat and jockey in one piece with heavy roll or bound cantle. Lariat strap on off side.

SKIRTS—28 inches long, about 13½ inches wide, wool lined with round corners; laced under the saddle with heavy lace strings; the wool lining makes it soft and easy on the horse's back.

TIE STRAPS—1⅝-inch long tie strap on the near side to tie with buckle tongue, and 2 inches wide on the off side to buckle.

RIGGING—Heavy iron leather covered cinch rings with extra heavy double rigged, solid rigging over the back.

CINCHES—Hard twisted cotton cord front cinch, 4-inch belting web rear cinch, with leather chafes and connecting straps; extra leather stay strap from chafe to chafe on the cotton cord front cinch.

STIRRUP STRAPS—3 inches wide, extra long to lace with large fender 9 inches wide and 17 inches long attached. Leather covered steel stirrups.

$30.59

LEATHER—This saddle is made out of extra high grade Dundee oak russet saddle skirting, soft velvet finish. Looks nicer, wears better, than any other skirting made.

WORKMANSHIP—The making of this saddle is a special art. The building up of the tree, the finishing up of the saddle, the adjusting the cinch rigging to have it in the proper place, requires good judgment on the part of the mechanic to have the saddle set just right on the horse's back and a man must know exactly where to place each and every part of the saddle. We have covered all the points necessary to make a high grade, well made stock saddle. This saddle is humane on the horse's back.

STAMPING—The edges of the straps are fancy stamped.

When you order this saddle, remember that you are getting one of the best high grade stock saddles that it is possible to make for $30.59. We are saving you $10.00 to $25.00 on this saddle. Weight of saddle, about 33 pounds; packed for shipment, about 43 pounds.

No. 10K1410   Price.........$30.59

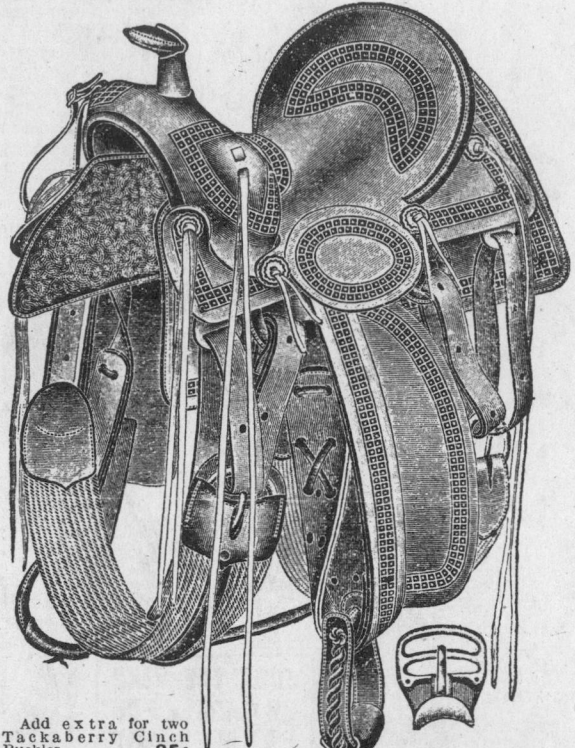

Add extra for two Tackaberry Cinch Buckles..........25c

HUMANE ON HORSE'S BACK.

ONE OF OUR ROSEBUD SWELL FORK STOCK SADDLES, $27.99

REDUCED IN PRICE FROM $29.95.

One of Our Exceptionally Big Bargains.

FREE—16-inch bucking roll style, heavy steel fork and hide covered, cantle slants the proper shape to make tree easy on the rider and on the horse's back.

SKIRTS—30 inches long, sheepskin wool lined and laced to the tree, heavy lace strings with leather rosettes.

SEAT—Seat and jockey are made in one piece, roll or bound cantle.

CINCH RIGGING—Heavy solid front and rear

$27.99

rigged, heavy rings, leather covered, 1¾-inch extra long tie straps on the near side to tie and buckle and 2 inches wide on the off side to buckle.

STIRRUP STRAPS—3 inches wide, extra long to lace with large fender attached, steel stirrups, leather covered.

CINCHES—20-strand white hard twisted cotton front cinch with leather stay strap and 4-inch belting web rear cinch with connecting straps; leather chafes. Lariat strap on the off side and long head string on the near side.

LEATHER—The best Dundee oak saddle skirting is used in this saddle.

WORKMANSHIP—The very best mechanics work on this saddle, special attention is given to the building up of the seat (making it easy for the rider) and adjusting of the double rigging so the saddle rides easy on the horse's back.

FINISH—Edge creasing, fancy stamped hood and seat.

Weight of saddle, about 31 pounds; packed for shipment, about 42 pounds.

No. 10K1433   Price..........................$27.99
Add extra for two Tackaberry Cinch Buckles......................25

OUR "JEFFERSON" IMPROVED STOCK SADDLE

REDUCED IN PRICE FROM $28.55 TO $26.99

TREE—15-inch hide covered, steel fork, high horn, high cantle, especially constructed for this improved saddle.

SEAT—Seat and jockey in one piece, rawhide bound or roll cantle, lariat strap on off side.

SKIRTS—25 inches long, about 13 inches wide, sheepskin wool lined, laced to the tree with heavy lace strings, fancy scaloped leather rosettes. The saddles ride easy on the horse's back.

CINCH RIGGING—Made extra strong with heavy rings, leather covered, solid front and rear rigging.

TIE STRAPS—1½ inches extra long on the near side to tie and buckle, and 1¾ inches on the off side to buckle.

CINCHES—20-strand Angora hair, leather

$26.99

chafes and connecting straps with buckle tongues.

STIRRUP STRAPS—3 inches wide, extra long to lace with fenders 8 inches wide and 16 inches long attached, with our heavy brass bound 2½-inch Moran style stirrup, leather lined and capped.

LEATHER—The best high grade Dundee oak saddle skirting.

WORKMANSHIP—The very best workmen are employed in making this saddle. It requires experience and knowledge to make a high grade, well made stock saddle, to adjust the rigging so the saddle will set on the horse's back properly.

FINISH—The finish on this saddle, fancy beaded stamp pommel, fancy stamped seat, and edge creasing throughout, with the edges of the straps all well finished. Weight of saddle, about 29 pounds; packed for shipment, about 40 pounds. Taking into consideration the quality of the saddle that we give you when comparing with saddles of a similar price in the local stores, we save you from $10.00 to $15.00.

No. 10K1443   Price.........................$26.99
Add extra for two Tackaberry Cinch Buckles......................25

HUMANE ON HORSE'S BACK.

Our Indian Prince Stock Saddle, $23.99.

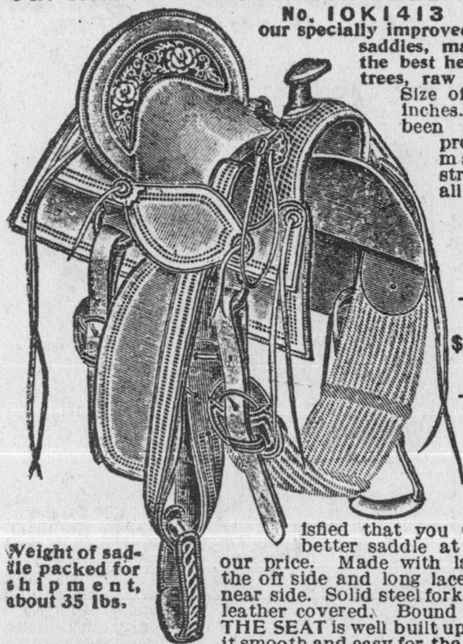

No. 10K1413 This is one of our specially improved heavily built saddles, made on one of the best heavy steel fork trees, raw hide covered. Size of the tree, 15 inches. This tree has been specially improved being made extra strong to stand all kinds of roping. We have used the very best grade of Dundee oak russet saddle

$23.99

skirting and given particular attention to the way the saddle is made and are satisfied that you cannot buy a better saddle at anything like our price. Made with lariat strap on the off side and long lace string on the near side. Solid steel fork tree and horn, leather covered. Bound or roll cantle. THE SEAT is well built up, which makes it smooth and easy for the rider. Extra large seamed jockey. Heavy 2½-inch STIRRUP LEATHERS to lace, with a large 16-inch fender attached; steel leather covered STIRRUPS; heavy double rigged saddle, solid over the front and rear, with leather covered steel rings; long 1½-inch TIE STRAPS on the near side to buckle and 1¾-inch short ties on the off side to buckle; heavy hair CINCHES with leather chafes and connecting straps, buckle tongues in the cinches; the SKIRTS are sheepskin wool lined, 25 inches long. Remember that this is one of the best bargains in this style of a saddle that you can buy. Popular priced and within the reach of everybody who wants a strictly up to date saddle.

Weight of saddle packed for shipment, about 35 lbs.

Price $23.99

Our Light Weight Stock Saddle, $15.27.

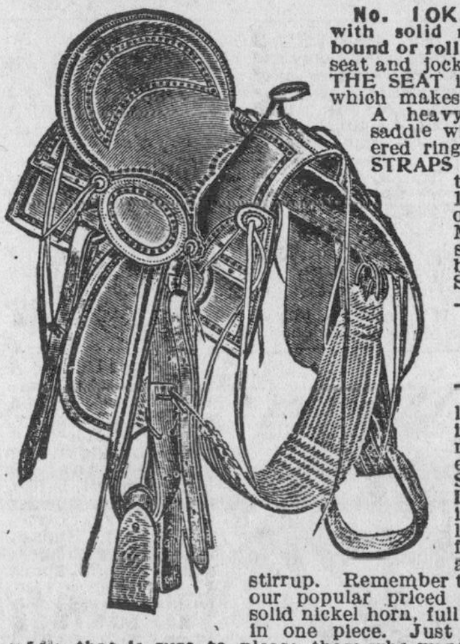

No. 10K1429 Made with solid nickel horn in bound or roll cantle. A solid seat and jockey in one piece. THE SEAT is well built up, which makes it very strong. A heavy double rigged saddle with leather covered rings; 1⅜-inch TIE STRAPS on the near side to buckle and 1½-inch on the off side to buckle. Mexican cotton strings with buckle tongues. Sheepskin wool

$15.27

lined skirts 23 inches long which makes it very easy on the horse. STIRRUP LEATHERS—2 inches wide to lace with 14-inch fender attached and Texas bolt stirrup. Remember that this is one of our popular priced saddles with a solid nickel horn, full seat and jockey in one piece. Just the style of a saddle that is sure to please those who want a light weight, medium priced stock saddle. Weight of saddle, packed for shipment, about 30 pounds. Price $15.27

Our Fancy Stamped Popular Priced Stock Saddle, $21.19.

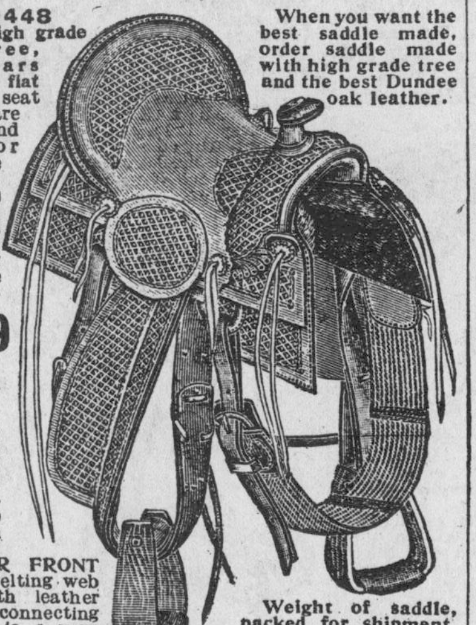

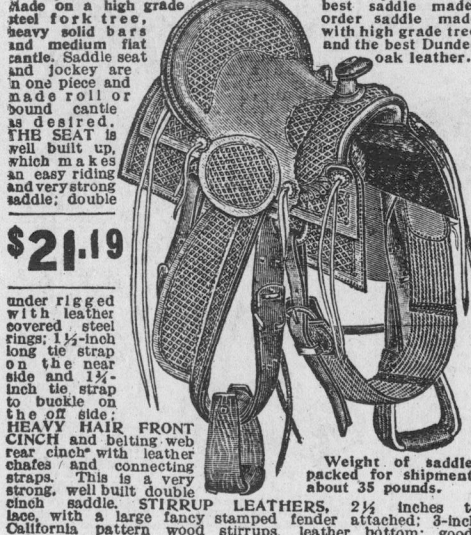

No. 10K1448 Made on a high grade steel fork tree, heavy solid bars and medium flat cantle. Saddle seat and jockey are in one piece and made roll or bound cantle as desired. THE SEAT is well built up, which makes an easy riding and very strong saddle; double

When you want the best saddle made, order saddle made with high grade tree and the best Dundee oak leather.

$21.19

under rigged with leather covered rings; 1½-inch long tie strap on the near side and 1¾-inch tie strap to buckle on the off side; HEAVY HAIR FRONT CINCH and belting web rear cinch with leather chafes and connecting straps. This is a very strong, well built double cinch saddle. STIRRUP LEATHERS, 2½ inches to lace, with a large fancy stamped fender attached; 3-inch California pattern wood stirrups, leather bottom; good, well made 26½-inch sheepskin wool lined skirts laced to the tree. Remember that we make this saddle in roll or bound cantle with seat and jockey in one piece. A strictly up to date, high grade, full stamped saddle. Price, $21.19

Weight of saddle, packed for shipment, about 35 pounds.

Our Full Stamped Wild West Stock Saddle, Improved and Reduced in Price from $40.87 to $38.99.

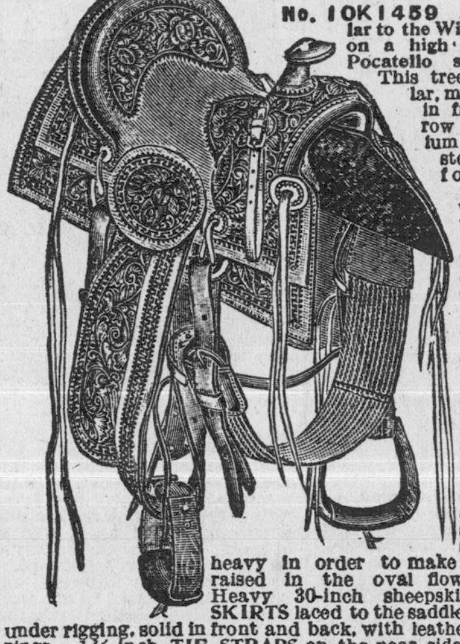

No. 10K1459 A saddle similar to the Wild West, made on a high grade 16-inch Pocatello steel fork tree. This tree is very popular, made extra wide in front, and narrow seat and medium flat cantle, steel horn and fork, covered with rawhide, which makes it very strong.

$38.99

The stamping on this saddle is all handwork by a highly skilled mechanic. We use the very best Dundee russet oak saddle skirting in this saddle, the stock is all very heavy in order to make the stamping raised in the oval flowered pattern. Heavy 30-inch sheepskin wool lined SKIRTS laced to the saddle, heavy double under rigging, solid in front and back, with leather covered steel rings. 1¾-inch TIE STRAPS on the near side to buckle and 2 inches on the off side to buckle; hard twisted cotton cord front cinch and heavy belting rear cinch with leather chafes and connecting straps, making a very strong double cinch saddle. We make this seat and jockey in one piece, roll or bound cantle; seat is well built up, making an easy riding saddle. STIRRUP LEATHERS, 3 inches, double California, to lace on top of heavy fancy stamped fender, ox bow brass bound leather bottom stirrups. Lariat strap is on the off side and a long lace string on the near side. A very handsome full stamped heavy weight stock saddle. Remember that we make this saddle roll or bound cantle and solid seat and jockey in one piece. Weight of saddle, packed for shipment, about 50 pounds. Price $38.99

Lady's or Gentleman's Park Saddle, $13.95.

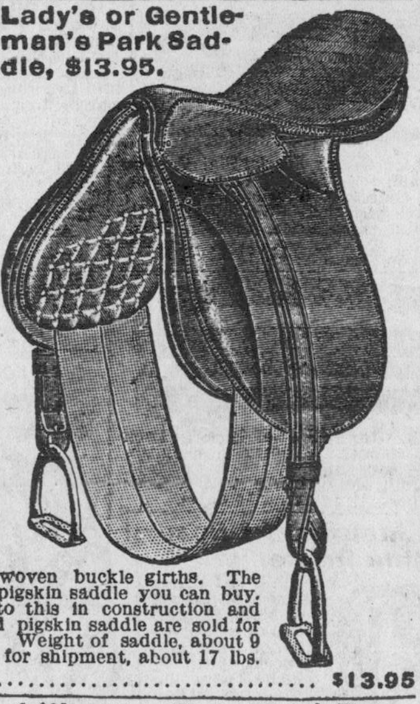

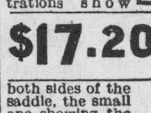

No. 10K1465 Made on a genuine English 16-inch cut back tree, patent stirrup bar, that will allow the stirrup strap to fly loose in case of accident and being thrown from the horse.

MATERIAL—Imported pigskin seat, jockey and skirt, raised knee puff and thigh puff; skirts

$13.95

are double and stitched.

PAD—Serge cloth quilted, leather bound.

STIRRUP LEATHERS—1 inch, with English buckle, with iron stirrups.

GIRTH—Double worsted woven buckle girths. The best full covered pigskin saddle you can buy. Saddles similar to this in construction and not a full covered pigskin saddle are sold for $25.00 to $35.00. Weight of saddle, about 9 pounds. Packed for shipment, about 17 lbs.

Price $13.95

Our Special Western Cow Girls' Side Saddle, $17.20.

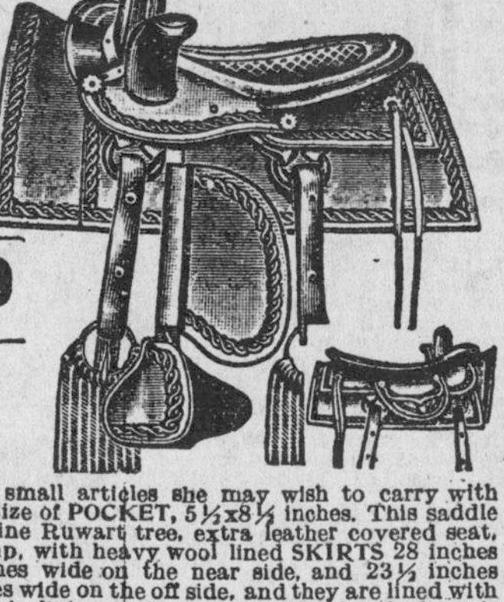

No. 10K1467 This saddle is intended to stand hard and rough riding. It is well built and well rigged. Made of heavy oiled California skirting, double rigged, with leaping horn and heavy roll cantle. Illustrations show

$17.20

both sides of the saddle, the small one showing the pocket, which every lady will find a very handy place to put papers or any other small articles she may wish to carry with her when riding. Size of POCKET, 5½x8½ inches. This saddle is made on a genuine Ruwart tree, extra leather covered seat, basket weave stamp, with heavy wool lined SKIRTS 28 inches long and 12½ inches wide on the near side, and 23½ inches long and 12½ inches wide on the off side, and they are lined with heavy wool sheepskin lining acting as protection for the horse's back. If you want a good, substantial, easy riding and stylish looking saddle we would recommend this one for your use. A personal inspection will demonstrate this to you. STIRRUP STRAPS are extra heavy leather, ⅞ inch wide to buckle, with 2¾-inch wood stirrup, leather covered, sheepskin lined. The cinches are Angora soft hair with iron rings and buckle tongues. The TIE STRAPS are heavy leather, 1½ inches to buckle on the off side and 1½ inches to buckle on the near side. This saddle is made with fender. Weight of saddle, packed for shipment, about 30 pounds. Price $17.20

Our Special Fancy Ladies' Side Saddle, $7.47.

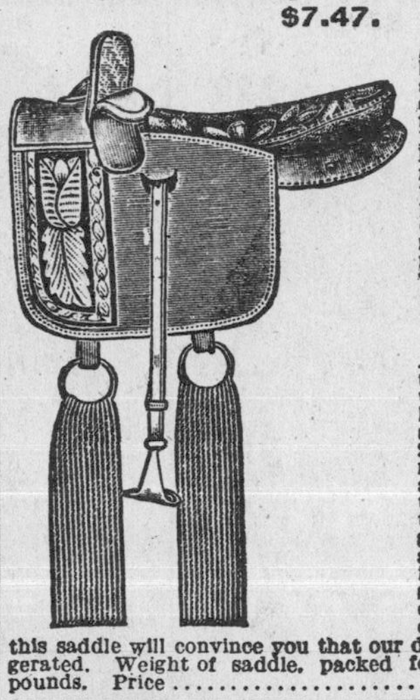

No. 10K1469 Made on an 18-inch Ruwart tree, fancy pigskin impression skirts stamped on one side, fancy figured seating. Detachable leaping horn, padded and well finished. The bars on this saddle are well padded, so as to be comfortable both for rider and horse. It is made with a 1⅛-inch

$7.47

tie strap to tie, with two cinches, soft woven hair. ¾-inch stirrup strap with metal shoe STIRRUP. We would recommend not to buy a cheaper saddle than this one at this exceptionally low price. We guarantee to ship you a saddle better in quality, workmanship and style than can be purchased elsewhere. A careful examination of this saddle will convince you that our description is not exaggerated. Weight of saddle, packed for shipment, about 21 pounds. Price $7.47

Our New Improved Saddle, $11.37.

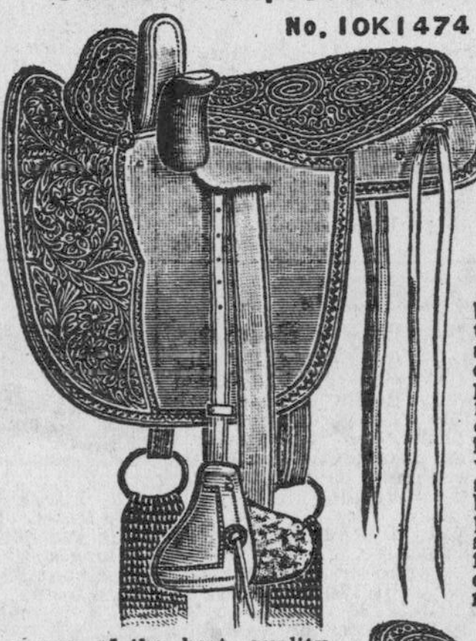

No. 10K1474 We have found this saddle to be one of the most popular on the market today. It is a good, comfortable, easy riding saddle, well made throughout, no expense having

$11.37

been spared to put in the best workmanship and material. At our exceptionally low price we are sure that it cannot be duplicated elsewhere. The illustrations herewith show both sides of the saddle, but in order to appreciate its value it should be carefully inspected. This saddle is made

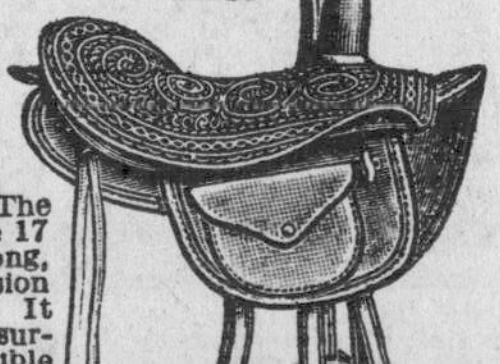

on one of the best quality Ruwart trees with the bars of the saddle padded with sheepskin so as to be easy and comfortable on the horse. Seating is made of fine buckskin with fancy stitching. The SKIRTS on this saddle are 17 inches wide and 15 inches long, made of fine pigskin impression leather, stamped and creased. It has 1¾-inch heavy leather surcingle to buckle and heavy double woven hair CINCHES with iron rings; ¾-inch stirrup strap, with wood leather bottom hooded stirrup. The leaping horns in this saddle are buckskin lined. Heavy under rigging with 1½-inch tie straps on each side. Large, fancy pocket on the off side, which is very handy for carrying papers and any other small articles. If you want a good saddle at a low price we can fully recommend this saddle. Weight of saddle, packed for shipment, about 25 pounds.

Price $11.37

Our Boys' Saddle, Double Cinch, $5.99

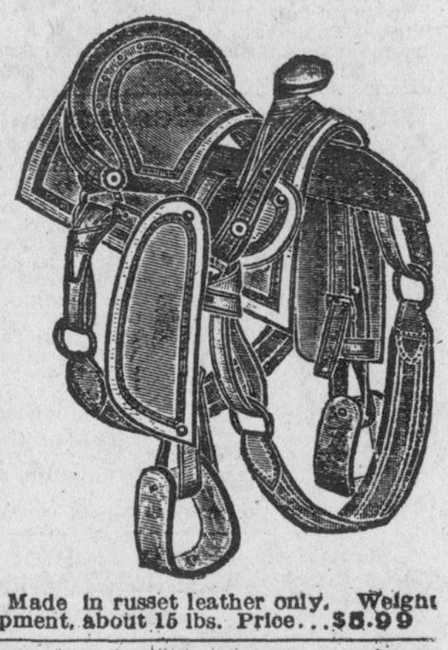

No. 10K1476 At this exceptionally low price we offer a good, strong, serviceable boys' saddle, made of heavy russet leather, well rigged and double cinch. This saddle is fitted with 3-inch cotton back band web cinches and 1¼-inch STIRRUP STRAPS with

$5.99

heavy fenders, and 3½-inch wood stirrups. The TIE STRAPS are made of 1⅛-inch heavy leather, 4 feet long. The tree of this saddle is 12½ inches with a good solid fork. The SKIRTS are 20 inches long. We have this season improved this saddle and we are sure you cannot make a mistake if you order. Made in russet leather only. Weight of saddle, packed for shipment, about 15 lbs. Price... $5.99

Oquawka, Ill.

Sears, Roebuck & Co.,
Chicago, Ill.

Gentlemen: The saddle recently purchased from you has given entire satisfaction, and I am much pleased with the purchase. I saved at least 50 per cent by purchasing this saddle of you instead of the local dealer. The quality is rather better than I expected, and I can readily recommend it as the best low priced saddle I have ever seen.

Yours truly,
R. R. BANTA.

Our Special Round Skirt Boys' Saddle, $3.98.

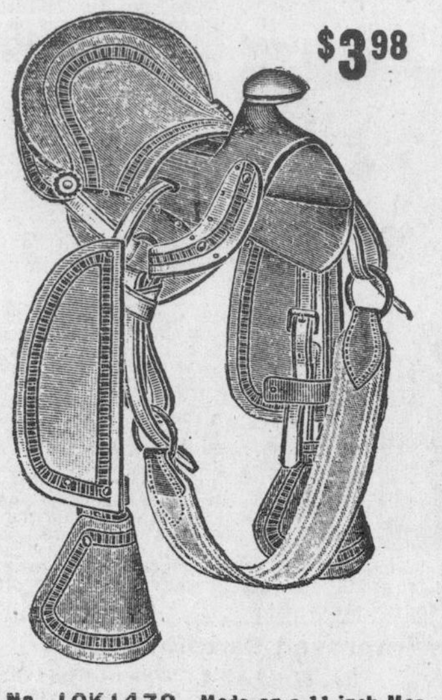

$3.98

No. 10K1479 Made on a 11-inch Morgan hide covered tree with stirrup straps, 1 inch, with heavy fenders riveted on, 1-inch tie straps and with 3½-inch heavy single web girth. Wood, leather covered, stirrups to prevent the boy's foot from slipping through. It is made in russet leather only, and at our exceptionally low price we consider it to be the best saddle on the market. Weight of saddle, packed for shipment, about 12 pounds.
Price...............................$3.98

Our Extra Heavy Boys' Stock Saddle, $9.97.

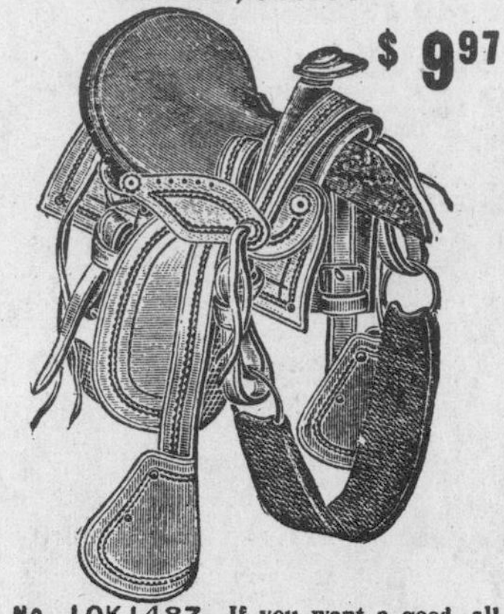

$9.97

No. 10K1487 If you want a good, all around saddle that will stand hard usage we would recommend this as being one of the best double cinch boys' saddles on the market. Made on a 12-inch steel fork hide covered tree. Half leather seat with jockey laced and screwed on. Made in roll cantle only. The SKIRTS on this saddle are 19 inches long, unlined. TIE STRAPS are 1⅛ inches to tie with 4-inch soft hair cinches with iron rings. STIRRUP STRAPS are 1½ inches to buckle with heavy fenders riveted on; 3-inch wood STIRRUPS, leather covered. We can fully guarantee this saddle in every respect. Weight of saddle, packed for shipment, about 22 pounds.
Price...............................$9.97

Be sure to give catalogue number in full when you order from this catalogue.

$10.99 Side Saddle.

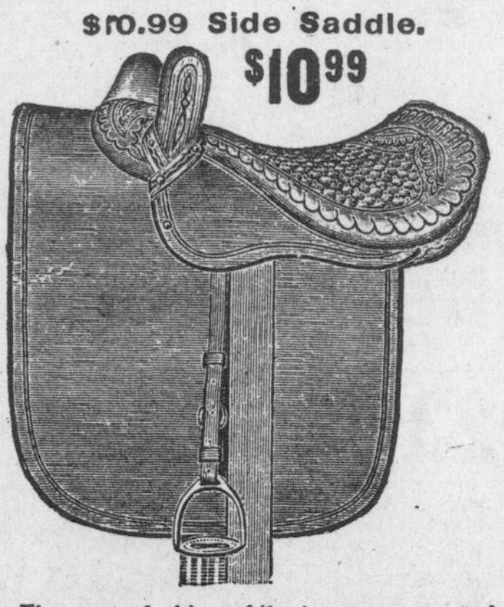

$10.99

The seat of this saddle is so constructed that it is very easy for the rider to sit in this saddle with the greatest comfort. The lady using this saddle will find it one of the easiest riding saddles that can be made, as the seat is so constructed as to give the rider plenty of room. The cantle is slanting, so as to protect from slipping backward. The horns are so constructed as to be easy on the limb. This style of tree is used in all high grade English saddles and gives the best satisfaction. TREE, 18-inch old style tree; SEAT, calfskin leather, silk stitched, hand raised; SKIRTS, large leather skirt, hogskin impression and embossed edges, leather jockey, leather stirrup strap, iron stirrup, web cinch and a leather surcingle over the skirt; PAD, sheepskin lined pad, serge bottom, hair stuffed, making the saddle easy on the horse's back; GIRTH, cotton cord girth to buckle on each side, leather surcingle to buckle on the off side, adjustable stirrup strap with iron stirrup. Weight, packed for shipment, about 25 pounds.
No. 10K1575 Price of saddle..$10.99

Sears, Roebuck & Co. Old Style Side Saddle, $7.35.

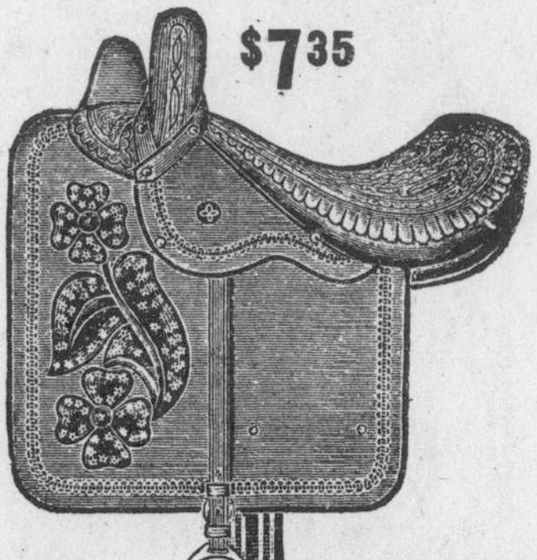

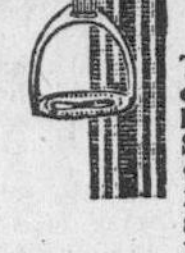

$7.35

No. 10K1496 This saddle is made on a famous and well known Somerset tree. Seat with slanting cantle. This saddle is strongly and substantially made along the lines necessary to make it a good, comfortable, easy riding saddle, suitable for heavy people. The SEAT is calfskin, quilted and hand raised with fancy stitching. The SKIRTS are embossed russet leather, with iron stirrups. The TREE is 17 inches. Special style skirts are large and heavy. The seating is made of calfskin, silk stitched and fancy finish. The PAD is made of heavy drill, hair stuffed and quilted. It is made single cinch only, with cotton girth to buckle on each side. If you want a good, neat appearing, comfortable, easy riding saddle, we would recommend this. Weight of saddle, packed for shipment, about 20 pounds.
Price...............................$7.35

BRIDLES.

Our Special Cowboy Bridle.

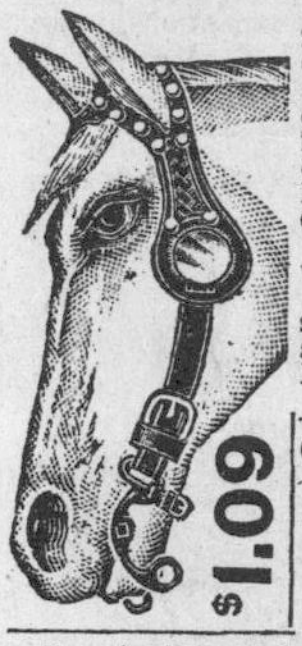

$1.09

No. 10K1700 Our Special Two-Ear Flat Russet Cowboy Bridle. ⅞-inch double cheeks, adjustable on both sides, with large nickel ornament. Spotted crown piece with two ear holes. Weight, about 14 ounces.
Price of bridle without bit.......$1.09
For price on bridle reins see Nos. 10K1709, 10K1712 and 10K1713.
If by mail, postage extra, 18 cents.

Our $1.65 Cowboy Bridle.

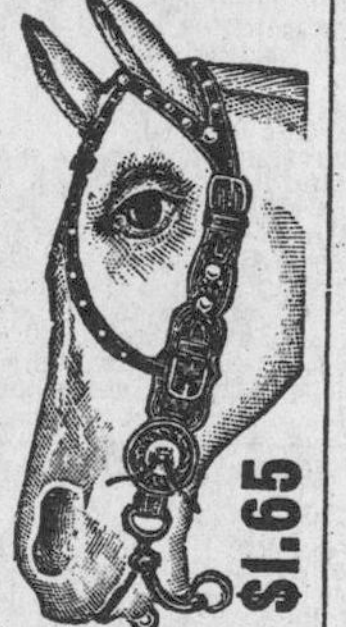

$1.65

No. 10K1701 Our Special Two-Ear Cowboy Bridle, with spotted face piece and fancy stamped scalloped cheeks, adjustable on each side. Nickel buckles and ornaments. Bridle is made out of russet oiled leather. Weight, about 16 ozs.
Price, of bridle without bit.......$1.65
For price on bridle reins see Nos. 10K1709 10K1712 and 10K1713.
For price on bit for bridle, see page 149.
If by mail, postage extra, 20 cents.

Our Great Western Bridle.

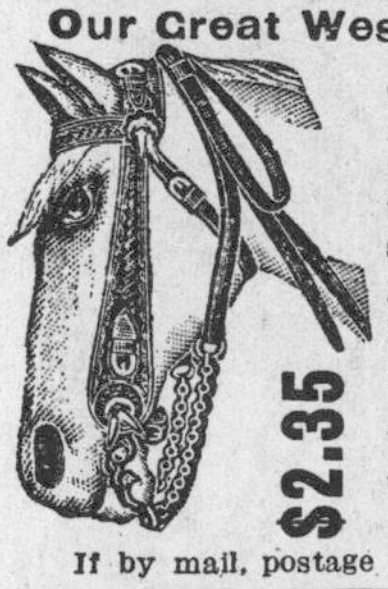

$2.35

No. 10K1702 Our Great Western Cowboy Bridle, made with wide pointed fancy stamped cheek, adjustable crown and throat latch. Fancy stamped brow band. Nickel buckles and ornaments. One of the new, up to date Western bridles; ⅞-inch by 6 feet reins, to loop in. Weight, about 24 ounces.
Price of bridle with bit...........$2.75
Without bit 2.35
If by mail, postage extra, 33 cents.

Braided Bridle Reins.

No. 10K1709 Our Special Braided Bridle Reins, made of fine quality calfskin, extra long with romal and quirt ends. These reins are made in three sizes: 4-plait, 6-plait and 8-plait. Weight, about 10 ounces.
Price, for 4-plait...................$1.13
Price, for 6-plait...................1.45
Price, for 8-plait...................1.81
If by mail, postage extra, each, 12 cents.

Flat Bridle Reins.

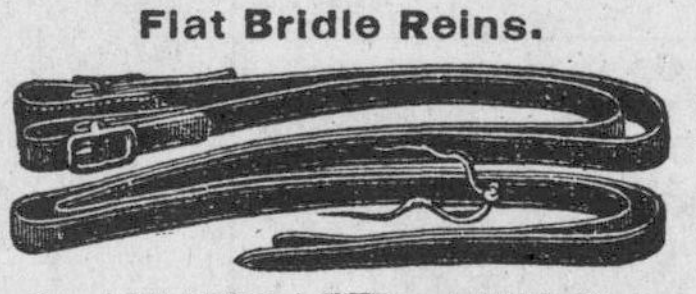

No. 10K1712 Our Special Flat Cowboy Bridle Reins. Made of ⅞-inch russet leather, buckle and billet ends to buckle in the bit, 7 feet long with lace string. Weight of bridle reins, about 12 ounces. Price, per pair, for one bridle...............72c
If by mail, postage extra, 14 cents.

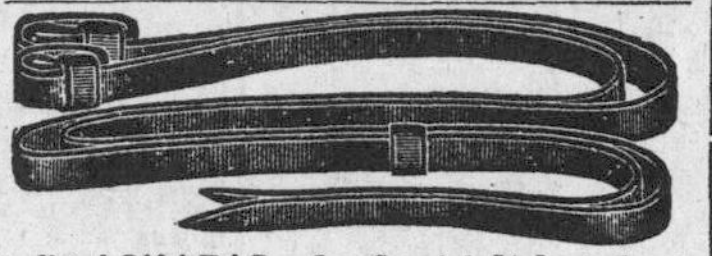

No. 10K1713 Our Special ⅞-Inch Loop End Bridle Rein, smooth, round edge finish, russet leather, 6½ feet long.
Price, per pair, for one bridle.......81c
If by mail, postage extra, 14 cents.

Our Rocky Mountain Special Riding Bridle.

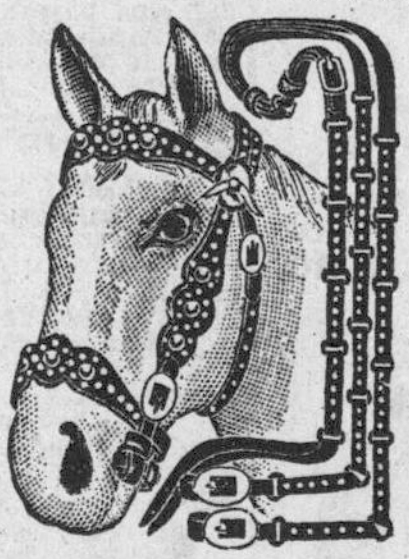

HEAD STALL—Made of russet or black leather, scalloped noseband, front and cheeks, cut 1⅞ inches wide on the large scallop and tapering to ¾ inch with nickel buckles. Three large nickel spots and as many small nickel spots as we can get on the leather around the edges of the scallops. Nickel spots on the throat latch and crown piece.

REIN—⅝-inch billets with nickel cart buckles. The front part of the rein has six double and stitched links connecting with nickel rings and are all nickel spots in center of each link. The hand part ¾ inch by 21 inches with quirt end buckled to the hand part and consists of four links, double and stitched with a row of nickel spots through the center to match the front part of the rein. The quirt is double end, ½ inch wide and 18 inches long. The rein measures full length including quirt to buckles, 7 feet. Weight of bridle, 34 ounces. Be sure to state whether you want black or russet.
No. 10K1715 Price of head stall only...............................$2.65
No. 10K1719 Price of rein only, 1.38
No. 10K1721 Price of bridle complete, head rein and bit.................$4.18
If by mail, postage extra, 48 cents.

Our Pony Bridle.

No. 10K1812 Our Shetland Pony Bridle. Only made pony size. Flat, with bar buckles, solid crown piece, with throat latch and cheeks to buckle on. XC buckles and full snaffle bit. ¾-inch bridle and reins, 4½ feet long. Made in russet or black. Weight, about 1 pound.
Price...............................$1.11
If by mail, postage extra, 25 cents.

$2.97 Round Pelham Bridle.

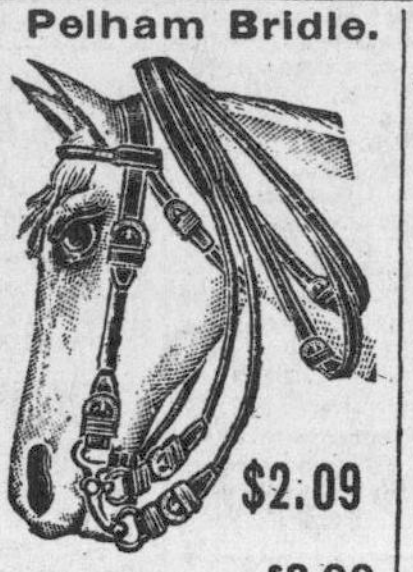

$2.09

No. 10K1813 Round Pelham. Superfine round russet leather bridle, round cheeks, front and two round reins, narrow loops, leather covered buckles, fine 4-ring XC port, bit and curb strap. Weight, about 32 ounces.
Price...$2.97
If by mail, postage extra, 37 cents.

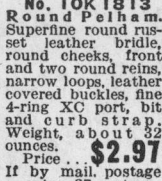

No. 10K1815 Same style as No. 10K1813, only single reins in place of double reins. Price...............$2.09
If by mail, postage extra, 27 cents.

Improved Stallion Bridle.

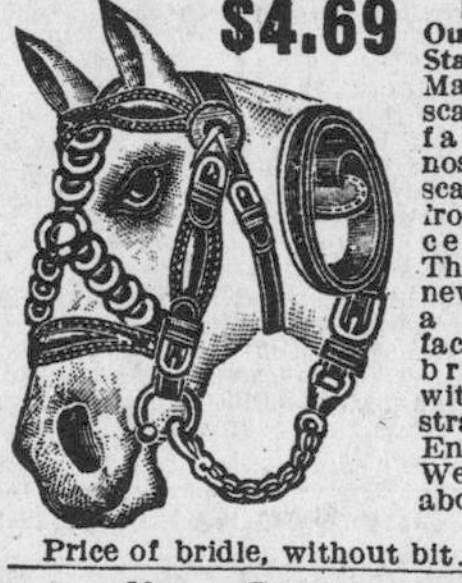

$4.69

No. 10K1817 Our Improved Stallion Bridle. Made with fancy scalloped cheeks, fancy scalloped nose band, fancy scalloped bridle front, with fine celluloid face. This is something new in the way of a fancy trimmed face piece stallion bridle, complete with 13-foot lead strap and 20-inch English lead chain. Weight of bridle, about 3 pounds.
Price of bridle, without bit......$4.69

New Stallion Bridle.

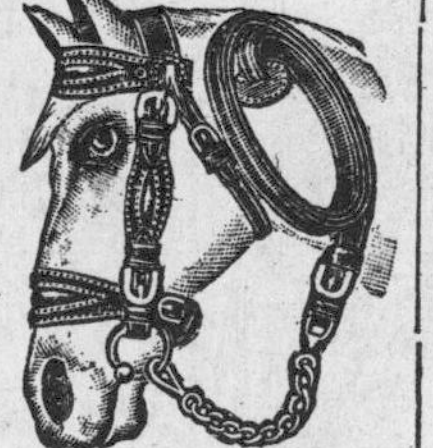

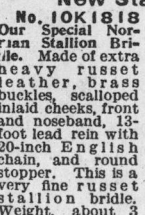

No. 10K1818 Our Special Norman Stallion Bridle. Made of extra heavy russet leather, brass buckles, scalloped inlaid cheeks, front and noseband, 13-foot lead rein with 20-inch English chain, and round stopper. This is a very fine russet stallion bridle. Weight, about 3 pounds.
Price of bridle without bit.......$3.54

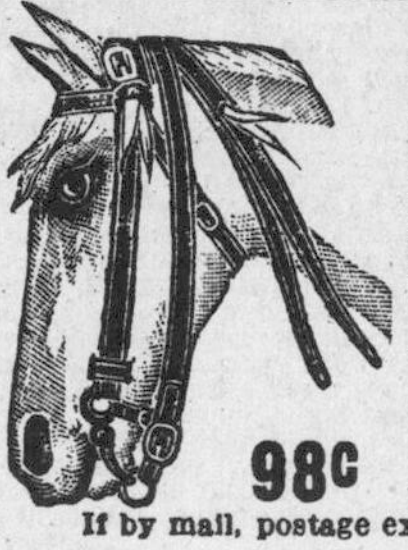

98c

No. 10K1821 Made of heavy Dundee oiled tanned leather. ¾-inch double head stall to buckle on top; ¾-inch reins, 6 feet long to loop in bit, XC buckles, port bit and curb strap. Weight, about 1½ pounds.
Price, without bit..............$0.98
Price, with bit...............1.04
No. 10K1822 ⅞-inch bridle with bit. Price.$1.33
If by mail, postage extra, 34 cents.

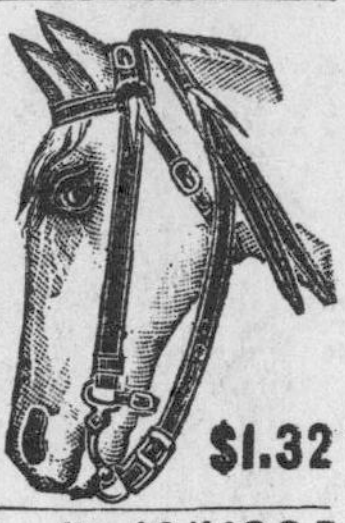

$1.32

No. 10K1323 Made extra heavy and strong, Oregon oiled tanned leather. ⅞-inch double head stall to buckle on top, ⅞-inch reins, to buckle in bit, 6 feet long, XC buckles, port bit curb strap. Weight, about 1½ lbs.
Price, without bit..........$1.32
Price, with XC port bit... 1.42
If by mail, postage extra, 33 cents.

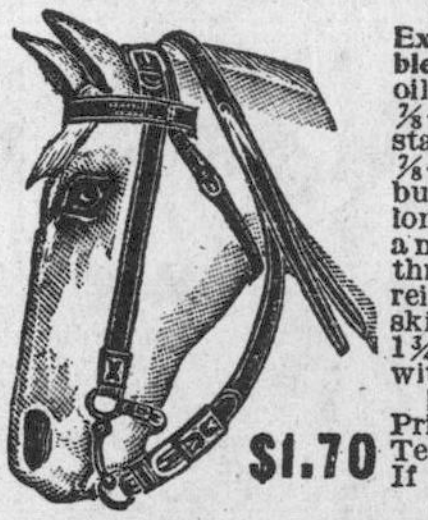

$1.70

No. 10K1825 Extra fine and durable. Made of Oregon oiled tanned leather, ⅞-inch double head stall to buckle on top; ⅞-inch reins, to buckle in bit, 6 feet long; nickel buckles and box loops throughout. Ends of reins laced with buckskin. Weight, about 1¾ pounds. Price, without bit..$1.70
No. 10K1826 Price, with blued Texas port bit;$1.84
If by mail, postage extra, 38 cents.

Extra Heavy Cowboy Bridle.

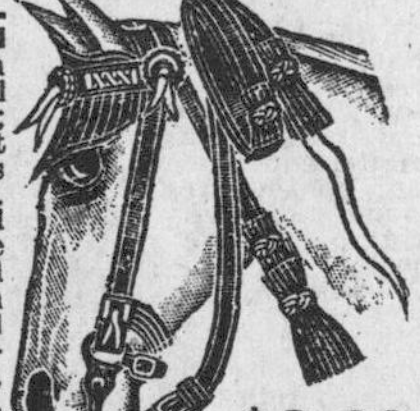

$2.69

No. 10K1827 Extra heavy Oregon oiled tanned leather, 1-inch double head stall to buckle on top; 1-inch reins, 6 feet long, laced at ends with buckskin. Heavy fringed front, fringed slide loops on cheeks and throatlatch, ⅝-inch curb strap. Nickel buckles and ornaments. Weight, about 2¼ pounds.
Price, without bit.........$2.69
No. 10K1829 Price, with blued Texas port bit....(Postage extra, 55c)....$2.83

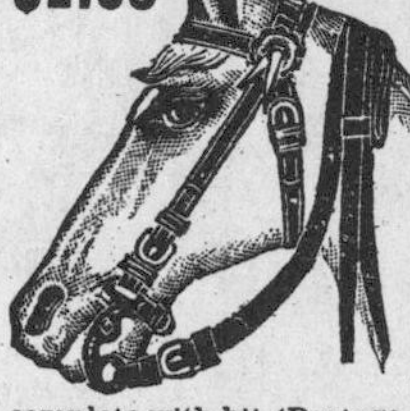

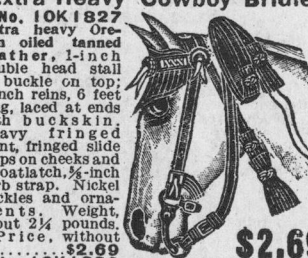

$2.08

No. 10K1830 ⅝-inch black leather. This is a very light hand made bridle, smooth, round edge finish, buckles on the crown piece, buckle and billet at the bit; ½-inch throat latch, chin strap; 6½-foot, ⅝-inch reins. A strictly California style bridle furnished complete with blued port Texas bit. Price, complete with bit (Postage extra 30c)$2.08
No. 10K1832 Same style bridle as No. 10K1830 quoted above, only made out of white California latigo, smooth, round edge finish, ⅝-inch bridle throughout. A very light riding bridle. Made of pure white leather with 6½-foot, ⅝-inch bridle reins, buckle and billet at the bit. This is a hand made bridle throughout. Price, complete with bit $1.73
If by mail, postage extra, 30 cents.

California Style Bridle.

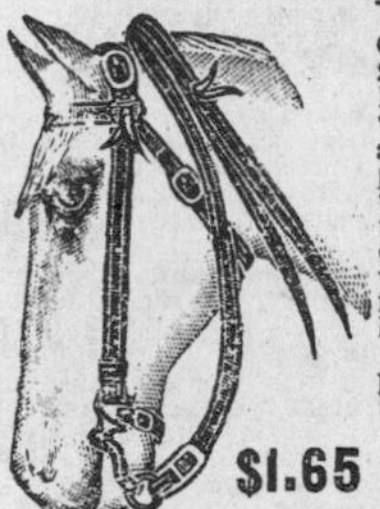

No. 10K1834 Our Special California Style White Latigo Riding Bridle, made with ⅝-inch double adjustable crown piece with buckle on top; ½-inch throat latch with curb strap; ⅞-inch white latigo rein; 6½ feet long; pure white latigo bridle.
Price, bridle complete with bit, each... **$1.65**
If by mail, postage extra, 30 cents.

$1.65

Heavy Fringed Front Bridle.

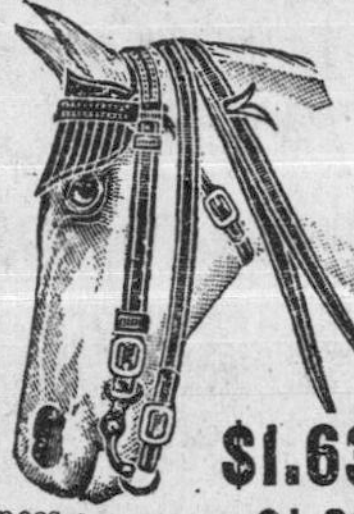

No. 10K1835 Fringed Front Bridle. This bridle is made with long, heavy bridle reins with quirt end, ⅞-inch double cheeks, to buckle in bit and looped into ring on crown piece, heavy fringed front sewed in ring on crown piece, crown has wide scalloped chafe with layer, making one of the best of cowboy bridles. Weight, about 23 ounces.
Price, without bit, each.......... **$1.63**
If by mail, postage extra, 32 cents.

$1.63

Special Mexican Diamond Braided Bridles.

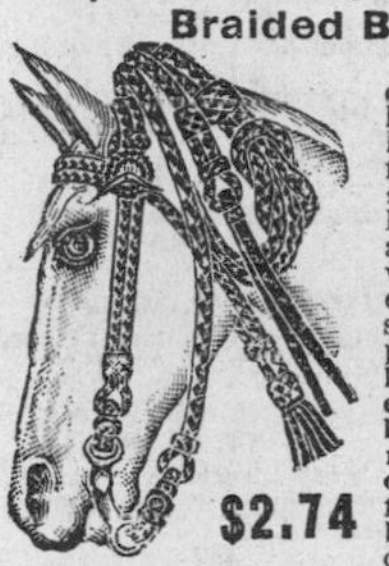

Our Special Mexican Cowboy Fine Diamond Braided Bridle, made of extra fine oil tanned calfskin, 8-plait, double head, double cheeks and double front, with fancy rosettes; extra braided billets, self adjusting crown piece, fancy braided knots and frills, extra fine long braided reins with round loop and romal or quirt ends. The finest fancy diamond braided bridle ever offered to our many customers. Equal, if not superior, to bridles which retail at $12.00 to $15.00. Weight, about 16 ounces.

$2.74

No. 10K1841 Eight-plait without bit. Price, each.......... **$4.24**
No. 10K1843 Same style of bridle as No. 10K1841, only six-plait. Without bit. Price, each.......... **$3.49**
No. 10K1844 Same style as No. 10K1841, only four-plait. Without bit. Price **$2.74**
(If by mail, postage extra, 25 cents.)

Buggy Bridles.

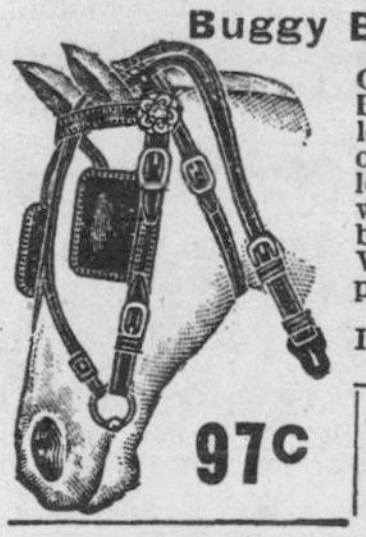

No. 10K1895 Our ⅝-inch Cheap Buggy Bridle (no box loop), overdraw check or side rein, patent leather blinds, flat winker braces, XC buckles throughout. Weight, about 2 pounds.
Price, each... **97c**
If by mail, postage extra, 38 cents.

97c

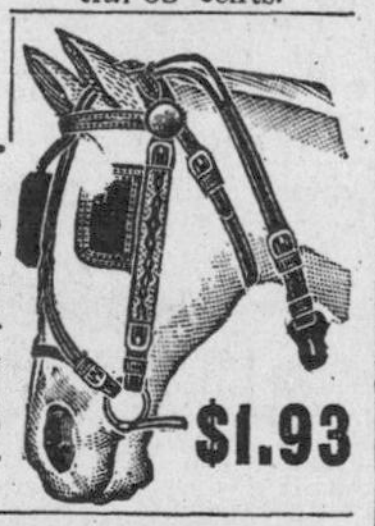

No. 10K1896 Our ⅝-inch Box Loop Cheek Buggy Bridle. Patent leather blinds, round winker braces, XC trimming, overcheck or side rein. Weight, about 2¼ pounds.
Price, each. **$1.93**
If by mail, postage extra, 48 cents.

$1.93

Williams' Humane Buggy Bridle, Kimble Jackson Check.

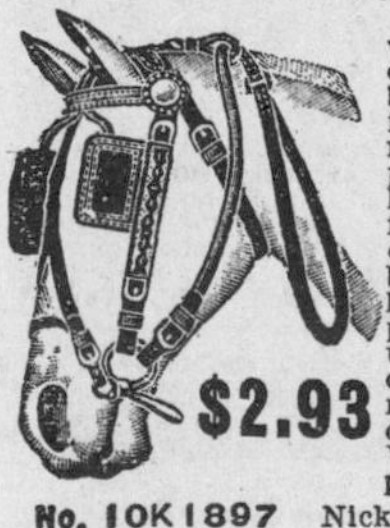

This bridle is made with side check and overcheck with nose band combined, ⅝-inch box loop cheeks, round winker stays, patent leather blinds, light round side check, fancy front, layer on crown; a very easy bridle on horse; holds head in correct position, and once used you will have no other. Trimming, nickel, Davis rubber or genuine rubber. Weight, about 2½ pounds.

$2.93

No. 10K1897 Nickel bridle. Price, each.......... **$2.93**
No. 10K1898 Davis rubber bridle. Price, each.......... **2.93**
No. 10K1900 Genuine rubber bridle. Price, each.......... **3.29**
If by mail, postage extra, 56 cents.

Our Fine Chicago Track Bridle.

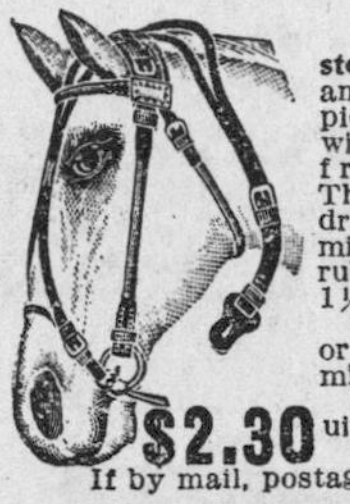

Made of selected stock, cheeks loop in bit and buckle-on crown piece, light overcheck with nose band, light front and rosettes. The finest grade of light driving bridle. Trimmings, nickel or Davis rubber. Weight, about 1½ pounds.
No. 10K1905 Nickel or Davis rubber trimmings. Each.... **$2.30**
No. 10K1909 Genuine rubber trimmings. Price, each.... **$2.53**

$2.30

If by mail, postage extra, 30 cents.

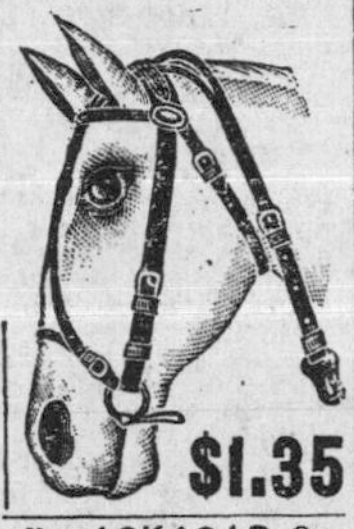

No. 10K1911 Our fine ⅝-inch Flat Cheek Open Bridle, overcheck with nose band, nickel or Davis rubber trimming. Weight, about 1¼ pounds.
Price, each. **$1.35**
If by mail, postage extra, 29 cents.

$1.35

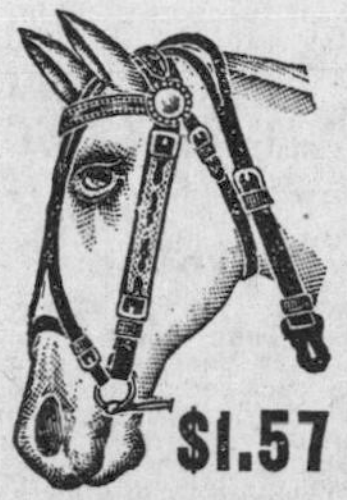

No. 10K1913 Our fine Open Bridle, ⅝-inch box loop cheeks, layer on crown piece, overcheck with nose band or side rein, fancy front, nickel or Davis rubber trimmings. Weight, about 1½ pounds.
Price, each. **$1.57**
Postage extra, 38c.

$1.57

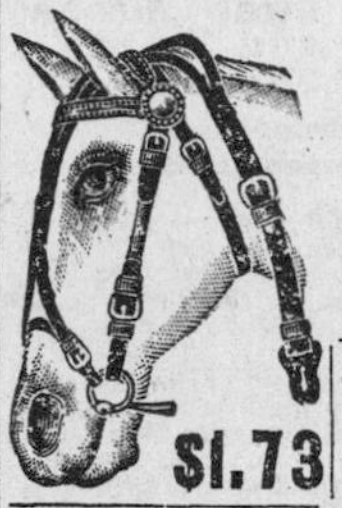

No. 10K1915 Our Extra Fine Round Open Bridle, overcheck with nose band or round side rein, long layer on crown piece, fancy front. Nickel or Davis rubber trimmings. Weight, about 1½ pounds.
Price, each. **$1.73**
If by mail, postage extra, 33 cents.

$1.73

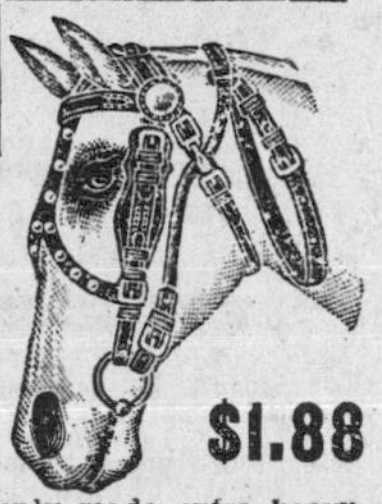

No. 10K1922 Our Fine Open Round Rein XC Team Bridle, ¾-inch scallop cheeks, harness leather front and spotted face piece. Weight, about 2¼ pounds.
Price, each **$1.88**
Postage, extra, 53c.

$1.88

No. 10K1923 Same style open bridle as No. 10K1922, only made extra heavy, ⅞-inch open cheek with spotted face piece. Weight, about 2½ pounds.
Price, ea. **$2.08**
If by mail, postage extra 56 cents.

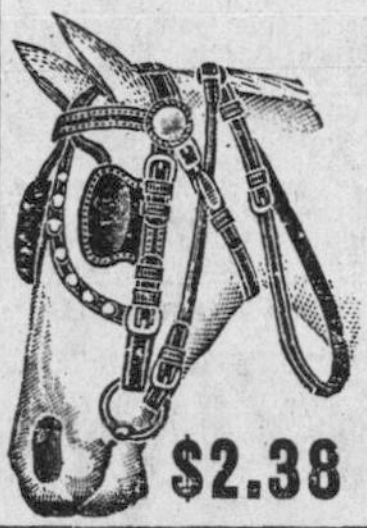

$2.38

Our $2.38 Team Bridle.

No. 10K1924 Our Fine Round Rein, Long Check, Sensible Blind Team Bridle. Face piece with spots. Extra good team bridle for team work. Weight, 3¼ pounds.
Price, ea. **$2.38**
If by mail, postage extra, 64 cents.

Our Long Cheek Team Bridle.

$1.89

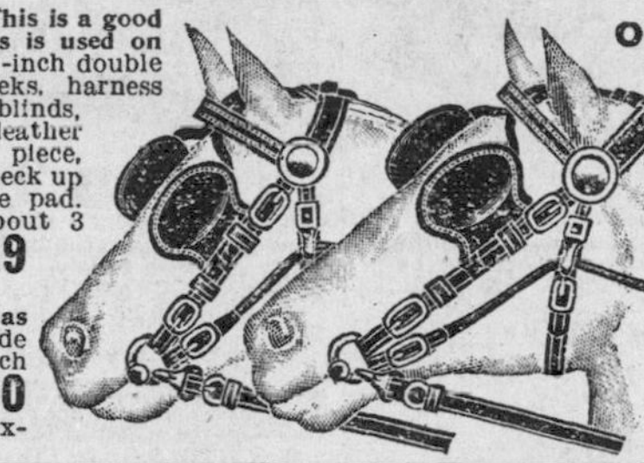

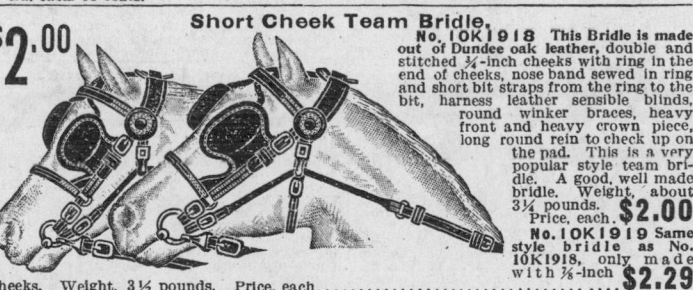

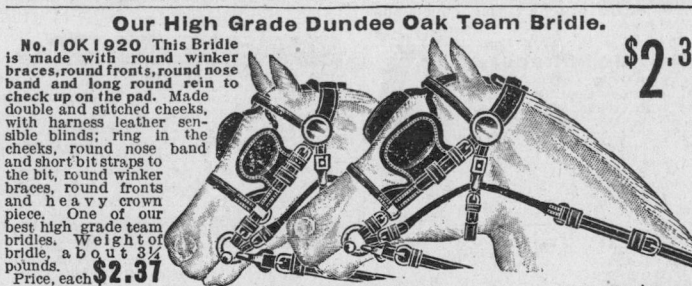

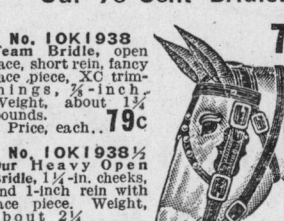

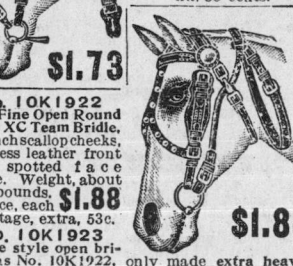

No. 10K1916 This is a good Team Bridle, such as is used on the farm. Made ¾-inch double and stitched cheeks, harness leather sensible blinds, round winker braces, leather front, heavy crown piece, long round rein to check up on the hook on the pad. Weight of bridle, about 3 pounds.
Price, each. **$1.89**
No. 10K1917 Same style bridle as No. 10K1916, only made with heavy ⅞-inch cheeks.
Price, each. **$2.10**
If by mail, postage extra, each, 63 cents.

Short Cheek Team Bridle.

$2.00

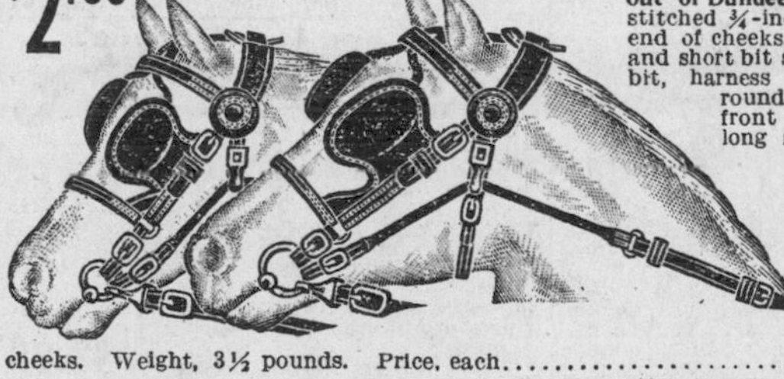

No. 10K1918 This Bridle is made out of Dundee oak leather, double and stitched ¾-inch cheeks with ring in the end of cheeks, nose band sewed in ring and short bit straps from the ring to the bit, harness leather sensible blinds, round winker braces, heavy front and heavy crown piece, long round rein to check up on the pad. This is a very popular style team bridle. A good, well made bridle. Weight, about 3¼ pounds.
Price, each. **$2.00**
No. 10K1919 Same style bridle as No. 10K1918, only made with ⅞-inch cheeks. Weight, 3½ pounds. Price, each.......... **$2.29**

Our High Grade Dundee Oak Team Bridle.

$2.37

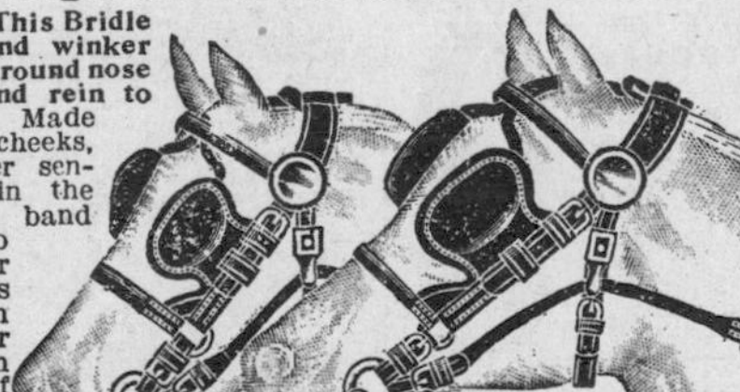

No. 10K1920 This Bridle is made with round winker braces, round fronts, round nose band and long round rein to check up on the pad. Made double and stitched cheeks, with harness leather sensible blinds; ring in the cheeks, round nose band and short bit straps to the bit, round winker braces, round fronts and heavy crown piece. One of our best high grade team bridles. Weight of bridle, about 3¼ pounds.
Price, each **$2.37**
No. 10K1921 Same style bridle as No. 10K1920, only made extra heavy, ⅞-inch cheeks. Weight about 3½ pounds, each. Price, each.......... **$2.60**

Round Team Bridle.

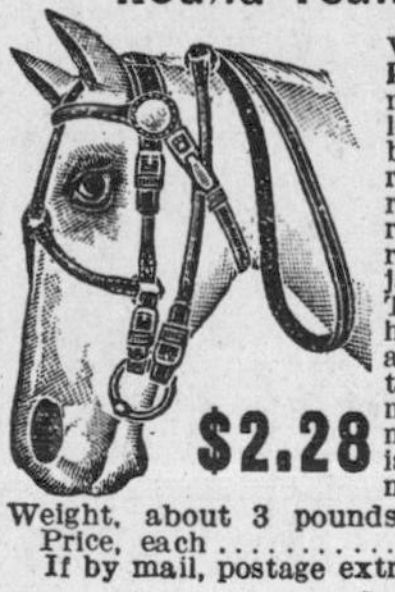

No. 10K1936 Williams' Celebrated Round Team Bridle, made of Dundee oak leather, with round bridle front, short round cheeks, with ring and bit strap, round face piece with ring, long round rein, japan roller buckles. The best, nicest and handsomest all around heavy open team bridle on the market, with japanned bit. This bridle is made with japanned buckles only. Weight, about 3 pounds.
Price, each.......... **$2.28**
If by mail, postage extra, each, 54 cents.

$2.28

Our 79-Cent Bridle.

79c

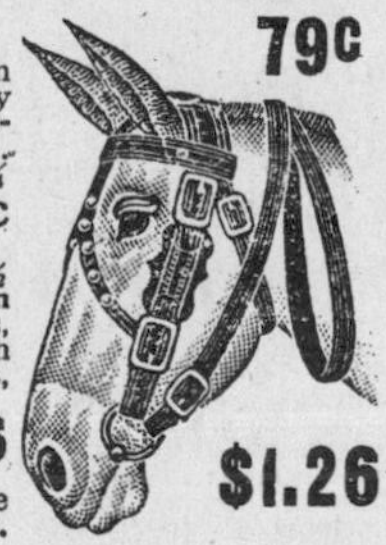

No. 10K1938 Team Bridle, open face, short rein, fancy face piece, XC trimmings, ⅝-inch. Weight, about 1¾ pounds.
Price, each.. **79c**
No. 10K1938½ Our Heavy Open Bridle, 1¼-in. cheeks, and 1-inch rein with face piece. Weight, about 2¼ pounds.
Price, each **$1.26**
If by mail, postage extra, each, 50 cents.

$1.26

Extra Heavy Bridle.

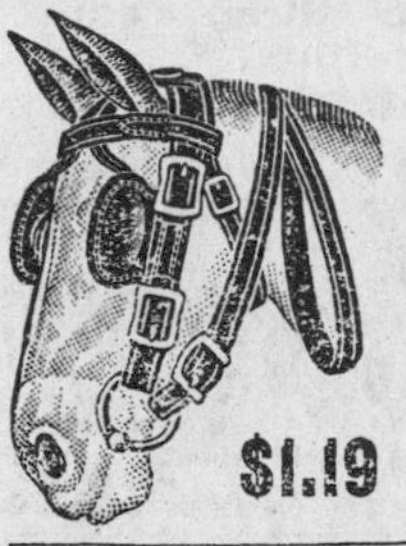

No. 10K1940 Our Extra Heavy Southern Bridle, made with large sensible blinds, 1¼-inch cheeks and 1-inch flat rein to throw over the hame. Flat winker braces, solid leather crown piece and front. Weight of bridle, about 3 pounds.
Each.. **$1.19**
If by mail, postage extra, each, 60c.

$1.19

Our 59-Cent Bridle.

No. 10K1943 Our Short Flat Rein, Pigeon Wing Blind Bridle, XC trimming, ¾-inch cheeks and rein, harness leather front. Weight, about 1¾ pounds.
Price, each.. **59c**
If by mail, postage extra, 35 cents.

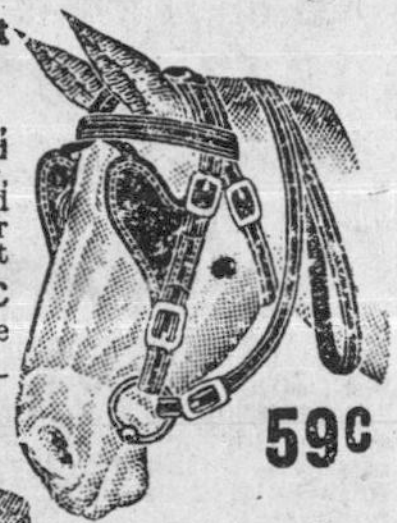

59c

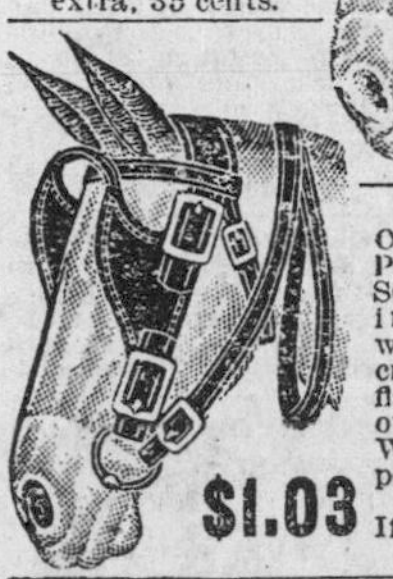

$1.03

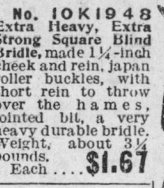

No. 10K1945 Our Extra Heavy Pigeon Wing Bridle. Southern style, 1¼-inch cheeks, flat winker braces, heavy crown piece and front; flat reins to throw over the hames. Weight, about 2½ pounds.
Price, each **$1.03**
If by mail, postage extra, 54 cents.

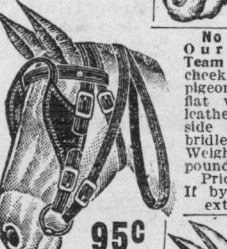

No. 10K1948 Extra Heavy, Extra Strong Square Blind Bridle, made 1¼-inch cheek and rein, japan roller buckles, with short rein to throw over the hames, jointed bit, a very heavy durable bridle. Weight, about 3¼ pounds.
Each.... **$1.67**

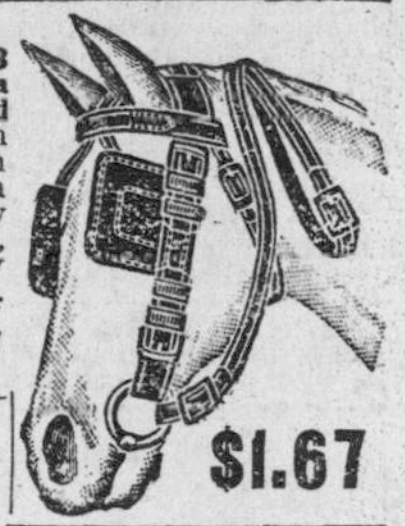

$1.67

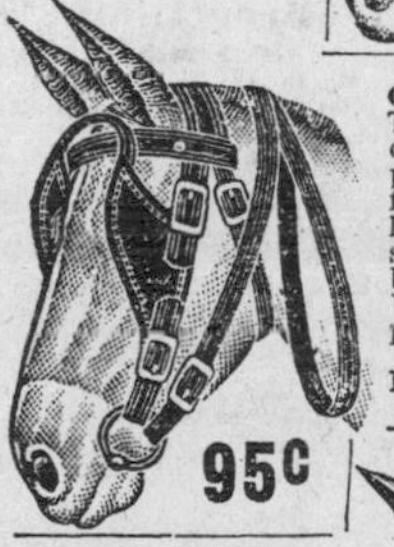

95c

No. 10K1951 Our Jenny Lind Team Bridle, ⅞-inch cheek, with cupped pigeon wing blinds, flat winker braces, leather front, flat side rein. A farm bridle. XC trimmed. Weight, about 2¼ pounds.
Price, each... **95c**
If by mail, postage extra, 50 cents.

No. 10K1952 Our Fine Open Bridle, made with ⅞-inch cheeks, with scallop chafe, ¾-inch nose band, ¾-inch double chin strap with ring, leather front, long round rein, the best open team bridle made. Weight, about 3 pounds.
Each.. **$1.89**
If by mail, postage extra, 58 cents.

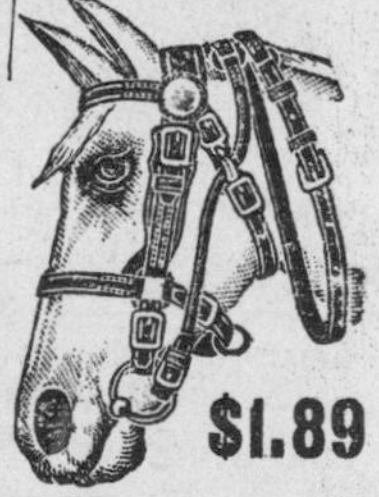

$1.89

Our Heavy Concord Team Bridle, $2.10.

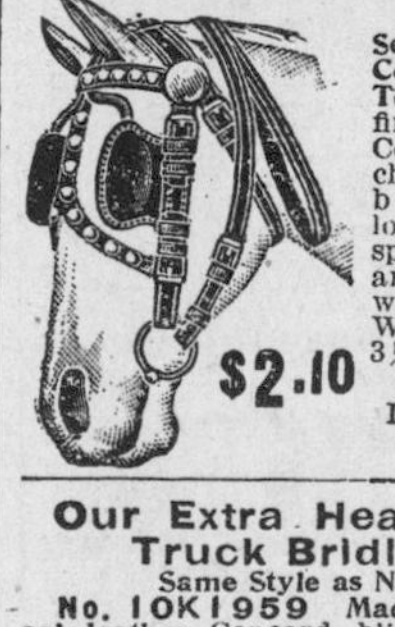

No. 10K1957 Sears, Roebuck & Co.'s Fine Dakota Team Bridle, made of fine Dundee oak leather. Concord blinds, ⅞-inch checks, japan roller buckles, four small loops, face piece brass spotted, brass front and rosettes, round winker braces, flat rein. Weight, about 3½ pounds.
Price, each.. **$2.10**
If by mail, postage extra, 60 cents.

$2.10

Our Extra Heavy Team or Truck Bridle, $2.73.

Same Style as No. 10K1957.
No. 10K1959 Made of fine Dundee oak leather, Concord blinds, 1¼-inch cheeks, with short loops, japan roller buckles, brass spotted face piece, heavy brass spotted front, round winker braces, ⅞-inch flat reins; one of the heaviest bridles we make. Weight, about 2½ pounds.
Price, each (Postage extra, 75c.), **$2.73**

Sig. 9—1st Ed.

Double Back Strap Team Breeching.

No. 10K2480 Made of well selected oak tan leather. Folded body with heavy layer, 1-inch double back straps running to ring in hames, 1-inch hip straps, 1-inch double side straps. Weight, about 12 pounds.
Price, per set, for two horses... **$8.63**

Dakota Team Breeching.

$9.69

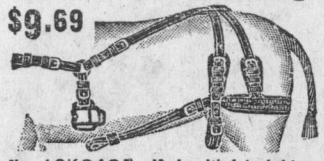

No. 10K2485 Made with 1-inch hip and back strap, with short straps to run to hame from ring on side, ⅞-inch breeching strap to snap under horse in ring on martingale. Heavy fold with wide layer, two rows stitching full length of breeching. Weight, about 12½ pounds.
Price, per set, for two horses... **$9.69**

No. 10K2486 Our Heavy 1½-inch, Japanned Buckle Dakota Breeching, 1¼-inch hip and back straps, 1¼-inch side straps, heavy fold body with wide layer. Weight, about 15 pounds.
Price, per set, for two horses... **$10.97**

Jersey Folded Breeching.

Jersey folded Breeching, made in two sizes, with a folded body, double and stitched layer, double hip straps and double back straps, with snaps in the ring. Weight, about 8 pounds.

No. 10K2487 Price, per set, for two horses, ⅝-inch double hip straps, 1-inch double back straps... **$4.23**

No. 10K2488 Price, per set, for two horses, 1¼-inch double hip straps, 1¼-inch double back straps... **$5.36**

Our Heavy Team Breeching.

$3.18

This team breeching is made with heavy harness leather folded body, with a heavy layer, double and stitched full length of the breeching, with breeching ring at each end, double and stitched breeching braces, with lead up strap to buckle on the hip strap and heavy side straps, with snaps to snap in the martingale ring.

No. 10K2490 Heavy Team Breeching, ⅞-inch side straps. Weight, about 5 pounds. Price, per set, for double harness, for **$3.18**

No. 10K2495 1-inch side straps, specially made throughout. Weight, about 5¾ pounds. Price, per set, for two horses, for **$4.38**

Our Team and Buggy Hip Breeching.

No. 10K2505 Made 1½-inch body, ⅞-inch side straps, to snap in pole strap under belly. Weight, 2¼ pounds. Price, per set, for two horses... **$2.16**

$2.16 **$2.23**

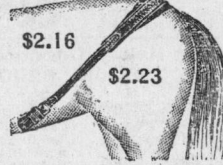

No. 10K2510 Made with a single strap body, with ¾-inch side straps of selected stock; made up to correspond with fine buggy harness. Weight, about 29 ounces. Price, per set, for two horses... **$2.23**

Single Buggy Breeching for One Horse.

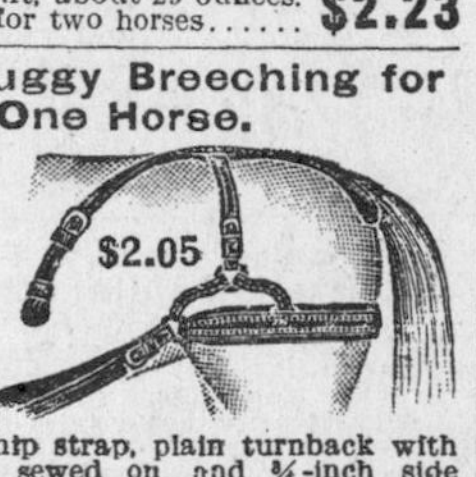

No. 10K2515 Common Single Buggy Breeching, made with folded body, straight layer, stitched, with two ring breeching stay, ⅞-inch hip strap, plain turnback with round crupper sewed on, and ¾-inch side strap, XC trimmings. Weight, about 40 ounces. Price, each, for one horse... **$2.05**

$2.05

Single Strap Breast Collar and Traces, V Shaped.

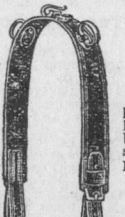

No. 10K2560 S., R. & Co.'s Special V Shaped Breast Collar and Traces, made of extra fine Delhi oak tanned leather, with 2½-inch V shaped body breast collar and 1⅛-inch single strap traces attached with ⅝-inch single strap neck strap. Weight, about 2½ pounds.
Price, each... **$2.58**

No. 10K2565 Same style of breast collar as No. 10K2560, only made with an extra heavy 3-inch V shaped single strap breast collar, with 1¼-inch single strap traces attached and ¾-inch single strap neck strap. Weight, about 2¾ pounds.
Price, each... **$3.28**

Hames and Single Strap Traces Attached.

No. 10K2570 Sears, Roebuck & Co.'s Special Hames and Single Strap Traces Attached, with three holes in back end. The hames are 3½-pound wrought iron, with 1⅛-inch traces riveted to the hames. Be sure to state the length of hames wanted to fit your collar. Trimmings, full japanned or XC. Weight, about 5 pounds. Price, per pair, including hame straps... **$2.61**

No. 10K2573 Price, per pair, for one horse, with nickel terret hames, with 1⅛-inch trace... **$2.72**

No. 10K2577 Same style of hames and traces as quoted above, only fine japanned body with nickel terrets, 1¼-inch single strap traces riveted to hames, with three holes in the back end. Weight, about 5½ pounds. Price, per pair, for one horse, including hame straps... **$2.91**

Our Alabama Slip Harness.

No. 10K2582 Consists of the pad, shaft tugs, bellybands, and double hip strap breeching only. The pad is wide patent leather top, stiff bottom pad, single strap skirts, double and stitched shaft tugs and single bellybands, double hip strap breeching. Hip straps 1 inch, side straps 1 inch, harness leather folded breeching body with layer double and stitched. A medium grade slip harness. Weight, per set, 7 pounds. Price, per set, as illustrated **$4.10**

$4.10

Our Extra Heavy Georgia Slip Harness.

$5.24

No. 10K2583 Made with solid harness leather pad with iron self adjusting tree, stuffed leather bottom pad and single strap harness leather skirts. The pad is 4 inches wide, double and stitched shaft tugs, double and stitched bearer; single strap bellybands, double hip strap breeching, 1-inch double hip straps and 1-inch side straps; double harness leather breeching body, double and stitched full length. Weight, about 9½ pounds... **$5.24**

Cow Bell Straps.

No. 10K2601 Our Fine Black Leather Cow Bell Strap, made with roller buckle and loop. State size of strap wanted. Weight, 8 ounces. Price, each.
Size, 1½ inches... 27c
Size, 2 inches... 39c
Size, 3 inches... 54c
If by mail, postage extra, 14 cents. For full line of Cow Bells, see Index.

Swiss Cow Bells.

These Swiss Cow Bells are made from Swiss bell metal. They are celebrated for their pure musical tone, which can be heard a long distance, and sound entirely different from common bells.

Catalogue No.	Diameter at mouth	Widest strap that can be used	Wt.	Price, Each
9K4950	3 5-16 in.	1½ in.	¾ lb	$0.37
9K4950	4 in.	1⅝ in.	1 lb	.52
9K4950	5 in.	2¼ in.	1¾ lbs	.97
9K4950	6 in.	3 in.	3 lbs	1.48

Plow Back Bands.

No. 10K2615 S., R. & Co.'s Dundee Oak Leather Plow Back Bands, made in three sizes with heavy leather loop for trace chain to run through. The best back band made. Weight, about 1¾ pounds.
Price, each, 3 in. $0.75
Price, each, 3½ in. .88
Price, each, 4 in. .99

Our Flat Leather Team Pad.

No. 10K2617 Our Flat Leather Team Pad with drop hook and terrets, 1¼-inch buckle and billet end, 3-inch solid leather body. Weight, per pair, 3½ pounds.
Price, each... **$1.43**

Chain Piping.

No. 10K2625 Leather Pipes, 24 inches long, to cover trace chains for plow harness. Weight, about 3 pounds. If you want the best chain pipes, order No. 10K2630.
Price, per set of four, for two horses... **$1.46**

No. 10K2630 S., R. & Co.'s Heavy Chain Piping, made of fine Dundee oak leather, put up in sets of four for two horses. Bound ends, made in three sizes. This is the best chain piping made. Weight, about 4½ pounds.
Price, per set of four, for two horses, piping 30 inches, per set... **$2.00**
Price, per set of four, for two horses, piping 36 inches, per set... **$2.33**
Price, per set of four, for two horses, piping 42 inches, per set... **$2.54**

No. 10K2631 Price, per set of four, for two horses, 5 feet chain piping. Weight, about 4 pounds... **$3.60**

Bellybands.

34c

No. 10K2635 Bellyband for Chain Traces, made with loop on each end for chain to go through, with one buckle on near side. Made in three sizes. Weight, 8 to 12 ounces.

Size, inches... 1¼ 1½ 2
Price, each... 34c 43c 56c
If by mail, postage extra, 15 cents.

No. 10K2645 Our Fine Double Bellyband, made of fine oak leather, heavy single strap, with ⅞-inch slip strap, fastened with loop in center. This bellyband is for old style shaft tug with billets. Weight, about 10 ounces. Price, for one horse... **67c**
If by mail, postage extra, 12 cents.

Team Bellybands.

No. 10K2650 Team Bellyband, folded and stitched; 18 inches long, with 1¼-inch buckle on each end. Weight, each, 17 ounces.
1¼-inch team bellyband. Price, each, 48c
1½-inch team bellyband. Price, each, 54c

Hip and Back Straps.

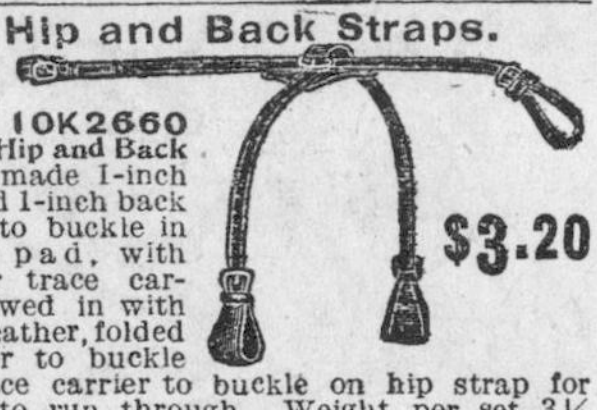

No. 10K2660 Team Hip and Back Strap, made 1-inch hip and 1-inch back strap, to buckle in back pad, with Cooper trace carrier sewed in with wear leather, folded crupper to buckle on, trace carrier to buckle on hip strap for traces to run through. Weight, per set, 3½ pounds.
Price, per set, for two horses... **$3.20**

$3.20

Team Traces.

Our Clip Cockeye Team Trace, made of good heavy leather, with two rows stitching and cockeye riveted on, making a very strong trace. Weight, about 8½ pounds.
No. 10K2700 1½ inches by 6 feet. Weight, about 8½ pounds.
Price, per set of four... **$4.69**
No. 10K2701 1¾ inches by 6 feet. Weight, about 9¾ pounds.
Price, per set of four... **$5.49**

Our Fine, Light Team Trace, made of good, heavy leather, with two rows stitching, cockeye sewed in.
No. 10K2705 1½ inches by 6 feet 6 inches, flat trace. Weight about 10 pounds. Price, per set of four... **$5.59**
No. 10K2710 S., R. & Co.'s Special Team Trace, made of fine Dundee oak leather, 1½ inches by 6 feet 6 inches long. This trace is used for slip tug team harness or for extra long horses. Weight, per set, about 9½ pounds. Price, per set of four traces for two horses... **$6.59**
No. 10K2712 Price, per set, 1¾ inches by 6 feet 6 inches, for two horses. Weight, about 10 pounds... **$7.73**
No. 10K2715 1¼-inch raised trace, 6 feet 6 inches long. Weight, per set, about 6 pounds.
Price, per set of four traces... **$5.95**
No. 10K2720 Made from good heavy oak tan stock, well stitched, 6 feet long, 1½ inches wide. Weight, per set, about 8½ pounds. Price, per set of four... **$5.99**
No. 10K2725 1¾-inch traces, 6 feet long. Weight, per set, about 10 pounds. Price, per set of four... **$7.59**

Single Strap Concord Trace.

No. 10K2740 Single Strap Concord Trace. Made from the very best selected heavy cuts of oak tan stock, 1½-inch points, 2½-inch body, 6 feet long. Weight, per set, about 8¼ pounds. Price, per set of four traces... **$6.40**
No. 10K2745 1¾-inch points, 2½-inch body, 6 feet long. Weight, per set, about 9 pounds. Price, per set of four traces... **$7.40**
No. 10K2746 2-inch points, 2½-inch body, 6 feet long. Weight, per set, about 10 pounds. Price, per set of four traces... **$8.90**
For Concord Toggles in place of cockeyes, add 50 cents.

Heavy Concord Truck Traces.

Concord Truck Traces. Made from the very best extra heavy selected oak tan stock, very heavy and strong, doubled and stitched, two rows of stitching, swell safe, 1½-inch bellyband billets, 6 feet long, with 12-inch heel chains, for use on a bolt hame.
No. 10K2750 Weight, about 14 lbs. 1½-inch, per set of four **$10.80**
No. 10K2755 Weight, about 17 lbs. 1¾-inch, per set of four, **$11.95**
No. 10K2756 Weight, about 20 lbs. 2-inch, per set of four, **$13.71**

Single Buggy Traces.

No. 10K2765 Machine Stitched Traces, 6 feet long, good, sound stock.
Size, inches... 1¼ 1⅛
Weight, per pair, about... 41 ozs. 31 ozs.
Price, per pair... $1.88 $1.74
No. 10K2770 Best Machine Stitched Traces, 6 feet long, raised center, hand smoothed round edge, selected stock.
Size, inches... 1¼ 1⅛
Weight, per pair, about... 38 ozs. 31 ozs.
Price, per pair... $2.16 $1.95

Double Buggy Traces.

No. 10K2775 Machine Stitched Traces, 6 feet 4 inches long, selected stock.
Size, inches... 1¼ 1⅛
Weight, per pair, about... 46 ozs. 42 ozs.
Price, per pair... $2.15 $1.94
No. 10K2780 Best Machine Stitched Traces, 6 feet 4 inches long, raised center, hand finished round edge.
Size, inches... 1¼ 1⅛
Weight, per pair, about... 41 ozs. 34 ozs.
Price, per pair... $2.51 $2.23

Our Special Single Strap Buggy Traces.

This trace is made of extra quality Dundee oak trace leather, double and stitched point and double and stitched heel; the balance or the body of trace is single strap. The trace is made in two sizes.
No. 10K2781 Size, 1⅛ inches, 6 feet long. Weight, per pair, 1½ pounds. Price, per pair... **$1.39**
No. 10K2782 Size, 1¼ inches, 6 feet long. Weight, per pair, 1¾ pounds. Price, per pair... **$1.74**

Our Special Single Strap Double Buggy Traces.

No. 10K2783 Size, 1⅛ inches, 6 feet long. Weight, per pair, about 1¾ pounds. Price, per pair, for one horse... **$1.51**
No. 10K2784 Size, 1¼ inches, 6 feet 6 inches long. Weight, per pair, about 2 pounds. Price, per pair, for one horse... **$1.88**

Gig Saddles.
For Single Harness.

No. 10K2800 Gig Saddle, made of patent leather, japanned metal seat, enameled cloth pad, 2½ inches wide, with ⅞-inch shaft bearer straps and ⅞-inch bellyband straps. Japanned or XC trimmed. Weight, about 2½ pounds. Price, each... **$1.05**
No. 10K2801 Gig Saddle, made of patent leather, japanned metal seat, enameled cloth pad, 3 inches wide, with 1-inch shaft bearer straps and ⅞-inch bellyband straps. Japanned or XC trimmed. Weight, about 3 pounds. Price, each... **$1.23**

3-Inch Single Strap Skirt Gig Saddle.

No. 10K2803 Enameled covered seat, long patent leather jockey, nickel hook, terrets and pad screw, 1-inch double and stitched bearer, 2-inch single strap harness leather skirt, ⅞-inch bellyband billets, patent leather pad, nickel trimmed only. Weight, about 3 pounds. Price, each, **$1.90**

Our Flexible Gig Saddle.

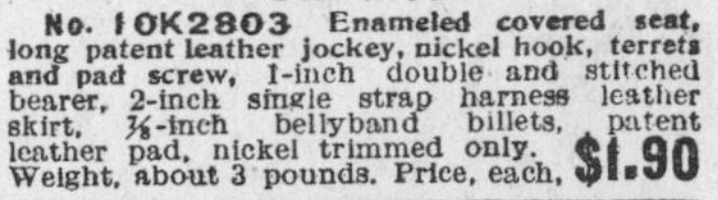

No. 10K2808 Made with a solid leather flexible tree, long patent leather jockey, 1-inch swinging bearer with ring and metal loop, swelled patent leather skirt, enameled leather pad laced in, ⅞-inch billet, brass trimming only. Size, 2½ inches; weight, 3 pounds. Price, each... **$3.57**

Full Patent Leather Gig Saddle

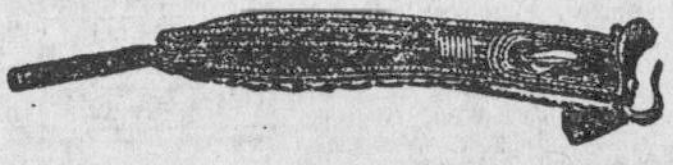

No. 10K2809 3-inch machine skirt, enamel leather pad laced in, long patent leather jockey, japanned seat, 1-inch double and stitched bearer, ⅞-inch billet. Weight, about 3¾ pounds. Price, each.... **$3.43**

Moline Loop End Harness Pad.

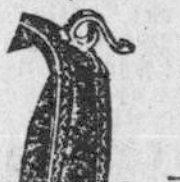

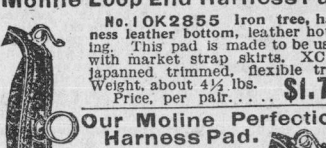

No. 10K2855 Iron tree, harness leather bottom, leather housing. This pad is made to be used with market strap skirts. XC or japanned trimmed, flexible tree. Weight, about 4½ lbs. Price, per pair.... **$1.72**

Our Moline Perfection Harness Pad.

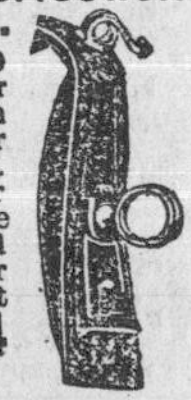

No. 10K2860 This pad is made for 1⅜-inch skirts, iron flexible tree, leather pad, leather housing. The best pad for team harness; the skirts are inserted in tree, and fastened with pad screw. XC or japanned trimming. Weight, about 5½ pounds.
Price, per pair **$1.74**

Hook and Terret Team Pad.

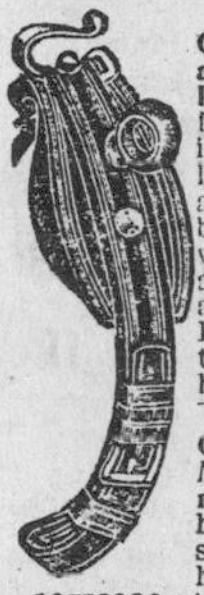

10K2980

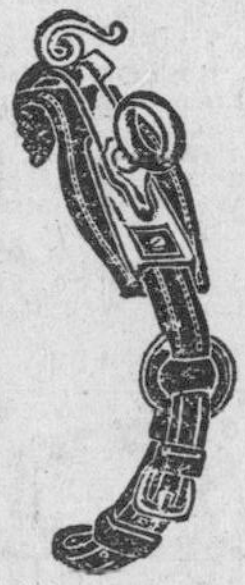

10K2986

No. 10K2980 Our Fine Hook and Terret Team Pad, made with folded body 1¼-inch layer, three loop and buckle and billet, turtle bottom fastened with pad screw and terrets. Wt., about 6 pounds. Price, per set for two horses **$3.47**

No. 10K2986 Our Special Style Moline Tree Harness Pad. Solid harness leather, stitched bottom, hair stuffed, with the adjustable Moline tree, short folded skirt with dee and 2¼-inch market strap to the trace buckle. This pad will not make the horse's back sore, as the ring on the side prevents the pad from wearing on the horse's back. Weight, about 7½ pounds.
Price, per set, for two horses... **$3.96**

Our Drop Hook and Terret Flat Pad.

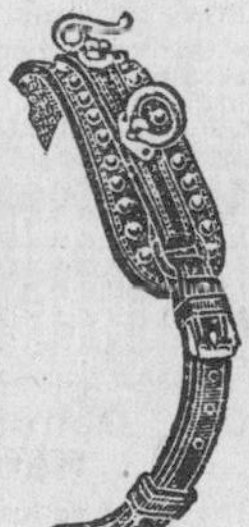

No. 10K3003 Made with harness leather housing, felt lined, nickel spots around the edge of the housing, drop hook and terrets riveted on; 1¼-inch layer double and stitched the full length with ring in each end, and heavy 1¼-inch market strap to buckle in the trace buckle. XC drop hook and terrets with nickel spots. Weight, about 4½ pounds.
Price, per set, for two horses........ **$3.15**

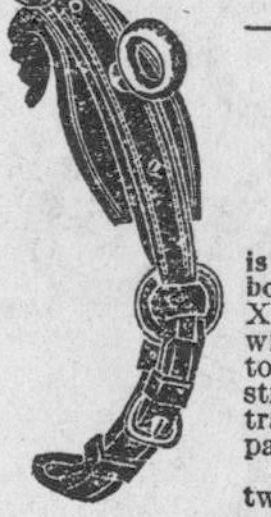

Kansas Double Team Harness Pad.

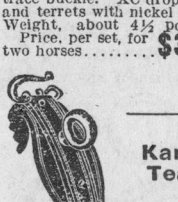

No. 10K3000 This Pad is made with heavy folded body with ring and chafe. XC hook and terret. Style, wide hair stuffed turtle bottom, short 1¼-inch market strap from ring in pad to trace buckle. Weight, per pair, about 6 pounds.
Price, per set, for two horses........ **$3.95**

Our Colorado Concord Pad.

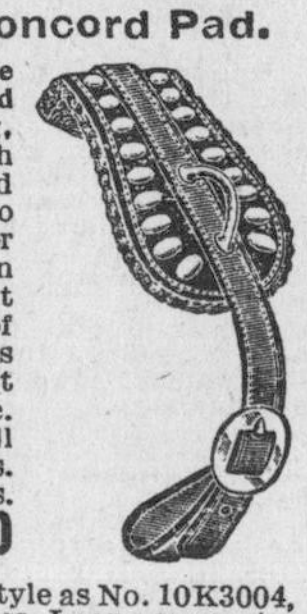

No. 10K3004 Made with a wide scalloped harness leather housing, heavy felt lined, 1¼-inch layer double and stitched the full length, with two Colorado brass loops for double back straps to run through. Brass peanut spots around the edge of the pad. Heavy brass buckle on the loop that fastens in the trace buckle. Pad is adjustable and will fit ordinary size horses. Weight, about 4½ pounds.
Price, per set, for two horses... **$4.80**

No. 10K3006 Same style as No. 10K3004, only made with one Brass Loop, on center for single back strap to run through to hames. Weight, about 4½ pounds.
Price, per set, for two horses.... **$4.40**

Our Fine Slip Tug Team Pad.

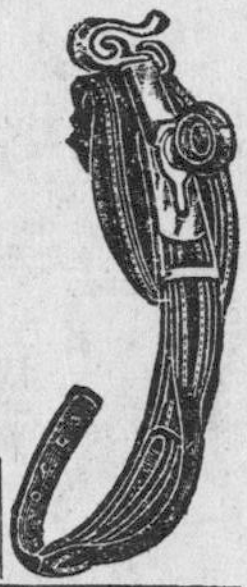

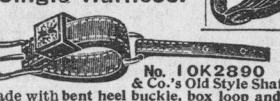

No. 10K3015 This Pad is made with heavy skirts with round loop on side to run the trace through, with good Moline tree. You cannot make a pad any better than we make this; 1¼-inch billets for bellyband. Weight, about 8¼ pounds per pair.
Price, per set, for two horses....... **$4.75**

Shaft Tugs for Single Harness.

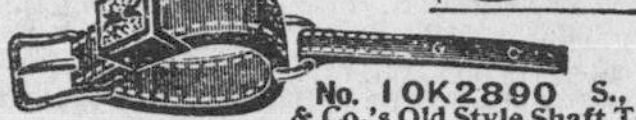

No. 10K2890 S., R. & Co.'s Old Style Shaft Tug, made with bent heel buckle, box loop and billet. Fine nickel or Davis rubber buckles. A shaft tug to be used with two bellybands. Weight, 12 ounces.
Price, ⅞ inch, per pair.............64c
Price, 1 inch, per pair.............67c
If by mail, postage extra, 12 cents.

Hame Tugs for Slip Tug Harness.

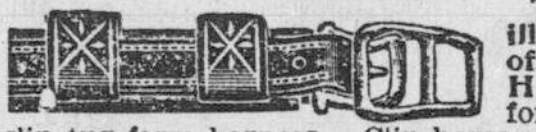

This is an illustration of our special Hame Tug for common slip tug farm harness. Clip hame with Champion trace buckle. A new and desirable hame tug, just introduced, and one which will be found superior to anything sold. Sold only in sets of four, in the following sizes:

No. 10K2905 Size, 1¼ inches, with box loop and Champion trace buckle, for light double harness. Weight, 2¼ pounds.
Price, per set of four, for two horses..$1.94

No. 10K2910 Size, 1½ inches, with two short loops. Weight, per set, 3 pounds.
Price, per set of four...............$1.99

No. 10K2915 Size, 1¾ inches, with two short loops. Weight, per set, 4 pounds.
Price, per set of four...............$2.25

Our Team Harness Hame Tugs.

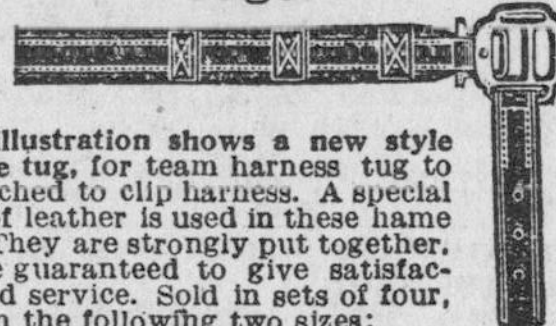

The illustration shows a new style of hame tug, for team harness tug to be attached to clip harness. A special grade of leather is used in these hame tugs. They are strongly put together, and are guaranteed to give satisfaction and service. Sold in sets of four, made in the following two sizes:

No. 10K2920 Size, 1½ inches. Weight, per set, 5 lbs. Price, per set of four...$3.15

No. 10K2925 Size, 1¾ inches. Weight, per set, 6 lbs. Price, per set of four...$3.49

Lace Box Loop Hame Tugs.

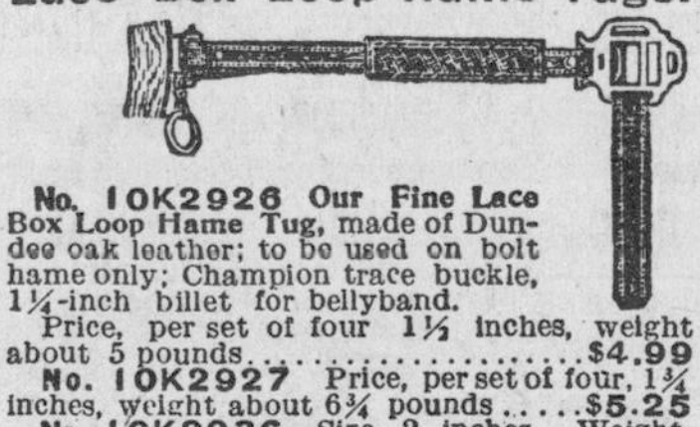

No. 10K2926 Our Fine Lace Box Loop Hame Tug, made of Dundee oak leather; to be used on bolt hame only; Champion trace buckle, 1¼-inch billet for bellyband.
Price, per set of four 1½ inches, weight about 5 pounds......................$4.99

No. 10K2927 Price, per set of four, 1¾ inches, weight about 6¾ pounds.....$5.25

No. 10K2936 Size, 2 inches. Weight, per set, about 8 pounds.
Price, per set of four................$6.98

Buggy Hame Tugs.

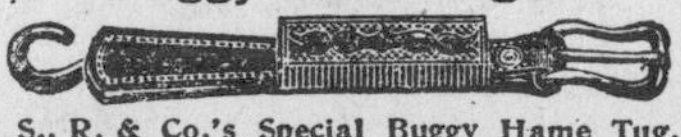

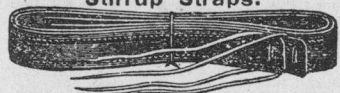

S., R. & Co.'s Special Buggy Hame Tug, made with box loop, open eye clip. Can be used on any iron hame for single or double harness. Extra strong; made in XC or japan. Price is for pairs for one horse with hame strap.

No. 10K2955 XC or japanned buckles.

Size, inches	1⅛	1¼
Weight, about	24 oz.	25 oz.
Price, per pair	91c	$1.07

Stirrup Straps.

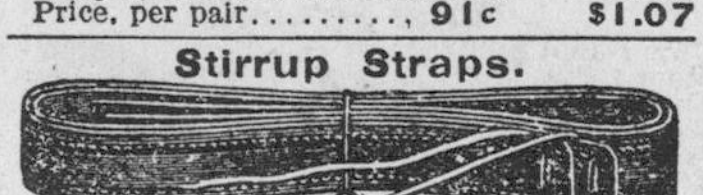

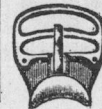

No. 10K3035 Stirrup Straps. 4 feet 4 inches long, with buckle, either black or russet leather. Be sure to state color wanted. Weight, 1 pound.
1 inch. Price, per pair...............64c
1¼ inches. Price, per pair...............87c
If by mail, postage extra, 19 cents.

No. 10K3040 California Style Stirrup Straps, cut from the best Dundee oak russet skirting leather, 5 feet 6 inches long, with lace strings. Extra heavy stirrup straps. Weight, 2¾ pounds.
2 inches. Price, per pair.............$1.60
2½ inches. Price, per pair.............2.10
3 inches. Price, per pair.............2.65
If by mail, postage extra, 49 cents.

Tackaberry Patent Cinch Buckle.

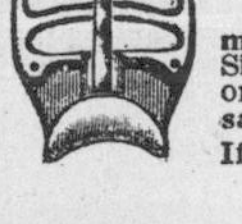

No. 10K3278 Made of malleable iron. XC plated. Size, 2-in. loops. To be used on cinches for Cowboy saddles. Price, each....... **13c**
If by mail, postage extra, 6 cents

Latigos.

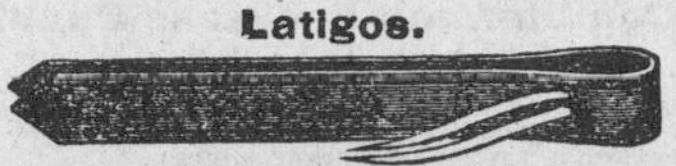

No. 10K3045 Latigo Straps, 2 inches wide, for buckle cinch ring, cut from the best Oregon oiled skirting leather, with lace string to fasten. Weight, 1¾ pounds. Length for draw side, 5 feet 6 inches. Price, per pair..$1.40
If by mail, postage extra, 27 cents.
Length for off side, 2 feet 8 inches.
Price, per pair 80
If by mail, postage extra, 17 cents.

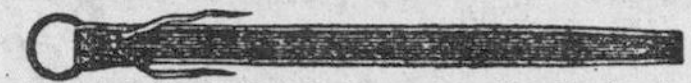

No. 10K3050 Latigos for tie cinch rig with lace strings to fasten to saddle rings. Weight, 15 ounces.
1¼ inches, 5 feet long. Price, per pair, 69c
1½ inches, 5 feet long. Price, per pair, 84c
If by mail, postage extra, 18 cents.

Cowboys' Riding Pants.

FANCY STAMPED WAISTBAND.

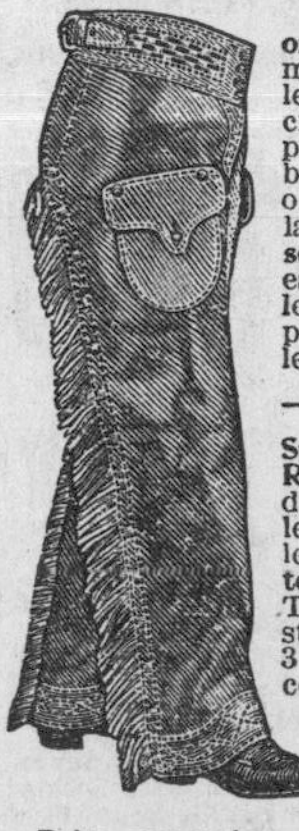

No. 10K3086 Chaps or Cowboys' Riding Pants, made of oiled chaparejos leather, stock being especially prepared for this purpose, stamped leather waistband, laced together, fringe on outside of each leg, thong laced, two pockets. Made for service. Sizes, 28 to 34 inches. Be sure to give inside leg measure. Weight, 4 to 5 pounds, according to length.
Price, per pair. **$9.25**

No. 10K3091 Our Special Denver Chaps or Riding Pants, made of heavy double twilled brown duck, leather waistband to lace, leather pockets, leather bottomed and leather fringe. This is an extra good, strong riding chap. Weight, 3 pounds. An ideal pair of cowboy riding pants. Everyone likes them because they are light and easy. Give length of leg wanted, inside measurement.
Price, per pair................. **$3.07**
If by mail, postage extra, 52 cents.

Horse Hobbles.

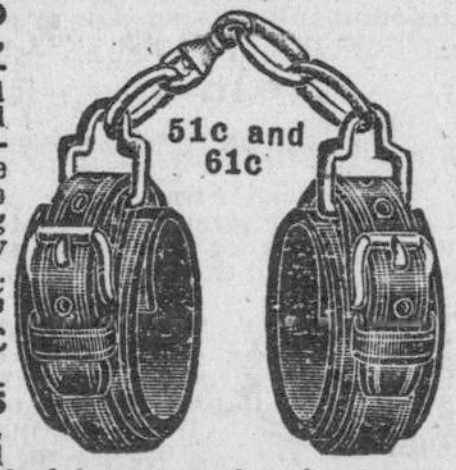

No. 10K3100 Front Hobbles, two leather anklets connected by a short swivel chain, to be attached to the fore legs of a horse to prevent running or straying away when loose. Weight, 1½ pounds.
Per pair, **51c**
Postage, 25 cents.

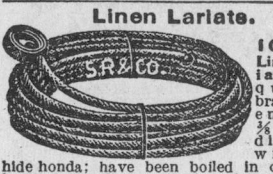

No. 10K3105 Side Hobbles, with chain and strap to be attached from one fore leg to one hind leg. Weight, 24 ounces.
Price, per pair.......... **61c**
If by mail, postage extra, 27 cents.

Linen Lariats.

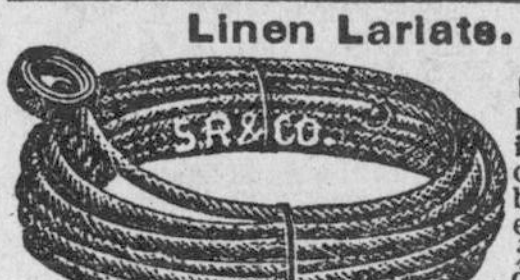

No. 10K3110 Linen Lariats, extra quality braided linen rope, ⅜ inch in diameter, with rawhide honda; have been boiled in oil, which keeps them soft and pliable and renders them waterproof; will not kink or snarl. Ends are patent grip fastened. Weight, about 3 pounds.
Length, 40 feet. Price, each......$2.13
Length, 50 feet. Price, each......2.53
½-inch linen lariat, 40 feet long, heavy and strong. Price, each...... 2.98

Manila Lariat Rope.

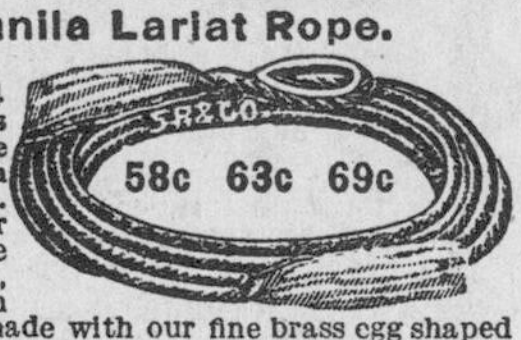

No. 10K3124 S., R. & Co.'s Special Fine Manila Lariat Rope. Made of four strands pure manila rope, 7-16 inch in diameter; made with our fine brass egg shaped honda. Braided on with braided tassel at the hondas and 8-inch tassel at the back end of lariat. This lariat is having a great sale throughout the country. This rope makes a very strong lariat.

Made in lengths..	30 feet	35 feet	40 feet
Weight, about...	2¼ lbs.	2¾ lbs.	3 lbs.
Price, each......	58c	63c	69c

If by mail, postage extra, 58 cents.

Riding Cuffs.

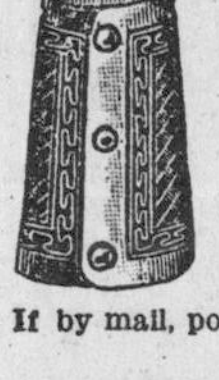

No. 10K3170 S., R. & Co. Special Hand Stamped Russet Leather Cuffs, made of extra fine russet leather, with three large glove buttons, which makes a fastening much better, neater and stronger than the buckle. Can be worn with or without coat. Length of the cuff, 7 inches. Weight, per pair, about 10 ounces. We do not break pairs.
Price, per pair.......... **86c**
If by mail, postage extra, per pair, 14 cents.

Riding Cuffs.

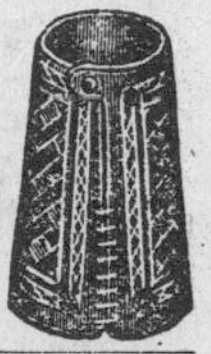

No. 10K3175 Our Fine Western Riding Cuffs, fancy stamped body 7 inches long, lace body and one button at the wrist. This cuff is made of extra fine russet cuff leather, and will fit over the coat sleeve. Weight, about 10 ounces. Price, per pair. **$1.00**
If by mail, postage extra, per pair, 14 cents.

No. 10K3180 Our Trinidad Cowboy Cuff, made with handsomely stamped body, scalloped top, lace at top for about 2 inches and buckle at the wrist. This is a cuff that we have had a very large demand for, and one we feel you will be perfectly satisfied with. This cuff is 7 inches long, made of extra fine russet cuff leather. No rider's outfit is complete without a pair of S., R. & Co.'s riding cuffs. We do not break pairs. Weight, about 10 ounces. Price, per pair...... **99c**
If by mail, postage extra, per pair, 14 cents.

COLLAR TOP PADS.

Collar Pads.

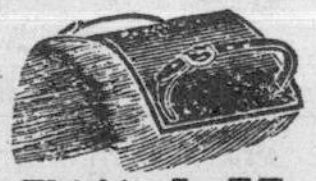

No. 10K3600 Collar Pad, made of heavy harness leather, lined with deerskin, tanned with the hair on; 9 inches long, 7 inches wide; ⅝-inch straps 18 inches long, to buckle around collar. Weight, 7 ounces. Price, each............. **57c**
If by mail, postage extra, 9 cents.

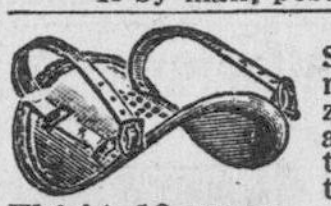

No. 10K3603 Curtis' Star Zinc Collar Pad, made of heavy galvanized zinc, with perforated top and double strap, one of the most healing pads to the neck on the market. Weight, 12 ounces.
Price, each............... **28c**
If by mail, postage extra, 18 cents.

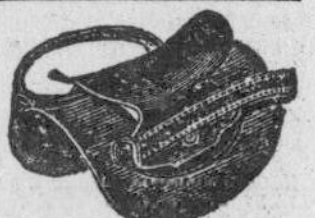

No. 10K3604 Oscillating Top Perforated Center Collar Pad, stamped out of heavy skirting, perforated top with steel saddle, which takes the weight of the collar off the horse's neck. One of the best top collar pads on the market. Weight, 12 ounces.
Price, each............ **34c**

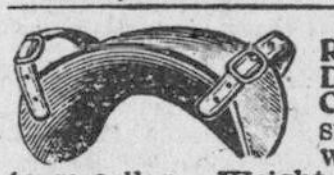

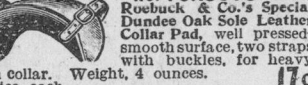

No. 10K3610 Sears, Roebuck & Co.'s Special Dundee Oak Sole Leather Collar Pad, well pressed, smooth surface, two straps with buckles, for heavy team collar. Weight, 4 ounces.
Price, each................ **17c**
If by mail, postage extra, 9 cents.

COLLARS.

Our Dolphi Duck Collar.

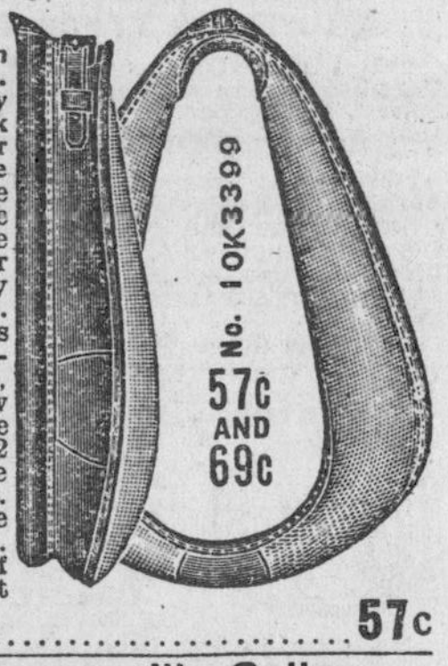

No. 10K3399 A Southern Plow Collar. Made of heavy cotton duck with leather chafes on the side where the chain or trace attaches to the hame. Leather pad, heavy canvas welt. This collar is used throughout the South, a good plow collar. Made in sizes 17 to 22 inches, inside measurement. Be sure to state size wanted. Weight of collar, about 4 pounds.
Price, each.............. **57c**

Our Brownsville Collar.

No. 10K3402 Our Cheap Farm Collar. We make this collar with a split rim and shoulder and heavy cotton duck face. One of the best heavy split leather and canvas collars we can make, a style that is used largely throughout the South and Southwest for a cheap farm collar. Made in sizes from 17 to 22 inches. Be sure to state size wanted. Weight of collar, about 4½ pounds.
Price, each.............. **69c**

Our Tompkins Farm Collar.

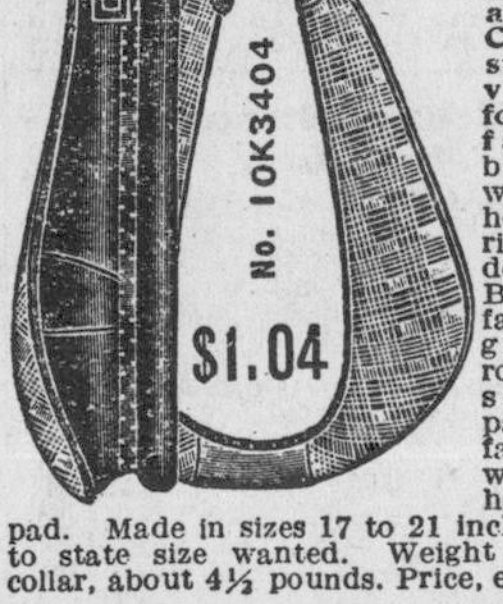

No. 10K3404 Our Baker Face Split Rim and Shoulder Collar. This style collar is very popular for a cheap farm collar, being made with good heavy split rim and shoulder and strong Baker cloth face. Extra good hame room, thong sewed, with patent collar fastener on top with good heavy leather pad. Made in sizes 17 to 21 inches. Be sure to state size wanted. Weight of collar, about 4½ pounds. Price, each, **$1.04**

Trace Chains.

No. 10K4080 Trace Chains, made of size No. 2, ½-inch wire, 7 feet long. Weight, per pair, 6½ pounds. Price, two chains for one horse **45c**

Twisted Trace Chain.

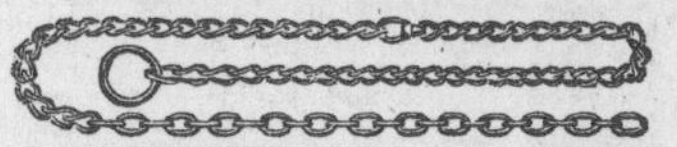

No. 10K4085 Sears' Special Heavy Twisted Link Trace Chains, made 7½ feet long. No. 0, 5-16-inch wire, twisted links. This is the best trace chain made. Weight, per pair, 10½ pounds. Price, for one horse, **98c**

Drop Hook and Terret.

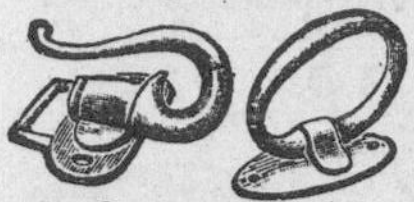

Hook. Terret.

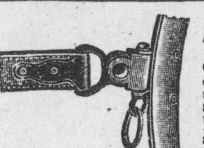

S., R. & Co.'s Special Drop Hooks and Terrets. To be riveted on flat pads. A hook that will lay flat on pad. Made in XC finish only. Weight of 2 hooks and 4 terrets, 25 ounces.

No. 10K4239 XC Terret, No. 303. Price, 4 terrets for **22c**

No. 10K4241 XC Drop Hook, No. 304. Price, 2 hooks for **12c**

If by mail, postage extra for 2 hooks, 20 cents.

Concord Clip Attachment.

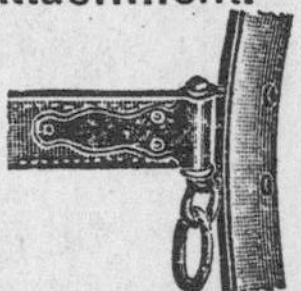

No. 10K4088 Our Concord Clip, to use on long staple or bolt hame, so you can clip your trace to hame. This is a big seller and the best to repair bolt hame tug or bolt traces that are broken at hame. Made in sizes as follows:

Width of hame bolt	1½	1¾	2	2¼
Weight, about each	5 oz.	6 oz.	6 oz.	8 oz.
Price, 4 for	**15c**	**20c**	**23c**	**25c**

Clip Attachment.

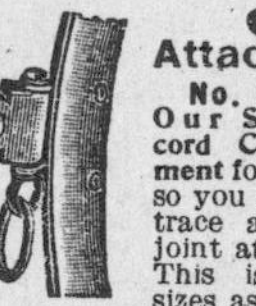

No. 10K4089 Our Special Concord Clip Attachment for bolt hame, so you can clip the trace and have a joint at the hame. This is made in sizes as follows:

Width of hame bolt	1½	1¾	2	2¼
Weight, about, each	12 oz.	12 oz.	14 oz.	16 oz.
Price, 4 for	**35c**	**38c**	**44c**	**47c**

Four is one set for two horses.

Our Joint Trace Splice.

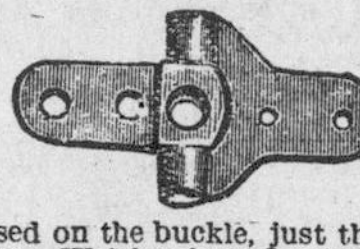

No. 10K4090 Our Joint Trace Splice, the only one that you can use when the trace is broken at the buckle. Will be as strong as ever and the same length as before and can be used on the buckle, just the same for any size trace. Weight, about 2 ounces each.

Price, per dozen, 75c; each **7c**

The Improved Trace Carrier.

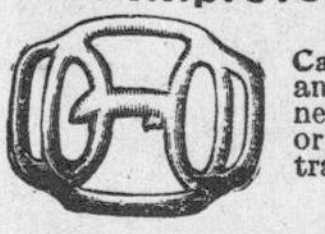

The Improved Trace Carrier to sew in back strap, and hip strap, of team harness. XC plate, white metal or japanned finish. The best trace carrier you can use.

No. 10K4132 Price, 2 for **8c**

No. 10K4133 Price, per box, 1 doz. **25c** Weight, 2¼ pounds per dozen.

Breast Strap Roller Snaps.

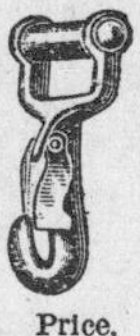

No. 10K4105 This special Breast Strap Roller Snap is used on team harness breast straps and snaps in the neckyoke ring; will roll on the strap and take the jar off the horse's shoulder. XC plate finish. Made in three sizes, 1½, 1¾ and 2 inches. Order by number and state size wanted.

Size, inches	Weight, about	Price, 2 Snaps for	Price, per doz.
1½	8 oz.	**19c**	**$0.95**
1¾	10 oz.	**21c**	**1.15**
2	12 oz.	**22c**	**1.25**

Bristol Breast Strap Roller Snaps.

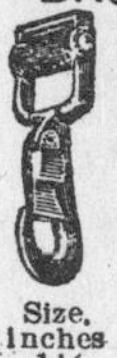

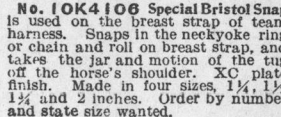

No. 10K4106 Special Bristol Snap is used on the breast strap of team harness. Snaps in the neckyoke ring or chain and roll on breast strap, and takes the jar and motion of the tug off the horse's shoulder. XC plate finish. Made in four sizes, 1¼, 1½, 1¾ and 2 inches. Order by number and state size wanted.

Size, inches	Weight, about	Price, each
1¼	9 oz.	**14c**
1½	10 oz.	**15c**
1¾	11 oz.	**16c**
2	13 oz.	**18c**

Combination Neckyoke Snap.

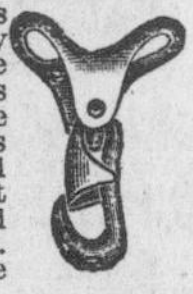

No. 10K4110 This Combination Neckyoke Snap and Slide is used on the breast straps of any heavy harness. Snaps in the neckyoke ring or chain and slides on the breast strap and takes the jar of the tug off the horse's shoulder. This snap is easily and quickly adjusted and the best combination neckyoke snap and slide on the market. XC finish. Order by number and state size wanted.

Size, inches	Weight, about	Price, 2 Snaps and Slides for	Price per doz.
1½	10 oz.	**23c**	**$1.15**
1¾	11 oz.	**25c**	**1.30**
2	12 oz.	**29c**	**1.43**

Breast Strap Slides.

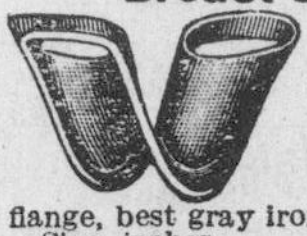

No. 10K4115 Gray Iron Breast Strap Slide is made from our special pattern. It fits the strap, will not cut at loop and works easy on the strap. A very heavy slide, wide flange, best gray iron, fine japanned finish.

Size, inches	1½	1¾	2
Weight, per dozen	4½ lbs.	6 lbs.	6¾ lbs.
Price, each	**2c**	**3c**	**4c**

XC Halter Trimming Sets.

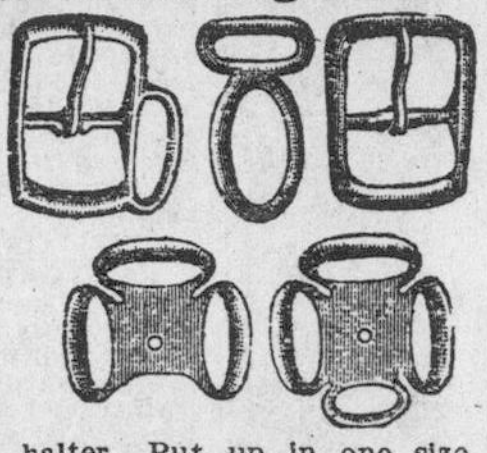

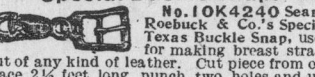

This Halter Trimming is put up in sets, six pieces to the set, for one halter, with rivets; you can make your halter with short pieces of leather by using this set of halter trimming, and will make a good strong leather halter. Put up in one size, 1¼ inches. Weight, per set, 8 ounces.

No. 10K4126 Price, per set **$0.14**

No. 10K4128 Price, per doz. sets **1.20**

Special Buckle Snap.

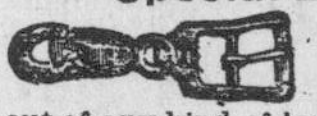

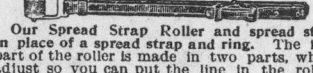

No. 10K4240 Sears, Roebuck & Co.'s Special Texas Buckle Snap, used for making breast straps out of any kind of leather. Cut piece from old trace 2½ feet long, punch two holes and use this buckle snap and make your breast strap. Size of buckle, 1½ inches only. Weight, about 1 pound. Price, per pair (2 snaps) .. **$0.13**

Price, per dozen pairs (24 snaps) ... **1.25**

Spread Strap Rollers.

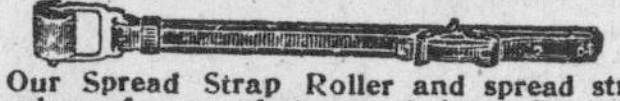

Our Spread Strap Roller and spread strap in place of a spread strap and ring. The iron part of the roller is made in two parts, which adjust so you can put the line in the roller.

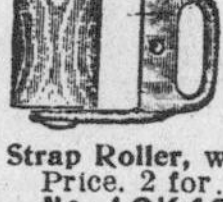

With this roller a line never becomes twisted but is held in the proper shape. They are very popular and are very satisfactory on a spread strap. Weight, 2 ounces.

No. 10K4258 Spread Strap Roller, with spread strap. Price, 2 for **27c**

No. 10K4260 Spread Strap Roller, without strap. Price, per dozen **53c**

If by mail, postage extra, dozen, 8 cents.

Check Springs.

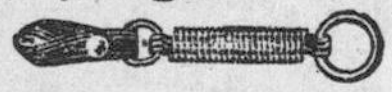

No. 10K4286 Check Spring for overcheck on buggy bridles. This illustration represents the flexible spring used on overcheck or side rein. The spring is so constructed that it takes the jar off the check rein and does not cut the horse's mouth or break the water hook. Made in one size only. Weight, 1 ounce. Every spring guaranteed for five years.

Price. (If by mail, postage extra, 4 cents). **18c**

Extra Heavy Harness Hooks.

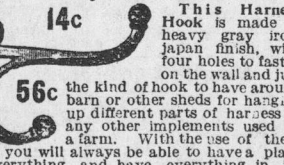

14c

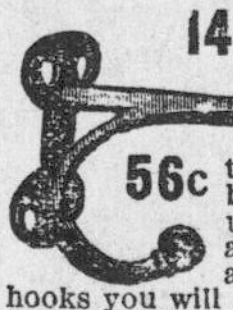

56c

This Harness Hook is made of heavy gray iron, japan finish, with four holes to fasten on the wall and just the kind of hook to have around barn or other sheds for hanging up different parts of harness or any other implements used on a farm. With the use of these hooks you will always be able to have a place for everything and have everything in its place. They are very handy, strong, and well made. The price is for four hooks of one size. Made in three lengths, 6, 8, or 10½ inches. Weight, each, 10, 17 and 44 ounces.

No. 10K4294 Price, four 6-inch hooks for **14c**

No. 10K4296 Price, four 8-inch hooks for **17c**

No. 10K4297 Price, four 10½-inch hooks for **56c**

COMPARE —THE— LOWER PRICES

IN THIS BOOK WITH THE PRICES QUOTED BY US IN

PREVIOUS CATALOGUES

AND WITH THE PRICES QUOTED BY ANY OTHER HOUSE, AND NOTE HOW MUCH WE SAVE YOU ON ANY NEEDED ARTICLE

Special Overcheck Loop.

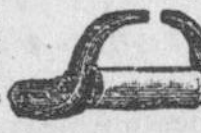

No. 10K4275 S., R. & Co.'s Special Overcheck Loop, made with roller and rivets to crown piece. The best overcheck loop made. Weight, about 4 ounces per dozen.

Price, per dozen **23c**

If by mail, postage extra, per dozen, 6 cents.

Harness Loops.

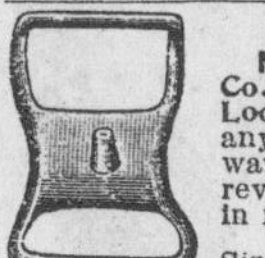

No. 10K4285 S., R. & Co.'s Special Conway Harness Loops, fine XC plate, used on any strap where you do not want to put a buckle; you only reverse the end of strap. Made in four sizes.

Size	¾ in.	⅞ in.	1 in.	1¼ in.
Weight, dozen	4 oz.	6 oz.	8 oz.	16 oz.
Price, per dozen	**14c**	**16c**	**21c**	**29c**

If by mail, postage extra, per dozen, 16 cents.

German Harness Snaps.

By size of snap we mean the width of strap that can be used.

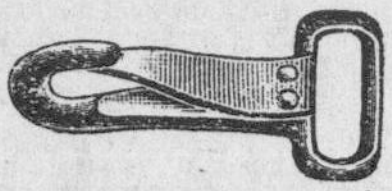

No. 10K4295 German Harness Snaps, bronzed finish. We handle only the heaviest and best snaps of this style made. ⅞ and 1-inch snaps are used on lines and side straps. The 1¼ and 1½-inch snaps are generally used on breast straps.

Size	Weight, per dozen	Price, per dozen
⅞ in.	11 oz.	**13c**
1 in.	12 oz.	**14c**
1¼ in.	26 oz.	**25c**
1½ in.	32 oz.	**32c**

Sears' Improved Flat Spring Triumph Harness Snaps.

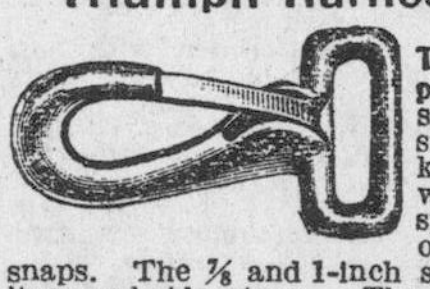

No. 10K4300 This snap is very popular and is considered the best snap on the market today. If you want the best flat spring harness snap order Triumph snaps. The ⅞ and 1-inch snaps are used on lines and side straps. The 1¼, 1½, 1¾ and 2-inch snaps are generally used on breast straps.

Size	Weight, per dozen	Price, per dozen
¾ in.	12 oz.	**17c**
⅞ in.	14 oz.	**18c**
1 in.	19 oz.	**19c**
1¼ in.	25 oz.	**36c**
1½ in.	28 oz.	**40c**
1¾ in.	32 oz.	**44c**
2 in.	37 oz.	**50c**

Banner Bolt Harness Snaps.

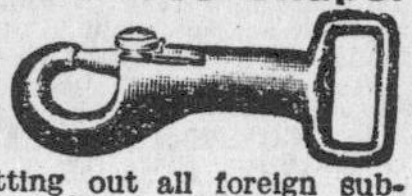

No. 10K4305 Banner Bolt Snaps. The principal feature of this snap lies in the spring being entirely covered, shutting out all foreign substances. The ⅞ and 1-inch snaps are used on lines and side straps. The 1¼, 1½, 1¾ and 2-inch are generally used on breast straps.

Size	Weight, per dozen	Price, per dozen
⅞ in.	16 oz.	**22c**
1 in.	18 oz.	**23c**
1¼ in.	24 oz.	**36c**
1½ in.	26 oz.	**41c**
1¾ in.	35 oz.	**45c**
2 in.	44 oz.	**51c**

Sears' Improved Harness Snaps.

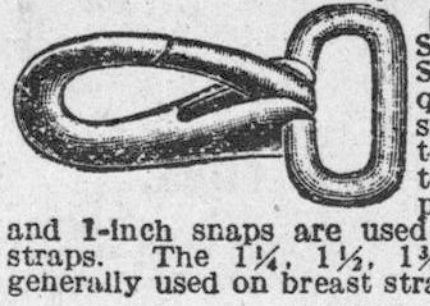

No. 10K4310 Sears' Improved Snaps, strictly first quality. Every snap is thoroughly tested in the factory before being packed. The ⅞ and 1-inch snaps are used on lines and side straps. The 1¼, 1½, 1¾ and 2-inch are generally used on breast straps.

Size	Weight, per dozen	Price, per dozen
⅞ in.	14 oz.	**24c**
1 in.	16 oz.	**25c**
1¼ in.	20 oz.	**40c**
1½ in.	32 oz.	**44c**
1¾ in.	38 oz.	**50c**
2 in.	46 oz.	**58c**

Rope Snaps.

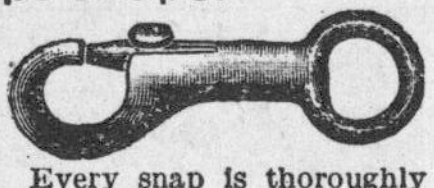

No. 10K4325 Round Eye Bolt Snaps for rope, XC finish. Polished on the loop and milled at the nose of the hook. Every snap is thoroughly tested.

Size	⅝	¾
Weight, per dozen, ounces	15	18
Price, per dozen	**24c**	**26c**

Open Eye Bolt Snaps.

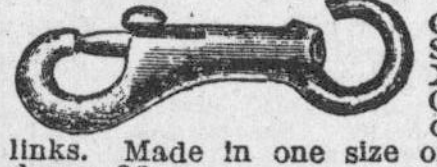

No. 10K4345 Open Eye Bolt Snap, made of XC malleable iron. Can be used on chain or open eye links. Made in one size only. Weight, per dozen, 36 ounces.

Price, per dozen **61c**

Swivel Eye Bolt Snaps.

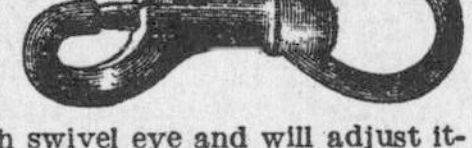

No. 10K4347 Swivel Eye Bolt Snap. Made of XC malleable iron. Round eye for rope. Snap made with swivel eye and will adjust itself to the twist of the rope. Made in three sizes. Weight, per dozen, ⅝ inch, 1¾ pounds.

Size, inch	⅝	¾	1
Price, per dozen	**46c**	**56c**	**89c**

Harness Soap.

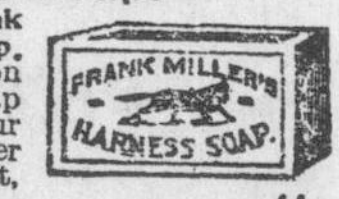

No. 10K4348 Frank Miller's Harness Soap. This is without question the best harness soap made. By using it your harness will wear longer and look better. Weight, per cake, 12 ounces.

Price, each **11c**

If by mail, postage extra, each, 14 cents.

Loop Roller Bar and Rein Buckle.

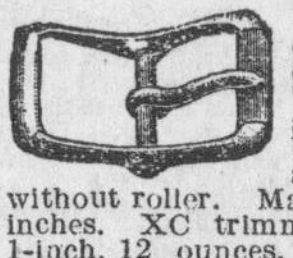

Made same style as the common bar rein buckle, only with metal roller. This buckle never peels the strap. It is easier unbuckled than any other style of buckle of this kind without roller. Made in sizes from ¾ to 1½ inches. XC trimming. Weight, per dozen, 1-inch, 12 ounces. Known as No. 150.

No. 10K4350 XC Harness Buckle, No. 150

Size, inches	¾	⅞	1	1¼	1½
Price, per dozen	**10c**	**12c**	**14c**	**21c**	**26c**

Our special reduced price on harness buckles sold in full boxes, ½ and ¼ gross. This style of buckle is known as No. 150 XC white metal with roller.

	Gross	Inch	Price
No. 10K4351	½	¾	**53c**
No. 10K4352	½	⅞	**61c**
No. 10K4353	½	1	**77c**
No. 10K4354	¼	1¼	**55c**
No. 10K4356	¼	1½	**69c**

We do not break boxes; full package only.

Our Improved Champion Trace Buckle.

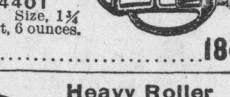

Three-Loop Japanned or XC Finish.

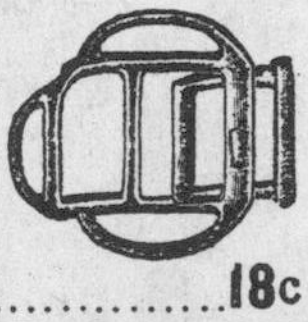

No. 10K4400 Three-Loop Champion Trace Buckles, made of best malleable iron, japanned finish. Size, 1½ inches. Weight, 5 ounces.

Price, 4 for **17c**

No. 10K4401 Japanned. Size, 1¾ inches. Weight, 6 ounces.

Price, 4 for **18c**

Heavy Roller Buckles.

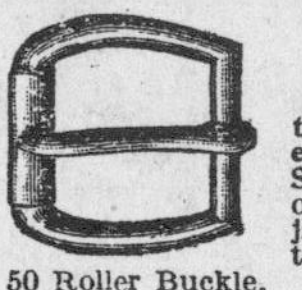

This buckle is used by the leading harness makers throughout the United States, has a heavy roller on front bar, made in japanned only, sold by the dozen. Known as No. 50 Roller Buckle.

No. 10K4445 Japanned Roller Buckles, No. 50.

Size, inch	¾	⅞	1	1¼
Price, per dozen	**7c**	**8c**	**9c**	**11c**
Size, inch	1½	1¾	2	
Price, per dozen	**13c**	**16c**	**20c**	

Our special price on No. 50 japanned harness buckles. The price is for full box of one size; we do not break boxes; order full package only, by catalogue number.

	Gross.	Inch.	Price.
No. 10K4446	1	¾	**56c**
No. 10K4447	1	⅞	**68c**
No. 10K4448	1	1	**78c**
No. 10K4449	½	1¼	**54c**
No. 10K4451	½	1½	**65c**
No. 10K4452	¼	1¾	**41c**
No. 10K4453	¼	2	**49c**

Our Genuine Pure Celluloid Harness Rings.

The price is for four rings of any one size.

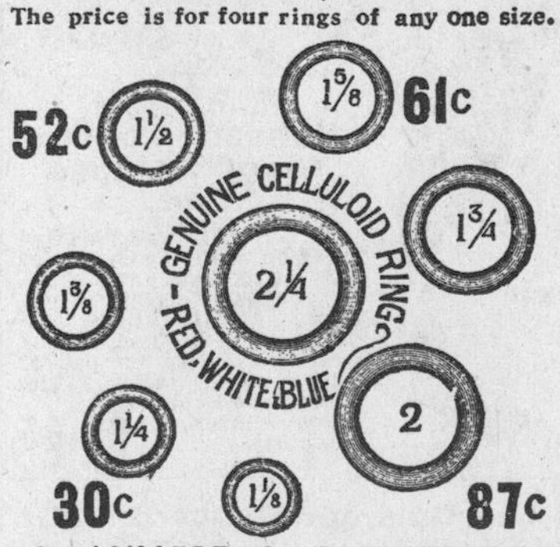

No. 10K4535 Our Genuine Pure Celluloid Harness Rings. We show eight sizes of rings, from 1⅛ to 2¼ inches. Be sure to state the size ring you want. Made in three colors, red, white and blue. With the use of these celluloid rings and celluloid loops you can make any style of spreader strap wanted for your harness. Be sure to state the color wanted, catalogue number and the size of the ring wanted. This superior Celluloid Ring is made for us out of the very best grade and highest quality celluloid, not an imitation, but the genuine. The price is for four rings of any one size.

What size do you want? Price is for 4 rings of any one size.

Size, inches	Weight, for 4 rings	Price, 4 for
1⅛	1	**26c**
1¼	2	**30c**
1⅜	2	**45c**
1½	3	**52c**
1⅝	3	**61c**
1¾	3	**75c**
2	4	**87c**
2¼	5	**98c**

If by mail, postage extra, 8 to 14 cents.

Harness Rings.

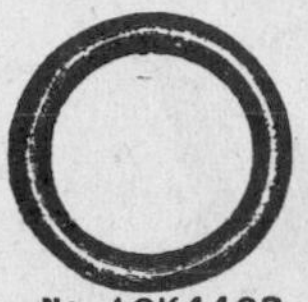

Made of fine quality of iron. This ring is used in the manufacture of all kinds of harness and halters and any other kind of work that wants good iron rings. Diameter of ring is the size.

No. 10K4493 Japanned Wrought Harness Ring.

Size of wire	No. 4	No. 3	No. 3	No. 1
Size of ring	1¼	1½	1¾	2
Per dozen	6c	8c	10c	15c

Celluloid Loops.

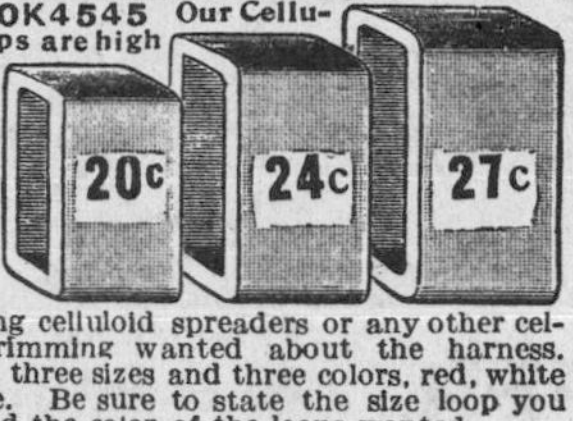

No. 10K4545 Our Celluloid Loops are high quality and are made to use in connection with our celluloid rings, in making celluloid spreaders or any other celluloid trimming wanted about the harness. Made in three sizes and three colors, red, white and blue. Be sure to state the size loop you want and the color of the loops wanted.

Diameter, inch	⅝	¾	⅞
Price, per dozen	20c	24c	27c

If by mail, postage extra, per dozen, 3c, 4c, 5c.

Celluloid Spreaders.

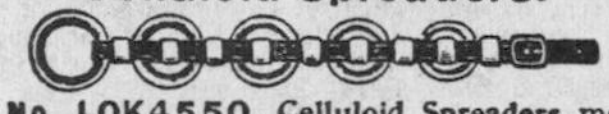

No. 10K4550 Celluloid Spreaders, made of five celluloid rings and nine celluloid loops on each strap; straps are 32 inches long. Weight, 9 ounces. Price, each 92c
If by mail, postage extra, 11 cents.

No. 10K4551 Pattern, 8 inches long, full length, large celluloid ring, four celluloid loops, three small rings and snap, all white. Weight, about 6 ounces. Price, each 48c
If by mail, postage extra, 10 cents.

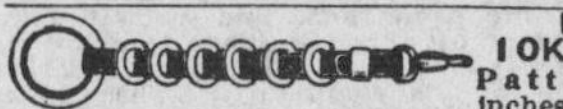

No. 10K4552 Pattern, 12 inches long, full length, large celluloid ring, seven celluloid loops, six small celluloid rings, snap, all white or fancy colors. Be sure to state color wanted. Weight, about 8 ounces. Price, each 67c
If by mail, postage extra, 10 cents.

Celluloid Spreaders.
LOOPED TOGETHER.

No. 10K4553 Our Fine Celluloid Union Spreaders, made with five celluloid rings, connected together with celluloid loops; all white or assorted color rings. Size of rings from 2 inches to 1¼ inches. The price is for each string, not pairs. Weight, about 4 ounces. Price, each $1.03
If by mail, postage extra, 6 cents.

Brass Ring Spreaders.

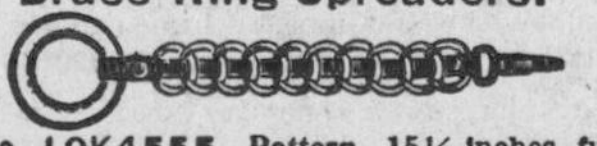

No. 10K4555 Pattern, 15½ inches, full length, large wood ring, ten brass rings or nickel rings, snap, made in brass or nickel. Wt., about 16 ozs. Price, each. 44c
If by mail, postage extra, 20 cents.

Large Wood Trimming and Center Ring.

No. 10K4582 Our Special Large Wood Center Ring. Made of hardwood. Colors, red, white or blue. Be sure to state color wanted. Size of ring, 2 inches in diameter. The best large wood center ring on the market. Weight, per doz., 1½ lbs. Price, each.... 4c
If by mail, postage extra, per dozen, 26 cents.

Our National Martingale Ring.

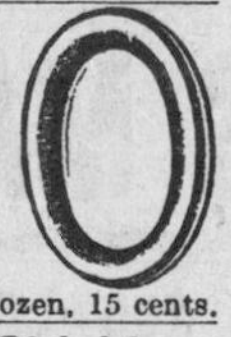

No. 10K4583 Very strong, well finished. Colors, red, white or blue. Be sure to state color wanted. Size, 1⅝ inches. Packed ¼ gross in box. Weight, per dozen, about 7 ounces. Price, per dozen.. 24c
If by mail, postage extra, per dozen, 15 cents.

Buckle Shield.

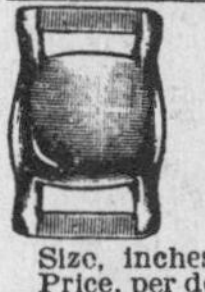

No. 10K4595 Stamped from solid brass, highly polished, edges smooth so they will not cut the straps. Made in brass or nickel. Weight, per dozen, 4 to 19 ounces.

Size, inches	¾	⅞	1	1⅛	1¼
Price, per dozen	27c	33c	43c	52c	62c

If by mail, postage extra, per dozen, 6 to 14 cents.

Banner Clipper at 67 Cents.

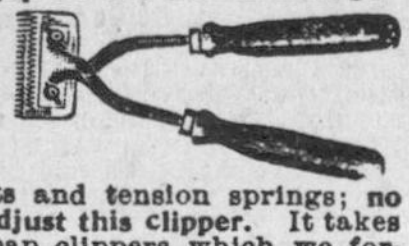

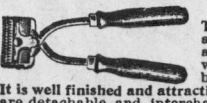

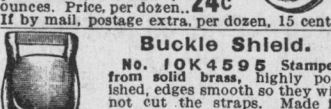

No. 10K4800 The Banner. It is a new clipper and a leader. The plates are detachable and interchangeable; has two thumb nuts and tension springs; no wrench needed to adjust this clipper. It takes the place of the cheap clippers which we formerly imported. Weight, 16 ounces. Price, each 67c
If by mail, postage extra, 20 cents.

The Crown Clipper for 90 Cents

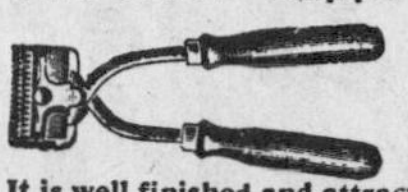

No. 10K4805 The Crown. This is a standard clipper and a great favorite with horsemen; has bright red handles. It is well finished and attractive. Cutting plates are detachable and interchangeable. Weight, 18 ounces. Price 90c
If by mail, postage extra, 22 cents.

Our High Grade Fetlock or Dog Clipper, 78 Cents.

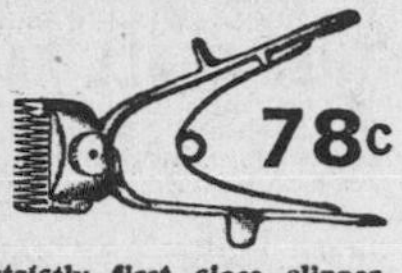

78c

No. 10K4815 Our 78-cent Leader Fetlock or Dog Clipper, made of extra fine tool steel plates, well ground and polished, wide milled teeth, handsomely nickel plated, fine piano steel spring. A strictly first class clipper. Dealers sell for $1.50. Weight, about 8 ounces. Price 78c
If by mail, postage extra, 10 cents.

Our Improved High Grade Newmarket Clipper, $1.00.

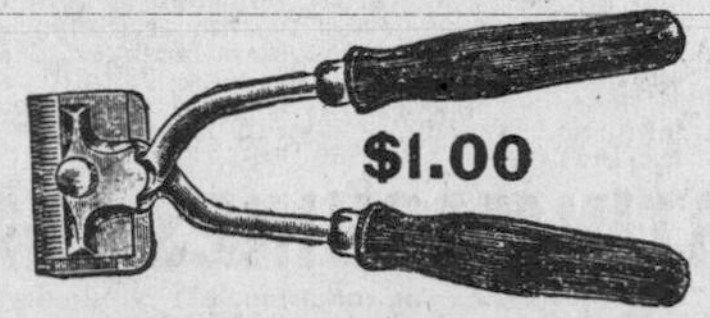

$1.00

No. 10K4820 Our Special Newmarket Clipper. One of the most popular styles hand horse clipper on the market. It is easily adjusted and cuts the finest hair smooth and even. The clipper plates are made out of imported tool steel, finely ground, the teeth are even and milled so that the hair fits into the clipper very even and the top cutters work so smoothly that the clipping becomes a pleasure with this Special Newmarket Clipper. Every horse owner should have a pair of these Newmarket Clippers in his stable. All parts of the clipper are interchangeable. Remember when you want a hand clipper for clipping horses, one that will give perfect satisfaction, order the Newmarket. Weight, about 20 ounces. Price $1.00
If by mail, postage extra, 22 cents.

O. K. Horse Clipper, $1.64.

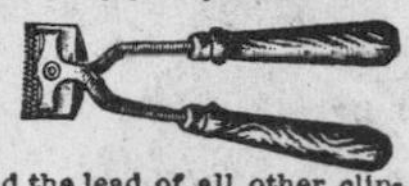

No. 10K4825 The O. K. No. 63. Our old reliable; nickel plated; an excellent cutter, bright polished handles, and has had the lead of all other clippers for several seasons. Cutting plates detachable and interchangeable. Weight, 16 ounces. Price $1.64
If by mail, postage extra, 22 cents.

The Best, Our Improved Ball Bearing Horse Clipper, $1.32.

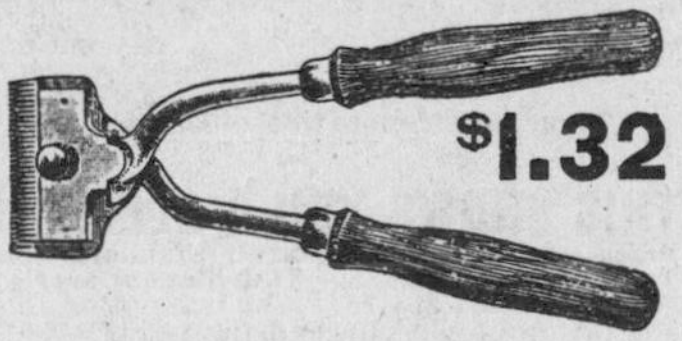

$1.32

No. 10K4830 Our Special Improved Ball Bearing Clipper. This clipper is an improvement on the Newmarket. It is ball bearing. The top cutter runs with ball bearing action. This makes the clipper work easy and cut smooth. The cutting parts of this ball bearing clipper are highly tempered tool steel. The teeth are milled in such a way that the hair gathers in the clipper and makes it easy for the operator to cut smooth with the least amount of friction. Finely nickel plated parts, polished handles and one of the best high grade hand clippers made. Every owner of a horse should have this special ball bearing clipper as it is one of the easiest working clippers made. Weight, about 18 ounces. Price $1.32
If by mail, postage extra, 22 cents.

The Best Fetlock Clipper, $1.05
Improved Handles and Tension Nut.
The Best Cutting Clipper Made.

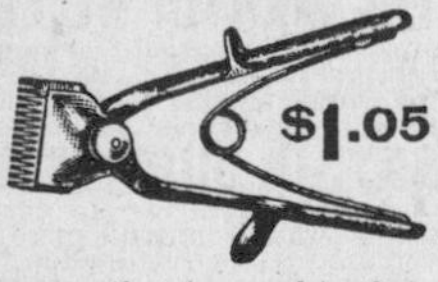

$1.05

No. 10K4835 One-Handed Horse or Dog Clipper. For trimming about the ears and fetlocks requires a keen cutting one-handed clipper with strong, elastic spring. You will find this is the one that is sought after. Plates detachable and interchangeable. Weight, 10 ounces. Price $1.05
If by mail, postage extra, 13 cents.

No. 10K4837 Extra springs. Price.. 9c
The parts of all our clippers are interchangeable and can be promptly duplicated.
If by mail, postage extra, each, 3 cents.

Our Imported English Double Bow Sheep Shears.

THEY WILL CUT THE FULL LENGTH OF THE BLADE. SOME SHEARS CUT AT THE HEEL BUT WILL NOT CUT GOOD AT THE POINT. THIS SHEAR IS GUARANTEED TO CUT AS WELL AT THE POINT AS IT DOES AT THE HEEL.

$1.04 6½ INCH

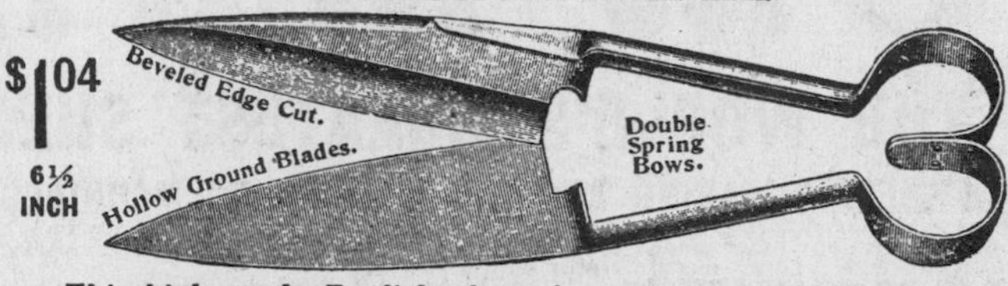

$1.24 7-INCH

This high grade English shear is made in Sheffield, England The steel used in this double bow shear is the best quality and highest grade razor steel. This shear has no equal for quality of material used and the way the shear is made, highly tempered, hollow ground blades, beveled edge cut, double bow spring. It is the leading shear used in Australia and all the leading sheep countries of Europe, and has gained the highest reputation with wool growers in the United States. We guarantee each shear to be perfectly constructed and tested, and guarantee each one to be superior to any other sheep shear on the market. This is the standard Sheffield English sheep shear. Made in two sizes, 6½ and 7 inches. Weight of shear, about 14 ounces.

No. 10K4661 Price, 6½-inch shear $1.04
No. 10K4662 Price, 7-inch shear 1.24
If by mail, postage extra, 22 cents.

Our Straight Blade Horse or Mule Shear.

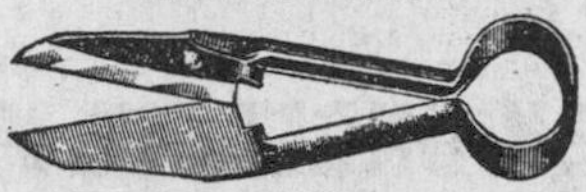

No. 10K4838 This Horse or Mule Shear is made with straight blades from the very best double shear cutlery steel, carefully hammer forged, and made the proper shape for hand shearing in roaching the mane, tail and fetlocks. Short blades, which make it easily handled. Blades are 4 inches long. Full length of shear, 9 inches. Weight of shear, 7 ounces. Price 33c
If by mail, postage extra, 10 cents.

Our Curved Blade Horse or Mule Shear.

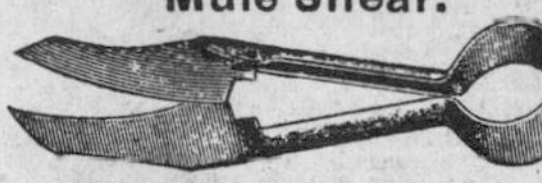

No. 10K4839 The blades on this shear are curved so you can clip the fetlocks clean or wherever a curved blade is necessary. Made of the very best double shear cutlery steel, perfectly tempered, hammered in oil. We guarantee this horse or mule shear to be the very best on the market. Excellent cutters and easily handled. Length of blade, 4 inches. Full length of shear, 9 inches. Weight, 7 ounces. Price 32c
If by mail, postage extra, 10 cents.

Sheep Shears.

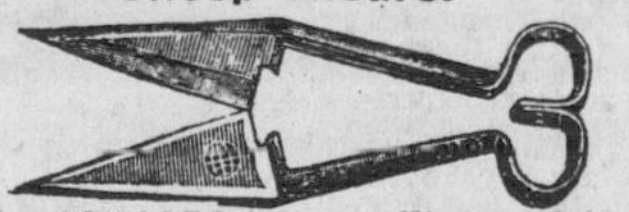

No. 10K4652 Great Western Sheep Shears. Double bow. Straight back and edge. Full polished blades. The shape and style used by professional shearers of the West. Don't let our low price cause you to doubt the quality of these shears. They are etched on blade as follows: "If this shear does not prove as good or better than any shear you ever had return it and money will be refunded." Weight, 11 to 14 ounces.

Length of blade, inches	6	6½
Price	74c	79c

If by mail, postage extra, 20 cents.

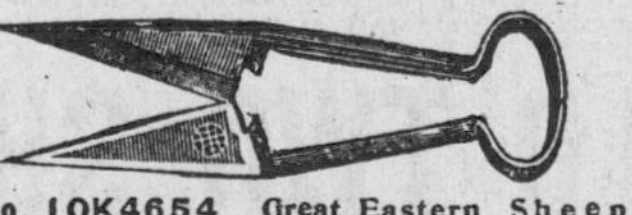

No. 10K4654 Great Eastern Sheep Shears. Single bow. Bent handles. Full polished and swaged. The shape and style used in the Central and Eastern States. Same quality, workmanship and finish as described under preceding number. Weight, 10 to 11 ounces.

Length of blade, inches	6	6½
Price	81c	85c

If by mail, postage extra, 20 cents.

The Celebrated Burgon & Ball's BBA Hollow Ground Sheep Shears.

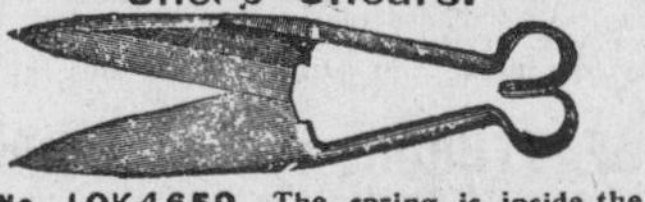

No. 10K4659 The spring is inside the bows with straight patent hollow ground blades, which insure it to be the best cutting shear on the market. It is the great champion shear; all professionals prefer this. It is also one of the finest examples of the steel worker's art. It is always cheapest to buy the best Burgon & Ball shear. We guarantee perfect satisfaction. Weight, 14 ounces.

Size, inches	6½	7
Price	$1.23	$1.43

If by mail, postage extra, 22 cents.

REDUCED PRICE ON CURRY COMBS.

Eight-Bar, Solid Back Curry Comb.

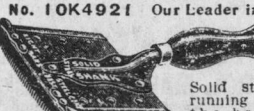

No. 10K4921 Our Leader in an eight bar, solid back curry comb. Solid steel shank running through the handle and riveted. Made from cold rolled steel, pressed steel shank and knockers, lacquered finish. Weight, about 12 ounces.
Price, per dozen, $1.10; each 10c
If by mail, postage extra, each, 14 cents.

Special 11-Cent Open Back Curry Comb.

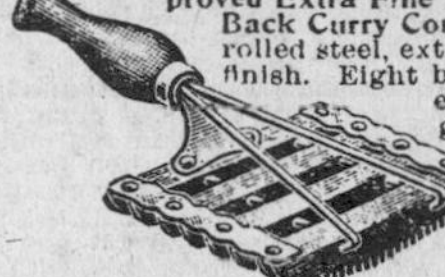

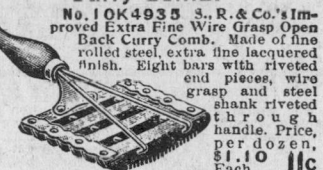

No. 10K4935 S., R. & Co.'s Improved Extra Fine Wire Grasp Open Back Curry Comb. Made of fine rolled steel, extra fine lacquered finish. Eight bars with riveted end pieces, wire grasp and steel shank riveted through handle. Price, per dozen, $1.10 Each.... 11c
If by mail, postage extra, 13 cents.

Our New Steel Bon Ton, Rustless and Plain Steel Curry Combs. The Best.

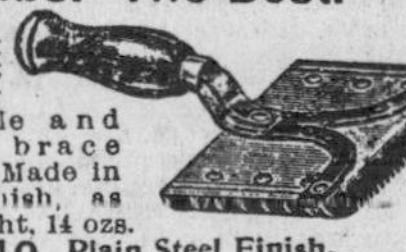

Made solid back, eight bars, wrought shank running through handle and riveted, strong brace and knocker. Made in three styles finish, as follows. Weight, 14 ozs.

No. 10K4940 Plain Steel Finish. Price, per dozen, $1.25; each 13c
No. 10K4941 Rustless. Galvanized steel. Price, per dozen, $1.87; each 18c
No. 10K4943 Bon Ton. Oxidized finish. Price, per dozen, $2.00; each 19c
If by mail, postage extra, each, 18 cents.

Our Reform Curry Comb.

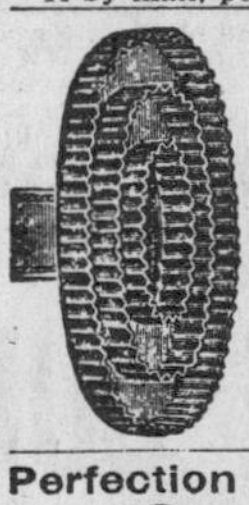

No. 10K4946 Our Reform Curry Comb is perfectly self cleaning, has no place for the hair to lodge, and requires but a gentle tap on its face to rid it of all dirt. Steel comb, with leather handle. Weight, 7 ounces.
Price, per dozen, $1.70; each 15c
If by mail, postage extra, 10 cents.

Perfection Steel Curry Combs.

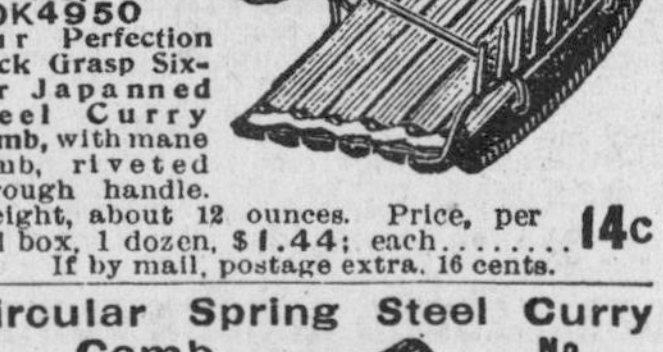

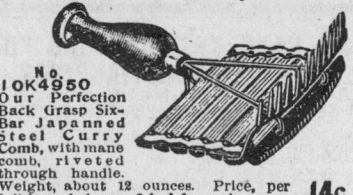

No. 10K4950 Our Perfection Back Grasp Six-Bar Japanned Steel Curry Comb, with mane comb, riveted through handle. Weight, about 12 ounces. Price, per full box, 1 dozen, $1.44; each 14c
If by mail, postage extra, 16 cents.

Circular Spring Steel Curry Comb.

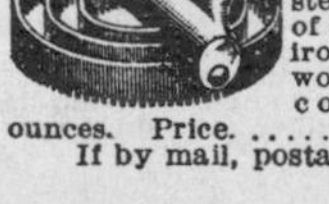

No. 10K4960 Circular Spring Steel Curry Comb. Three complete circles of steel, working independent of each other, attached to an iron back by a hinge joint; wood handle, a good solid comb. Weight, 10 ounces. Price 12c
If by mail, postage extra, 14 cents.

The Martin Wizard

THE WORLD'S GREATEST SHEARING AND CLIPPING MACHINES

MARTIN SHEEP SHEARING AND HORSE CLIPPING MACHINES so far excel all other shearing or clipping machines upon the market that to compare a Martin Machine with any other made, regardless of name, make or price, is like comparing a corn cultivator with a hoe, a modern reaper with a scythe.

THERE IS NO COMPARISON. Our genuine Martin Machines are really cheaper at double our price than any other machine on the market would be if sold at $5.00.

YOU CAN PROVE TO YOURSELF the immense superiority of the Martin Machines. Just send us an order for a Martin Wizard at $18.75, then order any other sheep shearing machine on the market at any price, of any make, with the other machine adjusted to shear an angora goat and attempt to remove the fleece. Then adjust it in any way you like, or any way the manufacturers tell you and try to shear a heavy wooled rambouillet, or better still, a Spanish merino, and note results. If you have ever tried it you know that there is not a machine on the market, except the Martin Wizard, that will do it.

THEN IN ALL FAIRNESS do the same thing with the Martin Wizard. That will tell our story mighty quick. The Martin Wizard will cut the wool by a clean scissor like cut, not depending upon terrific tension like the grinding machines. It will shear an angora goat, or the rambouillet, or Spanish merino, with perfect ease; it requires so little tension and runs so easily that a child can operate it (for instance, read this letter. We have hundreds like it).

Medford, Wisconsin.

Sears, Roebuck & Co., Chicago, Ill.

The Martin Sheep Shearing Machine is the best machine I have ever used. It works excellently. A child ten years old can turn it. We would not be without it.

(Signed) W. H. ZABEL.

OUR GREAT FREE TRIAL OFFER

SEND US AN ORDER for any one of our Martin Sheep Shearing Machines or Martin Horse Clippers. Include the price, whatever it may be, and we will send you the machine ordered, with the perfect understanding and agreement that it must reach you promptly, in perfect condition, that you can give it a fair trial, that if it doesn't prove perfectly satisfactory, that if it isn't better than any other machine on the market, that if it will not convince you that it will save its own cost in the first shearing in the difference in the cost of labor, and in the extra amount of wool that you will get as compared with any other machine made; if you are not convinced that the Martin Machine is cheaper at double our price than any other machine on the market would be at any price; in short, if you are not convinced that it is the only real shearing or clipping machine made, you can (we will expect you to, and, in short, we want you to) return the machine to us at our expense, and we will immediately refund your money, together with all freight charges that you have paid, and the free trial offer will not have cost you one cent. Ask any other sheep shearing machine manufacturer, dealer, firm or individual if they will let you try one of their machines on the same liberal terms. If they won't, they show a lack of confidence in their own machine; if they will, just order one of theirs from them and order the Martin from us. Try them side by side and return the machine that does not prove to be the best.

WHY AND HOW THESE WONDERFUL MARTIN MACHINES CAME INTO EXISTENCE

THOMAS A. MARTIN, the inventor of the Martin Shearing and Clipping Machines, has lived all his life in the great Northwest, where individual flocks of sheep of ten to fifty thousand were quite the common thing and are by no means scarce today. Mr. Martin has all his life been associated with the sheep industry and knows the hardships and difficulties that the sheep shearer had to contend with.

INNUMERABLE ATTEMPTS had been made for years to devise a machine that would satisfactorily shear all kinds of sheep, a machine that would be economical in the saving of wool, could be operated easily and would shear fast so as to minimize the cost of labor in shearing. Hundreds of machines were devised. Out of the hundreds perhaps a dozen were manufactured and put upon the market. None of them had ever proved satisfactory, and Mr. Martin, who devoted his time to shearing sheep during the shearing season, experienced the same trouble, disappointment and discouragement caused by these machines that everyone else had experienced. He knew and appreciated the absolute necessity of a machine that would do the work economically and quickly; he also knew to his sorrow that none of the machines on the market were satisfactory; that while some of them would shear a sheep after a fashion, they were one and all extremely crude. One machine would shear a few sheep and then become dull and useless another would take so much power to run it that it was impractical; another would literally shake itself to pieces; another would run so hot that it would actually burn the hand, and some were so dangerous that they would oftentimes kill the sheep. Once in a while one would be found that would shear a heavy wool, but not fine; none of them would work in dirty wool, and none would work in a fleece grown sheep.

MR. MARTIN HAPPENED TO BE MORE THAN A SHEEPMAN; he was also a first class mechanic, endowed with more than ordinary genius, and out of the shearing season owned and ran a machine shop. He realized the ever increasing demand for a satisfactory sheep shearing machine, and knew the enormous success with which such a machine would meet. Being familiar as he was with all the machines on the market, knowing just what was needed, and, above all, being a first class mechanic, he spent several years in experimenting, building machine after machine, trying each one in the field, correcting this and that little difficulty, until finally in 1887 he made application for and was granted a patent on what proved to be the only satisfactory sheep shearing machine that had ever been made up to that time. Every other machine on the market then and now ground the wool off instead of cutting it.

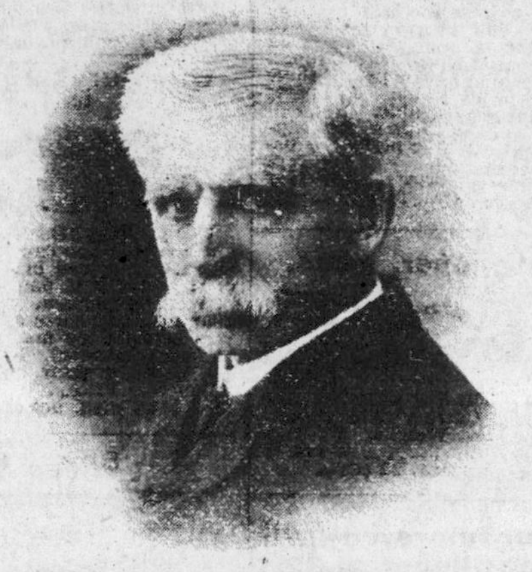

THOMAS A. MARTIN

MR. MARTIN'S MACHINE CUT, and it cut because Mr. Martin never lost sight of the fact that the grinding or chewing principle would never prove satisfactory, at least not in the form in which it was applied by all other manufacturers, which was fundamentally wrong. When we stop and think of the matter the absurdity of it can readily be seen. In spite of this fact, however, every machine on the market today, except the Martin Wizard, grinds or literally chews the wool off, the shearing mechanism being two steel plates, one pressing flat upon the other, and enormous tension applied to the cutter by the thumbscrew situated above the cutter. The very method of applying this tension in itself invited trouble. To make this type of machine shear at all the cutter would have to be screwed down to the comb so tightly that the wool would simply not pass between the two, thus literally grinding or chewing the wool off instead of cutting it.

NO BETTER CUTTING DEVICE has ever been invented than the principle in an ordinary pair of scissors. Mr. Martin realized this and it remained for him to apply the cutting principle of the ordinary scissors to a sheep shearing machine. It required years of experimenting and research and he finally succeeded, and it is that principle that makes the Martin Wizard the only real shearing machine on the market. It is by far the simplest machine manufactured, and will shear the finest wooled cashmere goat and the heaviest wooled Spanish merino or rambouillet with equal ease.

SHEAR YOUR FLOCK WITH ANY OTHER SHEEP SHEARING MACHINE MADE, then let us take the Martin Wizard and go over the same flock, and we will take from one-half to three-quarters of a pound more wool off of every sheep, which would be left on by any other sheep shearing machine made, and, mark you, we will complete this shearing in one-third of the time it takes to do it with any other sheep shearing machine made. (Witness this letter to substantiate our statement):

Iola, Illinois.

Sears, Roebuck & Co., Chicago, Ill.

I believe the Martin Sheep Shearing Machine is the best out. It can shear as fast as I can handle the sheep; shears the closest of any machine I have ever used; does not get out of order or choke up.

(Signed) E. L. CRUSE.

SHEAR YOUR SHEEP BY HAND and we will go over the same flock in one-tenth of the time, and get one pound to a pound and a half more wool from every sheep. Just figure this saving alone.

HERE IS WHAT THE MARTIN SHEEP SHEARING MACHINE WILL SAVE YOU IF YOU OWN 200 HEAD OF SHEEP.

THIS MACHINE WON'T COST YOU A CENT. Instead it will actually show a net profit, the amount of that profit depending upon the size of your flock. Let us suppose that your flock is small, consisting, say, of only 200 head. Compared with the cost of hand shearing, the saving made by a Martin Sheep Shearing Machine would appear in this manner:

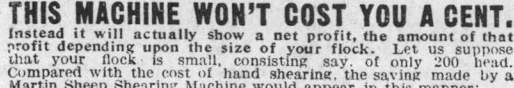

To shearing 200 sheep by hand at 15 cents each	$30.00
To shearing 200 sheep with the Martin Wizard (two men one and one-half days at $2.50 per day each)	7.50
Saving in labor	$22.50
To one pound more wool off of each sheep, 200 pounds in all, at 25 cents per lb.	50.00
Total saving	$72.50

THIS SHOWS YOU A CLEAR PROFIT OF $72.50, or over 35 cents apiece for every sheep you own. The Martin Standard Sheep Shearing Machine will cost you $12.75, the Martin Wizard, $18.75. Thus the net profit to you, if the shearing were done with a Martin Wizard will be $53.75. You will not be able to work quite so fast with the Martin Standard, and the profit will not, perhaps, be over $40.00, but that is big extra money—more than you can make with any other sheep shearing machine made.

ACCEPT OUR GREAT FREE OFFER of a trial of either one of these machines, and prove that our statement is correct. If it isn't, ship them back under the terms of our great free offer, previously explained.

WHY WE BUILD TWO SHEEP SHEARING MACHINES

WE HAVE TWO REASONS FOR OFFERING TWO STYLES OF SHEEP SHEARING MACHINES. First, our knowledge and experience gained through years of selling machinery tell us that two classes or styles of machines are absolutely necessary to satisfy all of our customers. Some of them want and are satisfied with a machine that requires little or no mechanical knowledge—a machine that is set up in our factory ready to operate, and that positively cannot get out of order. Another class of our customers want the highest grade of machine they can buy, and to such a machine they are willing to give the attention that any finely constructed machine requires. They appreciate the fact and know that to manufacture such a machine requires the application of mechanical principles that make it necessary to give it more or less care and attention; but, because of the superior work and service that they can obtain from such a machine they are more than willing to pay the extra price.

OUR SECOND REASON FOR MANUFACTURING AND OFFERING TWO MACHINES is that Mr. Martin has, to our mind, developed in his Martin Standard Sheep Shearing Machine one that is little short of marvelous in its simplicity and efficiency, that (excepting only the Martin Wizard) it is the best sheep shearing machine in the world, barring none; that it is miles ahead of any other machine manufactured, regardless of name, make or price (excepting only the Martin Wizard); that we have in the Martin Wizard the highest class, the best sheep shearing machine in the world; that in the Martin Standard we have (excepting the Martin Wizard) the best sheep shearing machine in the world. We thus not only have the best sheep shearing machine in the world to offer you, but also the second best machine in the world, and any other machine offered you by any firm or individual, regardless of name, make or price, is inferior to either of these machines and must become a third rate machine as compared with these two wonderful Martin Machines.

ANYONE WITHOUT MECHANICAL KNOWLEDGE OR INGENUITY, anyone who has not the facilities and does not care to give a fine piece of machinery only ordinary attention, anyone who wants the most simple, who wants a machine that is less liable to get out of order, requires less adjustment, less mechanical attention than any other sheep shearing machine in the world and a machine that (excepting only the Martin Wizard) will shear faster, easier, smoother, better than any other machine, and anyone who has never become accustomed to running the machines, or who wants a machine that requires absolutely no attention, WE MOST URGENTLY ADVISE TO BUY A MARTIN STANDARD.

THE MARTIN WIZARD, the highest grade machine we make, stands in a class by itself, and embodies mechanical principles not found in any other sheep shearing machine made. To anyone who will give a fine piece of machinery only reasonably fair care and attention, to anyone who wants the best sheep shearing machine in the world, barring none, a machine that will shear closer, faster, with less power, the easiest running machine in the world, we unqualifiedly urge them to buy the Martin Wizard.

BUT, IN JUSTICE TO OURSELVES, and in justice to this wonderful mechanical device, and especially out of consideration for our customers, WE BELIEVE IT OUR DUTY, unless you are prepared to give this wonderful piece of mechanical mechanism reasonable care and attention, unless you are prepared and willing to give it the adjustment that it requires (which is very simple), to say to you that it is not the machine for you to buy. On the other hand, if you want the best machine in the world, and are willing to give it the care and attention that the best machine in the world should have, order it by all means. Lack of space does not permit us going into detail for our reasons regarding this matter, but they are fully explained in our Special Sheep Shearing Machine Catalogue, which will be sent you free if you want additional information.

MARTIN HORSE CLIPPERS. What we have said regarding the Martin Wizard and Martin Standard Sheep Shearing Machines will apply with equal force to the wonderful Martin Wizard and Martin Standard Horse Clippers that we show pages 144 and 145.

Wizard Sheep Shearing Machine $18.75

THE WIZARD SHEEP SHEARING MACHINE PAYS FOR ITSELF

AND NETS YOU A PROFIT OF SEVERAL TIMES THE COST OF THE MACHINE BESIDES, THE FIRST SEASON, IN COST OF LABOR AND VALUE OF EXTRA WOOL PROCURED. DON'T WASTE TIME AND MONEY IN CLIPPING YOUR SHEEP BY HAND

THIS MACHINE COSTS YOU NOTHING, as explained on the opposite page. Observe our figures showing that you can save $72.50 the first season on a flock of 200 sheep, as against the hand shears method, saving almost four times the price of the machine. Even with 100 sheep it will pay for itself about twice over; thus not only costing you nothing but netting you a substantial profit.

THE MARTIN WIZARD IS IN A CLASS BY ITSELF. No other machine on the market can compare with it in the amount of work it will do and the speed with which it will perform its work under all conditions. With it you can shear the heaviest wooled Spanish Merino with perfect ease. It won't clog, no matter how greasy the wool or how fast you shear. It cuts faster than you can handle the sheep and never needs to be forced through the wool. It shears every part of the sheep, leaving no part to be finished with the hand shears, from the heaviest matted wool on the brisket to the fine wool around the head. It makes an absolutely complete and perfect job. We have the utmost confidence in the Martin Wizard and predict that every wide awake sheep man in the United States will be using the Wizard Machine inside of five years. We will be more than pleased to ship this machine on our free trial plan as explained on the opposite page.

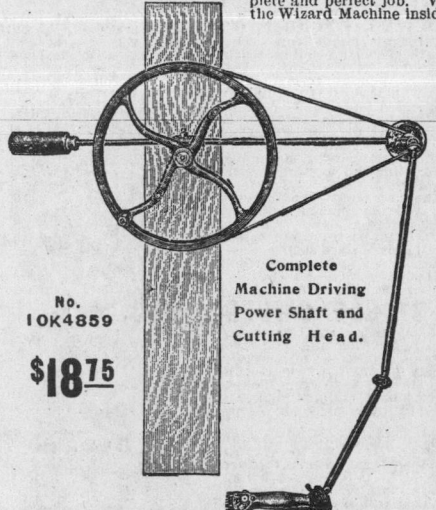

No. 10K4859

Complete Machine Driving Power Shaft and Cutting Head.

$18.75

THE QUALITY AND CONSTRUCTION OF THE MARTIN WIZARD. Nothing but the very best qualities of material and the finest expert labor enter into the Martin Wizard construction. We know the American farmer insists on getting the best, because it pays in the long run; we know that on the successful operation and the lasting qualities of our machine depends our entire sheep shearing machine business, and we have spared no expense to insure that only the best material and most perfect workmanship are put into it. The large balance wheel is made from specially toughened iron carefully turned in the lathe to secure accuracy and free running. It is mounted on Bessemer steel roller bearings of our own design which are guaranteed to run easier and wear longer than any ball bearing or any other roller bearing in the world. The bearings and shaftings are machined true to 1-1000 part of an inch. All shafting is specially cold rolled steel carefully case hardened by the cyanide process, insuring long life and easy running. The frame is the best wrought tubing. The shaft and casing the finest cold drawn steel tubing. All gears are cut from a solid bar of steel and each tooth milled separately and accurately. The cutter levers or the part carrying the upper knives is manganese bronze, with a tensile strength of 65,000 pounds to the inch. This material costs ten times as much as steel, only being used up to the present time on exclusively high priced machinery such as automobiles, etc. No other sheep shearing machine on the market contains it. The comb and cutter, the most important parts of a shearing machine are the best imported Swedish razor steel, far superior to any other knives on the market, specially tempered by our own process and ground absolutely perfect to 1-5000 part of an inch. Many of our customers write and tell us they shear as high as 80 to 100 head without changing knives. 40 head is, however, a fair average.

THE MARTIN WIZARD is the only machine based on absolutely correct principles. The cutting device is patterned after the ordinary pair of scissors. There being no better cutting device than scissors was ever invented. The Martin Wizard cutting device cuts the wool fiber with a clear scissors-like motion, just as your hand shears do it, only that it cuts with a marvelous speed, there being 1,600 strokes to the minute. Furthermore, the comb has sixteen perfect cutting edges, each one corresponding to one side of your hand shears, making eight perfect pairs of shears. The upper cutter consists of two prongs so gauged as to fit perfectly in between the cutting edges of the comb. Mark this! It is between and not on top of. Every time they travel across the comb, they drop in between the cutting edges and are brought against the cutting edge of each of the cutting edges with a drawing scissors-like motion which cuts the fiber. Thus, you have in effect eight pairs of hand shears, cutting each of the 1,600 times the cutters cross the comb, making 12,800 perfect, clean, scissors-like cuts a minute. So you see how it is impossible to clog the Wizard. Besides, as the knives are guarded, it is impossible either to cut yourself or to injure the sheep. Every experienced sheep shearer who has used hand shears knows how frequently sheep are injured in cutting with the hand shears. The Wizard way is the humane way to shear sheep.

THE WIZARD IS THE EASIEST RUNNING SHEEP SHEARING MACHINE ever invented and absolutely noiseless. It saves its cost almost the first day in the saving in cost of labor alone. Two men can easily shear 150 head a day. At $2.25 a day this makes your shearing cost but 3 cents a head; hand sheep shearing costs 12 to 15 cents a head, and adding the extra wool you get in using the Martin Wizard, it runs your saving up to over the cost of the machine and makes you a clear net profit. You certainly cannot afford to be without the Martin Wizard or afford to invest in any other type of machine.

Side View of the Famous Cutting Head of the Martin Wizard Sheep Shearing Machine.

SATISFACTION OR MONEY REFUNDED.

That means exactly what it says. We absolutely guarantee that the Martin Wizard will do everything that a perfect sheep shearing machine can do. We guarantee it against defects in material and workmanship. We guarantee that you will find it a satisfactory and profitable investment, and if you do not find it to be all of these things we want you to return it and get your money back as well as all transportation charges you may have paid.

No. 10K4860 Martin Wizard Driving Power with Martin Standard Head, ready to attach to post or wall. Price..........**$15.75**
No. 10K4863 Comb Guard Attachment for the Wizard Head, enabling the shearer to leave from 1/4 to 3/4 of an inch of wool on the sheep's back to protect it from the sun. Price..........**1.00**

No. 10K4859 The Martin Wizard Sheep Shearing Machine, complete, ready to attach to post. Weight, packed ready for shipment, 85 pounds. Price. **$18.75**
No. 10K4864 Martin Wizard Sheep Shearing Head, with extra comb and cutter. Price..........**$9.50**

EXTRA COMBS AND CUTTERS.
No. 6 Comb or Under Plate. Price..........75c
No. 7 Cutter or Upper Plate. Price..........35c

MARTIN STANDARD SHEEP SHEARING MACHINE, $12.75

WITH THE SINGLE EXCEPTION OF THE MARTIN WIZARD (ABOVE ILLUSTRATED AND DESCRIBED) THE MARTIN STANDARD IS ABSOLUTELY THE HIGHEST GRADE, STRONGEST, SIMPLEST, EASIEST RUNNING, CLOSEST CUTTING AND MOST PERFECT WORKING MACHINE EVER PRODUCED

No. 10K4857

$12.75

YOU CAN GET THE MARTIN STANDARD ABSOLUTELY FREE, simply because it pays for itself several times over on the first day's work it does for you. It will pay for itself in the extra wool you get off the first 50 sheep you shear and there is a saving of labor to consider as well, because any inexperienced man can shear anywhere from 75 to 150 sheep per day. Think of it! What a wonderful saving this is against the hand shearing method, and certainly no other sheep shearing machine (except only our Wizard) can compare with it for effective and rapid work. Don't leave the best part of the fleece on the sheep's back. Get a record breaking clip this year by using one of our machines. Figure this for yourself; the first 50 sheep you shear will pay for the machine and leave you a handsome profit. You will get 75 to 100 pounds more wool off the first 50 sheep. At 25 cents per pound, this means $19.00 to $25.00 in extra money, and our price is but $12.75.

READ HOW THIS MACHINE IS CONSTRUCTED. All heavy parts are made from special gray iron exceedingly tough and strong. SHAFTS are cold rolled steel carefully case hardened by the cyanide process, insuring long wear and perfect bearings. GEARS are not cast as many others are but are all cut from solid bar steel, each tooth milled separately and accurately. COMBS AND CUTTERS are the finest Swedish razor steel carefully tempered and ground by our secret process, insuring not only a perfect cutting edge, but enabling them to outwear any other comb ever manufactured. It cuts on the same principle as the Martin Wizard and embodies many of the fine features of that wonderful machine. In fact, the Martin Standard is second only in mechanical perfection to the wonderful Martin Wizard. Any other machine on the market is a third rate machine as compared with these two machines. It is so simple and easy to run that a twelve-year old boy can turn it. You cannot injure or cut yourself or the sheep. You take no chances whatever with the Martin Standard. While running at full speed the wear of the comb and cutter can be taken up. There is no cumbersome mechanism or adjusting above the comb and cutter; neither sand nor dirt can enter the working parts.

SEND TODAY FOR THE MARTIN STANDARD ON OUR GUARANTEE PLAN. We guarantee to satisfy you or refund your money, both price and any transportation charges you paid. Stop losing money, stop wasting money, stop wearing yourself out by using the slow hand shears, and save labor and money by letting this machine do your work.

WHY WE SELL THESE MACHINES AT SUCH A LOW PRICE. If you could buy a machine equal to the Standard at a dealer's, it would cost you at least $25.00, because it would have added to it many selling expenses and profits which would amount to more than the original cost of manufacturing the machine. When you buy from us, you get all the best of it and save money by getting these machines on the same basis as you get all the rest of our merchandise from us. We ask you to pay us just the actual manufacturing cost with but one very small margin of profit added. Whatever you pay, over and above our price, for other machines, is an absolute loss to you; and furthermore, it does not bring you as good a machine. Our selling methods enable you to get the best machines at away less than what the imperfect machines on the market would cost you. Remember, we guarantee to satisfy you or refund your money.

Side View of the Martin Standard Shearing Head.

No. 10K4857 The Martin Standard Sheep Shearing Machine, complete, ready to operate and ready to attach to post or wall. Weight, packed for shipment, about 70 pounds. Price..........**$12.75**
No. 10K4858 Martin Standard Sheep Shearing Head with extra Comb and Cutter. Price..........**$7.00**
EXTRA COMBS AND CUTTERS.
No. 310 Cutter or Upper Plate. Price, each..........50c
No. 311 Comb or Under Plate. Price, each..........80c

THE Martin Wizard Ball Bearing Horse Clipper $14.95 REDUCED FROM $16.95

FARMERS AND LIVERY STABLE OWNERS, ALL OWNERS OF HORSES, HERE IS A GREAT MONEY SAVER, A GREAT LABOR SAVER FOR YOU. BLACKSMITHS AND OTHERS WHO MAKE A BUSINESS OF CLIPPING HORSES, HERE IS A BIG MONEY MAKER FOR YOU

THE MARTIN WIZARD MARKS A NEW ERA IN HORSE CLIPPERS. It has made a revolution in the field of horse clipping. Like our Martin Wizard Sheep Shearing Machine, it is radically different from all other machines and is in a class by itself. It is years in advance of any other make on the market. **It clips closer, runs easier, faster, smoother and at less than half the expense of any other machine.**

IT PAYS FOR ITSELF IN THE COST OF CUTTERS ALONE. Few cutters of other machines cost less than $1.00 each; many cost more. Their construction is expensive; but cutters for the Wizard cost only $2.25 per dozen, $1.25 per half dozen, 25 cents each; or from one-sixth to one-fourth as much as others. In this item alone you make enough to save the cost of this machine.

LEADING AUTHORITIES ON LIVE STOCK agree that clipping is decidedly beneficial to the horse. It is now so thoroughly established that it is hardly necessary to mention it; but as some horse owners may not have given the subject any particular attention, we will mention a few points for your information:

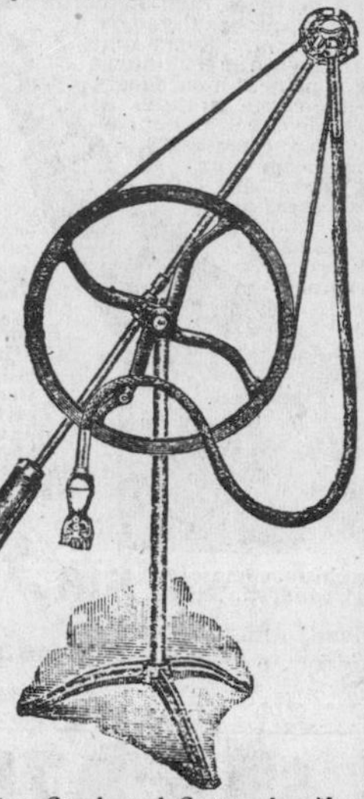

MANY DISEASES TO WHICH HORSES ARE SUBJECT are due to their perspiring freely when hard worked and then standing for hours at a time in their wet, soggy coats of hair. They catch cold and this rapidly leads to pneumonia, rheumatism, distemper, or some other of the scores of complications. Clipping insures against such conditions. It is humane to thus make your horse free from such conditions and make him comfortable, as well as a good business proposition from your standpoint. You will get more work out of him and prevent the expense of veterinary surgeons' bills. Remember the old saying, "An ounce of prevention is worth a pound of cure."

THE CLIPPED HORSE IS A WELL HORSE that does his work well, is always up and coming; he is free from perspiration, which always makes him uncomfortable and eventually chills him. He digests his food better and gets the benefit of all he eats. He will not waste his food. A clipped horse dries out rapidly after a hard day's work; he rests more comfortably at night and comes to his work refreshed the following day. As an experienced owner of horses, you know, and it stands to reason, that the horse with a thick coat of hair, wet and soggy with perspiration, **does not get a comfortable night's rest** in the stable, especially in the cool spring nights, and cannot therefore be as refreshed as a clipped horse. You can see clearly how he is liable to be seized with disease.

THERE IS PLEASURE IN RIDING BEHIND A CLIPPED HORSE, as he does not shed his hair. You have never the experience of getting horse hair in your mouth, or having your clothing covered with dead hair, from which nature is trying to relieve the animal. The clipped horse is in the pink of condition, bright, fresh and spunky and travels beautifully. **Assist nature;** clip your horse and keep him comfortable; enjoy your drive; protect him against disease, and you will never have any trouble with him.

Extra Comb and Cutter for Martin Wizard Horse Clipping Machine:

No. 56 Comb and Bottom Plate. Price, each........$1.50
No. 57 Top Cutter. Price, each........ .25
No. 68 Martin Wizard Head. Price........ 7.50

THE MARTIN WIZARD is absolutely the highest grade horse clipper on the market. We are willing to have you test this on our free trial plan. We guarantee it runs easier, cuts faster and smoother, and does more beautiful work than any other machine invented. If it does not do just as we claim upon a fair trial, we ask you to return it to us at our expense and we will refund the price and any transportation charges you paid.

HOW THE WIZARD IS MADE. All heavy parts are made of our special extra tough iron. The frame is the best wrought pipe, which never breaks or wears out. The large **balance wheel** is mounted on Bessemer steel rolls of our special design, without question the easiest running, longest wearing bearing in the world. The small transmission pinions are made of the finest cold rolled steel, cut from a solid bar and hardened by the cyanide process. This machine has ball bearings of our own patented design and is exceptionally easy running and noiseless. **The shaft** is made of the best Bessemer steel wire and covered with our specially woven braided fabric. **The head of the Wizard** is in itself a real marvel. Instead of having innumerable teeth, there are but two suspended from a common axis, thus always equalizing the pressure. Both **comb and cutter** are made of the finest Swedish razor steel, carefully tempered and ground. They are constructed to do twice the work of ordinary clippers, and the machine will pay for itself many times over in the saving of repairs alone. The top cutters cost but 25 cents each, while others cost from four to six times that price and are inferior to our Martin Wizard cutter. Consider the make and quality of this machine; compare it with what you know of other machines, consider our low price—only $14.95, and let us send you this machine on our free trial plan.

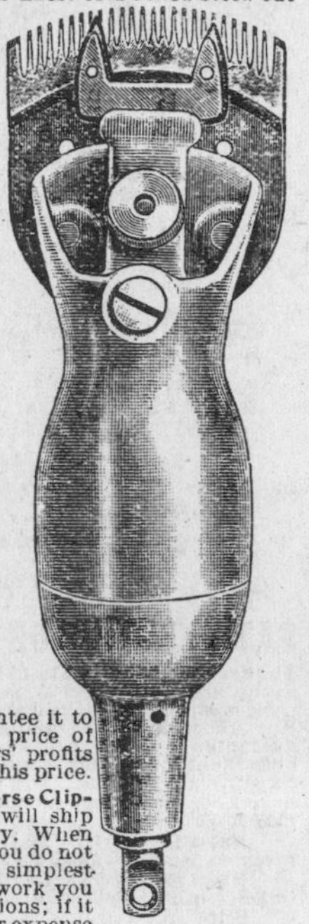

Top Vew of Cutting Head of Martin Wizard Horse Clipper.

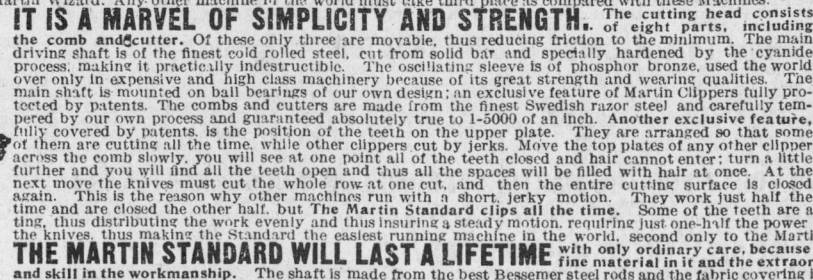

ARE YOU A LIVERY STABLE OWNER or a farmer, or do you own a number of horses? Remember, the regular price for clipping horses is $2.50 each and you save that much on each horse by buying this clipper. You can see how very quickly this machine will pay for itself. Even if you are the owner of but one horse, it will save you money because it saves you the cost of the job of clipping, makes a cleaner and more perfect job than any other machine; keeps your horse well and free from all disorders.

ARE YOU A BLACKSMITH or do you clip horses for profit? With the Wizard Machine you can clip faster and easier than with any other machine known. You can clip for $1.50 to $2.00 per horse; thus cutting the regular price and earn more than you can with any other machine per day at that. This will give you all the business in your locality and make the Wizard a big paying proposition for you. With a boy helper you can clip from six to eight horses a day easily and make from $10.00 to $20.00 per day.

OUR PRICE represents just the actual manufacturing cost and one small margin of profit. Don't imagine because the price is only $14.95 that it cannot be as good as the machines offered for fancy prices elsewhere. Remember, we guarantee it to be the best machine on the market regardless of name, make or price of other machines. If sold on the usual basis where agents' or dealers' profits and expenses would be added, it would cost you more than double this price.

OUR GUARANTEE Ask for No. 10K4874 Martin Wizard Horse Clipper, enclose our price, $14.95, and we will ship the machine strongly and carefully boxed, guaranteeing safe delivery. When received, take it out to your stable, put it into operation, and if you do not find it the easiest running, fastest and smoothest cutting and the simplest machine that you know of; if it does not do the most beautiful work you ever saw, or if it in any way does not measure up to your expectations; if it is not all that we claim for it, we want you to return it to us at our expense and we will refund to you both the price and any transportation charges you paid on it.

No. 10K4874 The Martin Wizard Horse Clipper complete with stand (as illustrated). Price........ **$14.95**

No. 10K4880 The Martin Wizard Power, with Martin Standard Clipping Head. Price........$14.25

Weight, packed for shipment, about 100 pounds.

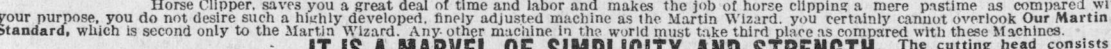

$10.75 THE MARTIN STANDARD BALL BEARING HORSE CLIPPER

SECOND ONLY TO THE MARTIN WIZARD THE MARTIN STANDARD BALL BEARING HORSE CLIPPER IS THE STRONGEST, FASTEST CUTTING, EASIEST RUNNING AND THE MOST PERFECT WORKING HORSE CLIPPING MACHINE YOU CAN BUY.

WHILE WE SPECIALLY RECOMMEND THE MARTIN WIZARD Ball Bearing Horse Clipper, above illustrated and described, because its fine high class mechanism enables you to do the finest work ever done by any Horse Clipper, saves you a great deal of time and labor and makes the job of horse clipping a mere pastime as compared with the work of other machines, yet, if for your purpose, you do not desire such a highly developed, finely adjusted machine as the Martin Wizard, you certainly cannot overlook **Our Martin Standard,** which is second only to the Martin Wizard. Any other machine in the world must take third place as compared with these Machines.

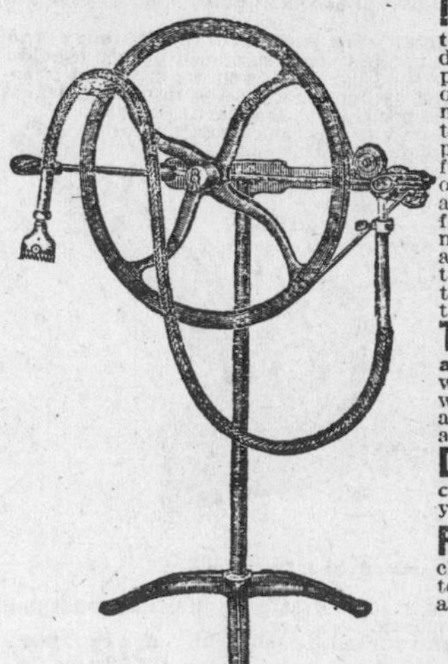

IT IS A MARVEL OF SIMPLICITY AND STRENGTH. The cutting head consists of eight parts, including **the comb and cutter.** Of these only three are movable, thus reducing friction to the minimum. The main driving shaft is of the finest cold rolled steel, cut from solid bar and specially hardened by the cyanide process, making it practically indestructible. The oscillating sleeve is of phosphor bronze, used the world over only in expensive and high class machinery because of its great strength and wearing qualities. The main shaft is mounted on ball bearings of our own design; an exclusive feature of Martin Clippers fully protected by patents. The combs and cutters are made from the finest Swedish razor steel and carefully tempered by our own process and guaranteed absolutely true to 1-5000 of an inch. **Another exclusive feature,** fully covered by patents, is the position of the teeth on the upper plate. They are arranged so that some of them are cutting all the time, while other clippers cut by jerks. Move the top plates of any other clipper across the comb slowly, you will see at one point all of the teeth closed and hair cannot enter; turn a little further and you will find all the teeth open and thus all the spaces will be filled with hair at once. At the next move the knives must cut the whole row at one cut, and then the entire cutting surface is closed again. This is the reason why other machines run with a short, jerky motion. They work just half the time and are closed the other half, but **The Martin Standard clips all the time.** Some of the teeth are always cutting, thus distributing the work evenly and thus insuring a steady motion, requiring just one-half the power to operate the knives, thus making the Standard the easiest running machine in the world, second only to the Martin Wizard.

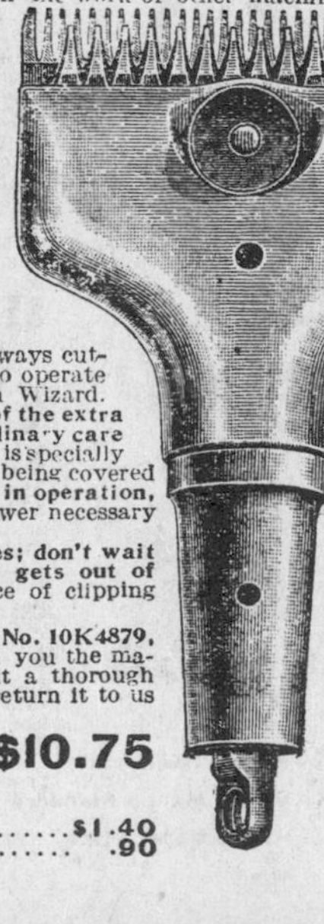

Top View of Cutting Head of the Martin Standard Horse Clipper.

THE MARTIN STANDARD WILL LAST A LIFETIME with only ordinary care, because of the extra fine material in it and the extraordinary care and skill in the workmanship. The shaft is made from the best Bessemer steel rods and the fabric covering it is specially woven for us by one of the largest eastern mills. It is a beautifully finished, fine appearing machine, the head being covered with heavy nickel plated copper and the frame finished with our specially air dried enamel. **It is noiseless in operation,** as there are no gears to rust and break. The machine runs so easily that a light belt transmits all the power necessary and the belt never slips.

DON'T FORGET THAT CLIPPING YOUR HORSE INSURES HIM against diseases; don't wait until the horse gets out of condition before using this method to better his health conditions. If you have not made a practice of clipping your horses, don't let $10.75 stand in your way.

REMEMBER, WE ASK ONLY A FAIR TEST for this machine. Send us your order, ask for No. 10K4879, enclose our price, $10.75, and we will send you the machine, thoroughly well boxed, guaranteeing it to arrive in perfect condition. When you receive it, give it a thorough test, and if you don't find it the best horse clipping machine you ever tried, you are at perfect liberty to return it to us at our expense, and we will refund to you both the price and any transportation charges you paid on it.

No. 10K4879 The Martin Standard Horse Clipper, complete with stand (as illustrated). Price........ **$10.75**

Weight, packed for shipment, about 90 pounds.

Extra Combs and Cutters for Martin Standard Horse Clipping Machine.

No. 206 Comb or Under Plate. Price, each........$1.40
No. 207 Cutter or Upper Plate. Price, each........ .90

Martin Enclosed Gear Horse Clipper

HAND POWER $14.95

IF YOU PREFER A GEARED MACHINE TO THOSE DRIVEN BY BELTS, WE OFFER YOU THIS HIGH GRADE
MARTIN ENCLOSED GEAR MACHINE

THE POWER IN THIS MACHINE is transmitted in the same manner as the power on a chainless bicycle and it runs just as easily. All working parts are enclosed in a dustproof case and run in hard oil and graphite. The large gear is made of our special tough iron with chilled surface, making it practically everlasting. The small pinions are cut from a solid bar of steel; each tooth milled separately to insure accuracy, and hardened by the cyanide process. The casing is of fine grained gray iron and the entire machine is finished with our specially air dried enamel. The small balance wheel serves to steady the motion of the machine and insures a steady, even motion. The shaft is made from Bessemer steel wire and is covered with our specially braided fabric.

WE EQUIP THESE MACHINES with either our Martin Standard or Martin Wizard Head, the same heads as shown on the preceding page. If you have much clipping to do you should buy this machine by all means. It will pay for itself many times over and will last a lifetime. We offer it on the same liberal guarantee as we do our other horse clipping and sheep shearing machines. When you receive this machine and give it a fair test and it does not give you the best of satisfaction, does not prove itself to be the best Horse Clipping Machine on the market, you are perfectly at liberty to return it to us at our expense and we will refund you both the price and any transportation charges you paid.

No. 10K4893 Martin Enclosed Gear Horse Clipper on stand (as illustrated) with Martin Wizard Head and extra comb and cutter. Price $18.75
No. 10K4898 Martin Enclosed Gear Horse Clipper with Martin Standard Head, extra comb and cutter. Price 14.95
Weight of each of the above outfits packed ready for shipment, about 90 pounds.
For prices on Heads and extra Combs and Cutters, see opposite page.

No. 10K4898
PRICE,
$14.95

FACE PLATE TO SHARPEN COMBS AND CUTTERS.
No. 10K4861 This is a specially prepared face plate with which anyone can sharpen the teeth or the comb and cutter of any of our sheep shearing machines or horse clippers. It gives a true, even surface. Do not put clipper plates of any kind on a grindstone or emery wheel, as it will spoil them. One Martin Face Plate and small box of emery powder with full directions. Price.......................$2.00

COMB GUARD.
No. 10K4863 This is a guard to be fastened to our Martin Wizard Sheep Shearing Machine to regulate the length of stubble, enabling the shearer to leave from one-quarter to three-quarters of an inch of wool on the sheep's back, so as to protect it from the sun. Price.................$1.00

$6.45 BUYS THE SHARP HORSE CLIPPER

GUARANTEED THE BEST LITTLE HORSE CLIPPER ON THE MARKET, BETTER THAN ANY OTHER MACHINE OF OTHER MAKES MADE TO SELL AT AS HIGH AS $10.00

AT $6.45 WE OFFER YOU A MACHINE, our Sharp Horse Clipper, made in our Martin Horse Clipping and Sheep Shearing Machine factory, and embodying many of the best principles of our higher grade machines, and which will do a finer class of work than any machine offered elsewhere for $10.00. We offer it on the same liberal terms as those on which we offer the Martin Wizard and Martin Standard Horse Clippers. You can give it a fair and thorough test. If it does not prove itself to be the best little horse clipper in existence, you are perfectly at liberty to return it to us at our expense and we will refund your money.

THE SHARP HORSE CLIPPER IS AN ENCLOSED GEAR MACHINE. The frame is so constructed as to enable it to be taken apart easily and packed in a case for traveling, and adjustable so that it can be raised or lowered as desired by the party turning the machine. The power is transmitted from the enclosed gear to the cutting head through our flexible shaft. The flexible shaft is made of the best Bessemer steel wire and the casing is a woven fabric providing ample protection. The knives are made of Swedish steel and the head is constructed to prevent interference from the accumulation of dust, dirt or hair. The bearings run in oil. It embodies many of the general principles of our Martin Wizard and Martin Standard Machines, and will do a clean, neat and perfect job.

IF FOR YOUR PURPOSE YOU DO NOT REQUIRE such highly developed and finely constructed machines as either our Martin Wizard or Martin Standard Horse Clippers; if you have not a great deal of horse clipping to do, if you want a practical, perfectly working machine for your own use or if you don't need such speedy machines as our Martin Wizard or Martin Standard, we especially recommend our Little Sharp Horse Clipper. With ordinary care it will last a lifetime. It is strongly constructed, well finished and will do the work required of it easily, smoothly and in a most acceptable manner.

WE WOULD LIKE YOU TO COMPARE the Sharp Horse Clipper with any machine sold for as high as $10.00 or even more, and you will then see the value we are offering in this machine. Machines at about $10.00 elsewhere are very imperfect and impractical machines. They are made largely to sell and without due regard for the purposes for which they are to be used. They are little better than worthless; while in the Sharp Horse Clipper we offer you a tried, tested and proven successful machine and are willing to leave it in your hands to say whether it is what you want or not. If you are not satisfied on giving it a fair test, we want you to return it and we will give you back both the price and any transportation charges you paid.
No. 10K4876 Price for the Little Sharp Horse Clipper, complete, ready to operate.................$6.45
Weight, packed ready for shipment, about 37 pounds.

No. 10K4876
Price,
$6.45

THE MARTIN HAS EVERYTHING THAT MAKES A PERFECT SHEARING MACHINE.
Mount Holly, N. J.
Sears, Roebuck & Co., Chicago, Ill.
Gentlemen:—We have given the Martin Sheep Shearing Machine what we believe to be a fair trial and find it does all you have claimed it will do. We find it will shear as close as can be cut to the skin, leaving nothing but the roots to grow again. We also find it does just as good work in close wool as in open wool, and will cut through all kinds of wool, no matter how greasy or dirty. It shears fast, cuts clean, runs easy; in fact, it has everything that makes a shearing machine perfect, and we will recommend it to anyone who is in need of such a machine.
Yours truly,   C. F. PARKER.

Kyles, Ohio.
Sears, Roebuck & Co., Chicago, Ill.
Gentlemen:—I received the Martin Horse Clipping Machine and find it satisfactory to me, for it is the very closest clipping machine that I know of and is the safest to use on horses. I consider it the best and it is easy to handle and can clip as fast as I can handle the horse.
Yours truly,   W. H. HARMON.

CUTS FASTER AND CLOSER THAN ANY MACHINE HE HAS EVER USED.
Lewisburg, Tenn.
Sears, Roebuck & Co., Chicago, Ill.
Gentlemen:—I received the Martin Sheep Shearing Machine several days ago and have tested it thoroughly, and find it to be the best machine on the market, simple to operate, does not get out of order, cuts faster and closer than any machine I have ever used and I can recommend it to anyone wanting a good machine.
Yours respectfully,   W. M. BOBO.

Seneca Falls, N. Y.
Sears, Roebuck & Co., Chicago, Ill.
Gentlemen:—The Martin Horse Clipping Machine that I bought of you is first class in every respect and considered by a very prominent dealer in Seneca Falls, who has clipped a hundred horses to my one, to be superior to all others on the market.
Yours very truly,   A. T. DILTS.

THE MARTIN ENCLOSED GEAR SHEEP SHEARING AND HORSE CLIPPING MACHINES
EQUIPPED FOR RUNNING BY POWER.

IF YOU HAVE A GREAT DEAL OF SHEARING TO DO, you will find this machine a splendid investment. We furnish it equipped with either the Martin Wizard Shearing Head or the Martin Standard Shearing Head. Transmission of power is by direct means. It is equipped with tight and loose pulleys. Pulley face 1½ inches, diameter 10 inches. Runs 75 to 100 revolutions per minute. It can be operated with a small electric motor, steam engine, gasoline engine, tread mill, windmill or horse power. It is equipped with brackets enabling you to firmly bolt it to a post or wall.
No. 10K4869 Martin Enclosed Gear Sheep Shearing Machine, equipped with Martin Wizard Shearing Head and extra Comb and Cutter, and tight and loose pulleys. Price.................$21.75
No. 10K4871 Martin Enclosed Gear Sheep Shearing Machine, equipped with Martin Standard Shearing Head and extra Comb and Cutter, and tight and loose pulleys. Price.................17.00
No. 10K4895 Martin Enclosed Gear Horse Clipper with Wizard Head, equipped with tight and loose pulleys for power attachment. Price.................21.57
No. 10K4901 Martin Enclosed Gear Horse Clipper with Martin Standard Head, extra comb and cutter, equipped with tight and loose pulleys for power attachment. Price.................17.00
Weight of each of the above outfits, packed ready for shipment, about 90 pounds.
For price of extra Combs and Cutters, etc., see page 144.

IF YOU WISH CRANK IN ADDITION TO PULLEYS SO YOU CAN TURN BY HAND WHEN DESIRED, ADD $1.00 EXTRA.

HORSE BRUSHES

We guarantee our line of Palmetto, Rice Root and Leather Back Horse Brushes strictly high grade, our bristle brushes the finest and the very best that labor and quality of material can produce.

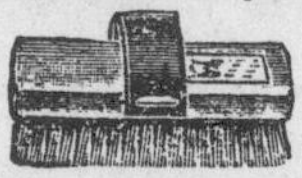

No. 10K5000 Mexican Rice Root Horse Brush, wood back with strap; 3 inches wide and 7 inches long. Weight, 8 ounces. Price........... **8c**
If by mail, postage extra, 12 cents.

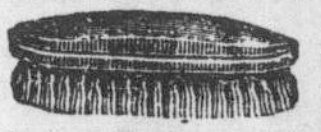

No. 10K5015 Sears, Roebuck & Co.'s India Fiber Horse Brush, wood back, with pointed ends. Fiber 1½ inches long. Size of brush, 2¾ by 10 inches. Weight of brush, 9 ounces. Strictly first class. Price **15c**
If by mail, postage extra, 13 cents.

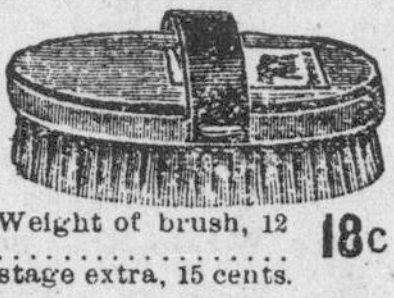

No. 10K5050 Our Heavy Wood Back India Fiber Horse Brush. 2-inch long India fiber. Size of brush, 8½ inches long and 3½ inches wide, with leather strap. Weight of brush, 12 ounces. Price........... **18c**
If by mail, postage extra, 15 cents.

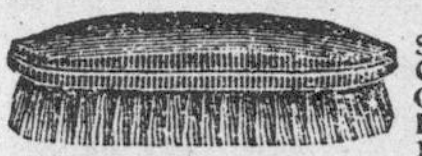

No. 10K5070 Sears, Roebuck & Co.'s Special Grade of India Fiber Horse Brush, 1½ inches long, double wood back, screw top, highly polished, 10½ inches long by 3 inches wide; pointed ends; the best grade of India fiber brush. Weight of brush, 14 ounces. Price.... **22c**
If by mail, postage extra, 17 cents.

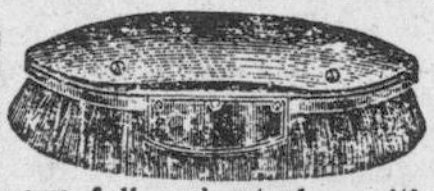

No. 10K5091 Sears' Special Extra High Grade Italian Rice Root Brush, made out of the very best quality rice root. Brush is very full and stocky with leather thumb and finger guards. Brush is 10 inches long and is considered by all horsemen to be the best rice root brush made. Weight of brush, 16 ounces. Price.... **80c**
If by mail, postage extra, 20 cents.

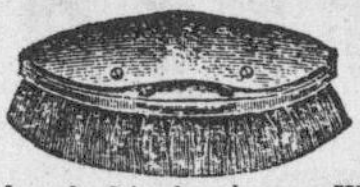

No. 10K5093 Sears' Special Jockey Size Dandy Brush, made out of the best imported Italian rice root. A very full stocky brush. Size of brush, 8 inches long. Weight, 12 ounces. This is one of the best Jockey Size Dandy Brushes made. Price........... **43c**
If by mail, postage extra, 15 cents.

S., R. & Co.'s Horse Brushes.

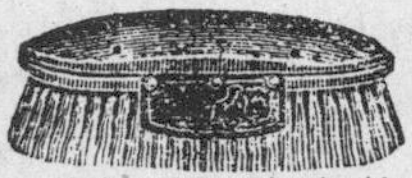

No. 10K5090 Sears, Roebuck & Co.'s Special Quality Extra High Grade Rice Root Horse Brush. Size of brush, 10 inches long and 2¾ inches wide; double polished top, pointed ends, leather thumb and finger guards. A strictly high grade brush. Weight of brush, 12 ounces.
Price........... **40c**
If by mail, postage extra, 17 cents.

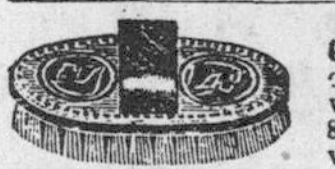

No. 10K5094 Nine-Row Horse Brush, made of tampico, heavy back with patent leather strap, 8½ inches long, 4¼ inches wide. Weight, 8 ounces. Price........... **15c**
If by mail, postage extra, 10 cents.

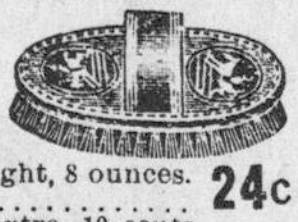

No. 10K5095 Gray Mixed Tampico Center Horse Brush with outside row of bristles. A good 11-row brush with heavy leather strap. 8½ inches long, 4½ inches wide. Weight, 8 ounces. Price........... **24c**
If by mail, postage extra, 10 cents.

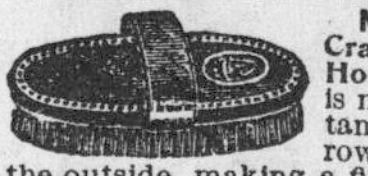

No. 10K5096 Our Crawford Leather Back Horse Brush. This brush is made with dark mixed tampico center, with two rows of white tampico on the outside, making a fifteen-row brush. The brush is made about 9 inches long and 4½ inches wide, with a good leather strap. Weight, 9 ounces. A good leather back horse brush. Price........... **42c**
If by mail, postage extra, 13 cents.

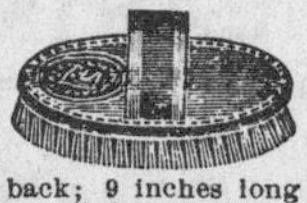

No. 10K5097 Our Evansville Leather Back Horse Brush. One row of white bristles outside and nine rows of good mixed tampico in center; a good eleven-row horse brush; good, heavy grain leather back; 9 inches long and 4½ inches wide, with good heavy strap; stitched all around with good heavy thread. Weight, 10 ounces. Price.... **46c**
If by mail, postage extra, 13 cents.

Lincoln Army Brush.

No. 10K5099 Leather Back Horse Brush. Made with flexible leather back, wire stitched. Fifteen rows of mixed tampico and bristles. Outside row of gray bristles; body of brush extra fine quality of gray tampico. Looks like an all bristle brush. A good flexible leather back army brush. Weight, 10 ounces. Size, 9 inches long and 4¼ inches wide.
Price........... **79c**
If by mail, postage extra, 13 cents.

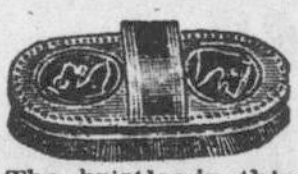

No. 10K5103 This Brush contains 15 rows of all pure Black Chinese Bristles, finished with heavy leather back and leather strap, flat face. The bristles in this brush, though of medium stiffness, will stand up under wear and will outlast several ordinary fiber brushes. The brush is 8½ inches long and 4 inches wide. Weight, 9 ounces. Price........ **49c**
If by mail, postage extra, 12 cents.

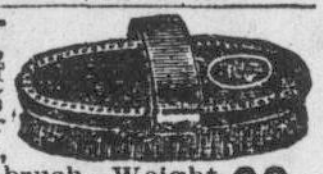

No. 10K5109 Leather Back Oval Shape, Tampico Center. Size of brush, 9 inches long, 4½ inches wide, with leather strap, length of tampico, 1 inch. Extra good cheap brush. Weight of brush, 12 ounces. Price........... **68c**
If by mail, postage extra, 15 cents.

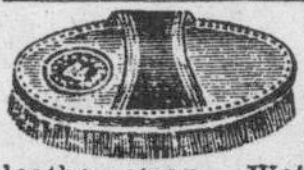

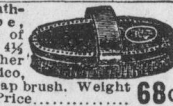

No. 10K5110 Oval Shape Horse Brush, warranted all bristles, oval face, 15 rows of sewed stub bristles. Size of brush, 9 inches long, 4 inches wide, leather strap. Weight of brush, 10 ounces. Price........... **93c**
If by mail, postage extra, each, 13 cents.

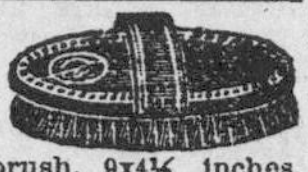

No. 10K5120 Our fine quality of Mixed Bristle Brush, flat face, fine quality of mixed black and brown bristles, flexible leather back, leather strap. Size of brush, 9x4½ inches. Weight of brush, 10 ounces.
Price........... **99c**
If by mail, postage extra, 13 cents.

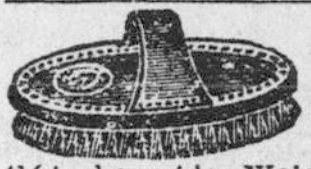

No. 10K5130 Sears, Roebuck & Co.'s Special All Black Bristle Horse Brush, 19 rows of black bristles. Flat face. Size, of brush, 9 inches long, 4½ inches wide. Weight of brush, 10 ounces. Price........... **$1.57**
If by mail, postage extra, 13 cents.

The Bonner. Only $1.60.

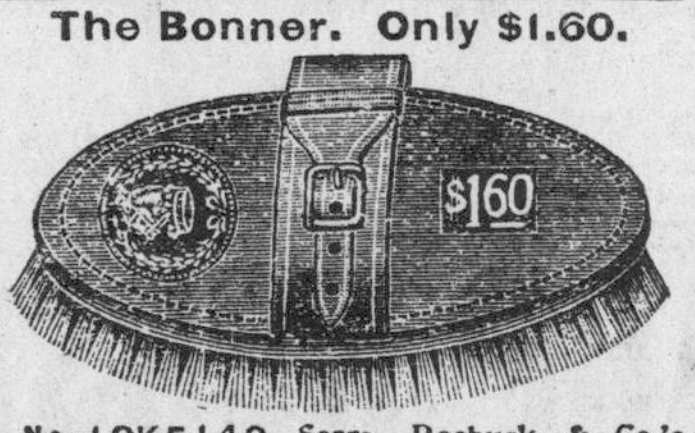

No. 10K5140 Sears, Roebuck & Co.'s Special Bonner Warranted All White Bristle Oval Faced Brush. 19 rows of bristles, adjustable strap, leather back. Size of brush, 9 by 4½ inches. Extra fine horse brush. Weight of brush, 12 ounces, packed in single box.
Price........... **$1.60**
If by mail, postage extra, 15 cents.

The Best $2.51 Horse Brush.

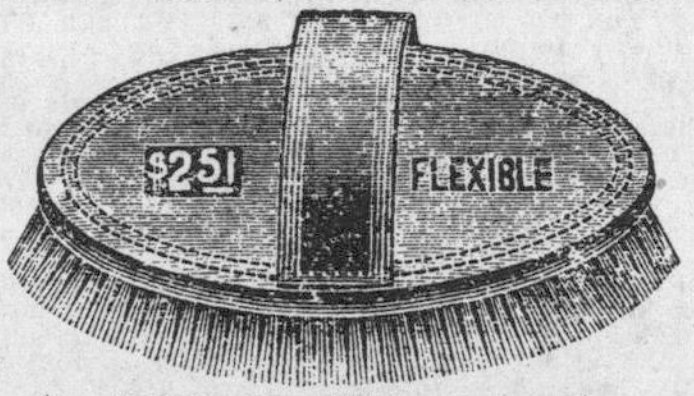

No. 10K5143 This brush is made on a solid sole leather flexible block, flat face, 19 rows of the very stiffest butt cut gray India Bristles. Trimmed, stands out 1⅛-inch from the block; outside row of bristles sewed through the back with copper wire; heavy russet leather top and strap sewed with heavy linen thread. This brush is flexible and will bend in the hand; when brushing the horse's legs it will curl right around. The brush adjusts itself to the horse by the pressure of the hand. This is an extra quality of the best gray bristles. The brush is penetrating and will clean the horse as no other brush will. This brush is one of the highest standards of horse brushes made. If not found perfectly satisfactory and you do not think you have one of the best brushes that can be made, you can return the brush at our expense and we will cheerfully refund your money. The brush is 9½ inches long and 4½ inches wide. Weight, 13 ounces. Price........ **$2.51**
If by mail, postage extra, 18 cents.

Our Jumbo Broom.

53c

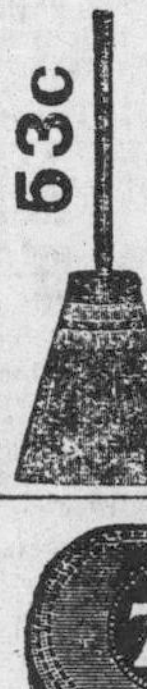

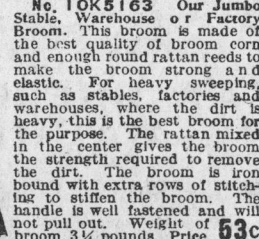

No. 10K5163 Our Jumbo Stable, Warehouse or Factory Broom. This broom is made of the best quality of broom corn and enough round rattan reeds to make the broom strong and elastic. For heavy sweeping, such as stables, factories and warehouses, where the dirt is heavy, this is the best broom for the purpose. The rattan mixed in the center gives the broom the strength required to remove the dirt. The broom is iron bound with extra rows of stitching to stiffen the broom. The handle is well fastened and will not pull out. Weight of broom, 3¼ pounds. Price, **53c**

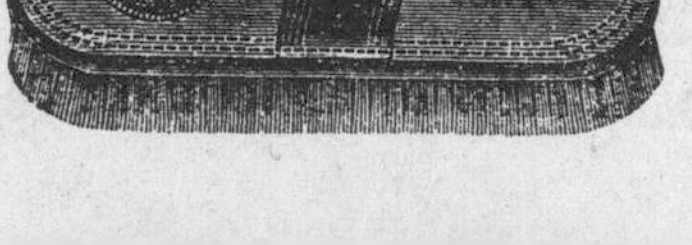

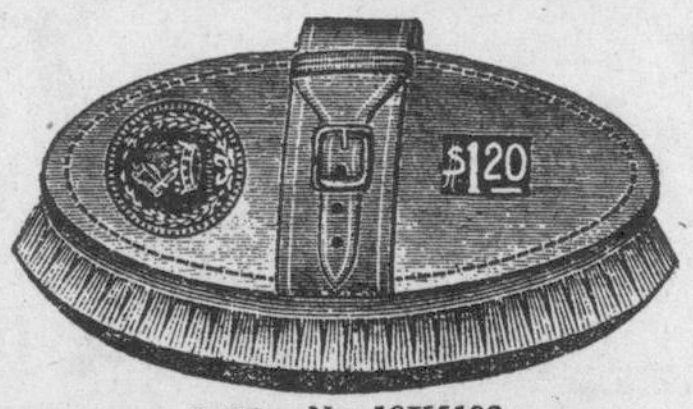

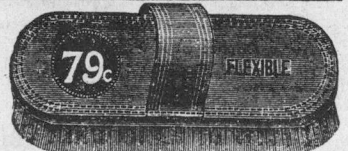

BACK. No. 10K5102

Morning Star Low Cut Quarter Boot, $1.91.

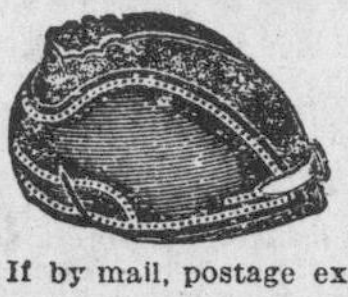

No. 10K5335 Morning Star Low Cut Quarter Boot. One strap, with spur strap, felt lined; one of the best boots made. This is a special with us. Weight, per pair, 12 oz. Price, per pair........... **$1.91**
If by mail, postage extra, per pair, 16 cents.

S., R. & Co.'s Shin and Ankle Boot, $1.90.

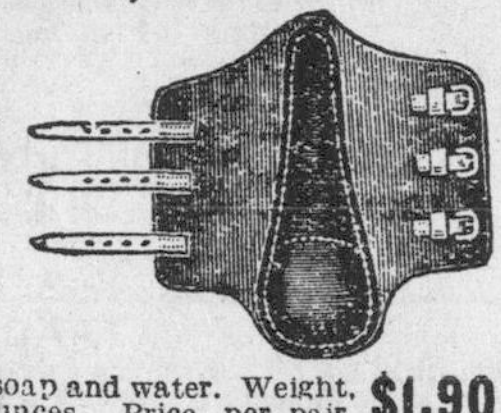

No. 10K5380 S., R. & Co.'s Shin and Ankle Boot is made of fine russet leather, cupped bottom, padded shin, calfskin lined, three-strap. This boot can be washed with soap and water. Weight, per pair, 8 ounces. Price, per pair, **$1.90**
If by mail, postage extra, per pair, 12 cents.

Interfering Device, 30 Cents.

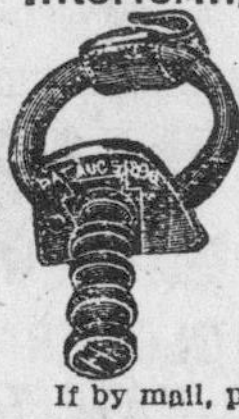

No. 10K5450 This device has been used for some time, has never failed to stop the most obstinate case of interfering, and in most cases can be dispensed with after ten days or two weeks. They will spread the colt's gait and make him a wide traveler. Every horseman will understand the merits of them when seen. Weight, each, 4 ounces. Price, each........... **30c**
If by mail, postage extra, each, 7 cents.

Stable or Street Broom, 49c.

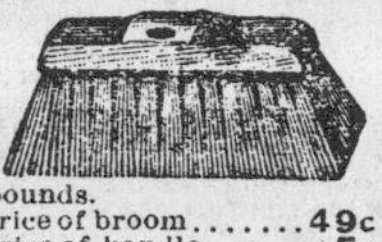

This is made with 14-inch wood back, four rows rattan splints. Should be used in every stable. Furnished with or without handle. Weight, 2 pounds.
No. 10K5165 Price of broom........49c
No. 10K5170 Price of handle...... 5c

Our Acme Bass Broom.

Made with heavy wood back, the brush part made of fine bass fiber. The brush will last for years. Furnished with or without handle. Weight, 2 pounds.
No. 10K5175 Price of broom........64c
No. 10K5180 Price of handle........ 5c

Common Sense Toe Weights.

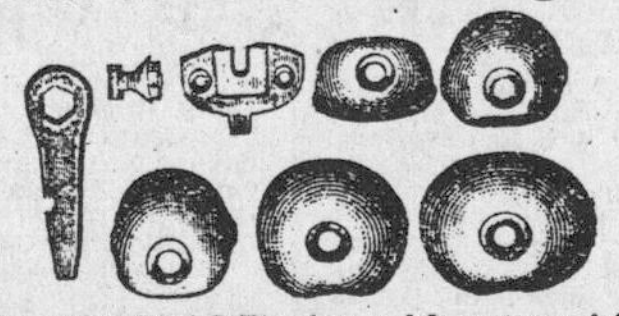

No. 10K5612 The demand for a toe weight that is easily and quickly adjusted, from one ounce to six, is so great that we have had made for us this special toe weight set, consisting of a pair of spurs and five pairs of weights, 2, 3, 4, 5 and 6 ounces. The spur itself weighs 1 ounce. You will be able, therefore, to weight your horse with 1, 2, 3, 4, 5 and 6-ounce weights. The Common Sense Toe Weight is the best. Nickel plated. We furnish as many pairs of spurs as you want at 15 cents per pair, and bolts and screws extra, per pair, 15 cents. This set of weights you can use on five horses at one time, with extra spurs. The most complete set of toe weights on the market. If not satisfactory, you can return them. Weight, 2 pounds.
Price, per set........... 48c
Common Sense Spurs, extra, per pair.... 15c
Bolts and screws, extra, per pair........ 15c
If by mail, postage extra, per set, 32 cents.

Brass Toe Weights.

No. 10K5613 Our Solid Brass Common Sense Toe Weights. Five pairs of solid brass weights and one pair of brass spurs and flat headed brass screw bolts, the same style as No. 10K5612, only made of solid brass, highly polished. Price, per set........... $1.04
Extra spurs, per pair........... .15
Bolts and screws, extra, per pair........ .15
When ordering sets of toe weights, and wanting extra spurs, bolts and screws be sure to allow the extra price for spurs, bolts and screws.
If by mail, postage extra, 32 cents.

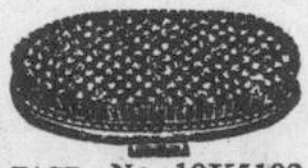

No. 10K5102 Our Improved All Bristle Brush, 15 rows, and every other tuft white and black bristles. The black bristles are long and the white bristles are short, FACE. No. 10K5102 which gives the brush a chance to penetrate the hair. Leather back and adjustable leather strap handle. This is one of the latest improved brushes, and if not found entirely satisfactory can be returned at our expense. Size, 9 inches long, 4½ inches wide. Weight, 11 ounces. We show face and back of this brush.
Price........... **$1.20**
If by mail, postage extra, 15 cents.

The Old Reliable Springsteen Shield.

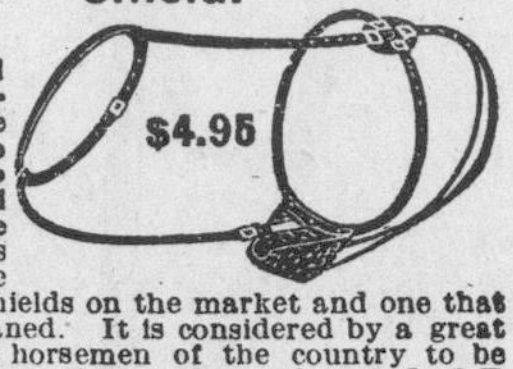

No. 10K5631 This Shield is easily adjusted, the harness so made as to raise and lower the pouch. It is one of the best made shields on the market and one that is easily cleaned. It is considered by a great many of the horsemen of the country to be superior to any other on the market.
Price........... **$4.95**
If by mail, postage extra, 45 cents.

Pacing and Trotting Hopple.

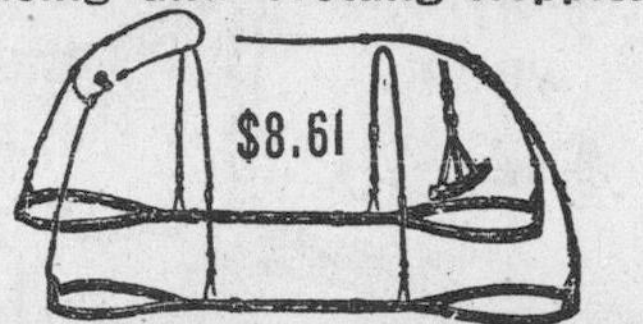

No. 10K5640 A Genuine Sears, Roebuck & Co.'s Hopple, made with laced rawhide connecting straps, extra strong loops, covered with very fine calfskin so as not to wrinkle, made for trotting or pacing horses, strong but light weight. Finely finished, with snap adjustment, made to put on and take off the horse very quickly. This is positively the finest hopple made. Neck, hip and quarter straps complete ready for use. Medium weight hopple. Weight, about 4 pounds.
Price........... **$8.61**

Standard Tail Holder.

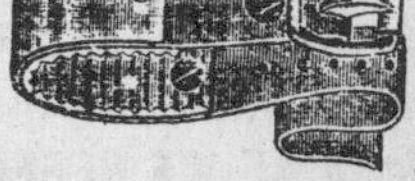

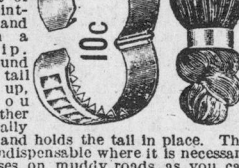

No. 10K5665 Our Standard Tail Holder. This tail holder is made with a leather body, nickel plated spring, and corrugated rubber lined, and buckles around the tail. Braid the tail, loop it up, and buckle the Standard Tail Holder as tight as you can buckle it. The corrugated rubber lining prevents the holder from slipping on the tail. A great many like this tail holder better than they do our Common Sense Metal Tail Holder. With the use of this tail holder the horse's tail will not become matted with mud. Weight, about 2 ounces. Price........... **8c**
If by mail, postage extra, 3 cents.

Common Sense Tail Clasp.

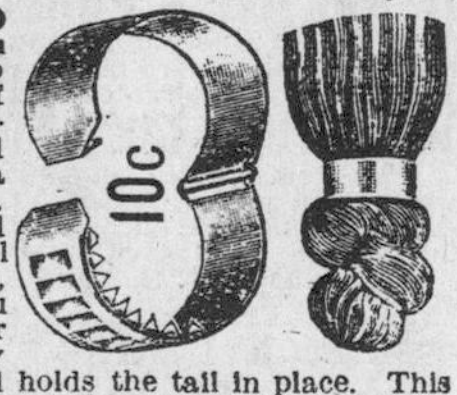

No. 10K5670 This Common Sense Tail Clasp is made out of solid brass, jointed center, and fastens with a notched clip. Spring it around the tail after tail is doubled up, and as you squeeze together it automatically fastens itself and holds the tail in place. This tail clasp is indispensable where it is necessary to drive horses on muddy roads, as you can always keep the tail clean when you use the Common Sense Tail Clasp. Weight, about 2 ounces. Price, each........... **10c**
If by mail, postage extra, 3 cents.

Our Lindsey Blanket Pins.

Made of Brass Wire. Will Not Rust. Nickel Plated. The Best Blanket Pin Made.

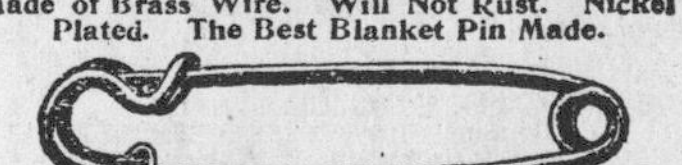

No. 10K5675 This blanket pin is made out of brass wire nickel plated, the old reliable Lindsey pattern, 3¼ inches long and is the best blanket pin on the market. Brass nickel plated pins do not rust. It is a better blanket pin than a steel nickel plated pin, because the steel pin will rust.
Price, per dozen........... **22c**
If by mail, postage extra, per dozen, 8 cents.

Our Handy Blanket Pin.

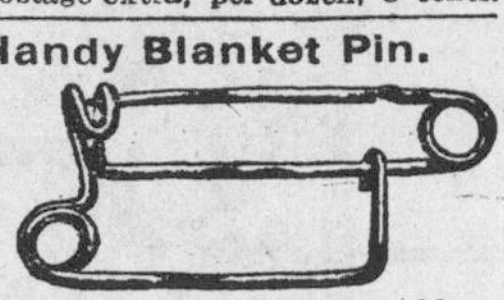

No. 10K5679 Made the same style as a blanket pin with extra safety loop to fasten around the traces, which prevents the blanket from blowing off the horse. This pin can be fastened to the blanket and when placed on the horse can be fastened around the traces, which will prevent the blanket from blowing off the horse. Price, per dozen........... **29c**
If by mail, postage extra, per dozen, 8 cents.

Canvas Feed Bags.

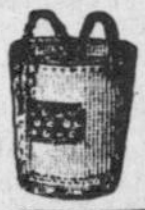

No. 10K5695 Canvas Feed Bags. Leather bottom, perforated side, with adjustable strap running over head.
Price, each.......... **49c**
If by mail, postage extra, 13 cents.

Bridle Plumes.

Made of hair switches, metal tipped with hook to fasten to the bridles. These hair tassels are used for trimming on harness, bridles or spreaders.
Made in three sizes and three colors.

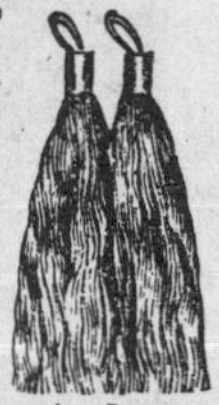

No. 10K5750 Bridle Plumes, colors, red or yellow, about 9 inches long.
Price, per pair........ **26c**
No. 10K5755 Bridle Plumes, colors, red or blue, about 11 inches long.
Price, per pair........ **29c**
No. 10K5760 Bridle Plumes, colors, red or green, about 13 inches long.
Price, per pair........ **32c**
Always state color wanted.
Weight, per pair, 3, 4 and 5 ounces.
If by mail, postage extra, per pair, 5 cents.

Rosette Bridle Plume.

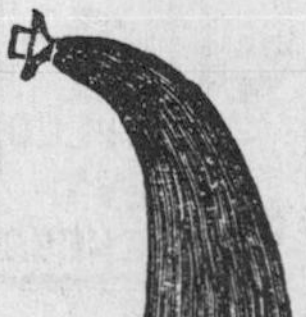

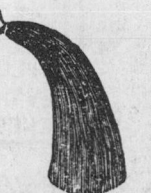

No. 10K5765 Sears' Special Rosette Drop Bridle Plume. This rosette is fastened to the bridle by the front and is strictly first class hair plume, being made out of cattle tails. Furnished in large size and one color, red only.
Price, per pair, **45c**
If by mail, postage extra, per pair, 10c.
We do not break pairs. Pairs are always one color. We only furnish bridle plumes as listed. No other color or size.

Gents' Saddle Blanket.

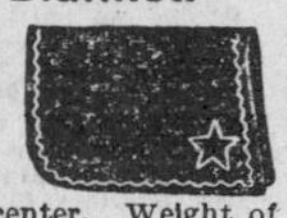

No. 10K5810 Our Gents' Felt Saddle Blanket, fancy scalloped border with star corner, plain colored body with assorted fancy braid, scalloped edge. Size of blanket, 24 inches long and 16 inches wide from center. Weight of blanket, 12 ounces.
Price, each.......... **54c**
If by mail, postage extra, 14 cents.

Gents' Fine Saddle Blanket.

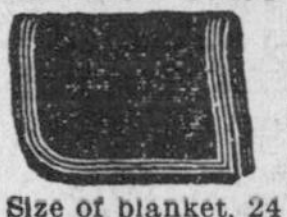

No. 10K5815 Our Extra Fine Gents' Saddle Blanket, made of a good quality of plain felt with bound and braided edge. One of the best gents' light saddle blankets we handle. Size of blanket, 24 inches long and 16 inches wide from center. Weight of blanket 12 ounces. Price, each.......... **89c**
If by mail, postage extra, 14 cents.

Our Roosevelt Saddle Blanket.

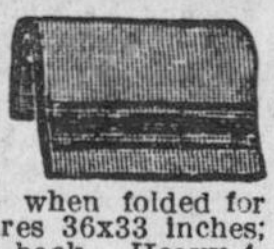

No. 10K5816 This is one of our specials, having been recommended by some of the best rough riders in the country as being the only saddle blanket to be used with heavy stock saddles; is 36x66 inches. This blanket when folded for use under the saddle measures 36x33 inches; soft and easy on a horse's back. Heavy 4-pound blanket.
Price, each.......... **$1.05**

No. 10K5817 Our Indian Red Saddle Blanket with black stripes. This blanket is woven the same as a horse blanket. Body part is red filling with black stripes. Blanket when folded is just the size for a large saddle. Blanket is made so as to fold four different sides, giving a clean blanket each day for the horse. This is the same style blanket as No. 10K5816. Blanket is about 34x66 inches. Weight about 30 oz. Price, each.... **$1.24**
If by mail, postage extra, 35 cents.

Cowboy Fine Woven Hair Saddle Blanket.

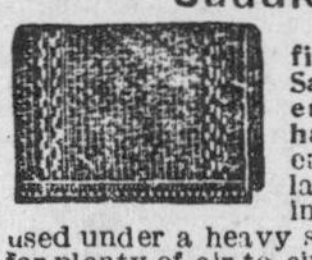

No. 10K5845 Our fine heavy woven hair Saddle Blanket, bound ends, pure white Angora hair, with light stripes on ends. This is an extra large saddle blanket, 30x40 inches. This blanket when used under a heavy stock saddle leaves room for plenty of air to circulate between the saddle and horse's back, preventing any galls or sore back. It is used universally throughout the western country, and has given the very best satisfaction. Weight of this blanket is 3½ pounds. Price, each........ **$1.65**
If by mail, postage extra, 60 cents.

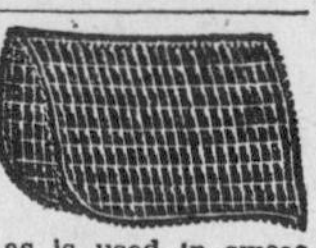

No. 10K5850 Our Special Quilted Saddle Blanket, made of heavy old gold drill with fancy stitched edge, with nine rows quilting. This pad is stuffed with high grade composite stuffing such as is used in sweat pads. A stuffed saddle blanket, full quilted is the easiest kind of saddle blanket on the horse's back. The saddle will not gall the horse's back. Size of blanket, 26 inches long, 34 inches wide. Weight, about 4 pounds. Price, each.......... **54c**

WONDERFUL VALUES IN WHIPS.

REDUCED PRICES.

Jumbo Express Whip.

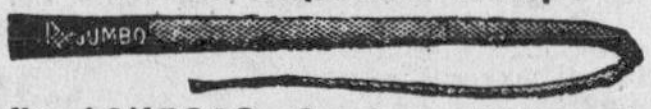

No. 10K5893 Our Jumbo Whip is the best imitation gut color. The heaviest and best Jumbo whip made. Weight, about 6 ounces. Price.......... **22c**

Tiger Brand.

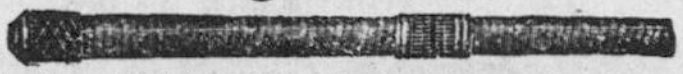

No. 10K5901 Stocked java, black, wine and imitation gut. Star finish, loaded, linen lined, one 1½-inch chased mount, 4-stitch head button, rubber cushion cap, Boston snap. Length, 6 feet. Weight, about 7 ounces. Price.......... **34c**

The Elk Rawhide Whip.

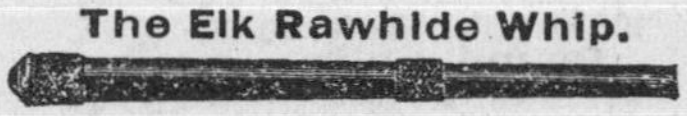

No. 10K5902 Full rawhide protruding through cap. Straight, black and wine, star finish, linen lined, two 4-stitch black buttons, japanned cap, Boston snap. Length, 6 feet. Price.......... **36c**

Phoenix Rawhide Whip.

No. 10K5904 Rawhide. Straight, old gold and nankeen, 4-plait cover mixed. Star finish, wire wound, linen lined, two 8-stitch long old gold buttons, rubber cushion cap, English snap. Length, 6 feet. Weight, about 8 ounces. Price.......... **69c**

Calash Rawhide Whip.

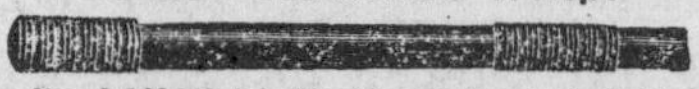

No. 10K5941 The Calash Rawhide Whips give the best satisfaction. Wine finish, waterproof under cover, 2½-inch panel and beaded black head and ferrule, rubber cushion cap, half silk English snap. Made in three sizes, 6, 6½ and 7 feet. Weight, about 8 to 10 ounces.

Length, feet	6	6½	7
Price	77c	81c	89c

The Mayflower Rawhide Buggy Whip.

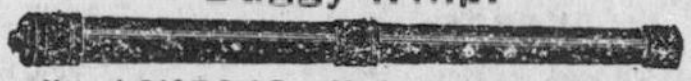

No. 10K5942 Made of the best twisted rawhide center, well stocked, one solid piece rawhide entire length of whip, black star finish, waterproof under cover, two braided buttons, half silk English snap. One of the best full rawhide buggy whips we can make. Length, 6 feet. Weight, about 8 ounces. Price.......... **84c**

Our Best Full Rawhide Whip.

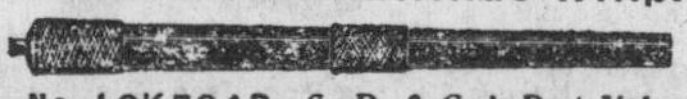

No. 10K5943 S., R. & Co.'s Best Value Rawhide Whip, full length rawhide from point to handle, rubber lined and waterproof cover, extra quality of heavy rawhide throughout, fine black star finish, fine braided button, English snap. A handsomely finished whip, made in the one length only, 6 feet. One of our best rawhide buggy whips. Weight, about 10 ounces. Price.......... **$1.14**

Crown Point Rawhide Whip.

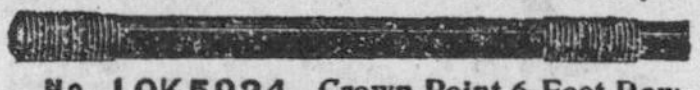

No. 10K5924 Crown Point 6-Foot Rawhide Whip. Rawhide running the entire length of whip and through a loaded butt at end of whip, giving it weight; two handsome buttons; Boston snap. One of the best rawhide center whips ever offered. Weight, about 8 ounces. Price.......... **52c**

Our Tim B Full Rawhide Whip.

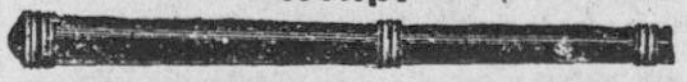

No. 10K5926 Tim B Whip. Never before offered for the money. A black thread covered rawhide through whip, rawhide from snap, extending through the cap at butt end of whip, two buttons, Boston snap. Length, 6 feet. Extra good rawhide buggy whip. Weight, about 6 ounces. Price. **49c**

Our New Radium Rawhide.

No. 10K5927 A 6-Foot Black Thread Covered Whip, with two pretty double buttons, rubber cap, Boston snap, and a wire woven under cover, giving strength and durability to the whip. Double eelskin loop for snap, which will not pull out. Weight, about 10 ounces. Price.......... **69c**

Our Knickerbocker Special, Full Length Rawhide Buggy Whip.

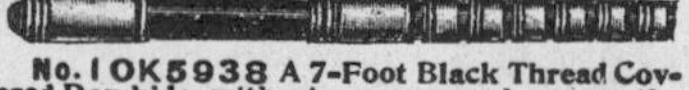

No. 10K5938 A 7-Foot Black Thread Covered Rawhide, with wire woven under cover the entire length of whip; rawhide runs from snap through cap at end of whip. The whip has eighteen beautiful nickel ferrules and a long nickel head mount. The best mounted rawhide whip we can make. Boston snap. A very showy whip. Weight, about 14 ounces. Price.......... **$1.11**

Half Length Rawhide Center Full Leather Covered Team Whip.

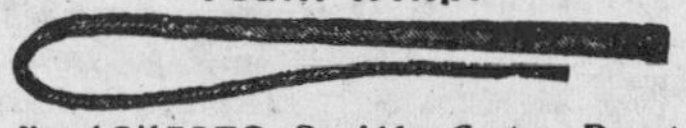

No. 10K5972 Rawhide Center, Russet Covered Team Whip. 4-plait buckskin. Full length of whip, 8 feet. Weight, about 10 ounces. Price.......... **84c**

No. 10K5973 Our Special Heavy Rawhide Center Team Whip. Fine yellow calfskin covered, buck stitched, 6-plait braided buckskin point. Full length of whip, 8 feet. Weight, about 10 ounces. Price.......... **$1.05**

Whip Lashes.

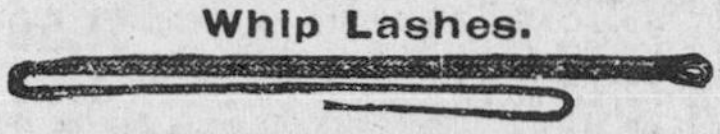

No. 10K6000 Our 6-Plait Genuine Buck Braided Whip Lash. All hand made, well tapered, extra quality.

Length, feet	5	6	7
Price	26c	31c	37c

If by mail, postage extra, 3 cents.

No. 10K6005 Our 4-Plait Genuine Buck Braided Whip Lash. All hand braided, best quality.

Length, feet	5	6	7	8
Price	20c	25c	28c	45c

If by mail, postage extra, 3 cents.

No. 10K6007 Our Special 8-Plait California Style Buck Lash, with silk snap. Made in two lengths.

Length, feet	10	12
Price	83c	95c

If by mail, postage extra, 4 cents.

No. 10K6011 Our Special 12-Plait Genuine Braided Buck Stage Lash. All hand braided, plain tapered lash from loops, extra quality lash. We sell the best.

Length, feet	10	12	16
Price	$1.34	$1.61	$2.24

If by mail, postage extra, 4 cents.

No. 10K6012 Our Special 16-Plait Genuine Braided Buck Stage Lash. The best, all hand braided, well tapered. The best quality buckskin used in our high grade buck lashes.

Length, feet	10	12	16
Price	$1.80	$2.15	$2.95

If by mail, postage extra, 4 cents.

Hickory Whip Stocks.

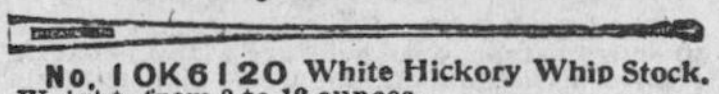

No. 10K6120 White Hickory Whip Stock. Weight, from 8 to 12 ounces.

Length, feet	3½	4½
Price	19c	21c

Whip Crackers.

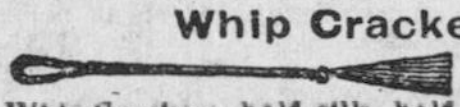

No. 10K6133 Whip Crackers, half silk, half cotton, 7 inches long. Price, per dozen.......... 14c
No. 10K6135 Whip Crackers, all silk, best quality, 7 inches long. Price, per dozen, 21c
No. 10K6140 Cotton Whip Crackers, 7 inches long. Price, per dozen.......... 5c
We do not break dozens. Weight, 2 ounces.
If by mail, postage extra, per dozen, 2 cents.

Fancy Rawhide Whip.

No. 10K6150 Our Rawhide black German braided cover, fancy basket handle, two braided buttons, japanned cap, fancy plaited English wrist loop. Weight, 5 ounces.
Price.......... **45c**

Solid Leather Team Whips.

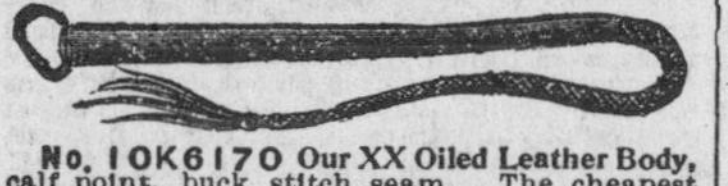

No. 10K6170 Our XX Oiled Leather Body, calf point, buck stitch seam. The cheapest leather team whip made. Weight, about 14 ounces.

Length, feet	5	6	7
Price	40c	42c	53c

XXXX Team Whips.

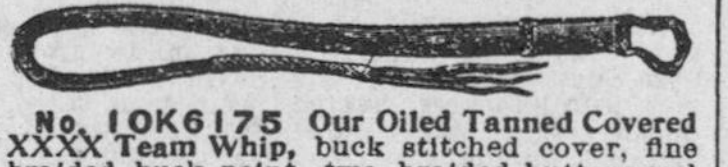

No. 10K6175 Our Oiled Tanned Covered XXXX Team Whip, buck stitched cover, fine braided buck point, two braided buttons and hand loop. Weight, about 18 ounces.

Length, feet	6	6½	7
Price	56c	62c	67c

No. 10K6176 Sears' Special Extra Heavy Double XXXX Team Whip. The best leather team whip that can be made. We are making a special run on this whip. If you want the best, take this whip. Weight, about 18 ounces.

Length, feet	6	6½	7
Price	71c	78c	85c

San Antonio Quirt.

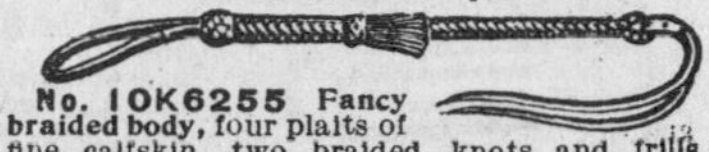

No. 10K6255 Fancy braided body, four plaits of fine calfskin, two braided knots and frills. Length of body, 18 inches; total length of quirt, 33 inches. Weight, about 6 ounces.
Price, each.......... **34c**
If by mail, postage extra, each, 9 cents.

Brown's Improved Australian Drover Cattle Whip.

REDUCED PRICES ON IMPROVED CATTLE WHIP.

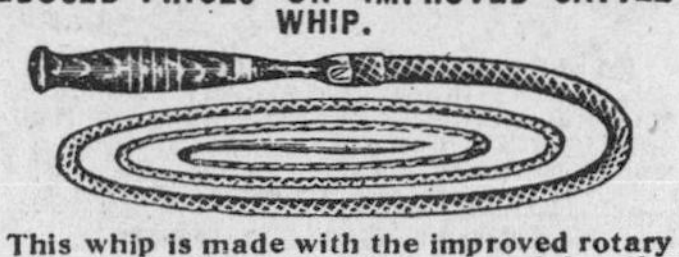

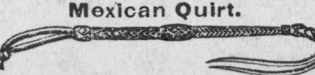

This whip is made with the improved rotary handle, brass front revolving in wood handle. The Australian knot is so attached to the handle that it prevents it from breaking down or breaking loose, being attached with a rawhide fastener, making a revolving, flexible, non-breakable, Australian knot. This whip is made in three patterns.

No. 10K6240 8-plait calfskin body with buckskin point.

Length, feet	10	12	14
Price, each	$1.69	$1.81	$1.93

No. 10K6241 8-plait buckskin body with buckskin point.

Length, feet	10	12
Price, each	$1.68	$1.85

No. 10K6242 12-plait rawhide body with buckskin point.

Length, feet	10	12	14
Price, each	$2.40	$2.50	$2.60

If by mail, postage extra, 30 cents.

Mexican Quirt.

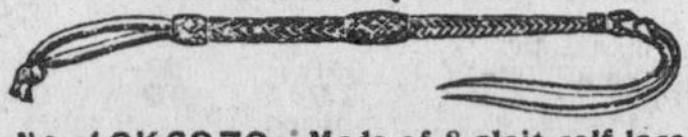

No. 10K6270 Made of 8-plait calf lace leather. Iron spike, heavy braided knots, leather hand loop. Length of body, 19 inches; total length of quirt, 34 inches. Weight, about 12 ounces. Price.......... **73c**
If by mail, postage extra, each, 13 cents.

Dallas Quirt.

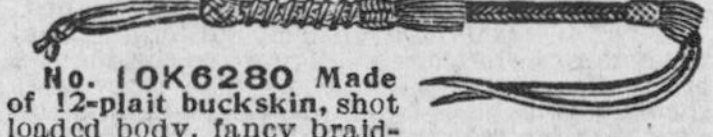

No. 10K6280 Made of 12-plait buckskin, shot loaded body, fancy braided, corded handle, three braided knots and frills. Length of body, 20 inches; total length of quirt, 33 inches. Weight, about 16 ounces. Price.......... **99c**
If by mail, postage extra, each, 16 cents.

Our Western Mule Skinner.

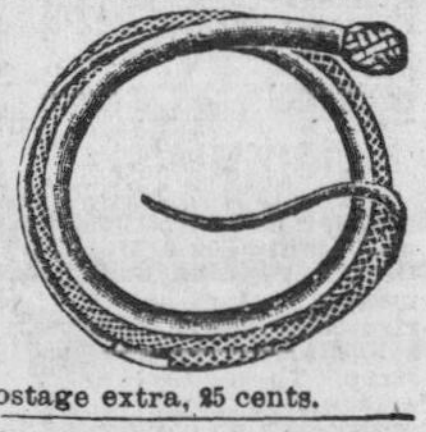

No. 10K6290 Made of fine latigo leather body, buck stitched, braided buckskin point, heavy braided knot, shot loaded. The best mule skinner on the market. Weight, about 25 ounces.
Price, 6 ft.. **$1.18**
Price, 7½ ft. **1.43**
If by mail, postage extra, 25 cents.

S., R. & Co.'s Australian Cattle Whip.

Made with adjustable double loop fastener, revolving handle, shot loaded, warranted not to break down at handle or break the shot sack, can be easily repaired when worn out, or if you break the handle, you can put it in yourself. This is the best cattle whip made. Made in calfskin, buckskin or rawhide. Leather tanned expressly for fine cattle whips. Order by number and state length.

REDUCED PRICES ON CATTLE WHIP.

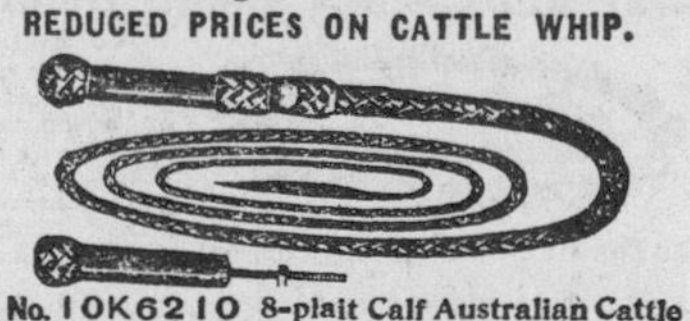

No. 10K6210 8-plait Calf Australian Cattle Whip.

Length, feet	10	12	14
Price	$1.50	$1.69	$1.79

No. 10K6220 8-plait Genuine Buckskin Australian Cattle Whip.

Length, feet	10	12	14
Price	$1.55	$1.68	$1.89

No. 10K6225 12-plait Genuine Buckskin Australian Cattle Whip.

Length, feet	10	12	14
Price	$1.70	$1.90	$2.10

No. 10K6235 12-plait Oiled Rawhide Australian Cattle Whip. Weight, about 24 ounces.

Length, feet	10	12	14
Price	$2.00	$2.20	$2.30

If by mail, postage extra, 30 cents.

Improved Rotary Jacksonville Drovers' Whip.

WE HAVE IMPROVED OUR LEATHER WHIPS AND REDUCED THE PRICES.

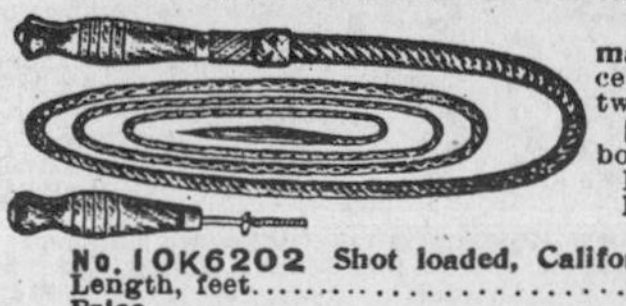

This whip is the most perfect drovers' whip on the market, light and easily handled, wrought iron bolt center, with maple wood revolving handle, made in two styles, as follows:

No. 10K6201 California Style, fine 8-plait latigo body, with buck point. Not shot loaded.

Length, feet	10	12	14
Price	$1.20	$1.43	$1.60

If by mail, postage extra, 27 cents.

No. 10K6202 Shot loaded, California style, 8-plait latigo body, buck point.

Length, feet	10	12
Price	$1.40	$1.61

If by mail, postage extra, 29 cents.

Boys' Drovers' Whip.

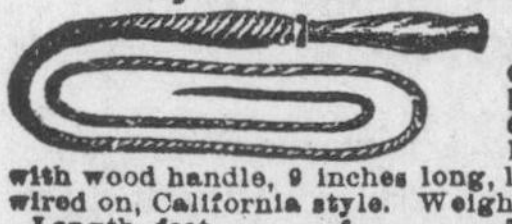

No. 10K6180 Our Boys' Drover Whip, 6-plait, oiled kip, made with wood handle, 9 inches long, lash strongly wired on, California style. Weight, 16 ounces.

Length, feet...	6	7	8
Price	34c	41c	48c

If by mail, postage extra, 15 cents.

Oklahoma Quirt.

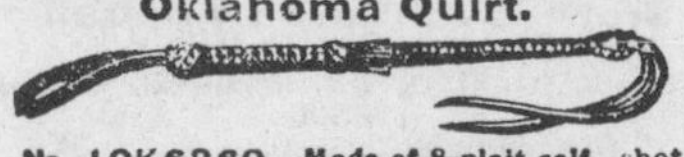

No. 10K6260 Made of 8-plait calf, shot loaded body, fancy braided quirt, three braided knots and frills. Length of body, 20 inches; total length of quirt, 33 inches. Weight, about 14 ounces. Price 47c

If by mail, postage extra, 18 cents.

Loose Sleigh Bells.

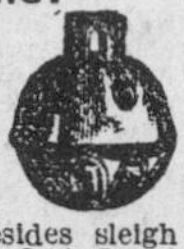

No. 10K7260 "King Henry" Sleigh Bells. Made of polished bell metal with a loop to go through the strap, and are fastened by wire fasteners. This is a very easy and convenient bell for those wishing to make their own straps of sleigh bells. They are also used for a great many other purposes besides sleigh bells. Made in seven sizes, 0, 1, 2, 3, 4, 5 and 6. Plain bell metal finish. Sold and priced by the dozen for each size. You can make a fine strap of sleigh bells by using this No. 10K7260 bell and three or four or more of the No. 10K7265 Swedish bells. (Rim sleigh bells, without wire fasteners.)

Number	0	1	2	3
Diameter, inches	1	1⅛	1¼	1⅜
Weight, per dozen, about, ounces	9	12	13	15
Price, per dozen	31c	35c	47c	62c

Number	4	5	6
Diameter, inches	1½	1⅝	1¾
Weight, per dozen about, ounces	20	26	32
Price, per dozen	75c	90c	99c

Postage extra, per dozen, 19 to 40 cents.

Loose Swedish Sleigh Bells.

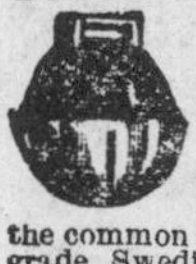

No. 10K7265 Our Special Swedish Sleigh Bells. Made of the genuine high grade cast bell metal, polished. Each bell has a distinct tone in itself and using 7, 9, 11, 13 and 15, each bell chimes with the other. These bells are entirely different from the common sleigh bell. They are the highest grade Swedish bells made. The loop goes through one strap and another small strap runs through the loop, fastening the bell to the straps. Three, four, or more of these Swedish bells used with a few of the No. 10K7260 bell make one of the best straps of sleigh bells you can buy. These Swedish bells are also used in a great many sections of the country as cow bells or sheep bells.

Numbers	7	9	11	13	15
Diameter, inches	2	2¼	2½	2¾	3¼
Weight each, about oz.	7	8	9	11	14
Price, each	28c	32c	47c	56c	64c

If by mail, postage extra, each, 10 to 20 cents.

Sleigh Bells.

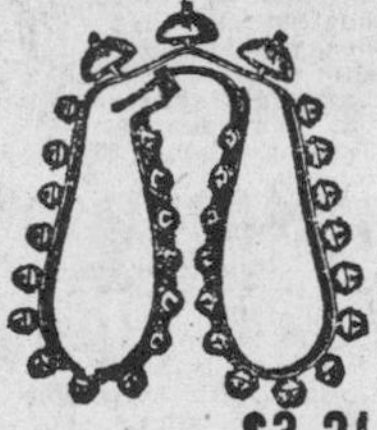

No. 10K7200 Dexter Body Strap with Chimes, 30 extra tinned, genuine bell metal Dexter bells, riveted on high grade solid harness leather strap. These bells must not be compared with cast iron or stamped steel bells which are being largely sold this season.

Price, per strap $3.21

No. 10K7201 Dexter Body Strap with Chimes. Same as No. 10K7200, genuine bell metal, heavily nickel plated and polished. Price, per strap $3.65

If by mail, postage extra, 54 cents.

Our Jack Frost Sleigh Bells.

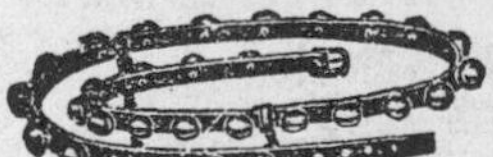

We make this strap of sleigh bells on a good heavy 1-inch black harness leather strap, using 30 fine nickel plated pressed steel bells, 1⅛-inch diameter, riveted to the strap also make it with 30 1¼-inch nickel plated bells riveted to the strap. These two styles of sleigh bells are very popular and are considered great value. All the bells are finely nickel plated and all have clear ringing tone. Order Jack Frost Bells.

No. 10K7204 Price, per strap of 30 1⅛-inch bells $1.35

If by mail, postage extra, 36 cents.

No. 10K7207 Price, per strap of 30 1¼-inch bells $1.50

If by mail, postage extra, 48 cents.

The "Beaver Dam" Sleigh Bells.

This Special "Beaver Dam" Sleigh Bells is one of the best straps of sleigh bells it is possible to make. We use 30 fine polished, nickel plated bells, riveted on a heavy harness leather strap, also make it with 36 bells, polished, and nickel plated, riveted on a black harness leather strap. We could not make you any better straps of sleigh bells no matter what price you paid for them, than the four styles we list under Nos. 10K7204, 10K7207, 10K7216 and 10K7219. They are the best straps of sleigh bells that we handle, our special make. Order your bells by catalogue number and allow the price.

No. 10K7216 Price, per strap of 30 bells $3.12

If by mail, postage extra, 56 cents.

No. 10K7219 Price, per set, strap of 36 bells $3.50

If by mail, postage extra, 64 cents.

Our Brewster Sleigh Bells.

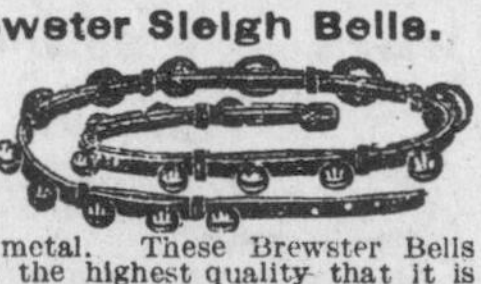

This Body Strap consists of 19 polished Brewster Sleigh Bells, made out of pure cast bell metal. These Brewster Bells are considered the highest quality that it is possible to make in this priced bell. The tone and ring is clear and distinct, and from small to large bells the tone increases. Made with double russet harness leather strap with bells fastened to the strap by wire. Size of bells 1¼ inches to 1¾ inches in diameter. Also made with 23 round polished Brewster Bells fastened to a heavy double russet strap with wire fasteners, assorted sizes, diameter, 1⅛ to 2⅛ inches.

No. 10K7235 19 Brewster Bells. Price, per strap $1.58

No. 10K7240 23 Brewster Bells. Price, per strap 2.36

If by mail, postage extra, 48 cents for the 19 bells and 57 cents for the 23 bells.

Neck Strap Sleigh Bells.

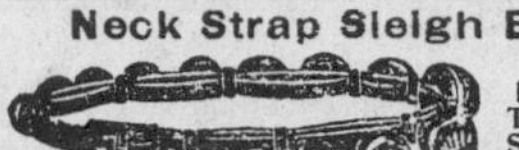

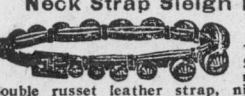

No. 10K7250 This Neck Strap is made with double russet leather strap, nine polished genuine bell metal bells fastened to the straps with wire fasteners. The liner protects the horse's neck from the fasteners of the bells. Made in assorted sizes from 1 to 5 and diameter is 1⅛ to 1⅝ inches. The bells are from light to heavy tone. Price, per strap of nine bells 66c

If by mail, postage extra, 28 cents.

Pole or Shaft Chimes

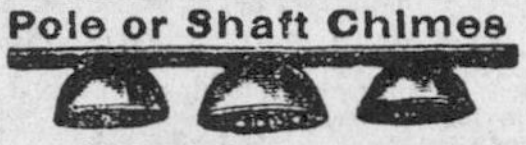

No. 10K7274 This special Shaft Chime has three nickel plated, beaded edge shaft bells with iron knockers, open bell riveted to an iron strap that is fastened underneath the shafts. Clear, ringing tone. Set in two straps with six bells.

Price, per set 45c

If by mail, postage extra, 30 cents.

Shaft or Pole Chimes.

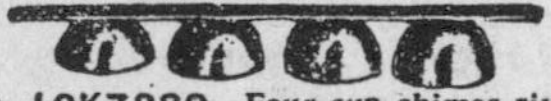

No. 10K7280 Four cup chimes riveted to an iron strap, open bell face with knockers, electro nickel plated; one of the highest grade steel bells and has earned its reputation for a clear tone. These Pole or Shaft Chimes are fastened to the shaft by screw in each end of the strap and on the lower side of the shaft. The set consists of two straps of eight bells, four bells to the strap.

Price, per set 90c

If by mail, postage extra, 45 cents.

Mikado Chimes.

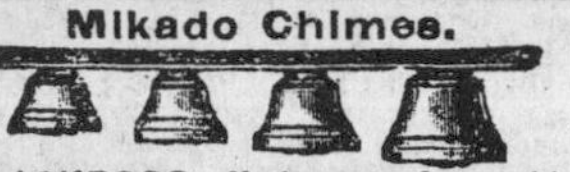

No. 10K7288 Made out of pure high grade cast bell metal, finely polished and nickel plated, open bell with iron knockers, gives clear ringing tone and is considered the best shaft or pole chime made. Dealers everywhere get a high price for this pole chime because of the excellent quality of the bells and their tone. Each set consists of two straps of bells, four bells on each strap. Price, per set $1.89

If by mail, postage extra, 60 cents.

Swiss or Shaft Chime.

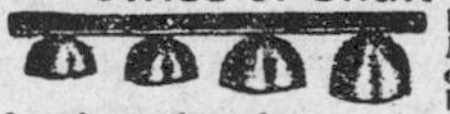

No. 10K7297 Made with four open face chime bells with iron knockers riveted to an iron strap, musical tones from light to heavy. Made out of pure bell metal, highly nickel plated, four different size chime bells riveted to the strap. The set consists of two straps of bells, four bells on each strap, making eight bells to the set. Price, per set $3.15

If by mail, postage extra, 62 cents.

Swiss Pole Chimes.

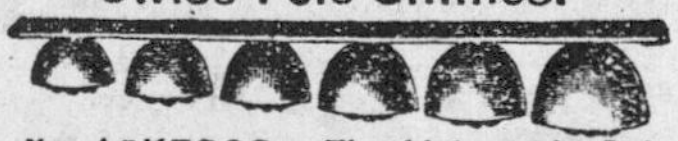

No. 10K7303 The high grade Swiss Pole Chime, harmonized sound, made out of pure Swiss bell metal, six Swiss bells, open face, iron knockers, riveted to an iron strap, nickel plated, highly polished. The best six-bell pole chime you can buy. Dealers ask a very high price for this Swiss Pole Chime because the quality of the bells and their tone is very rich. This pole chime has six harmonized graduated Swiss bells, and the price is for one strap of six bells.

Price, for six bells on one strap $1.73

If by mail, postage extra, 52 cents.

Russian Saddle Chimes.

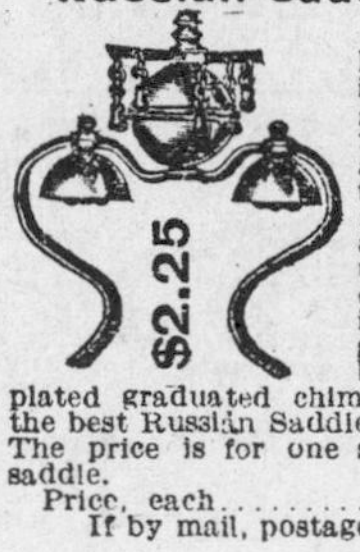

No. 10K7335 This Russian Saddle Chime is made with metal gong and two open face bells attached to a fancy brace that fastens to a saddle by removing the terrets and running them through the saddle chime braces, fastening the chimes to the gig saddle. These bells are highly nickel plated graduated chimes, iron knockers and the best Russian Saddle Chime we can make. The price is for one set of chimes for one saddle.

Price, each $2.25

If by mail, postage extra, 48 cents.

Harness Makers' Collar Awls.

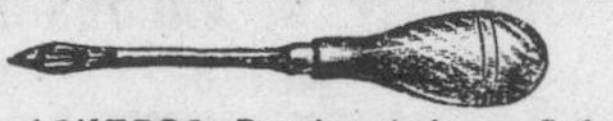

No. 10K7520 Drawing Awls, or Collar Awls, as they are called, are made with large eye for sewing horse collars with leather thongs or whangs. The awl is made of the best tool steel, highly tempered. Length, from 8 to 9 inches. Weight, 4 ounces.

Price 30c

If by mail, postage extra, 5 cents.

Leather Gauge Knife.

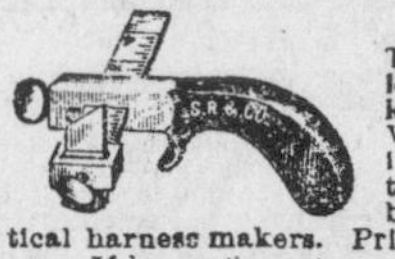

No. 10K7550 This is the best hollow iron handle gauge knife on the market. Will cut from ⅛ to 4 inches in width. It is the same knife used by all practical harness makers. Price 95c

If by mail, postage extra, 21 cents.

Harness Makers' Round Knife.

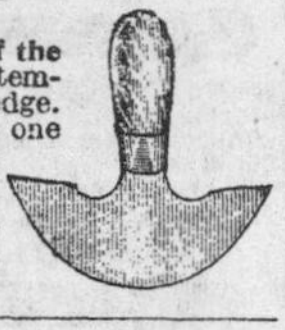

No. 10K7595 Made of the best tool steel elegantly tempered to take very sharp edge. Rosewood handles. Every one is guaranteed. Blades measure 5 inches. Weight, 5 oz.

Price, 5 inches. Each 65c

If by mail, postage extra, each, 7 cents.

Square Point Trimming Knife.

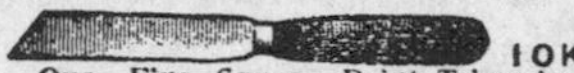

No. 10K7605 Our Fine Square Point Trimming Knife. Round handle with a fine blade made from fine tool steel. Weight, 3 ounces. Price 9c

If by mail, postage extra, 4 cents.

Revolving Spring Punches.

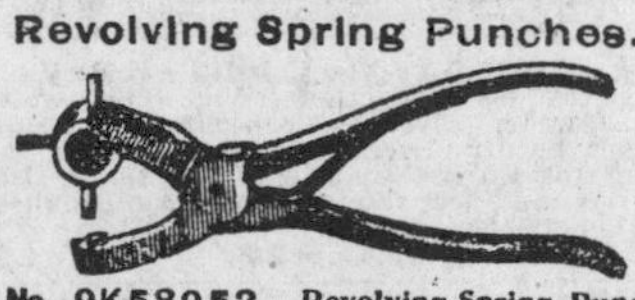

No. 9K58952 Revolving Spring Punch, with four tubes of different sizes. Weight, 14 ounces. Price 36c

No. 9K58954 Revolving Spring Punch, with six tubes of different sizes. Weight, 14 ounces. Price 45c

Harness or Belt Rivets.

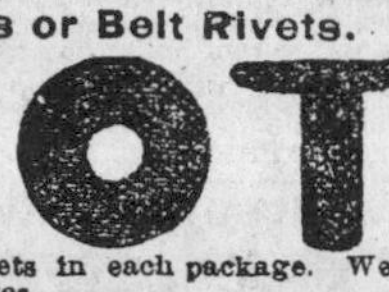

We only sell this in the one size. No. 8 is the size used for all kinds of work. There are enough burrs for the rivets in each package. We do not break packages.

No. 9K58940 Coppered Iron Rivets and Burrs. Made of soft iron, heavily coppered. Put up in ½-pound packages containing about 60 rivets and burrs. Size No. 8, assorted lengths. Price, per package 7c

Price per dozen packages 75c

S., R. & Co.'s Special Harness Repair Kit, $3.95.

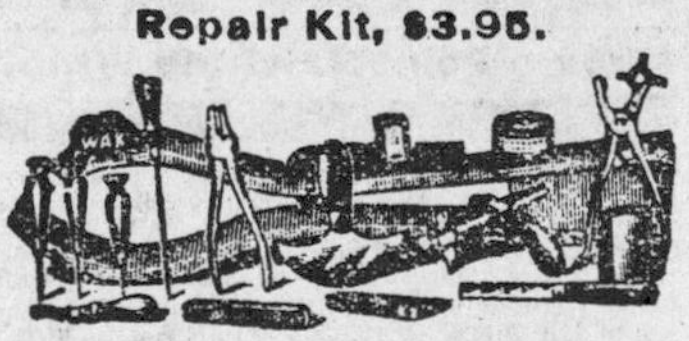

No. 10K7671 This repair kit is made up so that anyone can repair his old harness or make a new set. The following items are in this set:

One wood clamp for holding the leather to stitch	Three awls and handles
One round knife	One edging tool
One gauge knife	One double wood creaser
One 4-tube punch	One collar awl
One square point trimming knife	One rivet set
One paper of needles	One box of assorted rivets
One ball of thread	One pair of pliers
One ball of wax	

This is a very complete set and sold only as listed, no parts being omitted. In a nice box so that the tools will always be in the box when you want to use them. Weight, 13 pounds. Price $3.95

Riveting Machines.

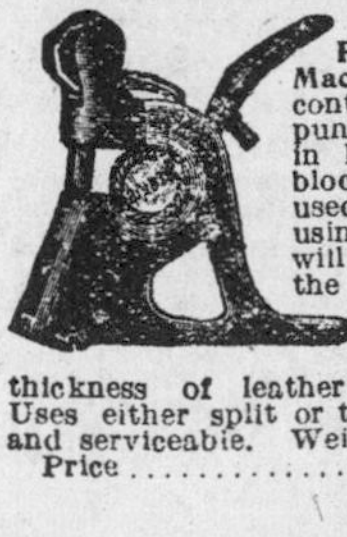

No. 9K58912 Fulton Special Riveting Machine, with pocket to contain rivets and hollow punch for punching holes in harness or straps. A block of wood should be used under the tube when using punch. This machine will do its work equal to the highest priced machine made. It is instantly adjustable to any length of rivet or any thickness of leather within its capacity. Uses either split or tubular rivets. Strong and serviceable. Weight, 2¼ pounds.

Price 46c

Hollow Tubular Steel Rivets.

No. 9K58922 Hollow Tubular Steel Rivets, japanned, for use with No. 9K58912 or similar riveting machines, put up in boxes containing 50 rivets, assorted lengths, from 3-16 to ½ inch long, for general repair work on harness, etc. Price, per box .. 3c

No. 9K58924 Hollow Tubular Rivets, japanned, put up in boxes containing 100 rivets, all the same length.

Length, inch	3-16	4-16	5-16	6-16	7-16
Price, per box	7c	8c	9c	10c	11c
Length, inch	8-16	9-16	10-16	11-16	12-16
Price, per box	12c	13c	14c	15c	16c

Slotted Rivets.

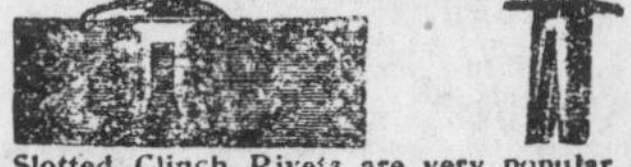

Slotted Clinch Rivets are very popular, as no set or other tool is required except a common hammer. Put up in packages containing 100 rivets. We do not break packages. Made of coppered annealed steel.

No. 9K58930 Slotted Rivets. Size No. 9, Assorted lengths. 100 rivets in each package.

Price, for 3 packages 8c

Price, for 12 packages 27c

Harness Needles.

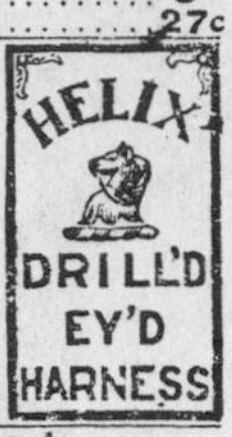

No. 10K7685 Harness Needles. 25 in paper, assorted sizes, from 0 to 4.

Price, per paper 5c

If by mail, postage extra, per paper, 2 cents.

Wax.

No. 10K7690 Wax. Price, 7 balls for 5c

If by mail, postage extra, 5c.

Harness Thread.

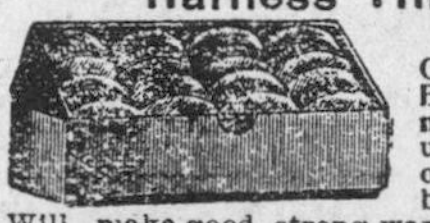

No. 10K7695 Our American Brand No. 10 Harness Thread. Natural linen color, 2-ounce balls, eight balls to pound. Will make good strong wax ends.

Price, per ball 12c

If by mail, postage extra, per ball, 3 cents.

Harness Awl Blades.

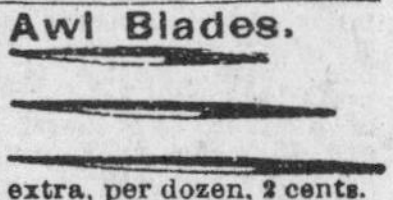

No. 10K7710 Harness Awl Blades, to be used in extra handles. Per dozen 20c

If by mail, postage extra, per dozen, 2 cents.

Wood Awl Handles.

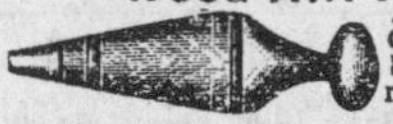

No. 10K7715 Common Wood Awl Handles, with ferrule.

Price, 4 for 6c

If by mail, postage extra, for 4, 5 cents.

Harness Horse.

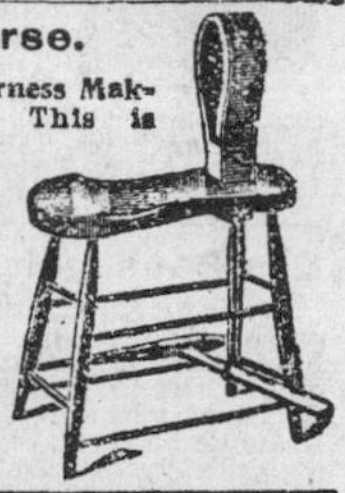

No. 10K7741 Harness Makers' Stitching Horse. This is something every horse owner should have. Any man can do his own repairing and save his time, as well as his money. Made of good sound wood. Weight, 18 pounds. Price for stitching horse without jaw strap $2.75

With jaw strap, 3.00

LEATHER.

NOTE—Owing to the uncertainty of the leather and hide market, the prices on these goods are subject to change without notice.

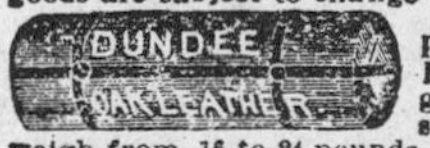

No. 10K7760 Pure Dundee Oak Harness Leather, good B grade, whole sides only; sides weigh from 16 to 24 pounds. Price, per pound 38c

No. 10K7765 Extra Quality No. 1 Dundee Oak Tanned Leather, black; weight, per side, from 16 to 24 pounds. Price, per pound 40c

No. 10K7771 Harness Leather Bellies, weighing from 3 to 5 pounds, used for repairing or making cheap strap work. Price, per pound 27c

Will send as near the weight wanted as possible.

NOTE—All of our different grades of Harness Leather are selected from packers' steer hides, and our weights run from 16 to 24 pounds and we will give you as near the weight that you order as we can.

Mexican Spurs.

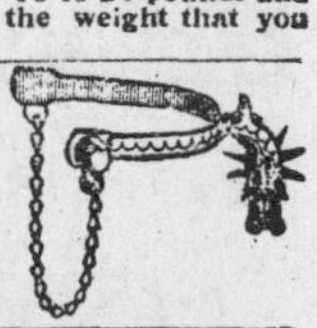

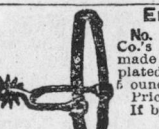

No. 10K8015 Chased and filed, with single chain and ball. Length, 1⅜-inch rowel. Weight, about 12 ozs. Price, per pair 24c

If by mail, postage extra, per pair, 14 cents.

English Spurs.

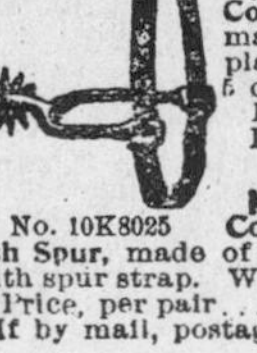

No. 10K8025

No. 10K8025 S., R. & Co.'s Special English Spur, made of malleable iron, XC plated, with spur strap. Wt., 6 ounces.

Price, per pair 30c

If by mail, postage extra, per pair, 9 cents.

No. 10K8030 S., R. & Co.'s Fine, Heavy Brass English Spur, made of solid brass, highly polished, with spur strap. Weight, 5 ounces.

Price, per pair 35c

If by mail, postage extra, per pair, 9 cents.

YOUR MONEY WILL BE IMMEDIATELY RETURNED TO YOU FOR ANY GOODS NOT PERFECTLY SATISFACTORY. 99

Mexican Curb Bridle Bits.

We always carry a large stock of bits on hand, as we do the largest business in this line to the consumer of any house in America.

No. 10K8140 Fine Blued Mexican Curb Bits, with short port on mouth bar. Weight, 11 oz. Price, each........13c

No. 10K8141 Blue Port Bit, same as No. 10K8140, only made with roller in port. Price, each..15c

If by mail, postage extra, each, 16 cents.

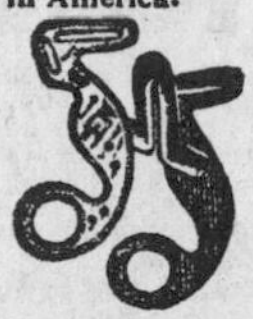

Our Improved Low Port Nickel Bit.

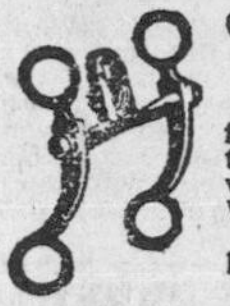

No. 10K8119 So many call for low port bits that we had this extra good nickel bit made; very strong and well finished. Weight, 10 ounces. Price, each...........69c

If by mail, postage extra, each, 14 cents.

Racine Nickel Driving Bit.

No. 10K8130 Made with solid mouth bar, half check snaffle. This is one of the best nickel driving bits on the market and one that we have a very large sale on. Stiff or jointed. We always send jointed unless ordered stiff. Weight, 8 ounces. Price, each..........15c

If by mail, postage extra, each, 12 cents.

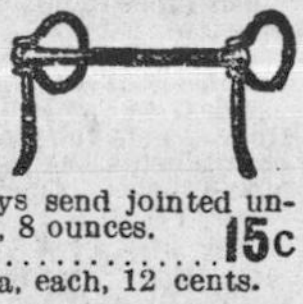

Dexter Driving Bit.

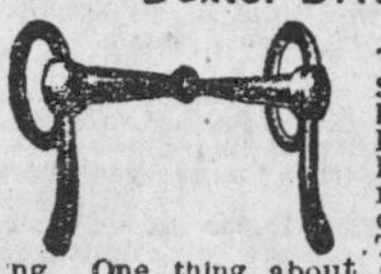

No. 10K8135 This is the finest Steel Driving Bit we handle. Large, heavy cheeks. Large heavy, tapered mouthpiece, jointed or stiff, as wanted. The best nickel plating. One thing about a bridle that should be the very best is the bit. We recommend this as being the best, most handsome, solid driving bit we handle. Weight, 14 ounces. Price, each..........45c

If by mail, postage extra, each, 15 cents.

California Bit.

No. 10K8245 California Bit. XC plated, plain finished, patent port, complete rein chains and roller. Wt., 18 ounces. Price, each....31c

If by mail, postage extra, 24 cents.

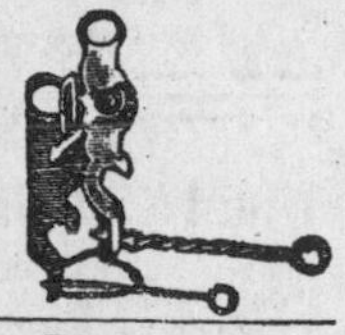

Wilson Bit.

No. 10K8270 Wilson Bit. For holding hard mouthed horses. The bit pulls on the upper jaw of the horse in place of the under jaw, and will hold the most vicious horse. Weight, about 10 ounces.

XC plate. Price, each..........11c

Nickel plate, wrought iron. Each....29c

If by mail, postage extra, each, 15 cents.

Our Special Port Bit.

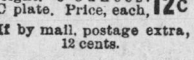

No. 10K8150 Our Special Malleable Port Bit. Made of fine malleable iron, highly XC plated, with straight posts, low port. Weight, 8 ounces. XC plate. Price, each, 12c

If by mail, postage extra, 12 cents.

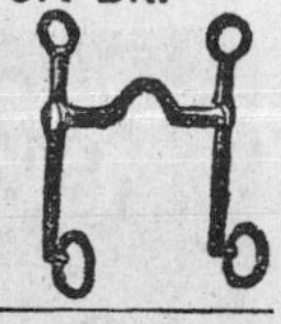

Imperial Driving Bit.

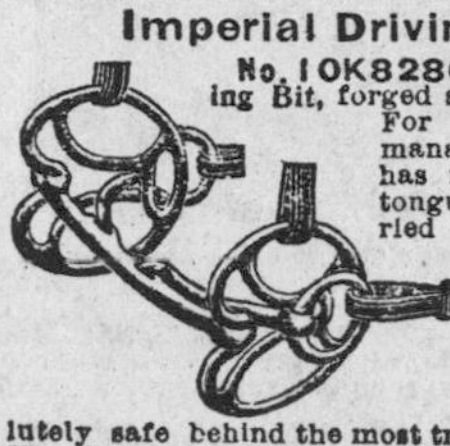

No. 10K8280 Imperial Driving Bit, forged steel mouth bar. For vicious and unmanageable horses it has no equal. The tongue cannot be carried over the top of the bit. Its peculiar construction gives the driver such leverage that he is absolutely safe behind the most treacherous horse. Weight, about 11 ounces.

XC plate. Price, each..........40c

Fine nickel plate. Price each.......90c

If by mail, postage extra, 15 cents.

The Jay-Eye-See Bit.

No. 10K8285 For pullers and vicious horses it is unexcelled. Weight, 11 ounces. Fine XC plate. Price, each, 15c

Full nickelplate. Price, each, 30c

If by mail, postage extra, 15 cents.

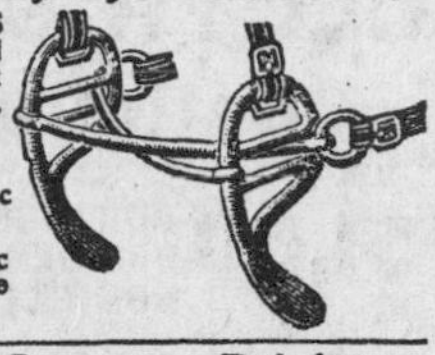

Improved Success Driving Bit.

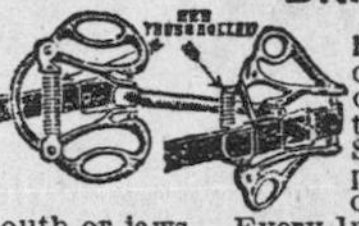

One of the best humane bits. No other bit has more controlling power than the Improved Success Bit without punishing the horse or lacerating the mouth or jaws. Every Improved Success Bit has a wrought steel bar, and is finished in XC and nickel. Weight, about 15 ounces.

No. 10K8291 XC finish. Each..50c

No. 10K8292 Nickel finish. Each..95c

If by mail, postage extra, 19 cents.

Twisted Wire Bits.

No. 10K8305 Double Twisted Wire Bit, jointed mouth, XC plate. Weight, 6 ounces. Price, each....10c

No. 10K8310 Single Twisted Wire Bit. Jointed mouth, 2¼-inch ring. Weight, 5 ounces. Price, each...(Postage extra, 8 cents.)..7c

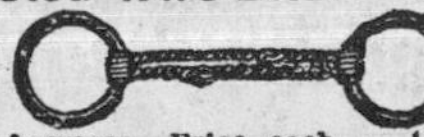

Stiff Ring Bit.

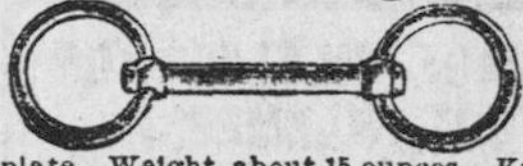

No. 10K8315 Solid Head Stiff Ring Bit. 3-inch ring, XC plate. Weight, about 15 ounces. Known as No. 90. Each, (Postage extra, 17 cents) 13c

Jointed Bridle Bit.

No. 10K8320 Stiff or Jointed Bridle Bit, 2¾-inch ring, XC plate. Weight, 8 ounces. Known as No. 47. Price, each............7c

If by mail, postage extra, 10 cents.

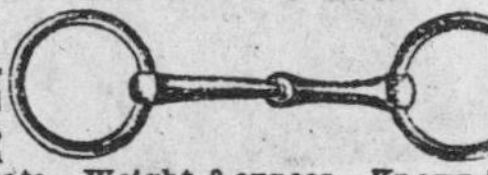

Overcheck Bit.

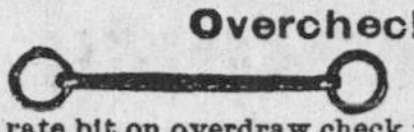

No. 10K8330 Overcheck Bit, to be used as a separate bit on overdraw check reins. Weight, 2 oz.

XC plate. Price, 2 for..........8c

Nickel plate. Price, 2 for.........10c

If by mail, postage extra, 4 cents.

Rubber Mouth Bit.

No. 10K8340 Squire's Flexible Rubber Mouth Bit, nickel, half cheek snaffles. Weight, 7 ozs. Each, 29c

If by mail, postage extra, 10 cents.

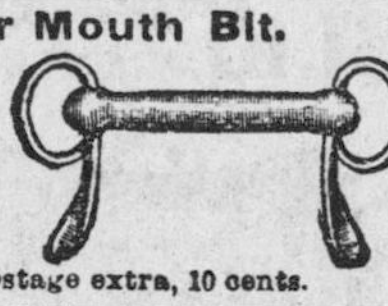

The Celebrated Humane Bit.

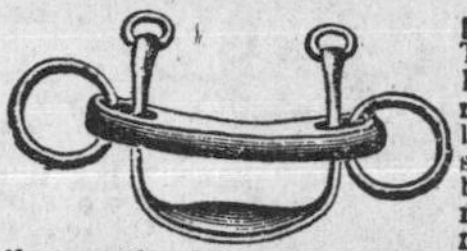

No. 10K8343 The Celebrated Humane Bit is made of solid leather, the strongest and best bit on the market, and cannot pull through the mouth. With this bit you do not need any overdraw bit, the overdraw buckles in small rings, and pulls from under jaw, making it very easy on horse. Nickel plated rings. Weight, about 16 ounces. Price, each. 65c

If by mail, postage extra, 11 cents.

Solid Leather Bit.

No. 10K8349 This bit is made of solid leather, with steel forged rings; a very easy bit on a tender mouth horse and one that gives universal satisfaction. Nickel plated. Weight, about 9 ounces. Price, each............34c

If by mail, postage extra, 12 cents.

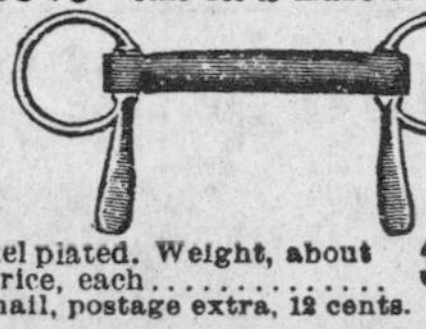

THE LOWER PRICES QUOTED IN THIS CATALOGUE will be more interesting to you than the prices quoted by any other firm or individual.

OUR COTTON AND LEATHER FLY NETS

We recommend to all drivers of horses to use some kind of fly net on their horses during the fly season. We show several styles of the very best patterns of fly nets.

Cotton Mesh Buggy Nets are illustrated under No. 10K9015, No. 10K9021, No. 10K9025, No. 10K9031 and No. 10K9050.

Round Leather Express Nets are illustrated under No. 10K9069, No. 10K9074 and No. 10K9081, three styles of nets. Make your selection by catalogue number.

The greatest bargain in Light Round Leather Buggy Nets are those listed under No. 10K9096, No. 10K9097, No. 10K9098 and No. 10K9099.

Heavy Upper Leather Team Nets are listed under No. 10K9231, No. 10K9237, No. 10K9245, No. 10K9251 and No. 10K9253.

Cotton Cord Team Nets are No. 10K9001, No. 10K9006, No. 10K9113 and No. 10K9117. Team nets made out of high grade belting leather under No. 10K9183 and No. 10K9125.

We also handle a full line of burlap and scrim fly covers. Our styles of burlap fly covers are the popular selling styles and the best values for the money ever offered, are cool and light on the horse.

70c COTTON CORD MESH TEAM NET FOR WORK HORSES.

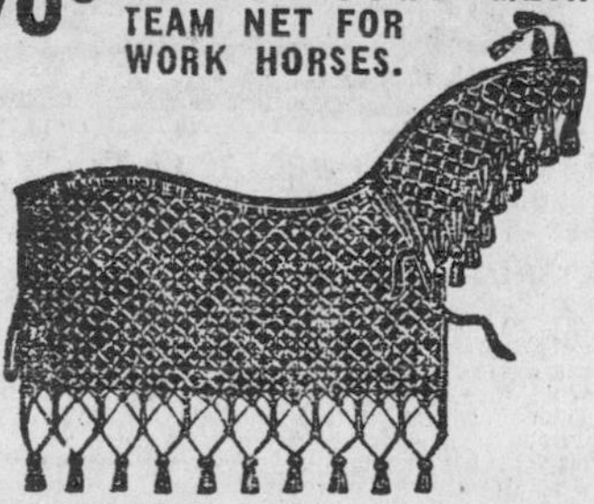

Our Cotton Cord Team Net. Body, neck and ear tips; diamond knotted mesh, woven center bar; neck part snaps to body; fancy colored body, border and tassels. An extra good cheap mesh net. Weight, 17 ounces each.

No. 10K9001 Price, each..........70c

If by mail, postage extra, 22 cents.

87c COTTON CORD MESH TEAM NET FOR WORK HORSES.

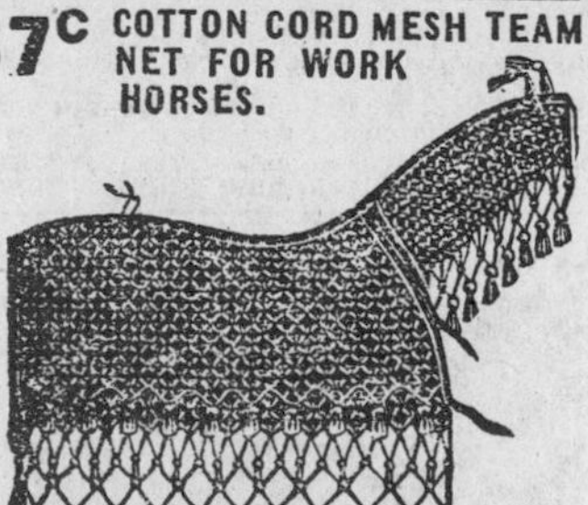

Our Special Cotton Cord Team Net. Diamond knotted mesh, heavy cord, woven center bar; body, neck and ear tips; neck snaps to body; 1½-inch mesh. A good everyday team net. Made in two patterns. Pattern No. 1, black body, lemon border and black tassels. Pattern No. 2, green body, lemon border and red tassels. State pattern wanted. Weight, each, 17 ounces.

No. 10K9006 Price, each.......87c

If by mail, postage extra, 22 cents.

$1.12 OUR PURE ALL WHITE NET FOR BUGGY HORSE.

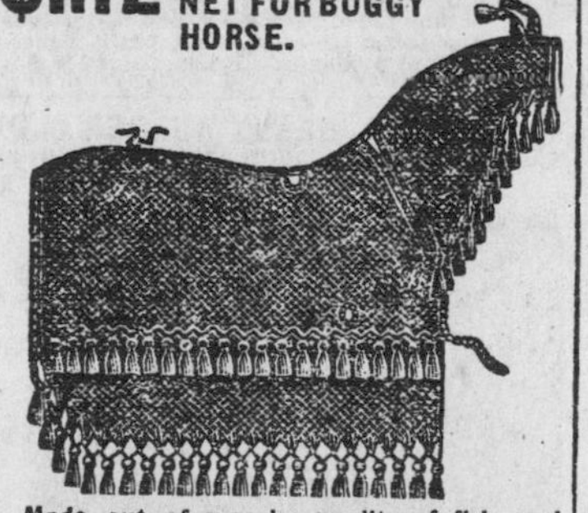

Made out of superior quality of fish cord cotton woven mesh body with fancy knotted neck piece, detachable, with mesh ear tips and tassels. This net is one of the best all white nets that we make. Has double row of tassels, one row on the border and one row on the side of the net. Woven center bar, braided terret holes and braided shaft holes. This net is a closely knotted border, making a small mesh which keeps the flies off the horse. Remember, this net is all white. Weight of net, about 16 ounces.

No. 10K9015 Price, each......$1.12

If by mail, postage extra, 20 cents.

ASSORTED PATTERN, FANCY COLORS, ONE OF THE MOST POPULAR BUGGY NETS.

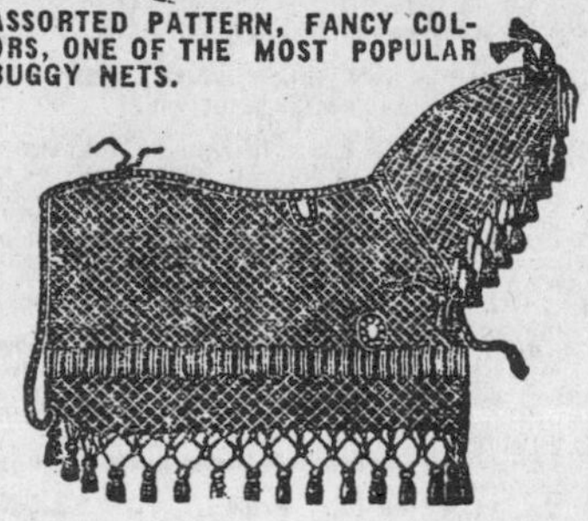

$1.63 OUR NEW PATTERN SHAFT NET FOR BUGGY HORSE.

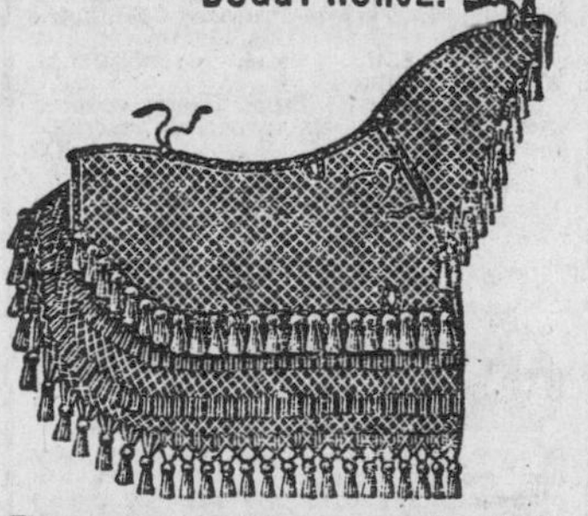

These nets are made to use on single or double horses. Made with shaft hole so that the shafts will not tear the net. The meshes are small diamond woven mesh with double row of tassels, extra fancy woven round border with heavily knotted fringe. Diamond mesh body with extra neck piece, mesh ear tips with tassels to keep the flies off the ears. We make this net all black with two rows white tassels. It is a very handsome net. Weight of net, 27 ounces.

No. 10K9031 Price, each......$1.63

If by mail, postage extra, 33 cents.

$1.19 OUR LIGHT MESH FLY NET.

This net is made out of fish cord cotton, knotted mesh body, and detachable neck piece, cotton ear tips with tassels to keep the flies off the horse's ears and fancy woven knotted border with one row of tassels. Braided terret holes and braided shaft holes. This net is made in fancy colors, red body with green and yellow stripes, green border, yellow and green tassels. A net that is very popular and one that looks well on a horse. It is one of our cheapest buggy nets. Weight of net, about 17 ounces.

No. 10K9021 Price, each......$1.19

If by mail, postage extra, 22 cents.

DOUBLE THE VALUE OF YOUR DOLLAR by purchasing needed articles from us at our greatly reduced prices.

$1.48 LIGHT COTTON FLY NET FOR BUGGY HORSE.

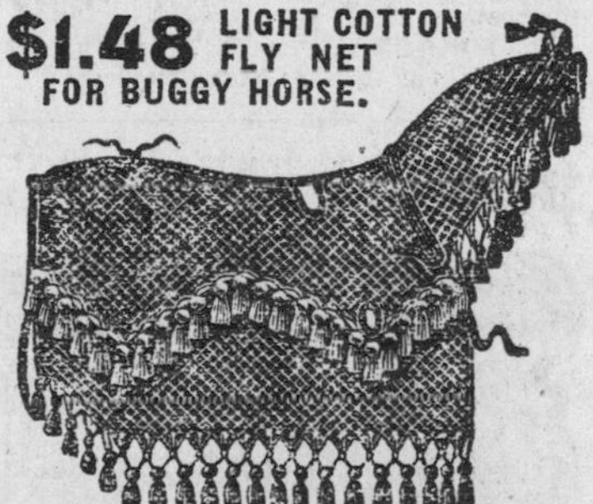

One of the best light cotton fly nets that we handle. The style of this net and the way it is made make it a very popular net. The meshes are very fine, closely woven and knotted. It is made with body and neck pieces with ear tips with tassels, which keep the flies off the ears. Has double row of tassels, zigzag row along the side of the horse and lower one on bottom of the net. These tassels come in variegated colors and the body of the net is apple green with lemon tassels. It is one of the handsomest and best cotton fly nets we can make. Weight of net, 17 ounces.

No. 10K9025 Price, each....$1.48

If by mail, postage extra, 22 cents.

$1.93 OUR SPECIAL THREE-ROW TASSEL TUG NET.

If you want a good net try this one for buggy horse.

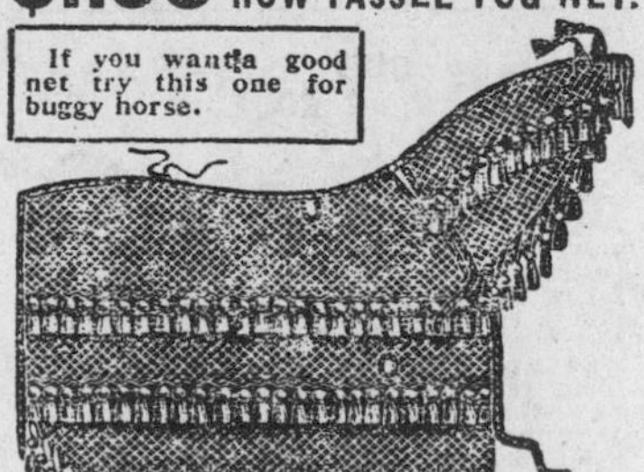

This net is made with extra neck piece and ear tips with two rows of tassels on the neck piece and three rows of tassels on the body. It is a very handsome net and looks very stylish on the horse. It is made with green body with olive green tassels and border to match. Mesh body and neck piece, terret holes and shaft holes. Three rows of tassels on the body and two rows on the neck. The neck piece is detachable. One of the best fly nets on the market. Weight of net, 28 ounces.

No. 10K9050 Price, each....$1.93

If by mail, postage extra, 34 cents.

FANCY MOMIE CLOTH BUGGY LAP ROBES—Continued.

$1.10 OUR HIGH GRADE MOMIE CLOTH LAP ROBE.

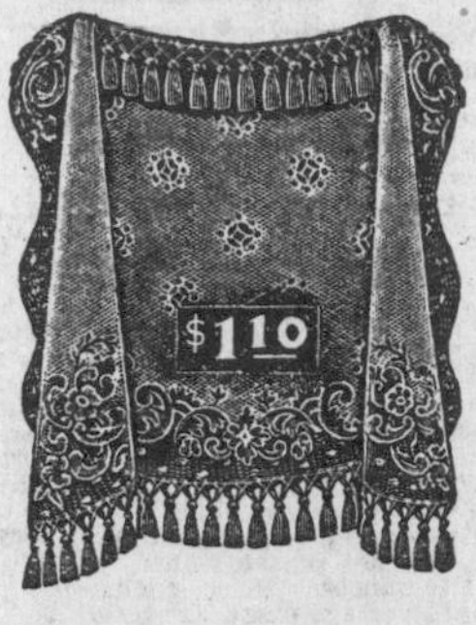

MATERIAL—Extra heavy momie cloth yarn, woven in fancy jacquard pattern. A very beautiful design.
COLORS—Olive green, old rose and light brown. Closely woven.
SIZE—52x60 inches; weight about 16 ounces.

No. 10K9932 Price..........$1.10
If by mail, postage extra, 18 cents.

$1.18 JACQUARD PATTERN LAP ROBE.

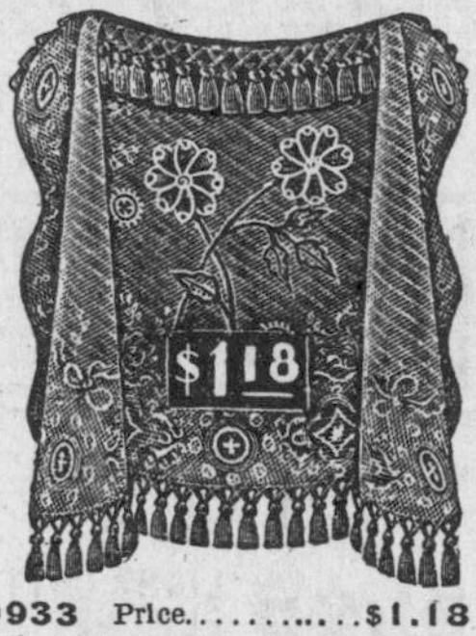

MATERIAL—Momie cloth yarn woven in fancy jacquard pattern, fancy rich colored body.
EMBROIDERED—Fancy embroidered zephyr yarn representing two roses.
SIZE—50x60 inches; weight, about 16 ounces.

No. 10K9933 Price..........$1.18
If by mail, postage extra, 18 cents.

$1.15 OUR BROWN AND WHITE LAP ROBE.

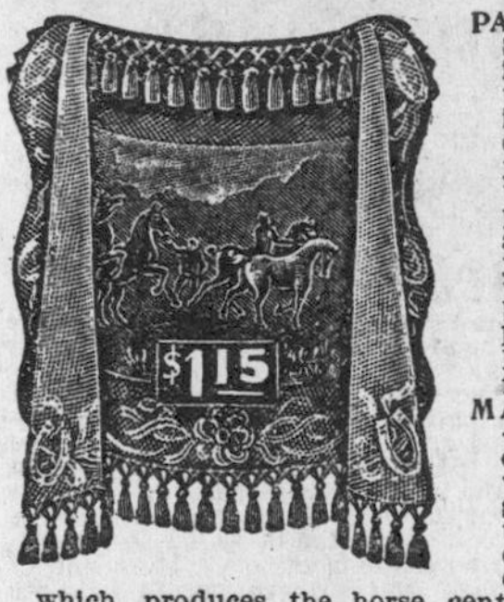

PATTERN—Six horses in the center woven in the cloth by jacquard weaving process and fancy jacquard woven border, heavy knotted fringe.
MATERIAL—Momie cloth yarn woven together on the jacquard machine, which produces the horse center in the weaving of the robe.
SIZE—48x60 inches; weight, about 18 ounces.

No. 10K9934 Price..........$1.15
If by mail, postage extra, 21 cents.

$1.25 OUR BEST BUGGY LAP ROBE.

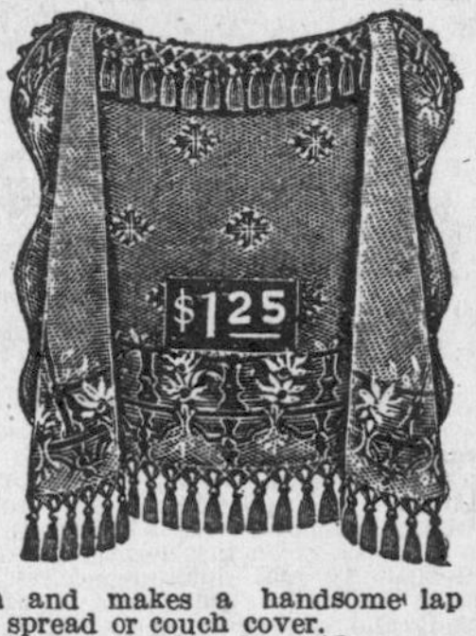

MATERIAL—Momie cloth yarn woven together in a fancy jacquard woven pattern, plain center with jacquard stars through the body, fancy woven border.
COLORS—Olive green, red, and old gold; a very beautiful design and makes a handsome lap robe, table spread or couch cover.
SIZE—50x62 inches; weight, about 18 ounces.

No. 10K9936 Price..........$1.25
If by mail, postage extra, 21 cents.

$1.50 OUR HIGH GRADE EMBROIDERED CENTER MOMIE CLOTH LAP ROBE

MATERIAL—Momie cloth yarn, woven on a jacquard loom, jacquard fancy drop stitch pattern.
EMBROIDERED CENTER—Fancy color zephyr yarn, fancy flowered center in rich colors, assorted patterns. Heavy knotted fringe, fancy borders. Rich design.
SIZE—48x60 inches; weight, 17 ounces.

No. 10K9940 Price..........$1.50
If by mail, postage extra, 20 cents.

CARRIAGE HEATERS OR FOOT WARMERS.

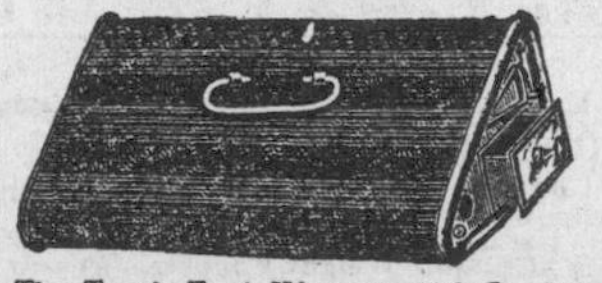

The Tropic Foot Warmer and Carriage Heater is the best made. Most economical to operate. Makes driving comfortable in the coldest weather at a cost of less than ¼ cent per hour. Burns 12 to 16 hours with one filling. $3.75 is the regular price of this heater when sold under its regular copyrighted name. Our price for same heater sold under the name of Tropic is $1.74.

Both ends are made of light castings, in an ornamental triangular shape, fitted with adjustable ventilators, which regulate the heat. Handsomely bronzed. Has removable fire box with brass ends. Fire can be extinguished by tightly closing ventilators and drafts (doing away with the inconvenience of pouring water on the coal as is necessary with other heaters).

The sides are made of heavy sheet iron, asbestos lined, and covered with heavy Brussels carpet. It is entirely fireproof, will not scorch the blankets or clothes. Can be carried about. Burns without flame, no soot nor odor. Burns any kind of prepared coal. Best results can be had by using the Perfect Prepared Coal, listed below. Remember, this identical heater retails for $3.75. Size, 14x8x5 inches. Weight, 7 pounds.

No. 10K3753 Tropic Heater, covered with fancy Brussels carpet, as described above. Price..........$1.74

PERFECT CARRIAGE HEATER.

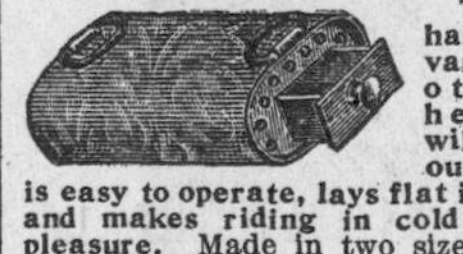

This Heater has many advantages over other style heaters; it will not get out of order, is easy to operate, lays flat in the buggy and makes riding in cold weather a pleasure. Made in two sizes, 14 inches long, weight, about 5½ pounds, and 20 inches long, weight, about 7¼ pounds. Heavy galvanized iron side, top and bottom, metal ends, and perforated metallic drawer working on a slide and held in place by a spring, which holds the prepared coal, and when placed in the heater requires no further attention and burns without flame, smoke, odor or dirt from twelve to fifteen hours, and can be extinguished with water and used again if desired. The heavy galvanized iron sides are covered with heavy asbestos paper and covered with an extra quality velvet Brussels carpet. This protects the robe, blanket or skirt from the heater. Remember that these two heaters would retail in the regular way for $3.75 and $4.75. At the price we are making you on these two heaters we are saving you more than enough to buy the coal to last you through the season. If two people are going to use the heater, we recommend the 20-inch size.

No. 10K3756 Price, 14-inch heater..........$1.60
No. 10K3758 Price, 20-inch heater..........2.95

Perfect Prepared Coal, for above heaters. Fully guaranteed to burn without smoke, odor, flame or soot, and can be extinguished and relighted at any time. Put up in boxes containing 1 dozen cakes each, size 7¼x2½x1¼ inches.

No. 10K3760 Price, per box of 1 dozen cakes..........59c

PLUSH ROBES

WHEN YOU WANT TO BUY a plain Plush Lap Robe, you first look for the price robe you want to buy, then you look for the size and description of this robe. We show you five distinct styles and grades of Plain Plush Robes. Our No. 10K13459 or No. 10K13461 at $1.25 and $1.45 is a single plush robe and just the style robe for spring and fall use or any time you want a light weight plush robe. For a heavy, warm, durable double green plush robe order No. 10K13464 or No. 10K13469, the best $2.15 and $2.49 plush robes you can buy. Robes similar to this but not as good quality are sold for from $1.00 to $1.50 more than our price.

THE ROBE we send you under No. 10K13472 is an extra large size and extra heavy plush robe the best $3.54 robe you can get. Remember, this robe is extra large size and will go over the laps of two people and tuck under the side.

FOR AN EXTRA HEAVY and extra large size robe, order our No. 10K13476 at $4.95. This robe is not generally handled by other dealers because of the high quality and the price they must sell the robe for. Do not take a lighter robe or a cheaper quality robe and think you are getting as good a robe as we are selling you for $4.95, because you cannot get it. Order this and get the best. If you want a heavy double green plush robe with rubber interlining, order our No. 10K13479 at $4.50. This is an extra large size robe with an interlining of rubber cloth, which makes it wind and waterproof. When you order your plush robes from Sears, Roebuck & Co., you always get the best, and for less money than you can buy the same quality anywhere.

GRAY AND FANCY COLOR SINGLE AND DOUBLE PLUSH ROBES $1.25 TO $4.95.

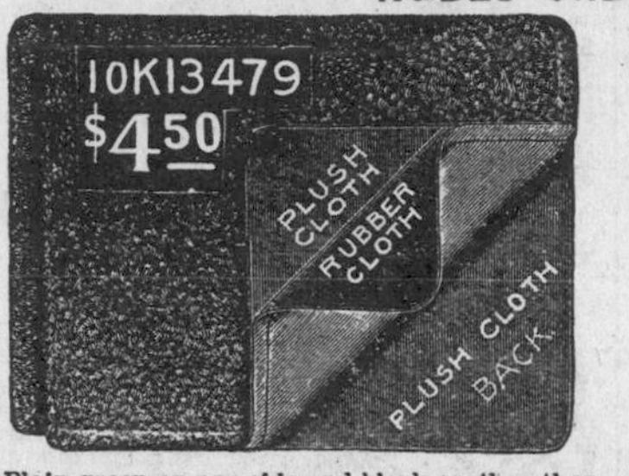

Our line of fine single and double green plush robes includes all the best patterns, and all sizes, from $1.25 to $4.95. Our fine rubber face robes, with plush backs, wind and waterproof, for $2.50 and $3.59.

Our Gray and Fancy Color Single Plush Buggy Robe. This robe is made of soft gray and colored plush stock, bound around edges. Size, 50x60 inches. Weight, about 3 pounds.

No. 10K13459 Price, gray..........$1.25
No. 10K13461 Price, fancy..........1.45

No. 10K13464 The London Special Double Plain Green Plush Carriage Robe. Plain green pattern on one side and plain black on the other side. A very handsome, stylish and well made plush robe. Size of robe, 50x60 inches. Weight of robe, about 6 pounds. Price..........$2.15

No. 10K13469 The Astoria Special, Extra Heavy Double Green Plush Lap Robe. Plain green on one side and black on the other. This is an extra quality of fine plush robe. Size, 50x60 inches. Weight, about 6½ pounds. The best kind of a robe for everyday use. Always looks neat and clean. Price..........$2.49

No. 10K13472 The Bisbee Special Double Green and Black Plush Robe. Raised black plush on one side, raised green plush on the other. The Bisbee is our new robe. Fine soft raised plush. This robe is extra large size, 54x72 inches. Weight, about 8 pounds. Price..........$3.54

No. 10K13476 The Edinburgh. Extra Heavy Double Green Plush Robe. Superfine quality of plain green silk plush on one side and handsome shade of black on the other side. Double, extra large. Size, 54x72 inches. Weight, about 8½ pounds. This is the largest, handsomest and most durable double green plush robe we handle. One of the best sellers in our line. Price..........$4.95

THE AMERICAN RUBBER INTERLINED PLUSH ROBES.

No. 10K13479 The American Rubber Interlined Plush Robe. Green plush robe, 54x72 inches. Rubber interlined, making it windproof and very warm. All robes with rubber interlining are very warm and strong. Weight, about 12 pounds. Price..........$4.50

WATERPROOF LAP ROBES. Plush Robes, Rubber Face, $2.50 and $3.59.

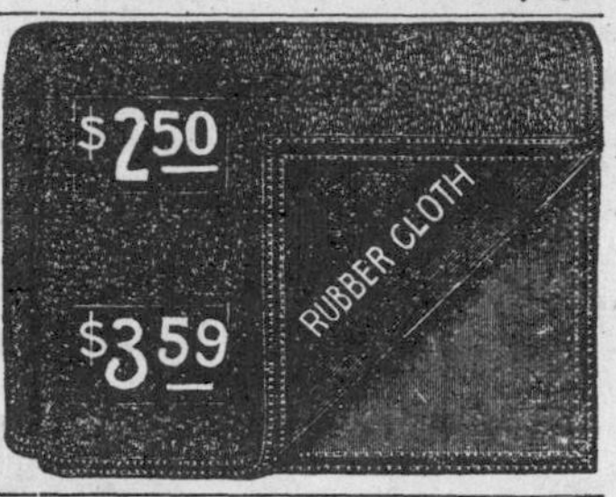

No. 10K13481 The Special Heavy, Rubber Lined Waterproof Lap Robe. This robe is made with a fine plush back, facing of rubber, made for all kinds of stormy weather. **Can be used with either plush or rubber side up.** Size, 50x60 inches. Weight, about 5¾ pounds. Price..........$2.50

No. 10K13483 The Special Plush Lined, Rubber Faced Storm Lap Robe. This lap robe is made of an extra quality of rubber facing and superfine plush back. **Nothing better ever made in a storm lap robe.** Size, 50x72 inches. Weight, about 6 pounds. Price..........$3.59

$6.30 HEAVY RUBBER CLOTH INTERLINED ROBES. OUR AMERICAN BISON ROBE IS ONE OF THE BEST HEAVY ROBES YOU CAN BUY. $7.30

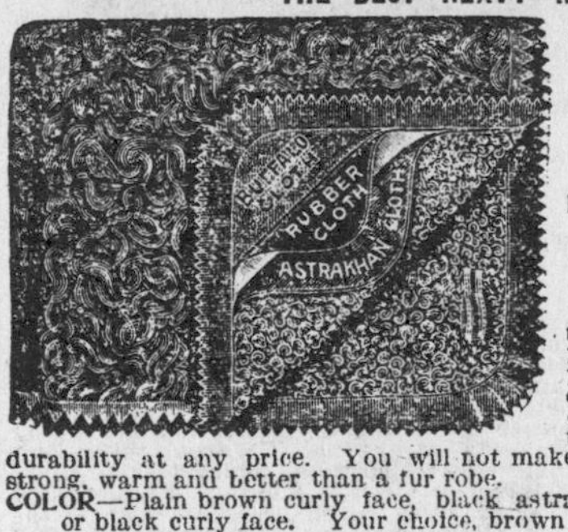

MATERIAL.—The material used in this high grade American Bison Robe is a fine long carded wool and hair mixed body, woven together with a heavy double warp back, making a very strong, solid body with long curly wool face. The back of the robe is made of a very heavy astrakhan cloth, curly face, woven with extra heavy cotton warp.

LINING—An interlining of heavy rubber cloth with double row stitching around the robe and with a double pinked felt border, black and red. This robe is stronger and warmer than his fur robe.

We guarantee the robe to be wind, water and mothproof and to outwear any skin robe that you can buy and always be soft and pliable. If you get this robe wet from snow or rain it will dry quickly and not be hard like most of the cheap fur robes. There is no robe in the world that will compete with this robe for warmth and durability at any price. You will not make any mistake in buying this robe because it is strong, warm and better than a fur robe.

COLOR—Plain brown curly face, black astrakhan cloth lined, red and black pinked border or black curly face. Your choice, brown or black. State color desired.

No. 10K14503 Size, 54x62 inches. Weight, about 10 pounds. Price..........$6.30
No. 10K14509 Size, 54x72 inches. Weight, about 11½ pounds. Price..........7.30

$3.05 EXTRA HEAVY SINGLE PLUSH ROBE FOR BUGGY AND CARRIAGE USE.

If you want a nice single plush buggy robe try this special $3.05 robe.

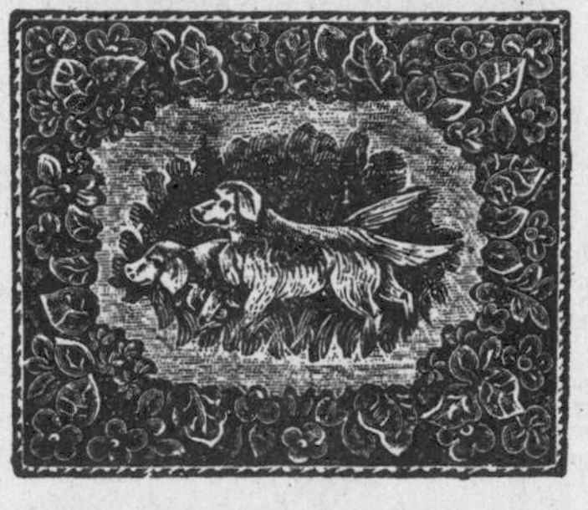

SINGLE PLUSH—Extra heavy and full raised plush on each side. It is as heavy as a double plush robe would be if made in two pieces. This robe at $3.05 is the greatest bargain ever offered in a full raised plush single quality robe. A very thick plush robe.

PATTERN—Dog center, fancy flowered border, braided bound edge.

COLORINGS—Red and black and seal brown pattern on one side and plain black on the other side. You will note by the weight of the robe that it is a very heavy single plush robe.

SIZE—50x60 inches. Weight, about 5½ pounds.

No. 10K14512 Price..........$3.05

$3.99 THIS EXCELLENT QUALITY BEAUTIFUL DEER HEAD DOUBLE PLUSH ROBE IN NATURAL COLORS FOR LESS THAN THE AVERAGE DEALER PAYS AT WHOLESALE.

Remember the Quality of Plush makes the price of our Robes.

THIS POPULAR ROBE is made of two plies of good wearing plush, with a good standing nap, equal in every way to the grades used in robes selling at $5.75 at retail. The plies are strongly sewed together and the back is the plain black plush, while the front is of a strikingly beautiful pattern in colors that are perfectly natural to the scene presented. The design shows the head of a deer in the center of the robe and in the natural shades of tan and yellow. The deer is in the attitude of taking a rest, his tongue hanging out and shown in red. The head is set in a background of rich green and surrounded by a border of the trunks and branches of trees in their natural colors, dark brown with touches of yellow to represent the sunshine that comes through the foliage, thus showing the deer as through a clump of trees. This is a reproduction of a picture that is greatly admired everywhere and is brought out perfectly on this robe, making as rich an effect as anybody would care to see in a lap robe. While the quality of material and make guarantees you a robe of great durability and is practically coldproof, yet if you want a perfectly windproof and waterproof robe the next number below with the same deer head design and the same quality of plush with rubber interlining is recommended for your consideration. Size of this robe, 48x60 inches. Weight, about 5½ pounds.
No. 10K14528 Deer Head Double Plush Robe. Price....................$3.99

$5.25 OUR DEER HEAD DOUBLE PLUSH ROBE WITH RUBBER INTERLINING.

THIS ROBE IS MADE of the same good wearing quality of plush, double ply and the same size exactly as our above No. 10K14528, only that this one has an interlining of rubber between the two plies of plush which makes the robe wind and waterproof and stronger. This rubber lined robe is selling at retail for about $6.75. Take your choice of either this one or the one above. They are exceptional qualities in point of material and design and remember that our price is lower than the average dealer pays for the equal at wholesale. We are giving you the same excellent values on each and every robe in our line. Weight, about 8½ pounds.
No. 10K14533 Rubber Interlined Deer Head Double Plush Robe. Price....$5.25

$3.35 PLUSH ROBE.

PATTERN—River bank and shrubbery showing three deer coming out of the thickets to water; a very beautiful design.
COLOR—Dark shaded colors; black, old gold and red; fancy scroll border.
MATERIAL—Raised plush, soft nap, woven body, double plush sewed together, plain black on one side and medallion fancy pattern on the other side.
No. 10K14515 Size, 50x60 inches. Weight, about 6 pounds.
Price..................................$3.35
No. 10K14518 Size, 60x70 inches. Weight, about 8½ pounds.
Price..................................$4.99

$3.59 PLUSH ROBE.

MATERIAL—A heavy cotton warp back and long nap raised plush face, solid black plush on one side and this handsome medallion pattern on the other, backed together and hemmed around the edge, making a double plush robe.
PATTERN—A pair of hunting dogs, representing man's favorite companions on a hunting trip.
COLORS—Dark shaded combination colors, black, red, green, brown and light blues.
SIZE—About 50x60 inches. Weight, about 6 pounds.
No. 10K14523 Price........$3.59

$5.37 OUR NAVAJO SPECIAL PATTERN INDIAN ROBE.

MATERIAL—Woven plush body, plain black on one side and medallion raised plush on the other.
COLOR—Plain black on one side, green, red, and white diamond figure on the other side.
STYLE—A reproduction of the Navajo Indian blankets. This pattern has been very popular and one of the best selling patterns we handle.
SIZE—The robe is made in extra large size, 60x70 inches, and weighs about 9¼ pounds. Will go over the laps of two people and tuck under at the sides and plenty long enough to fold under the feet. A warm, double plush robe.
No. 10K14538 Price..........$5.37

$3.58 OUR SPECIAL DEER AND DOG CENTER PLUSH ROBE.

PATTERN—A running deer and dog, a large and beautiful design.
COLOR—Dark and light green, black, red, seal brown and tan and fancy colored border.
MATERIAL—Raised plush with a woven back, two pieces backed together and hemmed around the edges. This robe is strong and warm and the greatest value ever offered for $3.58.
SIZE—50x60 inches. Weight, about 6 pounds.
No. 10K14541 Price,........$3.58

$5.87 OUR KENTUCKY BELLE DOUBLE PLUSH ROBE.

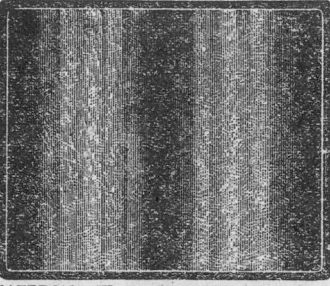

MATERIAL—Woven plush with a heavy cotton warp back and fine raised plush face, soft and silky.
STYLE—Double plush robe, two pieces of plush backed together and hemmed around the edge making a heavy double robe.
PATTERN—Two patterns; color dark shaded brown, and dark shaded green.
SIZE—Extra large, 60x70 inches; will go over the laps of two people and tuck under at the sides. Weight, about 9 pounds. Entirely new robe, blended colors from dark to light shaded to dark. A handsome combination.
No. 10K14543 Dark shaded green pattern Price.....................$5.87
No. 10K14548 Dark shaded brown color. Price.....................$5.87

$4.49 THE BEST ROBE THAT YOU CAN BUY.

MATERIAL—Heavy woven, cotton back, raised plush face, soft nap, two pieces of plush backed together and hemmed edges, making a warm double plush robe.
PATTERN—Deer head center with dog heads and horns, representing hunting scene; combination fancy border.
COLORS—Plain black on one side and handsome medallion pattern on the other; red, brown, green, white and yellow, very striking colors and combinations, a rich looking $4.49 robe.
SIZE—50x60 inches. Weight, about 6 pounds.
No. 10K14558 Price........$4.49

$4.25 IF YOU WANT A GOOD ROBE, TRY THIS ONE.

MATERIAL—Raised plush, solid cotton warp back, soft and warm; two pieces of plush backed together and hemmed around the edges, making a strong, durable plush robe.
COLORS—Red, brown, yellow, light green and purple; a beautiful combination of blending colors.
PATTERN—Scroll design.
SIZE—50x60 inches. Weight, about 6 pounds.
No. 10K14563 Price.........$4.25
The same robe made with rubber faced drill between the two pieces of plush, hemmed around the edges, making the robe windproof, rainproof and mothproof. The same pattern as No. 10K14563.
No. 10K14568 Price.......$5.43

$4.69 PLUSH ROBE.

MATERIAL—Heavy woven plush body, heavy cotton warp back, raised napped plush face, solid woven black plush back; two pieces plush backed together and hemmed around the edge, a very strong, well made robe.
PATTERN—Two beautiful spotted hunting dogs.
COLORS—The robe is shaded green, red, white, light and dark brown with scroll border of red roses; dogs are light colored body with dark brown spots. The combination of colors is very soft, blending into beautiful shades.
SIZE—50x60 inches. Weight, about 7 pounds.
No. 10K14573 Price.......$4.69

$4.50 BUYS THIS FINE QUALITY SPLENDID WEARING DOUBLE PLUSH ROBE WITH THIS HANDSOME MEDALLION PATTERN, WORTH $7.00 RETAIL.

THE RICH DESIGN IS TAKEN FROM A WORLD FAMOUS PAINTING OF TWO HORSES IN THE STRIKINGLY NATURAL ATTITUDE OF TERROR BEFORE AN APPROACHING THUNDER STORM. ONE OF THE MOST BEAUTIFUL PICTURES EVER USED ON A ROBE.

THE MATERIAL in this lap robe consists of two plies of heavy strong wearing plush, stoutly sewed together. This plush has strong nap that stands up and does not lay flat like in the average plush robe offered at retail at much higher prices than we quote for this one. We guarantee this robe for many seasons' wear, and assure you it could not be duplicated at retail under $7.00. We quote less than the usual wholesale price on robes. The back is plain black plush and the front shows the following rich design in colors. The design—The centerpiece is reproduced from a justly celebrated painting showing two horses (one brown and the other white) in the attitude of terror before an approaching thunder storm, and is as true to life as one could ever hope to see in a picture. It is the most handsome production ever seen in a robe. This is set in a background of shaded blue with the hills appearing in the distance and surrounded by a border of red, green and yellow, representing wild roses, and their foliage in their natural colors. Certainly you would look a long time before you would find another robe with all the merits of this one, in point of quality and design.

WHILE RECOMMENDING THIS EXCELLENT LAP ROBE for your special consideration, we wish to remind you that we have selected our entire line with the same great care as we have shown in selecting this one. The qualities and designs are the best ever made and remember that you can suit your own particular taste from our line and be sure of getting the greatest value it is possible for the consumer to obtain. You pay no retail profits or expenses in our prices. Size of this robe is 50x60 inches and weighs about 7 pounds.
No. 10K14553 Price...........................$4.50

$2.29 NAVAJO INDIAN PLAID HORSE BLANKET.

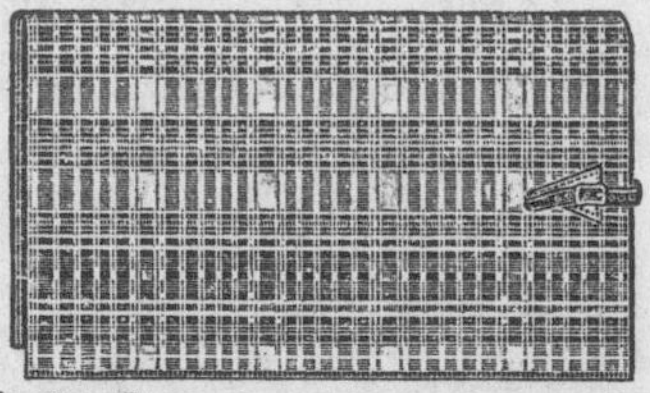

$2.29 Our Navajo Indian Plaid Horse Blankets are made in two fancy patterns; handsome drop box plaid, alternate colors, new pattern for our line for this season; heavy double warp, fine soft long blanket filling, very bright fancy colors. Made in one size, 76x80 inches. Weight, about 5 pounds.

Buyers of horse blankets we know are always looking for a horse blanket that is strictly up to date both in quality of material, pattern and finish. This Navajo Indian Plaid Blanket is something entirely new and you cannot help but see the great value we offer you in this 76x80-inch blanket at $2.29. Remember the quality of material used in a horse blanket makes the price the blanket must sell for and if you bought this same blanket of your local dealer it would cost you from $3.00 to $3.25.

MATERIAL—Long carded blanket stock, mixed with wool filling spun to yarn, woven together with hard twisted double warp, making a strong warm body.

PATTERN—Black and green, alternate drop box plaid, wide fancy heading, purple, green and white stripes in border. One of our best grade plaid blankets. Fancy Navajo Indian box plaid, combination headings.
SIZE—76x80 inches. Weight, about 5 lbs.
No. 10K16494 Price, each $2.29

PATTERN—Red and black, alternate drop box plaid body, fancy colors, red, black, white and orange, stripe and plaid, extra wide heading. Very new pattern this year.
SIZE—76x80 inches. Weight, about 5 lbs.
No. 10K16499 Price, each $2.29

$2.69 HIGHBALL HORSE BLANKET.

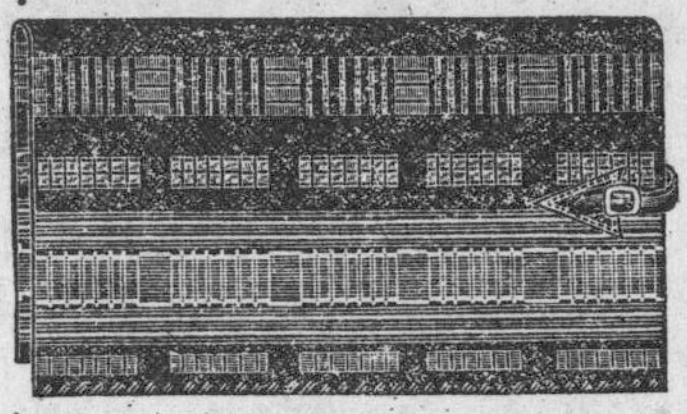

$2.69 In making up our line and our selection of horse blankets from one of the largest blanket mills in the United States, at the suggestion of the manufacturer we selected this high grade box plaid, wool finish horse blanket. One size and made in three patterns. Size, 80x84 inches, weight, about 6 pounds, the size generally used for medium size buggy horse. There is no blanket in our line or on the market today that will give better wear and hold its color better than this Special $2.69 Blanket. Remember the quality of blanket stock makes the price of the blanket. We have other cheap plaid blankets, but this is a high quality of material and a work of art in patterns.

MATERIAL—Long carded blanket filling handsomely dyed, spun into yarn and woven together with heavy double warp, making a very strong and high finished blanket. Read descriptions of the patterns carefully and select the color you like best by catalogue number.

PATTERN—Our Highball, drop box plaid, alternate green, brown and white body, fancy red, white, green and brown heading. A handsome selection for a horse blanket.
SIZE—80x84 inches. Weight, about 6 lbs.
No. 10K16504 Price, each....$2.69

PATTERN—Our Highball, drop box plaid, alternate wine body, red, white, green and lemon body stripes; lemon, red, green, white and black plaid heading. One of our best selections. What is your choice?
SIZE—80x84 inches. Weight, about 6 lbs.
No. 10K16509 Price, each $2.69

PATTERN—Our Highball box plaid pattern, gold, black and green reversible plaid body, fancy plaid heading; red, black, white and green stripes alternate. Make two selections when you order above blankets. If we are out of one we can give you the other.
SIZE—80x84 inches. Weight, about 6 lbs.
No. 10K16515 Price, each....$2.69

LEATHER USED IN SADDLES

WE make the Dundee Russet Oak Saddle Skirting that is used in our saddles. Other large manufacturers have asked us to furnish them with the Dundee oak saddle skirting we make so their saddles would be as good in quality as the saddles we sell in our catalogue. We do not make leather for any other manufacturer, but use all the leather we make in our own saddles and harness, which makes our saddles and our harness superior in quality to any other harness or saddles on the market. If you doubt our statement, order a saddle or harness, examine it yourself, or get your friends to examine it and if their judgment is different than our statements return harness or saddle to us at our expense and we will gladly refund your money and pay the transportation charges.

$2.39 OUR SPECIAL BOSTON PLAID, AND JACQUARD WEAVE HORSE BLANKETS, SOMETHING NEW, TRY THEM. $2.98

ONE OF OUR GREAT BARGAINS IN FANCY PLAID HORSE BLANKETS. HIGH GRADE WOOL BLANKET FILLINGS. BRIGHT COLORS. STRONG AND WARM.

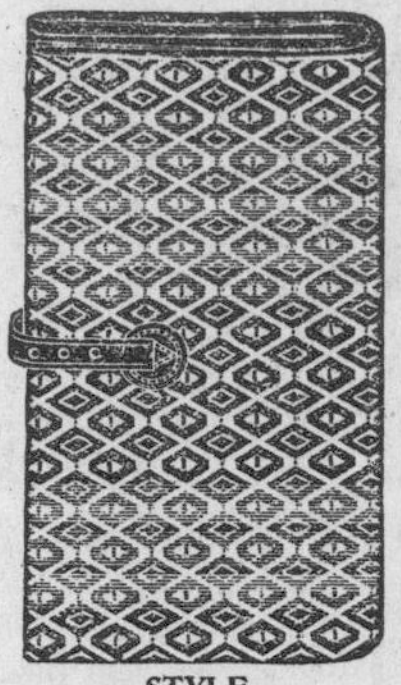

STYLE
No. 10K16476
No. 10K16481

We know our customers always want the latest patterns in Horse Blankets, the best blanket they can buy for the money. The quality of material that is used in this blanket, the way this blanket is made, makes it one of our best styles.

$2.39 The quality of the material, the amount of colored stock used in this high grade plaid blanket, if sold in local stores would sell for from $3.50 to $4.00. We show this blanket in four patterns, four colored bodies and two sizes, giving two patterns to each size to make your selection from. Read carefully the description of each number and make your selection of color to suit your fancy.

No. 10K16476 Green and black jacquard body; fancy green checkered stripes; red, old gold, white and black fancy striped border. SIZE—76x80 inches. Weight, about 5 pounds. Price, each....$2.39

No. 10K16481 Old gold and silver jacquard body; white, orange, black and red stripes; fancy shaded body of white, orange, black and red. SIZE—76x80 inches. Weight, about 5 pounds. Price, each....$2.39

$2.98 No. 10K16485 Tan and white jacquard body; square block plaided body. Color, tan and white, the Horse Show Blanket looks like an all wool blanket. Shaded border. One of the best patterns. SIZE—84x90 inches. Weight, about 7 pounds. Price, each....$2.98

No. 10K16490 Black and white checkered plaid gray body; black and white stripes and border. A very handsome blanket. Looks like wool blankets, square block plaided body. If you want a swell horse blanket this is the one. SIZE—84x90 inches. Weight, about 7 pounds. Price, each....$2.98

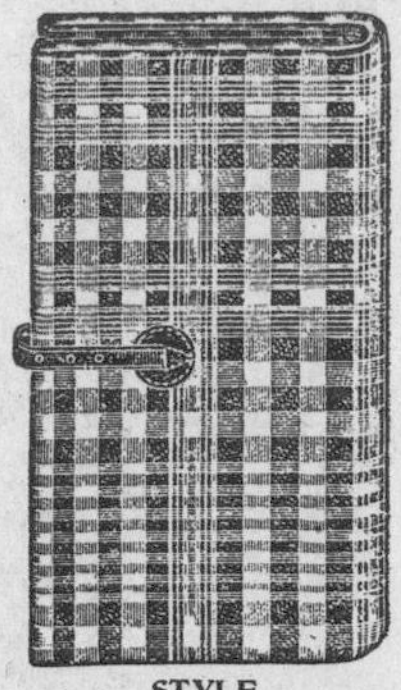

STYLE
No. 10K16485
No. 10K16490

NO SUCH PRICE REDUCTIONS have ever been made by any firm or individual as we have made in the pages of this Big Catalogue on the HIGHEST GRADE MERCHANDISE.

$2.99 LADY SAVOY HORSE BLANKET.

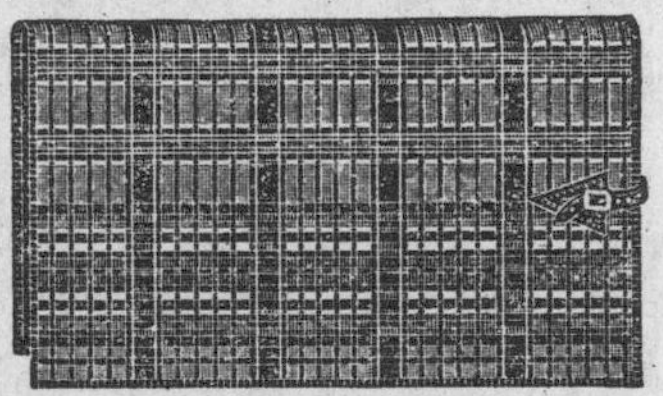

$2.99 When looking for the greatest value you can buy in a drop box plaid body and extra large size blanket, 84x90 inches, weight, about 7 pounds, read carefully the descriptions of the three patterns we list under this number. The quality of the material and fancy colors, strong woven body with extra heavy double warp, the drop box plaid making one color on one side and reversible color on the other; something entirely new. Buy this blanket if you want $1.25 in value for every dollar the blanket costs you. Remember, this blanket is made in three patterns. Read the descriptions carefully and select the pattern you like best.

PATTERN—Wine and green body, drop plaid, alternate wine and green, fancy heading, color, white, orange, red and lemon. Fancy plaided body.
SIZE—84x90 inches. Weight, about 7 lbs.
No. 10K16520 Price, each $2.99

PATTERN—Old gold and tan color plaid body alternate extra wide plaid heading, red, black, green and white color. One of the finest horse blankets we make in this style. New this year for us.
SIZE—84x90 inches. Weight, about 7 lbs.
No. 10K16523 Price, each $2.99

PATTERN—Brown body, alternate plaid, fancy heading, red, white and sage green; dark color horse blanket; very handsome. State your second choice when ordering.
SIZE—84x90 inches. Weight, about 7 lbs.
No. 10K16527 Price, each $2.99

$2.89 WESTERN HORSE BLANKET.

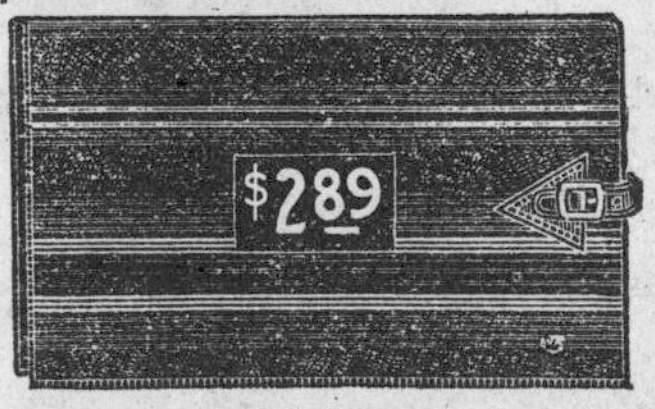

If you are looking for the best horse blanket you can buy for $2.89, in a brown body or a black body, do not overlook these two patterns. They are the greatest value in horse blankets we have been able to make at $2.89. This same blanket if purchased from other dealers would cost you from $3.75 to $4.00. Compare these two blankets with any blankets of a like price offered by any dealer and if this blanket is not better in every respect, better quality, and better style and a better made blanket, we want you to return it to us and we will refund your money and the transportation charges. Made in one size only, extra large, 84x90 inches and weighs about 7 pounds. Two special patterns.

PATTERN—Brown body with heavy orange, green, black and lemon stripes and border.
SIZE—84x90 inches. Weight, about 7 pounds.
No. 10K16531 Price, each....$2.89

PATTERN—Black body, solid green stripes, fancy green striped border.
SIZE—84x90 inches. Weight, about 7 pounds.
No. 10K16535 Price, each $2.89

$2.35, $2.79, $3.20, $3.99. OUR GREAT EASTERN FAWN SQUARE HORSE BLANKET.

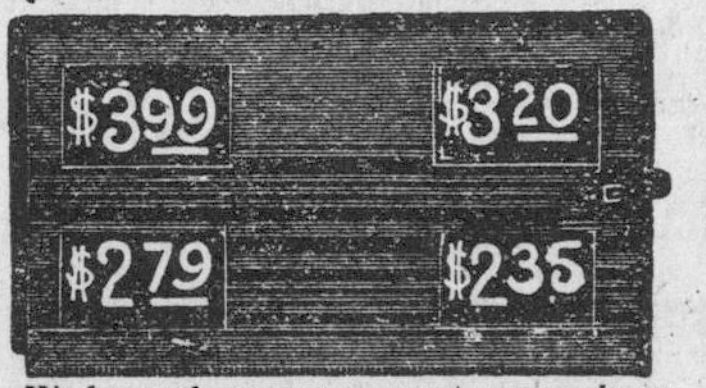

We know there are a great many cheap, shoddy, poorly colored fawn blankets offered for sale at reduced prices. We have seen these blankets; we know how they are manufactured, we know the quality of material used in them and we know they will not give good satisfaction. We know when we offer you this special, high grade eastern fawn blanket that we are giving you a higher quality of blanket filling, long carded blanket stock, and the genuine fawn color body with bright red headings. This blanket has no equal when quality of material and coloring is compared. Order this special fawn blanket, compare it with any other fawn blanket of about the same price and if our blanket is not the best blanket, a better colored and a better made blanket, a firmer and softer blanket, we want you to return the blanket and we will refund your money and the transportation charges. You do not want to buy a cheap, poorly colored fawn blanket when you can buy this high grade eastern fawn blanket at the prices we quote. Made in four sizes. Order the blanket you want by catalogue number. Looks like wool blanket and does not cost as much and will wear just as good.

No. 10K16542 Size, 76x80 inches. Weight, about 5 pounds. Price, each, $2.35
No. 10K16546 Size, 80x84 inches. Weight, about 6 pounds. Price, each, $2.79
No. 10K16551 Size, 84x90 inches. Weight, about 7 pounds. Price, each, $3.20
No. 10K16555 Size, 90x96 inches. Weight, about 9 pounds. Price, each, $3.99

$2.69 AND $3.46 BLUE BODY HORSE BLANKET.

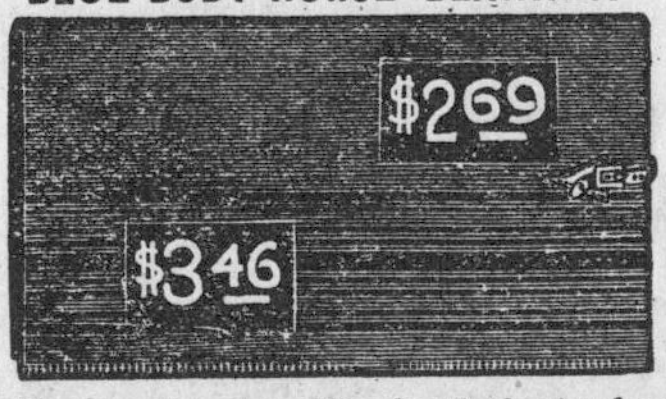

You are always looking for the best values you can get when buying a solid blue body horse blanket. This special army blue blanket that we make is considered by our customers who use it to be the best blanket for the money that they have ever used. There are a great many cheap blue horse blankets. The quality of material used in making our blanket makes the price of the blanket. The cheaper the quality of material the cheaper we can sell the blanket. Material, blue mixed wool blanket filling, carded and spun, making a solid cord, woven together with double hard twisted warp, long nap, soft filling blanket.

STYLE—Two patterns. (No. 1 is the blue body made with heading of red stripes and No. 2 is the blue body with the green stripe heading) a very handsome pattern. Always buy high grade blue blankets if you want the best.

No. 10K16560 Size, 84x90 inches. Weight, about 7 pounds. Price, each, $2.69
No. 10K16564 Size, 90x96 inches. Weight, about 9 pounds. Price, each, $3.46

DOUBLE THE VALUE OF YOUR DOLLAR by purchasing needed articles from us at our greatly reduced prices.

OUR GREAT CHALLENGE VALUE PLAIN GREEN HORSE BLANKETS AT $2.68 TO $4.89

Nothing to equal this blanket sold in retail stores for less than 50 per cent higher price.

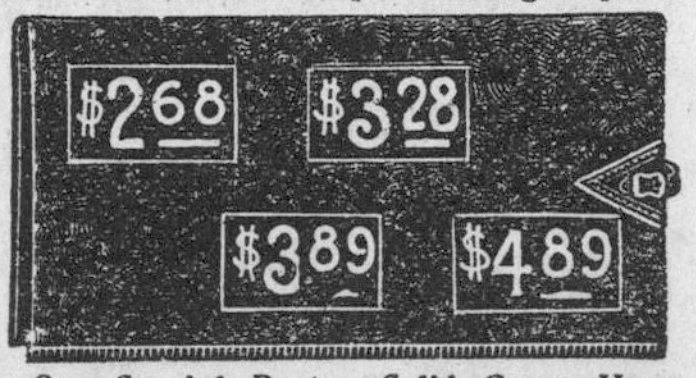

Our Special Boston Solid Green Horse Blanket, made of fine all green blanket filling, heavy hard twisted green warp, making a very strong and serviceable blanket; one solid color. No stripes in this blanket. Plain solid green body, strong warp, a warm, durable and handsome blanket. Our prices, as shown below, will interest dealers everywhere, for we know they cannot buy a blanket to equal this from the jobber at as low prices as we quote. Made in four sizes.

No. 10K16571 Size, 76x80 inches. Weight, 5 pounds. Price, each....$2.68
No. 10K16575 Size, 80x84 inches. Weight, 6 pounds. Price, each....$3.28
No. 10K16582 Size, 84x90 inches. Weight, 7 pounds. Price, each....$3.89
No. 10K16586 Size, 90x96 inches. Weight, 9 pounds. Price, each....$4.89

Mt. Kisco, N. Y.
Sears, Roebuck & Co., Chicago, Ill.
Gentlemen— I could not have been more satisfied than I was with the set of harness I received from you. We have a very bad horse when he is in harness, and the first time I took him out with that harness on, I never thought it would stand the test, but it did, and I never saw a set of harness put together so well before. I have had quite a few sets of harness, but none of them suited me as well as this one and I will recommend its purchase to others. I do not think you could improve the harness any as it is satisfaction right through. Wishing you luck, I remain, Yours very truly,
J. BRUNK.

R. F. D. No. 1, Blakesburg, Iowa.
Sears, Roebuck & Co.
Gentlemen—Am well pleased with the saddle bought of you and saved about $4.00 on it. The quality was better than I expected and will be glad to recommend the saddle to others. I do not know of any improvements you could make. A few years ago, when leather was much cheaper than now, I paid $14.00 for a saddle in Ottumwa that was not as good as the one you sent me for $10.27.
Yours very truly,
BEN ABEGG.

R. F. D. No. 3, Raymond, Ill.
Sears, Roebuck & Co., Chicago, Ill.
Gentlemen—I am well pleased with the harness I received from you some time ago. I saved about $12.00 on the harness, buying it from you. The quality is better than I expected and found every piece and part solid leather, trimming extra quality. It is a better harness than you usually see in this section of the country at any price. Would recommend this harness to anyone who wants a first class harness. Do not think you could better it at any price. Thanking you for courteous treatment and prompt shipment, I remain, Yours very truly,
WALTER ATKINSON.

Andover, Ohio.
Sears, Roebuck & Co., Chicago, Ill.
Gentlemen—The harness purchased from you was received promptly and I am pleased to inform you that it was in every respect as recommended and is very much better than I expected to receive and is entirely satisfactory in every respect. I saved from $5.00 to $10.00 by placing this order with you in place of purchasing of home dealers. Very respectfully,
CHAS. D. AINGER.

WOOD MANTELS, ART TILE AND HOUSE FURNACES

FREE **FOR THE ASKING.** The biggest, most comprehensive and complete catalogue of wood mantels, art mantel tile, house heating and ventilating furnaces ever issued by us or any other manufacturer, will be sent to you FREE UPON REQUEST.

IT TELLS YOU all about the high quality of material we use in the construction of these wonderful household values, how we are able to make the lowest prices quoted by any manufacturer for like high grade goods; why we can live and do business on the one small conscientious margin of profit we add to the cost of material and labor, and why we are able to out-distance all competition.

WE ARE THE MANUFACTURERS of the most beautiful quarter sawed, parlor car finish, as well as plain solid oak mantels, and our foundry produces the highest grade of mantel grates, coal or gas fire places, and house heating and ventilating furnaces, at a cost to us of only the material and labor, to which we add only our one small conscientious margin of profit, and quote our prices direct from shop to fireside at our famous "Live and let live prices" named in this big free catalogue illustrated on this page.

ON A POSTAL CARD or in a letter, say "Send me your big free Catalogue of Wood Mantels, Art Tile and House Furnaces," and it will go forward to you promptly by mail, postpaid, containing a full complete description of every mantel we manufacture, of tiling for mantel facing and hearth, of coal and gas fire places, and house heating and ventilating furnaces.

THIS BIG FREE CATALOGUE contains too many beautiful illustrations, shows too many things you ought to know, and gives you such simple, plain instructions about how you can install wood mantels and hot air house furnaces for us to duplicate all this valuable information in these pages of our General Catalogue.

EVERY BUILDER, every contractor and every house owner, anyone who contemplates the erection or the remodeling of a home, cannot afford to be without the information it contains.

$2.38 AND UPWARD

$2.38 When we tell you we can furnish a solid oak base mantel with shelf and top apron at $2.38; when we tell you we can furnish you a solid oak, elegant mantel with mirror for $7.60; when we tell you we not only carry these grades in the best quality possible to furnish for these prices, but that we also make the finest line of medium priced, and the most elegant line of magnificent quarter sawed, full luster polished and palace car finished wood mantels ever offered by us or any other manufacturer, you will agree with us that you cannot afford to be without this big free catalogue illustrated on this page.

THE MANTEL ILLUSTRATED to the left is one of our rich, simple conventional styles, and is sold direct from shop to fireside at the wonderfully low price of $22.98 in massive, full quarter sawed solid oak.

DO NOT BE DECEIVED when told we cannot furnish palace car finish, quarter sawed mantels at $13.20 to $39.48, and plain sawed solid oak mantels from $2.38 to $12.67, but send for our big free Mantel Catalogue, and learn that if we ship you a mantel and it is not all and more than we claim for it, the best value you ever saw at anything like the price, you can hold it subject to our disposal, and your money will be promptly refunded, including any freight charges you may have expended.

ART TILE FOR FIREPLACE FACINGS AND HEARTH

OUR BEAUTIFUL MULTI-COLORED

first quality enameled tile, tinted in more beautiful shades than were ever known before in the mantel business, and finished in the most beautiful enameled glazes. Price, 33½ cents per square foot packed in barrels. We furnish them for any mantel openings with any size hearth and quote our wonderfully low prices for a few sizes of mantel openings and hearths.

No. 61K1220 Set complete, to be used in a mantel woodwork opening, 36x36 inches, with a hearth 60 inches long by 18 inches deep. Price.....**$4.00**

No. 61K1221 Set complete, to be used in a mantel woodwork opening, 39 inches high, 42 inches wide, with a hearth 60 inches long by 18 inches deep. Price.................................**$4.83**

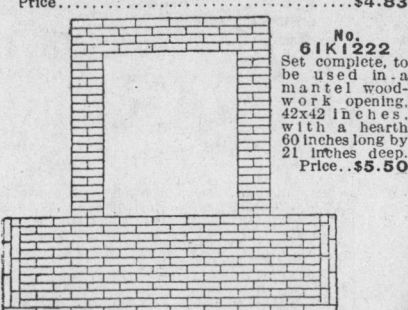

No. 61K1222 Set complete, to be used in a mantel woodwork opening, 42x42 inches, with a hearth 60 inches long by 21 inches deep. Price..**$5.50**

WONDERFUL VALUES in dull unglazed encaustic mantel tile, furnished either in a dark brick red or a beautiful smooth brick buff color. Price, 22 cents per square foot packed in barrels.

No. 61K1223 Set complete, to be used in a mantel woodwork opening, 36x36 inches, with a hearth 60 inches long by 18 inches deep. Price.....**$2.67**

No. 61K1224 Set complete, to be used in a mantel woodwork opening, 39 inches high, 42 inches wide, with a hearth 60 inches long by 18 inches deep. Price.................................**$3.23**

No. 61K1225 Set complete, to be used in a mantel woodwork opening, 42x42 inches, with a hearth 60 inches long by 21 inches deep. Price.....**$3.67**

CERAMIC MOSAIC FLOOR TILE

DO YOU KNOW you can have a beautiful ceramic mosaic tile floor in your vestibule, your bath room or any other room at such small cost you cannot afford to be without it? Send for our beautiful color plate book, showing this wonderful material in beautiful color designs with borders and center pieces most artistic for vestibules, or in plain white hexagons for bath room floors.

20c PER SQUARE FOOT and upward for the most sanitary and best fireproof floor ever laid. A floor that will outwear the house itself. The cleanest, sweetest, prettiest bath room floor you ever saw when laid in pure white.

OUR COLOR PLATE BOOK will tell you all about the simple method of preparing, leveling and laying ceramic mosaic tile; will expose the mysterious secret of how to lay it without the services of an expert tilewright, and enable you to determine for yourself that any workman who can level a Portland cement bed can lay the floor. You will learn that a tile floor can be overlaid on any wooden floor with the use of our Patent Tile Cement.

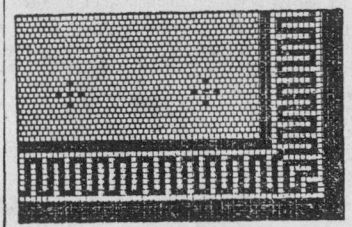

CONTRACTORS, BUILDERS, AND OWNERS of your own homes, do not overlook this opportunity for a beautiful, aseptic sanitary floor at prices hitherto unheard of, and offered to you with simple, straightforward instructions how to lay it and how to avoid the high priced tile setter so unnecessary to this work under our directions for setting.

WRITE FOR OUR COLOR BOOKLET showing our beautiful assortment of designs. Make your selection and send us your order with a sketch of the floor to be tiled, and we will ship it to you prepared in flexibly connected sections of two square feet, ready for laying, accompanied by a perfect plan and thorough instructions so that no one may make a mistake in laying it perfectly.

HOUSE HEATING AND VENTILATING

We heat your house. We ventilate your house. We keep the warm air pure and in constant circulation.

SOFT COAL $25.11 TO $78.40, according to the cubic capacity of the house, we furnish our Acme Hummer soft coal and wood burning furnace.

HARD COAL $27.79 TO $82.24 according to the capacity required, we furnish our Acme Tropic anthracite coal burning furnace. We are manufacturing the best line of hard coal, soft coal and wood furnaces, and at prices so low as to attract orders from dealers everywhere, on account of the high quality, scientific construction, durability and efficiency in ventilating and heating.

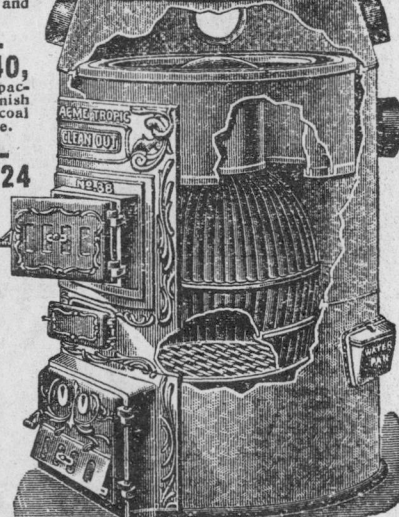

WRITE FOR OUR FURNACE CATALOGUE, or better still, send us a rough sketch of the floor plans of your house, showing the points of the compass or which direction the house fronts, giving accurate measurements of all rooms, regardless of which are to be heated; giving the location of the chimney flue, the height of the cellar, or remodeling an old one, you cannot afford to be without our prices. Get our estimate now and order early. While we can ship furnaces alone very promptly, if you want the full equipment of pipes and registers, it will take two weeks to get out your order. Write now.

GRANITE AND MARBLE MEMORIALS

SEND FOR OUR BIG FREE BEAUTIFULLY ILLUSTRATED SPECIAL CATALOGUE OF MONUMENTS, TOMBSTONES, GRAVE MARKERS, FOOT STONES, CORNER POSTS FOR CEMETERY LOTS, ORNAMENTAL IRON AND STEEL FENCING FOR LAWNS AND GRAVE LOT ENCLOSURES, WIRE GRAVE GUARDS, ORNAMENTAL LAWN VASES AND SETTEES.

THIS WONDERFUL BOOK FREE FOR THE ASKING

ITS WONDERFUL VALUES offered, its beautiful illustrations of memorial art, and the fund of information it gives to the uninitiated about to buy a tombstone or monument, stamp it as the greatest book of its kind ever issued. It tells you how much profit other granite companies and granite dealers try to make out of you, how they take advantage of your total unfamiliarity with work of this kind to obtain from you extraordinary high prices for the most ordinary material and workmanship.

IT IS A BIG BOOK OF NEARLY 150 PAGES, beautifully illustrated direct from photographs of the monuments themselves, just as they will appear when erected in your cemetery. It contains full and accurate descriptions of the largest, handsomest and most beautiful line of monuments and tombstones ever combined in a single catalogue. Only a postal card is required to obtain one for the asking.

OUR PRICES ARE SO LOW, our method of doing business direct from quarry to cemetery is so modern, our guarantee of safe arrival at destination, free from mar, scratch or injury, and our open proposition and convincing offer that if it does not please you in every particular, your money will be refunded, are all so original and daring that it is worth your while to read this book, whether you buy from us or not. It gives you all the reasons why we are able to undersell all other monument dealers, and clearly explains why, if you have any idea of ordering a tombstone, monument, grave marker, a cemetery lot enclosure, or anything else in this line, you should be sure to send for this, our big, free catalogue with all its wealth of interesting information, and its beautiful designs from which to make your selection. Whether you order from the pages of this, our big, free special monument catalogue, or from someone else, this book will give you a fund of information indispensable to making your selection, and the prices we quote will give you an accurate knowledge of the real value of the stone you intend to purchase.

IT WILL BE A REVELATION. It will give you such an insight into the methods commonly followed by others in this business, explaining without reservation the present prevailing, old fashioned, long profit methods of handling, by which methods you pay the profits and expenses of the wholesaler, the profits and expenses of the retailer, and a large commission to the salesman who visits you and encourages you to buy from him at his high prices. This wonderful book of values points the way direct from quarry to cemetery, eliminating all these intermediate expenses and profits, giving you the benefit of the cost of the rough quarried marble or granite, plus only the cost to cut, carve, shape, polish and letter, with but our one conscientious margin of profit between quarry and cemetery. Vermont may seem a long distance from your home station, but we guarantee safe arrival, free from mar, scratch or injury in transportation; guarantee it will be lettered exactly as you instruct us, and in the most approved, workmanlike manner; guarantee you will find you have made a saving of at least 50 per cent, even after you have paid the low rate of freight on monumental work.

SEE NEXT PAGE ABOUT OUR **BEST BARRE GRANITE.**

ACME BLUE VERMONT MARBLE. This material, when polished, develops a dark blue gray beautifully veined mirror surface, susceptible to strong, clear, sharp tracing, carving and lettering, is the nearest to the color of dark granite and is the most popular color for marble memorials. It will stand severe weather exposure for a greater length of time than the best imported Italian marble.

WHITE ACME RUTLAND ITALIAN. This wonderfully beautiful white clouded marble is as handsome as the most expensive and highly celebrated Italian marble, and for lasting qualities is far superior to it. It withstands weather exposure longer and in every way is the ideal marble for cemetery work. All marble work requires four to six weeks to finish, letter and ship. Then allow ample time for it to reach you.

WE POSITIVELY REQUIRE THAT EVERY PIECE of granite or marble which enters into any of our beautiful monuments, tombstones or markers shall be carefully inspected before it is cut and polished, and even after much expense of time and labor is put in the stock, if any flaws should appear or defects in quality are found, the block is immediately rejected. By using all the precautions known to our highly trained craftsmen and their most skilled methods, we deliver to our customers a class of cemetery work such as is seldom seen in stocks of retail marble companies.

SEND US YOUR ORDER for any tombstone or monument shown on these pages or in our big free Tombstone Catalogue, and we will make it to your order for you, shaping, carving, polishing, tracing and finishing it exactly as described, lettering it according to the inscription you furnish us, boxing it carefully and shipping it from the works in Vermont to your home station, with the distinct understanding and binding agreement that if it is not all and more than we claim for it, finished exactly as illustrated and described, lettered exactly as you have ordered it, you can hold it subject to our disposal at our own total loss, and we will refund you the money you have remitted us, together with any freight charges you may have paid. We guarantee it to reach you free from mar, scratch or injury in transportation. This convincing offer and open proposition of insurance against disappointment places all the risk on us and should convince you that you cannot afford to order a tombstone or monument elsewhere. We do all the lettering for you. The tombstone reaches you complete ready for setting up in the cemetery.

LETTERS ON MARBLE. Ordinary sunk verse letters, 2½ cents per letter. Ordinary sunk inscription letters, 1½ inches and under, 6 cents per letter. Letters 2 inches and under, raised ⅛ inch in panel, 18 cents per letter.

$4.90 and Upward Includes the Traced Lettering Shown In This Design.

Delivered on the cars at our Vermont works.

Give us four to six weeks to finish, letter and ship.

Dimensions: Nos. 61K540 and 61K541. Total height, 16 inches. Base, 14x8x6 inches. Tablet, 10x10x4 inches. Shipping weight, 138 pounds.
No. 61K540 Price, Acme Blue Dark Vein Marble............$4.90
No. 61K541 Price, White Acme Rutland Italian Marble............$5.25

Dimensions: Nos. 61K542 and 61K543. Total height, 20 inches. Base, 16x8x8 inches. Tablet, 12x12x4 inches. Shipping weight, 192 pounds.
No. 61K542 Price, Acme Blue Dark Vein Marble............$5.95
No. 61K543 Price, White Acme Rutland Italian Marble............$6.43

A Sleeping Lamb, a Beautiful Symbol of Innocence, $10.00 Dark, $11.25 White.

Recommended in White Acme Rutland Italian at $11.25, but very beautiful in Acme Blue Dark Vein Marble, at $10.00. Delivered on the cars at our Vermont works.
Dimensions: Nos. 61K690 and No. 61K691. Total height, 26 inches. Bottom base, 18x10x5 inches. Upper base, 14x6x4 inches. Tablet and lamb, 14x12x4 inches. Shipping weight, 275 pounds.
No. 61K690 Price, Acme Dark Vein Marble..$10.00
No. 61K691 Price, White Acme Rutland Italian Marble............$11.25
Give us four weeks to finish, letter and ship.

W. O. W. Camps.

Your trust will be faithfully kept when you obtain the greatest possible monumental value for the grave of your deceased brother.

Woodmen beneficiaries, get the worth of your $100.00.
Woodmen, it's your bounden duty to see to it that they do.
Beneficiaries are widows and children. They need your guiding care in making this one selection of their life.
Woodmen, all, send for our prices on the Sovereign Committee's Official designs and be sure to also ask for this big, free Monument Catalogue in which we tell you how you can be your own contractor under the constitution and by-laws of your benevolent order; how you can get a bigger, better, Dark Barre Granite Monument for your $100.00 than you can possibly obtain elsewhere; how you can have the contract coming to the protecting requirements of your noble order and its Sovereign Monumental Committee.

Wondrous Art, and a Memorial Breathing Sweet Innocence in its Every Line, $38.40 Dark, $40.20 White.

Our sculptor's genius here represents inspiring art in all the beautiful soft lines of this design, carved from our world famous White Acme Rutland Italian Marble.
Dimensions: Nos. 61K730 and 61K731. Total height 26 inches. Bottom base 20x12x8 inches. Upper base 16x8x4 inches. Shell cove die 14x16x6 inches. Shipping weight, 384 pounds.
No. 61K730 Price, Acme Blue Dark Vein Marble...$38.40
No. 61K731 Price, White Acme Rutland Italian Marble...$40.20
Give us four weeks to finish, letter and ship.

$20.48 and Upward.

Dimensions: Nos. 61K760 and 61K761. Total height, 30 inches. Bottom base, 26x12x8 inches. Upper base, 21x7x4 inches. Tablet, 18x18x4 inches. Shipping weight, 500 pounds.
No. 61K760 Price, Acme Blue Dark Vein Marble..................$20.48
No. 61K761 Price, White Acme Rutland Italian Marble............$22.72
Dimensions: Nos. 61K762 and 61K763. Total height, 40 inches. Bottom base, 32x14x10 inches. Upper base, 28x10x6 inches. Tablet, 24x24x6 inches. Shipping weight, 1,075 pounds.
No. 61K762 Price, Acme Blue Dark Vein Marble............$31.80
No. 61K763 Price, White Acme Rutland Italian Marble............$38.10
Dimensions: Nos. 61K764 and 61K765. Total height, 44 inches. Bottom base, 34x18x12 inches. Upper base, 23x12x8 inches. Tablet, 24x24x8 inches. Shipping weight, 1,530 pounds.
No. 61K764 Price, Acme Blue Dark Vein Marble............$43.80
No. 61K765 Price, White Acme Rutland Italian Marble............$49.23

THE BEST VALUES EVER OFFERED IN DARK BARRE GRANITE

BEST BARRE GRANITE MONUMENTS AND MARKERS

at heretofore unheard of prices. We only illustrate a few here. Send for our big, free Special Tombstone Catalogue, and examine the most wonderful line of granite designs ever offered by us or any other granite company, and at the most wonderful values you ever saw.

WORLD FAMED DARK BARRE GRANITE

for cemetery work is so indestructible by weather exposure that history does not furnish a single instance of the slightest deterioration from time or weather. There are many kinds and colors of so called granites offered to the public in monumental work under fancy names and false descriptions of merit, but none of them will compare with the wonderful product of the Barre Hills in Vermont for hardness, durability and stability of color. This wonderful material is so hard that cutting from the quarry, sawing, shaping, polishing, carving, tracing and lettering, require the most laborious

WOODMEN OF THE WORLD

You cannot afford to be without our prices on your Sovereign Committee's Official Designs, and our big Free Granite Monument Catalogue.

The best $4.60 worth of Barre Granite Marker ever offered by any producer or dealer. Rock face four sides. Mirror polished top surface. No. 61K500 Dimensions, without stub, 12x12x6 inches. Estimated weight 95 pounds. Price....$4.60 If wanted with 12-inch stub add 75 cents.

AT $4.60 AND UPWARD

pages of our big free Special Tombstone Catalogue. The wonderful growth of our tombstone and monumental business in the last few years is caused by our using only the best blocks of the highest grade of material from the oldest and deepest quarries in these great Barre Granite Hills coupled with our modern theory, principle and practical method of eliminating the intermediate expenses and long profits of the old, high priced method of selling tombstones, furnishing them direct from quarry to cemetery, saving you the long expenses and high profits of the wholesaler, the retailer and large commissions of the traveling agent or local salesman.

SEND FOR OUR BIG FREE TOMBSTONE CATALOGUE

and examine its beautiful variety of monuments, tombstones and markers, or better still, SEND US YOUR ORDER for one of the designs shown on this page, and we guarantee to furnish it exactly as illustrated and described, letter it exactly as you instruct us, guarantee its safe arrival at your home station free from mar, scratch or injury, and if you do not find it all and more than we claim for it, the best value you ever saw at anything like the price, you can hold it subject to our orders for disposal, and we will refund you the full amount you have remitted us, together with any freight you may have paid.

WE DO ALL THE LETTERING FOR YOU.

Send us the inscription exactly as you desire it placed on the tombstone or monument, and we will resubmit it to you typewritten for your approval while we are carving and polishing the block ready to receive the lettering.

INSCRIPTIONS ON GRANITE. Ordinary V sunk letters, 1 inch or under, 12 cents each; 1½ inches or under, 15 cents each; 2 inches or under, 17 cents each, and other sizes in proportion, as determined by the size of the marker or monument. Raised letters: 1½ inches and under, 45 cents each; 2 inches and under, 48 cents each; 3 inches and under, 60 cents each, and other sizes in proportion.

efforts by pneumatic tools and machines. Our reputation is long since established for delivering direct from quarry to cemetery the highest of high grade monumental work, both marble and granite, and we have made and sustained this reputation by furnishing just such material as best Dark Barre Granite at the wonderful values quoted on this page and in the

---

ROYAL VALUE IN A ROYAL SARCOPHAGUS OF BEST DARK BARRE GRANITE.

$110.67 AND UPWARD, ACCORDING TO YOUR SELECTION FROM THE FIVE SIZES QUOTED BELOW.

Royal in value, royal in design, royal in quality, and royal in its elaborate workmanship and finish.

$110.67 AND UPWARD means exactly as illustrated, with its fine hammer carved apex; with its fine hammered top with pediments on all four sides and at all four corners of the cap; with polished surfaces on all four sides of the cap and the initial of the family name and other tracing on the front pediment; with the fine hammered inner curve of the cap, fine hammered chamfered corners and tracing on all four sides of the monument block, finishing with its beautifully polished upper base, with pediment in the front, giving ample space for the family name in large letters, and with its fine hammered bottom base, all making the most splendid specimen of our art and granite handicraft.

EXAMINE THE ILLUSTRATION;

observe its proportion; take careful note of the measurements given below opposite each catalogue number and price; then compare it with anything of like size and style of finish offered you by any other granite company or local dealer, and learn for yourself where you can obtain 50 per cent greater value for your investment than you can anywhere else in the world.

SELECT THE SIZE YOU DESIRE,

and send us your order for one of these royal specimens of our granite monuments. We guarantee to make it to order for you, finish it exactly as we illustrate and describe it, letter it exactly as you instruct us, and guarantee its safe arrival at your station free from mar, scratch or injury in transportation. We bind ourselves that you will find it all and more than we claim for it, a great saving to

you in the purchase price, even after you pay the low rate of freight, or you can hold the shipment subject to our disposal, and your money will be refunded, together with any freight charges you have paid.

No. 61K210 Total height, 4 feet 6 inches. Bottom base, 36x19x12 inches. Upper base, 31x14x10 inches. Monument, 27x18x10 inches. Cap, 32x15x14 inches. Estimated weight, 2,480 pounds. Price....**$110.67**
Give us nine weeks to finish, letter and ship.

No. 61K211 Total height, 5 feet. Bottom base, 42x22x14 inches. Upper base, 36x16x11 inches. Monument, 32x20x12 inches. Cap, 37x17x15 inches. Estimated weight, 3,820 pounds. Price....**$125.00**
Give us nine weeks to finish, letter and ship.

No. 61K212 Total height, 5 feet 5 inches. Bottom base, 48x26x15 inches. Upper base, 41x19x12 inches. Monument, 36x22x14 inches. Cap, 42x20x16 inches. Estimated weight, 5,560 pounds. Price....**$155.63**
Give us ten weeks to finish, letter and ship.

No. 61K213 Total height, 5 feet 10 inches. Bottom base, 54x32x16 inches. Upper base, 45x23x13 inches. Monument, 38x24x16 inches. Cap, 46x24x17 inches. Estimated weight, 7,480 pounds. Price....**$186.88**
Give us twelve weeks to finish, letter and ship.

No. 61K214 Total height, 6 feet 3 inches. Bottom base, 60x37x17 inches. Upper base, 50x26x14 inches. Monument, 42x26x18 inches. Cap, 51x27x18 inches. Estimated weight, 8,550 pounds. Price....**$241.88**
Give us twelve weeks to finish, letter and ship.

ONLY $72.00 AND UPWARD FOR THIS BIG BARRE GRANITE MONUMENT

IN ALL ITS RUGGED BEAUTY AS ILLUSTRATED

$72.00 AND UPWARD includes the fine hammered apex cap with its rock face broad edge on all four sides, the rock face pediment on the front and the fine hammer curved undercut joining the monument block. It includes the monument block, polished and traced on the face, as illustrated, and the back full polished without tracing. Both ends of the monument block are rock faced. The upper base is rock faced on four sides, excepting when the family name is desired in raised letters, as illustrated. The bottom base is rock faced all around and the wash cut bevels are fine hammered.

SEND FOR OUR BIG FREE MONUMENT CATALOGUE,

where we illustrate the most complete line of granite tombstones and monuments; or, better still, make your selection from this page, where we show a few choice designs. Send us your order for one of these big Barre Granite monuments at these heretofore unheard of prices of $72.00 to $134.00, according to the size selected.

EXAMINE THE SIZES AND PRICES

carefully quoted below, compare them with anything of like size and quality of material offered by any other granite company or your local dealer, and learn that we save you at least 50 per cent, even after you have paid the low rate of freight on monumental work.

HOW WE MAKE THE PRICES.

These wonderfully low prices are only made possible by our modern equipment for taking the rough stock from the quarry, modern machinery for handling it in the granite works, the selection of the highest grade of granite craftsmen to operate the pneumatic power tools for shaping, carving, polishing and lettering the work, all combined with our modern method of "direct from the quarry to cemetery" at only our one conscientious margin of profit. We avoid all the intermediate expenses of the wholesaler, the retailer and the big commissions paid to traveling agents by the old time method of selling tombstones and monuments.

SEND US OUR CATALOGUE PRICE,

adding enough to cover the cost of lettering, and we will shape, polish, carve hammer and letter this splendid granite monument, box it carefully and guarantee its safe arrival at your home station. If after examining it you do not find it is all and more than we claim for it, finished exactly as illustrated and described, lettered exactly as instructed, and arrives free from mar, scratch or injury in transportation, you can hold it subject to our disposal and we will refund you the money you have paid us, together with any freight charges expended.

No. 61K230 Total height. 4 feet 4 inches. Bottom base, 40x22x14 inches. Upper base, 33x15x10 inches. Monument, 28x16x10 inches. Cap, 34x16x12 inches. Estimated weight, 2,890 pounds. Price....**$72.00**
Give us eight weeks to finish, letter and ship.

No. 61K231 Total height, 4 feet 8 inches. Bottom base, 46x30x14 inches. Upper base, 36x20x10 inches. Monument, 30x18x14 inches. Cap, 37x21x12 inches. Estimated weight, 4,200 pounds. Price....**$94.00**
Give us nine weeks to finish, letter and ship.

No. 61K232 Total height, 5 feet. Bottom base, 52x32x14 inches. Upper base, 42x22x12 inches. Monument, 36x20x16 inches. Cap, 42x22x14 inches. Estimated weight, 5,100 pounds. Price....**$110.00**
Give us ten weeks to finish, letter and ship.

No. 61K233 Total height, 5 feet 6 inches. Bottom base, 60x36x16 inches. Upper base, 49x25x12 inches. Monument, 42x22x18 inches. Cap, 49x25x16 inches. Estimated weight, 8,000 pounds. Price....**$134.00**
Give us eleven weeks to finish, letter and ship.

WRITE FOR OUR SPECIAL CATALOGUE OF ORNAMENTAL FENCING

For lawns, parks, cemeteries and grave lot enclosures, which also illustrates single grave guards and a big assortment of large cast iron lawn vases and lawn settees of wood, wire and steel.

Bicycles

WE CHALLENGE ANY OTHER MANUFACTURER OR DEALER IN THE WORLD TO EQUAL OUR BICYCLES IN QUALITY AND PRICE

WE ARE THE LARGEST RETAILERS OF BICYCLES in the world and our sales for 1907 show a larg : increase over the sales for 1906. Our highest grade bicycles are known to bicycle riders in practically every community in the United States; well and favorably known because of their superior construction, their durability, their grace and beauty of design and their easy riding qualities. We have been manufacturing the world's best bicycles for years. In our Napoleon and our Elgin King we have been selling two of the most famous models in bicycle history; models which a few years ago sold at the very highest prices—$125.00 to $150.00 in the days of the great popularity of the bicycle. These models, vastly improved by us over the old patterns, have been steadily reduced in price, our guarantees have covered a longer period of time, until today in the matter of qualities, finish, adjustment, ease of running and lowness of price, the wheels we offer in the pages of this catalogue outdistance and outclass all competition.

THE BICYCLE WILL BE INCREASINGLY POPULAR IN 1908. There is every evidence that the sales will be larger than in 1907 by a very large percentage. The bicycle has settled down to a sound commercial basis. While it is not the fad it once was, it is an important factor in the daily life of thousands of people, and to those who need a bicycle, or those who contemplate purchasing for the pleasure there is in the ownership of a high grade wheel, we offer you in these pages an exceptionally fine line of the world's best bicycles at a wide range in price and carrying such guarantees as no other manufacturers or dealers offer on the wheels they make and sell.

YOU WILL FIND MANY IMPROVEMENTS on the models offered for 1908 which were not to be had in 1907. Our automatic coaster brake, the new style tires and very rigid frame construction, positive alignment and many other special features distinguish our wheels for 1908 and put them in a class by themselves; and if you have any thought of purchasing a bicycle this year, we ask you to read our bicycle proposition very carefully, because under our liberal terms and in view of our long time guarantees you cannot afford to place an order for a bicycle with any other firm or individual at home or elsewhere.

WE MAKE EVERY PIECE AND PART that enters into the construction of our bicycles, insuring absolute uniformity of construction, an important factor which should not be overlooked. Many so called bicycle manufacturers are merely assemblers, as they make up frames from tubing, lugs, tees, stamped heads, seat post clusters, forks, crowns and other parts which they secure from various manufacturers on the open market. As these parts so assembled are not made specially for each other, it stands to reason that a bicycle so constructed cannot possibly be as easy running, as strong and durable as a wheel made by one manufacturer who strives to excel in his product and produce the best to be had in each and every individual part of the machine he sells. Every part which enters into the construction of our bicycles is tested before it is used. We own our own dies and patterns, we own many expensive special machines which no other bicycle manufacturer could afford to buy and operate because his limited output and sale would not justify the investment, but with our enormous output, greater than the combined sales of any other five mail order houses, we can well afford to equip and operate the finest bicycle factory in the world, filled with special machines, special equipment designed to produce the various parts which enter into our bicycles. It is because of this splendid factory equipment, these special machines and special equipment that we are able to turn out the high grade, first quality bicycles that we offer in these pages, and put such value into them that no other wheels offered anywhere can begin to compare with them. These are the reasons that we are able to give you better bicycles than others, and at the same time save you from $10.00 to $25.00 on your purchase. If you want the very best bicycle that money will buy, if you want every up to date feature to be had on any bicycle, and many special features not to be had except on the wheels manufactured by us, if you want a long lived bicycle, one that is easy running, as carefully built as a watch, and at the same time wonderfully low in price, you will make no mistake in ordering either our Elgin King, our Napoleon, or our Peerless Bicycle, as illustrated and described in these pages.

MANY NEW AND ATTRACTIVE FEATURES HAVE BEEN ADDED TO OUR BICYCLES

THIS YEAR, AND THE MOST IMPORTANT OF THESE ARE OUR AUTOMATIC PEERLESS COASTER BRAKE AND OUR NEW AMERICA TIRE.

OUR AUTOMATIC PEERLESS COASTER BRAKE.

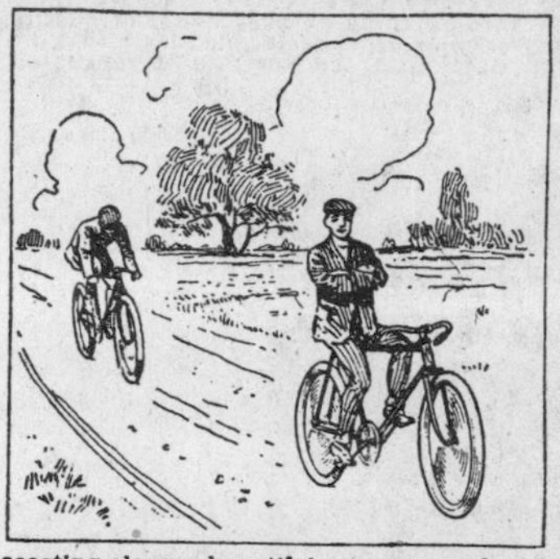

THREE-FOURTHS OF OUR BICYCLES SOLD LAST YEAR were equipped with a coaster brake. The introduction of the coaster brake has done more to revive bicycling than any improvement in bicycle construction in recent years. If you once ride a coaster brake model, you will never go back to the old style bicycle. Realizing the importance of the feature of bicycle construction, we have incorporated in our equipment the PEERLESS AUTOMATIC COASTER BRAKE. It was first introduced by us last fall, and in the short period of six months the sales were so great that our coaster brake factory was unable to supply brakes fast enough to take care of the demand. The Peerless Brake, without exception, is giving absolute satisfaction, as it is a radical improvement over any other coaster brake on the market. Owing to the enormous sales which we expect this season, we have arranged to equip our bicycles with a coaster brake at a never before heard of low price of $3.00 in addition to the cost of our regular roadster models. The sensation is great to be coasting along a beautiful country road with a gentle breeze at your back, or on a slightly down road without any exertion on your part, not even the moving of the pedals, while the other fellow, riding a bicycle without a coaster brake, is seen sweating and panting from exertion and the heat of the day. Try the coaster brake once and you will never go back to the old way. For detailed description of our Peerless Brake, see page 169.

OUR AMERICA TIRE. Never before in the history of our tire business has a tire achieved the popularity, reached the enormous sales and given the entire satisfaction in the short space of a single season, as has our new America Tire. Notwithstanding these facts we have been particularly anxious to surpass its construction, if possible, and produce a tire with puncture proof qualities without detracting from its light, easy running and resilient qualities, and thereby be superior.

WE HAVE SUCCEEDED far beyond our expectations, as we have been able to incorporate in our Improved America Tire such features as will make it practically puncture proof, in fact, as puncture proof as a tire can be without being constructed solid, and, further, be the fastest, strongest, easiest running and most resilient tire ever produced. These are factors which have never before been so successfully incorporated in the construction of a pneumatic tire. Further we have been successful in manufacturing a new tread and in our new link chain, non-skid tread we have the handsomest and most scientific tread ever put on a tire. It will positively conform to any road condition, and it is entirely free from that holding back sensation often experienced when riding certain tires.

MANY DEALERS PUT THE CHEAPEST TIRE which they possibly can secure on their bicycles, so as to increase their profit on each bicycle sold. Not so with us. We equip our bicycles with the best tire that we handle, and the best tire that money can buy. We fully realize that while we do not make as much money on each bicycle, yet we more than make up for our small profit by the quantity we sell. Do not forget that in purchasing this tire you are fully protected by our written binding guarantee, and if you do not find this tire exactly as we represent it, if not satisfactory because of defective material or imperfect workmanship, regardless of time and service, we will replace or repair free of charge, or refund your money together with transportation charges both ways. We cannot make you a more liberal offer to induce you to try our New America Tire.

Read carefully the detailed description of our America Tire, as found on page 169.

TAKING INTO CONSIDERATION these and many other important improvements which are incorporated in our Peerless, Napoleon, Elgin King, Kenwood and Josephine Bicycles, they are the finest products that experience and inventive genius, coupled with scientific methods of manufacture, can produce.

SO POSITIVE ARE WE that our bicycles are superior to other makes, regardless of price, that we guarantee them for two years, and we know that we are perfectly safe in doing this, as these bicycles are not constructed to last two years, but to last a lifetime.

WE ARE SO CONFIDENT that, if it were possible for you to visit our factory and follow the making of our bicycles from the designers' planning to the finished details, see the many steps in the manufacture of the various pieces that go to make up a bicycle, and the many improvements which are necessary to bring each bicycle to our required standard, see the actual work and the experienced help that this line of work demands, it would be especially interesting to you. You would note how critically each bicycle is inspected before it leaves our factory, and after such a visit and inspection, there would not remain the slighest doubt in your mind but that our line represents the highest product in bicycle manufacture; you would readily see why we have chosen to manufacture such bicycles as we sell, and you would be just as enthusiastic as we are, and agree with us fully in our claim that our bicycles are the best ever produced.

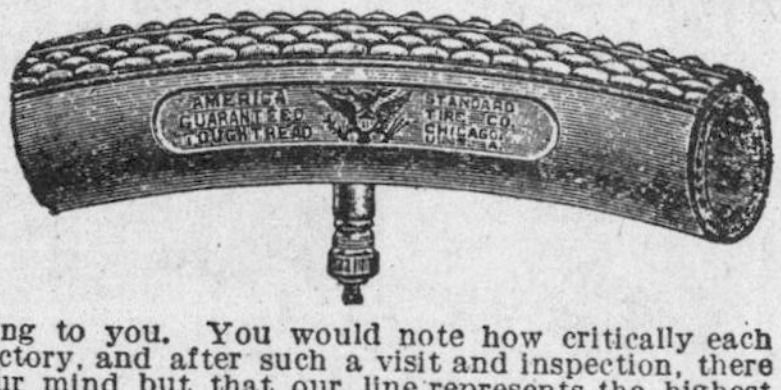

IF YOU COULD FULLY APPRECIATE the above conditions, we know that you would not hesitate a moment in placing your orders with us for your requirements in this line. You are positively protected by our written binding guarantee, and if for any reason after you have received the bicycle you do not find it exactly as we have represented and illustrated it, and if for the slightest reason you desire to return the bicycle, we will refund your money, together with transporation charges both ways.

KENWOOD BICYCLES

NOTE. WE CANNOT FURNISH KENWOOD BICYCLE WITH COASTER BRAKE.

OUR KENWOOD BICYCLES compare favorably with bicycles sold by other dealers at $15.00 to $18.00. We have sold the Kenwood Bicycle for years and it is a very well known make. At $11.95 it is unquestionably one of the greatest values offered in the bicycle on the market, values such as no other dealer has ever been able to offer. It is the best bicycle we can turn out for the money. This bicycle will give satisfaction. It is well made and contains good material. It is fully covered by our binding two-year guarantee and while it is a better bicycle than you could obtain from any other dealer from one-quarter to one-half more money, at the same time, of course, it is not as good a bicycle as our Peerless, Napoleon or Elgin King. In the latter named bicycles we have spared no expense. The 1908 Model Peerless and celebrated Napoleon boast many improvements and many features of value which we could not possibly afford to embody in our Kenwood Bicycles at $11.95 apiece. Inasmuch as our Kenwood Bicycle cannot be furnished with coaster brake, we therefore recommend that before placing your order, you carefully read the description of our 1908 Model Peerless, our celebrated Napoleon and Elgin King.

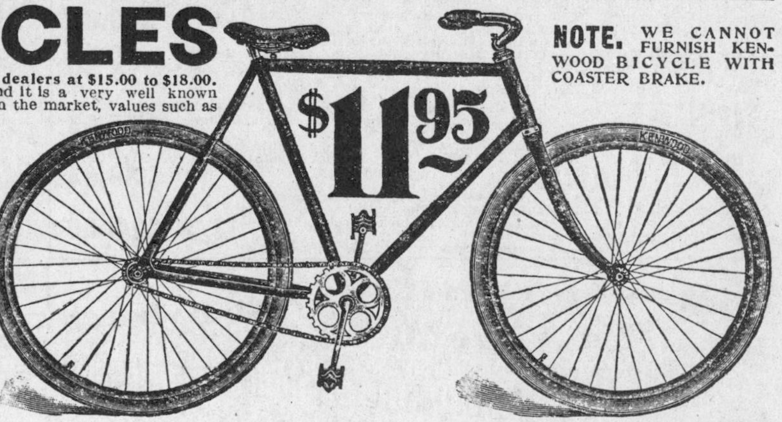

DETAILED DESCRIPTION

FRAME is made of fine seamless 1-inch steel tubing, flush at every joint. Made in 22-inch frame only. THE FORK is fitted with nickel plated, heavy square crown, and is enameled jet black, contrasting nicely with the nickel plated front and rear sprockets and nickel plated cranks, pedals and handle bars. One-piece hanger, 7-inch round cranks, rat trap ball bearing pedals, adjustable handle bars, with leather grips, full size padded leather saddle. Kenwood single tube pneumatic tires. The price of $11.95 does not include the tool bag. We can furnish a tool bag with wrench, pump and tube of quick tire repair cement at an additional charge of 50 cents.

No. 19K1403 Men's Kenwood Bicycle. Price $11.95

THE FAMOUS RED HEAD ELGIN KING

THE ADVANCE 1908 MODEL ELGIN KING, as illustrated, is probably the best known bicycle on the market today. It is not only widely known, but also very favorably known. It is a bicycle which we have manufactured continuously for a great many years, and there is hardly a town or hamlet in the United States where the Elgin King bicycle with its characteristic red head and red center tube is not in use today and known to bicycle riders. Before we controlled this bicycle and manufactured it in our factory with our improved facilities, it was sold for $125.00, and yet the old original Elgin King bicycle that sold for $125.00 is not to be compared with our famous Elgin King, which we sell today for $14.95. The Elgin King is a better wheel today because important improvements have been embodied in its construction, and we have kept it thoroughly up to and in fact ahead of the times. In addition, it possesses many features that are distinctly its own, and which are not found in any other bicycle. The many little details that enter into its construction have been given very careful attention, and it is this attention to detail that has made the Elgin King famous. We desire that you note carefully the detailed description of the Elgin King as given below.

$14.95

RED HEAD

RED CENTER TUBE

DETAILED DESCRIPTION

FRAME, size 20, 22 and 24-inch, as desired. Made of 1-inch 20-gauge, best quality Shelby seamless cold drawn steel tubing, finished flush at all joints. The construction and lines of this frame are mechanically correct. Its construction is such as to equalize and distribute all weight and strain. There is absolutely no chance of this frame being forced out of alignment or buckling, and it is specially designed for the use of the Peerless Coaster Brake.

FORK is fitted with heavy square forged crown. We show an illustration on this page.

WHEELS are standard 28-inch, fitted with the celebrated straight center, specially constructed Elgin King guaranteed hub, which is conceded to be one of the finest hubs made.

RIMS are made of selected one-piece rock elm, by the Mutual Rim Co., recognized to be the best manufacturers of high grade rims. All rims are enameled with black center, with red edges, delicately outlined with a gold stripe to match the red head and red center tube.

SPOKES are manufactured by the Birmingham Needle Co., and are laced according to our own special method, which insures the wheels on an Elgin King bicycle never getting out of true.

BEARINGS are extra large size, turned from the solid bar, and are tempered. We use no soft bearings in our bicycles. The bearings are all tested by micrometer and are guaranteed accurate to the one-thousandth part of an inch. The bearings are all dustproof, a distinctive feature which insures their lasting and easy running qualities.

SPROCKET. Handsome design, as shown in the above illustration. Stamped from the finest steel boiler plate, finely finished, heavily nickel plated.

HANGER. The celebrated one-piece Duplex hanger, the simplest and strongest hanger made. Fitted with 7-inch, one-piece, drop forged and tempered steel cranks.

PEDALS. Elgin King specially constructed rat trap pedals. Full ball bearing, heavily nickel plated and polished. One of the finest pedals made.

TIRES. Our Elgin King bicycles are equipped with our Improved America Tire, the newest and best single tube tire on the market, the manufacture and sale of which is controlled exclusively by us. See page 169 for full description of the America Tire.

SADDLE. Fine seal grain, full size, oil tanned saddle. Nicely padded and form fitting shape.

HANDLE BARS. Adjustable, fitted with Hercules expander, which firmly holds the bar in position, yet can be quickly loosened. The bar is heavily nickel plated, and is fitted with the best quality laminated leather grips.

TOOL BAG, made of heavy specially tanned seal grain leather, and contains a fine steel wrench, polished brass, quick action hand pump, and a tube of Seroco Quick Tire Repair Cement.

GEAR. 81-gear is regular equipment, and is always furnished unless otherwise specified. While we can furnish 72 or 91-gear upon order, experience has long since demonstrated that 81-gear, with 26-tooth front and a 9-tooth rear sprocket, gives by far the best results and is most universally used.

FINISH. The finish of the Elgin King bicycle is fully up to the other sterling qualities of this bicycle. It is furnished with a red head and red center tube. The balance of the frame is enameled in jet black, and is unquestionably one of the finest and most handsomely finished bicycles on the market today, and is second only to our Improved Peerless and Napoleon models. The enormous success attained by our Elgin King bicycle has caused many manufacturers to imitate it in finish, but there is only one Elgin King bicycle, and while there are others that are enameled to imitate it, there is no bicycle that looks like the Elgin King, or that will give you the satisfaction and wear that the genuine Elgin King bicycle will. The frame is enameled with four coats of Eclipse American enamel, baked under high temperature, in a dustproof oven. The head and center tube, as shown in illustration, are enameled in a rich vermilion red, which forms a handsome contrast with the jet black. The red head is further offset by graceful darts which extend on the upper and lower tubes, which are delicately outlined with a gold stripe.

No. 19K1417 Elgin King, Roadster Model. Price.. **$14.95**
No. 19K1418 Elgin King, Coaster Model. Price.. **17.95**

THIS ILLUSTRATION shows you a sectional view of our Elgin King hanger and frame attachments. Note the reinforced lugs which extend several inches into the tubing, thereby reinforcing the frame so that the bearings, driving chain and all running gear will remain absolutely in line, which causes it to run very freely and the cranks to revolve with little or no exertion. You will see that this additional reinforced construction, placed as it is in that part of the bicycle which receives the most strain, gives great strength at this point. In all of its adjustments, the cones, bearings and parts, the Elgin King is a particularly satisfactory bicycle.

THE FOLLOWING ILLUSTRATION will give you a good idea of the strength of our forged fork crown. Note the heavy steel forgings with extra tubing. This construction does entirely away with any danger of our front forks becoming seriously damaged or bent, should you by accident run against some obstruction. This style of construction is a particularly satisfactory one and you cannot imagine any construction which would insure longer wear or better satisfaction than that employed in our Elgin King.

DO NOT OVERLOOK OUR PEERLESS AUTOMATIC COASTER BRAKE in purchasing a Peerless, Napoleon or Elgin King Bicycle. For the small additional sum of $3.00 we furnish our Peerless, Napoleon or Elgin King models with the most perfectly constructed, positive acting, and easiest riding coaster brake ever produced. If you have never ridden a coaster brake bicycle we know that if you will try it, you will be just as enthusiastic as we are. The additional pleasure which you derive by being able to coast down slight or steep and dangerous hills with absolute safety can in no way be contrasted with the old method of back pedaling to control your speed while going down a steep hill, as back pedaling is as tiresome as riding up the next hill.

OUR PEERLESS COASTER BRAKE is absolutely positive in its action, and the rider can stop the wheel on the steepest hill by a slight backward pressure on the pedal. In fact, you have your wheel under such perfect control that you can ride down a hill which you would not dare to attempt on the old style bicycle and coast at such speed that in most cases if you are not compelled to stop instantly, you will coast down the hill and nearly to the top of the next without pedaling. You are thus able to secure frequent short intervals of rest, and finish your ride as fresh as when you started.

SO CONFIDENT ARE WE that a cyclist who has had the pleasure of riding a wheel fitted with our Peerless Coaster Brake would not ride a regular bicycle of any kind, that we want you to order a bicycle fitted with our Peerless Coaster Brake, and if after riding it for ten days you do not care for this great improvement and prefer the regular hub, you can return the rear wheel with coaster brake to us, and we will exchange same for a regular rear wheel, allowing you transportation charges both ways, and refunding you the difference between our coaster model and our regular model, that of $3.00, so that this experiment will be entirely at our expense.

OUR NAPOLEON BICYCLE

OUR NAPOLEON BICYCLE IS ONE THAT HAS ABSOLUTELY MAINTAINED ITS STANDING

IN THE ACCOMPANYING ILLUSTRATION we have endeavored to show you the relative difference between our head construction as employed in our famous Napoleon and the construction used by other manufacturers. We make the head out of one heavy seamless carbon steel tube, the lugs being brazed in, instead of punched, and are especially fitted with flared ends which offer an additional brazing surface, which renders this construction more than twice as strong as the head construction offered by others. Note the long arms of the lugs which extend a considerable distance into the tubing so that with a quick twist or a heavy fall the strain is equally distributed and does not come on any particular point. Note the plain head as used by many manufacturers which is

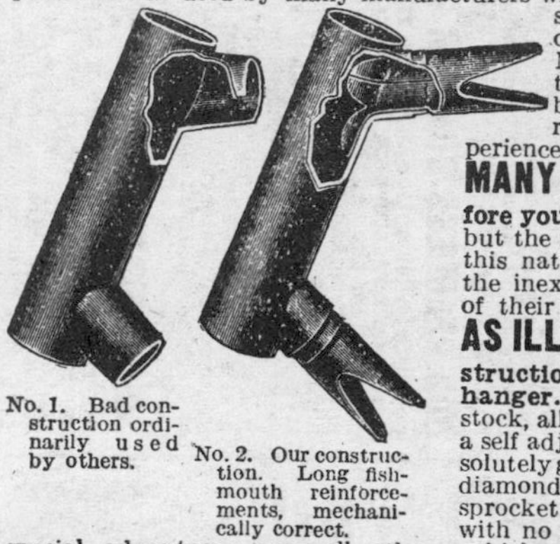

No. 1. Bad construction ordinarily used by others.

No. 2. Our construction. Long fishmouth reinforcements, mechanically correct.

since the early days of bicycling, when it was recognized as one of the leading high grade wheels, which reputation it has always held and maintained to this day. Many of the features embodied in our Napoleon Bicycle are controlled exclusively by us. For this reason our competitors have been attempting to imitate our Napoleon, but it is impossible for you to purchase a genuine Napoleon Bicycle except from us. It has been kept strictly up to date by many late improvements and it is today a recognized leader. We have sold thousands of them within the past few years and there are probably more Napoleon Bicycles ridden today than any other bicycle in the market. We absolutely guarantee the construction employed and will replace any bicycle which through defect of material or workmanship proves unsatisfactory within two years' time. We further send these bicycles on a TEN-DAY FREE TRIAL and if at the end of ten days you are not entirely satisfied with the bicycle and do not think you have secured the greatest value you could possibly get from any other dealer, if you think it differs from our catalogue description or if not all we claim it to be, you have the privilege of returning it to us and your money, together with transportation charges, will be refunded in view of the many 1908 improvements, it is a greater value than ever.

simply bent together and brazed, which makes it undesirable because it cannot be reinforced. Our fittings, as shown in illustration No. 2, are more expensive, as compared with the one shown in illustration No. 1. The ordinary heads used on bicycles sold by others can be stamped out in one operation, while our heads require expensive machinery, improved dies and the best experienced help to manufacture.

MANY OF THESE FEATURES are deserving of a very careful consideration on your part before you make a selection of a bicycle, as not only the life of the wheel but the rider's safety is dependent on seemingly unimportant details of this nature. Any bicycle can have a fine, high polished finish and to the inexperienced the frame may look as good but in actual use the secrets of their imperfect construction are quickly told.

AS ILLUSTRATED ON PREVIOUS PAGE is our new model Diamond drop forged, one-piece, all steel construction is the special feature of our Napoleon construction hanger. The cranks are diamond shaped and are made from full crucible stock, all cones being turned from the solid bar. The stationary cone acts as a self adjusting locknut in securing the bracket to the cranks. We can absolutely guarantee that you will never find a loose sprocket on our Napoleon diamond hanger, as the small lug built in the right crank which engages the sprocket gives the rider the greatest possible power in driving the bicycle with no possible danger of its becoming disengaged. This hanger has special advantages over all others, which explains the durability and easy running qualities of the Napoleon. Owing to the perfect construction of the bearings and the rigidity of the frame, it is impossible to get this hanger out of alignment. The cranks can be removed from the frame without removing the sprocket.

OUR NAPOLEON HUB as illustrated on the Previous page is one of the strongest and most satisfactory hubs known and its special construction permits the use of large cones which insure smooth running qualities. These hubs are fitted with the latest improved ball retainers and dustproof devices. We desire to particularly call to your attention our most ingeniously devised cones. With these cones the balls run one-third higher up than on any other cone. This does away with the danger of the cones breaking off on the edges or the breaking of the balls as frequently happens with the other style hubs.

THE BEARINGS of our Napoleon are made of the best grade tool steel turned to shape. You will never find any soft bearings in our bicycles. The older they get the smoother they operate. Part for part you will find our bearings to be heavier gauge material than is used in any other bicycle. We know of no manner in which we could improve the quality of the material or construction of the bearings used on our bicycles. They are absolutely the best. Quality and improvements considered, we are selling our bicycles lower than ever before.

THE CHAINS used on our bicycles are especially made for us by one of the most reliable and best known chain manufacturers in this country, the Duckworth Detachable Chain Co., whose name alone stands for everything that is best in the manufacture of high grade chains, as they are the original detachable chain manufacturers. We have selected the Duckworth chains because in the history of their manufacture of over twenty years, they have never turned out a quantity of chains in which the material used for the blocks and sides of the chain has not been carefully tested and thoroughly tried before shipment. This gives us a chain which will stand great strain, and one which we can fully guarantee.

It is not necessary, should your chain break, to drag your bicycle blocks, or possibly miles, to a blacksmith shop to have it repaired, for, as our illustration shows, you can detach the links by hand and by simply by carrying an extra link in the tool bag, which you will rarely need, you can effectively repair your chain with the loss of a very few minutes.

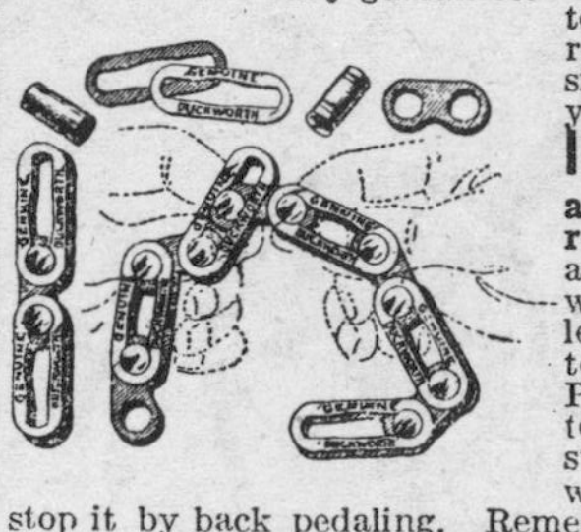

IN PLACING YOUR ORDER overlook the fact that you can secure a coaster brake model bicycle for only $3.00 additional to our regular roadster model price. Our Peerless Coaster Brake does not change the appearance of the bicycle as the entire mechanism is contained in the rear hub which is slightly larger than the regular rear hub. There are absolutely no levers or parts of any kind to think about when using a coaster. All you have to do is to make the same motion as though you are riding an ordinary bicycle. Pedal forward when you want to go ahead and press slightly back when you want to stop. When you want to rest, simply stop pedaling and the bicycle goes forward on its own momentum, until you stop it by back pedaling. Remember, there is no danger of your feet flying off the pedals when descending a steep hill and thereby losing control of your wheel, resulting in a more or less disastrous fall, if you use our Peerless Coaster Brake. With our coaster brake you have that positive assurance, regardless of the speed you are traveling that you have the bicycle under complete control at all times, and to stop, all you have to do is to simply press slightly back on the pedal and the machine will be brought to a full stop in just a few feet.

DETAILED DESCRIPTION OF OUR FAMOUS NAPOLEON BICYCLE

FRAME—20, 22 or 24 inches, made of the highest quality 1-inch Shelby seamless drawn tubing, finished flush at every joint. All joints are doubly reinforced with an additional inside tube or sleeve, which greatly increases the strength, and makes this wheel almost again as strong as wheels of ordinary construction offered in competition.

OUR REINFORCED CONSTRUCTION—So called on account of the extra long, cold pressed steel fishmouth reinforcements which extend far into the tubing. Napoleon reinforcements have long been noted for their marvelous strength, and this special construction adds greatly to the strength and absolutely prevents any vibrations and strains in all directions to a minimum all uncomfortable vibrations, and the points in our Napoleon fine construction. This frame is especially adapted for the use of a coaster brake.

WHEELS are laced according to our improved method, which insures long wear. Rims are made of one piece rock elm, handsomely enameled and striped to match the frame, with blue centers and black sides, gracefully outlined with a gold stripe.

OUR IMPROVED MODEL is equipped with the straight center genuine Napoleon improved specially constructed long distance, wearproof hubs. Heavily nickel plated, with large hardened steel bearings, cups, and cones, which positively insure long wearing qualities.

HANGER—Improved 20th Century Diamond, one-piece drop forged, with 7-inch steel cranks, fitted with Star ball retainers. This hanger can be easily removed from the frame without removing the sprocket. The ball race on our hanger is so ingeniously devised that the hanger is always in alignment. It is absolutely the smoothest and most frictionless hanger ever placed in a bicycle.

THIS BICYCLE is furnished with our Improved America Single Tube Tire, which is today the finest, fastest, easiest riding puncture proof pneumatic tire ever placed on the market. The satisfaction that has attended the introduction of this tire since it was first placed on the market makes it a worthy addition to our Napoleon Bicycle. We have incorporated in this tire a radical new construction, and we know that we have not taken from its resiliency and easy running qualities by the introduction of our New Puncture Proof Tread. The nonskid link chain tread which we are this years introducing on our America Tire is positively the most scientific and practical tread ever put on a tire.

AS ILLUSTRATED ON PREVIOUS PAGE we use the well known Improved Model Napoleon specially constructed, full ball bearing, high grade Rat Trap pedals, which are manufactured exclusively for us, one of the easiest running and best wearing pedals in existence. This pedal is specially made for us by the Standard Pedal Mfg. Co., of Torrington, Conn., and it is a well known fact that they excel all other pedal manufacturers in their highly finished, long wearing and easy running qualities.

HANDLE BARS—Full adjustable, with combination expander, which holds the handle bar firmly in position, and at the same time allows the bar to be quickly released to allow changes, forward extension stem which positively insures a more comfortable and easy riding position than any other handle bar used. For pleasure the bar can be adjusted in an upturned position, and when desired for racing purposes can, in the short space of a minute, be turned down, giving a most advantageous position for those desiring speed.

SADDLE—Full sized selected leather saddle, specially tanned, finely padded and finished. Guaranteed to hold its shape, fitted with adjustable clamp. While we could secure a saddle for far less money, we have not done so as we desire to fit our Napoleon Bicycle with the very best equipment, so as to keep it positively ahead of any other bicycle on the market.

GEAR—81-gear is the regular equipment, and furnished unless otherwise specified. We can furnish 72 or 91 upon order. Long experience has demonstrated the 81-gear, with 26-tooth front and a 9-tooth rear sprocket, gives the best results, and is most universally used.

TOOL BAG—Made of heavy, specially tanned leather, as illustrated on previous page, and contains fine steel wrench, polished brass quick action hand pump, and a tube of Seroco Quick Repair Tire Cement.

FINISH—The New Improved Model Napoleon is one of the finest finished wheels on the market. It is only surpassed by our 1908 Model Peerless. It is handsomely enameled in a rich jet black, with a delicate artistic double panel gold stripe, which beautifully offsets its jet black body. It is further illuminated with heavy nickel plated fork crown, handle bars, and stem, seat post stem, sprockets, hand rubbed finish, this bicycle is specially finished in anti-rust enamel, with a hard rubbed finish, the same as any high grade piano. It is further decorated with handsome rims the same as any high grade bicycle, with a broad blue stripe in center to match blue in name plate, as illustrated on previous page.

No. 19K1430 NAPOLEON IMPROVED MODEL. Price **$15.95**

No. 19K1431 NAPOLEON IMPROVED MODEL, fitted with Peerless Coaster Brake. Price **18.95**

THE 1908 PEERLESS $17⁹⁵

THIS BEAUTIFUL BICYCLE, OUR 1908 PEERLESS, IS STRONG AND RIGID, THE MOST RELIABLE, LIGHTEST RUNNING BICYCLE EVER PRODUCED

During the past year we introduced the Peerless Bicycle to the public, and in the very short space of one season it has secured a reputation and created a demand previously unknown in the bicycle manufacturing business. Never before in the history of bicycles, has any bicycle on its own merits, sprung into such prominence as has our Peerless bicycle. It took our experience of over a quarter of a century in the manufacture of bicycles, many months of study, and the best brains that were ever engaged in the manufacture of bicycles for this bicycle, but it took but one season for the experience, time, efforts and money spent in its production. We sold thousands of these wheels last season; in fact, the sales of the Peerless bicycle alone were greater than the entire bicycle sales of any other dealer, and we predict for this bicycle the greatest success that was ever attained by any bicycle since their early days. We have made many changes and alterations in its construction, and we know that our 1908 model will be more popular than ever before. The sales on this bicycle this year will indicate the appreciation of the bicycle riders for a bicycle built on the sterling qualities of our Peerless.

ONE OF THE STRONG FEATURES

THE MOST VITAL PART OF A BICYCLE

THE ILLUSTRATION ON PREVIOUS PAGE

THE ILLUSTRATION OF OUR PEERLESS FORK CROWN

PEERLESS ARCHED CENTER HUBS

THE RIGIDITY OF OUR PEERLESS FRAME CONSTRUCTION

TWICE THE PLEASURE

IN OUR IMPROVED AMERICA TIRE

DETAILED DESCRIPTION OF OUR 1908 MODEL PEERLESS

FRAME — 20, 22 and 24-inch, 22 and 24-inch standard, 20-inch recommended for people under 5 feet 6 inches in height.

HANGER —

PEDALS —

WHEELS —

TIRES —

HANDLE BARS —

TOOL BAG —

GEAR — 81 gear is our regular equipment.

FINISH —

No. 19K1444 Improved Model Peerless Bicycle, Road Model. Price..........$17.95
No. 19K1445 Improved Model Peerless Bicycle, Coaster Model, equipped with the Famous Peerless Coaster Hub and Brake. Price..........20.95

Sig. 11—1st Ed

OUR 1908 MODEL JOSEPHINE $16.65

NEATEST, MOST PERFECT DESIGNED, ELEGANT FINISH.

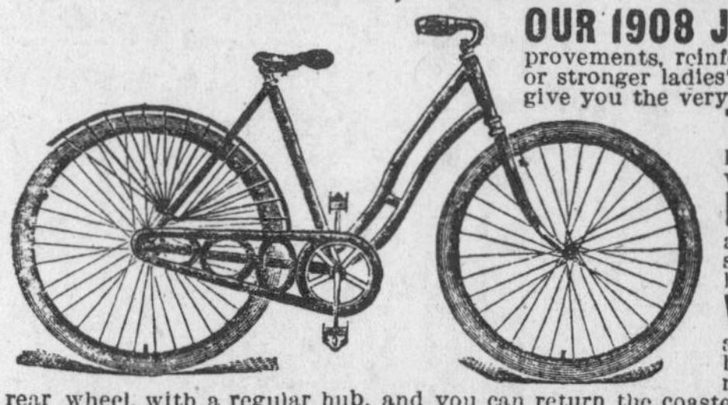

OUR 1908 JOSEPHINE is the highest quality and most beautiful ladies' bicycle ever produced. Peerless construction; made same as our High Art Peerless, and embodies all the improvements, reinforcements and special features identified with our Peerless Bicycles. There is no finer, easier riding or stronger ladies' bicycle made at any price. We strongly recommend this bicycle in preference to all other ladies' wheels. We know that it will give you the very best of satisfaction.

THE EQUIPMENT OF OUR JOSEPHINE is the same as Our Model Peerless, with the exception that it is equipped with the ladies' drop frame, special ladies' saddle, our 1908 ladies' adjustable handle bar and our combination rubber pedals. For further detailed description of our Josephine Bicycle, we would refer you to the description of our Peerless.

FINISHED in a handsome jet black enamel, beautifully off set by heavy nickel plated handle bars, hubs, crown and sprocket. It is furnished with a 22-inch frame, which is standard size. At our $16.65 price it is a marvel of value, and we protect all purchasers of this bicycle for a period of two years with our written binding guarantee. Furthermore, we ship our Josephine on ten days' trial with the understanding that if it is not satisfactory and the greatest value ever offered in a ladies' bicycle it may be returned to us and your money will be immediately refunded.

WE FURTHER REQUEST that before you place your order with us for a Josephine Bicycle you read fully our detailed description of our Peerless Coaster Brake, and if there is any question in your mind as to the advisability of paying the small sum of $3.00 extra for a coaster brake, we suggest by all means that you order a coaster brake bicycle and after you have used it for thirty days, remember, that if it does not come up to your fullest expectations, if it does not increase your pleasures in bicycling over one half, notify us immediately, and we will ship promptly a regular rear wheel, with a regular hub, and you can return the coaster brake rear hub and wheel to us, and we will refund you the difference, $3.00, plus transportation charges. We cannot do more to induce you to try the coaster brake on your bicycle.

No. 19K1432 Ladies' 1908 Josephine Bicycle, road model. Price.. $16.65
No. 19K1433 Ladies' 1908 Josephine Bicycle, coaster model, equipped with our Peerless Coaster Brake. Price...... 19.65

IDENTICAL IN CONSTRUCTION AND MADE WITH THE SAME CARE AND PRECISION AS OUR FAMOUS ELGIN KING RED HEAD.

JUVENILE BICYCLES

THE MOST SATISFACTORY PRESENT FOR BOYS AND GIRLS. FOR DETAILED DESCRIPTION SEE ELGIN KING WRITE UP.

BOYS' RED HEAD BICYCLES.

$13.60

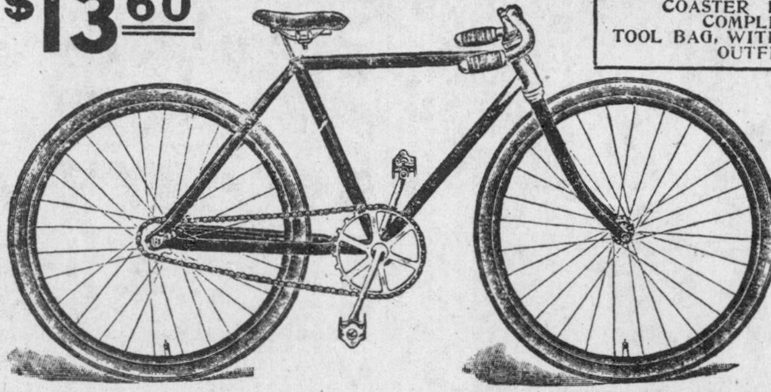

OUR JUVENILE, EQUIPPED WITH PEERLESS COASTER BRAKE, MAKES A MOST COMPLETE CHILD'S BICYCLE. TOOL BAG, WITH WRENCH, PUMP AND REPAIR OUTFIT, 50 CENTS EXTRA.

GIRLS' RED HEAD BICYCLES.

$13.60

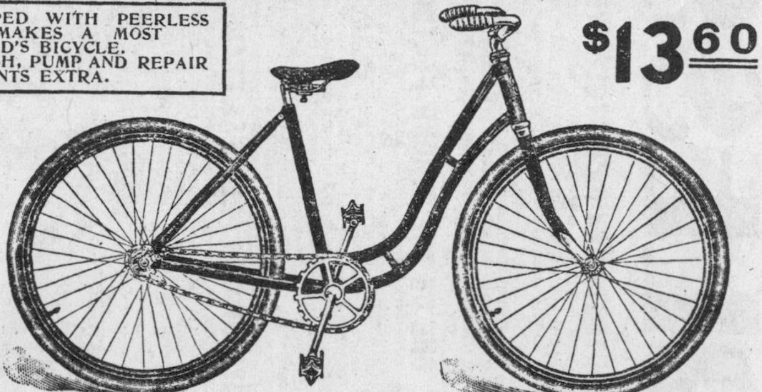

No. 19K1460 Boys' Red Head Bicycle, road model, 16-inch frame, 24-inch wheels. Price $13.60
No. 19K1461 Boys' Red Head Bicycle, coaster model, 16-inch frame, 24-inch wheels. Price.............$16.60
No. 19K1463 Boys' Red Head Bicycle, road model. 18-inch frame, 26-inch wheels. Price $13.95
No. 19K1464 Boys' Red Head Bicycle, coaster model. 18-inch frame, 26-inch wheels. Price $16.95

CAUTION. Be careful, when ordering, to order a wheel that is the right size. In order to arrive at the proper size, take inseam measurement from crotch to heels, allow 5½ inches for the length of the crank, 3 inches for the saddle above the frame. Thus a 16-inch frame would answer for a boy or girl having an inseam measurement up to 24 inches. An 18-inch frame, inseam measurement from 24 to 28 inches. For a boy or girl having an inseam measurement greater than 28 inches, we recommend our regular 20-inch Elgin King or Improved Josephine Bicycles, fully described on the preceding pages.

No. 19K1466 Girls' Red Head Bicycle, road model. 16-inch frame, 24-inch wheels. Price $13.60
No. 14K1467 Girls' Red Head Bicycle, coaster model. 16-inch frame, 24-inch wheels. Price $16.60
No. 19K1469 Girls' Red Head Bicycle, road model. 18-inch frame, 26-inch wheels. Price............$13.95
No. 19K1470 Girls' Red Head Bicycle, coaster model. 18-inch frame, 26-inch wheels. Price............$16.95

IF IN DOUBT order our coaster brake model. For our special offer, see Peerless Coaster Brake described on page 163.

BICYCLE TIRES

WE ARE THE LARGEST HANDLERS OF BICYCLE TIRES IN THE WORLD. Our business in bicycle tires is larger than that of any other five mail order houses combined. We take the output of several factories. This enormous business enables our manufacturers to purchase raw materials at a less cost, which in turn permits us to sell bicycle tires at far lower prices than any other dealer; and, furthermore, insures our having a stock on hand at all times that is fresh and clean, and you need have no fear of receiving tires from us in which the elasticity of the rubber has been destroyed or has died of dry rot.

$3.10 PER PAIR NAPOLEON SINGLE TUBE TIRES

THE BEST TIRE EVER MADE FOR $3.10 PER PAIR. NEW CONSTRUCTION, BETTER VALUE, LONGER WEAR.

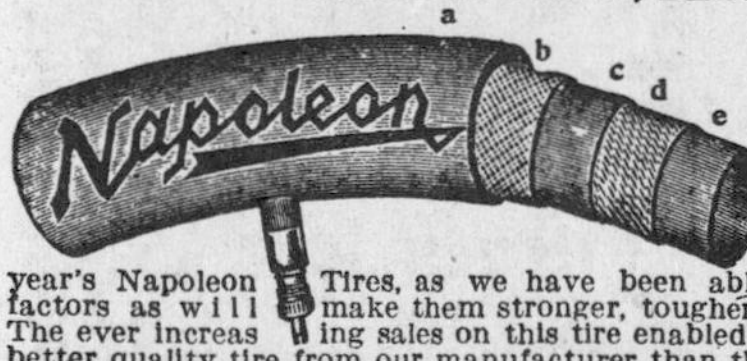

NAPOLEON TIRES. There are in use today many thousand more Napoleon Tires than any other one tire made. Thousands of bicycle riders throughout the country will testify today to the high qualities of this tire. They are, in fact, so well and favorably known they hardly need an introduction. We have been particularly successful in improving the construction of our this year's Napoleon Tires, as we have been able to incorporate in their construction such factors as will make them stronger, tougher, longer wearing and just as resilient as ever. The ever increasing sales on this tire enabled us to demand this better construction and better quality tire from our manufacturer than they have heretofore supplied.

WE HAVE ATTEMPTED TO GIVE YOU SOME IDEA in the accompanying illustration of the new five-piece method in making our Napoleon tire, which practically makes five different tires vulcanized together.

(a) Shows the outer tread or friction layer of rubber, thick, heavy and hard to puncture.
(b) Fabric woven and sealed together with special vulcanizing compound.
(c) The thin layer of pure gum rubber which thoroughly vulcanizes, when heated, both layers next to it into one solid flexible piece.
(d) Layer of tough, interwoven Armor fabric.
(e) Is airtight reinforced pure gum inner tube, the part that contains the air. Each portion of this tire is made separately. Then vulcanized into one mass, which makes complete tire. It is a good construction and one which gives very satisfactory results.

We desire that you do not judge this tire by its price, for the raw material that enters into the construction of this tire costs more than the entire construction of most tires. Our Napoleon construction is a particularly good construction and one which giv unusually satisfactory results.

EACH YEAR FOR THE PAST THREE YEARS this tire has doubled its sales and this increase in sales has enabled us to radically improve the Napoleon construction, namely, to add a layer of tough interwoven Armor fabric made of good quality of Sea Island cotton and an additional layer of pure gum rubber between the two fabric layers so as to insure resiliency without materially adding to the cost of the tire, so that we are still able to sell you this high grade and satisfactory tire at the old price of $3.10. This new construction should render the Napoleon Tire more popular than ever before. We will gladly repair or replace any Napoleon Tire which is defective, providing same is sent us prepaid for inspection.

No. 19K1808 Improved Napoleon Single Tube Tires. Size, 28x1½ inches. Shipping weight, 6 pounds. Price, per pair........ $3.10

NAPOLEON TIRES FOR CHILDREN'S WHEELS. Our Juvenile Tires are in quality and construction identical with the larger sizes. Do not order juvenile tires unless you want them for use on a boy's or girl's bicycle. Then follow the table of instructions for ordering tires shown elsewhere.

No. 19K1813 Improved Napoleon Juvenile Tires. Size, 26x1½ inches. Shipping weight, 2 pounds. Price, per pair........ $3.10
No. 19K1815 Improved Napoleon Juvenile Tires. Size, 24x1½ inches. Shipping weight, 2 pounds. Price, per pair........ $3.10

$2.85 PER PAIR GENUINE KENWOOD SINGLE TUBE TIRES

TOUGH TREAD, RESILIENT, EASY RIDING.

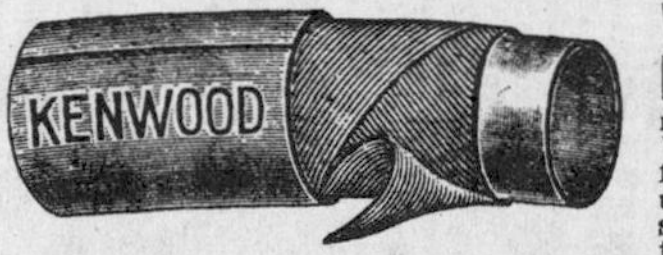

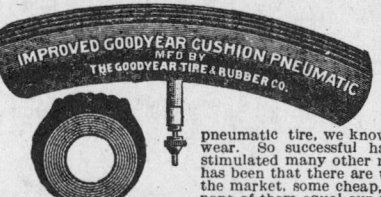

WE OFFER HEREWITH OUR GENUINE KENWOOD TIRES. Tires which we have sold for a number of years with highly satisfactory results. While we sell these tires at a phenominally low figure, yet they are by no means a cheap tire. The unusual high price of pure gum rubber and the scarcity of Sea Island cotton has led most manufacturers to substitute reclaimed rubber and mineral compound, which is secured from secondhand rubber products, rubber being separated from the fabrics by chemical process, and the rubber which they derive by this process is rubber in name only, as its elasticity has been destroyed. For Sea Island cotton they have substituted army canvas, which is by no means as satisfactory. We use in our Kenwood Tires only the finest materials and they are further constructed on scientific principles. Pure gum rubber, selected Sea Island cotton and the best quality of friction fabric are the only materials used in our Kenwood Tires and we fully guarantee them to be perfect in every respect. We suggest before you purchase a tire that you look over our Napoleon and more especially our Improved America Tires, as for the additional amount of money they are vastly superior to any other tire.

No. 19K1820 Kenwood Tires. Size, 28x1½ inches. Price, per pair........ $2.85

$7.95 PER PAIR IMPROVED GOODYEAR CUSHION PNEUMATIC TIRES.

HEAVY TREAD, EXTRA STRONG, WEAR RESISTING.

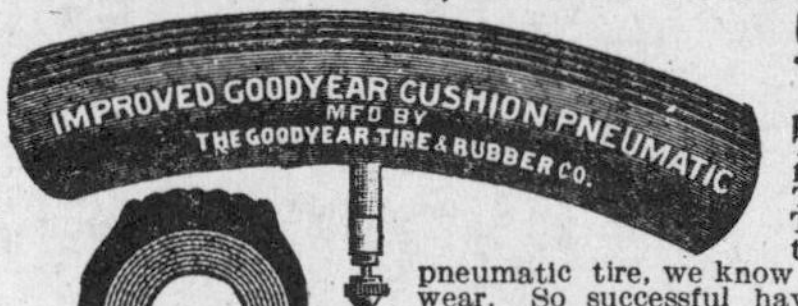

OUR CUSHION PNEUMATIC TIRES. For the past number of years we have taken the entire output of our Cushion Pneumatic Factory. These tires have been constructed by a firm that has made Cushion Pneumatic Tires a specialty for the last twenty years. The result has been that wherever we see the name "Goodyear" today in a cushion pneumatic tire, we know it stands for quality, efficiency and long wear. So successful have our manufacturers been that it has stimulated many other manufacturers to imitate them. The result has been that there are today many cushion pneumatic tires on the market, some cheap, and many of them more expensive, yet none of them equal our Goodyear Cushion Pneumatic Tire.

AS ITS NAME IMPLIES it is a combination of pneumatic and a cushion tire, embodying all the good features of other cushion tires and none of their defects. The material entering into the construction of these tires is the very best. They are made entirely of new rubber and the finest Sea Island cotton fabric, cut on the bias, thus insuring a longer wearing and more resilient tire than any other cushion pneumatic tire on the market. They are entirely free from that heavy, hard pulling sensation. The heavy walls are protected by additional layers of cotton fabric, as shown in the illustration, and our improved thread makes it as nearly puncture proof as it is possible to make a tire which contains air. The walls are so thick that it is practically impossible for any nail or tack to reach the air tube. Within the heavy walls run an air chamber ¾ of an inch in diameter, lined with pure rubber, thus insuring an exceptionally easy riding tire, one that is much softer, and more elastic than the ordinary solid or cushion tire, and one which only needs to be pumped up once or twice a season. The construction of this tire renders you immune to all tire troubles, such as broken glass, tin cans, nails, and the like.

No. 19K1828 Improved Cushion Pneumatic Tires. Price, per pair........ $7.95

We will attach these tires to any of our bicycles, in place of our regular tires, at $5.00 additional.

$4.10 FOR A PAIR OF OUR IMPROVED AMERICA TIRES

FAST, EASY RIDING, RESILIENT, PRACTICALLY NON-DESTRUCTIBLE

OUR AMERICA TIRE FOR 1908 is an entirely new production and a decided improvement over any other tire on the market. It is constructed for us by one of the most experienced manufacturers in the world and possesses all the features of tire construction that stand for service, durability and satisfaction, and, in addition, has many new and radical improvements. The America Tire which we furnished during the season just past was in construction superior to any other tire and its sales were far greater than any other one tire on the market, and, while it gave entire satisfaction, yet we were not satisfied and set out to produce a puncture proof tire. After months of research and experiment we have succeeded in producing a tire that is practically puncture proof and, in fact, as puncture proof as a tire can be without being constructed solid, and yet not detract in the least from the fast, easy riding and resilient qualities of the ordinary pneumatic tire.

WE HAVE GONE A STEP FURTHER in our construction. We have added to this tire a link chain non-skid tread, the most practical and scientific tread ever made. It will positively do away with that holding back sensation so frequently experienced while riding certain tires, as it positively conforms to any roadbed, and owing to its special construction and the thick layers of pure gum rubber we have been able to absolutely maintain its phenomenal speed, lightness and great resiliency.

ON THE RIM SIDE of the tire we have added a flannelette strip, which is vulcanized thoroughly to tire, which serves a double purpose, not only protects the rim of tire from becoming rim worn, but its wooly nap on the rim side enables our tires to be cemented to the rims in such a manner that there is no danger of their slipping or creeping.

IT IS SELF HEALING. By a special process known only to us the inside rubber air tube is chemically treated in such a manner that practically all punctures are self closing and self healing, so that, should the puncture proof fabric be punctured by any accident, the inside air chamber will quickly close and thus prevent the escape of the air.

IF YOU DO NOT FIND them just exactly as we represent them, if they are not the handsomest, most substantial, easiest riding and most resilient tires that you ever saw, we request that you return them to us, and we will refund your money, both the price and any transportation charges you paid.

MADE $5.00 BETTER at no additional cost to you. We challenge any manufacturer to produce a $10.00 tire, or a tire at any price, to compare with our America in resiliency, toughness, mechanical construction and long wearing qualities.

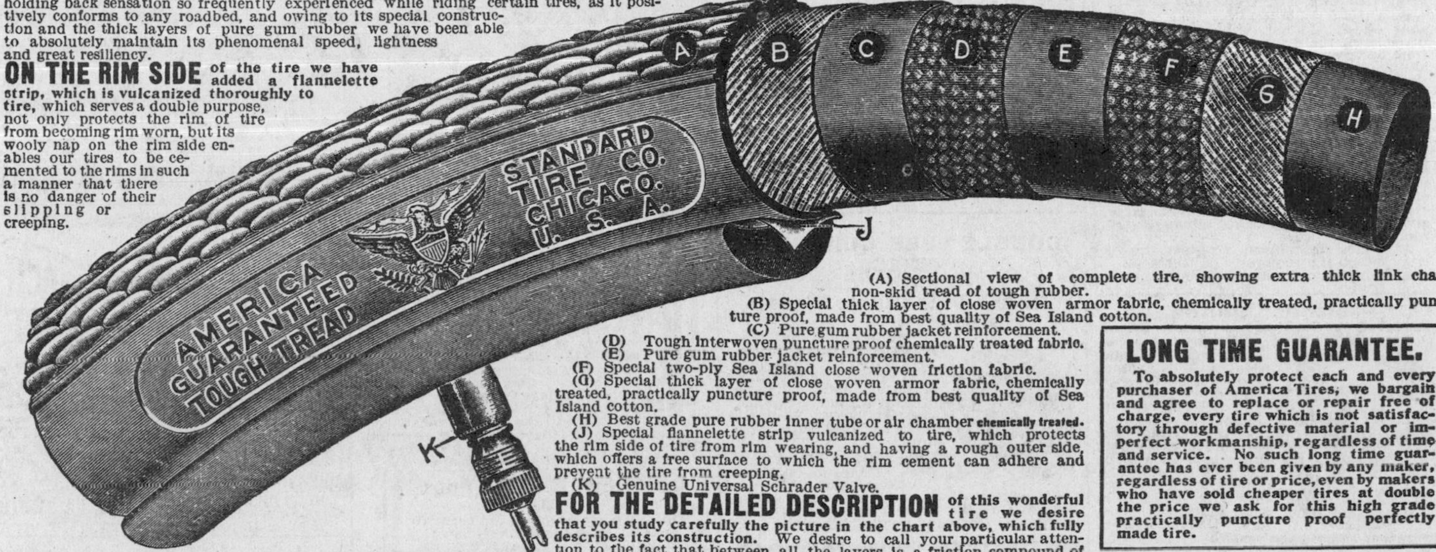

(A) Sectional view of complete tire, showing extra thick link chain non-skid tread of tough rubber.
(B) Special thick layer of close woven armor fabric, chemically treated, practically puncture proof, made from best quality of Sea Island cotton.
(C) Pure gum rubber jacket reinforcement.
(D) Tough interwoven puncture proof chemically treated fabric.
(E) Pure gum rubber jacket reinforcement.
(F) Special two-ply Sea Island close woven friction fabric.
(G) Special thick layer of close woven armor fabric, chemically treated, practically puncture proof, made from best quality of Sea Island cotton.
(H) Best grade pure rubber inner tube or air chamber chemically treated.
(J) Special flannelette strip vulcanized to tire, which protects the rim side of tire from rim wearing, and having a rough outer side, which offers a free surface to which the rim cement can adhere and prevent the tire from creeping.
(K) Genuine Universal Schrader Valve.

LONG TIME GUARANTEE.

To absolutely protect each and every purchaser of America Tires, we bargain and agree to replace or repair free of charge, every tire which is not satisfactory through defective material or imperfect workmanship, regardless of time and service. No such long time guarantee has ever been given by any maker, regardless of tire or price, even by makers who have sold cheaper tires at double the price we ask for this high grade practically puncture proof perfectly made tire.

FOR THE DETAILED DESCRIPTION of this wonderful tire we desire that you study carefully the picture in the chart above, which fully describes its construction. We desire to call your particular attention to the fact that between all the layers is a friction compound of the very finest washed upper river Para rubber in semi-liquid form, so that each layer of pure rubber and Sea Island fabric as laid one upon the other is thoroughly cemented together, which practically makes one piece of these many parts. The many parts of the whole construction are then vulcanized by an improved slow method which positively does not injure the elasticity and resiliency of the rubber. Many manufacturers vulcanize tires by a rapid method, subjecting the tires to extreme heat for a very few moments. This process many times actually burns the very life out of the rubber, which causes the tire to lose its resiliency. With our method the life of the rubber is preserved, and one part is as elastic as the other. Not an ounce of reclaimed rubber enters into the construction of our tires. Every one is tested and inspected before it leaves our factory. Owing to the construction of our non-skid, link chain tread and the quality of our heavy armor fabric, nails, tacks, glass, sharp stones and splinters will not puncture this tire, as they are likely to puncture an ordinary tire.

NOTICE. Ladies' and men's bicycles always require 28-inch tires. Do not order tires of a smaller size unless wanted for a juvenile bicycle.

No. 19K1803 Famous America Tires. Size, 28x1½ inches. Shipping weight, 6 pounds. Price, per pair........ **$4.10**

OUR PEERLESS AUTOMATIC COASTER BRAKE

REMODEL YOUR BICYCLE TO A COASTER BRAKE MODEL

By Buying Either the Coaster Brake Only and Using It in Place of Your Regular Rear Hub, or Buying the Rear Wheel Complete with Coaster Brake.

THE MOST VALUABLE INVENTION IN THE HISTORY OF BICYCLING IS OUR PEERLESS COASTER HUB AND BRAKE.

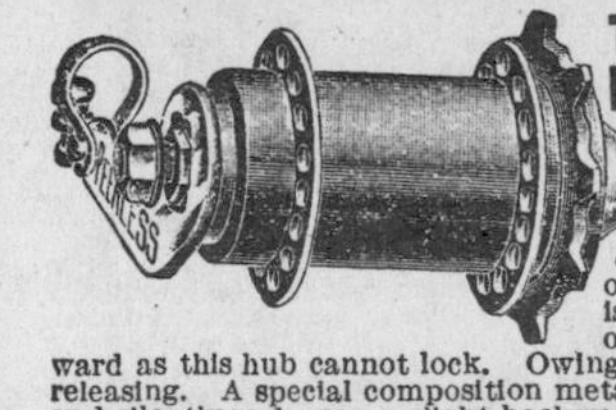

THE PEERLESS COASTER HUB AND BRAKE is considered as great an invention and improvement as the pneumatic tire, as it combines all the elements of ease and comfort as well as safety as a brake. It embodies all the good points of other coaster hubs, with none of their defects, with many new and important features found only in this hub. It has no ratchets, cams or clutches, therefore cannot slip in changing from one operation to another; it is positive in its action. There is absolutely no friction in its bearings in either driving or coasting. Wheel is always free to go forward or backward as this hub cannot lock. Owing to the ingenious construction of the brake, it is self releasing. A special composition metal is used for the braking shoe, which works perfectly and silently and upon a slight backward movement of the pedals automatically the rider can bring into play a powerful metal to metal brake which immediately controls the speed of the wheel by the backward pressure, regardless of the speed or steepness of the hill. Our Peerless has fewer parts than any of the other coaster brakes made. All parts are accurately turned from the highest quality of tool steel, finely finished.

ONE OF THE MOST IMPORTANT FEATURES of our coaster brake is that it can be adjusted without being removed from the frame. With the ordinary coaster brake the rider is compelled to detach the wheel, remove the chain from the sprockets, and in doing this lose the entire adjustment of the back wheel, in order to slightly tighten or loosen the adjustment of the coaster brake. This is the only hub having this feature. In the operation of the Peerless Hub and Coaster Brake it requires no special knowledge, as it is entirely automatic in its action. The Peerless Coaster Brake and Hub has been pronounced the greatest brake ever produced, due to the special construction of the braking surfaces. The braking shoe offers resistance in opposite directions, which gives the maximum of braking power with the minimum of exertion.

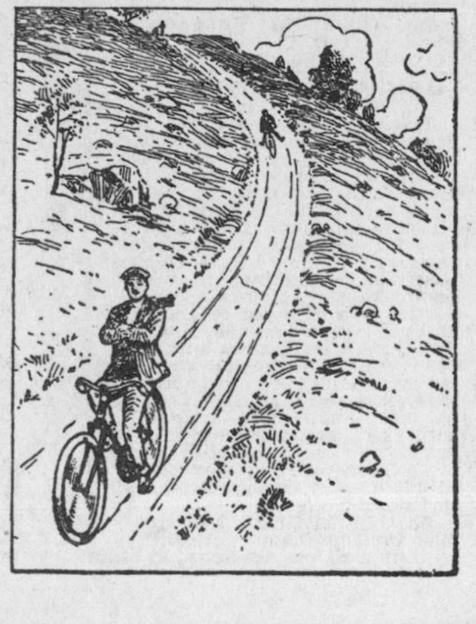

REMEMBER, THE PEERLESS COASTER BRAKE is a great labor saving device. You can ride fifty miles and coast twenty-five miles and thereby save nearly one-half of your strength. We desire that you note the picture herewith, which shows you the ease, grace, speed and comfort derived from the use of the coaster brake, while going down a steep hill, as contrasted with the use of the old hub, as the rider of the old style hub, if he is conservative, will walk down a steep hill, which means he will have to walk up the next hill, while the other fellow with a regular hub may decide to ride down, with the result that about two-thirds the way down he is traveling at such a terrific speed that he has lost his pedals and the smallest stone in the road or a bend at the bottom will cause a more or less disastrous fall. There is no hill too steep to coast safely if your bicycle has a Peerless Coaster Brake.

IF YOU HAVE BEEN A RIDER but have given it up, or if you are today riding a bicycle equipped with an old style rear hub we suggest that you get a coaster brake bicycle or coaster brake hub for your bicycle and try it, and we know that you will fully agree with us in our claims for our coaster brake. We know that if you will but make the test that you will agree with us that the coaster brake has done more to revive bicycling than any other invention.

IF YOU WILL BUT STOP AND THINK of your past bicycle experiences you will recall many times that life or limb depended upon the slightest mishap when you have been riding down steep hills or possibly when you have been making corners quickly and you found yourself immediately confronted with a team or automobile coming toward you at a high rate of speed, and you have had to use all your strength and ingenuity to avoid an accident. If you will think over your past experiences carefully you will realize how your troubles would have ended with a coaster brake; it would have saved you many accidents, disagreeable experiences, dollars in repairs to your bicycle and many a long walk home.

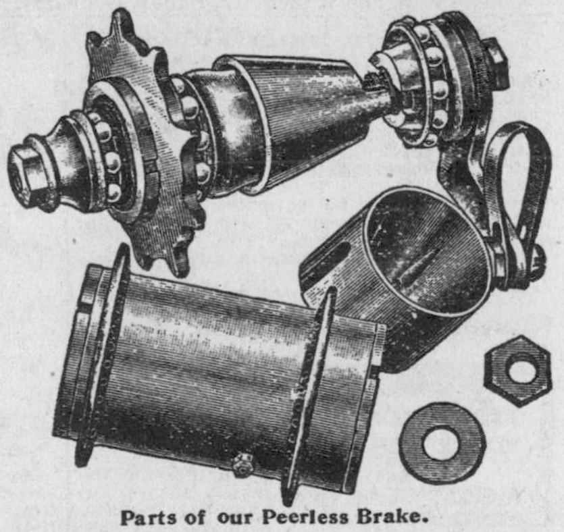

Parts of our Peerless Brake.

WE OFFER OUR PEERLESS COASTER BRAKE with our binding guarantee that it will give absolute satisfaction in every respect. We further suggest that if you are considering purchasing a bicycle, that if you have not fully made up your mind to buy a bicycle with the coaster brake, that you borrow a bicycle with coaster hub, ride it from four to five miles and we are positive that you would not buy anything but a coaster brake bicycle after this trial. We further bargain and agree if you secure one of our coaster brake bicycles and after using it ten, twenty or thirty days and you are not then fully satisfied with our coaster hub, if for any reason you desire to return it to us we will immediately express to you a rear wheel, charges prepaid, fully equipped for your bicycle, and refund you the difference of $3.00 between the coaster brake model and the roadster model. We know that we are taking no chance in making you this liberal offer as we know that they will give you entire satisfaction. We can furnish these hubs complete with clip for fastening brake arm to lower fork of bicycle, drilled for 32 or 36 spokes, with 7, 8, 9, 10 or 11-tooth sprockets, for either 3-16 or ¼-inch chain. Be sure in ordering to specify number of spokes and size of sprocket.

Unless otherwise specified, we will ship you hub for 36 spokes with 9-tooth sprocket. Weight, 3¼ pounds.

NOTE. This hub can be attached to a bicycle by any repairman or equipped to any of our other bicycles at an additional charge of $3.50. Thousands of our bicycles will be equipped with the famous hub and coaster brake this season with the most satisfactory results.

No. 19K1995 Peerless Coaster Hub and Brake. Price........ **$3.50**
No. 19K1997 Rear Wheel, complete with coaster brake hub, spokes properly laced, wheel trued up ready to attach to your frame, size 28 inches. Price, without tires.. **$4.05**
No. 19K1998 Wheels for clincher tires, such as the G.&J. or the Dunlop. Price, **4.25**

$3.55 PER PAIR IMPERIAL DOUBLE TUBE TIRES. RELIABLE.

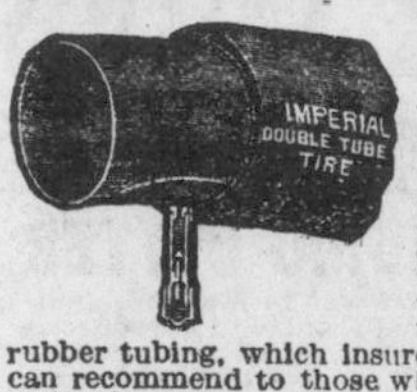
IMPERIAL
DOUBLE TUBE
TIRE

THE SALES ON OUR IMPERIAL TIRE have shown that it is fully up to the expectations of the riders who desire double tube tires. In fact the demand for these tires is rapidly increasing, as they are a strictly high grade double tube tire. There is no double tube tire on the market today, regardless of price, that is superior to our Imperial Tire. They are capable of withstanding hard service, and at the same time have sufficient life to make them comfortable to ride. They are unusually well constructed for a double tube tire, as special attention has been given to the tread, which is the part of the tire most likely to wear. It is constructed with the improved heavy raised tread, making it difficult to puncture. The inner tube is made of exceptionally good quality pure rubber tubing, which insures stability, and will give the best of satisfaction. It is a tire that we can recommend to those who desire a double tube tire and those who give considerable thought to the importance of their tire equipment. It is the best of the kind that can be produced.

No. 19K1846 Imperial Double Tube Tires. 28x1½ and 28x1⅝ inches. Be sure to state size desired. Shipping weight, 5½ pounds.
Price, per pair........ **$3.55**

See our Improved Cushion Pneumatic Tires, as illustrated on preceding page, for a heavy tread, high grade, wear resisting tire.

Instructions For Ordering Tires.

Be careful to order tires that will fit your wheel. In measuring, measure the diameter of the tire blown up or inflated from outer edge to opposite outside edge, also measure width of tire. Usually the size can be obtained from the old tires, as nearly all tires have size branded on the side but when this information cannot be obtained it becomes necessary to measure the rim. It is not always understood by the rider that the size of tires is governed by the outside diameter when inflated, which explains why a rim measuring 25 inches in diameter from edge to edge requires a 28-inch tire, and other sizes as per our explanatory table given below. **Measuring diameter of rim, edge to edge.**
A 21-inch rim requires a 24-inch tire.
A 23-inch rim requires a 26-inch tire.
A 25-inch rim requires a 28-inch tire.

Protection Bands.

Will Make Your Old Tires Last Another Season.

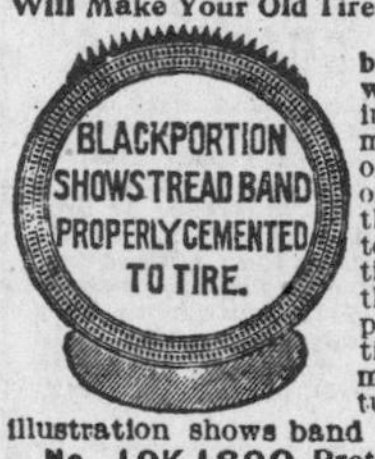
BLACKPORTION
SHOWS TREAD BAND
PROPERLY CEMENTED
TO TIRE.

These are heavy rubber bands, 1¼ inches wide, made extra thick in one piece, to be cemented over the tread of any 28-inch tire with ordinary rubber cement, thus enabling the rider to secure more use from tires which are worn on the tread. Will also prolong the life of new tires and make them more difficult to puncture. Dark portion in illustration shows band on tire.

No. 19K1890 Protection Band. Price, each........ **44c**
If by mail, postage extra, each, 10 cents.

$5.47 PER PAIR GOODRICH SINGLE TUBE TIRES.

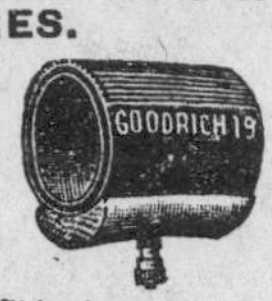
GOODRICH 19

THESE GOODRICH TIRES are preferred by many riders, and are good, serviceable, high grade tires. No pump or kit included.

No. 19K1835 Goodrich No. 19 Tires. Size, 28x1½ or 28x1⅝ inches. Shipping weight, 2 pounds. Price, per pair... **$5.47**

DOUBLE TUBE CLINCHER TIRES.

G. & J. Detachable Tires.

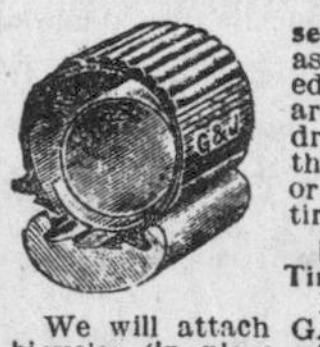

Note that prices are quoted separately for tires and rims, as the latter are not included in price of tires. Rims are natural finish, and come drilled with thirty-two and thirty-six holes. No pump or kit included with these tires.

No. 19K1875 G. & J. Tires. 28x1⅝ in. Price, per pair... **$7.31**

We will attach G. & J. tires to any of our bicycles (in place of regular tires) at $4.90 additional. Shipping weight, 8 pounds.

No. 19K1877 Casings, 28x1⅝ inches. Price, each........ **$2.57**
If by mail, postage extra, each, 50 cents.

INNER TUBES.

Guaranteed Butt End Tubes.

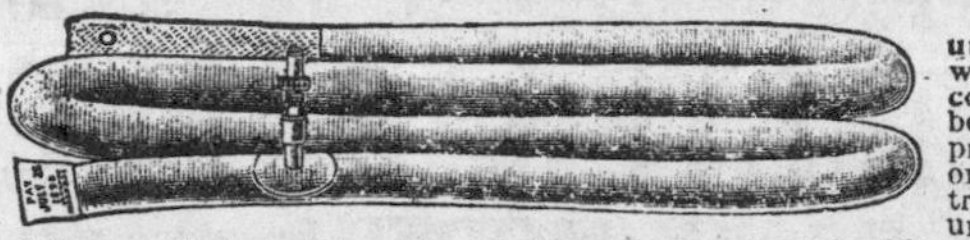

We are the largest distributors of inner tubes in the world, selling direct to the consumer. We know we have better inner tubes at lower prices than anyone else, and only ask that you give them a trial. All of our tubes are made under our special specifications of the very best quality of Upper River Para rewashed rubber, with doubly reinforced butt ends, and improved standard cloth inserted valve stem construction. The ends are closed by a special process known as the butt end method of closing, and are positively warranted not to blow out. Every tube is guaranteed to give satisfaction, and if not satisfactory in every way, may be returned and we will replace it. If you have an old tire that is porous, single or double tube, one of these inner tubes will enable you to place it in good riding condition.

Napoleon Inner Tubes.

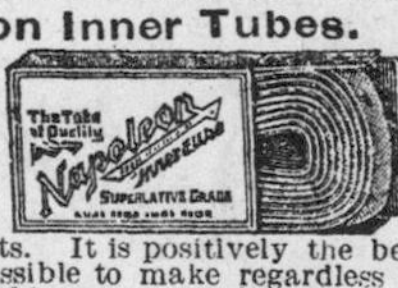
Napoleon
Superlative Grade

They are well and favorably known. For years we have sold the Napoleon Inner tubes with the most satisfactory results. It is positively the best tube that it is possible to make regardless of price. Any tube blown out will be cheerfully replaced without charge.

No. 19K1909 Napoleon Inner Tubes, 28 inches. Price, each........ **89c**
If by mail, postage extra, each, 12 cents.

Monarch Guaranteed Inner Tubes.

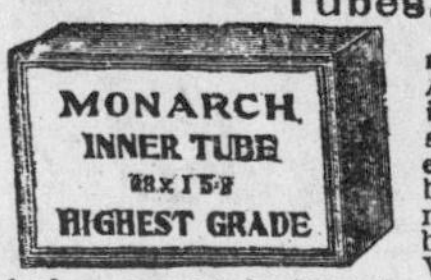
MONARCH
INNER TUBE
28x1⅝
HIGHEST GRADE

These tubes are made from pure African rubber, reinforced valve construction and patented ends. The best tube for the money it is possible to produce. Will fit any 28-inch cemented double tube tire.

No. 19K1905 Monarch Inner Tubes, 28 inches. Price, each........ **65c**
If by mail, postage extra, each, 12 cents.

Morgan & Wright Patent No. 1 Inner Tubes.

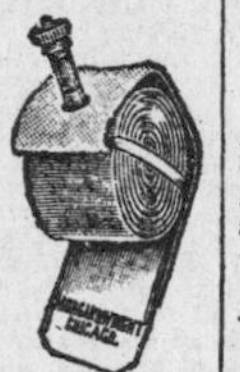

These tubes are well known and have always given good satisfaction. They are guaranteed in every way.

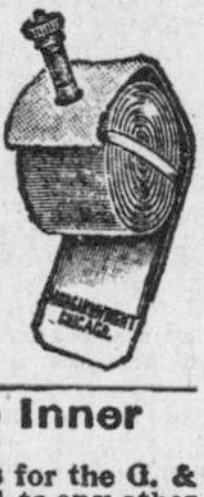

No. 19K1906 M. & W. Patent No. 1 Inner Tubes.
Price, each, 28 inches ..**72c**
Price, each, 26 inches ..**73c**
Price, each, 24 inches ..**74c**
If by mail, postage extra, each, 12 cents.

G. & J. and Dunlop Inner Tubes.

No. 19K1916 Inner Tubes for the G. & J. and Dunlop Tires, not adapted to any other tire, 28x1⅝ inches.
Price, each..(Postage extra, 12c).. **$1.19**

Valves for Single and Double Tube Tires.

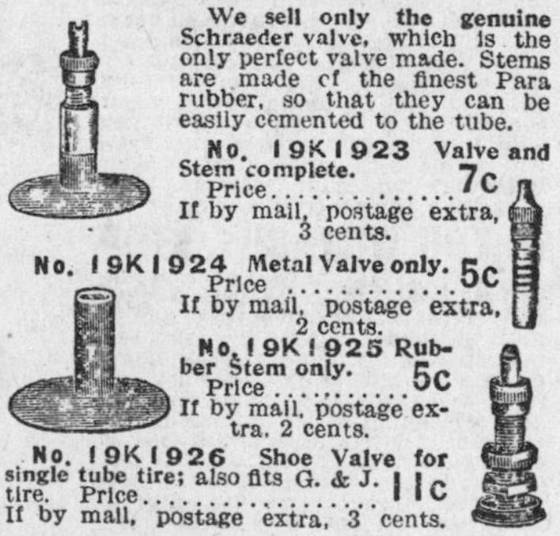

We sell only the genuine Schraeder valve, which is the only perfect valve made. Stems are made of the finest Para rubber, so that they can be easily cemented to the tube.

No. 19K1923 Valve and Stem complete.
Price........ **7c**
If by mail, postage extra, 3 cents.

No. 19K1924 Metal Valve only.
Price........ **5c**
If by mail, postage extra, 2 cents.

No. 19K1925 Rubber Stem only.
Price........ **5c**
If by mail, postage extra, 2 cents.

No. 19K1926 Shoe Valve for single tube tire; also fits G. & J. tire. Price........ **11c**
If by mail, postage extra, 3 cents.

Bicycle Pumps

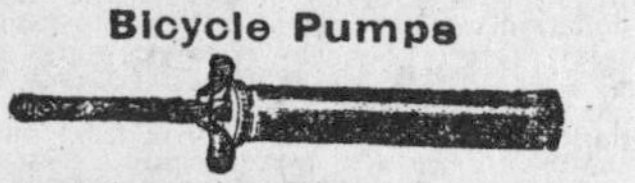

A Good Serviceable Pump, made of strong material, and will last two or three seasons. The favorite style and size. Compound action, including hose connection which will fit all valves, having an universal inside thread.

No. 19K1938 Pump.
Price......(Postage extra, 5c)........ **9c**

Keno Pump Connection.

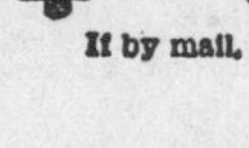
KENO

The Best Right Angle Connection Made.

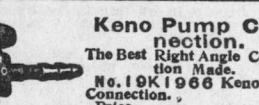

No. 19K1966 Keno Pump Connection.
Price........ **11c**
If by mail, postage extra, 3 cents.

BICYCLE LAMPS.

In making your selection kindly bear in mind that our oil lamps are made to burn common kerosene or coal oil, obtainable everywhere. The gas lamps use calcium carbide.

NOTE—All of our lamps are of standard make, guaranteed against all imperfections in material and workmanship. Read carefully, instructions furnished with each lamp. We cannot accept for credit or exchange lamps that have been used unless they are positively defective.

ADVANCED 1908 COLUMBIA GAS LAMP.

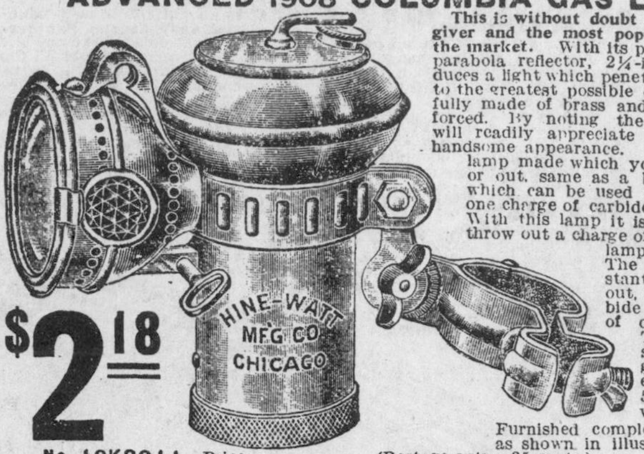
HINE-WATT
MFG. CO.
CHICAGO

$2.18

This is without doubt the greatest light giver and the most popular gas lamp on the market. With its powerful aluminum parabola reflector, 2¼-inch lens, it produces a light which penetrates the darkness to the greatest possible distance. Beautifully made of brass and every part reinforced. By noting the illustration you will readily appreciate the exceptionally handsome appearance. It is the only gas lamp made which you can turn down or out, same as a barn lantern, and which can be used continuously with one charge of carbide until exhausted. With this lamp it is not necessary to throw out a charge of carbide when the lamp is turned out. The lamp lights instantly, does not jar out, and uses less carbide than the majority of other gas lamps. This lamp, while smaller in size, gives a very powerful light. It is 5½ inches high; weight, 18 ounces. Furnished complete with bracket, as shown in illustration.

No. 19K2011 Price........(Postage extra, 35 cents.)........ **$2.18**

The Giant Foot Pump.

NEW COMPOUND ACTION.

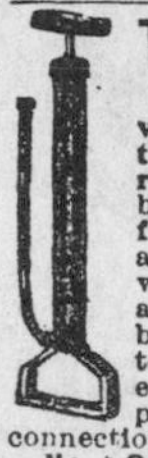

The Giant Foot Pump is made of the very finest quality of seamless tubing and positively will neither rust nor corrode. It has a 1⅛x12-inch barrel, detachable hose, with a powerful plunger, having at its lower end a patented device whereby the leather washer is continually expanded against the sides of the barrel, thereby making it impossible for the barrel to leak air, thus making it much easier to inflate a tire than with other pumps. The hose is fitted with a connection that will fit all modern valves.

No. 19K1942 Giant Foot Pump. Price........ **25c**
If by mail, postage extra, 22 cents.

Our New Marvel Foot Pump.

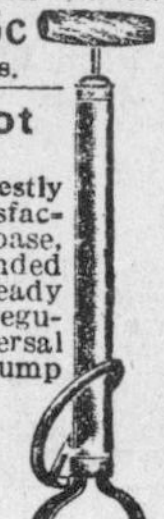

This is a pump which we can earnestly recommend, having proved very satisfactory. Fitted with strong cast iron base, wide enough to stand alone; intended for those requiring a heavy pump ready at all times. Has 12-inch barrel, regular heavy rubber hose, having universal connection that will fit all valves. Pump is beautifully plated; double compound action.

No. 19K1944 New Marvel Foot Pump. Price........ **35c**
If by mail, postage extra, 29 cents.

The Giant Pocket Pump.

38c

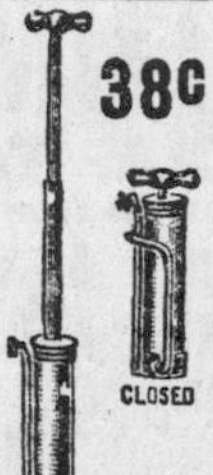
CLOSED
EXTENDED

A combination hand or foot pump, very powerful. Illustration shows pump extended for use as a foot pump, also when telescoped ready to carry in pocket. Made of seamless brass, finely nickel plated. Size, when closed, 6½ inches; extended, 15½ inches. Has universal valve connection to fit any standard tire.

No. 19K1950 Giant Pocket Foot Pump. Price........ **38c**
If by mail, postage extra, 10 cents.

The Improved Telescope Bicycle Pump.

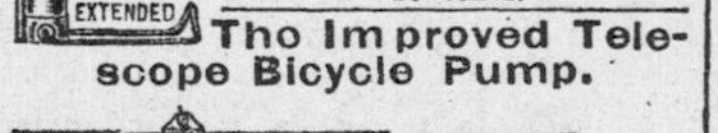

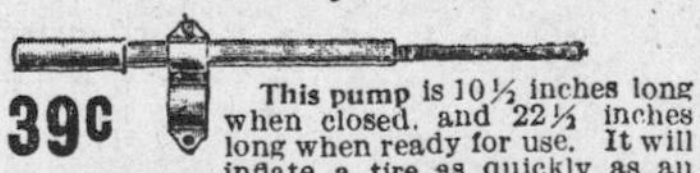

39c

This pump is 10½ inches long when closed, and 22½ inches long when ready for use. It will inflate a tire as quickly as an ordinary foot pump. Can be attached to frame by means of clamp accompanying every pump. Made on scientific principles, being small and compact, but very powerful, entirely of brass, handsomely nickel plated. Every rider ought to have one of these pumps.

No. 19K1954 Telescope Pump. Price........ **39c**
Postage extra, 10 cents.

Baldwin High Pressure Pump.

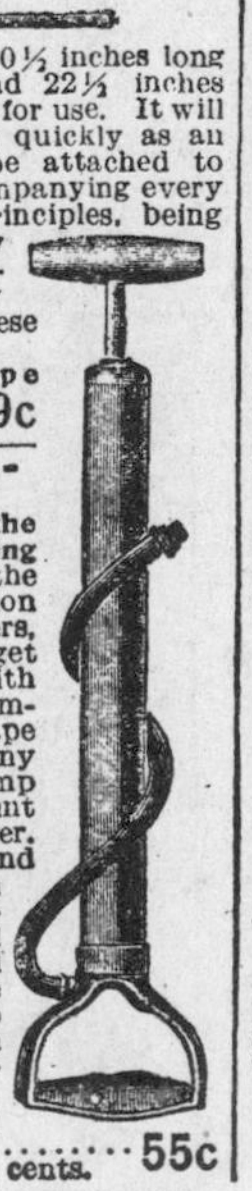

This pump is made to fill the demand for a powerful pump having a very high pressure. It is of the new triple compound, double action type, with expanding washers, which enables the operator to get an extremely high pressure with very little exertion. It is an impossibility for any air to escape past the plunger, as in many pumps, causing the user to pump considerably more air on account of the air escaping past the plunger. The barrel is made extra long, and of a special alloy of metal which is guaranteed not to rust or corrode, extra thick, so that it will not bulge out or dent, is fitted with extra quality rubber hose having universal connection to fit all tires, and is strong enough to inflate heavy carriage or vehicle tires, if desired.

No. 19K1956 Baldwin High Pressure Pump. Price........ **55c**
If by mail, postage extra, 45 cents.

SEARCHLIGHT GAS LAMP.

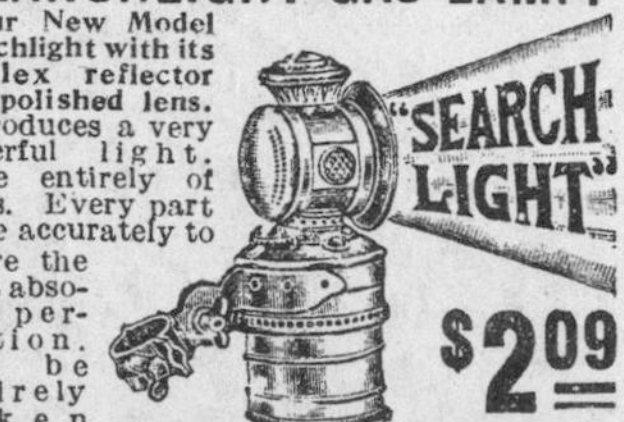
"SEARCH LIGHT"

$2.09

Our New Model Searchlight with its Duplex reflector and polished lens. It produces a very powerful light. Made entirely of brass. Every part made accurately to insure the most absolute perfection. Can be entirely taken apart for cleaning. Has removable lens, protected reflector, imported tip and needle valve. The bracket is adjustable to fit any bicycle. Size, 8 inches high.

No. 19K2003 New Searchlight Gas Lamp. Price........ **$2.09**
If by mail, postage extra, each, 35 cents.

Carbide.

NOTE—**In order to conform with the insurance laws, which prohibit the handling of high explosives and combustible materials in connection with other lines of merchandise, we are unable to furnish carbide. The same ruling applies to other explosives and combustibles, such as gunpowder, dynamite and flashlight powder.**

The 20th Century Oil Headlight.

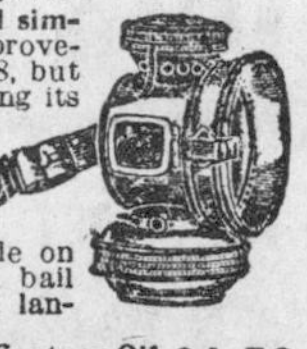

It is smaller, lighter, and simpler than ever, many improvements being made for 1908, but all with a view to increasing its already great light giving capacity. It has the parabola reflector, self locking wick, cannot jar out. Rigid bracket, adjustable to fit any angle on fork or head, also has a bail handle, for use as a hand lantern. Burns kerosene.

No. 19K2020 20th Century Oil Lamp. Price..(Postage extra, 39c).. **$1.52**

OIL LAMPS.

Our Light Weight Lamp.

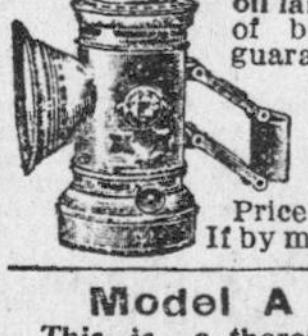

Positively the best low price oil lamp made. Made entirely of brass, handsomely plated, guaranteed to give satisfaction. No solder to melt, or parts to come loose. Burns kerosene oil. 5 inches high.

No. 19K2018 Light Weight Lamp.
Price........ **75c**
If by mail, postage extra, 20 cents.

Model A E-Z Saddles.

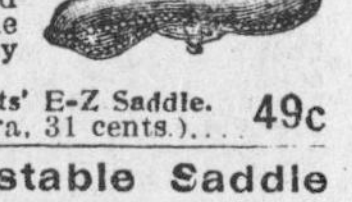

This is a thoroughly up to date saddle, well padded, specially formed, made of grain leather, with nickel spring, and clamp, and, as the name implies, is a very easy rider.

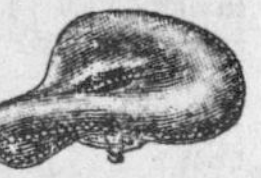

No. 19K2025 Gents' E-Z Saddle.
Price.....(Postage extra, 31 cents.)........ **49c**

Standard Adjustable Saddle Spring.

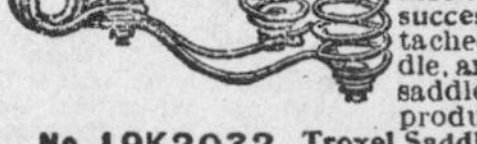

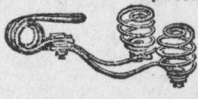

This is something entirely new and is meeting with great success. Can be attached to any saddle, and is the easiest saddle spring ever produced.

No. 19K2032 Troxel Saddle Spring.
Price.....(Postage extra, 24c)........ **37c**

Rubber Pump Tubing.

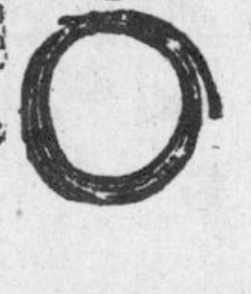

The best quality, as used on all hand and foot pumps, ⅜-inch, in 3-foot lengths (without connections).

No. 19K1960 Tubing. Price, for 3 feet........ **11c**
If by mail, postage extra, per foot, 3 cents.

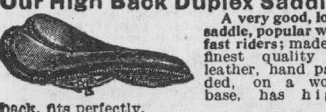

Our High Back Duplex Saddle.

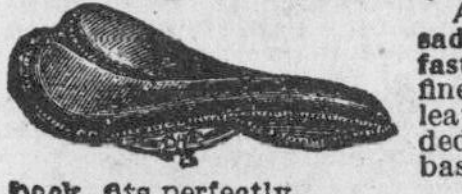

A very good, long saddle, popular with fast riders; made of finest quality of leather, hand padded, on a wood base, has high back, fits perfectly.
No. 19K2036 Men's High Back Duplex Saddle. Price.......... 83c
If by mail, postage extra, 30 cents.

Our Triple Coil Spring Saddle.

One of the Finest, Easiest Riding Saddles Made.

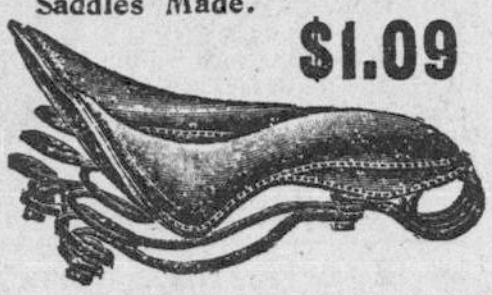

$1.09

This saddle is shaped to fit the form, full size saddle, with large tempered steel coil springs, just lively enough to absorb all vibration and jar, thereby preventing rough roads from detracting from the enjoyment of riding. The saddle is made of fine russet grain leather, hand padded, sewed on a patent lock stitch machine, thereby preventing ripping. There is no more comfortable saddle to be had at any price.
No. 19K2042 Triple Coil Spring Saddle. Price..(Postage extra, 39c.).. $1.09

Expander Seat Post.

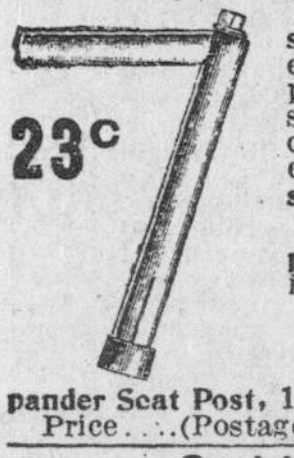

23c

Made of best seamless steel tubing, fitted with expander, elegantly nickel plated. We supply these seat posts either 13-16, ⅞ or 15-16 inches in diameter. State diameter desired plainly.
No. 19K2047 Expander Seat Post, 5 inches long. Price.. 23c
If by mail, postage extra, 14 cents.
No. 19K2048 Expander Seat Post, 10 inches long. Price....(Postage extra. 19 cents.)... 35c

Saddle Clamp.

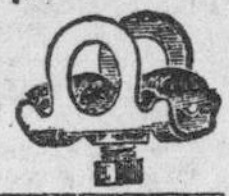

Well and strongly made, will fit any two-spring saddle. Nicely nickel plated.
No. 19K2052 Saddle Clamp. Price.... 5c
If by mail, postage extra, 6 cents.

Our Import Pedals.

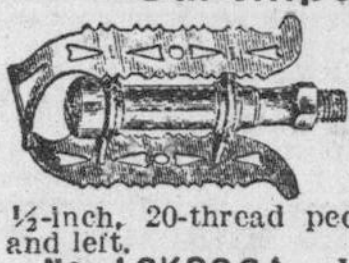

Elegant in design, first class in finish and fully guaranteed. The best low priced pedal made. Nickel plated and polished. Made in standard size, with ½-inch, 20-thread pedal pin. Mated right and left.
No. 19K2061 Import Rat Trap Pedal. Price, per pair........ 57c
If by mail, postage extra, per pair, 16 cents.

Matchless Bridgeport Pedals.

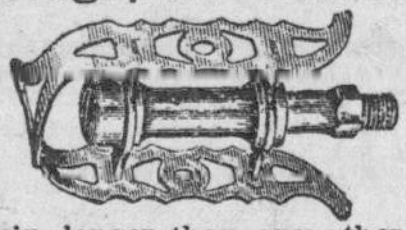

Strongest, handsomest and easiest running pedal ever made. Nothing but the finest material used throughout. When properly adjusted and lubricated it will spin longer than any other pedal made. It is absolutely dustproof and the bearings may be adjusted from the outside. It appeals to the rider today because it is the lightest running and the longest square pedal now on the market.
No. 19K2065 Bridgeport Pedal. Price, per pair........ 85c
If by mail, postage extra, per pair, 18 cents.
No. 19K2066 Combination Pedals. Price, per pair........ 95c
If by mail, postage extra, per pair, 25 cents.

Never Slip Pedal Rubbers.

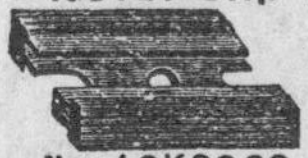

Can be attached to any pedal in a moment. Do not rattle; give good satisfaction. Four rubbers constitute the set.
No. 19K2069 Pedal Rubbers. Price, per set of four........ 18c
If by mail, postage extra. per set of four, 5c.

Thiem's Toe Clips.

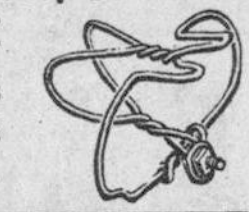

Made of crucible wire. Nothing but a severe accident will put it out of shape.
No. 19K2072 Thiem's Toe Clips. Price, per pair...... 12c
If by mail, postage extra, per pair, 7 cents.

The Standard Toe Clips.

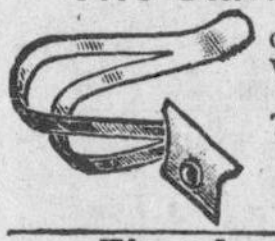

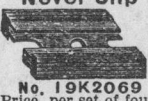

These Toe Clips are made of tempered steel and are very popular clips.
No. 19K2074 Standard Toe Clips. Price, per pair........ 7c
If by mail, postage extra, per pair, 3 cents.

Fine Leather Tool Bag.

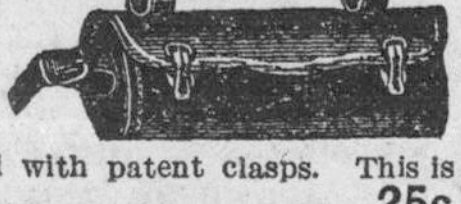

Excellent quality, large and roomy, thoroughly well made of oak tanned leather, ends reinforced, nicely embossed, fastened with patent clasps. This is a fine bag.
No. 19K2078 Tool Bag. Price.... 25c
If by mail, postage extra, 7 cents.

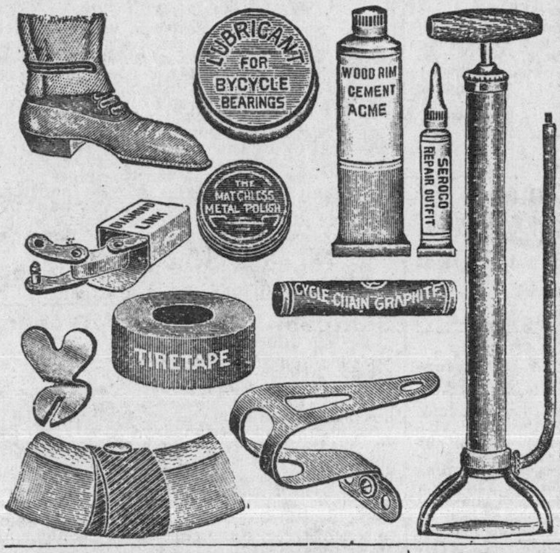

OUR WONDER COMPLETE CYCLISTS' OUTFIT 69c

This is a complete, up to date outfit, and contains everything necessary for the rider. Has been selected with great care and only such articles as are necessary and of real merit have been included.

WHAT THE OUTFIT CONTAINS.

High Grade New Era Heavy Foot Pump, one full size stick of Acme Chain Lubricant, one large tube Wood Rim Cement, Quick Tire Repair Outfit and Emergency Puncture Band, full size roll of Tire Tape, one set of Diamond Chain Repair Links, package of Lubricant for bicycle bearings, Spoke Grip to keep your spokes tight, box High Grade Polish, one pair of Standard Toe Clips and one pair Trousers Guards.
No. 19K1993 Wonder Complete Cyclists' Outfit. Price.............. 69c
Unmailable.

Grain Leather Tool Bag.

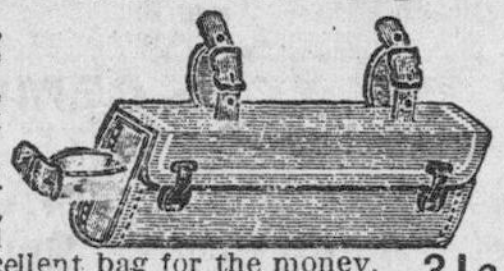

An elegant, attractive tool bag. Well made of good quality grain leather, ends reinforced, extra large and roomy. Excellent bag for the money.
No. 19K2080 Tool Bag. Price... 31c
If by mail, postage extra, 10 cents.

Tourist Bicycle Case.

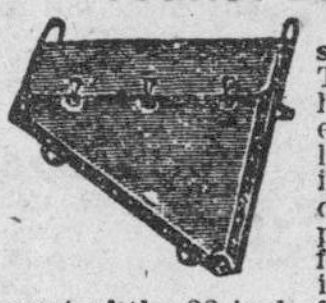

Made in triangular shape, as per illustration. This case is made of heavy press board, covered with canvas and linen lined. The cover is fastened with patent clasps, and straps are provided for attaching to frame. It will fit any 24-inch diamond frame and most of the 22-inch frames, unless the latter have very short heads. Weight, 2 pounds.
No. 19K2079 Tourist Bicycle Case. Price.......... 78c
If by mail, postage extra, each, 35 cents.

HANDLE BARS.

Adjustable Handle Bar.

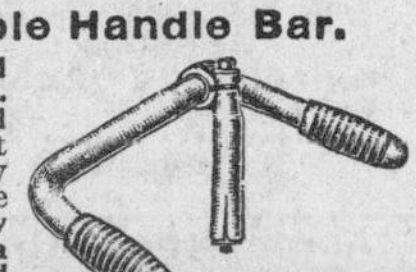

Sometimes called Reversible Bar. Made of best steel tubing, with patent forged stem. By loosening bolt the bar can be instantly changed from a drop to a raised position, or vice versa. Made only 20 inches wide, ⅞-inch expander stem, and fitted with good grips, securely cemented.
No. 19K2082 Adjustable Bar. Price. 52c
If by mail, postage extra, 30 cents.
No. 19K2083 Extra Stems. Price. 32c
If by mail, postage extra, 15 cents.

Extension Stem Adjustable Bar.

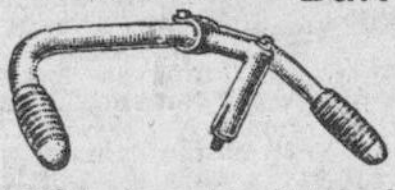

Similar to No. 19K2082 bar, but with 2½-inch forward extension stem ⅞ inch in diameter, with expander. The upper is 20 inches wide, fitted with good grips.
No. 19K2086 Extension Bar. Price. 89c
If by mail, postage extra, 35 cents.

The Kelly Handle Bar.

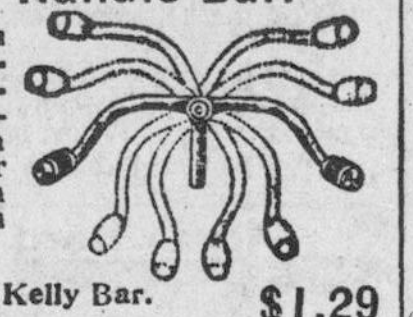

This well known bar permits an endless variety of adjustments, the arms being separate. Each bar fitted with a pair of good grips. Stem is ⅞ inch only, with expander.
No. 19K2089 Kelly Bar. Price........ $1.29
If by mail, postage extra, 45 cents.
We also furnish the Kelly Bar with 2½-inch forward extension stem, especially adapted for tall riders. Stem, ⅞ inch only, with expander. Each bar fitted with a pair of good grips.
No. 19K2090 Extension Bar. Price...(Postage extra, 45 cents.).. $1.41

Handle Bar Buffer.

The Rubber Handle Bar Buffer goes on over frame and prevents your handle bar from knocking off the enamel. Every cyclist should have one
No. 19K2110 Handle Bar Buffer. Price......(Postage extra, 3 cents.).... 5c

Wound Leather Grips.

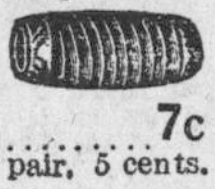

These grips are made from genuine sole leather, and are certainly the most durable made.
No. 19K2112 Leather Grips. Price, per pair.......... 7c
If by mail, postage extra, per pair, 5 cents.

Sewed Leather Grips.

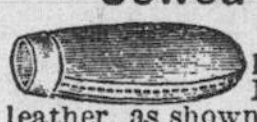

This grip is the easiest and lightest grip in the market. Made of oil tanned, cowhide leather, as shown in illustration. The leather covering of this grip is first stitched and then turned outside in, thereby leaving seam on the inside. The cover is then drawn over a wooden core, the seams fitting into a groove in the wood, thereby making a perfectly smooth outside. The open end has fine nickel plated ferrule.
No. 19K2114 Sewed Leather Grips. Price, per pair.............. 29c
If by mail, postage extra, per pair, 5 cents.

Our 14-Cent Bell.

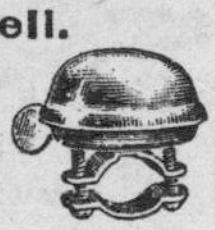

Handsomely nickel plated, 1¾-inch gong, of pure bell metal. Has rotary electric movement.
No. 19K2120 Nickel Plated Bell. Price...... 14c
If by mail, postage extra, 8c.

Shield Bell.

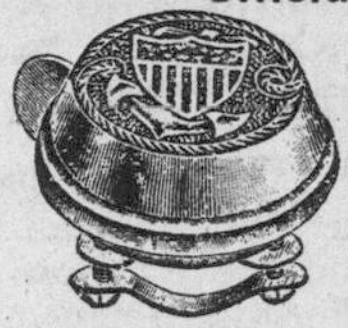

A very pretty design, 1¾-inch gong, with the shield handsomely enameled in colors, all other parts being finely nickel plated. This bell has rotary electric movement.
No. 19K2122 Shield Bell. Price........ 21c
If by mail, postage extra, 8 cents.

Continuous Ringing Bell, With Flag Top.

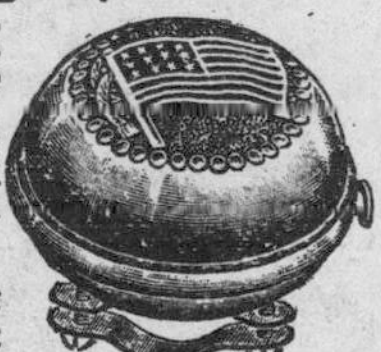

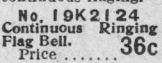

This is a very handsome bell, having 2¾-inch gong the top being enameled, showing the national emblem in natural colors. The mechanism is ratchet electric, continuous ringing.
No. 19K2124 Continuous Ringing Flag Bell. Price....... 36c
If by mail, postage extra, 12 cents.

Tire Chimes.

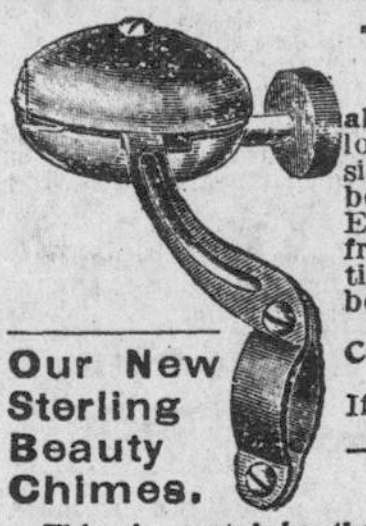

A loud, musical double alarm, continuing as long as rider wishes—simply pull a string, bell does the rest. Easily attached to any front fork as per directions packed with each bell.
No. 19K2127 Tire Chimes. Price.......... 49c
If by mail, postage extra, 12 cents.

Our New Sterling Beauty Chimes.

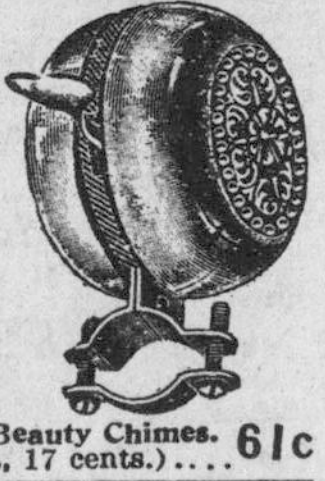

This is certainly the most beautiful chimes bell ever produced. The mechanism is perfect, no rewinding, continuous rotary movement, double gong, non-revolving, making a very loud and harmonious alarm. The gongs are of genuine bell metal, 2¼ inches, handsomely decorated. Suitable for use on bicycles, tandems and automobiles.
No. 19K2129 New Beauty Chimes. Price....(Postage extra, 17 cents.).... 61c

Our New Model Cycle Horn.

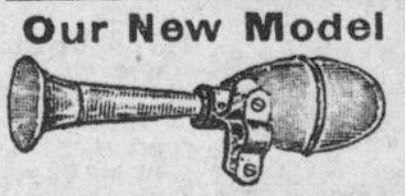

This new horn is made entirely of brass, beautifully nickel plated, with imported metal reed, and latest style sure grip rubber bulb. Gives a very shrill and melodious alarm, which can be heard a great distance. Horn is 6½ inches long, fully tested and is attached to bicycle by means of special metal clamp.
No. 19K2130 New Model Cycle Horn. Price..(Postage extra, 8 cents.) 38c

Bicycle and Motor Cycle Horn.

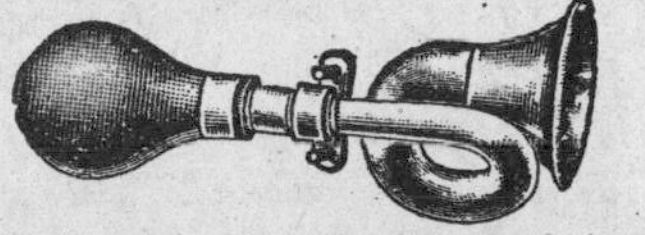

This is a high class horn of the bugle type. Gives a deep melodious alarm, and can be heard at an extreme distance. Made of finest spun brass, 7½ inches total length, 2½ inches diameter at mouth, beautifully plated, sure grip, india rubber bulb.
No. 19K2131 New Imported Horn. Price.....(Postage extra, 12 cents.).... 86c

Bicycle Wheels.

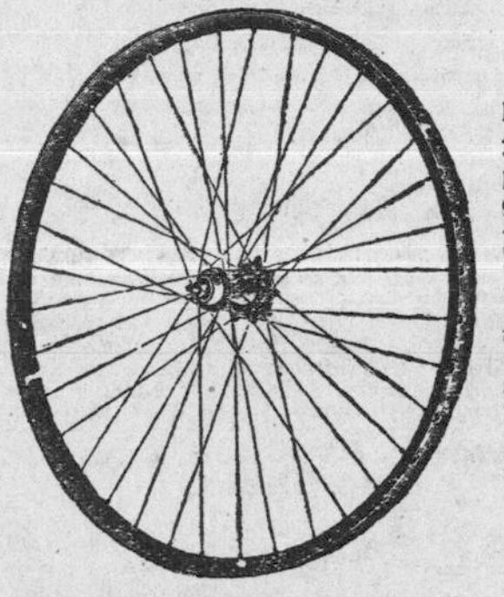

NOTE. All wheels have a coat of XX hard cement, which when moistened with gasoline or benzine is ready for tire.

These wheels are especially well constructed and if you have an old bicycle in which the hubs are giving trouble, a pair of them will enable you to put it in first class condition. Rims, spokes and hubs are guaranteed to be high grade. Rims are all standard crescent shape to take 28-inch tires such as Napoleon, Kenwood, M. & W., etc. The bearings of these wheels are especially well constructed to give good service. Cones and cups extra well hardened, hubs heavily nickel plated. The spokes are also heavily plated, and of great tensile strength. We cannot furnish or build odd sizes of wheels. Weight, about 2½ pounds each.

Wheels for 28-Inch Cemented Tires Only.

No. 19K2141 Rear Wheel only. Price.......... $1.49
No. 19K2142 Front Wheel only. Price.......... 1.44

Wheels for Clincher Tires.

No. 19K2143 Rear Wheel only for G. & J. Tire. Price.......... $1.95
No. 19K2144 Front Wheel only for G. & J. Tire. Price.......... 1.85
For price on G. & J. tires, see page 170.
No. 19K2156 Rear Wheel only for Dunlop Tire. Price.......... $1.95
No. 19K2157 Front Wheel only for Dunlop Tire. Price........ 1.85

Bicycle Hubs.

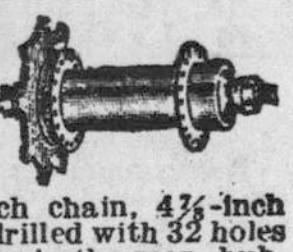

The bearings are of three-point contact, cups and cones are extra heavy, carefully hardened and fitted with ball retainers and oilers. Sprockets can be had 7, 8, 9 or 10-tooth for 3-16-inch chain, 4⅜-inch tread. We can supply hubs drilled with 32 holes in the front hub or 36 holes in the rear hub.
No. 19K2159 Rear Hub only. Price....(Postage extra, 17 cents.)... 64c
No. 19K2160 Front Hub only. Price....(Postage extra, 10 cents.)... 37c

Concave Center Hubs.

Same as above, except concave centers.
No. 19K2162 Rear Hub only. Price.......... 79c
If by mail, postage extra, 16 cents.
No. 19K2164 Front Hub only. Price.......... 49c
If by mail, postage extra, 11 cents.

Bolton's Hub Straps.

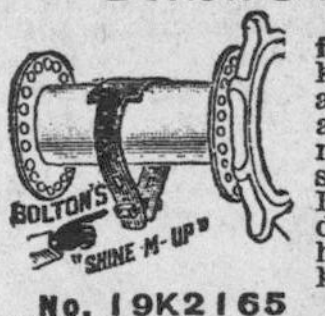

This article fills a long felt want, as it positively keeps your hub polished at all times. A neat, attractive little article made of leather with a small weight at bottom. Hangs loosely on hub, does not revolve with the hub, therefore the hub is kept bright and polished.
No. 19K2165 Bolton's Hub Straps. Price, per pair........ 11c
If by mail, postage extra, per pair, 5 cents.

Wood Rims.

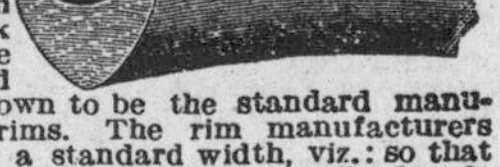

Our rims are all one piece, made from selected rock elm, by the Mutual Wood Rim Co., known to be the standard manufacturers of rims. The rim manufacturers have adopted a standard width, viz.: so that a rim to fit a 28x1⅜-inch tire will also fit a 28x1½-inch tire. We cannot supply rims of special color or drill other than 32 and 36 holes.
No. 19K2170 Front Rim, 32 holes. Price (Postage extra, 25 cents.).. 39c
No. 19K2171 Rear Rim, 36 holes.. Price.....(Postage extra, 25 cents). 39c

Rims for Clincher Tires.

Dunlop Wood Rims, 28x1⅜ inches.

No. 19K2174 Rim for Front Wheel. Price........ 49c

No. 19K2175 Rim for Rear Wheel. Price........ 50c

G. & J. Rims, 28x1⅜ inches.

No. 19K2177 Rim for Front Wheel. Price........ 49c

No. 19K2178 Rim for Rear Wheel. Price........ 50c

NOTE.—Dunlop rims can only be used with Dunlop detachable tires, and G. & J. rims can only be used with G. & J. clincher tires. Do not order these rims for any other make of tires.

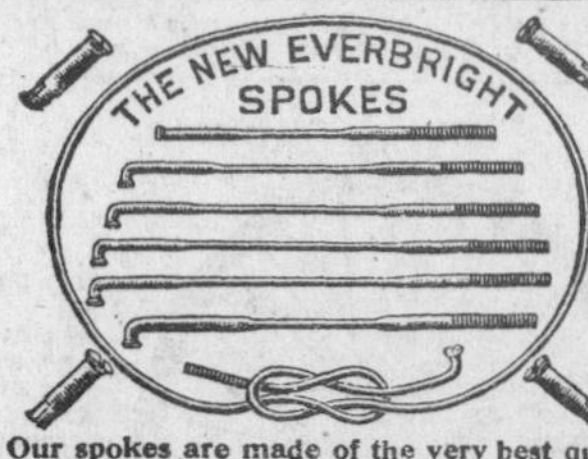

Our spokes are made of the very best quality of piano wire and are of great tensile strength. They are finely plated and are standard gauge. We furnish spokes complete with the nipples and washers, one dozen in each package.

No. 19K2180 Spokes complete with Nipples and Washers. Price, per dozen... 9c

If by mail, postage extra, 7 cents.

Duckworth Patented Detachable Chain.

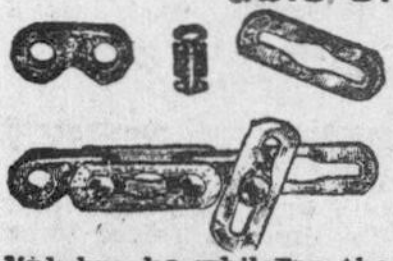

This is the genuine Duckworth all steel detachable chain. Any link can be taken apart and put together in a very few moments. It is indispensable, as if a link breaks while on the road it may be removed and the next link coupled up.

No. 19K2192 Detachable Chain, 60 links, 3-16-inch. Price........ 74c

If by mail, postage extra, 25 cents.

No. 19K2193 Extra links for same. Price........ 3c

If by mail, postage extra, 3 cents.

Diamond Chain Repair Links.

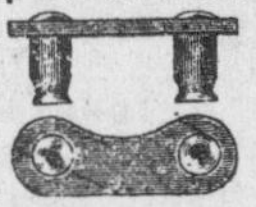

Invaluable to every rider. Put up in neat box containing two links, with full instructions. No tools required.

No. 19K2194 Diamond Repair Link. Price 8c

If by mail, postage extra, 3c.

Neverbreak Steel Balls.

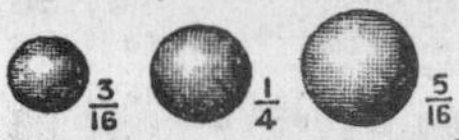

3/16 1/4 5/16

Steel Balls, highest grade, guaranteed true to gauge. Made of the finest tool steel.

	Size, inch	Price, two dozen	Postage extra, two doz.
No. 19K2200	⅛	5c	4c
No. 19K2201	5-32	7c	4c
No. 19K2202	3-16	9c	5c
No. 19K2203	¼	13c	6c
No. 19K2204	5-16	15c	6c

Sprocket Lock.

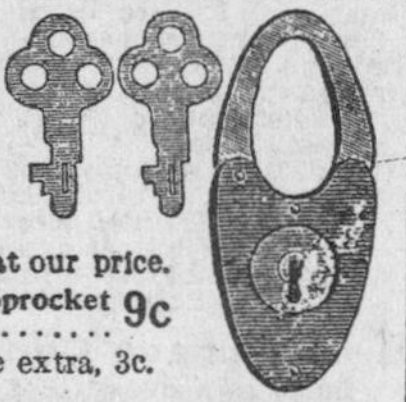

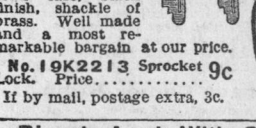

A very handsome appearing lock, steel case, black finish, shackle of brass. Well made and a most remarkable bargain at our price.

No. 19K2213 Sprocket Lock. Price........ 9c

If by mail, postage extra, 3c.

Bicycle Lock With Chain.

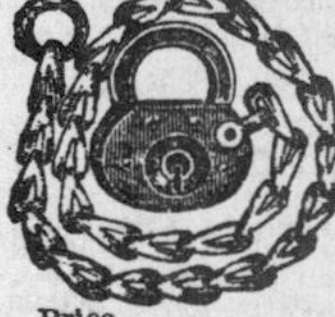

A chain lock is desired by many riders, and we herewith offer one that fills the bill, and is not too heavy for the pocket when not in use. Has steel case, black finish, brass shackle and chain, with one key.

No. 19K2217 Lock and Chain. Price........ 13c

If by mail, postage extra, 5 cents.

The Security Cyclometer.

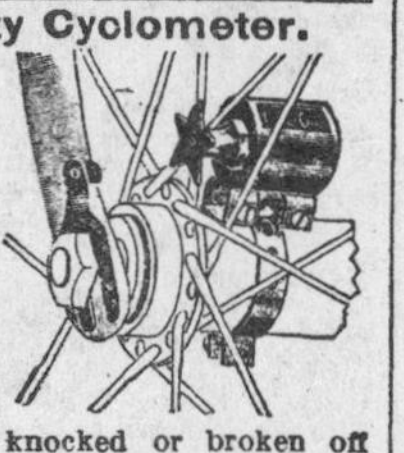

Every rider should have a good, accurate cyclometer which will tell how far he rides. The Security Cyclometer for 28-inch wheels. Positively the most durable cyclometer ever presented to the rider. It fits around the barrel of front hub between the flanges and cannot be knocked or broken off in falls. The interference pin is placed on inside of fork, out of danger. Its mechanism is perfect with a total register of 10,000 miles. It is finely nickel plated and thoroughly first class in every way.

No. 19K2220 The Security Cyclometer. Price........ 72c

If by mail, postage extra, 5 cents.

Pocket Parcel Carrier.

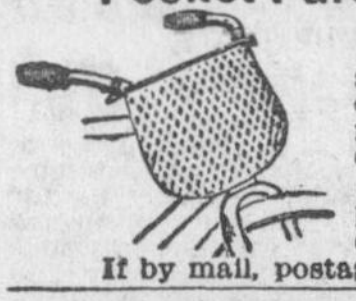

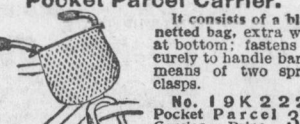

It consists of a black netted bag, extra wide at bottom; fastens securely to handle bar by means of two spring clasps.

No. 19K2224 Pocket Parcel Carrier. Price.. 32c

If by mail, postage extra, 6 cents.

Our Triumph Oiler.

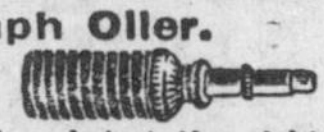

In this oiler we present one of the neatest patterns on the market, well made, nicely plated, and just the right size to go in tool bag.

No. 19K2226 Triumph Oiler. Price........ 5c

If by mail, postage extra, 2 cents.

Automatic Liquid Pistol.

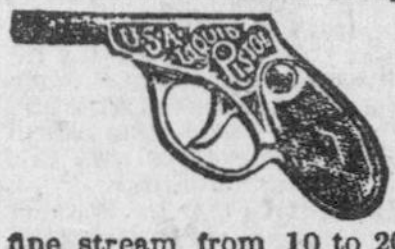

This is the genuine U. S. A. pistol. Can be used with water or any liquid. By operating the trigger it may be loaded or discharged as often as desired. Throws a fine stream from 10 to 20 feet, and is a very practical defense against vicious dogs or tramps. A good protection for the cyclist.

No. 19K2229 Liquid Pistol. Price........ 40c

If by mail, postage extra, 9 cents.

Patent Trousers Guard.

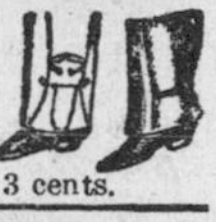

A neat and handy device.

No. 19K2232 Patent Trousers Guard. Price, per pair........ 3c

If by mail, postage extra, 3 cents.

BICYCLE TOOLS.

Combination Tool.

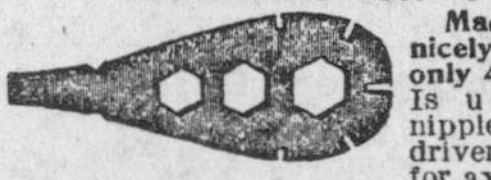

Made of steel nicely nickel plated, only 4 inches long. Is useful as a nipple grip, screwdriver and wrench for axle nuts.

No. 19K2237 Combination Tool. Price........ 9c

If by mail, postage extra, 3 cents.

Pincers For Inserting Plugs.

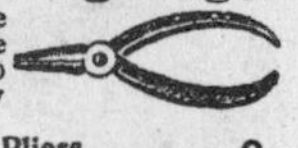

These pliers are made for inserting plugs in single tube tires, but are also found useful for many other purposes.

No. 19K2239 Plug Pliers. Price........ 6c

If by mail, postage extra, 5 cents.

S., R. & Co.'s Bicycle Wrench.

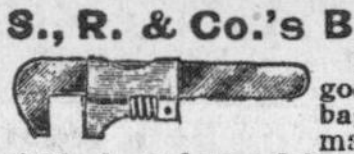

Every rider needs a good wrench for his tool bag. This wrench is made of best quality steel, hardened jaws, handsomely nickel plated, 5 inches long.

No. 19K2240 Bicycle Wrench. Price........ 11c

If by mail, postage extra, 6 cents.

The Columbian Wrench.

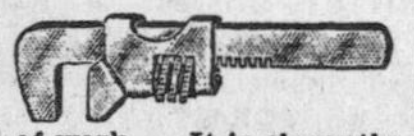

An extra heavy forged wrench, with wide, carefully hardened steel jaws, suitable for almost any kind of work. It is elegantly polished and nickel plated in the finest possible style and is a very fancy wrench, 5½ inches long.

No. 19K2241 Wrench. Price........ 17c

If by mail, postage extra, 10 cents.

Handy Nipple Grip.

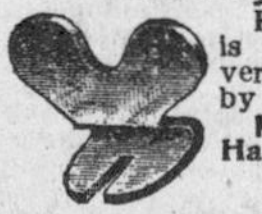

Fits the pocket and tool bag, is nicely nickel plated and a very handy little article, needed by every rider.

No. 19K2250 Handy Nipple Grip. Price.. 7c

If by mail, postage extra, 2 cents.

Seroco Tire Repair Outfit.

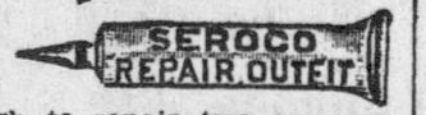

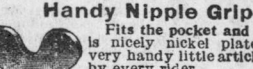

This is an excellent article for repairing punctures in single tube tires. Each tube contains enough to repair two or more punctures. One of these carried in your tool bag when on a trip will eliminate a great deal of your tire troubles. Tube has needle point for inserting in puncture when injecting cement.

No. 19K2254 Seroco Single Tube Tire Cement. Price........ 7c

If by mail, postage extra, 3 cents.

No. 19K2255 Goodrich Jiffy Outfit. Price........ 14c

If by mail, postage extra, 6 cents.

No. 19K2256 Double Tube Outfit. 10c

If by mail, postage extra, 4 cents.

The Cox Single Tube Tire Repair Outfit.

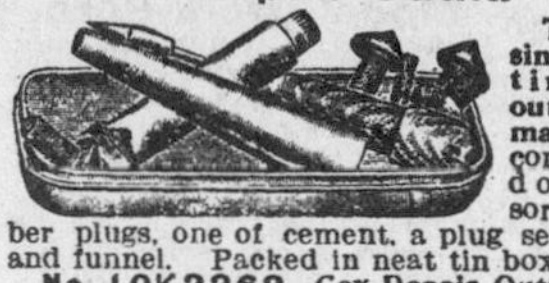

The best single tube tire repair outfit on the market. It consists of ½ dozen assorted rubber plugs, one of cement, a plug setting tool and funnel. Packed in neat tin box.

No. 19K2262 Cox Repair Outfit. Price........ 19c

If by mail, postage extra, 6 cents.

Wald Repair Tool.

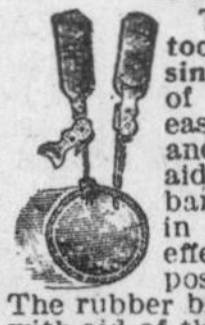

The simplest and most effective tool on the market for repairing single tube tires. This tool is made of steel, is 4¾ inches long, can be easily carried in tool bag or pocket, and weighs but 1 ounce. With the aid of this tool and a few rubber bands, a puncture can be repaired in a single tube tire in a far more effective manner than you could possibly repair it with rubber plugs. The rubber band is forced into the puncture with aid of the slotted needle at the end of the tool, and is released by simply pressing on the trigger as shown in the illustration. Complete instructions furnished with each tool.

No. 19K2264 Wald Repair Tool. Price........ 16c

If by mail, postage extra, 3 cents.

Sampson Puncture Closer.

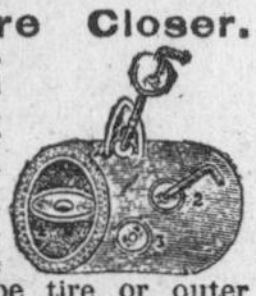

As per illustration, consists of brass with threaded stem. In case of puncture, one disc is forced through the puncture, the other is screwed down tight, the stem cut off. Full instructions accompany the outfit. This is the only thing that will perfectly close holes or cuts in a single tube tire or outer casing which has been filled with "Neverleak" or other tire fluid. Made entirely of brass, very effective and easy to apply. Sold in sets of three, containing large, medium and small sizes.

No. 19K2266 Sampson Puncture Closer. Price, 2 sets for........ 36c

If by mail, postage extra, 5 cents.

BICYCLE CEMENT, VARNISH, TIRE SOLUTION AND ENAMEL.

Acme Rubber Cement.

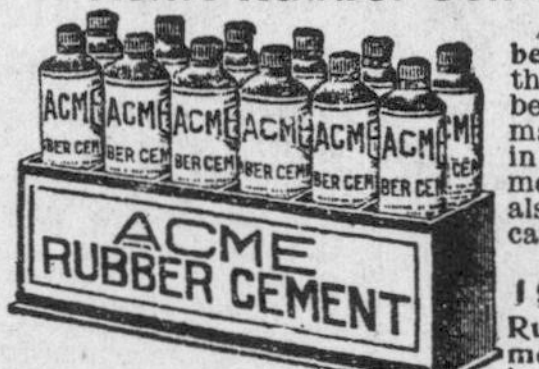

Acme Rubber Cement, the best rubber cement made, put up in collapsible metal tubes, also 4-ounce cans.

No. 19K2270 Rubber Cement, ¾x4-inch collapsible tubes. Price, each........ 3c

If by mail, postage extra, 5 cents.

No. 19K2272 Rubber Cement, 1x6-inch collapsible tubes. Price, each.... 5c

If by mail, postage extra, 10 cents.

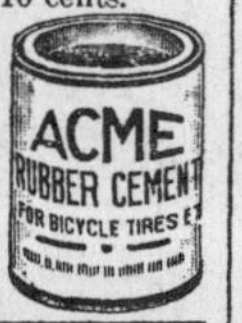

No. 19K2275 Rubber Cement in 4-ounce cans. Price........ 7c

If by mail, postage extra, 11 cents.

No. 19K2276 Rubber Cement, ½-pint cans. Price........ 12c

Not mailable.

Acme Wood Rim Cement.

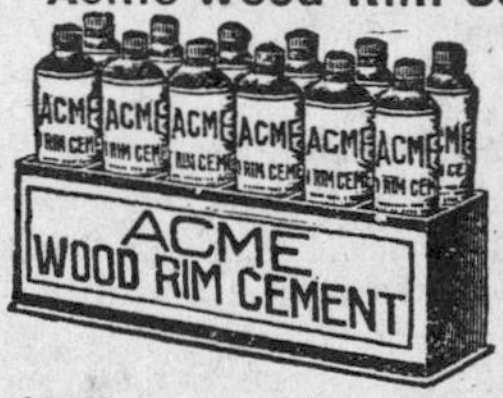

Wood Rim Liquid Cement, the famous Acme brand, the finest cement made for cementing tires to rims. This cement is to be used where the rim already has a coating of hard cement. Where new rims are used which have not been previously cemented, use Acme Hard Cement, Catalogue No. 19K2287.

No. 19K2280 Wood Rim Liquid Cement, 1x6-inch collapsible tubes. Price, each........ 5c

If by mail, postage extra, 9c.

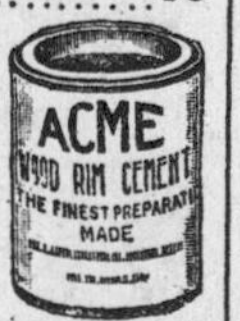

No. 19K2281 Wood Rim Liquid Cement, 4-ounce cans. Price........ 7c

If by mail, postage extra, 11 cents.

No. 19K2282 Wood Rim Liquid Cement, ½-pint cans. Price........ 9c

Not mailable.

Acme Hard Cement.

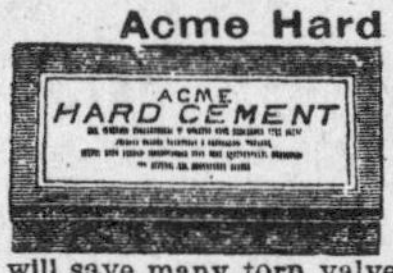

For cementing tires, grips, etc. All rims should have a good heavy coat of hard tire cement to insure the tires from becoming loose. This will save many torn valve stems.

No. 19K2287 3-ounce cakes. Price, 2 for........ 9c

If by mail, postage extra on 2 cakes, 9 cents.

No. 19K2288 1-pound cakes. Price........ 18c

If by mail, postage extra, 18 cents.

Sure Shot Repair Solution.

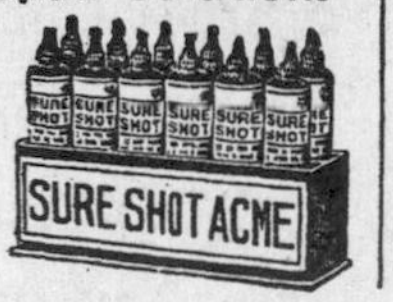

For repairing punctures in single tube tires this cement is very satisfactory. Tubes, ⅜x4 inches.

No. 19K2294 Sure Shot Solution. Price, per tube........ 9c

If by mail, postage extra, 5 cents.

Acme Patching Rubber.

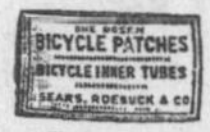

Acme Patching Rubber, made from pure Para rubber, 1 dozen sheets in package.

No. 19K2297 Acme Patching Rubber. Price, per package........ 16c

If by mail, postage extra, 3 cents.

Puncture Band.

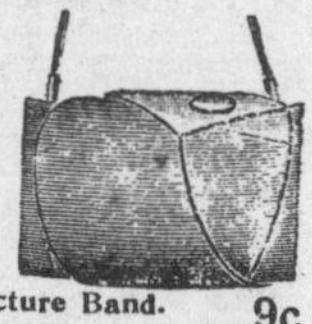

Intended for temporary repairs when rider is away from home. It is 9½ inches long, 1½ inches wide, made of vulcanized rubber; will go around tire two or three times and button on under side of rim, thus enabling rider to inflate damaged tire and ride home.

No. 19K2304 Puncture Band. Price........ 9c

If by mail, postage extra, 3 cents.

Everlasting Tire Tape.

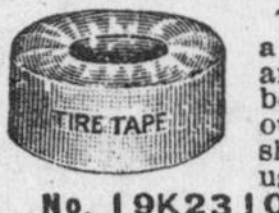

This Tape is manufactured by a new patent method, is guaranteed to not dry out, hold better and last longer than any other tape made. No cyclist should be without this very useful part of repair outfit.

No. 19K2310 Tire Tape. Price, 3 rolls for........ 5c

If by mail, postage extra, 4 cents.

Neverleak Tire Fluid.

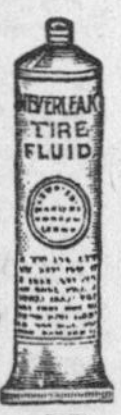

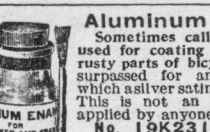

One tube of this fluid injected into a single tube tire will render it absolutely leakproof. Furnished in 4-ounce collapsible tubes, with connection which screws into valve. Very handy to use. It overcomes all trouble on account of tire being porous and subject to tread leaks. Guaranteed not to injure a tire. It does not prevent patching, plugging, vulcanizing or other repairs. Do not wait until your tire leaks, but put it into your tires at once, thus prevent any danger of a leak while riding, as it is a self healing puncture fluid.

No. 19K2312 Neverleak Tire Fluid. Price, per 4-ounce tube........ 19c

If by mail, postage extra, 12 cents.

Aluminum Lacquer.

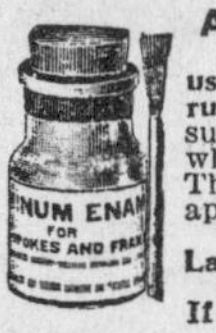

Sometimes called Nickelplater, used for coating and retouching rusty parts of bicycles, etc. Unsurpassed for any purpose for which a silver satin finish is desired. This is not an enamel. Easily applied by anyone.

No. 19K2317 Aluminum Lacquer. Price, per bottle........ 9c

If by mail, postage and tube extra, 9 cents.

Acme Bicycle Enamel.

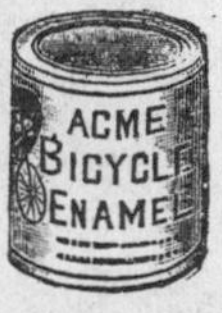

Air drying, does not require baking. Bright, true to color, and dries in ten hours with a beautiful deep luster. Can be applied by anyone. Made in royal blue, jet black, Brewster green, carmine, bright vermilion, chrome yellow or snowy white. State color.

No. 19K2320 Bicycle Enamel. 4-ounce cans. Price, per can........ 9c

If by mail, postage and tube extra, 10 cents.

Acme Chain Lubricant.

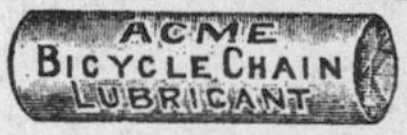

All chains should be kept clean and lubricated. This lubricant will make your bicycle run easier and your chain last longer. Should be used by every up to date cyclist.

No. 19K2324 Chain Lubricant. Price, 2 for........ 5c

If by mail, postage extra for two, 3 cents.

Acme Air Drying Varnish.

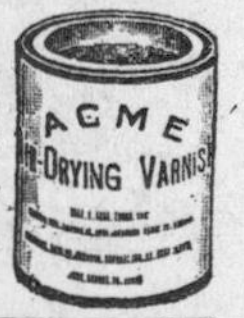

To be applied over enamel to preserve it and to brighten old enamel.

No. 19K2326 Acme Air Drying Varnish, in ¼-pt. can. Price, per can........ 10c

If by mail, postage and tube extra, 10 cents.

Genuine Acme Oil.

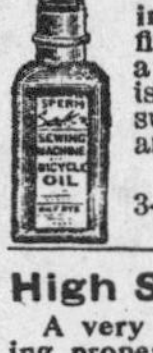

Especially prepared for those desiring a high grade oil, for all kinds of fine machinery, bicycles, etc. Acts as a rust preventive, lubricant and polish, also used for cleaning any polished surface. Is perfumed, making it pleasant to handle.

No. 19K2329 Acme Oil, 3-ounce bottle. Price........ 11c

Not mailable.

High Speed Bicycle Oil.

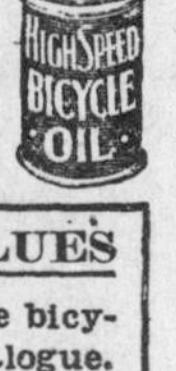

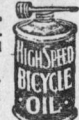

A very necessary article in taking proper care of a bicycle and its bearings. "Acme Brand."

No. 19K2332 Bicycle Oil, ½-pint can. Price........ 12c

Not mailable.

WONDERFUL VALUES

are offered in our advance bicycles, shown in this catalogue.

HARRIS 20TH CENTURY RAILROAD ATTACHMENT.

$5.45

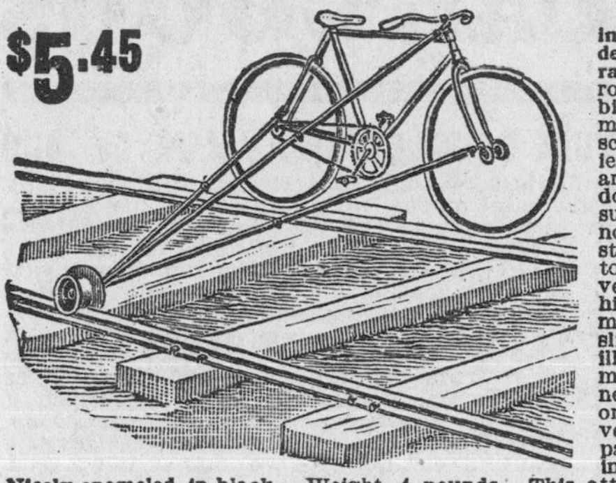

This transforms the ordinary bicycle into the most practical and durable device for obtaining high speed on railroad tracks, making a regular railroad velocipede out of an ordinary bicycle. It consists of three braces made of seamless steel tubing, telescoped into each other for convenience in adjusting or carrying. They are attached to a steel wheel with double flanges and rubber covered surface, which makes it absolutely noiseless in operation. It is light, strong and simple, and can be attached to or detached from the bicycle in a very few moments. Either a low or high rate of speed can be very easily maintained, and it is impossible to slip, owing to the rubber tires. Our illustration plainly indicates the manner of attaching, and when not needed it can be very easily carried on the handle bars, as it takes but a very small amount of space. The parts are substantially made, and intended to have great durability. Nicely enameled in black. Weight, 4 pounds. This attachment has become very popular with railroad and telegraph employes, both male and female.

No. 19K1639 Harris 20th Century Railroad Attachment. Price.......... $5.45

Harris No. 2 Flyer Attachment. Same as above, with extra wheels to be placed in front and behind bicycle. Especially constructed for persons desiring to secure a high rate of speed, as it will hold the curves better, and sustain heavier loads than the No. 1. Weight, 11 pounds.

No. 19K1640 Harris No. 2 Flyer Attachment. Price.......... $7.70

VELOCIPEDES.

BIG VALUES.

$1.25

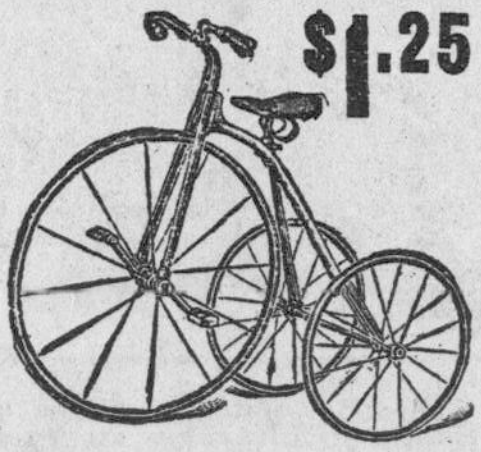

These velocipedes have extra heavy spokes, all parts are made extra strong. They are built for service and wear. They are fitted with comfortable grain leather spring saddle, and at our price undoubtedly represent the greatest values offered in this line. They are furnished with either steel or rubber tires and in various sizes. Select the size required according to inseam measurement, measuring from crotch to heels.

READ WHAT WE HAVE TO SAY ABOUT OUR PEERLESS VELOCIPEDES BEFORE YOU BUY.

Catalogue No.	Front Wheel	Inseam Measurement	Shipping Weight	Steel Tires	Rubber Tires
19K1621	16-inch	14-inch	13 pounds	$1.25	$2.50
19K1622	20-inch	17-inch	14 pounds	1.50	2.90
19K1623	24-inch	19-inch	17 pounds	1.85	3.50
19K1624	26-inch	21-inch	18 pounds	2.50	3.95

OUR PEERLESS VELOCIPEDES.

BALL BEARING CONSTRUCTION.

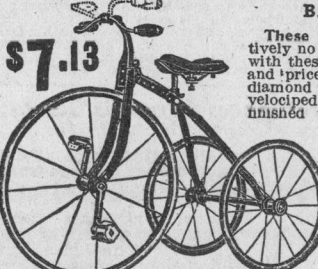

$7.13

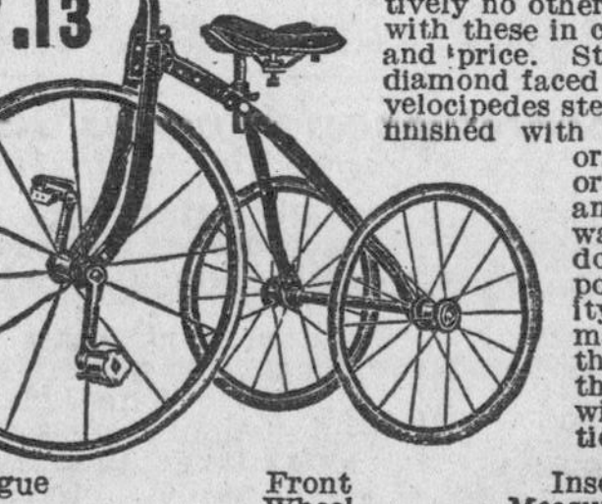

These velocipedes are built just like a bicycle. Positively no other velocipede on the market that will compare with these in construction, long wear, easy running qualities and price. Steel ball bearing pedals, ball bearing hubs, diamond faced cranks, curved front forks, which make these velocipedes steer and run easier than any others. They are finished with beautiful maroon enamel, baked. Double orange stripe on fork and backbone and fancy orange head. Genuine bicycle saddle, sewed and padded. Handle bars can be given backward or forward, as well as upturned and downturned positions. Pedals, cranks, seat posts, handle bars are finished with good quality nickel plating. Wheels are the strongest made, fitted with ¾-inch rubber tires. While these velocipedes cost you a little more money than the ordinary cheap velocipedes, yet they will more than make up for their slight additional cost in their years of service.

Catalogue No.	Front Wheel	Inseam Measurement	Shipping Weight	Price
19K1636	16-inch	14-inch	30 pounds	$7.13
19K1637	20-inch	17-inch	35 pounds	7.49
19K1638	24-inch	19-inch	40 pounds	7.93

NOTICE—Select the size required according to inseam measurements, measuring from crotch to heels.

$4.73 FOR BOYS' IMPROVED FARM WAGON WITH DETACHABLE SEAT, HANDLE AND SHAFTS.

$4.73

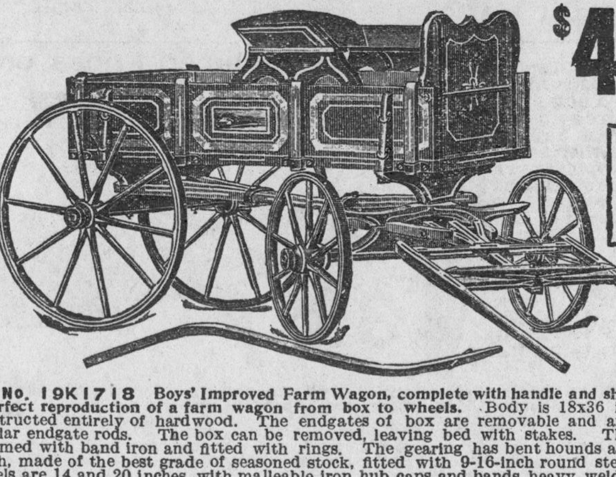

Pole and Whiffletree 75 Cents Extra

No. 19K1718 Boys' Improved Farm Wagon, complete with handle and shafts. **This is a perfect reproduction of a farm wagon from box to wheels.** Body is 18x36 inches, frame constructed entirely of hardwood. The endgates of box are removable and are fitted with regular endgate rods. The box can be removed, leaving bed with stakes. The stakes are trimmed with band iron and fitted with rings. The gearing has bent hounds and adjustable reach, made of the best grade of seasoned stock, fitted with 9-16-inch round steel axle. The wheels are 14 and 20 inches, with malleable iron hub caps and bands, heavy welded tires, and made with dodged or staggered shaved spokes, thus insuring a strong and substantial wheel. All parts are strongly ironed and braced. The gearing and wheels are painted in bright red and hand striped in black. The box is painted in Brewster green, set off by handsome landscape and scrollwork. It is the handsomest, strongest and best boys' wagon on the market. Shipping weight, about 68 pounds. For goat or dog harness, see index. Price.......... $4.73

BOYS' WAGONS.

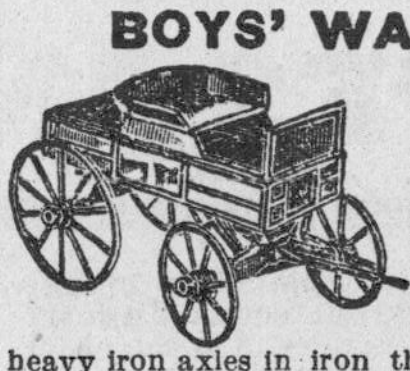

No. 19K1720 Iron Axles; body, 14x28 inches; wheels, 12 and 16 inches. Hardwood paneled body, landscape painting, scrolled and varnished, hub caps, high seat and dashboard. Iron braced, heavy iron axles in iron thimble skein, oval tires welded and shrunk on. Same as illustration. Shipping weight, 28 pounds. Price.......... $1.94

Boys' Express Wagons.

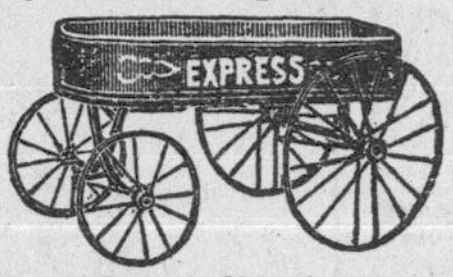

Boys' Steel Wagon. The best and strongest steel wagon made; finely painted and ornamented steel box, malleable iron gear, tinned steel wheels.

Catalogue No.	Body	Size of Wheels	Shipping Weight	Price
19K1726	14x25	11x14	18 lbs.	$1.30
19K1730	15x30	12x15	20 "	1.50
19K1734	16x32	13x16	27 "	1.95
19K1738	18x36	14x18	35 "	2.75

No. 19K1738 made of heavier material, extra well made, and best suited for heavy work.

The Defiance Coaster Wagon.

$2.95

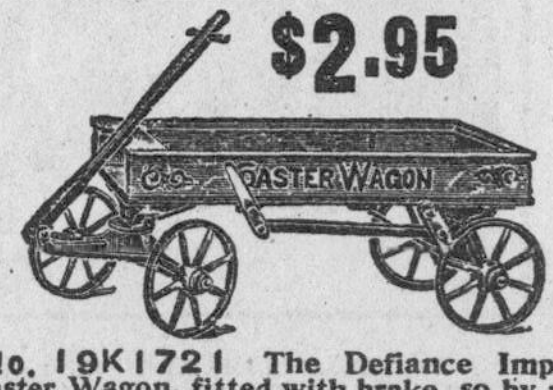

No. 19K1721 **The Defiance Improved Coaster Wagon, fitted with brake, so by pressing upon the lever of brake the boy can control the speed of wagon while coasting.** Body constructed of well seasoned hardwood, with detachable sides and ends. Gear is of No. 1 selected stock, securely braced to body by 7-32x¾-inch round edge iron, 9-16-inch round steel axle. Steering gear, as shown in illustration, of heavy malleable iron and hardwood. Wheels are extra heavy, with shaved spokes, rims ¾x½-inch bent rock elm, tires ¾x⅛-inch rough steel welded and shrunk on. Strong malleable iron hub caps and bands. Body and gear varnished on a natural wood, decorated in black and red. Wheels painted in bright red. Length, 36 inches; width, 16 inches; height, 16 inches. Shipping weight, about 35 pounds. Price.......... $2.95

20th Century Steel Frame Hand Car.

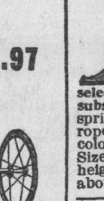

$3.97

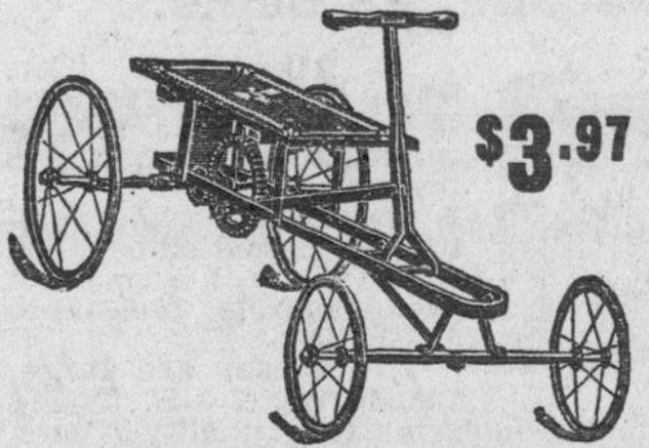

No. 19K1770 **The 20th Century Flyer is a new production and is the best and strongest car on the market.** Constructed entirely of steel, except seat and handle bar, built to withstand hard usage, guaranteed to support 200 pounds. This car is propelled by a lever which is attached to a crank with a frictionless cogged gear action. The fastest, most positive and easiest propelling gear ever placed on a hand car. This car is steered by the feet placed on either side of the axle. The frame is made of bar steel, well braced and bolted together, enameled black. Axles, ⅝-inch hardened steel. All steel wheels, extra heavy spokes, galvanized and shod with best ½-inch rubber tires. Handle bar and seat are made of selected oak, covered with three coats of green paint and varnish, beautifully decorated in red and gold. The gearing is so protected that there is no danger of catching fingers and clothing. While it is great sport for the child, it is also a great physical developer. While riding this car the entire body is brought into use, thus developing the muscles of back, shoulders, neck, arms and legs. Shipping weight, about 35 pounds. Price $3.97

The Irish Mail Hand Car for Boys and Girls.

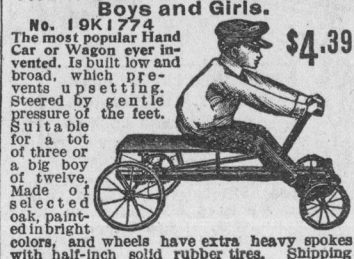

$4.39

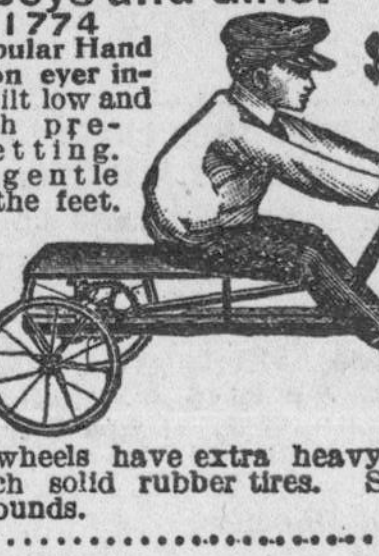

No. 19K1774 **The most popular Hand Car or Wagon ever invented. Is built low and broad, which prevents upsetting. Steered by gentle pressure of the feet.** Suitable for a tot of three or a big boy of twelve. Made of selected oak, painted in bright colors, and wheels have extra heavy spokes with half-inch solid rubber tires. Shipping weight, 30 pounds. Price.......... $4.39

Automobiles.

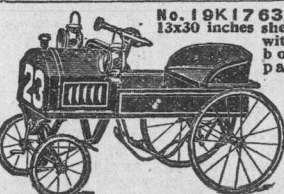

$3.93

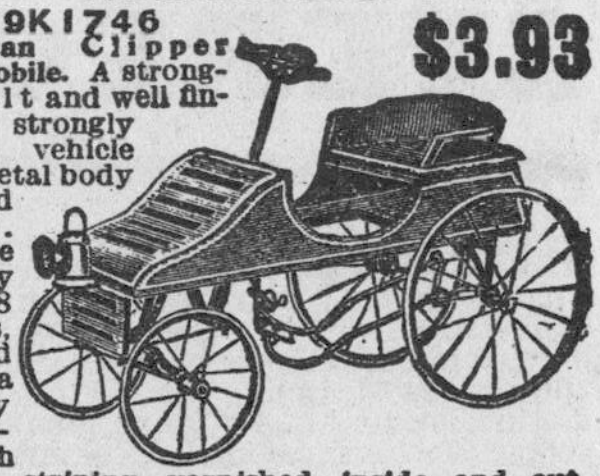

No. 19K1746 **American Clipper Automobile. A strongly built and well finished, strongly geared vehicle with metal body and seat.** The body is 13x28 inches, painted in a pretty vermilion with yellow striping, varnished inside and out. Wheels are 16 and 8 inches, with ¾-inch rubber tires. Has special wheel steering device. Shipping weight, 40 pounds. Price, without lamp or horn.......... $3.93

No. 19K1748 **The Winner Automobile.** Of same construction as above but larger size. The body is 14½x35½ inches; wheels, 18 and 12 inches, has ½-inch rubber tires. Shipping weight, 45 pounds. Price, without lamp or horn.......... $4.73

No. 19K1749 **Signal Horns for attaching to above automobiles.** Shipping weight, 1 pound. Price.......... 46c

No. 19K1752 **Brass Lamps to fasten on automobiles.** Shipping weight, 4 pounds. Price.......... $1.00

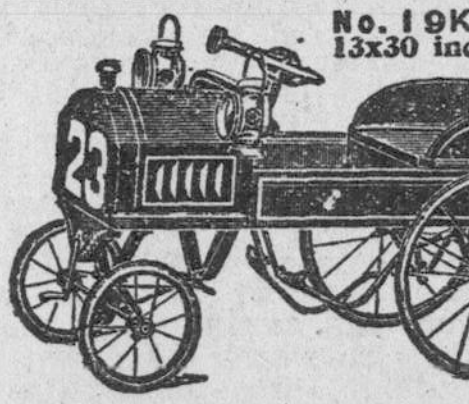

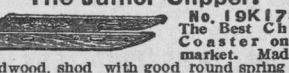

No. 19K1763 **Body, 13x30 inches sheet steel with wood bottom, painted dark auto red with light auto gray striping. Number in yellow. Ratchet starting crank and license number. Seat hinged, making package compartment underneath.** Gear, wrought steel, with patent steering device and bridle brace on front gear, finished with black baked enamel. Wheels, 8-inch front, 14-inch rear. ½-inch rubber tire, finished in green enamel. Shipping weight, 40 pounds. Price.......... $5.27

Lamp and horn extra. See above.

SLEDS.

The Junior Clipper.

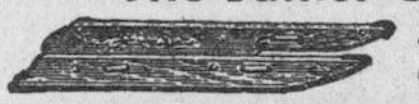

No. 19K1789 The Best Cheap Coaster on the market. Made of hardwood, shod with good round spring runners, hand holes on sides. Nicely painted and decorated. Size: length, 37 inches; width, 10¾ inches; height, 4 inches. Shipping weight, about 9 pounds. Price.......... 39c

Spring Shod Clipper.

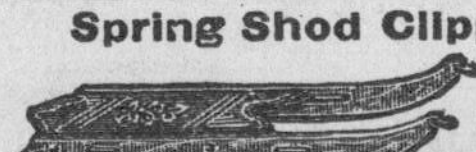

No. 19K1791 An Ideal Coaster, made from selected hardwood put together in a most substantial manner, shod with full round spring runners. Fitted with rings in front for ropes. Top is handsomely decorated in bright colors, runners varnished in natural wood. Size: length, 43 inches; width, 11½ inches; height, 3½ inches. Shipping weight, about 12 pounds. Price.......... 93c

Steel Favorite.

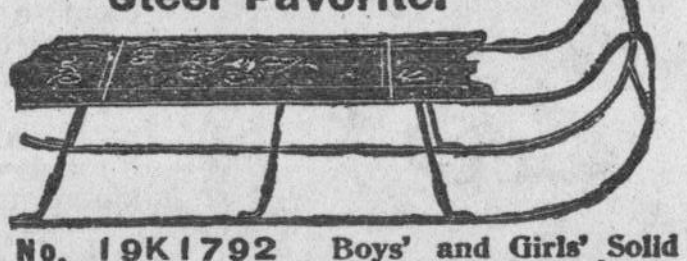

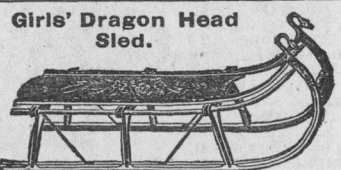

No. 19K1792 Boys' and Girls' Solid Steel Frame Sled, three-ply veneered top, beautifully decorated. Frame and runners made of half oval steel, enameled in black and green. This sled is made with three steel knees securely riveted to the runners. Handsome design, very strong and durable, and made to stand the racket. Length, 30 inches; width, 10 inches; height, 7 inches. Shipping weight, about 10 pounds. Price.......... 91c

Girls' Dragon Head Sled.

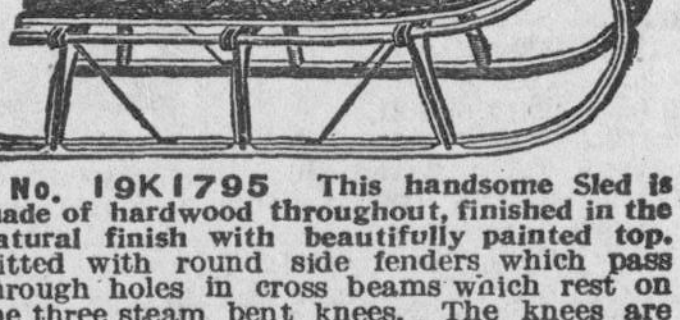

No. 19K1795 **This handsome Sled is made of hardwood throughout, finished in the natural finish with beautifully painted top.** Fitted with round side fenders which pass through holes in cross beams which rest on the three steam bent knees. The knees are neatly mortised into the steam bent runners, which are shod with half oval steel shoes. In addition to the two diagonal steel braces, it is also fitted with three upright braces on each side, which are specially bent to fit over the end of cross beams and securely fastened, extending down along the knees and firmly attached to the runner, thus rendering this the strongest girls' wood frame sled on the market. Size: length, 33 inches; width, 15 inches; height, 8 inches. Shipping weight, about 10 pounds. Price.......... $1.15

STEREOSCOPES AND OPTICAL GOODS

SEEN THROUGH THE STEREOSCOPE, a stereoscopic view brings the original scene directly before us in a way that seems almost like magic, so wonderful is the effect of distance, depth, relief and solidity. The marvelously true to life appearance, everything seemingly of full natural life size, the wonderful detail, the perspective, the figures springing up in the foreground as distinct and real as if alive, make the stereoscopic view a most delightful entertainment.

SEEN FOR THE FIRST TIME, the effect is almost startling, and if you have never looked through the scope at one of these wonderful pictures you have still before you one of the real pleasures of life.

HOW STEREOSCOPIC PICTURES ARE MADE. At first thought a stereoscopic view seems to be simply a double photograph, two photographs mounted side by side on one card. Apparently the two photographs are just alike, but in reality there is a wonderful difference in these two pictures, these two photographs that form the stereoscopic view, and the whole secret of the superiority of a stereoscopic picture over any other form of photograph lies in this fact—that the two pictures are not exactly alike.

STEREOSCOPIC VIEWS ARE MADE WITH A DOUBLE CAMERA, a special camera fitted with two lenses, which makes two simultaneous pictures of the same subject side by side on the same plate, these two pictures differing from each other, because the two lenses are about three inches apart, and therefore the picture which one lens makes is from a slightly different view point than the picture made by the other lens. One lens sees, or takes a little more of the right hand side of the subject, the other lens a little more of the left hand side. When these two pictures are combined by the prismatic lenses of the stereoscope we get that wonderful stereoscopic effect, that effect of reality, of distance, of perspective and of relief which has puzzled the scientists and excited the admiration of everyone since the day of the discovery of the stereoscope by Prof. Wheatstone and Sir David Brewster, away back in the first half of the 19th century.

THE STEREOSCOPE IS AN OPTICAL INSTRUMENT for viewing stereoscopic pictures. It is provided with two powerful prismatic magnifying lenses. When the stereoscopic view is looked at through the stereoscope the prismatic lenses of the instrument combine the two pictures into one and at the same time cause a wonderful transformation in the appearance of the view. The two ordinary looking photographs, the two pictures, apparently just alike, become, when seen through the stereoscope, a single picture, life size, with everything standing out in relief, just exactly as though you were looking at the object itself instead of a picture.

THE EDUCATIONAL VALUE OF OUR STEREOSCOPIC VIEWS

COMPLETE DESCRIPTIONS WITH EVERY VIEW. Ours is the only line of views on the market in which each and every view is accompanied by a full description, complete information regarding every picture in our big line of 1,260 subjects.

THIS DESCRIPTIVE FEATURE DOUBLES THE VALUE OF OUR VIEWS. Views sold by other dealers, without descriptive matter of any kind, or simply with the name of the view printed at the bottom, may be interesting for a time. The pictures may be beautiful, may prove a source of amusement, but to be of real value, to be of lasting interest, every stereoscopic view should be accompanied by a complete, accurate and carefully written description.

LET US SELECT AT RANDOM one of the pictures from our big set of 100 views of the World, say, for example, No. 287, which is entitled, "**Interior of the Coliseum, Rome, Italy.**" Seen through the stereoscope this is a beautiful picture. As we look at it we seem to be actually in Rome, looking at this most famous of ancient Roman buildings, but no matter how perfect this picture may be, no matter how natural in appearance it is, no matter how true an idea it gives us of the exact appearance of the Coliseum, our interest is very greatly increased and the picture assumes a new and greater value when we turn it over and read on the back that the Coliseum is the largest and most magnificent stone amphitheater ever built, that its erection was commenced by Vespasian, A. D. 72, that it was opened during the reign of Titus, but not completed until the time of Domitian, that 12,000 captive Jews were the workmen and that the Christian martyr Gaudentius was the architect; that this wonderful amphitheater was used for gladiatorial combats and fights of slaves and Christians with wild beasts; that St. Ignatius was the first martyr that was here devoured by lions, and that a cross in the arena now marks the spot where the early Christians suffered. We read that outwardly the building shows four stories, supported respectively by Doric, Ionic and Corinthian columns, on which the arches of each story rested. We learn that five elliptic, massive walls carried spaces for the spectators in the interior, and we learn of the marvelous ingenuity in the arrangement of the passages through which the multitudes reached the 87,000 seats; we learn how the name Coliseum is derived from the Italian word Colosseo, that it was first used in the eighth century, and probably derived from the colossal statue of Apollo-Nero, located near by.

WITH THIS FUND OF INFORMATION BEFORE US, the picture takes on new interest, and when you remember that each and every one of the 1,260 views, constituting our great Educational Series, comes with full and complete descriptive matter, some idea of the genuine and lasting value of this series of views may be gained.

ABOUT POSTAGE, EXPRESS OR FREIGHT on stereoscopic views. If sent by mail, the postage on one set of 100 views and stereoscope is 35 cents, or on the views alone, 20 cents. If more than one outfit is ordered it is cheaper to ship by express, and to most points within 500 miles of Chicago it is cheaper to ship even one outfit by express. If you include with your order for views goods from other departments sufficient to make a freight shipment, the cost of transportation on the views will be so small that it is not worth considering.

This Standard Stereoscope, 28 Cents.

No. 20K2500 This Standard Stereoscope is a first class instrument, guaranteed to give perfect satisfaction, and is exactly the same quality that is sold all over the country by dealers and agents at from 75 cents to $1.00.

The lenses are large, measuring 1 3-16 by 1⅜ inches; specially ground from a fine quality of pure, clear, optical glass accurately adjusted and firmly mounted.

The frame is made from selected hardwood; the lens board composed of five pieces carefully mortised together to prevent warping, and the hood is of three-ply hardwood veneer, nicely finished and varnished.

Price, each..........................$0.28
Per dozen.............................3.25
If by mail, postage extra, each, 19 cents.

28ᶜ

Our Large Lens Walnut Stereoscope for 60 Cents.

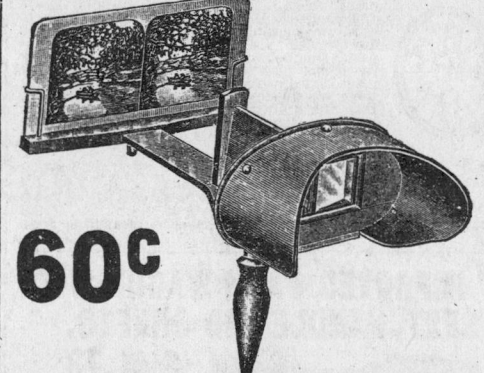

No. 20K2506 This Stereoscope is made from solid black walnut throughout, varnished walnut hood, brass trimmings and patent folding handle. The lenses in this walnut stereoscope are extra large; the very highest grade stereoscopic lenses made, specially ground from the best clear optical glass and accurately adjusted. Best workmanship and carefully selected materials throughout; an extra good stereoscope.

Price, each....$0.60
Per dozen......6.95
If by mail, postage extra, each, 19 cents.

60ᶜ

Our Special Aluminum Stereoscope for 49 Cents.

No. 20K2503 This elegant Stereoscope is made with fine aluminum hood, beautifully engraved and bound with dark red velvet. The frame is of cherry wood, carefully finished and varnished, with patent folding handle. The lenses are extra quality, of good size, carefully ground from the highest grade of fine, clear glass, accurately adjusted and firmly held in place by latest patented aluminum lens lock. Our Special Aluminum Stereoscope is a universal favorite with canvassers, who find that the elegant appearance and sterling good qualities which it possesses, make it a very ready seller. The very low price which we quote on this stereoscope is made possible only by the fact that we have contracted for the largest quantity of high grade stereoscopes ever handled by any one dealer, and have thus been enabled to reduce the manufacturing cost to the lowest possible figure. Price, per dozen, $5.64; each........................49ᶜ

If by mail, postage extra, each, 19 cents.

**VARNISHED CHERRY FRAME.
ENGRAVED ALUMINUM HOOD.
PATENT LENS LOCK.**

Greatly Reduced Prices on Stereo-Graphoscopes

The Stereo-Graphoscope is an instrument made upon a new principle by means of which it can be adjusted for either regular stereoscopic views or single photographs and other pictures by simply reversing the lenses. The manner in which the lenses are mounted and the shape of the hood shuts out all light, making a dark chamber around the eyes and giving a very clear, beautiful effect to the picture.

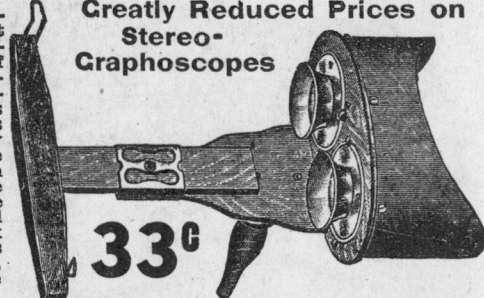

33ᶜ

No. 20K2510 Stereo-Graphoscope, cherry frame, varnished cherry hood, brass trimmings and wood screw handle. Medium size lenses of best quality.
Price, per dozen, $3.80; each...............................33ᶜ
If by mail, postage extra, each, 25 cents.

No. 20K2511 Stereo-Graphoscope, cherry frame, varnished mahogany hood, brass trimmings and patent folding handle. Best grade lenses of large size, a first class instrument throughout. Price, per dozen, $5.20; each...............................45ᶜ
If by mail, postage extra, each, 25 cents.

No. 20K2512 Our Best Stereo-Graphoscope, made with oiled cherry frame, fine varnished mahogany hood, all trimmings nickled plated and highly polished, patent folding handle, first quality materials and best workmanship throughout. Extra large lenses of very highest quality. Price, per dozen, $7.50; each...............................65ᶜ
If by mail, postage extra, each, 25 cents.

50 STEREOSCOPIC VIEWS 35c
OF THE GREAT PLANT OF SEARS, ROEBUCK & CO.
$177,619.00 EVERY WORKING DAY FOR THE YEAR 1906

THIS IS THE TREMENDOUS AMOUNT OF MONEY that tells the story of the vast volume of business which comes to Sears, Roebuck & Co. from its millions of customers in the United States. A fortune every hour passes through our counting room and the interesting processes by which this enormous volume of business is handled by more than nine thousand and employes working in the great buildings are faithfully told in pictures in this wonderful set of fifty stereoscopic views which we are anxious for every customer of ours to possess. If you could just follow your order from the time it reaches our house, when it passes into the mail opening department where the letter is opened by machinery, then to the readers, and from their hands to the auditing and the order writing, the routing, the merchandise departments, then to the shipping room, it would prove a wonderful revelation to you as to the most modern, up to date methods of handling a great business, and this is exactly what you will be able to do if you possess a set of these fifty stereoscopic views. You can follow the order through the house, you will understand just how it is handled in the several departments, because each stereoscopic view of a department in this great store is fully described in detail on the back of the view. After you have looked at the picture through the stereoscope then you turn it over and read the full story of the picture, just what the hundreds of employes shown in the picture are doing, how they do it and why it is done. These wonderful stereoscopic views will show you the vast shipping rooms, where the goods are packed and handled and loaded on the cars and started on their journey to you. They will show you how we have handled 28,000 shipments by mail in a single day, 25,000 shipments by express in one day and 10,000 shipments by freight in one day, a volume of business which keeps several train crews busy setting the empty cars on the tracks in our train shed and hauling the loaded ones to the several railroads which center in Chicago. These pictures will show you the wonderful automatic weighing and package filling machinery in the grocery department, how our coffee is weighed and put up by machinery, how rice is sacked and the bags sewed by machinery. It will show you the wonderful printing department where the great catalogue which we send our customers free, is set in type, printed, bound and mailed; the most wonderful printing plant in the world, the largest of its kind in existence, an equipment which enables us to send 6,000,000 of our 1,200-page catalogues a year to our customers throughout the length and breadth of the United States.

THESE FIFTY STEREOSCOPIC VIEWS SHOW YOU the methods in vogue in the greatest merchandise institution in the world, methods which have enabled us to sell you the highest grade merchandise at lower prices than have ever been quoted in the history of merchandising, methods which enable us to make your dollar reach further, whether it be expended for necessities or luxuries, than it has ever gone before. That you may know us more intimately, that you may know how your order is handled after it reaches us, we have had this set of stereoscopic views manufactured, and offer them to you at just a part of their cost. We have believed that our customers would enjoy this set of views, they would be glad to know something of this great institution which is endeavoring to serve them economically and satisfactorily, the institution which is reaching out and breaking up combinations and associations designed to secure exorbitant prices and entirely unnecessary profits at the expense of the farmer and other producers. We want you to know about this institution, we want you to know everything it is possible to know about it, and for these reasons we are anxious to have this set of fifty stereoscopic views in your home, believing it will be decidedly to our mutual advantage, giving you a tangible idea of the magnitude of this business and at the same time showing to your friends how well and how satisfactorily we could serve them if they are not already our customers.

WE WOULD LIKE TO SEND THESE VIEWS FREE to every one who is dealing with us, but we have more than six million customers on our list at the present time, and the expense of sending a set of these pictures to every one of these six million people would amount to a tremendous sum of money, an expense far greater than it is possible for us to assume. We feel, however, that everyone who has dealt with us, must take an interest in our great institution, and we want our customers to know just as much about our business as possible. For this reason we are offering this set of stereoscopic views of our plant for sale at a price just sufficient to barely cover the actual cost of having the original pictures made, including the cost of the copper plates from which they are reproduced, the cardboard, the boxing, etc.

ON THE BACK OF EACH IS PRINTED the full story of the picture, telling just what the hundreds of employes are doing, how they do it, and why they do it. You will find in this set of pictures the most interesting story you have ever heard, and it will give you new ideas regarding the great things that may be accomplished in the world of business by original ideas and square dealing.

A LIST OF THE PICTURES IN THIS SET OF STEREOSCOPIC VIEWS.

No. 1 Mr. R. W. Sears, President of Sears, Roebuck & Co., at his desk. The gentleman who founded this great institution.

No. 2 General view of Sears, Roebuck & Co. A scene on the streets at the morning hour.

No. 3 Main Entrance to the Merchandise Building, the busiest hive of industry in this country.

No. 4 The Merchandise Building, the largest building in the world devoted to housing merchandise.

No. 5 Sunken Garden with the Merchandise Building in the distance, a glimpse of the beautiful gardens.

No. 6 The Railroad Yards, where hundreds of cars are shipped daily, bearing thousands of tons of merchandise.

No. 7 Automatic Weighing and Bag Sewing Machines in the Grocery Department. Putting up rice, coffee, teas, spices, etc., by automatic machines.

No. 8 Watchmaking in the Jewelry Department. Skillful men adjusting and fitting movements, setting diamonds, engraving, etc.

No. 9 Cutting 18 Suits of Clothes at One Operation with Electricity, in the Ready Made Clothing Department.

No. 10 Talking Machine Records. A million solos, duets, quartets, the richest band, mandolin and guitar music piled on shelves in the Merchandise Building.

No. 11 Packing Goods for Shipment. Showing how the great shipping room is able to handle a hundred thousand orders daily.

No. 12 Mail Packing in the Shipping Room where thousands of dollars are paid to Uncle Sam daily to carry watches, jewelry and the lighter articles by mail to our customers.

No. 13 The Train Shed where we can load 200 carloads of merchandise daily and start it on its way to our customers.

No. 14 The Long Distance Telephone Switch Board. The marvelous apparatus through which thousands of messages pass daily.

No. 15 Automatic Telephone Switch Board. The famous Automatic Telephone Girl, the newest thing in telephone engineering.

No. 16 Pneumatic Tube Station, shooting written messages through miles of tubing by compressed air.

No. 17 In the Bowels of the Earth. The great tunnels extending under all the buildings of our forty-acre plant.

No. 18 Playtime on the streets at noon.

No. 19 A Glimpse of the administration Building. Largest exclusive office building in the world used by a single firm or individual.

No. 20 Another Glimpse of the Administration Building.

No. 21 Magnificent Marble Entrance of the Administration Building.

No. 22 Where Money Checks, Drafts, and Money Orders are handled by the armful.

No. 23 520 Girls Preparing Our Customers' Orders for the Order Fillers in the Merchandise Building.

No. 24 Hundreds of Employes indicating the Railroad, Express Company or Steamship Company which will carry the customer's order to its destination.

No. 25 Talking to Our Customers. The Correspondence Department answering the thousands of inquiries received daily.

No. 26 How we use the Talking Machine and the Typewriter in answering letters received from our customers.

No. 27 Keeping a Record of every Dollar and ever order you send us.

No. 28 Counting the Money received daily and preparing it for deposit in the banks.

No. 29 The great rush at the close of the business day when our more than 9,000 employes leave the buildings for home.

No. 30 Setting the Type for the Great Catalogue.

No. 31 The Wonder of the Printing Industry, the Automatic Typesetting Machine.

No. 32 Making Printing Plates by Electricity.

No. 33 Sending 437,000 miles of white paper through the great printing presses.

No. 34 Making Typewritten Letters at the rate of 7,000 an hour.

No. 35 A Wonderful Machine, with 44 arms and 44 pairs of fingers doing more wonderful work than the human hand can do.

No. 36 Automatic Catalogue Gathering Machine in the Printing Plant.

No. 37 Machine with Razor Edged Knives cutting through 2,500 sheets of paper in the twinkling of an eye.

No. 38 A Boiler room without Coal Shovelers, in which the coal falls into the furnace and out again.

No. 39 A Million Dollars' worth of Engines, dynamos, air compressers, pumps, etc; furnishing heat, light and power.

No. 40 Great Switch Board in the Engine Room where a child could control with one hand more than 12,000-horse power.

No. 41 A Picture of the Main Dining Room where we entertain our customers who visit the plant.

No. 42 One of the great restaurants where we can serve 1,200 employes at one time.

No. 43 Preparing the Food for 9,000 employes.

No. 44 Tons of Meat and other Provisions hanging in the great refrigerators connected with the restaurant.

No. 45 The Most Beautiful Sunken Garden in Chicago, where every tree, shrub and flower known to this climate is grown in season.

No. 46 The Fountains and Artificial Lake where visiting customers may pass a cool and pleasant hour in the summer time.

No. 47 The Grecian Pergola. A revival of one of the architectural masterpieces of the Ancients.

No. 48 Where New Employes become qualified to handle our customers' orders and letters.

No. 49 A Fire Drill by the Fire Company, showing how we protect the lives of our employes and the property of the Company.

No. 50 The Free Hospital in the Merchandise Building where injured or sick employes are given the services of the most skilled physicians and trained nurses. Price 35c

50 views in leatherette case and good quality hardwood stereoscope. Price....... 50c

No. 20K2519 Sears, Roebuck & Co. Views. 50 views in leatherette case, without stereoscope. If by mail, postage extra, 12 cents.

No. 20K2518 Sears, Roebuck & Co. Views. If by mail, postage extra, 27 cents.

100 CHILDREN'S STORY VIEWS

THE MOST NOVEL AND INTERESTING COLLECTION OF COLORED STEREOSCOPIC VIEWS AND EXCELLENT CHILDREN'S STORIES EVER PRODUCED.

SOMETHING FOR THE LITTLE ONES

98c

The Queen of the Home.

EVERY BOY OR GIRL will enjoy this big set of one hundred beautiful, colored, stereoscopic views more than anything they have ever seen. The pictures are all clean, wholesome, up to date views, showing the children engaged in their youthful sports and pastimes. On the back of every one of these views there is printed a complete story relating to the subject of that view. These stories have been written by the best known literary men and women, and form the most interesting collection of children's stories that have ever been brought together. The stories have all been prepared especially for this set of views and will never fail to make glad the heart of every boy and girl who reads them. We have printed a few of the stories on this page. Be sure to read these stories to the children, and remember that there are ninety-six other stories, many of them far more interesting than those that are printed on this page.

LOTS OF JOLLY FUN can be had in the evening with this big set of colored stereoscopic views. The children will never tire of looking through the wonderful stereoscope and seeing their little playmates engaged in all the fun and frolic of innocent childhood. These views will help to pass many a rainy day, and the excellent stories will ever be remembered in later years, as one of the most pleasant recollections of childhood's golden hours. The well written style and literary merit of these stories will develop an interest for good literature in the minds of the boys and girls who read them, as every story is full of life and fun, sparkling with the choicest gems of childish wit and humor.

MOTHERS, give the children a real big treat. Think for a minute how much you enjoy seeing a good stereoscopic picture yourself, and then realize how much more the children will appreciate this big set of colored views which has been especially prepared for them. Every picture is one that will be sure to interest the boy or girl who sees it. Some of the pictures are the most unique that have ever been produced by the stereoscopic camera, and the stories on the back of every picture will prove a source of never tiring interest. The bright eyes and happy faces of the children, as they gaze in wonder at this wonderful set of stereoscopic views will bring back memories of the old school days.

An Evening at Home With the Little Ones.

THE OLD SCHOOL DAYS when we picnicked in the woods, built miniature railways in the backyard, played "hare and hounds" through the meadows and over the fields. There are pictures of snow fights, showing the brave assault made by the boys on the big snow fort, and the valiant manner in which its noble defenders fought to save the day. The bright days we spent among the flowers of the field or romped with childish delight beneath the shadows of the big oak trees are memories that will never fade from our fondest recollections. Every view in this big set is made from an actual photograph, and the colors are so exquisite, the effect so beautiful, as to far surpass anything heretofore produced in stereoscopic views.

FAIRY STORIES are probably more fascinating to the children than anything else. How well every one remembers the breathless anticipation with which we waited to hear the "Once upon a time" which we knew was the beginning of some wonderful tale that was to lead us into unknown realms where a brave prince was to rescue some beautiful young lady who was in danger, and how they all lived happy, ever afterward. Yet these tales of idle fancy do not begin to equal in interest the real, everyday, wide awake stories that are printed on the back of these views. The stories are every one right up to date, and deal with the boys and girls of our own land, and the things they do every day of the year.

SOME OF THE INTERESTING STORIES

LAST SUMMER MINNIE AND MARIE, who live in the big city, came out into the beautiful country to visit their cousins, Jane and Katie. One day they went fishing on the river, and the very first thing Katie did was to put a big, fat angle worm on her hook and drop the line down into the deep pool and get a bite. She jerked quickly and up from the water came a big eel, wiggling and twisting. After lunch they started fishing again, and Marie, who had caught the idea, proceeded to tie the empty sardine can on her line and cast it into the water. "What are you doing, Marie?" asked Katie. "Why," explained Marie, "you put a wiggly worm on your hook and caught a great big wiggly worm, so I'm going to put this sardine can on mine and catch a great big can of sardines."

WAR HAS BEEN DECLARED. The first heavy snow storm has covered the ground a foot deep with soft, sticky snow, and the Snow Birds, at the first warning, sent out scouts into the enemy's country and the scouts came flying back with the alarming news that the South Siders, under their terrible leader, Jack Rabbit Smith, are preparing to descend upon the Snow Bird country. Gen. Tommy Clark at once takes steps toward resistance. Feverishly the Snow Birds roll gigantic balls of snow and pile them high upon each other, while others, armed with spades and snow shovels, throw up masses of snow, which hastily is packed between the crevices. The younger Snow Birds are put to work making ammunition, and cautioned to make the snow balls hard, but not to soak them in water, which is against the rules of warfare. Finally the fort is complete, and with a cheer the flag is run up, the fort christened Fort Lucius. Scouts come flying back, reporting the advance of the South Siders. Inside the walls of the fort the defenders crouch low, to deceive their opponents as to their real fighting strength. Slowly the invaders advance. The redoubtable Jack Rabbit never has succeeded in capturing the stronghold of the Snow Birds, but this time he is determined. His sled loads of ammunition are wheeled into position and his men, acting quickly under his orders, spread themselves in a half circle and rush onward until Fort Lucius is surrounded entirely and all avenues of escape cut off. Suddenly the South Side warriors stoop, unlace their snow shoes, and holding them as shields, begin the advance from all directions, firing as they advance. Shot and shell rain upon Fort Lucius which fires a volley that checks the advance. One of Jack Rabbit's well aimed shots knocks General Tommy from the ramparts, but he is up in a moment, fighting grandly and encouraging his men. Fiercely the battle rages, charges are made and repelled. Finally at one supreme dash, the enemy leaps over the walls in the face of the terrible rain of snowballs, and the brave defenders, their ammunition exhausted, are compelled to surrender the fort to their captors. But it was fun while it lasted, and next week there will be another fight—if the snow still stays.

ONCE UPON A TIME there was a little boy who didn't like to say his prayers. One day he sat down and wrote his prayers out on a piece of paper and tacked them upon the wall over the bed and at night he would kneel down real quick and say: "Oh Lord, them's my sentiments," and jump right under the covers. There was another little boy and his sister, who were mischievous, and one night, while little Robbie was saying his prayers, his sister kept tickling the soles of his bare feet. He kept right on with his prayers as long as he could and then he said, "Oh Lord, excuse me a minute while I lick the stuffin' out of Susie."

THERE WAS ONCE SOME LITTLE BOYS who never wanted to do anything but swim. Their papa told them they must go in only twice a day during the real hot weather, but they were very naughty boys, and when their papa hid their bathing suits they used to pretend they were just going to play in the woods and then they would run away and go swimming. One day Jimmy and Jerry, which were the names of these two naughty little boys, went swimming, and Jerry got his shirt on inside out when he dressed. His papa noticed it, and said, "Jerry, have you been swimming?" "No, sir," said Jerry, who didn't know it was worse to tell a fib than to be switched. "How did your shirt get wrong side out?" asked his papa. "I guess I did it climbing through a hole in the fence backwards," said Jerry. And his papa switched him twice, once for disobeying and going swimming, and a harder one for telling a lie. And he didn't let them go in swimming for two whole days.

WONDERLAND and all its mysteries were never so fascinating as will be this big set of beautiful, colored stereoscopic views. The children will see their little friends at the seashore, playing on the beach and in the sand. They will laugh over the pillow fights of the little girls in the morning. They will feel sorry for the poor little girl who got her face so dirty that her own mamma did not know her, and will never tire of looking at the beautiful snow pictures, with the children engaged in their winter sports and pastimes. Remember that these pictures are not taken in some unheard of and far away land, but represent the real children in this great wonderland of our own country.

HAPPY CHILDHOOD HOURS will be made doubly interesting to the little ones by this big set of stereoscopic views that have been especially prepared for them. The colors in these beautiful pictures are marvels of the photographic art; they show each view in all of its wonderful, natural beauty, as vivid and as lifelike as though the actual scene itself appeared before us. What seem to be only white specks in the picture of a snow scene, when seen through the wonderful stereoscope, instantly burst forth into a myriad of glittering crystals, reflecting the sparkling sunlight into our eyes. So natural and so realistic are these views that the exclamations of wonder and amazement from the little ones will make glad the hearts of every loving mother.

THE CHARMING STORIES only serve to add to the interest of these beautiful pictures. Don't fail to read the stories, that are printed on this page, to the children, and remember that there are one hundred of these stories, one story on the back of every view. If you want to make the little ones happy, if you want to afford them countless hours of childish fun and recreation, you will not fail to order this wonderful set of children's story views. Instruct us to include it in your next shipment, or send us an order for this set by mail at once; you will be repaid a thousand times by the bright eyes and eager faces of the children, as they gaze at these beautiful pictures and read the fascinating stories printed on the back of every view.

No. 20K2540 Children's Story Views. Complete set of 100 views, all different, with printed stories on the back of every view, including fine hinged cover, imitation leather box for views. Price, with stereoscope............ **$1.13**
Price, without stereoscope.. **98c**

Be sure to state whether you want stereoscope. For cost of postage, express or freight charges, see note on page 178.

THE SIEGE OF PORT ARTHUR

100 COLORED STEREOSCOPIC VIEWS
THE MOST THRILLING AND REALISTIC PICTURES EVER MADE
OF THE JAPANESE-RUSSIAN WAR

WAR IS AWFUL

85c

BUT THE JAPANESE have set before the world an example of scientific and business like warfare which has never been equaled by any other nation. They engaged German officers of high rank to drill their army, and planned their campaign with a passion for detail and unerring precision, against which no amount of valor could prevail. Scientific in everything they did, their army was handled with the greatest regard to hygiene and sanitation. We have views showing them boiling their drinking water in camps. We see their sentries stationed at the rivers to prevent contamination of the water. Their hospital service was an example to the entire world in caring for the wounded upon the battlefield. In one instance, the same operation was performed on a Japanese soldier that was performed upon President McKinley. The stomach of this man was removed and sewed up while Russian shot and shrapnel were flying overhead. Yet two weeks later this soldier was homeward bound and told by the surgeons that his recovery was almost certain. A marked characteristic of the little Jap is his intense patriotism. Their empire could never be invaded except by the extermination of every living man.

THE WAR OF MODERN TIMES.

When the Japanese realized that they were not to take Port Arthur by storming the fortifications, they prepared a campaign which was to take more than a year in its execution. Trenches were dug in a zig-zag fashion, each one getting a little nearer to the fortifications. As these trenches neared the walls of the fort, the danger became extreme, and it was only through the smallest loopholes that the Japanese were able to keep a watch on the Russian movements. A soldier was stationed in the trench, with his eye to this small hole in the embankment, but so accurate was the aim of the hidden Russians that many of the Japanese fell at these loopholes, pierced with a bullet through the eye. A war correspondent, standing by when a man fell, asked the commander how many had been killed at the same hole during that day. "Twenty," was the reply. While these trenches were being dug eighteen immense guns, like the one shown on this page, were brought from the Island of Japan and mounted upon solid concrete foundations before the fortifications of Port Arthur. These guns were nicknamed by the war correspondents "The Osaka Babies."

THE MOST REALISTIC SET OF VIEWS

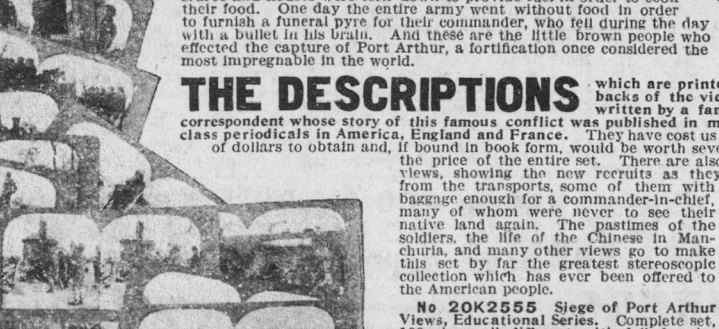

ever produced. We see the gunners at work, who never saw the fortifications they were aiming at. Yet, each shell struck exactly where it was intended and within a space of 12 feet square. These mathematical calculations were determined by the outlook on 203 Meter Hill. The story of taking this famous hill is one of the most tragic in the entire conflict. Two thousand men were lost in storming this hill, and during the night of the assault Lieutenant-General Oshima sat in his tent all night weeping. So terrible had been the Russian fire that it was necessary for the Japanese to use the bodies of their dead and wounded comrades in protecting themselves from this deadly hail of bullets. At another time during the siege firewood became very scarce and houses were torn down to provide fuel in order to cook their food. One day the entire army went without food in order to furnish a funeral pyre for their commander, who fell during the day with a bullet in his brain. And these are the little brown people who effected the capture of Port Arthur, a fortification once considered the most impregnable in the world.

THE DESCRIPTIONS

which are printed on the backs of the views were written by a famous war correspondent whose story of this famous conflict was published in many high class periodicals in America, England and France. They have cost us hundreds of dollars to obtain and, if bound in book form, would be worth several times the price of the entire set. There are also comedy views, showing the new recruits as they arrived from the transports, some of them with baggage enough for a commander-in-chief, many of whom were never to see their native land again. The pastimes of the soldiers, the life of the Chinese in Manchuria, and many other views go to make this set by far the greatest stereoscopic collection which has ever been offered to the American people.

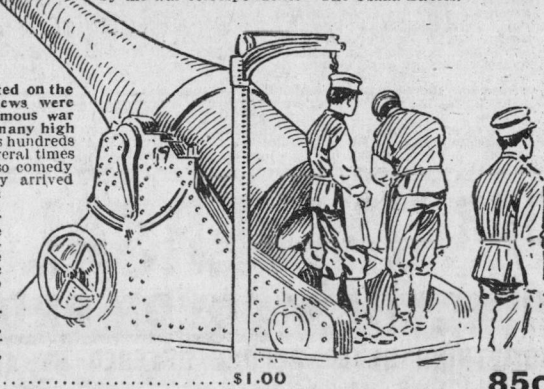

No 20K2555 Siege of Port Arthur Views, Educational Series. Complete set, 100 views all different, with full descriptions of each view, in fine, hinged cover, imitation leather box.
Price, with stereoscope..................$1.00
Price, without stereoscope..................85c
Be sure to state whether you want stereoscope.
For cost of postage, express or freight charges, see note on page 178.

FAIR JAPAN—100 COLORED VIEWS 85c
SHOWING THE WONDERFUL BEAUTY OF
THE ISLAND EMPIRE OF THE SEA

THERE IS NO NATION which is more interesting than that of the little brown people. Older, almost, than any country in the world, these people are today observing the spirit of progress that bids fair to outrival many a larger nation in its accomplishments. It is in this set of views on Japan that the full value of the colored stereoscopic view becomes apparent. Nowhere is such a wealth of color so prevalent on every hand as we find in Japan. There are views taken in their parks and gardens, showing the beautiful fields of iris and chrysanthemums. And then we have views showing that famous volcano, Fujiyama, which rears its lofty peak from the center of this island. It is one of the most unique sights of the world, standing 12,000 feet high, and seeming, from a distance, to rise directly from the sea itself. We also see the ancient treasure houses, many of them built five hundred years ago, containing the antique heirlooms of this peculiar people. Many other views showing the tea gardens, fisheries, and quiet home life of the island are also included in this set.

THE "GEISHA" GIRLS,

or singing girls of Japan, are one of the most interesting features of the island's social life. The vivacity and pleasing unconstraint of the beautiful young women has led to many a match with an enamored, though poor, student of Japan. The following is said frequently to happen: The young student declares his affection, and his friends, hearing what they deem to be evil courses, stop supplies. The singing girl supports her lover, who thereupon passes his examinations brilliantly and obtains an official post. They are married, and he rises to be one of the leading men of the Empire, while she, of course, is a great lady with her carriage and her weekly reception day. The descriptions on the back of our views abound in interesting anecdotes as well as in vivid descriptions of this wonderful country which centuries ago was known as

No. 20K2525 Views of Japan, Educational Series. Complete set, 100 views, all different, with full descriptions of each view, in fine, hinged cover, imitation leather box.
Price, with stereoscope.........$1.00
Price, without stereoscope..................85c
Be sure to state whether you want stereoscope.
For cost of postage, express or freight charges, see note on page 178.

"THE LAND OF THE RISING SUN"

A FEW OF THE 100 SUBJECTS

Treasure House—500 years old.
The Thousand Lanterns—At temple.
Ancient Stone Dog—Guarding temple.
Worshipping Fox at Shrine.
The Garden of Sleep.
Egyptian Lotus in Full Bloom.
Gorgeous Fields of Iris.
Busy Scene in Rice Fields.
Theater Street—A mile long.
A Rosary Shop—Osaka.
Potato Dealer's Stall—Yakohama.
Japanese Girls at Flower Show.
Dancing Girls and Refreshments.
At the Crater of Fujiyama.
A Rough Trail Across Lava.
Japan—From above the clouds.

HOW THIS CHURCH DOUBLED ITS ATTENDANCE

THROUGH THE USE OF OUR "HOLY LAND"

SET OF COLORED STEREOSCOPIC VIEWS

READ THIS CAREFULLY

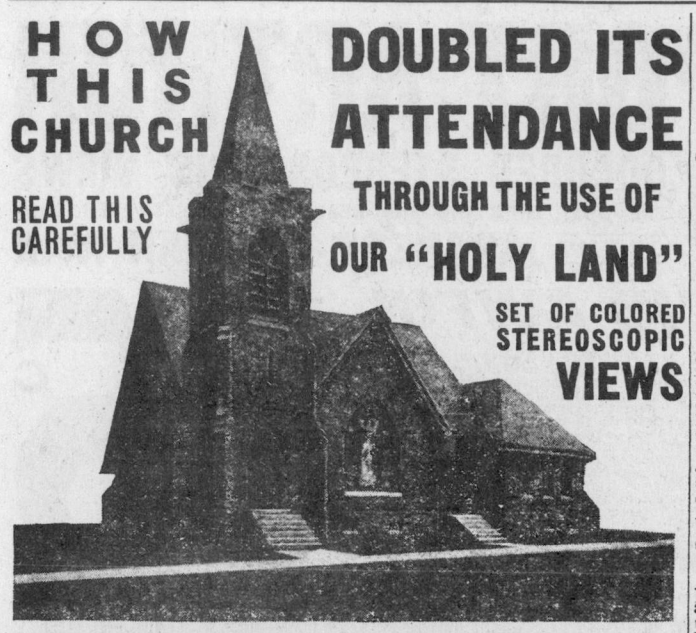

OUR PLAN

It is a well established fact that the finances of a church or Sunday school depend largely upon the attendance of its members. One church has evolved a plan by which the punctual attendance of its Sunday school members has been brought about in a very interesting manner. They purchased a dozen sets of our "Holy Land" views, including the stereoscopes, and on the first morning their attendance was only about twenty-five at the opening hour. The announcement made was as follows: "Every scholar who arrives before the opening of the school at 9:30 will be given a colored stereoscopic view free. If you arrive after the school has commenced you do not get a stereoscopic view. When you have fifteen of these colored stereoscopic views, you will then be given a beautiful stereoscope free, which will complete your set and enable you to enjoy your collection of views." This plan aroused such interest and enthusiasm among the young people that the next Sunday the attendance was over forty when the school opened. The following Sunday the attendance was greater yet, and over sixty views were needed to supply those present at the opening hour. The attendance rapidly increased, and with this increase of attendance came a corresponding increase in the collection, so that the cost of these views was rapidly made up in this manner. There was another very important effect which this plan produced. It stimulated a real interest in the lessons of the day, for everyone in the family, from the old folks to the children, take an interest in these wonderful colored stereoscopic views, and home study is developed to a greater extent and made far more interesting and helpful than by any other plan that has ever been devised.

100 COLORED STEREOSCOPIC VIEWS OF THE HOLY LAND, 85¢

OF THE PLACES MADE SACRED THROUGH BIBLE HISTORY.
PRINTED DESCRIPTIONS ON THE BACK OF EVERY VIEW.

FOR BIBLE STUDY. These views are all made from actual photographs and were taken at great expense. Many of them are scenes which have never before been reproduced in photographic form. There are views of the great city wall of Damascus and the traditional spot where Paul was let down by night from the wall in a basket. We see the River Jordan and can almost imagine John, The Baptist, still standing there, baptizing the people of the land of Palestine. And then there are the beautiful temples and also views of the narrow streets in Jerusalem, one of which it is claimed was the way Christ passed on his way to the crucifixion. There is a picture of the Jaffa Gate in the western wall of Jerusalem, where swarms of traders and repulsive beggars crouch at the entrance, and a view of the lepers, showing the crippled and horrible condition in which this dreadful disease has left them. Then there is the "Hangman's Tree" under which it is said Absalom rode on a mule, the story with which we are all so familiar.

THE ANCIENT LAND OF PALESTINE

with its many harbors and wonderful views of the great Plains of Sharon are also included in this set. There is a view of Hasbeych where the darkest blot on the history of Damascus was enacted when 6,000 Christians were murdered by a Mohammedan mob in 1860. We behold the vine clad houses of Nazareth, nestling among the beautiful green hills that rise high above the surrounding plains. The Garden of Gethsemane with the Olive Tree which is supposed to be nineteen hundred years old, and the tomb of the Virgin at the foot of Mt. Olive, are seen in this wonderful set, and many other interesting views of places, the names of which we are all familiar with.

THE LOW PRICE at which we can sell this great set of colored stereoscopic views places it within the reach of every man, woman and child who is interested in the study of the Bible. Do not hesitate to order this set. You will get more real, actual good out of these beautiful colored views and the Bible stories and interesting descriptions that are printed on the back of every view than from any other investment you can make. The descriptions have all been prepared by a man who is a profound student of Bible history, and these descriptions in themselves, if bound into a volume, would form a most interesting and instructive book on the Holy Land and its people.

No. 20K2535 Holy Land Views, Educational Series. Complete set, 100 views, all different, with full description of each view, in fine, hinged cover, imitation leather box. **85¢**

Price, with stereoscope, **$1.00**; without stereoscope.................

Be sure to state whether you want stereoscope.

For cost of postage, express or freight charges, see note on page 178.

OUR UNIVERSAL SERIES 200 OLEOGRAPH COLORED STEREOSCOPIC VIEWS. $2.30

MADE BY AN ENTIRELY NEW COLOR PROCESS

SOMETHING NEVER BEFORE OFFERED BY ANY DEALER.

THESE VIEWS comprise a series of subjects taken from every part of the world. There are views showing the great cities of the old continent, the magnificent scenery and famous edifices that occupy so prominent a place in the world's history. Many of the views are taken in our own land of America, showing the wonders of the Western Hemisphere. The great forests of the North and the thousands of cattle grazing on the western plains, form interesting pictures that have never before been presented to the public in any stereoscopic set. We visit the islands of the sea, tour through tropical climes and explore the snow covered lands of the polar regions. There is no subject which is not included in this wonderful set of two hundred magnificent views. We have pictures of the immense battleships of our navy, showing the gigantic guns which have wrought such havoc among the navies of the world. There are pictures of plant life, showing most interesting studies in natural history. There are views of hunting and fishing in many lands. We see the moon with all the wonderful effect it presents when seen through an immense telescope. It stands out in relief before us, a great globe floating majestically in the heavens, so vivid and so real that we can study every line on its vast surface, just as do the astronomers through the huge telescopes in our observatories. If you really want a set of stereoscopic views in which every picture is one of the greatest interest, you will not fail to order this big set.

THE COLORING of these pictures is done by a new process, the latest development in color photography, and enables us to reproduce the original picture with every detail clear and sharp, on full calendered paper and mounted on smooth round cornered cards. The surface of the photographs are highly polished and given a glossy finish which adds greatly to the beauty of the picture and also enhances the stereoscopic effect. The life of the picture is also longer when finished in this beautiful manner. Pictures among the woodlands and forests show the trees and vines with all the effect of sunlight and shadow that can be obtained with an artist's brush. The coloring of these pictures is so exquisite, the stereoscopic effect so marvelous and the views themselves so beautiful as to command the admiration of anyone who appreciates the real artistic possibilities of color photography.

UNIVERSAL SERIES GENERAL SUBJECTS

Famous Cities of the World.
Wonderful Yellowstone Park.
Cattle Grazing on Western Plains.
Beautiful Niagara Falls.
Giant Forests of America.
Gold Mining in Alaska.
Life in the Philippine Islands.
The Orient: Its Cities and People.
Ruins of Ancient Egypt.
Sphinx and Pyramids.
Castles of Switzerland.
Hunting and Fishing in Many Lands.
Old Fortifications of Cuba.
Immense Battleships of our Navy.
Studies in Plant Life.
The Moon Seen Through a Telescope.

200 BEAUTIFUL COLORED VIEWS

THE DESCRIPTIONS on the back of every view are interesting and intelligent writings about each of the different subjects of the set. These descriptions have cost an immense amount of money to obtain and are the work of the best literary people of the day. The time and labor involved in writing them would be sufficient to prepare a large volume of two hundred pages, and they are worth many times the price we ask for the entire set. We also include free of charge a beautiful leatherette case which is just the size of the views. It is dustproof and will protect your views from injury and preserve them for many years. You will find that an evening spent with this wonderful collection of colored views and their well written descriptions will prove a source of never ending enjoyment and afford an education which would cost hundreds of dollars to obtain.

200 OLEOGRAPH VIEWS WITH LEATHERETTE CASE FOR VIEWS, $2.30

No. 20K2520 Oleograph Stereoscopic View Outfit, consisting of 200 new process Oleograph colored stereo views, exactly as illustrated, described and listed above, every view with complete history and description printed on the back, all contained in a handsome leatherette case, with first grade hardwood stereoscope. Shipping weight, 5½ pounds. Price, complete..................**$2.45**

No. 20K2521 Oleograph Stereoscopic Views, 200 views in case, same as No. 20K2520, but without scope. Price.. (Shipping weight, 4½ lbs., unmallable account weight.)..**$2.30**

ST. LOUIS WORLD'S FAIR

100 BEAUTIFUL COLORED STEREOSCOPIC VIEWS OF THIS WONDERFUL AND MAGNIFICENT EXPOSITION **85¢**

THIS SET IS WORTH $500.00 TO YOU. If you visited the great exposition at St. Louis, you will, no doubt, remember that it cost you, what seemed at the time, an exorbitant sum of money for the admission fees that were required. In order to see the wonderful sights of the fair grounds. If you did not visit the Fair, you have, no doubt, regretted it many times since, and this set affords you the opportunity of seeing the magnificent buildings, beautiful lagoons, and also every one of the various attractions on the fair ground. There is a picture of your own state building in this wonderful set, showing how the visitors from your state were made welcome and afforded a resting place while on the grounds. We see the gigantic bird cage, the largest ever built in the world. There are views of the fair grounds by night, showing the myriad of electric lights, which enchanted thousands of people with their festive radiance. We see the great clock made entirely of flowers, and we stroll through the big machinery hall, filled with the latest inventions of modern engineering. Then there is the corn exhibit, the most wonderful spectacle ever produced. The famous cascades in all their grandeur are brought before us through the stereoscope, and we seem to be standing in the very midst of these mammoth fair grounds, to which thousands of people came every day of the seven long months

ON THE "PIKE". Here we find scenes of real interest, showing the Midway with all of its many attractions. We see the beautiful reproduction of the Tyrolean Alps and the pretty girls who brought us refreshments while we rested ourselves in the quaint old taverns. We see the Philippine Village, with the native men and women engaged in the occupations of their far off land. We see that magnificent work of art called "Creation," which excited the wonder of everyone who visited it; the Streets of Cairo, as natural as the ancient city itself; Battle Abbey, Japanese Houses; Cliff Dwellers, and all of the other multitudinous attractions of this great Midway are seen with the actual thrill of appreciation and excitement of a personal visit to the attraction. The following list contains a few of the many subjects which are included in this big set of colored views. Every picture has a description printed on its back that forms a reliable and interesting history of one of the greatest fairs ever held in the world.

SPORTING SERIES

100 COLORED STEREOSCOPIC VIEWS **85¢**

WORLD'S FAIR SET. PARTIAL LIST OF SUBJECTS

MAGNIFICENT BUILDINGS

Festival Hall
Palace of Electricity
Palace of Mines and Metallurgy
Terrace of States
Government Building
Illinois State Building
Iowa State Building
Minnesota State Building
Michigan State Building
New York State Building
Pennsylvania State Building
Indiana State Building
Missouri State Building
Kansas State Building
Arkansas State Building
Louisiana State Building
Texas State Building
Alaska Building and Totem Poles
England Building and Gardens
Royal Gateway—China Exhibit
Ben Chama Temple—Siam

WONDERFUL EXHIBITS

"Lone Star" of Texas (Grains)
Nebraska Corn Display
Indiana and Missouri Exhibit
Moose—Minnesota Game Exhibit
California's Exhibit of Fruit
War Department Exhibit
Bethlehem Steel Co.'s Exhibit

ALONG THE "PIKE"

Entrance to the "Pike"
General View of the "Pike"
Three Magicians
Gateway to "Court of Asia"
Gateway to "Tyrolean Alps"
Castle in the Tyrolean Alps
Bon Bon Girls in Alpine Village
Entrance to "Creation"
The "Cliff Dwellers"
Japanese Tea House and Gardens
Planting Rice, Philippine Village
"Battle Abbey," on the Pike
Moorish Street, "City of Jerusalem"
Sea Fowls at "Hagenbech's"

CASCADE AND GARDENS

Grand Stairway of Cascade
Sunken Gardens
Statue of Marguerite—French Gardens
The Great Floral Clock
Mammoth Bird Cage
Happy Family in Bird Cage
Festival Hall at Night
Countless Thousands of Electric Lights
Bird's Eye View from Observation Wheel

AND FIFTY OTHERS

SPECIAL

THE TERRIBLE SAN FRANCISCO EARTHQUAKE AND FIRE

THE STORY of the San Francisco disaster is one that will ever live in the minds of American people. On the memorable day of April 18, 1906, at the peaceful morning hour when the inhabitants of beautiful San Francisco slumbered in their homes, this terrible catastrophe descended upon the silent city. Without warning the earth suddenly began to tremble and rock as though shook by the hand of some mighty giant. The immense front of the Columbia Theater ponderously swayed out into the street and toppled to the ground with a terrific crash. The James Flood building swung outward on its foundations and then slowly settled back into place. The phenomena was so uncanny, the spectacle so wierd and gruesome that it filled the mind like a horrible nightmare. Following the earthquake came the fire, and engines dashed by in every direction. People fled from the burning districts, dragging their trunks and possessions with them, and it seemed like the entire city, the homes of thousands of people, was to be utterly wiped off the map.

HAVOC OF DEATH. Law and order vanished, but military power soon took command of the city and Mayor Schmitz issued his famous proclamation "to kill any man on the spot found stealing or committing any other crime." An observer tells of seeing two men caught red handed in their theft. They were marched up the street and faced about, confronting the soldiers. A volley of firearms rung out and the culprits pitched forward on their faces, never to rise again. The heroic bravery of the firemen has never before been equaled. Many of them lost their lives trying to rescue men and women from the burning structures. At one time four men appeared at the top of a towering building which had become a seething mass of flames. Their escape was cut off, and rather than suffer the living death of cremation they ordered the soldiers to shoot them, and as the volley of muskets rang out, they pitched back into the fiery furnace and were never seen again.

THE RUINS OF A GREAT CITY were all that remained of once beautiful San Francisco. In some places magnificent brown stone residences with ivy covered walls stood like the ruins of an ancient castle in some foreign land. The work of reconstructing was begun at once, and food and money began to pour into the city from all parts of the country. As an illustration of the efficiency of the soldiers the following incident is narrated: A bakeshop was selling bread at 75 cents a loaf when a sergeant brought the butt of his musket down on the counter and announced that bread would hereafter be sold at 10 cents a loaf or there would be one baker less to the public. These views are the most interesting collection that has ever been offered to the public. They are all taken from actual photographs made during and directly after the great fire and form a series of views that excel anything heretofore produced.

FLEEING REFUGEES. Pictures taken of people as they fled before the fire, driven into the parks and surrounding cities to find resting places. Many were compelled to cook in the street and millionaire and beggar stood side by side in the famous bread line. These views bring before us in the most vivid and realistic manner the terrible desolation which spread over this devastated territory. There is a printed description on the back of every view, recording the experiences of many of those who passed through this awful calamity. There are statistical facts which form a complete and valuable collection for reference. These descriptions alone, if bound in book form, would readily sell for many times the price of the outfit. San Francisco has now begun its work of rebuilding the city from its ruins, and no other pictures will ever be made of this awful earthquake and fire. Don't fail to order this wonderful set of 100 colored stereoscopic views, now.

75¢

No. 20K2560 San Francisco Earthquake Series. 60 beautiful colored stereoscopic views, 60 historic descriptions printed on the backs, 1 leatherette case for the 60 views. Price, as above described ...(Postage extra, 13 cents)...............**90¢**
Price, with stereoscope included.............(Postage extra, 28 cents)..............**90¢**

A FEW OF THE MANY SUBJECTS

WITH THE HUNTERS

Unlucky Antelope
"Sorry I Killed Him"
Skinning a Prong Horn Buck
On the Trail with the Spoils
A Prong Horn Going to Camp
Fawn Hidden in the Underbrush
"The Drop" on a Bunch of Elk
A Yearling in Hard Luck
The Last Buffalo (dead)
Walking Upon the Point
Backing Up the Point
A Very Dead Sand Hill Crane
After Quail in Our Automobile
The Young Trappers
"Jennie," Our Pet Pack Mule

AFTER THE DUCKS

Duck Hunter Getting Under Cover
Decoys Out; Ready for Business
A Fall Morning Over Decoys
Just Out of Range
Turning Loose from Point Blind
The Ducks Must Suffer
Picking up a Double
A Nice Morning's Shoot
The Return at Evening
The Landing—All in

UP QUIET STREAMS

Landing a Small Mouth Bass
Picking Them Out of the Pool
The Strike; "A Big One, Sure'
Hooked but Not Netted
Taking Him in Out of the Wet
Landing a Four-Pound Rainbow
Still Water on Kinnikinnick
Never a Prettier Stream
Could Water be More Promising
A Risky Crossing
A Fine String of Black Bass

AMONG THE INDIANS

Braves in Full Leather
Passing the Pipe of Peace
Blackfoot Squaw and Papoose
Squaws Braiding Rush Mats
Gray Eagle and His Lodge
Sioux Rider and Racing Pony
Indian Rider and Medicine Man
A Real Live Cowboy
Our Guide "Jack and His Pony"

IN THE CAMP

Lean-to Camp by the River
"Want Some Supper, Bob"
Camping on the Marsh
Snug Camp Among Foot Hills
Camp Fire Dreams

ALSO FIFTY OTHER VIEWS

HUNTING AND FISHING.

Did you ever catch a fish or shoot a duck? Every lover of outdoor sports, whether it be hunting big game among the dense forests and mountains of the West or catching the gamy black bass or the wary trout in some secluded nook, will enjoy this magnificent set of colored views. There are pictures, showing the snow fields of the North; of quiet inland streams on balmy summer days; of mountain forests, so dense that a passage seems impossible and showing the methods by which the hunter and trapper secure their game. We see them bringing down the prey, carrying it into the camp, oftentimes busy explaining why the bag is not fuller, each one with a better story than the other.

INDIANS AND COWBOYS

of the Western plains are also depicted in this great set. We see the young Sioux Indian with his racing pony; the medicine man in his wierd incantations. We see the Blackfoot squaw at home with her papoose and old Gray Eagle himself, the best known Indian of the Sioux Nation standing before his lodge. The cowboy's life on the western plains is also brought before us in vivid reality. It is this life that has produced such men as our great President Roosevelt, and it is with the keenest interest that we watch these cowboys of the plains performing their daily tasks on the great cattle ranches of the west.

CAMP FIRE MEMORIES

and pleasant days spent in the quiet woods or among the marshes with dogs and ponies, are ever a source of pleasant recollection. These views will bring back the pleasant days when we stayed in some "blind" with the decoys spread, and brought down the ducks as they descended so unsuspectingly into our trap. There are pictures of many kinds of camps, one view showing a "one man camp," built in the hollow of a log. Many other interesting subjects are included in this set. Descriptions and stories are printed on the back of every view, which make them of double value and a source of lasting pleasure for the many days to come.

TEST QUESTIONS.

No. 1. What is your age?
No. 2. Have you ever worn glasses before, and if so, how long and what number were they?
No. 3. Do your eyes stand out prominently or are they sunken?
No. 4. Do your eyes become tired after slight use?
No. 5. Does the light hurt your eyes?
No. 6. How long is it since your sight began to fail?
No. 7. Do you suffer from headaches or pain over the eyes?
No. 8 Can you see well at a distance without glasses?
No. 9. Do you desire glasses for reading or for seeing at a distance?
No. 10. Can you read test type No. 8 at a distance of 10 feet without glasses? If not, what number can you see at this distance?
No. 11. What is the number of the **smallest type** that you can easily and distinctly read, when holding this page at a distance of 12 inches from the eyes, without glasses?
No. 12. What is the **greatest possible distance** at which you can easily and distinctly read paragraph No. 26, without glasses?

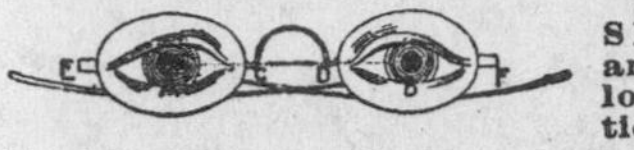

If you desire SPECTACLES answer the following three questions:

No. 13. What is the distance between the pupils (A to B)?
No. 14. What is the width of nose at base (C to D)?
No. 15. What is the distance between the temples (E to F)?

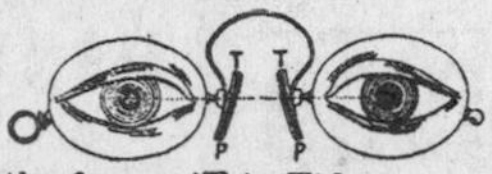

If you desire EYE-GLASSES answer the following four questions.

No. 16. What is the width of nose (T to T)?
No. 17. What is the width of nose (P to P)?
No. 18. Is the bridge of your nose prominent or flat?
No. 19. What is the distance from the center or pupil of one eye to the center or pupil of the other eye?

TYPE FOR TESTING THE EYES.

60

The smallest size letters on this card should be read easily at fifteen inches from the eye. If you cannot do so you should wear spectacles. It does not pay to buy cheap spectacles.

52

They distort the rays of light, disturb the angles of vision, cause pain and discomfort and injure the eyesight. When it is necessary to hold work or reading matter farther than fifteen inches from the eyes

44

in order to see distinctly, it is a sure sign of failing vision, and much annoyance, discomfort and pain will be prevented

40

by having a pair of glasses fitted. Pain in the eyes when wearing spectacles is usually caused

36

either by improperly fitted lenses, or from the centres of the lenses not corresponding with

32

the centres of the eyes. To be perfect, a lens must be made with highly polished surfaces

26

of accurate curvatures. Our crystalline lenses are the best in the market.

22

They are made from the clearest and finest material obtainable

20

AND ARE WARRANTED TO BE OF ABSOLUTELY

18

PERFECT CONSTRUCTION.

16

BUY NO OTHER KIND.

13

CRYSTALLINE

11

LENSES

10

ARE THE

8

B E S T.

SPECTACLES AND EYEGLASSES

WE WILL REFUND YOUR MONEY IN FULL IF THE SPECTACLES WE SEND YOU DO NOT FIT YOUR EYES PERFECTLY.

INSTRUCTIONS FOR ORDERING.

Give the catalogue number of the style of Spectacles or Eyeglasses you want, and answer very carefully the test questions in the first column on this page.
When ordering spectacles or eyeglasses of any kind to be sent by mail, include 5 cts. extra for postage.

RIDING BOW SPECTACLES.

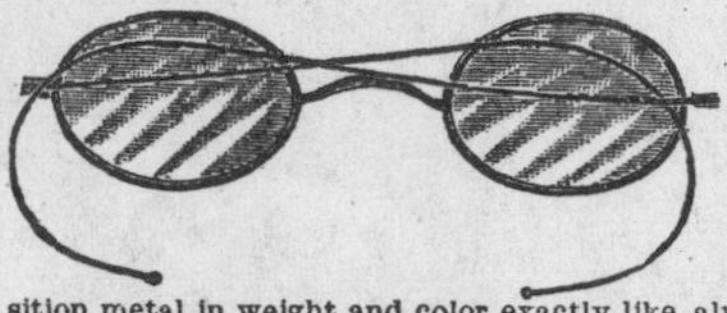

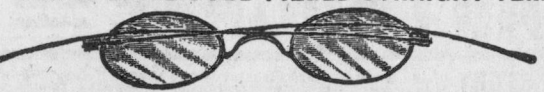

The Riding Bow Spectacles, known also as Hook Bow, are to be preferred in all cases where the glasses are to be worn constantly, or nearly so. The shape of the temples prevents the spectacles falling off, and also keeps the lenses more exactly in the proper position all the time.

No. 20K3000 Steel Spectacles, first quality, riding bow temples, finely tempered, with good quality lenses. Price, with leather case.......... **48c**

No. 20K3005 Best Grade Steel Spectacles, the very best riding bow steel spectacle made, nickel plated, finely finished, perfectly tempered and warranted in every respect. These spectacles are fitted with the **finest quality crystalline lenses,** carefully ground and accurately centered. Price, with leather case. **88c**

No. 20K3010 Alumnico Spectacles, riding bow temples, light and well finished, with fine accurately centered crystalline lenses. Alumnico is a composition metal in weight and color exactly like aluminum. **Warranted not to tarnish.** Price, with leather case....... **$1.00**

No. 20K3016 Solid Gold Spectacles, riding bow temples, perfection joints, highly polished and fitted with the finest accurately centered crystalline lenses. Price, with leather case, 14-karat, **$3.30;** 10-karat, with leather case...... **$2.50**
If by mail, postage extra, 5 cents.

STRAIGHT TEMPLE SPECTACLES.

Straight Temple Spectacles are most suitable for those who wear glasses for near work only, and therefore remove them frequently from the eyes.

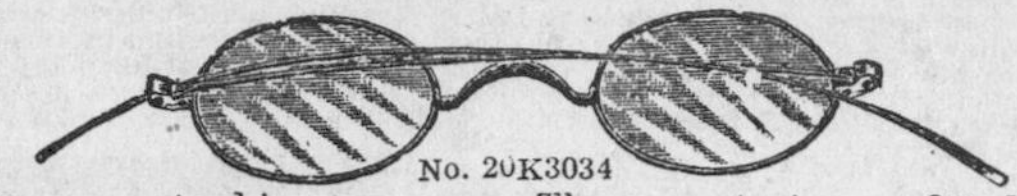

No. 20K3034

No. 20K3024 Steel Spectacles; first quality, straight temples, finely tempered, with good quality lenses. Price, with leather case........... **45c**

No. 20K3029 Best Grade Steel Spectacles, the best straight temple steel spectacle that can be manufactured, full nickel plated, perfectly tempered, elegantly finished, both frame and lenses guaranteed in every way. These spectacles are fitted with the very best quality of **accurately ground crystalline lenses,** carefully adjusted.
Price, with leather case.......................... **85c**

No. 20K3034 Alumnico Straight Temple Spectacles for 95 cents. We offer these genuine Alumnico Straight Temple Spectacles as the most satisfactory, most durable and most comfortable straight temple spectacle made, except the solid gold or gold filled styles. They are far superior to steel, as alumnico is a light, silvery metal that **will never rust or tarnish,** but will always keep its fine bright color. These frames are as carefully finished as our best solid gold, and fitted with our highest grade crystalline lenses.
Price, with leather case.... .... (If by mail, postage extra, 5 cents.)............ **95c**

OUR SPECIAL GOLD FILLED STRAIGHT TEMPLE SPECTACLES, AT $1.65.

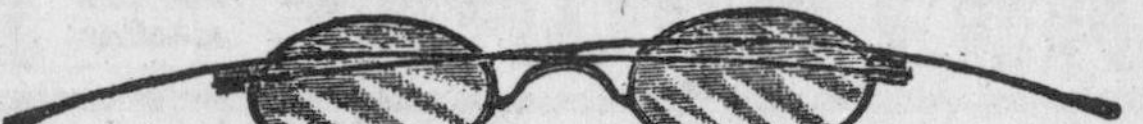

No. 20K3039 We furnish these extra high grade Straight Temple Spectacles as absolutely the best straight temple gold filled spectacle that can be manufactured. They are genuine gold filled, made with two plates of extra heavy solid gold over an inner plate of hard composition metal, and we will replace without charge any pair that discolors, tarnishes or wears through to the composition metal in ten years. Equal in appearance to solid gold, beautifully finished and fitted with the very highest grade crystalline lenses. Price, with leather case.................. **$1.65**

No. 20K3044 Solid Gold Spectacles; straight temple bows, perfection joint, highly polished, heavy weight, fitted with the finest accurately centered crystalline lenses. Price, with leather case, 14-K., **$3.45;** 10-K., with leather case **$3.20**
If by mail, postage extra, 5 cents.

BIFOCAL LENSES.

The illustration shows appearance of Bifocal Lenses. We recommend Bifocal Lenses in cases where spectacles are required for both near and distant vision. **We furnish these lenses in the style known as cemented bifocal lenses,** which are the latest, best and most satisfactory style made. Any of the spectacles or eyeglasses in this catalogue (except the rimless) can be furnished with bifocal lenses for **50 cents extra;** for example, spectacle No. 20K3034, the regular price of which is **95 cents,** would be **$1.45** with bifocal lenses.

FLEXIBLE GUARD EYEGLASSES.

The Flexible Guard Eyeglasses are generally preferred when glasses are not constantly worn, as they are easily adjusted to the nose.

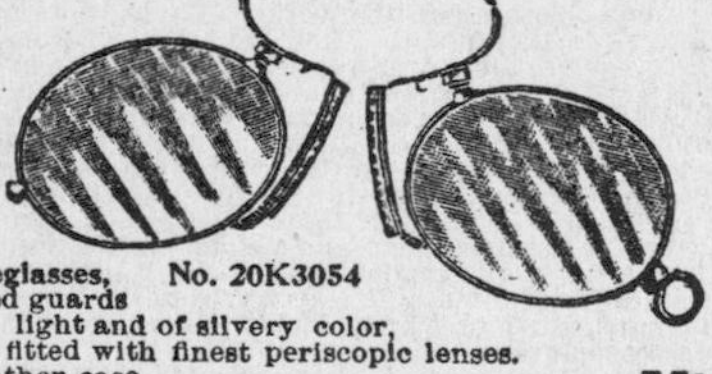

No. 20K3054

No. 20K3051 Alumnico Eyeglasses, flexible cork lined guards and oval spring, light and of silvery color, will not tarnish, fitted with finest periscopic lenses.
Price, with leather case.................................. **75c**

No. 20K3054 Gold Filled Eyeglasses, flexible cork lined guards and oval spring, warranted for ten years, fitted with finest crystalline lenses. The very highest grade gold filled flexible guard eyeglass frame that can be produced.
Price, with leather case.............................. **$1.25**
If by mail, postage extra, 5 cents.

OFFSET GUARD EYEGLASSES.

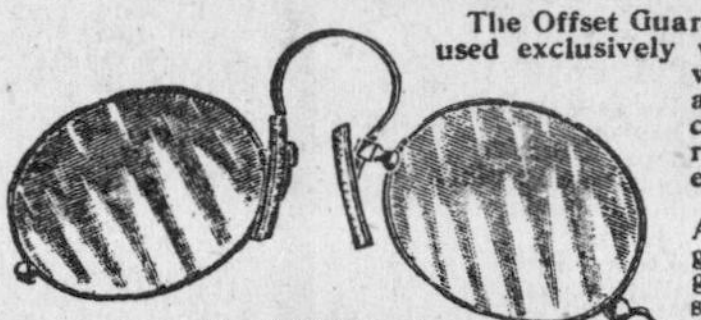

No. 20K3063

The Offset Guard Eyeglasses are used exclusively when glasses are worn constantly, as they are specially adapted to remain in a fixed position.

No. 20K3061 Alumnico Eyeglasses, offset guards, cork or shell lined, hoop spring, light and of silvery color, warranted not to tarnish, fitted with finest periscopic lenses.
Price, with leather case.................................. **75c**

No. 20K3063 Gold Filled Eyeglasses offset guards, either cork or shell lined, round hoop spring warranted for ten years, fitted with finest crystalline lenses. The very highest grade offset guard gold filled eyeglass frame that can be produced.
Price, with leather case **$1.25**

COLORED SPECTACLES.

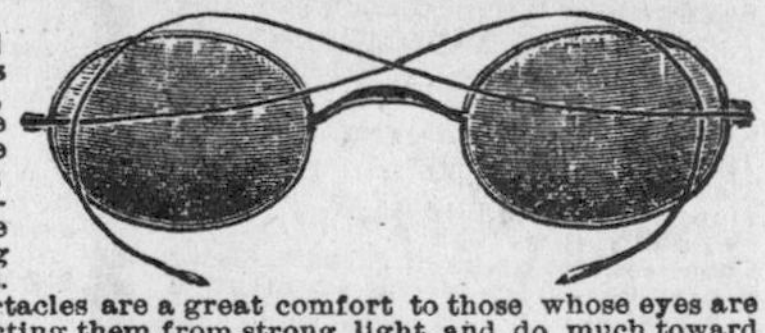

No. 20K3071 Colored Lens Spectacles, a high grade steel frame spectacle; with best colored coquille lenses, riding bow temples. **Colored spectacles are a great comfort to those whose eyes are weak, protecting them from strong light, and do much toward preserving the sight. Furnished with either smoke or blue lenses.** Price, with leather case.......................... **32c**
If by mail, postage extra, 5 cents.

COMBINATION OFFER

GOLD FILLED RIMLESS EYEGLASSES AND GOLD FILLED AUTOMATIC CHAIN $2.48, LATEST IMPROVED AUTOMATIC EYEGLASS CHAIN, HIGHEST GRADE RIMLESS EYEGLASSES, MOST STYLISH AND SATISFACTORY OUTFIT.

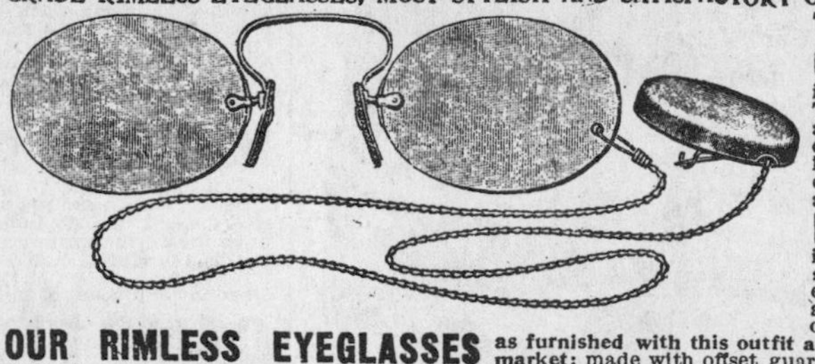

THE AUTOMATIC EYEGLASS CHAIN consists of a small neat case which may be pinned to the coat or the waist and in which is enclosed a spring controlling the chain. The chain is easily drawn out to its full length, and automatically winds itself up again in the case when it is given a slight twitch. This chain is of best quality gold filled, solid 10-karat gold over an inner white composition metal, fully guaranteed.

NO OTHER EYEGLASS CHAIN is so convenient, and no other eyeglass chain is so neat and stylish in appearance. It is suitable either for ladies' or gentlemen, usually being attached to the vest when worn by a gentleman, or to the waist when worn by a lady.

OUR RIMLESS EYEGLASSES as furnished with this outfit are the highest grade rimless eyeglasses on the market; made with offset guards lined with tortoise shell, the most comfortable style of guard to wear. All the metal parts of these eyeglasses are made from the highest grade gold filled stock, made with two heavy plates of solid gold over an inner plate of hard composition metal, beautifully finished and highly polished. As to quality, we guarantee that these rimless eyeglasses are genuine American Optical Company's goods, made from the very best stock, genuine 10-karat gold over an inner plate of composition metal, the very best gold filled eyeglasses that it is possible to produce.

THE LENSES. We fit these eyeglasses with extra high class crystalline lenses made from the very purest optical glass carefully selected and accurately centered.

OUR GUARANTEE. We send out this complete outfit, these high grade rimless gold filled eyeglasses with tortoise shell guards and gold filled automatic eyeglass chain and holder under our binding ten years' guarantee, under the terms of which we agree to replace this outfit or any part of it that gives out through defective materials or poor workmanship at any time within ten years.

No. 20K3090 Special outfit complete with Rimless Eyeglasses and Automatic Chain as illustrated and described above, together with fine, spring cover, leather case for the eyeglasses.
Price..(If by mail, postage extra, 6 cents.).......................... **$2.48**

OUR $1.85 GOLD FILLED SPECTACLES.

$1.85

OUR TEN-YEAR GUARANTEE. We put out every pair of these spectacles under our binding ten years' guarantee, and if they wear through, tarnish, discolor or give out by reason of defect in material or poor workmanship at any time within ten years, we will replace them with a new pair or refund the amount paid for them.

WHY WE CAN SELL SPECTACLES AT PRICES SO MUCH LOWER THAN ARE CHARGED BY OTHERS.

It has always been customary for opticians to make enormous profits and the prices asked are always entirely out of proportion to the actual value of the goods themselves. Opticians attempt to justify their extortionate prices on the plea that their customers are paying them for their skill, their time and their knowledge.

WE ARE ABLE, however, by reason of the enormous number of orders we receive for spectacles, to sell these goods on our regular staple merchandise small profit plan.

ABOUT THE QUALITY. Spectacles offer a greater opportunity for unscrupulous dealers to impose upon their customers than is found in any other line of merchandise. Spectacles, and particularly spectacle lenses, are made in a great variety of qualities, ranging all the way from the highest class of optically perfect goods down to trash that is not only worthless but liable to result in permanent injury to the wearer's eyesight. We could offer to our customers gold filled spectacles at $1.50 per pair, or $1.25, or $1.00, in fact, we could even sell gold filled spectacles, all complete, at 75 cents per pair if we used a low grade of lenses, cheap frames, and allowed our orders for spectacles to be filled by cheap incompetent workmen. We believe, however, that quality is more important, perhaps, in spectacles than any other line of merchandise. We believe that the very best is none too good, and when we offer you our special gold filled spectacle at $1.85, we absolutely guarantee that it is the highest grade gold filled spectacle that can be made. We guarantee that it is genuine 10-karat gold over the highest grade composition metal, made by the most expert and experienced workmen and fitted with the very highest grade, the very best quality centered crystalline lenses. We not only guarantee this gold filled spectacle to be the very best gold filled spectacle that can be made, but we guarantee it to be equal in every respect to gold filled spectacles sold by opticians at from $5.00 to $8.00 per pair.

WE GUARANTEE that the frame of our $1.85 gold filled spectacle is a genuine American Optical Co. frame, made by the American Optical Co., makers of the highest grade spectacle frame in the world.

REMEMBER, we send these glasses out with the understanding that if they are not perfectly satisfactory in every way, if they do not fit your eyes perfectly, enable you to see better than any other glasses you have ever worn, they can be returned to us at our expense, and we will refund your money.

No. 20K3080   Gold Filled Riding Bow Spectacles. Price, with leather case..$1.85
If by mail, postage extra, 5 cents.

CABLE BOW GOLD FILLED SPECTACLES FOR $1.98.

CABLE RIDING BOW SPECTACLES are the most comfortable and most satisfactory style of spectacles that can be worn. The secret of their comfort lies in the fact that the bows or temples are of a peculiar twisted construction made from the very highest grade fine gold filled wire twisted together like the strands of a rope, this peculiar construction being plainly shown in our large illustration. This method of making the bows renders them very flexible and somewhat larger than the regulation style, making it impossible for them to cut into the flesh back of the ears, thereby entirely doing away with the discomfort which is often experienced with the ordinary style.

$1.98

ABOUT THE QUALITY. In our cable bow gold filled spectacles at $1.98 we maintain exactly the same high standard of quality that we do in our $1.85 gold filled spectacles. We guarantee that the frame is a genuine American Optical Co. frame, the highest grade frame that can be manufactured, solid 10-karat gold over an inner white composition metal, exactly the same as our No. 20K3080 gold filled spectacles, except that the bows are made from fine, gold filled, twisted wire instead of the one-piece gold filled wire. We guarantee that the lenses are the very highest grade genuine crystalline lenses, accurately centered.

OUR 10-YEAR GUARANTEE. We send these spectacles out with the understanding and agreement that the gold will not wear off, discolor nor tarnish in ten years' constant use. If these spectacles give out, through any defect in material or through poor workmanship, or if they tarnish, discolor or wear off at any time within ten years, we will replace them with a new pair absolutely free of charge.

OUR CABLE RIDING BOW GOLD FILLED SPECTACLES are fitted with the highest grade periscopic crystalline lenses, accurately centered, carefully selected, in accordance with your answers to our best questions, and, if they do not fit your eyes perfectly, if you do not find them better than any other spectacles you have ever worn, they can be returned to us at our expense, and we will refund your money, including postage both ways.

No. 20K3083 Cable Riding Bow Gold Filled Spectacles. Price, with leather case, $1.98
If by mail, postage extra, 5 cents.

RIMLESS SPECTACLES AT $2.14.

$2.14

STYLISH AND ELEGANT. Rimless spectacles are the very latest and most stylish spectacles made. They are light and elegant in appearance, comfortable to wear and contribute in no small measure towards giving the wearer a neat and dressy appearance.

ABOUT THE QUALITY. Our rimless spectacles, like all of our other high grade spectacles, are genuine American Optical Co. goods, both the lenses and the frames manufactured in this celebrated factory, the very highest grade frames and the very highest grade genuine crystalline centered lenses that are made. There are cheap rimless spectacles on the market, the same as there are cheap spectacles of all kinds, and by handling these cheap second quality goods we could very easily sell rimless spectacles at any price from $1.00 up, but we believe that it pays to handle only the very highest grade of spectacles and to sell the very highest grade at about one-fourth the price which the ordinary optician is compelled to charge for similar goods.

OUR 10-YEAR GUARANTEE. These rimless spectacles are guaranteed against discoloration or tarnishing, and if the gold wears off, if they discolor or tarnish, or give out in any way, through poor materials or workmanship at any time within ten years we will send you a new pair or refund your money. You take absolutely no chance in ordering spectacles from us, as we will return your money immediately if the spectacles are not in every way satisfactory.

IF YOU ALREADY HAVE A PAIR OF SPECTACLES that suit your eyes and would like to own a pair of our high grade, gold filled, rimless spectacles, we suggest that you tell us the number of your lenses, if you know it, or, if not, that you send us your spectacles, and we will select from our stock a pair of these high grade, gold filled spectacles, with lenses of exactly the same strength as your own and of the same dimensions, so that they will fit you just as well as the old pair.

No. 20K3086 Gold Filled Rimless Spectacles, as described and illustrated above.   Price with leather case............(If by mail, postage extra, 5 cents)..............$2.14

OUR RIMLESS EYE GLASSES FOR $1.65.

OUR RIMLESS EYE GLASSES are made with offset guards, lined either with cork or tortoise shell, the mountings are the very highest grade gold filled stock, guaranteed, made with two heavy plates of fine, solid gold over an inner plate of hard composition metal, beautifully polished and finished. The lenses are extra high grade crystalline lenses, accurately centered, made from the very purest optical glass, carefully selected to meet the requirements indicated by your answers to our test questions.

ABOUT THE QUALITY. We guarantee that our rimless eye glasses are genuine American Optical Co. goods, made from the very finest stock, genuine 10-karat gold, highest grade centered crystalline lenses, both the lenses and the frames made by the American Optical Co. By departing from our regular high standard of excellence we could put up a pair of rimless eye glasses that would apparently look just as good as our regular style, and sell them for $1.50 or $1.00; or by using a gold plated frame and cheap non-centered lenses we could even make the price considerably below $1.00, but we do not believe that our customers wish to risk their eyesight for the sake of saving a few cents on a pair of glasses.

EVERY PAIR OF OUR RIMLESS EYE GLASSES is sent out under our binding ten years' guarantee, under the terms of which we agree to replace any pair that tarnish, wear off, or give out through defective materials or poor workmanship in ten years. A pair of carefully adjusted high grade gold filled rimless eye glasses gives the wearer a distinguished and prosperous appearance which is entirely lacking with the ordinary styles of spectacles.

$1.65

REMEMBER every order for either spectacles or eye glasses receives the careful personal attention of our expert optician, a graduate of the Northern Illinois College of Ophthalmology, who has for years made a special study of fitting spectacles by mail.

REMEMBER that every pair of spectacles or eye glasses which we sell is sent out with the distinct understanding and agreement that if they are to fit your eyes perfectly, if you do not find the glasses entirely satisfactory in every way, if they do not enable you to see better than any other glasses you have ever worn, they may be returned to us and your money will be refunded, including postage both ways.

No. 20K3089 Rimless Eye Glasses. Price, with leather case.. $1.65
If by mail, postage extra, 5 cents.

Eyeglass Chains.

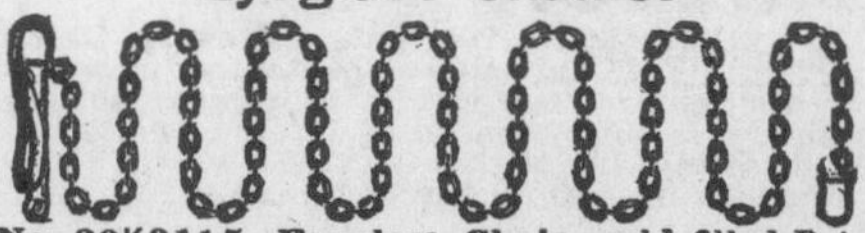

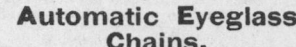

No. 20K3115 Eyeglass Chain, gold filled. Price, with snap and hook, 35c; with snap and hairpin, 33c; with snap and earloop........32c

No. 20K3117 Eyeglass Chain, extra quality, gold filled, fully guaranteed. Price, with snap and hook, 58c; with snap and hairpin, 55c; with snap and earloop........51c

No. 20K3119 Eyeglass Chain, best quality, solid 10k gold. Price, with snap and hook, $1.35; with snap and hairpin, $1.50; with snap and earloop........80c

Postage extra on any style chain, 2 cents.

Automatic Eyeglass Chains.

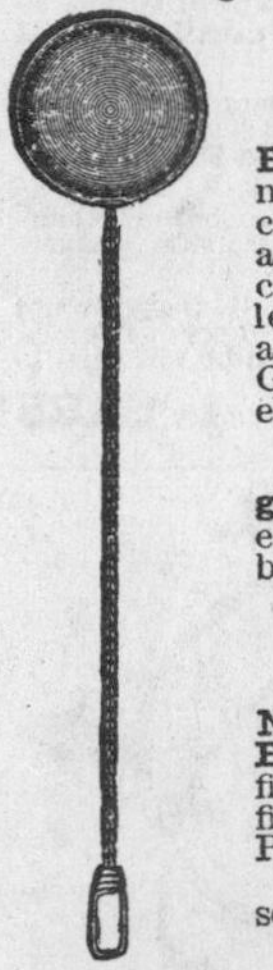

No. 20K3121 The Automatic Eyeglass Chain consists of a small neat case which may be pinned to the coat or waist and in which is enclosed a spring controlling the chain. The chain is easily drawn out to its full length, and upon a slight twitch it automatically returns to the case. German silver chain with black enameled case. Price........45c
If by mail, postage extra, 2 cents.

No. 20K3122 Automatic Eyeglass Chain. Same as No. 20K3121, except that both chain and case are best quality gold filled. Guaranteed. Price........$1.29
If by mail, postage extra, 2 cents.

Eyeglass Hooks.

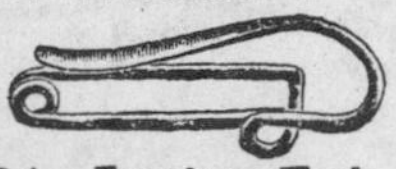

No. 20K3129 Eyeglass Hook, fine quality gold filled. Price......15c

No. 20K3131 Eyeglass Hook, solid gold, extra quality. Price....62c
If by mail, postage extra, 2 cents.

Murine Eye Remedy.

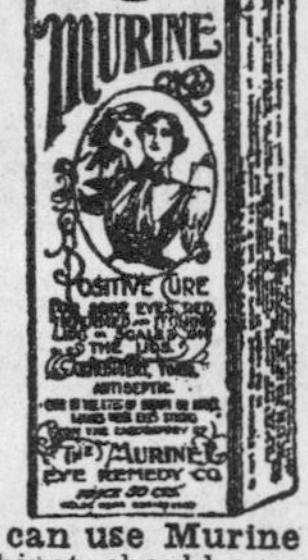

No. 20K3140 Murine is a preparation for the relief of diseased conditions of the eye, an absolutely harmless, pure distilled product. Murine is good for weak eyes, inflamed eyes, sore eyes, relieves tired eyes, watering eyes, granulated lids, removes floating spots in eyes, clears vision, brightens dull eyes, relieves pain in injured eyes. Murine can be used by anybody, may be used as often as desired; it always benefits the eyes, and never harms them. School children's eyes are strengthened by Murine, professional men find relief from eye strain in Murine. Farmers, railroadmen and others exposed to wind and weatherare greatly benefited by Murine. Everybody can use Murine to advantage, and every medicine cabinet should contain a bottle of it. We know Murine is the best eye medicine in the world.

Price per bottle, complete with dropper........40c
Extra for postage and mailing case, if sent by mail, 10c.

Eye Shades.

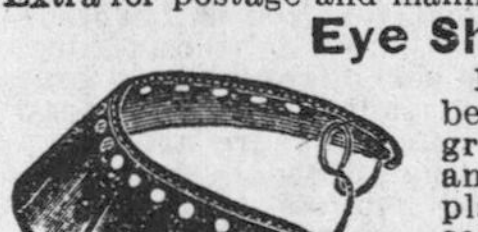

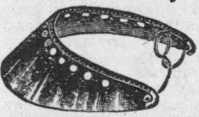

No. 20K3160 Eye Shade, best grade transparent green celluloid, very light and comfortable. Held in place by light elastic cord, self adjusting. Price.....7c
Postage extra, 2 cents.

Goggles and Eye Protectors.

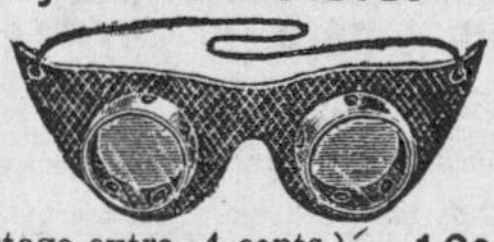

No. 20K3166 Fine Leather Goggles, with lenses in perforated aluminum mountings, so as to allow perfect ventilation. High grade clear lenses, 1½ inches in diameter. Price....(Postage extra, 4 cents.)...12c

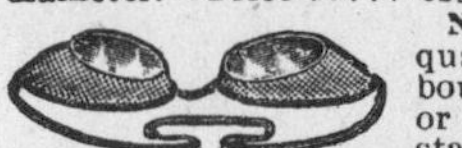

No. 20K3169 Goggles, good quality, wire gauze, velvet bound edges, with smoke, blue or clear glasses. Be sure to state color of glasses desired. Each pair in cloth bound box. Price........20c
If by mail, postage extra, 3 cents.

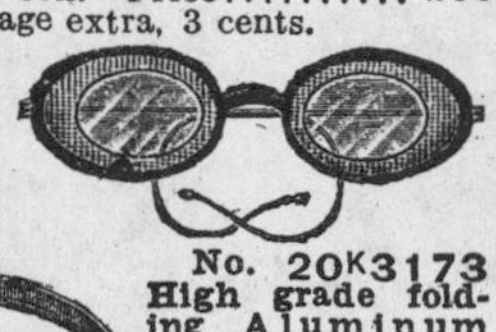

No. 20K3171 Goggles, steel frame, velvet bound, finely finished, with stiff nose piece and tempered riding bow temples. Extra fine wire gauze and highest grade light smoke lenses. Price...95c
If by mail, postage extra, 4c.

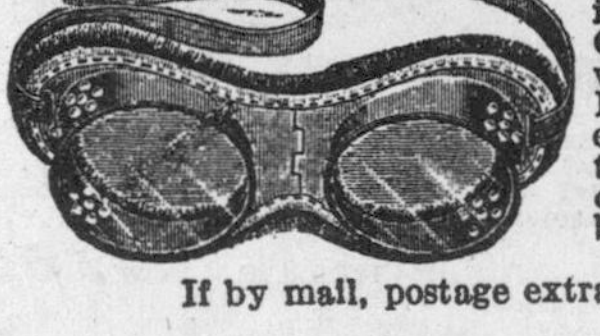

No. 20K3173 High grade folding Aluminum Goggles. Bound with silk chenille. Mountings perforated to allow ventilation. Extra large, clear lenses. Elastic band and clasp. Price......60c
If by mail, postage extra, 4 cents.

Automobile Goggles, 95 Cents.

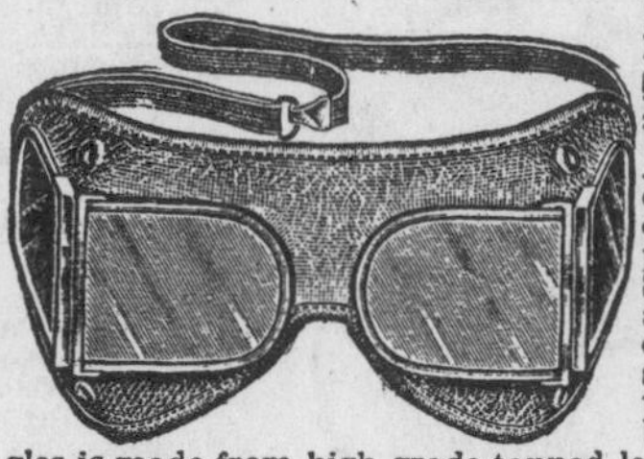

No. 20K3176 Extra high grade, four lens, Automobile Goggles. All lenses are detachable and can be easily replaced if broken. Side lenses enable one to see clearly to the side as well as to the front. The body of the goggles is made from high grade tanned leather, and lined with silk. Holes for ventilation. Elastic band and clasp. Price........95c
If by mail, postage extra, 5 cents.

Scenery or Shooting Spectacles.

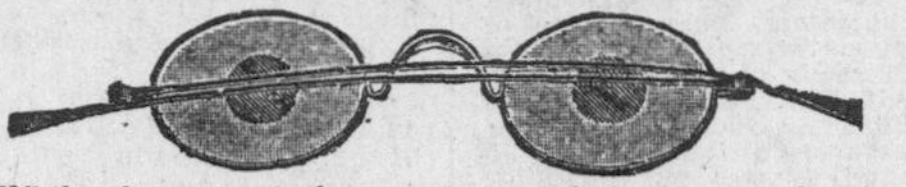

While these spectacles are commonly known as shooting spectacles, they are largely used by tourists in looking at scenery, especially where the light is bright and dazzling or when the ground is covered with snow, which reflects the light and tires the eyes.

The peculiar amber tint of the lenses, not only improves the view but enables one to see more plainly at a distance, and is very pleasant and soothing to the eye. The lenses are known as diaphragm lenses, being sanded or ground in such a manner as to exclude the view except through the clear circle in the center of each lens.

No. 20K3187 Shooting Spectacles, steel frames, straight temples, good quality, nickel plated, amber tinted diaphragm lenses. Price........16c

No. 20K3189 Shooting Spectacles, steel frames, straight temples, best quality, finely tempered with bronze finish. Best amber tinted diaphragm lenses. Price........29c

No. 20K3191 Shooting Spectacles, steel frames, same as illustration, but with riding bow temples, fine quality, extra finish, with best grade amber tinted diaphragm lenses. Price........35c

No. 20K3193 Shooting Spectacles, steel frames, straight temples, best quality, finely tempered and extra finish, with best grade smoke tinted diaphragm lenses. Price.......42c
If by mail, postage extra, any style, 5 cents.

Our 75-Cent Dust Protector.

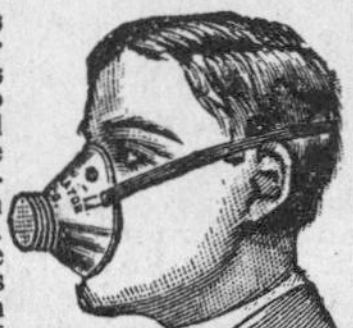

No. 20K3201 Against dust it is the greatest protector ever made. For thrashers, grain men, millers, farmers and everyone whose duties call him into dusty places. It is worth a thousand times its cost as a protection to the lungs, to the general health and comfort. Thousands of men are saved from consumption by the use of this protector. It protects the nose and mouth from the intrusion of dust which is so injurious to the head and lungs. No miller, grain buyer, thrasher or farmer is safe without one. They afford perfect protection with perfect ventilation. Made of fine metal, handsomely nickel plated, bound with chamois skin, adjustable to anyone by strong elastic band, absolutely indestructible and worth a thousand times the trifling cost as a safeguard to health. Each protector comes packed in a neat box with full instructions for use. Price........75c
If by mail, postage extra, 5 cents.

Conversation Tubes.

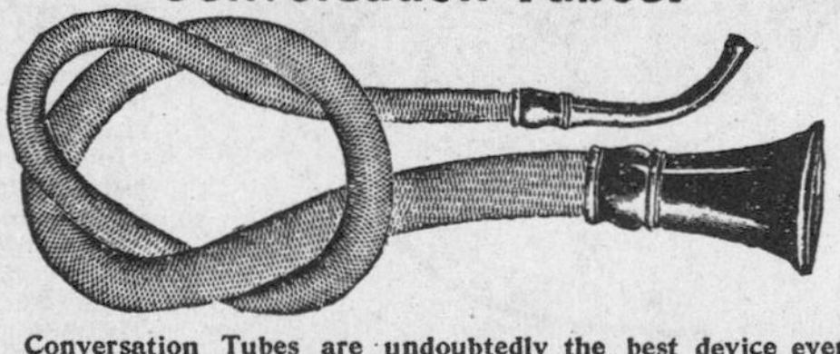

Conversation Tubes are undoubtedly the best device ever made for the relief of deafness, and these are the very highest grade of conversation tubes made; finely constructed throughout, with a peculiar metallic spiral lining, which gives the tube great flexibility and at the same time keeps it fully distended in any position.

No. 20K3250 Mohair Conversation Tube, medium size, tapered, covered with flexible mohair, hard rubber ear piece and bell. Price........$1.30
If by mail, postage extra, 13 cents.

No. 20K3251 Mohair Conversation Tube, same as No. 20K3250, but larger size, 3 feet in length. Price.....$1.40
If by mail, postage extra, 20 cents.

No. 20K3255 Silk Conversation Tube, very highest grade manufactured, covered with finest quality black silk, tapered tube, medium size. Price........$1.60
If by mail, postage extra, 13 cents.

No. 20K3256 Silk Conversation Tube, same style and quality as No. 20K3255, but larger size, 3 feet in length. Price.....(If by mail, postage extra, 20 cents)......$1.75

Miss Greene Hearing Horn, $1.25.

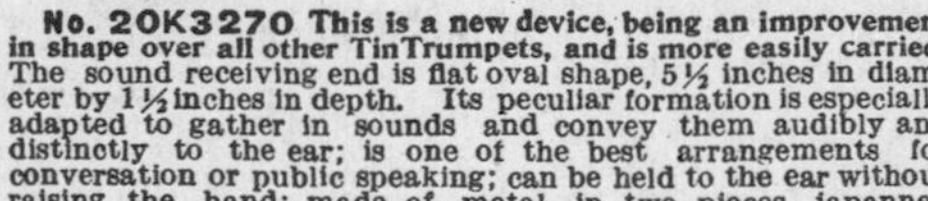

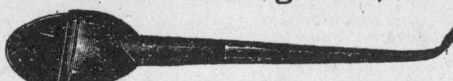

No. 20K3270 This is a new device, being an improvement in shape over all other TinTrumpets, and is more easily carried. The sound receiving end is flat oval shape, 5½ inches in diameter by 1½ inches in depth. Its peculiar formation is especially adapted to gather in sounds and convey them audibly and distinctly to the ear; is one of the best arrangements for conversation or public speaking; can be held to the ear without raising the hand; made of metal, in two pieces, japanned black. Price........$1.25
If by mail, postage extra, 13 cents.

Hearing Horns.

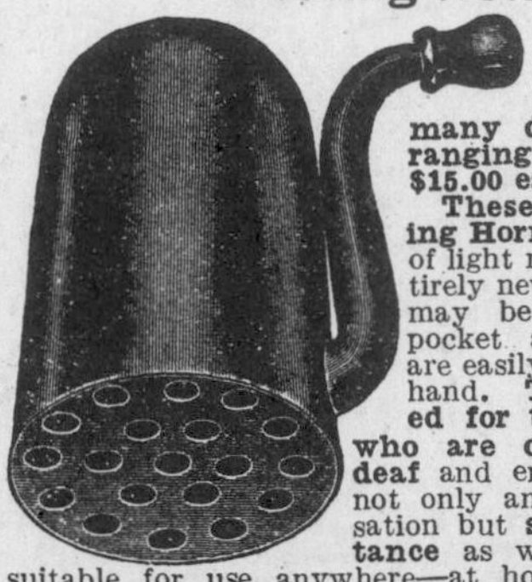

These horns are exactly the same as those advertised by many dealers at prices ranging from $8.00 to $15.00 each.

These London Hearing Horns are constructed of light metal upon an entirely new principle. They may be carried in the pocket and when in use are easily concealed in the hand. They are designed for the use of those who are only moderately deaf and enable one to hear not only an ordinary conversation but sounds at a distance as well, making them suitable for use anywhere—at home, in church, or public entertainments.

Made in Two Sizes, with Black Oxidized Finish.

No. 20K3265 London Hearing Horn, medium size, 2½ inches in length. Price........$1.20
If by mail, postage extra, 7 cents.

No. 20K3267 London Hearing Horn, large size, 4 inches in length. Price........$1.30
If by mail, postage extra, 8 cents.

Your money will be promptly refunded if the horn does not give entire satisfaction.

Highest Grade French Reading Glasses.

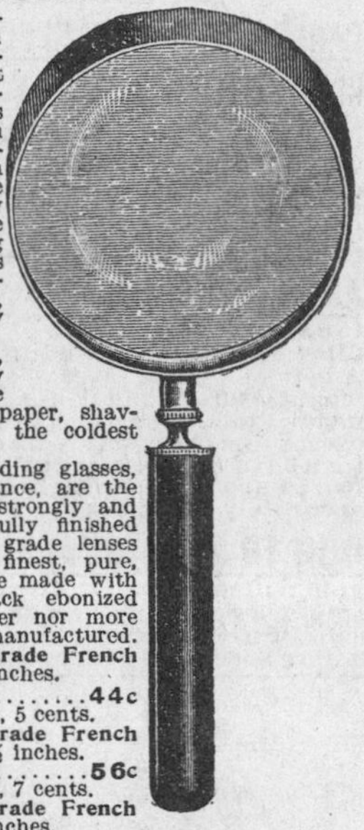

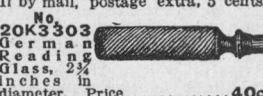

These finely made, beautifully finished and powerful reading glasses are very desirable for reading small print and for general use in looking at pictures, small objects or for any purpose for which a magnifying glass is required. Old people find them especially desirable, as the large range of vision they afford is very restful to the eyes. These reading glasses bring out the details of photographs or other pictures in a wonderful manner, adding greatly to their beauty and interest.

Used as Burning Glasses, these reading glasses are very powerful, readily setting fire to light materials, such as paper, shavings or dry leaves, even in the coldest winter weather.

Made in Paris. These reading glasses, which are made in Paris, France, are the best readers manufactured, strongly and substantially made, beautifully finished and fitted with extra high grade lenses specially ground from the finest, pure, clear optical glass. They are made with nickel plated rims and black ebonized handles. There are no better nor more powerful glasses than these manufactured.

No. 20K3319 Best Grade French Reading Glass, diameter, 2 inches. Price........44c
If by mail, postage extra, 5 cents.

No. 20K3321 Best Grade French Reading Glass, diameter, 2½ inches. Price........56c
If by mail, postage extra, 7 cents.

No. 20K3323 Best Grade French Reading Glass, diameter, 3 inches. Price........72c
If by mail, postage extra, 9 cents.

No. 20K3326 Best Grade French Reading Glass, diameter, 4 inches. Price........$1.25
If by mail, postage extra, 14 cents.

No. 20K3328 Best Grade French Reading Glass, diameter, 5 inches. Price........$2.10
If by mail, postage extra, 22 cents.

Pearl and Gold Reading Glass, $2.60.

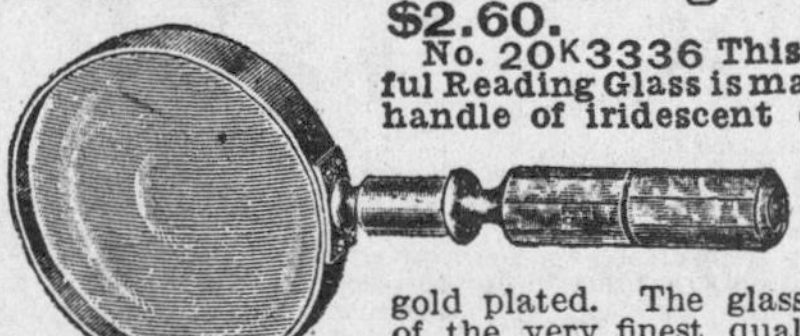

No. 20K3336 This beautiful Reading Glass is made with handle of iridescent oriental pearl, and all metal parts heavily gold plated. The glass itself is of the very finest quality, 3½ inches in diameter, making an instrument that is not only serviceable and useful to the fullest extent, but at the same time of the richest and most ornamental appearance. Price....$2.60
If by mail, postage extra, 15 cents.

German Reading Glasses.

These reading glasses, Nos. 20K3301 to 20K3311, inclusive, are suitable for the same purposes as our best grade French reading glasses, but are not so finely made and not quite so powerful.

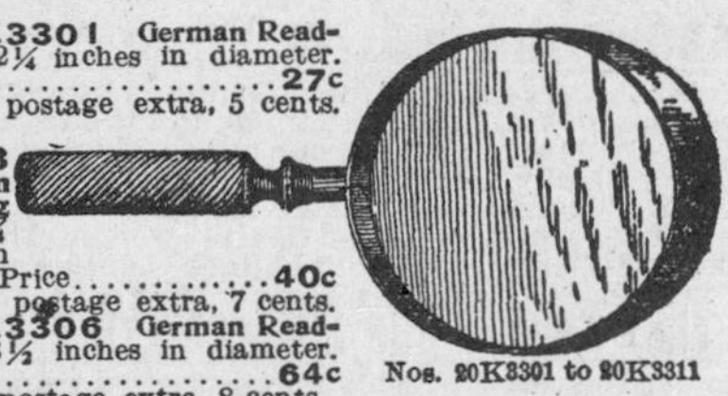
Nos. 20K3301 to 20K3311

No. 20K3301 German Reading Glass, 2¼ inches in diameter. Price........27c
If by mail, postage extra, 5 cents.

No. 20K3303 German Reading Glass, 2¾ inches in diameter. Price........40c
If by mail, postage extra, 7 cents.

No. 20K3306 German Reading Glass, 3½ inches in diameter. Price........64c
If by mail, postage extra, 8 cents.

No. 20K3309 German Reading Glass, 4 inches in diameter. Price....(If by mail, postage extra, 13 cents.)..70c

No. 20K3311 German Reading Glass, 5 inches in diameter. Price....(If by mail, postage extra, 16 cents)..$1.40

OPERA GLASSES.

Chevalier Opera Glass, $2.25.

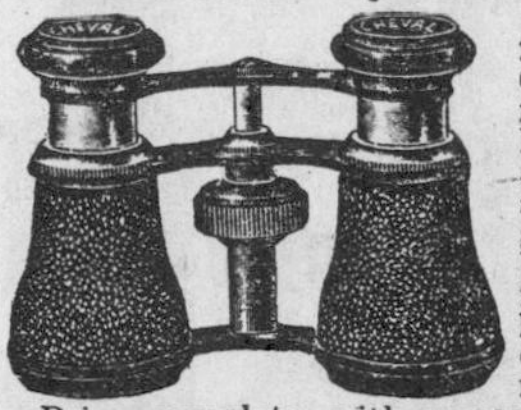

No. 20K3402 **This is a genuine Chevalier Opera Glass,** made with first quality achromatic lenses, 1⅛ inches in diameter. The center bar and the draw tubes are gold plated. The cross bars and tops are finished in black enamel and the leather covering is a fine quality of black pebbled morocco.

Price, complete, with morocco case.........**$2.25**
If by mail, postage extra, 10 cents.

Marchand Opera Glass, $2.75.

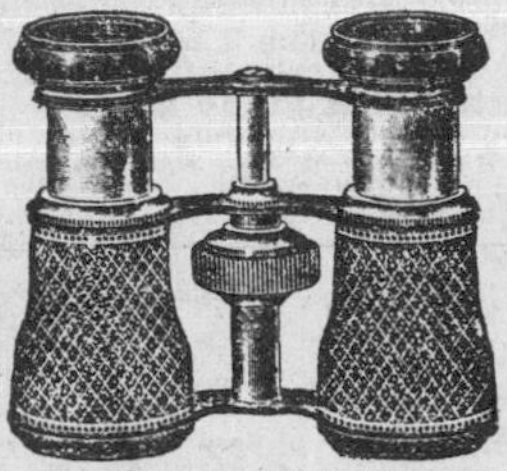

No. 20K3407 **This Opera Glass is made by Marchand, Paris,** and fitted with fine achromatic lenses, 1⅛ inches in diameter. The barrels are covered with dark maroon leather and ornamented with two narrow, beaded gold bands. The center bar, draw tubes and other trimmings are gold plated and the tops and cross bars are finished in bright, black enamel. This opera glass is made with extra large eyepieces and is a good, serviceable instrument, at a very low price.

Price, complete, with morocco case.........**$2.75**
If by mail, postage extra, 12 cents.

Marchand Pearl Opera Glass, $4.20.

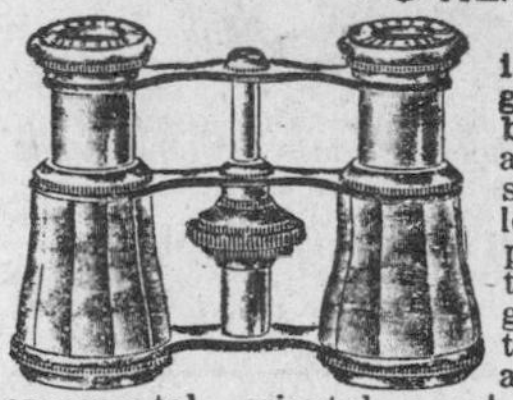

No. 20K3412 **This is a beautiful pearl and gold Opera Glass, made by Marchand, Paris,** and one of the best instruments ever sold for so low a price. All metal parts, including draw tubes and cross bars are gold plated. The bodies, tops and focusing screw are covered with highly ornamental, oriental pearl, and the first quality achromatic lenses are 1 inch in diameter.

Price, complete, with morocco case.........**$4.20**
If by mail, postage extra, 10 cents.

Colmont's Gold Banded Pearl Opera Glass, $7.90.

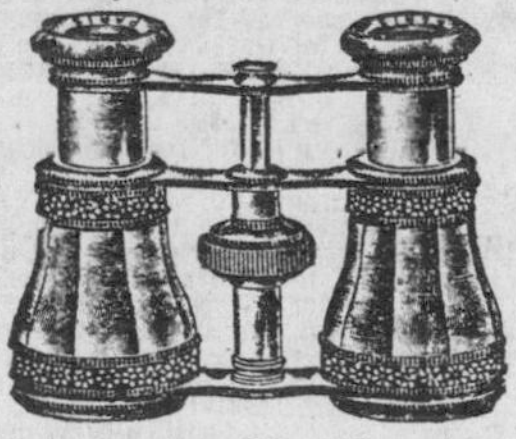

No. 20K3417 **This is the very highest grade Opera Glass that we handle,** a genuine Colmont beautifully made, fitted with the very highest quality of achromatic lenses, exquisitely finished throughout in pearl and gold. Colmont's opera glasses are recognized as instruments of the highest grade, and this is one of the most popular styles produced by this maker. The pearl is an extra quality, pure iridescent white. The barrels are further ornamented by two highly decorative openwork gold bands. A beautiful glass for ladies' use; of the highest degree of optical perfection, and as beautiful as a piece of jewelry.

Price, complete, with morocco case.........**$7.90**
If by mail, postage extra, 14 cents.

FIELD GLASSES.

Chevalier Field Glass at $2.80.

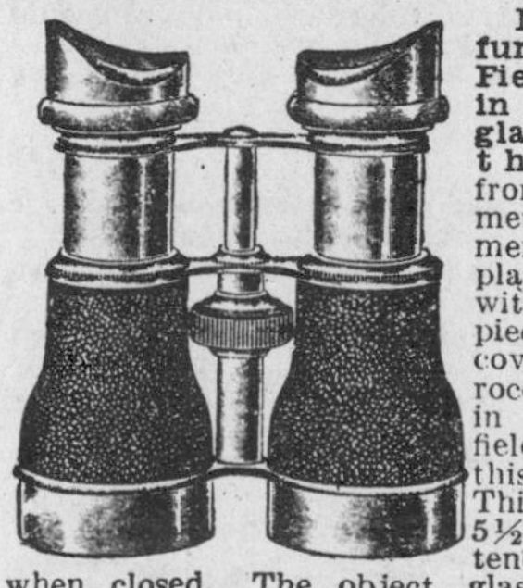

No. 20K3430 **We furnish this Chevalier Field Glass as the equal in every way of field glasses sold all through the country** at from $5.00 to $8.00. All metal parts of this instrument are heavily nickel plated, and it is made with special hooded eyepieces. The barrels are covered with black morocco leather, and it is, in our opinion, the best field glass ever sold at this exceedingly low price. This field glass measures 5½ inches high when extended, 4⅜ inches high when closed. The object glasses are 19 lignes in diameter. The weight is 16½ ounces, and the magnifying power, three times.

Price, complete, with leather case and strap. **$2.80**
If by mail, postage extra, 39 cents.

Genuine Marchand Field Glass, $5.95.

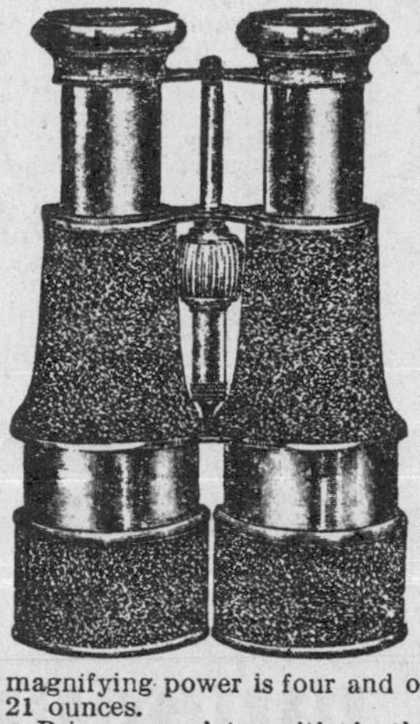

No. 20K3435 **This genuine Marchand Field Glass is fitted with high class achromatic lenses, extra large eyepieces.** All metal parts are finished in bright, black enamel, and the covering is a fine quality of black pebbled morocco leather. As compared with other field glasses sold at moderate prices, this instrument is better made, better finished, and gives finer definition and greater clearness than glasses ordinarily retailed at from $10.00 to $12.00. This glass is made with extension sun shades, and measures 7 inches high when extended, 5½ inches when closed. The object glasses are 24 lignes in diameter and the magnifying power is four and one-half times. Weight, 21 ounces.

Price, complete, with leather case and shoulder strap.........................**$5.95**
If by mail, postage extra, 39 cents.

Genuine Colmont Field Glass, $7.95.

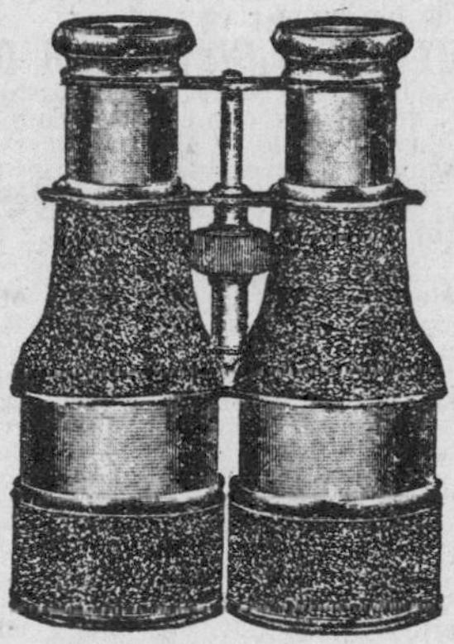

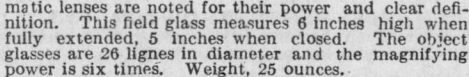

No. 20K3445 **The name "Colmont" is in itself a guarantee of quality,** and we can recommend this instrument to anyone desiring a strictly high class field glass of the best optical qualities. It is strongly and substantially made, good materials and workmanship throughout insuring strength and durability. This glass is made with extension sun shades, all metal parts finished in bright, black enamel, the leather covering is the best quality of black morocco leather, the eyepieces are extra large, making it an easy glass to use, and the fine achromatic lenses are noted for their power and clear definition. This field glass measures 6 inches high when fully extended, 5 inches when closed. The object glasses are 26 lignes in diameter and the magnifying power is six times. Weight, 25 ounces.

Price, complete, with leather case and shoulder strap.........................**$7.95**
If by mail, postage extra, 47 cents.

$6.80 Buys a $15.00 Field Glass.

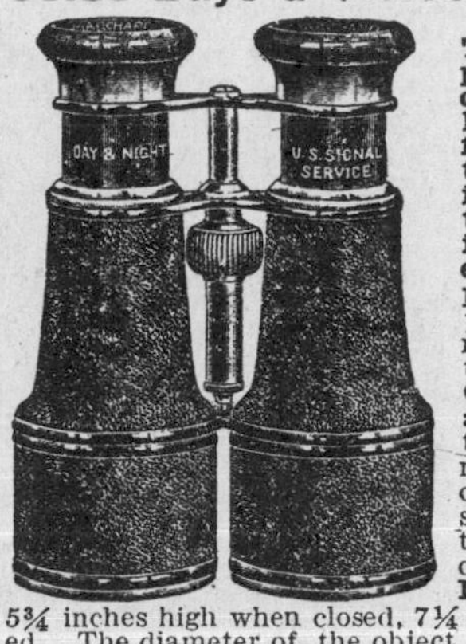

No. 20K3440 **This Field Glass is provided with first quality achromatic lenses, carefully fitted; the draw tubes are finished in dead black and the trimmings are in bright black enamel and nickel plate.** This glass possesses higher magnifying power than the Marchand Field Glass, and the lenses are of better quality, thus giving finer definition and greater clearness. Workmanship and materials throughout are first class. **Our $6.80 Field Glass** measures 5¾ inches high when closed, 7¼ inches when extended. The diameter of the object glasses is 24 lignes, the magnifying power is five times and the weight is 22 ounces.

Price, complete, with leather case and strap.**$6.80**
If by mail, postage extra, 36 cents.

Jena Special Tourists' Field Glass, $10.80.

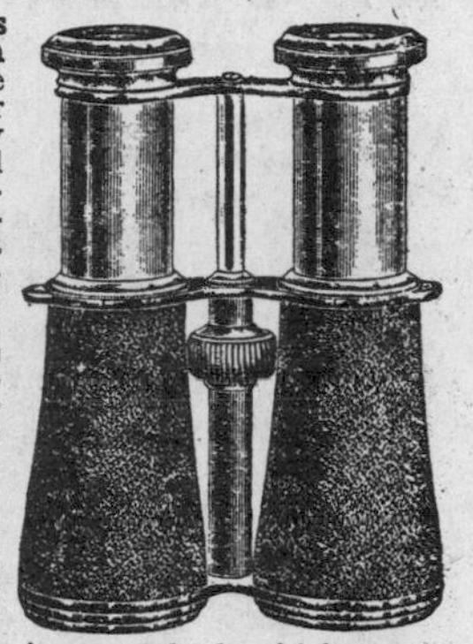

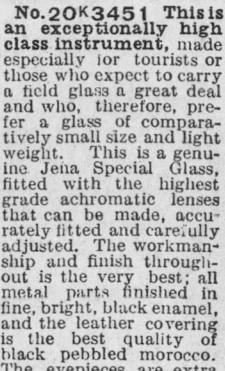

No. 20K3451 **This is an exceptionally high class instrument,** made especially for tourists or those who expect to carry a field glass a great deal and who, therefore, prefer a glass of comparatively small size and light weight. This is a genuine Jena Special Glass, fitted with the highest grade achromatic lenses that can be made, accurately fitted and carefully adjusted. The workmanship and finish throughout is the very best; all metal parts finished in fine, bright, black enamel, and the leather covering is the best quality of black pebbled morocco. The eyepieces are extra large and the high grade achromatic object glasses, made from genuine Jena special glass, are noted for their definition and clearness. This Jena Special Tourists' Field Glass measures 6¾ inches high, when fully extended and 4⅜ inches high, when closed. The object glasses are 19 lignes in diameter and the magnifying power is five times.

Price, complete, with leather case and shoulder strap.........................**$10.80**
If by mail, postage extra, 32 cents.

THE SURPRISINGLY LOW REDUCED PRICES prevailing in this catalogue mean **GREATER SAVINGS TO OUR CUSTOMERS than ever before.**

$12.95 For Our Highest Grade Genuine Jena Special Field Glass.

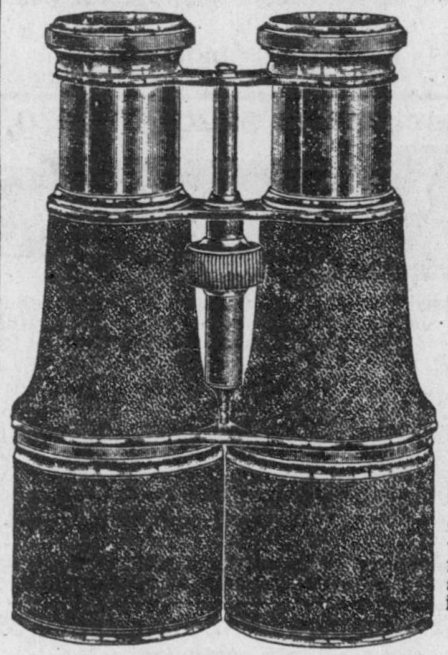

No. 20K3454 **This large illustration, engraved by our artist direct from a photograph, will give you an idea of the appearance of our JENA SPECIAL FIELD GLASS. The lenses of this field glass are ground from the famous Jena special optical glass, made in the Jena glass factory in Germany.**

IT IS FROM THIS SPECIAL NEW GLASS, this latest result of the experiments and investigations of the most skilled and scientific glass makers of Europe, that the lenses for our Jena Special Field Glasses are ground. They are ground by the most skilled lens grinders, they are fitted with the utmost care, and they are accurately adjusted. **These lenses combine, to a degree never before attained, the highest power with the most marvelous definition and clearness.**

WE OFFER THE JENA SPECIAL FIELD GLASS, not merely as the equal of glasses sold by other dealers at several times our price, but we offer it as absolutely the best field glass that can be obtained at any price. We sell this glass under a positive guarantee, and if you do not find it superior to any field glass to which you may compare it, you may return it at our expense and we will refund your money.

BEAR IN MIND that our special $12.95 price, is for the large size Jena Special Field Glass with lenses 26 lignes in diameter. This field glass measures 6 inches high when closed and 7¾ inches when extended, weighs 33 ounces, and the magnifying power is seven times. The draw tubes, cross bars, tops and trimmings are all finished in fine black enamel and the covering is the best grade of morocco leather.

Price, complete, with fine case and strap............**$12.95**
If by mail, postage extra, 64 cents.

No. 20K3455 **OUR JENA SPECIAL ALUMINUM FIELD GLASS.** Exactly the same as our No. 20K3454, except that **all metal parts are made of aluminum,** thus reducing the weight and adding to its handsome appearance. The highly polished draw tubes are finished in the natural silvery color of aluminum, all trimmings are finished in black and the covering is morocco leather. Weight, only 18 ounces.

Price, complete, with fine case and strap.................................**$15.60**
If by mail, postage extra, 42 cents.

Maxim Binocular Telescope for $19.25.

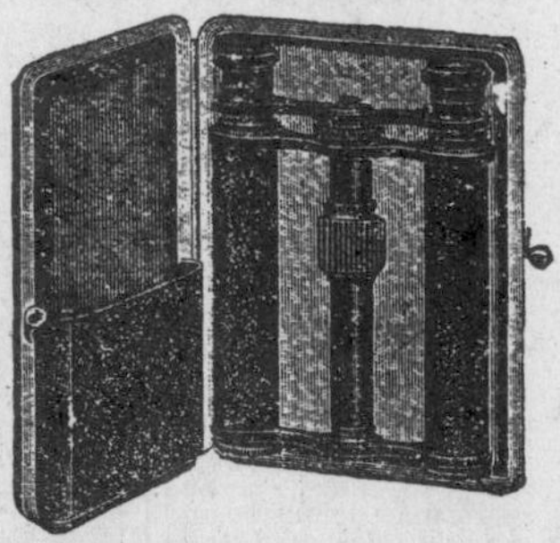

An exceedingly small and compact instrument of high magnifying power. This is a genuine Maxim Double Telescope, made by Maxim, the celebrated Paris telescope maker, and is the handiest and most efficient instrument of this kind ever devised. It is an ideal glass for tourists, farmers, hunters, ranchmen, stockmen or anyone requiring **a powerful instrument which at the same time is small in size, light and compact. Our special Binocular Telescope weighs only 9 ounces and is so compact that it may be carried in the coat pocket as easily as a pocketbook, yet has a magnifying power of nine times or one-half again as high a power as the best field glasses.** Our illustration shows the glass in the fine silk lined morocco leather pocket case, which is included without extra charge. **When closed our Special Binocular Telescope measures only 4¾ inches high, the distance from side to side is only 3½ inches and the barrels are only ¾ of an inch in diameter. The length when extended for use is 6¾ inches.** The lenses with which our Special Binocular Telescope is fitted are the best quality achromatic, accurately fitted and adjusted. Diameter of field of view at 1,000 yards is 210 feet. The magnifying power is nine times and the definition is exceptionally fine.

No. 20K3460 Maxim Double Telescope. Price, complete with morocco pocket case, as shown in illustration....**$19.25**
If by mail, postage extra, 22 cents.

Nine-Power Busch Prism Binocular, $33.50.

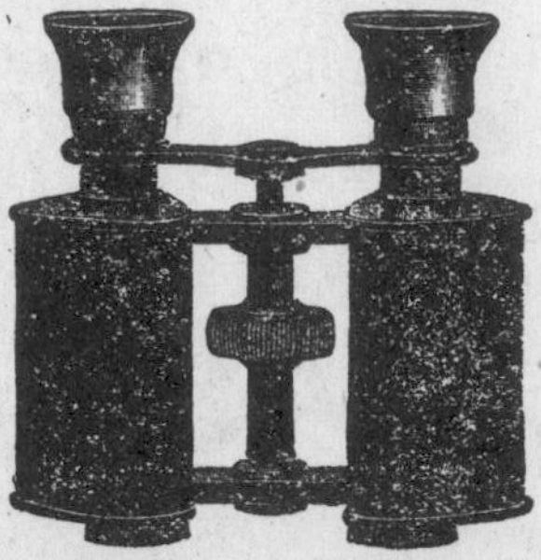

The Busch Prism Binoculars are made with a view to securing the greatest possible solidity and durability combined with the necessary portability, ease of manipulation and lightness of weight.

The bars and bodies are made from one solid casting of an especially hard alloy of aluminum. The working parts are of brass. This form of construction makes it possible to use fewer parts, fewer screws, and renders it almost **impossible for the glass to get out of optical adjustment. The bodies** are covered with the very finest black pebbled morocco leather and all exposed metal parts are finished in fine bright black enamel, highly polished.

The Busch Prism Binocular is adjustable for pupillary distances in a simple way by bending the hinged bars to the necessary width. The focus screw is large and centrally located, as shown in our illustration. The eyepiece of the right barrel is made movable to allow for adjustment of differences in the power of the users' eyes.

These Binoculars are made by the RATHENOWER OPTISCHE INDUSTRIE-ANSTALT, one of the largest optical concerns in Europe, noted for the production of extra high grade goods.

No. 20K3465 9-Power Busch Prism Binocular. Linear magnifying power, 9 diameters. (Superficial power, 81 times). Real field of view, 4.6 deg. Diameter field of view at 1,000 yards, 240 feet. Price, with solid sole leather case and shoulder strap....**$33.50**
If by mail, postage extra, 38 cents.

BUSCH TERLUX PRISM BINOCULAR $55.00

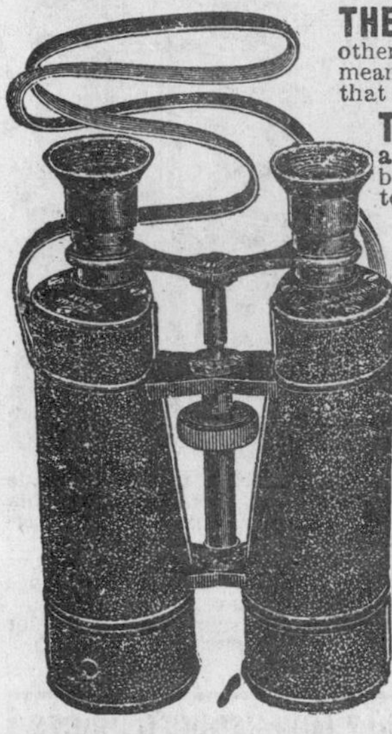

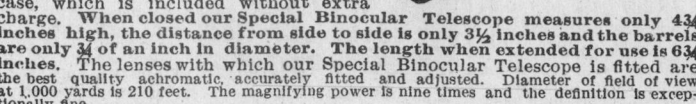

THE OBJECTIVE LENSES of the Busch Terlux Prism Binocular are one and three-eighths inches in diameter, almost twice the diameter of any other prism binocular glass made, and as the illumination increases in proportion to the square, this means that the Busch Terlux Prism Binocular glass admits almost four times the volume of light that is admitted by any other binocular glass made.

THE BUSCH TERLUX PRISM BINOCULAR GLASS is so designed as to secure the greatest possible solidity and durability, compatible with ease of manipulation and lightness of weight. The bodies and crossbars are made from one solid casting, of an especially hard alloy of aluminum, to secure the greatest possible solidity and rigidity, thus insuring permanent alignment, with the least possible weight. The working parts are brass, the bodies are covered with the very finest black pebbled morocco leather and all exposed metal parts are finished in fine, bright, black enamel, highly polished. The Busch Terlux Prism Binocular is adjustable for pupillary distances, in a most simple and convenient way, by bending the hinge bars until the two barrels are just exactly the right distance apart to fit the user's eyes. The eyepiece of the right barrel is made movable, to allow for adjustment of possible differences in the powers of the user's eyes. There are other high grade binocular glasses which equal this instrument in certain particulars, but there is no instrument made which equals this instrument in **all respects.** The magnifying power is high, the field of view is large, the illumination is far greater than possessed by any other glass, and the definition is better than with any other glass. There is no glass more highly corrected for spherical and chromatic aberration. The design is handsome, the construction strictly high class in every particular and the finish most excellent. For the use of tourists, farmers, hunters, ranchmen, stockmen, or anyone requiring a very powerful, very high class instrument, this binocular glass is absolutely the best. It is an ideal instrument for astronomical purposes, giving beautiful views of the moon, showing many of the double stars, and other interesting astronomical phenomena. The linear magnifying power of this binocular is 12 diameters (superficial power, 144 times); the diameter of the field of view at 1,000 yards is 180 feet. Weight, without case, 21 ounces. Size, 7 inches high by 4⅛ inches wide.

No. 20K3475 Busch Terlux Prism Binocular, 12-Power (engraved "Prisma Binocle, Terlux D. R. C. M.), complete with solid sole leather case and shoulder strap. Price.....(Shipping weight, 4 pounds)......**$55.00**

ADMIRAL LORD CHARLES BERESFORD'S OPINION.

The following letters received by the manufacturer of the Busch Terlux Binocular are self explanatory:

First Letter. H. M. S. "Bulwark," Mediterranean.
At Sea, 20th June, 1906.

Admiral Lord Charles Beresford's compliments to Mr. Busch. Lord Charles has been looking through a pair of Mr. Busch's glasses which had engraved on them "Prisma Binocle, Terlux D. R. C. M." Lord Charles during his long experience at sea has never before looked through so good a pair of glasses. If Mr. Busch will send Lord Charles a pair of these glasses, together with the account of their price, Lord Charles will be very glad. The address will be: H. M. S. "Bulwark," Mediterranean Fleet.

The glasses belong to Mr. Charles Larios of Gibralter and were given to Mr. Larios by Mr. Muller.

Second Letter. H. M. S. "Bulwark," Mediterranean.
At Venica, 20th August, 1906.

Gentlemen—Thank you for your letter of the 13th August. I now have a pair of your Prism Binoculars. They are certainly by far the best glasses I have ever used.

To Messrs. Emil Busch, A. G.
Rathenower Optische Industrie-Anstalt,
Rathenow, Prussia, Germany.

Yours faithfully,
CHARLES BERESFORD,
Admiral.

USED BY WELLMAN POLAR EXPEDITION.

Headquarters, Wellman Record-Herald Polar Expedition, Danes Island, N. W. Spitzbergen, Latitude 79 degrees, 40 minutes North.

Sears, Roebuck & Co., Chicago, Ill.

After exhaustive tests of the various imported Standard Binocular Field Glasses submitted for test and use of the Wellman Polar Expedition, every officer of the Expedition is unanimous in the approval of the Busch Terlux, submitted by your firm, after three months of steady use and comparison with even the finest glasses used by the largest steamship lines, Military and Naval Glasses, for both land and marine purposes, in temperate and extreme Northern latitudes, minimum and maximum ranges. For field of vision, clearness of details and sharpness, no other glass, (and we have the most famous glasses made) has been found to even approach it.

Under every extreme of light, distance, weather, shore or marine use, in over 7,000 miles of travel and use, to the very ice fields of the Polar circle and 80 degrees latitude, no glass as yet put up against it has been found to equal it in any respect.

Faithfully yours,
FRANCIS A. BUZZACOTT,
Member Wellman Polar Expedition.

June, 1906.

Achromatic Sun Shade Telescopes at $1.90 to $4.70, According to Size.

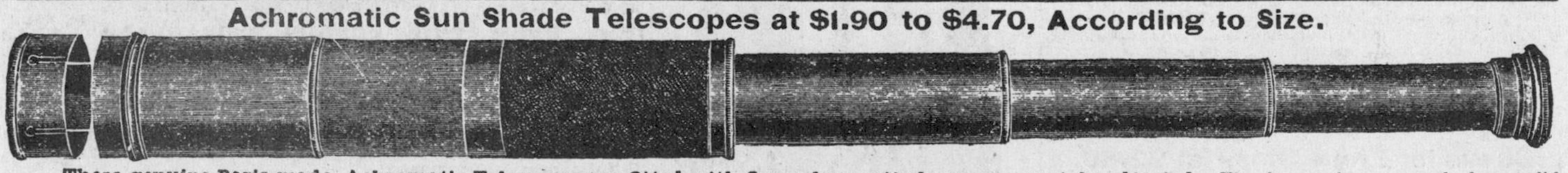

These genuine Paris made, Achromatic Telescopes are fitted with fine achromatic lenses, accurately adjusted. The draw tubes are made from solid brass, highly burnished. The trimmings, including the extension sun shade and the cap, are made from lacquered brass, and the covering is the best black, pebbled morocco leather. These achromatic telescopes are made with extension sun shades, which add greatly to their efficiency, brass caps for front lenses and sliding covers for the eyepieces.

No. 20K3500 Achromatic Sun Shade Telescope. Diameter, 10 lignes; length, closed, 5 inches; extended, 15½ inches; magnifying power, ten times. Price....(If by mail, postage extra, 12 cents.)....**$1.90**

No. 20K3501 Achromatic Sun Shade Telescope. Diameter, 12 lignes; length, closed, 6½ inches; extended, 19 inches; magnifying power, twelve times. Price....(If by mail, postage extra, 13 cents.)....**$2.25**

No. 20K3502 Achromatic Sun Shade Telescope. Diameter, 14 lignes; length, closed, 7 inches; extended, 20¾ inches; magnifying power, sixteen times. Price....(If by mail, postage extra, 18 cents.)....**$2.80**

No. 20K3503 Achromatic Sun Shade Telescope. Diameter, 16 lignes; length, closed, 8½ inches; extended, 26 inches; magnifying power, nineteen times. Price....(If by mail, postage extra, 24 cents.)....**$4.20**

No. 20K3504 Achromatic Sun Shade Telescope. Diameter, 19 lignes; length, closed, 9¾ inches; extended, 32 inches; magnifying power, twenty-four times. Price....(If by mail, postage extra, 31 cents.)....**$4.70**

Nickel Cap Pocket Telescope, $3.65.

No. 20K3510 This new Nickel Cap Pocket Telescope is an exceedingly convenient instrument to carry in the pocket, the rounded nickel plated caps making it absolutely dust-proof and affording perfect protection to the lenses. This Nickel Cap Pocket Telescope is fitted with extra quality achromatic lenses. The draw tubes are burnished brass, the caps heavily nickel plated and the body covered with the best black morocco leather. Length, closed, 6¾ inches; extended, 16¾ inches; magnifying power, twenty times.

Price....(If by mail, postage extra, 15 cents)....**$3.65**

No. 20K3510 partly extended.

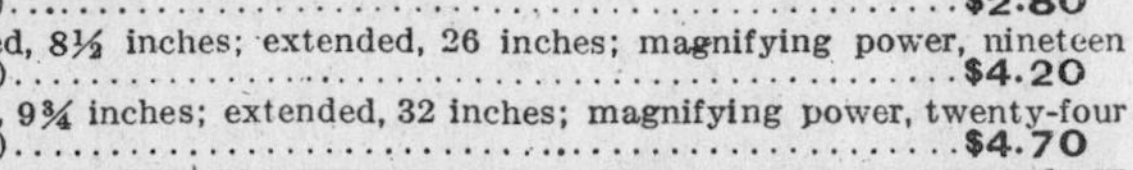

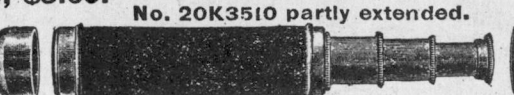

Our New Hinge Cap Telescope, $3.95.

No. 20K3515 We recommend this glass particularly to those who are willing to pay a little more money for the sake of quality. This instrument comes from a Paris maker, who is noted for the **quality** of his telescopes, particularly the lenses, which are of higher grade and better quality than the lenses used by other makers. The object glass in this telescope is a very fine achromatic lens, insuring high magnifying power and fine definition. This instrument is strongly and substantially made throughout, finely finished, fitted with the special patented hinge cap, sliding cover in the eyepiece, draw tubes of highly burnished brass, and trimmings of bronzed brass, lacquered. Length, closed, 6⅝ inches; extended, 16¾ inches; magnifying power, twenty times; diameter of object glass, 14 lignes. Price..................(If by mail, postage extra, 15 cents).................$3.95

This Big Marine Telescope, $5.55.

No. 20K3520 This telescope, although designed especially for use on shipboard, is a fine instrument for general purposes. It is a one draw telescope, the draw tube made of highly burnished brass, and all exterior metal work of lacquered brass. Both the object lens and the eyepiece are protected by sliding covers, and the body is covered with a special corded material made from pure linen, ornamental in appearance, and even stronger and more durable than leather. The diameter of this telescope is 2½ inches. The length, closed, is 14½ inches; extended, 24 inches; the magnifying power, twenty-two times. Price..................$5.55

No. 20K3520 partly extended.

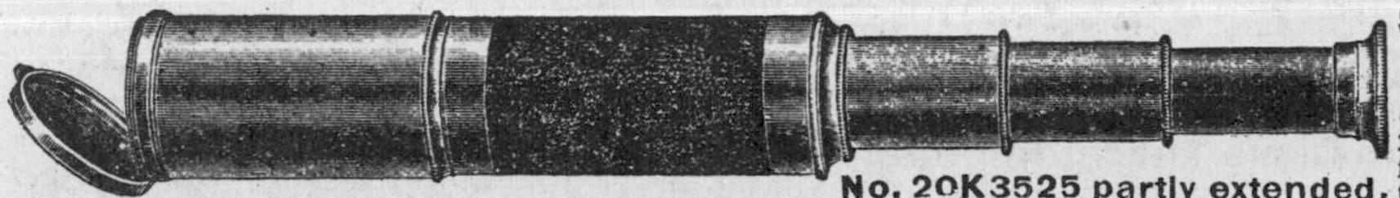

If by mail, postage extra, 37 cents.

Special Gun Metal Hinge Cap Telescope, $8.40.

No. 20K3525 partly extended.

No. 20K3525 This special hinge cap telescope is an exceptionally good telescope in every way, material and workmanship the very best, extra quality achromatic lenses, carefully and accurately adjusted, giving high power and fine definition. The metal parts, including the outside trimmings and the draw tubes, are made with the finest gunmetal finish, a finish that never tarnishes and which insures smooth and perfect working of the draw tubes so long as the instrument may be used. The patented hinged cap affords perfect protection to the object glass and the eyepiece is perfectly protected by a sliding cover. This telescope is made with extension sun shade, by means of which the object glass is perfectly protected from the direct rays of the sun when viewing objects where it is necessary to look toward the west in the evening, and toward the east in the morning. This telescope measures 8 inches long when closed, and 23⅜ inches long when fully extended. The diameter of the object glass is 16 lignes, and the magnifying power is 24 diameters. Price..................$8.40

If by mail, postage extra, 22 cents.

Our Special Strap Telescope, $11.95.

No. 20K3530 This high grade, first quality telescope, made with leather caps and shoulder strap, is an ideal instrument for rough work, carrying on horseback, etc., the leather caps and the strong leather covering affording perfect protection to the instrument, no matter how roughly it may be handled. The body of this telescope is covered with fine quality, pebbled morocco leather. The caps are of the same durable material, made extra heavy and strong. The metal parts are all made with dead black oxidized finish and the workmanship throughout is the best. This telescope is provided with specially ground achromatic lenses of the highest degree of excellence, carefully and accurately adjusted, and we particularly recommend this telescope to anyone desiring a serviceable, strongly made instrument, of the highest degree of optical perfection. The diameter of the object glass is twenty-two lignes; the length, closed and with the caps on, is 10¾ inches; the length when fully extended is 35¾ inches, and the magnifying power is thirty diameters.
Price..................(If by mail, postage extra, 47 cents.)..................$11.95

This illustration shows the telescope partly extended.

Large Field Extra Luminous Telescope, $17.25.

No. 20K3540 partly extended.

No. 20K3540 This telescope is the highest grade telescope that can be manufactured, representing the very highest degree of excellence in instruments of this kind.

IT IS FITTED WITH GENUINE ANASTIGMAT LENSES, lenses that are perfectly corrected, not only for spherical and chromatic aberration, but also for astigmatism, thereby securing the finest possible definition, combined with the highest possible magnifying power.

THIS TELESCOPE embraces a wider angle of view than any other telescope made of corresponding size and power, and the peculiar construction of the lenses, both the objective lens and the lenses in the eyepiece, is such as to admit an unusually large amount of light, from which fact the instruments are known as "**Extra Luminous.**" This desirable quality is particularly advantageous on dark, cloudy days or when using the instrument along toward evening.

UNDERSTAND, that so far as magnifying power and definition are concerned this is the best telescope that can be manufactured, fully equal in its optical and mechanical perfection to the very finest astronomical telescopes.

THE WORKMANSHIP, FINISH AND MATERIALS used in this telescope are made to correspond with its unsurpassed optical qualities, all metal parts, both the draw tubes and the external fittings, being made with the finest gunmetal finish and the covering is a very fine quality of blue levant leather. Made with patented hinge cap for protection of the object glass, sliding cover for the eyepiece, two draws length, closed, 10¾ inches; extended, 24 inches; diameter of object glass, 19 lignes; magnifying power, thirty diameters. Price..................$17.25

If by mail, postage extra, 33 cents.

25-Ligne Hinge Cap Telescope, $19.70.

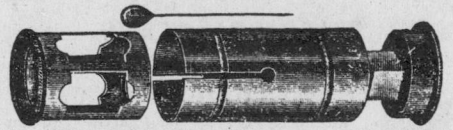

No. 20K3545 This is the most powerful telescope that we handle, a much higher grade telescope than is to be found in the best optical stores in the United States. **It is the lenses** which make this instrument so much superior to ordinary telescopes, these lenses being especially ground from the finest optical glass, very carefully centered and accurately adjusted. They are made to combine to the greatest possible extent the finest definition and highest magnifying power. **For astronomical work** this telescope forms an ideal instrument, showing clearly and distinctly the interesting changes and mysterious spots on the surface of the sun, the wonderful mountain ranges and apparently extinct craters of the moon, the satellites and the surface markings of the planet Jupiter, the wonderful rings of Saturn, the canals on the planet Mars, nebulae, double stars, etc. **For the observation of the sun** a dark glass is mounted in the slide cover of the eyepiece. **The magnifying power is 50 diameters.**

The draw tubes, trimmings, and all exposed metal parts are made with fine gunmetal finish, the very best and most expensive finish known for optical instruments. This fine steel **blue gunmetal finish will never tarnish** nor rust and the draw tubes always work smoothly and easily. The body of the instrument is covered with a fine grade of pebbled morocco leather. **This telescope is made with sunshade,** and instead of the ordinary cap it is provided with a hinged metal cover which affords perfect

Astronomical Eyepiece, $5.20.

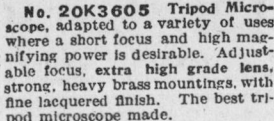

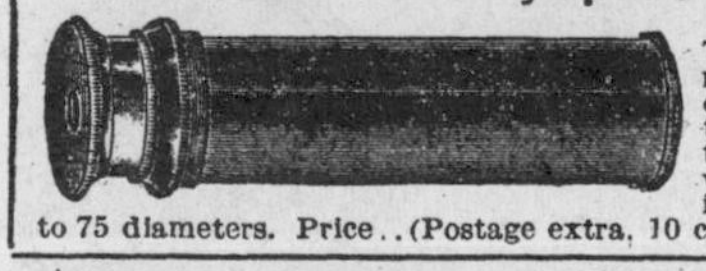

No. 20K3546 This Eyepiece is made for use with our No. 20K3545 telescope, for astronomical observations only and increases the power to 75 diameters. Price..(Postage extra, 10 cents.)....$5.20

protection to the object glass. The length, when extended, is 41½ inches; when closed, 12¼ inches. Weight, 50 ounces. The diameter of the object glass is 25 lignes (2¼ inches) and the magnifying power 50 diameters. Price, complete..................$19.70

Genuine Stanhope Lens Floroscope, 30 Cents.

No. 20K3600 This Microscope is fitted with an exceedingly powerful Stanhope lens, by means of which the animalculae in stagnant water, entirely invisible to the naked eye, can be distinctly seen. A drop of vinegar seen by this instrument is found to be swarming with living creatures, and yeast water is alive with wriggling germs. Besides the high power Stanhope lens, this Floroscope is also fitted with an ordinary long focus magnifying glass for the examination of insects, flowers, etc. An intensely interesting instrument. Finished in lacquered brass.
Price...(If by mail, postage extra, 3 cents) .30c

Tripod Microscope.

No. 20K3605 Tripod Microscope, adapted to a variety of uses where a short focus and high magnifying power is desirable. Adjustable focus, extra high grade lens, strong, heavy brass mountings, with fine lacquered finish. The best tripod microscope made.

Price..................29c
If by mail, postage extra, 5 cents

Double Lens Miners' Glass, $2.25.

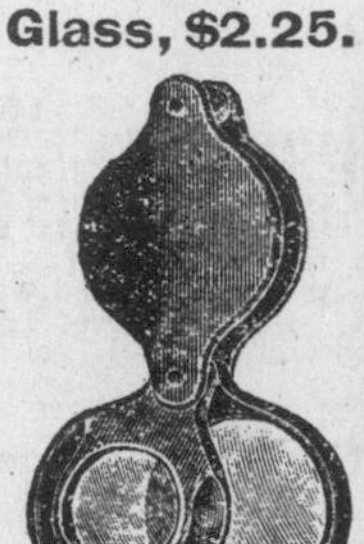

No. 20K3610 This is a powerful and substantially constructed magnifier, made by the Bausch & Lomb Optical Co., especially for prospectors' use. The case is extra heavy, made of polished hard rubber, the two lenses are of high magnifying power and large diameter, the smaller one 1 inch and the larger one 1½ inches.
Price....................$2.25
If by mail, postage extra, 2c.

Miners' Magnifying Glass, $1.35.

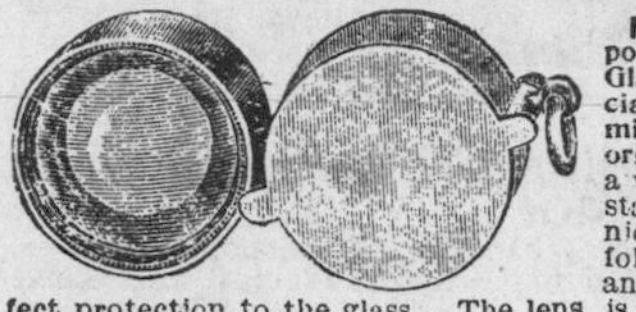

No. 20K3615 This powerful Magnifying Glass is made especially for the use of miners and prospectors, being mounted in a very strong and substantial metal case, nickel plated, the lens folding into the case and thus affording perfect protection to the glass. The lens is 1¼ inches in diameter and very powerful. Price....................$1.35
If by mail, postage extra, 3 cents.

Triple Lens Magnifiers.

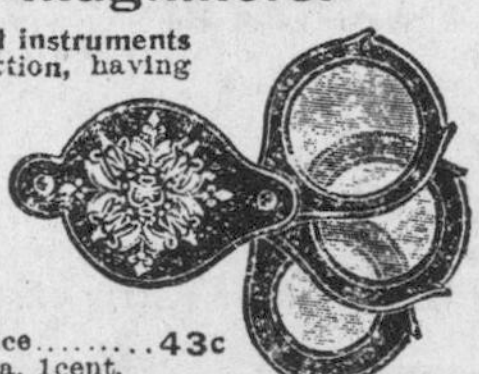

These are the most powerful instruments made in this style of construction, having three extra fine quality magnifying glasses, which can be used separately or all together as desired, thus giving a range of power. The three lenses used together form an extra powerful magnifier. Mounted in finely finished rubber cases.

No. 20K3620 Diameter of lenses, ⅝, ⅜ and ⅜ inch. Price..........43c
If by mail, postage extra, 1 cent.

No. 20K3622 Diameter of lenses, ⅝, ⅝ and ⅞ inch. Price...(Postage extra, 1 cent)..........51c

No. 20K3624 Diameter of lenses, ¾, ⅞ and 1 inch. Price..........(If by mail, postage extra, 2 cents)..........64c

Folding Coddingtons.

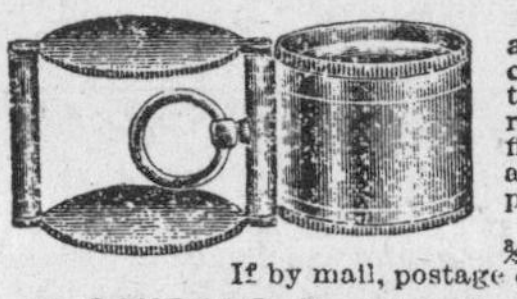

These Coddington Magnifiers are made with folding metal cases, nickel plated, making them very convenient for carrying in the pocket. They are fitted with very fine double achromatic lenses of high power.

No. 20K3630 Diameter, ⅝ inch. Price..........$0.75
If by mail, postage extra, 2 cents.

No. 20K3632 Diameter, 1 inch. Price.......... 1.00
If by mail, postage extra, 3 cents.

No. 20K3634 Diameter, 1¼ inches. Price.......... 1.25
If by mail, postage extra, 6 cents.

No. 20K3636 Diameter, 1⅜ inches. Price.......... 1.40
If by mail, postage extra, 8 cents.

Gem Microscope, $1.90.

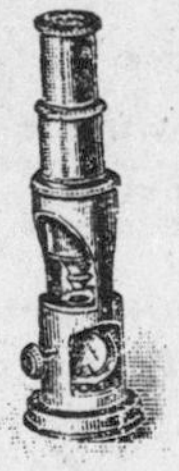

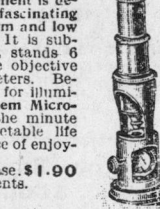

No. 20K3650 This little instrument is designed especially for beginners in this fascinating study, and its simplicity, compact form and low price make it a very popular style. It is substantially made of brass throughout, stands 6 inches high, has one eyepiece and one objective giving magnifying power of 20 diameters. Beneath the stage a mirror is provided for illumination of transparent objects. The Gem Microscope has sufficient power to render the minute objects in mineral, animal and vegetable life distinctly visible and will prove a source of enjoyment and profitable instruction.
Price, complete in polished wood case.$1.90
If by mail, postage extra, 14 cents.

THERMOMETERS.

Tin Case Outdoor Thermometers.

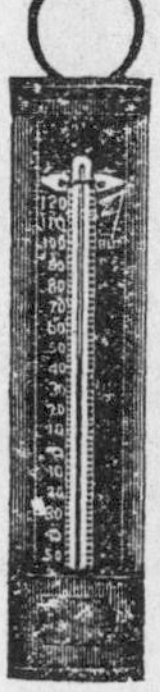

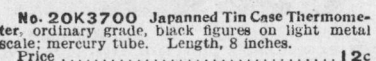

No. 20K3700 Japanned Tin Case Thermometer, ordinary grade, black figures on light metal scale; mercury tube. Length, 8 inches.
Price..........12c
If by mail, postage extra, 4 cents.

No. 20K3703 Japanned Tin Case Thermometer, extra quality, heavier, better made and more accurate than the preceding style; seasoned tubes of standard size, mercury only; a good reliable thermometer for ordinary use. Length, 8 inches. Price..........25c
If by mail, postage extra, 5 cents.

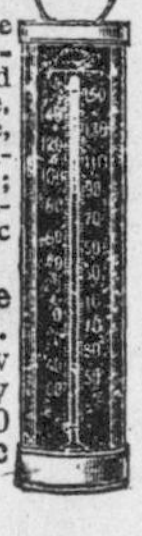

No. 20K3706 Guaranteed Tin Case Thermometer, best grade made, ("Accuatus" trademark), white figures and graduations upon black oxidized scale, thoroughly seasoned tubes of large size, good material and workmanship throughout, and guaranteed absolutely accurate; mercury only. Length, 10 inches. Retails everywhere at $1.50. Price...85c
If by mail, postage extra, 7 cents.

No. 20K3710 Polished Copper Case Thermometer for indoor or outdoor use. Red spirit tube graduated to 60 degrees below zero, in large, easy reading figures. Carefully tested for accurate readings. Length, 10 inches. Price..........55c
If by mail, postage extra, 10 cents.

Distance Reading Thermometers.

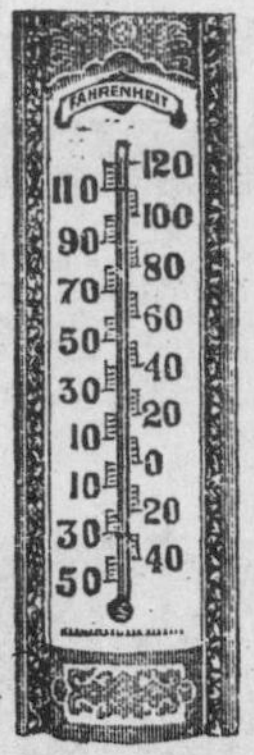

In the Distance Reading Thermometers the scale and figures are large and very distinct, the tube magnifies the column of red spirit, and the temperature is therefore easily read at a distance of from 15 to 25 feet. They are very convenient and present a handsome appearance.

No. 20K3715 Distance Reading Thermometer, enameled metal case, large black figures, red spirit tube, 7¼ inches long.
Price..........13c
If by mail, postage extra, 6c.

No. 20K3716 Distance Reading Thermometer, same style as 20K3715, but 2¾ inches wide by 9½ long, with extra large and plain figures, easily read at a distance of 25 feet. Price.....17c
If by mail, postage extra, 7c.

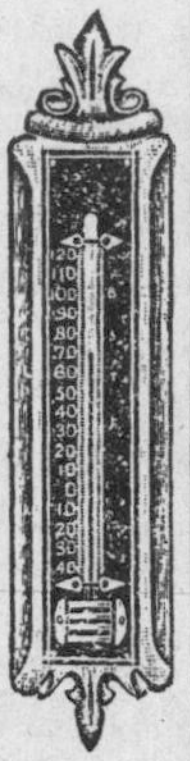

No. 20K3720 First Quality Cabinet House Thermometer. Guaranteed seasoned tubes. White figures on black background. Reading from 40 degrees below zero to 120 degrees above zero. Fancy carved oak back. Length of scale, 8 inches. Can also be used out of doors. Price..........85c
If by mail, postage extra, 11 cents.

Storm Glass Thermometers.

No. 20K3730 The Old Original Poole's Barometer, a combined storm glass and thermometer, mounted upon varnished wood case, 3 inches wide by 9 inches long. This storm glass foretells the weather with a fair degree of accuracy for 24 hours in advance, and the thermometer shows correct temperature.
Price..........18c
If by mail, postage extra, 8 cents.

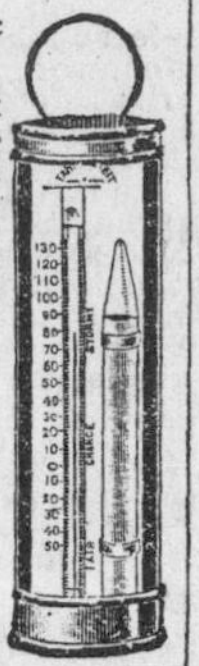

No. 20K3733 Antique Oak Storm Glass and Thermometer combined, mounted upon carved oak back with fancy beaded edge, black oxidized metal scale to thermometer with brass mountings, extra large storm glass with etched lettering. A reliable and handsome instrument.
Price..........58c
If by mail, postage extra, 15 cents.

No. 20K3736 Copper Case Storm Glass and Thermometer, case made of polished copper, silvered metal scale, high grade thermometer with standard size tube, mercury. A very serviceable instrument for outdoor use. Price..50c
If by mail, postage extra, 9 cents.

Fever Thermometers.

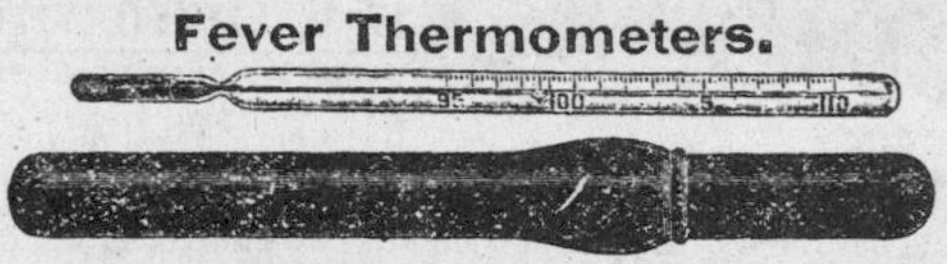

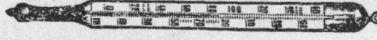

Clinical or fever thermometers are used, as the name implies, for taking the temperature in cases of sickness. No family should be without a good fever thermometer, and we handle only the highest grade, as a cheap or inaccurate instrument is worse than useless.

No. 20K3745 Fever Thermometer, 4 inches long, magnifying tube, self registering, in hard rubber case, very accurate and guaranteed. A certificate of accuracy given with each one. Price......(If by mail, postage extra, 4 cents.)..........78c

No. 20K3746 Fever Thermometer, 4 inches long, self registering, in hard rubber case, magnifying tube, very carefully tested and guaranteed, registers in one minute. Each thermometer accompanied by certificate of accuracy.
Price......(If by mail, postage extra, 4 cents)..........98c

No. 20K3747 Fever Thermometer, 4 inches long, self registering; in black enameled case with gold trimmings, chain and clasp; cannot be lost out of pocket; magnifying tube; very carefully tested and certificate of accuracy with each one.
Price......(If by mail, postage extra, 4 cents.)..........89c

Dairy Thermometers.

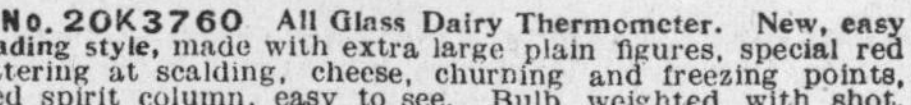

No. 20K3760 All Glass Dairy Thermometer. New, easy reading style, made with extra large plain figures, special red lettering at scalding, cheese, churning and freezing points. Red spirit column, easy to see. Bulb weighted with shot, stands upright in cream. Very accurate. Price..........13c
If by mail, postage extra, 4 cents.

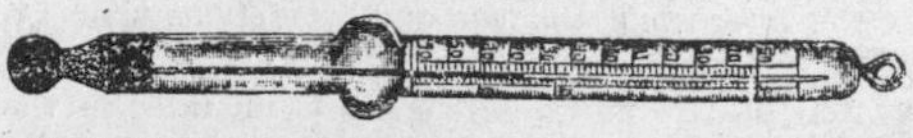

No. 20K3763 Dairy Thermometer, all glass. This thermometer floats in the cream in upright position with entire scale exposed to view. Scale is hand graduated and very accurate. Red spirit magnifying tube, making it very easy to read. Price....(If by mail, postage extra, 7 cents).....39c

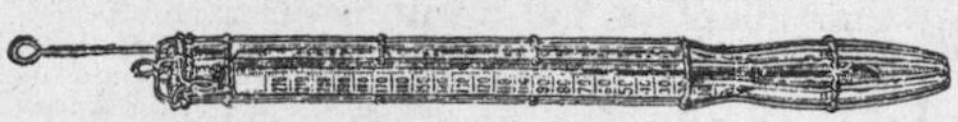

No. 20K3765 Extra High Grade Glass Dairy Thermometer in wire case to prevent damage. The scale is carefully lettered and gives all of the thirteen standard readings necessary to the dairy business. The tube is carefully seasoned and is magnifying on a yellow background, so that the readings can be easily made. Length of scale, 10 inches. Price..........65c
If by mail, postage extra, 9 cents.

Incubator Thermometers.

No. 20K3770 Incubator Thermometer on legs, extra large bulb and tube, very sensitive, white graduations on black oxidized metal plate. Absolutely accurate; 4 inches long. Price..........45c
If by mail, postage extra, 4 cents.

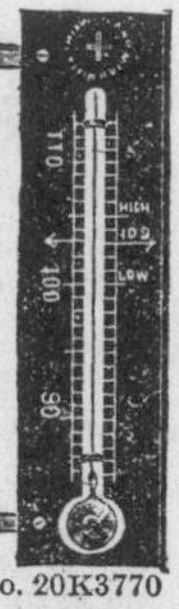

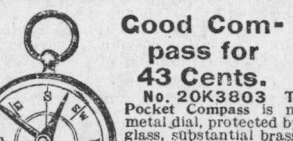

No. 20K3770

No. 20K3772 Incubator Thermometer, same quality as preceding style, but triangular in shape, 4 inches long, will stand upright among the eggs with scale showing plainly.
Price..........44c
If by mail, postage extra, 4c

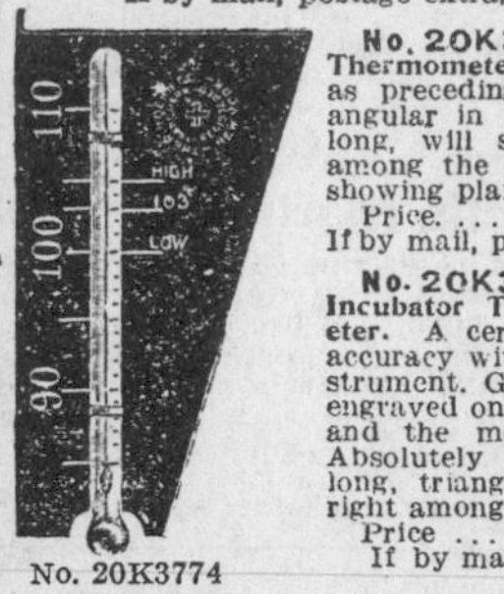

No. 20K3774

No. 20K3774 Standard Incubator Thermometer. A certificate of accuracy with each instrument. Graduations engraved on both tube and the metal back. Absolutely guaranteed. Four inches long, triangular in shape, to stand upright among the eggs.
Price..........95c
If by mail, postage extra, 3 cents.

POCKET COMPASSES.

Watch Style, 18 Cents.

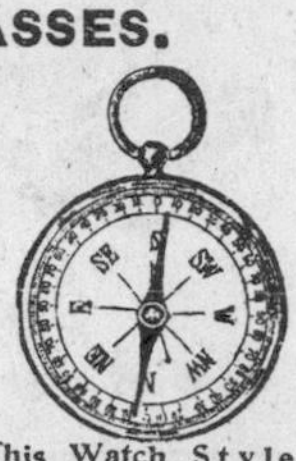

No. 20K3800 Pocket Compass, watch style, open face, bevel edge glass, paper dial, brass case. Diameter, 1½ inches.
Price...(Postage extra 2 cents)....18c

Good Compass for 43 Cents.

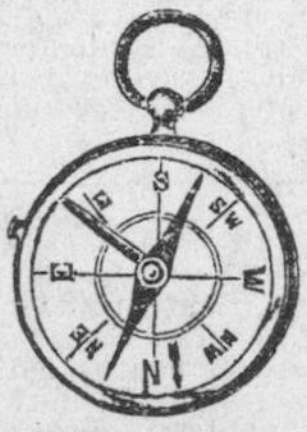

No. 20K3803 This Watch Style Pocket Compass is made with silvered metal dial, protected by heavy bevel edged glass, substantial brass case and provided with sliding stop. Diameter, 1¾ inches.
Price..........43c
If by mail, postage extra, 3 cents.

Jeweled Compass, 80c

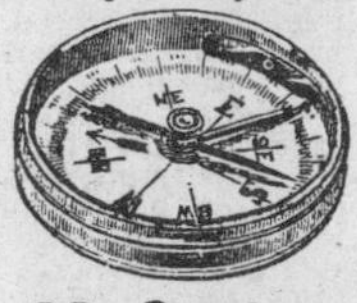

No. 20K3806 This fine Pocket Compass has strong brass case with cap cover, heavy bevel edged glass, silvered metal dial, with full circle divisions, sliding stop and jeweled cap to needle. Diameter, 1¾ inches. An extra good compass at a very low price. Price..........80c
If by mail, postage extra, 3 cents.

Jeweled Compass, 98 Cents.

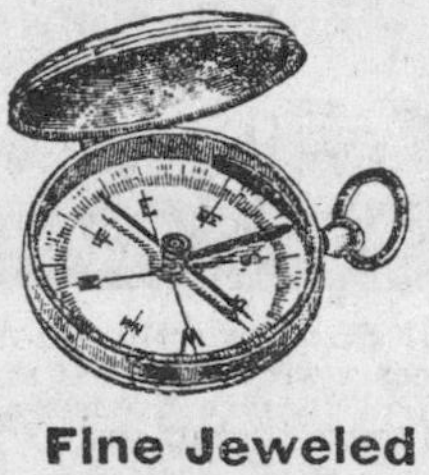

No. 20K3809 Our Watch Style Jeweled Pocket Compass is made with finely finished strong brass case with hinged cover, heavy beveled edge glass, silvered metal dial with full circle divisions and sliding stop. The needle is very sensitive and mounted with jeweled cap. Diameter 2 inches. A compass that will last a lifetime and give perfect satisfaction under any conditions.
Price..........98c
If by mail, postage extra, 5 cents.

Fine Jeweled Compass, $1.65.

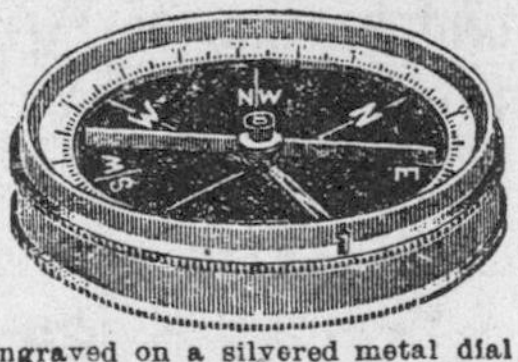

No. 20K3813 An extra high grade pocket compass, made throughout in the most careful and accurate way. Strongly made lacquered brass case, 2⅜ inches in diameter, with cap cover, extra heavy beveled glass, automatic stop and best grade jewel mounted English bar needle. Bottom of compass is oxidized in black, with white lettering, and the full circle divisions are engraved on a silvered metal dial raised to level of needle. Price..(Postage extra, 5c)..$1.65

High Grade Compass, $2.15.

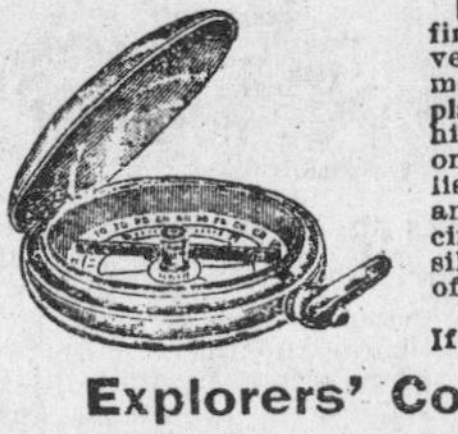

No. 20K3816 This is a very fine, compact compass, very convenient for carrying in pocket, made like a watch with nickel plated, dustproof case, spring hinged cover, opened by pressing on stem, best jewel mounted English bar needle, automatic stop and heavy beveled glass. The full circle divisions are engraved on a silvered metal dial raised to level of needle. Diameter, 2 inches.
Price..........$2.15
If by mail, postage extra, 3 cents.

Explorers' Compass, $1.95.

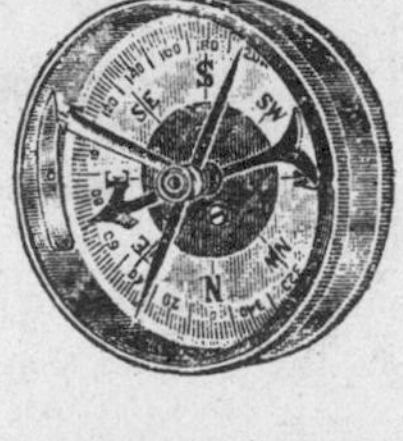

No. 20K3824 This Compass is made with a special hand which, by rotating the bottom of the compass, can be caused to point in any direction. The user, after getting his bearings, revolves the bottom of the compass until the hand points exactly in the direction which he desires to go, making it a very practicable and efficient instrument in every way. The case is made of solid brass, very strong and substantial, fitted with a heavy beveled edge glass, silvered metal dial, with full circle divisions, jeweled cap to needle and sliding stop. Diameter, 1¾ inches.
Price..........$1.95
If by mail, postage extra, 6 cents.

SURVEYORS' INSTRUMENTS.
Surveyors' Compasses with Levels

No. 20K3900 Surveyors' Compass with folding hooked sights, fine English bar needle, jewel mounted, with sliding stop, full circle divisions engraved on silvered metal dial, raised to level of needle. This compass is fitted with two spirit levels, greatly increasing the accuracy and efficiency. Length of needle, 2½ inches. Price, complete, including Jacob Staff mounting with ball and socket joint as shown in illustration.............$8.40
If by mail, postage extra, 22 cents.

No. 20K3902 Surveyors' Compass, same as No. 20K3900, but larger. Length of needle, 3 inches. Price, complete.....$9.45
If by mail, postage extra, 30 cents.

Surveyors' Vernier Compass.

$16.45 AND $18.95

No. 20K3910 Surveyors' Vernier Compass. Best English make, finest materials and workmanship throughout, bronze finish. Made with two very sensitive spirit levels for accurate adjustment. A fine vernier for close readings. Best agate mounted English bar needle and set screw stop. The full circle divisions are engraved on a silvered metal dial raised to level of needle. Length of needle 3½ inches. Shipping weight, 4 pounds. Price, complete, including ball and socket joint mounting, suitable for either Jacob Staff or tripod...........$16.45

No. 20K3912 Surveyors' Vernier Compass, same as No. 20K3910, but larger. Length of needle, 4½ inches. Shipping weight, 5 pounds. Price, complete....................$18.95
NOTE—Tripods are not included at above prices. See No. 20K3927 for prices on suitable tripods.

Extra High Grade Vernier Compass.

$32.40

No. 20K3918 This Surveyors' Vernier Compass is an extra high grade instrument, made throughout in the most careful and accurate manner, the very best compass on the market at any price.

The sights, which are detachable, are very firm and rigid, and graduated for taking angle of elevation and depression.

The vernier for adding or subtracting magnetic variations of the needle is placed under the glass. Two straight levels, very sensitive, are provided for adjustment, and the entire construction throughout is very heavy and substantial, highly finished and accurately adjusted.

The needle is 5 inches long, made of special magnetic steel, swung on a jeweled center and very sensitive.

This Compass is put up in a substantial, finely finished mahogany box with lock and carrying strap. Shipping weight, 25 pounds. Price, without tripod....................$32.40

No. 20K3919 Jacob Staff Mountings to fit above compass, No. 20K3918 only. Price....................$1.50
NOTE—If compass is to be used with tripod, the Jacob Staff mountings will not be needed.
See No. 20K3929 for prices on suitable tripod.

Compass Tripods and Jacob Staffs.

No. 20K3925 Jacob Staff, a straight, hardwood stick with metal shoe and tapered top, suitable for any of the compasses previously described. Price.............75c

No. 20K3927 Compass Tripod, light weight, good quality, suitable only for compasses Nos. 20K3910 and 20K3912. Price...........$3.90

No. 20K3929 Compass Tripod, extra quality, heavy, made especially for compass No. 20K3918. Price...................$4.60

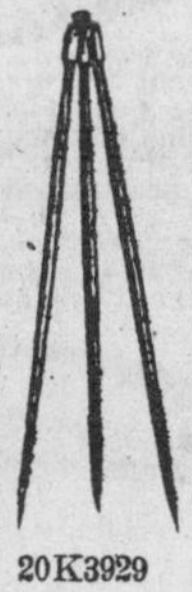

20K3927   20K3929

Hand Level, $3.25.

No. 20K3940 Surveyor's Hand Level for preliminary or estimate leveling. Can also be used for drainage work. Made of the finest materials and fitted with an accurately ground level bubble. Length, 5 inches. Price..(Postage extra, 4c.)..$3.25

Drainage Level, $23.90.

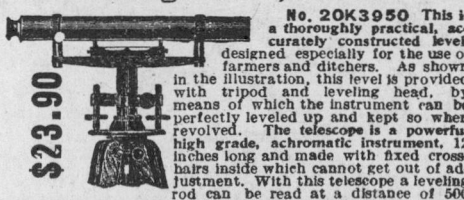

No. 20K3950 This is a thoroughly practical, accurately constructed level, designed especially for the use of farmers and ditchers. As shown in the illustration, this level is provided with tripod and leveling head, by means of which the instrument can be perfectly leveled up and kept so when revolved. The telescope is a powerful high grade, achromatic instrument, 12 inches long and made with fixed crosshairs inside which cannot get out of adjustment. With this telescope a leveling rod can be read at a distance of 500 feet. The telescope carries a carefully ground spirit level, adjustable by two nuts and so sensitive that a difference of ½ of an inch in 100 feet can be easily determined. The entire instrument is constructed of bronze metal, finely finished, with best workmanship throughout. Shipping weight, 12 pounds. Price, complete with tripod and box...........$23.90

Drainage Level, $28.00.

No. 20K3951 Drainage Level, same as No. 20K3950 but fitted with horizontal circle so that angles reading to single degrees can be turned off, thus making a very suitable instrument for builders.
Price, complete with tripod and carrying case.....$28.00

Architects' Level, $44.75.

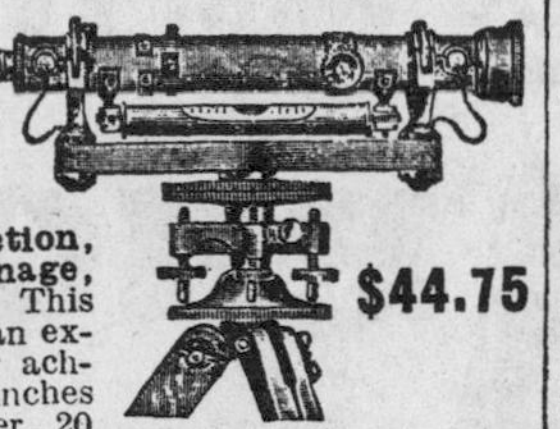

$44.75

No. 20K3955 This level exactly meets the requirements of architects, builders, millwrights, engineers, surveyors or others engaged in construction, sanitary work, drainage, road leveling, etc. This level is provided with an extra high grade perfectly achromatic telescope; 12 inches long, magnifying power 20 diameters, fitted with fine crosshairs, and adjustable eyepiece for precise focusing of the crosshairs. With this telescope a leveling rod can be read at a distance of 600 feet. The instrument revolves upon a horizontal circle 3⅝ inches in diameter, graduated from 0 to 90 each way and is read to 5 minutes by vernier fixed to spindle. The level ground absolutely true with very sensitive bubble, is graduated and securely mounted under the telescope. We furnish this level complete with metal trivet, substantial tripod, instruction book and fine mahogany case with lock and strap. Shipping weight, 22 pounds.
Price, complete...................$44.75

Engineers' "Y" Level, $75.00.

$75.00

No. 20K3960 This is a strictly high grade instrument, constructed throughout of bronze metal, equipped to meet with requirements of surveyors and railroad engineers who wish to do extremely accurate work. Achromatic telescope 16 inches long, extending to 18 inches, with dust cap and sunshade. Objective, 1¼ inches in diameter, focused with rack and pinion movement. Magnifying power is 30 diameters. Erecting eyepiece, with spiral adjustment, for focusing crosshairs. With this telescope readings can be made at 1,000 feet. Level vial is 6 inches long, cylindrically ground, carefully graduated and extremely sensitive. There are four leveling screws and clamp and tangent movement with opposing spring. Instrument sets on heavy, substantial base. Comes in mahogany finished case, with adjusting pins, instruction book, and includes fine hardwood tripod. Weight, with tripod, 14 pounds. Shipping weight, 25 pounds.
Price, complete.......................$75.00

Vernier Transit Compass, $69.00.

No. 20K3965 This Transit is an ideal instrument for county surveyors or others who want to do good land surveying, but do not care to invest the large amount usually charged for a transit. This instrument is provided with a very substantial leveling arrangement, with two straight levels, a powerful telescope 8 inches long with fine crosshairs and rack and pinion focus movement; the compass is 6¼ inches in diameter, with variation plate inside the circle. Length of needle, 5½ inches. Provided with clamp and tangent screw to center. This instrument is no heavier than an ordinary compass, the weight without tripod being only 8 pounds. We include with this instrument a good tripod, plumb bob, shade, adjusting pin, screwdriver, instruction book, magnifying glass and substantial mahogany box with lock and carrying strap. Shipping weight, 28 pounds. Price, complete...............$69.00

Vernier Transit Compass, $82.00.

No. 20K3966 Vernier Transit Compass, same as No. 20K3965, but with level and clamp to telescope, making instrument available for regular leveling work. Shipping weight, 28 lbs. Price, complete...$82.00

Engineers' and Mining Transit, $98.00.

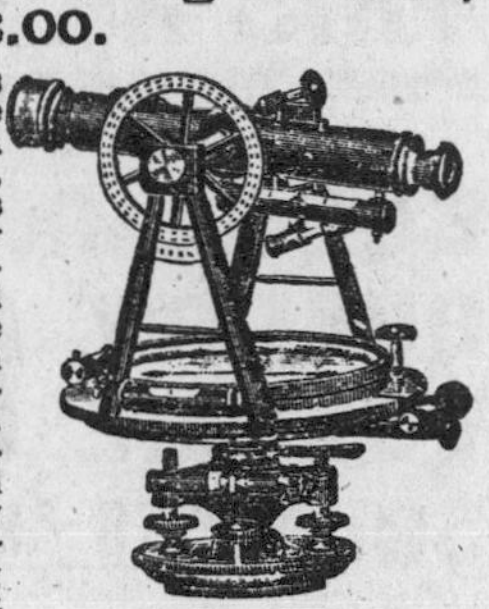

No. 20K3970 This instrument is a complete engineer's transit and level of the best type, reading horizontal angles on the limb and vernier circle to one minute, vertical angles on the vertical circle and vernier to five minutes, and is fitted with a fine leveling attachment and shifting center.

The limb is six and one-half inches in diameter and can be set to zero degrees by the lower clamp and tangent screw. It is read by one double vernier right and left, to single minutes. The graduations are in silver from 180°-0°-180°.

The compass is supplied with variation plate, set with rack and pinion and clamp, and angles can be turned off without using the needle. The needle is five inches long. The vernier plate has two finely ground levels at right angles.

The telescope is 9 inches long, and is equipped with a fine achromatic objective and erecting eyepiece with spiral adjustment by which the cross hairs can be focused. The objective is focused by a rack and pinion. The telescope is mounted on two standards, one of which is adjustable to make the telescope axis absolutely horizontal. The telescope axis has a clamp and tangent screw and fastened along the telescope is a finely ground sensitive level, 4½ inches long, properly graduated. This instrument is also provided with a vertical circle, 3½ inches in diameter, and with its vernier reading right and left, vertical angles can be read to five minutes. The instrument weighs 11 pounds and is fitted out complete in a finely finished mahogany case, containing plumb bob, adjusting pins, reading glass, sun shade, screwdriver and full directions for adjustment of instrument. Shipping weight, 30 pounds.
Price, complete with fine hardwood tripod, $98.00

Chesterman Chains.

No. 20K4000 Iron Chain, made of best iron wire, with two oval rings between links, brass swivel handles, brass tallies.

Length, 2 poles.	Price....$1.60
Length, 4 poles.	Price.... 2.50
Length, 50 feet.	Price.... 1.80
Length, 100 feet.	Price.... 2.75

NOTE—The 2-pole and 4-pole chains are divided into links and tallied every 10th link. The 50-foot and 100-foot chains are divided into feet and tallied every 10 feet.

STEEL TAPES AND ARROWS.
Rivetless Steel Tape.

No. 20K4005 Hodgeman Steel Tape; strongest tape made, and used by all railroads. Made of the very best tempered, polished and blued steel ribbon, 100 feet long, ¼ inch wide and .0015 inch in thickness. Numbered every foot with plain figures on an alloy, doing away with rivets or etchings, which are very apt to weaken the tape. End feet are divided into 10ths. Equipped with two fine strap handles and wound on a wooden reel. Price, complete............$3.90
Price, without reel............ 3.40

Marking Pins, 85c per Set.

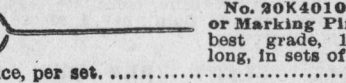

No. 20K4010 Arrows or Marking Pins, steel, best grade, 15 inches long, in sets of eleven.
Price, per set....................85c

Plumb Bob, $1.20.

No. 20K4015 Plumb Bob. Brass finish. Very carefully made and absolutely accurate. Weight, 8 ounces. Length, 3¾ inches. Price...................$1.20
If by mail, postage extra, 18 cents.

Leveling Rods and Poles.

No. 20K4025 Philadelphia Rod, heavy hardwood, divided into feet and 10ths, vernier reading to 100ths, with target, vernier and clamp. 7 feet long, sliding out to 13 feet. Price...................$9.90

No. 20K4028 Architects' Rod, hardwood, divided into feet, inches and ⅛ inches; with target, vernier and clamp, 5½ feet long, sliding out to 10 feet. Price........$5.10

No. 20K4031 Ranging Pole, best seasoned wood; octagonal, painted red and white, alternating every foot. Price, 10 feet, $2.12; 8 feet, $1.92; 6 feet............$1.70

Surveyors' Guide, $1.35.

No. 20K4035 By Andrew Duncan, C. E., containing necessary information to make any person a finished land surveyor without the personal aid of an instructor. The book is cloth bound, size 5x8 inches. Contains over two hundred pages of instructive matter, with all necessary illustrations and tables. Price....................$1.35
If by mail, postage extra, 16 cents.

THIS NEW FLEXIBLE ARM OXFORD CYLINDER PHONOGRAPHS

EQUAL IN TONE QUALITY AND VOLUME OF SOUND TO ANY $30.00 MACHINE EVER SOLD

$14.95

The biggest Talking Machine Bargain that we have ever offered. Less than one-half the price at which machines of this type have ever before been sold.

THIS NEW OXFORD TALKING MACHINE is made with the latest improved flexible arm and extra large, perfectly constructed flower horn. These improvements, this new flexible arm, and the big flower horn, result in a tone quality, a genuine musical quality heretofore possessed only by the highest priced machines. Not until you have heard this machine can you appreciate the wonderful power, the softness, the sweetness, and full round volume of sound, the marvelously exact reproduction of the human voice and instrumental music of all kinds, including even the largest choruses, bands, and orchestras.

THE IMPROVED FLEXIBLE ARM represents the very highest development of sound-reproducing mechanisms. This hollow and flexible arm, combined with the large flower horn, gives to the reproduction a beauty and naturalness of tone, a mellowness and genuine musical quality that is unequaled by talking machines of the older types. This combination of hollow flexible arm and flower horn results in special acoustic properties that enable this machine to bring out more fully than has ever before been accomplished with cylinder talking machines, the full and exact tone quality of the original music. This flower horn is so attached to the machine that it can be swung around and pointed in any direction without moving the machine itself, a great convenience when using the machine where a number of people are listening to the music.

THE LARGE FLOWER HORN is of an entirely new shape, this design being the result of a series of experiments to determine the exact shape that would produce the most natural and beautiful tone. It is made upon true acoustic principles, resulting in a volume of sound and fullness and richness of tone that is surprising. The body of this horn is made from the best sheet steel with fine black enamel finish, and resembles in shape a huge morning glory.

THE NEW SPRING CONTACT REPRODUCER, with button shaped sapphire, enables this machine to bring out tones heretofore entirely indistinguishable. The shape of the sapphire button and the fact that it is held closely in contact with the surface of the record at all times, greatly increases the volume of sound and enriches the quality. This reproducer is the exact same style now furnished with the expensive $30.00 and $40.00 machines, the best reproducer that can be made.

THE MOTOR with which this new Oxford Talking Machine is equipped is powerful, absolutely smooth running, noiseless and made with the latest type of speed regulator and governing device. It is made throughout from the best tool steel and brass, carefully and accurately assembled, made with machine cut gears, latest style of start and stop arrangement, and is thoroughly enclosed in the handsome oak cabinet as a protection from dust or injury. The motor can be wound while playing, a feature found only in high priced machines.

No. 20K5002

THE CABINET is made from solid quarter sawed oak, finely finished, all corners dovetailed, giving strength and durability, and is provided with a handsome bent oak cover, as shown in the illustration, to protect the machine from injury when not in use.

YOU CAN PAY A HIGHER PRICE for a graphophone if you prefer and you may get a machine that is finished a little finer than this one, a machine that may be a little more elaborately ornamented and that may perhaps look like a finer and handsomer piece of "furniture," but no matter what price you pay you cannot get any kind of a cylinder record talking machine that will produce any better music than this new Oxford machine. You cannot get a machine at any price that will have more real musical quality, that will reproduce the human voice with more perfect fidelity or that will render instrumental music with any greater degree of perfection.

IT TALKS, IT SINGS, IT LAUGHS, IT PLAYS, and all so naturally that it seems impossible that it can be a mere machine. As an entertainer nothing in the world equals a good talking machine as it brings to your home the same musicians, the same entertainers, the great bands and orchestras that amuse, delight and entertain great audiences in our most famous theaters. You can sing to its accompaniment, you can dance to its music, you can play to its songs.

COMPLETE OUTFIT, FLEXIBLE ARM OXFORD CYLINDER GRAPHOPHONE AND $16.95
TWO DOZEN GENUINE COLUMBIA P RECORDS

At $16.95 we offer this new Flexible Arm, Oxford Cylinder Talking Machine, complete with two dozen standard size genuine Columbia P records. Your own selection of subjects.

YOU CAN SELECT YOUR OWN RECORDS. The 24 records included with this wonderful Oxford Talking Machine Outfit are the famous Columbia P Records, standard size wax cylinder records and you can make your own selection of titles from the big list given on pages 199 and 200. You can pick out any selections you want, vocal solos, quartettes, bands, orchestras, instrumental solos, vaudeville and talking selections, exactly the kinds and titles that you like best and the only condition we make is that you make your selection from the Columbia P Records, from the lists given on pages 199 and 200.

IF YOU PREFER TO LEAVE THE SELECTION TO US we will give you the very finest assortment offered by our stock of more than 1,000,000 records, and by leaving it to us you may get an even more desirable collection than you would by selecting each title yourself, as we are thoroughly familiar with all the best titles and often have in stock selections of particular merit that may not be shown in our regular list.

No. 20K5002 Flexible Arm Oxford Cylinder Talking Machine, complete, just as illustrated and described, with large flower horn, spring contact reproducer, etc. Price, without records........**$14.95** Shipping weight, 35 pounds.

No. 20K5003 Complete Outfit, consisting of Flexible Arm Oxford Cylinder Talking Machine and 24 Columbia P Records. Price.......(Shipping weight, 40 pounds.)..**$16.95**

24 GENUINE COLUMBIA P RECORDS AND THE OXFORD JR. TALKING MACHINE ALL COMPLETE

YOUR OWN SELECTION OF SUBJECTS

$8.75

THE NEW OXFORD JR. TALKING MACHINE IS A STRICTLY HIGH CLASS TALKING MACHINE FOR REPRODUCING STANDARD SIZE WAX CYLINDER RECORDS. IT IS A THOROUGHLY WELL MADE MACHINE AND NOT TO BE COMPARED IN ANY WAY WITH THE CHEAP MACHINES THAT HAVE BEEN SO EXTENSIVELY ADVERTISED RECENTLY.

IT IS A HIGH CLASS MACHINE, MADE IN AMERICA, made by expert and experienced workmen in one of the largest and most successful talking machine factories in the world. It is made of good materials throughout, fitted with a high class spring motor, with machine cut gears, everything about it strong and substantial. It is made with patent feed device which holds the reproducer firmly in place as it travels along over the surface of the record. There are cheap talking machines made without feed device, and with such machines the reproducer slips and slides off the surface of the record, but this trouble is entirely prevented in the Oxford Jr. Talking Machine, as the reproducer is held firmly and guided in its course over the surface of the record by the patent feed device, exactly the same as the highest priced machines. This machine is made with heavy, solid and substantial iron base, finished in black enamel, with gold stripe decorations. It is made with standard size tapered mandrel, and will use any standard size of wax cylinder record, Columbia, Edison or any other standard make.

THE REPRODUCTION of the human voice or of instrumental music, as rendered by the Oxford Jr. Talking Machine, is just exactly as good as with machines costing ten and fifteen times the price which we ask for this machine. It is made with a high grade, aluminum style D 1 reproducer, with mica diaphragm and Brazilian sapphire reproducing point. It is equipped with black and gold horn with large extra wide bell, the body of the horn made of the best sheet steel, with fine black enamel finish; the bell made of solid brass, highly polished, giving the machine a most handsome and ornamental appearance. The tone qualities of this large black and gold horn are unexcelled, adding greatly to the volume of sound and naturalness and sweetness of tone.

THE OXFORD JR. TALKING MACHINE is not a toy. It is a high class machine, a machine that cannot be purchased in the ordinary market at less than double our price. Made of good materials all the way through, strong and substantial, easy to operate, made with fine clock work motor, automatic feed device and extra large black and gold horn.

FIFTY THOUSAND RECORDS PER MONTH. Under our new contracts with the largest manufacturer of records in the world they are to furnish us for these outfits 50,000 high class standard size wax cylinder records per month, genuine Columbia P Records, the exact same records that have for years been sold at 50 cents, and today cannot be purchased in any other market for less than 25 cents each. By contracting for this enormous quantity of one million records (more than fifty car loads), the largest order ever placed for talking machine records by any dealer anywhere in the world, we have succeeded in reducing the cost to us just the merest fraction over the actual cost of labor and materials, the lowest cost at which high class graphophone records have ever been purchased by any dealer, and in making up these outfits, consisting of the OXFORD JR. TALKING MACHINE AND TWENTY-FOUR OF

THESE HIGH CLASS STANDARD SIZE RECORDS AT $8.75, we are giving you the benefit of the saving which we effect by means of our tremendous purchasing power.

UNDERSTAND, OUR SPECIAL PRICE $8.75 includes the 24 Columbia P Records, the Oxford Jr. Talking Machine complete with clock work motor, style D 1 aluminum reproducer, large black and gold horn, an outfit that a few months ago could not have been purchased for less than $15.00.

No. 20K5010 Oxford Jr. Talking Machine and 24 Columbia P Records, complete outfit, just as illustrated and described above. Shipping weight, 20 pounds. Price.....$ 8.75
No. 20K5011 Oxford Jr. Talking Machine Outfit, consisting of Oxford Jr. machine as illustrated and described above and 48 Genuine Columbia P Records. Price......12.95
Shipping weight, 30 pounds. Make your selection of Records from the list on pages 199 and 200, the list of genuine Columbia P Records.

THE TYPE F H HARVARD DISC TALKING MACHINE

$15.90

The Large Flower Horn with which this machine is equipped, possesses, to an unusual degree, the magnificent acoustic or tone qualities which are peculiar to the latest type of flower horns. The unusual musical qualities of the flower horn, its ability to reproduce sound more absolutely true to the original music, is due to the peculiar curves and the extra wide flaring bell, which avoids the usual retardation of the sound waves, thereby giving a deep, clear and natural tone to every note.

THIS HORN is made with fine baked on enamel finish, ornamented with gold stripes, and besides the great improvement which it makes in the musical quality of the machine, also contributes greatly to the beautiful appearance of the outfit.

THE MELLOWNESS OF TONE AND REAL MUSICAL QUALITY of the reproduction, as rendered by the Type F H Harvard Talking Machine, is due partly to the new sound analyzing reproducer with which it is equipped and partly to the special acoustic properties of the flower horn, or rather to the combination of these two features. This reproducer is the latest product of the largest talking machine manufacturer in the world and represents the result of years of constant experiment and improvement. It is called the "sound analyzing" reproducer because of its ability to bring out every tone clearly and with the exact tone quality of the original music. It not only increases the volume of sound, but enriches the quality and reveals tones which with the earlier and less perfect types of reproducers were lost entirely. It is equipped with the automatic needle holder by which the needle is clamped into place and held securely by a spring lever; a slight pressure upon this lever instantly releases the needle, thus avoiding the use of the annoying set screw arrangement used in other reproducers.

GENERAL CONSTRUCTION. The Type F H Harvard Disc Talking Machine is made with golden oak cabinet of plain but elegant design, substantially made, all corners dovetailed and with removable top to afford access to the motor for oiling or occasional cleaning. The swinging arm and bracket, supporting the horn and reproducer, are beautifully designed and made from aluminum, highly ornamental and non-tarnishable. The turntable, of a special composition metal, is 10 inches in diameter, the cabinet measures 11¼ inches square by 5¼ inches high, the horn is 19 inches long with bell 17 inches in diameter. This machine is equipped with a powerful spring clock work motor, made throughout from brass and the best quality of steel, all gears and pinions machine cut to insure absolutely even and smooth running qualities. Perfectly uniform speed, essential to perfect reproduction, is obtained by the improved automatic governor and worm gear, perfect control of the speed is obtained by the new tension screw speed regulator, and the motor is stopped or started simply by pressing in or pulling out a small knobbed rod.

USES ANY KIND OF DISC RECORD. This machine is adapted to any style, any size or any make of flat disc record. Just think of the great variety of selections available for use with this machine and the wonderful possibilities for entertainment which it affords.

No. 20K5048 The Type F H Harvard Disc Talking Machine, with golden oak cabinet, large flower horn, sound analyzing reproducer, exactly as illustrated and described above. Shipping weight, 35 pounds. Price..$15.90

THE NEW PURPLE LABEL OXFORD RECORDS

THE LOW PRICES at which we are able to offer the Purple Label Oxford Disc Records may lead some to doubt their high quality. Many who have been accustomed to paying from 35 cents to $1.00 each for disc records may think that perhaps the Purple Label Oxford Disc Records at only 21 cents each may not be as good as the records which they have been accustomed to buying. But this enormous reduction in the price of disc records is made possible by the fact that we handle these records on exactly the same small percentage of profit plan upon which we sell the most staple merchandise. **We do not need to make a big profit on records.** Our sales are so enormous, not only in this line, but in all other lines of merchandise, that we can afford to be content with an exceedingly **small percentage of profit,** and as a result of our ability to sell records on our regular staple merchandise small profit plan, we can offer the Purple Label Oxford Disc Records, the very highest grade disc records that can be made, at prices which have heretofore been absolutely impossible.

THE MASTERS from which the Purple Label Oxford Disc Records are made are produced in New York City, in one of the most completely equipped laboratories for sound reproduction, situated in the heart of the theater district, where the very best artists, the best singers, the best speakers, the best entertainers of all classes are always at hand. In making good records it is essential to employ good artists, and as there is no city in the world where there are so many good artists to be had as in New York, the laboratory for making the Oxford record masters has been located there.

THE MATERIAL from which a disc record is made is also a most important consideration. The best material naturally produces the finest results, and in the making of the Purple Label Oxford Disc Records we use the very best material that it is possible to procure.

EVERY PURPLE LABEL OXFORD DISC RECORD that we sell is sent out with the express understanding and agreement on our part that if it does not meet with your entire approval, if it does not prove satisfactory in every way, it may be returned to us at our expense, and your money will be refunded.

No. 20K5115 Purple Label Oxford Disc Records, 7-inch, your own selection of titles. Price, per dozen, $2.50; each........ **21c**

21¢ EACH $2.50 PER DOZEN

MADE ONLY IN 7-INCH SIZE.

BARITONE SOLOS WITH ORCHESTRA ACCOMPANIMENT.
7656 Armorer's Song (from "Robin Hood")
71053 Behind the Clouds the Sun is Ever Shining
71054 Heidelberg Stein Song (from the musical comedy, "The Prince of Pilsen")
71650 I'm Wearing My Heart Away for You
71014 In the City of Sighs and Tears
7940 In the Good Old Summer Time
73018 Kalamazoo Is No Place for You
71052 Tale of the Sea Shell, The (from the musical comedy of "The Prince of Pilsen")
73029 Vacant Chair, The
7730 What the Brass Band Played

BARITONE SOLOS WITH PIANO ACCOMPANIMENT.
7378 Ain't Dat a Shame (coon song)
7346 Any Old Place I Can Hang My Hat Is Home, Sweet Home to Me
7872 Bill Bailey, Won't You Come Home (coon song)
7563 Birds Sing Sweeter, Lad, at Home, The
7689 Break the News to Mother
7151 Brown October Ale (from "Robin Hood")
71617 By the Sycamore Tree
73033 By the Watermelon Vine (piano accompaniment)
7405 Carrie Nation in Kansas (with ax effect)
7701 Come Back to Erin
73034 Come Take a Trip in My Airship
71050 Could You Be True to Eyes of Blue If You Looked Into Eyes of Brown
71057 Down Where the Wurzburger Flows
777 Fare Thee Well, Molly Darling
71190 Gambling Man, The (coon song)
73036 Good Bye, Eliza Jane
7381 Good Morning, Carrie
7377 Go 'Way Back and Sit Down (comic)
71579 Hiawatha
744 Home, Sweet Home
7726 I'll Come Back When the Hawthorn Blooms Again
71441 I'm Thinking of You All of de While (coon love song)
73037 I've Got a Feelin' for You
7190 Love's Old Sweet Song
7710 Minstrel Boy, The
7400 My Japanese Cherry Blossom (from "Hoity Toity")
71523 On a Moonlight Night
7106 On a Sunday Afternoon
7892 Rip Van Winkle Was a Lucky Man
73076 She's Just a Little Different from the Others that I Know
71519 She's My Girl (from "The Runaways")
71250 Since That I Met You (from the "Sultan of Sulu")
7857 Tale of a Bumble Bee, The (from "King Dodo")
71117 Under the Rose
71574 Up in the Cocoanut Tree
7194 Wearing of the Green
7375 Wedding of the Reuben and the Maid, The
7558 When You Were Sweet Sixteen
7403 Where the Sweet Magnolias Bloom
7700 Ye Banks and Braes o' Bonnie Doon
71600 You're as Welcome as the Flowers in May

TENOR SOLOS WITH PIANO ACCOMPANIMENT.
7221 Absence Makes the Heart Grow Fonder
73074 By the Old Oak Tree
7113 Good Bye, Dolly Gray
757 Good Bye, Sweet Dreams, Good Bye
7326 He Laid Away a Suit of Gray to Wear the Union Blue
7230 Hello, Central! Give Me Heaven
7324 I Can't Tell Why I Love You, But I Do
7114 I'm a Philosopher (comic)
755 In the House of Too Much Trouble
786 Just Because She Made Dem Goo Goo Eyes (coon song)

TENOR SOLOS WITH PIANO ACCOMPANIMENT—Continued.
7356 Killarney
73038 Little Boy Called "Taps"
75 Lost Chord, The
73171 My Cosy Corner Girl
7320 My Old Kentucky Home
7411 Noreen Mavourneen
7175 Sally in Our Alley
7488 What Do You Think of O'Hoolihan? (comic two voice specialty)
71525 When I Hold Your Hand in Mine
753 When the Harvest Days are Over
7199 Where Is My Wandering Boy Tonight?
7111 Who Threw the Overalls in Mistress Murphy's Chowder?

YODLE SONGS. TENOR
7591 Hi! Le! Hi! Lo!
706 Life in the Alps
7588 Medley of Emmett's Yodles
7709 Roll On, Silver Moon
7586 Sleep, Baby, Sleep
7589 Snyder, Does Your Mother Know You're Out?

BASS SOLOS WITH PIANO ACCOMPANIMENT.
7157 Asleep in the Deep
7433 Beyond the Gates of Paradise
7432 Kathleen Mavourneen
7429 My Home Is Where the Heather Blooms (from "Rob Roy")
7145 Sentinel Asleep, The
7156 Warrior Bold, A

BARITONE AND TENOR DUETS.
73027 Down on the Brandywine (piano accompaniment)
71616 Hiawatha, Parody on
73028 Heinie (comic German dialect song)
7792 I Never Trouble Trouble Until Trouble Troubles Me
7262 Just as the Sun Went Down
7259 'Mid the Green Fields of Virginia
7970 Under the Bamboo Tree
7261 While the Leaves Came Drifting Down
7790 Whoa! Bill (comic Rube duet)

VOCAL TRIOS. MALE VOICES.
7649 Camp Meeting
7652 In Front of the Old Cabin Door
7653 Mocking Bird Medley, The

VOCAL QUARTETTES. MALE VOICES.
These are deservedly among the most popular of records. The songs are finely rendered, and the effect is so natural that no stretch of the imagination is required to bring the singers so strongly forward in spirit that their actual presence seems to be achieved.
7716 Annie Laurie
7891 Barbecue in Old Kentucky, A
7511 Carry Me Back to Old Virginia
7890 Characteristic Negro Medley, A
7449 Church Scene (from "The Old Homestead")
7456 Coon Wedding in Southern Georgia
7451 Dixie Land
7822 Down on the Farm
7455 Farmyard Medley (with farmyard fowl and animal imitations)
7753 I'se Gwine Back to Dixie
7448 My Louisiana Lou
7512 My Old Kentucky Home
7650 Nationality Medley
7458 Night Trip to Buffalo
7752 Plantation Songs, Medley of
7715 Sally in Our Alley
7450 Sleigh Ride Party, The
745 Soldier's Farewell
73082 St. Patrick's Day at Clancy's (unaccompanied)
7454 Steamboat Medley
7818 Suwanee River
7514 Tenting Tonight on the Old Camp Ground
7521 The Old Oaken Bucket
7457 Trip to the County Fair, A
7714 Way Down Yonder in the Cornfield

VOCAL SOLOS IN GERMAN.
71159 Das Haidenroeslein
71168 Der Rattenfaenger
7123 Deutschland, Deutschland
7108 Die Wacht am Rhein
7131 Ich Weiss Nicht Was Soll es Bedeuten
71385 Maedchen mit dem Rothen Muendchen
71123 Vater, Mutter, Schwestern, Brueder

MINSTRELS.
Each record includes overture with bones, new jokes and witty sayings, interspersed with laughter and applause, and ends with song given in the title, accompanied by the orchestra and vocal quartette.
7641 Coon, Coon, Coon
733 Dese Bones Shall Rise Again
7642 Hear Dem Bells
7643 High Old Time, A
7798 I've a Longing in My Heart for You, Louise
7644 Laughing Song, The
7805 My Old Kentucky Home
7804 Old Folks at Home
7645 Old Log Cabin, The
7802 Tell Me

LAUGHING SONGS
7105 And Then I Laughed (Rube song)
722 I'm Old, but I'm Awfully Tough (Rube song)
7210 Negro Laughing Song (an old standard)
7759 Ticklish Reuben (Rube song)
73046 When the Circus Comes Around

SPECIAL TALKING RECORDS.
7833 Address by the late President McKinley at the Pan-American Exposition
7160 Lincoln's Speech at Gettysburg

COMIC TALKING SELECTIONS.
721 Arkansaw Traveler, The
7398 Backyard Conversation Between Two Jealous Irish Washerwomen (full of real comedy and back talk)
7884 "Blazing Rag" Concert Hall, The (introducing the Bouncer, the Tipsy Soubrette, the Professor and a Fight—very realistic)
7851 Dissertation on Love
7887 Dog Fight, The
7854 Football Match, A
719 Husking Bee Dance
735 Negro Sermon, A
7845 On Sweethearts
7847 On Trousers
7850 Political Meeting, A
73020 Reuben Haskins' Trip Through the New York Subway
723 Schultz on Kissing (Dutch dialect)
726 Schultz on the Man behind the Gun (Dutch dialect)

COMIC TALKING SELECTIONS.—Continued.
727 Schultz's Trip to Chicago (Dutch dialect)
734 Stump Speech on Love

THE FAMOUS UNCLE JOSH WEATHERBY'S LAUGHING STORIES.
71408 Uncle Josh at a Camp Meeting
71409 Uncle Josh on a Street Car
768 Uncle Josh in a Department Store
770 Uncle Josh's Arrival in New York
771 Uncle Josh at a Baseball Game
772 Uncle Josh on a Bicycle
774 Uncle Josh and the Lightning Rod Agent
776 Uncle Josh's Troubles in a Hotel
71868 Uncle Josh and the Insurance Company
71140 Uncle Josh and Aunt Nancy Smith on a Visit to New York
71518 Uncle Josh on an Automobile
73021 Uncle Josh on Jim Lawson's Horse Trade

BAND SELECTIONS.
7285 America
7188 American Republic March—Thiele
7928 Arkansaw Husking Bee, An
7406 At a Georgia Camp Meeting
787 Boston Commandery March (introducing "Onward, Christian Soldiers")
71372 "Cavalleria Rusticana," Selections from—Mascagni
7239 Coronation March (from the "Prophet")—Meyerbeer
7325 Dancing in the Dark (song and dance with clogs)
7354 Die Wacht am Rhein
7361 Dixie
71375 Down South (American sketch with clog dances—a winner)
7388 El Capitan March—Sousa
7389 Evening Chimes in the Mountains
7946 "Faust," Ballet Music from (No. 1, Tempo di Valse)
785 "Faust," Soldier's Chorus from—Gounod
7244 "Florodora," March from—Stuart
7870 Hail to the Bride March
7420 High School Cadets March—Sousa
7422 "Il Trovatore," Selections from
7427 In the Village Tavern (song and dance with clogs)
7428 Irish Airs, Medley of
71587 Jack Tar March (introducing sailor' hornpipe, eight bells, boatswain' whistle)
7436 Jolly Cadet, The (march characteristic
7478 Liberty Bell March (with bell effect—Sousa
7185 "Lohengrin," Bridal March from—Wagner
7495 Love's Dreamland Waltz
7507 Marching Through Georgia
7509 Marriage Bells (with cornet solo)
7240 Mendelssohn Wedding March
779 Mosquito Parade, The ("A Jersey Review")

LIST OF NEW PURPLE LABEL OXFORD RECORDS CONTINUED ON NEXT PAGE.

THE NEW PURPLE LABEL OXFORD RECORDS.—Continued.

BAND SELECTIONS—Continued.

7522 Mr. Thomas Cat (march comique—trombone imitations)
71897 Noisy Bill (characteristic march)
7537 O, Promise Me, (from "Robin Hood," with cornet solo)
71009 Paderewski's Famous Minuet
783 "Poet and Peasant," Overture to—Von Suppe
7549 Scotch Airs, Medley of
7555 Star Spangled Banner
7972 Stradella Overture—Flotow
782 Tell Me, Pretty Maiden (from "Florodora")
7678 Thunderer March
7564 Till We Meet Again Waltz
7674 Turkish Patrol, The

ORCHESTRA SELECTIONS.

71186 "Broadway Hits," Medley March
7592 Bugler's Dream, The
7595 Circus Gallop
7330 Creole Bells (with violin)—J. B. Lampe
7596 Dancing in the Kitchen (song and dance with clogs)
7600 Darkey Tickle (plantation medley, with clogs, shouts, etc.)
71431 Dixieland March (introducing "Dixie" and "Old Black Joe")
7602 Down on the Suwanee River
7263 Echoes of the Forest (descriptive, with bird effects)
7233 Espanita Waltz
7247 Forge in the Forest, The (descriptive, with cock crow, anvil, etc.)

ORCHESTRA SELECTIONS—Continued.

7337 Go 'Way Back and Sit Down
7607 Hands Across the Sea March—Sousa
7608 Happy Days in Dixie (plantation medley, with clogs, shouts, etc.)
7129 He Laid Away a Suit of Gray to Wear the Union Blue
71155 Hiawatha (a summer idyl)
7392 Hungarian Dance—Brahms
7609 Husking Bee
71548 In Cheyenne Joe's Cowboy Tavern
7242 Jolly Coppersmith (descriptive, with anvil effect and vocal chorus)
7616 Kentucky Jubilee Singers (plantation medley, with clogs, shouts, etc.)
7618 La Serenata Waltz (with castanets)
71571 Laughing Water—F. W. Hager
71043 Medley March (from the musical comedy, "The Prince of Pilsen," introducing "The Tale of the Sea Shell" and "The Stein Song")
7243 Night Alarm
7621 On the Midway (descriptive, introducing the fakirs and theatre)
71111 Spring Blossoms (caprice gavotte)
7629 Stars and Stripes Forever March—Sousa
71689 Uncle Sammy (march and two step)
71679 Winona Two Step

INSTRUMENTAL SOLOS.

7218 El Miserere (from "Il Trovatore," violin solo)
7217 Waltz from "Faust"—Gounod (violin solo)

INSTRUMENTAL SOLOS—Continued.

7212 Schubert's Serenade (violin solo)
7216 Then You'll Remember Me (violin solo)
71199 The Last Rose of Summer (cornet solo)
798 Intermezzo from "Cavalleria Rusticana" (clarionet solo)
7140 I'll Follow Thee—Bolero (flute solo)
7498 A Rag Time Skedaddle (piccolo solo)
7461 A Coon Band Contest (banjo solo)
7292 Coon Songs (banjo solo)
7465 Creole Belles (banjo solo)
7463 "When Mr. Shakespeare Comes to Town" and "Go 'Way Back and Sit Down" (banjo solo)
7640 Bugle Calls of the United States Army (bugle)
7638 Bugle Calls of the Rough Riders in Their Charge Up San Juan Hill (bugle)

SACRED SELECTIONS.

7146 Calvary (baritone solo)
7846 For All Eternity (tenor solo, violin accompaniment)
7447 The Holy City (with voice and organ, chimes)
7149 The Holy City (baritone solo)
7453 Hymns and Prayer from the Funeral Service Over President McKinley (vocal quartette, male voices)
7195 I Heard the Voice of Jesus Say (baritone solo)
73023 Jesus, Lover of My Soul (organ accompaniment, tenor solo)

SACRED SELECTIONS—Continued.

7396 Lead, Kindly Light (baritone solo, organ accompaniment)
7510 Lead, Kindly Light (vocal quartette, male voices)
7397 Nearer, My God, to Thee (baritone solo, organ accompaniment)
7438 Nearer, My God, to Thee (chimes)
7518 Nearer, My God, to Thee (vocal quartette, male voices)
73022 Ninety and Nine (organ accompaniment, tenor solo)
7394 "Onward, Christian Soldiers" and "Old Hundred" (with organ, orchestra)
7664 The Twenty-third Psalm and the Lord's Prayer (talking selection)

MISCELLANEOUS SELECTIONS.

7637 Over the Waves Waltz (Vienna orchestra)
7894 Tales from the Vienna Woods Waltz (Vienna orchestra)
73025 Dance of the Lightning Bugs (piano accompaniment, orchestra bells)
71821 Pretty as a Butterfly (orchestra accompaniment, orchestra bells)
71184 Oh, That We Two Were Maying (contralto and baritone duet)
7211 The Whistling Coon (the old favorite, song with whistling chorus)
7660 Clever Imitations of Well Known Actors (vaudeville)
71108 Uncle Jefferson (negro shout)

No. 20K5115 Purple Label Oxford Disc Records, seven inch. Your own selection of subjects from the list of this and preceding pages. Price, per dozen, **$2.50**; each **21c**

GENUINE COLUMBIA P RECORDS

18 CENTS EACH, $2.15 PER DOZEN.

STANDARD SIZE WAX CYLINDER RECORDS THAT CAN BE USED ON ANY GRAPHOPHONE, PHONOGRAPH OR OTHER STYLE OF TALKING MACHINE USING THE REGULAR STANDARD SIZE WAX CYLINDER RECORDS.

EVERY RECORD GUARANTEED. **We send out these genuine high class Columbia P Records, at 18 cents each, or $2.15 per dozen,** your own selection of subjects, with the distinct understanding and agreement that they can be carefully compared with other records, tested on any kind of a wax cylinder graphophone, phonograph or other style of talking machine, and if not found entirely satisfactory in every way, the equal in volume of sound, naturalness of tone, musical quality, and all other points whereby a record is judged; if they are not equal in all respects to any wax cylinder record, regardless of price, with which they may be compared, they can be returned to us at our expense, including transportation charges, and your money in full will be refunded. **Bear in mind that these records,** although sold at the lowest price ever known for standard size wax cylinder records, your own selection of subjects, are strictly high grade, first quality records, records that will compare with records sold by other dealers at 25 cents, 35 cents and 50 cents each.

SELECT YOUR OWN SUBJECTS from the following complete list. Pick out the exact selections you like best. Our stock of subjects contained in the following list is very complete, and you can order with full assurance that you will get exactly what you send for, records that you will like, records that are sure to please you, and at less than one-half the price you pay for records of corresponding quality elsewhere.

No. 20K5100 Columbia P Records. Price, per dozen, **$2.15**; each **18c**

VOCAL SOLOS WITH PIANO ACCOMPANIMENT.

531549 Absence Makes the Heart Grow Fonder. Tenor
531677 Ain't Dat a Shame (coon song). Baritone
56318 And the Parrot Said (comic). Tenor
531786 Bill Bailey, Won't You Come Home? (coon song). Baritone
54586 Break the News to Mother. Baritone
532089 C-h-i-c-k-e-n; That's the Way to Spell Chicken. Baritone
531338 Columbia, the Gem of the Ocean. Baritone
531603 Coon, Coon, Coon (coon song). Baritone
54615 Darling Nellie Gray. Baritone
532323 Down on the Farm (ballad). Baritone
55851 Fatal Rose of Red, The. Baritone
57181 Girl I Loved in Sunny Tennessee, The. Baritone
531311 Good Bye, Dolly Gray. Baritone
531649 Go 'Way Back and Sit Down. Tenor
531671 He Laid Away a Suit of Gray to Wear the Union Blue. Tenor
531628 Hello, Central; Give Me Heaven (sentimental). Baritone
55801 Holy City, The. Baritone
56309 I Couldn't (comic). Tenor
531706 If Time Was Money, I'd Be a Millionaire (coon song). Baritone
532335 I Like You, Lil, for Fair. (Tough song from "Peggy from Paris"). Tenor
54672 I'll Come Back When the Hawthorn Blooms Again. Baritone
531698 I'm the Man That Makes the Money in the Mint (comic). Tenor
531725 I Need the Money (comic). Tenor
531635 I've a Longing in My Heart for You, Louise. Tenor
532163 I've Got to Go Now, 'Cause I Think It's Going to Rain (comic coon song) Baritone
54592 I Want to Go Tomorrow (intensely funny). Baritone
57184 Just as The Sun Went Down. Baritone
531795 Letter Edged in Black, The. Baritone
54282 Little Bit Off the Top, A (comic). Baritone
531776 Mansion of Aching Hearts, The. Baritone
56365 Miss Helen Hunt (comic). Tenor
531779 Mister Dooley (as sung in "The Chinese Honeymoon"). Tenor
56301 Oh, Don't It Tickle You? (comic). Tenor

VOCAL SOLOS WITH PIANO ACCOMPANIMENT—Continued.

532245 On a Moonlight Night (waltz song). Baritone
531755 On a Sunday Afternoon. Baritone
531788 Please Let Me Sleep (coon song). Baritone
531726 Rip Van Winkle was a Lucky Man (from "The Sleeping Beauty and the Beast"). Tenor
54085 Safe in the Arms of Jesus. Baritone
532244 She's My Girl (song hit of "The Runaways," the latest Broadway success). Baritone
54254 Strike Up the Band, Here Comes a Sailor (comic). Tenor
532140 Things Ain't the Same, Babe, I'm Coming Home (a great coon movement). Baritone
531676 Way Down Yonder in the Cornfield (new ballad). Baritone
54275 Way to Kiss a Girl, The. Tenor
55068 What Do You Think of O'Hooligan? (comic). Tenor
532143 When It's All Going Out, and Nothing Coming In (coon song, as sung by Williams and Walker before His Royal Highness, King Edward VII.) Tenor
531724 When the Roses Bloom Again
531699 Yarns the Captain Told the Mate (comic). Tenor
56355 You Didn't Tell Me That Before We Married (comic). Tenor

VOCAL SOLOS WITH ORCHESTRA ACCOMPANIMENT.

532545 All Aboard for Dreamland (The latest New York waltz song). Tenor
532382 Always in the Way. Baritone
532515 Blue Bell (Marching Song and Chorus) A big success. Tenor
532471 For Sale, a Baby (by the composer of "Always in the Way"). Tenor
531750 Good Bye, Dolly Gray. Baritone
532539 Good Bye, Eliza Jane (A popular coon hit). Baritone
532546 Good Bye, Little Girl, Good Bye (A popular hit). Tenor
532512 Good Bye, My Lady Love. (One of the latest hits). Tenor
532508 Hannah, Won't You Open That Door? (A big hit). Baritone
532509 He Done Me Wrong, or The Death of Bill Bailey. Baritone
532397 I'm Just Barely Living, Dat's All (A hard luck tale of a speculative coon). Baritone

VOCAL SOLOS WITH ORCHESTRA ACCOMPANIMENT—Continued.

531879 In the Good Old Summer Time. Baritone
532540 I've Got a Feelin' for You (popular coon song). Baritone
531752 Little Boy in Blue, A. Baritone
532488 Meet Me in St. Louis, Louis. Tenor
532495 McGinty at the Living Pictures. Tenor
532456 The Man Behind. (Lew Dockstader's big hit). Tenor
532318 When Mamie, Sweet Mamie's a Bride. Tenor
532459 You're Always Behind, Like an Old Cow's Tail (from Dockstader's minstrels). Baritone
532384 Under the Anheuser Bush (This one is extra good)

VOCAL SOLOS WITH BANJO ACCOMPANIMENT.

57200-c Hot Time in the Old Town Tonight.
531403 If You Love Your Baby Make Them Goo Goo Eyes. Baritone
57200-h Little Old Log Cabin in the Lane. Baritone

YODLE SONG—TENOR.

The Yodling is distinct and agreeable, with good voice effect.

58902 Snyder, Does Your Mother Know You're Out?

SONGS WITH WHISTLING CHORUS.

531696 Whippoorwill Song, The (with bird imitations)
512653 Whistling Susanna

LAUGHING SONGS.

With Rube Laughing Chorus.

531756 And Then I Laughed
57601 Negro Laughing Song. (An old standard)
531764 Ticklish Reuben
514032 I'm Old, But I'm Awfully Tough

NEGRO SHOUTS.

Songs with laughing and whistling choruses.

57711 Bye Bye, Ma Honey
57713 Negro Songs, Medley of
57703 Turkey in the Straw

VOCAL SOLOS IN GERMAN.

532096 Das Haidenroeslein
58206 Die Wacht Am Rhein
532104 Der Rattenfaenger
58218 Es Hat Nicht Sollen Sein (Nessler)

SOPRANO AND CONTRALTO SOLOS.

Wonderful reproductions of the female voice.

56601 Ben Bolt. Soprano
531761 I'll Be Your Rainbeau. Soprano
56608 Old Kentucky Home. Soprano
531715 Stay in Your Own Backyard. Soprano
532519 Toyland (with male chorus, as sung in "Babes in Toyland"). Contralto

VOCAL DUETS WITH ORCHESTRA ACCOMPANIMENT.

532551 Down on the Brandywine (with chime effects). Very tuneful and catchy. Baritone and tenor
532531 Listen to the Mocking Bird (with bird imitations). Contralto and baritone.

VOCAL DUETS WITH PIANO ACCOMPANIMENT.

58416 Almost Persuaded. Baritone and tenor
58404 Bye and Bye You Will Forget Me. Baritone and tenor
531343 I Loved You Better Than You Knew. Baritone and tenor
532209 It's a Lovely Day for a Walk (seriocomic). Contralto and baritone
531878 Jerry Murphy Is a Friend of Mine. Baritone and tenor
531703 McManus and the Parrot (comic Irish song). Baritone and tenor
532517 'Possum Pie, or the Stuttering Coon. Baritone and tenor
531611 Reuben and Cynthia (a duet interspersed with humorous dialogue between male and female characters. One of Hoyt's great successes). Soprano and baritone
58420 Shadow of the Pines, In the. Baritone and tenor
532409 Under the Anheuser Bush. Baritone and tenor
531910 Under the Bamboo Tree (as sung by Miss Marie Cahill in the musical comedy "Sally in Our Alley"). Baritone and tenor
532267 Two Rubes in an Eating House. Baritone and tenor
58421 While the Leaves Came Drifting Down. Baritone and tenor
531684 Whoa, Bill! (a trombone extravaganza). Baritone and tenor

LIST OF COLUMBIA P RECORDS CONTINUED ON NEXT PAGE.

LIST OF COLUMBIA P RECORDS—Continued.

VOCAL TRIOS.

57707 Camp Meeting (opening with chorus by trio, followed by a negro sermon and ending with song by trio)
57705 Mocking Bird Medley, The (tenor solo, whistling, chorus by trio)

VOCAL QUARTETTES—Male Voices.

These songs are finely rendered, and the effect is so natural that no stretch of the imagination is required to bring the singers so strongly forward in spirit that their actual presence seems to be achieved.

59014 Annie Laurie
59071 Blue and The Gray, The
59067 Camp Meeting Jubilee (negro shout)
59068 Carry Me Back to Old Virginia (coon song)
59039 Church Scene from "The Old Homestead" (with church bell effect)
59046 Coon Songs, Medley of
532242 Coon Wedding in Southern Georgia, A
59037 Farmyard Medley (imitation of fowls, cattle, etc.)
59049 Fireman's Duty, The (descriptive—bells, horses' hoofs, gallant rescue, etc.)
531654 Hymns and Prayer from the Funeral Service Over President McKinley
59070 I'd Leave My Happy Home for You (coon song)
59010 I'se Gwine Back to Dixie (coon song)
531693 Laughing Quartette, The
531668 Lead, Kindly Light
59015 Little Alabama Coon (with baby cry and clog)
59033 Massa's in the Cold, Cold Ground (coon song, with banjo imitation)
59008 Moonlight on the Lake
59019 My Old Kentucky Home
59045 My Old New Hampshire Home
59012 Nearer, My God, to Thee
59050 Old Black Joe (coon song)
59030 Old Folks at Home, The
59018 Old Oaken Bucket, The
532241 Plantation Songs. Medley of (introducing "In the Evening by the Moonlight," "Down in the Cornfield," "Carry Me Back to Old Virginia" and "My Old Cabin Home")
59011 Rocked in the Cradle of the Deep
59064 Rock of Ages
59040 Sleigh Ride Party, The (descriptive)
531548 Soldier's Farewell, The
59041 Steamboat Medley (descriptive)
532236 St. Patrick's Day at Clancy's ("Loike Ould Times in Kilkenny, Begorra")
59048 Tenting on the Old Camp Ground
59038 Trip to the County Fair (imitation of railway, fakers and Rubes)
59029 Way Down Yonder in the Cornfield (coon song)
59061 Where Is My Wandering Boy Tonight?
59069• Where the Sweet Magnolias Bloom

MENDELSSOHN QUARTETTE—Mixed Voices.

532074 Good Night, Good Night, Beloved
532332 Home, Sweet Home, by John Howard Payne
532238 The Lord's Prayer and Gloria Patria

VOCAL SEXTETTE—Mixed Voices.

531604 Tell Me, Pretty Maiden (from "Florodora")

MINSTRELS.

These records each embrace overture, new jokes, laughter and applause, and end with song given in title, with orchestra and vocal quartette.

532045A Introductory Overture by the entire company
532045D End Man Song, "I'm a Nigger That's Living High," by Billy Golden
532045E Jokes Between Interlocutor and End Man
532045F I'm Wearing My Heart Away for You. Tenor solo by George J. Gaskin, with chorus by the entire company.
532045G Jokes between Interlocutor and End Man
532045L Banjo Solo, "Yankee Doodle," by Vess L. Ossman, with orchestra accompaniment
531609 Coon, Coon, Coon
513000 Dese Bones Shall Rise Again
531608 Good Bye, Dolly Gray
513005 Hear Dem Bells
532392 Squash Town Minstrels. Amateur (The local talent attempts to emulate the "reg'lar professionals," exceptionally funny)
531691 I'd Leave My Happy Home for You

BAND RECORDS.

51544 Admiral's Favorite March
51514 America
532311 Anona (intermezzo two step) by Mabel McKinley
532362 Any Rags (schottische)
531867 Arkansaw Husking Bee, An
532389 Bedelia, medley march (introducing "He Was a Sailor")
51505 "Bohemian Girl," Selections from
5533 Bride Elect March, The
531530 Bunch of Blackberries (cake walk)
51637 Charge of the Light Brigade March
5569 Circus Gallop (descriptive)
531486 Colored Major, The (ragtime march)
51550 Columbia Phonograph Co. March
5538 Coon Band Contest
5529 Dancing in the Dark (song and dance with clogs)
51518 Die Wacht Am Rhein
5518 Directorate March

BAND RECORDS—Continued.

51516 Dixie
523274 Dixie Girl Two Step
51508 El Miserere, from "Il Trovatore"
5535 Hands Across the Sea March
5501 High School Cadets March
5526 Honeymoon March
51642 International Cake Walk
532297 Jack Tar March (Sousa's latest, introducing sailor's hornpipe, eight bells, boatswain's whistle).
5507 Jolly Coppersmith (descriptive)
5506 King Cotton March
5500 Liberty Bell March (bell effect)
531625 Love's Dreamland Waltz
5537 Man Behind the Gun March
5519 Manhattan Beach March
51638 Marching Through Georgia
51522 Nearer, My God, to Thee (with cornet solo)
51539 Rock of Ages
5516 Say Au Revoir, But Not Good-Bye
531526 Sousa's Band's Coming (descriptive patrol)
531626 Spring and Love Waltz
51512 Star Spangled Banner
5532 Stars and Stripes Forever March
51588 Till We Meet Again Waltz
5520 Washington Post March

ORCHESTRA RECORDS.

515132 Angels' Serenade (piccolo and cornet duet)
515194 Battle of Manila (descriptive)
515162 Blue Danube Waltz
515206 Bugler's Dream, The (descriptive—introducing "Just Before the Battle, Mother," Bugle Calls, etc., and ending with "Nearer, My God, to Thee")
515191 Capture of Santiago (descriptive—The Bugle Call, Fall In, March, Opening of the Battle, In the Thick of the Fight, Caring for the Wounded, Cease Firing, The Battle Won, Patriotic Music)
531689 Creole Belle
515010 Dancing in the Kitchen (song and dance with clogs)
515145 Darky's Dream (with clogs)
515159 Darky Tickle (plantation medley, with clogs, shouts, etc.)
515229 Dewey's Return (descriptive, with steamboat whistles, cheers, etc. Music, "See The Conquering Hero Comes")
532191 Dixieland March, introducing "Dixie" and "Old Black Joe"
515064 Down on the Suwanee River (descriptive—pulling in the gang plank, steamboat bells, whistle, dance on board, with negro shouts and clogs)
515114 Flora Waltz (cornet solo, with full orchestra accompaniment)
515202 Georgia Camp Meeting, At a (march and two step)
532460 Gondolier (intermezzo two step, the latest popular success)
515007 Happy Days in Dixie (plantation medley, with clogs, shouts, etc.)
515142 Husking Bee (descriptive, introducing rural characters and scenes, with country dance and call in dialect)
532283 Laughing Water
515121 Let Her Rip (quadrille, with figures called)
515139 Limited Express, The (descriptive)

ORCHESTRA RECORDS—Continued.

515063 Night Alarm (with all the familiar descriptive effects, representing a fire alarm at night—fire bells, cries, horses' hoofs, winding of hose reel, whistle of engine, ending with firemen's chorus)
515195 Roosevelt's Rough Riders, Charge of
515044 Rose from the South Waltz
515220 Smoky Mokes March
515059 Virginia Skedaddle (plantation medley, with clogs, shouts, etc.)
515203 Whistling Rufus
531794 When Mr. Shakespeare Comes to Town

RECORDS BY VIENNA ORCHESTRA.

The Violin Effects of a String Orchestra Are Here Shown to Their Best Advantage.

531681 Life in Vienna Waltz
531847 Night in Venice Waltz, A
531683 Over the Waves Waltz

ORCHESTRA BELLS.

512516 Chiming Bells
512517 Mill in the Forest, The

CORNET RECORDS.

52807 Home, Sweet Home, duet
532491 Marriage Bells, (with chimes effect), solo
52814 Mid' the Green Fields of Virginia, duet
52813 My Old Kentucky Home, duet
52812 Nearer, My God, to Thee, duet
52815 She Was Bred in Old Kentucky, duet
532030 Sweet Sixteen Waltz, solo

FOUR WINNERS

SPECIAL COLUMBIA RECORDS AT 18c EACH.

The Arkansaw Traveler.

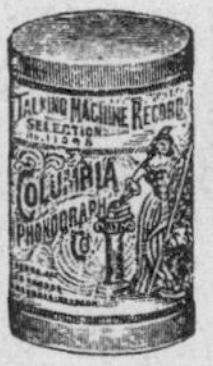

No. 511098 This is a talking and musical selection descriptive of an Arkansaw native sitting in front of his cabin door, scraping his fiddle, and replying to the questions of a traveler with a great variety of witty sallies. "Well, how do you do, boss, what might your name be?" "Say, what made you think I was boss heah?" "Oh I just guessed it!" "Well, jest guess what my name is!" This record is full of jokes and laughter and humorous fiddling. Don't overlook this one in making up your list.

Backyard Conversation Between Two Jealous Washerwomen.

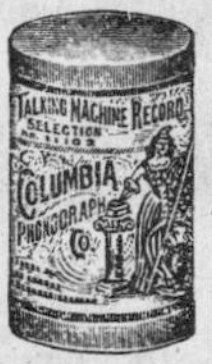

No. 511102 A record that is full of real comedy and back talk. "Good marnin', Mrs. Reilley and how are yez this marnin'?" "Mind yer bizness Mrs. Finnegan and pay yer rint!" "Here, here, you do be gittin' pretty smart this marnin', if I had a husband like that old coward of yours, do you know what I'd do with 'im?" "And what would ye do with 'im, Mrs. Finnegan?" "I'd have 'im arristed fer croolty to animiles." "You would, would ye? And what for?" "For batin' the likes of you, Mrs. Reilley." "Here, here, Mrs. Finnegan, my husband and I have been married fer tin years and niver had a fight in the house yit!" "No, ye always go out in the backyard to do yer fightin'." "Well, if I had such a dog faced tarrier fer an auld man as that husband of yours, you know what I'd do with 'im?" "And what would ye do with 'im, Mrs. Reilley?" etc. Get this record and hear the finish of the scrap.

Uncle Josh's Husking Bee Dance.

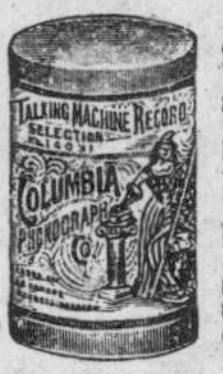

No. 514031 This is one of Cal Stewart's (Uncle Josh Weatherby's) biggest hits, and gives a most humorous imitation of a good old fashioned barn dance. "Well, neow, all you boys and gals get out th're on the barn floor and be ready to shake yourselves—Be ye all ready? Well, let 'er go." Then to the merry strains of Money Musk the dance goes on, "Honor Your Partners," "Right Hands Round," "All Join Hands," "Circle to the Center," and so on, Uncle Josh playing the fiddle in his inimitable style, calling and punctuating the figures of the dance with his famous and infectious laugh, "Oho! Ha, Ha, Ha, Haw, Well now I'll be gol darned ef that wa'n't pretty good. Now then you boys git to shucking corn; first boy that finds a red ear corn gets to kiss the purtiest gal on the barn floor."

The Night Alarm (Orchestra).

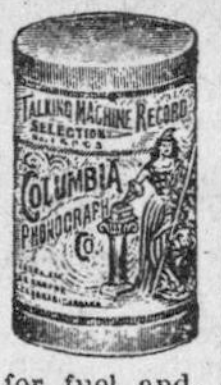

No. 515063 A wonderful descriptive selection by the full Columbia orchestra, representing an alarm of fire at night. The cry of Fire! Fire! is followed by the clang of the engine bells, the captain's shouted orders, "Box 32, let 'er go, Bill." Then comes the run to the fire, the steady beat of the horses' hoofs on the pavement, the arrival at the scene of action, the unwinding of the hose reel, the shrill whistling for fuel and, finally, the return to the engine house, ending with a characteristic chorus by the firemen on their way home, tired but happy in the knowledge of duty performed. A record that is full of excitement and inspiring music.

VIOLIN SOLOS.

527002 Ben Bolt (special arrangement)
527013 El Miserere, from "Il Trovatore"
531492 Holy City
527006 Imitation of Bagpipes and Scotch Airs, special arrangement.

CLARIONET SOLO.

53409 My Old Kentucky Home (with variations)

XYLOPHONE SOLOS.

512020 Dancing in the Sunlight
512009 Mocking Bird, The

PICCOLO SOLOS.

523501 Darkies' Jubilee
523505 Hornpipe Polka

DRUM, FIFE AND BUGLE CORPS.

512801 Marching Thro' Georgia, and Dixie
512800 The Girl I Left Behind Me and Auld Lang Syne

BUGLE CALLS.

53769 Rough Riders in Their Charge Up San Juan Hill, Bugle Calls of the
53768 United States Army, Bugle Calls of the

BANJO SOLOS.

53861 Bunch of Rags
531412 Coon Band Contest, A
53816 Darky's Dream
53825 El Capitan March
53856 Eli Green's Cake Walk
53860 Old Folks at Home (with variations)

BANJO SOLOS—Continued.

53830 Rag Time Medley (introducing "All Coons Look Alike to Me," and "Oh, Mr. Johnson")
53859 Whistling Rufus
531780 Whoa, Bill!

WHISTLING SOLOS.

512604 Home, Sweet Home
57701 Mocking Bird, The (with bird imitations running throughout the record)

TALKING RECORDS.

531666 Address of the late President McKinley at the Pan-American Exposition
511098 Arkansaw Traveler, The (descriptive of a native sitting in front of his hut scraping his fiddle and answering the interruptions of the stranger with witty sallies. Record is full of jokes and laughter)
531836 Auction Sale of a Bird and Animal Store (with bird and animal effects)
511102 Backyard Conversation Between Two Jealous Irish Washerwomen (full of real comedy and back talk)
511024 "Blazing Rag" Concert Hall, The (introducing the bouncer, the tipsy soubrette, the professor, and the fight—very realistic)
510501 Stump Speech on Love
531839 Daybreak at Calamity Farm (with animal effects)
511021 Dog Fight, The
531838 Passing of the Circus Parade, The (with animal and band effects)
510006 Sale of Household Furniture. (The leather lunged auctioneer)
510001 Sale of Pawn Broker's Goods. (The leather lunged auctioneer)
531694 Scene in a Police Court
531837 Trip to the Circus, A (with animal and band effects)

UNCLE JOSH WEATHERBY'S LAUGHING STORIES.

514000 Arrival in New York, Uncle Josh's
514005 Base Ball Game, Uncle Josh at a
514011 Bicycle, Uncle Josh on a
514023 Chinese Laundry, Uncle Josh in a
514004 Department Store, Uncle Josh in a
514008 Fifth Avenue Bus, Uncle Josh on a
514031 Husking Bee Dance, Uncle Josh's (giving a correct imitation of a New England dance on the barn floor, with the fiddler playing appropriate music and Uncle Josh calling the figures)
531574 Jim Lawson's Horse Trade, Uncle Josh on
531765 Last Day of School at Pumpkin Center, The
514029 Lightning Rod Agent, Uncle Josh and the
531573 Meeting of the Ananias Club at Pumpkin Center, Uncle Josh at a
532406 Ohio. Uncle Josh on the (descriptive with bells and steamboat imitations)
532405 Political Meeting at Pumpkin Center. (Introducing speech by Uncle Josh, national airs by county band and the Pumpkin Center Glee Club)
514027 Society, Uncle Josh in
532403 Threshing Time at Pumpkin Center (with imitation of steam thresher, song with banjo and chorus by the farm hands)

DESCRIPTIVE.

532461 Clarence the Copper. (Clarence leaves his beat to call on his best girl. The sergeant appears and Clarence is transferred)
532462 Leander and Lulu. (Leander attempts to propose while riding down town on elevated railway. Charlie Onthespot, his hated rival, is on the spot as usual)

SACRED SELECTIONS.

55801 Holy City, The. Baritone solo, piano accompaniment
54085 Safe in the Arms of Jesus. Baritone solo, piano accompaniment
531359 All Hail the Power of Jesus' Name. Baritone solo with church organ accompaniment
532496 I Need Thee Every Hour. Tenor solo with church organ accompaniment
531364 Jesus, Lover of My Soul. Baritone solo with church organ accompaniment
531356 Nearer, My God, to Thee. Baritone solo with church organ accompaniment
531358 Rock of Ages. Baritone solo with church organ accompaniment
531367 There is a Fountain. Baritone solo with church organ accompaniment
531357 Where Is My Wandering Boy Tonight? Baritone solo with church organ accompaniment
58416 Almost Persuaded. Baritone and tenor duet with piano accompaniment
531654 Hymns and Prayer from Funeral Service Over President McKinley. Vocal quartette, male voices
531668 Lead, Kindly Light. Vocal quartette, male voices
59012 Nearer, My God, to Thee. Vocal quartette, male voices
59064 Rock of Ages. Vocal quartette, male voices
59061 Where Is My Wandering Boy Tonight? Vocal quartette, male voices
532238 The Lord's Prayer and Gloria Patria —Mendelssohn, mixed quartette
51522 Nearer, My God, to Thee (with cornet solo) Band
51539 Rock of Ages. Band
52812 Nearer, My God, to Thee. Cornet duet
531492 Holy City, The. Violin solo

No. 20K5100 Columbia P Records. Your own selection of subjects, any of the titles shown in the list on this and the preceding pages. Price, per dozen, **$2.15**; each **18c**

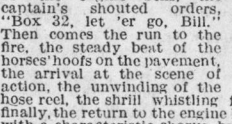

Flower Horns.

$1.20

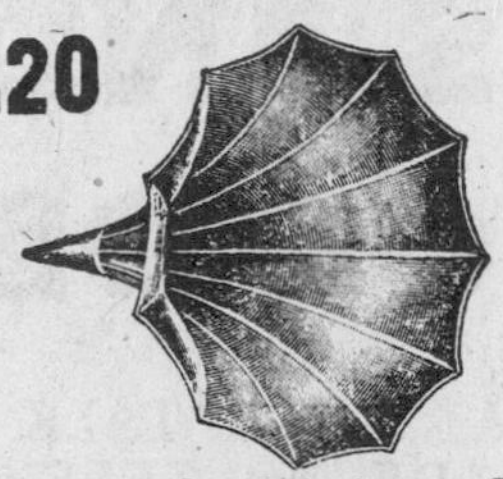

These new floral design or flower horns are the handsomest and most ornamental horns made for talking machines. In shape and design they are like an immense morning glory, and they are beautifully finished with a special enamel, either in black or in colors, with gold stripes or fancy decorations inside. This finish is baked on and is absolutely permanent and durable. These horns are made by a new process in such a way that all strain comes on the ribs, which are made of four thicknesses of metal, giving them great strength. The acoustic properties are unexcelled, giving full, rich, soft tones of great volume and clearness. **One size only, 31 inches long, with 22¼-inch bell.**

No. 20K5150 Flower Horn, black, with gold stripes. Price. $1.20

No. 20K5151 Flower Horn, maroon, with gold stripes. Price. $1.30

No. 20K5152 Flower Horn, blue, with gold stripes. Price. $1.30

No. 20K5153 Flower Horn, black, decorated inside. Price. $1.50

No. 20K5154 Flower Horn, maroon, decorated inside. Price. $1.60

No. 20K5155 Flower Horn, blue, decorated inside. Price. $1.60

Shipping weight, 25 pounds.

Hand Decorated Flower Horns.

$2.00

These new Flower Horns are the most beautiful horns made, decorated by expert artists with beautiful designs, chrysanthemums, white roses, pansies, pink roses, wild roses, etc.; the body of the horn finished in black, maroon or blue.

The tone qualities of the flower horns are superior to all other horns. The great diameter of the horn in proportion to its length gives a richness of tone produced by no other style of horn. While these horns are more ornamental than any other horns, more beautiful in appearance, and for this reason alone very desirable, their greatest value lies in the improved reproduction, the increase in musical qualities and naturalness of tone.

No. 20K5165 Black Flower Horn, decorated with chrysanthemums. Price. $2.00

No. 20K5166 Black Flower Horn, decorated with white roses. Price. $2.00

No. 20K5167 Maroon Flower Horn, decorated with pansies. Price. . $2.25

No. 20K5168 Maroon Flower Horn, decorated with white roses. Price. $2.25

No. 20K5169 Blue Flower Horn, decorated with pink roses. Price. $2.25

No. 20K5170 Blue Flower Horn, decorated with white roses. Price. $2.25

Shipping weight, 25 pounds.

Note—We ship these horns in strongly made hardwood crates, and guarantee them to reach destination in perfect order.

60c

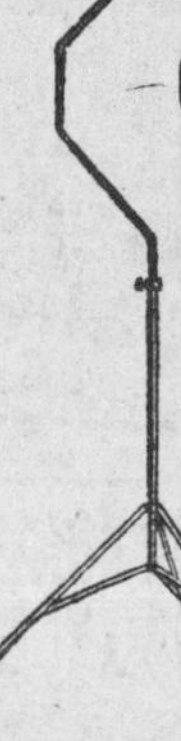

Folding Horn Stand.

No. 20K5180 Folding Horn Stand, fully nickel plated, strongly made, and adapted to carry any size horn up to 42 inches. Price. . . 60c

Folding Horn Cranes.

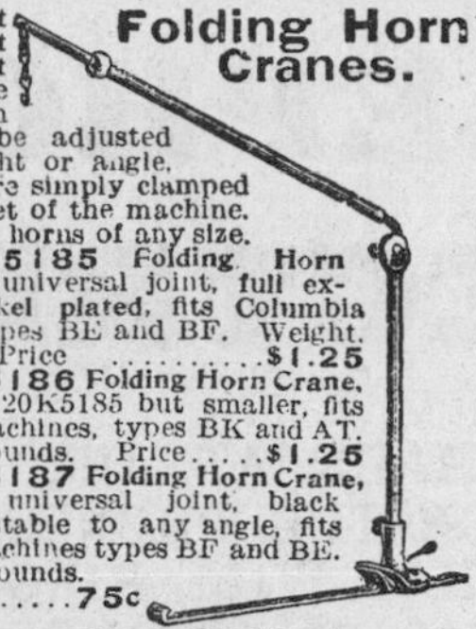

The most convenient horn support made. These new horn cranes can be adjusted to any height or angle, and in use are simply clamped to the cabinet of the machine. Will support horns of any size.

No. 20K5185 Folding Horn Crane, with universal joint, full extension, nickel plated, fits Columbia Machines, types BE and BF. Weight, 5 pounds. Price $1.25

No. 20K5186 Folding Horn Crane, same as No. 20K5185 but smaller, fits Columbia Machines, types BK and AT. Weight, 5 pounds. Price. $1.25

No. 20K5187 Folding Horn Crane, with semi-universal joint, black finish, adjustable to any angle, fits Columbia Machines types BF and BE. Weight, 4 pounds. Price. 75c

Cases for Cylinder Records.

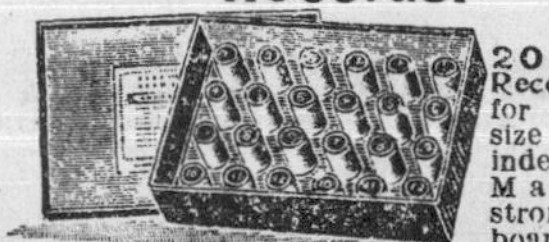

No. 20K5199 Record Boxes for standard size wax cylinder records. Made of strong pasteboard; covered with imitation leather, affording a convenient means of keeping the records safe and easily accessible.

No. 1 holds 12 records. Size, 11½ in. long, 8½ in. wide, 4½ high. Price 23c

No. 2 holds 24 records. Size, 17 in. long, 11½ in. wide, 4½ in. high. Price 40c

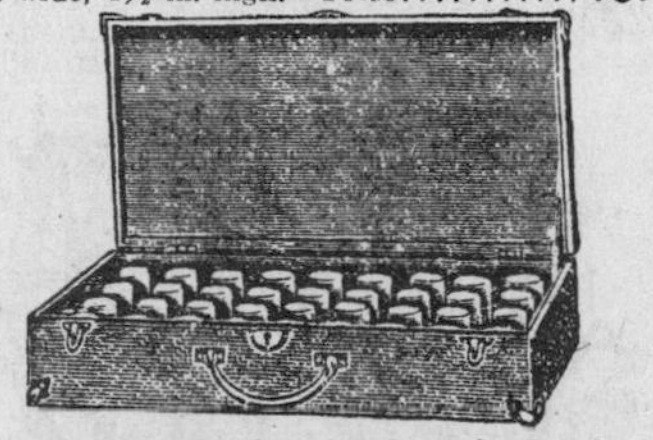

No. 20K5200 Carrying Cases for Standard Size Wax Cylinder Records, black seal grain covering, with improved pegs for records, full nickeled trimmings, two snap locks and lock and key. Best record cases made.

No. 2 holds 36 standard size records. Size, 16¾ in. long, 16¾ in. wide, 5 in. high. Price $2.25

No. 3 holds 72 standard size records. Size, 16¾ in. long, 16¾ in. wide, 9½ in. high. Price $3.90

Disc Record Cases.

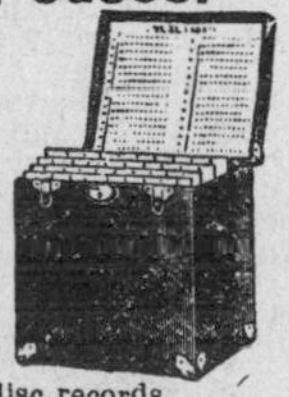

No. 20K5205 Disc Record Cases, strongly and substantially made from wood, covered with black seal grain imitation leather, nickel plated trimmings, two snap catches, lock and key and leather handle. Provided with numbered separators and numbered blank on inside of cover for list of selections, so any desired record may be instantly found.

No. 1 holds 50 7-inch disc records. Price $1.35

No. 2 holds 50 10-inch disc records. Price $1.55

Disc Record Trays.

Disc Record Trays, made of quarter sawed oak, thoroughly seasoned and kiln dried, hand rubbed and beautifully finished in golden oak. Holds fifty 7 or 10-inch records. This tray keeps your records in perfect condition, no scratching or damaging. Easy to move and by having the grooves that hold the records alternately countersunk takes up the least possible space, and at the same time makes each record accessible at any time. The selection No. is marked along the edge telling you the record in each slot. A handsome ornament and a money saver in one.

No. 20K5210 Disc Record Tray. For 7-inch records. Size, 14x9x5½. Weight, 8 lbs. Price $1.50

No. 20K5211 Disc Record Tray. For 10-inch records. Size, 14x12x5½. Weight, 10 lbs. Price $1.75

The New $5.00 Columbia D Reproducer for $3.00 (in exchange).

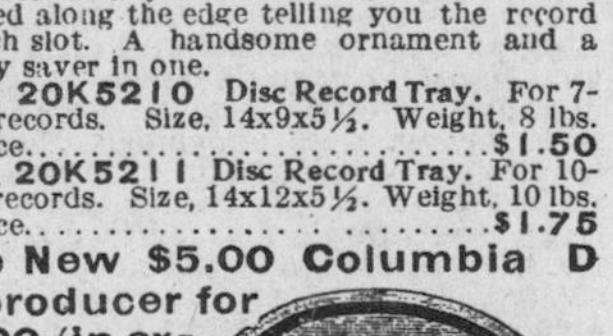

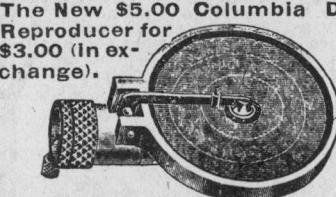

This is the latest improved Columbia D Reproducer, the same as now furnished with the AT and AO graphophones. It is made with practically indestructible, built up mica diaphragm, all metal parts of aluminum and the best tool steel, and is 1¼ inches in diameter. **In volume, sweetness and naturalness of tone, it is a source of astonishment and delight to all who hear it.**

No. 20K5225 Latest Columbia D Reproducer. Price $5.00

The regular price is $5.00, but **if you will send us your old reproducer and $3.00 in cash we will forward the new style D reproducer, just as described above.** Remember, your old reproducer, no matter what style and no matter how old it is, and $3.00 in cash will put you in possession of one of these new, up to date, $5.00 reproducers.

The Latest Columbia $5.00 Analyzing Reproducer or Sound Box for $2.00 (in exchange).

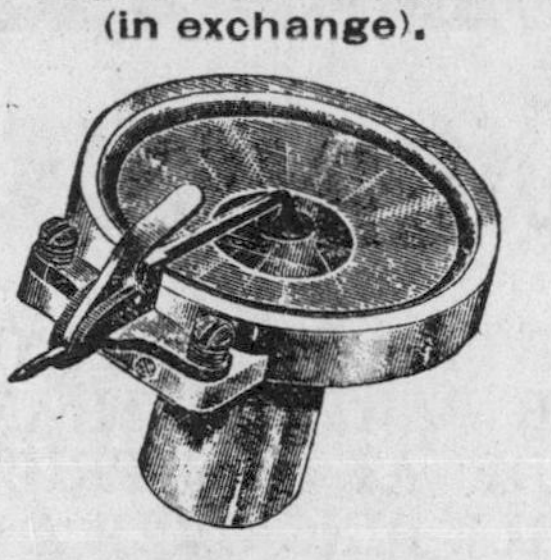

This Reproducer or Sound Box for disc talking machines, is the very latest production of the Columbia Phonograph Company. It is made with the reproducer bar pivoted on delicate points, practically eliminating all friction. This new form of construction enables the reproducer to reveal tones heretofore entirely indistinguishable. It greatly increases the volume of sound and enriches the quality. **The New Automatic Needle Holder with which this reproducer is equipped constitutes one of its very great advantages.** The needle is inserted or removed simply by pressing a little lever, as shown in the illustration, doing away entirely with the old fashioned screw, which was not only a nuisance to use, but was frequently lost, thus rendering the graphophone useless for the time being.

No. 20K5226 Columbia Analyzing Reproducer, or Sound Box for disc talking machines, latest style, just as described above. Price $5.00

$5.00 is the very lowest price we can make on this instrument, when sold in the regular way, but **if you wish to send us your old sound box and $2.00 in cash** we will send you the new reproducer, exactly as described above, thus putting you in possession of the very latest, most up to date sound box for only $2.00 in cash.

Miscellaneous.

No. 20K5250 Recorder, for Q, QC, QQ, Q Special or our Special Home Graphophone. Price. $2.50

No. 20K5252 Recorder, for BX, AT, AO, Harvard Senior, or Gem Graphophone. Price. $5.00

No. 20K5254 Reproducer, for Q, QC, QQ, Q Special, or our Special Home Graphophone. Price. $2.50

No. 20K5260 Diaphragm Glasses, best French glass, for recorders and old style reproducers, 1 5-16 inches diameter.

Price, per dozen, 30c; each. 4c

No. 20K5262 Mica Diaphragms, for D reproducers only, best quality, built up. Price, each. 19c

No. 20K5264 Mica Diaphragms, for sound boxes of any style Disc Graphophone. Price, each. 10c

No. 20K5266 Rubber Gaskets, for reproducers or recorders. Price, per set of three, ordinary size. 5c

Per set of two, for large D reproducer. 4c

No. 20K5270 Reproducer Ball, made of Brazilian pebble, but sold by many dealers as sapphire.

Price, each. 20c

No. 20K5272 Reproducer Ball, made of genuine sapphire, highest grade. Price, each. 75c

No. 20K5275 Governor Springs, for types Q, QC, QQ, BX, AB, Q special, Harvard Jr. and Sr. and our Special Home Graphophones. Price. 10c

No. 20K5278 Governor Springs, for types AK, AJ, AH, AR, AY, BH, BI, BD and Harvard Disc Talking Machines. Price. 15c

No. 20K5280 Governor Spring, for types AT, AO, AZ, AW, BK, BE, BF, BG. Price, each. 15c

No. 20K5285 Recorder Points, made of Brazilian pebble, but often sold as sapphire.

Price, each, in setting, flat edge. . 52c

Price, ea., in setting, cupped edge. 60c

No. 20K5290 Main Spring, single, for Q, QC, QQ, BX, AB and our special Home Graphophones. Price, each, 18c

No. 20K5292 Main Spring, for Oxford or Harvard No. 5. Price, each, 60c

State kind of Graphophone for which spring is wanted.

No. 20K5294 Main Spring, single, for Columbia Machines, types AT, AK, AJ, AH, BH, BI, and all Harvard Disc Talking Machines. Price, each. . 45c

No. 20K5300 10-inch Turn Tables to fit any Columbia Disc Machine.

Price, each $1.75

No. 20K5302 Speaking Tube, for use in record making, mohair covered, with spiral spring, lining and hard rubber mouthpiece; 22 inches long. Price. . 75c

No. 20K5304 Camel's Hair Brushes, 1½ inches wide, for dusting records

Price, each. 15c

No. 20K5306 Blank Cylinders, for record making. Standard size, same as P or XP records. Price, each. 15c

Standard Needles.

1,000 for 35 Cents.

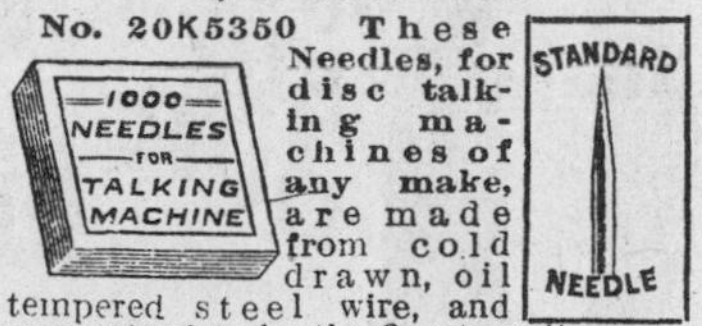

No. 20K5350 These Needles, for disc talking machines of any make, are made from cold drawn, oil tempered steel wire, and guaranteed to be the finest needles manufactured.

Price, per 100 (put up in envelopes of 100 each). 4c

If by mail, postage extra, 2 cents.

Price, per 1,000 (put up in boxes of 1,000 each) 35c

If by mail, postage extra, 8 cents.

Soft Tone Needles.

500 for 25 Cents.

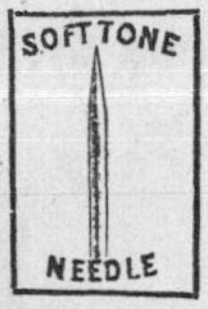

No. 20K5355 These **Soft Tone Needles are noted for the soft, sweet and natural tone which they produce,** making them particularly suitable for use in small rooms, where the standard needle reproduces the record too loudly. Put up only in packages of 500.

Price, per package (500 needles) 25c

If by mail, postage extra, 4 cents.

Spear Point or Double Tone Needles.

250 for 25 Cents.

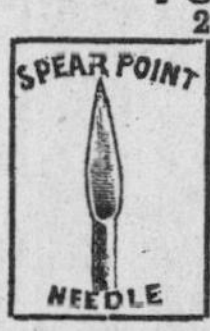

No. 20K5360 These new Spear Point **Needles are particularly desirable, as the tone and volume of sound can be varied at will,** giving either a soft or loud reproduction. With this needle the high notes are brought out with a sweet melody not obtainable with any other needle. Put up only in packages of 250.

Price, per package 25c

If by mail, postage extra, 3 cents.

Horn Connections.

No. 20K5365 Rubber Hose, large size, for connecting large horns to any style talking machine.

Price, per foot. 16c

No. 20K5371 Rubber Connection, for attaching large horns to any cylinder record machine. Price. . . 5c

No. 20K5372 Rubber Connection, L shaped, for connecting large horns to any disc machine. Price. 8c

We can furnish repair parts for any Columbia Graphophone or Harvard Talking Machine, but you must send us the broken or worn out part as a sample when ordering, except on items listed above. Put your name and address plainly on the package when you send us samples.

The Thompson Modifier.

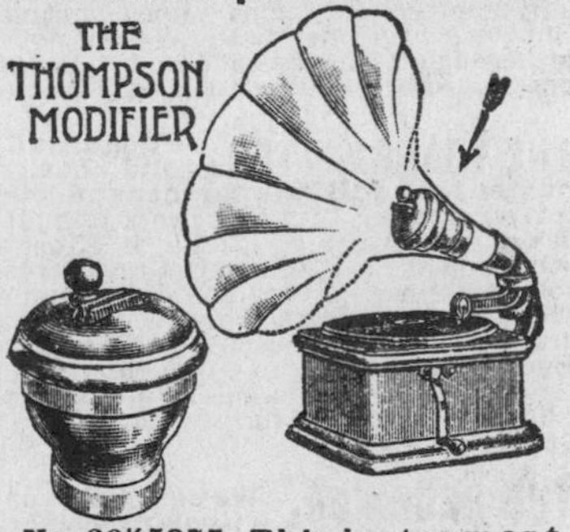

No. 20K5375 This instrument softens the tone, eliminates the metallic sound, takes all the scratch out, and makes the reproduction as soft, smooth and harmonious as the original. Modern disc records are frequently so true to the original, reproducing the sound practically in all its original volume that they are too loud to be pleasant in small rooms, and this Thompson Modifier, inserted in the horn of the machine softens the sound, making it pleasant and agreable even in the smallest of rooms. The Thompson Modifier is strongly and substantially made of brass, nickel plated, fitted with rubber at points where it touches the horn, and instantly put into place or as quickly removed.

There is no talking machine included with this modifier. It is simply an attachment to put into the horn of your own machine.

Price. 75c

$9⁹⁵ BUYS OUR 5 MAGNET TELEPHONES AND 1600 OHM ELECTRIC GOODS

THERE ARE NO TELEPHONES MADE AT ANY PRICE THAT WILL TALK PLAINER OR FARTHER THAN OUR TELEPHONES. THERE ARE NO TELEPHONES MADE AT ANY PRICE THAT WILL RING MORE BELLS ON A LINE OR THAT WILL RING OVER A GREATER DISTANCE THAN OUR TELEPHONES.

OUR FIVE-MAGNET BRIDGING TELEPHONES are built for use on lines with from thirty to forty instruments installed, and are equally suited to smaller lines. They are equipped with our extra powerful five-magnet generators, tested and guaranteed to ring through 125,000 ohms resistance, tested and guaranteed to ring through fifty telephones on the same line, **more power** than is ever required in actual practice. If you are building a new line, no matter how many telephones are to be installed, we advise the purchase of our powerful five-magnet 1,600-ohm compact, or 2,000-ohm Southwestern style bridging telephones, as this equipment is standard throughout the country. If you are buying telephones to put on a line already equipped, then it will be best to select instruments equipped with generators and ringers to match those already on the line. Prices on our bridging telephones, with both four and five-magnet generators and ringers of 1,000, 1,600 or 2,000 ohms resistance will be found at the bottom of this and the following page.

THE CABINETS. Our Compact Telephones are put up in cabinets of very ornamental design, very compact and made throughout of the best selected kiln dried oak. The corners are rounded and dovetailed, the screw holes are provided with metal bushings and the finish is a fine golden oak with piano polish. This cabinet measures 23¼ inches high by 5½ inches deep by 8⅝ inches wide. We put up our Southwestern style of telephone in an extra large, substantially made cabinet, with sufficient space in the lower compartment for two full sized wet batteries. We recommend this cabinet particularly for use in engine rooms, creameries, etc., and especially in warm, dry climates, where dry batteries are not satisfactory. This cabinet measures 32 inches high, 12 inches wide and 7 inches deep. It is made throughout of the finest selected kiln dried oak, with piano polish.

THE TRANSMITTER. We equip all our telephones with our latest improved solid back long distance transmitter, a transmitter that will talk farther and louder and plainer than any other transmitter made. The framework is built of heavy brass castings making it absolutely solid, and the carbon cup is turned from a solid brass bar. The carbon diaphragm and the granulated carbon are the very finest grade of carbon that we can import from Europe, and before going into the transmitter, are subjected to a special process of polishing which still further improves the quality.

THE RECEIVER. We equip all our telephones with our latest improved bi-polar receiver, a receiver that is the result of years of study, experiment and constant improvement. It is made with concealed connections, the coils are wound with **double silk** insulated magnet wire, the magnets are made from the

highest grade **imported** magnet steel, and the cords, which are made extra heavy to prevent any possibility of cord trouble, are attached with a special, wide contact which cannot work loose.

SWITCH HOOK. We equip all our telephones with our special long lever switch hook made with heavy German silver springs, and pure platinum contacts. This hook is so constructed that no current whatever passes through the frame and there is no chance of a shock when removing the receiver from the hook. The greatest attention is paid to securing perfect connections, every joint being soldered, and the general construction and design of this switch hook is such as to prevent any possibility of trouble from this source.

THE GENERATOR. Our generators are made from the best imported magnet steel, and are guaranteed to retain their magnetism and power longer than any other generator made. There is more steel, more wire and more power in our five-magnet generator than in any five or six-magnet generator on the market. The steel is the best imported magnet steel. The wire on the armature is the best double silk insulated magnet wire. Our five-magnet generator weighs 10½ pounds, and this weight is made up of the best imported magnet steel that can be bought, and the best double silk insulated copper magnet wire, the best magnet wire we can buy. **There is plenty of reserve power in this generator,** more power than you will ever need in actual practice. The resistance of an ordinary line, 25 or 30 miles in length, with 30 bridging telephones installed, **even if poorly constructed and put up with small wire,** is less than 60,000 ohms, and we absolutely guarantee our five-magnet generator to ring through 125,000 ohms resistance, more than double the work which it will **ever** be called upon to do, and from three to four times the work which it will ordinarily be required to perform. **There is plenty of reserve power in our big five-magnet generator, and it will always ring every bell on the most heavily loaded lines.** The gear wheels are solid brass castings with milled gears and reinforced spokes, made extra wide to insure strength and durability, and the shunt springs are of heavy German silver.

THE LIGHTNING ARRESTER Our New Two-Path Carbon Lightning Arrester is the most perfect protection from lightning as well as sneak currents, that has ever been devised. This lightning arrester is made up of three heavy brass punchings, the binding posts sweated on to insure perfect contact, the carbon extra large, presenting ample surface to the ground plate, and the mica insulated washers carefully perforated so that the shortest possible air gap is maintained between the carbon and the ground plates.

THE RINGER. Our telephones are all equipped with the latest improved ringers, made with adjustable armatures, the coils wound with **double silk** insulated magnet wire, and with magnets of the best imported magnet steel, heavily nickel plated and polished.

PRICES ON COMPACT BRIDGING TELEPHONES

No.	Description	Price, with two dry batteries, 6 for	each
No. 20K5500	Five-Magnet Compact Bridging Telephone, with 1,000-ohm ringer.	$56.45;	$ 9.70
No. 20K5501	Five-Magnet Compact Bridging Telephone, with 1,600-ohm ringer.	57.90;	9.95
No. 20K5502	Five-Magnet Compact Bridging Telephone, with 2,000-ohm ringer.	59.36;	10.20
No. 20K5506	Four-Magnet Compact Bridging Telephone, with 1,000-ohm ringer.	54.70;	9.40
No. 20K5507	Four-Magnet Compact Bridging Telephone, with 1,600-ohm ringer.	56.17;	9.65
No. 20K5508	Four-Magnet Compact Bridging Telephone, with 2,000-ohm ringer.	57.62;	9.90

Shipping weight of Compact Telephones, 43 pounds.

YOUR MONEY WILL BE IMMEDIATELY RETURNED TO YOU FOR ANY GOODS NOT PERFECTLY SATISFACTORY.

137

5 MAGNET 2000 OHM SOUTHWESTERN TELEPHONE $10.80
BRIDGING

GENERAL CONSTRUCTION

ONLY THE VERY BEST MATERIALS and only the very highest class of skilled labor is employed in the construction of our telephones. They are mechanically and electrically perfect in every detail, correctly and scientifically designed. We spare no expense that will in any way improve the quality. Our object is to produce the most perfect, the most serviceable and the most satisfactory telephone that can be manufactured. Every part that enters into the make up of these telephones is as good as expert designers and skilled workmen can produce. There is not a loose joint in the entire instrument, every connection being soldered, making a solid circuit that cannot possibly get out of order. The workmen engaged in the construction of these telephones are men of the highest degree of skill—men of long and practical experience in actual telephone construction.

SIMPLE AND EASY TO INSTALL. Our telephones are made with the greatest possible simplicity, all complicated parts having been eliminated. They are easy to put up and easy to keep in order after they are put up. They are easy to repair if by accident any part becomes damaged or broken. Any one without the slightest electrical knowledge or telephone experience can put up a telephone line and install our telephones. There is nothing complicated about them—nothing hard to understand. The instruments are simple, they are right in every way, they reach you in perfect order, and they come to you with simple and easily understood directions, so that it is easy for anyone, without the slightest previous experience, to put up a line and install these instruments with perfect assurance that the line will give good service.

TESTS AND MATERIALS. Every telephone that we sell is tested before it leaves the factory by ten different electrical experts. Not an instrument is allowed to go out that does not test better by 25 per cent than the standard established by the National Interstate Telephone Association. Our lumber is all air dried for months and afterward kiln dried, before it is made up into cabinets. Every lot of new material that comes to the factory is tested chemically and mechanically before it is accepted. There are no cheap materials used in our telephones. We could use American steel for the magnets of the generator, the receiver and the ringer, and make very substantial reductions in the cost, but imported magnet steel is better than American magnet steel, therefore every magnet that enters into the construction of our telephones is made from the highest grade of imported magnet steel. We use only first quality magnet wire, with double silk insulation, the most expensive magnet wire that we can buy. We use the very highest priced, the most expensive granulated carbon and carbon diaphragms that we can import. All of these things count, and count very much in determining whether a telephone is a good telephone or not. When you buy a telephone, you want one that you can rely upon all the time, under all conditions, and such a telephone must be made right all the way through. It must be put up by good workmen; it must be properly designed, and it must be made throughout from the very best materials. Our telephones comply with all these requirements.

MADE COMPLETE IN ONE FACTORY. There are many dealers in telephones today who pretend to be manufacturers, but who are merely assemblers, purchasing the various parts wherever they can buy the cheapest. They buy their generators from one factory, their transmitters from another and their receivers from another. The cabinet is made in still another factory, probably a factory where nothing is known of actual telephone requirements. All the various small parts are purchased here and there, and then these odds and ends of telephone construction are assembled or put together in this so called "telephone factory." It is impossible to produce a dependable, reliable telephone in this way, because the various parts come first from one source of supply and then another. They are always subject to variation because different manufacturers never produce articles exactly alike, and the purchaser of such a telephone never knows whether he can secure repair parts, never knows whether he can replace a worn out or broken part, and if the instrument is not satisfactory he finds that he has no redress, but must accept the loss and buy another telephone from some reliable dealer. Our telephones are made complete, from start to finish, in one factory. The generators, switchhooks, ringers, transmitters, receivers, cabinets, everything, even the smallest screws and washers which enter into the construction of our telephones, are made in one factory. Every part is interchangeable, and we can furnish at any time in the future, ten, fifteen or twenty years from now, exact duplicates of every part. Every part is interchangeable and we can replace, at any time, any part that may wear out in service or become damaged in any way.

PROMPT DELIVERIES. We carry in stock, right here at our store in Chicago, the largest stock of telephones that is carried by any dealer or manufacturer in the United States. We have thousands of telephones on hand at all times, packed and ready for immediate shipment; and whether you send us an order for one telephone or for one hundred telephones, you may send it with perfect confidence that shipment will be made at once and there will be no waiting, no delay. The instruments will go forward at once, carefully packed and guaranteed to reach you in perfect condition.

OUR GUARANTEE AND TWELVE MONTHS' FREE TRIAL OFFER. As the astonishing low prices which we quote on these telephones may, very naturally, lead some to doubt the high quality of the instruments, we send with every telephone our signed guarantee, under the terms of which we become responsible for the quality, material and workmanship of every telephone we sell, and we accept your order with the distinct understanding and agreement that you can put the telephone up, use it for twelve months, compare it with any other telephones in your neighborhood, telephones that may have cost twice the amount that we ask you for ours, and if at the end of the year you have any fault whatever to find with this telephone, if you do not find it better than any other telephone in your locality and if you do not feel that you have secured a better telephone and saved money, you can pack it up and return it to us at our expense. We will refund, without question, the entire purchase price, and reimburse you for all transportation charges.

OUR NAME does not appear on our telephones in any way. We find that occasionally customers who would like to take advantage of the low prices and high quality of our telephones, hesitate to do so because of the antagonism of local companies or other interested parties, and for this reason we do not put any name plate or any identifying mark of any kind on our telephones. You can send us your order for telephones with perfect assurance that the transaction is in every way strictly confidential, and that no marks will appear on the telephones inside or outside to show where you bought them.

PRICES ON SOUTHWESTERN STYLE BRIDGING TELEPHONES.

No. 20K5515 Five-Magnet Bridging Telephone, Southwestern Style, with 1,000-ohm ringer.
Price, with two dry batteries, 6 for $59.35; each $10.20
Price, with two wet batteries, 6 for $60.75; each 10.44

No. 20K5516 Five-Magnet Bridging Telephone, Southwestern Style, with 1,600-ohm ringer.
Price, with two dry batteries, 6 for $61.10; each 10.50
Price, with two wet batteries, 6 for $62.50; each 10.74

No. 20K5517 Five-Magnet Bridging Telephone, Southwestern Style, with 2,000-ohm ringer.
Price, with two dry batteries, 6 for $62.85; each 10.80
Price, with two wet batteries 6 for $64.25; each 11.04

No. 20K5521 Four-Magnet Bridging Telephone, Southwestern Style, with 1,000-ohm ringer.
Price, with two dry batteries, 6 for $55.30; each 9.50
Price, with two wet batteries, 6 for $56.70; each 9.74

No. 20K5522 Four-Magnet Bridging Telephone, Southwestern Style, with 1,600-ohm ringer.
Price, with two dry batteries, 6 for $57.05; each 9.80
Price, with two wet batteries, 6 for $58.45; each 10.04

No. 20K5523 Four-Magnet Bridging Telephone, Southwestern Style, with 2,000-ohm ringer.
Price, with two dry batteries, 6 for $58.80; each 10.10
Price, with two wet batteries, 6 for $60.20; each 10.34

Shipping weight, Southwestern Style Telephones, 54 pounds.

SERIES TELEPHONES. Series Telephones are made for use on lines where only two instruments are to be installed or for use on lines having a switchboard and an operator at a central office. Our Series Telephones are made throughout in the same perfect manner as our Bridging Telephones; every detail has exactly the same rigid inspection, and exactly the same high standard of excellence is maintained throughout the instrument. We put up our Series Telephones with the same high grade long distance transmitter, bi-polar receiver, long lever switch hook, improved ringer, etc., exactly the same as furnished with our highest grade Bridging Telephones. Our Series Telephones are equipped with three-magnet generators and 80-ohm ringers, will talk over lines of any length, and the generators are guaranteed to ring a bell over a 30-mile single line.

No. 20K5530 Compact Series Telephone. Price, including two dry batteries, 6 for $45.40; each $7.80
Shipping weight, 41 pounds each.

No. 20K5532 Southwestern Style Series Telephone. Price, including two dry batteries, 6 for $47.75; each 8.20
Price, including two wet batteries, 6 for $49.10; each.............. 8.44
Shipping weight, 52 pounds each.

No. 20K5532

No. 20K5530

SEE NEXT PAGE FOR DESK TELEPHONES.
Sig. 13—1st Ed.

OUR DESK TELEPHONES.

SUITABLE FOR ANY KIND OF A LINE, SERIES OR BRIDGING.

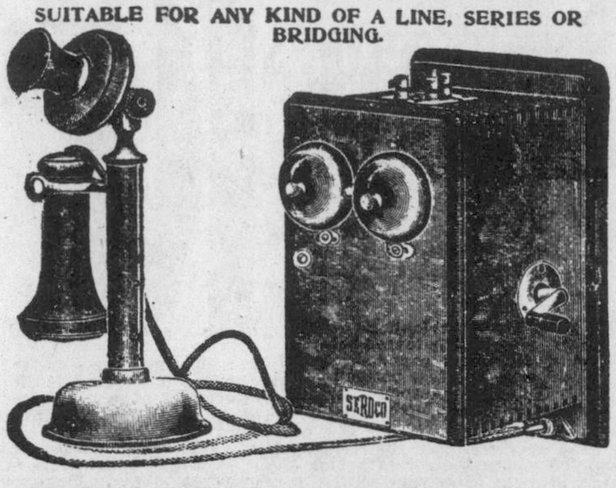

OUR DESK TELEPHONE is made with exactly the same high grade equipment as all the other styles of our telephones, either bridging or series, exactly the same high power generators, long distance transmitters, improved bipolar receivers, etc., embodying in all essential points every good quality represented in our various types of wall telephones.

THE GENERATOR AND RINGER are mounted in a neat golden oak cabinet, made with rounded, dovetailed corners and piano polish. This cabinet can be mounted on the wall near a table or desk, or on the side or underneath the table, where it is practically out of sight.

No. 20K5550 Series Desk Telephone, three-magnet generator, 80-ohm ringer, suitable for use on single lines where only two instruments are installed and also for lines having a switchboard and central operator. It cannot be used on bridging or party lines.
Price, each, with two dry batteries $12.20
Six, complete for 71.00

No. 20K5553 Bridging Desk Telephone, four-magnet generator, 1,600-ohm ringer, suitable for use on bridging lines when not more than 18 instruments are installed.
Price, each, with two dry batteries $13.65
Six, complete for 79.45

No. 20K5556 Bridging Desk Telephone, five-magnet generator, 1,600-ohm ringer, suitable for use on bridging lines with from 30 to 50 instruments installed.
Price, each, with two dry batteries $14.45
Six, complete for 84.10

No. 20K5560 Bridging Desk Telephone, five-magnet generator, 2,000-ohm ringer, suitable for bridging lines, with from 30 to 50 instruments installed.
Price, each, with two dry batteries $14.80
Six, complete for 86.15
Shipping weight of desk telephones is 35 pounds.

Pony Magneto Call Telephone.

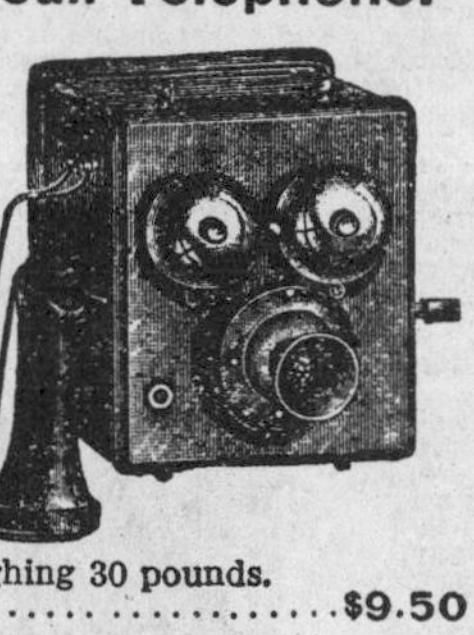

No. 20K5570 **This telephone is built for use on short lines of from 50 feet to 5 miles.** It can be used with copper or iron wire or even with fence wire. It is equipped with a high grade transmitter, receiver and three-magnet pony generator. It is put up in a handsome oak case, and all parts are heavily nickel plated. We furnish an outfit complete, consisting of two telephones, four batteries, weighing 30 pounds.
Price $9.50

Telephone Parts.

No. 20K5600 Our Solid Back Transmitter, the best long distance transmitter on the market. Our transmitters talk. Each one guaranteed. Price, each $1.20
If by mail, postage extra, 24 cents.
No. 20K5605 Our Bipolar Receiver is the result of twenty years' experience. They are in use on 150,000 telephones today. Each one guaranteed. Price, each 90c
If by mail, postage extra, 20 cents.
No. 20K5610 Five-magnet Bridging Generator, guaranteed to ring through 100,000 ohms. Made of the best imported steel. Price, each $3.95
No. 20K5612 Four-magnet Bridging Generator, guaranteed to ring through 50,000 ohms. Made of the best imported steel. Price, each $3.30
No. 20K5614 Three-magnet Series Generator, guaranteed to ring through 25,000 ohms. Made of the best imported steel. Price, each $2.40
No. 20K5619 80-ohm Series Ringer. Silk wound coils, imported steel magnet. Easily adjusted and fully guaranteed. Price, each 95c
No. 20K5621 1,000-ohm Bridging Ringer. Silk wound coils, imported steel magnet. Easily adjusted and fully guaranteed. Price, each $1.60
No. 20K5623 1,600-ohm Bridging Ringer. Silk wound coils, imported steel magnet. Easily adjusted and fully guaranteed. Price, each $1.85
No. 20K5625 2,000-ohm Bridging Ringer. Silk wound coils, imported steel magnet. Easily adjusted and fully guaranteed. Price, each $2.30
No. 20K5635 Nickel plated Gongs and Stands. Price, per set 20c
No. 20K5640 Long Lever Switch Hook. German silver springs, platinum contacts. All nickel plated. Price, each 50c

Telephone Switchboards.

No. 20K5575 50-line express type, automatic self restoring drop switchboard with five talking circuits, ten cords and plugs, five ringing out drops, switchboard generator, night alarm circuit, complete operator's set and fifteen feet of cable.
Price, without drops $78.50
No. 20K2310 Series drops installed. Price, each 1.65
No. 20K2320 Bridging drops installed. Price, each 2.10
We can furnish any kind or size of switchboard wanted. Tell us what you want and we will quote prices that will save you money.

No. 20K5655 250-ohm Induction Coil. Silk wound, square fiber ends. Price, each 45c
No. 20K5657 500-ohm Induction Coil. Silk wound, square fiber ends. Price, each 60c
Extension Bells, as an additional call for noisy places, and in other rooms away from the telephone, must be same size as telephone ringer.
No. 20K5670 80-ohm Extension Bell. Price, each $1.50
No. 20K5671 1,000-ohm Extension Bell. Price, each 2.50
No. 20K5672 1,600-ohm Extension Bell. Price, each 2.65
No. 20K5673 2,000-ohm Extension Bell. Price, each 2.85
No. 20K5680 Adjustable Arm with transmitter and coil, all complete. Price, each $2.10
No. 20K5685 Receiver Cords, worsted, 36 inches long. Price, per pair 16c
No. 20K5690 Telephone Mouthpieces. Male or female thread. Price, each 11c
If by mail, postage extra, 3 cents.

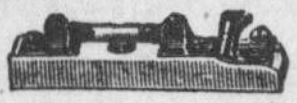

No. 20K5725 Single Pole Fuse Block with Carbon Lightning Arrester. Porcelain base and brass mountings, upright carbons, with mica insulation. Western Union or Postal style.
Price, each, with one dozen copper fuses 25c
No. 20K5727 Double Pole Fuses Blocks with Carbon Lightning Arrester, either Western Union or Postal style.
Price, each, with one dozen copper fuses 35c
No. 20K5729 Veribest Glass Inclosed Fuses, for Western Union fuse blocks.
Price, per 100 .... $1.40; each 1½c
No. 20K5731 ¼-Ampere Fuses, tipped with tinfoil, Western Union or Postal style.
Price, in lots of 100 .... $1.00; per dozen 12c
No. 20K5733 ¼-Ampere Fuses, tipped with copper. Western Union or Postal style.
Price, in lots of 100 ...... $1.25; per dozen 15c

Galvanized Telephone Wire.

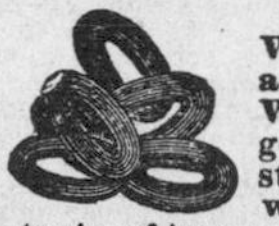

Our Double Galvanized Steel Line Wire is especially made for telegraph and telephone use. IT IS NOT FENCE WIRE. We guarantee this wire to be genuine BB and steel and to stand any standard test. **For long spans, steel wire,** which has double the breaking strain of iron wire, **is always preferable.** The No. 10 wire will weigh about 275 pounds to the mile, the No. 12, 165 pounds, and the No. 14 about 96 pounds.
This wire is sold in half-mile coils only. Prices subject to change without notice. All shipments made direct from our factory in Central Indiana.

	B.W.G. Gauge	Price, per 100 pounds on BB Iron Wire	Price, per 100 pounds on Steel Line Wire
No. 20K5750	No. 10	$3.87	$3.62
No. 20K5751	No. 12	4.00	3.75
No. 20K5752	No. 14	4.12	4.00

Write for special prices on large quantities.
We do not recommend fence wire for telephone use, but can furnish it at the lowest market price. Write for quotations.

Rubber Covered Telephone Wire.

No. 20K5760 Double Conductor Rubber Covered, braided, twisted, and covered with a saturated braid No. 19. Price, per hundred feet ... $1.57
No. 20K5765 Rubber Covered Braided, twisted pair telephone wire No. 19; for inside use.
Price, per hundred feet $1.35

Office and Annunciator Wire.

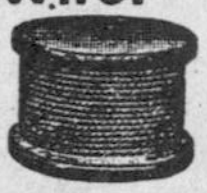

No. 20K5770 Annunciator Wire, No. 18, in ½ and 1-pound coils. 150 feet to the pound. Price, per pound 32c
No. 20K5772 Office Wire, No. 18, in 1-pound coils. Price, per pound 40c

Magnet Wire, B. & S. Gauge.

No. 20K5775 Belden Double Cotton Covered Magnet Wire. One piece only on a spool. Insulation and wire is perfectly uniform.

Size	1-oz. Spool	2-oz. Spool	4-oz. Spool	8-oz. Spool	1-lb. Spool	5-lb. Spool per lb.
16	....	......	......	.....	$0.57	$0.53
18	....	......	......	.....	.64	.60
20	....	......	......	$0.42	.74	.70
21	....	......	......	.47	.83	.77
22	....	......	......	.48	.86	.81
23	....	......	......	.50	.90	.85
24	....	......	$0.27	.52	.97	.92
25	....	......	.30	.58	1.06	1.01
26	....	$0.25	.38	.63	1.15	1.10
30	$0.25	.27	.45	.87	1.62	1.56
32	.27	.31	.52	.99	1.87	1.80
34	.30	.40	.70	1.36	2.52	2.42
36	.40	.50	.95	1.83	3.45	3.30

Note—Above prices include the spool and cost of spooling. The wire is furnished only on sized spools given. We can furnish single cotton, single and double silk covered in 5-pound lots. Prices on application.

Insulators, Brackets, Etc.

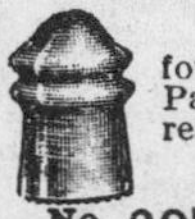

No. 20K5800 Pony Glass Insulator for telephone, telegraph and fire alarm work. Packed 400 in a barrel. Weight, per barrel ready for shipment, 300 pounds.
Price, per barrel, 400 insulators .. $6.30
Price, each, in less than barrel lots .01¾
No. 20K5805 Double Groove Pony Glass Insulator for telephone transposition work, packed 400 in a barrel. Weight, per barrel, ready for shipment, 300 pounds. Price, per barrel, 400 insulators $6.30
Price, each, in less than barrel lots .... .01¾

No. 20K5810 Porcelain Insulator No. 4½, new code; requiring 1 inch space between bottom and groove. Height, 1⅞ inches; diameter, 1¼ inches; hole, ⁵⁄₁₆ inch; groove, ⁷⁄₁₆ inch.
Price, per 100 .... 70c
Price, per standard package of 1,000 .... $6.65
No. 20K5815 Porcelain Insulator No. 5½, new code; requiring 1 inch space between bottom and groove. Height, 1⅞ inches; diameter, 1 inch; hole, ¼ inch; groove, ⁵⁄₁₆ inch. Price, per 100 .... $0.42
Price, per standard package of 1,000 .... 3.90

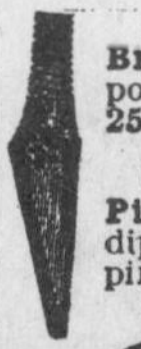

No. 20K5820 Pony Oak Telephone Bracket, painted and dipped, weight 1 pound each. Price, per sack containing 250 brackets $3.30
Price, each, in less than sack lots .. .01½
No. 20K5825 1¼-inch Pony Oak Pins, for telephone work, painted and dipped. Price, per sack, containing 250 pins $1.98
Price, each, in less than sack lots .. .01

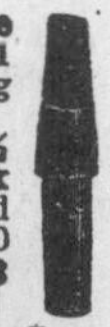

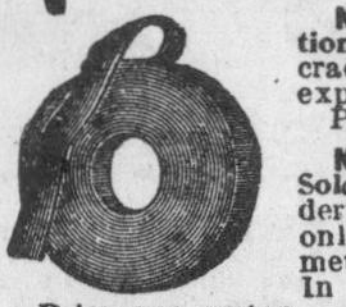

No. 20K5835 Black Insulating Friction Tape, will not vulcanize with heat, nor crack nor harden and become defective by exposure and use; ¾ inch wide.
Price, per pound 36c

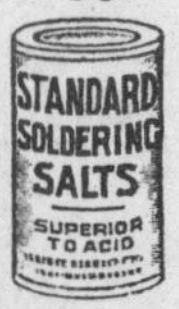

No. 20K5840 Standard Soldering Salts, for making soldering acid. Mixed with water only. Will not corrode the finest metal. Directions on package. In ½-pound cartons.
Price, per carton 21c
No. 20K5845 Soldering Stick, a soldering flux in solid form, superior to any style of acid, very portable, used by applying on heated joint.
Price, per stick 14c
No. 20K5850 Soldering Paste, 2-ounce box.
Price, per box 9c

10 lbs. Wire Solder for $1.98.

No. 20K5855 Wire Solder, best grade, for all electrical work. Price, per pound $0.21
Per 5-lb. coil .... $1.00 Per 10-lb. coil 1.98

Baby Knife Switches.

FOR TELEPHONE AND BATTERY WORK.

No. 20K5875 15-ampere, single pole, single throw. Price 25c
No. 20K5877 15-ampere, single pole, double throw. Price 33c
No. 20K5879 15-ampere, double pole, single throw. Price 30c
No. 20K5881 15-ampere, double pole, double throw. Price 40c

Tackle Block Wire Stretcher.

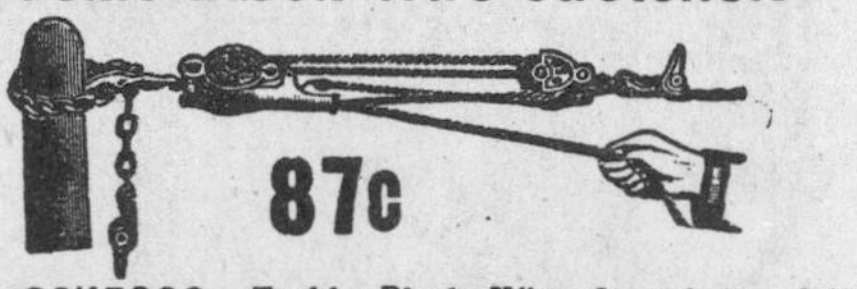

87c

No. 20K5900 Tackle Block Wire Stretcher. Self locking at any point. This stretcher is provided with all malleable iron grapples for stretching barbed wire strands and woven wire fencing and telephone wire. It is also a complete safety rope hoist for ordinary use with which one man can raise 500 pounds. Weight, 4½ pounds.
Price, complete with 16 feet of ⅜-inch rope 87c

Bull Dog Wire Grip.

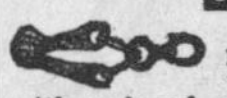

No. 20K5905 Bull Dog Wire Grip. The more you pull, the tighter it grips. Used with a tackle block with an ordinary wire stretcher, or with a hand spike and chain. It never slips, and does not injure the wire. Price, each 22c

Linemen's Tools.

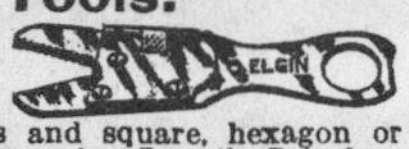

No. 20K5910 The Elgin Adjustable Linemen's Wrench. Made of the very best tool steel, heavily nickel plated. It will hold pipe nipples, collars, round or square rods and square, hexagon or round nuts. Guarantee with each wrench. Length, 7 inches. Weight, 10 ounces. Price 75c
No. 20K5915 Extra jaws for above. Price 25c

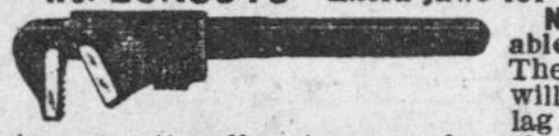

No. 20K5920 Adjustable Wrench for lag screw. The jaws are drop forgings; will hold square or hexagonal lag screws, conduit, or pipe. An exceptionally strong and well made wrench. Length, 9 inches. Price 62c

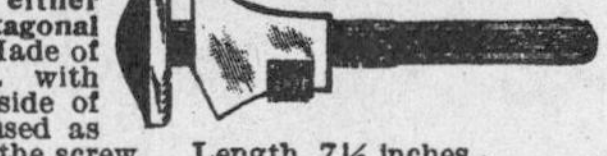

No. 20K5925 Combination Wrench for either square, round or hexagonal lag screw or bolts. Made of the best tool steel, with drop forged jaws, one side of which is plain, to be used as a hammer for starting the screw. Length, 7½ inches.
Price 65c

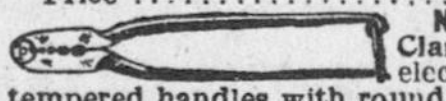

No. 20K5930 Linemen's Clamps or Connectors. Made from electro boracic Swedish steel. Spring tempered handles with round edges; will not wear out clothes. The best that mechanical skill can produce. Fully warranted. Length, 11 inches; full polished; for No. 8 wire and smaller, B. & S. gauge. Two oval and two round holes.
Price $1.35

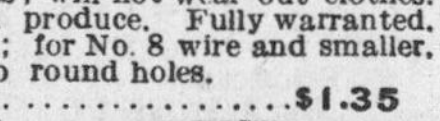

No. 20K5935 Linemen's Clamps; same grade as above. Length, 11 inches; full polished; for No. 8 wire and smaller, B. & S. gauge. Four round holes. Price $1.35

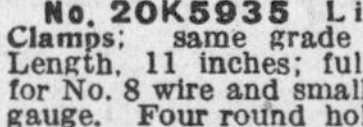

No. 20K5940 Linemen's Side Cutting Pliers. Made of the best tool steel properly tempered, raised cutters, polished finish.
Price, 8-inch .... $1.15; 7-inch 95c

Hargraves' Climbers.

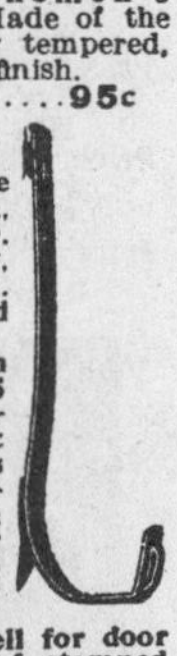

We guarantee these climbers to be made of the very best steel, perfectly tempered, finely finished, the very best, strongest and safest climbers made. We carry these climbers in standard lengths, namely, 15, 15½, 16, 16½, 17 and 17½ inches in stock. State length wanted. No straps are furnished with our climbers at prices as listed below.
No. 20K5945 Hargraves' Climbers, Eastern Pattern. Price, per pair, with spurs $1.85
No. 20K5946 Extra Spurs, for Eastern Pattern Climbers. Price, per pair with rivets 38c
No. 20K5950 Climber Straps. These straps are furnished with a large leather pad, which prevents the climber from digging into the knee. Can be used with any make of climber, either Eastern or Western. Price, per set of four $1.10

Iron Box Bells.

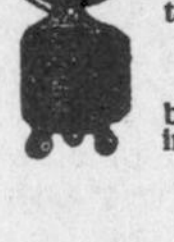

No. 20K6000 3-inch Iron Box Bell for door and call bell use. The box is made of stamped sheet metal, has cast gong and German silver contacts. Will ring 50 feet on one cell of battery.
Price, each 28c
If by mail, postage extra, 10 cents.
No. 20K6002 4-inch Iron Box Bell. This bell is larger and heavier than the 3-inch and is intended for use where a louder call is necessary.
Price, each 38c
If by mail, postage extra 14 cents.

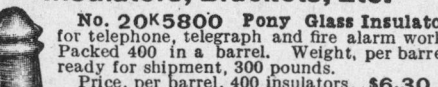

Ecco Buzzers.

No. 20K6006 Ecco Buzzer No. 0. A very small buzzer. Size, 1¼x¾ inches. Dust and bug proof, with spring cover, fully nickel plated, finely finished throughout. Platinum contact points. Will operate equally well on one or ten cells of battery. Price, each 43c
If by mail, postage extra, 5 cents.

No. 20K6008 Ecco Buzzer No. 4. Same as above, but larger. Size, 1⅞x3¼ inches. Japanned finish. Price..43c
If by mail, postage extra, 9 cents.

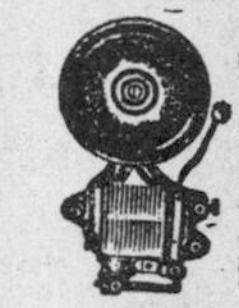

Skeleton Bell, for fire and burglar alarm. Has a heavy cast frame finished in black enamel, gold striped. The gongs are of cast bell metal, heavily nickel plated. It has the largest volume of sound with clearest ringing tone. Magnets are wound with double insulated wire, has a pivoted armature with two adjustable bearings. Binding posts are the patent Never Turn. We sell both Class A and Class B. Class B bells are second quality. Class A are highest grade made, superior in workmanship, finish and wearing qualities. Many dealers sell Class B bells at Class A prices, saying nothing about the class.

No. 20K6010 Skeleton Bell, with 4-inch gong. Price, Class A, $1.40; Class B..........$1.10

No. 20K6011 Same as above, with 6-inch gong. Price, Class A, $2.16; Class B..........$1.65

No. 20K6012 Same as above, with 8-inch gong. Price, Class A, $3.60; Class B..........$3.00

Electric Bell Outfits.
For Door and Call Bell Service.

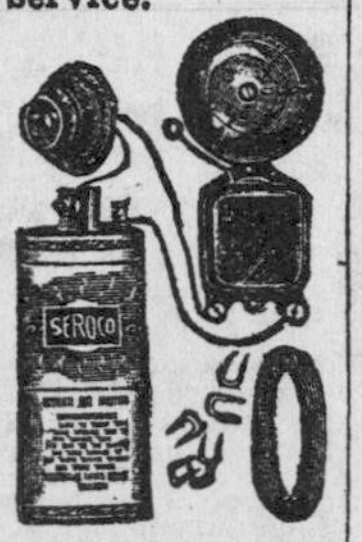

No. 20K6020 Electric Bell Outfit, complete, consists of one cell of Seroco dry battery, wood push button, one 3-inch iron box bell, 75 feet of annunciator wire and necessary staples. Weight, 3½ pounds when packed. Price. 68c

No. 20K6022 Electric Bell Outfit, consists of one Seroco dry battery, one bronze push button, one 3-inch iron box bell, 75 feet of annunciator wire and necessary staples. Weight, 3½ pounds when packed. Price..............78c

No. 20K6024 Electric Bell Outfit, consists of one cell of Seroco wet battery, one bronze push button, one 3-inch iron box bell, 75 feet of annunciator wire and necessary staples. Weight, 4¾ pounds when packed. Price..............................85c

No. 20K6026 Electric Bell Outfit, consists of two cells of Seroco dry battery, one bronze push button, one 3-inch iron box bell, 150 feet of annunciator wire and necessary staples. Weight, 5½ pounds when packed. Price................................$1.15

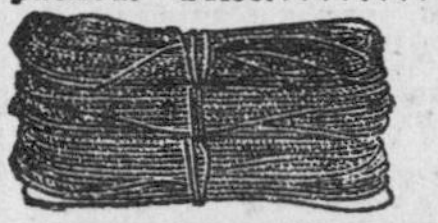

No. 20K5770 Annunciator Wire, No. 18, in ½ or 1-pound coils (150 feet to the pound).
Price, per pound..............32c

No. 20K6030 ½-Inch Brass Bell Wire Staples. Sold in 1-pound packages only.
Price, per pound..............12c

Our Seroco Wet Battery.

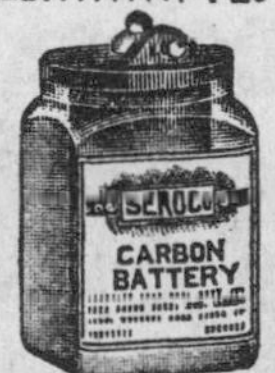

No. 20K6040 Our Special Seroco Wet Battery is a strictly first class open circuit battery for door bells, telephones, surgical and dental outfits, etc., easily recharged when exhausted, consists of round carbon, square zinc and jar and one charge of sal ammoniac. Price, complete..............28c
Weight, 4½ pounds when packed. Cannot be sent by mail.

No. 20K6041 Square Zinc, one zinc will last from one to six months, depending on the use.
Price, per dozen, 35c; 3 zincs......10c

No. 20K6042 Sal Ammoniac. Price, per charge, 5c
Per pound..............................15c

National No. 2 Battery.

The National No. 2 Open Circuit Battery is a good battery for open circuit work, as it has removable carbon elements; the depolarizer, when exhausted, can be emptied from the cup and filled with fresh material and screwed in place, which makes the battery as good as new. It is a first class battery for electric bells, burglar alarms and telephone use and gives good results for gas engine work. The battery consists of a Le Clanche jar, carbon cup and cover, circular zinc, rubber rings and a charge of sal ammoniac.

No. 20K6050 National No. 2 Battery. Complete. Price......................................63c
No. 20K6051 Zinc. Price..........................15c
No. 20K6052 Depolarizer. Price..............12c
No. 20K6053 Sal Ammoniac for battery. Price, per pound, 15c; per charge..............5c

Gravity Battery.

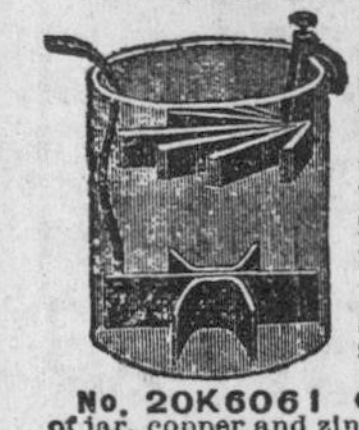

The Gravity Battery is a closed circuit battery used almost entirely for telegraph work. It can be used for operating electric bells, small motors, etc. Each battery requires about three pounds of blue vitriol or blue stone to charge it. Full directions for charging are given in the Manual of Telegraphy, sent with each telegraph instrument.

No. 20K6060 Gravity Battery. Size, 5x7 inches; consisting of jar, copper and zinc. Weight, 5 pounds.
Price, complete..............................42c

No. 20K6061 Gravity Battery. Size, 6x8 inches; consisting of jar, copper and zinc. Weight, 6 pounds. Price, complete..55c
NOTE—Blue Vitriol is not furnished with these batteries. It is always sold extra. Gravity batteries cannot be sent by mail.

No. 20K6062 Battery Jar, glass, 5x7. Price..........13c
No. 20K6063 Battery Jar, glass, 6x8. Price..........15c
No. 20K6064 Zinc, for 5x7 battery. Price..........25c
No. 20K6065 Zinc, for 6x8 battery. Price..........34c
No. 20K6066 Copper, for 5x7 battery. Price..........7c
No. 20K6067 Copper, for 6x8 battery. Price..........7c
No. 20K6068 Blue Vitriol. Price, per pound..........10c

Gas Engine Batteries.

No. 20K6075 The Fuller Battery. An ideal wet battery for gasoline engine work. It consists of a large carbon, porous cup, and very heavy zinc, all made to fit in a 6x8-inch gravity jar the same as No. 20K6061. Full directions for charging are sent with each cell. It requires about four of these cells to spark an ordinary gas engine on one charge for nine months. Price of battery complete..............$1.25

No. 20K6076 Renewals for Fuller Battery, consisting of zinc and a can of salt. Price..............................56c

No. 20K6077 Electropion Salt, for charging Fuller Battery. Price, per can..............................22c

Seroco Dry Battery.

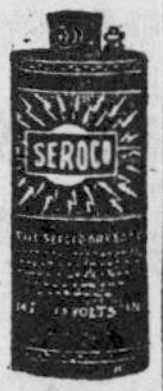

No. 20K6085 The Seroco Dry Battery is made especially for us by one of the largest dry battery manufacturers in the country. It is the best low priced battery on the market today. It is 2½x6 inches in size and weighs about 2 pounds. Is adapted for door bell and call bell use and for dry cell medical batteries. It is also one of the best telephone batteries made. Price, each...$ 0.16
Per dozen......................................1.80
Per barrel (125 batteries)................16.85
If by mail, postage extra, each, 35 cents.

Stand-By Batteries.

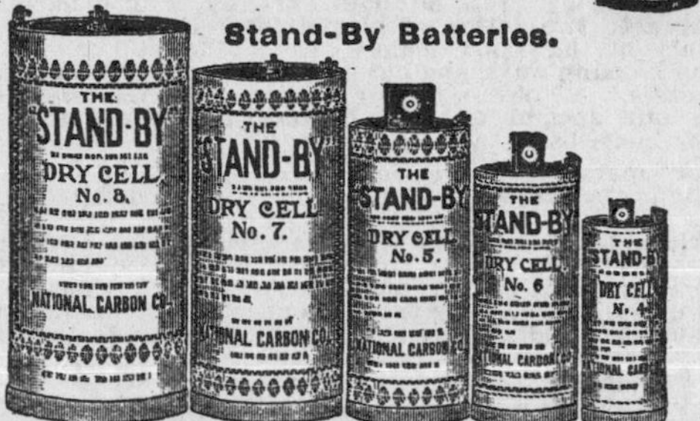

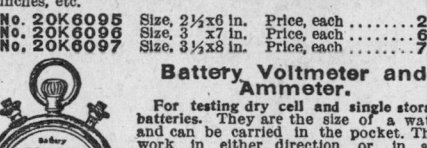

The Stand-By Dry Batteries are extra high grade batteries and tests will show them to be superior to all others. They will produce more current and last longer than any other dry cell batteries of their size on the market. The Stand-By Batteries live up to their name. They are made in five sizes suitable for different kinds of experimental work and the larger sizes are adapted especially to gas engine work where heavy discharges are necessary for short periods only.

	Size, inches	Weight	Price
No. 20K6090	1½x4	9 ozs.	16c
No. 20K6091	2 x5	1 lb. 2 ozs.	18c
No. 20K6092	2½x6	2 lbs.	21c
No. 20K6093	3 x7	3 lbs. 7 ozs.	50c
No. 20K6094	3½x8	5 lbs.	58c

The 1½x4-inch size can be shipped by mail, postage, 12 cents extra, but the larger sizes are too heavy for mail shipment and must be sent by express or freight.

Stand-By "Special" Dry Batteries.
With Blue Labels and Red Tops.

The Stand-By "Special" Cell is designed particularly for ignition work, so constructed that it gives an unusually heavy discharge, and consequently a hotter spark. It is undoubtedly the best dry battery made for ignition work, and is suitable for stationary engines, automobiles, launches, etc.

No. 20K6095 Size, 2½x6 in. Price, each..........26c
No. 20K6096 Size, 3 x7 in. Price, each..........60c
No. 20K6097 Size, 3½x8 in. Price, each..........75c

Battery Voltmeter and Ammeter.

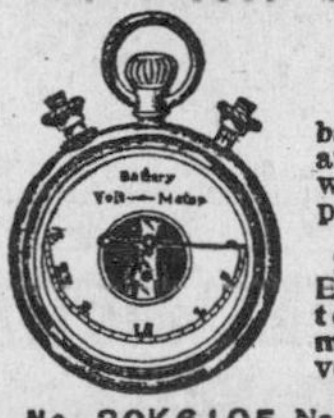

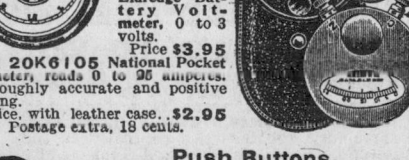

For testing dry cell and single storage batteries. They are the size of a watch and can be carried in the pocket. They work in either direction or in any position.

No. 20K6100 Eldredge Battery Voltmeter, 0 to 3 volts.
Price $3.95

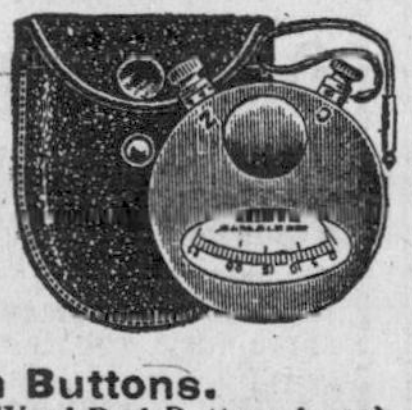

No. 20K6105 National Pocket Ammeter, reads 0 to 35 amperes. Thoroughly accurate and positive reading.
Price, with leather case..$2.95
Postage extra, 18 cents.

Push Buttons.

No. 20K6115

No. 20K6115 Wood Push Buttons, in oak, ash or walnut. German silver springs, porcelain center. Price, each..............................6c
Per dozen..............................70c
If by mail, postage extra, each, 4c

No. 20K6120

No. 20K6120 Solid Cap Stamped Brass Buttons.
Price..............................13c
If by mail, postage extra, 4c.

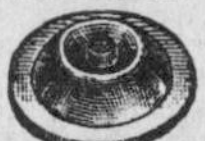
No. 20K6125

No. 20K6125 Anti-Wood Push Buttons. A metal push button cheaper than wood. Very neat and serviceable.
Price, per dozen, 50c; each..............5c
If by mail, postage extra, each, 4 cents.

Kenco Battery Fan Motor.

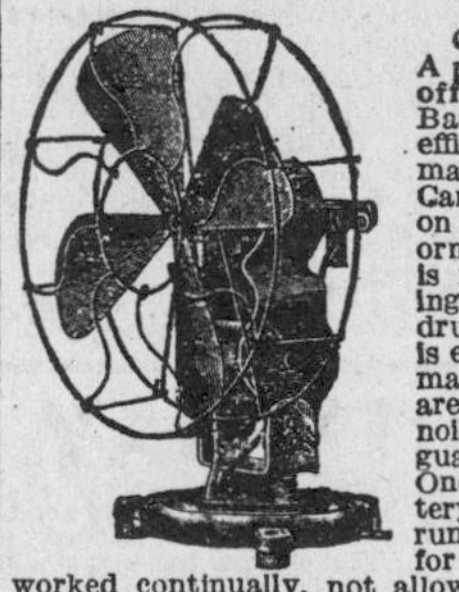

Costs 1 cent per hour to run. A portable fan motor for the home, office and sick room. The Kenco Battery Fan Motor is the most efficient motor of its kind on the market. Is adjustable on any angle. Can be attached to the wall or set on a desk, stand or shelf. It is an ornament to any room. The field is made of electrical steel punchings, the armature is of the six-slot drum type, brushes are adjustable, is equipped with oil cups with automatic feed. The base and frame are finished in black enamel; the noiseless bearings, 8-inch fan and guard are heavily nickel plated. One set of twenty cells of dry battery wired in multiple series will run this motor three hours per day for about three months. If worked continually, not allowing the battery to recuperate, the total number of hours the battery will operate the fan motor is greatly reduced. Where constant service is required, we recommend the use of two or three sets of batteries. When the batteries are exhausted, they are no longer of any use and must be thrown away. A new set, however, will make the fan outfit as good as new. The fan motor itself should last for years.

No. 20K6150 The Motor complete, with fan, guard, 20 feet of cord and twenty dry cells wired and packed in a neat case ready to connect to the motor when received. Weight complete, 52 pounds. Price..............................$8.75

No. 20K6151 Motor, with fan and guard, without batteries and cord. Weight, 7 pounds. Price..............$4.90

No. 20K6152 Battery for this motor, consisting of twenty high grade dry cells, packed in a neat wooden case, completely wired, ready to connect to motor. Weight, 45 pounds. Price..............................$3.95

Wood Base Switches.

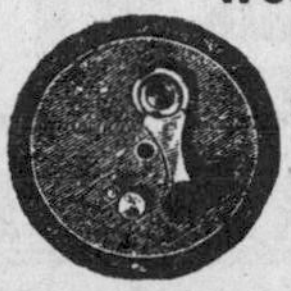

For use on telephones, closed circuit bell systems, burglar alarms and battery circuits in general. Has a hardwood base, with rubbed oil finish. Stamped lever, wood handle, painted with black insulated paint.

No. 20K6135 Price, 1 point..........9c
No. 20K6136 Price, 2 point..........10c
No. 20K6137 Price, 3 point..........12c
No. 20K6138 Price, 4 point..........13c
If by mail, postage extra, 2 cents.

Sure Waker Alarm Clock with Switch.

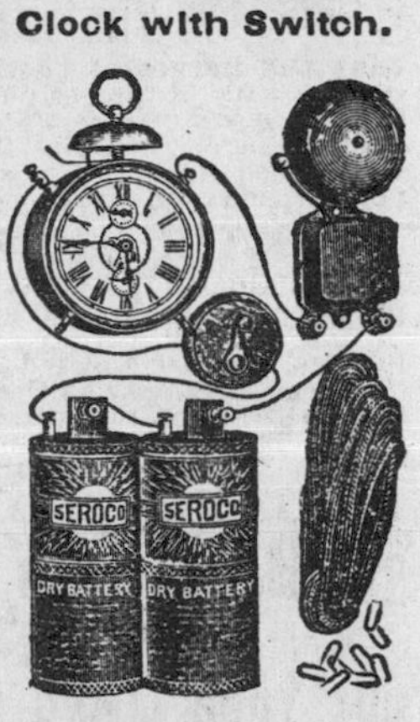

No. 20K6175 This is an Alarm Clock which, when placed in the circuit of an ordinary bell outfit, using a switch in place of a push button, will wake the soundest sleeper. Price of clock with switch..........$1.15
If by mail, postage extra, 24c.

No. 20K6176 The Sure Waker Alarm Clock Outfit consists of our Sure Waker alarm clock, 3-inch iron box bell, one wood base switch, two cells of Seroco dry battery and 75 feet of annunciator wire with necessary staples. The diagram shows the method of connection, which is very simple and can be made by anyone. Just the thing for the farmer, who can place the bell anywhere in the house and wake the occupant of the room at the same time he awakens. The bell will continue to ring until the switch is shut off. Weight, 5 pounds.
Price, all complete..$1.95

Genuine Ever Ready Flash Light.

SHOULD BE IN EVERY HOME.

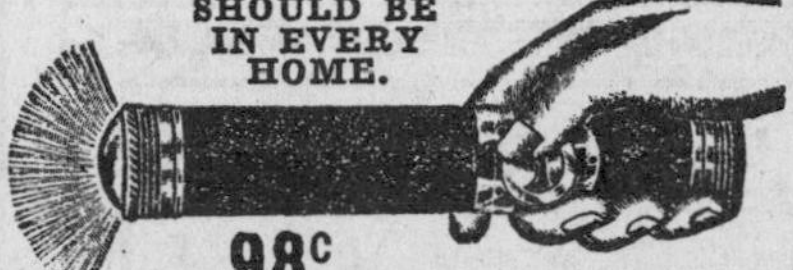

98c

No wires, no chemicals, no oil, smoke or odor, no danger. This search light is of the very latest design. Cylinder is made of heavy cardboard and covered with imitation morocco. The lamp is lighted by pressing the ring on the side against the ferrule. The lamp can be used at any angle and in any direction. It is not designed for steady use and if burned steadily will last about two hours. If used at intervals of a few seconds, will last from 60 to 90 days. **We guarantee a fresh battery with each light.**

No. 20K6200 No. 1 Ever Ready Searchlight, 8½ inches long, 1½ inches in diameter, good for from 4,000 to 5,000 flashes. Weight, 1 pound.
Price....(If by mail, postage extra, 24 cents)..98c

No. 20K6201 Extra battery for No. 1 Ever Ready. Price....(If by mail, postage extra, 14 cents)..21c

No. 20K6202 Extra lamp for No. 1 Ever Ready. Price...(If by mail, postage extra, 2 cents)....19c

No. 20K6206 No. 3 Ever Ready Searchlight, extra large, 1½x13 inches, contains a 5½-volt lamp; the most powerful searchlight of its kind on the market. Weight, 2 pounds. Price..............$1.60
If by mail, postage extra, 32 cents.

No. 20K6207 Extra battery for No. 3 Ever Ready. Price...(If by mail, postage extra, 20 cents)..38c

No. 20K6208 Extra lamp for No. 3 Ever Ready. Price......If by mail, postage extra, 2 cents)..25c

Genuine Ever Ready Vest Pocket Searchlights.

No one should be without one of these lights. Can be carried into a cellar of leaking gas or put into a keg of gunpowder without any danger. Always ready for use by simply pressing the button. Adopted by all the large police and detective agencies in the world. Endorsed and used by the United States Army and Navy. Indispensable to anyone making night calls, going into dark granaries, stables, etc. Size, 2⅛x2¾x1 inch. Weight, 12 ounces. **We guarantee a fresh battery with each light.**

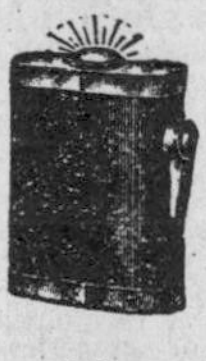

No. 20K6215 Ever Ready Vest Pocket Searchlight. Strong metal case, with handsome copper oxidized finish.
Price, complete with battery....55c
If by mail, postage extra, 15 cents.

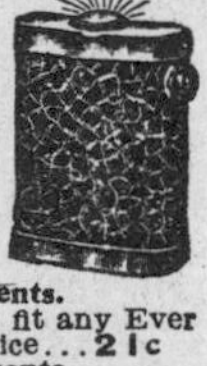

No. 20K6217 Ever Ready Vest Pocket Searchlight. Case made of strong metal, covered with imitation alligator leather, nickel plated trimmings.
Price, complete with battery, 75c
If by mail, postage extra, 15 cents.

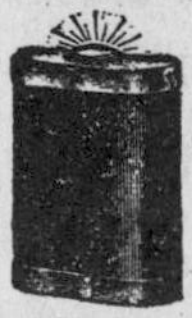

No. 20K6219 Ever Ready Vest Pocket Searchlight. Case made of highly polished fiber, waterproof, nickel plated trimmings.
Price, complete, with battery, 85c
If by mail, postage extra, 15 cents.

No. 20K6225 Extra Battery to fit any Ever Ready Vest Pocket Searchlight. Price....21c
If by mail, postage extra, 10 cents.

No. 20K6226 Extra Lamp to fit any Ever Ready Vest Pocket Searchlight. Price....19c
If by mail, postage extra, 2 cents.

Genuine Ever Ready Coat Pocket Light.

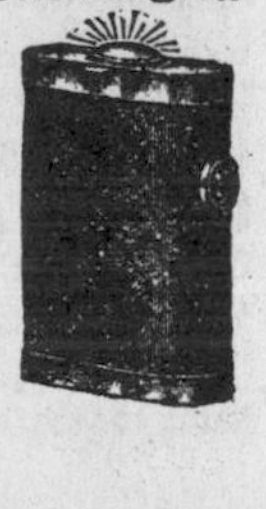

The Ever Ready Coat Pocket Searchlight is built in the same shape as the vest pocket light, only larger. It has a larger lamp, a better reflector and will last longer because of the larger battery. It has a metal leatherette covered case with nickel plated trimmings, size, 1⅛x3⅞x5 inches. Weight, 22 ounces.

No. 20K6230 Coat Pocket Light. Price, complete..............................95c
If by mail, postage extra, 24 cents.

No. 20K6231 Extra Battery for coat pocket light..............................29c
If by mail, postage extra, 22 cents.

No. 20K6232 Extra Lamp for coat pocket light. Price..............................19c
If by mail, postage extra, 2 cents.

$2.95 BUYS THIS ONE-CELL ELECTRIC MEDICAL BATTERY

A FAVORITE BATTERY FOR HOME USE

THE VALUE OF ELECTRICITY in the treatment of disease has been conclusively proven by Prof. Michael Faraday, who discovered that the nerves of the body are extremely sensitive to the action of electricity. Even after death, if electricity is properly applied, the muscles will act in the same manner as if life still remained. This discovery of Prof. Faraday has been improved upon in many ways, and our most prominent physicians are today using electricity in their treatment of many diseases. All of our electric medical batteries have been constructed upon the most improved principles, and our special one-cell battery is one of the most popular and well made style of batteries designed for home use.

THIS OUTFIT is shipped complete, all ready for operation as soon as it arrives. The dry cell is encased in a nickel plated cylinder, and the case is made of polished hardwood, fitted with strong clasp and handle for carrying. All metal parts are richly nickel plated, and the contact screw has a platina point, firmly held in place by lock nut. We include with this outfit a complete equipment consisting of one pair silk battery cords, one pair metal handles, one pair sponge electrodes, two wooden insulating handles, one nickel plated foot plate, directions for operating the battery, and our special instruction book, "Medical Electricity at Home." Everything is complete, so that you have only to connect the cords with the machine, turn on the switch, and the battery is in instant operation, and you can begin treatments immediately. This is by far the most popular outfit that has ever been placed upon the market.

No. 20K6300 Our Special One-Cell Medical Battery. Price, complete .... (Shipping weight, 6½ pounds.) **$2.95**

OUR GROCERY CATALOGUE IS FREE

CUT YOUR LIVING EXPENSES IN HALF

IF YOU WILL SEND FOR OUR GROCERY PRICE LIST you will be astonished to note the wonderful prices quoted therein on every grocery item. In fact, the prices we quote are the very lowest wholesale quotations on the very highest grade of seasonable groceries, and if you are at all interested in reducing your living expenses, won't you please send today for a copy of our Free Grocery Price List? And we will send it by return mail free and postpaid.

OUR GROCERIES SELL THEMSELVES.
We have been preaching the doctrine of highest quality and lowest prices for so many years, we have been supplying hundreds of thousands of our customers with all of their grocery needs so satisfactorily for so long a period of time and our methods of doing business have been so fully endorsed by our customers that it is not surprising that this grocery business has doubled and trebled from year to year. We feel that this increase in our grocery business, greater now than ever before, has been entirely due to the high quality of merchandise we sell, the extremely low prices which we quote and our sustained endeavor to carefully, promptly and satisfactorily fill every order for groceries received by us.

IT IS NOT SURPRISING that we supply the grocery needs of so many thousands of people at our money saving prices when you understand that our method of handling groceries cuts out a long row of profits to middlemen. We manufacture a very large percentage of the goods we offer, we import teas and coffees, we take the entire product in certain lines and we get such price concessions that our prices to our customers are less than the retailer pays his wholesaler for goods of equal quality. If you pay any dealer at home or elsewhere more than we ask for articles you need from day to day, you are paying a profit to the manufacturer, the jobber, the importer and the wholesaler.

IF YOU HAVE NEVER GIVEN US AN OPPORTUNITY to show you how much we can save you on the very best groceries, if you have never sent us an order for groceries, won't you please send today for a copy of our Free Grocery Price List? It contains our special propositions on groceries, our guarantees, and the most complete line of high grade groceries offered by any firm or individual. You cannot afford to purchase any bill of groceries until you have received this free book.

Send today for a copy of our Big Free Grocery List.

$6.80 BUYS THIS BIG IMPROVED DOUBLE CELL MEDICAL BATTERY
OUR TWO-CELL BATTERY

BEST VALUE FOR THE MONEY ever offered by any dealer. Our sales on this battery have been enormous, and we have received the most gratifying letters from our customers, expressing their entire satisfaction with the operation of this machine. It has a beautiful appearance, the case being made of hardwood, highly polished, and fitted with strong metal clasps and handle for carrying. The two dry batteries are concealed in the lower part of the cabinet and the cover is provided with a compartment for carrying the various electrodes. All metal parts are nickel plated, and the entire outfit finished in the very best possible manner. The battery has a regulator for controlling the strength of the current, a pole changer for reversing the poles from positive to negative when desired, and a three-point switch which allows the use of either one or both batteries at the same time. We also include the complete equipment of one pair silk battery cords, one pair metal handles, one pair sponge electrodes, two wooden insulating handles, one electric hair brush, one metal foot plate, directions for operating the battery, and our special instruction book, "Medical Electricity at Home." For a moderate priced machine, one adapted for professional use as well as home treatment, this outfit stands absolutely without an equal.

No. 20K6305 Improved Double Cell Medical Battery. Price, complete .... (Shipping weight, 10 pounds.) **$6.80**

OUR THREE-CELL MEDICAL BATTERY $9.95

THIS BATTERY IS THE MOST POWERFUL and completely equipped machine on the market. It presents the acme of perfection in medical batteries. It is furnished with three dry cell batteries concealed in the lower part of the cabinet and connected by a switch so that either one, two, or three of the batteries can be used at one time. It has a pole changer for reversing the current from positive to negative and there is also a circular carbon rheostat for regulating the strength of current, gradually increasing it from the very mildest vibrations to any strength desired. A special feature not found in other batteries, is the **Wheeled Rheotome** which allows the interval between vibrations to be regulated to any speed required. This feature is of the greatest importance in the treatment of many diseases by electricity. The outfit has a full equipment of one pair silk battery cords, two metal handles, one pair sponge electrodes, two wooden insulating handles, one electric hair brush, one metal footplate, complete directions for operating the battery, and our special instruction book, "Medical Electricity at Home." The complete equipment of this battery, its elegant finish and beautiful design, recommend it to those who desire the best battery obtainable for either professional use or home treatment. Size, 8x8x11 inches.

No. 20K6310 Our Three-Cell Medical Battery. Price, complete .... (Shipping weight, 18 pounds.) **$9.95**

OUR THIRTY-DAY FREE TRIAL OFFER

SELECT THE BATTERY YOU WANT and send us your order, enclosing our special price, $2.95, $6.80 or $9.95, according to style selected, and we will ship the battery at once, guaranteeing it to reach you in perfect order. You can try the battery in your own home for thirty days, test it in every way that you wish to, give it a fair and thorough trial, and if at the end of thirty days you are not entirely satisfied with the battery, you may return it to us at once, and we will cheerfully refund every cent you have paid us, including all transportation charges on the shipment.

THIS IS THE MOST LIBERAL PROPOSITION ON MEDICAL BATTERIES ever made by any dealer, and offers you an opportunity to try one of our batteries at your own home and entirely without expense if the results are not in every way satisfactory to you. We know our batteries are the best on the market, because they are made under our directions, according to our own specifications, and every battery is carefully tested by an expert inspector before it is allowed to leave the factory. Every metal part is of the very highest grade, every piece of lumber is carefully selected, the workmanship that enters into these batteries make them the most perfect, durable, high grade batteries that can be built.

REMEMBER THAT IT WILL NOT COST YOU A CENT to try this battery for yourself. Hundreds of customers have written us, telling the wonderful effect these batteries have had in their cases, but we want to prove to you exactly what it will do in your case.

IF YOU WANT TO TAKE ADVANTAGE of this wonderful offer and try this battery in your home for thirty days—send us your order at once, enclosing the full amount for the outfit you select, and the goods will be shipped to you without delay.

YOUR MONEY WILL BE IMMEDIATELY RETURNED TO YOU FOR ANY GOODS NOT PERFECTLY SATISFACTORY.

141

INCREASE YOUR SALARY BY LEARNING TELEGRAPHY

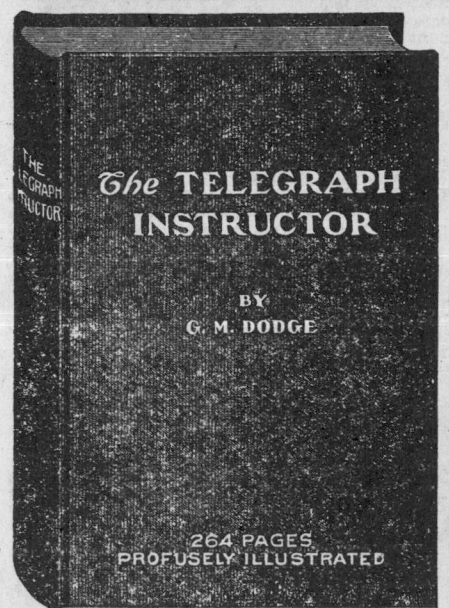

IT MEANS MONEY TO YOU

65c

TURN YOUR SPARE MOMENTS INTO DOLLARS. OUR BIG INSTRUCTOR TELLS YOU HOW. SEND FOR IT TODAY.

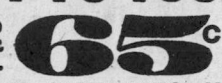

IT MEANS MONEY FOR— YOU

The TELEGRAPH INSTRUCTOR

BY G. M. DODGE

264 PAGES. PROFUSELY ILLUSTRATED

OUR BIG 264-PAGE "TELEGRAPH INSTRUCTOR" covers every branch of telegraphic work and is full of the most useful hints and suggestions that have ever been put into printers' ink. It contains complete instructions for setting up the instruments, line construction, installation of switchboards, care of batteries, etc., etc. It gives the Morse code in full, with hundreds of abbreviations that are in general use. The duties of every railroad employee from the superintendent down to the engineer, conductor, and switchman are fully explained in this big book.

YOU CAN BECOME A STATION AGENT, equipped with all the knowledge of an old time railroad man, as soon as you have mastered the contents of "The Telegraph Instructor." The various train signals and interlocking switch devices are fully explained and illustrated by diagrams. Much other valuable information, such as the Block system for handling trains, and many other modern systems and devices used in railroading are fully explained in this big book.

A COMMERCIAL TELEGRAPHER'S POSITION can be quickly secured if the instructions and suggestions given in this book are carefully followed out. "The Telegraph Instructor" contains a list of the one hundred rules now in use by the large commercial companies, and clearly explains every detail of the work so that you can assume the duties of a commercial operator with all the knowledge and confidence of an experienced telegrapher. The telegraphic field offers unlimited opportunities to the young man who desires to fit himself for the achievement of great success in the business world.

AS A BUSINESS TRAINING, telegraphy has proven the stepping stone by which many men have attained the highest pinnacles of success. Andrew Carnegie, the steel king, began as a railroad telegraph operator, and his training in this work enabled him in later years to build up and control the greatest industrial organization the world has ever known. Thomas A. Edison, "The Wizard of Menlo Park," early in life started as a telegraph operator. He is now a multimillionaire, and stands preeminent among the scientific men of the world. But his marvelous achievements are largely due to the early training he received at the key and sounder. Thomas B. Clowry, President of the Western Union Telegraph Company, started as an ordinary telegraph operator, and is now the head of this great company employing many thousands of men. Richard W. Sears, President of Sears, Roebuck & Company, the greatest mercantile institution in the world, employing in their store and the various factories which they own and control, nearly twenty thousand people, started his business life as station agent and telegraph operator in the little town of Redwood Falls, Minnesota. Scores of other such instances might be mentioned, but these few are only offered in proof that there is something about the duties of a telegraph operator that fits him to undertake and accomplish great things in the modern commercial world.

BIG SALARIES are paid to telegraph operators who become expert. Twenty years ago there were less than 25,000 operators in the country. Today they number more than 75,000 as compared with 120,000 lawyers, 115,000 preachers, and 150,000 doctors. The demand for telegraph operators is rapidly increasing every day and the beginner usually receives a salary of $50.00 to $60.00 per month. Positions with commission houses on the Board of Trade where accuracy and speed are absolutely necessary, pay as high as $4.00 and $5.00 per day, and the chief dispatchers of many railroads receive an annual salary of thousands of dollars and have the very best opportunity for promotion to the highest executive offices of the company.

SEND FOR OUR BIG BOOK AND LEARN ALL ABOUT THIS FASCINATING AND RAPIDLY GROWING BUSINESS.

No. 20K6477 "The Telegraph Instructor," just as illustrated and described above. Price..................(If by mail, postage extra, 8 cents).............**65c**

OUR COMPLETE LEARNER'S TELEGRAPH OUTFIT 1 35

OUR LEARNER'S OUTFIT CONSISTS OF OUR REGULAR 4-OHM LEARNER'S INSTRUMENT COMPLETE WITH ONE DRY BATTERY, CONNECTING WIRES, AND OUR "OPERATOR'S MANUAL."

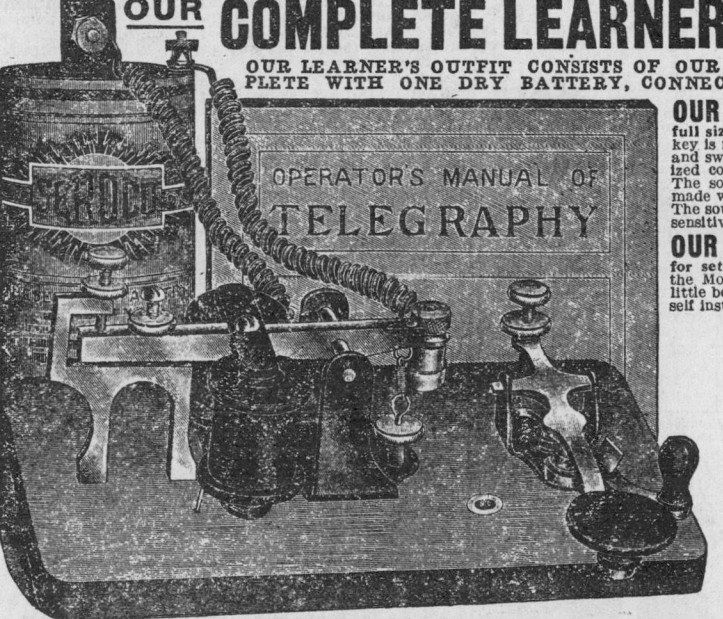

OPERATOR'S MANUAL OF TELEGRAPHY

OUR 4-OHM LEARNER'S INSTRUMENT, as included in this outfit, consists of a full size key and sounder, mounted on polished quarter sawed oak base. The key is made with nickel bar, latest thumb nut adjustment, composition key knob and switch handle, platina contact points and stamped frame finished in oxidized copper. The sounder has covered magnets wound to 4 ohms resistance. The sounding bar and sounder frame are nickel plated and highly polished, made with latest thumb nut adjustments and stamped trunnion stand with oxidized copper finish. The sounder frame and key base, being stamped from one solid piece of metal, insures an easy working, sensitive instrument which cannot get out of adjustment.

OUR "OPERATOR'S MANUAL" which we include free of charge with this outfit, is a sixteen-page book, containing full instructions for setting up and operating this outfit. It also contains instructions for telegraphing, explaining the Morse code fully, gives a number of practice exercises and a lot of general information. This little book teaches you how to send and receive messages, and gives you the essentials necessary for self instruction in telegraphy.

No. 20K6450 Learner's Telegraph Outfit, complete as illustrated and described above. Shipping weight, 4½ pounds. Price...............**$1.35**

No. 20K6452 Our Special Learner's Telegraph Outfit, consisting of 4-Ohm Learner's Instrument with battery, connecting wires, etc., just exactly the same as outfit No. 20K6450 except that instead of the small "Operator's Manual," we include a copy of our big 264-page book, "The Telegraph Instructor," as illustrated and described above. Price.................**$1.95**

No. 20K6454 Our Double Learner's Telegraph Outfit. This outfit consists of two of our 4-ohm instruments, four cells of dry battery, and three hundred feet of insulated copper wire. With this outfit the instruments can be installed in two different rooms in the house, and two operators can practice the Morse alphabet, sending and receiving messages from each other. Shipping weight, 15 lbs. Price, complete........**$3.75**

No. 20K6460 4-Ohm Learner's Instrument, without battery or connecting wire. Price..............**1.20**

If by mail, postage extra, 30 cents.

No. 20K6462 20-Ohm Learner's Instrument. This is exactly the same as our regular 4-Ohm Learner's Instrument except that the magnets are wound to 20 ohms resistance, making the instrument suitable for lines of any length up to fifteen miles. No connecting wire or battery is included. Price............**$1.45**

If by mail, postage extra, 30 cents.

EXTRA HIGH GRADE PRIVATE LINE INSTRUMENTS.

$1.98

No. 20K6470 4-Ohm Private Line Instrument, for practice on short lines. This instrument consists of an extra high grade aluminum lever sounder and fine steel lever key, mounted on highly polished quarter sawed oak base.

Materials and workmanship are the best. The sounder magnets are wound to 4 ohms resistance and covered with polished hard rubber, the sounding bar is made from aluminum, and for tone, loudness and quick action is unsurpassed. The fine steel lever key has hardened platina points and thumbscrew trunnion adjustments. The sounder frame and key are heavily nickel plated. Price...............**$1.98**

If by mail, postage extra, 38 cents.

No. 20K6475 20-Ohm Private Line Instrument, exactly the same as No. 20K6470, except that the sounder magnets are wound to 20 ohms resistance, making the instrument suitable for long distance work. Can be used on lines one-half mile or more in length. Price........**$2.20**

If by mail, postage extra, 38 cents.

ALUMINUM GIANT LEVER SOUNDERS.

$1.70

Our new Aluminum Giant Sounders excel all other sounders in tone, loudness and quick action, being in every respect the finest and best sounders made. The sounding bar is made from aluminum, the balance of the instrument is of brass, heavily nickel plated. The magnets are specially wound to insure perfect insulation and covered with polished hard rubber. The base is of highly polished oak, and the instrument is finished with the most careful attention to details and appearance. Special attention is directed to the way in which the wooden base is connected to the instrument, an open space being left between the wood and the metal, which greatly increases the sound and improves the tone.

No. 20K6480 Aluminum Lever Giant Sounder, as described and illustrated above, with magnets wound to 4 ohms resistance, for lines one-quarter mile or less in length. Price..............**$1.70**

If by mail, postage extra, 30 cents.

No. 20K6481 Aluminum Lever Giant Sounder, as described and illustrated above, with magnets wound to 20 ohms resistance for lines one-half mile or more in length. Will work on lines up to fifty miles in length. Price..............**$1.85**

If by mail, postage extra, 30 cents.

NICKEL PLATED STEEL LEVER KEYS.

90c

No. 20K6485 Steel Lever Key, legless. This is the standard key of the latest and most improved type, the lever and trunnions being made of solid steel, nickel plated, instead of brass, as in the old type of instrument. The same strength is secured with much lighter weight and the liability of loose trunnions completely avoided. This is, without doubt, one of the handsomest and best working keys on the market. Price..............**90c**

If by mail, postage extra, 10 cents.

No. 20K6486 Steel Lever Key, with legs. A standard key, just the same in general construction, material, workmanship and efficiency as No. 20K6485, but made with two legs which go through the table, clamping it firmly from below. Price..............**$1.00**

If by mail, postage extra, 10c.

THE SURPRISINGLY LOW REDUCED PRICES prevailing in this catalogue mean GREATER SAVINGS TO OUR CUSTOMERS than ever before.

EXPERIMENTAL APPARATUS AND ELECTRICAL TOYS.

The Toy Electric Engine.

The very latest thing in electric toys. This is the cheapest and most efficient toy electric engine ever built. It will run on one cell of a dry battery for from 75 to 100 hours, and will give a speed of from 300 to 1,000 revolutions per minute, a speed which can be controlled. The engine is mounted on a gray iron cast base, finished in baked black enamel. The magnets have double cotton covered magnet wire on special wrought iron cores. All the bearings are adjustable, and work on a pivot. The engine presents a neat, attractive appearance, and is the best engine ever put on the market for operating small mechanical toys. A complete booklet of instructions on the use of this engine, fully explaining the principles on which it is built, is furnished with each machine. Weight, when packed, 4 pounds.

No. 20K6350 Toy Electric Engine, with one cell of dry battery. Price..................$1.25

Electrohit.

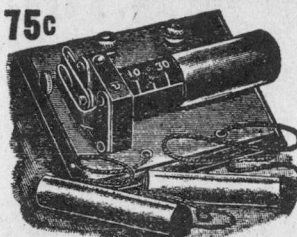

75c

No. 20K6355 The Electrohit is a coil mounted on a wood base, with binding posts and full instructions. It is the best coil on the market for the money. Many interesting and amusing tricks can be played with this instrument. For instance, partly fill a metallic basin with water, drop in a coin, hold one handle against the basin, ask a person to take the other handle and reach for the coin. The results will be interesting. This coil is especially made for those who are interested in the construction of induction coils and in performing small experiments. Price, without battery..(Postage extra, 10c).75c

NOTE—One Seroco Dry Battery, price 16 cents, will operate this coil perfectly.

Magneto Electric Thriller.

80c

No. 20K6360 Magneto Electric Thriller, is mounted on a neat wooden base, finished in red enamel, with full nickel plated trimmings, fitted with flexible cords and nickel plated handles. It shows the principles of the magneto electric machine, and affords great amusement as well as instruction. The current can be so regulated that it will make a strong man tremble, or so mild as not to injure a child. Price, 80c.

If by mail, postage extra, 25 cents.

Little Hustler Motor.

85c

No. 20K6365 The Little Hustler Motor, which we show here, is the finest small motor ever produced, for those to whom the study of electricity has an attraction. The principles governing the use of electricity which are made use of in dynamo and motor construction are strikingly shown. It is made from the best grade of Swedish iron, has three-part armature, extra long bearings, binding posts and grooved pulley. It is mounted on a neat wood base, is finished in black enamel, with nickel plated trimmings. This motor will run on a single cell of dry or wet battery. Price..................85c

If by mail, postage extra, 15 cents.

No. 20K6366 Little Hustler Motor. With two cells of dry battery. Price, $1.13

Cannot be sent by mail.

No. 20K6367 Nickel Plated 5-inch Fan, for Little Hustler Motor only.
Price..................19c

19c

If by mail, postage extra, 2 cents.

Little Hustler Motor Parts, 68c.

Build your own motor and learn the principles of motor building.

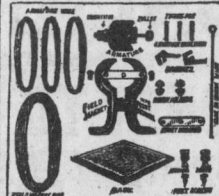

No. 20K6378 Little Hustler Motor Parts. For boys and others interested in experimental electrical work no better method of learning the principles of electric motor construction exists than by being able to build one. We furnish a set of motor parts, which are complete with the necessary wire for winding armature and field as well as all the screws, etc., necessary to put the machine together. With the instructions which accompany each set, anyone can construct a motor. Price, complete..................68c

If by mail, postage extra, 15 cents.

Baby Dynamo.

No. 20K6385 Baby Dynamo, built for experimental work only. It is not large enough for practical electric lighting of houses and buildings. At 3,000 revolutions it has an output of 5½ volts, 2½ amperes. Under full load it gives 6 volts and 2½ amperes. It will light three 4-candle power miniature lamps, will decompose water and can be used for nickel plating. By reversing the brushes it can be used as a motor and this is done almost instantly. This makes the machine one of the best for school laboratories or anyone interested in physics. The brush holder has rocker arm for adjusting the brushes, is equipped with oil cups, has a 1-inch groove pulley and is mounted on a handsome enameled stamped base. The field is finished in green enamel, trimmings are all nickel plated. Weight, 4½ pounds.

Price for dynamo, complete..................$3.75

Permanent Horseshoe Magnets.

No. 20K6400 We furnish Horseshoe Magnets in two qualities, the ordinary quality, made in Germany, and the best quality, made in England.

NOTE—When placing orders for Horseshoe Magnets, be sure to state plainly if German or English are wanted.

Length		German	Best English
2 inches.	Price	$0.04	$0.10
3 inches.	Price	.08	.14
4 inches.	Price	.14	.25
6 inches.	Price	.20	.50
8 inches.	Price	.68	1.05
10 inches.	Price	.98	1.75
12 inches.	Price	1.52	2.50

No. 20K6402 Square Bar Magnet, best quality, not as powerful as horseshoe magnets, but preferred in many cases on account of the shape.
Price, 6 inches long, 18c; 4 inches long..................12c

No. 20K6404 Lodestone or Natural Magnet. A naturally magnetic iron ore, very interesting as a curiosity and useful in certain peculiar arts and sciences. Ours is the genuine article. Price, per ounce..................10c
Per pound..................50c

Miniature Battery Lamps.

No. 20K6410 Miniature Lamps for experimental purposes. Be sure to give catalogue number and number of lamp when ordering.

Number	Volts	Amperes	Candle Power	No. of Cells Required	Price Each
33	3½	.40	1	3	20c
34	4	.25	1	3	20c
36	6	.25	2	5	20c
38	8	.25	3	7	20c
39	6	.95	4	7	22c
42	10	.60	6	9	22c

Above prices do not include receptacles.
If by mail, postage extra, per lamp, 2 cents.

No. 20K6420 Round Miniature Lamp Receptacles. Will fit any miniature lamp. Price..................6c
If by mail, postage extra, 2 cents.

No. 20K6422 Miniature Weatherproof Pendant Socket. Will fit any miniature lamp. Price, each..................12c
If by mail, postage extra, 2 cents.

Miniature Fruit Lamps.

No. 20K6425 Miniature Fruit Lamps, representing peaches, pears, apples, oranges, etc., in their natural colors. One lamp will burn on three cells of dry or wet battery. The latest and most novel form of table decorations.
Price, per dozen, assorted fruits, $2.75; each..................25c
If by mail, postage extra, each, 14 cents.

Miniature Table Lamp Outfit.

No. 20K6430 Miniature Table Lamp Outfit consists of three cells of Seroco dry battery, one miniature lamp receptacle, one 1-point switch, 30 feet of wire. This is a cheap outfit which illustrates thoroughly the principles of electric lighting by battery power. The lamp furnished is one-candle power. Weight, all complete, 6½ pounds.
Price, complete outfit..................82c

Gas Engine Igniters.

Magneto Gas Engine Igniter, designed to ignite gasoline engines and reduce the wear on the batteries. It is constructed with a permanent magnetic field and drum type armature. Its speed is regulated by a governor. For make and break engines it is operated by friction drive. For jump spark ignition it is operated with a belt. Will work on any gasoline engine fitted with sparking contacts. It runs the engine in either direction and ordinarily will ignite on one revolution of the fly wheel. Size of the base is 4 by 7 inches; height, about 8 inches; weight, 12 pounds. It can be used without a spark coil, although to obtain the best results it is best to use one. We guarantee this igniter thoroughly and can ship it on a 30-day free trial.

No. 20K6501 Gas Engine Igniter, for make and break ignition. Operated by friction drive.
Price..................$11.95

No. 20K6502 Gas Engine Igniter, for jump spark ignition. Operated with a belt.
Price..................$11.95

Jump Spark Coil.

No. 20K6510 Jump Spark Coil. This coil is one of the best on the market. It gives an intensely hot fat spark with very little battery consumption. The coils are wound with silk wire and are absolutely moistureproof. The coils work best on four cells of battery. Size, 3½x3½x9 inches over all. Weight, 4½ pounds.
Price..................$3.95

Empire Spark Plug.

No. 20K6520 Empire Spark Plug, the only self cleaning spark plug on the market. This is accomplished by means of the reserve gas cylinder which is part of the plug. Made for standard half-inch thread. Fully guaranteed. Price, each, 95c

No. 20K6525 Duplex Plug Attachment for Automobiles and Motor Boats. The Duplex Plug Attachment will make any spark plug fire, no matter how foul; it fits any plug. With this attachment on your spark plug, when your motor plugs miss fire, pull switch, without even stopping your motor, and you will have no further trouble. Guaranteed to save current and fuel. Price, each..................$2.50

No. 20K6530 Duplex Spark Plugs with Duplex Switch Device. Made with standard half-inch thread imported porcelain bushes; guaranteed not to crack or crumble. When this plug fails to work, all that is necessary is to pull the switch to which it is attached, without stopping your engine.
Price, each..................$2.00

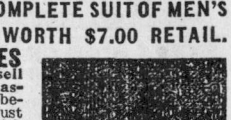

MUSICAL INSTRUMENTS

FULL ILLUSTRATIONS AND DESCRIPTIONS OF THE ENTIRE LINE OF BECKWITH PIANOS AND ORGANS, WITH SPECIAL FREE TRIAL OFFERS, ETC.

OUR NEW AND REMARKABLE OFFER No 1. We want you to try a Beckwith Piano or Organ, and so well convinced are we that these instruments are the finest made, we have such confidence in their ability to please the most critical musicians, that we are making a more liberal offer than ever. You can try a Beckwith Piano or Organ without investing a single penny with us, either for the instrument or for the freight charges.

DON'T SEND A PENNY WITH YOUR ORDER. **It is not necessary to deposit anything in advance or send us any money. Just send your order to us for a Beckwith and we will ship it to you, freight charges prepaid. Read this offer carefully.** It will convince you that we take the risk because you do not obligate yourself or promise anything or sign any agreement at all. We take all the risk, and all we ask as an evidence of good faith, after the instrument is received at your station is that you will deposit the cost and the freight charge with your banker, to be held for you for full thirty days while you try the instrument, with the understanding that if it is not all that you can possibly desire in a high class musical instrument, if after you have had all of your musical friends and neighbors and the most prominent, disinterested musical experts try it, then if it is not satisfactory, send it back to us, go to your banker, and he will hand you back all of your

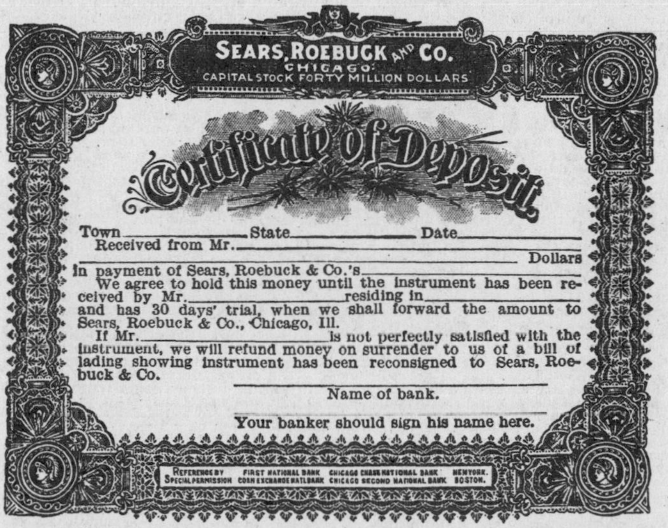

SEARS, ROEBUCK AND CO.
CHICAGO.
CAPITAL STOCK FORTY MILLION DOLLARS

Certificate of Deposit

Town________State________Date________
Received from Mr.________
________Dollars
in payment of Sears, Roebuck & Co.'s________
We agree to hold this money until the instrument has been received by Mr.________residing in________
and has 30 days' trial, when we shall forward the amount to Sears, Roebuck & Co., Chicago, Ill.
If Mr.________is not perfectly satisfied with the instrument, we will refund money on surrender to us of a bill of lading showing instrument has been reconsigned to Sears, Roebuck & Co.

____
Name of bank.
____
Your banker should sign his name here.

REFERENCE BY SPECIAL PERMISSION FIRST NATIONAL BANK CORN EXCHANGE NAT'L BANK CHICAGO CHASE NATIONAL BANK CHICAGO SECOND NATIONAL BANK NEW YORK. BOSTON.

money. This offer fully protects you because you do not deposit a penny until after the goods reach you and **all during your trial term your money is at your own bank under your complete control waiting for you to decide.** When sending your order under this offer, it is absolutely necessary that you give us the name of the bank where you will make your deposit after the instrument reaches you. Before writing your order, before instructing us to send a piano or organ to you under this liberal offer, please be sure to read **our 7 per cent interest bearing Offer No. 2.**

WHEN ORDERING AN INSTRUMENT under this plan, be sure to send us the name of the bank where you expect to deposit the money for the instrument and freight charges, after it arrives at your local station. Immediately upon receipt of your order, we will enter it at our factory and ship it at the earliest possible date, which will be inside of a few days. Under this plan of shipment we take absolutely all the risk, you run no risk whatever. You are not called upon to promise anything or agree to anything or to obligate yourself in any way whatever; all we ask is your permission to show you the wonderful quality represented by the Beckwith Pianos and Organs; we only ask you to test one for 30 days in your own home, and at the end of 30 days either buy it or send it back to us at our expense. Remember that if for any reason whatever you should return the shipment, you need not wait one moment for the return of your money in full; because **all during your trial term your money is at your own bank under your complete control.**

OUR 7 PER CENT INTEREST BEARING OFFER No. 2. **If you prefer not to let the banker or anyone else know what you pay for a Beckwith, if you wish to send the money with the order, then do so and we will deposit it for you in our Banking Department** where it will be held subject to your trial of the instrument and be returned to you if you are not satisfied after a 30-day trial. This Offer No. 2 has many great advantages over our Offer No. 1, but we will gladly ship a piano or organ without a dollar being sent to us just to show you the utmost confidence we have in the superb quality and great value of the Beckwith Pianos and Organs. At the same time there are many of our friends who would not order a Beckwith on the deposit plan and to these we say that in making our liberal Offer No. 1, **we are not withdrawing our Offer No. 2,** but you still have the privilege of sending the money with your order to us direct, to be returned to you **in full with interest added at the rate of 7 per cent a year** if you are not more than pleased with the instrument, if you do not keep it after a thorough test. While we will gladly ship a piano or organ on the deposit plan, yet it is really to your advantage to send the money with the order, because you are just as well protected as though the money was left in your own bank. Our entire institution, our enormous paid up capital, our forty-acre plant, our buildings, our millions of dollars' worth of merchandise, our well known reputation for honest dealing, are back of all our promises and agreements, are back of our guarantee under which we agree to refund all of your money down to the last penny if you are not satisfied at the end of a 30-day trial. **Another good reason** why the money should accompany the order is because the purchase of a piano or organ means more than the purchase of any ordinary merchandise, and most everyone prefers that the matter be treated confidentially between us. They do not care for the banker or anyone else to know what they pay for this high grade instrument. If you are one of these, we say, send your money with the order and you will be just as fully protected as though it was deposited in your own bank. Then again, while you are trying the instrument, your money is deposited in our Banking Department and is earning interest at the rate of 7 per cent a year for you. If you should return the instrument as unsatisfactory, not only would we hand you back the cost of the instrument in full but we would also include in our remittance the interest that this money had been earning for you during your trial term. You would also receive back every penny for freight charges and every penny advanced by you for cartage. In other words, we hold you free of every legitimate expense of every nature.

THESE OFFERS REMOVE ALL RESPONSIBILITY FROM YOU. **We take all the risk and you take none. We cannot understand what more liberal proposition could possibly be made to you. You do not take any chances at all.** We do not ask you to bind yourself, to obligate yourself or agree to anything; all we ask is that you let us show you the matchless quality of the Beckwith instruments under our liberal terms, allowing you full 30 days' trial without any risk on your part. We only ask as an evidence of good faith that you leave the cost of the instrument and the freight charges which we will gladly advance for you, with your local banker after it arrives, there to remain and to be held for you all the time you are trying the instrument. It is true that the majority of our friends do send the money with their orders, but we do not ask this. It is not necessary, but if you prefer to send the money and take advantage of the 7 per cent interest clause, as explained in our Offer No. 2, please accept this as our personal binding guarantee, our pledge to refund to you every penny of your money and hold you free of every reasonable expense of every nature whatsoever if you should return the instrument after a 30 days' test. It is our purpose to make this trial as favorable to you as we can, and knowing the Beckwith Pianos and Organs as we do, we willingly place the entire matter in the hands of yourself and your friends, gladly accepting your decision without question.

OUR BINDING 25-YEAR BOND OF INDEMNITY covers every piano and organ which we ship. A copy of this Bond of Indemnity is reproduced below. This is undeniably the strongest, most binding bond ever issued covering a piano or an organ and has more back of it than any guarantee or bond of indemnity offered by any other dealer, manufacturer or agent. We are glad to show this Bond of Indemnity and are proud of the fact that we can guarantee the Beckwith Pianos and Organs for 25 years, a full quarter of a century. We would not issue such a binding guarantee on any piano or organ unless we positively knew that the material in it was of the highest class, that it represented the best workmanship, that it represented quality in every way, quality of tone and wearing quality and all that makes a 25-year guarantee possible. Those who have been led to believe, who have been taught to believe that a high price is necessarily a guarantee of quality, should consider the terms of this Bond of Indemnity and should specially match it up word for word with those bonds of indemnity, warrants or guarantees issued by manufacturers who sell instruments of the same grade for about twice the price we ask. This is the most convincing argument we know of, that a high price is not a guarantee of excellence, because this Bond of Indemnity, covering the Beckwith Pianos and Organs, instruments of the best grade, the equal of any made, sold at double our price, is stronger by far, more protection to the purchaser, than any guarantee issued by those manufacturers who secure double our price and more for instruments of the same quality. It is to your interest to bear this fact in mind.

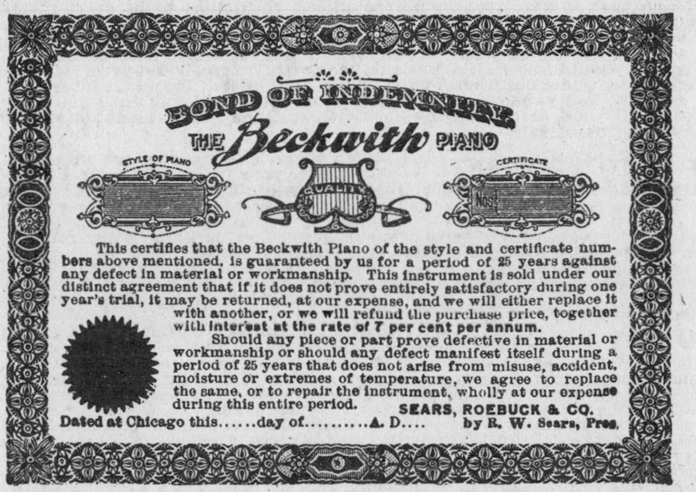

BOND OF INDEMNITY.
THE Beckwith PIANO
STYLE OF PIANO
QUALITY
CERTIFICATE Nos.

This certifies that the Beckwith Piano of the style and certificate numbers above mentioned, is guaranteed by us for a period of 25 years against any defect in material or workmanship. This instrument is sold under our distinct agreement that if it does not prove entirely satisfactory during one year's trial, it may be returned, at our expense, and we will either replace it with another, or we will refund the purchase price, together **with interest at the rate of 7 per cent per annum.**

Should any piece or part prove defective in material or workmanship or should any defect manifest itself during a period of 25 years that does not arise from misuse, accident, moisture or extremes of temperature, we agree to replace the same, or to repair the instrument, wholly at our expense during this entire period.

SEARS, ROEBUCK & CO.
Dated at Chicago this......day of..........A. D.... by R. W. Sears, Pres.

OUR ONE-YEAR TRIAL OFFER

is full protection to the purchaser. While we do ask that the Beckwith instrument be accepted or refused at the end of a 30 days' trial, yet, so as to remove every possible chance from your side of the transaction, we bind ourselves in our Bond of Indemnity, to which your attention is invited, to refund every penny of your money with interest added at the rate of 7 per cent per annum if you are not wholly satisfied with the instrument at any time within one year from the date of purchase. Could you ask for better protection? Could you ask for a more liberal offer? Could you ask for greater opportunity of judging the Beckwith than the full year that this offer gives you?

ASK YOURSELF THIS QUESTION. **If you are in the market for an instrument and if the Beckwith represents standard quality in every way, if our prices are lower than have ever before been attempted, and furthermore, if we take all the risk, don't your personal interests demand that you favor us with a trial order before considering any other instrument of any other make?** We claim without any fear of successful contradiction that the Beckwith Pianos and Organs represent quality in every line and in every part. We claim that the tone will satisfy the most critical musician, that the action is responsive and finely adjusted, that the finish is beautiful and that the material and workmanship are of the very best. Our prices are lower than have ever before been attempted on instruments of the highest grade, as a reference to the following pages will prove, and if you will read our liberal terms, our 30-day free trial offer, our send-no-money offer, the agreement contained in our guarantee, allowing you to return the instrument at any time within a year, when we will refund all your money, together with interest added at the rate of 7 per cent, you must be convinced that **we take the risk and you take none.** All of these facts should appeal to you, and you should not consider the purchase of any other instrument before trying a Beckwith under the liberal terms as shown on this page, and determining for yourself whether or not it is one to please you. If it is your purpose to own a piano or organ, and it is your ambition to have as fine an instrument as can be found in any mansion in the land, then you should send us your trial order under our liberal offers and take a Beckwith into your home for a full 30-day trial at the hands of yourself and any unprejudiced, unbiased musician.

READ EVERY WORD IN THE PAGES THAT FOLLOW. **It is very necessary that you read all about our pianos and organs and our liberal terms so that it will enable you to make the best selection.** Before deciding upon which piano or organ to order on trial, we ask you to see the illustration and description of every instrument shown, and especially those of our higher grades. **It will pay you** to invest all you can spare in a piano or organ, thus securing the best we can offer. We give you back every extra dollar that we are compelled to charge you for our higher priced instruments, in greater value, greater quality and, therefore, in greater satisfaction in the years to come. Make your selection from these pages and remember, you are protected because we bind ourselves to fulfill every promise and agreement. We guarantee that you will find everything exactly as illustrated and described and if you are not wholly pleased we will expect you, under our agreement, to return the instrument at our expense when we will refund all of your money.

IF WE COULD SEE YOU PERSONALLY **and could show you a Beckwith, we know that you would feel compelled to take it into your home for a 30-day trial,** and at the end of that time we know you would be so well satisfied with it, you would not only buy it, but would recommend it in the highest terms. Remember, we take all the risk and you take no chances at all. If anyone advises you not to buy a Beckwith under our liberal terms, it must be that they are trying to influence you for their own pecuniary gain. If anyone insists that you do not send for a Beckwith, saying it is not all we recommend it to be, you should look upon this advice with suspicion, because you must admit that our prices are very much lower than any others and because if the Beckwith represents all we claim, then you surely want to try one to find out if our claims are true. Send your trial order anyway so as to prove whether such advice is correct or not. If anyone advises you that the Beckwith Piano or Organ is not all we represent it to be, then if they are sincere and honest in their advice, they should also advise you by all means to send for one on trial so as to prove the truth of their claim. If they will not, you may rest assured they are not advising you for your own personal interests, because we will place an instrument in your hands all at our risk, so that you can see just what a Beckwith really is. Your interests demand that you do send for a Beckwith Piano or Organ before considering any other instrument in the market, owing to the quality so apparent in them, the fine tone which has been developed to such a wonderful degree, the wonderful saving our prices represent and **our extremely liberal trial terms and offers.**

WE GUARANTEE **that our Colonial Art or Special Concert Grand Pianos will compare in every way with other pianos of well known makes sold through other channels for as high as $500.00, and we guarantee that our Imperial Grand Organ, which is sold at from $46.80 upward, is an instrument the equal of those sold through ordinary channels for from $125.00 to $175.00. This saving is all yours, if, after a complete 30-day trial in your own home, you should buy the Beckwith under our liberal terms.**

THE BECKWITH PIANOS

A STANDARD LINE OF HIGH GRADE INSTRUMENTS AT PRICES LOWER THAN EVER BEFORE.
A FEW POINTERS ON THE ESSENTIALS OF A HIGH GRADE PIANO.

We wish we could tell you face to face all about the superlative merit, the exquisite tone quality, the fine finish and wonderful piano value represented by the Beckwith. We are many miles apart, and therefore the following pages in this catalogue must tell you what WE want you to know, what YOU want to know, and what you OUGHT to know about the Beckwith. You must read every page if you would know all about the Beckwith piano, the way it is made, the liberal terms under which it is sold, its marvelous tone quality, its delightfully responsive action and its many other satisfying qualities. We want you to see and try a Beckwith piano. You ought to try it as a matter of justice to yourself, because of the great saving that our price to you represents. Where could you better try a piano than in your own home? You are not here for us to show you the instrument, hence we will gladly put the piano in your own parlor, there to be tried by you and by your musical friends and your neighbors for full thirty days, entirely at our risk.

The fact that you are reading this page convinces us that you are interested in pianos. We feel that it is your intention to purchase one. If so, it is but natural that you should wish to buy the best instrument that it is possible to make, and we say to you that we can offer you a greater saving than anyone else, giving you a piano of the highest quality, a piano that is admitted by unprejudiced musicians to be of the first grade. If you would secure a piano of the highest type, an instrument of acknowledged superiority, worthy the place of honor in any home, at a larger saving in price to you than has ever before been attempted, then you should know all about the Beckwith. You should favor us with a trial order under our liberal thirty days' trial offers. If you are interested in a piano, you cannot afford to lay down this catalogue until you have read every word describing the Beckwith and the full explanation of our liberal terms of sale.

IT IS TO YOUR INTEREST to weigh every statement we make. It is to your interest to order a Beckwith piano on trial under our liberal offers, because of the wonderful saving our prices represent to you, and because the matter rests entirely in your hands to prove to yourself that the Beckwith is the equal of any piano made, regardless of price. If you agree to buy the piano after thirty days' trial, remember our promise and guarantee, to which we refer you, under the provisions of which you have a right to return the piano at any time within one year if you become dissatisfied, and have all your money refunded, together with interest at the rate of 7 per cent per annum. Could you ask for a more liberal offer or better protection?

DO NOT BE DECEIVED by the extremely low prices which we are enabled to quote on the Beckwith piano. It is a mistaken idea to measure the quality of an instrument by the price the manufacturer, dealer or agent seeks to secure for it. The cost to make any fine piano is not a large amount, and it would be an injustice to attempt to measure the quality of the Beckwith by our low prices. Forget the small amount we are willing to accept for this high grade instrument and order one under our liberal trial offer. Remember that it is the system under which most pianos are sold which increases the price but does not add one single thing of value to the quality. In paying the large price demanded by others for other makes of pianos you are not securing better quality or more value; you are only paying the unnecessarily large profits, commissions and expenses of the many dealers through whose hands it passes on its way to you. You will not find anything in any piano of any value that is not developed in the fullest degree in the Beckwith.

WE INVITE COMPARISON OF QUALITY as well as price. You cannot do us a greater favor than to order any instrument in this catalogue, comparing it with any like instrument in your neighborhood which has been sold at double our price. If you will do this, you will be convinced that a high price does not indicate any larger degree of quality but it does prove that the ordinary way of selling a piano or organ through jobbers, agents, dealers, etc., is a very expensive method of sale to the man who buys the goods. In buying a Beckwith you save this useless expense to yourself, you pay only the actual manufacturing cost with our one extremely small margin of profit added.

MAKING A PIANO is not an easy task. A successful piano manufacturer realizes that time is just as essential in the making of a good piano as perfect material and unexcelled workmanship. He knows that it is impossible to have quality in a finished product, no matter how fine the raw material and workmanship, unless time is allowed for its construction. It is not a question of two, three, four or five weeks, but a question of from five to seven months in making a good piano and then after it is complete it must receive its final voicing, tone and touch regulation and the other finishing touches that are absolutely essential to the life of the piano. This final treatment will alone take two or three weeks when it is done properly or as it is done in the Beckwith piano. This very fact makes it necessary for our factory to always have a large number of pianos on hand completed, awaiting your order and the final treatment usual before shipment. If you buy a Beckwith, you are sure of receiving an instrument that is made of the best material and by the most skilled workmen. You are also positive it has not been thrown together in a hurry, that it was not made in three or four weeks but that months have passed since it was first started in the factory and that each and every part has been handled with tender care. The result is an instrument of rare musical beauty.

THE SCALE of a piano is the scientific division and sub-division of the strings, giving them their proper length, determining just where they shall cross the sounding board and the exact striking line, where the hammers are to strike the strings. It is one of the most important points to be considered in the construction of a piano and is the fundamental principle upon which the construction of the instrument depends. The drawing of the scale and the scale itself is very fully and clearly set forth on page 218, to which your attention is invited.

THE ACTION is that portion of the instrument, through the medium of which the tone is produced. It contains many small levers, many separate pieces of felt, springs, etc. All centers or bearings must be adjusted so perfectly that they respond with the same elasticity to a delicate touch as they would to a strong stroke on the key. The Beckwith piano action, the material used in the construction of all its parts, is of the best quality, selected with the utmost care. The Beckwith is noted for the repeating quality of the action, the reliability of the action, which is to be depended upon under all conditions. Each bearing is bushed with genuine wool felt and **not** with so called military cloth; hence there is no point of contact in the entire action that is not felted so as to overcome over vibration or a harmonic tone.

THE METAL FRAME is another important feature of the instrument and it is necessary that it be so constructed as to give the least weight with the greatest degree of tensile strength. In the ordinary piano there is between nineteen and twenty tons pressure, and the metal frame and back must support this immense strain. If the plate is not properly cast and constructed of the finest grade of composition metal, it could not stand this strain but would "buckle" and the piano would be ruined. The metal plate used in the Beckwith is one of its strongest features, free from traces of sulphur, blow holes, and other imperfections.

THE STRINGS are of the highest grade of genuine Poehlmann piano wire, the finest strings in the market. Each piano has three strings to a tone in the upper register. All bass strings are carefully wound on a steel core and all but a few of the lowest ones which are single, are two strings to a tone. All pianos have overstrung bass.

THE SOUNDING BOARD mellows and increases the tone of the strings. The Beckwith sounding board is scientifically bellied and is made of the choicest selected mountain grown spruce, ribbed with braces of the same material. These ribs are dovetailed into the solid back. It is the most perfect sounding board possible to construct.

THE CASES are all works of art and a glance at the illustrations on the following pages must convince you of the extreme care and deep thought given to these designs by the artists. They stand alone as representing the highest advancement in the fine art of piano case designing, while the finish is most beautiful. Every case has from seven coats of varnish upward. Each coat of varnish is allowed to stand from eight to ten days in order to become thoroughly dried before another coat is put on. Each coat of varnish is hand rubbed so that the finished piano glistens like a mirror. It is not generally known that it requires about three months to properly varnish and rub up a piano case. Upon the thoroughness of this process depends the extremely high class finish for which the Beckwith cases are noted. Every Beckwith piano case (except the Home Favorite) is double veneered inside and outside, these veneers being cross banded, so there are actually five thicknesses of wood in the case. This is a positive guarantee that there will be no splitting or cracking at any time under natural conditions.

BUYING FROM A DEALER. The dealer or agent is not able to offer you as low a price on a high grade piano as we are. Where he buys four or five pianos on consignment or pays for them by turning in the notes you have given for the piano on the installment plan, we arrange by contract for from two thousand to three thousand at one time on a spot cash basis, thus securing the lowest possible cost. You take advantage of every bit of this saving if you buy a Beckwith after thirty days' trial. No dealer can compete with us nor can any dealer save you as much money as we can, in the following manner: We can best prove to you the saving that is yours when you buy a Beckwith. Order any one of the pianos listed in the following pages and you will find them to be all as represented by us. We guarantee if you order our $89.00 piano you will secure one exactly the same kind in tone and quality as dealers sell for $175.00 to $200.00. Order one of our $128.00 Beckwiths and you will find it exactly the same kind in tone and quality as dealers sell for about $250.00. Order one of our $168.00 Beckwith pianos and you will find it is the equal of those sold by agents at $350.00. Order one of our $189.00 or $195.00 Beckwith pianos and we positively guarantee you will find it the equal of any instrument regardless of name or make that sells for $500.00. We sell so many pianos at one time that we can afford to accept a very low margin for ourselves and still have a profitable business. There is no expense of selling pianos on the installment plan or making allowances for exchange. All of our transactions are figured on a cash basis, not necessarily cash with the order, but at the end of a thirty-day trial. All of these expenses you avoid, and they add nothing to the value of the instrument. The dealer is compelled to charge you all of these unnecessary expenses and if he did not do so, his business would not be profitable. He has very many expenses to meet that we entirely avoid and which must be paid by the buyer of his instrument. He must live and has his expenses to pay. Owing to the limited number of pianos he sells he must have what looks to you to be a large profit. That is his misfortune. The dealer's customers are few and far between because his trade is confined perhaps to a village or a township, or at most to a county. We sell pianos over the entire country from Maine to California and from the Great Lakes to the Gulf, and we sell more pianos in one day than the ordinary dealer will sell in six months.

STOP AND THINK how many pianos an agent will sell each year. How much store rent does he pay? How many bad debts does he have when he sells on the installment plan? What does he lose on articles he accepts in exchange? How much does he lose when discounting the notes he holds for installment sales? Figure what his honest living expenses are. His expense for his family, his expense for his salesmen. You will readily note by this that he is compelled to charge a large price over the actual cost, even without making any allowance for laying up a dollar for a rainy day.

IF ANYONE ASKS YOU TO PAY MORE THAN $195.00 for the highest grade, finest piano made, you are simply asked to pay not only the large profit which he must ask to make the business profitable, not only the actual cost to make the instrument at the factory, not alone the freight charge on the instrument, but also the profits and selling expenses of other men through whose hands the piano passed before it reached him. If anyone offers you a piano "just as good" as our Colonial Art Piano, described on page 214, or our Special Concert Grand Piano, described on page 216, for anywhere near our price, do not be deceived. We sell more pianos than anyone else.

REMEMBER that we offer you pianos at practically wholesale prices, and you positively avoid all intermediate and useless profits, expenses and commissions when you purchase a Beckwith piano after a complete trial. We give you the benefit of our enormous purchasing power, our complete knowledge of pianos, piano construction, piano values, the result of years of experience, all of which is yours without cost if you take advantage of our offers and purchase a Beckwith after a thirty-day trial.

THE FREIGHT CHARGES on a piano are exactly the same whether paid by the customer or the dealer. In quoting prices we do not include the freight charge. This must be borne by the buyer but when you buy a Beckwith you know exactly what you are paying for the piano and what you pay for the freight charge. If you buy a piano with the freight charges included in the price, you will never know the actual value of the piano and what is allowed for freight. If you buy from the dealer you are paying the freight charges just the same. No matter how you buy the instrument, you pay these charges when you pay them actually yourself and know just what they are or when you pay them in the form of the very greatly increased and large price demanded. We guarantee to give you a piano of sterling quality and save you at least one-half what others charge for pianos of the same grade, and we take all the risk of a thirty days' trial.

THE BECKWITH MOUSE PROOF PEDAL.

THIS IS ONE OF THE MOST IMPORTANT IMPROVEMENTS in piano construction and is a distinct Beckwith feature. It is a new departure and can be secured only in the Beckwith piano. We herewith show an illustration of this great improvement, to which we refer you. There are no other pedals made that are mouse-proof, although it is claimed for some that they are. The fact remains that this claim is not entirely justified. The only actual mouse proof pedal action made is that which is illustrated on this page. Mice enter pianos under the pedals at the points marked AAA in the illustration, but in the Beckwith piano they can go no farther, because the pedal action is absolutely

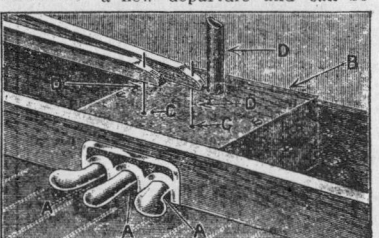

shut off from the balance of the piano by an ingeniously arranged covering, marked B, at the end of the pedals. This covering is chemically treated inside and the mice will not gnaw through it. In the top there are three openings, marked CCC in the illustration, through which the attachment rod and the pedal connecting rods, DDD, run. The openings in this mouse proof covering are all bushed with bushing felt. They fit snugly, but not so tight as to bind the rods, yet tight enough to prevent mice from getting inside of the piano. This is one of the most important improvements in piano construction in recent years, and to those who have been troubled with mice in their piano, its value will be at once apparent. This is a Beckwith improvement and can be secured only in a Beckwith piano.

$87.00 THE BECKWITH HOME FAVORITE PIANO

THE PRICE INCLUDES THE PIANO, A SOLID WOOD STOOL AND COMPLETE INSTRUCTION BOOK.

LOWER IN PRICE THAN EVER.

In this, our $87.00 Home Favorite Piano, we are offering a sample of the wonderful value to be found in every instrument in the Beckwith line of pianos illustrated and described in the pages which follow. This extremely low figure convincingly proves our ability to furnish pianos at a lower price than any other dealer. The piano illustrated on this page is in every way the equal in appearance, tone and quality, of those sold by others for as high as $150.00. We are today offering you better pianos, better values and at more attractive money saving prices than can be obtained from any other dealer. While we can sell this piano at the lowest price ever quoted on an instrument of this size and character, therefore, at a greater saving to you, it is but another example of our ability to quote extremely low prices on merchandise of the highest grade. While this is undeniably low, lower than quoted by any other dealer, on the other hand, every piano illustrated in this book is sold at just as low a price proportionally, at just as much of a money saving figure as this, when taking into consideration the extremely high quality and unexcelled piano value of the better and high grade instruments. In our Colonial Art and Special Concert Grand styles guaranteed by the manufacturer and by us for a full quarter of a century, 25 years, we offer pianos, the equal of any sold by any dealer anywhere for $500.00 and we can conscientiously place either one of these magnificent instruments in competition with those ordinarily sold at $500.00, enjoying world wide reputation and with absolutely no fear as to the ultimate outcome. We solicit your order for any piano illustrated in these pages, from this, the Home Favorite piano up to the Special Concert Grand, but we nevertheless urge you to read the description of every instrument shown before finally writing your order. While this is the lowest price ever quoted on a guaranteed piano of like grade, we ask you specially to remember that the price on the best piano in this line is proportionally just as low and while it is true we ask more for the pianos in the following pages than we do for this one, we are compelled to do so owing to the extra cost for the better pianos, at the factory. The difference in price that we ask you for the other pianos is the extra amount that we, ourselves, are compelled to pay to the factory for the higher grades, for the greater tone value and quality they represent. Whether you buy this, our cheapest piano, or the best in this book, they are all sold at the actual factory cost to make them, with our one uniformly small margin of profit added. When you buy a Beckwith you are taking advantage of our enormous purchasing power, our ability to quote low prices on pianos of the highest quality. and hence it is to your interest to purchase the best that your means will allow.

MUSIC IN THE HOME is at once a refining influence and a great aid in character building.

Music adds more to the enjoyment of home life than any other feature. It has much to do with the development of the finer sensibilities, the higher qualities of character in the growing child. One of the fondest recollections of a grown man or woman is a memory of the pleasant evenings of childhood in the old home; evenings of music, song, laughter and joy given over to singing of the grand old hymns and playing of the good old fashioned tunes. These fond recollections never die. They are woven into our very lives and will last as long as life remains. The memory at just the right moment of the happy hours at home all brought back by hearing some old familiar tune, has saved many a youth who was about to take his first downward step. Music is a refining influence and it has come to be almost an essential element in the upbuilding of the home. The charm of music is never so strong as when played upon a piano and if music is such a power for good in the home life, how essential it is, in making our selection of a piano, that we should select the very best that it is possible for us to secure. The Beckwith Piano offers such great possibilities in the saving of money on the purchase of a high grade piano, it seems that all those who read this page with a view of making a selection of a piano at some future time, should consider the greater merits, the greater value, the greater worth, of the pianos illustrated in the pages which follow. A piano is largely a life companion and we should choose our companions with rare discrimination. Every Beckwith Piano is guaranteed for twenty-five years except the Home Favorite which is guaranteed for five years only. It is the greatest value ever offered at anywhere near $87.00. It is a piano that would easily sell for $150.00 if sold through agents or dealers. If you are satisfied to purchase such a piano as dealers sell at $150.00, if you will be satisfied to make such a piano a permanent feature of your home life, a life friend as it were, then favor us with an order for this piano. But if you feel, as we hope you will feel, that you want the best that it is possible to buy, a piano the equal of the finest piano in any mansion in the land, an instrument that you will point to with pride, and will enjoy for years, even beyond the time for which it is guaranteed, then refer to the other pages which follow and select your piano there.

We hope that you will realize the immense saving that we offer and that the saving represented by our $189.00 or $195.00 pianos, the equal of any $500.00 instrument in the market, will appeal to you so strongly that you will at least make a strong effort to favor us with a trial order for one of them.

FULL DESCRIPTION.

Our HOME FAVORITE PIANO is tastefully designed and substantially built, and is a most remarkable value at the price named.

THE CASE is of a handsome design, as the illustration, taken direct from a photograph, will show. The panel in the duet or continuous music desk is ornamented with a handsome scroll and extends the full length of the piano. It is finished in either mahogany or walnut finish, but is not veneered, therefore we can only guarantee it for five years. This piano is fitted with the latest style of rolling fall board.

THE SCALE is a regular full 7⅓ overstrung scale, the same as will be found in any piano offered by others at $200.00. It is not harp strung but is overstrung in the regular manner, thus giving the greatest possible length to the string.

THE PIN BLOCK is built up of several pieces of rock maple, which holds the tuning pin firmly.

THE STRINGS are of a very fine quality, thoroughly tested, and the piano is fitted with overstrung, wound bass strings.

THE KEYS are genuine ivory and ebony, very finely polished.

THE SOUNDING BOARD is made of selected mountain grown spruce, scientifically braced.

THE METAL FRAME is as strong as it is possible to have in a piano of this size, and is large enough to withstand the strain in this piano when it is tuned to pitch.

THE TONE is very full, sweet and melodious and of ample power for all ordinary requirements.

THE SIZE. Height, 4 feet 6 inches; length, 5 feet 1 inch; depth, 2 feet 2 inches. Weight, boxed for shipment, 750 pounds.

WITH THIS PIANO we will include, without any extra charge, either the mandolin attachment or the practice pedal, which are fully described on page 212. It will be necessary for you to advise us which attachment you desire, but we advise you to order the practice pedal. The price includes a substantial stool and complete instruction book.

REMEMBER that this piano has full 7⅓ octaves, overstrung scale, ivory and ebony keys, and is the most marvelous value ever offered at this price. Owing to the size of the piano, however, the strings are not so long nor as heavy, the action is not so strong nor as large as in our better grades, the case is not double veneered but is only finished, hence, we are compelled to guarantee this piano for five years only.

THIS PIANO IS NOT MOUSEPROOF. ALL OTHER BECKWITH PIANOS ARE.

No. 46K1 Our Home Favorite Beckwith Piano. Price, $87.00.

GUARANTEED FOR FIVE YEARS ONLY,

but sold to you under our liberal terms with the privilege of returning it any time within one year if it is not found to be exactly as represented.

WE GIVE YOU BACK EVERY DOLLAR

that we are compelled to charge you for our better instruments. We give it back to you in greater piano value, quality and tone. We offer you this Home Favorite for $87.00, but if you pay us $128.00 for the Conservatory Cabinet Grand, $168.00 for the Empire Cabinet Grand, or $189.00 for our Colonial Art Piano, and $195.00 for our Special Concert Grand Piano, the equals of any in the market regardless of name, we give you back every extra dollar that we are compelled to ask you in extra quality and extra value. Therefore it is your own personal interest to buy the best that your means will allow, and if possible, to secure our Colonial Art or Special Concert Grand, instruments of matchless beauty and the equal of any in the market.

If, however, $87.00 is all that you care to invest, then favor us with your order, and we will give you better value than anyone else can offer at anywhere near this price. But in justice to yourself, and in justice to the low prices which our immense purchasing power makes it possible for us to quote you, you ought to take advantage of these low prices to the extent of investing all that you can spare, and if possible, order the Colonial Art or Special Concert Grand Piano described on pages 214 to 218.

THIS CUSTOMER SAYS THAT HE SAVED ONE-HALF IF NOT MORE WHAT HE WOULD HAVE HAD TO PAY FOR A PIANO OF THE SAME QUALITY TO AN AGENT.

Atlanta, Ga.

Sears, Roebuck & Co., Chicago, Ill.

Sirs:—I have instructed the bank to forward the money to you in payment for the Beckwith Special Concert Grand Piano received by me. I am more than delighted with the instrument. It is the prettiest case I have ever seen, while the tone is wonderfully sweet and flexible. I now know that I have saved one-half, if not more, of what I would have been compelled to pay for the same quality of a piano here. You remember that I said it was "up to you" to do what the dealers here said you could not do. You have done it and you have done them good I think. Wishing you all success possible with the Beckwith Piano, I am,

Respectfully, W. H. SMITH, 457 Houston St.

$195.00 BECKWITH SPECIAL CONCERT GRAND PIANO

ENTIRELY NEW IN DESIGN, BEAUTIFUL IN FINISH AND SPLENDID IN TONAL QUALITY.

A piano of the very highest possible attainment and sold by us under our great money saving method. Piano agents, retailers and other dealers easily secure from $450.00 to $500.00 for exactly the same kind of a piano.

WE OFFER THIS INSTRUMENT as the finest type of the art of piano construction, of the same grade and quality as the very best and most widely advertised concert pianos on the market, at a price never before attempted, and which means only the bare factory cost of the piano, with but our one usual small margin of profit added, all useless expenses of every nature being saved to you.

ONE GLANCE AT THE ILLUSTRATION WILL CONVINCE YOU that so far as the appearance is concerned, this piano is equal in every respect to the very

highest grade of concert pianos now on the market. No engraving, no description, however fine, can give you an adequate idea of the beautiful finish, the artistic appearance of the piano and the splendid tonal qualities it possesses. It must be seen and heard to be fully appreciated and the opportunity of testing the instrument is yours under our great 30 days' free trial, and wholly at our own risk as explained on page 209.

BY CAREFULLY READING THE DETAILED DESCRIPTION on the following pages you will see that every point in the manufacture of this instrument has received the utmost consideration and we assure you none but the finest material and the best workmanship enter into its construction. In offering this piano, our Special Concert Grand style of the celebrated Beckwith make, we are offering an instrument which represents the acme of piano perfection.

SEND NO MONEY.

Deposit nothing in advance. We will ship this piano, freight charges prepaid, for a full 30 days' free trial, as explained on page 209.

Just send your trial order and write us the name of the bank where you wish to deposit the cost of the piano and the freight charges after it is received at your local station, and we will ship promptly. If the piano does not please you, send it back at our expense and the bank will refund your money. Remember, you assume no risk because every dollar of your money will be at your own bank waiting for you.

We could not make such liberal offers unless we knew that the Beckwith Piano was all and more than we claim for it. Try this Special Concert Grand Piano in your own home for thirty days and if you do not find it the equal of any $500.00 piano in the market, send it back and your money will be refunded at once.

Veneered in quarter sawed oak, French burled walnut or San Domingo mahogany. Be sure to state veneer wanted.

Height, 4 ft. 10 in. Length, 5 ft. 6 in. Width, 2 ft. 4 in.

Shipping Weight, 1,000 pounds.

No. 46K13 The Beckwith Special Concert Grand, $195.00. Guaranteed with a written, binding guarantee for quality and workmanship for 25 years. Price includes a fine solid wood modern piano stool, also a handsome velour scarf and complete instruction book.

IN PURCHASING THIS PIANO FROM US you pay exactly what any high grade standard piano could be sold for if sold at the actual cost to make it at the factory, with but one small margin of profit added. No piano made costs more for its construction than this one and any price over that asked by us pays for nothing that is not found in the fullest degree in this instrument, and represents only useless expense and numerous abnormal profits. When we ask $195.00 for this piano, we are charging only for the high class workmanship and material entering into its construction, with but one small margin of profit added. The tone is as clear and liquid as running water from one end of the keyboard to the other. This tone is the combination of skilled workmanship of the highest class and of fine selected material used in making the piano, but unlike any other dealers, we ask you absolutely nothing for this superior tone. We place no fancy price on the instrument on account of its superlative tone quality, but are willing to accept $195.00 for it, which represents only the actual factory cost for material and labor, with but our usual one small margin of profit added.

WITHOUT FEAR OF CONTRADICTION we unhesitatingly claim and guarantee to prove to your complete satisfaction during 30 days' free trial at our risk that this piano is in every way the equal of any instrument sold in the market today for $500.00.

THIS PIANO IS MOUSE PROOF, as it is fitted with the exclusive Beckwith special mouse proof pedal action, which is a guarantee that the mice cannot get into the instrument around the pedals. This device is fully explained on page 210, to which we invite your special attention. It can only be secured in a Beckwith Piano.

THE MUFFLER OR PRACTICE PEDAL. This piano is of such fine grade, is such a magnificent instrument in every way that we furnish it only with the muffler or practice pedal. We do not furnish it with the mandolin attachment because the mandolin attachment is positively injurious to the tone. This is too fine a piano to put the mandolin attachment in it. This instrumental or mandolin attachment is nothing but a novelty; it is really a toy and in time will ruin the tone of any piano, as fully explained elsewhere in this book, and while we will cheerfully furnish it, providing our customers really request it, in our cheaper pianos, under no circumstances do we include it in either our Colonial Art Piano or this splendid Concert Grand Piano.

No. 46K13 Beckwith Special Concert Grand Piano. Price.............$195.00

THE BECKWITH SPECIAL CONCERT GRAND PIANO

FULLY GUARANTEED FOR 25 YEARS by the strongest, safest, most binding guarantee ever issued, under the terms of which you can return the piano any time within one year and have your money refunded with interest added at the rate of 7 per cent and which protects you against any damage arising from imperfect material or workmanship for full 25 years.

THE HIGHEST ATTAINMENT IN THE ART OF PIANO MAKING

No. 46K13 Price - - - - - - - - AS ILLUSTRATED ON PREVIOUS PAGE. **$195.00**

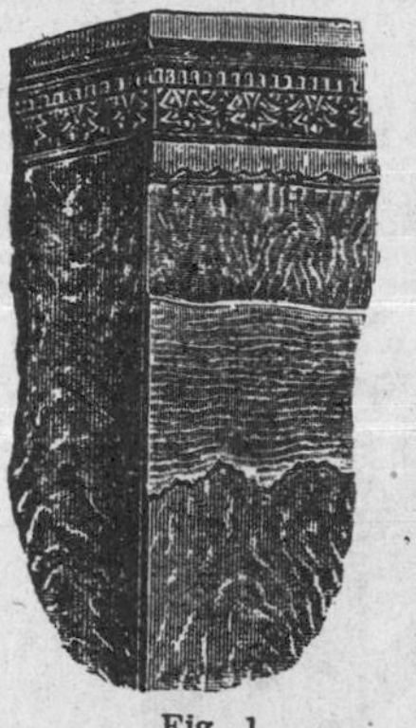

Fig. 1.

THE CASE. **The case of this piano is artistic in the highest degree. This beautiful design is entirely new, and was only adopted after the keenest competition on the part of several of the best piano designers in the country.** It is ornamented and tastefully decorated with handsomely executed genuine hand carving. There is not a particle of stained wood in the case; it is double veneered inside and outside in genuine woods and all pilasters, trusses, etc., are made of genuine solid oak, walnut or mahogany. All carvings are on natural wood. It is fitted with rolling fall cover with continuous hinges and has a handsome automatic two-thirds music desk. We believe it to be the most elegant piano that has yet been offered to the public, and will be glad to have you see it and examine it for yourself. The keyboard is supported by massive double pilasters and the latest style horn pedals of symetrical design are durably nickel plated and polished. The panels are very artistic and in perfect harmony with the richness of the very finely designed case. Each one of these cases is given an extremely high finish which takes from 70 to 90 days to apply. Each case is double veneered inside and out, and cross banded so that it cannot crack, warp or split under any natural conditions. Cross banding means that the first or inner layer of veneer is glued to the base wood of the case under an enormous pressure, while the second or outer layer is glued in a like manner across the grain of the inner veneer, so that it will not be affected by climatic changes, no matter how severe. The engraving which accompanies this, marked Figure 1, shows how the veneer is placed on the piano case. These pianos are given a very high finish, each coat of varnish being allowed to become thoroughly dry, then being rubbed down before the next coat of varnish is applied. These successive coats of varnish give the case that smooth, glassy appearance so much admired in all fine pianos. As this varnish is perfectly transparent, of the very highest grade and most expensive kind, the delicate grain of the wood shows through it in all its natural beauty. In most cheap pianos the finish of the case is entirely superficial. This part of a cheap commercial piano is slighted just as all the rest of it is, and only about one-third the number of coats of varnish are applied as is applied to the Beckwith and the varnish itself is of a very low grade. **The design of these cases is everything that can be desired and will harmonize with the furnishings of any parlor.** We furnish them in English quarter sawed oak, French burled walnut, and San Domingo mahogany. Each case is thoroughly hand rubbed and carefully inspected before being turned out of the factory.

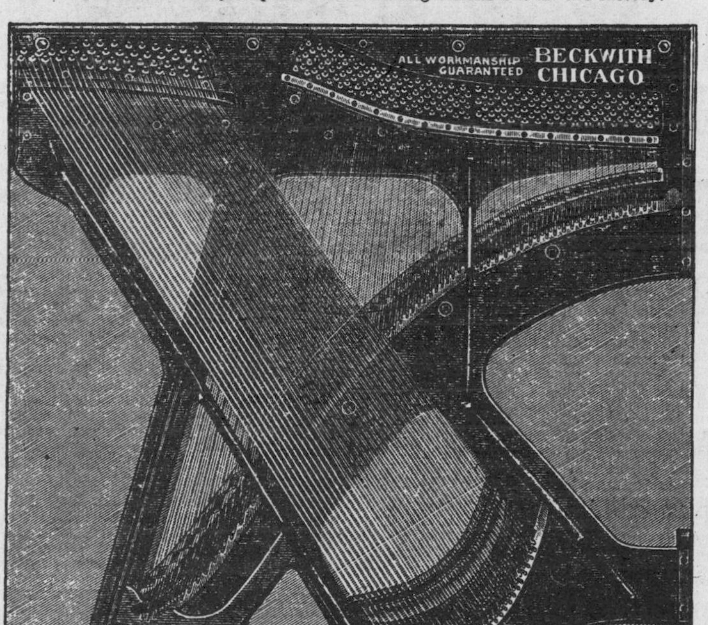

Fig. 2.

THE METAL PLATE **of this piano is of the pattern known as a full metal plate.** There is no cap upon it, but it is cast in one solid piece and is of the strongest possible construction. It must be strong to resist the tension of the strings when tuned to pitch, and with the extra strong back shown in another illustration, this metal plate makes a piano of unrivaled strength and durability, powerful enough to stand, if necessary, twice the strain that is put upon it. Examine this plate closely and you will find it has bushed tuning pins, ample reinforcements and braces, and with the extra strong back it will be seen at once, by a reference to Figure 2, that with this foundation the instrument is as strongly made as human ingenuity can make it. The metal plate in this piano receives the most careful consideration. Not one single plate is accepted until it receives the most searching inspection at the hands of experts. The fault with many cheap pianos is, that, to the manufacturer, a metal plate is a metal plate, and neither the quality of the workmanship or the quality of the casting receives any consideration whatever. The ordinary manufacturer of the ordinary piano is content to buy a metal plate at the lowest possible price, whereas, in the Beckwith the price is the last consideration. The quality and fitness of the plate must not only represent the highest quality in material, the most scientific casting, and be perfect in every way, but it must be the best that money can buy regardless of the price asked for it. Each plate is cast in the most approved manner and is thoroughly examined for any flaw or other imperfection. In casting the plate, allowances must be made for any tendency to warp in cooling, otherwise as the plate cools it naturally contracts, and in obedience to well defined natural laws the contraction would follow the line of least resistance and the plate would warp; this is guarded against in the casting of the perfect Beckwith plate. Should a plate be found which contains a so called blow hole, no matter how small or insignificant it might be, the plate is broken up. In the metal plate of the cheap commercial piano blow holes are numerous, because the manufacturer of such an instrument does not look upon the piano as an object of pride. To such a manufacturer the making of a piano resolves itself merely into the getting of dollars, and when an instrument has once passed out of his hands, with its many imperfections adroitly covered, it is forgotten. If a guarantee is issued with such a piano, it is of doubtful value and is more ornamental than it is useful; it is no protection to the purchaser because there is neither reputation nor financial resource back of it. Not so with the Beckwith piano. This Special Concert Grand Piano is guaranteed with a written and binding guarantee running for a period of twenty-five years, backed by unlimited capital and a reputation of years of honorable dealing. We could not assume the responsibility of such a guarantee if we did not positively know that it is impossible to purchase a better grade or better quality of material than enters into its construction. The best of everything goes into this piano. Finely figured veneers, the very best imported German steel piano strings, genuine high grade ivory and ebony keys, skilled workmanship of the best class, the highest priced and best selected piano felts and all that goes to make a recognized, standard, high grade, artistic piano. The plate is extra strong and very handsomely finished in gold bronze. From the illustration, which is necessarily small on account of our limited space, it is nevertheless easy to see how massive it is, how well it is braced and how securely it is fastened and bolted, together with the sounding board, to the extra strong foundation and frame.

PIN BLOCK. **The pin block is one of the most important features of a piano.** It is that part of the instrument which is built into the upper part of the foundation or back frame and into which the tuning pins are set. This pin block is also known among piano makers as a "wrest plank" and is made up of a number of separate layers of rock maple, as this is the best wood for this purpose. Each piece of wood is laid so that the grain runs in a different direction, and this in turn, presents to the tuning pins, as they go through the different layers of wood, a different face or grain. This binds the tuning pin and holds it firmly. In this piano is the very latest method of piano construction. It is equipped with what is known as "bushed" tuning pins. The metal plate of this piano is cast in one solid piece and extends from the bottom to the top of the piano, covering the pin block completely. Openings are drilled through this solid metal into which a plug, or "wood bushing" of hard maple is driven and through this bushing the heavily nickel plated, extra long tuning pin extends into the pin block. It is claimed that this prevents overvibration, overbrilliancy of tone, and also aids in holding the pin firmly, and by this method of construction the best tonal results are obtained. The pin block in this piano is of an extra strong construction, as a glance at Figure 3 will convince you. It is necessary to make it very strong and to use an extra strong nickel plated tuning pin on account of the strain when the piano is tuned to pitch, which in this instrument is over twenty tons. It is one of the finest and most scientific pin blocks ever constructed.

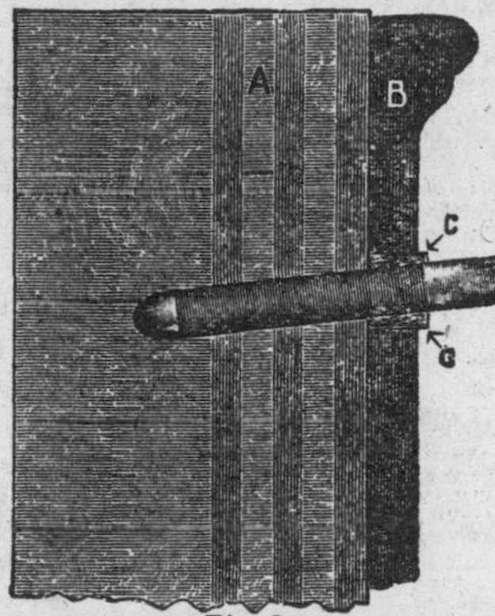

Fig. 3.
A—Built Up Pin Block.
B—Full Metal Plate.
C, C—Wood Bushing in Metal Plate.

SOUNDING BOARD. **This may be called the heart or soul of the piano and occupies the entire back of the instrument.** A good sounding board is made of the very choicest quality of selected materials, and every rib is dovetailed into the solid back. Over the sounding board the strings are stretched and the vibration of the strings is reinforced and the sonorousness is increased. It improves the quality of the tone and starts the vibration of the string running through all parts of the instrument and out from it, when the string is struck by the hammer. Without the sounding board there would be no tone, the sounding board is, as you might say, the tone center. The importance of a good tone center is therefore essential. In the Beckwith piano only the finest selected spruce is used for both the sounding board itself and for the ribs or braces. Every piece of wood used in the Beckwith sounding board is carefully examined and tested. The making of a good sounding board is a delicate operation; especially constructed rooms and appliances must be used to bring out the most perfect results. The temperature is a large factor in its construction, as well as the proper consistency and the color of the glue used. Glue enters largely in the making of sounding boards and only the finest glue should be used. Furthermore, in gluing the sounding boards the parts must be heated to a high degree of temperature so as to take the glue properly. In the Beckwith piano the sounding board is of the highest type; it is thoroughly air and kiln dried until the wood from which it is made becomes as resonant as the top of an old violin. In some pianos the sounding board has a great number of ribs on it, and while these are necessary to protect it against warping or splitting, yet no more ribs should be placed on the sounding board than are absolutely necessary to protect it against these dangers. In the Beckwith pianos there are just enough ribs placed on the sounding board, no more and no less, and the exact number of these is mathematically determined by study and experience. We guarantee that the sounding board of this piano will not become weak or cracked, as is often the case with other pianos, and if this instrument is compared with other pianos costing from $500.00 upwards, we know that the customer will find that in volume and sweetness of tone the Beckwith is the equal of any other piano made.

THE ACTION **is that part of the piano, through the medium of which the tone is produced. It means the keys, the hammers, and all the mechanism that transmits the stroke on the keys to the hammer, and thus produces the tone.** The Beckwith piano is famous for its even tone and the remarkable quickness with which it responds to every touch of the performer. The Beckwith piano is fitted with a repeating action and the hammers come back into position ready for the repeat with marvelous rapidity. On a great many pianos it will be found that if you attempt to strike a succession of notes on one key, the hammer refuses to register any, except the

first stroke, but when the same experiment is tried upon the key of a Beckwith each tone is distinctly marked; in fact, it is impossible to strike the notes with such rapidity that the hammer fails to respond. **Each piece and part is selected with extreme care and is assembled only by experts.** Every bearing in the entire action is bushed with specially prepared bushing felt. All of the felt in the hammers and the action itself is of the very highest grade possible to secure of all wool piano felt. After the action is assembled and before it is placed in the piano it is given a most searching examination. Every piece and part is gone over. After it is placed in position and fastened into the piano it is then given a most severe test for responsiveness, for quick action, and is adjusted and voiced to perfection. This action is equipped with a very strong brass flange. The latest improvement in action construction.

THE SCALE. **This is the underlying or fundamental principle upon which all pianos are built.** It is a so called "lay out" of the strings, and in drawing the scale, the scale maker or designer determines, by mathematical calculation, the exact position that each particular string of the entire 7⅓ octaves must occupy across the sounding board; the exact point where the lower bridges must rest upon the sounding board, the exact curve in the upper bridge just below the tuning pins, the size and length of strings to be used for each tone; must determine exactly where each particular hammer is to strike each particular string so as to bring out the fundamental tone. If these points are not very carefully considered, the result would be an uneven scale, and there would be what is called a "dead string" here, or perhaps a "wild tone" there, and that is what you find in cheap pianos of the commercial grade. Such tones are to a piano what flaws are to a diamond, and the peerless Beckwith piano can be likened to a diamond that is absolutely flawless, as no such tone will be found in it. The scale is as clear and as liquid as running water from one end of the piano to the other. To give some idea of what is required of a scale maker in drawing or designing a perfect scale, it is necessary for him to know the number of vibrations per second of each string. For example, when pianos are tuned to international pitch, middle "A" vibrates at the rate of 435 vibrations to a second. The least number that the ear can detect runs to about 24 per second, the highest number that the human ear can detect is about forty thousand per second. All this he must know and he must proportion the strings accordingly. He must know the exact point on each string where the hammer must strike to produce the true piano tone; he must remember that sound travels at the rate of 1,090 feet per second in the air and that these sound waves can be reflected, refracted, or deflected exactly as light waves are. Scientific research carried on by the best piano makers in the early history of piano building and years of subsequent experience demonstrates that by striking the string practically upon a nodal point produces the best quality of tone. The most desirable quality, the pure piano tone, is best brought out by striking the string at a point about one-eighth of its entire length below the upper bridge. This point is exactly between two nodes, or upon a nodal point. The string vibrates in waves. These waves or curves are called nodes. If the hammer strikes on one of these nodes, it will bring out a light, peculiar tone; or what is called a harmonic tone. Strange as it may seem, there is really more than one tone in a string, and unless care is used in determining the striking line, more than the fundamental tone will be heard. The lighter qualities of a piano string are known as "upper partials," whereas, the required tone, the true tone, is known as a "fundamental" tone. The surface of the hammer dampens or kills the "upper partials," allowing the fundamental tone to ring out in all its purity. The point of contact of the hammer on the string determines the tone quality, and experience and mathematical precision have determined in the Beckwith the one only true point of contact, and this desirable quality is a feature of this and the Colonial Art Piano. The scale of the Beckwith is as close to perfection as human knowledge, experience and ingenuity can make it.

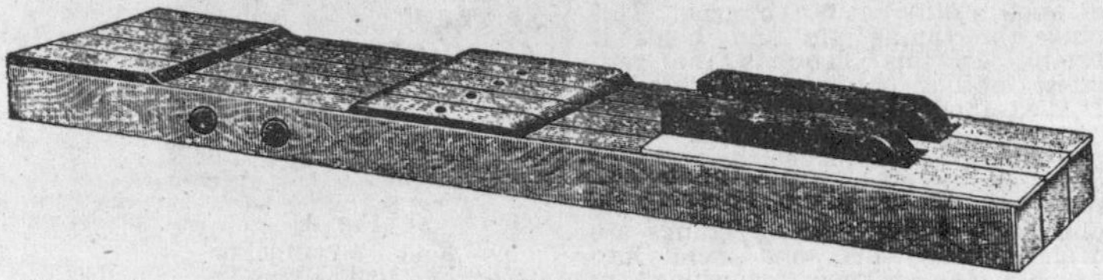

Fig. 4.

KEYS. **Figure 4 illustrates five Beckwith keys and shows how they are constructed.** A well made piano key must be made of thoroughly seasoned and kiln dried wood of perfect grain and absolutely free from any imperfection. This is the quality of wood used in the Beckwith piano keys. The ivory used is of the best grade of tusk ivory which is glued on to the wood under enormous pressure. The sharps are of genuine ebony highly polished. The keys are so evenly balanced that they fall back to their position instantly, after being struck by the performer, ready for the repeat. It is through the medium of the keys that the hammers strike the strings, or in other words, it is through the keys that the performer plays the piano, and this is one of the points of the Beckwith that receives the utmost care in construction and the most searching scrutiny and inspection when the piano is completed.

THE PIANO HAMMER **in this, our largest and best piano, is a genuine 14-pound hammer,** the greatest size and weight possible in any piano. This extra size, shown in Figure 5, is demanded by a larger sounding board area and longer and heavier strings. All these features, combined, give greater volume and purity of tone, and the increased striking surface in this hammer lessens the liability (which, however, is very slight in the Beckwith) of the felt hardening.

A hardened hammer means a hard and unsympathetic tone. The tone, and the scale, after all, is the piano, and as the hammer is what produces the tone, too much care cannot be given to it. No matter how fine a grade of string is used, the string does not vibrate unless made to do so by the striking of the hammer. The better the hammer in weight, the more nicely it is poised, the larger the striking surface, the better the quality of felt, the more perfect it is in construction, then naturally, the better the tone. It gives the string a chance to be heard to advantage. All of these essential points are combined in the hammer which is shown in the illustration and which we use in this and the Colonial Art Piano. The felt used is of the finest quality, genuine imported German felt; the shank is large enough to withstand the hardest blow, but is not unwieldy and does not burden the action with superfluous weight. Each hammer is voiced by an expert, special care being used to soften the face or striking surface of the hammer in the most scientific and approved manner, so as to bring out in the fullest degree the fine singing quality of tone. This piano is famous for the excellence of its tonal quality. The illustration shows the new, special two-piece felt hammer, the very latest advancement in hammer head construction, as well as a section of the brass flange. It is the finest hammer that it is possible to make, and the peculiar quality in the felt gives it an elasticity which is a large factor in producing a most beautiful quality of tone.

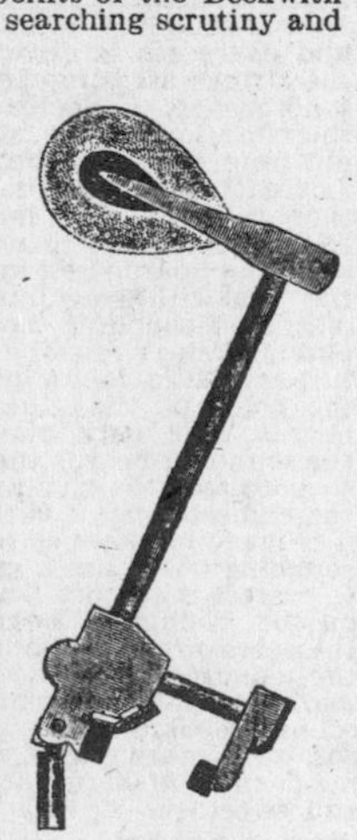

Fig. 5.

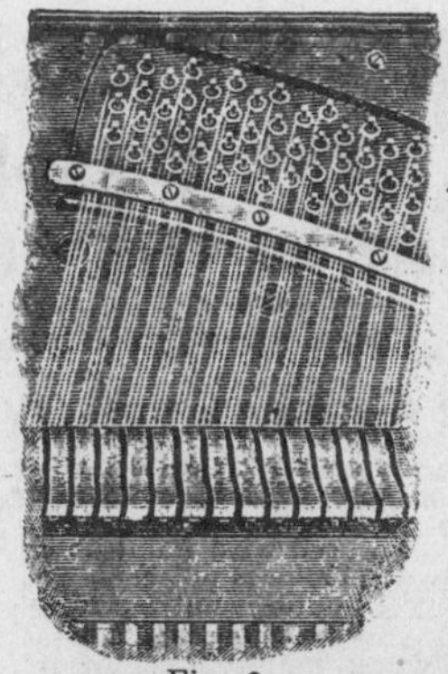

Fig. 6.

THE STRINGS. **This instrument has an overstrung scale, and is what is known as a three-string unison, each treble note having three strings, all of which are tuned in unison.** Figure 6 illustrates the way the instrument is strung. Each one of the strings placed in this piano is thoroughly inspected and properly tested before it is placed in position. The bass, or lower, part of the scale is what is called a two-string unison. All strings in the Beckwith pianos are of the very finest quality Poehlmann piano steel wire. Each string is tested for strength, size, and perfect formation before being accepted. They must all be free from any trace of phosphorus or sulphur, otherwise they would be brittle and liable to crack. An imperfect string produces an imperfect tone, and destroys the uniformity of tone so much desired in a fine piano. **A good string is a very important part of a piano, as the string when struck by the hammer vibrates and produces the tone.** The sounding board vibrates in harmony with the string and increases the volume of tone; therefore, if the string is poor the piano will produce a poor quality of tone. The bass strings in this instrument are all copper wound on a steel core and the materials in the strings are the best it is possible to secure. All these strings are wound specially to order for this instrument

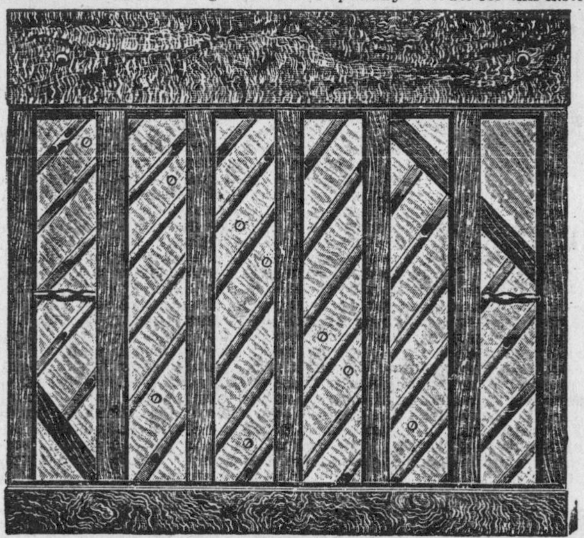

Fig. 7.

THE BACK FRAME. **This is sometimes known as the foundation and is a very important part of a piano, as it must bear its just proportion of the strain upon it when the piano is tuned to pitch.** The illustration, Figure 7, shows the seven massive uprights which are mortised into the top and bottom of the frame and shows the veneer on the two cross pieces as well as the scientifically ribbed sounding board. Into this back or foundation the pin block is built, and in a large piano, such as the Special Concert Grand, such a strong back is really essential. While the back of the piano really has nothing to do with the tonal production, yet many manufacturers give no thought to this important part and the relation it bears to the piano proper. Many piano makers use too few uprights in the back; others use too many and make them too heavy. It is unwise to burden a piano with superfluous weight, and a careful manufacturer, or one who studies this part of a piano, determines exactly the proper bracing to be used according to the size of the piano, the length of strings and other important features. The foundation or frame of a piano bears somewhat the same relationship to the instrument as a foundation of a building does to the superstructure, and therefore the maker of a high class piano bestows every consideration upon the back.

The wood in the Beckwith piano back is carefully selected and thoroughly seasoned. It really is a source of gratification to have every intending purchaser of this piano take the time and trouble to examine the back of this instrument, the uprights, the veneered upper and lower cross pieces, the general appearance of the back, the material, workmanship, finish, etc. If you will do this you will be convinced that the back receives the same tender care and attention as do the more delicate parts of the interior construction. It should do much to impress you with the quality of the piano as a whole.

REMEMBER, **you run no risk of any sort whatever in sending your order to us for a piano today, making your selection from the pages of this, our General Catalogue,** because we promise, agree and guarantee that you will find everything exactly as represented, illustrated and described, or we will cheerfully and willingly refund every dollar of expense on your part attending the transaction.

If you are in the market for a high grade, fine piano, then you cannot afford to place your order elsewhere, or consider the purchase of any other piano, no matter what the maker's name may be, before trying the high grade Beckwith of superlative quality under our great 30 DAYS' FREE TRIAL OFFER.

No. 46K13 Beckwith Special Concert Grand Piano.
Price.. **$195.00**

EASILY CAN COMPARE WITH THOSE SOLD BY AGENTS FOR $350.00.

Sears, Roebuck & Co., Chicago, Ill. Dumont, Iowa.
Gentlemen:—We received the piano ordered from you in good condition, and are well pleased with same. It is more than I expected for the money, and it can easily be compared with the ones the agents here sell for $350.00. Thanks. I'll do my best for you. Everyone who has seen it thus far has been well pleased with the instrument.
Yours truly, H. C. SCHMIDT.

A TUNER TOLD THIS CUSTOMER THAT THE BECKWITH PIANO WAS AN A1 FIRST CLASS INSTRUMENT IN EVERY RESPECT.

Sears, Roebuck & Co., Chicago, Ill. Columbus, Miss.
Gentlemen:—The Beckwith Piano purchased of you is a perfect instrument in every respect. It is all, and I confidently believe more than you claim it to be. The tuner whom I had to examine it says it is an A1, first class instrument in every respect. At the price I paid, he thought I almost had it given to me, as he says he has seen pianos that cost the owners $400.00 and upward that were not a bit better than mine. The agents who were "knocking" the Beckwith Piano have put down their little hammers and have gone "way back to sit down." They now say they cannot remember the name of the customer who bought a Beckwith which was unsatisfactory and which they claim was the case when they tried to get me to buy their piano. You can use my name in any way you wish as recommending the Beckwith.
Very truly yours, E. M. McKISSICK.

BECKWITH ORGANS
HIGHEST AWARD ST. LOUIS WORLD'S FAIR ~ AND JAMESTOWN EXPOSITION

A MAGNIFICENT LINE OF REED ORGANS

Manufactured in the most modern, up to date and best equipped organ factories in the world, and which for durability of construction, refinement and elegance of appearance, beauty of finish and musical capacity, are superior to any other organs made.

THE BECKWITH ORGAN COMPANY have established two of the very largest organ factories in the world for the sole purpose of manufacturing these splendid instruments. These factories are complete in every detail. In them they have installed the very latest, most improved labor saving organ making machinery and the very best system of handling material. They have enormous quantities of selected lumber on hand going through the long process of air seasoning. They have immense dry kilns, thus insuring wood for use in the organs that is absolutely and perfectly bone dry. They employ the most skillful, most experienced workman and use the most rigid system of inspection. These organ factories are located at two points, one at Louisville, Kentucky, the other at St. Paul, Minnesota, and in this way we are in a position to make a very large saving on the freight charges on any organ ordered from us. Our enormous organ business is not the result of chance or a favorable combination of circumstances, but has been built up through a most careful and conscientious attention to the smallest detail, unremitting and untiring efforts to maintain the exalted quality of these organs, which years ago secured recognition from prominent authorities as the finest organs in the world. The result is the most enviable reputation enjoyed by any like instruments in the market.

THE BECKWITH ORGANS are manufactured under our direct supervision, are fully guaranteed by us for twenty-five years and are sold only from factory to customer direct and in no other way, at the actual factory cost with our uniformly one small margin of profit added; under the most liberal terms and free trial offers ever made, as fully explained in detail on page 209 of this catalogue. You are fully protected when you place an order for a Beckwith Organ from the following pages. You secure every benefit that we, ourselves, can secure in the way of price reducing methods of manufacture. Every bit of saving that can be effected in any way goes to you because we are content to receive our usual one small margin of profit and, therefore, this organ, which is the standard of organ quality for the world, is placed in your home at actually less cost to you than others ask for inferior instruments of much less musical capacity.

THE MATERIALS are all the best that can be purchased by experts in their line. Each piece of wood is selected for its fitness, perfection of grain and fiber before it is accepted as fit for use in the Beckwith. All felts, reeds, springs, even the glue, varnish, etc., are all carefully inspected before accepted and the methods of construction and the check upon the quality of material purchased, put into effect by the Beckwith Organ Company, enable us to unqualifiedly guarantee these organs against any defect in their material or workmanship for a full quarter of a century.

THE QUESTION OF QUALITY is one that you should fully consider before you place your order. An agent unknown to you may place an organ in your home today that looks and sounds well, and to all appearances you have every reason to believe that it will prove "a thing of beauty and a joy forever," but tomorrow, next week, next month, perhaps, after the agent has gone, then the real trial of the organ will begin. Will it prove entirely satisfactory? Is there a lasting quality to its tone? If any defect should manifest itself, if you have any complaint to make of any nature, to whom will you go for redress? What guarantee do you hold? Where is the agent or manufacturer who gave the guarantee? What satisfaction will you secure in case you have any grievance to make? These things should all be considered when you place your order. If you do not favor us, then you should be sure of the guarantee. Buy an organ that is guaranteed by a responsible company who has money invested in a business, who will be here today, next year, twenty-five years from today, a concern backed by a large capital, responsibility and a reputation for fair dealing and you will run no risk. But in justice to yourself you ought first to try a Beckwith under our liberal terms before considering any other organ of any other make. Simply because our prices represent more of a saving to you than any other prices quoted by anyone on a **high grade** organ, and because we positively take the risk.

Facsimile of the great Diploma of Merit awarded the Beckwith Organs at the St. Louis World's Fair.

THE GOLD MEDAL UNANIMOUSLY VOTED TO THE BECKWITH ORGANS

ALL DOUBT AS TO THE QUALITY of the Beckwith has been forever removed, because of the special honors heaped upon it at the two greatest exhibitions of the product of man's ingenuity of recent years. It received the highest medal and diploma of merit and other honors at the St. Louis World's Fair and at the great Jamestown Exposition just closed, the Gold Medal was unanimously conferred upon this organ by the judges, together with other very special honors that fully attests its superlative quality. The magnificent line of Beckwith Parlor, Church and Chapel Organs shown at these two great exhibits attracted world wide attention and in each instance the highest honors were unanimously voted them in competition with a number of other organs of world renowned make, thus removing for all time all doubt, if any doubt had existed, as to the wonderfully high quality and the exalted excellence represented in the

IF YOU WISH TO SAVE MONEY, if you desire to take advantage of our great money saving prices and liberal offers, testing the organ in your own home for full thirty days at our risk, then do not let any agent or anyone else interested in seeing you buy some other organ at a profit or commission to themselves, argue you out of it. Do not be deceived by those who advance arguments against your own interests, who advise you not to save money on the purchase of an organ, but who advise you to buy elsewhere at a larger price. There is no mystery or secret processes in making an organ and we challenge the world to produce an organ equal to the Beckwith in quality and tone. Remember that those who would advise you not to try a Beckwith at our risk, with the understanding that you are not asked to buy it unless it represents a wonderful saving, are not advising you for your own interests. All we ask of you is that we be permitted to answer any argument made against the Beckwith. If you

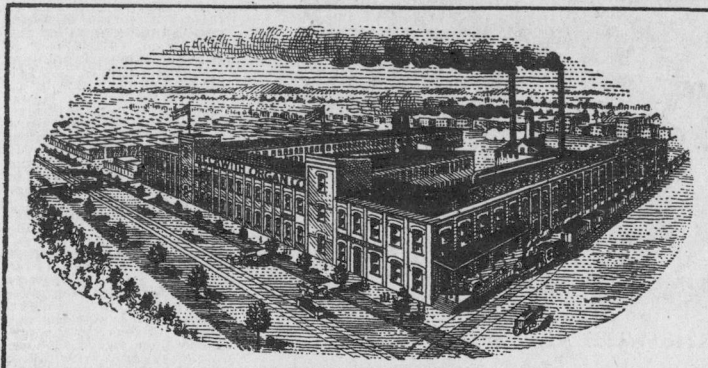

LOUISVILLE FACTORY.

ST. PAUL FACTORY.

Beckwith. This organ stands upon the highest pinnacle of musical excellence, and to question the quality in this organ means to cast reflection upon the integrity, honesty of purpose and sound judgment of the two great international juries, made up of the most distinguished and eminent authorities on organ construction and quality, who were unanimous in conferring these honors upon the Beckwith Organ, not only at the St. Louis World's Fair, but the Jamestown Exposition as well. Wherever the Beckwith Organ has been entered in competition with other well known makes, it invariably carries off the highest honors and it is recognized and acknowledged to be the standard of organ quality for the entire world. Others may copy the Beckwith Organ cases and the magnificent finish and appearance they represent, but no manufacturer has yet been able to imitate the wonderful tone quality.

WHY ARE YOU READING THIS PAGE? We feel sure that it is because you are interested either today, tomorrow or at some future time in the purchase of an organ. We would be very much pleased to prove to you the truth of our claims regarding the Beckwith Organ, to prove to you the excellence of these instruments by sending any one you may select for a complete thirty-day trial under our "send no money offer." If you will consent to our placing one of these organs in your home on trial, we are so sure that you will agree to keep it at the end of the trial term and give it your heartiest endorsement as well, that we will be perfectly willing to accept your order under our liberal terms and send it to you, freight charges prepaid, taking all the risk and responsibility without a single penny being advanced by you, as fully described on page 209. It has been proved that wherever we sell a Beckwith Organ we make a great many good friends, and the consequence is increased orders for this instrument. Therefore, it is very profitable to us to accept a very little margin of profit on each instrument, owing to the thousands and thousands we sell every year.

will order an instrument on trial at our risk, you would soon be convinced that if anyone advises you not to buy a Beckwith, but to buy some other make of organ at double our prices, that they are not advising you for your own welfare. They are not advising you to buy where you can get the greatest degree of satisfaction and value at the smallest possible price, therefore at the greater saving to you.

LET US PROVE THAT IT IS THE FINEST INSTRUMENT EVER OFFERED. This you can easily do without any risk to yourself. Try a Beckwith Organ at our risk, and if you do not find it all we claim it to be, then send it back and buy from someone else at a much larger price, therefore, at a larger cost to you. You owe it to yourself to take advantage of our prices and liberal offers. If any argument is advanced as to why you should not save for yourself all that our prices mean, then let us answer every statement made to you against our money saving prices and liberal terms. If you are looking for an organ at all, it is only natural that you should be looking for the best it is possible to secure. Remember the special honors conferred on the Beckwith at the St. Louis World's Fair and the Jamestown Exposition. Again, it is natural that you want to save as much money as is possible in the transaction. That being the case you cannot afford to overlook our offers. Nowhere can you get such a fine organ and so much value and musical capacity at such a saving in price. In view of these facts, in view of the liberal shipping terms, under which we gladly send out the Beckwith Organs, in view of our strong guarantee backed by Forty Million Dollars' worth of capital, do you not owe it to yourself, you who are reading this page, to order a Beckwith Organ on trial, so as to prove to your complete satisfaction whether or not our claims are true, whether or not we can save you one-half on the purchase of a high grade instrument?

$68.00 THE BECKWITH HOME QUEEN PIANO-ORGAN

No. 46K217

Order by Number.

NEVER HERETOFORE OFFERED FOR LESS THAN $69.00. THIS INSTRUMENT IS MAGNIFICENT AND SATISFYING IN TONE QUALITY AND PERFECT IN CONSTRUCTION.

WE ARE PROUD TO HAVE YOU COMPARE this piano-organ with any other offered by any other dealer or maker, knowing that this comparison will only convince you that this is the finest piano-organ offered, that it represents greater value than any other like instrument, that its tone is the most satisfying, most beautiful tone ever found in any piano cased organ, and that in every conceivable manner it leads the world as a standard piano-organ of all makes. The price, $68.00, places this beautiful piano-organ within the reach of all, and this price has never been approached by any other dealer for an instrument having the same wonderful capacity, the same beautiful tone, the same exquisite finish, representing the same value. Our price, $68.00, represents the actual cost to make this instrument with our one small margin of profit added, and you could not duplicate this organ or secure an organ approaching anywhere near its quality or capacity through other channels for under $150.00 to $175.00. If you are in the market for a piano-organ and desire the finest that was ever built, then you should order this one on trial under our liberal trial terms. You cannot afford to overlook the immense value, this wonderful saving that the Home Queen Piano-Organ represents. In appearance it is an exact counterpart, an exact duplicate, of a fine $400.00 upright piano, and the case glistens like a mirror.

SEND NO MONEY but refer to the liberal terms of shipment on page 209 wherein we explain how we will ship this organ to you without any money paid to us, direct, for a full thirty days' free trial, all freight charges prepaid. We are perfectly willing to advance the freight charges for you, to be paid by you with the cost of the organ if at the end of thirty days you find it all we claim it to be and one you will be proud to own.

THE CASE is in every way an exact duplicate of a piano in appearance and can be furnished in San Domingo mahogany, or French burled walnut. It is veneered both inside and outside, the veneers being cross banded, which is a guarantee it cannot warp, crack or split under any natural conditions. It is finished with the finest grade of transparent piano varnish, hand rubbed and shines like a mirror. Fitted with a duet music desk, regular piano fall board, piano pedals and pedal guards of modern design, handsomely nickel plated and polished.

PATENT AUTOMATIC COUPLER is another feature of this instrument which avoids the necessity of placing two extra stops in the organ. By a gentle pressure on the middle pedal, the treble and bass couplers are thrown into position and another slight pressure on the key instantly releases it. You will recognize this as a notable improvement. This middle pedal gives the effect of a practice pedal on a piano, further enhancing its piano appearance.

THE ACTION is the finest that years of experience can produce. The reeds are all of extra width, length and thickness, the largest found in any reed organ. They are Grand Orchestral reeds, which means that the tone is full, round, delightfully sweet, faultless in its matchless quality. These reeds are all controlled by the ingeniously arranged stops, which are noticeable to the casual observer. These stops you will note are immediately above the name on the organ, being almost concealed in the music shelf. The tongues of the reeds are double riveted to the solid reed block and are bent, tuned and voiced by hand specially for this instrument, and we guarantee that their volume of sweetness is unsurpassed by any piano-organ. Each part of the action is felted in the most approved manner, which guarantees there will be no rattle in the action. It contains full 7½ octaves of keys, the same as any grand piano made and any music written for a piano can be played upon it. This is a fine organ in a piano case, but is not in any sense a piano and cannot be made to produce a piano tone. GUARANTEED FOR 25 YEARS by a binding guarantee for quality.

GRAND PNEUMATIC SWELL. A very important improvement is this Pneumatic Swell, which avoids the necessity of having the unsightly knee swells showing on the organ. When it is

Beckwith Cabinet Grand Chicago

THIS IS AN EXACT REPRODUCTION OF STYLE No. 46K218 WITH THREE STOPS.

desired to increase the volume of tone it is only necessary to pump the organ a little harder, when this swell automatically opens; and to close the swell, it is only necessary to stop pedaling for a moment and it will close automatically. This is a wonderful improvement in organ construction, as it does not open suddenly, but gradually, giving a very beautiful effect to the music.

THE PIPE SWELL ATTACHMENT modifies the tone and produces a close imitation of the tone of a pipe organ. It is fitted over the reeds in the back of the organ, qualifying their tone in a most effective manner. This is a very important feature of the organ and one that commends itself to the musician.

THE BELLOWS is extremely large, therefore, has wonderful power. It occupies the entire width of the organ, which gives greatly increased size. It is constructed of three-ply built up stock and therefore cannot warp, crack or split under any natural conditions. It is covered with the finest quality of silk rubber cloth which is a guarantee against leaking. The bellows in this organ is always to be relied upon.

THE STOPS on the organ are not noticeable. There are three of them within easy reach of the performer and by a judicious use of these stops a number of very harmonious combinations are possible. The stops are immediately above the center of the organ as shown in the illustration, but are hardly discernible on the instrument.

THE MATERIAL in this organ is of the highest grade. The workmanship is the most skilled and we are so confident of the excellence of the instrument that we gladly send it out, as we do all Beckwith Pianos and Organs, under our liberal "send no money" offer.

THE VENEER used in this instrument is all selected and shows a fine figure. We furnish it in either San Domingo mahogany, or French burled walnut, as desired. Be sure to state veneer wanted.

A MAGNIFICENT STOOL FREE with this organ. It is beautifully finished in piano finish to match the case. The legs are handsomely turned and polished and are fitted with brass claws and glass balls for feet. The seat is full 14½ inches in diameter and can be easily raised and lowered to suit the convenience of the performer. It is very solid and substantially made and is varnished and hand polished.

A HANDSOME VELOUR SCARF FREE with the organ in a beautiful pattern of the latest artistic design, genuine all silk fringe. This scarf makes a handsome addition to the appearance of the organ and is full size, being 24 inches wide and 7 feet long.

A COMPLETE INSTRUCTION BOOK IS FREE with the organ. This is very complete in every way and will be a valuable acquisition to any student's library.

No. 46K217 BECKWITH HOME QUEEN PIANO-ORGAN. Full 7½ Octaves, 176 Grand Orchestral Reeds
controlled by two stops, stool, scarf and book. Price.. **$68.00**
No. 46K218 BECKWITH HOME QUEEN PIANO-ORGAN. Full 7½ Octaves, 238 Grand Orchestral Reeds
controlled by three stops, stool, scarf and book. Price... **73.00**

BECKWITH ORGANS

HIGHEST AWARD ST. LOUIS WORLD'S FAIR AND JAMESTOWN EXPOSITION

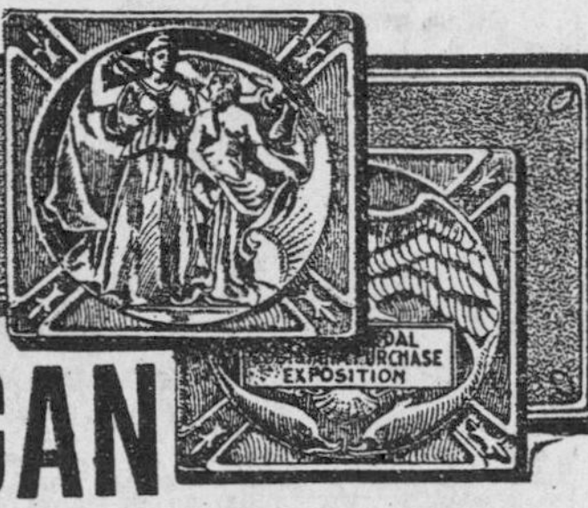

THE NEW BECKWITH IMPERIAL GRAND ORGAN

FULLY GUARANTEED FOR 25 YEARS, A QUARTER OF A CENTURY, BY THE STRONGEST, MOST BINDING GUARANTEE EVER GIVEN. SEE A COPY OF THIS GUARANTEE ON PAGE 209. ILLUSTRATED ON OPPOSITE PAGE.

THIS IS THE FINEST ORGAN MADE. It represents the very highest attainment in organ manufacture. This fact is universally admitted by everybody familiar with organ value. It is also proved by the thousands of unsolicited testimonials which we receive, praising it in the most unqualified terms. The reputation of the Beckwith Organ is not the result of any favorable combination of chances, but by the manufacturer holding to high ideals, by patient endeavor and progress during the years that this organ has held a prominent and enviable place in popular esteem.

GOLD MEDAL AWARDED TO THE BECKWITH. The highest award ever given to any organ was conferred upon the Beckwith at the Jamestown Exposition just closed, together with many other distinctive and special honors that were heaped upon it. The Special Jury of Awards at the St. Louis World's Fair also conferred upon the entire line of Beckwith Organs the highest medal and other flattering honors. These two awards, the greatest given to organ manufacturers in recent years, unanimously voted to the Beckwith, remove forever any doubt, if doubt could possibly exist, as to the sterling worth, the high quality and the magnificent tone of these organs.

THE BECKWITH IMPERIAL GRAND ORGAN is a beautiful instrument. It is not only a wonderfully fine piece of furniture, but the magnificent, majestic, rich, deep tone quality, which is its great characteristic, places it in a class all by itself, outstripping all competition for all time. You have it within your power to prove the truth of our claim. We are willing that you should try this organ for full thirty days at our risk without any money being advanced by you to us during this period. Remember that we do not ask you to be influenced by any description of this organ we may give you or by what we say, but we do ask you to judge the instrument yourself by a thorough examination of the organ at our risk, remembering you are the one to be pleased and that you are to accept it or reject it, entirely uninfluenced by any advice or suggestion made by us, basing your action altogether upon your own opinion of the organ.

THE CASE. The beautiful design is one which instantly charms all who have seen it, and was selected from many drawings submitted to us by the best organ designers of the world. Entirely new and distinctively original, dignity, richness and power are apparent in every line. It is well balanced and the proportions and lines are particularly attractive. The rich ornamentation, the carved brackets upholding the massive canopy are not only new in form but are entirely Beckwith ideas. The graceful sweep of the handsomely carved truss supporting the key bed, together with other special features, gives it a richness unapproached by any other organ design. All carvings of every nature are hand executed by experts. The wide top, the beautiful ornamentations, all combine, not only to make this case artistically beautiful, but impressive and imposing as well. The top is ornamented with a gracefully shaped French plate glass beveled edge mirror, which lends much to the appearance of the instrument. The back opens up like a door, making the action easily accessible if this is desired for any purpose. The music desk acts as a cover for a very large and convenient music cabinet. The organ is provided with a very handsome paneled fall board with lock and key, ornamental handles and casters. The pedals are covered with Brussels carpet with metallic pedal frames, highly nickel plated and burnished.

THERE IS A REASON WHY You should try a Beckwith Organ before considering any other organ. No matter how you send a trial order you are not buying the organ unless you decide to keep it at the end of thirty days. The Beckwith represents more value than any other organ. Our prices for a high grade organ that has received the Gold Medal at the Jamestown Exposition and the highest medal at the St. Louis World's Fair represents a greater saving to you than any other make. We will send an organ to you on trial absolutely at our risk for thirty days, as explained on page 209. Can you afford to overlook this liberal money saving offer?

FURNISHED IN OAK OR WALNUT. We give you two choices of wood in this organ. It is furnished either in beautifully figured oak with full quarter sawed front, or genuine selected American black walnut. While the case receives the requisite number of coats of varnish, yet each coat is carefully rubbed down with rotten stone by hand, and is finally finished in a very handsome oil rubbed finish, giving it that dainty, beautiful satin effect. Thus all the distasteful gloss is removed. This finish is extremely popular and is only found upon high class furniture.

GRAND ORCHESTRAL ACTION is the finest combination of stops and reeds of matchless quality ever combined in an organ. While all Beckwith Organs are fitted with a superior grade of reeds, in the Grand Orchestral Action is used a reed of extra breadth, thickness and width, which allows of a very much larger vibrating tongue, producing the most delightful organ tone ever heard from a reed. Each piece and part of this action is carefully felted with all wool felt of extra quality. There is not a particle of cotton faced or shoddy felt in the action. Every part where there could be vibration has been felted in the most approved fashion, which is a positive guarantee that there never will be any cause for complaint on this score.

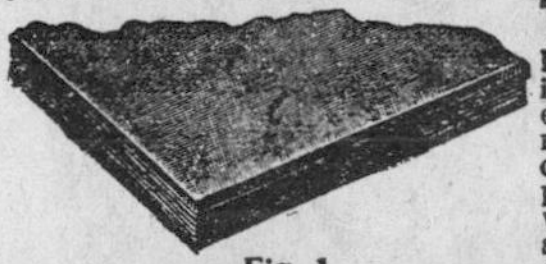

Fig. 1

THE BELLOWS. The bellows in the Beckwith Organ is built in strict accordance with Beckwith ideas and are as nearly automatic as man's ingenuity can make them. The consequence is wonderful ease in pumping and an absolute guarantee that there will never be that spasmodic or jerky sound so often found in other reed organs. The wood forming the bellows is threeply built up stock, which is a guarantee that it can never warp, crack or split under any natural condition. Fig. 1 shows a section of the bellows stock, illustrating how the different sections of wood are glued together, showing the grain of these pieces of wood running in opposite directions. The bellows is covered with extra quality silk cloth, heavily rubber coated, specially made for this purpose. Fig. 7 shows the bellows attached to the foundation board and illustrates a very important improvement in organ construction, which is only found in the Grand Orchestral Action. In an ordinary organ there is a brace running down from the foundation board, marked HH in the illustration, to the front part of the bellows. This reinforces the bellows to a certain degree, but in the Grand Orchestral Action the Beckwith improvement consists of one massive solid piece of hardwood, which is screwed and glued to the middle board and foundation board as well, (indicated by the letter J in Fig. 7), which makes the bellows and the foundation board absolutely one piece, which is a guarantee against the loosening of the bellows at the throat and a number of other complaints common to the ordinary bellows.

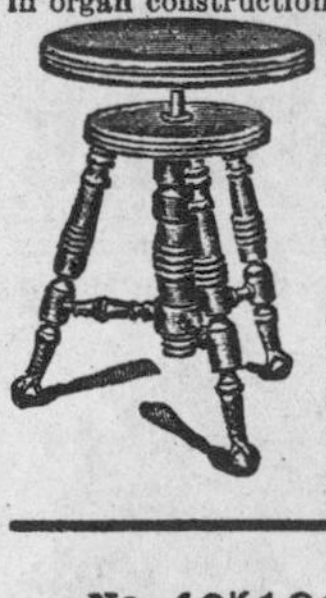

THE REED CELLS. In the Grand Orchestral Action the manufacturer is compelled by the added breadth, length and thickness of the reed to build a cell of larger dimensions to accommodate the increased tone caused by the larger vibrating tongue. By the peculiar shape of these reed cells and by reducing the thickness of the wood of which they are made to the proper degree, the tone has been modified or qualified so that, together with correct bending of the tongues of the reeds, a most delightful quality of tone is produced, a perfect imitation of the tones of the pipe organ.

THE REEDS are of unusual size, as large a reed as is used in any reed organ. The vibrating tongues of brass are double riveted to the strong and solid reed block. These reeds give a quality of tone that instantly charm everyone. These reeds are all cut, bent, tuned and voiced according to the tone quality which they are destined to produce. Each reed is subjected to the most careful test before it is accepted for the Grand Orchestral Action. A great deal of care and study have been given to the construction of these reeds, and the makers have succeeded in combining that singing quality so desirable in an organ, with the grand pipe-like tone which can alone give solidity and dignity to the harmony. Every reed, from the largest to the smallest is carefully inspected, bent, tuned and voiced by hand. This operation is performed by only the most careful, skillful and experienced workmen. The reed depends for its tone upon the peculiar formation given it by the bender. The reeds in the Grand Orchestral Action are all bent by experts who have combined years of experience with a strong, natural faculty for this work. Figures 2, 3, 4 and 5 illustrate some of the reeds in this action, but the reeds in the illustration are only about one-third the actual size.

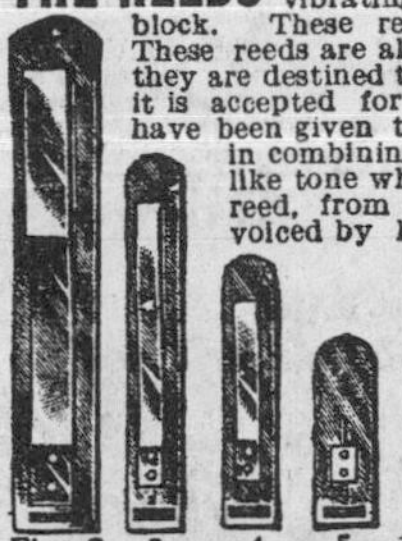

Figs. 2 3 4 5

2—A ponderous Sub-Bass reed.
3—A Diapason reed.
4—A Flute reed.
5—A Piccolo reed.

THE VALVE. A notable feature of the Beckwith Grand Orchestral Action is the attention given to the valve, a very important part of an organ, as its function has much to do with controlling the tone, and upon its construction depends the rapidity with which the organ responds to a pressure on a key. The Grand Orchestral valve has extra width and strength, but a great difference between this valve and the valves used on other organs of other makes is found in the construction of the facing of the valve. A glance at Fig. 6 will convey to you some idea of its construction. The foundation of the valve is straight grained cork pine of the highest grade. On top of this foundation is placed a very thick pad of all wool felt of great resiliency, and this in turn is faced, not with the ordinary oilcloth or rubber cloth facing used in many other makes of organs, but with genuine high grade selected sheepskin leather. The consequence is, that the valve perfectly closes the opening leading to the reed cells. This in turn guarantees that the organ will never give ground for complaint owing to leaking valves. The material on the valves is glued down the center only, leaving the edges free so that owing to the loose edges of the cushion, the valve will "seat" properly and prevent the reed from speaking unless the key is pressed.

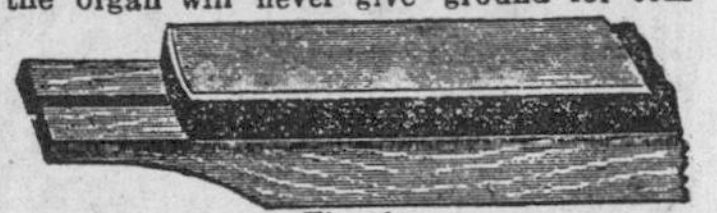

Fig. 6

THE INTERIOR CONSTRUCTION. The mechanical part of the Imperial Grand and Cathedral Chapel Organs is most perfectly constructed, durably built and skillfully adjusted. Fig. 7 shows a full view of the Grand Orchestral Action, complete, ready to be placed in an organ. "AA" shows the feeder valves, "BB" the pedal straps, "C" the stop connections, "DD" the swell rods. "E" the coupler rods, which is also a new idea and avoids many of the complications incident to the coupler actions found on other organs. The illustration shows the right hand coupler board raised, coupling the treble side of the instrument. "G" shows the guide pins which hold the keys in place, and "F" illustrates the tracker pins, which connect the keys with the valves of the organ. "HH" is the foundation board, "I" shows the excess pressure valve.

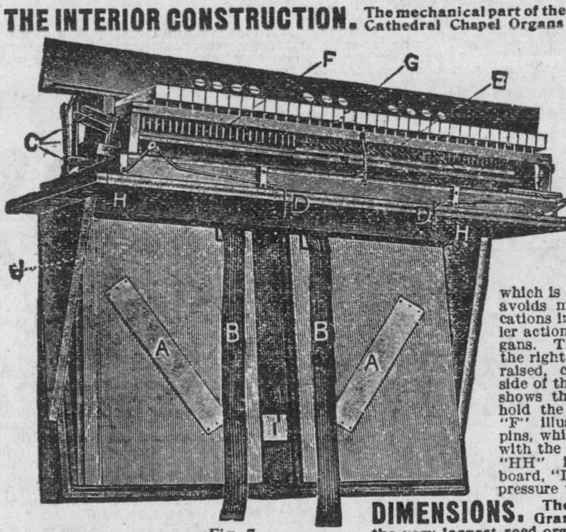

Fig. 7

DIMENSIONS. The Beckwith Imperial Grand Organ is one of the very largest reed organs on the market, being 87½ inches high, 46 inches long, and 24½ inches deep, in five octaves; and 87½ inches high, 53 inches long and 24 inches deep, in six octaves. It weighs, boxed and packed for shipment, in five octaves, 495 pounds, and in six octaves, 575 pounds.

FREE. We send absolutely free with each one of these organs a fine stool, made in wood to match the case of the organ, with handsome turned legs, brass claws fitted with glass balls. We also send a complete instruction book for the organ. The illustration shows you the stool which we give with this instrument.

NUMBERS, PRICES AND ACTIONS

The Imperial Grand Organ is furnished in five different styles, each style fitted with the Grand Orchestral Action, as follows:

No. 46K161 GRAND ORCHESTRAL ACTION A, 5 OCTAVES, 11 STOPS, OAK. Price **$46.80**

Four sets of extra heavy, extra quality reeds, as follows: One full set of Principal reeds, 24 notes; one full set of Melodia reeds, 37 notes; one full set of Diapason reeds, 24 notes; one full set of Celeste reeds, 37 notes; 122 extra heavy, extra quality reeds in all. These reeds are entirely under the control of the performer at all times by the use of eleven necessary stops, as follows: Principal, Diapason, Dulciana, Melodia, Celeste, Cremona, Diapason Forte, Principal Forte, Treble Coupler, Bass Coupler and Vox Humana.

No. 46K163 GRAND ORCHESTRAL ACTION B, 5 OCTAVES, 15 STOPS, OAK. Price **$52.80**

The same as No. 46K161, Grand Orchestral Action A, with the addition of one full set of Flute reeds, 37 notes; one full set of Bourdon reeds, 24 notes; 183 reeds in all. It is equipped with fifteen stops, eleven stops as in 46K161, but with an addition of four stops as follows: Bourdon, Viola, Flute and Dulcet.

No. 46K165 GRAND ORCHESTRAL ACTION C, 5 OCTAVES, 17 STOPS, OAK. Price **$55.80**

The same as No. 46K163, with an addition of one full set of Clarionet reeds, 24 notes; one full set of Cornet Echo reeds, 37 notes; a total of 244 reeds in all. These reeds are controlled by seventeen stops, the same stops as No. 46K163, omitting the Dulcet stop, but with the three following stops added: Clarionet, Cornet and Cornet Echo.

No. 46K167 GRAND ORCHESTRAL ACTION D, 6 OCTAVES, 11 STOPS, OAK. Price **$54.80**

The same as No. 46K161, except that it has one additional octave of reeds in the two treble sets, making a total of 146 reeds in all, controlled by the same stops as described under No. 46K161.

No. 46K169 GRAND ORCHESTRAL ACTION E, 6 OCTAVES, 17 STOPS, OAK. Price **$61.80**

This is the same as the action described under No. 46K165, except that it has one greater octave compass. The four treble sets contain four reeds, making a total of 292 reeds in all. The above prices are for oak only. If you desire the organ in walnut case, you must add $2.00 to the prices given.

$1⁸⁵ VIOLINS $26⁹⁵

AT $1.85 TO $26.95

WE OFFER A SPLENDID LINE OF VIOLINS. GOOD MATERIALS, MODELS, CORRECT PROPORTIONS AND EXPERT WORKMANSHIP, EACH AND EVERY ONE REPRESENTING A WONDERFUL VALUE. QUALITY AND PRICE COMPARED, WE CHALLENGE ALL COMPETITORS.

THE VALUE OF A VIOLIN. There is no article in the world, the value of which is so little known as the violin, and it has, therefore, been the custom of dealers to charge as much as the customer was willing to pay, basing their prices on fictitious or imaginary qualities the instruments were supposed to possess. There are only two fundamental things which determine the actual value of a violin: materials and workmanship. Upon the grades of materials, (wood, varnish, etc.) and the workmanship (model, proportion, construction, etc.) depend the ultimate results of whether the instrument will have a good tone, or not. Nobody but an expert is truly able to judge as to these two qualities. The manager of our Musical Department has made a life study of violins and relative values, and is, therefore, competent to judge them down to the smallest detail.

A WORD ABOUT PRICES. Our prices were never so low, and we were never in a position to offer greater values than we are at present. The prices we are asking for our violins are based strictly upon the cost to us, which is the actual cost of production, with but our very small percentage of profit added. Our sales are continually on the increase and, owing to our increased purchasing power, we have made wonderful reductions in price through our line. Our prices, consistent with quality, are positively lower than quoted by other dealers. Some dealers are offering violins as low in price as 75 cents, but these cannot be considered musical instruments. We know that in offering a violin at $1.85, we are striking the very lowest limit at which an instrument can be offered containing any merits whatsoever.

OUR LINE OF VIOLINS was never so complete and of such high grade as at the present time. From the lowest to the highest priced violin in our line, it represents the best value that can possibly be offered for the money. Our instruments are all constructed in accordance with the best known principles and of the best possible materials. Quality is never sacrificed to price. We earnestly solicit a comparison of our violins with those offered by other dealers, and we absolutely guarantee to give a better looking, better constructed, and better toned instrument at about one-half of their price. Our instruments are carefully tested and examined before shipping.

OUR LIBERAL TERMS OF SHIPMENT make it possible for you to order any of our violins, compare it with anything offered by other dealers, try it in your home for ten days, and if you are not satisfied with it for any reason whatever, return it to us, and we will refund your money and transportation charges. No fairer offer could be made by any dealer.

THE BOWS AND FITTINGS which we give with our violins are in every way equal to the instruments themselves.

OUR STUDENTS' VIOLIN

FULL SIZE. No. 12K213 $3.75   FRONT VIEW.

FULL SIZE. No. 12K213 $3.75   BACK VIEW.

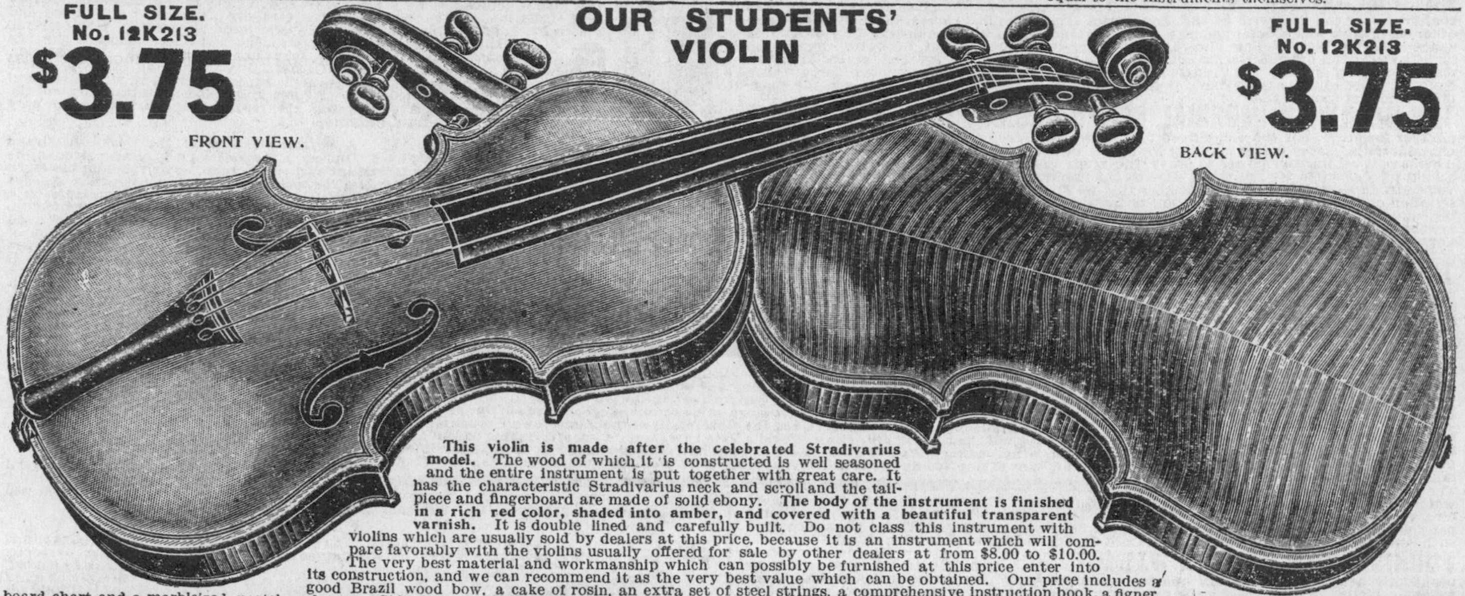

This violin is made after the celebrated Stradivarius model. The wood of which it is constructed is well seasoned and the entire instrument is put together with great care. It has the characteristic Stradivarius neck and scroll and the tailpiece and fingerboard are made of solid ebony. The body of the instrument is finished in a rich red color, shaded into amber, and covered with a beautiful transparent varnish. It is double lined and carefully built. Do not class this instrument with violins which are usually sold by dealers at this price, because it is an instrument which will compare favorably with the violins usually offered for sale by other dealers at from $8.00 to $10.00. The very best material and workmanship which can possibly be furnished at this price enter into its construction, and we can recommend it as the very best value which can be obtained. Our price includes a good Brazil wood bow, a cake of rosin, an extra set of steel strings, a comprehensive instruction book, a finger board chart and a marbleized pasteboard case. Shipping weight, 10 pounds.

No. 12K213   Full size.   Price...$3.75
No. 12K213¾   Same as above in every respect except three-quarter size. Suited for young students. Price...........$3.75

OUR $1.85 WONDER   No. 12K210   MAGGINI MODEL   No. 12K216

$1⁸⁵

This violin is made of good materials and accurate proportions, and we guarantee it is equal to instruments usually sold by other dealers for $2.50 to $3.00. However, we do not especially recommend it, as any of the other violins in our line at a trifle higher price represent by far a better investment. Shipping weight, about 10 pounds.
No. 12K210   Price...................$1.85

This violin is an exact copy of the celebrated Maggini violins and the characteristic Maggini double purfling gives it a very trim, graceful appearance. The back is made of two pieces of beautiful flamed maple, and the sides of the same material. The top is made of old well seasoned spruce and the soundholes are evenly and gracefully cut. The tailpiece, fingerboard and pegs are of solid ebony and the scroll is the characteristic neat Maggini model. The body of the instrument is finished in golden red blending into the natural color of the wood. The varnish is transparent and highly polished bringing out the grain of the wood in a very effective manner. This is one of the very best values that we have to offer in a moderate priced violin and in beauty of appearance, excellence of tone and durability of construction it cannot be equaled by any violin on the market at anywhere near this price. We furnish with this violin a very nicely finished, serviceable bow, which is in every way as good a value as the violin itself, a box of rosin, an extra set of steel strings, a complete instruction book, fingerboard chart and a marbleized pasteboard case. Shipping weight, about 10 pounds.
No. 12K216   Our new reduced price...........................$4.25

OUR STAINER MODEL

QUALITY THE SAME   PRICE LOWER THAN EVER BEFORE

This violin which we formerly sold for $5.15 is an exact copy of the famous Stainer violins, a characteristic of which is the bulging top and back and a long flat scroll. The original Stainer violins are today much sought after by artists on account of their exceedingly beautiful tone. Great care has been used to pattern this instrument exactly after this celebrated model. The back of the instrument is made of two pieces of very highly flamed, well seasoned maple and the sides are of the same material. The top is made of well seasoned, resonant silver spruce, the soundholes are graceful and very sharply and neatly cut and the purfling is accurately and evenly inlaid. The body of the violin is a deep red color blending into the natural color of the wood. The tailpiece, fingerboard and pegs are of solid ebony. If you will compare it with the violins usually sold by dealers throughout the country you will find that you cannot purchase an instrument of this grade elsewhere for less than $10.00 to $12.00.

THIS VIOLIN GOES COMPLETE with well made, durable bow of good pattern and finely finished, a complete instruction book, a box of rosin, an extra set of steel strings, a fingerboard chart and a very nice marbleized pasteboard case. Shipping weight, 10 pounds.
No. 12K218   Price..................

$4.95

TWO EXTRA SPECIAL HIGH GRADE VIOLINS

THE MOST REMARKABLE VIOLIN OFFER EVER MADE

VIOLINS MADE BY TWO OF THE GREATEST MODERN VIOLIN MAKERS NOW OFFERED YOU AT LESS THAN ONE-HALF THE PRICE USUALLY CHARGED FOR INSTRUMENTS OF THIS CLASS.

OUR SPECIAL REDUCED PRICES

Owing to the reduced cost of labor and materials entering into the construction of the splendid volin cases and trimmings given away with these two instruments, we, following our usual method, are giving our customers the benefit of this saving.

THERE IS NO ARTICLE SO DECEPTIVE IN VALUE as a violin, as the intrinsic value is difficult to determine. A large part of the price usually charged for violins, especially of high grade, is paid by the purchaser for values which are purely imaginary, and unless the buyer is a competent judge himself he generally is obliged to pay many times the price for which he could procure a strictly high grade instrument made by an expert violin maker. The manager of our violin department is not alone a player of exceptional ability, but is also acknowledged a judge of violins of all classes. After several years of continuous search, he has at last succeeded in arranging with two of the best known violin makers of Italy and Germany to provide us with their choice instruments, which, in the judgment of our expert, are the equal of violins generally sold at from $150.00 to $300.00, but in keeping with our general policy we offer these violins to our customers at a great saving in price, based on the cost of the instrument, and with only our usual small profit added. Do not make the mistake of comparing these violins with the instruments offered by dealers generally at these prices, because they are not handled by any other dealers. These makers are able to produce only a limited number of violins during a year and by our arrangement with them we get all of the instruments they make.

IT IS A WELL KNOWN FACT that strictly high grade new violins will increase in value from year to year, whereas a poor instrument is sure to deteriorate in quality. Such violins as the two we are offering on this page are sure to increase in value, as they are the product of two of the world's best known violin makers. The actual value of a new violin depends entirely upon the skill with which it is constructed and the materials which are used. If these two qualities are not of the highest grade and not embodied in the instrument, it will never develop in tone nor increase in value. We guarantee that the violins of the two makers, Vincenzo Pisani and Robert Nurnberger, embody all of the qualities essential to a fine violin. The choicest of wood, which has been carefully conserved and treasured for years before being put into these instruments, and selected with the greatest care and eye to the requirements of a fine violin, and then modeled and executed by the hands of such artists, is a guarantee that we are placing within reach of our customers such instruments as they may consider themselves fortunate to possess, and which will represent a splendid investment. It has been generally stated and considered as an accepted fact that violin making is a lost art, but we firmly believe that the violins of this class made in the present century are sure to become as valuable, in years hence, as the old masterpieces of Cremona are today.

$45.00 OUR GENUINE PISANI STRADIVARIUS MODEL VIOLIN $45.00

FRONT VIEW BACK VIEW

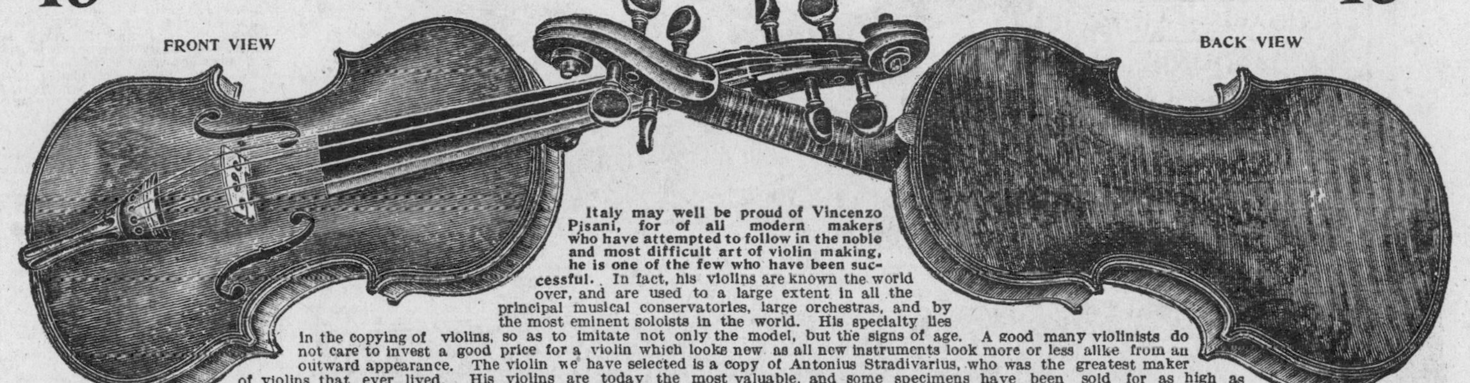

Italy may well be proud of Vincenzo Pisani, for of all modern makers who have attempted to follow in the noble and most difficult art of violin making, he is one of the few who have been successful. In fact, his violins are known the world over, and are used to a large extent in all the principal musical conservatories, large orchestras, and by the most eminent soloists in the world. His specialty lies in the copying of violins, so as to imitate not only the model, but the signs of age. A good many violinists do not care to invest a good price for a violin which looks new, as all new instruments look more or less alike from an outward appearance. The violin we have selected is a copy of Antonius Stradivarius, who was the greatest maker of violins that ever lived. His violins are today the most valuable, and some specimens have been sold for as high as $10,000. By special arrangement with Signor Pisani we will be able to obtain a very limited number of these instruments every year, as every one, of course, has to be made by hand, and to the smallest detail by himself. The back is made of one piece of the best possible maple obtainable, a wood which is well known for its sonorous qualities. The sides are made of the same material as the back, and the top is of Cremona silver spruce. It is needless to say that the best attention has been given to the lining, blocking, measurements, and everything connected with the making of this violin a perfect musical instrument. The maker has not only succeeded in these points, but by a special process has succeeded in producing an instrument which shows plainly the marks of age to the slightest degree. In fact, no one but an expert can distinguish the difference between this violin and instruments from one hundred and fifty to two hundred years old. Not only has he succeeded in duplicating the appearance, but also the beautiful, rich tone of the old instruments. If you wish to be the possessor of an instrument which looks in every respect like the old Stradivarius instruments, which have brought in recent years the fabulous price of $10,000.00 each, an instrument which will in the course of due time be worth a large amount of money, we would unhesitatingly recommend this instrument. With this violin we give a very fine Pernambuco bow, well balanced and such as will give satisfaction under all conditions. This bow has a stick of very fine grain, which will not warp, and the best quality ebony frog with pearl eyes and slide, and full trimmed with solid silver. A case made of four plies veneers, covered with black morocco leather, full velvet lined, with nickel plated trimmings and a set of our excellent Verona strings. Shipping weight, 9 pounds.

No. 12K288 Specially reduced price, complete........................ **$45.00**

$69.00 OUR NURNBERGER SOLOIST VIOLIN $69.00

FRONT VIEW BACK VIEW

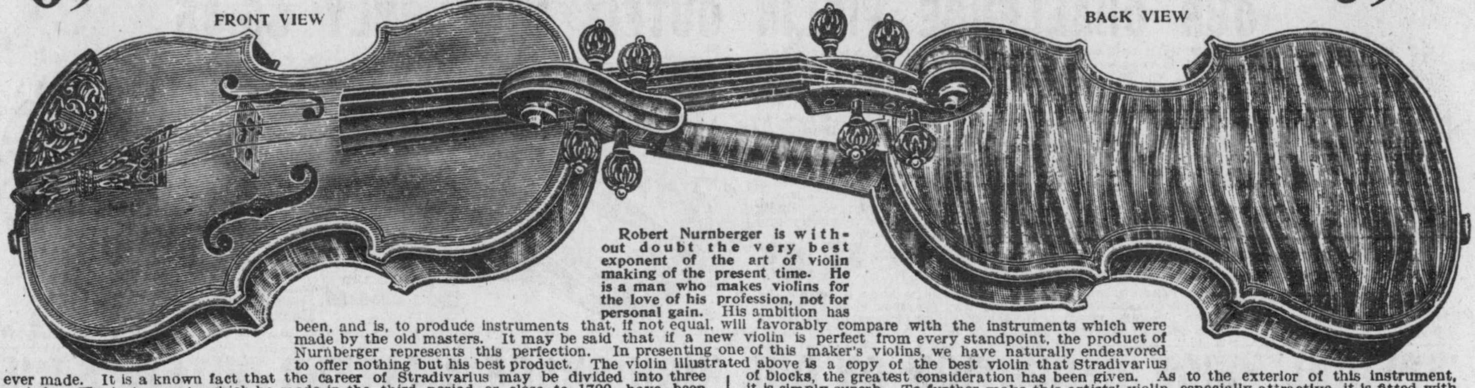

Robert Nurnberger is without doubt the very best exponent of the art of violin making of the present time. He is a man who makes violins for the love of his profession, not for personal gain. His ambition has been, and is, to produce instruments that, if not equal, will favorably compare with the instruments which were made by the old masters. It may be said that if a new violin is perfect from every standpoint, the product of Nurnberger represents this perfection. In presenting one of this maker's violins, we have naturally endeavored to offer nothing but his best product. The violin illustrated above is a copy of the best violin that Stradivarius ever made. It is a known fact that the career of Stradivarius may be divided into three periods. The instruments which he made in the third period, or close to 1700, have been pronounced by experts and by their actual musical value have proven to be the best. The material entering into the construction of a violin is a very important, in fact, vital consideration. The material which is employed by Mr. Robert Nurnberger is of the very choicest kind, which he has had in his possession for a number of years for the purpose of seasoning. Having all the important requisites for the making of a perfect instrument, we say with confidence that the violins made by Mr. Robert Nurnberger are without any question the best that can be produced. Technically speaking, this violin has a one-piece back, made of especially highly flamed maple, sides of the same material. The top is made of the very best Tyrolian spruce obtainable. This spruce, on account of the high altitude in which it grows, is of a peculiar strength and of vibrous variety. The grain is not too close, but even, and such as will act as the best conductor of sound. The edges and corners of this violin are rounded. The purfling is very carefully inlaid and sharply brought to a point at the corners. The neck is of especially fine curly maple, and the scroll purely Stradivarius, worked out with utmost accuracy. The finish on this instrument is a rich light red, with the edges brought to a natural finish, and the back shaded toward the center to its natural color. While the ingredients which the old masters employed in the making of their varnish have been a secret for centuries and are a secret to this day, we will say that the varnish used by Nurnberger on these instruments is the closest imitation of the original, a varnish that, while it will cover the instrument with a glassy and transparent coating, will not impair the tone-giving qualities of the wood. It is a known fact that the thickness of the wood should be in accordance with its peculiar quality. No one but the maker himself is capable of judging on these points. If the top is too thick, or too thin, the tone will be impaired. The same thing applies to the back and sides. To reach perfection the proper degree of thickness must be arrived at, thus the top will be thicker at the lower bout of the instrument, and thinner at the upper. To these important points of construction, including the lining and proper size of blocks, the greatest consideration has been given. As to the exterior of this instrument, it is simply superb. To further make this artists' violin especially attractive, it is fitted with an ebony tailpiece, very richly carved in a beautiful floral design, a genuine ebony chin rest, beautifully carved with a lyre, a sheet of music and a wreath. The pegs are also ebony, carved and tipped with gold plated pins. The fingerboard is of the finest quality ebony, dull in finish.

If you are interested in a real high class instrument which is superb from a tone, as well as from an appearance standpoint, you can do no better than purchase this instrument. It represents the best investment that one can make, as an instrument of this grade is sure to improve with age, and should, in the course of years, be worth many times the price paid for it. To protect the public from impostors who may be offering violins under the name of Nurnberger, we send with each of these instruments a letter bearing the authentic signature of the maker.

Albert Nurnberger, brother of the violin maker, makes a limited number of bows, and as a fitting companion for these violins, we have selected a bow of the Tourte model. Too much cannot be said of the value of a fine bow. In fact, all great artists will lay as much stress on the qualities of the bow as they do upon the violins. The finest and rarest bows are made of Pernambuco wood, carefully modeled and shaped by hand. Pernambuco wood is ofttimes used on cheaper bows, but the very finest quality, with the best of grain and the proper weight, is the kind employed on this bow, which is beautifully made and finished. The frog is handsomely trimmed with genuine silver and with mother-of-pearl slide. Such a bow as we furnish with this violin cannot be furnished at retail regularly for less than $10.00 to $15.00. To complete the outfit we also give a handsome violin case. This is made of four plies veneers, which prevents the case from ever getting out of shape, and is covered with rich seal grain leather, black in color. It is lined on the inside with beautiful silk plush and fitted with patent nickel plated catch and trimmings. We also give an extra set of our unequaled Verona strings, including a genuine silver G string.

No 12K290 Our wonderfully new low price, complete................ **$69.00**

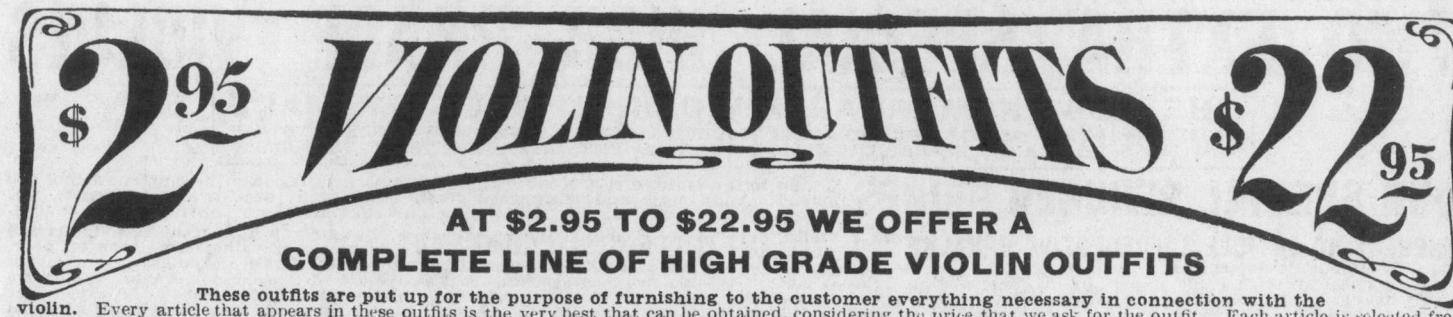

$2.95 VIOLIN OUTFITS $22.95

AT $2.95 TO $22.95 WE OFFER A COMPLETE LINE OF HIGH GRADE VIOLIN OUTFITS

These outfits are put up for the purpose of furnishing to the customer everything necessary in connection with the violin. Every article that appears in these outfits is the very best that can be obtained, considering the price that we ask for the outfit. Each article is selected from our own stock, which is a guarantee of quality, and each violin is selected for its peculiar fitness according to the price asked.

THE VIOLINS used in preparing these outfits were selected from the best workshops of Europe by our manager (who is an expert judge of musical merchandise) while on his annual buying trip. Together with this ability as a buyer, the large contracts made and our one small margin of profit, we are able to put on the market better violin outfits at lower prices than our competitors.

WE OFFER the same liberal terms of shipment on these outfits that we are offering upon all our other violins. Each one of these violins is strictly hand made.

OUR COMPETITION VIOLIN OUTFIT

THIS OUTFIT IS THE BEST VALUE ever offered for the money and anyone desiring a complete outfit for general use should not fail to examine this famous bargain. It must not be compared with the outfits offered generally by dealers at this price, because an outfit of this grade is sold by dealers generally at from $6.00 to $8.00. The violin we furnish with this outfit is a genuine Stradivarius model violin, with two-piece curly maple back, sides of the same material and top of silver spruce. The body of the instrument is finished in brown shaded to yellow. The violin is double lined.

This outfit has become very popular with beginners, and those not wishing a high priced outfit until they become proficient on the violin. Our sales on this outfit have been enormous and the quality of it has led to a great many sales on higher grade instruments.

THIS OUTFIT INCLUDES:
One Stradivarius model violin.
One Brazilwood bow, with ebony frog, inlaid with dots.
One marbleized pasteboard case.
One extra set of steel strings.
One piece of rosin, good quality.
One instructor. Simplest and most complete published.
One lettered fingerboard chart.

FOR THIS OUTFIT OTHER DEALERS ASK FROM $6.00 TO $8.00.

SEND $2.95 with your order and we will send you this outfit by express, and if you do not find it the greatest bargain you ever saw or heard of and perfectly satisfactory to you in every respect, you can return it to us at our expense and we will cheerfully refund your money.

No. 12K300 Our price.................... **$2.95**
Shipping weight, 7 pounds.

OUR CHALLENGE VIOLIN OUTFIT NOW ONLY $5.45

THE VIOLIN which we offer with this outfit is modeled after the celebrated Maggini violin, and is very skillfully and durably made. It has the characteristic double purfling of the well known Maggini model and is the very best violin ever offered in an outfit at this price. The back is made of two pieces of very nicely flamed maple and the sides are constructed of the same material. The top is made of a carefully selected piece of thoroughly seasoned silver spruce, and the tailpiece, fingerboard and pegs are made of solid ebony. The body of the instrument is finished in a dark red color, covered with fine transparent varnish. The neck is curly maple, very finely finished, and the scroll is neatly and gracefully cut.

THIS OUTFIT INCLUDES:
One Maggini model violin.
One genuine Brazilwood bow.
One canvas, fleece lined, leather bound case.
One extra set of steel strings.
One piece of rosin.
One complete instruction book.
One fingerboard chart.

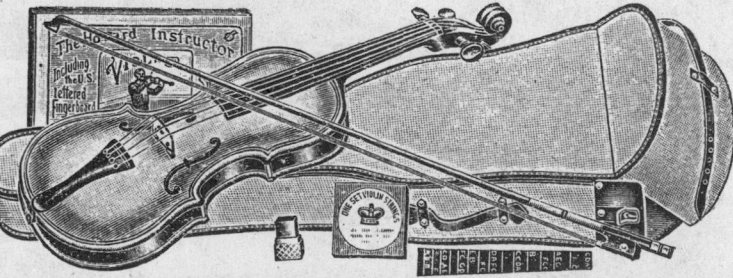

Equal to other dealers' outfits at from $11.00 to $13.00. **$5.45**
No. 12K306 Our price...(Shipping weight, 7 pounds)....

WE SHIP THIS OUTFIT to the customer with the assurance that it cannot be purchased in the regular way for less than $11.00 to $13.00. We are willing to have the purchaser compare it with anything his local dealer has to offer at these prices, and if he does not find that it is equal, and in many points superior, he can return the entire outfit to us, we will refund the money paid and pay the express charges both ways.

SPECIAL PRICE REDUCTION ON OUR HIGH GRADE AMATEUR OUTFIT $7.15

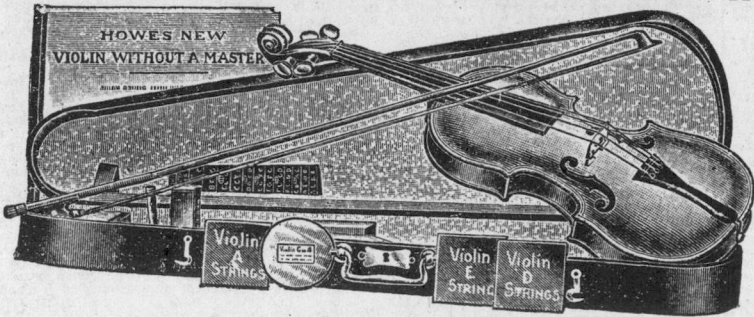

THIS OUTFIT IS OFFERED to those who desire to invest a little more money in an outfit than we ask for the above. Every article which it contains is the very best which can possibly be supplied for the price we ask, the entire outfit has been gotten up with great care so as to insure the customer receiving something which will be perfectly satisfactory to him and fully supply his needs.

THE VIOLIN which we give with this outfit is a genuine Stradivarius model, very handsomely and durably made. The back is made of two pieces of beautifully curled and flamed maple. The sides are made of a very pretty piece of maple and the top of a well selected piece of close grained silver spruce. The tailpiece, fingerboard and pegs are made of solid ebony, the scroll is very nicely cut and the body of the instrument is finished in yellowish brown color very nicely blending into yellow.

THIS OUTFIT INCLUDES:
One Stradivarius model violin.
One bow made of Brazilwood, with ebony frog, German silver trimmings.
One case, made of solid wood, has lock, handle and hook.
One extra set of Acme gut strings.
One instruction book.
One fingerboard chart.
One "A" tuning pipe.

Music dealers ask $15.00 and more for the same grade. **$7.15**
No. 12K308 Our price ....
Shipping weight, 10 pounds.

OUR SPECIAL CONSERVATORY OUTFIT

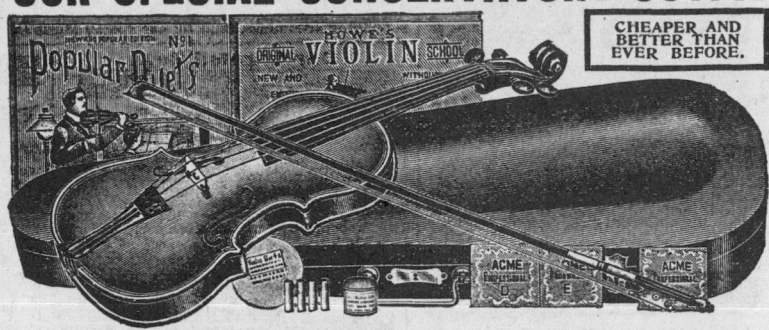

CHEAPER AND BETTER THAN EVER BEFORE.

THIS OUTFIT is a little higher in price than those preceding it and is fully as great a bargain as any in our line. Each article which goes to make it up is carefully selected and is of the very best, considering the price of the outfit. Do not make the mistake of comparing this outfit with the outfits sold generally by dealers throughout the country at this price, as this is a regular $20.00 outfit, and cannot be purchased for less than that amount from any dealer in the country. Our buying advantage is so great that we are in a position to get the very lowest possible prices upon all classes of goods, and as we import all of these goods from Europe we are able to quote the actual importing price with but our one small percentage of profit added. Every bit of advantage we can gain either in buying or selling, we give to our customers in low prices. That is the reason why we can sell this $20.00 violin outfit at $9.75. The outfit contains one special high grade Guarnerius model violin, with a beautifully flamed two-piece back made of selected and well seasoned maple. The sides are made of maple and the top of especially selected Cremona spruce. The sound-holes are of the characteristic Guarnerius pattern and the purfling is perfectly and tastefully inlaid. The instrument is a deep, rich brown throughout, covered with a splendid transparent amber varnish and highly polished. The tailpiece, fingerboard and pegs are of solid ebony, and the scroll is accurately and gracefully cut. The freight will be nothing if you have the outfit sent to you with a freight shipment of other goods.

THIS OUTFIT INCLUDES:
One Guarnerius model violin.
One imitation snakewood bow, carved ivory frog.
One wood case, with lock, handle and spring clasps, flannel lined.
One piece of Bernardel rosin.
One book, "Howe's Original Violin School."
One extra set Acme professional strings.
One set of violin tuning pipes E, A, D, G.
One book, "Popular Duets, No. 1."
One fingerboard chart.

This outfit retails elsewhere at $20.00 to $23.00. **$9.75**
No. 12K314 Our new reduced price.................
Shipping weight, 10 pounds.

OUR PROFESSIONAL VIOLIN OUTFIT

THIS OUTFIT is regularly sold by dealers throughout the country for from $25.00 to $30.00. We have been furnishing this outfit for the past five years, and it has given the greatest satisfaction to every purchaser. WE ARE OFFERING this outfit in response to a demand from professionals who desire an outfit for general work and do not wish to pay the usual high prices asked by dealers generally for outfits of this grade.

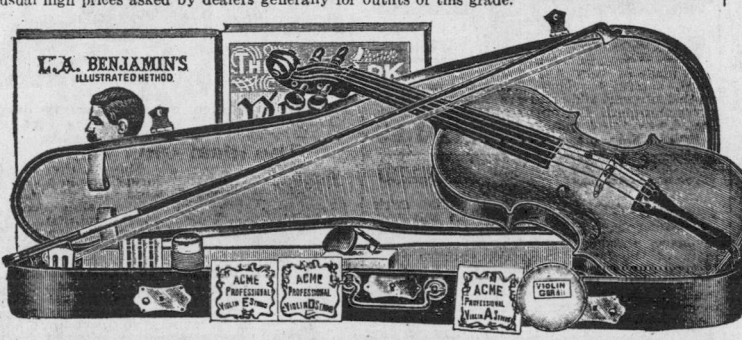

THE VIOLIN which we furnish with this outfit is a genuine Stradivarius model and is very elegant in appearance. It has two-piece back of highly flamed, well seasoned maple. The sides are made of a very good quality of maple, and the top is made of a carefully selected piece of close grain Cremona spruce. The tailpiece, fingerboard and pegs are made of solid ebony, the neck of curly maple, and the scroll is carefully and tastefully cut. The body of the instrument is finished in a very rich, brownish red color. It is the most elegant violin ever offered at the price. Express charges on this violin outfit will be very low, but if sent with a freight shipment of other goods it won't cost a penny extra for freight.

THIS OUTFIT INCLUDES:
One Stradivarius model violin as described.
One Tourte model bow, full German silver trimmings and best quality Brazil wood stick.
One solid wood case, exposition shape, full flannel lined, lock and spring clasps.
One piece of genuine Gustave Bernardel rosin.
One instruction book complete.
One extra set of Acme professional strings.
One latest patent chin rest.
One fingerboard chart.
One set of tuning pipes, E, A, D, G.
One violin mute, German silver.
One choice collection of violin music.

Other dealers ask $25.00 and $30.00 for inferior outfits. **$13.85**
No. 12K317 Our price.................
Shipping weight, 10 pounds.

OUR GENUINE HEBERLIN OUTFIT

FOR ONLY **$16.95** we are now offering this magnificent outfit. This reduction is the result of our favorable new agreement made possible by our large sales.

THIS OUTFIT INCLUDES:
One Heberlin violin as described.
One genuine snake wood Vuillaume model bow with handsomely carved genuine ivory frog, double pearl eye, German silver lining and ivory buttons.
One violin case, covered with a durable waterproof material, made in perfect imitation of alligator skin, full lined with velvet, leather handles, nickel link clasps and nickel spring lock.
One piece genuine Gustave Bernardel rosin.
One Henning's school for the violin, one of the most complete instruction books published. 101 pages printed on fine paper, bound in boards.
One mammoth collection of violin music with 350 selections.
One extra set of Acme professional strings.
One latest patent violin chin rest.
One violin mute.
One fingerboard chart.
One set tuning pipes, E, A, D, G.

THIS OUTFIT is high grade in every respect, and every article in it is fully guaranteed by us. The maker of the violin which we send with this outfit is among the best known violin makers of Europe and we have been able to arrange with him to furnish us with a limited number of these instruments, which we can supply in an outfit at this exceptionally low price. The violin is guaranteed to be perfect in every respect and is accompanied by a numbered certificate countersigned with the autograph of the maker. Should anyone attempt to sell you a Heberlin violin you can easily detect the fraud by asking for the certificate. We are showing herewith the facsimile of the certificate which goes with every one of these violins.

Certificate of Guarantee.

THE VIOLIN is a genuine Stradivarius model, has two-piece, highly flamed maple back, nicely figured maple sides and top of old, well seasoned Cremona silver spruce. The edges of the top, bottom and scroll are finished in natural wood, adding greatly to the instrument's appearance. The fingerboard and tailpiece are of solid ebony and the pegs of rosewood. The violin is double lined throughout and carefully blocked. The body is a very deep, rich wine red. An elegant instrument in every respect, and one which will please amateur and professional alike. Freight charges will be nothing if you order it shipped with other goods.

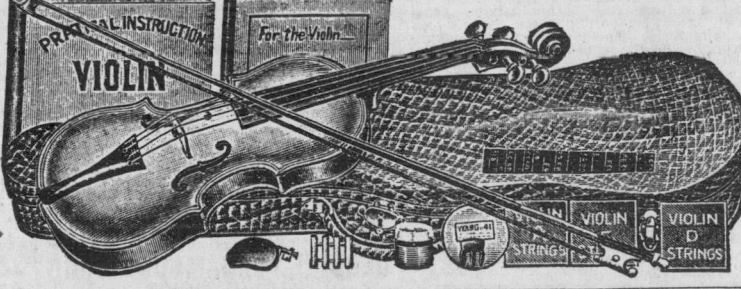

Outfit of the same merits cannot be procured from anyone but us for less than $32.00. **$16.95**
No. 12K321 Our price.................
Shipping weight, 12 pounds.

NEVER BEFORE have we offered this exceedingly high grade outfit at such a low price. Our wonderfully large sales enabled us to obtain concessions from the maker, and we give the benefit to our customers in the way of a reduction in price.

WE CANNOT BEGIN TO DESCRIBE the elegant and graceful appearance of this instrument, as it must be seen to be appreciated. The violin is of the well known Stradivarius model, perfect in copy and measurements. The back and sides are made of two pieces of very close grain, highly flamed maple, and the top is made of old Cremona silver spruce, thoroughly seasoned. The neck and scroll is made of curly maple, the scroll being very artistically and neatly cut, and is branded with the words "Chadwick's London Violin" on the back. This violin is golden yellow in color, and is covered with a transparent Cremona varnish, giving it a beautiful and brilliant luster. The fingerboard, tailpiece and pegs are made of ebony, nicely finished. This is undoubtedly the most elegant violin we furnish with any outfit in our catalogue.

OUR GENUINE CHADWICK (LONDON) OUTFIT

THIS IS AN EXTREMELY HIGH GRADE VIOLIN OUTFIT which we have made up for the use of professionals and high class amateurs, and which we are prepared to furnish at the present time at a price never before heard of. This is one of the very best outfits we have ever offered to our customers, and its sale up to the present time proves that it is destined to become as popular as any of our other high grade outfits. If you are looking for a violin outfit which will be strictly high class in every respect and in which every article will be of the very best, you will make no mistake in purchasing this. You will not find an outfit of this grade offered for sale by any of your local dealers. The violin which we furnish with this outfit is made under the direct supervision of Chadwick, the famous London violin maker, and we guarantee its beauty of appearance, the durability of its workmanship and the quality of its tone. As we are the sole agents for Chadwick violins, and as very few dealers carry an outfit of this grade (for which they are obliged to ask $45.00 to $50.00) we cannot ask you to compare it with other makes, but we ask you to do this: Purchase one of these outfits, give it a ten days' trial, and if you find that the workmanship, quality and tone is not worth $50.00 to you, return it to us, and we will refund your money together with all charges you may have paid.

THIS OUTFIT INCLUDES:
One Chadwick violin as described.
One Tourte model bow, full German silver trimmed, and of the very best quality Pernambuco wood.
One pulp case, covered throughout with a fine grade of leather, velvet lined and nickel trimmed. See illustration.
One genuine automatic telescope music stand.
One piece genuine Gustave Bernardel rosin.
One Mazas' Complete Violin Instructor.
Two volumes of Schradieck's Violin Studies.
One extra set of Verona Italian strings.
One latest pattern chin rest.
One set of tuning pipes, E, A, D, G.
One violin mute.
One fingerboard chart.

This outfit would retail at $45.00 and $50.00 if sold by other dealers. **$22.95**
No. 12K330 Former price, $23.45; our price now.
Shipping weight, 14 pounds.

VIOLIN CASES.

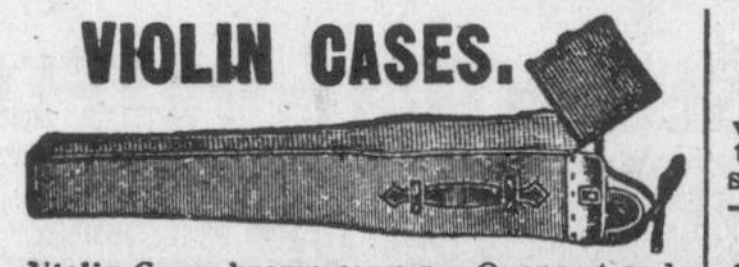

Violin Case, brown canvas. Opens at end. Leather bound edges, flannel lined, leather handle. Shipping weight, 7 pounds.
No. 12K4528 Price........... **68c**

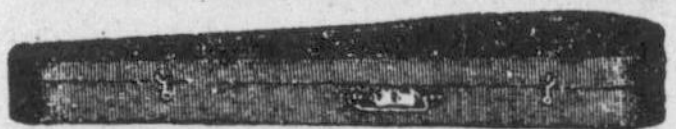

Violin Case, common shape, well made of wood and half lined with flannel, complete with handle, hooks and lock. Shipping weight, 8 pounds.
No. 12K4530 Price........... **98c**

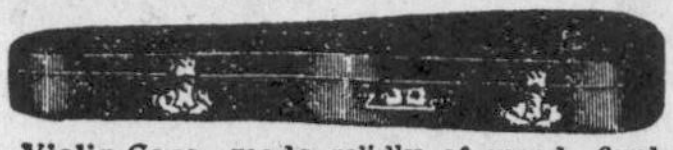

Violin Case, made solidly of wood, finely varnished black, exposition shape, full lined throughout with flannel; complete with lock, handle and spring clasps. Shipping weight, 8 pounds.
No. 12K4534 Price......... **$1.78**

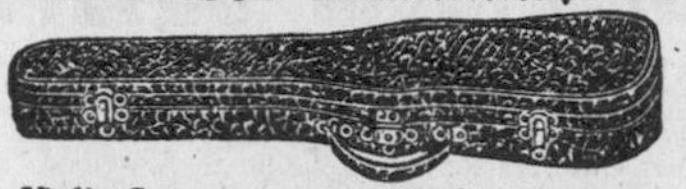

Violin Case, covered with durable waterproof material, made in perfect imitation alligator skin, full lined with velvet, leather handle, nickel link clasps and nickel spring lock. Shipping weight, 8 pounds.
No. 12K4535 Price........ **$3.25**

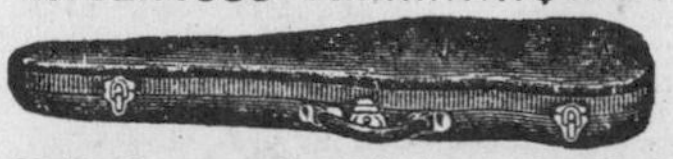

Violin Case, made of leather pulp, black finish, waterproof, fleece lined, has leather handle, nickel plated trimmings and patent spring lock. A very strong, durable and light case. Shipping weight, 8 pounds.
No. 12K4536 Price........ **$2.95**

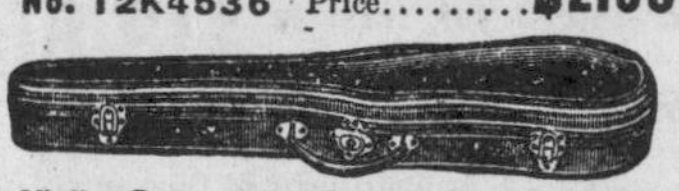

Violin Case, covered with black morocco leather, fitted with iron valance which renders case water and dustproof, and full lined with velvet, leather handle, nickel plated lock and hook hasps. **Especially good value.** Shipping weight, 8 pounds.
No. 12K4538 Price........ **$3.85**

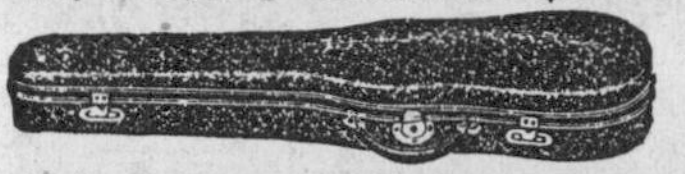

Violin Case, covered with heavy seal grain leather, lined throughout with silk plush, has hand sewed valance, leather handle, nickel plated burnished spring clasps, patent lock and trimmings. This is the best case manufactured. Retails regularly at $9.00 to $11.00. Comes in black only. Shipping weight, 8 pounds.
No. 12K4541 Price........ **$5.95**

VIOLIN BOWS.

If by mail, postage extra, each, 15 cents.

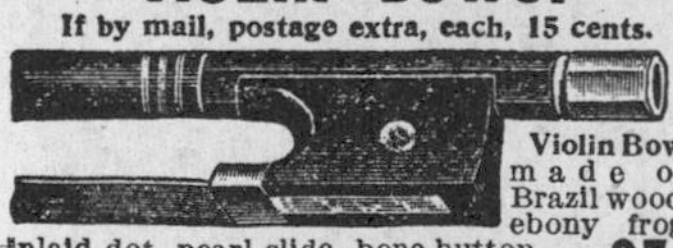

Violin Bow, made of Brazil wood, ebony frog, inlaid dot, pearl slide, bone button.
No. 12K4543 Price.......... **37c**

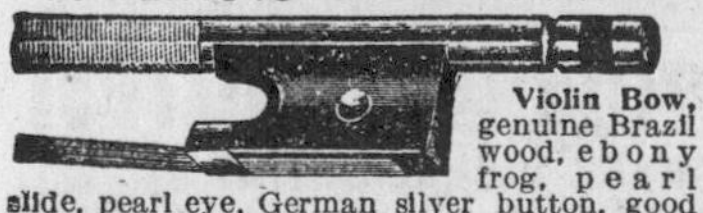

Violin Bow, genuine Brazil wood, ebony frog, pearl slide, pearl eye, German silver button, good quality bow hair.
No. 12K4546 Price........... **48c**

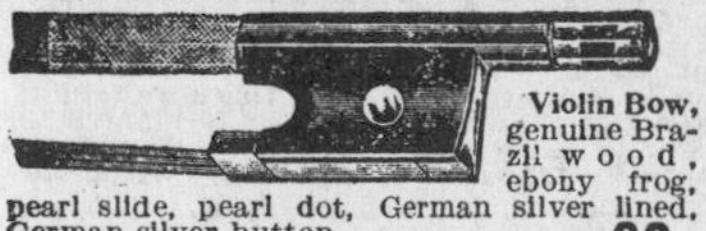

Violin Bow, genuine Brazil wood, ebony frog, pearl slide, pearl dot, German silver lined, German silver button.
No. 12K4547 Price.......... **69c**

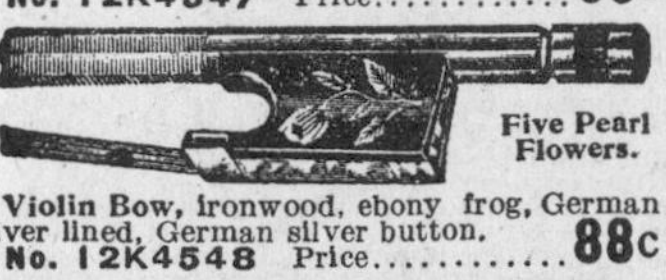

Five Pearl Flowers.

Violin Bow, ironwood, ebony frog, German silver lined, German silver button.
No. 12K4548 Price.......... **88c**

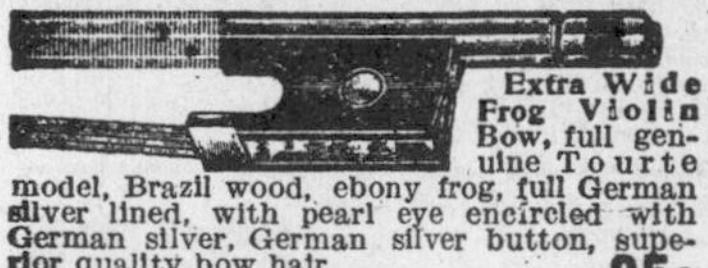

Extra Wide Frog Violin Bow, full genuine Tourte model, Brazil wood, ebony frog, full German silver lined, with pearl eye encircled with German silver, German silver button, superior quality bow hair.
No. 12K4550 Price.......... **95c**

VIOLIN SUPPLIES.

Our violin supplies and trimmings are selected from the best foreign and domestic workshops and are guaranteed to be of the highest quality considering the price we ask for them. On this page we quote only the articles most necessary to violinists. For additional supplies or trimmings, send for our Special Music Catalogue.

Our Curatoli Bow.

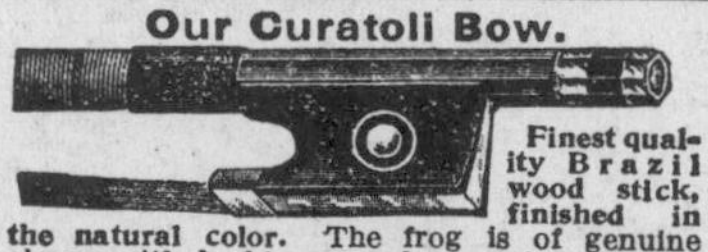

Finest quality Brazil wood stick, finished in the natural color. The frog is of genuine ebony, with double eye and pearl slide. Trimmings on the frog and button are of German silver, gold plated. It has fancy winding with leather grip. This is a very nicely balanced bow, and one that we can recommend without hesitancy.
No. 12K4551 Price.......... **$1.65**

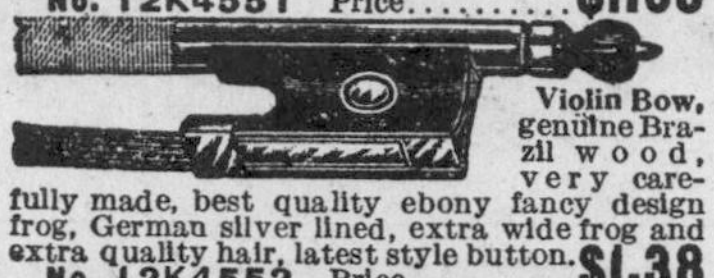

Violin Bow, genuine Brazil wood, very carefully made, best quality ebony fancy design frog, German silver lined, extra wide frog and extra quality hair, latest style button.
No. 12K4552 Price.......... **$1.38**

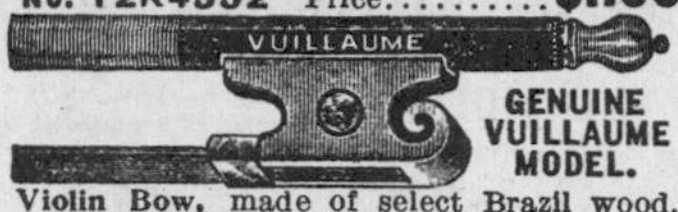

GENUINE VUILLAUME MODEL.

Violin Bow, made of select Brazil wood, imitation of snakewood. Has imitation ivory frog and button, double pearl eye, and is German silver lined. Best bow hair. An exceptional value.
No. 12K4553 Price.......... **$1.18**

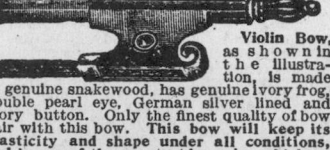

Violin Bow, as shown in the illustration, is made of genuine snakewood, has genuine ivory frog, double pearl eye, German silver lined and ivory button. Only the finest quality of bow hair with this bow. This bow will keep its elasticity and shape under all conditions, and is one of the greatest bargains which we offer in violin bows.
No. 12K4554 Price.......... **$2.35**

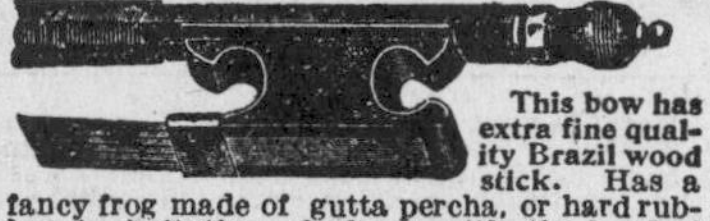

This bow has extra fine quality Brazil wood stick. Has a fancy frog made of gutta percha, or hard rubber in imitation of ebony with the head of Paganini carved on one side and a violin with music on the other. It has a genuine mother of pearl slide, German silver ring and lining, gutta percha thumbscrew ornamented with German silver. It has first quality bow hair and ivory tip. A very artistic and excellent bow in every respect.
No. 12K4555 Price.......... **$1.95**

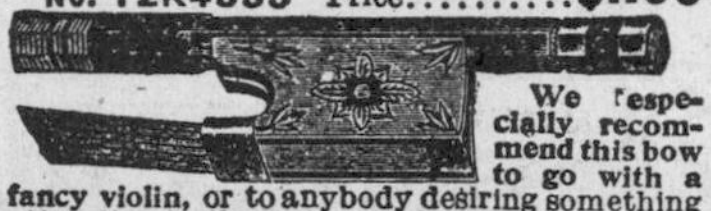

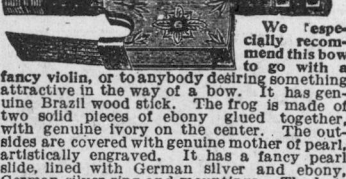

We especially recommend this bow to go with a fancy violin, or to anybody desiring something attractive in the way of a bow. It has genuine Brazil wood stick. The frog is made of two solid pieces of ebony glued together, with genuine ivory on the center. The outsides are covered with genuine mother of pearl, artistically engraved. It has a fancy pearl slide, lined with German silver and ebony, German silver ring and mountings. The button is made of ebony, octagon in shape, German silver mounted, inlaid with pearl, and with little German silver dots on each side. It has fancy windings with genuine leather grip, first quality bow hair and ivory tip.
No. 12K4556 Price........ **$2.45**

GENUINE PERNAMBUCO WOOD VIOLIN BOWS.

Important Facts About Our Genuine Pernambuco Wood Violin Bows.

It is a fact not generally understood by violinists that Pernambuco wood, which comes from Brazil in South America, has been for years considered the very best for making fine violin bows. This fact was discovered in the year 1780 by Francis Tourte, who became as celebrated as a bow maker as Stradivarius was as a maker of violins. The present form of violin bows is the one finally adopted by him after years of experiment and study, and his long life of research proved that Pernambuco wood is practically the only wood which possesses sufficient stiffness and lightness for the manufacture of fine violin bows. When it is understood that in many cases eight to ten tons of this wood will seldom produce more than a very few pieces with a grain sufficiently straight for the purpose, the value of the wood will become apparent. Each one of the bows offered below is made of genuine Pernambuco wood, carefully selected and skilfully made. These bows will retain their elasticity and shape under all circumstances. Each stick is thoroughly heated during the process of bending, and this is one of the requisites of a good violin bow.

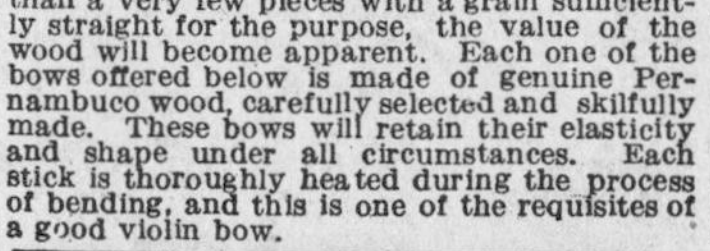

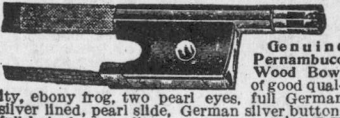

Genuine Pernambuco Wood Bow, of good quality, ebony frog, two pearl eyes, full German silver lined, pearl slide, German silver button, full hair, best quality.
No. 12K4557 Price.......... **$1.85**

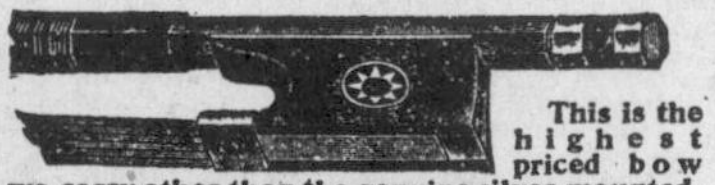

This is the highest priced bow we carry other than the genuine silver mounted. The stick is made of very good Pernambuco wood, has genuine ebony frog with pearl slide, and full German silver mountings. The frog is inlaid with a circle of German silver, containing a very fine star made of various colored pearl. It has ebony button, German silver mounted, inlaid with pearl, fancy silk winding with leather grip, extra fine quality Russian bow hair and ivory tip. We recommend this bow to be first class in every respect.
No. 12K4559 Price......... **$2.80**

Pure Silver Mounted Bows.

Genuine Pernambuco Wood Bow, round stick of extra well selected quality, very highly finished in a reddish color. It has fine ebony frog with pearl eyes and trimmed with solid silver, mother of pearl slide, and excellent quality bow hair. Silver winding, with leather grip.
No. 12K4560 Price........ **$2.85**

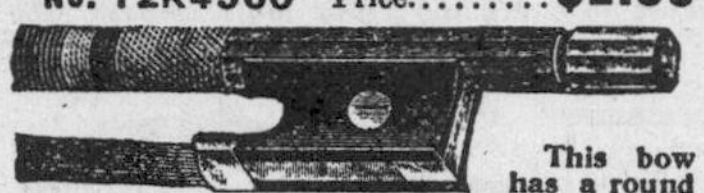

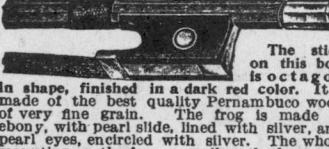

This bow has a round stick made of very fine quality Pernambuco wood, carefully selected, ebony frog, with mother of pearl slide and eye. Full genuine silver mounted. The entire button is of silver. Fitted with finest quality bow hair.
No. 12K4561 Price........ **$3.80**

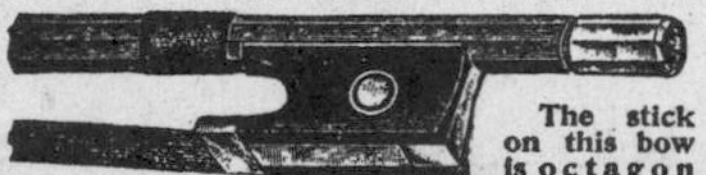

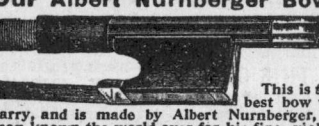

The stick on this bow is octagon in shape, finished in a dark red color. It is made of the best quality Pernambuco wood of very fine grain. The frog is made of ebony, with pearl slide, lined with silver, and pearl eyes, encircled with silver. The whole mounting on the frog, as well as the button is also of solid silver. It has fancy winding, with leather grip. Extra fine quality Russian bow hair. This bow retails regularly at $10.00.
No. 12K4562 Our price...... **$4.85**

Our Albert Nurnberger Bow.

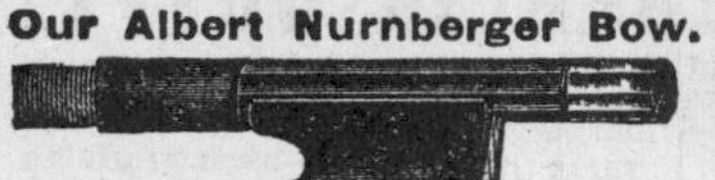

This is the best bow we carry, and is made by Albert Nurnberger, a man known the world over for his fine violin bows. The stick is round, of the very finest quality Pernambuco wood, finished in the natural color. Extreme care has been taken in selecting a firm and springy stick that will properly balance. The frog is made of the very finest quality ebony, with mother of pearl slide and German silver mounting. The button is of solid sterling silver. It has fancy winding, with leather grip. Finest quality Russian bow hair. This bow is very skilfully made and would ordinarily retail for $15.00 to $20.00.
No. 12K4565 Our price..... **$8.75**

Violin Patent Heads.

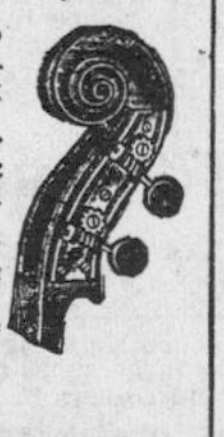

Made of solid brass, with handsome engraving on sides, black buttons.
No. 12K4570 Price, per set.......................... **23c**
As above, only nickel plated and polished.
No. 12K4572 Price, per set.......................... **28c**
If by mail, postage extra, 4 cents.
NOTE—Patent heads are made in full size only. Pins are set 1 3-16 inches distance from each other.

Violin Pegs.

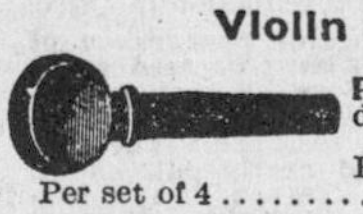

Solid Ebony Violin Peg, hollow shape, pearl dot in head.
No. 12K4582
Price, each........ **3c**
Per set of 4............................ **10c**

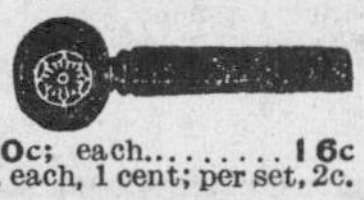

Solid Ebony Violin Peg, highly polished, handsomely inlaid with pearl.
No. 12K4589
Price, per set of 4, **60c**; each.......... **16c**
By mail, postage extra, each, 1 cent; per set, 2c.

The Champion Key.

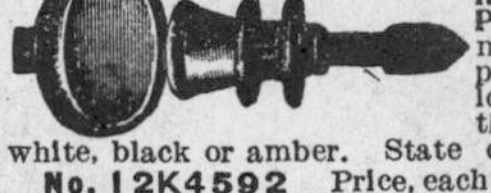

Genuine Celluloid Violin Peg, made of metal nickel plated, celluloid, polished thumb piece, white, black or amber. State color desired.
No. 12K4592 Price, each......... **20c**
Per set of 4.............................. **78c**
If by mail, postage extra, per set, 6 cents.

Violin Mute.

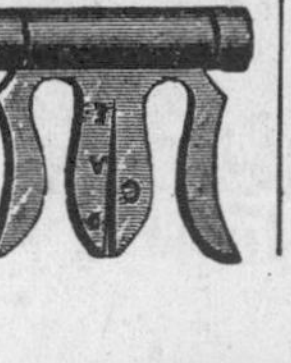

Violin Mute, as illustrated, is made of German silver and has tuning pipe A and string gauge.
No. 12K4636
Price.............. **15c**
If by mail, postage extra, 1 cent.

Becker Friction Pegs.

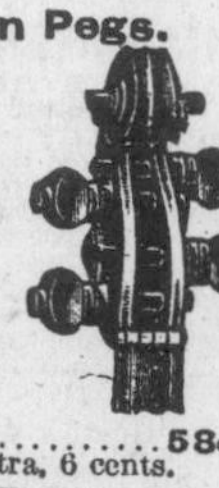

These pegs are an entirely new idea, and are so arranged that they do not injure the tone of the violin whatever. They are of great value to ladies and younger scholars especially, who find difficulty in turning up the pegs of their violin. The great advantage of these pegs is that they never slip and when the string is once tuned up to the pitch it remains there.
No. 12K4594
Price, per set.................... **58c**
If by mail, postage extra, 6 cents.

Violin Chin Rests.

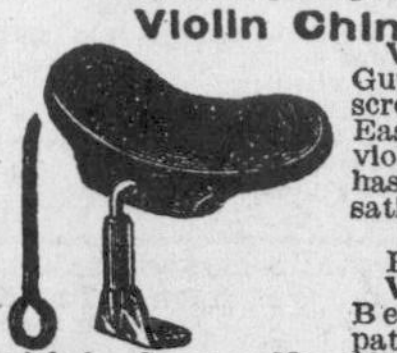

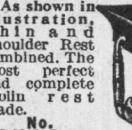

Violin Chin Rest, Gutta percha; single screw; double acting. Easily adjusted to any violin, a chin rest which has been found very satisfactory.
No. 12K4603
Price............**18c**
Violin Chin Rest, Becker's celebrated patent. Ebonite and nickel. Same as No. 12K4606, but without shoulder rest.
No. 12K4604 Price............. **26c**
If by mail, postage extra, 6 cents.

Chin and Shoulder Rest.

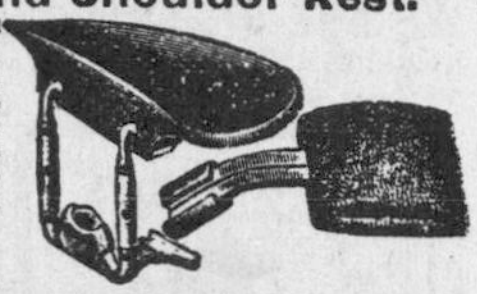

As shown in illustration, Chin and Shoulder Rest combined. The most perfect and complete violin rest made.
No. 12K4606
Price........................... **54c**
If by mail, postage extra, 6 cents.

The Ideal Chin Rest.

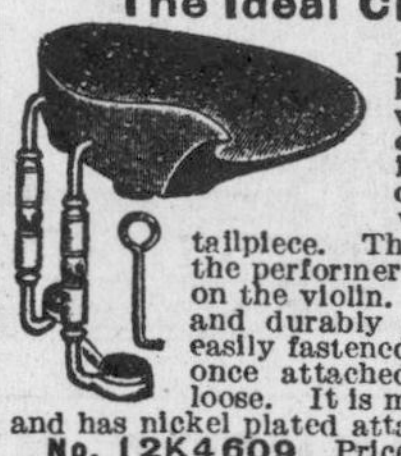

This is the very latest idea in a Chin Rest and one which will certainly please every violinist. It is made with a very deep cup and a horn which fits over the tailpiece. This gives the chin of the performer a very strong grip on the violin. It is very carefully and durably made, and is very easily fastened to the violin. When once attached it will not work loose. It is made of solid ebony, and has nickel plated attachments.
No. 12K4609 Price........... **58c**
If by mail, postage extra, 7 cents.

Violin Tailpieces.

If by mail, postage extra, each, 2 cents.

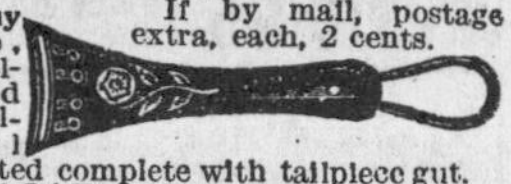

Solid Ebony Tailpiece, highly polished, inlaid with five colored pearl flowers. Fitted complete with tailpiece gut.
No. 12K4617 Price............ **23c**

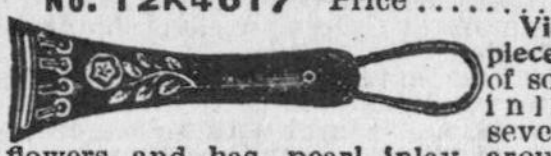

Violin Tailpiece; is made of solid ebony, inlaid with seven pearl flowers and has pearl inlay around string holes. Complete with tailpiece gut.
No. 12K4618 Price.............. **45c**

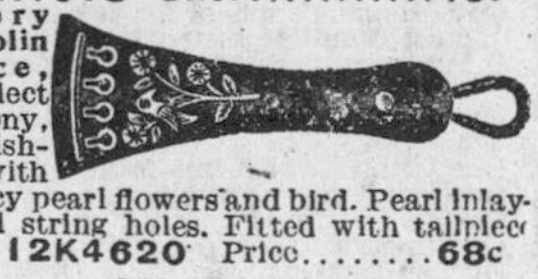

Our very finest **Violin Tailpiece**, made of selected solid ebony, highly polished, inlaid with eleven fancy pearl flowers and bird. Pearl inlaying around string holes. Fitted with tailpiece gut.
No. 12K4620 Price........ **68c**

Violin Bridges.

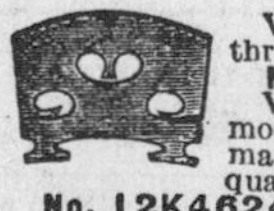

Violin Bridge, made of maple, three scrolls, good quality.
No. 12K4622 Price. **3c**
Violin Bridge, Vuillaume model, made of extra select maple, three scrolls, very fine quality.
No. 12K4624 Price.................. **8c**
Violin Bridge, made of selected maple. Superfine quality, three scrolls. Made for artists' use.
No. 12K4626 Price............. **14c**
If by mail, postage extra, each, 1 cent.

Violin Bow Rosin.

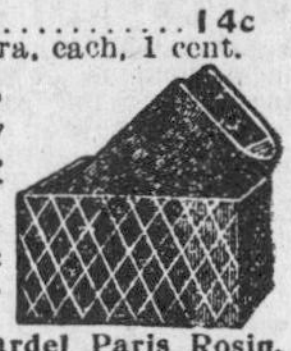

Large Sized Cakes Bow Rosin, in neat wood case, to be used without removing from case.
No. 12K4674
Price....................... **5c**
If by mail, postage extra, 2 cents.

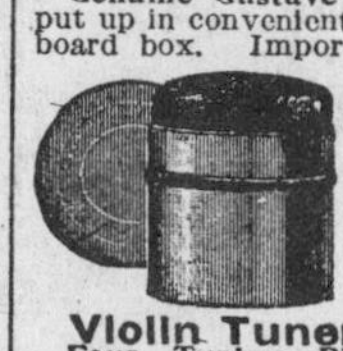

Genuine Gustave Bernardel Paris Rosin, put up in convenient form in fine round pasteboard box. Imported direct from France. Nothing better made.
No. 12K4678
Price.................. **13c**
Same rosin as No. 12K4678, put up in fine metal box.
No. 12K4679
Price.................. **19c**
If by mail, postage extra, 2 cents.

Violin Tuner.

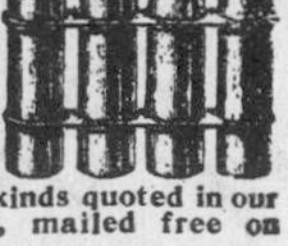

Four Tuning Pipes, E, A, D, G, combined, for tuning violin. Made of German silver and tuned to concert pitch.
No. 12K4690
Price.................... **16c**
Postage extra, 3 cents.
Violin trimmings of all kinds quoted in our Special Music Catalogue, mailed free on application.

$1.89 Guitars $28.15

AT $1.89 TO $28.15 WE OFFER THIS MATCHLESS LINE OF HIGH GRADE GUITARS

OUR LINE OF GUITARS is more than usually complete this year, and we are glad to be able to offer to our customers such especially wonderful values in this line. We wish to say that we could offer for sale guitars as low in price as $1.25, but the reputation which we have been so many years in building up is much too valuable for us to sacrifice for the sake of a few cents profit on the sale of such an instrument. Do not allow yourself to be misled by the apparently lower prices offered by others upon these instruments, because a careful examination and comparison will at once convince you that such instruments are not by any means what they appear to be, and that the guitar which we offer at $1.89 is superior in every way to those offered by others at a much higher price.

WE CONTROL the entire output of the largest and most modern factory in the United States and are, therefore, able to offer the instruments at the actual cost of production with only our small margin of profit added.

ALL OUR INSTRUMENTS are made by the most expert mechanics, according to the best principles of construction, are perfect in model and measurements, thoroughly braced and lined. The materials used are well seasoned and the best that money and experience can buy. We guarantee our instruments for one year against splitting or warping and will make good by exchange or refund any instrument that may show either of these defects. The finish of all our guitars, from the cheapest to the highest, is the very best consistent with the price charged.

AS A MATTER OF JUSTICE to yourself and to us, we ask you to carefully compare our instruments with those offered by other dealers. We fear no competition. We know we can give you a better made, better finished, and better looking and sounding guitar at a lower price than any other dealer.

THE DIMENSIONS OF THE DIFFERENT SIZES of guitars are as follows: STANDARD SIZE—Length of body, 18½ inches; total length, 37 inches; width, small end, 9⅛ inches; width, large end, 12¼ inches; depth, small end, 3⅛ inches; depth, large end, 3⅞ inches.

CONCERT SIZE—Length of body, 18¾ inches; total length, 37¾ inches; width, small end, 9⅝ inches; width, large end, 13¼ inches; depth, small end, 3⅛ inches; depth, large end, 3⅞ inches.

GRAND CONCERT SIZE—Length of body, 19 inches; total length, 38 inches; width, small end, 10 inches; width, large end, 14 inches; depth, small end, 3⅜ inches; depth, large end, 4 inches.

AUDITORIUM SIZE—Length of body, 19½ inches; total length, 38¾ inches; width, small end, 10⅜ inches; width, large end, 14⅞ inches; depth, small end, 3⅜ inches; depth, large end, 4 inches. **The auditorium size guitars are made to order only, and require from two to three weeks' time.**

WE SELL ALL OF THESE GUITARS upon the same liberal terms upon which we sell all other musical instruments, and give every purchaser ten days' trial.

WITH EACH GUITAR we send an extra set of strings, one Magic Capo d'Astro, one book of Guckert's chords and one lettered fingerboard chart. Shipping weight, 12 pounds.

$3.95 THE "VICTORIA" GUITAR OUTFIT

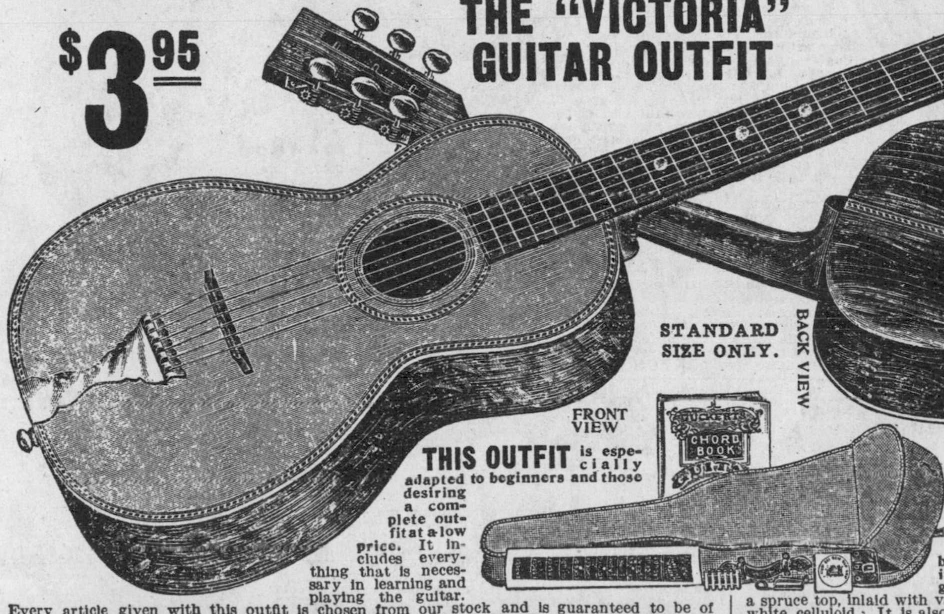

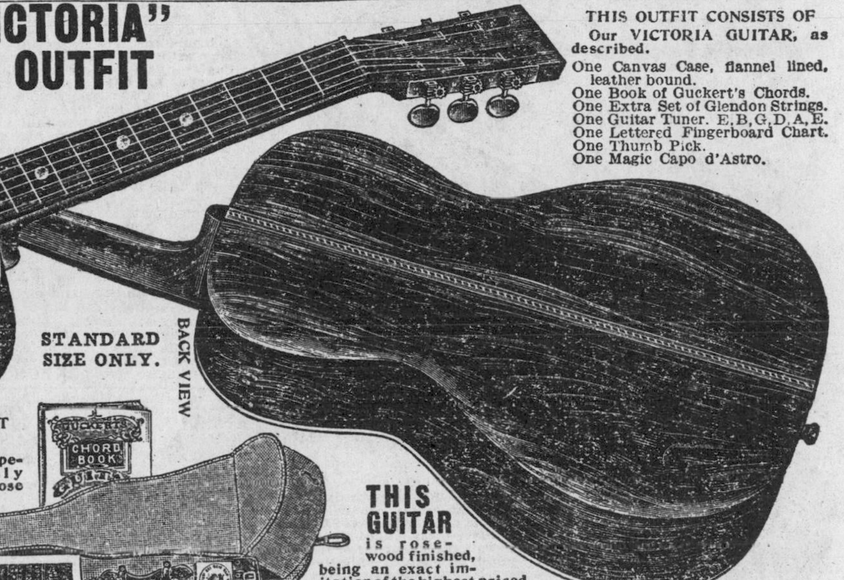

THIS OUTFIT CONSISTS OF

- Our VICTORIA GUITAR, as described.
- One Canvas Case, flannel lined, leather bound.
- One Book of Guckert's Chords.
- One Extra Set of Glendon Strings.
- One Guitar Tuner. E, B, G, D, A, E.
- One Lettered Fingerboard Chart.
- One Thumb Pick.
- One Magic Capo d'Astro.

STANDARD SIZE ONLY.

FRONT VIEW

THIS OUTFIT is especially adapted to beginners and those desiring a complete outfit at a low price. It includes everything that is necessary in learning and playing the guitar.

Every article given with this outfit is chosen from our stock and is guaranteed to be of the highest quality consistent with the price we ask for the outfit. By buying in large quantities, we are enabled to sell this outfit at the extremely low price quoted below. This outfit will more than favorably compare with those sold by other dealers at prices from $7.00 to $10.00. To prove this statement, purchase one of these outfits, compare the material and construction of it with dealers' outfits of the same grade, give it a thorough ten days' trial, and if not perfectly satisfactory, and you find that you have not saved from $3.00 to $5.00 on this outfit, return it to us, and we will refund every cent of your money together with all charges you may have paid.

THIS GUITAR is rosewood finished, being an exact imitation of the highest priced genuine rosewood. It has a spruce top, inlaid with variegated wood around the edge and soundhole, and bound with white celluloid. It is also inlaid down the back with a strip of different colored woods. The fingerboard is made of genuine rosewood with pearl position dots and raised frets. It has the best quality of American made patent head, nickel plated metal tailpiece and ebony bridge. **We furnish these guitars in standard size only.** Shipping weight, about 12 pounds.

No. 12K605 Our bargain price, standard size only **$3.95**
No. 12K606 We can also furnish this guitar in quarter sawed oak, exactly as described above, complete with outfit. Price ....

OUR $1.89 GUITAR

STANDARD SIZE ONLY.

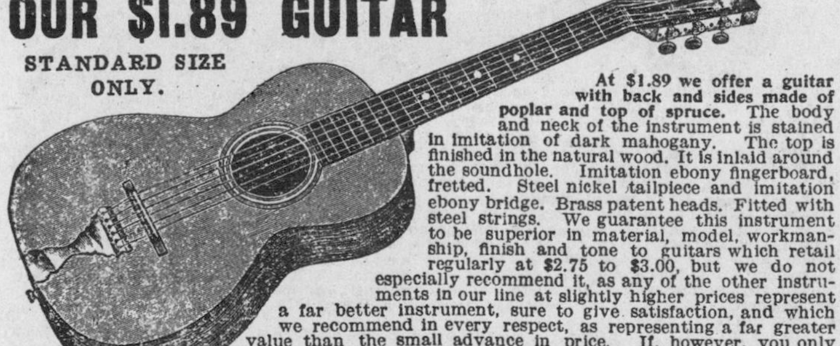

At $1.89 we offer a guitar with back and sides made of poplar and top of spruce. The body and neck of the instrument is stained in imitation of dark mahogany. The top is finished in the natural wood. It is inlaid around the soundhole. Imitation ebony fingerboard, fretted. Steel nickel tailpiece and imitation ebony bridge. Brass patent heads. Fitted with steel strings. We guarantee this instrument to be superior in material, model, workmanship, finish and tone to guitars which retail regularly at $2.75 to $3.00, but we do not especially recommend it, as any of the other instruments in our line at slightly higher prices represent a far better instrument, sure to give satisfaction, and which we recommend in every respect, as representing a far greater value than the small advance in price. If, however, you only care to invest $1.89 in an instrument, you can get the best grade of these instruments in the market by buying this guitar from us. **Standard size only.**

No. 12K590 Price.......... (Shipping weight, about 12 pounds.) **$1.89**

THE "SERENATA"

Standard Size Only.

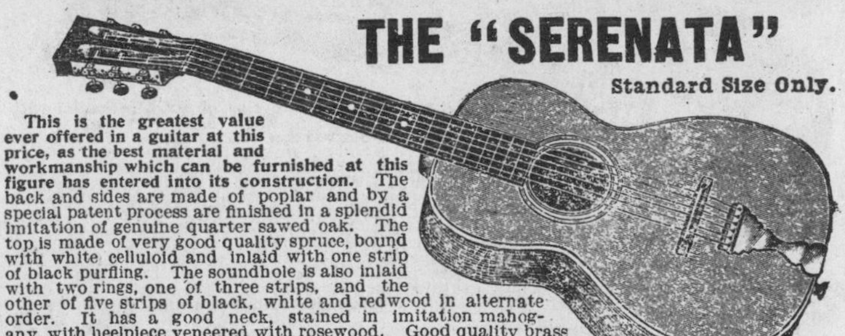

This is the greatest value ever offered in a guitar at this price, as the best material and workmanship which can be furnished at this figure has entered into its construction. The back and sides are made of poplar and by a special patent process are finished in a splendid imitation of genuine quarter sawed oak. The top is made of very good quality spruce, bound with white celluloid and inlaid with one strip of black purfling. The soundhole is also inlaid with two rings, one of three strips, and the other of five strips of black, white and redwood in alternate order. It has a good neck, stained in imitation mahogany, with heelpiece veneered with rosewood. Good quality brass patent heads with celluloid buttons. Hardwood fingerboard in imitation ebony, with raised frets and three pearl position dots. Nickel plated tailpiece. Ebonized bridge and steel strings. Is easy to play, accurately fretted and possesses a splendid tone. **Standard size only.**

No. 12K602 Price .... (Shipping weight, 12 pounds.) **$2.45**

THE "TOREADOR" $3.15 A SPECIAL VALUE

STANDARD SIZE ONLY.

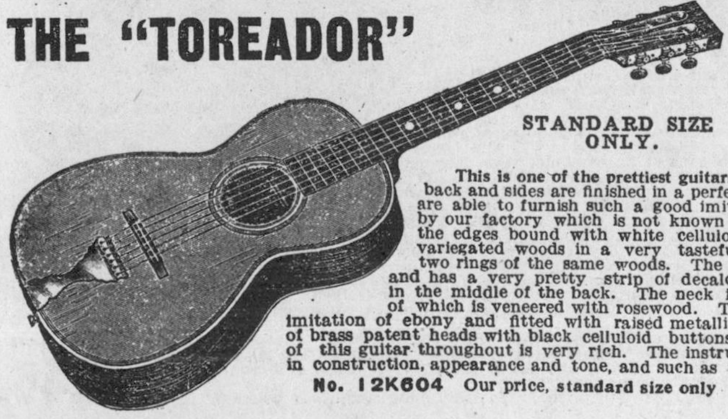
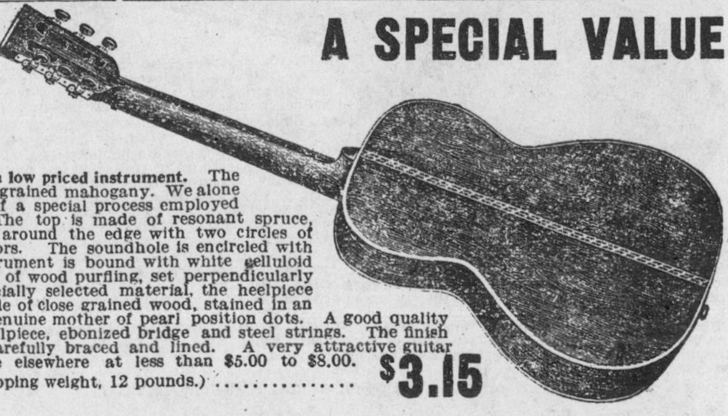

This is one of the prettiest guitars we have to offer in a low priced instrument. The back and sides are finished in a perfect imitation of finely grained mahogany. We alone are able to furnish such a good imitation on account of a special process employed by our factory which is not known to other makers. The top is made of resonant spruce, the edges bound with white celluloid. It is also inlaid around the edge with two circles of variegated woods in a very tasteful assortment of colors. The soundhole is encircled with two rings of the same woods. The back edge of the instrument is bound with white celluloid and has a very pretty strip of decalcomania, in imitation of wood purfling, set perpendicularly in the middle of the back. The neck is also made of especially selected material, the heelpiece of which is veneered with rosewood. The fingerboard is made of close grained wood, stained in an imitation of ebony and fitted with raised metallic frets. Has three genuine mother of pearl position dots. A good quality of brass patent heads with black celluloid buttons. Nickel plated tailpiece, ebonized bridge and steel strings. The finish of this guitar throughout is very rich. The instrument is also very carefully braced and lined. A very attractive guitar in construction, appearance and tone, and such as you could not procure elsewhere at less than $5.00 to $8.00.

No. 12K604 Our price, standard size only .... (Shipping weight, 12 pounds.) **$3.15**

$1⁹⁵ MANDOLINS $19⁸⁵

AT $1.95 TO $19.85 WE OFFER THIS SPLENDID LINE OF MANDOLINS.

GREATEST VALUE FOR THE MONEY is the keynote of these mandolin offerings. By exercising the greatest care in selection, we have gathered a line of mandolins that we believe to be unsurpassed in the country. We have not included in our offerings the cheapest possible instrument. We could offer mandolins as low as $1.25 and while they would be equal to those usually sold at $2.25 to $2.50 by most dealers, we do not believe they would give satisfaction to our customers, and therefore omit them from our line. When other dealers offer you a mandolin a little below our prices, don't fail to compare the instruments and you will immediately see that we offer you far greater value for your money.

OUR MANDOLINS are all made by expert mandolin makers, the highest paid mechanics in the country, and are all put up with the greatest care and on the most scientific principles and should not be compared with the cheap class of mandolins generally offered by other dealers. When you compare prices you should also compare the mandolins, and only then will you appreciate how far superior our instruments are to those offered by any other dealer, at any price.

OUR TERMS OF SHIPMENT are as liberal upon our mandolins as upon all of our other instruments. We allow any mandolin purchased from us to be tried and tested for ten days, and will receive it back and cheerfully refund the price paid, together with transportation charges, if it does not prove satisfactory.

WITH EACH ONE OF THESE MANDOLINS we give an extra set of strings, complete instruction book, a very nice pick and a fingerboard chart. Weight of mandolins, about 7 pounds.

THE CONQUEROR

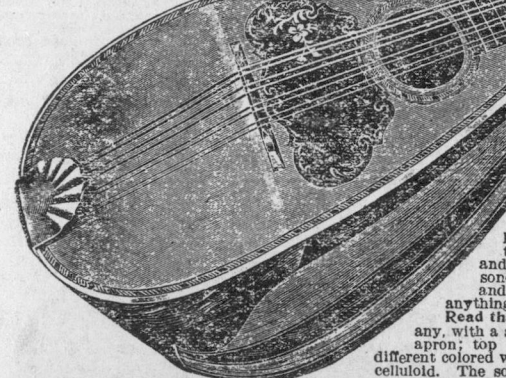

This is the greatest mandolin bargain ever offered by any concern in the world, and we would like to have you compare this instrument in every way with what is offered by other dealers, as we know it cannot be duplicated for any less than $8.00 to $10.00. Compare the number of ribs, the materials they are made of, the grain of the wood of the top, the beautiful and elaborate inlay we have around the edge of the top and around the soundhole, the rich and artistic guard plate we use, the neck, fingerboard, patent heads, in fact every part entering into its construction, the careful way it is built and braced, the splendid finish, and above all its powerful, sweet tone, due to thoroughly seasoned, carefully selected materials, perfect model, measurements and expert workmanship, and you will find it so far superior to anything you ever saw before that there will be no comparison whatever. **Read the description.** It has eleven ribs of alternate rosewood and mahogany, with a strip of white holly between each rib. It has solid rosewood cap and apron; top of resonant spruce, inlaid around the edge with a broad strip of different colored woods set in a very ornamental and elaborate design, and bound with white celluloid. The soundhole has a ring around it of the same ornamentation as the edge. The guard plate is very handsome and unique in design. Its body is black, surrounded by a Florentine ornament of a rich brick red and at the extreme left is inlaid a fine bouquet of flowers in woods of different colors. The neck is well cut and graceful, with the front of the head ebonized and polished. It is fitted with best quality brass American screw patent heads. The fingerboard is rosewood with raised, genuine German silver frets and real mother of pearl position dots. It has a nickel plated tailpiece and sleeve protector. It is coated with fine transparent varnish, which brings out the splendid and effective grain of the wood; very highly hand rubbed and polished. Solid rosewood bridge. **No. 12K706** Our price....(Shipping weight, 11 pounds.)............... **$3⁹⁵**

THE DEFIANCE.

This mandolin is not to be compared with the poorly constructed instruments usually sold at from $3.00 to $4.00, as it is superior in every respect. It has nine ribs of alternate maple and walnut, with strips of red inlaying between. The apron is made of imitation rosewood, the top of spruce, and has black fiber guard plate. Around the soundhole it is inlaid with four strips of different colored woods. The neck and head are made of imitation mahogany, fitted with solid brass patent heads. It has an ebonized fingerboard, inlaid with white pearl position dots and accurately fretted. The sleeve protector is of the nickel plated shell pattern with separate hooks for each string. **No. 12K701** Our price......(Shipping weight, 11 pounds)........... **$1.95**

THE COMPETITION.

Has nine ribs of alternate maple and mahogany, with thin strips of black wood between; imitation rosewood cap and apron and top of silver spruce inlaid around the edge with a strip of colored wood and bound with white celluloid. It has a ring of colored wood around the soundhole and an imitation tortoise shell guard plate with a very pretty floral design in colored woods. The neck is imitation mahogany; the patent heads of good quality brass; the fingerboard is rosewood with raised metallic frets and inlaid pearl position dots. It has a nickel plated sleeve protector and is very highly finished. **No. 12K703** Our price......(Shipping weight, 11 pounds)........... **$2.65**

THE SOVEREIGN.

Has thirteen ribs of solid rosewood with fine strips of white holly between. It has solid rosewood cap and apron, top of fine silver spruce, inlaid around the edge with a strip of different colored wood and bound with white celluloid. The soundhole is inlaid around with a ring of different colored wood to match the edges and bound with white celluloid. The guard plate is a beautiful imitation of tortoise shell and inlaid with a beautiful and classic design of various colored woods. The neck is of solid mahogany. The neck is veneered on the front with rosewood; the patent heads are of best American screw pattern; the fingerboard is solid ebony; has raised metallic frets and inlaid pearl position dots. The sleeve protector is highly nickel plated and the bridge is solid ebony. **No. 12K716** Our price........(Shipping weight, 11 pounds)....... **$4.95**

THE TROUBADOUR.

This Mandolin has fifteen ribs of solid rosewood with white holly inlaying between each rib. Cap of rosewood bound with celluloid. The top is of spruce, edges inlaid with strips of different colored woods and bound with white celluloid. The soundhole is bound with a strip of white celluloid and inlaid to match the edge of the top. It has a black guard plate with a design of flowers and vines in four colors. The neck is made of solid mahogany, and the front of the head is ebony veneered. The fingerboard is made of ebony bound with white celluloid, inlaid with four pearl position dots and is accurately fretted with rounded German silver frets. The instrument is fitted with the combination arm rest and sleeve protector. For purity, volume, sweetness of tone, workmanship and finish, this instrument will more than favorably compare with mandolins sold at from $12.00 to $15.00. **No. 12K720** Our price........(Shipping weight, 11 pounds)........ **$6.25**

THE IMPERIAL.

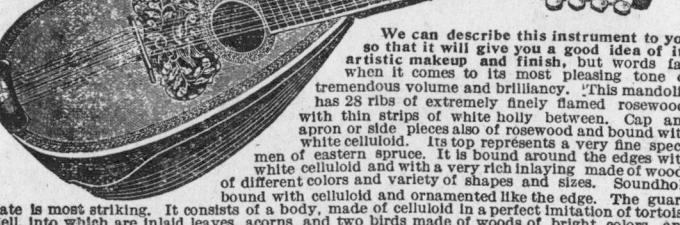

We can describe this instrument to you so that it will give you a good idea of its artistic makeup and finish, but words fail when it comes to its most pleasing tone of tremendous volume and brilliancy. This mandolin has 28 ribs of extremely finely flamed rosewood, with thin strips of white holly between. Cap and apron or side pieces also of rosewood and bound with white celluloid. Its top represents a very fine specimen of eastern spruce. It is bound around the edges with white celluloid and with a very rich inlaying made of woods of different colors and variety of shapes and sizes. Soundhole bound with celluloid and ornamented like the edge. The guard plate is most striking. It consists of a body, made of celluloid in a perfect imitation of tortoise shell, into which are inlaid leaves, acorns and two birds made of woods of bright colors and beautifully assembled. The neck is solid mahogany with the front of its head veneered with rosewood and inlaid with fine mother of pearl ornaments of the sunken covered pattern, nickel plated and polished, with white ivorite buttons. The fingerboard is of solid ebony, bound with celluloid, fretted and ornamented with position marks made of pearl. Tailpiece and arm rest combined, nickel plated and burnished. A splendid instrument in every respect and a bargain at double the price we ask. **No. 12K726** Our price....(Shipping weight, 11 pounds)........ **$9.95**

THE CARMENCITA.

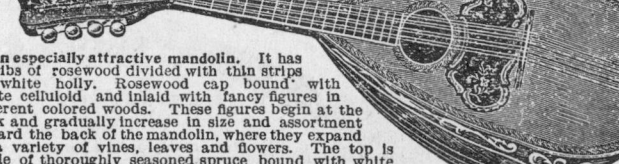

An especially attractive mandolin. It has 28 ribs of rosewood divided with thin strips of white holly. Rosewood cap bound with white celluloid and inlaid with fancy figures in different colored woods. These figures begin at the neck and gradually increase in size and assortment toward the back of the mandolin, where they expand in a variety of vines, leaves and flowers. The top is made of thoroughly seasoned spruce bound with white celluloid and inlaid with a very broad strip of purfling of different colored woods set in an artistic design. The soundhole is bound with white celluloid and ornamented with the same inlay as the edge of this instrument. The guard plate is of a strictly new design and is made of celluloid in imitation of tortoise shell surrounded by ornaments made of ebony, tulip wood and white celluloid in a Florentine design. The left corner of the guard plate is ornamented with a small bouquet of flowers inlaid in different colored woods. The neck is solid mahogany. The top of the head is veneered with ebony and decorated with inlaid ornaments of different colored woods. The fingerboard is of ebony, bound with celluloid and fitted with bone nut. It is very carefully fretted and has mother of pearl position dots. The patent heads are of the best quality covered style, nickel plated and highly polished. The tailpiece is a combination of a tailpiece and sleeve protector, is made of brass, nickel plated and highly burnished. **No. 12K753** Our price........(Shipping weight, 11 pounds)....... **$12.45**

THE 20TH CENTURY.

$5.95

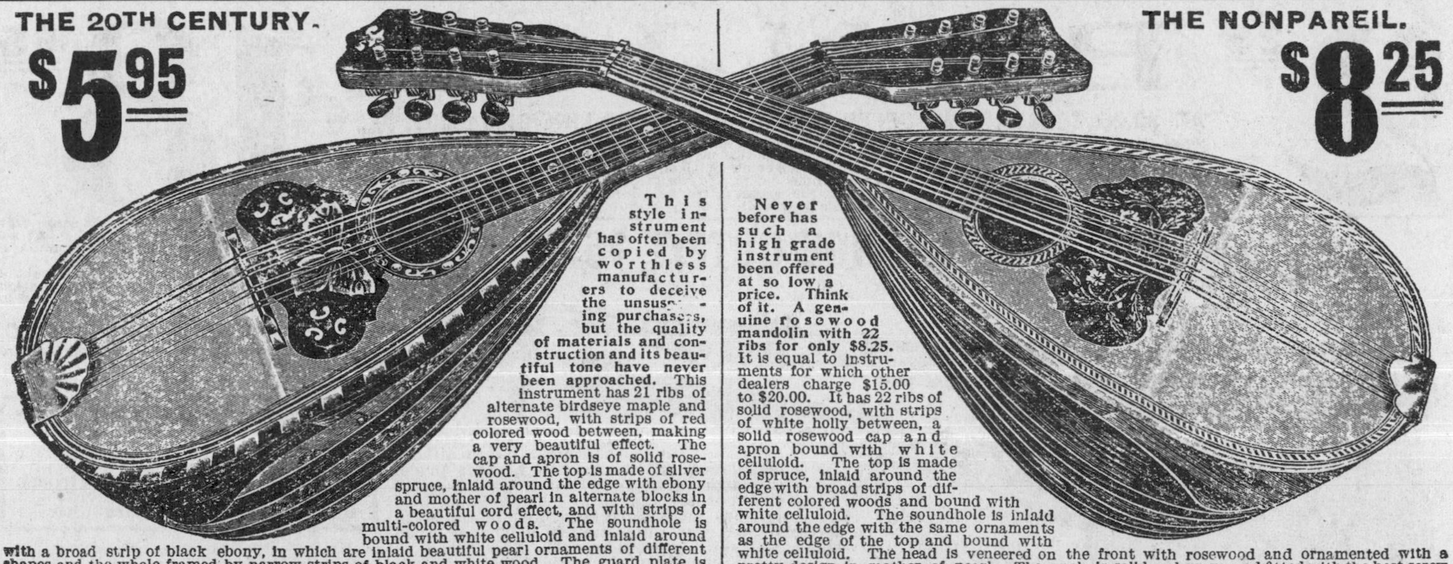

This style instrument has often been copied by worthless manufacturers to deceive the unsuspecting purchasers, but the quality of materials and construction and its beautiful tone have never been approached. This instrument has 21 ribs of alternate birdseye maple and rosewood, with strips of red colored wood between, making a very beautiful effect. The cap and apron is of solid rosewood. The top is made of silver spruce, inlaid around the edge with ebony and mother of pearl in alternate blocks in a beautiful cord effect, and with strips of multi-colored woods. The soundhole is bound with white celluloid and inlaid around with a broad strip of black ebony, in which are inlaid beautiful pearl ornaments of different shapes and the whole framed by narrow strips of black and white wood. The guard plate is in imitation tortoise shell inlaid with a splendid butterfly design in mother of pearl, in bright shades. The head is veneered on the front with rosewood, the neck is solid mahogany, and has the best screw pattern patent heads. The fingerboard is rosewood, with raised German silver frets and pearl position dots. The sleeve protector is nickel plated.

We guarantee this instrument to be of perfect construction, fine materials, accurate scale, and with a splendid tone of great volume, and with a fine piano finish. If your dealer were handling this grade of mandolin, he would be compelled to charge you $10.00 to $12.00 for same.

No. 12K718 Our price........(Shipping weight, 11 pounds)........ **$5.95**

THE NONPAREIL.

$8.25

Never before has such a high grade instrument been offered at so low a price. Think of it. A genuine rosewood mandolin with 22 ribs for only $8.25. It is equal to instruments for which other dealers charge $15.00 to $20.00. It has 22 ribs of solid rosewood, with strips of white holly between, a solid rosewood cap and apron bound with white celluloid. The top is made of spruce, inlaid around the edge with broad strips of different colored woods and bound with white celluloid. The soundhole is inlaid around the edge with the same ornaments as the edge of the top and bound with white celluloid. The head is veneered on the front with rosewood and ornamented with a pretty design in mother of pearl. The neck is solid mahogany and fitted with the best screw patent heads, highly nickel plated and burnished. The fingerboard is solid ebony, with raised metallic frets, ornamented with designs in mother of pearl and bound with white celluloid. The binding makes the performing on the instrument extremely easy as the frets do not protrude over the width of the fingerboard and do not interfere with the quick sliding of the hand from one position to another, besides adding immensely to the attractiveness of the instrument. It has a very handsome black guard plate inlaid with a very elaborate design of vines and flowers, made of woods of different colors, beautifully shaded. The sleeve protector is separable and highly nickel plated. The tone is very rich and powerful, every string even and ringing.

No. 12K724 Price ......(Shipping weight, about 12 pounds)........ **$8.25**

THE GENOA.

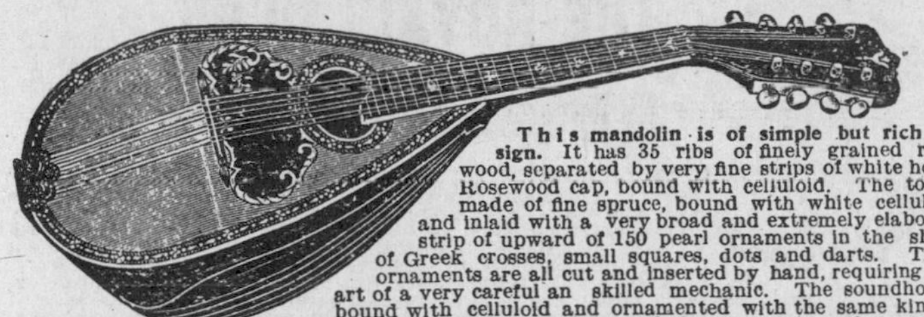

This mandolin is of simple but rich design. It has 35 ribs of finely grained rosewood, separated by very fine strips of white holly. Rosewood cap, bound with celluloid. The top is made of fine spruce, bound with white celluloid, and inlaid with a very broad and extremely elaborate strip of upward of 150 pearl ornaments in the shape of Greek crosses, small squares, dots and darts. These ornaments are all cut and inserted by hand, requiring the art of a very careful an skilled mechanic. The soundhole is bound with celluloid and ornamented with the same kind of purfling as the edge. The guard plate is an innovation, and we are proud to say that we are the first to offer it to the public. It is made of celluloid in imitation of tortoise shell, and is surrounded by pearl ornaments of French design. In the left corner is a fine ornament in mother of pearl, consisting of flowers, leaves and vines. The neck is made of mahogany, veneered on the back of the head with rosewood and on the front with ebony. The front is ornamented with a design in mother of pearl. The fingerboard is of the new extension pattern, which allows the performer three more notes on the scale than the ordinary mandolin. It is made of ebony, bound with white celluloid, carefully fretted, and inlaid with fine ornaments of pearl as position dots. Patent heads are of the covered style, engraved, nickel plated, with white celluloid buttons. The tone produced by this instrument is powerful and rich. Good clear high notes and powerfully deep bass. We furnish with this instrument, besides the usual outfit, a fine canvas flannel lined and leather bound case.

No. 12K757 Price.........(Shipping weight, 11 pounds).......... **$16.45**

THE CAMPANELLO.

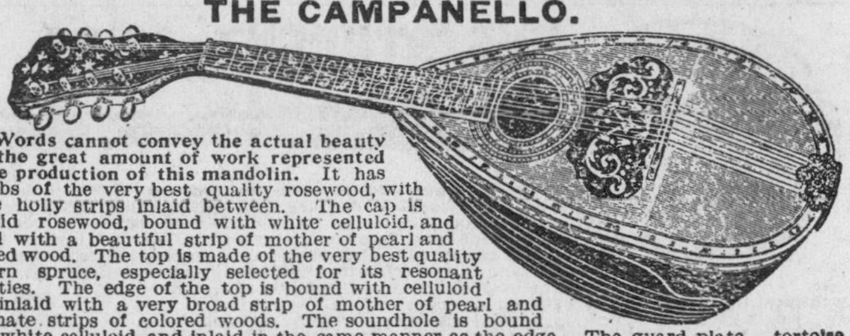

Words cannot convey the actual beauty and the great amount of work represented in the production of this mandolin. It has 44 ribs of the very best quality rosewood, with white holly strips inlaid between. The cap is of solid rosewood, bound with white celluloid, and inlaid with a beautiful strip of mother of pearl and colored wood. The top is made of the very best quality eastern spruce, especially selected for its resonant qualities. The edge of the top is bound with celluloid and inlaid with a very broad strip of mother of pearl and alternate strips of colored woods. The soundhole is bound with white celluloid and inlaid in the same manner as the edge. The guard plate tortoise shell, inlaid with a very tasteful design in mother of pearl. The neck is made of mahogany, elaborately carved. The head of the neck, front and back, is veneered with three layers of rosewood, white holly and ebony. The front of the head is inlaid with stars, crescents, diamonds, and flower shaped designs in mother of pearl. The fingerboard is made of solid ebony, bound with white celluloid, inlaid with a beautiful design in metal and mother of pearl, representing a flowerpot, vines, leaves and lilies and has raised metallic frets, carefully set and tested so that no muffled sound will be produced by the strings touching the frets when performing. Patent heads are of the best covered style, artistically engraved, gold plated and burnished, fitted with white celluloid buttons in a perfect imitation of ivory. The tailpiece is engraved to correspond with the patent heads, gold plated and polished. This is a regular $45.00 instrument. We furnish this instrument with a canvas case, leather bound and flannel lined.

No. 12K764 Price.......(Shipping weight, 11 pounds)........... **$19.85**

MANDOLINETTOS.

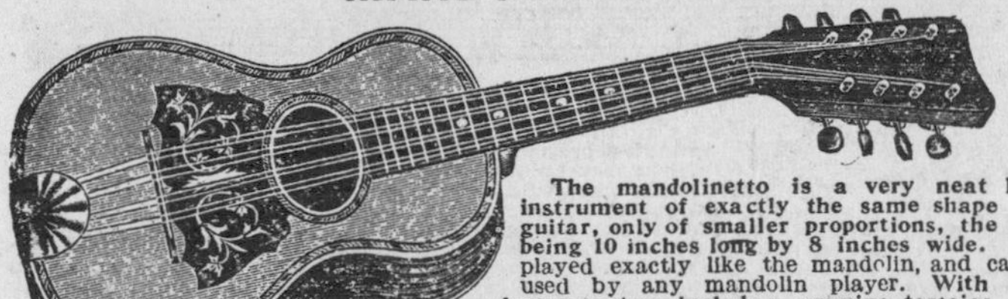

The mandolinetto is a very neat little instrument of exactly the same shape as a guitar, only of smaller proportions, the body being 10 inches long by 8 inches wide. It is played exactly like the mandolin, and can be used by any mandolin player. **With each instrument we include a genuine tortoise shell pick, one complete instruction book, and one leather bound, flannel lined case.** Shipping weight of these instruments about 7 pounds.

No. 12K913 **This instrument is very fine, being made of genuine rosewood.** The top is made of Eastern spruce, bound with white celluloid and inlaid with a broad strip of purfling in alternate colors and set in a very artistic design. The soundhole is also bound with white celluloid and inlaid around with a broad ring of the same inlay as the top. The guard plate is of celluloid, in a perfect imitation of tortoise shell, and inlaid with a very beautiful design of different colored woods. The back edge of this instrument is also bound with celluloid, and down the center of the back is inlaid a fine strip of purfling of the same variety as the top. The neck is made of genuine mahogany. The front of the head is veneered with rosewood. Patent heads are of the finest quality brass, screw pattern, with black celluloid buttons. The fingerboard is made of genuine ebony and very carefully fretted with German silver frets. It has genuine mother of pearl position dots. Tailpiece is highly nickel plated and polished. The finish of this instrument is magnificent.

No. 12K913 Price......... (Shipping weight, 12 pounds)......... **$6.25**

No. 12K911 **The body of this instrument is made of maple, finished by a patent process in a perfect imitation of quarter sawed oak.** The top is made of spruce, bound with white celluloid and inlaid around the edge and soundhole with strips of vario-colored wood purfling. It has a black celluloid guard plate. The neck is finished in imitation mahogany, with brass patent heads and black celluloid buttons. Fingerboard is made of hard wood in imitation of ebony, and is very carefully fretted. It has four pearl position dots. Nickel plated tailpiece and sleeve protector.

No. 12K911 Price.......... (Shipping weight, 12 pounds)......... **$3.35**

BANJO MANDOLINS.

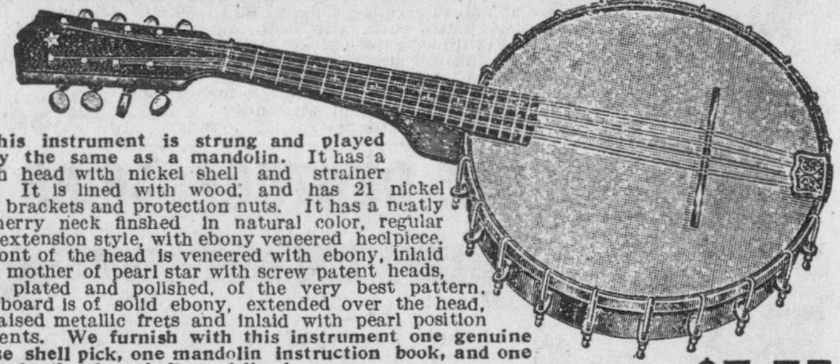

This instrument is strung and played exactly the same as a mandolin. It has a 10-inch head with nickel shell and strainer hoop. It is lined with wood, and has 21 nickel plated brackets and protection nuts. It has a neatly cut cherry neck finshed in natural color, regular banjo extension style, with ebony veneered heelpiece. The front of the head is veneered with ebony, inlaid with a mother of pearl star with screw patent heads, nickel plated and polished, of the very best pattern. Fingerboard is of solid ebony, extended over the head, with raised metallic frets and inlaid with pearl position ornaments. **We furnish with this instrument one genuine tortoise shell pick, one mandolin instruction book, and one canvas, leather bound, flannel lined case.**

No. 12K916½ Price ....(Shipping weight, 12 pounds)......... **$7.75**

Same as No. 12K916½ but with 7-inch shell and 17 brackets. We furnish this instrument with exactly the same outfit as No. 12K916½.

No. 12K916 Price..........(Shipping weight, 12 pounds)............... **$6.95**

OUR $7.85 ACME PROFESSIONAL BANJORINE.

Banjorines are now used very extensively by all the best and up to date banjo clubs and orchestras. It is tuned one-fourth higher than the regular instrument, and takes the leading part, same as the flute or oboe in an orchestra. The cadenzas and embellishments are taken up by this instrument. Is 11 inches in diameter, has nickel plated rim with spun wire edge, 24 brackets, heavy band or strainer hoop, and best quality calfskin head; 12-inch neck, highly polished, solid ebony extension fingerboard, 20 raised frets, rosewood veneered head inlaid with pearl, ebony pegs, six inlaid position dots, nickel plated tailpiece, and fine canvas case, leather bound and flannel lined. **A strictly high grade instrument.**

No. 12K914 Price........(Shipping weight, 15 pounds.).................. **$7.85**

MANDOLIN SUPPLIES.

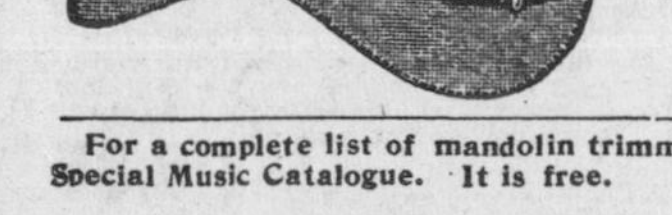

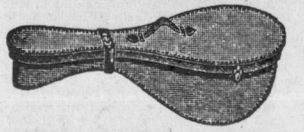

Mandolin Case, brown canvas with leather bound edges, flannel lined, handle and patent fastenings. Shipping weight, 5 pounds.

No. 12K5460 Price **65c**

For a complete list of mandolin trimmings and supplies, send for our Special Music Catalogue. It is free.

The Latest Invention in Mandolin Cases.

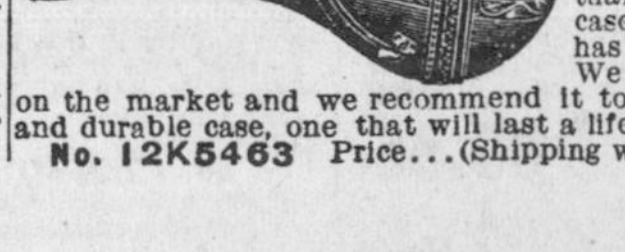

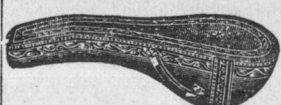

Mandolin Case, made of a secret composition of leather pulp, covered with black morocco leather, making it stronger, lighter and more graceful in appearance than the sole leather case. This case is flannel lined inside and it has a hand sewed leather handle. We are the first to place this case on the market and we recommend it to those desiring a handsome and durable case, one that will last a lifetime.

No. 12K5463 Price...(Shipping weight, 6 pounds) .. **$3.85**

Mandolin Picks.

If by mail, postage extra, each, 1 cent.

No. 12K5480 **Genuine Tortoise Shell.** Price...........2c

No. 12K5482 **Same, extra large, extra quality.** Price.....4c

Celluloid Mandolin Picks, in fine imitation tortoise shell. Very pliable and well adapted for tremolo.

No. 12K5485

Price, per dozen............ **10c**

If by mail, postage extra, per doz. 2c.

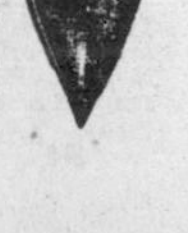

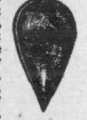

$2²⁵ BANJOS $18⁹⁵

AT $2.25 TO $18.95 WE OFFER THIS INCOMPARABLE LINE OF BANJOS.

We want you to make a careful comparison between the instruments which we are offering in this line and those offered by any other house. Such a comparison will convince you at once that no dealer can sell banjos which are in any way equal to ours at anywhere near the price we are quoting. We could sell banjos at much lower prices than we are offering, but they could not possibly prove satisfactory to our customers, and they would prove very poor advertisements for our line of musical goods. From the highest to the lowest priced banjos in this line each one contains the very best workmanship and material which it is possible to put into it at the price.

OUR CHALLENGE OUTFIT $5.75

SEND US YOUR ORDER, enclose our price and we will send the banjo promptly; give it ten days' trial and if you are not perfectly satisfied in every way, return the instrument to us and we will promptly return your money and transportation charges. We guarantee complete satisfaction in every transaction.

WE FURNISH, FREE, WITH EACH BANJO one set of Glendon strings, one instruction book of Guckert's chords, and one lettered fingerboard chart.

THIS OUTFIT CONSISTS OF THE FOLLOWING:
One Challenge Banjo.
One Extra Set of Glendon Strings.
One Book of Guckert's Chords
One Lettered Fingerboard Chart.

This is one of the best and most complete banjo outfits ever placed on the market at this price. Every article that goes to make up this outfit is the very best that possibly can be procured for the price asked. The banjo has an 11-inch head, with nickel shell, with both edges spun over wire, strainer hoop and wood lined. It has thirty-nine nickel plated hexagon brackets, a well made neck, finished in mahogany. The front of the head is veneered with wood finished in ebony; the fingerboard is ebony, fitted with raised metallic frets and inlaid pearl position dots. It is a very acceptable instrument and cannot be duplicated anywhere in the country for less than double the price we are asking. We would be glad to have you order this banjo and outfit and compare it with anything your dealer has to offer at from $10.00 to $12.00, and if you do not find it to be superior in every respect it can be returned to us and we will cheerfully refund your money. **Remember** that this outfit goes to you strictly on trial and if you are not fully satisfied that it is a great bargain in every respect we will gladly receive it back and refund every cent you have paid, including transportation charges. Shipping weight, about 12 pounds.

This splendid outfit could not be purchased elsewhere for less than $12.00.
No. 12K822   Price **$5.75**

THE STUDENT, $2.25

We would like to have you compare this banjo with any ordinarily sold by dealers throughout the country for $5.00 and $6.00. It has a 10-inch nickel plated shell, wood lined, with the lower edge spun over wire. The neck is made in imitation mahogany, and ebonized fingerboard fitted with raised German silver frets with three pearl position dots. It has eleven brackets, and is carefully and thoroughly made. It is a musical instrument in every sense of the word.
No. 12K810   Price ....(Shipping weight, 12 pounds) **$3.35**
This banjo is similar to the above, but is fitted with only nine brackets, has no position dots, and the edges of this instrument are not spun on wire, and while not as carefully finished, is superior to any on the market at $3.00 to $4.00.
No. 12K808   Price..........(Shipping weight, 12 pounds) **$2.25**

THE STAR, $4.35

This banjo is generally sold throughout the country at prices ranging from $7.00 to $9.00. It has an 11-inch nickel plated shell, with both edges spun on steel wire, and is fitted with seventeen nickel plated hexagon brackets. The neck and head are neatly cut and finished in mahogany color, and the head covered with a layer of ebony veneer. The fingerboard is made of ebony, one-eighth of an inch thick, nineteen inches long, fitted with twenty-two German silver frets and four pearl position dots. Calfskin head.
No. 12K813   Price ....(Shipping weight, 12 pounds) **$4.35**

THE CENTURY, $6.85

This is a regular $12.00 banjo and is sold at that price generally throughout the country. It has an 11-inch brass shell with both edges spun over wire and heavily nickel plated and polished, nickel strainer hoop of special design, preventing the hooks from cutting through the head. The shell is wood lined. It has an extension removable neck with metal truss and is tightened by two ebony keys. It has twenty-five hexagon brackets and genuine ebony fingerboard fitted with raised metallic frets and diamond and flower shaped position dots inlaid in mother of pearl. The front of the head is ebony veneered and fitted with ebony pegs. This instrument is fitted with special nickel plated patent tailpiece. Shipping weight, about 12 pounds.
No. 12K824   Price **$6.85**

THE GEM, $9.65

This banjo has an 11-inch heavy nickel shell with carefully wired spun edges and cherrywood lining. It has thirty-one nickel plated special pattern brackets with protection nuts and center grooved straining hoop which prevents the hooks of the brackets from cutting through the head. The head of the neck is veneered with ebony and inlaid with star, crescent, and flower shaped designs in mother of pearl. It has white celluloid patent keys and genuine ebony fingerboard with square and diamond shaped inlaid pearl position dots. The very best calfskin head is used on this instrument and in all our high grade ones. WE CAN RECOMMEND THIS BANJO as being first class in every respect and an instrument which will give the best of satisfaction under all conditions. Other dealers charge $18.00 to $20.00 for the same grade.
No. 12K858   Price ....(Shipping weight, 12 pounds) **$9.65**

THE ROYAL, $11.95

This banjo is a strictly professional instrument and one which we can highly recommend to all who desire a banjo for concert purposes. It has an 11-inch heavy nickel shell with both edges spun over wire, the entire metal parts of instrument highly burnished. It has nickel strainer hoop, and is cherry-wood lined. It has thirty-one nickel plated special artistic design brackets with protection nuts. The head is veneered on the front, fitted with patented friction pegs with celluloid buttons and is ornamented on the front with star, crescent, diamond and flower shaped figures inlaid in mother of pearl. The fingerboard is of solid ebony with raised metallic frets and star and square shaped position dots inlaid in mother of pearl. The neck is mahogany, nicely hand carved and veneered with ebony on the heel, a metal stay piece and ebony wedges. This is a very pleasing instrument, both from the standpoint of tone and general appearance. Shipping weight, about 12 pounds.
No. 12K862   Price **$11.95**

THE PEARL, $15.75

This is the first time a pearl fingerboard banjo of this grade has been offered for less than $25.00. It has an 11-inch heavily nickel plated shell, with both edges spun on heavy steel wire, and is lined with cherry, finished in mahogany. It is fitted with thirty-one nickel plated special pattern brackets, with closed ball and nuts, which serve as a protection for the sleeve. The straining hoop is of the improved center grooved pattern, five-eighths inches wide, artistically chased, giving it a rich appearance. The brackets fit into this center groove, which prevents them from cutting the head. The neck is of the extension pattern, made of cherry, and finished in San Domingo mahogany, it being fitted with ebony veneered heel and head, the latter inlaid with a beautiful design in mother of pearl. The real beauty of this instrument lies in the mother of pearl fingerboard, which is nineteen inches long and fitted with twenty-two raised German silver frets. The distance between each fret is inlaid with a block of white mother of pearl, bound with a one-eighth inch strip of ebony, making a very striking and beautiful contrast. The positions are marked by eight dark green pearl ornaments of various designs. This banjo is fitted with the best quality calfskin head. Not only is this a beautiful instrument, but it has a tone which is both sweet, powerful and responsive. Shipping weight, about 12 pounds. No. 12K864   Price **$15.75**

THE GLEE CLUB, $18.95

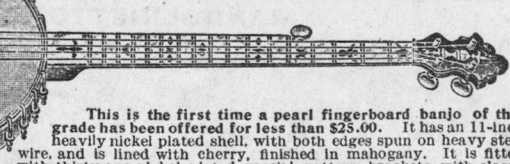

This banjo is artistic in every respect. It has an 11-inch head, heavy German silver shell, nickeled and burnished, both edges of which are wired and spun, lined with red stained birds-eye maple. Nickel plated grooved straining hoop. It has thirty-one standard pattern brackets with protection nuts. The head and fingerboard are veneered with three layers of different colored wood, capped with a heavy layer of genuine ebony. The front of the head is profusely inlaid with star, crescent and flower shaped figures in mother of pearl. The fingerboard is fitted with raised German silver frets and ornamented with beautiful designs inlaid in white metal and mother of pearl, representing a flowerpot, vines, leaves and lilies running the full length of the fingerboard. The instrument is fitted with patent friction pegs with white celluloid buttons. The heel of the neck is heavily hand carved and inlaid with different layers of colored wood, capped with ebony, as shown in illustration. The banjo is elegantly finished throughout. We would be glad to send you this instrument and give you an opportunity to compare it with anything your dealer has to offer in this line, and if you do not find, after the most critical comparison and examination, that it is much superior to anything you can buy from any local dealer for less than $40.00 to $45.00, you can box it up and return it to us and we will cheerfully refund every cent you have paid, including transportation charges. Shipping weight, about 12 pounds.
No. 12K870   Price **$18.95**

THE AUTOHARP

has become one of the most popular of small musical instruments. Our trade in these instruments has become enormous, and is largely due to two points: our extremely low prices and the general excellence of the instruments we handle. These are favorite musical instruments, because little practice is required to play upon them, and the music is of the very highest order. Anyone who can read English and possesses ordinary intelligence can play upon an autoharp, because the music that we furnish is simply and plainly figured and the player will find no difficulty in following it. **With each autoharp we give a complete instruction book with many different selections of music.** Each one of these instruments is finished in the most beautiful manner, and carefully and durably constructed. If your time will not allow you to learn to play upon a violin, piano or other instrument of this class, we would by all means advise you to purchase one of these instruments.

$2.95

23 Strings, 5 Bars.

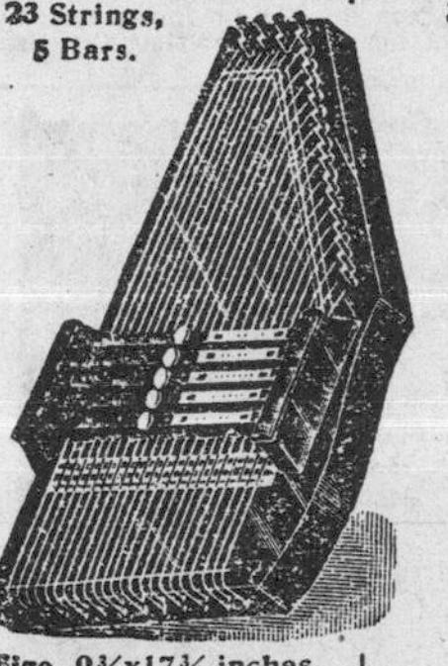

Size, 9¾x17¾ inches.

Our $2.95 Autoharp has 23 strings, 5 bars, and produces 5 chords. The possibilities of this beautiful instrument are unbounded, and while but little practice is needed for the beginner to play nicely, constant practice will enable the performer to produce very difficult music. Weight, packed for shipment, 6 pounds.

No. 12K902 Price......$2.95

$4.95

32 Strings, 8 Bars.

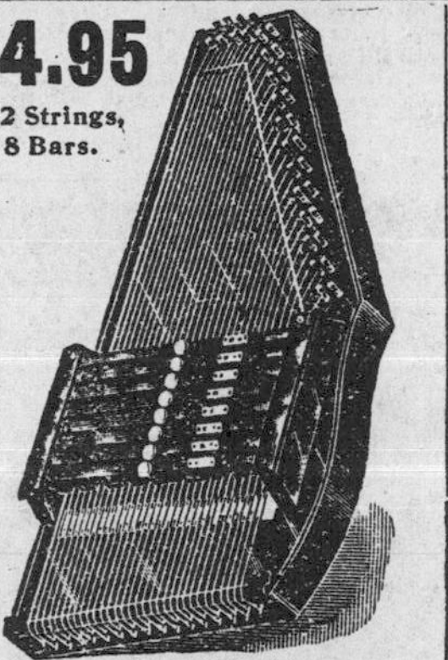

Size, 10½x21 inches.

For $4.95 we offer an autoharp that is entirely new, strictly first class in workmanship and susceptible of wonderful manipulation. This special autoharp is complete with 32 strings and is fitted with 8 bars, as it has 8 chords, as follows: C major, G seventh, F major, C seventh, Bb major, B minor, A seventh and G minor. The range of different music is very great and the possibilities of the instrument are beyond that of any other of similar construction and much higher price. You cannot purchase this autoharp from any other dealer for less than from $8.00 to $10.00. Weight, packed for shipment, 10 pounds.

No. 12K904 Price......$4.95

$6.45

37 Strings, 12 Bars.

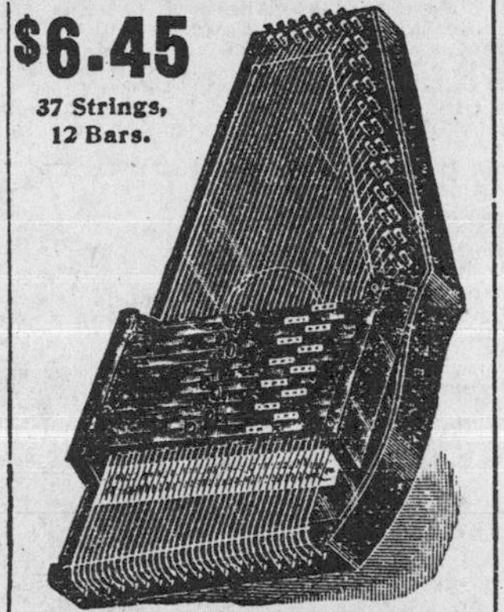

Size, 11¾x21 inches.

This Autoharp is the very latest product of the manufacturers, and is destined to become the most popular style of their entire list. It has 37 strings and 12 chord bars; these bars are placed close together, making the manipulation of them exceedingly easy. They produce 12 chords, as follows: G major, E seventh, C major, A minor, G seventh, E seventh, F major, D minor, C seventh, A seventh, Bb major and G minor. It is strung and tuned in a perfect chromatic scale. The finish is beautiful; highly polished ebony finish; altogether a handsome useful musical instrument. Weight, packed for shipment, 11 pounds.

No. 12K906 Price........$6.45

THE IDEAL HARP

$5.45

41 Strings, 5 Chords.

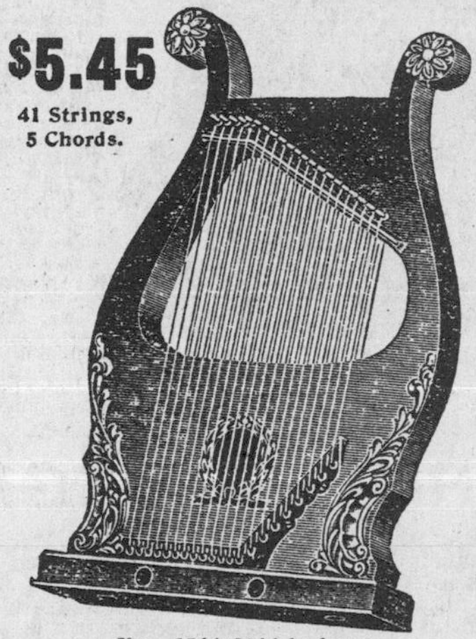

Size, 15½x23½ inches.

THIS HARP REPRESENTS THE LATEST INVENTION IN THE MARKET, and is built upon the principle of all simplified zithers and a combination of the Italian harp. The instrument is very graceful in form and artistically decorated. It is an innovation in design, resembling the beautiful lyre. The tone effect produced by this harp is of very pleasing quality and surprising volume, due to the base of the instrument which acts as a sound box. It furnishes genuine pleasure for the performer as well as the audience and is so easy to learn that anybody can, with a little study, become an expert in a very short time.

The body of the harp, which is 23½ inches high and 15½ inches wide, is made of thoroughly seasoned spruce, a wood best known for its musical qualities, and is decorated with beautiful carvings around the sound hole, lower edges and on the extreme top. The entire instrument is beautifully gilded and coated with a special transparent varnish which does not alter the brightness of the gilt, but prevents it from rubbing off, or becoming tarnished. It has nickel plated tuning pins and bridges of special design, insuring strength, as well as elegance. It has two sets of strings, one of them placed on each side of the instrument. One forms the melody or solo part which is played with the right hand, while the reverse side carries the bass, or accompaniment part, and is played with the left hand. A guide or indicator is placed on the opening of the harp, between the two sets of strings, and shows exactly the names and numbers of the strings, corresponding with the music published for this harp. The melody side has twenty-one strings of two octaves, with three sharps in each octave, representing the diatonic scale. The bass consists of twenty strings, forming five different chords, towit, C, G, F, D and A. If you are thinking of purchasing an instrument that you can learn without the aid of a teacher, an instrument with a beautiful tone, we cannot too highly recommend this harp, as besides these two splendid qualifications, the high finish, artistic outline, and decorations, makes this harp an ornament of exceptional beauty. We furnish with this instrument a complete instruction book, which will tell you exactly how to tune, and how to learn to play it. Weight, packed for shipment, 12½ pounds.

No. 12K910 Our price for this high grade harp..............$5.45

GUITAR ZITHERS.

The Guitar Zither is an improved and simplified German zither upon which may be rendered the most difficult music without the aid of a teacher. Our method of instruction is so easy that anyone can learn to play the instrument in a very short time. The bass notes are tuned in groups of chords. This is a very attractive feature because the various chords of the key are ready to be picked without effort. As an accompaniment of the voice these chords are invaluable. In connection with the violin, piano or other musical instrument, the guitar zither is especially delightful. It rewards individual skill more than any other harp in existence. These are musical instruments which charm alike the home circle and the concert audience.

$1.95

31 Strings, 4 Chords.

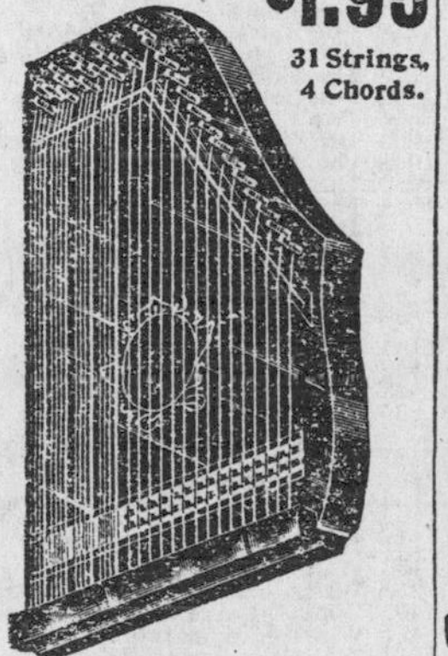

Size, 12¾x19 inches.

This is a splendid Guitar Zither, and is made of maple, ebonized and beautifully finished. It is inlaid around the soundhole with beautiful ornamentations, has 31 strings, 4 chords, namely, C, G, F major and G minor. Complete with instruction book, key and ring. This instrument will be found by players to be handsome in every respect, and possesses a deep tone which never fails to delight the listener. It is new in our line, and we highly recommend it for its many excellent qualities. Shipping weight, about 9 pounds.

No. 12K923 Price...$1.95

$2.95

41 Strings, 5 Chords.

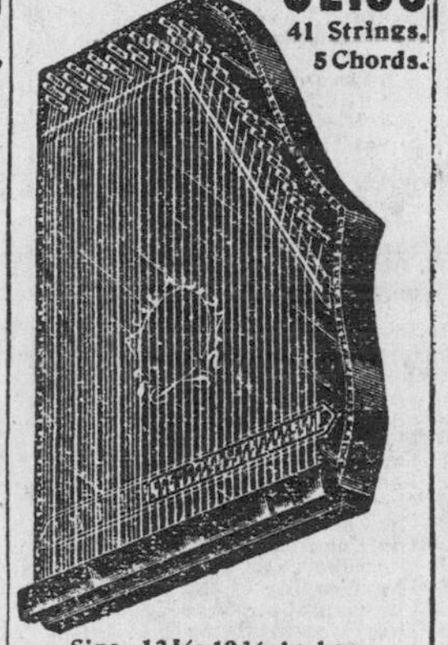

Size, 13⅜x19⅜ inches.

This Guitar Zither is made of maple, ebonized and handsomely finished, and is beautifully inlaid around the soundhole, has 41 strings, 5 chords, namely, C, G, F, D and A major. It is beautifully ornamented around the edge of the sounding board and is an instrument of which one may well be proud. We furnish a chart also with this instrument, which can be laid under the strings, giving the position of every note. It comes complete, with instruction book, key and ring. Shipping weight, about 9½ pounds.

No. 12K925 Price..$2.95

$3.95

51 Strings, 6 Chords.

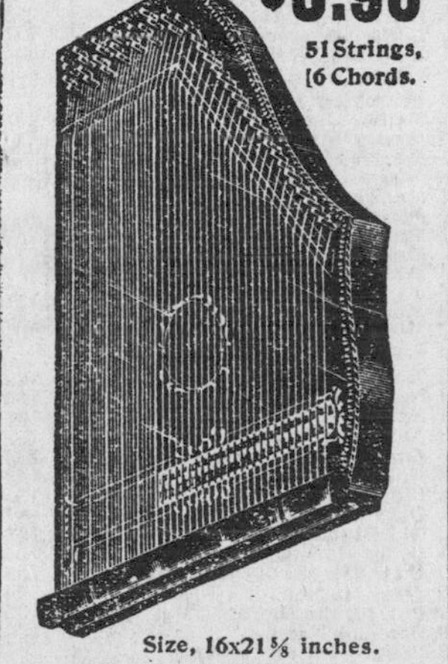

Size, 16x21⅝ inches.

This is a particularly fine instrument of great musical capacity. It is made of maple, ebonized, has hand rest, highly polished, and beautifully inlaid around the soundhole and the edge of the sounding board. Has nickel plated tuning pins, full chromatic scale with 51 strings, 6 chords, namely, C, G, F, D major and A and E minor. It has a deep, full, rich tone, and by the aid of the chart and instruction book which we send, it can be easily learned. We send it complete with chart, instruction book, key and ring. Shipping weight, about 11½ lbs.

No. 12K927 Price......$3.95

$3.35

41 Strings, 5 Chords.

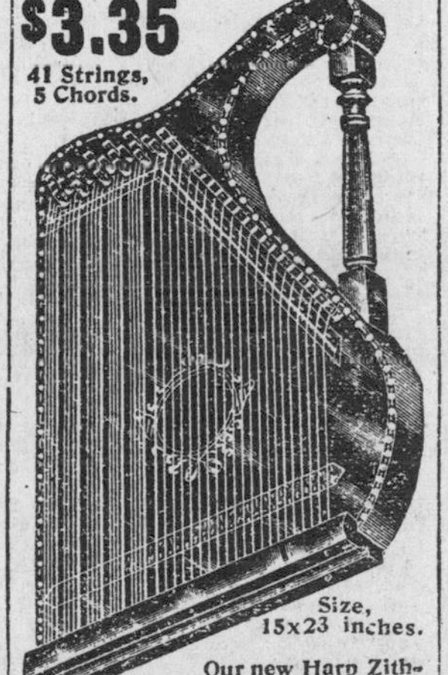

Size, 15x23 inches.

Our new Harp Zither. It is beautifully made and handsomely finished in imitation ebony. In appearance it perfectly resembles a beautiful Italian harp and has 41 strings with 5 groups of chords, as follows: A, D, F, G and C. It has nickel plated tuning pins, hand rest and chart under the strings, showing exactly what each string and chord represents. We furnish it with tuning hammer and instruction book. It is 15 inches wide and 23 inches high and the shipping weight, about 12 pounds.

No. 12K929 Price ..$3.35

MARX PIANO HARP.

Anyone, within a short time, can produce beautiful music on this instrument without the aid of a teacher.

$2.65

23 Strings, 7 Hammers.

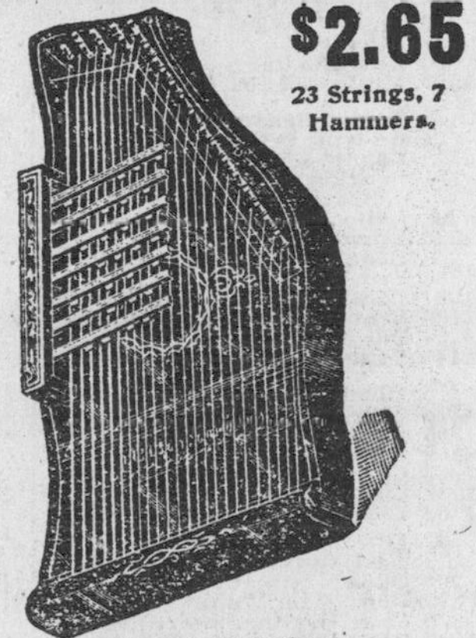

Size, 11x20 inches.

This instrument is picked with the right hand, same as an ordinary autoharp, while the hammers are manipulated with the left hand. These hammers are so arranged as to produce the chords of C major, G seventh, F major, C seventh, and their relative minors. The figured music which is used on this piano harp is the simplest ever offered in any instrument of this kind. It has 23 strings and 7 hammers. It differs from the ordinary autoharp in the important particular that there are no dead strings over which the performer has to play. It is 11 inches long and 20 inches wide, and weighs, boxed for shipment, 9 pounds. With this instrument we furnish one tuning key, one pick, one music holder and 30 pieces of figured music.

No. 12K947 Price.......$2.65

AUTOHARP AND GUITAR ZITHER CASES 85c

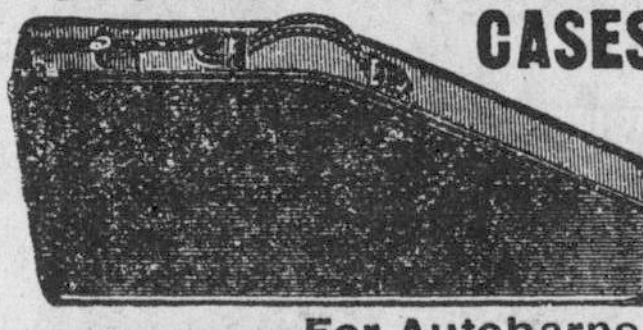

Superior model, made of good quality brown canvas, edges bound with leather. Inside flannel lined. Stitched leather handle.

For Autoharps.

No. 2, catalogue No. 12K902; No. 72⅞, catalogue No. 12K904; No. 73, catalogue No. 12K906.

No. 12K5584 Autoharp Case. Price............85c

For Guitar Zithers.

No. 2½, catalogue No. 12K923; No. 2½, catalogue No. 12K925; No. 3½, catalogue No. 12K927.

No. 12K5585 Guitar Zither Case. Price........85c

No. 12K5587 Harp Zither Case, for our No. 12K929. Price............$1.00

No. 12K5588 Ideal Harp Case. Price........ 1.50

Autoharp Tuning Pins.

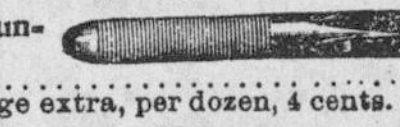

No. 12K5578 Autoharp Tuning Pins, made of blued steel. Price, per dozen..........5c

If by mail, postage extra, per dozen, 4 cents.

Tuning Keys.

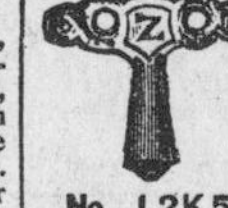

No. 12K5570 Tuning Keys, malleable iron. Price..........7c

If by mail, postage extra, 2 cents.

Autoharp Picks.

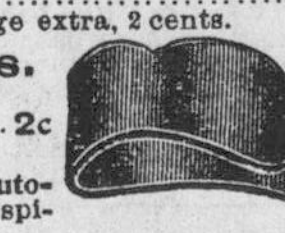

No. 12K5572 Picks, celluloid. Price..........2c

If by mail, postage extra, 2 cents.

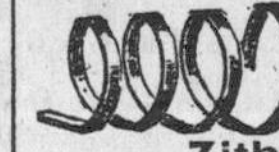

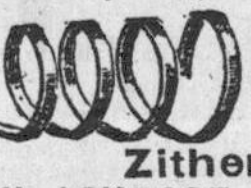

No. 12K5576 Autoharp Picks, brass, spiral. Price..........2c

If by mail, postage extra, 1 cent.

Zither Ring.

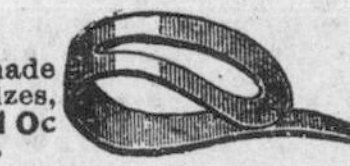

No. 12K5627 Zither Ring, made of steel, nickel plated, new model. Sizes, 1 to 6. Price 10c

If by mail, postage extra, 2 cents.

Autoharp Strings.

No. 12K4350	Set for No. 71	20c
No. 12K4352	Set for No. 2¾ (No. 12K902)	25c
No. 12K4354	Set for No. 72⅞ (12K904) or 3, 4, 5	30c
No. 12K4358	Set for No. 6	35c
No. 12K4359	Set for No. 73 (No. 12K906)	40c
No. 12K4360	Steel strings. Price, each	3c
No. 12K4362	Bass or wound strings. Price, each	5c

If by mail, postage extra, single string, 1 cent; per set, 4 cents.

When ordering single strings always mention number of harp, letter of string, and whether bass, low, middle, high or highest.

Guitar Zither Strings.

No. 12K4390	Set for No. 0½	48c
No. 12K4392	Set for No. 2 (No. 12K923)	48c
No. 12K4394	Set for No. 2½ (No. 12K925)	55c
No. 12K4396	Set for No. 3½ (No. 12K927)	75c
No. 12K4398	Plain strings. Price, each	3c
No. 12K4400	Wound strings. Price, each	5c

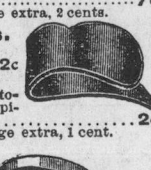

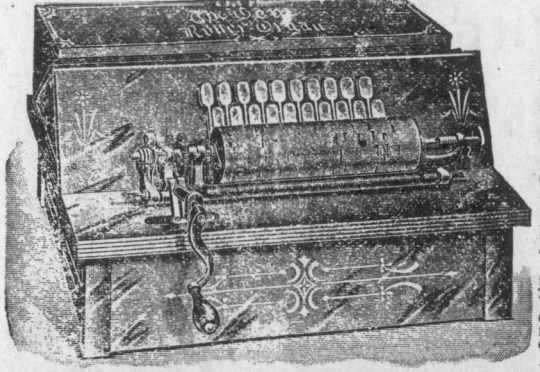

GEM ROLLER ORGAN

THE GEM ROLLER ORGAN is an excellent instrument in every respect. It is durably made, beautifully finished, handsome in appearance and wonderful in tone. It is so simply arranged that a child can operate it and no previous knowledge of the music is necessary in order to play the most delightful pieces on this beautiful little organ. The music is produced by the turning of the crank, shown on illustration, which sets in motion a roller which has teeth or pins like the cylinder of a regular Swiss music box. These pins operate upon valve keys, allowing the air to pass through and thus producing the different tones.

ALL THE WORKING PARTS of the instrument are easily accessible, and are made of solid metal, the rollers and keys being mounted on castings. Nothing has been omitted to give these instruments their crowning qualities of extreme simplicity and durability. They are beautifully finished, making a handsome parlor ornament, and are genuine musical instruments which are recommended by good musicians. Full sized organ reeds are used, and the volume of sound will fill any ordinary sized hall.

THEY WILL PLAY hymns and popular airs with clearness and accuracy, and furnish acceptable music for any occasion. For dances, lodges, etc., they are most admirable. Perfect execution of music is obtained without the services of a skilled musician. There is no limit to either kind or quality of music they will play, and they are the most perfect mechanical musical instruments in design, operation and effect that have been produced.

THE GEM ROLLER ORGAN is 14¼ inches long, 12 inches wide and 7¾ inches high. No. 12K985 Gem Roller Organ, including three rollers. Price. Order by number. Shipping weight, 12 pounds. **$3.45**

Size, 14¼x7¾x12 inches.

CONCERT ROLLER ORGAN, $7.60

THIS ORGAN is of somewhat higher grade than the Gem Roller Organ, has greater musical capacity, is much better constructed and a finer instrument in every way. The case of this instrument is 17 inches long, 13¾ inches wide and 12 inches high. The cylinder and all of the mechanism are enclosed and covered with a glass door, which effectually excludes dust and dirt. It is operated in the same way as the Gem Roller Organ and uses the same cylinder, so that in ordering cylinders for this organ you can make your selections from the list below.

THIS IS A VERY DESIRABLE INSTRUMENT, produces delightful music, and as the cylinders are removable, a great many different pieces can be played. The tone is similar to that of a parlor organ, as the tone is produced by reeds operated by a cylinder containing teeth, which open and close the valves. It is made of fine golden oak, nicely finished.

Five Tunes furnished Free with each Concert Organ.

No. 12K988   Concert Roller Organ.   Price........ **$7.60**

Weight, packed for shipment, 30 pounds.   Golden Oak Case. Size, 17x12x13¾ inches.

COMPLETE LIST OF THE BEST ROLLERS FOR GEM AND CONCERT ROLLER ORGANS.

Series No. 12K986 Order by Number. Always give second choice so if out of first we can substitute without delay. Price, per dozen, $1.98; each. (If by mail, postage extra, each, 6 cents) **18c**

90 All the Way My Saviour Leads	433 Flying Trapeze	603 Knocking, Knocking, Who is There?	67 Rock of Ages	246 The Irish Washerwoman
22 Almost Persuaded	1110 Flower Song	734 Lead, Kindly Light	91 Rescue the Perishing	247 The Devil's Dream
14 America	452 Fresh Life, Waltz	25 Let the Lower Lights be Burning	279 Red, White and Blue	273 The Star Spangled Banner
721 Anywhere With Jesus	617 God Be With You	147 Leap Year Waltz	456 Racquet Waltz	280 Tenting on the Old Camp Ground
126 Auld Lang Syne	726 Glory to His Name	158 Listen to the Mocking Bird	68 Sweet Hour of Prayer	283 The Old Oaken Bucket
135 Annie of the Vale	444 Galop—Jolly Brothers	166 Little Old Log Cabin	634 Shall We Gather at the River	295 The Way to be Happy—Waltz
146 Annie Laurie	200 I	286 Little Maggie May	108 Sweet Violets	301 The Girl I Left Behind Me
151 Alice Polka	201 II	335 Little Annie Rooney—Waltz	122 Sailors' Hornpipe	375 Take Me Back to Home and Mother
600 After the Ball	202 III Gay Life Quadrilles	553 Little Fairy Gallop	152 See-Saw Waltz	
1087 All Coons Look Alike to Me	203 IV	1020 Little Alabama Coon	253 Spanish Cavalier	390 The Battle Cry of Freedom
78 Beulah Land	204 V	1141 Laughing Water	297 St. Patrick's Day	577 The High School Cadets' March
4 Bringing in the Sheaves	222 General Boulanger's March	1146 Lindy	336 Sweetbriar Waltz	578 The Skirt Dance
136 Bonnie Eloise	347 Good Luck Mazurka	109 Marching Through Georgia	368 Schottische—Little Beauty	1004 The Bowery
181 Brucker Camp March—Brucker Lager Marsch	480 General Grant's Grand March	217 Medley Jig	406 Schottische—Always Smiling	1006 Two Little Girls in Blue
208 Belle Mahone	1107 Georgia Camp Meeting	243 Money Musk	420 Schottische—Happy-go-Lucky	1009 The Washington Post March
226 Bring Back My Bonnie to Me	1130 Good Bye, Dolly Grey	275 Maryland, My Maryland	476 Silver Threads Among the Gold	1038 The Sidewalks of New York
258 Bonnie Doon	17 Hold the Fort	298 Miss McLeod's Reel	1036 Sweet Marie	1039 The Fatal Wedding
1058 Ben Bolt	18 He Leadeth Me	446 Manhattan Polka	1071 Sweet Rosie O'Grady	1054 The Honeymoon March
1084 Bombasto March, Two Step	123 Home, Sweet Home	460 Myosotis	1096 Stars and Stripes Forever—March	1070 The Darkies' Dream
1102 Break the News to Mother	130 Hunter's March—Mikado	617 Mary and John		1086 There'll Come a Time
1138 Bill Bailey	277 Hail Columbia	1019 Molly and I and the Baby	1100 Sunnyside Clog	1133 Tale of the Kangaroo
1140 By the Sycamore Tree	635 Happy Day	1024 March of the Men of Harlech	1101 She was Bred in Old Kentucky	1168 Tammany
115 Climbing Up the Golden Stairs	1112 Hello, Ma Baby	1069 My Old Kentucky Home	1114 Smoky Mokes	1065 Up the Street
213 College Hornpipe	1113 High Born Lady	1129 Mosquito Parade	1124 Sunny Tennessee	1144 Under the Anheuser Bush
268 Comin' Thro' the Rye	1128 Holy City	1137 Mister Dooley	1127 Soldiers in the Park	119 Vienna Polka
450 Clayton's Grand March	1139 Hiawatha	1163 My Irish Molly O	1152 Silver Heels	23 Where Is My Boy Tonight
1066 Cosmos	1083 Hot Time in the Old Town	2 Nearer, My God, to Thee	1 The Sweet Bye and Bye	65 What a Friend We Have in Jesus
1132 Creole Belle	19 I Need Thee Every Hour	144 Nellie Gray	20 The Home Over There	81 We Shall Meet Beyond the River
1162 Cheyenne	21 Is My Name Written There	1121 Narcissus	729 The Haven of Rest	101 Waltz—Les Roses
127 Die Wacht am Rhine	27 I Will Sing of My Redeemer	1169 Napoleon's March	109 The Soldiers' Joy	103 When the Swallows Homeward Fly
173 Darling Bessie of the Lea	1030 In Love With the Man in the Moon	6 Onward, Christian Soldiers	124 The Marseillaise Hymn	111 Waltz—My Queen
205 Dixie	1135 I Left Because I Love You	26 Only an Armor Bearer	132 The Dreamland Waltz	150 Waltz—German Hearts
349 Dairy Maid Waltz	1136 In the Good Old Summer Time	112 Old Uncle Ned	138 The Parade March	234 Waltz—Cricket on the Hearth
370 Dear Evalina, Sweet Evalina	1145 In the Shade of the Old Apple Tree	121 Old Folks at Home	149 The Last Rose of Summer	407 Waltz—Loves' Dreamland
1027 Daddy Wouldn't Buy Me a Bow-wow	13 Just as I Am	262 Old Black Joe	155 The Beautiful Blue Danube	457 Waltz—Estudiantina
1134 Down Where the Cotton Blossoms Grow	73 Jesus, Lover of My Soul	443 O My Darling Clementine	161 The Blue Bells of Scotland	1116 Whistling Rufus
730 Everlasting Arms	260 Jingle Bells	1090 On the Banks of the Wabash	163 The Wearing of the Green	1153 Wait Till the Sun Shines, Nellie
1115 Eli Green's Cake Walk	278 Juanita	72 Pass Me Not	164 The Campbells Are Coming	
1125 El Capitaine—No. 1	399 John Brown [Me	29 Pull for the Shore	183 The Flyaway Galop	1161 You're a Grand Old Flag
4 From Greenland's Icy Mountain	1058 Just Tell Them That You Saw	30 Precious Name	194 The Golden Slippers	1167 You Look Awful Good to Father
	1117 Just as the Sun Went Down	153 Polka—On the Wing	195 The Quilting Party	190 Yankee Doodle
	1118 Just One Girl	262 Peep-O-Day—Polka	206 Till We Meet Again—Waltz	1119 Zenda Waltzes
		1106 Premiere March	207 The Arkansas Traveler	
			209 The Kiss Waltz	
			229 Tramp, Tramp	

VIOLONCELLOS.

Weight packed, about 45 pounds.

With each Violoncello we furnish FREE:
ONE perfect fitting canvas bag.
ONE good quality violoncello bow.
ONE large piece of rosin.
ONE complete instruction book.

VIOLONCELLO of good quality and tone, fitted with iron patent head. One which usually retails at about $15.00.
No. 12K400   Price.................... **$9.25**

VIOLONCELLO of better grade than the above. It has inlaid edges, and comes fitted with good quality patent head, and complete set of the best strings.
No. 12K406   Price.................... **$11.95**

OUR HIGH GRADE VIOLONCELLO. The sides and back are made of maple and the top of evenly grained seasoned spruce. It has ebony fingerboard, tailpiece and pegs. The tone, finish and construction of this instrument are such as you would naturally expect only on violoncellos which sell in retail stores at from $25.00 to $30.00.
No. 12K420   Price.................... **$16.75**

OUR HIGHEST GRADE VIOLONCELLO. The back and sides of this instrument are made of maple and the top is made of old well seasoned spruce. The fingerboard and tailpiece are of good quality ebony. The purfling is very carefully and neatly inlaid throughout, giving the instrument a handsome appearance. It is fitted with the best quality patent head, on brass double lined throughout. The tone of this instrument is pure, sweet and very powerful. Dealers that carry a violoncello of this grade usually ask from $30.00 to $40.00.
No. 12K422   Price.................... **$19.85**

DOUBLE BASS VIOLS.

Weight packed, about 125 pounds.

Our $22.45 One-Half Size Double Bass Viol.

At $22.45 we offer a Four-String Double Bass Viol, one-half size, with bow, and complete instruction book. This double bass viol is of the very best model, is dark red shaded, very highly polished, and is superior quality in every respect. Best patent head.
No. 12K450   Price.................... **$22.45**

Our Three-Quarter Size Double Bass Viol, $24.35.

A High Grade Three-Quarter Size Double Base Viol for $24.35. This double bass viol has four strings, finest iron patent head and is beautifully shaded and colored. In finish it is wonderfully fine, being highly polished throughout.
No. 12K462   Price.................... **$24.35**

$28.95 Three-Quarter Size Double Bass Viol.

This Double Bass Viol has four strings, high grade iron patent head, solid ebony fingerboard. The inlaid purfling adds greatly to the attractiveness of the instrument, giving it the appearance of the most expensive viols on the market. We furnish FREE with each instrument a good double bass bow, and complete instruction book.
No. 12K466   Price.................... **$28.95**

OUR BÖHM LINE OF SOVEREIGN ACCORDIONS

A FINE LINE OF LOW PRICED ACCORDIONS. We assure all admirers of the accordion that they will find in these instruments the greatest values ever offered in low priced accordions. They are made especially for us by a maker who has an international reputation for manufacturing these instruments. They are all well and thoroughly made throughout, and we know by actual comparison that our prices are far lower than what other dealers will ask for the same grade of instruments. We ship them upon the same terms that we ship out other musical goods and allow full ten days' trial. They are all handsomely finished and ornamented and are instruments which we can conscientiously recommend to our customers. This is a line of old favorite accordions and we have been so successful in handling them that we have come to look upon them as a staple article in the accordion line. By comparing quality and price of this line with any other dealer's accordions of the same grade, it will show where they suffer by such comparisons. If you are looking for an accordion of sterling merit, handsome in appearance, well made and beautifully toned, at prices one-half lower than you can obtain elsewhere, we will recommend any accordion in this line.

WITH EACH ACCORDION WE GIVE A COMPLETE INSTRUCTION BOOK.

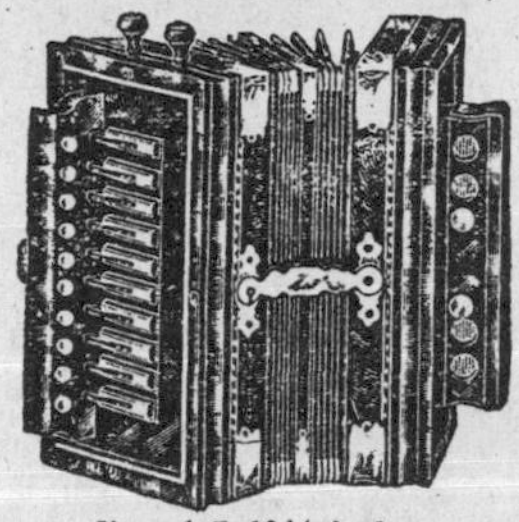

Size, 6x7x10¼ inches.

This is a very fine accordion, is highly polished and finished with fancy fluted mouldings, and has double bellows, eight folds, with corner protectors and nickel clasps. It is very prettily ornamented with nickel strips on the inside of the panels and is fitted with ten keys and two sets of reeds and stops. We can recommend this accordion very highly as being a durable and splendidly made instrument, and has great volume and mellowness of tone. We sell all accordions under our offer to refund your money and pay the express charges both ways should you decide that you did not care to keep it after a thorough trial and examination. It is exactly such an accordion as those for which you would be compelled to pay your local dealer from $3.50 to $4.00. We are satisfied that you will gladly admit this, if you could see it and test it, which you can do under our liberal offer. Weight, boxed, about 5½ lbs.

No. 12K994 Price...... **$1.85**

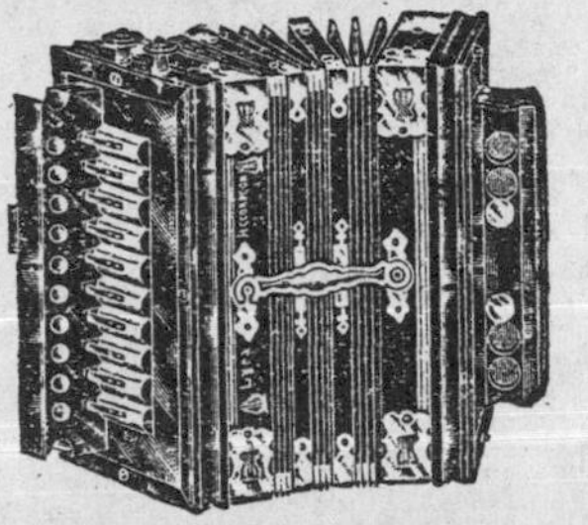

Size, 5¾x7x10¼ inches.

This is a very fine accordion with fluted, ebonized mouldings and dark red panels, triple bellows, nine folds, in three alternate colors, red, black and green. Highly ornamented corner protectors, ten nickel plated keys, two sets of reeds, two stops, fancy gold paper ornamentations around the frame. Nickel plated clasps and trimmings throughout. Fitted with strips of fancy webbing. A beautiful instrument at a low price. Should you purchase an accordion of this same grade from your local dealer he will charge you from $4.00 to $4.50 for it. Give us an opportunity of placing this splendid instrument in your hands for examination, with the understanding that we will receive it back and refund your money if it does not prove satisfactory in every particular. We guarantee the instrument to be a high class accordion in every respect. We have sold many thousands of these instruments and they have given universal satisfaction. Weight, boxed, about 7 pounds.

No. 12K995 Price....... **$2.15**

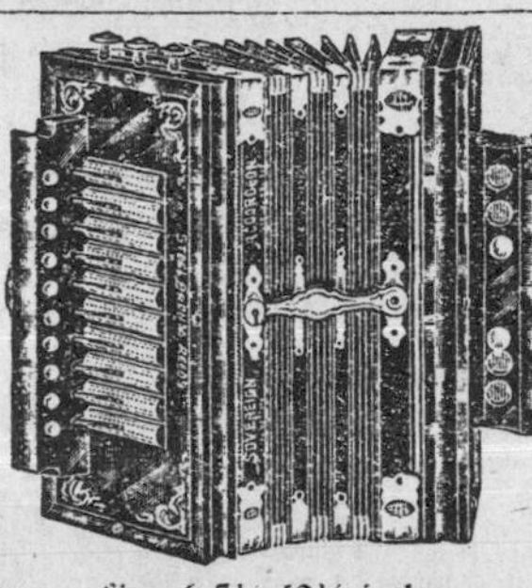

Size, 6x7¼x12¼ inches.

Fancy fluted mouldings finished in imitation ebony. Keyboard also in imitation ebony: rich deep blue panels, with gold decorations. Triple bellows of nine folds with corner protectors, bellows and all leather work being in two colors, green and brown, with rich Turkish red paper between the folds. Ten long nickel keys, three sets of steel bronze reeds, three stops. We will be glad to have you compare it with any accordion your local dealer has to offer in the same grade at double the price. We offer it to you as one of the greatest bargains that has ever been offered in such an instrument. We sell this accordion with the understanding that if you do not find when you receive it, that you have saved at least $3.00 on your purchase, that it is the greatest bargain you ever saw, you are to return it to us, and we will refund your money and pay the express charges. Weight, boxed, about 8 pounds.

No. 12K996 Price..... **$2.95**

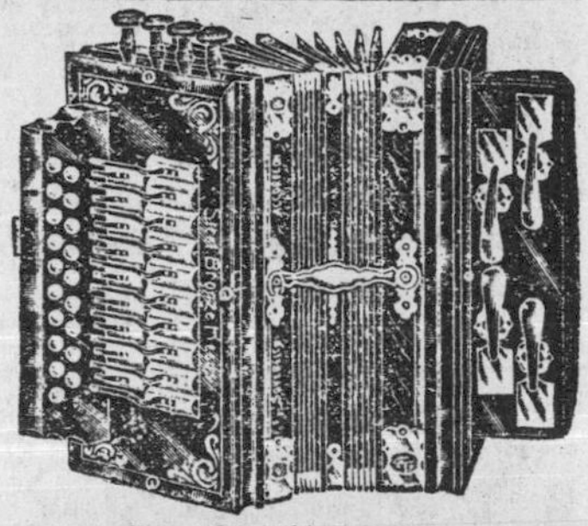

Size, 6⅝x11¾x7 inches.

This is undoubtedly the best double row accordion for the money yet placed on the market. It is finished with fancy fluted mouldings, highly polished ebonized keyboard, and is also furnished in imitation ebony, beautiful green panels ornamented with impressed gold designs, double bellows of ten folds, and each fold is protected by metal protectors. The clasps are all nickeled, and it is trimmed in three colors, red, black and green. It contains four sets of reeds, nineteen keys, four stops and four basses. This accordion is sold under our guarantee for quality and is shipped out with the distinct understanding and agreement that if it is not all that you expect or if it is not entirely satisfactory after a thorough trial and examination, it is to be returned to us at our expense and all money paid by you is to be refunded in full. Weight, boxed, about 9 pounds.

No. 12K997 Price..... **$4.25**

The same accordion as described above except that it has twenty-one keys. Weight, boxed, about 9 pounds.

No. 12K998 Price........... **$4.65**

OUR SPECIAL ACCORDIONS

THE INSTRUMENTS LISTED BELOW, WE HAVE SELECTED AS THE FAVORITE STYLES OF THREE WELL KNOWN MANUFACTURERS OF HIGH GRADE ACCORDIONS.

FOUR GENUINE PITZSCHLER ACCORDIONS. These accordions are celebrated throughout the world for their remarkable richness and purity of tone, ease of action and their handsome appearance. The workmanship and material are of the highest grade. Our prices represent the actual factory cost, plus our small margin of profit, and are lower than what is generally asked by our competitors for instruments of no reputation or merits whatsoever.

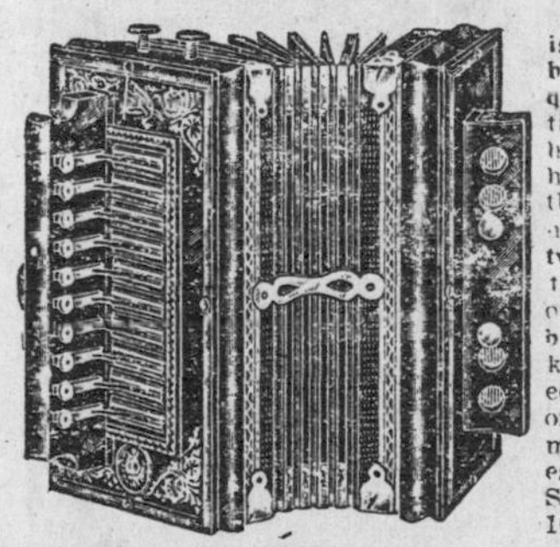

Size, 6½x13x7½ inches.

This accordion is low in price, but high in quality, is beautifully made and highly polished; has nine folds in the bellows with nickel corners; two stops and two sets of reeds, open action, two basses. The keys are mounted in mother of pearl buttons making them easily operated. Shipping weight, 10 pounds.

No. 12K1080 Price............ **$3.45**

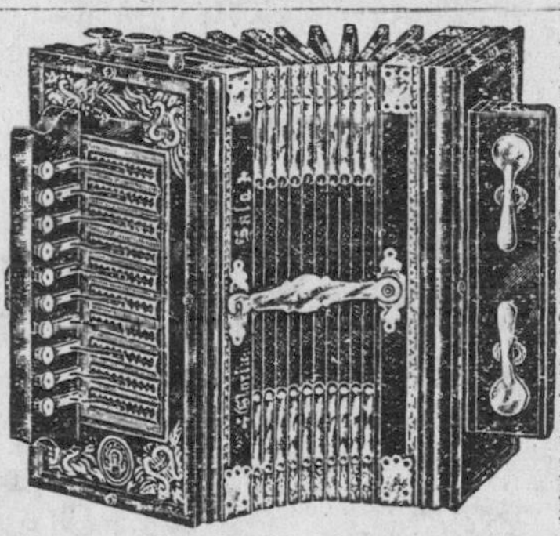

Size, 7x9x13½ inches.

Our Pitzschler Favorite. This accordion is one of the latest designs. The mouldings are all finished in imitation ebony, highly polished and beautifully decorated. Has ten-fold extra broad single bellows. The ends of the bellows are entirely covered with nickel and the corners are mounted with beautiful fancy brass caps, making this one of the handsomest accordions ever offered by any music dealer. This instrument has a sunken keyboard with open action. The keys are all mounted with mother of pearl buttons. This accordion has three sets of reeds, three stops and two basses, and produces a beautiful and powerful tone. No illustration however good can convey its real beauty and splendid tone. We include with this accordion a complete instruction book. Every instrument is carefully packed. Shipping weight, 11 lbs.

No. 12K1084 Price............ **$5.80**

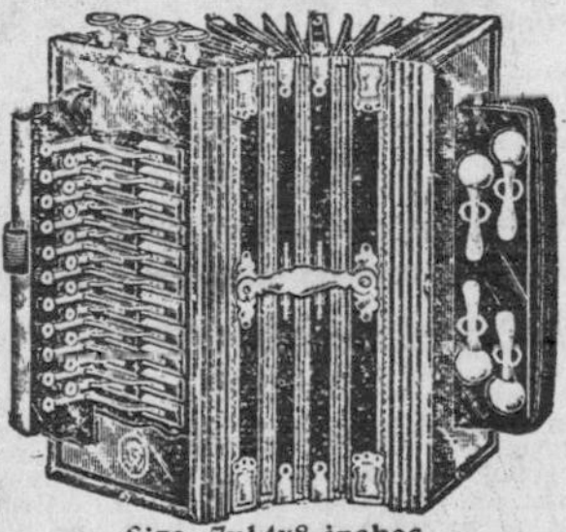

This is the finest Pitzschler Accordion we handle. It has fine fluted mouldings in imitation mahogany; panels genuine mahogany; all wood work finely polished and finished; sunken open action keyboard; double row, nineteen nickel keys; four basses; heavy double bellows, with nickel protectors; nickel plated corners and clasps; four stops; four fine sets of reeds. Pearl buttons. Size, 14 inches by 8 inches. A complete instruction book free.

Size, 7x14x8 inches.

No. 12K1088 Price........ **$6.65**

The same in every way as No. 12K1088, described above, but has twenty-one nickel plated keys.

No. 12K1090 Price........ **7.65**

Weight, packed, about 20 pounds.

THREE OTTO WEIDLICH ACCORDIONS. ON ACCOUNT OF THE HIGH GRADE WORKMANSHIP AND MATERIAL AT SUCH LOW PRICES, WEIDLICH ACCORDIONS HAVE BECOME POPULAR IN THIS COUNTRY.

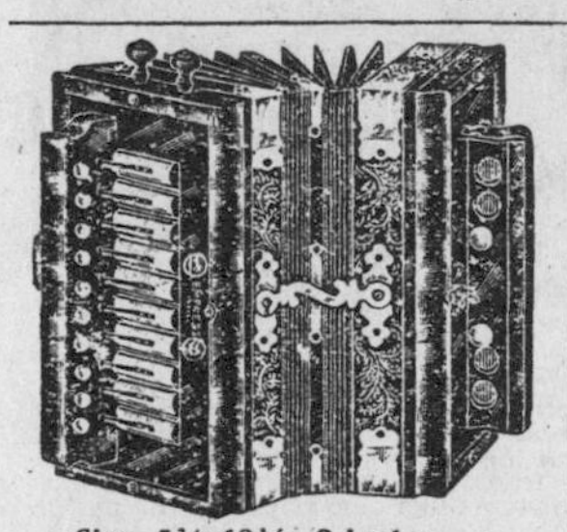

Size, 5¾x10¼x 9 inches.

Genuine Weidlich Empress Accordion. The frame is beautifully made with highly polished ebonized mouldings with gilt lines; has nickel corners and clasps, ten nickel keys, leather straps, two ebonized stops, powerful double bellows with the center folds protected with nickel corners. The space will not allow us to dwell with any great length upon the merits of this instrument. It has two sets of extra broad reeds, giving it a specially strong and beautiful quality of tone. Weight, boxed for shipment, about 10 pounds.

No. 12K1003 Price............... **$2.25**

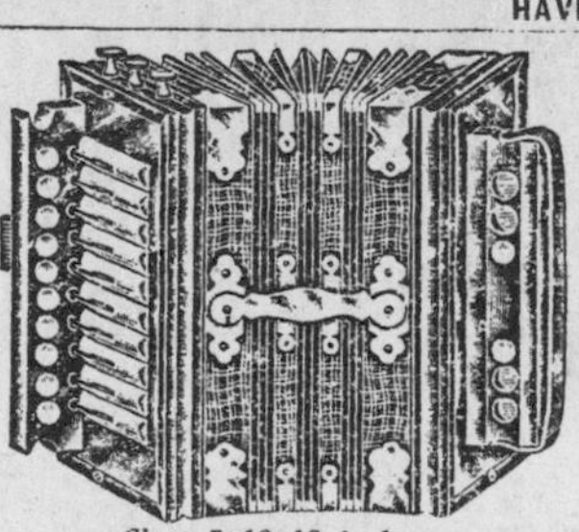

Size, 5x10x10 inches.

Our Special Weidlich United States Advance Accordion is a particularly striking little instrument in every respect. The frame is made of hardwood, finished in black enamel. The bellows are of triple style of nine folds, with corner protectors. It has three stops, controlling three sets of powerful steel bronze reeds. Two basses and ten keys, with nickel plated caps. The bellows folds are covered with very pretty snakeskin leatherette. All trimmings are highly nickel plated and polished. Weight, packed for shipment, 7 pounds.

No. 12K1007 Price, with instruction book................ **$2.45**

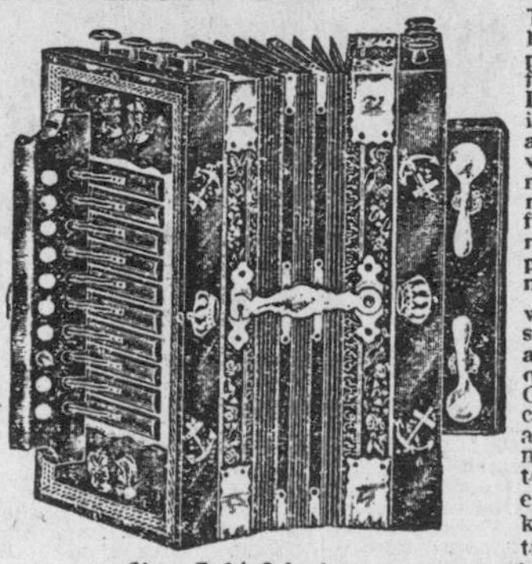

Size, 7x14x8 inches.

The Weidlich Empress Professional Insrument is a large accordion, with broad mahogany moulded frame, mahogany panels ornamented with handsome gilt and nickel ornaments. Clasps and corners are fully nickel plated, sunken open keyboard, triple bellows, with nine folds, ten keys, eight stops, four sets of reeds tuned in chords. The volume and quality of tone are especially desirable. We have sold hundreds of these accordions during the past nine years, and all have given unqualified satisfaction. Complete instruction book free. Shipping wt., 11 pounds.

No. 12K1022 Price......... **$6.40**

KALBE TREMOLO ACCORDION

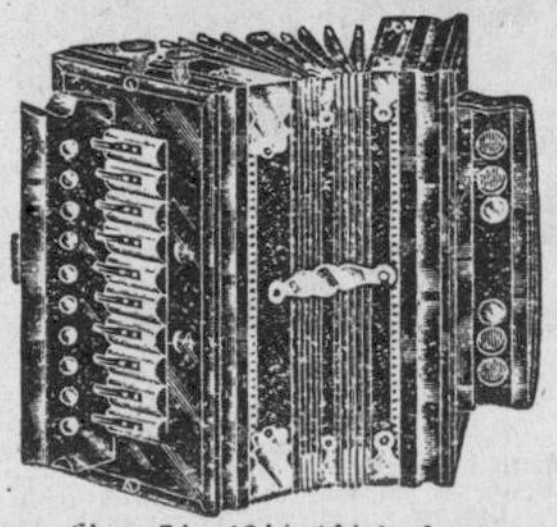

Size, 5½x10¼x6¾ inches.

This is a splendid Kalbe instrument with an ebonized maple frame very handsomely finished. It is very highly polished and is ornamented with fluted moulding. It has a powerful double bellows of eight folds, with nickel plated corner protectors. Highly polished nickel trimmings and clasps, ten keys, two basses, two sets of reeds and two stops. This accordion is fitted with a tremolo or vox humana attachment which gives the tone a wavy and undulating effect in imitation of the human voice. The tremolo can be thrown in and out of action at the will of the player by means of a lever operated by the thumb of the right hand. The instrument is splendidly fitted throughout and will be sure to satisfy all players upon the accordion. Weight, boxed for shipment, about 10 pounds.

No. 12K1100 Price....... **$2.95**

OUR NEW LINE OF M. HOHNER ACCORDIONS.

Free With Each Hohner Accordion.

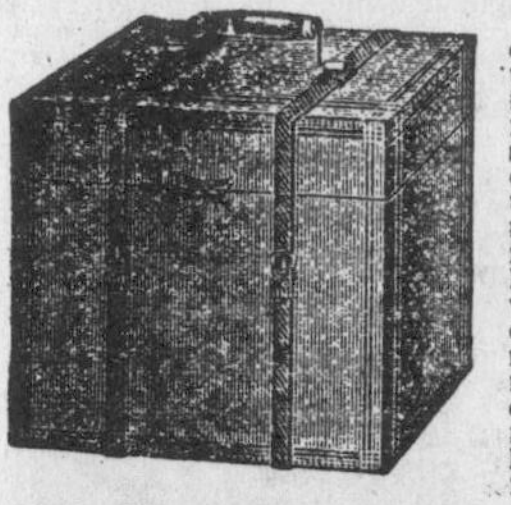

With each one of these accordions we send, without extra charge, a splendid carrying case, made to fit the different sizes of accordions shown on this page. These cases are made especially for us, and can be obtained with no other accordions on the market. They are made of heavy pasteboard, covered with a very durable covering of beautiful imitation of black morocco leather. They are fitted with two straps, made of a good quality of leather, fitted with buckles and a handle for carrying the case in the hand.

WE ARE SHOWING ON THIS PAGE OUR MAGNIFICENT LINE OF HOHNER ACCORDIONS, and we know that performers on these popular instruments will find them a welcome addition to our already large line of accordions. There are no accordions which are so thoroughly and carefully made as those which are manufactured in the Hohner factory. Every piece of woodwork is polished and finished to the last degree of perfection. Every joint is accurately fitted and solidly glued. There are no ragged edges or unfinished parts, and when you purchase one of these instruments you have the assurance that you are buying the very best that can be had at any price. The high grade and thorough finish on these accordions take them out of the line of novelties and place them among the standard musical instruments of the world. Each instrument is fitted with the very best quality of steel bronze reeds, and it is a well known fact that no accordions are tuned so accurately and harmoniously as the instruments of this splendid line. From the cheapest to the most expensive instruments, each one will be found to be the very best that can possibly be made at the price asked. We will be glad to have you compare these instruments with anything that your dealer has to offer in the same line and our liberal terms of shipment give you the fullest opportunity to do this.

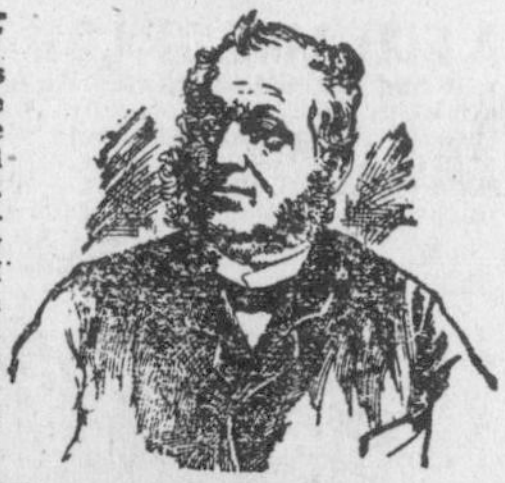

WE SEND A COMPLETE INSTRUCTION BOOK WITH EACH ACCORDION.

Each one of these instruments is fitted with pearl keys, so designed, rounded and finished as to be most agreeable to the fingers of the player. This feature is found upon no other line of accordions. The measurements given below do not include keyboards.

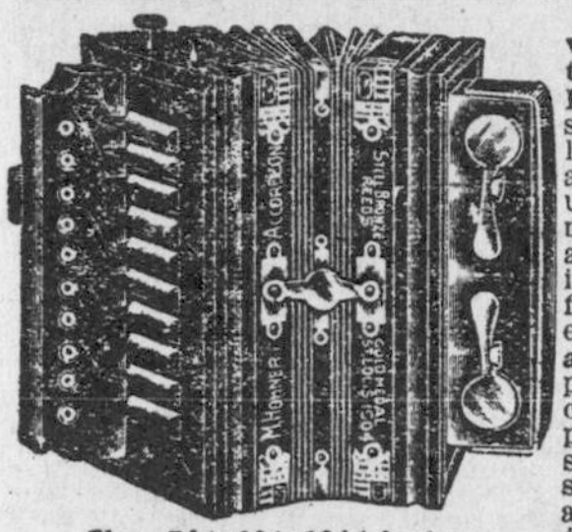

Size, 5½x6⅜x10¼ inches.

This accordion is a very neat and substantial little instrument. Has double bellows of six folds of fine quality leatherette. The corners are protected with the usual ornamental Hohner corner protectors, and the woodwork of the instrument is beautifully finished in black and blue enamel. **It has ten keys and two powerful basses,** patent spring, nickel clasps and the usual pearl buttons. It has two stops controlling two sets of steel bronze reeds and is so arranged that it can easily be taken apart. It possesses the usual high grade Hohner quality of tone and we offer it as the very best value ever placed on the market at this price. **This is an accordion for which the local dealer will ask you from $4.00 to $6.00, and if we should be favored with your order for one of these instruments and you do not find by comparison that this is true, we will gladly receive it back and refund your money.** Weight, packed for shipment, 6 pounds.

No. 12K1198 Price.................. **$2.45**

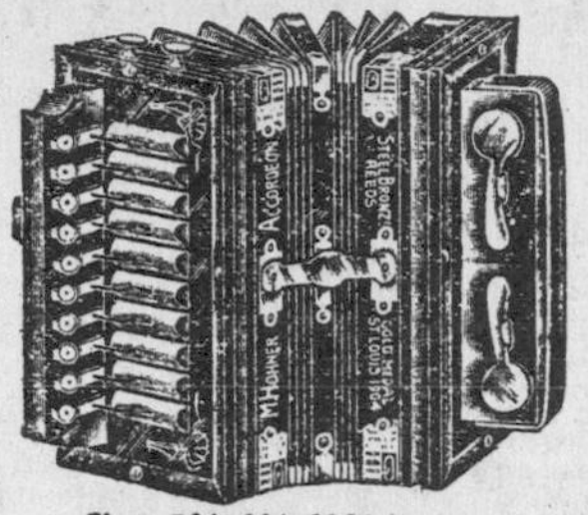

Size, 5¾x6½x10⅝ inches.

Hohner Accordion. This is a very fine accordion, handsomely finished in black and red enamel, highly polished. It has a double bellows of eight folds, each fold protected by special metal corner guards. It is fitted with patent spring clasps, **has two full sets of steel bronze reeds with two basses.** The keys are all fitted with mother of pearl buttons and the valves are nickel plated. Each reed plate is separate and securely fastened with metallic fasteners. It is one of the accordions which has given M. Hohner his great reputation and an instrument which will never disappoint the purchaser. It is an instrument which will stand comparison with any accordion your dealer has to offer at more than double the price, and we recommend it to all who desire a neat, compact and durably made instrument, which will prove satisfactory under all conditions. Weight, packed for shipment, 9½ pounds.

No. 12K1200 Price.................. **$3.45**

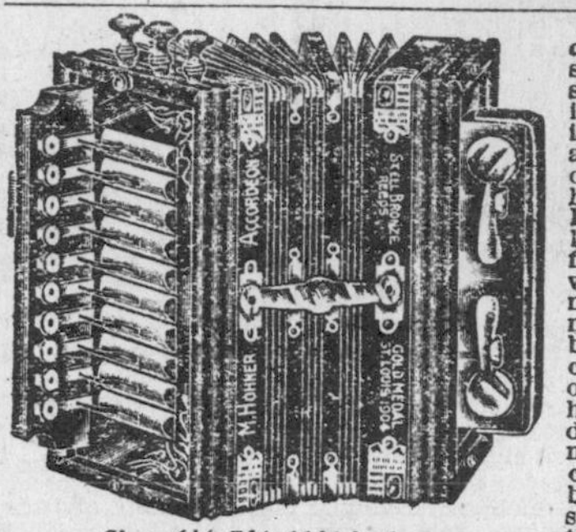

Size, 6¼x7⅝x11⅜ inches.

M. Hohner Accordion. This instrument is a splendid concert instrument, finished in black enamel with silver ornaments, very highly polished. It has triple bellows of nine folds, finished in red with brass corners. The instrument is protected by nickel plated corners throughout and is a very handsome and durable instrument. The top can be taken off by simply unscrewing two thumbscrews, making it very easy to repair in case anything should get out of order. It has patent spring clasps, pearl keys and three stops controlling three full sets of steel bronze reeds. For concert purposes it is unexcelled, as it has great depth and volume of tone and great musical capacity. It has two rich basses. Weight, packed for shipment, 11½ pounds.

No. 12K1204 Price.................. **$5.40**

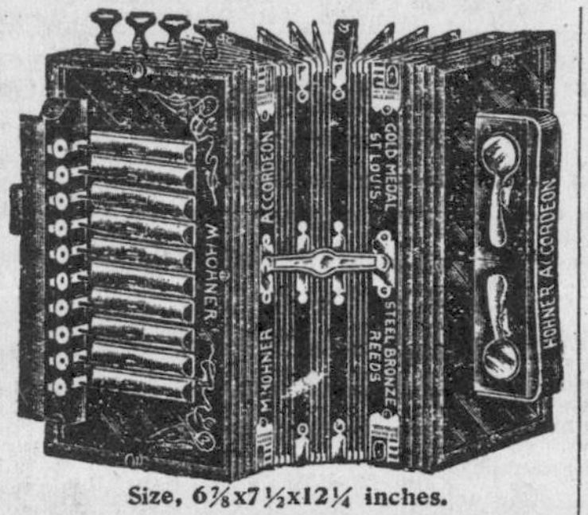

Size, 6⅞x7½x12¼ inches.

This beautiful Hohner accordion is finished in rosewood, with gold impressed ornaments. All woodwork brought to a fine piano finish. It has triple bellows of nine folds finished in different colored leatherette with brass corner protectors. Has four stops controlling four sets of steel bronze reeds. It is fitted with two powerful basses and the keys are fitted with elegant mother of pearl buttons and the valves are finished in gold enamel. The reeds in this accordion are tuned to thirds, making possible a succession of beautiful chords, and wonderfully increasing the capacity of the instrument. **If you will buy this accordion and compare it with any accordion which your dealer has to offer for from $8.00 to $10.00, you will not only find that it is in every way equal, but also in many points superior, and** if you are not perfectly satisfied with your bargain you can return it and we will cheerfully refund your money. Weight, packed for shipment, 11½ pounds.

No. 12K1208 Price.................. **$6.55**

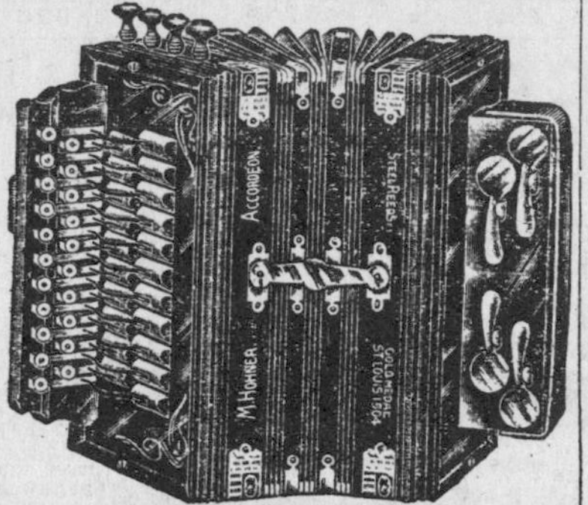

Size, 7⅝x7⅝x13½ inches.

Hohner Grand Concert Accordion. This is certainly a grand concert instrument, as it is fitted with a triple bellows of nine folds, four stops controlling four sets of steel bronze reeds. It has two rows of keys, nineteen in all, fitted with handsome mother of pearl buttons with valves finished in gold enamel. The entire instrument is finished in black and mahogany panels, and bright colored bellows cloth. The bellows folds are protected by heavy brass corner protectors. It has four powerful, deep, rich, basses accurately tuned with the treble reeds. The instrument is trimmed throughout with nickel plated trimmings and fitted with patent spring clasps. Weight, packed for shipment, 14½ lbs.

No. 12K1214 Grand Concert Accordion, 19 keys. Price.................. **$8.75**

No. 12K1216 Grand Concert Accordion, 21 keys. Price.................. **9.80**

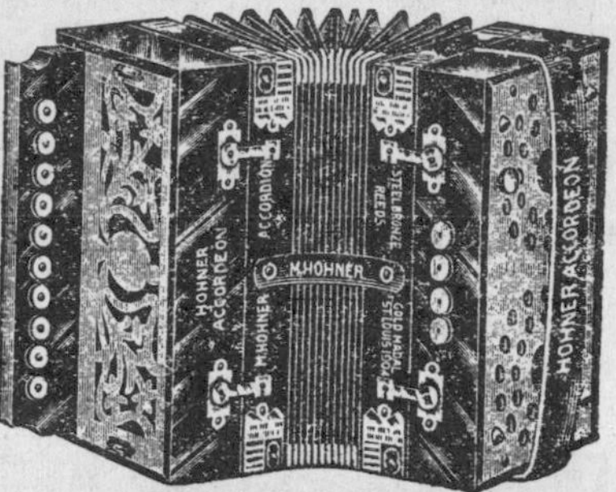

Size, 5¾x9¼x10¼ inches.

Hohner Italo-Bohemian Accordion. This is a splendid Italian accordion handsomely finished in black enameled wood frame and white maple panels. It has a powerful bellows of ten folds of black pebble leatherette, protected by brass corner protectors. It has four basses and ten keys fitted with handsome mother of pearl buttons. The scroll plate over the valves is lined with handsome green cloth and can be removed instantly by turning the catches, shown in the illustration. The entire instrument can be taken apart in a moment and the interior construction is first class. Weight, packed for shipment, 10 pounds.

No. 12K1220 Price.................. **$4.95**

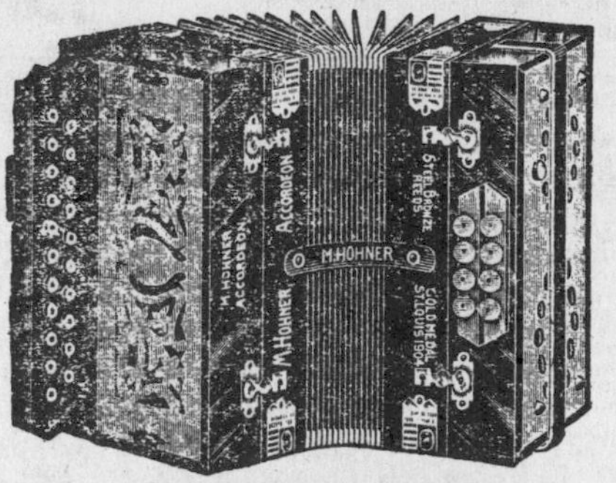

Size, 6⅛x11⅜x11½ inches.

Genuine Hohner Italian-Bohemian Accordion. It is made of a thoroughly seasoned spruce, a wood which is best known for its sonority, veneered in walnut and finished in imitation of mahogany, very highly polished. The panels are made of fancy openwork of beautiful design with green cloth lining, giving the accordion a very beautiful and rich appearance. The keyboard is invisible. The keys are made of pearl, shaped like a button, making them agreeable to the touch. It has a single bellows of fourteen folds, leather bound and with patent metal corner protectors. **It has twenty-one keys, eight basses** and all trimmings are nickel plated and very highly polished. The construction of this instrument is the same as the construction of the No. 12K1220 shown at the right and it has the same movable device by which the different complete sets of reeds can be taken from the instrument for repairs. The accordion is separable and can be taken apart instantly, should repairs be necessary. Weight, packed for shipment, 13½ pounds.

No. 12K1224 Price.................. **$8.75**

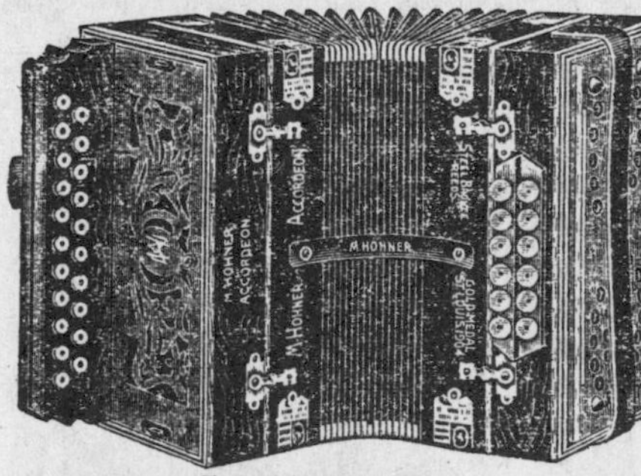

Size, 6x11x11⅜ inches.

Hohner Special Italian-Bohemian Accordion. It is made of genuine rosewood of a deep brown shade and rich flaming. It is inlaid throughout in natural wood, and fitted with nickel plated trimmings. It has a large and powerful bellows of sixteen folds, **twelve powerful basses and twenty-one keys fitted with elegant mother of pearl buttons.** This instrument is fitted with the new improved air valve in shape of a bar which runs nearly the entire length of the panel, and which can easily be opened with the thumb. Like all our Italian accordions it is separable and can be taken apart instantly. Each reed is set on a separate plate and securely fastened without the use of wax, by means of metallic clamps. The different sets of reeds are so arranged that they can be instantly taken out of the instrument in case any repairs should be necessary. Both the outside and inside construction is the very best that has ever been placed in an accordion. The twelve basses with which this accordion is fitted together with the four sets of reeds gives it a compass and power of tone not possessed by any other accordion. Weight, packed for shipment, 15 pounds.

No. 12K1228 Price.................. **$11.45**

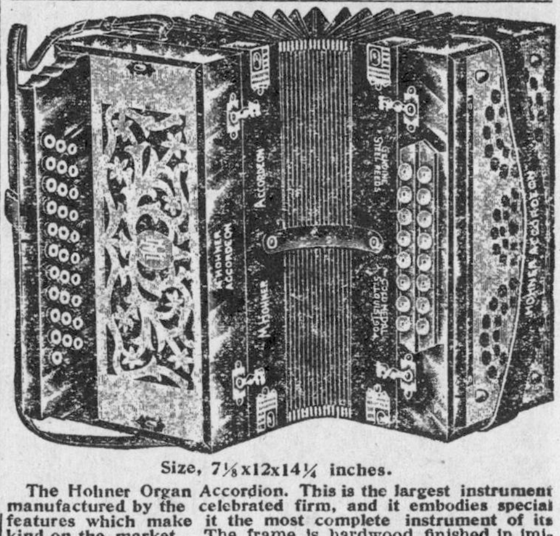

Size, 7⅛x12x14¼ inches.

The Hohner Organ Accordion. This is the largest instrument manufactured by the celebrated firm, and it embodies special features which make it the most complete instrument of its kind on the market. The frame is hardwood finished in imitation ebony, brought to a very fine piano polish. The panels are made in a fancy scroll work of maple, finished in natural color and ornamented with the Hohner monogram in silver letters. It has a bellows of sixteen folds, of black leatherette with brass corner protectors. The metal trimmings of this accordion are of brass, highly nickel plated and burnished. It has thirty-one invisible keys arranged in three rows and fitted with genuine mother of pearl button keys. These keys are recognized the best, as they permit the performer to run with greater rapidity up and down the keyboard. It has six sets of bronze reeds and sixteen basses. One of the features of this accordion is the air valve which, in the shape of a bar of the entire length of the panel, can be easily opened. It is also furnished with a very strong leather shoulder strap, as the accordion is very heavy. The tone of this instrument is so powerful as to resemble a parlor organ in every respect. With this instrument we give a very substantial wooden carrying case, covered with black imitation morocco leatherette, and complete with clasps and leather strap. Weight, boxed for shipment, 32 pounds.

No. 12K1230 Price.................. **$23.45**

THE CELEBRATED CH. WEISS HARMONICAS

CH. WEISS IS ONE OF THE MOST CELEBRATED OF ALL HARMONICA MAKERS and his instruments are in use by professionals and amateurs alike throughout the entire world. The principal characteristics of these instruments are elegance of finish, durability of construction and beauty of tone. To both professionals and amateurs we unhesitatingly recommend this line of harmonicas as something which will prove perfectly satisfactory in every respect. The line offers a great variety from which to select and each instrument is strictly high grade. We have now been handling this celebrated line of harmonicas for some years, and the fact that we are still handling them is conclusive proof that they have given universal satisfaction. Why should you buy a harmonica in the usual way from a local music dealer when you can buy a harmonica which is in every way equal, and in many points superior to harmonicas which you will buy in that way, paying double the price which we ask? Remember, that we promise to save you at least one-quarter on your purchase and all of these harmonicas are sold under this condition. Each instrument is furnished with a beautiful case, as shown in the illustrations, they are all easy blowing and accurately tuned to concert pitch. The harmonica is becoming a very popular instrument, because the musical public is beginning to realize that it is an instrument of real musical capacity and power. All of our harmonicas are beautifully and delicately tuned, are furnished with the very highest grade of bell metal reeds and are guaranteed satisfactory in every respect. The harmonica is an instrument which can be carried very handily in the pocket, and always helps to pass away the time very pleasantly. They are very easily learned and a wide range of music can be played on them.

EVERY HARMONICA IS FULLY GUARANTEED BY US. Each instrument shown in this line is suitable for the highest class of concert playing and can be used with splendid effect in playing with other instruments. Give us an opportunity to place one of these splendid instruments in your hands for approval, and we are sure that you will be so well satisfied with it that you will recommend it to all of your friends.

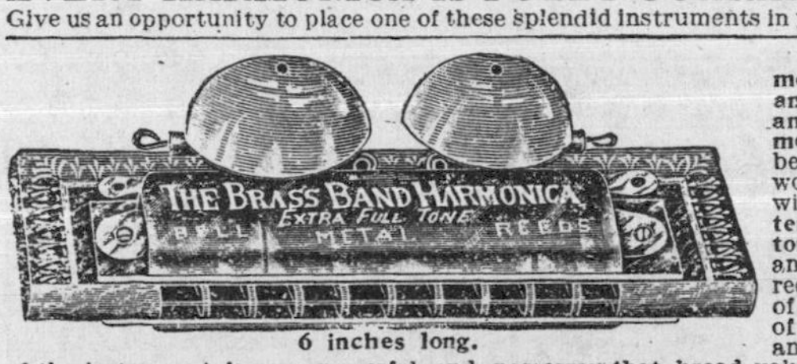

6 inches long.

The Brass Band Bell Harmonica is made by Ch. Weiss and is a splendidly finished and beautifully tuned instrument. It is fitted with tuned bells, which can be used with wonderful effect in connection with the instrument. It has **ten double holes, forty finely toned reeds,** accurately tuned and mounted on heavy brass reed plates. The bells are of the very best quality, made of the very best bell metal and highly polished. The tone of the instrument is very powerful and possesses that broad volume so much desired in a harmonica.

No. 12K1402 Price **67c**

Same as No. 12K1402, but has one bell, ten holes and twenty reeds. 5½ inches long.

No. 12K1404 Price.......(If by mail, postage extra, 8 cents) **36c**

Our Celeste Harmonica. This harmonica is made expressly for us by the celebrated maker, Ch. Weiss. It is made of the very finest material, and is intended for those who desire an instrument of great musical capacity and a splendid volume of tone. It has heavy nickel covers decorated with hand painted flowers. The panels are gold finished and give a rich appearance to the instrument. It has a wood frame, highly enameled in beautiful imitation of ivory. It is double sided, fitted with **twenty double holes, forty reeds on each side, making eighty reeds in all.** It comes in a splendid leatherette covered richly embossed case. This is a new instrument and one which we are prepared to recommend to all who desire something particularly fine in this line. The price which we quote on this harmonica represents simply what the harmonica costs us, with but our one small percentage of profit added, and is figured down so low that you cannot purchase a harmonica of this grade from any other dealer for less than twice the price we are making you.

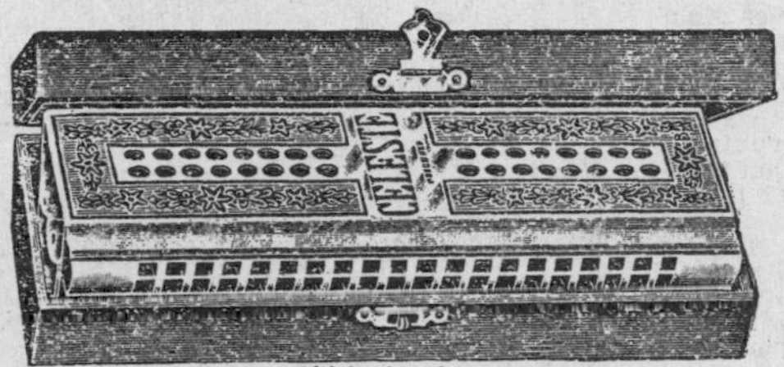

6¼ inches long.

No. 12K1414 Price **95c**

If by mail, postage extra, 15 cents.

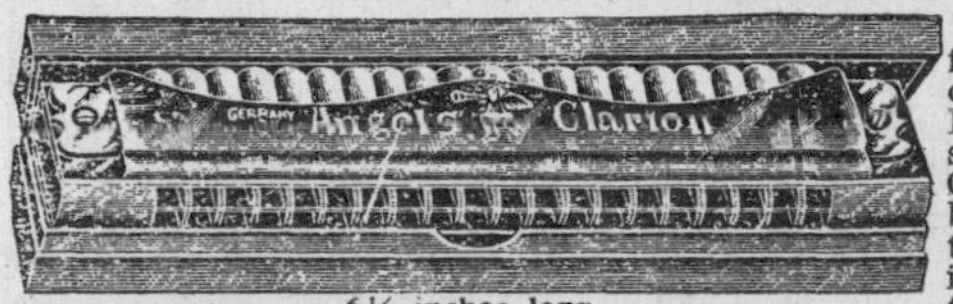

6¼ inches long.

Angel's Clarion. Manufactured by Ch. Weiss, maker of the celebrated Brass Band Harmonica. This harp resembles the Brass Band Clarion in some respects, but is so constructed as to produce peculiar, vibrating, organ-like tone not found in any other harmonica. It has **twenty double holes, with forty brass reeds,** and mounted on heavy brass reed plates. Has the clarion pipes and nickel covers. Packed in neat case. Every harmonica player should own one of these harps. This is a neat and compact instrument, suited for either amateur or professional playing, and one with which any harmonica player will be more than delighted. Our sales on this instrument have been enormous and are the best proof that it is an instrument of the very highest merit.

No. 12K1428 Price **60c**

If by mail, postage extra, 8 cents.

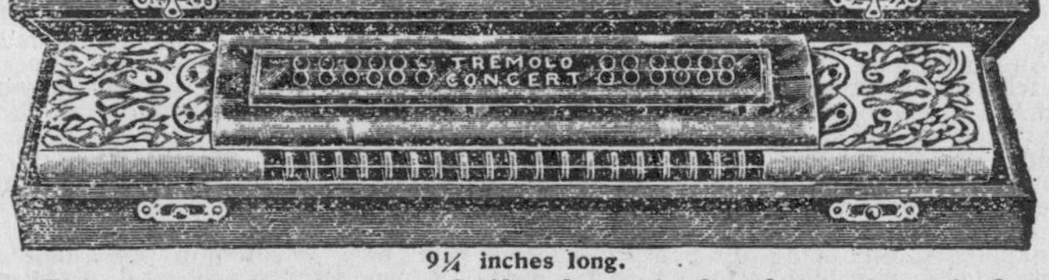

9¼ inches long.

This harmonica is one of the largest, handsomest and finest toned instruments made. Coming, as it does, from Europe, direct from the factory of the celebrated maker, Ch. Weiss, is a guarantee as to its quality. The illustration gives but a faint idea of what an exceptionally fine harmonica it really is. The wood frame is white enameled with gilt decorations. Has brass reed plates, highly polished nickel covers, **forty holes on each edge, eighty best bell metal reeds** accurately tuned to concert pitch, each side in a different key. As illustrated, it is packed in a handsome wood case with leatherette covering, satin lining and nickel clasps. Makes a beautiful ornament as well as a perfect musical instrument.

No. 12K1436 Price **90c**

If by mail, postage extra, 14 cents.

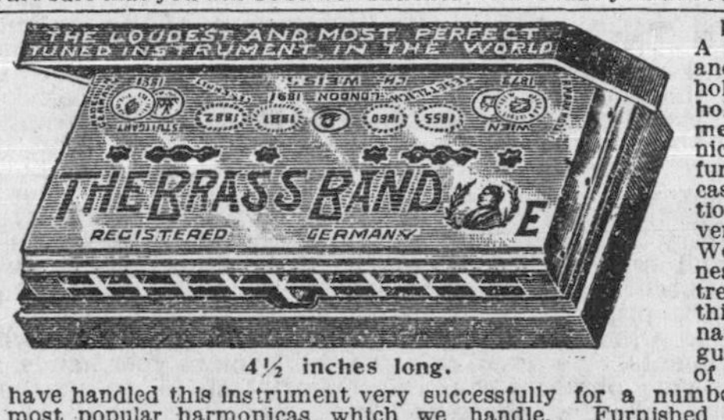

4½ inches long.

Brass Band Concert Harmonica. A double instrument of powerful and pleasing tone. Has ten double holes on each edge, twenty double holes in all; eighty fine bell metal reeds, brass reed plates, nickel covers. This harmonica is furnished with a very handsome case, as shown in the illustration, and is very handy and convenient for carrying in the pocket. We recommend it to all who wish a neat, compact harmonica at an extremely low price. The fact that this harmonica is stamped with the name of Ch. Weiss is a sufficient guarantee that it is an instrument of high grade in every respect. We have handled this instrument very successfully for a number of years and it is one of the most popular harmonicas which we handle. Furnished in the following combinations: A-D, C-F, C-G and A-E. State key wanted.

No. 12K1408 Price.........(If by mail, postage extra, 8 cents) **69c**

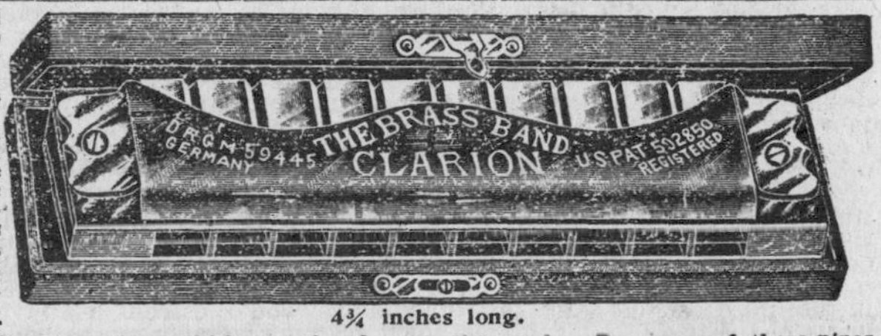

4¾ inches long.

The Brass Band Clarion Harmonica, manufactured by Ch. Weiss. A new invention in harmonicas. The brass reed plates and bell metal reeds are the same as those used in the celebrated Brass Band Harmonica which has gained such a world wide reputation. The new idea or invention is in the organ pipes, which are placed over the reeds. By means of these pipes the performer is enabled to change the tone at will, giving imitations of the flute, church organ or trumpet calls. Its construction makes it the most powerful toned harmonica as well as the easiest blowing and most attractive that has ever been placed on the market; pronounced as such by professionals throughout the country. Concert or large size harmonica has **ten double holes and forty reeds.** Packed in handsome heavy red leatherette case having substantial hinge and nickel plated fastener. Furnished in A, B, C, D, E, F and G. Be sure to state key wanted.

No. 12K1416 Price.........(If by mail, postage extra, 8 cents) **50c**

Brass Band Clarion Harmonica, has ten holes and twenty reeds. Packed in handsome red leatherette case. 4⅛ inches long.

No. 12K1420 Price.........(If by mail, postage extra, 6 cents) **23c**

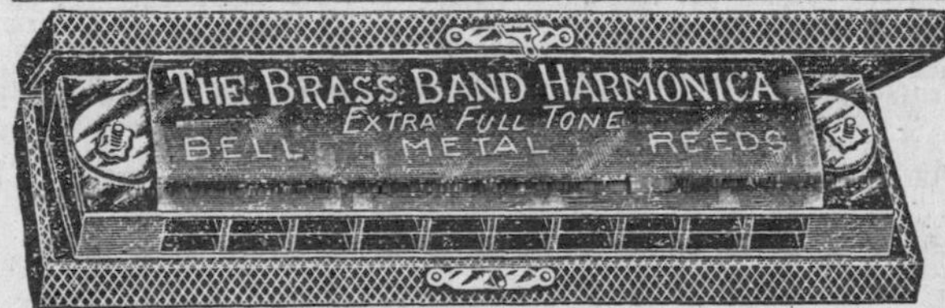

4¾ inches long.

Brass Band Harmonica. The reeds are made of the finest bell metal and are extremely sensitive, producing a remarkably smooth tone. The covers are flaring at the back and are made of solid brass, heavily nickel plated and are consequently of unusual strength, thus protecting the reeds perfectly. Accurately tuned to concert pitch. The Brass Band Harmonica has **ten double holes, forty bell metal reeds,** brass reed plates and extension ends. We include a handsomely lined wood case, as shown in illustration. Furnished in A, B, C, D, E, F and G. State key wanted. Retails for $1.00 and is worth every cent of it.

No. 12K1432 Price.........(If by mail, postage extra, 8 cents) **65c**

Same harmonica as No. 12K1432, but is 4⅛ inches long and has **ten holes and twenty reeds,** and comes packed in a neat pasteboard case.

No. 12K1434 Price.........(If by mail, postage extra, 6 cents) **19c**

7½ inches long.

This is the very latest harmonica produced by the celebrated maker, Ch. Weiss. It is made with **twenty-four double holes on each side, forty-eight double holes in all, and ninety-six reeds,** four heavy brass reed plates, and fancy nickel plated covers. This harp is especially constructed for the vibrato tone, making it sweet and powerful and similar to the tremolo of a parlor organ. For concert or parlor playing it cannot be surpassed. No player should be without one. Like all other Weiss harmonicas it is fully guaranteed. This harmonica comes in leatherette case, handsomely lined and nickel clasps.

No. 12K1440 Price.........(If by mail, postage extra, 15 cents) **$1.15**

THE PIPEOLION, 95c

Ch. Weiss, the manufacturer of the celebrated Brass Band Harmonicas, has invented this wonderful little instrument, which we consider the best and simplest musical instrument ever produced. It is not only easy to blow but the easiest of all reed instruments to learn to play. Any child who can count can learn to play the Pipeolion. The body of the instrument consists of wood finished in a rich dark color, embossed with gold designs. The mouthpiece is made of nickel plated metal, devoid of all sharp edges, permitting the performer to run from the bass to the melody part of the instrument with great rapidity. It has ten holes and ten corresponding trumpets, tempered the same as brass band instruments.

These trumpets are fitted with two reeds, enabling the performer to produce twenty different notes. The peculiar feature of this instrument lies in the fact that the reeds are built right into the trumpets, and in producing the sound it has to come out through the bell of the pipe, thus giving it a peculiar trumpet and organ like tone. The entire instrument is finished very beautifully, the trumpets being burnished, and the woodwork varnished and highly polished.

7⅞ inches long.
3¼ inches wide.

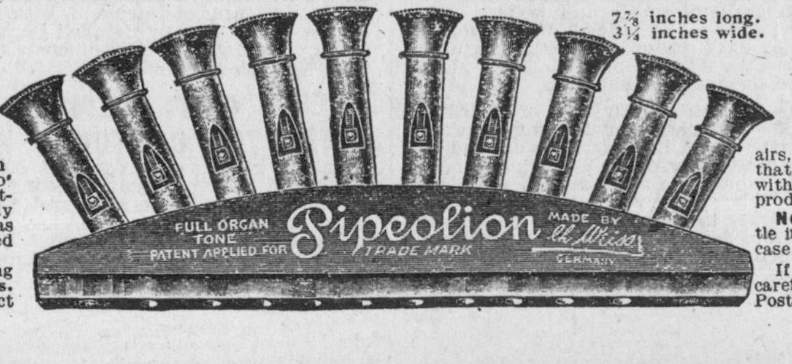

With each instrument we give a complete set of instructions of how to play, including four popular airs, written in a special copyrighted system, so easy that anybody, even a child, can in a short time and with little practice, learn to play the instrument and produce beautiful music with it.

No. 12K1450 Our price for this wonderful little instrument complete, in neat and substantial case **95c**

If sent by mail, we pack this instrument very carefully, insuring delivery in perfect condition. Postage, 12 cents.

OUR BAND INSTRUMENT DEPARTMENT

FOUR MAGNIFICENT LINES OF BRASS INSTRUMENTS SOLD EXCLUSIVELY BY US. A COMPLETE LINE OF WOOD WIND INSTRUMENTS, DRUMS, AND GENERAL BAND SUPPLIES. EVERY INSTRUMENT COVERED BY OUR WRITTEN BINDING GUARANTEE.

OUR FREE SPECIAL BAND INSTRUMENT CATALOGUE

THE MOST COMPLETE AND COMPREHENSIVE CATALOGUE OF BAND INSTRUMENTS EVER ISSUED WILL BE SENT TO YOU ABSOLUTELY FREE ON REQUEST.

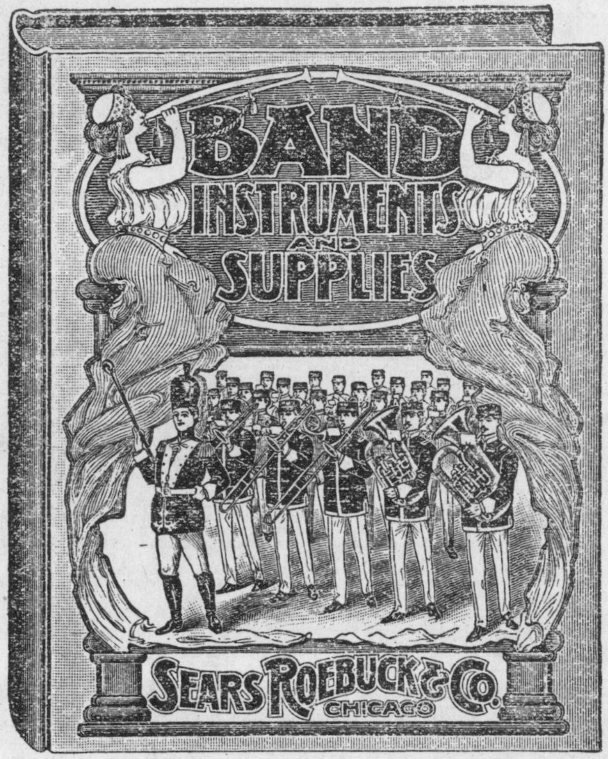

WE ARE SHOWING ON THIS PAGE an illustration of the splendid special catalogue which we are now issuing, containing illustrations and descriptions of band instruments and supplies, showing the most complete line ever offered to the bandmen of the United States. This book contains large illustrations and full descriptions of our four splendid lines of brass instruments; also **clarionets, saxophones, flutes, oboes, bassoons, drums and all kinds of band instrument supplies.** It also tells you how to select and purchase your band instruments, how to organize and manage your band, and gives a table showing the correct instrumentation for bands of all sizes, together with many suggestions in regard to the care of band instruments. This book should be in the hands of every bandman in the United States, as it marks a startling revolution in the purchase and sale of all kinds of band instruments. It fully explains the reasons why we are able to sell high class band instruments for one-half the prices asked by others. It tells you why the prices on band instruments have been so high in the past, and gives valuable information which will prove a great advantage to you when you are ready to purchase your instruments. We desire to place this book in your hands, but will say that if you are ready to make your purchase you are perfectly safe in making your selection of band instruments from the following pages, and it is much preferable for you to do so rather than cause a delay by writing for our Special Band Catalogue. The illustrations which we give on the following pages are faithful reproductions of the instruments themselves from photographs, and the descriptions are as complete as we can possibly make them in the small space allowed for this purpose. As the true and final test of any article ordered from us is the examination and trial which you give it after it is received, and as you are not asked to accept it until after a thorough trial you are fully satisfied that it is everything that you desire and a great bargain in every respect, you will see that you have the same advantages in ordering from this big catalogue that you would have in ordering from the special catalogue. If, however, you desire illustrations and descriptions of our complete line before ordering, we will be glad to send you this special catalogue, and it will only be necessary for you to send us a postal card saying, "Please send me your Special Band Catalogue," when it will be forwarded to you absolutely free. We are now the largest band instrument dealers in the world selling directly to users, and we are in a better position than any other house in the country to furnish you instruments of a high grade at the same small margin of profit which we make on groceries, dry goods, etc. If you are not particularly interested at the present time in the purchase of band instruments, we would esteem it a favor if you would send us the name of the band leader in your town, or some member of the band who will be interested in these goods. You probably know of some band about to be organized, and you will not only do us a great favor, but you will also do them a great service as well by sending us the name of the leading member, so that we may place this catalogue in his hands.

WE WANT ALL BANDMEN TO KNOW that we are now the largest band instrument dealers in the country selling directly to the user. Last year we furnished over 500 bands with complete sets of instruments besides selling an immense number of single instruments of all kinds, and this year our business will undoubtedly be doubled. The reason for the growth of this immense business is easily explained. Our methods of sale have worked the same revolution in this line of goods as in all other lines. We sell our instruments directly to the user adding but one small percentage of profit to the maker's price, and in this way the cornet which was formerly sold at $50.00 is now sold at $20.00, and a proportional saving is made throughout the entire line of band instruments. As our business has grown in this line and we have sold these instruments in greater quantities, we have been able to reduce the prices from time to time, so that now we are selling all classes of band instruments at prices ranging from one-third to one-half lower than any other dealers are able to offer. We ask you to compare all the instruments and prices shown in our catalogue with those offered by other dealers and you will find the above statement to be absolutely true in every particular. The fact that we send all of our instruments out with the understanding that the purchaser is to be the sole judge of their merits and decide for himself whether or not they are everything we claim for them and high grade instruments in every respect, will remove all doubt in regard to the truthfulness of the statements we make. It is our desire and intention to make our Band Instrument Department headquarters for band instruments and supplies in the United States, and we certainly could not do this by misrepresenting our goods in any way. There is no class of goods so susceptible to false valuation as musical instruments. The true value of such an instrument can only be fixed by one who is expert in its manufacture or handles it constantly in buying or selling. The fact that a man is a musician does not always make him a good judge of musical instrument values. He can judge of tone or ease of execution, but as to the material and workmanship contained in the instrument he is often the poorest kind of a judge. These are points for which the purchaser has to take the dealer's word absolutely, and, as a general rule, is entirely at the mercy of the man from whom he purchases. **The value of every musical instrument which we handle is accurately determined by an expert at the time we purchase it.** We base our prices upon the value determined at that time and sell the instrument to the customer under our binding guarantee, so that the purchaser is always sure of receiving an instrument the real value of which is in proportion to the price we charge. There are many so called high class cornets on the market today for which the manufacturer is charging from $50.00 to $100.00, when as an actual fact the real cost of manufacturing the instrument does not exceed $15.00 at the outside. He is able to fix and receive this large price because he has established a reputation, possesses a monopoly and is absolutely without competition. The price is fixed without any reference whatever to the real value of the instrument, but with the idea of getting as much as the unsuspecting customer is willing to pay.

THE MARCEAU BAND INSTRUMENTS are certainly the very finest line of low priced band instruments ever offered to American bandmen. They are fully warranted by us, shipped under our ten days' trial offer and we ship them with the distinct understanding and agreement that the buyer must be perfectly satisfied or they can be returned entirely at our expense. They are especially suitable for beginners or amateurs who are playing a medium grade of music and desire a set of instruments which will give satisfactory service at a low price. We have sold hundreds of sets of these instruments and they have proved universally satisfactory. They are all of the very best models with French pattern silver piston valve and are thoroughly tested and inspected by us before shipping.

OUR DUPONT BAND INSTRUMENTS. This is our line of medium priced band instruments and we are willing to have them compared with band instruments offered by other dealers and sold at more than double our prices. These instruments are especially suitable for the better grade of amateur bands and thousands of testimonials which we receive every year sufficiently prove that they give satisfaction in every case. We have handled them for the last five years, and during that time have furnished them to hundreds of bands. They are instruments which will meet every demand made upon them, are of the very best model, and are fitted with French light action piston valves. If you are figuring on purchasing a new set of instruments for your band and desire a set of instruments at a low price, which will give satisfaction under all conditions, we especially recommend them for your consideration.

TOURVILLE & CO. BAND INSTRUMENTS. This is certainly the most magnificent line of band instruments ever sold in this country. We are the sole American agents for these splendid instruments, and while we have only been selling them for about three years our sales have grown to enormous proportions. They will compare favorably with the very highest class of band instruments made in this country, and in many instances they have been selected in preference to several well known makes of instruments manufactured in this country. They are of beautiful model, handsome chased reinforced joints, splendidly made and fitted with the French light action silver piston valves. We recommend them to all bands who desire to do the very finest kind of concert playing, as they will meet every demand made upon them and prove satisfactory under all conditions. They are superb instruments in every respect and all we ask is an opportunity to place one or more of them in your bands for trial and examination, and if you do not find that they are up to your expectations in every way, and that the price you have paid is only about one-half what you would have to give any other dealer for the same grade of instruments, we will not ask you to keep them, but you can return them entirely at our expense and we will cheerfully refund your money. We have equipped some of the largest concert bands in the country with these splendid instruments, and in almost every case they have been selected in preference to well known and highly priced instruments of American make. All of these instruments are of the latest improved short model with high and low pitch attachments, pearl value buttons, handsomely ornamented with chased bands around the joints, made of the very best material and by the most skilful workmen. They are all imported from France, the home of modern high grade band instruments. We desire an opportunity to place a set of these magnificent instruments in your hands for trial and examination.

LAMOREAUX FRERES have devoted their time, thought and energy for twenty-five years to the manufacture of cornets and trombones exclusively. By putting their efforts into the making of these instruments, they have at last succeeded in producing cornets and trombones which, for the tone, workmanship, and model (which other manufacturers are vainly trying to copy) are superior to any other make and are recommended by artists of this country and Europe. On page 252 we give a good description of the cornets. For detailed descriptions and for illustrations, which show to better advantage the perfect models of these instruments, send for our Band Catalogue, which also includes the trombones.

OUR TEN DAYS' TRIAL OFFER.

AFTER THE CUSTOMER HAS RECEIVED THE INSTRUMENT we allow him to try it for ten days, and if at any time within that period it should prove unsatisfactory, it can be returned to us and we will refund the full price paid and pay express charges both ways. This fully protects the customer against any possible loss, and we make him the sole judge of the merits of the instruments. We ship all our band instruments and musical goods upon these terms, as we desire our customers to be perfectly satisfied before finally accepting their purchase.

OUR CELEBRATED MARCEAU BAND INSTRUMENTS.
GREATEST BARGAINS IN BAND INSTRUMENTS EVER OFFERED TO THE BANDMEN OF AMERICA.

THIS IS ONE OF THE FINE LINES of band instruments which we have been handling for years and which have given such immense satisfaction.

MUSIC RACKS and INSTRUCTION BOOKS are sent with all of these instruments.

WE GUARANTEE EVERY INSTRUMENT in this line and sell them on the same terms that we sell all of our other band instruments. Each horn is fitted with celebrated French piston light action valves and is splendid in model and finish. Beware of the cheap lines of instruments handled by dealers throughout the country. They only sell a very limited quantity of goods, and no manufacturer of any reputation whatsoever can entrust his agency to them.

Marceau E Flat Cornet.

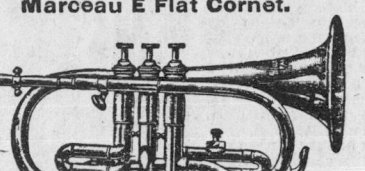

A clear toned, splendid instrument for the use of leaders. Guaranteed in every way. Beautiful in model, perfect in tune and tone. The E flat cornet is never used except for playing in a band. If you wish a cornet for general playing, you should order a B flat cornet.

No. 12K7980 Brass, highly polished. **$6.65**
No. 12K7981 Nickel plated, highly polished 7.55

Marceau B Flat Cornet.
SINGLE WATER KEY.

This is a fine B Flat Cornet in every way and is suitable for use in either band or orchestra. We send with it an A shank for use in orchestra, and it is a splendid instrument in every way.

No. 12K7984 Brass, highly polished. . . . **$6.85**
No. 12K7985 Nickel plated, highly polished 7.75

Marceau C Cornet.

We can also furnish this cornet in the key of C at the following prices:

No. 12K7988 Brass. Price. **$6.95**
No. 12K7989 Nickel plated. Price. 7.85

Marceau B Flat Cornet.
DOUBLE WATER KEY.

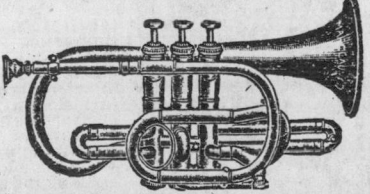

This Double Water Key Cornet has been a favorite with bandmen for a long time on account of its beautiful model and splendid new appearance. It is furnished with an A shank for use in orchestra and is a fine instrument in every way.

No. 12K7992 Brass, polished. Price. **$7.95**
No. 12K7994 Nickel plated, highly polished. Price. 8.95

Marceau Solo Altos.

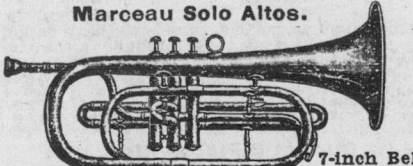

7-inch Bell.

These instruments are manufactured for solo alto purposes and have been great favorites ever since their appearance. They are easy blowing, have a splendid tone and a handsome appearance.

No. 12K8011 Brass, highly polished. **$10.45**
No. 12K8012 Nickel plated, highly polished. . . . 11.95

Marceau E Flat Altos and B Flat Tenors.

Altos
8-inch
Bell.

Tenors
8½-inch
Bell.

These instruments are splendid for harmony work in a band, and we recommend them highly for those who desire fine altos and tenors at extremely low prices. They have a splendid tone, a beautiful model and a handsome appearance. They are perfect in tune and tone and so well constructed that they will last a lifetime. The action of the valves is extremely light and either one of these instruments can be used very nicely for solo purposes. We guarantee them to be satisfactory, and we believe that alto and tenor players will find in these instruments just what they desire at a very small cost. We desire to place them in the hands of all who are looking for something in this line at a moderate price, and we do not ask the customer to take any chances as we assume all the risk of shipping them.

No. 12K8013 Alto, brass, polished. **$10.75**
No. 12K8014 Alto, nickel plated, polished. 12.25
No. 12K8015 Tenor, brass, polished. 12.60
No. 12K8016 Tenor, nick'l plat'd, polish'd 14.70

For Band Instrument Supplies of all kinds, send for our Special Band Instrument Catalogue

---

Marceau B Flat Baritone.

9½-inch Bell.

These instruments have been used with great success in all sorts of solo playing and general band work. A large number of bandmen have pronounced them the finest baritones on the market for less than double the price given below. Their tone is full and sonorous without being dull, and is light and clear without being too snappy. The model is handsome and the general workmanship on the instruments is all that can be desired. We recommend these baritones highly to baritone players throughout the country and we are always willing to have them compared with instruments offered by other dealers for twice the price.

No. 12K8017 Brass, highly polished. **$14.15**
No. 12K8018 Nickel plated, highly polished. Price. **$16.65**

Marceau F Circular Alto. 10-inch Bell.

This style of alto horn has become very popular with all kinds of military and concert bands in the last few years on account of its beautiful mellow tone. It is used almost exclusively by all of the larger bands and we recommend its use to all bandmen. Its circular model makes it a very easy blowing and sensitive instrument and not only does it add to the appearance of the band, but it gives the music a coloring which can be obtained in no other way. It is made by the same celebrated makers who manufacture the balance of this line, and is a valuable addition to the well known Marceau & Co. band instruments which we have handled so successfully for years. If your band does not possess altos of this model you should by all means procure them without delay, and you will find that the beautiful effect which you will obtain will much more than compensate for the small expense incurred. It is furnished with three additional crooks, Eb, D and C; thus enabling the performer to play in four different keys. All crooks are fitted with water key, enabling the performer to quickly remove the accumulation of saliva, a feature to be found only on our instruments.

No. 12K8033 Brass, highly polished. **$19.95**
No. 12K8034 Nickel plated. Price, 22.45

Marceau B Flat Bass.

10¼-inch Bell.

These instruments can be used with excellent effect to fill in between the E Flat Bass and the B Flat Baritone. They are very effective when used in the bass solos which frequently occur in band selections, and they serve to balance up the instrumentation in excellent shape. Their tone is everything that could be asked for in an instrument of this nature and in model and finish they are splendid in every way.

No. 12K8019 Brass, highly polished. **$15.40**
No. 12K8020 Nickel plated, highly polished. Price. . . . **$17.95**

Marceau E Flat Bass.

11½-inch Bell.

We wish to call your attention particularly to this instrument and will say without fear of contradiction, that it has never been equaled, price considered. It has a deep, rich tone and furnishes an excellent fundamental bass for any brass band. It has enough volume to answer for a large instrumentation and the tone is full and sweet enough for use, if desired, in orchestras. The model is fine and the tubing is so thoroughly braced and reinforced that it will not break down under severe use. The valves are all quick and responsive and we guarantee the instrument to be satisfactory in every particular.

No. 12K8021 Brass, highly polished. Price. . **$21.25**
No. 12K8022 Nickel plated, highly polished. Price. **$25.15**

Marceau E Flat Contra-bass. 15-inch Bell.

This instrument is of exactly the same splendid model and construction as our No. 12K8021, only it is of extra large proportions, and is very deep and rich in tone. We recommend it very highly to all band organizations. The bell of this instrument is of a flaring model.

No. 12K8021½ Brass, highly polished. **$24.60**
No. 12K8022½ Nickel plated, highly polished 28.60

Marceau Valve Trombones.
SPECIAL HILLYARD LONG MODEL.

No. 12K8023 6½-inch Bell.   No. 12K8029 7-inch Bell.

These Trombones are all fine in every respect and have that deep, rich tone so peculiar to trombones. Each should be fitted with at least two of these, as they give a coloring harmony, which could be obtained in no other way.

No. 12K8023 E Flat Alto Trombone, brass. Price. **$11.65**
No. 12K8024 E Flat Alto Trombone, nickel plated. Price. 13.15
No. 12K8029 B Flat Tenor Trombone, brass. Price. 13.55
No. 12K8030 B Flat Tenor Trombone, nickel plated. Price. 15.45

Marceau Slide Trombones.

7-inch Bell.

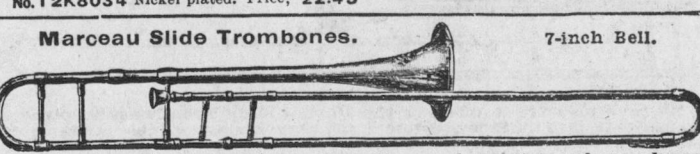

We know that these instruments will appeal to all trombone players who desire good, serviceable trombones at an extremely low price. For band and orchestra use they will be found equal to all requirements. For solo playing they have given general satisfaction. The slide works with ease and rapidity and the tone is mellow and powerful.

No. 12K8031 Brass, highly polished. Price. **$6.85**
No. 12K8032 Nickel plated, highly polished. Price. 8.55

OUR WORLD RENOWNED DUPONT BAND INSTRUMENTS

Dupont E Flat Cornet.

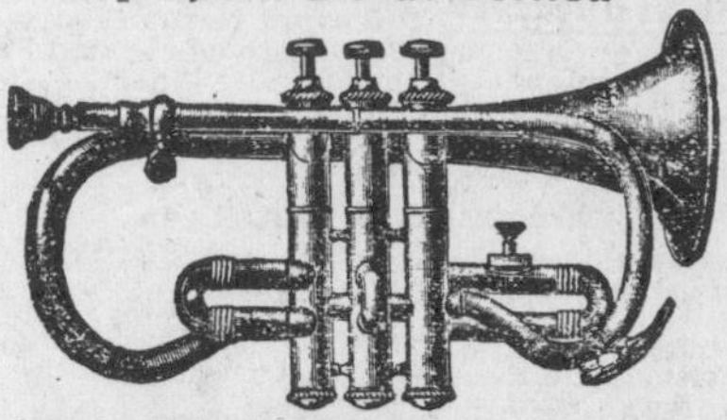

This is an especially fine instrument, and is so constructed that many of the objectionable features to be found in other E flat cornets have been entirely avoided. The E flat cornet is never used except for playing with a band. If you want a cornet for general playing you should order a B flat cornet.

No. 12K8040 Brass, polished........ $8.20
No. 12K8042 Nickel plated........ 9.45
No. 12K8044 Silver plated, satin finish........ 12.45
No. 12K8046 Silver plated, polished........ 14.65

Dupont B Flat Cornet, Single Water Key.

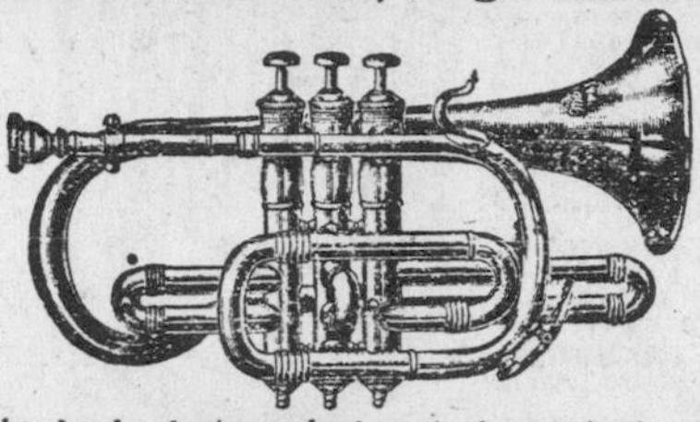

For band and orchestra work where steady, conscientious results are required, this cornet is particularly desirable.

No. 12K8047 Brass, polished........ $8.95
No. 12K8048 Nickel plated........ 10.20
No. 12K8049 Silver plated, satin finish........ 13.20
No. 12K8050 Silver plated, polished........ 15.45

Dupont C Cornet.

We can also furnish the above cornet in the key of C, thus avoiding the necessity of transposing the music when playing from piano or vocal scores. Complete with B flat crook.

No. 12K8039 Brass, polished........ $8.90
No. 12K8041 Nickel plated........ 10.15
No. 12K8043 Silver plated, satin finish........ 13.15
No. 12K8045 Silver plated, polished........ 15.40

Dupont B Flat Cornet, Double Water Key.

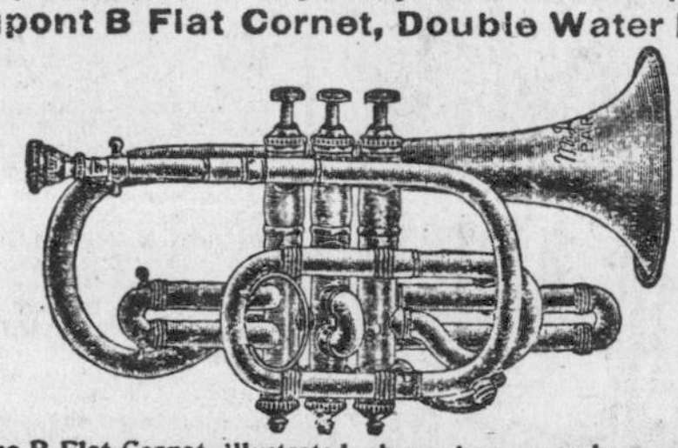

The B Flat Cornet, illustrated above, has never been excelled in playing qualities by any band instrument ever made. The material of which it is made is of the very finest, and the skill of the maker is splendidly shown in the beautiful model and excellent finish.

No. 12K8052 Brass, polished........ $10.95
No. 12K8054 Nickel plated........ 12.15
No. 12K8056 Silver plated, satin finish........ 15.20
No. 12K8058 Silver plated, polished........ 17.45

The Dupont B Flat Trumpet.

19 inches long.

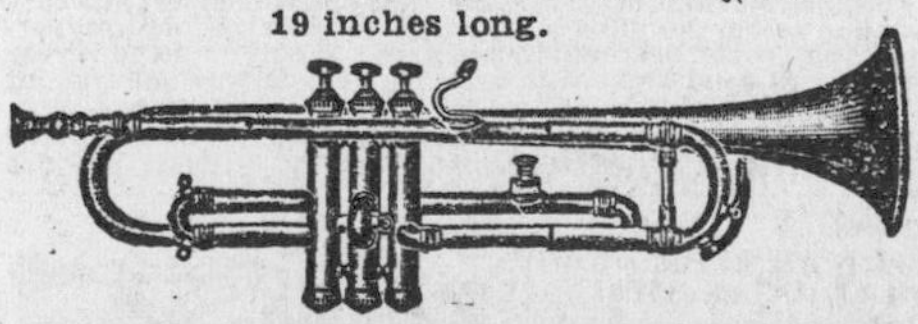

The B Flat Trumpet is becoming more popular every day, and is rapidly replacing the E flat and in many cases the B flat cornets. It has a peculiar tone, blending between the tone of the E flat and B flat cornets, and is very useful in certain compositions where the trumpet quality of tone is desired. These trumpets are used very extensively by large band organizations throughout the country. To play in the key of A extend tuning slide about 1¾ inches.

No. 12K8051 Brass, highly polished........ $10.45
No. 12K8053 Nickel plated........ 11.70
No. 12K8057 Silver plated, satin finish........ 14.65
No. 12K8059 Silver plated, burnished........ 16.95

FOR SAXOPHONES, OBOES, BASSOONS, ALTO AND BASS, CLARIONETS, KETTLE DRUMS AND A COMPLETE LINE OF BAND INSTRUMENTS AND SUPPLIES, SEND FOR OUR FREE BAND CATALOGUE.

Dupont Solo Alto.

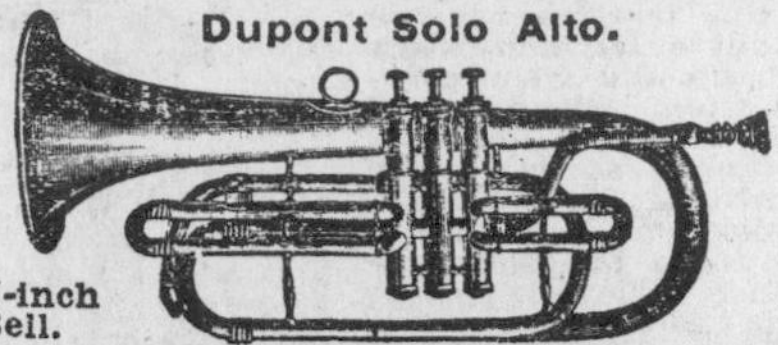

6¾-inch Bell.

This instrument is intended for use as a solo alto, and while it can be used as a harmony instrument it is best adapted for use on solo alto parts in band music which have been so popular of late years.

No. 12K8076 Brass, polished........ $12.15
No. 12K8078 Nickel plated........ 14.15
No. 12K8080 Silver plated, satin finish........ 18.65
No. 12K8082 Silver plated, polished........ 22.15

Dupont "F" Concert Alto (Symphony Horn.)

10⅜-inch Bell.

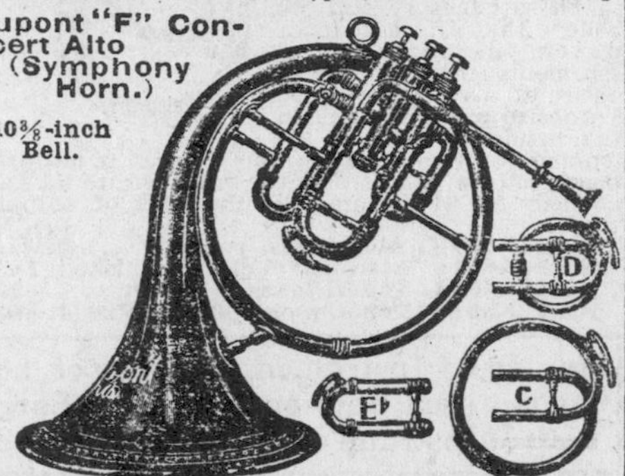

This is fast becoming a very popular instrument, both in bands and orchestras. It adds a dash of color to the harmony in band music, which can be obtained in no other way, and is fast supplanting the regular upright alto as an accompaniment horn. In orchestra it is considered valuable because it does not require the constant practice which is required on the French horn, and its tone is every bit as mellow and sweet. Anyone who has learned to play a cornet or alto can play this instrument, because it fingers exactly the same as a cornet and blows exactly the same as the alto. It is furnished in the key of F, with C, E flat and D crook. Every crook is furnished with water key, permitting the removal of saliva, without the trouble and inconvenience of removing the crooks. This improvement is not to be found on any other make. When used in a band it is always played in E flat, and when used in the orchestra, the F and D crooks are used. The C crook is very useful, as it throws the instrument into a key which enables the performer to play right along with the piano or organ without transposing the music It is the beautiful French horn model and is furnished complete, with music rack, mouthpiece and instruction book. We especially recommend this instrument and we know it will prove acceptable to all band and orchestra men who use it.

No. 12K8075 Brass, polished........ $24.95
No. 12K8077 Nickel plated........ 27.45
No. 12K8079 Silver, satin finish........ 32.45
No. 12K8081 Silver, polished........ 37.75

Dupont Altos and Tenors.

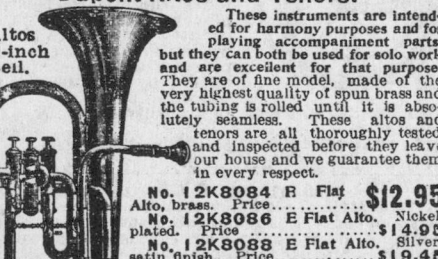

Altos 7¾-inch Bell.

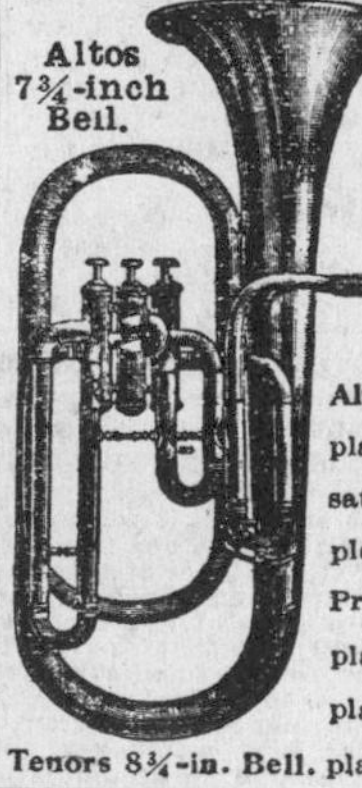

Tenors 8¾-in. Bell.

These instruments are intended for harmony purposes and for playing accompaniment parts, but they can both be used for solo work and are excellent for that purpose. They are of fine model, made of the very highest quality of spun brass and the tubing is rolled until it is absolutely seamless. These altos and tenors are all thoroughly tested and inspected before they leave our house and we guarantee them in every respect.

No. 12K8084 B Flat Alto, brass. Price........ $12.95
No. 12K8086 E Flat Alto. Nickel plated. Price........ $14.95
No. 12K8088 E Flat Alto. Silver, satin finish. Price........ $19.45
No. 12K8090 E Flat Alto. Silver plated, polished. Price........ $22.95
No. 12K8092 B Flat Tenor, brass. Price........ $14.80
No. 12K8094 B Flat Tenor, nickel plated. Price........ $16.95
No. 12K8096 B Flat Tenor, silver plated, satin finish. Price........ $22.75
No. 12K8098 B Flat Tenor, silver plated, polished. Price........ $26.20

Dupont B Flat Baritone.

10½-inch Bell.

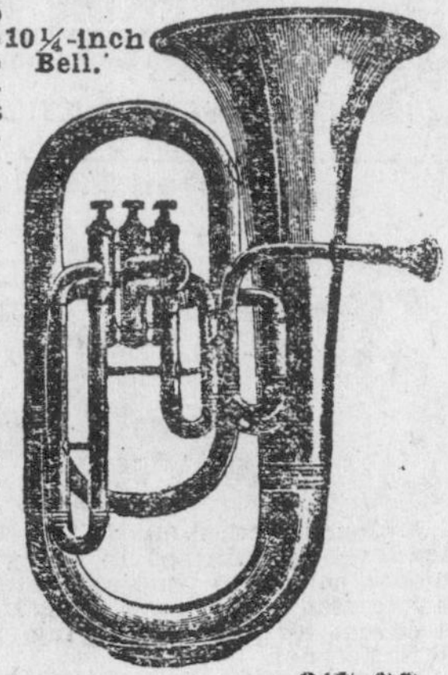

We take pleasure in bringing to the notice of baritone players the magnificent instrument shown in the engraving opposite. We have supplied these instruments to a large number of bands, and in every case they have called forth the unstinted praise of the player. The tone is round, full and deep, and in solo playing it leaves nothing to be desired. Particular care has been used by the manufacturer in the production of this instrument, and we do not hesitate to say that it is certainly one of the best baritones made today.

No. 12K8100 Brass, polished........ $17.60
No. 12K8102 Nickel plated........ 20.30
No. 12K8104 Silver plated, satin finish. 36.55
No. 12K8106 Silver plated, polished........ 32.60

Dupont B Flat Bass. 11-inch Bell.

This instrument is particularly adapted for shading and blending the deep diapason tones of the tuba, and forms a connecting link in the harmony between that instrument and the baritone. It produces an excellent effect in the heavy bass solos of modern street marches and selections, and serves to blend and distribute the harmony of the bass section.

No. 12K8108 Brass, polished........ $18.80
No. 12K8110 Nickel plated........ 20.60
No. 12K8112 Silver plated, satin finish... 30.80
No. 12K8114 Silver plated, polished........ 36.80

Dupont E Flat Bass.

12¾-inch Bell.

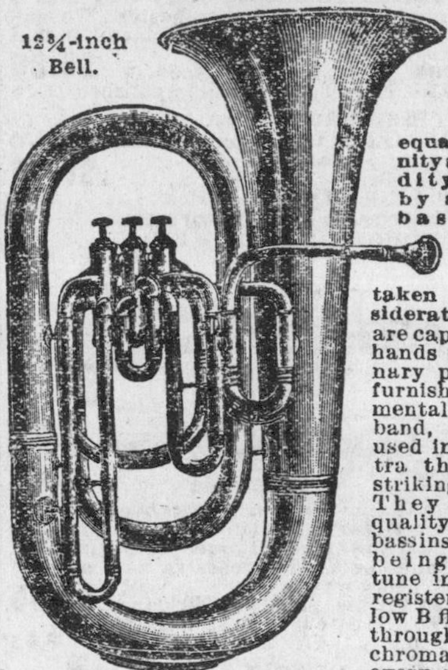

We do not believe that these instruments have ever been equaled for dignity and profundity of tone by any other basses ever made, where the price is taken into consideration. They are capable, in the hands of an ordinary player, of furnishing a fundamental bass for any band, and when used in an orchestra the effect is striking and grand. They possess the quality so rare in bass instruments of being in perfect tune in the upper register, and from low B flat clear up through the entire chromatic scale, every note is full, accurate and in perfect tune. We have supplied a great many bass players throughout the country with these instruments and in every instance they have called forth the loudest praise.

No. 12K8116 Medium, brass, polished........ $25.25
No. 12K8118 Medium, nickel........ 29.25
No. 12K8120 Medium, silver, satin finish.. 40.25
No. 12K8122 Medium, silver, polished........ 48.25

Dupont E Flat Contrabass.

13½-inch Bell.

This bass is of the same splendid model as the one quoted above, but is much larger in size and with an extra large size bell. It is extremely powerful. A bass that can be used with any organization no matter how large.

No. 12K8124 Contrabass, brass........ $27.15
No. 12K8126 Contrabass, nickel........ 31.35
No. 12K8128 Contrabass, silver, satin finish, 43.15
No. 12K8130 Contrabass, silver, polished.. 50.15

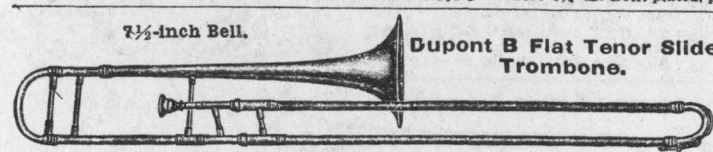

Dupont B Flat Tenor Slide Trombone.

7½-inch Bell.

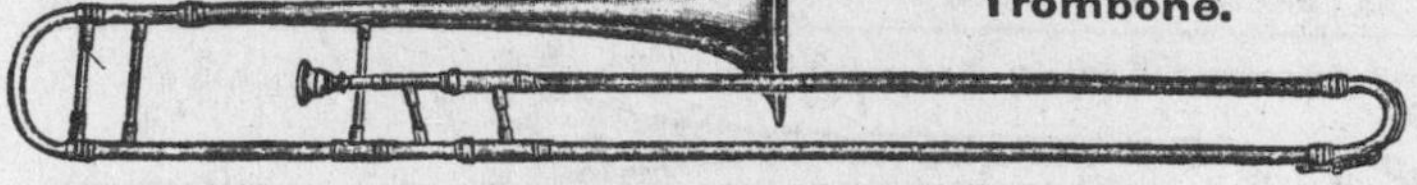

We take pleasure in offering the Dupont Slide Trombones to players because we believe that they represent the very highest possible attainments in this line, considering the extremely low prices which we are able to make. Great care and study has been given to their manufacture, and the result has been gratifying, indeed.

No. 12K8156 Brass, polished........ $7.95
No. 12K8158 Nickel plated........ 9.70
No. 12K8160 Silver plated, satin finish........ 13.20
No. 12K8162 Silver plated, polished........ 15.95

Dupont Valve Trombone.

8-inch Bell.

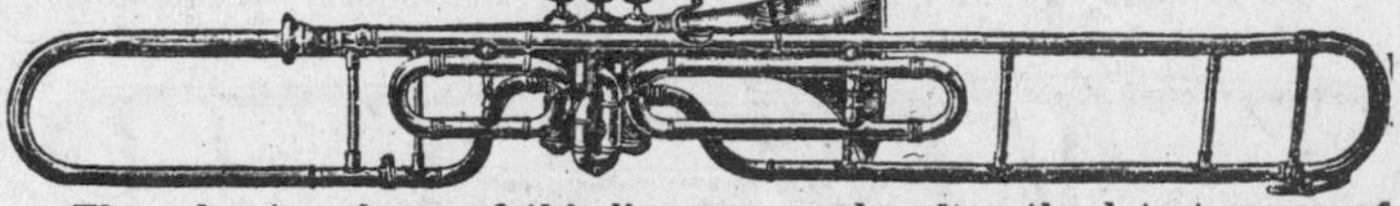

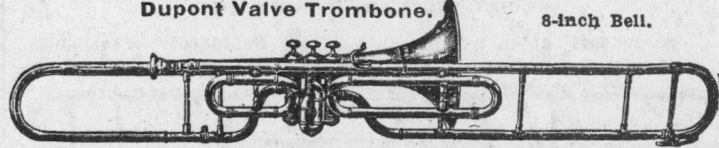

The valve trombones of this line are made after the latest approved models and are fine instruments in every respect.

No. 12K8132 E Flat Alto Trombone, brass, polished........ $12.90
No. 12K8134 E Flat Alto Trombone, nickel plated........ 14.90
No. 12K8136 E Flat Alto Trombone, silver plated, satin finish.... 19.40
No. 12K8138 E Flat Alto Trombone, silver plated, polished........ 22.90
No. 12K8140 B Flat Tenor Trombone, brass, polished........ 12.95
No. 12K8142 B Flat Tenor Trombone, nickel plated........ 15.20
No. 12K8144 B Flat Tenor Trombone, silver, satin finish........ 20.95
No. 12K8146 B Flat Tenor Trombone, silver plated, polished........ 24.45

OUR SPLENDID LINE OF TOURVILLE & CO. BAND INSTRUMENTS

MADE BY TOURVILLE & CO., OF PARIS, FRANCE,

AND THE ENTIRE LINE FITTED WITH MOTHER OF PEARL VALVE BUTTONS AND THE WONDERFUL TOURVILLE LOW PITCH ATTACHMENT.

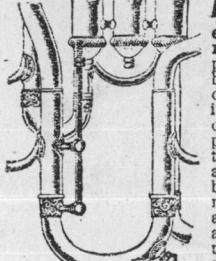

AN EXAMINATION OF THE ILLUSTRATIONS SHOWN BELOW will show you that each one of these splendid instruments is now fitted with a low pitch attachment, enabling the performer to change the instrument instantly from high to low pitch. This is of immense advantage, because the performer never knows when it will be necessary for him to change his instrument from one pitch to another, and with ordinary band instruments it would be necessary to possess both a high and low pitch instrument in order to be prepared for every emergency. With this attachment only one instrument is necessary. As all pianos manufactured nowadays are tuned to low pitch, and as the large majority of band instruments used throughout the country are tuned to high pitch, a great deal of confusion arises and professional musicians have always found it necessary to own both a high and low pitch instrument in order to be fully prepared for every emergency. With the Tourville instruments this is not necessary, as the low pitch attachment makes it easy to change from one pitch to another. The engraving which we show herewith illustrates how this appliance is attached to upright horns. It adds to the appearance of the instrument and is one of the most valuable improvements ever made in brass instruments. The addition of this attachment to these instruments has not in any way affected the price, and the low prices which we have always quoted on this splendid line places this great improvement easily within your reach. All of the cornets are fitted with extra low pitch slides, which can be inserted instantly if necessary to change from one pitch to another.

E Flat Cornet.
PEARL VALVE BUTTONS.

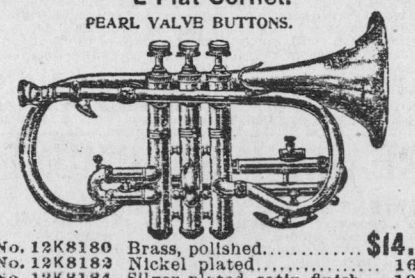

No. 12K8180	Brass, polished	**$14.95**
No. 12K8183	Nickel plated	16.20
No. 12K8184	Silver plated, satin finish	19.45
No. 12K8190	Silver plated, polished	20.95

Leaders' B Flat Cornet. Double Water Key.
PEARL VALVE BUTTONS.

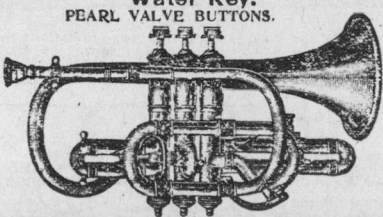

This cornet is a splendid instrument for general street and concert work, an ideal cornet for leaders who use a B flat cornet in their work.

No. 12K8201	Brass, polished	**$17.35**
No. 12K8202	Nickel plated	18.60
No. 12K8203	Silver plated, satin finish	21.85
No. 12K8204	Silver plated, polished	23.85

Artists' B Flat Cornet.
PEARL VALVE BUTTONS.

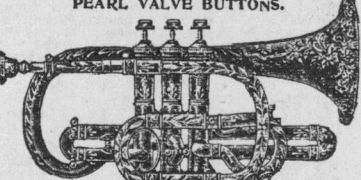

We offer this instrument as something particularly fine for soloists and those who desire a cornet of the highest grade in both looks and playing qualities.

No. 12K8205	Brass, polished	**$19.45**
No. 12K8206	Nickel plated	20.70
No. 12K8207	Silver plated, satin finish, gold lined bell	23.95
No. 12K8208	Silver plated, polished, gold lined bell	25.95

Another Improvement on our Tourville Line.

Every instrument from our E flat cornet to our BB flat bass is fitted with beautiful mother of pearl valve buttons, at no additional cost to our customers.

Solo E Flat Alto.
Pearl Valve Buttons.

6½-Inch Bell.

This is a favorite model with Alto players and is one which we highly recommend as handsome and durable. This instrument is easily the equal of other instruments of this line, and is very acceptable for playing solo alto parts.

No. 12K8192	Brass, polished	**$16.95**
No. 12K8194	Nickel plated, polished	18.95
No. 12K8196	Silver plated, satin finish	23.45
No. 12K8198	Silver plated, polished	27.45

Tenors and Altos.

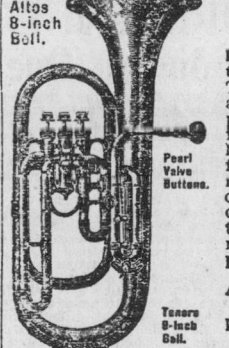

Altos 8-inch Bell.

Pearl Valve Buttons.

Tenors 9-inch Bell.

These are by far the best harmony instruments ever turned out by any maker. Their tone is peculiarly adapted for accompaniment parts and is heavy enough for solo work. As great care has been used in their manufacture as is used in the manufacture of the finest cornets of this line, and we do not hesitate to say that they are the best instruments of their kind ever produced.

No. 12K8210	Alto, brass polished	**$17.90**
No. 12K8212	Alto, nickel plated	$19.95
No. 12K8214	Alto, silver, satin finish	$24.40
No. 12K8216	Alto, silver, polished	28.45
No. 12K8218	Tenor, brass, polished	20.55
No. 12K8220	Tenor, nickel plated	22.80
No. 12K8222	Tenor, silver, satin finish	29.05
No. 12K8224	Tenor, silver, polished	32.55

We furnish each one of these instruments with a

MUSIC HOLDER AND INSTRUCTION BOOK

and offer the complete line as being unsurpassed by any line of Band Instruments on the market today.

B Flat Baritone. 11-Inch Bell.
PEARL VALVE BUTTONS.

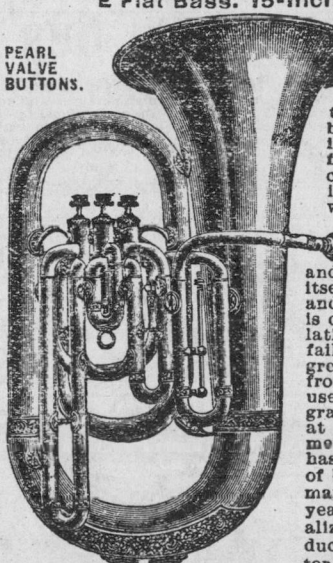

Of all brass instruments the baritone is perhaps the most difficult to make, for the reason that great depth and breadth of tone are required, combined with the lightest possible action. This happy combination is fully realized in this baritone. The valve action in this instrument is the result of much special thought and experiment, and the maker has succeeded in so regulating the air pressure as to produce the lightest valve action ever known.

No. 12K8226	Brass, polished	**$23.75**
No. 12K8228	Nickel plated	$26.85
No. 12K8230	Silver plated, satin finish	$32.75
No. 12K8232	Silver plated, polished	$39.75

B Flat Bass. 11¼-Inch Bell.

No. 12K8234	Brass, polished	**$25.25**
No. 12K8236	Nickel plated	28.25
No. 12K8238	Silver plated, satin finish	37.95
No. 12K8240	Silver plated, polished	46.25

E Flat Bass. 15-Inch Bell.

The Tuba shown in the illustration is without any question the finest E flat bass ever made in tone, tune and finish. Too much cannot be said in its praise, but we would prefer to place it in the hands of bass players and let it speak for itself. In tone, tune and valve action it is certainly a revelation, and never fails to receive the greatest praise from all who may use it. It has that grand, sonorous and at the same time mellow tone which has been the dream of both player and manufacturer for years, and only realized in this production of the master hand.

No. 12K8242	Brass, polished	**$35.35**
No. 12K8244	Nickel plated	39.65
No. 12K8246	Silver plated, satin finish	51.35
No. 12K8248	Silver plated, polished	59.85

Helicon E Flat Bass. 15½-Inch Bell.

We can furnish Helicon Basses in this line fitted with pearl valve buttons and an extra low pitch slide, at the following prices:

No. 12K8258	Brass, polished	**$60.65**
No. 12K8260	Nickel plated	65.90
No. 12K8262	Silver plated, satin finish	81.65
No. 12K8264	Silver plated, polished	88.85

BB Flat Bass. 16¾-Inch Bell.

To very large organizations we cannot recommend too highly this splendid instrument. Its tone is profound, compact and flexible. It is perfect in tune and tone throughout the entire register from the lowest to the highest note. This instrument we only furnish in the upright model, same as our E flat bass No. 12K8242. Fitted with pearl valve buttons.

No. 12K8250	BB Flat Bass, brass, polished	**$45.85**
No. 12K8252	BB Flat Bass, nickel plated, highly polished	52.15
No. 12K8254	BB Flat Bass, silver plated, satin finish	66.85
No. 12K8256	BB Flat Bass, silver plated, highly polished	74.45

Valve Trombones.
PEARL VALVE BUTTONS. 7-Inch Bell.

The Trombones of this line are all well balanced and easy to hold, and the model is one which has received the approval of both maker and player. Owing to the peculiarly sweet tone they possess, they are favorite instruments in all brass bands.

No. 12K8266	E Flat Alto Trombone, brass, polished	**$17.65**
No. 12K8268	E Flat Alto Trombone, nickel plated	19.55
No. 12K8270	E Flat Alto Trombone, silver plated, satin finish	24.15
No. 12K8272	E Flat Alto Trombone, silver plated, polished	28.15
No. 12K8274	B Flat Tenor Trombone, brass, polished	19.45
No. 12K8276	B Flat Tenor Trombone, nickel plated	21.30
No. 12K8278	B Flat Tenor Trombone, silver plated, satin finish	27.95
No. 12K8280	B Flat Tenor Trombone, silver plated, polished	31.45

B Flat Tenor Slide Trombones.
7½-Inch Bell.

In this instrument the maker has succeeded in combining the profound tone of the old German instruments with the light, airy tones of the more recent French trombones, thus realizing a dream which has haunted both maker and player for so many years. The tone of this trombone is mellow and rich, and the style of action is perfection itself.

No. 12K8282	Brass, polished	**$13.75**
No. 12K8284	Nickel plated	15.65
No. 12K8286	Silver plated, satin finish	19.25
No. 12K8288	Silver plated, polished	22.45

Our Engraved Marceau Bb Cornet $8.45

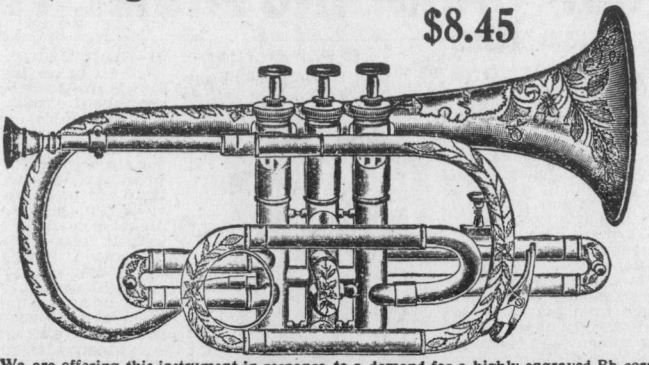

Our Engraved Double Water Key Marceau Cornet $13.15

COURTOIS MODEL.

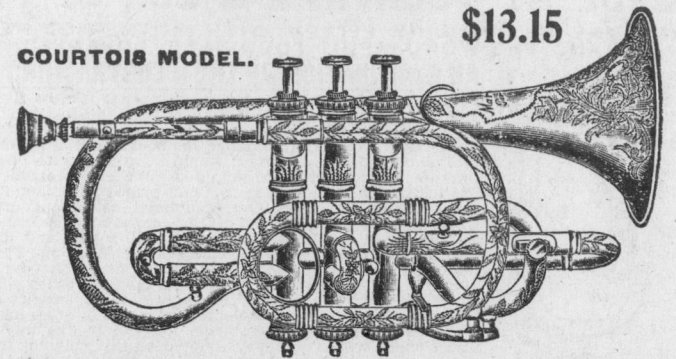

We are offering this instrument in response to a demand for a highly engraved Bb cornet at a moderate price. We can say, without fear of contradiction, that never before in the history of the band instrument business has a fully engraved Bb cornet been offered at any where near the price which we are quoting on this instrument. This cornet is one of our Marceau line, handsomely and completely engraved, and an instrument which is sure to please you in every way. It is fitted with French piston light action valves, the model is very handsome and the instrument is very carefully and skilfully made. If you desire a fine looking instrument, one which is easy blowing, and has a beautiful tone, we will unhesitatingly recommend this cornet to you. The engraving gives but a very poor idea of the appearance of this splendid instrument and nothing but an examination and trial will bring out all of its good qualities. Compare this instrument with any cornet of the same grade offered by any other dealer and you will find at once that we are offering it to you at one-half the price generally charged throughout the country. Complete with "A" set piece and instruction book.

No. 12K7850	Brass, polished. Price		$ 8.45
No. 12K7852	Nickel plated. Price		9.45
No. 12K7854	Silver plated, satin finish. Price		12.45
No. 12K7856	Triple silver plated, polished. Price		15.15

This is one of our double water key Marceau cornets, Courtois model, engraved especially in response to a demand for a cornet of handsome appearance and good tone at a moderate price. We are pioneers in offering instruments of this high grade at the exceedingly low prices quoted below. Up to the time we began to offer these instruments to the public the prices on all engraved band instruments were exceedingly high and were so fixed and maintained by the dealers, as it was to their interest to do so. We found that by importing the instruments directly from Europe and selling them with our one small margin of profit added we could furnish these beautifully engraved instruments at prices in many cases two-thirds lower than the dealers could afford to make.

No. 12K7860	Brass, highly polished. Price	Complete with	$13.15
No. 12K7862	Handsomely nickel plated. Price	"A" set piece	14.15
No. 12K7864	Triple silver plated, satin finish, gold bell. Price	and instruction	17.45
No. 12K7866	Triple silver plated, polished, with gold bell. Price	book.	19.65

MARCEAU ENGRAVED TROMBONES, QUOTED IN OUR BAND CATALOGUE, SENT FREE ON APPLICATION.

OUR ARTISTIC LINE OF LAMOREAUX INSTRUMENTS

UNQUESTIONABLY THE BEST AND MOST BEAUTIFUL LINE OF INSTRUMENTS ON THE MARKET.

In every industry, there is always one manufacturer who stands alone above all competitors, on account of the numerous valuable and special features in the articles of his production. In presenting the Lamoreaux instruments to the professional musicians of the country, we do so with the firm conviction that in securing the sole agency for America of the famous Lamoreaux Freres instruments we were certainly fortunate. The instruments made by the celebrated makers are models of perfection and Lamoreaux Freres of Paris are recognized as the masters of cornet and trombone makers. The reason why we consider their instruments the very best that the market can produce is because for the last twenty-five years they have been engaged in the sole manufacture of cornets and trombones, making a study of them, and giving them their entire efforts. No expense has been spared by them in securing the best materials capable of producing the best sound, and tempered to that degree which gives band instruments that silvery and voice-like tone. By reasons of the wonderful skill of their mechanics under their personal supervision, of the quality of the material, of their knowledge of the principles of sound, and of their model, we can state without fear of contradiction that the results are easier blowing instruments, so perfect in tune and of such marvelous tone, unsurpassed or even equaled by any other make in the world, regardless of price.

NOTICE. Since introducing these instruments in this country, the market has been flooded with cheap imitations made by makers of no reputation whatsoever. They have copied our model, but their instruments lack tune, tone, and blowing qualities, which is the life of an instrument. BEWARE OF THESE SPURIOUS SUBSTITUTES.

Our New HIGH and LOW Pitch Cornet, Four in One, $24.95

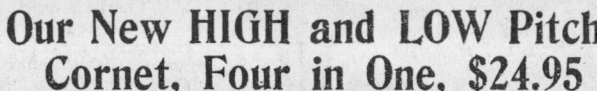

This splendid instrument is the finest cornet that we have so far offered to bandmen, and imported directly by us. It has many improvements, the most important of which is the screw device shown in the engraving for regulating the pitch of the cornet. It is not necessary to carry around a Bb and A shank with this cornet, because the instrument is accurately tuned in Bb and in order to throw it into the key of A, it is only necessary to reach down with the thumb of the right hand and push out the A slide by using the knob shown in the engraving. By using the screw attachment shown in the engraving the pitch of the instrument can be regulated to the very finest shade of tone, and you have a Bb and A cornet complete without the use of shanks, which are liable at any time to get loose or mislaid. We furnish also with this instrument a set of low pitch slides, so that the cornet can be changed from high pitch by pulling out the Bb slides and inserting these slides in their places. You will realize the importance of this addition, as pianos generally are tuned in low pitch, and band instruments of most all organizations are still in high pitch, thus compelling the performer to have two instruments in case he desires to play with a band organization and with a piano or orchestra. Special attention has been given to the valves so as to make them perfectly airtight and at the same time responsive to the touch, thus enabling you to perform the most difficult music with accuracy and precision. The bell of the instrument is handsomely engraved, as shown in the illustration, and the valve buttons are decorated with beautiful pearl tips. This instrument is furnished complete in a fancy seal grain covered case, lined with silk plush and silk, also a fine white satin ribbon across the cover with the name of the manufacturer stamped in gold letters. All metal trimmings on this case are made of brass heavily nickel plated and burnished.

This illustration shows the screw regulating device with which this cornet is fitted. Its many good points can be seen at a glance.

No. 12K7877	Brass, polished. Price	$24.95
No. 12K7879	Nickel plated. Price	26.20
No. 12K7881	Silver plated, satin finish, with gold plated bell, highly burnished. Price	30.45
No. 12K7883	Silver plated, polished, with gold plated bell, highly burnished. Price	33.05

If interested in Lamoreaux Trombones, send for our Special Band Catalogue.

OUR LAMOREAUX ARTIST TRIO CORNET $26.45

PRACTICALLY SIX INSTRUMENTS IN ONE. THE LATEST AND POSITIVELY THE ONLY PRACTICAL INVENTION OF ITS KIND.

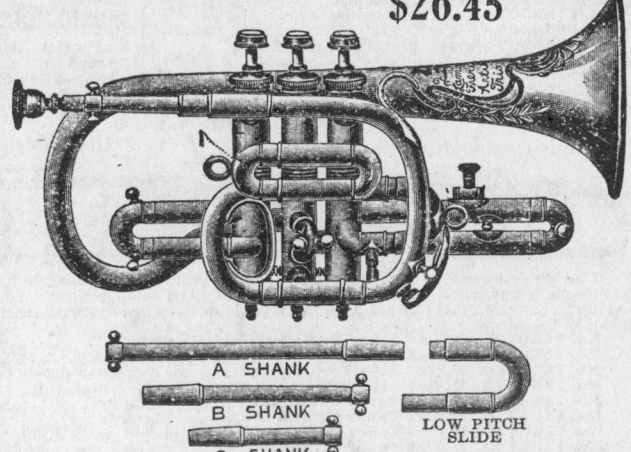

We present the latest invention in the market, a cornet which is perfect in the key of C, in the key of Bb and in the key of A, and can be played in high, as well as low pitch, and will be perfect in every key. Instruments of this nature have been brought into market before, but fell short of the purpose for which they were intended. It was for Lamoreaux Freres to invent an instrument which is not an experiment, but an assured success. The illustration given opposite shows the cornet adjusted to the key of C. That portion of the tubing marked No. 1 is blind and is not an air passage. By a very quick changing of the position of the tuning slide and the tubing of the blind coil, the instrument is immediately brought to the key of Bb. It becomes an A cornet, by using the A shank, same as on the regular Bb instrument. A very strong feature is also the fact that no matter in which key the performer may be playing, it is transformed from high pitch to low pitch, or visa versa, by the change of a little slide. Generally to obtain these results, not only the tuning slide has to be changed, but also the individual slides corresponding with each piston. The advantages of this improved idea can be easily understood. The amateur, as well as the professional musician, will appreciate the importance of an instrument which will enable him to play in a band, an orchestra, or a choir, in the home, with a piano or organ without transposing the music, also to be able to change his cornet to suit the pitch of instruments used by the different organizations he may come in contact with. The quality of this cornet is of the Lamoreaux grade, the finest of materials, and the highest of workmanship. This instrument has pearl buttons on the valve tips, and the bell of the instrument is artistically engraved.

We furnish this cornet complete in a case of the same grade as we give with the other Lamoreaux cornet quoted above. Do not be deceived by cheap substitutes.

No. 12K7885	Brass. Price	$26.45
No. 12K7887	Nickel plated. Price	27.70
No. 12K7889	Silver plated, satin finish, with gold plated bell. Price	31.95
No. 12K7891	Silver plated, polished, gold plated bell. Price	34.55

A SHANK

B SHANK

C SHANK

LOW PITCH SLIDE

OUR FINE LINE OF FLUTES AND PICCOLOS

All of these Flutes and Piccolos are made of grenadilla wood, selected stock, accurately bored and handsomely finished. They are fitted with pure German silver keys, highly polished and we guarantee them absolutely as to tone, tune and wearing qualities. These instruments are all made by one of the most celebrated European flute makers, and we take pleasure in offering them to American musicians. Remember that we send out all of these flutes with the understanding that if they do not prove satisfactory in every way, and up to your expectations in every particular, we will refund your money and pay the express charges both ways. The prices which we make on these flutes are less than one-half the prices which other dealers are asking for instruments of inferior grade, and these prices are only made possible by the fact that we ship them directly from our house to the customer. They are suitable for bands or orchestras, and can be used right along with piano or violin if the proper key is selected. Do not class these instruments with the different cheap flutes which local dealers are offering throughout the country, because these are high class instruments in every way, and when we ship them to our customers they go with our absolute guarantee of quality. If you are looking for a good flute at a very small price, we highly recommend these instruments to your consideration. We can furnish anything in this line from one-key flutes to the very finest Boehm instrument with a guarantee to sell them for lower prices than any other dealer can make.

OWING TO THE PECULIAR CHARACTER of the construction of wood wind instruments, they are liable to crack at any time, and no music dealer can give a guarantee for any length of time. We, however, guarantee that these instruments will reach you in perfect condition and should they be cracked when you receive them we will replace them with others in perfect condition. If, however, they are in perfect condition when you receive them we could not be responsible for their checking or cracking, as this depends entirely upon atmospheric conditions and is not governed in any way by the high or low quality of the material of which they are constructed.

$1.55

No. 12K9070 Genuine cocoa wood, German silver trimmed, tuning slide, 1 key. Price........$1.55

$2.10

No. 12K9072 Grenadilla wood, German silver trimmed, tuning slide, 4 keys. A very serviceable instrument at an unusually low price. Price........$2.10

$2.85

No. 12K9074 Grenadilla wood, tuning slide, cork joints, 6 keys, German silver caps and trimmings. A fine instrument. Price........$2.85

$3.95

No. 12K9076 Grenadilla wood, tuning slide, cork joints, 8 keys, German silver caps and trimmings. An exceptional bargain. Price........$3.95

$4.25

No. 12K9078 Grenadilla wood, tuning slide, cork joints, 8 keys, German silver caps and trimmings and metal embouchure. This flute is finely trimmed, handsomely finished and well made. Price........$4.25

$8.85

No. 12K9079 Grenadilla wood body with genuine American ivory head lined with brass. Tuning slide, cork joints, 8 German silver keys and German silver caps and trimmings. In pasteboard case. Price........$8.85

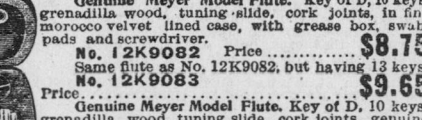

Genuine Meyer Model Flute. Key of D, 8 keys, grenadilla wood, tuning slide, cork joints, in fine morocco, velvet lined case, with grease box, swab, pads and screwdriver.
No. 12K9080 Price........**$6.35**

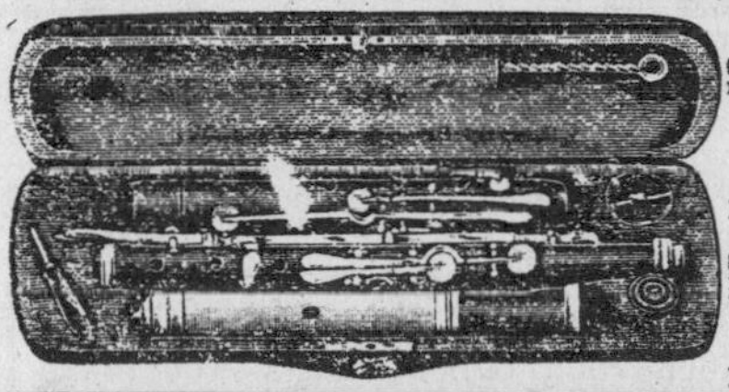

Genuine Meyer Model Flute. Key of D, 10 keys, grenadilla wood, tuning slide, cork joints, in fine morocco velvet lined case, with grease box, swab, pads and screwdriver.
No. 12K9082 Price........**$8.75**

Same flute as No. 12K9082, but having 13 keys.
No. 12K9083 Price........**$9.65**

Genuine Meyer Model Flute. Key of D, 10 keys, grenadilla wood, tuning slide, cork joints, genuine ivory head in velvet lined morocco case, with grease box, swab, pads and screwdriver.
No. 12K9084 Price........**$13.95**
No. 12K9085 Same flute as No. 12K9084, but with 13 keys. Price........**17.35**

Piccolos.

Key of D or E flat. Be sure to state key wanted. In pasteboard box.

No. 12K3392 Cocoa wood, 1 key, German silver trimmed. Price........**45c**

No. 12K3394 Grenadilla wood, with tuning slide and 4 keys, German silver trimmed. Price........**$1.10**

No. 12K3395 Grenadilla wood, with tuning slide, 6 keys, German silver trimmed, cork joints. Price........**$1.65**

If by mail, postage extra, 15 cents.

Meyer Pattern Piccolo.

Grenadilla, ivory head, 6 keys, with slide cork joints and German silver trimmed, in fine velvet lined morocco case, as shown in illustration. Key of D or E flat. Be sure to state key wanted.
No. 12K3396 Price........**$4.55**

If by mail, postage extra, 16 cents.

THREE SPLENDID LINES OF CLARIONETS.

We furnish our clarionets in high and low pitch.
In ordering be sure to state pitch desired.

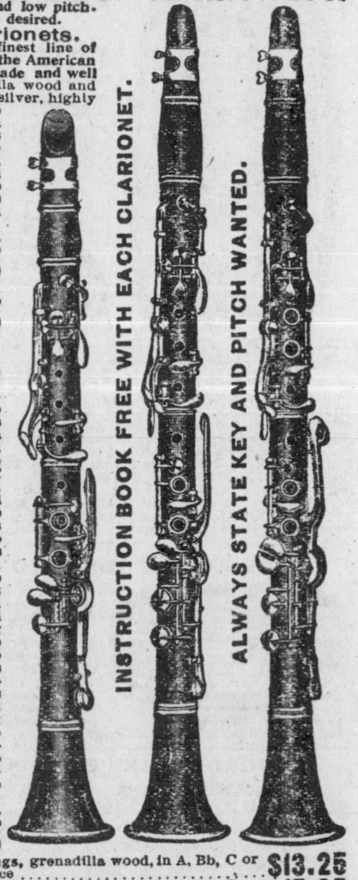

INSTRUCTION BOOK FREE WITH EACH CLARIONET.

ALWAYS STATE KEY AND PITCH WANTED.

LaFayette & Co.'s Clarionets.

These clarionets are certainly the finest line of low priced clarionets ever offered to the American bandmen. They are substantially made and well finished. They are made of grenadilla wood and all of the trimmings are pure German silver, highly polished. We promise to save the purchaser from $5.00 to $10.00 upon each one of these clarionets bought from us, and will ask our friends to compare them and the prices we ask, with the instruments and prices offered by other dealers. LaFayette & Co. have been manufacturing these clarionets for years. They have always given the greatest satisfaction.

No. 12K8850 13 keys, 2 rings, grenadilla wood, in A, Bb, C or Eb. Be sure to state key wanted. Price........**$9.95**

No. 12K8852 15 keys, 2 rings, grenadilla wood, in A, Bb, C or Eb. Be sure to state key wanted. Price........**$11.95**

Shipping weight, 50 ounces.

J. B. Martin Clarionets.

This is the line of favorite clarionets which we have handled for years, and which have given such universal satisfaction. We do not believe that there is a line of moderate priced clarionets on the American market today which in any way equals them in tone and finish. They are all made of genuine grenadilla wood, with trimmings of pure German silver, highly polished. They are bored through cleanly and evenly and are accurately made throughout. We guarantee them as to tune and tone and are prepared to take back any instrument which does not give satisfaction in every way. These clarionets, as well as the balance of our line, are fitted with the Albert system, and we can furnish them in all of the different keys. Bear in mind that you take no chances in purchasing one of these instruments, because we send them out on approval and we do not ask you to accept them unless you are perfectly satisfied in every respect. Many expert clarionet players have been surprised at the wonderful degree of superiority demonstrated by these clarionets. Bandmen desiring to furnish their reed sections with clarionets, and who are not prepared to pay a large amount for such instruments, cannot do better than purchase a set of these splendid clarionets.

No. 12K8854 13 keys, 2 rings, grenadilla wood, in A, Bb, C or Eb. Be sure to state key wanted. Price........**$11.25**

No. 12K8856 15 keys, 2 rings, grenadilla wood, in A, Bb, C or Eb. Be sure to state key wanted. Price........**$13.25**

No. 12K8858 15 keys, 4 rings, grenadilla wood, in A, Bb, C or Eb. Be sure to state key wanted. Price........**15.35**

Shipping weight, 13 keys, 50 ounces. Shipping weight, 15 keys, 64 ounces.

Tourville & Co.'s Universelle Clarionets.

Tourville & Co.'s Universelle Clarionets are considered by experts to be the finest in the world. We are offering these instruments in response to a demand for a line of clarionets which will be as fine as can be procured. We are willing to say without question that no clarionet, however costly, can excel these instruments in tune, tone and wearing qualities. They are used by all the finest concert bands of Europe and are meeting with an enthusiastic reception from clarionet players in this country. They are all made of the finest selected grenadilla wood, accurately and evenly bored, with the intervals absolutely perfect. The trimmings are all pure German silver, highly polished and strongly made. Because we are offering these clarionets at such extremely low prices, we do not want you to make the mistake of classing them with the different lines of low-class clarionets which are offered throughout the country by dealers today. The reason we are able to make such extremely low prices upon these instruments is because we purchase them directly from the manufacturer in France, and sell them by our usual method directly to the customer. No clarionet should cost over $20.00, and when you pay a higher price than this you are simply paying for the name of the maker, which in many cases adds no value to the clarionet in any way.

No. 12K8860 13 keys, 2 rings, grenadilla wood, in A, Bb, C or Eb. Be sure to state key wanted. Price........**$13.95**

No. 12K8862 15 keys, 2 rings, grenadilla wood, in A, Bb, C or Eb. Be sure to state key wanted. Price........**16.45**

No. 12K8866 15 keys, 4 rings and 4 roller keys. Price........**19.45**

Shipping weight, 13 keys, 70 ounces. Shipping weight, 15 keys, 72 ounces.

We can ship all accessories for clarionets. For prices send for our special Free Band Catalogue.

FIFES.

Key of B flat or C only. Be sure to state key wanted. Instruction Book, 12 cents.

No. 12K3358 Solid rosewood; brass ferrules. Price........**25c**

No. 12K3359 Cocoa wood; German silver ferrules. Price........**27c**

No. 12K3361 Solid ebony; nickel plated ferrules. Price........**48c**

No. 12K3362 Solid ebony; long metal ferrules. Crosby model; extra fine quality. Price........**68c**

If by mail, postage extra, 9 cents.

Nickel Plated Fifes.

Highly Nickel Plated Fife, for beginners, with mouthpiece adjusted all ready for playing. A very fine instrument for those who desire to learn the fife. Key of B flat or C. Be sure to state key wanted.
No. 12K3363 Price........**19c**

If by mail, postage extra, 7 cents.

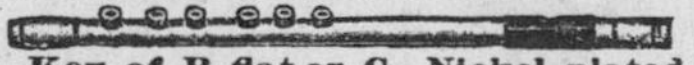

Key of B flat or C. Nickel plated with raised finger holes, with gutta-percha embouchure. Be sure to state key wanted.
No. 12K3364 Price........**55c**

If by mail, postage extra, 9 cents.

Our Special Acme Hand Made Fife.

Metal nickel plated, strictly high grade Fife for professional players. Made in two pieces. Easy blowing, perfect in scale. None better made. Key of C or B flat. Be sure to state key wanted.
No. 12K3365 Price........**95c**

If by mail, postage extra, 10 cents.

Atlas Flageolets.

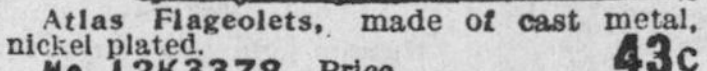

Atlas Flageolets, made of cast metal, nickel plated.
No. 12K3378 Price........**43c**

If by mail, postage extra, 12 cents.

Multiflutes.

Multiflute, the latest French novelty. Is a combination instrument. It is made of cast metal, nickel plated, and has three distinct mouthpieces, as shown in the illustration. The instrument is of French manufacture and imported by us direct from France. It is accurately tuned in key of F, and is easy to play.
No. 12K3391 Price........**58c**

If by mail, postage extra, 16 cents.

CLARIONET, FLUTE AND PICCOLO FURNISHINGS.

Clarionet Cases.

Made of case leather, handsomely embossed, round leather handle, flannel lined, nickel catch, for clarionets in all keys. Shipping weight, 10 ounces. Be sure to give key of clarionet.
No. 12K5708 Price........**88c**

Valise form, covered with seal grain leather, leather handle, flannel lined, nickel lock, hooks and name plate. Made to carry three clarionets. Shipping weight, 4 pounds.
No. 12K5710 Price........**$2.30**

Reeds. 4c to 16c

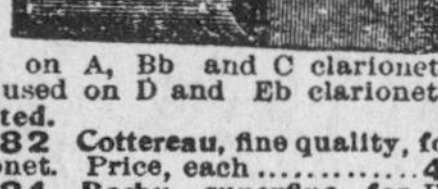

Imported Clarionet Reeds, best models.

Note—Bb reeds are used on A, Bb and C clarionets, Eb reeds are used on D and Eb clarionets. State key wanted.

No. 12K5682 Cottereau, fine quality, for Bb or Eb clarionet. Price, each........4c

No. 12K5684 Barbu, superfine, for Bb or Eb clarionet. Price, each........6c

No. 12K5685 Genuine Martin Freres, for Bb or Eb clarionet. Price, each........9c

No. 12K5686 Our Special Fournier Waterproof Clarionet Reeds. These reeds are strictly waterproof, and model and quality are particularly desirable. They are made for any key clarionet. Price, each........11c

No. 12K5688 Artists' Cabinet Reeds, a grade of reed that is the best that can be secured at any price. Made for Bb or Eb clarionet. Price is the same. Price, each...16c

If by mail, postage extra, 2 cents.

Clarionet Reed Cases.

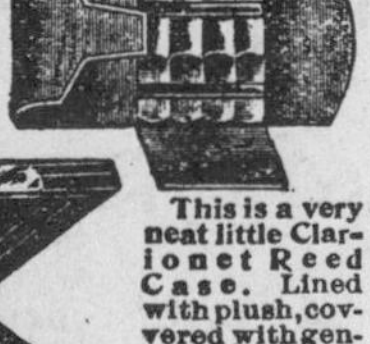

Leather Pocket Case, for six reeds.
No. 12K5694 Price........**22c**
Postage extra, 5 cents.

This is a very neat little Clarionet Reed Case. Lined with plush, covered with genuine leather, nicely finished and fitted with nickel plated spring clasp. The reeds are held in place on a glass plate by a broad band of silk elastic. The case is deep enough to hold from 8 to 10 reeds.
No. 12K5696 Price........**38c**

If by mail, postage extra, 5 cents.

Mouthpieces made of composition metal and with screw adjustment.

Note—Before ordering, measure instrument and be sure measurements are within sizes specified below.

No. 12K5650 For Piccolo, 2¼ to 2⅜ inches in circumference. Price........5c

No. 12K5651 For Fife, 2⅜ to 2⅝ inches in circumference Price........5c

No. 12K5655 For Flute, 3½ to 3¾ inches in circumference. Price....(Postage extra, 2 cents.)...9c

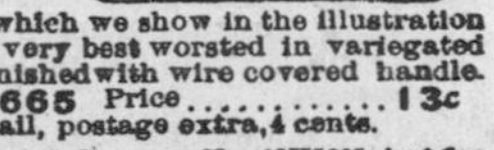

The Cleaner which we show in the illustration is made of the very best worsted in variegated colors and furnished with wire covered handle.
No. 12K5665 Price........**13c**
If by mail, postage extra, 4 cents.

No. 12K5666 Same as No. 12K5665, but for piccolo. Price....(Postage extra, 4c.)...9c

ACME PROFESSIONAL DRUMS

Fitted With Our New Patent Rods and Cord Hooks.

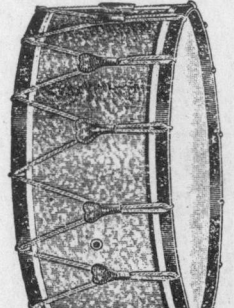

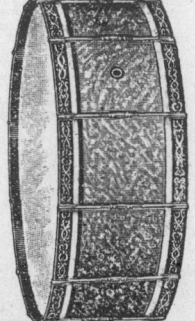

THESE WONDERFUL NEW INVENTIONS are certainly the greatest improvements that have ever been made in bass and snare drums. We know that they will be gladly welcomed by drummers all over the country, and they can only be secured on our drums. A glance at the illustration will show you at once how vast an improvement OUR NEW PATENT DRUM ROD is over the old fashioned device. It is stamped out of sheet steel and nickel plated. It is tightened by a double screw in the center and can be operated with almost any wrench. It fits snugly on the strainer hoops of the drum, and, unlike the old fashioned drum rod, does not allow the end to stick up beyond the hoop to catch on the clothing. It is very much neater in appearance than the old fashioned drum rod, and imparts a graceful appearance to the instrument, which cannot be obtained with any other drum rod. One of the greatest advantages which it possesses is that it makes the drum very much lighter than when fitted with the old fashioned drum rod. This increase in lightness makes a wonderful improvement in the tone of the instrument and adds 100 per cent to its responsiveness. REMEMBER, you can only obtain these drum rods with our Acme Professional Drums, and if you are thinking of purchasing a drum do not purchase elsewhere without having first given us an opportunity to place one of these instruments in your hands and demonstrate to you what a wonderful improvement these drum rods are. All of our Prussian pattern bass and snare drums are fitted with these patent drum rods, and we do not add anything extra to the price in order to give our customers the benefit of this wonderful invention.

THE NEW PATENTED DRUM HOOK is another remarkable invention for the improvement of the Regulation Pattern Drums. They are made of white metal and are very durable. Like the drum rods they can be obtained only from us and will be found only upon our Acme Professional Drums. Instead of having an eye for the cord to run through, like the old fashioned drum hooks, they are furnished with an open hook, which holds the cord securely in its place. Should it be necessary to fit the drum with a new cord or repair the cord when broken, it is not necessary to remove all the hooks, as with the old fashioned pattern, but it is only necessary to loop the cord over the hooks and tighten it up. All of our Regulation Drums are fitted with this new cord hook and you can obtain them from no one else and upon no other line of drums.

REGULATION PATTERN.   PRUSSIAN PATTERN.

REGULATION PATTERN.—ACME PROFESSIONAL TENOR OR SNARE DRUMS—PRUSSIAN PATTERN.

No. 12K8500 This is the regulation pattern with a shell 14 inches in diameter, made of birdseye maple, varnish finish, 8 inches high, cord hooks, with seven braces. The hoops are of maple, finished in imitation ebony or rosewood; best of calfskin heads, six snares, new pattern snare strainer, nickel plated hooks. Weight packed, about 15 pounds.
Price, including one pair of sticks.................$6.10
No. 12K8502 Regulation pattern, but with a 16-inch shell, 9½ inches high, made of birdseye maple with maple hoops, finished in ebony or rosewood. Shell has fine varnish finish, eight braces, best calfskin heads, new pattern snare strainers, nickel plated hooks.
Price, including one pair of rosewood sticks.................$6.50
No. 12K8504 The same description as No. 12K8502, but has a shell made of rosewood, fine varnish finish, nickel plated hooks. Price.................$6.85

OUR ACME PROFESSIONAL ORCHESTRA DRUMS.

These drums answer the same description as our Prussian Pattern Tenor or Snare Drums. They have shells 4 inches high, which renders them very sharp and responsive.
No. 12K8520 16-inch brass shell. Two calfskin heads. Price.................$6.65
No. 12K8522 Same as above, only with nickel plated shell. Price.................$6.95
No. 12K8524 This is our best orchestra drum. 16-inch nickel plated shell. The hoops are inlaid with a fine white metal band ½ inch wide, giving the drum a very handsome and striking appearance. With this drum we give ebony sticks instead of rosewood. Price.................$7.55

No. 12K8524

QUADRUPLEX BAND AND ORCHESTRA DRUM.

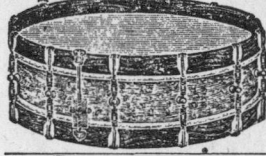

For band or orchestra, in a concert room or on the street, this drum has no equal. Its advantages, when used as a street drum, lies in the lightness of construction and the penetrating, yet brilliant tone. For orchestra playing, which is a severe test on snare drums, it is far superior to any drum made, regardless of price. It responds to the lightest touch of the sticks, so that from the softest to the loudest roll it can be played with remarkable ease and rapidity. The main feature of this drum is the quadruplex rod, so constructed that each head can be tightened separately (see illustration.) This drum has a highly polished birdseye maple shell, 4 inches high, 16 inches in diameter, fitted with twelve latest improved quadruplex rods, made of brass and stamped sheet metal, highly nickel plated and burnished. The hoops are finished in rosewood color. Has two of the best quality transparent calfskin heads, and twelve waterproof snares and nickel plated strainer. With this drum we include one pair of ebony sticks and webbed sling.
No. 12K8525 Price.................$16.45

THESE DRUMS have a shell made of birdseye maple, rosewood or brass (see descriptions below), carefully braced, 6 inches in height and 16 inches in diameter, except No. 12K8506, which is 14 inches in diameter. They are fitted with ebonized hoops, and with the exception of No. 12K8506, which has seven rods, they all have eight of our special pattern nickel plated rods, nickel plated snare strainer and a set of eight snares. They are all furnished with best quality calf or sheepskin heads, as per descriptions given below; special belt hook and knee rest. We furnish with each one of these drums a sling of good quality webbing and a pair of rosewood sticks. Weight, packed, about 15 pounds.

No. 12K8506 14-inch maple shell, seven rods, one calf and one sheepskin head. Price.................$5.45
No. 12K8508 16-inch maple shell, one calf and one sheepskin head. Price. 6.20
No. 12K8512 Same as above, but with two calfskin heads. Price. 6.65
No. 12K8510 16-inch brass shell, one calf and one sheepskin head. Price. 6.25
No. 12K8514 Same as No.12K8510, but with two calfskin heads. Price. 6.75
No. 12K8516 Rosewood shell, two calfskin heads. On this drum the hoops are very nicely decorated with fancy decalcomania ornamentations. Price.................$6.85
No. 12K8518 Of exactly the same description as the above, with the exception of the shell, which is made of brass and heavily nickel plated and polished. Price.................$7.25

DRUMMERS' DELIGHT—SINGLE HEADED DRUMS.

No. 12K8526 This drum has been designed to meet the requirements of drummers wishing a very sharp drum. It is quick in responding to the lightest touch of the sticks. It has a birdseye maple shell, highly polished, 14½ inches diameter, 3¾ inches high, including hoop, twelve special banjo bracket pattern nickel plated rods, highly polished, silk snare, with special patent adjuster. Best quality transparent head. The real thing for trap drummers. Easily carried. Occupies little space.
Price, including a pair of genuine ebony sticks, $7.95

Quadruplex   Drum Rod.

ACME PROFESSIONAL BASS DRUMS.

We furnish bass drums in either the Regulation or the Prussian pattern. See illustrations on top of page and read descriptions below.

OUR REGULATION DRUMS. All of our regulation pattern bass drums have a shell 12 inches high, with the exception of Nos. 12K8527, 12K8528, 12K8529 and 12K8530. Made of fine birdseye maple or imitation mahogany. Maple hoops finished in imitation ebony or rosewood. They are fitted with the special drum hooks described above and best quality drum cord, leather braces, and fitted with either one calfskin and one sheepskin head or with two calfskin heads. This is stated in each description.

OUR PRUSSIAN PATTERN answers the same description as our regulation, except that the shell is 9 1-2 inches high, and they are fitted with our special patent drum rods. The maple hoops are finished in imitation ebony and are decorated with fancy decalcomania ornamentations. With all our drums we furnish a webbing sling and a buckskin head stick. The number of rods for the different size drums is as follows: 24-inch drums, 9 rods; 28-inch drums, 11 rods; 30-inch drums, 12 rods; 36-inch drums, 15 rods.

We furnish bass drums in either imitation mahogany or birdseye maple at the same price. Party ordering will please use the number in the column stating at its head the kind of material desired. For instance, if a 30-inch, two calfskin head, imitation mahogany drum is wanted, the number will be 12K8538. If the same is wanted in the birdseye maple, the number will be 12K8537.

IMPORTANT. Bass drums are made in Regulation and Prussian patterns (see illustrations above). WE CANNOT FILL YOUR ORDER UNLESS YOU STATE WHICH PATTERN YOU DESIRE.

Birdseye Maple Shell No.	Imitation Mahogany Shell No.	
12K8527	12K8528	24 inches in diameter, 10 inches high. One calfskin and one sheepskin head. Price.................$8.85
12K8529	12K8530	Same as above. With two calfskin heads. Price.................9.60
12K8531	12K8532	Shell, 28 inches in diameter, 12 inches high. One calfskin and one sheepskin. head. Price.................10.75
12K8533	12K8534	Same as above. With two calfskin heads. Price.................11.85
12K8535	12K8536	Shell, 30 inches in diameter, 12 inches high. One calfskin and one sheepskin head. Price.................11.95
12K8537	12K8538	Same as above, with two calfskin heads. Price.................13.15
12K8539	12K8540	Shell, 36 inches in diameter, 12 inches high, with two calfskin heads. Price.................$17.95

OUR LINE OF BUGLES AND TRUMPETS.

These instruments are all of regulation pattern, size and key, and are fully guaranteed by us. They are all made of the very highest grade of spun brass and are tempered just to the proper point where they become the best medium for the transmission of musical sounds. They are all of good model, handsomely finished and splendid tone.

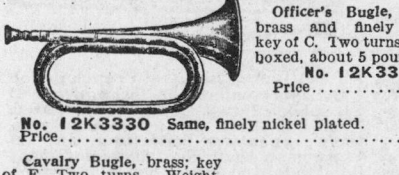

Officer's Bugle, made of brass and finely finished; key of C. Two turns. Weight, boxed, about 5 pounds.
No. 12K3329 Price.................$1.35
No. 12K3330 Same, finely nickel plated. Price.................1.90

Cavalry Bugle, brass; key of F. Two turns. Weight, boxed, 6 pounds.
No. 12K3334 Price.................$1.85
No. 12K3335 Same, nickel plated. Price.................2.35

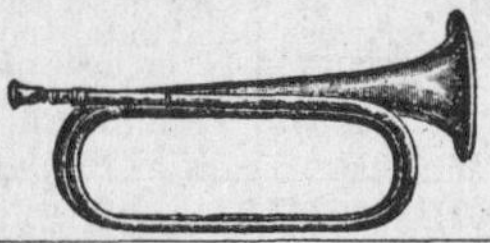

Infantry Bugle, brass; key of C. with B flat crook. Weight, boxed, 6 pounds.
No. 12K3341 Price.................$1.95
No. 12K3342 Same, nickel plated. Price.................2.45

Genuine Hunting Horn, brass; one turn.
No. 12K3345 Price.................60c
If by mail, postage extra, 18 cents.
Genuine Hunting Horn, brass; three turns.
No. 12K3346 Price.................95c
If by mail, postage extra, 22 cents.

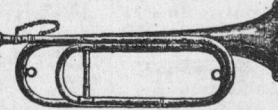

Cavalry Trumpet, key of F, made of brass, with tuning slide.
No. 12K3347 Price.................$2.25
No. 12K3348 Same, nickel plated. Price.................2.85

This Cavalry Trumpet is in the key of G, but the tuning slide is long enough so that it can be tuned to F. We furnish this trumpet with two mouthpieces. 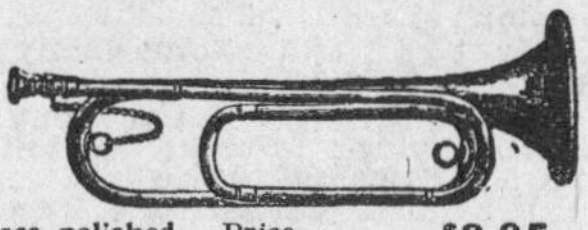
No. 12K3350 Brass, polished. Price.................$2.95
No. 12K3352 Same, nickel plated. Price.................3.50
Weight, boxed, 8 pounds.

Folding Drum Stand.

No. 12K3600 Seroco Patent Folding Drum Stand. It is made of the best quality of steel, highly nickel plated. It is the neatest and most compact drum stand manufactured, very solid in construction yet very light. Will fit any size drum. Shipping weight, 4 pounds. Price. $2.25

Triangles.

Steel, nickel plated, with hammer.
No. 12K3686 6-in. Price. 26c
Postage, 9 cents.
No. 12K3688 7-inch. Price.................32c
If by mail, postage extra, 13c.
No. 12K3690 8-inch. Price. (If by mail, postage extra, 15c.).......38c

Triangle Beater.

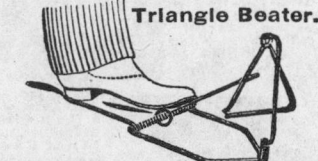

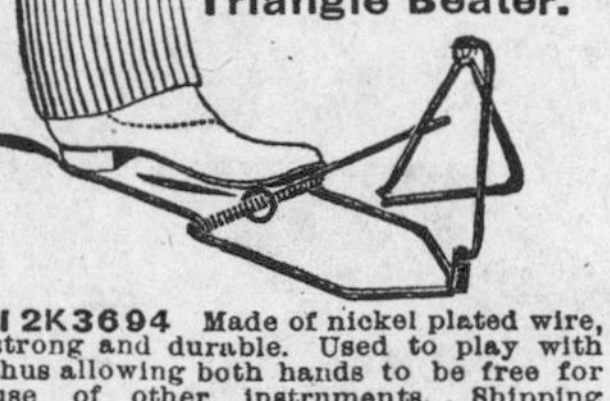

No. 12K3694 Made of nickel plated wire, very strong and durable. Used to play with foot, thus allowing both hands to be free for the use of other instruments. Shipping weight, 10 ounces.
Price, without triangle.................55c

For Band Furnishings send for **OUR SPECIAL CATALOGUE**

Drum and Cymbal Beater.

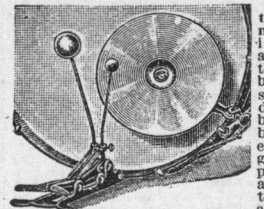

Made entirely of metal. An important advantage of this beater is being able to strike the drum or cymbal alone or both together, also with greater rapidity and accuracy than with any other make on account of its quick action and simple construction. Easy to carry, as it is easily put together and packed. Shipping weight, 5 pounds.
No. 12K3668 Price.................$2.53

CYMBALS.

Brass Cymbals with Leather Handles.

No. 12K3660 10-inch. Wt., 35 ounces. Per pair..$1.32
No. 12K3662 12-inch. Wt., 45 ounces. Per pr.$1.75
No. 12K3663 13-inch. Weight, 50 ounces. Price, per pair.................$1.98
Imitation Turkish Cymbals. Made of fine composition metal, hammered by hand, powerful in tone, complete with leather handles.
No. 12K3664 8-inch. Weight, 35 ounces. Price, per pair.................$2.65
No. 12K3666 12-inch. Weight, 65 ounces. Price, per pair.................$4.15

Glendon Steel Strings.

These strings are made of good quality Damascus steel and are not to be classed with the cheap trade strings which flood the market at the present time.

Glendon Violin Strings.

Silvered steel. Each string one full length.

		Doz.	½ Doz.
No. 12K4172	E	5c	
No. 12K4174	A	5c	
No. 12K4176	D, covered	11c	6c
No. 12K4178	G, covered	11c	6c
No. 12K4180	Set of four		4c

If by mail, postage extra, per set or dozen, 2c.

Glendon Banjo Strings.

Silvered steel. Each string one full length.

		Doz.	½ Doz.
No. 12K4220	B and E	5c	
No. 12K4222	G	5c	
No. 12K4224	E	5c	
No. 12K4226	A	22c	12c
No. 12K4228	Set of five		5c

If by mail, postage extra, per set or dozen, 2c.

Glendon Guitar Strings.

Silvered steel. Each string one full length. G, D, A and E strings silvered wire wound on steel.

		Doz.	½ Doz.	Each
No. 12K4270	E	5c		
No. 12K4272	B	5c		
No. 12K4274	G	11c	6c	
No. 12K4276	D	22c	12c	
No. 12K4278	A	33c		3c
No. 12K4280	E	44c		4c
No. 12K4282	Set of six			12c

Postage extra, per set, 2 cents; per dozen, 4c.

Glendon Mandolin Strings.

Silvered steel. Each string one full length.

		Doz.	½ Doz.
No. 12K4290	E	5c	
No. 12K4292	A	5c	
No. 12K4294	D	11c	6c
No. 12K4296	G	11c	6c
No. 12K4298	Set of eight		6c

If by mail, postage extra, per set, 3 cents; per dozen, 4 cents.

Cornet Cases.

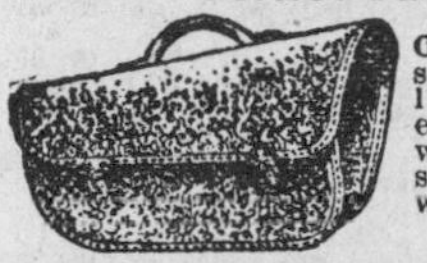

No. 12K5713 Gray Canvas, satchel form, leather bound edges, flannel lined, with shoulder strap. Shipping weight, 30 ounces. Price.......70c

No. 12K5715 Made of black pebble leather, very fine, satchel form, as illustrated; flannel lined, nickel plated trimmings, with shoulder strap. Shipping weight, 30 ounces. Price......98c

No. 12K5716 Trumpet case. Same description as No. 12K5715 but 31 inches long, made to fit the trumpet cornet. Shipping weight, 54 ounces. Price.......$1.25

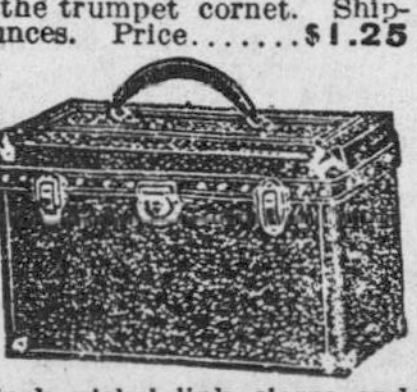

Cornet case, valise form, made of wood covered with an indestructible waterproof material made in perfect imitation of seal leather, handsomely embossed, trimmed with nickel corners, leather handle, nickel spring lock, nickel link clasps and nickel hinges. Lined inside with velvet, partitioned off for cornet and various parts. One of the best cornet cases made. Shipping weight, 6 pounds.

12K5717 Price.................$3.15

Trombone Cases.

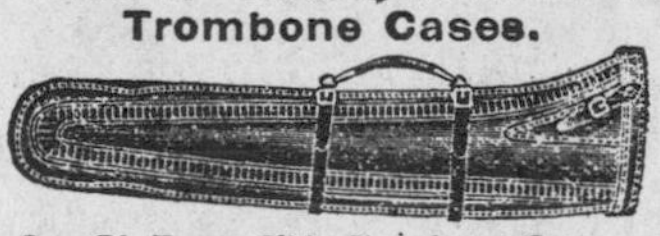

Our Bb Tenor Slide Trombone Cases are made of black sole leather, very artistically embossed and lined with red flannel. They have metal end protectors, strong carrying straps and handle. Suitable for either high or low pitch instruments. Furnished with extra inside pocket for low pitch slide. Shipping weight, 6 pounds.

12K5718 Price.................$5.95

We can furnish cases for instruments of all kinds. Send for Special Band Instrument Catalogue.

Calfskin Heads.

For Drums, Banjos and Tambourines.

Catalogue No.	Size, inches	For	Price
12K5770..	12	10-inch Shell	$0.25
12K5772..	13	11-inch Drum Shell	.33
12K5774..	14	11½-inch Shell	.43
12K5776..	15	12-inch Shell	.52
12K5778..	16	13-inch Shell	.63
12K5782..	18	15-inch Drum	.77
12K5783..	19	16-inch Drum	.81
12K5784..	20	17-inch Drum	.92
12K5785..	22	19-inch Drum	1.05
12K5786..	28	24-inch Bass Drum	2.05
12K5787..	30	26-inch Bass Drum	2.30
12K5788..	32	28-inch Bass Drum	2 55
12K5789..	34	30-inch Bass Drum	2.75
12K5790..	36	32-inch Bass Drum	3.00
12K5792..	38	34-inch Bass Drum	3.50
12K5794..	40	36-inch Bass Drum	3.95

Extra Quality Special Banjo Heads.

Genuine Rogers. First Quality.

No. 12K5796 13-inch, white, for 11-inch banjo. Price.......................69c

No. 12K5797 14-inch, white, for 11½-inch banjo. Price.......................79c

No. 12K5798 16-inch, white, for 13-inch banjo. Price.......................94c

Shipping weight, 12 to 20-inch head, 4 ozs.
Shipping weight, 20 to 28-inch head, 9 ozs.
Shipping weight, 30 to 36-inch head, 20 ozs.
Shipping weight, 36 to 40-inch head, 24 ozs.

Genuine Bell Brand Strings.

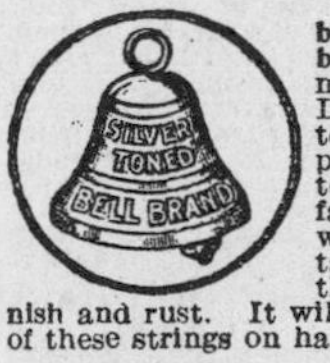

These strings are celebrated for their silver bell-like tone. They are made of the finest quality Damascus steel, carefully tested and heavily silver plated, giving them the tone which has made them famous. Each string is wrapped in ribbed anti-tarnish paper, protecting them from moisture, tarnish and rust. It will pay to keep a supply of these strings on hand at all times.

Bell Brand Violin Strings.

Steel, triple silver plated and polished. Each string one full length.

		Doz.	½ Doz.	Each
No. 12K4182	E	22c	12c	
No. 12K4184	A	22c	12c	
No. 12K4186	D, cov'ed	33c		3c
No. 12K4188	G, cov'ed	44c		4c
No. 12K4190	Set of four			11c

If by mail, postage extra, per set or dozen, 3c.

Bell Brand Banjo Strings.

Steel, triple silver plated and polished. Each string one full length.

		Doz.	½ Doz.	Each
No. 12K4230	B and E	22c	12c	
No. 12K4232	G	22c	12c	
No. 12K4234	E	22c	12c	
No. 12K4236	A	44c		4c
No. 12K4238	Set of five			12c

If by mail, postage extra, per set, 3 cents.

Bell Brand Guitar Strings.

Steel, triple silver plated and polished. Each string one full length. G, D, A and E strings silvered wire wound on steel.

		Doz.	½ Doz.	Each
No. 12K4283	E	22c	12c	
No. 12K4284	B	22c	12c	
No. 12K4285	G	44c		4c
No. 12K4286	D	55c		5c
No. 12K4287	A	66c		6c
No. 12K4288	E	77c		7c
No. 12K4289	Set of six			23c

If by mail, postage extra, per set, 3 cents; per dozen, 5 cents.

Bell Brand Mandolin Strings.

Steel, triple silver plated and polished. Each string one full length.

		Doz.	½ Doz.	Each
No. 12K4310	E	22c	12c	
No. 12K4312	A	22c	12c	
No. 12K4316	D	33c		3c
No. 12K4318	G	44c		4c
No. 12K4320	Set of eight			22c

If by mail, postage extra, per set or doz., 3c.

Our Special High Grade Transparent Heads.

No. 12K5802 13-inch for 11-inch shell. Price.......53c

No. 12K5805 14-inch for 11½-inch shell. Price.......62c

No. 12K5808 16-inch for 13-inch shell. Price.......76c

FOR DRUMMERS' SUPPLIES, TRAPS, TAMBOURINES, ETC., SEND FOR SPECIAL BAND CATALOGUE.

Music Stands.

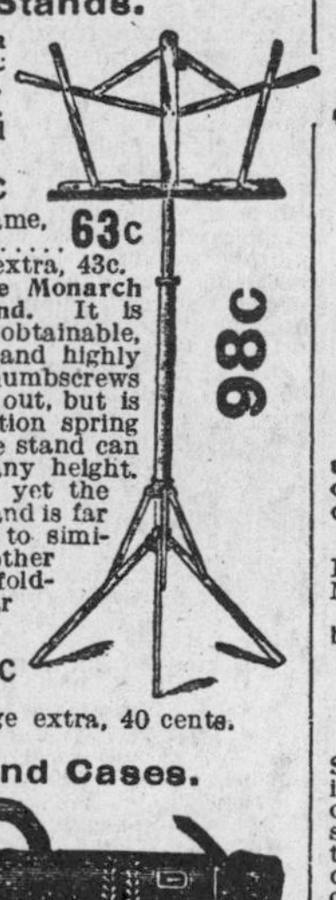

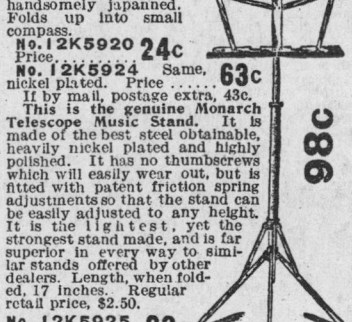

Our Special Umbrella Pattern Folding Music Stand, made of iron, handsomely japanned. Folds up into small compass.

No. 12K5920 Price........24c

No. 12K5924 Same, nickel plated. Price......63c

If by mail, postage extra, 43c.

This is the genuine Monarch Telescope Music Stand. It is made of the best steel obtainable, heavily nickel plated and highly polished. It has no thumbscrews which will easily wear out, but is fitted with patent friction spring adjustments so that the stand can be easily adjusted to any height. It is the lightest, yet the strongest stand made, and is far superior in every way to similar stands offered by other dealers. Length, when folded, 17 inches. Regular retail price, $2.50.

No. 12K5925 Our price......98c

If by mail, postage extra, 40 cents.

Music Stand Cases.

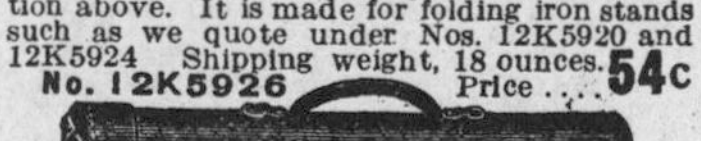

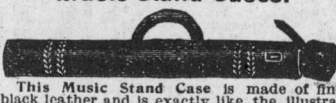

This Music Stand Case is made of fine black leather and is exactly like the illustration above. It is made for folding iron stands such as we quote under Nos. 12K5920 and 12K5924. Shipping weight, 18 ounces.

No. 12K5926 Price......54c

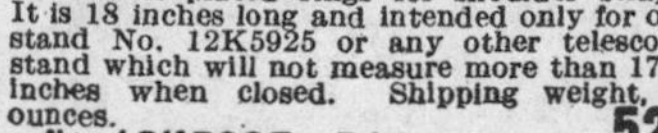

This Music Stand Case is made of black leather, with extra strong hand sewed handle and nickel plated rings for shoulder straps. It is 18 inches long and intended only for our stand No. 12K5925 or any other telescope stand which will not measure more than 17½ inches when closed. Shipping weight, 14 ounces.

No. 12K5927 Price..........52c

IMPORTED GUT AND SILK STRINGS.

WE IMPORT DIRECT FROM EUROPEAN MANUFACTURERS and handle none but the best strings made. Not an inferior string sold by us at any price. We guarantee every one to be perfectly made of the best quality and material. WE DO NOT GUARANTEE THEM AGAINST BREAKING, but they will last as long as can be expected of the best strings made. We solicit your orders in this particular line, knowing that we can please you in the fullest degree and save you from 50 to 60 per cent on every purchase.

Silk Violin E Strings.

No. 12K4125 Muller's Celebrated Eternelle. Most reliable string in existence.......Doz. $1.10, Each 10c

If by mail, postage extra, 2 cents.

Extra Quality Violin Strings.

All E strings have 4 lengths, A and D strings 2½ lengths and G strings 1 length.

		Doz.	Each
No. 12K4130	E, polished	76c	7c
No. 12K4132	E, rough finish	76c	7c
No. 12K4134	A	76c	7c
No. 12K4136	D	99c	9c
No. 12K4138	G	65c	6c
No. 12K4139	Set of four		25c

If by mail, postage extra, per set, 2 cents.

No. 12K4140 G string, extra fine quality, pure silver wire wound on gut. Each...40c

If by mail, postage extra, 2 cents.

Our Special Waterproof Violin Strings.

By virtue of a special preparation these are purer in tone than the ordinary strings. They are made scientifically correct and absolutely unsusceptible to climatic influences. They are especially desirable for players who are troubled with moist fingers, as they possess extraordinary durability. Every string is fully tested and warranted. All E strings have 4 lengths, A and D strings 2½ lengths and G strings 1 length.

		Doz.	Each
No. 12K4141	E	$1.54	14c
No. 12K4142	A	1.54	14c
No. 12K4143	D	1.76	16c
No. 12K4144	G	.88	8c
No. 12K4145	Set of four		52c

If by mail, postage extra, per set, 2 cents.

Our "Verona" Brand Violin Strings.

Special attention is called to this splendid line of strings, as they are unquestionably as fine as any Italian strings made. They are made of the very best quality of sheep gut, and particular attention is called to the way they are wrapped, which insures them against injury in transmission through the mails. We recommend them to all who are looking for fine violin strings at a reasonable price. All E strings have 4 lengths, A and D strings 2½ lengths and G strings 1 length.

		Doz.	Each
No. 12K4146	E	$1.76	16c
No. 12K4147	A	1.76	16c
No. 12K4148	D	2.09	19c
No. 12K4149	G	1.10	10c
No. 12K4150	Set of four		61c

If by mail, postage extra, per set, 2 cents.

Our Special "Verona" Brand Silver G String.

This string is made of the same high grade genuine Italian gut and by the same process as all the other strings, but is wound with genuine silver wire and brought to a high polish. We guarantee this string absolutely against rattling or buzzing. The tone of this string is very rich, melodious and of great carrying power.

No. 12K4152 Verona G String. Price, each...................85c

If by mail, postage extra, 2 cents.

Metronomes.

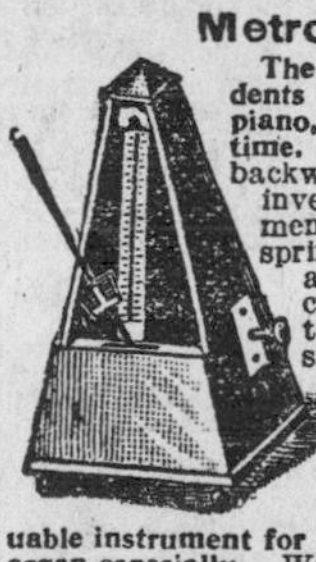

The Metronome is used by students of music, especially of the piano, to indicate the tempo or time. The upright rod moves backward and forward like an inverted pendulum, the movement being actuated by a spring which is wound up with a key. The time is indicated both to eye and ear, the movement being in sight and ticking similar to a clock. The time is regulated fast or slow by the sliding weight on the pendulum, while the latter has a graduated scale. This is an invaluable instrument for pupils of the piano and organ especially. Weight, 2 pounds. We sell only the very finest French make.

No. 12K3807 Metronome. Genuine French make, solid mahogany case. Maelzel system. Price..........$1.95

No. 12K3808 Same as No. 12K3807, but with bell attachment. Price..........$2.95

Organ and Piano Charts.

Campfield's Piano and Organ Chart and Scientific Music Table. By the aid of this ingenious and remarkable chart you can at once learn to play all the cords in any key at sight without the aid of a teacher. It also teaches 115 scientific points about music, including all the notes, elementary harmony, composition, modulation and transportation, besides illustrating the relationship between the different keys, as well as between the major and minor keys. A volume of valuable musical information condensed in this chart, endorsed by the leading pianists and organists throughout the United States and protected by United States copyright.

No. 12K6994 Price..........25c

Piano Tuning Hammer.

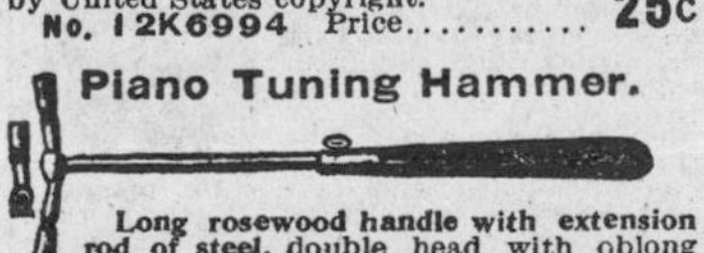

Long rosewood handle with extension rod of steel, double head with oblong and square holes and single star head. Extra quality, warranted. Weight, 1 pound.

No. 12K3801 Price..........$1.28

Extra Quality Acme Professional Violin Gut Strings.

All E strings have 4 lengths, A and D strings 2½ lengths and G strings 1 length.

		Doz.	Each
No. 12K4162	E	$0.99	9c
No. 12K4164	A	.99	9c
No. 12K4166	D	1.21	11c
No. 12K4168	G	.76	7c
No. 12K4170	Set of four		36c

If by mail, postage extra, per set, 2 cents.

No. 12K4171 G string, pure silver wire wound on gut, burnished, superfine quality. Price, each..................50c

If by mail, postage extra, 2 cents.

Extra Quality Acme Professional Banjo Gut Strings.

Each string one full length. The same string is used for both first and fifth on the banjo.

		Doz.	Each
No. 12K4194	B and E	76c	7c
No. 12K4196	G	84c	8c
No. 12K4198	E	99c	9c
No. 12K4200	A	65c	6c
No. 12K4202	Set of five		35c

If by mail, postage extra, per set, 2 cents.

Professional Guitar Strings.

The E, B and G strings are of superior quality gut and the D, A and E or 6th string are silver wire wound on silk.

All of these strings are of the very highest quality. Each string one full length.

		Doz.	Each
No. 12K4240	E	$0.88	8c
No. 12K4242	B	.88	8c
No. 12K4244	G	1.10	10c
No. 12K4246	D	.44	4c
No. 12K4248	A	.55	5c
No. 12K4250	E	.66	6c
No. 12K4252	Set of six		41c

If by mail, postage extra, per set, 3 cents.

Extra Quality Acme Professional Guitar Gut Strings.

D, A and E strings silvered wire on silk, plush knots.

		Doz.	Each
No. 12K4260	E	$0.99	9c
No. 12K4262	B	.99	9c
No. 12K4264	G	1.20	11c
No. 12K4265	D	.88	8c
No. 12K4266	A	.99	9c
No. 12K4267	E	1.10	10c
No. 12K4268	Set of six		56c

If by mail, postage extra, per set, 3 cents.

Best Quality Double Bass Strings.

The G and D strings are of high grade Italian gut, the A strings can be furnished either in plain gut or wound with silvered wire and the E strings wound with silvered wire on gut.

		Each
No. 12K4321	G	$0.66
No. 12K4323	D	.88
No. 12K4325	A, wound	1.10
No. 12K4327	A, plain	.95
No. 12K4329	E	1.35

If by mail, postage extra, single string, 4 cents; per set, 12 cents.

Acme Violoncello Strings.

These strings are the very best quality and we highly recommend them in every respect.

		Each
No. 12K4340	A	11c
No. 12K4342	D	17c
No. 12K4344	G	8c
No. 12K4346	C	9c
No. 12K4348	Set of four	40c

If by mail, postage extra, single string, 2 cents; per set, 5 cents.

Music Rolls and Bags.

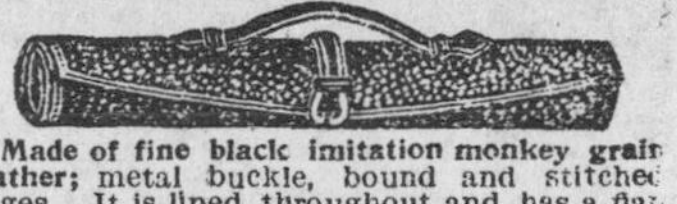

Made of fine black imitation monkey grain leather; metal buckle, bound and stitched edges. It is lined throughout and has a flap at the bottom to hold music. Size, open, 14¾x15½ inches.

No. 12K5990 Price..........27c

If by mail, postage extra, 13 cents.

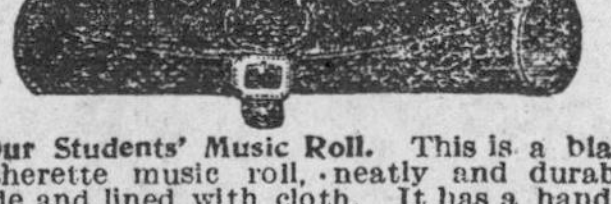

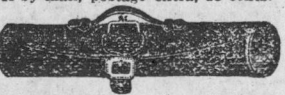

Our Students' Music Roll. This is a black leatherette music roll, neatly and durably made and lined with cloth. It has a handle strap and nickel plated buckle, and is furnished with a purse.

No. 12K5992 Price..........35c

If by mail, postage extra, 15 cents.

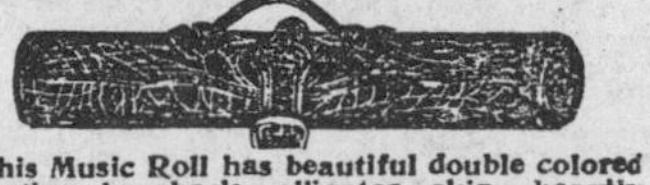

This Music Roll has beautiful double colored imitation hornback alligator skin, heavily lined, with stitched handle, wide lined and stitched strap and fine nickel buckle. It is lined throughout, and has a flap at the bottom to hold music in place. Bound and stitched all around. Size, open, 14¾x15 ins.

No. 12K6004 Price..........48c

If by mail, postage extra, 15 cents.

Genuine Leather Music Rolls.

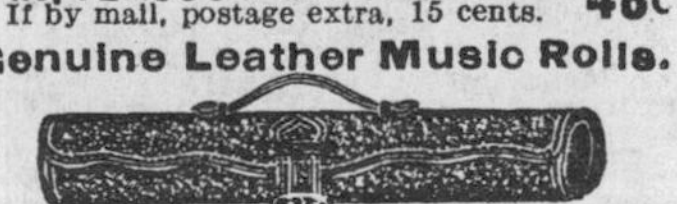

A Very Fine Seal Grain Leather Roll, has leather handle, wide strap and fancy buckle. We furnish this roll in either orange or black. Be sure to state color wanted.

No. 12K6007 Price..........65c

If by mail, postage extra, 14 cents.

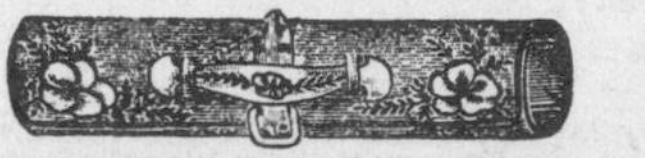

Our New Burnt Leather Music Roll. This is one of the tastiest music rolls ever placed on the market and is decorated with pretty designs burnt on the leather, with an imitation white rose on each end made of white velvet. We know you will like it. Fitted with strap and handsome nickel plated buckle. Leather handle ornamented with tasty design.
No. 12K6008 Price.......... **85c**
If by mail, postage extra, 13 cents.

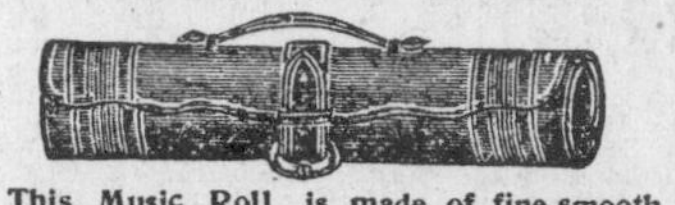

This Music Roll is made of fine smooth polished cowhide leather in orange or black, beautiful creased sides, and has an inside flap to keep the music in place, wide strap and finely plated harness buckle. Be sure to state color wanted. Size, 14¾x15 inches.
No. 12K6011 Price.......... **$1.15**
If by mail, postage extra, 15 cents.

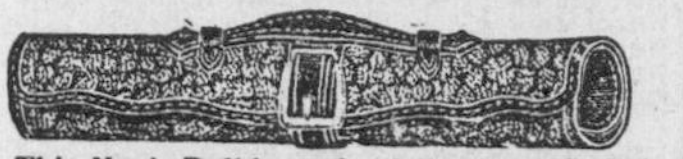

This Music Roll is made of fine black buffalo grain leather, leather lined, bound and stitched edges, heavy double stitched handle, wide lined and stitched strap and fine nickel buckle. It has an inside flap at bottom to hold music in place. Size, open, 14¾x15½inches.
No. 12K6009 Price.......... **$1.30**
If by mail, postage extra, 15 cents.

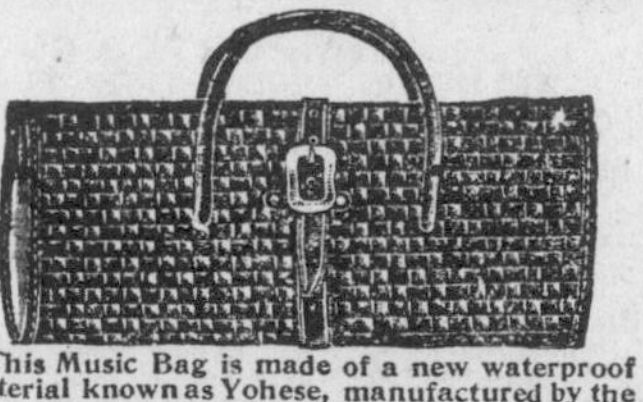

This Music Bag is made of a new waterproof material known as Yohese, manufactured by the Japanese by a secret process, and is a perfect imitation of genuine leather. It is pressed to imitate woven basket work, has black straps, nickel plated buckle and is lined with fancy material. It opens flat and takes a full size sheet of music, which is held in place by two flaps of special design. It is bound and stitched and is the very latest article in music bags. It comes in black only.
No. 12K6021 Price.......... **67c**
If by mail, postage extra, 12 cents.

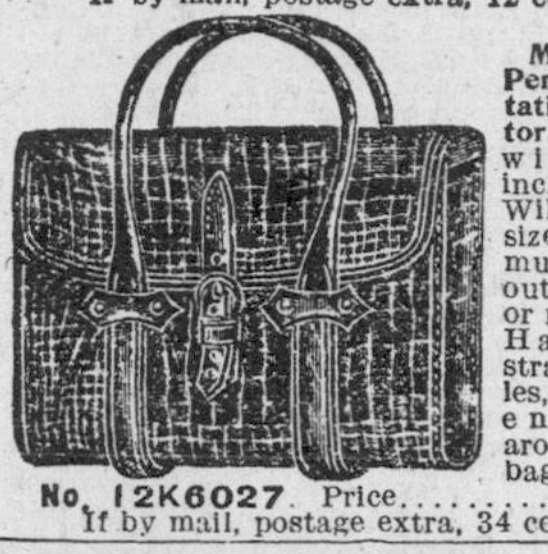

Music Bag. Perfect imitation alligator, 15 inches wide, 12 inches high. Will hold full size sheet music without folding or rolling. Has strong strap handles, reaching entirely around the bag.
No. 12K6027. Price.......... **$1.15**
If by mail, postage extra, 34 cents.

Piano and Organ Stools.

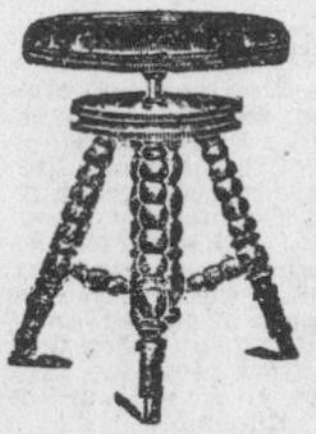

Piano or Organ Stool, made of solid oak, walnut or mahogany finish, round polished top, 12½ inches in diameter; three legs; very strong. Shipping weight, about 15 pounds. Be sure to state finish desired.
No. 12K6062 Price.......... **$1.45**

Special Value at $1.65.

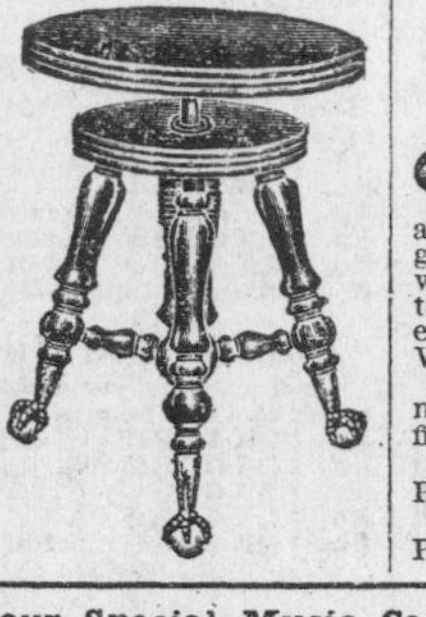

Piano or Organ Stool, made of solid oak or in ebony, walnut and mahogany finish; nicely polished round top, 13½ inches in diameter; three legs, with brass feet and glass balls. Shipping weight, about 25 pounds. Be sure to state finish desired.
No. 12K6068 Price.......... **$1.65**
Same description as No. 12K6068, but with four legs.
No. 12K6070 Price.......... **$2.05**

The Best Piano Stool Made for the Money.

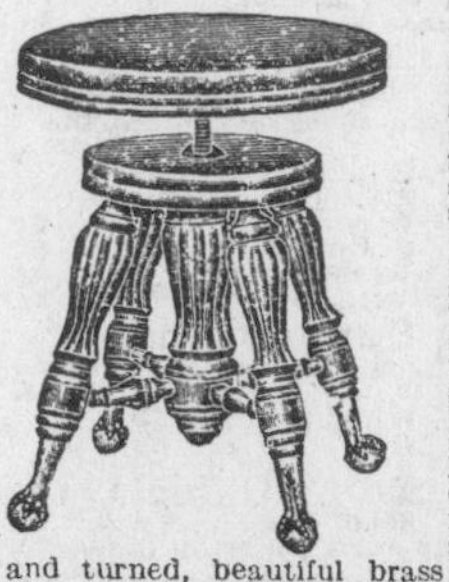

This stool is the most massive and substantially built piano stool we have ever been able to furnish. This stool is made of solid wood, has a 15-inch round polished top with shaped edges. The top is made of two pieces of wood glued together so that it becomes doubly strong. The base has a massive center post and four legs, handsomely fluted and turned, beautiful brass claw feet with glass balls. Only the best kiln dried hardwood lumber is used throughout, and only the best quality of screws; nuts and bolts enter into the construction of this stool. Weight, packed for shipment, 25 pounds.
No. 12K6071 Mahogany, rosewood, walnut or ebony finish. Be sure to state finish desired. Price.......... **$2.35**
No. 12K6074 Solid oak. Price.......... **2.65**
No. 12K6076 Solid walnut. Price.......... **3.10**

NOTE: In our Special Music Catalogue, which is mailed free of charge on application, we show a very complete line of instrument parts or trimmings; also larger line of music rolls, books, etc. Don't forget to send for it if interested.

SHEET MUSIC CATALOGUE.

WE SHOW HEREWITH but a few of the instruction books and folios which we are prepared to supply, just to show the difference between the regular retail price and our price. If you are interested in instruction books, folios and publications of any kind, we would advise that you send for our Special Sheet Music Catalogue, quoting a very large and complete line of instruction books for all instruments, vocal folios, instrumental collections, orchestra and band selections and songs of all kinds. We can furnish anything in the line of music, whether in sheet or book form, American or foreign publication, and if you will send for this Special Sheet Music Catalogue you will be startled at the astonishingly low prices quoted therein. **The prices which we quote in our catalogue are lower than what dealers usually term "teachers' prices."**

Our Department of Publications is the largest in the country, dealing directly with the consumer, and our buying power, together with our method of selling (our small margin of profit added to original cost), enables us to make these prices lower than any ever made before by any dealer. After looking over the few books shown below as an illustration of what we can do, then if you do not find what you desire, be sure to send for our Special Sheet Music Catalogue before making your purchases elsewhere, as we can save you from 30 to 50 per cent on any publication that you may want to buy.

PIANO INSTRUCTION BOOKS.

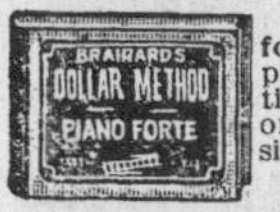

Brainards' New Easy Method for Piano. Containing complete and thorough instructions; also a choice selection of vocal and instrumental music. Regular retail price, $1.00.
No. 12K6955 Our price.......... **40c**
If by mail, postage extra, 8 cents.

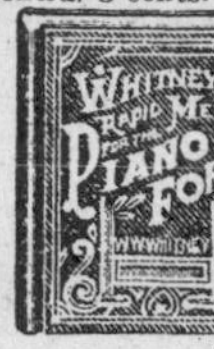

Whitney's Rapid Method for the Piano Forte. A thorough, progressive course of lessons presented in an easy and attractive form; with illustrations showing proper position of the hands and finger on the keyboard. Also contains a great variety of instrumental pieces. Bound in board. Regular retail price, $2.00.
No. 12K6959 Our price.......... **80c**
If by mail, postage extra, 20 cents.

The Rapid Piano Instructor.

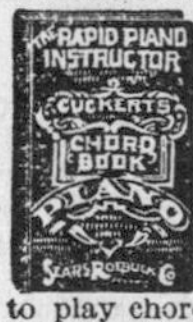

Chord Book for Piano. This book was especially compiled for us by the celebrated instructor and composer, E. N. Guckert. It contains illustrations of the piano keyboard, showing the fingers to be used in each chord, besides many other valuable illustrations and instructions for the beginner or advanced pupil. This book will teach anyone how to play chords and accompaniments without the aid of a teacher. Our own edition.
No. 12K6961 Price.......... **$1.00**
If by mail, postage extra, 20 cents.

Organ Instruction Books.

Chord Book for the Organ. This book was especially compiled for us by E. N. Guckert, the celebrated instructor and composer. It contains 24 illustrations of the keyboard of the organ showing the fingers used in each chord, besides other valuable instructions for the beginner or advanced pupil. This book will teach anyone how to play chords and accompaniments without the aid of a teacher. Our own edition.
No. 12K6968 Price.......... **$1.00**
If by mail, postage extra, 16 cents.

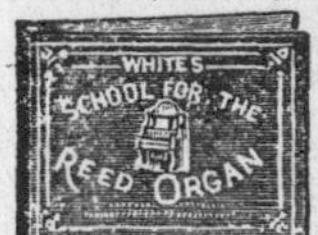

White's School for the Reed Organ. Contains a full and comprehensive method of instruction, also scales, studies, exercises, voluntaries, songs, marches, waltzes, polkas, opera melodies, hymns, tunes, etc., arranged for the reed organ, melodeon or harmonium, by C. A. White and Charles C. Blake. Contains 152 pages. Bound in board. Retail price, $1.50.
No. 12K6982 Our price.......... **65c**
If by mail, postage extra, 14 cents.

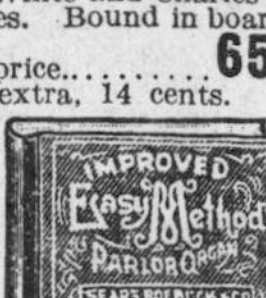

Whitney's Improved Easy Method for the Parlor Organ. This is a new and attractive system by which the pupil may rapidly learn to play the organ. Besides a thorough course in music, this book contains a choice collection of vocal and instrumental pieces. Retail price, $1.50.
No. 12K6988 Our price.......... **50c**
If by mail, postage extra, 13 cents.

VIOLIN INSTRUCTION BOOKS.

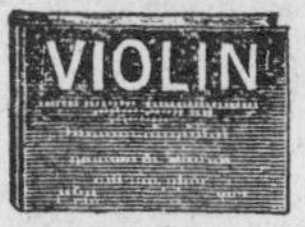

Howe's Violin Without a Master. Containing new and complete rules and exercises, with full directions in bowing and all necessary instructions to perfect the learner in the art of playing the violin; to which is added a large selection of popular airs and dance music, as well as operatic airs, with several pieces arranged as duets.
No. 12K6996 Price.......... **22c**
If by mail, postage extra, 3 cents.

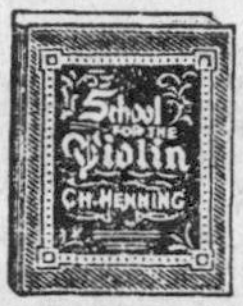

Henning's School for the Violin. Specially revised, with bow and finger marks added. In three parts, complete in one book; 101 pages, printed on fine paper, bound in board.
No. 12K7004 Price, complete.......... **80c**
If by mail, postage extra, 15 cents.

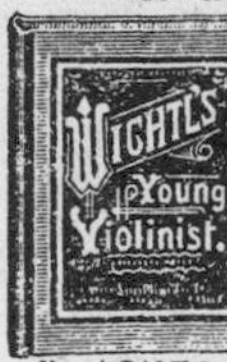

Wichtl's Young Violinist. Contains the first instruction in the violin line, including 100 progressive exercises in the first position through all intervals and keys with the second violin part for the teacher. It contains also Pleyel's celebrated violin duets. English, German and French text. Retail price, $1.00.
No. 12K7016 Our price.......... **38c**
If by mail, postage extra, 15 cents.

Guitar Instruction Books.

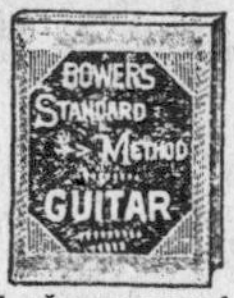

Bowers' Standard Method for the Guitar. Positively the most popular instruction book for the guitar ever published; bound in paper. Retail price, 50 cents.
No. 12K7030 Our price.......... **25c**
If by mail, postage extra, 5c.

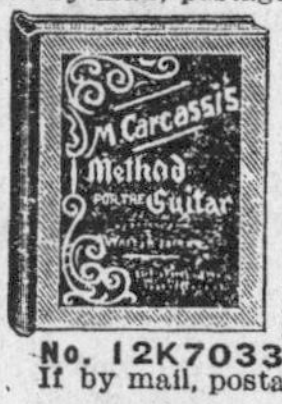

New and Improved Method for the Guitar. By Carcassi, the celebrated guitarist. The number of popular songs in each of the different keys, together with the masterly instructions of Carcassi, make this a desirable method to both teacher and scholar. Retail price, $1.00.
No. 12K7033 Our price.......... **50c**
If by mail, postage extra, 17 cents.

Banjo Instruction Books.

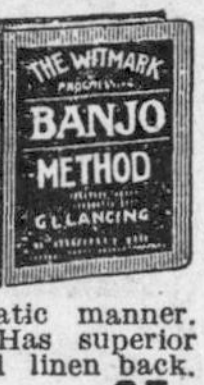

Witmark's Progressive Banjo Method. Written and compiled by G. L. Lansing. Complete, progressive, thoroughly up to date method. The elementary or first part will enable the pupil to progress so as to play the popular selections of today within a short time. The entire work is arranged in a most progressive and systematic manner. The book contains 88 pages. Has superior quality paper, flexible cover and linen back. Retail price, $1.00.
No. 12K7053 Our price.......... **65c**
If by mail, postage extra, 10 cents.

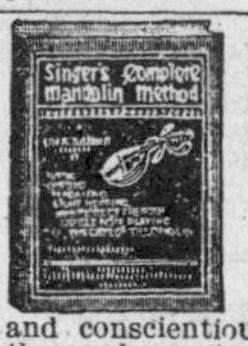

Singer's Complete Mandolin Method. Thoroughly and carefully explains all the technicalities in connection with the mandolin. It is not only filled with instructions and exercises, but contains many beautiful tunes arranged for solos and duets. It is complete in every respect and any student who will use it patiently and conscientiously will certainly become a thorough master of the instrument. Special attention is devoted to tuning, shifting, memorizing, sight reading, tremolo playing, double note playing and the care of the mandolin, besides other important subjects. Retail price, $1.50.
No. 12K7078 Our price.......... **$1.00**
If by mail, postage extra, 12 cents.

MISCELLANEOUS INSTRUCTION BOOKS.

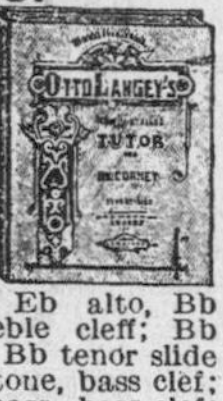

Otto Langey's Celebrated Instructors for any Instrument. These books have a world wide reputation as being among the finest instructors ever published, being easily understood, yet complete in every detail, so that a beginner using one of these books, can with practice easily master any instrument. Published for cornet, Eb alto, Bb tenor, bass clef; Bb tenor, treble cleff; Bb tenor slide trombone, bass clef; Bb tenor slide trombone, treble clef; Bb baritone, bass clef; Bb baritone, treble clef; Bb bass, bass clef; Bb bass, treble clef; Eb bass, clarionet, flute, piccolo, violin, viola, violoncello, double bass, guitar, mandolin, banjo, saxophone, oboe, bassoon, French horn, drums, fife, tympany, orchestra bells, xylophone and piano. Best and most complete edition. Regular retail price, $1.00.
No. 12K7119 Our price, each book....(Postage extra, 12 cents.).... **38c**

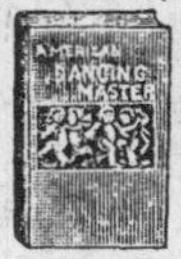

Howe's New American Dancing Master, containing 400 dances and including 100 figures of the German. The latest and most fashionable dances are included, with full explanations of the latest and most approved figures and calls for the different changes, as well as rules on deportment, toilet and etiquette of dancing; 140 pages. Retail price, 50 cents.
No. 12K7152 Our price.......... **30c**
If by mail, postage extra, 3 cents.

Gospel Hymns.

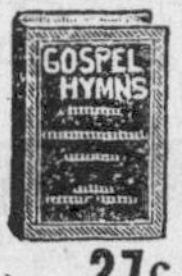

No. 12K6690 Consolidated Nos. 1, 2, 3 and 4. Large type, words and music; 400 pages. Price.......... **67c**
If by mail, postage extra, 10c
No. 12K6694 Words only. Nos. 1, 2, 3 and 4. Price.......... **17c**
If by mail, postage extra, 4c.
No. 12K6696 Gospel Hymns, No. 5, with words and music. Price....(Postage extra, 6 cents.).... **27c**
No. 12K6700 No. 6. Price....(Postage extra, 6 cents.).... **25c**
No. 12K6701 No. 6. Christian Endeavor edition. Price.......... **29c**
If by mail, postage extra, 6 cents.
No. 12K6704 Nos. 5 and 6 combined. Price.(Postage extra, 8 cents.).... **55c**
No. 12K6706 Nos. 5 and 6. Words only. Price..(Postage extra, 4 cents.).... **18c**
No. 12K6707 Nos. 1 to 6. Complete, with words and music in one volume. Bound in cloth. Price.......... **86c**
If by mail, postage extra, 20 cents.
No. 12K6709 Nos. 1 to 6. Words only, cloth cover. Price.......... **17c**
If by mail, postage extra, 3 cents.

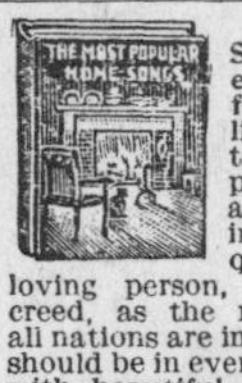

The Most Popular Home Songs. This is one of the finest collections of the old famous songs which we always like to sing and hear. It contains 135 beautiful songs of a patriotic, sentimental, sacred and humorous character. It is intended to meet with the requirements of every music loving person, regardless of nationality or creed, as the most famous compositions of all nations are in the book. One of these books should be in every home. Printed on fine paper with beautiful two-color lithographed cover. Retail price, 50 cents.
No. 12K6550 Our price.......... **35c**
If by mail, postage extra, 5 cents.

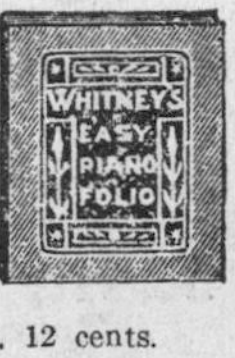

Whitney's Easy Piano Folio. Very fine and desirable collection of easy piano pieces, especially adapted for beginners. Nothing hard to finger or read. Waltzes, marches and everything herein contained arranged in a very easy and progressive manner. Retail price, 50c.
No. 12K6715 Our price.......... **30c**
If by mail, postage extra, 12 cents.

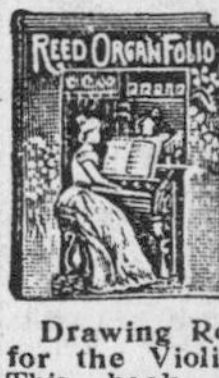

Reed Organ Folio. A new collection of the best and most popular music of the day, arranged especially for the five-octave organ. Over 60 pieces, full sheet music size; paper cover. Retail price, 50 cents.
No. 12K6808 Our price.......... **25c**
If by mail, postage extra, 11c.

Drawing Room Collection for the Violin and Piano. This book contains 121 pages of the best violin music by the most celebrated composers, and is a most desirable book for violin players. The pieces are arranged especially for beginners and amateurs. Retail price, 50c.
No. 12K6824 Our price.......... **30c**
If by mail, postage extra, 12 cents.

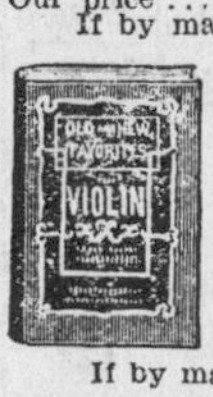

Old and New Favorites for Violin. This is just what its name signifies and is a splendid collection of favorite music for the violin, both old and new. It contains over 150 pages of dance and operatic music and is bound up in the most handy form for convenient use. Retail price, 50 cents.
No. 12K6848 Our price.......... **16c**
If by mail, postage extra, 5 cents.

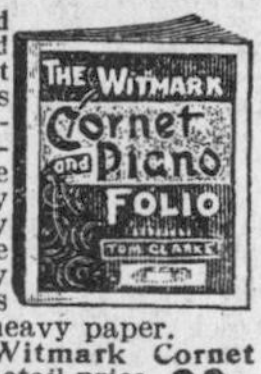

The Witmark Cornet and Piano Folios are splendid collections of the latest popular music, arranged as duets for these two instruments. We can safely promise that the purchaser will be perfectly satisfied with every selection contained in any of these folios. They are all handsomely and durably bound and the music is printed from new plates on heavy paper.
No. 12K6903 The Witmark Cornet and Piano Duets, No. 1. Retail price, 50 cents. Our price.......... **23c**
If by mail, postage extra, 7 cents.

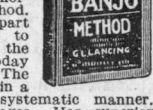

WATCHES, DIAMONDS, AND JEWELRY

WHEN YOU BUY A GOLD FILLED CASE by all means we would advise you to select our new Plymouth gold filled case. This case is recommended above all other makes, being made of extra plates of solid gold over an inner composition metal and will wear longer than any other gold filled case made and is the handsomest and best fitting of any. We have discontinued the sale of the Sears gold filled case and the Sears, Roebuck & Co. brand of special cases. The Plymouth case is manufactured by the same company especially for us for the benefit of our customers who sometimes prefer a differently named case so that they in turn can sell it or trade it to better advantage. With every Plymouth gold filled case we issue our unqualified written binding guarantee. You are protected in the purchase of this case to the very letter. Unlike any other guarantee written or sent with any gold filled case, our guarantee unqualifyingly guarantees our gold filled cases to be as represented. Sears, Roebuck & Co. as an institution stands behind every Plymouth filled case.

IN SELECTING A MOVEMENT we would advise by all means that you pick out as the best possible value one of the Edgemere or one of the Plymouth Watch Co. movements, illustrated on pages 259 and 260, and quoted throughout the following pages in the various sizes and grades. For a gentleman's watch, the 21 jeweled Prince of Wales, in 16-size, both open face and hunting, and the 21 jeweled King Edward, in 18-size, open face or hunting, both movements manufactured by the Plymouth Watch Co., stand out pre-eminently the best values and the most accurate timekeepers in this entire department. No pains or expense were considered in their making. In everything that constitutes a fine watch, timekeeping, finish and size, these movements are undoubtedly the finest in the American market.

MAIL AND EXPRESS SHIPMENTS. We recommend sending watches by express, as they do not receive the hard usage as when sent by mail. Our statistics show that 90 per cent of breakages in watches happens while in transit through the mails; therefore, we again advise you to have watches shipped by express, and all other small jewelry by mail, as it is perfectly safe and far the cheapest. Postage is 1 cent per ounce. A watch packed for shipment weighs from 6 to 8 ounces; chains, rings and other small articles of jewelry, about 2 ounces. Packages amounting to $1.00 or over should be registered, which costs 8 cents extra, as this is the safest method. **25 cents will carry any watch to any part of the United States by express.**

ENGRAVING. Cash in full must accompany all orders when goods are marked with engraving. We charge for engraving in script on jewelry, watches, etc., 2½ cents per letter; in Old English, small, 5 cents per letter. Monograms on silverware and jewelry are all the rage. Prices for two or three-letter combinations, script or ribbon style, as follows:

	Script	Ribbon
½-inch size	20c	$0.25
¾-inch size	30c	.35
1 -inch size	50c	.75
1½-inch size	65c	1.35

In writing orders when goods are to be engraved, write or draw plain letters, so as to avoid mistakes. We cannot exchange goods after they have been engraved.

MERCHANDISE ENGRAVED ACCORDING TO INSTRUCTIONS. We must caution you that under no circumstances will we exchange or refund money on any merchandise that has been engraved according to instructions with letters, dates or monograms. The merchandise is of no value to us after it has been so marked. Our goods are as shown and we have described them as carefully and as accurately as we could. Therefore, should you desire any article engraved you must do so on your own risk. But remember, we guarantee the quality of every article in our catalogue to be exactly as described and we are willing at any time to refund your money, together with transportation charges both ways, whether the goods are marked or not, when the quality proves different than is claimed.

REGARDING ENGRAVINGS ON WATCH CASES. It sometimes happens that we are out of the exact engraving on watch case ordered, but we aim to carry exact designs. When the exact engraving cannot be had, we always have a very similar one, which we will take the liberty of sending, rather than delay your order, it being understood you can return same if not perfectly satisfactory.

WATCH REPAIRING. We have a thoroughly equipped mechanical department, which is fitted with all the latest tools and appliances for the repairing of all kinds of watches. Our charges are about one-half what is usually charged by the retail dealers, and the work will be done in a very superior manner. We cannot give an accurate estimate of the cost of repairs without a thorough examination of the work. Our charges are merely enough to cover cost of material and labor. In sending a watch for repairing, be sure to send it by registered mail; mark on the outside of the package your name and address, and write us at the same time that you have done so, giving full explanation regarding trouble with watch. **DO NOT FAIL when sending anything to us for repairs to PLAINLY WRITE YOUR NAME AND ADDRESS ON PACKAGE.**

OUR BINDING GUARANTEES.

WATCH CASE GUARANTEE. Where a watch case in this catalogue is described as guaranteed for life, 25, 20, 10 or 5 years, it applies to gold filled watch cases, and means that the case is covered by plates of solid gold over an inner plate of hard composition metal, and the gold is guaranteed to wear and retain its perfect color for the time stated, and if the gold in any piece or part of the case wears through within the stipulated time mentioned in the description and in the guarantee, the case will be replaced with a new case free of cost to you.

OUR PLYMOUTH LIFE GUARANTEE.

Where we describe any gold filled case or article of jewelry or silverware as carrying our PLYMOUTH LIFE GUARANTEE, we mean that should any of these articles fail in any part to be exactly as warranted, we will exchange same at any time within your natural life, whether you have owned the article five years, twenty years or fifty years. Return it to us, and we will upon receipt of it send another one of the same quality FREE OF CHARGE.

MOVEMENT GUARANTEE. Where we guarantee a watch movement for five years, the guarantee is absolute and binding upon us to replace or repair, free of cost to you, any piece or part of the watch movement that may become defective by reason of imperfect material or workmanship at any time within five years; and while this guarantee does not include removing dirt, cleaning of movement or repairing, free of cost, any piece or part that may be broken or damaged through careless or improper handling, it is the widest, longest and strongest watch movement guarantee ever issued, and if you buy any movement from us and on the last day of the fifth year the watch stops or fails to keep accurate time, and this failure is in any way due to imperfect material or workmanship, it will be repaired by us or replaced with a new movement free of any cost to you. Our written guarantees which accompany every watch and movement are so written over our own signature that there can be no question of your absolute security in the purchase of any watch case, watch movement or complete watch from us.

DIAMOND GUARANTEE. Our Refund, Exchange and Guarantee Certificate. With every diamond we issue a written, binding guarantee with a further agreement that you can at any time return any diamond you may select, where weight and quality are quoted, and exchange it for any other diamond or other article of jewelry at the same or higher price.

We further agree on the return of any diamond purchased from us within sixty days of purchase, when so requested, to refund in cash your full purchase price, and we further agree at any time after sixty days, on return of any diamond to us, when requested to do so, to refund your full purchase price less 10 per cent.

JEWELRY GUARANTEE. Where we describe any article of jewelry as solid gold, gold filled or gold plated, where we describe it as 18, 14 or 10-karat or solid silver or silver plated, the article of jewelry is covered by our binding guarantee, guaranteeing it to be in every way exactly as represented by us, and if after received, and examined and put to any kind of test, acid or otherwise, it should prove any different, should fall short in the slightest degree of the representation made in this catalogue, we will replace the article purchased with a new article or refund your money, as you may direct.

TECHNICAL TERMS USED IN DESCRIBING JEWELRY AND SILVERWARE.

BRIGHT POLISH is a finish on silver and gold showing the bright polished surface of the metal itself without coloring, and always has a bright and shining surface.

SATIN FINISH. The finishing of jewelry and silverware by sand blasting or a scratch brush, which dulls the surface and gives it a peculiar satiny effect and shows the dull color of the metal without any other coloring.

ROMAN COLOR is the absolutely pure color of virgin gold. It is pure gold plated upon a lower karat of gold and is of a rich, bright yellow or canary color, the same color as nuggets of pure 24-karat gold. Two methods are used in putting this color on, the electro plating process and the acid process. The acid process is used only on 14 and 18-karat jewelry. When Roman color is used the article is generally satin finished after.

HAND ENGRAVING. When stated that the article is hand engraved, we mean that the article is beautified, as the illustration of the article shows, by bright cutting done by hand with an engraving tool.

GOLD FILLED STOCK. Gold filled stock is made of stock that is gold filled, the outside or visible surface being a sheet of solid gold of substantial thickness, hard soldered on a plate of base metal.

ROLLED GOLD PLATE. Rolled gold plate is made very similarly to gold filled stock, with the exception that the plate is rolled to a thinner degree and has not the wearing ability of gold filled stock.

ELECTRO PLATE. Electro plate is a process of gold plating by electricity. This is the cheapest and quickest method of gold plating. Electro plated jewelry cannot be guaranteed, and will wear but a short time. It is very difficult to recognize electro plated jewelry from rolled plate or gold filled. Only one well versed and educated in the jewelry business can recognize the difference.

TECHNICAL TERMS USED IN DESCRIBING WATCHES.

FULL ADJUSTMENT. A high grade watch is fully adjusted when it is adjusted to heat, cold, isochronism and to six positions.

ADJUSTED TO TEMPERATURE. As a watch is only as perfect as the balance wheel and hairspring is perfect, and as these parts are made of metal, and the metal contracts and expands with the variations in temperature, a watch to be adjusted to temperature must have the balance wheel so constructed as to allow for extreme cold or extreme heat. In other words, the balance wheel must be so constructed that one metal will expand to such an amount as can be taken up by the other metal used in its makeup. When the balance wheel is so constructed that this variation does not affect it, it is known then to be adjusted to temperature.

ADJUSTED TO ISOCHRONISM is an adjustment of the hairspring by which it vibrates with the balance wheel in perfect uniformity; that is, when the long and short arcs of a balance wheel are caused to perform in the same time by means of the hairspring. This assures accuracy in timekeeping.

ADJUSTED TO POSITION. This adjustment can only be brought about by having the balance wheel in perfect poise and absolutely trued. The watch is run and timed in six different positions and corrections are made from time to time until the watch runs in each position without any variation in time.

BREGUET HAIRSPRINGS. This hairspring differs from the old style flat hairspring in having the outer coil adjusted above the other coil and tempered in this position. This arrangement insures a condition for perfect adjustment of the hairspring in all positions, thus obviating all chances of its becoming misplaced and entangled, as has always been the case with flat hairsprings.

PATENT REGULATOR is a device for controlling the vibrations of the hairspring, and by its use a watch can be regulated to the smallest fraction of time.

STEM WIND AND STEM SET. All watches that are set by turning the winding crown, whether they are set by pulling out a setting lever or by pressing in a push pin, are known as stem set and stem wind watches.

PENDANT SET. All watches that are set without setting lever or push pin are known as pendant set watches, being set by pulling out the winding crown, which is located at top of pendant or neck, as it is sometimes called; the hands may be set by simply turning the crown, which is pushed back into place when the hands are in desired position.

TIMING SCREWS. With the use of these screws a watch can be brought down to accurate time without in any way changing the position of the hairspring. Only a watchmaker can manipulate these screws. Care must be taken in the use of them in timing a watch, together with great skill, as a well poised balance wheel is very delicate and easily put out of true and is often spoiled by incompetent workmen.

CUT BALANCE. The cut or expansion balance is the most reliable for accurate time. They are so constructed that there can be only a minimum amount of variation by any climatic change, whereas the solid balance wheel, by contraction or expansion, will vary when used where variations of temperature are met with.

RUBY JEWELS are used in the high priced, fine finished watches. By ruby jewels we mean the jewels are of genuine ruby. **Garnet jewels** are mostly used in the average middle priced watches, and are made of garnet, and cheap imported watches are sometimes fitted with glass jewels.

DOUBLE SUNK DIALS are made of three pieces: The outer part on which the numerals are placed, the center or plain field, and the small circular disc for registering the seconds. This construction is a great advantage over the plain dials as a preventive of the hands catching, thereby causing the watch to stop.

SAFETY PINION is a patent device on the center wheel arbor of a watch, the purpose of which is to protect the train wheels and mainspring barrel from damage in cases where the mainspring breaks.

WATCHMAKERS', WIRE WORKERS' AND JEWELERS' TOOLS AND MATERIALS

ONLY $1.18 FOR THIS WIRE WORKERS' OUTFIT.

We have endeavored to give the weights on the articles listed on this page, or the exact postage required to mail each article. Where no postage is given, article can be mailed for 4 cents.

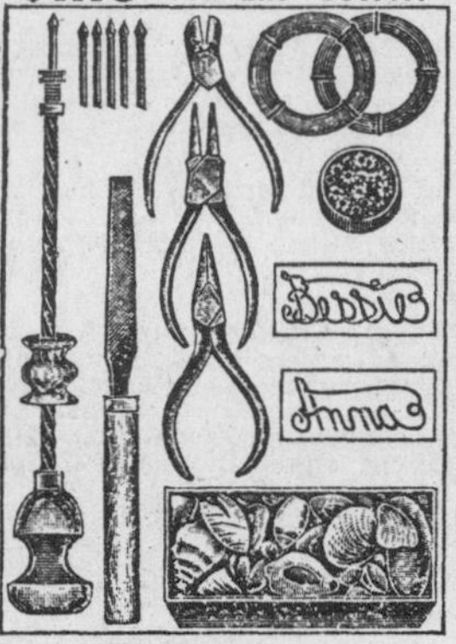

No. 4K2 Wire Artists' or Wire Workers' Tool Set for $1.18.

SEND US $1.18 and we will ship you by express our entire Wire Workers' Outfit, exactly as illustrated, and if after you have carefully examined it you do not find it equal or better than sets offered for $1.95 and $2.25, return it and we will refund your money, together with the express charges. This outfit consists of the following items: 1 pair snipe nose pliers, 1 pair round nose pliers, 1 pair side cutting pliers, 1 file with handle, 1 ounce gold plated wire (½-ounce round and ½-ounce square), ½-gross plated washers, assorted, 1 lot assorted shells, 1 drill, 2 sample names. Follow the principle used in making these names and you will know the entire art. Shipping weight, about 1¾ pounds. Order by number.

No. 4K2 Price.................. $1.18
If by mail, postage extra, 18c.

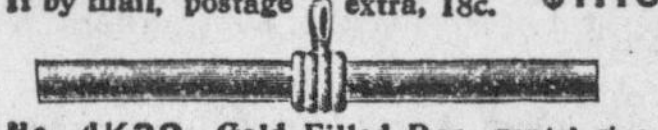

No. 4K32 Gold Filled Bar, gents' size. Price..................15c
No. 4K33 Gold Filled Bar, ladies' size. Price..................15c

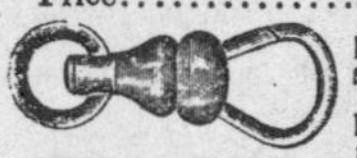

No. 4K38 Gold Filled Swivel, gents' size. Price.........22c
No. 4K39 Gold Filled Swivel, ladies' size. Price.........22c

Prices of Gold Plated Wire and Wire Workers' Material.

We cannot sell any of this material in smaller quantities than quoted.

No. 4K4 1st quality round wire. Sizes, 16 to 21 gauge. Price, per ounce..........62c
No. 4K6 2d quality round wire. Sizes, 16 to 21 gauge. Price, per ounce..........43c
No. 4K8 3d quality round wire. Sizes, 16 to 21 gauge Price, per ounce......18c
No. 4K10 1st quality square wire. Sizes, 18 to 22 gauge. Price, per ounce......62c
No. 4K12 2d quality square wire. Sizes, 18 to 22 gauge. Price, per ounce..........43c
No. 4K14 3d quality square wire. Sizes, 18 to 22 gauge. Per ounce......18c

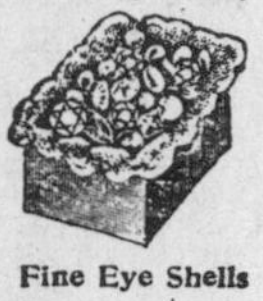

No. 4K94 Jobbing Stones, assorted. Containing all colors and sizes in imitation of genuine. Price, per gross......72c

No. 4K96 Fine Eye Shells for Hat Pins. Price, per dozen.........28c

No. 4K98 Shells Assortment. In box Price......14c

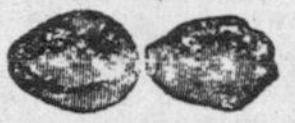

No. 4K100 Money Cowrie Shells for Cuff Buttons. Price, per 100, 34c

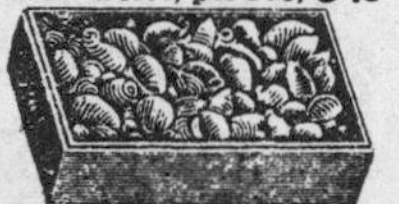

No. 4K102 Coffee Shells. Price, per 100 22c

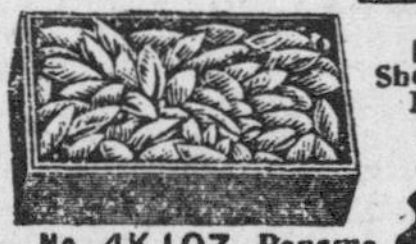

No. 4K104 Rice Shells. Price, per 100. 16c

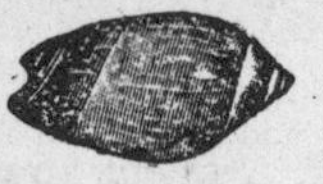

No. 4K107 Panama Shells. Price, per 100, $1.00

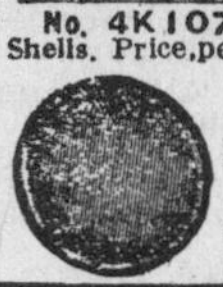

No. 4K120 Large Brown Sea Beans. Price, per dozen..........18c
No. 4K122 Large Red Sea Beans. Price, per 100..........38c

THE TOOLS AND IMPLEMENTS

we herewith illustrate are the most necessary in the equipment of a watchmakers' kit. The material of our tools is made of the very finest procurable.

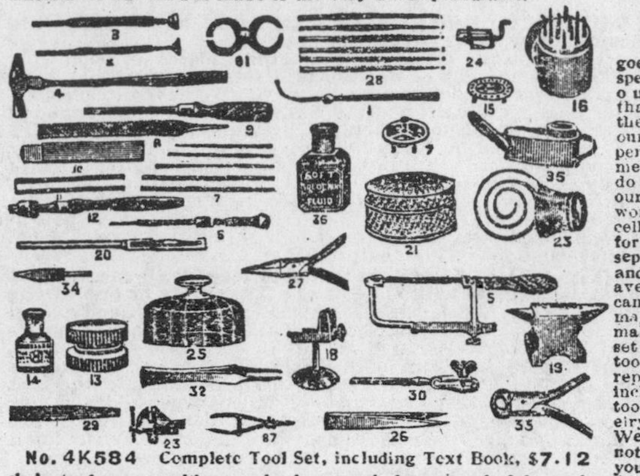

EACH TOOL

goes through a rigid inspection before leaving our establishment, so that we are assured of them being received by our customers in perfect condition. Our mechanics here who do our watch work use our own tools, and the work done by us is excelled by none. This set for $7.12 consists of 47 separate and distinct pieces and text book. Any man of average mechanical skill can learn to rectify the majority of causes that make a watch stop. The set not alone includes tools necessary for watch repairing, but likewise includes a complete set of tools for silverware, jewelry and clock repairing. We know that you would not fail to be pleased with your purchase if you conclude to favor us with an order for one of these wonderful watchmakers' and jewelers' sets.

No. 4K584 Complete Tool Set, including Text Book, $7.12. Shipping weight, 12 pounds.
No. 4K584 Price for complete set, including text book.......................... $7.12

OUR SPECIAL DRIVE IN TOOLS.

WATCHMAKERS', JEWELERS' AND SILVERSMITHS' OUTFITS FOR..... $3.30

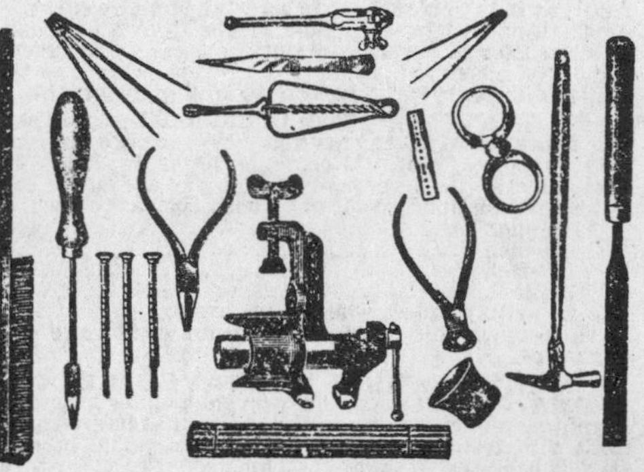

No. 4K124 Our Special Drive in Tools. A Watchmakers', Jewelers' and Silversmiths' Outfit for $3.30, consisting of twenty-four distinct tools, each one being used to perform certain important work. This set can be used not only by beginners, but by anyone wishing to repair watches, clocks or silverware. A splendid set to practice with. You can always add from time to time necessary tools from our list of watchmakers' tools described on this page. This set consists of twenty-four separate and distinct tools and appliances, as follows: One jewelers' flat file with handle, 1 watchmakers' hammer with handle, 1 watchmakers' rubber magnifying eyeglass, 1 pair jewelers' cutting pliers, 1 pair calipers, 1 watchmakers' riveting stake, 1 small bench vise, 1 pair soldering tweezers, 1 pair watchmakers' tweezers, 1 pair of jewelers' flat pliers, 1 watchmakers' or jewelers' pin vise, 3 watchmakers' screwdrivers, each being a different size, 1 jewelers' soldering copper, 1 watchmakers' or clockmakers' brush, 4 needle files, very important for watchmakers and jewelers; 1 bundle peg wood, 3 pivot broaches; to this complete set of twenty-four distinct and separate tools is likewise added, 1 cube of refined jewelers' chalk, one bottle of watchmakers' oil, 1 bundle of watchmakers' pith wood, 1 bundle of brass wire, 1 text book. This book gives recipes, new methods, and much valuable information regarding watch repairing, stone setting and other valuable pointers.

No. 4K124 Price, complete, with all above mentioned additions, and boxed in a neat wooden box. (Weight, complete, about 6 pounds.)........ $3.30

WE DO NOT carry any other watch and clock material for sale except that quoted and illustrated on this page. Should you desire balance staffs, hole jewels, mainsprings, etc., and you are not positive of the exact size of watch that you want it for, send a sample to us and state the make of the watch and the movement number and the size in inches and fractions of an inch, write us that you have sent the sample and enclose in the package your name and address so as to prevent possible loss and confusion. **REGARDING WATCH CRYSTALS.** We carry two kinds, the Geneva crystal used in hunting style cases and the mi-concave crystal or the thick beveled edge style for open face watches. These crystals vary in sizes and heights. The sizes vary 1-16 of a millimeter in diameter and the heights range from 4 to 8 millimeters. Therefore, it will be absolutely necessary, and we will undertake to fill no orders unless the exact sizes and heights are given. If you do not know these send us the bezel of the watch to be fitted with a crystal.

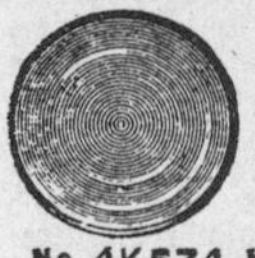

No. 4K570 Watch Glasses, hunting style. Price, per gross.....$4.00
No. 4K572 Watch Glasses, thick for open face. Price, per gross......$4.00

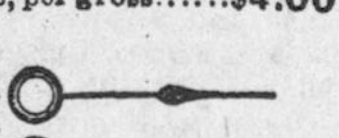

No. 4K574 Hands, steel, for watches, hour and minute, for all sizes of American and imported watches. Price, per dozen pairs..........22c
No. 4K575 Hands, for clocks, all lengths. Price, per dozen pairs..........20c
No. 4K576 Hands, steel, seconds, for all sizes American and imported watches. Price, per dozen..12c
No. 4K578 Mainsprings, for watches, all styles and sizes. Price, per dozen........96c
No. 4K580 Mainsprings, for clocks, 1-day. Price, each..........14c
No. 4K582 Mainsprings, for clocks, 8-day. Price, each..........35c
No. 4K0590 Elgin Balance Staffs, all sizes. Price, per dozen........$1.25
No. 4K0591 Waltham Balance Staffs, all sizes. Price, per dozen........$1.25
No. 4K0592 Hampden, Springfield, Seth Thomas, Plymouth, New York Standard, Trenton or Rockford Balance Staffs, all sizes. Price, per dozen........$1.25
No. 4K0593 Hole Jewels, plate or cock and foot for Elgin, Waltham, Hampden, Springfield, Rockford, Plymouth, New York Standard, Trenton or Seth Thomas, for all sizes. Price, per dozen........$1.00
No. 4K0594 Cap or End Stones for Elgin, Waltham, Hampden, Springfield, Rockford, Plymouth, New York Standard, Trenton or Seth Thomas, all sizes. Doz..75c
No. 4K0596 Roller Jewels or Ruby Pins for Elgin, Waltham, Hampden, Springfield, Rockford, Plymouth, New York Standard, Trenton or Seth Thomas, all sizes. Doz...60c

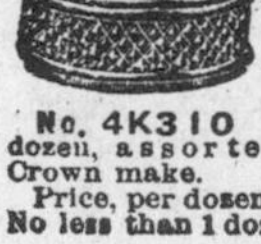

No. 4K250 Alcohol Cup. Glass. Height, 1⅜ inches. Diameter, 3 inches. Price..................18c
Postage extra, 11 cents.

No. 4K310 Drills, 1 dozen, assorted sizes. Crown make. Price, per dozen....21c
No less than 1 dozen sold.

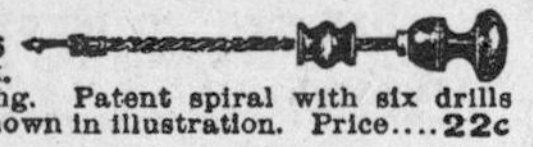

No. 4K316 Drill Stock. 10 inches long. Patent spiral with six drills extra, not shown in illustration. Price....22c

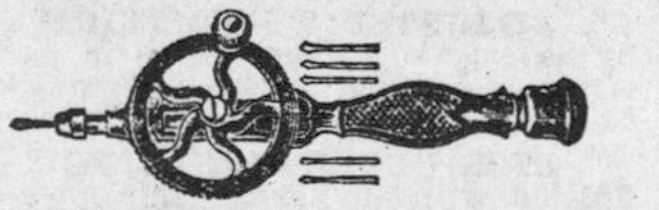

No. 4K318 Drill Stock, patent geared with adjustable split chuck; top of drill unscrews and has receptacle for holding drills; 10½ inches long. Price..(Postage, 16c)....79c

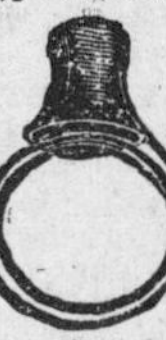

No. 4K330 Eye Glass, hard rubber with coil spring; 2 to 5-inch focus. Price.....34c
No. 4K332 Eye Glass, plain, hard rubber, without spring; 2 to 5-inch focus. Price..........22c
No. 4K333 Eye Glass, plain, without spring; 2 to 5-inch focus; aluminum frame. Price..........23c

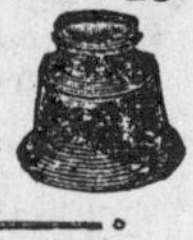

No. 4K334 Eye Glass, double lens. Very powerful, used for very accurate work. Price..................40c

No. 4K340 Files, needle; any shape shown above. Length of file complete with handle, 4 inches. Price, set of six.....45c
No. 4K344 Files, screw head for filing slots in screw heads. Length, 3½ inches. Price..................18c

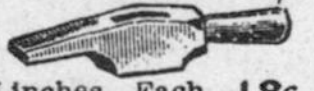

No. 4K374 Hammers, Swiss.

2 inches. Each.	14c	2¾ inches. Each..	18c
2¼ inches. Each.	14c	3¼ inches. Each..	18c
2½ inches. Each.	14c	3¾ inches. Each..	23c

No. 4K366 Handles, for hammers. Maple. Price..................5c

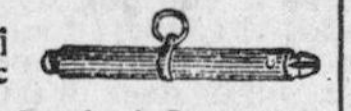

No. 4K388 Keys. Birch patent key; will wind any watch. Price.8c

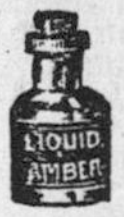

No. 4K384 Jewelers' Cement. For cementing china, glass, ivory, beads, pearls, jewels, etc. Price, per bottle.......... 23c
No. 4K385 Granite Hold Fast Cement. Price, per bottle........14c

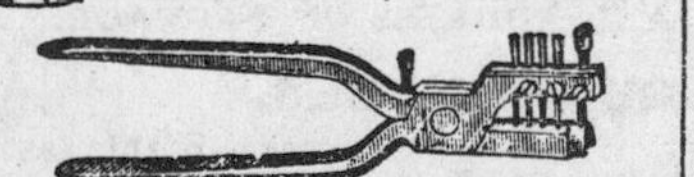

No. 4K400 Punch, mainspring with four punches and mainspring barrel hook punch, nickel plated. Length, 7 inches. Price..$1.08
If by mail, postage extra, 12 cents.

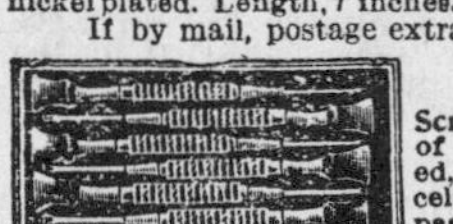

No. 4K472 Screwdrivers, set of six, nickel plated, with colored celluloid heads; in pasteboard box. Set of six.$1.25

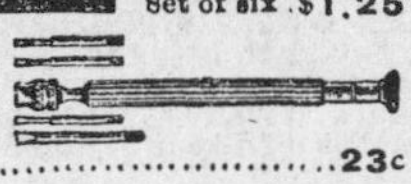

No. 4K474 Screwdriver, adjustable, nickel plated, with four different sized blades. Price..........23c

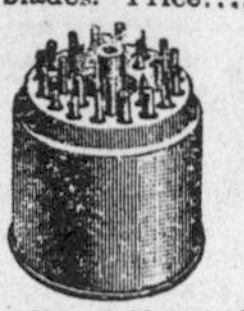

No. 4K480 Staking and Punching Set. 24 punches and hollow steel stake in boxwood box with cover. Ea...$1.08
If by mail, postage extra, 8 cents.

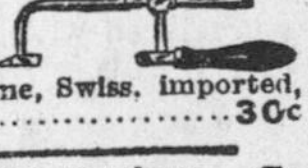

No. 4K500 Saw Frame, nickel plated, extra quality. Price..............80c
No. 4K501 Saw Frame, Swiss, imported, not nickel plated. Price..........30c
No. 4K502 Saws. Price, per dozen....7c
No less than 1 dozen sold.

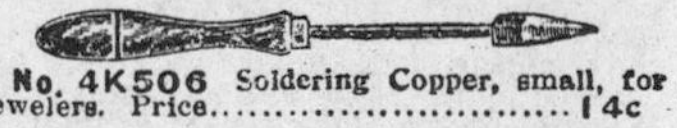

No. 4K506 Soldering Copper, small, for jewelers. Price..........14c

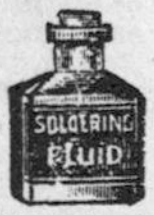

No. 4K510 Soldering Fluid. Price, per bottle..........14c
No. 4K511 Anti-Oxidizer, used for retaining the color on metal when hard soldering. Price, per bottle..........14c

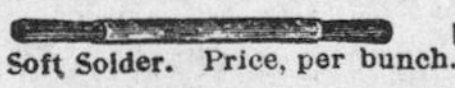

No. 4K512 Soft Solder. Price, per bunch..........5c

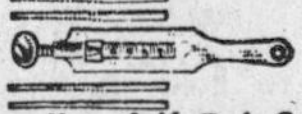

No. 4K514 Screw Stock and Dies, with four taps, imported. Price..........85c

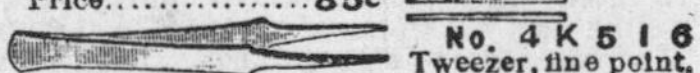

No. 4K516 Tweezer, fine point, nickel plated. Price..........12c

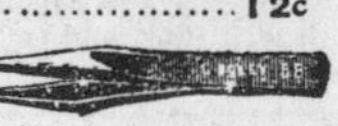

No. 4K517 Tweezer, hollow handle, genuine Boley make, very light, with fine points, for hairsprings and other fine work. Price.................24c

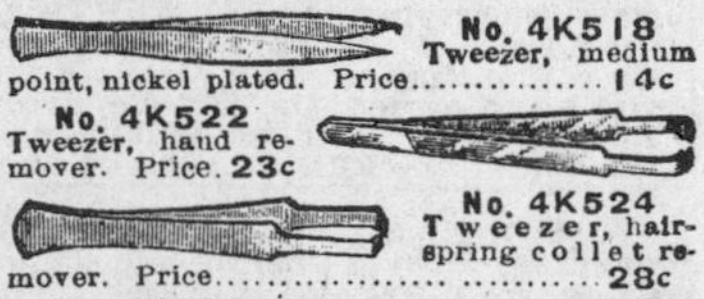

No. 4K518 Tweezer, medium point, nickel plated. Price..........14c
No. 4K522 Tweezer, hand remover. Price. 23c
No. 4K524 Tweezer, hairspring collet remover. Price..................28c

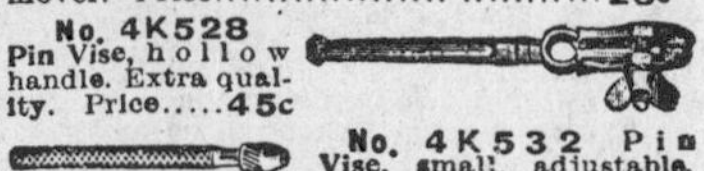

No. 4K528 Pin Vise, hollow handle. Extra quality. Price.....45c
No. 4K532 Pin Vise, small, adjustable. Price..................14c

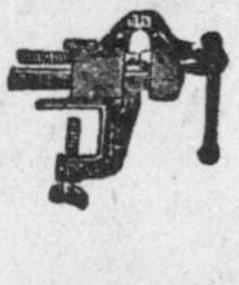

No. 4K536 Vise, 1½-inch steel jaws, clamp vise, handy to adjust to any work bench. Weight, 2½ lbs. Price...70c
No. 4K537 Same size jaws as above, but with swivel bar base. Weight, 3 pounds. Price..................94c

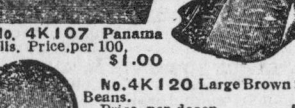

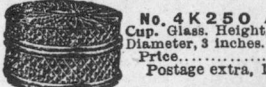

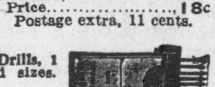

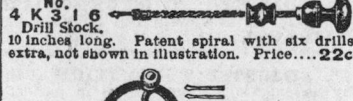

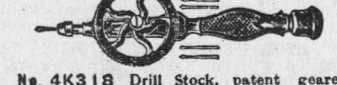

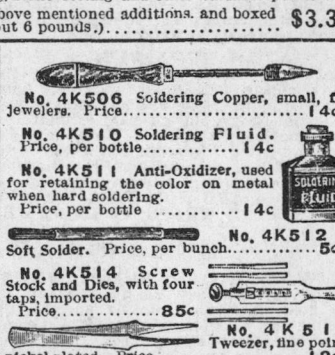

DESCRIPTION OF WATCH MOVEMENTS WE RECOMMEND

ILLUSTRATED AND DESCRIBED HERE AND QUOTED THROUGHOUT THE FOLLOWING PAGES

THE MOVEMENTS WE RECOMMEND, **listed throughout our watch department and priced complete in various cases, are made especially for us by watch companies known to be the largest and most reliable in America.** Watch movements bearing the manufacturer's name are sold by the manufacturer at a fixed price, subject to certain fixed discounts. The quantity the wholesaler purchases, whether a dozen or a thousand at a time, does not alter this fixed price. The very smallest purchaser can buy as cheaply as the very largest, which means the manufacturer makes a very handsome profit; purchasing ability and outlet, which should enter into the proposition, does not; so, in order to equalize this and make it possible for our customers to reap all the benefits that our immense outlet and purchasing ability should bring about, we have had various movements (described and illustrated here) made without the stamp of the manufacturer's name, using instead a name that we ourselves selected. The manufacturers, therefore, agreed that on condition we would take a large per cent of the movements that they produce in their factories, and stamped with a name that we should select, and not their own, we could buy these movements at a cost approximately the same as if we owned the factories ourselves. We therefore are quoting and selling these movements, grade for grade compared with the manufacturer's own named movements, at about 33⅓ to 50 per cent less than the prices they put upon them. The manufacturer of our movements takes this position, in which he is quite correct, that if we were permitted to put the movements he manufactures under his own name and sell them, including the cases, at the price we do, it would ruin his business with every wholesale and retail watch dealer in America.

OUR 7 JEWELED EDGEMERE LINE THE BEST VALUE EVER OFFERED IN THE UNITED STATES.

NOTE THE ILLUSTRATIONS **and descriptions of our 18-size, 16-size and 6-size Edgemere movements,** and note especially the very low prices at which we furnish these movements fitted complete in the various cases as shown and quoted in the following pages, and bear in mind that in spite of the low price we guarantee this 7 jeweled Edgemere movement line the equal of any 7 jeweled movement made at 25 to 33⅓ per cent more than we ask, regardless of name, make or price. Above everything, don't compare this 7 jeweled Edgemere line of movements with the cheap 7 jeweled lines now on the market. We have discontinued the sale of the Trenton, Standard and Century 7 jeweled movements, since our contract enables us to offer you one of the highest grade 7 jeweled movements made at a lower price than other houses can sell even the cheap grade of the 7 jeweled movements. Our five-year binding guarantee goes out with the 7 jeweled Edgemere line. In running and lasting qualities these movements are worth more than double any of the cheap 7 jeweled movements. If you are looking for a watch at a very moderate price, order one of these movements, and if you are not satisfied and it is not worth double what others are asking for cheap 7 jeweled movements, you can return the watch and we will refund your money.

OUR PLYMOUTH WATCH COMPANY FULL ADJUSTED LINE.

POSITIVELY THE HIGHEST GRADE **17 and 21 jeweled American made movements made in the United States.** Note the illustration and description. If you are looking for positively the highest order of watches, most accurate timekeeping, by all means order our Plymouth Watch Company brand. We recommend them above all other makes. Grade for grade, we are quoting them at one-half the price the manufacturer gets from the wholesaler for movements bearing the factory name. Our five-year binding guarantee goes with every one of these movements. If the watch does not prove exactly as described, exactly as illustrated, an accurate timekeeper, perfectly finished and timed in every way, you can return it to us and we will, upon its receipt, instantly refund your money without parley or waste of time.

OUR OTHER SPECIAL MOVEMENTS.

THE OTHER SPECIAL MOVEMENTS **we offer in the different sizes and grades illustrated and described in these pages are movements that we own on the basis of actual cost of material and labor,** and to which we add but one small percentage of profit; we therefore can furnish you any of these watches at about one-half the price that we can offer a watch of equal grade bearing the manufacturer's name.

OUR FIVE-YEAR GUARANTEE. **Every one of these movements, the movements that we recommend,** is covered by our binding five-year guarantee covering every piece and part that enters into its make, and if any part should fail to perform its duty within five years through defective material or workmanship it will be replaced or repaired by us free of charge.

Gents' 18-Size, Open Face or Hunting Case, Stem Wind, 17 Jeweled, Adjusted Plymouth Watch Co. Movement.

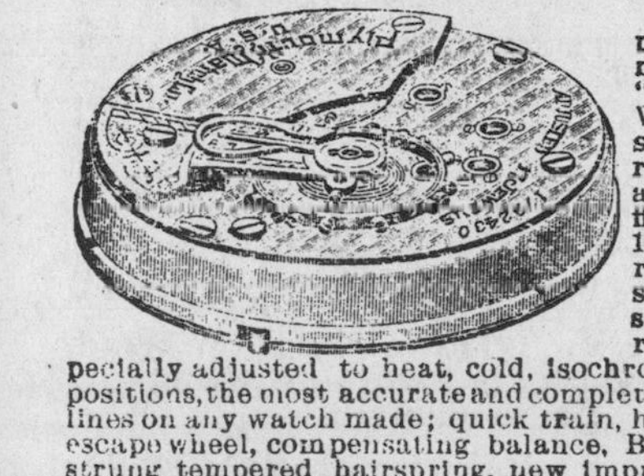

This movement is marked "Plymouth Watch Co.," is solid nickel, richly damaskeened and finished, has 17 ruby jewels, raised gold settings with screws, accurately and especially adjusted to heat, cold, isochronism and all positions, the most accurate and complete adjustment lines on any watch made; quick train, hand finished escape wheel, compensating balance, Breguet overstrung tempered hairspring, new improved patent micrometer regulator barrel arbor pivots, double sunk glass enamel dial with marginal figures. This 17 jeweled, full adjusted, full plate movement is gotten out for us with a view to furnishing a higher grade adjusted movement than is made and sold by any watch company in America. While we furnish it at a much lower price than you can buy a 17 jeweled adjusted movement bearing the manufacturer's name, if you order this movement and do not find, after giving it a thorough trial, that it gives better satisfaction than any other 17 jeweled movement made, you can return it to us at our expense and we will immediately refund your money.

Gentlemen's 18-Size, Stem Wind, Lever Set, Open Face or Hunting Style, 21 Jeweled King Edward Movement, Manufactured by the Plymouth Watch Co.

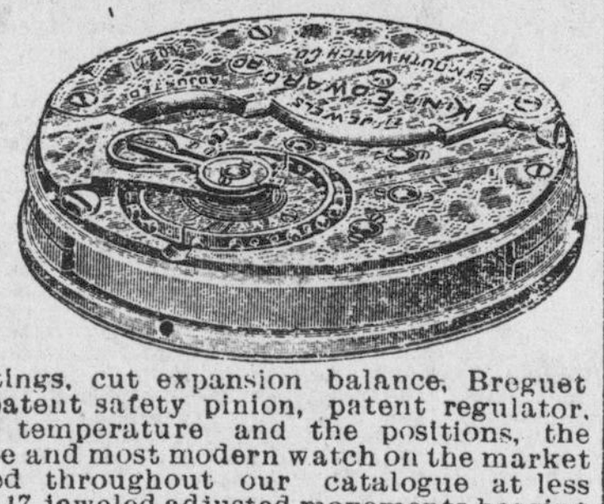

This movement, procured by us under a new deal and in an immense quantity, represents the highest perfection in watchmaking. It has 21 fine ruby jewels in gold settings, cut expansion balance, Breguet hairspring, patent safety pinion, patent regulator, adjusted to temperature and the positions, the most accurate and most modern watch on the market today, quoted throughout our catalogue at less cost than the 17 jeweled adjusted movements bearing the makers' name. This watch we can recommend as being perfection in the watchmaking art, and is made with the idea not to equal any 21 jeweled watch on the market but to have something better than has been heretofore manufactured. By all means, if you want the best watch manufactured, we would advise either the Prince of Wales in the 16-size or the King Edward in the 18-size.

Gents' 18-Size, Open Face or Hunting Case, 7 Jeweled Edgemere Movement.

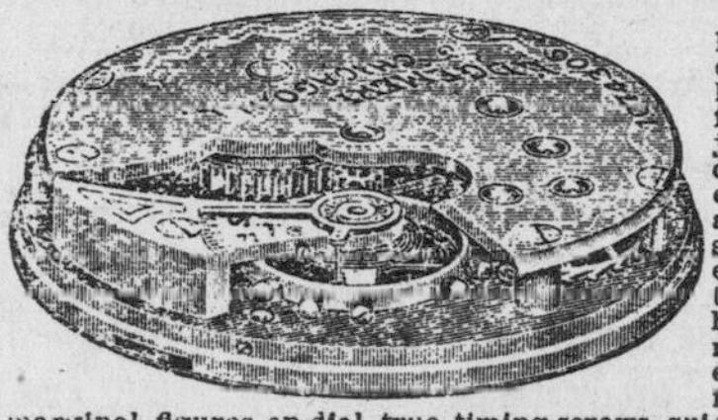

Gents' 18-size Edgemere, open face or hunting case, full nickel, 7 jeweled, neatly damaskeened, expansion balance, hairspring hardened and tempered, highly finished regulator, patent pinion, polished screws, marginal figures on dial, true timing screws, quick train, worth double any of the cheap 7 jeweled movements and guaranteed the equal of any 7 jeweled movement made.

NOTE—We sell this high grade 7 jeweled movement complete in any case for less than others sell the cheap grades of 7 jeweled movements.

TRAINMEN'S SPECIAL.

This is a Cheap Trading Watch, Made to Look Like the Most Expensive 23 Jeweled, Adjusted Railway Watch Made.

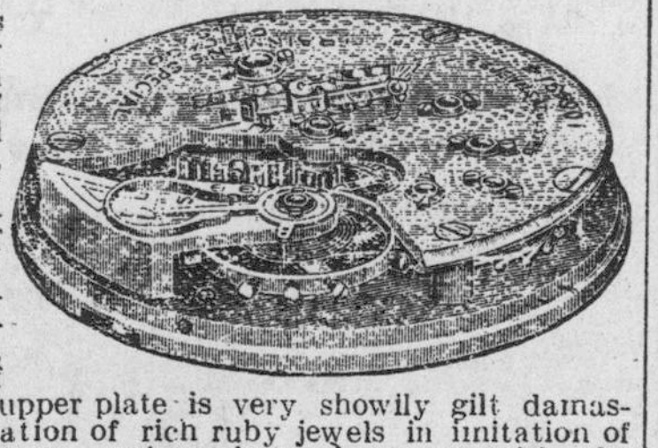

While it is in interior construction a plain 7 jeweled movement, to give to it all the appearance of the highest priced railway movement made, it is made of nickel, the upper plate is very showily gilt damaskeened, imitation of rich ruby jewels in imitation of solid gold screw settings have been set with the screws over the pinion places of the entire top of the plate, including all pinion spots, center first; second and third wheels and balance; has a patent regulator, it is stamped "23 jewels, adjusted;" it is also stamped with a locomotive on the plate and on the front or dial and is named "Trainmen's Special." It is essentially a trading watch. We have sold thousands of these movements to auctioneers, horse traders and other traders, peddlers, jewelers, publishers and scheme houses for premiums, etc., for while we sell it for just what it is, in interior construction a plain 7 jeweled American movement, it has all the appearance of a movement that you would pay $25.00 or more for. It is especially popular in our No. 4K1114 Alaska metal stem wind case, and all for $3.20, making an ideal trading watch or watch that really has the appearance of a $50.00 gold filled, 23 jeweled, adjusted watch, but you buy the complete watch for $3.20. Many of our customers among the traveling men carry them as a side line and sell them at from $5.00 to $20.00, adding from $5.00 to $25.00 a week to their net income. If you want a very showy watch for trading purposes there is nothing that will match this watch.

Gentlemen's 16-Size, Open Face or Hunting Style, 7 Jeweled, Nickel Edgemere Movement.

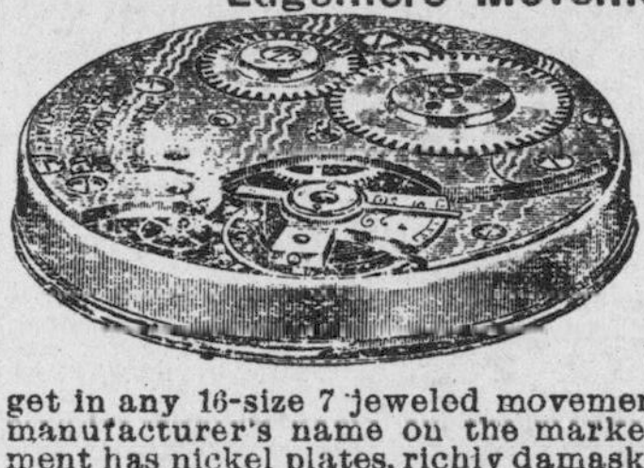

This movement is made for us under contract, and at our price, fitted with any 16-size case as shown on the following pages, will give you double the value that you can get in any 16-size 7 jeweled movement bearing the manufacturer's name on the market. This movement has nickel plates, richly damaskeened, exposed high polished winding wheels, non-magnetic balance and hairspring, full polished pinions, handsome double pressed dial with red marginal figures, is stem wind and pendant set and positively gives the best satisfaction of any 7 jeweled cheap watch on the market. Its equal cannot be procured for twice what we ask for it.

Gentlemen's 16-Size, Open Face or Hunting Style, 15 Jeweled, Patent Regulator Edgemere Movement.

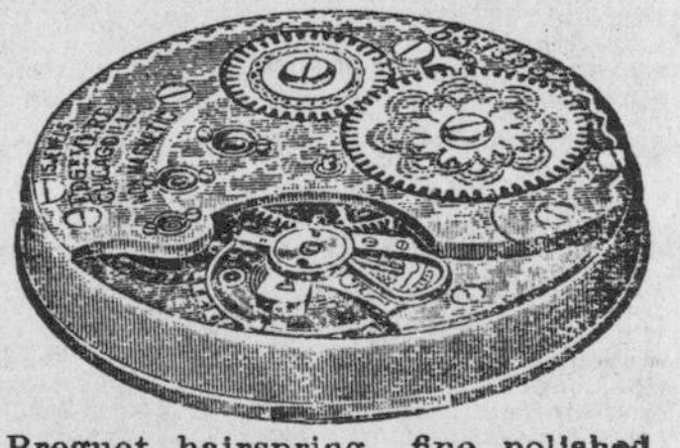

This movement is made under our new arrangement, is highly finished and an accurate timekeeper, has full nickel plates, jewels in screw settings, high polished exposed winding apparatus, cut expansion balance, with Breguet hairspring, fine polished patent regulator, the equal of any 15 jeweled movement manufactured bearing the makers' name and, different from any other make, this movement is anti-magnetic, guaranteed by the maker. By reason of our new contract we are able to quote it in this catalogue on the various pages at less than we ask for 7 jeweled movements bearing the makers' name. If you want a good and accurate timekeeper, we would advise you to select this watch above all other 16-size movements with 7 jewels, stamped with the makers' name.

Gents' 16-Size, Open Face or Hunting Case, 17 Jeweled, Adjusted Plymouth Watch Co. Movement.

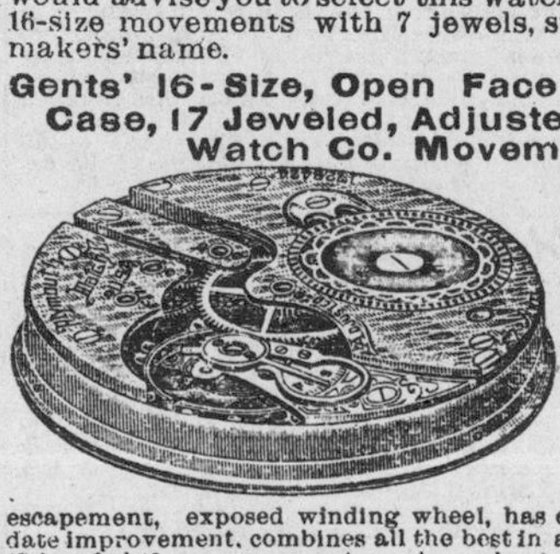

This is our gents' 17-jeweled adjusted 16-size movement, each movement stamped "Plymouth Watch Co." It is 17 jeweled, all jewels in screwed settings, accurately adjusted to heat, cold, position and isochronism; has the latest patent micrometer regulator, patent pinion and escapement, exposed winding wheel, has every new and up to date improvement, combines all the best in all the highest grade 17 jeweled 16-size movements made, and yet we offer it at a lower price than we can offer any other 17 jeweled movement.

Gentlemen's 16-Size, Open Face or Hunting, 21 Jeweled, Nickel, Patent Regulator Prince of Wales Movement, Manufactured by the Plymouth Watch Company.

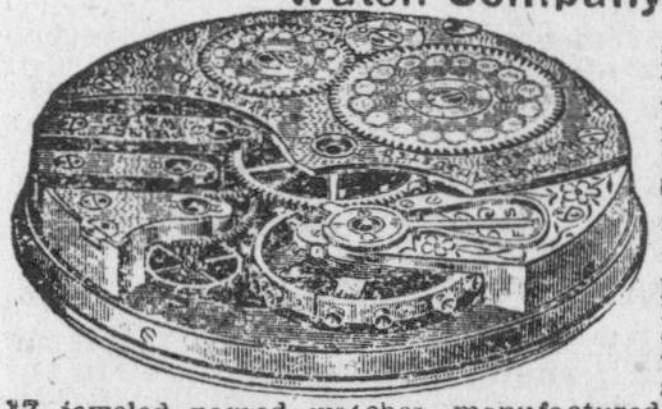

This movement is a new addition to our exceptional value page and represents positively the highest grade watch in 21 jeweled manufactured. A new deal with a new company for an immense quantity enables us to sell this watch to you at less money than 17 jeweled named watches manufactured by others. This watch has full nickel plates, jewels all in settings, cut expansion balance, double sunk dial, patent regulator; in fact, all modern improvements, adjusted to temperature and positions, in fact, a watch such as cannot be compared with any other watch quoted or illustrated in our catalogue. If you purchase this watch you are making a saving of not less than $12.00 to $15.00 and are getting the best production of modern watchmaking.

Gentlemen's 12-Size, Open Face or Hunting Style, Solid Nickel, 7 Jewel, Stem Wind and Pendant Set Edgemere Movement.

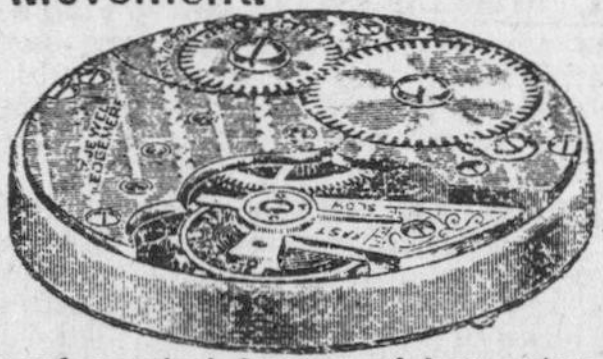

This movement is made especially for us. It is stamped "7 jewel Edgemere." Has straight line lever escapement, fine bright polished exposed winding wheels, bright polished screw heads, richly damaskeened nickel plates, fine selected white enamel dial with red marginal figures, and better than any other 7 jeweled movement, this our Edgemere movement are all fitted with anti-magnetic hairspring. The manufacturers claim they are absolutely impervious to magnetism, one of the greatest difficulties to overcome in accurate timekeeping. If you order this watch movement you are selecting the best 7 jeweled extra thin model, stem wind and pendant set watch on the market and at a price which means a saving of no less than from $2.50 to $3.50 to what regular named 7 jeweled watches bring on the market. We conscientiously recommend this watch above all other 12-size thin model 7 jeweled grades.

Gentlemen's 12-Size, Open Face or Hunting Style, 15 Jeweled, Stem Wind and Pendant Set Edgemere Movement.

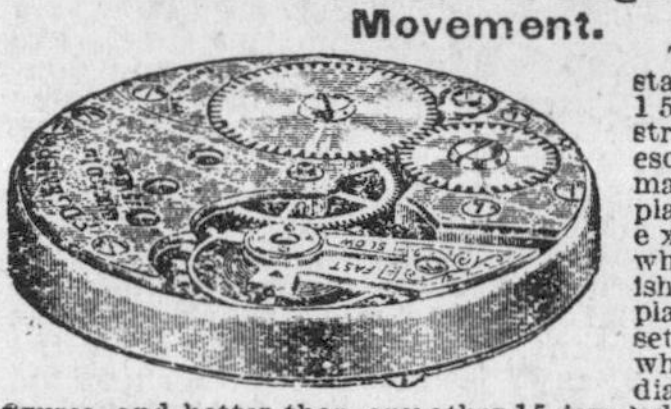

This movement is stamped "Edgemere, 15 jewels," has straight line lever escapement, fine damaskeened nickel plates, high polished exposed winding wheels, bright polished screw heads, all plate jewels in screw settings, fine selected white hard enamel dial, red marginal figures, and better than any other 15 jeweled, 12-size extra thin model movement on the market, this our Edgemere movement is fitted with a genuine anti-magnetic hairspring. The manufacturers claim this makes the movement impervious to magnetism. By this improvement one of the principal causes of watches running inaccurately has been overcome. If you are selecting the 15 jeweled, 12-size watch, by all means buy this one. We recommend it above all other makes of the same grade. If you order this watch, you not only will make a saving of from $2.00 to $5.00 on the price, but will be getting a more accurately running and more dependable watch.

Gentlemen's 12-Size, 17 Jeweled, Open Face or Hunting Style, Stem Wind and Pendant Set Plymouth Watch Co. Movement.

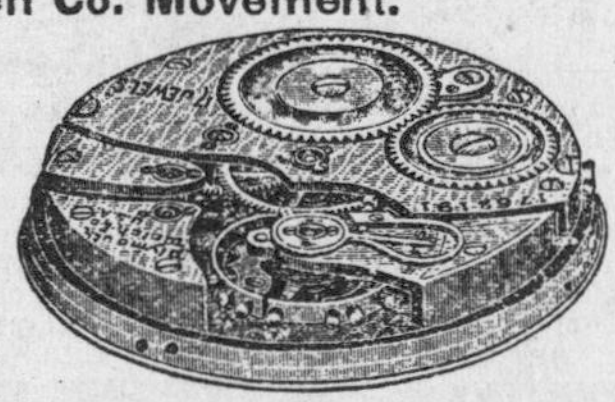

As positively the acme of perfection in 17 jeweled, 12-size movements, we offer this, our latest production from the factory. This movement is stamped "Plymouth Watch Co.," and represents the highest order in this grade above all other makes. This movement is adjusted, trued and timed before leaving the factory to the very closest possible degree. It has high polished exposed winding wheels, Breguet hairspring, true timing screws, patent safety pinion, handsomely damaskeened nickel plates and patent regulator, jewels in screw settings; in fact, every detail in watchmaking has been covered and perfected. While this movement stands pre-eminent for timekeeping and perfection of finish, still, by our new contract, in placing our immense order, we are able to sell it at less than watches stamped with the maker's name throughout these pages. We would advise, if you are looking for a small size extra thin gents' watch in a high jeweled grade, to positively select this one to the exclusion of all other grades and makes.

Gentlemen's 12-Size, 21 Jeweled, Adjusted Stem Wind and Pendant Set, Highest Grade Movement.

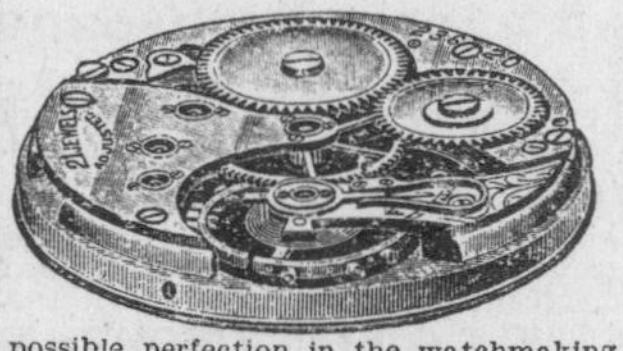

This movement is imported by us, for the express use of our customers who wish a high grade, accurate timekeeping, perfectly finished Swiss watch at a price much less than an American made watch of equal grade. This movement represents the highest possible perfection in the watchmaking art. It is extra thin model, has fine finished nickel plates, lever escapement, 21 fine ruby jewels in solid goldine composition metal, each plate setting fastened with screws, fine high polished exposed winding wheels, fine tapered regulator and regulator bar, cut expansion balance, true timing screws, genuine Breguet hairspring. The dial is of fine white enamel, with plain figures, fine blue tapered steel hands and red marginal figures. In fact, such a watch as cannot be duplicated in the United States in any factory, bearing the maker's name, for twice what we ask. Yet we are able, by importing these movements direct, to place in the hands of our customers a new, up to date, extra thin model, high grade, 12-size watch at not less than 50 per cent saving over the same grade made in the United States.

Remember, in selecting a watch, if you want the highest possible grade in the 12-size containing 21 jewels and adjusted, that nothing excels the Swiss production. The home of watchmaking, celebrated for the perfection and accurate timekeeping qualities of their watches. Our unqualified guarantee for a term of five years goes with this movement and we suggest and recommend this watch if you want a high grade gentlemen's size time watch.

Ladies' 6-Size, Hunting Case, Stem Wind and Pendant Set, 7 Jeweled Edgemere Movement.

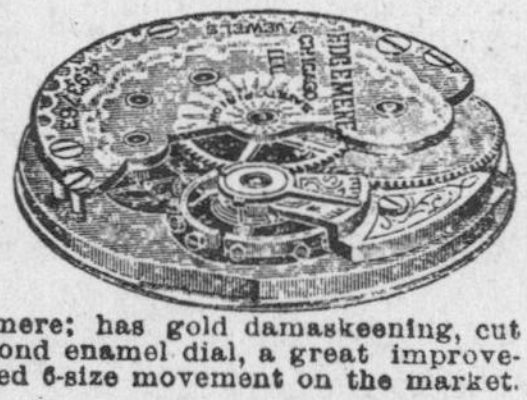

Like the gents' 18-size movement, we guarantee this 7 jeweled movement the equal of any 7 jeweled 6-size movement made, and worth two of any of the cheap 7 jeweled movements on the market. It is the highest grade 7 jeweled movement made, and in selecting a ladies' watch, we would especially recommend that you select our 7 jeweled Edgemere; has gold damaskeening, cut expansion balance, sunk second enamel dial, a great improvement over any other 7 jeweled 6-size movement on the market.

Ladies' 6-Size, Hunting Style, Stem Wind and Pendant Set Countess Janet Movement, Stamped 17 Jewels.

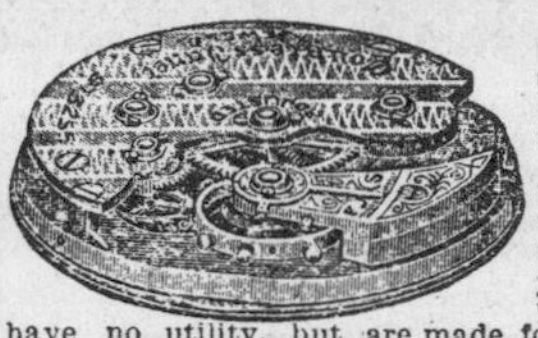

This watch is made for a trading watch in ladies' size. Never before has a ladies' size watch been placed on the market for this purpose. It looks exactly like a high grade 17 jeweled or 19 jeweled watch; is richly nickeled; has 17 large imitation ruby jewels screwed on the plates, which, however, have no utility, but are made for show only. The movement itself is merely a good 7 jeweled American made movement, manufactured for our express use by one of the big watch companies. As a timekeeper will keep only fair time. It is richly damaskeened so as to make a beautiful appearance; is stem wind and pendant set. Our 18-size cheap trading watch for travelers has met with exceptionally fine sale. The profit from a watch of this sort cannot be estimated. Never before have they been placed on the market. They have the appearance of a watch being worth twenty times more than what we ask. This watch is particularly attractive for the purposes of watch trading, for peddlers' use, publishing houses, scheme houses, partial payment houses, in fact, any one wanting a watch having the appearance of the very highest grade for next to nothing in cost.

Ladies' 6-Size, Hunting Case, Stem Wind, 17 Jeweled Adjusted Movement.

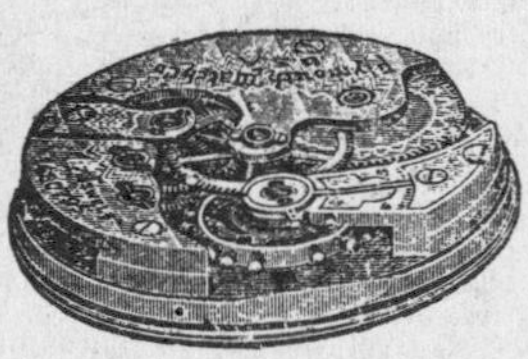

These movements are marked "Plymouth Watch Co." They are positively the highest grade 17 jeweled 6-size movements made. Solid nickel, richly damaskeened in gold, full 17 jewels, finest ruby jewels in gold settings, settings set with screws, compensating cut balance, balance adjusted with true timing screws, finest overstrung patent Breguet hairspring, polished center wheel, quick train, patent pinion. Movement is accurately adjusted to heat, cold, position and isochronism, combining everything that you could get in any movement that you would pay three times the price for if sold by any manufacturer under the manufacturer's name and number; so in selecting the very finest thing in a ladies' 6-size watch we would especially recommend that you select this movement, and we will furnish it to you, quality for quality, at one-half the price you could buy any other make.

Ladies' 0-Size, 7 Jeweled, Stem Wind and Pendant Set Swiss Movement.

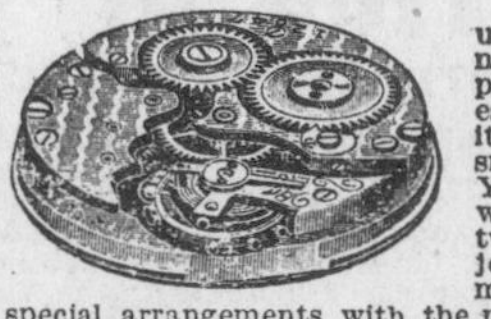

This movement is made for us under contract. It is full nickel, quick train, 7 jewels, patent pinion and patent lever escapement, and we guarantee it the highest grade 7 jeweled small 0-size movement made. You will find this movement will keep better time and last twice as long as any other 7 jeweled 0-size movement on the market, and yet, under our special arrangements with the manufacturer, we can furnish this in a much higher grade 7 jeweled movement than you could get elsewhere at less than the ordinary 7 jeweled movements are sold by others. In selecting a very small watch for a lady in an 0-size, unless you want to get our high grade 15 Jeweled Edgemere 0-size movement, we would especially advise that you select this in preference to any other 7 jeweled 0-size movement made.

Ladies' 0-Size, 15 Jeweled, Stem Wind and Pendant Set, Patent Regulator Edgemere Movement.

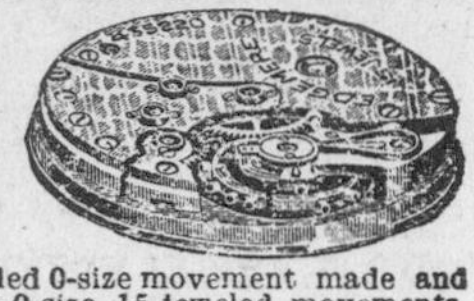

This small 0-size ladies movement is solid nickel, richly finished, full 15 jeweled, jewels in beautiful settings, full screwed. It is very elaborately finished, has the latest patent micrometer regulator, cut expansion balance, finest patent straight line lever escapement, quick train, patent pinion; in short, it is the highest grade 15 jeweled 0-size movement made and will outwear two of the ordinary 0-size 15 jeweled movements, and yet, under our special arrangements with the manufacturer, owning this movement, as we do, on the basis of the actual cost of material and labor, we can, after adding our one small percentage of profit, furnish it to you at a much lower price than we can furnish a 15 jeweled movement of other makes bearing the manufacturer's name and grade.

Ladies' 0-Size, 15 Jeweled, Patent Regulator Plymouth Watch Co. Movement.

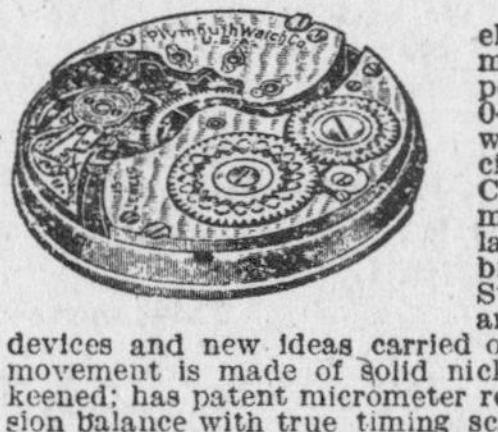

Ladies' small 0-size 15 jeweled Plymouth Watch Co. movement. For the highest possible perfection in 15 jeweled small 0-size ladies' watch movements we recommend this, our specially made Plymouth Watch Co. movement, above all other makes. This movement is the latest production of one of the biggest factories in the United States. All latest improvements are embodied in it; all new devices and new ideas carried out to the fullest extent. The movement is made of solid nickel, plates beautifully damaskeened; has patent micrometer regulator; has full cut expansion balance with true timing screws; has the latest straight line patent lever escapement, highly polished and ornamented exposed winding wheels. The movement is stem wind and pendant set, and has 15 fine ruby and garnet jewels, each jewel in screw setting. The dial is selected, no blemish, no dust spots, as inferior watches sometimes show. In fact, it is the best 15 jeweled American made movement ever turned out, and if you want to buy a ladies' 0-size small watch, and want a 15 jeweled, high grade, fine running and accurate timekeeping movement, by all means select this movement above all other makes. We bar none made.

Ladies' 0-Size, 17 Jeweled, Stem Wind and Pendant Set Plymouth Watch Co. Movement.

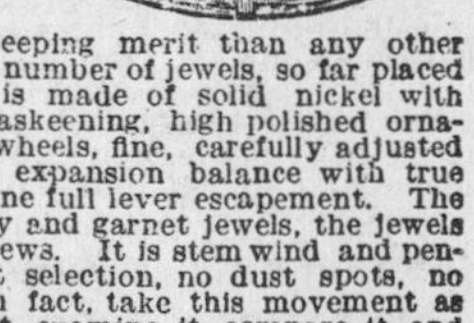

Ladies' small 0-size 17 jeweled adjusted patent regulator movement, absolute perfection turned out at last by the watch company that makes our special movement. It is our especially made Plymouth Watch Co. movement, manufactured by one of the biggest makers in the United States, and we claim it to have more accurately running and timekeeping merit than any other 0-size movement, no matter the number of jewels, so far placed on the market. The movement is made of solid nickel with handsome moire antique damaskeening, high polished ornamented steel exposed winding wheels, fine, carefully adjusted micrometer regulator, full cut expansion balance with true timing screws, latest straight line full lever escapement. The movement contains 17 fine ruby and garnet jewels, the jewels firmly and securely set with screws. It is stem wind and pendant set. The dial is the first selection, no dust spots, no blemish, absolutely perfect. In fact, take this movement as a whole, dissect it, take it apart, examine it, compare it, and it will stand the most rigid inspection. It will be found perfect in every detail and positively give entire and absolute satisfaction. If you are looking for a ladies' watch that will be dependable, one that she can catch trains by and will not vary in time, one day running fast, the next day running slow, and the third day not running at all, by all means select this one. We recommend it and can sincerely say that it is the best 0-size 17 jeweled movement ever placed on the market.

Fancy Dial.

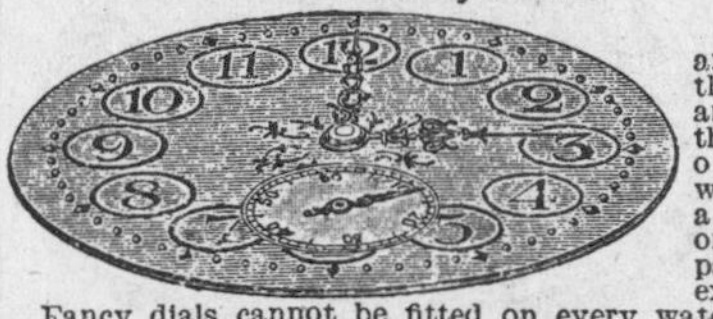

We show here an illustration of the fancy dial and gold hands that we furnish on different watches quoted and illustrated on the following pages at 90 cents extra.

Fancy dials cannot be fitted on every watch in our catalogue. We caution you only to order them on such watches where it is clearly stated on the page that we can furnish fancy dials. The illustration merely gives you an idea of how the fancy dial will look. They are not all exactly as this picture shows, as they vary in design. They come in various tints, with floral decorations and gold work, and all of them beautiful.

The illustration is a dial made to fit 18-size watches. We furnish any size, 18, 16, 12, 6 and 0-size for American watches.

Prices of Elgin and Waltham Movements Without Cases.

For the accommodation of our customers only, and so as to avoid inquiries for prices, we herewith quote our prices on Elgin and Waltham movements without cases. When ordering be sure to give the size and make of case, whether open face or hunting movement required; also keep in mind that only an open face movement will go in an open face case and the hunting style movement in the hunting case, and that we can furnish only stem wind movements. Stem wind movements cannot be fitted in key wind cases. Do not fail to plainly write your name and address on package when sending a watch case to us for a new movement.

18-size, 7 jeweled Elgin or Waltham, gilded plates	$3.85
18-size, 7 jeweled Elgin or Waltham, nickel plates	4.40
18-size, 15 jeweled Elgin or Waltham, nickel plates	5.50
18-size, 17 jeweled Elgin or Waltham, nickel plates, not adjusted	6.60
18-size, 17 jeweled C. M. Wheeler or P. S. Bartlett, Waltham	8.80
16-size, 7 jeweled Elgin or Waltham, nickel plates	5.50
16-size, 15 jeweled Elgin or Waltham	7.70
16-size, 17 jeweled No. 241 Elgin	$12.65
12-size, 7 jeweled Elgin and Waltham, nickel plates	5.50
12-size, 15 jeweled Elgin or Waltham, nickel plates	7.70
12-size, 17 jeweled No. 275 grade Elgin	15.12
6-size, 7 jeweled Elgin or Waltham, nickel plates	4.95
6-size, 15 jeweled Elgin or Waltham, nickel plates	6.15
0-size, 7 jeweled Elgin or Waltham	7.15
0-size, 15 jeweled Elgin or Waltham	8.80
0-size, 17 jeweled Elgin	14.30

DO NOT OVERLOOK THE FACT that all of the watches illustrated and described on this and the previous page carry with them our written binding guarantee that amply secures and protects you for a term of five years. You positively take no chance, you run no risk when buying watches from us.

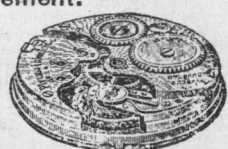

A GREAT PRICE REDUCTION IN WATCHES THROUGHOUT OUR WATCH DIVISION.

59c AND UPWARD FOR American WATCHES

Nickel, Metal, Electro Plate, Silver, Gold Filled and Solid Gold Watches. Our prices are prices unknown to others. A great saving to buyers. Remember, we are always ready to refund your money if our goods are not found at all times as represented.

59c 87c

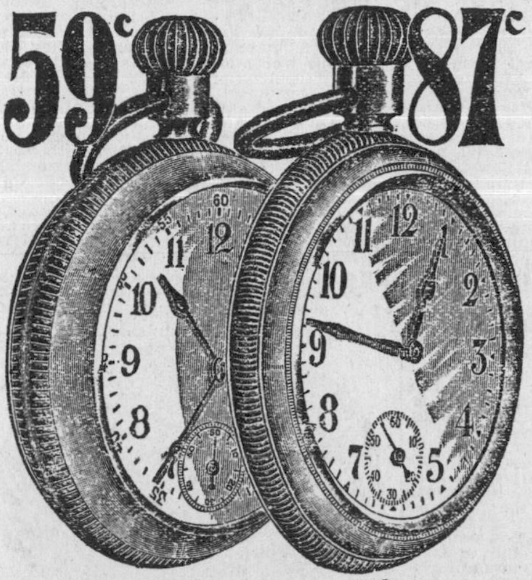

No. 4K790 No. 4K794

Your choice of American made watches for 59 cents or 87 cents, advertised and sold throughout the United States for $1.00 and $1.25. Different from the advertised dollar watch, our watch is stem wind and pendant set. No need to open the case to wind or set the hands. **This watch for 59 cents** is nickel plated, stem wind and pendant set, open face, patent lever movement, runs thirty to thirty-six hours with one winding. We guarantee it to reach destination in perfect going order.

No. 4K790 Price 59c

Our 87-cent watch, as illustrated, No. 4K794, is the watch we recommend. Better than any $1.25 watch sold. This watch is guaranteed American made, is stem wind and pendant set, small 16-size model, made thin and is up to date in every detail. The case is nickel plated, plain polished, open face, as illustration shows. The movement is a lever escapement and is guaranteed. Each one is accompanied by the manufacturer's guarantee for one year. We in turn give our unqualified guarantee backing his. You are doubly secured. Nothing would please your boy better than a watch, and you will be training him how to handle and how to carry a watch at very little cost.

No. 4K794 Price....................................87c

ALASKA METAL ALL AMERICAN OPEN FACE WATCH AND CHAIN

$2.56

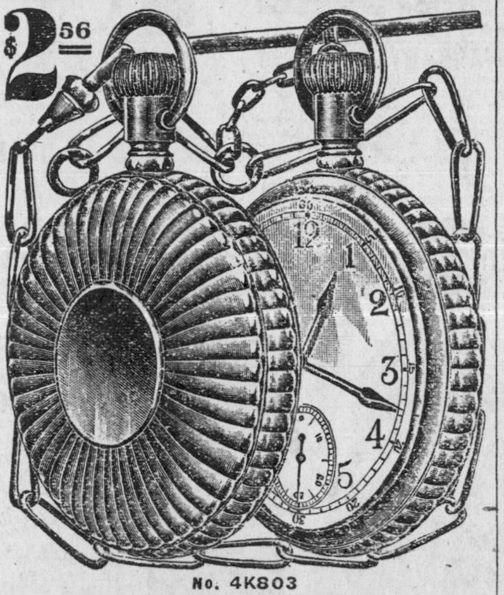

No. 4K803

Snap back and snap bezel genuine Alaska metal all American thin model open face watch (the illustration shows both the front and back of watch), **complete with a good guaranteed rolled gold plate gentlemen's vest chain.** $2.56 for a good genuine American stem wind and stem set nickeled movement fitted in a genuine Alaska metal open face snap back and bezel extra thin model case, together with a fine rolled gold plate, full 12-inch soldered link gentlemen's vest chain, guaranteed for six years, is a price unheard of before. With every watch sold, together with the guarantee on the chain, is sent our five-year written binding watch guarantee. This handsome case as illustrated is made of Alaska metal, a composition of several metals, giving the watch the appearance of solid coin silver. It has the appearance in every way of a very high grade solid silver watch, and in every way except in intrinsic value is its equal. It will wear and retain its solid silver color for a lifetime. The case is handsomely finished in the corrugated pattern with a heavy beaded edge. It is open face, full 18-size, stem wind and pendant set. It is fitted with a very heavy beveled edge French crystal. At $2.56 we furnish this complete outfit, case, movement and chain. The movement fitted in this watch is a genuine American made movement. It has 7 jewels, is stem wind and stem set, made and sold exclusively by us, and is the output of one of the most representative and well known movement makers in the United States.

No. 4K803 Price, for complete outfit, including chain....................................$2.56

No. 4K805 The same case as No. 4K803, and chain, but fitted with a 7-jeweled Elgin or Waltham movement.. $4.93

18-SIZE, THIN MODEL, NICKEL OPEN FACE WATCH.

$1.68

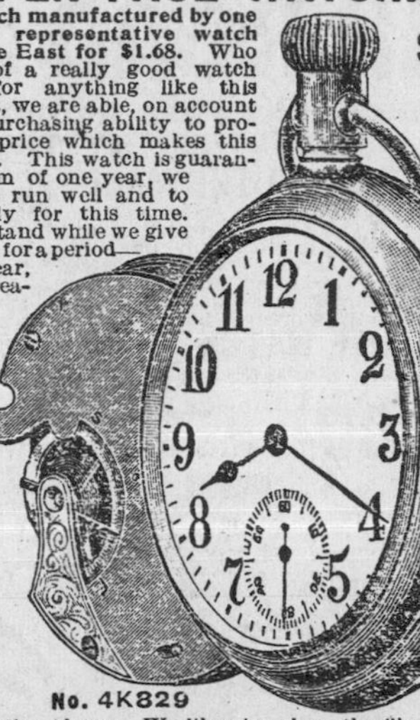

No. 4K829

A new watch manufactured by one of the most representative watch makers in the East for $1.68. Who ever heard of a really good watch being sold for anything like this money? Yet, we are able, on account of our vast purchasing ability to procure it at a price which makes this price possible. This watch is guaranteed for a term of one year, we warrant it to run well and to run accurately for this time. Please understand while we give our guarantee for a period—of only one year, there is no reason that we know of why this watch will not run well and accurately for five or ten years. It all depends on the care you give the watch. It is stem wind and stem set, is jeweled, has fine porcelain dial, the case is nickel open face, is thin 18-size model, the exact same size as illustration shows. We likewise show the illustration of the movement. It is made of strong metal plates, the same watch under certain names brings at any retail store from $2.50 to $3.00. This astonishing offer is made by us and can be made by us only by reason of our omitting the manufacturer's name. Please don't ask it. You will observe we have carefully erased the manufacturer's name from the plate of the movement as well as from the dial. It runs from 30 to 36 hours with but one winding, we know that you will be more than pleased with it, we know that you will be much surprised. Send us $1.68 together with 14 cents, the registry mail charges, a total of $1.82, and we will mail you this watch by registered mail. If you do not find it in every way satisfactory and in every way as described, you can return it and we will refund your money together with all transportation charges.

No. 4K829 Price....................................$1.68

GENTLEMEN'S SMALL EXTRA THIN MODEL SOLID NICKEL WATCH.

$2.58

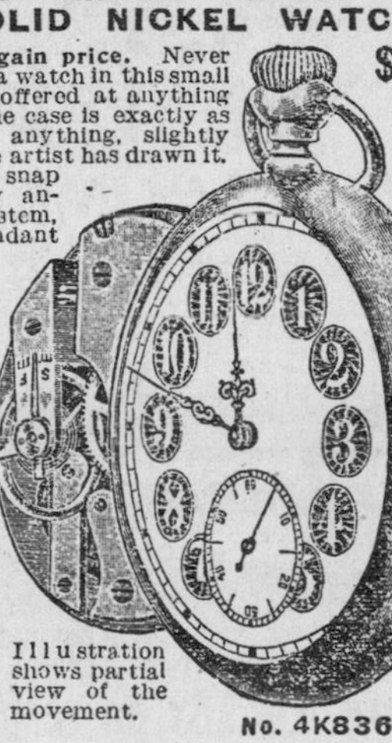

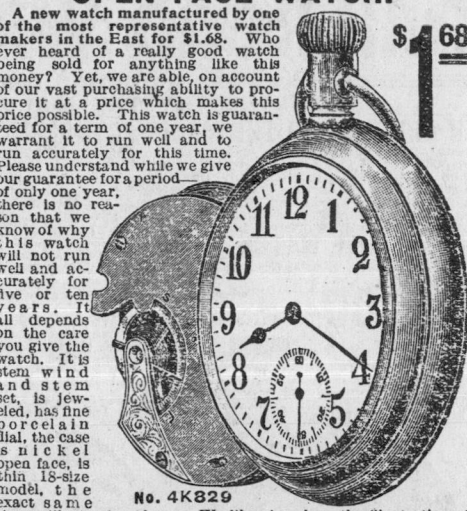

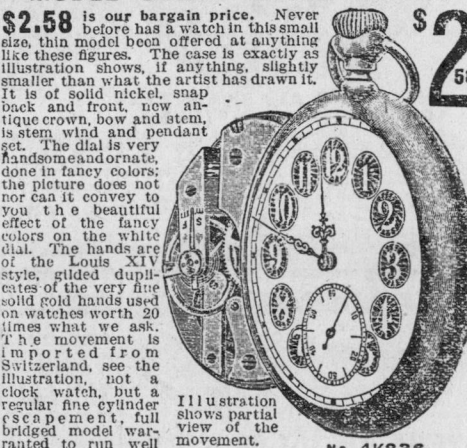

Illustration shows partial view of the movement.

No. 4K836

$2.58 is our bargain price. Never before has a watch in this small size, thin model been offered at anything like these figures. The case is exactly as illustration shows, if anything, slightly smaller than what the artist has drawn it. It is of solid nickel, snap back and front, new antique crown, bow and stem, is stem wind and pendant set. The dial is very handsome and ornate, done in fancy colors; the picture does not nor can it convey to you the beautiful effect of the fancy colors on the white dial. The hands are of the Louis XIV style, gilded duplicates of the very fine solid gold hands used on watches worth 20 times what we ask. The movement is imported from Switzerland, see the illustration, not a clock watch, but a regular fine cylinder escapement, full bridged model warranted to run well and accurately. This watch is especially attractive to young men or those desiring a cheap but unpretentious yet modest watch, one that will last a lifetime if properly cared for.

No. 4K836....................................$2.58

WATCH REPAIRS AT ONE-HALF THE PRICE ASKED BY OTHERS

REMEMBER that a watch should not run longer than one and one-half years without having the oil cleaned off and fresh oil applied. An engine or sewing machine will be oiled several times a day, but we have known people to carry a watch for ten years without having it cleaned or fresh oil applied. Usually a movement thus treated is of **no value, being entirely worn out.** Our charge for cleaning and oiling is **50 cents.** The regular price is $1.50. We give below a list of charges for repairs which will be subject to changes in some cases. For example: Old fusee watches, made some fifty or sixty years ago in England, the material of which is difficult to procure.

Balances, American Expansion............$1.50 to	$2.75
Balances, American Steel or Nickel	.50
Balances, English, Steel or Composition	1.00
Balances, Swiss, Composition	.75
Balances, Swiss, with Screw	1.25
Balances, Swiss, Expansion, cut	3.00
Cleaning, ordinary Swiss, Duplex or American	.50
Cleaning, ordinary English	1.00
Demagnetizing Watch Movements, ordinary	.75
Demagnetizing Watch Movements, finer grades ....$1.00 to	2.00
Dials, Swiss, without seconds	1.00
Dials, Swiss, with seconds	1.50
Dust Bands, American	.25
Hairsprings, ordinary flat	.75
Hairsprings, Breguet	1.50
Hands, common, each	.10
Hands, fine, each	.20
Jewels, American, Cock or Foot (with settings)	.50
Jewels, American, 3d, 4th or 'Scape ....50c to	.75
Jewels, Endstone, in setting	.50
Jewels, Cap, Swiss (with plate)	.25
Jewels, Swiss, 3d, 4th, 'Scape or Balance, set in plate	.50
Jewels, Swiss, 3d, 4th, 'Scape or Balance Fine Ruby	1.50
Jewels, Swiss, Center, Fine Ruby in Gold Set	3.00
Jewels, Roller	.35
Jewels, Pallet, Set in Old Settings, American	.75
Mainsprings, Swiss	.50
Mainsprings, English, with hook	$0.75
Mainsprings, American	.50
Mainsprings, Repeaters, etc.............$1.00 to	1.50
Pallets, Fork and Arbor, complete, ordinary	3.00
Pallets, Fork and Arbor, complete, American ....$1.25 to	2.50
Pinions, American, 3d, 4th or 'Scape	.75
Pinions, American Center	1.00
Pinions, American, Center, Patent, complete with Wheel	2.00
Pinions, Cannon	.50
Pinions, Swiss, 3d, 4th or 'Scape, ordinary	1.00
Pinions, Swiss, 3d, 4th or 'Scape, fine.......$1.75 to	2.00
Pinions, Swiss, Center, ordinary	1.50
Pinions, Swiss, Center, fine	2.00
Pinions, Swiss, Cannon	.50
Ratchets, English, Swiss or American	.50
Staffs, Balance, American..........75c to	1.25
Staffs, Balance, Howard, etc	2.50
Staffs, Balance, English, ordinary	1.25
Staffs, Balance, English, fine..........$1.50 to	2.50
Staffs, Balance, Swiss, ordinary	1.25
Staffs, Balance, Swiss, fine	2.50

CHANGING KEY WIND CASES TO STEM WIND.

Silver Cases	$1.50
Gold Cases	2.50

WHEN WATCHES are sent with instructions to put them in good order we will do everything necessary to put them in good running condition, but when the instructions are to repair a certain particular part of a watch, the repairs will be strictly confined to the part or parts specified and we cannot hold ourselves responsible for anything further than may be necessary to insure correct running of the watch. In sending any part of a watch, if your intention is to fit same yourself, do not instruct us to fit same, but kindly use the word "select." This prevents misunderstanding your wishes. If an idea of the cost cannot be obtained from this list, send the watch to us and on receipt of same we will examine it, quote cost of repairing and hold for instructions.

SHIPPING DIRECTIONS. When shipping watches or jewelry for repairs or exchange, mark plainly as follows: "Sears, Roebuck & Co., Watch Repair Department, Chicago, Ill.," and in upper left hand corner put your own name and address, prefixing the word "From". Also enclose a card in the package with your own name and address and stating that the watch is for repairs. If you send a watch or small piece of jewelry by mail, be sure to put letter postage (2 cents an ounce) on it, because the writing on the card put inside the package makes it subject to first class mail charges. It is safer to send it as first class mail anyway, and it would be better to register it for 8 cents additional. The government guarantees safe delivery of registered mail. At the same time you send the package write us a separate letter, stating that you have sent a watch (by mail or express) for repairs, what repairs you want made, or that you wish us to quote cost of repairing.

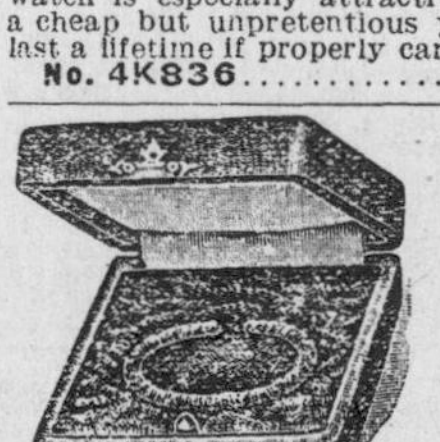

THIS FINE WATCH BOX FOR 23 CENTS.

No. 4K588 This picture, made from a photograph, shows one of our fine lined and leatherette covered watch boxes that we supply for 23 cents extra with any watch purchased of us. In ordering, state what size watch the case is intended for.

Price....................23c

If by mail, postage extra, 2 cents.

CUT PRICE, 23 CENTS.

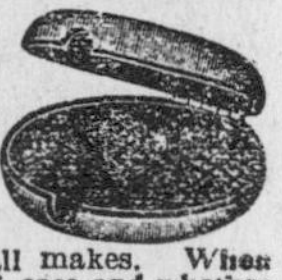

No. 4K586 The Ajax Watch Insulator or Protector protects your watch. It is made of a secret compounded metal, beautifully enameled and lined with velvet. **Order by number.** The maker guarantees that this insulator protects the watch case from wear and the movement from all ordinary magnetic influence. It fits all size watches, open face or hunting style of all makes. **When ordering, don't fail to give size and make of case and whether open face or hunting style is wanted.** Price...........23c

If by mail, postage extra, 2 cents.

PACKING FOR SHIPMENT. **Watches should be wrapped in some soft material** (cotton batting is good), and packed in a strong box, about 2x3x3 inches. **Do not try to ship more than one watch in a box of this size,** as it requires considerable packing about each watch to insure safe shipment.

CASH WITH THE ORDER **must be sent for all repair work.** If you do not know what the cost will be, send what you think will more than cover it and we will refund the balance. If to be returned by mail, send 7 cents for each watch for postage and 8 cents extra for registry.

WE BUY OLD GOLD AND SILVER and pay the highest market price, namely, 18-karat gold, 72c; 14-karat gold, 56c, and 10-karat gold, 40c per pennyweight. Silver fluctuates in value, but at the present time is worth 50c per ounce. In all cases we hold old metal **until we are advised by customers that estimate of value is satisfactory.**

18-SIZE, LEVER SET, OPEN FACE RAILROAD WATCHES

THAT PASS RAILROAD INSPECTION GUARANTEED BY THE MANUFACTURERS

$18.00 TO $68.00

IN ADDITION TO THE MANUFACTURER'S WARRANT, we send you our own personal guarantee on both case and movement. The movements we list pass railroad inspection. If you are a railroad man or an individual that wants a watch such as railroad men carry, you can select any one here. It is safer to buy a railroad watch from us than anywhere else on earth. Our movements come direct from the factory in their original boxes and never have been fitted into any other case but the one you select. It has been tried and tested, no watchmaker has tampered with it and you are getting a movement that is fresh, clean, untarnished and absolutely adjusted the same as when it left the adjuster's hands at the factory.

THE 18-SIZE WATCH has been selected in preference to any other size. While 16-sizes are accepted by some railroads, the majority decided on the 18-size. Statistics show that more than 90 per cent are 18-sizes, as compared to the 16-sizes used by the railroad men. The best case for a railroad man to carry is a case so constructed that the time can be readily read, one that will not collect dirt or grease, a case that is absolutely dust and dampproof, and above all, a case that is an absolute protection to the movement. Our cup cases fill the bill. They are perfect railroad men's watches, will keep accurate time, are open face, screw bezel, solid back cup case with a regular round bow and fitted with the new patent screw nut pendant device and perfectly plain bright polished. You may have a choice of material, they are all constructed alike.

SEE THE ILLUSTRATIONS OF MOVEMENTS. According to our judgment, they are the best manufactured in the United States, grade for grade. Read the descriptions of them. We have copied the company's own statement, you are getting the words of the manufacturer direct. See the illustrations which do not by one-half do them justice. After reading carefully the description of our cases and after making the selection of the movement you want and reading our quotations on same, you have discovered a saving of no less than from 15 to 20 per cent. On railroad watches, this saving means considerable. On any other watch in our catalogue, we save you much more. We have many watches, our 17 jeweled Plymouth watch and our 21 jeweled Prince of Wales and King Edward are good running, accurate time keeping watches. We do not know why, but they are not accepted by the inspectors of various railroads. On these we can save you larger profits. 15 to 20 per cent is a handsome amount considering the close price made on these types of watches. All we ask is a careful comparison of prices and a careful investigation and we know our more interesting figures will win your patronage.

$18.00 AND UP.

Twenty-five cents will carry any watch to any part of the United States by express. We recommend sending watches by express, as they do not receive the hard usage as when sent by mail. If sent by mail, postage extra, including registry fee, 14 cents.

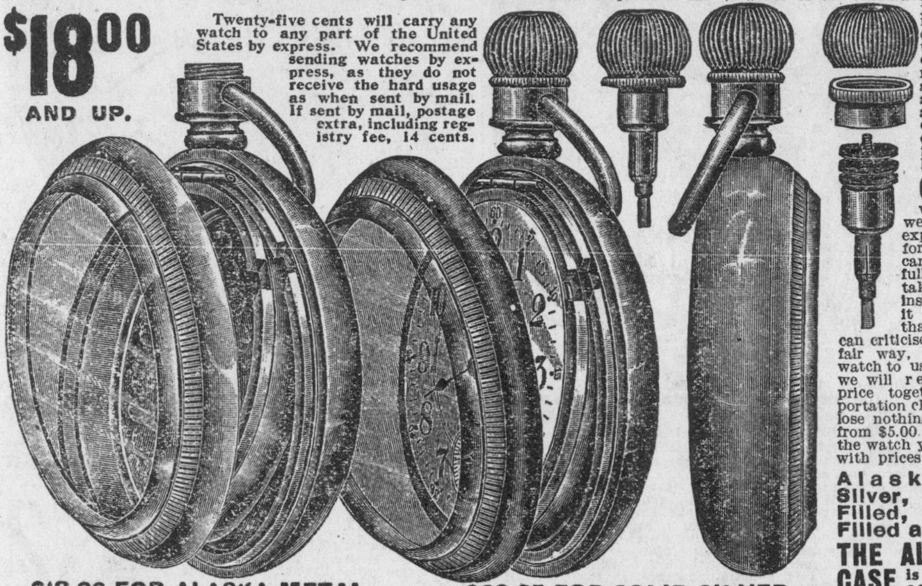

$18.00 FOR ALASKA METAL.
$21.40 FOR GOLD FILLED.
$22.35 FOR SOLID SILVER.
$53.25 FOR SOLID GOLD.

The above illustrations show you various views of our railroad plain polished, solid back, screw bezel, patent screw nut cup cases. The first illustration of the case shows you its various parts—the bezel is unscrewed, the swing ring is lifted up and exposed to view, the screw nut, crown, sleeve and stem removed. The second illustration shows you the crown, screw nut and stem fitted on the case and the movement fitted into the swing ring. The third illustration shows you the movement dropped back into place in the swing ring and the bezel screwed into place.

OUR LIBERAL OFFER. Convince yourself if our argument has not convinced you. Order any one of the watches described on this page, select the case you want to fit it into; we will send it to you by express. You can wear it for a week or a month, you can examine it as carefully as you like, you can take it to any jeweler or inspector and if he finds it in any way different than described, and can criticise it in any legitimate, fair way, you can return the watch to us and upon its receipt, we will refund the purchase price together with all transportation charges. You stand to lose nothing, you stand to save from $5.00 to $10.00 according to the watch you select as compared with prices asked by others.

Alaska Metal, Solid Silver, 20-Year Gold Filled, 25-Year Gold Filled and Solid Gold.

THE ALASKA METAL CASE is made from a secret composition metal manufactured exclusively for our use, it resembles solid silver in every way but in intrinsic value and has the same white silverlike color through and through, is tough, close grained and exceedingly hard. The case weighs from 3½ to 3¾ ounces.

THE SOLID SILVER CASE. This case is made of solid silver, weighs three ounces solid silver of the highest quality; that is 925-1000 fine, all of the case with the exception of the swing ring is solid silver. It is not practical to construct this ring of solid silver.

THE GOLD FILLED CASE, guaranteed for 20 years' continual wear, is made of the very finest gold filled stock, manufactured by the Illinois Watch Case Co., of Elgin, Ill., plainly struck in the back with the terms of the guarantee signed by the company themselves.

THE GOLD FILLED CASE guaranteed for 25 years' continual wear. This case is manufactured of gold filled stock, warranted to retain a solid goldlike appearance for a term of 25 years, the back of the case is struck with the terms of the guarantee signed by the manufacturers.

THE SOLID GOLD CASE. This case is manufactured by the Brooklyn Watch Case Co., of Brooklyn, N. Y., is of solid 14-karat gold, every piece and particle entered in its make except the swing ring is solid gold. It is not practical to make this device of gold. Each case is plainly stamped with its quality, the United States Stamping Law Protection.

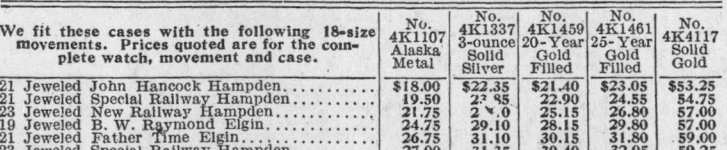

We fit these cases with the following 18-size movements. Prices quoted are for the complete watch, movement and case.	No. 4K1107 Alaska Metal	No. 4K1337 3-ounce Solid Silver	No. 4K1459 20-Year Gold Filled	No. 4K1461 25-Year Gold Filled	No. 4K4117 Solid Gold
21 Jeweled John Hancock Hampden	$18.00	$22.35	$21.40	$23.05	$53.25
21 Jeweled Special Railway Hampden	19.50	23.85	22.90	24.55	54.75
23 Jeweled New Railway Hampden	21.75	2[illegible].0	25.15	26.80	57.00
19 Jeweled B. W. Raymond Elgin	24.75	29.10	28.15	29.80	57.00
21 Jeweled Father Time Elgin	26.75	31.10	30.15	31.80	59.00
23 Jeweled Special Railway Hampden	27.00	31.35	30.40	32.05	59.25
21 Jeweled Veritas Elgin	30.75	35.10	34.15	35.80	66.00
23 Jeweled Veritas Elgin	35.75	40.10	39 15	40.80	68.00

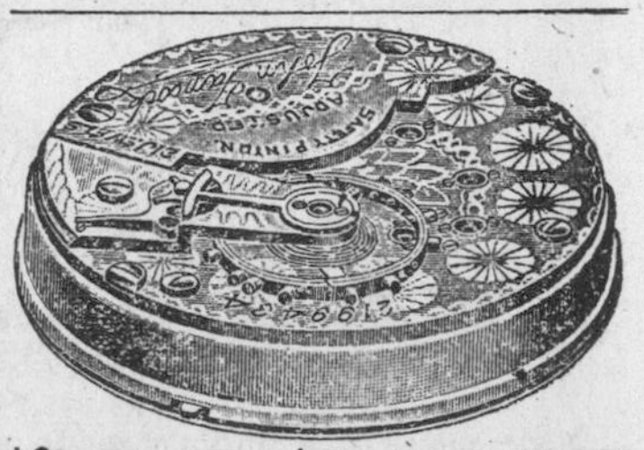

$18.00 TO $53.25 COMPLETE IN CASE.

The above is an illustration of the 18-size John Hancock 21 Jeweled Hampden Movement. It has 21 fine ruby and sapphire jewels in gold setting, escape cap jewels, compensating balance, gilt screws, adjusted to temperature, isochronism and five positions, steel escapement wheel, Breguet hairspring, mean time screw, new model stud, patent micrometer regulator, bright bevel head screws, patent center pinion, polished steel work, double sunk glass enameled dial, finely damaskeened and finished throughout, gold lettering. Nickel.

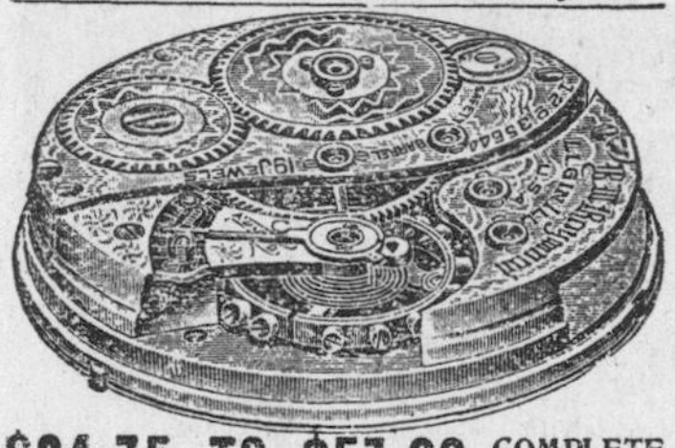

$24.75 TO $57.00 COMPLETE IN CASE.

The above is an illustration of the 18-size 19 Jeweled B. W. Raymond Adjustable Elgin Movement. It has 19 fine ruby jewels (raised gold settings); adjusted to temperature, isochronism and positions, steel escape wheel, exposed pallets, compensating balance, Breguet hairspring, micrometric regulator, patent safety barrel with spring box rigidly mounted on bridge, barrel arbor pivots running in jewels, display winding work, patent recoiling click, patent self locking setting device, double sunk glass enamel dial, dust ring, damaskeened plates, closely timed and finely finished throughout.

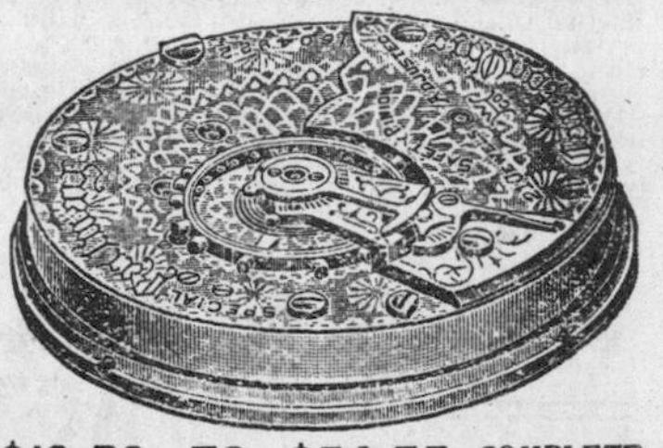

$19.50 TO $54.75 COMPLETE IN CASE.

The above is an illustration of the 18-size 21 Jewel Special Railway adjusted Hampden Movement. It has 21 fine ruby and sapphire jewels in solid gold setting, jeweled center escapement, cap jewels, conic pivots, beveled head, gilt screws, micrometer regulator gold screws, compensating balance, accurately adjusted to temperature, isochronism and five positions, double sunk glass enameled dial with red marginal figures, steel escapement wheel, Breguet hairspring, new model stud, mean time screws, steel work highly polished, patent center pinion, elegantly engraved and damaskeened, fine escapement, Fleur de Lis hands, and first quality Hampden mainspring. Nickel.

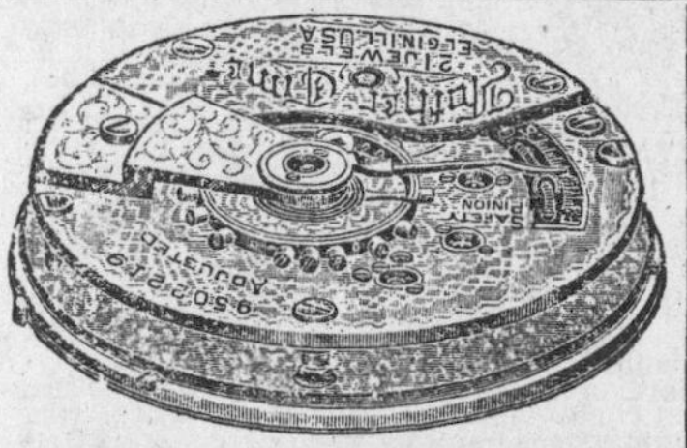

$26.75 TO $59.00 COMPLETE IN CASE.

The above is an illustration of the 18-size 21 Jeweled Father Time Adjusted Elgin Movement. It has 21 fine ruby jewels (gold settings), adjusted to temperature, isochronism and positions, steel escape wheel, pallet arbor and escape pinion cone pivoted and cap jeweled, exposed pallets, compensating balance, Breguet hairspring, micrometric regulator, patent recoiling click, double sunk glass enamel dial, dust ring, damaskeened plates, carefully timed and finely finished throughout.

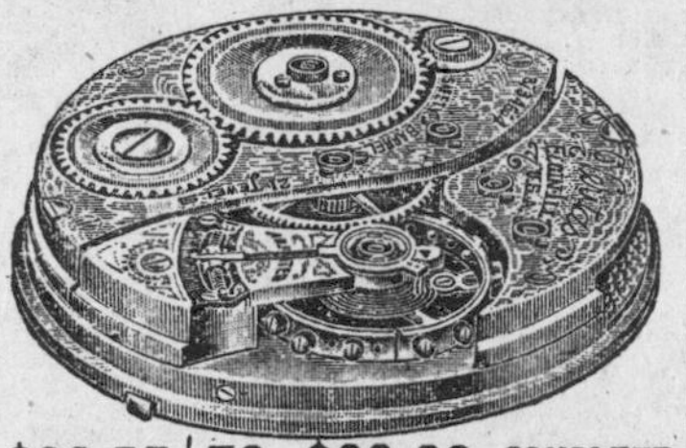

$30.75 TO $66.00 COMPLETE IN CASE.

The above is an illustration of the 18-size 21 Jeweled Veritas Adjusted Elgin Movement. It has 21 fine ruby jewels (raised gold settings), adjusted to temperature, isochronism and positions, steel escape wheel, pallet arbor and escape pinion cone pivoted and cap jeweled, exposed pallets, compensating balance, Breguet hairspring, micrometric regulator, patent safety barrel with spring box rigidly mounted on bridge, display winding work, patent recoiling click, patent self locking setting device, double sunk glass enamel dial, dust ring, damaskeened plates, closely timed and finely finished throughout.

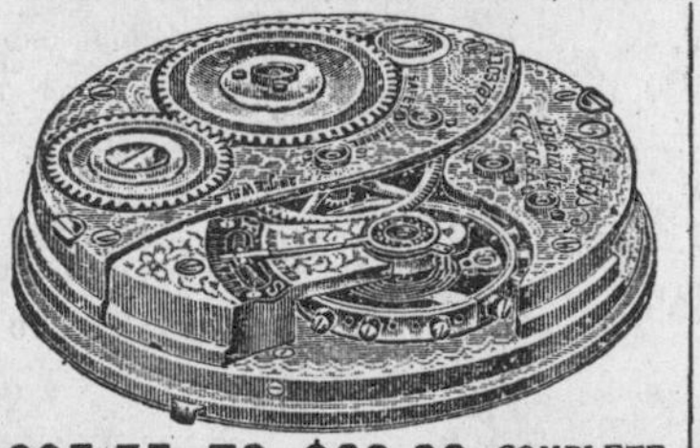

$35.75 TO $68.00 COMPLETE IN CASE.

The above is an illustration of the 18-size 23 Jeweled Veritas Adjusted Elgin Movement. It has 23 extra fine ruby jewels (raised gold settings) adjusted to temperature, isochronism and positions, double roller escapement, steel escape wheel, poised pallet and fork, pallet arbor and escape pinion cone pivoted and cap jeweled, exposed pallets, compensating balance, Breguet hairspring, micrometric regulator, patent safety barrel with spring box rigidly mounted on bridge, barrel arbor pivots running in jewels, display winding work, patent recoiling click, patent self locking setting device, double sunk glass enamel dial, dust ring, plates beautifully damaskeened, closely timed and parts finely finished throughout.

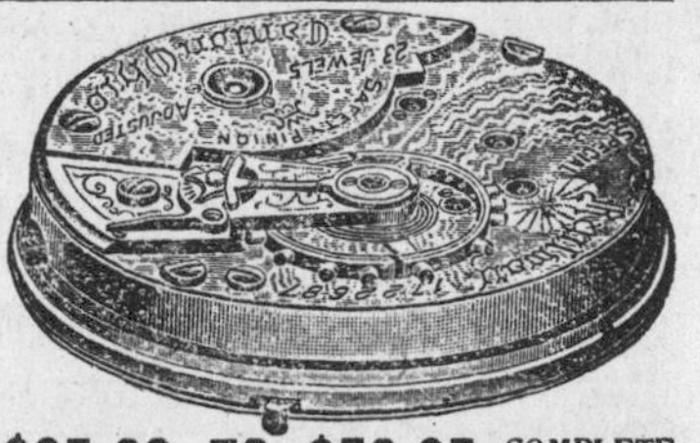

$27.00 TO $59.25 COMPLETE IN CASE.

The above is an illustration of the 18-size 23 Jeweled Special Railway Hampden Adjusted Movement. It has 23 extra ruby and sapphire jewels in solid gold setting, bar arbor and center staff jeweled with the finest of sapphire escapement, cap, jewels, conic pivots, finely graduated micrometer regulator, compensating balance, gold screws, steel escapement wheel, Breguet hairspring, mean time screws, new model stud, accurately adjusted to temperature, isochronism and five positions, patent center pinion, beveled head, gilt screws, highly polished steel work, fine double sunk glass enamel dial, best Fleur de Lis hands, elegantly engraved and damaskeened in two colors, gold lettering, nickel. The handsomest, most finely finished and closely timed movement made in America.

SOLID SILVER OPEN FACE OR HUNTING STYLE GENTLEMEN'S 18-SIZE NEW MODEL WATCHES AT CUT PRICES

WE GUARANTEE EACH CASE illustrated on this page to be solid silver. Our written binding guarantee goes out with each one. If you do not wish to own a gold filled or solid gold watch, by all means select one of these. Silver is a metal that will not tarnish in the pocket, is tough and will wear for the term of your natural lifetime. For those who desire a good watch, a watch that is not too pretentious we advise solid silver.

THE BEST PLAIN SILVER CASE illustrated on this page we believe to be No. 4K1336 or No. 4K1338, the new dust and dampproof, screw nut, gold reflector solid back cup case. It is the most perfect model of a solid silver case. The illustration shows the screw bezel off and the swing ring fitted with the movement slightly raised up. In closing the watch merely drop the swing ring back into the body of the case and then screw on bezel. Railway men or those that wish a watch to be absolutely free of dust and damp usually select this type of case.

$4⁹⁸ AND UP

For 90c extra we will furnish a fancy dial and gold hands on the silver watches on this page.
For 23 cents we furnish a beautiful Leatherette Presentation Case to fit anywatch. See No. 4K58 on page 261.

PRICES REDUCED
MORE THAN YOUR MONEY'S WORTH.

See pages 259 and 260 for the descriptions and beautiful illustrations of our special lines of **MOVEMENTS,** Plymouth Watch Co. and Edgemere line of Watch Movements.

25 CENTS will carry any watch to any part of the United States by express.

$5⁹⁸ AND UP

Open Face, Screw Back and Bezel.	Open Face. Jointed Front and Back.	Hunting Style.	Solid Gold Inlaid. Open Face.	Open Face, Screw Back and Bezel. Hand Engraved Box Joints.
No. 4K1304 3-ounce, Plain Polished Case.	No. 4K1312 3-ounce, Plain Polished Case.	No. 4K1320 3-ounce, Plain Polished Case.	No. 4K1340 3-ounce Case, open face, screw back and bezel, gold inlaid stag.	No. 4K1348 3-ounce, Hand Engraved.
No. 4K1306 3-ounce, Hand Engraved.	No. 4K1314 3-ounce, Hand Engraved.	No. 4K1322 3-ounce, Hand Engraved.	No. 4K1342 3-ounce Case, open face, screw back and bezel, gold inlaid engine.	No. 4K1349 4-ounce, Hand Engraved.
No. 4K1308 4-ounce, Plain Polished Case.	No. 4K1316 4-ounce, Plain Polished Case.	No. 4K1324 4-ounce, Plain Polished Case.	No. 4K1344 4-ounce Case, stag inlaid.	
No. 4K1310 4-ounce, Hand Engraved.	No. 4K1318 4-ounce, Hand Engraved.	No. 4K1326 4-ounce, Hand Engraved.	No. 4K1346 4-ounce Case, engine inlaid.	

We fit these cases with the following 18-size movements. Prices quoted are for the complete Watch, Movement and Case.	No. 4K1304	No. 4K1306	No. 4K1308 4K1340 4K1342	No. 4K1310	No. 4K1312	No. 4K1314	No. 4K1316	No. 4K1318	No. 4K1320	No. 4K1322	No. 4K1324	No. 4K1326	No. 4K1344 4K1346	No. 4K1348	No. 4K1349	No. 4K1336	No. 4K1338
7 JEWELED EDGEMERE, nickel plates, special make.	$4.98	$5.58	$6.25	$6.49	$5.51	$5.55	$6.29	$6.53	$5.58	$5.90	$6.30	$6.70	$7.05	$5.98	$7.00	$6.38	$7.28
7 Jeweled Elgin or Waltham, gilt	7.45	7.78	8.45	8.69	7.71	7.75	8.49	8.73	7.78	8.10	8.50	8.90	9.25	8.25	9.20	8.65	9.45
7 Jeweled Elgin or Waltham, nickel	8.00	8.33	9.00	9.24	8.26	8.30	9.04	9.28	8.33	8.65	9.05	9.45	9.80	8.80	9.75	9.20	10.00
15 Jeweled Waltham, gilt plates.	8.55	8.88	9.55	9.79	8.81	8.85	9.59	9.83	8.88	9.20	9.60	10.00	10.35	9.35	10.30	9.75	10.55
15 Jeweled Elgin or Waltham, nickel	9.10	9.43	10.10	10.34	9.36	9.40	10.14	10.38	9.43	9.75	10.15	10.55	10.90	10.85	10.30	11.10	
17 Jeweled Elgin or Waltham.	10.20	10.53	11.20	11.44	10.46	10.50	11.24	11.48	10.53	10.85	11.25	11.65	12.00	11.00	11.95	11.40	12.20
17 JEWELED PLYMOUTH WATCH CO., nickel plates, special make.	12.15	12.48	13.15	13.39	12.41	12.45	13.19	13.43	12.48	12.80	13.20	13.60	13.95	12.95	13.90	13.35	14.15
17 Jeweled G. M. Wheeler Elgin, or P. S. Bartlett Waltham.	12.40	12.73	13.40	13.64	12.66	12.70	13.44	13.68	12.73	13.05	13.45	13.85	14.20	13.20	14.15	13.60	14.40
21 JEWELED KING EDWARD PLYMOUTH WATCH CO., patent regulator, adjusted, nickel plates, special make.	18.60	18.93	19.60	19.84	18.86	18.90	19.64	19.88	18.93	19.25	19.65	20.05	20.40	19.40	20.35	19.80	20.60
21 Jeweled John Hancock Hampden.	20.90	21.23	21.90	22.14	21.16	21.20	21.94	22.18	21.23	21.55	21.95	22.35	22.70	21.70	22.65	22.10	22.90
21 Jeweled Special Railway Hampden	22.35	22.68	23.35	23.59	22.61	22.65	23.39	23.63	22.68	23.00	23.40	23.80	24.15	23.15	24.10	23.85	24.35
23 Jeweled Special Railway Hampden	29.85	30.18	30.85	31.09	30.11	30.15	30.89	31.13	30.18	30.50	30.90	31.30	31.65	30.65	31.60	31.35	31.85
TRAINMEN'S SPECIAL, stamped 23 jewels, adjusted, special make.	5.95	6.28	6.95	7.19	6.21	6.25	6.99	7.23	6.28	6.60	7.00	7.40	7.75	6.75	7.70	7.15	7.95
19 Jeweled Adjusted B. W. Raymond No. 240 Grade Elgin, made in open face only	27.60	27.93	28.60	28.84	27.86	27.90	28.64	28.88	Not made	Not made	Not made	Not made	29.40	28.40	29.35	29.10	29.60
21 Jeweled Father Time Elgin	29.60	29.93	30.60	30.84	29.86	29.90	30.64	30.88	29.93	30.25	30.65	31.05	31.40	30.40	31.35	31.10	31.60
21 Jeweled Veritas Elgin.	33.60	33.93	34.60	34.84	33.86	33.90	34.64	34.88	33.93	34.25	34.65	35.05	35.40	34.40	35.35	35.10	35.60
23 Jeweled Veritas Elgin. Made in open face style only	38.60	38.93	39.60	39.84	38.86	38.90	39.64	39.88	Not made	Not made	Not made	Not made	40.40	39.40	40.35	40.10	40.60

$11⁶⁸

$11.68 for a gold filled center, solid silver sided watch, fitted with genuine Elgin or Waltham movement, a high grade 15 jeweled perfect finished watch. A startling value, new and never before made. Send us $11.68 and we will send you this fine 18-size, hunting style, extra thin model, stem wind and stem set, antique crown, bow and stem, solid silver sided gentlemen's watch, by registered mail. Do not fail to add to your remittance the mail charges of 14 cents.

THE CASE is as illustration shows, extra thin model, beautifully ornamented by variegated floral sprays in solid gold. The back lid and front lid of this case is solid silver and solid gold ornamented. The center, that part of the watch that the lids are fitted upon, is of high grade gold filled stock, and guaranteed to wear and give good satisfaction for a term of twenty years.

THE MOVEMENT that we fit in this handsome case at $11.68 is genuine Elgin or Waltham 15 jeweled, very latest up to date model.

OUR WRITTEN BINDING GUARANTEE for a term of five years is sent with every one sold, protecting you against defect in both material and workmanship.

THE CASE is remarkable for its artistic beauty. Just imagine a watch with gold center, beautiful silver sides fixed on this center. These sides are handsomely ornamented in solid floral work of variegated colors and then to complete the picture the case is fitted with the very latest antique crown, bow and stem. This description can only give you the faintest idea of the beauty of this case. It must be seen to be appreciated.

We fit this case with any of the following 18-size movements that you may desire for the price quoted:
No. 4K1390 Fitted with the 15 jeweled Elgin or Waltham movement. Price. **$11.68**
No. 4K1391 Fitted with the 17 jeweled Plymouth Watch Co. movement, which represents the highest perfection of any 17 jeweled movement, is finer finished, more accurately running and has more modern improvements than any other 17 jeweled watch. Price. **$14.65**

18-Size, Hunting Style.
Solid silver with solid gold ornamentation.
No. 4K1392 Fitted with the G. M. Wheeler Elgin or P. S. Bartlett Waltham movement. Price. **$14.65**
No. 4K1393 Fitted with the 21 jeweled King Edward Plymouth Watch Co. movement, which represents the highest grade, most perfectly running 21 jeweled movement made in the United States, embodying the most modern improvements of any watch manufactured in the United States. Price. **$21.50**

This illustration shows you how the 17 jeweled Plymouth Watch Company movement and the 21 jeweled King Edward Plymouth Watch Company movement look. The 17 jeweled movement represents the highest perfection of any 17 jeweled watch in 18-size yet placed on the market quoted with this handsome case for $14.65. The 21 jeweled King Edward movement illustrated at the top is the best 21 jeweled adjusted movement ever manufactured in the United States. It is the most accurate, best timekeeping watch that it is beyond criticism. Experts claim that it is beyond criticism.

For $21.50 we fit this high grade 21 jeweled movement in the handsome case illustrated to the left.

PRICES REDUCED $6³⁸ AND UP

No. 4K1336 Open Face, 3-ounce, Heavy Plain Polished Screw Bezel and Solid Silver Back Case. Has gold reflector and dampproof crown with screw nut.
No. 4K1338 Open Face, 4-ounce, same style as No. 4K1336.

$3⁹⁷

25 cents will carry any watch to any part of the United States by express.

HORSE TIMER AT A CUT PRICE.

NEW, UP TO DATE, solid nickel, Bassene style, stem wind, jeweled horse timer. This timer is operated from the crown by merely pressing down the same mechanism as used in horse timers worth hundreds of dollars. It has start, stop and fly back arrangements, also, as illustration shows, has a minute register. The escapement is jeweled, reducing friction to a minimum and increasing the accuracy of the timer. The case is of solid nickel, new Bassene style, no rough edges or joints. Bright polished. The movement is imported from Switzerland, straight line cylinder escapement and worth three times what we ask. The dial is of fine white porcelain, the second marks and figures plainly and accurately named. Fine blued steel sweep second hands and fine blued steel minute register hands.

No. 4K1450 Price...............$3.97
No. 4K1452 Same style as above but with fine jeweled lever escapement movement. Price...............$5.95

A WATCH WITHOUT HANDS AT A CUT PRICE $7⁹⁸

Illustration showing the dial.

Illustration showing the back lid.

OUR NEW SOLID SILVER SMALL 18-SIZE OPEN FACE NOVELTY WATCH. The center circle shows the hour and the oval the minute. It is wound and set the same as any other watch, but is less complicated and less liable to get out of order. You will never be bothered on account of the hands catching or dropping off, or finding that your watch does not keep accurate time on account of the hands being too loose. This watch comes in a size smaller than the regular 18-size. The case is solid silver, .925 fine, in other words, solid sterling silver stem wind and stem set; comes in open face only. The dial is a beautiful silver dial with rich raised gold ornamentation, exactly as illustration shows. The movement is imported from Switzerland. It has 15 fine ruby jewels, straight line lever escapement, and is perfectly finished in every detail, a watch that we can recommend, being an accurate timekeeper.

No. 4K1454 Solid silver. Price...............$7.98
No. 4K1456 Same as No. 4K1454, but with black oxidized steel gunmetal case. 6.80

CUT PRICE $5.08 FOR THIS COMPLETE LADIES' OUTFIT,

WATCH, CASE AND CHATELAINE PIN. Procured from Any Other Source Would Cost Double This Amount.

SEND US $5.08 and 25 cents extra for express charges, $5.33 in all, and we will send to you, prepaid, this gold filled hunting style, 0-size, beautifully engraved ladies' watch, gold filled chatelaine pin and swivel, in leather covered velvet lined case. The case is gold filled, made of two plates of solid gold overlaying an inner layer of composition metal and is guaranteed by the manufacturer for a term of 5 years. The engraving consists of sprays of flowers with vermicelli border work, has the antique bow and pendant, is stem wind and pendant set, finished and perfected in every detail. Don't ask for the maker's name. According to our contract, one of the principal conditions was that we were not to mention the manufacturer's name, on account of the wonderfully small figures we are asking for this watch, although each one is stamped plainly and distinctly in the inside of the case and each one carries the maker's personal guarantee. This maker is one of the most representative and best known case manufacturers in the United States.

THE MOVEMENT we fit in this watch for $5.08 is a good 7 jeweled lever. It has exposed winding wheels. It has solid nickel plates, double depressed fine white select enameled dial and cut expansion balance, which insures accuracy in timekeeping. The chatelaine pin is gold filled, beautifully hard enameled, gold filled swivel to hang watch on, making a combination seldom equaled.

$8.10 if you want a high grade 15 jeweled movement fitted in this case. Illustration shows the 15 jeweled Edgemere. It has 15 fine ruby jewels, all the plate jewels in screw settings, cut expansion balance, fine whiplash patent regulator with micrometric screw, stem wind and pendant set, in every way a fine high grade movement. Straight line lever escapement, fine selected white dial. Its equal sold by any merchant or any other concern for no less than $10.00 to $12.00. $8.10 complete, case, fine 15 jeweled Edgemere movement, pin and box.

No. 4K1468 Complete outfit as described and illustrated above, with 7 jeweled lever movement. Price...............$5.08
No. 4K1471 Same outfit illustrated and described above, but fitted with a genuine 15 jeweled Edgemere movement. Price...............8.10

No. 4K1468 0-Size, Hunting Style.

$5⁷⁷

$5.77 and $7.75

OUR CUT PRICES 18-SIZE, OPEN FACE, SOLID BACK, SWING RING, GOLD FILLED WATCHES.

GUARANTEED for 20 and 25 years' continuous wear. The Illinois Watch Case Co., of Elgin, Ill., manufacturer of these cases, agrees to replace with a brand new gold filled case of same style and grade any one of these cases worn through to the base metal within 20 or 25 years.

The swing ring, a new improvement on gold filled cases, makes it possible to produce an absolutely dust and dampproof watch case. You can examine the movement in a swing ring case without difficulty. See illustration. The front or bezel screws off. The back is solid, made of one piece. The movement is fastened in the center ring, which is securely joined to the case by a strong hinge. To examine the works, lift up the swing ring (illustration shows the ring partially lifted); to replace in case, let ring drop back in first position and screw on bezel.

THE ILLUSTRATION of movement above shows the movement we fit in this watch for $12.35 or $14.25 according to guarantee of case. $12.35 for this high grade adjusted movement and this dust and dampproof gold filled case is a wonderful offer. The movement has 17 fine ruby jewels, cut expansion balance, overstrung Breguet hairspring, patent safety pinion, straight line lever escapement, true timing screws, fine double sunk dial, adjusted to heat, temperature and position, in fact the complete watch represents

18-Size. the value purchased anywhere else of no less than $25.00 to $30.00. This is a watch we recommend if you are looking for a watch to keep accurate time.

$19.20 FOR A 21 JEWELED WATCH. To railway men, train starters and all others wanting a reliable timepiece, one that can be depended upon, we can recommend the 21 jeweled King Edward Plymouth Watch Co. movement. It has solid nickel plates, patent regulator, Breguet hairspring, and is especially adjusted, fitted in one of the new dustproof swing ring cases as an absolute protection against dust and damp.

No. 4K1458	Gold filled.	Guaranteed for 20 years.	Plain polished or engine turned.
No. 4K1460	Gold filled.	Guaranteed for 25 years.	Plain polished or engine turned.
No. 4K1462	Gold filled.	Guaranteed for 25 years.	Hand engraved.
No. 4K1464	Gold filled.	Guaranteed for 20 years.	Hand engraved.

We fit these cases with the following 18-size movements. Prices quoted are for the complete watch, movement and case.	Nos. 4K1458 4K1464	Nos. 4K1460 4K1462
7 JEWELED EDGEMERE, nickel plates, special make	$ 5.77	$ 7.75
7 Jeweled Elgin or Waltham, gilt plates	7.87	9.77
7 Jeweled Elgin or Waltham, nickel plates	8.40	10.30
15 Jeweled Waltham, gilt plates	8.93	10.83
15 Jeweled Elgin or Waltham, nickel plates	9.45	11.35
17 Jeweled Elgin or Waltham, not adjusted	10.50	12.40
17 JEWELED PLYMOUTH WATCH CO., patent regulator, adjusted, nickel plates, special make	12.35	14.25
17 Jeweled G. M. Wheeler Elgin or P. S. Bartlett Waltham, patent regulator, adjusted, nickel plates	12.60	14.50
21 JEWELED KING EDWARD PLYMOUTH WATCH CO., patent regulator, adjusted, nickel plates, special make	19.20	21.10
21 Jeweled John Hancock Hampden, patent regulator, adjusted, nickel plates	21.40	23.05
21 Jeweled Special Railway Hampden, patent regulator, adjusted, nickel plates	22.90	24.55
23 Jeweled Special Railway Hampden, patent regulator, adjusted, nickel plates	30.40	32.05
Full 19 Jeweled Adjusted, B. W. Raymond No. 240 Grade Elgin	28.15	29.80
Full 21 Jeweled Adjusted, Father Time Elgin	30.15	31.80
Full 21 Jeweled Adjusted, Veritas Elgin	34.15	25.80
Full 23 Jeweled Adjusted, Veritas Elgin	39.15	40.80
TRAINMEN'S SPECIAL, stamped 23 jewels, adjusted, special make	6.55	8.45

CUT PRICE $4.82 FOR THIS $10.00 OUTFIT.

SEND US $4.82 and we will send you this thin model, gold filled watch, handsomely engraved beaded center, antique bow and pendant, fitted with a genuine American 7 jeweled movement, together with this gold filled, soldered link, fancy stone set slide chain.

THE CASE is 6-size, hunting style. Don't compare this ladies' watch and chain with watches extensively advertised as gold filled watches, gold stiffened watches, rolled gold plate watches or like advertisements. This is a genuine gold filled watch, made of two solid gold plates soldered over an inner plate of composition metal, and is guaranteed not alone by the manufacturer, but we ourselves, knowing the quality of these goods, send our own written binding guarantee, backing up the manufacturer's, which protects you for a term of five years. You are doubly protected, first by the manufacturer's guarantee, then by our own guarantee.

THE MOVEMENT in this watch is stem wind and pendant set, is American made, has full nickel plates, has 7 fine jewels, cut expansion balance, in fact, a movement that will give entire and absolute satisfaction.

THE CHAIN is gold filled, bright polish, fancy soldered links, exactly as illustration shows, is 48 inches long and fitted with a very handsome oval shaped fancy stone set, gold front slide.

No. 4K1473 6-Size, Hunting Style.

No. 4K1473 Price for complete outfit, including watch, movement, chain and case...............$4.82
If by registered mail, postage extra, 14 cents.

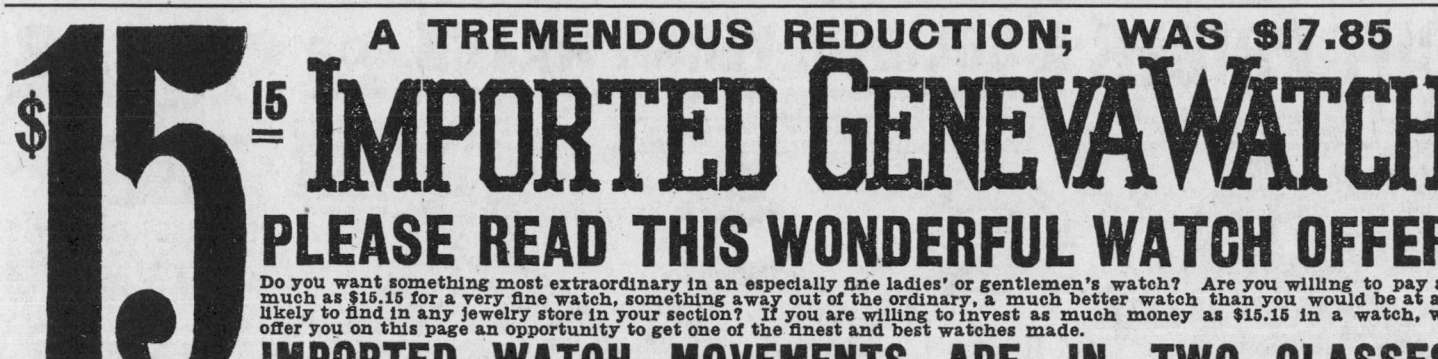

A TREMENDOUS REDUCTION; WAS $17.85

$15.15 IMPORTED GENEVA WATCH

PLEASE READ THIS WONDERFUL WATCH OFFER

Do you want something most extraordinary in an especially fine ladies' or gentlemen's watch? Are you willing to pay as much as $15.15 for a very fine watch, something away out of the ordinary, a much better watch than you would be at all likely to find in any jewelry store in your section? If you are willing to invest as much money as $15.15 in a watch, we offer you on this page an opportunity to get one of the finest and best watches made.

IMPORTED WATCH MOVEMENTS ARE IN TWO CLASSES

namely, very common and very high grade. The very common or even common imported watch movements we do not sell, for in the more common grade movements the cheaper American made movements, such as Edgemere, Elgin, Waltham, etc., are far better timekeepers than the common imported movements. Practically every very fine watch movement made is imported from Europe.

GENEVA, SWITZERLAND, EUROPE, turns out the very finest watch movements of the world. Go into the very finest jewelry store in Chicago, New York, or any other large American city, and you will scarcely see an American made movement offered for sale. The movements they offer are all made in Geneva, Switzerland, but in such stores they get very fancy prices. Scarcely one Geneva watch is offered for less than $50.00 and from that figure they run at once up into the hundreds. All very fine watch movements, even one of the very special split second, repeaters, striking, chronograph, and especially fine made thin model movements, all the very finest watch movement work is done in, and therefore must come from Geneva, Switzerland, Europe.

WE ARE THE FIRST HOUSE **in the world to bring the genuine high grade Geneva watch movements before the American public at anything like a low price.** The first house to make a price low enough to bring such a fine watch within reach of all. No longer is it necessary to pay $50.00 to $100.00 to own a Geneva watch, for by a most wonderful and absorbing watch movement contract made by us, strange as it may seem, we are just now able to take the very highest grade life guaranteed, full engraved American gold filled watch case made and fit into this case a very fine genuine Geneva Swiss movement in your choice of two sizes for men, or one size for women, and, strange as it must seem to everyone who reads this, and much as watch dealers will wonder, we can offer these marvelously fine watches for only $15.15.

DON'T BUY ONE OF THESE FINE WATCHES **and then treat it as you would a dollar nickel watch.** If you are at times engaged at dirty or heavy work; if your work takes you at times into dusty fields behind the harvester, or to the railroad section; if your work at times takes you otherwise into dirty or dusty places and when at work your watch is jammed and roughly used, on such occasions don't wear as fine a watch as this for the purpose. In such cases **don't buy this watch at all,** or buy this watch and also a cheap heavy watch for a dollar or so, using the cheap watch when at very dirty or rough work.

THIS GENEVA WATCH **is the rubber tired, beautifully hand finished, painted and trimmed runabout buggy or surrey of your stable,** the beautiful, easy riding, comfort giving, and always dependable rig that you so much like to hitch to on proper occasions and for proper use, but you wouldn't make a farm or lumber wagon or truck wagon of such a rig, you wouldn't use it to haul manure, hay, dirt, etc., and unless absolutely necessary you would not drag such a beautiful rig miles through deep mud. These fine Geneva watches are the fine rubber tired, hand made, delicate and beautifully finished, yet strong, reliable and practically everlasting fancy runabout rigs of the watch making industry of the world.

FOR WONDERFUL TIMEKEEPING QUALITIES **and rare specimens of beauty,** and for those who are willing to give a fine watch just reasonable care, only the reasonable care that such a fine piece of machinery deserves, these fine Geneva watches are the only watches to buy.

THE LADIES' BEAUTIFUL SMALL SIZE **is the only watch for any lady to buy, and the men's 16 or 12-size watch is the only fine watch for any man to buy or wear** if engaged in anything but the heaviest work, and a thoroughly fine watch for any man to buy, even if engaged at times in heaviest and dirtiest work, provided you are willing to be just a little careful of this most beautiful and perfect piece of watch machinery.

BUY THIS GENEVA WATCH AT $15.15 **in either gentlemen's or ladies' styles and no American watch even at $50.00 in price will compare with it.** Let your friends see, examine and compare your Geneva watch with their watches and every judge will pronounce your $15.15 watch worth $50.00 to $100.00.

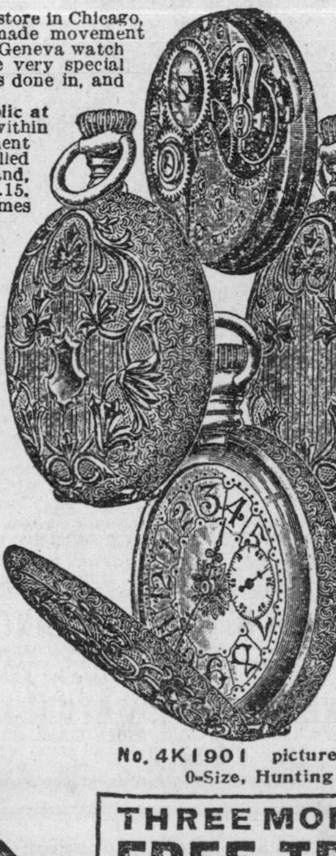

These illustrations show front, back and open view of case, also movement of ladies' 0-size watch, fitted with genuine Geneva movement. The pictures are life size.

No. 4K1901

0-Size, Hunting Style.

THE SIZES OF THESE GENEVA WATCHES

THE PICTURES HEREON **show the exact size of these watches. The largest, 16-size gents' watch, just as illustrated, is 2 inches wide.** The 12-size gents' watch, just as illustrated, is 1⅞ inches wide. The ladies' 0-size, just as illustrated, is 1⅜ inches wide. All are made especially thin, neat and dainty, and all have unique antique bows. They are all smaller, thinner, lighter, neater and in every way handsomer and finer than what you can buy in American made watches; the 12 or 16-size, the ideal size, shape and style for the carrying timepiece of a real gentleman, and the 0-size is just the watch in size, thickness and weight for the most exacting, most fashionable lady to wear, and as for timekeeping dependability they are unequaled. The three illustrations on this page will give you just a little idea of the appearance of our Geneva watch and the several sizes in which it comes. The largest size, the 16-size for gentlemen, we offer for the first time in the history of the watch making industry in a genuine imported Geneva movement for only $15.15. One of the pictures in the group of three shows the front of the watch with its handsome Geneva special dial or face and gold hands. Another picture shows the back of the watch detailing the gold filled case with its beautiful engraving and elaborate finish. The third picture in the group shows the wonderful Geneva movement, and these three pictures are engraved by our artist direct from photographs and are exact in size and appearance.

THE GENTLEMEN'S 12-SIZE WATCH, **one size smaller than the 16-size and two sizes smaller than the common sized (18-size) American watches, a handsome, light, thin, neat model is truly a real gentlemen's timepiece.** This is the size now so popular among the most fashionable city men, the size, style and kind sold so largely in the most fashionable retail jewelry stores in the largest cities. This watch is truly a beauty in every respect. It's to a cheap big clumsy 18-size American watch like a $3,000.00 automobile to a lumber wagon. If you can possibly afford to pay $15.15 for a watch, then by all means order this, the finest, the most genteel timepiece we have ever been able to offer.

THESE ILLUSTRATIONS **at the top (the smallest pictures) show the ladies' 0-size genuine Geneva Hunting (or double) case life guaranteed watch which is offered for only $15.15.** One picture shows the back of this watch closed and one picture shows the watch open, giving you an idea of the beautiful fancy gold and enameled finish gold hands and dial. In style and quality this case is exactly the same as the two gentlemen's cases, only smaller, and hunting case (or double case) in place of open face like the two gents' watches. The genuine Geneva movement which we fit in this beautiful case is in every respect exactly the same as the gentlemen's watches described, only that it is much smaller, being the neat, small, thin, light, ladies' size at $15.15.

THESE GENEVA MOVEMENTS **in all three sizes, 16, 12 and 0, are all alike, except for size, all made from very finest decarbonized nickel,** all are full 17 jeweled, red, hand turned ruby jewels in gold settings, jeweled both sides throughout, including centers; all adjusted to heat, cold, position and isochronism; patent regulators, patent escapement, patent pinion, patent dust protector, quick train cut balance wheel, Breguet hairspring, compensating balance, Geneva compensating system, all hand finished and polished parts, all the movements the very best in every respect.

THE LIFE GUARANTEED **gold filled cases in all three sizes, 16, 12 and 0-size, are all American made and the highest grade gold filled cases manufactured.** Cases are made of heavy thick plates of fine solid gold over inner plates of hard composition metal and are guaranteed to wear and retain their pure gold color for a lifetime. They are most elaborately engraved, finished and decorated, wonderfully well finished, all fitted with genuine antique bows, all stem wind and patent pendant setting. The gentlemen's watches, the 16 and 12-sizes, are open face only, the 0-size ladies' watches are double or hunting case.

FANCY DIALS **or faces. These Geneva watches all have very fancy dials** (see illustrations), the most beautiful dials made, finished with gold and colored ornamentations and fancy gold hands.

IF YOU WANT A VERY FINE WATCH, **something away out of the ordinary,** then order a watch to hand down to your children and from them to your children's children. Order either the gents' 16-size Geneva watch or the one size smaller, the 12-size, or if you want something very fine in a ladies' watch then order the ladies' 0-size illustrated on this page.

BE SURE TO ORDER BY NUMBER.

No. 4K1901	Ladies' small size watch. Price..	$15.15
No. 4K1903	12-size gentlemen's watch. Price.	15.15
No. 4K1905	16-size gentlemen's watch. Price.	15.15

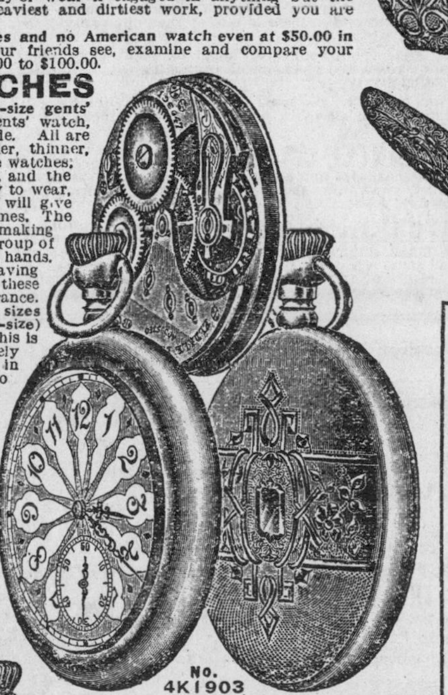

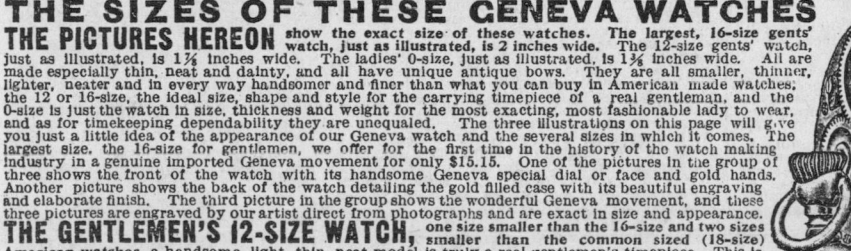

No. 4K1903

12-Size, Open Face, Screw Back and Screw Bezel.

These illustrations are life size and show front, back and movement of the gentlemen's 12-size watch with genuine Geneva movement.

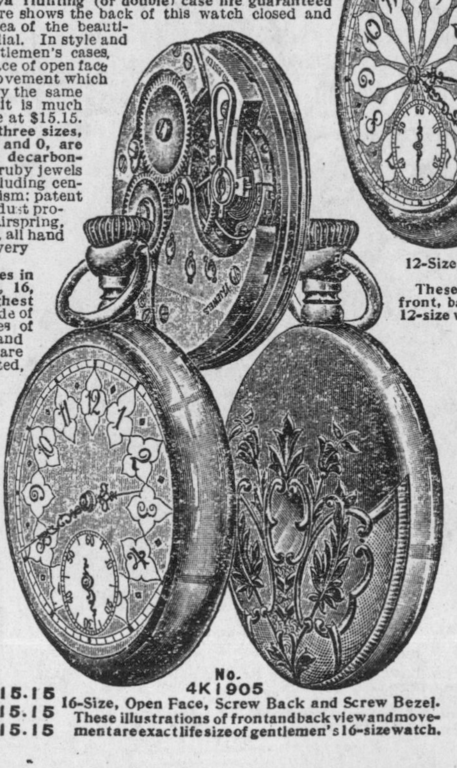

No. 4K1905

16-Size, Open Face, Screw Back and Screw Bezel.

These illustrations of front and back view and movement are exact life size of gentlemen's 16-size watch.

THREE MONTHS' FREE TRIAL AND GUARANTEE OFFER

Send us $15.15, state whether you want us to send you the gentlemen's 16 or 12-size, or whether you want the ladies' 0-size genuine Geneva watch and we will send the watch you order to you with the distinct understanding and agreement that you can use the Geneva watch three months, during which time you may put the Geneva watch to every test, compare it with any American made watch you can buy at from $50.00 up, and if you are not perfectly satisfied with your purchase, you can return the watch to us at our expense and we will immediately refund your $15.15.

OUR LIFE GUARANTEE. We send with every Geneva watch a written binding guarantee, guaranteeing the gold filled case to wear and retain its gold and gold color for life and we guarantee the Geneva movements as accurate timekeepers for five years.

IF YOU WANT A GENTLEMEN'S OR LADIES' WATCH WE ADVISE YOU TO DO THIS:

IN A LETTER TO US **say which one of these three watches you want, inclose our great offer price, $15.15,** let us send you the watch with our written binding guarantee and with the understanding and agreement that you can use any one of these watches you may order, for three months, during which time you can put it to every possible test, compare it with the highest grade American watches, let your friends see and examine it and let any disinterested watch expert examine it that you may have his opinion, and if for any reason you should become dissatisfied with your purchase at any time within three months, you can return the watch to us at our expense and we will immediately return your money, together with any express charges you may have paid.

IN YOUR OWN INTEREST, **if you feel you can afford to invest as much as $15.15 in the highest grade gold filled case made in America and in one of the highest grade stem wind,** pendant set movements made in the world, a genuine Geneva movement, made in Geneva, Switzerland, then by all means, in preference to any of the more common watches, watches that are retailed generally at $15.00 to $30.00, by all means send us your order for this gold filled Geneva watch. Remember, it comes in three sizes exactly as illustrated and described, two sizes for gentlemen (the smaller of the two is 12-size and the larger 16-size); and the ladies' watch is one of the handsomest watches ever produced. It's the standard 0-size. The movements are all the same grade; they differ only in size, so whether you wish a watch for a gentleman or a lady, before buying elsewhere rather than invest $5.00, $10.00 or $15.00 for a watch, endeavor to add just a little to the amount you have decided to spend, send us $15.15 and let us send you one of these wonderful Geneva timepieces in the best gold filled case made!

CUT PRICES A SOLID SILVER 16-SIZE WATCH FOR $4.38

25c will carry any watch to any part of the United States by express. We recommend sending watches by express as they do not receive the hard usage as when sent by mail. If sent by mail, postage extra, including registry, 16 cents.

For 90c extra we will furnish a fancy dial and gold hands on the silver watches on this page.

See pages 259 and 260 for the descriptions and beautiful illustrations of our special lines of movements, Plymouth Watch Co. and Edgemere line of watch movements.

LOOK HERE! Your choice of any one of these solid silver watches, new 16-size, extra thin model, in open face or hunting case, for $4.38 and upward. Think of it! $4.38 for solid silver, open face case, screw back and screw bezel, dust and dampproof, new antique crown, bow and pendant, bright polished throughout, extra thin model watch. Just the kind of a model watch that you are looking for, fitted with a good 7 jeweled Edgemere movement, stem wind and pendant set, covered by our written, binding five-year guarantee, all for $4.38.

A GOLD FILLED CENTER CASE with solid silver lids inlaid in solid gold for $6.95. Who ever heard of the like! The center of the case, that is, every part of the watch that the hinges fit upon, is of gold filled metal, and the crown, stem and bow of the antique style made to match it. The lids, the front and the back are made of solid silver inlaid with pure gold in various colors to imitate nature and the landscape effects properly, complete with the movement. A good timer, and one that we guarantee against defective material and workmanship. Remember the price; all we ask is $6.95 for this handsome watch.

No. 4K2152 Solid Silver Hunting Style, solid gold ornamented inlaid, hand engraved, gold filled fancy center.   **No. 4K2154** Solid Silver, screw back and bezel.   Open Face.   **No. 4K2156** Solid Silver Hunting Style, plain polished.   **No. 4K2158** Solid Silver, engine turned, Hunting Style.

JUST WHAT THESE CASES ARE

THE FIRST WATCH has a gold filled center with gold filled crown and stem, the bow is solid silver, the lids are solid silver, both front and back. Lids are inlaid and ornamented with solid gold in various tints and colors. The case is fitted with inside protecting cap, well made bezel, especially grooved so as to securely hold the crystal.

THE SECOND WATCH shows the open face, screw back and screw bezel, bright polished extra thin model style. Has antique crown, bow and stem. Bezel fitted with a very fine thick crystal. This is one of the popular styles for a cheap watch in solid silver and worth double what we ask.

THE THIRD WATCH is hunting style, plain polished, made of solid silver. Has antique bow, crown and stem, inside protecting cap, well made especially grooved bezel for securely holding the crystal.

THE FOURTH WATCH is hunting style also, the same in all ways as the third watch, but instead of being plain polish is engine turned. Many watch owners prefer the engine turned case.

OUR WRITTEN BINDING GUARANTEE goes with every one of these cases, and warrants the case to be solid silver through and through. Together with this guarantee and embodied in same is the guarantee on any movement that you select, which warrants the watch free from all defects of material and workmanship for a term of five years.

ORDER ONE OF THESE WATCHES. Send us $4.38 up to $28.80, according to style of case and grade of movement, and we will upon receipt of your order make shipment at once. After you get the watch, examine it, compare it with any watch of same size and material offered by any merchant or owned by any one of your friends or neighbors, and if our watch, grade for grade, size for size, material for material, does not excel the watch you have looked at at the merchant's or your friend's watch, considering the price paid by him and the price paid by you, you can return it and we will upon its receipt at once refund your money, together with all transportation charges. If sent by mail, postage extra, including registry, 16 cents.

THE TWO MOVEMENTS that we advise your selecting, fitted in any one of these four cases we illustrate here, our 17 jeweled Plymouth Watch Company movement and our 21 jeweled Prince of Wales movement, both of these movements representing the highest possible perfection in watch making. The 17 jeweled movement that we fully describe on page 260 positively gives accurate time. The 21 jeweled movement, likewise described on page 259, is recognized by watch authorities as being the most perfect 21 jeweled movement ever manufactured in the United States. Notwithstanding that these two movements are the best made, the cases the most up to date on the market, for those who desire purchasing the new thin model 16-size solid silver watches, yet, on account of our close connection with one of the largest watch factories in the United States, on account of purchasing ability where we make quantity count, we are able to offer your choice of any one of these cases fitted with either of these two movements at the astonishingly low price of $14.42 to $21.60.

We fit these cases with the following 16-size movements. Prices quoted are for the complete watch, movement and case.

	No. 4K2152 16-Size, Hunting Solid Silver, Gold Ornamented	No. 4K2154 16-Size, Open Face, Screw Back and Screw Bezel	No. 4K2156 16-Size, Hunting Style, Plain Polished	No. 4K2158 16-Size, Hunting Style, Full En- gine Turned
7 JEWELED EDGEMERE, nickel plates, special make	$6.95	$4.38	$4.85	$4.85
7 Jeweled Elgin or Waltham, nickel plates	10.10	7.62	8.00	8.00
15 JEWELED EDGEMERE, patent regulator, nickel plates, special make	9.60	7.12	7.50	7.50
15 Jeweled Elgin or Waltham, nickel plates, patent regulator	12.30	9.82	10.20	10.20
17 Jeweled Elgin or Waltham, not adjusted	14.50	12.02	12.40	12.40
17 Jeweled No. 241 Grade Elgin, adjusted	17.25	14.77	15.15	15.15
17 JEWELED PLYMOUTH WATCH CO., nickel plates, patent regulator, adjusted	16.90	14.42	14.80	14.80
17 Jeweled No. 243 Grade Elgin, adjusted, nickel plates	28.80	26.32	26.70	26.70
21 JEWELED PRINCE OF WALES, PLYMOUTH WATCH CO., full adjusted, patent regulator, nickel plates	21.60	19.12	19.50	19.50

SOLID GOLD 14-KARAT AND GOLD FILLED, NEW THIN MODEL, DUEBER-HAMPDEN WATCHES

OPEN FACE AND HUNTING STYLE. 16-SIZE, 25-YEAR WARRANTED GOLD FILLED AND 14-KARAT SOLID GOLD.

THESE CASES ARE MADE BY THE DUEBER WATCH CO. They are the correct thing, the right size and shape, hand engraved and in every respect perfect. The movements are all new models manufactured by the Hampden Watch Company, each one guaranteed an accurate timepiece for five years. Note the prices and compare them with what others ask for the same watch.

SELECT THE WATCH YOU WANT in solid gold or in gold filled, open face or hunting style. The gold filled cases of the John C. Dueber factory are known to be exactly as represented, guaranteed for 25 years and so stamped on the inside lid. You are amply protected in selecting a John C. Dueber watch.

THE SOLID GOLD CASES manufactured by the same firm are noted throughout the world for their beautiful finish and artistic designs. These cases are solid gold, 14-karat fine. Every piece and particle that goes into the case is of this quality. The engravings are all hand work. The greatest care exhibited on details. The latest English idea of antique crown, bow and stem used in these cases.

IF YOU SELECT THE OPEN FACE WATCH we will send you the new dust and dampproof, screw back and screw bezel case. Not jointed, but the latest idea in open face case making.

THE HUNTING STYLE CASES are the Bassene type, close jointed, no raw or unsightly edges.

OUR GUARANTEE goes out with the John C. Dueber cases and the Hampden movements. We back this guarantee with our own written, binding guarantee, protecting you against defective material or faulty workmanship. Every watch is carefully inspected and oiled before it leaves our establishment. You are sure of getting a brand new, accurately running watch in every instance when you buy from us.

$17.00

Gold Filled.
No. 4K2171   No. 4K2173
This illustration shows the hunting and open face style, gold filled, warranted for 25 years, 16-size Dueber-Hampden watches.
No. 4K2171   Open Face.
No. 4K2173   Hunting.

$32.50

Solid Gold.
No. 4K2175   No. 4K2177
This illustration shows the hunting and open face style, solid 14-karat gold, 16-size Dueber-Hampden watches.
No. 4K2175   Open Face.
No. 4K2177   Hunting.

Prices quoted are for the complete watch, movement and case.	No. 4K2171 Gold Filled, Open Face, Warranted for 25 Years	No. 4K2173 Gold Filled, Hunting Style	No. 4K2175 Solid Gold, Open Face	No. 4K2177 Solid Gold, Hunting Style
Full 17 jeweled General Stark movement	$17.00	$18.00	$32.50	$38.00
Full 17 jeweled William McKinley movement	19.50	21.00	34.70	39.70
Full 21 jeweled William McKinley movement	32.00	34.00	45.75	50.75

SPECIAL DRIVES IN AMERICAN WATCHES

$3.16 A CUT PRICE IN GENUINE ALASKA METAL 16-SIZE SWING RING CUP CASE WATCH

Solid silver and Alaska metal, extra thin model, 16-size, swing ring dust and dampproof watches. Perfection has arrived at last—$3.16 for an absolutely dust and dampproof case means that you have a watch that will last a lifetime. Dampness and dust are the banes of watches. It is from these two causes that most watch troubles arise.

$3.16

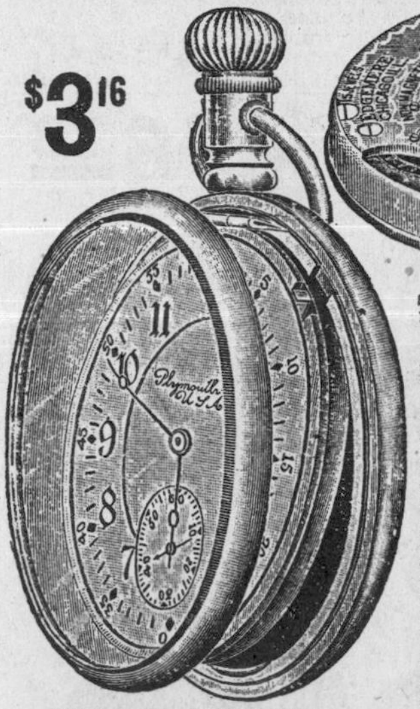

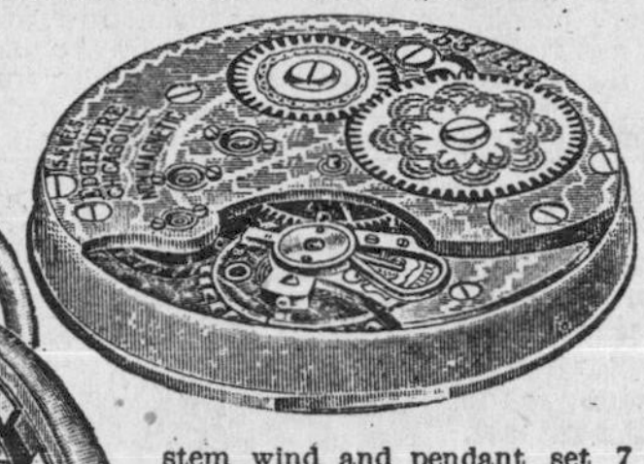

OPEN FACE SWING RING.
No. 4K2160 16-Size, Solid Silver, Open Face, Swing Ring.
No. 4K2162 16-Size, Alaska Metal, Open Face, Swing Ring.

OUR $3.16 OFFER

Send us $3.16, together with the mail charges of 14 cents extra, and we will ship you, upon receipt, one of these solid Alaska metal watches, the nearest approach to solid silver yet discovered, fitted with a thin model, stem wind and pendant set 7 jeweled Edgemere movement.

BUY THE SWING RING CASE. It is the best. Note the illustration, which shows the front bezel unscrewed and the swing ring slightly raised. When the watch is closed this swing ring falls back and the bezel is tightly screwed on. This makes the front and back of the watch absolutely dust and dampproof. The watch is protected from above by a new patent screw nut stem; the extra nut being used for filling the crevices on the inside of the watch between the crown and the stem makes it impossible for the dust and damp to filter through. No part has been overlooked to bring about this perfect dust and dampproof arrangement.

$4.95 FOR THE SAME WATCH IN SOLID SILVER. Think of it! $4.95 for this absolutely dust and dampproof solid silver watch. Competition defied when prices of such astonishing figures are being made. See the list of movements printed below. Particularly note the 15 jeweled Edgemere movement illustrated here, fitted in Alaska compound metal case for $5.85, or in the solid silver case for $7.60. In this movement you have a 15 jeweled, fine finished, accurately running watch which only costs you $5.85, or $7.60, but if you wish to own the best 17 jeweled movement manufactured in the United States, a movement that is stem wind and pendant set, containing 17 fine ruby jewels, with all modern improvements, a movement that will run accurately, one that can be guaranteed, a movement that you will be proud of, select the **17 jeweled Plymouth Watch Company movement** quoted at **$13.15** and **$14.90**, according to case. In this case and in this movement you have the perfection of the watch world. **For other movements, Elgin, Waltham, etc., see quotations listed below:**

We fit these swing ring cases with the following 16-size movements. Prices quoted are for the complete watch, movement and case.	No. 4K2162	No. 4K2160
7 JEWELED EDGEMERE, nickel plates, special make	$ 3.16	$ 4.95
7 Jeweled Elgin or Waltham, nickel plates	6.35	8.10
15 JEWELED EDGEMERE, patent regulator, nickel plates, special make	5.85	7.60
15 Jeweled Elgin or Waltham, nickel plates, patent regulator	8.55	10.30
17 Jeweled Elgin or Waltham, not adjusted	10.75	12.50
17 Jeweled No. 241 Grade Elgin, adjusted	13.50	15.25
17 JEWELED PLYMOUTH WATCH CO., nickel plates, patent regulator, adjusted	13.15	14.90
17 Jeweled No. 243 Grade Elgin, adjusted, nickel plate	25.05	26.80
21 JEWELED PRINCE OF WALES, PLYMOUTH WATCH CO., full adjusted, patent regulator, nickel plates	17.85	19.60

CUT PRICE $2.76 OR $3.20 FOR A GENUINE ALASKA COMPOUND METAL, 16-SIZE, EXTRA THIN MODEL WATCH

$2.76 for the open face, screw back and screw bezel, antique crown, stem and bow, or $3.20 for the hunting style case, inside protecting cap, especially made crystal bezel holder, either one representing values for which the competitor asks double our price. We want you to be the judge. Either of these watches quoted at $2.76 to $25.05, according to movement. Enclose with your remittance 14 cents extra to defray the registered mail charges. Upon receipt of your order we will make shipment of the watch at once. Examine it carefully, especially look at the movement that we send you, then compare it with similar watches offered by your local jeweler or offered by any other catalogue firm, or compare it with the watch owned by your neighbor or friend, and if our watch, considering all factors, does not show you a saving of 20 to 33⅓ per cent, in other words, from $1.00 to $5.00 on the purchase by all means return the watch to us and we will, upon receipt, refund your money, together with the transportation charges that have been incurred both ways.

$2.76

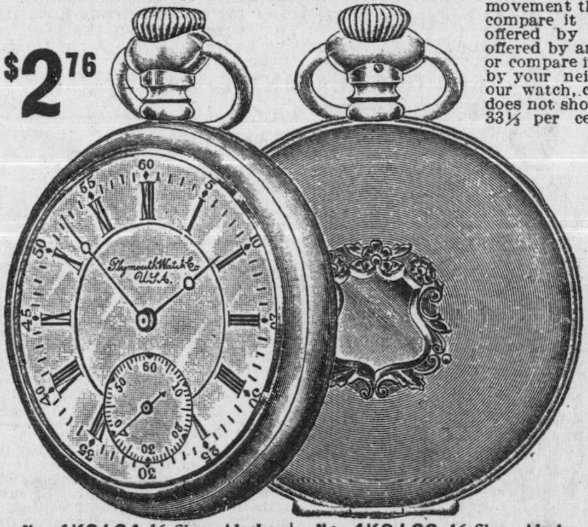

No. 4K2164 16-Size, Alaska Metal Back and Screw Bezel. | No. 4K2166 16-Size, Alaska Metal, Hunting Style Case.

SEE ILLUSTRATION. They are both bright polish. No. 4K2164 shows open face, screw back and screw bezel watch. No. 4K2166 shows hunting style watch. Both extra thin models, the very latest up to date style, new antique crown, stem and bow. They are stem wind and pendant set, snappy, up to date watches in every respect.

WHY WE ARE ABLE TO MAKE THIS OFFER. All price precedents have been swept aside and we own them at a figure just as though we own the factory. The factory absolutely produces these cases for us at cost. They do not make one cent of profit, and they supply them to us only because of our wonderful purchases of other goods from them and so as to give our customers a special bargain on a staple article, at the same time enabling them to keep their workmen busy in such seasons when the sale of watches is light, thereby keeping their organization together. This wonderful purchase of cases, together with the movement contract that we have, places us in such a safe position that we can sincerely and conscientiously make the offer.

We fit these 16-size Alaska metal cases with the following 16-size movements. Prices quoted are for complete watch, movement and case.	No. 4K2164	No. 4K2166
7 JEWELED EDGEMERE, nickel plates, special make	$ 2.76	$ 3.20
7 Jeweled Elgin or Waltham, nickel plates	5.95	6.35
15 JEWELED EDGEMERE, patent regulator, nickel plates, special make	5.45	5.85
15 Jeweled Elgin or Waltham, nickel plates, patent regulator	8.15	8.55
17 Jeweled Elgin or Waltham, not adjusted	10.35	10.75
17 Jeweled No. 241 Grade Elgin, adjusted	13.10	13.50
17 JEWELED PLYMOUTH WATCH CO., nickel plates, patent regulator, adjusted	12.75	13.15
17 Jeweled No. 243 Grade Elgin adjusted, nickel plates	24.65	25.05
21 JEWELED PRINCE OF WALES, PLYMOUTH WATCH CO., full adjusted, patent regulator, nickel plates	17.45	17.85

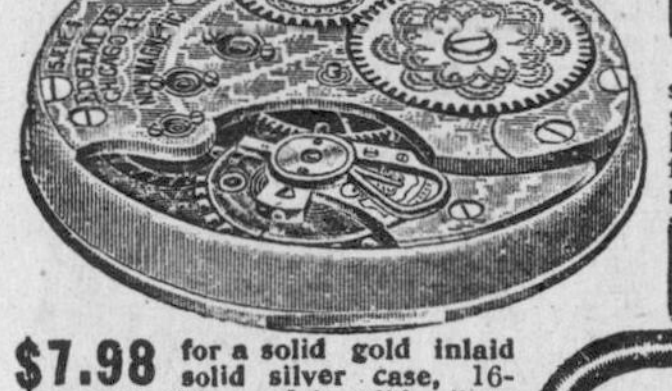

$7.98

This illustration shows the handsome 15 jeweled, lever escapement, fine finished movement we fit in this case for

$7.98

$7.98 for a solid gold inlaid solid silver case, 16-size extra thin model solid silver case, screw back and screw bezel, stem wind and stem set, the inlaying done in various colors of gold to represent different floral designs with a solid gold shield in the center in varicolored gold border.

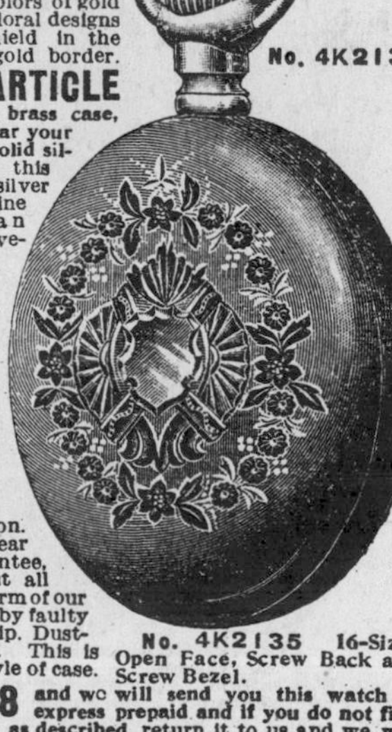

No. 4K2135

THE GENUINE ARTICLE

Not a filled case, not a brass case, but a case that will wear your natural lifetime, being solid silver. $7.98 complete, this solid gold inlaid solid silver case fitted with a genuine 15 jeweled American model movement, a movement that we guarantee for five years, is one of our challenge offers. This movement is stem wind and pendant set, has 15 jewels in gold screw settings, Breguet hairspring, patent pinions, patent regulator, beautiful nickel damaskeened plates, in fact a high grade, up to date thin model movement, such as we know will give entire satisfaction. It carries our five-year written binding guarantee, protecting you against all breakages during the term of our guarantee when caused by faulty material or workmanship. Dustproof and dampproof. This is only possible in this style of case.

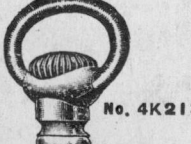

No. 4K2135 16-Size, Open Face, Screw Back and Screw Bezel.

SEND US $7.98 and we will send you this watch by express prepaid and if you do not find it in every way exactly as described, return it to us and we will upon its receipt return your money, together with the transportation charges. No. 4K2135 Price.........$7.98

$7.96 AND UP

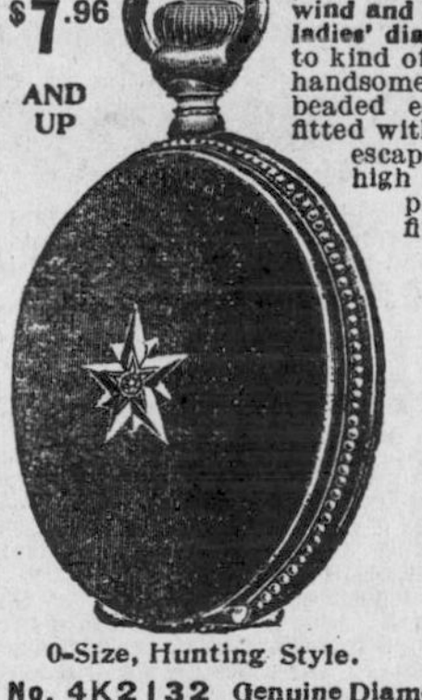

0-Size, Hunting Style.

$7.96 TO $17.50 for this gold filled twenty-year stem wind and pendant stem set guaranteed ladies' diamond set 0-size watch, according to kind of movement. $7.96 for this very handsome plain polished, thin model, beaded edge, genuine diamond set case, fitted with an imported 7 jeweled lever escapement movement, means selling high grade watches at unheard of prices. $11.15 for the same case fitted with a 15 jeweled movement.

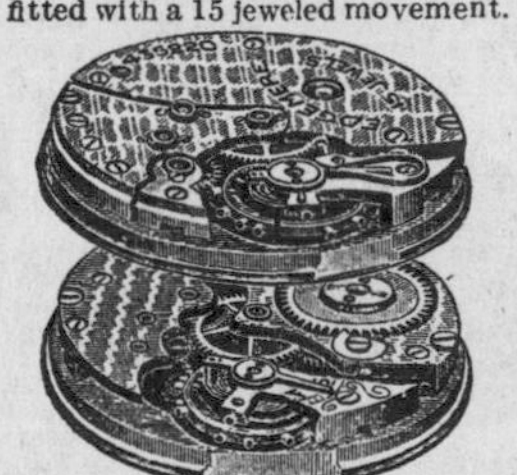

No. 4K2132 Genuine Diamond Set, Small 0-size, Gold Filled, Twenty-Year Guaranteed Watch.

JUST THINK OF IT! You can make a very handsome present or own for your own personal use a watch that you can well be proud of. The case is our Kingston gold filled case. It is guaranteed to wear and retain its solid gold appearance for a term of twenty years. The diamond set in this watch is warranted to be genuine, brilliant and just large enough to be beautiful and attractive.

THE MOVEMENT, as illustrated above, has 7 fine jewels, well set, has lever escapement, exposed winding wheels, nickel damaskeened plates and is a good, accurate timekeeper. We send with it our own personal binding guarantee for a term of five years.

THE 15 JEWELED MOVEMENT, manufactured especially for us, has 15 fine jewels, exposed winding wheels, bridged, as illustration shows. Nickel plates very handsomely damaskeened, Breguet hairspring, the latest 0-size 15 jeweled movement made at nearly double the price. Each one carries with it our five-year guarantee for quality and accuracy. The top movement in the illustration shows how this movement appears.

Fitted with 7 jeweled Swiss Lever movement	$ 7.96
Fitted with 7 jeweled American movement	9.15
Fitted with the 15 jeweled Edgemere, our own specially made movement	11.15
Fitted with the 7 jeweled Elgin or Waltham	11.85
Fitted with the 15 jeweled Elgin or Waltham	13.10
Fitted with the 15 jeweled Plymouth Watch Co.	12.85
Fitted with a 17 jeweled Plymouth Watch Co. movement, which represents the highest possible perfection in watch making (no other 17 jeweled watch movement can compare with it in timekeeping and general finish)	17.50

CUT PRICE. A 12-SIZE WATCH AT AN UNHEARD OF PRICE.

Boys' or Gentlemen's Hunting Style Genteel, Thin, 12-Size

GOLD FILLED WATCHES.

Illustration shows the watch partially opened and also side view of watch showing extreme thinness of same.

$6.98

No. 4K2150 12-Size Hunting Style.

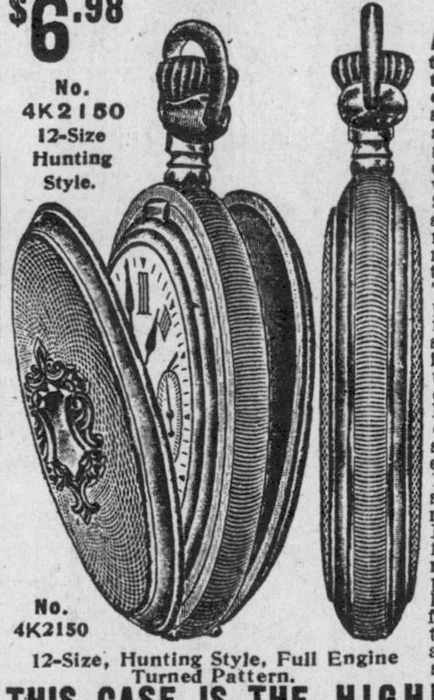

No. 4K2150

12-Size, Hunting Style, Full Engine Turned Pattern.

A SMALL, thin, genteel, high grade, twenty-year gold filled watch, the coming size, thickness, shape and style for boy or gentleman; the neatest, most perfect watch made. Price, $6.98 and upward, according to grade of movement. All the movements we fit in this case are 6-size. The case is made especially for that size movement. This 12-size gold filled hunting style case is gotten up in imitation of the very finest 14-karat solid gold case, extra thin model, 12-size, two sizes smaller than the regular 16-size and three sizes smaller than the regular 18-size. Plenty large enough for any gentleman; not a load in the pocket, but a thin, light, neat watch and far more sensible than a heavy watch, also a very popular size for boys.

THIS CASE IS THE HIGHEST GRADE GOLD FILLED warranted for twenty years, a certificate of guarantee accompanying each case. It is hunting style, fine engine turned in perfect imitation of solid gold, has solid gold antique bow and crown. We fit in this case the following 6-size movements:

7 JEWELED EDGEMERE, special make	$6.98
COUNTESS JANET, stamped 17 jewels, adjusted	7.38
7 Jeweled Elgin or Waltham, gilt plates	8.70
7 Jeweled Elgin or Waltham, nickel plates	9.22
15 Jeweled Elgin or Waltham, nickel plates	10.28
16 Jeweled Lady Waltham, nickel plates	12.90
17 JEWELED PLYMOUTH WATCH CO., nickel plates, patent regulator, special make	12.65

A LADIES' HUNTING STYLE GOLD FILLED $15.00 WATCH FOR $6.28

$6.28 FOR YOUR CHOICE OF ANY ONE OF THESE GOLD FILLED 20-YEAR GUARANTEED CASES ILLUSTRATED HERE, COMPLETE WITH A 7 JEWELED AMERICAN MADE MOVEMENT.

WE ILLUSTRATE only four cases of the most popular designs, but they are four of the handsomest watches that can be procured, copied after solid gold patterns. In selecting one of these watches you will own a watch that has every appearance of being solid 14-karat gold. Each case has been selected with a view of putting in the hands of our customers a perfect article. Each case is perfectly finished in detail, special attention being given to the joints, no rough edges, no unsightly parts. The very latest, up to date antique bow, stem and crown. Finely finished, jointed inside protecting cap, perfectly finished inside bezel, well grooved, so that it holds the crystal of the watch securely.

$6.28 MAY SEEM A SMALL SUM OF MONEY for a high grade gold filled watch, but it is made possible only because of our immense purchasing power, together with the fact that these cases are made by one of the largest watch companies in the United States, branded with the name "Kingston," all useless expense being cut out. All of these advantages we are offering to you in this our $6.28 gold filled ladies' size watch offer.

$6.28 REDUCED IN PRICE

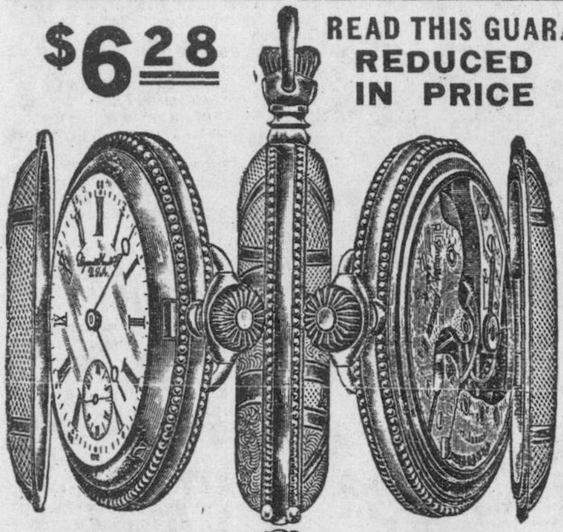

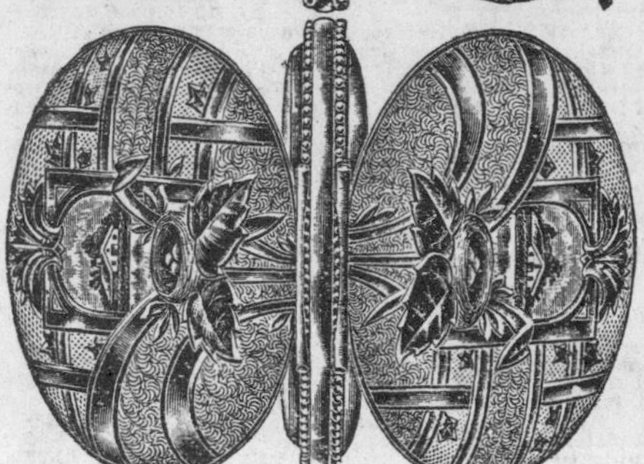

No. 4K2813 6-Size, Hunting Style.

This illustration shows our full engraved case and is engraved on perfectly bright, plain polished surfaces, ornamented with beautiful vermicelli work, floral sprays and landscapes, selected with a view to please those who desire full engraved cases.

READ THIS GUARANTEE. The illustration shows a facsimile of the guarantee that goes out with each case. Together with this case guarantee is our own written binding guarantee that we, as a firm, send out, which protects you for a term of twenty years.

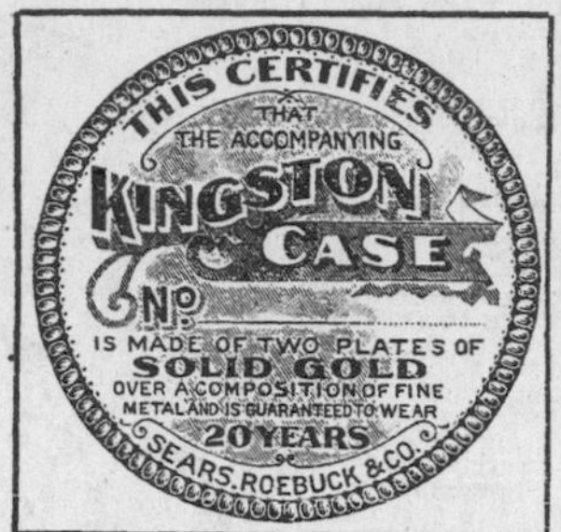

OUR KINGSTON BRAND 6-SIZE CASES, guaranteed for twenty years, considering the price, leads them all. Made of plates of solid gold, rolled to the proper thickness, covering a composition metal, not cheap or shoddy, but the genuine article.

You have noted no doubt that there are but four varieties of cases illustrated on this page. Several of the illustrations merely show you the different views of the same watch so as to give a correct idea of how the watch will appear. Be sure to order by number and to plainly state the kind of movement wanted, inclosing with your order the correct amount of money, together with the mail charges. 12 cents will carry any one of these watches to any part of the United States by registered mail.

THE CASES shown on this page are copies of solid gold designs and the equal of any solid gold case in general appearance, engraving, finish, and, in fact, the equal of a solid gold case in everything except intrinsic value. None but an experienced jeweler would know but that they were solid gold.

25 cents will carry any watch to any part of the United States by express. We recommend sending watches by express as they do not receive the hard usage as when sent by mail. If sent by mail include 12 cents extra for postage and registry fee.

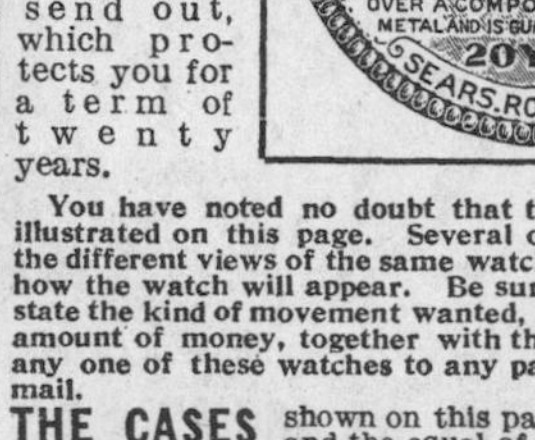

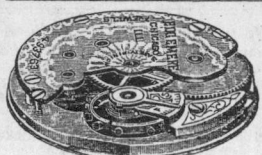

$6.28 For this movement fitted in the case you select. This our 7 jeweled Edgemere movement, plates beautifully damaskeened, contains 7 jewels and is equal to any 7 jewel movement made. Worth two of the cheap movements being sold at 30 to 40 per cent more on the market now. Is stem wind and pendant set, has cut expansion balance, sunk second dial, improved in every way over cheap 7 jeweled watches quoted anywhere.

LOOK AT THIS!

$6.60 For any one of these cases fitted with our Countess Janet movement. Could any movement be made handsomer? Could any movement be made more attractive? It is stamped "17 jewels, adjusted," the plates are beautifully damaskeened, shows handsome jewel settings on the plate, yet we are able to sell you this watch complete with one of the four cases that you select and this movement for $6.60. As a matter of fact, though, the movement is merely 7 jeweled American made. Is stem wind and pendant set, a good timer, will give good satisfaction, as good satisfaction as any 7 jeweled movement.

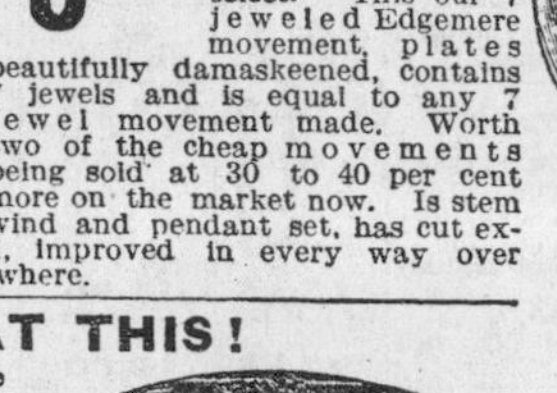

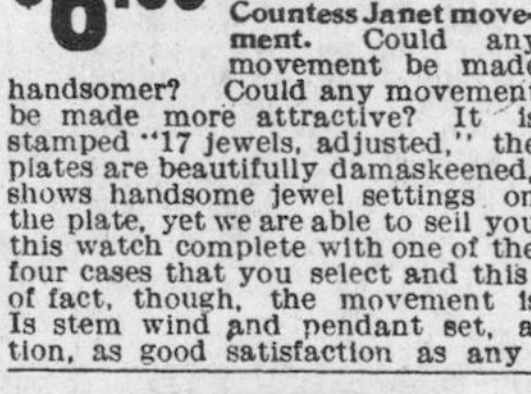

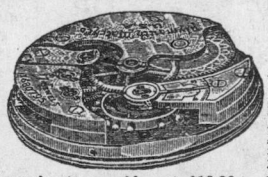

$11.90 For this movement fitted in the watch case you select. In this watch you have the acme of perfection. This watch is stem wind and pendant set, has 17 fine ruby jewels, and if you are looking for a watch that is an accurate timekeeper, positively the best 17 jeweled watch possible to manufacture, by all means select this movement. It is worth twice what we ask and retail merchants would get $18.00 to $20.00 for this watch and consider that they are selling a bargain. Seventeen ruby jewels we guarantee this watch to contain, each jewel in screw setting. Has full protecting dust band, bridges beautifully damaskeened, cut expansion balance, overstrung Breguet hairspring, full polished screw heads, safety pinions, fine white select dial; in fact, we know no piece or part that has been overlooked.

We have listed here a complete line of movements that we can fit in either one of the four cases that you select at the prices quoted.

Should you, after reading the descriptions of the cases and the movements, decide to order one of these watches, remember to include 12 cents extra for the mail charges, as we will then send it to you by registered mail, and if after you have examined the watch and you do not find it in every way as we have described it, both movement and case, and if you do not find it is the value such as we claim for it, or for any other criticisms that you may have you do not desire it, you can return it to us and we will at once upon its receipt refund your money, together with the mail charges both ways. Such an offer as this absolutely must assure you how sincere we are in the value we offer. We do not ask you to take our word; use your own judgment. Compare the watch after you receive it, with any friend's watch or any watch shown by any jeweler and prove to yourself our statements are true.

We fit any case shown on this page with the following 6-size movements. Prices quoted are for the complete watch, movement and case.

7 JEWELED EDGEMERE, special make	$6.28
COUNTESS JANET, stamped 17 jeweled, adjusted	6.60
7 Jeweled Elgin or Waltham, gilt plates	7.95
7 Jeweled Elgin or Waltham, nickel plates	8.47
15 Jeweled Elgin or Waltham, nickel plates	10.53
16 Jeweled Lady Waltham, nickel plates	12.15
17 JEWELED PLYMOUTH WATCH CO., nickel plates, patent regulator, special make	11.90

$6.28 REDUCED IN PRICE

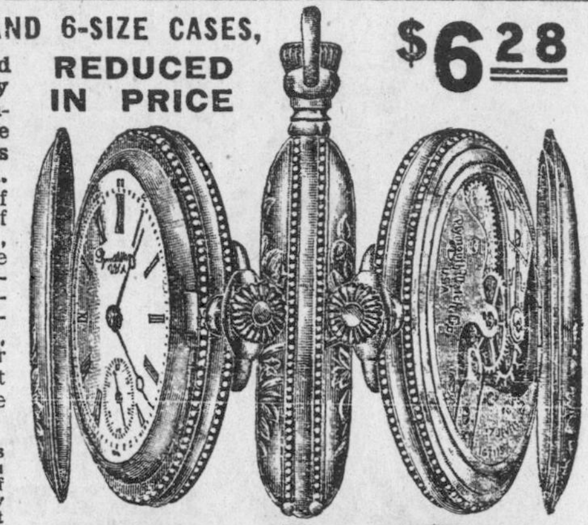

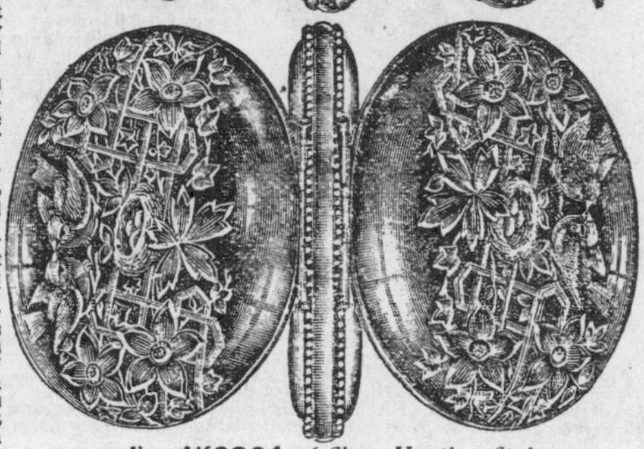

No. 4K2804 6-Size, Hunting Style.

This is our solid gold pattern bird design with ribbon engraved center effect, built after the Juergenson style. The center of the case is beaded. The top and bottom of the case are bright polished. Through the center runs a beautiful ribbon design with double bird engraving, making the design novel and unique.

For 90 cents extra we can furnish a fancy dial and gold hands on any watch on this page. See illustration on page 260.

REDUCED IN PRICE

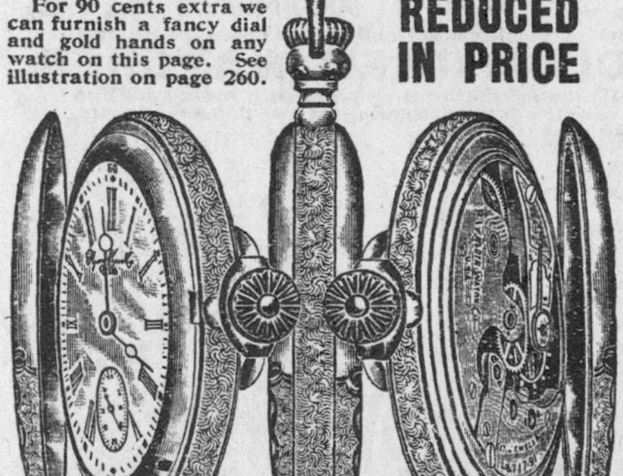

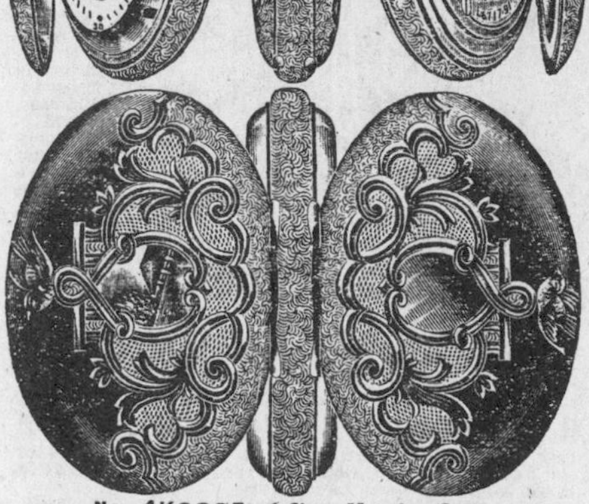

No. 4K2805 6-Size, Hunting Style.

This case is one of the Bassene style. The lids are so constructed that when closed no space or edge is seen between the lid and the center, just the same as solid gold cases are made. Note the engraving. This style is patterned after solid gold designs, floral half engraved. The bottom shows beautiful vermicelli work, the top being bright polished.

REDUCED IN PRICE

For 23 cents we furnish a beautiful Leatherette Presentation Case to fit any watch. No. 4K588 on page 261.

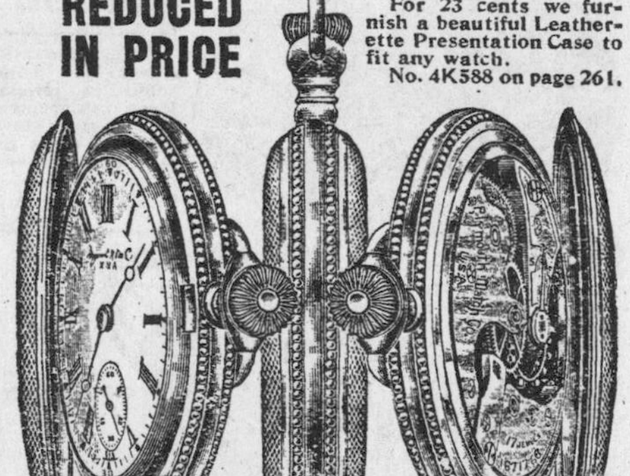

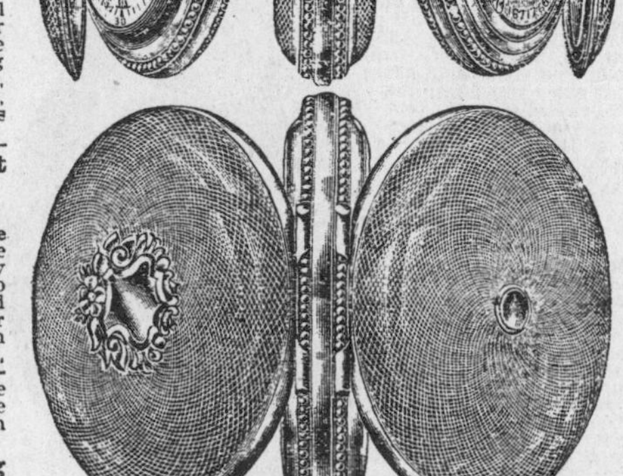

No. 4K2801 6-Size, Hunting Style.

This is our Juergenson engine turned, bright effect, solid gold pattern. Case selected with a view of pleasing those who wish a plain and simple case. This case never shows mars or scratches and can be worn a lifetime without obliterating. The design is as popular and up to date as it was 100 years ago, when it was brought out. It is considered one of the staple designs.

LADIES' 6-SIZE GOLD FILLED WATCHES

$6 65 GUARANTEED FOR 20 AND 25 YEARS $6 65
AND FOR THE TERM OF YOUR NATURAL LIFETIME

THREE GRADES OF GOLD FILLED CASES illustrated on this page, the 20 and 25-year guaranteed gold filled cases manufactured by the most representative makers in the United States, the Illinois Watch Case Co. and the John C. Dueber Watch Case Co. We protect every guarantee with our own written binding warrant, in other words, select one of these cases guaranteed for 20, 25 years or for life, and together with the manufacturer's guarantee, we send our own binding warrant giving you a double protection. **WHEN YOU SELECT A WATCH,** we advise you by all means, selecting the best. For a very little more money you can buy the Plymouth life guaranteed watch.

YOU WILL OBSERVE THAT WE SHOW AND DESCRIBE THE MOST REPRESENTATIVE MAKERS, JOHN C. DUEBER, THE ILLINOIS WATCH CASE CO., AND THE PLYMOUTH WATCH CASE CO. YOU CAN MAKE NO MISTAKE IN SELECTING ANY ONE OF THE THREE BRANDS.

WHAT WE MEAN BY THE LIFE GUARANTEE is simply this, that these cases are guaranteed to be gold filled, of the very highest quality and the nearest approach to solid gold cases manufactured, and that the solid gold sheets that cover them will wear for the period of your natural lifetime; should any one at any time wear down to the inner composition metal, and expose it in any place or part, you can return it to us and we will exchange the case for a brand new one, free of all charges. **IF YOU** desire expending a small sum of money, then select the Plymouth 20-year guaranteed case. We believe this the best value for your money as compared to any other 20-year gold filled case on the market.

LIFE GUARANTEE — $8 40 — $8 40 — LIFE GUARANTEE

No. 4K3100 PLYMOUTH. 14-Karat Gold Filled. Diagonal Engraving. Warranted for life. **No. 4K3102** Same make, but engine turned.

No. 4K3108 DUEBER. 14-Karat Gold Filled. Warranted 25 years. **No. 4K3109** Same make. Plain engine turned.

No. 4K3110 Illinois Watch Case Co. 14-Karat Gold Filled. Warranted 25 years. **No. 4K3112** Same make. Plain engine turned.

No. 4K3114 Illinois Watch Case Co. 14-Karat Gold Filled. Warranted 25 years. Set with genuine brilliant cut diamond. Raised ornamentation.

No. 4K3116 Illinois Watch Case Co. Warranted 25 years. Plain polished. Set with five genuine rose diamonds.

No. 4K3118 PLYMOUTH. 14-Karat Gold Filled. Full engraved. Warranted for life.

$6 65 AND UP — $6 65 AND UP

Illustrations on this page show exact size.

For 23c we furnish a beautiful leatherette presentation case to fit any watch. See No. 4K588 on page 261.

For 90 cents extra we can furnish fancy dial and gold hands on any watch on this page. For illustration see page 260.

25 cents will carry any watch to any part of the United States by express.

You will not be disappointed in the timekeeping qualities of the Plymouth Watch Co., U.S.A., Special Movement.

PLYMOUTH. No. 4K3120 10-K. Gold Filled, 20 years guaranteed.

PLYMOUTH. No. 4K3122 10-K. Gold Filled, 20 years guaranteed.

PLYMOUTH. No. 4K3124 10-K. Gold Filled, 20 years guaranteed.

ILLINOIS WATCH CASE CO. No. 4K3126 10-K. Gold Filled, 20 years guaranteed.

DUEBER. No. 4K3128 10-K. Gold Filled, 20 years guaranteed.

ILLINOIS WATCH CASE CO. No. 4K3130 10-K. Gold Filled, 20 years guaranteed.

LIFE GUARANTEE — LIFE GUARANTEE

No. 4K3132 PLYMOUTH. 14-Karat Gold Filled. Full Engraved. Warranted for life.

No. 4K3134 PLYMOUTH. 14-Karat Gold Filled. Warranted for life. Genuine diamond set. Plain polished.

WE FIT ABOVE CASES WITH THE FOLLOWING 6-SIZE MOVEMENTS. PRICES QUOTED ARE FOR THE COMPLETE WATCH, MOVEMENT AND CASE.	25-year Warrant. Nos. 4K3108 4K3109 4K3110 4K3112	Diamond Set, 25-year Warrant. No. 4K3116	Diamond Set, Ornamented, 25-year Warrant. No. 4K3114	Life Guarantee Nos. 4K3100 4K3102 4K3118 4K3132	Life Guarantee Diamond Set. No. 4K3134	20-year Warrant. Nos. 4K3120 4K3122 4K3124 4K3126 4K3128 4K3130
7 JEWELED EDGEMERE, special make	$ 7.40	$ 8.65	$15.15	$ 8.40	$11.40	$ 6.65
COUNTESS JANET, stamped 17 jewels, adjusted	7.60	8.85	15.35	8.60	11.60	6.85
7 Jeweled Elgin or Waltham, gilt plates	8.95	10.20	16.70	9.95	12.95	8.20
7 Jeweled Elgin or Waltham, nickel plates	9.47	10.72	17.22	10.47	13.47	8.72
15 Jeweled Elgin or Waltham, nickel plates	10.53	11.78	18.28	11.53	14.53	9.78
16 Jeweled Lady Waltham, nickel plates	13.15	14.40	20.90	14.15	17.15	12.40
17 JEWELED PLYMOUTH WATCH CO., nickel plates, patent regulator, special make	12.90	14.15	20.65	13.90	16.90	12.15

This is an illustration of our 6-Size Plymouth Watch Co. 17 Jeweled Movement. We guarantee this movement to give you absolute satisfaction. Fitted in the Plymouth case at $12.15 makes it a rare bargain.

Illustration of our 7 Jeweled, 6-Size Edgemere.

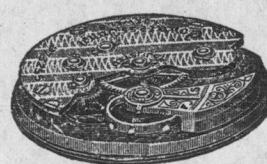

Illustration of the Countess Janet Movement.

LADIES' SMALL O-SIZE SOLID 14-KARAT GOLD WATCHES

$10.95 REDUCED IN PRICE

$12 FOR THIS SOLID GOLD, 14-KARAT, OPEN FACE, 80 EXTRA SMALL SIZE

REDUCED IN PRICE $17.45

LADIES' CHATELAINE WATCH

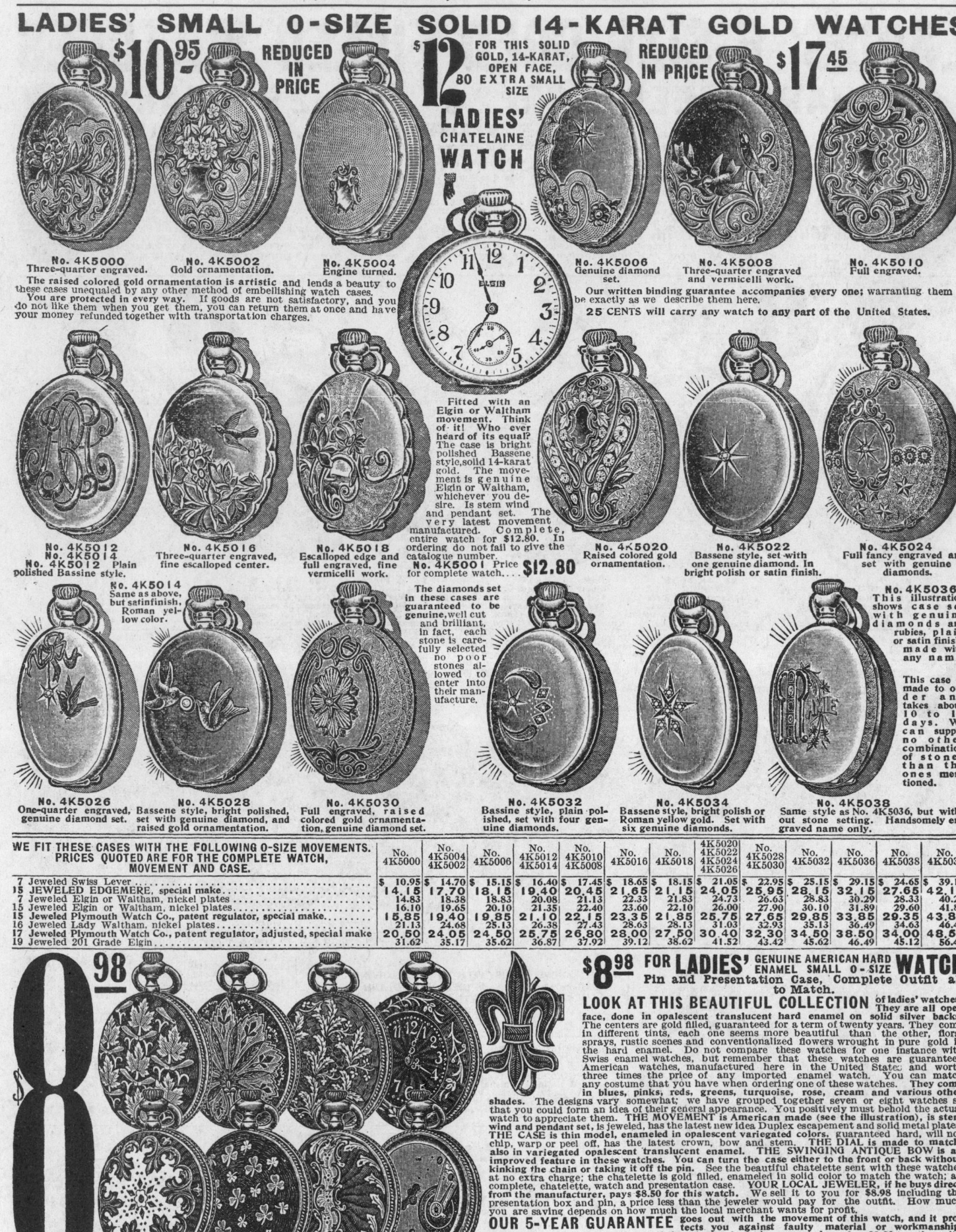

No. 4K5000 Three-quarter engraved.

No. 4K5002 Gold ornamentation.

No. 4K5004 Engine turned.

The raised colored gold ornamentation is artistic and lends a beauty to these cases unequaled by any other method of embellishing watch cases. You are protected in every way. If goods are not satisfactory, and you do not like them when you get them, you can return them at once and have your money refunded together with transportation charges.

No. 4K5006 Genuine diamond set.

No. 4K5008 Three-quarter engraved and vermicelli work.

No. 4K5010 Full engraved.

Our written binding guarantee accompanies every one; warranting them to be exactly as we describe them here.

25 CENTS will carry any watch to any part of the United States.

No. 4K5012
No. 4K5014
No. 4K5012 Plain polished Bassine style.
No. 4K5014 Same as above, but satin finish, Roman yellow color.

No. 4K5016 Three-quarter engraved, fine escalloped center.

No. 4K5018 Escalloped edge and full engraved, fine vermicelli work.

Fitted with an Elgin or Waltham movement. Think of it! Who ever heard of its equal? The case is bright polished Bassene style, solid 14-karat gold. The movement is genuine Elgin or Waltham, whichever you desire. Is stem wind and pendant set. The very latest movement manufactured. Complete, entire watch for $12.80. In ordering do not fail to give the catalogue number.
No. 4K5001 Price for complete watch.... **$12.80**

The diamonds set in these cases are guaranteed to be genuine, well cut and brilliant, in fact, each stone is carefully selected no poor stones allowed to enter into their manufacture.

No. 4K5020 Raised colored gold ornamentation.

No. 4K5022 Bassene style, set with one genuine diamond. In bright polish or satin finish.

No. 4K5024 Full fancy engraved and set with genuine diamonds.

No. 4K5036 This illustration shows case set with genuine diamonds and rubies, plain or satin finish, made with any name.

This case is made to order and takes about 10 to 12 days. We can supply no other combination of stones than the ones mentioned.

No. 4K5026 One-quarter engraved, genuine diamond set.

No. 4K5028 Bassene style, bright polished, set with genuine diamond, and raised gold ornamentation.

No. 4K5030 Full engraved, raised colored gold ornamentation, genuine diamond set.

No. 4K5032 Bassine style, plain polished, set with four genuine diamonds.

No. 4K5034 Bassene style, bright polish or Roman yellow color. Set with six genuine diamonds.

No. 4K5038 Same style as No. 4K5036, but without stone setting. Handsomely engraved name only.

WE FIT THESE CASES WITH THE FOLLOWING O-SIZE MOVEMENTS. PRICES QUOTED ARE FOR THE COMPLETE WATCH, MOVEMENT AND CASE.

	No. 4K5000 4K5002	No. 4K5004	No. 4K5006	No. 4K5012 4K5014	No. 4K5010 4K5008	No. 4K5016	No. 4K5018	No. 4K5020 4K5022 4K5024 4K5026	No. 4K5028 4K5030	No. 4K5032	No. 4K5036	No. 4K5038	No. 4K5034
7 Jeweled Swiss Lever	$ 10.95	$ 14.70	$ 15.15	$ 16.40	$ 17.45	$ 18.65	$ 18.15	$ 21.05	$ 22.95	$ 25.15	$ 29.15	$ 24.65	$ 39.15
15 JEWELED EDGEMERE, special make	14.15	17.70	18.15	19.40	20.45	21.65	21.15	24.05	25.95	28.15	32.15	27.65	42.15
7 Jeweled Elgin or Waltham, nickel plates	14.83	18.38	18.83	20.08	21.13	22.33	21.83	24.73	26.63	28.83	30.25	28.33	40.39
15 Jeweled Elgin or Waltham, nickel plates	16.10	19.65	19.95	21.35	22.40	23.60	22.15	26.00	27.90	30.10	31.89	29.60	41.59
15 Jeweled Plymouth Watch Co., patent regulator, special make	16.85	19.40	19.85	21.10	22.15	23.35	21.85	25.75	27.65	29.85	33.85	29.35	43.85
16 Jeweled Lady Waltham, nickel plates	21.13	24.68	25.13	26.38	27.43	28.63	28.13	31.03	32.93	35.13	36.49	34.63	46.49
17 Jeweled Plymouth Watch Co., patent regulator, adjusted, special make	20.50	24.05	24.50	25.75	26.80	28.00	27.50	30.40	32.30	34.50	38.50	34.00	48.50
19 Jeweled 201 Grade Elgin	31.62	35.17	35.62	36.87	37.92	39.12	38.62	41.52	43.42	45.62	46.49	45.12	56.49

$8.98

$8.98 FOR LADIES' GENUINE AMERICAN HARD ENAMEL SMALL O-SIZE WATCH Pin and Presentation Case, Complete Outfit all to Match.

LOOK AT THIS BEAUTIFUL COLLECTION of ladies' watches. They are all open face, done in opalescent translucent hard enamel on solid silver backs. The centers are gold filled, guaranteed for a term of twenty years. They come in different tints, each one seems more beautiful than the other, floral sprays, rustic scenes and conventionalized flowers wrought in pure gold in the hard enamel. Do not compare these watches for one instance with Swiss enamel watches, but remember that these watches are guaranteed American watches, manufactured here in the United States and worth three times the price of any imported enamel watch. You can match any costume that you have when ordering one of these watches. They come in blues, pinks, reds, greens, turquoise, rose, cream and various other shades. The designs vary somewhat; we have grouped together seven or eight watches so that you could form an idea of their general appearance. You positively must behold the actual watch to appreciate them. THE MOVEMENT is American made (see the illustration), is stem wind and pendant set, is jeweled, has the latest new idea Duplex escapement and solid metal plates. THE CASE is thin model, enameled in opalescent variegated colors, guaranteed hard, will not chip, warp or peel off, has the latest crown, bow and stem. THE DIAL is made to match, also in variegated opalescent translucent enamel. THE SWINGING ANTIQUE BOW is an improved feature in these watches. You can turn the case either to the front or back without kinking the chain or taking it off the pin. See the beautiful chatelette sent with these watches at no extra charge; the chatelette is gold filled, enameled in solid color to match the watch; all complete, chatelette, watch and presentation case. YOUR LOCAL JEWELER, if he buys direct from the manufacturer, pays $8.50 for this watch. We sell it to you for $8.98 including the presentation box and pin, a price less than the jeweler would pay for the outfit. How much you are saving depends on how much the local merchant wants for profit.

OUR 5-YEAR GUARANTEE goes out with the movement of this watch, and it protects you against faulty material or workmanship. Here is our offer to convince you if there is any doubt in your mind; send us $8.98 together with mail charges 14 cents, a total of $9.12, and we will send you the watch that we here describe. You can examine it, compare it with any watch of the same kind displayed in your local merchant's store at $12.00 to $15.00, and if we have not saved you from $4.00 to $6.00, return the watch and we will refund your money together with transportation charges. (In ordering, state the shade you desire.)

No. 4K4960 Price for complete outfit, watch, box and pin **$8.98**

19 C AND UP

REDUCED PRICES
GENTLEMEN'S VEST CHAINS

SOLID NICKEL, ROLLED GOLD PLATE, SOLID SILVER AND WHITE METAL. SOLDERED LINKS THROUGHOUT, EXCEPT WHERE OTHERWISE STATED.

OUR CHOICE OF ANY WATCH CHAIN ILLUSTRATED HERE FOR 19 CENTS AND UPWARD, ACCORDING TO MATERIAL, QUALITY, ETC.

NEVER BEFORE has such an astonishing offer on gentlemen's watch chains been offered. We wish to impress you particularly with the fact that every one of the chains quoted on this and the following pages is positively exactly as represented. All chains, unless otherwise stated, are 12 inches long. Each chain is complete as illustration shows with bar, swivel or catch and locket attachment, sometimes called the toggle chain. If by mail, postage on gentlemen's chains, 3 cents extra; registry, 8 cents extra.

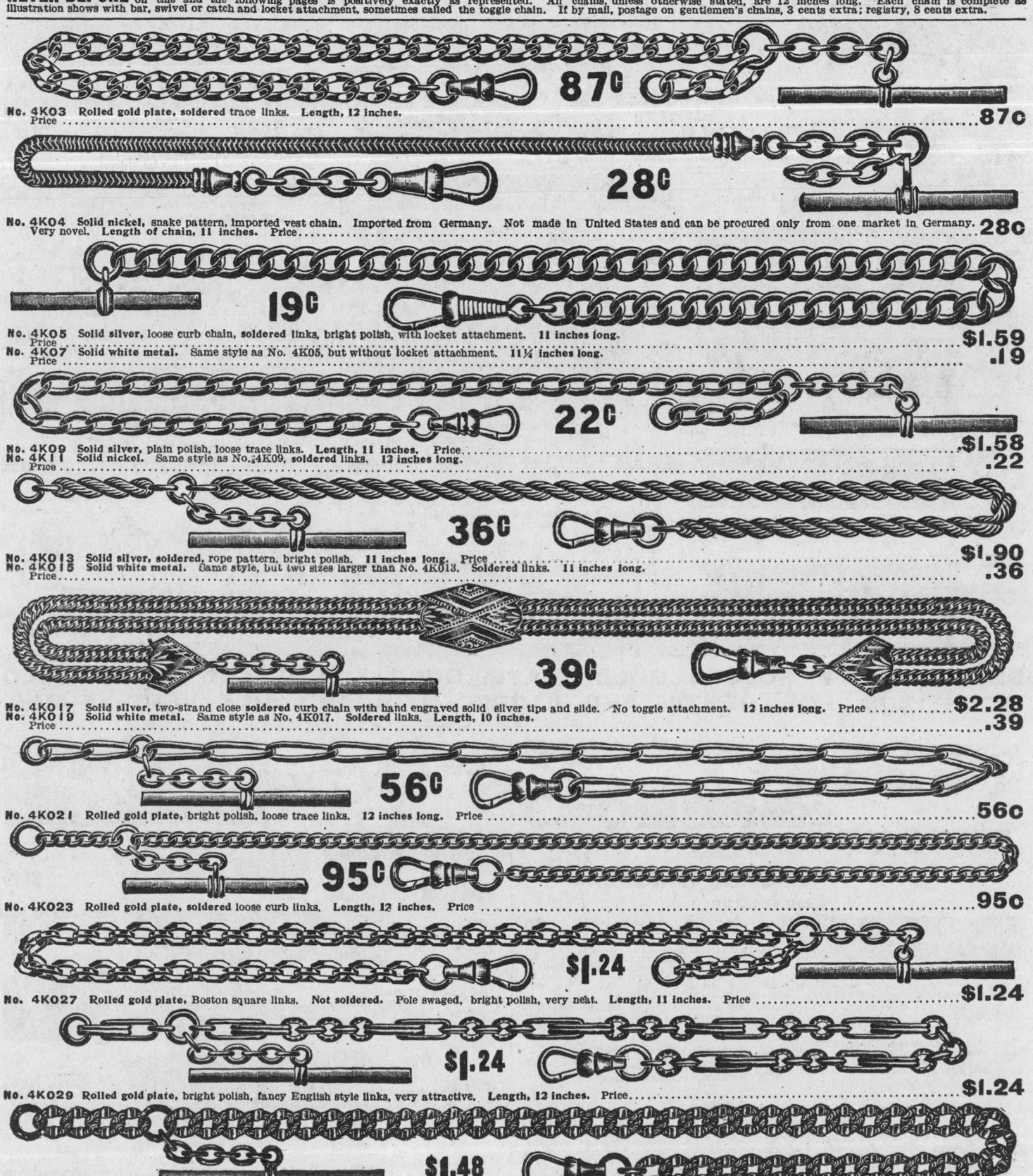

87c

No. 4K03   Rolled gold plate, soldered trace links.   Length, 12 inches.
Price ....**.87c**

28c

No. 4K04   Solid nickel, snake pattern, imported vest chain.   Imported from Germany.   Not made in United States and can be procured only from one market in Germany. Very novel.   Length of chain, 11 inches.   Price ....**.28c**

19c

No. 4K05   Solid silver, loose curb chain, soldered links, bright polish, with locket attachment.   11 inches long.
Price **$1.59**
No. 4K07   Solid white metal.   Same style as No. 4K05, but without locket attachment.   11¼ inches long.
Price ....**.19**

22c

No. 4K09   Solid silver, plain polish, loose trace links.   Length, 11 inches.   Price **$1.58**
No. 4K11   Solid nickel.   Same style as No. 4K09, soldered links.   12 inches long.
Price ....**.22**

36c

No. 4K013   Solid silver, soldered, rope pattern, bright polish.   11 inches long.   Price **$1.90**
No. 4K015   Solid white metal.   Same style, but two sizes larger than No. 4K013.   Soldered links.   11 inches long.
Price ....**.36**

39c

No. 4K017   Solid silver, two-strand close soldered curb chain with hand engraved solid silver tips and slide.   No toggle attachment.   12 inches long.   Price **$2.28**
No. 4K019   Solid white metal.   Same style as No. 4K017.   Soldered links.   Length, 10 inches.
Price ....**.39**

56c

No. 4K021   Rolled gold plate, bright polish, loose trace links.   12 inches long.   Price **56c**

95c

No. 4K023   Rolled gold plate, soldered loose curb links.   Length, 12 inches.   Price **95c**

$1.24

No. 4K027   Rolled gold plate, Boston square links.   Not soldered.   Pole swaged, bright polish, very neat.   Length, 11 inches.   Price **$1.24**

$1.24

No. 4K029   Rolled gold plate, bright polish, fancy English style links, very attractive.   Length, 12 inches.   Price **$1.24**

$1.48

No. 4K031   Rolled gold plate, engraved fancy links, bright polish, soldered.   Length, 12 inches.
Price **$1.48**

GENTLEMEN'S WATCH FOBS

Your choice of any fob on this page for 39 cents and upward according to design, size and quality. Nothing better manufactured, nothing more up to date, the choice specimens picked from thousands of designs. Most beautiful styles in nickel, silk, leather or woven wire effects that we show this season. If by mail, postage on gentlemen's fobs, 3 cents; registry, 8 cents extra.

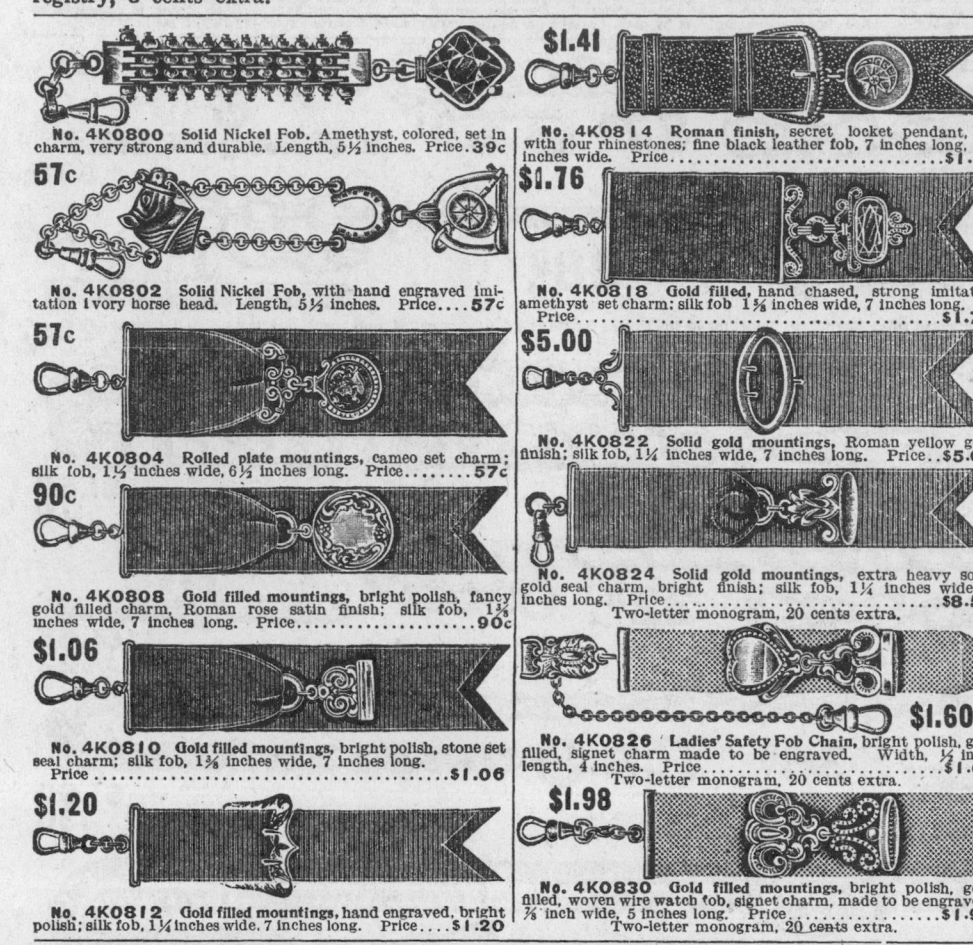

No. 4K0800 Solid Nickel Fob. Amethyst, colored, set in charm, very strong and durable. Length, 5½ inches. Price. 39c

57c

No. 4K0802 Solid Nickel Fob, with hand engraved imitation ivory horse head. Length, 5½ inches. Price.... 57c

57c

No. 4K0804 Rolled plate mountings, cameo set charm; silk fob, 1½ inches wide, 6½ inches long. Price........ 57c

90c

No. 4K0808 Gold filled mountings, bright polish, fancy gold filled charm, Roman rose satin finish; silk fob, 1⅜ inches wide, 7 inches long. Price.................... 90c

$1.06

No. 4K0810 Gold filled mountings, bright polish, stone set seal charm; silk fob, 1⅜ inches wide, 7 inches long. Price.. $1.06

$1.20

No. 4K0812 Gold filled mountings, hand engraved, bright polish; silk fob, 1¼ inches wide, 7 inches long. Price.... $1.20

$1.41

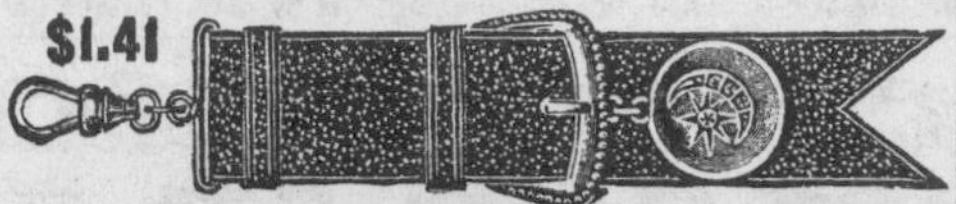

No. 4K0814 Roman finish, secret locket pendant, set with four rhinestones; fine black leather fob, 7 inches long, 1¼ inches wide. Price.. $1.41

$1.76

No. 4K0818 Gold filled, hand chased, strong imitation amethyst set charm; silk fob 1⅜ inches wide, 7 inches long. Price.. $1.76

$5.00

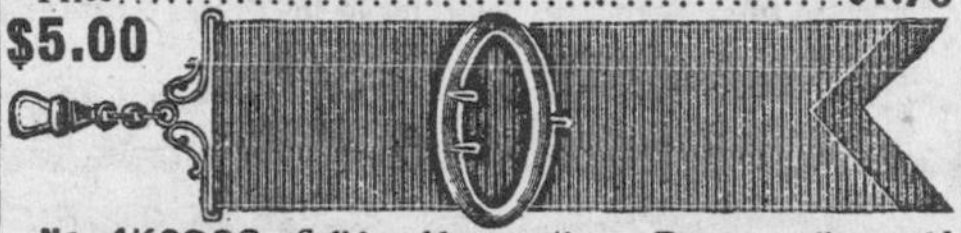

No. 4K0822 Solid gold mountings, Roman yellow gold finish; silk fob, 1¼ inches wide, 7 inches long. Price.. $5.00

No. 4K0824 Solid gold mountings, extra heavy solid gold seal charm, bright finish; silk fob, 1¼ inches wide, 7 inches long. Price.. $8.50
Two-letter monogram, 20 cents extra.

$1.60

No. 4K0826 Ladies' Safety Fob Chain, bright polish, gold filled, signet charm made to be engraved. Width, ½ inch; length, 4 inches. Price.. $1.60
Two-letter monogram, 20 cents extra.

$1.98

No. 4K0830 Gold filled mountings, bright polish, gold filled, woven wire watch fob, signet charm, made to be engraved; ⅞ inch wide, 5 inches long. Price.. $1.98
Two-letter monogram, 20 cents extra.

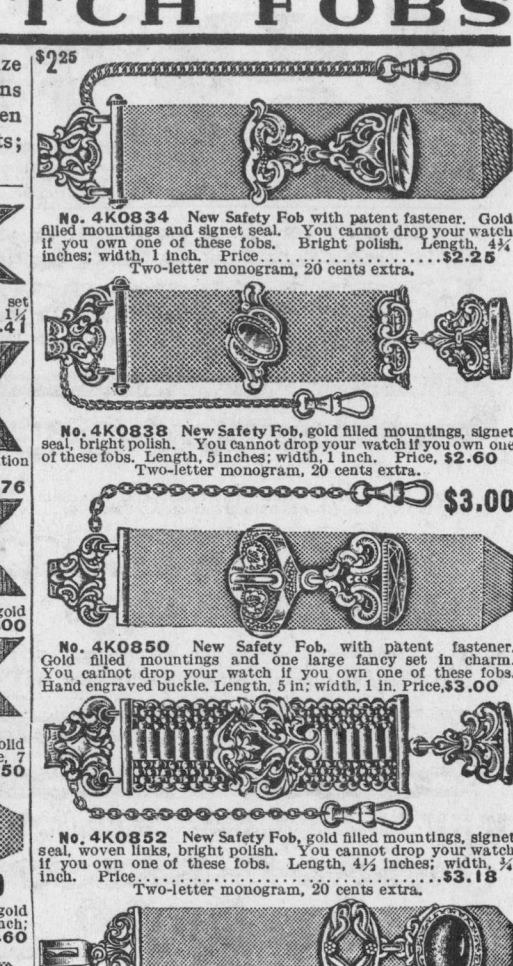

$2.25

No. 4K0834 New Safety Fob with patent fastener. Gold filled mountings and signet seal. You cannot drop your watch if you own one of these fobs. Bright polish. Length, 4¾ inches; width, 1 inch. Price.. $2.25
Two-letter monogram, 20 cents extra.

No. 4K0838 New Safety Fob, gold filled mountings, signet seal, bright polish. You cannot drop your watch if you own one of these fobs. Length, 5 inches; width, 1 inch. Price, $2.60
Two-letter monogram, 20 cents extra.

$3.00

No. 4K0850 New Safety Fob, with patent fastener. Gold filled mountings and one large fancy set in charm. You cannot drop your watch if you own one of these fobs. Hand engraved buckle. Length, 5 in; width, 1 in. Price, $3.00

No. 4K0852 New Safety Fob, gold filled mountings, signet seal, woven links, bright polish. You cannot drop your watch if you own one of these fobs. Length, 4½ inches; width, ¾ inch. Price.. $3.18
Two-letter monogram, 20 cents extra.

No. 4K0858 New Patent Safety Vest Pocket Fob. You cannot drop your watch if you own one of these fobs. Gold filled mountings, gold filled wire fob and bright polish flat signet charm made to engrave. Lgth., 4½ in; width, 1¼ in. Price,... $5.50
Two or three-letter monogram engraved, 20 cents extra.

BEST QUALITY ROLLED GOLD PLATE, GOLD FILLED AND SOLID GOLD MOUNTINGS, FOR GENTS' AND LADIES' HAIR AND SILK VEST CHAINS.

No. 4K0662 Gold filled, set with pearl and two garnets. Price, per set, including bar, toggle and swivel. 90c

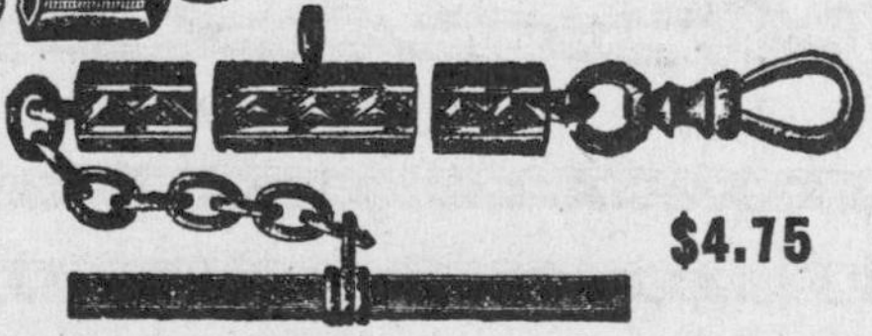

No. 4K0664 Fine solid gold. Price, per set, including bar, toggle and swivel.... $4.75

$4.75

HAIR CHAINS.

No. 4K0666 Hair Chain braided to order, like illustration. Price..... $1.00

Requires about 1½ ounces hair combings to braid a chain. Is made in two pieces, and together with mountings is 12½ inches long. We do not do this braiding ourselves. We send it out; therefore we cannot guarantee same hair being used that is sent us; you must assume all risk. When you send in your hair to be braided be sure to write us when you do so and put your name and address on package. No extra charge for mounting the hair chain when the mountings are purchased from us.

No. 4K0661 Same as above; two strands. For mounting see No. 4K0667. Price.. $1.50

No. 4K0784 Best quality, gold filled, fluted pattern, engraved. Price, per set, including, bar, toggle and swivel.................. 76c

$1.19

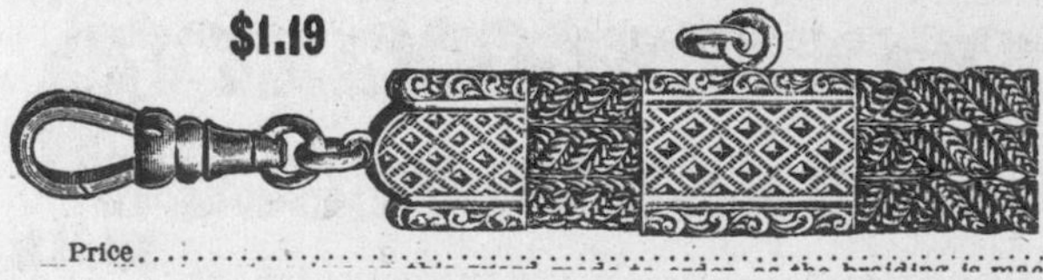

No. 4K0668 Fancy Woven Three - Strand Hair Vest Guard, 8½ inches long with very fancy rolled gold plate tips, slide bar and swivel. Price.. $1.19

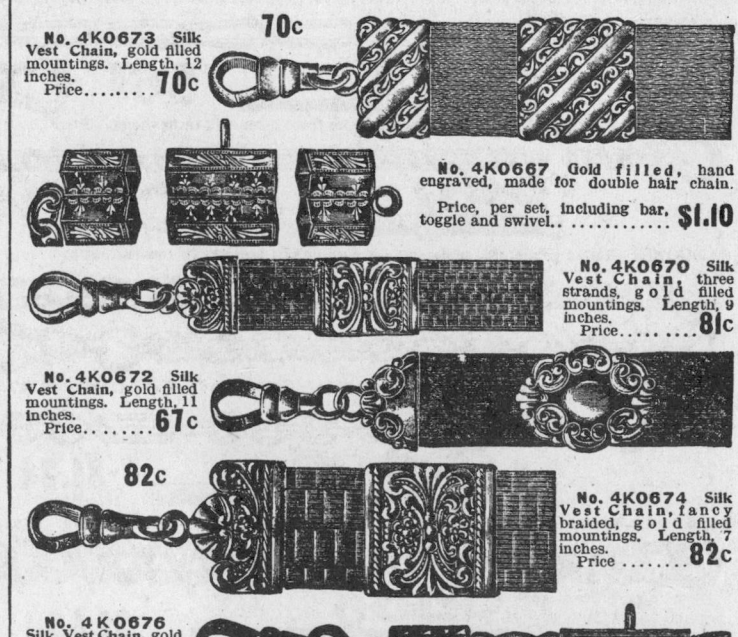

No. 4K0673 Silk Vest Chain, gold filled mountings. Length, 12 inches. Price......... 70c

70c

No. 4K0667 Gold filled, hand engraved, made for double hair chain.

Price, per set, including bar, toggle and swivel.. .... $1.10

No. 4K0670 Silk Vest Chain, three strands, gold filled mountings. Length, 9 inches. Price.......... 81c

No. 4K0672 Silk Vest Chain, gold filled mountings. Length, 11 inches. Price......... 67c

82c

No. 4K0674 Silk Vest Chain, fancy braided, gold filled mountings. Length, 7 inches. Price 82c

No. 4K0676 Silk Vest Chain, gold filled mountings. Length, 9 inches. Price. $1.20

SEE OUR NEW PRICES ON GENTLEMEN'S 10 AND 14-KARAT SOLID GOLD CHAINS

YOU CAN WEAR any one of these Solid Gold Chains for your natural lifetime and keep it in the family forever. If by mail, postage extra, 3 cents; 8 cents extra for registered or insured mail.

THE PRICES on Gentlemen's Vest Chains vary on account of the weight of gold in them. The lighter the chain the less it costs, although the cheapest chain shown is strong enough to protect any watch.

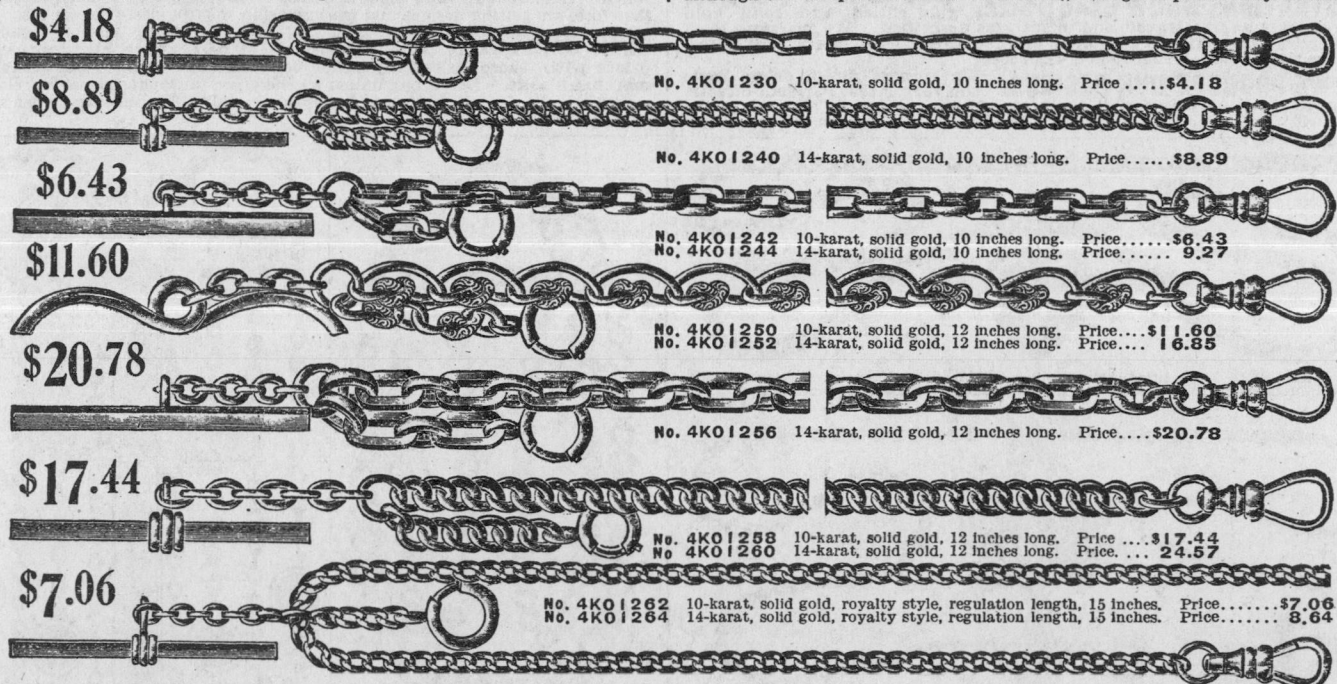

$4.18 No. 4K01230 10-karat, solid gold, 10 inches long. Price.....$4.18

$8.89 No. 4K01240 14-karat, solid gold, 10 inches long. Price......$8.89

$6.43 No. 4K01242 10-karat, solid gold, 10 inches long. Price......$6.43
No. 4K01244 14-karat, solid gold, 10 inches long. Price...... 9.27

$11.60 No. 4K01250 10-karat, solid gold, 12 inches long. Price...$11.60
No. 4K01252 14-karat, solid gold, 12 inches long. Price... 16.85

$20.78 No. 4K01256 14-karat, solid gold, 12 inches long. Price....$20.78

$17.44 No. 4K01258 10-karat, solid gold, 12 inches long. Price ...$17.44
No. 4K01260 14-karat, solid gold, 12 inches long. Price... 24.57

$7.06 No. 4K01262 10-karat, solid gold, royalty style, regulation length, 15 inches. Price......$7.06
No. 4K01264 14-karat, solid gold, royalty style, regulation length, 15 inches. Price...... 8.64

BEST QUALITY LADIES', MISSES' AND CHILDREN'S NECK CHAINS in solid gold, gold filled and amber. We war-

rant each one to be exactly as illustrated and described and satisfaction guaranteed in every instance unless otherwise stated. Stones used on this page are the finest imitations, the same as is generally used in high grade jewelry. If by mail, postage on neck chains 3 cents extra; 8 cents extra for registered mail.

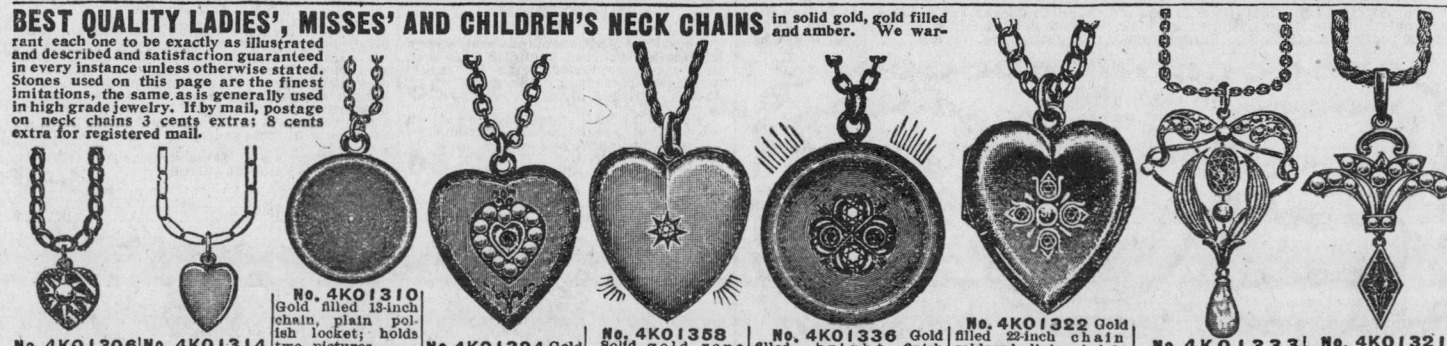

No. 4K01306 Gold filled 13-inch chain, fancy heart pendant, set with genuine opal. Price...$1.52

No. 4K01314 Solid gold 13-inch chain, Roman finish, fancy links. Price...$1.90

No. 4K01310 Gold filled 13-inch chain, plain polish locket; holds two pictures. Price.....$1.68
No. 4H01312 Same as No. 4K01310. Solid gold. Price...$5.95

No. 4K01324 Gold filled 13-inch chain, satin finish, locket holds two pictures, set with pearls and ruby. Each..$1.78

No. 4K01358 Solid gold rope chain, 18 inches long, Roman satin finish heart charm, set with genuine cut diamond. Price.......$6.00

No. 4K01336 Gold filled, bright finish chain, 22 inches, soldered links, satin finish, locket holds two pictures, set with two rhinestones and two rubies. Each.$2.24

No. 4K01322 Gold filled 22-inch chain soldered links, bright polish, heart shaped locket, to hold two pictures, set with one genuine opal and four ruby doublets. Price.$2.14

No. 4K01333 Solid gold, 14-inch neck chain with fancy pendant, set with genuine pearls and one ruby doublet. Price......$5.50

No. 4K01321 Solid gold soldered links, 18-inch rope chain, pendant set with fine blue stone and pearls. Price..$6.75

$1.75 No. 4K01342 Gold filled, bright polish, new festoon necklace, set with pearls and turquoise. Length, 13 inches. Price........$1.75

No. 4K04005 Neck Chain Locket. Bright polish, gold front, hand engraved, holds two pictures. Price......48c

$8.80 No. 4K01344 Solid gold, new festoon necklace, pendant hard enameled, set with genuine pearls and one emerald doublet. Length, 14 inches. Price...$8.80

No. 4K04009 Neck Chain Locket. Gold front, bright polish, hand engraved, rhinestone set, holds two pictures. Price.............56c

No. 4K01390 Solid gold, 13-inch soldered rope chain, no pendant. Price....$2.46
No. 4K01392 Same style as No. 4K01390, 22-inch. Price...$4.04

No. 4K01394 Gold filled, 22-inch soldered rope chain, no pendant. Price....$2.05
No. 4K01396 Same style as No. 4K01394, solid gold. Price...$5.00

No. 4K01348 First Quality Genuine Amber Bead Necklace. Beads with hand cut facets, strung on linen cord with screw clasp. Length, 12 inches. Price 95c
No. 4K01350 First Quality Genuine Amber Bead Necklace. Same style as No. 4H01348, 14 inches long. Price $1.14
No. 4K01352 First Quality Genuine Amber Bead Necklace. Hand cut facets. Same style as No. 4K01348, but 15 to 16 inches long. Price $1.34
It is said by some that genuine amber beads prevent croup and other throat troubles in children.

$2.36 No. 4K01346 Solid gold, 13-inch, Roman finish, soldered trace links, three heart pendants, each set with turquoise. This chain is particularly adapted for babies and children. Price........$2.36

No. 4K01406 Gold filled, 22-inch chain, no pendant. Price ...$1.44
No. 4K01408 Same style as No. 4K01406, solid gold. Price....$4.98

$2.14 No. 4K01376 Gold filled, 14-karat, finest bead necklace; bright polish. Same size bead as illustration shows. This is the regulation, up to date, popular size. Length, 13 inches. Price..................................$2.14
No. 4K01378 Solid gold, 14-karat, warranted bead necklace; Roman yellow satin finish. Size slightly smaller than illustration shows. Length, 14 inches. Price....$5.98

No. 4K01379 Same style as No. 4K01378, but bright polish. Price....$5.98
No. 4K01380 Gold filled, 14-karat, bright polish bead necklace. One size larger than illustration shows as No. 4K01376. Length, 13½ inches. Price....$2.48
No. 4K01382 Solid Gold 14-karat Bead Necklace, satin Roman finish, same style and size exactly as No. 4K01380. Length, 14 inches. Price....$11.50

THE ABOVE NECK CHAINS, both the solid gold and the gold filled, are of the 14-karat stock. We can guarantee them not to discolor or tarnish the neck. Any quality less than this is bound to do so. Exceptions to the rule: It sometimes happens that through the use of certain drugs, such as sulphur, etc., where there is much salt in the perspiration, the neck chain will discolor the neck, whether it is solid gold, 14-karat or absolutely 18-karat gold. The highest grade of the gold will make little or no difference in this condition.

HIGHEST QUALITY NECK CHAINS

ILLUSTRATIONS SHOW EXACT SIZE. Made in rolled gold plate, gold filled and solid gold stock, exactly as illustrated and exactly as described. We guarantee them to give entire satisfaction. The latest Parisian effects. We particularly direct your attention to Nos. 4K01316 and 4K01364.

HOW WE PROCURE OUR DESIGNS. We import direct from Paris the very latest Parisian effects. These new designs are sent to the factory with instructions to duplicate them and to create an article at a price which invariably represents half the cost of the imported article. You really, therefore, are getting designs and workmanship worth twice what we ask.

READ CAREFULLY THE DESCRIPTIONS, note the designs and, above all, compare our prices with those asked by other concerns and what your local retail merchant asks. Don't buy unless we show you a wonderful saving either in money or value. Mail charges on ladies' neck chains, 3 cents extra; 8 cents extra for registered or insured mail.

No. 4K01300 Gold filled, bright polish, soldered neck chain. 14 inches long. Gold filled, bright polished enamel turquoise set locket attached; holds two pictures. Price... **$1.28**

No. 4K01316 Gold filled, bright polish, gold soldered cable links. 13-inch chain. Pendant is beautiful Roman yellow rose color. Set with fine brilliant rhinestones, genuine pearls and amethyst. Parisian effect, very attractive. Price... **$2.25**

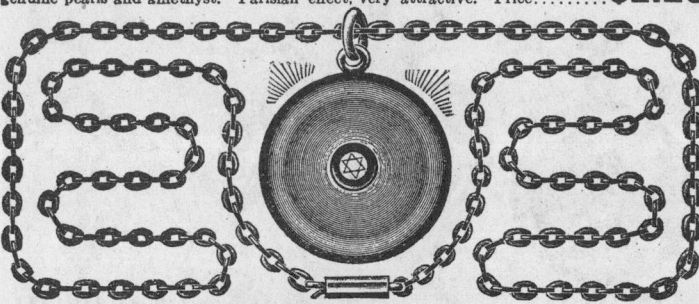

No. 4K01328 Gold filled, guaranteed, bright polish, gold soldered, fancy gnarled cable links. 22-inch chain. Locket gold filled, bright polish, set with fine brilliant rhinestone; holds two pictures. Price... **$2.28**
No. 4K01330 Same style as No. 4K01328. Bright polished locket, without stone setting. Price... **2.08**

No. 4K01332 Gold filled, bright polish, gold soldered, square Boston links. 22 inches long. Locket holds two pictures; is satin finish, set with fine brilliant rhinestones and genuine opal. Price... **$2.62**

No. 4K01334 Gold filled, bright polish, gold soldered, square Boston links. 22 inches long. Locket holds two pictures; is satin finish, set with fine brilliant rhinestones and genuine opal. Price... **$2.98**

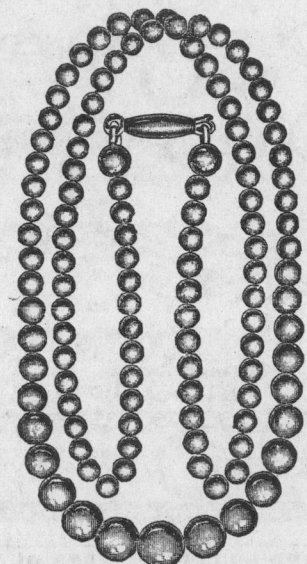

No. 4K01337 Genuine Coral, strung on fine linen thread, complete with snap and catch, graduated beads for ladies' wear; length of chain, 18 inches. Price... **$3.25**

No. 4K01335 Same style as shown above, but smaller beads, particularly adapted for infants and misses up to 16 years of age; length of chain, 18 inches. Price... **$2.50**

No. 4K01364 Gold filled, gold soldered, bright polish, fancy chased, lapped cable links, set with amethysts. Length, 22 inches. Cross gold filled, Roman yellow satin finish, hand engraved and bright cut. Set with amethyst doublets. Length of cross, 2½ inches. This is one of the most attractive and biggest values ever offered in a complete outfit of fancy stone set necklace with cross pendant. Price... **$3.48**

No. 4K01366 Same style as No. 4K01364, but set with imitation rubies. Price... **3.48**

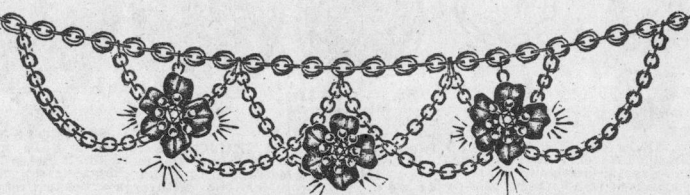

No. 4K01339 Ladies' gold filled soldered link festoon necklace, 16 inches long, bright polished chain with three fancy pendants, each pendant set with fine imitation diamonds. Price... **$2.45**

No. 4K01360 Solid gold, bright polish, soldered neck chain, with heart charm. Roman satin finish, set with one genuine cut diamond. Length of chain, 13 inches. Price... **$3.75**

No. 4K01398 Gold filled, bright polish, gold soldered, neck chain. 22 inches long. No pendant. Patent octagon snap. Price... **$1.12**
No. 4K01400 Same style as No. 4K01398, but in solid gold, bright polish. Very light weight, nearly invisible. Price... **2.30**
No. 4K01401 Same style as No. 4K01398, but in solid gold, same weight and size and finish. Price... **4.68**

LADIES' GUARD OR LORGNETTE CHAINS
MADE OF THE BEST ROLLED GOLD PLATE, GOLD FILLED STOCK.

ALL CHAINS ILLUSTRATED ON THIS PAGE ARE EXACTLY AS DESCRIBED. FULL REGULATION LENGTH, 48 INCHES.

WE TAKE PARTICULAR PRIDE IN OUR SELECTION OF LADIES' GUARD CHAINS. Each one has been tried and tested — the most reliable manufacturer in the United States is represented in this line. Your choice of any lorgnette chain on this page according to style and quality for 16 cents to $3.98. Please remember that our chains are all guaranteed to give absolute satisfaction, that we guarantee them to be made of the best rolled gold plate and gold filled stock that money can buy. All of these chains are complete as in illustration of Nos. 4K0964. Postage on ladies' guard chain, 4 cents; 8 cents extra for registered mail. Unless otherwise stated, the stones used in the various settings on this page are the finest imitations, the same as is generally used in high grade jewelry.

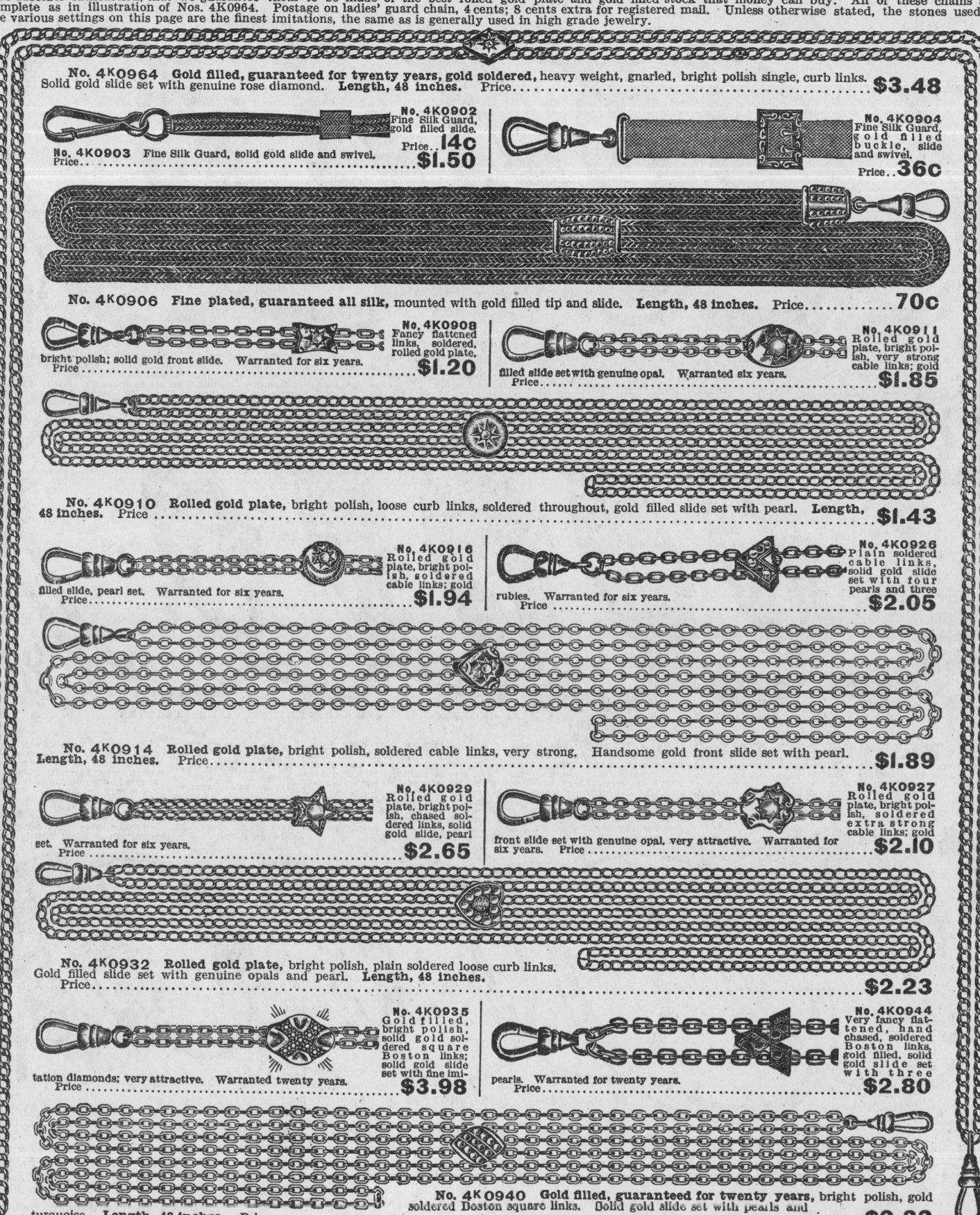

No. 4K0964 Gold filled, guaranteed for twenty years, gold soldered, heavy weight, gnarled, bright polish single, curb links. Solid gold slide set with genuine rose diamond. **Length, 48 inches. Price**................**$3.48**

No. 4K0902 Fine Silk Guard, gold filled slide. **Price**..**14c**

No. 4K0903 Fine Silk Guard, solid gold slide and swivel. **Price**..**$1.50**

No. 4K0904 Fine Silk Guard, gold filled buckle, slide and swivel. **Price**..**36c**

No. 4K0906 Fine plated, guaranteed all silk, mounted with gold filled tip and slide. **Length, 48 inches. Price**............**70c**

No. 4K0908 Fancy flattened links, soldered, rolled gold plate, bright polish; solid gold front slide. **Warranted for six years. Price**...........**$1.20**

No. 4K0911 Rolled gold plate, bright polish, very strong cable links; gold filled slide set with genuine opal. **Warranted six years. Price**........**$1.85**

No. 4K0910 Rolled gold plate, bright polish, loose curb links, soldered throughout, gold filled slide set with pearl. **Length, 48 inches. Price**..................**$1.43**

No. 4K0916 Rolled gold plate, bright polish, soldered cable links; gold filled slide, pearl set. **Warranted for six years. Price**..................**$1.94**

No. 4K0926 Plain soldered cable links, solid gold slide set with four pearls and three rubies. **Warranted for six years. Price**..................**$2.05**

No. 4K0914 Rolled gold plate, bright polish, soldered cable links, very strong. Handsome gold front slide set with pearl. **Length, 48 inches. Price**..................**$1.89**

No. 4K0929 Rolled gold plate, bright polish, chased soldered links, solid gold slide, pearl set. **Warranted for six years. Price**..................**$2.65**

No. 4K0927 Rolled gold plate, bright polish, soldered extra strong cable links; gold front slide set with genuine opal, very attractive. **Warranted for six years. Price**..................**$2.10**

No. 4K0932 Rolled gold plate, bright polish, plain soldered loose curb links. Gold filled slide set with genuine opals and pearl. **Length, 48 inches. Price**..................**$2.23**

No. 4K0935 Gold filled, bright polish, solid gold soldered square Boston links; solid gold slide set with fine imitation diamonds; very attractive. **Warranted twenty years. Price**..................**$3.98**

No. 4K0944 Very fancy flattened, hand chased, soldered Boston links, gold filled, solid gold slide set with three pearls. **Warranted for twenty years. Price**..................**$2.80**

No. 4K0940 Gold filled, guaranteed for twenty years, bright polish, gold soldered Boston square links. Solid gold slide set with pearls and turquoise. **Length, 48 inches. Price**..................**$2.32**

LADIES', MISSES' AND CHILDREN'S GOLD FILLED AND SOLID GOLD NETHERSOLE BRACELETS

GUARANTEED TO GIVE ENTIRE SATISFACTION. THE ILLUSTRATIONS SHOW EXACT SIZES

EACH BRACELET is fully described as to size, finish, stone setting, etc. We are particularly proud of this very complete line of bracelets, selected from hundreds of patterns, made by the most representative and dependable manufacturers in the United States. Each one was selected with a view of procuring the best bracelet of this type for the money. Bracelets not as good in quality, not as fine finished, not so up to date are selling at double the prices we are quoting. All joints, all seams, all stone setting, engraving, etc., the finest that workmen can do. The tubing from which these bracelets are made is the exact size as illustrations show, although the diameter of the bracelet is slightly larger than what the illustrations would convey. Today bracelets are the latest fashion. No costume complete without a bracelet, so thoroughly has this new jewelry been adopted.

If by mail, postage on bracelets, 4 cents extra; insurance or registry, 8 cents extra.

EVERY ONE OF THESE BRACELETS COMES FITTED IN A FINE LINED, ENAMELED TOP CASE OR IN A FINE SATINY FINISHED CANTON FLANNEL BAG, MADE ESPECIALLY TO HOLD THE BRACELET.

$2⁴⁸   **$1³⁸**

No. 4K07701   No. 4K07703   No. 4K07705   No. 4K07707   No. 4K07709   No. 4K07711

No. 4K07701 Gold filled, plain polish, jointed bracelet. Oval tubing. 2½ inches in diameter. Each..$2.48

No. 4K07703 Gold filled, bright polish, engraved and hand chased jointed bracelet. Oval tubing. 2½ inches in diameter. Each....$2.85

No. 4K07705 Gold filled, bright polish, jointed bracelet. Large oval tubing. 2½ inches in diameter. Price, each........$2.80

No.4K07707 Gold filled, bright polish, engraved and hand chased jointed bracelet. Large oval tubing. 2½ inches in diameter. Each..$2.90

No. 4K07709 Gold filled, bright polish, engraved and hand chased jointed bracelet. 2½ inches in diameter. Medium size oval tubing, set with three fine imitation diamonds. $3.18

No.4K07711 Gold filled, Roman polish, patent spring, jointed bracelet with signet top. Round tubing, 2½ inches in diameter. Each..$1.38
Two or three-letter monogram, engraved, 20 cents extra.

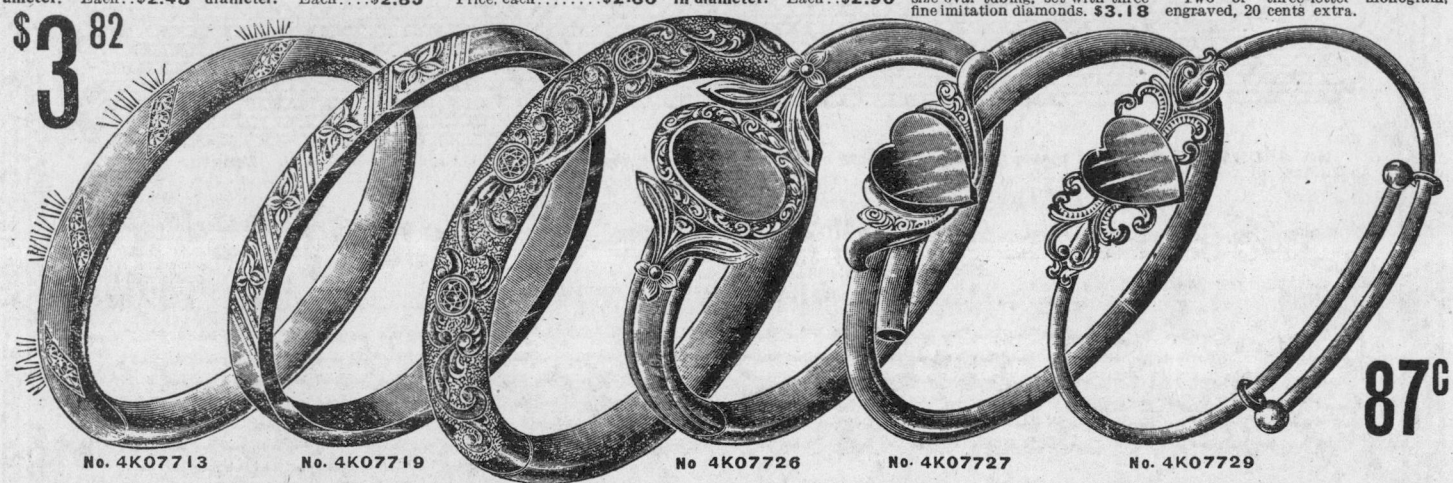

$3⁸²   **87c**

No. 4K07713   No. 4K07719   No 4K07726   No. 4K07727   No. 4K07729

No. 4K07713 Gold filled, bright polish, patent pull-out spring bracelet. Oval tubing. 2½ inches in diameter. Set with fine brilliant rhinestones. It is a very artistic and fine bracelet. We can recommend it. Price, each $3.82

No. 4K07719 Gold filled, bright polish, jointed bracelet. Square tubing, hand engraved; exact copy of solid gold. New this season. 2½ inches in diameter. Ea. $3.45

No. 4K07720 Gold filled, bright polish, hand engraved and hand chased finish, highest possible grade jointed Nethersole bracelet. Large size oval tubing. 2½ inches in diameter. Set with three amethysts; most artistic bracelet illustrated on this page. We can especially recommend this bracelet. Each $4.25

No. 4K07726 Gold filled, bright finish, signet top, patent pullout spring bracelet. It is one of the most artistic bracelets we show, manufactured by positively the best bracelet maker in the United States. We especially recommend this one to those who desire a most artistic effect. Diameter, 2½ inches. Each, $4.25
Two or three-letter monogram, engraved, 20 cents extra.

No. 4K07727 Gold filled, bright polish, round tube bracelet. Signet top. 2½ inches in diameter.

Price, each...$1.49

Two or three-letter monogram, engraved, 20 cents extra.

No. 4K07729 Rolled gold plate, Roman yellow ornamentation, with signet top, bright polish spring bracelet. Especially adapted for young ladies or misses. 2½ inches in diameter, but can be made to fit smaller wrists.

Price, each.........87c

Two or three-letter monogram, engraved, 20 cents extra.

$1⁰⁶   **$1⁶⁰**

No. 4K07733   No 4K07739   No. 4K07741   No. 4K07743 / No. 4K07745   No. 4K07747   No. 4K07749

No. 4K07733 Rolled gold plate, bright polish and yellow satin finish young ladies' or misses' bracelet, set with two fancy doublets. Will fit young ladies from 15 to 25 years of age; can be adjusted to the different size wrists. Each, $1.06
Two or three-letter monogram, engraved, 20 cents extra.

No. 4K07735 Solid gold, jointed, oval tubing bracelet, bright polish or yellow satin finish, according to choice. Be sure to state in your order without fail whether you desire bright polish or Roman yellow satin finish style. 2½ inches in diameter.
Price, each........$6.98

No. 4K07739 Solid gold, bright polish child's bracelet; fits any child from 3½ to 7 years of age. Set with finest enamel turquoise. One of the daintiest and prettiest bracelets shown this year. 1¾ inches in diameter.
Price, each....$4.60

No. 4K07741 Solid gold, Roman yellow satin finish signet bracelet. Especially made for children from 3 to 7½ years of age. 1¾ inches in diameter.
Price, each..$3.60
Two or three-letter monogram, engraved, 20 cents extra.

No. 4K07743 Gold filled, bright polish, engraved and hand chased babies' jointed bracelet. 1¾ inches in diameter. Will fit infants up to 3½ years of age.
Price, each $1.10
No 4K07745 Same style, size and shape as No. 4K07743, but plain polish, with no engraving or chasing.
Price, each............85c

No. 4K07747 Rolled gold plate, bright finish, signet, spring bracelet, for children from 3½ to 7½ years of age. 1¾ inches in diameter.
Price, each......78c
Two or three-letter monogram, engraved, 15 cents extra.

No. 4K07749 Infants' rolled gold plate automatic adjustable bracelet. Fits an infant from one to four years of age.
Each..$1.60

ROLLED GOLD PLATE AND GOLD FILLED PATENT SPRING AND JOINTED BRACELETS.

that you will be more than pleased with the artistic appearance and fine wearing qualities of our bracelets Prices smashed. Your choice of any bracelet on this page for $1.65 and upward. Postage on bracelets, 4 cents; if by registered mail, 8 cents extra.

Will fit any wrist. The latest and most sensational on the market. Quality positively warranted. We know

$1⁹⁵⁵

No. 4K07751 Gold Filled Child's Bracelet, bright polish and Roman finish, non-complicated spring bracelet. Child's size, fits any child from 3½ to 7 years of age. 7-16 of an inch wide. Price, each........$1.65

No. 4K07753 Gold Filled, bright polish and Roman finish flexible spring bracelet. Fits any wrist. Simply constructed. 7-16 of an inch wide. Price, each........$2.00

No. 4K07755 Gold Filled, bright polish, engraved, flexible spring bracelet. Fits any wrist. Massive and attractive. Simply constructed and cannot get out of order. 7-16 of an inch wide. Price, each........$2.10

No. 4K07759 Gold Filled, bright polish, non-complicated signet center spring bracelet. Fits any wrist. Massive and attractive. 7-16 of an inch wide. Two or three-letter monogram, extra, 25 cents. Price, each, $2.65

No. 4K07769 Gold Filled, bright polish, rose yellow finish, adjustable spring bracelet fits any wrist, is set with fancy amethyst doublets. This is one of the latest bracelets on the market. Price, each........$2.50

No. 4K07766 Ladies' Reversible Flexible Double Stone Set Rolled Gold Plated Bracelet, 3½ inches in diameter, opens with a clasp, different from any other bracelet on the market. You cannot blacken your arm in hot weather using this bracelet. The inside, as illustration shows, is set with mother of pearl. Stone set shown on the outside is, according to taste, either fancy red, green or amethyst colored. Be sure to mention color you desire when ordering. Each bracelet comes in a handsome cloth lined box. Each..$1.90

$2⁸⁵

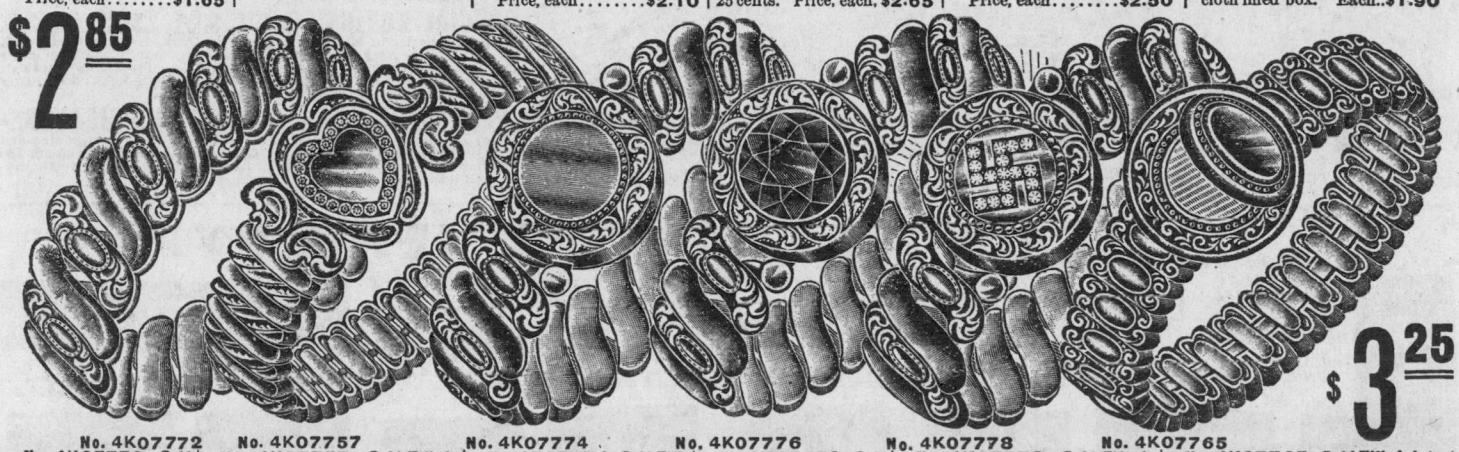

$3²⁵

No. 4K07772 Gold Filled, patent adjustable spring bracelet, bright polish. Fits any wrist. Cannot get out of order. Price, each....$2.85

No. 4K07757 Gold Filled, bright polish and Roman finish, signet center, adjustable spring bracelet. Fits any wrist. Cannot get out of order. Each..$2.85 Two or three-letter monogram engraved, 25 cents extra.

No. 4K07774 Gold Filled, bright polish, signet center, adjustable spring bracelet. Fits any wrist. Cannot get out of order. Each..$3.25 Two or three-letter monogram, 25 cents extra.

No. 4K07776 Gold Filled, bright polish, adjustable spring bracelet. Cannot get out of order. Fits any wrist. Set with large fancy red stones. Price, each....$3.00

No. 4K07778 Gold Filled, latest idea patent adjustable spring bracelet, bright polish. Set with imitation diamonds with Swastika emblem, supposed to bring good luck. Fits any wrist. Price, each..........$4.25

No. 4K07765 Gold Filled, latest fad, patent adjustable flexible spring bracelet, bright polish. Roman finish, with patent signet locket top to hold picture. Fits any wrist. Each, $3.25 Two or three-letter monogram, 25 cents extra.

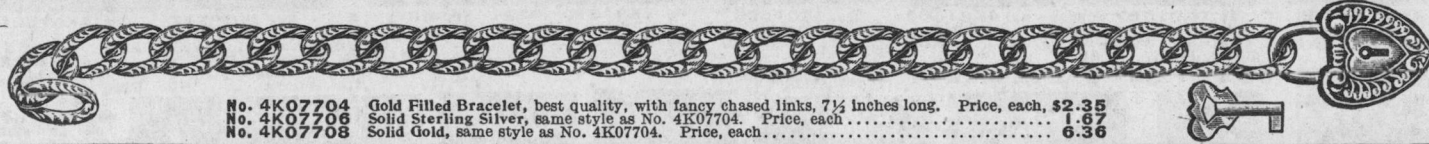

No. 4K07704 Gold Filled Bracelet, best quality, with fancy chased links, 7½ inches long. Price, each, $2.35
No. 4K07706 Solid Sterling Silver, same style as No. 4K07704. Price, each........................1.67
No. 4K07708 Solid Gold, same style as No. 4K07704. Price, each................................6.36

LADIES' HIGH GRADE BACK COMBS.

IF BY MAIL, POSTAGE EXTRA, 3 CENTS; REGISTRY, 8 CENTS EXTRA.

FOR CHEAPER COMBS SEE NOTION DEPARTMENT

No. 4K01650 Ladies' Back Comb. Patent safety device so comb cannot be lost from the hair. Gold filled, Roman yellow finish mounting. Width of comb, 4 inches. Price, each.......$1.50

No. 4K01652 Ladies' Back Comb. With safety device so that comb can never be lost from the hair. Roman yellow satin finish gold filled mounting, set with imitation amethysts. Width of comb, 4½ inches. Each.............$1.60

No. 4K01654 Ladies' Back Comb. Gold filled, bright polish mounting. Width of comb, 4½ inches. Price, each............$1.85

No. 4K01656 Ladies' Back Comb. With safety hold device, latest style. Solid gold inlaid work. Width of comb, 4½ inches. Price, each............$2.00

No. 4K01658 Ladies' Back Comb. Gold filled, bright polish mounting, set with imitation pearls. Width of comb, 4 inches. Price, each..........$2.50

  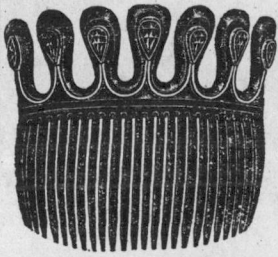 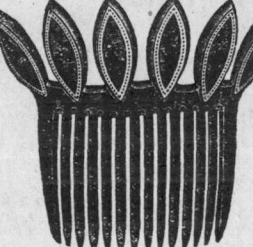

No. 4K01662 Ladies' Back Comb. Gold filled, Roman yellow finish mounting, set with imitation amethysts. Width of comb, 4 inches. This comb is one we recommend, being one of the most artistic placed on the market this year. Price, each...............$3.75

No. 4K01660 Ladies' Back Comb. Roman rose gold filled mounting, set with imitation amethysts, very artistic. Width of comb, 4 inches. Price, each............$3.00

No. 4K01664 Ladies' Back Comb. Parisian importation. Roman yellow finish gold filled mounting, set with imitation amethysts. Handsomest comb gotten out this year. Width of comb, 4¼ inches. Price, each.........$3.75

No. 4K01666 Ladies' Back Comb. French pattern, bright polish, gold filled mounting. Width of comb, 4½ inches. Price, each...$3.85

For a complete line of Hair Barrets see page 322.

HOW TO FIND CORRECT SIZE OF RING YOU WANT

It is very important when you order a finger ring from us that you send us the correct size, and to help you find the correct measurement so that we can send a ring which will exactly fit your ring finger, we give you the following information. We give five different methods below, and we would recommend that you use two of the methods described, and we further recommend that you send us your measurements according to Methods No. 1 and No. 2, which we believe to be the best.

METHOD No. 1. If you now own a ring which fits the finger on which you propose to wear the new ring, or if you do not own a ring yourself and can borrow one from a friend or a neighbor which fits your ring finger, you can ascertain the size you will need by following these directions: The circles which we show herewith numbered from 00 to 13 represent standard ring measurements. Place the ring you own or the one you have borrowed which fits your finger over these circles until you find the one that just fits inside the ring, and the number of that circle is the size ring you will require. If one circle should be slightly smaller and the next one slightly larger than the inside of the ring which fits your finger, this would indicate that you want a size between the two. For example: If size 6 is just a little small and size 7 just a little large, you will want the size between these two, or No. 6½. This is a most satisfactory method of getting your ring size and we recommend that you use it.

METHOD No. 2. Cut a narrow strip of paper about one-eighth inch wide, as shown in the illustration Fig. 1, wrap this narrow strip of paper around the finger at the joint (illustration Fig. 2 shows the correct position) and cut it off with the scissors so that the ends of the paper will exactly meet (illustration Fig. 3). Pin this little piece of paper to your order or enclose it in a little envelope and attach this envelope to your order and say in your letter that you have enclosed the slip of paper in the envelope and attached it to your order.

METHOD No. 3. If you own or can borrow a ring which fits you, a flat or plain band ring, that is to say a ring that has no setting in it, lay it on a piece of white paper, and with a pen, or better still, a very sharp pointed pencil, draw the inside circle of the ring and send this drawing to us, either pinned to your order or in a separate envelope pinned to your order.

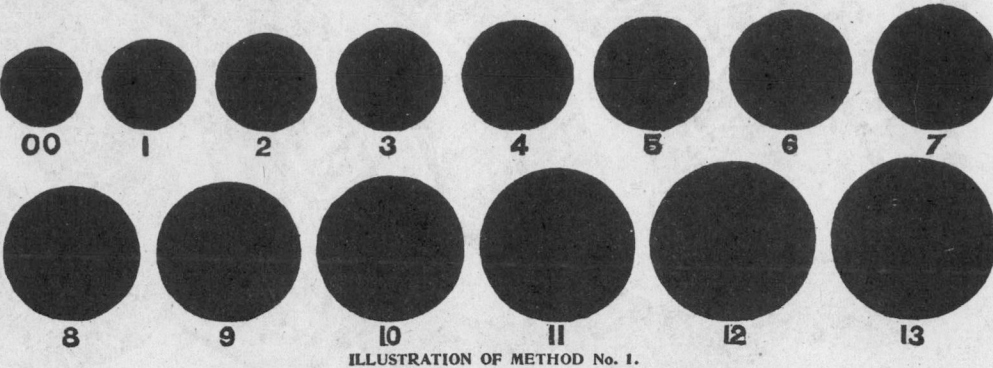

ILLUSTRATION OF METHOD No. 1.

METHOD No. 4. Take a soft piece of thin copper wire, or even a hairpin will serve the purpose, and wind it around the finger at the middle joint, then twist it together, making a complete ring with the wire, and enclose this wire in your order, attaching it to the paper to prevent its becoming lost.

METHOD No. 5. If you have time to wait a few days, write us and ask us to send you our ring gauge, and upon receipt of your letter we will at once mail it, together with full instructions, free of charge.

SPECIAL NOTICE. In ascertaining the finger size by using the strip of paper method, which is Method No. 2, or the wire ring method, which is Method No. 4, be sure to remember that very frequently the middle joints of one's fingers are larger than the finger between this point and the knuckles, and therefore you should be sure to use the middle joint of the finger as the place to take the ring measurement.

Figure 1   Figure 2   Figure 3

ILLUSTRATION OF METHOD No. 2.

IF YOU WILL BE VERY CAREFUL IN TAKING THE MEASUREMENTS by any one of these methods, we will be sure to have your correct ring size and the ring we send you will be sure to fit your finger. It is very easy to get the ring size by any of these methods, and if you will follow our instructions carefully, we guarantee that the ring you order will fit you.

CRYSTALLINE DIAMOND JEWELRY

No. 4K01548 Solid gold studs, plain mounting. Price. $1.20
No. 4K01550 Same style, gold filled. Price.....46c

DON'T FAIL TO GIVE EXACT SIZE OF RING WANTED.

Rings, Scarf Pins, Studs, Earrings and Brooches in Solid Gold, Solid Silver and Gold Filled Mountings, Set With Crystalline Diamonds. You Must See Them to Appreciate Them.

Crystalline Diamonds are worn by actors and actresses and those wanting the most perfect imitation diamonds known. We have thousands of professional people, actors and actresses, throughout the United States, who buy our Crystalline Diamonds to wear instead of using the genuine article. Postage extra on rings, earrings, studs and scarf pins, 2 cents; brooches, 4 cents; registration, 8 cents extra on any.

No. 4K01584 Gold filled. Price.....98c
No. 4K01585 Same style as No. 4K01584, but solid silver. Price.....$1.12

No. 4K01500 Solid gold. Price......$2.15

No. 4K01502 Solid gold. Price....$3.58
No. 4K01504 Rolled plate. Price....48c

No. 4K01506 Solid gold. Price......$2.38

No. 4K01508 Solid gold. Price..... $3.80

No. 4K01510 Solid gold. Price.....$2.75
No. 4K01512 Rolled plate. Price.....48c

No. 4K01514 Solid gold. Price......$2.85
No. 4K01516 Rolled plate. Price.....56c

No. 4K01518 Solid gold. Price......$2.85
No. 4K01520 Rolled plate. Price.....57c

No. 4K01521 Solid gold. Price........$3.65
No. 4K01522 Rolled plate. Price........65c

DON'T FAIL TO GIVE SIZE OF RING WANTED.

No. 4K01538 Solid silver, gold finish, ruby doublet center. Price.......75c

No. 4K01552 Solid gold studs, plain mounting. Price...$1.90
No. 4K01554 Same style, gold filled. Price.57c

No. 4K01523 Solid gold. Price....$3.32

No. 4K01524 Solid gold. Price.$2.70

No. 4K01541 Gold filled Scarf Pin. Price.$1.30

No. 4K01540 Gold filled Scarf Pin, 1 Parisian pearl. Price.$1.14

No. 4K01542 Gold filled Scarf Pin. Price.......$1.02

No. 4K01544 Solid gold studs, plain mounting. Price....84c
No. 4K01546 Same style, gold filled. Ea..33c

No. 4K01562 Solid gold. Per pair....$1.90

DON'T FAIL TO GIVE SIZE WANTED.

No. 4K01556 Solid gold Ear Knobs. Per pair....$1.45
No. 4K01557 Same style, gold filled. Per pair..57c

No. 4K01590 Gold filled. Price........$1.80

No. 4K01632 Solid silver, gold finish. Price.$1.44

No. 4K01558 Per pr. $1.78

No. 4K01568 Gold filled. Per pair.......76c

No. 4K01560 Solid gold. Per pair.$2.40

No. 4K01570 Gold filled. Per pair.......48c

No. 4K01572 Gold filled. Per pair....72c

No. 4K01604 Gold filled. Price....$1.08

No. 4K01600 Gold filled. Price.....64c

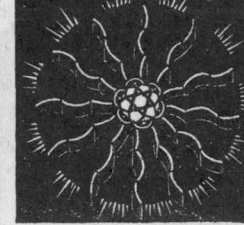

No. 4K01576 Solid gold. Price......$3.52

No. 4K01602 Gold filled. Price.....72c

No. 4K01624 Gold filled. Price....$2.28

FINEST QUALITY SOLID GOLD WEDDING RINGS IN 10, 14 AND 18 KARAT.

We are leaders in wedding rings. The wedding rings we quote here and show are the finest manufactured and different than shown by others; these wedding rings are absolutely seamless, made without a seam. No discolorations or marring where the ring is joined. In fact, an absolutely one piece ring, as wedding rings should be. We guarantee them the finest finished and highest in quality ever offered.

DON'T FAIL TO GIVE SIZE OF RING WANTED. SEE PAGE 308 FOR HOW TO ARRIVE AT THE EXACT SIZE YOU WANT.

For Prices on Engraving See Page 257.

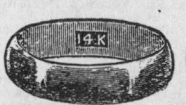

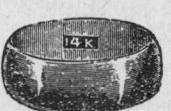

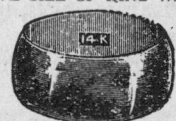

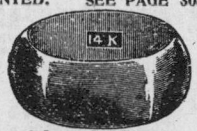

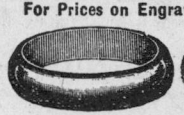

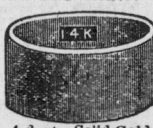

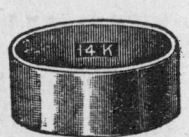

2 dwt. Solid Gold
No. 4K02200 10-karat..$1.19
No. 4K02202 14-karat..$1.59
No. 4K02204 18-karat..$1.99

3 dwt. Solid Gold
No. 4K02206 10-karat..$1.79
No. 4K02208 14-karat..$2.39
No. 4K02210 18-karat..$2.99

5 dwt. Solid Gold
No. 4K02212 10-karat..$2.99
No. 4K02214 14-karat..$3.99
No. 4K02216 18-karat..$4.99

6 dwt. Solid Gold
No. 4K02218 10-karat......$3.59
No. 4K02220 14-karat......$4.79
No. 4K02222 18-karat......$5.99

4 dwt. Solid Gold Tiffany style.
No. 4K02232 14-karat..$3.19
No. 4K02234 18-karat..$3.99

5 dwt. Solid Gold Tiffany style.
No. 4K02238 14-karat..$3.99
No. 4K02240 18-karat..$4.99

4 dwt. Solid Gold
No. 4K02248 10-karat..$2.39
No. 4K02250 14-karat..$3.19
No. 4K02252 18-karat..$3.99

6 dwt. Solid Gold
No. 4K02254 10-karat.$3.59
No. 4K02256 14-karat.$4.79
No. 4K02258 18-karat.$5.99

GENTLEMEN'S FINEST QUALITY SOLID GOLD INITIAL AND EMBLEM RINGS, WITH AND WITHOUT DIAMOND SET.

WE SUPPLY —ANY— INITIAL.

These rings furnished with Odd Fellows, Masonic, Knights of Pythias, Modern Woodmen of America, F. O. Eagles, Woodmen of the World, Elks or Knights of the Maccabees' emblems at same price as quoted for initials.

DO NOT FAIL TO GIVE EXACT SIZE OF RING AND INITIAL OR EMBLEM WANTED.

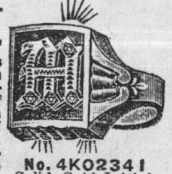

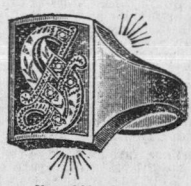

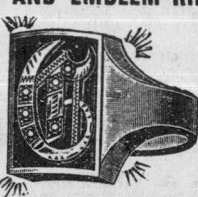

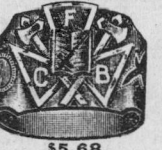

No. 4K02341 Solid Gold Initial. Price.......$1.85
No. 4K02343 Solid Gold Initial, set with 4 diamonds. Price.........$3.84

No. 4K02345 Solid Gold Initial. Price...........$4.12
No. 4K02347 Solid Gold Initial, set with 5 diamonds. Price..$6.60

No. 4K02349 Solid Gold Emblem or Initial. Price..........$4.12
No. 4K02351 Solid Gold Emblem or Initial, set with 5 diamonds. Price.........$6.60

No. 4K02353 Solid Gold Initial. Price..........$4.95
No. 4K02355 Solid Gold Initial, set with 6 diamonds. Price.........$8.25

No. 4K02357 Solid Gold Initial. Price$6.15
No. 4K02359 Solid Gold Initial, set with 6 diamonds. Price.$8.75
No. 4K02361 Solid Gold Initial, set with 13 diamonds. Price$11.75

No. 4K02363 Solid Gold Emblem or Initial; can be furnished with any emblem quoted on this page; cannot be supplied with diamond set tops. Price....$4.65

No. 4K02365 Solid Gold Initial or Emblem; cannot be furnished with diamond top. Price.....$4.20

$3.79

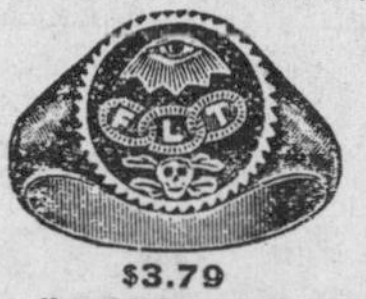

Solid gold, medium weight, any emblem as listed below. Price, each..........$3.79
No. 4K02130 Odd Fellows.
No. 4K02132 Masonic.
No. 4K02134 Knights of Pythias.
No. 4K02136 Modern Woodmen.
No. 4K02138 Woodmen of the World.
No. 4K02140 Red Men.
No. 4K02142 United Workmen.
No. 4K02144 Knights of Maccabees.
No. 4K02146 Elks.

DO NOT FAIL TO GIVE EXACT SIZE AND EMBLEM WANTED.

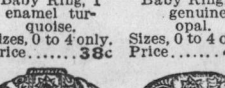

$5.68

Solid gold, heavy weight, any emblem listed below. Price, each..........$5.68
No. 4K02148 Knights of Pythias.
No. 4K02150 Odd Fellows.
No. 4K02151 Masonic.
No. 4K02152 Modern Woodmen.
No. 4K02153 Woodmen of the World.
No. 4K02154 Red Men.
No. 4K02155 United Workmen.
No. 4K02156 Knights of Maccabees.
No. 4K02157 Fraternal Order of Eagles.
No. 4K02158 Elks.

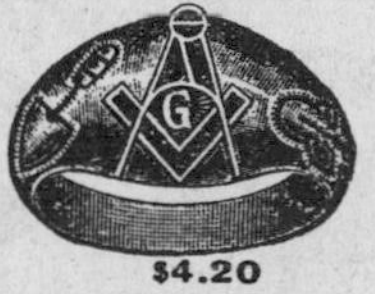

$4.20

Solid gold ring, heavy weight, any emblem as listed below. Price, each..........$4.20
No. 4K02162 Masonic.
No. 4K02164 Odd Fellows.
No. 4K02166 Knights of Pythias.
No. 4K02168 Modern Woodmen.
No. 4K02170 Woodmen of the World.
No. 4K02172 Red Men.
No. 4K02174 United Workmen.
No. 4K02176 Knights of Maccabees.
No. 4K02180 Elks.

POSTAGE ON RINGS IS 2 CENTS; IF BY REGISTERED MAIL, 8 CENTS EXTRA.

BABIES', CHILDREN'S AND MISSES' SOLID GOLD SET AND BAND RINGS.

BABY RINGS ARE MADE IN SIZES FROM 0 TO 4. MISSES' RINGS TO FIT MISSES AND BOYS, AGES 14 TO 16 YRS., IN SIZES FROM 5 TO 8 ONLY.

For full instructions for measurement of ring sizes, see page 308. When cash in full is sent with order the rings can be sent by mail, postage, 2 cents; registered mail, 8 cents extra.

RINGS Nos. 4K02380 TO 4K02444 IN SIZES 0 TO 4 ONLY.

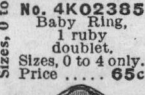

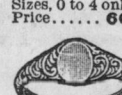

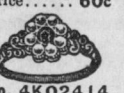

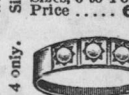

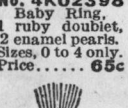

No. 4K02380 Baby Ring, 1 enamel turquoise. Sizes, 0 to 4 only. Price......38c

No. 4K02382 Baby Ring, 1 genuine opal. Sizes, 0 to 4 only. Price......47c

No. 4K02384 Baby Ring, 3 garnets. Sizes, 0 to 4 only. Price......47c

Sizes, 0 to 4 only.

No. 4K02385 Baby Ring, 1 ruby doublet. Sizes, 0 to 4 only. Price.......65c

No. 4K02390 Baby Ring, 1 emerald doublet. Sizes, 0 to 4 only. Price.......60c

No. 4K02392 Baby Ring, 1 emerald doublet. Sizes, 0 to 4 only. Price.......60c

No. 4K02394 Baby Ring, 1 garnet doublet. Sizes, 0 to 4 only. Price......62c

Sizes, 0 to 4 only.

No. 4K02396 Baby Ring, 1 enamel turquoise. Sizes, 0 to 4 only. Price......62c

No. 4K02398 Baby Ring, 1 ruby doublet, 2 enamel pearls. Sizes, 0 to 4 only. Price.......65c

No. 4K02402 Baby Ring, 2 enamel turquoise, 1 enamel pearl. Sizes, 0 to 4 only. Price....70c

No. 4K02404 Baby Ring, 1 enamel turquoise. Sizes, 0 to 4 only. Price.......76c

No. 4K02406 Baby Ring, 1 genuine garnet. Sizes, 0 to 4 only. Price......76c

No. 4K02408 Baby Ring, 1 genuine opal, 2 enamel pearls. Sizes, 0 to 4 only. Price......80c

Sizes, 0 to 4 only.

No. 4K02410 Baby Ring. Rose finish, hand carved, for initial. Sizes, 0 to 4 only. Price.....80c

No. 4K02412 Baby Ring, Roman rose color for initial. Sizes, 0 to 4 only. Price......95c

No. 4K02414 Baby Ring, 1 emerald doublet, 8 enamel pearls. Sizes, 0 to 4 only. Price......95c

No. 4K02416 Baby Ring, Roman rose color, for engraving initial. Sizes, 0 to 4 only. Price...$1.00

Sizes, 0 to 4 only.

No. 4K02419 Baby Ring, 3 genuine opals. Sizes, 0 to 4 only. Price......85c

No. 4K02424 Baby Ring, 1 genuine rose diamond. Sizes, 0 to 4 only. Price...$1.10

No. 4K02426 Baby Ring, 1 genuine rose diamond, 2 genuine garnets. Sizes, 0 to 4 only. Price..$1.10

DON'T FAIL TO GIVE SIZE OF RING WANTED.

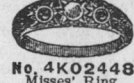

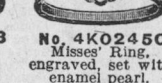

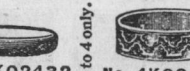

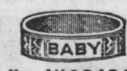

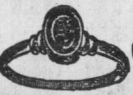

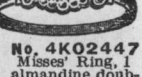

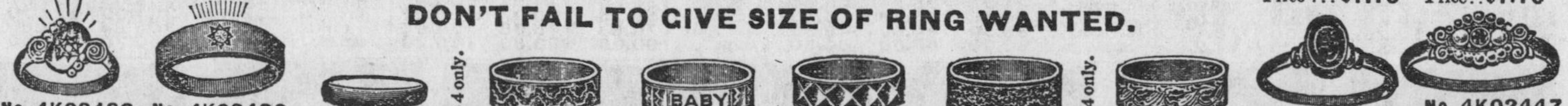

No. 4K02428 Baby Ring, 1 genuine rose diamond. Sizes, 0 to 4 only. Price....$1.42

No. 4K02430 Baby Ring. Extra heavy, 1 genuine cut diamond. Sizes, 0 to 4 only. Price....$2.05

No. 4K02432 Baby Ring. Sizes, 0 to 4 only. Price......28c

Sizes, 0 to 4 only.

No. 4K02434 Baby Ring. Sizes, 0 to 4 only. Price......38c

No. 4K02436 Baby Ring. Sizes, 0 to 4 only. Price......38c

No. 4K02438 Baby Ring. Sizes, 0 to 4 only. Price......54c

No. 4K02440 Baby Ring. Sizes, 0 to 4 only. Price......58c

Sizes, 0 to 4 only.

No. 4K02444 Baby Ring. Sizes, 0 to 4 only. Price......62c

No. 4K02446 Misses' Ring, 1 imitation carbuncle. Sizes, 5 to 8 only. Price.......76c

No. 4K02447 Misses' Ring, 1 almandine doublet, 2 enamel pearls. Sizes, 5 to 8 only. Price......84c

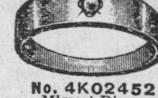

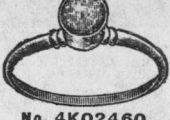

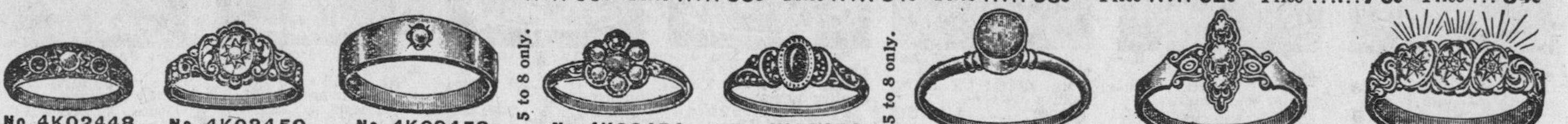

No. 4K02448 Misses' Ring, enamel pearl and turquoise. Price.......84c

No. 4K02450 Misses' Ring, engraved, set with enamel pearl. Price...........84c

No. 4K02452 Misses' Ring, 1 enamel turquose. Price..........92c

Sizes, 5 to 8 only.

No. 4K02454 Misses' Ring, enamel pearls and turquoise. Price.........95c

No. 4K02456 Misses' Ring, 1 imitation ruby. Price.........92c

Sizes, 5 to 8 only.

No. 4K02460 Misses' Ring, 1 genuine opal. Price.............$1.35

No. 4K02462 Misses' Ring, fancy shank, set with 3 genuine pearls. Price..............$2.50

No. 4K02464 Fancy Mounting, set with 3 genuine rose diamonds. Price..........$4.50

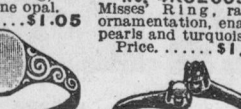

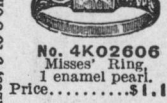

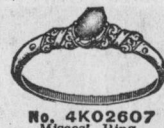

No. 4K02600 Misses' Ring, 1 genuine opal. Price.........$1.01

No. 4K02602 Misses' Ring, 1 genuine opal. Price..........$1.05

No. 4K02603 Misses' Ring, raised ornamentation, enamel pearls and turquoise. Price........$1.20

Sizes, 5 to 8 only.

No. 4K02606 Misses' Ring, 1 enamel pearl. Price..........$1.19

No. 4K02607 Misses' Ring, fancy shank, genuine opal. Price...........$1.20

Sizes, 5 to 8 only.

No. 4K02608 Misses' Ring, 3 amethyst doublets. Price...........$1.24

No. 4K02610 Misses' Seal Ring, Roman satin finish. Price........$1.20 2-letter monogram, engraved, 15c extra.

No. 4K02612 Misses' Ring, 3 enamel turquoise. Price..........$1.26

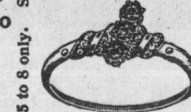

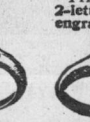

No. 4K02614 Misses' Ring, 1 genuine opal. Price..........$1.29

No. 4K02616 Misses' Seal Ring, Roman finish. Price........$1.31 3 letter monogram, engraved, 20c extra.

No. 4K02618 Misses' Ring, 1 genuine pearl, 1 sapphire doublet. Price.........$1.32

Sizes, 5 to 8 only.

No. 4K02619 Misses' Ring, plain shank, cup setting, genuine pearl. Price.........$1.35

No. 4K02620 Misses' Ring, 1 almandine doublet. Price..............$1.43

Sizes, 5 to 8 only.

No. 4K02621 Misses' Ring, fancy mounting, 3 ruby doublets. Price, $1.40

No. 4K02622 Misses' Ring, 3 enamel turquoise, 4 enamel pearls. Price, $1.43

No. 4K02624 Misses' Ring, 3 ruby doublets, 4 enamel pearls. Price.......$1.43

GENUINE DIAMONDS AND SOLID GOLD 14-CARAT MOUNTINGS

WITH EVERY DIAMOND we issue a written, binding guarantee, with a further agreement that you can at any time, within one year, return any diamond you may select from this catalogue, and exchange it for any other diamond or other article of jewelry at the same or a higher price.

WE FURTHER AGREE on the return of any diamond purchased from us within sixty days of purchase, when so requested, to refund in cash your full purchase price, and we further agree, at any time, within one year after sixty days, on return of any diamonds to us, when requested to do so, to refund your full purchase price, less 10 per cent.

YOU CAN BUY A DIAMOND from us today at $2.19 to $460.00 and you can keep it for three months or longer, and if you so desire, return it to us, any time within one year, and we will refund you in cash the full amount of money you paid us for it, less 10 per cent. But we must caution you that we positively will not exchange, refund, or allow credit for any diamond purchased from us unless it is in or with the original setting, and is accompanied by our guarantee and refund certificate that was sent with the diamond.

DIAMONDS ARE ADVANCING IN PRICE. The greatest authorities in New York, London, Antwerp, Paris and Amsterdam claim they are being sold today cheaper than they will ever be sold again. The supply is limited, the demand is becoming greater and it will be impossible in a very short time to fill orders at double the price at which diamonds are being sold for today. They are absolutely a safe investment. We advise you as friends, if you contemplate buying a diamond, by all means buy it now. The longer you wait the more it will cost.

EXCEPTIONS where we do not give our refund and exchange certificate with a purchase. This ruling applies to such items plainly marked "no refund certificate," and is made necessary for the reason that where we allow a refund certificate, the cost of making the mounting is but a small item of cost and the gold value is the principal one. Where we do not give our refund certificate, the actual gold value amounts to but little and the principal cost is in the making and the cost of the pearls, fancy stones, etc., and as we melt up all returned mountings, our loss would be too great where the cost of making the article is the principal expense. However, we will allow for the diamond without the mounting. On most of our diamond mounted jewelry we quote quality and weight. Where quality and weight are not given we do not allow refunds or exchange after goods have been worn.

GRADES OF DIAMONDS.

FIRST QUALITY. These stones are perfect in color, proportion, brilliancy and shape. Specially picked with the idea of selecting the best stones from original papers. Best in every way for brilliancy, shape, color and perfection.

SECOND QUALITY. The second quality diamonds are in every particular the same as the first quality, except the color, or because of a very slight imperfection, not large enough to be called a flaw and only perceptible to an expert. We will send you either one you may desire—a perfect, slightly off color diamond, or a very white diamond with a very slight imperfection. Most of the diamond merchants sell this, our second quality diamond, and particularly the ones that have a very slight imperfection, as first quality. They do not recognize this very sight fault as an imperfection at all.

With every diamond we send a plush covered and plush lined case for same FREE.

THIRD QUALITY. A third quality diamond is one that is brilliant and well cut, but has some imperfection or blemish, generally so small and so slight that it requires one high in the knowledge of diamonds to be able to detect the imperfection at all. Our own third quality diamonds are practically perfect in cut and shape. The color may be the same as in our first or second quality, but by close examination it is possible to detect a blemish of some sort. Our third quality diamonds never have cracks in them or large, unsightly chunks or pieces knocked out of them. The same quality that we sell for third quality is sold by some monthly payment houses and by small dealers as first quality stones. These people either buy and sell them as first quality because they are unable to judge diamonds, or they are fully aware of the imperfections and are simply misrepresenting the goods.

WE ASK A CAREFUL COMPARISON of our goods with those shown by other concerns, which will do more toward showing the value we give than any other argument.

THESE ILLUSTRATIONS show various diamond mountings and various size diamonds according to weight. The mountings vary in sizes according to the weight of stone to be mounted. All diamond ring mountings are guaranteed 14-carat gold, hand made by skilled workmen. So that our customers may have a wider range of diamonds and diamond mountings to select from different than those illustrated and described already mounted upon the following pages, we have quoted the diamonds and the diamond mountings separately, arranging the mountings grouped around the diamond illustrations.

WE DO NOT CHARGE FOR THE WORK of setting the diamonds in the mountings. In writing your order for any of the following mountings, be sure to give the exact catalogue number of the mounting wanted together with the weight of stone you desire buying. As example:—Diamond mounting No. 4K08002 price, $5.00; set with ¾-carat diamond, first quality, price, $136.50; cost of diamond ring complete, $141.50.

TO ARRIVE AT THE COST OF RING COMPLETE, add the cost of the mounting which is plainly printed under each one, to the cost of the diamond as quoted in the table below. You will note that we have given the size of diamond the various mountings will take. Do not select a mounting with different size stone than is suggested by the weights as quoted under each mounting.

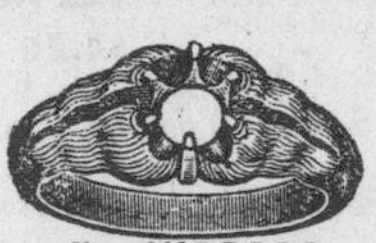
No. 4K08000
1 to 1½ carats.
Price..........$7.50

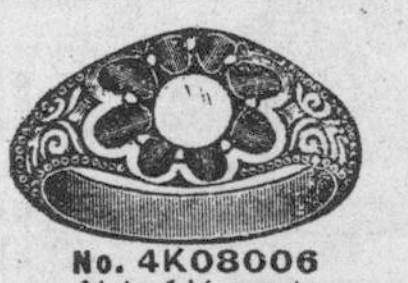
No. 4K08006
¾ to 1¼ carats.
Price..........$7.00

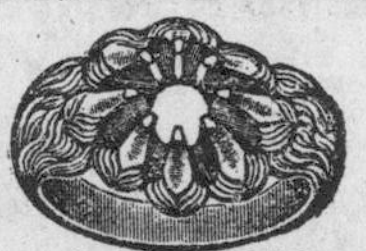
No. 4K08010
5-16 to ½ carat.
Price..........$7.00

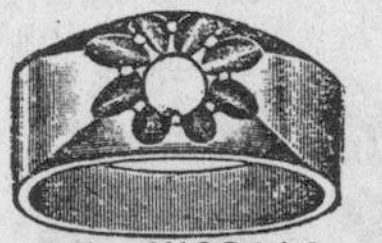
No. 4K08014
1⅛ to 2 carats.
Price..........$7.00

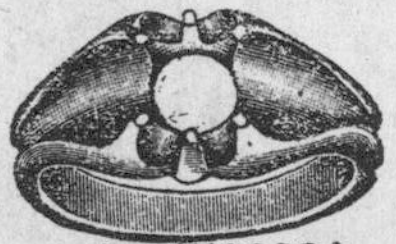
No. 4K08004
⅞ to 1½ carats.
Price..........$7.50

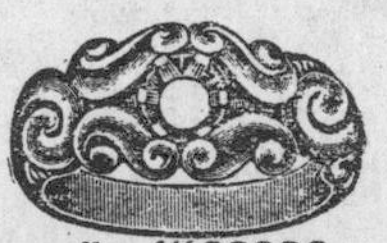
No. 4K08030
¼ to ¾ carat.
Price..........$6.50

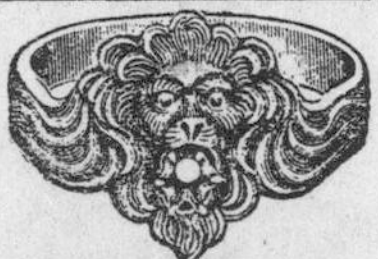
No. 4K08028
1-16 to ¼ carat.
Price..........$9.00

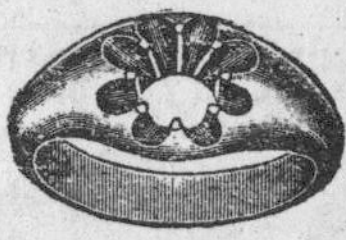
No. 4H08002
⅝ to 1½ carats.
Price.......$5.00

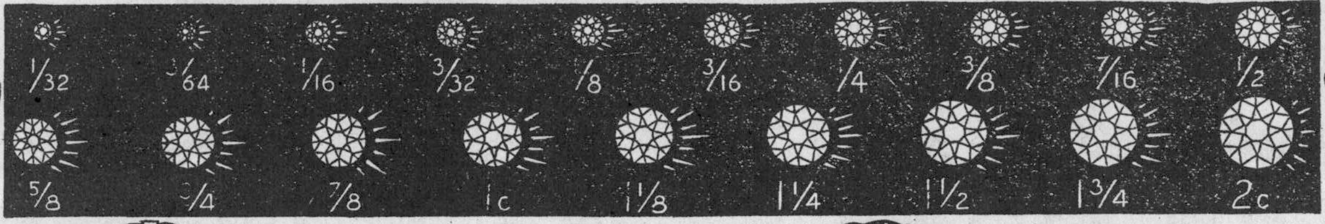

1/32
1/64
1/16
3/32
1/8
3/16
1/4
3/8
7/16
1/2
5/8
3/4
7/8
1c
1 1/8
1 1/4
1 1/2
1 3/4
2c

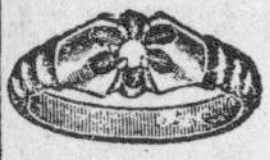
No. 4K08018
1-32 to 5-32 carat
Price..$2.75

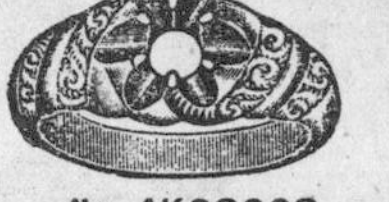
No. 4K08008
⅝ to 1 carat.
Price..........$5.75

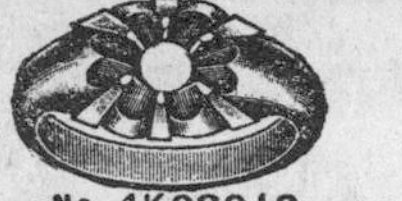
No. 4K08012
5-16 to ½ carat.
Price..........$3.75

No. 4K08016
1-32 to ⅛ carat.
Price..........$2.65

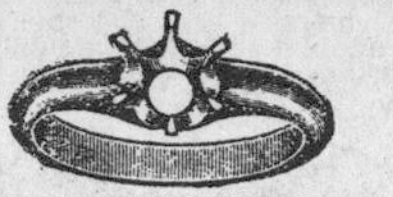
No. 4K08026
1⅝ to 2 carats.
Price..........$4.50

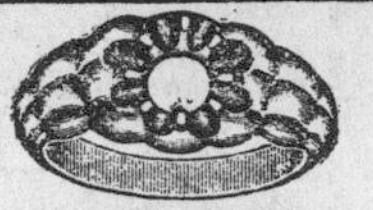
No. 4K08024
¾ to 1¼ carat.
Price..........$8.00

No. 4K08022
1-16 to ¼ carat.
Price..........$3.00

No. 4K08020
1-32 to 5-32 carat.
Price..........$3.00

PRICES OF DIAMONDS ONLY.

	First Quality	Second Quality	Third Quality
1-32 carat....	$ 3.28	$ 2.66	$ 2.19
3-64 carat....	4.59	3.75	3.05
1-16 carat....	6.13	5.00	4.06
5-64 carat....	7.66	6.25	5.08
3-32 carat....	9.19	7.50	6.09
⅛ carat......	12.25	10.00	8.13
5-32 carat....	16.88	13.75	11.25
3-16 carat....	$20.25	$16.50	$13.50
¼ carat......	30.75	27.25	20.00
9-32 carat....	37.13	31.78	22.50
5-16 carat....	41.25	35.94	25.94
⅜ carat......	54.38	45.38	36.75
7-16 carat,...	66.50	54.69	45.50
½ carat......	80.00	66.00	54.50
9-16 carat.	$ 93.94	$ 75.38	$ 65.81
⅝ carat ..	104.38	83.75	73.13
11-16 carat	125.13	105.38	95.26
¾ carat ..	136.50	114.97	103.95
⅞ carat ..	159.25	135.97	121.27
15-16 carat	170.63	145.68	129.94
1 carat ...	190.00	163.80	145.20
1 1-16 carats	$201.88	$174.03	$154.27
1⅛ carats ..	213.75	185.45	170.77
1¼ carats ..	242.50	210.00	189.76
1½ carats ..	294.00	263.02	250.80
1⅝ carats ..	321.75	284.90	271.70
1¾ carats ..	402.50	306.84	292.60
2 carats....	460.00	350.70	334.40

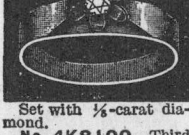

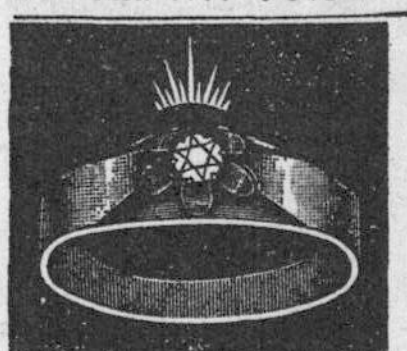
Set with ⅛-carat diamond.
No. 4K8100 Third quality diamond.
Price........$10.38
No. 4K8102 Second quality diamond.
Price........$12.25
No. 4K8104 First quality diamond.
Price........$14.50

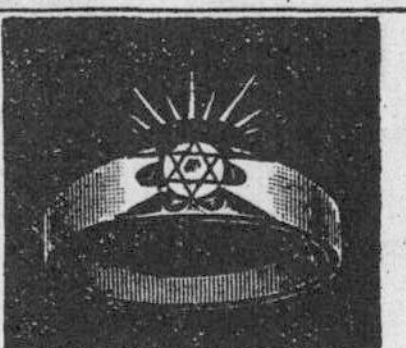
Set with 3/16-carat diamond.
No. 4K8106 Third quality diamond.
Price........$16.00
No. 4K8108 Second quality diamond.
Price........$19.00
No. 4K8110 First quality diamond.
Price........$22.75

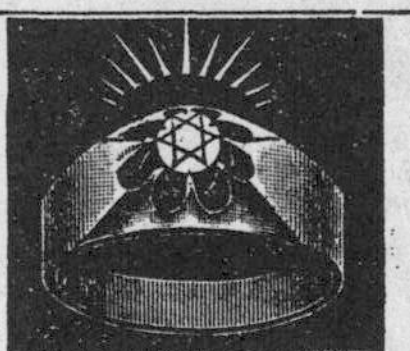
Set with ¼-carat diamond.
No. 4K8112 Third quality diamond.
Price........$22.50
No. 4K8114 Second quality diamond.
Price........$29.75
No. 4K8116 First quality diamond.
Price........$33.25

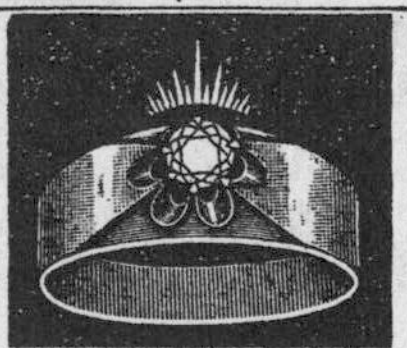
Set with 5/16-carat diamond.
No. 4K8118 Third quality diamond.
Price........$29.44
No. 4K8120 Second quality diamond.
Price........$39.44
No. 4K8122 First quality diamond.
Price........$44.75

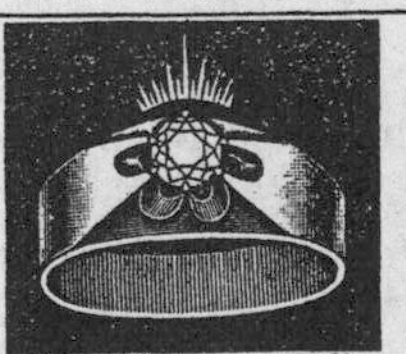
Set with 7/16-carat diamond.
No. 4K8124 Third quality diamond.
Price........$49.25
No. 4K8126 Second quality diamond.
Price........$58.44
No. 4K8128 First quality diamond.
Price........$70.25

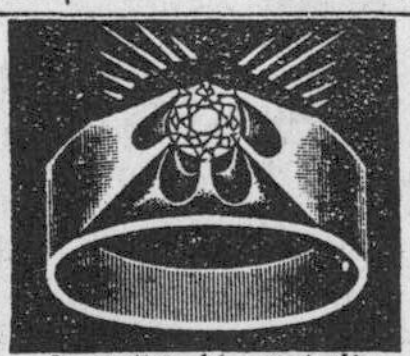
Set with ½-carat diamond.
No. 4K8130 Third quality diamond.
Price........$58.50
No. 4K8132 Second quality diamond.
Price........$70.00
No. 4K8134 First quality diamond.
Price........$84.00

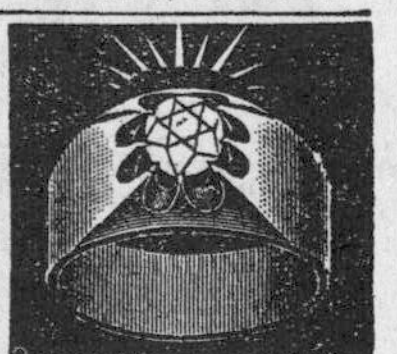
Set with 9/16-carat diamond.
No. 4K8136 Third quality diamond.
Price........$69.81
No. 4K8138 Second quality diamond.
Price........$79.38
No. 4K8140 First quality diamond.
Price.....$97.94

BE SURE TO GIVE RING SIZE.

BE SURE TO GIVE RING SIZE.

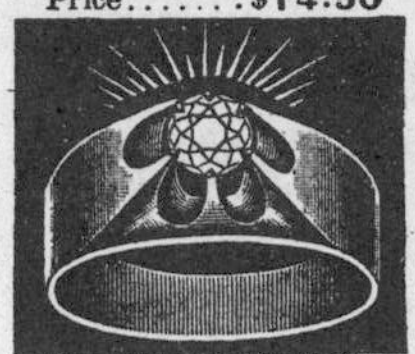
Set with ¾-carat diamond.
No. 4K8142 Third quality diamond.
Price......$108.45
No. 4K8144 Second quality diamond.
Price......$119.00
No. 4K8146 First quality diamond.
Price......$141.00

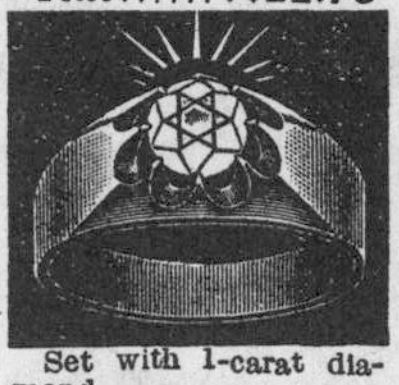
Set with 1-carat diamond.
No. 4K8154 Third quality diamond.
Price......$150.20
No. 4K8156 Second quality diamond.
Price......$168.80
No. 4K8158 First quality diamond.
Price..... $195.00

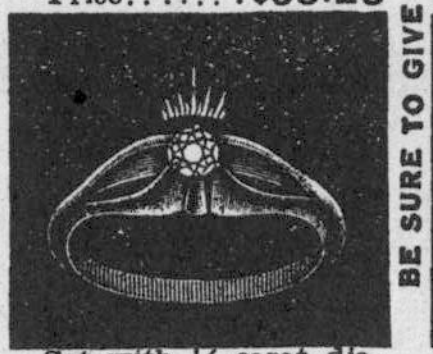
Set with ⅛-carat diamond.
No. 4K8208 Third quality diamond.
Price........$11.13
No. 4K8210 Second quality diamond.
Price........$13.00
No. 4K8212 First quality diamond.
Price........$15.25

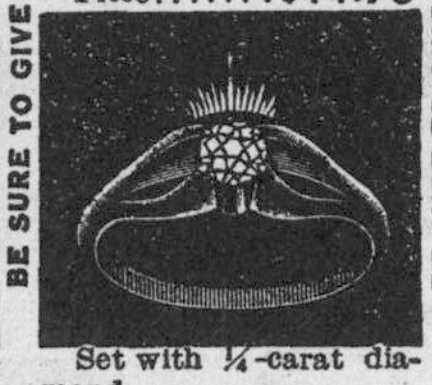
Set with ¼-carat diamond.
No. 4K8214 Third quality diamond.
Price........$23.25
No. 4K8216 Second quality diamond.
Price........$30.50
No. 4K8218 First quality diamond.
Price........$34.00

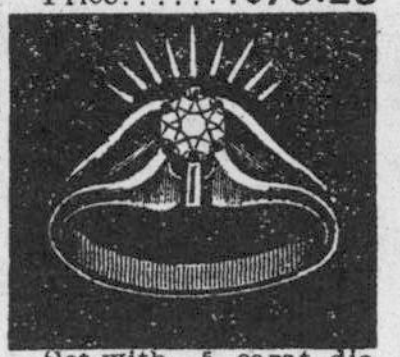
Set with 5/16-carat diamond.
No. 4K8220 Third quality diamond.
Price........$29.69
No. 4K8222 Second quality diamond.
Price........$39.69
No. 4K8224 First quality diamond.
Price........$45.00

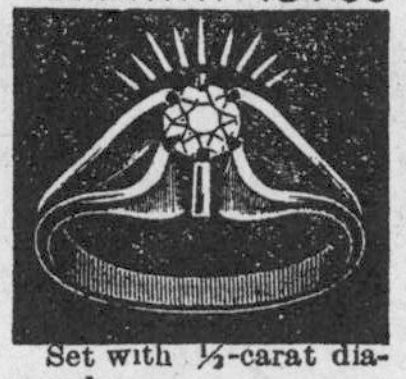
Set with ½-carat diamond.
No. 4K8226 Third quality diamond.
Price........$59.00
No. 4K8228 Second quality diamond.
Price........$70.50
No. 4K8230 First quality diamond.
Price........$84.50

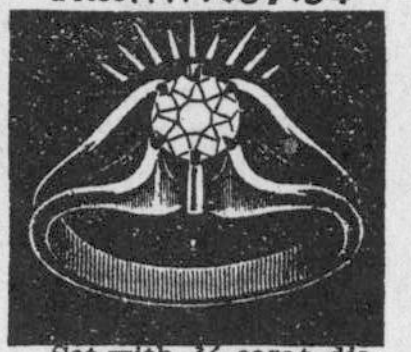
Set with ¾-carat diamond.
No. 4K8232 Third quality diamond.
Price... $109.45
No. 4K8234 Second quality diamond.
Price.... $120.47
No. 4K8236 First quality diamond.
Price.... $142.00

FINE ROLLED GOLD PLATE AND GOLD FILLED GENTS' CHARMS

Postage on Charms, 3 cents extra; 5 cents extra if sent by insured mail.

No. 4K03804 Gold filled Compass, fancy mounting, no toy, but scientifically accurate. Price.........$1.03

No. 4K03814 Gold filled, fancy Horseshoe and Horse. Price.........53c

No. 4K03816 Rolled gold plate, bright polish, fancy views. Price.....24c

No. 4K03820 Rolled gold plate, fine compass. Price.....28c

No. 4K03832 Gold filled Compass, fancy mounting, very accurate. Price.....78c

No. 4K03834 Gold filled, hand carved Horse, heavy gold plate, with ruby eyes. Price.................$1.20

No. 4K03836 Rolled gold plate, bright finish. Faith, Hope and Charity. Price.......42c

GOLD FILLED AND GOLD FRONT SMALL SIZE LOCKETS

USED FOR NECK CHAINS, FOR CHILDREN OR FOR LADIES; OR FOR GENTLEMEN DESIRING A SMALL SIZED LOCKET TO HOLD PHOTOGRAPHS.

No. 4K04004 Bright polish, rolled gold plate, one rhinestone. Holds two pictures. Price....45c

No. 4K04005 Bright polish, gold front, hand engraved, holds two pictures. Price...48c

No. 4K04007 Bright polish, gold front, hand engraved, holds two pictures. Price....48c

No. 4K04009 Bright polish, hand engraved, rhinestone set, holds two pictures. Price....56c

No. 4K04010 Bright polish, gold filled. Holds two pictures. Price....59c

No. 4K04011 Gold front, bright polish, handengraved, rhinestone set, holds two pictures. Price....56c

No. 4K04012 Gold filled, bright polish, set with enamel pearl. Holds two pictures. Price....78c

No. 4K04013 Gold front, fancy mounting, hand engraved. Holds two pictures. Price....72c

No. 4K04014 Gold filled, bright polish, set with enamel pearl. Holds 2 pictures. Price....80c

No. 4K04015 Gold filled, bright polish, imitation diamond set. Holds two pictures. Price........95c

LOCKETS AND SOCIETY EMBLEM CHARMS, Gold and Gold Filled.

> WE CAN SUPPLY ANY ORDER QUOTED UNDER ILLUSTRATIONS. TO AVOID MISTAKES, GIVE CATALOGUE NUMBER AND STATE THE EMBLEM WANTED. ILLUSTRATIONS SHOW EXACT SIZE AND DESIGN.

Gold filled locket, bright polish; holds 2 pictures. Hard enameled emblem. Any of the following orders:
Price....$1.65
No. 4K04166 Odd Fellows.
No. 4K04168 Masonic.
No. 4K04172 Modern Woodmen of America.
No. 4K04176 United Workmen.
No. 4K04178 Knights of the Maccabees.

Gold filled trimmings, set with black enamel onyx center, emblem in colored enamel.
Price....89c
No. 4K04200 Odd Fellows.
No. 4K04202 Masonic.

Gold filled, bright polish, hard enameled emblem. Price....$1.68
No. 4K04212 Modern Woodmen of America.
No. 4K04214 Woodmen of the World.
No. 4K04216 Masonic.
No. 4K04218 Knights of Pythias.
No. 4K04220 Odd Fellows.
No. 4K04222 United Workmen.
No. 4K04224 Knights of Columbus.

Solid gold, hard enameled emblem, bright mounting. Price....$2.98
No. 4K04262 Woodmen of America.
No. 4K04264 Woodmen of the World.
No. 4K04266 Masonic.
No. 4K04268 Odd Fellows.
No. 4K04270 Knights of Pythias.
No. 4K04272 Knights of Maccabees.

Gold filled, bright polish, hard enameled emblem. Price..82c
No. 4K04300 Masonic.
No. 4K04302 Odd Fellows.
No. 4K04304 Knights of Pythias.
No. 4K04306 Knights of Maccabees.
No. 4K04308 Knights of Columbus.

No. 4K04310 Gold filled, Masonic and Odd Fellows, combined. Each....85c
No. 4K04312 Same as above, solid gold. Price, each...$3.20
No. 4K04314 Solid gold, Masonic only. Price, each...$2.15

No. 4K04316 Solid gold, Knights Templar. Extra heavy black enamel onyx, 9 ruby doublets and 4 genuine rose diamonds. Each.....$13.10

No. 4K04318 Knights of Pythias, solid gold, hard enameled. Price, each..$6.62
No. 4K04320 Same as No. 4K04318, but gold filled. Price, each....$4.08

No. 4K04406 Gold filled, enameled, Woodmen of America. Price........95c
No. 4K04408 Gold filled, Woodmen of the World. Price........95c

No. 4K04468 Gold filled, enameled and engraved, G. A. R. Price.....72c
No. 4K04470 Same style, but solid gold. Price...$3.10

> THE SURPRISINGLY LOW REDUCED PRICES prevailing in this catalogue mean greater savings to our customers than ever before.

ALWAYS ORDER BY NUMBER.

No. 4K04486 Solid gold, enameled, Odd Fellows. Price....$1.90

No. 4K04462 Gold filled, Improved Order of Red Men. Price.....72c

No. 4K04324 Solid gold, stone center, Masonic. Price.... $3.40
No. 4K04326 Same style, but gold filled mounting. Price, $1.04

No. 4K04452 Solid gold, enameled, Knights of Pythias. Price...$1.88

No. 4K04464 Gold filled, Woodmen of America. Price....92c
No. 4K04466 Woodmen of the World. Price.92c

No. 4K04480 Gold filled, Elks. Price....$1.14
No. 4K04482 Solid gold, Elks. Price,..$9.50

No. 4K04382 Gold filled, enameled and engraved, Independent Order of Odd Fellows. Price....$1.04
No. 4K04384 Same as above, solid gold. Price......$6.50

No. 4K04398 Blue enameled, gold filled, Masonic. Price....$1.10
No. 4K04399 Same style as No. 4K04398, but in cheaper quality. Price....88c
No. 4K04400 Same as above, solid gold. Price, $2.98

PLEASE NOTE WE CARRY MANY DIFFERENT EMBLEMS QUOTED UNDER EACH DESIGN SHOWN.

SOLID GOLD AND GOLD FILLED EMBLEM PINS AND BUTTONS

WE WARRANT THEM TO GIVE ENTIRE SATISFACTION. TO AVOID MISTAKES PLEASE GIVE NUMBER AND STATE EMBLEM WANTED.

TWO CENTS WILL CARRY ANY ONE OF THESE PINS TO ANY PART OF THE UNITED STATES OF AMERICA BY MAIL, INSURANCE OR REGISTRY EXTRA.

Illustrations on this page show exact size.

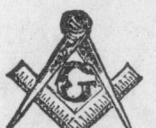

No. 4K04600 Gold filled, Masonic engraved. Price.......26c
No. 4K04602 Solid gold, same as above. Price........52c

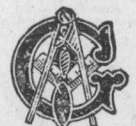

No. 4K04604 Gold filled, Masonic, enameled and engraved. Price..43c
No. 4K04605 Solid gold, same as above. Price.......68c

No. 4K04606 Gold filled, Masonic, enameled. Price........48c
No. 4K04608 Solid gold, same as above. Price........85c

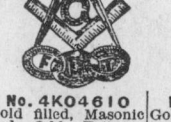

No. 4K04610 Gold filled, Masonic and Odd Fellows, enameled. Price,35c
No. 4K04611 Solid gold, same as above. Price..58c

No. 4K04612 Gold filled, Odd Fellows, enameled. Price........33c
No. 4K04614 Solid gold, same as above. Price..62c

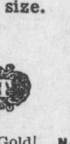

No. 4K04616 Gold filled, Odd Fellows, enameled. Price..38c
No. 4K04618 Solid gold, same as above. Price.........66c

No. 4K04620 Gold filled, Odd Fellows, engraved. Price......36c
No. 4K04622 Solid gold, same as above. Ea. $1.00

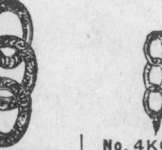

No. 4K04624 Gold filled, Odd Fellows. Price......19c
No. 4K04626 Solid gold, same as above. Price......38c

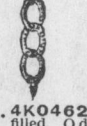

No. 4K04628 Gold filled, Ladies of the Maccabees. Price.......63c
No. 4K04630 Solid gold. Same as above. Price...$1.15

No. 4K04670 Gold filled, Independent Order of Foresters. Price......48c
No. 4K04672 Solid gold, same as above. Price.......85c

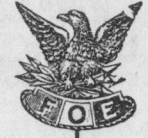

No. 4K04678 Gold filled, Fraternal Order of Eagles. Price. 50c
No. 4K04680 Solid gold, same as above. Price........72c

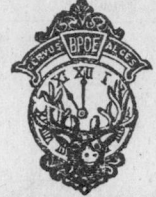

No. 4K04682 Gold filled, Elks. Ea..63c
No. 4K04684 Solid gold, same as above. Price.........$1.37

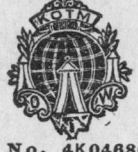

No. 4K04686 Gold filled, Maccabees. Price........48c
No. 4K04688 Solid gold, same as above. Price........85c

No. 4K04690 Gold filled, Christian Endeavor. Price 48c
No. 4K04692 Solid gold, same as above. Price........90c

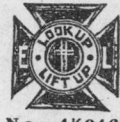

No. 4K04694 Gold filled, Epworth League. Price.......43c
No. 4K04696 Solid gold, same as above. Price.......72c

No. 4K04632 Gold filled, Knights of Pythias. Price........53c
No. 4K04634 Solid gold. Same as above. Price.....$1.10

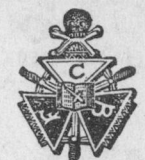

No. 4K04636 Gold filled, Knights of Pythias. Price, 40c
No. 4K04638 Solid gold, same as above. Price..78c

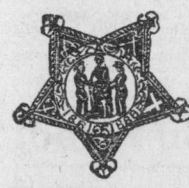

No. 4K04640 Gold filled, G. A. R. enameled. Price..........48c
No. 4K04641 Solid gold, same as above. Price...........95c

No. 4K04642 Gold filled, Modern Woodmen. Price.........38c
No. 4K04644 Solid gold, same as above. Price..72c

No 4K04648 Gold filled, Modern Woodmen. Price....34c
No. 4K04650 Solid gold, same as above. Price..78c

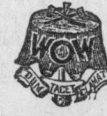

4K04655 Gold filled, Woodmen of the World. Price..48c
4K04657 Solid gold, same as above, price each...70c

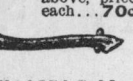

No. 4K04654 Gold filled, Woodmen of America. Price........46c
No. 4K04656 Solid gold. Same as above. Price, 68c

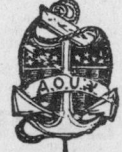

No. 4K04658 Gold filled, Ancient Order United Workmen. Price.....38c
No. 4K04660 Solid gold, same as above. Price..........72c

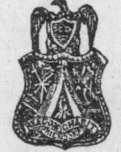

No. 4K04662 Gold filled, Red Men. Price..43c
No. 4K04664 Solid gold, same as above. Ea.82c

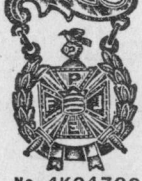

No. 4K04700 Gold filled, Rathbone Sisters. Price..62c
No. 4K04702 Solid gold. As above. Price.....$1.32

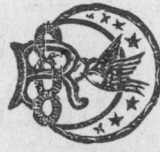

No. 4K04704 Gold filled, Daughters of Rebekah. Price.......48c
No. 4K04706 Solid gold, same as above. Price......95c

No. 4K04651 Gold filled. Woodmen of the World. Each 34c
No. 4K04646 Solid gold, same as above. Price..72c

No. 4K04645 Gold filled. Woodmen of the World. Price 38c
No. 4K04652 Solid gold, same as above. Price..78c

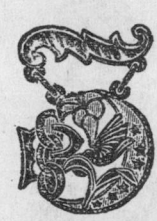

No. 4K04708 Gold filled, Daughters of Rebekah. Price........72c
No. 4K04710 Solid gold. As above. Price.......$1.32

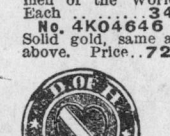

No. 4K04712 Gold filled, Degree of Honor. Price.......42c
No. 4K04714 Solid gold, same as above. Price 85c

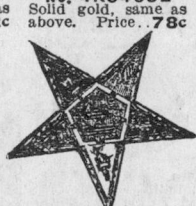

No. 4K04716 Gold filled, Eastern Star. Price..........48c
No. 4K04718 Solid gold. Same as above. Price..........$1.10

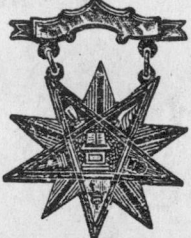

No. 4K04720 Gold filled, Eastern Star. Price..........72c
No. 4K04722 Solid gold, same as above. Price..........$1.68

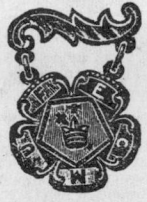

No. 4K04724 Gold filled, Royal Neighbors. Price.......72c
No. 4K04726 Solid gold. Same as above. Price....$1.42

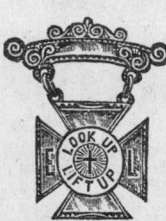

No. 4K04728 Gold filled, Epworth League. Price.........72c
No. 4K04730 Solid gold. Same as above. Price..........$1.24

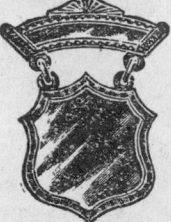

Class or Trophy Pins.
No. 4K04731 Solid Gold. Price.....96c
No. 4K04732 Solid Silver. Price......30c
No. 4K04734 Gold Filled. Price......34c

Class or Trophy Pins
No. 4K04736 Solid Gold. Price.....96c
No. 4K04737 Solid Silver. Price......34c
No. 4K04738 Gold Filled. Price ...48c

WE ENGRAVE any inscription wanted at the rate of 2½ cents per letter for script, 5 cents per letter for Old English, or 3 cents per letter for block. This price for engraving is for badge work only. In engraving badges two kinds of lettering are usually used, script and block, or script and Old English.

SOLID GOLD AND GOLD FILLED EMBLEM BUTTONS. HALF SIZE BUTTONS MADE IN SOLID GOLD ONLY.

ORDER BY NUMBER AND NAME EMBLEM.

Illustrations on this page show exact size.

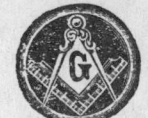

Masonic.
No. 4K04740 Gold filled. Price.......26c
No. 4K04742 Solid gold. Price.......70c

Odd Fellows.
No. 4K04746 Gold filled. Price 26c
No. 4K04748 Solid gold. Price 70c

Knights of Pythias.
No. 4K04752 Gold filled. Price 35c
No. 4K04754 Solid Gold. Price 70c

Ancient Order United Workmen
No. 4K04758 Gold filled. Price 35c
No. 4K04760 Solid gold. Price 70c

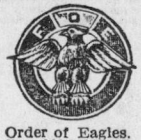

International Association of Machinists.
No. 4K04764 Gold filled. Price 65c
No. 4K04766 Solid gold. Price 80c

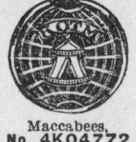

Order of Eagles.
No. 4K04768 Gold filled. Price 60c
No. 4K04770 Solid gold. Price....$1.35

Maccabees.
No. 4K04772 Gold filled. Price 26c
No. 4K04774 Solid gold. Price 70c

No. 4K04860 Masonic. Small size, solid gold. Price......48c

No. 4K04862 Odd Fellows. Small size, solid gold. Price..48c

No. 4K04864 Knights of Pythias. Small size, solid gold. Price. 48c

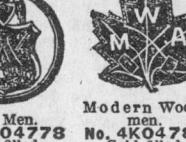

Red Men.
No. 4K04778 Gold filled. Price 26c
No. 4K04780 Solid gold. Price 70c

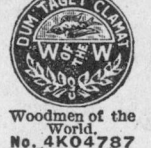

Modern Woodmen.
No. 4K04784 Gold filled. Price 26c
No. 4K04786 Solid gold. Price 70c

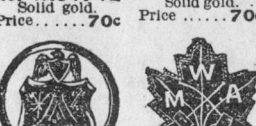

Woodmen of the World.
No. 4K04787 Gold filled. Price 26c
No. 4K04789 Solid gold. Price 70c

Elks.
No. 4K04788 Gold filled. Price 54c
No. 4K04790 Solid gold. Price.....$1.20

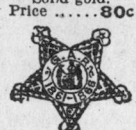

G. A. R.
No. 4K04836 Gold filled. Price 35c
No. 4K04838 Solid gold. Price 62c

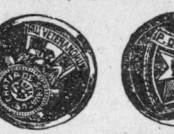

Sons of Veterans.
No. 4K04840 Gold filled. Price 37c
No. 4K04842 Solid gold. Price 70c

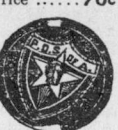

Patriotic Sons of America.
No. 4K04844 Gold filled. Price 26c
No. 4K04846 Solid gold. Price 70c

No. 4K04866 Modern Woodmen. Small size, solid gold. Price..48c

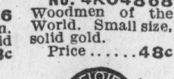

No. 4K04868 Woodmen of the World. Small size, solid gold. Price......48c

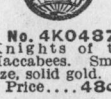

No. 4K04870 Knights of the Maccabees. Small size, solid gold. Price.....48c

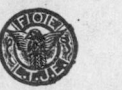

No. 4K04872 Red Men. Small size, solid gold. Price......48c

No. 4K04874 Order of Eagles. Small size, solid gold. Price..48c

No. 4K04876 Knights of Columbus. Small size. Solid gold. Price....48c

LADIES' LACE PINS, CUFF PINS, BABY PINS AND PIN SETS.

MAIL CHARGES on Lace Pins, Brooches, Cuff Pins, Baby Pins and Sets, 2 cents extra; 8 cents extra by insured or registered mail.

No. 4K06010 Baby Pin, gold filled, Roman and bright finish. Price..............43c
Engraving 2½ cents per letter extra if desired.

No. 4K06012 Baby Pin, gold filled, Roman and bright finish. Price..........38c
Engraving, 2½ cents per letter extra if desired. We charge 2½ cents per letter for script engraving; 5 cents for Old English.

No. 4K06018 Gold front, raised ornamented ends. Price, per pair.34c

No. 4K06021 Solid gold, bright polish. Per pair....83c

No. 4K06023 Solid gold, Roman yellow color, set with genuine pearls. Pr.$1.31

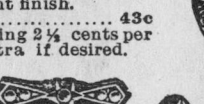

No. 4K06024 Solid gold front, Roman color, hand engraved. Per set of 3....90c

No. 4K06026 Solid gold front, bright finish, set with pearls and enamel turquoise. Per set of 3.$1.13

No. 4K06028 Gold filled, hand engraved, bright finish, soldered chain. Price...................58c

No. 4K06030 Solid gold front, Roman finish, bright engraved, soldered chain. Price...................$1.15

No. 4K06034 Gold front, bright finish, hand engraved, soldered chain. Price...................75c

No. 4K06036 Solid gold front, Roman finish, bright hand engraving, soldered chain. Price...............93c

No. 4K06039 Solid gold, bright polish, raised ornamented ends, soldered links. Price, each...............$1.70
3 for............4.59

No. 4K06041 Solid gold, Roman yellow color, set with genuine pearls, soldered links. Price, each....$2.25
3 for............6.08

No. 4K06000 Gold front, bright polish, hand engraved, bar pin. Price...................56c

No. 4K06003 Gold front, bright polish, hand engraved, bar pin. Price...................83c

No. 4K06025 Gold front, bright polish, hand engraved, set with enamel pearls. Price, per set of three.87c

No. 4K06027 Gold front, bright polish. Price, per set of three.........96c

No. 4K06031 Gold front, hand engraved, bright polish, soldered chain. Price...................$1.35

No. 4K06033 Gold front, hand engraved, bright polish, soldered chain. Price...................$1.10

FINEST QUALITY ROLLED GOLD PLATE AND SOLID GOLD EARRINGS AND DROPS.

POSTAGE EXTRA, 2 CENTS. REGISTERED MAIL, 8 CENTS EXTRA.

No. 4K06061 Bright polish, solid gold front, hand engraved, ball pendants. Price, per pair.......51c

No. 4K06063 Bright polish, solid gold front, hand engraved, ball pendants. Price, per pair......68c

No. 4K06065 Solid gold fronts, hand engraved, ball pendants. Per pair......72c

No. 4K06067 Solid gold, set with seven genuine Bohemian garnets. Per pair.......91c

No. 4K06069 Solid gold, pearl center, ball pendants. Per pair....95c

No. 4K06071 Solid gold, plain setting, set with imitation pearls. Per pair. $1.11

No. 4K06073 Solid gold, plain polished ball. Per pair......$1.18

No. 4K06075 Solid gold, fancy cup setting, genuine pearl set. Per pair......$1.52

No. 4K06077 Solid gold, set with 12 rhinestones, 1 enamel turquoise. Per pair....$3.18

THE GREAT REDUCTIONS IN THE PRICES shown in the pages of this catalogue we feel sure will be very pleasing to our millions of customers.

No. 4K06043 Rolled gold plate hoop earrings, engraved, solid gold wires. Per pair. 31c

No. 4K06045 Rolled gold plate hoop earrings, engraved, solid gold wires. Per pair. 39c

No. 4K06047 Solid gold earrings, bright polish. Per pair.......62c

No. 4K06049 Solid gold hoop earrings, faceted and polished. Per pair......93c

No. 4K06051 Solid gold plain hoop earrings. Per pair.......95c

No. 4K06053 Solid gold hoop earrings, extra quality, faceted and polished. Per pair....$1.05

No. 4K06055 Solid gold hoop earrings, extra quality, faceted and polished. Per pair......$1.40

No. 4K06057 Solid gold fronts, hand engraved, ball pendants. Per pair.......48c

No. 4K06059 Bright polish, solid gold front, hand engraved, ball pendants. Price, per pair.....53c

SOLID SILVER, GOLD FILLED, ROLLED GOLD PLATE AND SOLID GOLD CROSSES.

Illustrations Show Exact Size.   Postage on Crosses, 3 cents extra.   Registry, 8 cents extra.

No. 4K06079 Solid silver. Price........20c
No. 4K06081 Gold filled, bright burnished. Price26c
No. 4K06083 Solid gold. Price.....$1.18

No. 4K06085 Rolled plate, engraved. Price.........21c

No. 4K06087 Solid silver. Price.........30c
No. 4K06089 Gold filled, set with enamel turquoise. Price.........33c
No. 4K06091 Solid gold. Price.....$1.37

No. 4K06093 Gold filled cross, set with imitation pearls and ruby center. The latest idea, very fashionable. Price..90c

No. 4K06095 Solid gold front, fancy engraved, satin finish. Price..76c

No. 4K06097 Gold filled, set with almandine doublets and one brilliant. Price.......85c

No. 4K06098 Solid gold, bright polish, perfectly made. Price. $1.15

No. 4K06099 Fine solid gold, fancy engraved, satin finish. Price....$1.40

HEAVY SOLID SILVER NOVELTIES

NOTHING MORE APPROPRIATE FOR A GIFT. EVERY NOVELTY ILLUSTRATED ON THIS PAGE IS OF SOLID SILVER, EXCEPT WHEN OTHERWISE STATED, AND HEAVIER THAN ANY OTHER LINE ON THE MARKET AT PRICES MORE THAN DOUBLE WHAT WE ASK.

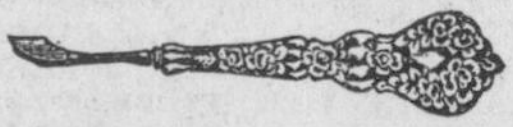

No. 4K06800 Solid Silver Cuticle Knife, Rose pattern, 4½ inches long. Price.......59c
If by mail, postage extra, 4 cents.

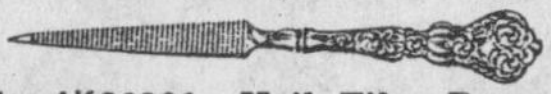

No. 4K06801 Nail File, Rose pattern, 6 inches long. Price.........59c
If by mail, postage extra, 4 cents.

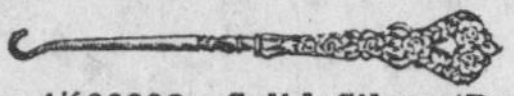

No. 4K06802 Solid Silver Button Hook, Rose pattern, 6½ inches long. Price.......59c
If by mail, postage extra, 4 cents.

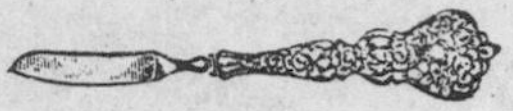

No. 4K06804 Solid Silver Desk Knife, Rose pattern, 5½ inches long. Price.......59c
If by mail, postage extra, 4 cents.

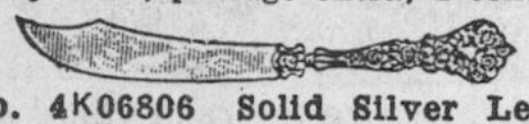

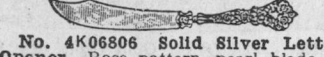

No. 4K06806 Solid Silver Letter Opener, Rose pattern, pearl blade, 8 inches long. Price.......79c
If by mail, postage extra, 5 cents.

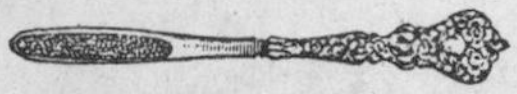

No. 4K06808 Solid Silver Tooth Brush, Rose pattern, 6½ inches long. Price.......59c
If by mail, postage extra, 4 cents.

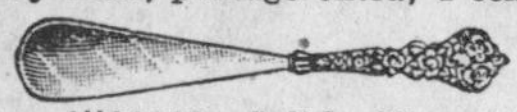

No. 4K06812 Solid Silver Shoe Horn, Rose pattern, 7 inches long. Price.......59c
If by mail, postage extra, 6 cents.

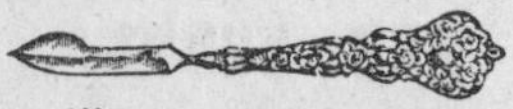

No. 4K06814 Solid Silver Ink Eraser, Rose pattern, 5½ inches long. Price.......59c
If by mail, postage extra, 4 cents.

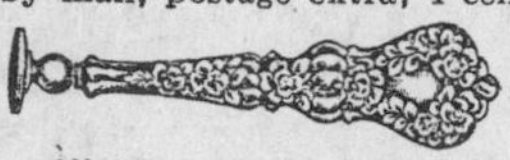

No. 4K06815 Solid Silver Letter Seal, Rose pattern, 3½ inches long. Price.......62c
10 cents extra for deep engraved letter.
If by mail, postage extra, 4 cents.

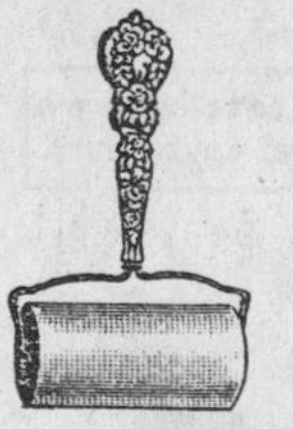

No. 4K06816 Solid Silver Roller Writing Blotter, roller style, Rose pattern, 5½ inches long. Price.... 59c
If by mail, postage extra, 5 cents.

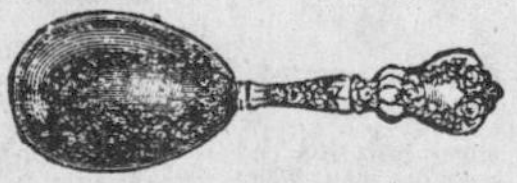

No. 4K06818 Solid Silver Stocking Darner, Rose pattern, 6 inches long. Price.......59c
If by mail, postage extra, 5 cents.

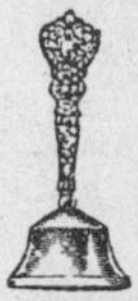

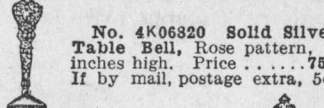

No. 4K06820 Solid Silver Table Bell, Rose pattern, 5 inches high. Price......75c
If by mail, postage extra, 5c.

No. 4K06852 Table Bell, Colonial pattern, 4½ inches high. Price.......68c
Postage extra, 5 cents.

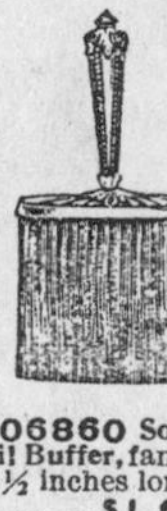

No. 4K06854 Solid Silver Hat Brush, Colonial pattern, 6 inches long. Price.......98c
By mail, postage extra, 4c.

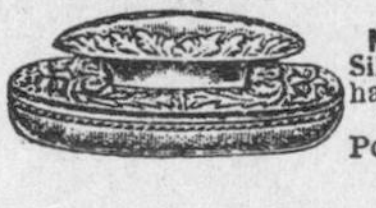

No. 4K06860 Solid Silver Nail Buffer, fancy handle, 4½ inches long. Price......$1.60
Postage extra, 4 cents.

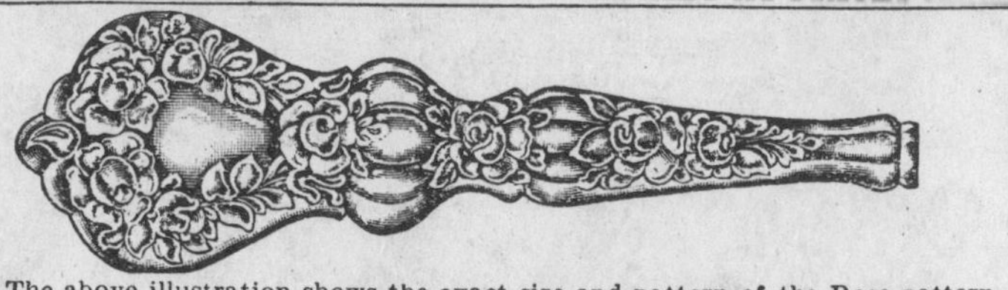

The above illustration shows the exact size and pattern of the Rose pattern handle used on silver novelties illustrated on this page.

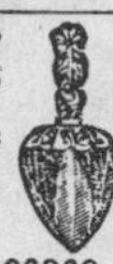

No. 4K06862 Solid Silver Needle Emery, fancy handle, 3 inches long. Price.......38c
If by mail, postage extra, 6 cents.

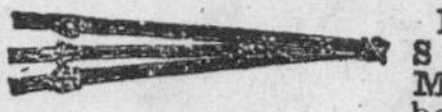

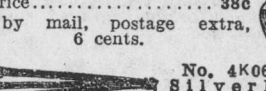

No. 4K06868 Silver Book Mark. Silk ribbon, sterling silver mounted book mark. Price . . 19c
If by mail, postage extra, 2 cents.

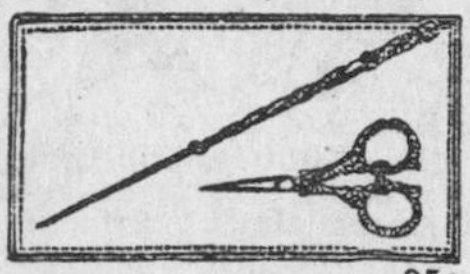

No. 4K06870 Solid Silver Crocheting Set. Needle, 7 inches; scissors, 3½ inches. Price.......95c
If by mail, postage extra, 10 cents.

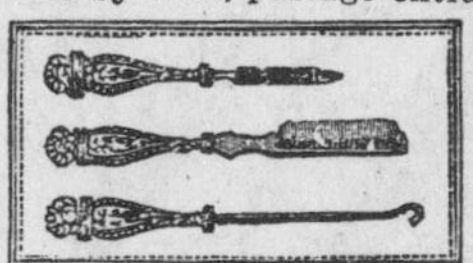

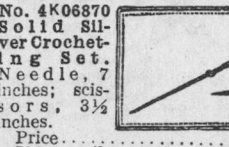

No. 4K06872 Solid Silver Toilet Set. Button hook, 6 inches; tooth brush, 6 inches; nail file, 4½ inches. Price.......76c
If by mail, postage extra, 10 cents.

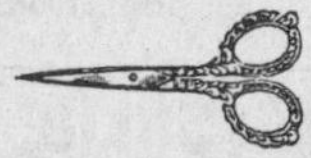

No. 4K06876 Solid Silver Embroidery Scissors, fancy handles, 4 inches long. Price.......75c
If by mail, postage extra, 4 cents.

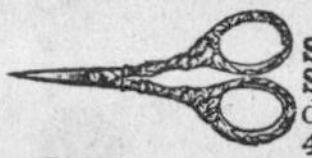

No. 4K06877 Solid Silver Manicure Scissors, fancy handles, curved blades, 4½ inches long. Price.......90c
If by mail, postage extra, 4 cents.

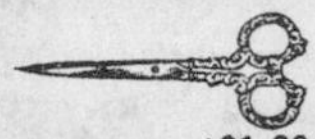

No. 4K06879 Solid Silver Sewing Scissors, fancy handles, 6 inches long. Price.......$1.20
If by mail, postage extra, 5 cents.

WE ONLY QUOTE AND ILLUSTRATE MATCH BOXES OF GOOD, DURABLE WEIGHT.

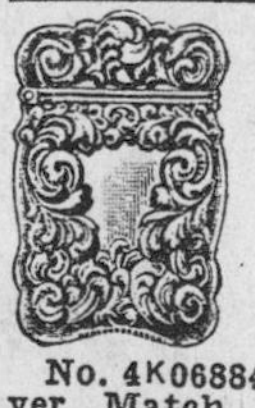

No. 4K06882 Solid Silver Match Box, medium weight, 2¼ inches long. Price $1.20
If by mail, postage extra, 3 cents.

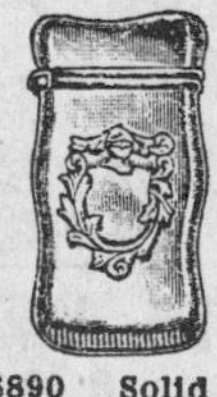

No. 4K06884 Solid Silver Match Box, extra heavy, plain polish, 2½ inches long. Price .. $1.65
If by mail, postage extra, 5 cents.

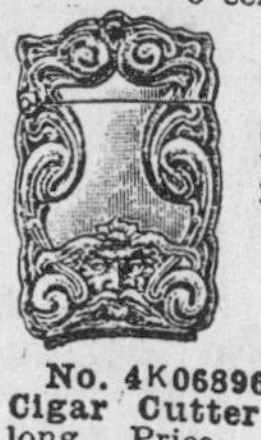

No. 4K06890 Solid Silver Match Box, extra heavy, bright polish, 2½ inches long. Price.......$2.25
If by mail, postage extra, 3 cents.

No. 4K06896 Solid Silver Cigar Cutter, 1½ inches long. Price.......62c
If by mail, postage extra, 3 cents.

No. 4K06900 Solid Silver Stamp Box. Price.......49c
If by mail, postage extra, 3c.

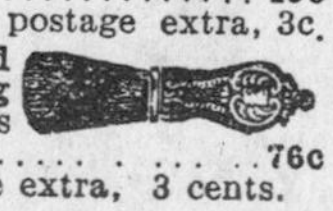

No. 4K06902 Solid Silver Shaving Brush, 4¼ inches long. Price.......76c
If by mail, postage extra, 3 cents.

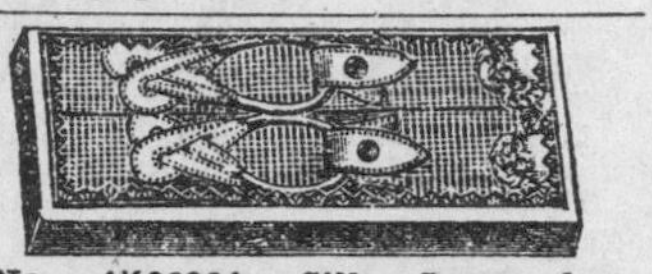

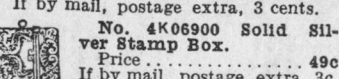

No. 4K06904 Silk Suspenders, solid silver buckles, in fine glass covered box. Price.......$1.46
If by mail, postage extra, 25 cents.

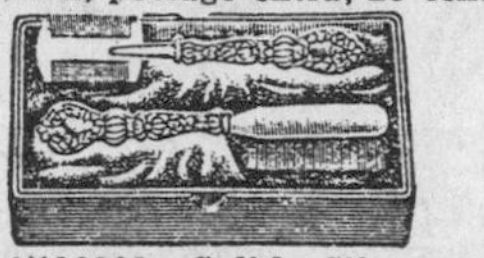

No. 4K06908 Solid Silver Rose Pattern Baby Set. Brush, 6 inches long; comb, 5½ inches long. Price, complete in box.......$2.00
If by mail, postage extra, 6 cents.

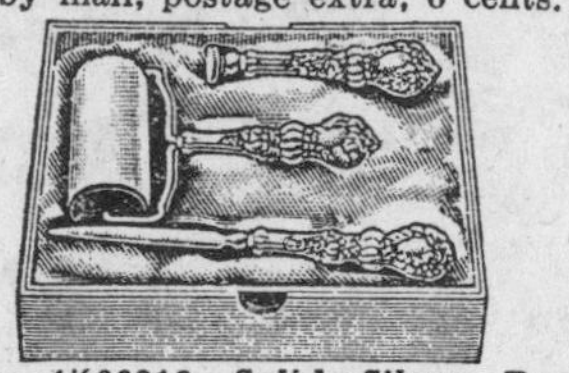

No. 4K06916 Solid Silver Desk Set, Rose pattern. Paper cutter, 6½ inches long; blotter, 5 inches long; letter seal, 3¾ inches long. Price, complete in box.......$1.95
If by mail, postage extra, 10 cents.

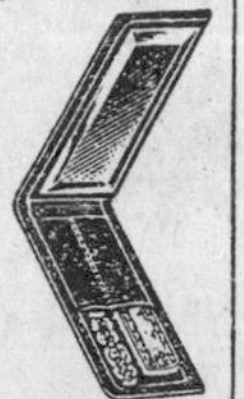

No. 4K06918 Gentlemen's Vest Pocket Toilet Set, in mirrored case. Solid silver comb and nail file. Length of case, 3½ inches; width, 2 inches. Price.....95c
If by mail, postage extra, 5 cents.

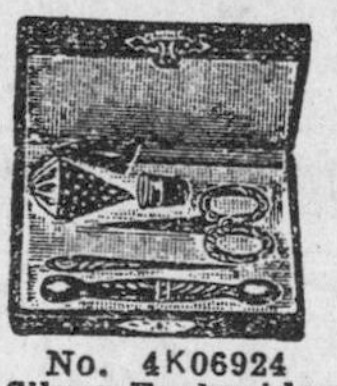

No. 4K06922 Solid Silver Glove Set, five pieces, box 5x4 inches, complete. Price......$1.58
If by mail, postage extra, 10 cents.

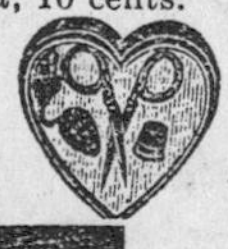

No. 4K06924 Solid Silver Embroidery Set, three pieces. Price, 98c
If by mail, postage extra, 6 cents.

No. 4K06926 Garters, Solid Silver mountings, set with fancy stone, fine silk web; in box. Price, per pair......$1.90
If by mail, postage extra, 6 cents.

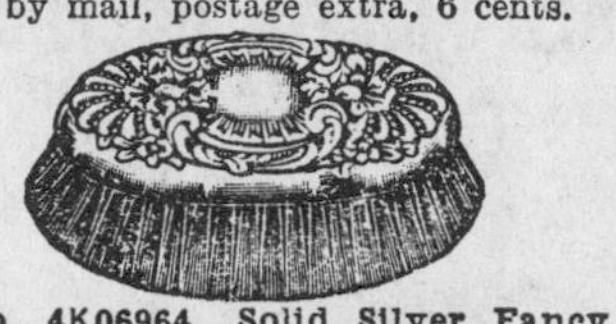

No. 4K06964 Solid Silver Fancy Raised Ornamented Military Brush, 4½ inches long, 2¾ inches wide. Price, per pair.......$4.65
If by mail, postage extra, 8 cents.

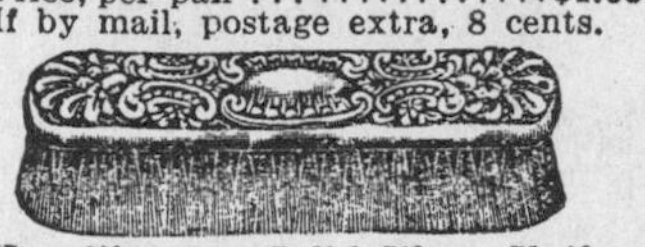

No. 4K06962 Solid Silver Clothes Brush, fancy top, 6½x1⅝ inches. Price.......$1.98
If by mail, postage extra, 10 cents.

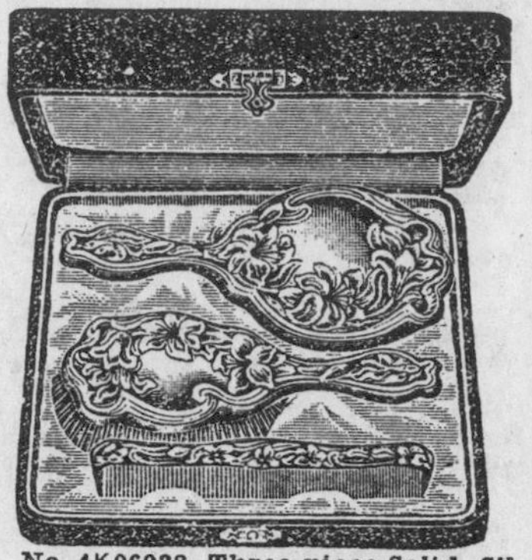

No. 4K06938 Three-piece Solid Silver Tiger Lily Pattern Toilet Set, in pretty lined leatherette covered case. Mirror, 9½ inches; brush, 8½ inches; comb, 7½ inches. This is an extra heavy weight toilet set, and one of the handsomest on the market. Shipping weight, 4 pounds. Price... . $11.69

No. 4K06940 Mirror alone, not mailable. Price.......$6.71

No. 4K06942 Brush alone. Price.......$3.71
If by mail, postage extra, 12 cents.

No. 4K06944 Comb alone. Price.......$1.23
If by mail, postage extra, 4 cents.

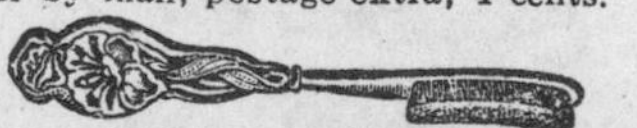

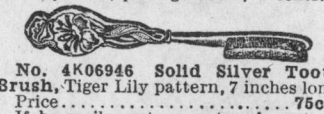

No. 4K06946 Solid Silver Tooth Brush, Tiger Lily pattern, 7 inches long. Price.......75c
If by mail, postage extra, 4 cents.

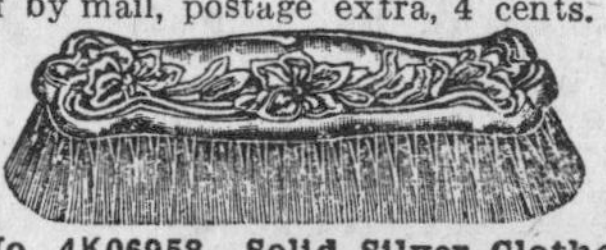

No. 4K06958 Solid Silver Clothes Brush, Tiger Lily pattern, 7x2¼ inches. Price.......$3.00
If by mail, postage extra, 10 cents.

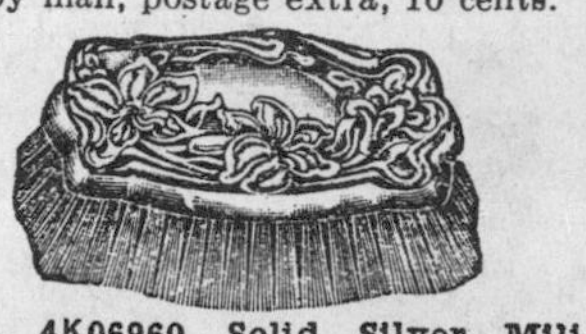

No. 4K06960 Solid Silver Military Hair Brush, Tiger Lily pattern, 4⅛x3 inches. Price, per pair..$6.00
If by mail, postage extra, 8 cents.

BEATRICE SILVER PLATED TOILET SETS.

A brand new pattern on the market, and the biggest value ever offered for the money. To satisfy the popular demand for toilet sets and manicure pieces, we contracted for a large quantity of the very handsome articles illustrated below. They are silver plated on white metal, strong, substantial and good for practical purposes. They are all full sizes, in fact, run larger in size than similar articles quoted on this page in solid silver. Complete in box, as illustration shows.

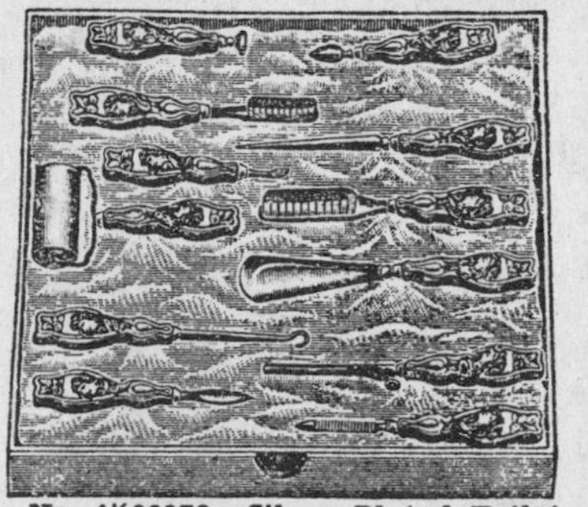

No. 4K06970 Silver Plated Toilet Set, consisting of the twelve following pieces: nail brush, hand brush, nail file, cuticle knife, paper cutter, roller blotter, letter seal, ink eraser, curling iron, button hook, shoe horn and corn knife. Shipping weight, 2½ pounds.
Price, complete in white paper cloth lined box.......$2.78

CUT PRICES IN SOLID GOLD PENS AND PEARL HOLDERS

MADE UNDER CONTRACT FOR US, THE SPECIFICATIONS ARE CARRIED OUT IN EVERY DETAIL.

OUR PENS AND HOLDERS are the best on the market. The pearl sticks, gold filled holders and noses are made and selected from the best stock to be purchased. Illustrations are exact size. The actual size of pens and holders are from 6 to 7 inches long. Don't be misled by fancy prices asked by others. We warrant our pens and holders the equal of any and better than the most. Postage on pen holders, if by mail, 5 cents extra; registry, 8 cents extra.

No. 4K07050 Genuine silk plush covered, plush lined pen box. Size, 8 inches. Price, each (with any pen you select) 19c

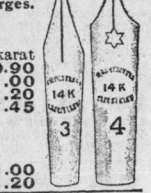

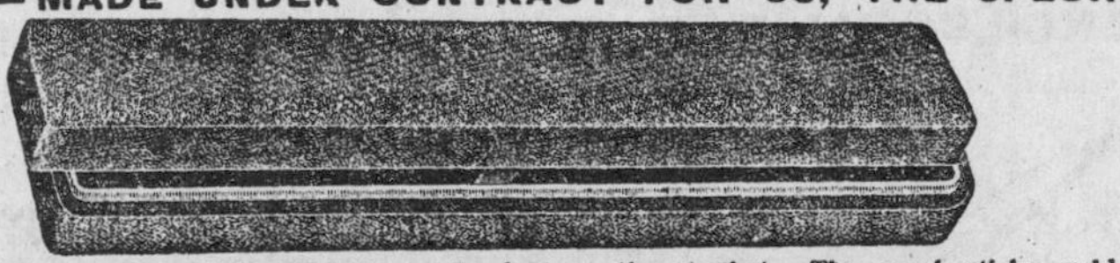

HIGHEST QUALITY SOLID GOLD PEN POINTS.

Illustration shows No. 3 Long Nib Pen and No. 4 Stub Pen. We sell these pens in the various sizes as quoted in 10 and 14-karat gold. Be sure to order by number. Gold Pens repointed for 22 cents each. 2 cents extra for mail charges.

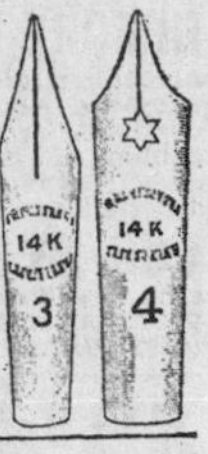

Finest Quality Solid Gold Pens. LONG NIBS.

No.	No.	10-karat	14-karat	No.	No.	10-karat	14-karat
4K07351	1	35c	45c	4K07359	5	$0.65	$0.90
4K07353	2	40c	50c	4K07361	6	.75	1.00
4K07355	3	45c	65c	4K07363	7	.90	1.20
4K07357	4	50c	75c	4K07365	8	1.10	1.45

STUB. Made in 14-Karat Only.

No.	No.		No.	No.	
4K07367	4	75c	4K07371	6	$1.00
4K07369	5	90c	4K07373	7	1.20

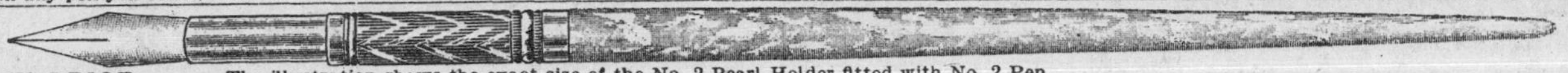

REDUCED IN PRICE.

The illustration shows the exact size of the No. 2 Pearl Holder fitted with No. 2 Pen.

BEST QUALITY GOLD PEN IN GOLD FILLED AND PLAIN PEARL DESK HOLDER.

		No. 1 Pen	No. 2 Pen	No. 3 Pen	No. 4 Pen	No. 5 Pen	No. 6 Pen
No. 4K07068	10-karat gold Pen with Holder	62c	$0.94	$0.98	$1.10	$1.30	$1.48
No. 4K07071	14-karat gold Pen with Holder	93c	1.10	1.26	1.48	1.75	1.97

The illustration shows the exact size of the No. 4 Pearl Holder fitted with No. 4 Pen.

SOLID GOLD PEN IN BEST QUALITY GOLD FILLED AND PLAIN PEARL SLIDE HOLDER.

		No. 1 Pen	No. 2 Pen	No. 3 Pen	No. 4 Pen	No. 5 Pen	No. 6 Pen
No. 4K07072	10-karat gold Pen with Holder	$1.05	$1.21	$1.25	$1.46	$1.57	$1.78
No. 4K07075	14-karat gold Pen with Holder	1.20	1.44	1.57	1.75	1.92	2.19

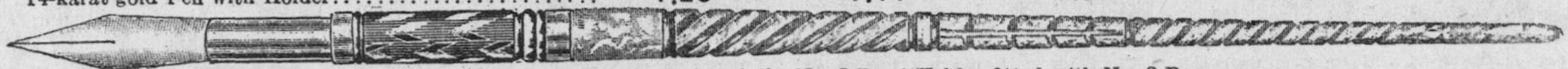

The illustration shows the exact size of the No. 2 Pearl Holder fitted with No. 2 Pen.

SOLID GOLD PEN IN BEST QUALITY GOLD FILLED AND FANCY HAND TURNED PEARL DESK HOLDER.

		No. 1 Pen	No. 2 Pen	No. 3 Pen	No. 4 Pen	No. 5 Pen	No. 6 Pen
No. 4K07080	10-karat gold Pen with Holder	$1.10	$1.26	$1.43	$1.59	$1.81	$2.03
No. 4K07081	14-karat gold Pen with Holder	1.27	1.50	1.73	1.96	2.19	2.42

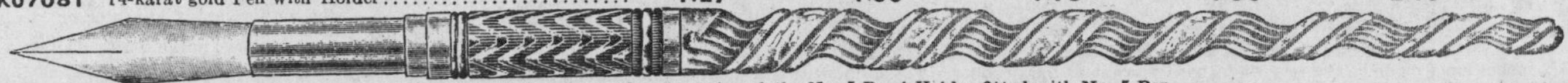

The illustration shows the exact size of the No. 5 Pearl Holder fitted with No. 5 Pen.

SOLID GOLD PEN IN BEST QUALITY GOLD FILLED AND FANCY FULL TWIST PEARL DESK HOLDER.

		No. 1 Pen	No. 2 Pen	No. 3 Pen	No. 4 Pen	No. 5 Pen	No. 6 Pen
No. 4K07076	10-karat gold Pen with Holder	$1.05	$1.21	$1.37	$1.54	$1.76	$1.98
No. 4K07079	14-karat gold Pen with Holder	1.20	1.43	1.66	1.89	2.12	2.35

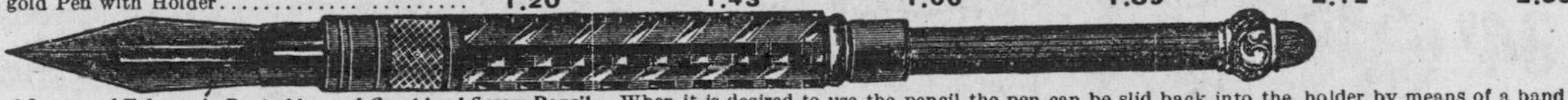

No. 4K07089 Gold Filled Improved Telescopic Penholder and Combined Screw Pencil. When it is desired to use the pencil the pen can be slid back into the holder by means of a band on the outside, and the pencil can be brought into position. 14-karat Pen with Holder. Price, No. 3 Pen, $1.70; No. 4 Pen, $1.95; No. 5 Pen, $2.10; No. 6 Pen $2.45

BEST QUALITY SOLID GOLD PEN IN GOLD FILLED AND EBONY DESK HOLDER.

The illustration shows the exact size of the No. 1 Holder fitted with No. 1 Pen.

		No. 1 Pen	No. 2 Pen	No. 3 Pen	No. 4 Pen	No. 5 Pen	No. 6 Pen	No. 7 Pen
No. 4K07090	10-karat gold Pen with Holder	$0.60	$0.65	$0.70	$0.72	$0.88	$0.98	$1.20
No. 4K07093	14-karat gold Pen with Holder	.77	.83	.99	1.10	1.26	1.36	1.64

Sterling Silver Desk Set, $1.16.

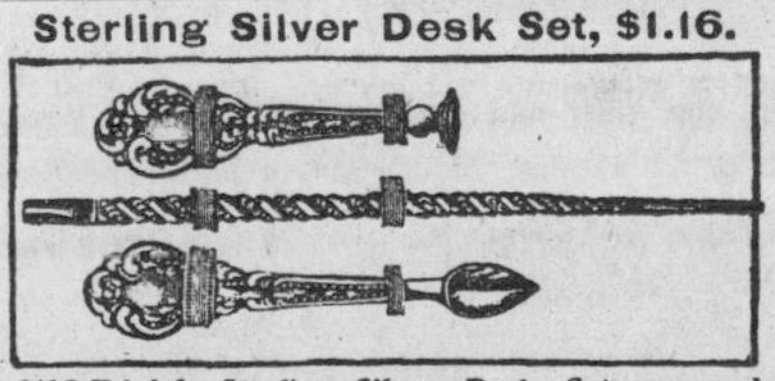

No. 4K07144 Sterling Silver Desk Set on card. Set consists of silver penholder, 6 inches long; silver handled ink eraser, 3¾ inches long; silver handled letter seal, 3 inches long. Price, complete set $1.16
If by mail, postage extra, 6 cents.

Combination Desk Set, $1.80.

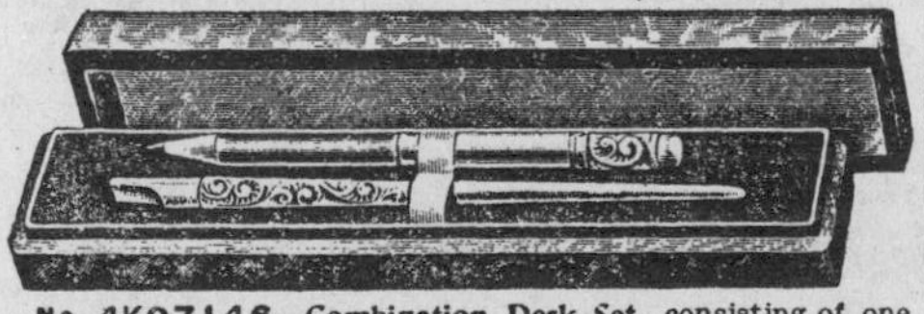

No. 4K07146 Combination Desk Set, consisting of one solid silver penholder, 6¼ inches long, and one solid silver lead pencil holder with rubber eraser attached, 2¾ inches long; entire length, with pencil, 5 inches. Complete in hardwood polished oak box, silk plush lined. Price, per set $1.80
If by mail, postage extra, 6 cents.

Our $1.72 Combination Desk Set.

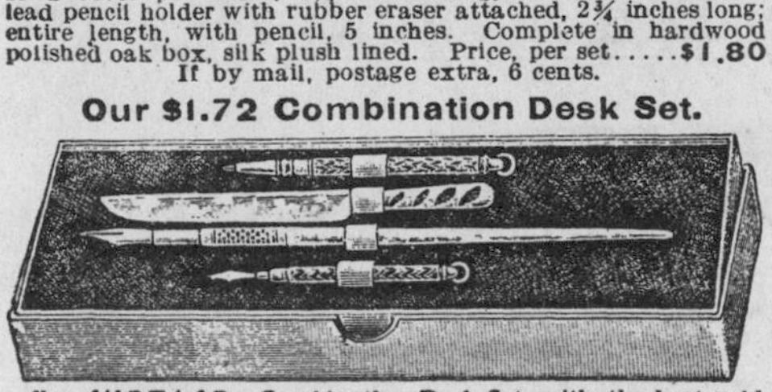

No. 4K07148 Combination Desk Set, with the best gold filled mountings, consisting of one pearl letter opener, 4¼ inches long; one pen and penholder, pen, solid gold; entire length, 6¼ inches; one fancy screw toothpick, full extended length, 2¾ inches; and one screw pencil, full extended length, 3 inches. Price, complete in enameled paper velvet lined box .. $1.72
If by mail, postage extra, 4 cents.

Combination Desk Set, $1.82.

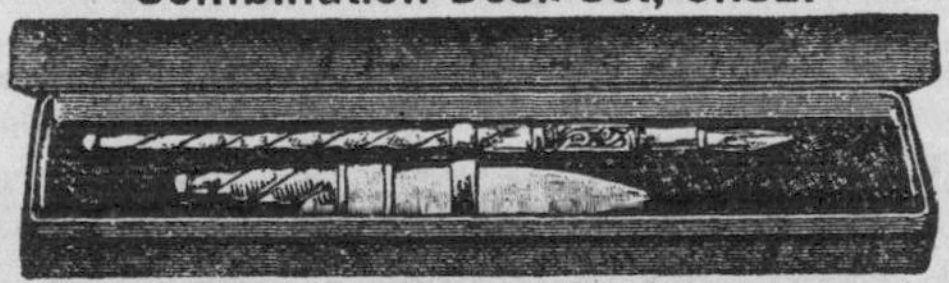

No. 4K07151 Desk Set, consisting of pearl paper cutter and pearl handled penholder and solid gold 14-karat No. 1 pen. Cutter and penholder made to match, ornamented with gold filled wire work. Price, with box complete $1.82
If by mail, postage extra, 3 cents.

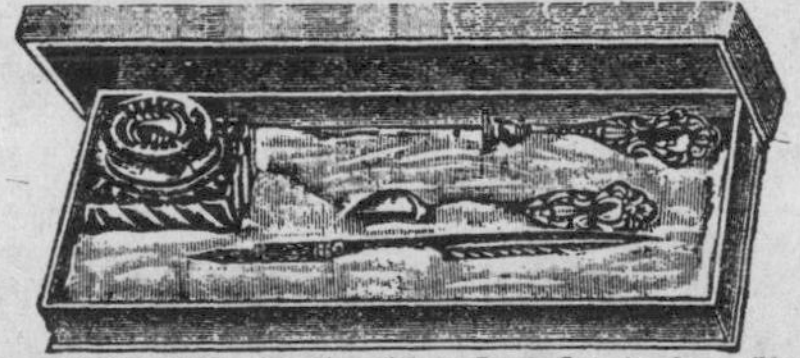

No. 4K07152 Sterling Silver Desk Set, in fine silk lined paper box. Set consists of silver covered fluted square ink well, 1½x1½x1½ inches; silver handled letter seal, 2½ inches long; pearl penholder with solid No. 1 gold pen, 5 inches long; silver handled ink eraser, 3¼ inches long. Price, for complete set ... (Postage extra, 8 cents.) ... $1.76

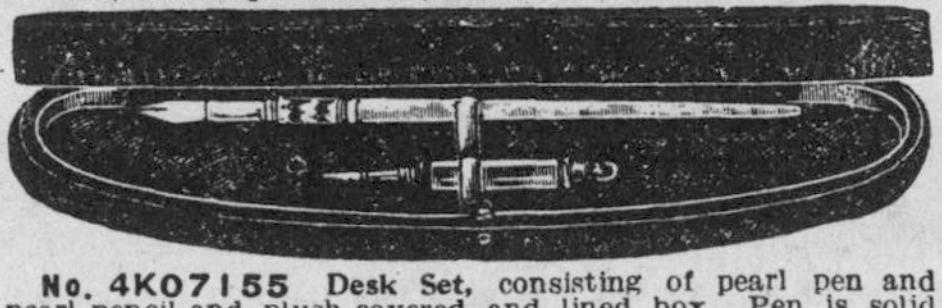

No. 4K07155 Desk Set, consisting of pearl pen and pearl pencil and plush covered and lined box. Pen is solid gold, 14-karat, No. 1 size; pencil is pearl with gold filled trimmings. Price, for complete set $2.42
If by mail, postage extra, 4 cents.

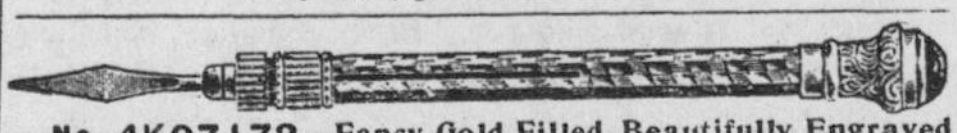

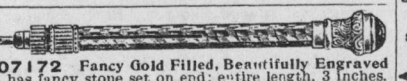

No. 4K07172 Fancy Gold Filled, Beautifully Engraved Toothpick, has fancy stone set on end; entire length, 3 inches. Toothpick can be slid back into case. Illustration shows pick ready for use. Price ...... (Postage extra, 2 cents.) 65c

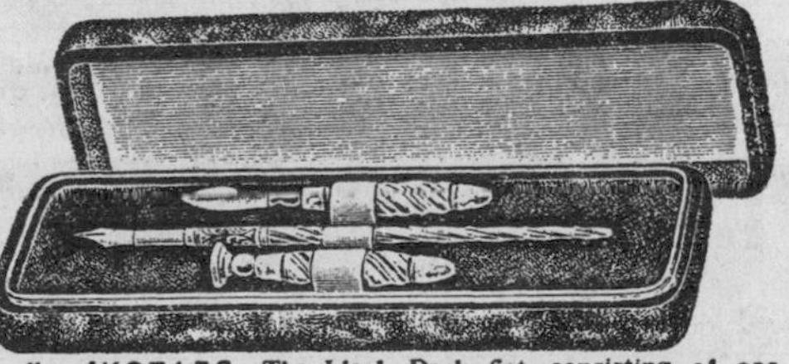

No. 4K07156 The Ideal Desk Set, consisting of one fine pearl letter seal, 2½ inches long; one fine pearl hand turned penholder with solid silver nose, fitted with a solid gold pen; full length of penholder and pen, 6¼ inches, and one pearl handled steel eraser; full length, 3¾ inches. Price, complete in beautiful silk plush box, velvet lined $2.96
If by mail, postage extra, 4 cents.

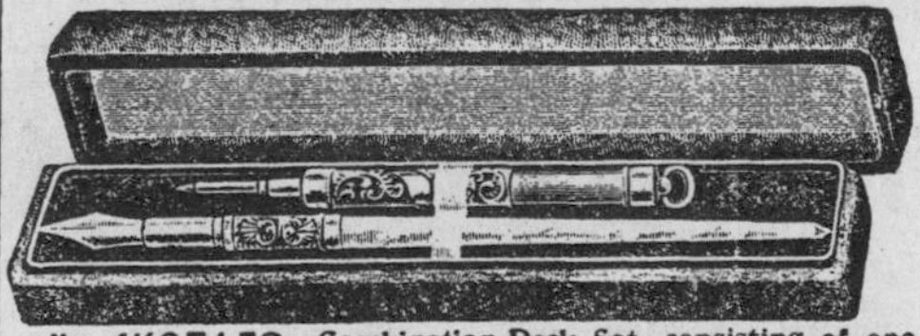

No. 4K07158 Combination Desk Set, consisting of one gold filled magic pencil, full extended length, 5 inches; one pearl penholder with gold filled nose, fitted with large size solid gold pen; full length of penholder, including pen, 7½ inches. Price, complete in beautiful silk plush box, velvet lined ..... (If by mail, postage extra, 4 cents.) $3.09

Screw Pencils.

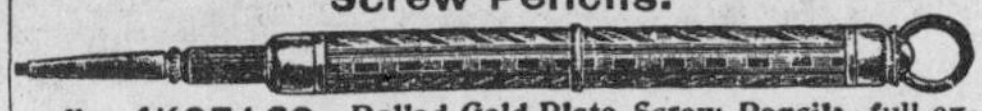

No. 4K07160 Rolled Gold Plate Screw Pencil; full extended length, 2¾ inches. Price 15c
If by mail, postage extra, 2 cents.

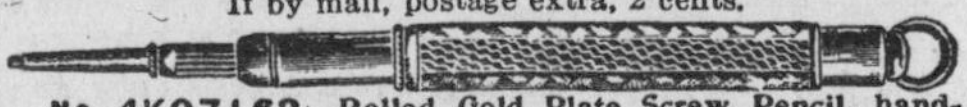

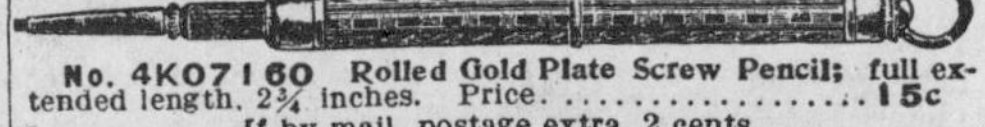

No. 4K07162 Rolled Gold Plate Screw Pencil, handsomely engraved; full extended length, 4 inches. Price ...... (If by mail, postage extra, 2 cents.) 46c

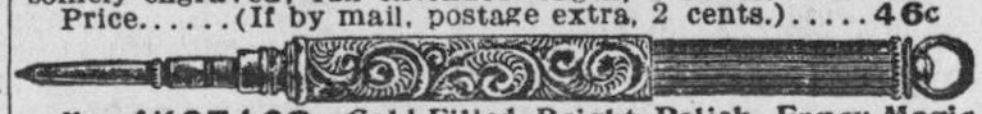

No. 4K07168 Gold Filled, Bright Polish, Fancy Magic Pencil; full extended length, 6 inches. Price .... (If by mail, postage extra, 2 cents.) $1.38

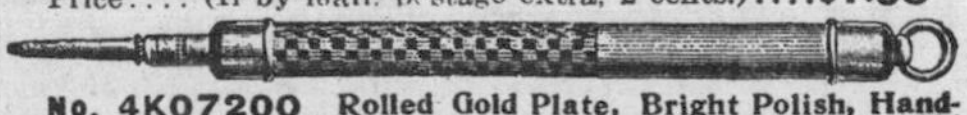

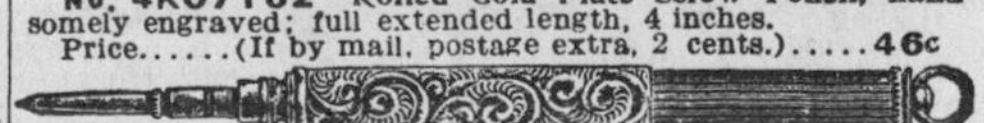

No. 4K07200 Rolled Gold Plate, Bright Polish, Handsomely Engraved Magic Pencil; full extended length, 4¾ inches. Price ... (If by mail, postage extra, 2 cents.) ... 68c

No. 4K07170 Fine Gold Filled, Fancy Chased Toothpick and Ear Spoon. Entire length, 4 inches. Pick and spoon can be shoved back in case when not in use. Price $1.18
If by mail, postage extra, 2 cents.

FOUNTAIN PENS AND STYLOGRAPHIC PENS

ANOTHER ASTONISHING CUT IN THE PRICES OF

—SOMETIMES CALLED INK PENCILS—ILLUSTRATIONS SHOW EXACT SIZE—

BEFORE LISTING A FOUNTAIN OR STYLOGRAPHIC PEN we have carefully and thoroughly investigated the mechanism of all the various makes and have selected the pens we illustrate as the most perfect on the market. Our pens are non-leakable; the joints are made a little tighter than other makes. The rubber used is the very finest Para rubber, not scraps and fillings of inferior quality. The feeds we can especially recommend as being the best of their type. The gold points used in our fountain pens are a little heavier, a little longer and a little thicker than are used in competing brands.

OUR STYLOGRAPHIC, OR INK PENCILS, lead the pen world for quality and price. Twenty to 40 per cent saved on the purchase of any pen illustrated on these pages. We actually put in your pocket, if you select a pen from us, by reason of the cut prices we are offering, 50 cents to $2.50, according to the price and the pen you select. We positively save you the entire

retailer's profit and some of the jobber's besides. Our fountain pens are made in proportion. When a No. 2 pen is quoted we wish it understood that a No. 2 barrel is used, and when a No. 4 pen is quoted a No. 4 barrel is used. Many unscrupulous concerns use a No. 2 barrel and fit a No. 4 pen.

THIS HANDSOME FOUNTAIN PEN PROTECTOR FREE. With every fountain pen illustrated on this page, we send FREE, without cost to you, one of these patent clips. It is adjustable; fits any pen on this page. By its use you cannot lose your fountain pen or drop it from your pocket.

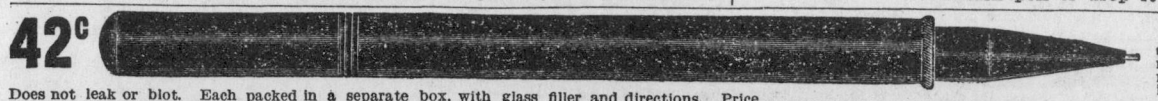

42c
Does not leak or blot. Each packed in a separate box, with glass filler and directions. Price..........

Stylographic Pens.
No. 4K07250 Stylographic Fountain Pen. Made of vulcanized hard rubber, tapering to a round point, flow regulated by a steel needle. Will make impression through three carbons. **42c**

98c
The stylographic pen is the best and most practical pen made for carbon copy work. It will make an impression through three carbons and is especially adapted for addressing. Price, complete, with detachable spring clip, filler and cleaner, together with full directions..........

No. 4K07251 Our Congress Regulation Stylo Pen or Ink Pencil, is made of black, hard vulcanized Para rubber, beautiful engine turned barrel, has latest spring principle, patent sleeve, covered air chamber vent. **98c**

79c
The stylographic pen is the best and most practical pen made for carbon copy work. It will make an impression through three carbons and is especially adapted for addressing. Price, complete, including detachable patent clip, filler and cleaner, together with full directions..........

No. 4K07253 Our Black and Tan Stylo Pen, sometimes called ink pencil. Our Black and Tan Stylographic Pen when point is covered by the cap, measures 3¾ inches, and holds a full complement of ink. This pen is made of the very finest black and red hard Para rubber. The stylo needle is solid gold tipped, has the spring principle stylo, the latest improvement. **79c**

$1.23
point is 3¾ inches long, made of the very finest hard vulcanized Para rubber. The stylo or writing point is gold, iridium tipped, has the latest spring stylo principle non-leakable, tight jointed, perfect in every respect. similar pens are bringing on the open market from $2.00 to $2.50 each. The stylographic pen is the best and most practical pen made for carbon copy work and general writing. It will make an impression through three carbons and is especially adapted for addressing. Price, complete with patent detachable clip, filler, cleaner, and full directions..........

No. 4K07255 Our Tan Teddy Stylographic Pen, sometimes called ink pencil. We have had this pen made with a view of surpassing anything on the market for quality and perfection of make. We can conscientiously recommend this pen; nothing finer manufactured in the United States of its style. This pen with cap over **$1.23**

94c
A Leader.
No. 4K07254 Our Leader Fountain Pen, the greatest value ever offered for the money. Extra large, hand chased barrel and cap of the best quality hard rubber, fitted with large solid gold pen, and a newly patented under feed. The workmanship is absolutely perfect and we guarantee it to be non-leakable. Fitted with No. 3 pen. State whether you desire pointed, medium or stub pen. Price, complete, including detachable patent clip, filler and cleaner, together with full directions..........**94c**

94c
Excelsior Self Filling Fountain Pen.
No. 4K07256 A High Grade Self Filling Fountain Pen, at one-half the lowest price ever made by any dealer. The barrel is extra large and made of the best quality hard rubber, fitted with No. 2 solid gold pen, with self feed. The simplest self filling pen made. Price, complete, including detachable patent clip, filler and cleaner, together with full directions..........**94c**

$1.08
Non-Breakable Cap.
No. 4K07258 Our New Wabash, with patent, non-breakable cap; something brand new in the fountain pen line. The cap has a ferrule of rolled gold plate, as illustration shows, which makes it practically non-breakable. The cap is the weak point on the fountain pen. The case is perfectly plain and has non-leakable screw nozzle, medium length and fitted with a No. 2 solid gold pen. Comes only medium pointed, a pen well selected for general work. Price, complete, including detachable patent clip, filler and cleaner, together with full directions. **$1.08**

63c
pen only furnished. We guarantee this pen to be equal to any sold by others for $1.00 to $1.75. Price, complete, including detachable patent clip, filler and with full directions.

No. 4K07260 The Wabash. Plain case, screw nozzle, medium length, fitted with a No. 2 medium solid gold pen; medium cleaner, together **63c**

$1.46
Patent Clip Fountain Pen.
No. 4K07261 Extra large hand chased barrel, best quality rubber, fitted with large No. 4 solid gold pen, newly patented safety clip. You cannot drop your pen from your pocket with this attachment. Furnished in medium or stub pen. Price, complete, including detachable patent clip, filler and cleaner, together with full directions..........**$1.46**

$1.02
Perfection Fountain Pens.
Absolutely perfect. These pens cost more to make than any other pen sold. All this cost goes into the material and the workmanship, and not into ornamentation. The barrels are hand made. This insures perfect proportions. Of the finest grade vulcanized hard Para rubber. The gold pens are solid gold, extra heavy and extra long, under feed, and the construction and interior mechanism of the highest order. The best fountain pen made regardless of price. State whether you want pointed, medium or stub pen.

No. 4K07262 Fitted with No. 3 (as large as other manufacturers' No. 4) solid gold pen. Price, complete, including detachable patent clip, filler and cleaner together with full directions..........**$1.02**

No. 4K07264 Fitted with No. 4 (as large as other manufacturers' No. 5) solid gold pen. Price, complete, including detachable patent clip, filler and cleaner together with full directions..........**1.25**

No. 4K07266 Fitted with No. 5 (as large as other manufacturers' No. 6) solid gold pen. Price, complete, including detachable patent clip, filler and cleaner with full directions..........**1.50**

No. 4K07268 Fitted with No. 6. Price, complete, including detachable patent clip, filler and cleaner, together with full directions..........**1.90**

$1.12
Ready-Fill Self Filling Fountain Pen.
No. 4K07276 Ready-Fill Self Filling Fountain Pen, just as described. With patent sleeve and self filler. Fills, cleans and adjusts itself. Fills in one second. Writes the moment it touches the paper, never blots, does not get out of order. Made with patent hand feed, and fitted with No. 2 gold pen and hard rubber barrel. Price..........**$1.12**

TABLEWARE

A NEW WARE MADE BY A NEW PROCESS. YOU CAN SCOUR IT WITH A BRICK.

THE CHEAPEST AND BEST FLATWARE MADE. The Alaska Tableware is not plated, but is the same solid metal through and through, and will hold the same color as long as there is any portion of the goods left. Do not be deceived by any dealer who undertakes to sell you any of the numerous imitations of this ware that are sold on the market for more money than we ask for the genuine. The genuine Alaska Tableware can be had only of us. **BEFORE TAKING HOLD OF THIS NEW DISCOVERY** we left nothing undone to thoroughly investigate the properties of this metal and to test the same in every conceivable manner, to satisfy ourselves that it was all that it was represented to be. After having made all sorts of experiments, and it stood all tests, we made a contract with the factory to handle the goods. It has now been about seven years since we began to handle this line,

and it has not only proved from experiment to be as represented, but with seven years of actual service in the hands of many thousands of our customers, who send us the most flattering recommendations in praise of these goods, and with the rapidly increasing sales, we feel that we cannot recommend it too highly. **THE METAL IS VERY DENSE AND TOUGH,** is almost as white as genuine silver, takes a beautiful polish and requires much less care than does silver plated ware. **THE FANCY PATTERN** is equal in appearance and artistic finish to any of the best silver plated or solid silver goods on the market. The immense quantities of these goods we handle, and the conditions of our contract direct with the factory, puts us in a position to furnish this genuine Alaska Tableware at a slight advance over cost to manufacture.

$1.18 FOR A SET OF SIX REGULAR DINNER SIZE KNIVES.

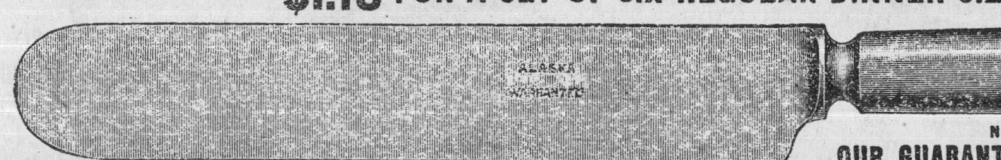

No. 5K332 Medium Alaska Knife.

OUR GUARANTEE. ALASKA METAL KNIVES ARE NOT PLATED. They are the same metal and color through and through. They are proof against all table and fruit acids. They will not rust. They will not tarnish. They will cut and cut well. They can be ground and sharpened like a steel knife, and we guarantee them for the term of your natural lifetime.

$3.65 ALASKA TABLEWARE SET.

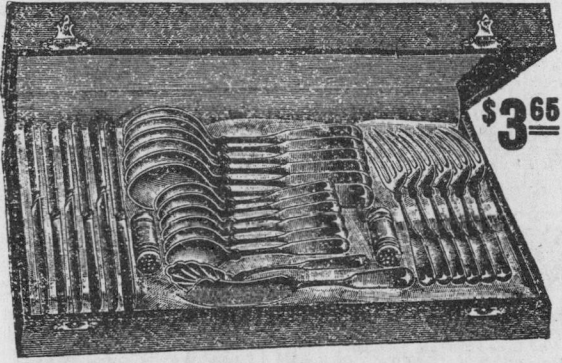

$3.65

28-piece Set of Alaska Tableware in fancy lined leatherette case, consisting of six medium size knives, six medium size forks, six tablespoons, six teaspoons, one butter knife, one sugar shell and one salt and one pepper shaker. Complete set made of Alaska metal, the nearest approach to solid silver yet discovered, the same composition metal through and through. This set will last you your natural lifetime, you can keep it clean without any expense, scour it with sand. Shipping weight, 6½ pounds.

No. 5K352 Tipped Pattern, 28-piece set, plain knives. Price, $3.65
No. 5K354 Shell Pattern, 28-piece set, plain knives. Price, 3.65
No. 5K356 Fancy Pattern, 28-piece set, plain knives. Price, 4.34
The knives in the above set have plain handles, as illustration shows.

A POINT OF INFORMATION. Pure solid silver will tarnish. Coal gas, smoke, even the atmosphere will cause silver to oxidize, that is, turn dark. This does not denote that it is of inferior grade or poor manufacture. Silverware, to be kept bright and clean, should be polished from time to time.

No. 5K198 Silver Sunshine Polish, paste form, is unquestionably the purest and best silver polish made, contains no acid and will not scratch. Price, per ½-pint bottle......22c
Cannot be sent by mail.
No. 5K200 Silver Sunshine Powder, for silverware, cut glass, china, etc. Contains no acid and will not scratch. Price, 3 boxes for........21c
If by mail, postage extra, per box, 8 cents.

On account of space we are compelled to illustrate these teaspoons in reduced size. These teaspoons are made in the regular size, 6 inches long.

Relative lengths of Alaska Metal Teaspoons, 6 inches; dessert spoons, 7½ inches; tablespoons, 8¼ inches; medium forks, 7½ inches; medium knives, 9 inches; sugar shells, 5¾ inches; butter knives, 7 inches.

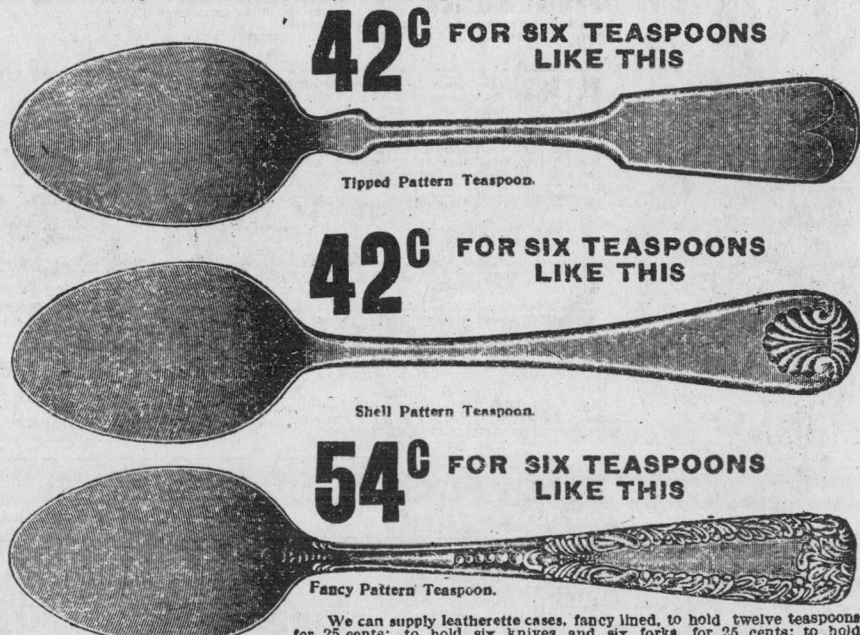

42c FOR SIX TEASPOONS LIKE THIS
Tipped Pattern Teaspoon.

42c FOR SIX TEASPOONS LIKE THIS
Shell Pattern Teaspoon.

54c FOR SIX TEASPOONS LIKE THIS
Fancy Pattern Teaspoon.

We can supply leatherette cases, fancy lined, to hold twelve teaspoons for 25 cents; to hold six knives and six forks, for 25 cents; to hold twelve teaspoons, butter knife, sugar shell and pickle fork, for 25 cents; to hold twelve teaspoons and six tablespoons, for 38 cents, to hold one dozen tablespoons, for 25 cents. Cases only supplied when goods are ordered to fill same from us.

OUR SPECIAL PRICES.

Any of these goods can be sent by mail on receipt of price and additional amount named for postage.

		Tipped Pattern	Shell Pattern	Fancy Pattern
No. 5K326	Teaspoons. If by mail, postage extra, 8 cents. Price, set of ½ dozen......	$0.42	$0.42	$0.54
No. 5K327	Dessert Spoons. If by mail, postage extra, 12 cents. Price, set of ½ dozen......	.74	.74	.90
No. 5K328	Tablespoons. If by mail, postage extra, 15 cents. Price, set of ½ dozen......	.84	.84	1.08
No. 5K329	Medium Forks. If by mail, postage extra, 15 cents. Price, set of ½ dozen......	.84	.84	1.08
No. 5K332	Knives. See illustration above. If by mail, postage extra, 34 cents. Price, set of ½ dozen...	1.18	Not Made	Not Made
No. 5K333	Sugar Shells. If by mail, postage extra, 2 cents. Price, each......	.13	.13	.17
No. 5K334	Butter Knives. If by mail, postage extra, 2 cents. Price, each......	.14	.14	.18

The standard of quality and finish of the above goods are guaranteed by the manufacturers to us, and we guarantee them to our customers. You run no risk whatever in purchasing this ware, for if you do not find it to be exactly as represented, it can be returned to us and your money will be refunded. Be sure to state catalogue number and pattern wanted when you order. WE DO NOT MAKE ANY OTHER PIECES OF ALASKA METAL TABLEWARE THAN THOSE MENTIONED ON THIS PAGE.

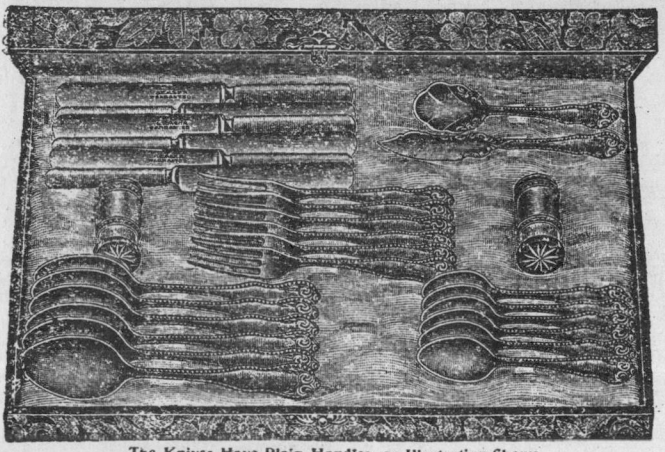

The Knives Have Plain Handles, as Illustration Shows.

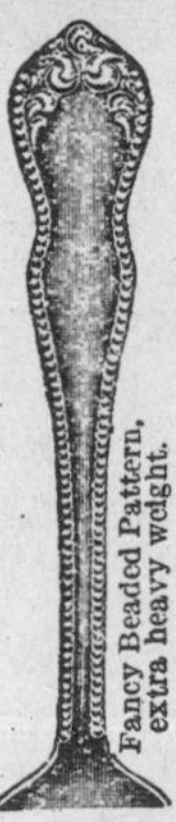

Fancy Beaded Pattern, extra heavy weight.

$5.38 ALASKA METAL TABLEWARE SET IN A FANCY PRESENTATION BOX.

Fancy extra heavy weight Beaded Pattern 28-Piece Alaska Metal Set in a fancy plush coverd silk lined presentation box for $5.38. On account of the many inquiries for a heavier weight Alaska metal set we have had this beautiful pattern made in heavier weight than has ever been offered in any composition metal set. Two more pieces in our set than offered by others. The two extra pieces consist of salt and pepper shakers. They are Alaska metal tops with glass salt and pepper holders, serviceable and good. The balance of the set, twenty-six pieces, is of our guaranteed silver like metal, branded Alaska metal, and is fully guaranteed and warranted. Twenty-eight pieces in all, consisting of six full size knives, six full size dinner forks, six full size extra heavy weight teaspoons, six full size extra heavy weight tablespoons, butter knife, sugar shell, and salt and pepper shakers. Every piece made to match, every piece a picture of perfection. Our margin of profit is so small that we cannot sell any of the pieces separately, as the profit on any part of this set would be so small we would lose money on account of the packing and shipping costs. $5.38 does not represent one-half what this set is truly worth. For beauty and for utility, for everything that goes to make a silverware set you have positively the best that money can buy. Shipping weight, 6½ pounds.

No. 5K368 Price for complete Fancy Beaded Pattern Alaska Metal Tableware Set, in plush covered case.........**$5.38**

REDUCED PRICES ON
SOLID SILVER KNIVES, FORKS AND SPOONS
POSITIVELY NO BETTER QUALITY MANUFACTURED
SOLID SILVER FLAT WARE IN THE LATEST AND MOST UP TO DATE PATTERNS.

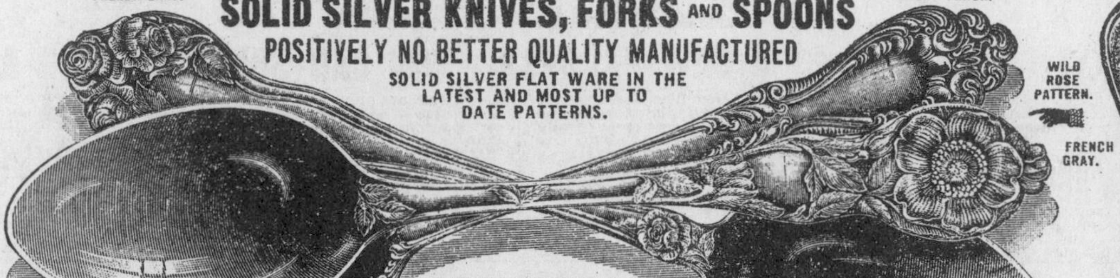

PRINCESS PATTERN. BRIGHT FINISH.

WILD ROSE PATTERN. FRENCH GRAY.

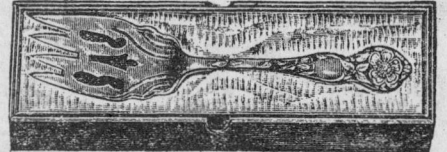
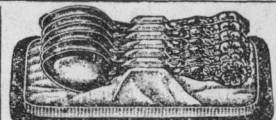

SIX SOLID SILVER TEA-SPOONS FOR $3⁶⁶

Orange Blossom Pattern. French Gray.
We charge for engraving, 2½ cents per letter for Script and 5 cents per letter for Old English.

THE DEMAND

for solid silver tableware has increased each year, and in order to give our customers the latest styles we have secured new patterns just out this season. The die work of these new patterns is the best that skilled labor can turn out. The workmanship is the best. Note the edges, trimming and finish of these spoons; nothing better made, nothing better finished in any factory, and at prices 10 to 15 per cent less than a wholesaler can purchase from us. Buy a set of solid silver tableware and you will have a set that you can hand down from generation to generation, because it will last forever.

FINISH. Notice that we furnish three patterns in the latest French gray finish and two in a bright finish. From these patterns we know that you can make a selection that will please you. While the light weight teaspoons will give you excellent service, we recommend the medium and heavy weight, as these are heavier and will stand rougher usage. The price of silver bars has steadily advanced during the past three years, but our low prices are figured on the actual cost of material and manufacture with only one small per cent of profit added. Please note that all fancy pieces, such as sugar shells, butter knives, cream ladles, berry spoons and cold meat forks, come in a fancy lined box for which we make no extra charge. When ordering, be sure to state pattern wanted.

SPECIAL NOTICE. We cannot exchange or refund money on silverware after being engraved, as it is positively of no value to us; therefore, when you order silverware engraved you do so with the understanding that the goods are not to be exchanged or a refund asked for.

Postage on Teaspoons, per set of six ... 8 cents
Postage on Tablespoons, per set of six ... 15 cents
Postage on Medium Forks, per set of six ... 15 cents
Mount Vernon Pattern. Bright Finish.

SIX SOLID SILVER TEA-SPOONS FOR $4⁷²

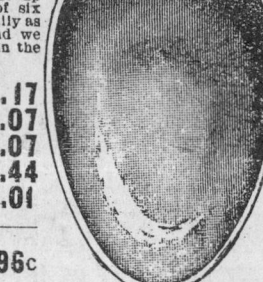

Catalogue No.		Princess Rose	Wedding Rose	Mount Vernon	Orange Blossom	Wild Rose
5K1502	Teaspoons, light weight, per set of six....	$ 3.09	not made	not made	$ 3.66	not made
5K1504	Teaspoons, medium weight, per set of six...	4.12	$ 4.72	$ 4.72	4.82	$ 4.82
5K1506	Teaspoons, heavy weight, per set of six....	5.14	5.79	5.79	6.07	6.07
5K1508	Teaspoons, extra heavy weight, per set of six...	not made	6.82	6.82	7.21	7.21
5K1510	Tablespoons, medium weight, per set of six...	10.28	not made	not made	12.62	12.62
5K1512	Tablespoons, extra heavy weight, per set of six..	not made	13.96	13.96	14.43	14.43
5K1516	Medium Forks, medium weight, per set of six....	10.80	not made	not made	12.62	12.62
5K1517	Medium Forks, extra heavy weight, per set of six..	12.46	13.96	13.96	14.43	14.43

No. 5K1544 Cold Meat Fork. Gilt tines, Princess pattern, solid silver, heavy weight. Length, 7½ inches. Price.... **$3.12**

No. 5K1546 Wild Rose, Wedding Rose, Mt. Vernon or Orange Blossom Pattern. Solid silver, extra heavy weight. State pattern desired. Price.... **$4.66**
If by mail, postage extra, 10 cents.

Solid Silver Teaspoons, in a fancy lined satin covered case. We made up this set, consisting of six teas in a case, especially as a presentation set, and we will furnish this set in the following patterns:

No. 5K1561 Wild Rose Pattern. Solid silver, medium weight. Price, per set of six, in box... **$5.17**
No. 5K1563 Wedding Rose Pattern. Solid silver, medium weight. Price, per set of six, in box... **5.07**
No. 5K1565 Mt. Vernon Pattern. Solid silver, medium weight. Price, per set of six, in box... **5.07**
No. 5K1567 Princess Pattern. Solid silver, light weight. Price, per set of six, in box... **3.44**
No. 5K1571 Orange Blossom Pattern. Solid silver, light weight. Price, per set of six, in box... **4.01**
If by mail, postage extra, 15 cents.

No. 5K1552 Solid Silver Sugar Shell, Poppy pattern, medium weight, French gray handle, gilt bowl. Length, 5¼ inches. Price.... **96c**
If by mail, postage extra, 4 cents.

Solid Silver Hollow Handled Knives with steel blades heavily silver plated. Knives are 9½ inches long. These knives are positively the finest manufactured.

No. 5K1519 Princess Pattern. Price, per set of six, in box... **$10.04**
No. 5K1521 Wedding Rose and Mount Vernon Pattern. Price, per set of six, in box... **14.55**
No. 5K1523 Orange Blossom and Wild Rose Pattern. Price, per set of six, in box... **13.36**
If by mail, postage extra, 32 cents.

No. 5K1520 Sugar Shell. Gilt bowl, Princess pattern, solid silver, heavy weight. Length, 5½ inches. Price.... **$1.49**

No. 5K1522 Wild Rose, Wedding Rose, Mt. Vernon or Orange Blossom Pattern. Solid silver, extra heavy weight. State pattern desired. Length, 6 inches. Price.... (If by mail, postage extra, 4 cents.) **$2.09**

No. 5K1524 Butter Knife. Plain blade, Princess pattern, solid silver, heavy weight. Length, 6¼ inches. Price.... **$1.66**
No. 5K1526 Wild Rose, Wedding Rose, Mt. Vernon or Orange Blossom Pattern. Solid silver, extra heavy weight. State pattern desired. Length, 6½ inches. Price.....(If by mail, postage extra, 5 cents.).... **$2.25**

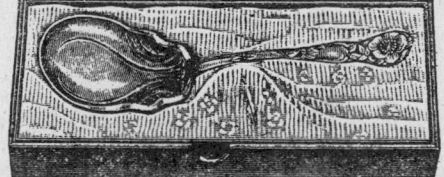

No. 5K1532 Berry Spoon. Gilt bowl, Princess pattern, solid silver, heavy weight. Length, 8 inches. Price.... **$3.64**
No. 5K1534 Wild Rose, Mt. Vernon or Orange Blossom Pattern. Solid silver, extra heavy weight. State pattern desired. Length, 8¾ inches. Price.... **$5.52**
No. 5K1535 Wedding Rose Pattern. Solid silver, extra heavy weight only. Length, 8¾ inches. Price....(If by mail, postage extra, 12 cents.).... **$6.88**

Poppy pattern is made in medium weight only.

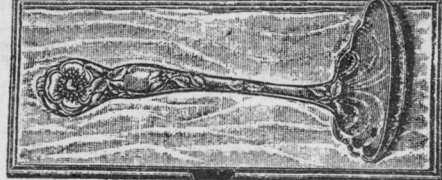

No. 5K1536 Cream Ladle. Gilt bowl, Princess pattern, solid silver, heavy weight. Length, 4¾ inches. Price.... **$1.76**
No. 5K1538 Wild Rose, Wedding Rose, Mt. Vernon or Orange Blossom Pattern. Solid silver, extra heavy weight. State pattern desired. Length, 5¼ inches. Price.....(If by mail, postage extra, 5 cents.).... **$2.59**
No. 5K1540 Gravy Ladle. Gilt bowl, Princess pattern, solid silver, heavy weight. Length, 5¾ inches. Price.... **$2.99**
No. 5K1542 Wild Rose, Wedding Rose, Mt. Vernon or Orange Blossom Pattern. Solid silver, extra heavy weight. State pattern desired. Length, 6 inches. Price.....(If by mail, postage extra, 10 cents.).... **$3.87**

No. 5K1554 Solid Silver Sardine or Meat Server. Poppy pattern, medium weight. French gray handle, gilt tines. Length, 5¼ inches. Price.... **96c**
If by mail, postage extra, 4 cents.

No. 5K1558 Solid Silver Baby Spoon in the Poppy pattern, medium weight, French gray finish, with a fancy ornamented bowl representing the different figures interesting to children. Price.... **96c**
If by mail, postage extra, 4 cents.

No. 5K1566 Solid Silver Pickle Fork. Poppy pattern, French gray handle, gilt tines. Length, 6¼ inches. Price.... **96c**
If by mail, postage extra, 4 cents.

No. 5K1572 Solid Silver Cold Meat Fork. Poppy pattern, medium weight, French gray handle, gilt tines. Length, 7½ inches. Price.... **$2.49**
If by mail, postage extra, 6 cents.

No. 5K1568 Solid Silver Jelly Server. Poppy pattern, medium weight, French gray handle, gilt blade. Length, 7½ inches. Price.... **$1.92**
(Postage extra, 4 cents.)

No. 5K1556 Solid Silver Cream Ladle. Poppy pattern, medium weight, French gray handle, and gilt bowl. Length, 5½ inches. Price.... **96c**
If by mail, postage extra, 5 cents.

No. 5K1574 Solid Silver Berry Spoon. Poppy pattern, medium weight, French gray handle, gilt bowl. Length, 7½ inches. Price.... **$2.59**
If by mail, postage extra, 6 cents.

No. 5K1576 Solid Silver Gray Ladle. Poppy pattern, medium weight, French gray handle, gilt bowl. Length, 6 inches. Price.... **$1.96**
If by mail, postage extra, 5 cents.

No. 5K1564 Solid Silver Olive Spoon. Poppy pattern, medium weight, French gray handle, gilt bowl. Length, 6¼ inches. Price.... **96c**
(Postage extra, 4 cents.)

$4.66 FOR THIS 28-PIECE GENUINE SOLID ALASKA METAL INITIAL TABLEWARE SET

SIX FULL SIZE DINNER FORKS, SIX FULL SIZE DINNER KNIVES, SIX FULL SIZE TABLESPOONS, SIX FULL SIZE TEASPOONS, ONE BUTTER KNIFE, ONE SUGAR SHELL, ONE SALT AND-PEPPER SHAKER. 28 PIECES IN A FINE CASE, AS ILLUSTRATED, ALL COMPLETE.

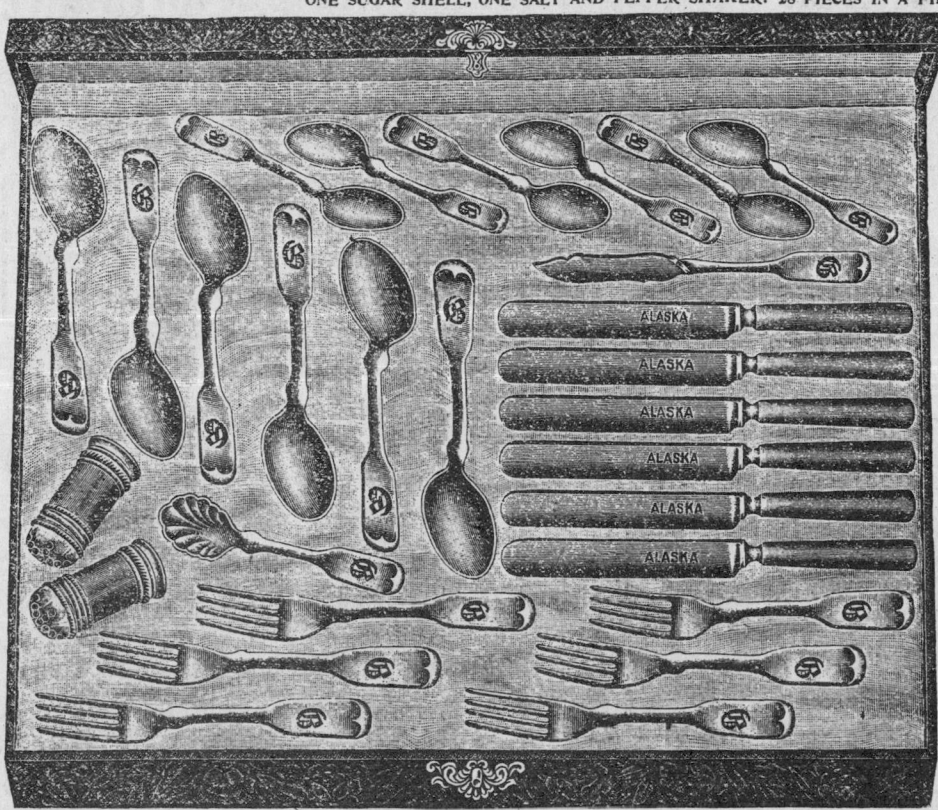

THE ENGRAVING. Each piece comes engraved, according to the initial you desire. State plainly in your order the exact letter, write it plainly and distinctly so that no mistakes can be made. To have a set of silverware engraved with a beautiful large letter alone would cost you $2.00 to $3.00. We will give splendid work. The letter is most exquisite, it will please you and costs you nothing.

THE CASE COSTS YOU NOTHING, provided you purchase the entire set, 28 pieces in all. Should you desire any of the pieces separately please order by number as quoted in the table below. We do not sell less than six at any one time. The case that we send absolutely free of charge if you buy this set is beautifully covered with figured plush with a fine silk lining, and so built that the pieces can be set in racks, making a very beautiful presentation case, or enables you to keep correct count of all the pieces.

ALASKA METAL is a secret composition metal made especially for us under our own formula. The purpose of Alaska composition metal is to imitate solid silver at a fraction of the cost of solid silver. Our Alaska metal is the nearest approach to solid silver yet discovered; equals it for wearing qualities and appearance. It is difficult for experts to see the difference between solid silver and this Alaska composition metal. Our set at $4.66, made in sterling silver, would cost no less than $60.00 to $75.00.

THE KNIVES ARE BETTER THAN SOLID SILVER. You can scour them with a brick, are impervious to acid, impervious to any of the wear and tear that solid silver and silver plated knives are subject to, and they will take a good cutting edge. You can sharpen them as frequently as you like and never injure them. They will not break by dropping them on the floor as steel knives do. Neither are they soft. Solid silver knives are soft and will bend out of shape. They will not rust. Can be scoured and should be scoured with any polish.

OUR ALASKA METAL COMPOSITION TABLEWARE is not plated tableware, but the genuine article. The same metal through and through, but like solid silver must not be left for any length of time, twelve hours or more, in vinegar or in foods that contain acid or salt, such as butter, etc.

UNDERSTAND, they are highly efficient, the same as solid silver, but must not be left over night in any acid foods, fats or grease.

THE PROCESS in the making of this composition metal is only known to us and the manufacturer that follows our formula. It is necessary for us to buy immense quantities to be able to furnish our customers with this wonderful set for the price quoted, $4.66.

ABOVE ALL, do not compare this solid silver-like genuine Alaska metal initial set with any other quoted on the market. There is no comparison. There is no set that equals it, no composition metal that is like our composition metal for the nearest approach to solid silver. For a metal that you can actually scour with a brick, for a metal that will not tarnish, ours leads them all. See the price, $4.66. Metal sets furnished by others, but not one-half as good, are sold at a higher price than we ask.

Shipping Weight 7½ Pounds.

POSTAGE on these goods, if to go by mail, will be extra, as follows: Teaspoons, 6 cents; tablespoons or forks, 15 cents; sugar shell or butter knife, 2 cents; knives, 34 cents.

THE EXPRESS CHARGES will amount to next to nothing as compared to what you will save in price. Express charges will average for five hundred miles, 35 cents; one thousand miles, 75 cents; greater distances in proportion.

No. 5K1480	**ALASKA TABLEWARE SET,** complete with case. Price, 28 pieces,		**$4.66**
No. 5K1482	Teaspoons. Price, per set of six.		.60
No. 5K1483	Tablespoons. Price, per set of six		1.20
No. 5K1484	Table Forks. Price, per set of six		1.20
No. 5K1488	Sugar Shell. Price, each		.18
No. 5K1489	Butter Knife. Price, each		.26
No. 5K332	Table Knives. Price, per set of six		1.18
No. 5K1491	Salt and Pepper Shakers. Price, per pair		.22

NEVER IN THE HISTORY OF THE UNITED STATES

have Souvenir Spoons been so popular. The demand is increasing daily, as the souvenir spoon fills a long felt want, being particularly adapted for whist prizes, souvenir gifts, birthday presents, in fact, appropriate for any occasion where a small gift is required. We selected the State Souvenir Spoon as the most fitting for all requirements. Each spoon is so engraved, so constructed as to represent a different state. Each spoon carries a beautiful design showing the seal of the state it represents, the state motto and the principal product. Illustration shows the State of Iowa, the coat of arms and the state motto, "Our liberties we prize and our rights we will maintain," all surmounting a fine bas relief of the Hawkeye Indian, Iowa being the Hawkeye State. As its chief product is wheat, the spoon is designed with a sheaf of wheat and shows a soldier in uniform holding the stars and stripes. This same scheme is carried out on all the various states. We can furnish spoons for every state in the Union.

BE SURE to name the state desired. The spoons are of solid silver, 5 inches long, gray oxidized French finish, with gilt bowls. The die work, finishing and gold work are beyond criticism. Choice of any souvenir spoon.
No. 5K1367   Price.   (If by mail, postage extra, 4 cents) **79c**

79C FOR A SOLID SILVER, GOLD BOWL, STATE SOUVENIR SPOON.

We furnish a State Spoon for every state in the Union.

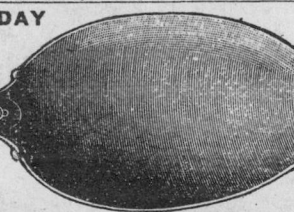

95C FOR A SOLID SILVER, GOLD BOWL BIRTHDAY SOUVENIR SPOON, WORTH $1.50

No. 5K1369 Solid Silver Birthday Souvenir Spoons representing the twelve different months. Illustration shows the January spoon. We have selected these souvenir spoons from hundreds of patterns. They are the heaviest, most artistic and best finished spoons for the money in the market. The spoon is 5 inches long, handle is French gray finish with gold plated bowl. The ornamentation is handsome repousse die work. The sign of the zodiac or sign of the month is wrought upon each spoon according to the month. Below this in bas relief is a figure of a baby cherub. The name of the month is carved out on the shank while the back of the spoon is ornamented with a floral design. These spoons are being extensively purchased for birthday presents, souvenir gifts or to be given as prizes at card parties. When ordering, do not forget to mention the name of the month wanted. Price ....(If by mail, postage extra, 6 cents.).... **95c**

HIGH GRADE, SECTIONAL SILVER PLATE 26-PIECE GENUINE $9.28 ROGERS BRAND DINNER SET

SECTIONAL PLATE CONSTRUCTED.

HOW THIS SECTIONAL QUADRUPLE SILVER PLATED WARE IS MADE.
Blanks of high grade nickel are rolled out to the proper shape, the heaviest stock on the market being used, with the result that the teaspoons, tablespoons, forks, etc., are extra heavy weight. From these blanks spoons, forks, etc. are constructed in the rough, this rough piece then is put into the pattern press where the pattern is struck upon it. After the blank receives the pattern it is properly finished and stoned down. When this is done the highest paid mechanics plate portions of the spoon that receive the greatest wear, such as the high point at the bottom of the bowl, the lip of the bowl, the high point on the back part of the handle and the high point on the front of the handle. These places covered with solid silver, are then made level and smoothed down to the pattern of the article. It is then silver plated in the regular way, producing a double wearing quality.

SET CONSISTS OF 26 PIECES, in French gray finish and, as shown in illustration at side of box, is one of the latest and handsomest designs, which we have named the "Lexington." Six full size teaspoons, six full size tablespoons, six full size table forks, full size sugar shell, full size butter knife and six full size table knives, all the pieces matching perfectly. This set is manufactured by the Wm. Rogers Manufacturing Co.; it is known as their Anchor Brand and is produced with the idea of furnishing discriminating users of silverware with the longest wearing, finest appearing silverware for the least amount of money.

OUR MARGIN OF PROFIT is based on our one small per cent profit system. We buy direct from the manufacturer, we sell direct to the user, which saves the wholesaler's and retailer's profits. The case that we send with this set, free of all cost, is cloth lined and leatherette covered, and is so constructed that the twenty-six pieces are set in racks, so that they do not come in contact one with the other, thus preventing marring and scratching.

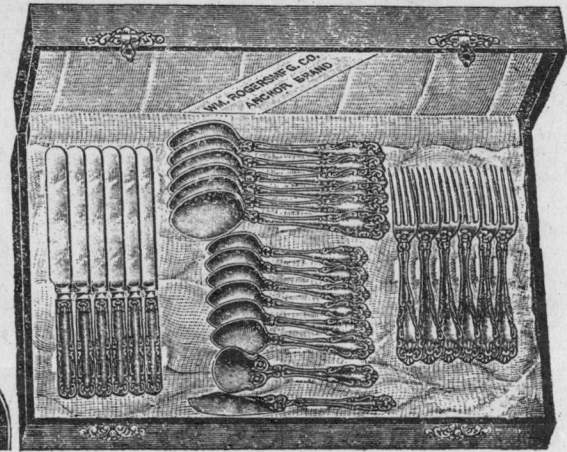

No. 5K193   26-Piece Sectional Plate Rogers Brand Silverware Set. Price...... **$9.28**
This set weighs, boxed ready for shipment, about 7½ pounds.

PRICES REDUCED OUR QUADRUPLE SILVER PLATED TABLEWARE DEPARTMENT

OUR SILVERWARE IS SOLD WITH A FIVE-YEAR INSURANCE GUARANTEE.

IN THIS DEPARTMENT we have added many new designs and bettered the quality of every piece. The growing demand for the highest possible grade silver plated tableware has indicated to us the advisability of bettering our present lines and increasing the number of pieces. We have investigated this branch of merchandise along entirely new lines with this result, that we are able to offer this new line made especially for us, a higher grade silver plated tableware than has ever before been offered at prices 20 to 30 per cent less than asked by others for inferior goods. We believe that qualities count and through the bettering of this line, that is, by increasing the silver deposit, using a higher grade of Britannia metal, will result in increase of sales and therefore greater business for us.

A FIVE-YEAR INSURANCE with our silver plated tableware. Every piece of tableware, when so stated, is covered by one of our five-year written binding guarantees. This guarantee goes out with every piece of silver plated tableware, except when otherwise stated. It is far reaching. It protects you in every direction, makes you absolutely assured that you are owning the best quadruple silver plated ware procurable.

OPPOSITE is practically a facsimile of the guarantee that goes out with our insurance guaranteed silver plated tableware. Different from any other firm in the United States, we know how our tableware is made. Different from any other merchant, we know our tableware is positively quadruple silver plated. Different from any other dealer, we have compared our line of silver plated tableware with practically every other line that is shown or comes to Chicago or New York markets, which practically includes every maker, and ours stands pre-eminently the best. Therefore, we feel perfectly safe in making this offer, that is, to give a five-year insurance. Notwithstanding the reason of a special arrangement with the manufacturer, by reason of our one small percentage of profit system, our prices are less than the trashy premium stuff, so called the triple, double or quadruple silver plated ware offered by others at 30 to 40 per cent more than we ask for ours, which is the very best. Every piece purchased from us represents a double saving to you; a money saving first, because you save money in the original purchase, and because it will outwear from three to four times silver plated ware of inferior quality.

OUR BINDING GUARANTEE.

WE GUARANTEE this piece of tableware to be quadruple plated and to be made of genuine Britannia metal of the very highest quality white metal compound, plated with absolutely pure silver and we warrant it to retain its silver like appearance, if properly cleaned and used in ordinary domestic service, for a term of five years. We further agree to take back at any time within five years from date of purchase and exchange for new any piece of silver plated tableware sold under this guarantee that shows the silver worn off and exposes the Britannia metal underneath, if used as described above.

SEARS, ROEBUCK & CO.

No. 5K1604 Pickle Caster. Triple plated, floral ornamented cover, fancy embossed base, hand burnished fancy handle and floral design pickle tongs. Height, 10½ inches. Shipping weight, 4 pounds. Price.. **$1.18**

No. 5K1605 Pickle Caster. Quadruple silver plated, hand burnished base and cover, fancy fleur de lis pattern handle and pickle tongs, ruby glass with gold decorations. Height, 9½ inches. Shipping weight, 5 pounds. Price...... **$2.25** Guaranteed for five years.

$1.74

No. 5K1621 Cracker Jar. Quadruple silver plated on genuine Britannia metal. Height, 8¾ inches. Is extra heavily made with a fluted edge, satin finish with bright cut engraving. The cover is bright finish, hand burnished with beaded repousse ornamentation. The handle is well made with a conventional design ornamentation. This cracker jar is our leader, made especially for us with the idea of furnishing our customers with the best in this class of merchandise, and in order to introduce our silver plated hollow ware we are selling this cracker jar at an extremely low figure. Your local merchant would ask from $2.50 to $3.00 for one not so good. Shipping weight 7 pounds. Price.................. **$1.74** Guaranteed for five years.

$2.36

No. 5K1637 Dinner Caster. Five bottles, quadruple silver plated on genuine Britannia metal, satin finish with hand engraved ornamentation. Height, 15¾ inches. Shipping weight, 7½ pounds. Price........... **$2.36** Guaranteed for five years.

$1.12

No. 5K1632 Dinner Caster. Triple silver plated, embossed floral design, rim and base hand burnished, satin finish, fancy handle with five diamond cut pattern bottles. Height, 14 inches. Shipping weight, 7½ pounds. Price.............. **$1.12**

$2.18

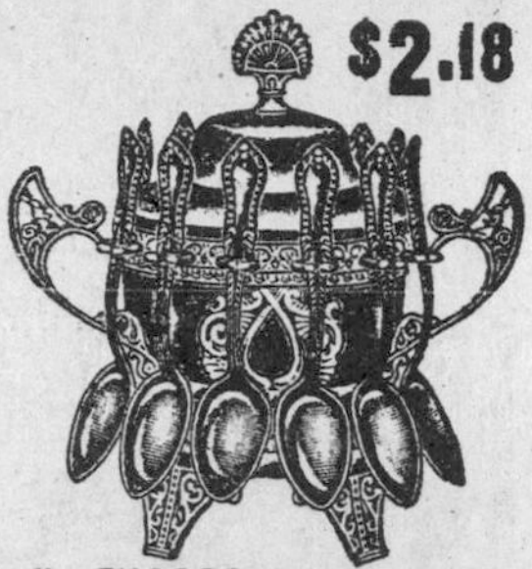

No. 5K2333 Our Combination Sugar Bowl and Spoon Holder. The sugar bowl is of ruby glass, set in a fine triple plated silver stand with a silver plated cover. Stands 9 inches high, 8½ inches wide from handle to handle. Surrounding the bowl, properly arranged, is a rack fitted with twelve silver plated beaded pattern teaspoons of good serviceable quality and weight. Shipping weight, 5 pounds. Price, including 12 teaspoons.............. **$2.18**

No. 5K2332 Sugar Bowl only, without teaspoons. Price.............. **$1.30**

No. 5K1630 Toothpick Holder. Bright finish, repousse ornamentations, fancy handles and feet; gold lined. Height, 2½ inches. Price.............. **87c** If by mail, postage extra, 6 cents. Guaranteed for five years.

No. 5K1611 Spoon Tray. Quadruple silver plated, extra heavily made, hand burnished, with ornamented feet and beaded edge. Britannia wire handle with oak leaf ornamentation; center of tray is satin finished and gold lined. Length, 7½ inches. Made especially for us in order to convince our customers what a high grade line of hollow ware we carry and at what remarkably low prices we are able to sell. Nothing more useful or appropriate for a gift. Shipping weight, 5 pounds. Price.. **$1.69** Guaranteed for five years.

Silver Sunshine Powder will make old silverware look like new. **No. 5K200** In powder form. Price, **21c** 3 boxes........ Postage, extra, 8c.

No. 5K1611............$1.69

$1.90

No. 5K2101 Crumb Set. Quadruple silver plated on the best Britannia metal, beautiful beaded edge with hand engraved center. Length of scraper, 9½ inches. Weight, 3 pounds. Price.............. **$1.90** Guaranteed for five years.

$1.42

No. 5K1619 Individual Caster. Quadruple silver plated, satin finish, with repousse ornamentation; bottles are genuine cut glass. Ht., 3¾ inches. Price.............. **$1.42** Postage extra, 22 cents. Guaranteed for five years.

$9.65

No. 5K1671 Candelabrum. Five lights, 11 inches high, quadruple silver plated on genuine Britannia metal. Design represents a woman in Grecian costume. The figure is well executed and splendidly finished. The workmanship is the best with French gray effects. With this candelabrum we furnish silk shades, red candles, candle holder and a mica shade that protects the silk and silver from the flame. The candle holder is self adjusting. The entire outfit makes a most attractive ornament for a dining room. Shipping weight, 10 pounds.

Price of candelabrum with five complete shades, as illustration shows.............. **$9.65**

We sell the shades separate when desired.

No. 5K1673 Price of shade with candle holder, complete, each..........(Postage, 16c).............. $1.20

No. 5K1670 Price of candelabrum without shades......(Shipping weight, 7 pounds).............. 4.45

Guaranteed for five years.

A Handsome Wedding Gift, $1.90.

No. 5K2128 Combination Salt Set. Quadruple silver plated salt cups with a beaded border, handsome designed feet and handle. Height of cup, 1¾ inches; length of salt spoon, 2¾ inches. Comes in a neat lined box. Price........... **$1.90** If by mail, postage extra, 12c. Guaranteed for five years.

No. 5K2125 Cake Basket. Triple silver plated, fancy rococo border, fancy ornamented feet and handle. Center is gold lined, with bright finished border. Diameter is 8 inches; height, 9¾ inches. Shipping weight, about 7 pounds. Price.... **$1.69**

OUR VERY BEST CAKE BASKET, $3.38

No. 5K2133 Cake Basket. Quadruple silver plated on genuine Britannia metal, fluted design, with daisy floral repousse ornamentation, hand burnished. Height, 8 inches; diameter, 9¾ inches. The most handsome cake basket ever offered, must be seen to be appreciated. Shipping weight, 7 pounds. Price.............. **$3.38** Guaranteed for five years.

No. 5K1822 Child's Cup. Quadruple silver plated, satin finish, engraved "Baby," gold lined. Height, 2¼ inches. Price..(Postage, 6c)..... **86c** Guaranteed for five years.

No. 5K1802 Child's Cup. Satin finish, engraved center, hand burnished base, gold lined. Height, 2⅜ inches. Price..(Postage, 6c).. **48c**

No. 5K1849 Napkin Ring. Quadruple silver plated, satin finish, very handsomely engraved. Width, 1⅜ in. Price..(Postage, 6c).... **54c** Guaranteed for five years.

No. 5K1855 Napkin Ring with base. Quadruple silver plated, hand burnished, hand engraved napkin ring. Supported by two finely executed cupid figures. Height, 2¾ inches. Price.............. **$1.20**

Silver Dip.

The new lightning cleaner. Sixty seconds cleans your silverware; no rubbing, no scratching, no half a day waste of time. A tin pan holding about a gallon of water and a tablespoonful of our Sixty Seconds Lightning Silver Polish heated to the boiling point, submerge your tarnished silverware, rinse it in hot water and wipe with a soft canton flannel cloth. No acid, no poison, absolutely harmless, yet one of the best silver polishes placed on the market.

No. 5K199 Price, per can, **21c** If by mail, postage extra, 10 cents.

OUR LEADER, $3.20.

No. 5K2119 Bread Tray. Quadruple silver plated on genuine Britannia metal, 13½ inches long. Very heavily made with a beautiful floral design ornamentation, finished in French gray with your initial engraved in Old English in the center of the tray. Comes in a beautiful lined presentation case. For a gift nothing could make a better show, considering the price. They are guaranteed for five years' continual wear. Please note that we only engrave one initial but any initial which you may desire. Shipping weight, 4 pounds. Price of bread tray in neat lined presentation case, with one initial...(Guaranteed for five years)... **$3.20**

No. 5K2772 Toilet Set, three pieces, quadruple silver plated on genuine Britannia metal, ornamented with a four-leaf clover design, finished in French gray, 5-inch French beveled glass mirror; genuine Russian bristles in hair brush; nothing finer made, nothing more beautiful. By all means if you want the best set on the market select this one. Price, per set, in box.... **$6.58** If by mail, postage extra, 42 cents. Guaranteed for five years.

A Splendid Wedding Gift, $3.68

No. 5K2149 Sugar and Cream Set. Quadruple silver plated on genuine Britannia metal, fluted design, fancy rococo border. Both are gold lined. Height, 4 inches. Comes in a neat lined presentation case. Nothing is more serviceable, nothing is more acceptable than a high grade silver plated sugar and cream set. Shipping weight, 4 pounds. Price of complete set in presentation case................ **$3.68** Guaranteed for five years.

No. 5K2107 Bread Tray. Triple silver plated, embossed with a grape vine ornamentation, finished in a French gray finish; length, 12½ inches. Shipping weight, 2 pounds. Price...................... **$1.22**

No. 5K1618 Cracker Jar. Imported prism cut, pink tinted glass with quadruple silver plated floral leaf design cover. Height, 6½ inches. Shipping weight, about 7 pounds. Price................. **$1.20**

No. 5K2114 Bread Tray. Triple silver plated, bright finish, fancy embossed border, hand engraved, length, 12 inches. Shipping weight, 3 pounds. Price.................. **$1.36**

No. 5K2301 Syrup Pitcher, quadruple silver plated lid and imitation cut glass base. This syrup pitcher is very handsome in design. Stands 6½ in. high. Shipping weight, 1½ pounds. Price................ **84c**

CRUCIFIX, CANDLESTICKS AND CANDELABRUM

Made by one of the best silverware manufacturers in the United States. They are all made of genuine Britannia metal. The die work is exceptionally fine.

No expense spared to make these the finest ever manufactured. They are quadruple plated and then lacquered, which prevents tarnishing.

98c   52c $2.18   75c   70c

No. 5K10921   No. 5K10905   No. 5K10941   No. 5K10927 No. 5K10917

No. 5K10921 Crucifix, made of genuine Britannia metal, quadruple silver plated. The base of this crucifix is satin finished with raised letters. Height, 10½ inches. Shipping weight, about 3 pounds. Price............ **98c**

No. 5K10905 Crucifix, made of genuine Britannia metal, quadruple silver plated. Stands 8½ inches high. Shipping weight, about 3 pounds. Price............ **52c**

No. 5K10941 Crucifix, Candelabrum and Holy Fount, all combined, made of Britannia metal. The die work is exceptionally fine. Stands 13 inches high, is quadruple silver plated and lacquered, which insures the candelabrum from tarnishing. A special feature of this candelabrum is the holy water fount, which is detachable, something never placed on the market before. You can use it as a candelabrum and by attaching the holy water fount you have a complete crucifix, candelabrum and holy water fount. Shipping weight, 7 pounds. Price.................. **$2.18**

No. 5K10927 Candlestick, made of genuine Britannia metal, quadruple silver plated in a beautiful embossed design. Height, 8¾ inches. Shipping weight, about 2 pounds. Price.................. **.75**

No. 5K10917 Crucifix, made of genuine Britannia metal, quadruple silver plated. Stands 10 inches high. Shipping weight, about 3 pounds. Price......... **.70**

No. 5K10919 Same as No. 5K10917, but gold plated. Price.................. **1.24**

$4.15 FOR THE VERY NEWEST UP TO DATE VIATICUM CABINET OR SICK CALL OUTFIT.

MADE ESPECIALLY FOR US OF THE HIGHEST GRADE METAL, SOLID SILVER PLATED, AND GUARANTEED TO RETAIN ITS SILVERLIKE APPEARANCE IF PROPERLY USED.

This Viaticum Cabinet or Sick Call Outfit is the official and rubrical household sacramental service, and is recommended and approved of by the highest in the church. It is particularly adapted to most of the religious services and is ready for use in the home during the administration of the sacrament. It is made to satisfy and comfort the aged and infirm, and to serve as a family altar around which the members of the family may gather at the appropriate time. The cabinet is so constructed that it contains a place for each particular article necessary in the various ceremonies and is always ready at all times. Each cabinet contains a combination silver crucifix 13 inches high, holy water fount and candelabrum. The holy water fount, different from all other founts in combination with crucifix and candelabrum, is detachable and attachable, as are also the candle sockets and crucifix. A silver handled holy water sprinkler and glass bottle with screw top for holy water, two fine beeswax candles, positively rubrical and can be blessed, a linen napkin and a linen communion cloth, a supply of fine cotton used by the priest, a silver plated gold lined spoon cup, our own pattern, something absolutely new for administering the holy water to the communicant, two beautifully engraved silver plated plates, the entire outfit exactly as illustration shows in each and every detail. The cabinet itself is made of hard polished wood, lined with purple satin, the front doors hung on hinges, well made, and positively will last a lifetime. Especial attention and the greatest care has been exercised on each piece and part to make it positively the finest ever produced. Shipping weight, about 12 pounds. **No. 5K10946** Price...................................... **$4.15**

PRAYER OR ROSARY BEADS.

WITH SOLID SILVER AND GOLD FILLED CONNECTIONS.

Our rosaries are made by one of the most reputable gold filled chain manufacturers in the United States. We guarantee them to give entire satisfaction and to be exactly as described and illustrated.

No. 5K10676 Mother of Pearl Rosary Beads. The beads are large and fine with a beautiful luster, exact size as shown at side of box. White metal chain. Length, 16 inches. Comes in a fancy plush lined box. Price.................. **75c** If by mail, postage extra, 4 cents.

No. 5K10698 Mother of Pearl Rosary Beads. This bead is well rounded, exact size as shown at side of box, having a very fine luster. Gold filled chain and crucifix, guaranteed for five years. Length, 17 inches. In a fancy plush lined box. Price.................. **$1.45**

No. 5K10699 Same Chain and Crucifix as No. 5K10698, with imitation Amethyst Beads. Price.................. **$1.45**

No. 5K10700 Same Chain and Crucifix as No. 5K10698, with imitation Ruby Beads. Price.................. **$1.45** If by mail, postage extra, 4 cents.

This Rosary is made with a very fine large perfectly cut faceted bead, exact size as shown at side of box, has solid silver connections and crucifix. Is 16½ inches long. Comes in a lined box.

No. 5K10678 Imitation Ruby Beads. Price.................. **$1.25**

No. 5K10682 Imitation Amethyst Beads. Price.................. **1.25**

No. 5K10684 Jet Beads. Price.................. **1.25** If by mail, postage extra, 4 cents.

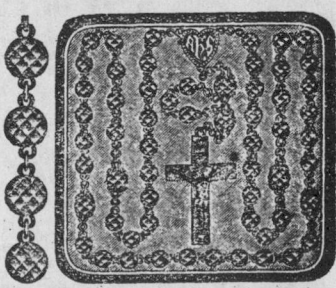

No. 5K10692 Our Finest Imitation Amethyst Rosary Beads, exact size as shown at side of box. Chain and crucifix are gold filled, guaranteed for ten years. Length of chain, 17 inches. We can conscientiously recommend this rosary as being the finest made and one which would cost you double the price from your local jeweler. Comes in a fancy lined box. Price.................. **$1.85**

No. 5K10693 Same Chain and Crucifix as No. 5K10692, with imitation Ruby Beads. Price.................. **$1.85** If by mail, postage extra, 4 cents.

CLOCKS

THE BEST CLOCK MAKERS in the United States are represented. They are the oldest and most reliable makers. The Waterbury Clock Co., the Gilbert Clock Co., the New Haven Clock Co. and the Ansonia Clock Co., stand pre-eminent. Every clock we sell is guaranteed by the manufacturers, and we personally warrant every clock sold to give entire and absolute satisfaction. For the biggest value for the money, for clocks that we can and do give our written binding guarantee with every one sold, we would direct your attention to the following clocks. Each one is made under special contract for us. They are manufactured by one of the makers named, but on account of the very low price, we cannot print the maker's name. However, each one of these clocks carries our binding guarantee. For an alarm clock we recommend the Reliable Alarm, No. 5K2915, at 74 cents; our new Luminous Radium, No. 5K2907, at 89 cents; or our Sure Get Up Long Alarm, No. 5K2949, price, $2.26. For a cabinet clock we would recommend our No. 5K3096, price, $2.18, or if this design does not suit you, and you wish a calendar attachment together with a thermometer and barometer, we would direct your attention to our No. 5K3099, price, $2.59, or the Prophet, No. 5K3126, price, $3.18. If you want a mantel clock, something very fine, the greatest value for the money, you can surely make a selection from the following clocks. The movements are of the highest standard. It is only a question of design in the case. No. 5K3291, Rough Rider, at $5.38; No. 5K3202, our Prince Elias, at $3.62; No. 5K3614, our Lexington, price, $4.55; No. 5K3602, our Lady Isabelle, price, $4.22; or No. 5K3626, the John Cabot, price, $5.05.

49 Cents or 68 Cents; Your Choice of Either One.

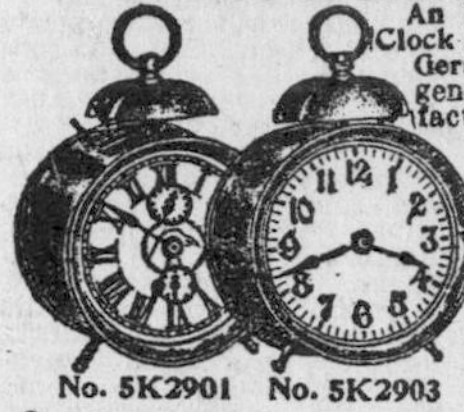

No. 5K2901 No. 5K2903

An Imported alarm Clock manufactured in Germany. They give generally fair satisfaction. The only difficulty with the imported clock is the fact that when it gets out of order it is impossible to get the material to repair it properly. No. 5K2903 at 68 cents, is an American production, and considering the price is a marvel of value. We guarantee it for one year, but conscientiously believe that it should wear and give good satisfaction for many years if properly handled. Both of these clocks stand 6½ inches high. Both have 4-inch dials. The imported German clock has Roman numerals and the American made clock has Arabic numerals. Both alarm continuously for one-half minute. Weight of clock, packed ready for shipment, about 2 lbs.

No. 5K2901 Imported Alarm Clock. Price 49c

No. 5K2903 American Made Alarm Clock. Price 68c

89c

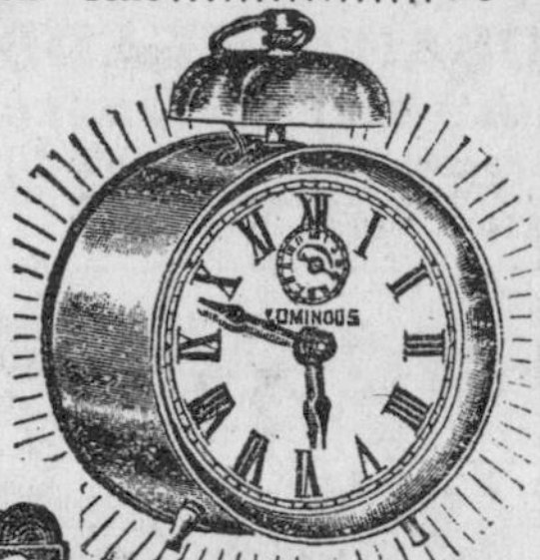

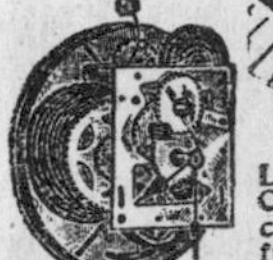

No. 5K2907 Our New Luminous Radium Alarm Clock, made under special contract, with the idea of furnishing our customers with a better alarm clock than any other on the market at a price within the reach of all. By a secret process the dial is covered with a luminous substance which causes the dial to throw out a ray of light like a ball of fire when placed in the dark. This enables you to see the time from any part of the room. This clock is an excellent timekeeper and will give entire satisfaction. 6½ inches high, has 4-inch dial. We know exactly how it is made, how it is adjusted and regulated, and therefore send our two-year guarantee with each clock. SEE THE MOVEMENT as illustrated. It is made of brass with oil tempered steel parts, is the latest model in this style of clock and built on anti-friction principles. Runs 30 hours with one winding, alarms 30 seconds on a clear nickel bell. Different from any other concern, we show you the movement, so that you know exactly what you are getting. Price....... 89c

If by mail, postage extra, 31 cents.

$1.26

No. 5K2911 Our New Interval Alarm Clock, made especially for us with the idea of producing a clock for less money equal to any sold on the market for from $1.75 to $2.00. This clock is made under our own specifications. Stands 6 inches high, has a 4-inch dial with Roman numerals, blue steel hands, and a 4-inch bell on the back. The best alarm clock on the market.

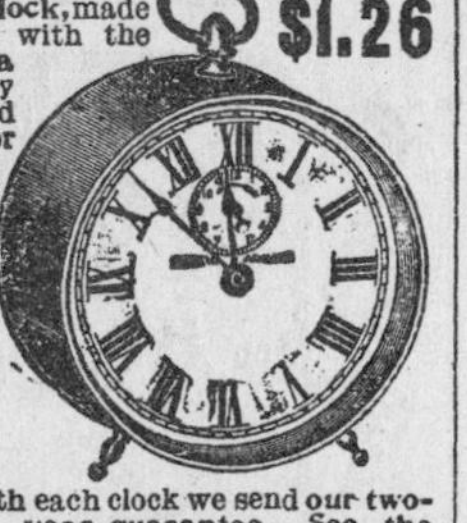

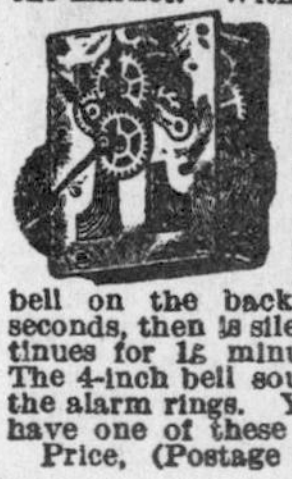

With each clock we send our two-year guarantee. See the movement in this clock. We illustrate it here. It runs for 30 hours with one winding. Made of hand wrought brass and oil tempered steel parts, polished pivots and pinions which reduces friction to a minimum, thereby insuring accurate timekeeping. The 4-inch bell on the back of the clock rings for 40 seconds, then is silent for 20 seconds and continues for 15 minutes unless you shut it off. The 4-inch bell sounds like a fire gong when the alarm rings. You cannot oversleep if you have one of these clocks.

Price, (Postage extra, 35 cents.).. $1.26

92c Calendar Alarm Clock.

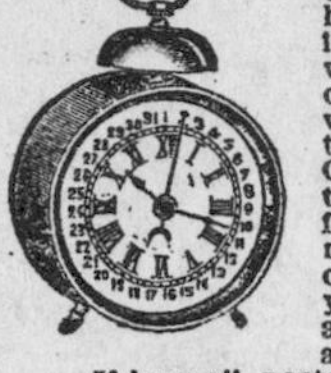

No. 5K2914 Nickel Calendar Alarm Clock, height 6¼ inches, dial 4 inches, runs 30 hours with one winding, has a calendar attachment as well as alarm, is made by the New Haven Clock Company and is guaranteed to give entire satisfaction. Has a large nickel bell on top. This clock automatically tells you the day of the month as well as being an alarm clock. Price, 92c

If by mail, postage extra, 31 cents.

Reliable Alarm. A SURE SLEEP BREAKER FOR 74c

No. 5K2915 Nickel Alarm Clock made especially for us by one of the largest clock companies in the United States, but on account of the low price at which we sell it we cannot give the maker's name. The movement is of the latest lever escapement, made of brass, and oil tempered steel parts. Each clock is thoroughly examined and tested for accurate timekeeping and running durability before leaving the factory. It is again examined in our house before shipping, which insures you an accurate timekeeper. Stands 6½ inches high. Dial is 4 inches in diameter.

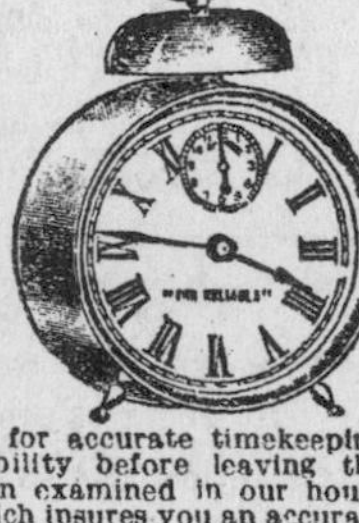

Price....... 74c

If by mail, postage extra, each, 32 cents.

$1.52 Strike Alarm Clock.

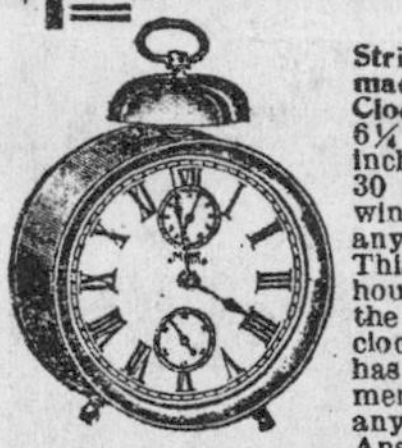

No. 5K2925 Strike Alarm Clock, made by the Ansonia Clock Company, height, 6¼ inches, dial, 4½ inches, movement runs 30 hours with one winding, different from any other alarm clock. This clock strikes the hours and half hours the same as a mantel clock. In addition it has an alarm attachment which alarms at any time set. The Ansonia Clock Company is known for the excellent clocks which they manufacture and we guarantee this clock to be an excellent timekeeper and to give entire satisfaction.

Price....... $1.52

If by mail, postage extra, 36 cents.

Our Sure Get Up Alarm Clock, $2.26

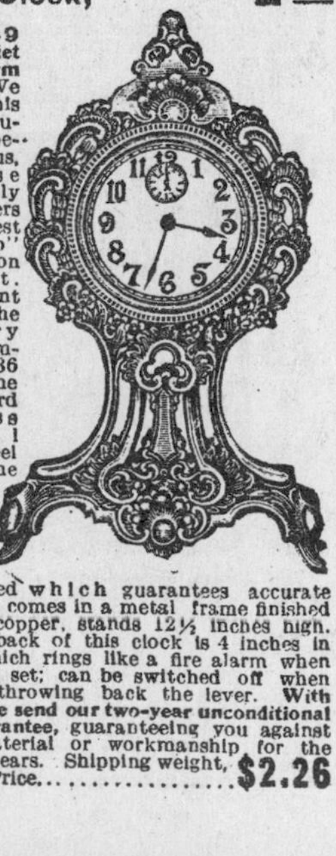

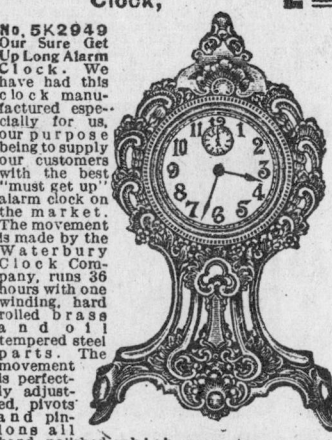

No. 5K2949 Our Sure Get Up Long Alarm Clock. We have had this clock manufactured especially for us, our purpose being to supply our customers with the best "must get up" alarm clock on the market. The movement is made by the Waterbury Clock Company, runs 36 hours with one winding, hard rolled brass and oil tempered steel parts. The movement is perfectly adjusted, pivots and pinions all hand polished which guarantees accurate timekeeping, comes in a metal frame finished in oxidized copper, stands 12½ inches high. Bell on the back of this clock is 4 inches in diameter, which rings like a fire alarm when the alarm is set; can be switched off when desired by throwing back the lever. With each clock we send our two-year unconditional binding guarantee, guaranteeing you against defective material or workmanship for the term of two years. Shipping weight, 9 pounds. Price....... $2.26

96c Boudoir Alarm Clock.

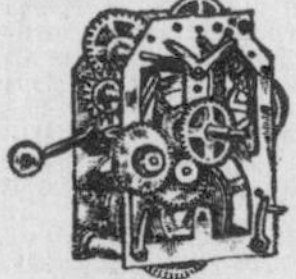

No. 5K2941 Boudoir Alarm Clock. Our gilt cupid design Boudoir Alarm Clocks for 96 cents. Never before in the history of boudoir clocks has anything like the handsome little clock, here illustrated, been offered at anything like this price. The immense quantity purchased is the only reason that makes this price possible. Clock stands 10 inches high, 8½ inches wide at base, dial is 2¼ inches in diameter, fitted with a French beveled crystal. The frame is made of metal representing the figure of cupid with two dragon head side ornaments. Different from all other boudoir clocks, this one has an alarm attachment. The movement (see the illustration) runs 30 hours with one winding, is an excellent timekeeper, has an alarm attachment and rings the same as any alarm clock. The alarm bell is ingeniously hidden on the back of the clock.

Price....... 96c

Weight, boxed ready for shipment, 6 pounds.

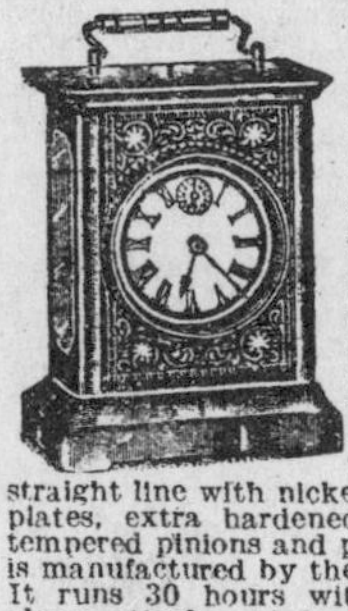

No. 5K2932 Nickel Plated Glass Paneled High Grade Alarm Clock. Stands 6 inches high, 4¾ inches wide at base and 3 inches deep, has fine glass panels. You can observe the working of the movement through the sides. The dial is 2¾ inches in diameter, has plain Roman numerals. This clock is beautified by gilt arabesque panel work in the front of the clock. The movement is straight line with nickel plated front and back plates, extra hardened brass wheels and oil tempered pinions and pivots. The movement is manufactured by the Waterbury Clock Co. It runs 30 hours with one winding. The alarm attachment is invisible, being placed underneath the clock. This clock is not alone an alarm clock, but also strikes the hours and half hours on a bell. Weight, packed ready for shipment, about 4 pounds.

Price....... $2.30

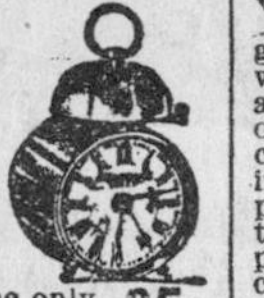

No. 5K2931 Wasp Alarm Clock, lever escapement, runs one day with one winding; stands 3¼ inches high; dial 2 inches in diameter; is manufactured by the Waterbury Clock Company and is guaranteed to keep correct time.

Price....... $1.20

If by mail, postage extra, 16c.

No. 5K2933 Same as No. 5K2931, but without alarm; time only. Price....... 85c

$2.48 For a Musical Alarm Clock.

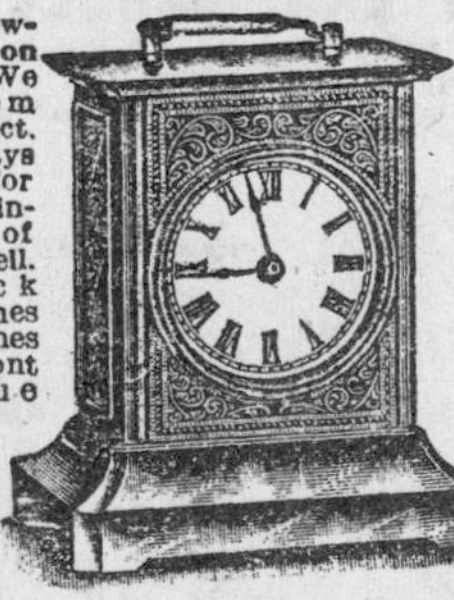

One of the newest novelties on the market. We import them ourselves direct. This clock plays one tune for about ten minutes instead of ringing a bell. This clock stands 7 inches high, 5 inches wide with front arabesque ornamentation around dial, full nickel plated frame with glass sides so that the movement and its action is visible at all times. The movement is a fine one. The illustration shows the movement as well as the music attachment which is ingeniously hidden at the bottom of the clock, and so arranged that when the clock is set at a certain time, instead of an alarm bell being heard, a beautiful tune is played. The device is simple and strong in construction and the danger of getting out of order is very remote. With care, that is, if the clock is not handled or played with but merely wound and set and placed on the mantel shelf or bureau, it should last for many years and give entire satisfaction. $2.48 is a remarkably low figure for such a unique piece of clock mechanism, and this price is only possible on account of our one small percentage of profit system. Weight of clock, packed ready for shipment, about 2½ pounds.

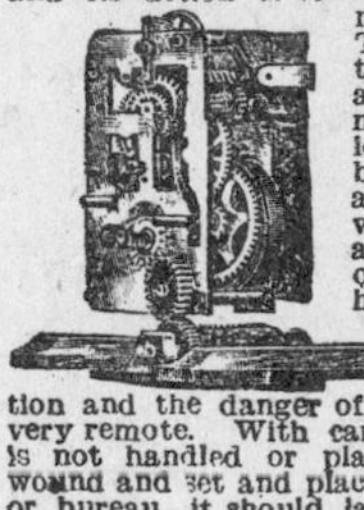

No. 5K3048 Musical Alarm Clock. Price....... $2.48

$1.85 For This Eight-Day Cabinet Clock.

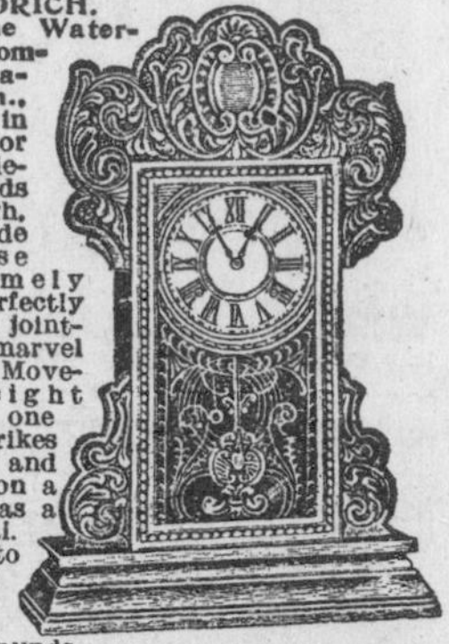

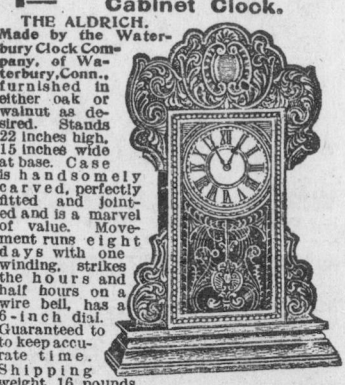

THE ALDRICH. Made by the Waterbury Clock Company, of Waterbury, Conn., furnished in either oak or walnut as desired. Stands 22 inches high, 15 inches wide at base. Case is handsomely carved, perfectly fitted and jointed and is a marvel of value. Movement runs eight days with one winding, strikes the hours and half hours on a wire bell, has a 6-inch dial. Guaranteed to keep accurate time. Shipping weight, 16 pounds.

No. 5K3102 Strikes on a wire bell. Price....... $1.85

No. 5K3104 Strikes on a wire bell, with an alarm attachment. Price....... $2.30

No. 5K3108 Strikes on a gong bell, with an alarm attachment. Price....... $2.45

$2.98 New Mission Style Solid Oak Dark Weathered Finish Clock.

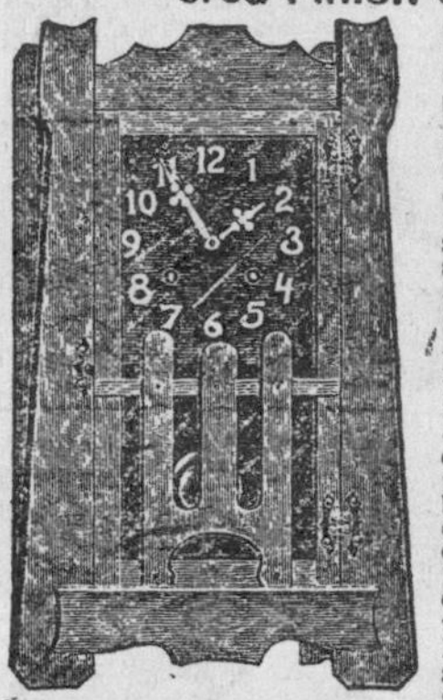

No. 5K3158 It stands at the highest point 20½ inches high, width at the base 12 inches. The dial is plain and is also made of solid oak with bright metal numerals and bright metal hands. The movement runs for eight days with but one winding, manufactured by the renowned New Haven Clock Co., of New Haven, Conn., strikes the hours and half hours on a sweet toned cathedral wire gong. Do not compare this finely built clock with similar clocks offered on the market; ours at a lesser price, compared with similar clocks offered on the market, is far better. We have contracted for an immense number; an immense quantity has made this astonishing price possible. We again offer you the advantage of the saving, adding only our own small per cent of profit to the original cost. This clock boxed, ready for shipment, weighs about 18 pounds. Price....... $2.98

$3.45 Is a Wonderful Offer in a Fancy Cabinet Clock.

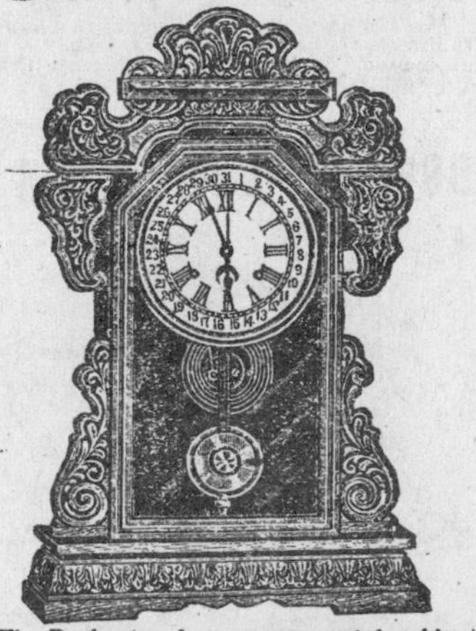

The Rochester fancy ornamental cabinet clock, made of solid black walnut, handsomely hand carved; height, 26½ inches. Different from any other cabinet clock, this clock has an 8-inch dial, a 2-inch larger dial than an ordinary cabinet clock, which makes it easy to see the time from any part of the room. It is fitted with an eight-day movement made by the Waterbury Clock Co., hand wrought brass and oil tempered steel parts, strikes the hours and half hours. In addition it has a calendar attachment which automatically registers the day of the month. Shipping weight, about 20 pounds.

No. 5K3151 Strikes on wire bell. Price....... $3.45

No. 5K3153 Strikes on cathedral gong. Price....... 3.75

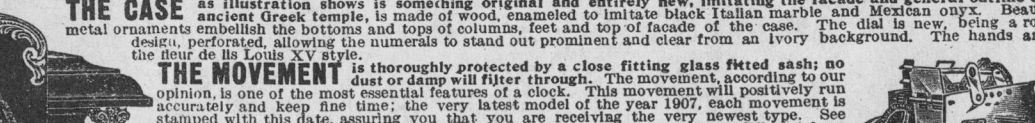

THE ROUGH RIDER CLOCK.

$5.38

FOR THIS MASSIVE, HANDSOME MANTEL CLOCK, COMPLETE, AS ILLUSTRATION SHOWS.

Read this description, then compare it with any clock you have seen advertised or exhibited in any store at 40 per cent more than we ask.

If our clock does not represent better value, if our clock is not the handsomer ornament to grace any parlor, then, by no means, buy it.

THIS CLOCK is one of the latest productions of the Waterbury Clock Co., of Waterbury, Conn., and they guarantee it, we, in turn, warrant it. The reputation of the Waterbury Clock Company is second to none. When you buy a clock of their production you are owning a clock made as finely as skilled labor and high grade material will allow, considering the price. We call this clock our Rough Rider Clock because of the beautiful figure done in bronze of a western cowboy with lariat in hand, gracefully posed on a galloping broncho.

PLEASE OBSERVE the beautiful lines of this clock, take particular note of the handsome bronze metal side ornaments and metal feet. See the metal dial sash and frame done in Arabesque rococo work; the dial is white with Roman numerals 5¾ inches in diameter, plain and distinct, easily seen from any part of the room. The clock, including the figure, is 19½ inches high, width at base, 17½ inches, depth 8 inches.

THE CASE is made of fine seasoned wood, guaranteed not to warp, covered by a secret prepared enamel to imitate black marble and Mexican onyx; this preparation is guaranteed not to crack, peel or chip off. A cloth slightly moistened with sweet oil gently rubbed over this clock will keep it as new forever.

A MANTEL CLOCK is as good as the movement that is fitted into it; the movement that is fitted into this clock is as fine as can be made of wrought brass and tempered steel, runs eight days with one winding, strikes the hours on a cathedral gong and the half hours on a cup bell. Each one is timed and adjusted before being fitted in the case and again after fitted.

$5.38 does not represent one-half the true value of this clock. We have reduced our very small percentage of profit again; we must unload, we bought an immense quantity and are giving you the advantage of our wonderfully close buying. The clock comes complete, boxed, ready to be set up, with full instructions plainly printed on the back of the clock, how to hang the pendulum, how to wind, how to set and various other important instructions.

No. 5K329   Price, including figure $5.38
No. 5K330   Price, figure alone .... .78
Boxed, ready for shipment, weighs about 25 pounds.

$3.25 for a Drop Octagon Office Clock.

The case is made of oak, 24 inches high. The case is ornamented with a beautifully carved moulding which lends a richness to this clock seldom equaled. The dial is made of white enameled paper, plain Roman numerals painted exceedingly large. The hands are made of blued steel fleur de lis pattern. The dial is ornamented with a plain polished gilt sash. The movement is made by the Waterbury Clock Co., of hand wrought brass and oil tempered steel. Pinions and pivots are hand polished, assuring accurate timekeeping. The clock is guaranteed to us by the manufacturers and we in turn guarantee it to our customers. Shipping weight, 20 pounds.

No. 5K3519   10-inch dial, time only. Price..............$3.25
No. 5K3521   10-inch dial, time with calendar. Price........$3.40
No. 5K3523   10-inch dial, time with strike. Price..........$3.50
No. 5K3525   12-inch dial, time only. Price................$3.50
No. 5K3527   12-inch dial, time with calendar. Price........$3.65
No. 5K3529   12-inch dial, time with strike. Price..........$3.78

No. 5K3519   No. 5K3521
No. 5K3525   No. 5K3527

Others Cannot Meet This Price. $4.46

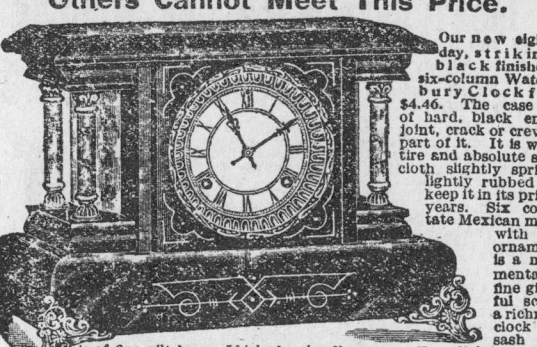

Our new eight-day, striking, black finished, six-column Waterbury Clock for $4.46. The case is of hard, black enameled wood, not a joint, crack or crevice to be found in any part of it. It is warranted to give entire and absolute satisfaction. A woolen cloth slightly sprinkled with sweet oil lightly rubbed over this clock will keep it in its pristine beauty for many years. Six columns, made to imitate Mexican marble and ornamented with gilt tops and bases, ornament the sides. This is a new idea in clock ornamentation. The feet are of fine gilt metal with beautiful scroll work, which lends a richness and charm to this clock rarely equaled. The sash which holds the dial is of fine gilt brass, 5¾ inches in diameter. The dial is plain and distinctly marked with Roman numerals and fitted with fine fleur de lis hands. The clock stands 10¾ inches high; the base from foot to foot, 15½ inches wide; depth, 7 inches. The movement is manufactured by the Waterbury Clock Co., of Waterbury, Conn., and is trued and timed and guaranteed in every respect; runs eight days with one winding; strikes the half hours on a brass bell and the hours on a cathedral toned gong. It is made of fine hard wrought brass, oil tempered steel parts, and with care will wear and keep time for a lifetime. Weight, packed for shipment, about 20 pounds.

No. 5K3900   Price....................$4.46

$5.90 INVESTIGATE THIS OFFER.

QUEEN OF THE NIGHT PARLOR MANTEL CLOCK.

$5.90 for this eight day, striking, metal ornamented Parlor Mantel Clock. A masterpiece of clock making. Our very latest creation. Designed especially for us by one of the greatest clock companies in the United States. We cannot give you the maker's name on account of special price. Never before has such a magnificent specimen of clock been sold for twice what we ask. The clock runs eight days with one winding. Strikes the hours on a cathedral gong and the half hours on a cup bell. We guarantee this clock. With each one we send our written binding guarantee, which insures and protects you for a term of five years against defective material or workmanship. We are able to do so only because we know how this clock has been constructed, and why it is superior to any that is on the market at anything near the price.

Five-Year Guarantee sent with this Clock.

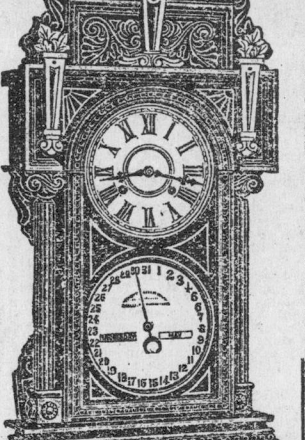

Different from any other concern, we show you the movement. Please note the illustration. The movement is made of solid brass, extra toughened oil tempered pivots, pinions and intricate steel parts. Different from all other clock movements. This movement is made after anti-friction models. All friction in these clocks has been reduced to a minimum and while we only guarantee it to give good time for a term of five years, it should last your natural lifetime if properly handled. The case is made of fine hardwood, finished by a secret enameling process representing black and pink Mexican onyx. It stands 13 inches high; width, 18 inches; depth, 6¾ inches. The front of the clock is ornamented by six imitation marble columns with gilt metal tops and bases. The sides have two conventionalized gilt metal floral designed ornaments. The feet, as illustration shows, are artistic, massive and in splendid proportion, finished in gilt metal. The dial is gilt, perforated and ornamented in floral design, and is protected by a heavy French glass set in a rococo ornamented gilt sash. The numerals are Arabic style, plain and distinct, yet in keeping with the ornamental design. The hands are of blue steel of Henry VI style. This clock can be kept like new by applying a soft cloth or a piece of cotton flannel slightly dampened with sweet oil. $5.90 is the price arrived at after figuring exact cost of material in the case, exact cost of the movement and exact cost of making and handling with one small percentage of profit added. The clock company's profit, the jobber's profit and the retailer's profit have all been eliminated and you are the gainer by no less than $4.00 to $6.00 by this method of figuring. This clock, boxed ready for shipment, weighs about 21 pounds.

No. 5K3934   Price.................$5.90

$6.75 Eight-Day Perpetual Calendar Clock.

Our Eight-Day Perpetual Calendar Clock, with 8-inch dial, manufactured especially for us by the Waterbury Clock Co., of Waterbury, Conn. The clock is made of oak, stands 28½ inches high. The case is beautifully embossed and carved throughout. Beautiful ornaments adorn the top and sides of this case. On either side are two massive oak columns which lend a richness to this clock that cannot be excelled. The case is made of extra heavy hardwood, kiln dried. All joints are perfectly fitted, protecting this movement from dust and dampness. The glass of door is decorated in black and gold. The movement is the latest straight line verge escapement, made of hard wrought brass and oil tempered, steel pinions and pivots, no burred edges to interfere with the timekeeping qualities of the clock. Runs eight days with one winding. Strikes the hours and half hours on a sweet toned gong. The clock is guaranteed to us by the manufacturer and we in turn guarantee it to our customers, and with proper care it should last you your natural lifetime. Shipping weight, 25 pounds.

No. 5K3580   Price...............$6.75

Actually Priced at One-Half Value.

$5.50 for this solid iron black enameled Eight-Day Parlor Clock. The case is made of iron enameled by a patent process, is guaranteed not to mar, peel or chip. It would require an expert to know the difference between this patent enamel iron clock and the genuine black Italian marble imported from Italy. Clock stands 10½ inches high, 15½ inches wide at base, 7 inches deep. Gilt front ornaments, gilt lion head side ornaments, gilt feet and dial sash lend a richness and artistic value to this clock unequaled by any other. The dial is its most handsome feature, having a gilt finished rim richly ornamented by a fancy rococo chased border with genuine mother of pearl inlaid figures. The numerals are plain and distinct, easily seen and exactly as illustration shows. The dial is 6 inches in diameter. The hands are of the Henry VI style, well made of blue steel. The movement fitted in this case manufactured by the celebrated New Haven Clock Co., of New Haven, Conn., runs eight days with one winding, is made of fine hard wrought brass and oil tempered steel parts. Hand polished pinions and pivots make this clock in running ability second to none.

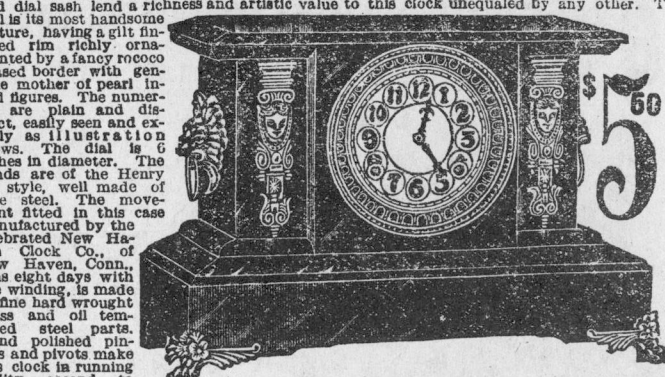

The latest improved, straight line verge escapement, friction reduced, non-burred wheels, simple in construction, perfectly finished and perfectly adjusted, insures this clock to run and give absolute satisfaction. Strikes the hours and half hours on a sweet toned gong. The clock is warranted to us by the manufacturers and we in turn warrant it to you to give entire and absolute satisfaction. Weight, packed ready for shipment, about 35 pounds.

No. 5K3932   Price, complete................$5.50

CROCKERY AND GLASSWARE

THE DINNER SETS AND GLASSWARE herein shown consist only of the best goods made by the world's foremost potters and glass makers, and include French, German, Austrian, English and American ware.

WE HAVE REDUCED OUR PRICES wherever possible. In pursuance of our recognized policy, wherever we have been able to make a saving in the cost of our goods, we have given our customers the benefit of this saving in the form of reduced prices. Sometimes the saving we effect is small and sometimes large, but in every case the customer gets the benefit of it.

COMPARE OUR PRICES with those asked by your local dealer and you will readily appreciate that every dinner set herein offered represents a saving of from $2.50 to $25.00. DO NOT BE DECEIVED by allowing your dealer to lead you to believe that our goods are second quality, which is his only excuse for our low prices.

WE SELL NO SECONDS in any of these wares, and only handle the finest and most carefully selected goods the market affords.

ABOUT FREIGHT CHARGES. Nearly all railroad companies carry crockery and glassware at second class rate, and sometimes as low as third class, depending on the section of the United States to which it is shipped. The second class rate averages from 40 to 50 cents per 100 pounds for 500 miles. You will find that the freight charges will amount to next to nothing as compared to what you will save in price.

FOR 5 CENTS each we send, postpaid, an individual butter plate of any dinner set, excepting our Haviland china, for which a charge of 10 cents is made. This sample, though small, will show the quality of the ware and give a fair idea of the decoration of the set.

OUR BINDING GUARANTEE

WE ABSOLUTELY GUARANTEE every piece of our crockery and glassware listed in this catalogue.

WE GUARANTEE that in each class and grade of ware the articles we list are better in quality and lower in price than can be obtained from any other dealer.

WE GUARANTEE to replace free of all charges, any piece that may prove defective in material and workmanship.

WE ALSO GUARANTEE safe delivery and will replace free of charge all breakage in transit.

AMERICAN DINNERWARE.

WE SELL ONLY THE FINEST QUALITY. We offer to our customers the best American china that is made. We do not sell ironstone or low grade china dinner sets. Our American dinner sets are made by the famous Homer Laughlin China Company, and are composed entirely of semi-vitreous china and porcelain, which means ware made from the best imported clays, finely ground and mixed in such a manner as to make smooth, pure white ware, and is guaranteed to last forever without crazing or discoloring. We do not attempt to sell first class, specially selected stock for less money than some other houses are selling seconds, i. e., defective stock. We could sell seconds at less money than any of our competitors if we dealt in that class of merchandise.

NOTE—ALL PLATTERS ARE MEASURED FROM EDGE TO EDGE.

UNDER THE ILLUSTRATION AND DESCRIPTION OF EACH STYLE OF AMERICAN DINNERWARE will be shown the combination which can be furnished of that kind. BEFORE PURCHASING REFER TO THIS PAGE to see exactly what pieces are contained in each set.

100-Piece Dinner Set.

12 Tea Cups	1 Oval Open Vegetable Dish
12 Tea Saucers	1 Round Open
12 Dinner Plates	Vegetable Dish
12 Tea Plates	1 Covered Vegetable Dish
12 Pie Plates	(2 pieces)
12 Sauce Dishes	1 Covered Sugar
12 Butter Plates	Bowl (2 pieces)
1 Platter, 12-inch	1 Sauce Boat
1 Platter, 14-inch	1 Pickle Dish
	1 Covered Butter Dish (3 pieces)
	1 Bowl
	1 Cream Pitcher
	1 Pitcher, quart size

101-Piece Dinner Set.

12 Tea Cups	1 Round Open Vegetable Dish
12 Tea Saucers	2 Covered Vegetable Dishes (4 pieces)
12 Dinner Plates	1 Platter, 12-inch
12 Tea Plates	1 Platter, 14-inch
12 Soup Plates	1 Covered Sugar Bowl (2 pieces)
12 Sauce Dishes	1 Cream Pitcher
12 Butter Plates	1 Pickle Dish
1 Oval Open Vegetable Dish	1 Bowl
	1 Covered Butter Dish, (3 pieces)
	1 Sauce Boat

56-Piece Dinner Set.

6 Tea Cups	1 Platter, 10-inch
6 Tea Saucers	1 Platter, 12-inch
6 Dinner Plates	1 Oval Baker
6 Tea Plates	1 Covered Vegetable Dish (2 pieces)
6 Pie Plates	1 Sauce Boat
6 Sauce Dishes	1 Pickle Dish
6 Butter Plates	1 Covered Butter Dish (3 pieces)
	1 Sugar Bowl (2 pieces)
	1 Cream Pitcher
	1 Bowl

80-Piece Dinner Set.

12 Tea Cups	1 Platter, 12-inch
12 Tea Saucers	1 Platter, 14-inch
12 Dinner Plates	1 Round Open Vegetable Dish
12 Pie Plates	1 Oval Open Vegetable Dish
12 Sauce Dishes	1 Covered Vegetable Dish (2 pieces)
12 Butter Plates	1 Sauce Boat
	1 Pickle Dish

$3.69 — THE ANGELUS PLAIN WHITE DINNER SET

THE FINEST PURE WHITE SEMI-VITREOUS CHINA. Our Angelus Dinner Set is the most up to date and best modeled plain white dinner service made. Every piece included in these sets is very richly embossed and artistically modeled, as shown in the illustration. Every piece is very white and thin, and equal to the best grades of English semi-porcelain ware.

ITS WEARING QUALITIES ARE UNSURPASSED, as the body of the ware is composed of the finest grades of clays, fired to a flinty hardness, and covered by a deep, glossy milk white glaze. We guarantee that this set is pure milk white, perfect in selection, without mishaps or small impractical pieces. We formerly sold a cheap, low grade set. Solely on account of our customers we have discontinued it. A low grade plain white set is expensive at any price. It has neither beauty nor quality to recommend it, and anyone who purchases one will never purchase another. At a slight difference in cost we sell you this fine quality high grade set. Shipped direct to our customers from the pottery in East Liverpool, Ohio. Sold only in complete dinner sets as listed.

No. 3K203 Angelus Pure White Semi-Porcelain Dinner Sets.

56-Piece Dinner Set.	Shipping weight, 50 pounds.	Price	$3.69
80-Piece Dinner Set.	Shipping weight, 60 pounds.	Price	4.45
100-Piece Dinner Set.	Shipping weight, 85 pounds.	Price	5.89
101-Piece Dinner Set.	Shipping weight, 90 pounds.	Price	6.45

For number and style of pieces see descriptive matter at the top of this page. When ordered with the regular sets, we can furnish the following pieces:

Coffee Cups and Saucers.	Price, per dozen	$1.35
Individual Vegetable Dishes.	Price, per dozen	.95
Soup Plates, new coupe shape.	Price, per dozen	.83

$4.65 — OUR ARBUTUS FLORAL DINNER SET.

While it is not as good as the sets listed on pages 351 and 352, which are the very best and most beautiful sets of American china made, yet is an excellent value, and for those who want a low priced set this is the best set ever offered. The decoration is exceptionally handsome print consisting of dainty clusters and sprays of arbutus flowers and foliage, delicately shaded and artistically applied. The decoration is furnished in either of two colors, a rich shade of green or a rich deep pink. When ordering, state color desired. The ware is light and thin and is carefully selected, and has a glossy white glaze. It has a new and attractive shape which has never before been offered in a dinner set so low in price. All pieces are handsomely modeled and embossed. These sets are shipped direct to our customers from the pottery in East Liverpool, Ohio.

No. 3K214 Our Arbutus Semi-Vitreous Dinner Sets.

56-Piece Dinner Set.	Shipping weight, 50 pounds. Price	$4.65
80-Piece Dinner Set.	Shipping weight 60 pounds. Price	$4.95
100-Piece Dinner Set.	Shipping weight, 84 pounds. Price	$6.85
101-Piece Dinner Set.	Shipping weight, 87 pounds. Price	$7.45

For number and style of pieces in the above sets, see top of this page.

$6.45 — OUR WOOD VIOLET GOLD STIPPLED DINNER SET

is the highest American semi-porcelain, clear, white and glossy, made of the best quality of material and decorated in the most artistic manner. The shape is new. Each piece is artistically embossed in new design.

BEAUTIFULLY DECORATED with sprays of purple wood violets, with delicate green leaves and here and there a red brown nasturtium, all in their natural colors, making an exceedingly dainty combination of colors and a most attractive decoration. The knobs, handles and edges of all pieces are heavily stippled with coin gold, as shown in the illustration, giving the set a very rich appearance. We guarantee every piece to be of the very best quality, especially selected to wear. Shipped from the pottery in East Liverpool, Ohio. We furnish the set in the combinations shown at the top of this page.

No. 3K290 Wood Violet Dinner Sets.

56-Piece Dinner Set.	Weight, 50 lbs.	Price $6.45
80-Piece Dinner Set.	Weight, 60 lbs.	Price 7.85
100-Piece Dinner Set.	Weight 85 lbs.	Price 9.90
101-Piece Dinner Set.	Weight, 90 lbs.	Price 10.75

IMPERIAL FAIENCE DINNER SET $5⁸⁵

"FAIENCE" IS THE BEST QUALITY OF SEMI-VITREOUS CHINA
CLUSTERS OF PINK ROSES. SPRAYS OF COIN GOLD. NEW IN DESIGN, SHAPE AND ORNAMENTATION.
SCALLOPED EDGES WITH BEAUTIFUL LACE EMBOSSING.

An Illustration of our Imperial Faience 100-Piece Dinner Set, one-twelfth actual size.

OUR IMPERIAL FAIENCE DINNER SET is a splendid value in American China Dinner Sets. For fear that some of our customers do not understand what "Faience" means, we would state that Faience is the best grade of semi-vitreous china. The body of this ware is pure white, medium thin and light in weight, yet strong and durable. This set is graceful in shape. Every piece is daintily scalloped with embossing around the edges in lace design.

PINK ROSE DECORATION. The decoration of this set is particularly attractive. It consists of clusters of delicately shaded pink roses in full bloom and rosebuds, with a background of green leaves and foliage in their natural colors. The flowers are artistically placed around the edges and extend toward the center.

FULL GOLD TRIMMED. Between each floral cluster is a genuine gold floral scroll ornament in the form of a spray, composed of roses and leaves outlined in bright gold, which adds immensely to the richness of the set. In addition every handle and knob on all the pieces is elegantly hand traced in bright coin gold.

ANOTHER REDUCTION IN PRICE. Although we have been selling this set exceedingly close and on a very small margin of profit, nevertheless, on account of the tremendous popularity of this set, we are enabled to buy it in even larger quantities than heretofore, and thus effect a slight saving in cost, which saving we give entirely to our customers. In the reduced prices we quote. If you want the best American china dinner set, and one that is equal to the very best grades of English porcelain, let us send you "Our Finest" Dinner Set No. 3K285, but if you do not want a set as fine as No. 3K285, you cannot do better than buy our "Imperial Faience" Dinner Set.

No. 3K256 Our Imperial Faience Dinner Set.

56-Piece Dinner Set.	Shipping weight, 50 pounds. Price	$ 5.85
80-Piece Dinner Set.	Shipping weight, 70 pounds. Price	6.89
100-Piece Dinner Set.	Shipping weight, 85 pounds. Price	9.58
101-Piece Dinner Set.	Shipping weight, 90 pounds. Price	10.39

For number and style of pieces included in the above dinner sets, see page 349.
When ordered with the dinner set, we can furnish the following pieces:

Coffee Cups and Saucers. Weight, 8½ ounces each. Price, per dozen	$1.75
Soup Plates, new coupe shape. Size, 8 inches. Price, per dozen	1.25
Individual Vegetable or Side Dishes. Size, 5½ inches. Price, per dozen	1.30

Each set shipped from our warehouse in East Liverpool, Ohio.

$7⁴⁸ WHITE AND GOLD DINNER SET

FINEST QUALITY OF CHINA—HAVILAND SHAPE
FULL GOLD DECORATIONS. A SOLID BURNISHED EDGE AND LACE BORDER
A REFINED SET IN PERFECT STYLE AND EXQUISITE TASTE

Illustration of our White and Gold 100-Piece Dinner Set, one-twelfth actual size.

WHITE AND GOLD is considered to be the most artistic and refined decoration used in dinner ware. It is always in the very best of taste; it has always a rich appearance on the table. Flower decorations may change and go out of style, but a white and gold dinner set is always fashionable and always in style.

SPECIAL SELECTED QUALITY. The ware from which this dinner set is made, is of the highest grade of pure white American porcelain, specially selected. This means that our White and Gold Dinner Set is equal to the best grade of English porcelain ware and is absolutely perfect in every respect.

NEW HAVILAND SHAPE. The shape of this set is the same as that of "Our Finest" Decorated American China Dinner Set, No. 3K285. It is a copy of the newest Haviland shape. Each piece is the acme of gracefulness and beauty, and is light and thin, yet very strong and durable. Each piece is elaborately embossed in ornamental design and the shape of the handles gives an appearance of extra lightness to the covered ware. It is a set that appeals to people of refined taste.

DECORATED WITH BURNISHED COIN GOLD. The exquisite gold decoration of this set makes it, without question of a doubt, the handsomest white and gold American china dinner set ever sold. The edge of every piece is decorated with a broad band of burnished coin gold, supplemented with an inside lace border of coin gold, which follows the outline of the rich embossing. All the handles are elaborately hand traced with gold. In ordering, please mention the number of pieces desired. Shipped from the pottery in East Liverpool, Ohio.

No. 3K280 White and Gold Dinner Set.

56-Piece Dinner Set.	Shipping weight, 50 pounds. Price	$ 7.48
80-Piece Dinner Set.	Shipping weight, 60 pounds. Price	8.75
100-Piece Dinner Set.	Shipping weight, 84 pounds. Price	10.95
101-Piece Dinner Set.	Shipping weight, 90 pounds. Price	11.75

For number and style of pieces included in the sets quoted above, see page 349.
When ordered with regular sets, we can furnish the following pieces:

Coffee Cups and Saucers. Price, per dozen	$1.98
Individual Vegetable Dishes. Price, per dozen	1.65
Soup Plates, new coupe shape. Price, per dozen	1.48

YOUR MONEY WILL BE IMMEDIATELY RETURNED TO YOU FOR ANY GOODS NOT PERFECTLY SATISFACTORY.

215

ROSE GARLAND DINNER SET $12.45

GENUINE BAVARIAN TRANSLUCENT CHINA. BEAUTIFULLY DECORATED WITH GARLANDS OF PINK ROSES AND GREEN FOLIAGE. ELABORATELY TRIMMED WITH GENUINE COIN GOLD

THE BEAUTIFUL DECORATION consists of a full border pattern composed of dainty garlands of pink roses and green foliage in their natural colors. In the center of each plate, dish, etc., is a medallion of roses and green leaves, and on all the platters, in addition there are festoons of roses scattered about. The inside of each cup also is decorated with a full border of roses.

EXTRA ELABORATELY FULL GOLD TRIMMED. In addition to this delicate, exquisite floral decoration, no expense has been spared to have every piece in this set elaborately hand traced in genuine coin gold. Every piece in this set has two gold lines completely surrounding it, one on each side of the embossed border, and in addition all the handles are hand traced with gold.

Illustration of our 100-Piece Rose Garland Bavarian China Dinner Set, One-Twelfth Actual Size.

NEWEST AND MOST FASHIONABLE SHAPE. The shape of the Rose Garland Bavarian Dinner Set is one of its most attractive features. By referring to the illustration you will see how beautifully each piece is modeled, how graceful is the design and how delicate the appearance. Each piece is charmingly embossed around the edges in a Grecian design, known as the "Walls of Troy." The edges of each piece are artistically fluted and the handles are in bow knot ribbon design. The body of this set is made of the finest quality of extra light and translucent Bavarian china, equal in appearance to the best grades of Haviland dinner wares. We sell this dinner set in both 56-piece and 100-piece sets. The composition of the 56-piece set is the same as given on page 354. The composition of the 100-piece set differs from the regular composition, and is as follows:

12 Tea Cups	1 Platter, 11½ inches	1 Sauce Boat and Stand—
12 Saucers	1 Platter, 15½ inches	(2 pieces)
12 Dinner Plates	2 Open Vegetable Dishes	1 Covered Butter Dish—
12 Breakfast Plates	1 Covered Vegetable Dish—	(3 pieces)
12 Tea or Pie Plates	(2 pieces)	1 Cream Pitcher
12 Sauce Dishes	1 Covered Sugar Bowl—	1 Pickle Dish
12 Individual Butters	(2 pieces)	1 Large Salad Bowl

No. 3K378 Rose Garland Genuine Bavarian China Dinner Set. 56-piece set. Shipping weight, 50 pounds. Price............$12.45
100-piece set. Shipping weight, 90 pounds. Price............18.85

$13.95 100-PIECE CARLSBAD CHINA DINNER SET

THIS SET is made of genuine translucent china. The shape is new and attractive, being embossed and gracefully outlined. The cups, sugars, creamers, etc., are modeled so light and thin in shape that they are termed egg shell china, yet are very strong and durable. The decoration consists of a dainty pink floral spray with green leaves and vines forming the background. The decoration consists of beautiful flowers and foliage in their natural colors. In addition all the knobs and handles on every piece are full gold traced. This set is furnished only in the 100-piece combination. At the low price we sell this set it is a great bargain and a splendid value.

No. 3K371 100-Piece Dinner Set, complete. Shipping weight, 90 pounds. Price............$13.95

$15.50 BUYS THIS 100-PIECE ROYAL CHINA DINNER SET

THE CHINA is extra thin and light, handsomely modeled. Every piece is most graceful in outline and handsomely embossed. The decoration is exceedingly pretty, consisting of dainty pink floral sprays and green foliage, in colors true to life. Each spray is gracefully arranged, making a pattern which is far more handsome than many patterns sold at double the price. The handles and knobs on every piece are full gold traced. Furnished only in regular 100-piece combination, with this exception, that it contains breakfast plates instead of coups soup plates.

No. 3K372 100-Piece Dinner Set, complete. Shipping weight, 90 pounds. Price............$15.50

GENUINE HAVILAND CHINA

WE SELL ONLY THE GENUINE THEODORE HAVILAND
French China Dinner Sets, which is the best Haviland China made. Every piece of china that we represent in our catalogue to be Haviland china, will be found to bear the registered trade mark of Theodore Haviland.

THE EXTREMELY LOW PRICES at which we sell our genuine Haviland French China Dinner Sets, are made possible by the fact that we buy direct from Theodore Haviland at Limoges, France, and import this china ourselves, and the saving that we make in brokers' commissions, jobbers' profits and the like, we give to our customers.

Theodore Haviland
Limoges
FRANCE
Trade Mark of the Genuine
Theodore Haviland China.

The composition of the Genuine Haviland Dinner Sets listed in this catalogue consists of the following pieces:

56-PIECE DINNER SET.

6 Tea Cups	6 Sauce Dishes, 5-inch
6 Tea Saucers	6 Individual Butter Dishes, 3⅛-inch
6 Dinner Plates, 10-inch	1 Meat Platter, 14-inch
6 Tea Plates, 7½-inch	1 Open Vegetable Dish (oval)
6 Coupe Soup Plates, 7½-inch	1 Covered Vegetable Dish (oval)
1 Sauce Boat and Stand	1 Sugar Bowl
1 Covered Butter Dish	1 Cake Plate, 12-inch	1 Cream Pitcher

100-PIECE DINNER SET.

12 Tea Cups	12 Individual Butter Dishes,	1 Vegetable Dish, covered (round)
12 Tea Saucers	3⅛-inch	1 Sauce Boat and Stand
12 Dinner Plates, 10-inch	1 Meat Platter, 12-inch	1 Covered Butter Dish
12 Tea Plates, 7½-inch	1 Meat Platter, 16-inch	1 Pickle Dish, 9-inch
12 Coupe Soup Plates, 7½-inch	1 Vegetable Dish, open (oval)	1 Sugar Bowl
12 Sauce Dishes, 5-inch	1 Vegetable Dish, covered (oval)	1 Cream Pitcher

Each set is carefully packed by expert packers. We furnish round sample individual butter plates, postpaid, to any of our Haviland sets, on receipt of 10 cents. While this butter plate will not do full justice to the sets it will give an idea of the beauty of the ware and the delicacy of the decoration.

CAKE PLATE.

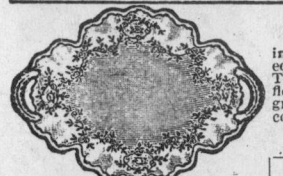

Made of the finest quality of genuine Haviland China in an oval shape, with elaborately fluted and embossed edges, these edges being hand traced with two gold lines. The handles are open and incrusted with gold. The floral decoration consists of a border of pink roses with green foliage, this border being in graceful festoon design, completely surrounding the inside edge of the plate.
No. 3K414 Cake Plate. Price............$1.48
Weight, packed for shipment, 2 pounds.

SALAD OR BERRY SET.

Contains one large salad bowl, measuring 8½ inches and six individual salad saucers, each measuring 5 inches. The china used in this set is Theodore Haviland's finest china, with the sides delicately fluted and the edges scalloped. A solid band of incrusted yellow Roman gold is around the edge, with a fine inside hand traced gold line following the details of the embossing. The flower decoration consists of garlands of pink roses and is placed both on the outside and on the inside of the bowl and the inside of every saucer.
No. 3K422 7-Piece Haviland Salad Set. Price.....(Weight, 4 pounds.)....$4.98

INDIVIDUAL SERVICE SET.

Made of the finest genuine Haviland china, decorated with a border of pink roses and green foliage; the outside edge incrusted with yellow Roman gold. The set consists of an 8-inch plate, an oatmeal or mush bowl, an individual cream pitcher and a cup and saucer. This set makes an ideal present, besides having the advantage of being extremely useful.
No. 3K418 Individual Service Set.
Price....................$2.85
Weight, packed for shipment, 3½ pounds.

See page 357 for our beautiful genuine Haviland Chocolate Set and genuine Haviland Tete-a-Tete Set.

$23.50 — 100-PIECE HAVILAND DINNER SET

Theodore Haviland
Limoges
FRANCE

THIS GENUINE HAVILAND SET is of a new and handsome shape, in that pure translucent white, delicately decorated, and made only by Theodore Haviland, of Limoges, France. Haviland china is always very thin, light in weight, perfect in color, great in strength, perfect in finish and beautiful in decoration. The decoration of this set consists of a very delicate pink wild crabapple blossom with light green moss fern background. It has the genuine coin gold knobs and handles, adding richness to the set. $23.50 is the lowest price ever asked for a full dinner set of **GENUINE Haviland China—100 pieces.** This kind of ware must be seen to be appreciated. Very carefully packed in small imported casks. Shipping weight, 100 pounds.
No. 3K415 100-Piece Haviland Dinner Set.
Price....................**$23.50**

100-PIECE ROSE SPRAY HAVILAND DINNER SET — $27.69

SPRAYS OF DELICATE PINK ROSES with green foliage artistically arranged on all pieces, and French gray scrolls, make an exceptionally delicate and pretty decoration. All handles are decorated with pure coin gold, greatly adding to the richness of the set.
No. 3K409 100-Piece Haviland Dinner Set. Price..................

THE VINCENNES SHAPE and the graceful embossing in a fancy festoon pattern on every piece sets off very effectively the decoration. The ware is light and thin, made from genuine Theodore Haviland translucent china.
$27.69

100-PIECE ROSE WREATH HAVILAND DINNER SET — $31.98

DAINTY PINK CLIMBING ROSES, entwined with delicate green foliage and leaves, gracefully arranged, form a complete border, encircling the edge of each piece. Every piece is adorned with a beautiful jewel center composed of four rose sprays. All handles and knobs are elegantly hand stippled with pure coin gold. The shape of pieces is particularly attractive. It is one of Haviland's newest and most popular shapes.
No. 3K401 100-Piece Haviland Dinner Set. Price...........

MADE OF FINE QUALITY genuine Theodore Haviland translucent china, pure white, very light and thin. Each piece, in addition to being decorated as described, is artistically embossed with festoon border of bow knot design. The larger pieces are delicately fluted, with edges and feet to match. The shape is known as Lambelle pattern.
$31.98

OUR MAMMOTH GENUINE CHINA ASSORTMENT $3.38

38 PIECES OF THE CHOICEST OF CHINAWARE FOR LESS THAN 9 CENTS EACH.

DECORATED WITH DELICATE PINK FLOWERS WITH GREEN LEAVES. FULL GOLD TRIMMED.

DEAR TO THE HEART of every housekeeper is beautiful, handsomely decorated china. How much more will this set of fancy china appeal to the housekeeper when every piece is useful. Beautiful on the table or in the china closet. **THIS IS THE MOST WONDERFUL BARGAIN** ever offered in high grade imported china. An assortment of thirty-eight of the choicest pieces of chinaware for slightly less than 9 cents for each piece. You can make no mistake by sending us your order for this **mammoth assortment**, as all the pieces included in this set cannot be bought in a retail store for less than $5.00. Every piece is made of the finest extra thin translucent Bavarian china, handsomely embossed and beautifully decorated with pink roses and other flowers. Each piece is elegantly trimmed with bright gold. All pieces are guaranteed to please you in every respect.

The assortment includes the following pieces:

- 1 Large 10-Inch China Cake Plate
- 1 9-Inch China Salad Bowl
- 6 5¾-Inch China Fruit or Sauce Dishes to match
- 6 8-Inch China Tea or Cake Plates
- 6 China Fancy Cups and Saucers
- 1 3-Piece China Mustard Pot
- 1 China Sugar Bowl and Cover
- 1 Large China Celery Tray
- 1 3-Piece China Butter Dish
- 1 China Spoon Holder
- 1 China Toothpick Holder
- 1 China Pitcher

Packed in a strong box. Shipping weight, 35 pounds.

No. 3K1612 Mammoth China Assortment. Price **$3.38**

BREAD AND BUTTER AND TEA PLATES.

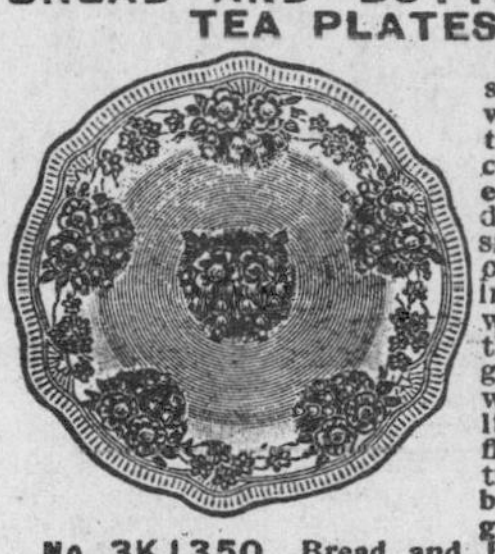

Made of selected pure white thin translucent china, neatly embossed. The decoration consists of borders of pink roses, intermingled with lilies of the valley, and green leaves, with a medallion center of flowers. Edges trimmed with bright coin gold.

No. 3K1350 Bread and Butter Plates. Size, 6¼ in. Weight, per half dozen, 3 pounds. Price, per dozen, **$1.15**; half dozen..**63c**

No. 3K1355 Tea Plates. Size, 7¾ inches. Weight, per half dozen plates, 4 pounds. Price, per half dozen.......**$0.83**
Per dozen **1.48**

No. 3K1365 Large Tea Plates. Size, 8½ inches. Weight, per half dozen, 5 pounds. Price, per dozen, **$1.65**; half dozen, **88c**

FANCY SALAD OR BERRY SET.

Made of fine translucent Austrian china richly scalloped and embossed. Decorated with a large cluster of roses with a background of green foliage. The edges are elaborately stippled with bright gold. Set consists of one 8½-inch salad bowl and six 5¼-inch sauce dishes to match. Weight, per set, 8 pounds.

No. 3K1555 Price, per set.....**$0.98**
Per half dozen sets.............. **5.65**

BREAD OR CAKE PLATE.

Made of select quality translucent china, richly embossed and has scalloped edge and open handles. The decoration consists of large clusters of roses intermingled with lilies and a background of fern leaves. The outer edges are handsomely gold traced. Size, 10½ inches. Weight, 1½ pounds.

No. 3K1390 Price, each.......**$0.49**
Per dozen........................ **5.75**

BREAD OR CAKE PLATE.

Elaborately ornamented with gold. Decorated with fruits and flowers. It is made of the very finest quality of translucent Bavarian china, handsomely embossed. It has open handles on each side. Size, 9½ inches. Weight, each, 1½ pounds.

No. 3K1395 Price, each.......**$0.45**
Per dozen........................ **2.69**

SALAD OR BERRY BOWL.

Made of translucent German china; neatly embossed and decorated with four pink floral sprays and green foliage. Size, 8½ inches. Weight, each, 1¼ lbs.

No. 3K1570 Price, each.......**$0.23**
Per dozen........................ **2.25**

TEA AND FRUIT PLATES.

Made of genuine pure white translucent china. Decorated with large cluster of American beauty roses and green foliage. The scalloped edge is ornamented with full gold lace border.

No. 3K1370 Tea or Fruit Plates. Size, 8 inches. Weight, per half dozen, 4 pounds. Price, per half dozen, **$1.19**
Per dozen **2.29**

No. 3K1380 Tea or General Utility Plates. Size, 10 inches. Weight, per half dozen, 6 pounds. Price, per half dozen.....**$1.74**
Per dozen........................ **3.39**

TEA OR FRUIT PLATES.

CHRYSANTHEMUM DESIGN. VERY HANDSOME.

Made of genuine translucent Bavarian china with scalloped edges, handsomely embossed. Decorated with clusters of pink, yellow and white chrysanthemums, with a background of green ferns. The edges are richly stippled with coin gold. Size, 9 inches. Weight, per half dozen, 4 pounds.

No. 3K1375 Price, per half doz..**$1.55**
Price, per dozen..................... **2.89**

AMERICAN BEAUTY BOWL.

Made of Bavarian china handsomely embossed. Decorated with a border of American beauty roses with beautiful lace gold edges. Size, 10 inches. W'ght, 2 lbs.

No. 3K1575 Price, each.....**$0.53**
Per half dozen **2.98**

IRIDESCENT LUSTER BOWL.

Made of the most select Bavarian china, handsomely embossed in paneled designs and lace border edges. Tinted in pearl gray and pink luster. All embossments are hand traced in bright gold. Decorated with large floral sprays and green foliage. Size, 11 inches. Weight, each, 1½ pounds.

No. 3K1580 Price, each....**$0.82**
Per half dozen.................. **4.85**

CHOCOLATE SET.

Extra fine quality of Bavarian china beautifully modeled and handsomely embossed. Decorated with beautiful clusters of American beauty roses and rosebuds, with a background of green leaves. The body is handsomely tinted in green, which shades from a dark grass green at the top to a light green at the bottom. The handles and edges are heavily clouded with genuine gold. One 10-inch chocolate pot, and six 3½-inch cups with saucers. Weight, per set, 4½ pounds.

No. 3K1595 Price, per set....**$1.98**

OUR FINEST SALAD OR BERRY SET.

Made of the finest translucent Bavarian china. The decorations consist of sprays of pink and yellow roses, intertwined with lilacs with a background of green foliage. The scalloped edges are elaborately embossed and decorated with genuine coin gold, in a floral rose design. The set consists of one 10¾-inch, extra deep bowl and six 6-inch sauce dishes to match. Weight of set, 10 pounds.

No. 3K1560 Price, per set **$1.85**
Per half dozen sets.......................**10.98**

FOUR-PIECE TABLE SET.

This set consists of a large Sugar Bowl, Creamer, Butter Dish with drainer, and Spoon Holder. It is made of fine quality of translucent china, embossed and decorated with sprays of roses, with background of green leaves. The sides are decorated with sprays of bright coin gold. The edges are scalloped. Height of sugar bowl with top, 4½ inches.

No. 3K1440 China Four-Piece Table Set.
Price per set (Weight, per set, 8½ pounds)......**75c**

USEFUL TABLE ASSORTMENT.

Contains: 1 Large Cracker Jar, 1 Olive or Bon Bon Dish, 1 Celery Tray (12 inches), 1 Syrup Pitcher with Plate, 1 Pickle Dish or Spoon Tray (9 inches)

Have these useful pieces handy, but when not in use they will be an ornament to any china closet. Made of fine white translucent Bavarian china, in fancy fluted shapes, elaborately embossed around the edges. On each piece is a cluster of pink flowers with green foliage, and the trays are stippled with gold, while the cracker jar has a gold line around the edge.

No. 3K1588 Table Assortment. Price.........**$1.18**
Each set packed complete in a box. Weight, 4½ pounds.

No. 3K1515 Cracker Jar only. Price............**39c**
No. 3K1525 Syrup Pitcher only. Price..........**27c**
No. 3K1490 Celery Tray only. Price.............**32c**
No. 3K1485 Pickle Dish or Spoon Tray only. Price. **23c**
No. 3K1480 Olive or Bon Bon Dish only. Price...**10c**

BREAD AND BUTTER PLATES.

Made of fine translucent china, delicately embossed. Decorated with large American beauty roses, and elaborately ornamented with a rich, genuine gold lace border. These are exceptionally pretty plates. Size, 6¼ inches. Weight, per half dozen, 3 lbs.

No. 3K1360 Price, per half dozen...................**$0.79**
Per dozen............................ **1.44**

CEREAL AND SPICE SET.

Housekeepers' fine German China Cereal and Spice Jars, pure white body heavily glazed and decorated in rich flow blue in neat scroll floral design, with names of spices or cereals on each jar as shown in the illustration. The set is composed of thirteen useful pieces, consisting of six large cereal jars, measuring 7½ inches high by 5½ inches wide, and six assorted spice jars, 4 inches high by 3 inches wide, all being fitted with covers to match; also a large size salt box which has a hardwood polished cover. Shipping weight, 16 pounds.

No. 3K560 Cereal and Spice Set. Price......**$2.69**

No. 3K561 Cereal and Spice Set, exactly like above, excepting that a salt jar, similar to the cereal jars, is furnished in place of the salt box. Weight, 16 pounds. Price...**$2.58**

$3.85 GENUINE HAND DECORATED CHINA PLATE RAIL SET

AN EXCEPTIONAL VALUE. This is the chance of a lifetime to obtain a gorgeous plate rail set, consisting of six genuine china plates of the finest quality, hand decorated in natural colors by famous artists, at a price that is less than half what you have been compelled to pay for this same set heretofore.

EACH PLATE IS DESIGNED BY AN ARTIST and hand decorated by him in as many as fifty different colors on one plate. These colors are exceptionally rich and brilliant and include such rare colors as royal purple, crimson, sapphire blue, emerald green, topaz, etc. The outer edge of each plate is handsomely trimmed with full gold. The colors are all true to life and every detail is brought out. The diameter of each plate is 9¼ inches. Retail price, $2.50 per plate.

No. 3K1620 Price, per set, six artistic plates, each a separate design... **$3.85**
Weight, packed for shipment, per set, 5½ pounds.

CHILDREN'S DECORATED CUPS AND SAUCERS.

Made of White Translucent China in Fancy Embossed Pattern, tinted in pleasing colors shading to white. The decoration consists of a spray of flowers with green leaves. Neatly stippled in gold. Height of cup, 2⅜ inches. Weight, per half dozen, 3 pounds.

No. 3K1305 Price, per half dozen. 54c
Price, per dozen 97c

AFTER DINNER CUPS AND SAUCERS.

Made of the Finest Quality Hand Decorated Imported Translucent China. They are light and thin, delicately embossed and beautifully moulded in the new, fashionable shape. Decorated with sprays of flowers and tinted in pleasing iridescent colors. Full gold trimmed. Height of cup, 2 inches. Weight, per half dozen, 2 pounds.

No. 3K1310 Price, per half dozen. $1.45
Price, per dozen 2.69

TEA CUPS AND SAUCERS.

Made of Fancy Imported China. A good, practical, medium size cup, in new crimped design. Cup and saucer richly decorated with bands of iridescent colors, handles stippled with bright gold. The bottom of the cup and center of saucer is fancily fluted. Height of cup, 3 inches. Weight, per dozen, 6 pounds.

No. 3K1315 Price, per half dozen, $0.69
Price, per dozen 1.25

LARGE CUPS AND SAUCERS.

They are made of White Translucent China and are decorated with large clusters of flowers and green leaves. Each cup and saucer is stippled with bright gold. Height of cup, 3½ inches. Weight, per half dozen, 2½ pounds.

No. 3K1320 Price, per half dozen, $0.89
Price, per dozen 1.65

No. 3K1345 Extra Large Cups and Saucers (like No. 3K1320, excepting that they are extra large). Height of cup, 3⅝ inches. Weight, half dozen, 3 pounds.
Price, per half dozen $1.33
Price, per dozen 2.48

OUR FINEST CUPS AND SAUCERS.

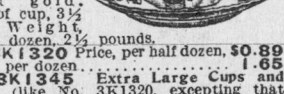

Made of the Finest Quality of Thin Translucent China, richly embossed, elegantly tinted in rich green, which shades from a light to a dark green; decorated with large red American beauty roses, buds and foliage, handles and edges heavily clouded with coin gold. An exact reproduction of hand painted china. Height of cup, 2⅔ inches. Weight (cup and saucer), 10 ounces.

No. 3K1335 Price, per pair (2 cups and 2 saucers) $0.95
Price, per half dozen 2.75

MUSTACHE CUPS AND SAUCERS.

Made of Imported China. Beautifully decorated with pink chrysanthemums and green leaves, fully trimmed with gold, edges and handles stippled with bright gold. Height, 3⅛ inches. Weight, per dozen, 6 pounds.

No. 3K1325
Price, per half dozen, 88c; each 16c

SUGAR AND CREAM SET.

Made of Translucent China in the New Fluted Haviland shape. Decorated with clusters of pink roses and green leaves. Edges and handles are handsomely ornamented in bright gold. 3½ inches high. Weight, 14 ounces.

No. 3K1415 Price, per set...... $0.23
Price, per half dozen sets 1.29

SUGAR AND CREAM SET.

Finest Quality of Austrian China. Medium size, pure white, richly embossed. The decoration consists of panels of garlands of roses, connected with iridescent green bands, highly illuminated with bright gold, with gold lace borders. The handles and edges are heavily covered with coin gold. 2¾ inches high. Weight, 8 ounces.

No. 3K1425 Price, per set..... $0.75
Price, per half dozen sets 4.25

THREE-PIECE TABLE SET.

Fine Bavarian China. Consists of sugar, creamer and teapot. Handsomely modeled in a new French shape and neatly embossed: beautifully decorated with roses, and green leaves, and has full traced gold handles, knobs, lace border. Height, 5 inches. Weight, 2 lbs.

No. 3K1430 Price, per set..... $0.59
Price, per half dozen sets 3.48

THREE-PIECE OATMEAL SET.

Made of German China, handsomely embossed. The decoration consists of large sprays of flowers. The set consists of one 6¼-inch plate, 4½-inch bowl and fancy pitcher. 3 inches high. Weight, per set, 1¼ pounds.

No. 3K1445
Price, per half dozen sets. $1.19; per set, 22c

THREE-PIECE OATMEAL SET.

Consists of 7-inch plate, 6-inch oatmeal bowl and one-half pint pitcher, which measures 3¼ inches high. This set is made of selected Bavarian china, richly decorated with large sprays of pink and yellow flowers. The edges are heavily clouded with bright coin gold. Weight, per set, 1½ pounds.

No. 3K1450 Price, per set..... $0.75
Price, per half dozen sets 4.48

MEDALLION BERRY BOWL.

Made of the choicest Bavarian china, richly embossed, with portrait medallion centerpiece and beautiful lace border. Richly tinted in dark green and elaborately trimmed with coin gold. 10 inches. Weight, each, 2 pounds.

No. 3K1585 Price, each...... $0.95
Per dozen 10.50

JAPANESE CHINA.

CUPS AND SAUCERS.

Thin China Cups and Saucers, decorated in artistic flow blue, Jap designs, very neat and dainty. Weight, per dozen, 5½ pounds.

No. 3K1800 Price, per half dozen, $0.80
Price, per dozen 1.49

Fine Thin China Cups and Saucers, medium size, beautifully hand decorated with Jap roses, gold illuminated and traced. Weight, per dozen, 6 pounds.

No. 3K1805 Price, per half dozen. $1.18
Price, per dozen 2.25

Finest Quality Thin Jap China Cups and Saucers, beautifully decorated by hand both inside and out with pretty pink and blue floral design, fully gold scroll illuminated and gold traced edges. Weight, per half dozen, 3 pounds.

No. 3K1810 Price, per half dozen. $1.55
Price, per dozen 2.95

PLATES.

Japanese China 6-inch Plates, decorated in artistic flow blue, Jap figured designs; suitable for serving cake, fruit dessert or ice cream. Weight, 4½ pounds.

No. 3K1820 Price, per half dozen 53c
Price, per dozen.. 95c

Japanese China 7-inch Plates, decorated in artistic flow blue, Jap designs, very neat and handsome. Packed one dozen in original Jap straw packages. Weight, 9 pounds.

No. 3K1825 Price, per half dozen. $0.75
Price, per doz. 1.39

SALT AND PEPPER SHAKERS

Fine Jap China Shakers, hand decorated with roses, green tinted neck, full gold traced, complete with cork stopper. Weight, per set, 8 lbs.

No. 3K1832 Price, per set, two pieces 19c

Exceptionally Handsome Salts and Peppers, hand decorated with Jap roses, rich royal blue neck and bottom, full gold traced, with cork stopper. Weight, per set, 8 ounces.

No. 3K1835 Price, per set, two pieces 25c

SUGAR AND CREAM SETS.

Fine Jap China Sugars and Creamers. Exceptionally handsome design with royal blue tinted edges and handles, hand decorated rose floral decorations, and full scroll gold tracings. Weight, 2½ pounds.

No. 3K1840 Price, per set 49c

Fine Thin China Sugars and Creamers, beautiful new French pattern, with dark royal blue tinted edges and handles, hand decorated floral design, full gold scroll tracings. Weight, 2⅔ lbs.

No. 3K1842 Price, per set 79c

TEAPOT TILES.

German China, handsomely tinted in dark green, decorated with large floral sprays. Embossed edges stippled with gold. Diameter, 6¼ inches. Weight, ½ pound.

No. 3K1465 Price, each 9c
Price, per dozen 95c

OATMEAL BOWL.

Japanese China Bowls, decorated Japanese flow blue figured designs; very suitable for serving oatmeal, desserts, broths, etc. Packed one dozen in original Jap straw packages. Weight, 9 pounds.

No. 3K1830 Blue and White Bowls.
Price, per half dozen 43c
Price, per dozen 75c

SALAD OR BERRY SET.

Fine Thin Jap China Salad Set, consisting of 9½-inch salad bowl and six 5-inch nappies to match, beautifully decorated by hand, with pink daisies and violets; has rich royal blue scalloped edges, fully gold traced and rich lattice scrolls of dull gold. Regular $3.00 value. Weight, 9 pounds.

No. 3K1860 Price, per set... $1.98

CHOCOLATE SET.

Fine Jap China Chocolate Set, consisting of two-pint chocolate pot and six cups and saucers. Decoration consists of hand painted pink Jap roses and forget me nots. All pieces are ornamented with rich bright gold scrolls and edges are tinted in light green. Weight, 10 pounds.

No. 3K1870 Price, per set... $1.48

TEA SET.

Nine-Piece Tea Set, consisting of teapot, sugar bowl, cream pitcher, and six large tea cups and saucers. It is handsomely decorated with Jap roses and forget me nots and green foliage. The edges are delicately tinted with rich green, and all pieces are handsomely illuminated with scrolls and lattice work of bright gold. The cups are decorated both inside and outside. The value speaks for itself. Neatly packed in original Japanese box. Weight, 10 pounds.

No. 3K1884 Price, complete $2.29

AWATA VASES.

Genuine Japanese Awata Vase. Measures 10 inches in height; made from Japanese porcelain beautifully decorated with large Japanese wild roses and foliage in bold relief, fully outlined in bright gold, with leaves in natural colors, on rich dark blue body. Exceptional value. Packed one pair in a package. Weight, each, 5 pounds.

No. 3K1890
Price, each 59c

HAIR RECEIVER.

Bavarian China, scalloped shape, neatly embossed, decorated with large rose sprays and green foliage, with fancy gold lace edge. Diameter, 4½ inches. Weight, 6 ounces.

No. 3K1475 Price, each..... $0.23
Price, per half dozen 1.35

$3²⁵ OUR ENGRAVED INITIAL GLASS ASSORTMENT

An Absolutely New Idea.   The Swellest Thing in Glassware.

SCINTILLATING CRYSTAL GLASS.   BEAUTIFUL HAND ENGRAVED INITIALS.

WOULD YOU LIKE TO OWN THIS SET? What do you think of a glass set made of the finest crystal glass, in an exceptionally swell shape, each piece bearing your own initial, surrounded by a wreath, the initial and wreath engraved on the glass by hand? Wouldn't you like to own a set of this kind?

FINEST CRYSTAL GLASS. Refined, elegant shape. When we determined to offer to our customers an initial glassware set, we went to the glass manufacturer who in our opinion made the finest and most perfect clear, bright glass, and explained to him what we wanted, and told him that we must have an absolutely new, elegant shape; something different from what has ever been offered before, and a shape that would be an ornament to any table. If you will refer to the illustration you will agree with us, that the manufacturer has done his part.

EVERY INITIAL ENGRAVED BY HAND. Please bear in mind that the initial on every piece, and the beautiful wreath surrounding the initial, are engraved into the glass itself. That is, it is cut right into the glass, so that it can never wear off or grow faint. The initial will outlast the glass itself. By reference to the illustration, you will see that the initial is exceptionally swell and elegant, viz., in old English lettering, and that the wreath surrounding it is particularly dainty and ornate.

A SET WITH INDIVIDUALITY. Do you want a glassware set that has a striking personality? A set that gives to the table particular individuality? Why do people have their knives and forks, their silverware, their dinnerware, etc., marked with their initials, unless it is that it gives an appearance of elegance and a distinct personality to the ware not obtainable in any other manner? If this is the case, why should not glassware be so marked? Why should not your butter dish, your spoon holder, your water pitcher, your glasses, salad bowl, etc., bear your initial? This set contains the following 32 pieces of the finest quality of glassware, each piece having your own initial engraved on by hand.

1 Water Pitcher	1 Salad or Berry Bowl	1 Butter Dish (2 pieces)	1 Sugar Bowl (2 pieces)
12 Tumblers	12 Saucers	1 Spoon Holder	1 Cream Pitcher

No. 3K510 Our Initial Glass Assortment. Shipping wt., 35 lbs. Price....$3.25

OUR SUPERB PRESSED CUT GLASS ASSORTMENT $3³⁹

STYLISH   **ELEGANT**

THIS GREAT BIG ASSORTMENT of pressed cut glassware is considered more nearly like genuine cut glass than any other set of glassware. No one will be able to say positively when they see it or handle it, whether it is genuine cut glass, or not, for a closer likeness has never been produced.

IT IS SO PERFECT IN DESIGN AND FINISH, so clear and brilliant that even those who are best posted readily believe this ware to be genuine cut glass. It cannot be surpassed in beauty, finish, style and workmanship. This superb assortment is made from the best quality of crystal and is pressed in steel moulds which are made from the finest cut glass models. It is made extra thick and rich, which makes it exceedingly brilliant and also strong and durable. It has all the richness, all the luster, all the depth of cut, all the brilliancy, all the accuracy of design, of shape, of style, and beautiful effect of genuine cut glass.

A GENUINE CUT GLASS SET similar to the one we offer, containing all the pieces that this one does, 48 in number, would cost you not less than $150.00. Why should you pay $150.00 for a set when you can obtain one for $3.48 that nine-tenths of the people will think is genuine cut glass, that it is just as pretty, just as attractive and just as elegant as cut glass?

48 MASSIVE, BRILLIANT, STYLISH, DEEPLY CUT PIECES are contained in this assortment. Never before have as many or as beautiful or as useful pieces been put up in one assortment. The same care, the same workmanship has been devoted to making this set as in making the very finest cut glass outfits. The salt and pepper shakers have heavy genuine silver plated tops.

No. 3K515 Our Superb Pressed Cut Glass Assortment (48 pieces), consisting of:

1 Sugar Bowl	1 Oil Cruet	1 8-Inch Salad Bowl	1 Salt Shaker
1 Creamer	1 Celery Tray	1 ½-Gallon Pitcher	1 Pepper Shaker
1 Butter Dish	1 Spoon Holder	12 Tumblers	1 8-Inch Footed Fruit Bowl
12 4-Inch Nappies		1 Footed Jelly Stand	12 Individual Salts

Shipping weight, 40 pounds. Price, complete.............$3.39

$3⁶⁸ OUR GENUINE COLONIAL PRESSED CUT ASSORTMENT

REFINED, ARTISTIC, BEAUTIFUL GLASSWARE

THIS IS JUST THE ASSORTMENT YOU ARE LOOKING FOR. Heretofore the Colonial cut has been used only on the very finest grades of genuine cut glass. There is a richness and elegance about this style that is hard to describe. The set must be seen to be appreciated. The design is the new convexed panel or Colonial design which brings out all the fire and brilliancy so characteristic of high grade crystal glass. The set is made from the very finest quality pure crystal glass. It is exceedingly heavy, and all the edges have been finely finished and burnished by hand.

GENUINE CUT GLASS IN COLONIAL PATTERN is an article that has heretofore only been found in the homes of the rich. It is a luxury that only the finest home could afford. In making genuine cut glass in Colonial pattern a finer and more select grade of glass must be used than in any other style of cutting, for the reason that the plain surface of the Colonial cut would show up any defect that might be covered in more elaborate cutting.

EACH PIECE IS HEAVILY ORNAMENTED at the bottom in embossed design. This embossing around the bottom of each piece adds a wonderful richness to the effect and sets off the Colonial cutting to great advantage.

THIS MAMMOTH ASSORTMENT CONSISTS OF 37 SEPARATE PIECES, including a syrup jug with genuine silver plated hinge top, and salt and pepper shakers, each with genuine silver plated perforated tops.

No. 3K520 Genuine Colonial Pressed Cut Glass Assortment. The assortment consists of 37 pieces, as follows: Shipping weight, 62 pounds.

1 Water Pitcher (½ gallon)	1 Celery Tray	12 Tumblers	1 Sugar Bowl
1 Spoon Holder	1 Berry Dish	12 Nappies	1 Fruit Stand
1 Salt Shaker	1 Cream Pitcher	1 Jelly Jug	1 Vinegar Cruet
1 Syrup Jug	1 Pepper Shaker	1 Butter Dish	

Packed complete in box.   Price........$3.68

Water Set. Made of hand finished nile green glass, hand decorated in three delicate tints, 12½-inch tankard pitcher, which has a fancy fluted top and is decorated with a white amethyst band, covered with white enamel scroll pattern and six hand finished tumblers decorated to match.

No. 3K573 Green Glass Decorated Water Set. Price, per set.....97c. Shipping weight, 15 pounds.

GENUINE RUBY GLASS HAND PAINTED WATER SET

RICHEST OF ALL THE RICH.   WILD ROSE AND GOLD DECORATED.

THIS BEAUTIFUL HAND PAINTED WATER SET is made of the finest quality ruby glass of beautiful shade and quality. It consists of one ½-gallon water pitcher and six ½-pint tumblers. It is made in the new French shape.

THE ELEGANT DECORATION consists of wild roses with their stems and leaves in their natural colors. These flowers are painted on by hand in a great variety of colors. In addition, each piece is hand traced with bright coin gold. The water pitcher is blown in a new French bell shape, with graceful handle and spout, the neck of the pitcher being fluted. The tumblers are decorated to match the pitcher.

REMEMBER, THIS IS A $5.00 SET, and we are offering it to our customers for $1.89. Can be used on the table for water or lemonade, and in the china closet or on the parlor table it will add a richness to the room not otherwise obtainable.

No. 3K575 Genuine Ruby Glass Hand Decorated Water Set, consisting of one pitcher and six tumblers. Shipping weight, 15 pounds. Price, per set.....$1.89

$5.00 Water Set for $1.89

GENUINE CUT GLASS

SALAD, BERRY AND SAUCE DISH.

Cut in the delicate and beautiful chrysanthemum pattern. The cutting is exceedingly rich, heavy and elaborate, consisting of 6 hob stars of 20 points each, 6 sections of silver basket cutting, and other beautiful and effective decorations. Scalloped edge. Weight, packed, 4 to 7 pounds, according to size.

No. 3K2000	5-inch Dish.	Price	$1.35
No. 3K2002	6-inch Dish.	Price	1.65
No. 3K2001	7-inch Dish.	Price	2.39
No. 3K2011	8-inch Dish.	Price	3.18
No. 3K2021	9-inch Dish.	Price	4.25

HANDLED NAPPY.

Cut in the chrysanthemum pattern to match dish described above. This nappy has the same brilliant and beautiful cutting. For olives, jelly, pickles, nuts, etc. Weight, packed, 4 to 5 pounds

| No. 3K2032 | 5-inch Handled Nappy. | Price | $1.39 |
| No. 3K2034 | 6-inch Handled Nappy. | Price | 1.68 |

VENUS SALAD OR BERRY BOWL.

8 inches in diameter, extra heavy weight, in the Sunburst pattern with scalloped edge. The cutting is extremely deep and the design is very popular. This bowl is on a 10-inch beaded plateau. Shipping weight, 9 pounds.

| No. 3K2044 | Bowl, with plateau. | Price | $5.48 |
| No. 3K2046 | Bowl, without plateau. | Price | 4.35 |

FRUIT, SALAD OR BERRY BOWL.
Unexcelled in Brilliancy of Design and Elaborateness of Ornamentation.

This bowl is conspicuous because of its remarkable brilliancy and elaborateness of the cutting. The design consists of four hearts with 33 six-sided raised points, each point projecting ¼ of an inch, set within a conventional design of heavily mitered lines with a star on the bottom. Diameter is 8 inches. French mirror plate glass, 10-inch plateau with jewel notched edges and metal back. Weight, carefully packed for shipment, 8 pounds.

| No. 3K2055 | Bowl, with plateau. | Price | $5.98 |
| No. 3K2056 | Bowl, without plateau. | Price | 4.85 |

SALT AND PEPPER SHAKERS.

In beautiful sunburst pattern. Genuine solid sterling silver embossed screw tops. Richly and deeply cut with two sunbursts and four notched prisms on each one. Weight, packed, 1¼ pounds.

No. 3K2070 Consisting of one salt and one pepper shaker. Price, per set... **$1.25**
If by mail, postage extra, 16 cents.

SPOON TRAY.

One of the handsomest small pieces made. Can also be used for olives, pickles, bon bons, etc. The design consists of 4 hob stars, fan and silver cutting. 8 inches long by 4 inches wide. Weight, packed, 2½ pounds.
No. 3K2031 Genuine Hand Cut Tray. Price.. **$1.85**

WATER SET.
Exquisite Design and Purity of Color.

The most beautiful Water Set ever offered for less than $30.00. Finest quality pure white crystal glass, guaranteed to be without flaw or defect. The elaborate and intricate cuttings on the bottle consists of five sunburst stars of 15 deep cut points on a stem, with heavily mitered lines, smaller hob stars, fan ornamentation and silver cutting forming the balance of the design. On the bottom is a large, deeply cut diamond star, 4¼ inches in diameter, with 32 points. The neck of the bottle is octagonal shape, with jewel notched cuttings. The bottle stands 8½ inches high. Holds nearly 3 pints. The TUMBLERS are 4 inches high, holding ½ pint, are an exact duplicate of the bottle in design, only smaller. French bevel plate glass, 14-inch plateau with jewel notched edges, and metal back. Weight, packed for shipment, 29 pounds.

No. 3K2082	Imperial Water Set, complete, including water bottle, 6 tumblers and plateau. Price	$13.75
No. 3K2083	Water Bottle only. Price	5.48
No. 3K2086	Tumblers only. Price, per ½ doz.	7.69

TOILET SETS

All toilet sets shown on this page are made up in assortments of TWELVE useful and necessary pieces as follows:
Large Covered Slop Jar (2 pieces).   Large Covered Chamber (2 pieces).   Large Roll Edge Wash Bowl (1 piece).
Tooth Brush Holder (1 piece).   Large Water Pitcher (1 piece).   Fancy Shaped Mug (1 piece).
Medium Hot Water Pitcher (1 piece).   Soap Dish with cover and strainer (3 pieces).

We have discontinued the sale of Six and Ten-Piece Toilet Sets. This action is taken entirely in our customers' interests, as most people ordering the smaller assortment, usually request at some later date a large slop jar, which is one of the most necessary pieces in a toilet set. Sets containing less than 12 pieces are invariably furnished without a slop jar.

OUR 12-PIECE WHITE AND GOLD TOILET SET, $5.98
ELABORATELY DECORATED WITH COIN GOLD.

NEW SWELL SHAPE. Our new Edgemont shape toilet set is the acme of style and elegance. The shape is absolutely new and particularly attractive. It is made of the very finest quality of semi-porcelain with a deep, rich glaze. The ware is exceptionally tough and strong and is the equal of the very best English toilet ware. No home is too rich for this set.

RICHLY DECORATED WITH GOLD. This set is particularly rich in gold treatment. Each piece is surrounded by a border of burnished coin gold in floral design, and inside of this border are sprays outlined and hand traced in gold. The quality of gold used is the best quality of burnished coin gold.

YOU CANNOT BUY A BETTER TOILET SET than our White and Gold. You cannot buy one that will wear better or look handsomer. The decoration is one that will match any furniture or wall paper, no matter what the style or color.

No. 3K463 Our 12-Piece White and Gold Toilet Set. Price...... (Shipping weight, 65 pounds.)...... **$5.98**

$6.69 OUR 12-PIECE AMERICAN BEAUTY ROSE TOILET SET
ELABORATELY TRIMMED WITH BURNISHED GOLD.

OUR 12-PIECE AMERICAN BEAUTY ROSE TOILET SET is made of the finest quality American white semi-porcelain, heavily embossed, with a high lustrous glaze, in the new swell shape and will be found to be an ornament to any room.

SUPERB DECORATIONS. The decoration very closely resembles genuine hand painted china. It consists of large clusters of red American beauty rose buds and green foliage and stems in colors.

BURNISHED GOLD TRIMMING. This is the most elaborately gold decorated set sold. All the edges, handles and bottoms are solidly covered with bright burnished gold. The dark part of the illustration indicates the gold. In addition each piece is handsomely embossed in scroll design.

IF YOU WANT A VERY ELEGANT TOILET SET, something rich and massive, elaborately decorated, let us send you this toilet set. Shipped from our pottery in Ohio. Weight, packed for shipment, 65 pounds.
No. 3K477 Our 12-Piece American Beauty Rose Toilet Set. Price...... **$6.69**

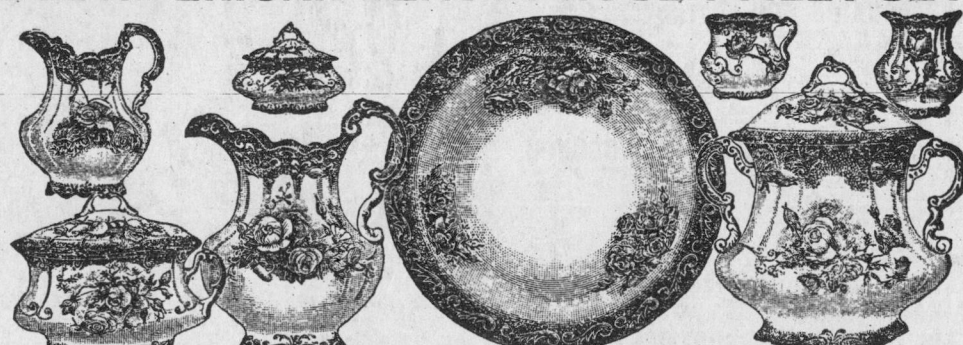

OUR HARVARD 12-PIECE TOILET SET, $4.95

Handsomely tinted in light blue, light green or pink, at both upper and lower extremities of each piece, indicated by the dark shading in the illustration, and decorated with gold medallions, between the tinted edges. Be sure to state color wanted. Made of American semi-porcelain, in one of the newest shapes. These sets are shipped from our pottery in Ohio.
No. 3K439 12-Piece Toilet Set, as illustrated, with jar. Price...... **$4.95**
Shipping weight, 60 pounds.

OUR YALE 12-PIECE TOILET SET, $3.89

Our Yale Toilet Set is made of American semi-porcelain ware. The decoration is in one color and is printed on. It consists of very large and beautiful jack roses, prettily entwined with foliage. We can furnish the decoration in green, blue or pink. Be sure to specify color of decoration desired. Shipped from our pottery in Ohio. Shipping weight, 60 lbs.
No. 3K411 12-Piece Toilet Set, as illustrated, with jar. Price...... **$3.89**

$4.45 OUR BORDEAU PARLOR LAMP

EXCEPTIONALLY ATTRACTIVE. HIGHEST GRADE OF WORKMANSHIP. BEAUTIFUL DESIGN IN NATURAL COLORS.

OUR BINDING GUARANTEE

WE GUARANTEE that our lamp will outwear, will give a better light and is handsomer in appearance than any other lamp of similar design.

DO NOT CONFUSE this lamp with imitations made in the same style and which look the same in an illustration. Our lamp represents the highest grade of workmanship and the very finest materials, while the cheap lamps of the same pattern are most inferior, both as regards workmanship and quality.

ELEGANTLY EMBOSSED, decorated in natural colors. This beautiful lamp is made of the very finest quality of translucent porcelain. The body of the globe and base are richly tinted in brown, which shades into dark orange. The embossing is in the form of large clusters of grapes and leaves with panel scrolls in bold relief. The grapes and leaves are colored true to life, giving an exceedingly rich and elegant appearance to the lamp. The bottom of the base and the crown on the base are made of heavy gold plated solid brass in open work filigree design. No other lamp made with so rich and elaborate trimmings.

100-CANDLE POWER Success central draft burner, No. 1 Belgian chimney. We have equipped this lamp with an extra heavy candle power burner, so as to insure it giving a brilliant and livable light. Many of the parlor lamps have small burners and many statements are made regarding the candle power, which are not borne out by using. It has a solid brass oil pot which fits in the china base, and solid brass burner. Most of the cheap parlor lamps have no oil pot. The oil is poured into the base, which sooner or later gives the base a greasy and ugly appearance.

EXTRAORDINARY VALUE. We say, without fear of contradiction, that this lamp is extraordinary value, and not only is it perfect in workmanship and design, but it is made of only the very finest and richest materials. It stands 26 inches high and is equipped with a full 10-inch globe, which insures its safe delivery. Shipping weight, 32 pounds.

No. 3K1009 Our Bordeau Parlor Lamp.
Price........................$4.45

Beauty Special, $3.59.

This is the handsomest Rose Design Parlor Lamp made. This decoration consists of beautiful, dark, American Beauty roses, with their buds, leaves and stems in their natural colors in large clusters on both sides of the lamp and globe on a tinted green background. The large American Beauty roses are put on by hand in the deep red color, making the flowers stand out distinct from the lamp. The crown and base are of solid cast brass in open work design and the fount holder has a solid brass drawn ring. The removable oil fount is of brass and has the No. 2 100-candle power center draft burner, taking No. 2 Rochester chimney and round wick. Shipping weight, 30 pounds.

No. 3K980 Beauty Special Parlor Lamp. Price........................$3.59

New Style Lilac, $3.89.

Our New Style Lilac in the Romeo shape, decorated with hand painted lilacs, is the newest and most fashionable thing in parlor lamps. It is extra large and shapely throughout. The decoration consists of large hand painted lilacs, highly enameled, with light green leaves. Richly tinted in a dark green and when lighted the beautiful lilacs appear true to life. The burner is the highest grade central draft type, produces a 100-candle power, complete with No. 2 Rochester chimney and wick. 27½ inches high and has a large 10-inch globe and is adorned with heavy brass crown and base finely gold lacquered. Securely packed in a box. Shipping weight, 30 pounds.

No. 3K988 New Style Lilac Parlor Lamp. Price........................$3.89

OUR LEADER SOLID BRASS STUDENT LAMP.

SATIN FINISH—DUPLEX BURNER—IMPORTED GREEN DOME SHADE.

$6.95 THIS IS THE FINEST STUDENT LAMP MADE.

It is in a new artistic design, very ornamental and strikingly handsome. Made of solid brass. Elegantly burnished in the rich French satin finish. This is the newest finish. The ornamented oil pot and the lamp proper are made in the new cone shape. The lamp is fitted with a stand made of French satin finished brass, which consists of a rod 21 inches long and an extra weighted base, so that the lamp will not upset. The lamp can be raised, lowered or turned on the rod, to any position to suit the user.

60-CANDLE POWER DUPLEX (DOUBLE WICK) BURNER.

This lamp is fitted with an extra powerful burner, with patent extinguisher. This burner will produce a 60-candle power light, which will give a light of great brilliancy, and is just the thing to save the eyes when reading. The oil pot holds 1¼ pints of oil, and will burn 10 hours with one filling. The lamp is complete with a large full 10-inch elaborate green dome shade with white lining, and the finest quality genuine lead glass Duplex chimney.

BEAR IN MIND that this lamp is made of genuine solid brass. No composition or bronze metal is to be found in it, as is the case with many students' lamps usually sold at $15.00. Do not confuse this lamp with cheap students' lamps although they may try to imitate our shape. Shipping weight, 30 lbs.

No. 3K764 Our Leader Solid Brass Student Lamp. Price........................$6.95

ELEGANT EMBOSSED AND DECORATED BANQUET OR PARLOR LAMPS

WE TAKE PLEASURE IN PRESENTING AN ENTIRELY NEW AND COMPLETE LINE OF PARLOR OR BANQUET LAMPS AND

——GLOBES——

which were selected with the greatest care after long and careful investigation. **We feel confident that we are offering the best line of lamps made.** Every lamp is made of the finest quality of china, heavily embossed with **solid brass trimmings,** and is carefully tinted and decorated by the most skilled artists. Every lamp is equipped with the best quality burner, wick and chimney. **Our prices** are from 33 to 50 per cent less than quoted by the regular crockery dealers. Each lamp is carefully packed in box or barrel to insure safe delivery.

American Beauty, $3.18.

This is one of the prettiest lamps shown this season. Do not confuse this lamp with the cheap parlor lamps in American Beauty design. This one is better, handsomer, more elaborately decorated and in every way superior. The globe measures 10½ inches in diameter; the vase or cylinder to match is of equal size. The lamp measures 26 inches high. The hand painted decorations consist of beautiful American Beauty roses and foliage on a blue tinted background. The crown and bottom of base are made of richly polished brass in open work design. It has the improved Success central draft burner and takes No. 1 Belgian chimney and round wick. It produces a strong and steady 80-candle power light. This lamp compares favorably with those sold by crockery dealers at $4.50 to $5.00. Shipping weight, 25 pounds.

No. 3K976 American Beauty Parlor Lamp Price........................$3.18

Royal Poppy, $1.95.

This beautiful Parlor or Banquet Lamp is exceptionally large and attractive for the price we ask. It is complete with 9-inch globe and vase, and measures 21 inches high. The decoration consists of large hand painted poppies in pink, purple and white. The globe and also the vase are delicately tinted at the top in light green and the bottom in pink. It has a heavy brass plated metal foot of scroll design. It is equipped with No. 3 Climax burner, No. 3 wick and No. 2 Electric chimney, and produces 60-candle power light. Shipping weight, 20 pounds.

No. 3K967 Royal Poppy Parlor Lamp. Price........................$1.95

Imperial Cardinal, $3.45.

This Banquet Lamp is made of ruby glass and when lighted produces a rich ruby glow. It is handsomely embossed in large scrolls of floral design, the embossing being of satin finish cardinal glass. The combination of highly polished ruby glass for the body of the lamp and satin finish cardinal glass embossing makes an exceedingly rich, attractive and handsome lamp. It is furnished with improved Success central draft burner, 80-candle power, and wick and No. 1 Belgian chimney. It has a solid brass removable fount and brass plated crown. Height, 26 inches, and has a 10-inch globe. Shipping weight, 28 pounds.

No. 3K978 Imperial Cardinal Parlor Lamp. Price........................$3.45

OUR IMPERIAL PARLOR LAMP $6.39

ROSE PINK COLOR. WILD GEESE DECORATION.
GENUINE GOLD PLATED SOLID BRASS TRIMMED

THE VERY NEWEST and smartest design in parlor lamps. We are exceedingly fortunate in being able to offer our customers the very latest design, the most fashionable coloring and shape. This lamp is made of the very finest quality of translucent porcelain, tinted a delicate rose pink. This color is sometimes called old rose. Bands of Japanese ebony black encircle the top and bottom of the shade and base, with horizontal lines running up and down the shade and base.

A FULL 5-INCH FRINGE of pink translucent beads hangs from the shade ring which is 12 inches in diameter and made of solid brass, with four heavy supports. The advantage of the fringe of beads is not only that it adds richness and elegance to the light but that it tones down and softens the light that comes from under the shade and it also covers up the more unattractive part of the burner. The base is heavy open cast, in filigree design, and is made of the finest quality of genuine gold plated solid brass.

100-CANDLE POWER Success central draft solid brass burner is used in this lamp, with a chimney of the very best quality of lead glass. The shade measures fully 15 inches and the lamp stands 26 inches high. It has a solid brass oil pot which fits into the china base.

SUPERB DECORATION. The decoration on this lamp consists of flying wild geese in ivory white, with feet, head and wings tinted in their natural colors. This decoration is hand painted by artists and is one of the richest and most effective decorations that we have ever seen. It cannot be adequately described or shown by the illustration. The lamp must be seen to be appreciated. Not only is this an exceptional value, but it is one of the most beautiful and graceful as well as newest designs on the market. A richer or more effective lamp when lighted, with the light streaming through the rose pink shade with ivory white decoration and through the deep fringe of opalescent pink beads, cannot be imagined. Rose color is the most becoming of any light. A regular $20.00 value.

No. 3K1025 Our Imperial Japanese Parlor Lamp. Price........................$6.39

GAS FIXTURES

LET US SAVE YOU MONEY WHEN YOU BUY YOUR GAS FIXTURES. All we ask is that you make a selection from this catalogue, and after you have received them, if you are not satisfied that you have saved 50 per cent on your purchase, return them to us at our expense and we will gladly refund your money together with all transportation charges both ways.

THE PROFESSIONAL GAS FITTER, PLUMBER OR MECHANIC will do well to buy his fixtures from us. We can save him money and at the same time furnish him with fixtures that will give satisfaction to his customers. Our exclusive designs

cannot fail to please even the most critical and the fixtures have a rich, expensive appearance.

OUR GUARANTEE. We guarantee that the fixtures are made of the best quality of highly polished brass. We guarantee that these fixtures are well made, strong and durable. Every fixture is tested before leaving our house to insure against leakage. We claim our fixtures are superior in quality, finish and durability and we guarantee them to give perfect satisfaction.

NATURAL GAS AND ACETYLENE GAS TIPS. The prices quoted here are for fixtures fitted complete with tips for artificial or manufactured gas. We can furnish gas fixtures for natural gas at an extra cost of 8 cents for each tip or with acetylene tips for 25 cents each tip.

Swing Gilt Brass Gas Bracket.

Made of excellent quality of brass in ribbed design. Furnished complete with wall plate, pillar, tip, and with one or two arms, either

No. 3K2211 with burner cup or with white crystal glass shade in richly cut design and brass shade holder.

No. 3K2202 Single Swing Gilt Brass Gas Bracket with burner cup.
Price, per ½ dozen, $2.18; each 37c

No. 3K2203 Single Swing Gilt Brass Gas Bracket with white crystal glass shade and brass shade holder.
Price, per ½ dozen, $3.08; each 53c

No. 3K2210 Double Swing Gilt Brass Gas Bracket with burner cup.
Price, per ½ dozen, $3.48; each 61c

No. 3K2211 Double Swing Gilt Brass Gas Bracket with white crystal glass shade and brass shade holder.
Price, per ½ dozen, $4.45; each 78c

One and Two Light Polished Brass Pendant.

Suitable for kitchen, cellar, back hall and other places where a fancy gas fixture is not necessary. All brass tubing nicely polished, neat and well constructed. Furnished complete with burner cup, pillar and gas tip. No globe or globe holders furnished at prices quoted below.

No. 3K2225

No. 3K2235 One-Light Pendant, 30 ins. long. Price 49c

No. 3K2236 One-Light Pendant. Price........54c

No. 3K2225 Two-Light Pendant, 36 inches long. Price....$1.15

One-Light Fancy Gas Pendant Polished Brass.

One of the neatest and most artistic pendants on the market. It is made of polished brass with fluted cup and fancy carved leaf ornaments and fancy gas stop cock. The pendant is very well constructed, and is an ornament to any room. Furnished complete with brass ceiling plate, pillar and gas tip and in one length only, 36 inches. We can furnish this pendant either with or without a globe and holder.

No. 3K2234 Fancy Gas Pendant, with burner cup. Price..$1.12
No. 3K2238 Fancy Gas Pendant, fitted with white crystal shade in very rich looking design, and brass burner plate. Price........$1.23

Hall Gas Fixture.

A very neat and effective fixture for little money. Made of highly polished brass tubing, in graceful design. Comes complete as shown in illustration with ceiling plate, pillar, gas tip, globe, globe holder and fluted ceiling protector hanging over the light. Length of fixture, 30 inches. We can furnish this light with either opalescent or red globe.

No. 3K2245 Price, with opalescent globe....$1.49
No. 3K2246 Price, with red globe........$2.08

$2.39 OUR LEADER HALL LIGHT

NEW DESIGN. VERY ARTISTIC. A GREAT BARGAIN.

THIS BEAUTIFUL FIXTURE is made of solid brass tubing, very highly polished with heavy weight brass ornamentation. We consider this fixture the greatest value in hall lights ever offered for the money.

A HANDSOMELY EMBOSSED CROWN is fitted around the top of the globe. On either side of the frame, just above the light, a wrought brass spray projects, adding greatly to the graceful design. A fluted ceiling protector hangs over the light, while above it is a center ornament in the form of a brass cup, and above that the brass ceiling plate. The globe is of opalescent glass, fluted in a graceful design cylinder shape. An openwork key to turn on and off gas completes the light.

THIS HALL FIXTURE IS FURNISHED COMPLETE with globe, brass globe holder, pillar, lava gas tip and ceiling plate, just as shown in the illustration. The fixture, when you receive it, is all complete and ready to screw into ceiling. Bear this in mind. Our price is for the fixtures complete. It includes all the parts.

No. 3K2255 Our Leader Hall Gas Fixture, just as described above. Price............$2.39
No. 3K2256 Our Leader Hall Gas Fixture, just as described above, but with transparent red globe. Price..................$3.18

"The Star" Gas Chandelier.

$2.89

Made of highly polished brass with exceedingly attractive ornamentation. Consisting of fancy fluted ball ornament and pear shaped pendant. The curved arms project from this ring and have cast brass ornaments in dull finish. Fitted complete, as shown in the illustration, with beautiful pebbled crystal glass shades, ornamented with cut stars. It is also fitted with brass shade holders, pillar, lava gas tips and brass ceiling plate. We can furnish with two or three lights. Length of fixtures, 36 inches. Spread of arms, 19 inches.

No. 3K2275 Two-light fixture. Price........$2.89
No. 3K2276 Three-light fixture. Price..$3.88

Imperial Gas Chandelier.

A well made finely finished chandelier and exceedingly attractive to look at. It has a graceful design, being made of extra fine brass tubing, highly polished, with fluted cup, pear shape ornament. Around the center of the pear shape ornament runs a beaded band, from which project the arms. The arms are in graceful descending curves with solid cast brass ornaments in fern design. The delicately etched shades add greatly to the beauty of the chandelier. This fixture can be furnished with two or three lights and comes complete with etched shades, brass shade holders, pillar, lava gas tips and ceiling plate.

$3.35

No. 3K2280 Two-light fixture. Price....$3.35
No. 3K2281 Three-light fixture. Price..$4.50

$3.48 PEERLESS GAS PORTABLE LAMP.

A high grade reading lamp for parlor and library, furnished complete, green shade and tubing. The lamp is all ready to use when you receive it. All that is necessary to do is to remove the gas tip from the fixture and slip in the gooseneck. Then turn on the gas and light it. The price we ask includes all the parts, including burner, which is of best quality, being made of polished brass; high grade cap mantle, opaque chimney globe with air holes, green shade (green outside, white inside) fitted with a heavy green bead fringe to match, and six feet of the best quality of mohair tubing fitted with brass gooseneck. A high grade lamp. We are able to offer our customers a high grade reading lamp, and for those desiring a high grade lamp we believe this outfit will give perfect satisfaction. The stand is made of metal, finished in a rich black color. The metal is highly ornamented and trimmed in polished brass. A lamp of this quality and finish together with all the fittings we give has never been sold before for less than $5.00 and more often at $7.50.

No. 3K2191 Peerless Lamp, complete and ready to light. Price............$3.48

Gilt Gas Chandelier.

For people desiring a low price fixture this is just what they want. Made of polished brass, corrugated design with brass ball ornament in satin finish and artistic loop design. Furnished with two or three lights. Length of fixture, 36 inches. Spread of arms, 36 inches. Remember the prices quoted below are for the fixture complete with crystal glass globes in rich design, brass globe holders, pillar, gas tips and ceiling plate, all complete and ready to put up.

$1.78

No. 3K2265 Two-light fixture. Price....$1.78
No. 3K2266 Three-light fixture. Price..$2.38

"Au Fait" Polished Brass Gas Chandelier.

$1.89

The very best low price chandelier made. It is made of polished brass in a simple and classical design, yet at the same time most artistic. It is ornamented with two octagonal shaped balls with beaded centers, just above where the arms connect. The lower ball has a flattened octagonal top with a rounded embossed lower part; and the arm connection and keys are of dull finished brass. Furnished with either two or three lights and is complete with white crystal shades in richly cut design, brass shade holders, pillar, lava gas tips and brass ceiling plate. Length of fixture, 36 inches. Spread of arms, 19 inches.

No. 3K2270 Two-light fixture. Price, $1.89
No. 3K2271 Three-light fixture. Price, $2.49

OUR SPECIAL EXTRA VALUE LEADER CHANDELIERS

Solid Heavy Brass Tubing, Highly Polished, Elaborately Ornamented, Satin Finish Trimmings.

EXQUISITE IN DESIGN AND DETAIL.

Do not be deceived by the price we ask for this chandelier. The only thing cheap about it is the price.

WE GUARANTEE THIS FIXTURE to be of the best materials. It is made of heavy brass tubing, very highly polished. Part of the tubing is corrugated, giving the fixture a very rich appearance. The fixture has a fluted ceiling plate and is ornamented with a fluted cup in satin finish surmounting a ball with beaded band and large pineapple shaped pendant. This pendant is extra large and elegant, and has attached to it at the bottom a fluted ball in satin finish brass. From this ball five heavy cast brass leaves reach up and are appliqued on the pendant. A ribbed band of satin finish brass surrounds the pendant, from which band project the arms, which have a graceful downward curve and are ornamented with heavy solid cast brass ornaments in dull finish. The keys are fancy openwork in the same finish.

$4.18

THE CHANDELIER IS FITTED complete with fluted brass ceiling plate, pillars, best quality of lava gas tips, brass shade holders and beautiful new swell shape silver frosted shades, with embossed edges and angel design, having delicate tracery work etched around the figures. Elegant parlor, library or dining room chandelier.

No. 3K2295 Our Leader Chandelier, with TWO lights. Price................$4.18
No. 3K2297 Our Leader Chandelier, with THREE lights. Price..................$5.19
No. 3K2298 Our Leader Chandelier, with FOUR lights. Price......................$6.15

FURNITURE

THERE ARE CHEAPER CHAIRS MADE AND SOLD THAN WE OFFER—BUT THE QUALITY OF SUCH CHAIRS IS CHEAPER ALSO.

We offer our customers only chairs of standard size. When you buy from us you get the best chair in the market. We do not cut the quality in order to reduce our price. If you are led to believe from a picture that another chair is cheaper than ours, we invite comparison of the goods, and you will readily see that our chairs are far superior in every way. We guarantee our prices on chairs and other furniture, QUALITY CONSIDERED, are lower than you can get from any dealer or other catalogue house.

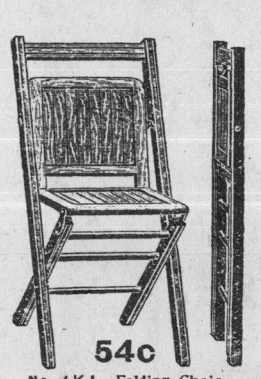

54c

No. 1K1 Folding Chair, made of hardwood, has slat seat and back. Folds absolutely flat, 1½x16x40 inches. Cannot fold accidentally when in use. Illustration shows chair open and closed. A strictly high grade chair. Just the thing for entertainment halls—easy to stack up when not in use. Weight, 10 pounds.

Price, each........$0.54
Per dozen 6.45
Per hundred, shipped direct from factory ..$50.00

38c 64c

This is a high grade chair, bow back, made of Wisconsin hickory rock elm, finished in rich golden color. Bow back is steam bent, and has four spindles. Seat, back, spindles and posts are neatly striped, making a handsome appearance. Chair is suitable for either dining room or kitchen. Shipping weight, each, 10 pounds.

No. 1K5 As illustrated.
Each......Per doz.......Per 100
64c......$7.50......$61.50

No. 1K3 Similar to No. 1K5, but with veneer seat and not striped.
Price, each..................38c

78c

No. 1K7 Our special kitchen chair. Made of Wisconsin hickory rock elm, finished in golden oak, with seat, posts and spindles fancy striped. Chair is extra strong, with steam bent bow back. Posts and spindles ornamented by fancy turnings. As a substantial and cheap chair for all around use it cannot be equaled. Shipping weight, 12 pounds.

Price, each......$ 0.78
Per dozen 9.20
Per hundred 75.00

64c

No. 1K11 A durable dining chair at a very low price. Carved top with heavy turned back posts and turned spindles. Made of well seasoned elm, finished a handsome golden oak color. Substantial veneered wood seat with a strong base and turned front stretchers. Shipping weight, 8 pounds.
Price.........64c

73c

No. 1K15 A new design of exceptional value. Made specially attractive with five fancy turned spindles in the back. Broad carved top. Heavy back posts. Built up veneered seat. Strong stretcher base. Constructed of elm, thoroughly well seasoned, and has a rich golden finish. Shipping weight, 9 pounds.
Price.........73c

84c

No. 1K17 A very substantial dining chair, made of elm, in rich golden oak finish. Has a broad carved top and heavy back posts, with strong, curved brace arms. The handsomely turned spindles in the back are securely fitted into the seat frame. The seat is made of heavy built up veneered stock, and has a strong stretcher base with turned front. This is a far better chair of its kind than usually sold by others at $1.25. Shipping weight, 10 pounds.
Price.........84c

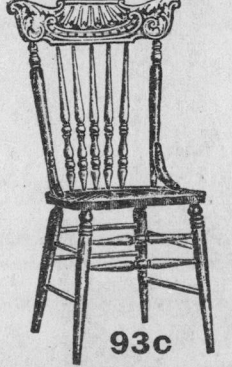

93c

No. 1K19 We call particular attention to the heavy, carved top of this chair which adds greatly to its appearance and comfort. The heavy, turned posts and spindles are strengthened by curved brace arms. Made of selected elm, with built up veneered seat. Heavy base with turned front. Well finished to match golden oak. Shipping weight, 10 lbs. Price. 93c

98c

No. 1K21 This dining chair is made of thoroughly air seasoned and kiln dried elm, high gloss golden finish. Note the roomy seat and deep, smooth cut handsome carved panels in back. Spindles, legs and posts smooth turned and finished. Exceptional value. Weight, 12 pounds. Price.......98c

$1.05

No. 1K27 A very massive, handsomely carved dining chair. The broad back with wide carved top is filled with nine fancy turned spindles. Made of kiln dried Northern elm, high gloss golden oak finish. Built up veneered seat with strong stretcher base. Shipping weight, 12 pounds. Price..........$1.05

$1.12

No. 1K25 Extra heavy, bolted post dining chair. Very wide carved top. Flat shaped spindles in the back. Bent posts securely bolted to the seat. Golden oak finish. Substantial turned base, with built up veneered seat. Very strong construction. Shipping weight, 11 lbs. Price...........$1.12

$1.25

No. 1K23 This attractive dining room chair, made of selected thoroughly seasoned elm, finished golden, has a broad, roomy shaped seat, full braced arms and legs, making it as strong and durable as a chair can be made. Panels and spindles artistically ornamented, as shown in illustration. Weight, 12 pounds. Price.....$1.25

$1.34

No. 1K29 This is the latest thing out in a medium price veneered saddle seat diner, made of selected, thoroughly seasoned elm, golden finish. Back is neatly carved, as shown in the illustration, and firmly braced to seat, making entire chair strong and substantial. Weight, 12 pounds. Price...........$1.34

$1.42

No. 1K33 This extra large diner is made of selected elm finished in golden color. Wide embossed top and lower panel, back strengthened by one slat and four spindles. Seat made of veneered elm and securely braced to the long back posts. This is an exceptionally heavy and well constructed chair, handsome in design and will give good service. Wt., 12 lbs. Price.. $1.42

$1.53

No. 1K35 The very latest design for a veneered seat dining room chair, made of quarter sawed oak, golden finish. High back with three broad flat spindles and top panel deeply carved. Extra wide saddle seat with back posts securely braced to seat. A very strong and durable chair. Weight, 14 pounds. Price.....$1.53

$1.72

No. 1K38 This veneered saddle seat dining room chair has handsomely carved panels connected by flat spindles, giving it a handsome and attractive appearance. The best quality of veneering is used in the construction of the saddle seat. Has long back posts firmly braced to the seat, making a very strong and durable chair. Wt., 12 lbs. Price.....$1.72

$1.85

No. 1K45 This plain, richly designed saddle seat dining chair is made of quarter sawed golden oak. The large size and comfort giving back, combined with a handsome finish, make this a very desirable chair. Long back posts securely braced to seat make it very strong and durable. Exceptional value. Price..........$1.85

$1.95

No. 1K43 This handsome diner is made of quarter sawed oak, thoroughly seasoned, finished golden and highly polished. Wide back panel is quarter sawed with just enough carving to give it an artistic effect. Seat is saddle shaped and made of best quality of veneer. Legs and back are strongly braced, making it as durable as it is beautiful. Weight, 12 pounds. Price.........$1.95

$2.10

No. 1K48 Beautiful design, extra large and heavy. Broad shaped top. Wide, ornamental, sawed panel back. Heavy bent posts, braced with short curved arms. Made of finest quarter sawed golden oak, handsomely finished. Saddle shaped veneered seat. Strong stretcher base. Very comfortable. Price..$2.10

Solid Oak Box Seat Dining Chairs
GENUINE LEATHER SEATS

$1 95
PRICE EACH

FULL BOX SEAT
DINING ROOM CHAIR
No. 1K121
ORDER BY NUMBER

Made of selected oak, upholstered with genuine No. 1 leather with quarter sawed back, finished in a rich golden gloss finish for $1.95 each, a price never before attempted and only made possible by our having contracted with one of the largest box seat chair factories in the country for 10,000 chairs at the actual cost of material and labor, and we are giving you the benefit of this purchase, enabling you to buy a strictly up to date first class box seat diner at a lower price than it costs most factories to manufacture. Remember this is not a cheaply constructed chair, but honestly made of best selected oak and full sized.

THE WOOD used in the construction of this box seat diner is selected northern oak thoroughly air seasoned and kiln dried. The back panel and top slats are made of beautifully figured quarter sawed oak.

THE WORKMANSHIP is first class throughout; all joints are mortised, doweled and glued. The dowel pin holes are concealed by wood button heads rounded on the edges. The braces are square and perfectly fitted and the top and back panels are all neatly rounded.

THE FINISH is a rich golden color in a high gloss; each piece is thoroughly sandpapered to produce a perfectly smooth surface and coated with a high grade varnish. The result is that our high gloss finish is as good as most of the so called polished chairs.

THE SEATS are full size and upholstered with genuine leather fitted perfectly to the seat frame and trimmed with gimp and black enameled tacks. Most box seat diners sold by others at higher prices are under size and have very small leather seats.

THE LEGS. The handsome shaped legs are cut out of selected stock, mortised and doweled to seat frame and are firmly braced by the square stretchers.

THE ILLUSTRATION. While it will enable you to form some idea of the beauty and elegance of this chair it is possible to give you but a small idea of the great value in quality. We call your special attention to the heavy shaped legs, square stretchers and beautifully shaped quarter sawed back and top panels. Our designer has devoted a great deal of time to bringing out a design that would not only be pleasing to the eye but present a chair that would be well built, strong and comfortable.

OUR OFFER. We propose to make this chair a standing advertisement for our box seat dining room chair line and if you are considering the purchase of a set of dining room chairs you cannot afford to place your order elsewhere. Send us your order for as many of these chairs as you may require at $1.95 each. We will ship them promptly on receipt of your order, securely packed to insure safe delivery and when you get them compare them with other box seat diners sold by other dealers at double our price and if you are not satisfied that you have received a better chair, a chair worth double the price we ask you for it, or if you are not satisfied in every way, you can do us no greater favor than to return the chairs to us and we will cheerfully refund you your money together with all freight charges.

OUR LINE OF BOX SEAT DINERS. In addition to this No. 1K121 chair at $1.95 each, we show on page 369 a complete line of latest designs in box seat dining room chairs at prices ranging from $1.75 to $5.95 each, every one of which represents as great a bargain as the set illustrated on this page—space alone preventing our showing them all in large illustrations.

CANE SEAT DINING ROOM CHAIRS.

AT 77 CENTS TO $1.78 we are offering a line of cane seat diners that for quality, style and finish cannot be duplicated by other dealers for almost double our price. There may be other chairs sold at cheaper prices but the quality is also cheaper. Our cane seat chairs are made of thoroughly seasoned stock; the seats are full sized, the turnings are smooth and the carvings are all deep cut. **The seats** are caned by hand and are far superior to the machine caned seats used by other manufacturers. **The finish.** Every piece is thoroughly sanded before finishing, and as we use nothing but the best No. 1 varnish the result is a beautiful golden high gloss finish, as good a finish as most of the so called polished chairs have. **The construction** is first class in every detail, every joint and every spindle is examined and secured in place by glue reinforced by steel screws. Back posts braced to seats with little wood arms, making in all a solid substantial chair.

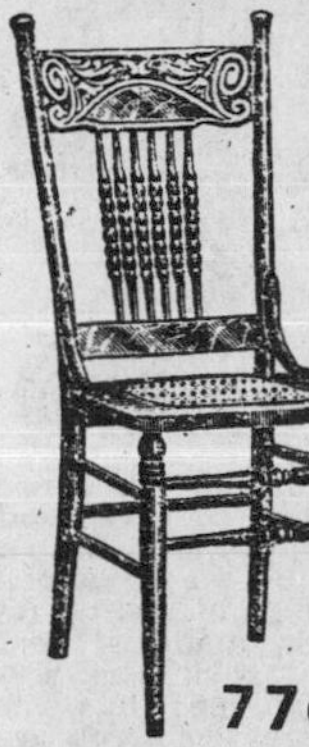

77c

No. 1K85 This cane seat dining room chair is made throughout of seasoned hardwood with golden finish. Has high back with ornamented top panel and fancy spindle. We do not guarantee this chair to be the equal of solid oak chairs, but offer it to show what can be done in the way of good values at a low price. Shipping weight, 10 lbs.

Price, each........$0.77
Set of 6 chairs..... 4.60

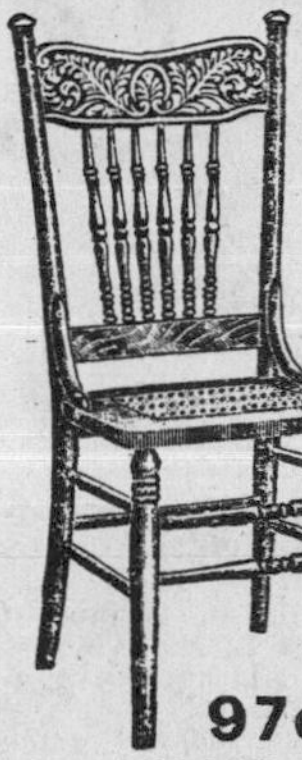

97c

No. 1K90 This large, handsome cane seat dining room chair has quartered oak panels, golden finish, high back, firmly braced to seat, ornamented with fancy carving and spindles, as shown in the illustration. Legs are solid and substantial. The equal of chairs sold by other dealers at double our price. Weight, 10 pounds.

Price, each........$0.97
Set of 6 chairs..... 5.75

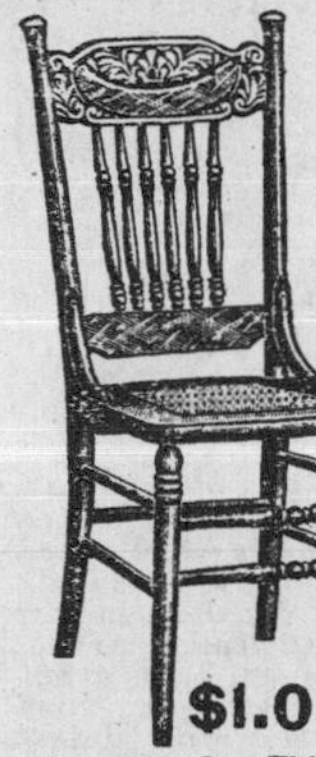

$1.07

No. 1K93 This large cane seat diner is made of selected material, quarter sawed oak panels and hand woven cane seat. Extended posts, spindles and legs all handsomely turned. Has deep carved top panel. Seat is firmly braced to back posts, making a very strong and substantial chair. Weight, 11 pounds.

Price, each........$1.07
Set of 6 chairs..... 6.25

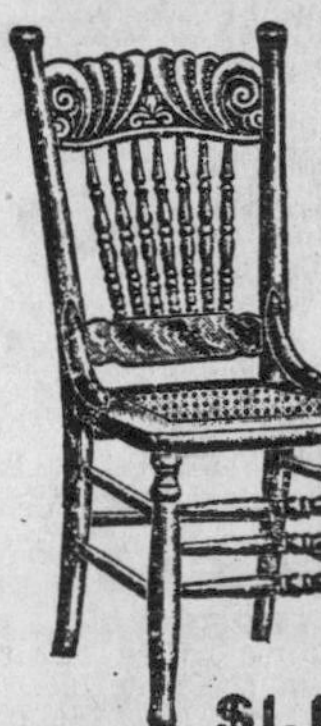

$1.17

No. 1K97 Large hand woven cane seat diner, has solid oak seat and back, with handsome deep embossed quarter sawed oak top panel. Back is firmly braced to seat; spindles, braces and legs are hand turned of neat design. Is a strictly high grade chair, not to be compared with the cheap chairs usually offered at this price. Weight, 11 pounds.

Price, each........$1.17
Set of 6 chairs..... 6.85

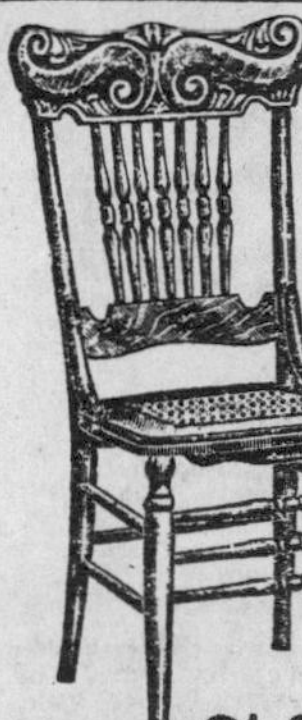

$1.37

No. 1K101 The best constructed and cheapest hand woven cane seat dining room chair on the market. Made of oak, golden finish. Back panels quarter sawed and beautifully carved legs and spindles all hand turned. Back posts securely braced, wide and comfortably shaped seats. Exceptional value at our very low price. Weight, 12 pounds.

Price, each........$1.37
Set of 6 chairs..... 8.10

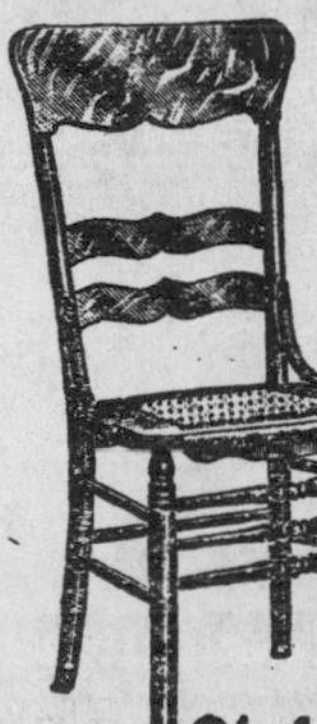

$1.47

No. 1K104 An unusually attractive dining room chair, made of solid oak, golden finish, with back panels quarter sawed. Has wide shaped seat, hand caned, thoroughly braced to back posts, as shown in the illustration. This is one of the most popular designs on the market. Weight, 12 pounds.

Price, each........$1.47
Set of 6 chairs..... 8.60

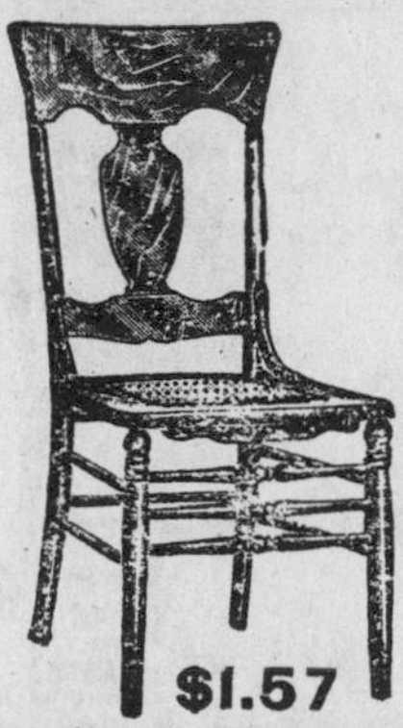

$1.57

No. 1K108 This chair is one of our most popular patterns. Made of oak, thoroughly seasoned, golden finish, panels quarter sawed. Wide shaped hand caned seat with apron front, well braced to back posts. Legs firmly joined to seat, making a very solid and substantial chair. Weight, 12 pounds.

Price, each........$1.57
Set of 6 chairs..... 9.20

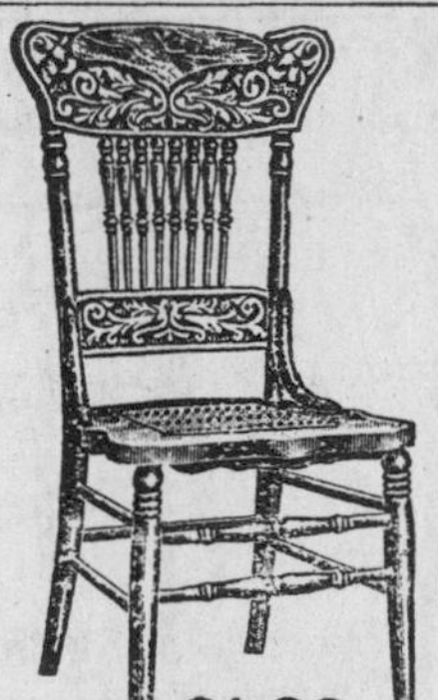

$1.63

No. 1K112 The best chair ever shown for the money, made of seasoned oak, rich golden finish. Has a high back, handsomely carved panels and spindles, wide shaped seat covered with best quality of hand woven cane. Legs and back are strong and well braced. Just the chair to stand constant use. Weight, 12 pounds.

Price, each........$1.63
Set of 6 chairs..... 9.50

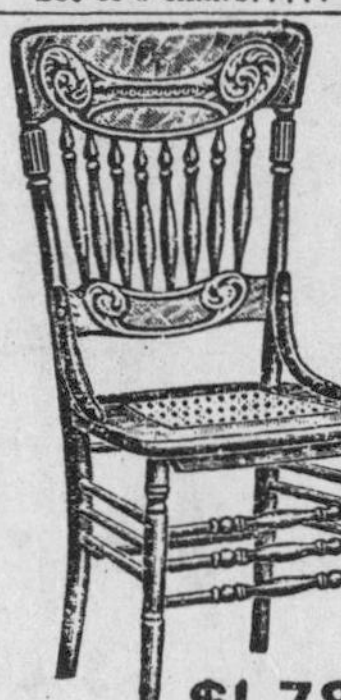

$1.78

No. 1K116 This dining room chair is a special design with extra large back and hand caned seat. It is made of selected oak, high gloss golden finish. Back panels are quarter sawed with deep carvings. Heavy turned spindles in back and legs. Thoroughly braced throughout. It makes a handsome serviceable chair. Weight, 14 pounds.

Price, each......$ 1.78
Set of 6 chairs... 10.50

HIGH GRADE BOX SEAT DINING CHAIRS.

IN OFFERING our line of high grade box seat diners we do so with the knowledge that we are the leaders in price, quality, style, and workmanship. **The quarter sawed oak** used in the construction of these high class diners is the best that can be procured (special attention is given to the flaky grain), and is thoroughly dried before being cut up into stock sizes. **The frames** are mortised and doweled, the dowel holes concealed by a wood button head countersunk in the frame. Joints are all trued with rounded edges, giving to the frame a handsome and finished appearance. **The seats** are upholstered by hand with best quality No. 1 leather over a tightly stretched heavy webbing (with the exception of No. 1K120), and this construction is acknowledged by all manufacturers to be better and stronger than leather over cane and is used in all high class chairs. **The finish** is the best that first class material and skilled workmen can produce, and as each chair is finished by hand the result is a higher polish than usually seen in the best quality of chairs.

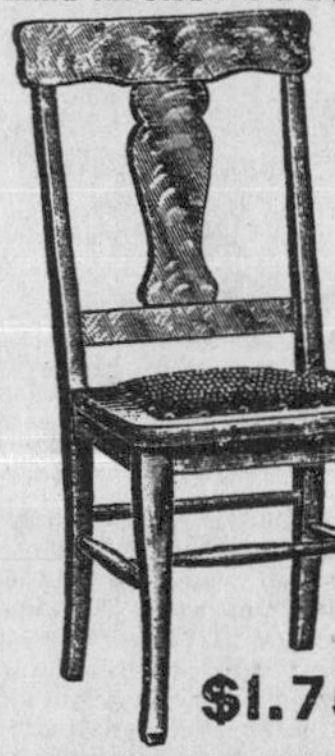

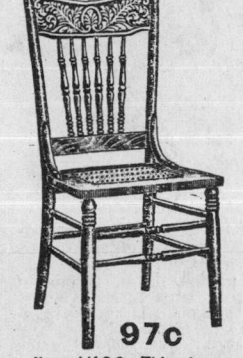

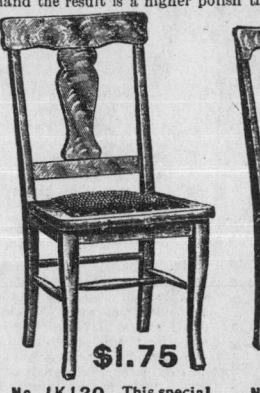

$1.75

No. 1K120 This special box seat diner is made of selected thoroughly seasoned oak with quarter sawed back, finished in a high gloss golden color. The seat is mortised and braced and upholstered with **chase leather**, a perfect imitation of genuine leather. A strong durable chair, a better chair than is sold by other dealers at $2.25 to $2.75 each. Weight, 14 pounds.

Price..............$1.75

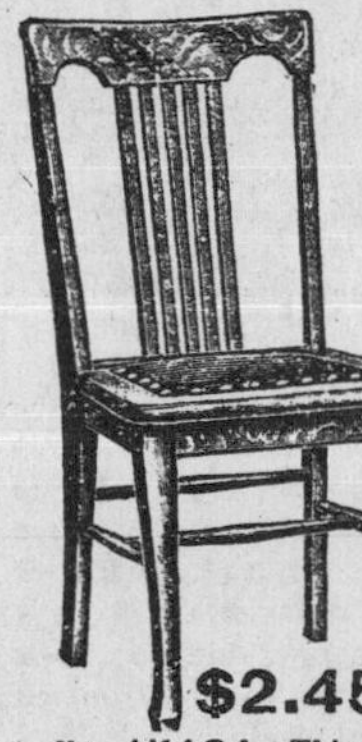

$2.45

No. 1K124 This handsome box seat diner is made of selected quarter sawed oak, with a high gloss golden finish. Seat is mortised and doweled and covered with cane, hand woven or genuine leather. Heavy shaped legs, high back fitted with five flat spindles, as shown in illustration. Weight, 15 pounds.

Price, cane seat....$1.95
Price, leather seat.. 2.45

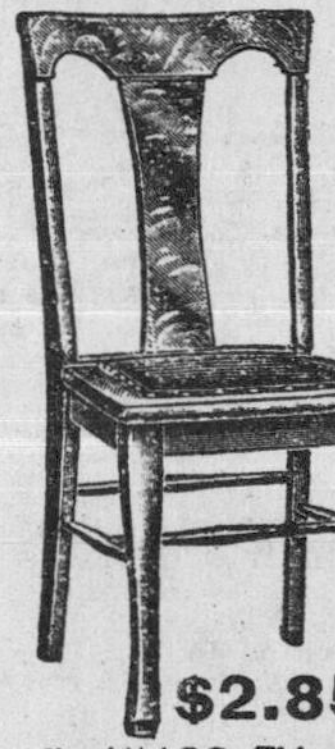

$2.85

No. 1K128 This serviceable box seat diner is made of thoroughly seasoned quarter sawed oak, finished in a golden color and highly polished. Seat is mortised and doweled and covered with patent seat, upholstered in genuine leather. Shaped legs and high paneled back. A strong serviceable chair at a very low price. Weight, 15 pounds.

Price, leather.....$2.85

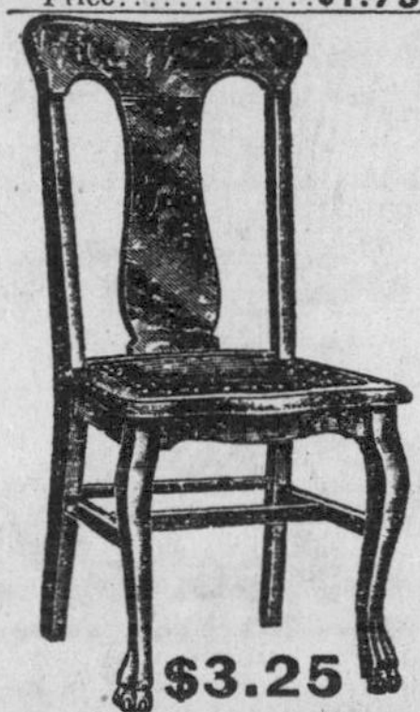

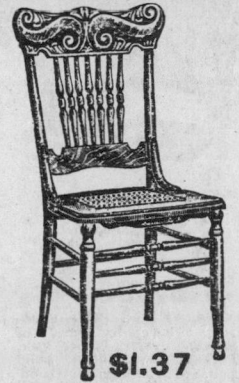

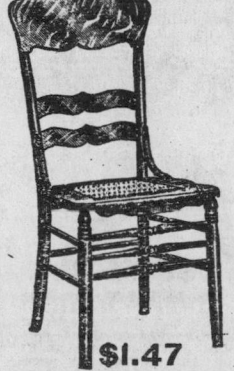

$3.25

No. 1K130 An extra heavy full box seat diner, made of best quality flaky grained quarter sawed oak, thoroughly seasoned, finished in golden color and hand polished. Has a shaped seat, doweled and mortised, upholstered in genuine leather. Heavy French shaped legs with claw feet; wide panel back. Strongly constructed and specially recommended for its strength and beauty. Shipping weight, 18 pounds.

Price, leather seat...$3.25

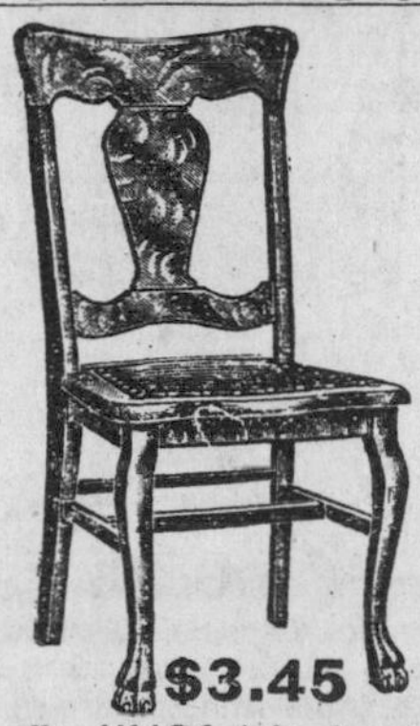

$3.45

No. 1K134 A handsome full box seat diner, made of thoroughly seasoned and selected quarter sawed oak in golden finish and hand polished. Heavy French shaped legs with claw feet. Mortised seat, covered with heavy webbing and upholstered in genuine leather, or covered with superfine cane, woven by hand. Double cross panels and heavy paneled back. Weight, 18 pounds.

Price, cane seat....$2.95
Price, leather seat.. 3.45

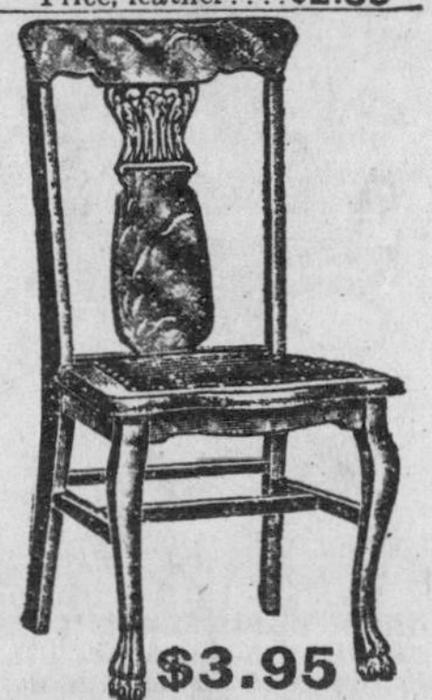

$3.95

No. 1K138 A heavy box seat diner, made of selected quarter sawed oak, hand polished, rich golden finish. Mortised frame, shaped seat, upholstered in genuine leather over a heavy webbing. Heavy French shaped legs. Back panel ornamented with a deep die carving (as shown in illustration). A chair built for service, strong, durable and ornamental. Shipping weight, 18 pounds. Price.... $3.95

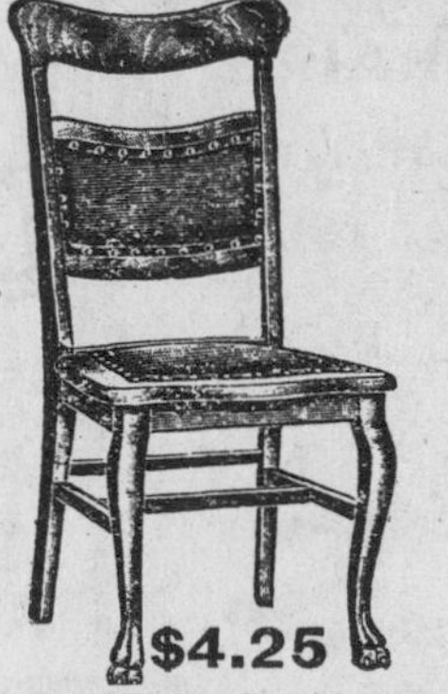

$4.25

No. 1K140 One of our specially designed full box seat diners. Seat and back upholstered in genuine No. 1 leather. French shaped legs with claw feet. Frames made of selected quarter sawed oak, finished golden color and highly polished. Construction and finish first class in every detail. A handsome, serviceable chair. Must be seen to be fully appreciated. Shipping weight, 18 pounds.

Price..............$4.25

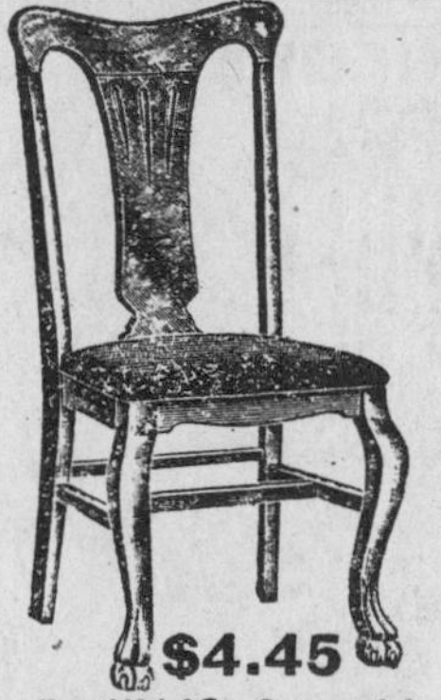

$4.45

No. 1K142 Our special upholstered slip seat diner, made of thoroughly seasoned quarter sawed oak, finished in a rich golden color, highly polished. The frame of chair is mortised and braced. The all leather seat is full width of chair and upholstered over a separate form, fitting snugly over frame. Extra heavy French legs, claw feet and ornamental back. A solid, well constructed chair of the latest pattern. Weight, 18 pounds.

Price..............$4.45

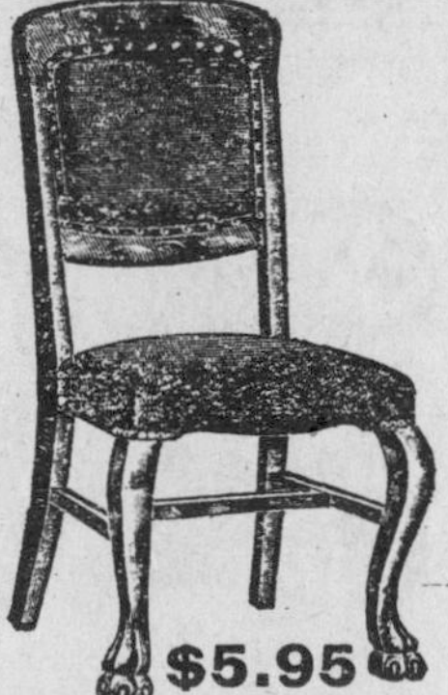

$5.95

No. 1K144 A high grade upholstered diner, with a genuine No. 1 leather upholstered seat and back. Made of selected quarter sawed oak, with a rich golden finish, and highly polished. Frame is mortised, and thoroughly braced. Extra heavy French legs with deep carved claw feet. The finish and construction of this chair is first class in every respect and we especially recommend it for durability and style. Weight, 18 pounds. Price .$5.95

OFFICE CHAIRS AT BIG REDUCTION IN PRICES

  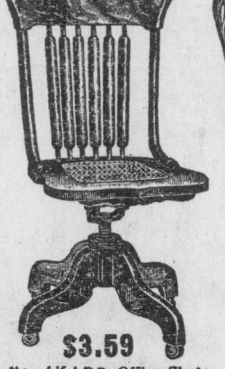 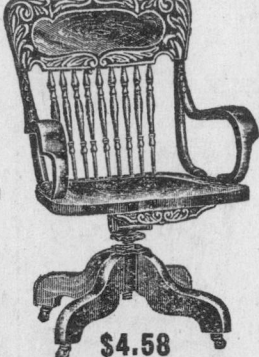 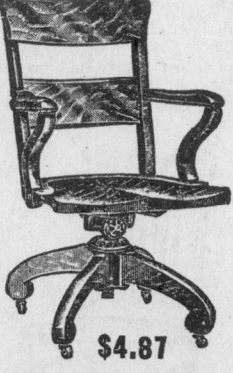 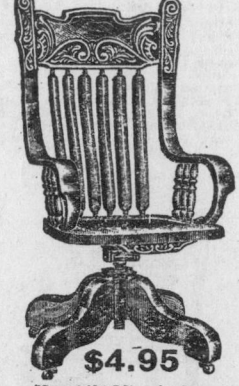

$1.69

$2.19

$3.59

$4.58

$4.87

$4.95

No. 1K175 This popular design Douglas office chair is thoroughly well made of Wisconsin hickory rock elm, high gloss, golden finish. The back and arms are extra well braced with fancy turned spindles. The chair is decidedly comfortable, and after being once used is considered an absolute necessity. Wood seat, perfectly finished. Shipping weight, 14 pounds. Price.......... **$1.69**

No. 1K179 A large high back, comfortable office chair, made of elm, finished golden. Steam bent hickory rock elm arms, securely bolted to seat and back. Legs thoroughly braced, making it extra strong and durable. A splendid chair for home or hotel use. Shipping weight, 16 pounds. Price **$2.19**

No. 1K185 Office Chair. Is very comfortable, thoroughly well made and handsome in appearance. The back posts are well bolted to seat. Cane seat is hand woven, and the spring may be adjusted to any degree of tension desired, while the chair may be raised or lowered by means of the screw in steel plate. This chair is made of the very finest rock elm and finished golden oak. Complete with casters. Shipping weight, 30 pounds. Price..... **$3.59**

No. 1K193 A neat, comfortable office chair, made of selected elm, golden finish. Back of chair is medium height and beautifully carved. Has steam bent arms, back posts and wood seat, fitted with latest style spring and revolving attachment. Complete with casters. Shipping weight, 35 pounds. Price **$4.58** Price, arm chair to match.. 2.48

No. 1K197 This saddle seat office chair, made of selected oak, golden finish, is one of our most attractive new designs. It has the regular Bank of England arm, and curved back fitted with cross panels. Solid oak base and latest patent revolving screw and spring attachment. Built for comfort and durability. Complete with casters. Shipping weight, 30 pounds. Price **$4.87**

No. 1K195 A large comfortable and roomy high back office chair; carved top and front, bent slats in back, made of best selected rock elm, finished golden; has the best patented screw and spring base, and is strong and durable. Complete with casters. Shipping weight 38 pounds. Price.. **$4.95** Price, arm chair to match. 3.15

$5.35

$6.35

$6.45

$8.75

$7.95

$8.65

No. 1K199 This office chair has a full saddle shaped seat. It is made of choice highly figured quarter sawed oak; golden finish. The arms are securely fastened to the seat and back posts by bolts. The base is fitted with the best adjustable rotary spring attachment, adjustable to any height. It has shapely arms and heavy paneled back. The construction and finish strictly high grade. Complete with casters. Shipping weight, 35 pounds. Price .. **$5.35** Price, arm chair to match.......... 3.90

No. 1K230. This is one of the most comfortable office chairs we have ever offered, made of selected quarter sawed oak, golden finish, highly polished. Saddle seat, medium height back and Bank of England arm. Base is fitted with best rotary spring attachment and adjustable to any height. Construction is first class in every detail. Complete with casters. Shipping weight, 35 pounds. Price. **$6.35**

No. 1K221 This office chair is made of selected quarter sawed oak, polished finish. Has the best screw and spring attachment. Neatly shaped arms and back, strictly first class throughout. Will match any high grade desk. It has wood seat, saddle shape and very comfortable. Complete with casters. Shipping weight, 30 pounds. Price, **$6.45** Price, arm chair to match, 4.85

No. 1K235 Revolving office chair with Bank of England arm. Made of selected quarter sawed oak, hand polished. Back is shaped to fit the form and the curved arms permit chair being drawn close to desk. Seat adjustable to any height desired by means of a hand screw, which allows seat to revolve without changing height. Complete with casters. Shipping weight, 35 pounds. Price, saddle wood seat...............$ 8.75 Price, perforated leather seat........... 10.15 Price, arm chair.... 7.50 Price, perforated leather seat........ 8.65

No. 1K236 This handsome office chair is made of selected quarter sawed oak, dark golden finish and hand polished. The high back is upholstered in best quality of leather. Furnished in either solid wood saddle seat or perforated leather laid over cane. Seat is adjustable to any height, by means of our patent adjustable screw. Construction throughout is first class, insuring a comfortable and durable chair. Furnished complete with casters. Shipping weight, crated, 55 pounds. Price, wood seat .....$7.95 Price, leather seat.... 9.85 Price, arm chair to match, wood seat only, 6.85

No. 1K238 This handsome office chair is one of the very latest designed, made of highly figured quarter sawed oak, golden finish and polished. Large roomy seat, continuous bent arm, flat spindles in back, very strong and durable. Patent revolving spring attachment, solid wood seat or perforated leather seat. Complete with casters. Shipping weight, 40 lbs. Price, wood seat, **$8.65** Price, perforated leather seat.. 9.95

CHILDREN'S CHAIRS

98c

$1.55

$2.50

$1.15

$1.58

$2.15

No. 1K248 This nursery chair is made of selected reeds. We formerly sold the same style chair made of willow at 69 cents, but it was not a satisfactory chair. The frame of this chair is exceptionally strong and durable. A convenient article for the home and will be fully appreciated by all mothers. Shipping weight, about 5 pounds. Price. **98c**

No. 1K252 This handsome child's rocker is made of selected elm finished in rich golden color. Fancy turned spindles, deep carved ornaments in back with a fine deep seat. Rocker is strongly built and will give good service. It is made in the same manner as our full sized rockers which is a guarantee of its lasting qualities. Weight, 10 pounds. Price.. **$1.55**

No. 1K255 This beautiful child's reed rocker is made of best quality of German reed. The workmanship and material is the same as used in our high grade full sized rockers which is a guarantee of its wearing qualities. Frame is of selected stock, thoroughly seasoned. Strongly constructed throughout. Weight, 8 pounds. Price...... **$2.50**

No. 1K258 This chair is made of the best rock elm, kiln dried and thoroughly seasoned. You will see from the illustration that it is strongly built and very handy. Adjustable table, which swings over the child's head so that the child can be placed in the chair before adjusting the table. The chair is finished either in red or golden, as may be desired. Weight, 12 pounds. Price......... **$1.15**

Our latest style child's high chair, as here illustrated, is made with either wood or cane seat. It has large drop table and is made of thoroughly seasoned golden elm, highly finished, making it one of the best grades on the market. The back panel is deeply and elegantly carved. Weight, 13 pounds. No. 1K261 Wood seat. Price **$1.58** No. 1K262 Cane seat. Price 1.79

No. 1K264 This child's high chair is made of selected oak, with choice of wood or best quality of cane seat. Back posts are braced and top and back panels are made of quarter sawed oak. It has a large size drop table, which prevents child from falling out. In making up the chair special attention is given to construction, making it very substantial, as well as neat and attractive in design. Weight, 12 pounds. Wood seat. Price..$2.15 Cane seat. Price.... 2.25

No. 1K265½ This combination chair is made of golden oak, gloss finish. Has broad quarter sawed oak panel back and flat spindles. Open cane seat. Can be quickly changed into low go-cart mounted on metal wheels. Best table and guard attachment to hold child securely in seat. Weight, 18 lbs. Price **$3.35**

WONDERFUL VALUES IN ROCKERS

BIG REDUCTION IN PRICES

AT $1.20 TO $15.10, WE OFFER THE MOST WONDERFUL VALUES IN ROCKERS. NEW AND UP TO DATE DESIGNS, STRICTLY DEPENDABLE IN MATERIAL, CONSTRUCTION AND FINISH. BETTER IN QUALITY AND LOWER IN PRICE THAN CAN BE BOUGHT ELSEWHERE. EVERY ROCKER ON THIS AND THE FOLLOWING PAGES AT THE PRICE WE ASK MEANS A SAVING TO OUR CUSTOMERS OF 30 TO 40 PER CENT, AS AGAINST THE PRICE FOR THE SAME QUALITY OFFERED BY OTHER DEALERS.

OUR ROCKERS embody all the new, up to date ideas in rocker construction. The designs are exceptionally attractive, selected with a view of combining the greatest strength and solidity with a handsome appearance. They are the product of years of experience and we offer them to our customers with the positive assurance and guarantee that in no retail store or other catalogue can they be excelled in elegance of design, perfection of construction and finish. **YOU WILL FIND EACH ROCKER** made of better material, better in finish, better constructed in every detail, more dependable and durable, and in fact, in every way more satisfactory than rockers made by the average factory and sold by the average dealer. **EVERY POST, PANEL, SPINDLE, ARM AND SEAT** is made of thoroughly seasoned stock, perfectly framed, constructed, fitted and finished. **WE GUARANTEE** every rocker to be lower in price than the same quality of goods can be found elsewhere. If any other firm meets or cuts our price on any rocker, they do it at the expense of quality. You are especially requested to return our goods at our expense if you do not find this true by comparison of the goods.

OUR SOLID COMFORT ROCKER

THIS EXTRA LARGE MASSIVE QUARTER SAWED OAK ROCKER is a splendid example of the wonderful values we offer in our chair and rocker line. An exceptionally popular design, first class in construction and finish, comfortable and durable, and at our low price, $3.85, represents a big saving to our customers. Quality for quality, this magnificent rocker cannot be purchased elsewhere for less than $6.00 to $7.00.

$3.85

THIS MAGNIFICENT ROCKER has a broad back, 27 inches high from seat to top, with extra large top panel and small bottom panel reinforced by eleven fancy turned spindles. The high, shapely curved arms are firmly attached to the seat by five solid turned spindles. We call your special attention to the extra large and exceptionally comfortable form fitting, deep and wide **veneered roll seat**, size 20x20 inches, with ornamental deep carved front. The massive, continuous front posts from arms to rockers are deeply embossed. The connecting spindles beneath the seat are turned from extra selected solid oak. Each piece and part framed and fitted in a perfect manner. All surfaces smoothed, sanded, rubbed and finished in a clear, transparent, high gloss golden color.

A SPECIAL FEATURE of this rocker is the patent knocked down construction. The seat and arms are fastened securely to the posts by means of heavy bolts and can be easily put together by anyone. This method of construction not only improves the quality, but eliminates the liability to damage and reduces the freight charges about one-half.

WE CHALLENGE ANY DEALER IN CHICAGO, your own home, or elsewhere, to furnish this same high quality solid oak rocker at anywhere near our $3.85 price. Send us your order for this splendid rocker, for we know you will be more than well pleased and will say that you never saw its equal at the price. Everyone will admit that it is certainly a big bargain. Weight, 30 pounds.

No. 1K297　Price.................................**$3.85**

No. 1K297
ORDER BY NUMBER

OUR PEERLESS HOME COMFORT ROCKER

A STRIKINGLY HANDSOME AND ATTRACTIVE NEW DESIGN, HIGH GRADE ROCKER. Quality for quality, the equal of those generally offered by others at $7.50 to $8.50. **THE WOOD** is thoroughly seasoned quarter sawed oak, selected for the beauty of the highly figured grain and finished in a clear, transparent, high gloss golden color. The posts, panels, arms, spindles and seat are framed and fitted in a perfect manner. The wide, deep, roomy, form fitting roll seat and high, shapely curved comfortable back are made of three-ply veneer stock transversely laid and guaranteed not to warp, check or split. The seat is 20 inches wide and 20 inches deep. The back from seat to top is 30 inches high and 23 inches wide. **THE BROAD CURVED** arms are firmly supported by the large corner posts and ten fancy turned spindles. **THE PATENT KNOCKED DOWN CONSTRUCTION** by which the seat and arms are fastened to the posts by heavy bolts, give this splendid rocker additional strength and rigidity and permit its shipment in a package 33 inches long, 28 inches wide, 10 inches thick, insuring its safe delivery by the transportation company and reducing the freight charges fully one half.

WE EXPECT TO SELL THOUSANDS of these magnificent rockers, for every order we receive will mean many more orders from the friends and neighbors of every customer who gets this splendid rocker at the wonderfully low price $4.45. We know that every rocker we send out will prove an advertisement for us and that every customer who receives this rocker will be astonished at the value. Every pleased customer is the means of getting another and in return for this generous response, we give them the benefit of every advantage we possess in buying and selling goods and always make our prices far below all others for strictly dependable merchandise.

No. 1K377　Price..**$4.45**

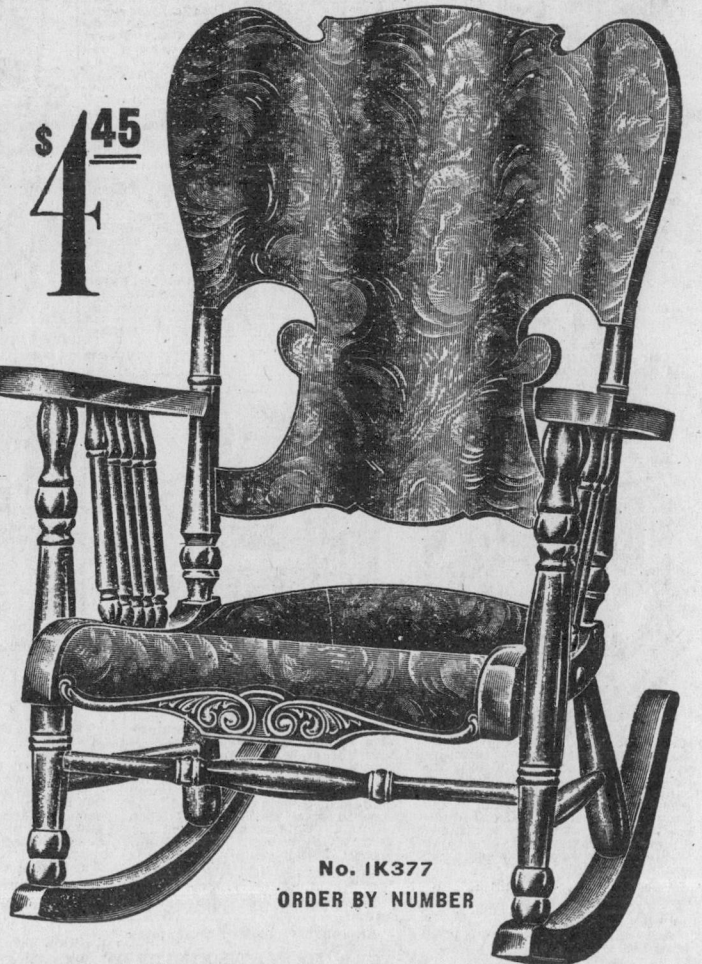

$4.45

No. 1K377
ORDER BY NUMBER

FIVE HANDSOME ROMAN CHAIRS

$4.95

$6.35

$7.75

$8.65

$9.55

No. IK423 A handsome Roman Seat, very popular as an odd corner piece, made of selected material in either quarter sawed oak, golden finish or birch imitation mahogany finish and highly polished. Has a curved arm rest, comfortable seat, and is strongly constructed throughout. Our price is about one-half the regular retail price. Shipped direct from factory in Western New York or Chicago. Shipping weight, 15 pounds.
Price, quartered oak...**$4.95**
Price, mahogany finish..............5.10

No. IK425 This beautiful Roman Chair is constructed with a view to style, comfort, and durability. It is made of selected material in either quarter sawed oak, golden finish or birch imitation mahogany, hand polished. Wide comfortable seat, two panels in back, top panels handsomely carved. Must be seen and compared with other chairs of same quality to appreciate its full value. Shipped direct from factory in Western New York or. from Chicago. Shipping weight, 20 pounds.
Price, quartered oak....**$6.35**
Price, Imitation mahogany..............6.45

No. IK427 This exceptionally handsome Roman Chair is made of oak, quarter sawed, golden finish, or birch, imitation mahogany finish, and highly polished. Material specially selected and strongly constructed. Has neat carvings on back top panel, arms are bent and seat curved, resting on solid wood bases. For a medium priced chair it cannot be equaled for comfort and beauty. Shipped direct from factory in Western New York or Chicago. Shipping weight, 29 pounds.
Price, quartered oak..............**$7.75**
Price, mahogany finish..............7.95

No. IK428 This Roman Chair is the very latest design, made of selected material in either quarter sawed oak, or birch in imitation mahogany and highly polished. Wide comfortable seat, curved arms and heavy claw feet on front legs. Back posts and top panel have deep handsome carvings. Strongly constructed throughout, it makes a stylish, durable chair that cannot be duplicated for double the money at any retail store. Shipped direct from factory in Western New York or Chicago. Shipping weight, 35 pounds.
Price, quartered oak....**$8.65**
Price, imitation mahogany..............8.75

No. IK430 A masterpiece in a Roman Chair. The latest design, made in quarter sawed oak or imitation mahogany, highly polished. Material and workmanship of the very best. Back is extra heavy, with deep carving. Arms bent, seat curved, and resting on handsome French shaped legs. The whole piece is solid, substantial and comfortable. Shipped direct from factory in Western New York or Chicago. Shipping weight, 30 pounds.
Price, quartered oak....**$9.55**
Price, mahogany finish....9.75

SPECIAL VALUES IN MISSION FURNITURE.

THIS STYLE OF FURNITURE is no longer an experiment, but after the test of years is now one of the most popular styles on the market for all who appreciate beauty and simplicity of design combined with strength and comfort. It derives its name from the original pieces found in an old Spanish Mission in Southern California and has been approved and accepted by the Arts and Crafts Societies of the United States and England. Prominent architects throughout the country recommend and specify this style and finish.

THE WOOD is solid oak, specially selected, thoroughly air seasoned and kiln dried, special attention being given to the grain of the wood. Absolutely guaranteed not to warp, check or shrink.

THE FINISH is familiarly known as weathered and is obtained by special treatment by use of preservative stains which produce a rich brown effect showing the beautiful grain of the wood with a rich sheen, which, in certain lights, gives an effective glow to the surface and will not scratch or mar and does not become blurred by changes in the temperature. We also furnish each piece in a beautiful golden finish. Be sure to state finish desired or we will ship weathered oak.

THE CONSTRUCTION of each piece is strictly first class; every post and bar, joint and tenon perfectly framed and joined, the best that modern machinery and skilled workmanship can produce.

THE GENUINE No. 1 leather, imitation Spanish leather and leatherette used on our Mission furniture is the best quality. The color of the genuine No. 1 leather and leatherette is black, tinged with a shade of dark olive green. We furnish the imitation Spanish leather in dark red, olive green or dark golden brown, as desired. In ordering be sure to state color desired, otherwise we will ship dark golden brown.

No. IK3910 This high back, comfortable Rocker is offered at half the price you would have to pay an ordinary furniture dealer. Made of solid oak throughout, of the strongest construction, a beautiful Mission design, with upholstered back and full spring seat. The broad panels in the back and under the arms are artistically designed and the wide arms and front posts are carefully shaped. The heavy box framed seat and curved back posts add to the strength, and the entire rocker is so constructed that it can be shipped knocked down, thereby insuring the lowest freight rate. Be sure to state whether you want weathered oak or golden oak when ordering. Shipped direct from our factory in Western New York. Weight, 42 pounds.
Price, upholstered with black leatherette..............**$4.65**
Price, upholstered with imitation Spanish leather..............5.35
Price, upholstered with genuine leather..............6.95

$4.65
Be sure to state the finish desired.

No. IK3924 This extra large Massive Rocker is made of specially selected quarter sawed oak in golden or weathered finish as desired. Note the roomy seat with roll front, the broad curved arms and shaped front posts. Each side of rocker has six turned beaded spindles. Extra high back and roomy seat. Upholstered in best quality No. 1 genuine black leather or dark red, mottled olive green or golden brown fabricoid, as desired. This rocker cannot be purchased in retail stores for less than double the price we ask. Shipping weight, about 50 pounds. Be sure to state finish of wood and color of leather desired.
Price, weathered or golden oak, fabricoid..**$6.75**
Price, weathered or golden oak, genuine No. 1 leather..............8.45

$6.75

No. IK3952 Massive Mission Rocker with loose cushion back and loose cushion seat. A rocker built to give solid comfort and last a lifetime. Compare this with any rocker offered at double our price. Covered with genuine leather, thick soft cushions, extra large frame, made of heavy solid oak. Has wide arms and front with box frame seat. Finished weathered or golden oak. Shipped direct from our factory in Western New York.
Weight, 40 pounds. Price, genuine leather..**$9.85**
Arm chair to match, same price as rocker.
Sofa to match, genuine leather. Weight, 65 pounds.
Price..............**$16.85**

$9.85

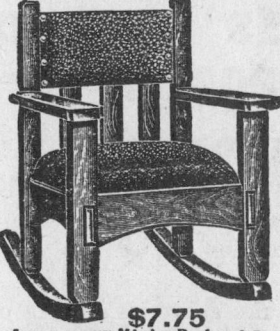

$3.85

$4.65

$5.65

$7.75

$6.35

No. IK3928 A strong, substantial Rocker, built on the lines that have made Mission furniture so popular. Made of solid oak, finished either weathered or golden oak. Be sure to state finish desired. Has broad ornamental panel in the back and under each arm, full upholstered seat with heavy box frame. Shipped direct from our factory in Western New York. Weight, 40 pounds.
Price, imitation Spanish leather..............**$3.85**
Price, genuine leather.... 4.95
Arm chair to match, same price as rocker.

No. IK3930 A very comfortable upholstered back and seat Mission Rocker with wide arms and heavy sides. Made of solid oak, finished weathered or golden, built to give good service. Thoroughly well made and strongly constructed. Be sure to state finish desired when ordering. Shipped direct from our factory in Western New York. Weight, 38 pounds.
Price, upholstered with imitation Spanish leather..............**$4.65**
Price, upholstered with genuine leather..............5.35
Arm chair to match, same price as rocker.

No. IK3934 A strictly Mission Rocker, reproduced from the original found in an old Spanish Mission in Southern California. The comfort and style of this rocker has been often imitated but never equaled. We control the exclusive sale of this rocker. Made in the most careful manner of selected oak with heavy square posts and wide arms. Broad overstuffed upholstered seat. An exceptionally strong, durable and comfortable rocker at a big saving in price. Shipped direct from our factory near Chicago. Weight, 25 pounds.
Price, genuine leather. **$5.65**

Large, roomy Mission Rocker, can be furnished with full spring seat or loose cushion seat filled with elastic cotton felt. Has upholstered back with broad panels. Wide arms and front and heavy box framed seat. Made of selected oak finished weathered or golden. Be sure to state finish desired. Very comfortable. Shipped direct from factory near Chicago. Weight, 45 pounds.
No. IK3938 Price, genuine leather spring seat..............**$7.75**
No. IK3942 Price, genuine leather loose cushion seat........**$8.35**
Arm chair to match, same price as rocker.

No. IK3946 Morris Chair, with adjustable back and upholstered side head rests. Has wide heavy arms and front with openwork panels under the arms and is made of solid oak throughout. High upholstered back with full spring seat. Finished either Mission weathered or rich golden oak. Be sure to state finish desired.
Price, imt. Spanish leather **$6.35**
Price, genuine leather..**$11.25**

BE SURE TO STATE FINISH OF WOOD AND COLOR OF COVERING MATERIAL DESIRED.

YOUR MONEY WILL BE IMMEDIATELY RETURNED TO YOU FOR ANY GOODS NOT PERFECTLY SATISFACTORY.

229

$1 75 REED CHAIRS - ROCKERS $6 65

AT $1.75 TO $6.65 WE SHOW LATER DESIGNS AND BETTER VALUES THAN WE HAVE EVER BEFORE BEEN ABLE TO OFFER. PRICES LOWER THAN THE LOWEST. LESS THAN RETAIL DEALERS PAY AT WHOLESALE. EVERY CHAIR GUARANTEED FOR QUALITY.

OUR REED CHAIRS AND ROCKERS are made of the best quality, specially selected imported reed, and the frames of thoroughly seasoned hardwood. Each piece is perfectly framed and fitted in a perfect manner. We guarantee our reed chairs and rockers never to wear loose in the joints.

OUR PRICES. Look out for low catchy prices. Many dealers, and especially catalogue houses, in a vain effort to compete with us are sacrificing quality in order to name an apparently low price. We know that no other dealer can give you the same value, the same high standard of quality for the same low price as we give you.

$2.75 FOR THIS IMPERIAL REED ROCKER. It will please you immensely; you will find it to be a big, roomy, comfortable, well made, high grade rocker, a constant source of comfort, and an ornament to the room. We could not send out any article that would better represent us, for on the quality of this rocker, the satisfaction it will give every purchaser we are willing to stand or fall. We are perfectly willing for you to judge us throughout, to form your opinion of the quality of everything we offer from your judgment of this $2.75 rocker. It is our big leader, our example of all our values, our challenge to competition, our proof of superiority. By making this illustration larger you can get a better idea of the value we offer and can see how nearly the cost of the material and labor in this piece must represent the entire price we ask you, namely, $2.75. It is a price less than you can buy a chair of this kind from any other catalogue house, less than retail dealers can buy such a chair in any quantity.

No. 1K460 Price..................(Shipping weight, 14 pounds.)..............**$2.75**

WE MAKE THIS STANDING OFFER which is open for you to take advantage of at all times. If you see an article in any other catalogue, a reed rocker for example, that looks like this, our big $2.75 leader for as low a price or lower, order both articles, get them both for comparison, you be the judge, and if you do not see immediately that we give you greater value for your money, furnish you better quality at a lower price, we are willing for you to return our goods at our expense and get your money back at once. We could easily cheapen this handsome reed rocker 25 cents, 35 cents, 50 cents or even 75 cents, and still show you a very attractive picture. But if you examined it closely, compared it with this chair, you would quickly see the difference in quality. Such a chair cut in quality to the extent of 25 cents, 50 cents or 75 cents would not give you satisfaction. It would be a poor investment compared with the article we offer, but many dealers and catalogue houses are willing to do this. We will not do it.

No. 1K456 This large comfortable reed rocker has extra high back and wide seat, closely woven with double strand reeds. Has full continuous roll around back and arms. The frame is made of thoroughly seasoned hardwood, natural shellac finish. This rocker is firmly constructed and is exceptional value. Compared with other rockers at anywhere near the same price it is worth double the money. Shipping weight, 15 pounds. Price. **$2.23**

No. 1K454 Same design as above, but made of cheaper reed. Shipping weight, 15 pounds. Price............... **$1.75**

$2.75 OUR LEADER

No. 1K458 This ladies' cane seat rocker is of the very best pattern. It has a high back with continuous arms, full reed wrapped. Cane seat and a reed apron front. Frame is firmly constructed of thoroughly seasoned maple, finished in shellac. We invite comparisons both as to quality and price. We compare the goods of other dealers with our goods and always find when the price is the same or lower, the quality of the goods is much lower. We are the largest buyers of reed rockers in this country and we have advantages by reason of this purchasing power that other dealers cannot offer you. Shipping weight, 12 lbs. Price.............**$2.62**

$2.62

$2.89

No. 1K459 This splendid rocker has a large full round continuous roll on back, sides, arms and across the front. Seat is made of best hand woven cane. The frame is made of thoroughly seasoned hard white maple, natural shellac finish. Attractive in design, firmly constructed, and exceptionally comfortable. A big saving in price to our customers. Shipping weight, 14 pounds. Price.... **$2.89**

$3.23

No. 1K461 This large size gentlemen's or ladies' rocker is one of the latest designs, and constructed with a view to comfort and durability. It has a wide roll seat, full wrapped continuous arms and posts, and made over a maple frame, thoroughly seasoned. Every rocker and chair in our line is carefully wrapped and packed and safe delivery guaranteed. Shipping weight, 15 pounds. Price.... **$3.23**

$3.32

No. 1K463 This is without a doubt the best value in a ladies' rocker ever offered. It has the continuous roll arm, extending to the front and beneath the seat, forming a curtain or apron front. The seat is best hand woven cane and the woodwork of frame is maple, well seasoned. Weight, 12 pounds. Price.... **$3.32**

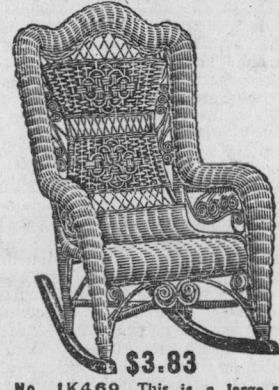

$3.65

No. 1K468 This handsome cane seat rocker is exceptionally well made with low back, heavy rolls extending from back to the seat with basket front, finished in shellac. It is one of the newest patterns and is exceptional value at the price we ask. Shipping weight, 12 pounds. Price..... **$3.65**

$3.83

No. 1K469 This is a large size ladies' or gents' rocker, latest design and constructed with a view to comfort and durability. Has a wide roll seat with back beautifully ornamented. Continuous roll extending from back and covering front legs of rocker. Thoroughly well constructed and guaranteed to be the best value ever offered. Shipping weight, 12 pounds. Price............... **$3.83**

$4.22

No. 1K451 This splendid rocker is made of specially selected imported reeds, and has extra high back, wide seat closely woven with double strand reeds. It has big, full, round, continuous roll around back and arms. Extra strong hard white maple frame, natural shellac finished. Exceptionally strong and comfortable. Sells in stores at $6.00 to $7.00. Shipping weight, 14 pounds. Price............ **$4.22**

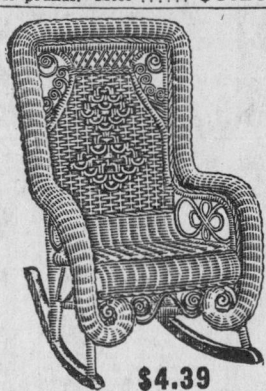

$4.39

No. 1K470 This is a specially designed gents' rocker, strong and comfortable, made of very best material throughout. It has continuous arms extending under seat, forming ram's horn effect, as shown in illustration. Fancy scroll front, full wrapped, finished in shellac. Sells in stores at $8.00 to $9.00. Shipping weight, 15 lbs. Price............ **$4.39**

$5.28

No. 1K473 This handsome ladies' rocker is made of best selected reed on a thoroughly seasoned frame of hardwood, fancy grill work in back and under front of seat. Seat is covered with the best grade of cane. Legs thoroughly braced, seat and back posts wrapped with rattan, making an extra strong and durable chair. Weight, 10 pounds. Price............ **$5.28**

$5.30

No. 1K474 This rocker has been specially designed for us, and nothing has been overlooked in quality and beauty of design. Full roll seat with continuous roll extending from back and under seat. Beautifully ornamented with fancy scroll work. For comfort and durability we recommend this rocker. Shipping weight, 15 lbs. Price............ **$5.30**

$6.65

No. 1K481 This extra large comfortable rocker is one of the handsomest designs we have to offer. It is made of best selected reed over a thoroughly seasoned hardwood frame. Large roomy saddle seat with basket front, and a continuous roll extending over back and arms; exposed parts all wrapped with rattan. Honestly constructed and a bargain at our price. Weight, 15 pounds. Price............ **$6.65**

A Beautiful Design In a Highly Ornamental Reception Chair.

Handsome Ornamental Corner or Reception Piece.

No. 1K486   No. 1K490   No. 1K488

$3.93

$4.92

THE ABOVE ILLUSTRATION shows our special three-piece suite. Each piece is made over a frame of thoroughly seasoned hardwood with best quality of selected reed and seats covered with superfine cane. Well constructed by expert workmen. We can furnish pieces separate or in suites as desired, and either with or without cushions. THE CUSHIONS are made of high grade crush plush filled with good grade of hair; tied on with tassels as shown in illustration. THE CUSHIONS can be furnished in dark red, blue, green or old gold, and can be ordered in assorted colors if preferred. Be sure to state color of cushions desired. Seat of settee is 37 inches long by 17 inches deep. Seat of chair, No. 1K486 and rocker, No. 1K488, measure, 17 inches by 17 inches. Suite is light, easily handled—from the point of beauty and durability cannot be excelled. Weight of three pieces, 50 pounds.

No. 1K498 Ladies' Ornamented Reception Chair, made of the very best reed. Has a cane seat and finished in shellac. Posts and braces are all hand wrapped with reed, making altogether a very strong and durable chair, suitable for a parlor or reception room. Weight, 7 pounds. Price............ **$3.93**

No. 1K499 This handsome Reception and Corner Chair is exceptionally attractive in design; durable and comfortable. It is made of the best quality of specially selected reed, natural shellac finish and is very strong; fit to adorn any parlor. Weight, 10 pounds. Price.... **$4.92**

	Price, without cushions	Price, with cushions
No. 1K486 Price for chair	$ 4.85	$ 6.25
No. 1K488 Price for rocker	4.90	6.30
No. 1K490 Price for settee	8.40	10.50
No. 1K493 Price for complete suite	18.15	23.05

$5^{35} KITCHEN CUPBOARDS $9^{75}

BIG REDUCTION IN PRICES.

AT $5.35 TO $9.75 WE SHOW WONDERFUL VALUES IN KITCHEN CUPBOARDS. VALUES THAT CANNOT BE EQUALED. OUR LOW PRICES ARE NOT MADE AT THE EXPENSE OF QUALITY.

$9.75 FOR THIS EXTRA LARGE MASSIVE HIGH GRADE

KITCHEN CUPBOARD

made of specially selected, thoroughly air seasoned and kiln dried stock, high gloss and golden finish. The entire front is made of solid oak, the sides of Northern elm, the two woods best adapted for kitchen cupboard construction. It stands 90 inches high, 42 inches wide; the base is 17 inches deep and the top section 12 inches deep. For convenience in handling and shipping and to provide a roomy platform on the base, it is made in two sections. The top section is fitted with two doors with extra thick glass panels. Inside has two spacious shelves for dishes. The base has two roomy drawers for linen and cutlery and a spacious cupboard with double door below. Ornamented with neatly designed scroll carvings. The material, construction, and finish of this splendid kitchen cupboard is strictly first class throughout. The doors, drawers and panels are perfectly framed and fitted, every post and piece the best that skilled workmanship can produce. You will find this cupboard, as well as every other cupboard on this page, made of better material, better construction and better finish than is generally sold by other dealers.

THE PRICE represents a saving to our customers of fully 30 to 40 per cent as against the price asked by others. We accept your order with the distinct understanding that if when you have received and examined this splendid kitchen cupboard, it is not perfectly satisfactory in every respect and that you have saved considerable money, you may return it to us and we will return your money together with all transportation charges.

SECURELY PACKED and shipped direct from factory in Central Ohio, or from our warehouse nearest your railroad station as mentioned in the price list.

HOW WE ARE ABLE TO MAKE QUICK DELIVERY AND SAVE TIME AND FREIGHT CHARGES TO OUR CUSTOMERS.

OUR SALES on this magnificent high grade Kitchen Cupboard have grown so large from every section of the country that, in order that we may be able to get one of these splendid and deservedly popular kitchen cupboards to our customers in the WEST and NORTHWEST in a day or two from the date we receive your order, to insure its reaching you in perfect condition, to remove the liability of breakage or damage and reduce the freight charges to the smallest possible amount, we have arranged warehouse facilities at St. Paul, Minn., and Kansas City, Mo. We ship this kitchen cupboard in solid car lots, receiving from the railroad company the very lowest carload freight rates, so that when we receive your order here in Chicago for this Kitchen Cupboard No. 1K510, we immediately send your order by special mail delivery to the warehouse nearest you and order this kitchen cupboard shipped to your railroad station on your order at once. It will leave the warehouse in perfect condition and will reach you in a few hours to a day or two at the farthest from the time it leaves the warehouse, and when you get it you will only need to pay the small freight charges for the short distance from the warehouse to your railroad station. The total cost of this splendid kitchen cupboard to our customers in the WEST and NORTHWEST will amount to considerably less than if shipped to you singly as one shipment from the factory in Ohio to your nearest railroad station. Shipping weight, 150 pounds.

No. 1K510   Price at factory in Central Ohio **$9.75**

No. 1K510   Price at warehouse in Kansas City, Mo. **11.52**

No. 1K510   Price at warehouse in St. Paul, Minn. **11.38**

This Cupboard is made of thoroughly seasoned Northernhardwood, solid oak front, high gloss golden finish. Substantial in construction. It stands 6 feet 7 inches high, 39 inches wide and 15 inches deep. Double thick heavy glass doors, two drawers with pulls. Lower cupboard is made with double doors, with lock and key. Inside of cupboards have shelves. We also furnish this cupboard with all hardwood, golden oak finish. Shipped direct from factory in Central Ohio or Southern Indiana.

Shipping weight, 130 pounds.
No. 1K502   Price, oak front.. **$6.25**
No. 1K501   Price, all hardwood, golden oak finish. **5.35**

No. 1K503 This Splendid Kitchen Cupboard is the equal of those generally offered by other dealers at $11.00 to $12.00. It is made of thoroughly seasoned northern hardwood with solid oak front, high gloss golden finish. Is 6 feet 7 inches high, 42 inches wide and 15 inches deep; has two drawers and shelves in top and cupboard. Shipped direct from factory in Central Ohio. Shipping weight, 140 pounds.

Price **$6.85**

No. 1K505   Same as above, with glass doors. Price **7.25**

No. 1K506 This High Grade Patent Kitchen Cupboard is made of thoroughly seasoned oak, high gloss golden finish. Height, 76 inches; width, 38 inches; depth, 15 inches. Double paneled ends hinged to back. Front securely fastened by screw bolts to the end panels, a patent method of construction which gives additional solidity and durability. Upper doors fitted with double strength glass panels, below which are two drawers and a spacious compartment with double paneled doors built of three-ply stock. Shipped knocked down in single package, securely crated, from factory in Central Indiana.

Shipping weight, 125 pounds.
Price **$7.75**

No. 1K508 This New Design Cupboard is made of thoroughly seasoned Northern hardwood with solid oak front, high gloss golden finish. Base contains one cupboard, two large drawers, four spice drawers and flour bin 12 inches wide, 24 inches deep. Height, 6 feet 7 inches; width, 3 feet 2 inches; depth, 16 inches. Double thick glass in doors. Strictly first class in construction throughout. Shipped direct from our factory in Central Ohio.

Shipping weight, 140 lbs. Price. **$8.85**

WE GUARANTEE OUR KITCHEN CUPBOARDS NOT TO WARP, CHECK OR SHRINK. THE LUMBER IS CAREFULLY SELECTED AND THOROUGHLY SEASONED.

$2⁹⁵ KITCHEN CABINETS $18⁴⁵
BIG REDUCTION IN PRICES
AT $2.95 TO $18.45 WE OFFER WONDERFUL VALUES IN KITCHEN CABINETS

New in design, strictly high grade in material, construction and finish. Better in quality and lower in price than can be bought elsewhere. We challenge any firm on earth to furnish Kitchen Cabinets the equal of ours in quality at the price we ask

KITCHEN CABINETS are the most wonderful invention ever devised for assisting the housekeeper. The many weary steps they save will be fully appreciated by every housekeeper. When first introduced a few years ago the sale was limited. As soon as they were put on the market and offered at popular prices, their convenience and usefulness was quickly recognized and the sale of them has jumped from the hundreds to the thousands. The use of the Kitchen Cabinet in the United States has become so general that one of these economical and labor saving devices is to be found in nearly every community. Don't fail to secure this great convenience for yourself without delay. We know there is not a more convenient and satisfactory piece of furniture for the home than a good Kitchen Cabinet. You will be surprised what a convenience a Kitchen Cabinet is, the variety of uses it can be put to, how completely it takes care of the materials used in the kitchen and in such convenient shape; a place for everything and everything in its place.

OUR KITCHEN CABINETS are made for us under contract by the largest, best known and most reliable manufacturers in this country, whose long experience in the designing and making of cabinet work enables them to give us the benefit of every good idea, whose modern machinery and skilled workmanship combine to produce better goods than are turned out by other manufacturers. All the latest and best improvements in design and construction are embodied in our Kitchen Cabinets. Every article used in the kitchen is provided a place in our Kitchen Cabinet within easy reach of the busy housewife.

THE MATERIAL used in the construction of our Kitchen Cabinets is thoroughly air seasoned and kiln dried, hardwood throughout, except the platform of the base, which is made of white wood for ease and convenience in cleaning. We absolutely guarantee every cabinet against warping, checking or shrinking. We use no "culls." Every piece of lumber is carefully selected and guaranteed free from all defects.

THE CONSTRUCTION of our Kitchen Cabinets is the best that modern machinery and skilled workmanship can produce. Every post and panel, joint and tenon perfectly framed and fitted. The doors are perfectly fitted; the drawers and bins run smoothly without friction. The same high grade workmanship is used in the lowest priced as well as in the highest priced cabinet. The bins and drawers are so constructed that they can be easily taken out and cleaned, which is not the case with most cabinets made by other manufacturers. Each cabinet is fitted with one or two sliding removable kneading and chopping boards, both sides smooth and even, which can be taken out and placed on top of the table for convenience in using.

THE FINISH. The very best grade of materials is used in the finishing of our Kitchen Cabinets. Special care is taken in the entire process of finishing, special attention being given to the preservation of the wood.

THE TRIMMINGS. The handles used on our Kitchen Cabinets are genuine brass, French lacquered to prevent tarnishing. The hinges, fasteners, locks and knobs are the best quality obtainable.

THE PACKING. Every Kitchen Cabinet is firmly and securely crated for shipment. The special feature of our Kitchen Cabinets is that they are so constructed that the lower part of the legs can be removed and placed inside the cabinet for convenience in packing and can be easily put on by anyone. This feature is not found in any cabinets of other manufacturers. This method of construction insures safe handling and a much lower freight rate by the transportation company. We absolutely guarantee every cabinet to arrive at your home in the same perfect condition in which it leaves the factory.

THE BASE OF OUR KITCHEN CABINETS without the top section makes a highly satisfactory, convenient and useful cabinet by itself. The flour, sugar and meal bins, the linen and cutlery drawers, pot and pan cupboards, and the removable kneading and chopping board, together with the roomy basswood top, will be fully appreciated by every housekeeper. We quote prices for the base alone (without the top section) in several of our cabinets on pages following.

OUR PRICES in every case are figured on factory cost. We have secured unusually advantageous prices because of the immense quantity we sell, which represents very little more than cost of raw material and labor. Our selling prices on all our cabinets represent the narrowest kind of a profit above first cost to us, and as a result you can buy a high grade Kitchen Cabinet from us for the same or less money than most dealers pay at wholesale. Do not be misled by the low prices. Do not feel that because our prices are very low, the quality of our cabinets is not the very best. Quality is a watchword with us, and we never take one penny out of the quality to make a "catchy price." Every cabinet we sell is strictly high grade, and while dealers and others may advise you against sending your order to us and say we cannot furnish good furniture at such low prices, we want you to be the judge by sending us your order for one of our Kitchen Cabinets and proving our claim, and at the same time relieve you of all risk. If you do not find our Kitchen Cabinets all that we claim, and that you have not only saved considerable money and secured an article that is perfectly satisfactory, you are specially requested to return it to us and we will refund your money together with all transportation charges.

$8⁹⁵ THIS MAGNIFICENT HIGH GRADE KITCHEN CABINET $8⁹⁵
REDUCED IN PRICE FROM $9.65 TO $8.95.

CONVENIENT, COMPACT AND CAPACIOUS. STRIKINGLY ATTRACTIVE IN DESIGN. STRICTLY HIGH GRADE IN CONSTRUCTION AND FINISH. THE EQUAL OF KITCHEN CABINETS GENERALLY SOLD AT $14.00 TO $16.00.

Without question the best value ever offered by any dealer in a strictly high grade solid white maple Kitchen Cabinet. It is a splendid example of convenience of arrangement, a place for everything used in the kitchen, within easy reach of the busy housewife. It is made of specially selected hard white maple, thoroughly air seasoned and kiln dried, finished natural color. Entire height of cabinet, 60 inches.

THE BASE has a white wood top with moulded edges, size 25x48 inches. It has a large dustproof flour bin holding 50 pounds of flour, above which are two drawers for cutlery and a convenient sugar bin. Note the roomy cupboard for pots and pans and the two linen drawers above. Fitted with one kneading and one chopping board, finished on both sides, can be removed and placed on the top for convenience in using. The legs are detachable, the turned part being doweled into the square posts which adds to the convenience in handling.

THE TOP SECTION combines excellence and beauty of design with a convenient and practical arrangement which cannot be excelled. Cupboards with the drawers affording ample space for dishes, spice cans, coffee and tea canisters and a variety of packages and commodities within easy reach of the busy housewife.

THE FINISH of this Kitchen Cabinet is a light natural white maple color, no coloring being used. The surface is perfectly sanded and smooth and given several varnish coatings, which brings out the beautiful natural grain of the wood and has an appearance of purity and cleanliness.

THE CONSTRUCTION of this splendid Kitchen Cabinet is strictly first class throughout. The doors, drawers and bins are perfect fitting. All the drawers and bins can be easily taken out for cleaning and airing—a convenience seldom found in cabinets made by other manufacturers. The posts and panels are perfectly framed and joined, every post and piece the best that skilled workmanship can possibly produce.

REDUCED IN PRICE FROM $9.65 TO $8.95. On account of the universal satisfaction these cabinets have given our customers and the big increase in volume of sales during the past year, we have been enabled to make a new contract at a substantial reduction in price, and we give our customers the benefit of the reduced cost.

No. 1K518

THE ARTICLES DISPLAYED ARE NOT INCLUDED WITH THE CABINET.

HOW WE ARE ABLE TO MAKE QUICK DELIVERY AND SAVE TIME AND FREIGHT CHARGES TO OUR CUSTOMERS ON THIS KITCHEN CABINET.

Our sales on this magnificent high grade Kitchen Cabinet have grown so large from every section of the country that in order that we may be able to get one of these splendid and deservedly popular Kitchen Cabinets to our customers in the WEST and NORTHWEST in a day or two from the date we receive your order, to insure its reaching you in perfect condition, to remove the liability of breakage or damage and reduce the freight charges to the smallest possible amount, we have arranged warehouses in St. Paul, Minn., and Kansas City, Mo. We ship this Kitchen Cabinet in solid car lots, receiving from the railroad company the very lowest carload freight rates, so that when we receive your order here in Chicago for this Kitchen Cabinet No. 1K518, we immediately send your order by special mail delivery to the warehouse nearest you and order it shipped to your railroad station on your order at once. It will leave the warehouse in perfect condition and will reach you in a few hours to a day or two at the farthest from the time it leaves the warehouse, and when you get it you will only need to pay the small freight charges for the short distance from the warehouse to your railroad station. The total cost of this Kitchen Cabinet to our customers in the west and northwest will amount to considerably less than if shipped to you singly as one shipment from the factory in Michigan to your nearest railroad station. Shipping weight, 205 pounds.

No. 1K518 Price at factory in Grand Rapids, Mich.......... **$8.95**

No. 1K518 Price at warehouse in Kansas City, Mo....... **$10.73**

No. 1K518 Price at warehouse in St. Paul, Minn....... **$10.52**

EXCEPTIONAL VALUES IN HIGH GRADE KITCHEN CABINETS

COMPARISON OF OUR KITCHEN CABINETS WILL SHOW EVERY ONE LOWER IN PRICE THAN THE SAME QUALITY CAN BE PURCHASED ELSEWHERE. WE CHALLENGE ANY FIRM ON EARTH TO FURNISH KITCHEN CABINETS —THE EQUAL OF OURS IN QUALITY AT THE PRICE WE ASK—

THE KITCHEN CABINETS we display this season, for beauty of design, high quality of material, construction and finish and convenience of arrangement and extraordinary value are positively unequaled. The excellent features embodied in the design and construction of our kitchen cabinets are the result of practical experience and careful study. They supply the need for every article used in the kitchen. Each cabinet is provided with ample bin drawer and shelf space. You will find every kitchen cabinet from the cheapest to the highest priced is perfectly constructed from specially selected materials and extra well finished. You will find every kitchen cabinet we sell to be made of better material, better constructed and better finished, more lasting and in every way more satisfactory than kitchen cabinets turned out of the average factory and sold by the average retail dealer. The illustrations will give you some idea of the convenience of arrangement and general appearance, but they must be seen, examined and compared with kitchen cabinets that sell at much higher prices to understand and appreciate the wonderful values.

OUR DESIGNS are strictly up to date. They are the result of the most careful and painstaking efforts. We offer you the same advantage of selection as you can find in any of the largest furniture stores in the cities with the added convenience of making your selection in your own home. The excellent practical features embodied in these splendid kitchen cabinets will be readily recognized by every housekeeper. While it is impossible for any illustration to bring out the beauty of design, the color, or the handsome smooth carvings, yet by a careful reading of the descriptions and close examination of the illustrations, which are exact reproductions of the photograph of the article, you can form a correct idea of the design.

THE WONDERFUL UTILITY of all of these splendid high grade Kitchen Cabinets will be readily recognized. A place is provided for everything used in the kitchen. Everything needed for the preparation of the meal is within easy reach of the busy housewife.

THE FINISH. The finish is a light natural color. The surface is perfectly sawed and smooth and the varnish coating brings out the beautiful natural grain of the wood.

READ WHAT WE SAY ABOUT OUR KITCHEN CABINETS ON PRECEDING PAGE.

Our Big Bargain Cabinet

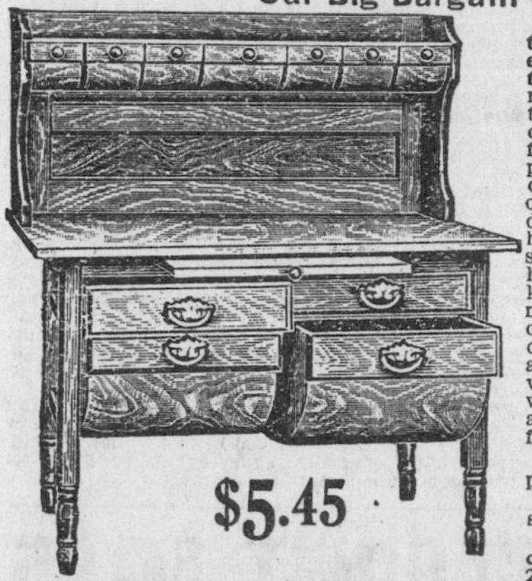

$5.45

No. 1K512 This Cabinet is an illustration of the wonderful saving to our customers, not only in this article, but in every other that we offer. Base is made of white maple, natural finish, with a white basswood table top. Size, 25x45 inches. Height of entire cabinet, 50 inches. It has two dustproof flour bins with wooden bottoms, two drawers partitioned for cutlery, and a removable carving and kneading board. Lower part of legs are detachable and placed inside drawers for convenience in shipping. Top has a double paneled back, a roomy top shelf, below which are seven drawers for holding various commodities used in the kitchen. We furnish the base of this cabinet without the top section if desired. Order one of our cabinets, place it beside any other cabinet offered at anywhere near our price, and if you do not find our cabinet double the value of the other, return it to us and we will cheerfully refund your purchase price and transportation charges. Shipped direct from factory in Southern Michigan.

Price, complete cabinet. Shipping weight, 135 pounds........ **$5.45**
Price, without top section, shipping weight, 95 pounds...... **3.65**

No. 1K511 We can furnish this Kitchen Cabinet without the top section, size, 25x44 inches. It is made of birch, natural finish. While we are confident that it will prove far superior in quality to any cabinet offered by any other dealer at the price, we do not recommend it. At the slight difference in price, order one of the better grade maple cabinets which you will find a far better investment and which difference in price is actually represented in the cost of material and labor. Shipping weight, 95 pounds. Price.......... **$2.95**

Kitchen Cabinet, Reduced from $7.95 to $6.98.

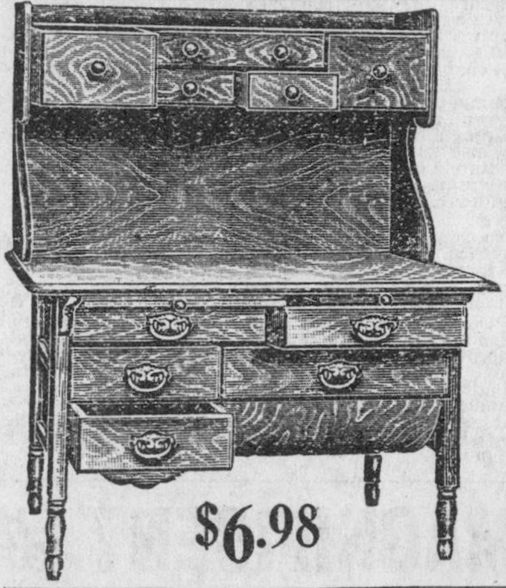

$6.98

No. 1K514 This handsome high grade Kitchen Cabinet is made of specially selected, thoroughly air seasoned and kiln dried hard white maple, natural finish. The table top on the base, size, 25x48 inches, is made of basswood, with moulded edges. Height entire cabinet, 55 inches. Base has large dustproof flour bin with wooden bottom, holding 60 pounds of flour, to the left are two roomy drawers for utensils and commodities. The two top drawers are for cutlery, linen, etc., fitted with two sliding chopping and kneading boards which can be taken out and placed on top for convenience in using. Top section has roomy top shelf, one large and two small drawers and two deep drawers for spice cans, packages, utensils, and various commodities used in every kitchen. All drawers and bins are perfect fitting and can be taken out for airing and cleaning. This cabinet cannot be bought in stores for less than $1?.00 to $12.00. Shipped direct from factory near Grand Rapids, Michigan.

Price, complete cabinet. Shipping weight, 185 pounds.... **$6.98**
Price, without top section. Shipping weight, 125 pounds.... **5.25**

$7.85 for This High Grade Kitchen Cabinet.

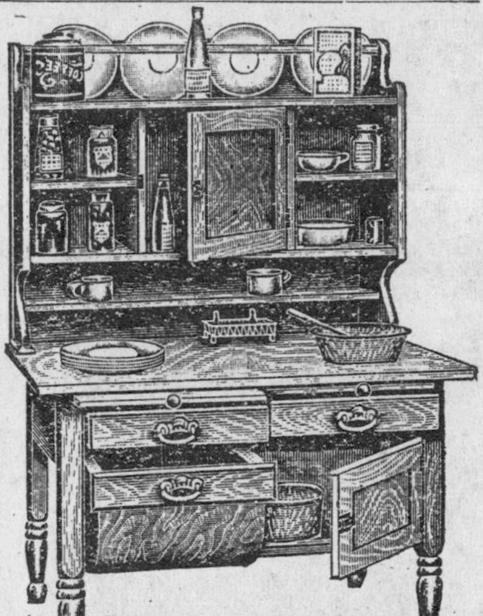

The articles displayed are not included with the cabinet.

No. 1K538 This Kitchen Cabinet at $7.85 is the equal of any cabinet offered by others at $12.00 to $13.00. Made of selected thoroughly seasoned hard white maple, natural finish, with a white basswood table top, with moulded edges on the base section. Size, 28x44 inches. Entire cabinet is 66 inches high. It has a large dustproof sliding bin which holds 70 pounds of flour, a spacious cupboard for pots, pans, etc., a cutlery drawer, linen drawer and a removable carving and kneading board finished on both sides. Top section has a roomy cupboard, four small shelves, a large shelf, and a combination shelf and plate rack on top. The construction is strictly first class throughout. Convenient and commodious arrangement will be fully appreciated by every housekeeper, as a place is provided for almost every article needed in the kitchen. The legs are detachable, the turned part being doweled into the frame posts which adds to the convenience in handling and using. Securely crated and shipped direct from factory near Grand Rapids, Mich. Our price for this kitchen cabinet represents a big saving to our customers.

Price, complete cabinet. Shipping weight, 155 pounds.... **$7.85**
Price, without top section. Shipping weight, 95 pounds.... **4.65**

This Splendid Kitchen Cabinet, $10.85.

No. 1K521 This High Grade Kitchen Cabinet is made of white maple, natural finish. Base has a 26x48-inch table top, with moulded edges, made of basswood for ease in cleaning. Entire cabinet is 60 inches high. Extra large bin has wooden bottom and will hold 60 pounds of flour. Note the five roomy drawers for linen, knives, forks and various utensils and commodities. Has a removable kneading and chopping board, smooth finished on both sides, which can be taken out and placed on top of the base for convenience in using. Top section has a broad shelf, below which are six drawers for sugar, spices, packages, etc., and a large cupboard for coffee cans, bottles, etc. Drawers and bins can be removed for cleaning and airing. The high quality of cabinet construction, together with the practical arrangement, makes this strictly high grade kitchen cabinet wonderful value at our price. Compare this kitchen cabinet with those generally sold by others at $16.00 to $18.00. Shipped direct from factory in Grand Rapids, Mich. Shipping weight, about 195 pounds.

Price, complete cabinet.. **$10.85**

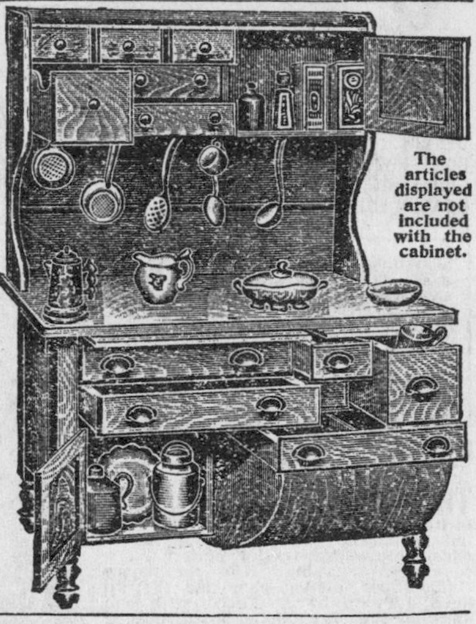

The articles displayed are not included with the cabinet.

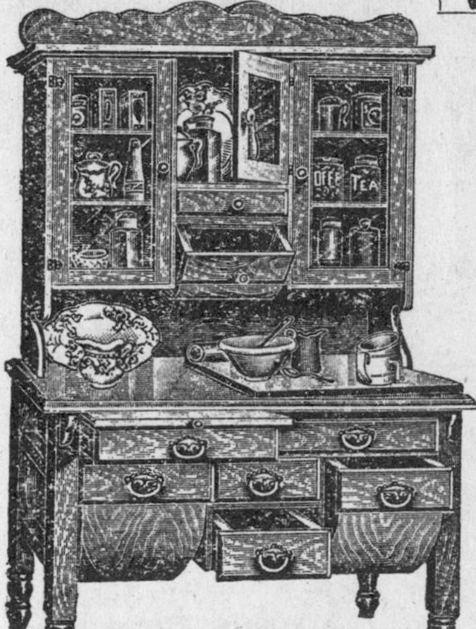

The articles displayed are not included with the cabinet.

No. 1K523 This high grade Kitchen Cabinet is a splendid example of convenience of arrangement in kitchen cabinet construction. It is made of specially selected hard white maple, thoroughly air seasoned and kiln dried, finished natural color. Entire height of cabinet, 72 inches. The base has a white wood top with moulded edges, size 25x50 inches. It has two dustproof flour bins with wood bottoms each holding 50 pounds of flour, between which are two deep drawers for linen and packages. Two long drawers above are convenient receptacles for cooking spoons, knives, forks and various other utensils used in every kitchen. Fitted with one kneading and one chopping board finished on both sides and can be removed and placed on top for convenience in using. The legs are detachable, the turned part being doweled into the square posts, which adds to the convenience and safety in handling and shipping. The top section combines excellence and beauty of design with a convenient and practical arrangement, which cannot be excelled. Cupboards with shelves and glass doors affording ample space for dishes, spice cans, coffee and tea canisters and a variety of packages and commodities within easy reach of the busy housewife. Note the tilting sugar bin in the center and spacious shelf below. Shipped direct from factory in Southern Michigan.

Price, as illustrated Shipping weight, 240 pounds.......... **$11.75**
Price, base only. Shipping weight, 130 pounds.......... **5.85**

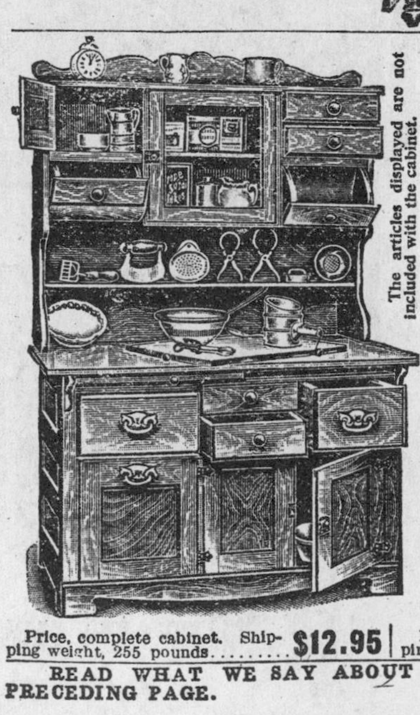

The articles displayed are not included with the cabinet.

This Magnificent High Grade Kitchen Cabinet Reduced from $13.45 to $12.95.

No. 1K525 Exceptionally attractive in design, strictly high grade in material, construction and finish, the equal of kitchen cabinets generally sold at $20.00 to $22.00. Made of specially selected, thoroughly air seasoned and kiln dried hard white maple, with a white wood platform on base with moulded edges. Entire height of cabinet, 70 inches; width of base, 25x50 inches. We call your special attention to the spacious and convenient arrangement of the compartments in the base. A roomy cupboard with double doors, to the left of which is a large flour bin which will hold 75 pounds of flour. In center two drawers for knives, forks, spoons, etc., either side of which is a spacious drawer for utensils, linen, etc. It has two removable chopping and kneading boards. In the top section is a cupboard with glass door and shelf, two tilting bins for sugar and salt, two drawers and a small cupboard. In the convenient and commodious arrangement, high quality of material and construction. This cabinet cannot be excelled. Remember the freight charges on a kitchen cabinet will amount to almost nothing as compared to what you will save in price when you buy from us. Comparison of our kitchen cabinets will show every one 30 to 40 per cent lower in price than the same quality can be bought elsewhere. Shipped direct from factory near Grand Rapids, Mich.

Price, complete cabinet. Shipping weight, 255 pounds.......... **$12.95**
Price, without top section. Shipping weight, 160 pounds.......... **$7.95**

READ WHAT WE SAY ABOUT OUR KITCHEN CABINETS ON PRECEDING PAGE.

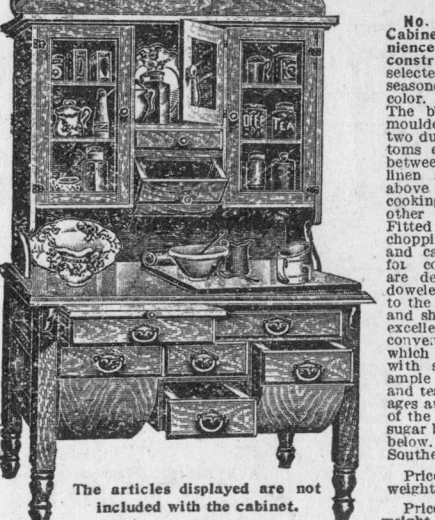

YOUR MONEY WILL BE IMMEDIATELY RETURNED TO YOU FOR ANY GOODS NOT PERFECTLY SATISFACTORY.

233

THE WILSON KITCHEN CABINETS

THE BEST KITCHEN CABINETS MADE REGARDLESS OF NAME, MAKE OR PRICE

THE KITCHEN AND THE KITCHEN CABINET. The kitchen is the workshop of the home. The work of the kitchen rightly understood and properly done is the most important of the entire household. System in the office, the store and the factory is a very valuable asset. Why is it not valuable in the kitchen? The housewife without the help of a kitchen cabinet with the cooking utensils and materials within easy reach, takes ten steps where one should suffice. The hours of drudgery will be turned into minutes of pleasure with the convenience of one of our Wilson Kitchen Cabinets. Our Wilson Kitchen Cabinet does for the woman and her kitchen what modern machinery and labor saving devices do for the bread winners of the family. Our Wilson Kitchen Cabinet holds, in a convenient and practical way, all the materials and utensils used in cooking. Any one of these cabinets is, in fact, a whole kitchen, occupying the floor space of a kitchen table, making the cooking easy, sanitary and economical, insuring the best results. Every workman does better work with good tools than with poor ones.

IN THESE FOUR WILSON CABINETS is attained the absolute perfection of kitchen cabinet construction. The newest and best ideas of arrangement have been carefully and conscientiously worked out. Embodied in their splendid detail of arrangement are practical suggestions from thousands of America's best housekeepers. Compact, roomy and convenient, a place for everything in the kitchen and everything always in place. We challenge any other firm on earth to furnish kitchen cabinets their equal in solidity of construction, elegance of design, completeness of detail, honesty of material, beauty of finish and painstaking workmanship. Made in Grand Rapids, Michigan, by one of the best, most favorably known and reliable makers of strictly high grade, dependable furniture. They are the perfect product of the best skilled workmanship from the highest grade materials obtainable at any price.

THE SATIN WALNUT used in the construction of these splendid kitchen cabinets is a thoroughly air seasoned and kiln dried Northern hardwood, specially adapted to kitchen cabinet construction, possessing perfect strength, solidity and a beautiful grain. The so called "satin walnut finish," offered by many other dealers, is but a poor imitation of the genuine satin walnut used in our Wilson Kitchen Cabinets.

It is a coarser, softer wood and does not possess the perfect wearing qualities and handsome close grain of genuine satin walnut. The genuine satin walnut used in our Wilson Kitchen Cabinets is specially selected from the choicest lumber, thoroughly tested; will not warp, check or split and will hold its color for a lifetime.

THE FINISH on these magnificent kitchen cabinets is a beautiful color with a rich high gloss golden brown. It has a velvety sheen which harmonizes with all surroundings and to produce which requires special care by the best skilled and experienced workmen. The surfaces are carefully rubbed and sanded until perfectly even and smooth, after which the best wood filler and special finishing coatings are applied. The resulting surface is as smooth as glass and when thoroughly dry and hardened will not be affected by the varying temperature and steam in the kitchen.

THE WORKMANSHIP. Each cabinet is so constructed that the top section can be detached from the base section for convenience and safety in handling and shipping. Every panel, bar, post, drawer side and drawer bottom, is framed and fitted in the most perfect manner. The doors are perfect fitting, the drawers and bins slide without friction or binding. THE BINS are made entirely of wood, the bottoms of three-ply stock and laid transversely, a big improvement over metal bottoms as they will not dent or corrode and flour will not mold in them. They can be easily removed for airing and cleaning.

THE TRIMMINGS are the best quality cast brass with French lacquer to prevent tarnishing. The doors have patent spring fasteners that work without friction.

IF THERE IS ANY DOUBT IN YOUR MIND of the superior super-extra quality of these splendid kitchen cabinets, of the purity and high quality of material, the perfection of construction or the beauty of finish, send us your order with the distinct understanding that if they are not all we claim them to be, the best in construction, the best in finish, the finest kitchen cabinet made, regardless of name, make or price; if, when you have received any one of them, examined, tested and compared it with any other cabinet made, you are not more than satisfied, your money will be immediately returned to you.

No. 1K530 The convenient and practical arrangement of this splendid Kitchen Cabinet will be readily recognized. It is 75 inches high. The base has a 27x44-inch top and is fitted with our patent drop bins, one to hold 60 pounds flour, the other partitioned for meal and sugar. Bins are supported by wheels attached to their sides and run on a track reducing the friction and permitting the bins to be easily moved when filled. Each bin can be readily taken out for cleaning and airing. Above bins are two roomy drawers for linen and cutlery. The two kneading and chopping boards can be easily removed and placed on top for convenience in using. Top section has a roomy china cabinet with glass paneled doors and spring fasteners. Below china compartment are two cupboards and two roomy shelves for packages, utensils and various commodities used in every kitchen. Bins, drawers and doors fitted with best quality cast brass handles. This cabinet holds in a convenient and practical way all the necessary commodities and cooking utensils used in the preparation of the meals. This splendid high grade kitchen cabinet we guarantee superior in quality of material, workmanship, finish and convenient arrangements to any kitchen cabinet generally offered by others at $20.00 to $25.00. Securely crated and shipped from factory in Grand Rapids, Michigan. Shipping weight, 300 pounds. Price.............. **$13.25**

Articles displayed are not included with the cabinet.

No 1K537 This splendid Kitchen Cabinet is 75 inches high. The varied assortment and arrangement of drawers, bins, china cabinets, shelves, etc., furnish a place for every utensil and commodity used in the kitchen. The base has a 27x44 inch top, a roomy cupboard for pots, pans, a large flour bin to hold 50 pounds of flour and two drawers for knives, forks, spoons and other kitchen cutlery. The kneading and chopping board can be taken out and placed on top when used. The top section has a china cabinet, with glass doors and spring fasteners. Note the convenient cupboard for corn starch, oatmeal and similar packages, the tilting bins for sugar and salt and pockets on the doors for small packages, etc. Below is a broad shelf for tea, spice and coffee cans and other necessary utensils. Drawers and bins easily removed for airing and cleaning. The doors perfectly fitted, the drawers and bins when filled, move without binding or friction. Roomy, convenient, sanitary, made of the best material, constructed and finished to last a lifetime, this magnificent labor saving kitchen cabinet will be fully appreciated by every housewife. A finer kitchen cabinet in every way than is generally offered by other dealers at $22.00 to $28.00. Shipped direct from factory in Grand Rapids, Mich. Shipping weight, 310 pounds. Price...... **$15.65**

Articles displayed are not included with the cabinet.

No. 1K543 The wonderful utility, convenience and roominess combined in this Kitchen Cabinet will be fully appreciated in every home. Entire cabinet, 76 inches high. The base has a 27x44-inch top and contains a large bin to hold 60 pounds of flour, above which is a cutlery drawer and removable kneading and chopping board. The roomy cupboard to the left with broad shelf will hold pots, pans, etc. The inside of the door fitted with an upper rack holding four spice cans and a lower rack for packages of various kinds. The top section has a large cupboard with broad shelf for dishes, packages and various commodities used in every kitchen. Note the drop bin for sugar in the center, each side of which are two roomy drawers. The inside of door on the right has an upper rack with three spice cans, below which is a rack with coffee and tea cans. The outer side of the door has a "Daily Reminder" and a "Card Index." The door on the left is fitted with two racks for packages, bottles, etc. All drawers and bins easily removed for convenience in cleaning. Every commodity used in the modern kitchen is provided for in this magnificent kitchen cabinet. A place for everything and everything in place. Shipped direct from factory in Grand Rapids, Mich. Shipping weight, 310 pounds. Price.......... **$17.45**

Articles displayed are not included with the cabinet.

No. 1K548 This is the most complete Kitchen Cabinet ever offered by any dealer. A place is provided for every utensil and commodity used in the modern up to date kitchen. Entire cabinet is 78 inches high. Base has a 27x44-inch top. The large drawer in the base has a bread and cake compartment with hinged metal covers, above which are two drawers for linen and cutlery. The inner side of cupboard door has a rack with four cereal cans, below which is a convenient shelf for packages, etc. The kneading and chopping board can be placed on top for convenience in using. We call your special attention to the top section with the china cabinet in the center, to the left of which is a bin to hold 50 pounds flour, with flour sifter beneath. On the right is a spacious cupboard and tilting sugar bin. The inside of door has a rack with tea and coffee cans, a "Daily Reminder" for recording the need of new supplies from the grocery, "A Card Index" and a rack with four spice cans. A splendid combination of drawers, shelves, bins, racks, etc., all easy of access, and by their location make this kitchen cabinet a whole kitchen in itself, reducing the labor of cooking and producing sanitary and economical results. This cabinet has no equal in the superior excellence of its material, workmanship and finish, and in its compact, convenient and orderly arrangement.

Shipped direct from factory in Grand Rapids, Michigan.

Shipping weight, 325 pounds. Price....... **$19.85**

Articles displayed not included with the cabinet.

$4.45 REFRIGERATORS AND ICE CHESTS $29.45

ODORLESS, SANITARY, CLEANABLE AND DURABLE. THE COLDEST REFRIGERATORS MADE AND EVERY DEGREE OF COLDNESS UTILIZED IN THE PERFECT PRESERVATION OF THE FOOD.

OUR REFRIGERATORS are made for us by the largest, best and most favorably known manufacturer of refrigerators in the United States. They are the result of years of valuable experience in refrigerator construction. In them is embodied every scientific principle and practical idea. We challenge any firm on earth to furnish a refrigerator the equal of ours in solidity, cleanliness, convenience and durability, a refrigerator that will use as small an amount of ice and produce as cold a temperature and every degree of this coldness utilized in the perfect preservation of the food. They save the ice, are easy to keep clean, they preserve everything entrusted to their care in the hottest weather, they produce a pure, germproof, dry, cold atmosphere; they are handsomely designed and scientifically and perfectly constructed and they will last a lifetime.

THE MATERIALS used in the construction of our refrigerators, have been selected after years of valuable experience, on account of their perfect adaptation to perfect refrigerator construction. Durability and strength, cleanliness and perfect insulation, are the qualities needed in the refrigerator materials. Refrigerators generally sold by other dealers frequently have serious defects in the material used, invariably cracking and breaking, failing to retain the cold, and offering shelter for dirt and impurities.

THE WOOD. The outside case of our refrigerator is made of the very best quality of northern ash and elm, the two best woods for outer case refrigerator construction, specially selected and thoroughly air seasoned and kiln dried and absolutely guaranteed not to warp, crack, check or shrink. The inner wood section of the case is made of thoroughly seasoned hardwood selected for its special adaptation to a cold temperature.

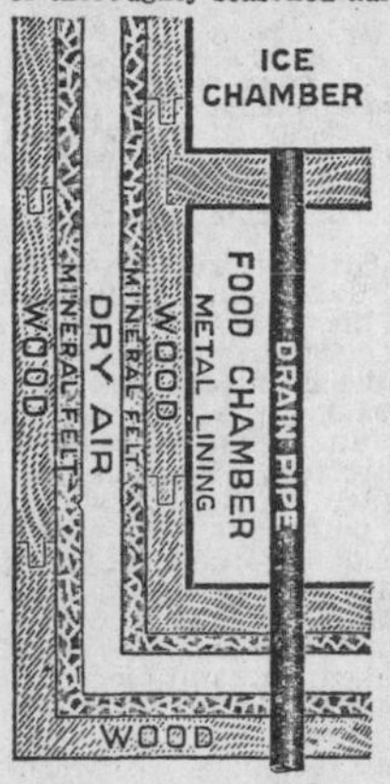

THE CONSTRUCTION. This illustration shows the construction of one of the walls of our refrigerators, a part of the floor of the ice chamber and the sanitary drain pipe, and the arrangement of the materials which enter into its construction. Each section of the wall is a perfect non-conductor of heat or cold, making it absolutely impossible for heat to penetrate or cold to escape. Each wall is made with an outside wood section, a thick sheet of mineral felt, a dry air space, another sheet of mineral felt, a section of wood and the metal lining. Note especially that two sections of mineral felt are used in the walls of our refrigerators and read what we say about mineral felt. Each wood section is framed and fitted in the most perfect manner. The tongue and groove joining is used, instead of miter joints, making it absolutely impossible for the joint to break loose. The zinc lining and galvanized steel lining are fastened securely to the inner wood casing, covering it entirely and rendering it impossible for the water to come in contact with the wood in any part of the chambers. There are no cracks, or crevices for the accumulation of dirt or impurities. The mineral felt is held in place against the wood section by strong cleats. Solidity, cleanliness and durability are combined with perfect sanitary and germproof inner chambers. A perfect dry cold air circulation and every degree of this coldness utilized in the perfect preservation of the food.

THE DRIP CUP as shown in the illustration, is made of cast steel and is hinged to the bottom of the refrigerator and held in place beneath the drain pipe. The water fills the cup and overflows into the pan below. The lower end of the drain pipe is immersed in this water in the cup and prevents air from the outside entering the refrigerator through the drain pipe.

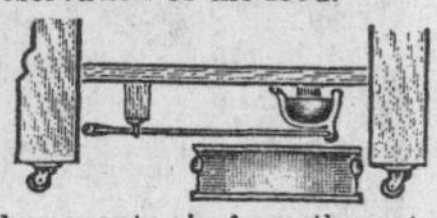

MINERAL FELT is absolutely the most perfect insulator for refrigerators. It can not settle in the walls, leaving the ice chamber unprotected; nor can it sift through the inner walls soiling the provision chamber, as does mineral wool or charcoal. It is a combination of mineral wool, asbestos and hair felt, compressed or "felted" into thick sheets, making a perfect insulator not only for the walls of the refrigerator, but the doors and lid as well, which can not be done with a filling in the lump or powdered form, such as mineral wool or charcoal. This is a very important feature, as the door or front of the refrigerator, being always exposed, requires the same insulation as the side walls of the case.

THE ICE CHAMBER is lined with the best quality galvanized steel, absolutely guaranteed not to corrode and cannot be broken or dented by the weight of the ice. We call your special attention to the solid metal ice rack, as shown in the illustration. It is made of heavy, galvanized, corrugated steel. Its construction permits a free circulation of the pure cold, dry air. The wonderful improvement over the wooden racks used by many other makers, will be readily recognized. Water soaked wood absorbs the odors from the provision chamber and interferes with the flow of water to the drainage pipe. Our solid metal rack is supported by bands of galvanized steel riveted to the under corrugated surface of the galvanized steel platform, gives greatest strength, durability and a much larger condensing surface than any other ice rack made.

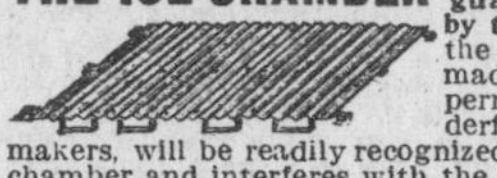

THE FOOD CHAMBER. The top, sides and bottom of the provision compartment are lined with the best quality zinc. The bottom (or floor) is on a level with the bottom of the doors making it easy to keep clean should anything be dropped or spilled thereon. The shelves are made of galvanized steel bars with a small open space between them through which the cold air currents pass freely downward and upward. Shelves made by most manufacturers have small perforated holes in the solid shelf, thereby impeding the circulation of the air and often stopping the circulation entirely when the food or food plates cover the holes. The cold, dry air circulation in our food chamber is rendered perfect by our galvanized steel bar shelves.

THE COLD DRY AIR. The air inside of our refrigerators is not damp and lifeless, but intensely cold, absolutely dry and constantly moving in duplex currents (as shown in the illustration below) from the ice downward, passing and repassing in and through the food, carrying all the impurities upward, depositing them on the ice, which, in melting, sends them out of the refrigerator through the sanitary drain pipe from which there can be no backward flow of moisture or odor. All within is clean, sweet and pure.

THE SAVING OF ICE. A refrigerator that wastes ice is dear at any price, no matter how cheap the first cost may be. We have given the question of insulation and ice saving careful study. In a comparative test made with several refrigerators made by other manufacturers, our refrigerator produced a lower temperature with an equal amount of ice, under the same conditions, proving in a practical way that our refrigerator is without question the best and most scientific in its insulation and ice saving properties. In other words, a 50-pound cake of ice in our refrigerator will last as long as a 75-pound cake in the ordinary refrigerator.

THE ICE CAPACITY. A cake of ice cut the exact dimensions of the ice chamber will weigh the full number of pounds given in the description of each of our refrigerators. We recommend the selection of a refrigerator with an ice capacity large enough to hold not only the amount of ice you may wish to use, but to accommodate the unmelted portion of the previous cake, as well as milk bottle, water bottle and other products generally placed beside the ice. For example, a refrigerator to accommodate a 50-pound ice cake and the small unmelted part of the previous cake should have a capacity of at least 65 pounds.

THE PRICES at which we offer each refrigerator in our line is on the basis of actual cost of material and labor in its production. We have carefully investigated, compared and tested the question of quality and price, and in every case have found that at the price we are able to quote on each and every refrigerator in our line, we are saving our customers 30 to 40 per cent as against the prices asked by other dealers for refrigerators of inferior quality. Send us your order for one of our high grade refrigerators, and when you have received it, examined it and tested it, you do not find that you have a refrigerator that is much better in every detail of material, construction and finish than you could possibly have purchased elsewhere, and at a big saving in price, we ask you to return it to us and we will refund the price, together with all transportation charges.

$15.85 THIS MAGNIFICENT PURITAN WHITE REFRIGERATOR

THE LEADER OF OUR REFRIGERATOR LINE, COMPACT, CONVENIENT AND A CAPACIOUS ICE AND FOOD CHAMBER.

THIS SPLENDID HIGH GRADE REFRIGERATOR is one of the most popular designs, tall and deep, it requires but little floor space, yet has generous shelf room in the food chamber and is adapted for use in every home and especially convenient for apartment houses or flats. The large door of the ice chamber permits easy filling of the compartment, while the top can be used as a sideboard shelf.

THE OUTSIDE CASE is made of specially selected, thoroughly air seasoned and kiln dried, northern ash, in a beautiful high gloss golden finish. The doors have thick, raised panels and are fitted with heavy solid brass hinges and locks.

THE LOCKS on all our refrigerators have adjustable strikes, permitting the door to be closed with a slam and drawing the door into an airtight joint. The strike runs on a screw and is readily and easily adjusted, so the door always closes air tight.

THE INTERIOR. The inner walls of the ice chamber and the ice rack are made of best quality heavy galvanized steel.

THE LINING of the provision chamber, the shelves and drain pipe, are enameled with a pure white sanitary odorless enamel, a mineral compound containing no white lead, oil or turpentine. It is applied in three coats, each coat thoroughly baked and hardened in ovens under a high temperature, and after cooling, a coating of white shellac is applied, which gives it a high glossy finish and can be cleaned with warm water. Many other manufacturers use ordinary white enamel, containing white lead, turpentine, oils and other poisonous ingredients, which are foul smelling and unsanitary. We absolutely guarantee our white enamel to be odorless. It cannot taint the food and gives always a clean sanitary, snowy white interior.

THE PRICE at which we offer this strictly high grade refrigerator represents a saving to our customers of fully 30 to 40 per cent as against the price generally asked for similar refrigerators by other dealers. Send us your order for one of these magnificent refrigerators, place it in your home, compare it with any refrigerator offered by any other dealer, and if you are not perfectly satisfied in every respect and have saved considerable money, you may return it to us and we will immediately refund the purchase price, together with all transportation charges.

No.	Width, inches	Depth, inches	Height, inches	Ice Capacity, pounds	Shipping Weight, pounds	Price
1K592	28¾	20	53¾	65	175	$15.85
1K593	31⅛	21⅞	56⅛	100	210	18.20

The above prices are for these refrigerators at factory in Southern Michigan.

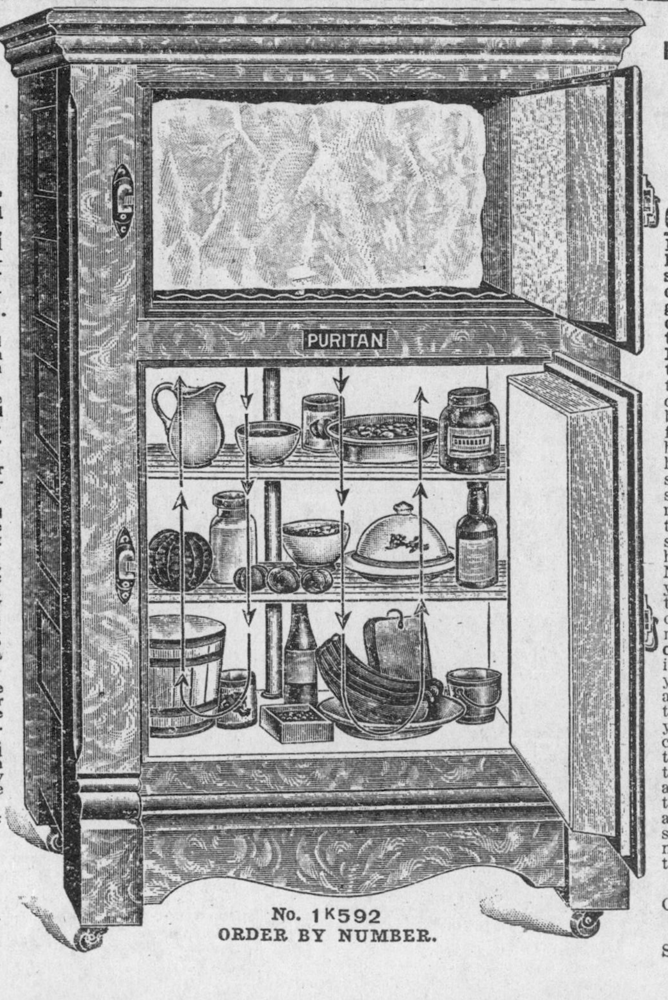

No. 1K592
ORDER BY NUMBER.

HOW WE ARE ABLE TO MAKE QUICK DELIVERY TO OUR CUSTOMERS IN THE WEST AND NORTHWEST ON REFRIGERATOR No. 1K592

OUR SALES on this magnificent high grade Puritan Refrigerator, No. 1K592, have grown so large from every section of the country that, in order that we may be able to get one of these splendid and deservedly popular refrigerators to our customers in the West and Northwest in a day or two from the date we receive your order, to insure its reaching you in perfect condition, to remove the liability of breakage or damage and reduce the freight charges to the smallest possible amount, we have arranged warehouse facilities at St. Paul, Minnesota and Kansas City, Missouri. We ship this refrigerator in solid car lots, receiving from the railroad company the very lowest carload freight rates, so that when we receive your order here in Chicago for this refrigerator, No. 1K592, we immediately send your order by special mail delivery to the warehouse nearest you and order the refrigerator shipped to your railroad station on your order **at once.** It will leave the warehouse in perfect condition, and will reach you in a few hours to a day or two at the most from the time it leaves the warehouse, and when you get it you will need to pay the small freight charges for the short distance from the warehouse to your railroad station. The total cost of this refrigerator, No. 1K592, to our customers in the WEST and NORTHWEST, will amount to considerably less than if shipped to you singly as one shipment from the factory in Michigan to your nearest railroad station.

Price at warehouse in Kansas City, Mo. $17.37

Price at warehouse in St. Paul, Minnesota..... 17.37

$4.45 ECONOMY REFRIGERATORS AND ICE CHESTS $17.95

At $4.45 to $17.95 we offer wonderful values in this line of Economy Refrigerators and Ice Chests. Solid cast brass trimmings, galvanized steel inside linings and shelves, removable drain pipe, patented drip cup and swinging front baseboard. Convenient in arrangement, they are excellent preservers of food with an economical consumption of ice. Constructed on the best scientific principles, with a perfect insulation and circulation, they combine utility, cleanliness, solidity and durability.

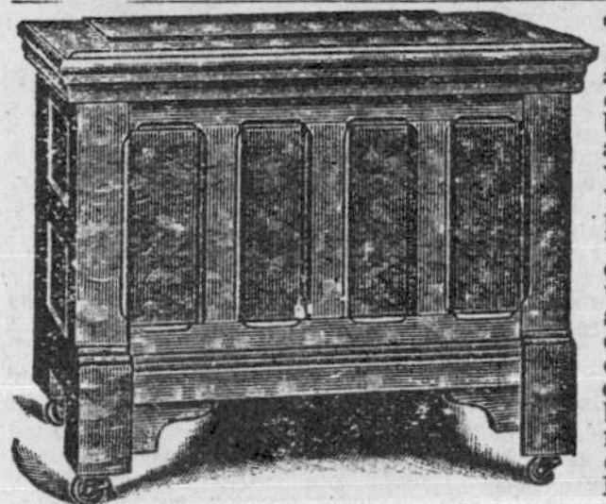

THIS ICE CHEST we furnish in five different sizes, all built with a thick outer case of thoroughly seasoned northern elm, high gloss golden finish. The inner walls are built in the same perfect manner as the refrigerators and are economical in the use of ice. They are lined with a good quality galvanized steel and have galvanized steel shelves and ice rack. They are equipped with drain pipe, drip cup and finished first class throughout. While an ice chest does not have the cold dry air circulation like our refrigerators, yet they are excellent preservers of food and will give satisfaction. We recommend the purchase of one of our high grade refrigerators because of the greater convenience in handling the food and ice, the cold dry air circulation which keeps the provision chambers perfectly dry, always cold and will preserve the food better with less consumption of ice. Securely crated and shipped direct from factory in Southern Michigan.

Catalogue No.	Width	Depth	Height	Shipping Weight	Price
1K551	24⅞ inches	16¾ inches	24½ inches	70 pounds	$ 4.45
1K553	31¾ inches	21⅛ inches	25¾ inches	93 pounds	6.75
1K555	36¾ inches	24¾ inches	30⅞ inches	130 pounds	9.45
1K556	40¾ inches	26¾ inches	33⅛ inches	185 pounds	11.25

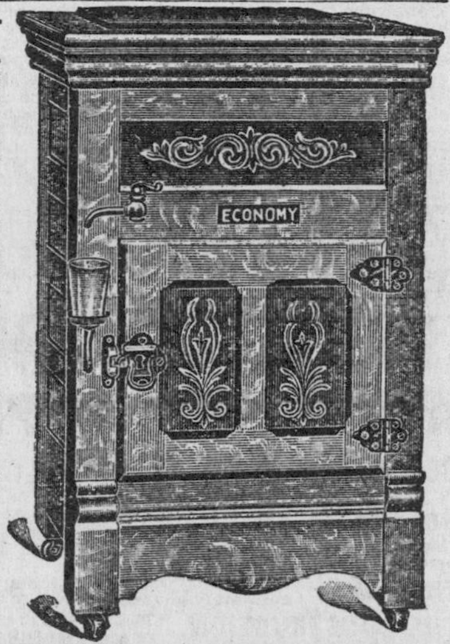

THIS IS A CONVENIENT, attractive and desirable refrigerator, substantially built and has our perfect insulated walls by which the ice is protected and the food preserved. The ice chamber is lined with galvanized steel and the bottom protected by a corrugated ice rack.

THE FOOD CHAMBER is lined with a good quality of galvanized steel and has double paneled door with heavy cast brass hinges and patent lock, with adjustable strike which allows the door to close with a slam, making an airtight joint; fitted with patent drain pipe and drip cup.

THE OUTER CASE is made of thoroughly seasoned northern elm, high gloss golden finish and having a swinging front baseboard. We use better material, the galvanized steel linings are heavier, the hardwood case better constructed, and the insulation and circulation of the cold dry air more perfect than the ordinary refrigerators sold by other dealers. The preservation of the food and the saving of ice will almost equal the value of the refrigerator in a single season.

SELECT ANY REFRIGERATOR from this line and send us your order, subject to ten days' trial, and we will guarantee the refrigerator which we will send you to give splendid satisfaction.

Catalogue No.	Width	Depth	Height	Ice Capacity	Shipping Weight	Price
1K560	24¾ inches	16⅛ inches	39¼ inches	35 pounds	100 pounds	$6.85
1K561	26⅞ inches	17⅞ inches	41¼ inches	45 pounds	110 pounds	8.75
1K562	27⅞ inches	18½ inches	43⅛ inches	60 pounds	125 pounds	9.65

We furnish No. 1K562 refrigerator with a porcelain lined water cooler, faucet and glass holder as shown in the illustration at $2.50 extra. The water cooler reduces the capacity of the ice chamber.

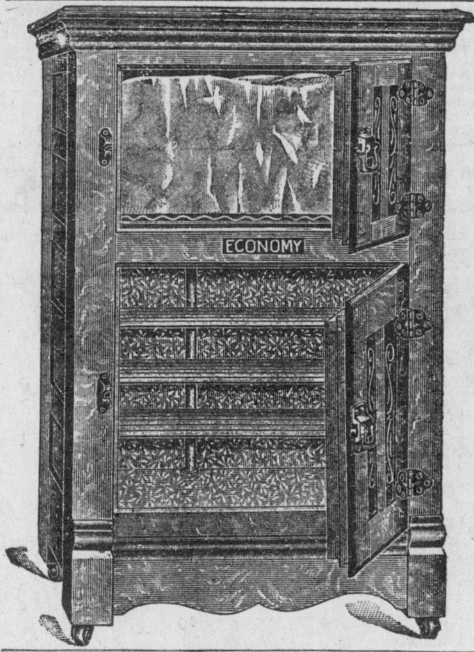

ACCESSIBLE, CLEANABLE, DURABLE.

THIS REGRIGERATOR requires but a small floor space, yet has roomy ice and provision chambers. An ice saver, a food saver and a space saver. The outer case is made of thoroughly seasoned northern elm, high gloss golden finish. Note the massive double paneled doors fitted with heavy cast brass hinges and our patent locks and strike. The doors can be closed with a slam and the joints are airtight. The ice chamber door opens from the front, a convenience in filling and chopping the ice. The floor of the food chamber is on a level with the bottom of the door, making it easy to clean. The ice and food chambers are lined with galvanized steel and fitted with drain pipe and drip cup. Has swing front baseboard.

THE INSULATED inner walls, the perfect system of dry air circulation, keep the provision chamber cold, dry and wholesome. An excellent preserver of the food with an economical consumption of ice; built to give superiority in general construction, convenience and refrigeration; securely crated and shipped from factory in Southern Michigan.

Catalogue No.	Width	Depth	Height	Ice Capacity	Shipping Weight	Price
1K571	24⅛ inches	18 inches	49¾ inches	50 pounds	120 pounds	$10.25
1K572	28 inches	19 inches	55½ inches	75 pounds	160 pounds	12.75

ECONOMY REFRIGERATOR $14.35

ECONOMY LARGE DOUBLE DOOR FAMILY REFRIGERATOR

COLD, DRY AND ROOMY. PERFECT INSULATION, PERFECT CIRCULATION AND PERFECT PRESERVATION OF THE FOOD.

THE REFRIGERATOR has an ice capacity of 100 pounds and is a splendid size for large families. It has beautifully carved northern elm case, in high gloss golden finish. Solid brass hinges and locks, and the best quality galvanized steel linings, galvanized ice rack and provision shelves. It has a removable waste pipe and our improved trap to prevent the entrance of warm air. A swinging front baseboard.

IT HAS OUR PERFECT SCIENTIFIC INSULATION, which makes it wonderfully economical for natural or artificial ice. The ice chamber is of ample capacity. The double doors to the provision chamber assist in maintaining a low temperature, as well as saving in ice, as when but one door is open at a time less warm air enters the refrigerators. Built with a view to convenience, economy and satisfactory service and every inch of space carefully utilized.

THIS REFRIGERATOR IS SURE TO PLEASE YOU.

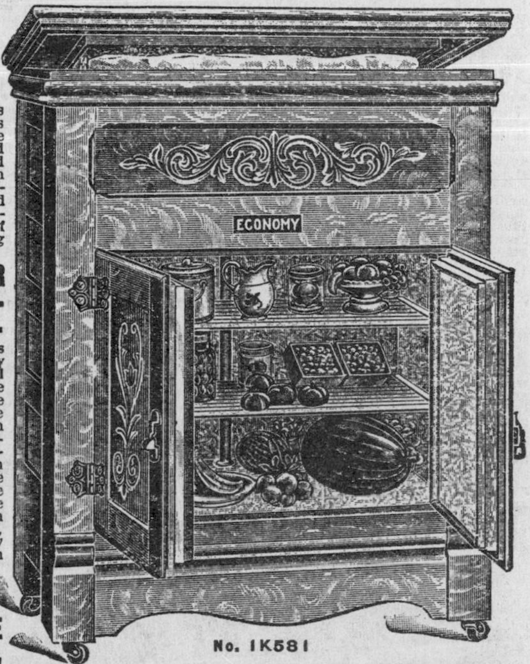

No. 1K581

It is solid and substantial in appearance and elegant in finish and the decorations add greatly to its appearance.

Catalogue No.	Width	Depth	Height	Ice Capacity	Shipping Weight	Price
1K581	35¾ inches	21⅛ inches	45¾ inches	100 pounds	165 pounds	$14.35

ECONOMY REFRIGERATOR $17.95

LARGE DOUBLE DOORS. CONVENIENCE, CLEANLINESS, COLDNESS.

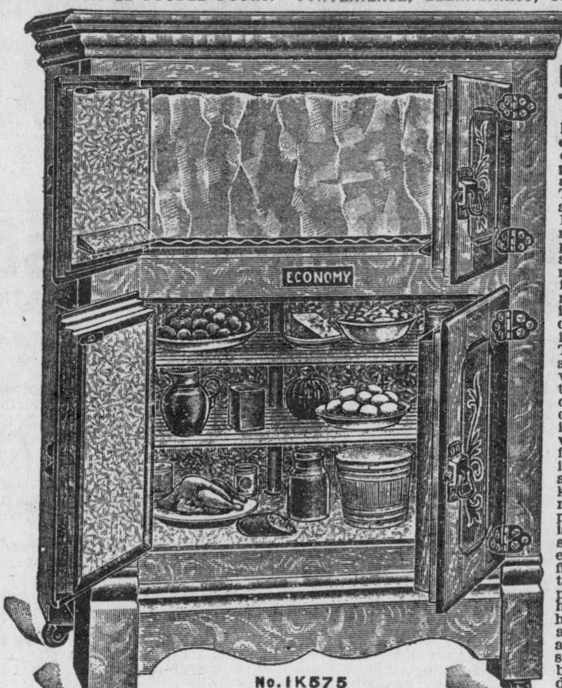

No. 1K575

DO NOT BUY A REFRIGERATOR TOO SMALL. It should be large enough to hold several days' supply of provisions and an ample supply of ice. This refrigerator has an ice capacity of 125 pounds and will readily hold a 100-pound piece of average dimensions with room to spare. The food chamber is large, roomy and convenient. The ice chamber doors in front make it easy of access. The perfectly insulated walls and galvanized steel linings, the perfect duplex circulation of the cold dry air from the ice chamber downward through the food chamber, passing and repassing in a constant flow, will keep provisions and milk fresh, sweet and pure. The outer case is made of thoroughly seasoned northern elm, high gloss golden finish. Doors have thick raised moulded panels and fitted with heavy cast brass hinges and patent adjustable locks and strikes. Has swing front baseboard, removable drain pipe and hinged drip cup. Shipped direct from factory in Southern Michigan.

Catalogue No.	Width	Depth	Height	Ice Capacity	Shipping Weight	Price
1K575	36¾ inches	19⅜ inches	50¾ inches	125 pounds	195 pounds	$17.95

$3.65 EXTENSION TABLES $29.45

SUBSTANTIAL REDUCTIONS IN PRICE.

AT $3.65 TO $29.45 WE OFFER A SPLENDID LINE OF EXTENSION TABLES.

High Grade in Material, Construction and Finish. Wonderful Saving in Price. Compare Our Goods. Compare Our Prices. Quality and Prices Compared, We Challenge all Competition.

THE FACTORIES devoted to the manufacture of our tables are factories that are thoroughly equipped with the latest type of machinery, employ only the highest class of workmen, and there are no factories in the country better equipped to turn out a higher quality of goods and at the same time at the very minimum of cost. Orders for plain oak tables from customers in the east and southeast will be filled direct from factory located in the east. Orders for plain oak tables from western customers will be shipped from our factory in Indiana. Orders for quarter sawed oak tables will be filled from factories in the East or Middle West. By so doing the cost of unnecessary handling is eliminated and the lowest possible freight charges are secured to all customers. Every table is shipped knocked down, carefully crated with the legs detached and accepted by the railroad company at the lowest freight rate.

ABOUT THE LOCATION OF OUR FACTORIES. The immense quantity of extension tables which we sell and the steadily increasing volume of our business enables us to make contracts with the largest, most favorably known and best makers of high grade extension tables whose factories are located in the Eastern, Northern, Southern and Middle Western parts of the United States. In most cases we have a factory located near your town, which means a very small freight charge, and hence a big saving to you which should be considered in making your selection and comparing our goods with those offered by any other dealer.

FACTORY INSPECTION. Thoroughly experienced and competent inspectors, men who are expert cabinetmakers and finishers, are employed at each of our factories, to carefully inspect every article. Every detail of the construction and finish is rigidly examined before the article is packed for shipment. Each article, after being thoroughly inspected as to material, construction and finish, is securely wrapped, burlapped or crated, whichever style of packing is best suited to the style of article, in order to insure safe delivery at destination in the same perfect condition. We guarantee safe delivery.

QUALITY AND PRICE GUARANTEE. We guarantee every article in this catalogue to be lower in price than the same quality of goods can be bought elsewhere. If any other house meets or cuts our prices on any article they do it at the expense of quality. If you do not find this is so by comparing the goods, or if you ever buy anything from us that is not lower in price than the same quality of goods can be bought from any other house, you are especially requested to return our goods at our expense and get your money back at once.

ABOUT FREIGHT CHARGES. The freight charges on an extension table will amount to next to nothing as compared with what you will save in price. The freight on an average extension table for a distance of 500 miles will amount to from 75 cents to $1.25. Don't let the item of freight charges prevent you from ordering, for we positively guarantee that after you have paid all freight charges you will find that you have saved considerable money by sending your order to us. The freight charges are exactly the same if paid by you as when paid by us, and we recommend that you pay the freight at your station when the goods arrive, as it will enable us to make more prompt delivery. If there is no agent at your station, do not fail to send enough money with your order to prepay the freight charges; otherwise we cannot make shipment without first writing you

for the money. Should you send more money than is required to pay the freight charges, the difference will be refunded to you. On pages 13 to 17 we give a table of freight rates which will enable you to calculate about what the freight will amount to.

OUR STYLES are up to date. The extension tables which we illustrate and describe on the following pages represent the newest and choicest designs of today. The selection represents the experience of years and careful study, and has been chosen with a view to giving our customers a line of tables as stylish in design, high grade in construction and finish as can be found anywhere, and to give them the privilege of sitting at home and selecting from our catalogue a table that is the equal in quality of any to be found in any store in the world, and at the same time give them the advantage of buying such a class of goods, usually sold at high prices, at the very low price of factory cost with but one small percentage of profit added.

THE WOOD used in the construction of our tables is especially selected, thoroughly air seasoned and kiln dried and absolutely guaranteed not to warp, check or shrink.

THE CONSTRUCTION of our tables is absolutely the best that modern machinery and skilled workmanship can produce. Every part and piece is thoroughly well made, inspected and carefully fitted before being passed to the finishing department. The legs are fastened to the top by a very simple, strong and durable device. They are easily detached for convenience in moving or shipping.

THE FINISH of our tables is strictly first class and only the best grade of wood filler and varnish is used that is obtainable. The top of every table is rubbed until perfectly even and smooth, which prevents the finish from being affected by hot plates or dishes which may be set upon it. The beauty of the finish must be seen to be fully appreciated. To obtain a smooth surface and better luster and a finish that will not craze, check or blister, facilities are employed by which each coat of this finish is allowed to thoroughly dry and harden before applying the succeeding one.

THE LEAVES of our dining room tables are made of plain oak, golden finish, but are not as highly finished as the tops, this being a rule adopted by all manufacturers for the reason that when in use they are covered by the tablecloth.

HOW TO ORDER. Fill out one of our regular order blanks or write your order on any plain paper; state the catalogue number of the goods you want; enclose our price with your order, sending us either a postoffice money order, an express money order, a bank draft or registered letter. If you live on a rural route, you can give your letter and the money to the rural carrier who will either write out a money order for you or give you a receipt for the money and get a money order at the postoffice and mail it in your letter. The goods will be sent to you with the understanding and agreement that if they do not prove perfectly satisfactory they can be returned to us at our expense of freight charges and we will promptly return your money including what you paid for freight. Our reputation for reliability and responsibility is so thoroughly established in every section of the country that no one can hesitate to send his order and his money with the order, since we agree that everything must prove perfectly satisfactory to you or we will return all your money and pay all freight charges and you will not be out one cent by the transaction

---

THIS SPLENDID SOLID OAK EXTENSION TABLE $6.65

A BIG SAVING IN PRICE

GENERALLY SOLD AT ALMOST DOUBLE THE PRICE WE ASK.

No. 1K626 ORDER BY NUMBER   42-INCH TOP

No. 1K626 This Extension Table is without question one of the greatest values ever offered, the equal of dining room tables generally sold by others at almost double the price we ask. Attractive in design, strictly dependable in material, construction and finish.

THE WOOD is specially selected, thoroughly air seasoned and kiln dried solid oak, absolutely guaranteed not to warp, check or shrink.

THE CONSTRUCTION. The top is 42 inches square when closed and can be extended to a convenient length as noted in the list below. It has a full boxed rim beautifully shaped with perfectly framed and mitered corners. The top is supported by five massive, beautifully turned and fluted legs, 4 inches thick, securely fastened to the top by a strong and durable device and can be readily detached for moving or shipping.

THE FINISH is a beautiful high gloss golden color which brings out perfectly the handsome grain of the wood. The top and legs are perfectly sanded and smoothed and the filler and varnish used to fill the pores, to preserve and protect it, are the best that can be obtained.

EACH TABLE is furnished with a set of good quality casters and a crate for the extra leaves and is securely packed in a strong crate to insure safe delivery at your railroad station.

SEND US YOUR ORDER for this splendid extension table with the distinct understanding that upon receiving it, if you are not more than satisfied with your purchase and that you have a table that cannot be bought elsewhere for less than one-third to one-half more than the price we ask, you can return the table to us and we will refund your money together with the freight charges. Shipped direct from factory in East or West according to location of customer thereby insuring the lowest possible freight charge.

Shipping weight	125 pounds	145 pounds	165 pounds	185 pounds
Size	6-foot	8-foot	10-foot	12-foot
Price	$6.65	$7.65	$8.65	$9.65

$6.95 FOR THIS HANDSOME SOLID OAK EXTENSION TABLE

MASSIVE ROPE TWIST CARVED LEGS. A VALUE THAT CAN NOT BE EQUALED ELSEWHERE FOR LESS THAN $10.00 TO $12.00

No. 1K628 This Magnificent Solid Oak Extension Table is exceptional value at the price. Handsome in design, strictly first class in construction and finish, generally sold in stores at $10.00 to $12.00.

THE WOOD is thoroughly seasoned oak, specially selected for its handsome grain effects. Guaranteed not to warp, check or shrink.

THE CONSTRUCTION throughout is strictly first class. It has a 42x42-inch top with moulded edges and wide boxed rim with perfectly mitered corners. Note the handsome rope turned and fluted legs, 4 inches thick, firmly fastened to the top.

THE FINISH is a beautiful high gloss golden color which brings out the handsome grain of the wood and smooth surface and bright luster. The extra leaves are carefully fitted into each other by dowel pins and a strong crate is furnished with each set of leaves.

OUR PRICE, $6.95 TO $9.95, according to length of table desired, means a big saving to our customers. In fact, we offer this table at a lower price than most dealers pay wholesale. Remember, quality in material, quality in construction and quality in finish of our extension tables is without doubt or question the best obtainable.

EVERY TABLE is shipped under our binding guarantee. We guarantee it to reach you in the same perfect condition it leaves us, and prove entirely satisfactory to you, otherwise you can return it to us at our expense of freight charges, and we will immediately return your money. The freight charges on this extension table will amount to next to nothing as compared to the great saving in price. Shipped direct from factory in East or West according to location of customer thereby insuring the lowest possible freight charge.

Shipping weight	125 pounds	145 pounds	165 pounds	85 pounds
Size	6-foot	8-foot	10-foot	12-foot
Price	$6.95	$7.95	$8.95	$9.95

No. 1K628 ORDER BY NUMBER   42-INCH TOP

THIS MASSIVE SOLID OAK PILLAR EXTENSION TABLE REDUCED IN PRICE TO $11.85.

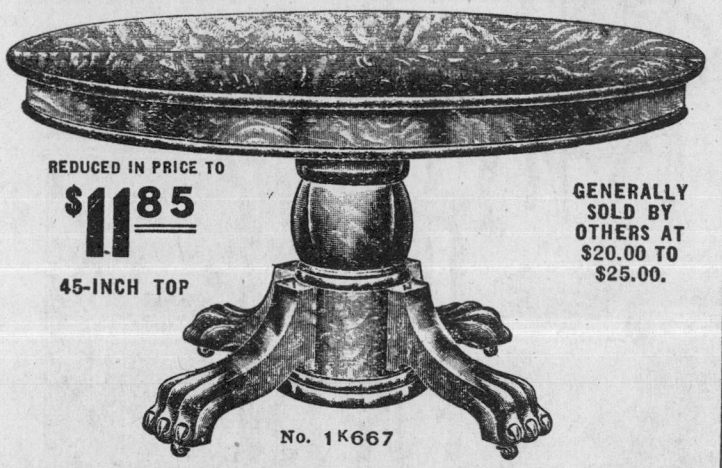

REDUCED IN PRICE TO
$11⁸⁵
45-INCH TOP

GENERALLY SOLD BY OTHERS AT $20.00 TO $25.00.

No. 1ᴷ667

No. 1ᴷ667 This strikingly handsome massive high grade solid oak pillar Extension Table is a splendid example of up to date design, high grade construction and finish. Made from thoroughly air seasoned specially selected stock, carefully inspected, perfectly framed and fitted. **The top** is 45 inches in diameter, has wide boxed rim and moulded edges. **The base** has a massive center pedestal 11 inches thick securely framed to the top and fitted with patent locking device to prevent spreading. The massive legs have deep smooth cut hand carved claw feet. The finish is a rich golden color which brings out the handsome flaky grain of the wood. Each table is furnished with a set of good quality casters, and a separate crate for the extra leaves. The price, $11.85 to $15.95, according to length of table desired represents a big saving to our customers. This splendid table cannot be purchased in retail stores for less than one-third to one-half more than the price we ask. Securely crated and shipped direct from factory in Eastern Ohio or Western Indiana, the point nearest your railroad station, thereby insuring the lowest possible freight charges.

Size	6-ft.	8-ft.	10-ft	12-ft.
Shipping weight	200 lbs.	220 lbs.	240 lbs.	260 lbs.
Price	$11.85	$13.25	$14.65	$15.95

THIS HANDSOME QUARTERED OAK EXTENSION TABLE REDUCED TO $18.45.

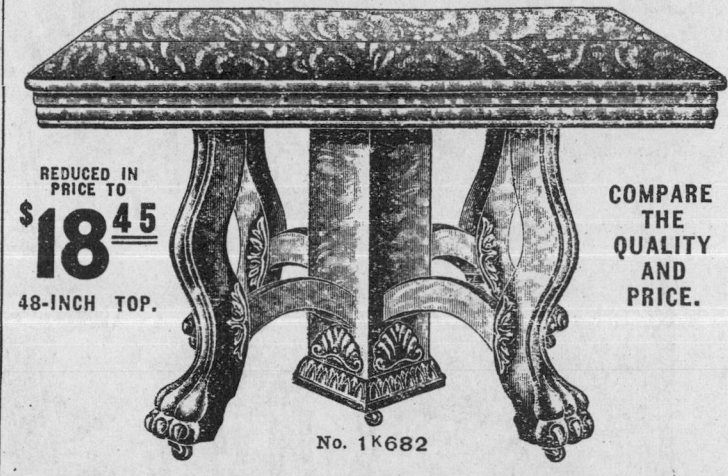

REDUCED IN PRICE TO
$18⁴⁵
48-INCH TOP.

COMPARE THE QUALITY AND PRICE.

No. 1ᴷ682

No. 1ᴷ682 This magnificent Extension Table will please those who like **massiveness of design,** combined with high quality of material, construction and finish. **The wood** is highly figured quarter sawed oak, thoroughly seasoned and kiln dried. **The finish** is a beautiful golden color, highly polished. **The top** is 48x48 inches and has moulded edges and wide box rim with mitered corners. **The base** consists of a heavy center pedestal and four massive shapely designed legs with genuine hand carved claw feet. The workmanship is strictly first class in every detail. Durability and strength are combined in this splendid table. Our price $18.45 to $21.45 according to length desired represents a saving to our customers of $10.00 to $12.00 as against the prices generally offered by other dealers. Remember our low prices are not made at the expense of quality, you will find this to be so by comparing the goods and the prices. We want you to be the judge of the quality and the price. Securely packed, the top and base in a separate crate. Shipped direct from factory in Indiana and guaranteed to reach you in perfect condition.

Size	8-ft.	10-ft.	12-ft.
Shipping weight	260 lbs.	280 lbs.	300 lbs.
Price	$18.45	$19.95	$21.45

MASSIVE SOLID OAK NON-DIVIDING CENTER PILLAR EXTENSION TABLES

EXCEPTIONALLY ATTRACTIVE AND MASSIVE IN DESIGN, HIGH GRADE IN CONSTRUCTION AND FINISH.
MADE BY ONE OF THE LARGEST AND MOST RELIABLE MAKERS OF DINING ROOM FURNITURE IN THE UNITED STATES.

THE WOOD used in the construction of these magnificent extension tables, is thoroughly air seasoned and kiln dried, specially selected for the beauty of its grain.

THE CENTER PILLAR of these massive extension tables, as shown in the illustrations below, is securely attached to a cross bar firmly fastened to the top. It does not divide in the center and remains stationary when the table is spread for extra length; a method of construction which combines solidity and durability with a strikingly handsome appearance.

THE MASSIVE LEGS have a perfect, broad curve and decorated with genuine, extra large massive claw feet. The legs are firmly fastened to the top and can be readily detached for convenience in shipping.

THE TOPS have neatly rounded and moulded edges and deep, full boxed rims perfectly framed and fitted.

THE FINISH is a beautiful golden color, highly polished, the grain of the wood being brought out in a perfect manner.

REDUCED IN PRICE TO
$12⁷⁵
45-INCH TOP.

No. 1ᴷ669

THIS PICTURE shows how the Non-Dividing Pillar Extension Tables illustrated above, look when extended. The solid center pedestal is bolted to the slides and remains stationary in the center of the table. This method of construction gives additional solidity and durability.

REDUCED IN PRICE TO
$15³⁵
48-INCH TOP.

No. 1ᴷ675

No. 1ᴷ669 This massive, high grade Extension Table is made of specially selected thoroughly air seasoned and kiln dried oak, highly polished golden finish. It has a 45-inch round top with moulded edges and with wide box rim, finished in a perfect imitation of highly figured flaky grained quarter sawed oak. The large non-dividing center pedestal is 11 inches in diameter. The massive shapely curved legs, size, 4x3¾ inches, have extra large, deep, smooth cut, finely executed, hand curved claw feet. The workmanship is strictly first class in every detail, each piece and part perfectly framed and fitted. Handsome and massive in design, beautiful in finish and represents at the price we ask a saving of 40 to 50 per cent to our customers as against the price asked by others. Securely crated and shipped knocked down from factory in Indiana.

Size	6-foot	8-foot	10-foot	12-foot
Shipping weight	170 lbs.	200 lbs.	230 lbs.	260 lbs.
Price	$12.75	$14.25	$15.75	$17.25

No. 1ᴷ675 This magnificent high grade Extension Table is strikingly handsome in design, strictly first class in material, construction and finish. A design that ranks with the best productions of the day and at the price we ask represents wonderful value. Made of specially selected, thoroughly air seasoned and kiln dried oak, highly polished golden finish. Large round top, 48 inches in diameter, is made of highly figured, flaky grained, quarter sawed oak and has moulded edge and full box rim. The large non-dividing center pedestal is 11 inches in diameter. Note the massive shapely curved legs, size, 6x3¼ inches, securely fastened to the top, with extra large, smooth cut, hand carved claw feet. Fitted with best quality casters. Securely crated and shipped, knocked down direct from factory in Ohio.

Size	6-foot	8-foot	10-foot	12-foot
Shipping weight	175 lbs.	205 lbs.	235 lbs.	265 lbs.
Price	$15.35	$17.15	$18.85	$20.65

9 piece Dining Room Suite

$62 35/~

French Design

No. 1K705

A STRIKINGLY HANDSOME NINE-PIECE DINING ROOM SUITE, exceptionally attractive in design, the equal of those generally offered by others at $90.00 to $100.00. A reproduction of a deservedly popular French design. Graceful and symmetrical outline, first class in material, construction and finish. This splendid dining room set ranks with the best productions of the day and at our price, $62.35, represents wonderful value which will be readily recognized when seen, examined and compared with sets offered in retail stores at almost double the price we ask.

THE WOOD is thoroughly air seasoned and kiln dried, specially selected for the quality of the grain. The workmanship is first class throughout, the doors perfect fitting, the drawers dovetailed on the sides and grooved on the bottoms, smooth running and non-binding. The ornamental carvings are hand made, clean cut and finely executed. The finish is a beautiful high gloss golden, with a rich lustrous sheen.

THE EXTENSION TABLE is made of solid oak, has a 48-inch top made of specially selected highly figured quarter sawed oak, with molded edge and wide box rim, supported by a massive non-dividing center pedestal 11 inches in diameter, as shown in illustration on page 389, and extends to 6-foot length. If 8-foot length is desired, add $1.75 to price of complete set. The large shapely curved legs have massive, genuine, smooth cut, hand carved claw feet.

No. 1K705 Price, complete set, nine pieces $62.35
Price for the set includes the 6-foot length extension table. If 8-foot length is desired, add $1.75 to price of set,

THE BUFFET SIDEBOARD, made of solid oak, finished in a perfect imitation of highly figured quarter sawed oak, is 56 inches high and has a 24x48-inch top, a large top drawer and three small drawers with full swell front, each side of which is a roomy cupboard, with glass doors with lattice panels. Mirror in top is best quality French bevel plate, size, 14x36 inches, above which is a spacious shelf, supported by shapely designed standards with hand carved claw feet to match the legs.

THE CHINA CABINET, made of solid oak, finished in a perfect imitation of highly figured quarter sawed oak, is 66 inches high, 44 inches wide and 15 inches deep. Has full swell double thick bent glass ends and front. Note the massive, shapely designed front posts and extra large, smooth cut, hand carved claw feet. Top section has best quality French bevel plate, size, 6x24 inches above which is a roomy shelf supported by curved standards, to match the base.

THE DINING ROOM CHAIRS are made of highly figured quarter sawed oak with extra large full box framed seats, securely blocked, mortised and joined by handsome turned stretchers. Upholstered in the best quality of genuine No. 1 black leather. The shapely curved legs have hand carved claw feet. Note the shapely designed top and center panels in the back. This dining room set is carefully packed and shipped direct from factory in Southern, Ohio. Shipping weight, about 550 lbs.

Colonial Dining Room Suite Complete

9 Pieces

$72 45/

No. 1K708

THIS MASSIVE DINING ROOM SET is an exact reproduction of an old Colonial design. It is made especially for us by one of the largest manufacturers of dining room furniture in the United States and is a design that combines simplicity of outline with excellent wearing qualities. An exceptionally popular style sold only in the most fashionable and exclusive city retail furniture stores at fancy high prices; in fact, you will find upon careful comparison that a Colonial dining room suite of this style cannot be bought in a retail store for less than $150.00 to $200.00. Our contract for a large quantity of these magnificent Colonial dining room sets enables us to offer them to our customers at a price below what your retail dealer can buy them at wholesale. This magnificent dining room set is without question the greatest value we have ever been able to offer to our customers and it must be seen and examined to be fully appreciated.

THE WOOD is thoroughly air seasoned and kiln dried, carefully selected for the quality of the grain.

THE WORKMANSHIP is first class throughout, the drawers dovetailed on the sides and grooved on the bottoms, and smooth running. The doors perfect fitting.

THE FINISH is a rich dark golden. Each piece has a perfect smoothly, glossy, transparent, highly hand polished surface attained by the use of only the best wood filler and varnish.

THE MASSIVE SIDEBOARD is made of solid oak, finished in a perfect imitation of highly figured quarter sawed golden oak, highly polished. It has a 24x50 inch top, two serpentine double curved top drawers, one of which

No. 1K708 Price, table only ...... 8-foot, $19.45; 10-foot... $21.25
Price for the set includes the 8-foot length extension table.

is lined for silverware, a large linen drawer and roomy cupboard. Note the massive round corner posts and the large hand carved claw feet. Mirror best quality French bevel plate, size, 18x36 inches. Broad top shelf supported by large columns, to match the base.

THE LARGE AND ROOMY CHINA CABINET is made of solid oak, finished in a perfect imitation highly figured flaky grained quarter sawed oak, highly polished. It is 72 inches high, 44 inches wide and 16 inches deep. Has full swell glass ends and front. Note the large front columns and massive, deep, smooth cut hand carved claw feet. Mirror in top ornament, size, 6x38 inches and mirror in top shelf, size, 10x36 inches, both best quality French bevel plate.

THE EXTENSION TABLE has a 48-inch highly figured quarter sawed oak top with molded edge and wide boxed rim, supported by a massive center pedestal 10 inches in diameter and four large columns 4 inches thick securely framed into a broad massive base with extra large hand carved claw feet and extends to 8-foot length. If 10-foot length is desired, add $1.75 to price of complete set. The base is finished in a perfect imitation of highly figured flaky grained quarter sawed oak to match the top. Highly polished.

THE CHAIRS are made of specially selected highly figured flaky grain quarter sawed oak. Seats are full box frame, securely mortised and joined and upholstered in the best quality of No. 1 genuine leather. Note especially the broad, shapely panel back and handsome front legs with hand carved claw feet. This dining room set is securely packed and shipped direct from factory in Southern Ohio. Shipping weight, about 600 pounds.

No. 1K708 Price, complete set, nine pieces $72.45
If 10-foot length is desired, add $1.75 to price of full set.

SIDEBOARDS

NEW AND UP TO DATE IN DESIGN

MATERIAL, WORKMANSHIP, FINISH — HIGH GRADE —

BIG REDUCTION IN PRICES

THE MOST WONDERFUL VALUES EVER OFFERED IN HIGH GRADE SIDEBOARDS AT $7.95 to $35.95

OUR SIDEBOARDS THIS SEASON, for beauty of design, high quality of construction and finish, for convenience in arrangement and for extraordinary value, are positively unequaled. They embody all the new ideas in sideboard construction, the designs are greatly improved over any previous season and every one represents the product of the most up to date and modern machinery, the best material to be obtained and are put together by the most skilled workmanship that money can buy. We have been able to constantly improve the quality and reduce the price; today we call more than ordinary attention to this magnificent line of sideboards, presented on this and the following pages, and do so with the assurance that we are in a position to furnish our customers greater values than were ever offered before, much better goods than they can secure from other dealers and all at prices about one-third less than goods of equal quality are sold in regular furniture stores. Whether you want a cheap sideboard or one of the best that money can buy you can be suited from these pages, and no matter which sideboard you select you may feel sure that you are saving one-third in price. Our entire line of sideboards, from the cheapest to the best, every sideboard we handle, is thoroughly well made from carefully selected material and extra well finished. You will find every sideboard we furnish to be of better material, better finish, better fitting, more lasting and in every way more satisfactory than those turned out from the average factory and sold by the average retail dealer. You will find our designs strictly up to date and, in fact, we offer you the same advantage in selection as if you were in one of the largest city furniture stores, with the difference that the price you pay us is fully one-third lower than the price the same quality sideboard would cost you in the city furniture store.

THE WOOD used in the construction of our sideboards is thoroughly air seasoned and kiln dried and specially selected for the beauty of its highly figured grain. Every panel, post and piece is the highest quality obtainable.

THE CONSTRUCTION of our sideboards is perfect in every detail. The best skilled workmanship and modern machinery are used in the construction of every sideboard in our line. The frame work is carefully mortised and joined, the drawers dovetailed on the sides and grooved on the backs and bottoms. The panels are built up transverse layers of specially selected highly figured stock which prevents warping or checking or shrinking. In fact, every part and piece is perfectly fitted and joined. The drawers work smoothly without friction. Each sideboard is the perfection of construction throughout and guaranteed no matter how severe the climatic changes and conditions.

THE FINISH on every sideboard is a rich dark golden color, which brings into strong relief the beautiful highly figured grain of the wood perfectly. The materials used in the finishing process are the best obtainable. Each coating, from the filler of the wood to the last coat of varnish, is given plenty of time to harden and dry before being polished and rubbed down and the result is a perfectly smooth glossy transparent polished surface that will not wear off in a short time, as ordinary finishes do, but will last a lifetime.

THE MIRRORS used in our sideboards are the very best quality a perfectly beveled edge and a perfect reflection. We do not use any cheap domestic plate mirrors, and no "seconds" or "shocks" or mirrors with hair line scratches are to be found in our sideboards.

FACTORY INSPECTION. Thoroughly experienced and competent inspectors, men who are expert cabinetmakers and finishers, are employed at each of our factories to carefully inspect every sideboard. Every detail of the construction and finish is rigidly examined before the article is packed for shipment. Each article, after being thoroughly inspected as to material, construction and finish, is securely wrapped, burlapped or crated, whichever style of packing is best suited to the style of article in order to insure safe delivery at destination in the same perfect condition. We guarantee safe delivery.

OUR GREAT VOLUME OF BUSINESS enables us to contract with the best furniture factories located in all parts of the United States, all of these factories frequently making the same article for us, so that customers living in the vicinity of the factory will have very much less freight to pay than would otherwise be possible. We call particular attention to the location of our factories and the points from which our sideboards are shipped.

THE CARVINGS on our sideboards are exceptionally attractive in design, being deep, smooth cut and finely executed. Not the cheap, coarse, rough made and carelessly finished carving found on sideboards made by most manufacturers.

THE TRIMMINGS are the best quality obtainable. The handles are made of genuine cast brass highly burnished and lacquered. Drawers fitted with locks and keys, and each piece has good quality casters.

$14 65 FOR THIS SIDEBOARD

This handsome, high grade, massive sideboard $14.65. Without question the best value ever offered by any dealer in a strictly high grade, hand carved, massive designed solid oak sideboard. A sideboard that sells in retail furniture stores at $22.00 to $25.00.

DESCRIPTION.

No. 1K915 This magnificent, high grade massive sideboard is 45 inches long by 22 inches wide, and is made of specially selected thoroughly air seasoned and kiln dried oak. High gloss golden finish. The double top drawers and large linen drawer below have double serpentine curved veneered quartered oak fronts. One of the top drawers is lined for silverware. The cupboard as shown in the illustration is large and roomy and fitted with double doors, ornamented with deep smooth cut carvings. Note the carved front claw feet. The handsome top has a roomy shelf, supported by shapely curved standards to match the legs and bracket shelves. Fitted with best quality French bevel plate mirror, size, 18x30 inches. The construction is strictly first class throughout, the frame work perfectly joined and the trimmings the best quality.

OUR PRICE, $14.65, for this magnificent Sideboard represents a saving to our customers of fully 40 per cent, as we are offering you this magnificent sideboard at a lower price than most dealers pay at wholesale. Order one of these splendid sideboards, compare it with any sideboard offered by any retail furniture store at $22.00 to $25.00 and if you do not find it made of better quality of material, higher grade in construction and finish, you may return it to us and we will immediately return your money together with transportation charges. This sideboard is securely packed to insure delivery in the same perfect condition as it leaves the factory.
No. 1K915 Price............(Shipping weight, 225 pounds),............**$14.65**

No. 1K915   Always order by Number.

ALL ORDERS FROM CUSTOMERS IN THE EAST will be filled from our factory in Eastern Pennsylvania. Orders from customers in the West, Middle West and South will be filled from factory in Indiana, the factory located nearest your railroad station, thereby insuring the lowest possible freight charges in every case.

No. 1K901 This Sideboard is made of thoroughly seasoned oak, high gloss golden finish. The base, 20x42 inches, has two top drawers, one lined for silverware. A large drawer underneath, suitable for table linen, etc. Has two cupboards at the bottom. Fitted with cast brass fancy knobs, handles and locks. The mirror is French bevel plate, 14x24 inches. This sideboard is handsomely ornamented with raised carvings. Fitted with best quality casters. Shipped direct from factory in Pennsylvania or Central Indiana. Exceptional value at the price we ask. Shipping weight, 150 pounds. Price...... **$7.95**

No. 1K905 This handsome Sideboard is made of solid oak, high gloss golden finish. The base is 22x44 inches and has double top drawers with swell fronts, one lined for silverware, a large linen drawer and roomy cupboard with double doors. Broad top shelf supported by shapely curved standards and bracket shelves. Mirror, best quality French bevel plate, size, 14x24 inches. Carvings hand made and finely executed. In fact, this is not a cheap sideboard, but a high grade sideboard at a low price and should be compared with sideboards sold at $14.00 to $15.00. Material, construction and finish first class. Securely packed and shipped direct from factory in Pennsylvania or Central Indiana. Shipping weight, about 160 pounds. Price................ **$9.85**

No. 1K906 This Sideboard is made of thoroughly air seasoned and kiln dried oak. High gloss, golden finish. The base has a 22x44-inch double top. It has two top drawers with serpentine fronts, one lined for silverware, a large linen drawer and cupboard with double doors below. Fitted with locks, cast brass handles and best quality casters. Mirror is best quality French bevel plate, size, 16x26 inches. The roomy top shelf is supported by neatly curved standards. Compare this sideboard with those sold by others at $18.00 to $20.00 and you will find it exceptional value at the price we ask. Shipped direct from factory in Central Indiana or Pennsylvania. Shipping weight, 200 pounds. Price...... **$10.85**

No. 1K907 This Sideboard is made of solid golden oak, high gloss finish. The base is 23 inches wide and 45 inches long. Has full swell front, containing two top drawers, one of which is lined for silverware, a roomy drawer and a linen cupboard below. Has 16x26-inch French bevel plate mirror. Decorated with hand made carvings finely executed. Fitted with locks, keys and best quality cast brass handles and casters. Carefully packed and shipped direct from factory in Pennsylvania or Central Indiana, thereby insuring lowest possible freight charges. Securely crated to insure safe delivery. Shipping weight, 175 pounds. Price.................. **$12.25**

No. 1K910 This Sideboard is made of thoroughly seasoned oak, high gloss golden finish. Base has a shaped double top, size 21x44 inches, in a perfect imitation of quarter sawed oak grain. One of the top drawers is lined for silverware. Entire front is richly figured, quarter sawed oak, hand carved claw feet. Mirror is best quality, French bevel plate, size 16x28 inches. Broad top shelf supported by handsome curved standards. Decorated with finely executed hand carvings. Fitted with locks, cast brass handles and best quality casters. Thoroughly well made throughout. Compare this sideboard with those offered by others at $20.00 to $25.00. Shipped direct from factory in Western Pennsylvania or Indiana. Shipping weight about 200 lbs. Price. **$13.25**

No. 1K912 This massive Sideboard is made of thoroughly air seasoned and kiln dried oak, high gloss golden finish. Height, 72 inches. Base has 45x22-inch shaped top with moulded edge and contains two swell front top drawers, one of which is lined for silverware, a large linen drawer and roomy cupboard fitted with locks, keys and best quality cast brass handles. Mirror best quality French bevel plate, size, 18 x 30 inches. Note especially the massive, shapely, curved front corner posts of the base with large, deep, smooth cut, hand carved claw feet. Broad top shelf supported by handsomely designed standards to match the corner posts. Strictly first class in material, construction and finish. Shipped direct from factory in Southern Ohio. Shipping weight, 200 pounds. Price................. **$14.35**

No. 1K915 This Sideboard is made of thoroughly seasoned oak, high gloss golden finish. Base has a 22x45-inch top, shaped to correspond to the double serpentine curved fronts of the drawers. One of the top drawers lined for silverware. Note the shapely French legs with hand carved claw feet. Has full paneled ends and back. Mirror best quality French bevel plate, size, 18x30 inches. The massive Colonial style standards supporting the broad top shelf have hand carved claw feet to match the base. Carvings hand made and finely executed. Thoroughly well made in every detail of construction. Shipped direct from factory in Ohio or Pennsylvania. Shipping weight, about 200 pounds. Price, **$14.65**

No. 1K921 This Sideboard is made of solid oak, thoroughly air seasoned and kiln dried. High gloss golden finish. Base, 24x48 inches; has three top drawers, center drawer lined for silverware; below which is a large linen drawer and spacious cupboard, with serpentine curved doors. Mirror best quality French plate, size, 18 x 30 inches. The top is decorated with two veneered quartered oak rolls, and clean, smooth cut hand made carvings. Best quality cast brass trimmings and casters. This sideboard should be compared with those offered in stores at $25.00 to $30.00. Shipped direct from factory in Central Indiana. Shipping weight, about 220 pounds. Price, **$15.65**

No. 1K923 This Sideboard is made of specially selected oak, with a perfect imitation of quartered oak grain, high gloss golden finish. Base has 24x48-inch top, three fullswellfront center drawers, one of which is lined for silverware, either side of which are spacious closets. Below is a large linen drawer. Supported by curved legs with hand carved claw feet. Mirror is best quality French bevel plate, size 18 x 36 inches. Broad top shelf supported by shapely veneered standards with hand carved claw feet to match the base. Fitted with locks, keys and best quality cast brass handles and casters. Shipped direct from factory in Ohio. Shipping weight, about 220 pounds. Price.................... **$16.75**

No. 1K924 This Sideboard is made of solid oak with a perfect imitation of quartered oak grain in a beautiful golden finish, polished. It has double top, size, 22x48 inches. One of the top drawers lined for silverware. All drawers have shaped fronts. Note the massive standards with cross banded veneering decorated with hand carved lion heads. Mirror, best quality of French bevel plate, 18x36 inches. Fitted with locks, cast brass handles and best quality of casters. Thoroughly well made in every detail of construction and finish. Shipped direct from factory near Grand Rapids, Mich., or Pennsylvania. Shipping weight, about 230 pounds. Price.. **$17.45**

No. 1K925 This Sideboard is made of selected quarter sawed oak with a polished golden finish. Base is 22x48 inches, has full paneled ends and back. It has three center drawers with full swell fronts, one lined for silverware. Note the spacious cupboards at the sides, large linen drawer below. Fitted with locks, keys and cast brass handles. Front posts have hand carved claw feet. Mirror is best quality French bevel plate, size, 18x32 inches. Decorated with ornamental carvings, hand made and finely executed. Construction and finish best grade throughout. Shipped direct from factory in Pennsylvania or Indiana. Shipping weight, about 230 pounds. Price. **$17.65**

No. 1K926 This Sideboard is made of thoroughly air seasoned and kiln dried solid oak, with highly figured quarter sawed oak front. Popular golden finish. Has a 22x48-inch double top, shaped to correspond with the serpentine curved front of the drawers. One upper drawer is lined for silverware. Lower part of base contains linen drawer and spacious cupboard with double doors. Best quality French bevel plate mirror, 18x32 inches. Best quality casters and cast brass knobs and handles. Shipped direct from our factory in Indiana or Pennsylvania, according to location of customer, thereby insuring lowest freight rates. Shipping weight, 250 pounds. Price............... **$17.75**

$8.75 CHINA CABINETS $32.25
STRICTLY FIRST CLASS IN MATERIAL, CONSTRUCTION AND FINISH.
NEW AND UP TO DATE IN DESIGN. A BIG SAVING IN PRICE.

OUR CHINA CABINETS from the lowest price to the highest price, as illustrated below, are made of thoroughly air seasoned and kiln dried oak. The wood is specially selected for the beautiful highly figured quality of the grain.

THE MATERIAL, WORKMANSHIP AND FINISH are strictly first class. The posts, panels, bars and doors perfectly framed and fitted. The doors are perfect in alignment and non-binding. The carvings deep smooth cut and finely executed. The shelves have grooves on the back edge for holding plates upright. The finish is a clear transparent golden color which brings out the grain of the wood and each piece has a smooth, glassy surface attained by the use of the best finishing materials obtainable.

QUALITY AND PRICE. Our low prices are not made at the expense of quality. Our prices are based on factory cost and the selling price in each instance represents a saving to our customers of fully 30 to 40 per cent as against the prices asked by other dealers. If you do not find this so by comparing our goods you are specially requested to return them to us and get your money back at once.

EXCEPTIONAL VALUE.

No. 1K1070 This Handsome China Cabinet is made of thoroughly seasoned and kiln dried quarter sawed oak in a golden finish. It is 64 inches high, 36 inches wide by 14 inches deep. Fitted with three grooved shelves. It has double thick bent glass ends and large glass door. Thoroughly well made in every detail. Ornamental in design, beautiful in finish. It must be seen to be appreciated. Shipped direct from factory in Southern Ohio or Northern Illinois. Shipping weight, 150 pounds. Price.......**$8.75**

The Chinaware shown is not included with this Cabinet

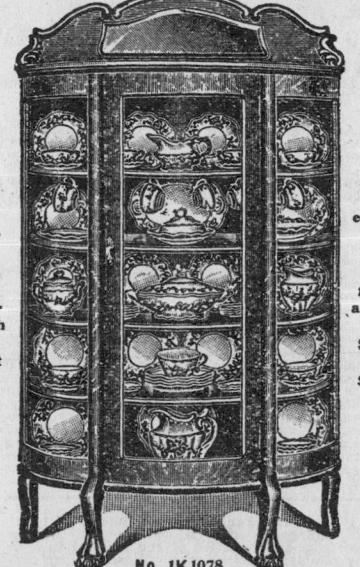

No. 1K1078

The equal of China Cabinets generally sold at $20.00 to $22.00

No. 1K1078 This China Cabinet has full swell double thick bent glass ends and front. The wood is thoroughly air seasoned and kiln dried, specially selected, highly figured quarter sawed oak, polished golden finish. Height, 67 inches; width, 36 inches; depth, 16 inches; mirror on top, 6x18 inches. Finished back, double grooved shelves. Handsome in design, high grade in construction, beautiful in wood and finish.
Price, as illustrated, at factory in Northern Illinois..$12.25
Price, with mirror in top decoration and back of
top shelf, at factory in Northern Illinois...........13.85
Price, with mirror in top decoration and back of
top shelf, at warehouse in Kansas City, Mo.........14.78
Price, with mirror in top decoration and back of
top shelf, at warehouse in St. Paul, Minn..........14.83

HOW WE ARE ABLE TO MAKE QUICK DELIVERY AND SAVE TIME AND FREIGHT CHARGES TO OUR CUSTOMERS.

Our sales on this magnificent China Cabinet No. 1K1078 have grown so large in every section of the country that in order to enable us to get one of these splendid China Cabinets to our customers in the West and Northwest in a day or two from the date we receive your order and to reduce the freight charges to the smallest possible amount, we have arranged warehouse facilities at Kansas City, Mo., and St. Paul, Minn., and we ship it to you from the warehouse nearest your railroad station. It will leave the warehouse in perfect condition and will reach you in a few hours to a day or two at the farthest from the time it leaves the warehouse, and when you get it you will need to pay only the small freight charge for the short distance from the warehouse to your railroad station. The total cost of this splendid China Cabinet to our customers in the West and Northwest will amount to considerably less than if shipped to them singly from the factory in Illinois to their nearest railroad station. Read what we say on page 398 about how we are able to make quick delivery and save time and freight charges to our customers.

No. 1K1081 This China Cabinet is made of solid oak thoroughly air seasoned and kiln dried, high gloss golden finish. Height, 66 inches; width, 41 inches; depth, 15 inches. Has double thick full swell bent glass ends and front. Note the massive shapely curved front posts and the large hand carved claw feet. Mirror in ornamental top, best quality French bevel plate, size, 6x24 inches. Shelves have moulded edges and grooved backs. The hand carved decorations are deep, smooth cut and perfectly executed. Best quality French plate mirror furnished for back of any shelf at $2.25 per shelf extra. Shipped direct from factory in Southern Ohio or Northern Illinois. Shipping weight, 180 pounds.
Price, mirror in top ornament only..**$13.45**
Price, mirror in top ornament and top shelf........**$15.45**

No. 1K1084 This splendid China Cabinet is made of solid oak thoroughly air seasoned and kiln dried, high gloss golden finish. Height, 66 inches; width, 44 inches; depth, 15 inches. Has full swell double thick bevel glass ends and front, full paneled back and grooved shelves with moulded edges. Note the massive shapely curved front posts and large hand carved claw feet. Top section has best quality French bevel plate mirror, size 6x24 inches, above which is a roomy shelf supported by handsome designed standards. Best quality French plate mirror furnished for back of any shelf for $2.25 per shelf extra. Sells in stores at $20.00 to $25.00. Shipped direct from factory in Southern Ohio or Northern Illinois. Shipping weight, 180 pounds.
Price, mirror in top ornament only, $14.65
Price, mirror in top ornament and top shelf.........**$16.90**

No. 1K1086 This handsome China Cabinet is made of thoroughly air seasoned and kiln dried highly figured quarter sawed golden oak, high gloss golden finish. It is 40 inches wide; 72 inches high; 14 inches deep. Full swell bent glass ends with top panels made of best quality leaded glass. Grooved shelves with rounded corners and finished back. Mirror in top decoration, size, 8x18 inches; best quality French plate. Note the ornamental bracket shelves on top. Strictly high grade throughout. French plate mirror furnished for back of any shelf, $2.25 extra. Sells in stores at $22.00 to $26.00. Shipped direct from factory in Northern Illinois. Shipping weight, about 175 pounds. Price, without leaded glass.....**$16.75**
Price, as illustrated, with leaded glass and mirror in top ornament........**$18.35**

No. 1K1089 This massive Colonial Design China Cabinet is made of specially selected, thoroughly air seasoned and kiln dried oak, in a perfect imitation of highly figured flaky grain quarter sawed oak, high gloss golden finish. Height, 72 inches; width, 44 inches; depth, 16 inches. Has double thick full swell bent glass ends and door. Note the massive round columns and the large deep, smooth cut hand carved claw feet. Mirror in top ornament, best quality French bevel plate. Size, 6x38 inches. Shelves have moulded edges and grooved backs. French plate mirror furnished for back of any shelf at $2.25 per shelf extra. An exact reproduction of an old Colonial design. Strictly first class in construction and finish. Shipped direct from factory in Southern Ohio. Shipping weight, 190 pounds. Price, mirror in top ornament and top shelf........**$20.95**

This China Cabinet, $19.85.

No. 1K1092 Exceptionally attractive new design, high grade China Cabinet made of highly figured quarter sawed golden oak, highly polished. Height, 72 inches; width, 44 inches. Has double thick bent glass ends and front. Note the hand carved and fluted columns each side of door, the French shaped hand carved claw feet and ornamental mirror frame with heavy top roll. Mirror in top ornament, best quality French bevel plate, size, 8½x38 inches. French plate mirror back any shelf, $2.25 per shelf. A cabinet that is perfect in construction, made of selected material and beautifully finished. Sells in retail furniture stores at $30.00 to $35.00. Shipped direct from factory in Northern Illinois. Shipping weight, about 215 pounds. Price, mirror in top ornament only.....$19.85
Price, as illustrated, two mirrors.....$22.35

Our $21.65 China Cabinet.

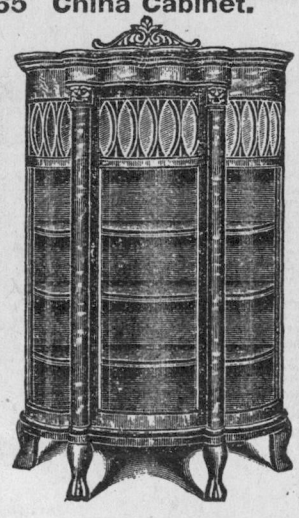

No. 1K1094 This China Cabinet must be seen to be fully appreciated. Made of specially selected thoroughly seasoned, highly figured quarter sawed oak, golden finish, highly polished. It is 43 inches wide; 70 inches high; 15 inches deep. Note the beautiful columns surmounted with hand carved Dragon Heads on each side of swell front door and the beautiful leaded glass panels in door and bent glass end. Fitted with grooved shelves with rounded edges. Double paneled finished back. French plate mirrors for back of any shelf, $2.25 per shelf. High grade in every detail of wood construction and finish. Sells in retail stores at $28.00 to $30.00. Shipped direct from factory in Northern Illinois. Shipping weight, about 175 lbs.
Price, without leaded glass.......$21.65
Price as illustrated........$24.95

No. 1K1099 This high grade China Cabinet is made of highly figured quarter sawed golden oak, specially selected for the beauty of the grain, highly polished. Height, 82 inches; width, 48 inches. Has double thick bent glass ends and front; hand carved canopy top; has two mirrors, 8x12 inches; center mirror, 8x24 inches, all best quality French bevel plate. Note the large veneered columns, hand carved claw feet. Front edge of base and top cross banded veneered to match the columns. French plate mirror back of any shelf, $2.50 per shelf extra. Shipped direct from factory in Northern Illinois. Shipping weight, about 255 pounds. Price, wood top rail without canopy......$24.35
Price, mirror in top only....$29.65
Price, as illustrated.....$32.25

$7⁹⁵ COMBINATION $27⁴⁵
BOOKCASES

BIG REDUCTION IN PRICES.

AT $7.95 TO $27.45 WE SHOW THE FOLLOWING HANDSOME HIGH GRADE, NEW STYLE COMBINATION BOOKCASES; THESE VALUES CANNOT BE EQUALED.

OUR LOW PRICES ARE NOT MADE AT THE EXPENSE OF QUALITY. WE GUARANTEE EVERY BOOKCASE LOWER IN PRICE THAN THE SAME QUALITY OF GOODS CAN BE BOUGHT ELSEWHERE.

No. 1K1113

OUR COMBINATION BOOKCASES this season, for beauty of design, high quality of construction and finish, and convenience in arrangement and for extraordinary value, are positively unequaled. They embody all the new ideas in bookcase construction, the designs are greatly improved over any previous season and every one represents the product of the most up to date and modern machinery, the best material to be obtained and put together by the best skilled workmanship that money can buy.

THE WOOD used in the construction of our combination bookcases is specially selected, highly figured oak. It is thoroughly air seasoned and kiln dried before being put through the factory. Great care is taken to get the highest quality and the choicest flaky grained lumber.

THE CONSTRUCTION of our combination bookcases is strictly high grade, the best that modern machinery and skilled workmanship can produce. The framework is carefully joined and mortised evenly together and grooves carefully fitted. The drawers are dovetailed on the sides and grooved on the backs and bottoms. The panels are made of transverse layers of highly figured, flaky grained oak, which prevents warping or shrinkage. Every part and piece is carefully and perfectly fitted. The drawers all work smoothly without friction, and the doors close without binding. The hand carving is finely executed and new and original in design.

THE MIRRORS used in our combination cases are the very best quality of genuine heavy thick French bevel plate, with a perfect beveled edge and a perfect reflection. We do not use any cheap, domestic plate mirrors.

$10.85 FOR THIS MAGNIFICENT NEW DESIGN high grade combination bookcase. Is made of specially selected, thoroughly air seasoned and kiln dried oak, high gloss golden finish, exceptionally attractive in design, high grade in construction and beautiful in finish; without question the most wonderful value ever offered. The equal of combination bookcases generally sold at $16.00 to $18.00. It stands 75 inches high and 38 inches wide. New design pattern shaped mirror is best quality French bevel plate, size 12x12 inches. Writing desk has drawer and pigeonholes for stationery, etc. Below desk is a roomy drawer and spacious cupboard; book compartment has full swell bent glass door and adjustable shelves to fit any size books. Note especially the ornamental head made carvings on the top and the bric-a-brac shelf below mirror. Fitted with locks, keys and best quality cast brass handles and casters. The workmanship is strictly first class throughout, doors and drawers perfectly fitted and entire frame extra well constructed, perfectly rigid and strong. Our price $10.85 at which we offer our customers this beautiful combination bookcase and writing desk, a price that is possible only by reason of our advantageous and extremely large contract direct with the manufacturer and because we add but the narrowest kind of a profit to the actual cost of material and labor. Shipping weight, 140 pounds.

HOW WE ARE ABLE TO MAKE QUICK DELIVERY of this bookcase and save time and freight charges to our customers. Our sales on this magnificent high grade combination bookcase have grown so large from every section of the country that, in order that we may be able to get one of these splendid and deservedly popular combination bookcases to our customers in the WEST and NORTHWEST in a day or two from the date we receive your order, to insure its reaching you in perfect condition, to remove the liability of breakage or damage and reduce the freight charges to the smallest possible amount, we have arranged warehouse facilities at St. Paul, Minn., and Kansas City, Mo. We ship this combination bookcase in solid car lots receiving from the railroad company the very lowest carload freight rates, so that when we receive your order here in Chicago for this combination bookcase, No. 1K1113, we immediately send your order by special mail delivery to the warehouse nearest you and order the combination bookcase shipped to your railroad station on your order at once. It will leave the warehouse in perfect condition and will reach you in a few hours to a day or two at the farthest from the time it leaves the warehouse, and when you get it you will need to pay the small freight charges for the short distance from the warehouse to your railroad station. The total cost of this combination bookcase to our customers in the WEST and NORTHWEST will amount to considerably less than if shipped to you singly as one shipment from the factory in Illinois to your nearest railroad station. Shipping weight, 140 pounds.

No. 1K1113 Price at factory in Northern Illinois...$10.85
Price at warehouse in Kansas City, Mo. 11.78
Price at warehouse in St. Paul, Minn. 11.75

No. 1K1101 This Combination Bookcase is made of thoroughly seasoned oak, high gloss golden finish. Height, 72 inches; width, 34 inches. Mirror is best quality French bevel plate, size, 10x12 inches. Writing desk has drawer, pigeonholes and pen rack. Below desk is a spacious cupboard and imitation drawer. Roomy book compartment has four adjustable shelves and double strength glass door. Best quality cast brass knobs and casters. Sells in retail stores at $11.00 to $12.00. Exceptional value at the price we ask. Shipped direct from factory in Northern Illinois. Shipping weight, 125 pounds. Price.... **$7.95**

No. 1K1103 This New Design Combination Bookcase and Writing Desk is made of solid oak, high gloss golden finish. Height, 72 inches; width, 36 inches. Pattern shaped mirror, size, 12x12 inches; is best quality thick French bevel plate. Note the bracket shelf below mirror and convenient arrangement of interior of writing desk. Below writing desk is a spacious compartment with imitation drawer. Book section has adjustable shelves to fit any size books and will hold 100 to 125 ordinary size books. Sells in stores at $15.00 to $16.00. Shipped direct from factory in Northern Illinois. Shipping weight, 130 pounds. Price...... **$9.45**

No. 1K1110 This Handsome Combination Bookcase and Writing Desk is made of quarter sawed oak with a high gloss golden finish. Height, 72 inches; width, 39 inches. Fitted with pattern shaped French bevel mirror, size, 12x12 inches. Inside of desk is provided with drawer and pigeonholes for envelopes, writing paper, etc. Below desk is a convenient drawer and roomy cupboard for books, magazines, newspapers, etc. Ornamented with smooth cut handsomely designed hand carvings. Adjustable shelves, to fit any size book, thoroughly seasoned. Fitted with locks, keys and best quality of cast brass handles and casters. Shipped direct from factory in Northern Illinois. Shipping weight, 130 pounds. Price.... **$10.65**

No. 1K1105 This Combination Bookcase and Writing Desk is made of selected oak with a high gloss golden finish. Height, 72 inches; width, 36 inches. Interior of desk is fitted with drawer and pigeonholes. Below desk is an imitation drawer and spacious cupboard. Book section has double thick glass door. Shelves adjustable to any size book. Fitted with best quality of French plate mirror, size, 12x12 inches. Note the ornamental deep smooth cut, hand carved decorations and French shaped front legs. Fitted with the best quality cast brass handles, locks and casters. Sells in retail stores at $12.00 to $14.00. Securely crated and shipped direct from factory in Northern Illinois. Shipping wt., 135 lbs. Price.... **$8.95**

No. 1K1106 Full Swell Bent Glass Door Combination Bookcase at $9.85, the equal of those offered in retail stores at $15.00 to $16.00. Made of thoroughly seasoned quarter sawed oak, except the ends, which are made of plain oak. High gloss golden finish; height, 72 inches; width, 37 inches. Writing desk has drawer, pigeonholes and pen rack. Book compartment fitted with four adjustable shelves and will hold 125 average size books. Mirror is best quality French bevel plate, size, 12x12 inches. Material, construction and finish first class. Fitted with locks, keys, cast brass handles and casters. Shipped direct from factory in Northern Illinois. Shipping weight, 130 pounds. Price...... **$9.85**

No. 1K1116 This Combination Bookcase and Writing Desk is made of quarter sawed oak in a high gloss golden finish. Height, 72 inches; width, 39 inches. Interior of desk is arranged for stationery, below which are three spacious drawers. Pattern shaped French bevel plate mirror, size, 12x14 inches. Shelves adjustable to any size book. Note the convenient shelf above mirror. Decorated with ornamental smooth cut hand carvings. High grade in construction, beautiful in wood and finish. Fitted with best quality of cast brass handles, locks and casters. Exceptional value at our price. Shipped direct from factory in Northern Illinois. Shipping weight, 135 pounds. Price..... **$12.45**

49c—HIGH GRADE PARLOR TABLES—$12.75
AT GREATLY REDUCED PRICES

AT 49c TO $12.75 WE SHOW WONDERFUL VALUES IN PARLOR AND LIBRARY TABLES, new and up to date in design, strictly first class in material, high grade in construction and finish, better in quality and lower in price than can be bought elsewhere.

Folding Table.
No. 1K1198 This folding table is made of wavy grained birch in a fine golden finish. The legs are hinged securely to the top, and when open are held in place with a strong flexible brace which extends entirely across the top. Size of top, 24x31 inches. Retails regularly at $2.25. Adapted for lunch, sewing, writing, card parties, etc. Shipping weight 20 pounds.
Price, golden birch..................$1.15

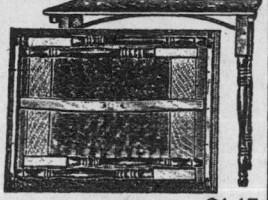

Parlor Stand.
No. 1K1200 This pretty parlor stand is an exceptionally useful piece of furniture, suitable for lamp or ornament. Made of oak, finished golden. Is 29 inches high with 12-inch top. Shipped knocked down, thereby greatly reducing the freight charges. Can be easily put together with screws, which are provided. Shipping weight, 15 pounds. Price..................49c

49c

No. 1K1202 This parlor table is made of solid oak, in a high gloss golden finish, or in birch or mahogany finish. It is 32 inches high and has a top 17x17 inches. The heavy, full boxed top is supported by handsome turned legs. Extra well constructed in every detail. It combines beauty, strength and durability, a combination of qualities hard to find in small parlor tables. Crated and shipped direct from our factory in Chicago. Shipping weight, 25 pounds.

	Golden Oak	Mahogany Finish
Price..	$1.54	$1.52

$1.54

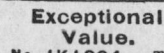

Exceptional Value.
No. 1K1204 This parlor table is made of solid oak, high gloss golden finish. Top is 24x24 inches, and has a mitered rim. Has roomy lower shelf securely fastened to high fancy turned legs. It is substantial in construction, attractive in design and is generally sold by others at $1.50 to $1.75. Exceptional value at the price we ask. Shipped knocked down. Shipping weight, 25 lbs.
Price...........$1.15

$1.15

No. 1K1207 This Parlor Table is made of thoroughly seasoned oak, high gloss golden finish. It has a 22x22-inch top with a moulding beneath the edge to prevent top from warping. The shapely curved French shaped legs are firmly dovetailed into the top and supported by a roomy shelf. Substantial in construction and exceptional value at the price we ask. Shipped knocked down from Chicago. Shipping weight, about 25 pounds. Price..... $1.39

$1.39

Our Leader.
A Genuine Quartered Oak Table for $1.68.
No. 1K1208 The best value ever offered in a parlor table at so low a price. Made of quarter sawed oak, high gloss golden finish. Top, 24 x 24 inches. Broad, shapely lower shelf, smoothly turned, fancy designed legs securely fastened into the top. A table that sells in retail stores for $2.25 to $2.50. Shipping weight, 30 lbs.
Price.......................$1.68

$1.68

No. 1K1210 This parlor table is made of quarter sawed oak, high gloss, golden finish. Fancy shaped top, size 24x24 in., has broad pendant apron, which prevents top from warping, polished. The shapely turned legs are securely fastened to the top and firmly attached to broad lower shelf. Sells at retail stores at $3.00 to $3.25. Shipping weight, 30 pounds.
Price..... $1.89

$1.89

No. 1K1217 This parlor table must be seen to be fully appreciated. Made of selected quarter sawed oak, golden finish or in birch in imitation of mahogany, polished. It has a double curved edge top, size, 24x24 inches, with embossed rim securely fastened with screws to prevent warping. Has French curved legs and full shaped lower shelf. Shipping weight, 30 pounds.

	Oak	Mahogany Finish
Price..	$2.26	$2.21

$2.26

No. 1K1212 This parlor table is made of quarter sawed golden oak or birch imitation mahogany finish, highly polished. The top is 24x24 inches with rounded edges and beautifully embossed rim. Securely framed beneath the top. The shapely turned legs are firmly attached to the top, strengthened by the spacious and neatly designed lower shelf. This table is generally sold in stores at $3.75 to $4.00. Shipping weight, 35 pounds.

	Quartered Oak	Mahogany Finish
Price brass claw feet	$2.49	$2.43
Price, wood feet	2.14	2.08

$2.49

No. 1K1214 This Parlor Table has a 24x24-inch shaped top, as shown in the illustration. Made of highly figured quartered golden oak or fine imitation mahogany finish, highly polished. Has neat beaded moulding underneath which is screwed to the top, thereby preventing it from warping; shaped lower shelf. Has turned legs fitted with brass claw feet with glass balls. This table sells in furniture stores at $3.50. Shipping weight, 25 lbs.

	Oak	Mahogany Finish
Price, brass claw feet.....	$2.68	$2.63

$2.68

Round Top Table.
No. 1K1218 This parlor table has a round top 24 inches in diameter with full boxed rim. It is made of highly figured quarter sawed oak, golden finish or birch, in a perfect imitation mahogany finish, highly polished. The roomy shaped lower shelf is supported by neatly turned legs. Strictly high grade in construction; attractive in design and finish. Shipping weight, 35 pounds.

	Quartered Oak	Mahogany Finish
Price, brass claw feet....	$2.85	$2.80
Price, wood feet	2.48	2.43

$2.85

No. 1K1219 This parlor table is made of thoroughly seasoned oak, high gloss, golden finish, or in birch, perfect imitation mahogany finish. Curved top and full box rim. Size top, 24x24 in. The shapely curved legs are securely framed into the top and given additional strength by the broad lower shelf. Material, construction and finish first class throughout. Sells in retail stores at $4.00. Shipping weight about 50 pounds.

	Golden Oak	Mahogany Finish
Price..................	$2.89	$2.85

$2.89

No. 1K1221 This Parlor or Library Table is made of solid golden oak, high gloss finish. Has full boxed top. Size, 22x30 inches, with shaped edges and spacious drawer. The smooth turned legs are firmly framed into the top. Note the broad convenient lower shelf. This table is specially adapted for the parlor, library or bedroom and is wonderful value at our price. Shipping weight, about 40 pounds.
Price, Golden Oak................$2.95

$2.95

No. 1K1222 This is one of the choicest patterns in a parlor table ever designed. The shapely curved 24x24-inch top, ornamented by broad shaped rim richly hand carved in a highly artistic manner. The spacious lower shelf is securely fastened to heavy rope shaped legs. We furnish it in specially selected quarter sawed oak, golden finish, or in choice grained birch in perfect imitation of mahogany, highly polished. Shipping weight, 35 pounds.

	Oak	Mahogany
Price, brass claw feet........	$3.10	$3.06
Price, wood feet.........	2.72	2.68

$3.10

No. 1K1224 The wood in this parlor table is selected quarter sawed golden oak or birch finished in perfect imitation of mahogany, highly polished. It has a 24x24-inch top with curved rounded edges and a carved box rim. The shapely French legs are securely fastened to the top with patent bolt construction. Compare this table with those sold by others at $4.50 to $5.00. Shipping weight, 35 pounds.
Price, Quartered Oak, $3.07; Mahogany Finish, $3.04

$3.07

No. 1K1226½ This parlor table is made of choice, specially selected highly figured flaky grained quarter sawed oak, golden finished, piano polished. Top, size 24x24 inches; has rounded edges and broad moulded rim. Spacious lower shelf. Handsome turned legs 2½ inches thick with genuine cast brass claw feet with glass balls. Strictly high grade in every detail. Should be compared with tables offered in retail stores at $4.75 to $5.50. Shipping weight, 35 pounds.
Price, quartered oak........$3.39

$3.39

HANDSOME IN DESIGN

PARLOR CABINETS

BIG REDUCTION IN PRICES

The Handsome New Design Up to Date Parlor Cabinets Which We Illustrate Below Are Made By the Largest and Best Known Manufacturer of High Grade Goods of This Kind in the United States.

THE WOOD used in the construction of our Parlor Cabinets is thoroughly air seasoned and kiln dried. Selected especially for the beauty of the grain, and will please the most exacting and cultivated taste.

THE CONSTRUCTION of our Parlor Cabinets is strictly high grade in every detail. Every joint and tenon carefully and perfectly fitted. The corners and edges are carefully rounded.

THE FINISH. The materials used in the finishing of our Parlor Cabinets are the very best grade obtainable, from the filler, hardwood oil, to the polishing coats of varnish. Special care is taken to bring out the beautiful grain of the wood. Plenty of time is given each coating and polishing process to harden and dry, in order to produce the best possible finish, a smooth surface and bright luster. A finish that will last a lifetime instead of the ordinary finish that fades away in a short time.

THE DESIGNS are new and strikingly handsome. They are graceful in outline and make an attractive addition to any parlor. No parlor is furnished complete without one of our new and handsome parlor cabinets. The illustration gives you but a slight idea of the handsome effect worked out in these cabinets.

THE PRICE at which we offer these beautiful cabinets is 40 to 50 per cent less than you can purchase similar cabinets in retail stores.

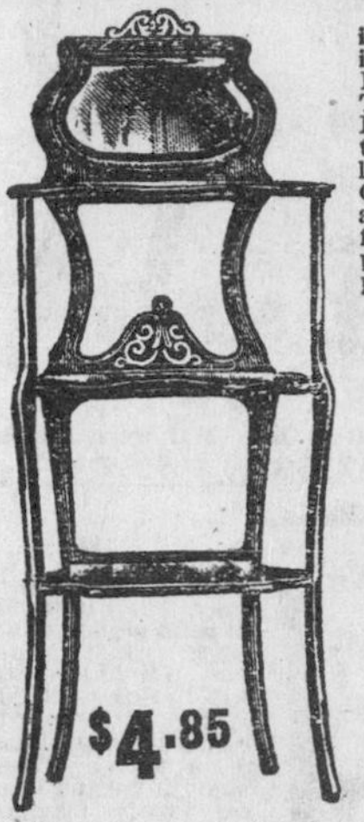

No. 1K1301 This Parlor Cabinet is made of select birch finished in perfect imitation of mahogany. Height, 55 inches; width, 22 inches. The ornamental pattern shaped French beveled plate mirror in the top is 8x14 inches. Has three shapely shelves. Piano polish finish. Others ask double the price we ask for this cabinet. Shipped direct from factory near Chicago. Shipping weight, crated, 50 pounds. Price **$4.85**

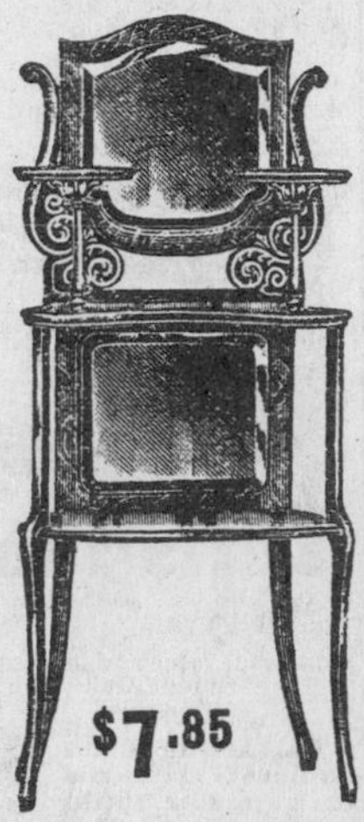

No. 1K1305 This handsome, artistic hand carved, piano polished Cabinet is 55 inches high, 24 inches wide; fitted with two genuine French beveled plate mirrors 14x14 inches. This cabinet has two roomy fancy shaped shelves securely fastened into the back and front legs. Note the ornamental, convenient bracket shelves on each side of the mirror. We call special attention to the perfect imitation mahogany polish finish on all our Parlor Cabinets, so closely resembling genuine mahogany that it is almost impossible to distinguish the difference. Strictly high grade in material and construction. Sell in retail stores at almost double the price we ask. Shipping weight, 50 pounds. Securely crated to insure safe delivery and shipped direct from factory near Chicago. Price **$7.85**

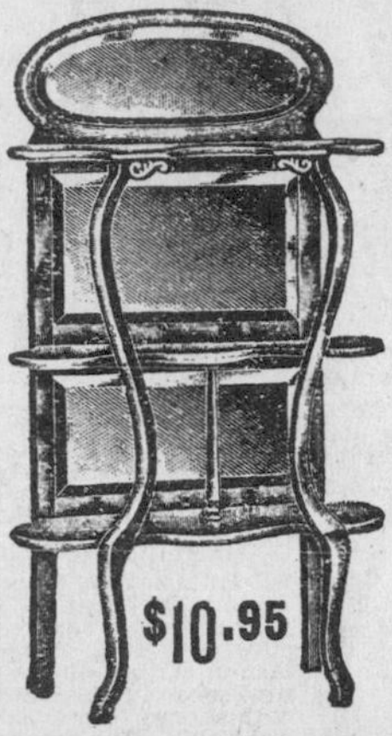

No. 1K1302 This is one of the choicest designs in Parlor Cabinets. No parlor is completely furnished if it does not contain a handsome parlor cabinet. Made of finest quality of selected birch, given the highest hand polished mahogany finish. It stands 54 inches high, 28 inches wide. The mirror in the ornamental top is 8x22 inches. The mirror beneath the top shelf is 12x20 inches. The mirror beneath the middle shelf is 10x20 inches. All the best quality of French beveled plate. Shipped direct from factory near Chicago. Shipping weight, 60 pounds.
Price, without mirror back of lower shelf **$9.65**
Full mirror back, three mirrors, as illustrated **$10.95**

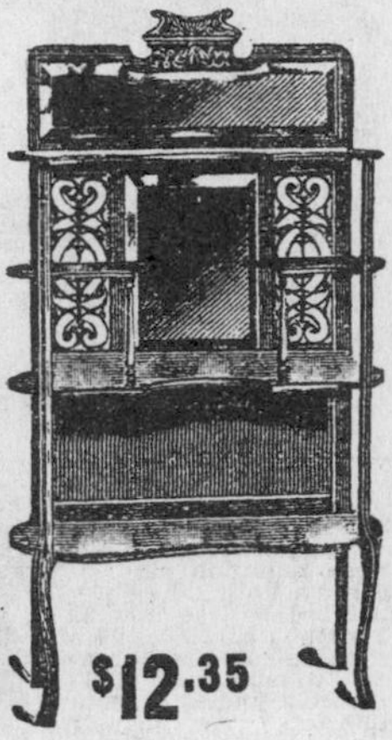

No. 1K1306 This Handsome and Attractive Parlor Cabinet is made of the finest birch with a rich mahogany finish, with pretty ornamental shelves and two bevel plate French mirrors, one 7x26 inches and one 12x16 inches; is 60 inches high and 32 inches wide; is graceful in outline and a welcome and beautiful addition to a parlor. No parlor is properly furnished if it does not include one of our new and handsome cabinets. The illustration will give you some idea of the beautiful effect worked out in this new cabinet. To fully appreciate the high quality of material, the beauty of outline and perfect imitation mahogany polish finish, you must see, examine and compare our Parlor Cabinets with those offered by others at one-third to one-half more than the price we ask. Shipping weight, 60 pounds. Shipped direct from factory near Chicago. Price.. **$12.35**

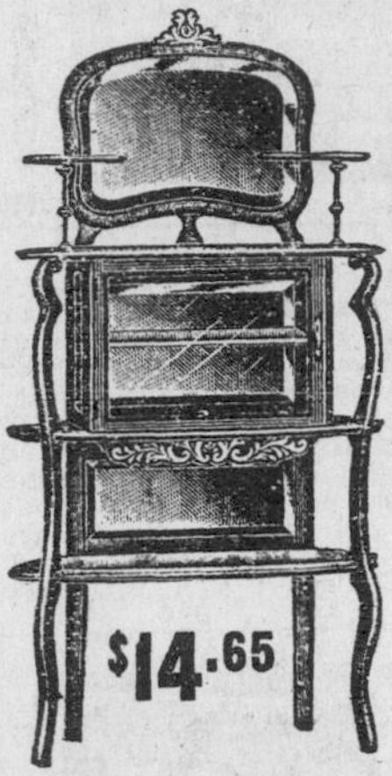

No. 1K1308 This Parlor Cabinet cannot be purchased in retail stores for less than $18.00 to $20.00. The wood is specially selected, thoroughly seasoned birch in a perfect imitation mahogany finish, highly polished. Height, 65 inches; width, 26 inches. Mirror on top is 14x14 inches. Mirror behind lower shelf, 8x14 inches. Enclosed cabinet in center has 12x14-inch mirror in back, double thick glass door and heavy plate glass shelf. All mirrors best quality French bevel plate. Handsome in design, perfect in construction, beautiful in finish. Shipped direct from factory near Chicago. Shipping weight, about 60 lbs.
Price, as illustrated.. **$14.65**

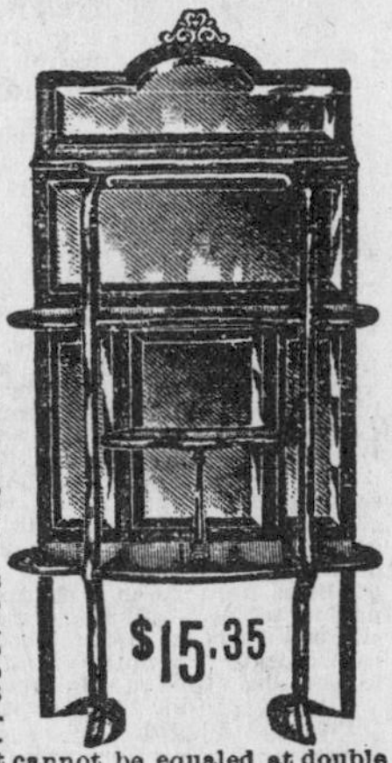

No. 1K1310 We offer this handsome new Parlor Cabinet as the equal of any parlor cabinet you can buy anywhere at $20.00 to $22.00. The wood is the finest wavy grained selected birch in the highest hand polished mahogany finish. It is 61 inches high, 32 inches wide. It has five French beveled plate mirrors of the best quality in the back. The mirror on the top is 8x24 inches; the mirror under the top shelf is 10x26 inches; the mirror in the center back of lower shelf is 18x21 inches; the two mirrors to the right and left of the mirror in the back of lower shelf are each 6x18 inches. For high quality of construction, beauty in finish and attractiveness of design this cabinet cannot be equaled at double the price. Thoroughly well packed and safe delivery guaranteed. Shipped direct from factory near Chicago. Shipping weight, 65 pounds.
Price, complete with five mirrors **$15.35**

HIGH GRADE MATERIAL

MUSIC CABINETS

AT GREATLY REDUCED PRICES

MUSIC CABINETS AND LADIES' DESKS. Our new and up to date line of Music Cabinets, which we illustrate on this page, are made by the largest, oldest and best known manufacturer of high grade goods of this kind in the United States. THE WOOD used in the construction is thoroughly air seasoned and kiln dried, selected especially for the beauty of its grain and will please the most exacting and cultivated taste. THE CONSTRUCTION is strictly high grade in every detail. Every joint and tenon carefully and perfectly fitted. THE FINISH.—This highly figured quarter sawed golden oak, the handsome birch and the rare and beautiful mahogany, are each given a high grade piano polish finish. No photograph or illustration can show the beautiful grain of this wood or the highly polished surface. THE DESIGNS are new, artistic and strikingly handsome, and at the prices we offer them represent a saving of 35 to 40 per cent to our customers.

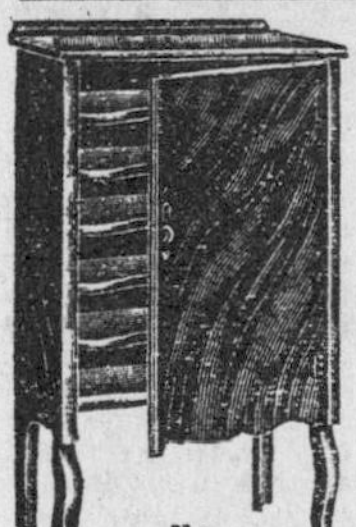

No. 1K1316

No. 1K1316 This is wonderful value in a High Grade Music Cabinet. We furnish it in solid golden oak with a highly figured quarter sawed oak front and top, or in selected birch in a perfect imitation of mahogany, polished like a piano. Height, 41 inches; width, 19 inches. High grade in every detail of construction. Shipped direct from factory in Chicago. Shipping weight, about 50 pounds.

	Oak	Mahogany Finish
Price..............	**$4.60**	**$4.65**

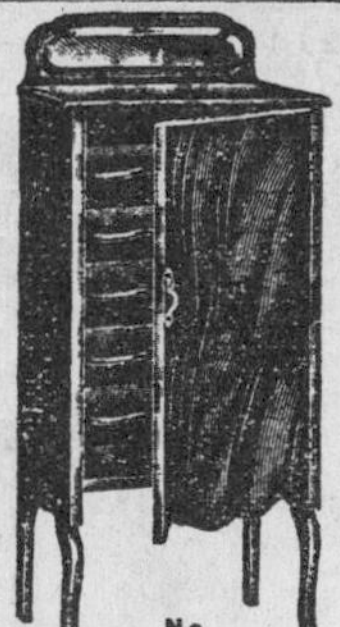

No. 1K1317

No. 1K1317 This Music Cabinet is made of thoroughly air seasoned and kiln dried birch in a perfect imitation of mahogany, polished like a piano. It stands 43 inches high and 19 inches wide. A spacious and convenient arrangement of shelves for music. Ornamented with a genuine French plate mirror; size, 4x16 inches. Thoroughly well made in every detail of construction and finish. A perfect match for mahogany piano. Shipped direct from factory in Chicago. Shipping weight, about 60 pounds.

	Oak	Mahogany Finish
Price, as illustrated	$6.15	$6.25
Price, wood top rail....	4.75	4.80

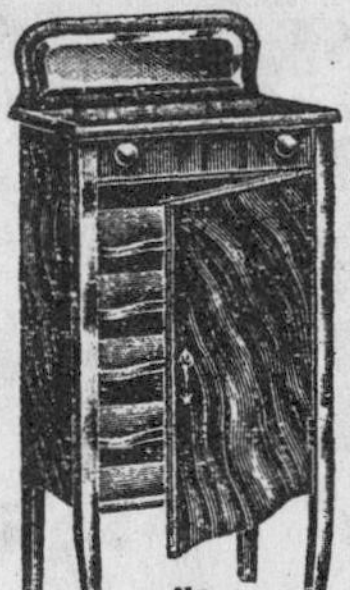

No. 1K1318

No. 1K1318 This Music Cabinet is 45 inches high, 19 inches wide. It is made in solid oak with a highly figured quarter sawed oak front and top, or in birch in a perfect imitation of mahogany, piano polished. The top is ornamented with a French plate mirror; size, 4x16 inches. It has a roomy drawer above the spacious cupboard. The wood, construction and finish strictly first class. Shipped direct from factory in Chicago. Shipping weight, about 55 pounds.

	Oak	Mahogany Finish
Price, as illustrated.......	$7.25	$7.15
Price, with wood top rail..	6.30	6.20

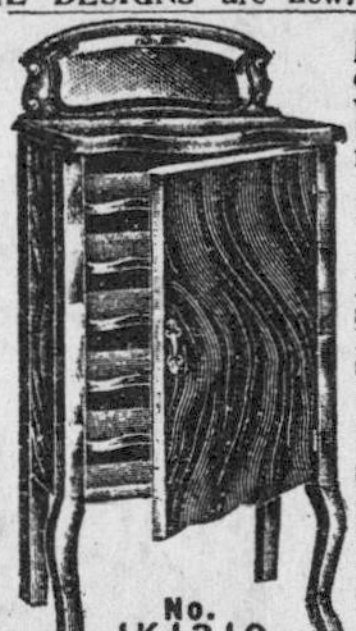

No. 1K1319

No. 1K1319 This Music Cabinet is made of highly figured black walnut or selected birch, with a genuine mahogany front and top. It stands 45 inches high, 19 inches wide. Pattern shape mirror is the best quality French beveled plate; size, 6x14 inches. Double curved French shaped front legs. Inside similar to No. 1K1317. Handsome in design, high grade in construction and has a polished finish like a piano. Shipped direct from factory in Chicago. Shipping weight, about 55 lbs.

	Walnut	Mahogany Finish
Price, as illustrated......	$9.95	$8.25
Price, wood top rail......	8.75	7.65

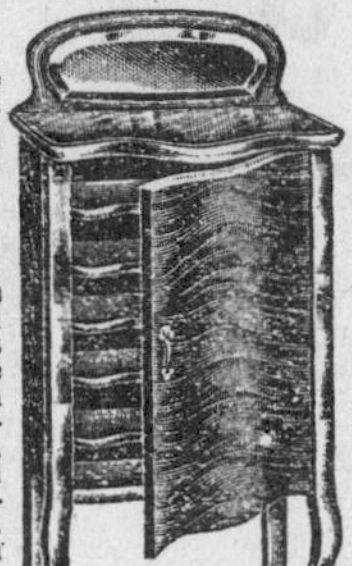

No. 1K1319½

No. 1K1319½ This Handsome Music Cabinet is made of highly figured quarter sawed oak or of selected birch in a perfect imitation of mahogany finish, highly polished. Height, 45 inches; width, 19 inches; depth, 16 inches. Door has full swell front fitted with lock, key and cast brass handle. Note the handsome French shaped front legs. Inside similar to No. 1K1317. Strictly high grade in material, construction and finish. Shipped direct from factory in Chicago. Shipping weight, about 60 pounds.

	Oak	Mahogany Finish
Price, as illustrated........	$9.25	$9.35
Price, wood top rail	8.35	8.45

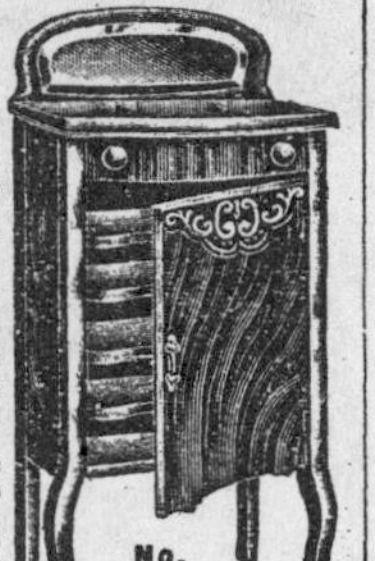

No. 1K1320

No. 1K1320 This Music Cabinet has a genuine mahogany front and top. Highly polished finish, a perfect match for mahogany piano. The height is 45 inches, the width 19 inches. It has double curved genuine French front legs. A full swell top drawer and a convenient arrangement of shelves inside, similar to No. 1K1317. The door is decorated with genuine hand carvings, finely executed. The ornamental mirror is the best quality French beveled plate; size, 6x16 inches. Shipped direct from factory in Chicago. Shipping weight, about 60 pounds.

	Oak	Mahogany Finish
Price, as illustrated....	$10.25	$10.65
Price wood top rail....	9.15	9.50

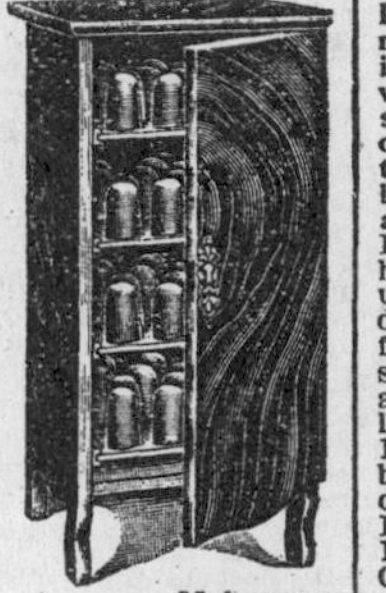

No. 1K1324 This Graphophone Record Cabinet, made of solid oak with front and top of highly figured quarter sawed oak, golden finish, or in birch, perfect imitation mahogany finish, highly polished. Inside has four sliding shelves with maple pegs for 56 records. We also furnish this cabinet with partitions for 130 discs 12 inches in diameter, as shown in illustration of No. 1K1326. Height, 34 inches; depth, 16 inches; width, 16 inches. Shipped direct from factory in Chicago. Shipping weight, 50 pounds.

	Oak	Mahogany Finish
Price, disc records	$5.65	$5.50
Price, cylinder records..	6.45	6.30

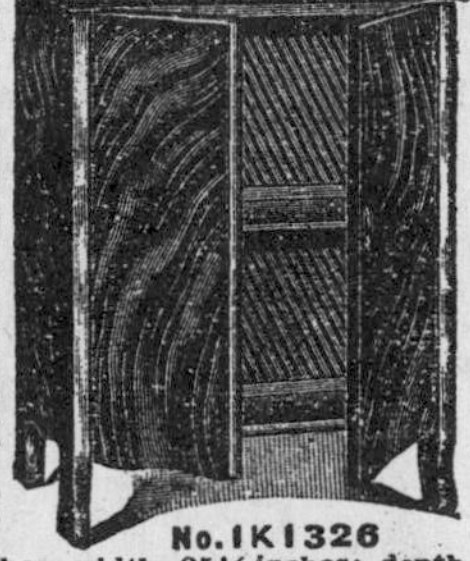

No. 1K1326

No. 1K1326 This Large Graphophone Record Cabinet we furnish in solid oak with quarter sawed golden oak front and top; or in birch, mahogany finish. Partitioned to hold 220 discs up to 12 inches diameter. Also furnished with sliding shelves and pegs similar to No. 1K1324 to hold 200 cylinder records. Height, 35 inches, width, 25½ inches; depth, 18 inches. Shipped direct from factory in Chicago. Shipping weight, 65 pounds.

	Oak	Mahogany Finish
Price, disc records ...	$10.35	$10.30
Price, cylinder records.	11.65	11.60

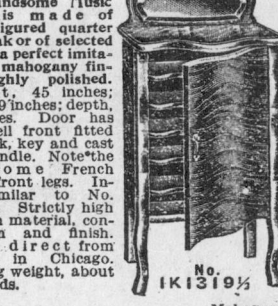

PARLOR DESKS

$3.75   ATTRACTIVE IN DESIGN   **PARLOR DESKS**   EXCEPTIONALLY LOW IN PRICE   **$12.35**

THIS SPLENDID LINE OF PARLOR DESKS combine utility and convenience with first class material, construction and finish. Our sales of this deservedly popular line of desks have increased steadily from season to season, and we have been able to constantly improve the quality, and reduce the price, until this season we are able to call more than special attention to this magnificent line of Parlor Desks, with the assurance that we are able to furnish our customers greater values than have ever been offered before by any dealer, much better goods than they can secure from other dealers and all at prices about one-third less than goods of equal quality are generally sold.

THE WOOD used in our Parlor Desks shown on this page is carefully selected, thoroughly air seasoned and kiln dried. Every piece of wood used is guaranteed against warping, checking or shrinking.
THE CONSTRUCTION is first class throughout. Every joint, post, bar and panel is carefully framed and fitted. The drawers nonbinding and smooth running.
THE FINISH. The best quality of finishing materials obtainable are used in the finishing of each desk, special care being taken to bring out the grain of the wood in the most perfect manner.

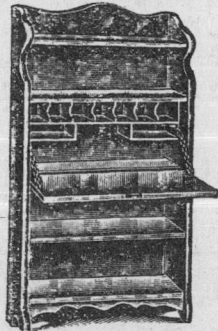

No. 1K1600 This Handsome Combination Bookcase and Secretary is made of oak, thoroughly seasoned, high gloss golden finish. It is 60 inches high and 30 inches wide. Drop leaf and bookcase proper, 22 inches deep. Interior is partitioned with pigeonholes. Shipped direct from factory in Southern Indiana. Exceptional value at the price we ask.
Shipping weight, 60 pounds.
Price.................. **$3.75**

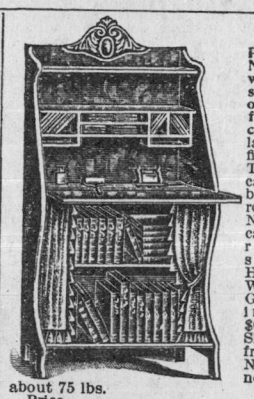

No. 1K1603 Parlor Desk. Neat design, well made of select golden oak, high gloss finish, prettily carved. Has large drop leaf fitted with lock. The lower part can be used for books, and has rod for curtain. Note the hand carved top and roomy top shelves. Height, 60 in. Width, 30 in. Generally sold in store at $6.50 to $7.00. Shipped direct from factory in Northern Illinois. Weight, about 75 lbs. Price. **$4.25**

No. 1K1606 Parlor Desk. Neat design, well made of select golden oak, high gloss finish, prettily carved. Has large drop leaf fitted with lock. The lower part can be used for books and has rod for curtain; also has a French beveled plate mirror and a large shelf in upper part. Height, 60 in., width, 30 inches. The equal of desks generally sold at $6.75 to $7.00. Shipped direct from factory in Northern Illinois. Weight, about 75 lbs. Price. **$4.85**

No. 1K1609 Parlor Desk. Made of select golden oak, high gloss finish. Width, 30 inches, height, 60 inches. Has a large drop leaf and shelves below for books. Has a rod for curtain. Top is ornamented with bracket shelves and a 10x24-inch French beveled plate mirror. Securely crated and shipped direct from factory in Northern Illinois. Weight, 80 pounds. Price. **$5.75**

No. 1K1612 This Desk is made of solid oak, high gloss golden finish. Height, 56 in.; width, 30 in. Below desk are three large drawers fitted with locks, keys and cast brass handles. Material, construction and finish first class throughout. Exceptional value. Shipped direct from factory in Northern Illinois. Shipping weight, 95 pounds. Price. **$6.35**

No. 1K1615 This Combination Desk and Bookcase is made of golden oak, high gloss finish. Height, 63 inches; width, 30 inches; depth, 13 inches. Ornamental top has 8x10-inch pattern French beveled mirror. Inside desk fitted with pigeonholes. Below desk is a curtain rod. Shipped direct from factory in Northern Illinois. Shipping weight, 100 pounds. Price. **$6.95**

No. 1K1618 Parlor Desk. A graceful and sensible design. Made of select golden oak stock, high gloss finish. Width, 30 inches; height, 63 inches. Has a large drop leaf, a roomy drawer and shelves below for books. Has a rod for curtain. Top is ornamented with bracket shelf and an 8x14-inch French beveled plate mirror. Securely crated and shipped direct from factory in Chicago or Southern Indiana. Weight, 85 pounds. Price. **$7.45**

No. 1K1621 This Combination Desk and Bookcase is made of golden oak with quarter sawed oak front, high gloss golden finish. Height, 63 in.; width, 30 in. Mirror in top, best quality French beveled plate, size, 8x12 inches. Below desk is a spacious bookcase fitted with glass doors. Inside of desk has convenient arrangement of pigeonhole space. Shipped direct from factory in Northern Illinois. Shipping weight, 90 pounds. Price. **$8.65**

No. 1K1624 This Combination Desk and Bookcase is made of golden oak with quarter sawed oak front, high gloss golden finish. Height, 60 inches; width, 30 inches. Note the book compartment with lattice paneled doors. Below desk are three roomy drawers. Inside of desk has drawer, convenient arrangement of pigeonhole space. Fitted with best quality cast brass handles, locks and casters. Shipped direct from factory in Northern Illinois. Shipping weight, 100 pounds. Price..... **$9.85**

No. 1K1627 This Splendid Desk is made of golden oak with quartered oak front. It is 44 inches high, 31 inches wide and 16 inches deep. The interior is arranged for books and stationery, as illustrated. The lid of writing desk is supported, when open, by a brass arm at each side. The lower part of desk has one large drawer, two smaller drawers and a cupboard in which is a small drawer and three letter files. Knobs, locks, cabinet work and finish first class. Shipped direct from factory in Northern Illinois. Shipping weight, 125 lbs. Price. **$10.45**

$6.45

No. 1K1630 This Desk is made of solid oak in fine golden finish. It is 32 inches long, 44 inches high and 22 inches deep. It contains thirteen pigeonholes, two book stalls, and one drawer in the top section, center drawer in the base. It is fitted with a patent flexible dustproof curtain like a regular office desk. A very substantial, attractive and useful desk, designed to fill the requirements of a home desk different from the usual pattern. Carefully packed and shipped direct from our factory in Chicago. Shipping weight 100 pounds. Price **$6.45**

No. 1K1633 This extra large Desk is made of quarter sawed oak, high gloss golden finish. Height, 48 inches; width, 30 inches; depth, including fall lid, 30 inches. Inside fitted with convenient pigeonhole space and drawers. Note the two large drawers below desk; fitted with locks, keys and cast brass knobs. Has shapely curved French legs. Material, construction and finish first class throughout. Compare this desk with those offered in retail stores at $12.00 to $14.00. Shipped from factory in Central Indiana. Shipping weight, 100 pounds. Price, as illustrated **$8.75**
$8.75 As illustrated.
Price, without mirror............... 7.45

No. 1K1636 Ladies' Desk; 4 feet 10 inches high, 29 inches wide, with 8x14-inch French beveled plate mirror. This desk is made of solid oak, with quartered oak front. Also made in birch, perfect imitation mahogany. High gloss finish. Fitted with roomy pigeonhole case. Has two large drawers and upper shelf. Decorated with genuine carving, finely executed. Best quality casters. Securely crated and shipped direct from factory near Chicago. Shipping weight, 90 pounds.

	Quartered Oak	Mahogany Finish
Price	$9.35	$9.30

$9.35

No. 1K1639 This large, handsome Desk is made of solid golden oak with highly figured quarter sawed oak front, highly polished. Height, 56 inches; width, 28 inches; depth, 17 inches, with writing lid 14x30 inches. Note the ornamental canopy top with genuine French beveled plate mirror, size 6x22 inches. Base has three large full swell front drawers and shaped French curved legs. Fitted with best quality cast brass handles, locks, keys and casters. High grade in material, construction and finish. Shipped direct from factory near Chicago. Shipping weight, 110 pounds. Price, as illustrated... **$12.35**
Price, without canopy top.. $10.45

$12.35

$5.95 OFFICE DESKS $26.95

BIG REDUCTION IN PRICES

AT $5.95 TO $26.95 WE SHOW WONDERFUL VALUES IN NEW AND UP TO DATE DESIGNS OF OFFICE DESKS.

WE CHALLENGE THE WORLD ON QUALITY AND PRICE. A LOWER PRICE THAN OURS MEANS POORER QUALITY.

THE OFFICE DESKS WE DISPLAY THIS SEASON represent a line made for us under special contract by the largest, oldest and best desk manufacturers in this country, manufacturers whose long experience in the manufacture of desks enables them to give us the benefit of every good idea, whose modern machinery and skilled workmanship combine to produce better goods than are turned out by other manufacturers and whose contract with us, by which we take practically the entire output of the factory, enables us to offer these desks to our customers on the basis of manufacturing cost, the cost of material and labor with but our one small percentage of profit added. By this method and this connection we are able to eliminate from the selling price every unnecessary item and the price to you, the price printed in this catalogue, is as low or even lower than most retail dealers would pay at wholesale for these goods.

FACTORY INSPECTION. Thoroughly experienced and competent inspectors, men who are expert cabinet makers and finishers, are employed at each of our factories who carefully inspect every article. Every detail of the construction and finish is rigidly examined before the article is packed for shipment. Each article after being thoroughly inspected as to material, construction and finish, is securely wrapped, burlapped or crated, whichever style of packing is best suited to the style of article, in order to insure safe delivery at destination in the same perfect condition. We guarantee safe delivery.

THE WOOD used in our office desks is specially selected fine grained oak. It is thoroughly air seasoned and kiln dried. Absolutely guaranteed not to warp, shrink or check. The panels and polished writing bed are constructed of the three-ply wood, perfectly joined together with the grain crossing, thereby insuring great strength and preventing warping or shrinkage.

THE CONSTRUCTION of our office desk is the very best that skilled workmanship and modern machinery can produce. Every part of the framework is perfectly fitted and joined by mortise and tenon. The drawers are dovetailed on the sides and grooved on the bottoms and backs, carefully and perfectly fitted with guides, making them easy moving and free from friction.

THE FINISH of our office desk is strictly high grade in every detail. The color a beautiful golden. The materials are the best obtainable from hardwood oil to the polishing coat of varnish. Special care is taken to bring out the highly figured grain of the wood. Plenty of time is given each coating and polishing process in order to produce a better and smoother surface, a brighter luster and a finish that will preserve its beauty for a lifetime instead of the ordinary finish produced by other makes that fade away in a few months.

OUR PATENT DUSTPROOF ROLL CURTAIN. The ribs of the curtain are perfectly fitted, preventing the catching and retaining of dust and grit, so detrimental and annoying to all other makes of flexible curtains; perfectly noiseless, free and easy action and graceful appearance while in motion, as though possessed of life. No friction caused by dust or grit accumulating between grooved slats. Easily kept clean with an ordinary dusting brush. We guarantee the durability of our curtain and claim that no other curtain now on the market can be raised or lowered as easily and gracefully. No creaking, cracking noises or jerky motion while operating our curtain. THE PATENT DUSTPROOF CURTAIN used on all our roll top desks is undoubtedly superior to any other make and an exceptionally desirable feature.

THIS SPLENDID OFFICE DESK $15.65

The Equal of Office Desks Sold Generally at $22.00 to $25.00.

THIS ROLL TOP DESK is wonderful value at our price. It is made of carefully selected, thoroughly seasoned oak in a beautiful golden finish. It is 48 inches long, 45 inches high and 30 inches wide. The right hand pedestal in the base contains a private drawer with Yale lock; dimensions, 9½ inches long, 9½ inches wide and 3¾ inches deep. A bookstall 19½ inches high, 12½ inches deep and 4 inches wide, two index letter files, 12½ inches high, 11 inches wide, 3 inches thick, and two pigeonhole compartments for stationery. The left pedestal contains four drawers, each 23 inches long, 12½ inches wide and 4¼ inches high. Above each pedestal is a sliding adjustable arm rest, which adds to the convenience and table surface of the desk. The top section contains six wood front filing boxes, 9 inches deep, 3 inches high and 4 inches wide, two large pigeonholes in the center, two bookstalls, each 12 inches high, 9 inches deep, 3 inches wide, two convenient drawers 9 inches long, 5½ inches wide and 3 inches high. Also pen racks, blotter holder, etc. The spacious bed and splendid arrangement of drawers, index files, pigeonhole space make this desk the equal in comfort and convenience of office desks generally sold at more than double our price. This desk is fitted with a dustproof flexible curtain that is noiseless, free and easy of action and graceful in appearance. Shipping weight, 240 pounds.

ORDER BY NUMBER.
No. 1K1665

HOW WE ARE ABLE TO MAKE QUICK DELIVERY AND SAVE TIME AND FREIGHT CHARGES TO OUR CUSTOMERS ON THIS OFFICE DESK.

Our sales on this magnificent high grade office desk have grown so large from every section of the country that, in order that we may be able to get one of these splendid and deservedly popular office desks to our customers in the West and Northwest in a day or two from the date we receive your order, to insure it reaching you in perfect condition, to remove the liability of breakage or damage and reduce the freight charges to the smallest possible amount, we have arranged warehouse facilities at the places named in the list below. We ship this office desk in solid car lots, receiving from the railroad company the very lowest carload freight rates, so that when we receive your order here in Chicago for this office desk, No. 1K1665, we immediately send your order by special mail delivery to the warehouse nearest you and order this office desk shipped to your railroad station on your order AT ONCE. It will leave the warehouse in perfect condition and will reach you in a few hours to a day or two at the farthest from the time it leaves the warehouse, and when you get it you will need to pay only the small freight charges for the short distance from the warehouse to your railroad station. The total cost of this office desk to our customers in the West and Northwest will amount to considerably less than if shipped to you singly as one shipment from the factory in Ohio to you nearest railroad station.

No. 1K1665 Price at factory in Chicago.. **$15.65**
Price at warehouse in Kansas City, Mo....... **17.24**
Price at warehouse in St. Paul, Minn........ **17.12**

Wonderful Value, $5.95.

This Flat Top Office Desk is made of thoroughly air seasoned and kiln dried oak, high gloss golden finish. We furnish it in two lengths, as noted below. It is 30 inches wide. The pedestal contains three drawers, each 23 inches long, 11¼ inches wide, 3¼ inches deep, and one large drawer 23 inches long, 11¼ inches wide and 9¼ inches deep. Each drawer fitted with separate lock and key. The drawers have the best dovetail construction grooved on the bottoms and backs. Carefully fitted with guides and are perfect fitting and smooth running. The panels are made of three-ply built up stock to prevent warping or shrinkage. The cabinet construction in every detail is strictly first class. This desk has all the convenience of a regular flat top desk generally sold in stores at $10.00 to $12.00. This desk is without doubt or question the most wonderful value ever offered by any dealer in a flat top office desk, and if you will compare carefully the sizes, description and prices of our office desks with those offered by other dealers you will readily recognize the big saving it is possible for you to make by placing your order with us. This desk is shipped direct from factory in Central Indiana. Shipping weight, about 100 pounds.

No. 1K1647 Price, 3 feet 6 inches long........................$5.95
No. 1K1648 Price, 4 feet long..................................6.45

Oak Flat Top Desk, $10.25.

This Flat Top Office Desk is made of oak, golden finish. It is 4 feet 6 inches long, 2 feet 6 inches wide and 30 inches high. The left pedestal contains three drawers, each 23 inches long, 11¼ inches wide, 3¼ inches high, and one drawer same length and width, 9 inches high. The right pedestal contains one drawer 23 inches long, 11¼ inches wide and 3¼ inches high, and a spacious cupboard containing five pigeonholes, each 4 inches wide by 3¾ inches high, and two bookstalls, 13¾ inches deep, 19 inches high and 4 inches wide. The distance between the pedestals in the 54-inch size desk is 24 inches, and in the 4-foot size 17½ inches. The top of this desk is made of transverse layers, insuring it against warpage or shrinkage. Construction and finish are strictly high grade. Our low prices are not made at the expense of quality. We guarantee this office desk and every other office desk in this catalogue lower in price than the same quality of goods can be bought elsewhere. Shipped direct from factory in Southern Indiana. Shipping weight, 150 pounds.

No. 1K1650 Price, 4 feet 6 inches long........................$10.85
No. 1K1651 Price, 4 feet long..................................10.25

Roll Top Curtain Desk, $11.95.

This Office Desk is made of thoroughly air seasoned and kiln dried oak, high gloss golden finish. It is 44 inches long, 45 inches high and 30 inches deep. The left pedestal contains two drawers, each 23 inches long, 10 inches wide and 3½ inches deep, and one large drawer 23 inches long, 10 inches wide and 9¾ inches deep. The right pedestal contains three book stalls, each 19 inches high, 13½ inches deep, and 3 inches wide. Above pedestals are two extension sliding arm rests. Bed of the desk is built of transverse layers of three-ply stock securely framed by a solid rim, prevents shrinkage or warping. Top section contains eight pigeonholes, each 3x4 inches and two center pigeonholes for stationery, etc. The distance between the pedestals is 18¾ inches. Fitted with our patent flexible dustproof curtain with Yale lock. Curtain closed locks the drawers automatically. Shipped direct from factory in Southern Indiana. Shipping weight, about 200 pounds.

No. 1K1654 Price...$11.95

$20.00 Office Desk for $12.95.

This Office Desk is without question the most wonderful value ever offered in a roll top curtain desk. It is made of specially selected oak, high gloss golden finish. Length 46 inches, height 45 inches, depth 30 inches. The left hand pedestal contains three drawers, each 21 inches long by 9 inches wide. Top drawer is 4¼ inches high. Middle drawer 6¼ inches high. Bottom drawer 7¾ inches high. The right hand pedestal is fitted with three book stalls 17 inches high and a spacious shelf above, for large books and stationery. Above each pedestal is a sliding adjustable arm rest which adds to the

convenience and table surface of the desk. The top section contains nine pigeonholes, 4½ inches high, 2¾ inches high and 9 inches deep; two drawers, pen racks, blotter holder, etc. The spacious bed surface and convenient arrangement of pigeonhole case make this desk an equal in comfort and convenience of desks at double the price we ask. Fitted with our patent dustproof flexible curtain preventing the catching and retaining of dust and grit so detrimental and annoying to all other makes of curtains. This curtain is perfectly noiseless, free and easy of action and graceful in appearance. Shipping weight, 185 pounds.

No. 1K1658 Price...$12.95

Our $13.85 Roll Top Office Desk.

No. 1K1662 This splendid Roll Top Office Desk is made of choice grained selected oak in a beautiful golden finish. It is 4 feet long, 30 inches wide and 46 inches high; it has four drawers in the left pedestal, each 20½ inches long, 10 inches wide and averages 4½ inches high. The right hand pedestal contains one drawer 20½ inches long, 10 inches wide and 4½ inches high and a spacious book cupboard containing two bookstalls for large books and four pigeonholes for stationery, etc. Above each pedestal is a sliding adjustable arm rest which adds to the convenience and table surface of the desk. The top section contains twelve pigeonholes for envelopes, stationery, etc., two drawers, two penracks, blotter holder, etc. It has a full paneled closed back and is finished all around. The drawers are dovetailed and the entire frame of the desk is mortised and joined in the most perfect manner possible. The easy moving and perfect fitting drawers, the flexible dustproof curtain, the spacious and convenient cupboard and pigeonholes, together with handsome highly figured oak wood with beautiful golden finish make this high grade desk one of the most wonderful bargains we have ever offered. The curtain is fitted with a Yale lock with two keys. The curtain locks the drawers in the left pedestal automatically. The door of the cupboard has a separate lock and key. This desk is mounted on patent chilled steel frame casters. Shipped direct from factory in Southern Indiana thereby insuring lowest freight charges. Shipping weight, 220 pounds.

Price...$13.85

An Absolutely First Class Desk, $21.85.

No. 1K1672 This High Grade Office Desk is 50 inches long, 47 inches high, 31 inches deep, made of thoroughly seasoned golden oak with a highly figured quarter sawed oak front and writing bed. Four drawers in left pedestal, each 23 inches long, 12 inches wide, 4½ inches high inside. Right pedestal has cupboard containing five indexed letter drawer files, each 10 inches long, 12 inches wide, 3 inches high, above which is a drawer of same size as those in left pedestal. Convenient center drawer between pedestals 23 inches long, 17½ inches wide, 2½ inches deep. Top section has two drawers and wood front pigeonhole filing boxes, 9 inches by 4½ inches by 2¾ inches, between which are four pigeonholes and small cupboard. Vertical bookstalls are 14 inches high, 9 inches deep, and 3 inches wide. Distance between pedestals, 18½ inches. Fitted with our patent dustproof flexible curtain with Yale lock which locks drawers in base automatically. Extension arm slide above top drawer in each pedestal. Strictly high grade in wood, construction and finish. Sells in retail stores for $35.00 to $40.00. Shipped direct from factory in Central Indiana. Shipping weight, about 225 pounds. Price, as illustrated.................$21.85

Exceptional Value at Our Price, $23.95.

This Desk, 60 inches long, 52 inches high, 33½ inches wide, is made of solid oak except the platform of the base, which is made of built up three-ply veneer stock. The top and front highly figured quarter sawed, grain specially selected. Three upper drawers in each pedestal are each 24½ inches long, 11¼ inches wide and 3¼ inches deep. Two lower drawers in each pedestal are each 24½ inches long, 11¼ inches wide and 9 inches deep. Top section contains sixteen pigeonholes

Wood front filing boxes, each, 20 cents extra in this desk.

3x4 inches, four pigeonholes 3x5½ inches, two bookstalls, each 17 inches high, 4 inches wide and 8½ inches deep, four special pigeonholes for stationery and two drawers. Fitted with our patent flexible dustproof curtain with Yale lock, which locks the drawers in the base automatically. Has an extension arm slide above drawers in each pedestal. The handsome columns on the front of the base, the beautiful hand carved drawer pulls, the full paneled closed back and ends, the strictly high grade construction and finish, make this desk wonderful value. Shipped directly from our factory in Southern Indiana. Shipping weight, 300 pounds. Oak.

No. 1K1676 Price, 54 inches long.................$23.95
No. 1K1677 Price, 60 inches long.................25.75

This High Grade Office Desk, $26.95.

No. 1K1680 This Office Desk should be compared with those offered by others at $40.00 to $45.00. It is made of specially selected thoroughly air seasoned and kiln dried oak. Entire front, bed and top are made of highly figured quarter sawed oak, golden finish. It is 54 inches long, 31 inches wide and 48 inches high. Each pedestal in the base has four roomy drawers with raised fronts, between which is a convenient drawer for large papers, etc. The top section has eleven pigeonholes, wood filing boxes with quartered oak fronts, two bookstalls, one indexed letter file, one card index, three small drawers, one tray drawer beneath letter file, and one private compartment with door fitted with lock and key. Extension arm slides above each pedestal. Fitted with our patent flexible dustproof curtain with Yale lock, which locks the drawers automatically. Strictly high grade in material, cabinet construction and finish. The convenient arrangement of the top section cannot be fully appreciated until seen and carefully examined. This magnificent desk combines all the features of the highest grade office desks usually offered in the stores at double the price we ask. Shipped direct from factory in Central Indiana. Shipping weight, about 225 pounds. Price...$26.95

OFFICE CHAIRS.
On page 370 we show a choice assortment of strictly high grade office chairs which we guarantee to be better in quality and lower in price than any similar chairs offered by any other dealer. We invite a careful comparison of the goods as only in that way can the superior quality of our desks and chairs be fully appreciated.

$14.95 BEDROOM SUITES $43.95
BIG REDUCTION IN PRICES
AT $14.95 TO $43.95 WE SHOW THE GREATEST VARIETY OF HANDSOME SUITES
THE MOST ASTONISHING VALUES EVER OFFERED IN BEDROOM SUITES.

WITH OUR LINE OF BEDROOM SUITES enlarged, greatly improved, brought right up to date to include the very newest styles for this season and at greatly reduced prices, we are prepared to save you so much money we feel you cannot afford to buy a bedroom suite elsewhere.

HOW WE ARE ABLE TO MAKE THE PRICES SO LOW, and how it is possible for us to reduce our prices on bedroom suites below any previous quotations: Our bedroom suites are made for us under contract by the best manufacturers in this country, and our output has increased to such an extent that we are able to contract in each case for a very large part of the output of the factory, and these factories, desiring to run at full capacity the year around, are willing to take our contract at the cost of material and labor, as it facilitates the working of their factories and enables them to run every working day at full capacity, and thus reduce the cost, not only on the suites they make for us, but on the suites they sell to other people. As a result, we obtain our bedroom suites this season, including all the newest designs at about the cost of material and labor, to which we have added only our usual small percentage of profit.

QUALITY AND PRICE GUARANTEE. We guarantee every article in this catalogue to be lower in price than the same quality of goods can be bought elsewhere. If any other house meets or cuts our prices on any article they do it at the expense of quality. If you do not find this is so by comparing the goods, or if you ever buy anything from us that is not lower in price than the same quality of goods can be bought from any other house, you are especially requested to return our goods at our expense and get your money back at once.

ABOUT THE LOCATION OF OUR FACTORIES. The immense quantity of bedroom suites which we sell and the steadily increasing volume of our business enable us to make contracts with the largest, most favorably known and best makers of high grade bedroom suites, whose factories are located in the Eastern, Northern, Southern and Middle Western parts of the United States. In most cases we have a factory located near your town, which means a very small

freight charge and hence a big saving to you, which should be considered in making your selection and comparing our goods with those offered by any other dealer.

FACTORY INSPECTION. Thoroughly experienced and competent inspectors, men who are expert cabinet makers and finishers, are employed at each of our factories, who carefully inspect every article. Every detail of the construction and finish is rigidly examined before the article is packed for shipment. Each article, after being thoroughly inspected as to material, construction and finish, is securely wrapped, burlapped or crated, whichever style of packing is best suited to the style of article, in order to insure safe delivery at destination in the same perfect condition. We guarantee safe delivery.

PROMPT SHIPMENT. At each of our factories we have prepared immense warehouse room. The goods are made up, carefully finished, inspected and placed in a perfectly dry and thoroughly ventilated storage room, ample time being given for the finish to thoroughly set, dry and harden before being packed for shipment. We are thus enabled to make shipment within a few days after receiving your order.

ABOUT FREIGHT CHARGES. The freight charges on a bedroom suite will amount to next to nothing as compared to what you will save in price. The freight on an average bedroom suite for a distance of 500 miles will amount to $1.75 to $2.25. Don't let the item of freight charges prevent you from ordering, for we positively guarantee that after you have paid all freight charges you will find that you have saved considerable money by sending your order to us. The freight charges are exactly the same if paid by you as when paid by us, and we recommend that you pay the freight at your station when the goods arrive, as it will enable us to make more prompt delivery. If there is no agent at your station, do not fail to send enough money with your order to prepay the freight charges; otherwise we cannot make shipment without first writing you for the money. Should you send more money than is required to pay the freight charges, the difference will be refunded to you. On pages 13 to 17 we give a table of freight rates which will enable you to calculate about what the freight will amount to.

Wonderful Value, Reduced from $15.95 to $14.95

No. 1K1706 This Bedroom Suite should not be compared with suites offered by other dealers at anywhere near our price. It is the equal in quality and finish of suites sold by others at $25.00 to $30.00. Made of thoroughly air seasoned and kiln dried oak. High gloss, golden finish. Bed, 73 inches high, 54 inches wide. Note the broad top panel decorated with attractive, ornamental hand made carvings, smoothly cut and finely executed. Dresser measures 19x40 inches and has double deck shaped top with rounded edges and corners. It has full panel ends and back. Top drawers have fine swell fronts. The handsome mirror is best quality French bevel plate, size, 20x24 inches. Washstand has a double top, with small top drawer to match dresser. Fitted with locks, best quality cast brass handles and casters. Every detail of construction is first class throughout. Drawers perfect fitting and smooth running. Shipped direct from factory in Western New York or Central North Carolina, the point nearest your railroad station, to insure lowest freight charges. Shipping weight, 300 pounds.
Price, complete suite..**$14.95**

Exceptional Value, Reduced to $17.45

No. 1K1718 This Bedroom Suite should be compared with suites sold in retail stores at $25.00 to $30.00. Made of thoroughly seasoned solid oak, high gloss, golden finish. Bed is 76 inches high, 73 inches long, 54 inches wide. Dresser has double deck top, with rounded corners and edges, size, 20x42 inches. Top drawers have curved fronts. Mirror is best quality French bevel plate, size, 22x28 inches. Washstand has a double deck top, size, 18x32 inches, and matches dresser. Fitted with best quality locks, cast brass handles and casters. Bed and dresser ornamented with perfectly matched, smooth cut ornamental carvings. Construction and finish first class throughout. Shipped direct from factory in Pennsylvania, Central Indiana or North Carolina, according to location of customer, thereby insuring the lowest possible freight charges. Shipping weight, 320 pounds.
Price, complete suite..**$17.45**

This Solid Oak Bedroom Suite, Reduced to $16.35

No. 1K1712 In this solid oak Bedroom Suite we offer wonderful value. It must be seen to be fully appreciated. The bed is 74 inches high, 4 feet 6 inches wide and 6 feet 1 inch long. The dresser has a shaped double top, 20x40 inches, two swell front top drawers, with two large drawers below, all fitted with best quality cast brass trimmings, locks and keys. The mirror is French bevel plate, size, 20x24 inches. Mirror frame and standards have rounded edges. The washstand has 18x32-inch double top and matches the dresser. The handsome hand carvings on the bed and dresser are new in design and finely executed. The finish is beautiful golden, the construction first class, the design very attractive. Shipped direct from our factory in Indiana or North Carolina, the point nearest customer, to insure lowest freight charges. Shipping weight, 310 pounds.
Price, complete suite..**$16.35**

This Splendid Bedroom Suite, Reduced to $18.75

No. 1K1724 This Suite should be compared with suites sold in retail stores at from $30.00 to $35.00. It is made of thoroughly air seasoned and kiln dried oak, high gloss golden finish. The bed is 6 feet 6 inches high, 4 feet 6 inches wide, 6 feet 1 inch long. The base of the dresser is 20x42 inches. It has full panel ends. Drawers perfect fitting, move without friction. Fitted with locks, keys and best cast brass handles. The mirror is the best quality of French bevel plate, size, 22x28 inches. The washstand matches the dresser and has an 18x32-inch double top and swell top drawer. The bed and dresser are decorated with beautiful hand carvings, original in design and finely executed. Note the massive roll on foot end of bed. Fitted with best quality casters. Shipped direct from factory in Pennsylvania, Central Indiana or North Carolina, according to location of customer, thereby insuring the lowest freight charges. Shipping weight, 320 pounds.
Price, complete suite..**$18.75**

HIGH GRADE BEDROOM SUITE $24⁸⁵

NEW AND UP TO DATE IN DESIGN, HIGH GRADE IN CONSTRUCTION AND FINISH AT A BIG SAVING IN PRICE.

THE EQUAL OF BEDROOM SUITES GENERALLY SOLD AT $45.00 TO $50.00.

THE FINISH on this high grade bedroom suite is a rich dark golden color, which brings into strong relief the beautiful, highly figured grain of the wood perfectly. The materials used in the finish of this bedroom suite are the best obtainable. Each coating, from the filler of the wood to the last coat of varnish is given plenty of time to harden and dry before being polished and rubbed down, and the result is a perfectly smooth, glossy, transparent polished surface that will not wear off in a short time as ordinary finishes do, but will last a lifetime.

THE BED is regular full size, 78 inches high, 74 inches long and 54 inches wide. We call your special attention to the broad, highly figured, three-ply veneer panel and extra large roll on the foot end. The ornamental deep, smooth cut, hand made carvings on these three pieces are finely executed.

THE WOOD used in the construction of this bedroom suite is the best grade of oak, and is thoroughly air seasoned and kiln dried and especially selected for beauty of its highly figured grain. Every panel, post and piece is the highest quality obtainable.

THE CONSTRUCTION of this magnificent bedroom suite is perfect in every detail. The best skilled workmanship and modern machinery are used in the construction of this high grade bedroom suite. The framework is carefully mortised and joined, the drawers dovetailed on the sides and grooved on the backs and bottoms. The panels are built up of transverse layers of specially selected highly figured stock which prevents warping or checking or shrinking. In fact, every part and piece is perfectly fitted and joined. The drawers work smoothly without. Each bedroom suite is the perfection of construction throughout and guaranteed not to warp, check or split, no matter how severe the climatic changes and conditions.

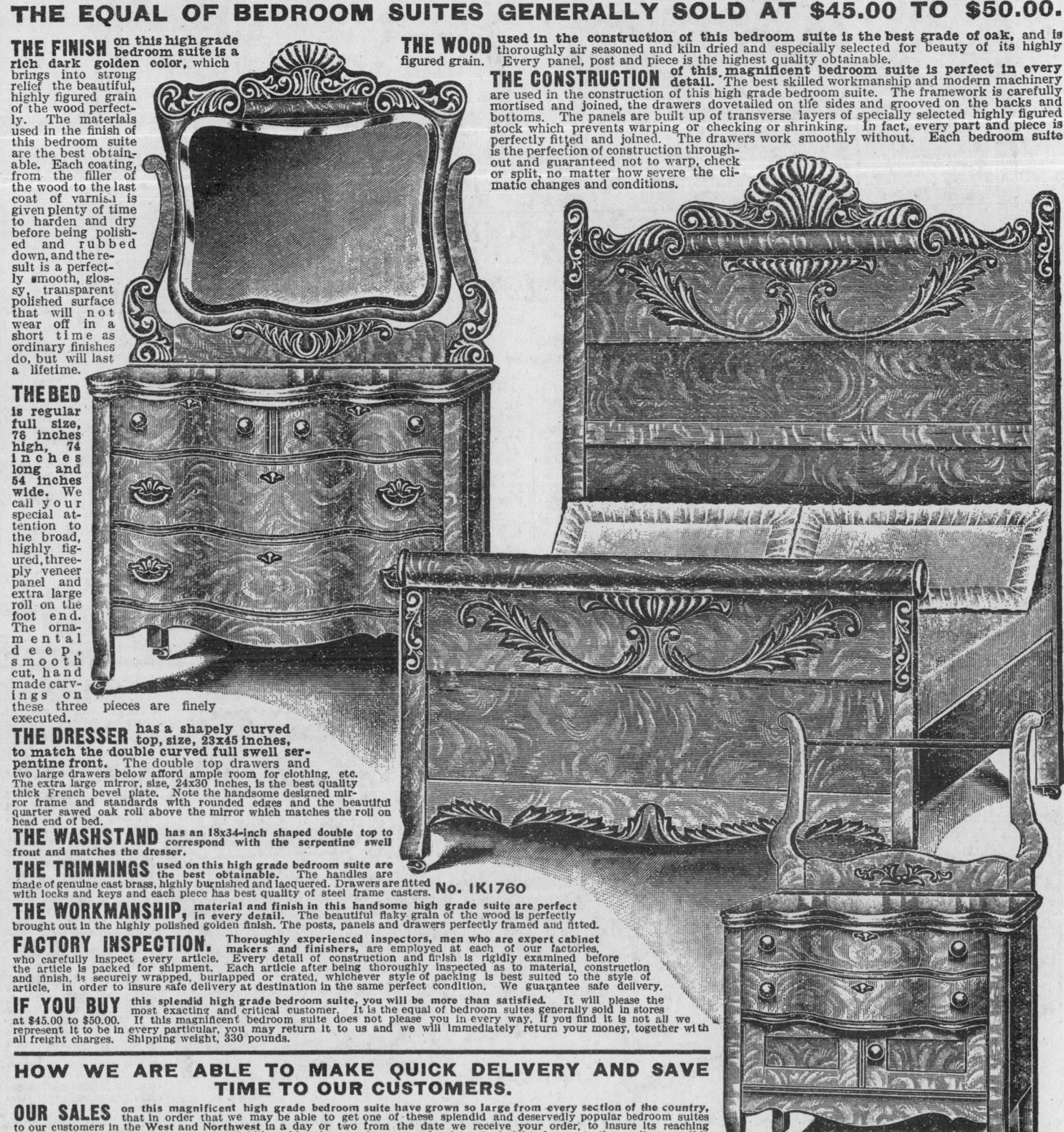

No. IK1760

THE DRESSER has a shapely curved top, size, 23x45 inches, to match the double curved full swell serpentine front. The double top drawers and two large drawers below afford ample room for clothing, etc. The extra large mirror, size, 24x30 inches, is the best quality thick French bevel plate. Note the handsome designed mirror frame and standards with rounded edges and the beautiful quarter sawed oak roll above the mirror which matches the roll on head end of bed.

THE WASHSTAND has an 18x34-inch shaped double top to correspond with the serpentine swell front and matches the dresser.

THE TRIMMINGS used on this high grade bedroom suite are the best obtainable. The handles are made of genuine cast brass, highly burnished and lacquered. Drawers are fitted with locks and keys and each piece has best quality of steel frame casters.

THE WORKMANSHIP, material and finish in this handsome high grade suite are perfect in every detail. The beautiful flaky grain of the wood is perfectly brought out in the highly polished golden finish. The posts, panels and drawers perfectly framed and fitted.

FACTORY INSPECTION. Thoroughly experienced inspectors, men who are expert cabinet makers and finishers, are employed at each of our factories, who carefully inspect every article. Every detail of construction and finish is rigidly examined before the article is packed for shipment. Each article after being thoroughly inspected as to material, construction and finish, is securely wrapped, burlapped or crated, whichever style of packing is best suited to the style of article, in order to insure safe delivery at destination in the same perfect condition. We guarantee safe delivery.

IF YOU BUY this splendid high grade bedroom suite, you will be more than satisfied. It will please the most exacting and critical customer. It is the equal of bedroom suites generally sold in stores at $45.00 to $50.00. If this magnificent bedroom suite does not please you in every way, if you find it is not all we represent it to be in every particular, you may return it to us and we will immediately return your money, together with all freight charges. Shipping weight, 330 pounds.

HOW WE ARE ABLE TO MAKE QUICK DELIVERY AND SAVE TIME TO OUR CUSTOMERS.

OUR SALES on this magnificent high grade bedroom suite have grown so large from every section of the country, that in order that we may be able to get one of these splendid and deservedly popular bedroom suites to our customers in the West and Northwest in a day or two from the date we receive your order, to insure its reaching you in perfect condition, to remove the liability of breakage or damage, and reduce the freight charges to the smallest possible amount, we have arranged warehouse facilities at St. Paul, Minnesota and Kansas City, Missouri. We ship this bedroom suite in solid car lots, receiving from the railroad company the very lowest carload freight rates, so that when we receive your order here in Chicago for this bedroom suite, No. IK1760, we immediately send your order by special mail delivery to the warehouse nearest you and order it shipped to your railroad station on your order at once. It will leave the warehouse in perfect condition and will reach you in a few hours to a day or two at the most from the time it leaves the warehouse, and when you get it you will need to pay the small freight charges for the short distance from the warehouse to your railroad station. The total cost of this Bedroom Suite to our customers in the West and Northwest will amount to considerably less than if shipped to you singly as one shipment from the factory in Michigan to your nearest railroad station. Shipping weight, 330 pounds.

No. IK1760 Price at factory in Grand Rapids, Mich	**$24.85**
Price at warehouse in Kansas City, Mo	**27.65**
Price at warehouse in St. Paul, Minn	**27.75**

THIS HANDSOME FOUR-PIECE BEDROOM SUITE $39.25

QUARTERED OAK, BIRDSEYE MAPLE OR NATURAL MAHOGANY.
WE CHALLENGE EVERY FIRM ON EARTH IN QUALITY AND PRICE.

No. 1K1796

The illustration shows the suite made of mahogany. Note the handsome grain of the wood.

NO. 1K1796 This handsome high grade Bedroom Suite we furnish in suite or separately in natural mahogany, birdseye maple or quarter sawed golden oak. The **South American Mahogany** used in this suite is specially selected and finished in a natural color, a beautiful light brown, which brings out perfectly the handsome grain of this rare wood. This finish is popularly known to the trade as "Toona Mahogany." The **Birdseye Maple** is one of the handsomest grained woods of which furniture is made. The birdseye grain is exceptionally attractive, the color a beautiful white, slightly tinged with yellow, and is specially adapted for guests' or young ladies' rooms. **THE QUARTER SAWED GOLDEN OAK** is specially selected, highly figured, flaky grained, carefully matched and finished in a beautiful golden color. Compare this suite with those offered in retail stores at double the price we ask.

THE BED is 54 inches high, 73 inches long, 54 inches wide. Note the handsome broad panels and curved roll on head and foot end. **The Dresser** has a 20x42-inch top, two curved front top drawers, below which are two large drawers. Mirror best quality French bevel plate; size, 22x28 inches, with rounded frame and standards. **Chiffonier** has 18x32-inch top, two small top drawers and four large drawers. Mirror best quality French bevel plate, size 12x18 inches, and matches the dresser. **Commode** has 18x32-inch top and matches the dresser and chiffonier. Fitted with locks, keys, best quality cast brass handles and casters. Shipped direct from factory in Western New York or Grand Rapids, Michigan.

	100 lbs. Bed	120 lbs. Dresser	100 lbs. Chiffonier	50 lbs. Commode	370 lbs. Suite
Shipping weight					
Price, Natural Mahogany	$9.85	$12.65	$11.35	$5.95	$39.80
Price, Birdseye Maple	9.80	12.60	11.30	5.90	39.60
Price, Quartered Oak	9.75	12.55	11.25	5.85	39.25

MASSIVE HIGH GRADE BEDROOM SUITE REDUCED FROM $44.95 TO $43.95

COMPARE OUR GOODS, COMPARE OUR PRICES, WE WANT YOU TO BE THE JUDGE OF THE QUALITY AND THE PRICE.

No. 1K1799

No. 1K1799 This massive high grade Bedroom Suite is made of specially selected high figured, flaky grained quarter sawed golden oak, or birch, in a perfect imitation mahogany finish, rubbed and polished.

THE BED is regular full size, 76 inches high, 74 inches long and 54 inches wide. We call your special attention to the broad, highly figured three-ply veneer panel and extra large roll on the head and foot end. The shapely designed corner posts are rounded at the top. The ornamental deep, smooth cut, hand made carvings on these three pieces are finely executed.

THE TRIMMINGS used on this high grade Bedroom Suite are the best obtainable. The handles are made of genuine cast brass, highly burnished and lacquered. Drawers are fitted with locks and keys and each piece has best quality of steel frame casters.

THE DRESSER has a shapely curved top, size 22x44 inches, to match the double curved full swell serpentine front. The double top drawers and two large drawers below afford ample room for clothing, etc. The extra large mirror, size 26x32 inches, is the best quality thick French bevel plate. Note the handsome designed mirror frame and standards with rounded edges and the beautiful quarter sawed veneered roll above and below mirror, which matches the roll on head and foot end of bed.

THE WASHSTAND has a 23x34-inch shaped double top to correspond with the serpentine swell front and matches the dresser.

THE WORKMANSHIP, material and finish in this handsome high grade suite are perfect in every detail. The beautiful flaky grain of the wood is perfectly brought out in the highly polished golden finish. The posts, panels and drawers perfectly framed and fitted.

THE PRICE. This magnificent, high grade massive Bedroom Suite cannot be purchased in retail furniture stores for less than $60.00 to $70.00. It will please the most exacting and critical customer. Carefully packed and shipped direct from factory near Grand Rapids, Michigan.

	160 lbs. Bed	230 lbs. Dresser	70 lbs. Commode	460 lbs. Suite
Shipping weight				
Price, quarter sawed oak	$14.95	$21.75	$8.95	$43.95
Price, mahogany finish	14.85	21.70	8.90	43.85

$5⁴⁵ DRESSERS $27⁶⁵
A BIG SAVING IN PRICE
AT $5.45 TO $27.65 WE OFFER WONDERFUL VALUES IN DRESSERS.
HANDSOME IN DESIGN, FIRST CLASS CONSTRUCTION AND FINISH.

THESE DRESSERS which we offer this season are made by the largest and most reliable manufacturers in the country. The designs are all new and up to date, they are shipped direct from the factory enabling us to make the lowest price possible, based on the actual cost to manufacture, with but our one small percentage of profit added. Almost every style of dresser made is illustrated on the following pages. The value we give you and the immense saving will only be fully appreciated when you compare these dressers with those offered by others at prices 30 to 40 per cent higher than we ask.

THE WOOD used in the construction of our dressers is thoroughly air seasoned and kiln dried before being put through the factory; it is carefully selected, special attention being given to the high quality of the grain.

THE CONSTRUCTION of our dressers is strictly high grade throughout, the drawers all dovetailed, the panels built of transverse layers of three-ply stock, the posts and crossbars mortised and framed in the most perfect manner. In fact, every part and piece is thoroughly well made and fitted, the best that modern machinery and skilled workmanship can produce. All the drawers move easily. The bevel plate glass mirrors we use in our dressers are the very best obtainable. We use none of the cheap domestic plate. Every dresser is fully trimmed and castered and absolutely guaranteed in every detail of construction. The very best quality of material is used in the finishing of our dressers. The hardwood, oil, the glue and the varnish are the highest grade obtainable. Experienced and skilled workmen only are employed in the factory which makes these goods. The color is a beautiful golden, rich mahogany or natural birdseye maple as noted in each description, which brings out the handsome grain of the wood.

FACTORY INSPECTION. Thoroughly experienced and competent inspectors, men who are expert cabinet makers and finishers, are employed at each of our factories, who carefully inspect every article. Every detail of the construction and finish is rigidly examined before the article is packed for shipment. Each article, after being thoroughly inspected as to material, construction and finish, is securely wrapped, burlapped or crated, whichever style of packing is best suited to the style of article, in order to insure safe delivery at destination in the same perfect condition. We guarantee safe delivery.

QUALITY AND PRICE GUARANTEE. We guarantee every article in this catalogue to be lower in price than the same quality of goods can be bought elsewhere. If any other house meets or cuts our prices on any article they do it at the expense of quality. If you do not find this is so by comparing the goods, or if you ever buy anything from us that is not lower in price than the same quality of goods can be bought from any other house, you are especially requested to return our goods at our expense and get your money back at once.

WE GUARANTEE OUR QUALITY BETTER AND OUR PRICE LOWER THAN THE SAME DRESSERS CAN BE BOUGHT ELSEWHERE.

THIS MAGNIFICENT DRESSER $13²⁵

QUARTER SAWED SWELL FRONT, STRIKINGLY HANDSOME IN DESIGN, FIRST CLASS IN MATERIAL, CONSTRUCTION AND FINISH.
A BIG SAVING IN PRICE

THIS HANDSOME DRESSER made of specially selected, thoroughly seasoned oak, in a beautiful golden finish. It has a 22x44 inch shaped top, to correspond with the double curved full swell serpentine front and contains four roomy drawers. Entire front is made of highly figured, flaky grained quarter sawed oak. The mirror is the best quality thick French beveled plate, size, 24x30 inches. The mirror frame has rounded edges and standards decorated with genuine raised hand made carvings, ornamental and finely executed. The drawers are dovetailed, perfect fitting and smooth running. Every post and panel carefully framed and fitted in the best manner possible. The durability and construction we guarantee to be the equal of any dresser made. The wood used in the construction of the dresser is specially selected from fine grained oak and guaranteed not to warp, shrink or check. The finish is strictly high grade, special attention being given to bringing out the grain of the wood most effectively. The contract for a large quantity of these dressers enables us to offer them at a very low price, a price below what your retail dealer can buy them for in car lots.

DEALERS MAY SAY OUR PRICES ARE TOO LOW because they are actually less than what the dealer is obliged to pay for the goods at wholesale, but we are able to make these low prices because we contract for a very large part of the output of each factory, and these factories, desiring to run at full capacity all the year around are willing to take our contract at a price representing practically only the cost of material and labor, as it facilitates the working of the factory and enables them to reduce the cost of their goods. We give you the benefit of this great saving. In addition thereto, we save you all the intermediate agents' and jobbers' commissions and profits, all of which adds to the cost, but does not improve the quality. Shipping weight, 175 pounds.

How We Are Able to Make Quick Delivery of This Dresser and Save Time and Freight Charges To Our Customers.

OUR SALES on this magnificent high grade quartered oak front dresser have grown so large from every section of the country that, in order that we may be able to get one of these splendid and deserved popular dressers to our customers in the West and Northwest in a day or two from the date we receive your order, to insure its reaching you in perfect condition, to remove the liability of breakage or damage and reduce the freight charges to the smallest possible amount, we have arranged warehouse facilities at Kansas City, Mo., and St. Paul, Minn. We ship this dresser in solid car lots, receiving from the railroad company the very lowest carload freight rates, so that when we receive your order here in Chicago for this dresser, we immediately send your order by special mail delivery to the warehouse nearest you and order this dresser shipped to your railroad station on your order at once. It will leave the warehouse in perfect condition and will reach you in a few hours to a day or two at the farthest from the time it leaves the warehouse and when you get it you will need to pay the small freight charges for the short distance from the warehouse to your railroad station. The total cost of this dresser to our customers in the West and Northwest will amount to considerably less than if shipped to you singly as one shipment from the factory in Indiana to your nearest railroad station. Shipping weight, 175 pounds.

NOTE: We show our lower priced dressers on next page.

No. 1K1858 Order by number.

No. 1K1858
Price at factory in Indiana or North Carolina.....................$13.25
Price at warehouse in Kansas City, Mo.............................14.89
Price at warehouse in St. Paul, Minn.............................14.94

No. 1K1974 This extra large size Chiffonier is made of selected, thoroughly seasoned oak, high gloss golden finish. Base has double top with rounded edges and corners; size, 22x42 inches. Above three large drawers are four small drawers and cupboard with full swell quarter sawed oak fronts. Mirror is best quality French bevel plate, size, 16x26 inches. Decorated with smooth cut hand made carvings, cabinet construction high grade, drawers perfect fitting. Fitted with locks, keys and best quality cast brass handles and casters. This chiffonier cannot be purchased in retail stores for less than $15.00 to $16.00. Shipped direct from factory in North Carolina or Ohio. Shipping weight, about 185 pounds. Price..... **$11.85**

This High Grade Chiffonier, $14.80.

No. 1K1977 This is an exceptionally handsome Chiffonier. Especially designed to go with brass or iron beds. Made of selected quarter sawed oak, golden finish, birdseye maple or genuine mahogany veneered front. Has serpentine shaped front, double top 20x34 inches, full panel ends. French legs. Best quality French bevel plate circular pattern mirror, 18x20 inches. Best quality cast brass handles and locks. Complete with casters. Throughout a strictly high class piece of furniture. Sells in stores at $22.00 to $25.00. Shipped direct from factory near Grand Rapids, Mich. Shipping weight, 180 pounds.

Price, quartered oak..... **$14.80**
Price, mahogany front..... **14.90**
Price, birdseye maple..... **15.00**

No. 1K1979 This high grade Chiffonier is made of especially selected thoroughly air seasoned golden oak, highly polished. The double swell serpentine curved front is made of highly figured, flaky grained quarter sawed oak, specially selected for the beauty of grain. Base is 22x37 inches. Mirror best quality thick French bevel plate, size 16x20 inches. Note the handsome design mirror frame and standards with rounded edges, decorated with genuine smooth cut hand made carvings. Fitted with locks, keys and best quality cast brass handles. This cabinet construction is first class throughout, the drawers perfect fitting and smooth running. Exceptional value. Sells in retail stores at $20.00 to $22.00. Shipped direct from factory in Central Indiana. Shipping weight, 150 pounds. Price......... **$15.25**

No. 1K1980 This Chiffonier has a double curved serpentine front; size, 20x33 inches. We furnish it in selected quarter sawed oak, birdseye maple or genuine mahogany veneered front, ends and top, all highly polished. The mirror frames and standards are highly figured wood like the base. The base contains five large drawers fitted with locks, key and best quality of cast brass handles and casters. The beautiful pattern shaped mirror is the best quality French bevel plate; size, 16x20 inches. The shapely curved standards and mirror frame are hand carved, thoroughly well made throughout and matches dresser No. 1K1872, illustrated on page 417, and commode No. 1K1906. Illustrated below. Shipped direct from factory in Western Pennsylvania or Grand Rapids, Mich. Shipping weight, 150 pounds.

Price, oak........ **$13.25**
Price, mahogany ... **13.35**
Price, birdseye maple..... **13.45**

No. 1K1988 This strictly high grade Chiffonier is made in three different woods: quarter sawed oak, genuine mahogany veneered front, ends and top, and birdseye maple, specially selected for beauty of the grain of the wood and highly polished. It is 34 inches wide, 20 inches deep, 74 inches high. It has a full swell front, solid panel ends and with two top drawers double curved. The mirror frame and standards are made of same kind of wood as the base, not imitation finish. The handsome designed mirror is the best quality of French bevel plate, size, 18x24 inches. The drawers have locks, keys and best quality cast brass handles. This chiffonier matches dresser No. 1K1873. Shipped direct from our factory in Western New York or Grand Rapids, Mich. Shipping weight, 160 pounds.

Price, oak...... **$15.95**
Price, mahogany . **16.05**
Price, birdseye maple..... **16.15**

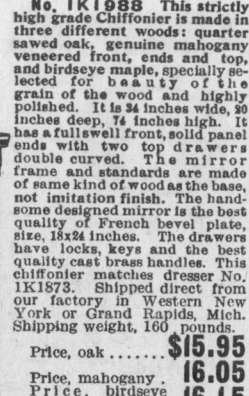

No. 1K1989 This extra large handsome Chiffonier is made of highly figured quarter sawed golden oak, thoroughly air seasoned and kiln dried, highly polished. The double top, size, 20x40 inches, is shaped to correspond with serpentine front. It has five large drawers, above which are two small drawers fitted with locks, keys and cast brass handles. It has massive round front corner posts and heavy hand carved claw feet. The pattern shaped mirror is the best quality French bevel plate, size, 16x26 inches. Mirror frame has rounded edges. The shapely curved standards are decorated with finely executed hand carvings. Complete with best quality casters. High grade in every detail of construction and finish. Sells in retail stores at $25.00 to $30.00. Shipped direct from factory in Pennsylvania or Indiana. Shipping weight, 175 pounds.

Price, quarter sawed oak........ **$19.65**

$2.59

$4.25

$4.85

$5.75

$7.10

$8.45

No. 1K1901 This Commode is made of seasoned northern hardwood, golden oak finish. It has a 17x30-inch top, a roomy top drawer and cupboard with double doors. Fitted with good quality casters. Built for service and at the price we ask is exceptional value. Generally sold by other dealers at $4.00 to $4.50. Shipped direct from factory in Ohio or North Carolina, according to location of customer. Shipping weight, 60 pounds. Price......... **$2.59**

No. 1K1904 This Washstand we furnish in white enamel, golden oak or mahogany finish. Especially adapted for use with our iron beds, in white enamel, matches dresser No. 1K1822 on page 416. It has curved top, 18x32 inches. Fitted with best quality cast brass trimmings and casters. Shipped from factory near Grand Rapids, Mich., or Pennsylvania. Shipping weight, 70 pounds.
Price, oak finish.... **$4.25**
Price, mahogany **4.35**
Price, enamel **4.95**

No. 1K1905 This Washstand is made of thoroughly seasoned solid oak, high gloss golden finish. Has an 18x34 inch shaped top to correspond with the double swell serpentine curved top drawer. Front top drawer made of highly figured, flaky grained quarter sawed oak. Fitted with best quality cast brass handles and casters. Matches dresser No. 1K1858, illustrated on page 415. Shipping weight, 70 pounds.
Price......... **$4.85**

No. 1K1906 This Washstand matches No. 1K1872 Dresser and No. 1K1980 Chiffonier. Made in quarter sawed golden oak, genuine mahogany or birdseye maple. Top is 18x28 inches. Towel rack is made of same wood as base, and is not imitation finish. High grade in construction. Shipped from factory in Western Pennsylvania or Grand Rapids, Mich. Shipping weight, 65 pounds.
Price, quartered oak.. **$5.75**
Price, mahogany..... **5.85**
Price, birdseye maple. **5.95**

No. 1K1907 Made in quarter sawed golden oak, genuine mahogany or birdseye maple, specially selected, highly figured and highly polished. Base is 20x32 inches. Towel rack is made of same wood as the base, not imitation finish. Fitted with locks and keys and the best quality cast brass trimmings. Shipped from factory in Western Pennsylvania or Grand Rapids, Mich. Shipping weight, 75 pounds.
Price, quartered oak.. **$7.10**
Price, mahogany..... **7.15**
Price, birdseye maple. **7.20**

No. 1K1912 We furnish this high grade Washstand in highly figured quarter sawed golden oak, birdseye maple or mahogany. Highly polished. Extra large top, size 20x37 inches, shaped to correspond with the full serpentine curved front. Strictly high class in material, construction and finish. Fitted with best quality cast brass trimmings and casters. Shipped direct from factory in Grand Rapids, Mich. Shipping weight, 80 pounds.
Price, quartered oak.. **$8.45**
Price, mahogany..... **8.95**
Price, birdseye maple **9.25**

THREE SPECIAL HOTEL WASHSTANDS.

No. 1K1914 This Toilet Washstand is especially adapted for small bedrooms and hotels. Made of well seasoned northern hardwood, golden oak finish and furnished with large roomy drawer and large compartment below the drawer. Top is 18x32 inches. Mirror good quality bevel plate glass, 12x20 inches in size. Casters are best quality. Shipped direct from factory in Western Ohio or North Carolina. Shipping weight, 70 pounds.
Price.......... **$4.90**

No. 1K1915 This Stand is especially constructed for hotel use, but also makes a very attractive piece of furniture for the home. It is made of hardwood, golden oak finish. Has 18x32-inch double top and 14x24-inch bevel plate mirror. Serpentine shaped front drawer, roomy cupboard below. Cast brass handles and knob. Mounted on casters. Shipped direct from factory in Western Ohio or North Carolina. Shipping weight, 80 pounds.
Price........ **$5.35**

No. 1K1917 This Hotel Stand is made of solid oak, high class golden finish. Has full swell front top drawer with two drawers and a cupboard below. Has 18x32-inch double top. The mirror is best quality bevel plate, 14x24 inches. Knobs and handles are cast brass. Complete with casters. Shipped direct from factory in Western Ohio or North Carolina. Shipping weight, 85 pounds.
Price....... **$6.90**

No. 1K1918 This Bedroom Commode is made of thoroughly seasoned oak, golden finish. The top is 16x16 inches. Cabinet construction first class. Has hinged top with removable granite vessel. Thoroughly well made and finished. Shipping weight, about 25 pounds. Price........ **$3.85**

No. 1K1900 This Washstand is made from thoroughly seasoned northern hardwood, golden oak finish, and has one drawer and lower shelf. Top, 16x23 inches. Weight, 35 pounds. Price.......... **$1.85**

$6²⁵ CHIFFOROBES AND WARDROBES $27⁹⁵

COMPARISON OF OUR WARDROBES WILL SHOW EVERY ONE LOWER IN PRICE THAN THE SAME QUALITY OF WARDROBE CAN BE PURCHASED ELSEWHERE.

THE CHIFFOROBES as illustrated on this page are in use only a short time. Their wonderful utility has been quickly recognized and the demand has become greater and greater every season. They are exceptionally serviceable on account of the number of ways in which they can be used. They embody all the new ideas in chiffonier and wardrobe construction. Each article possesses the essential features of both wardrobe and chiffonier. They have been given a well recognized superiority by reason of their practical and commendable new features. Provided with ample drawer space and wardrobe compartment for use in homes where lack of space renders impossible the use of the two separate pieces.

THE WARDROBES illustrated on this page are made with the best knocked down construction. A piece of furniture with knocked down construction is made in sections. Each piece or section is perfectly framed and fitted and can be readily put together by anyone without the use of any tools except a screwdriver. This feature not only improves the quality, but eliminates the liability to damage and reduces the freight charges about one-half.

WE SHIP all our Wardrobes direct from the factory to our customers and our No. 1K2021 from the factory or warehouse nearest your railroad station. We guarantee safe delivery.

OUR LEADER $14³⁵

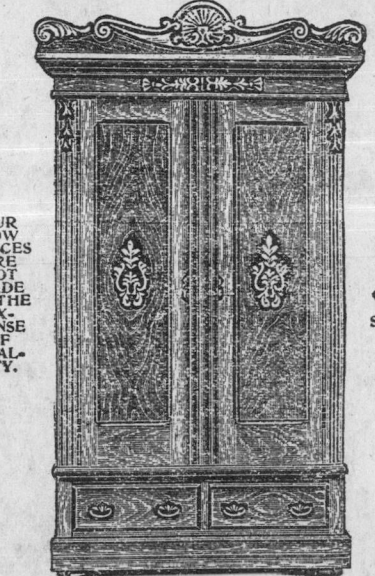

OUR LOW PRICES ARE NOT MADE AT THE EXPENSE OF QUALITY.

THE EQUAL OF WARDROBES GENERALLY SOLD AT $20.00 TO $25.00.

No. 1K2021 No. 1K2021 This high grade Wardrobe is made of solid oak, thoroughly seasoned and kiln dried. The double doors are fitted with three-ply panels to prevent shrinkage. The base contains two roomy drawers. This wardrobe is 92 inches high, 46 inches wide, 18 inches deep. Inside it is fitted with broad top shelf with double hooks. Top section and panels decorated with finely executed hand carvings. Can be shipped knocked down or set up. Shipping weight, 190 pounds.
Price at factory in Central Ohio............$14.35
Price at warehouse in Kansas City, Mo..........15.87
Price at warehouse in St. Paul, Minn..........16.15

No. 1K2007 This Wardrobe is made of northern hardwood and has oak front; Golden gloss finish. Height, 89 inches, 39 inches wide and 16 inches deep. Doors have three-ply oak panels. Inside fitted with broad shelf and clothes hooks. Note the convenient drawers in the base. Made with knocked down construction. We guarantee this wardrobe as well as every other wardrobe shown on this page lower in price and better in quality than you can find elsewhere. Our prices mean a saving to our customers of 30 to 40 per cent as against the prices asked by other dealers. Shipping weight, about 125 pounds.
Price............$7.45
No. 1K2001 Same wardrobe, hardwood, golden oak finish, 82 inches high.
Price............$6.25

No. 1K2012 This Wardrobe is made of thoroughly seasoned oak, high gloss golden finish. Height, 73 inches, 40 inches wide and 16 inches deep. Doors have three-ply panels. Base has a roomy drawer. Inside fitted with broad shelf with hooks. The special feature of this wardrobe is the patent folding construction. The sides are hinged to the back and fold inward, and the front securely fastened to the side panels by screw bolts. A method of construction which gives exceptional durability with added convenience in shipping. Securely packed in a single crate and shipped direct from factory in Central Indiana. Shipping weight, 120 pounds.
Price............$8.65

No. 1K2012½ Strictly high grade solid oak Wardrobe in a beautiful golden finish, at a big reduction in price, a price below what ordinary dealers pay at wholesale. Dimensions, 84 inches high, 40 inches wide, 16 inches deep. The extension base has two drawers. The double doors are fitted with transverse three-ply oak panels. The handsome top is decorated with genuine hand carvings. The construction is strictly high grade. Can be taken apart for convenience in moving. Securely packed and shipped direct from our factory in Western Ohio. Shipping weight, 175 pounds.
Price.....$10.45

No. 1K2014 This Wardrobe is made of thoroughly seasoned northern hardwood with selected oak front. High gloss golden finish. Board panels in the doors are made of three-ply stock. Base has two roomy drawers. Inside fitted with spacious shelf and clothes hooks. Similar to No. 1K2012. Note the ornamental top and smooth cut carvings. Height, 90 inches, width, 45 inches, depth, 16 inches. Material, construction and finish first class. Shipped knocked down. Shipping weight, 160 lbs. Price..$11.85

No. 1K2022 This handsome Wardrobe is made of choice grained oak with highly figured quartered oak panels in the doors. The beautifully moulded base is fitted with two drawers. Inside of wardrobe is partitioned with three removable shelves on one side and single shelf with double hooks on other side. The ornamental top and side posts are hand carved. Absolutely dustproof and finished on the inside. Dimensions, 94 inches high, 52 inches wide; 18 inches deep. Knocked down construction. Strictly high grade in construction and hand polish golden finish. Well packed and shipped direct from our factory in Western Ohio. Shipping weight, 250 pounds.
Price...$20.85

HOW WE ARE ABLE TO MAKE QUICK DELIVERY, SAVE TIME AND FREIGHT CHARGES FOR OUR CUSTOMERS.

OUR SALES on this magnificent, high grade wardrobe No. 1K2021 have grown so large from every section of the country, that in order to enable us to get one of these splendid wardrobes to our customers in the WEST and NORTHWEST in a day or two from the date we receive your order, and to insure its reaching you in perfect condition and reduce the freight charges to the smallest possible amount, we have arranged warehouse facilities at the following places: St. Paul, Minn., Kansas City, Mo. We ship this wardrobe from the warehouse nearest your railroad station. Read what we say on page 428 about the great saving in time and freight charges to our customers.

No. 1K2026 A strikingly attractive high grade Wardrobe, made of thoroughly seasoned oak, highly polished golden finish. Height, 82 inches; width, 50 inches; depth, 18 inches. Doors fitted with best quality of French bevel plate mirrors, size, 12x48 inches, or with highly figured quartered oak panels. Inside of wardrobe is fitted with a removable shelf with double hooks for clothing. Note the handsome cross banded veneered rolls on the corner posts and top ornament. Has broad extension base with two drawers and massive shapely curved legs. Fitted with best quality of cast brass trimmings, locks and keys. Strictly high grade in material, construction and finish. Compare this handsome high grade wardrobe with those sold in stores at $40.00. Shipped knocked down from factory in Western Ohio. Shipping Wt., 230 lbs.
No. 1K2026 Price, as illustrated............$27.95
No. 1K2027 Price, panel doors............18.25

No. 1K2004 This Chifforobe is made of thoroughly air seasoned and kiln dried Northern hardwood in a perfect imitation of highly figured flaky grained quarter sawed oak, high gloss golden finish. The beautiful imitation grain is so perfect that experts find it difficult to distinguish it from the genuine quarter sawed oak. Height, 58 inches; width, 39 inches; depth, 20 inches. It has five roomy drawers and a spacious cupboard. Above the top drawer is a genuine French bevel plate mirror, size, 8x10 inches, securely hinged to a slide and when not in use, falls forward and can be pushed backward into the space above the top drawer. Fitted in the top of the spacious wardrobe are sliding coat hangers suspended from a horizontal metal rod. Inside of full paneled door is fitted with a patent metal pants hanger. Shipped direct from factory in Southern Ohio. Shipping weight, about 200 pounds. Price.............$15.35

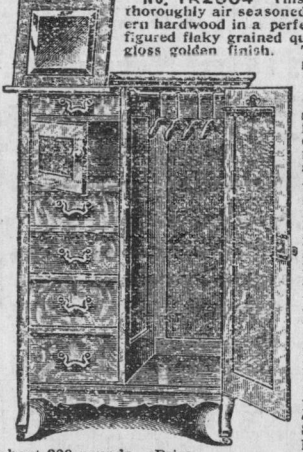

No. 1K2006 This extra large Chifforobe is made of thoroughly air seasoned and kiln dried Northern hardwood in a perfect imitation highly figured flaky grained quarter sawed oak, high gloss, golden finish. Height, 58 inches, width, 44 inches, depth, 22 inches. It has five large drawers for shirts, underwear, etc., two small drawers for collars, neckwear, etc., and a convenient hat box. Above the top drawer is a genuine French bevel plate mirror, size, 12x12 inches, securely hinged to a perfectly framed slide and when not in use can be folded into the space above the drawer. The roomy wardrobe is fitted with metal rod with patent sliding coat hangers. Note the patent metal trouser hanger attached to the inside of the door, all of which preserve to form and improve the appearance of the clothing. Shipped direct from factory in Ohio. Shipping weight, about 200 pounds............$16.95

HALL RACKS

No. IK2203 New design hall rack is made of highly figured quarter sawed oak, golden finish. Height, 74 inches; width, 22 inches. The mirror is the best quality French bevel plate; size, 10 x 10 inches. The double hat and coat hooks are genuine cast brass. Shipping weight, 80 pounds. Price. **$4.85**

No.IK2205 Artistic and highly ornamental hall rack. Made of selected quarter sawed golden oak. Height, 76 inches; width, 24 inches. Mirror is best quality French bevel plate; size, 12 x 12 inches. Roomy box with lid in seat. Shipping weight, 90 lbs. Price. **$6.65**

No.IK2209 This hall rack is made of specially selected highly figured quarter sawed oak, high gloss golden finish. Height, 76 inches; width, 24 inches. Mirror best quality French bevel plate; size, 10x17 ins. Seat has a roomy box with lid, for rubbers, etc. Shipping weight, about 100 lbs. Price. **$8.35**

No. IK2215 This hall rack is made of highly figured quarter sawed golden oak, handsomely carved. Height, 80 inches; width, 28 inches. Mirror is the best quality French bevel plate; size, 12x20 inches. Seat has spacious box with lid for rubbers, etc. Shipping weight, about 110 pounds. Price. **$9.85**

No. IK2224 This hall rack compares with those offered by others at $18.00 to $20.00. Made of highly figured quarter sawed oak, highly polished. Height, 80 inches; width, 34 inches. Mirror, best quality French bevel plate; size, 16x24 inches. Seat has a spacious box with lid. Construction high grade. Must be seen to be appreciated. Shipping weight, about 115 pounds. Price. **$11.45**

Each Hall Rack on this page is fitted with cast brass double coat and hat hooks and umbrella holder.

Add 6 inches to width of each Hall Rack on this page to include umbrella holder.

No.IK2226 This handsome massive hall rack is 80 inches high, 34 inches wide. Made of solid quarter sawed golden oak, high gloss, golden finish. The beautiful pattern shaped mirror is the best quality French bevel plate; size, 18x30 inches. Large box with lid in seat. Shipping weight, 130 pounds. Price. **$13.65**

No. IK2230 This hall rack is made of highly figured quarter sawed oak, high gloss golden finish. Height, 83 inches; width, 34 inches. Mirror is best quality French bevel plate; size, 18x40 inches. Roomy box in seat with lid. Decorated with genuine hand carvings. Construction high grade. Shipping weight, 140 pounds. Price. **$14.75**

No. IK2235 This hall rack cannot be fully appreciated until seen. Made of selected highly figured quarter sawed oak, high gloss golden finish. Height, 79 inches; width, 36 inches. Mirror is best quality French bevel plate; size, 20x24 inches. Large box in seat with lid. Shipping weight, about 140 pounds. Price. **$16.35**

No. IK2237 Extra large hall rack made of highly figured quarter sawed golden oak, high gloss golden finish. Height, 81 inches, width, 38 inches. Extra-large mirror; size 18x40 inches, best quality French bevel plate. Note the massive cross banded veneered roll and genuine hand carvings. Seat has roomy box with lid. Shipping weight, 160 pounds. Price. **$17.85**

No.IK2253 The wood of this hall seat and mirror is selected quarter sawed golden oak, highly polished; seat, 32 inches long, 36 inches high, 18 inches deep; spacious compartment with lid in the seat for rubbers, etc. Mirror is best quality French bevel plate. Shipping weight, about 100 pounds.
Price, mirror 10x14 .... **$1.75**
Price, mirror 12x20 .... **2.55**
Price, seat in golden oak **6.45**
Price, seat in weathered oak. .. **6.35**

MIRRORS

Our mirrors as illustrated on this page except No. IK2262 in the regular quality as noted are made of the very best quality, extra thick imported genuine French plate absolutely guaranteed free from all defects, with a plain or beveled edge and a perfect reflection. Every mirror except No. IK2262 which we ship to our customers is carefully and critically examined by our expert inspector of years of experience and is shipped under our binding guarantee of quality.

We do not use any of the so called "seconds or shocks." They are defective mirrors with imperfections which make them almost worthless.

We do not use mirror plates with "hair line scratches" or "air bubbles" in the surface.

We do not use mirror plates with the "cheap composition imitation silver mixture." The "silvering" on the back of our mirrors is absolutely the purest and best quality obtainable, guaranteed not to become dull or "peel off."

We do not use any frame finished in so called "imitation gold bronze or dutch metal." Our gold finished frames are finished with genuine gold bronze and gold leaf ornamentation.

As an illustration of quality note carefully in the list, the comparative prices on No. IK2262 for the "regular quality" generally offered by other dealers and the best quality imported French plate mirrors. Such a difference in price means a larger reduction in quality and we offer the "regular quality" of No. IK2262 in competition with mirrors sold by many dealers but we do not recommend them.

No. IK2245 The frame of this hall mirror is made of thoroughly air seasoned and kiln dried, highly figured quarter sawed oak, golden finish, polished or in dull weathered oak finish. The pattern shaped mirror is the best quality thick French bevel plate, size, 12x18 inches. Extreme outside measurements of frame, 21x29 inches. Note the heavy cast double hooks. Shipping weight, about 20 lbs. Price, quartered golden oak. **$4.75**
Price, quartered weathered oak **4.65**

No. IK2262 We furnish this mirror with a golden oak frame in the regular quality of plain French plate, which we offer as the equal of those generally sold by other dealers or in the very best quality genuine thick imported French plate with plain or beveled edge with handsome cast brass gold lacquered ornaments on the corners as noted in the list below. The imported French plate mirror in plain or beveled edge we guarantee to be absolutely the highest quality obtainable, free from all defects and with a perfect reflection.

Width of Frame, inches	Size of Plate, inches	Regular quality, French plain	Best quality imported French plain, brass corners	Best quality imported French bevel brass corners
1½	9x12	$0.33	$0.55	$0.75
1½	10x14	.45	.75	.95
1½	12x20	1.05	1.33	1.60
2	14x24	1.35	1.84	2.25
2	16x28	2.00	2.95	3.35
3	18x36	3.00	4.45	4.85
3	18x40	3.50	5.75	6.25

No. IK2268 This handsome Florentine design parlor mirror has a frame 4 inches wide, beautifully carved, with cut out openings. Finished in gold bronze with shaded ornaments. The mirror is the best quality genuine thick imported French bevel plate. Strictly high grade.
Price, size, 16x20 inches **$2.60**
Price, size, 18x40 inches **5.85**

We guarantee our mirrors to be all specially selected and carefully inspected—free from defects. We do not sell so called "seconds or shocks" which are generally sold at lower prices.

No. IK2272 This mirror has a 6-inch frame, finished in green and gold or white and gold with heavy raised ornamental stem and lining; both sides of stem are finished fine green bronze or enamel. Best quality French bevel plate. Size, 18x40 inches. Price, French plain mirror. **$5.65**
Price, French bevel plate. **6.25**

No. IK2276 Frame is 7 inches wide, finished in pearl green and tinted with gold; gold burnishes on the heavy ornamented corners. Fitted with the best imported French plate mirror, 18x40 inches. Price, plain mirror. **$6.30**
Price, bevel mirror. **6.75**

No. IK2280 This parlor mirror is made of the best quality genuine French bevel plate; size, 18 x 40 inches. Mounted in a handsome oak frame, decorated with raised carvings, finished in all gold or in black with gold ornaments.
Price, all gold... **$6.45**
Price, black and gold. **6.40**

No. IK2284 This parlor mirror is fitted with a beautiful oak frame, finished in all gold with new raised carvings with tips gold burnished, best quality genuine French bevel plate; size, 18x40 inches. It must be seen to be fully appreciated. Sells for $10.00 in retail stores. Our price. **$7.50**

No. IK2288 This mirror has heavy, solid golden oak frame, or imitation mahogany, with heavy top carving of rich pattern, and fluted column on frame and is very ornamental. Size of plate, 18x40 inches. Price, French plain mirror. **$6.75**
Price, French bevel mirror. **7.65**

No. IK2292 Frame of this handsome mirror is 7½ inches wide, made of quarter sawed oak, finished all gold or black and gold with beautiful hand carved decorations; burnished gold corners. Fitted with best quality French bevel plate, 18 x 40 in. Price, all gold. **$9.15**
Price, black and gold. **9.10**

$2²⁵ EXCEPTIONAL VALUES IN WOOD BEDS $15⁹⁵
NEW IN DESIGN, FIRST CLASS IN MATERIAL, CONSTRUCTION AND FINISH.

THE MATERIAL used in the construction of our wood beds is thoroughly air seasoned and kiln dried and guaranteed not to warp, check or shrink.

THE WORKMANSHIP in every detail is strictly first class. The panels, intervening bars and posts are carefully and perfectly framed and fitted. The carvings are hand made, clean, smooth cut and nicely executed.

THE FINISH of the solid oak beds is a beautiful high gloss golden. These hardwood beds are finished in a perfect imitation of highly figured flaky grained quarter

sawed golden oak, so perfect that experts find it hard to distinguish it from the genuine quarter sawed oak.

OUR WOOD BEDS are carefully and securely crated, the slats belonging to each bed being used for the crate frame, and each bed is guaranteed to arrive at destination in the same perfect condition as it left the factory. Special care should be taken not to destroy the slats when unpacking the bed. Each bed is furnished with a set of good quality of casters.

No. 1K2300
This bed is made of hardwood, thoroughly air seasoned and kiln dried in a perfect imitation of quarter sawed golden oak. High gloss golden finish. Height, 3 feet 6 inches. We furnish it in 3 feet 6 inches or 4 feet 6 inches wide. Substantial in construction. Shipped from factory in Southern Indiana or Chicago, thereby insuring lowest possible freight charges. Shipping weight, 100 pounds.

Width	3½ feet	4½ feet
Price	**$2.25**	**$2.35**

No. 1K2302
Wood bed made of hardwood in a perfect imitation of quarter sawed golden oak, thoroughly seasoned and beautifully finished. Height, 4 feet; length, 6 feet; width, 3 feet 6 inches or 4 feet 6 inches. Construction first class. A bargain at our price. Shipped direct from factory in Southern Indiana or Chicago. Shipping Wt., 90 pounds.

Width, 4½ feet. Price............ **$2.65**
2.75

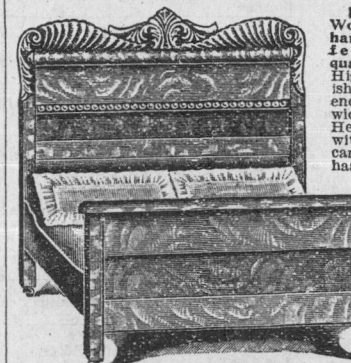

No. 1K2304
Wood bed made of hardwood in a perfect imitation of quarter sawed oak. High gloss golden finish. Height of head end, 5 feet 2 inches; width, 4 feet 6 inches. Head end decorated with genuine hand carvings. Foot end has broad top rail. Thoroughly well made and beautifully finished. Shipped direct from factory in Southern Indiana or Chicago. Shipping weight, 95 pounds.
Price, **$3.85**

No. 1K2306
This bed is made of thoroughly seasoned hardwood. In a perfect imitation of quarter sawed golden oak. High gloss finish. Head end is 5 feet 9 inches high and handsomely decorated with genuine hand carvings. Foot end has broad top rail. Length, 6 feet; width, 4 feet 6 inches. Construction strictly first class. Shipped direct from factory in Southern Indiana or Chicago, thereby insuring lowest possible freight charges. Shipping weight, 110 pounds. Price...... **$4.40**

No. 1K2308 This handsome wood bed is made of hardwood, in a beautiful and perfect imitation of quarter sawed golden oak. High gloss finish. Height of head end, 6 feet 2 inches; width (slat), 4 feet 6 inches. Note the genuine and artistic hand carving on head and foot end. High grade in construction. Shipped from factory in Southern Indiana or Chicago, thereby insuring lowest possible freight charges. Shipping weight, 120 pounds. Price, **$4.90**

No. 1K2310 This handsome bed is made of solid oak thoroughly seasoned and kiln dried, high gloss golden finish. It is 74 inches high, 54 inches wide and 73 inches long, inside measurements. Broad center panels in head and foot end made of three-ply stock to prevent warping and shrinking. Ornamented with new design, hand made smooth cut carvings. Strictly first class in every detail of material, construction and finish. Sells in stores at $8.00 to $10.00. Shipped direct from factory in Pennsylvania, Indiana or North Carolina, according to location of customer. Shipping weight, 125 pounds.
Price, **$5.45**

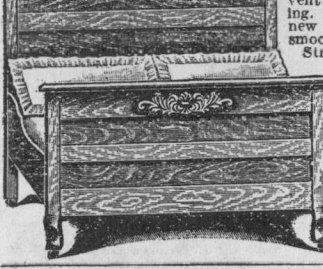

No. 1K2312
Handsome high grade wood bed, made of thoroughly seasoned oak, high gloss golden finish. Height, 74 inches; width, 54 inches, and length 74 inches. Broad panels in the head and foot end made of three-ply veneered stock. Note especially the massive half roll on the foot end and the head end. Decorated with clean, smooth cut, genuine hand carvings. Exceptionally attractive in design, high grade in construction and finish. Compare this bed with those generally sold in stores at $12.00 and $14.00. Shipped direct from factory in Indiana or North Carolina, according to location of customer. Shipping weight, 125 pounds.
Price............ **$5.85**

No. 1K2314 This wood bed is made of specially selected, thoroughly seasoned solid oak, finished in a beautiful high gloss golden color. It is 76 inches high, 54 inches wide and 73 inches long. Full panel head and foot end made of three-ply veneered stock to prevent warping or shrinking. Every post, panel and bar is perfectly framed and fitted. Ornamented with genuine hand made carvings. Exceptionally attractive in design, strictly first class in material, construction and finish. Generally sold in stores at $12.00. Securely packed and shipped direct from factory in Indiana or North Carolina, according to location of customer. Shipping weight, 125 pounds. Price............ **$6.10**

No. 1K2316
This handsome new design wood bed is regular size, 76 inches high, 54 inches wide and 73 inches long. The finish is a high gloss golden color. Note especially the massive quarter sawed veneered roll of the foot end and the ornamental new design hand made carvings. Broad panels in head and foot end are made of highly figured, flaky grained, quarter sawed oak. Compare this splendid bed with those offered by others at 30 per cent to 40 per cent more than the price we ask. Securely packed and shipped direct from factory in Indiana, North Carolina or Pennsylvania, according to location of customer. Shipping weight, 130 pounds.
Price............ **$6.55**

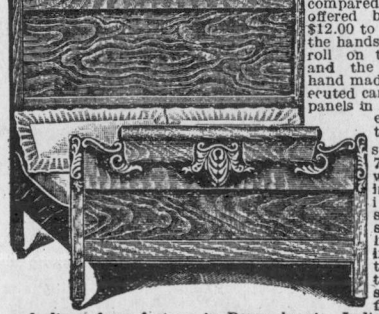

No. 1K2318
This magnificent high grade bed is made of carefully selected, thoroughly seasoned solid oak, high gloss golden finish. Quality for quality it must be compared with beds offered by others at $12.00 to $14.00. Note the handsome veneered roll on the foot end and the ornamental, hand made, finely executed carvings. Broad panels in head and foot end made of three-ply stock. Height, 78 inches; width, 54 inches. Strikingly handsome in design, strictly high grade in every detail of material, construction and finish. Shipped direct from factory in Pennsylvania, Indiana or North Carolina, point nearest your railroad station. Shipping weight, 140 pounds. Price..... **$6.85**

No. 1K2320
This massive high grade bed is exceptional value. Made of specially selected thoroughly seasoned, solid oak, high gloss, golden finish. Height, 78 inches; width, 54 inches; length, 74 inches. We call your special attention to the broad panels in the head and foot end made of three-ply built up stock of highly figured, flaky grained quarter sawed oak and the massive quarter sawed oak veneered roll on the head and foot end. The ornamental hand made carvings are finely executed. Strictly first class in every detail of material, construction and finish. Shipped direct from factory in Indiana. Shipping weight, 125 pounds. Price............ **$7.35**

Napoleon Bed.

No. 1K2322
This magnificent high grade Napoleon bed is made of specially selected, highly figured quarter sawed golden oak or mahogany. Highly polished. Height, head end, 54 inches. Height, foot end, 38 inches. Note the handsome veneered roll on head and foot end and the shapely curved legs with hand carved claw feet. This beautiful design derives its name from its adoption by Napoleon the First. It combines beauty and simplicity of outline with high quality in material, construction and finish. Sells in stores at $25.00 to $30.00. Shipped direct from factory in Northern Illinois. Shipping weight, 125 pounds.

	Quartered oak.	Mahogany finish.
Price	**$15.85**	**$15.95**

WOOD FOLDING BEDS AT BIG REDUCTION IN PRICES

THE HIGH GRADE WOOD FOLDING BEDS
shown on this page are made for us by the largest and best known manufacturers of high grade folding beds in the United States.

THE NATIONAL SPRINGS
used in our folding beds are made of heavy steel wire links, joined by small steel plate. The fabric is attached to the end by high carbon steel spiral springs. Guaranteed not to sag and will last a lifetime.

REDUCED TO $9.35

No. 1K2324 Mantel Folding Bed is made of thoroughly seasoned hardwood, golden oak, high gloss finish. Height, 62 inches; width, 54 inches, closed. It is 48x72 inches, when opened. Fitted with the celebrated National springs, guaranteed not to sag. Has automatic end legs. Mattress to fit should be 46x72 inches. Shipped from factory in Indiana. Shipping weight, 245 pounds. Price, **$9.35**

No. 1K2326 This Folding Bed is made of hardwood, golden gloss finish. Built up front panels, ornamented with fancy carving. Top is fitted with a French bevel mirror; size, 10 x 12 inches. Size of bed when open is 48x72 inches. A mattress to fit should be 3 feet 10 inches wide, 6 feet long and 2½ inches thick, and to be flexible enough should be made of cotton, hair or felt. Fitted with National springs with steel spiral spring ends. The folding bed should be compared with those offered by others at $15.00 to $16.00. Shipped from factory in Indiana. Shipping weight, 250 pounds. Price, as illustrated **$11.75**

No. 1K2362 Mantel Folding Bed, oak front, built up oak panels, golden finish. Size, closed, 69 inches high, 54 inches wide, 19½ inches deep. Size, open, outside, 54 x 75 inches; inside, 48 x 72 inches. Mattresses to fit should be 3 feet 10 inches by 6 feet with a 2½-inch box, and to be flexible enough should be made of felt, hair or cotton. Illustration shows top of bed with two fancy brackets. French bevel mirror, 8x24 inches. To fully appreciate the wonderful value of this bed, compare it with those offered at $15.00 to $18.00 in retail stores. Shipped direct from factory in Indiana. Shipping weight (full size), 250 pounds. Price **$13.25**

No. 1K2328 This Mantel Folding Bed is made of thoroughly seasoned northern hardwood. High gloss, golden finish. Has broad oak veneered large front panel. Ornamental top, fitted with French bevel plate mirror, 12x18 inches, each side of which is a bric-a-brac shelf. Size bed open for use, 48x72 inches. Fitted with best quality woven wire springs with steel spiral supports. Mattress to fit should be 46 inches wide and 72 inches long with 2½-inch box edge and should be made of cotton, hair or felt. This folding bed should be compared with those offered by others at $18.00 to $20.00. Shipped direct from factory near Grand Rapids, Michigan. Shipping weight, 200 lbs. Price, as illustrated **$13.45**

No. 1K2330 Mantel Folding Bed, made of thoroughly air seasoned oak. Front panels, made of highly figured quarter sawed golden oak. The paneled front and ornamental top are decorated with attractive, finely executed hand carvings. The mirror is the best quality French bevel plate, size, 10x20 inches. On each side of mirror is a convenient bracket shelf. Fitted with National spring with steel spiral spring ends. Bed, when open for use, is 48x72 inches. Shipped from factory in Indiana. Shipping weight, 260 pounds. Price, as illustrated **$14.75**

No. 1K2332 This Folding Bed is one of our latest designs; has full panel sides and quartered golden oak front panel. The top and front are ornamented with heavy carvings, and French bevel mirror, size, 10 x 17 inches. The bed is 48x72 inches when opened for use. The mattress to fit bed should be 3 feet 10 inches wide, 6 feet long and 2½ inches thick, and to be flexible enough should be made of cotton, hair or felt. Fitted with National spring with steel spiral spring ends. Shipped from factory in Indiana. Shipping weight, 245 pounds. Price **$16.70**

No. 1K2337 This splendid Folding Bed is exceptional value at the price we ask. Note the highly figured quarter sawed oak front and top with ornamental carving and massive veneered rolls. Mirror best quality French bevel plate, size 10x32 inches. Size bed open for use, 72x48 inches. Fitted with National spring fabric. Mattress to fit should be 46x72 inches, with 2½-inch box edge. Shipped from factory in Indiana. Shipping weight, 250 pounds. Price **$18.25**

No. 1K2373 This handsome Folding Bed is made of oak throughout, with quarter sawed oak front and top, full panel sides, highly polished, golden finish. The front is decorated with heavy carvings and has a full swell in center panel. The top is the very latest design. It has a large French bevel mirror, size, 14x24 inches, supported by two elegantly carved standards, giving to the bed that artistic relief that has made it so popular. The bed when open is 48x72 inches. The mattress to fit should be made 3 feet 10 inches wide, 6 feet long and 2½ inches thick. We recommend a cotton, hair or felt mattress. Compare this bed with those offered at retail stores at $28.00 to $30.00. Shipping weight, 200 pounds. Price, with mirror top.. **$19.65** Price, with plain top rail.. **17.85**

No. 1K2336 Quartered oak, golden finish, swell front. Built up veneered oak panels, full panel sides. Size, closed, 73 inches high, 54 inches wide, 20 inches deep. Size, open, outside, 54x75 inches; inside, 48x72 inches. Mattress to fit should be 3 feet 10 inches by 6 feet, with a 2½-inch box, and to be flexible enough, should be made of felt, cotton or hair. Note the extra large French bevel plate mirror, size, 12x36 inches, below which are two ornamented bracket shelves. Fitted with National spring with steel spiral spring ends. Shipped from factory in Indiana. Shipping weight, 255 pounds. Price **$19.75**

No. 1K2340 This up to date new design Mantel Folding Bed is made of solid oak, high gloss, golden finish. Entire front and top section made of highly figured quarter sawed oak. Note especially the massive cross banded veneered roll, full swell center panel and imitation drawers. Top fitted with best quality French bevel plate mirror, size 12x20 inches. Height, closed, 58 inches. Bed open for use, 72x48 inches. Fitted with National spring fabric. Every detail of material, construction and finish strictly high grade. Sells in stores at $30.00 to $32.00. Shipped direct from factory in Southern Indiana. Shipping weight, 265 pounds. Price, as illustrated **$23.25**

No. 1K2342 This Upright Folding Bed has oak front, high gloss, golden finish. Mirror, best French bevel plate, size, 18x30 inches, fitted with self adjusting locking device to prevent closing up by accident. Size, closed, 78 inches high, 56 inches wide and 24 inches deep. Fitted with National spring fabric. The bed proper is 48x72 inches. Mattress to fit should be 4x6 feet, with 3-inch box. This folding bed cannot be bought in furniture stores for less than $25.00 to $30.00. Shipped from factory in Indiana. Shipping weight, 385 pounds. Iron weights, separate, 130 pounds. Price **$20.75**

No. 1K2344 New design solid oak Upright Folding Bed. Front is made of highly figured quarter sawed oak. High gloss, golden finish. Mirror, best quality French bevel plate, size, 18x40 inches. This bed is 78 inches high outside, 72x50 inches inside. Fitted with National springs and self adjusting locking device. The beautiful hand made carvings are clean cut and finely executed. Every detail of material, construction and finish strictly first class. Compare this bed with those offered in stores at $30.00 to $35.00. Shipped direct from factory in Southern Indiana. Shipping weight, 395 pounds. Iron weights, separate, 130 pounds. Price **$24.45**

No. 1K2346 This splendid new design high grade Upright Folding Bed is made of solid oak, high polished, golden finish. Entire front made of highly figured, flaky grained, quarter sawed oak or in birch, with figured mahogany front panel in a perfect imitation mahogany finish. Note the serpentine curved side panels and hand carved decorations. Size of bed open for use, 72x50 inches. Fitted with best quality woven wire spring with steel spiral spring supports and with patent self adjusting locking device to prevent closing up by accident. Mirror is best quality of French bevel plate, size, 18x40 inches. Shipped direct from factory near Grand Rapids, Michigan. Shipping weight, 365 pounds. Iron weights, separate, 180 lbs. Price, birch, mahogany finish **$31.65** Price, golden oak **31.75**

$3.60 SANITARY STEEL COUCHES, DAVENPORTS AND FOLDING BEDS $17.65

CONVENIENT, COMFORTABLE, VERMIN PROOF AND INDESTRUCTIBLE.

AT $3.60 TO $17.65 our Sanitary Steel Couches and Davenports, have been given a well recognized supremacy by reason of their many superior, practical and commendable new features. Absolutely clean, sanitary, light in weight, but strong, durable and comfortable. Adapted for use in every home.

THE FRAMEWORK is made of the best quality high carbon Bessemer steel, guaranteed not to bend or break. The rods, bars, posts and rails are securely welded or riveted in such manner as to give the maximum of strength.

THE SPRING WORK consists of our new special hair pin double fabric, made of the best quality heavy wire, interwoven and interlaced in such manner as to be absolutely non-sagging and noiseless. It is fastened at each end to the steel frame by a large number of high carbon steel coil helical springs, combining strength, comfort and durability.

This illustration shows our No. 1K2534 Davenport open as a bed. Each Sanitary Steel Davenport and Couch illustrated below can be opened into a full size bed in similar manner.

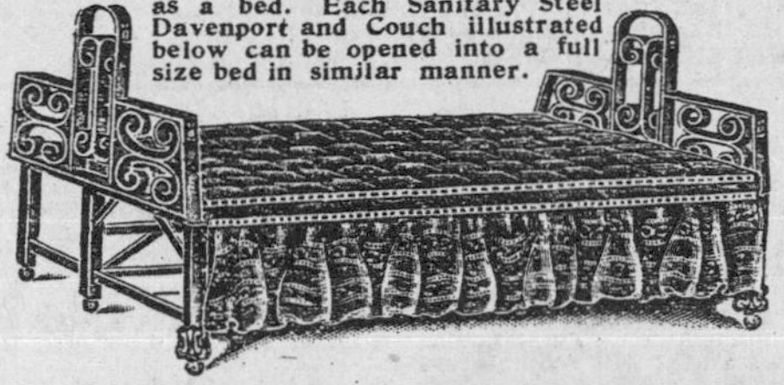

THE FINISH. We use the best quality gold bronze on these sanitary steel couches.

ELASTIC COTTON MATTRESS PADS used on our Sanitary Steel Couches and Davenports, are made of excellent quality white cotton, strictly sanitary and very comfortable, a soft, yet compact and durable mattress pad which easily conforms to the couch whether open or closed, fitted with strong tapes on all sides by which the mattress pad is securely tied to the outer edges of the couch or davenport. These elastic cotton mattress pads are covered with high grade art cretonne, handsomely tufted in biscuit form. The mattress pads used on our sanitary steel davenports are made with square box edges like a mattress, only thinner, so that they will conform to the shape of the davenport in any position. The mattress pads used on our sanitary steel couches are made with pillow stitched edges.

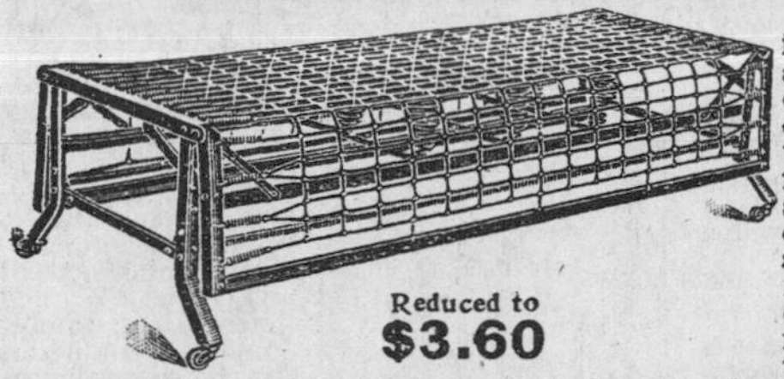

Reduced to **$3.60**

No. 1K2530 Steel Folding Bed Couch, either used as a couch when the sides are dropped and covered with a couch cover, or when opened, to be used as a very comfortable, large size bed. The sides may be lowered and, covered with a mattress pad and couch cover, it then makes a very handsome and comfortable couch. The sides may be raised with ease and the folded couch becomes a very comfortable and extra large size bed. It is convenient, takes up little room, is comfortable and attractive. The size of the couch when the sides are dropped down is 74 inches long and 26 inches wide. The size of the double bed when opened out to its full extent is 74 inches long and 50 inches wide. Finished in gold bronze. By referring to our Dry Goods Department you will find a very complete line of draperies, suitable for a cover which can be furnished at a very small price. Shipped from Chicago, Illinois. Shipping weight, 70 pounds.

Price, Steel Folding Bed Couch, without mattress pad or drapery....... $3.60
Price, Elastic Cotton Mattress Pad, with art cretonne covering. Weight, 18 pounds.. 2.95
Elastic Cotton Bolster, with art cretonne covering....... 1.05

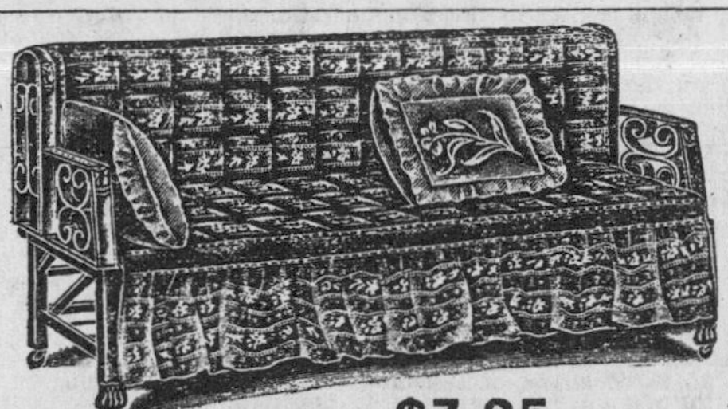

$7.25

No. 1K2534 This beautiful Sanitary Steel Davenport and Bed Couch is 72 inches long and 28 inches wide, as illustrated; back 20 inches high and 48 inches wide opened for use as a bed. The arms, posts and legs are made of 1¼-inch angle steel. The end bars, side rails and cross bars are made of heavy high carbon Bessemer steel, securely welded or riveted together. To form a bed the back automatically drops down, the seat slides forward, the arms remaining stationary, forming the head and foot of the bed. The special hair pin fabric used in the spring is very closely woven and attached at the ends to the frame by forty-two high carbon steel spiral springs, making an absolutely noiseless and perfectly comfortable bed that will not sag or stretch out of shape. Fitted with good quality casters. Beneath the seat is a convenient rack for holding bed clothing when not in use. Furnished in gold bronze. Generally sold by others at $12.00 to $14.00. Shipping weight, about 100 pounds.

Price, Sanitary Steel Sofa, without mattress pad....... $7.25
Price, Elastic Cotton Mattress Pad, with art cretonne cover with ruffle. Square box edges. Weight, 20 pounds....... $3.95

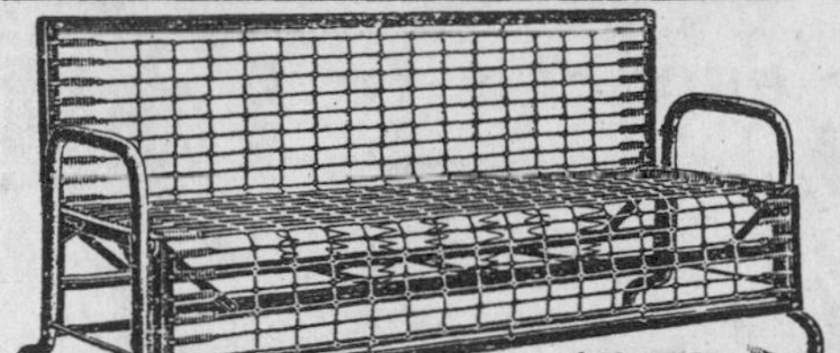

$5.35

No. 1K2532 This Folding Sanitary Steel Davenport Sofa Bed is 74 inches long; width open for use as a bed, 50 inches. Height, back over seat, 17 inches; width, seat, 21 inches. Posts, arms and legs are one solid piece of drawn tubing, 11-16 inch in diameter. Side rails, end rails and connecting rods are made of heavy, high carbon steel securely welded or riveted together, making a frame very strong and rigid. Back and front wing are raised and lowered by a simple ratchet attachment a child can operate. The new hair pin double fabric is made of the best quality heavy wire interwoven and interlaced in such a manner as to be absolutely non-sagging and noiseless. The fabric is fastened at each end by twenty-seven high carbon steel spiral springs. Finished in gold bronze. Simplicity of construction, attractiveness of design and wonderful strength and durability are combined in this article. Shipped from Chicago, Illinois. Shipping weight, 90 pounds.

Price, Sanitary Steel Davenport, without mattress pad....... $5.35
Price, Elastic Cotton Mattress Pad, with art cretonne cover, as shown on No. 1K2534. Square box edges. Weight, 20 pounds....... $3.45

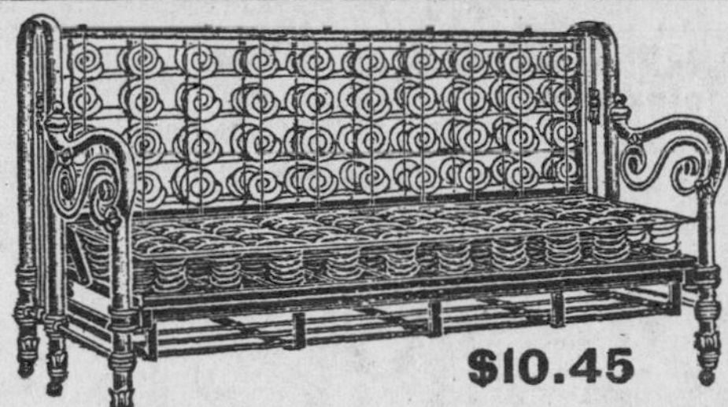

$10.45

No. 1K2535 This Sanitary Steel Davenport Bed is made of the best high carbon Bessemer rolled steel and drawn tubing 1½ inches thick. The joints are securely welded and riveted, guaranteed not to bend or break. As a davenport it is 75 inches long, 22 inches wide; back, 23 inches high. Open for bed, 75 inches long, 45 inches wide. Fitted with the best grade folding spring made of high carbon Bessemer steel coils with full spring edge, non-sagging and exceptionally comfortable. Note the convenient receptacle for bed clothing beneath seat. To form a bed the back automatically drops, seat slides forward, the arms remaining stationary forming the head and foot of bed. Finished in gold bronze. Shipped from Chicago, Illinois. Shipping weight, about 120 pounds. Price, Sanitary Steel Davenport, without mattress pad. $10.45
Price, Elastic Cotton Mattress Pad, extra thick, with art cretonne cover with ruffle, as shown on No. 1K2534. Weight, 25 pounds....... $4.35

OUR SANITARY STEEL FOLDING BEDS are a modern invention, having been in use but a short time. Their wonderful utility combined with absolute cleanliness, being vermin proof, has become so well known that the demand is greater and greater every season. They supply the need for an extra bed when it is impossible to have a regular standing bed, as the amount of room they require when closed is the same as an ordinary dresser.

THE FRAMEWORK is made of the best quality of high carbon Bessemer steel, securely fastened at the joints with bolts and rivets. The top section is made of thoroughly seasoned hardwood and finished to harmonize with the frame. The top, when the bed is folded, can be used as a mantel shelf for bric-a-brac, etc.

THE SPRINGS used on our mantel folding beds, except No. 1K2376, have the well known "National Fabric," which consists of heavy tinned or copper wires, each about 5 inches long, joined by small metal plates. The fabric is attached to the end bars of the bed by high carbon steel spiral springs. Absolutely guaranteed not to sag.

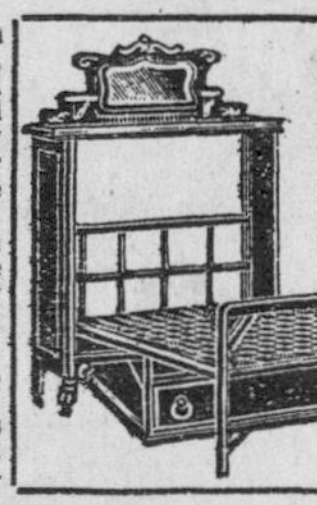

This small illustration shows our No. 1K2384 Folding Bed open. Each folding bed illustrated below can be opened in a similar manner.

THE FINISH. We furnish all our folding iron beds in either of the following colors: Gold bronze, or a perfect imitation of golden oak, as desired. In ordering be sure to state color desired, otherwise we will ship gold bronze.

MATTRESS FOR FOLDING BEDS. We especially recommend our Elastic Felt Mattress for use on our folding beds. The same quality of material and made in the same manner as our Elastic Felt Mattresses, illustrated and described on page 433. They are made 46x72 inches with a 2½-inch box edge which allows room for bed clothing in the bed when folded. We do not sell the so-called "wool mattresses," generally offered by other dealers, as they are made of ground rags and are unclean and unsanitary.

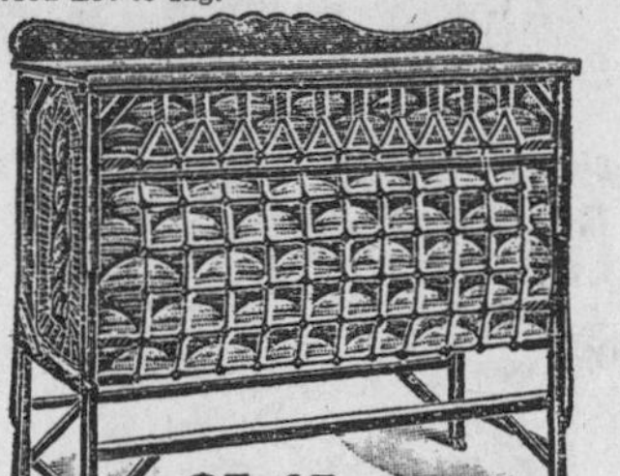

$5.45

Height, 44 inches. Depth, 20 inches.

No. 1K2369 This Folding Bed is built of high carbon Bessemer steel thoroughly braced, fitted with National spring fabric, is strong and durable **and absolutely non-sagging.** The finish is gold bronze with white enamel finished top. **This bed, in its recently improved form is the best made and best appearing low priced sanitary steel folding bed ever offered by any dealer. Exceptionally convenient, easily handled and comfortable. For mattresses to fit these beds, see page 434.**

Size, 3 feet 6 inches by 6 feet 2 inches; weight, 75 pounds. Price....... **$5.45**
Size, 4 feet by 6 feet 2 inches; weight, 90 pounds. Price....... **5.95**

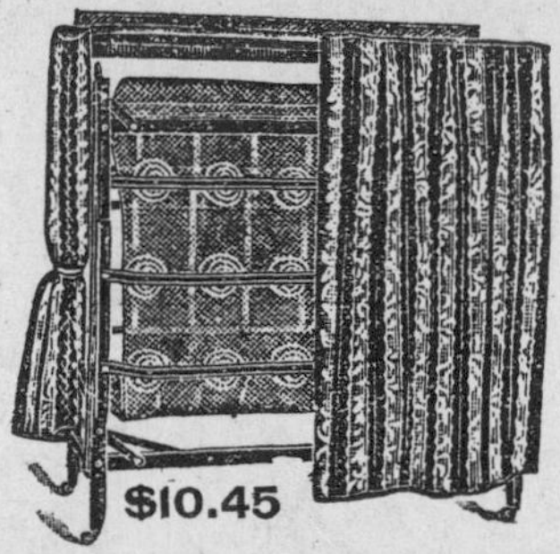

$10.45

No. 1K2376 This Steel Folding Bed is made with a fine woven wire fabric supported with fifteen of the best tempered coil springs making it impossible for the fabric to sag. The top is fitted with brass hooks ready to attach the curtains so that lower portion may be covered in the day time. The top of the bed is stationary and so arranged that when bed is opened it forms head piece. The foot piece folds under the top of the bed and in that position holds the mattress in place when bed is closed. There are no weights of any kind used in the bed, so it is impossible for it to close up when sleeping in it. Height, when closed, 50 inches; depth, 24 inches; length, open, 6 feet 2 inches. Finished in bronze colors. Shipping weight, 170 pounds.

Price, 4-foot bed without curtain **$10.45**

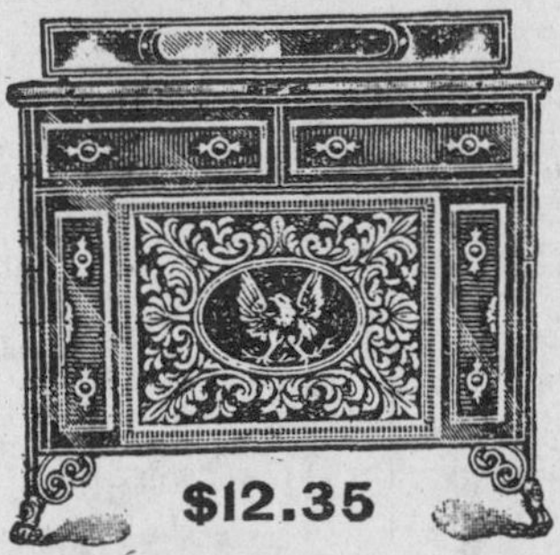

$12.35

No. 1K2377 This Metal Folding Bed combines neatness, lightness, comfort and cleanliness. It is made entirely of steel, except the top. Dimensions: closed, height, 45 inches; depth, 24 inches. Dimensions: open for use, length, 6 feet 2 inches; width, 4 feet. Fitted with the celebrated National spring. Front ornamented with large medallion of stamped steel. Top can be draped and ornamented with bric-a-brac, making an attractive article of furniture for the home. See page 433 for mattress to fit this bed. Shipping weight, 120 pounds.

Price, with mirror top....... **$12.35**
Price, with plain top....... **10.85**

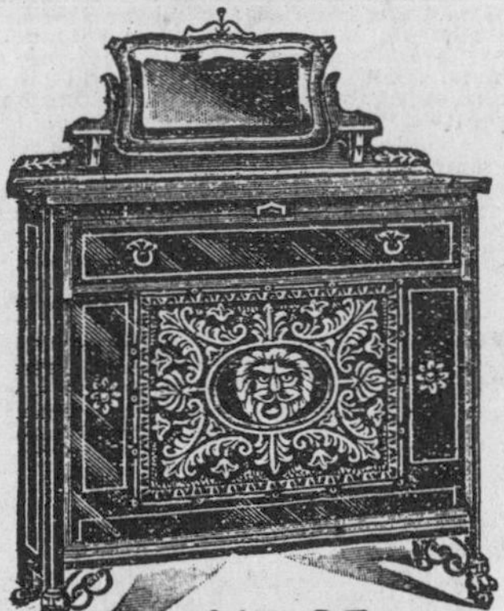

$17.65

No. 1K2384 This Magnificent Metal Folding Bed has genuine steel front and ends. The top is made of thoroughly seasoned hardwood finished to match the frame. Note the handsome pressed steel front panel with heavy oxidized medallion center. Mirror is best quality French bevel plate, size, 12x24 inches. Dimensions: closed, 52 inches high, 24 inches deep. Dimensions: open for use, 74 inches long, 48 inches wide. Fitted with high grade spring with National fabric, the most comfortable, best wearing, non-sagging spring made. Best quality casters. Finished in a perfect quality of golden oak, dead black or rich gold bronze. State color wanted. See page 434 for mattress to fit this bed. Shipping weight, 200 pounds.

Price, as illustrated....... **$17.65**
Price, wood panel back....... **14.65**

$1.39 IRON BEDS $12.75

BIG REDUCTION IN PRICES

AT $1.39 TO $12.75 We offer you finer iron beds than were ever before shown. Newest designs, first class material, construction and finish. Wonderful values. We challenge the world on quality and price. A lower price than ours means a poorer quality.
THEY ARE INDESTRUCTIBLE AND WILL NEVER WEAR OUT.

THE METAL USED in the construction of our beds is strictly high grade throughout. No rusty scrap iron or corroded refuse metals. The highest and best quality of malleable iron, rolled Bessemer steel and drawn brass tubing.

THE CONSTRUCTION of our metal beds is the best that modern machinery, science and skilled workmanship, can possibly produce. Every part and parcel is carefully modeled, framed and joined. The joints and chills carefully rounded and smoothed. The rails are made of Bessemer steel in angle shape and will not bend or break. Great care is taken in the fitting of the tongue and grooves by which the rail is fastened to the head and foot end. They stand firm and will support any weight of persons.

THE FINISH of our iron beds, we guarantee the best that can be made. The enamel which is used for the several coatings is the highest grade obtainable. Each coat, after being carefully and thoroughly applied, is baked in a large oven heated to a very high degree of temperature, then thoroughly smoothed and polished. This produces a finish that is impervious to water and all our iron beds can be cleaned of finger marks or other soiling by washing with soap and water.

THE BRASS TRIMMING which is used in the ornamentation and construction of our metal beds is of the highest quality of drawn brass tubing, highly polished and burnished, coated with the best quality of French lacquer, which absolutely preserves the polish and prevents tarnishing. Lacquer is to brass what varnish is to wood, it preserves the material.

COLOR BEDS. We furnish all our iron beds in white enamel unless ordered otherwise. Under the especial description of each bed it specifically states whether furnished in single solid color or in combination colors. Many designs of beds are much more attractive in single solid color only and for that reason we furnish certain patterns in single solid color only. When beds are ordered in colors, shipment will be made direct from factory near Chicago and from three days to one week's time is required before shipment can be made.

WE CALL YOUR SPECIAL ATTENTION to the fact that we furnish our iron beds shown on pages 428 and 429 in combination colors, with gilt decorated chills, as follows: Maroon and white, light blue and white, pea green and white, dark blue and white, pink and white, olive green and white or dark green and white. When you wish to order a bed in combination of colors, be sure to state colors desired.

WE ESPECIALLY RECOMMEND maroon and white, light blue and white, pea green and white, as the most effective and desirable combinations. When finished in combination colors the posts and top rods are finished in the first color mentioned above and the filling rods in white.

VERNIS MARTIN ALL GOLD FINISH. This beautiful high grade finish was introduced in this country recently and has become deservedly popular. It derives its name from its inventor, a Frenchman, Vernis Martin. It is a three-coat finish, consisting of a priming foundation coat thoroughly baked and hardened, a second coat of gold bronze and, lastly, a third coat of the best quality varnish. The finish color is a transparent, rich golden tint, closely resembling the high grade all brass beds. To produce this handsome finish requires great care by the best skilled workmen. Our Vernis Martin finish must be seen, examined and compared with that offered by other dealers to be fully appreciated. We absolutely guarantee it not to fade or tarnish.

THE SIDE RAILS on all our iron beds are made of the best high carbon Bessemer steel, angle shape. THEY ARE FITTED to the bed with the reverse side up to allow the use of wood slats or regular extension end bar springs as desired. TO SET UP IRON BEDS, place the rail in the groove, lay a piece of wood on the shank of the rail and drive into the groove with hammer by striking the wood.

HOW TO ORDER. When ordering a metal bed, be careful to state the width wanted, also the color, otherwise white will be shipped. We illustrate our beds made up with bolster, mattress and covering, but the price quoted is for the bed only. Springs, mattresses and pillows are illustrated and described on pages 431 to 435.

Adjustable Iron Bed Canopy.

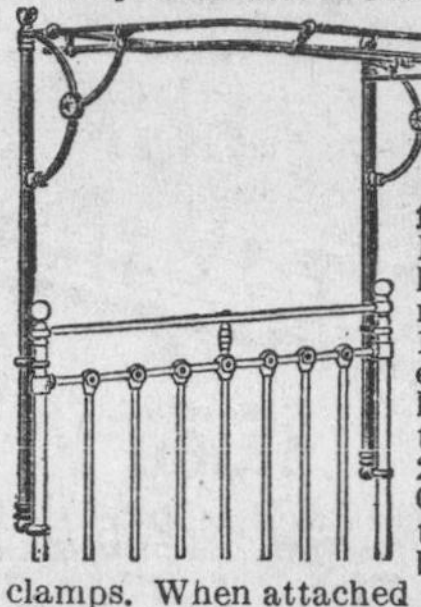

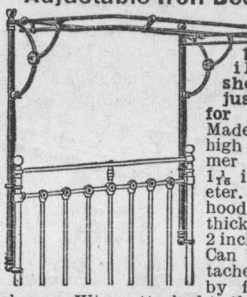

No. 1K2401 This illustration shows our adjustable canopy for iron beds. Made of best quality high carbon Bessemer steel. Posts, 1 1/16 inches in diameter. Solid steel hood rods, ⅜ inch thick. Brass knobs, 2 inches in diameter. Can be securely attached to bed posts by four patent clamps. When attached to the bed the top of canopy measures 86 inches from the floor. Finished in baked white enamel or any solid color. In ordering canopy be sure to give size of post, width of bed, and color wanted. Shipping weight, about 35 pounds.
Price, all sizes **$3.25**

$4.98 FOR THIS HANDSOME DESIGN HIGH GRADE, MASSIVE IRON BED complete with best quality steel springs.

The bed is one of our special three-piece combination beds which has no side rails. The long bar of the spring forms the side rail of the bed. One of the finest methods of construction known and offered exclusively by us. This method makes it possible to pack and ship the bed at less expense. We offer this combination outfit to show what it is possible for us to produce in a strictly high grade bed, spring and mattress at an extremely low price, which is offered only as a sample of the wonderful values we are giving in our entire bed line. Height of the head end of the bed, 56 inches, foot end, 44 inches. The corner posts are 1 5-16 inches in diameter and are mounted with massive smooth cast ornamental chills. The top rod and filling rods are ⅜ inch thick. These dimensions make an unusually substantial and massive bed. Finished throughout in best quality white enamel, thoroughly baked and hardened. The spring frame is made of high carbon steel angle bars, 1¼ inches wide. The fabric is made of best quality heavy tinned wire interwoven and interlaced in what is called hairpin style, making it absolutely non-sagging and noiseless. The fabric is fastened to the steel frame at each end by fifteen high carbon steel spiral springs. This spring combines the greatest comfort and lasting qualities it is possible to obtain. The mattress is the finest of its kind that skill and our knowledge of mattress construction could enable us to produce. A combination mattress never before offered, suitable for use in any climate. The filling is made of white basswood excelsior, thoroughly screened and freed from all impurities. This forms the inner filling only. One side is covered with a thick layer of the best quality sanitary sea moss, which is not excelled for its hygienic and comfort giving qualities. The other side of the mattress is covered with thick layers of elastic felt of good quality. This makes the mattress suitable for cold or warm weather and furnishes a firm or soft bed as may be desired. The ticking is extra quality heavy twill, closely stitched and full bound. The mattress is made in the very latest and most up to date manner. Diamond tufted with leather tufts, and we place it in competition with mattresses sold throughout the country at $6.00 to $7.00.

No. 1K2395 Full size only. Price, Iron Bed and Spring.....$4.98
Shipping weight, about 110 pounds.

No. 1K2395 Full size only. Price, Mattress only..........$3.98
Shipping weight, about 50 pounds.

REDUCED TO $4.98

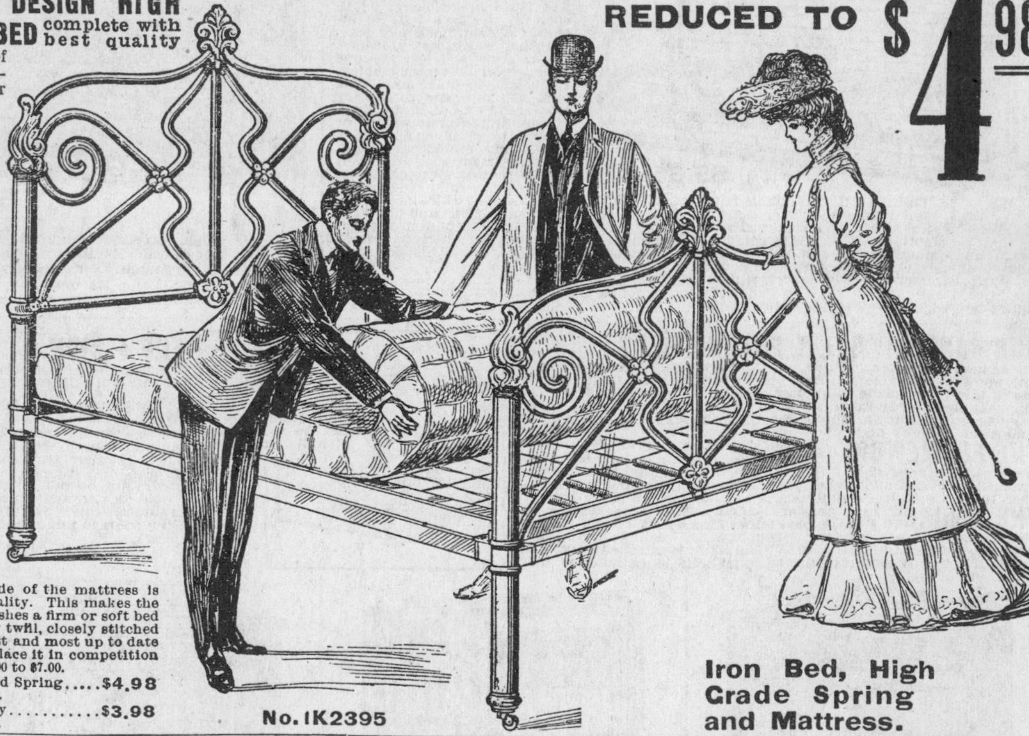

No. 1K2395

Iron Bed, High Grade Spring and Mattress.

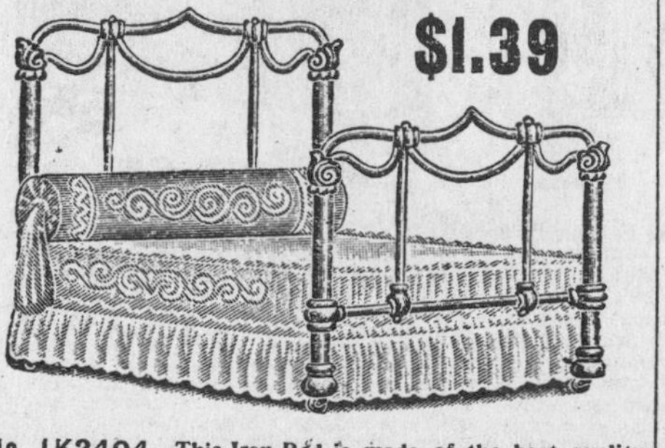

$1.39

No. 1K2404 This Iron Bed is made of the best quality malleable iron and high carbon steel. Height, head end, 48 inches; height, foot end, 38 inches; corner posts, ⅞ inch thick; filling rods, ⅜ inch thick; finished in white enamel only. Wonderful value at our price. Furnished in 3 foot 6 inch, or 4 foot 6 inch widths. Shipping weight, 55 pounds. Be sure to state size desired. Price, all sizes...... **$1.39**

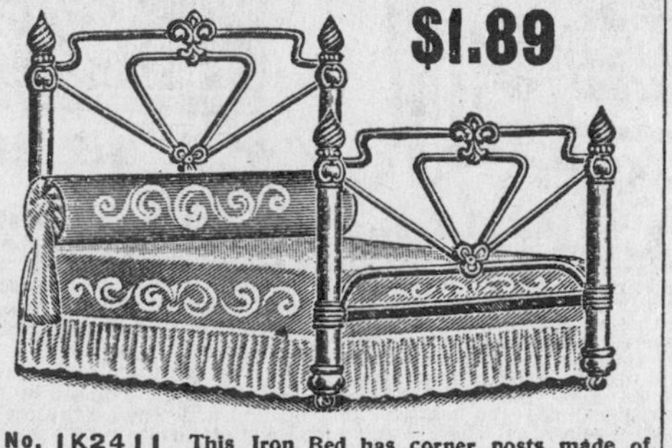

$1.89

No. 1K2411 This Iron Bed has corner posts made of drawn steel tubing ⅞ inch thick, filling rods, solid steel ⅜ inch thick. Height, head end, 50 inches; height, foot end, 45 inches. Finished in solid color white enamel only. Furnished in 3 foot, 3 foot 6 inch or 4 foot 6 inch widths. Exceptional value. Shipping weight, 60 pounds. Be sure to state size desired. Price, all sizes.......... **$1.89**

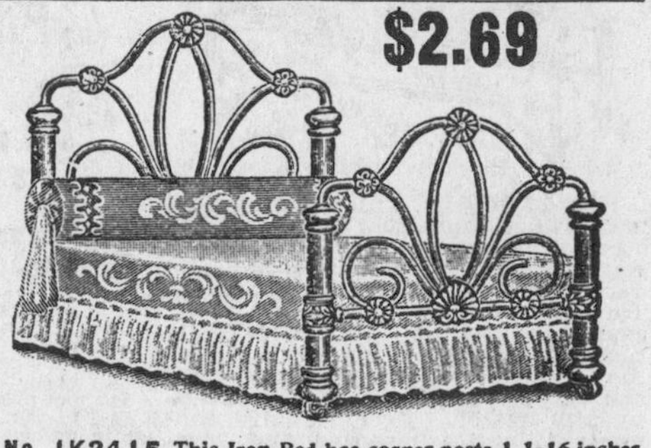

$2.69

No. 1K2415 This Iron Bed has corner posts 1 1-16 inches thick. Solid steel top rods and filling rods, ⅜ inch thick. Height, head, 64 inches; height, foot, 50 inches. Furnished only in solid color baked white enamel. Best quality casters. Made in 3 foot, 3 foot 6 inch, 4 foot or 4 foot 6 inch widths. Be sure to state size desired. Weight, 75 pounds. Price **$2.69**

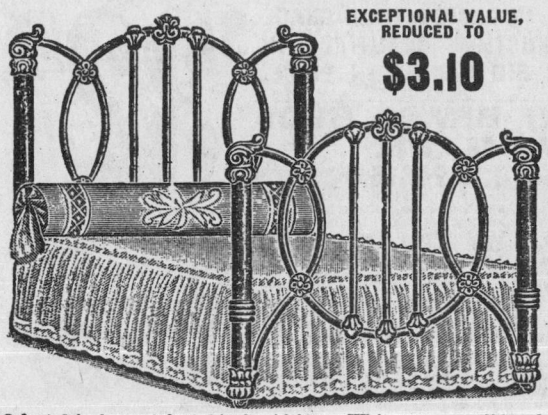

EXCEPTIONAL VALUE, REDUCED TO $3.10

No. 1K2416 This Bed is made of the best quality steel tubing with solid steel filling rods, cross rails and side rails. Corner posts, 1 1/8 inches thick. Filling rods, 3/8 inch thick. Height of head end, 62 inches. An exceptionally attractive new design, strong and substantial. A bed that sells generally in stores at $5.50 to $6.00. Furnished in 3 foot, $3.10

3 foot 6 inch or 4 foot 6 inch widths. White or any solid color enameled finish. Best quality steel frame casters. Shipping weight, 95 pounds. **Be sure to state size and color desired.** Price, any solid color............. **$3.10**

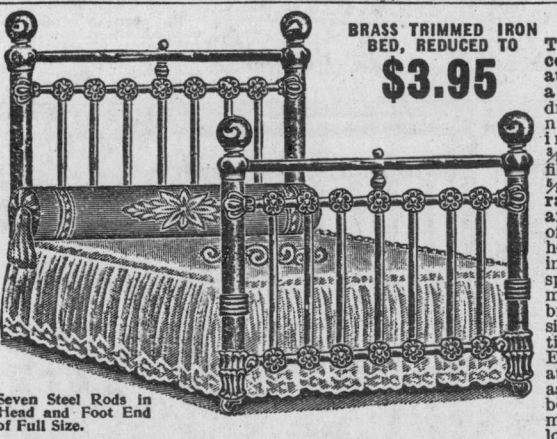

WONDERFUL VALUE, REDUCED TO $3.85

No. 1K2418 This Iron Bed has corner posts and top rods made of 1 1/4-inch tubes. Is 60 inches high at the head and 41 inches at the foot. The scroll rods are 7/16 inch thick, the bottom rods are 3/8 inch. Note the handsome chills on posts and filling rods. Finished in best quality baked white enamel or any solid color. Complete with best quality casters. Furnished in three widths: 3 foot 6 inch, 4 foot or 4 foot 6 inch. Generally sells in stores at Shipping $3.85

$6.00 to $6.50. **Be sure to state size and color desired.** weight, 95 pounds. Price, any solid color........................ **$3.85**

BRASS TRIMMED IRON BED, REDUCED TO $3.95

No. 1K2424 This bed is exceptional value at the price we ask. It has drawn steel corner posts 1 1/8 inches thick, 3/8-inch solid steel filling rods and 5/8-inch **brass top rail on both head and foot.** Height of head, 58 inches; height of foot, 42 inches. Has brass spindles and top mounts and four brass vases. Full size has seven vertical steel rods. Exceptional value at the price we ask. Fitted with best casters. Is made in the following widths: 3 foot, 3 foot 6 inch, 4 foot or 4 foot 6 inch. Shipping weight, 100 pounds.

Seven Steel Rods in Head and Foot End of Full Size.

Finished in white enamel or any solid color. **Be sure to state size and color desired.**
Price, any solid color........................ **$3.95**

A BARGAIN, REDUCED TO $4.13

No. 1K2429 Head is 57 inches high; 45 inches at the foot. Corner posts made of drawn steel tubing 1 1/8 inches thick. Solid steel filling rods 7/16 inch thick. Has brass knobs, brass vases and brass rosettes and full extension bow foot end. Finished in best baked white enamel or any solid color. Fitted with set of best casters. This bed is made in the following widths: 3 foot 6 inch or 4 foot 6 inch. This bed sells in stores at $6.50 or $7.00. Shipping weight, 90 pounds.

BOW FOOT

Be sure to state size and color desired. Price, any solid color....... **$4.13**
Sig. 27—1st Ed.

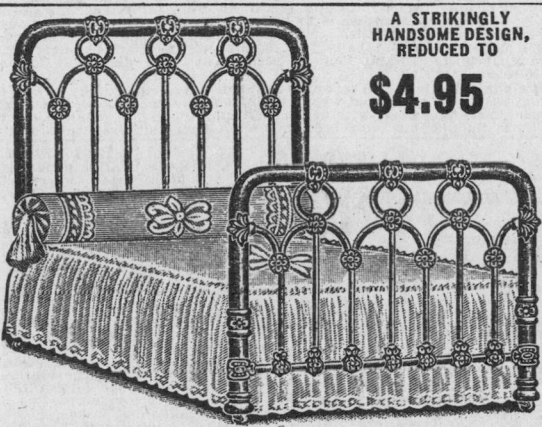

THIS SPLENDID DESIGN, REDUCED TO $4.20

No. 1K2432 This Iron Bed is strikingly handsome in design. Head is 67 inches high, foot 48 inches high. Corner posts made of drawn steel tubing 1 1/8 inches in diameter. Top rods 1/2 inch thick, bottom rods 7/16 inch thick, filling rods 3/8 inch thick. We call your special attention to the beautifully shaped and interlaced top and filling rods connected by large smooth cast and moulded chills. Finished in baked white enamel or any solid

color with gilt decorated chills. Made in 4 foot 6 inch width. Best quality casters. Shipping weight, 100 pounds. **Be sure to state color desired.** Price, any solid color........................ **$4.20**

A STRIKINGLY HANDSOME DESIGN, REDUCED TO $4.95

No. 1K2439 This Iron Bed is exceptional value. Corner posts and top rods made of drawn steel tubing 1 1/8 inches thick. Handsome designed solid steel filling rods and rings 3/8 inch in diameter. Ornamental smooth cast chills are decorated with gilt. Height head, 58 inches. Height foot, 38 inches. Made in 3 foot 6 inch, 4 foot or 4 foot 6 inch widths. Finished in baked white enamel or any solid color. Best quality casters.

Shipping weight, 115 pounds. **Be sure to state size and color desired.** Price, any solid color, with gilt chills........................ **$4.95**

A SPLENDID VALUE, REDUCED TO $5.06

No. 1K2442 An exceptionally attractive, new design, four-post Iron Bed. Height, head end, 61 inches. Corner posts made of drawn steel tubing 1 1/8 inches in diameter. Vertical and cross filling rods 3/8 inch in diameter are made of solid steel. Finished in any color baked enamel. Massive, smooth cast chills have gilt decorations. Made in 4 foot 6 inch size only. A strikingly handsome bed at an astonishingly low price. Sells

in stores at $8.00 to $9.00. Shipping weight, about 118 pounds. **Be sure to state color desired.**
Price, any solid color, with gilt chills........................ **$5.06**

BRASS TRIMMED IRON BED, REDUCED TO $5.75

No. 1K2446 This high grade Iron Bed represents a saving, at the price we ask, of $3.50 to $4.00, as against the prices generally offered by others. Height, head, 60 inches. Height, foot, 42 inches. Corner posts and top rods made of drawn steel tubing 1 1-16 inches thick. The solid steel vertical and scroll design filling rods 5-16 inch thick. Note heavy brass knobs 2 1/2 inches in diameter and the handsome, deep smooth cut chills with gilt decorations. Finished in baked white enamel or any solid color enamel or combination colors. We especially recommend olive green and white, light blue and white or pea green

and white with gilt chills. Made in 4 foot and 4 foot 6 inch widths. Shipping weight, 145 pounds. **Be sure to state size and color desired.**
Price, any solid color, with gilt chills........................ **$5.75**
Price, two colors, with gilt chills........................ **6.15**

$16.45 BRASS BEDS $32.95

HANDSOME IN DESIGN, HIGH GRADE IN CONSTRUCTION, BEAUTIFUL IN FINISH, A BIG SAVING IN PRICE.

WE INVITE MORE THAN ORDINARY ATTENTION to this splendid line of Brass Beds, as illustrated below. They are made for us by the largest and best known manufacturers of brass beds in the United States. You will find each bed is made of better material, better in finish, more perfectly fitted, more durable and in every way more satisfactory, than brass beds made by the average factory and sold by the average dealer. Every improvement in brass bed construction is embodied in the construction of our brass beds. They are the perfect product of the best skilled workmanship from the highest grade material obtainable at any price.

THE DESIGNS are strikingly attractive and graceful in outline. They embody all the new, up to date ideas in brass bed construction, selected with the view of combining the greatest strength and solidity with a handsome appearance, the product of years of experience, and we offer them to our customers with the positive assurance and guarantee that in no retail store or other catalogues, can they be equaled in elegance of design, perfection of construction, combined with beauty of finish.

THE METAL. The raw material which enters into the construction of our brass beds is specially and thoroughly tested before being worked up into the finished product. No rusty scrap or corroded stock is used. Every post, rod, knob, husk, rail and mounting is made from the choicest high grade stock. Thoroughly experienced and competent inspectors carefully inspect each piece and every piece of the raw material is rigidly examined. You will never find a defective part or piece in one of our brass beds.

THE FINISH of a brass bed is the most important feature next to the material and construction. Each piece, post, rod, husk, vase and knob is burnished and polished in the most perfect manner until the surface is as smooth as a mirror. To preserve this perfectly polished mirrorlike surface, the entire bed is given several coatings of the finest quality imported lacquer, which prevents the finish from tarnishing. In other words, lacquer is to polished brass what varnish is to polished wood. There are as many grades of lacquer as there are grades of varnish. We use none but the best. To produce this highly polished surface and apply the lacquer requires workmen skilled in the art. Our brass beds need no repolishing. To keep them in perfect condition, use a soft cotton cloth or chamois skin to remove the dust.

HOW OUR BRASS BEDS ARE MADE.

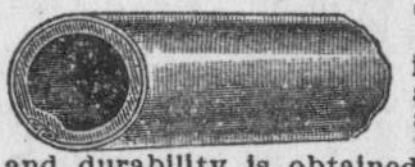

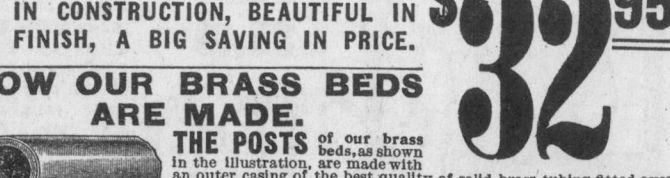

THE POSTS of our brass beds, as shown in the illustration, are made with an outer casing of the best quality of solid brass tubing fitted over an inner casing of the best high carbon Bessemer steel tubing. By this method of construction the greatest possible strength, rigidity and durability is obtained and the liability of denting the surface is practically eliminated.

WE CALL YOUR SPECIAL ATTENTION to the extra heavy steel shank perfectly framed on the posts, into which the angle steel side rails and end rails are fitted when the bed is set up. The tongue on the rail fits perfectly into the groove of the steel shank on the post. By this device the bed stands in a perfect alignment, rigidly and firm.

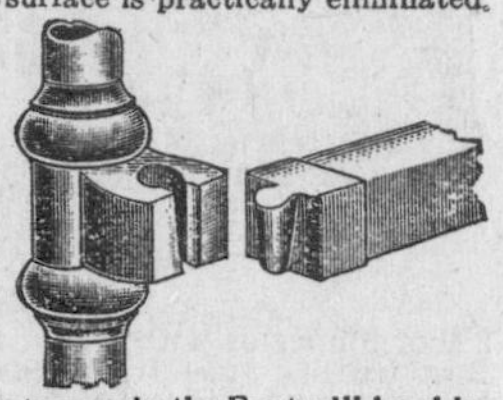

THE PACKING. We use especial care in the packing of our brass beds. Each bed is carefully wrapped in tissue paper and cotton flannel and securely packed in a strong wooden crate in such manner as to prevent any possibility of injury. We guarantee every bed to reach our customer in the same perfect condition it leaves the factory.

THE FREIGHT CHARGES. All orders from our customers in the East will be shipped from our factory in New York. All orders from our customers in the Middle West and West will be shipped from our factory near Chicago, thereby insuring the lowest possible freight charges. The freight charges on a brass bed amount to almost nothing as compared with the big saving in price. The freight charges on an average brass bed for a distance of 500 miles, will amount to $1.25 to $1.50. We always select the factory nearest to your railroad station. Remember that your local dealer must pay the same freight rate that you pay and that he includes the freight charges in figuring his selling price.

OUR PRICES. We challenge any firm on earth to furnish the same quality of brass beds at the same or anywhere near the price we ask. In fact, we know by actual comparison and test of the goods that we are saving our customers 35 per cent to 50 per cent as against the prices asked by other dealers. Many dealers, and especially other catalogue houses, in their efforts to compete with us are sacrificing quality in order to name a low price. Quality is a watchword with us. Remember, quality in material, quality in construction and quality in finish of our brass beds is absolutely and without doubt or question the very best obtainable at any price.

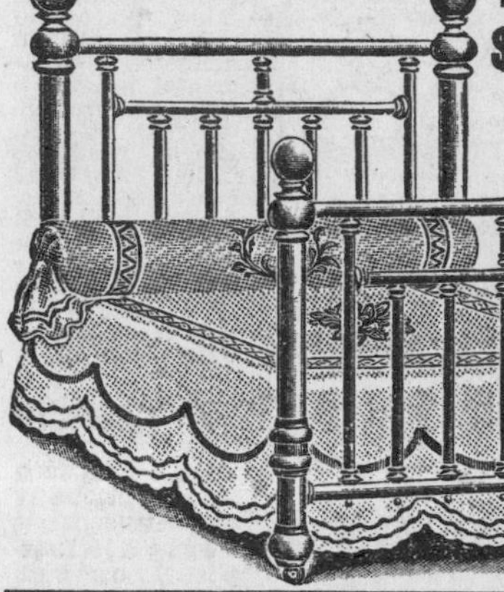

REDUCED TO $16.45

THIS HIGH GRADE BRASS BED is generally sold in retail stores at $22.00 to $25.00. Corner posts are 2 inches thick. Top rods on head and foot end, ¾ inch thick; bottom rods and vertical filling rods ⅝ inch thick. Head end stands 64 inches high, the foot end 43 inches high. The extra large brass balls on corner posts are 3 inches in diameter. Note the ornamental fancy designed husks in center, top and bottom of corner posts. Best quality ball bearing casters. We furnish this brass bed in four widths, 3 foot, 3 foot 6 inch, 4 foot, or 4 foot 6 inch. Length, 76 inches. Shipping weight, 180 pounds. Be sure to state size desired, otherwise we ship full size.

No. 1K2504 Price, all sizes, 1½-inch posts..... **$16.45**

No. 1K2506 Price, all sizes, 2-inch posts..... **$19.65**

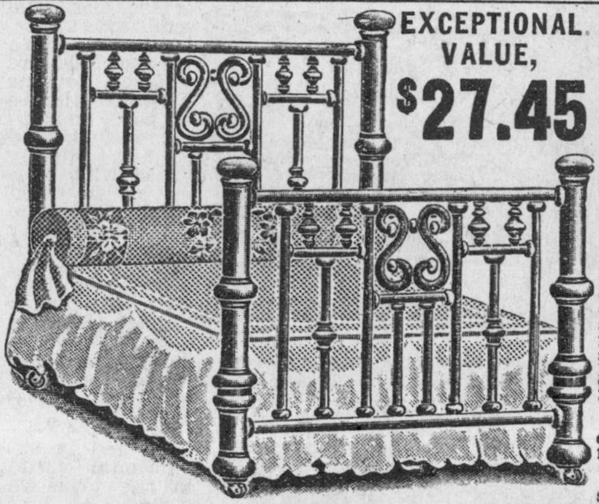

EXCEPTIONAL VALUE, $27.45

No. 1K2518 THIS MAGNIFICENT HIGH GRADE BRASS BED should be compared with those generally sold at $40.00 to $45.00. The head end stands 57 inches high, the foot end 38 inches high. The massive corner posts are 2 inches in diameter, surmounted with heavy brass knobs 2¼ inches thick. The top and bottom rods are made of 1-inch tubing, all other filling rods ¾ inch thick. Note the beautiful scroll center design in the head and foot end and the large husks and mounting on posts and filling rods. Made in 4 foot and 4 foot 6 inch widths. Best quality large ball bearing casters. Shipping weight, 240 pounds.

Be sure to state size desired, otherwise we ship full size.

Price, all sizes......... **$27.45**

No. 1K2512 EXCEPTIONAL VALUE IN A STRICTLY HIGH GRADE BRASS BED. Our price, $22.65, represents a saving to our customers of $10.00 to $12.00 as against the prices asked by others. The corner posts are the largest used on brass beds, being 2 inches in diameter, surmounted with heavy brass knobs 3 inches in diameter. Top rail on head and foot end ¾ inch thick; bottom rail and other filling rods ⅝ inch thick. Note the large husks on corner posts and the handsome scroll in top of head and foot ends. Five vertical filling rods in head and foot have large husk mountings in center. The head end stands 56 inches high, bow foot end 40 inches high. We furnish this bed in 3 foot, 3 foot 6 inch, 4 foot, or 4 foot 6 inch widths. Length, 76 inches. Securely wrapped and crated and shipped direct from factory in East or West, according to location of customer. Shipping weight, 180 pounds. Be sure to state size desired, otherwise we ship full size. Price, all sizes..... **$22.65**

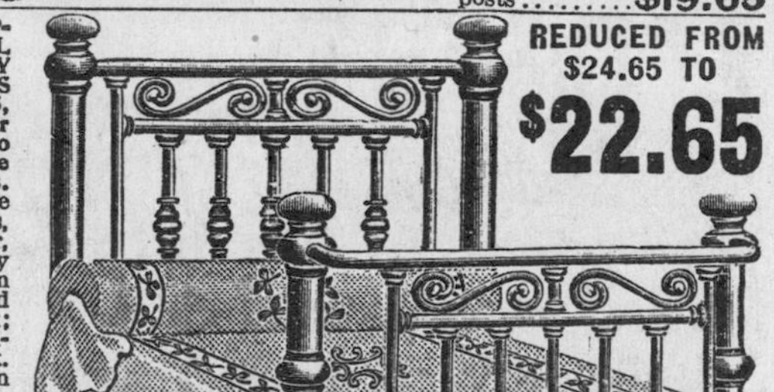

REDUCED FROM $24.65 TO $22.65

No. 1K2520 THIS MASSIVE HIGH GRADE CONTINUOUS POST BRASS BED cannot be excelled in design, material, construction or finish. The head end stands 61 inches high, foot end 42 inches high. The massive posts and top rails are 2 inches in diameter, cross fitting rods ¾ inch thick, vertical filling rods ⅝ inch in diameter. Note especially the beautiful rounded and beaded corners, the large husks in center and bottom of posts. Made in 3 foot 6 inch or 4 foot 6 inch widths. Best quality ball bearing casters. Securely wrapped and crated and shipped direct from factory in East or West, according to location of customer. Shipping weight, 200 pounds. Be sure to state size desired, otherwise we ship full size.

Price, all sizes **$28.85**

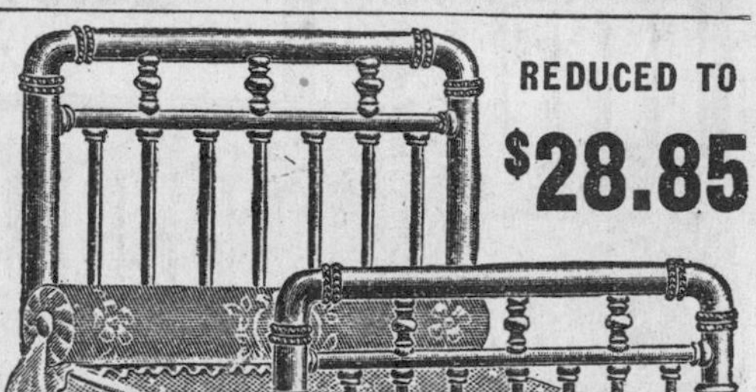

REDUCED TO $28.85

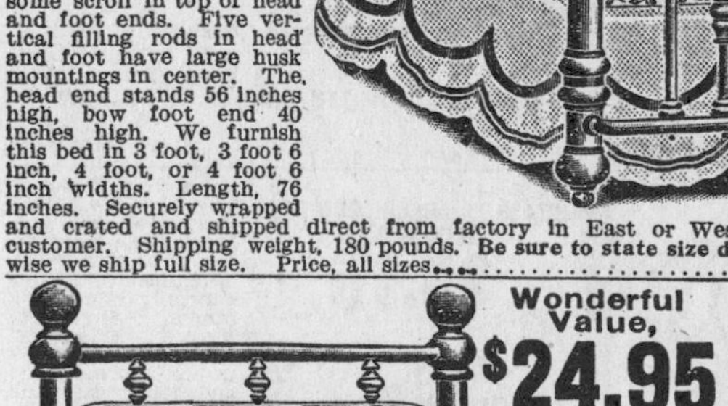

Wonderful Value, $24.95

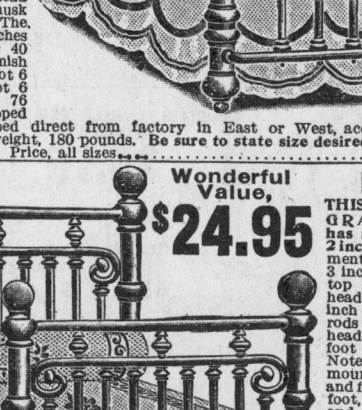

No. 1K2514 THIS SPLENDID HIGH GRADE BRASS BED has massive corner posts 2 inches in diameter, ornamented with heavy knobs 3 inches in diameter. The top and bottom rods on head and foot ends are ¾ inch thick, all other filling rods ⅝ inch thick. The head is 62 inches high, the foot end 42 inches high. Note the large husks and mountings on corner posts and filling rods. Made in 3 foot, 3 foot 6 inch, 4 foot and 4 foot 6 inch widths. Height, 76 inches. Best quality large ball bearing casters. Securely wrapped and crated and shipped from factory in East or West, according to location of our customers. Shipping weight, 240 pounds. Be sure to state size desired, otherwise we ship full size.

Price, all sizes......... **$24.95**

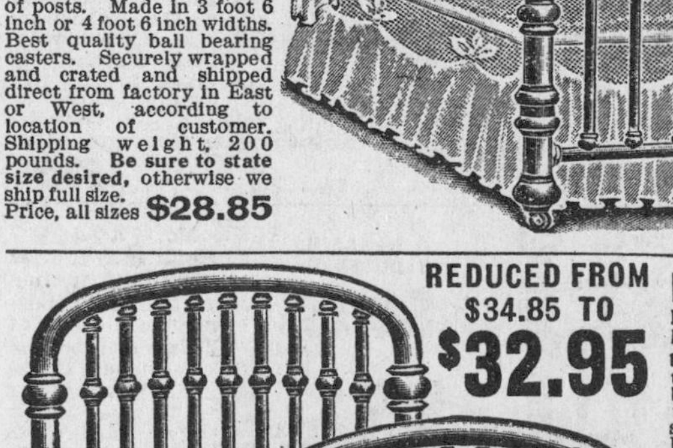

REDUCED FROM $34.85 TO $32.95

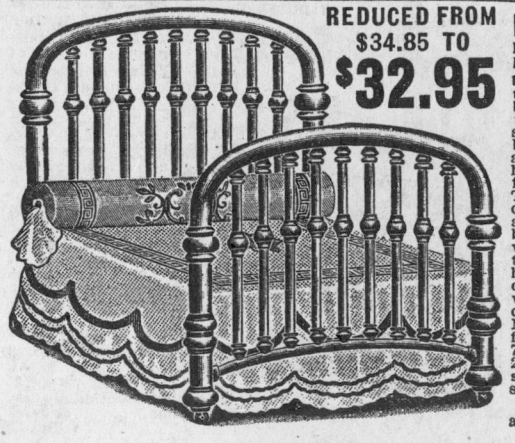

No. 1K2524 THIS MAGNIFICENT HIGH GRADE BRASS BED combines simplicity of design, perfection of construction and beauty of finish, and to be thoroughly appreciated should be compared with brass beds offered by others at $45.00 to $50.00. The head end is 62 inches high, foot end 43 inches high. The massive continuous corner posts and top rails are 2 inches in diameter, bottom rods ⅞ inch thick, vertical filling rods ¾ inch thick. Note the large husks in center and base of corner posts and on the 18 vertical filling rods. Best quality ball bearing casters. Made in 3 foot 6 inch or foot 6 inch widths. Length 76 inches. Shipping weight 200 pounds. Be sure to state size, otherwise we ship full size.

Price, all sizes...... **$32.95**

COTS AND CRIBS

We call special attention to the construction of our Cradles, Cribs and Folding Beds, as they are all made with screw construction so that when shipped they are packed in a condensed and small package, thereby greatly reducing the freight charges. Anyone can set up our cradles, cribs and folding beds without any difficulty, as the parts do not require special fitting. K. D. means knocked down, or in other words, in parts. By shipping goods knocked down the freight charges are greatly reduced.

OUR MATTRESSES FOR CRIBS AND COTS as described on page 434, are made throughout of the best quality of material obtainable. They are absolutely clean, sanitary, comfortable and durable. We especially recommend our elastic felt, sea moss and hair mattresses for use on cribs and cots.

Universal Woven Wire Cot.

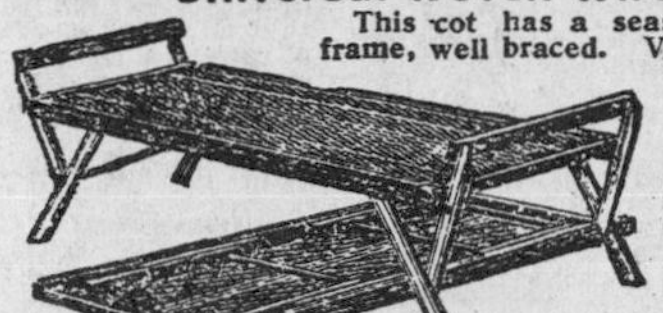

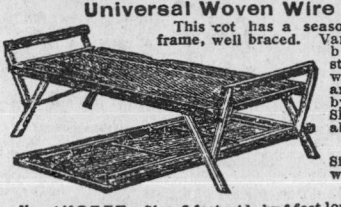

This cot has a seasoned hard maple frame, well braced. Varnish finish. The bed is made of strong single weave wire fabric. Head and foot are raised by opening legs. Shipping weight, about 30 pounds.

No. 1K2556 Size, 2 feet 6 inches wide by 6 feet long. Price........91c

No. 1K2557 Size, 3 feet wide by 6 feet long. Price....98c

Wonderful Value at $1.08.

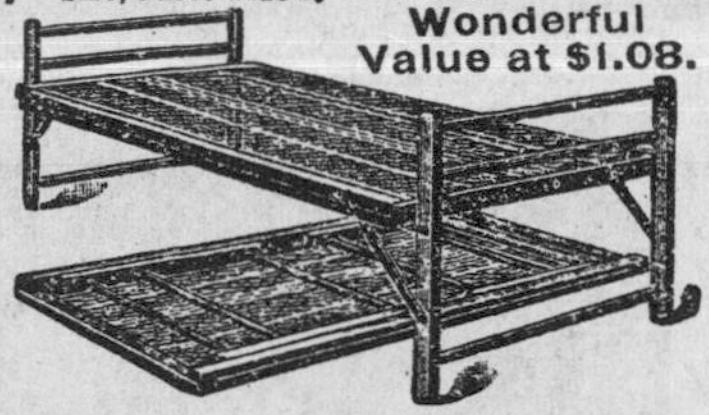

This is the best low priced, compact folding cot on the market. The frame is made of hard maple with upright posts, strongly braced. Varnish finish. The bed is made of strong single weave wire fabric, making the most comfortable and durable bed of its kind possible to produce. Shipping weight, about 35 pounds.

		Price
No. 1K2560	Size, 2 feet 6 inches wide by 6 feet long,	$1.08
No. 1K2561	Size, 3 feet wide by 6 feet long.........	1.17

An Excellent Cot for $1.73.

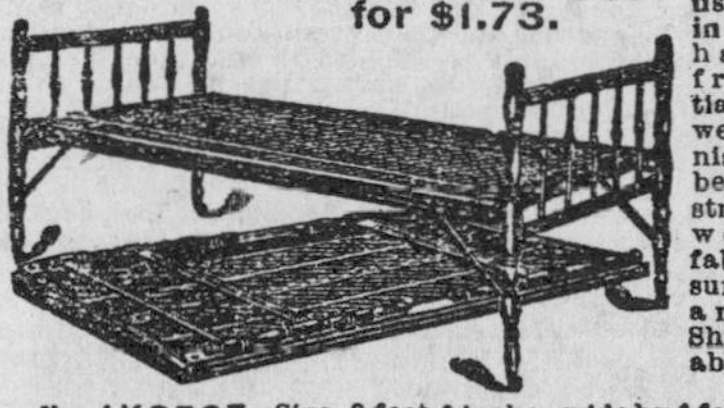

This cot is unusually attractive in design. Has a hard maple frame substantially made and well braced. Varnish finish. The bed is made of strong single weave wire fabric, which insures comfort and durability. Shipping weight, about 35 pounds.

		Price
No. 1K2565	Size, 2 feet 6 inches wide by 6 feet long,	$1.73
No. 1K2566	Size, 3 feet wide by 6 feet long.........	1.85
No. 1K2567	Size, 3 feet 6 inches wide by 6 feet long,	1.95

Steel Cot, $2.75.

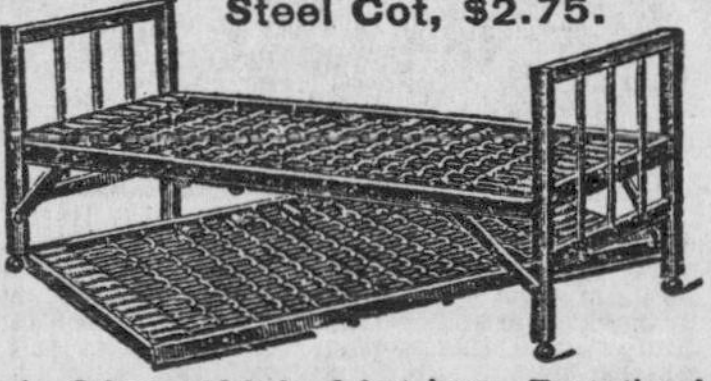

The frame of this folding cot is made of 1¼-inch angle Bessemer steel. It is fitted with our double hairpin fabric steel coil helical endsprings. Height of head and foot ends, 28 inches. Furnished in 2 foot 6 inch width by 6 feet long or in 3 foot width by 6 feet long. Exceptional value at the price we ask. Generally sold in stores at $4.00 to $4.25. Shipping weight, about 60 pounds. Be sure to state width desired.

No. 1K2569 Price, 2 foot 6 inch width.........$2.75
Price, 3 foot width.........................3.10

Steel Couch Cot, $3.85.

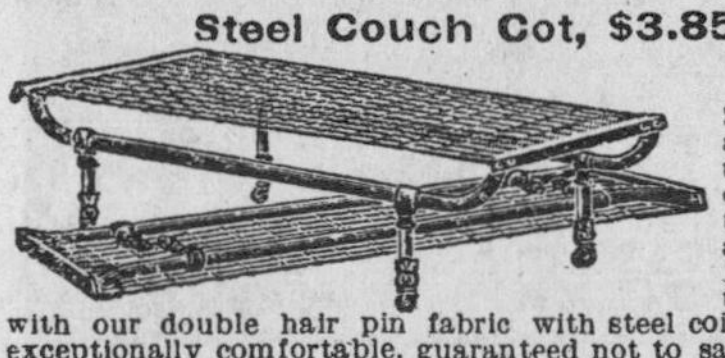

No. 1K2570 Specially adapted for use as a couch or bed. Continuous posts and top rods 1½ inches thick. Fitted with our double hair pin fabric with steel coil end springs; exceptionally comfortable, guaranteed not to sag. Height 17 inches, width 30 inches, length 75 inches. Finished in dead black or bronze. Fitted with best quality casters. Combines comfort, cleanliness and durability. Be sure to state finish desired. Shipping weight, 50 pounds. Price, **$3.85**

Steel Cot, $4.15.

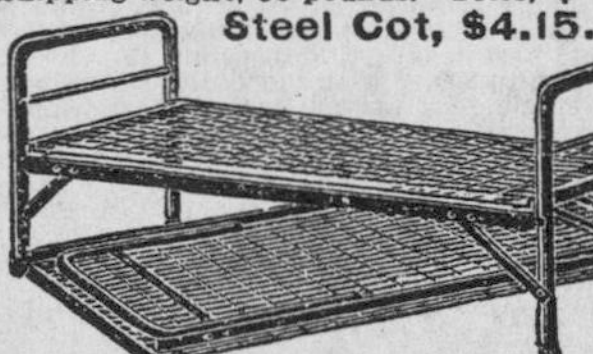

This Folding Steel Frame Cot has continuous posts and top rods 1⅛ inches thick, filling rods ⅜ inch thick. Angle steel side rails. Fitted with our hairpin fabric with steel coil spring ends, non sagging and noiseless. Head and foot 29 inches high, dead black finish. A splendid bed, will last a lifetime. Made in 2 feet 6 inch and 3 feet widths, 72 inches long. Shipping weight, about 65 pounds. Be sure to state width desired.

No. 1K2573 Price, 2 foot 6 inch width..........$4.15

No. 1K2574 Price, 3 foot width..........$4.55

Baby Tender and Walking Chair.

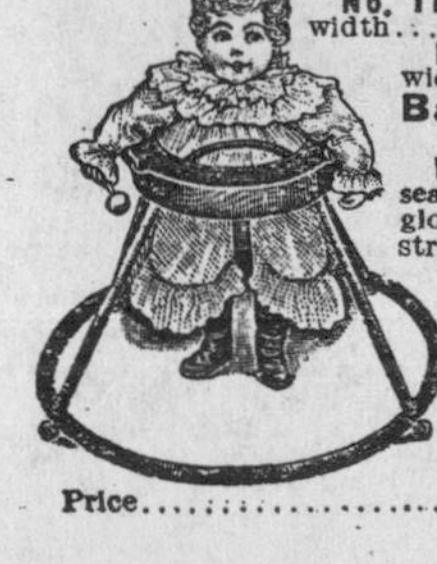

No. 1K2575 Made of thoroughly seasoned Northern hardwood, golden gloss finish. Seat is suspended by straps attached to four spiral springs and is adjusted by an elastic strap in front which compels the child to slip back on the seat and not remain astride the wooden bar as in other makes of baby walkers. This baby walker is endorsed by leading physicians and nurses. Shipped knocked down. Shipping weight, 10 pounds.

Price..**$2.21**

Our Cradle $1.75

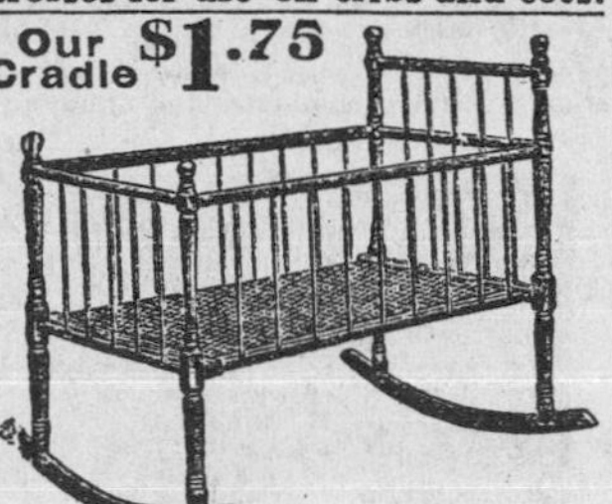

No. 1K2578 This is a very handsome, substantial cradle, furnished complete with woven wire spring. The frame is made of thoroughly seasoned selected white maple, finished in natural or imitation mahogany, as desired. Be sure to state finish desired. Has shaped posts and panel head. It is well constructed and fully guaranteed. Size, 24x44 inches. Shipped knocked down in small package, thereby greatly reducing freight charges. Easily set up. Shipping weight, about 17 pounds. Price **$1.75**

Our $3.45 Patent Swing Bed.

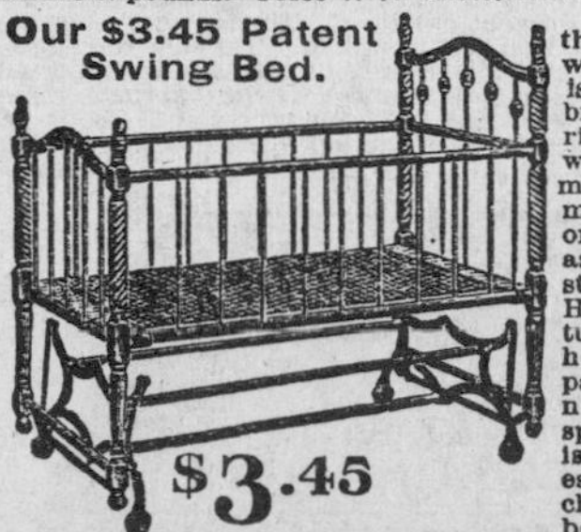

$3.45

It is so constructed that it remains level while rocking. The base is made of iron, well braced and perfectly rigid. Mounted on wheels. The frame is made of selected white maple, finished natural or imitation mahogany as desired. Be sure to state finish desired. Has handsome rope turned posts, shaped head and foot and panel head with ornamental spool spindles. The spring is a woven wire fabric, especially adapted for children's beds and will be found exceptionally comfortable and durable. Size, 24x44 inches. Shipped knocked down in small package, thereby greatly reducing freight charges. Easily set up. Shipping weight, 33 pounds.

No. 1K2585 Price..................................$3.45

No. 1K2586 Same crib as No. 1K2585, but made of solid oak, finished golden. Price..............$3.75

Our $1.47 Folding Crib.

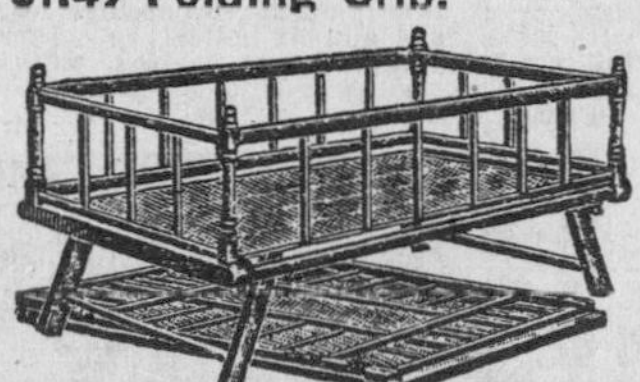

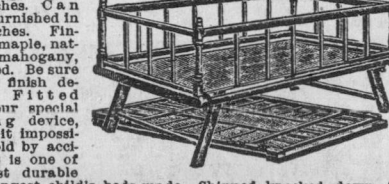

With woven wire spring. Size, 30x54 inches. Can also be furnished in 36x60 inches. Finished in maple, natural or mahogany, as desired. Be sure to state finish desired. Fitted with our special folding device, making it impossible to fold by accident. It is one of the most durable and strongest child's beds made. Shipped knocked down in small package, thereby greatly reducing freight charges. Easily set up. Shipping weight, about 25 pounds.

No. 1K2592 Price, size, 30x54 inches..............$1.47
No. 1K2593 Price, size, 36x60 inches..............1.62

White Maple Folding Crib, $2.35.

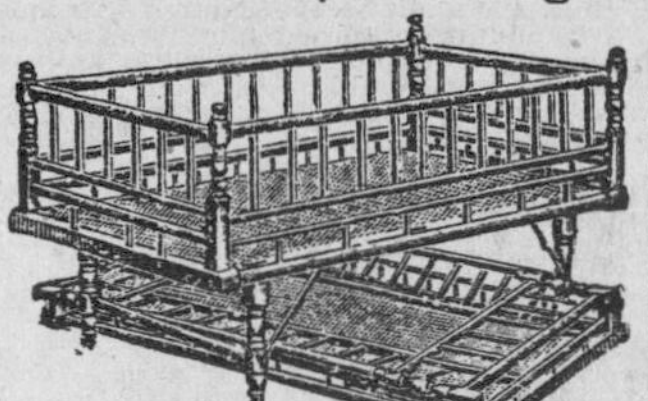

This Folding Crib is made of selected white maple. Has shaped posts and legs. Extra high sides and ends. Constructed so as to fold with bedding in place. Adjustable braces for firmly holding legs in place when open. Castings are all made of malleable iron and the springs of special crib fabric. We can furnish this crib finished in natural or imitation mahogany. Be sure to state finish desired. Shipped knocked down in small package, thereby greatly reducing freight charges. Easily set up.

No. 1K2596 Size, 30x54 inches Weight, 28 pounds. Price..$2.35

No. 1K2597 Size, 36x60 inches. Weight, 33 pounds. Price..2.60

An Excellent Child's Bed for $1.95.

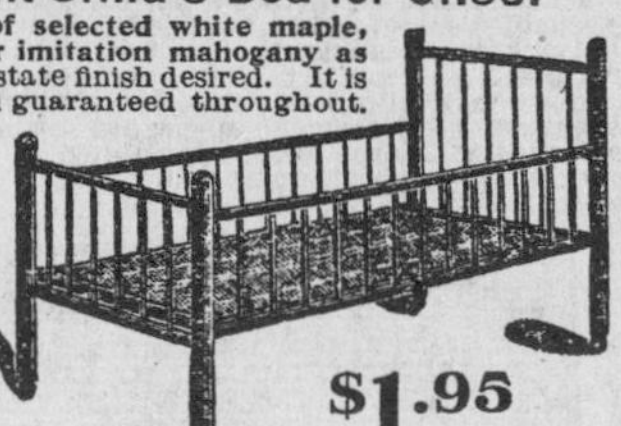

$1.95

This Bed is made of selected white maple, finished in natural or imitation mahogany as desired. Be sure to state finish desired. It is well constructed and guaranteed throughout. The spring is a woven wire fabric, especially adapted for children's beds, and will be found exceptionally comfortable and durable. Size, 30 inches wide, 60 inches long and 12 inches deep. Shipped knocked down in package 4½ inches thick, thereby greatly reducing the freight charges. Easily set up. Shipping weight, 25 lbs.

No. 1K2604 Price..................................$1.95

No. 1K2605 Size, 40 inches wide, 60 inches long and 12 inches deep. Shipping weight, 28 pounds. Price........$2.30

Be sure to state finish desired, otherwise we ship natural finish.

CHILDREN'S IRON CRIBS.

On page 433 we show a complete line of Children's Iron Cribs. **We guarantee our quality better and our prices lower than the same or similar cribs can be bought elsewhere.**

Child's Bed for $2.45.

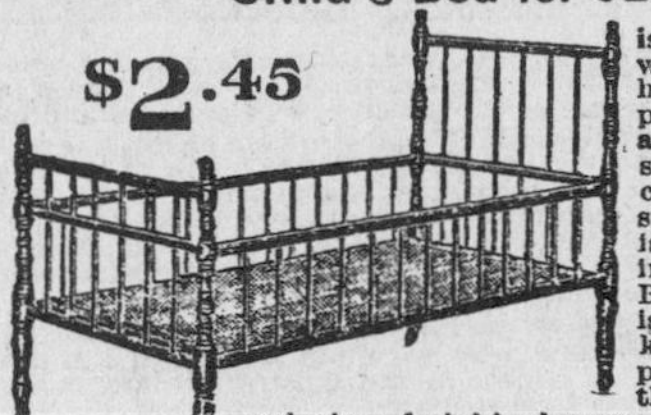

$2.45

This Child's Bed is made of selected white maple. Has handsome turned posts. Paneled head and foot. Spring of special crib fabric, comfortable and strong. The finish is natural color or imitation mahogany. Be sure to state finish desired. Shipped knocked down in package 4½ inches thick, thereby greatly reducing freight charges. Size, 30x60 inches. Shipping weight, 29 pounds.

No. 1K2606 Price........................**$2.45**

No. 1K2607 Size, 40x60 inches. Shipping weight, 33 pounds. Price. **2.95**

High Sides Wood Crib, $2.65.

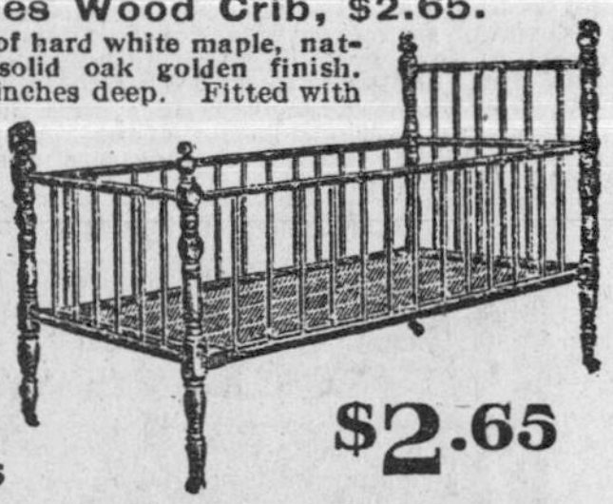

$2.65

This Bed is made of hard white maple, natural finish, or in solid oak golden finish. Extra high sides 16 inches deep. Fitted with high grade woven wire spring. Fancy turned posts, rails and spindles. Best quality casters. Shipped knocked down. Be sure to state size and wood desired. Shipping weight, 30 pounds.

No. 1K2610 Price, maple, size, 30x60......$2.65
Price, oak, size, 30x60......$3.15

No. 1K2611 Price, maple, size, 40x60 inches..................$3.25
Price, oak, size, 40x60 inches..................3.65

Handsome Child's Wood Bed, $3.40.

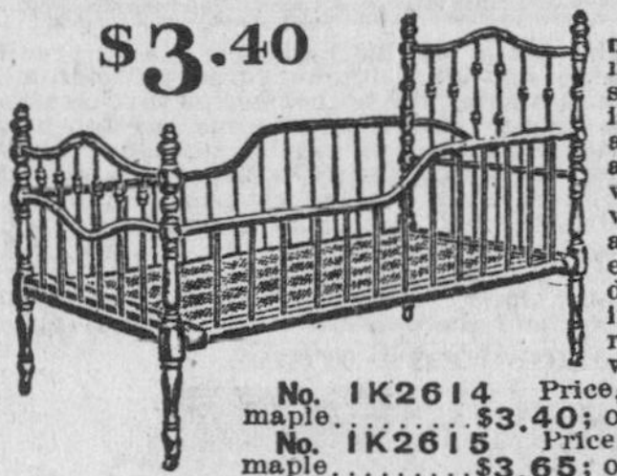

$3.40

This Child's Bed is made of white maple, natural finish or in solid oak golden finish. It has ornamental spindles in head and foot end. Fitted with a high grade woven wire spring and best quality casters. Shipped knocked down, thereby securing lowest freight rate. Shipping weight, about 35 lbs.

No. 1K2614 Price, size, 30x60, maple..........$3.40; oak..........$3.85

No. 1K2615 Price, size, 40x60, maple..........$3.65; oak..........4.15

Be sure to state size and wood desired.

Excellent Child's Folding Bed for $3.65.

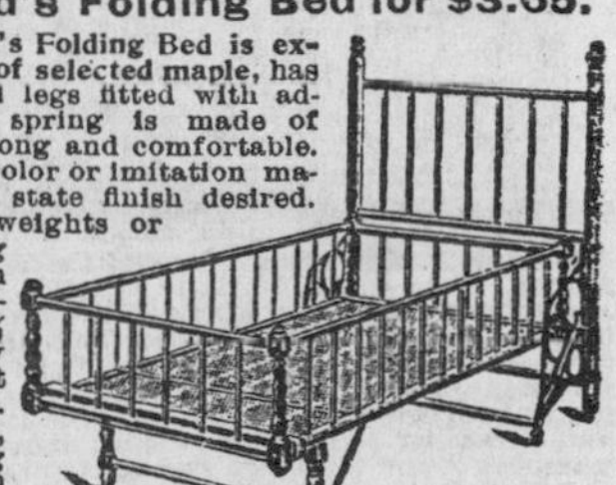

This beautiful Child's Folding Bed is exceptionally well made of selected maple, has fancy turned posts and legs fitted with adjustable braces. The spring is made of special crib fabric, strong and comfortable. The finish is natural color or imitation mahogany. Be sure to state finish desired. Folds up without weights or springs, straps holding bedding in place when folded. Shipped knocked down in package 4½ inches thick, thereby greatly reducing freight charges. Easily set up.

No. 1K2622 Size, 30x60 inches. Shipping weight, crated, 59 pounds. Price $3.65

No. 1K2623 Size, 40x60 inches. Shipping weight, crated, 70 pounds. Price. **$4.10**

Our Best Child's Folding Bed for $5.15.

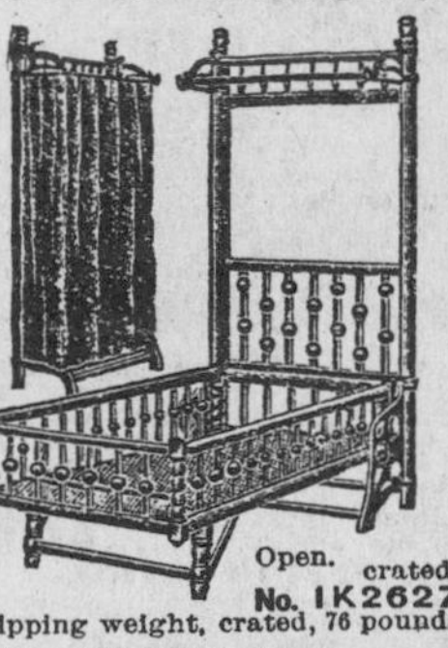
Closed. Open.

This is the best Child's Folding Bed in the market. Made of selected maple. Has fancy turned posts and legs and ornamental spool spindles. Neat, strong iron canopy, with rings for attaching drapery. Castings are all made of japanned malleable iron. The spring is made of special crib fabric. Two straps hold the bedding in place when bed is closed. Folds without weights or springs. Can be furnished in natural finish or imitation mahogany. Be sure to state finish desired. Shipped knocked down in small package, thereby greatly reducing freight charges. Easily set up.

No. 1K2626 Size, 30x50 inches. Shipping weight, crated, 68 pounds. Price...$5.15

No. 1K2627 Size, 40x60 inches. Shipping weight, crated, 76 pounds. Price 6.15

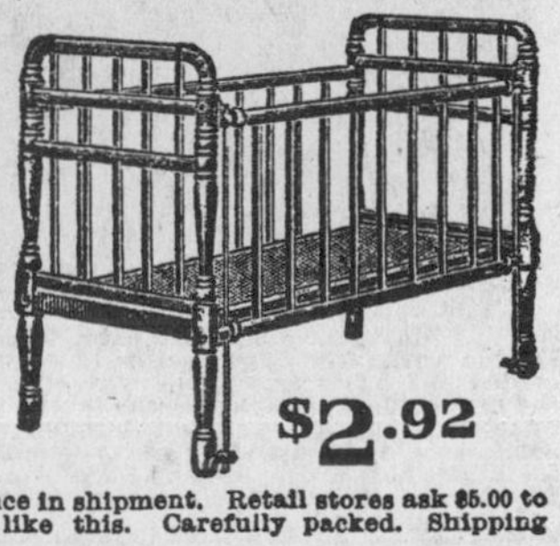

$2.92

No. 1K2628 This handsome Child's Bed is made of selected maple in either a natural or in a white enamel finish. It is fitted with the best woven wire spring. Outside measurement, 3 feet 6 inches long, 2 feet 2 inches wide. It has extra high sides, one of which raises and lowers on perpendicular metal rods. Strong and durable. It has 9 spindles on each side. Very smooth, round corners. Shipped knocked down for convenience in shipment. Retail stores ask $5.00 to $6.00 for child's bed like this. Carefully packed. Shipping weight, 25 pounds.

Price, in maple, natural finish..............................$2.92
Price, in white enamel.......................................3.32

89c BED SPRINGS $6.15

AT 89 CENTS TO $6.15 WE SHOW A COMPLETE LINE OF BED SPRINGS. REDUCED IN PRICE BUT NOT IN QUALITY.

OUR BED SPRINGS are made by the largest and best known manufacturers of this kind of goods in the world and our output has increased to such a large volume that we are able to contract for a very large part of the outputof such factory at the actual cost of material and labor. They embody all the new ideas in spring construction.

THE MATERIAL used in the construction of the frames of our bed springs is the highest and best grade obtainable. THE WOOD FRAMES are made of thoroughly air seasoned and kiln dried hard maple. Specially selected, free from all defects and guaranteed not to warp. THE METAL FRAMES are made of the best high carbon rolled steel and drawn tubing. Guaranteed not to bend or break.

THE FABRIC used on our bed springs is extra quality, closely woven and corded to prevent sagging and stretching. It is absolutely noiseless, the special construction positively eliminates the annoying squeak common to the ordinary make of bed springs.

THE STEEL COILS used in the construction of our all wire spiral bed springs, and in the suspension supports, as shown in the illustration are made of the best high carbon tempered steel.

HOW TO ORDER. When ordering a spring be sure and state whether spring is to be used on a wood or iron bed. Springs for iron beds (except No. 1K2814 and No. 1K2815), are made with extended sides, which rest on the side rail of bed and do not require bed slats. Springs for wood beds are made to fit inside bed rails and rest on the bed slats. Give exact size of bed inside. State whether for a wood or iron bed. If you want a spring 4 feet wide and 6 feet long, write it thus: 4-0 x 6-0. Never write 4x6. Our woven wire mattresses measure 1 inch less in width and 1½ inches less in length than marked. We cannot fill orders for springs unless you give exact size and state, whether for wood or iron bed.

A Bargain at 89 Cents.

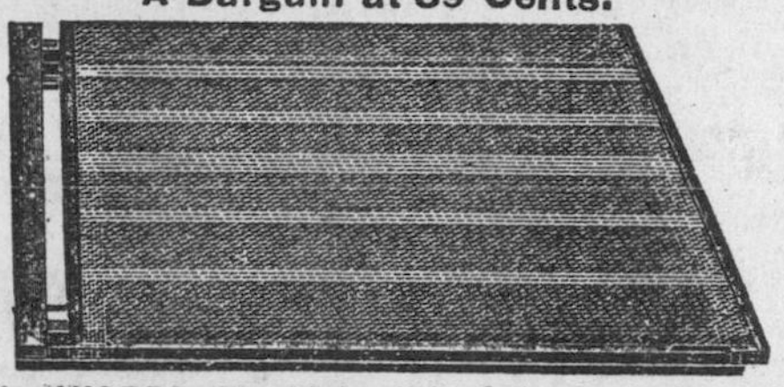

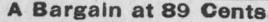

No. 1K2759 The fabric of this Spring is single pencil weave, with corded edges and thirteen inner cords. The frame is made of selected hard maple, with corner blocks that elevate the fabric above the frame. Has a double end bar and bolt extension device by which the weave can be tightened when necessary. The corners are strengthened with iron plates and the frame is coated with varnish, making an excellent finish. Shipping weight, about 58 pounds. Be sure to state size of bed for which spring is required when ordering.
Price, all sizes.............................. **$1.49**

No. 1K2755 Same spring as No. 1K2759, illustrated and described above, but without the extension end. Price..**89c**

An Excellent Spring.

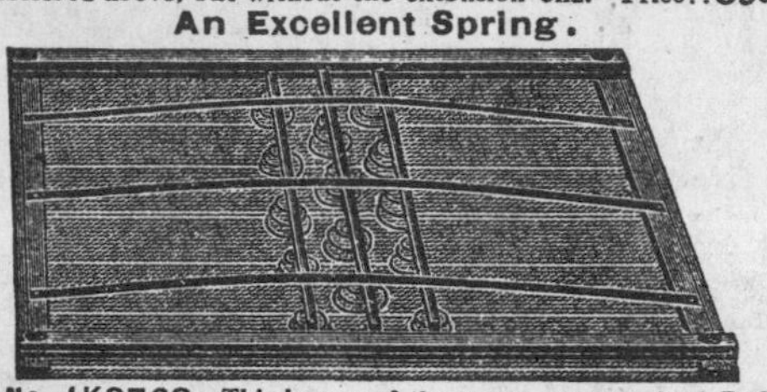

No. 1K2768 This is one of the very best low priced Bed Springs made. The fabric is closely woven with corded edges and thirteen additional cords in the body of the fabric, as illustrated. The frame is made of hard maple and strengthened with steel corner plates. The center of the spring is supported by fourteen spiral springs resting on wood slats and fastened to the frame with steel bands. The construction is perfect for comfort and durability. Shipping weight, about 42 pounds. Be sure to state size of bed for which spring is intended.
Price, all sizes.............................. **$1.58**

Wonderful Value.

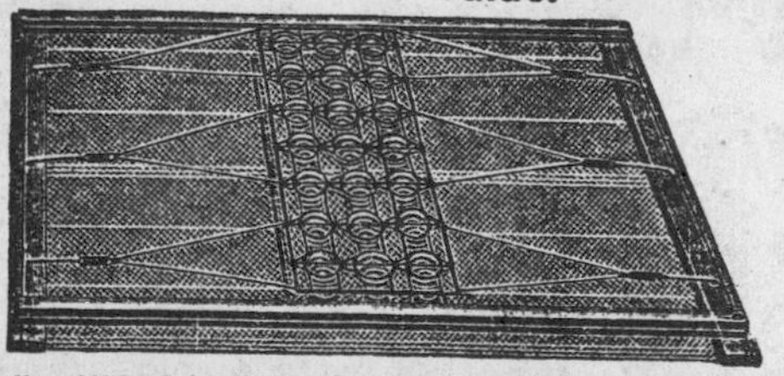

No. 1K2781 This Spring has a hard maple frame firmly bolted together. Strengthened with steel corner plates. This fabric is single weave with cord edges and fourteen inner cords and is supported by a spiral spring bed, made of the best grade of high carbon steel wire, and attached to the frame with steel rods and steel helical spiral springs. Furnished for all sizes except 3-foot width. Shipping weight, 50 pounds. State size wanted. Price.................. **$2.10**

Heavy, Hard Maple Frame Spring.

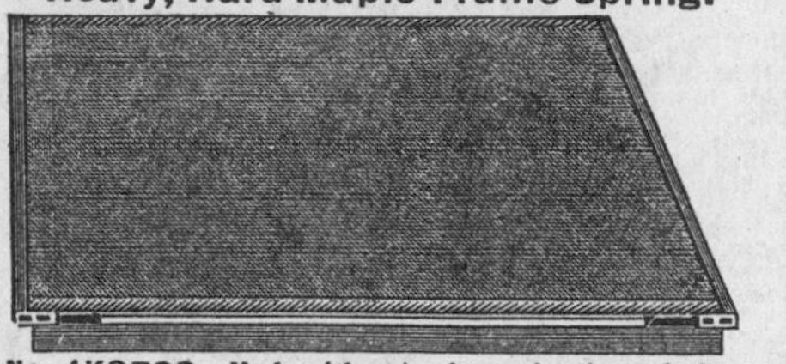

No. 1K2783 Made with extra heavy hard maple frame. Double woven wire fabric weighs 12 pounds, closely woven and corded and has a heavy rope wire edge. A special feature is the new method of fastening the fabric into the end bars with metal attachments. Perfect tension, exceptionally strong, comfortable and adapted for heavy weight persons. Furnished for all size beds except 3½ and 3-foot widths. Shipping weight, 60 pounds. Be sure to state size wanted.
Price.............................. **$2.45**

We cannot fill orders for springs unless you give the exact size and state whether for WOOD or IRON bed.

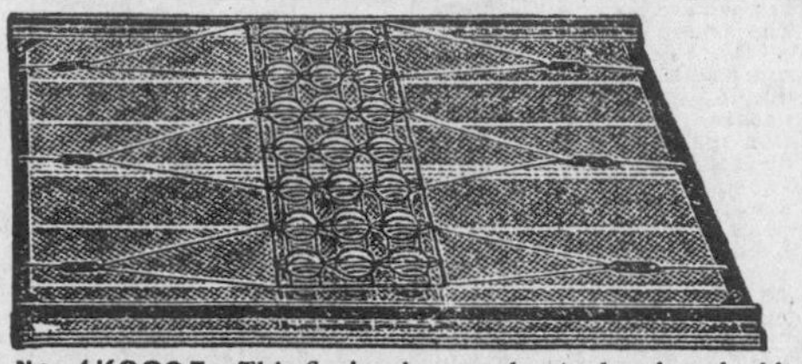

No. 1K2805 This Spring has angle steel end and side rails, with corners braced at one end and improved cast corner connections that prevent twisting. The fabric is alternate single and double weave, strongly corded. Has steel rod edges. The fabric is well elevated above the side rails and is supported by twenty-one steel spiral springs and six helical springs, making it impossible for it to sag. Shipping weight, about 56 pounds. Be sure to state size wanted. Price, all sizes.............................. **$2.58**

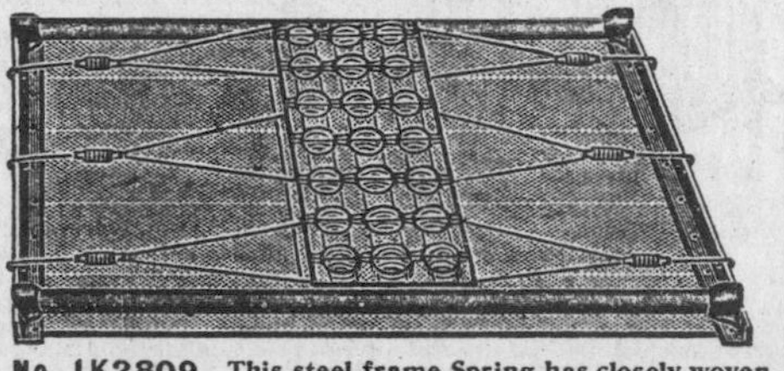

No. 1K2809 This steel frame Spring has closely woven, double fabric with corded edges. The tubular steel side rails are 1 1-16 inches in diameter and has angle steel ends, 1¼ inches wide. The fabric is well elevated above the side rails. Patent corner fastenings make the frame perfectly rigid. Has steel support of twenty-one spiral springs attached to the frame with steel rods and six helical spiral springs. Furnished in full size and 4-foot widths only. Shipping weight, largest size, 65 pounds. State size wanted.
Price.............................. **$3.05**

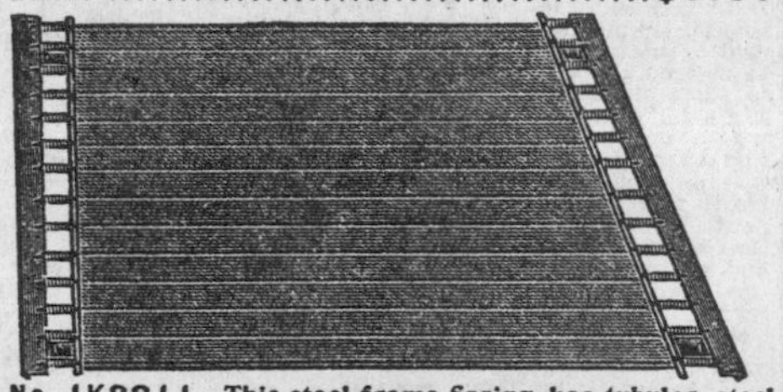

No. 1K2811 This steel frame Spring has tubular steel side rails 1¼ inches thick and angle steel end bars 1¼ inches wide. The closely woven and firmly corded fabric is attached to the end bars with twenty-eight spiral steel helical springs which distributes the weight equally. Furnished in full size and 4-foot widths only. Shipping weight, 65 pounds. Be sure to state size wanted. Price.............. **$3.35**

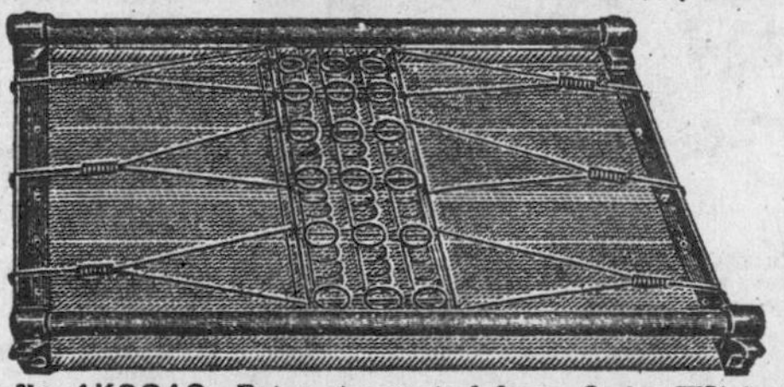

No. 1K2812 Extra strong steel frame Spring. It has heavy tubular steel side rails, 1 5-16 inches thick, and angle steel end bars, 1¼ inches wide, finished in bronze. The close "pencil" weave fabric is elevated 4 inches above side rails by heavy corner castings, making the entire surface of the spring extra soft and comfortable. Fabric has a heavy rope wire edge and a heavy coiled wire support, containing 18 highly tempered Bessemer steel springs, suspended by six steel coil springs attached to the end bars. Furnished in full size and 4-foot widths only. Guaranteed not to sag. Shipping weight, about 75 pounds. Price.............. **$3.85**

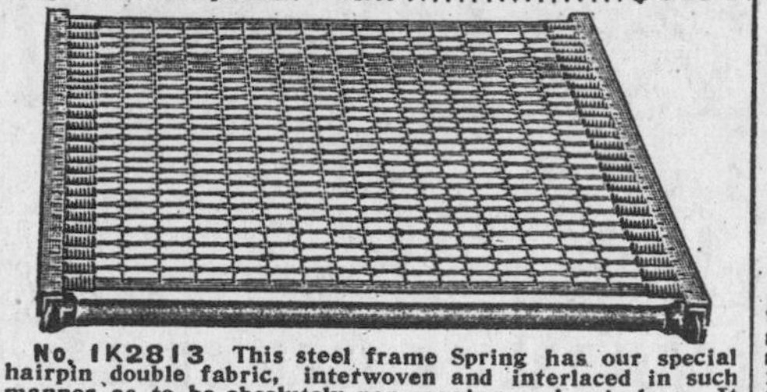

No. 1K2813 This steel frame Spring has our special hairpin double fabric, interwoven and interlaced in such manner as to be absolutely non-sagging and noiseless. It is fastened to the end bars by twenty-eight spiral steel springs. Side rails are 1½-inch steel tubing, angle steel end bars 1¼ inches wide. Fabric raised 4 inches above side rails by heavy corner casting. Bronze finish. Furnished in full size and 4-foot widths only. Shipping weight, about 65 pounds. State size wanted. Price.............. **$3.95**

Patent Interlocking Top.

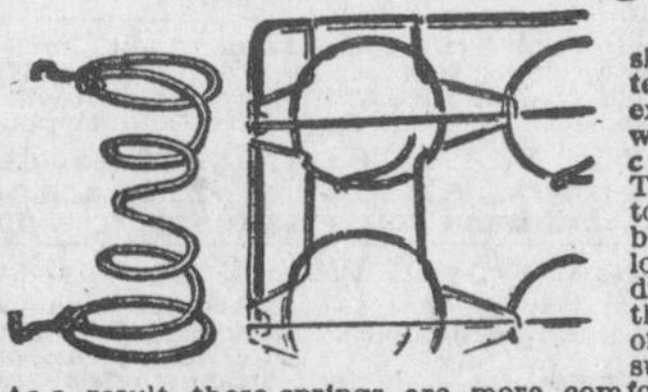

This illustration shows the patent interlocking top as used exclusively on our all wire bed springs, except No. 1K2814. They are fastened together at the top by continuous interlocking wire which divides the strain, so that no spiral, or set of spirals, is forced to support the weight. As a result, these springs are more comfortable and durable than any other all wire springs made.

Our Patent Bed Slat for Iron or Brass Beds.

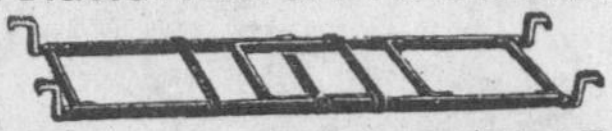

Adjustable Iron Bed Slat, to fit any size bed, to be used to support steel spiral springs when used on metal beds.

No. 1K2730 Price, per set of 4 slats.............. **$1.35**

No. 1K2731 Same slat as above, non-adjustable. Be sure to state width of bed when ordering this slat.
Price, per set of 4 slats.............. **$1.19**

All our springs can be furnished to fit iron beds without using slats, except No. 1K2814 and No. 1K2815.

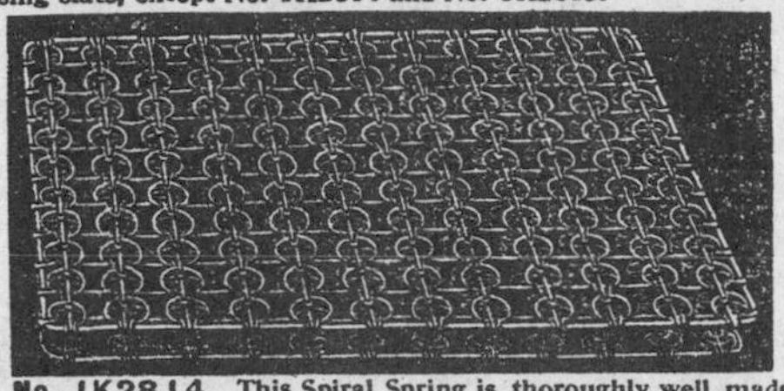

No. 1K2814 This Spiral Spring is thoroughly well made. The top and bottom surfaces are alike, the spiral spring being cone shaped so that the spring can be used either side up. Coils firmly braced by lengthwise and transverse steel wires, making it strong and comfortable. It is finished in black japan and is clean and sanitary. The full size spring has 120 double coils. Shipping weight, about 25 pounds. State size of bed when ordering. Price.............. **$1.45**

To fit this spring to iron bed it is necessary to purchase a set of slats.

We recommend especially No. 1K2822 Spring, for iron beds, it being superior in every way and so made that no slats are required.

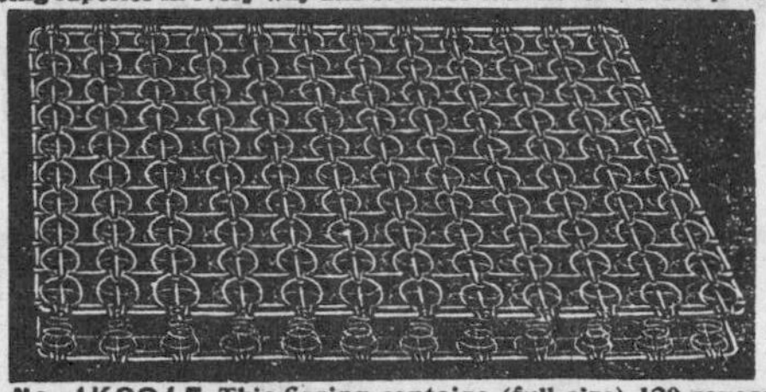

No. 1K2815 This Spring contains (full size) 120 reverse coils, made of the best quality high carbon Bessemer steel wire, oil tempered, joined with our Patent Interlocking Top, as illustrated above. Can be used either side up. Finished in black Japan. Highest degree of comfort and durability combined in this spring. Furnished in full size and 4-foot widths only. Shipping weight, about 28 pounds. To fit this spring to an iron bed it is necessary to purchase a set of steel slats. Price.............. **$2.85**

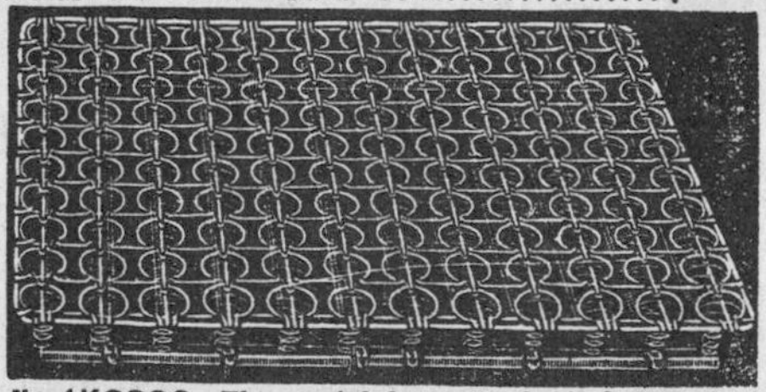

No. 1K2822 The special features of this Spring are the rigid base, unusual strength and extreme lightness in weight. The base is constructed with twelve steel bars joined together by three rows of steel braces. The top of the bed is composed of 120 highly tempered spiral springs bound together with our patent interlocking top, as illustrated and described above. The rigid base makes it impossible for the bed to get out of shape, and together with our interlocking top makes the most perfect single deck spring bed it is possible to produce. No slats are required with the spring when used on iron beds, and only three slats when used on wood beds. Finished in black japan. In ordering, be sure to state kind and size of bed for which you wish to use this spring. Shipping weight, about 47 pounds. Price, all sizes...... **$3.45**

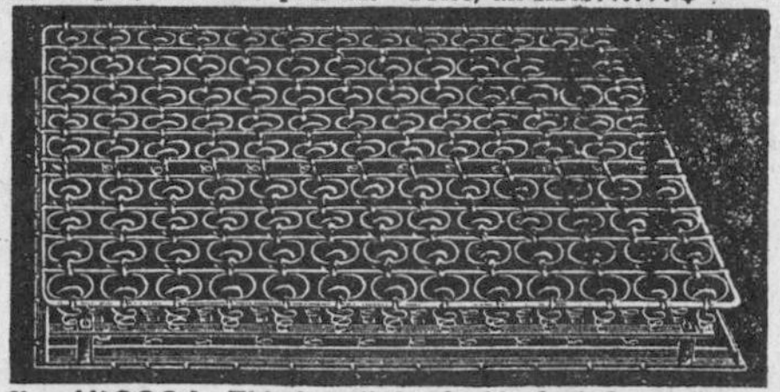

No. 1K2824 This is called a double deck Spring because the spiral springs are about one-third longer than the ordinary single deck spring, which gives the bed greater elasticity, consequently makes it the most comfortable and durable spring it is possible to construct. There are 117 of these deep, highly tempered springs used and the edge springs rest on a steel bar directly over the side rail of the bed. All springs are securely attached to a rigid steel frame and steel slats. Finished in black japan. Made for either iron or wood bed. Shipping weight, about 75 pounds. No slats required for this spring when used on iron beds. Price, as illustrated...... **$6.15**
Price, without steel frame for wood bed.......... **4.75**

BOX SPRING MATTRESSES

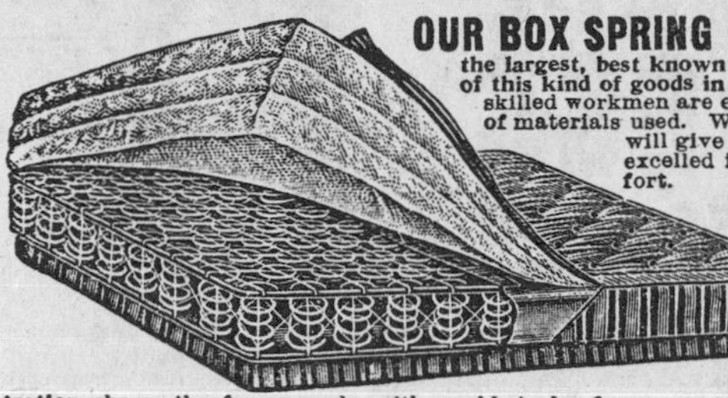

OUR BOX SPRING MATTRESSES are made for us by the largest, best known and most reliable manufacturer of this kind of goods in the world. Only the very best skilled workmen are employed and the highest grade of materials used. We absolutely guarantee that we will give you a box spring that cannot be excelled in strength, durability and comfort.

THE FRAME is made of thoroughly air seasoned and kiln dried northern hardwood, perfectly jointed and firmly bound crosswise with heavy slats. The joints are all glued and nailed, making them absolutely vermin proof. The illustration shows the frame made with a rabbet edge for use on metal beds. The extended edges rest upon the side and end rails, thus doing away with bed slats. For wood beds the edges are made straight.

THE SPRINGS are extra long, double cone shaped and made from the best high carbon steel, oil tempered. They are securely fastened to the cross slats of the frame by heavy staples and tied, cross tied eight ways and knotted at the top with best quality Italian hemp twine, and then covered with a clean burlap. A heavy rattan edge extends entirely around the spring to which the outer row of springs is firmly attached, giving a strength and durability much better than all other makes of springs. In our full size box mattresses, except in No. 1K2832, we use 80 springs and a proportionate number in the smaller sizes.

The width of upholstered springs for metal bedsteads is always the same as the outside measure of the rails, 4 feet 6 inches, 4 feet, 3 feet 6 inches, 3 feet, and the regular length is 6 feet 4 inches. Springs for a wood bed are regular 1-inch space all around. If the bed spring measures 4 feet 6 inches by 6 feet 4 inches, the regular size of spring for wood bed should be 4 feet 4 inches by 6 feet 2 inches. Be sure to state whether the spring is for a wood or iron bed. Shipping weight, about 100 pounds.

No. 1K2832 Box Spring with Flax Fiber and Cotton Top. The flax fiber used on the top of this mattress is made from the best quality flax, absolutely clean and wholesome. It is covered with a layer of cotton, and makes a very comfortable and satisfactory filling. Covered with a good grade of sateen ticking. Price........................ **$9.95**

No. 1K2833 Elastic Felt Top Box Spring. Elastic felt, as shown in the illustration used on our box mattresses, is made of pure, long staple white cotton, thoroughly cleaned, carded and woven into sheets or layers the full size of the mattress. These sheets are placed on a foundation of flax fiber and have great tensile strength, softness and resiliency and will not pack, spread or lump, which makes an exceptionally good bed. Covered with a good grade of heavy sateen ticking. Price........................ **$11.45**

No. 1K2835 Hair Top. The top of this mattress is made of good quality curled hair, on a foundation of fine Flax Fiber which makes an excellent filling for a box mattress. Read what we say on page 436 about hair. Highest grade heavy sateen ticking. Price, **$12.85**

No. 1K2836 Extra Fine, Long Curled Hair Top. The best box mattress in the market. Read what we say on page 436 about the hair used on the top of a fine flax fiber foundation in our mattresses. This box mattress is made up with the very best quality satin finished ticking obtainable. Price........ **$13.95**

SPECIAL VALUES IN FEATHERS AND PILLOWS

OUR FEATHERS AND PILLOWS. No class of merchandise offers so great an opportunity for deception as feather pillows. It is very difficult for most buyers to determine the exact quality of the feathers and the proportions. Our feathers from the lowest priced to the highest priced are the very best that can be obtained, the quality and proportions being determined by an expert of long years of experience. Everything that modern and strictly up to date methods of handling, cleaning and curing can do has been done to give our customers clean, sanitary, odorless feathers and pillows that cannot be purchased of other dealers for less than 40 to 50 per cent more than the price we ask.

OUR SPECIAL PROCESS. Every feather that we sell in bulk or in the pillow is put through a special process, which consists of subjecting them to alternating currents of steam, hot and cold blasts of air, which absolutely removes every particle of foreign

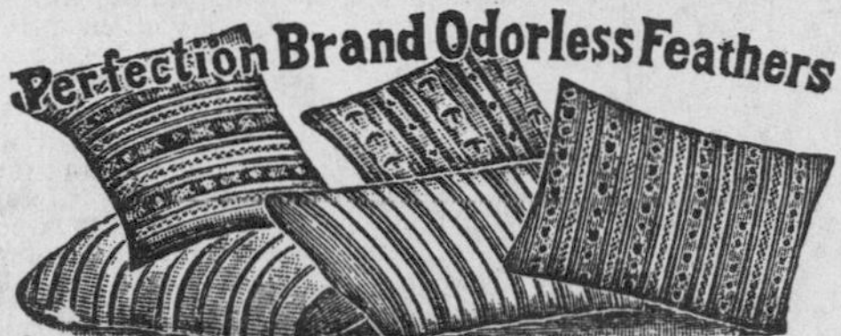

Feathers when taken from the fowl contain considerable quantities of oil and animal matter. If this is not entirely removed the decomposition which takes place renders the feathers foul smelling and unsanitary.

matter and renders the feathers odorless, wholesome, and hygienic. Renovating processes used by many others destroys the life and buoyancy of the feather. By our special process, the life, resiliency and buoyancy of the feathers is increased fully 50 per cent. This we absolutely guarantee in every grade of feathers we offer, from the lowest to the highest grade, whether in bulk or in the made up pillow. You cannot fully appreciate the high standard of our feathers and feather pillows, unless you make a close comparison with those offered by any other concern at fully 40 to 50 per cent higher in price than we ask. Should you favor us with an order, it will mean the sale of many more in your neighborhood.

OUR PILLOWS. The ticking which we use on our pillows is the very best quality of heavy sateen or Amoskeag twill ticking. We furnish them in a variety of sizes and weights. We especially recommend the 3 and 3½-pound weights. Each pillow is thoroughly filled and rounded out and will retain its life and buoyancy for years.

Steam Cured Feathers.

No. 1K2952 Grade C3. Mixed Feathers. Steam dressed and cured. A better quality than is offered by any other dealer at the price, but we do not recommend this grade. We especially recommend our No. 1K2955 as the best moderate priced feathers which are entirely satisfactory. Price, per pound........................ **31c**

No. 1K2955 Grade C2. A special mixture selected on account of the filling qualities. Makes a very comfortable pillow, absolutely odorless and clean, steam dressed and cured by our special process. A satisfactory grade. Price, per pound........................ **44c**

No. 1K2959 Grade C1. An extra selected mixture of blended odorless feathers, principally duck and goose. Steam dressed and air blast cured by our special process. An absolutely sanitary grade at very moderate cost. Excellent value. Price, per pound........................ **52c**

No. 1K2963 Grade B3. Goose and duck feathers. A mixture which produces a very resilient and buoyant pillow. Free from coarse quills. Sanitary steam dressed and air blast cured by our special process. Always satisfactory. Price, per pound........................ **58c**

No. 1K2966 Grade B2. Staple quality of goose feathers with slight mixture of duck feathers, thoroughly cured by our special process. Very buoyant. Guaranteed satisfactory in every respect. Price, per pound........... **67c**

No. 1K2969 Grade B1. Sanitary prime goose feathers, good color and buoyant, very soft and downy, odorless and sanitary. Steam dressed and air blast cured by our special process. A very fine quality. Price, per pound **76c**

No. 1K2971 Grade A2. Pure prime live goose feathers with down. Strictly high grade in every respect. Steam dressed and air blast cured by our special process. Sanitary and odorless. Free from all foreign substances. Very buoyant. Extra fine quality. Price, per pound........ **85c**

No. 1K2976 Grade A1. The very best, specially selected pure prime live goose feathers and white goose down, equal parts. Thoroughly cleaned, steam dressed and air blast cured by our special process. Cannot be excelled. Price, per pound........................ **97c**

Down.

No. 1K2983 Mixed gray and white goose down, good color, light and buoyant, strictly high grade throughout, odorless and sanitary, very fluffy. Cured by our special process of steam and air blast. Price, per pound........................ **84c**

No. 1K2986 Select choice white goose down. Steam dressed and air blast cured by our special process. Odorless, hygienic, and very buoyant. Extra fine quality. Price, per pound........................ **$1.23**

Pillows.

No. 1K3004 Superior Brand. Pure prime live goose feathers with down. Strictly high grade in every respect. Sanitary and odorless. Steam dressed and air blast cured by our special process. Extra fine quality. Gobelin art ticking.

Size........	21x27	23x28	24x29	26x30	27x31
Weight, each	2 lbs.	2½ lbs.	3 lbs.	3½ lbs.	4 lbs.
Price, each..	$1.95	$2.45	$2.95	$3.43	$3.90

No. 1K3006 Imperial Brand. Sanitary prime goose feathers, good color and buoyant, very soft and downy. Odorless and sanitary. Steam dressed and air blast cured. A very fine quality. Finest art ticking.

Size........	21x27	23x28	24x29	26x30	27x31
Weight, each	2 lbs.	2½ lbs.	3 lbs.	3½ lbs.	4 lbs.
Price, each..	$1.62	$2.02	$2.43	$2.83	$3.24

No. 1K3009 Royal Brand. Staple quality of goose feathers, an excellent filling. Thoroughly cured by our special process. Guaranteed satisfactory in every respect. Fancy striped satin finish ticking.

Size........	20x27	22x27	23x29	24x29	26x31
Weight, each	2 lbs.	2½ lbs.	3 lbs.	3½ lbs.	4 lbs.
Price, each..	$1.38	$1.72	$2.07	$2.41	$2.76

No. 1K3013 Ideal Brand. An extra fine selected mixture of blended odorless feathers, duck and goose. Steam dressed and air blast cured by our special process, which insures an absolutely sanitary grade at very moderate cost. Best satin finish ticking.

Size........	20x26	21x27	22x29	24x30	25x30
Weight, each	2 lbs.	2½ lbs.	3 lbs.	3½ lbs.	4 lbs.
Price, each..	$1.18	$1.47	$1.77	$2.06	$2.36

No. 1K3019 Diamond Brand. A special mixture selected on account of its excellent filling qualities. Makes a very comfortable pillow. Absolutely odorless and clean. Steam dressed and air blast cured. Best satin finish ticking.

Size....................	22x27	24x28	25x30
Weight, each............	3 lbs.	3½ lbs.	4 lbs.
Price, each.............	$1.20	$1.40	$1.55

No. 1K3025 Puritan Brand. Mixed feathers, free from any vegetable fiber. Odorless, steam dressed and air blast cured by our special process. A popular pillow mixture. Covered with a fine satin finish ticking.

Size.................	20x26	21x27	22x28
Weight, each.........	3 lbs.	3½ lbs.	4 lbs.
Price, each..........	85c	95c	$1.10

No. 1K3028 Crown Brand. Mixed feathers prepared in a sanitary manner, making a serviceable pillow, covered with 8-ounce Amoskeag A. C. A. ticking.

Size....................	18x25	20x26	21x27
Weight, each............	2½ lbs.	3 lbs.	3½ lbs.
Price, each.............	45c	52c	59c

Down Cushions.

No. 1K3022 Java Brand. Made of imported Japanese silk floss, non-absorbent, vermin proof, very resilient and elastic, odorless and hygienic. An ideal sofa cushion. Muslin covered.

Size...........	16x16	18x18	20x20	22x22	24x24	26x26
Price, each...	21c	26c	35c	47c	59c	70c

No. 1K3024 Leader Brand. Filled with a mixture of duck and turkey down, steam dressed, air blast cured, odorless and sanitary. Muslin covered.

Size...........	16x16	18x18	20x20	22x22	24x24	26x26
Price, each...	25c	32c	45c	58c	68c	95c

HIGH GRADE IN CONSTRUCTION

CHILDREN'S IRON CRIBS

BEAUTIFUL IN FINISH

Our All Iron Crib, Drop Sides, $4.65.

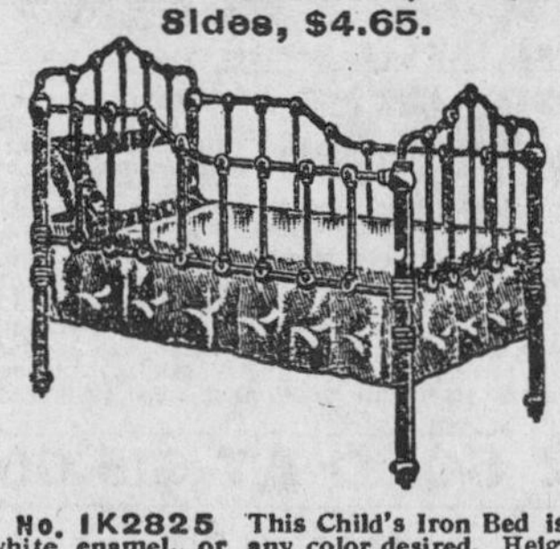

No. 1K2825 This Child's Iron Bed is in white enamel, or any color desired. Height, head end, 45½ inches; height, foot, 40½ inches. Corner posts, ⅞ inch. Filling rods, ⅜ inch thick. Made of best quality malleable iron and high carbon steel. Fitted with high grade woven wire spring. It has hinged drop sides. Sells in retail stores at $7.00 to $8.00. Shipped knocked down. Furnished in two sizes. Shipping weight, 115 pounds. Be sure to state color desired, otherwise we will ship white.
Size, 2 ft. 6 in. by 4 ft. 6 in. Price......**$4.65**
Size, 3 feet by 5 feet. Price........... **4.95**

Extra High Side Iron Crib, $5.95.

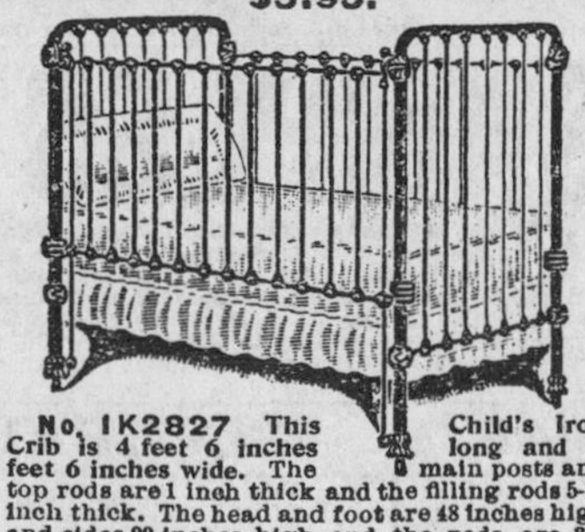

No. 1K2827 This Child's Iron Crib is 4 feet 6 inches long and 2 feet 6 inches wide. The 4 main posts and top rods are 1 inch thick and the filling rods 5-16 inch thick. The head and foot are 48 inches high and sides 22 inches high, and the rods are 3⅛ inches apart so that the child cannot stick its head through, climb over, fall out or otherwise harm itself. Fitted with woven wire springs. One stationary side and one vertical sliding drop side. Finished in white enamel or any color desired. Be sure to state color desired, otherwise white will be furnished. Shipped knocked down, well crated. Shipping weight, 125 pounds.
Size, 2 ft. 6 in. by 4 ft. 6 in. Price......**$5.95**
Size, 3 feet by 5 feet. Price........... **6.30**

Brass Trimmed High Sides Crib. $6.45

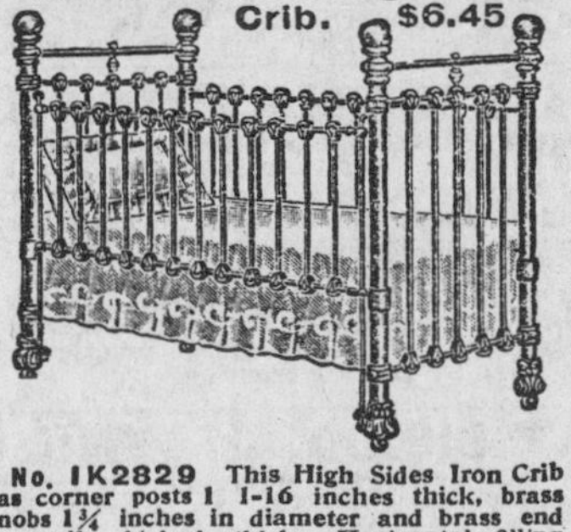

No. 1K2829 This High Sides Iron Crib has corner posts 1 1-16 inches thick, brass knobs 1¾ inches in diameter and brass end top rails ½ inch thick. Horizontal filling rods 7-16 inch, vertical filling rods ⅜ inch thick. Height head and foot, 43 inches. One stationary side and one vertical sliding drop side, each 18 inches high. Fitted with best quality spring and finished in baked white enamel or any color desired. Sells in retail stores at $9.00 to $10.00. Shipping weight, about 125 pounds. Be sure to state color desired, otherwise we ship white.
Size, 2 ft. 6 in. by 4 ft. 6 in. Price...**$6.45**
Size, 3 feet by 5 feet. Price....... **6.85**

New Design High Sides Iron Crib, $7.35.

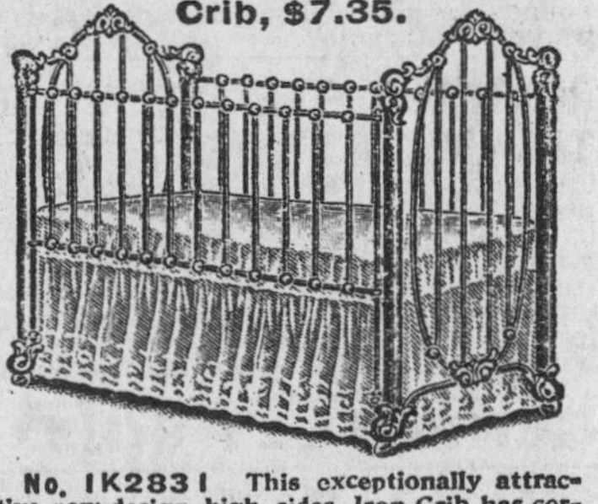

No. 1K2831 This exceptionally attractive new design high sides Iron Crib has corner posts 1⅓ inches thick. Top rails ⅝-inch thick, vertical filling rods ⅜-inch thick, horizontal filling rods ⅜-inch thick. Height of head and foot 48 inches. One stationary side and one vertical sliding drop side each 18 inches high. Fitted with best quality woven wire spring and finished in baked white enamel or any color desired. This crib can not be furnished in retail stores for less than $10.00 to $12.00. Shipping weight, 135 pounds.
Size, 2 ft. 6 in. by 4 ft. 6 in. Price, **$7.35**
Size, 3 feet by 5 feet. Price....... **7.95**

WE FURNISH THE GENUINE WHITMORE ELASTIC FELT MATTRESS

AS ADVERTISED FOR $10.95

A GOOD BED is a physical necessity. An absolutely even elastic surface, soft and springy yet firm, is the necessary quality of a good mattress. In this Genuine Whitmore Luxury Elastic Felt Mattress is attained the absolute perfection of mattress building. The elastic felt used in this mattress is of a special super extra grade, a snowy white fabric made from the choicest and longest fibers of pure white cotton of the greatest tensile strength and purity. These fibers are rigidly tested and carefully inspected as to their length and elastic strength and by a special scientific chemical process every trace of impurity is removed and rendered absolutely germproof, mothproof, verminproof and waterproof. The carefully prepared material is lightly blown apart and by mechanical rotary air pressure is made into loose, flaky sheets. The sheets are then placed into a mammoth felting machine, the fibers are drawn, curled and formed into double sheets, each joining and interlacing one within the other into a perfect single sheet wonderfully elastic, beautiful, light, airy and absolutely sanitary and perfectly non-absorbent. These thick, elastic, snowy white sheets are then laid one upon the other, compressed to about one-fifth their original thickness and inclosed in the best quality satin finished ticking, cut to match, top and bottom, sides and ends accurately stitched and tufted. In purity of stock, perfection of construction, comfort giving and wearing qualities this mattress cannot be excelled at any price. It has a standard 4-inch border, and the one-piece mattress 4-foot and 4-foot 6-inch sizes are fitted on both sides with handles, as shown in the illustration.

SANITARY ELASTIC WHITMORE FELT MATTRESS
SANITARY · WILL NOT MAT · VERMIN PROOF · NON-ABSORBENT · NON CONTAGIOUS · NEVER GETS LUMPY · HAND MADE FILLING · NEVER REQUIRE REMAKING

NONE GENUINE WITHOUT THIS TRADE MARK.

Every mattress bears a genuine Whitmore trade mark label, of which the above is an exact copy. Shipped direct from Chicago to our customers.

This illustration is copyrighted.

A photographic reproduction of the Whitmore Luxury Elastic Felt Mattress. This illustration shows the hand laid, snowy white sheeted filling laid in place and partially enclosed within the hand sewed ticking of the Whitmore Elastic Felt Mattress.

OUR SIX MONTHS' FREE TRIAL OFFER

Send us your order for this Genuine Whitmore Luxury Elastic Felt Mattress, inclose the price, $10.95, and when you have received it, compared, examined and tested it, by sleeping on it for six months, we give you the privilege of returning it to us and we will immediately return your money together with the freight charges.

BETTER STILL, at the same time you send us your order for this splendid mattress send your order to any other dealer for any other mattress regardless of **name, make or price,** and when you receive them place them side by side, examine the filling, the ticking, the sewing, the tufting, and if, after comparison, test and trial, you do not find our mattress far superior in every way you may return it to us and we will at once return your money together with the freight charges.

THE ILLUSTRATIONS OF ELASTIC FELT MATTRESSES generally shown are made from pen drawings or sketches. The artist and engraver exaggerates certain features of material and construction, picturing them as he thinks they should look and not as they really are, and the mattress you receive does not correspond with the picture. This illustration at the left is an exact photographic picture of a completed mattress opened at one end, and shows the precise relative thickness and elasticity of the snowy white fibrous sheets, the uniform tufting, binding, stitching and the ticking as it actually will be found in the Genuine Whitmore Luxury Elastic Felt Mattress when you receive it.

GENERALLY SOLD AT $15.00
— OUR PRICE —
$10.95

THE TUFTING of the Genuine Whitmore Luxury Elastic Felt Mattress is perfectly done. Each tuft is of the same size, space and tightness of tension. The finest quality of hemp twine and cotton "stays" absolutely guaranteed not to pull through or fall out. This insures an absolute uniformity of thickness, softness and elasticity, when every square inch exactly duplicates the other, making a perfect and ideal bed which brings comfort from head to foot. **THE BINDING** and the border of the Genuine Whitmore Luxury Elastic Felt Mattresses are accurately set on and double stitched, which not only improves the appearance but preserves the shapeliness of the finished mattress.

THE TICKING. The best quality heavy satin finish ticking is used on this Genuine Whitmore Luxury Elastic Felt Mattress. A very closely woven textile fabric in colors of white, blue and drab stripes exceptionally neat and attractive in appearance, will not soil easily, and wearing qualities cannot be excelled. Should the ticking become soiled through any cause, soap, brush and water will cleanse it thoroughly and will not hurt the filling, because it is nonabsorbent.

THE WORKMANSHIP. Perfect accuracy in the cutting and matching of the ticking, careful stitching and boxing of the border all combine to make the best mattress that human brain can devise and skilled workmanship produce.

45 POUNDS

A FULL WEIGHT MATTRESS SHOULD WEIGH 45 POUNDS. We call special attention to the weight of our mattresses. Our full size mattresses weigh 45 pounds unpacked and the smaller sizes in proportion, as noted in the list below. **All weights guaranteed.** Many other dealers offer mattresses as full weight which weigh only 40 pounds. We could sell our mattresses at still lower prices by reducing the weight, but a full size mattress which weighs only 40 pounds as offered by other dealers is too thin and will prove unsatisfactory.

No. IK3145
ORDER BY NUMBER
BE SURE TO STATE SIZE WANTED

This illustration is an exact photographic reproduction of our Luxury No. IK3145 Mattress ready for use.

REMEMBER, THE FREIGHT TO ANY RAILROAD STATION IN THE UNITED STATES on this mattress is but a very small item compared with what you save in price. We do not quote this mattress freight prepaid. If we did we would have to make higher prices so as to cover freight charges to the most distant points, and the customer living 100 miles away would be helping to pay the freight to the customer 500 miles away. This mattress weighs, packed for shipment, about 50 pounds. The freight for 100 miles from Chicago will be 25 cents, for 200 miles, 35 cents, for 300 miles, 40 cents, for 500 miles, 45 cents, and for 1,000 miles, $1.05, and greater or less distances in proportion, so you see the freight charges amount to practically nothing as compared with what you save in price by buying from us.

SAMPLES FREE.

If there is any doubt in your mind of the superior quality of the Whitmore Luxury Elastic Felt Mattress as compared with any other felt mattress, regardless of name, make or price, do not order any felt mattress until you have sent to us for a sample of the ticking and the super-extra grade of snowy white elastic felt, which we will be pleased to send to you upon request, postpaid and free of charge. Compare the felt and ticking furnished by any other dealer and you will find the elastic felt used in the Genuine Whitmore Luxury Elastic Felt Mattress so far superior in length and textile strength of the fiber, in springy softness and elasticity, and in the snowy white purity of color that it is in a class by itself, an unequaled and unrivaled mattress filling.

GENERALLY SOLD AT $15.00.		No. IK3145	GENERALLY SOLD AT $15.00	
4½ feet by 6 feet 3 inches.	4 feet by 6 feet 3 inches.	3½ feet by 6 feet 3 inches.	3 feet by 6 feet 3 inches.	3 feet by 5 feet.
$10.95	$10.65	$9.85	$8.95	$6.85
Actual weight mattress unpacked, 45 pounds. Two parts, 35 cents extra.	Actual weight, 40 pounds.	Actual weight, 35 pounds.	Actual weight, 30 pounds.	Actual weight, 16 pounds.

READ WHAT WE SAY ABOUT THE FREIGHT CHARGES. All mattresses are carefully packed in heavy paper and new burlap, and safe delivery guaranteed. For other elastic felt mattresses see next page. We have them as low as $5.85.

DEPARTMENT OF UPHOLSTERED FURNITURE

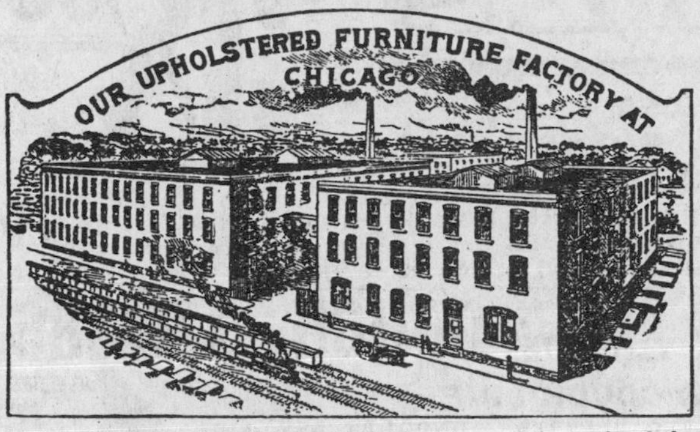

THIS DEPARTMENT has been greatly enlarged and improved, and following the very latest styles in upholstery, in frame work, covering and making, we present this new line of goods at prices based on the actual cost to produce, the cost of material and labor, with but our one small percentage of profit added.

OUR COUCHES AND PARLOR SUITES are made for us under contract by the most reliable manufacturers in the country. Only the most skilled mechanics are employed. **We have followed the very latest styles,** to give our customers the same style and grade of goods that are handled by the most fashionable city retail furniture dealers, where they are usually sold at fancy prices.

IN THE FRAME WORK, the coverings, the springs, the canvas and stuffing we use a higher grade of goods, a better class of material than is used by the average maker of upholstery, and you will find an upholstered couch, chair, divan or other piece you may buy of us will have a distinctiveness in style, workmanship and finish not found in the ordinary grade of goods. You will find our goods more lasting, more satisfactory, and at least one-third lower in price than anything furnished by others that will approach our goods in general appearance and style.

THE WOOD used in the construction of our upholstered furniture is specially selected, thoroughly air seasoned and kiln dried before being put through the factory. Great care is taken to get the highest quality and the choicest flaky grained lumber.

THE FINISH. The hardwood oil, the glue and the varnish used in the finishing of our upholstered furniture frames are of the highest grade obtainable. Special care is taken in the finishing of each frame, plenty of time being given for each coat to thoroughly harden and dry before rubbing and polishing down for the next coat. The color is a beautiful golden, which brings out the handsome flaky grain of the wood perfectly, or a perfect imitation of mahogany.

THE LEGS on all our couches and Roman divans are detachable, being fastened to the frame with heavy bolts, and are easily put on. They are shipped with the legs detached.

OUR GUARANTEE. In order that you need not feel that you are taking the slightest risk in sending to us for an upholstered piece of furniture, if you have any doubt as to the great values we offer, we wish to say that we stand ready to refund your money immediately and pay the freight charges both ways if the article you get from us is not perfectly satisfactory in every way.

THE COVERING MATERIALS.

To give our customers a better understanding of the materials which we use in upholstering our furniture, we give below a description of the texture of the different materials. When parlor suites are upholstered in Velour, Brocatelle or Silk Damask, each piece comprising the suite is upholstered in a different shade, but all shades are selected with great care so they will harmonize. We will furnish the entire suite in the same color throughout if desired, but we recommend a combination of colors except in materials which can be procured in only two colors, such as Brocaded Velour, Verona Plush, Crushed Plush and Car Plush. When these materials are used it is advisable to have the suite upholstered in the same color throughout.

FIGURED VELOUR.

Our high colored figured velour is a cloth universally known and is the kind of covering most generally used. It is woven like velvet, but with a higher and heavier pile, is soft and has the velvet effect. The high colorings are put into the ground of the cloth by an extract process. **The body colors are red, green or brown, and the pattern combinations of artistic colors, which make the total effect very striking.** There are many grades of velour on the market but **WE USE NONE BUT THE BEST.**

CORDUROY.

Corduroy is one of the best known and most staple of upholstery coverings. Its wearing qualities cannot be excelled. It is woven like velvet with parallel ridges instead of the plain surface which velour has. There are many grades of corduroy, but we use only the best imported grades, made from the best selected materials and guaranteed to give perfect satisfaction. **We furnish corduroy in solid color of myrtle green or dark red.** A couch covered with this material will prove exceptionally satisfactory.

PLAIN BROCADED VELOUR.

Plain brocaded velour is an entirely new covering for upholstering purposes, and has thus far proven to possess most excellent wearing qualities. The body of the cloth is woven in a block pattern of one solid color with a raised effect. It has a raised nap the same as in plush. An exceptionally desirable and attractive covering. **We can furnish plain brocaded velour in solid color of myrtle green, deep red or tobacco brown.**

FANCY BROCADED PLUSH.

This is one of the very latest and most desirable weaves in covering for upholstered furniture. The nap of the cloth, which is very long, is woven in fancy block patterns and combinations of green and black, red and black, tobacco brown and black with a solid color background in a Terry effect brown to correspond with the nap. This cloth is very heavy and made of selected materials and coloring, and is used only on high grade furniture. It is guaranteed to have exceptionally good wearing qualities and is such a handsome, striking material that it is sure to please everyone.

BROCADED VERONA PLUSH.

This luxurious fabric is one of the handsomest coverings for high grade furniture which it is possible to procure. It is made with a raised figure of handsome floral design in two colors, combinations of green and black or red and black with background to match the body of the cloth. The large floral figure is made with a long nap the same as the finest plush cloth and is extra heavy. Only the strongest colors are used, giving the furniture when finished a most luxurious appearance.

CRUSHED PLUSH.

Crushed plush is universally known. It is made in many grades, but the quality which we use is not to be compared to what is offered by many other manufacturers and dealers. The crushed plush which we furnish is made especially for us of a strictly high grade fur which has an exceptionally silky, lustrous appearance and is guaranteed to hold its color; even the finest wool will not compare with it in this respect. After the fur is woven into the cloth the entire piece is put through the process of crushing, which brings out the rich, shaded effects for which this cloth is so much sought after. **We can furnish crushed plush coverings in red, green, blue or brown, in solid colors only.**

BROCADED SILK PLUSH.

No upholstery material which we furnish can compare in richness and style with brocaded silk plush. The nap of the cloth is made of silk woven into handsome figures made on a backing slightly mixed with cotton, which makes it more durable than the all silk. The fur and the yarns used are dyed before being woven, which makes the colors absolutely fast. It has proven exceptionally satisfactory and is used only in the manufacture of the highest class parlor suites.

PLAIN SILK PLUSH.

Plain silk plush is one of the most popular upholstery materials used for parlor suites, fancy chairs and rockers. It is especially attractive when used as covering for cushions. The nap of the cloth is made of the finest silk yarns, woven very close, and has a rich, luxurious velvet sheen. It is all silk and the yarns are dyed before weaving, thus making the colors absolutely fast. **We furnish this handsome covering in olive green or dark red, solid colors,** either of which will harmonize with almost all surroundings.

FIGURED SILK DAMASK.

This material has been used for many years and has proven very desirable covering for parlor suites, fancy chairs and rockers. The cloth is made up in handsome flowered designs woven into the cloth and not printed. Yarns are well selected and dyed before being woven into the tapestry, thereby producing fast colors. Flowers are all silk on a mercerized background, giving it a rich and lustrous appearance that will outwear the all silk damask. The cloth is made up of colors to harmonize, and when made into suites, a different ground color is generally used on each piece. Our customers can select a color for each piece if desired, as all furniture is upholstered after the order is received, but we advise leaving selection of color to the manfacturer who employs the most skilled mechanics with many years experience.

PANNE PLUSH.

This is one of the most attractive and best wearing coverings used in the upholstering of furniture. It has a heavy linen warp with a silk nap, very closely woven. It has a rich, lustrous appearance. It is used only on high grade furniture and is specially adapted for the covering of loose cushions used on three-piece parlor suites. This cloth is very heavy and will please the most exacting taste. **We furnish this covering in dark olive green, solid color only,** which will harmonize with almost all surroundings.

CAR PLUSH.

Car plush is one of the oldest staple coverings that has ever been produced. It derives its name, car plush, from the fact that it is so extensively used in covering car seats and is especially selected for this purpose on account of its durability. Fabrics that look well, but do not wear well, soon go out of style, but a couch covered with car plush is always in style and will look well and wear like leather.

There are many grades of car plush, some being made with the pile of the cloth of wool and mohair mixed, others with cashmere and mohair mixed, or in other combinations which cheapen the cost of production. We use only the very best grade of genuine all mohair car plush, which is the only fabric that will hold its color absolutely, and there is no other fabric, even including wool, silk or linen, that will hold its color as well as mohair. **We guarantee it not to fade. We can furnish it either in deep red, myrtle green or tobacco brown colors.**

BE SURE TO READ THIS

We give above a description of the textures of some of the different materials used on our upholstered furniture, and while the descriptions will no doubt give an excellent idea of the nature of the materials, yet it is impossible to fully describe the handsome designs and harmonious colors of our five-piece parlor suites, or the beautiful new textures which are produced from season to season by the manufacturers who make this class of work a specialty. In order to make it possible for our customers to see exactly what materials are used we have made special arrangements with the manufacturers of the upholstering goods to supply **extra large samples** from which to make a selection.

HOW WE FURNISH OUR SETS OF EXTRA LARGE SAMPLES OF COVERING MATERIALS FREE.

By special arrangement with the manufacturers of the different materials used in our Upholstered Furniture Department we are able to furnish complete sets of the different kinds of materials in the different shades used on our upholstered furniture. These sets are made up of extra large pieces and will enable you to make a selection of the material and color which you desire, far better than you could without the samples or from a description only.

SET No. 1 consists of the sample coverings for Parlor Suites, odd Rockers and Chairs. This set contains samples of Figured Velour, Plain Brocaded Velour, Floral Brocaded Velour, Fancy Brocaded Velour, Brocaded Verona Plush, Crushed Plush, Brocaded Silk Plush, Silk Brocatelle, Silk Damask and many other new and novel coverings suitable for this class of furniture. The samples show the full pattern or figure of the goods and all the different colorings in each particular pattern. This complete set will be sent to you by mail or express, prepaid, on receipt of 50 cents **and when they are returned to us at our expense** we will return your 50 cents, or if you send us an order at the same time you return the set of samples we will allow you 50 cents on your order.

SET No. 2 contains sample coverings for Couches, Davenports, Roman Davenports and Bed Couches. This set consists of large pieces of Figured Velour, Corduroy, Plain Brocaded Velour, Fancy Brocaded Plush, Crushed Plush, Brocaded Verona Plush, Car Plush, and other new and handsome materials suitable for this class of furniture. These samples show the full pattern or figure of the goods and show all the different colors of each particular pattern. This complete set will be sent by mail or express, prepaid, on receipt of 50 cents **and when they are returned to us at our expense,** we will return your 50 cents, or if you send us an order at the same time you return the set of samples we will allow you 50 cents on your order.

BE SURE TO STATE whether you want Set No. 1, showing sample covering for Parlor Suites, Rockers and Chairs, or Set No. 2 for Couches, Davenports and Bed Couches, as the materials in these sets are not alike and we send but one set upon receipt of 50 cents.

If you want to order a Parlor Suite, Rocker or Chair and a Couch, Davenport or Bed Couch, we recommend that you send $1.00 and get both sets on the same conditions as we offer one set.

REMEMBER THAT IT COSTS YOU NOTHING to see the goods, as we refund your money in full or credit it on your order and the samples are sent prepaid and are returned at our expense. We would gladly furnish either of these complete sets of samples without asking the 50 cents deposit, but you can understand that there are a great many of these large samples in a set and a large amount of material is used to make one of these complete sets of samples and we are compelled to protect ourselves against loss.

IT IS REALLY NOT NECESSARY to delay your order by first writing for samples, since you can order from the descriptions given above of the different covering materials which we use in upholstering our furniture. We are willing that you should order direct from this catalogue and these descriptions without ordering or writing for samples and we will send the goods to you with the distinct understanding and agreement that they must reach you in perfect condition and that they must prove entirely satisfactory to you and that you will find that you have made a big saving in price; otherwise the goods can be returned to us and we will promptly return your money.

$3⁷⁵ COUCHES $38⁹⁵

BIG REDUCTIONS IN PRICES.
AT $3.75 TO $38.95 WE SHOW A WONDERFUL
VARIETY OF HANDSOME COUCHES

LATEST DESIGNS, HIGH GRADE IN CONSTRUCTION, NEW EFFECTS IN COVERING MATERIALS.
COMPARE OUR GOODS; COMPARE OUR PRICES

We challenge any house on earth to furnish as high quality Couches at prices as low as we ask.

THIS HANDSOME VICTORIA DESIGN HIGH GRADE COUCH, $7⁸⁵

THE LEADER OF OUR COUCH LINE.

THE MOST WONDERFUL COUCH VALUE EVER OFFERED. UNDOUBTEDLY AND WITHOUT QUESTION THE EQUAL OF COUCHES OFFERED BY OTHER DEALERS AT $15.00 TO $20.00.

This magnificent Victoria design, massive frame, beautifully carved, biscuit tufted Couch must be seen to be fully appreciated.

No. 1K3436 Order by Number

This illustration shows the Victoria Couch upholstered in Figured Velour, a very durable and satisfactory covering. For those wishing a better grade of covering we would recommend the Brocaded Verona Plush, it is beautiful in pattern and the combination of colors in green and black or red and black, with its good wearing qualities has made it very popular.

The number of this Couch is No. 1K3436. Always order by number and be sure to state the kind and color of covering desired.

Covering	Figured Velour	Plain Brocaded Velour	Fancy Brocaded Plush	Brocaded Verona Plush	Crushed Plush
Price	$7.85	$8.25	$8.55	$9.35	$10.45

THE MASSIVE FRAME is made throughout of specially selected northern hardwood, thoroughly air seasoned and kiln dried, veneered with highly figured flaky grained quarter sawed oak, especially selected for beauty of the grain. Length, 74 inches, width, 27 inches. Decorated with deep, smooth cut, hand made carvings, finely executed. Most of the strictly up to date furniture factories construct only what is known as veneered furniture, the kind in most popular demand. By this process the handsome effect of the finest high grade furniture can be obtained at a reduced cost by building up the frames of hardwood, using as the upper surface the highly figured flaky grained quartered oak. The shapely designed, handsome claw legs are detachable for convenience in handling and shipping, being fastened to the frame by heavy bolts and are easily put on.

IN THIS COUCH our factory has adopted the same method, thereby presenting the effect of the very best furniture made, and at the same time giving us this beautiful couch at a very low price, and guaranteed by us in every respect as durable as any couch made by the old method. This method can be employed only in the most up to date and dependable factories, and we take the lead, and consequently it is not being offered by any other dealer.

THE FINISH is a beautiful golden color, and brings out the handsome flaky grain of the wood perfectly. Great care is taken in the finishing process, special attention being given to the preservation of the wood. The best materials that can be obtained are used in order to produce a higher grade of finish, a more perfect luster and better surface, a finish that will not crack, peel, check or become dull.

THE CONSTRUCTION of this high grade Victoria Couch is the same as we use on all our high grade couches. We use our guaranteed indestructible, high carbon, all steel construction in this couch, as well as on almost all the other couches we sell. The springs are one of the most essential parts of a couch. If the spring work is poor, the couch soon loses its shape and wears out. The grade of wire used in our indestructible construction is alone a guarantee of the lasting qualities. The elasticity, durability and comfort of the springs depend on shape, height, weight and temper of the steel wire used. The body of the couch has 24 springs and the head 4, made of the best quality high carbon Bessemer steel. The springs on the bottom side are intercoiled into steel bands, which run crosswise on the bottom, and are fastened to the top side of the rail on each side of the couch and can never get loose, besides being reinforced with a steel wire running lengthwise on the bottom, into which the springs are also intercoiled. The tops of the springs are securely fastened together with steel wire (no twine being used), and the edge wire is clinched into the springs in such a manner that it can never get loose. Comfort, durability and lasting qualities are thus obtained in the most perfect manner. Springs are covered with heavy duck canvas instead of the cheap burlap used by most other manufacturers. The filling in this magnificent, high grade Victoria couch is the very best grade of fine flax fiber, with a clean, new cotton top, a filling that is more elastic, cleaner and more durable than the cheap hair filling used by many other manufacturers. Cheap, short hair is unclean, unsanitary and foul smelling, besides packing into a hard mass.

THE COVERING MATERIALS used on this couch are fully described on page 43. They include all the latest effects, harmonious colorings and best weaves. Each material is the most excellent quality, and no matter which you may select you will find a distinctiveness of style and pattern that cannot be excelled, and is guaranteed to prove exceptionally satisfactory. Only the strongest and fastest colors are used, giving the couch a luxurious appearance.

HOW WE MAKE THE PRICES SO LOW ON OUR STRICTLY HIGH GRADE COUCHES.

—much lower, in fact, than most dealers can buy—explained by the fact that we have for some time taken almost the entire output of two of the largest and best known couch factories in the United States. One is located in a suburb of Chicago, the other in Central New York, both on the main line of railroads, where ground is cheap, and have been able to meet the situation without a great outlay of money.

The Most Modern Machinery and Labor Saving Devices have been installed. The materials are purchased in carload lots. Year by year with the increasing output of the factory, the cost of production has been lowered, and we have all the time given our customers the benefit of the reduction by making couches cheaper in price and better in quality. We are offering you this handsome, high grade Victoria couch, with a handsome quarter sawed oak frame, beautifully hand carved, with massive claw feet, at a price lower than we have ever been able to offer such a couch. It is positively the most wonderful couch value ever offered by anyone. There is no other factory that can produce the couch in thousand lots at a cost of manufacture as low as the price we ask, $7.85.

COMPARE CAREFULLY. Read the description of our couches and carefully compare them with those offered by others at more than double the price we ask, and you will quickly recognize the saving it is possible for you to make by placing your order with us.

EVERY COUCH IS SENT OUT UNDER OUR BINDING GUARANTEE. We guarantee it to reach you in the same perfect condition it leaves us and to prove entirely satisfactory to you, otherwise you can return it to us at our expense of freight charges both ways and we will immediately refund your money. The couch weighs, packed for shipment, 110 pounds, and you will find the freight will amount to nothing as compared to what you will save in price.

DIRECT FROM FACTORY. This couch is shipped direct from our factory near Chicago, or from Central New York, thereby cutting out all intermediate cost of handling and intermediate profits, which, together with the favorable conditions outlined above, enable us to quote such an extremely low price as $7.85.

OUR GUARANTEED ALL STEEL SPRING CONSTRUCTION.

THIS ILLUSTRATION is a reproduction of a photograph of one of our couch frames and bodies, showing our celebrated all steel spring construction. This steel construction is used in all of our better grade couches as you will find described under each number. When no mention is made of the all steel construction, we use the old method of tying the springs with common twine; but in our better couches you will find that we are using this steel construction, which is in many respects far superior to the common twine tied construction. The number of springs used is mentioned in the description of each couch and varies according to the style. In connection with the steel construction, which is used in the body part of the couch, we use a number of double cone steel springs in the head of the couch. The springs, the most essential part of a couch, are cone shaped and are drawn from the best high carbon steel wire obtainable. The grade of wire used is alone a guarantee of the lasting qualities of this construction. The elasticity and durability of the spring all depend on the shape, height and weight of the steel wire used. Nothing has been spared in time or money, costly dies, etc., to construct this spring to give the best possible results. The springs on bottom side are intercoiled into steel band irons which run crosswise on bottom and are fastened to the top of side rail and can never get loose, besides being reinforced with a steel wire running lengthwise on the bottom, into which the springs are also intercoiled. The top of spring is tied, as shown in illustration, every spring securely fastened with steel wire, no twine, and edge wire is clinched into the springs in such a manner that it can never come off. Its neat appearance and sanitary features are especially desirable in a couch.

THIS MAGNIFICENT EMPRESS DESIGN HIGH GRADE COUCH $12.15

MASSIVE AND STRIKINGLY HANDSOME IN DESIGN, STRICTLY HIGH GRADE IN CONSTRUCTION, BEAUTIFUL IN FINISH. THE EQUAL OF COUCHES GENERALLY OFFERED BY DEALERS AT $20.00 TO $25.00.

Our low prices are not made at the expense of quality. We guarantee every couch lower in price than the same quality of goods can be bought elsewhere.

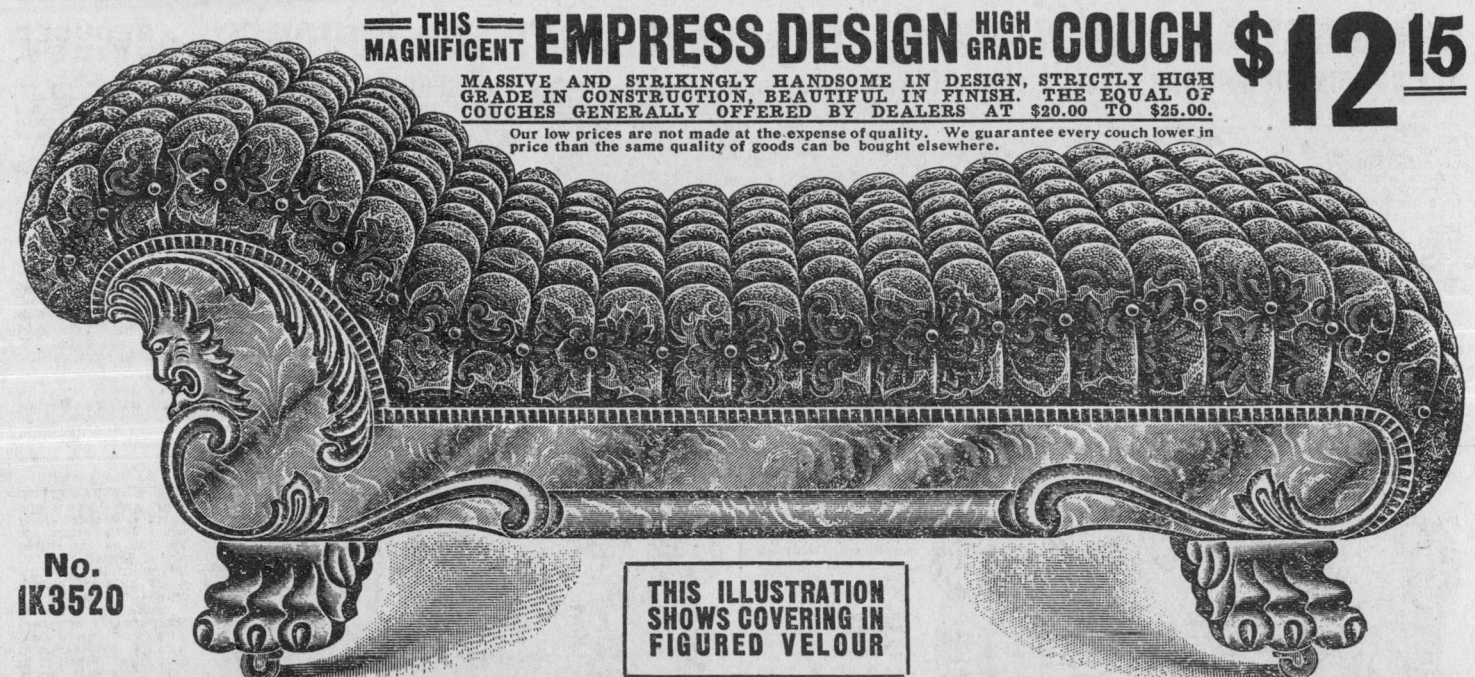

No. IK3520

THIS ILLUSTRATION SHOWS COVERING IN FIGURED VELOUR

No. IK3520 THIS MAGNIFICENT HIGH GRADE COUCH is made of specially selected and thoroughly seasoned hardwood, veneered with highly figured quarter sawed oak finished in a rich golden color and highly polished. Deep carvings made of oak and heavy claw feet. It is 78 inches long and 30 inches wide, spring edges with eight rows of deep tufts securely fastened with our celebrated Naper steel tufting buttons guaranteed not to pull out. This couch has our indestructible all steel construction as described on page 438, with twenty-eight springs in the body and nine springs in the head, thirty-seven springs in all. Springs are covered with heavy duck canvas. Filling is the best quality flax fiber and clean new cotton. The upholstering materials are carefully selected from the latest patterns as fully described on page 437. The workmanship on this couch is first class in every detail and no effort has been spared to put on the market the best couch possible at a price never before heard of. We invite comparison with other couches that are sold by other dealers at double our price. Casters furnished with each couch. Shipping weight, 105 pounds.

THE NUMBER OF THIS COUCH IS No. IK3520. Always order by number and be sure to state kind and color of covering wanted.

Covering	Figured Velour	Plain Brocaded Velour	Brocaded Verona Plush	Crushed Plush
Price at factory near Chicago or Central New York.	$12.15	$12.45	$13.55	$15.65
Price at warehouse in Kansas City, Mo.	12.82			
Price at warehouse in St. Paul, Minn.	12.98			

HOW WE ARE ABLE TO MAKE QUICK DELIVERY AND SAVE TIME AND FREIGHT CHARGES TO OUR CUSTOMERS

OUR SALES on these Magnificent High Grade Couches have grown so large from every section of the country that, in order that we may be able to get one of these splendid and deservedly popular Couches to our customers in the WEST and NORTHWEST in a day or two from the date we receive your order, to insure its reaching you in perfect condition, to remove the liability of breakage or damage and reduce the freight charges to the smallest possible amount, we have arranged warehouse facilities at Kansas City, Mo. and St. Paul, Minn., and will ship from these warehouses the No. IK3520 Couch, upholstered in figured green velour only and the No. IK3769 Couch, upholstered in fabricord (imitation leather) only. We ship these Couches in these two styles only of upholstering in solid car lots, receiving from the railroad company the very lowest carload freight rates, so that when we receive your order here in Chicago for either Couch No. IK3520 in green velour or No. IK3769 in fabricord, we immediately send your order by special mail delivery to the warehouse nearest you and order the Couch shipped to your railroad station on your order at once. It will leave the warehouse in perfect condition and will reach you in a few hours or a day or two at the farthest from the time it leaves the warehouse, and when you get it you need to pay the small freight charges for the short distance from the warehouse to your railroad station. The total cost of either of these couches to our customers in the WEST and NORTHWEST will amount to considerably less than if shipped to you singly as one shipment from the factory near Chicago to your nearest railroad station.

THIS HANDSOME HIGH GRADE GONDOLA COUCH $11.55

UPHOLSTERED IN FABRICORD LEATHER, OR GENUINE No. 1 HAND BUFFED LEATHER. BEAUTIFUL IN DESIGN, BETTER IN QUALITY AND LOWER IN PRICE THAN CAN BE BOUGHT ELSEWHERE.

Compare this couch with those generally offered by other dealers at ⅓ to ½ more than the price we ask.

No. IK3769

EVERY COUCH SOLD UNDER OUR BINDING GUARANTEE OF QUALITY

No. IK3769 THIS HANDSOME GONDOLA SHAPED COUCH is made of thoroughly seasoned hardwood, veneered in beautifully figured quarter sawed oak, finished in a rich golden color with deep oak carved moulding as shown in illustration. Heavy substantial legs, deep carved and fitted with good quality of casters. Couch is upholstered either in genuine hand buffed No. 1 leather or fabricord (imitation leather) with full spring edge, and small diamond tufts made with the Naper double prong steel tufting buttons. When upholstered in leather, the couch is filled with selected long, washed goat hair, when upholstered in fabricord, it is filled with an extra quality of fine tow with a cotton and hair top. Couch is 80 inches long and 30 inches wide and has the all steel spring construction illustrated and described on page 438. There are twenty-eight high carbon Bessemer steel springs in the body and nine in the head, making thirty-seven in all, covered with a heavy duck canvas. For an up to date serviceable couch, one guaranteed to give absolute satisfaction in every respect, this couch cannot be reproduced quality for quality, by other dealers and sold for double the price we ask. Shipping weight, 115 pounds.

THE NUMBER OF THIS COUCH IS No. IK3769. Always order by number and be sure to state kind of covering desired.

Covering	Fabricord	No. 1 Leather
Price at factory near Chicago or Central New York.	$11.55	$29.25
Price at warehouse in Kansas City, Mo.	12.32	
Price at warehouse in St. Paul, Minn.	12.38	

COMBINATION ROMAN DIVAN, SOFA, DAVENPORT AND COUCHES AT REDUCED PRICES.

THE COMBINATION ROMAN DIVAN, Sofa, Davenport and Couch has become so popular that we are paying special attention to this particular branch of our upholstering department. This combination piece is a modern invention but its general utility has been quickly recognized. It is exceptionally useful on account of the numerous ways it can be utilized. Either end can be lowered to any angle desired by an automatic attachment; in so doing there are no straps or strings to pull. When ends are lowered for use as a couch, as shown in illustration, it is as comfortable as any couch, being as long and wide as any regular couch. When in use as a divan or sofa it cannot be excelled for comfort.

OPERATION IS VERY SIMPLE.

In order to lower the arms, raise them to their upright position and by pushing them still a little higher the automatic ratchet will disconnect and the arm will lower to a level, and it can then be raised to any position desired.

THE CONSTRUCTION is strictly first class throughout, every joint and corner perfectly framed and fitted. In fact, nothing that skilled workmanship and modern machinery can do to produce a first class article has been overlooked.

THE SPRINGS are the best high carbon Bessemer steel coil springs securely fastened at the top and bottom and covered with a heavy duck canvas and filled with a fine grade of tow and thick layer of elastic cotton. The tufted couches have a deep biscuit tuft made with the celebrated metal Naper tufting buttons guaranteed not to pull out.

THE FRAMES are made of thoroughly seasoned wood, specially selected to secure a fine grain and we guarantee them not to warp or shrink.

THE COVERINGS used on our Roman Divan Sofas, Davenports and Couches are especially selected for their wearing qualities and the beautiful and harmonious effects are fully described on page 437. You will find our coverings are more lasting, more satisfactory and at least one-third lower in price than anything offered by other concerns that approach our goods in quality and style.

THE LEGS on all of our Roman Divans are detachable, being fastened to the frame by heavy bolts and are easily put on. Shipped with legs and back detached, thereby getting a much lower freight rate.

THE ILLUSTRATION shows one of our combination Roman Davenports as a couch. Each piece illustrated below can be made up in the same manner.

This illustration shows our combination Roman Davenport with arms lowered for use as a couch.

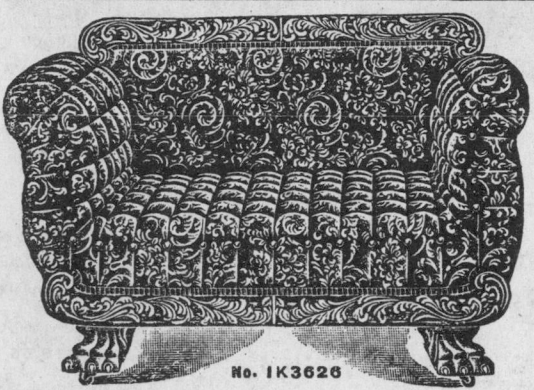

No. 1K3626 This combination Roman Divan is made of thoroughly seasoned hard wood. The deeply carved scrolls are of solid oak with a dark golden finish. Heavy claw feet. Length, 38 inches inside arms when used as a davenport and 74 inches long when both ends are lowered for use as a couch, as shown in illustration above. Width, 23 inches. Deeply tufted with spring edge front; coverings of the very latest designs as described on page 437. For a more detailed description of construction and operation, see article above on construction and operation. Shipping weight, 140 pounds.

No. 1K3626

| The number of this Roman Divan is No. 1K3626. Always order by number and be sure to state the kind and color of covering desired. | | | | |
Covering	Figured Velour	Plain Brocaded Velour	Fancy Brocaded Plush	Brocaded Verona Plush	Crushed Plush
Price	$8.85	$9.15	$9.95	$10.85	$12.85

No. 1K3638 This combination Roman Divan and Couch is 80 inches long when both arms are lowered, as shown in above illustration, 40 inches inside the arms when ends are raised, seat is 27 inches deep. Frame is made of thoroughly seasoned quarter sawed oak, heavy carvings and claw feet. Finished in golden oak and highly polished. Seat is built on our indestructible all steel construction, spring edge and deeply tufted with the Naper steel tufting buttons. Coverings are of the latest designs; for full description of covers see page 437. For a more detailed description of construction and operation. Shipping weight, 150 pounds.

No. 1K3638

| The number of this Divan is No. 1K3638. Always order by number and be sure to state the kind and color of covering desired. | | | | |
Covering	Figured Velour	Plain Brocaded Velour	Fancy Brocaded Plush	Brocaded Verona Plush	Crushed Plush
Price	$12.65	$12.95	$13.40	$13.95	$15.75

No. 1K3631 This handsome Roman Divan or Davenport Couch is 74 inches long when both arms are lowered for use as a couch, as shown in above illustration, and 40 inches between the arms when both arms are upright; width of seat, 23 inches. Frame is made of quarter sawed oak with beautiful carvings finished in a dark golden color. Full set high carbon Bessemer steel coil spring seat, spring edge and deeply tufted. Heavy claw feet. Coverings of the very latest patterns, as fully described on page 437. For a more detailed description of construction and operation, see articles above on construction and operation. Shipping weight, 140 pounds.

No. 1K3631

| The number of this Sofa is No. 1K3631. Always order by number and be sure to state the kind and color of covering desired. | | | | |
Covering	Figured Velour	Plain Brocaded Velour	Fancy Brocaded Plush	Brocaded Verona Plush	Crushed Plush
Price	$10.35	$10.65	$11.10	$11.85	$13.75

No. 1K3640 This combination Roman Divan and Couch is 78 inches long when converted into a couch by lowering the ends, and 36 inches between the arms when used as a divan. Seat is 27 inches wide. Frame is made of selected quarter sawed oak, handsomely carved back and claw feet. Finished in rich golden color and highly polished. Spring edge seat deeply tufted. Coverings are of the very latest designs. For description of cover see page 437. For a more detailed description of construction, see article above on construction and operation. Shipping weight, 150 pounds.

No. 1K3640

| The number of this Sofa is No. 1K3640. Always order by number and be sure to state the kind and color of covering desired. | | | | |
Covering	Figured Velour	Plain Brocaded Velour	Fancy Brocaded Plush	Brocaded Verona Plush	Crushed Plush
Price	$13.45	$13.95	$14.55	$14.95	$16.65

No. 1K3634 A very handsome combination Roman Divan and Couch. Frame is made of quarter sawed oak with heavy carvings, solid Roman legs finished in dark golden color and highly polished. Seat is 27 inches deep and 36 inches between the arms when ends are raised. When ends are extended, as shown in above illustration, it makes a couch 80 inches long. Seat has spring edge and is deeply tufted with the Naper steel tufting buttons. Coverings are of the very latest design. For a more detailed description of construction and operation, see article above on construction and operation. Shipping weight, 150 lbs.

No. 1K3634

| The number of this Divan is No. 1K3634. Always order by number and be sure to state the kind and color of covering desired. | | | | |
Covering	Figured Velour	Plain Brocaded Velour	Fancy Brocaded Plush	Brocaded Verona Plush	Crushed Plush
Price	$11.75	$12.05	$12.25	$12.85	$14.85

No. 1K3642 The latest design in Roman Divan and Davenport Couch. Frame is made of selected quarter sawed oak, highly polished and finished in a rich golden color. Deep smooth cut hand carvings. Has smooth top with ruffled spring edge. Measures 40 inches between arms, and 78 inches when arms are let down for use as a couch. Seat made on our indestructible all steel construction spring. For a detailed description, see article above on construction and operation. Coverings are of the latest designs and are fully described on page 437. Shipping weight, 150 pounds.

No. 1K3642

| The number of this Divan is No. 1K3642. Always order by number and be sure to state the kind and color of covering desired. | | | | |
Covering	Figured Velour	Plain Brocaded Velour	Fancy Brocaded Velour	Brocaded Verona Plush	Crushed Plush
Price	$14.85	$15.25	$15.65	$15.95	$17.85

THE ABOVE PIECES SHIPPED DIRECT FROM FACTORY IN CENTRAL NEW YORK OR NEAR CHICAGO, ACCORDING TO LOCATION OF CUSTOMER, THEREBY INSURING THE LOWEST FREIGHT RATES.

HIGH GRADE AUTOMATIC DAVENPORT BED SOFAS

DAVENPORT BED SOFAS. No home is complete without one. Their wonderful usefulness, and the extremely low prices we are offering them at, has made them so popular that the sales for the past season jumped into the thousands. They are useful and ornamental. You will be fully convinced if you purchase one of our davenport bed sofas.

THE FRAMES of our davenport bed sofas are made of thoroughly seasoned and kiln dried selected wood.

OPERATION. Each davenport is fitted with an automatic device by which they are easily converted into a large size bed, as shown in illustration, and back again to a davenport sofa. To change into a bed, raise the seat which is counterbalanced, when seat is raised the back lowers automatically, when back is on a level push seat up until the ratchet clicks. Then the seat can be lowered to a level, completing the bed. To change back to davenport raise the seat

AT REDUCED PRICES.

This illustration shows No. 1K3655 Automatic Davenport made up as a bed.

until ratchet clicks, then bear down on seat and the back will raise and the seat lowers automatically; simple and easy, nothing to get out of order and can be operated by a child.

THE CONSTRUCTION is strictly high grade throughout. The celebrated steel construction is used on all our davenports except No 1K3644 which has the hand tied construction. Filling is a fine grade of tow with a cotton top. Heavy duck canvas over springs. Deep tufting made with double prong steel tufting buttons. Below the seat of each davenport is a roomy box the full length and width of the seat for bed clothing, etc.

THE FINISH. Nothing is omitted in style or finish that can be accomplished by first class workmanship. The very best finishing materials are used on the frames and special care given to bring out figured grain of wood.

COVERINGS are all of the very latest design and first class material; for full description of design refer to page 437.

SHIPPING. Our davenports are made with detachable ends, easily set up, and shipped knocked down, securing lowest freight rates. Shipped direct from factory near Chicago or from Central New York.

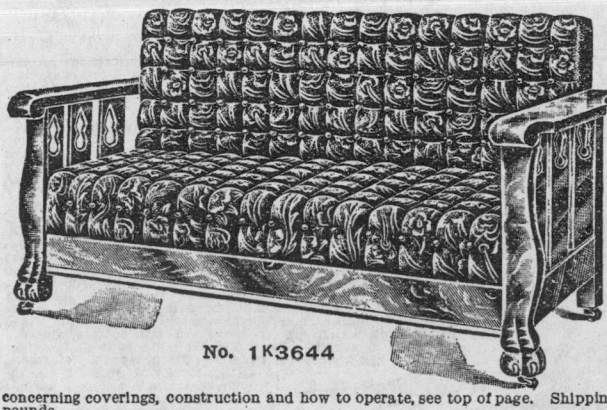

No. 1K3644 is made of oak golden gloss finish. As a davenport it measures 72 inches long and 23 inches wide between arms and 72 inches by 45 inches when opened as a bed. Has spring seat back and edge, contains 49 high carbon Bessemer steel springs. For full information concerning coverings, construction and how to operate, see top of page. Shipping weight, 200 pounds.

The number of this davenport is No. 1K3644. Always order by number and be sure to state the kind and color of covering wanted.

Covering	Figured Velour	Plain Brocaded Velour	Fancy Brocaded Plush	Brocaded Verona Plush	Fabricord Leather	Crushed Plush	Car Plush	No. 1 Genuine Leather
Price	$14.75	$15.35	$15.55	$16.45	$16.55	$19.45	$24.65	$34.85

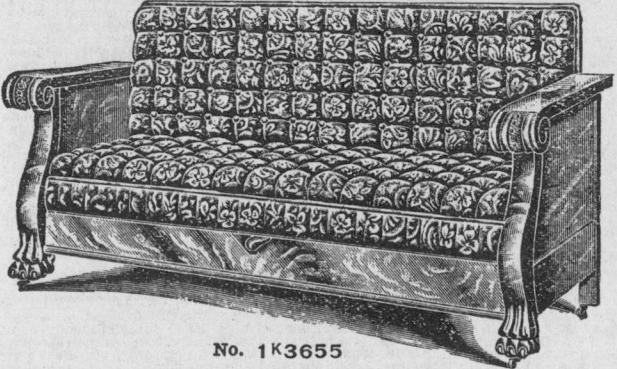

No. 1K3652 This Davenport Couch is 72 inches long and 23 inches wide, and 72 inches long and 45 inches wide when made into a bed. Frame is made of thoroughly seasoned oak, golden finish, hand carved and polished. Has full spring seat and back. Fitted with 48 high carbon steel springs. For further description of construction, coverings, and how to operate, see article at top of page. Shipping weight, 250 pounds.

The number of this davenport is No. 1K3652. Always order by number and be sure to state the kind and color of covering wanted.

Covering	Figured Velour	Plain Brocaded Velour	Fancy Brocaded Plush	Brocaded Verona Plush	Fabricord Leather	Crushed Plush	Car Plush	No. 1 Genuine Leather
Price	$17.25	$17.75	$17.95	$19.85	$19.95	$21.75	$26.85	$37.35

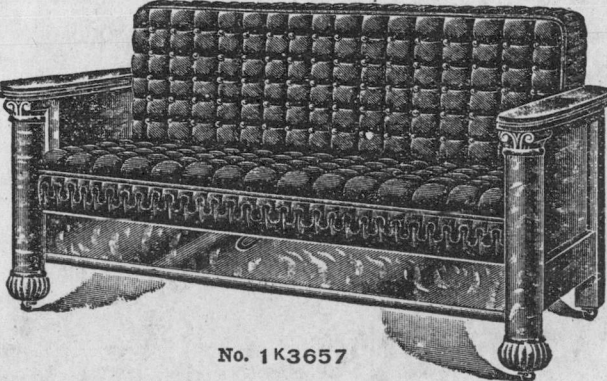

No. 1K3657 This Colonial style Davenport Bed and Sofa is made of special selected, thoroughly seasoned quarter sawed oak, highly polished and finished in rich golden color. Deep hand carvings on post. It is 72 inches long and 23 inches deep as a davenport, and when open for a bed measures 72 inches long and 45 inches deep. Full steel construction. Has spring seat and back containing 48 high carbon Bessemer steel springs. For further description concerning construction, coverings and how to operate, see article at top of page. Shipping weight, about 275 pounds. The number of this davenport bed sofa is No. 1K3657. Always order by number and be sure to state the kind and color of covering desired.

Covering	Figured Velour	Plain Brocaded Velour	Fancy Brocaded Plush	Brocaded Verona Plush	Fabricord Leather	Crushed Plush	Car Plush	No. 1 Genuine Leather
Price	$21.95	$22.45	$22.65	$23.55	$23.75	$26.35	$31.25	$42.35

No. 1K3658 This massive Davenport Bed and Sofa is made of quarter sawed oak, thoroughly seasoned, handsomely carved and polished, finished in golden color. As a sofa it is 72 inches long and 23 inches deep, and as a bed it is 72 inches long and 45 inches wide. Spring seat, spring back with ruffled front. Seat and back contain 54 high carbon steel coil springs. Illustration shows davenport upholstered in genuine leather. For more detailed information concerning construction, coverings and how to operate, see article at top of page. Shipping weight, 250 pounds.

The number of this davenport is No. 1K3658. Always order by number and be sure to state the kind and color of covering desired.

Covering	Figured Velour	Plain Brocaded Velour	Fancy Brocaded Plush	Brocaded Verona Plush	Fabricord Leather	Crushed Plush	Car Plush	No. 1 Genuine Leather
Price	$24.45	$24.85	$25.15	$25.75	$25.95	$28.65	$32.45	$44.85

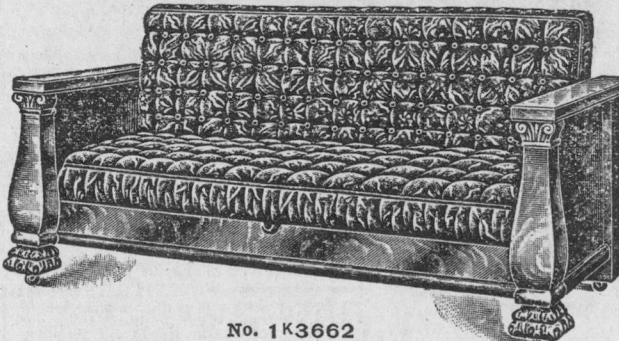

No. 1K3655 This high grade Davenport is made of beautifully figured quartered oak, golden finish, rubbed and polished, decorated with hand carvings. As a sofa it is 72 inches long and 23 inches deep, as a bed it is 72 inches long and 45 inches wide. Has a tufted spring seat and back containing 48 high carbon steel springs. For a more complete description of construction, coverings and how to operate, see article at head of page. Shipping weight, 250 pounds.

The number of this davenport bed sofa is No. 1K3655. Always order by number and be sure to state the kind and color of covering desired.

Covering	Figured Velour	Plain Brocaded Velour	Fancy Brocaded Plush	Brocaded Verona Plush	Fabricord Leather	Crushed Plush	Car Plush	No. 1 Genuine Leather
Price	$19.65	$20.15	$20.35	$21.25	$21.35	$23.95	$28.95	$39.85

No. 1K3662 This handsome Davenport Bed and Sofa is 72 inches long and 23 inches deep, and when opened for use as a bed measures 72 inches long and 45 inches wide. Has deep tufted spring seat and back with ruffled front. Contains 48 high carbon Bessemer steel springs. Frame is made of quarter sawed oak, highly polished with massive posts and deep hand carvings. For a more detailed description concerning construction, coverings and how to operate, see article at top of page. Shipping weight, about 275 pounds.

The number of this davenport bed sofa is No. 1K3662. Always order by number and be sure to state the kind and color of covering desired.

Covering	Figured Velour	Plain Brocaded Velour	Fancy Brocaded Plush	Brocaded Verona Plush	Fabricord Leather	Crushed Plush	Car Plush	No. 1 Genuine Leather
Price	$26.45	$26.65	$26.95	$27.85	$28.25	$30.85	$35.25	$46.85

THE ABOVE PIECES SHIPPED DIRECT FROM FACTORY IN CENTRAL NEW YORK OR NEAR CHICAGO, ACCORDING TO LOCATION OF CUSTOMER, THEREBY INSURING THE LOWEST FREIGHT RATES.

$3.65 MORRIS CHAIRS $16.95

AT $3.65 TO $16.95 WE SHOW WONDERFUL VALUES IN MORRIS CHAIRS AT GREATLY REDUCED PRICES.
OUR $3.65 MORRIS CHAIR WILL BE FOUND ON NEXT PAGE.

All the Newest Designs and Latest Improvements.

ON THE BASIS OF MANUFACTURING COST, with but our one small percentage of profit added, we offer you these high class Morris chairs, and you can buy them for less money than most retail dealers pay at wholesale. Never before have we been able to show such a splendid line of these popular chairs, or such fine, high grade chairs at such low prices.

THE MORRIS RECLINING CHAIR derives its name from the inventor, William Morris, a New England Yankee. It combines simplicity of construction with ease and comfort, as no other chair does. The spacious depth and width of the seat, the broad and high adjustable back, together with the broad arms, render the Morris chair the superior in ease and comfort of any chair devised. The frames are massive in design and are made to wear. The Morris chair has become so well known and the demand for them so great that the sale has jumped from the hundreds into thousands. No home can afford to be without one.

THE GREAT DEMAND for our Morris chairs enables us to make a contract for an immense quantity of them at a very low price, and our customers reap the benefit. In fact, the price which we quote is in almost every instance much lower than the ordinary dealer can buy them.

DESCRIPTION OF OUR LINE OF MORRIS CHAIRS. The wood used in the construction of our Morris chairs is the best quality of highly figured oak, or birch, imitation mahogany finish, as noted in the description of each chair, specially selected for the beauty of the grain of the wood. It is thoroughly air seasoned and kiln dried before being put through the factory. Every piece is guaranteed not to warp, shrink or check. The careful inspection and selection of the wood enables us to insure the best and most satisfactory results it is possible to obtain. Every chair is covered by our binding guarantee, and should it at any time prove defective or unsatisfactory we stand ready to refund the purchase price together with all transportation charges.

THE CONSTRUCTION of our Morris chairs is strictly high grade in every detail. The joints are mortised and joined in the most perfect manner. The bars are highly ornamental, spindles are carefully framed and turned, the edges and corners rounded; the seats are upholstered with highly tempered steel springs, which are absolutely indestructible. The old fashioned string tied spring construction we have discarded. Our new indestructible steel construction prevents the springs breaking loose and turning over. The seat of a Morris chair is the most essential part of it. We use the best grade of high carbon steel wire springs, intercoiled into steel band irons, which are crosswise on the bottom, and are fastened to the top of the side rails of the chair and can never get loose, besides being reinforced with a steel wire running lengthwise into which the coil springs are interlaced. Neat in appearance, sanitary and everlasting.

THE RATCHET ATTACHMENT. On the back of the chair is a ratchet attachment by which the back is raised or lowered, and locked in several positions. It works very easily, and is absolutely guaranteed not to get out of order.

THE FINISH of our Morris chairs is strictly first class. The highest quality of material obtainable is used. Special care is taken to produce a smoother surface, a better luster and finish, that will not crack, peel or blister, that will look better after years of use than the ordinary finish will in one month. Each coating is thoroughly rubbed down and allowed to dry and harden before applying the succeeding one.

THE CUSHIONS of our Morris chairs are thoroughly well made, the velour and verona and crushed plush coverings are the newest and best patterns. The colors are all guaranteed fast. They are closely stitched and button tufted. We furnish the cushions in the following colors: Dark green, dark red or brown, as best adapted to harmonize with all surroundings. The full box edge and firm stitching of our cushions make them more shapely and lasting than any other cushion made.

THE FABRICORD LEATHER used on our Morris chairs is one of the greatest inventions brought out in recent years. It serves as a substitute for leather in upholstering furniture, and can be produced at a very much lower cost. The body of the material is made of heavy sateen fabric, coated, finished and grained in exact imitation of the finest grade of hand buffed leather and is guaranteed by the manufacturers not to crack or peel off. The color is black.

THIS MORRIS CHAIR, without doubt, is the most attractive in design, the handsomest in outline, and most comfortable and substantial chair it is possible to produce. We are offering the greatest value ever shown in this kind of a chair. You cannot fully appreciate the wonderful value we are giving in this chair unless you see it and compare it carefully with Morris chairs that others sell at double the price we ask. The frame is thoroughly well constructed in every detail, every joint perfectly fitted.

The illustration shows stationary cushions covered in fabricord leather.

THE WOOD used in this Morris chair is made almost entirely of oak, thoroughly air seasoned and kiln dried. The finish is a beautiful golden color. The highly ornamental and finely executed carvings on the front bars and posts add to the beauty and attractiveness of our Morris chairs. The seats are built of our indestructible solid Bessemer steel construction, intercoiled into steel bars and fastened securely into the frame on the sides, besides being reinforced with a steel wire, running lengthwise, making the most durable spring seat it is possible to produce.

THE SEAT of this Morris chair is upholstered with our patent high carbon steel spring construction, guaranteed to last a lifetime. The stationary cushions used in this Morris chair are covered in fabricord leather as illustrated and described above. The reversible loose cushions we furnish in the best quality, imported French velour cloth in plain or figured pattern, in dark green, red or brown colors, as desired. BE SURE TO STATE WHEN ORDERING REVERSIBLE LOOSE CUSHIONS whether plain solid color or figured pattern is desired, also state color wanted.

THE BACK of this Morris chair is adjustable to four different reclining positions by means of a ratchet attachment, guaranteed against breakage.

WE FURNISH THIS MORRIS CHAIR IN STATIONARY FABRICORD LEATHER CUSHIONS OR WITH REVERSIBLE LOOSE CUSHIONS IN VELOUR, AS DESIRED

FITTED with best quality casters, packed and shipped direct from our factory near Chicago or Central New York. Shipping weight, 60 pounds.

5,000 MORRIS CHAIRS AT $4.45. We expect to sell 5,000 of these special chairs at $4.45 in oak during the following season. Our contract is made on that basis. We believe that all who want a Morris chair for little money and see this announcement, will send us their order; we believe they will recognize the extraordinary values that we are offering. Furniture dealers will admit when they see the chair that it is indeed a bargain and a wonder of value. The prices are very little more than the actual cost of material and labor, on enormous quantity basis, with our narrow margin of profit added. We illustrate this chair with a large picture, not only to direct attention to this Morris chair, but to emphasize the extraordinary values that our entire line of Morris chairs represent. You cannot afford to place your order elsewhere for a Morris chair if you will consider the values here illustrated and described.

WE SHIP this Morris chair with the distinct understanding and agreement, that if it is not perfectly satisfactory in every respect, and exactly as represented and described, that if you are not satisfied that you have a better Morris chair than you can purchase elsewhere at almost double the price we ask, you can return it to us and your money will be refunded together with all transportation charges.

No. 1K5562   Golden Oak, upholstered seat and back fabricord leather, stationary cushions as illustrated. Price..................$4.45
No. 1K5563   Golden Oak, seat and back fitted with reversible loose cushions in figured velour. Price..................5.45

NOTE—WE SHIP THIS MORRIS CHAIR DIRECT FROM FACTORY IN CENTRAL NEW YORK OR NEAR CHICAGO, ACCORDING TO LOCATION OF CUSTOMER, THEREBY INSURING THE LOWEST FREIGHT CHARGES. SHIPPING WEIGHT ABOUT 60 POUNDS.

No. 1K5565 The frame of this Morris Chair is made almost entirely of oak, high gloss golden finish. Broad shapely arms are 5 inches wide. Note the massive front posts with hand carved heads. Seat and back are upholstered in imitation leather, black color. Seat is 22½ inches wide by 20 inches deep, supported by our guaranteed all steel indestructible spring construction, containing six high carbon steel springs. Back is 26 inches high by 19 inches wide, adjustable to four different reclining positions. Strong, durable and comfortable. Sells in retail stores at more than double the price we ask. Shipped from factory in Central New York. Shipping weight, 50 pounds.
Price, golden finish, stationary cushion **$3.65**

No. 1K5569 A special design Morris Chair made of thoroughly seasoned oak, quarter sawed and finished in a rich golden color. Made with stationary cushions, with spring seat and back like illustration or with reversible cushions, upholstered in best quality velour, verona, red green or brown, or fabricoid (imitation leather). Back is adjustable to several positions by our patent automatic ratchet attachment. Strongly constructed, and no description could give any idea of the value we are offering in this chair. Must be seen to be appreciated. Shipped direct from factory in Western New York. Shipping weight, 60 pounds.

	Velour	Verona	Fabricoid
Price, stationary cushion...	$5.65	$6.15	$6.65
Price, reversible cushion....	6.25	6.75	7.15

No. 1K5637 This Colonial Style Morris Chair is made of oak, specially selected, thoroughly air seasoned and kiln dried. Polished golden finish. The broad, shapely arms, full swell front rail and massive round front posts are made of highly figured quarter sawed oak. Made with stationary hair filled cushions, deep tufted back and head rest. Seat fitted with our indestructible spring construction. Back adjustable to several comfortable positions by our patent ratchet attachment. Upholstered in verona, crushed plush, fabricoid and genuine No. 1 leather covering. Simplicity of outline is combined with comfort and durability in this high grade Morris chair. Sells in stores at 50 per cent more than the price we ask. Shipped direct from factory near Chicago or in Central New York. Shipping weight, 65 pounds.

	Verona	Crushed Plush	Fabricoid	Genuine No. 1 Leather
Price....	$8.35	$9.65	$9.85	$15.95

No. 1K5665 This beautiful massive Morris Chair is made of thoroughly seasoned and specially selected quarter sawed oak, highly polished and finished in a rich golden color. Note the massive carvings on the wide curved arms, heavy claw feet and curved front rail. Cushions are reversible and made of best quality of verona, crushed plush, fabricoid (imitation leather) and genuine leather, filled with hair and deeply tufted. Back is adjustable to several comfortable positions by our patent rod and ratchet attachment. Beauty of design is combined with solid construction, making this chair the most desirable piece we have ever offered. Shipped direct from our factory near Chicago or in Central New York. Shipping weight, 75 pounds.

	Verona	Crushed Plush	Fabricoid	Gen. Leather
Price...	$9.75	$11.25	$11.55	$16.95

EXCEPTIONAL VALUE.

1K5658

A SPLENDID CHAIR

No. 1K5659

THE DAVIS AUTOMATIC MORRIS CHAIRS

DESIGNED FOR THOSE WHO LIKE MASSIVENESS AND SIMPLICITY OF OUTLINE, COMBINED WITH STRICTLY HIGH QUALITY OF MATERIAL, CONSTRUCTION AND FINISH.

No. 1K5660

EACH CHAIR FITTED WITH FOOT REST ATTACHMENT AS SHOWN IN ILLUSTRATION.

UTILITY AND COMFORT OF EACH PIECE IS AN IMPORTANT CONSIDERATION

The frames are made of thoroughly seasoned quarter sawed oak, specially selected for the beauty of the grain, finished in a beautiful golden color, highly polished. Every post and bar, joint and tenon perfectly framed and fitted, the best that skilled workmanship can produce. The deep, broad roomy seats are 21½ inches wide by 23 inches deep, supported by high carbon Bessemer steel coil springs. The shapely curved, deep hand tufted back is 29 inches high by 21½ inches wide and can be adjusted to any reclining position by the automatic attachment by a slight pressure on the back and without moving from chair. Genuine hair filling. Covered in velour, corduroy, fabricoid, crushed plush or genuine No. 1 leather, as desired. See page 436 for description of the high grade covering. Each chair fitted with best quality casters. We invite the closest comparison of these special high grade Morris chairs with similar chairs offered by others and ours will be found better made, better finished and much lower in price. Shipping weight, about 65 pounds.

EMPIRE DESIGN

No. 1K5661

	Velour	Corduroy	Fabricoid (Im. Leather)	Crushed Plush	Genuine Leather
No. 1K5658 Price.........	$9.85	$10.60	$11.15	$11.80	$15.10
No. 1K5659 Price.........	10.75	11.50	12.15	12.80	16.15
No. 1K5660 Price.........	11.95	12.35	12.95	13.35	17.20
No. 1K5661 Price.........	12.10	12.85	13.45	14.15	16.95

See page 436 for description of Coverings used on all our Morris Chairs.

AN EXCEPTIONALLY COMFORTABLE RECLINING SWING CHAIR.

$6.25

THE MOST WONDERFUL VALUE EVER OFFERED IN A RECLINING SWING CHAIR.

No. 1K5738 This Adjustable Reclining Rocker is made of solid oak, thoroughly seasoned and kiln dried, in high gloss golden finish. The seat is attached to the platform base by heavy steel rods in such a manner that it gives a perfect swinging motion. The back is adjustable to any position by means of a steel rod attached to the arm on either side of rocker. This combined with the foot rest makes one of the most comfortable reclining chairs and an indispensable invalid chair. It has full spring seat and spring back, covered with a fine quality of flax fiber and clean, new cotton. Upholstered with the best quality of figured velour, fancy brocaded velour in red, green or brown colors, or fabricoid leather in black. Foot rest in illustration is shown extended and when not in use folds back beneath the chair out of sight. This reclining chair should be compared with those offered in retail stores at $12.00 to $15.00. Shipping weight, about 60 pounds. Shipped direct from our factory in Western New York. When ordering be sure to state color of cushions wanted.

THE EQUAL OF CHAIRS SOLD ELSEWHERE AT $12.00 TO $15.00

Price, Figured Velour.................................$6.25
Price, Fancy Brocaded Plush..................... 6.45
Price, Fabricoid Leather 7.15

No. 1K5652 This large massive Morris Rocker we furnish in choice selected quarter sawed oak, or in birch, mahogany finish, piano polished. The cushions are stationary with our full steel construction spring seat and back, upholstered in the best grade of velour or verona, red, green or brown, and fabricoid (imitation leather). The back is neatly tufted with head roll and adjustable to several comfortable positions by our patent ratchet attachment. Shipped direct from factory in Western New York. Shipping weight, 60 pounds. When ordering be sure to state the color of cushions and finish wanted.

$6.85

	Velour	Verona	Fabricoid (Imitation Leather)
Price, tufted cushions, oak or mahogany....	$6.85	$7.95	$8.25

Price, with foot rest attachment, as shown on No. 1K5656, $1.00 extra.
We can furnish this as a regular Morris chair, with claw feet, at 50 cents less than above prices.

No. 1K5656 This Morris Rocker combines elegance, comfort and durability. Made of the very best flaky grain quarter sawed oak, or birch, in mahogany finish, finely polished. The seat is supported by full steel spring construction, back neatly tufted, with head rest. Adjustable to several comfortable positions by our patent ratchet attachment and upholstered in best quality velour or verona, red, green or brown, and fabricoid (imitation leather). The hand carved swans' necks and broad shaped arms make it a very attractive design. Shipped direct from factory in Western New York. Shipping weight, 50 pounds. When ordering be sure to state color of cushions and finish wanted.

	Velour	Verona	Fabricoid (Imitation Leather)
Price, oak, imitation mahogany, stationary cushions, only........	$7.45	$8.15	$8.75

Price, with foot rest attachment, $1.00 extra.
We can furnish this as a regular Morris chair, with claw feet, at 50 cents less than above prices.

NEW DESIGN THREE-PIECE PARLOR SUITE WITH REMOVABLE CUSHIONS, $16.45.

NO. 1K5771 This handsome new design, high grade, Three-Piece Parlor Suite represents exceptional value at the price we ask. We call your special attention to the removable cushion seats. Each piece is fitted with a boxed edge, button tufted cushion, fitted perfectly and securely fastened at the corners by silk cords and tassels. The cushions rest on our all steel indestructible spring construction. They are readily removed for dusting and airing and will wear longer and prove more satisfactory than stationary upholstered seats. The beauty of design, high quality of workmanship and elegance of finish can only be fully appreciated when you see it. The substantial frames are made of specially selected birch, finished in perfect imitation of mahogany. The back is decorated with genuine hand carvings perfectly executed. Furnished in the various high grade coverings by the single piece or full suite as noted below. Shipped direct from factory in Chicago or Eastern Pennsylvania, according to location of customer. Shipping weight, about 100 pounds.

This illustration shows our Three-Piece Parlor Suite, No. 1K5771.

DIMENSIONS.

	Height	Length	Width	Number springs
Divan	38 inches	41 inches	19 inches	8
Arm chair	37 inches	24 inches	19 inches	4
Rocker	37 inches	24 inches	19 inches	4

PRICES FOR COMPLETE SUITE OF THREE PIECES.

The number of this Parlor Suite is No. 1K5771. Always order by number and be sure to state the kind and color of covering desired.

Covering	Fancy Brocaded Velour	Plain Silk Plush	Crushed Plush	Brocaded Silk Plush	Panne Plush
Price	$16.45	$17.95	$18.45	$19.65	$19.95

PRICES FOR SINGLE PIECES.

Covering	Fancy Brocaded Plush	Plain Silk Plush	Crushed Plush	Brocaded Silk Plush	Panne Plush
Divan	$7.15	$7.65	$7.85	$8.35	$8.65
Rocker	5.45	5.95	6.15	6.45	6.65
Arm Chair	4.95	5.45	5.65	5.95	6.15

No. 1K5781 THE STYLE.

The illustration shows one of the newest designs in a high grade Three-Piece Parlor Suite. The graceful curves shown in the top rail, arms and front legs appeal to the taste of those who admire simplicity of outline combined with beauty and strength.

THE FRAME is made of specially selected birch in a perfect imitation mahogany finish, piano polished. The shapely back panels are veneered with genuine mahogany, highly figured. The top rail, arms and front posts are continuous and have rounded edges. The construction is strictly first class in every detail.

THE SPRINGS in the seat are made of the best quality high carbon Bessemer steel, firmly fastened together with corrugated steel bands, interlaced at the top and bottom, and will last a lifetime.

THE CUSHIONS are made of fancy brocaded plush, crushed plush, plain silk plush, brocaded silk plush, or panne plush; either of which coverings you may select can be furnished in plain solid colors of dark olive green or dark red. Read what we say about the different kinds of upholstery materials on page 436. They are made with full box edge and are button tufted. They are securely fastened at the corners by silk cord with silk tassels, and rest on our all steel spring construction, as described above. They are easily detached for airing and cleaning. The added convenience, comfort and wearing qualities will be readily recognized by every housekeeper. Shipped direct from factory in Chicago or Eastern Pennsylvania. Crated to insure safe delivery, shipping weight, 175 lbs.

This illustration shows our Three-Piece Parlor Suite, No. 1K5781.

PRICES FOR COMPLETE SUITE OF THREE PIECES.

The number of this Parlor Suite is No. 1K5781. Always order by number and be sure to state the kind and color of covering desired.

	Fancy Brocaded Plush	Crushed Plush	Plain Silk Plush	Brocaded Silk Plush	Panne Plush
Price	$22.75	$24.45	$25.25	$25.95	$26.25

PRICES FOR SINGLE PIECES.

	Fancy Brocaded Plush	Crushed Plush	Plain Silk Plush	Brocaded Silk Plush	Panne Plush
Sofa	$9.85	$10.45	$10.85	$11.05	$11.25
Arm Chair	7.05	7.35	7.75	7.95	8.05
Rocker	7.55	7.95	8.35	8.45	8.65

This illustration shows four pieces of our No. 1K5786 Parlor Suite.

The fifth piece is a duplicate of the parlor chair which has no arms.

No. 1K5786

This beautiful Five-Piece Parlor Suite is a splendid example of up to date workmanship and finish, made of specially selected highly figured birch, in perfect imitation of mahogany. In every detail, workmanship and material is strictly high grade and guaranteed to please. It has deep hand tufted backs, carefully overlaid and fastened securely with metal buttons. The gimp and cord are made to match the coverings. Each piece is upholstered in the very best possible manner with different style of coverings, as noted opposite and described on page 436. Each piece has a full spring seat; springs of the best quality of high carbon Bessemer steel wire with the corrugated steel wire bottom instead of webbing. Our price on this suite represents the actual cost at the factory with but a small margin of profit added. By shipping direct from the factory we save the extra expense of handling, enabling us to quote a very low price. Weight of suite crated, complete, ready for shipment, 280 pounds. Shipped direct from factory in Chicago or Eastern Pennsylvania.

The number of this Parlor Suite is No. 1K5786. Always order by number and send the price which corresponds with the kind of upholstering you select. Be sure to state color desired.

PRICES FOR COMPLETE SUITE OF FIVE PIECES.

Covering	Figured Velour	Fancy Brocaded Plush	Brocaded Verona Plush	Crushed Plush	Brocaded Silk Plush	Silk Damask
Price	$29.75	$30.95	$31.90	$34.25	$35.45	$36.65

PRICES FOR SINGLE PIECES.

Covering	Figured Velour	Fancy Brocaded Plush	Brocaded Verona Plush	Crushed Plush	Brocaded Silk Plush	Silk Damask
Sofa	$10.55	$10.95	$11.35	$12.15	$12.35	$12.95
Arm Chair	6.65	6.95	7.15	7.75	7.95	8.35
Rocker	7.15	7.45	7.65	8.25	8.45	8.65
Reception Chair	3.55	3.65	3.80	4.10	4.15	4.35

HIGH GRADE FIVE-PIECE PARLOR SUITE, REDUCED TO $43.45

MADE IN QUARTER SAWED GOLDEN OAK OR BIRCH, IN PERFECT IMITATION MAHOGANY FINISH.

This illustration shows four pieces of our No. 1K5812 Parlor Suite. The fifth piece is a duplicate of the parlor chair which has no arms.

NO. 1K5812 This magnificent high grade Five-Piece Parlor Suite is generally sold in stores at $85.00 to $100.00. No illustration or description can do justice to this splendid parlor suite. Exceptionally handsome and massive in design, decorated with deep, smooth cut, hand made, finely executed carvings. Each piece has broad and deep seat and back, constructed according to the latest and best method known in the art of high grade upholstering.

THE FRAMES are exceptionally attractive and massive in design, perfect in every detail of material, construction and finish. Made of especially selected, highly figured, quarter sawed golden oak, or in birch, perfect imitation of mahogany finish. Polished like a piano. Note the heavy veneered roll on the back; the broad, shapely curved arms, with large, hand made, smooth cut, finely executed dragons' heads, and the massive hand carved claw feet. Strength, beauty, comfort and durability are combined in this splendid suite.

THE SPRINGS used in each piece are the very best quality high carbon Bessemer steel, securely fastened at the bottom to corrugated steel wire and covered with an extra quality duck canvas. Sofa has eighteen springs; easy chair, nine springs; rocker, nine springs; parlor chair, four springs. Each piece has soft spring edge.

THE COVERINGS used on this Parlor Suite comprise all the newest and latest effects in high grade textures, the choicest designs and harmonious colorings. The beautiful fabrics must be seen to be fully appreciated. Note the beautiful, deep, diamond tufted backs and corded front. Read what we say about our upholstering materials on page 436.

OUR PRICE, $43.45 to $62.95, according to the kind of covering selected, is much lower than most dealers pay wholesale for such a parlor suite. For some time we have utilized almost the entire capacity of one of the largest parlor suite factories in the United States. The immense volume of business we have been able to give them has enabled them to lower the cost of production from time to time and we are able to give our customers the full benefit of this reduction by making our parlor suites lower in price and better in quality. We challenge any other factory in the world to produce this high grade parlor suite at the price we ask. This parlor suite is securely wrapped and crated to insure safe delivery. Shipped direct from factory in Chicago or Eastern Pennsylvania. Shipping weight, 360 pounds.

DIMENSIONS.

	Height	Width	Depth	No. of Springs
Divan	42	49	22	18
Arm Chair	42	25	22	9
Rocker	40	25	22	9
Reception Chair	38	21	19	4

The number of this Parlor Suite is No. 1K5812. Always order by number and send the price which corresponds with the kind of upholstering you select. Be sure to give color of covering; whether golden quartered oak or mahogany finish is desired, otherwise we ship mahogany finish.

PRICES FOR COMPLETE SUITE OF FIVE PIECES.

Covering	Fancy Brocaded Plush	Brocaded Verona Plush	Crushed Plush	Brocaded Silk Plush	Silk Damask	Genuine No. 1 Leather
Price	$43.45	$46.95	$48.65	$51.25	$51.35	$62.95

PRICES FOR SINGLE PIECES.

Covering	Fancy Brocaded Plush	Brocaded Verona Plush	Crushed Plush	Brocaded Silk Plush	Silk Damask	Genuine No. 1 Leather
Sofa	$15.45	$16.65	$16.95	$18.35	$18.65	$22.65
Arm Chair	10.25	10.85	11.00	11.95	12.00	14.65
Rocker	10.75	11.35	11.50	12.45	12.50	15.15
Reception	4.85	5.45	5.55	5.75	5.95	7.35

THIS HIGH GRADE THREE-PIECE PARLOR SUITE, REDUCED TO $47.85

A MASSIVE AND HANDSOME DESIGN. WONDERFUL VALUE AT THE PRICE WE OFFER IT.

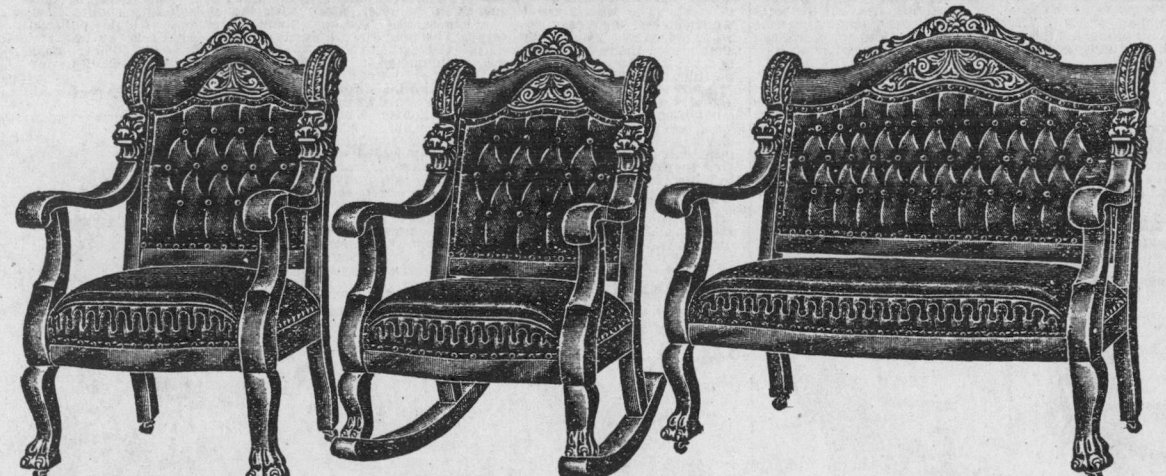

No. 1K5816 This beautiful Three-Piece Parlor Suite is strictly high grade and a suite of the same class would sell at the retail stores for $15.00 to $25.00 more than we ask for it.

THE ILLUSTRATION shows the suite upholstered in genuine leather and, while it conveys some idea of the richness and elegance of the suite, it does not begin to do it justice. It must be seen to be fully appreciated.

THE FRAMES are massive and of an exceptionally graceful design, beautifully decorated by the heavy carvings on the backs and arms. Made of selected birch and finished in a perfect imitation of mahogany with a regular piano polish. Strength, durability and comfort are all combined in this high class suite.

COVERINGS. In addition to the genuine leather, as shown in the illustration, we also furnish this suite in the several different coverings as named in the price column. We use nothing but the best material and the latest designs in covers. Read what we say about our upholstering material on page 436.

THIS SUITE is securely wrapped and crated to insure safe delivery and shipped direct from our factory in Chicago or Eastern Pennsylvania. Shipping wt., 335 lbs.

PERFECT CONSTRUCTION is everything in a high grade suite and we have accomplished that in this suite. The seats are made with a ruffled spring edge and the backs are tufted. We use in the seats only the best high carbon Bessemer steel springs fastened with corrugated steel wire and covered with heavy duck canvas.

IN OFFERING this suite at $47.85 to $63.45, according to the style of material selected for covering, we are giving you the benefit of the very low cost we are able to secure through our ability to take the entire output of one of the largest up to date upholstering factories in the country and we challenge any other factory to produce this high grade suite at the price we ask. You must see, examine and compare these three pieces with anything you could buy elsewhere at anything like the price to appreciate the value we are giving, and to make this possible and to guarantee you against any chance of loss, we offer to send you this or any suite, guaranteeing it to reach you in perfect order and giving you the privilege of using it in your own home for thirty days, and if for any reason you become dissatisfied with your purchase and do not feel that you have received a much better suite than you could have obtained elsewhere, even at much more money, you can return the suite to us at our expense and we will refund your money.

The number of this Parlor Suite is No. 1K5816. Always order by number and send the price which corresponds with the kind of upholstering you select. Be sure to give color of covering.

DIMENSIONS.

	Height, inches	Width, inches	Depth, inches	No. of Springs
Divan	49	49	22	18
Rocker	47	26	22	9
Arm Chair	47	26	22	9

PRICES FOR COMPLETE SUITE OF THREE PIECES.

Covering	Brocaded Verona Plush	Crushed Plush	Brocaded Silk Plush	Panne Plush	Genuine No. 1 Leather
Price	$47.85	$49.85	$53.35	$53.65	$63.45

PRICES FOR SINGLE PIECES.

Covering	Brocaded Verona Plush	Crushed Plush	Brocaded Silk Plush	Panne Plush	Genuine No. 1 Leather
Sofa	$19.95	$20.95	$22.35	$22.55	$26.95
Rocker	15.95	16.85	17.35	17.65	20.35
Arm Chair	15.35	16.25	16.75	17.05	19.75

BABY CARRIAGES AND GO-CARTS

MANY YEARS EXPERIENCE in the sale of childrens' vehicles has taught us the requirements of our customers in this line of merchandise, and, as a result, we offer in our 1908 line a selection of baby carriages and go-carts representing a combination of the most desirable features of all the best go-carts and carriages on the market, with the defects of none.

WE TAKE THE ENTIRE OUTPUT of one of the largest factories in the United States, and, consequently, are in a position to control absolutely the cost and quality of production. We sell more carriages and go-carts to the consumer direct than any other concern in the world, which demonstrates the fact that our prices must be much lower and the quality far better than that of any other dealer.

A CAREFUL COMPARISON OF THE GOODS will prove that our carriages and go-carts are handsomer in design, easier riding, more durable in construction and the lowest in price.

OUR PRICES represent the actual cost of material and labor which enter into the construction of each vehicle, with only a small margin of profit added. There are no salesmen's commissions or jobbers' profits included, hence our price to you is lower than what the retail dealer is obliged to pay.

THE MATERIALS used in our vehicles are the very best that can be obtained and are subjected to a careful inspection before being made up.

THE DURABILITY as well as the appearance of the carriage is always taken into consideration, so that all carriages or go-carts, even the lowest priced ones, are guaranteed to give satisfactory wear.

THE ATTACHMENTS AND GEARS which we furnish are strictly up to date in every respect and possess many special qualities which are not found in the carriages or go-carts offered by other manufacturers or dealers.

THE WORKMANSHIP AND CONSTRUCTION are guaranteed to be the very best throughout, as only expert workmen are employed at our factories and every vehicle undergoes a most rigid inspection.

THE FINISH throughout is in keeping with the high grade of material and workmanship which enters into the construction of our vehicles.

EVERY GO-CART AND BABY CARRIAGE is strongly crated in a small crate, the wheels and gears off. By shipping in this way the lowest transportation charges are obtained and safe delivery guaranteed. Our carriages and go-carts are so constructed that they can be easily assembled.

WE GUARANTEE PROMPT DELIVERY. Every upholstered go-cart and carriage is made up special after the order is received by us, which requires from three to six days, but under our contract with our manufacturers this year we are able to guarantee that every order will be filled within eight days after it is received at the factory. While it will be possible in nearly every instance to fill the order within two or three days after it is received, you should allow at least eight days after the order is sent us for shipment to be made.

25 CENTS TO $1.50 will pay the freight charges on a go-cart or carriage to any place in the United States located east of Fargo, N. D., Kansas City, Mo., or Little Rock, Ark. Freight to all other points proportionately low. We will be pleased to quote the exact freight or express charges to your railroad station on any vehicle you may select and you will find the charges to be but a very small amount as compared to what you will save in placing your order with us.

WE CALL SPECIAL ATTENTION to one of the weak points of most carriages and go-carts on the market, namely, the flimsy wheels and poor quality of rubber tires. It has been customary to make a showy design that will attract the eye of the purchaser and to slight the construction of the vehicle by the use of inferior wheels and poor quality of rubber tires, to keep the price down. In our line this year, we use extra heavy rubber tires of the best quality without having increased our selling price. All our wheels are made of best grade of steel with sufficient spokes to make them strong and rigid. Steel rims are made with deep grooves to prevent the tires from slipping off.

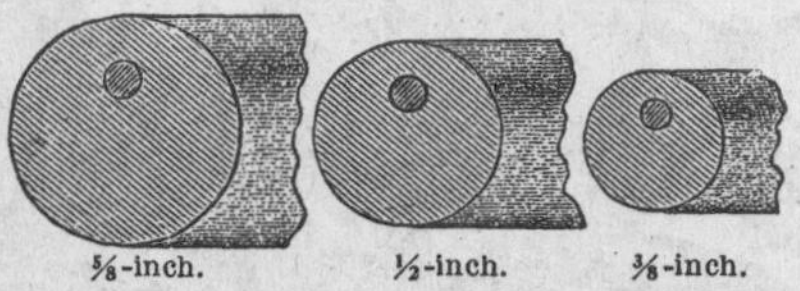

⅝-inch. ½-inch. ⅜-inch.

These illustrations represent the diameter or thickness of the tires we use. The ⅜-inch tire is used only on the smallest and lightest folding carts and cheapest go-carts and carriages. All others in our line have either ½-inch or ⅝-inch tire, according to the size and weight of the go-cart or carriage.

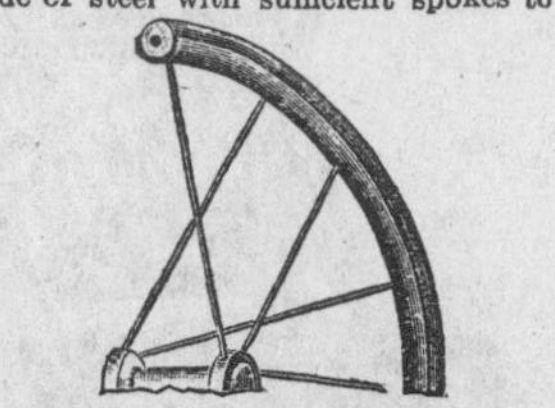

This illustration shows a section of our improved superior quality steel wheels. Note the deep groove or tire channel which prevents the tire from slipping off. Our wheels are the best on the market.

GRADES AND COLORS OF UPHOLSTERING.

DENIM. Good serviceable figured cotton fabric in bright colors; red, blue, myrtle, golden brown.

BEDFORD CORD. Extra strong and serviceable ribbed material made of tightly woven cotton, furnished in solid colors; red, blue, myrtle, drab, tan, golden brown.

NOVELTY CLOTH. Fancy figured soft material in brocaded effect; red, blue, green, golden brown.

TAPESTRY. Extra strong and heavy, finely finished mercerized cotton; in neat, bright oriental patterns. Colors, green, red, blue.

FIGURED VELOUR. A sort of velvet plush, silk finished material, high colored floral figures with solid color background; red, blue, green and golden brown.

CORDUROY. Silk finished, closely woven ribbed material, solid colors; red, blue, green, golden brown.

SIMILE LAMBELLE. Mercerized damask, beautifully figured with solid colored background. Very closely resembles silk; red, blue, green, golden brown, steel.

SILK DAMASK. Beautiful silk brocaded figures of contrasting colors on pure silk background; red, blue, green, steel.

PARASOLS listed below are the latest style and are of exceptional value. They are complete with frame and can be furnished in the following colors: green, blue, red, white or brown. The price quoted does not include rod and top ball. Parasols without rod and ball can be mailed, postage 16 cents, which must be prepaid.

Price of Rod and Top Ball 25c

Can only be shipped by express or freight.

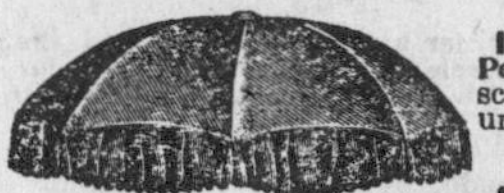

No. 1K6005 Percaline, with scalloped edge, unlined. Price.. 39c

No. 1K6006 Percaline (like No. 1K6005), lined with percaline. Price, 58c

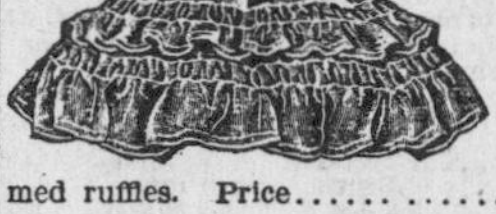

No. 1K6015 Extra quality mercerized sateen (looks exactly like fine quality of satin), with two shirred and hemmed ruffles. Price $1.25

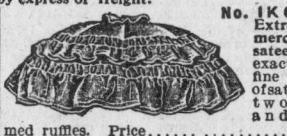

No. 1K6010 Good quality sateen, with deep scalloped ruffle. Best low priced parasol made.

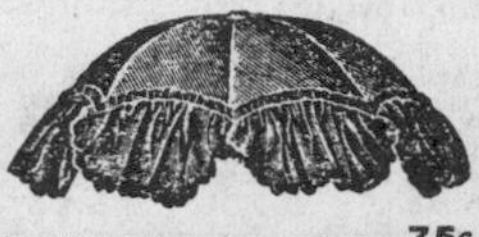

Price 75c

No. 1K6020 Satin, lined with percaline. Has deep tucked and hemmed ruffle. Very neat and rich. Price $1.65

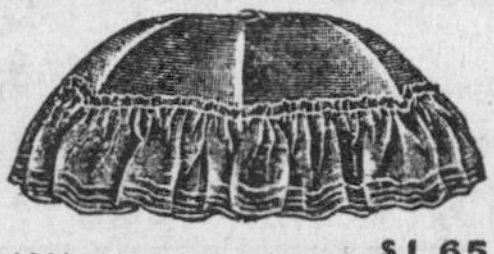

Be sure to order a rod and top ball if you haven't got one, as you cannot use the parasol without it.

LACE COVERS. A very select line of the most desirable patterns. All entirely new this season. Lace covers are used on parasols and do not have frames or linings. Therefore, you must have a parasol in order to use a lace cover. Can be shipped by mail, postage about 15 cents which must be prepaid.

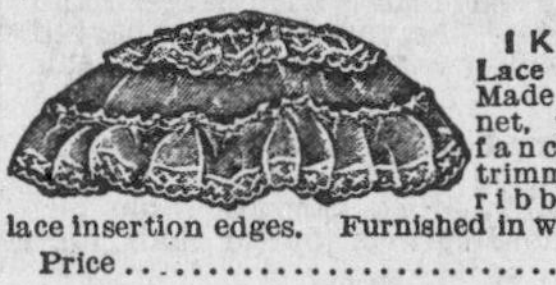

No. 1K6031 Lace Cover. Made of bobbinet, with two fancy ruffles, trimmed with ribbon and lace insertion edges. Furnished in white only.

Price 49c

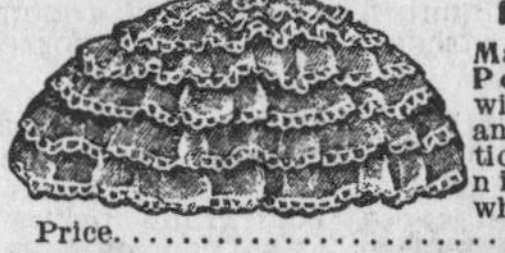

No. 1K6041 Made of Irish Point Lace, with six ruffles and lace insertion. Furnished in white only.

Price $1.23

No. 1K6036 Made of India lawn (imitation drawn work), with three deep ruffles and puff. Furnished in white only. Very handsome. Price 89c

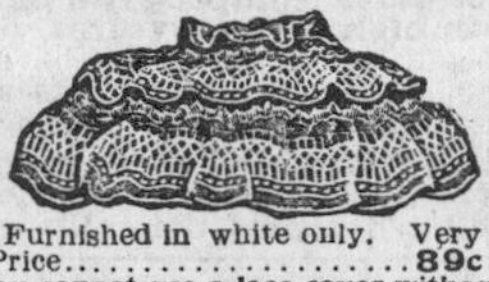

No. 1K6046 Made of fine quality Brussels Net, with two deep tucked ruffles with fancy lace stripes. Furnished in white only. An exceptionally high grade lace cover. Price $1.95

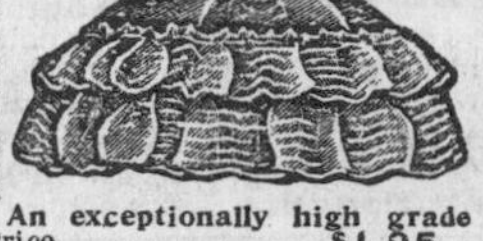

You cannot use a lace cover without a parasol; also, rod and top ball.

OUR SMALL FOLDING GO-CARTS ARE THE BEST MADE.

This illustration shows one of our carts compactly folded.

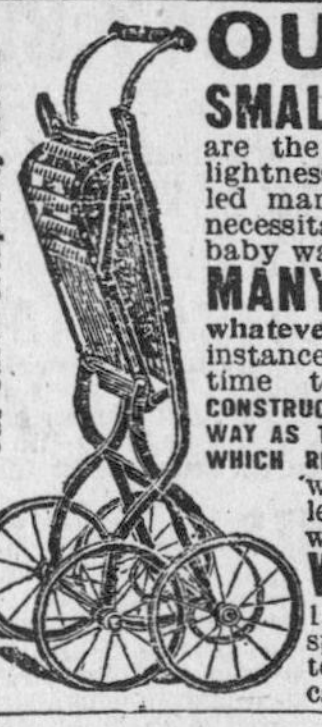

SMALL FOLDING GO-CARTS, recently introduced, have found exceedingly large sale, as they are the most practical little vehicles made for runabout use, due to their lightness and compact folding features. The extraordinarily large sale has led many manufacturers to produce a folding go-cart at a low price, which necessitated the sacrifice of quality to such a degree that the comfort of the baby was entirely ignored.

MANY OF THE FOLDING GO-CARTS offered this season have no springs whatever, causing the cart to continually jolt and jar, which in many instances causes severe injuries to the child which are not discovered in time to prevent deformity. OUR LINE OF FOLDING AND RECLINING GO-CARTS IS CONSTRUCTED WITH STEEL COILED SPRINGS PLACED DIRECTLY BELOW THE CART IN SUCH A WAY AS TO PRACTICALLY ELIMINATE ALL JAR AND JOLT, CAUSING AN EASY RIDING MOTION WHICH REMOVES ALL POSSIBILITY OF INJURY TO THE OCCUPANT. Folding go-carts without the above mentioned features are being condemned by the leading ladies' home societies and physicians throughout the country, who only approve and recommend a vehicle built on hygienic lines.

WE CAN FURNISH any of our small folding carts without springs at a lower price than any other dealer, see No. 1K6055, but considering the slight difference in price of cart without springs and one we quote with springs, and considering our customers' interests and the welfare of the child, we do not recommend the folding cart without springs.

THE MATERIALS USED in our small folding carts are the best that can be obtained. The entire framework, including axles and wheels, is made of steel. The wheels are 10 inches in diameter, fitted with the best quality rubber tires, which makes them easy riding and noiseless. The push handles are made of highly polished wood placed at a convenient height. The patent reclining device for the back is the best and simplest on the market. On all of the carts except No. 1K6055 and No. 1K6060 the dash is fitted with an adjustable device which makes it possible to raise or lower the dash to any position desired.

EACH CART is fitted with a substantial strap to keep the child from falling out. All metal parts of our carts are enameled in a handsome shade of green. All body parts, whether in wood or reed, are finished in natural color, coated with shellac. When folded, our carts occupy less room than any other cart on the market. Our carts can be folded so closely that they can be carried with the greatest ease, or transported in a buggy or street car, as they practically take up no space.

THE LOW PRICES quoted on our go-carts represent a big saving to our customers. In fact, the prices asked by us are the same or less than most retail dealers pay at wholesale. Send us your order with the distinct understanding that when you receive it, examine and compare it, you may return it to us and your money and freight charges will be refunded if you are not perfectly satisfied in every respect.

$4.45
$3.95

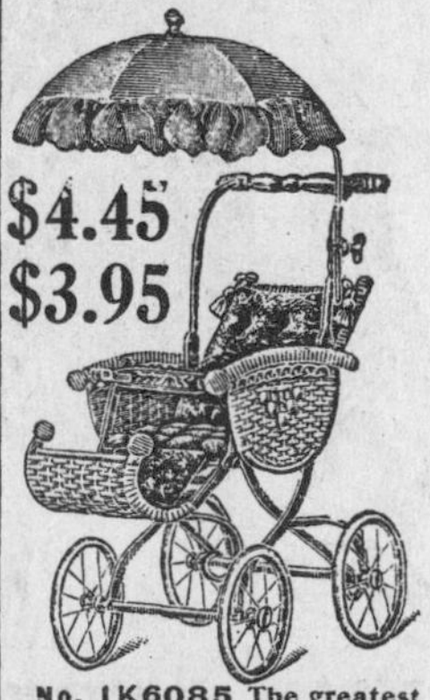

No. 1K6085 The greatest value of our entire line of small folding carts. Has shield design closely woven sides, with curved arm rests made of fancy turned maple ornamented with turned wood balls. Has percaline parasol and denim covered cushions on seat, back and dash. Parasol rod, top ball and clamp adjusted to any angle.

Price, complete, as illustrated $4.45

No. 1K6084 Price, without parasol and upholstery $3.95

$1.60

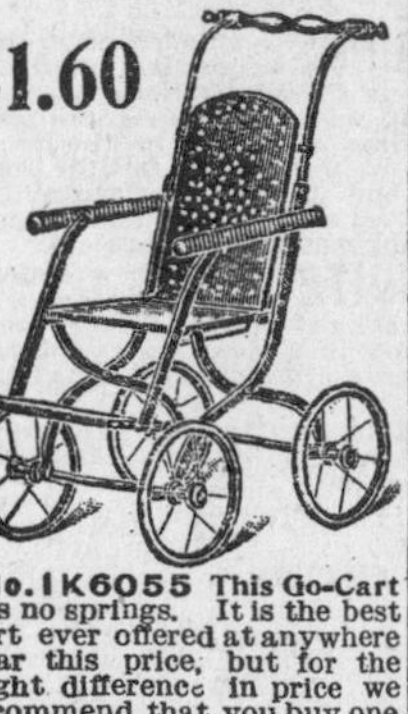

No. 1K6055 This Go-Cart has no springs. It is the best cart ever offered at anywhere near this price, but for the slight difference in price we recommend that you buy one of our better grade carts with springs.

Price, as illustrated . $1.60

$2.15

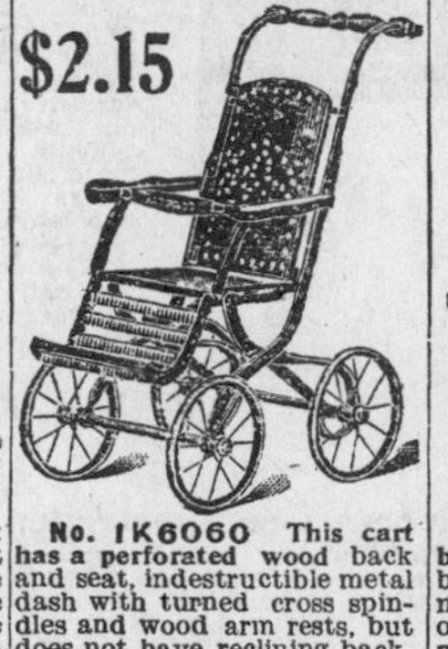

No. 1K6060 This cart has a perforated wood back and seat, indestructible metal dash with turned cross spindles and wood arm rests, but does not have reclining back. The best folding cart on the market for the money.

Price, Go-Cart $2.15

$2.45

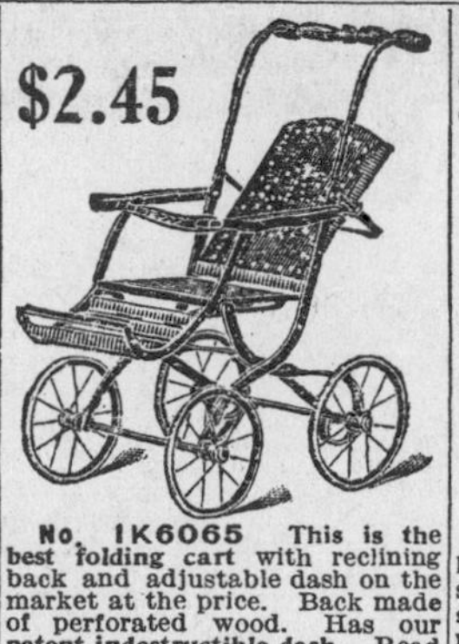

No. 1K6065 This is the best folding cart with reclining back and adjustable dash on the market at the price. Back made of perforated wood. Has our patent indestructible dash. Read what we say above about the construction of our folding carts.

Price, Go-Cart $2.45

$2.75

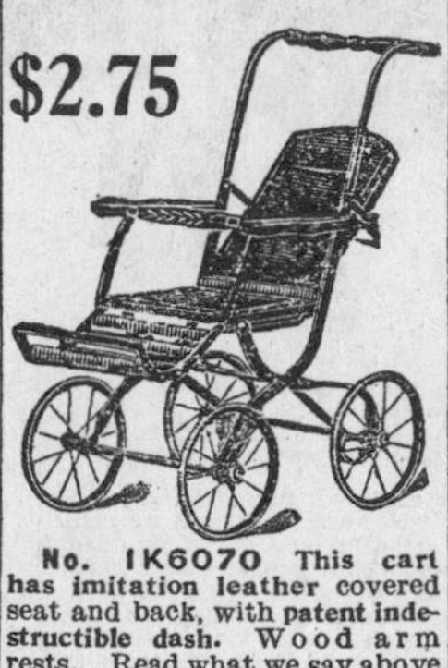

No. 1K6070 This cart has imitation leather covered seat and back, with patent indestructible dash. Wood arm rests. Read what we say above about the construction of our folding carts.

Price, Go-Cart $2.75

$3.45

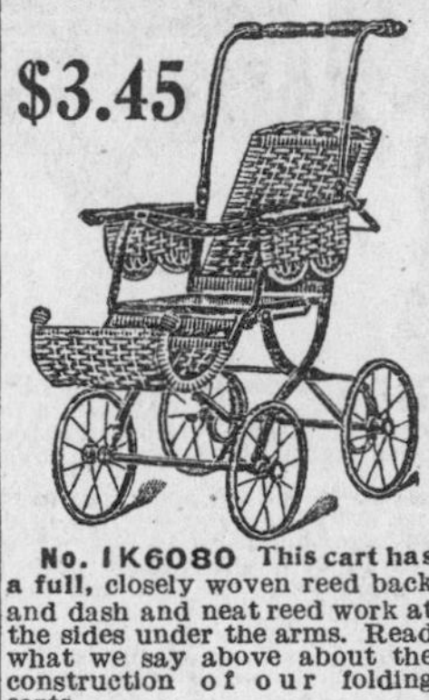

No. 1K6080 This cart has a full, closely woven reed back and dash and neat reed work at the sides under the arms. Read what we say above about the construction of our folding carts.

Price, Go-Cart $3.45

THESE FOLDING AND RECLINING CARTS are shipped direct from our factory at Toledo, Ohio, excepting when the order is with other goods taken from our Chicago stock, in which case they will be shipped together with the other goods, thus insuring lowest transportation charges. Each cart is well packed and should be received in same condition in which it leaves the factory. Shipping weight, each, 20 pounds.

$6.98 THE DAVIS COLLAPSIBLE GO-CARTS $6.98

HIGHEST QUALITY AND LOWEST PRICES, combined with durability, style and comfort in a folding go-cart that can be easily transported, make the Davis Collapsible Go-Cart the most desirable cart on the market. The most important consideration in a child's vehicle is comfort to the child. This feature is found only in the Davis Collapsible Go-Cart, which is fitted with two vertical springs, thereby preventing any jar or jolt, so injurious to the child. The reclining device in this cart is simple in construction and easily adjusted and permits the child to be placed in any position desired. In the construction of the Davis Collapsible Go-Cart nothing has been spared to make it the best cart of its kind it is possible to produce. The framework is made of thoroughly seasoned hardwood, finished in rich mahogany color, firmly braced with wrought metal.

A FOLDING GO-CART WHICH EMBRACES ALL THE BEST FEATURES OF ALL VEHICLES OF THIS CLASS ON THE MARKET, AND THE DEFECTS OF NONE.

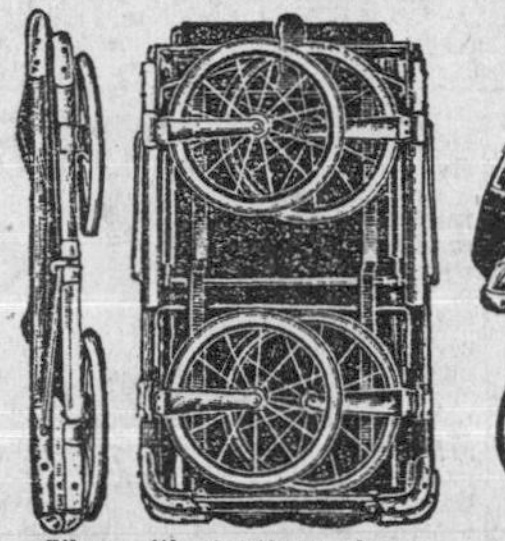

These illustrations show space occupied when cart is folded.

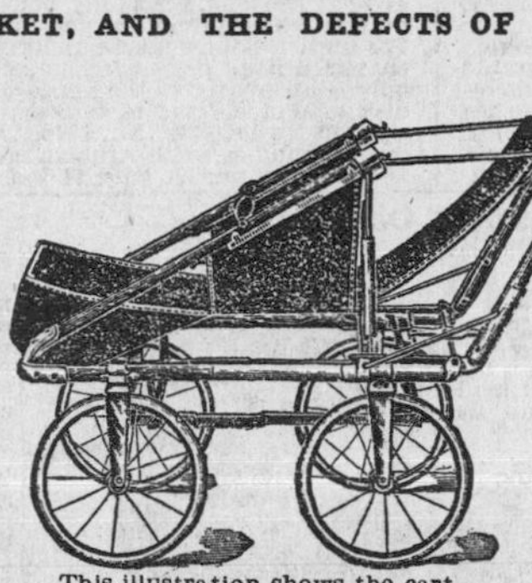

This illustration shows the cart in reclining position.

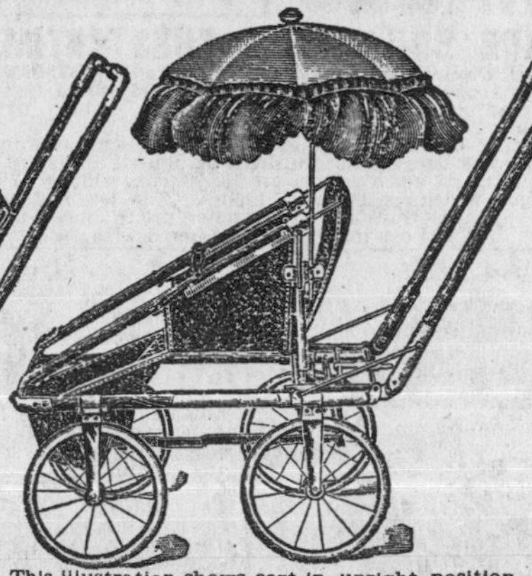

This illustration shows cart in upright position, complete with parasol and attachments. Price, as illustrated . . $6.98

ALL METAL TRIMMINGS AND PARTS are finished with what is known as oxidized finish, being a dark blue steel color with copper spots, making a perfect match in finish with the framework and upholstery. The wheels are all of the same size, 10 inches in diameter, and are fitted with heavy rubber tires which make the cart easy running and noiseless. The upholstery is the best grade of Chase leather, a material that has proven the most desirable for carts of this class. We use a handsome shade of maroon, which harmonizes perfectly with the finish of the framework and the metal trimmings. All we ask is a trial order. Let us send you one of the Davis Collapsible Go-Carts with the distinct understanding that if it does not please you in every way we will refund your money in full and pay transportation charges both ways.

No. 1K6090 Davis Collapsible Go-Cart, complete with parasol and attachments............$6.98

RECLINING AND FOLDING GO-CARTS

GREAT CARE has been taken to produce attractive patterns, which are substantially built and embody all the desirable features of the large reclining go-cart sleepers or folding go-carts. Even the smallest detail has been carefully considered. The back can be easily adjusted to an upright or reclining position and the dash raised or lowered independently of each other, as may be desired. These carts can be compactly folded, thereby taking little room when not in use, as shown in illustration of Cart No. 1K6156. They are light in weight and can easily be carried when necessary. Material throughout is the best that money can buy. The body has been considerably enlarged and stands at a convenient height. Framework is made of specially selected, thoroughly air seasoned and kiln dried maple. All joints are dovetailed, doweled and glued, making the frame strong and rigid. The handles are made of steel, gracefully bent and connected with the gear, placing the cart under direct control.

WITH EACH CART we furnish a handsomely embossed protection strap which prevents the child from falling out of the cart. All of the carts in this line have three mahogany finished hand grips, excepting the four highest priced carts, which are fitted with richly enameled Arabian green continuous hand grips, ornamented with nickel plated ferrules. There is a parasol clamp fastened to the pusher handle, which makes it possible to place the parasol when used with the cart at any angle. The reed work is entirely woven by hand from selected imported reeds. They are finished in light natural color with a heavy coat of waterproof shellac over two coats of transparent filler, making three coats in all; a far better finish than is put on any other go-cart in the market, and which insures absolute protection to the reeds.

ALL CARTS have strong, woven cane seats 10½ inches wide and 14½ inches long; the gear is equipped with the finest quality of elastic, oil tempered steel springs, which are arranged directly below the seat, thereby removing all jar and jolt. All our carts have four 12-inch wheels with grooved rims and patent hub caps and wheel fasteners, a device which detaches the wheels by the simple operation of a thumb spring, and are fitted with the latest improved automatic foot brake. We call special attention to the fact that we use ½-inch heavy rubber cushion tires except on the cheapest carts, whereas other dealers offer similar carts with 10-inch wheels and light rubber tires. This alone places our carts in a very much higher class and they will therefore give far better satisfaction and represent a much better investment. All gear parts are enameled in Brewster green, ornamented with stripes, which makes a handsome, durable and attractive finish.

Each cart is well protected with a paper wrapping and securely crated to insure safe delivery. Shipping weight, about 60 pounds.

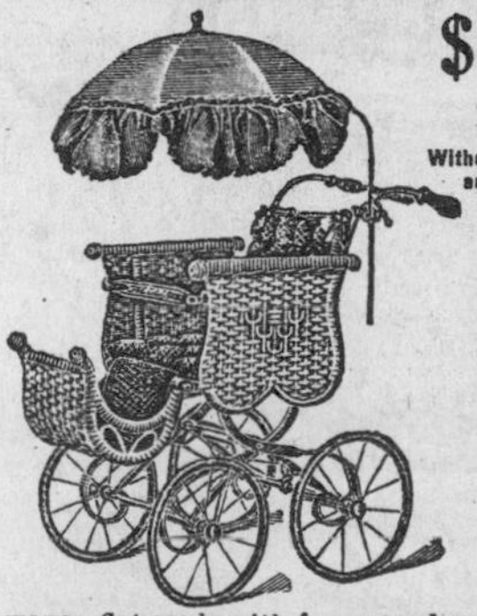

$4.25

Without Upholstery and Parasol.

Wonderful value. Compare it with carts offered by other dealers at $8.00 to $10.00. Exceptionally strong and well made. The sides and dash are made of closely woven flat reeds with fancy reed scrolls. Has mahogany finished hand grips, and 12-inch steel wheels with ⅜-inch rubber tires. Adjustable reclining back and dash. Read what we say about the size, construction and finish of this cart.

No. 1K6108 Go-Cart, without upholstery and parasol. Price........$4.25

No. 1K6109 Upholstered with cushions of Novelty Cloth covering on seat, back and dash, trimmed with cords and tassels. (See description of upholstery material on page 456.) Has sateen parasol with fancy deep scalloped ruffle; complete with rod, top ball and adjustable clamp. Price....................$6.25

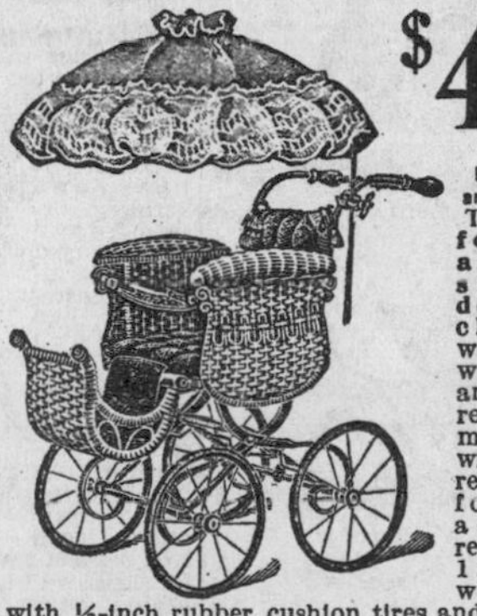

$4.85

Without Upholstery and Parasol.

The sides form an artistic shield design, closely woven with flat and round reeds, surmounted with round reed rolls, forming an arm rest. Has 12-inch wheels, with ½-inch rubber cushion tires and mahogany finished hand grips, independent adjustable back and dash. Read what we say about the size, construction and finish of this cart.

No. 1K6116 Go-Cart, without upholstery and parasol. Price..........$4.85

No. 1K6117 Upholstered with cushions of Bedford Cord, covering seat, back and dash, trimmed with cord and tassels. (See description of upholstery on page 456). Has percaline parasol with scalloped edges and lawn cover with deep fancy ruffle and puff. Complete, as illustrated, with rod, top ball and adjustable clamp. Price..........$6.95

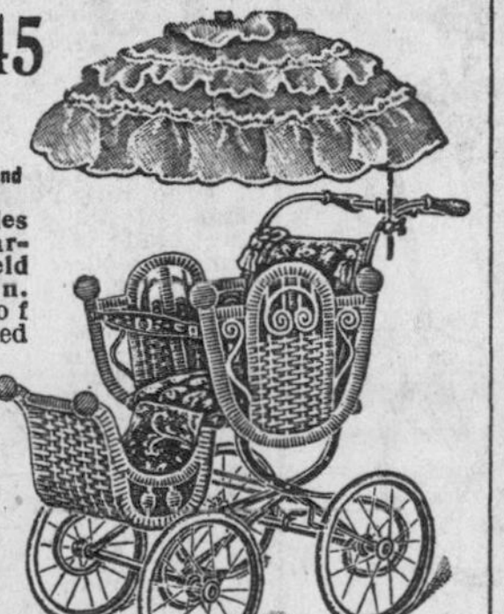

$5.45

Without Upholstery and Parasol.

The sides form an artistic shield design. Made of maple, filled in with spindles and reed scrolls. All projecting edges are ornamented with hand turned wood balls. Has adjustable back and dash, mahogany finished hand grips and 12-inch steel wheels with ½-inch rubber cushion tires. Read what we say above about size, construction and finish of this cart.

No. 1K6114 Go-Cart, without upholstery and parasol. Price...........$5.45

No. 1K6115 Upholstered with cushions of Novelty Cloth, covering seat, back and dash, trimmed with cord and tassels. (See description on page 456.) Has percaline parasol with scalloped edges and fancy bobbinet lace cover with deep ruffles and puff. Complete as illustrated, with rod, top ball and adjustable clamp. Price...........$7.65

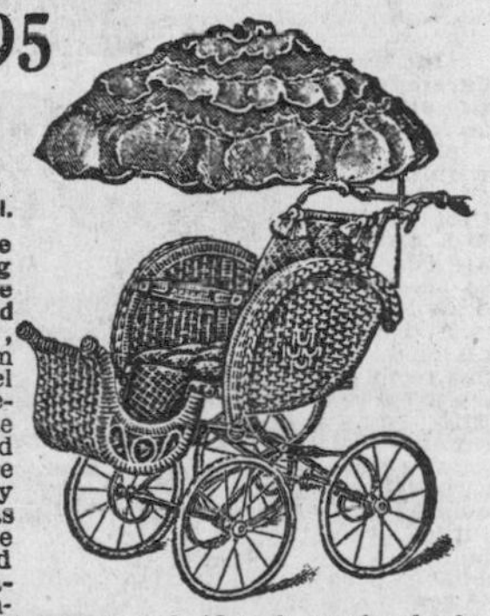

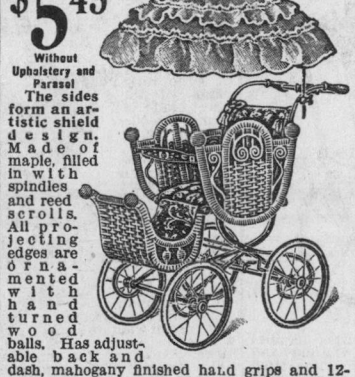

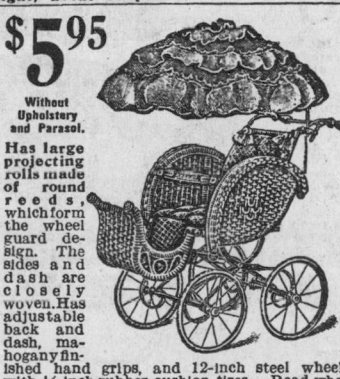

$5.95

Without Upholstery and Parasol.

Has large projecting rolls made of round reeds, which form the wheel guard design. The sides and dash are closely woven. Has adjustable back and dash, mahogany finished hand grips, and 12-inch steel wheels with ½-inch rubber cushion tires. Read what we say above about the size, construction and finish of this cart.

No. 1K6132 Go-Cart, without upholstery and parasol. Price.........$5.95

No. 1K6133 Upholstered with cushions of Bedford Cord, covering seat, back and dash, finished with fancy cords and tassels. (See description of upholstery on page 456.) Has percaline parasol with scalloped edge and fancy bobbinet lace cover with embroidered ruffles and puff. Complete as illustrated, with rod, top ball and adjustable clamp. Price........................$7.95

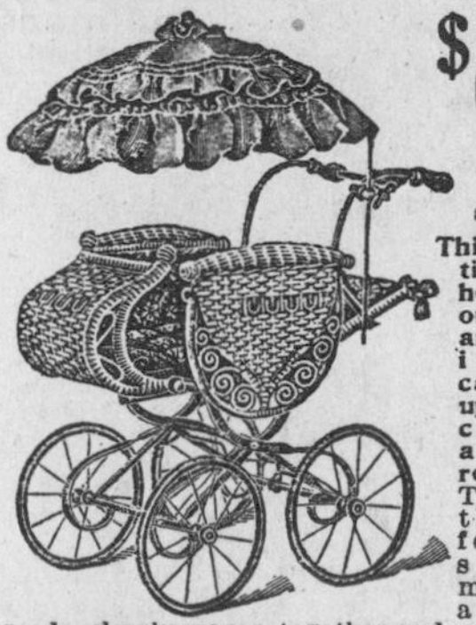

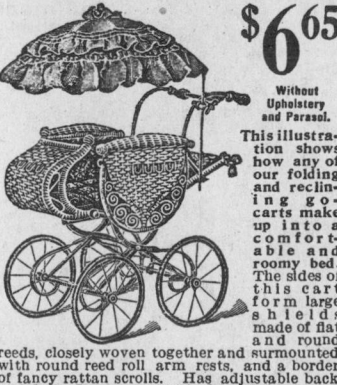

$6.65

Without Upholstery and Parasol.

This illustration shows how any of our folding and reclining go-carts make up into a comfortable and roomy bed. The sides of this cart form large shields made of flat and round reeds, closely woven together and surmounted with round reed roll arm rests, and a border of fancy rattan scrolls. Has adjustable back and dash, mahogany finished hand grips, and 12-inch steel wheels with ½-inch rubber cushion tires. Read what we say above about the size, construction and finish of this cart.

No. 1K6140 Go-Cart, without upholstery and parasol. Price.........$6.65

No. 1K6141 Upholstered with cushions of Tapestry, covering seat, back, sides and dash, trimmed with fancy cord and tassels. (See description of upholstery on page 456). Has good quality sateen parasol with two deep ruffles and puff. Complete, as illustrated, with rod, top ball and adjustable clamp. Price..........................$8.45

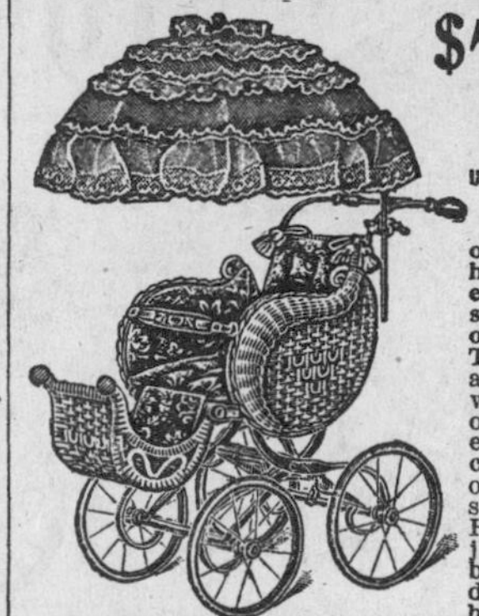

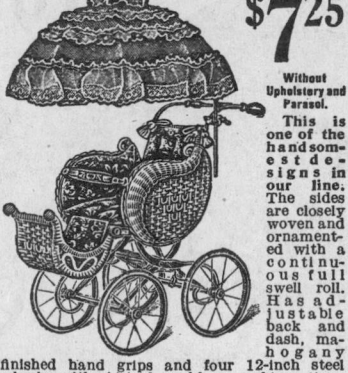

$7.25

Without Upholstery and Parasol.

This is one of the handsomest designs in our line. The sides are closely woven and ornamented with a continuous full swell roll. Has adjustable back and dash, mahogany finished hand grips and four 12-inch steel wheels with ½-inch rubber cushion tires. Read what we say above about the size, construction and finish of this cart.

No. 1K6148 Go-Cart, without upholstery and parasol. Price..........$7.25

No. 1K6149 Upholstered with cushions of Tapestry, covering on seat, back, sides and dash, trimmed with fancy cords and tassels. (See description of upholstery on page 456.) Has a green lined white percaline parasol with scalloped edges, and a fancy white bobbinet lace cover with three embroidered ruffles and puff. Complete, as illustrated, with rod, top ball and adjustable clamp. Price..........$8.95

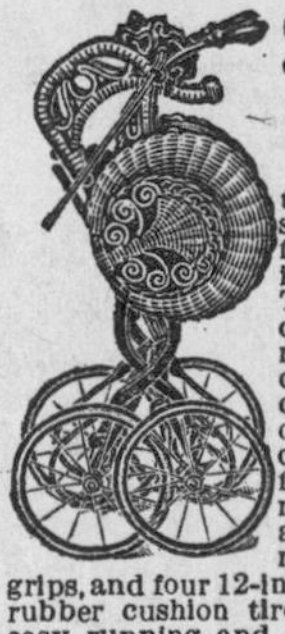

$7.85

Without Upholstery and Parasol.

Any of the go-carts in this line can be folded as shown in this illustration; floor space occupied 19x23 inches; height, 36 inches. They are light in weight and can be easily carried when necessary. The sides of this cart are made with large continuous rolls in the form of a circle, with fan design center—made of round and flat reeds with highly ornamental reed scrolls. Has adjustable back and dash, mahogany finished hand grips, and four 12-inch steel wheels with ½-inch rubber cushion tires which make these carts easy running and noiseless. The framework is made of specially selected and seasoned hard white maple. An exceptionally attractive design. Read what we say above about the size, construction and finish of this cart.

No. 1K6156 Go-Cart, without upholstery and parasol. Price.............$7.85

No. 1K6157 Upholstered with cushions of Novelty Cloth, covering back, sides, seat and dash, trimmed with fancy cords and tassels. (See description of upholstery on page 456). Has good quality sateen parasol same as illustrated and described on No. 1K6141. Complete with rod, top ball and adjustable clasp. Price...........................$9.65

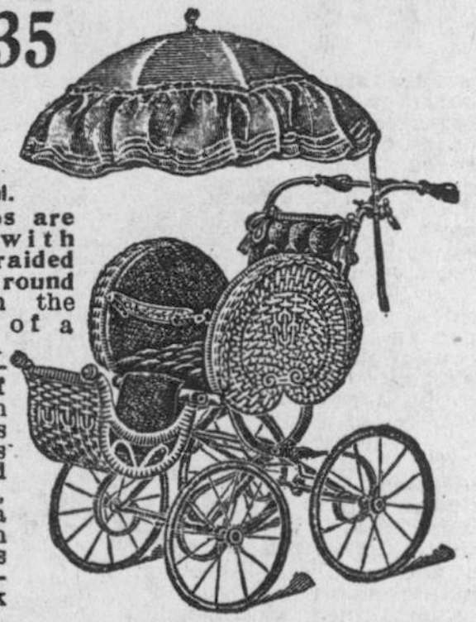

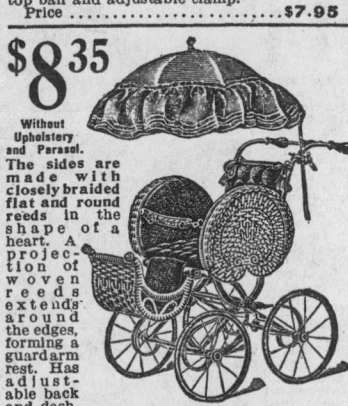

$8.35

Without Upholstery and Parasol.

The sides are made with closely braided flat and round reeds in the shape of a heart. A projection of woven reeds extends around the edges, forming a guard arm rest. Has adjustable back and dash, mahogany finished hand grips, and four 12-inch steel wheels with ½-inch rubber cushion tires. Read what we say above about the size, construction and finish of this cart.

No. 1K6164 Go-Cart, without upholstery and parasol. Price............$8.35

No. 1K6165 Upholstered with cushions of Tapestry, in seat, back, sides and dash trimmed with cord and tassels. Has fine quality satin parasol with deep scalloped ruffle and double hemmed edge. Complete, as illustrated, with rod, top ball and adjustable clamp. Price...................$10.95

BABY CARRIAGES

IN PRESENTING OUR NEW LINE OF BABY CARRIAGES WE ARE CONFIDENT THAT WE ARE SHOWING THE BEST BABY CARRIAGES EVER OFFERED AT ABOUT ONE-HALF THE USUAL PRICE QUOTED BY OTHER DEALERS.

ALL OUR CARRIAGES ARE BUILT VERY SUBSTANTIALLY, of the very best materials and have all the latest devices, such as the PERFECTION EASY RIDING GEAR, with patent automatic foot brake, patent hub caps and wheel fasteners, and are furnished with 16-inch regular ⅜-inch rubber tired, ½-inch cushion tired, or ⅝-inch heavy automobile cushion rubber tired steel wheels, as specified below. The double spiral springs are very elastic and arranged in such a manner as to produce easy, comfortable motion with no jar or jolt. The frame work is made of kiln dried maple, all joints are dovetailed, doweled and glued. The bottoms of all our carriages are 13½ inches wide by 27 inches long except the two cheapest carriages which are 14 by 25 inches. The low and medium priced carriages have maple bottoms ⅜-inch thick and the higher priced ones have cane bottoms, making them light and strong. All our carriages are upholstered with cushion seats, back and sides, with material to harmonize with the balance of the carriage and have the latest style parasol with rod and top ball, in fact, they are the best carriages made and are fully guaranteed in every respect. Each carriage, except Nos. 1K6307, 1K6309 and 1K6321 has long, gracefully bent steel push handles, securely attached to the axles and firmly braced, which brings the gear under direct control and makes it easy to guide the carriage. We furnish hollow steel handles made of bicycle tubing with new continuous Arabian green enameled hand grips with nickel plated ferrules on No. 1K6372 and No. 1K6382, which not only add greatly to the appearance of the carriage but are very light and strong. We furnish solid steel handles with mahogany finished grips and wheels with ½-inch rubber cushion tires on No 1K6332, No. 1K6342, No. 1K6352 and No. 1K6362. No. 1K6392 has solid steel pusher handles with Arabian green hand grips ornamented with nickel plated ferrules and 16-inch steel wheels with ⅝-inch automobile tires.

Our Leader at $4.25.

$4.25

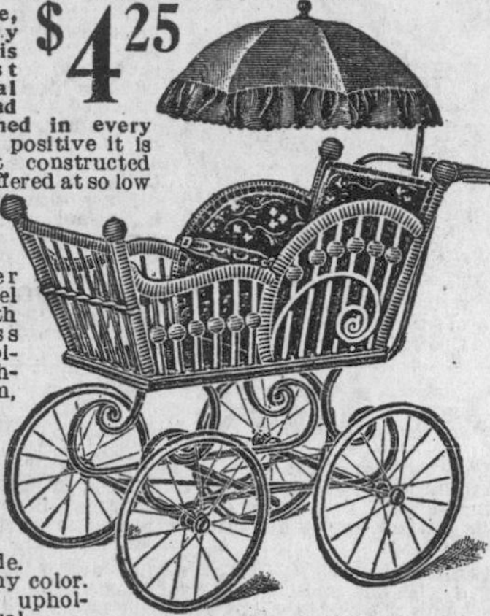

This carriage, although very low in price, is made of best quality material throughout and is well finished in every way. We are positive it is the very best constructed carriage ever offered at so low a price. Equipped with four 16-inch steel wheels with ⅜-inch rubber tires and steel pusher rods with maple cross handle. Upholstered with cushions of denim, covering seat, sides and back. (See description of upholstery on page 456.) Has a percaline parasol with fancy scalloped ruffle. Furnished in any color. Complete with upholstery and parasol.

No. 1K6309 Price, with rod, top ball and adjustable clamp..............**$4.65**

No. 1K6307 Same as above but with steel rim wheels, without rubber tires. Price, complete..............**$4.25**

Our $6.15 Carriage.

$6.15

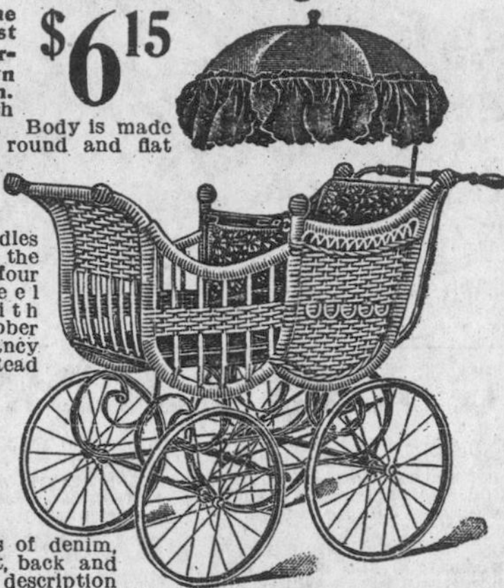

This is one of the finest low priced carriages shown this season. A value which can't be beat. Body is made of selected round and flat reeds woven into a handsome design. Has steel pusher handles attached to the body and four 16-inch steel wheels with ⅜-inch rubber tires and fancy hand grips. Read what we say at the top of this page about the size, construction and finish of this carriage. Upholstered with cushions of denim, covering seat, back and sides. (See description of upholstery on page 456.) Has a fine sateen parasol with fancy deep scalloped ruffle, furnished in any color.

No. 1K6321 Complete, with rod, top ball and adjustable clamp. Price..............**$6.15**

$7.85

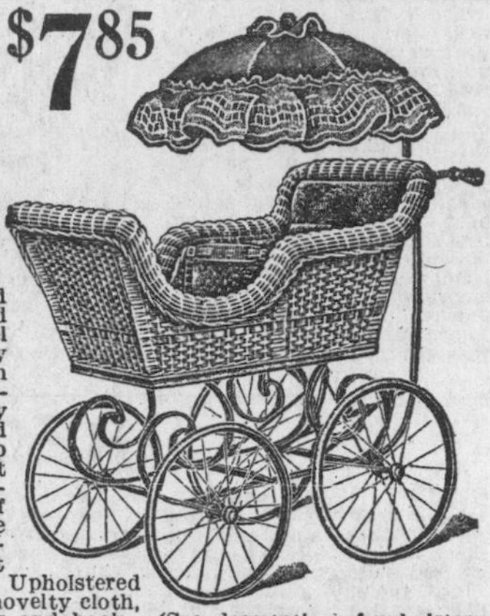

Special attention is drawn to the substantial manner in which this carriage is made. The entire body is closely woven with round and flat reeds, with a large reed roll surrounding the body. Has long, gracefully bent steel pusher handles attached to the axles and four 16-inch steel wheels with heavy ½-inch cushion tires and fancy imitation mahogany hand grips. Read what we say at top of this page about the size, construction and finish of this carriage. We guarantee the carriage to be the best value ever offered. Upholstered with cushions of novelty cloth, covering seat, sides and back. (See description of upholstery on page 456.) Has roll head rest made of fine silk plush. Has green lined white percaline parasol and lawn cover with fancy ruffle, furnished in white only.

No. 1K6332 Complete, with rod, top ball and adjustable clamp. Price..............**$7.85**

$8.95

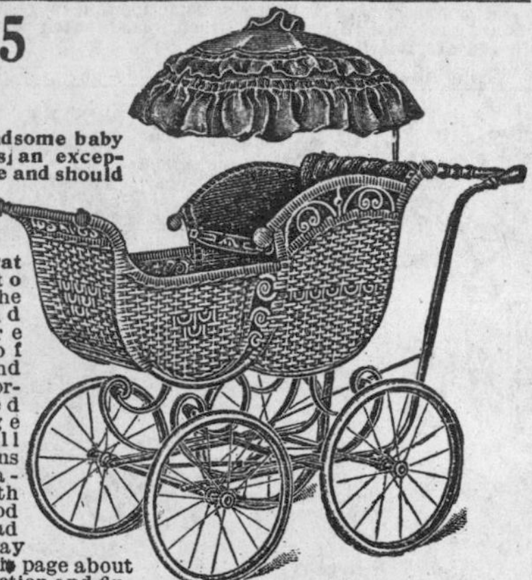

This handsome baby carriage is an exceptional value and should be compared with carriages that retail at $15.00 to $18.00. The sides and dash are made of round and flat reeds ornamented with large scrolls. All projections are ornamented with turned wood balls. Read what we say at top of this page about the construction and finish of this carriage. Has gracefully bent steel pusher handles attached to the axles, highly polished mahogany finished hand grips and four 16-inch heavy ½-inch rubber cushion tired wheels. It is upholstered with cushions of Bedford cord, covered sides, back and seat. (See description of upholstery on page 456.) Has fine quality mercerized sateen parasol, with two shirred ruffles and puff, furnished in any color.

No. 1K6342 Complete, with rod, top ball and adjustable clamp. Price..............**$8.95**

One of the Handsomest Carriages Made.

$10.45

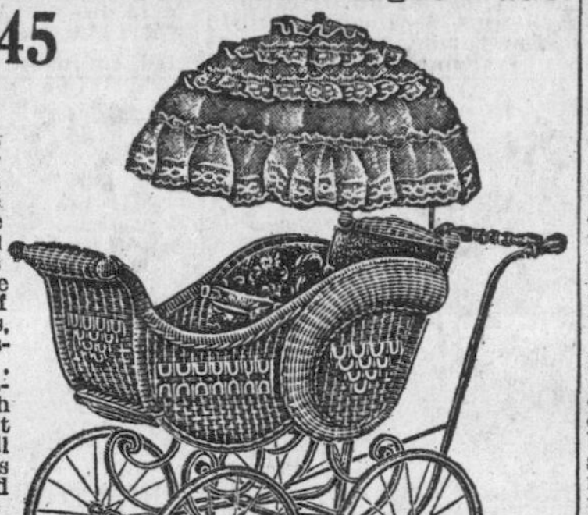

This carriage is very elaborate in design. The sides are composed of large rolls made of the finest grade of round reeds, forming a crescent design, neatly ornamented with mosaic effect center. All frame work is made of hard maple. It has a closely woven reed roll dash and an extra high back with large round reed roll surmounting the top. Read what we say at top of this page about the size, construction and finish of carriage. Has gracefully bent steel pusher handles attached to the axles and four 16-inch steel wheels with heavy ½-inch rubber cushion tires and highly polished mahogany finished hand grips. It is upholstered with tapestry, covering the sides and cushion seat. (See description of upholstery on page 456.) The high back is upholstered with cushions and head rest. Has a green lined white percaline parasol and handsome bobbinet lace cover with three fancy ruffles and puff trimmed with lace insertion edges.

No. 1K6352 Complete, with rod, top ball and adjustable clamp. Price..............**$10.45**

$12.65

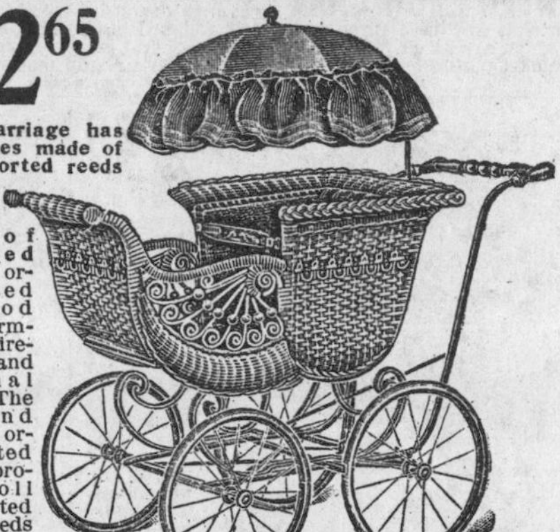

This carriage has swell sides made of fine imported reeds and a fancy open work of heavy reed scrolls, ornamented with wood balls, forming an entirely new and original design. The back and sides are ornamented with a projecting roll of selected round reeds forming a sort of arm rest neatly finished with closely braided edges. The extra large dash is surmounted at the top by a massive round reed roll. All projections are ornamented with hand turned wood balls. Read what we say at top of this page about the size, construction and finish of this carriage. Has gracefully bent steel pusher handles attached to the axles, continuous Arabian green hand grips with nickel plated ferrules and four 16-inch steel wheels with ½-inch rubber cushion tires. Upholstered with corduroy covering, sides, back and cushion seat. (See description of upholstery on page 456.) Has extra quality satin parasol with fancy double hemmed ruffle, lined with green percaline, furnished in any color.

No. 1K6362 Complete, with rod, top ball and adjustable clamp. Price..............**$12.65**

A New and Striking Pattern.

$14.85

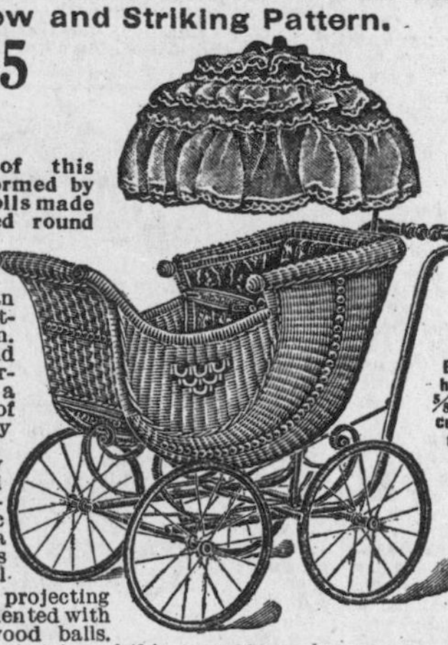

Extra heavy ⅝-inch cushion tires

The sides of this carriage are formed by massive swell rolls made of fine imported round reeds ornamented with maple bead work, forming an exceptionally attractive design. The back and sides are surmounted by a continuous roll of extra quality round reeds. Center of body is ornamented with neat triangular mosaic design and extra high dash has round reed roll at the top. All projecting points are ornamented with hand turned wood balls. Read what we say at top of this page about the size, construction and finish of this carriage. Has gracefully bent hollow steel handles of bicycle tubing firmly braced and attached to the axles, continuous Arabian green grip handles with nickel plated ferrules and four 16-inch extra heavy ⅝-inch rubber cushion tires. Upholstered with cushions of Simile Lambelle, covering seat, sides and back. (See description of upholstery on page 456.) Has white percaline parasol lined with green, and fancy Irish point lace cover with three deep ruffles and puff trimmed with ribbon and lace insertion edges, furnished in white only.

No. 1K6372 Complete, with rod, top ball and adjustable clamp. Price..............**$14.85**

At $16.95 We Offer One of the Finest Carriages Made.

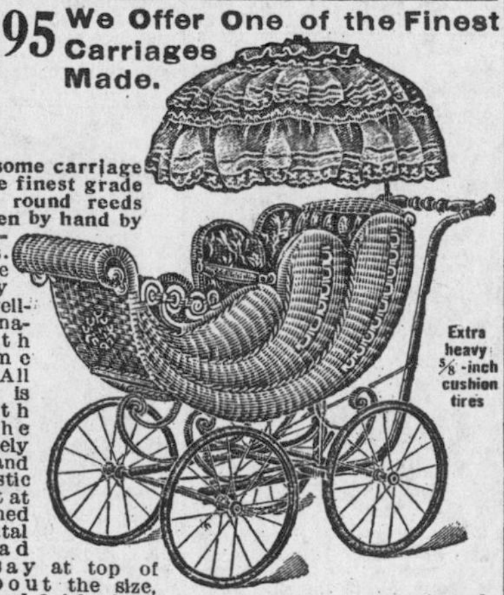

Extra heavy ⅝-inch cushion tires

This handsome carriage is made of the finest grade of imported round reeds entirely woven by hand by the most expert weavers. The sides are formed by three large swelled rolls, ornamented with handsome reed scrolls. All frame work is wrapped with rattan. The back is of closely woven reeds and dash has artistic reed roll effect at the top, finished with ornamental scrolls. Read what we say at top of this page about the size, construction and finish of this carriage. The handles are made of hollow steel bicycle tubing attached to the axles, and firmly braced, fitted with the latest continuous Arabian green enameled hand grips, trimmed with nickel plated ferrules. Wheels have extra heavy ⅝-inch rubber cushion tires. It is upholstered with fine quality silk damask cushions, covering seat and sides, with tufted cushion back. (See description of upholstery on page 456.) Has white percaline parasol lined with green and handsome extra quality Brussels net lace cover with three deep ruffles trimmed with fancy lace insertion edges.

No. 1K6382 Complete, with rod, top ball and adjustable clamp. Price..............**$16.95**

$19.45

Our Celebrated Pullman Sleeper.

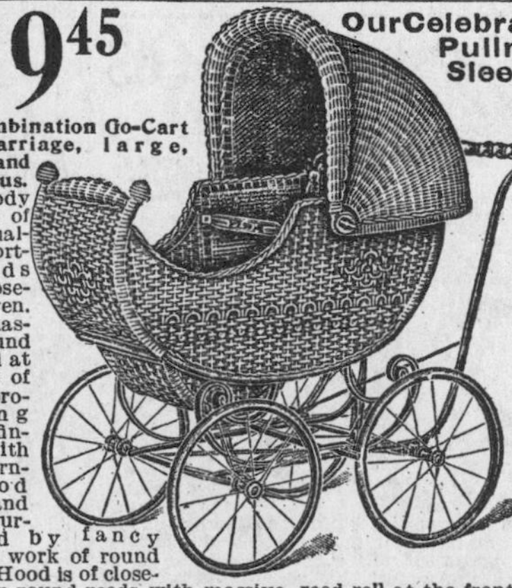

Extra heavy ⅝-inch cushion tires.

A combination Go-Cart and Carriage, large, roomy and luxurious. The body is made of extra quality imported reeds very closely woven. Has massive round reed roll at the top of dash, projecting points finished with hand turned wood balls and body surmounted by fancy braided work of round reeds. Hood is of closely woven round reeds with massive reed roll at the front. Can be adjusted to any position desired and affords ample protection in all kinds of weather. The large foot rest at the bottom of the body makes it possible for the occupant to sit in an upright position with the feet resting in a natural position. By pulling out the small slide which covers the foot rest when not in use, and adjusting the back, this carriage can be converted into a comfortable bed. Has our **Perfection easy riding gear,** four 16-inch steel wheels, extra heavy ⅝-inch cushion tires. Solid steel pusher handles, continuous Arabian green hand grips, and upholstery of corduroy for hood, sides and bed.

No. 1K6392 Price, complete, as illustrated..............**$19.45**

$2.73 FOR A COMPLETE OUTFIT OF ENAMELED WARE AND KITCHEN ITEMS $2.73

PEERLESS WARE IS HIGHEST GRADE. Extra heavy, double coated enamel. Each piece carefully inspected before sending out. Peerless ware is made of heavy sheet steel, coated with pure gray enamel, two coats, baked on under an intense heat which unites the enamel to the steel body in such a manner that it cannot chip off or crack, if properly used. The enamel used on Peerless Gray Ware is absolutely pure and will not discolor or peel with age.

YOU SAVE MONEY BY BUYING AN ASSORTMENT. We buy these sets in immense quantities and offer them to you at actual factory cost plus our one small percentage of profit. Buying from us you save at least 50 per cent on the price you would have to pay at retail and get better ware than you can get anywhere else.

PEERLESS GRAY WARE is durable and substantial, does not rust like tin or iron and is as easily cleaned as crockery. The use of good enamel ware cuts the kitchen work in half.

Price has been reduced.

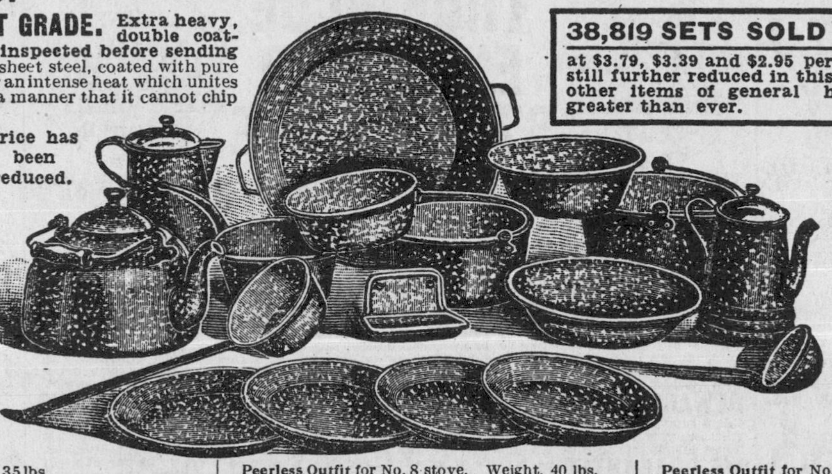

38,819 SETS SOLD BY US LAST YEAR

at $3.79, $3.39 and $2.95 per set. These low prices are still further reduced in this book along with over 3,000 other items of general hardware. Your saving is greater than ever.

We furnish these outfits in three different sizes, for No. 7, No. 8 and No. 9 stoves, each set containing the following articles:

1 Peerless Enameled Sauce Pan
2 Peerless Enameled Pudding Pans
1 Peerless Enameled Wash Basin
1 Peerless Enameled Windsor Pattern Dipper
4 Peerless Enameled Pie Plates, 9 inches in diameter
1 Peerless Enameled Soap Dish, to hang on the wall
1 Peerless Enameled Dish Pan
1 Peerless Enameled Soup Ladle
1 Peerless Enameled Tea Kettle
1 Peerless Enameled Coffee Pot
1 Peerless Enameled Teapot
2 Peerless Enameled Preserving Kettles

Peerless Outfit for No. 7 stove. Weight, 35 lbs.
No. 9K22007 Price, complete, as illustrated and described........ **$2.73**

Peerless Outfit for No. 8 stove. Weight, 40 lbs.
No. 9K22008 Price, complete, as illustrated and described........ **$3.18**

Peerless Outfit for No. 9 stove. Weight, 50 lbs.
No. 9K22009 Price, complete, as illustrated and described........ **$3.59**

68-PIECE ELITE KITCHEN AND STOVE WARE ASSORTMENT ONLY $7.98

INCLUDES TINWARE, IRONWARE, WOODENWARE AND EVERYTHING NEEDED ABOUT THE KITCHEN, STOVE OR LAUNDRY AT A PRICE SO LOW YOU CAN'T AFFORD TO DO WITHOUT.

OUR ELITE ASSORTMENTS contain the very finest grades of merchandise, including a solid copper nickel plated tea kettle, solid copper coffee and teapots, complete set of Potts' sad irons, and practically every necessary article in the kitchen or laundry. Read the entire list of articles contained in this immense assortment and you will find by figuring up the retail prices, that this outfit would cost you at least 50 per cent more if the items were bought separately in your best home store. We figure only one small profit on the entire lot instead of a separate profit on each item. We sell thousands of these assortments every year, buy the goods in immense quantities and offer them to you in these wholesale assortments at wholesale prices, prices lower than the average merchant pays for the goods he buys, which will not compare with ours for quality.

Three different sizes of Elite assortments, to fit No. 7, No. 8 and No. 9 stoves, each assortment containing the following articles:

1 Heavy IX Tin Copper Bottom Wash Boiler
1 Iron Stove Kettle
1 Tin Cover to fit
1 Nickel Plated Copper Tea Kettle
1 Iron Spider
1 Fry Pan, 10 inches
1 Basting Spoon
1 Stove Shovel, heavy steel
1 Nickel Plated Copper 5-pint Coffee Pot
1 Nickel Plated Copper 4-pint Teapot
1 Retinned Preserving Kettle
1 Cover to fit
1 Retinned Sauce Pan
1 Cover to fit
1 Tin Muffin Frame, 12 cups
½ Dozen Tin Pie Plates, 9 inches
1 Extra Heavy Retinned Dish Pan, 14 quarts
1 Pieced Tin Cup, 1 pint
1 Heavy Copper Bottom Water Dipper, 2 quarts
1 Flat Handled Skimmer

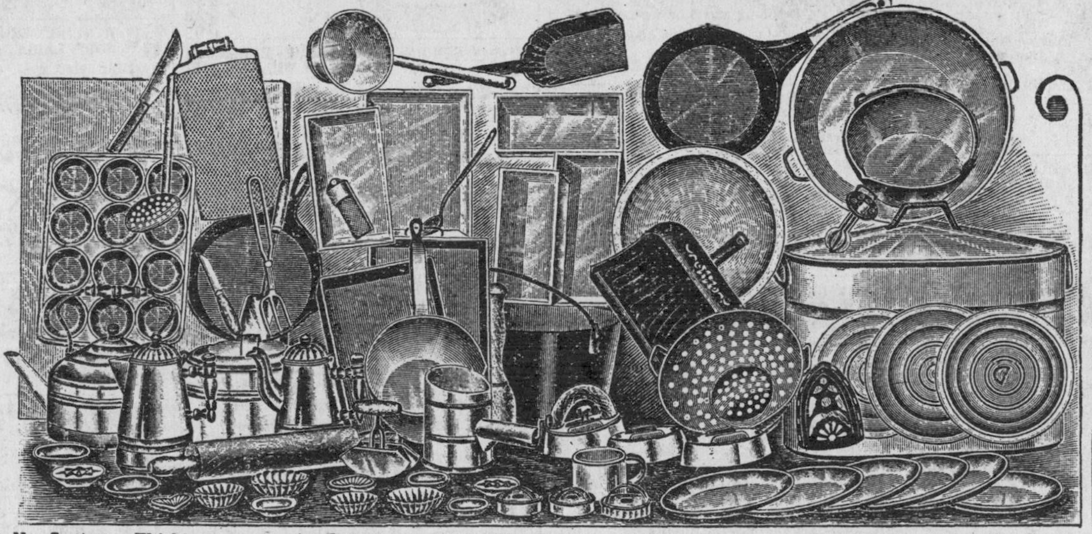

1 Vegetable Fork
3 Tin Bread Pans
2 Tin Cake Pans
2 Drip Pans, 10x12 and 10x14 inches
1 Dozen Assorted Patty Pans
1 Rolling Pin
1 Cake Turner
1 Retinned Colander
1 Cake Cutter
1 Biscuit Cutter
1 Doughnut Cutter
1 Nutmeg Grater
1 Large Grater
1 Revolving Flour Sifter
1 Dover Egg Beater
1 Covered Japanned Dust Pan
1 Butcher Knife
1 Paring Knife
1 Mincing Knife
1 Bread Board
1 Wood Potato Masher
1 Oval Hardwood Chopping Tray
1 Steamer
1 Set Mrs. Potts' Sad Irons, consisting of Three Irons, Handle and Stand

Sharp reduction in prices of these sets from the low prices named in our last catalogue.

Elite Assortment for No. 7 stove. Weight, 100 pounds.
No. 9K22027 Price........ **$7.98**

Elite Assortment for No. 8 stove. Weight, 105 pounds.
No. 9K22028 Price........ **$8.43**

Elite Assortment for No. 9 stove. Weight, 110 pounds.
No. 9K22029 Price........ **$8.86**

FORMER LOW PRICES FURTHER REDUCED.

WHITE PORCELAIN ENAMELED STEEL WARE

QUALITY HIGH AS HERETOFORE.

EVERY PIECE IS MADE SEAMLESS, of one piece of sheet steel, heavily coated inside and outside with pure white porcelain enamel and with edges or border a bright clear blue color. Every piece full size and made in the best and most practical shape. It cannot be broken, is not easily chipped and is less than one-half the weight of crockery. The enamel is not affected by acids, will not discolor and is as easily cleaned as china. We recommend White Porcelain Enameled Ware for ordinary household use, camping parties, miners and prospectors. It is more serviceable than crockery as it is unbreakable, does not chip and is light in weight. Every piece of White Porcelain Enameled Ware is guaranteed first quality and the best made regardless of price.

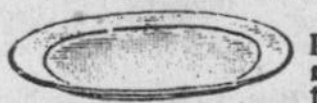

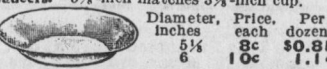

No. 9K24200 White Porcelain Enameled Dinner Plates. 8¾-inch is the popular size.

Diameter, inches....	8	8¾	9½
Price, each..........	$0.09	$0.11	$0.13
Per dozen..........	1.04	1.27	1.50

No 9K24202 White Porcelain Enameled Cups. 3⅛-inch is the best size.

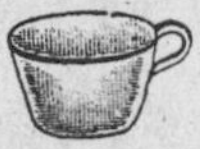

Diameter, inches	Price, each	Per dozen
3⅛	10c	$1 12
4	12c	1.36

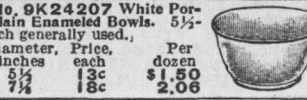

No. 9K24204 White Porcelain Enameled Saucers. 5⅛-inch matches 3⅛-inch cup.

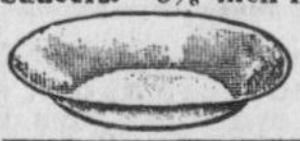

Diameter, inches	Price, each	Per dozen
5⅛	8c	$0.85
6	10c	1.14

No. 9K24207 White Porcelain Enameled Bowls. 5½-inch generally used.

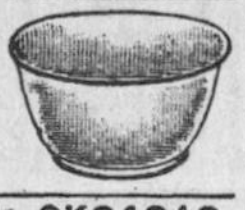

Diameter, inches	Price, each	Per dozen
5½	13c	$1.50
7⅛	18c	2.06

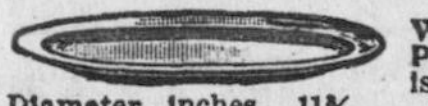

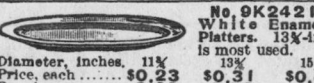

No. 9K24212 White Enameled Platters. 13⅝-inch is most used.

Diameter, inches.	11⅝	13⅝	15⅝
Price, each.......	$0.23	$0.31	$0.40
Per dozen..........	2.60	3.56	4.60

$2.33 FOR THIS COMPLETE PORCELAIN ENAMEL DINNER SET.

YOU SAVE ON THE COST OF EACH ITEM WHEN YOU BUY A COMPLETE SET.

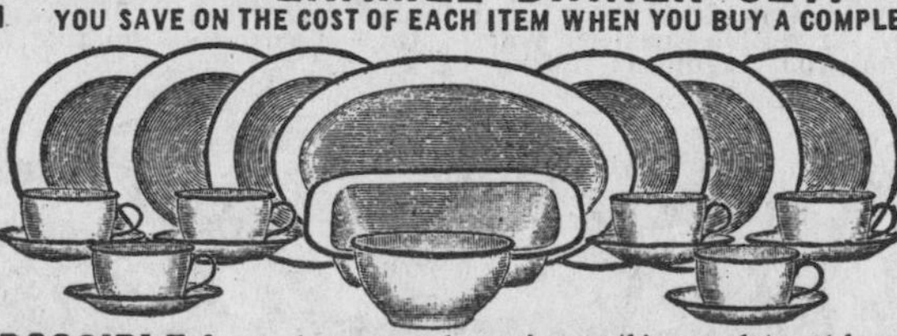

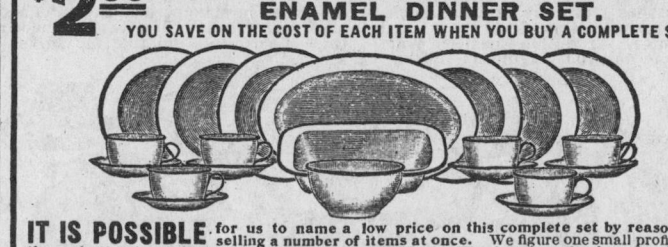

IT IS POSSIBLE for us to name a low price on this complete set by reason of selling a number of items at once. We figure one small profit on the entire lot, instead of a separate profit on each item. We give you the benefit of all the saving in selecting, handling and packing the goods. It is to your interest, therefore, to order a complete outfit at one time if you can possibly do so.

This matchless set of Porcelain Enamel Ware consists of 6 large dinner plates, 6 coffee cups, 6 saucers, 1 large oval platter, 1 large vegetable dish and 1 bowl.
No. 9K22016 Price, complete........ **$2.33**

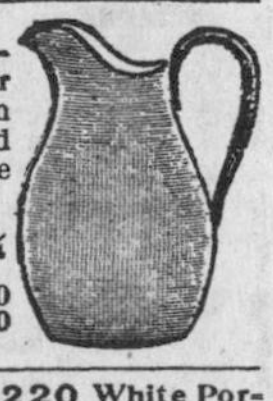

No. 9K24217 White Porcelain Enameled Ewers or Water Pitchers, drawn from one piece of steel, guaranteed seamless. We sell most of the 2-quart size.

Diam. in..	5½	6	6¾
Holds, qts.	1	1½	2
Price ea.,	$0.44	$0.59	$0.70
Per doz..	5.20	6.90	8.20

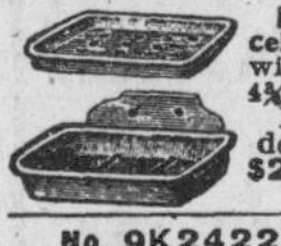

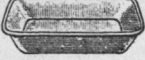

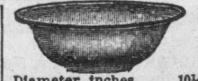

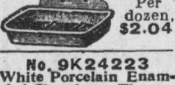

No. 9K24220 White Porcelain Enameled Soap Dishes, with removable drainers. Size, 4⅝x3⅝ inches. Price, ea.. 18c
Per dozen, $2.04

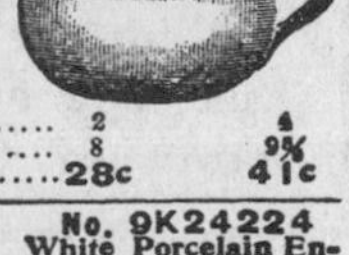

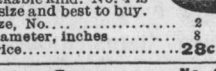

No. 9K24223 White Porcelain Enameled Chambers. The unbreakable kind. No. 4 is full size and best to buy.

Size, No....	2	4
Diameter, inches..........	8	9⅝
Price....................	28c	41c

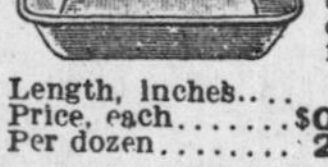

No. 9K24209 White Porcelain Enameled Vegetable Dishes. We recommend 10¼-inch size for families.

Length, inches....	9⅛	10¼	11
Price, each.......	$0.19	$0.21	$0.24
Per dozen.........	2.20	2.40	2.70

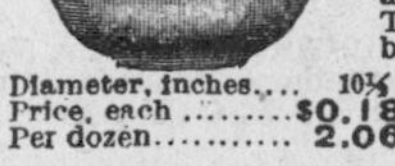

No. 9K24215 White Porcelain Enameled Wash Basins. The largest size is the best for most people.

Diameter, inches....	10⅛	12	13⅛
Price, each........	$0.18	$0.24	$0.30
Per dozen..........	2.06	2.65	3.45

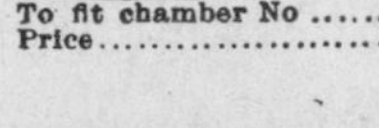

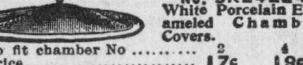

No. 9K24224 White Porcelain Enameled Chamber Covers.

To fit chamber No..........	2	4
Price....................	17c	19c

37c GENUINE TRUE BLUE ENAMELED TEAPOT, HOLDS 1 QUART.

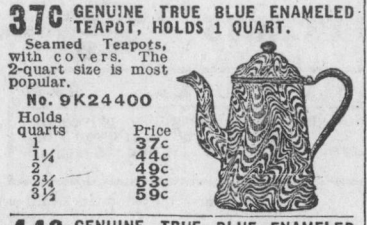

Seamed Teapots, with covers. The 2-quart size is most popular.

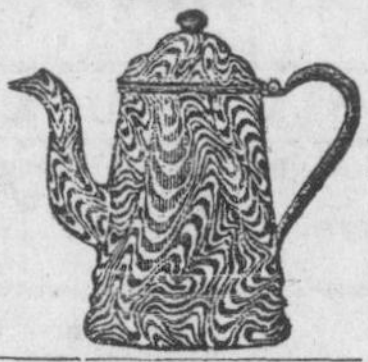

No. 9K24400

Holds quarts	Price
1	37c
1¼	44c
2	49c
2¾	53c
3½	59c

44c GENUINE TRUE BLUE ENAMELED COFFEE POT, HOLDS 1½ QUARTS.

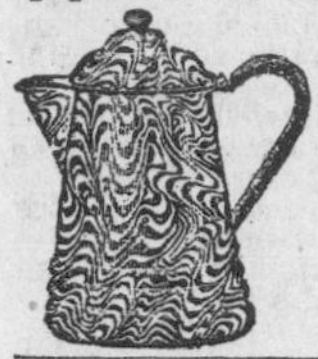

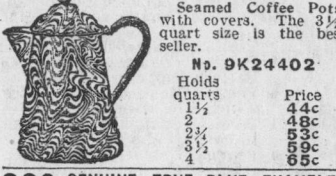

Seamed Coffee Pots, with covers. The 3½-quart size is the best seller.

No. 9K24402

Holds quarts	Price
1½	44c
2	48c
2¾	53c
3½	59c
4	65c

82c GENUINE TRUE BLUE ENAMELED COFFEE BOILER, HOLDS 6 QUARTS.

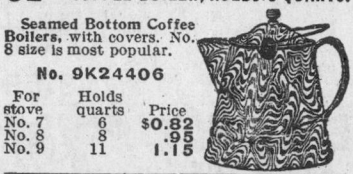

Seamed Bottom Coffee Boilers, with covers. No. 8 size is most popular.

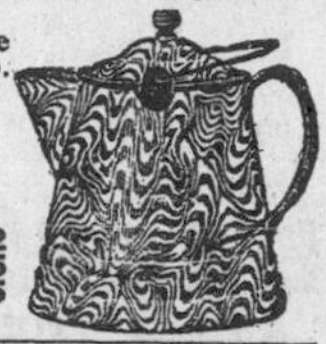

No. 9K24406

For stove	Holds quarts	Price
No. 7	6	$0.82
No. 8	8	.95
No. 9	11	1.15

76c GENUINE TRUE BLUE ENAMELED TEA KETTLE, HOLDS 4½ QUARTS.

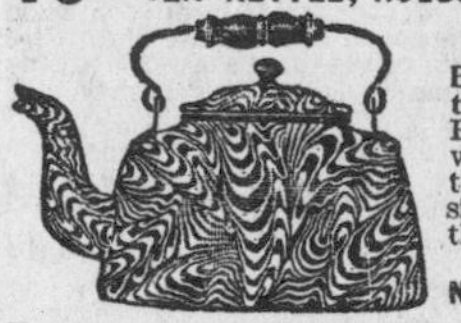

Seamed Flat Bottom Tea Kettles, with covers. Rustproof, and will not discolor the water. No. 8 size is used more than any other.

No. 9K24408

For stove	Holds quarts	Price
No. 7	4½	$0.76
No. 8	6	.87
No. 9	7½	1.03

21c GENUINE TRUE BLUE ENAMELED WASH BASIN, SMALL SIZE.

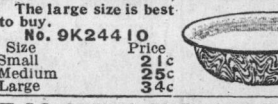

The large size is best to buy.

No. 9K24410

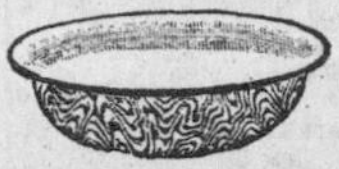

Size	Price
Small	21c
Medium	25c
Large	34c

54c GENUINE TRUE BLUE ENAMELED DISH PAN, HOLDS 9 QUARTS.

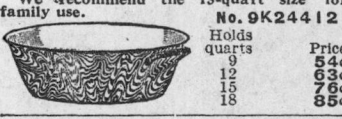

We recommend the 15-quart size for family use.

No. 9K24412

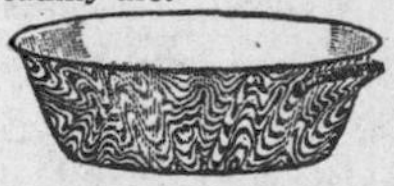

Holds quarts	Price
9	54c
12	63c
15	76c
18	85c

15c GENUINE TRUE BLUE ENAMELED SAUCE PAN, 1¼-QUART SIZE.

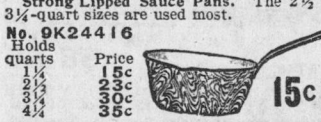

Strong Lipped Sauce Pans. The 2½ and 3¼-quart sizes are used most.

No. 9K24416

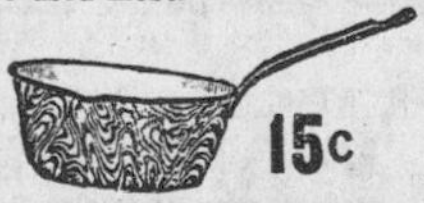

Holds quarts	Price
1¼	15c
2½	23c
3¼	30c
4¼	35c

LOW PRICES BEFORE, STILL LOWER NOW ON OUR LINE OF TRUE BLUE ENAMELED STEEL WARE

GENUINE TRUE BLUE ENAMELED WARE FINEST QUALITY WARRANTED

GENUINE TRUE BLUE ENAMELED WARE FINEST QUALITY WARRANTED

THE BEST ENAMELED WARE IT IS POSSIBLE TO MAKE, REGARDLESS OF COST. DO NOT THINK BECAUSE WE SELL TRUE BLUE WARE AT SUCH REMARKABLY LOW PRICES IT IS NOT AS GOOD AS OTHER BRANDS. BETTER QUALITY CANNOT BE PRODUCED.

WITH A FEW EXCEPTIONS as noted, every article in the entire line is made seamless with spun covers and knobs. True Blue Enameled Ware is made of cold drawn steel. Four coats of the finest grade of enamel are applied on both inside and outside to each article of True Blue Ware. The enamel used is guaranteed to be chemically pure, free from all poisonous or harmful ingredients, and positively will not discolor from the acids of fruits and vegetables. True Blue Enameled Ware will not peel off, is as easy to clean, but is not broken like earthenware or china; is durable but does not rust like tin or iron, will outlast any other enameled ware made and is an ornament to any kitchen. The outside blue mottled surface forms a strong contrast with the pure white inside and gives a finish which makes True Blue Enameled Ware the most beautiful kitchen ware made. We do not handle seconds, and each piece is guaranteed perfect.

BEWARE OF IMITATIONS of True Blue Enameled Ware. On account of the high quality of True Blue Ware many dealers offer for sale a blue mottled ware which bears some resemblance to the original True Blue, and they will tell you it is True Blue, or just as good. DO NOT BE DECEIVED. We are the only house offering True Blue Enameled Ware, and no one can buy a piece of it except from us.

WE GUARANTEE each piece of genuine True Blue Enameled Ware to be perfect, not to leak and to outwear any other enameled ware on the market. Order a lot of it; when it comes, examine it closely. If it is not superior to any you ever used, ship it back to us and we will refund your money and pay the transportation charges both ways. Remember, there is only one genuine True Blue Enameled Ware, and it can be had only from us.

NOTE: We guarantee every piece of True Blue Ware to hold the actual quantity we say it does. We list no "trade" sizes.

41c GENUINE TRUE BLUE ENAMELED BERLIN SAUCE PAN, 2½ QUARTS.

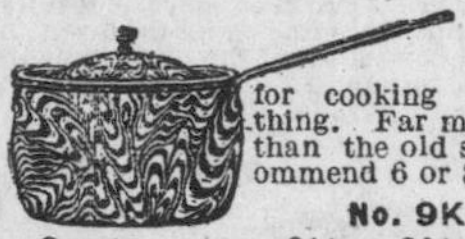

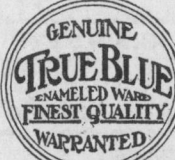

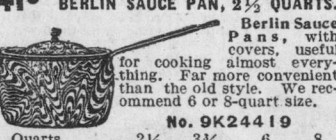

Berlin Sauce Pans, with covers, useful for cooking almost everything. Far more convenient than the old style. We recommend 6 or 8-quart size.

No. 9K24419

Quarts	2½	3¾	6	8
Price	41c	50c	59c	74c

49c GENUINE TRUE BLUE ENAMELED BERLIN KETTLE, 3¾ QUARTS.

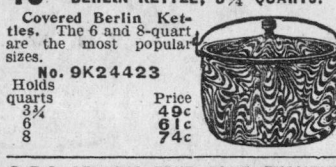

Covered Berlin Kettles. The 6 and 8-quart are the most popular sizes.

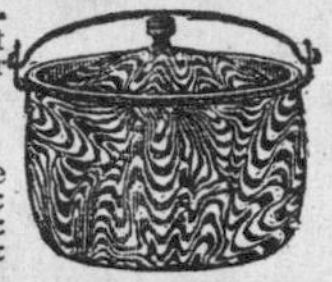

No. 9K24423

Holds quarts	Price
3¾	49c
6	61c
8	74c

30c GENUINE TRUE BLUE ENAMELED PRESERVING KETTLE, 3½ QUARTS.

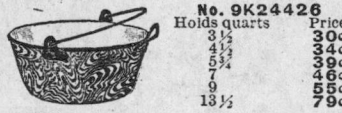

Strong Lipped Preserving Kettles. The 7 and 9-quart are the best selling sizes.

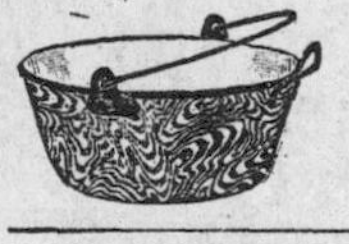

No. 9K24426

Holds quarts	Price
3½	30c
4½	34c
5¾	39c
7	46c
9	55c
13½	79c

14c GENUINE TRUE BLUE ENAMELED PUDDING PAN, HOLDS 1 QUART.

Extra Deep Pudding Pans. The 2½ and 3¼-quart are the most popular sizes.

No. 9K24432

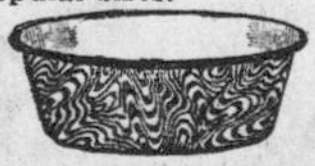

Holds quarts	Price
1	14c
1¾	18c
2½	20c
3¼	22c

22c GENUINE TRUE BLUE ENAMELED MILK PAN, HOLDS 2¾ QUARTS.

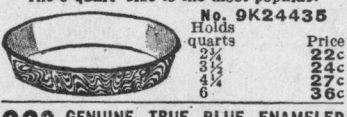

The 6-quart size is the most popular.

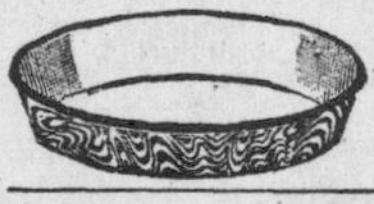

No. 9K24435

Holds quarts	Price
2¾	22c
3½	24c
4¼	27c
6	36c

66c GENUINE TRUE BLUE ENAMELED WATER PAIL, 8½ QUART SIZE.

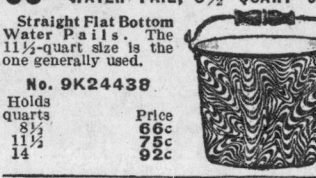

Straight Flat Bottom Water Pails. The 11½-quart size is the one generally used.

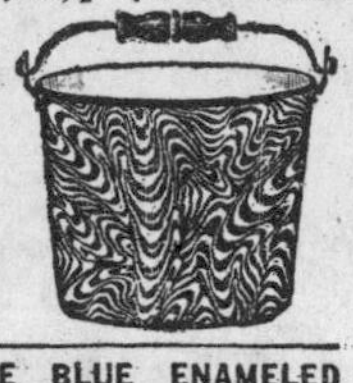

No. 9K24438

Holds quarts	Price
8½	66c
11½	75c
14	92c

10c GENUINE TRUE BLUE ENAMELED PIE PLATE, SIZE, 8x⅝ INCHES.

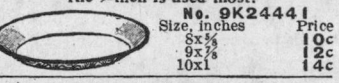

The 9-inch is used most.

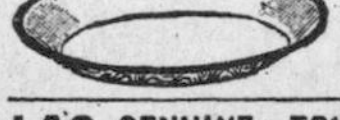

No. 9K24441

Size, inches	Price
8x⅝	10c
9x⅞	12c
10x1	14c

14c GENUINE TRUE BLUE ENAMELED DINNER PLATE, REGULAR SIZE.

Size, 8½ inches; which is full size.

No. 9K24445

Price, each....$0.14

Per dozen..... 1.55

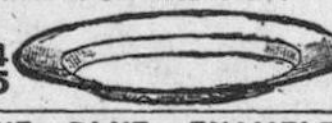

19c GENUINE TRUE BLUE ENAMELED CUP AND SAUCER, STANDARD SIZE.

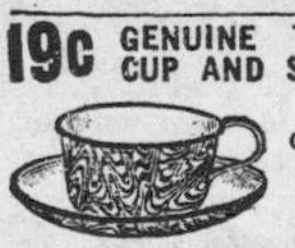

Cup is 4x2¼ inches, saucer is 5¾ inches.

No. 9K24450

Price, cups, each, $0.11

Per dozen 1.28

Saucers, each, 8c; per dozen...... .94

14c GENUINE TRUE BLUE ENAMELED SOUP BOWL, HOLDS 1½ PINTS.

The unbreakable kind.

No. 9K24452

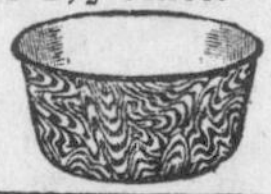

Holds pints	Price
1½	14c

49c GENUINE TRUE BLUE ENAMELED WATER PITCHER, 2-QUART SIZE.

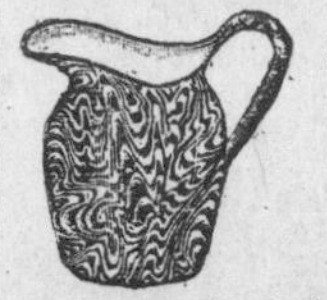

The handiest pitcher you ever used for milk. The 3-quart size is the best seller.

No. 9K24455

Holds quarts	Price
2	49c
2½	68c

62c GENUINE TRUE BLUE ENAMELED DOUBLE BOILER, HOLDS 1⅛ QTS

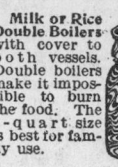

Milk or Rice Double Boilers with cover to both vessels. Double boilers make it impossible to burn the food. The 3-quart size is best for family use.

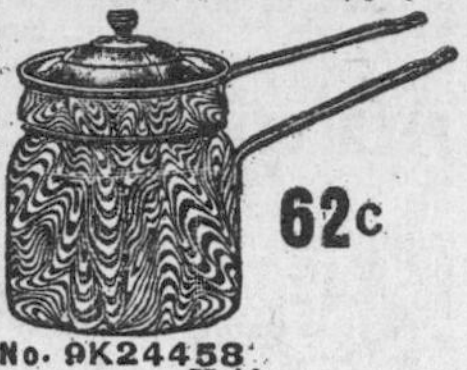

No. 9K24458

Holds quarts	Price	Holds quarts	Price
1⅛	62c	3	$1.04
1¾	82c	3½	1.26

19c GENUINE TRUE BLUE ENAMELED WINDSOR DIPPER, 1-PINT SIZE.

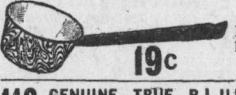

With strong, round handles. The 1½-pint size is most used.

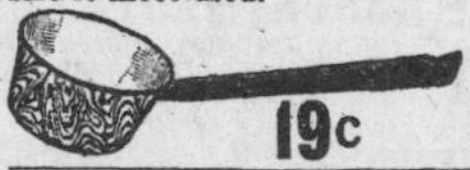

No. 9K24463

Holds pints	Price
1	19c
1½	22c

11c GENUINE TRUE BLUE ENAMELED SOUP LADLE, 14 INCHES LONG.

Regular size, 14 inches long.

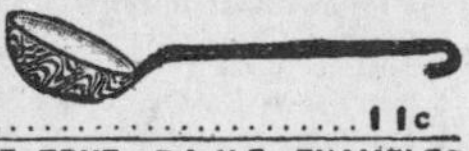

No. 9K24468

Price........................11c

10c GENUINE TRUE BLUE ENAMELED BASTING SPOON, 14 INCHES LONG.

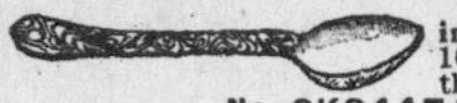

Threaded Basting Spoons. The 16-inch is worth the difference.

No. 9K24471

Size, inches	14	16
Price	10c	12c

17c GENUINE TRUE BLUE ENAMELED WALL SOAP DISH, FULL SIZE.

Wall Soap Dishes, with grates. Regular size, 6½x4x1½ inches.

No. 9K24477

Price............17c

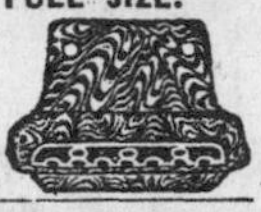

33c GENUINE TRUE BLUE ENAMELED CHAMBER, SMALL SIZE.

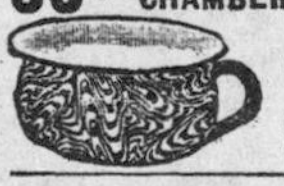

The large size is generally used.

No. 9K24485

Size	Small	Med.	Large
Price	33c	40c	48c

14c GENUINE TRUE BLUE ENAMELED CHAMBER COVER, SMALL SIZE.

No. 9K24486

Size	Small	Med.	Large
Price	14c	17c	21c

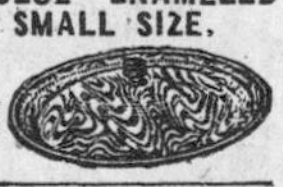

$4.58 COMPLETE OUTFIT OF TRUE BLUE ENAMELED WARE $4.58

YOU SAVE ON THE COST OF EACH ITEM WHEN YOU BUY A COMPLETE OUTFIT

WE SELECT THE ARTICLES in these outfits from our regular stock, they are the same high grade as those listed above and are covered by the same broad guarantee. True Blue Enameled Ware is made of sheet steel, quadruple coated inside and out, full weight and full size, is strong, durable, perfect in manufacture and finish and will not break. No other ware made will give you the same service as our True Blue. We furnish three assortments suitable for stoves Nos. 7, 8 or 9 containing the following articles:

YOU SAVE STILL MORE.

The low prices in our last catalogue have been still further reduced in this book on over 3,000 hardware items alone.

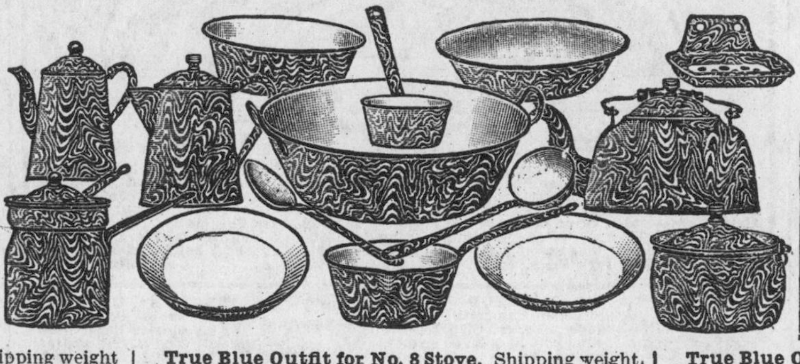

- 1 Tea Kettle.
- 1 Coffee Pot.
- 1 Teapot.
- 1 Berlin Kettle.
- 1 Sauce Pan.
- 1 Pudding Pan.
- 1 Wash Basin.
- 1 Double Boiler.
- 1 Dish Pan.
- 1 Soap Dish.
- 1 Basting Spoon.
- 2 Pie Plates.
- 1 Windsor Dipper
- 1 Soup Ladle.

By selling a complete set of True Blue Enameled Ware at one time, on a single order, we are enabled to quote a much lower price than if we sold each piece separately. True Blue is the highest grade made, each piece, covered by our GUARANTEE OF SATISFACTION OR YOUR MONEY BACK.

True Blue Outfit for No. 7 Stove. Shipping weight 43 pounds, as illustrated and described. No. 9K22012 Price.............. **$4.58**

True Blue Outfit for No. 8 Stove. Shipping weight, 50 pounds, as illustrated and described. No. 9K22013 Price.............. **$5.19**

True Blue Outfit for No. 9 Stove. Shipping weight 56 pounds, as illustrated and described. No. 9K22014 Price.............. **$5.79**

ACME OUTFIT OF IRONSTONE ENAMELED WARE

THE TOUGHEST AND MOST DURABLE ENAMELED WARE EVER OFFERED AT ANYTHING LIKE THE PRICE.

ACME IRONSTONE ENAMELED WARE is made of cold drawn steel, is covered with two heavy coats of vitrified enamel and then subjected to an intense heat, which unites the enamel to the steel so that it cannot peel off or crack. Ironstone Enamel Ware is a rich dark purple in color, mottled with white and has a glossy, pleasing finish. It is strong and durable, easily cleaned, will not discolor and will outlast any similar ware on the market at even double our price.

BUY AN ACME ASSORTMENT AND SAVE MONEY. By selling a large number of items at once we figure one small profit on the entire lot, instead of a separate profit on each item. We take the entire output of one of the largest manufacturers and actually offer these goods to you in wholesale assortments at less than ordinary wholesale prices. We handle three different sizes of Acme Ironstone Enameled Ware Outfits to fit No. 7, No. 8 and No. 9 stoves. Each outfit contains the following articles:

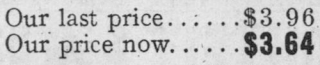

$3 64

BUYS THIS COMPLETE SET OF

ACME

IRONSTONE ENAMELED WARE.

NOTE THAT WE HAVE REDUCED PRICES.

Our last price......$3.96
Our price now......$3.64

One of more than 3,000 items in hardware alone in this book that have been reduced in this book. Your saving is greater than ever.

1 Tea Kettle
1 Coffee Pot
1 Teapot
1 Double Boiler for Rice or Milk
1 Berlin Kettle
1 Sauce Pan, medium
1 Sauce Pan, large
1 Preserving Kettle
3 Pie Plates
3 Jelly Plates
1 Dish Pan
1 Pudding Pan, medium
1 Pudding Pan, large
1 Milk Pan
1 Basting Spoon
1 Windsor Dipper
1 Ladle
1 Soap Dish to Hang
1 Drinking Cup
1 Wash Basin

EACH ARTICLE is guaranteed to be first quality. Order one of these assortments and if you do not find the goods to be exactly as represented, return them to us and we will refund your money.

Acme Ironstone Enameled Ware Outfit for No. 7 Stove. Shipping weight, 50 lbs. **$3.64**
No. 9K22004 Price, complete, as illustrated and described ....
Acme Ironstone Enameled Ware Outfit for No. 8 Stove. Shipping weight, 55 lbs. **4.37**
No. 9K22005 Price, complete, as illustrated and described ....
Acme Ironstone Enameled Ware Outfit for No. 9 Stove. Shipping weight, 60 lbs. **4.89**
No. 9K22006 Price, complete, as illustrated and described ....

54c DEED OR CASH BOX, COMPLETE WITH FIRST CLASS LOCK AND KEY.

Convenient for keeping and carrying valuable papers, cash, etc. Flat top, sunk handle, nicely japanned and hand striped. Size, about 12x8x5inches and large enough to receive deeds, bonds, insurance policies and all legal papers.
No. 9K26080 Price.......... **54c**

$4.63 DOUBLE WALL FIREPROOF CASH BOX, COMPLETE WITH LOCK.

The walls of this box are sufficiently thick to make it absolutely fireproof in any residence. Made on the same principle as a high priced fireproof safe. It is a perfectly safe receptacle for deeds, bonds, contracts, mortgages, notes, insurance policies, tax receipts, jewelry, etc. To test this box we had one subjected to an intense heat in a furnace. Not only was the iron heated red hot, but it reached a white heat, which is the point just before iron melts. The contents of box were not even marred. Every person who owns valuables of any nature ought to have one. Furnished with a first class padlock with two keys. Dimensions: Inside, 10 inches long, 6¼ inches wide, 3 inches deep. Approximate weight, 50 pounds.
No. 9K26094 Price.........$4.63

$3 84 OUR QUEEN 44-PIECE STOVE FURNISHING SET $3 84

THIS ASSORTMENT CONTAINS SUFFICIENT HIGH GRADE WARE TO OUTFIT YOUR KITCHEN, AND YOU CANNOT POSSIBLY GET AS GOOD QUALITY ELSEWHERE AT ANYTHING LIKE THE PRICE

THIS QUEEN OUTFIT contains among other goods, a copper bottom wash boiler, copper bottom tea kettle, cast iron stove kettle, iron spider, etc. Read the full list carefully, note the number of large pieces, the size and capacity of each. You could not duplicate this set at any retail store for double our price.

Note that we have reduced prices.

1 Copper Bottom Tin Wash Boiler
1 Copper Bottom Tin Tea Kettle
1 Cast Iron Stove Kettle
1 Cast Iron Spider
1 Wrought Iron Fry Pan, polished, 10 inches
1 4-pint Tin Teapot
1 5-quart Tin Coffee Pot
1 10-quart Retinned Dish Pan
1 Revolving Flour Sifter
2 Black Dripping Pans, 10x12 and 10x14 inches

WE GUARANTEE EVERY ARTICLE to be first quality and the best of its kind or grade. We do not carry seconds of any kind and if you order one of these assortments and do not find the goods to be exactly as represented you are at liberty to return the goods and we will refund your money.

1 Tin Bread Pan, 5¾x10¾x3 inches
2 Bread Tins, 7¾x11¾x1½ inches
1 Box Grater
1 Biscuit Cutter
1 Dover Egg Beater
1 Dozen 3-inch Plain Patty Pans
½ Dozen 9-inch Tin Pie Plates
1 14-in. Basting Spoon
1 Cake Turner
1 1-quart Tin Cup
1 Vegetable Fork
1 Tin Dipper
1 Flat Handled Skimmer
1 Fire Shovel
1 Tin Wash Basin
1 Tubed Cake Pan, 10-inch

Queen Assortment for No. 7 Stove. Weight, 60 lbs. **$3.84**
No. 9K22017 Price................
Queen Assortment for No. 8 Stove. Weight, 65 lbs. **$4.17**
No. 9K22018 Price................
Queen Assortment for No. 9 Stove. Weight, 70 lbs. **$4.42**
No. 9K22019 Price................

$1.39 DOUBLE WALL FANCY PATTERN WATER COOLER, HOLDS 2 GALS.

Double Wall, filled with non-conducting material, galvanized iron reservoir, handsomely decorated in various colors, side handles, nickel plated faucet. Requires less ice than any other, will not rust and will outlast any cooler on the market. The 4-gallon size is best for family use.
No. 9K26130
Gallons..2   4   8
Price, $1.39 $2.12 $3.13

14c FOR 4 FIREPROOF ASBESTOS STOVE MATS.

A household necessity. Made of asbestos of superior quality, scorch proof as well as fireproof. A cooking utensil used on one of these mats will not get too hot and the food will not scorch. Diameter, 9 inches.
No. 9K26990 Price, 4 for................14c

19c FOR A LIGHTNING BREAD TOASTER AND COFFEE BOILER COMBINED. REGULAR 35-CENT KIND.

Toasts four slices of bread in two minutes and boils tea or coffee at the same time on any gas, gasoline or oil stove, and for a quick meal beats a red hot coal fire. Heavy steel, braced and dovetailed at corners.
No. 9K26995 Price, reduced from 23 cents to................19c

Prices on hardware still further reduced in this book from the low prices named in our last catalogue. Over 3,000 hardware items cheaper than before.

OUR ECLIPSE IRONSTONE ENAMELED WARE OUTFIT

THE HIGHEST GRADE TWO-COAT ENAMELED STEEL WARE EVER OFFERED BY ANY HOUSE AT ANY PRICE. THE SAME HIGH GRADE WARE AS OUR ACME OUTFIT DESCRIBED ABOVE BUT WITH A LESS NUMBER OF PIECES.

DON'T TRY to put up with ironware and tinware any longer. Think of the time you waste scrubbing pots and pans to keep the rust off. Our Ironstone Enameled Ware does not rust, leak or crack and is as easily cleaned as china. Send us an order for a set of this enameled ware and do your work in half the time it now requires.

WHILE THIS ECLIPSE OUTFIT contains almost everything necessary about the kitchen, for a larger assortment we refer you to our Acme Outfit of Ironstone Enameled Ware shown at the top of this page. The quality of our Acme and Eclipse Outfits is identically the same, the Acme simply has more articles in it and is well worth the difference in price. Every item included in the larger set will be found useful about the kitchen.

WE CARRY THREE SIZES of Eclipse Ironstone Enameled Ware Sets to fit No. 7, No. 8 and No. 9 Stoves, each set containing the following articles:

$1 98 No. 7
$2 29 No. 8
$2 61 No. 9

1 Tea Kettle
1 Teapot
1 Coffee Pot
1 Preserving Kettle
1 Wash Basin
1 Pudding Pan
2 Pie Plates
1 Soap Dish to Hang
1 Ladle
1 Dipper
1 Sauce Pan
1 Basting Spoon
1 Drinking Cup

EACH ITEM covered by our binding guarantee to take back at our expense any article that is defective or that is not entirely satisfactory.
Eclipse Ironstone Enameled Ware Outfit for No. 7 Stove. Shipping weight, 25 lbs. **$1.98**
No. 9K22001 Price, complete, as illustrated and described................
Eclipse Ironstone Enameled Ware Outfit for No. 8 Stove. Shipping weight, 28 lbs. **2.29**
No. 9K22002 Price, complete, as illustrated and described................
Eclipse Ironstone Enameled Ware Outfit for No. 9 Stove. Shipping weight, 31 lbs. **2.61**
No. 9K22003 Price, complete, as illustrated and described................

WHITE HOUSE BREAD MIXER AND KNEADER, $1.79

OUR LAST CATALOGUE PRICES REDUCED. YOUR SAVING IS GREATER THAN EVER.

Will knead from one to eight regular sized loaves of the choicest bread in less than three minutes without touching the dough with the hands from start to finish.

THE WHITE HOUSE BREAD MIXER is built on the latest and most improved scientific principles. The dasher or kneader remains stationary; the entire receptacle revolves, thus forcing the dough against the mixer, causing compression as well as thorough mixing. The bucket and cover are made of the finest XX (heaviest quality) double thick non-rusting tin plate. The mixer or kneader is made of steel, heavily plated with pure block tin and will not rust. The White House Bread Kneader is simple, nothing to get out of order, and with ordinary care ought to last a lifetime. It is as easy to clean as a tin pail, can be clamped to any table and is the most convenient device of its kind ever invented. The White House is the cleanest bread mixer ever manufactured. Positively the hands do not come in contact with the dough. The cover is kept on the mixer while using it, which prevents dust, disease germs or insects from getting into the bread.

YOU ALWAYS MAKE GOOD BREAD with the White House Mixer, as it thoroughly and evenly mixes the batter, insuring the lightest, best bread you ever ate. The heavy tin pail holds twelve quarts and will knead from one to eight loaves as required. The White House Mixer is easy to turn, any child can operate it, and it only requires three minutes, instead of half an hour, as is necessary in the old way.

OUR LOW PRICE OF $1.79 is only possible because we take the entire output of the factory that manufactures the White House Bread Mixer. We sell tens of thousands of these machines every year direct from factory to consumer. The White House is the best bread mixer and kneader on the market; better than mixers offered by others at $4.00, $5.00 or even $6.00.

SEND US YOUR ORDER FOR A WHITE HOUSE BREAD MIXER, try it in your own kitchen, and if you do not find the White House Mixer kneads better bread with less labor, ship it back to us at our expense and we will immediately refund your money. You take no risk whatever. Don't delay; send your order NOW.

No. 9K25424   White House Bread Mixer and Kneader. Shipping weight, boxed, 23 pounds. Price............ **$1.79**

Former Low Prices Still Further Reduced. **$1.57** SANITARY, CONVENIENT FLOUR BIN AND SIFTER, HOLDS 25 POUNDS.

The most convenient bin and sifter ever invented; will pay for itself in a short time by the saving of flour which is ordinarily wasted if it is allowed to remain in the sack; keeps dust, insects and disease germs out and is the most sanitary method of handling of flour. Made of heavy IXX tin, japanned on the outside and absolutely rustproof throughout; handsomely decorated and is an ornament as well as a necessity to any kitchen or pantry. In the illustration part of front is cut away to show the shield, sifter, etc. The sifter is protected from pressure of the flour by our new shield, which enables the agitator to work easily and smoothly, and obviates all grinding through of foreign substances. A tin skirt below the sifter prevents the flour from scattering all over the bottom of the bin, but instead directs it into the proper receptacle. The 50-pound size is most convenient for ordinary family use; 100-pound size for large families.

No. 9K26002

Holds, pounds	25	50	100
Size, inches	10¼x23	12⅞x27¼	15½x34
Price	$1.57	$2.10	$2.98

WHITE HOUSE BREAD AND PASTRY MAKING OUTFIT $4.82

NOTE THE LOWER PRICE.

38 USEFUL ARTICLES, A COMPLETE ASSORTMENT FOR $4.82

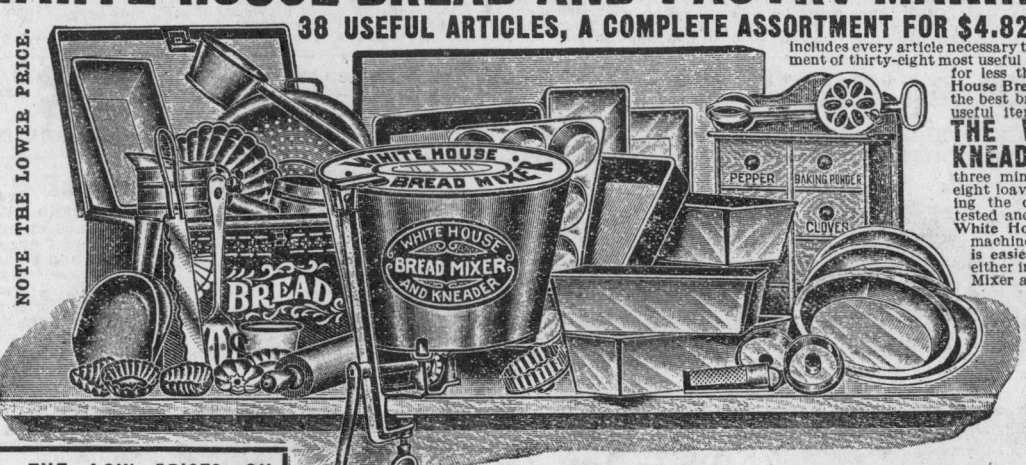

No housewife can well afford to do without this big assortment, includes every article necessary to make bread or cake, a grand assortment of thirty-eight most useful articles which cannot be duplicated for less than $10.00. The Famous White House Bread Mixer and Kneader, included in this assortment, is the best bread maker on the market and is only one of the many useful items included in this great big assortment of ware.

THE WHITE HOUSE BREAD MIXER AND KNEADER. Read the full description of this wonderful machine at top of this page. In less than three minutes it will knead thoroughly the materials to make eight loaves of white and fluffy bread, without the hands touching the dough. It is the very latest invention, completely tested and tried, and sure to give the best of satisfaction. The White House Bread Mixer kneads by compression, while other machines only mix the dough. The White House Bread Mixer is easiest to operate. It works so easy a child can operate it, either in a standing or sitting position. The White House Bread Mixer alone is worth the full price we ask for this outfit.

WE ALSO GIVE YOU, in addition to this White House Bread Mixer and Kneader, thirty-seven other valuable and useful articles, including a large Bread Box, Pastry Board, Wood Cabinet, Baking Tins, in fact every article that can be used in connection with a baking outfit. Read below; we give you the full list of the various items included in this mammoth assortment. Country agents and canvassers would ask you $5.00 for this Bread Mixer alone. We give you, in addition to this valuable piece, thirty-seven other useful articles which represent values which cannot be duplicated by your local dealer at double our prices.

THE LOW PRICES ON HARDWARE IN OUR LAST CATALOGUE ARE LOWER STILL IN THIS BOOK. OVER 3,000 HARDWARE ITEMS HAVE BEEN REDUCED.

No. 9K21995   White House Bread and Pastry Making Outfit (consisting of 38 pieces). Packed in a strong wood box. Shipping weight, about 50 pounds. Price...................... **$4.82**

1 White House Bread Mixer.	1 Forged Slotted Mixing Spoon.	1 Tin Muffin Pan, 12 Cups.
1 Set of 6 Patty Pans.	1 Egg Beater.	1 Retinned Scoop.
1 Tube Cake Pan, 8 inches.	1 Rolling Pin.	1 Serrated Edge Bread Knife.
6 Tin Pie Plates, 9 inches.	1 Tin Dipper, 1 quart.	2 Drip Pans, 10x12 inches.
1 Large Bread Box.	6 Tin Bread Pans, 10x6x3 inches.	1 Tin Graduated Measure, 1 quart.
1 Patent Rotary Flour Sifter.	1 Retinned Colander, 11½ inches.	

Additional items: 1 White Enameled Cup, 3 inches. 1 8-Drawer Wood Spice Cabinet. 1 Nutmeg Grater. 1 Set Biscuit, Cooky and Doughnut Cutters. 1 Large Bread or Pastry Board.

9C FAMILY SIZE, HOLT'S OR CYCLONE IMPROVED EGG OR CREAM BEATER. Just ask your dealer his lowest price.

Will whip a pint of cream fine in two to three minutes; beats eggs in twenty seconds. We guarantee it to beat eggs or whip cream in one-third the time of the best Dover beater. Is larger and stronger than the regular Dover beater, and has improved flaring dashers.
No. 9K26628   Family size. Length, 10½ inches. Price.............. 9c
No. 9K26629   Hotel size. Length, 12¼ inches. Price.............. 16c

4C FOR THIS EXTRA HEAVY RETINNED WIRE POTATO MASHER. 
Less than one-half dealers' price. Has hardwood handle, is well made and is the best masher on the market.
No. 9K26577   Price, each 4c

4C LARGE SIZE, FINE WIRE GAUZE ENAMELED HANDLE STRAINER.
The best strainer made. 
No.9K26607   Large, full size. Price.... 4c

4C EXTRA LARGE SIZE, TINNED WIRE HINGED TEA OR COFFEE BALL.
Complete with hinge and catch. Put the tea or coffee in the ball and drop it into the pot and boil in the usual way. You get the full strength of the tea or coffee without grounds or leaves, and no strainer is necessary.
No. 9K26613   Full size. Price....4c

ECONOMICAL STEAM COOKER, $4.87

AT THIS REDUCED PRICE YOUR SAVING IS GREATER THAN EVER.

CAN YOU AFFORD TO DO WITHOUT AN ECONOMICAL COOKER WHEN IT SAVES THREE TIMES ITS COST IN FUEL ALONE DURING THE YEAR?

YOU CAN COOK ONIONS, CABBAGE, POTATOES AND PUDDING in the Economical Cooker at the same time, and with less fuel than it would require to cook any one of them in the old way. Any combination of foods you desire can be cooked in this wonderful cooker with no danger of one smelling or tasting like another. The Economical Cooker is steam tight. The steam rises to the condensing dome at the top of the cooker, which is so constructed that the condensed steam runs back down the sides to the tank and does not drip on the food. It is impossible to burn or scorch food in the Economical Cooker, it requires but little attention, is equipped with whistle which begins to blow fifteen minutes before the tank boils dry, thus allowing ample time to refill the tank, and a self-regulating valve which holds the steam under pressure and makes it cook twice as quickly as the ordinary steam cooker. Food cooked in an Economical Steam Cooker loses nothing in evaporation, but retains all its savory juices.

THE ECONOMICAL STEAM COOKER is made of heavy XX (best grade) charcoal tin, has copper tank and with ordinary care will last a lifetime. It works equally well on wood, coal, oil, gas or gasoline stoves and has thick walls which retain the heat a long time after the fire is extinguished, thus keeping the food hot till it is ready to serve. The Economical has the greatest capacity of any cooker on the market. It is especially convenient for canning fruit. It will hold at one time a dozen 1-quart Mason jars, and cook the fruit perfectly. The Economical is easy to clean, and cuts the household work in half. The Economical Cooker has two swing doors, four compartments and we furnish with it two heavy seamless cooking pans. The Economical measures 12 inches square, 22 inches high and weighs, crated, about 20 pounds. Steam cookers that are in every way inferior to our Economical are sold by retailers and agents all over the country for from $8.50 to $10.00 each.

No. 9K23843   Economical Steam Cooker, complete with instruction book containing 200 tested recipes. Price.... **$4.87**

$2.08 FOR A 4-FOOT CRUCIBLE STEEL POND ICE SAW AND HANDLE.

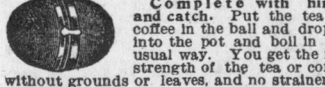

No. 9K29593   Sharpened and set. The best ice saw made.

Length, feet	4	4½	5
Price	$2.08	$2.43	$2.67

No. 9K29594   Extra Tiller Handles, for pond ice saws. Price........54c

51C DROP FORGED, FULL SIZE, WELL MADE SOLID STEEL ICE TONGS.

Our Ice Tongs are strictly first quality and are far superior to the tongs generally sold. The best size for family and wagon use; will easily handle a 200 pound block.
No. 9K29637   Price........51c

19C FOR AN ALUMINUM BOWL JAPANNED LEMON SQUEEZER.

Better than the 25-cent retail kind.

Japanned, with cast aluminum bowl to hold juice while squeezing. The best squeezer on the market. Not to be confused with the kind commonly offered.
No. 9K29682   Price........19c

THIS PAGE OF KITCHEN UTENSILS, LOW IN OUR LAST CATALOGUE, PRICED STILL LOWER NOW.

6c REFINED SMOOTH PLANISHED STEEL DRIPPING PANS, SIZE 7x10 INCHES.

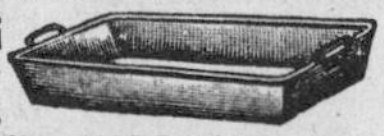

Made of heavy sheet, have wired edges and are nicely finished. State size wanted. 10x14 is the most popular size.

No. 9K23815

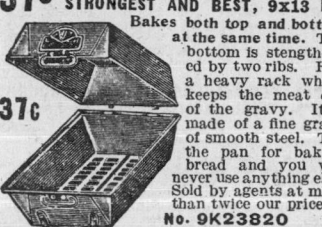

Size, in.	7x10	8x12	10x14	11x16	14x17
Price	6c	9c	12c	14c	17c

37c ACME COVERED ROASTING PAN, STRONGEST AND BEST, 9x13 IN.

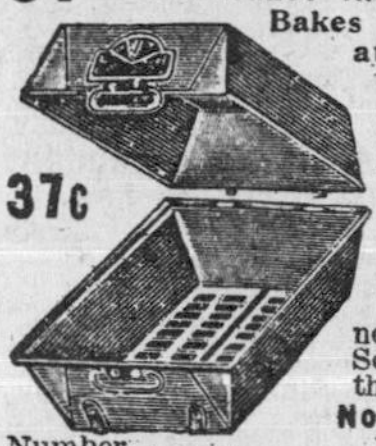

37c

Bakes both top and bottom at the same time. The bottom is stengthened by two ribs. Has a heavy rack which keeps the meat out of the gravy. It is made of a fine grade of smooth steel. Try the pan for baking bread and you will never use anything else. Sold by agents at more than twice our price.

No. 9K23820

Number	1	2	3	4
Width, inches	9	10	11	13
Length, inches	13	15	16	18
Height, inches	7½	7½	8½	9½
Price	37c	46c	54c	64c

25c FOR 12 ASSORTED ANIMAL CAKE CUTTERS.

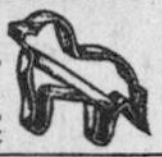

Just the thing for the children. Made of best IC tin.

No. 9K25038 Price, per dozen, assorted 25c

21c FOR 6 BEST GRADE TIN PASTRY CUTTERS.

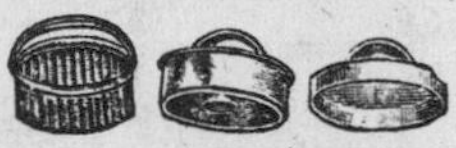

Consists of two biscuit, two doughnut and two cooky cutters. Well made, nicely finished.

No. 9K25043 Price, per set of six, 21c

9c PER SET CARD PARTY CAKE CUTTERS.

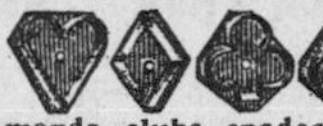

For cakes resembling the different denominations of cards, hearts, diamonds, clubs, spades.

No. 9K25050 Price, per set of four cutters 9c

8c FOR AN AUTOMATIC NUTMEG GRATER, SIMPLE, DURABLE AND ECONOMICAL.

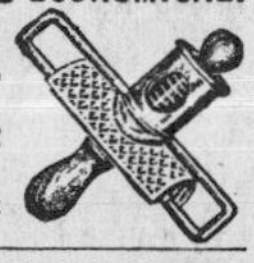

It will not clog, tear the fingers, nor drop the nutmeg. It grates very fine, and grates it all up, leaving no pieces.

No. 9K25119 Price, 8c

18c FOR A DOUBLE STEEL KNIFE COMBINED GRATER AND SLAW CUTTER.

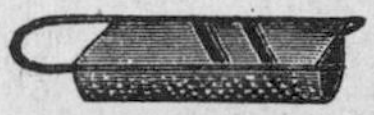

The slicer sheet is detachable. Two knives made of best quality of steel and can be resharpened.

No. 9K25126 Price 18c

52c ONE-PIECE SOLID CAST ALUMINUM HIGHLY POLISHED SOUP LADLE.

52c

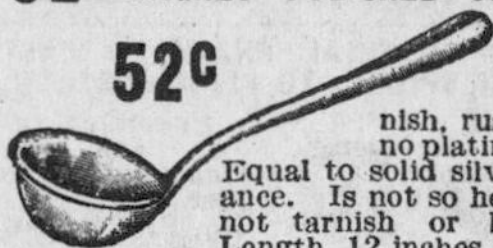

Strong, light and attractive. Will not tarnish, rust or corrode, no plating to wear off. Equal to solid silver in appearance. Is not so heavy and will not tarnish or become dull. Length, 12 inches.

No. 9K24646 Price 52c

8c FOR A SINGLE LOAF IDEAL BREAD PAN, MADE OF PLANISHED STEEL.

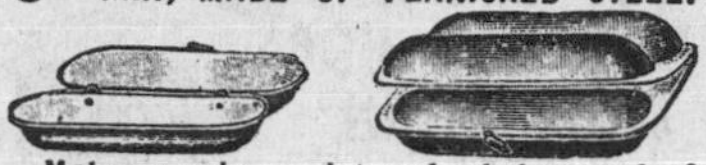

Makes a crisp, moist and wholesome loaf a certainty. It bakes evenly through and through. There is no danger of burning, and no special care is required. The crust is thin, smooth and even, and the loaf of beautiful shape, the bread is more nutritious, more tasty and more digestible.

		Size	Price
No. 9K25324	Double,	13⅝x10	18c
No. 9K25326	Single,	13⅛x5	8c

10c FOR AN 8-CUP SOLID FRAME HEAVY TIN MUFFIN PAN

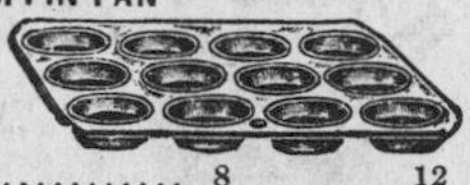

Size of cups, 3¼x1 inches.

No. 9K25396

Cups	8	12
Price	10c	16c

7c EXTRA HEAVY POLISHED TIN SANITARY BREAD PAN, No. 6.

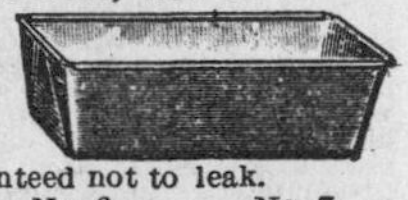

All corners and edges are rounded, no grease, dirt or dough can become embedded in them as in ordinary pans. Full wired. Guaranteed not to leak.

No. 9K25314	No. 6	No. 7
Size, inches	8½x4½x2¾	9½x4½x3½
Price, each	7c	9c
Per dozen	75c	90c
	No. 8	No. 9
Size, inches	10¼x6¼x2¾	11¼x7¼x2¾
Price, each	9c	$0.11
Per dozen	92c	1.15

7c FOR 12 ENAMELED COVER KNOBS, COMPLETE.

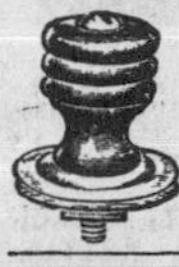

With washers and nuts. Anyone can apply. When ordering, state if wanted for tea kettle or coffee pot. Made of wood with tin flanges.

No. 9K25150

Price, per 100, 55c; per doz. 7c

17c EXTRA HEAVY IXXX POLISHED TIN GRADUATED QUART MEASURE.

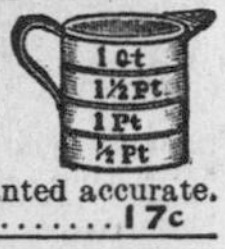

Made of the highest grade material heavily retinned. The best measure it is possible to produce. Will outlast a dozen of the light cheap kind. Especially recommended for dairymen, marketmen and family use. Warranted accurate.

No. 9K25163 Price 17c

$4.89 PRINCESS STOVE AND KITCHEN OUTFIT, 66 USEFUL ARTICLES $4.89

THIS COMPLETE ASSORTMENT CONTAINS MORE KITCHEN WARE THAN YOU CAN BUY IN A RETAIL STORE FOR DOUBLE OUR PRICE, AND THE PRICE IS EVEN LOWER THAN WE QUOTED IN OUR LAST CATALOGUE.

No inferior goods or seconds are included. Every article in this assortment is strictly high grade, and we guarantee the quality and size. Read the list of articles we furnish, note the copper bottom wash boiler, copper bottom tea kettle, coffee pot and tea pot, and the other large pieces, every one of the highest grade.

WE ARE ABLE TO OFFER these Princess assortments at the remarkably low prices we do because we sell thousands of them every year and are content to figure our profit on each outfit extremely low.

WE GUARANTEE EACH ITEM in the Princess outfit to be strictly high grade, full size and entirely satisfactory. Send us your order for one of these assortments, and if you are not entirely satisfied with it, ship it back to us and we will refund your money. The greatest value outfit of kitchen ware ever offered.

Three sizes, to fit No. 7, No. 8 and No. 9 stoves.

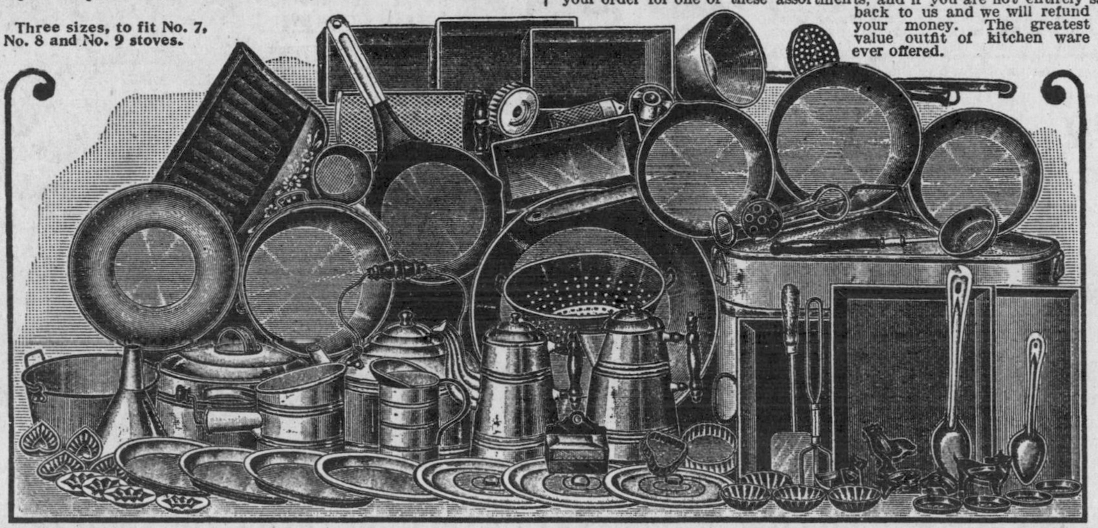

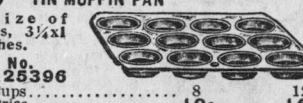

Each outfit contains:
- 1 IX Tin Wash Boiler, with flat copper bottom
- 1 IX Tin Tea Kettle, with flat copper bottom
- 1 IX Tin Coffee Pot, with copper bowl bottom and enameled wood handle
- 1 IX Tin Tea Pot, with copper bowl bottom and enameled wood handle
- 1 Retinned Wash Basin. 1 IX Tin Dipper, with heavy copper bottom
- 2 Heavily Retinned Preserving Kettles
- 1 Heavily Retinned Sauce Pan
- 2 Retinned Pudding Pans. 1 IC Tin Colander
- 1 Heavily Retinned Dishpan
- 1 IC Tin Steamer, with rimmed cover
- 4 Tin Pie Plates, 9 inches in diameter
- 3 Tin Bread Pans
- 1 Tin Oblong Pan
- 1 Deep Oblong Pan
- 1 Tin Measure, 1-quart size, graduated by one-half pints. 1 Tin Funnel
- 1 Tin Grater, with enameled wood handle
- 1 Retinned Soup Ladle, with enameled wood handle
- 1 Tin Gravy Strainer
- 10 Assorted Cake, Cooky, Biscuit and Doughnut Cutters.
- 1 Nutmeg Grater
- 1 Retinned Flat Handle Skimmer
- 1 Cake Turner with enameled wood handle
- 12 Assorted Tin Patty Pans
- 1 Patent Rotary Flour Sifter
- 1 Covered Japanned Dust Pan
- 2 Retinned Threaded Basting Spoons
- 1 Tinned Kitchen Fork, 3 prongs, length, 12½ inches
- 1 Dover Egg Beater
- 3 Assorted Tin Pot Covers, to fit kettles and saucepans.
- 1 Square Japanned Match Box
- 1 Polished Lipped Frying Pan, with always cool handle
- 2 Sheet Iron Dripping or Roasting Pans

Princess Stove and Kitchen Outfit for No. 7 Stove. Weight, 55 pounds.
No. 9K22037 Price, complete, as illustrated and described **$4.89**

Princess Stove and Kitchen Outfit for No. 8 Stove. Weight, 60 pounds.
No. 9K22038 Price, complete, as illustrated and described **$5.47**

Princess Stove and Kitchen Outfit for No. 9 Stove. Weight, 65 pounds.
No. 9K22039 Price, complete, as illustrated and described **$5.97**

9c SET OF 4 FULL SIZE BEST TIN PIE PLATES.

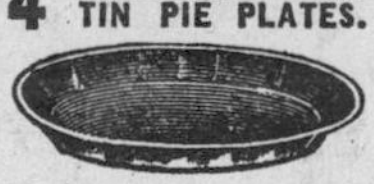

Made of good quality tin. Not the cheap light weight, easy to rust kind. 9 inches diameter, ⅞ inches deep, the popular size and the right kind to buy.

No. 9K25465 Price, per set of 4 .... 9c

6c SET OF 6 BEST TIN TART OR PATTY PANS.

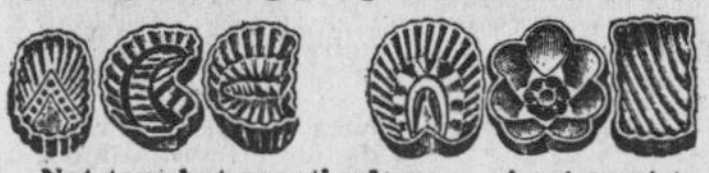

Not toys but practical pans. A set consists of one of each pattern shown in illustration; can also be used as individual jelly moulds.

No. 9K25494 Price, per set of 6 .... 6c

24c FOR 6 POT COVERS AND GALVANIZED RACK.

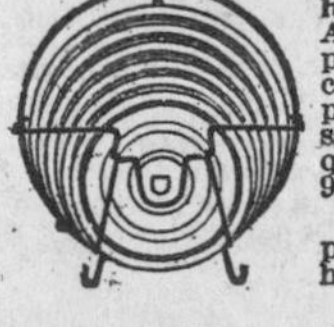

Handy outfit of one heavy galvanized wire holder and six pot covers. A cover to fit every size pot. Covers make food cook quicker and soon pay for themselves in saving of fuel. Good quality tin; one each 9, 9½, 10, 10½, 11, 11½-inch.

No. 9K25546 Price, per set, 6 covers and holder 24c

9c IXX TIN PLATE OLD RELIABLE HUNTER'S FLOUR SIFTER.

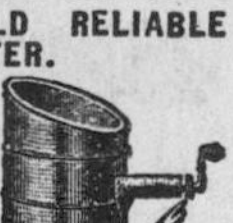

The genuine Hunter's flour sifter. Made of heavy tin plate. Also used as a scoop, measure or strainer.

No. 9K25529 Price.. 9c

19c THE FAVORITE SIFTER, HEAVILY NICKEL PLATED AND POLISHED.

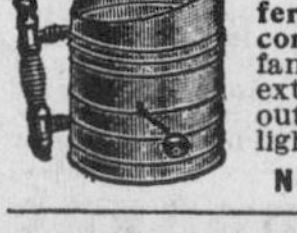

Well worth the slight difference in price we are compelled to charge. Has fancy enameled wood handle, extra strong and durable. Will outlast half a dozen cheap, light sifters.

No. 9K25533 Price. 19c

3c FOR THIS STEEL BLADE ENAMELED WOOD HANDLE CAKE TURNER.

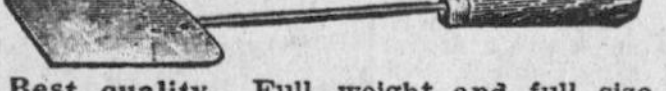

Best quality. Full weight and full size.

No. 9K25445 Price 3c

23c SET OF 4 LOOSE BOTTOM IXX CAKE PANS.

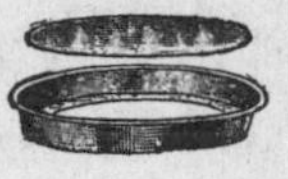

Made of good quality tin. 9 inches diameter, 1 inch deep. Prevents sticking and require no greasing.

No. 9K25505 Price, per set of 4 .... 23c

18c FOR THIS JAPANNED EXTRA HEAVY IXX TIN SHARP EDGE DUST PAN

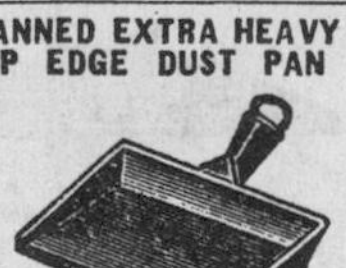

Rustproof handle well put on, can be hung on a nail when not in use. The best dust pan on the market. Built for wear, and will stand rough usage.

No. 9K26179 Price 18c

31c NICKEL PLATED CRUMB TRAY AND SCRAPER, POLISHED AND ETCHED.

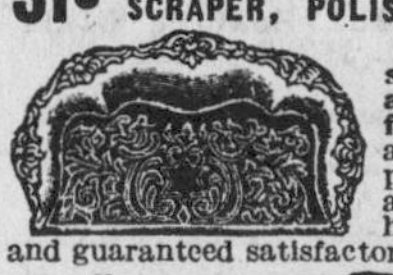

These trays and scrapers have the appearance of the finest silver. They are highly nickel plated and polished, are decorated in handsome designs and guaranteed satisfactory.

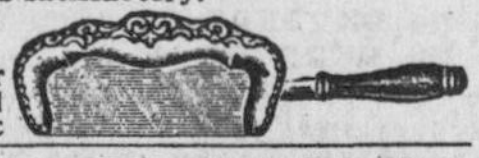

No. 9K26198 Price, for crumb tray and scraper .. 31c

11c FOR A JAPANNED OVAL TEA TRAY, 14 INCHES LONG.

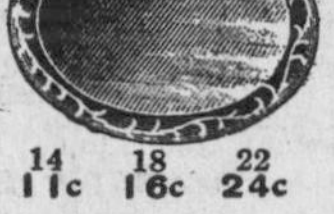

Has fancy scroll border decorated by hand, and is greatly superior in service to the light weight trays ordinarily sold. Well made of good material and nicely finished.

Length, inches	14	18	22
No. 9K26212 Price.	11c	16c	24c

8c RAT PROOF, MOUSE PROOF, AND DAMP PROOF METAL MATCH BOX HOLDER.

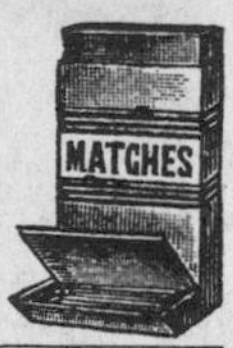

Holds full box of 200 matches. Made of heavy IXX tin plate. Nicely finished. Has sand paper to strike them on. Order one of these holders, put it up in a convenient place and stop groping around in the dark for a match.

No. 9K26055 Price, each 8c

6c RETINNED STEEL SLOTTED MIXING SPOON OR CAKE BEATER.

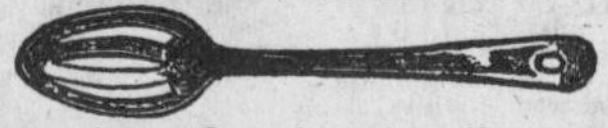

One piece. Smooth and easily cleaned. Length, 11½ inches.

No. 9K26552 Price 6c

17c HANDY KITCHEN SET, CONSISTING OF FORK, SPOON AND CAKE TURNER.

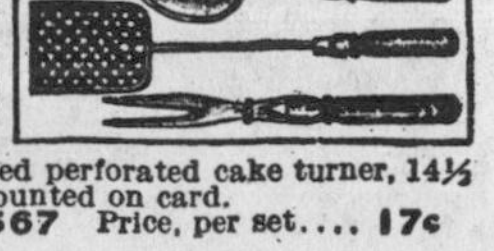

Consisting of one wood handle steel flesh fork, 11 inches long; one retinned wood handle basting spoon, 10¾ inches long, and one nickel plated perforated cake turner, 14½ inches long, mounted on card.

No. 9K26567 Price, per set 17c

IMPERIAL STOVE HOLLOW WARE.

No more dirty, smutty, greasy pots and kettles. Imperial Stove Hollow Ware is as easy to keep clean as china. It is made of smooth pure white porcelain and on the outside with mottled blue and white enamel, all of which is united with the cast iron at an intense heat, thereby forming a perfect union of the two, which no subsequent heating can destroy. It is pleasing in appearance, and we warrant every piece to give satisfaction. The numbers given designate the size of stove the article is intended for.

No. 7   No. 8   No. 9

74c   76c   78c

IMPERIAL ENAMELED CAST STOVE POTS.

White porcelain lined, mottled blue enamel on outside.

No. 9K23570

Number	7	8	9
Diameter at top, inches	9¼	10¾	11½
Depth, inches	6¾	7¾	8½
Price	74c	76c	78c

43c FOR IMPERIAL 4-QUART CAST IRON ENAMELED PRESERVING KETTLE.

Smooth as glass and as easy to clean as china. Ideal for preserving fruits, etc., as it is not affected by acids, does not stain and will not discolor anything cooked in it.

No. 9K23577

Capacity, quarts	4	6	8	10
Price	43c	53c	63c	68c
Capacity, quarts	12	16	20	24
Price	75c	98c	$1.23	$1.47

35c FOR IMPERIAL ENAMELED CAST IRON SPIDER, TO FIT No. 7 STOVE.

Enameled inside and out. Impossible to rust.

No. 9K23565

Number	7	8	9
Dimensions at bottom, inches	8½	9	9½
Price	35c	41c	44c

No. 7   No. 8   No. 9

67c   68c   69c

IMPERIAL ENAMELED CAST IRON KETTLES.

Easy to clean. Has heavy bail and enameled handle.

No. 9K23567

No.	Diam. at top	Depth inches	Price
7	9½ in.	6½	67c
8	10½ in.	7½	68c
9	11½ in.	8	69c

97c FOR IMPERIAL ENAMELED STOVE TEA KETTLE, TO FIT No. 7 STOVE.

Will not rust or discolor the water.

No. 9K23574

No.	Capacity	Price
7	5½ quarts	$0.97
8	6½ quarts	1.14
9	9 quarts	1.17

$1.19 PORCELAIN LINED IRON HAM OR WASH BOILER. SIZE No. 7.

Will not rust or discolor the clothes, and with ordinary care will last a lifetime. Size indicates the size stove it will fit.

No. 9K23585

Size	7	8	9
Length, inches	19	21½	24
Width, inches	9¾	11¾	13
Price	$1.19	$1.39	$1.65

$1.33 EXTRA HEAVY SUGAR OR WASH KETTLE, HOLDS 8 GALLONS.

Complete, with bails, milled and painted. The best kettle offered by anyone. We do not list "trade" sizes. Capacities given are actual.

No. 9K23776

Will Hold	Weight About	Price
8 gallons	30 lbs.	$1.33
14 gallons	42 lbs.	1.66
20 gallons	52 lbs.	2.37
27 gallons	85 lbs.	3.33

$6.23 FOR HAND MADE SEAMLESS 12-GALLON PURE COPPER KETTLE.

Made in the old fashioned way from one piece of pure copper. Will never rust; lighter than iron kettles and with proper use will last a lifetime.

No.	Size, gal.	Weight, about	Diam. on top	Depth, inside in.	Price
9K23780	12	21 lbs.	19 in.	13	$6.23
9K23782	16	23½ lbs.	20 in.	13¾	7.10
9K23786	20	29 lbs.	22 in.	14½	8.75
9K23787	25	31½ lbs.	23½ in.	15	9.45
9K23789	36	45 lbs.	26 in.	19	13.95

15c FOR ACME COLD HANDLE WROUGHT STEEL SEAMLESS FRYING PAN.

Large size, 11-inch top diameter, stamped from one piece steel. Full polished with side lip and cold handle. Flat bottom. Fit any stove.

No. 9K23830   Price.........15c

20c SEAMLESS UNBREAKABLE WROUGHT STEEL SKILLET WITH COLD HANDLE.

Large size, made of one piece solid unbreakable cold rolled steel, handle always cool, flat bottom, fits any stove. Diameter at top, 10½ inches.

No. 9K23833   Price.........20c

REGAL STOVE FURNISHING, KITCHEN AND LAUNDRY OUTFIT

THE GREATEST COMBINATION OF STOVE FURNISHINGS, HOUSEHOLD NECESSITIES AND KITCHEN UTENSILS EVER OFFERED FOR LESS THAN $10.00

$5.81   REDUCED PRICES MAKE YOUR SAVING GREATER THAN EVER

FOR ONLY $5.81 we will send you this mammoth assortment, each article guaranteed full size and the very best grade possible to make. It includes about everything necessary to equip your stove and to use about the kitchen and laundry. Read the list of articles carefully, note the enameled stove board, copper bottom wash boiler, set of sad irons, enameled ware utensils, cast iron pots and spiders, all of the highest grade. If you buy a cook stove or range from us, don't fail to include this set with your order, and if you buy the stove elsewhere, send us your order for this outfit anyway. There isn't an item in the set that is not needed from time to time in household work.

YOU SAVE MONEY by buying a complete outfit at one time. By selling forty items at once we are able to give you more for your money than if you bought each item separately. Instead of figuring a separate profit on each item in the set, we figure only one small profit on the entire lot. This Regal Outfit at $5.81 represents more real value than any assortment ever offered by anyone else at twice the price. We carry the Regal Outfit in three sizes to fit No. 7, No. 8 and No. 9 stoves. Each set contains the following items:

6 Stove Pipe, 6-inch	1 Jap. Coal Hod, 17-inch
1 Elbow, 6-inch	1 Stove Board, 30x30
1 Stove Pipe Damper, 6-in.	25 ft. Stove Pipe Wire
1 Pipe Collar, 6-inch	1 Polishing Mitten
1 Fire Shovel, 16-inch	1 Stove Brush
1 Fire Shovel, 22-inch	2 Boxes Stove Polish
1 Stove Lifter	3 Sensible Sad Irons (1 Sad
1 Bent Poker, 26-inch	Iron Handle, 1 Sad Iron
1 Straight Poker, 26-inch	Rest)
1 IX Copper Bottom Boiler	1 Acme Fry Pan
1 Enameled Steel Tea	1 Steel Drip Pan, 10x12
Kettle	1 Steel Drip Pan, 10x14
1 Enameled Steel Coffee Pot	1 Covered Roasting Pan,
1 Enameled Steel Teapot	11x16
1 Cast Iron Stove Pot	1 Match Safe
1 Cast Iron Spider	3 Pot Covers

Regal Stove Furnishing, Kitchen and Laundry Outfit for No. 7 stove. Weight, 100 pounds. No. 9K22022   Price, complete......... **$5.81**

Regal Stove Furnishing, Kitchen and Laundry Outfit for No. 8 stove. Weight, 105 pounds. No. 9K22023   Price, complete......... **$7.16**

Regal Stove Furnishing, Kitchen and Laundry Outfit for No. 9 stove. Weight, 110 pounds. No. 9K22024   Price, complete......... **$7.76**

ITEMS ON THIS PAGE PRICED LOW IN OUR LAST CATALOGUE, STILL FURTHER REDUCED NOW.

21c WROUGHT STEEL HINGED PANCAKE GRIDDLE, STRONG AND DURABLE.

Heats quickly and is lighter than any other griddle. The batter is first poured into the little round hinged pans. When done on the first side the round pans are turned over with a fork into the long pan, and while the cakes are finishing the round pans are refilled. Can bake six cakes a minute.

No. 9K23536   Price.........21c

64c FOR A BALL BEARING WAFFLE IRON. No. 8 STOVE SIZE.

No. 9K23712

Instantly taken apart for cleaning or greasing; fine, smooth castings, the best waffle irons made.

Size	8	9
Diameter, inches	7½	8½
Price	64c	78c

No. 9K23713   Waffle Irons. Exactly like the above, but without the ball bearing joint; otherwise this equal in every respect.

Size, inches	8	9
Price	53c	5 9

9c FOR EXTRA STRONG DOUBLE HANDLE STEEL STOVE SHOVEL.

Made extra strong. Unlike the cheap article ordinarily sold, the handle cannot be broken; it is hollow, of an oval shape, and fits the hand nicely; large, full size, 22 inches long.

No. 9K23381   Price.........9c

49c FOR CAST IRON JAPANNED ADJUSTABLE STOVE PIPE SHELF.

Cast iron, japanned is 18 inches square, made for 6-inch pipe. This shelf is complete in itself and is easily put up, raised and lowered. A heavy weight upon it only strengthens its grasp and assists in holding it in place, making it grip the pipe tighter.

No. 9K23374   Price.........49c

7c FOR BEST COLD HANDLE, NICKEL PLATED STEEL STOVE POKER.

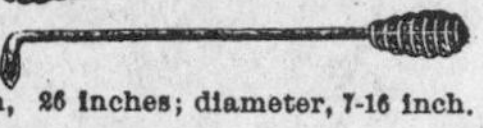

Extra Heavy, the kind that don't bend up when you want to use them. Length, 26 inches; diameter, 7-16 inch.

No. 9K23397   Straight. Price.........7c
No. 9K23398   Bent. Price.........7c

38c IMPROVED ADJUSTABLE CAST IRON FIRE BACK. FITS ANY STOVE.

Made from the very best quality of cast iron. It is so constructed that it can be adjusted either in width or height to the smallest fraction of an inch. Length adjusts from 14½ to 21 inches; the height, from 5 to 6½ inches.

No. 9K23495   Price.........38c

14c FOR THIS WELL MADE SHEEPSKIN POLISHING MITTEN AND DAUBER.

For polishing stoves, furniture, shoes, cleaning bicycles, etc. The finest polishing mitten made.

No. 9K23359   Price, for both.....14c

21c FOR 5 POUNDS

PLASTIC ASBESTOS STOVE LINING.

No. 9K23490 Composed of asbestos and other fireproof materials; is easily applied with a trowel and makes a durable and economical lining for cook stoves, useful for repairing broken brick or iron lining. Price, 5-pound pail, 21c; 10-pound pail, 41c

21c FOR 6 POUNDS

ACME FIREPROOF STOVE LINING CEMENT.

No. 9K23492 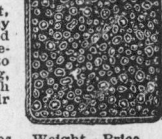 The Acme Stove Lining Cement for lining stoves, ranges, etc., and repairing old brick sets until it is burned. If directions are closely followed it will not crack or crumble. The 12-pound package will make a back. Full directions with each package so that no one can make a mistake. 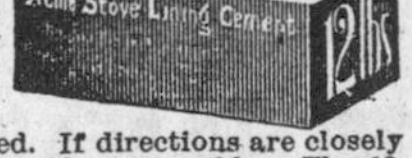
Price, per box, containing 6 pounds.........21c
Price, per box, containing 12 pounds.........39c

3c FOR THIS NICKEL PLATED COLD HANDLE STOVE LID LIFTER.

No. 9K23391   Price.............3c

62c MOSAIC ENAMELED STEEL STOVE BOARDS. SIZE, 26 INCHES SQUARE.

Not affected by heat, perfectly safe under any stove. Can be scrubbed like oilcloth and will retain their colors. Made to represent mosaic tiling, lined with wood, which makes them keep their shape.

No.	Size, inches	Weight	Price
9K23471	26 x 26	7½ lbs.	$0.62
9K23473	26 x 32	9½ lbs.	.72
9K23475	30 x 30	9½ lbs.	.80
9K23477	30 x 38	12½ lbs.	1.02
9K23478	36 x 36	12½ lbs.	1.13
9K23479	32 x 42	15½ lbs.	1.19

45c FOR COMPLETE NON-EXPLOSIVE SMOKELESS ALCOHOL STOVE.

For travelers, sick room, camp or nursery. Will boil a quart of water in nine minutes. Cannot explode. Is smokeless. Solid brass; nickel-plated.

No. 9K22830   Price.......45c

33c RUST PROOF, CRACK PROOF SOLID SPRING BRASS WASHBOARD.

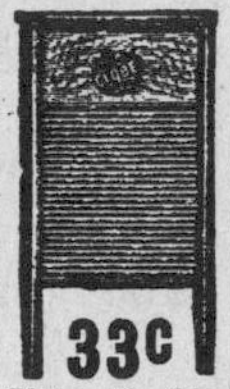

The rubbing surface is made of a sheet of hard spring brass; it will not corrode, crack or get out of shape; has the latest improved corrugated cable crimp and will do the washing with one-half the labor required on ordinary boards. It is not necessary to rub hard, the board will do the work. Has protector top and open back braced by bent truss rods so that rubbing surface can never sag.

No. 9K28085 Price 33c

The Old Reliable Banner Globe Double Washboard. Standard family size; double zinc surface; globe crimp on one side and plain crimp on the other; hardwood frame and stationary protector top; strong and well made.
No. 9K28090 Price 27c

Leader Washboard. Single zinc rubbing surface with globe crimp. Protector top. A strong and durable board at a small price.
No. 9K28096 Price 19c

43c FOR 100 FT. 1-4 INCH MANILA CLOTHES LINE.

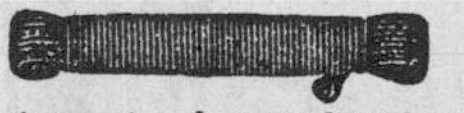

Manila Rope, ¼ inch diameter, 6-thread, makes the strongest and most durable clothes line you can get. 100 feet is the ordinary clothes line length.
No. 9K28101 Per 100 feet 43c

23c FOR GALVANIZED 100 FT. 6-WIRE REGULAR 50-CENT CLOTHES LINE.

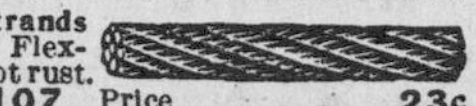

Made of six strands of No. 18 wire. Flexible, and will not rust.
No. 9K28107 Price 23c

33c FOR 6 DOZ. HOLD FAST CLOTHES PINS.

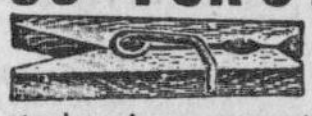

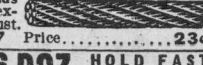

Will not tear the most delicate fabric. Easily removed when frozen to line. Has galvanized steel spring, warranted never to rust.
No. 9K28117 Price, per half gross .. 33c
Per gross 63c

58c PER BOX HARDWOOD CLOTHES PINS.

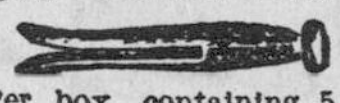

Full count. We do not sell less than a full box.
No. 9K28120 Per box, containing 5 gross 58c

11c FOR 4 HEAVY JAPANNED CLOTHES LINE HOOKS.

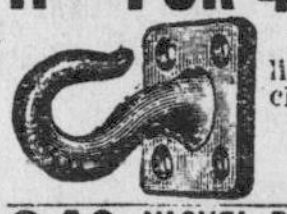

Rustproof, easy to slip line on hook. Screws not included.
No. 9K28125
Price, 4 for 11c

34c NICKEL PLATED SENSIBLE SLEEVE IRON, DETACHABLE HANDLE.

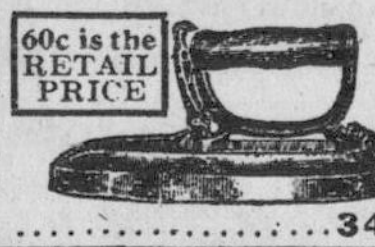

For laundering shirt waists and children's clothes. Will iron a plait or tuck to the seam. Weight, 4 pounds. Length, 8 inches.
No. 9K22059
Price 34c

87c SELF HEATING FAMILY CHARCOAL IRON.

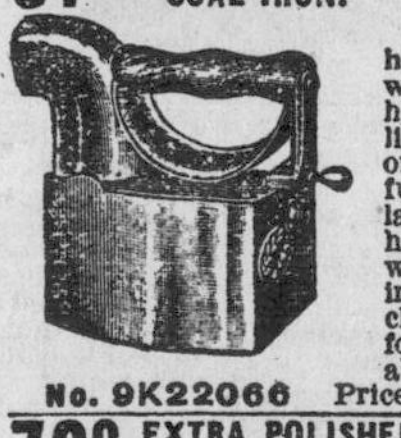

Removable top and hardwood handle with shield. Is self heating and requires little attention. Uses ordinary charcoal as fuel, is easily regulated to any desired heat and does away with the hot fire on ironing day. Agents charge $2.00 to $2.50 for this iron. Weight, about 7 pounds
No. 9K22066 Price 87c

70c EXTRA POLISHED FACE TAILORS' GOOSE, WEIGHT 12 POUNDS.

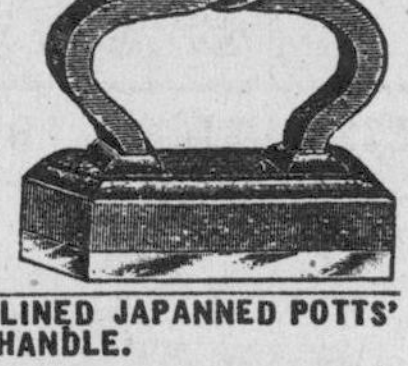

Well made and nicely balanced. Better than the kind others sell for 10c to 15c per lb.
No. 9K22070
Weight, 12 lbs. Price 70c
Weight, 16 lbs. Price 95c
Weight, 20 lbs. Price $1.18

9c ASBESTOS LINED JAPANNED POTTS' SAD IRON HANDLE.

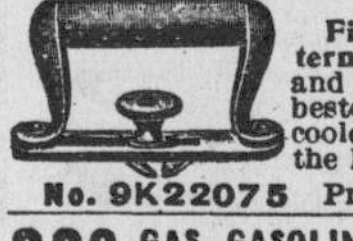

Fits any Mrs. Potts' pattern Sad Irons; is all steel and cannot be broken. Asbestos insulated and the coolest handle made. Fits the hand.
No. 9K22075 Price 9c

22c GAS, GASOLINE OR OIL STOVE SAD IRON HEATER.

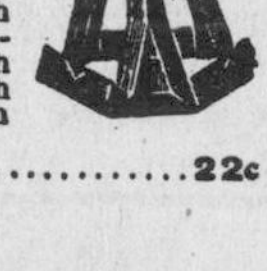

Will save fuel enough in a short while to pay for itself. Heats three irons at one time and will keep two rapid ironers supplied with hot irons. The heat coming in direct contact with the irons heats them much faster than can be done on heaters with closed sides.
No. 9K22085 Price 22c

$2.49 EXTRA HEAVY HIGH GRADE POLISHED SOLID COPPER WASH BOILER No. 8.

THE BEST WASH BOILER ON THE MARKET AT ANY PRICE.

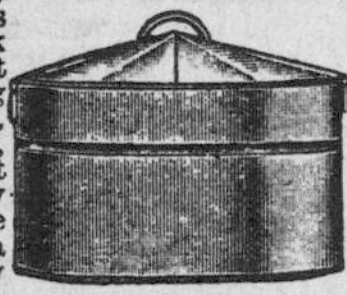

Will outlast half a dozen ordinary tin boilers. Because our price is 50 cents to $1.50 less than others ask for solid copper wash boilers, don't think the goods are not A1. Buying material in immense quantities, manufacturing the boilers ourselves, using the latest labor saving cost reducing machines, and adding only one small percentage of profit, we are enabled to offer them to you at a lower price than most jobbers pay for light inferior goods.

OUR ACME solid copper wash boilers are made of the best grade of heavy planished sheet copper, tinned inside and have heavy tin covers. They have flat copper bottoms, well riveted drop handles; are wired around the top and double seamed in such a manner they will never leak. All these details add to the original cost of manufacture, but no boiler is perfect that is made any other way.

WE GUARANTEE EVERY ACME SOLID COPPER WASH BOILER

we send out to be perfect in material and workmanship, not to leak and to give entire satisfaction. You take no risk in ordering a wash boiler from us; if it is not exactly what we claim it to be, or if it is not equal to boilers others ask $3.50 to $4.50 for, ship it back at our expense and your money will be promptly returned to you together with the amount of freight you had to pay.

No. 9K25007 No. 8, size 10¼x20½ inches. Weight, 6½ pounds. Price $2.49
No. 9, size 11½x22 inches. Weight, 8 pounds. Price 2.68

NOTE—Some wash boilers are sold that are not full size. No. 9 boilers are offered that are no larger than our No. 8. Our goods are full size, full weight and the best quality.

For the best line of clothes wringers sold by any house in the world, see page 588 of this catalogue.

71c IX TIN COPPER BOTTOM WASH BOILER, SIZE No. 7.

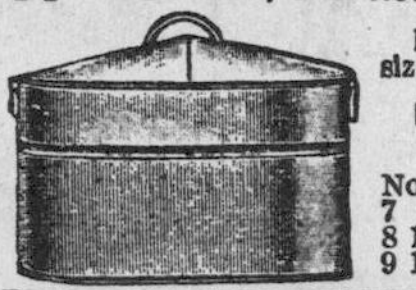

Flat bottom, full sizes. Drop handles.

No. 9K25000

No.	Inches	Weight lbs.	Price
7	9½x18½	5	71c
8	10¼x20¼	5½	77c
9	11½x22	6½	88c

$1.04 COPPER RIM AND BOTTOM IX TIN WASH BOILER, SIZE No. 8.

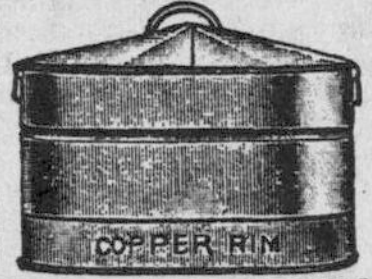

IX Tin top and cover, flat bottoms, full sizes. Drop handles.

No. 9K25002

No.	Inches	Weight lbs.	Price
8	10¼x20¼	6	$1.04
9	11½x22	6¾	1.24

39c OUR IDEAL CLEANER. EQUAL TO A WASHING MACHINE. OVER 1,000 DOZEN SOLD BY US LAST YEAR.

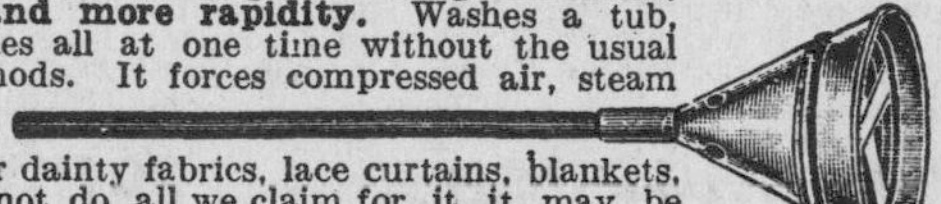

Does washing equal to any large washing machine, but with greater ease and more rapidity. Washes a tub, pail or boiler full of clothes all at one time without the usual wear and tear of old methods. It forces compressed air, steam and water through the clothes, quickly removing all dirt. Has no equal for dainty fabrics, lace curtains, blankets, woolens, etc. If it does not do all we claim for it, it may be returned and money will be refunded. Made of the best tin.
No. 9K2154 Price, per dozen, $4.40; each 39c

78c FOR A SET OF 3 MRS. POTTS' SAD IRONS, DETACHABLE HANDLE AND STAND, COMPLETE.

Bargain price elsewhere, 98 cents. Our price, per set, 78c
YOU SAVE MONEY WHEN YOU BUY HARDWARE OF US.

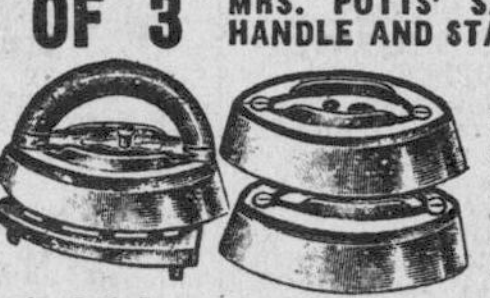

Set consists of one iron with rounded end, for polishing, weight, 4 pounds; two with regular ends, one weighing 5½ pounds and one 5⅜ pounds; one detachable wood handle, always cool, and one iron stand.

No. 9K22045 Mrs. Pott's Sad Irons, in sets of three, with detachable wood handle and iron stand, as above; finely polished. Packed one set in a box. Price, per set 78c

96c FOR A COMPLETE SET NICKEL PLATED POLISHED SENSIBLE SAD IRONS.

A handsome outfit, consisting of three highly nickel plated and polished solid sad irons, ground by perfect machinery, which makes every iron true; face shaped to make ironing easier than with the old style irons. These solid irons hold the heat longer than the ordinary Mrs. Potts' irons. The handle is the strongest and best

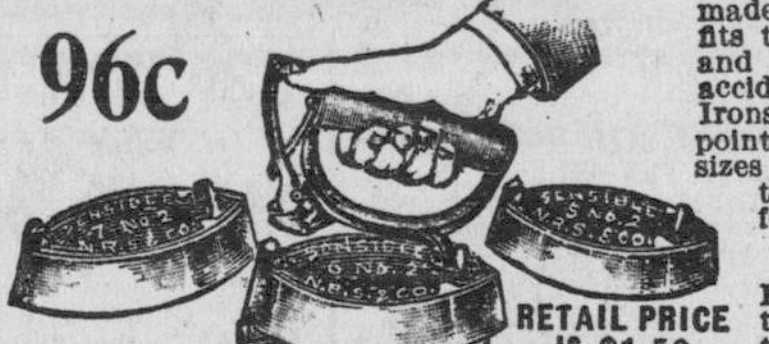

made; will not shake, fits the hand perfectly and cannot become accidentally detached. Irons are double pointed, one each, sizes 5, 6 and 7, just the right weights for family use.

No. 9K22056 Price, per set of three irons, detachable handle and stand ... 96c

55c CLOTHES LINE REEL OR DRYER. SUBSTANTIAL AND CONVENIENT.

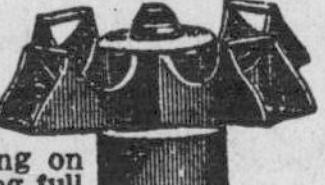

Has a socket which fastens over the top of a post. The reel revolves on this socket and is made for four bars. From 100 to 200 feet of line can be strung on bars and this can be hung full of clothes without moving basket. Bars not included.
No. 9K28035 Price 55c

97c FOLDING UMBRELLA CLOTHES BAR WITH 16 HARDWOOD ARMS.

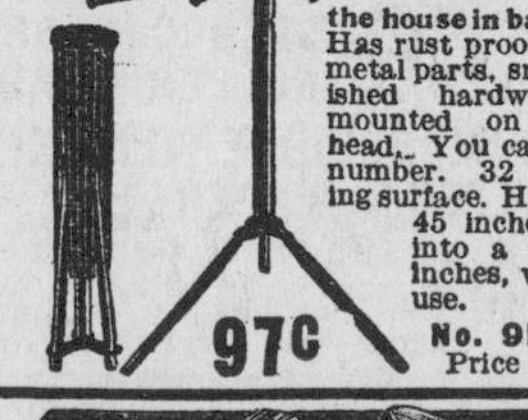

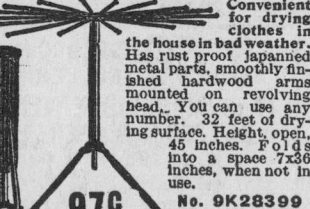

Convenient for drying clothes in the house in bad weather. Has rust proof japanned metal parts, smoothly finished hardwood arms mounted on revolving head. You can use any number. 32 feet of drying surface. Height, open, 45 inches. Folds into a space 7x36 inches, when not in use.
No. 9K28399
Price 97c

$1.24 ADJUSTABLE FOLDING CURTAIN STRETCHER AND QUILTING FRAME

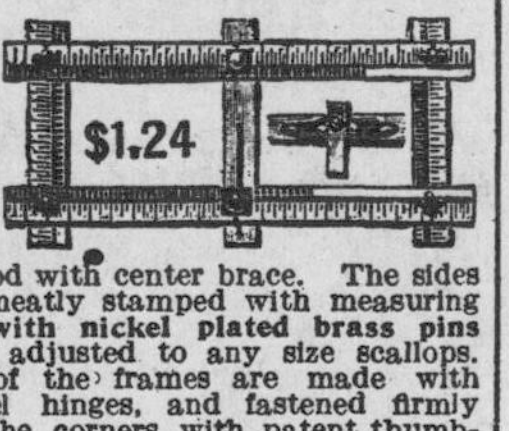

Finest frame made. Extends 6x12 feet, and will hold any ordinary size curtain. Made of choice 2-inch selected white basswood with center brace. The sides and ends are neatly stamped with measuring rule, fitted with nickel plated brass pins which can be adjusted to any size scallops. Connections of the frames are made with stamped steel hinges, and fastened firmly together at the corners with patent thumbscrews. When folded occupies the smallest amount of space. Usually retails for $2.00.
No. 9K28465 Price $1.24

Extends to 6x12 feet and will hold any curtain; made of 1⅜-inch stock with center brace, very light and strong. Rods stamped with measuring rule. Has nickel plated stationary pins 1 inch apart. For center connections of frames we use a stamped steel plate hinge; fastened to side rails by bolts. Can be folded into the smallest possible space when not in use.
No. 9K28461 Price 73c

$1.63 FOR A COMPLETE SET OF FINE HOUSEHOLD CLEANING BRUSHES.

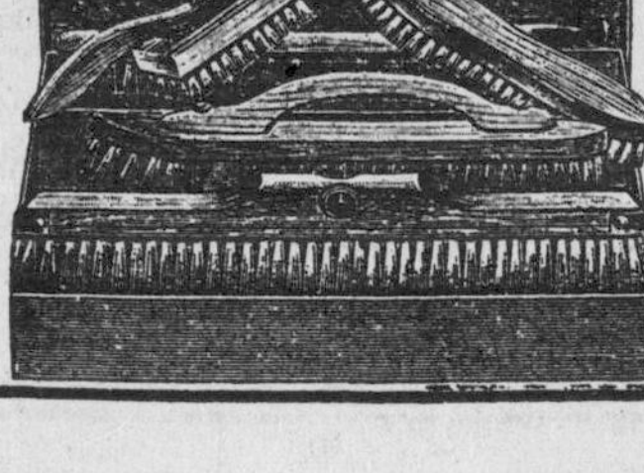

The greatest brush value ever offered, each article is the very best quality. Includes, 1 large bristle floor or sweeping brush with handle, worth retail $1.50; 1 good quality dusting brush, retailing at 50 cents; 1 scrub brush, retailing at 10 cents; 1 handy brush, retailing at 10 cents and 1 curved back stove brush, retailing at 25 cents. We pack the above assortment in a paper carton as illustrated. Cannot be duplicated in any retail store for less than $2.45. Order a set and end your brush troubles.
No. 9K22949 Price, complete $1.63

WE HAVE ALWAYS SOLD
GOOD HARDWARE
FOR LOWER PRICES THAN ANY OTHER HOUSE.
On over 3,000 hardware items PRICES ARE
STILL FURTHER REDUCED
IN THIS CATALOGUE.

77c FOLDING IRONING BOARD, ADJUSTABLE TO 3 DIFFERENT HEIGHTS.

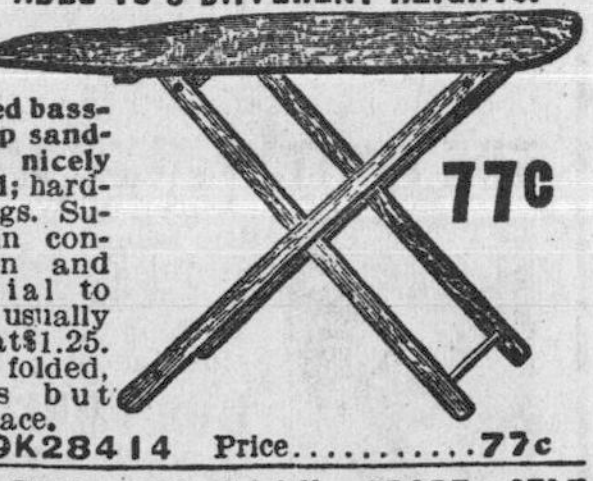

Selected basswood top sanded and nicely finished; hardwood legs. Superior in construction and material to boards usually offered at $1.25. When folded, occupies but little space.
No. 9K28414 Price 77c

27c FULL SIZE HIGH GRADE SELF WRINGING MOP.

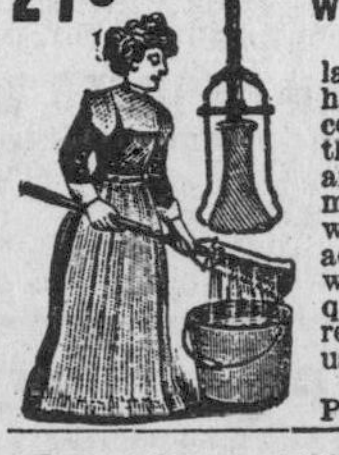

Made of cotton coils, large and full size. The hands do not come in contact with the water, the mop being wrung at arm's length. This permits using scalding water, which is an important advantage as the floor washes easier, cleaner and quicker and dries more readily when hot water is used.
No. 9K22120
Price 27c

10c FOR A MONARCH LARGE STIFF FIBER SCRUB BRUSH.

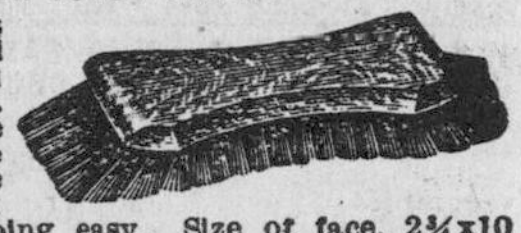

Reaches into and cleans all corners. Just the right shape to fit the hand and make scrubbing easy. Size of face, 2¾x10 inches. Solid back. Palmetto fiber.
No. 9K22910 Price 10c

19c TAMPICO AND RUBBER COMBINED SCRUB BRUSH AND SCRAPER.

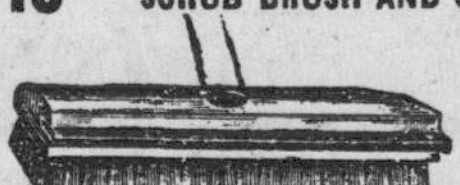

Size of block 11x3 inches, filled with best Mexican tampico with rubber scraper inserted in side.
No. 9K22920 Price 19c

3c WHITE TAMPICO HANDY HOUSE BRUSH WITH HANDLE. THE 10c KIND.

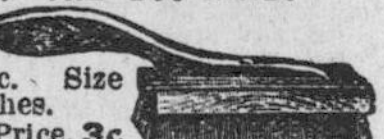

For scrubbing vegetables, cleaning wash basins, etc. Size of block, 4½x1¼ inches.
No. 9K22923 Price, 3c

13c CURVED BACK BEST TAMPICO STOVE BRUSH, HARDWOOD BACK.

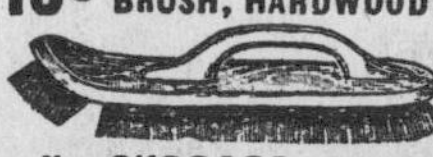

Five rows well filled with good stock. Varnished back. Length, 12½ inches
No. 9K22932 Price 13c

34c FOR A SELECTED BRISTLE OBLONG WINDOW BRUSH.

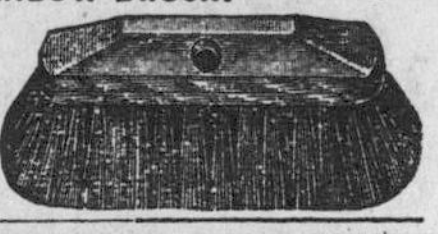

Length of block, 8½ inches; 7 rows bristles 2 inches long. Handle not furnished.
No. 9K22943
Price 34c

63c SELECTED BRISTLE FLOOR BRUSH, COMPLETE WITH HANDLE.

THE REGULAR $1.00 KIND.

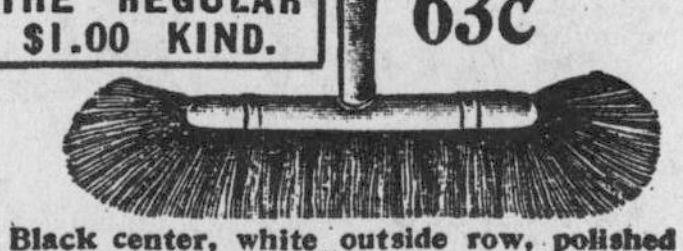

Black center, white outside row, polished back, best for hardwood or painted floors. Not suitable for use on carpets.
No. 9K22950

Length, inches	12	14	16
Price	63c	78c	$1.00

28c EXTRA HIGH GRADE COUNTER DUST BRUSH, GRAY AND WHITE.

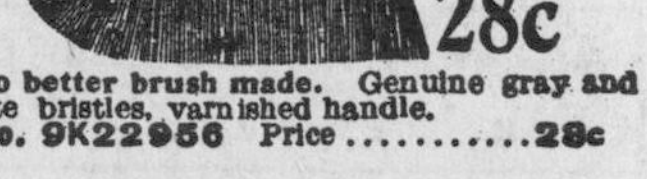

No better brush made. Genuine gray and white bristles, varnished handle.
No. 9K22956 Price 28c

69c FOR THE IMPROVED PURITAN CHOPPER COMPLETE WITH FOUR CUTTERS AND COOK BOOK

THE CHOPPER THAT SAVES YOU MONEY. THE ONLY ONE YOU CAN'T AFFORD TO DO WITHOUT.

THE BEST AND MOST CONVENIENT CHOPPER on the market at anything like our price. Chops all kinds of raw or cooked meats, vegetables, fruits, etc. Each size chopper has three hand forged steel knives or cutters: coarse, medium and fine for meats and vegetables, and one nut butter cutter.

THE IMPROVED PURITAN FOOD CHOPPER is made of the finest material throughout, each working part is carefully finished so it will run smoothly and all exposed parts are heavily retinned, which makes it rustproof, easy to clean and sanitary. It is as carefully constructed as if intended to sell for twice the price. Simple, has few parts, and does the most satisfactory work in half the time usually required by other choppers.

THE PURITAN possesses all the good features found in other choppers with several valuable improvements of its own. It has a perfect drip spout which catches and saves the juice and prevents soiling the table or floor. It has an improved table clamp which holds fast. It quickly chops all kinds of food, meat, vegetables, fruit, etc., fine or coarse, and does not choke up. It is so easy to operate that a 10-year old girl can easily turn it. It is strong, durable and substantial, and with ordinary care will last a number of years.

OUR PURITAN FOOD CHOPPER will pay for itself in a short time by making it possible to utilize cold meats, "left overs," etc. We furnish with each Puritan Chopper a copy of our Puritan Food Chopper Cook Book which contains over 200 tested recipes and explains how to save time, labor, money and food by using a Puritan Chopper.

EVERY PURITAN CHOPPER WE SELL is covered by our regular guarantee of "satisfaction or your money back." We recommend Size 1 for general family use.

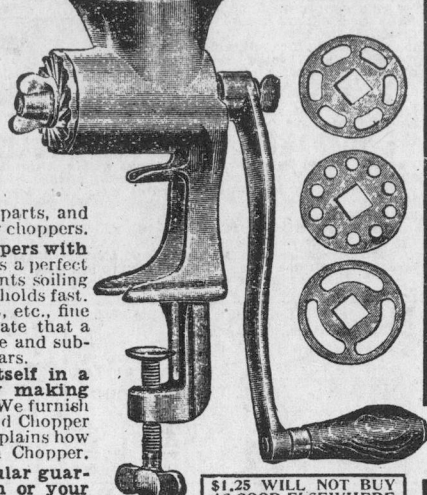

$1.25 WILL NOT BUY AS GOOD ELSEWHERE

No.	Size		Price
No. 9K29500	Size 0, chops 1¾ pounds meat per minute, 2⅜x2¾-inch hopper.	Price	$0.69
No. 9K29503	Size 1, chops 2 pounds meat per minute, 2½x3 -inch hopper.	Price	.87
No. 9K29504	Size 2, chops 2½ pounds meat per minute, 3 x4 -inch hopper.	Price	1.05
No. 9K29505	Size 3, chops 3½ pounds meat per minute, 4 x5 -inch hopper.	Price	1.37

ENTERPRISE FOOD CHOPPERS.

Cut like a pair of scissors; do not tear, grind or squeeze the meat; impossible for any strings, sinews or gristle to pass through without being chopped. The Enterprise can be taken apart in a few seconds and is easily cleaned. All parts are interchangeable and can be replaced at small cost. Knives and plates are made of finest steel and fully warranted.

96c BRONZE BEARING EASY TURNING ENTERPRISE FOOD CHOPPER.

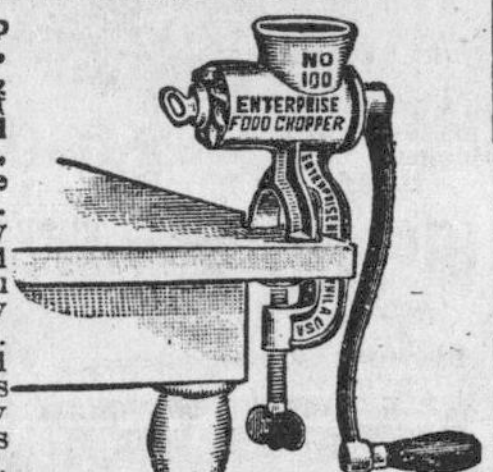

It will chop raw meat, cooked meat, vegetables of all kinds, bread and crackers, and will make peanut butter. It will chop any kind of food any size you wish for any kind of dish. Can be cleaned in a minute, is always ready and never gets out of order. Four knives, one each, fine, medium and coarse, and nut butter cutter furnished with each machine. The phosphor bronze bearing reduces the friction, makes the machine easier to turn and last much longer. Will chop two pounds of meat per minute.
No. 9K29502 Price............96c

$1.65 GENUINE ENTERPRISE TINNED ROTARY KNIFE FOOD CHOPPER.

Chops exactly as shown. The meat is fed into the hopper, and by the feed screws carried forward and forced into the plate, where it is cut off by the revolving knife. Small family size, with clamp (No. 5), chops 1½ pounds per minute.
No. 9K29506 Price............$1.65

$2.45 FOR A LARGE FAMILY SIZE ENTERPRISE MEAT CHOPPER.

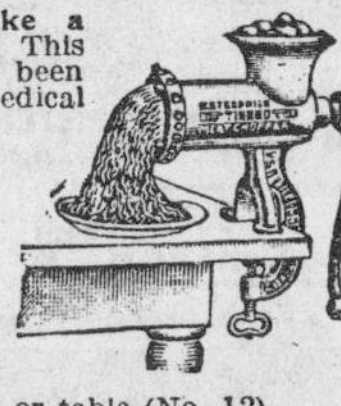

Cuts meat like a pair of scissors. This chopper has been adopted by the Medical Department of the United States army. With clamp (No. 10), chops 3 pounds per minute.
No. 9K29507 Price....$2.45
Same as above except with legs to screw to bench or table (No. 12).
No. 9K29508 Price............$2.24

Sausage Stuffing Attachments for Enterprise Meat Choppers.

Have new patented corrugated spout, prevents air entering casing, thus preserving the sausage. Made of spun brass, nickel plated. Made in two sizes of tube, namely: ¾ inch and 1¼ inches. When ordering, be sure to give number of chopper.

No. 9K29516 Price, with ¾-inch tube.		To fit chopper—		
No. 5	No. 10	No. 22	No. 32	No. 232
40c	43c	45c	55c	63c	65c

Price, with 1¼-inch tube. To fit chopper—				
No. 5	No. 10	No. 12	No. 22	No. 32	No. 232
65c	63c	72c	75c	$1.00	$1.05

$3.68 BUYS THIS HOTEL SIZE ENTERPRISE MEAT CHOPPER.

Noiseless, easy to turn, rapid. Absolutely chops everything that passes through. With legs to screw to table or bench (No. 22), chops 4 pounds per minute. Weight, 12 pounds.
No. 9K29509 Price............$3.68
Butchers' Size Enterprise Meat Chopper, with legs to screw to table or bench (No. 32), chops 5 pounds per minute. Weight, 18 pounds.
No. 9K29510 Price............$4.90

$7.93 BUTCHER'S SIZE MEAT CHOPPER WITH FLY WHEEL.

Does not heat or discolor the meat, is easy to turn, noiseless, and will cut any size desired. (No. 232), chops 5 lbs. per minute; weight, complete, 38 lbs.
No. 9K29512 Price....$7.93

Warranted Steel Knives for Enterprise Meat Choppers.

Made of best quality material, are sharp and nicely finished. Be sure to give number of chopper for which the knife is wanted.

No. 9K29517 Price, to fit chopper—				
No. 5	No. 10	No. 12	No. 22	No. 32	No. 232
23c	26c	29c	43c	65c	67c

Steel Plates for Enterprise Meat Choppers.

When ordering, be sure to give size holes and number of chopper for which the plate is wanted. The plate having 3-16-inch holes is most commonly used, and is what is furnished with choppers.
No. 9K29518 With 3-16, ¼, 5-16, or ⅜-inch holes. Price, to fit chopper—

No. 5	No. 10	No. 12	No. 22	No. 32	No. 232
30c	43c	45c	65c	90c	92c

8c BRONZED 5-INCH SINGLE ARM FLOWER POT BRACKET.

No. 9K22500 Strong enough to hold any flower pot not over 4 inches across the bottom. Shelf 4 inches in diameter. Price....8c

28c ENAMELED DOUBLE SHELF 12-INCH ARM FLOWER POT BRACKET.

No. 9K22510 Nicely finished, an ornament to any home. Diameter of dishes, one 4 inches and one 4¾ inches inside. Price............28c

58c ENAMELED 12-INCH DOUBLE ARM 4-POT BRACKET.

No. 9K22515 These brackets are well made, strong and substantial. Diameter of dishes, two 4 inches and two 4¾ inches inside, complete, as shown. Price............58c

$1.74 FOR A HIGH GRADE LEADER CARPET SWEEPER.

It has broom action, reversible bail, improved dumping device, the new improved braid band which never comes off, strictly pure bristle brush, handsomely finished case. The metal parts are japanned finish.
No. 9K22300 Price............$1.74

74c FOR A FAMILY SIZE JAPANNED IRON SAUSAGE STUFFER.

No. 9K29531 Size 1, for families. Price......74c
No. 9K29530 Size 0, for butchers. Price....$1.03

96c FOR THIS RUSTPROOF SPEEDY RAILROAD SAUSAGE STUFFER.

The castings are heavy and nicely japanned. Barrel is made of heavy tin plate. Suitable for family and hotel use. Capacity, 3½ pounds.
No. 9K29533 Price............96c

$1.37 FOR A 2-QUART SIZE LARD, WINE AND JELLY PRESS.

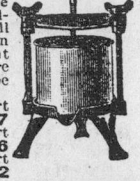

Made with special reference to strength and guaranteed against breakage under any fair usage. Cylinders are heavy tin and all parts tinned all over. Can be taken apart in a moment for cleaning. All parts are interchangeable and can be replaced.
No. 9K29538 2-quart size. Price............$1.37
No. 9K29539 4-quart size. Price............$2.76
No. 9K29540 10-quart size. Price............$4.12

$3.04 ENTERPRISE SAUSAGE STUFFER LARD AND FRUIT PRESS.

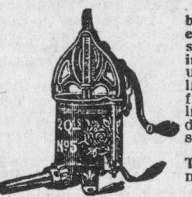

Unexcelled for butchers' or farmers' use for stuffing sausages and pressing lard. For kitchen use there is nothing like it for pressing fruit for making jellies, wine, etc. Full directions for use are sent with each press.
No. 9K29523 Two-qt. size, japanned, rack movement. Price....$3.04

$4.05 SCREW MOVEMENT ENTERPRISE STUFFER AND PRESS.

Used as a sausage stuffer, lard press, jelly press and wine press.
No. 9K29524 Four-quart size, japanned. Weight, 30 pounds. Price............$4.05
No. 9K29525 Eight-quart size, japanned. Weight, 44 pounds. Price....$5.68

$1.97 GENUINE BISSELL'S IMPROVED CHAMPION CARPET SWEEPER.

A high grade sweeper at a very low price. It has the Bissell broom action, reversible bail, new improved braid band furniture protector which never comes off. Bissell's new improved spring dumping device, pure bristle sweeping brush, handsomely finished case. All metal parts are nicely japanned.
No. 9K22305 Price............$1.97

LOW PRICES IN OUR LAST CATALOGUE STILL FURTHER REDUCED IN THIS BOOK ON OVER 3,000 HARDWARE ITEMS MAKE YOUR SAVING GREATER THAN EVER.

OUR MONEY SAVING PRICES ON HARDWARE STILL FURTHER REDUCED IN THIS BOOK.

68c FOR A RUSTPROOF, MASHPROOF, PERFECT CHERRY STONER.

Does not crush the cherry or cause any loss of juice; a perfect machine for large, small or California cherries. The seed extracting knife drives the seeds into one dish and throws the cherries into another. The mark of the knife can scarcely be seen on the seeded fruit. It seeds from 20 to 30 quarts per hour. Heavily tinned to prevent rust.

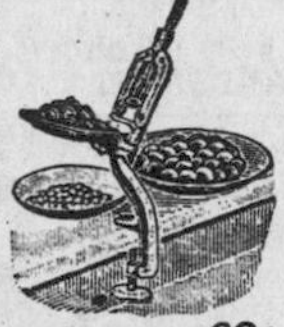

No. 9K22170 Price............68c

94c FOR AN ENTERPRISE, ADJUSTABLE, RAPID RAISIN AND GRAPE SEEDER.

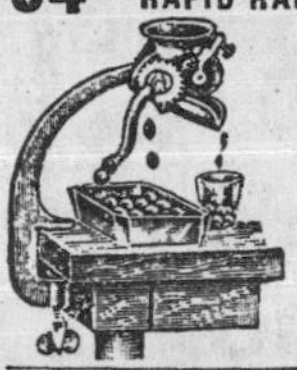

Simply constructed, adjustable to any size fruit, and does neat, clean work rapidly. Seeds raisins wet or dry, grapes for preserving purposes, and is the most satisfactory machine of its kind on the market. Will seed a pound in five minutes.

No. 9K22175 Price............94c

51c FOR AN ECONOMICAL VERMONT POTATO PARER AND EYE CLEANER.

Useful every day in the year in every household. Pares any shape or kind of potato better and easier than can be done by hand. By taking a thinner paring, saves at least 50 per cent of the outside of the potato that is ordinarily wasted. Very simple and durable. Also suitable for quinces and pears.

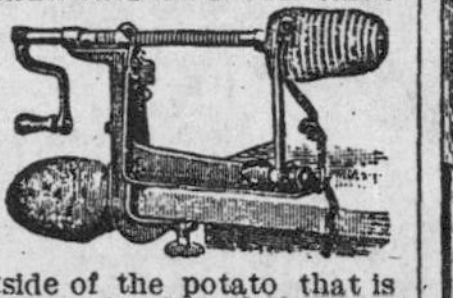

No. 9K22180 Price............51c

43c VERMONT APPLE PARER, WITH SLICING AND CORING ATTACHMENT.

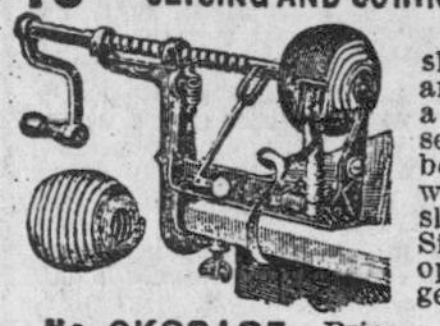

Pares, cores and slices the fruit, and pushes off apple and core separately, or can be used to pare without coring and slicing if desired. Simple and easy to operate. Cannot get out of order.

No. 9K22185 Price............43c

53c SIMPLEX HIGH SPEED, AUTOMATIC APPLE PARER, RAPID AND STRONG.

Pares very close to both ends of the apple, but does not core or slice. All parings fall clear of the machine. Has automatic push off, and after paring knife recedes so as to leave room to place another apple on the forks. Very rapid and strong and the best to use where paring only is desired.

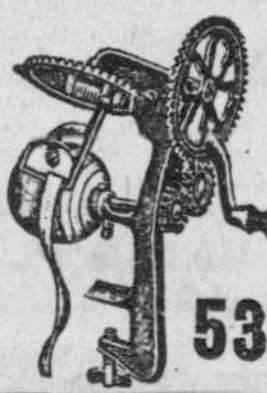

53c

No. 9K22190 Price............53c

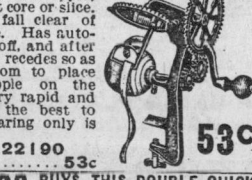

63c BUYS THIS DOUBLE QUICK APPLE PARER, SIMPLE AND SWIFT.

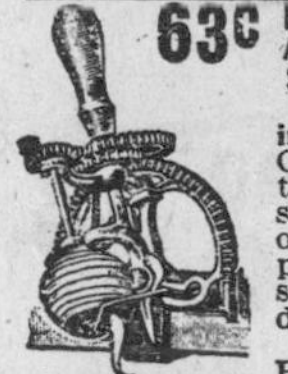

The most rapid hand paring machine in the world. One forward movement of the hand pares an apple from stem to blossom. A return of the handle pushes the apple off of the fork. Very simple, yet strongly built; does not core or slice.

No. 9K22195 Price............63c

14c COMBINED FRUIT AND VEGETABLE PRESS AND POTATO MASHER.

Useful for a variety of purposes. Is especially recommended for mashing potatoes. It is not necessary to peel the potatoes as it mashes and removes the skin of boiled potatoes in one operation.

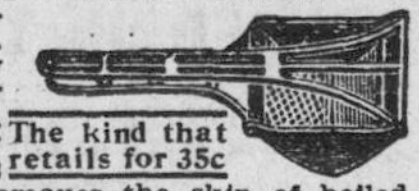

The kind that retails for 35c

No. 9K22125 Price............14c

$2.77 STRONG, SUBSTANTIAL FRUIT, WINE AND JELLY PRESS.

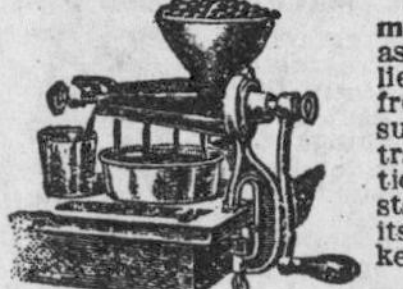

Can be used for many purposes, such as making wines, jellies and fruit butter from fruits, the entire substance being extracted in one operation. The most substantial machine of its kind on the market.

No. 9K29552 Price............$2.77

37c LIGHT AND DURABLE JAPANNED STEEL CARPET STRETCHER.

Simple in construction and powerful, easy to operate and is warranted not to injure the finest carpet. It holds the carpet in position after it is drawn to its proper place, giving the operator the free use of both hands with which to do the nailing.

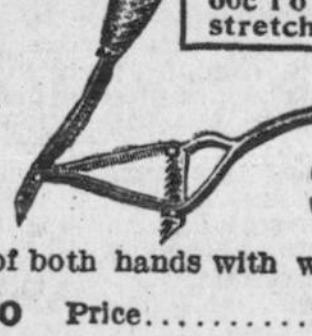

Others ask 60c for this stretcher.

37c

No. 9K22780 Price............37c

52c BUYS THIS ENCLOSED HOPPER NEW HOME BOX COFFEE MILL.

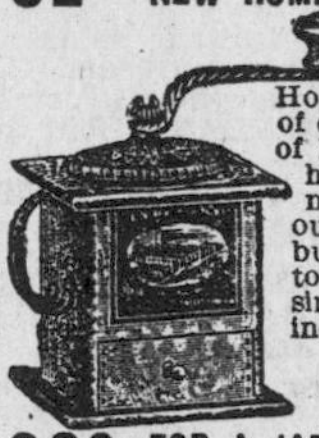

The best Box Mill made. Wood top, iron cover and side handle. Hopper holds over a pound of coffee. The box is made of hardwood, dovetailed, highly polished and varnished, and supplied with our improved grinding burrs, which are warranted to pulverize coffee, if desired. Size, 6¾ x 6¾ x 8 inches.

No. 9K22230 Price............52c

32c FOR A JAPANNED TIN CANISTER, STEEL BURR WALL COFFEE MILL.

Canister holds one pound of coffee, is practically airtight and moisture proof. By buying the coffee in the bean, and grinding it just as you need it, you secure the full strength, as it is well known that coffee rapidly loses its strength if allowed to stand after grinding. Has improved steel burrs and will grind coarse, medium or fine as desired.

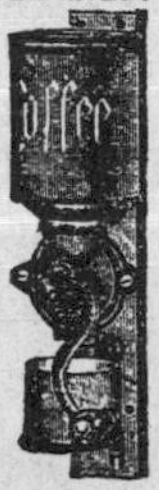

No. 9K22205 Price...32c

47c GLASS FRONT X-RAY WALL COFFEE MILL.

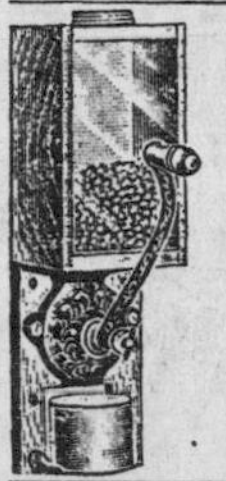

The X-Ray Mill has wood frame and wood hopper with glass front Hopper holds one pound, and the coffee is always in sight. Easily regulated to grind fine or coarse as desired. Turns easy. Grinds fast. The mill is well made, strong and durable and warranted to give satisfaction.

No. 9K22210 Price, 47c

$4.68 FOR A HIGH GRADE NATIONAL COFFEE AND SPICE MILL.

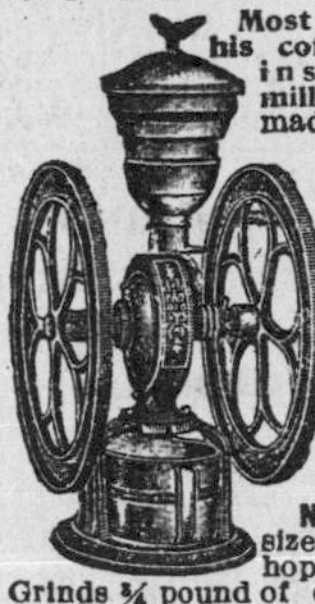

Most any merchant can double his coffee and spice sales by installing one of these mills. The grinders are made of steel and grind the kernels into uniform size; can be adjusted from fine to coarse or vice versa while in operation. Grinds quicker and easier than many mills offered at double the price. Handsomely finished in maroon and gold, an ornament to any store. Fully guaranteed in every respect. Sold in two sizes.

No. 9K22240 Medium size with 12-inch fly wheels; hopper holds 1¼ pounds. Grinds ¾ pound of coffee per minute. Height, 24½ inches. Shipping weight, 47½ pounds. Price............$4.68

No. 9K22245 Large size with 17-inch fly wheels; hopper holds 2 pounds. Grinds 2 pounds of coffee per minute. Height, 28 inches. Shipping wgt., 68 lbs. Price, $7.82

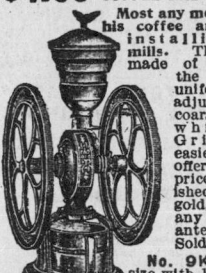

44c HARDWOOD BOX, RAISED HOPPER STEEL BURR COFFEE MILL.

Dovetailed and varnished. This mill is fitted with a spring between the grinding burrs which prevents them from rubbing together and dulling the teeth. Will grind coarse, medium or fine, as desired. Size, 7x7x5 inches.

A regular 75c mill.

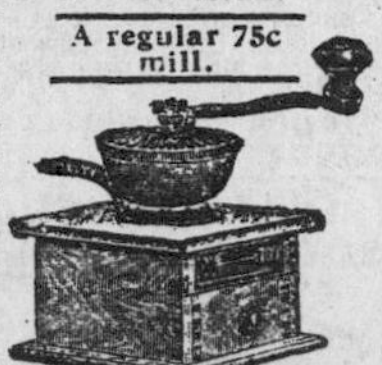

No. 9K22238 Price............44c

$1.92 FOR A FULL SIZE 3-QUART HIGHEST GRADE ALASKA ICE CREAM FREEZER.

THE ALASKA MAKES BETTER CREAM, FREEZES QUICKER, AND REQUIRES LESS ICE AND SALT THAN ANY OTHER FREEZER MADE

The Alaska Freezer is simple, has few parts, and is easy to operate and clean. Made of the best materials throughout. Tubs are clear kiln dried Northern pine, treated with a paraffine and oil preparation which makes them waterproof. Hoops are heavy galvanized steel and positively will not come loose. Cans are extra heavy charcoal tin plate with retinned iron tops and bottoms and will outlast any other freezer can made. Gearing is heavily galvanized and will not rust. The only freezer made with aerating spoon dasher, with slotted spoon shaped floats, mounted on the arms which carry the wood scrapers. As the can revolves the freezing mixture is removed from the sides and thrown to the center, where it is beaten and aerated until frozen into the smoothest and most delicious cream you ever tasted. The ice guard prevents ice or salt getting into the Alaska and the covered gear protects the fingers of the operator. Order an Alaska Freezer, give it a fair trial, and if you are not entirely pleased with it, return it to us in ten days and your money will be promptly refunded.

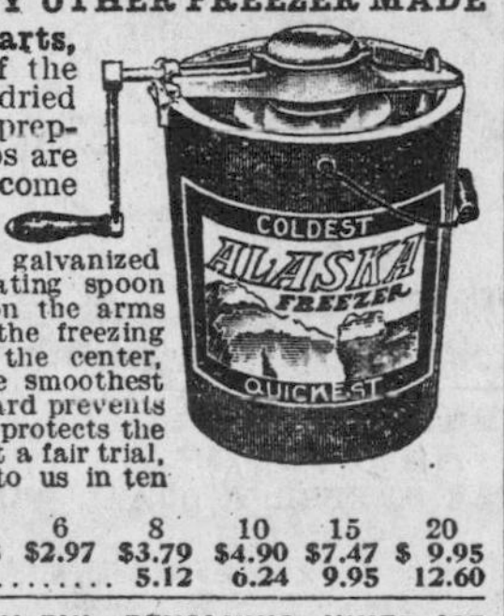

	Size, quarts	2	3	4	6	8	10	15	20
No. 9K29627	Price	$1.60	$1.92	$2.33	$2.97	$3.79	$4.90	$7.47	$9.95
No. 9K29628	With Fly Wheel. Price					5.12	6.24	9.95	12.60

10c IXX EXTRA HEAVY TIN, REVOLVING KNIFE ICE CREAM DISHER.

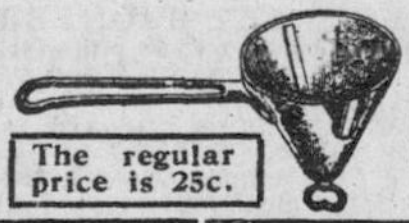

The regular price is 25c.

Has two revolving knives which cut the cream loose. Made of heavy tin, nicely finished and durable. Divides each quart into eight equal portions.

No. 9K29632 Price............10c

7c FOR A RUSTPROOF DOUBLE RING POT CHAIN AND SCRAPER.

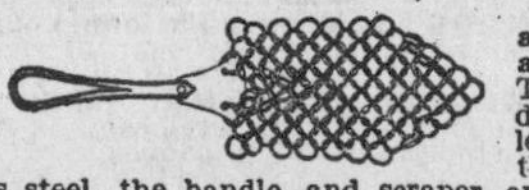

A new and useful article The handle is malleable iron, the blade is steel, the handle and scraper are tinned. With one of these you can clean your pots in half the usual time.

No. 9K22700 Price............7c

7c "QUICK AND EASY" STEEL BLADE, WOOD HANDLE CAN OPENER.

Opens any can, round or square, of any size, quicker and easier than others.

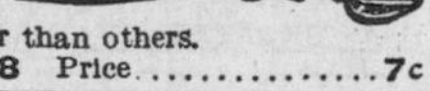

No. 9K22718 Price............7c

7c JAPANNED MALLEABLE IRON HANDLE STEEL BLADE MINCING KNIFE.

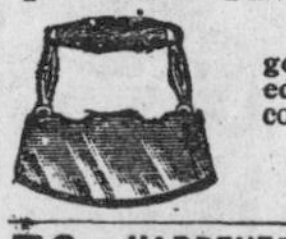

Ground sharp, made of good steel and will hold an edge. Handle can't split or come loose.

No. 9K22760 Price..7c

7c HARDENED BLUE STEEL HEAD, ALL METAL TACK HAMMER.

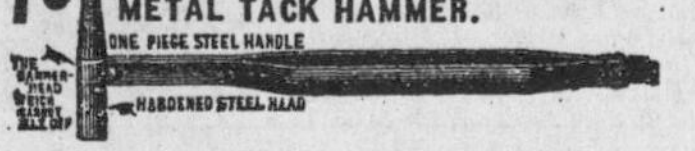

Handle polished steel, countersunk on head, which prevents head from coming off.

No. 9K22771 Price............7c

4c FORGED STEEL, POLISHED BLADE, STEEL TACK CLAWS AND PULLER.

Riveted tang, varnished wood handle. The best made.

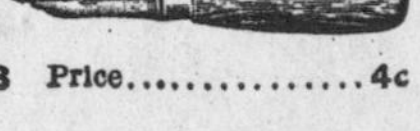

No. 9K22773 Price............4c

18c FOR 6 BRIGHT STEEL WIRE COAT HANGERS.

17 inches wide. Garments when hung on this device do not lose their shape as when hung on hooks or nails.

Retail, 10c each.

34c PER DOZEN.

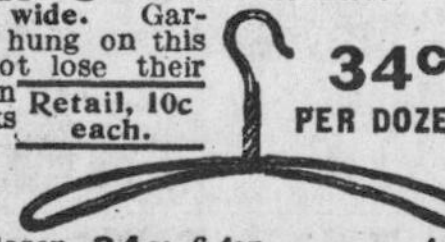

No. 9K26568 Price, per dozen, 34c; 6 for............18c

23c FOR 3 PANTS HANGERS. SAVE PRESSING.

Made of steel, neatly japanned. Hook folds up when not in use.

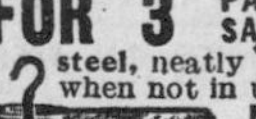

No. 9K26571 Price, 3 for...23c
Per dozen............85c

14c BRIGHT WIRE FOLDING CARD RACK AND PHOTO HOLDER

Useful for holding cards, photos, etc. It admits of very handsome decoration with ribbons. Just the thing for amateur photographers and post card collectors. Made of twisted steel wire, brightly tinned. It folds up into a small package and cannot be injured in shipping. Holds 91 pictures. Size, 20½x30 inches; weight, 6 ounces.

No. 9K26655 Price............14c

70c FOR 12 JAPANNED RUSTPROOF, VERMINPROOF WIRE HENS' NESTS, 13 INCHES DIAMETER.

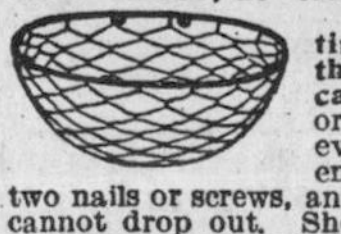

Made of poultry netting and are positively the best nests that money can buy. They are favored by poultry raisers everywhere. Can be fastened to the wall with two nails or screws, and are made so that eggs cannot drop out. Should be lined with hay or straw and supported at bottom. Size is outside diameter of nest. Sold only in dozen lots.

No. 9K26468 13-inch Hen's Nest. Price, per dozen............70c
No. 9K26469 15-inch Hen's Nest. Price, per dozen............96c

11c TOUGH FIBER IMITATION LEATHER CHAIR SEAT, 12 INCHES SQUARE.

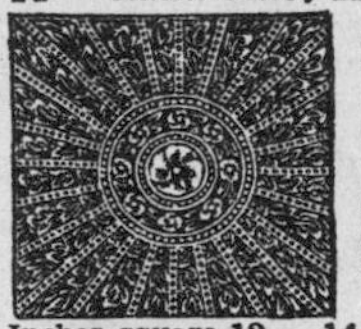

Made of tough fiber board in exact imitation of fancy embossed leather. Fine for reseating old cane or leather seated chairs. Can be cut to any shape and fastened with brass head tacks. Finished in dark green or turkish red.

No. 9K28575

Inches, square	12	14	16	18	20
Price	11c	15c	21c	27c	33c

7c FOR 100 SMALL SIZE SOLID BRASS HEAD NAILS.

For upholstering, nailing on chair seats, fancy work, etc. Price, per 100 Per 1,000

		Per 100	Per 1,000
No. 9K48671	Small size.	7c	55c
No. 9K48673	Large size.	9c	80c

69c FOR 1,000 FEET FINE WIDTH CHAIR CANE, IN HANKS.

All full lengths, in hanks of 1,000 feet. This is a high grade chair cane. We carry in stock fine, medium and common width.

No. 9K28579
Fine. Price, per hank............69c
Medium. Price, per hank............80c
Common. Price, per hank............84c

No. 9K28581 Binding Cane. Extra No. 1 grade, in hanks of 500 feet. Price..55c

7c FOR A DECORATED SPLASHER MAT.

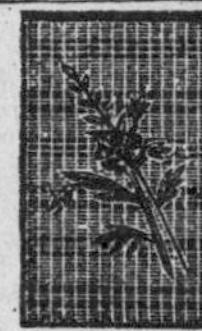

For protecting wall above washstand. Made of sewed wood splints with assorted centers. These are very attractive mats and are not easily soiled like linen splashers. Size, 17¾x29¼ inches.

No. 9K28640 Price............7c

38c FOR 4 NEATLY WOVEN PALM LEAF TABLE MATS.

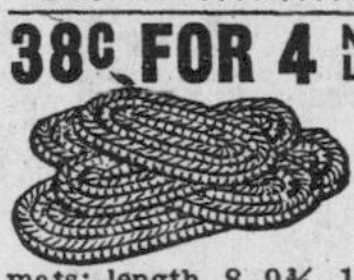

Light and attractive, for use under hot platters, etc. Prevents burning of tablecloth and marring finish of table. Set consists of four oblong mats; length, 8, 9¾, 11, 12¾ inches, respectively.

No. 9K28650 Price, per set, one each size............38c

20c LOADED BOTTOM SELF-RIGHTING NICKEL PLATED CUSPIDOR.

Size, 5x7½ inches.

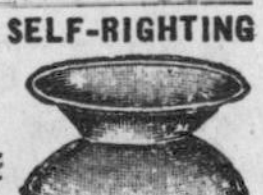

No. 9K26116 Price, 20c

42c LARGE SIZE CAST IRON WHITE ENAMELED INSIDE CUSPIDORS.

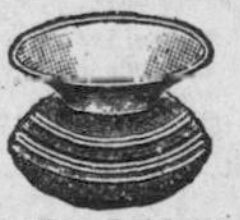

Outside painted, assorted colors, banded. Size, 8½x6 inches.

No. 9K26119 Price............42c

$1.17 GALVANIZED ODORLESS COMMODE AND SLOP BUCKET.

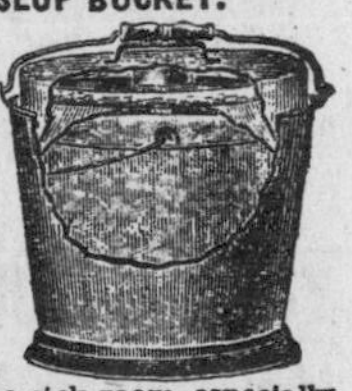

It is impossible for the foul air to escape, even when the lid is removed, as there is inside the lid a receptacle that holds a deodorizer which neutralizes all gases inside the commode. The disinfectant (2 tablespoonfuls of chloride of lime), needs only to be renewed once in two weeks at a small cost. It is indispensable in the sick room, especially in cases of contagious diseases and fevers. Does not have to be emptied until filled, no matter how long it stands. Illustration shows construction. Made of galvanized iron, heavily painted. Has removable inside bucket and also removable seat, etc. A convenient and sanitary device which should be in every home. Holds 9 quarts.

No. 9K26162 Price............$1.17

41c TOILET STAND COMPLETE WITH 12-INCH WHITE ENAMELED BASIN.

75c elsewhere

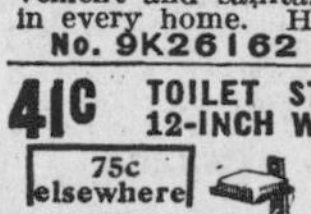

Easily attached to the wall, post or the side of a wooden pump. The wash basin can be removed, permitting the toilet stand frame to be folded up and put out of the way when not in use. Complete with soap holder and towel hook. The framework is made of steel, neatly japanned and is unbreakable. The basin alone is worth the price we ask for the entire outfit.

No. 9K26261 Price............41c

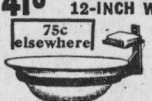

53c GALVANIZED CORRUGATED BOTTOM STEEL BUSHEL BASKETS.

Provided with extra heavy corrugated bottoms, insuring great strength. These baskets are more convenient than those made of wood as they hold water and can be used as a tub.

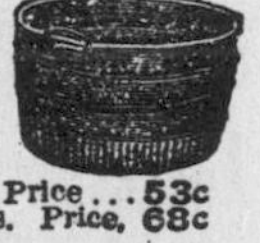

No. 9K26845 1 bushel. Price...53c
No. 9K26846 1½ bushels. Price, 68c

HOUSEHOLD AND COUNTER SCALES

Every person who buys or sells by weight ought to have a first class scale. You can't afford to take someone's word as to the weight of merchandise you buy or sell: Read the full descriptions of our scales, pick out the one that suits your needs and send us your order.

We guarantee every scale we sell to be accurate, reliable and satisfactory. Order a scale from us; when it comes, test it, and if it is not entirely satisfactory, ship it back to us and your money will be promptly refunded. **FOR WAGON AND PORTABLE PLATFORM SCALES SEE PAGES 563 TO 567.**

96c CRUCIBLE STEEL SPRING GUARANTEED FAMILY SCALE, WITHOUT SCOOP. CAPACITY, 24 POUNDS.

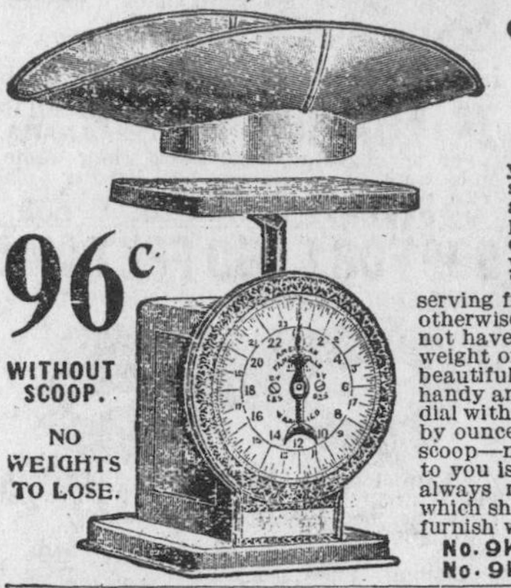

96c

WITHOUT SCOOP.

NO WEIGHTS TO LOSE.

CANNOT BE DUPLICATED IN THE ORDINARY RETAIL STORE FOR TWICE OUR PRICE.

The quality is absolutely the best, and if you are not entirely pleased with the scale we send you, you are at liberty to return it to us and we will refund the full amount of the price. Every family in the land ought to have one of these scales, and at the prices we quote you cannot afford to do without one. Saves "guesswork" in making cakes, mincemeats, preserving fruits, etc. Will detect mistakes (intentional or otherwise) in weights. With one of these scales you do not have to take anybody's word, but can verify the weight of every package you buy. Scale made of steel, beautifully finished and decorated; is unbreakable, light, handy and always ready. Has 5-inch white enameled dial with plain figures, easily read. Capacity, 24 pounds, by ounces. We furnish this scale either with or without scoop—note the prices below—but the difference in cost to you is so slight and a scoop is so very convenient we always recommend the purchase of scale No. 9K29901, which shows in the illustration the heavy tin scoop we furnish with it.

No. 9K29900 Price, without scoop........$0.96
No. 9K29901 Price, with heavy tin scoop... 1.12

$1.87 60-POUND, LARGE DIAL GENERAL PURPOSE SCALE, WITHOUT SCOOP.

A SCALE THAT YOU CAN'T DEPEND UPON IS WORSE THAN NO SCALE AT ALL. The U. S. Family Scale is entirely dependable and is one of the most practical general purpose scales on the market. Made of the best materials, by skilled workmen, and we buy them in such large quantities and sell them at such low figures that you can buy from us and save fifty per cent on the price you would have to pay your local dealer. The capacity of this scale is 60 pounds, by 2 ounces. The body is made of 18-gauge drawn steel finished in black enamel. The dial is extra size, finely enameled, and the figures are large and plain. This scale will not rust, tarnish or the enamel on the face become dull. The springs are of the best quality oil tempered steel and will retain their full strength for a lifetime. Scale furnished either with or without scoop, but a scoop is so convenient we recommend that you buy No. 9K299024 scale with scoop, as the saving in time will soon pay the slight difference in price.

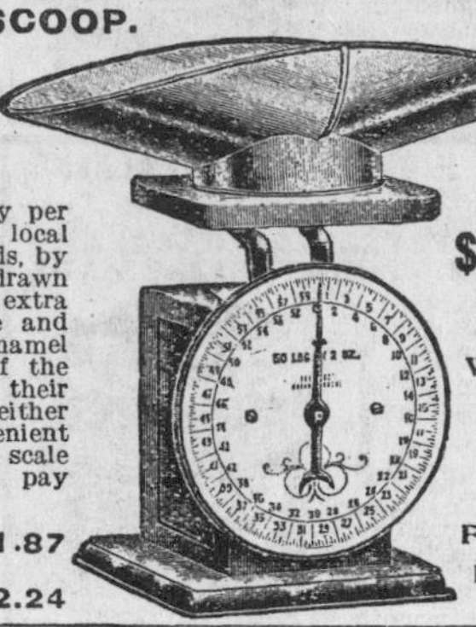

$1.87

Without Scoop.

Large Dial.

Plain Figures.

Easily Read.

No. 9K29902 Price, without scoop...$1.87
No. 9K299024 Price, complete, with scoop.......................... 2.24

74c FOR THIS JAPANNED EVEN BALANCE SCALE, COMPLETE WITH WEIGHTS AND SCOOP.

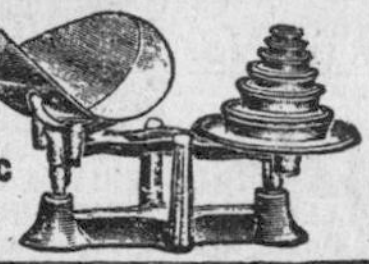

74c

SOME PEOPLE PREFER A SCALE WITH WEIGHTS.

We offer our 74-cent Even Balance at such a low figure no family in the country can afford to do without one. Even Balance Scale weighs 4 pounds, by half ounces. Warranted accurate and reliable. Made of cast iron, nicely japanned.

No. 9K29904 Price, complete, with weights and scoop.......74c

98c FOR A HEAVY, STRONG, ACCURATE AND RELIABLE 200-POUND SCALE BEAM WITH TWO POISES.

HEAVY, STRONG, ACCURATE AND RELIABLE.

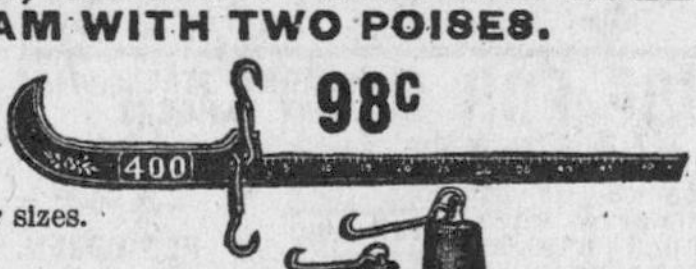

98c

Finished in black japan, striped and marked in bronze on both sides. Will weigh to full capacity and guaranteed satisfactory. The 400 and 600-pound beams are the most popular sizes.

No. 9K29883

Capacity, lbs....	200	250	400	600	1,000	1,200
Price, complete..	98c	$1.26	$1.97	$2.69	$4.45	$4.98

$1.98 FOR A BRASS BEAM COUNTER SCALE, COMPLETE CAPACITY, 25 POUNDS.

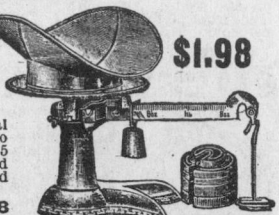

QUALITY CONSIDERED, THE CHEAPEST COUNTER BEAM SCALE ON THE MARKET.

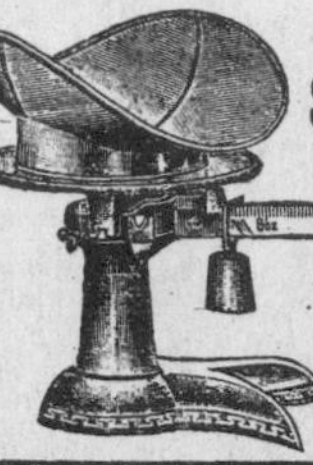

$1.98

Each scale is thoroughly tested, guaranteed to be accurate and entirely satisfactory in every respect. Better than similar scales offered by others at $2.50 to $3.50. They are made of the finest material by the largest scale manufacturer in the country. Our low price is possible only because we sell several thousands of this one scale each year and are content to add only a small profit to the first cost. Capacity, 25 pounds. Has heavy tin scoop and carefully graduated brass beam marked by half ounces; is handsomely painted and decorated, and presents a pleasing appearance.

No. 9K29905 Price, complete, with scoop..$1.98

THE INTERNATIONAL SCALE

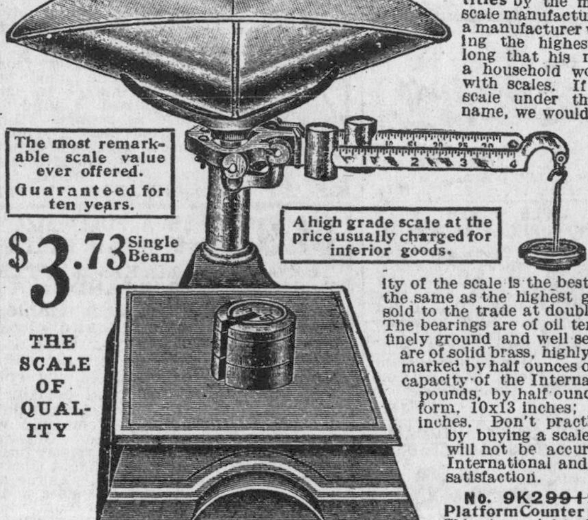

The most remarkable scale value ever offered. Guaranteed for ten years.

A high grade scale at the price usually charged for inferior goods.

$3.73 Single Beam

THE SCALE OF QUALITY

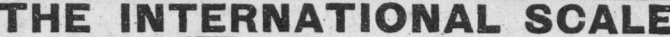

OUR INTERNATIONAL SCALES are made for us in immense quantities by the most widely known scale manufacturer in this country, a manufacturer who has been making the highest grade scales so long that his name has become a household word in connection with scales. If we sold this same scale under the manufacturer's name, we would be compelled to charge you double the price we ask as we can only buy them at this remarkably low price with the understanding that they shall be sold under our own brand. The quality of the scale is the best and is identically the same as the highest grade union scale, sold to the trade at double the price we ask. The bearings are of oil tempered tool steel, finely ground and well seated. The beams are of solid brass, highly polished and are marked by half ounces on both sides. The capacity of the International Scale is 240 pounds, by half ounces. Size of platform, 10x13 inches; scoop, 10½x19½ inches. Don't practice false economy by buying a scale so cheap that it will not be accurate, but buy the International and we guarantee you satisfaction.

No. 9K29912 International Platform Counter Scale, single beam. Shipping weight, 42 pounds. $3.73

No. 9K29913 International Platform Counter Scale, with double brass beam, as illustrated. Shipping weight, 44 pounds. Price.................... 4.18

$2.82 FOR THIS PIONEER UNION PLATFORM COUNTER SCALE WITH WEIGHTS AND SCOOP.

ONLY $2.82 FOR THE PIONEER UNION.

Weighs from ½ ounce to 240 pounds. Has nicely japanned frame and platform, tin scoop and solid brass beam, marked 44 pounds, by ½ ounces. This is a good, strong platform counter scale, and the same standard of quality usually offered at $5.00 to $6.00. It is as good as any scale on the market with the exception of our own International Scale, illustrated and described above. The Pioneer Scale will weigh correctly and give satisfaction, but the International Scale is so much better finished, more carefully adjusted and assembled that it is well worth the slight difference in price.

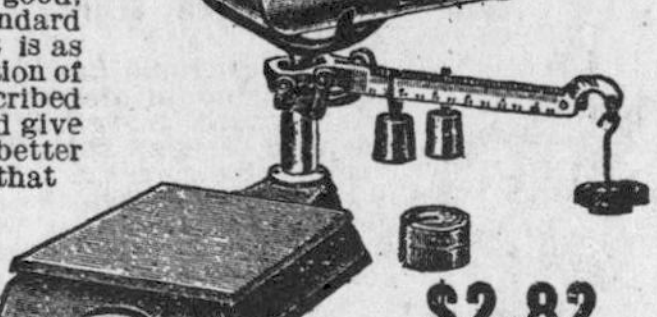

$2.82 Single Beam.

No. 9K29914 Pioneer Patform Counter Scale, single beam. Shipping weight, 40 pounds. Price..........................$2.82

No. 9K29915 Pioneer Platform Counter Scale, equipped with extra tare beam, as illustrated. Shipping weight, 42 pounds. Price..........................$3.17

YOUR SAVING IS GREATER THAN EVER; OVER 3,000 HARDWARE ITEMS REDUCED IN THIS BOOK

16c FOR A FLUTED FRUIT AND VEGETABLE SLICER.

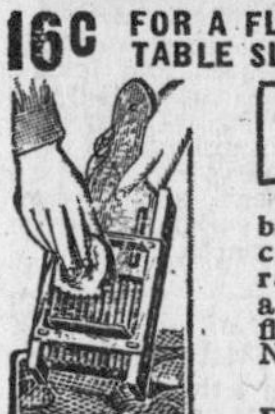

AGENTS AND OTHERS ASK 50C FOR THIS PERFECT SLICER.

For slicing apples, pears, bananas, potatoes, beets, carrots, cucumbers, turnips, radishes, etc. Makes dainty and attractive perforated flutings, Saratoga chips, etc. No waste; anybody can use it.

No. 9K28220 Price................16c

24c ADJUSTABLE HARDWOOD TWO-KNIFE SLAW AND VEGETABLE CUTTER.

For slicing cabbage, potatoes and all vegetables. Size, 17x6¼ inches.

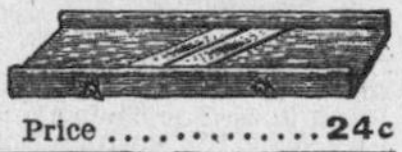

No. 9K28223 Price............24c

84c FOR AN ADJUSTABLE KNIFE KRAUT CUTTER, SIZE 8x24 INCHES.

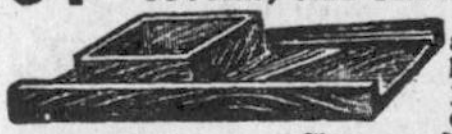

With slide box and tool steel knives easily adjusted to cut fine or coarse.

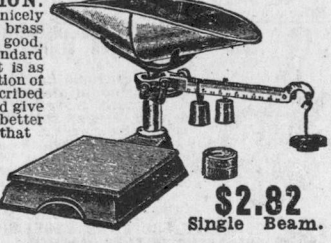

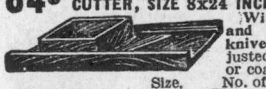

No.	Size, inches	No. of Knives	Price
9K28236	8x24	3	$0.84
9K28238	9x30	3	1.50
9K28239	12x36	4	2.96

8c FOR A THREE-ARM STEEL NICKEL PLATED TOWEL RACK.

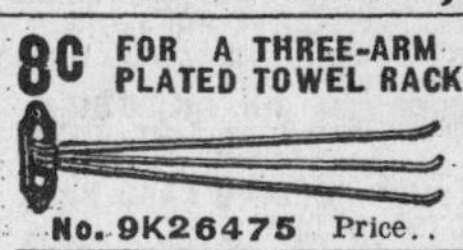

Swinging arms. 12½ inches long.

No. 9K26475 Price..............8c

9c FOR THIS CONVENIENT FIVE-ARM TOWEL BAR OR CLOTHES RACK.

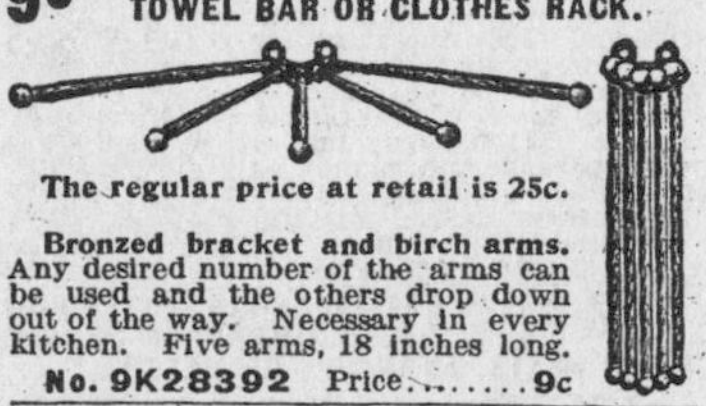

The regular price at retail is 25c.

Bronzed bracket and birch arms. Any desired number of the arms can be used and the others drop down out of the way. Necessary in every kitchen. Five arms, 18 inches long.

No. 9K28392 Price.........9c

8c FOR THIS HINGED COVER WHITE WOOD LARGE SIZE SALT BOX.

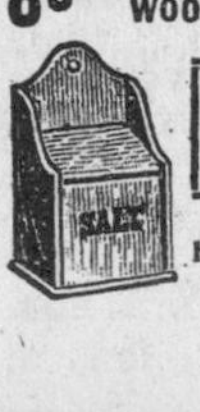

ELSEWHERE YOU PAY 25 Cents FOR ONE NOT AS GOOD.

Size, 4½x5 inches, and will hold two small bags of salt.

No. 9K28261 Price.....8c

13c VARNISHED HARDWOOD TOWEL ROLLER, STRONG AND ATTRACTIVE.

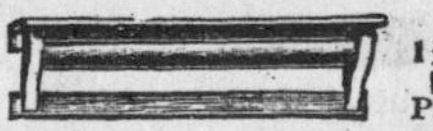

Size of roller, 1⅜x18 inches.

No. 9K28357 Price.........13c

48c FOR THIS HARDWOOD SPICE CABINET WITH EIGHT DRAWERS.

Others ask 75 cents for an inferior article.

A place for everything and everything in its place. Neatly constructed cabinet for holding and preserving spices. Eight drawers marked for contents. Best low priced cabinet on the market. Size, 12x18 inches.

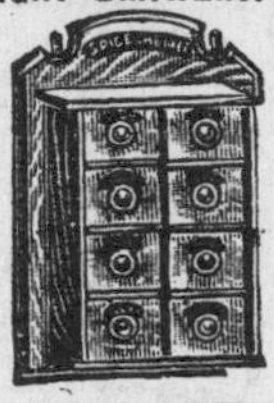

No. 9K28250 Price..........48c

38c FOR 2,000 ORANGE-WOOD HAND POINTED TOOTHPICKS.

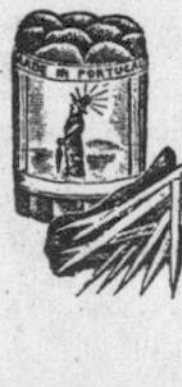

Imported from Portugal. The best toothpick made. Put up in bundles of 2,000 picks.

No. 9K28190 Price, per bundle...........38c

9c SELECTED SOLID MAPLE ROLLING PIN WITH REVOLVING HANDLES.

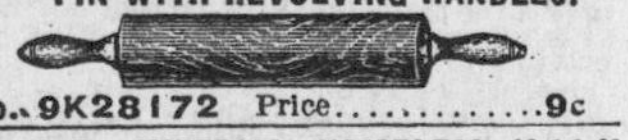

No. 9K28172 Price.............9c

$9.60 IMPERIAL NOISELESS MILK SHAKE MACHINE, COMPLETE.

Buy one of these machines and make it pay for itself in one day at your county fair. It is handsomely painted, has nickel plated trimmings and glass caps for tumblers. It can be securely fastened to the floor, and does not shake counter. This machine will soon pay for itself as it takes less milk to make milk shakes with it than it does by hand. One-half dozen tumblers furnished with each shaker, and directions for making syrups included. Weight, packed for shipment, 74 pounds.

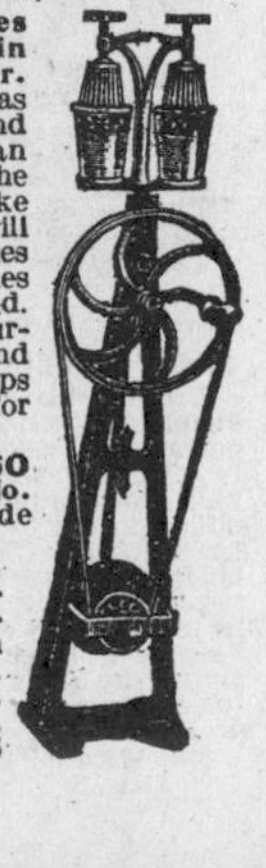

No. 9K29661 Price, $9.60

Same construction as No. 9K29661, except stand made to be used on counter or bar, and requires but little room. Packed complete with one-half dozen tumblers. Directions for making syrups with each machine. Weight, packed for shipment, 43 lbs.

No. 9K29660 Price, complete............$6.65

MILK CANS AND DAIRY SUPPLIES

YOU CAN SAVE MONEY BY BUYING YOUR DAIRY SUPPLIES FROM US. We sell thousands of milk cans, dairy pails, churns, etc., every month, we place enormous contracts with the largest manufacturers, and add only one small profit to the factory cost.

WE GUARANTEE EACH ITEM ON THIS PAGE to be first class in every particular. Order a lot of dairy supplies, when they are received, examine them closely; if you are not pleased with them, return them at our expense and your money will be promptly returned to you.

MONEY SAVING HARDWARE PRICES IN OUR LAST CATALOGUE STILL FURTHER REDUCED IN THIS BOOK

$1.55 FOR A 5-GALLON SILVER STEEL ELGIN PATTERN R. R. MILK CAN.

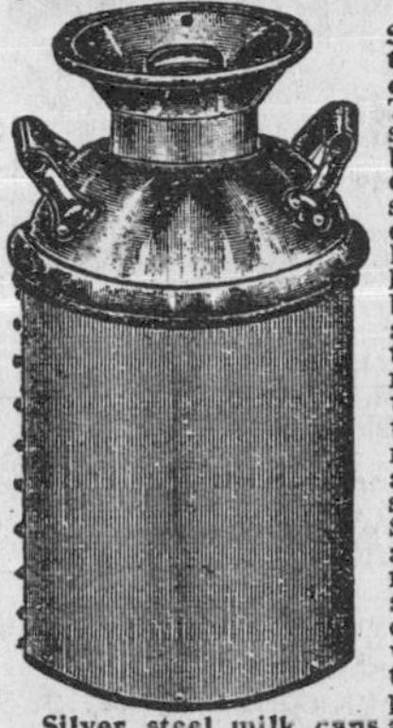

Our Heavy Silver Steel Milk Cans are the best shipping cans in the world. They are built of solid steel from bottom to cover, every part double seamed and riveted, then heavily loaded with best half and half solder by experts. They are tinned and retinned with as much pure block tin as the steel will take up. They cannot leak or rust, are strong and will stand hard usage. Silver steel cans are the heaviest made, are rigid and stiff, will not dent or cave in and you will never be troubled about repairs.

Silver steel milk cans are sanitary, have no seams or crevices to collect milk and dirt, breasts and bottoms are full rounded and you will save enough time in washing these cans to pay the slight difference in price.

Silver steel cans are cheapest in the end. Better than cans others ask $3.00 for; better than any cans made. Compare the weights of silver steel cans with the weights of others, think of the time saved in washing of the saving in repair bills, and remember that we fully guarantee these cans to please you and to be the best cans made.

No. 9K29006

Capacity, gals.	5	8	10
Average weight, lbs.	12	20½	23
Price, each	$1.55	$2.15	$2.30

$1.75 FOR AN 8-GALLON WISCONSIN PATTERN RIVETED MILK CAN.

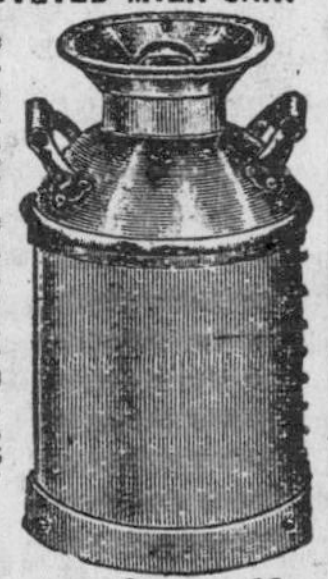

A splendid can for the money, adapted for hauling back and forth to the creamery, but not intended for heavy shipping purposes. Made of steel, with seamless neck, double seamed to the breast, riveted body and strong, heavy bottom hoop. This can is carefully tinned and retinned and inside seams are soldered, but not loaded as in our silver steel cans. Wisconsin pattern can has full rounded breast and bottom and is easy to clean.

No. 9K29000

Capacity, gallons	8	10
Average weight, pounds	15	16½
Price, each	$1.75	$1.90

Milk Can Links and Washers.

No. 9K29047 For attaching cover to can to prevent its being lost; fitted to any of our milk cans at an additional charge of, per can **5c**

Copper Milk Can Letters and Figures.

No. 9K29048 For marking cans. Size, 1⅜ inches, soldered onto can at, per letter or figure **1½c**

Brass Faucets for Milk Cans.

No. 9K29050 We fit a ¾-inch brass faucet to any milk can for delivery purposes, when desired, at an additional cost, including price of faucet and labor of **$1.40**

35c FOR A 10-QUART STEEL CLAD DAIRY PAIL. BEST MADE.

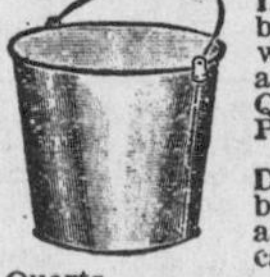

No. 9K25191 Made of IX tin. Well soldered with best solder. Patent bottom; will never leak. Sizes are actual capacity.

Quarts	10	12	14
Price	17c	21c	26c

No. 9K25194 Steel clad Dairy Pails. It is impossible to construct a better pail at any price. Sizes are actual capacity. Note the weights.

Quarts	10	12	14
Inches	11x9⅛	11¼x10	11¾x10¾
Weight, pounds	3¼	3½	3¾
Price	35c	38c	41c

$3.85 FOR AN IMPROVED MILK COOLER AND AERATOR, SIZE No. 2.

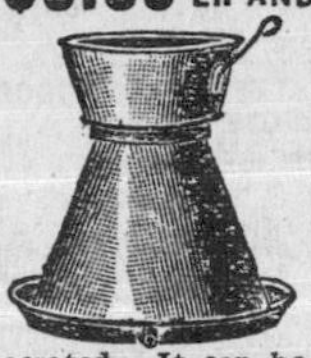

Improves the flavor of fresh milk and its products by drawing out the objectionable odors which new milk always contains. Makes the milk keep longer, takes out all animal heat and thoroughly cools and aerates it. Pour the milk into the hopper, and by the time you are through milking it is cooled and aerated. It can be used either with running water or filled from a well, spring or with ice. The milk will be cooled to within a few degrees of the temperature of the water. One filling with ice will cool 500 to 600 quarts of milk down to a temperature of 50 degrees. Attach rubber hose to water inlet and fill water compartment with cold water, or lift off top and fill from bucket. Be careful to place the cooler and aerator where there is plenty of pure fresh air. Use the agitator freely to draw the warm water from the sides. The water overflow will permit of your keeping a running stream of water constantly passing through, and this is desirable where such can be resorted to. Built of heavy tin plate with galvanized steel bottom and painted inside with two coats of best anti-rust paint. Prices include double cheese cloth strainer and spring pins. With little care, should last for years. Securely crated for shipment.

No. 9K29085

No.	2	3	4
Milk receiver, holds quarts	18	34	52
Number of cows	5 to 25	25 to 50	50 to 100
Weight, crated lbs.	31	37	40
Price, complete	$3.85	$4.52	$5.67

16c BRASS BOTTOM MILK STRAINER.

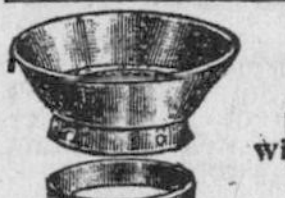

No. 9K25200 Complete with hoop. Size, 10 inches. Price **16c**

$1.73 FOR SIX CREAM SETTING CANS, 14-QUART SIZE.

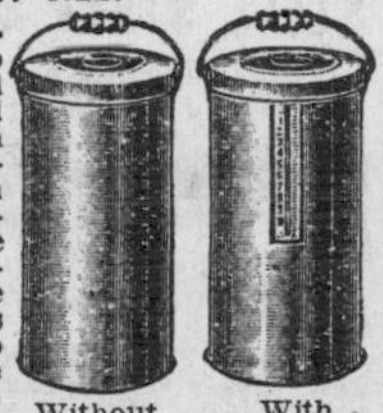

Without Gauge. With Gauge.

Have airtight covers. It requires no locking device to hold the cover down, and is the only cream can that can be completely submerged in water without leaking. Cream cans are much easier to handle than pans. The graduated glass gauge enables you to watch and measure the rising cream. We quote a special price in lots of six cans and do not sell less quantities.

No. 9K29100 Made of IX tin plate, without gauge.

Quarts	14	18	20
Weight, pounds	2½	3	3½
Per crate of six cans	$1.73	$1.92	$2.08

No. 9K29103 Made of IXX tin plate, with gauge.

Quarts	14	18	20
Weight, pounds	2¾	3¼	3¾
Per crate of six cans	$2.42	$2.63	$2.78

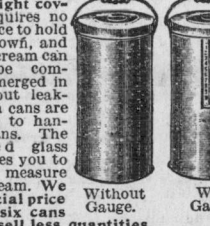

$3.19 IMPROVED DILUTION CREAM SEPARATOR, HOLDS 10 GALS.

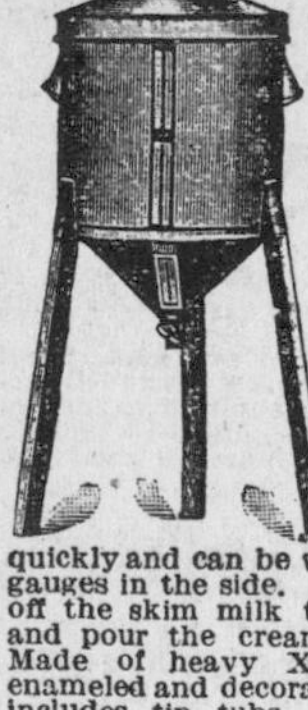

Separates cream from milk in thirty to fifty minutes and gives you sweet diluted milk, which is far superior to sour milk as a stock food. Saves several hours waiting for the cream to rise and gets 20 to 25 per cent more butter fat out of milk than the old way. To use, fill the separator half full of milk; an equal quantity of water is then poured in through a tube so that it enters at the bottom. As the water gradually mixes with the milk it separates the cream, which rises to the top. This process takes place quickly and can be watched through the glass gauges in the side. When all has risen, draw off the skim milk through faucet at bottom and pour the cream out in another vessel. Made of heavy XXX charcoal tin plate, enameled and decorated on the outside. Price includes tin tubs, strainer and everything necessary to use.

No. 9K29189

Capacity Gallons	Outside Measure	Shipping Weight	Price, Complete
10	12x30 in.	23 pounds	$3.19
14	14x30 in.	24 pounds	3.68
18	15x30 in.	28 pounds	3.93
21	16x30 in.	29 pounds	4.33
24	18x36 in.	30 pounds	4.90
28	19x38 in.	36 pounds	5.60

$3.21 ECONOMICAL DOUBLE CAN SEPARATOR, HOLDS 4 GALLONS.

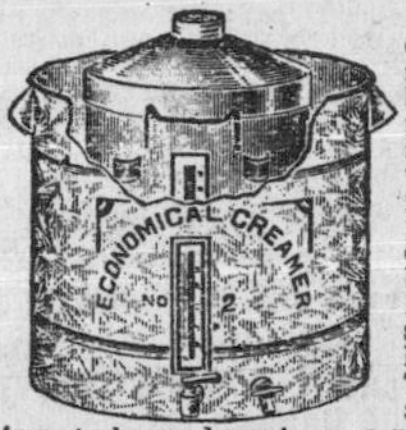

Will separate the cream from the milk in four to six hours and produce perfect separation in warm or cold weather. Has removable inner can, permitting thorough cleaning of both cans. No labor wasted in skimming, lifting or handling of crocks. The milk is aerated and ventilated and is not churned as in a centrifugal separator. Glass gauges at top and bottom enable you to watch the progress of the cream rising and to draw off the milk and cream separately through valve in bottom. Inner can is made of heavy tinned steel, painted on outside to prevent rust. Outer can made from galvanized iron with double seamed bottom, all carefully soldered. Cover is cone shaped and by reversing, forms a strainer.

No. 9K29190

Capacity of Inner Can	Size of Water Tank	Shipping Weight	Price
4 gals.	17½x14½ in.	20 pounds	$3.21
6 gals.	21½x14½ in.	23 pounds	3.72
8 gals.	21½x17½ in.	27 pounds	4.19
10 gals.	21½x18½ in.	30 pounds	4.54
12 gals.	23½x19 in.	33 pounds	4.79
15 gals.	28½x19 in.	38 pounds	5.15

$3.73 IMPROVED SANITARY UNION EASY TURNING ROTARY CHURN.

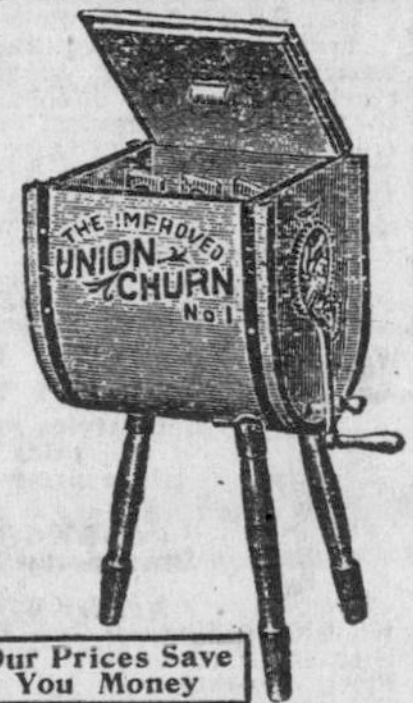

You can make, gather, work and salt your butter without removing it from the Union Churn, or without touching the butter with your hands. If hoops become loose they can be tightened by simply turning a nut. Dasher can be quickly removed and easily cleaned. The lid fits down tight and does not leak; the iron parts are all japanned and it is nicely painted. The cog gearing develops extra power which makes it churn quickly and turn so easily a child can operate it.

No.	Holds, Gals.	Churns, Gals.	Weight, Pounds	Price
9K29221	5	3	32	$3.73
9K29222	7	4	35	4.23
9K29223	10	6	38	4.95
9K29225	15	8	44	6.93

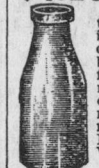

$1.98 OUR NEW STYLE WHITE CEDAR CYLINDER CHURN, SIZE No. 1.

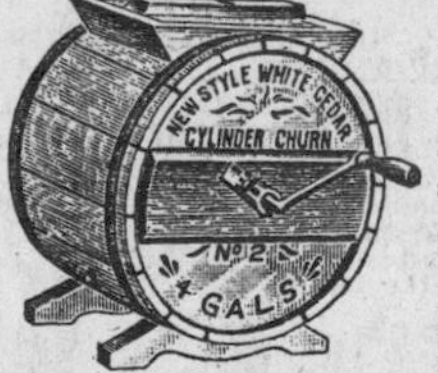

Made entirely of white cedar, the best wood known for churns; is easily cleaned and will not leak. The top is large and the dasher is easily removed. Has double dasher and the crank is locked to the churn with a clamp and thumbscrew. Hoops are galvanized iron and will not rust.

No. 9K29226

Nos.	1	2	3	4
Will hold, gals.	3	4	7	10
Will churn, gals.	2	3	4	5
Weight, lbs.	11	14	18	22
Price	$1.98	$2.35	$2.85	$3.25

$3.75 FOR A PHILADELPHIA BUTTER WORKER, QUICK AND EASY.

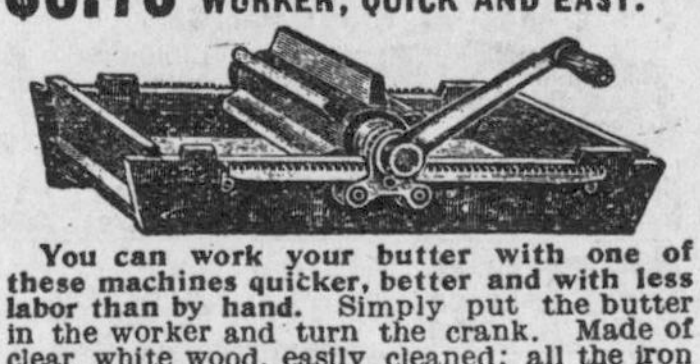

You can work your butter with one of these machines quicker, better and with less labor than by hand. Simply put the butter in the worker and turn the crank. Made of clear white wood, easily cleaned; all the iron parts are tinned and cannot rust.

No.	Size	Will Work	Wgt.	Price
9K29246	14x23 in.	10	24 lbs.	$3.75
9K29247	17x27 in.	20	30 lbs.	4.35
9K29248	20x36 in.	30	33 lbs.	4.90
9K29249	23x36 in.	50	41 lbs.	5.85

$2.57 OUR IMPROVED COVER STAR BARREL CHURN, 6-GALLON.

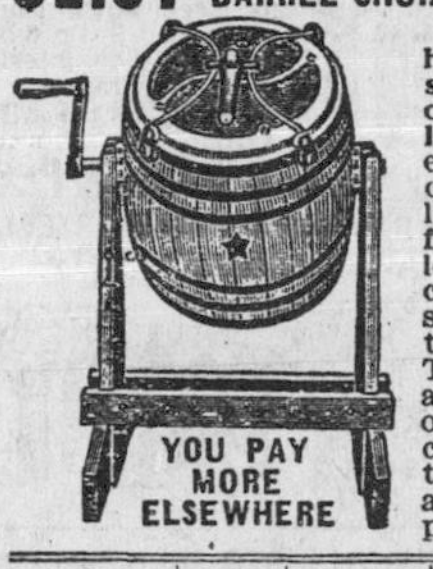

Made of selected hardwood. This style of churn is old, tried and reliable, easy to operate and keep clean; it is absolutely impossible for this churn to leak, as the wear can be taken up as simply as one can turn a thumb nut. The fasteners are attached to the outside of the churn, and clamp the cover with an anti-leak compound lever action.

No.	Holds Gals.	Churns Gals.	Weight, pounds	Price, as illustrated
9K29200	6	1 to 3	29	$2.57
9K29201	10	1 to 5	36	2.86
9K29202	15	1 to 7	43	3.23
9K29203	20	2 to 9	52	3.54
9K29204	25	2 to 12	71	4.43
9K29205	35	3 to 16	80	5.30

$2.95 BABCOCK HIGH SPEED MILK TESTING OUTFIT COMPLETE.

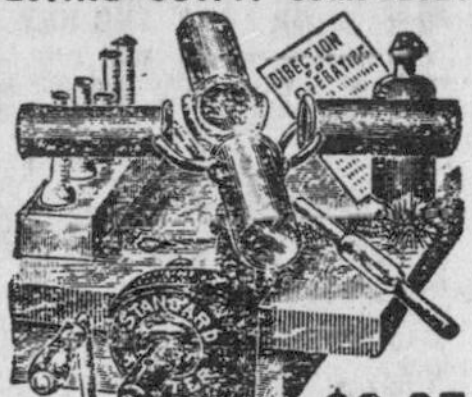

$2.95

It costs no more to feed a good cow than a poor one. To make dairying pay and to know the profit derived from each individual cow, it is necessary to test the milk. Our Babcock Milk Testers tell the exact quality of each cow's milk. A tester is absolutely necessary when buying cows as the quantity of milk a cow gives is not always an index to the value of the cow. You can save double the cost of one of our testers in buying a single cow. Our Babcock Tester has cut spiral gear wheel and steel spindle with worm thread enclosed in heavy case; is fitted with swinging pockets and malleable heads, and can be attached to any table or bench. Nicely finished in red enamel. Weight, boxed, about 15 pounds. Price includes bottle of acid, test bottles, brush, acid measure, pipette and full directions for making tests. No previous knowledge of milk testing necessary. Anyone who can read can learn to make a test.

No. 9K29270 2-bottle for milk. Price **$2.95**
No. 9K29271 4-bottle for milk. Price **$3.78**
No. 9K29272 2-bottle for milk and cream. Price **$3.23**
No. 9K29273 4-bottle for milk and cream. Price **$4.12**

$4.23 PER GRO. FLINT GLASS MILK JARS.

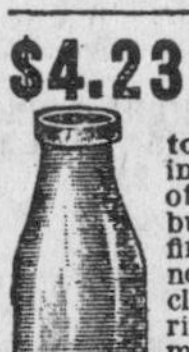

Your customers will be willing to pay more for milk if delivered in sealed bottles. Order a supply of us and get the cream of the business. Our bottles are made of first quality flint glass, and are not easily broken. They are smooth, clean and heavy. They have deep rim at top to hold stopper, large mouth and can be readily cleaned. Packed six dozen to the crate. We do not sell less than a crate.

No.	Size	Weight per gro.	Price, per crate of 6 doz.	Price, per gro.
9K29127	½-pints	116 lbs.	$2.15	$4.23
9K29129	Pints	185 lbs.	2.50	4.90
9K29128	Quarts	305 lbs.	3.50	6.85

$1.24 FOR 6,000 BEST WATERPROOF MILK BOTTLE CAPS.

No. 9K29130 They fit either size glass milk jars.
Price, per bushel basket containing 6,000 stoppers. Weight, 20 pounds **$1.24**
Price, per barrel containing 50,000 stoppers. Weight, 135 pounds **$9.45**

No. 9K29137 Our Big Leader Milk Jar Stoppers, medium weight, good quality stock, paraffined both sides, waterproof. Put up in barrels containing 50,000. We do not sell less than a barrel. Weight, 130 pounds.
Price, per barrel **$7.40**

11c FOR THIS BEST BRISTLE MILK BOTTLE CLEANING BRUSH.

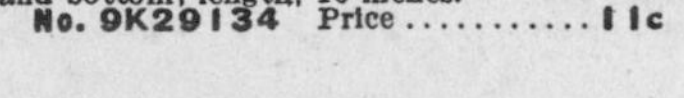

11c

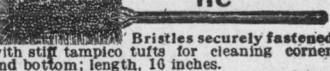

Bristles securely fastened, with stiff tampico tufts for cleaning corners and bottom; length, 16 inches.
No. 9K29134 Price **11c**

33c SECURE SELF LOCKING DOUBLE LINK IRON CHEST LOCKS.

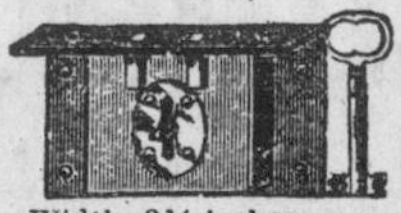

Made of iron with brass keyhole escutcheons. Double bitted keys, all different in a dozen.

No. 9K48107 Width, 2⅜ inches. Price, per dozen, $3.85; each 33c
No. 9K48109 Width, 4 inches. Price, per dozen, $4.75; each..........40c

66c SELF LOCKING DOUBLE LINK BRASS CHEST LOCK WITH TWO KEYS.

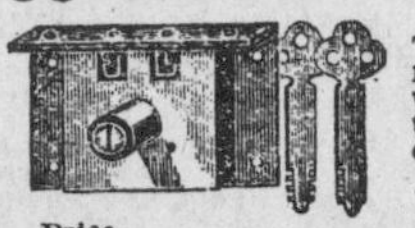

Brass Chest Lock. Two nickel plated flat steel keys. For wood 1 inch thick. The finest chest lock made.
No. 9K48123 Width, 3½ inches.
Price..........66c

17c FOR A BRASS CYLINDER STEEL DRAWER LOCK WITH TWO KEYS.

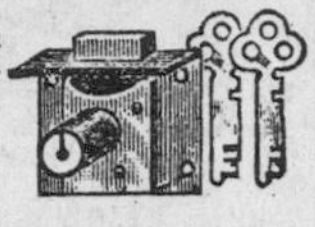

Steel, with brass cylinder, for wood ⅞ inch thick. Two nickel plated steel keys.
No. 9K48147 1¾ inches wide.
Price, each.....$0.17
Per dozen...... 2.02

23c BUYS THIS CYLINDER SOLID BRASS DRAWER LOCK FOR ⅞-INCH WOOD.

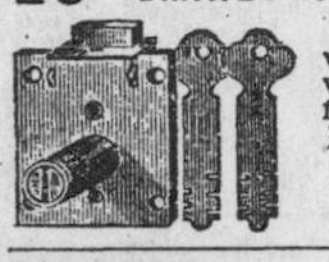

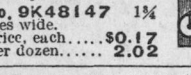

Put on without cutting wood. Size, 1⅝ inches wide. Two nickel plated flat steel keys. For wood ⅞ inch thick.
No. 9K48151
Price, each $0.23
Per dozen 2.72

4c IRON WARDROBE OR CUPBOARD DOOR LOCK AND KEY.

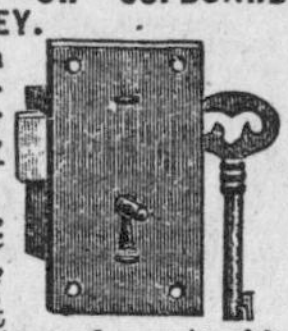

Intended to be put on without cutting the wood. Bolts shoot right and left. Width, 1¼ inches; length, 2⅜ inches. One iron tumbler, with one key.
No. 9K48173 Price, per dozen, 45c; each..4c
No. 9K48177 Width, 1⅜ inches; length, 2⅞ inches. Heavy iron bolt with two secure levers. A good serviceable lock. Price, each..........$0.23
Per dozen.......... 2.60

Carpet Tacks.

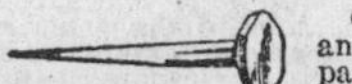

Guaranteed full size and strictly half weight papers.

No. 9K48681 Iron Cut Tacks.

Size, ounces	2	4	6	8	10	12
Per doz. papers	12c	16c	18c	22c	28c	34c

No. 9K48683 Tinned Carpet Tacks.

Size, ounces	6	8	10	12
Per dozen papers	22c	28c	34c	42c

No. 9K48685 Blued Staples or Double Pointed Tacks for matting, oilcloth or heavy carpet; size, 11 ounces in packages of 100.
Price, per dozen papers..........14c

Solid Brass Head Upholstering Nails, used for nailing on chair seats, upholstering furniture, etc.

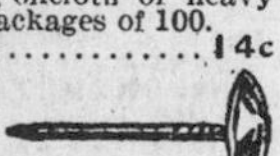

No. 9K48671 Small size.

Packages of	100 Nails	1,000 Nails
Per paper	7c	55c

No. 9K48673 Large size.

Packages of	100 Nails	1,000 Nails
Per paper	9c	80c

11c PER GROSS BRIGHT WIRE SCREW EYES No. 214.

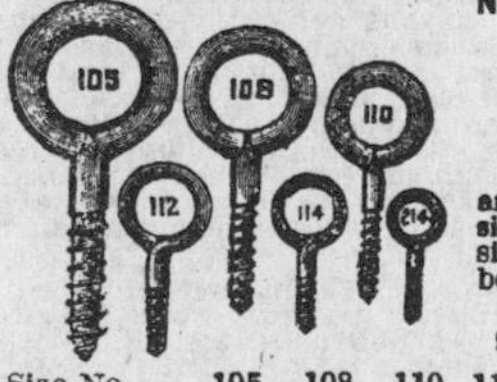

Illustrations are half actual size. Mention size and number.
No. 9K48601

Size No.	105	108	110	112	114	214
Per dozen	4c	3c	2c	2c	2c	2c
Per gross	39c	24c	19c	13c	12c	11c

2c FOR 12 BRIGHT WIRE SCREW HOOKS, SIZE No. 12.

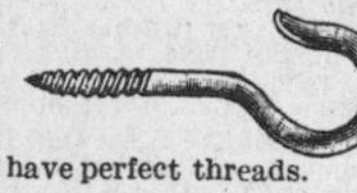

Bright Wire Screw Hooks. The size of wire is in proportion to length, the longer screw hooks being heavier wire. Nicely finished and have perfect threads.
No. 9K48605

Size No.	12	10	8	6½	5	0
Lengths	1½	1⅞	2¼	3	3½	4½
Price, doz.	2c	2c	3c	4c	6c	$0.15
Per gross	19c	22c	30c	44c	57c	1.60

Give number when ordering.

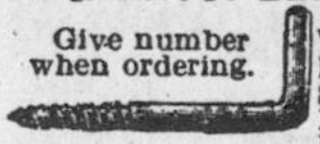

No. 9K48609 Bright Wire Straight Screw Hooks.

Size No.	114	112
Length, inches	1	1¼
Price, per doz.	2c	2c
Per gross	18c	19c

Size No.	110	108	106	104
Length, inches	1½	2	2½	3
Price, per doz	2c	3c	4c	6c
Per gross	22c	23c	46c	70c

$1.26 TROLLEY ROLLER BEARING STEEL BARN DOOR HANGERS.

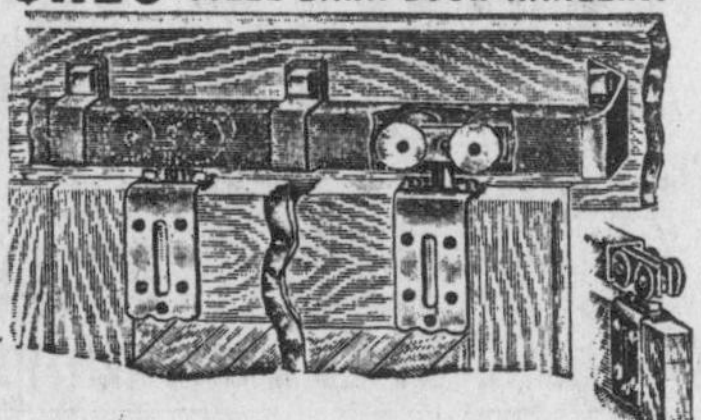

Waterproof, sparrowproof and jumpproof. The most satisfactory hanger made. Suitable for doors weighing up to 400 pounds and from 1½ to 2¼ inches thick. Set consists of two hangers, two end brackets, one center bracket and the necessary bolts and screws.
No. 9K48829 Price, per set, complete, without track..........$1.26

Trolley Track for hangers above. Price of track does not include center brackets.
No. 9K48831

Length, feet	4	5	6	8	10
Price, per length	40c	50c	60c	80c	$1.00

Center Track Brackets for Trolley Track. Center brackets should not be more than 3 feet apart.
No. 9K48833 Price, each..........10c

56c THE ROCKWELL HINGE JOINT BARN DOOR HANGER.

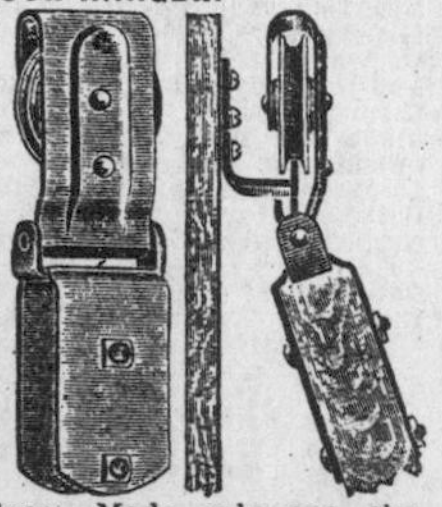

Steel roller bearings, every part except wheel made of steel. Wheel protected from storm. Made with a hinge joint and cannot bind when door is swung in or out. Has guard that runs under and inside the track, (and cannot jump the track). It runs easy on any length of track. Will carry any door. Made only one size, for doors 1¾ inches thick. (Will not run on the common track. For track for this hanger see next number.)
No. 9K48871 Price, per pair..........56c

Track for the Rockwell or any other barn door hanger. Made of round edge steel, 1¼x3-16 inches. Strong enough to carry the heaviest door. To put this track up it requires three screws to each foot. The diameter of each screw should be No. 12, the length either 1 inch or longer, as required. Screws are not furnished at price named.
No. 9K48873

Length, feet	4	6	8	10
Price, per length	19c	28c	37c	46c

6c PER DOZ. BRASS SCREW AND CUP HOOKS.

Both styles are same price. State size wanted.

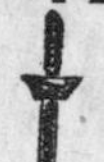

No. 9K48615 Brass Screw Hooks.

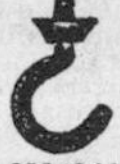

No. 9K48619
No. 9K48615 Brass Cup Hooks. No. 9K48619

Size, inch	½	⅝	¾	⅞	1
Price, per doz.	6c	6c	7c	7c	8c
Per gross	69c	70c	74c	78c	89c

18c FOR 12 WHITE PORCELAIN PICTURE KNOBS.

Complete with screw.

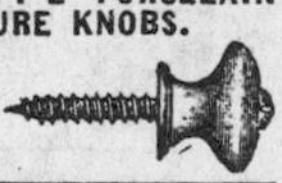

No. 9K48621 Price, per dozen..........18c

11c PER DOZ. PORCELAIN HEAD GILT RIM PICTURE NAILS.

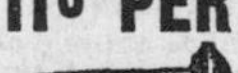

No. 9K48611 Price, per dozen..........11c

19c PER DOZ. BRASS WALL PICTURE HOOKS.

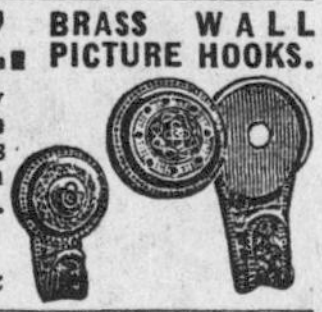

Put up with an ordinary wire nail. The round plate is removed while nail is being driven and when replaced covers the nail.
No. 9K48613
Price, per dozen, 19c

7c FOR 25 YDS. BRAIDED WIRE PICTURE CORD.

Silvered, guaranteed full length. (We do not cut coils.)
No. 9K48617 No. 2, suitable for medium weight pictures.
Price, per coil of 25 yards..........7c
6 coils for..........39c

7c FOR 2 3-INCH WROUGHT IRON HINGE HASPS.

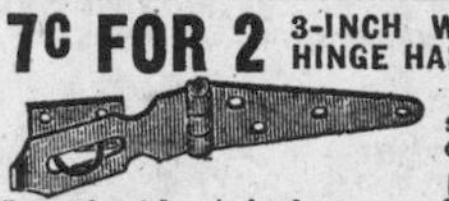

Complete as shown. Without screws.
No. 9K48979

Length of hasp, inches	3	6	8
Price, 2 for	7c	12c	14c
Per dozen	36c	60c	78c

6c FOR 3 STEEL HASPS AND STAPLES.

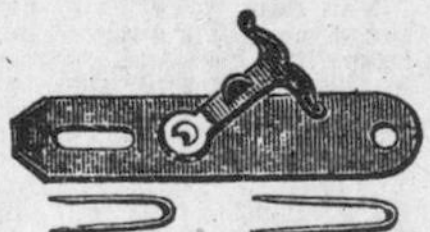

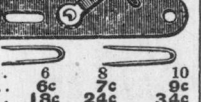

Complete as shown.
No. 9K48973

Length, inches	6	8	10
Price, 3 for	6c	7c	9c
Per dozen	18c	24c	34c

37c ROLLER BEARING ANTI-FRICTION STEEL BARN DOOR HANGER.

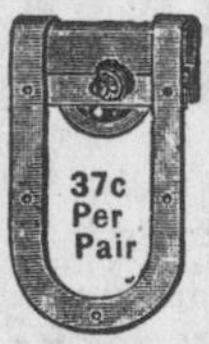

Has cold rolled steel axle and anti-friction bearings, which are fully covered to protect them from the weather. With the exception of the wheel, it is made entirely of wrought steel, is built to stand the roughest usage and can be used on any standard track. We do not furnish bolts at prices quoted on barn door hangers. All hangers require bolts 5-16 inch in diameter. For prices of bolts, see page 513.
No. 9K48837 For small doors. Frame, 4¾x11½ inches. Price, per pair..........37c
No. 9K48839 For ordinary sized doors. Frame, 6¼x12¼ inches. Price, per pair..46c
No. 9K48841 For heaviest doors. Frame, 7x14 inches. Price, per pair..........54c

51c ANTI-FRICTION STEEL BARN DOOR HANGER WITH LOOSE AXLE.

The kind that retails for 75 cents.

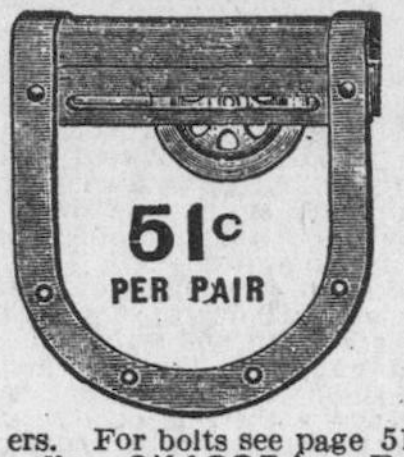

This hanger is made entirely of heavy steel, with the exception of the wheel, and is fully covered to protect it from snow and ice. Runs smoothly and is built to stand continuous hard service. The wheel has a deep groove to prevent jumping the track. Bolts are not furnished with hangers. For bolts see page 513.
No. 9K48851 For ordinary doors. Frame, 9x10¼ inches. 3-inch wheel, 8-foot run. Price, per pair..........51c
No. 9K48853 For wide doors. Frame, 11x11¾ inches. 4-inch wheel for 10-foot run. Price, per pair..........61c
No. 9K48855 For wide and heavy doors. Frame, 12x12¼ inches, 5-inch wheel for 11-foot run. Price, per pair..........83c

13c FOR 4 FEET FULL SIZE BRACED BARN DOOR TRACK.

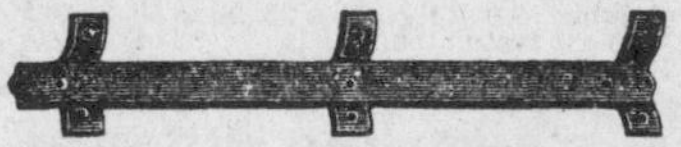

Standard size, 3-16x1 inch, made solid and strong, will carry the largest doors. Comes in 4, 6, 8 or 10-foot lengths. Requires No. 12 screws to fasten to building. Prices quoted do not include screws.
No. 9K48861

Length, feet	4	6	8	10
Price, per length	13c	19c	25c	32c

STEEL STRAP AND T HINGES.

You pay twice our prices at home.

Made of standard gauge wrought steel.

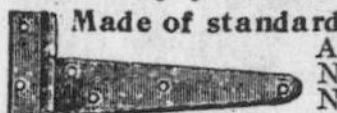

All full size and weight. No better hinges made. Not the cheap, thin, light weight kind offered by others.

NOTICE—Screws are not furnished with hinges at prices quoted. For screws see page 475.

No. 9K47851 Light Wrought Steel T Hinges. Size given is measurement from joint to end of hinge.

Size, in.	3	4	6	8
Price, per pair	3c	4c	6c	7c
Per dozen pairs	32c	40c	60c	70c

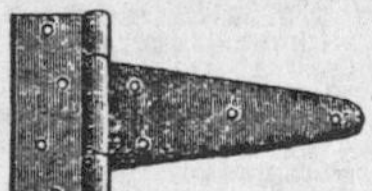

Extra Heavy Wrought Steel T Hinges. Size given is measurement from joint to end of hinge.
No. 9K47853

Size, inches	6	8	10	12	14
Price, per pair	9c	$0.16	$0.23	$0.31	$0.36
Per dozen pairs	95c	1.70	2.55	3.50	4.15

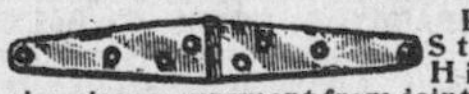

Light Wrought Steel Strap Hinges. Size given is measurement from joint to end of hinge.
No. 9K47855

Size, in.	3	4	5	6
Price, per pair	3c	4c	6c	7c
Per dozen pairs	33c	41c	62c	73c

Heavy Wrought Steel Strap Hinges, without screws.

No. 9K47857

Size, inches	6	8	10	12	14
Price, per pair	7c	$0.12	$0.17	$0.25	$0.34
Per dozen pairs	82c	1.42	1.98	2.94	4.03

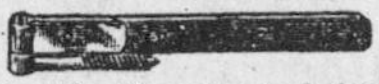

Wrought Steel Screw Strap Hinge. Requires two bolts ⅜ inch in diameter and four bolts 5-16 inch in diameter to put them on. Bolts not furnished. See page 513 for bolts.
No. 9K47861

Size, inches	10	12	14
Price, per pair	$0.16	$0.20	$0.24
Per dozen pairs	1.88	2.36	2.83

8c FOR 2 SECURITY COMBINED HOOK, HASP AND STAPLES.

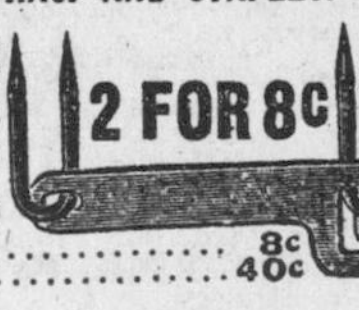

The most popular hasp on the market. Length, 8 inches. Complete with staples.
No. 9K48975
Price, 2 for..........8c
Per dozen..........40c

Retail dealers ask double our prices for most of the staple hardware shown on this page. The low prices in our last catalogue have been still further reduced on over 3,000 hardware items in this book.

10c EXTRA HEAVY JAPANNED IRON BARN DOOR LATCH.

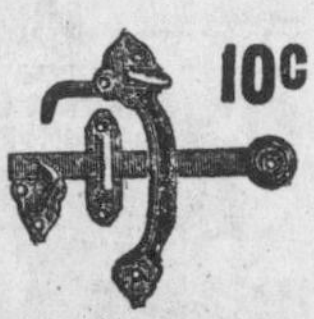

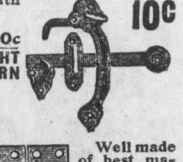

Strong, substantial and durable, with wrought latch.
No. 9K48885
Price..........10c

16c HEAVY WROUGHT JAPANNED BARN DOOR BOLT.

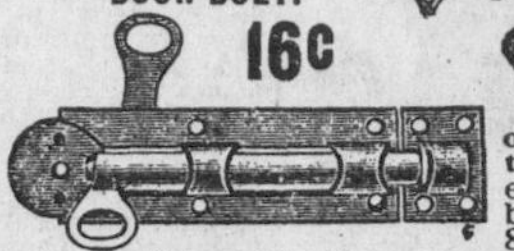

Well made of best materials. Has extra heavy bolt. Length, 8 inches.
No. 9K48891 Price..........16c

4c JAPANNED YANKEE DOOR CATCH. TO HOLD SWING DOORS OPEN.

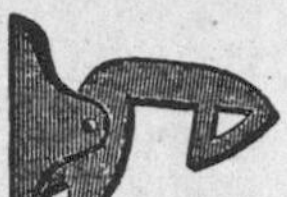

A very useful article for this purpose. Made of cast iron, japanned.
No. 9K48895
Price..........4c

3c EXTRA HEAVY JAPANNED IRON BARN DOOR PULL.

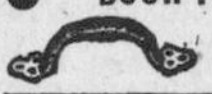

No. 9K48899 Price..3c

7c BARN DOOR STAY ROLLERS. ADJUSTABLE TO ANY THICKNESS OF DOOR.

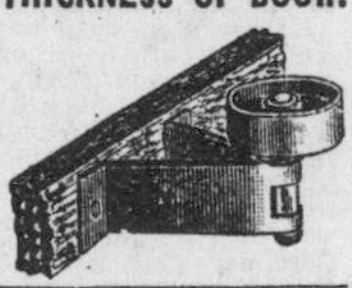

Barn Door Stay Rollers, adjustable to any thickness of door. Will always stay in the right position. The strongest adjustable stay in the market.
No. 9K48925
Price..........7c

26c PER SET SELF CLOSING GATE HINGES.

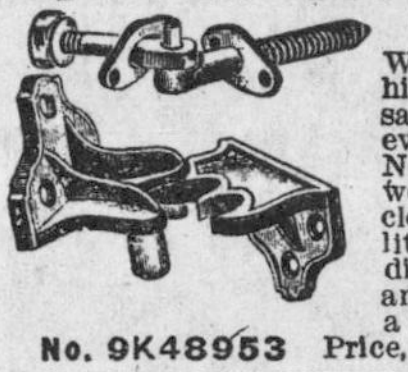

Swing both ways. Wrought upper hinge. The most satisfactory hinges ever put on a gate. Needs no spring or weight to keep it closed. Costs but little more than ordinary strap hinges and will outlast half a dozen pairs.
No. 9K48953 Price, per set.... 26c

7c FOR THIS RIGHT OR LEFT HAND GATE LATCH.

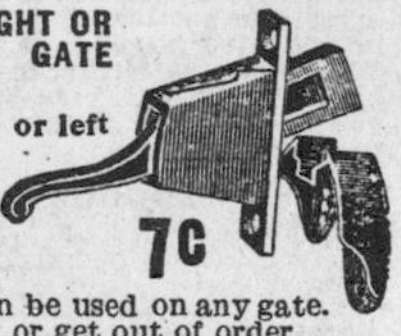

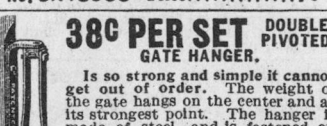

For either right or left hand gates, or gates that swing both ways. Especially recommended for use with No. 9K48953 hinges, though it can be used on any gate. No springs to break or get out of order.
No. 9K48955 Price..........7c

38c PER SET DOUBLE PIVOTED GATE HANGER.

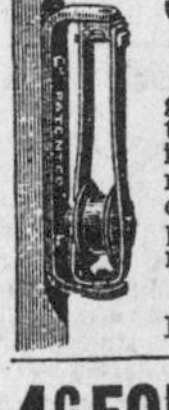

Is so strong and simple it cannot get out of order. The weight of the gate hangs on the center and at its strongest point. The hanger is made of steel and is fastened on outside corner near the center of the post with two lag bolts, and does not project or have weak points.
No. 9K48959
Price, per set..........38c

4c FOR 3 WROUGHT HOOKS AND STAPLES.

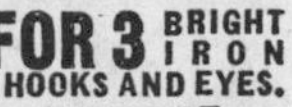

No. 9K48965

Length, inches	4	6
Price, 3 for	4c	6c
Per package, 3 dozen	40c	48c

2c FOR 3 BRIGHT IRON WIRE HOOKS AND EYES.

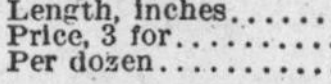

No. 9K48967

Length, inches	2	4
Price, 3 for	2c	3c
Per dozen	7c	11c

4c NEVER-RUST MALLEABLE SAFETY GATE HOOK AND STAPLES.

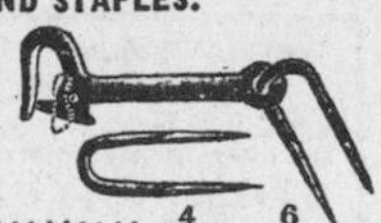

Malleable Hook with Steel Staples, all heavily tinned to prevent rusting.
No. 9K48969

Length, inches	4	6
Price, each	4c	6c
Per dozen	44c	64c

10c FOR 2 GALVANIZED HITCHING RINGS.

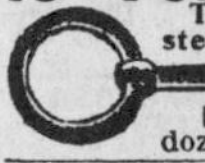

These rings have heavy wrought steel screw and malleable ring. Diameter of ring 2¼ inches.
No. 9K48983 Price, per dozen, 48c; 2 for..........10c

16c FOR 72 POLISHED WROUGHT IRON STAPLES.

Assorted lengths, from 1½ to 3 inches. Nicely finished, well pointed, full size. Six dozen in a box.
No. 9K48991 Price, per box....16c

$1.37 FOR A WROUGHT STEEL CORNER HAY RACK, HEIGHT, 3 FEET.

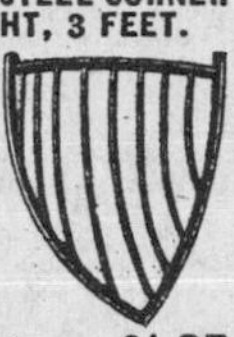

Will save hay enough to pay for itself in a short time. What is left is good for next feeding, not trampled on the floor as is the case when hay is fed in the old way. Made of round wrought steel rods, ½ inch in diameter. Frame, flat steel, 1¼x ⅜ inches. Height, 3 feet; projects from corner 2 feet. Weight, 25 lbs.
No. 9K49103 Price..........$1.37
Cast Iron Corner Hay Rack, projects from corner 22 in.; height, 27 inches; weight, 29 lbs.
No. 9K49101 Price..........$1.04

$1.06 CAST IRON CORNER FEED AND SALT BOXES, 10 INCHES DEEP.

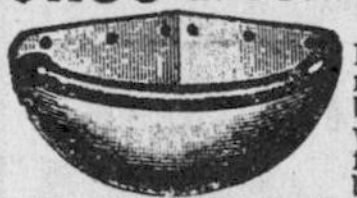

Very substantial. Horses and cattle cannot destroy these iron boxes like they can wood. The most satisfactory feed and salt boxes ever made.
No. 9K49111 Feed Box. Size, 16 inches on each side, 10 inches deep. Price....$1.06
No. 9K49113 Feed Box with heavy roll rim. Size, 16 inches on each side, 10 inches deep; weight, 28 pounds. Price........$1.36
No. 9K49117 Salt Box. Size, 6 inches on each side, 5 inches deep. Price......29c

8c FOR A FLUTED MALLEABLE IRON PICKET PIN WITH SWIVEL.

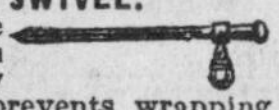

This fluted malleable Iron Pin is strong enough and long enough to hold any cow. Has swivel which prevents wrapping chain around pin. 15 inches long.
No. 9K49121 Price..............8c

42c FOR A 20-FOOT BRIGHT WIRE TIE OUT COW CHAIN.

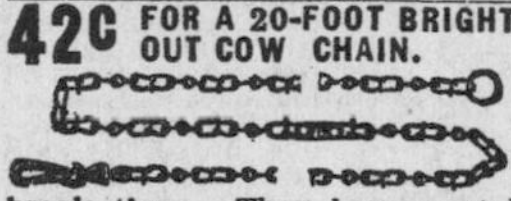

Light, but so strong that no ordinary strain will break them. They have a stake ring 3¼ inches in diameter on one end, a steel swivel snap on the other and a swivel in the center.
Length, feet.......... 20 30
No. 9K49125 Price..... 42c 62c

3c FOR A MALLEABLE IRON LARIAT OR ROPE SWIVEL, 3 INCHES LONG.

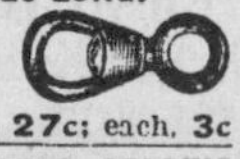

Stronger than any rope that will go in either eye; one eye ⅜ inch inside, the other ¾ inch inside.
No. 9K49129 Per doz., 27c; each, 3c

14c FOR AN OLD RELIABLE TYLER'S SAFETY WEANER, SMALL SIZE.

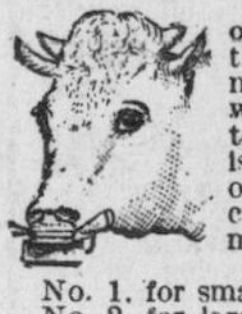

Has no sharp points to prick or gouge the cow. Does not go through or rub against the calf's nose and make it sore. The only weaner having side protection to prevent sucking sidewise and is warranted to wean the most obstinate case without injury or cruelty to calf or cow. Not mailable.
No. 9K49141
No. 1, for small calves. Price........14c
No. 2, for large calves. Price........16c
No. 3, for yearlings. Price........18c
No. 4, for 2-year olds and cows. Price..20c

32c ADJUSTABLE HOOSIER WEANER, FOR CALVES OR SMALL YEARLINGS.

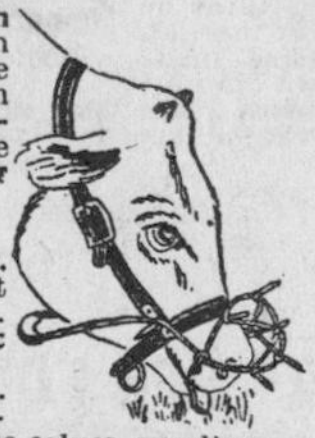

Does not interfere with feeding, but drops down over the mouth when the head is raised in position to suck. A very satisfactory weaner. Price includes good leather straps.
No. 9K49151
Hoosier Calf Weaner. Adjustable to fit smallest calves or small yearlings. Price..........32c
No. 9K49153
Hoosier Range Weaner. Same as above, only larger. Adjustable to fit large calves, yearlings or colts. Price..........38c
No. 9K49155 Hoosier Cow Weaner. Adjustable to fit large yearlings or largest cows. Halter is made of best oil filled waterproof leather, frame of wrought steel, all metal parts tinned to prevent rust. Price....48c

23c GALVANIZED WIRE BASKET WEANER WITH STRAPS, FOR CALVES.

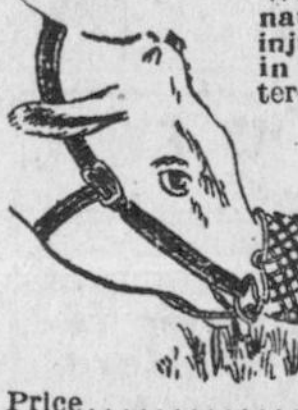

Will wean the most obstinate case without cruelty or injury, and give satisfaction in every way. Does not interfere with feeding, but when head is raised to suck, the wire basket drops over mouth. Made of heavy galvanized wire and has solid oil filled waterproof leather straps.
No. 9K49161
For calves. Price..23c
No. 9K49163
For yearlings. Price..........26c
No. 9K49165 For cows. Price..33c

$3.73 V SHAPE BLADE DEHORNING CLIPPERS. CUTS ALL AROUND THE HORN. IMPOSSIBLE TO CRUSH THE HORN. CUTS ON ALL SIDES AT ONCE. KNIVES CANNOT INTERLOCK OR CUT INTO EACH OTHER.

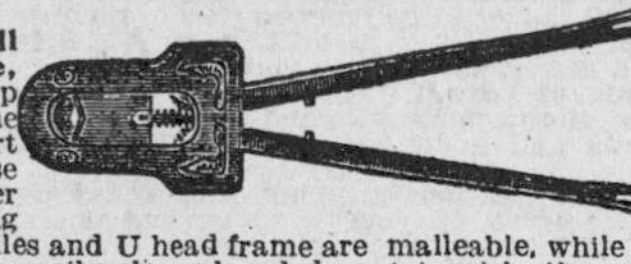

This style Dehorner in the large size will clip any size horn from cattle of any age, smooth and clean. The special size will clip any ordinary size horn. In opening the blades the handles do not go far enough apart to prevent the operator having ample purchase and twice the power of any other dehorner made. The material used in manufacturing this clipper is of the best quality. The handles and U head frame are malleable, while the knives are of the best crescent steel; can be easily cleaned and do not tarnish, thus preventing all possibility of blood poisoning. Twisting or prying will cause the blades to break. We will not replace blades broken from this cause.
No. 9K49201 V Blade Dehorner. Special size. Knives open 3 inches. Large enough for any ordinary stock. Price..........$3.73
No. 9K49203 Extra Sliding Knife, for special size V Blade Dehorner. Price, .39
No. 9K49205 Extra Stationary Knife, for special size V Blade Dehorner. Price, .38
No. 9K49211 V Blade Dehorner. Large size. Knives open 3½ inches. Price, 4.72
No. 9K49213 Extra Sliding Knife, for large size V Blade Dehorner. Price, .41
No. 9K49215 Extra Stationary Knife, for large size V Blade Dehorner. Price, .40

GENERAL REDUCTION IN PRICE ON HARDWARE ON THIS PAGE FROM THE EXTREMELY LOW PRICES IN OUR LAST CATALOGUE.

5c FULL SIZE MALLEABLE CATTLE LEADER WITH BRASS SPRING.

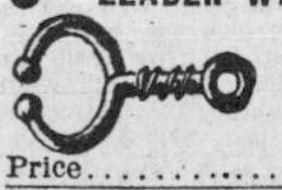

With brass spring; full size; regular goods, same as you pay double the price for or more.
No. 9K49261
Price..........5c

12c POLISHED COPPER BULL RING, 2½-INCH, WITH SCREWDRIVER.

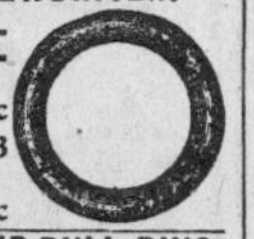

2½ inches in diameter; polished, complete with screwdriver to fit.
No. 9K49271 - Price, 12c
Same as No. 9K49271, 3 inches in diameter.
No. 9K49273 Price, 15c

15c SELF PIERCING COPPER BULL RING, SAVES TIME AND LABOR.

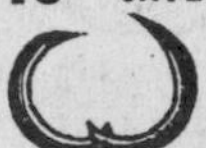

Cuts its own hole. Prevents accident and danger of making bull vicious. Diameter of ring, 2½ inches. Directions with each ring.
No. 9K49275 Price... 15c

24c PATENT LONG REACH BULL SNAP WITH 3-FOOT CHAIN.

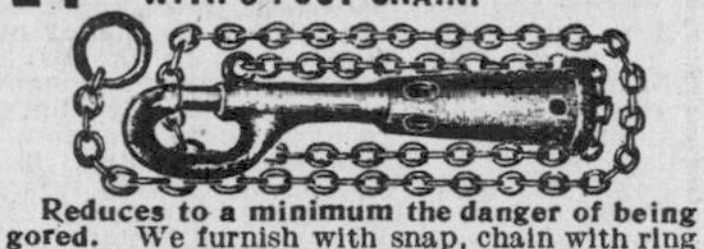

Reduces to a minimum the danger of being gored. We furnish with snap, chain with ring on end and three screw eyes. No wood handle furnished.
No. 9K49281 Price..........24c

54c "CAN'T ROOT" HOG CLIPPER AND EAR MARKER COMBINED.

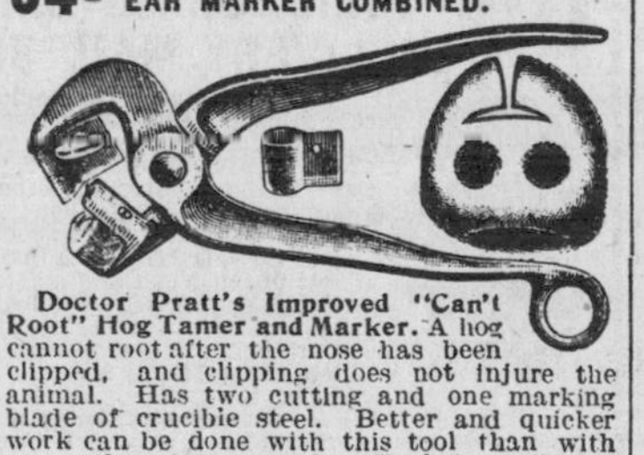

Doctor Pratt's Improved "Can't Root" Hog Tamer and Marker. A hog cannot root after the nose has been clipped, and clipping does not injure the animal. Has two cutting and one marking blade of crucible steel. Better and quicker work can be done with this tool than with any other tamer made. Tool is malleable iron with concealed spring and heavily nickel plated to prevent rust. Length, 10 inches.
No. 9K49365 Price..........54c

$1.54 STOCK MARKING PUNCH WITH BEST STEEL CUTTING DIES.

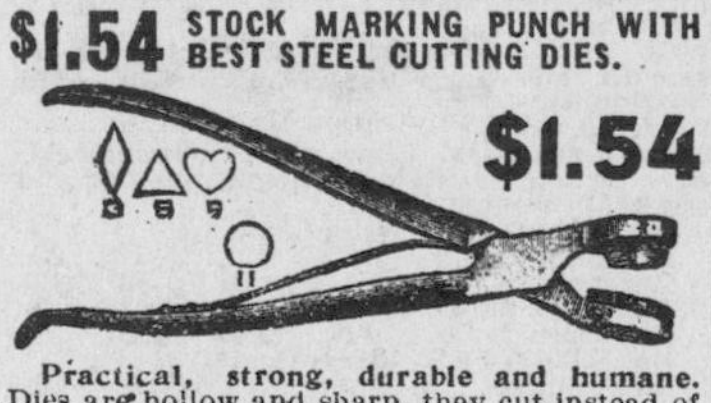

$1.54

Practical, strong, durable and humane. Dies are hollow and sharp, they cut instead of punching, as is the case when solid dies are used. Have strong malleable iron handles. The dies are from ¼ to 1 inch long; entire length of tool, 11¼ inches. When ordering, state the number of the die you prefer.
No. 9K49371 Price..........$1.54

11c FOR 4 OCTAGON PATTERN BRASS OX BALLS.

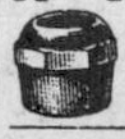

To put on the tips of the horns of vicious cattle. Medium size, ¾ inch.
No. 9K49283 Price, 4 for..11c

$1.50 FOR 100 METAL EAR LABELS.

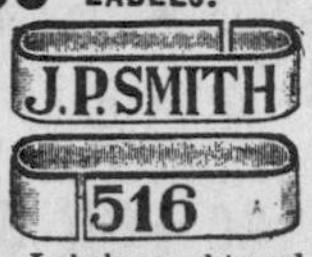

For sheep, cattle and hogs. Made with name on one side and any one number or consecutive numbers on reverse side. Not more than eleven letters in type as illustrated can be stamped on sheep labels, or fifteen on cattle or extra cattle sizes. Labels are shipped separately from other goods direct from factory only and customers should allow postage to cover same as follows: 13 cents per 100 on sheep and hog, 25 cents per 100 on cattle and 40 cents per 100 on extra cattle sizes. We cannot furnish less than 25 labels of one name and number.

When ordering give catalogue number, name and label numbers. Write plainly.	No. 9K49335 Sheep and Hog Size	No. 9K49337 Cattle Size	No. 9K49339 Extra Cattle Size
100 with one name and numbers...	$1.50	$2.00	$2.50
50 with one name and numbers...	1.00	1.25	1.50
25 with one name and numbers...	.65	.75	1.00
100, one name only or numbers only	1.00	1.50	1.75
50, one name only or numbers only	.75	1.00	1.25
25, one name only or numbers only	.50	.60	.80

75c OVAL HOLE EAR PUNCH FOR METAL LABELS. REGULAR SIZE.

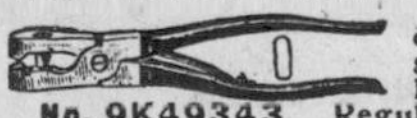

Punches small oval hole in ear, and closes the label.
No. 9K49343 Regular Cattle, Sheep and Hog Size Ear Punch. Price..........75c
No. 9K49341 Extra Cattle Size Ear Punch. Price..........$1.20
If by mail, postage on punch, extra, 10 cents.

$1.15 FOR 25 PURE ALUMINUM EAR BUTTONS.

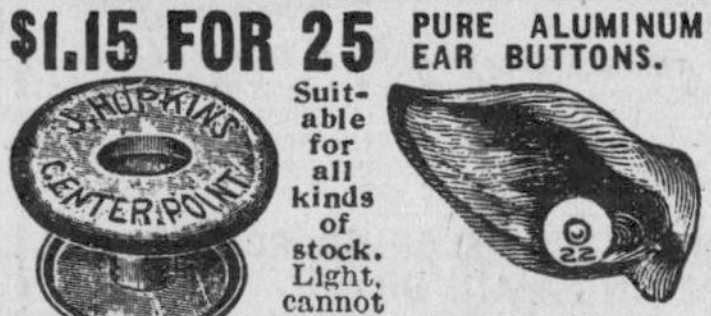

Suitable for all kinds of stock. Light, cannot pull out, do not rust or tarnish, positively the best stock buttons made. Furnished with name (not exceeding 19 letters) on one side and any number or series of numbers on reverse side.
No. 9K49351
With Name and No. Price, per 25.....$ 1.15
With Name and No. Price, per 50.... 1.75
With Name and No. Price, per 100... 3.25
With Name and No. Price, per 500.. 15.00
With Name and No. Price, per 1,000. 27.00
Buttons are made to order and shipped direct from factory only and cannot be forwarded with other goods. Customers must allow 10 cents per 100 for postage in addition to above prices unless ordered by express.
Punch and Plier combined for fitting above buttons to ears of animals.
No. 9K49353 Price..........$1.00
If by mail, postage extra, 10 cents.

$1.96 FOR A TATTOO STOCK MARKER, COMPLETE WITH ANY THREE LETTERS OR FIGURES.

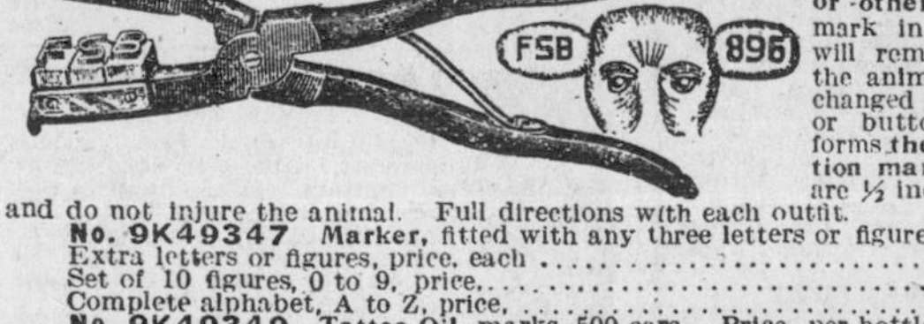

For marking the ears of horses, cattle, sheep, hogs, dogs or other animals. A tattoo mark in the skin of any animal will remain visible as long as the animal lives. It cannot be changed or removed as ear labels or buttons frequently are, and forms the only perfect identification mark. These tattoo letters are ½ inch in size, made instantly and do not injure the animal. Full directions with each outfit.
No. 9K49347 Marker, fitted with any three letters or figures. Price......$1.96
Extra letters or figures, price, each.......... .30
Set of 10 figures, 0 to 9, price.......... 2.72
Complete alphabet, A to Z, price.......... 6.21
No. 9K49349 Tattoo Oil, marks 500 ears. Price, per bottle.......... .47
No. 9K49350 Tattoo Oil, red, for extra dark skin. Price, per bottle.......... .49
If by mail, postage extra on marker, 5 cents; on oil, 8 cents.

41c FOR THIS JAPANNED DEHORNING SAW, COMPLETE WITH BLADE.

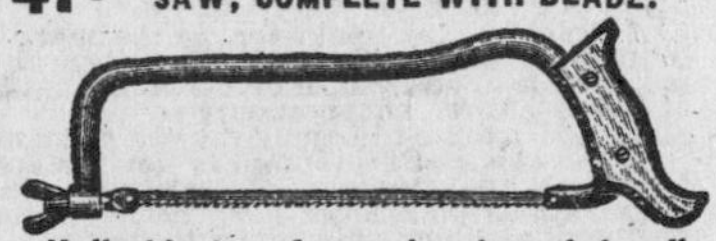

Malleable iron frame, beechwood handle, complete with 9½-inch blade, ¼ inch wide.
No. 9K49241 Price..........41c
Extra blades for this saw.
No. 9K49243 Price, 4 for......30c

17c HILL'S MALLEABLE IRON TONGS FOR HOLDING HOGS.

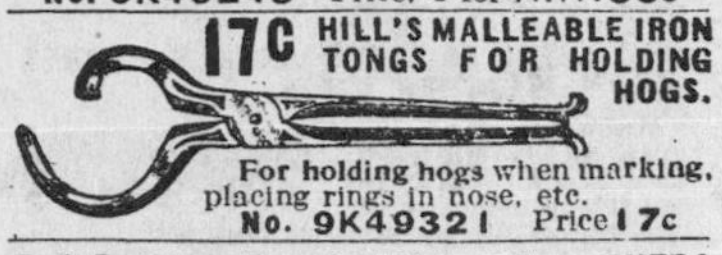

For holding hogs when marking, placing rings in nose, etc.
No. 9K49321 Price 17c

39c ONE-MAN DOUBLE END EXTRA STRONG JAPANNED HOG HOLDER.

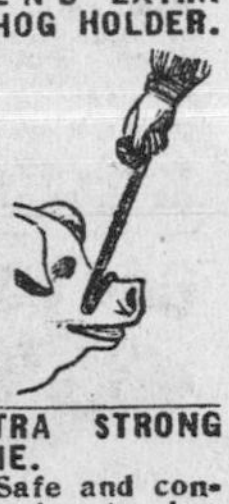

One man can hold and snout the largest hog, or hold the same while castrating. Pregnant sows can be snouted without injury to the animal. One end holds large hogs, the other small ones. No touching with the hands. No throwing down. We guarantee it to give entire satisfaction. Full directions sent with each holder.
No. 9K49323 Price, 39c

13c OHIO PATTERN EXTRA STRONG WIRE LINK COW TIE.

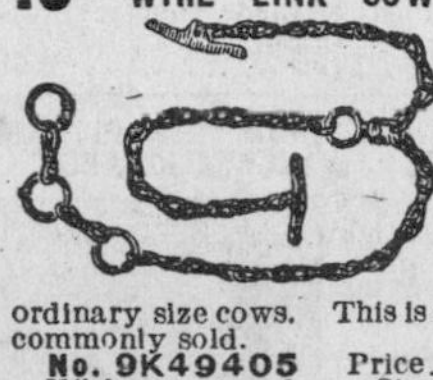

Safe and convenient, has smooth links and will not tangle. Allows great freedom to the animal's head. Easily put on and taken off. Has two toggles. Size, 2-0, suitable for ordinary size cows. This is the size and weight commonly sold.
No. 9K49405 Price..........13c
With two toggles. Size, 4-0, heavy and strong enough for the largest cow.
No. 9K49407 Price..........18c

16c OHIO PATTERN AMERICAN FLAT LINK STEEL COW TIE.

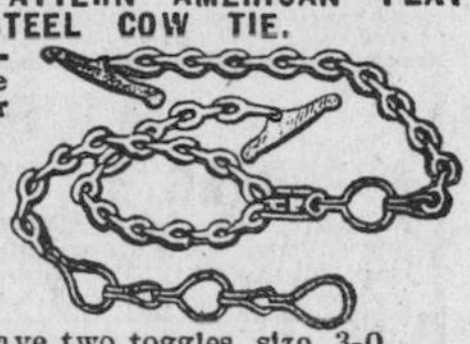

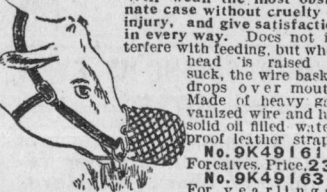

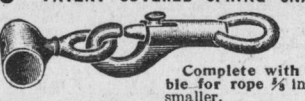

Rings and swivels are made of Bessemer steel, toggles always hang at right angles and do not get unfastened. Much larger and stronger than the size usually sold. Have two toggles, size, 3-0.
No. 9K49413 Price..........16c
With two toggles. Size, 5-0. The heaviest and strongest cow tie made.
No. 9K49415 Price..........23c

7c STEEL COW TIE FIXTURE, SAFE, STRONG AND CONVENIENT.

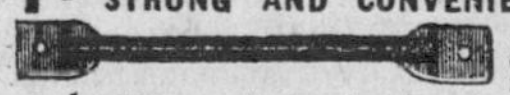

Strong, safe and convenient. Can be used with any tie having two toggles. Entire length, 16 inches. Width at ends, 2 inches.
No. 9K49435 Price..........7c

6c TINNED CATTLE TIE IRONS WITH PATENT COVERED SPRING SNAP.

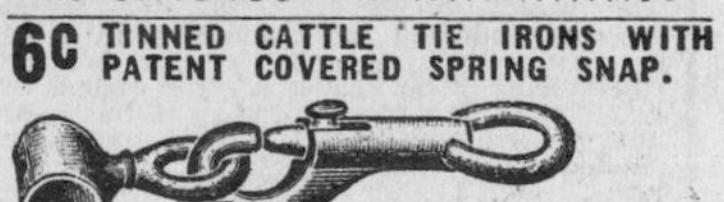

Complete with thimble for rope ⅜ inch or smaller.
No. 9K49289 Price..........6c

6c HILL'S MALLEABLE HOG RINGER, STRONG AND SUBSTANTIAL.

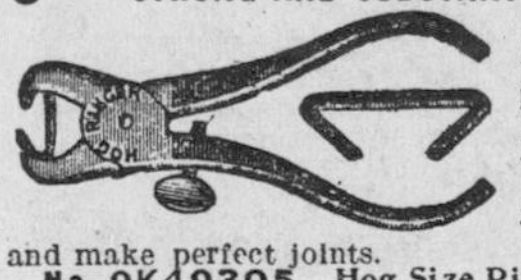

No. 9K49303 Hill's Malleable Hog Ringer. Price..6c
Rings are nicely made, well finished and make perfect joints.
No. 9K49305 Hog Size Rings. Price, per box of 100..........4c
No. 9K49307 Shoat Size Rings. Price, per box of 100..........4c
No. 9K49309 Pig Size Rings. Price, per box of 100..........4c
Per dozen boxes, any size..........43c

9c FOR AN IMPROVED PERFECTION HOG RINGER, NICELY JAPANNED.

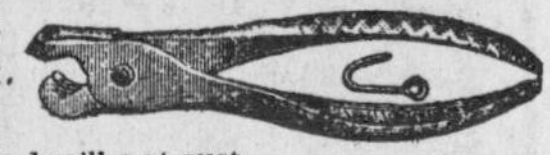

Made of best gray iron. Nicely japanned. Rings are coppered and will not rust.
No. 9K49311 Perfection Ringer. Price..........9c
No. 9K49313 Rings, to be used with above ringer; 100 in a box. Price, per box 7c
Per dozen boxes..........78c

6c PER DOZEN CAST IRON STOCK MARKS.

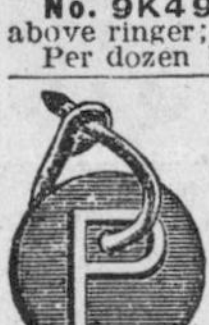

With raised letters—never wear out. Used with Perfection Ring and Ringer. Can furnish any single letter, A to Z.
No. 9K49331 Price, per dozen, without rings....6c
Per 100, without rings...38c

COLDPROOF WEATHER STRIP.

Keeps out the cold; keeps in the heat. You will save more than enough on fuel alone in a single winter to pay for weather stripping your house. The high grade line we sell is made of such superior material that it will not have to be renewed for a number of years. It is not necessary to pay a carpenter to put it on, as it is very simple all that is required to apply it being a hammer and a few small nails or tacks.

"An ounce of prevention is worth several pounds of cure." Your family will have fewer coughs, colds and doctor's bills, they will be more comfortable and you will enjoy your home as you never have before if the windows and doors are made windproof and dustproof with our superior weather strip.

You can save 50 to 75 per cent on the cost of weather stripping your house by ordering it from us and applying it yourself. Just measure up your windows and doors, send us your order and do away with the cold drafts, dust, etc., which come in even the most tightly constructed house if not properly fitted with high grade rubber or felt strip.

74c FOR 50 FEET FLEXIBLE RUBBER WEATHER STRIP.

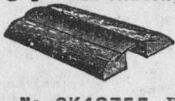

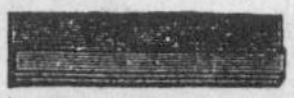

Made of best quality pure rubber; all fresh, new stock. We do not sell "worked over" rubber, or inferior strip of any kind. Carried in three sizes, the narrow width for windows, medium width for sides and tops of doors and the widest for bottoms of doors. Put up in packages of 50 feet.

No.	Width	Per ft.	Per pkg.
9K48735	½ inch	2c	$0.74
9K48737	¾ inch	2½c	.97
9K48739	1 inch	3c	1.23

54c FOR 50 FEET ALL FELT CUSHION WEATHER STRIP.

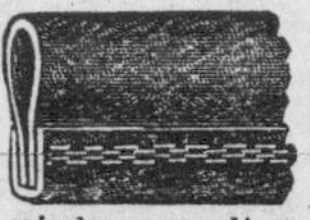

Made of best quality long fiber black wool felt, closely woven and very durable. As easy to put on as rubber and gives satisfactory service. Carried in three sizes, the narrow width for windows, medium width for sides and tops of doors and the widest for bottoms of doors. Put up in packages of 50 feet.

No.	Width	Per ft.	Per pkg.
9K48745	½ in.	1½c	$0.54
9K48747	⅝ in.	2c	.83
9K48749	¾ in.	2½c	1.08

64c FOR A 3-FOOT STORMPROOF RUBBER THRESHOLD.

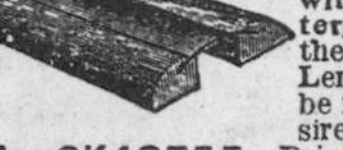

Two hardwood strips with pure rubber centerpiece. Keeps out the cold and snow. Length, 3 feet. Can be made shorter if desired.

No. 9K48755 Price............64c

45c FOR A 28-INCH IRON STORM THRESHOLD.

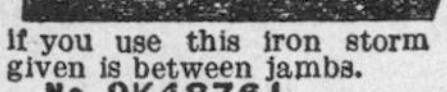

No rain or snow will beat under your door if you use this iron storm threshold. Size given is between jambs.

No. 9K48761

Size, inches	28	30	32	34	36
Price	45c	49c	52c	54c	57c

46c HEAVY CAST IRON ASH PIT OR FUEL DOOR, 8 INCHES SQUARE.

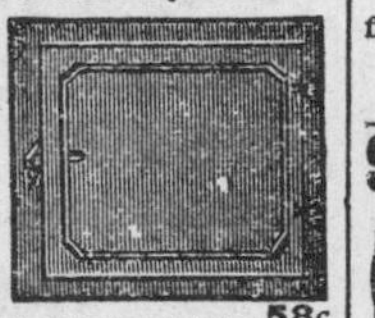

Well made, nicely finished, fits tight. Size indicates size of opening in inches. Price includes door and frame.

No. 9K48771

Size of Opening	Price
8x 8	46c
8x10	52c
10x12	58c
10x14	64c

14c FOR 3 UNBREAKABLE FOOT SCRAPERS.

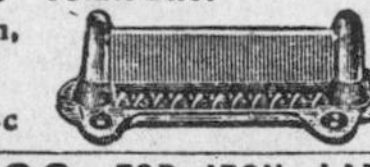

Heavy cast iron, finished in japan.

No. 9K48795
Price, 3 for...14c

98c PER 100 FOR IRON LADDER SOCKETS.

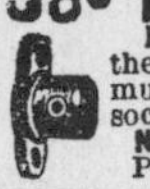

Iron Ladder Sockets. By use of these sockets ladders can be made much lighter and stronger. Hole in socket 1 inch in diameter.

No. 9K48801 Price, 24 for...30c
Per 100..........98c

R. F. D. MAIL BOXES.

APPROVED BY THE POSTMASTER GENERAL, and each box so marked.

When requested we put customer's name on box free of charge and send with the box a heavy cardboard stencil of name which will be found convenient for marking grain bags, implements, etc. You can save money by getting your neighbors to join you in an order for mail boxes. Buy a dozen or more at one time and get the benefit of the lower prices.

49c OUR LEADER, THE PLAINEST, SIMPLEST, STRONGEST FULL SIZE, HIGH GRADE MAIL BOX EVER MADE.

168,943 of these Leader Boxes Sold by Us Last Year.

Approved by the Postmaster General

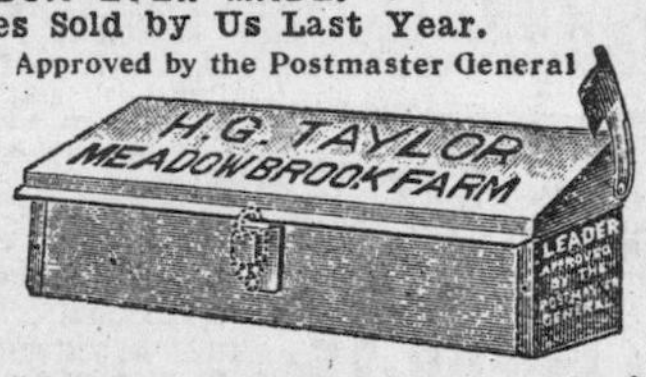

No frills or fancy work about it. No complicated patented mechanism to get out of order; nothing but a plain, everyday mail box at a plain everyday price. We have been selling this same style box ever since Rural Free Delivery was established, have sold hundreds of thousands of them, all of which are satisfactory, and consider it the best box on the market at anything like our price. The association of R. F. D. mail carriers recently endorsed top opening boxes in preference to all others as being safer and more convenient. The Leader is a top opener, safe and simple, the most convenient box made for carrier or patron. It is strongly made of heavy galvanized steel, then painted with rustproof aluminum paint, has turned edges, riveted joints, sloping roof, overhanging cover and is absolutely weatherproof and freezeproof. Our Leader Box has self setting flag signal, holder for outgoing mail, hasp for lock and is easy to put up. Size, 6 inches deep, 6 inches wide, 18 inches long; weight 6½ lbs.

No. 9K23100 Price, not including locks, per dozen, $5.65; each........49c

63c FOR OUR EUREKA ROUND BOTTOM, SLOPING ROOF, OVERHANGING COVER, TOP OPENING MAIL BOX.

Approved by the Postmaster General.

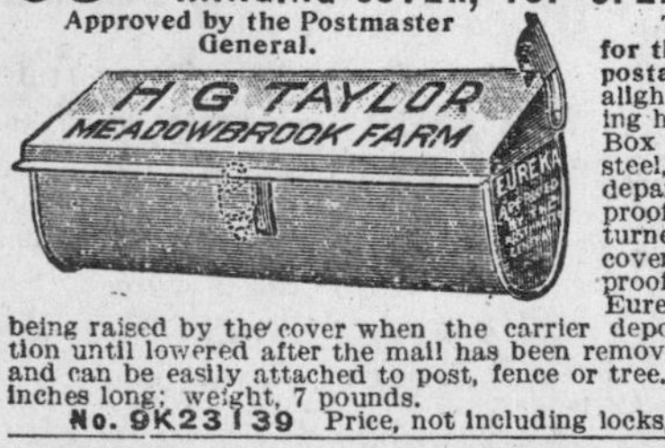

The most convenient box on the market for the carrier, as he can easily take letters, postals, money, etc., from the box without alighting from his wagon and without removing his gloves or mittens. Our Eureka Mail Box is made of extra heavy galvanized sheet steel, two gauges thicker than the postoffice department requires, then painted with rustproof aluminum paint; has seamed joints, turned edges, sloping roof and overhanging cover, which makes it absolutely weatherproof and freezeproof. The flag signal on our Eureka Mail Box is simple and perfect, it being raised by the cover when the carrier deposits the mail, and remains in that position until lowered after the mail has been removed. The Eureka has hasp for padlock, and can be easily attached to post, fence or tree. Size, 6 inches deep, 6 inches wide, 18 inches long; weight, 7 pounds.

No. 9K23139 Price, not including locks, per dozen, $7.36; each..........63c

DIETZ CELEBRATED TUBULAR LANTERNS.

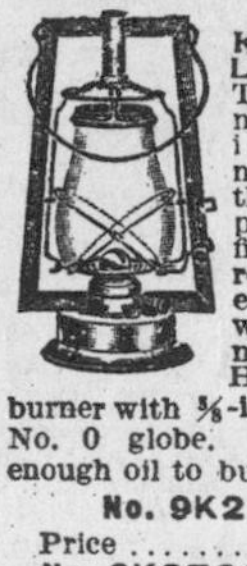

Dietz Victor Kerosene Side Lift Lantern. The best and most convenient lantern made at anything like our price. Can be filled, lighted, regulated and extinguished without removing globe. Has No. 1 burner with ⅝-inch wick and No. 0 globe. Fount holds enough oil to burn 17 hours.

No. 9K27002
Price..............45c

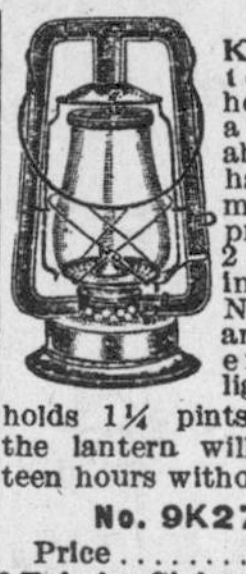

Dietz Royal Kerosene Lantern. Extra heavy, strong and serviceable. The best hand lantern made at any price. Has No. 2 burner, 1-inch wick and No. 0 globe, and gives an extra bright light. Fount holds 1¼ pints of oil, and the lantern will burn nineteen hours without refilling.

No. 9K27012
Price..............62c

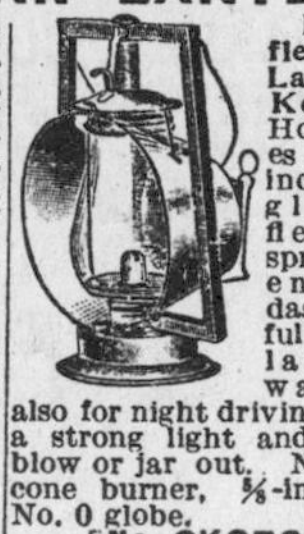

Dietz Reflector Dash Lantern for Kerosene. Hood 6 inches deep, 5-inch silvered glass reflector and spring fastening for dash. Useful as a hand lantern or wall lamp; also for night driving; throws a strong light and will not blow or jar out. No. 1 long cone burner, ⅝-inch wick, No. 0 globe.

No. 9K27027
Price..............$1.10

No. 9K27003 Dietz No. 0 Tubular Globes to fit any of the above lanterns. Each, 6c

HIGH GRADE PADLOCKS

$1.24 BRONZE METAL.

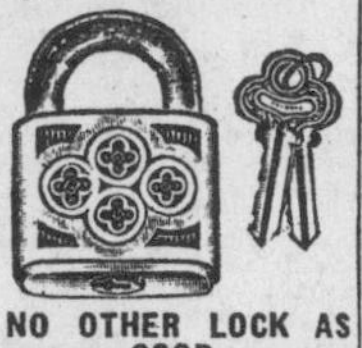

NO OTHER LOCK AS GOOD.

Rustproof and burglar proof, the strongest and most secure padlock made. Has heavy cast bronze metal case, bronze metal works, double locking hardened bronze shackle, pin tumbler, cylinder and two gold plated German silver keys. Width of case, 2 inches; length, including shackle, 3 inches.

No. 9K49001
Price..........$1.24

34c HARVARD SPRING SHACKLE, SELF LOCKING 6-LEVER PADLOCK.

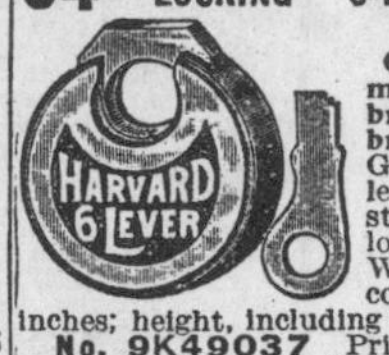

Genuine gun bronze metal case, phosphor bronze springs, solid brass inside works. Guaranteed full 6-lever. One of the strongest, most secure locks ever offered. Will never rust or corrode. Width, 2¼ inches; height, including shackle, 2½ inches.

No. 9K49037 Price..........34c

21c DEFENDER 3-LEVER.

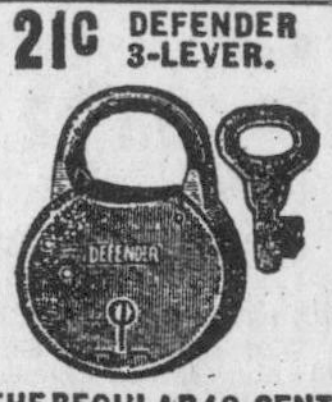

THE REGULAR 40-CENT KIND.

The largest and best 3-lever solid brass padlock ever offered for less than 40 cents. Is self locking, has heavy spring shackle and two flat steel keys. Will outlast half a dozen ordinary iron locks. Width, 2 inches; height, including shackle, 2⅞ inches.

No. 9K49004
Price..........21c

18c BRASS PLATED RUSTPROOF LIBERTY 6-LEVER PADLOCK.

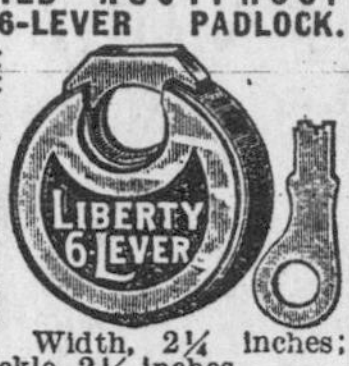

Handsome, strong and secure; the best lock ever offered at anything like this price. Case and shackle made of high grade malleable iron; brass plated inside and out. Has six secure brass levers, is self locking and has two flat steel keys. Width, 2¼ inches; height, including shackle, 2½ inches.

No. 9K49043 Price..........18c

69c NABOB BRONZE.

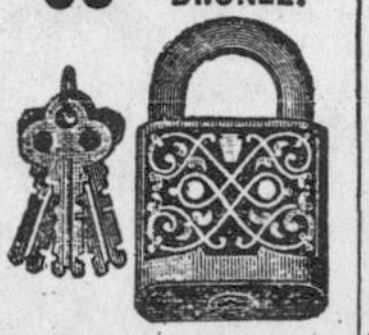

RETAILERS ASK $1.25

Our Nabob rustproof genuine phosphor bronze Self Locking Padlock. The handsomest and best padlock ever offered for less than a dollar. Bolt locks both sides of shackle, making it doubly secure. Each lock has three corrugated flat steel keys. Width, 2⅛ inches; height, including shackle, 2¾ inches.

No. 9K49011
Price..........69c

43c HARVARD EXTRA LONG SHACKLE 6-LEVER PADLOCK WITH CHAIN.

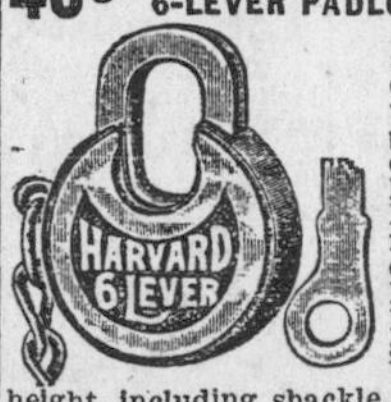

Extra long shackle Harvard 6-Lever Padlock with 9-inch nickel plated chain. No danger of losing or having this stolen. Especially recommended for store doors, gates, etc. Made of the same high class material as our 9K49037. Width, 2¼ inches, height, including shackle, 3 inches.

No. 9K49039 Price..........43c

15c INVINCIBLE 6-LEVER.

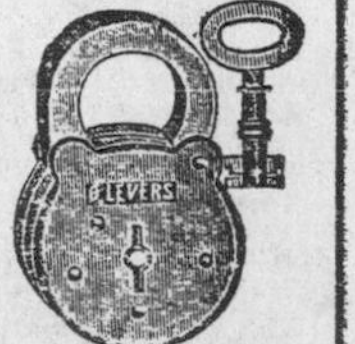

RETAIL PRICE, 30 CENTS EACH.

The strongest and best lock of its kind. Made of wrought steel, heavily brass plated, is self locking with spring shackle. Has six secure levers and two double bitted keys. Width 2 inches; length, 3½ inches. Undoubtedly the best lock ever sold at the price.

No. 9K49025
Price..........15c

24c ARMORY RUSTPROOF EXTRA HEAVY 8-LEVER SELF LOCKING PADLOCK.

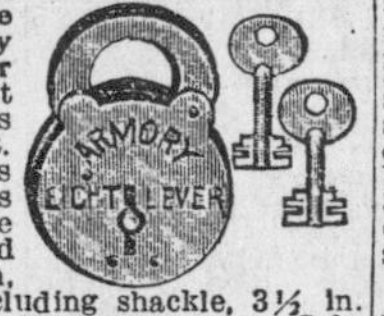

A secure rustproof lock that cannot be picked or opened by any key in your town. Solid wrought steel, heavily brass plated inside and out. Is self locking, has extra heavy brass plated spring shackle and two double bitted steel keys. Width, 2½ in.; height, including shackle, 3½ in.

No. 9K49005 Price..........24c

19c SOLID BRASS MASTER KEYED RURAL FREE DELIVERY MAIL BOX LOCK, WITHOUT CHAIN.

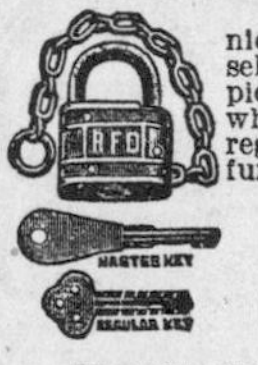

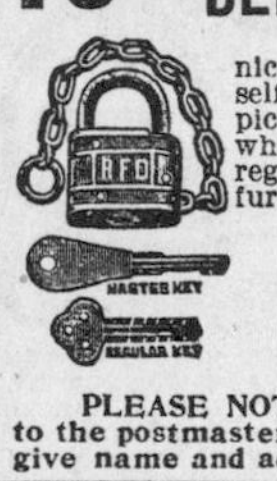

The best R. F. D. Locks ever offered. Made of heavy cast brass, nicely finished and will not rust or corrode. They have spring shackles, are self locking and the inside works are so constructed that they cannot be picked. Made especially for R. F. D. mail boxes, though they can be used wherever a good, strong, substantial lock is required. Price includes two regular keys to each lock. One master key for use of the mail carrier furnished with each dozen locks. Height of lock, including shackle, 2 inches.

No. 9K49060 Padlock without chain, with two keys. Price..$0.19
Per dozen, with one master key..........2.26
No. 9K49065 Padlock with chain as illustrated, and two keys. Price..........23
Per dozen, with one master key..........2.70
No. 9K49070 Extra Master Keys to fit any number of locks. Price..........10

PLEASE NOTE.—The government requires that all master keys be delivered by us to the postmaster of the town at which the rural route originates. In ordering please give name and address of postmaster to whom master key is to be sent.

5c PER YARD IRON JACK CHAIN No. 8.

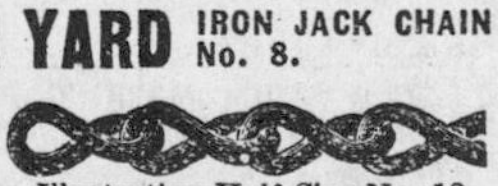

Illustration Half Size No. 12.

Strong and well made, smooth and flexible, useful for a variety of purposes. Links closed but not welded. Be sure to state catalogue number and size chain wanted.

No. 9K49451 Iron Chain.

Size number	8	12	16	20
Length, link, inches	1⅛	⅞	⅝	½
Price, per yard	5c	3c	2c	2c
Per dozen yards	45c	27c	20c	15c

No. 9K49453 Brass Chain.

Size number	8	12	16	20
Length, link, inches	1⅛	⅞	⅝	½
Price, per yard	$0.22	9c	5c	3c
Per dozen yards	2.45	98c	44c	27c

2c PER FOOT BRIGHT WIRE COIL CHAIN No. 6.

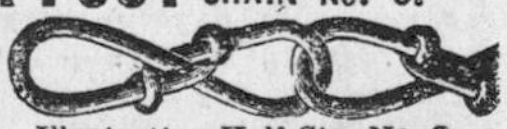

Illustration Half Size No. 2.

One of the strongest patterns on the market, links made without welds. The wire will break before the links will pull apart. State size chain wanted.

No. 9K49461

Size No.	Length, link, inches	Price, per foot	Per 100 feet
000	2½	3c	$2.85
0	2	2½c	2.16
2	1¾	2c	1.80
6	1⅜	2c	1.40

2c PER FOOT FLAT STEEL COIL CHAIN No. 6.

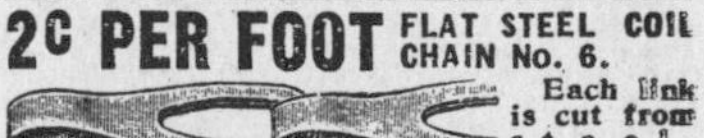

Illustration Half Size No. 0.

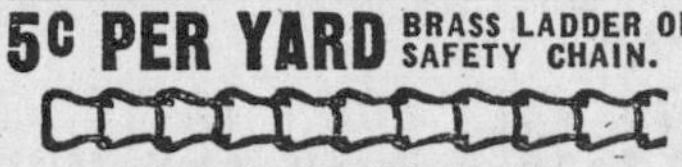

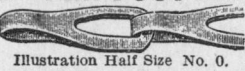

Each link is cut from steel, making a strong, smooth, flexible chain. State size chain wanted.

No. 9K49465

Size No.	Length, link, inches	Price, per foot	Per 100 feet
000	1⅞	4c	$3.80
0	1¾	3c	2.65
2	1½	2½c	1.96
6	1	2c	1.65

5c PER YARD BRASS LADDER OR SAFETY CHAIN.

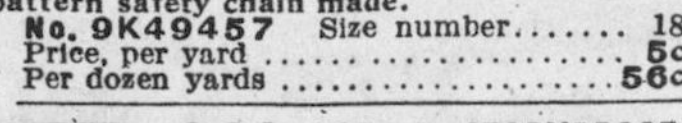

Illustration Half Size No. 18.

Well made, nicely finished and the best pattern safety chain made.

No. 9K49457 Size number....... 18
Price, per yard.......... 5c
Per dozen yards.......... 56c

38c FOR A STORMPROOF HOUSE MAIL BOX.

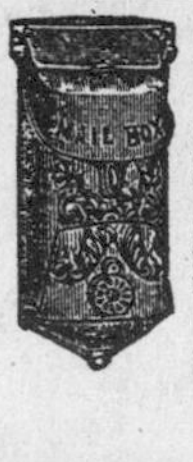

Made of cast iron, nicely japanned, with gilt decorations and letters. Has hinged slot cover and top, covered peephole and wire spring attachment to hold newspapers, etc. Size, 6x12 inches; weight, 4½ pounds. Cannot be used on rural routes.

No. 9K23150 Price, each 38c
Per dozen, not including locks..........$4.46

YOUR SAVING IS EVEN MORE

Low prices in our last catalogue still further reduced on over 3,000 Hardware Items in this book.

37c GENUINE SWISS BELL METAL COW BELLS; LOUD, CLEAR AND SWEET.

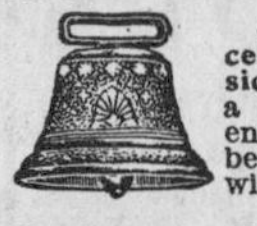

Cast from Swiss bell metal, celebrated for their pure musical tone, which can be heard a long distance and sounds entirely different from common bells. Prices given are for bells without straps.

Catalogue No.	Diameter at mouth	Widest strap that can be used	Price
9K49501	3 5-16 in.	1½ inches	$0.37
9K49503	4 inches	1⅝ inches	.52
9K49505	5 inches	2⅛ inches	.97
9K49507	6⅛ inches	3 inches	1.48

10c ELECTRO COPPER PLATED WROUGHT STEEL COW BELLS, 3⅜ INCHES.

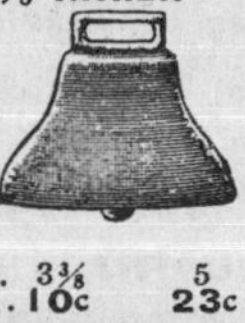

Made of one piece of solid steel, warranted not to crack. The tone is entirely different from the ordinary cow bell, and can be heard much farther. Heavily electro copper plated and looks like a copper bell. The smallest size makes a good loud team bell.

No. 9K49511

Diameter of mouth, inches	3⅜	5
Price	10c	23c

10c FOR A No. 5 WELL MADE, NICELY FINISHED, STANDARD COW BELL.

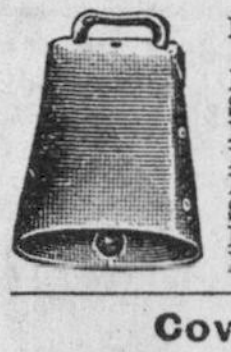

Will not rust or corrode. Have very loud tone.

No. 9K49515

Nos.	0	2
Size of mouth	6x4½	5½x3⅞
Height, inches	6½	5
Price	27c	18c
Nos.	3	5
Size of mouth	4½x3	3¼x2⅝
Height, inches	4¾	3¼
Price	13c	10c

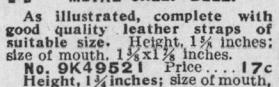

Cow Bell Straps.

Fine Black Leather Cow Bell Straps. Made with roller buckle and loop.

No. 10K2601

Width, inches	1½	2	3
Price	27c	39c	54c

17c FOR A SMALL SIZE CAST BELL METAL SHEEP BELL.

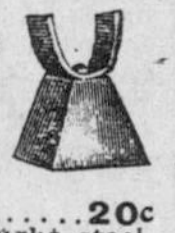

As illustrated, complete with good quality leather straps of suitable size. Height, 1⅝ inches; size of mouth, 1⅜x1⅛ inches.

No. 9K49521 Price....17c

Height, 1¾ inches; size of mouth, 1½x2 inches.

No. 9K49523 Price....20c

Round Sheep Bells. Made of wrought steel, malleable iron loop, copper plated, very durable; will not crack; with straps.

No. 9K49527

Diameter, inches	2 7-16	2⅞	3⅜
Price	12c	14c	17c

$3.20 PER 100 WIRE FENCE RATCHET AND TIGHTENER.

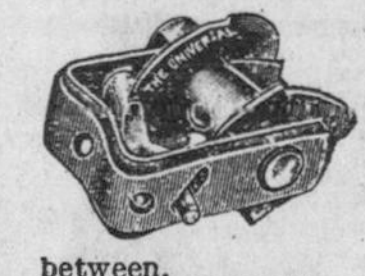

You can easily keep your fences tight in hot or cold weather with the Universal Ratchet. It is reversible and cannot get out of order. The frame is of steel. The lock is positive and automatic. Can be used at the posts or midway between.

No. 9K65611 Price, per dozen..$0.40
Per box containing 100..........3.20

78c IMPROVED TACKLE BLOCK WIRE STRETCHER AND SAFETY HOIST.

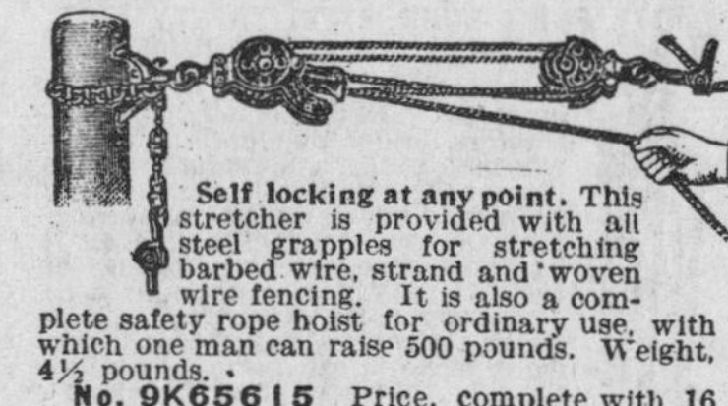

Self locking at any point. This stretcher is provided with all steel grapples for stretching barbed wire, strand and woven wire fencing. It is also a complete safety rope hoist for ordinary use, with which one man can raise 500 pounds. Weight, 4½ pounds.

No. 9K65615 Price, complete with 16 feet of ⅜-inch rope..........78c

19c IMPROVED NEVERSLIP WIRE GRIP, STRONG AND DURABLE.

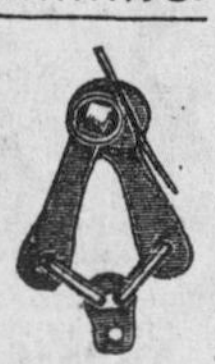

The more you pull, the tighter it grips the wire and never slips. When attached to a handspike it makes a splendid stretcher for either barbed or smooth wire. The grip can be attached to any wire stretcher.

No. 9K65619 Price, 19c

44c NOTCHED BAR WIRE STRETCHER, HEAVY AND POWERFUL.

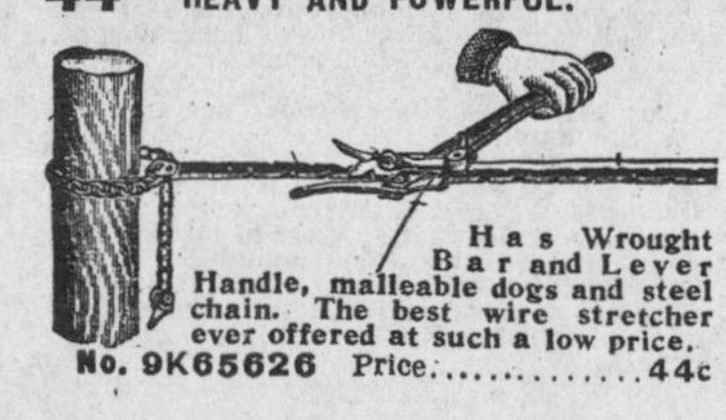

Has Wrought Bar and Lever Handle, malleable dogs and steel chain. The best wire stretcher ever offered at such a low price.

No. 9K65626 Price..........44c

FARM BELLS

OUR FAMOUS CRYSTALLINE COMPOSITION METAL BELL.

We take the entire output of the factory making CRYSTALLINE METAL BELLS. Nowhere else can you get as good a bell. They are the

SWEETEST TONED, CLEAREST RINGING, LOUDEST SOUNDING FARM BELLS IN THE WORLD.

MONEY SAVING PRICES RULE ON THIS PAGE.

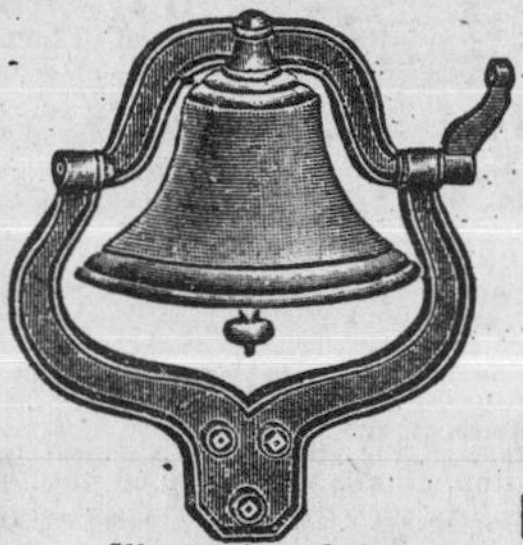

Illustration of sizes Nos. 1, 2, 3 and 8.

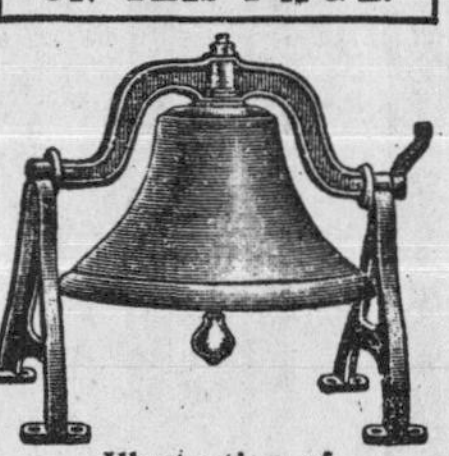

Illustration of Size No. 4.

YOU TAKE NO RISK IN BUYING A CRYSTALLINE METAL BELL.

SEND US YOUR ORDER for one of these high grade, perfect toned farm bells, use it thirty days, compare it with any composition bell you ever saw at any price, and if it is not entirely satisfactory, ship it back at our expense and we will promptly return your money.

OUR FAMOUS CRYSTALLINE METAL BELLS are clearer, sweeter and louder than any bells you ever heard. It is a pleasure to hear them ring. They are so proportioned and made of such good material that the tone is entirely free from the discords so common to other bells.

WE SELL THOUSANDS OF THESE BELLS EACH YEAR, add only one small profit to the bare cost of manufacture and actually offer them to you at prices 25 to 50 per cent lower than others ask for common cast iron bells. Every bell we sell is full weight and full size, and our price includes all the necessary fixtures for erecting.

	Size No.	Bottom Diameter	Weight, Complete	Price, Complete
No. 9K66051	1	14 inches	35 pounds	$1.04
No. 9K66052	2	16 inches	50 pounds	1.47
No. 9K66053	3	18 inches	70 pounds	1.99
No. 9K66054	4	19½ inches	90 pounds	2.64
No. 9K66058	8	19½ inches	90 pounds	2.63

For Schoolhouse, Factory, Church and Fire Alarm Bells, see page 552.

78c FOR THE LATEST IMPROVED COMBINATION FENCING PLIER.

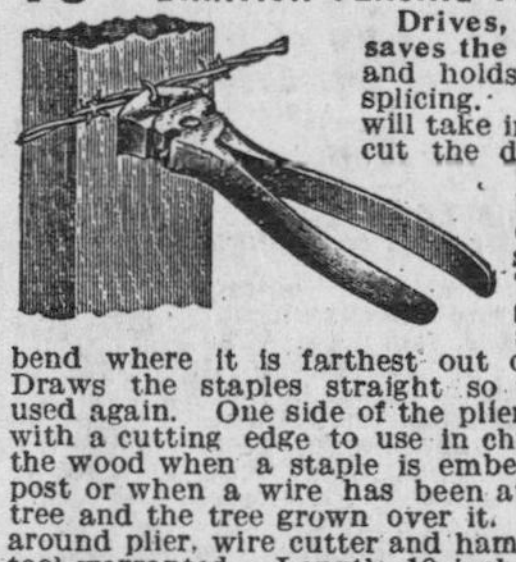

Drives, pulls and saves the staples; cuts and holds wire for splicing. The cutter will take in and easily cut the double and twisted barbed wire or No. 9 smooth wire. The jaws grasp the staple on its bend where it is farthest out of the wood. Draws the staples straight so they can be used again. One side of the plier is provided with a cutting edge to use in chipping away the wood when a staple is embedded in the post or when a wire has been attached to a tree and the tree grown over it. It is an all around plier, wire cutter and hammer. Every tool warranted. Length, 10 inches.

No. 9K65624 Price..........78c
If by mail, postage extra, 30 cents.

64c HANDY ANDY TEMPERED STEEL COMBINATION TOOL.

SAME EXACTLY AS SOLD BY AGENTS FOR $1.00 TO $1.25.

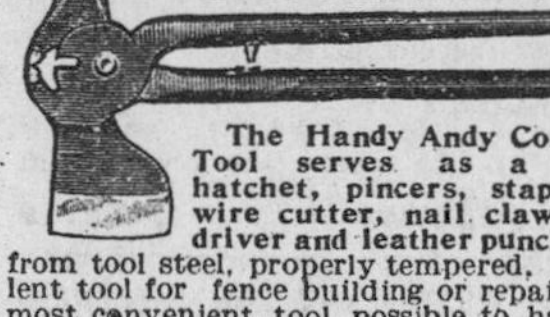

The Handy Andy Combination Tool serves as a hammer, hatchet, pincers, staple puller, wire cutter, nail claws, screwdriver and leather punch. Forged from tool steel, properly tempered. An excellent tool for fence building or repairing. The most convenient tool possible to have about the house. Length, 12 inches.

No. 9K65625 Price..........64c

HOW TO ORDER.

In ordering merchandise from the pages of this General Catalogue or any of our special catalogues, please be very careful to give catalogue number in full, and where the size or color is required to fill your order satisfactorily, please be careful to give the size and color wanted. If you will just give catalogue number in full, size and color, and any other special information we ask for when you order from us, you will be sure to get just exactly what you want without delay; but if you neglect to give catalogue number, size or color, we may have to write you for further information. Understand, it is a very simple matter to order goods by mail. Our descriptions are complete, we guarantee all our merchandise to be absolutely satisfactory, we guarantee that you will save money by ordering from us, and we are extremely anxious to serve you satisfactorily and promptly, and you can help us immensely to do this by following our instructions as closely as possible.

8c FOR A CLEAR TONED POLISHED BELL METAL TURKEY BELL.

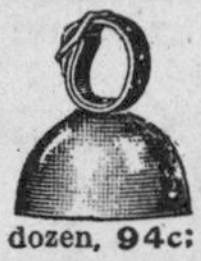

Diameter, 1¾ inches; enables the flock to be easily located, makes the foxes shy. Furnished complete with strap as shown. These bells also make desirable chimes for shafts, sleighs, etc.

No. 9K49531 Price, per dozen, 94c; each..........8c

9c FOR A No. 1 CAST BELL METAL SPUN AND POLISHED BELL.

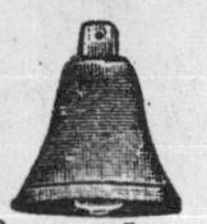

May be used for a variety of purposes; make good sheep bells, harness bells for milk wagons, drays, etc. Full weight goods. Best shape for sound. Not made with extra flare to increase diameter of mouth.

No. 9K49551

Nos.	1	3	5
Diam. of mouth, ins.	2⅛	2½	3⅛
Price, each	$0.09	$0.15	$0.24
Per dozen	1.04	1.68	2.80

17c CAST BELL METAL HAND OR DINNER BELL, SIZE No. 3.

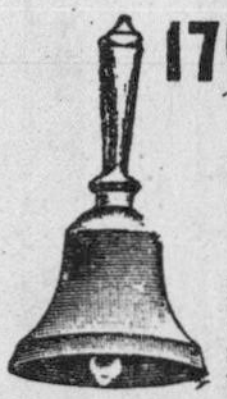

Made of high grade genuine cast bell metal, highly polished; ebonized wood handle, and a sweet, full, musical tone. Full size and weight.

No. 9K49555

No.	Diameter	Price
No. 3,	3 inches	$0.17
No. 7,	4⅜ inches	.52
No. 9,	5⅝ inches	.92
No. 13,	7⅝ inches	1.62

32c FULL SIZE, HIGHLY NICKEL PLATED TEA OR CALL BELL.

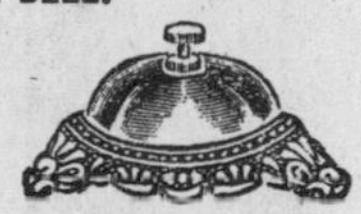

Highly nickel plated, 3¼-inch gong. Fancy aluminum bronzed base. Have a sweet, clear, pleasing tone.

No. 9K49559 Price..........32c

58c FOR A 4-INCH NICKEL PLATED TRIP GONG BELL, COMPLETE.

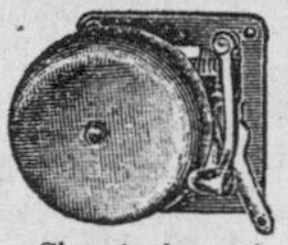

Have highly polished nickel plated cast gongs, brass springs and iron base; heavy, well made and have extra fine tone.

No. 9K49567

Size, inches	4	6	8	10
Price	58c	$1.18	$2.23	$3.92

PRICES ON HARDWARE STILL FURTHER REDUCED IN THIS BOOK FROM THE LOW PRICES NAMED IN OUR LAST CATALOGUE. OVER 3,000 HARDWARE ITEMS CHEAPER THAN BEFORE

REGISTERS, BORDERS AND FACES.

Our immense business on hot air registers, borders and register faces has increased from year to year till we now sell more of these goods than any one concern in the United States. We control the output of one of the largest independent factories and sell them at the actual cost of material and labor, plus our one small percentage of profit. All our hot air registers, borders and register faces are full size and full weight, not the cheaply constructed, light weight kind usually offered by retailers and builders' supply houses. Thousands of contractors, carpenters and owners buy their registers, etc., from us, not only on account of the superiority of our goods and the great saving in cost, but because we carry at all seasons a full assortment of sizes. Order a lot of hot air registers from us; compare them with any goods made; if ours are not equal in quality to registers others sell at prices 25 to 50 per cent higher than we do, return them to us and your money will be refunded.

41c FOR A 6x8-INCH BLACK JAPANNED HOT AIR REGISTER.

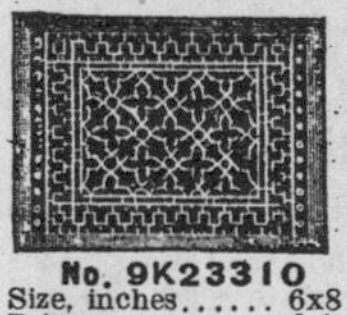

Black japanned; can be used in floor or side wall. We do not furnish borders with registers unless at an additional cost. These registers fit boxes of the size indicated.

No. 9K23310

Size, inches	6x8	8x10	9x12	10x12
Price	41c	46c	69c	80c
Size, inches	10x14	12x15	14x18	
Price	$1.30	$1.51	$2.98	

32c BLACK JAPANNED REGISTER BORDER FOR A 6x8-INCH REGISTER.

Black Japanned Register Borders, to match No. 9K23310 registers.

No. 9K23312

Size, in.	Price
6x8	$0.32
8x10	.34
9x12	.46
10x12	.49
10x14	.73
12x15	.81
14x18	1.44

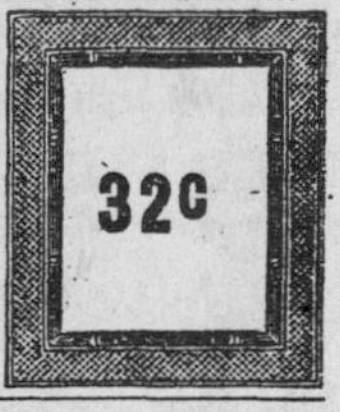

37c FOR A FULL WEIGHT, FULL SIZE, HIGH GRADE WHITE ENAMELED REGISTER FACE FOR CEILING, SIZE, 6x8 INCHES.

Finished in baked white enamel, in a very attractive pattern. Used extensively for side walls and ceilings.

No. 9K23314

Size, inches	6x8	8x10	9x12	10x12	10x14	12x15	14x18
Price	37c	41c	56c	63c	88c	$1.11	$1.88

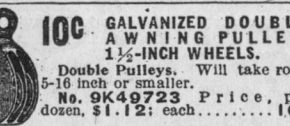

7c GALVANIZED RUSTPROOF AWNING PULLEY, 1½-INCH WHEEL.

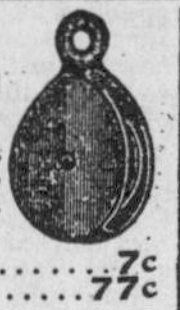

Single Pulleys. Useful for a great many purposes. Will not take rope larger than 5-16 inch diameter.

No. 9K49721 Price, each..........7c
Per dozen..........77c

10c GALVANIZED DOUBLE AWNING PULLEY, 1½-INCH WHEELS.

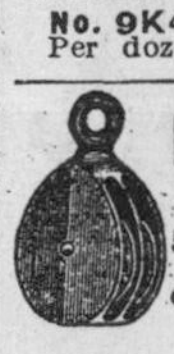

Double Pulleys. Will take rope 5-16 inch or smaller.

No. 9K49723 Price, per dozen, $1.12; each..........10c

4c FOR A 2-INCH WHEEL, JAPANNED IRON SCREW PULLEY.

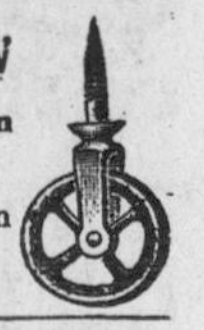

Will not take rope larger than 5-16 inch.

No. 9K49731

Size of Wheel	Price, each	Dozen
2 inches	4c	43c
3 inches	7c	79c

23c FOR A JAPANNED 10-INCH WELL WHEEL WITH FRAME.

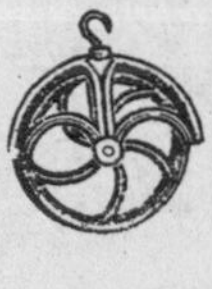

Size given is width of frame.

No. 9K49741 Price, 23c

TOOLS AND HARDWARE

ILLUSTRATIONS ARE ACTUAL SIZE.

40d 30d 20d 16d 10d 8d 6d 4d 3d 2d

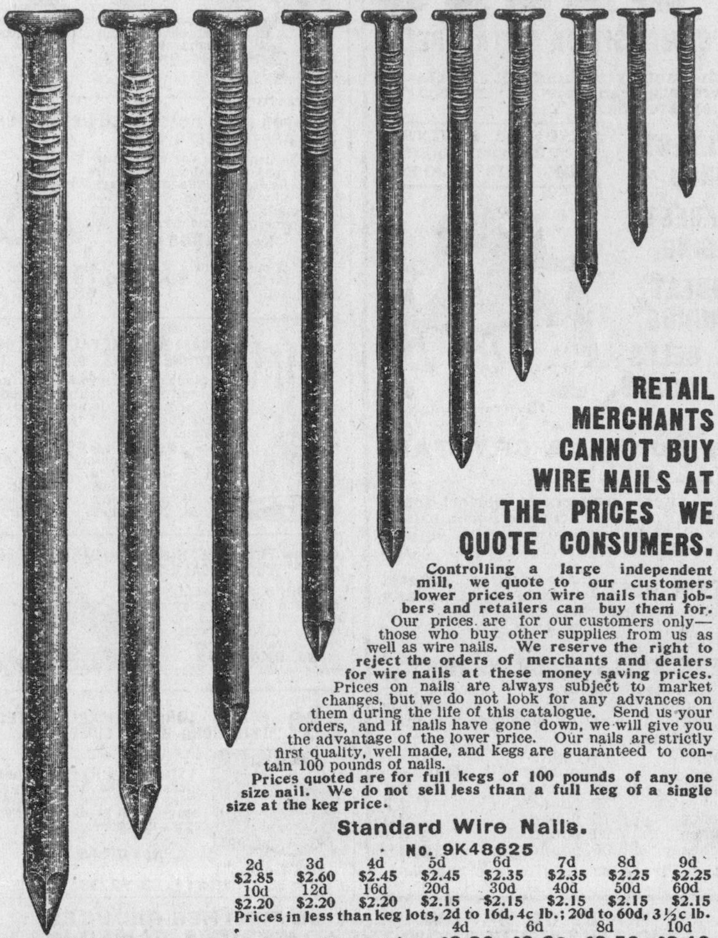

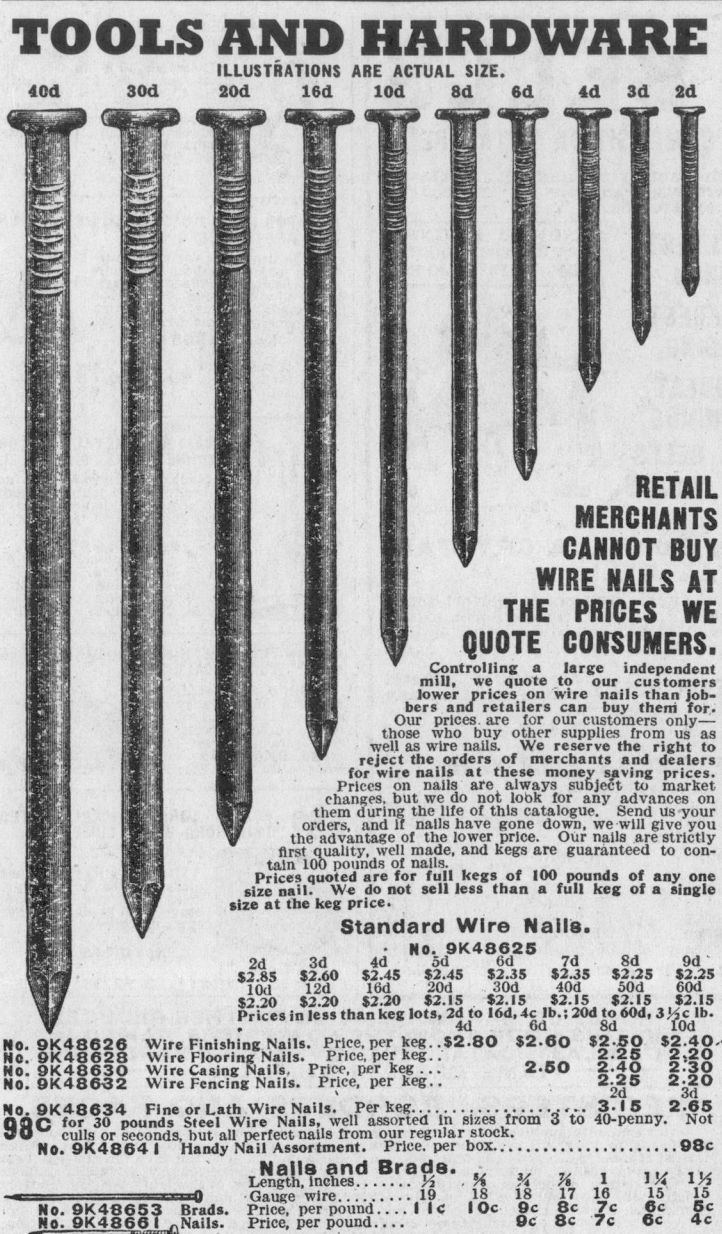

RETAIL MERCHANTS CANNOT BUY WIRE NAILS AT THE PRICES WE QUOTE CONSUMERS.

Controlling a large independent mill, we quote to our customers lower prices on wire nails than jobbers and retailers can buy them for. Our prices are for our customers only—those who buy other supplies from us as well as wire nails. We reserve the right to reject the orders of merchants and dealers for wire nails at these money saving prices. Prices on nails are always subject to market changes, but we do not look for any advances on them during the life of this catalogue. Send us your orders, and if nails have gone down, we will give you the advantage of the lower price. Our nails are strictly first quality, well made, and kegs are guaranteed to contain 100 pounds of nails.

Prices quoted are for full kegs of 100 pounds of any one size nail. We do not sell less than a full keg of a single size at the keg price.

Standard Wire Nails.

No. 9K48625

2d	3d	4d	5d	6d	7d	8d	9d
$2.85	$2.60	$2.45	$2.45	$2.35	$2.35	$2.25	$2.25
10d	12d	16d	20d	30d	40d	50d	60d
$2.20	$2.20	$2.20	$2.15	$2.15	$2.15	$2.15	$2.15

Prices in less than keg lots, 2d to 16d, 4c lb.; 20d to 60d, 3½c lb.

		4d	6d	8d	10d
No. 9K48626	Wire Finishing Nails. Price, per keg..	$2.80	$2.60	$2.50	$2.40
No. 9K48628	Wire Flooring Nails. Price, per keg..			2.25	2.20
No. 9K48630	Wire Casing Nails, Price, per keg ...		2.50	2.40	2.30
No. 9K48632	Wire Fencing Nails. Price, per keg..			2.25	2.20

		2d	3d
No. 9K48634	Fine or Lath Wire Nails. Per keg....................	3.15	2.65

98c for 30 pounds Steel Wire Nails, well assorted in sizes from 3 to 40-penny. Not culls or seconds, but all perfect nails from our regular stock.

No. 9K48641 Handy Nail Assortment. Price, per box....................98c

Nails and Brads.

	Length, inches......	½	⅝	¾	⅞	1	1¼	1½
	Gauge wire.........	19	18	18	17	16	15	15
No. 9K48653 Brads.	Price, per pound....	11c	10c	9c	8c	7c	6c	5c
No. 9K48661 Nails.	Price, per pound....			9c	8c	7c	6c	4c

Bill Posters' and Upholsterers' Tacks.

	2	3	4	6	8	10	12
Size, ounces..........................	2	3	4	6	8	10	12
No. 9K48691 Bill Posters'. Per lb.	$0.13	$0.12	$0.11	$0.10	$0.09		
Price, per 25-pound box..................	2.70	2.60	2.50	2.40	2.15		
No. 9K48695 Upholsterers'. Per lb.	.13	.10	.09	.09	.08	.08	.07
Price, per 25-pound box..................	2.80	2.40	2.15	2.05	1.90	1.80	1.65

For other tacks, see page 476.

$2.14 FOR A 2X12-INCH BELL BOTTOM JACK SCREW.

Wrought Iron Screws, lathe turned threads, cast iron stands. These are high class jack screws, well made, nicely finished, powerful and durable. We do not furnish levers with these screws.

$1.03 to $4.34 according to size.

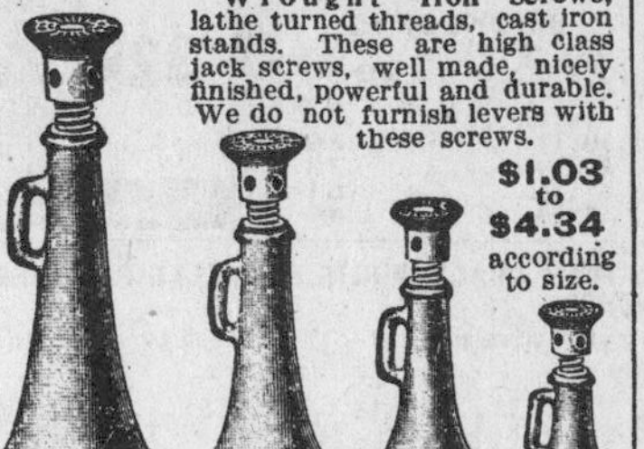

Capacity—1¼-inch screws, 10 tons; 1½-inch screws, 12 tons; 1¾-inch screws, 16 tons; 2-inch screws, 20 tons; 2½-inch screws, 28 tons.

No. 9K31355

Diam. of Screw, In.	Height of Stand, In.	Height over all, In.	Price	Diam. of Screw, In.	Height of Stand, In.	Height over all, In.	Price
1¼	8	11¼	$1.03	2	8	12	$1.78
1½	8	11½	1.27	2	10	14¼	2.03
1½	10	13½	1.43	2	12	16¼	2.14
1½	12	15	1.57	2	14	18	2.46
1¾	10	13¾	1.72	2	16	19¾	2.78
1¾	12	15½	1.87	2½	14	18¼	3.57
				2½	18	22½	4.34

$1.84 FOR A 20-INCH CAST IRON JACK SCREW.

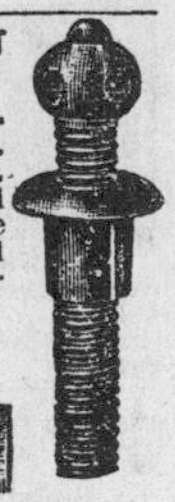

Strong and powerful, will last indefinitely and give satisfaction. Made with cast seamless threads, which make them very smooth and uniform. Recommended to house movers, contractors, builders and all others who require a strong, dependable screw.

No. 9K31365

Diam. of Screw	Height Over All	Price
3 inches	20 inches	$1.84
3 inches	24 inches	2.13
3 inches	30 inches	2.53
3 inches	36 inches	2.91

$3.07 HIGH GRADE ACME SPECIAL RATCHET JACK SCREW.

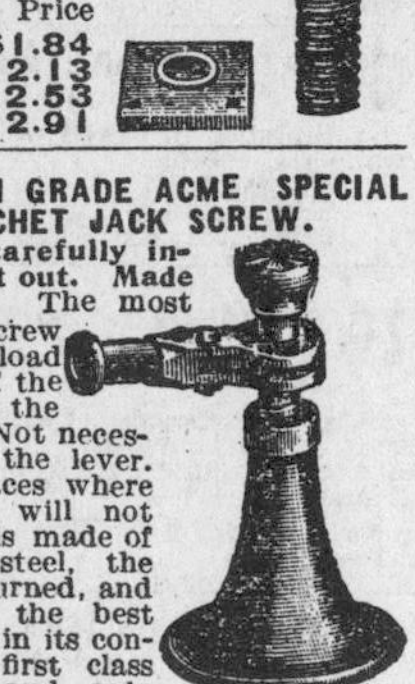

Every screw carefully inspected before sent out. Made in one size only. The most convenient jack screw ever invented. A load can be lifted in half the time required with the old style screw. Not necessary to pull out the lever. Can be used in places where an ordinary jack will not work. The screw is made of solid cold rolled steel, the threads are lathe turned, and throughout, only the best materials are used in its construction. It is first class in every respect and only costs a little more than the common jack screw. Capacity, 25 tons. Diameter of base, 10 inches; diameter of screw, 2 inches; height of stand, 10 inches; height over all, 19 inches.

No. 9K31375 Price, each......$3.07

PURE MANILA ROPE

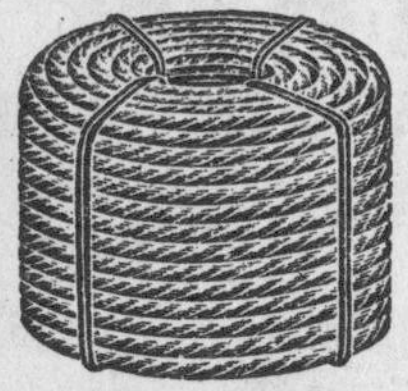

OUR MANILA ROPE is made of pure long manila fiber, unadulterated with sisal, jute or inferior material of any kind. It is full weight, all fresh, new stock and will stand 25 to 50 per cent more strain than the rope sold by most dealers. Many manufacturers adulterate their rope with clay, junk (old rope), sisal, etc. We guarantee every foot of rope we send out to be the finest grade, made of pure long fiber manila and to be satisfactory in every way.

HAY CARRIERS require the very best rope made. When ordering rope for hay carriers, order ⅜ inch for the check rope, and either ¾ inch, ⅞ inch or 1 inch for the carrier rope.

MANILA ROPE is never measured exact diameter, one-third of the circumference being considered the diameter. Can furnish in one piece any length up to 1,200 feet. State size wanted.

No. 9K71298 Pure Manila Rope.

Size, inches....................	3-16	¼	5-16	⅜	½	⅝
Price, per foot..................	¼c	⅜c	⅝c	⅞c	1½c	2¼c
Size, inches....................	¾	⅞	1	1⅛	1¼	1½
Price, per foot..................	3c	4¼c	5½c	6¾c	8c	10½c

PURE MANILA LARIAT ROPE.

Made of the same quality of stock as our regular manila rope. It is four-strand, hard laid and is absolutely the best lariat rope made. It will not kink, will run freely and will maintain a perfect loop until completely worn out.

No. 9K71280 7-16-inch Lariat Rope. Price, per foot..................1½c

18c TO $2.58, ACCORDING TO SIZE, WOOD TACKLE BLOCKS.

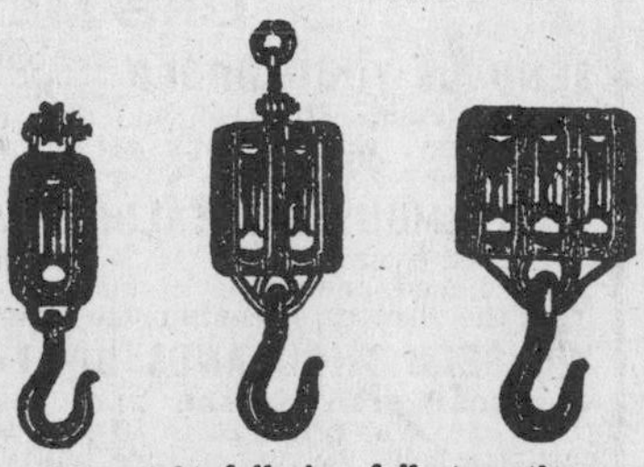

Full weight, full size, full strength, very best quality iron strap with iron sheaves and steel pins. Blocks with or without beckets are the same price. Order from list below and state which is wanted.

When two blocks are ordered for a set, one should be with becket and the other without.

No. 9K49601 With becket.
No. 9K49603 Without becket.

Size of Shell, inches	For Rope, inches	Single Pulley, Price	Double Pulley, Price	Triple Pulley, Price
3	5-16	$0.18	$0.32	$0.42
4	½	.21	.39	.52
5	⅝	.22	.43	.56
6	¾	.28	.49	.72
7	⅞	.32	.58	.85
8	1	.41	.69	1.02
10	1⅛	.67	1.10	1.63
12	1¼	1.09	1.80	2.58

19c TO $4.23, ACCORDING TO SIZE, METAL TACKLE BLOCKS.

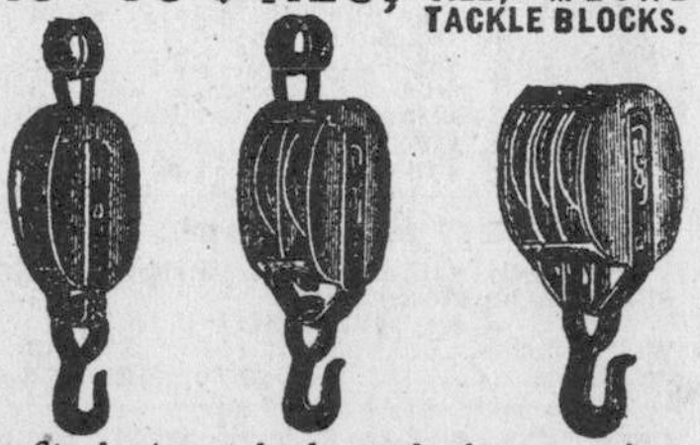

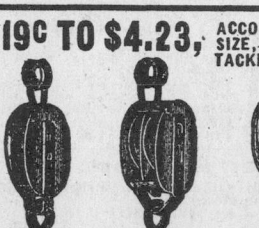

Steel straps, hooks and pins, gray iron sheaves; well made, strong and powerful. No better tackle blocks sold by anyone. Edges are rounded to prevent wearing of rope; straps extend below the pins, making them extra strong. No extra charge for beckets.

No. 9K49631 Without becket.
No. 9K49633 With becket.

Size of Shell, inches	For Rope, inches	Single Pulley, Price	Double Pulley, Price	Triple Pulley, Price
3	⅜	$0.19	$0.36	$0.47
4	½	.23	.44	.58
5	⅝	.25	.47	.62
6	¾	.29	.54	.77
7	⅞	.35	.65	.94
8	1	.44	.76	1.09
10 Heavy	1⅛	1.12	1.84	2.52
12 Heavy	1¼	1.80	2.97	4.23

$2.26 FOR A 7-INCH METAL SNATCH BLOCK. LIGHT AND STRONG.

Our Metal Snatch Blocks recommend themselves for their neatness, strength and convenience. They are almost as light as wood blocks, and yet 30 per cent stronger and stiffer.

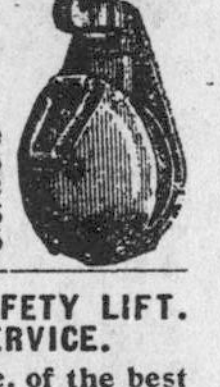

No. 9K49641

Length of Shell, inches	For Diameter Rope, inches	Size of Sheave, inches	Price
7	¾ to ⅞	3½x1¼	$2.26
8	1 to 1⅛	4 x1½	2.72
10	1¼ to 1⅜	5½x1⅞	4.05
12	1½ to 1⅝	7 x2	4.76

75c SECURITY AUTOMATIC ROPE HOIST. COMPACT AND POWERFUL.

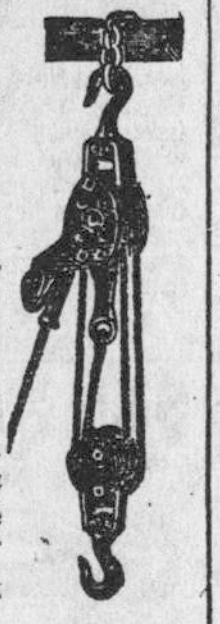

Convenient and safe; hoists, lowers, locks and unlocks without the bother of a trip rope. The heavier the load the tighter it locks. It can be used in any position, horizontal or perpendicular. Just the thing for erecting windmills, pumps, bridges, etc. It is made of the best malleable iron and fully warranted. All sizes have double lower block. Prices given do not include rope.

Made to take ⅜-inch rope. One man can lift 600 pounds. Capacity, 1,000 pounds.

No. 9K49691 Price, without rope......................75c

Made for ½-inch rope. One man can lift 600 pounds. Capacity, 1,500 pounds.

No. 9K49693 Price, without rope......................$1.51

Made for ¾-inch rope. One man can lift 600 pounds. Capacity, 2,500 pounds.

No. 9K49695 Price, without rope, $2.39

$9.24 WESTON PATTERN DIFFERENTIAL CHAIN HOIST, ½ TON CAPACITY.

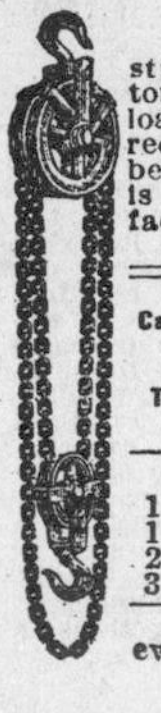

The most powerful hoist ever constructed. A boy of twelve can lift 2 tons with ease. Automatically holds load in any position. No brake or locks required. Made throughout of the very best material. Each pulley and chain is carefully tested before leaving the factory.

No. 9K49699

Capacity in Tons	Price Complete with Chain as Illustrated	Lift in Feet	Extra Chain, Price per Foot	Net Weight Complete Hoists, Pounds
½	$ 9.24	7	31c	29
1	11.94	8	33c	50
1½	16.35	8½	35c	87
2	20.44	9	37c	123
3	26.16	9½	44c	167

Four feet extra chain required for every foot of extra lift.

93c FOR A BURR STEEL SAFETY LIFT. STRONG, MADE FOR SERVICE.

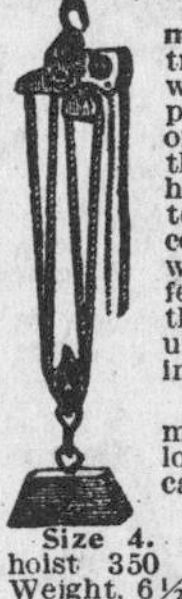

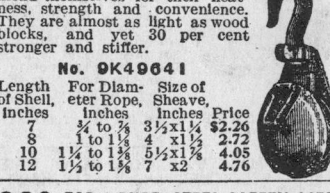

Made for hard usage, of the best material. Recommended for contractors, bridge builders and others who have use for a powerful hoist. No part of the lift can be worn out by ordinary usage, and it is far cheaper than the ordinary lock blocks, as it has no wedge, eccentric, springs or teeth to get out of order and need constant repairs. The brake against which the rope is locked being perfectly smooth, can in no way injure the rope. Prices given include upper and lower blocks but do not include rope.

Size 3. For ⅜-inch rope; one man can hoist 300 pounds. Double lower block. Weight, 4⅛ pounds; capacity, 800 pounds.

No. 9K49651 Price ..93c

Size 4. For ½-inch rope; one man can hoist 350 pounds. Double lower block. Weight, 6½ pounds; capacity, 1,500 pounds.

No. 9K49655 Price...........$1.74

Size 5. For ⅝-inch rope; one man can hoist 400 pounds. Double lower block. Weight, 11 pounds; capacity, 2,000 pounds.

No. 9K49659 Price...........$2.20

Size 6. For ¾-inch rope; one man can hoist 450 pounds. Double lower block. Weight, 17 pounds; capacity, 2,500 pounds.

No. 9K49663 Price...........$2.70

Size 4½. For ½-inch rope; one man can hoist 600 pounds. Triple lower block. Weight, 10 pounds; capacity, 3,000 pounds.

No. 9K49667 Price...........$3.18

Size 5½. For ⅝-inch rope; one man can hoist 700 pounds. Triple lower block. Weight, 20 pounds; capacity, 3,500 pounds.

No. 9K49671 Price...........$3.75

Size 6½. For ¾-inch rope; one man can hoist 850 pounds. Triple lower block. Weight, 28 pounds; capacity, 5,000 pounds.

No. 9K49675 Price...........$4.40

The above prices and weights include upper and lower block. No rope furnished at above prices.

KENWOOD STANDARD HAY CARRIER OUTFITS

OUR COMPLETE KENWOOD STANDARD Hay Carrier Outfits are carefully made up of such articles as our extensive experience teaches us make the most desirable and satisfactory outfits. In case you wish a longer outfit or an outfit in any way different from the outfits which we list, please make up your order from the individual items as described by us, giving catalogue number, quantity required and price of each separate item. If you want an outfit complete as listed and want additional items, then order the outfit under its catalogue number and price, and the additional items under their respective catalogue numbers and prices. The amount of hay carrier rope and check rope which we furnish in the barn outfits is ample for unloading at the center of the barn, or for unloading at one end with the horse hitched at the other end; but if you wish to unload at the end of the barn and hitch the horse at the same end, you will need additional carrier rope equal in feet to the length of the barn, and additional check rope equal in feet to one-half the length of the barn. We furnish ¾-inch manila carrier rope in our standard outfits because it is abundantly strong; but ⅞-inch or 1-inch manila rope can be furnished at extra price. Wire rope or larger manila rope cannot be used. **Only the highest quality pure manila rope furnished in these outfits.**

$8.35 KENWOOD STANDARD WOOD TRACK HAY CARRIER OUTFIT FOR A 30-FOOT BARN consists of 1 wood track hay carrier, 1 short tine double harpoon hay fork, 12 rafter brackets, 12 wood track hanging hooks, 4 floor hooks, 3 steel yoke knot passing pulleys, 90 feet of ¾-inch manila carrier rope and 35 feet of ⅜-inch manila check rope. For each 5 feet additional length of barn we add 2 rafter brackets, 2 wood track hanging hooks. 10 feet of ¾-inch manila carrier rope and 5 feet of ⅜-inch manila check rope. Wood track is not included in the Wood Track Outfits listed by us.

No. 9K71300	30-foot Outfit.	Weight, 100 pounds. Price	$ 8.35
No. 9K71301	35-foot Outfit.	Weight, 105 pounds. Price	8.85
No. 9K71302	40-foot Outfit.	Weight, 110 pounds. Price	9.35
No. 9K71303	45-foot Outfit.	Weight, 115 pounds. Price	9.85
No. 9K71304	50-foot Outfit.	Weight, 120 pounds. Price	10.35
No. 9K71305	55-foot Outfit.	Weight, 125 pounds. Price	10.85
No. 9K71306	60-foot Outfit.	Weight, 130 pounds. Price	11.35

$11.05 KENWOOD STANDARD STEEL TRACK HAY CARRIER OUTFIT FOR A 30-FOOT BARN consists of 1 steel track hay carrier, 1 short tine double harpoon hay fork, 30 feet of double angle steel track complete, 12 rafter brackets, 12 steel track hanging hooks, 4 floor hooks, 3 steel yoke knot passing pulleys, 90 feet of ¾-inch manila carrier rope and 35 feet of ⅜-inch manila check rope. For each 5 feet additional length of barn we add 5 feet of double angle steel track complete, 2 rafter brackets, 2 steel track hanging hooks, 10 feet of ¾-inch manila carrier rope and 5 feet of ⅜-inch manila check rope.

No. 9K71320	30-foot Outfit.	Weight, 175 pounds. Price	$11.05
No. 9K71321	35-foot Outfit.	Weight, 193 pounds. Price	11.90
No. 9K71322	40-foot Outfit.	Weight, 211 pounds. Price	12.80
No. 9K71323	45-foot Outfit.	Weight, 229 pounds. Price	13.75
No. 9K71324	50-foot Outfit.	Weight, 247 pounds. Price	14.75
No. 9K71325	55-foot Outfit.	Weight, 265 pounds. Price	15.65
No. 9K71326	60-foot Outfit.	Weight, 283 pounds. Price	16.60

$10.37 KENWOOD STANDARD WIRE CABLE TRACK HAY CARRIER OUTFIT FOR A 50-FOOT BARN consists of 1 reversible cable hay carrier, 1 short tine double harpoon hay fork, 50 feet of ½-inch steel hay carrier cable, 2 eye bolts, 2 ½-inch cable clamps, 4 floor hooks, 3 steel yoke knot passing pulleys, 130 feet of ¾-inch manila hay carrier rope and 55 feet of ⅜-inch manila check rope. For each 5 feet additional length of barn you should order and allow price for 5 feet of ½-inch steel hay carrier cable, 10 feet of ¾-inch manila hay carrier rope and 5 feet of ⅜-inch manila check rope. This style of outfit is generally selected for temporary use; that is, for moving from one barn to another.
No. 9K71330   50-foot Cable Track Outfit.   Weight, 120 pounds.   Price................$10.37

$12.89 KENWOOD STANDARD 50-FOOT HAY STACKING OUTFIT consists of 1 cable hay carrier, 1 short tine double harpoon hay fork, 150 feet of ½-inch steel cable for carrier track and guys, 2½-inch cable clamps, 2 square collars for ½-inch cable, 2 long bolts for top of posts, 3 steel yoke knot passing pulleys, 130 feet of ¾-inch manila carrier rope and 65 feet of ⅜-inch manila check rope. For each 10 feet additional length of outfit you should order and allow price for 10 feet of ½-inch steel cable, 10 feet of ¾-inch manila carrier rope and 10 feet of ⅜-inch manila check rope.
No. 9K71335   50-foot Stacking Outfit.   Weight, 165 pounds.   Price................$12.89

KENWOOD HAY CARRIERS AND TOOLS

OUR LINE OF hay carriers, forks, pulleys, etc., is complete in every respect, and every article in this line is the very best that can be produced. Our hay carriers and sling carriers are made to be used with either ¾-inch, ⅞-inch or 1-inch manila carrier rope and ⅜-inch manila trip rope. They cannot be used with larger than 1-inch carrier rope and cannot be used with wire carrier or wire trip rope. All hay carriers, outfits, etc., quoted on this page are shipped from Chicago. For Sulky Hay Rakes, see page 545.

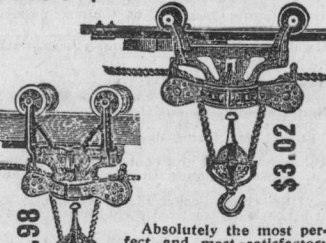

$2.98 KENWOOD STANDARD DOUBLE SWIVEL HAY CARRIER. $3.02 $2.98

Absolutely the most perfect and most satisfactory hay carriers made. They reverse by swiveling and will work either way from the stop and at either end of the barn without changing the rope or any part of the carrier, and the swivel is so perfectly constructed that it holds in line with the track as firmly as a plain reversible carrier, but is easily swiveled when desired. The wood track carrier will work on ordinary dressed 4x4-inch track. The steel track carrier is to run on our double angle steel track only. Price includes stop and fork pulley. Carrier will work with any style fork. If carrier is to be used with wagon slings, a sling pulley will be required. The sling pulley is extra, and is not included in the price of carrier.
No. 9K71200   Wood Track Hay Carrier. Weight, 33 pounds. Price.........$2.98
No. 9K71201   Steel Track Hay Carrier. Weight, 30 pounds. Price.........$3.02

$2.92 KENWOOD STANDARD REVERSIBLE CABLE HAY CARRIER. $2.92

This carrier is made to run on either ½-inch wire cable or ⅜-inch rod, and is reversible, adapting it especially for use with hay stacking outfits or with barn slings where it is not desirable to place a permanent track. Price includes stop and fork pulley. Carrier will work either way and with any style of fork. If carrier is to be used with wagon slings, a sling pulley will be required. The sling pulley is extra and is not included in price of carrier.
No. 9K71208   Cable Hay Carrier. Weight, 26 pounds. Price.........$2.92

$1.34 KENWOOD STANDARD SINGLE HARPOON HAY FORK. Single Harpoon Hay Fork. Full regular size and perfect in operation. Weight, 15 pounds.
No. 9K71215   Price.........$1.34

$5.88 KENWOOD STANDARD DOUBLE SWIVEL SLING HAY CARRIER. $5.92

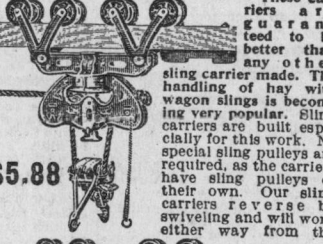

These carriers are guaranteed to be better than any other sling carrier made. The handling of hay with wagon slings is becoming very popular. Sling carriers are built especially for this work. No special sling pulleys are required, as the carriers have sling pulleys of their own. Our sling carriers reverse by swiveling and will work either way from the $5.88

$5.92

See those eight equalizing track pulleys.

stop and at either end of the barn without changing the rope or any part of the carrier, and the swivel is so perfectly constructed that it holds in line with the track as firmly as a plain reversible carrier, but is easily swiveled when desired. They draw the hay or grain up direct as the load stands. No twist in the rope or cramping of the pulleys. The wood track carrier will run on ordinary dressed 4x4-inch track. The steel track carrier is to run on our double angle steel track only. Slings can be locked and dumped at any height desired. Can also be used with any kind of hay forks and either one or two forks can be used at once.
No. 9K71210   Wood Track Sling Carrier. Weight, 72 pounds. Price.........$5.88
No. 9K71211   Steel Track Sling Carrier. Weight, 65 pounds. Price.........$5.92

LOW PRICES in our last catalogue still further reduced in this book on over 3,000 hardware items.

$1.46 FOR THIS KENWOOD STANDARD SELF LOCKING SLING PULLEY.

For use with our hay carriers only. Not required with sling carriers. Will lock at any place, no matter whether the sliding load be great or small. Cannot be used with sling carriers or with hay carriers of other makes. Weight, 10 pounds.
No. 9K71235   Price.........$1.46

86c KENWOOD STANDARD DOUBLE HARPOON HAY FORK.

Short Tine Double Harpoon Hay Fork, with 24-inch tines and 16 inches between points. The size and style of fork which is in general use and which we furnish in our regular hay carrier outfits. Made from best quality iron and steel. Weight, 18 pounds.
No. 9K71217   Price.........86c
Long Tine Double Harpoon Hay Fork. Same as above, except that tines are 30 inches long, adapting this fork for use in loose straw, etc. Weight, 21 pounds.
No. 9K71218   Price.........98c
Alfalfa Double Harpoon Hay Fork. Same as above, except that it is extra heavy and the tines are 34 inches long and 22 inches between points. This fork is especially adapted for handling alfalfa, straw, etc., but can be used for any kind of hay. Weight, 30 pounds.
No. 9K71219   Price.........$1.81

$3.96 KENWOOD STANDARD STEEL TINE GRAPPLE FORK. $3.96

Four-Tine Grapple Fork. For ordinary use. Weight, 35 lbs.
No. 9K71221   Price.........$3.32
Six-Tine Grapple Fork. Same as shown in illustration. For short hay, loose straw, etc. Weight, 55 lbs.
No. 9K71222   Price.........$3.96

$1.47 KENWOOD STANDARD ADJUSTABLE WAGON SLINGS.

The most rapid manner of handling hay, straw, corn stalks, etc., is with wagon slings. Three slings are generally used for the load. Prices are for single slings, not for sets. Our slings are adjustable to suit any length of rack and have reliable trip locks. 4-foot slings have two ropes between the cross bars; 5-foot and 6-foot slings have four ropes. The trip rope is long enough to allow you to trip the sling easily, and there is a small rope attached to each end ring so that you can pull the ends of the sling together without difficulty. Sling pulleys or sling carriers must be used with wagon slings.
No. 9K71227   4-Foot Wagon Sling. Weight, 18 pounds. Price.........$1.47
No. 9K71229   5-Foot Wagon Sling. Weight, 22 pounds. Price.........$1.84
No. 9K71228   6-Foot Wagon Sling. Weight, 25 pounds. Price.........$1.96

Kenwood Standard Hay Carrier Sundries.
Rafter Bracket. For hanging hay carrier track. Can be attached with nails or screws.
No. 9K71255   Price.........2c
Wood Track Hanging Hook. 14 inches long, under bend for hanging wood track.
No. 9K71257   Price.........5c
Steel Track Hanging Hook. For hanging our double angle steel track.
No. 9K71259   Price.........6c

Kenwood Standard Hay Pulleys.

Our hay pulleys can be used with any manila rope up to 1 inch, but cannot be used with wire rope.

Snatch Pulley Block. To shorten travel of horse without reducing power. Horse travels only half the distance hay is carried. Rope can be thrown off and returned to load in half the time. Has iron sheave.
No. 9K71237   Price.........45c 
Iron Yoke, Common Frame Pulley, with large loose hollow pin and 5½-inch maple sheave. A very popular pulley.
No. 9K71241   Price.........16c 
Steel Yoke Knot Passing Frame Pulley, with 5½-inch maple sheave. The most popular pulley made and recommended by us as the best selection. The style of pulley we furnish with hay carrier outfits.
No. 9K71247   Price.........18c

Swivel Rope Hitch. Made of malleable iron. Can be used on any manila rope up to 1 inch. Fastens anywhere. No cutting or tying of rope and no twisting.
No. 9K71251   Price.........13c

8½c PER FOOT KENWOOD DOUBLE ANGLE STEEL TRACK.

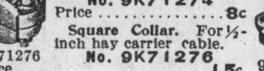

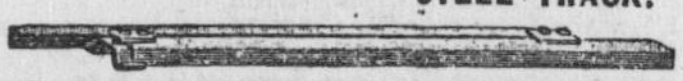

For our line of hay carriers and sling carriers only. Furnished only in multiples of 5 feet; that is, 10-feet main pieces with two 5-foot pieces to break joints. Price includes couplings and bolts, and with 30 feet or more two end bumpers are furnished. Price does not include rafter brackets or hanging hooks. Weight, 2½ pounds per foot.
No. 9K71253   Price, per foot...8½c

Kenwood Standard Hay Carrier, Hooks, Bolts, Etc. 
Jointed Hanging Hook. For hanging wood track to beams without using rafter brackets.
No. 9K71261   Price.........9c 
Floor Hook, ¾-inch diameter. To screw into floor or barn timbers to hold rope pulleys.
No. 9K71263   Price.........6c 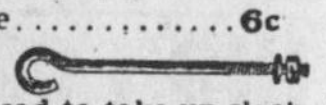
Eye Bolt. For fastening hay carrier cable to end of barn. Has long thread to take up slack.
No. 9K71269   Price.........23c 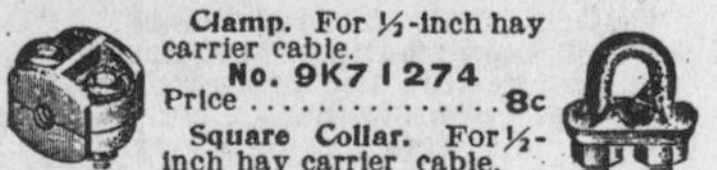
Clamp. For ½-inch hay carrier cable.
No. 9K71274   Price.........8c
Square Collar. For ½-inch hay carrier cable.
No. 9K71276   Price.........15c

Our Hay Carrier Cable is made up of seven strands of galvanized steel wire, tightly twisted together as shown in the illustration. ½-inch Hay Carrier Cable. For cable carrier track. Weight, ½ pound per foot.
No. 9K71278   Price, per foot...2½c

EVERY HARDWARE PRICE NAMED IN THIS BOOK WILL SAVE YOU MONEY.

MECHANICS' TOOLS

THOUSANDS OF CARPENTERS, BUILDERS AND OTHERS HAVE FOUND THAT THEY CAN BUY THE VERY FINEST MECHANICS' TOOLS FROM US AT PRICES 25 TO 50 PER CENT LOWER THAN OTHERS CHARGE FOR TOOLS NOT AS GOOD. ARE YOU BENEFITING BY THIS SAVING; CAN YOU AFFORD TO PAY HIGH PRICES ELSEWHERE WHEN YOU CAN GET BETTER GOODS FROM US FOR LESS MONEY?

THE SUPERIORITY of our Mechanics' Tools over all others is proven by our enormous sales; our business in this line is the largest of any concern in the United States. Our customers who buy most of these goods are the highest class workmen in their respective localities, men who know good tools and who will have no other kind. They send us order after order, saving the big difference between our price and prices charged by retailers.

THE INSPECTION of our Mechanics' Tools is very thorough; every tool coming into our establishment is carefully examined by an experienced inspector, and if it does not come up to the highest standard is sent back to the factory. We attribute our enormous sales to the fact that we never allow inferior tools to be shipped out on orders. All we ask you to do is read our guarantee, send us your order and give them a fair trial.

WE GUARANTEE EVERY MECHANICS' TOOL

quoted in this department to be free from flaws and defects and perfectly adapted to the work it is intended to do. We guarantee them to be superior to any tools of any other make at anything like our price. Buy tools of us and if you are not entirely satisfied that you are getting better value for less money than you could possibly obtain elsewhere, ship them back to us and we will promptly refund your money. Could we afford to make this liberal guarantee unless we KNEW our goods would stand your examination?

$15.93 OUR NEW VICTOR TOOL OUTFIT

GREATLY IMPROVED FOR THIS SEASON'S SELLING WITH A NEW SELECTION OF HIGH GRADE TOOLS PACKED IN A HARDWOOD CHEST.

THIS OUTFIT CANNOT BE MATCHED ELSEWHERE FOR LESS THAN $24.00 TO $27.00.

YOU SAVE

ON THE COST OF EACH ITEM WHEN YOU BUY HARDWARE FROM US. REDUCED PRICES ON OVER 3,000 ITEMS MAKE YOUR SAVING GREATER THAN EVER.

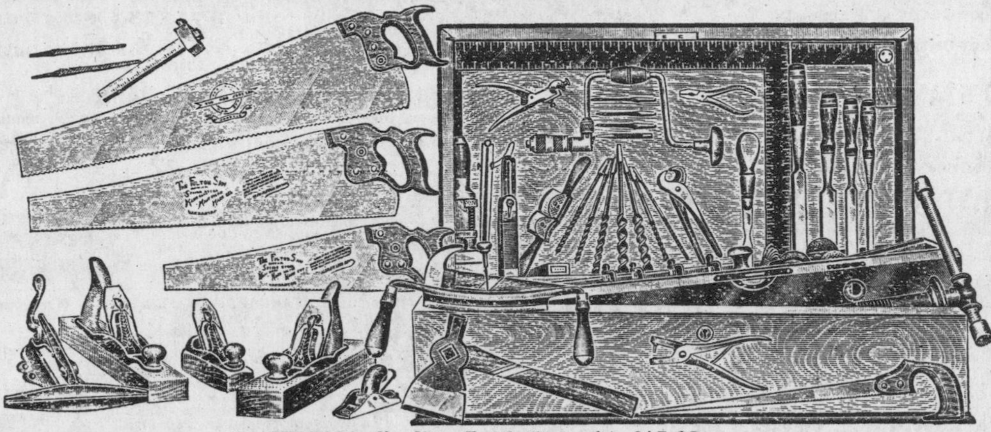

EVERY ITEM IN THIS OUTFIT COVERED BY OUR GUARANTEE OF "SATISFACTION OR YOUR MONEY BACK."

No. 9K55002 New Victor Tool Outfit, complete, $15.93.

OUR NEW VICTOR TOOL OUTFIT WILL PAY FOR ITSELF IN A SHORT TIME.

YOU CAN SAVE several times its cost by doing small jobs around the house, repairing furniture, etc. Most any man is handy with tools, provided he has the right kind. The tools in the new Victor set are all high grade, warranted articles selected from our regular line of mechanics' tools and put up in this convenient set for use of first class workmen. Our New Victor Outfit of tools is not surpassed by any outfit put up, with the single exception of our Improved Invincible Outfit illustrated on the next page and priced at the wonderfully low price of $25.23 for a complete set of tools that cannot be bought elsewhere for less than $50.00.

WHEN YOU SEND us an order for one of our New Victor Outfits, we pack the goods in a hardwood tool chest which is large enough to contain additional tools that you may select from time to time. This tool chest is well made and nicely finished, has a sliding tray and is fitted with good lock and hinges.

Read below the full list and description of high grade tools contained in our New Victor Outfit.

1 "Odd Jobs" Warranted Steel Rip Saw, 28 inches long.
2 High Grade Fulton Saws, 1 26-inch hand, and 1 18-inch panel.
1 Compass Saw. Steel blade, 14 inches in length.
4 Fulton Tool Co. Adjustable Planes. 1 wood smooth plane, length 8 inches; 1 wood jack plane, length 15 inches; 1 wood fore plane, length 20 inches, and 1 iron block plane, length 5½ inches.
1 Improved Morrill Pattern Saw Set. For setting hand, band, buck or meat saws.
1 Adjustable Iron Saw Clamp. Jaws, 9½ inches long.
2 Fulton Tool Co. Slim Taper Saw Files, 1 each 5 and 6 inches.
1 Steel Carpenters' Square, with 16-inch tongue, 2 inches wide, spaced ⅛, ¼ and 1 inch. With Essex new board measure.
1 Pair of Carpenters' Steel Pincers, length, 8 inches.
1 Combination Wire Cutter and Pliers, length, 5½ inches.
1 Knurled Steel Nail Set, with cup point.
1 Spring Tube Punch, for cutting holes in leather.
1 Box of 100 Assorted Slotted Rivets.
1 Wrought Iron Bench Screw, with patent collar.
1 Set of 4 Quilt Frame Clamps.
1 Beechwood Marking Gauge, with boxwood thumbscrew, steel point and graduated bar.
1 Pair of Wing Dividers, length 8 inches, polished steel with adjusting screw.
1 Chalk Line Reel and Awl.
1 Medium Size Braided Chalk Line.
12 Cakes of Carpenters' Chalk, assorted red, white and blue.
1 Carpenters' Extra Quality Lead Pencil.
1 Adjustable Plumb and Level, polished mahogany, arched top plates and two side views. Length, 28 inches.
1 Try Square with 6-inch blade, brass lined handle.
1 Sliding T Bevel, with brass tipped rosewood handle, 8-inch blade.
1 Carpenters' Boxwood Rule, 2-foot. Square joints, with brass edge plates. Spaced 8ths, 10ths, 12ths and 16ths, with drafting scale.
1 Solid Cast Steel Shingling Hatchet, weight, 23 ounces.
1 Forged Steel Nail Hammer, weight, 1 pound.
1 Standard Monkey Wrench, length, 10 inches.
1 Fulton Tool Co. Forged Steel Razor Blade Draw Knife, length of cut, 8 inches.
1 Iron Spoke Shave, with straight and concave steel cutters.
1 Fulton Tool Co. Socket Framing Chisel, width, 1 inch, with iron ring.
3 Fulton Tool Co. High Grade Socket Firmer Chisels, 1 each size, ¼, ½ and 1 inch, with leather tipped hickory handles.
1 Octagon Steel Cold Chisel, ½ inch.
1 Steel Blade Screwdriver, with beechwood handle and 6-inch blade.
1 Ratchet Brace, with head and handle of hardwood, with 10-inch sweep.
1 Set of Cast Steel Extension Lip Auger Bits, 1 each size, ¼, $\frac{5}{16}$, ⅜, ½, ⅝, ¾ and 1 inch.
3 German Pattern Gimlet Bits, 1 each, size $\frac{1}{16}$, ⅛ and $\frac{3}{16}$ inch.

OUR NEW VICTOR CHEST measures over 34 inches long, 18 inches wide, 10 inches deep, and is large enough to contain additional tools that may be bought from time to time. Weight, packed for shipment, 90 pounds.

No. 9K55002 The New Victor Chest and Tools, complete. Price........................ **$15.93**

GOOD HARDWARE IS PRICED STILL LOWER IN THIS BOOK THAN IN OUR LAST CATALOGUE.

$7.97 OUR "GOOD VALUE" TOOL SET

COMPLETE AS ILLUSTRATED, WITH HARDWOOD CHEST.

A PLACE FOR EVERYTHING AND EVERYTHING IN ITS PLACE.

ONE OF OUR WORLD FAMOUS ASSORTMENTS OF STRICTLY

HIGH GRADE TOOLS

TOOLS FOR ALMOST ANY PURPOSE that, if bought in the regular way, would cost you double the price we ask for them, tools that are first quality, correctly made and finished and every one fully warranted.

AT $7.97

this is the finest assortment of tools ever offered for the money, and a set which you could not buy elsewhere for less than $12.00 to $13.00.

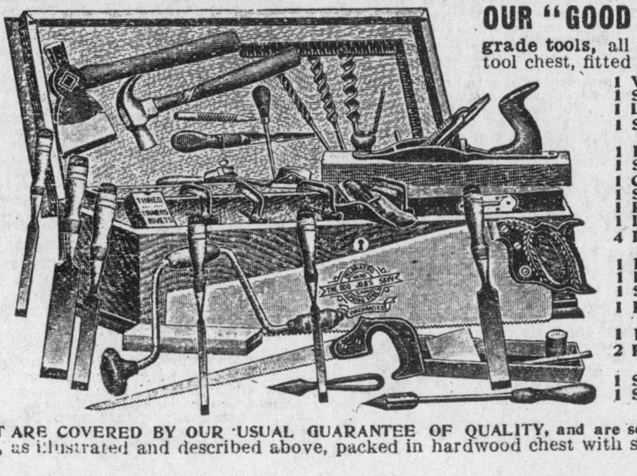

OUR "GOOD VALUE" OUTFIT consists of the following standard high grade tools, all packed in well made, nicely finished hardwood tool chest, fitted with lock and hinges:

1 Warranted Hand Saw, 24 inches.
1 Solid Steel Compass Saw.
1 Lever Saw Set.
1 Set of 6 Fulton Tool Co. High Grade Chisels, sizes, ¼ to 1½ inches.
1 Rapid Cutting Oil Stone.
1 Screwdriver, with 5-inch Forged Steel Blade.
1 Carpenters' Steel Square, nickel plated.
1 Soldering Outfit.
1 Package Mending Rivets, useful for many purposes.
1 Level, 12 inches, cherry finished.
4 Double Spur, Solid Cast Steel Auger Bits, sizes, ¼, ½, ¾ and 1 inch.
1 Knurled Nail Set.
1 Bit Brace, with 10-inch sweep.
1 Steel Scratch or Marking Awl.
1 Fulton Tool Co. High Grade Shingling Hatchet, with 3⅞-inch cutting bit.
1 Forged Steel Nail Hammer, size, 1½.
2 Fulton Tool Co. High Grade Planes, 1 each, 5½-inch block and 14-inch jack.
1 Set of 4 Japanned Quilt Frame Clamps.
1 Spoke Shave, with adjustable cap, crucible cast steel blade and enameled handles.

ALL TOOLS IN THIS "GOOD VALUE" OUTFIT ARE COVERED BY OUR USUAL GUARANTEE OF QUALITY, and are selected from our regular stock.

No. 9K55055 "Good Value" Outfit, as illustrated and described above, packed in hardwood chest with sliding tray. Price, complete.... **$7.97**

$25.23 IMPROVED INVINCIBLE TOOL OUTFIT

THIS IS THE COMPLETE OUTFIT. THE ONE THAT CONTAINS ALL THE TOOLS.

THE GREAT $50.00 SET ON WHICH WE GUARANTEE TO SAVE YOU BIG MONEY AT THE UNMATCHABLE PRICE OF $25.23.

REDUCED PRICES MAKE YOUR SAVING GREATER THAN EVER

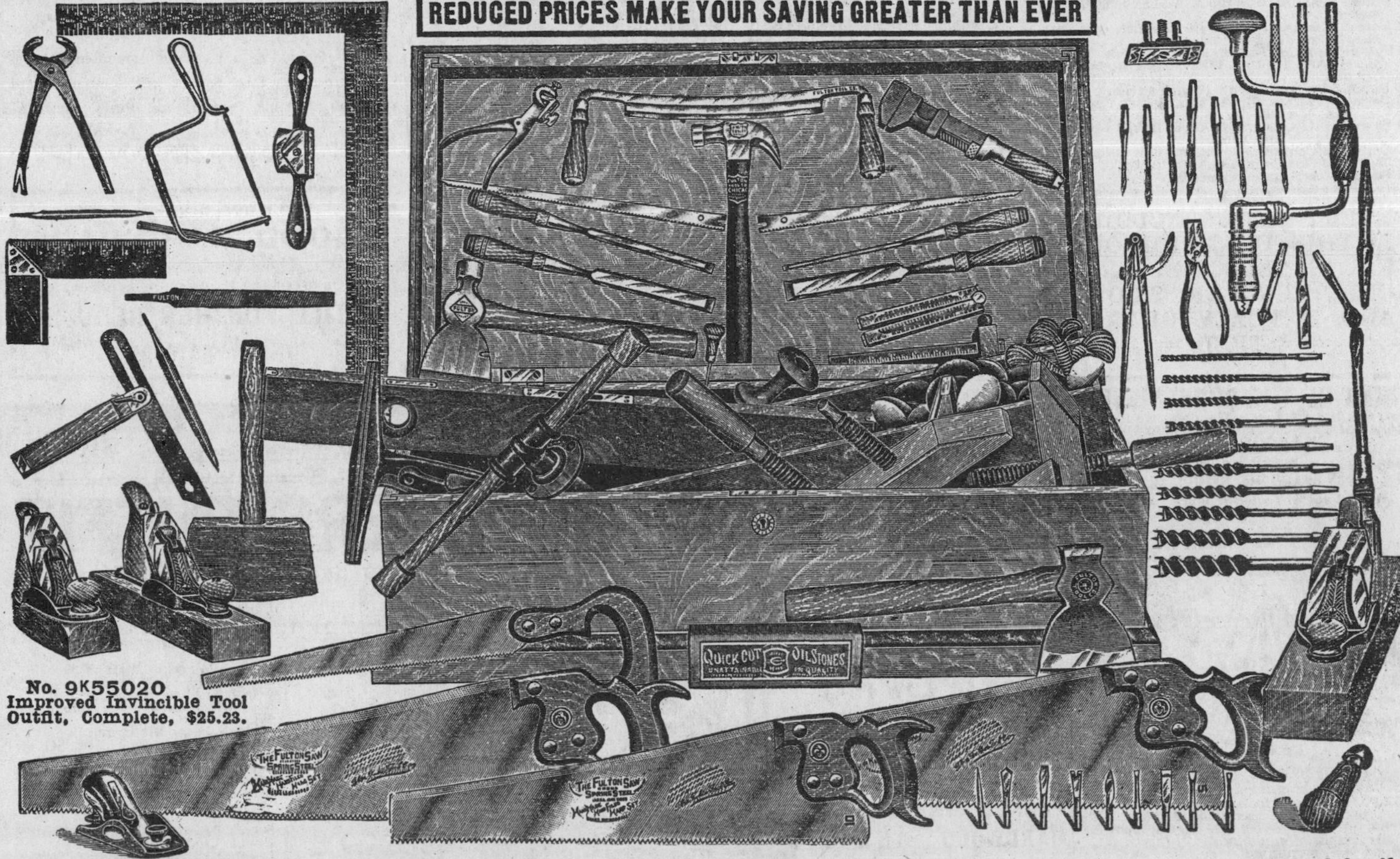

No. 9K55020 Improved Invincible Tool Outfit, Complete, $25.23.

THIS ILLUSTRATION shows the greatest, grandest and most complete selection of first quality, high grade tools ever assembled for the price. An outfit that positively cannot be bought for less than $50.00 in any hardware or tool supply house.

UNMATCHABLE IN SALES. UNMATCHABLE IN COMPLETENESS. UNMATCHABLE IN VALUE.

TAKE A LIST OF THE TOOLS contained in this outfit, price them at any first class store in your neighborhood, and you will find that you cannot buy them for less than $50.00. Then note that our price for the complete outfit as illustrated, packed in a hardwood chest, is only $25.23. If you need a set of tools send us your order for this] fine outfit and we guarantee to please you or refund your money.

OUR IMPROVED INVINCIBLE IS THE BIGGEST SELLING OUTFIT OF TOOLS IN THE WORLD.

ONLY THE FACT OF OUR ENORMOUS SALES and our tremendous purchasing power enables even us to offer for $25.23 this complete assortment of tools which positively cannot be purchased in any hardware or tool supply house for less than $50.00. Every one of our Invincible tool sets is sent out under a positive guarantee that the tools are the very best made, that they will thoroughly please you and that they are unmatchable at our price. Send us your order for one of these Invincible Tool Outfits for $25.23 and if after you get the goods you do not think they are positively the best value you ever saw and greatly superior to any assortment that you can buy elsewhere at even double the price you paid us, return the goods to us and we will cheerfully refund your money. We have been making this offer on our Invincible tool sets for years and have never heard of a dissatisfied customer.

OUR IMPROVED INVINCIBLE TOOL OUTFIT IS PACKED IN A BEAUTIFUL HARDWOOD TOOL CHEST, WEATHERED OAK FINISH.

THIS CHEST, which could not be bought at retail for less than $7.00 to $8.00 measures over 34 inches long, 18 inches wide and 10 inches high. It has a sliding tray and is fitted with a fine lock and strong hinges. It is made out of the best materials by skilled workmen and like the tools it contains cannot be made better.

STUDY THE ILLUSTRATION of this big and complete assortment of tools. You will note that every tool you can possibly need is included in this outfit. Remember in addition that every tool is fully guaranteed by us to be of the highest possible grade and that our price for the complete outfit including hardwood chest is only........................ **$25.23**

BELOW WE GIVE A COMPLETE LIST OF THE TOOLS PACKED IN OUR IMPROVED INVINCIBLE OUTFIT AND WHICH WE ASK YOU TO READ CAREFULLY.

1 **Fulton Tool Co. Shingling Hatchet,** solid steel 3⅜-inch cut.
1 **Fulton Tool Co. Broad Hatchet,** solid steel, 4½-inch cut.
1 **Fulton Tool Co. Nail Hammer,** size No. 1½, weight, 1 lb. Finely nickel plated, octagon neck and poll, ebony finished hickory handle.
4 **Fulton Tool Co. Socket Firmer Chisels.** Blades each 6 inches long with full beveled edges. Handles are finely polished fir[illegible] quality hickory, with leather tips. Chisels are one each ¼, ½, ¾ and 1 inch size.
1 **Fulton Tool Co. Carpenters' Drawing Knife.** Forged steel, 10-inch, finest razor blade.
3 **Fulton Tool Co. Saws,** one 28-inch Rip, one 26-inch hand, one 20-inch panel Fulton saws are hand made from finest steel and are warranted best saws in the world.
1 **Fulton Tool Co. Nest of Three Saws,** consisting of 1 handle, 1 keyhole blade, 1 compass blade and 1 pruning blade, all interchangeable.
1 **Square Hickory Mallet,** mortised handle. Head is 6½x2¾x3¾ inches.
6 **Cakes Assorted Color Carpenters' Chalk.**
1 **Beechwood Chalk Line Reel and Awl.**
3 **Hanks Braided Chalk Line.**
1 **Monkey Wrench.** Size, 10-inch. Strongly made and well finished.
4 **Fulton Tool Co. Carpenters' Planes,** 1 handled adjustable wood base smooth plane. Length, 9 inches. 1 wood base 15-inch handled jack plane; 1 wood base 26-inch jointer; 1 iron block plane 6⅜ inches long, with adjustable knuckle joint and nickel plated trimming. Fulton planes embody all the newest and best improvements and are superior to any other planes.
10 **Fulton Tool Co. Double Spur, Extension Lip Auger Bits.** Positively the best boring bit on the market. Heads are carefully fitted and bits finely finished. One each of the following sizes: ¼, 5-16, ⅜, 7-16, ½, 9-16, ⅝, ¾, ⅞ and 1 inch.
3 **Fulton Tool Co. Files.** These files are superior in cut and finish to any other file at any price. 1 each, 4 and 6-inch slim taper, and 1 8-inch mill.
1 **Adjustable Saw Clamp.** Can be instantly adjusted to any angle.
1 **Original Morrill's Pattern Saw Set,** with improved anvil; will set hand, panel, rip, meat, buck or band saws.
1 **Combined Try and Mitre Square.** 7½-inch blade, brass lined rosewood handle and graduated steel blade.
1 **Sliding "T" Bevel,** 10-inch blade, rosewood handle, brass tipped with flush adjusting screw and steel blade.
2 **Sets 10-Inch Hand Screw Clamps,** made of seasoned hardwood.
1 **2-foot Rule,** full brass bound, double arch joints, four-fold with drafting scale.
1 **Improved Marking Gauge,** made of beechwood with boxwood thumbscrew. Marked in inches.
1 **Quick Cut Oil Stone.** Size, 7x2 inches. Mounted in finished chestnut case.
1 **Awl and Tool Set,** with 10 forged steel awls and tools and hollow cocobolo handle which holds tools when not in use.
1 **Combined Plier and Wire Cutter,** 6-inch.
1 **Pair Carpenters' Pincers.** 8-inch, with claw on handle. Forged from superior steel.
1 **Wrought Iron Bench Screw.** 1 inch in diameter, with patent collar, double thread and wood handle.
1 **Extra Quality Steel Square.** Size of body 24x2 inches; size of tongue, 16x1½ inches. Marked in sixteenths, twelfths and fourths, and also with brace and Essex board measure.
1 **Adjustable Plumb and Level,** mahogany polished, proved glasses, arched top plates, brass tipped with two side views.
1 **10-inch Sweep Ratchet Brace.** Lignum vitae head. Well finished and heavily nickel plated.
8 **Forged Steel, German Pattern, Gimlet Bits.** 1 each of the following sizes: 1-16, 3-32, ⅛, 5-32, 3-16, 7-32, ¼ and 5-16 inch.
2 **Countersink Bits,** forged from steel and polished. 1 each, flat head for metal and snail head for wood.
1 **Screwdriver Bit,** for use in bit brace, 5½ inches long, forged from steel.
1 **Square Reamer Bit,** for use in bit brace, forged from steel.
3 **Knurled Cup Point Nail Sets.** Assorted sizes.
1 **Iron Handle Spoke Shave,** with 2⅛-inch steel cutter.
1 **Nickel Plated Coping Saw,** with 1 dozen extra blades.
1 **Bench Stop,** screw adjusting, with reversible cast steel head.
1 **Polished Forged Steel Wing Divider,** 8-inch.
1 **Warranted Tool Steel Machinists' Screwdriver.** 6-inch blade; round, corrugated, imitation rosewood handle.

WE CALL YOUR ATTENTION to the fact that more than half of the edged tools in this magnificent outfit are the celebrated Fulton Tool Co. goods. There are more tools sold under this well known brand than any other line in the world and every tool branded Fulton Tool Co. is absolutely guaranteed by us to be the best of its kind made. We will exchange or refund price on any article branded Fulton Tool Co. bought of us that does not give perfect satisfaction to our customer.

No. 9K55020 Improved Invincible Tool Outfit. Shipping weight, packed complete, 100 pounds. 'rice........................ **$25.23**

$10.13 OUR CHAMPION TOOL OUTFIT

A BIG LOT OF HIGH GRADE TOOLS COMPLETE IN A HARDWOOD CHEST

The tools we pack in our Champion Outfit for $10.13 are as follows:

2 High Grade Springfield Saws, 1 each, 24-inch hand and 26-inch rip.
1 Standard Cast Steel Blade Compass Saw, 12 inches.
1 Fulton Tool Co. Adjustable Wood Bottom Jack Plane, length, 15 inches.
1 Fulton Tool Co. Iron Block Plane, length, 7¼ inches.
1 Forged Steel Adze Eye Nail Hammer, with bell face. Weight, 1 pound.
3 Fulton Tool Co. Socket Firmer Chisels, 1 each, ¼, ½ and 1 inch. With leather tipped hickory handles.
1 Ratchet Bit Brace, with 10-inch sweep.
5 German Pattern Gimlet Bits, 1 each size, 1-16, ⅛, 3-16, ¼ and 5-16.
5 Extension Lip Cast Steel Auger Bits, 1 each size, ⅜, ½, ⅝, ¾ and 1 inch.
1 Cast Steel Countersink, with snail head for wood.
1 Cast Steel Flat Countersink, for metal.
1 Forged Steel Square Reamer Bit.

EVERY TOOL INCLUDED IN THIS CHAMPION OUTFIT IS SELECTED FROM OUR REGULAR STOCK AND IS FULLY GUARANTEED

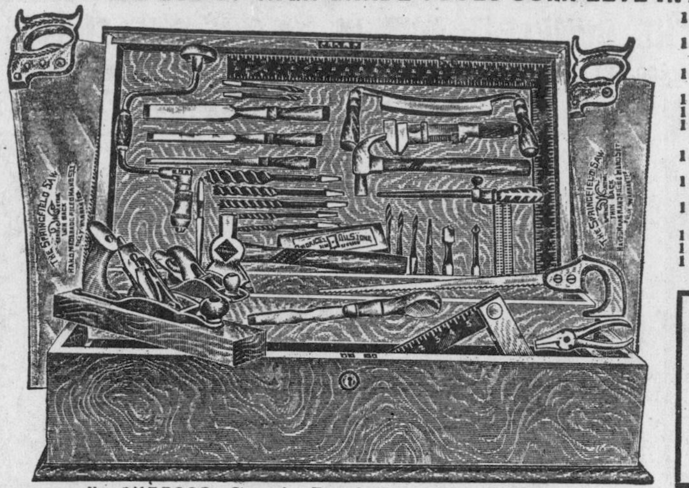

No. 9K55008 Champion Tool Outfit, complete, $10.13

1 Carpenters' Boxwood Rule, two-foot, fourfold with square joints and drafting scale.
1 Steel 6-inch Blade Try Square, with brass lined handle.
1 Screwdriver, with 5-inch cast steel blade, beech handle.
1 Knurled Steel Cup Point Nail Set.
1 Solid Steel Shingling Hatchet, with 4-inch cut.
1 Fulton Tool Co. Razor Blade Drawing Knife, 8-in. cut.
1 Oil Stone, length, 6 inches. Mounted in hardwood case.
1 Carpenters' Steel Square, with Essex board measure, 16-inch tongue marked on both sides.
1 Pair Button's Pattern Steel Pliers and Wire Cutters. Length, 6 inches.
1 Standard Monkey Wrench, length, 10 inches.
1 Fulton Tool Co. Slim Taper File, length, 6 inches.
1 Iron Tool and File Handle.

We have always sold **GOOD HARDWARE** at lower prices than any other house. On over 3,000 Hardware items prices are **STILL FURTHER REDUCED** IN THIS CATALOGUE.

THINK OF THE CONVENIENCE of having "the right tool at the right time," a tool that is strong and dependable. Our Champion Outfit of Tools is just the outfit for any man who wants a good set of tools for general purposes. The tools in our Champion Outfit cannot be duplicated at any retail store for less than $15.00 to $17.00. The chest we furnish with our Champion Outfit is made of hardwood, weathered oak finish, has strong substantial lock and hinges, and is large enough to contain additional tools that may be bought later if needed.

No. 9K55008 This Champion Set of high grade Tools, packed in hardwood chest, as illustrated. Weight, packed for shipment, 75 pounds. Price, complete **$10.13**

$2.39 FOR THIS 18-PIECE EVERYDAY WARRANTED TOOL SET.

A splendid set of tools for home use. Will save its cost on one job.

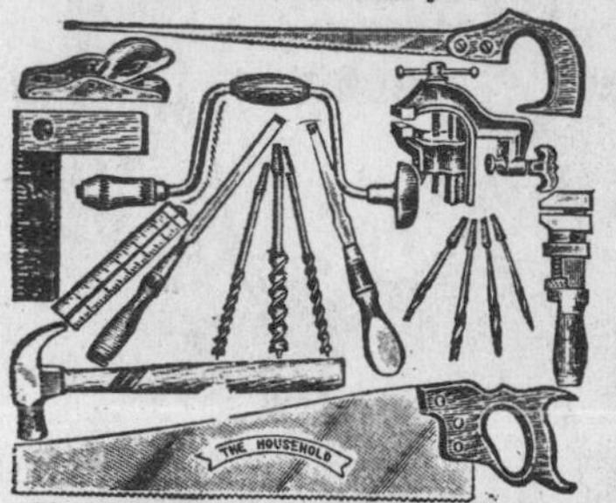

$2.39 for a set of tools you could not buy in any retail store for less than $3.50. This special set at $2.39 consists of the following strictly standard grade tools:

1 Hand Saw, warranted.
1 Nail Hammer, warranted.
1 Bit Brace.
4 Double Cut Gimlet Bits, assorted.
3 Warranted Double Spur Auger Bits, 1 each size, ⅜, ½ and ¾ inch.
1 14-inch Compass Saw which can also be used as a rip saw.
1 2-foot Boxwood Rule.
1 5-inch Forged Steel Screwdriver.
1 8-inch Monkey Wrench.
1 5½-inch Iron Block Plane.
1 ½-inch Socket Firmer Chisel, warranted.
1 Combination Anvil and Vise, 1½-inch jaws, open 1¾ inches.
1 6-inch Brass Lined Try Square.

No. 9K55036 18 tools. Price.. **$2.39**
Weight, packed for shipment, 15 pounds.

$6.16 OUR RELIABLE WOOD BUTCHERS' OUTFIT

THE MOST REMARKABLE VALUE EVER OFFERED IN A HIGH GRADE TOOL ASSORTMENT.

A FAMOUS ASSORTMENT OF TOOLS PRICED SO LOW THAT THE SALES RUN INTO THOUSANDS OF SETS EACH SEASON. PACKED IN A NEW HARDWOOD CHEST AND WITH IMPROVED TOOLS THIS YEAR.

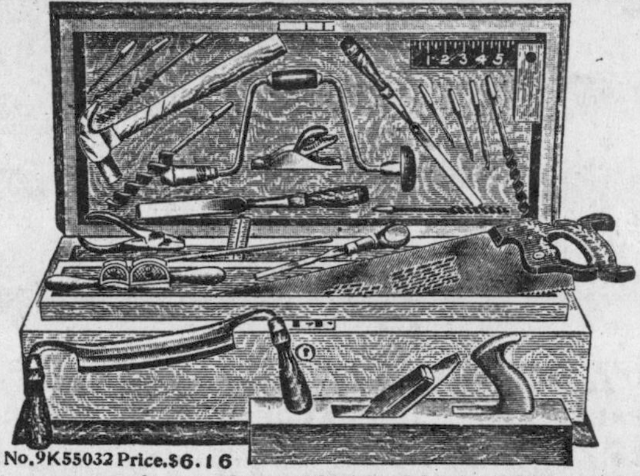

No. 9K55032 Price $6.16

OUR WOOD BUTCHERS' OUTFIT CONSISTS OF THE FOLLOWING TOOLS:

1 22-inch Warranted Hand Saw.
1 2-foot Rule.
1 6-inch Try Square, brass lined.
1 5½-inch Combination Plier and Wire Cutter.
1 10-inch Sweep Bit Brace.
4 Auger Bits, one each size, ⅜, ½, ¾, and 1 inch.
5 German Pattern Gimlet Bits, one each size, 1-16, ⅛, 3-16, ¼, and 5-16 inch.
1 Warranted Solid Steel Nail Hammer.
1 8-inch Drawing Knife.
1 Double Cutter Spoke Shave.
2 Leather Tipped Handle Socket Firmer Chisels, one each size, ½ and 1 inch.
1 5-inch Screwdriver.
1 Beechwood Jack Plane, with double iron cutter.
1 5½-inch Iron Block Plane.
1 Good Carpenters' Pencil.

THIS ASSORTMENT OF TOOLS is one of our oldest and best selling outfits. We sell thousands of these sets each year and they have never failed to please our customers. The tools in this Wood Butchers' Set are all selected from our regular stock and are strictly high grade goods. This season we have made an extremely careful selection of tools and pack them in an improved box made of hardwood and furnished with tray, hinges and lock. If you undertook to buy the tools contained in this outfit of the same high grade in a first class hardware store they would cost you no less than $10.00 or $11.00. We pack the outfit complete with chest as described, all for $6.16.

No. 9K55032 Wood Butchers' Tool Set and lock box as described. Weight, complete, packed for shipment, 40 pounds. Price.......... **$6.16**

$9.94 FOR THIS STRONG SUBSTANTIAL SOLID MAPLE CABINET MAKERS' BENCH.

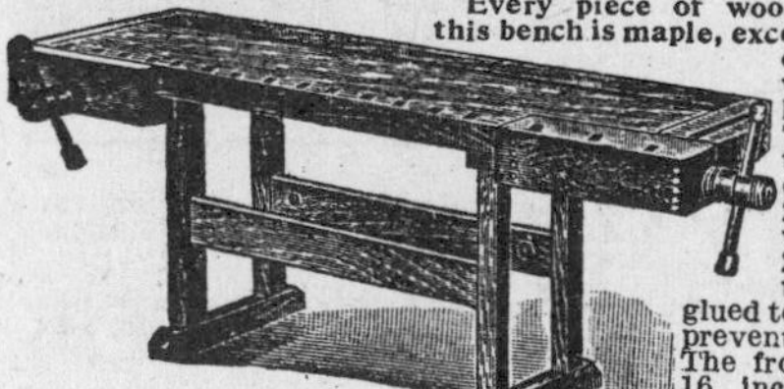

Every piece of wood used in this bench is maple, except handle of screw, which is hickory. The front top made of pieces 2½ inches wide and 2¾ inches thick, glued together to prevent warping. The front top is 16 inches wide and back top (which is recessed) is 8 inches wide. Screws are 24 inches long and 2½ inches in diameter over the thread. It is put together with bolts so that it may be tightened up when necessary. Length, 6½ feet; width, 2 feet; height 34 inches. Shipping weight, 190 pounds.

No. 9K55094 Price.......... **$9.94**

$6.98 FOR A HIGH GRADE SOLID MAPLE HANDY WORK BENCH.

The Handy Work Bench is intended for light work, amateurs, manual training schools, etc. It is made the same as the regular standard cabinet makers' bench except it is lighter. Top is made of hard maple strips 1⅞ inches thick, glued together to prevent warping. Furnished with two 2-inch maple bench screws. The stand is made of 2-inch maple, dressed to about 1¾ inches. The top is 20 inches wide (the back being recessed) and 42 inches long. Mortises for spring bench hooks are provided. Height, 31 inches. Shipping weight, 100 pounds.

No. 9K55096 Price.......... **$6.98**

72c PER PAIR STEEL SPRING BENCH HOOKS.

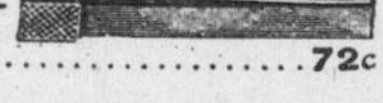

Made of steel, strong and substantial, suitable for above benches.

No. 9K55098 Price, per pair.......... **72c**

YOU PAY TWICE OUR PRICE AT RETAIL ON THOUSANDS OF HARDWARE ITEMS.

$4.68 CARPENTERS' HARDWOOD EMPTY TOOL CHEST WITH TWO SLIDING TRAYS.

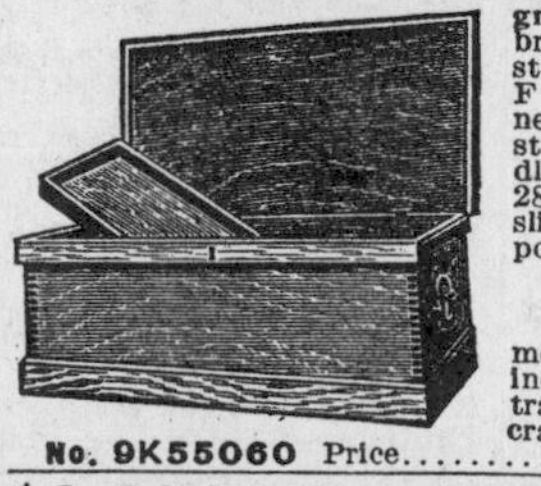

Made of select straight grained hardwood, strongly braced; sides of ⅞-inch stock, dovetailed and glued. Finished with moulding, neatly varnished, fitted with strong lock, hinges and handles. Inside measurements, 28x15x14 inches, with two sliding trays. Weight, 66 pounds.

No. 9K55056 Price.......... **$4.68**

Extra large size. Inside measurements, 32 x 18 x 16 inches. With two sliding trays and saw rack. Weight, crated, 82 pounds.

No. 9K55060 Price.......... **$6.12**

$2.63 SEASONED HARDWOOD CARPENTERS' SHOULDER TOOL CHEST.

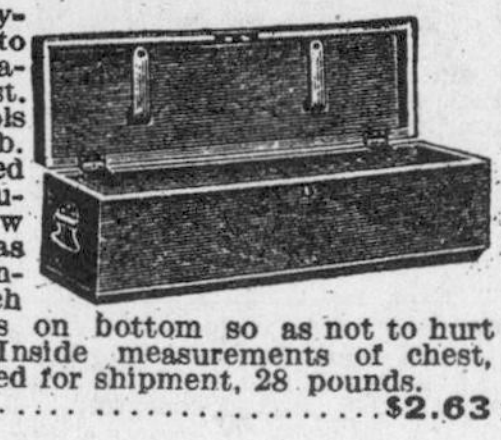

Very convenient for carrying tools from one place to another when it is not desirable to take a larger chest. Will hold all the ordinary tools necessary for any one job. Nicely varnished. With locked joints and fitted with good double link lock and brass elbow catch to hold cover open. Has saw rack and enameled handles. Chest is made of ⅝-inch stock and has rounded corners on bottom so as not to hurt shoulder when carrying. Inside measurements of chest, 32x8x8 inches. Weight, crated for shipment, 28 pounds.

No. 9K55068 Price.......... **$2.63**

$5.49 MACHINISTS' HARDWOOD EMPTY TOOL CHEST WITH TWO DRAWERS.

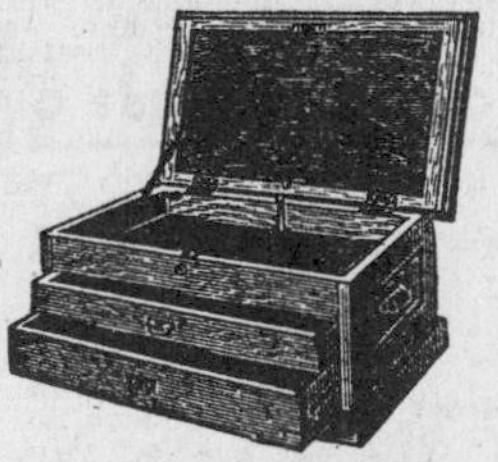

The highest grade tool chests made, such as are in general use among the highest class workmen and are not to be confused with the light, cheap, soft wood kind offered by others. These chests are made of selected hardwood and are furnished with Yale pattern locks, nickel plated drawer pulls and extra heavy enameled handles. Each chest is provided with a brass elbow to hold up lid, and a device to lock all the drawers at once automatically.

With two drawers. Outside dimensions, 20⅝ inches long by 13 inches wide by 9¾ inches high. Inside dimensions are as follows: Receptacle under lid, 18x10¼x3⅛ inches; first drawer, 16⅞x9x1¾ inches; second drawer, 16⅞x9x2⅝ inches; space under second drawer, 1 inch deep. Shipping weight, 30 pounds.

No. 9K55076 Price.......... **$5.49**

With three drawers. Outside dimensions, 23½ inches long by 14½ inches wide by 12 inches high. Inside dimensions are as follows: Receptacle under lid, 21x11¾x3⅛ inches; first drawer, 20x10½x1 inches; second drawer, 20x10½x1½ inches; third drawer, 20x10½x2½ inches; space under bottom drawer, 1⅜ inches. This is a high grade chest and should not be compared with cheap boxes made of gum wood of inferior quality. Shipping weight, 37 pounds.

No. 9K55080 Price.......... **$6.92**

IF YOU ARE A MECHANIC don't fail to look through these pages very carefully and compare our prices with those quoted by any other dealer on goods of equal quality. WE GUARANTEE OUR TOOLS TO BE THE BEST MADE.

8c FOR A 3½-INCH HIGH GRADE FULTON IRON BLOCK PLANE.

Not a toy but a practical tool for light work. 1-inch cutter. Weight, 9 ounces.

Price........8c

15c FOR A 5½-INCH FULTON IRON BLOCK PLANE.

Fulton planes are the finest made. Width of cutter, 1¼ inches; weight, 13 ounces.

No. 9K55320 Price........15c

24c FOR A 7½-INCH GUARANTEED FULTON IRON BLOCK PLANE.

Fulton planes are all full size and full weight. Width of cutter, 1¾ inches; weight, 1¼ pounds.

No. 9K55322 Price........24c

30c "DOUBLE HEADER" 7¾-INCH FULTON IRON BLOCK PLANE.

This plane has two slots and two cutter seats. It can be used as a block plane, or, by reversing the position of the cutter and the clamping wedge it can be used to plane close up into corners, or other difficult places; width of cutter, 1¾ inches; weight, 1½ pounds.

Price........30c

24c FOR A 5½-INCH FULTON ADJUSTABLE IRON BLOCK PLANE.

Fulton planes are larger, heavier and better constructed than planes you have heretofore considered standard. Width of cutter, 1½ inches; weight, 12 ounces.

No. 9K55326 Price........24c

33c FOR A 7½-INCH FULTON IRON ADJUSTABLE BLOCK PLANE.

Fulton planes are finished better than any other make. Width of cutter, 1¾ inches, weight, 1½ pounds.

No. 9K55328 Price........33c

55c DOUBLE ADJUSTABLE 6-INCH FULTON IRON BLOCK PLANE.

With screw adjustment to regulate the thickness of the shaving. It also has adjustment for opening or closing the throat as may be required for coarse or fine work. Width of cutter, 1¾ inches. Weight, 22 ounces.

No. 9K55330 Price........55c

65c KNUCKLE LEVER DOUBLE ADJUSTABLE FULTON IRON BLOCK PLANE.

Knuckle lever with screw adjustment and adjustable mouth. With patent side adjustment for exact adjusting of the cutter with the face of the plane. Nickel plated trimmings. Length, 6 inches; width of cutter, 1¾ inches. Weight, 24 ounces.

No. 9K55334 Price........65c

$1.82 ADJUSTABLE CIRCULAR PLANE WITH FLEXIBLE STEEL FACE.

The flexible steel face can be easily shaped to any required arc, either concave or convex by turning the knob on the front of the plane. Can also be used as a straight bottom plane. Length of face, 10¼ inches; width of cutter, 1¾ inches; weight, 3½ pounds.

No. 9K55534 Price........$1.82

$1.58 TONGUING AND GROOVING PLANE WITH TWO CUTTERS.

Commonly called a "match" plane. Handsomely nickel plated and well finished throughout. Can be changed instantly from one style to the other. Will match boards of any thickness from ¾ to 1¼ inches. Weight, 2½ pounds.

No. 9K55536 Price........$1.58
No. 9K55538 Will match boards any thickness from ⅜ to ¾ inch. Weight, 2¾ lbs.
Price........$1.57

97c FOR THIS DUPLEX RABBET PLANE AND FILLETSTER.

Remove the arm to which the fence is secured and a handled rabbet plane is had, and with two seats for the cutter, so that the tool can be used as a bull nose rabbet if required. The arm to which the fence is secured can be screwed into either side of the stock, thus making a superior right or left hand fillister with adjustable spur and depth gauge. Length, 3½ inches; 1¾-inch cutter. Weight, 3¼ lbs.

No. 9K55540 Price........97c

FULTON PLANES

CONSTRUCTED OF THE FINEST MATERIAL, PROPERLY PROPORTIONED AND ARE SUPERIOR TO ALL OTHERS IN CUTTING QUALITIES.

THE ADJUSTMENT is perfect and simple, the finish is unsurpassed and the tool steel cutters are tempered by an improved patent process, assuring the best results. Every Fulton plane sent out is thoroughly tested and if not found equal to or better than any other plane you ever saw, regardless of make, name or price, same can be returned to us at our expense and purchase price will be refunded.

Fulton Smooth Bottom Iron Bench Planes.

Made of strong, smooth, heavy castings. The face is ground perfectly. The working parts are all made by automatic machinery, and are interchangeable. The cutters are made from the best shear steel, carefully made, and tempered to cut and hold an edge. Every plane is guaranteed to give satisfaction in use.

> FULTON TOOLS ARE THE BEST MADE AT ANY PRICE.

> HARDWARE PRICES REDUCED IN THIS BOOK MAKE YOUR SAVING GREATER THAN EVER.

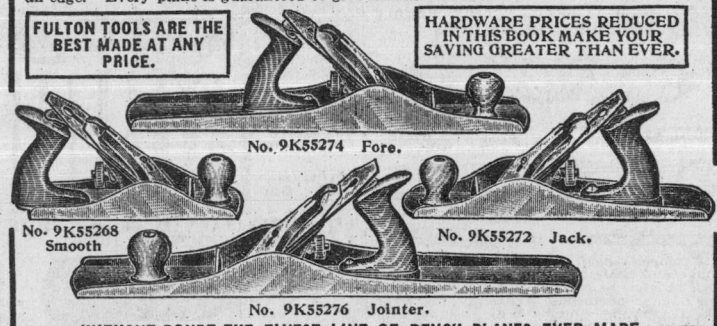

No. 9K55274 Fore.
No. 9K55268 Smooth
No. 9K55272 Jack.
No. 9K55276 Jointer.

WITHOUT DOUBT THE FINEST LINE OF BENCH PLANES EVER MADE.

Catalogue Number	Length, inches	Width of Cutter, inches	Weight, pounds	Price	Catalogue Number	Length, inches	Width of Cutter, inches	Weight, pounds	Price
9K55268	9 Smooth	2	3½	$1.24	9K55274	18 Fore	2⅜	7	$1.82
9K55272	14 Jack	2	4¾	1.46	9K55276	22 Jointer	2⅜	8½	2.12

No. 9K55282 Set of four Fulton Iron Planes, one each. No. 9K55268 Smooth; No. 9K55272 Jack; No. 9K55274 Fore and No. 9K55276 Jointer. Price, set....$6.33

Fulton Corrugated Bottom Iron Bench Planes.

EXACTLY THE SAME AS THOSE DESCRIBED ABOVE BUT WITH CORRUGATED BOTTOMS.

SATISFACTION OR YOUR MONEY BACK.

FULTON QUALITY THE BEST.

Some mechanics prefer to use a corrugated or grooved bottom plane, claiming that it sticks closer to the wood than a plane with a smooth bottom.

Catalogue Number	Length, inches	Width of Cutter, inches	Weight, pounds	Price	Catalogue Number	Length, inches	Width of Cutter, inches	Weight, pounds	Price
9K55294	9 Smooth	2	3½	$1.25	9K55300	18 Fore	2⅜	7	$1.83
9K55298	14 Jack	2	4¾	1.47	9K55302	21 Jointer	2⅜	8½	2.13

No. 9K55308 Set of four high grade Fulton Iron Bench Planes, with corrugated bottoms, one each. No. 9K55294 Smooth; No. 9K55298 Jack; No. 9K55300 Fore and No. 9K55302 Jointer. Price, per set........$6.34

WE HAVE ALWAYS SOLD GOOD HARDWARE

AT LOWER PRICES THAN ANY OTHER HOUSE. ON OVER 3,000 HARDWARE ITEMS PRICES ARE STILL FURTHER REDUCED IN THIS CATALOGUE.

Fulton Adjustable Wood Bottom Planes.

Positively the best and most reliable wood plane made. Works equally well in hard or soft wood. The bottoms are made of carefully selected air seasoned beech and castings are strong and smooth. The working parts are made by automatic machinery and all parts are interchangeable. The cutters are made from the best double refined English cast steel, tempered by the most improved process, highly polished and sharpened ready for use.

No. 9K55200 Smooth.

No. 9K55206 Handled Smooth.

Every cutter is fully warranted. All Fulton planes have our patent lateral or side adjustment for exact adjusting of cutter with the face of the plane.

No. 9K55212 Jack.

Catalogue Number	Length, inches		Width of Cutter, inches	Wgt., lbs.	Price
9K55200	8	Smooth	1¾	2¾	$0.75
9K55206	9	Hdld. Sm'h	2	3¼	.95
9K55212	15	Jack	2	3¾	.84
9K55214	15	Jack	2¼	4	.96
9K55218	20	Fore	2⅜	5¾	1.05
9K55224	26	Jointer	2⅜	7¼	1.19

No. 9K55230 Set of four Fulton Wood Planes, one each. No. 9K55200 Smooth; No. 9K55214 Jack; No. 9K55218 Fore and No. 9K55224 Jointer. Price, per set........$3.89

Fulton Beechwood Bench Planes.

Correctly made of selected straight grained beechwood, the best wood known for planes, are properly proportioned and fitted with high grade double steel cutting irons and polished ebony start. They are the best planes of their kind on the market, and are greatly superior to many cheap imitations sold in competition at low prices. Covered by the same guarantee as our Fulton iron and wood bottom planes quoted above.

Catalogue Number	Length, inches		Cutter, inches	Weight, pounds	Price
9K55242	8	Smooth	2½	2½	$0.59
9K55244	16	Jack	2¼	4½	.65
9K55246	22	Fore	2½	6½	1.10
9K55248	26	Jointer	2½	9	1.20
9K55250	28	Jointer	2½	10	1.30

No. 9K55254 Set of Four Planes, Smooth, Jack, Fore and 26-inch Jointer. Price, set........$3.40

67c PATENT ADJUSTABLE PLANE GAUGE. FITS ANY WOOD PLANE.

This gauge can be attached to any wood plane. Has all the features of the iron plane gauge but is for wood planes only. Does away with the continual use of a try square. Nickel plated. Illustration shows gauge attached to plane.

No. 9K55588 Price, gauge only, without plane........67c

$1.27 PATENT ADJUSTABLE JOINTER GAUGE FOR WOOD OR IRON PLANES.

This tool can be readily attached to any iron or wood plane, and will enable the operator to accurately plane either square or bevels of any desired angle, made entirely of iron and steel.

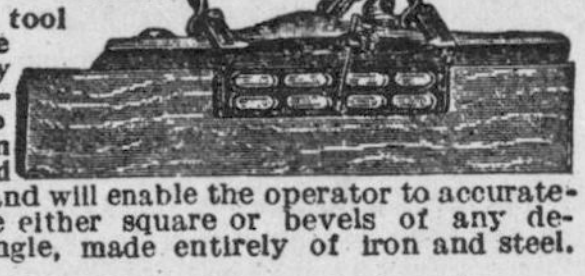

No. 9K55590 Price, without plane........$1.27

$1.23 FULTON ADJUSTABLE SCRAPER PLANE.

Fulton Adjustable Veneer Scraper. Unexcelled for scraping veneers, finishing cabinet work and removing old paint and glue. Crucible steel cutters, rosewood handle and knob, and without doubt the finest plane of its kind made. Length, 9 inches, with 3-inch cutter.

No. 9K55346 Price........$1.23

48c SKEW RABBET FANCY WOOD PLANE. SIZE, ½ INCH.

Made of selected straight grain hardwood, with warranted irons. State size wanted.

No. 9K55562 Skew Rabbet Plane.

Size, inch	¼	⅜	½	⅝	¾
Price	48c	49c	50c	51c	52c
Size, inches	1	1¼	1½	1¾	2
Price	56c	58c	70c	80c	

$1.52 JACK RABBET PLANE, WITH HANDLE AND SPUR CUTTERS.

Made of selected hardwood, finished in oil, with warranted irons. State size wanted, either 1½ or 2 inches.

No. 9K55564 Price........$1.52

88c PER PAIR HOLLOW AND ROUND PLANES.

Only finest grade of straight grained beechwood used in making these planes.

No. 9K55566

Nos.	1	2	3	4	5	6
Works, inch	¼	⅜	½	⅝	¾	⅞
Price, per pair						88c

No. 9K55568

Nos.	7	9
Works, inches	1	1¼
Price, per pair		1.02

No. 9K55570 No. 11 works 1½ inches. Price, per pair........1.21
Be sure to state what size you want in your order. We do not break pairs.

98c BEECHWOOD NOSING PLANE WITH WARRANTED IRONS.

No. 9K55572 The same high quality as our other fancy wood planes. For steps, to work ⅞, 1, 1⅛ or 1¼ inches; any one size. State size wanted.

Price........98c
No. 9K55574 To work 1⅜ or 1½ inches, any one size. State size wanted. Price........$1.07
Each plane works only one size.

8c FOR 3 BEECHWOOD JACK PLANE HANDLES.

No. 9K56082 Made of selected stock, nicely finished.
Price, each........3c
3 for........8c

12c FOR 3 FORE OR JOINTER PLANE HANDLES.

No. 9K56086 Beechwood. Price, each........5c
3 for........12c

Extra Quality Fulton Plane Irons.

For Fulton Planes. For wood bench planes and all iron planes. Best material and workmanship and finely tempered; warranted. The double irons have steel caps.

Irons for Fulton Patent Planes, with wood base or made of all iron with smooth or corrugated bottoms.

No. 9K55580 Single Irons.
No. 9K55582 Double Irons.

Width, inches	1¾	2	2¼	2⅜	2½
Single Irons	18c	20c	22c	24c	26c
Double Irons	31c	33c	35c	37c	39c

Irons for Common Beech Wood Bench Planes.

No. 9K55587 Single Irons.
No. 9K55587 Double Irons.

Width, inches	2	2¼	2½	2¾
Single Irons	26c	29c	35c	42c
Double Irons	52c	58c	68c	78c

Block Plane Irons for Fulton Block Planes.
No. 9K55584

Width, inches	1½	1¾
Price, each	12c	15c

PLEASE NOTE—In sending us orders for plane irons be sure and give us the number of the plane as well as the description and the size of the iron you want, to enable us to fill your order correctly. Also please note that we are not in position to furnish irons for any planes except those regularly listed by us. We cannot fill orders for irons made by manufacturers whose goods we do not handle.

60c RAISED HANDLE CABINET SCRAPER WITH TEMPERED STEEL BLADE.

Best scraper made. 11-inch handle, 2¾-inch blade.

No. 9K55602 Price..............60c

5c TEMPERED SAW STEEL CABINET SCRAPER. SIZE, 3X5 INCHES.

Edges finished ready for use. Better than the kind others sell for 10 cents.

No. 9K55624 Price, 5c

Jennings' Extra Quality Cabinet Scraper. Made from best saw steel, edges finished ready for use. Size, 3x6 inches.

No. 9K55628 Price..............17c

22c TEMPERED SAW STEEL SWAN NECK CABINET SCRAPER.

The shape makes it easy to hold, and does not cramp the hand like a square scraper. Size, 3½x6 inches. Smithed and blocked by hand.

No. 9K55632 Price, 22c

64c FOR A UNIVERSAL ADJUSTABLE HANDLED SCRAPER.

You Pay Twice Our Price at — Retail. —

The most convenient scraper ever invented. Has all edges ground perfectly square, any of which may be almost instantly brought into use. The blade may be readily adjusted to any angle, and the scraper will work into corners.

No. 9K55636 Price..............64c

55c WOOD SCREW CUTTER OR SCREW BOX CUTS ¼ INCH.

Hardwood box with tool steel cutters, for cutting threads on wood hand screws. Cuts both male and female thread.

No. 9K55642

Cuts, inch	¼	⅜	½	⅝	¾	1
Price	55c	56c	57c	69c	74c	92c

Cuts, inches	1¼	1⅜	1½
Price	$1.26	$1.59	$1.83

14c HIGH GRADE BOXWOOD MARKING GAUGE, BRASS THUMBSCREW.

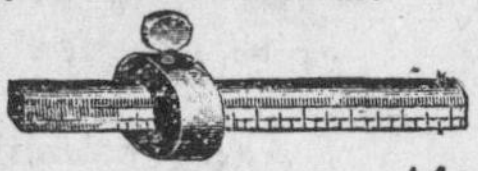

Has oval head and bar with steel points.

No. 9K55704

Price..............14c

38c SOLID MAHOGANY MORTISE AND MARKING GAUGE.

The finest finished best constructed gauge made, with screw slide, brass thumbscrew, steel points and plated head.

No. 9K55712 Price..............38c

48c IMPROVED NICKEL PLATED SOLID METAL POCKET BUTT GAUGE.

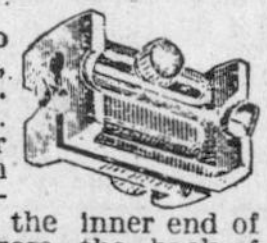

Every carpenter ought to have one of these light, handy, time saving tools. Will pay for itself on one job. Setting the cutter at the outer end of one bar for gauging on the edge of the door automatically sets the cutter at the inner end of the same bar for gauging from the back of the jamb. The second bar has a steel cutter for gauging the thickness of the butt.

No. 9K55726 Price..............48c

23c METALLIC BUTT GAUGE WITH ROTARY STEEL WHEEL MARKER.

Light and easily carried in the pocket. Made entirely of steel. Set one end for thickness of butts, the other for width, and avoid the use of two gauges.

No. 9K55730 Price..............23c

If ordered by mail, add 5 cents for postage.

27c SOLID STEEL NICKEL PLATED MARKING OR DEPTH GAUGE.

With hexagon head and bar. Steel marking point is attached to extreme end of bar to admit marking close up to corners, tool is finely polished and heavily nickel plated. Length, 6 inches. Accurately graduated to 32nds its entire length, a desirable tool and the most perfect gauge of its kind made.

No. 9K55732 Price..............27c

67c SOLID STEEL COMBINATION MARKING AND MORTISE ROLLER GAUGE.

Heavily nickel plated. Marker is a revolving steel wheel, which will not follow the grain.

No. 9K55738 Price..............67c

80c SOLID STEEL COMBINATION TRIPLE BEAM ROTARY MARKING GAUGE.

Every first class carpenter should have one of these gauges. It is a labor saver where either single, double or triple measurements are desired. The three beams are of different lengths, and each one is graduated. Whole tool polished and nickel plated.

No. 9K55742 Price..............80c

9c FOR A SOLID FORGED STEEL SOCKET SCRATCH AWL.

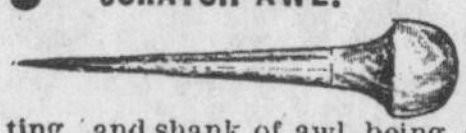

Polished beech handle. No danger of handle splitting and shank of awl being driven through your hand if you use this awl.

No. 9K55764 Price..............9c

4c HANDLED BRAD AWL WITH STEEL SHOULDER AND FERRULE.

Steel shoulder awl, polished handle with ferrule. Sizes, small, medium and large. State size wanted.

No. 9K55760 Price..............4c

96c HIGHEST GRADE HOLLOW HANDLE TOOL SET WITH TEN TOOLS.

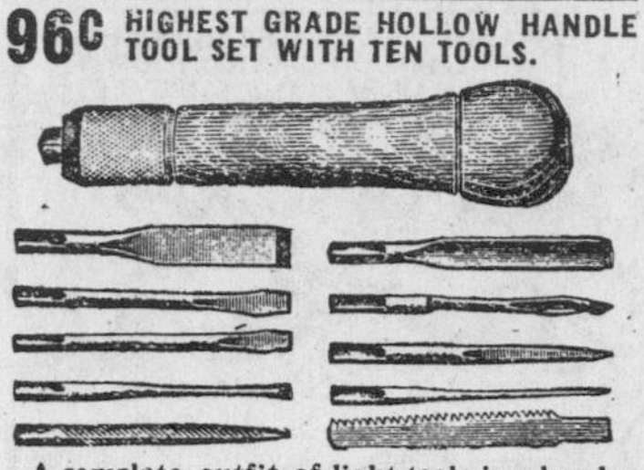

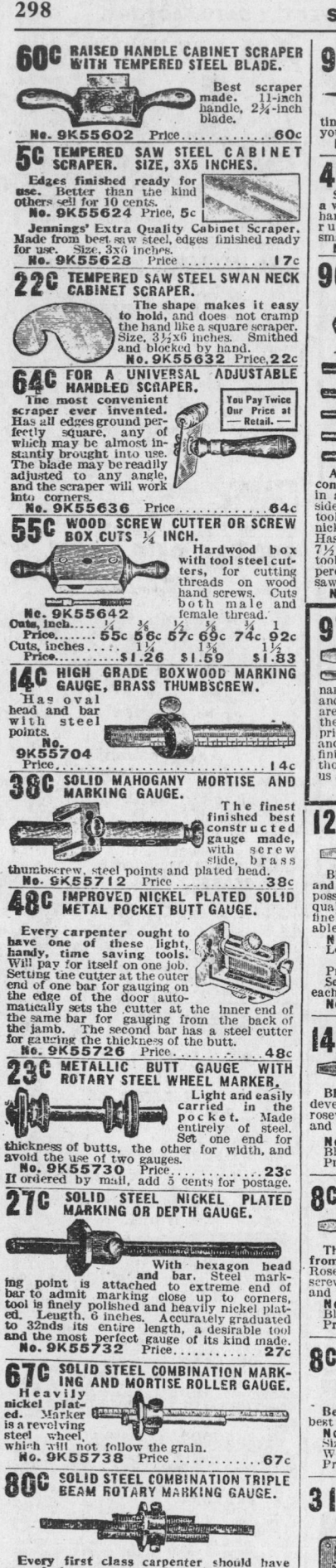

A complete outfit of light tools in a handy, convenient holder. Will save twice its cost in a short time in carpenter bills alone, besides the convenience of having "the right tool at the right time." With positive grip, nickel plated knurled sleeve and chuck. Has polished cocobolo handle, entire length, 7½ inches, and contains ten high grade steel tools, as shown, carefully hardened and tempered, about 4 inches in length, and keyhole saw 7 inches long. Will also hold other tools.

No. 9K55792 Price..............96c

29c FOR THIS HOLLOW HANDLE AWL TOOL SET COMPLETE.

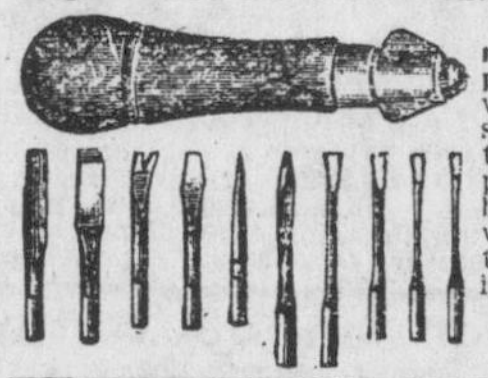

The best set made for the price, complete with forged steel awls and tools. Hollow polished cocobolo handle, which holds tools when not in use.

No. 9K55772 Price...29c

66c HOLLOW HANDLE FORGED STEEL TOOL SET COMPLETE.

Has strong, secure chuck, polished handle and 9 tools 4½ inches long, forged from tool steel, hardened in oil and carefully finished.

No. 9K55782 Price, 66c

17c LEATHER AWL SET COMPLETE WITH AWLS, NEEDLES AND THREAD.

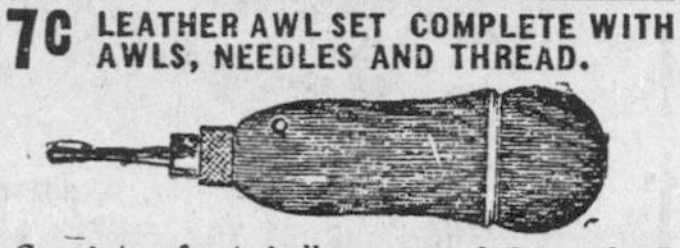

Consists of: A hollow enameled handle, 5 inches long. Inside the handle is a spool holding 50 feet of the best waxed linen shoe thread. Inside the spool are three awls and three needles of sizes commonly used.

No. 9K55798 Price..............17c

97c FULTON AUTOMATIC REVERSIBLE DOUBLE SPIRAL SCREWDRIVER WITH THREE BITS.

Intended for practical work. Locks automatically, and can be used as an ordinary screwdriver. The bits and working parts of this tool are made of the finest tempered steel and guaranteed to stand more real hard work than any screwdriver on the market. Handles are hardwood, tubes are highly polished, seamless brass, with swell sleeve. When you buy the Fulton Automatic Screwdriver you get full value in the article for every penny of the price. Most screwdrivers of this class are sold mainly on their manufacturers' reputations, and will not stand hard use. We guarantee this tool to be the best in workmanship and finish of any automatic screwdriver on the market, regardless of name or make. After a thorough trial if not perfectly satisfactory in every way, you are at liberty to return same to us and purchase price will be cheerfully refunded. Length closed, without bit, 10 inches.

No. 9K55828 Price, complete, with three bits..............97c

12c FOR A 3-INCH EVERLASTING HIGH GRADE SCREWDRIVER.

Blade passes entirely through the handle and is capped on the top, making it impossible to turn in handle. Blade is high quality tool steel. Handle is hardwood, finely finished. The best and most serviceable screwdriver made. Fully warranted.

No. 9K55802

Length of blade inches	3	4	5	6	8	10	12
Price, each	12c	15c	19c	23c	31c	37c	44c

Set of four Screwdrivers as above, one each 3, 5, 8 and 12 inches.

No. 9K55804 Price, per set.......97c

14c FOR A 3-INCH GUARANTEED GENUINE CHAMPION SCREWDRIVER.

Blade guaranteed no to turn, pull out or develop any imperfections. Handle is dyed rosewood and has a high gloss finish. Ferrule and blade polished. Fully warranted.

No. 9K55816

Blade, inches	3	4	5	6	8	10
Price, each	14c	19c	23c	25c	34c	43c

8c FOR A 3-INCH CHAMPION PATTERN FORGED STEEL SCREWDRIVER.

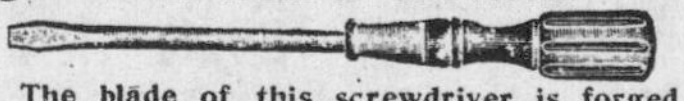

The blade of this screwdriver is forged from a very tough grade of crucible steel. Rosewood finished handle, steel ferrule. This screwdriver will stand the most severe usage and is warranted.

No. 9K55820

Blade, inches	3	4	5	6	8	10
Price, each	8c	9c	10c	12c	14c	16c

8c FOR A 6-INCH FORGED STEEL BLADE SCREWDRIVER.

Beechwood handle, brass cap ferrule. The best screwdriver ever offered for the price.

No. 9K55812

Size of blade, inches	2	4	6
Whole length, inches	5½	9	12½
Price	4c	6c	8c

31c FOR THIS TIME-SAVING ADJUSTABLE CLAPBOARD MARKER.

By moving this tool half an inch when placed in position as shown it will make a full line across the clapboard exactly over the edge of the corner board. Saw to the mark and you have a perfectly close joint. Has steel teeth, adjustable to take up wear.

No. 9K55756 Price..............31c

35c FOR A 4-INCH TOOL STEEL OIL TEMPERED RATCHET SCREWDRIVER.

The Goodell Ratchet Screwdriver excelled by none on the market. Blades, dogs and springs are made from tool steel, the ratchet teeth are cut directly into the stem of the blade; changes from right to left are made by turning the knurled ferrule. Sold strictly on its merits and the quality is the very best.

No. 9K55836

Size blade, ins.	4	5	6	8	10
Each	35c	40c	44c	50c	55c

69c AUTOMATIC INTERCHANGEABLE SCREWDRIVER WITH THREE BITS.

Goodell's Automatic Screwdriver can be used as a spiral, ratchet or a plain screwdriver. Three oil tempered blades. Has cherry stained handle and are practically unbreakable. Length, closed, 7½ inches; open 11½ inches.

No. 9K55844 Price, complete.....69c

$1.12 DOUBLE SPIRAL REVERSIBLE AUTOMATIC SCREWDRIVER.

Goodell's simplest, strongest and most practical Screwdriver. For both driving and drawing screws automatically; it cannot be excelled. It has two separate and distinct spirals, each working entirely independent of the other, furnished with three blades.

No. 9K55860 Price..............$1.12

45c DRILL ATTACHMENT FOR AUTOMATIC SCREWDRIVERS.

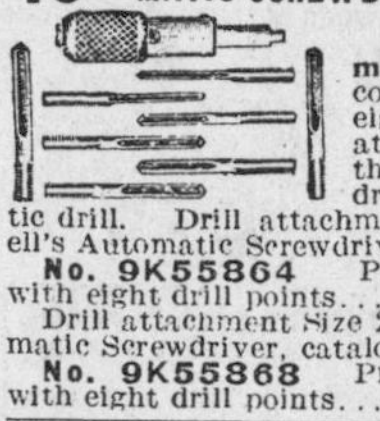

For Goodell's Automatic Screwdrivers, consists of a chuck and eight drill points. This attachment converts the automatic screwdriver into an automatic drill. Drill attachment Size 1, fits Goodell's Automatic Screwdriver No. 9K55844.

No. 9K55864 Price for attachment with eight drill points..............45c

Drill attachment Size 2, fits Goodell's Automatic Screwdriver, catalogue No. 9K55860.

No. 9K55868 Price for attachment with eight drill points..............47c

68c AUTOMATIC HAND DRILL COMPLETE WITH EIGHT DRILL POINTS.

Manufactured by Goodell, Pratt & Co. Length, 9½ inches, with cocobolo handle. This tool does not differ in the slightest degree from our more expensive styles; except it is left dull nickeled, affording considerable saving in cost.

No. 9K55906 Price, complete.....68c

$1.10 NICKEL PLATED, POLISHED HAND DRILL WITH EIGHT POINTS.

Goodell's highest grade Automatic Drill. Handle is knurled the entire length, the rotating cap through which the drill points are extracted is smooth and solid, is held in place by a spring bolt, and can be unlocked and rotated by moving the catch. The end nut by which the jaws are tightened is large, knurled the entire length, and cannot be turned off. Drill points properly fastened in the chuck cannot be pulled out when in use. Eight drill points from 1-16 to 11-64, furnished with each tool. 9½ inches long.

No. 9K55910 Price..........$1.10

42c MALLEABLE FRAME HAND DRILL COMPLETE.

Has hollow head with hardwood screw cap; containing six drill points. Length, 10½ inches.

No. 9K55926 Price..........42c

Extra Drill Points for above hand drill.

No. 9K55930 Price, per set of 6, 10c

$1.03 HIGH GRADE HAND DRILL WITH EIGHT FLUTED DRILL POINTS.

Has malleable iron frame, steel spindle and pinion, cut gears and chuck, taking from 0 to 5-32. Handle of cocobolo, is hollow and contains eight assorted size drills.

No. 9K55934 Price.........$1.03

Extra Drill Points for above hand drill.

No. 9K55938 Price, per set of 8..34c

$1.34 NICKEL PLATED HAND DRILL COMPLETE WITH EIGHT POINTS.

Steel frame, highly polished. All gears have cut teeth, the large gear has a wide face which can be used instead of crank handle for delicate work. Has three-jawed chuck. Capacity, 0 to 5-32 inch. Furnished with eight drill points from 1-16 to 11-64 and will hold any twist drill up to 5-32 inch. Length, 10 inches.

No. 9K55950 Price..........$1.34

$2.24 EXTRA LARGE HIGH GRADE DOUBLE GEARED HAND DRILL.

Goodell Pratt's Finest Hand Drill. Impossible to construct a better tool. Has double gears with cut teeth, two speeds, and a three-jawed chuck. Capacity, 0 to ⅜ inch. Has knurled nut, nickel plated, well made and accurate. Frame is malleable iron japanned with cocobolo handle. The head is hollow with screw cap. Spindle runs in a hardened steel cone bearing. No drill points furnished.

No. 9K55954 Price..........$2.24

39c PER BAR TINNERS' BEST SOLDER.

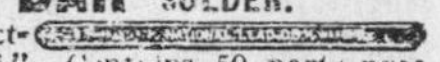

Guaranteed strictly "half and half." Contains 50 parts pure block tin and 50 parts lead. Bars contain about 1¼ pounds each. We do not cut bars.

No. 9K63254 Price, per bar.....39c

29c SQUARE POINT No. 1½ SOLDERING COPPER.

The best goods on the market. Made of solid copper with steel shanks. The number is just double the weight of a single iron, and the price is per single iron, not per pair. When ordering give number wanted.

No. 9K63250 No.	1½	2	3	4
Price, per single iron	29c	38c	57c	75c

2c BASSWOOD SOLDERING COPPER HANDLES WITH WIRE FERRULES.

No. 9K63251 Price, per dozen, 19c; each..........2c

52c FULTON 2-INCH WARRANTED SOLID STEEL TINNERS' SNIPS.

Length of cut is measured from the bolt.

Forged from one solid piece of steel and laid full length of cutting surface with finest cutlery steel. Warranted the most perfect snip made.

No. 9K63259

Full Length		Length of Cut		Price
8	inches	2	inches	$0.52
9	inches	2¼	inches	.65
10	inches	2½	inches	.77
11¾	inches	3	inches	.81
13	inches	3½	inches	1.12

$1.13 FULTON SPECIAL SOLID STEEL 3-INCH TINNERS' SNIPS.

For cutting scrolls and circles as well as straight lines. Especially adapted to cornice work. Blades are rounding front and back and very sharp pointed. Made of the best material, have forged handles and steel blades, and are fully warranted.

No. 9K63260 Cuts 3 inches. 3½ inches.

Price.......... $1.13 $1.42

MACHINISTS' TOOLS

All the tools listed on this page are made by manufacturers who have established the highest reputation for accuracy, workmanship, design and finish.

THESE TOOLS are made by skilled mechanics in modern, well equipped factories. Only the best materials enter into their construction. The parts of tools are carefully inspected at every stage of their manufacture, and each completed tool must also pass a rigid inspection before it is sent out.

EVERY ITEM quoted on this page is warranted accurate and reliable, and covered by our guarantee of "satisfaction or your money back."

For hardwood machinists' tool chests see page 484.

SOME PEOPLE stamp their names on tools, causing them to spring, and then write us they are defective. Stamping the name on them is the cause of their being "out." We cannot replace or exchange any tool on which a name has been stamped.

18c FOR A SPRING TEMPERED STEEL RULE, LENGTH, 2 INCHES.

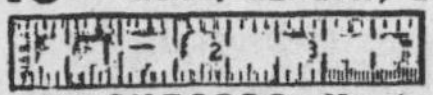

Thickness, 3-64 inch or No. 18 Gauge.

No. 9K56826 No. 4 graduation.
No. 9K56828 No. 1 graduation.

Lengths, ins.	2	3	4	6	12
Width, ins.	½	⅝	⅝	¾	1
Price	18c	25c	33c	47c	90c

Steel Rules. English Measure.

Graduations: Our rules are divided into parts of inches as follows:

No. 1 Graduation.	No. 4 Graduation.
1st corner, 10, 20, 50, 100	1st corner.......64
2d corner....12, 24, 48	2d corner.......32
3d corner....16, 32, 64	3d corner.......16
4th corner.......14, 28	4th corner.......8

31c SPRING TEMPERED GRADUATED STEEL CENTER GAUGE.

For use in grinding and setting screw cutting tools. Graduated, one corner; each in 32ds, 24ths, 20ths and 14ths.

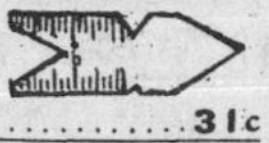

No. 9K56836 Price.............31c

63c KEY RING, INSIDE OR OUTSIDE SCREW PITCH GAUGE.

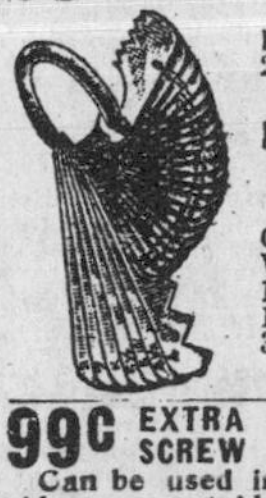

Made to carry in the pocket, light, accurate and reliable. 29 pitches, 4 to 40.
No. 9K56840 Price, 63c

Improved Screw Pitch Gauge.

Improved Screw Pitch Gauge. Can be used inside or outside. With 22 pitches, as follows: 9, 10, 11, 11½, 12, 13, 14, 15, 16, 18, 20, 22, 24, 26, 27, 28, 30, 32, 34, 36, 38, 40.
No. 9K56846 Price, 82c

99c EXTRA HIGH GRADE 24-PITCH SCREW PITCH GAUGE.

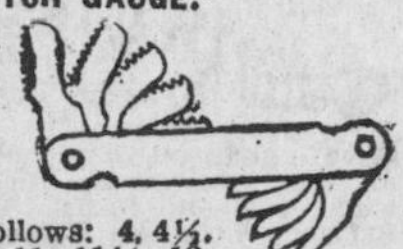

Can be used inside or outside; also as a 60-degree center gauge, and to test the grinding of either inside or outside threading tool. This gauge has 24 pitches, as follows: 4, 4½, 5, 5½, 6, 7, 8, 9, 10, 11, 11½, 12, 13, 14, 15, 16, 18, 20, 22, 24, 26, 27, 28, 30.
No. 9K56850 Price.............99c

$2.20 LATEST IMPROVED UNIVERSAL SURFACE GAUGE, SIZE A.

Has heavy steel, nicely finished case hardened base, grooved through bottom and end and is adapted for use on or against flat or circular surfaces. Very sensitive and accurate and can be used for a great variety of purposes.

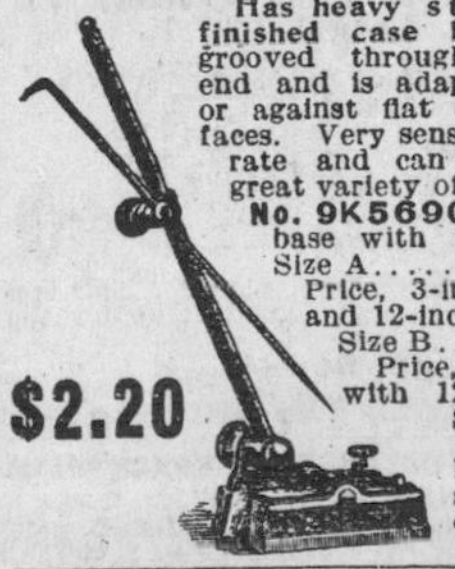

$2.20

No. 9K56902 Price, 3-inch base with 9-inch spindle. Size A..........$2.20
Price, 3-inch base with 9 and 12-inch spindles. Size B..........$2.40
Price, 3¼-inch base with 12-inch spindle. Size C..........$2.60
Price, 3¼-inch base with 12 and 18-inch spindles. Size D. $2.80

$1.19 NICKEL PLATED HIGH SPEED INDICATOR, WARRANTED ACCURATE.

This is a nicely made and finely working Indicator. The working parts are inclosed like a watch, and as well made. The graduations show every revolution, and with two rows of figures read both right and left, as the shaft may run. The instrument is nickel plated and has a rosewood handle, and frictionless bearing so that it will not heat the fingers when run at high speed. With rubber tips for both pointed and hollow centers.

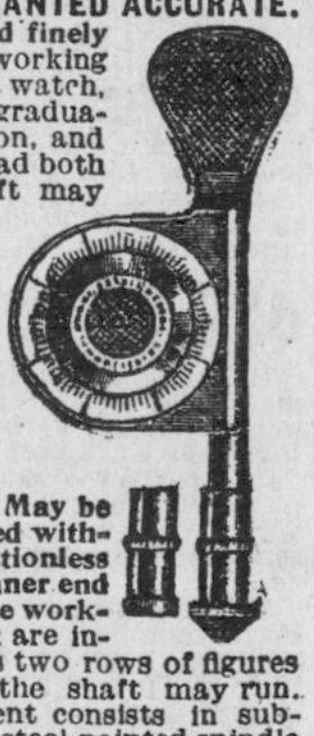

No. 9K56860
Price..........$1.19

High Speed Indicator. May be run at highest speed required without heating, as it has frictionless bearing against which the inner end of the spindle revolves. The working parts of this instrument are incased and the dial plate has two rows of figures reading right or left, as the shaft may run. An important improvement consists in substituting for the hardened steel pointed spindle and split caps, rubber tips for both pointed and centered shafts, which not only remove the jar and run smoothly, but produce a stronger frictional contact between the shaft and the instrument.
No. 9K56870 Price..........88c

Speed Indicator, devised to automatically register hundreds as well as units and tens. The instrument will register 5,000 revolutions and repeat. Has a hard rubber handle, making a safe insulator when used on electrical machinery. It has our new rubber tips for both pointed and hollow center.
No. 9K56880 Price..........$2.57

$2.06 TALLYING REGISTER OR COUNTING MACHINE, GUARANTEED ACCURATE.

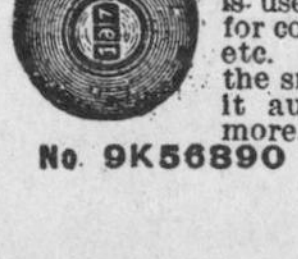

Registers from 1 to 1,000, and can be set to zero at will. Weight, 8 ounces, and can be easily carried in the pocket. It is used for checking or tallying, for counting cattle, sheep, poles etc. All you have to do is press the small lever on the side and it automatically registers one more. Nickel plated.
No. 9K56890 Price.........$2.06

$2.37 MACHINISTS' 9-INCH COMBINATION SCALE, MITRE HEAD, CENTER HEAD, PROTRACTOR HEAD AND LEVEL.

THE MOST COMPLETE MACHINISTS' COMBINATION SET EVER MADE.

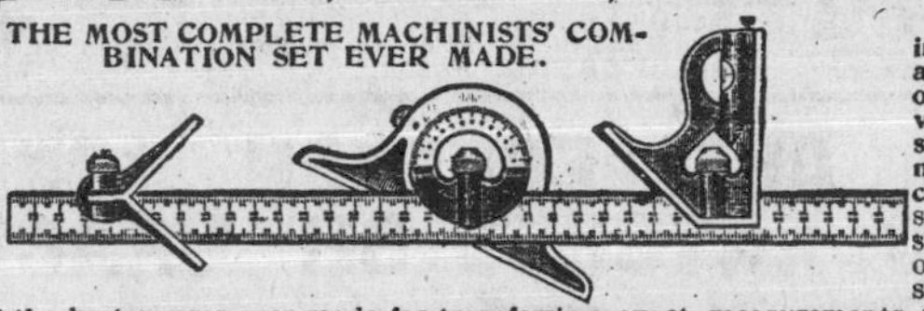

The adjustable scale in connection with attachments forms one of the most convenient and useful sets ever devised for machinists' or mechanics' use. This set complete is a substitute for a whole outfit of common try squares, and it is one of the best gauges ever made for transferring exact measurements or laying out work. It is most convenient for a depth gauge or to square in a mortise. As a mitre it is perfect, while with the auxiliary center head it forms a centering square, both inside and outside, which is perfectly accurate and for convenience has never been equaled. Each part may be instantly removed or replaced and used interchangeably with the scale. The scale is hardened and graduated, with heavy figures reading both ways. Illustration shows scale with all parts attached. At the left, first is the center head, next protractor head with level attachment and to the right the mitre head.

No. 9K56812 Combination Sets, consisting of scale, mitre head, center head, protractor head and level. Complete.

With scale, inches	9	12	18	24
Price, per set	$2.37	$2.67	$3.13	$3.62

No. 9K56814 Combination Square, consisting of scale, mitre head and center head.

With scale, inches	6	9	12	18	24
Price, per set	$1.10	$1.35	$1.53	$2.02	$2.56

No. 9K56818 Combination Square, consisting of scale and mitre head.

With scale, inches	6	9	12	18	24
Price, per set	79c	97c	$1.18	$1.67	$2.14

MONEY SAVING PRICES ON TOOLS AND HARDWARE ARE QUOTED ON EVERY PAGE. REDUCTIONS IN PRICE MAKE YOUR SAVING GREATER THAN EVER.

68c PERFECTED FIRM JOINT, SCREW ADJUSTING CALIPER, 4-INCH.

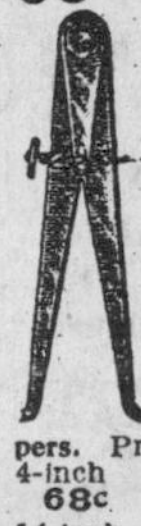

These high grade tempered steel calipers are far superior to the cheap riveted joint tools generally offered. The screw adjustment for fine measurements, the improved joint which may be set to any desired degree of uniform tension, the shape and stiffness of the legs, quickness and wide scope of adjustment, all go to make this caliper a leader in its line. Illustration shows No. 9K56906 inside caliper.

Prices for either Inside or Outside Calipers.

No. 9K56906 Inside Calipers.
No. 9K56908 Outside Calipers. Price, each.

4-inch	6-inch	8-inch	10-inch	12-inch
68c	75c	93c	$1.12	$1.41
14-inch	16-inch	18-inch	20-inch	24-inch
$1.51	$1.71	$1.87	$2.07	$2.67

28c FOR A 3-INCH IMPROVED FIRM JOINT TEMPERED STEEL CALIPER.

Illustration Shows No. 9K56912 Outside Caliper.

Prices for either Outside or Inside Calipers.

No. 9K56912 Outside.
No. 9K56914 Inside.

3-inch. Price, each.	$0.28
4-inch. Price, each.	.36
5-inch. Price, each.	.40
6-inch. Price, each.	.45
8-inch. Price, each.	.55
10-inch. Price, each.	.65
12-inch. Price, each.	.75
14-inch. Price, each.	1.05
16-inch. Price, each.	1.25

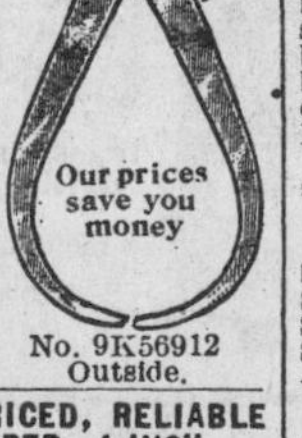

No. 9K56912 Outside.

60c SIMPLE, LOW PRICED, RELIABLE LOCK JOINT CALIPER, 4-INCH.

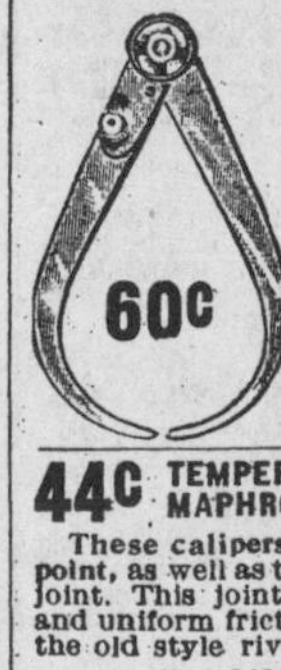

Can be instantly adjusted and quickly locked firm in the joint. Illustration shows No. 9K56916 outside caliper.

Prices for either Outside or Inside Calipers.

No. 9K56916 Outside.
No. 9K56918 Inside.

4-inch, Price, each..	$0.60
6-inch, Price, each..	.68
8-inch, Price, each..	.85
10-inch, Price, each..	1.10
12-inch, Price, each..	1.30

44c TEMPERED STEEL FIRM JOINT HERMAPHRODITE CALIPER, 4-INCH.

These calipers have adjustable point, as well as the improved firm joint. This joint, with its smooth and uniform friction, is superior to the old style riveted joint.

No. 9K56924

Size, in.	4	6	8	10
Price, each	44c	58c	74c	88c

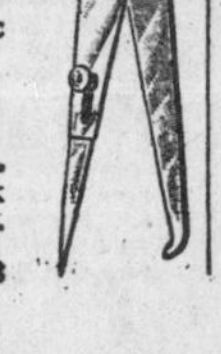

Hermaphrodite Calipers.

No. 9K56928 Same pattern as above, with improved lock joint and sensitive adjustment.

Size, in.	4	6	8	10
Each	73c	85c	98c	$1.18

72c FOR A 2½-INCH TEMPERED STEEL FAY PATTERN CALIPER.

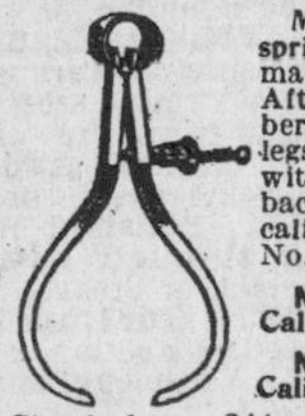

Made with either solid or spring nut. The bow is stiff, making the caliper reliable. After calipering inside a chambered cavity, by pressing the legs together they may be withdrawn, and as they spring back will show the exact size calipered. Illustration shows No. 9K56934 outside caliper.

No. 9K56934 Outside Calipers.
No. 9K56936 Inside Calipers.

Size, inches	2½	3	4	5	6
Solid Nut	72c	74c	82c	90c	$0.99
Spring Nut	81c	83c	91c	99c	1.08

43c YANKEE PATTERN TEMPERED STEEL CALIPER, SIZE, 2½ INCHES.

The Yankee Calipers and Dividers are not quite so heavy as those quoted in previous numbers and cost less. The bow is stiff, making the caliper reliable. After calipering inside of chambered cavity, by springing in the legs they may be withdrawn, and as they spring back, will show the exact size calipered. Illustration shows No. 9K56950 inside caliper.

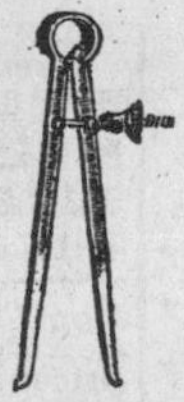

Prices for either inside or outside calipers.

No. 9K56950 Inside Calipers.
No. 9K56952 Outside Calipers.

Size, inches	2½	3	4	5	6	8
Solid Nut	43c	47c	50c	55c	58c	74c
Spring Nut	53c	57c	60c	65c	68c	84c

44c FOR A 2½-INCH YANKEE PATTERN SPRING DIVIDER.

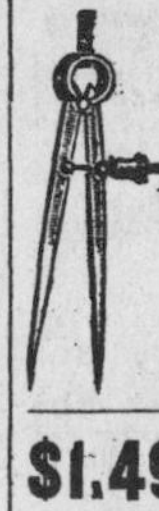

Points made of crucible forged steel, nicely tempered. These dividers are light, rigid, nicely finished and worth twice the price of the cheap malleable dividers offered by others.

No. 9K56986

Size, inches	2½	3	4
Solid Nut	44c	48c	52c
Spring Nut	54c	58c	62c
Size, inches	5	6	8
Solid Nut	59c	66c	80c
Spring Nut	69c	76c	90c

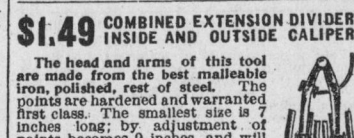

$1.49 COMBINED EXTENSION DIVIDER, INSIDE AND OUTSIDE CALIPER.

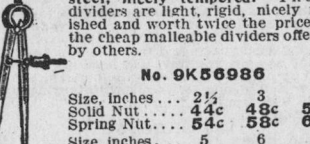

The head and arms of this tool are made from the best malleable iron, polished, rest of steel. The points are hardened and warranted first class. The smallest size is 7 inches long; by adjustment of points becomes 9 inches, and will scribe a 22-inch circle; will caliper 11 inches outside and 13 inches inside. The second size is 9 inches; by adjustment of points becomes 12 inches, will scribe a 30-inch circle, and caliper 14 inches outside and 16 inches inside.

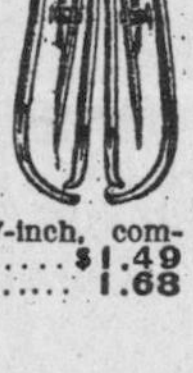

No. 9K56970 Price, 7-inch, complete..........$1.49
Price, 9-inch, complete..........1.68

87c DROP FORGED SOLID TOOL STEEL EXTENSION DIVIDERS, 6-INCH.

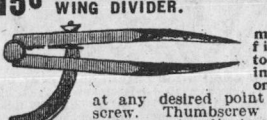

The same high grade goods as the balance of the tools shown on this page. Well made, finely finished and polished. Are light but strong and accurately adjusted. Has patent lock nut between the arms against which a spiral spring acts. Leg can be removed and ordinary lead pencil used instead of steel point if desired.

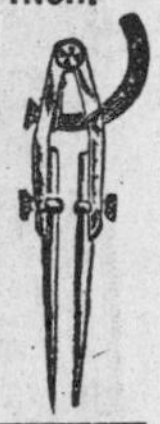

No. 9K56991

Size, inches	6	8	10
Will scribe circle, inches	20	27	35
Price	87c	$1.04	$1.21

15c FOR A 6-INCH POLISHED CAST STEEL WING DIVIDER.

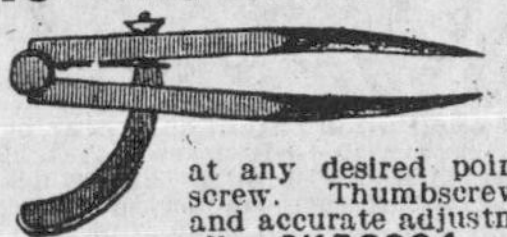

A well made, nicely finished tool, cheap in price only. Held at any desired point by a set screw. Thumbscrew for slight and accurate adjustment.

No. 9K56994

Size, inches	6	8	10
Price	15c	20c	26c

35c IMPROVED INTERCHANGEABLE POINT MECHANICS' SCRIBER.

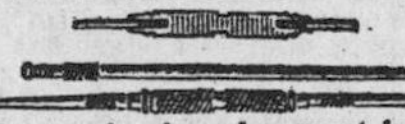

Made for mechanics who must have a reliable tool. These points are made of a high grade of steel, finely tempered. The knurled stock is of sufficient size to be easily held without cramping or turning in the fingers. The long bent point will be found useful for reaching through holes, etc. Length, with short bent point, 9 inches; with long point, 12 inches. The knurled sleeve is nickeled.
No. 9K57026 Price, complete..35c

36c STEEL BELL CENTERING TOOL, KNURLED AND NICELY POLISHED.

A very useful little tool; will soon pay for itself in time saved. Diameter, 1½ inches.

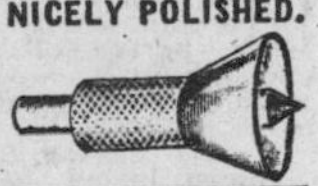

No. 9K57030
Price..........36c

26c MACHINISTS' INVOLUTE WRENCH, TAKES NUTS, FITTINGS AND PIPE.

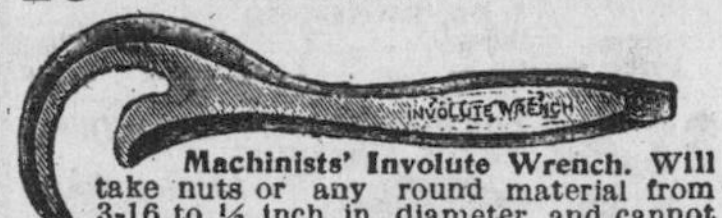

Machinists' Involute Wrench. Will take nuts or any round material from 3-16 to ½ inch in diameter and cannot slip. Has screwdriver on end and is full polished, well made, and perfectly tempered. Entire length, 5¾ inches.
No. 9K57034 Price..........26c

$1.49 "TIME SAVER" DRILL, TAP AND STEEL WIRE GAUGE.

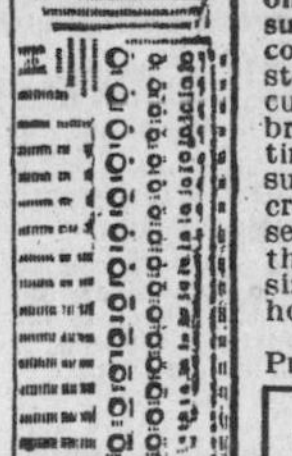

By the use of this gauge one is enabled to select at once the right sized drill to suit machine screw tap most commonly used, leaving just stock enough for the tap to cut a full thread without breaking, thus saving much time and uncertainty of result attending the former crude ways of making a selection. Figures designate the number of drill required, sizes agreeing with the holes.
No. 9K57038
Price..........$1.49

You pay twice our prices at retail on many Hardware Items.

83c FOR A 4-INCH STEEL PLUMB BOB FILLED WITH MERCURY.

These plumb bobs are made from solid steel, bored and filled with mercury. Noteworthy features are their great weight in proportion to size, low center of gravity, small diameter, hardened and ground points, knurling on body, and the simple and effective device at top for fastening end of line after winding up. Each is provided with a braided silk line. Nickel plated.

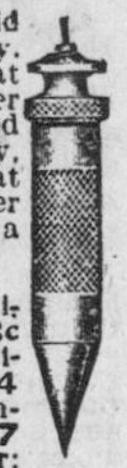

No. 9K57042
Price, 4 inches long, ½ inch in diameter; weight, 3½ ounces.......83c
Price, 5 inches long, ⅝ inch in diameter; weight, 6 ounces.......$1.24
Price, 5½ inches long, ⅞ inch in diameter; weight, 12 ounces.........$1.67
Price, 6 inches long, 1 inch in diameter; weight, 16 ounces.........$2.09

24c CAST BRASS PLUMB BOB, 6-OUNCE, WITH HARDENED STEEL POINT.

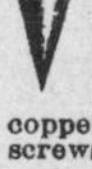

Has screw top so that cord can be properly fastened.

No. 9K57046

Weight, ounces	6	11½	16
Price	24c	40c	46c

Accurate and True Plumb Bobs. The body is turned from a solid steel bar, heavily nickel plated, over an electro copper plate. The points are hardened. The screws are solid brass.

No. 9K57050

Weight, ounces	4½	9½	17
Price	24c	40c	47c

10c HIGHLY POLISHED AND NICKEL PLATED IRON PLUMB BOB, 5-OZ.

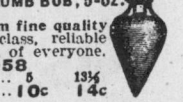

Accurately made from fine quality soft gray iron. First class, reliable tool, at a price in reach of everyone.

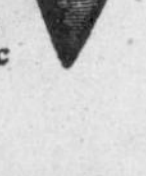

No. 9K57058

Weight, ounces	5	13½
Price	10c	14c

$6.86 FULTON SPECIAL BRACE AND BIT SET COMPLETE.

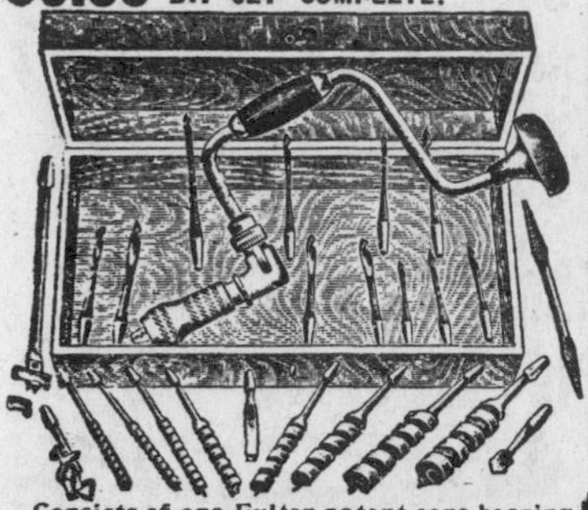

Consists of one Fulton patent cone bearing Ratchet Bit Brace with 10-inch sweep; eight Fulton special single twist auger bits, which will bore in any kind of wood quicker, smoother, and easier than any other bit made, one each, size ¼, 5-16, ⅜, ½, ⅝, ¾, ⅞ and 1 inch; one Steer's patent expansive bit with micrometer screw adjustment, the most perfect expansive bit made, boring holes from ⅞ to 3 inches. Eleven extra high quality German pattern gimlet bits, one each, size from 2-32 to 12-32; one crucible steel countersink with adjusting gauge for wood; one solid steel flat countersink for metal; one Fulton special screwdriver bit and one Fulton auger bit file. All packed in hardwood box with brass hinges and hooks.
No. 9K56585 Per set, complete..$6.86
Fulton Special Brace and Bit Set, as described above, but without expansive bit.
No. 9K56587 Price, per set....$5.31

46c FOR A HIGH GRADE BIT BRACE WITH 8-INCH SWEEP.

A finely finished, well made Bit Brace; has blued forged steel jaws, lignum vitae head and handle. Metal parts polished and heavily nickel plated.

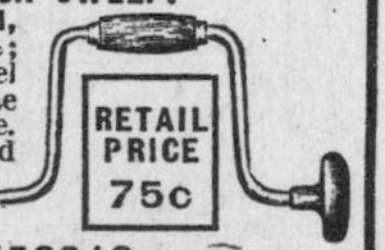

RETAIL PRICE 75c

No. 9K56012

Sweep, inches	8	10	12
Price, each	46c	49c	54c

Bit Brace with cold drawn steel sweep, stained hardwood head and handle.
No. 9K56062

Sweep, inches	8	10
Price, each	20c	24c

$2.42 FOR A COMBINATION RATCHET BRACE AND DRILL.

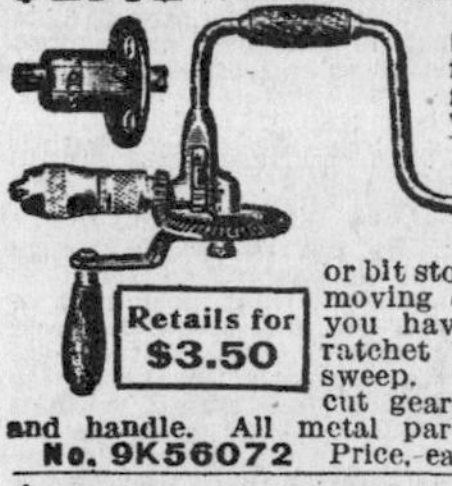

Retails for $3.50

Has ball bearing head, forged steel alligator jaws which will take round shank tools up to ½ inch and any auger bit or bit stock drill. By removing drill attachment you have a high grade ratchet brace, 10-inch sweep. Has accurately cut gears, cocobolo head and handle. All metal parts nickel plated.
No. 9K56072 Price, each......$2.42

$4.12 FOR ADJUSTABLE TWO-SPEED BORING MACHINE.

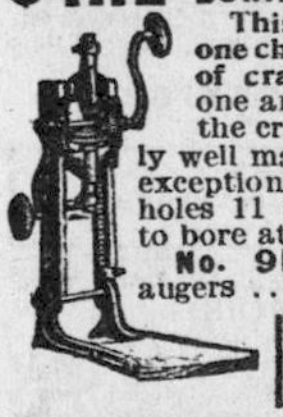

This machine gives speed on one chuck equal to two-thirds that of cranks. On the other chuck one and one-fourth the speed of the cranks. Machine is thoroughly well made, all iron and steel, with exception of wood base and will bore holes 11 inches deep. Is adjustable to bore at any angle.
No. 9K56116 Price, without augers..........$4.12

You pay $6.50 at retail for one not as good.

$2.35 BRACE AND BIT SET WITH BALL BEARING RATCHET BRACE.

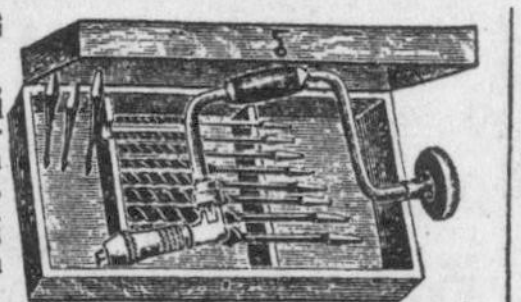

This outfit consists of one high grade ball bearing brace, 10-inch sweep, cocobolo wood parts, steel clad head and alligator jaws; eight extra selected cast steel double spur auger bits, sizes, ¼, 5-16, ⅜, ½, ⅝, ¾, ⅞ and 1 inch; three German pattern solid steel gimlet bits, sizes, 1-16, ⅛ and 3-16 inch, all packed in fancy hardwood box with brass hinges and hook.
No. 9K56551 Per set...........$2.35
Brace and Bit Set as described above, except has Irwin pattern auger bits with solid center stem.
No. 9K56553 Per set...........$3.05

$3.96 BRACE AND BIT OUTFIT WITH EXTENSION LIP AUGER BITS.

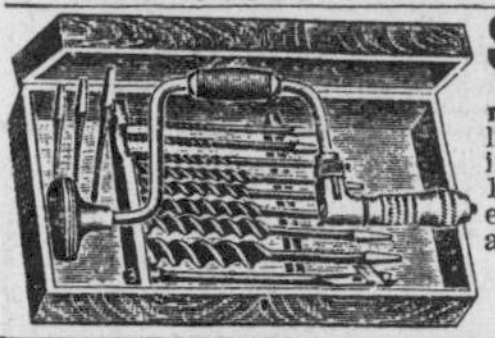

With this outfit we furnish one Fulton cone bearing ratchet brace, 10-inch sweep; eight Jennings pattern extension lip auger bits, one each, size ¼, 5-16, ⅜, ½, ⅝, ¾, ⅞ and 1 inch, three German pattern cast steel German gimlet bits, sizes; 1-16, ⅛ and 3-16 inch; one large size Fulton Clark's pattern expansive bit, cutting from ⅞ to 3 inches, all in neat, strong and substantial hardwood box with hinges and hook.
No. 9K56561 Price, per set..........$3.96
Brace and Bit Set as above, without expansive bit.
No. 9K56565 Per set..........$3.23

FULTON ANTI-FRICTION CONE BEARING RATCHET BIT BRACE

$1.35 FULTON BRACE

10-inch sweep. A better brace than you can buy elsewhere for $2.25.

Lignum Vitae Head with our easy running frictionless patent cone bearing.

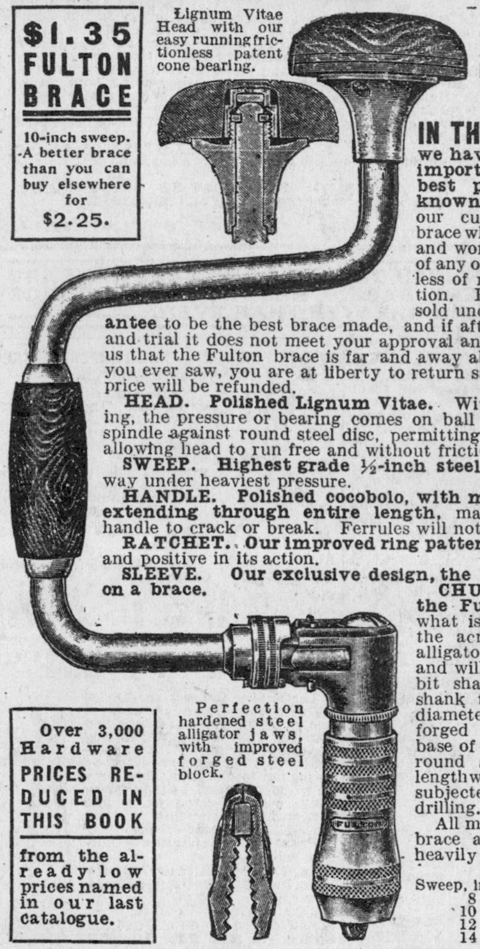

A BRACE WHICH IS ABSOLUTELY PERFECT IN EVERY DETAIL.

IN THE FULTON BRACE we have combined new and important features with the best points of other well known makes, and offer to our customers a ratchet bit brace which for beauty, strength and workmanship is far ahead of any other brace made, regardless of make, name or reputation. Every Fulton brace is sold under our **ironclad guarantee** to be the best brace made, and if after careful examination and trial it does not meet your approval and you do not agree with us that the Fulton brace is far and away ahead of any similar tool you ever saw, you are at liberty to return same to us and purchase price will be refunded.

HEAD. Polished Lignum Vitae. With our patent cone bearing, the pressure or bearing comes on ball shaped cone on end of spindle against round steel disc, permitting a fine adjustment and allowing head to run free and without friction.

SWEEP. Highest grade ½-inch steel, will not bend or give way under heaviest pressure.

HANDLE. Polished cocobolo, with metal bushing or tube extending through entire length, making it impossible for handle to crack or break. Ferrules will not slip.

RATCHET. Our improved ring pattern, accurately machined and positive in its action.

SLEEVE. Our exclusive design, the handsomest ever put on a brace.

CHUCK. In the chuck of the Fulton brace we have, what is considered by experts the acme of perfection. The alligator jaws are forged steel, and will take all regular shaped bit shanks as well as round shank tools up to ⅜-inch in diameter. Chuck is fitted with forged steel block located at base of jaws, preventing small round shank tools slipping lengthwise through jaws when subjected to heavy pressure in drilling.

All metal parts of the Fulton brace are finely polished and heavily nickel plated.

Perfection hardened steel alligator jaws, with improved forged steel block.

Over 3,000 Hardware PRICES REDUCED IN THIS BOOK from the already low prices named in our last catalogue.

No. 9K56033

Sweep, inches.	Price, each.
8	$1.22
10	1.35
12	1.47
14	1.59

$6.27 FOR OUR FULTON BRACE AND JENNINGS PATTERN BIT SET.

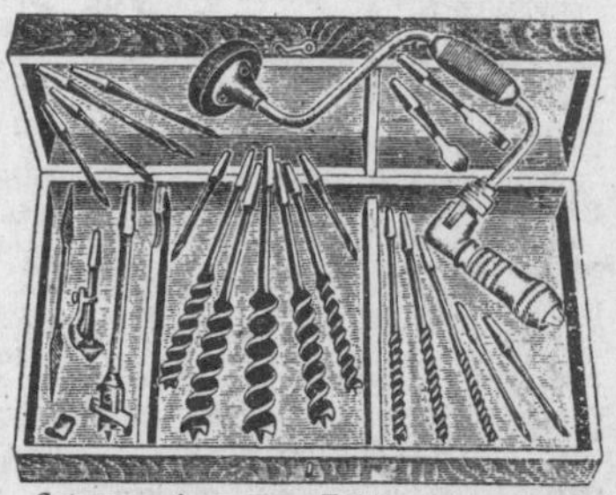

Set comprises one Fulton cone bearing ratchet brace, 10-inch sweep; eight Fulton-Jennings pattern auger bits, sizes ¼, 5-16, ⅜, ½, ⅝, ¾, ⅞ and 1 inch; one large size Steers' expansive bit, cutting from ⅞ to 3 inches; eight high grade German pattern gimlet bits, sizes 3-32 to 8-32; one forged steel screwdriver bit; one flat countersink bit for metal; one countersink for wood with adjusting gauge, one Fulton auger bit file, all put up in fancy hardwood box fitted with brass hinges and hook. An assortment which cannot be duplicated elsewhere for less than $8.00 to $9.00.
No. 9K56581 Price, per set..$6.27
The Fulton Brace and Jennings Pattern Bit. Set as described above, without expansive bit.
No. 9K56583 Price, per set..$4.84

$1.10 BALL BEARING RATCHET BIT BRACE WITH 8-INCH SWEEP.

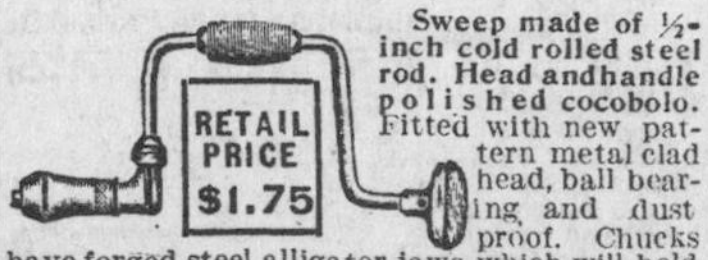

RETAIL PRICE $1.75

Sweep made of ½-inch cold rolled steel rod. Head and handle polished cocobolo. Fitted with new pattern metal clad head, ball bearing and dust proof. Chucks have forged steel alligator jaws which will hold all sizes, square shank and small sizes round shank bits and drills. This brace is finely finished; all metal parts fully polished and handsomely nickel plated and is the best brace possible to produce for the money.
No. 9K56021

Sweep, inches	8	10	12
Price, each	$1.10	$1.15	$1.20

79c NICKEL PLATED RATCHET BIT BRACE, 10-INCH SWEEP.

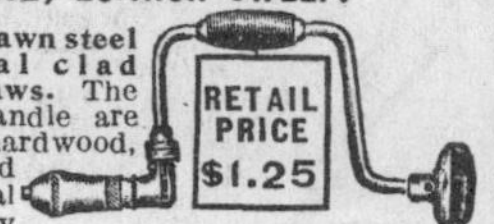

RETAIL PRICE $1.25

Has cold drawn steel sweep, metal clad head, steel jaws. The head and handle are made of hardwood, black ebonized finish. All metal parts nicely polished and heavily nickel plated. This is a very popular brace and a good value for the price.
No. 9K56019

Sweep, inches	10	12
Price, each	79c	89c

62c FOR A RATCHET BIT BRACE WITH HARDENED STEEL JAWS.

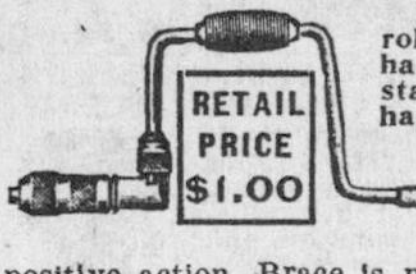

RETAIL PRICE $1.00

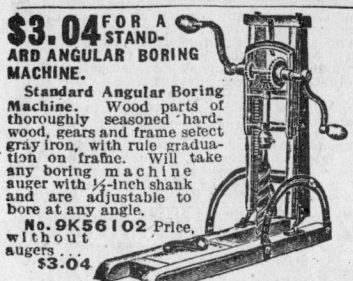

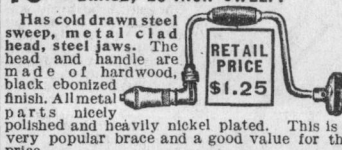

Has polished cold rolled steel sweep, hardwood mahogany stained head and handle, hardened jaws. The ratchet is operated by the ring method, insuring positive action. Brace is nicely finished and metal parts nickel plated. Made in 10-inch sweep only.
No. 9K56017 Price, each......62c

45c OUR IMPROVED RATCHET BIT BRACE WITH 10-INCH SWEEP.

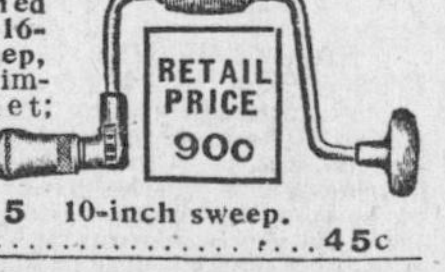

RETAIL PRICE 90c

Head and handle mahogany stained hardwood, has 7-16-inch steel sweep, hardened jaws, improved ratchet; a good brace for ordinary use.
No. 9K56015 10-inch sweep.
Price, each..........45c

75c FOR BEST QUALITY SPOFFORD BIT BRACE WITH 8-INCH SWEEP.

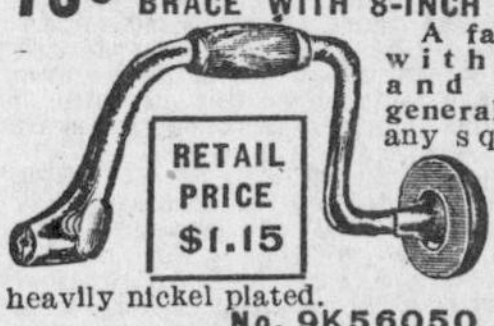

RETAIL PRICE $1.15

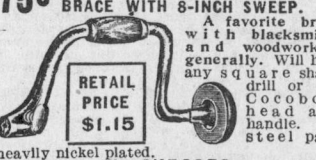

A favorite brace with blacksmiths and woodworkers generally. Will hold any square shank drill or bit. Cocobolo head and handle. All steel parts heavily nickel plated.
No. 9K56050

Sweep, inches	8	10	12	14
Price, each	75c	85c	95c	$1.05

$1.62 FOR PRATT'S PATENT AUGER HANDLE OR RATCHET DRILL.

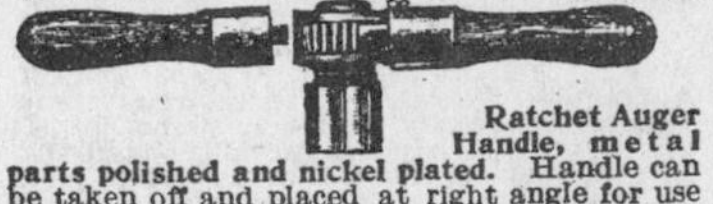

Ratchet Auger Handle, metal parts polished and nickel plated. Handle can be taken off and placed at right angle for use in close quarters. Wood on detachable handle revolves. Is also frequently used as a ratchet drill.
No. 9K56188 Price, each....$1.62

$3.04 FOR A STANDARD ANGULAR BORING MACHINE.

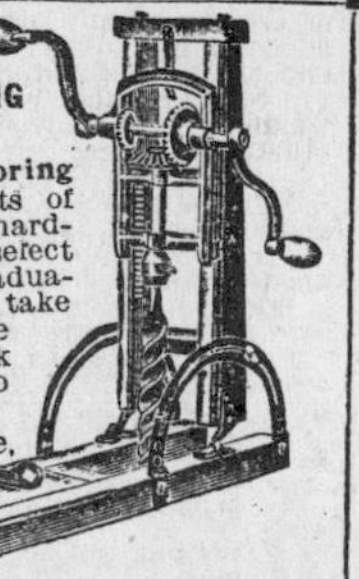

Standard Angular Boring Machine. Wood parts of thoroughly seasoned hardwood, gears and frame select gray iron, with rule graduation on frame. Will take any boring machine auger with ½-inch shank and are adjustable to bore at any angle.
No. 9K56102 Price, without augers..$3.04

$6.65 FOR THE WELL KNOWN MILLER FALLS BORING MACHINE.

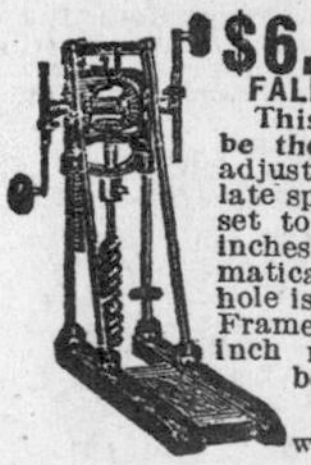

This machine is conceded to be the best of its kind. Has adjustable cranks which regulate speed and power. Can be set to bore any depth to 11¼ inches. Has device which automatically withdraws auger when hole is made, without reversing. Frame and braces made of 9-16-inch round steel rods. Will bore at any angle.
No. 9K56120 Price, without augers...$6.65

47c FOR A ¾-INCH FULTON SPECIAL BORING MACHINE AUGER.

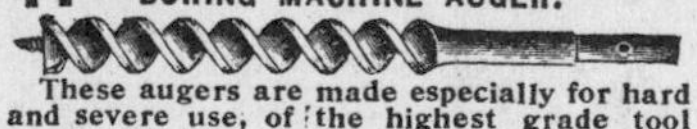

These augers are made especially for hard and severe use, of the highest grade tool steel. They are heavier and stronger than the standard augers and the twist is more open, giving greater clearance. The head is fitted and filed by hand. This tool will bore smoother, faster and deeper without withdrawing and with less friction than any other. Fully warranted.
No. 9K56150

Size, inches	¾	⅞	1	1¼
Price, each	47c	50c	53c	60c
Size, inches		1½	1¾	2
Price, each		67c	72c	80c

28c FOR A STANDARD GRADE 1-INCH BORING MACHINE AUGER.

This auger is made of solid crucible steel, nicely finished. The same as those sold by dealers as the highest grade. Fully warranted.
No. 9K56140

Size, inches	1	1¼	1½	1¾	2
Price, each	28c	35c	44c	51c	59c

16c FOR ADJUSTABLE INTERCHANGEABLE CARPENTERS' AUGER HANDLE.

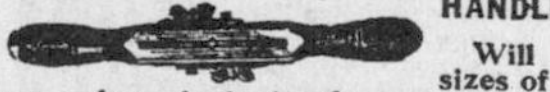

Will fit all sizes of nut augers and can be instantly removed. This handle is made of selected hard wood; is cheaper than the common handle as only one is required for full set of augers.
No. 9K56180 Price, each..........16c

43c FOR A ¾-INCH FULTON SPECIAL CARPENTERS' NUT AUGER.

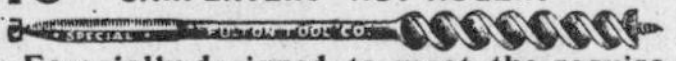

Especially designed to meet the requirements of carpenters, millwrights, car builders and other mechanics who must have first class tools. This auger is made extra heavy, and the head is fitted by hand by expert workmen. The hollow of twist is left natural temper color. It will bore deeper, easier and smoother than any similar tool made, and for appearance and actual hard work is the best and handsomest auger possible to produce. Fully warranted.
No. 9K56170

Size, inches	¾	⅞	1	1¼
Price, each	43c	46c	50c	54c
Size, inches		1½	1¾	2
Price, each		60c	67c	74c

20c FOR ¾-INCH STANDARD PATTERN CAST STEEL NUT AUGER.

Extra high grade cast steel, standard pattern carpenters' Nut Auger. Material and construction guaranteed. Nicely finished, full polished and fully warranted. Price does not include handle.
No. 9K56160

Size, inches	¾	⅞	1	1¼	1½	1¾
Price, each	20c	23c	26c	33c	40c	47c
Size, inches	2	2¼	2½	2¾	3	
Price, each	55c	75c	95c	$1.25	$1.68	

10c FOR 3 SELECTED HARDWOOD AUGER HANDLES.

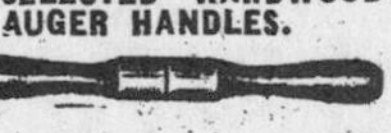

Common hardwood Auger Handles. State size when ordering.
No. 9K56184 Price, 3 for..........10c

7c FOR A ⅜-INCH STANDARD GRADE COMMON PATTERN AUGER BIT.

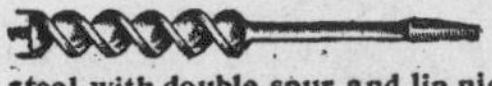

Every bit is made from extra tool steel, with double spur and lip nicely finished. For common use or in the hands of one who is not a mechanic, they will give good satisfaction.

No. 9K56202

Size, inch	3-16	¼	5-16	⅜
Price, each	7c	7c	7c	7c
Size, inch		7-16	½	9-16
Price, each		8c	9c	10c
Size, inch	⅝	11-16	¾	13-16
Price, each	11c	12c	13c	14c
Size, inch		⅞	15-16	1
Price, each		15c	16c	17c

Set of Six Standard Pattern Auger Bits. One each size, ¼, ⅜, ½, ⅝, ¾ and 1 inch. In plain box.
No. 9K56204 Price, per set......61c

Set of Eight Standard Pattern Auger Bits. One each size, ¼, 5-16, ⅜, ½, ⅝, ¾, ⅞ and 1 inch. In plain box.
No. 9K56208 Price, per set......83c

Set of Thirteen Standard Pattern Auger Bits. One each size, from ¼ to 1 inch. In plain box.
No. 9K56212 Price, per set....$1.41

10c FOR A ¼-INCH JENNINGS PATTERN EXTENSION LIP AUGER BIT.

These bits are made from the finest tool steel, and are designed for mechanics' use and are far superior to the cheap, poorly tempered bits sold by others. Warranted.

No. 9K56250

Size, inch		¼	5-16	⅜	7-16
Price		10c	11c	12c	14c
Size, inch		½	9-16	⅝	11-16
Price		15c	16c	17c	18c
Size, inch	¾	13-16	⅞	15-16	1
Price	19c	21c	23c	25c	27c

Set of Six Jennings Extension Lip Auger Bits, one each size, ¼, ⅜, ½, ⅝, ¾ and 1 inch. In finely finished, well made hardwood box.
No. 9K56252 Price, per set....$1.16

Set of Eight Jennings Pattern Extension Lip Auger Bits, one each size, ¼, 5-16, ⅜, ½, ⅝, ¾, ⅞ and 1 inch. In finely finished, well made hardwood box. Weight, per set, 2¾ lbs.
No. 9K56254 Price, per set...$1.37

Set of Thirteen Jennings Pattern Extension Lip Auger Bits, one each size from ¼ to 1 inch. In finely finished, well made hardwood box. Weight, per set, 5 pounds.
No. 9K56258 Price, per set....$2.28.

$1.23 STEERS' EXPANSIVE BIT WITH MICROMETER ADJUSTING SCREW.

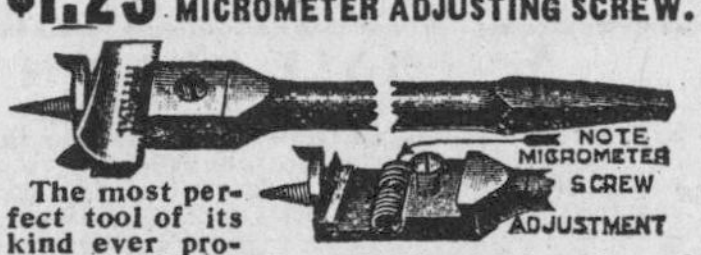

The most perfect tool of its kind ever produced. The stock or holder is drop forged from selected tool steel. The cast steel cutters are held firmly by the patent micrometer adjusting screws and cannot slip or creep. Is easily adjusted and operated. Handsomely finished and polished. Made in two sizes with two cutters. Small size cuts ⅝ to 1¾ inches. Large size, ⅞ to 3 inches. Entire length, small size 8 inches; large size, 9¼ inches. Will fit any bit brace.

No. 9K56470 Small size. Price...$1.23
No. 9K56474 Large size. Price... 1.47
No. 9K56480 Extra Cutters for Steers' Expansive Bit. Fits small size only.
No. 1 cuts ⅝ to 1⅛ inches. Price......18c
No. 2 cuts 1⅛ to 1¾ inches. Price...23c
No. 9K56484 Fits large size only.
No. 3 cuts ⅞ to 1¾ inches. Price.....31c
No. 4 cuts 1¾ to 3 inches. Price......35c
No. 5 cuts 3 to 4 inches. Price........73c

54c FOR A FULTON CLARK'S PATTERN EXPANSIVE BIT, ½ TO 1½ INCHES.

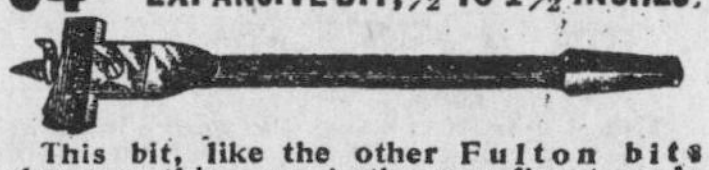

This bit, like the other Fulton bits shown on this page, is the very finest grade made. The cutters are made of the best quality tool steel, properly tempered and we guarantee it to do good work and be satisfactory. With this tool you can bore holes of any diameter between sizes mentioned. It is elegantly made and highly polished. Two sizes.

Small size, with two cutters, one boring from ½ to ⅞ in., the other from ⅞ to 1½ in.
No. 9K56450 Price, complete..54c

Large size, with two cutters, one boring from ⅞ to 1¾ inches, the other boring from 1¾ to 3 inches.
No. 9K56454 Price, complete..74c
No. 9K56460 Extra Cutters, only for small size Clark's Expansive Bits.
No. 1. Cuts from ½ to ⅞ inch. Price.... 9c
No. 2. Cuts from ⅞ to 1½ inches. Price... 13c
No. 9K56464 Extra Cutters, only for large size Clark's Expansive Bits.
No. 3. Cuts from ⅞ to 1¾ inches. Price.. 17c
No. 4. Cuts from 1¾ to 3 inches. Price . 19c
No. 5. Cuts from 3 to 4 inches. Price.....28c

FULTON EXTENSION LIP AUGER BITS

JENNINGS PATTERN.

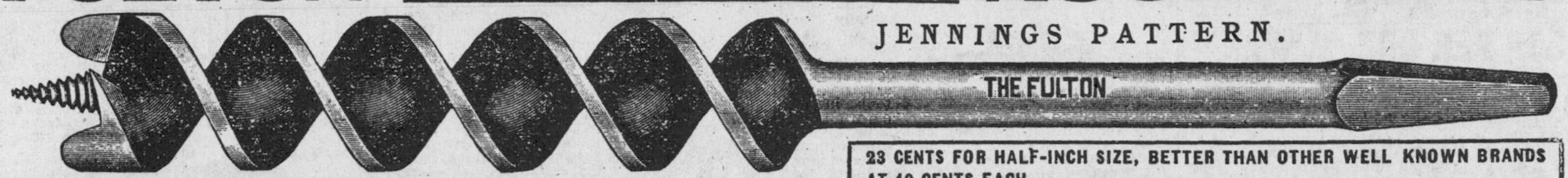

23 CENTS FOR HALF-INCH SIZE, BETTER THAN OTHER WELL KNOWN BRANDS AT 40 CENTS EACH.

THE BEST JENNINGS PATTERN EXTENSION LIP AUGER BIT MADE.

FULTON BITS ARE HAND MADE of the finest crucible cast steel, tempered by an IMPROVED PROCESS, and guaranteed to be superior to any on the market. These bits are finished with highly polished edges, natural temper color in the twist, and are the handsomest and most satisfactory extension lip bits made. Everything necessary to make it a perfect borer and cutter is done in its manufacture. The head is fitted and filed strictly by hand. Every bit is given careful inspection and cannot leave the factory unless it is absolutely perfect. The hollow of the twist is thoroughly cleaned out to give proper clearance. Screws have single thread.

REMEMBER, THAT FOR QUALITY OF BIT, appearance, finish, capacity and smooth boring we guarantee our Fulton Extension Lip Auger Bits to excel all others, and if you send us an order for these bits and are not thoroughly pleased with the goods in every way, return them to us in thirty days and we will refund your money and in addition will pay the transportation charges both ways.

No. 9K56230

Size, inches	¼	5/16	⅜	7/16	½	9/16	⅝	11/16	¾	13/16	⅞	15/16	1	1⅛	1¼	1⅜	1½
Price	14c	16c	18c	21c	23c	25c	28c	30c	32c	35c	38c	41c	44c	48c	53c	59c	66c

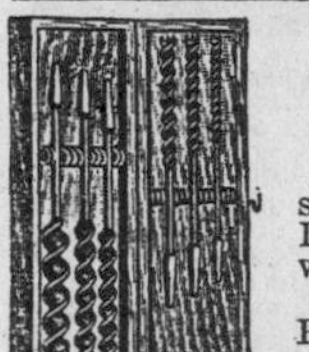

$1.73 SET OF 6 FULTON EXTENSION LIP AUGER BITS.

Jennings pattern. One each size, ¼, ⅜, ½, ⅝, ¾ and 1 inch. In well made, nicely finished hardwood box.
No. 9K56232
Price, per set..............$1.73

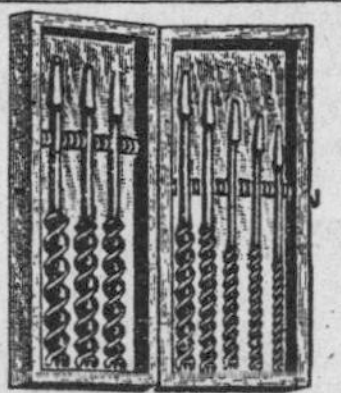

$2.11 SET OF 8 FULTON EXTENSION LIP AUGER BITS.

Jennings pattern. One each size, ¼, 5-16, ⅜, ½, ⅝, ¾, ⅞ and 1 inch. In well made and finely finished hardwood case.
No. 9K56234
Price, per set...........$2.11

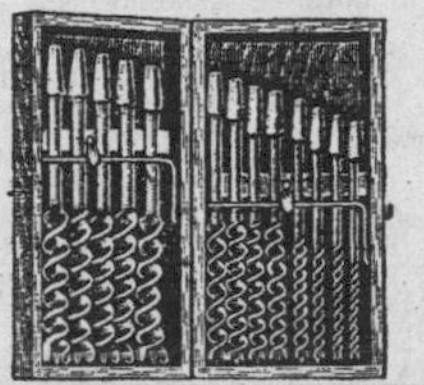

$3.59 SET OF 13 FULTON EXTENSION LIP AUGER BITS.

Jennings pattern. One each size, ¼ to 1 inch. In well made and finely finished hardwood case.
No. 9K56238
Price, per set.....$3.59

FULTON SPECIAL SINGLE TWIST EXTENSION LIP AUGER BITS

FASTEST CUTTING BIT MADE

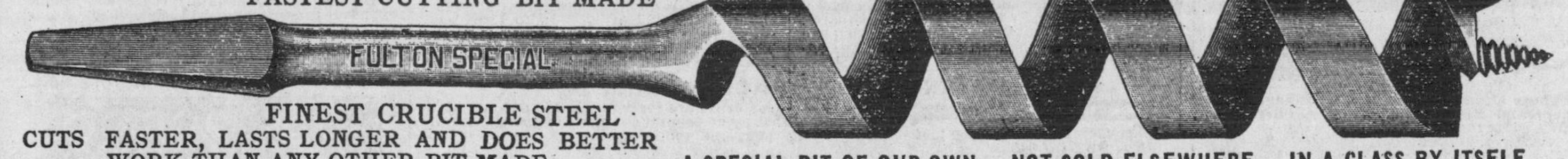

FINEST CRUCIBLE STEEL
CUTS FASTER, LASTS LONGER AND DOES BETTER WORK THAN ANY OTHER BIT MADE.

A SPECIAL BIT OF OUR OWN. NOT SOLD ELSEWHERE. IN A CLASS BY ITSELF.

MADE OF THE FINEST GRADE CRUCIBLE CAST STEEL, highly tempered, and will give entire satisfaction to anyone who wants the best. The only bit made that will absolutely clear itself in any kind of wood. Requires no pressure. Compare these bits with the best bit you ever used and you will find the Fulton Special outclasses them all. They bore equally well in dry, green or hard wood, knots or end boring. The only bit which will do all these kinds of boring. The head is fitted and filed by hand. The hollow of twist and shank of bit are natural temper color. The bits are tempered the entire length.

THE FULTON SPECIAL is positively the best auger bit made at any price for any kind of wood boring, and if not found so after a thorough test, bits can be returned to us at our expense, and purchase price will be returned. Every bit warranted.

No. 9K56280

Size, inches	4/16	5/16	6/16	7/16	8/16	9/16	10/16	11/16	12/16	13/16	14/16	15/16	16/16
Price	18c	20c	22c	25c	28c	31c	34c	37c	40c	43c	46c	49c	53c

Set of Six Fulton Special Single Twist Auger Bits, one each size, ¼, ⅜, ½, ⅝, ¾ and 1 incn. In well made, nicely finished hardwood box.
No. 9K56282 Price, per set..........$1.99

Set of Eight Fulton Special Auger Bits, one each size, ¼, 5-16, ⅜, ½, ⅝, ¾, ⅞ and 1 inch. In well made, finely finished hardwood case. Weight, 3 pounds
No. 9K56284 Price, per set..........$2.73

Set of Thirteen Fulton Special Auger Bits, one each size from ¼ to 1 inch. In well made and finely finished hardwood case. Weight, 5 pounds.
No. 9K56288 Price, per set..........$4.46

$5.85 SET OF 13 C. E. JENNINGS & CO.'S No. 1½ SINGLE TWIST EXTENSION LIP AUGER BITS.

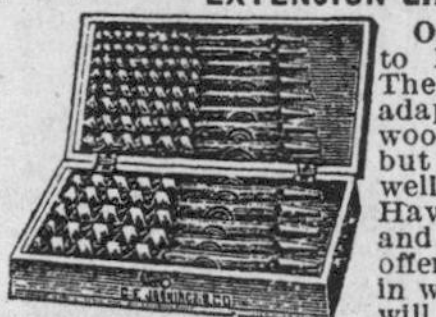

One each size. ¼ to 1 inch inclusive. The bit is especially adapted for hard wood and end boring but will bore equally well in soft wood. Having but one lip and one spur, they offer little resistance in working. They will lead into the end of hardwood without being forced. Put up in fancy hardwood box sold in sets only.
No. 9K56279 Price, per set....$5.85

$1.56 SET OF 6 IRWIN PATTERN EXTENSION LIP AUGER BITS, SOLID CENTER STEM.

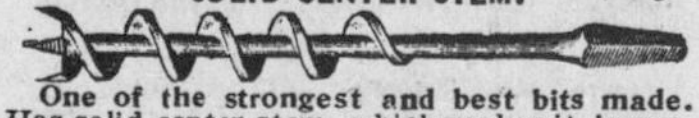

One of the strongest and best bits made. Has solid center stem, which makes it impossible to choke. They have double the clearing space of the ordinary bit and bore fast and easy. Fully warranted. One each size, ¼, ⅜, ½, ⅝ ¾ and 1 inch. In hardwood box.
No. 9K56275 Per set..........$1.56

Set of Eight Irwin Pattern Extension Lip Auger Bits. One each size, ¼, 5-16, ⅜, ½, ⅝, ¾, ⅞ and 1 inch. In hardwood box.
No. 9K56277 Price, per set....$2.07

Set of Thirteen Irwin Pattern Auger Bits. Each size, ¼ to 1 inch, in fancy hardwood box.
No. 9K56278 Price, per set....$3.47

$1.43 SET OF 6 COOK'S PATTERN FULTON RAPID BORER AUGER BIT.

With rounded lip, made with extra coarse double thread screw to lead fast into wood and for end boring. The head of this bit is fitted and filed by hand, is tempered the full length of the twist. Especially made for fast boring and end boring in soft wood and will bore faster than any auger bit made, but we do not recommend it for hardwood. Fully warranted. In hardwood boxes.

Set of Six, sizes, ¼, ⅜, ½, ⅝, ¾ and 1 inch.
No. 9K56304 Price, per set....$1.43

Set of Eight, sizes, ¼, 5-16, ⅜, ½, ⅝, ¾, ⅞ and 1 inch.
No. 9K56308 Price, per set....$1.89

Set of Thirteen, sizes, ¼ to 1 inch.
No. 9K56312 Price, per set....$3.01

$4.42 SET OF 13 GENUINE RUSSEL-JENNINGS AUGER BITS.

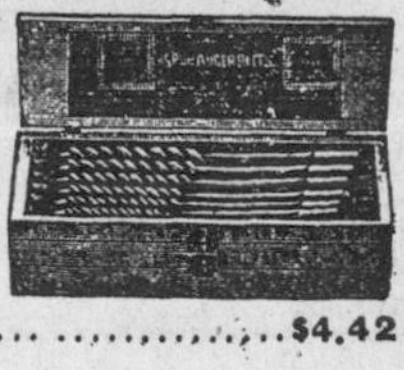

Preferred by many mechanics to any other, sold only in full sets. One each size, from 4-16 to 1 inch. Put up in a fancy hardwood box. Every bit warranted.
No. 9K56274
Price, per set......................$4.42

73c FOR A 12-INCH RAPID BRACE AND BIT EXTENSION.

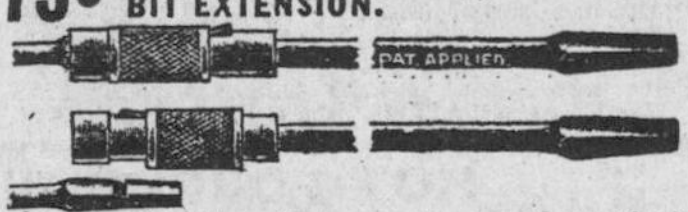

For boring deep holes or in any place that cannot be reached with an ordinary bit. This extension will follow into a hole ⅝-inch or larger. The bits can be put in and taken out quicker than with any other extension. Any bit brace tool can be used in this extension.

No. 9K56348

Length, inches	12	18	24
Price	73c	86c	98c

23c FOR A ¼-INCH TOOL STEEL SHIP AUGER BIT WITH SCREW.

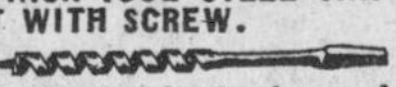

Has 5 or 6-inch twist, very strong, desirable for rough boring and boring in wood not seasoned.

No. 9K56370

Size, inch	¼	5-16	⅜	7-16	
Price	23c	24c	25c	26c	
Size, inch	½	9-16	⅝	11-16	
Price	27c	30c	33c	36c	
Size, inch	¾	13-16	⅞	15-16	1
Price	39c	43c	47c	51c	55c

26c FOR A 4-16-INCH SUPERIOR CAST STEEL CAR BIT, WARRANTED.

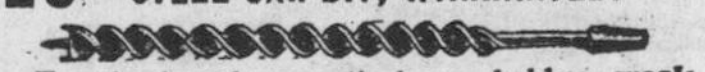

For boring heavy timbers, bridge work, mill work, etc. Has 12-inch twist.

No. 9K56380

Size, inch	4-16	5-16	6-16	7-16	8-16
Price	26c	28c	30c	33c	37c
Size, inch	9-16	10-16	11-16	12-16	13-16
Price	42c	47c	51c	55c	59c
Size, inch	14-16	15-16	16-16	17-16	18-16
Price	63c	68c	74c	80c	87c

36c FOR A 5-16-INCH GENUINE WATROUS SHIP AUGER CAR BIT.

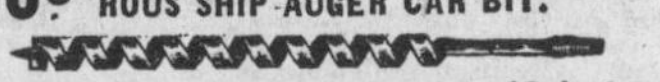

With screw. Length of twist, 12 inches. Used by car builders, millwrights, etc. The finest bit made for boring hardwood.

No. 9K56390

Size, inch	5-16	⅜	7-16	½	9-16	
Price	36c	39c	41c	43c	45c	
Size, inch	⅝	11-16	¾	13-16	⅞	
Price	49c	51c	54c	57c	60c	
Size, inch	15-16	1	17-16	1⅛	19-16	1¼
Price	63c	65c	69c	72c	74c	77c

YOU SAVE STILL MORE OVER 3,000 HARDWARE ITEMS IN THIS BOOK STILL FURTHER REDUCED FROM OUR LAST CATALOGUE.

21c ACCURATE BIT GAUGE, WILL FIT ANY SIZE BIT.

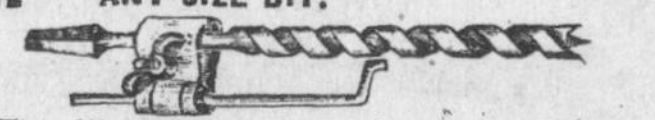

This illustration shows the gauge in all its parts. It will exactly gauge the depth of hole to be bored, will soon pay for itself in time saved.
No. 9K56352 Price, without bit..21c

$1.14 FOR A NICKEL PLATED ANGULAR BORING ATTACHMENT.

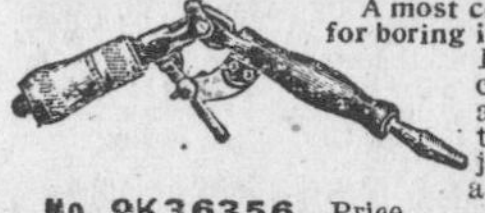

A most convenient tool for boring in corners, etc. Fits any brace, can be used as a straight extension or adjusted to any angle desired.
No. 9K36356 Price..........$1.14

6c BEST QUALITY FORGED TOOL STEEL CENTER BIT.

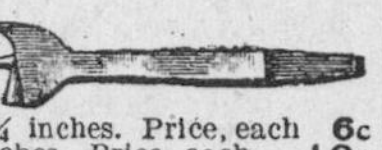

Straw color temper. State size wanted.
No. 9K56400
Sizes, ⅛, ½, ⅝, ¾ inches. Price, each 6c
Sizes, ⅞, 1, 1¼ inches. Price, each...10c
Sizes, 1½, 1¾, 2 inches. Price, each..15c
Set of 10 Extra Quality Center Bits. One each size from ⅜ to 2 inches.
No. 9K56408 Price, per set....74c

37c PER DOZ. DOUBLE CUT GIMLET BITS.

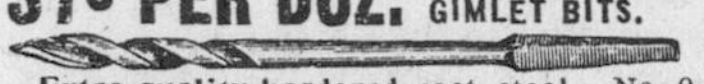

Extra quality hardened cast steel. No. 0 is about 1-16 inch. The other numbers increase gradually up to No. 6, which is about ¼ inch. Be sure to state size wanted.
No. 9K56412 Price, any size, Nos. 0, 1, 2, 3, 4, 5 or 6, per doz., 37c; each.....4c
A set of the above bits, one of each size. Weight, 10 ounces.
No. 9K56414 Price, per set of seven 24c

53c PER DOZ. GERMAN PATTERN GIMLET BIT.

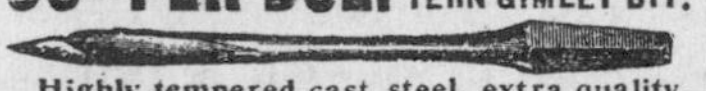

Highly tempered cast steel, extra quality. Will bore with small risk of splitting. The small sizes are easily broken if not handled right, and should be used carefully. Draw the bit when you have bored to depth of pod, and you will have no trouble then to bore as deep as bit will go. Sizes, 2-32, 3-32, 4-32, 5-32, 6-32, 7-32, 8-32 and 10-32 inch. State size.
No. 9K56416 Price, any size, per doz., 53c; each..........................5c
Set of eight of the above bits, one of each size.
No. 9K56420 Price, complete....35c
German Pattern Gimlet Bits. Special high grade. Made from a special steel, hardened and drawn to a very fine spring temper, especially for wagon makers and other workers in hardwood. Sizes, 2-32, 3-32, 4-32, 5-32, 6-32, 7-32, 8-32, 9-32, 10-32, 11-32 and 12-32 inch.
No. 9K56426 Price, each, any size. 6c
Per dozen, any size 69c
Set of eleven of the above bits, one of each size.
No. 9K56430 Price, complete....63c

10c HAMMER FORGED TOOL STEEL COUNTERSINK GIMLET BITS.

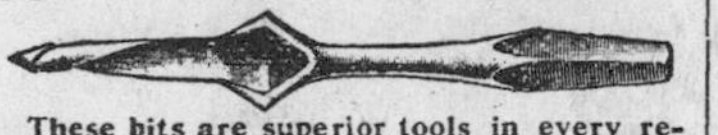

These bits are superior tools in every respect and far superior to those offered by other concerns.

Number	0	1	2	3	4
Bores, depth, ins.	¾	1	1¼	1½	1¾

No. 9K56440 Price, any size, each, 10c
No. 9K56442 Price, per set of five, 47c

16c FULTON SPECIAL CRUCIBLE STEEL SCREWDRIVER BIT, SMALL SIZE.

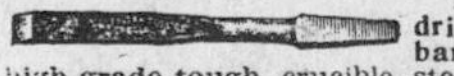

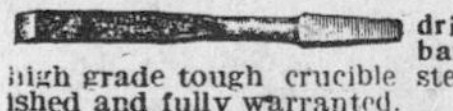

The best screwdriver bit made, bar none. Forged high grade tough crucible steel. Highly polished and fully warranted.
No. 9K56494

Sizes	Small	Medium	Large	Extra
Price	16c	18c	20c	22c

8c SQUARE REAMER BIT, FORGED FROM EXTRA CAST STEEL.

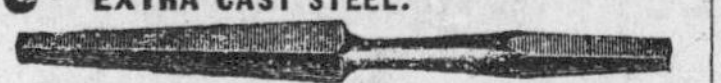

Better than bits sold at double our price.
No. 9K56500 Price.............8c

7c FORGED CAST STEEL FLAT COUNTERSINK BIT FOR METAL.

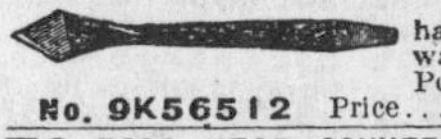

Tempered for hard service and warranted perfect. Polished.
No. 9K56512 Price..............7c

7c ROSE HEAD COUNTERSINK BIT FOR METAL OR WOOD.

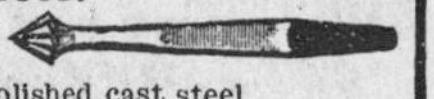

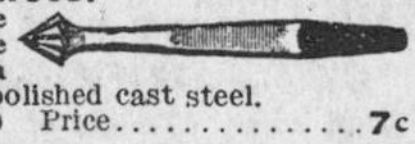

The angle of the head is the same as the taper on a screw. Made of polished cast steel.
No. 9K56520 Price..............7c

7c TEMPERED CAST STEEL SNAIL HEAD COUNTERSINK BIT FOR WOOD.

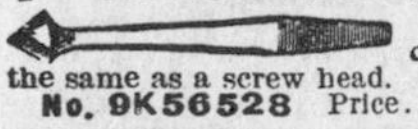

Makes a clear, clean cut, tapered the same as a screw head.
No. 9K56528 Price..............7c

16c CAST STEEL COUNTERSINK BIT FOR WOOD, WITH GAUGE.

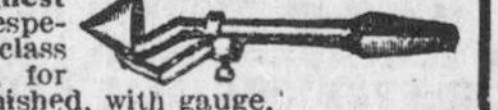

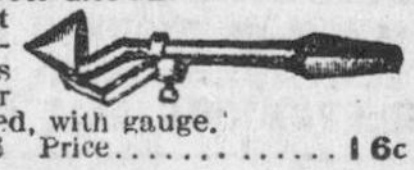

Made of highest grade steel, especially for first class mechanics, for wood, finely finished, with gauge.
No. 9K56536 Price..............16c

OVER 3,000 HARDWARE ITEMS IN THIS BOOK REDUCED IN PRICE FROM THE ALREADY LOW FIGURES QUOTED IN OUR LAST CATALOGUE.

BALL BEARING CHAIN DRILL.

Will put holes into iron, brass or other hard metals with less effort than the common brace and bit does in wood. Put the shank in a brace, loop the chain around the object to be drilled, fasten end of chain in slot to give pressure, screw upon the hand wheel and you have a portable drill press which is exceedingly easy to operate on account of the ball bearings. Furnished with 3 feet of chain.

No. 9K56634

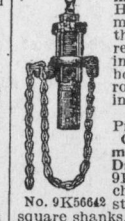

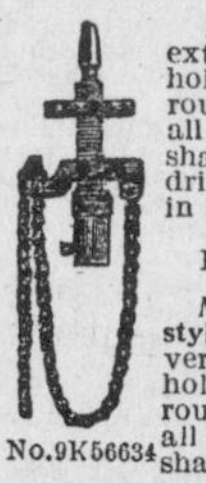

Marvel Chain Drill, style D, has extra long combination chuck, which holds standard ½-inch round shank drills and all sizes square, taper shank or bit stock drills. Drills are held in by set screw.
No. 9K56634
Price..............71c
Marvel Chain Drill, style C, fitted with universal chuck which holds ⅛ to ½-inch round shank drills and all sizes square, taper shank or bit stock drills.
No. 9K56638 Price, $1.04

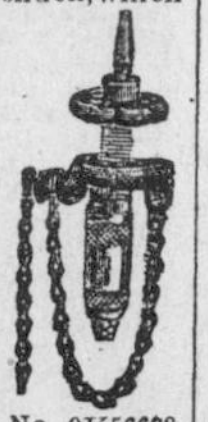

No. 9K56638

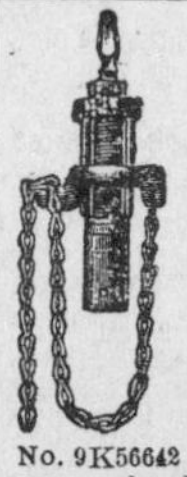

No. 9K56642

Goodell-Pratt Automatic Chain Drill. Has an entirely automatic feed; the end thrust has its friction reduced by ball bearings. The chuck will hold drills having round shanks ½ inch in diameter.
No. 9K56642
Price.......$1.37
Goodell-Pratt Automatic Feed Chain Drill. Same as No. 9K56642, except has chuck for holding bit stock drills with square shanks.
No. 9K56646 Price..........$1.73

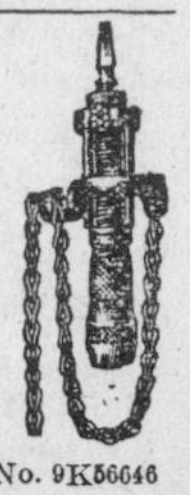

No. 9K56646

$2.34 TWO-SPEED BALL BEARING BREAST DRILL.

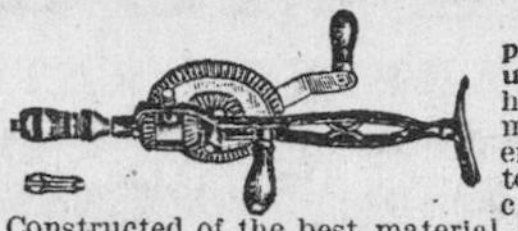

Made especially for us by the highest class manufacturer of these tools in the country. Constructed of the best material throughout. Has malleable iron frame, adjustable breast plate, cut gears and two speed adjustment. Nickel plated chuck, with two sets of jaws, one for ordinary bit stock drills, the other for round shank drills, 1-16 to 5-16 inch. Polished hardwood handles.
No. 9K56622 Price...........$2.34

$3.18 BALL BEARING DOUBLE GEARED BREAST DRILL.

$3.20

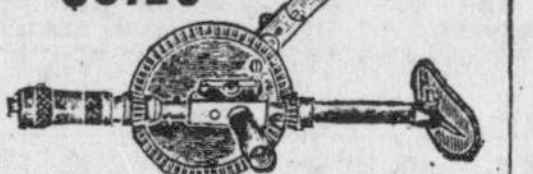

Well made, strong and durable. Has a 6-inch drive wheel giving speed 4½ to 1. The gearsare cut, the handles are cocobolo, and the stock and chuck nickel plated. Has a protected level attachment to show when the tool is being held true, also an extension crank. Has alligator jaws and will take all sizes bit stock and round shank drills ⅛ to ½ inch, inclusive.
No. 9K56626 Price.............$3.18

94c MECHANICS' BALL BEARING UNIVERSAL RATCHET HANDLE.

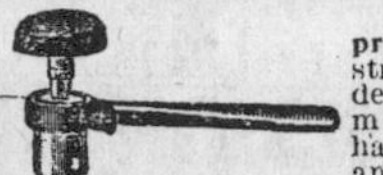

A most desirable and practical tool, constructed to meet the demand of first class mechanics, has iron handles 8 inches long, and a shifter operating the ratchet mechanism, which can be made either right or left hand. Has ball bearing lignum vitae head; the socket has square taper hole provided with set screw for fastening the bit.
No. 9K56676 Price...........94c

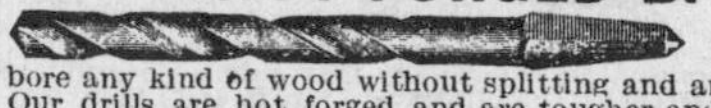

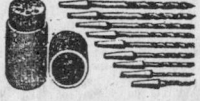

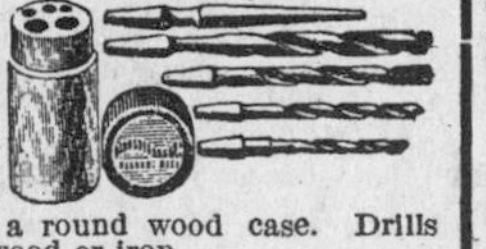

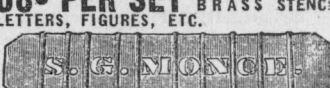

$4.34 BENCH DRILL, SOLID IRON FRAME AND VISE ATTACHMENT.

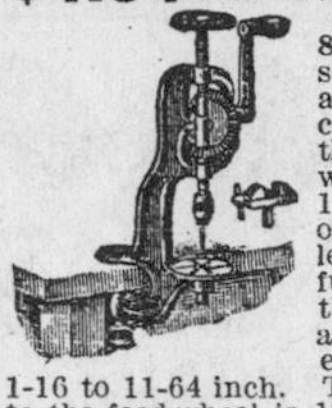

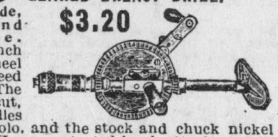

Goodell Bench Drill, No. 8½, cut gears, steel feed screw, adjustable table and a special vise, which can be used in place of the table for holding the work. The jaws open 1 3-16 inches and operate on a right hand and a left hand screw. It is furnished complete with three-jawed chuck, capacity 0 to ¼ inch, and eight fluted drills from 1-16 to 11-64 inch. The height from the table to the feed wheel is 13 inches. The machine will give good honest service. Weight, 15 lbs.
No. 9K56682 Price..........$4.34

$6.57 TWO-SPEED BENCH DRILL, WITH EIGHT DRILL BITS.

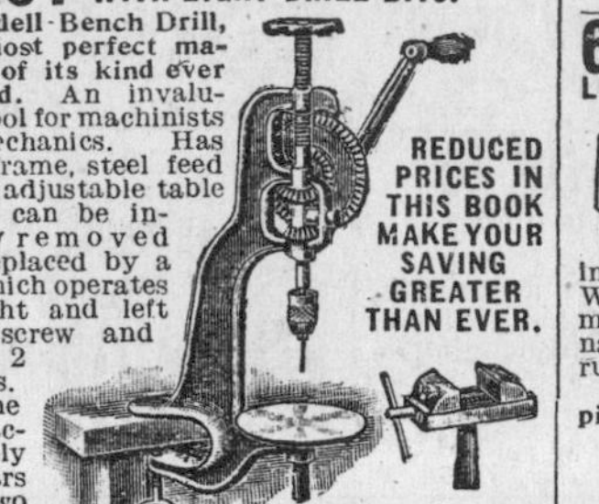

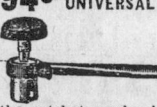

REDUCED PRICES IN THIS BOOK MAKE YOUR SAVING GREATER THAN EVER.

Goodell Bench Drill, the most perfect machine of its kind ever devised. An invaluable tool for machinists or mechanics. Has solid frame, steel feed screw, adjustable table which can be instantly removed and replaced by a vise which operates on right and left hand screw and opens 2 inches. Machine has accurately cut gears with two speeds, changed instantly by convenient shifter, is fitted with strong three-jawed chuck with capacity 0 to ⅜ inch, which will take regular straight shank drills. With each machine we furnish a set of eight fluted drills, 1-16 to 11-64 inch. The height from table to feed wheel is 18 inches. Weight, 18 pounds.
No. 9K56692 Price..........$6.57

PATENT WOOD BRACE DRILLS.

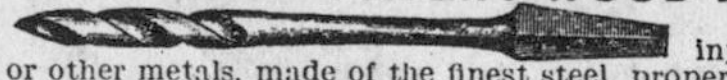

These drills are for wood only, but are not injured by accidental contact with nails, screws or other metals, made of the finest steel, properly tempered and accurately ground.
No. 9K56742

Size	⅛	5-32	3-16	7-32	¼	9-32	5-16	11-32	⅜	13-32	7-16	15-32	½	⅝	¾
Price	7c	8c	9c	11c	13c	15c	16c	17c	18c	19c	20c	21c	23c	25c	29c

No. 9K56748 Set of nine Wood Brace Drills, one each, ⅛, 5-32, 3-16, 7-32, ¼, 5-16, ⅜, 7-16 and ½-inch. Price, per set, complete $1.11

STRAIGHT SHANK TWIST DRILLS.

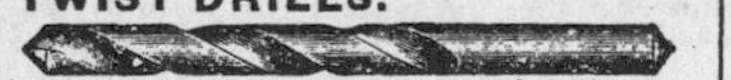

These drills cannot be be used in the ordinary bit brace. They must be used in a chuck made for round shank drills. The shank and twist are the same size. Hot forged from the finest steel, accurately ground and will outlast the ordinary milled drills offered by others two to one. We guarantee the quality equal to any made. Be sure to state size wanted.
No. 9K56760

Diam. in 64ths of inch	4	5	6	7	8	9	10	11	12	13	14	15	16	17	18
Length	2½	2⅝	2¾	2⅞	3	3⅛	3¼	3⅜	3½	3⅝	3¾	3⅞	4	4⅛	4¼
Price, each	3c	4c	4c	4c	5c	5c	6c	6c	7c	7c	8c	9c	9c	$0.10	$0.11
Price, per dozen	31c	34c	37c	41c	45c	50c	55c	61c	67c	74c	81c	89c	96c	1.04	1.12

Diam. in 64ths of inch	19	20	21	22	23	24	25	26	27	28	29	30	31	32
Length	4⅜	4½	4⅝	4¾	4⅞	5	5⅛	5¼	5⅜	5½	5⅝	5¾	5⅞	6
Price, each	$0.11	0.12	0.13	0.14	0.15	0.16	0.17	0.17	0.18	0.20	0.21	0.22	0.22	0.23
Price, per dozen	1.20	1.28	1.36	1.45	1.55	1.66	1.76	1.86	1.96	2.08	2.16	2.24	2.33	2.45

For BLACKSMITHS' DRILLS see page 511.

HOT FORGED BIT STOCK DRILLS.

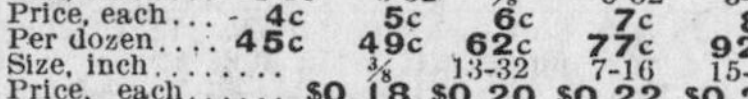

Bit stock drills will fit any bit brace and will drill steel, iron or other metal. Will bore any kind of wood without splitting and are not injured by contact with screws or nails. Our drills are hot forged and are tougher and stronger than milled drills as the best part of the steel is not thrown away. Our drills are accurately ground to micrometer gauge and sizes are exact. All our drills, 3-32 and larger, have solid forged steel shanks, thereby giving increased strength. Points of drills should be kept well oiled when drilling metal.
No. 9K56720

Size, inch	1-16	3-32	⅛	5-32	3-16	7-32	¼	9-32	5-16	11-32
Price, each	4c	5c	6c	7c	8c	$0.09	$0.11	$0.12	$0.14	$0.16
Per dozen	45c	49c	62c	77c	92c	1.06	1.16	1.29	1.52	1.78

Size, inch	⅜	13-32	7-16	15-32	½	⅝	¾	⅞	1
Price, each	$0.18	$0.20	$0.22	$0.24	$0.27	$0.39	$0.50	$0.57	$0.69
Per dozen	2.05	2.28	2.50	2.78	3.06	4.50	5.76	6.52	7.98

74c FOR 9 SMALL SIZE BIT STOCK DRILLS.

The most convenient way to buy drill bits, a separate hole for each size. 1 each size, 1-16, 3-32, ⅛, 5-32, 3-16, 7-32, ¼, 5-16 and ⅜ inch.
No. 9K56736 Price for complete set in round wood box..................74c

78c SET, 4 BIT STOCK DRILLS AND ONE SQUARE REAMER.

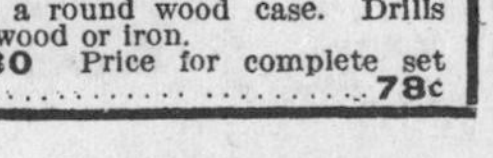

Consists of four Bit Stock Twist Drills, one each size, ¼, 5-16, ⅜ and ½ inch, and one extra quality square reamer bit. Put up in a round wood case. Drills will bore either wood or iron.
No. 9K56730 Price for complete set with box.......................78c

Hand Made Steel Stamps.

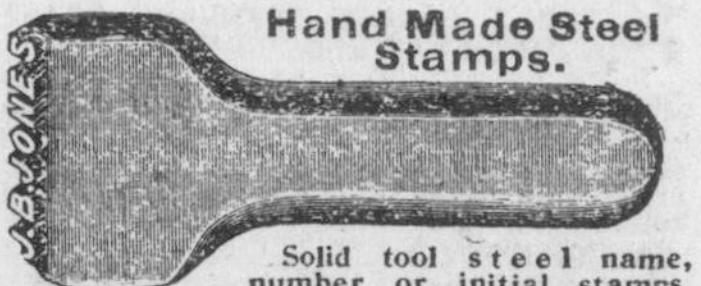

Solid tool steel name, number or initial stamps, made and finished by hand. Will outlast the cheap machine made kind two to one. For marking tools, etc. Made to order, one line only, any letters or figures desired. Prices given are per letter, not for stamp complete.
No. 9K57102

Size, letter, inch	1-16	3-32	⅛	3-16	¼
Price, per letter,	11c	12c	13c	15c	20c

Stamps mailed from factory only. Prices include postage.
Names for stamps should be written plainly as stamps made to order cannot be returned.

Hand Made Steel Letters and Figures.

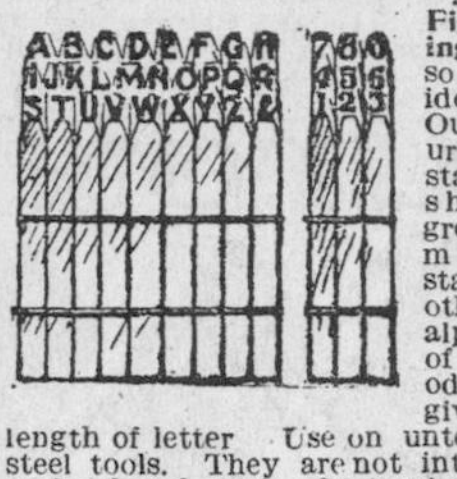

Steel Letters and Figures for stamping tools, etc., so you can always identify them. Our letters and figures are hand made, stamping clear and sharp and are greatly superior to machine made stamps sold by all other houses. An alphabet consists of 26 letters, 1 period and 1 &. Sizes given indicate the length of letter Use on untempered part of steel tools. They are not intended to stamp on hardened steel. State size wanted.
No. 9K57110

Size, letter, in.	1-16	⅛	3-16	¼	⅜
Wt. ozs. per set.	16	20	22	28	48
Price, each...	3c	3c	$0.04	$0.05	$0.08
Per alphabet.	73c	73c	1.02	1.25	1.95

No. 9K57114 Steel Figures.

Size, inch......	1-16	⅛	3-16	¼	⅜
Wt. ozs., per set	4	6	8	12	30
Per set of 9....	25c	27c	35c	42c	69c

By mail, postage extra, 1 cent per ounce.

68c PER SET 1-2-INCH SPRING BRASS STENCIL LETTERS, FIGURES, ETC.

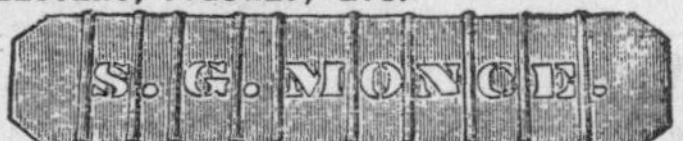

Interchangeable Locking Stencils, put up in fonts of letters assorted by printers' rules. We cannot break fonts nor change the assortment. As put up they will make any ordinary name. They are made of brass and will not rust or curl up as the ordinary letters do.
No. 9K57124 Complete Font of 70 pieces, consisting of letters, periods, figures, etc.

Size, inches	½	¾	1	1½
Price, per font	68c	74c	78c	$1.05

Black Stencil Ink.
A large box of highest grade stencil ink with sponge cup and sponge for above stencil sets.
No. 9K57128 Price, per box...22c
Bristle Stencil Brushes.
The best brush made for the price. Made of pure bristles and will not shed. Has seamless zinc ferrule.
No. 9K57136 Price..........11c

$5.12 KEY CHECK OUTFIT, COMPLETE IN HANDSOME HARDWOOD BOX.

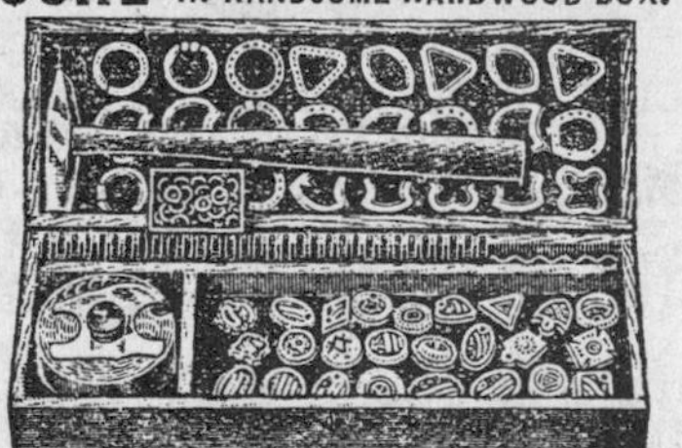

You can make this outfit pay for itself in a few hours at your county fair, or in any crowd. Checks cost you 1½ cents each, can be stamped in a few minutes and easily sell for 10 to 25 cents each. The work is simple, anyone can do it. This complete outfit consists of complete alphabet of 1-16-inch steel letters, a complete set of 1-16-inch figures a handsome nickel plated key check anvil with gauge for guiding dies when stamping all kinds of key checks, a steel hammer, 100 assorted German silver key checks, 24 assorted key rings, 144 small key check rings. Packed in fancy hardwood box, as illustrated.
No. 9K57150 Price, for complete outfit...................$5.12
Assorted German Silver Key Checks, with lodge emblems and other fancy designs, with scroll for name.
No. 9K57154 Price, per 100..$1.98
Assorted German Silver Key Checks, fancy shapes, plain.
No. 9K57158 Price, per 100..$1.49
Assorted German Silver Umbrella Plates, oblong and oval.
No. 9K57162 Price, per dozen..13c
Assorted Key Rings of different sizes and shapes.
No. 9K57166 Price, per doz.$0.25
Per gross.......................2.68
Small Key Rings, for fastening key check to key ring.
No. 9K57170

Diameter, inches..	⅜	7-16	½	⅝
Price, per gross..	34c	36c	39c	43c

Assortment of six Key Chains, different links, all with leather flap to attach to button on one end and spring snap on other end. Lengths, from 18 to 20 inches. In sets only.
No. 9K57174 Price, per set....45c

THE STEEL SQUARE AND ITS USES. $1.33

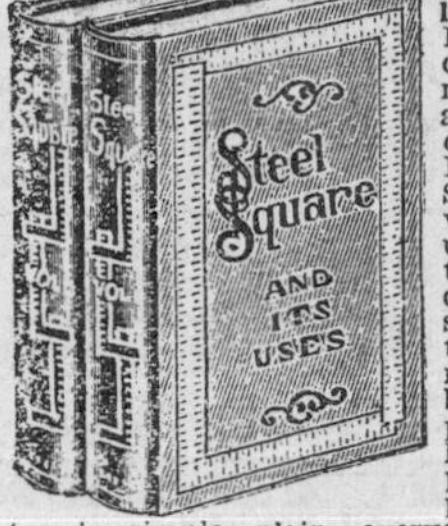

TWO VOLUMES. Edited by William A. Radford. In addition to containing all the matter that has appeared in the original Fred T. Hodgson's Steel Square books, revised and brought up to date, it contains several hundred pages of absolutely new matter that has never before been printed or placed in the hands of the practical carpenter. Written in simple, plain, everyday language so that it can be easily understood and followed. Contains a vast amount of new, practical, everyday information, such as is necessary for every progressive and successful carpenter to know.

THIS UP TO DATE AND PRACTICAL WORK on the application of the steel square treats of the laying out of rafters, finding the lengths of jacks, securing bevels, showing how to measure solids, surfaces and distances.

SPECIAL CHAPTERS are devoted to that part of stair building to which the steel square can be applied. Other chapters treat of heavy timber framing, showing how the square is used for laying out mortises, tenons, shoulders, etc. Each volume measures 6x9 inches and contains over 300 pages and 50 modern house plans. Over 300 illustrations. Bound in cloth.

No. 3K9110 Price, per set, two volumes $1.33
If by mail, postage extra, per set, 20 cents.

PRACTICAL CARPENTRY.

A Complete Up To Date Explanation of Modern Carpentry. Two Volumes. Edited by William A. Radford.

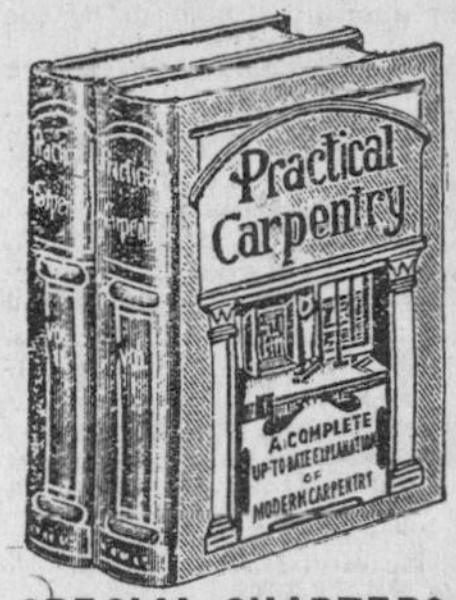

IT IS THE MOST COMPLETE, most accurate, most up to date and most practical work upon this subject. It contains the best and quickest methods for laying roofs, rafters, stairs, floors, hopper bevels, mitering, coping, splayed work, circular work, and, in fact, for forming all kinds of carpenter work.

SPECIAL CHAPTERS are devoted to building construction, which takes the carpenter from foundation to roof, with complete illustrations of each detail, such as foundation, windows, cornices, doors, roofs, porch work, etc. There are also special chapters devoted to good and faulty construction and all kinds of framing.

Over 400 illustrations, many of them cover an entire page. Each volume contains 50 modern house plans and over 300 pages. Size, 6x9 inches. Bound in cloth. For a full description of this work and other books of interest to the carpenter and builder see Book Department.

No. 3K252 Price, per set, 2 vols .. $1.33
Postage extra, per set, 30 cents.

11c FOR A 4½-INCH BRASS LINED TRY SQUARE, ACCURATE AND TRUE.

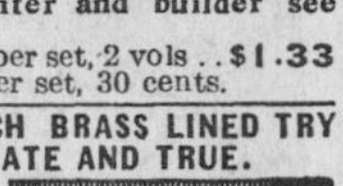

The spacing and marks on this special try square are cut in a graduating machine, being deep and plain and will not become dim with use. The handle is plain beechwood, brass lined with three rivets and a large heavy brass plate. We guarantee this try square to be perfectly satisfactory in every way and is not to be confused with the poorly constructed competition goods offered by others. The size designates length of blade from the handle.

No. 9K57402

Size, inches	4½	6	7½	9	12
Price	11c	12c	14c	16c	22c

$2.43 FULTON SPECIAL 25-FOOT STEEL TAPE LINE IN LEATHER CASE.

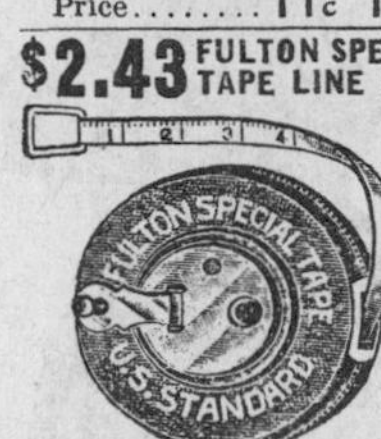

Like the other Fulton tools we sell, the best on the market; will not stretch like a linen or cotton tape and is not affected by moisture. Warranted rust-proof. The measurements are guaranteed accurate. The case is compact, very durable and will not break. The winding drum is large, has a long crank, winds easily and the handle folds nearly flush with the case. We can safely recommend this tape to the purchaser as an article which is first class, durable and perfectly accurate. Marked feet and twelfths (inches) and eighths.

No. 9K57482

To measure feet	25	50	75	100
Price	$2.43	$2.95	$3.90	$5.05

Metallic Warp Tape Line, is durable, reliable, accurate and strong. A metallic warp is woven in with the linen, which prevents stretching. Has a heavy red leather case, folding handle; spaced in feet and twelfths of feet.

No. 9K57490

To measure feet	50	75	100
Price	$1.96	$2.46	$3.06

CARPENTERS' STEEL SQUARES

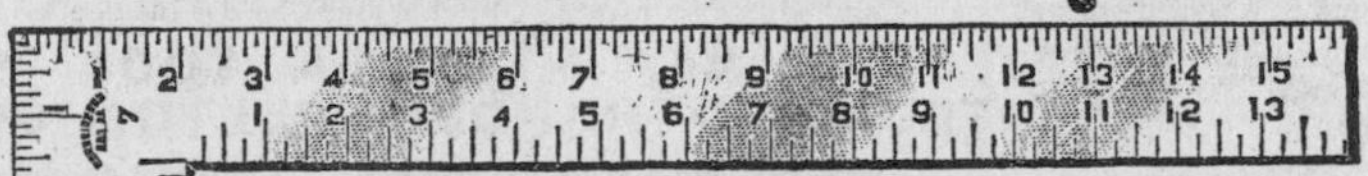
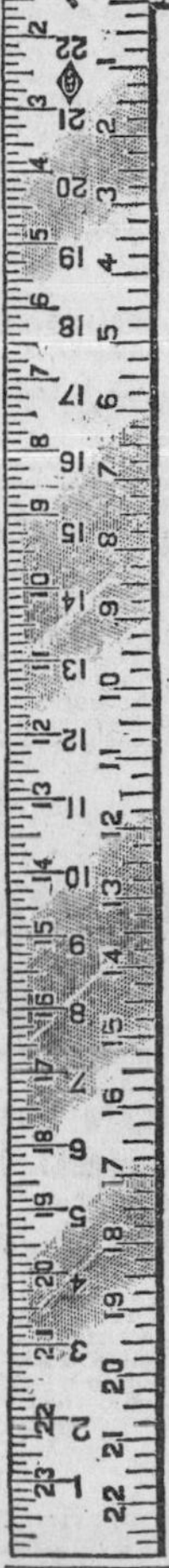

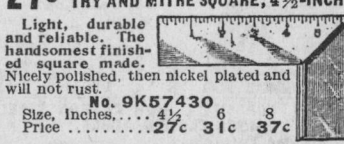

WELL MADE, NICELY FINISHED, ACCURATE AND TRUE; HAVE THE PROPER "HANG" AND WILL GIVE BETTER SATISFACTION THAN ANY OTHER SQUARES MADE.

A steel square unless it is true and properly made is worse than useless. Every steel square we send out is fully guaranteed for quality and warranted true. Our squares are made both body and tongue tapered, the ends being thinner. This gives strength where it is needed, at the same time making the square lighter and easier to handle. Remember, every steel square we send out is warranted perfect and better than any other make of similar pattern.

61c will buy a better Steel Square from us than $1.00 will buy at retail. All our prices save you money.

Our "Rustless" Royal Copper Finish Square, the most beautiful and complete square ever produced, is finished in "royal copper" with white enamel figures and graduations. Body of square 24x2 inches. Marked on face in sixteenths and eighths and on back in twelfths, thirty-seconds and hundredths. Has 16-inch tongue spaced on front in sixteenths and eighths, and on back in twelfths and tenths. In addition it has brace measure, eight square and the patent rafter table which gives the measure of rafter for any of seven pitches of roof, based on the length of horizontal measurements of building from center to outside. Full directions accompany each square.

No. 9K57324 Price, each $1.54

Blued Rustless Finish Steel Square. This is an extra quality square. The body measures 24x2 inches. The markings show brace measure, 8 square and Essex board measure, feet and inches in full. On face of square, body and tongue are both marked 1-16 and ⅛-inch spaces. On back of square, body is marked 1-12 and 1-32-inch spaces, tongue is marked 1-12 and 1-10-inch spaces. The blued, rustless finish on this square is very desirable and shows the figures clear and distinct. Length of tongue .... 16 inches 18 inches

No. 9K57334 Price, each 98c 99c

Steel Square. Polished Finish. Exactly the same as our square No. 9K57334, except the finish is polished steel, not blued.

No. 9K57338 Length of tongue .... 16 inches 18 inches
Price, each 79c 81c

Blued Rustless Finish Steel Square. One of the most popular squares ever manufactured. The body measures 24x2 inches. The face is marked, both body and tongue in 1-16 and ¼-inch spaces. The back is marked, both body and tongue in 1-12 and ¼-inch spaces. This square also carries brace measure and Essex board measure, with feet and inches in full and in addition shows rafter scale giving length, pitch and bevel of rafters. This scale will be easily understood by any carpenter, and is the most desirable and practical scale ever put on a steel square. Length of tongue, 16 inches.

No. 9K57344 Price, each 86c

Steel Square. Polished Finish. Just the same square as our No. 9K57344, except without rafter scale and finish is polished steel. The quality is the same as on the more expensive finish. Length of tongue, 16 inches.

No. 9K57354 Price, each 61c

Steel Square. Polished Finish. This is one of the best selling squares ever constructed on account of its low price and good quality. It is full size in body, measuring 24x2 inches. On both sides it is marked in ⅛, ¼ and 1-inch spaces. This square carries the Essex board measure, with feet and inches in full. For a low priced solid steel square this number cannot be excelled. Length of tongue, 16 inches.

No. 9K57364 Price, each 49c

Polished Iron Square. This is a large square, the body measuring 24 inches long by 2 inches wide. The tongue measures 12 inches long by 1½ inches wide. Square is marked in ⅛-inch spaces on both sides. This is the best iron square manufactured and is as accurate as a square can possibly be made at this price. It is not, however, warranted by us and we recommend the purchase of a steel square always.

No. 9K57388 Price, each 24c

21c FOR A 6-INCH COMBINED TRY AND MITRE SQUARE.

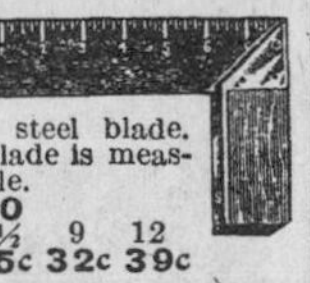

Made in the same careful manner as our steel framing squares. Has brass lined rosewood handle, graduated steel blade. Square inside and out. Blade is measured from outside of handle.

No. 9K57410

Size blade, inches	6	7½	9	12
Price	21c	25c	32c	39c

53c FOX ALL STEEL NICKEL PLATED COMBINED SQUARE AND MITRE.

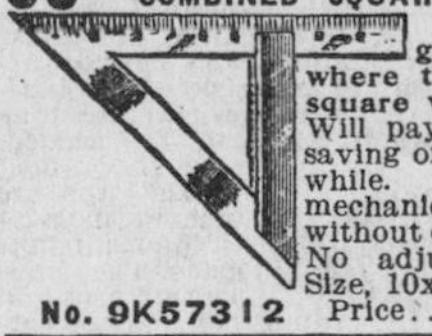

Can be used in a great many places where the ordinary try square would not work. Will pay for itself in the saving of time in a short while. No first class mechanic can afford to do without one of these tools. No adjusting necessary. Size, 10x10 inches.

No. 9K57312 Price 53c

27c FOX ALL STEEL NICKEL PLATED TRY AND MITRE SQUARE, 4½-INCH.

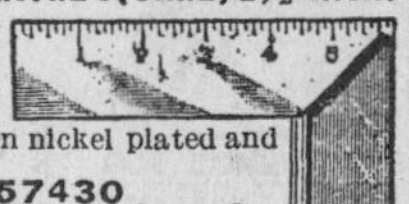

Light, durable and reliable. The handsomest finished square made. Nicely polished, then nickel plated and will not rust.

No. 9K57430

Size, inches	4½	6	8
Price	27c	31c	37c

16c RIGHT OR LEFT HAND SLIDING T BEVEL, 6 INCHES LONG.

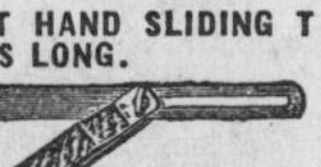

The finest T bevel sold by anyone. It has solid rosewood handle, brass tipped, flush adjusting screw, steel blade can be used right or left hand, either side up, which is a great convenience.

No. 9K57450

Length, inches	6	8	10	12
Price	16c	18c	20c	22c

$9.63 IMPROVED LEVELING INSTRUMENT, COMPLETE WITH SIGHT TUBE AND ADJUSTABLE EXTENSION TRIPOD.

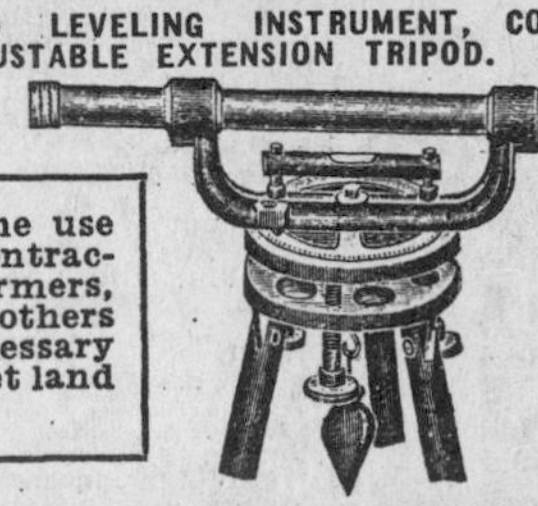

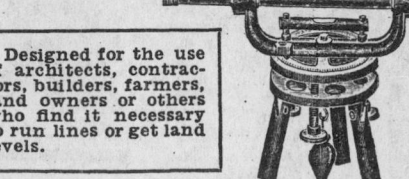

$9.63

Designed for the use of architects, contractors, builders, farmers, land owners or others who find it necessary to run lines or get land levels.

Our previous price $9.94 our price now ..... $9.63. Over 3,000 hardware prices reduced in this book make your saving greater than ever.

INVALUABLE FOR LEVELING FOUNDATIONS and walls, setting machinery, floor timbers and sills, running lines, ditches and drains, grading roads or hillsides and will more than save its cost on one job. Hiring a surveyor every time you want to run a line or get a land level is a waste of money when you can buy for our low price of $9.63 a complete instrument like this that will last a lifetime and always be ready for use just when you want it. Every builder or contractor should own one of these instruments as it is just the thing for getting building levels correctly and is a great time and money saver. The instrument, complete, consists of upper plate with graduated arc divided by degrees, tripod head, tripod with extension legs as noted, plumb bob and line. The sight tube, 12 inches long, is brass, nickel plated, with small eye aperture at one end and usual cross wires at the other. The level case and graduated arc are also nickel plated and the other parts are nicely japanned. There is no magnetic needle or complicated mechanism about this instrument and with the complete directions we furnish with each one, anyone can use it and get perfect results. Save money by ordering one of these fine instruments. Packed in nicely finished box for carrying.

No. 9K57224 Price, complete $9.63

$1.18 FOR A 12-INCH ADJUSTABLE IRON LEVEL WITH TWO PLUMBS.

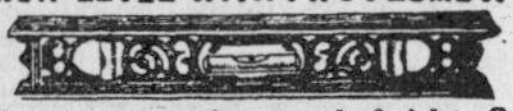

The top, bottom and ends of this level are ground absolutely true, japanned finish; 2 inches wide. Warranted accurate.

No. 9K57238

Length, inches	12	18	24
Price	$1.18	$1.33	$1.58

$1.87 DAVIS' ADJUSTABLE IRON PLUMB, LEVEL AND INCLINOMETER, 6-INCH.

Preferred by the best mechanics for their accuracy and reliability.

No. 9K57246

Length, in.	6	12	18	24
Price	$1.87	$2.41	$2.87	$3.36

43c FULL LENGTH POLISHED CHERRY PLUMB AND LEVEL.

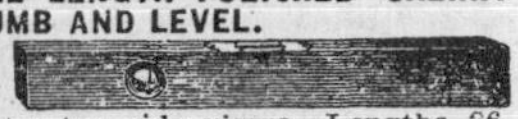

Proved glasses; not adjustable; arch top plate; two side views. Lengths, 26, 28 or 30 inches. State length wanted.

No. 9K57266 Price 43c

71c POLISHED MAHOGANY ADJUSTABLE PLUMB AND LEVEL.

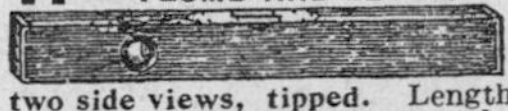

Proved glasses, arch top plates, two side views, tipped. Lengths, 26, 28 or 30 inches. State length wanted.

No. 9K57272 Price 71c

99c WARPPROOF AND SPRINGPROOF ADJUSTABLE PLUMB AND LEVEL.

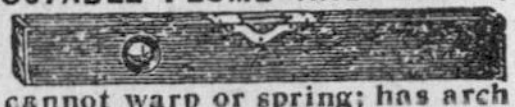

Made of three pieces glued together so it cannot warp or spring; has arch top plate; two ornamental brass lipped side views; proved glasses; hand polished and brass tipped ends. Lengths, 26, 28 or 30 inches. State length wanted.

No. 9K57274 Price 99c

$2.11 POLISHED MAHOGANY PLUMB AND LEVEL, WITH GROUND GLASSES.

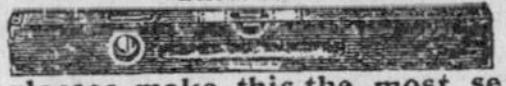

The superior ground glasses make this the most sensitive level made. Has arch top plate, two brass lipped side views, polished and tipped. Lengths, 26, 28 or 30 inches. State length wanted.

No. 9K57282 Price $2.11

$1.14 FOR A 42-INCH MASONS' ADJUSTABLE PLUMB AND LEVEL.

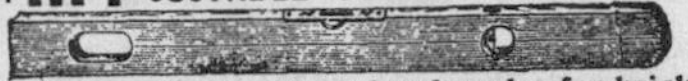

The most convenient level made, for brick or stone masons' use. Has arch top plate, two side views and adapted to be used with a plumb bob and line. Plumbs and level glasses are adjustable and can be trued up when necessary in a few moments with an ordinary screwdriver. 42 inches long.

No. 9K57286 Price $1.14

56c PER PAIR IMPROVED LEVEL SIGHTS.

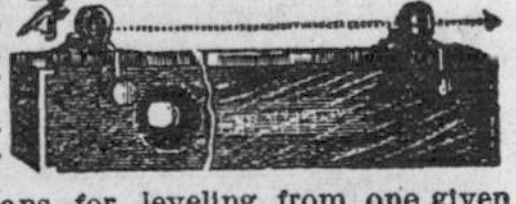

Can be quickly adjusted to an ordinary carpenters' level and afford a convenient and accurate means for leveling from one given point to another at a distance away. The price given below is for sights only. Level is not included.

No. 9K57288 Price, per pair, for wood levels 56c

8c FOR A HIGH GRADE POCKET LEVEL, PROVED AND WARRANTED TRUE.

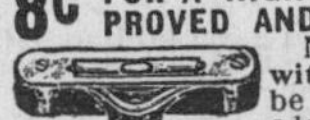

No mechanic should be without one of these. Can be quickly attached to the edge of a steel square or a straight edge. Body is iron, brass top plate.

No. 9K57296 Price 8c

28c FOR A 2½-INCH NICKEL PLATED HEXAGON POCKET LEVEL.

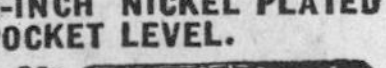

Very convenient, accurate and reliable. Have proved glasses and are warranted accurate.

No. 9K57298

Length, inches	2½	3½
Diameter, inches	⅜	7-16
Price	28c	35c

35c FOR A 3-FOOT POCKET STEEL MEASURING TAPE.

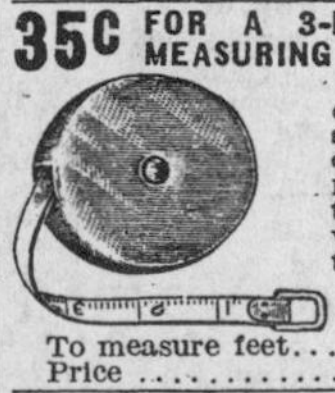

Nickel plated brass case, spring wind with stop. Marked one side only. ¼-inch tape, marked inches and sixteenths. Light and convenient for carrying in the pocket.

No. 9K57474

To measure feet	3	5	6
Price	35c	44c	56c

18c STANDARD MECHANICS' TAPE, 25 FEET, IN BRASS BOUND CASE.

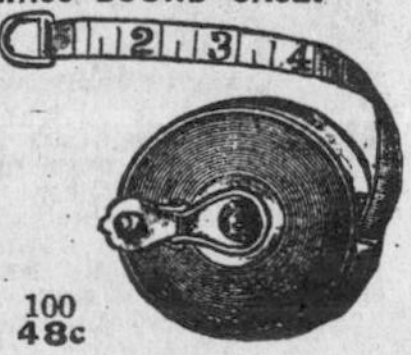

Has folding handle, with ½-inch cotton tape oiled to make it shrinkproof. This is a good low priced tape for ordinary use.

No. 9K57478

To measure feet	25	50	75	100
	18c	25c	38c	48c

CARPENTERS' BOXWOOD RULES.

Made of selected imported Turkish boxwood, nicely finished and accurately spaced. Figures and marks are cut plain and deep and will not become dim with age. Joints, edges and plates made of solid brass.

9C TWO-FOOT FOUR-FOLD ROUND JOINT BOXWOOD RULE.

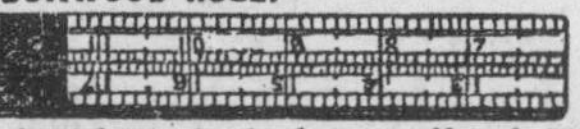

The best low priced rule ever offered. Has middle plates, spaced 8ths and 16ths, 1 inch wide.
No. 9K57502   Price..........9c

14C TWO-FOOT FOUR-FOLD SQUARE JOINT RULE, 1 INCH WIDE.

Cannot be duplicated at any retail store for less than 25c. Has edge plates at joints, spaced 8ths, 10ths, 12ths and 16ths, with drafting scale.
No. 9K57506   Price............14c

32C TWO-FOOT FOUR-FOLD FULL BRASS BOUND BOXWOOD RULE.

A strictly high class rule at a medium price. Has square joints, spaced 8ths, 10ths, 12ths and 16ths, and drafting scale, 1 inch wide.
No. 9K57524   Price............32c

47C TWO-FOOT FOUR-FOLD BRASS BOUND DOUBLE ARCH JOINT RULE.

Extra strong and substantial. Is spaced 8ths, 10ths and 16ths, drafting scale, 1½ inches wide. The best boxwood rule made.
No. 9K57530   Price............47c

43C E-Z RED TWO-FOOT FOUR-FOLD SQUARE JOINT RULE.

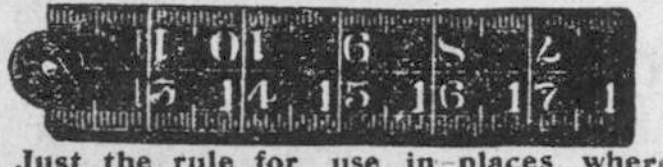

Just the rule for use in places where the light is dim or for men with poor eyesight. Has square joints spaced 8ths and 16ths, 1¾ inches wide; rule is light yellow with red figures.
No. 9K57534   Price............43c

$1.63 COMBINED RULE, SPIRIT LEVEL, SQUARE, PLUMB, BEVEL, ETC.

Can also be used as an inclinometer, brace scale, drafting scale, T-square, protractor, right angled triangle. Full directions for use with each rule. The most convenient tool a carpenter ever carried in his pocket. Useful dozens of times each day. Brass bound.
No. 9K57540   Price............$1.63

23C THREE-FOOT FOUR-FOLD ARCH JOINT BOXWOOD RULE.

Fills the bill when a 3-foot rule is needed. The quality is there. Has middle plates, spaced 8ths and 16ths, 1 inch wide.
No. 9K57544   Price............23c

38C ONE-FOOT FOUR-FOLD FULL BRASS BOUND CALIPER RULE.

Answers the purpose of a caliper and of a rule; light and easily carried in the pocket. Has arch joints, spaced 8ths, 10ths, 12ths and 16ths. Width, 1 inch.
No. 9K57548   Price............38c

16C SIX-INCH TWO-FOLD SQUARE JOINT CALIPER RULE.

Every man, whether he is a mechanic or not, ought to carry a rule. This light, low priced caliper rule is the very one for you. Spaced 8ths, 10ths, 12ths and 16ths. Width, ⅞ inch.
No. 9K57554   Price............16c

29C TWO-FOOT FOUR-FOLD ARCHITECTS' BEVELED EDGE RULE.

Used by contractors, builders, carpenters, etc., as well as architects. Has arch joints, edge plates, spaced 8ths, 10ths, 12ths and 16ths, with architects' drafting scale, 1 inch wide.
No. 9K57556   Price............29c

13C THREE-FOOT SIX-FOLD HARDWOOD ZIGZAG OR FOLDING RULE.

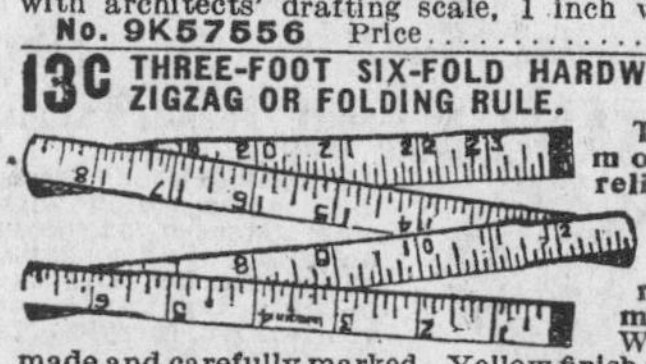

The most reliable low priced rule made. Well made and carefully marked. Yellow finish with black markings. Have spring joints, brass tips.
Length, feet...........1 2 3 4 5 6
No. 9K57560 Price. 13c 19c 24c 28c 36c

19C THREE-INCH INSIDE OR OUTSIDE POCKET CALIPER STEEL RULE.

Will caliper on the outside up to 2¾ inches. Inside up to 3½ inches. Is an extension rule from 3 to 5 inches. Makes a small steel square with 3½-inch tongue and 1½-inch body. In another form it makes a square with 3½-inch body and 1⅜-inch tongue. Graduated on both sides.
No. 9K57578   Price............19c

FULTON NAIL HAMMERS.

The best line of nail hammers offered by any concern in the United States. Made of finest tool steel, properly proportioned and tempered for service. They have the proper "hang" and will please any first class mechanic. Handles all made of selected straight grain hickory. Handles are well wedged and will not contract. Weights given do not include weight of handles.

67C FOR A No. 1½ EXTRA TOOL STEEL, NICKEL PLATED, EBONIZED HANDLE FULTON SPECIAL NAIL HAMMER.

The finest hammer it is possible to make. Because our price on this hammer is less than others charge for hammers similar in appearance, do not think for a moment our hammer is not equal to any made. This Fulton Special Hammer costs as much, or more, to manufacture than any hammer on the market. Only by selling thousands of hammers direct to the user and adding just one small profit to the original factory cost, are we able to quote a lower price than $1.00 each on these superior tools. The Fulton Special Hammer has octagonal neck and poll. Handsomely polished and nickel plated. They are proportioned right; hang right; claws are right shape to draw a nail without breaking, and the temper is right.

No. 9K57702   Size No..........1 1½ 2
Weight, without handle.........1⅛ lbs. 1 lb. 13 ozs.
Price............................68c 67c 66c

33C PER DOZ. HICKORY HAMMER HANDLES.

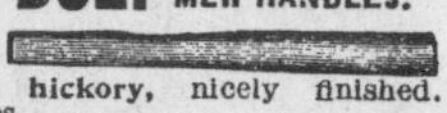

Made of selected straight grain seasoned hickory, nicely finished. Length, 14 inches.
No. 9K57741   Per doz., 33c; each, 3c

76C FOR THIS FULL SIZE HIGHEST GRADE NAIL HOLDING HAMMER.

With this hammer one can drive nails beyond ordinary reach. By the improved form of the groove this hammer will hold any wire nail not larger than 10d. Made from the best quality crucible cast steel, properly tempered and guaranteed perfect. Handles made of selected hickory, properly put in. Only one size and shape made. Weight 1 pound 2 ounces, without handle.
No. 9K57714   Price, with handle..76c

YOU PAY MORE ELSEWHERE.

25C FOR A No. 1½ SPRINGFIELD FORGED STEEL NAIL HAMMER.

The best hammer offered for the price. Made for mechanics' use and not to be compared with the cheap, poorly constructed cast goods sold by other concerns. These hammers are carefully made of select material and are much better than hammers usually sold at 48 to 60 cents each. Fitted with seasoned hickory handles. Every hammer warranted against flaws or imperfections and guaranteed to give excellent satisfaction.
No. 9K57726
Size..................1 1½ 2
Weight, ounces.......20 16 13
Price................27c 25c 23c

43C FOR SIZE 1½ BELL FACE FULTON SPECIAL NAIL HAMMER.

Forged from extra tool steel, properly tempered and not excelled in quality by any hammer on the market. Adze eye, bell face. Never-rust finish and selected hickory handle properly put in. Every hammer warranted to give satisfaction or money refunded.

RETAILERS ASK 75c FOR ONE NOT AS GOOD.

No. 9K57710
Size, No.............1 1½ 2
Weight, ozs..........20 16 13 7
Price...............44c 43c 42c 41c

FULTON GUARANTEED HATCHETS.

Correctly proportioned, properly tempered and the finest finished hatchets made. They are forged of the finest material, the cutting bit being of special formula, double refined crucible steel. The heads are of extra tough steel, made for that purpose, and guaranteed to stand the severest use. The cutting bit is inserted into the body of the hatchet and is tempered to cut and hold an edge. The handles are No. 1 selected hickory. Fulton hatchets are high grade tools, made for first class mechanics, and we positively guarantee them to be the best hatchets on the market, regardless of name or price. Order by number and give size.
PLEASE NOTE—All our hatchets have handles properly put in, but the weights given are the weights of hatchets only, before handles are put in.

44C FOR A SIZE 2 HIGH CARBON CRUCIBLE STEEL FULTON SHINGLING HATCHET, FINISHED IN COPPER BRONZE.

Regular Fulton Quality, absolutely the best. The strongest proof of the superiority of these hatchets over all others is in the immense quantities we sell. Our sales on this one number amount to far more than the entire business of a great many retailers. We buy them in immense quantities, add only one small profit to the bare cost of manufacture and actually offer them to you at a much lower price than the average local dealer pays for goods that will not compare in quality. These Fulton hatchets have polished bits, hickory handles and are finely finished and correctly tempered. Every Fulton hatchet we sell is covered by our guarantee of "satisfaction or your money back."

THE CUTTING BIT OF THIS HATCHET IS HIGH CARBON CRUCIBLE STEEL CAREFULLY TEMPERED AND FOR SERVICE - CANNOT BE EQUALED

No. 9K57750
Size..................1 2 3
Width of bit, inches..3½ 4 4½
Weight.......1 lb. 1 oz. 1 lb. 7 oz. 1 lb. 13 oz.
Price................40c 44c 48c

45C PER DOZ. HICKORY HATCHET HANDLES.

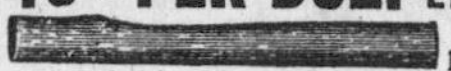

Made of selected straight grained hickory, nicely finished. Length, 14 inches.
No. 9K57791   Per doz., 45c; each..4c
Hickory Broad Hatchet Handles.
No. 9K57793
Length, inches......16 17 18
Price, each.........5c 6c 7c
Per dozen...........54c 60c 68c

71C FOR A SIZE 1 FULTON SPECIAL FULL POLISHED SHINGLING HATCHET.

Made especially for those mechanics who cannot afford to take risks where quality is concerned. Strong where strength is needed, have the proper "hang" and are without doubt the best hatchets made. They have octagon neck and round poll. High carbon crucible steel bit. Full polished, with extra select handle. Fully warranted.
No. 9K57770
Width of bit, Size in.   Wt.   Price
1   3½   1 lb. 5 oz.   71c
2   3⅞   1 lb 11 oz.   73c

41C FOR A SIZE 1 HIGH CARBON STEEL FULTON HALF HATCHET.

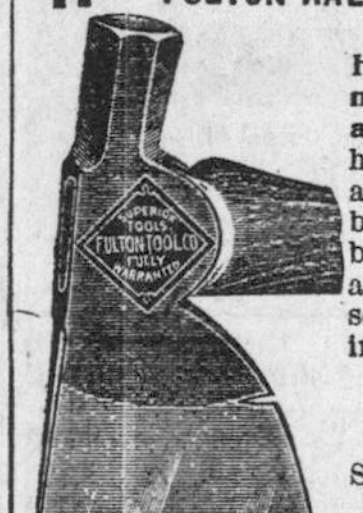

Like our other Fulton Hatchets, superior in material, workmanship and finish. The bits are highly tempered to cut and hold an edge. The body is finished in copper bronze, with polished bit and head. Handles are selected hickory, well put in. Fully warranted.
No. 9K57752
Width of bit, Size inches   Wt.   Price
1   3½   15 oz.   41c
2   3⅞   1 lb 5 oz.   44c
3   4   1 lb 11 oz.   48c

39C FOR A No. 1 CRUCIBLE STEEL FULTON LATHING HATCHET.

Cannot be duplicated elsewhere at the price. Others ask 60 cents to 75 cents for hatchets not as good as the Fulton. Handsomely finished in copper bronze, polished bit, hickory handle. Covered by our regular Fulton guarantee of satisfaction or your money back.
No. 9K57754
No.................1 2
Width, inches.....2¼ 2½
Weight........14 oz. 1 lb. 1 oz.
Price.............39c 42c

74C FOR A FULL SIZE POLISHED FULTON SPECIAL LATH HATCHET.

This hatchet is so handled that it has the proper balance or "hang." Haines Pattern, made of special high carbon crucible steel, carefully tempered. Full polished. Extra select hickory handles. Fully warranted in every particular. The handsomest lathing hatchet made. Width of bit, 2 inches. Weight, without handle, 14 ounces.
No. 9K57794
Price............74c

46C FOR SIZE 1 HIGH CARBON STEEL FULTON CLAW HATCHET.

Regular Fulton quality, finished in copper bronze, with polished bit, No. 1 hickory handle, weight does not include handle. Fully warranted.
No. 9K57756
Width of bit, ins.   3½
Weight....1 lb. 3 oz.
Price...........46c
No.................2
Width of bit, ins.   3¾
Weight....1 lb. 9 oz.
Price...........49c
No.................3
Width of bit, inches   4¼
Weight....1 lb. 15 oz.
Price...........53c

58C FOR SIZE 2 FULTON BROAD HATCHET OR CARPENTERS' BENCH AXE.

High carbon crucible steel bit finished in copper bronze, with polished bit, hickory handle. Weight does not include handle. Fully warranted.
No. 9K57758
No.................2
Width of bit, inches..4½
Weight.....1 lb. 12 oz.
Price.............58c
No.................3 4 5
Width of bit, in. 5 5½ 6
Weight...2 lbs. 2 oz. 2 lbs. 8 oz. 2 lbs. 14 oz.
Price......63c 71c 81c

$1.08 FOR A 3½-INCH CUT, EXTRA CAST STEEL FULTON CARPENTERS' ADZE.

The same high grade and finish as our other Fulton edge tools. Price does not include handle. No. 9K57840
Width of cut, inches.....3½ 4 4½
Weight, pounds...........3½ 3¾ 4
Price............$1.08 $1.11 $1.13
Fulton Tool Co. Ship Carpenters' Adze, with spur head. Warranted. No. 9K57842
Width of cut, inches.....4½ 5
Price...............$1.27 $1.29 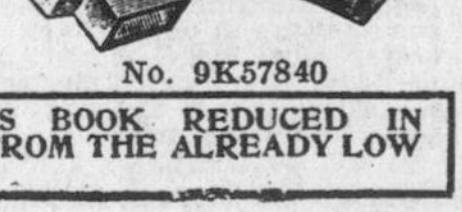
No. 9K57840

17C SELECTED QUALITY STRAIGHT GRAINED CARPENTERS' ADZE HANDLE.

Made of best seasoned stock, nicely finished. 34 inches long.
No. 9K57851   Price............17c

OVER 3,000 HARDWARE ITEMS IN THIS BOOK REDUCED IN PRICE FROM THE ALREADY LOW FIGURES QUOTED IN OUR LAST CATALOGUE.

FULTON GUARANTEED CHISELS

THE FINEST LINE OF CHISELS SOLD BY ANY CONCERN ANYWHERE. The material that goes into our Fulton chisels is the very best that money will buy. They are made by skilled workmen, finely finished, tempered right and fully guaranteed by us to be perfect in manufacture. If you buy Fulton chisels of us and find any defects in them in any way, return the goods to us within thirty days and we will refund your money. Fulton Chisels are made in a wide range of sizes and finishes as described below. We carry complete assortments of chisels in sets attractively put up and priced very low. By all means, buy a complete set as you save some money by buying them in sets and in addition get a handsome box, enabling you to properly take care of them.

FULTON SPECIAL HAND HONED LEATHER TIPPED BEVEL EDGE SOCKET FIRMER CHISELS.

THE HIGHEST GRADE, MOST CAREFULLY FINISHED CHISELS ON THE MARKET.

Made of solid cast steel, tempered by a superior process, ground and honed by hand, and will cut faster, and hold an edge longer than any other chisels made. Handles are made of extra selected white hickory tipped with four layers of solid leather. Fulton special chisels are superior to any on the market and we guarantee them to be entirely satisfactory.

No. 9K58102 Size, inches	¼	⅜	½	⅝	¾	⅞	1	1¼	1½	1¾	2
Price	28c	30c	32c	34c	36c	38c	40c	42c	44c	46c	48c	50c

$2.73 SET OF 6
FULTON SPECIAL FIRMER CHISELS.
One each size, ¼, ½, ¾, 1, 1½ and 2 inches. In fancy hardwood case fitted with hinges and hook and patent clasp to hold chisels in place.
No. 9K58104
Price, per set $2.73

$3.86 SET OF 9
FULTON SPECIAL FIRMER CHISELS.
One each size, ¼, ⅜, ½, ⅝, ¾, 1, 1¼, 1½ and 2 inches. In fancy hardwood box as illustrated.
No. 9K58105
Price, per set $3.86

$5.03 SET OF 12
FULTON SPECIAL FIRMER CHISELS.
One each size, ⅛ to 2 inches, in hardwood box as illustrated.
No. 9K58106
Price, per set $5.03

FULTON LEATHER TIPPED SQUARE EDGE SOCKET FIRMER CHISELS.

The same high grade material as our Fulton special chisels described above except that these have square edges and are not hand honed. For quality of material, finish and cutting qualities these chisels cannot be equaled at the price. They are high grade, first class tools. Warranted.

No. 9K58002

Size, inch	¼	⅜	½	⅝	¾
Price	19c	20c	21c	22c	23c	25c
Size, inches	⅞	1	1¼	1½	1¾
Price	26c	30c	31c	33c	36c	39c

Set of Six Fulton Tool Co. Socket Firmer Chisels, as described above. One each size, ¼, ½, ¾, 1, 1½ and 2 inches. Put up in neat hardwood box.
No. 9K58004 Price, per set $1.89
Set of Nine Fulton Tool Co. Socket Firmer Chisels. One each size, ¼, ⅜, ½, ⅝, ¾, 1, 1¼, 1½ and 2 inches in hardwood box.
No. 9K58005 Price, per set $2.73
Set of Twelve Fulton Tool Co. Socket Firmer Chisels, as described above. One each size, from ⅛ to 2 inches. In neat hardwood box.
No. 9K58006 Price, per set $3.49

FULTON SOCKET SLICK CHISELS.

Made of the same high grade material as our other Fulton chisels, and finished in the same superior manner. Complete with handle as shown in illustration. Length over all, about 31 inches.
No. 9K58080 Price, 3 inches $0.89
Price, 3½ inches 1.04

FULTON SOCKET FRAMING CHISEL.

Regular Fulton quality. No better goods made. Blades made of crucible cast steel properly tempered, have beveled edges and are full polished. Handles are made of selected hickory and have iron rings on end to prevent splitting. Warranted. No. 9K58060

Size, in.	⅜	½	¾	1	1¼	1½	2
Price	28c	31c	34c	37c	40c	43c	46c	49c

Set of Six Fulton Tool Co. High Grade Socket Framing Chisels, with bevel backs, hickory handles, iron rings on end. one each, ½, ¾, 1, 1¼, 1½ and 2 inches. In hardwood box.
No. 9K58062 Price, per set $2.67
Set of Eight Fulton Tool Co. Extra High Grade Socket Framing Chisels, with bevel backs. One each size, ⅜, ½, ¾, 1, 1¼, 1½ and 2 inches. In hardwood box.
No. 9K58064 Price, per set $3.56

$4.09 SET OF 12 MERRILL & WILDER'S SOCKET FIRMER CHISELS.

One each size, ⅛ to 2 inches inclusive. Blades forged from highest grade tool steel. Sharpened and hand honed ready for use. Blades measure 6 inches from shoulder. Finely polished with applewood handles. Fully warranted. Put up in fancy wood box.
No. 9K58179 With plain edges. Price, per set $4.09
No. 9K58181 With beveled edges. Price, per set 4.79

27c PER DOZEN SELECTED HICKORY CHISEL HANDLES. 
For socket framing or corner chisels, with malleable iron ferrule on end to prevent splitting.
No. 9K58210 Price, per dozen, 27c; each 3c

FULTON SPECIAL LEATHER TIPPED BUTT CHISELS WITH BEVEL EDGES.

Especially adapted for putting on hardware trim. The blades are about 3½ inches to shoulder, permitting the workman to get close to his work. The sockets are heavy and strong. They are furnished with a special shaped selected hickory handle, tipped with leather.

No. 9K58130 Size, inches	1	1¼	1½	1¾	2
Price	41c	43c	45c	48c	51c

$2.36 SET OF 5
FULTON SPECIAL BUTT CHISELS.
Made up from our regular stock of Fulton Special Butt Chisels, described above. One each size, in hardwood box, nicely finished with hinges and hook.
No. 9K58132
Price $2.36

FULTON SOCKET CORNER CHISELS.

Will pay for itself several times over by the time saved working in square mortises. Made of extra tool steel, polished outside, with handle. Handle has iron ring on end to prevent splitting. Size given is width of each face.
No. 9K58070 Price, ¾ inch 59c
Price, 1 inch 60c

36c PER DOZEN LEATHER CAPPED CHISEL HANDLES. 
Made of selected white hickory, with three layers of solid sole leather in cap. Socket firmer.
No. 9K58214 Price, per dozen, 36c; each 4c

14c FOR A SELECTED HICKORY MALLET COMPLETE WITH HANDLE.

The best mallet ever offered for such a low price. Head is 6¼x3⅛x2¾ inches; mortised handle. Weight, about 1½ lbs.
No. 9K58262 Price 14c
Square Lignum Vitae Mallets. Head is 6½x 3¾x3¾ inches. Weight, 3½ pounds.
No. 9K58264 Price 27c

37c FOR A 2-INCH FACE NEVER-SPLIT RAWHIDE BOUND MALLET. 
The handsomest, most durable and finest finished mallet ever made. The spring of the hide facing cushions the bowl.
No. 9K58272
2 -inch face. Price 37c
2½-inch face. Price 46c
3 -inch face. Price 58c

10c FOR A HALF-INCH FULTON CRUCIBLE TOOL STEEL COLD CHISEL. 
Forged from a special grade of tough steel, carefully tempered, have polished blades and turned polished heads. We could not produce a better chisel. Size indicates diameter of octagon stock from which chisel is made. No. 9K58310

Size, inch	½	⅝	¾
Price	10c	16c	22c

28c POLISHED NICKEL PLATED CAST STEEL TICKET OR CARD PUNCH.
The best punch on the market for the price. Has spring which keeps it open. Assorted holes; used for punching cards, tickets, etc.
No. 9K58354 Price 28c

The 50c kind.

38c FULTON 7-INCH RAZOR STEEL HOLLOW GROUND DRAWING KNIFE.

Forged from best cast steel tempered by a special process, and warranted to outcut and outlast any drawing knife made. Can be kept sharp with one-half the labor required for oval blade knives. Has selected hickory handles. No. 9K57602

Size out, inches	7	8	10	12
Price	38c	42c	46c	49c

22c SUPERIOR ADJUSTABLE SPOKE SHAVE WITH RAISED HANDLES. 
10 inches long, 2⅛-inch cutter.
No. 9K57630 Price 22c

16c ADJUSTABLE DOUBLE CUTTER IRON SPOKE SHAVE WITH CUTTERS.
1½-inch hollow and straight cutters, 10 inches long.
No. 9K57642 Price 16c

$3.58 OUR "PREMIER" OUTFIT OF FULTON GUARANTEED EDGE TOOLS.
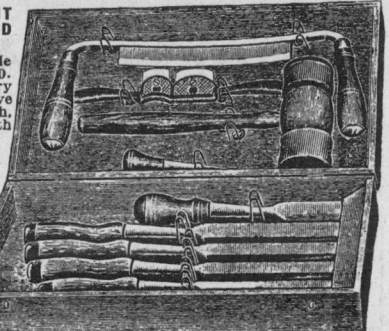
The most complete outfit of high grade edge tools ever offered for less than $5.00. Every item regular Fulton quality, every item fully guaranteed. Consists of five Fulton socket firmer chisels, one each, sizes, ¼, ½, ¾, 1 and 1¼ inches with leather top hickory handles. 1 Fulton special socket butt chisel, 1½-inch with bevel edges and four-layer leather top hickory handle. 1 Fulton 8-inch razor blade drawing knife, 1 Fulton spoke shave with straight and concave steel cutters. 1 forged steel square reamer bit, 1 steel socket awl and 1 mallet 2½-inch face with rawhide head. All in well made, strong hardwood box with hinges and hooks. An outfit which could not be bought anywhere for less than $5.00.
No. 9K57662
Price, complete, only $3.58

76c FULTON 8-INCH FOLDING HANDLE RAZOR BLADE DRAWING KNIFE.

RETAILERS ASK $1.35
A practical compact tool for the carpenter's outfit. Handles to protect cutting edge. Forged from best steel. Tangs extends through handles. Fully warranted.
No. 9K57606

Size cut, inches	8	10	12
Price	76c	88c	99c

65c GOODELL'S HIGH GRADE REMOVABLE HANDLE SPOKE SHAVE. 
Has polished rosewood handles, 2-inch cast steel cutter; either handle may be removed.
No. 9K57646 Price 65c

18c SET OF 4 KNURLED NAIL SETS. 
With cup or hollow point. Just the thing for starting screws which are rusty or have broken heads. Tempered at both ends. Size of points 2-32, 3-32, 4-32 and 5-32.
No. 9K58320
Price, each, any size 5c
Per dozen 53c
No. 9K58322 Set of Four Knurled Nail Sets. Assorted sizes, Price, per set 18c

7c TEMPERED CAST STEEL KNURLED PRICK PUNCH.
Better than the kind others sell for 10c to 15c. Diameter, ⅜ inch.
No. 9K58330 Price 7c

7c TEMPERED CAST STEEL KNURLED CENTER PUNCH. 
No better center punch made at any price. Diameter, ⅜ inch.
No. 9K58334 Price 7c

48c FOR A HEAVY SUBSTANTIAL ECONOMICAL NAIL PULLER. 
Saves time, labor, cases and nails. No merchant, carpenter or plumber can afford to be without a nail puller. It pays for itself.
No. 9K58370 Price 48c

88c THE GENUINE "CYCLOPS," THE HIGHEST GRADE NAIL PULLER MADE.

Forged from special grade of tool steel, hardened and tempered by perfected process to greatest resistance and toughness. The lever handle on this tool continues to form part of the foot. By use of this handle control is given over both jaws. It is impossible for jaw to slip with this tool, and it brings the nail out straight.
No. 9K58372 Price 88c

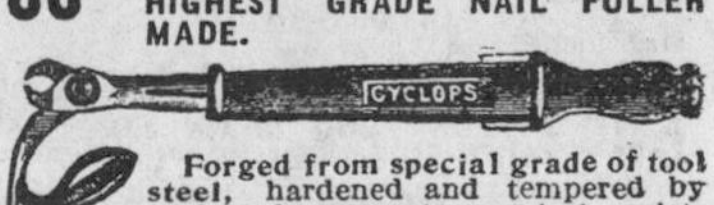

FULTON GUARANTEED FILES

MADE OF CRUCIBLE CAST STEEL, TEMPERED BY A SECRET PROCESS, AND ARE SUPERIOR TO ALL OTHERS.

FULTON FILES cut faster, last longer, wear better and give more general satisfaction than any other files made. They are made for service, sold on merit and by buying from us you pay no middlemen's profits. You get more **real value** for your money when you buy a Fulton file than when you buy any other kind. We sold over **40,000 dozen Fulton Guaranteed Files** last year, which is the strongest proof of the superiority of these files over all others. Thousands of mill men, machinists, etc., depend on us for their files and will not use any but a Fulton brand.

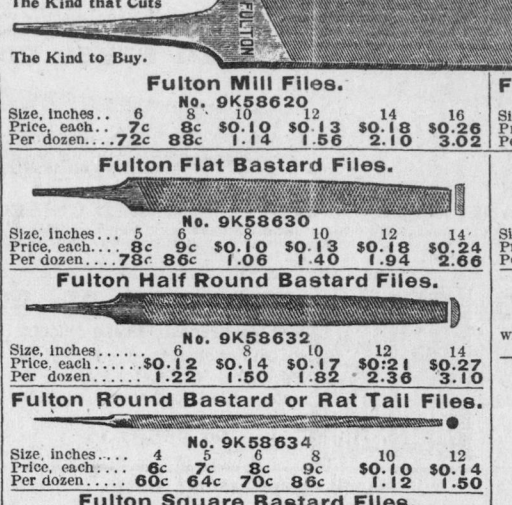

Over 3,000 items in Hardware alone have been still further reduced from the low prices in our last catalogue.

The Kind that Cuts

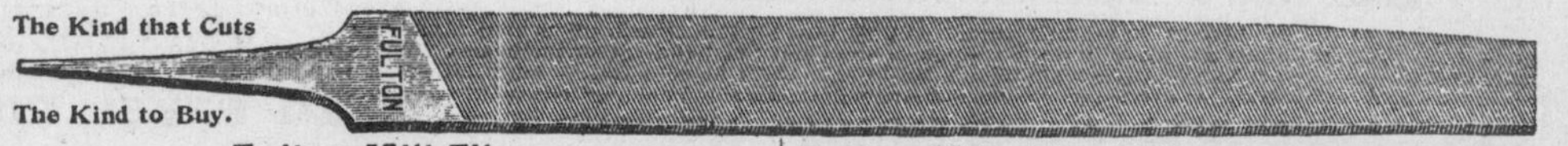

The Kind to Buy.

Fulton Mill Files.

No. 9K58620

Size, inches	6	8	10	12	14	16
Price, each	7c	8c	$0.10	$0.13	$0.18	$0.26
Per dozen	72c	88c	1.14	1.56	2.10	3.02

Fulton Mill Files With One Round Edge.

No. 9K58622

Size, inches	8	10	12	14
Price, each	$0.09	$0.12	$0.15	$0.22
Per dozen	1.04	1.38	1.74	2.58

Fulton Double End Taper Files.

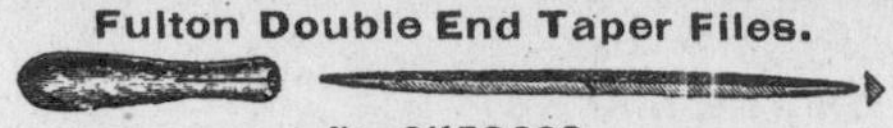

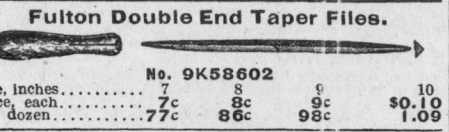

No. 9K58602

Size, inches	7	8	9	10
Price, each	7c	8c	9c	$0.10
Per dozen	77c	86c	98c	1.09

Fulton Flat Bastard Files.

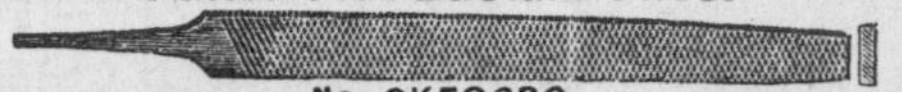

No. 9K58630

Size, inches	5	6	8	10	12	14
Price, each	8c	9c	$0.10	$0.13	$0.18	$0.24
Per dozen	78c	86c	1.06	1.40	1.94	2.66

Fulton Half Round Wood Rasps.

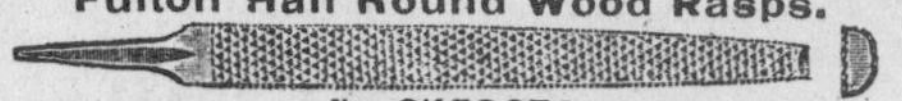

No. 9K58670

Size, inches	8	10	12	14
Price, each	$0.20	$0.27	$0.36	$0.47
Per dozen	2.28	3.10	4.10	5.50

Fulton Taper Files.

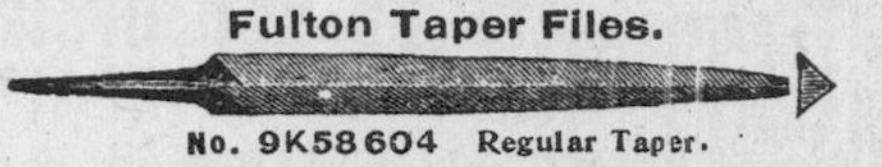

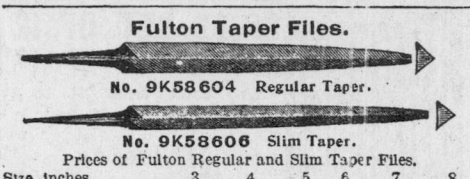

No. 9K58604 Regular Taper.

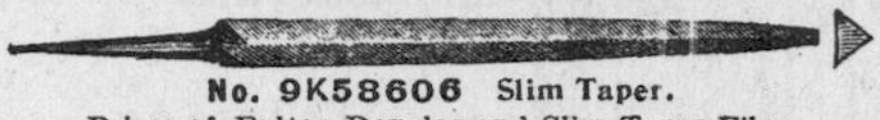

No. 9K58606 Slim Taper.

Prices of Fulton Regular and Slim Taper Files.

Size, inches	3	4	5	6	7	8
Price, each	4c	5c	6c	7c	8c	$0.10
Per dozen	42c	44c	52c	68c	86c	1.09

Fulton Half Round Bastard Files.

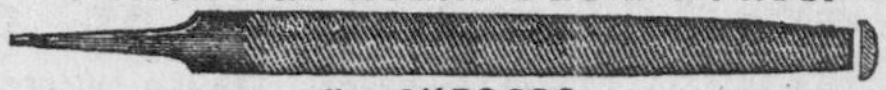

No. 9K58632

Size, inches	6	8	10	12	14
Price, each	$0.12	$0.14	$0.17	$0.21	$0.27
Per dozen	1.22	1.50	1.82	2.36	3.10

Fulton Auger Bit File.

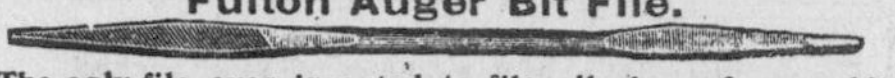

The only file ever invented to file all sizes of auger bits without filing the screw and lip and spoiling your tool.
No. 9K58692 Price, per dozen, 98c; each.......9c

Fulton Round Bastard or Rat Tail Files.

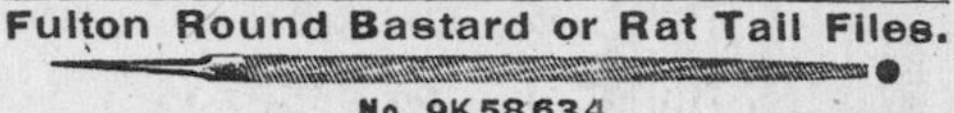

No. 9K58634

Size, inches	4	5	6	8	10	12
Price, each	6c	7c	8c	9c	$0.10	$0.14
Per dozen	60c	64c	70c	86c	1.12	1.50

Fulton Assorted Needle Files.

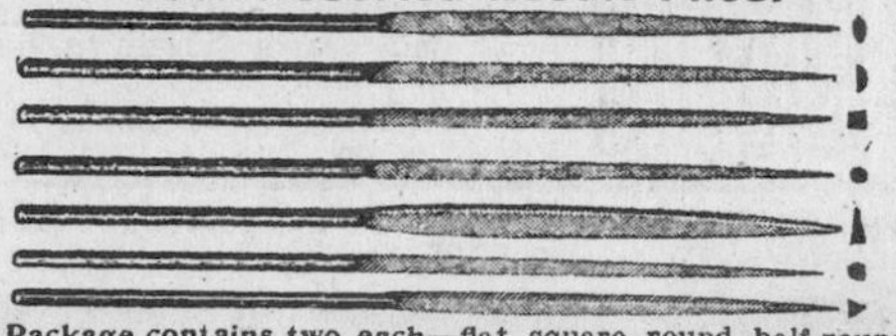

Package contains two each—flat, square, round, half round and oval; one each—three square and knife. We do not break packages.
No. 9K58694 Price, per dozen, assorted as above. 69c

Weed's Special Slim Blunt Hand Saw File.

A great favorite with professional saw filers.

No. 9K58610

Size, inches	5	5½	6
Price, each	8c	$0.09	$0.10
Per dozen	92c	1.02	1.12

Fulton Square Bastard Files.

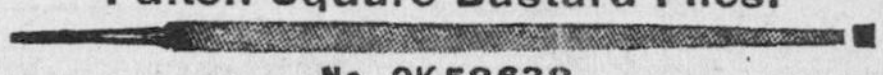

No. 9K58638

Size, inches	4	5	6	8	10	12
Price, each	7c	8c	9c	$0.10	$0.14	$0.18
Per dozen	76c	82c	92c	1.10	1.48	2.04

8c FOR A STEEL WIRE FILE BRUSH OR CLEANER.

The most durable file brush in the market.

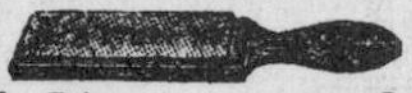

No. 9K58594 Price..........8c

12c PER DOZEN FILE HANDLES WITH FERRULES.

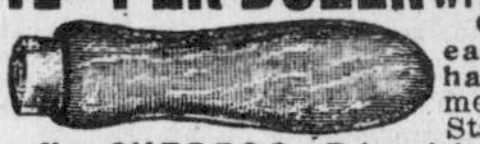

Others ask 5c each for these handles. Large, medium or small. State size.
No. 9K58596 Price, 4 for........5c
Per dozen..........12c

8c INTERCHANGEABLE FILE HANDLE AND TOOL HOLDER.

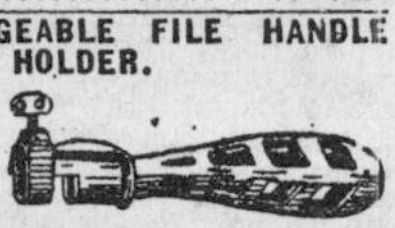

Made of malleable iron, 5 inches long, japanned finish. It will hold equally well all size files, twist drills, gimlets, screwdrivers and all tools with shanks less than ⅜ of an inch square, round or flat.
No. 9K58598 Price..........8c

16c CARPENTERS' COMBINED PINCERS, CLAW AND SCREWDRIVER, 6-INCH.

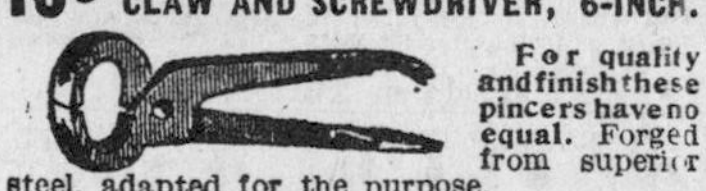

For quality and finish these pincers have no equal. Forged from superior steel, adapted for the purpose.
No. 9K58402

Size, inches	6	8	10	12
Price	16c	20c	24c	28c

19c FOR A 4-INCH FULTON FLAT NOSE BOX JOINT PLIER.

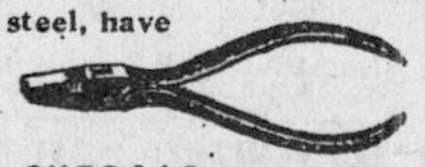

Made of forged steel, have polished jaws, and one of the best fitted and strongest pliers on the market.
No. 9K58410

Size, inches	4	5	6
Price	19c	23c	28c

36c FOR A 5-INCH FULTON SIDE CUTTING BOX JOINT PLIER.

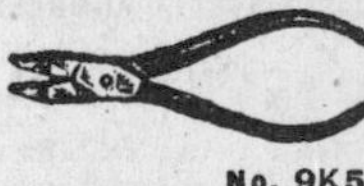

Made of the best tool steel. Has polished jaws and raised cutters. The strongest and most popular plier on the market today.
No. 9K58418

Size, inches	5	6	7	8
Price	36c	44c	53c	68c

93c FOR A 6-INCH FULTON SIDE CUTTING LINEMAN'S PLIER.

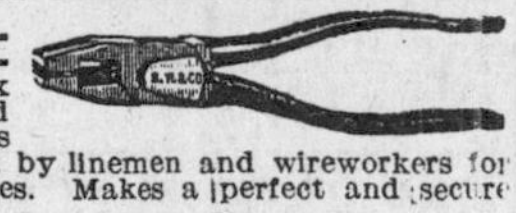

With splicing attachment. Box joint raised cutters. This plier is used by linemen and wireworkers for splicing wires. Makes a perfect and secure connection.
No. 9K58422

Size, inches	6	7	8
Price	93c	$1.20	$1.35

59c FULTON LONG CHAIN NOSE LAP JOINT SIDE CUTTING PLIERS.

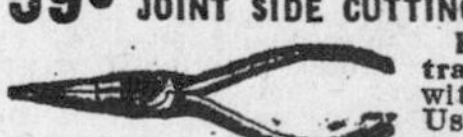

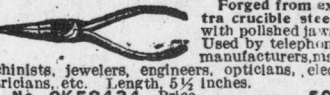

Forged from extra crucible steel, with polished jaws. Used by telephone manufacturers, machinists, jewelers, engineers, opticians, electricians, etc. Length, 5½ inches.
No. 9K58424 Price..........59c

23c FOR A 4-INCH FULTON HAND FORGED END CUTTING NIPPER.

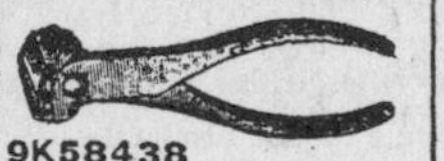

Lap joint, hand forged from crucible steel. The best end cutting nipper made.
No. 9K58438

Size, inches	4	5	6
Price	23c	29c	34c

15c FOR A HOUSEHOLD WIRE CUTTER AND GAS BURNER PLIER.

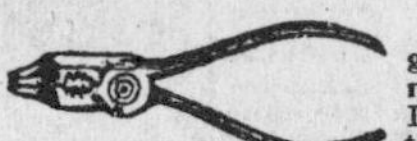

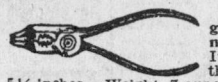

Well made, of good material and nicely finished. It's a good one for the money. Length, 5½ inches. Weight, 7 ounces.
No. 9K58450 Price..........15c

48c FOR A 6-INCH FULTON FORGED STEEL COMBINATION PLIER.

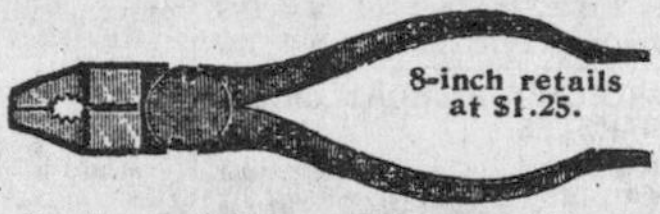

8-inch retails at $1.25.

Combination Burner, Wire and Side Cutting Pliers. A valuable tool in any household or shop. Has screwdriver and reamer on ends of handle, making this a tool suitable for all purposes.
No. 9K58454

Size, inches	6	8	10
Price	48c	65c	97c

33c COMPOUND LEVER FORGED STEEL END CUTTING NIPPERS.

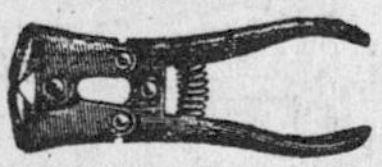

Well made and nicely finished. Have coil spring. Carefully tempered and tested. Will cut all kinds of soft wire, but not intended for piano wire. Length, 5½ inches.
No. 9K58466 Price..........33c

26c FULTON SPECIAL 6-INCH BUTTON PATTERN WIRE CUTTER AND PLIER.

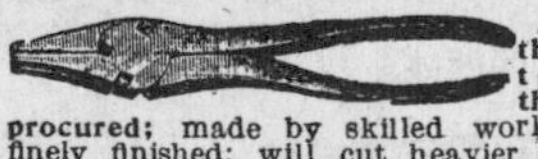

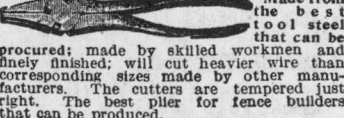

Made from the best tool steel that can be procured; made by skilled workmen and finely finished; will cut heavier wire than corresponding sizes made by other manufacturers. The cutters are tempered just right. The best plier for fence builders that can be produced.
No. 9K58472

Size, inches	4½	6	8	10
Price	22c	26c	34c	44c

43c PER DOZ. JAPANNED QUILT FRAME CLAMPS.

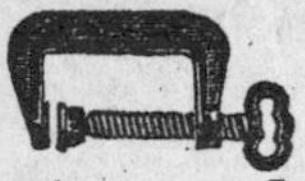

Made of malleable iron, nicely japanned, with improved ball and socket head on screw. Can be used as a cabinet clamp. 3-inch opening.
No. 9K58520
Price, per dozen, 43c; each..........5c

WE HAVE ALWAYS SOLD **GOOD HARDWARE** at lower prices than any other house. On over 3,000 Hardware items prices are **STILL FURTHER REDUCED** in this catalogue.

12c FOR A 3-INCH MALLEABLE IRON CLAMP WITH STEEL SCREW.

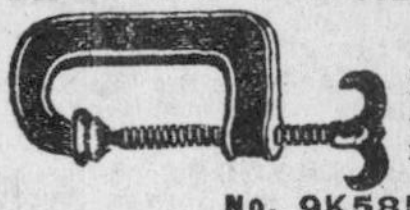

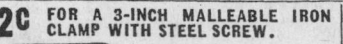

Has perfect swivel head, cut thread and is by far the best clamp made.
No. 9K58524

Opens, inches	Weight, lbs.	Price	Opens, inches	Weight, lbs.	Price
3	1½	12c	6	2	26c
4	1½	16c	8	3½	36c
5	1¾	20c	10	5¼	43c

35c FOR A 2½-INCH SELECTED HARDWOOD BENCH SCREW.

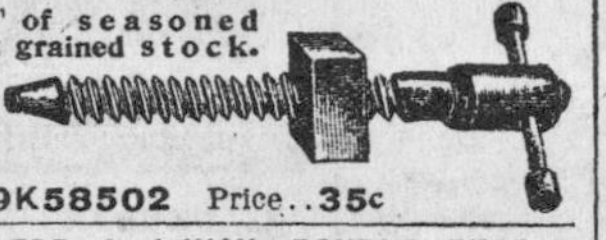

Made of seasoned straight grained stock. The best bench screw made.
No. 9K58502 Price..35c

27c FOR A 1-INCH DOUBLE THREAD WROUGHT IRON BENCH SCREW.

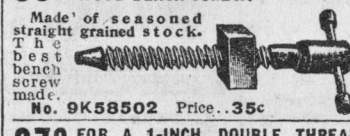

The threads on these bench screws are machine cut, they have wood handles and movable collars. They are in every way superior to the ordinary screws furnished by others, and we guarantee them to be entirely satisfactory.

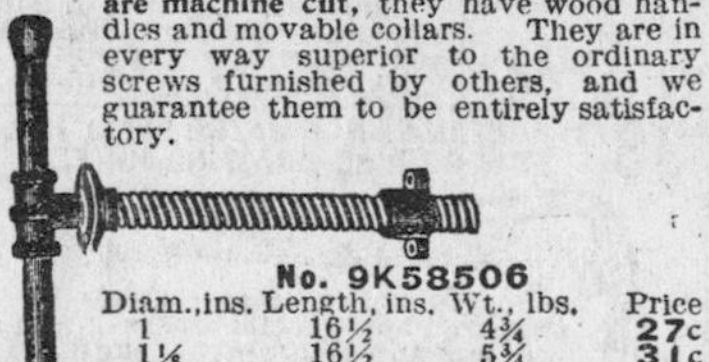

No. 9K58506

Diam., ins.	Length, ins.	Wt., lbs.	Price
1	16½	4¾	27c
1⅛	16½	5¾	31c
1¼	17½	6½	38c
1½	19½	10	62c

21c FOR AN 8-INCH JAW HARDWOOD HAND SCREW CLAMP.

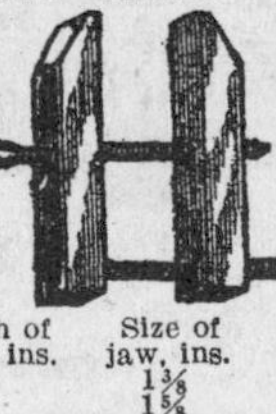

Twice Our Prices at Retail.

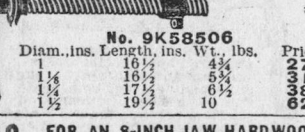

Made of selected seasoned stock, threads are accurately cut and tool is finished in a superior manner throughout. Illustration shows complete set.
No. 9K58540

Length of jaw, ins.	Length of screw, ins.	Size of jaw, ins.	Price, per set
8	10	1⅜	21c
10	12	1⅜	27c
12	14	1¾	31c
16	18	2¼	37c
20	24	2⅝	59c

49c FOR A 12-INCH CABINET MAKERS' STEEL BAR ECCENTRIC CLAMP.

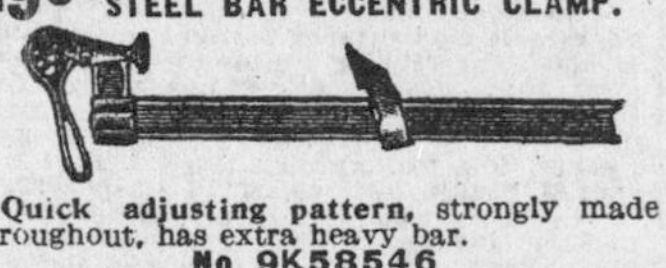

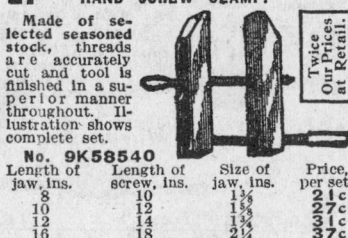

Quick adjusting pattern, strongly made throughout, has extra heavy bar.
No. 9K58546
Price, 12-in...49c Price, 30-in...75c
Price, 18-in...58c Price, 36-in...82c
Price, 24-in...66c Price, 48-in...97c

25c SCREW ADJUSTING REVERSIBLE CAST STEEL BENCH STOP.

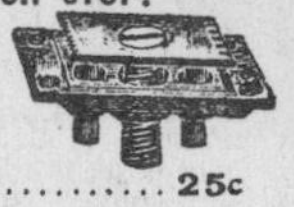

Made of best quality material. Will answer every purpose and give satisfaction.
No. 9K58514 Price..........25c

24c FOR A 1¼-INCH JAW HINGED HAND VISE.

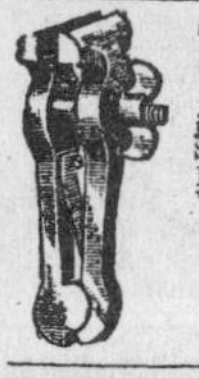

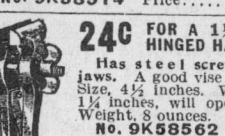

Has steel screw and chilled jaws. A good vise for the price. Size, 4½ inches. Width of jaws, 1¼ inches, will open 7-16 inch. Weight, 8 ounces.
No. 9K58562 Price, 24c

Reduced prices in this book make your savings greater than ever.

20c IMPROVED CLAMP VISE WITH STEEL SCREW AND CUT THREAD.

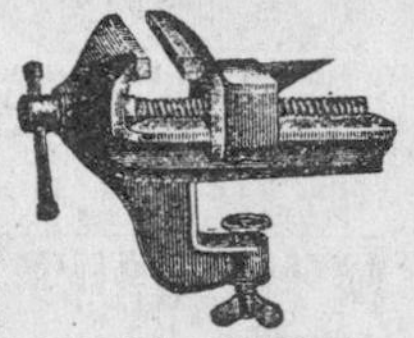

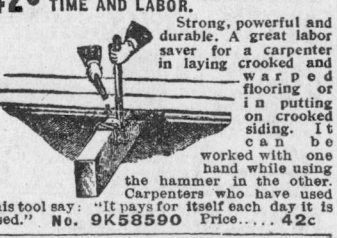

Far better than the cheap malleable or cast iron vises offered by others and will fully meet the requirements of jewelers, dentists, watchmakers, etc. Thread works smoothly. The jaws are true, the tops and ends of jaws being ground and polished. Lever is solid polished steel, body is enameled.

Catalogue Number	Width of Jaw, inches	Weight, pounds	Price
9K58570	1½	1¼	20c
9K58574	2	2	38c

42c PATENT FLOORING CLAMP SAVES TIME AND LABOR.

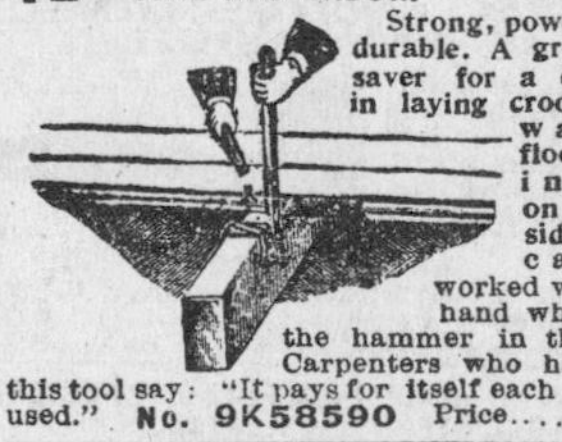

Strong, powerful and durable. A great labor saver for a carpenter in laying crooked and warped flooring or in putting on crooked siding. It can be worked with one hand while using the hammer in the other. Carpenters who have used this tool say: "It pays for itself each day it is used." No. 9K58590 Price.....42c

$1.78 PER DOZEN SPRING STEEL SHINGLING BRACKETS, LIGHT, STRONG, SAFE.

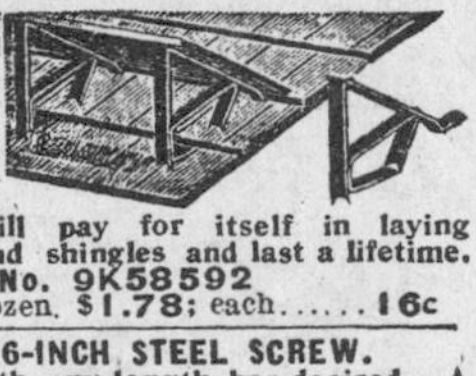

Made of spring steel firmly riveted together. Quickly put up and taken down, leaving no nail holes in the roof. Will pay for itself in laying twenty thousand shingles and last a lifetime.
No. 9K58592
Price, per dozen, $1.78; each......16c

45c GENUINE HERCULES CLAMP ATTACHMENT WITH 6-INCH STEEL SCREW.

Can be used with any length bar desired. A favorite with carpenters and cabinet makers. Has ⅝-inch steel screw. Castings are very strong and heavy. Will fit wood bar 1⅜x2½ inches.
No. 9K58552 Price, without wood bar, per dozen, $5.25; each..........45c

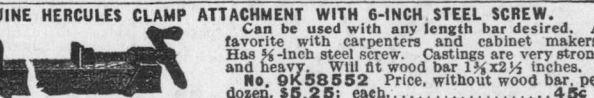

15c FOR A 6x2-INCH QUICK CUT OIL STONE IN HARDWOOD CASE.

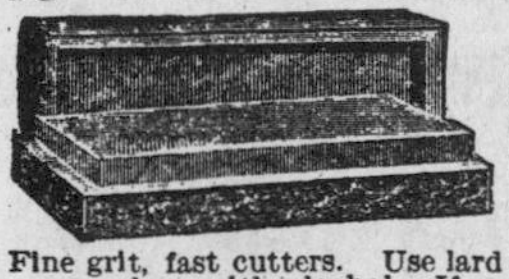

The best oil stones on the market for general purposes. Guaranteed to give satisfaction and not to glaze. Fine grit, fast cutters. Use lard oil; if necessary, reduce with alcohol. If used with water only they surpass the ordinary oil stones. Mounted in a finely finished chestnut case.
No. 9K58708

Size of stone, inches	3½x1¼	6x2	7x2	8x2
Price	8c	15c	17c	20c

34c FOR A 1-POUND GENUINE WHITE WASHITA OIL STONE.

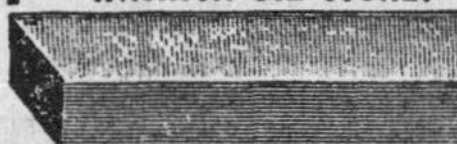

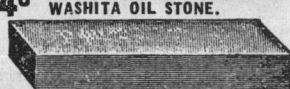

A fine tough grit, of uniform texture, no hard spots; free grit and a quick cutting stone. The most satisfactory stone for carpenters' and general woodworkers' tools, warranted not to glaze. Without case.
Weight, about, pounds 1 1½
No. 9K58720 Price..34c 52c
Extra White Washita Oil Stone, same as preceding number except medium hard, fine grit. For tools of hard temper requiring a very smooth edge.
Weight, about, pounds 1 1½
No. 9K58722 Price..35c 53c
Standard White Washita Oil Stone, extra selected quality, without case.
Weight, about, 1 pound.
No. 9K58730 Price............22c
Soft Arkansas Oil Stones, specially adapted for use on fine edged, delicate tools. The smoothest cutting stone on the market. Without case.
Weight, about, pounds 1 1½
No. 9K58740 Price........95c $1.33

14c SELECTED ROUND EDGE STANDARD WHITE WASHITA SLIP.

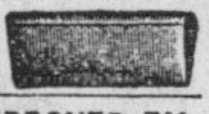

The same high quality as the Washita stones described above.
No. 9K58750 Price.. 14c

19c FOR AN 8x2-INCH IMPROVED EMERY OIL STONE.

A keen edge may be obtained in half the time required by the use of the quarried stone. Made with coarse and fine side, combining two stones in one, coarse side used for taking out nicks and for rapid cutting; fine side for putting on a fine, keen edge. Made of best sharp Turkish emery.
No. 9K58702 Size, 8x2 inches.
Price..............................19c

64c FOR A 6-INCH KITCHEN GRINDSTONE, WITH JAPANNED IRON FRAME.

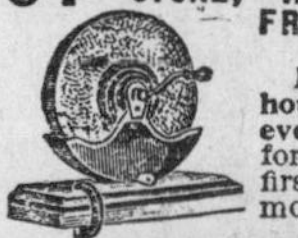

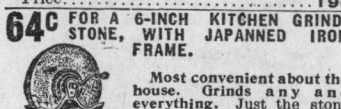

Most convenient about the house. Grinds any and everything. Just the stone for butcher knives, etc. Has first quality stone, well mounted.
No. 9K58780

Diam. of stone..	6 in.	8 in.	10 in.
Price	64c	73c	96c

$1.54 OUR QUICK AND EASY EMERY GRINDER, COMPLETE.

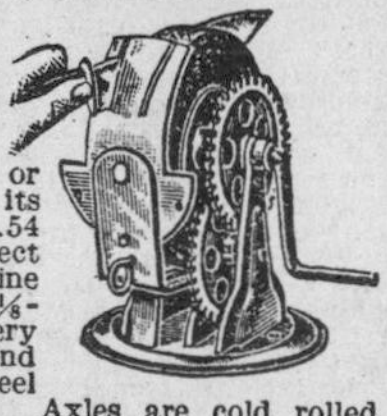

The strongest, most substantial and practical Emery Grinder ever built to sell at a price so low. Nothing else like it or as good for twice its price. For only $1.54 we offer this perfect little grinding machine complete with a 6x1⅛-inch high grade emery wheel. The frame and gears are solid steel and indestructible. Axles are cold rolled steel. Bearings are babbitted, and a speed of 1,500 revolutions per minute can easily be maintained without heating or binding. The Quick and Easy Emery Grinder will sharpen any small edged tool in one-fifth the time it takes to do the same work on a grind stone. Has a special attachment for holding knives at the right angle for perfect grinding and an adjustable rest for other tools. Especially recommended for grinding drill bits and other tools. Weight, complete, 4 pounds.
No. 9K58782 Price...........$1.54

$4.97 FULTON FOOT POWER STEEL FRAME EMERY GRINDER.

RETAIL DEALERS ASK $8.00

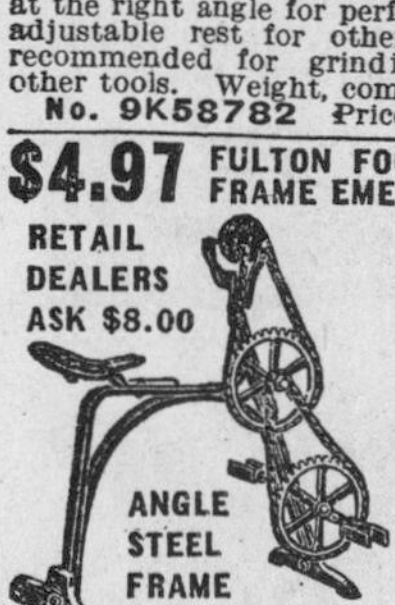

A thoroughly practical grinder for blacksmiths, repair shops or home use. Far superior to the cheaply constructed, light weight grinders offered by others. Frame and posts which support working parts are heavy channel steel. Provided with adjustable steel seat. Operated by compound sprocket gear. Has positive motion, no belts or ratchets, to slip and is strong and rigid. Tool rest adjustable as to height or bevel. Steel axle ⅝ inch, ½ inch between flanges. Will take wheels up to 6x1½ inches. Emery wheel 6x1¼ inches furnished with each machine. Polishing and buffing wheels can also be used. Full directions with each machine. Covered by our usual guarantee of "satisfaction or your money back." Weight, crated, 40 pounds.
No. 9K58784 Price, complete..$4.97

$3.04 IMPROVED QUICK CUT, DOUBLE TREADLE, BALL BEARING, ANGLE STEEL FRAME GRINDSTONE.

IMITATIONS RETAIL FOR $4.25.

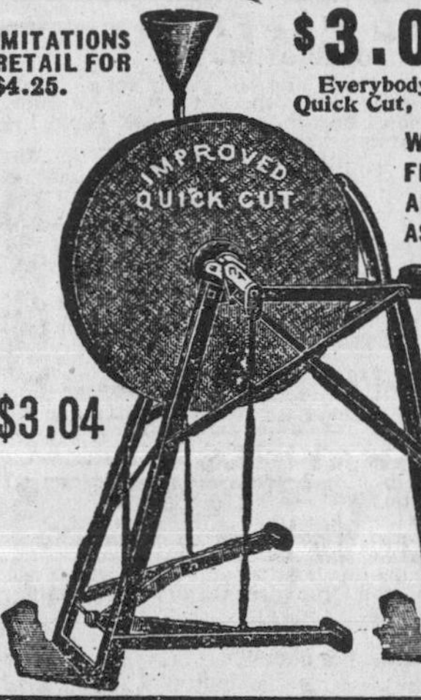

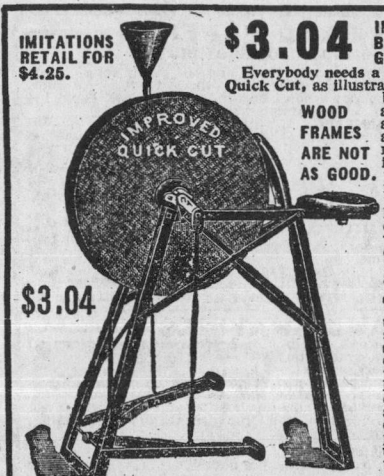

WOOD FRAMES ARE NOT AS GOOD.

$3.04

Everybody needs a Mounted Grindstone, and in our Improved Quick Cut, as illustrated, we offer for only $3.04 the biggest and best value ever put out. Frame is made of angle steel, so strong that it is indestructible and so rigid that there is no vibration. The axle is cold rolled steel, true as a die, and runs in ball bearings, which wonderfully increase the power of the machine and lighten the labor. Our Improved Quick Cut Stone runs so easy that the strength of a small boy will easily operate it and grind perfectly the hardest tool. Note the many good features of the Improved Quick Cut Mounted Stone with its angle steel frame and ball bearings, over all imitations.

SEE THE BICYCLE PATTERN — ADJUSTABLE SEAT —

the double tread pedals, the water cup and solid guard to protect the operator. The stone is the best Berea grit, 20 to 22 inches diameter and 2 to 2½ inches thick. Just the right size, true and perfect. Shipped knocked down and carefully crated with face of stone protected by wood strips. Weighs about 85 pounds, and we guarantee safe delivery. The Improved Quick Cut is the perfect stone and the one you want. Send us your order for one of these fine stones today. We guarantee it will please you.
No. 9K58760 Price..........$3.04

49c FOR A 40-POUND GENUINE BEREA GRIT UNMOUNTED GRINDSTONE.

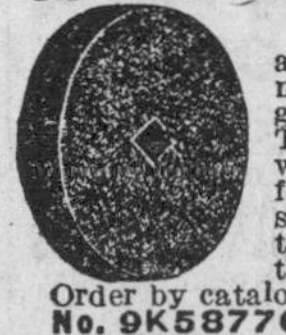

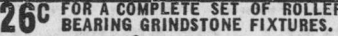

Our genuine Berea Stones are the quickest cutting, nicest finished, truest eyed grindstone on the market. There is no tool about the workshop or home more useful or necessary than a grindstone. The best costs but a trifle as compared with the time lost using a "dull" stone.
Order by catalogue number and size.
No. 9K58770

Size Number	Diameter, about, inches	Thickness, about, inches	Weight, about, pounds	Price, each
1	16	2	40	$0.49
2	18	2¼	50	.63
3	20	2½	60	.76
4	22	2½	80	.93
5	24	2¾	100	1.24
6	26	2¾	120	1.49
7	28	3	150	1.88
8	29	3¼	175	2.19
9	30	3½	200	2.48

29c HUNTINGTON PATTERN IMPROVED EMERY WHEEL DRESSER.

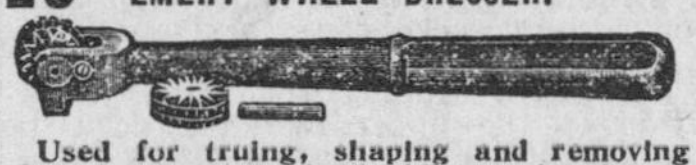

Used for truing, shaping and removing glaze from emery wheel while running, leaves the wheel clean and sharp and in the best possible condition for cutting.
No. 9K58810 Price, with two sets of cutters..............................29c
Extra cutters for emery wheel dressers, quality the best.
No. 9K58812 Price, per set........6c
Per dozen sets..........................69c

26c FOR A COMPLETE SET OF ROLLER BEARING GRINDSTONE FIXTURES.

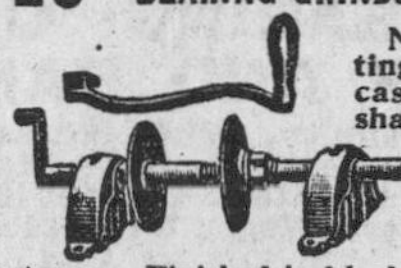

No danger of splitting stone, as is the case when a common shaft is used and held with wooden wedges. Adjustable for different thickness stones. Finished in black japan and are the best fixtures on the market for the price.
No. 9K58776

Length, inches..	15	17	19	21
For stone, pounds	40	60	80	100
Price, per set	26c	28c	30c	34c

59c PER SET IMPROVED BALL BEARING GRINDSTONE FIXTURES, COMPLETE.

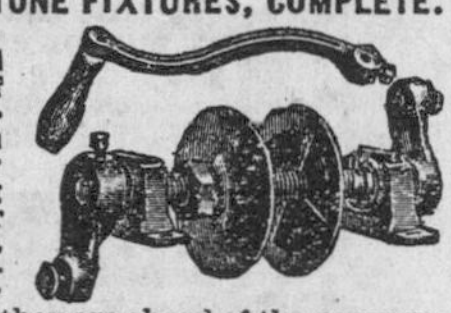

If your grindstone is mounted on a set of these ball bearing fixtures you will no longer dread grinding day. Mount your grindstone on a set of these fixtures and see for yourself how far they are ahead of the common fixtures generally sold. These fixtures save half the labor of grinding. They will support stones of varying thicknesses from 1½ to 3½ inches and can be mounted on any kind of a wood frame. Axle is solid steel and cannot break. Journal boxes are iron and journal cases are steel with finest ball bearings. Journal cases are so constructed that balls cannot possibly fall out and be lost. Flanges tighten up with two loose nuts, avoiding danger of breaking stone. Complete as illustrated with two cranks and one handle.
No. 9K58778 Price, per set.....59c

HOWARD CORUNDUM WHEELS.

Outcut and Outlast Any Emery Wheels Made.

Corundum is the greatest cutting substance known and is the cheapest when the amount of work done is considered. A man can do more grinding with a Howard Corundum Wheel than with any other wheel in existence. We sell thousands of Howard Corundum Wheels every year and have never had a dissatisfied customer. Send us a trial order for Howard Corundum Wheels and you will never use any other. In ordering always tell us what purpose wheel is to be used for so we can send you one adapted to the work you want to do. Be sure to mention size mandrel hole you want.

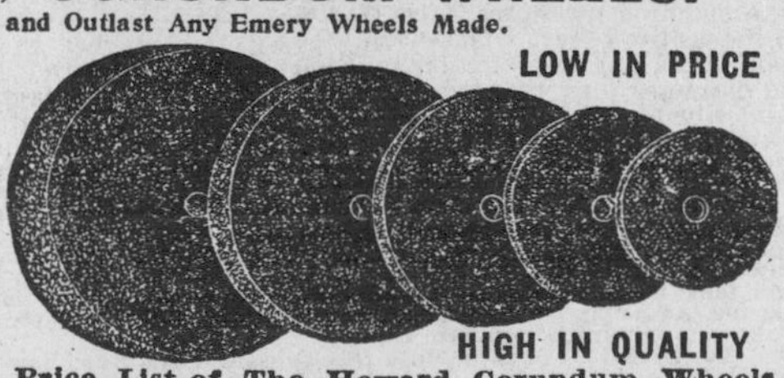

LOW IN PRICE

HIGH IN QUALITY

DIRECTIONS FOR ORDERING. In ordering always give the details of the work to be ground, whether iron or steel and whether surface or edge work and if for wet or dry grinding. ALSO GIVE THE DIAMETER, THICKNESS, SIZE OF HOLE, SHAPE OF FACE AND SPEED OF WHEEL.

Price List of The Howard Corundum Wheels.
No. 9K58806 Flat Face. No. 9K58808 Round Face

Diameter, inches	Thickness, inches ¼	⅜	½	¾	1	1¼	1½	2
2	$0.11	$0.14	$0.15	$0.18	$0.19	......	......	......
3	.15	.20	.24	.29	.33	......	......	......
4	.19	.24	.28	.34	.40	......	......	......
5	.25	.30	.35	.45	.55	$0.65	$0.75	......
6	.35	.40	.44	.60	.77	.93	1.09	$1.40
8	.53	.59	.65	.90	1.15	1.40	1.65	2.15
10	.75	.84	.92	1.25	1.59	1.93	2.25	2.90
12	.90	.95	1.00	1.50	1.85	2.25	2.65	3.50
14	......	1.29	1.56	2.12	2.65	3.20	3.70	4.80
16	......	......	......	2.70	3.40	4.10	4.80	6.20
18	......	......	......	3.30	4.25	5.10	6.10	7.90

14c FOR A No. 2 SEAMLESS RUSTPROOF COPPERIZED STEEL OILER.

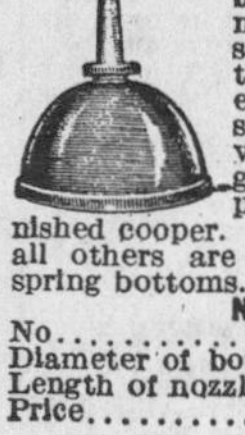

Think of the hundreds of times you need an oil can. Order one of these and get the best. They are strong, well made and durable. Equal to solid copper in everything but the price. They are heavy electro copper plated on the inside to prevent rust and to prevent the oil from becoming gritty. On the outside they perfectly resemble solid burnished copper. The 9-inch nozzles are bent; all others are straight. Have clock steel spring bottoms.
No. 9K26950

No.	2	4	6
Diameter of bottom..	3⅜	3⅝	4⅛
Length of nozzle, ins..	3	9	3
Price	14c	17c	25c

5c FOR A ½-PINT STRAIGHT OR BENT SPOUT OIL CAN.

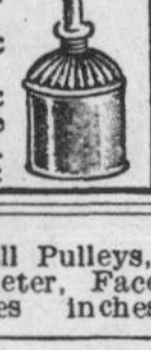

You can't afford to do without an oiler when you can get one at such a low price.
No. 9K26975 Bent spout. Price 5c
No. 9K26976 Straight spout. Price.............................5c
Seamless steel, copper plate inside and outside, holds about ½ pint.
No. 9K26983 Price..........14c

Over 3,000 hardware items in this book reduced in price from the already low figures quoted in our last catalogue.

$2.38 TWO-WHEEL EMERY WHEEL STAND, 2-INCH PULLEY.

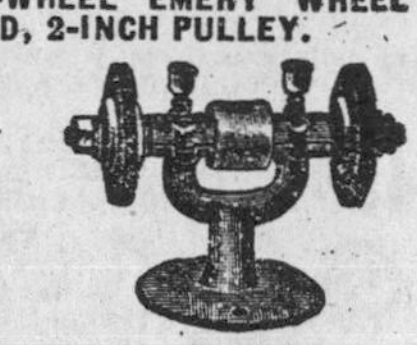

A good serviceable machine with dustproof oilers and adjustable bearings for power; will run two 6-inch emery wheels, 1 inch thick; has ¾-inch steel spindle, ½ inch between flanges. Pulley, 1⅜-inch on face. Price does not include emery wheels. Complete with lag screws. Weight, 9 pounds.
No. 9K58820 Price..........$2.38

$5.07 TWO-WHEEL EMERY WHEEL STAND, 2¼-INCH PULLEY.

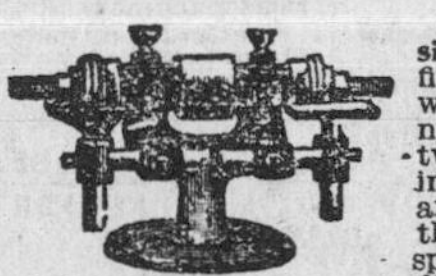

This is a full sized stand, nicely finished, strong where strength is needed. Will run two wheels 10 inches in diameter and 1½ inches thick, has steel spindle ⅝ inch in diameter in bearings, ¾ inch between flanges. The bearings are babbitted, 2 inches long and adjustable; mounted with brass oil cups. Pulleys 2¼ inches diameter, 1¾-inch face. Two adjustable knuckle joint rests, as shown. Complete with lag screw. Weight, 18 pounds.
No. 9K58822 Price..........$5.07

$7.58 TWO-WHEEL EMERY WHEEL STAND, 3½-INCH PULLEY.

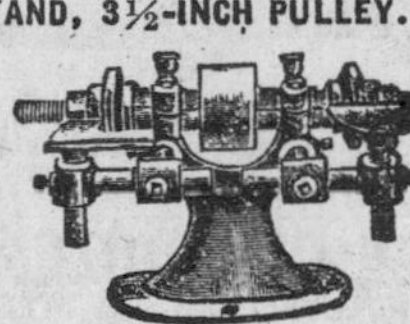

Order one of these stands and a couple of our corundum wheels. You will then be equipped for grinding anything that comes to hand. Will run two wheels 12 inches in diameter and 2 inches thick; has steel spindles 13 inches long and 1 1-16 inches diameter in bearings, 1 inch between flanges. The bearings are babbitted, 2¼ inches long and same style as engine lathe bearings, mounted with brass oil cups. Pulleys 3½ inches diameter, 2¼-inch face, complete with lag screws. Weight, 33 pounds.
No. 9K58824 Price..........$7.58

$9.66 TWO-WHEEL EMERY WHEEL STAND, 5-INCH PULLEY.

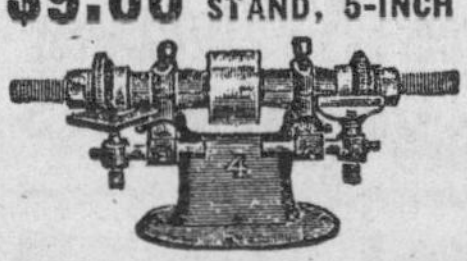

This Emery Wheel Stand is far superior to the cheap light weight stands offered by others. Will run two wheels 16 inches in diameter and 2½ inches thick, has steel spindles 1⅜ inches diameter in bearing, 1¼ inches between flanges. The bearings are babbitted 4 inches long and same style as engine lathe bearings, mounted with brass oil cups. Pulley, 5 inches diameter, 4¼-inch face, provided with two rests which are knuckle jointed and can be set at any desired angle. Complete with lag screws. Weight, 76 pounds.
No. 9K58826 Price..........$9.66

69c POLISHING HEAD FOR POWER, WITH TWO-INCH PULLEY.

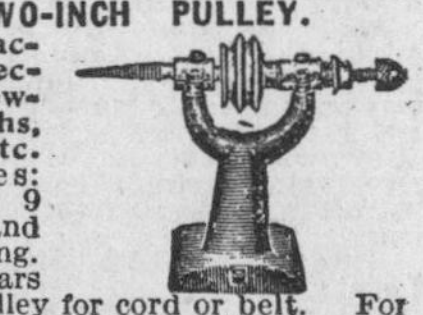

A thoroughly practical machine, recommended for jewelers, gunsmiths, model workers, etc. Height, 6 inches; length of spindle, 9 inches; taper left hand screw, 2½ inches long. Drill chuck and collars on other end. Pulley for cord or belt. For wheels not larger than 6 inches in diameter and ¾ inch thick. Complete with lag screws. Weight, 3 pounds.
No. 9K59630 Price..........69c

COUNTER SHAFTING.

We carry four sizes of counter shafts adapted for use with the grinders illustrated above and for general power purposes

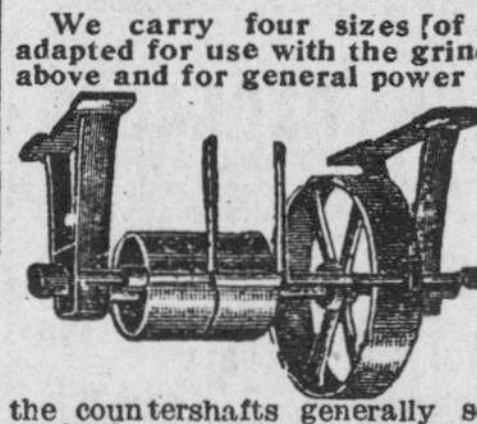

Our counter shafts are made by expert machinists, of the very best materials, carefully fitted and we guarantee them to be superior to the countershafts generally sold and to be perfectly satisfactory in use. All counter shafts are furnished complete as illustrated, with driving pulley, tight and loose pulleys, belt shifter, shifter rod and heavy, strong and rigid cast hangers. Order by number from list below. Price includes lag screws for attaching.

	Shaft, Diameter, inches	Small Pulleys, Diameter, inches	Small Pulleys, Face, inches	Drive Pulleys, Diameter, inches	Drive Pulleys, Face, inches	Weight, pounds	Price, Complete
No. 9K59620	⅞	3¼	1¾	8	1¾	21	$2.83
No. 9K59622	1⅛	5	2¼	10	2¼	34	4.23
No. 9K59624	1⅛	6	3	12	2¾	49	5.72
No. 9K59626	1¼	6	4½	16	4	75	7.96

19c FOR A COMPLETE SOLDERING OUTFIT, COPPER, SCRAPER, ETC.

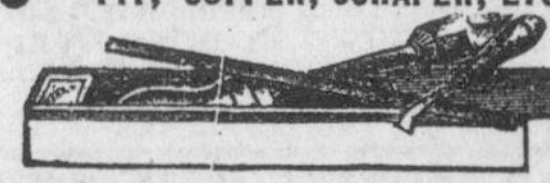

Will pay for itself in a short time mending pots, pans, etc. Consists of a small soldering copper, a scraper, a bar of solder and a box of resin.
No. 9K58906 Price..........**19c**

46c FULTON SPECIAL ADJUSTABLE RIVETING MACHINE.

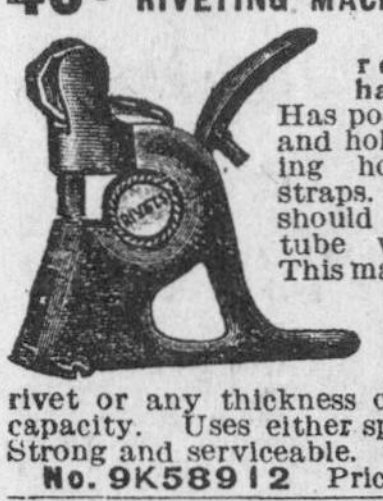

The regular 75-cent retail kind. The handiest riveter made. Has pocket to contain rivets and hollow punch for punching holes in harness or straps. A block of wood should be used under the tube when using punch. This machine will do its work equal to the highest priced machine made. It is instantly adjustable to any length of rivet or any thickness of leather within its capacity. Uses either split or tubular rivets. Strong and serviceable.
No. 9K58912 Price..........**46c**

23c LEVER RIVETING MACHINE FOR TUBULAR (HOLLOW) RIVETS.

YOU PAY MORE ELSEWHERE.

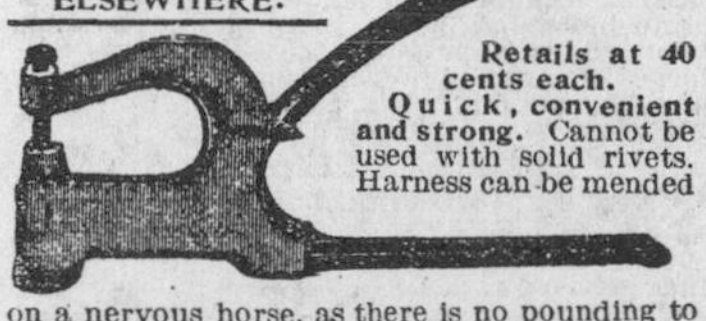

Retails at 40 cents each. Quick, convenient and strong. Cannot be used with solid rivets. Harness can be mended on a nervous horse, as there is no pounding to disturb it. Simply pulling down the lever punches the hole and completes the job. See No. 9K58922 for rivets to use with this machine.
No. 9K58914 Price..........**23c**

32c PER DOZEN BOXES
HOLLOW TUBULAR STEEL RIVETS.

Japanned, for use with above or similar riveting machines, put up in boxes containing 50 rivets, assorted lengths, from 3-16 to ½ inch long, for general repair work on harness, etc.
No. 9K58922 Price, per box..........**3c**
Per dozen boxes..........**32c**

Hollow Tubular Rivets, japanned, put up in boxes containing 100 rivets, all the same length.

No. 9K58924

Length, inch	3-16	4-16	5-16	6-16	7-16
Price, per box	7c	8c	9c	10c	11c
Length, inch	8-16	9-16	10-16	11-16	12-16
Price, per box	12c	13c	14c	15c	16c

26c PER DOZEN BOXES
SLOTTED STEEL CLINCH RIVETS.

Retails at 60c.

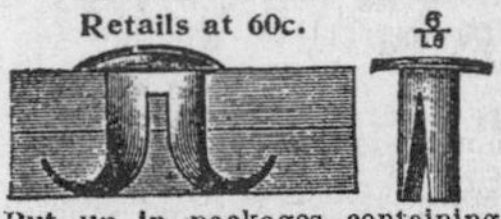

Made of coppered annealed steel. No set or other tool is required except a common hammer. Put up in packages containing 100 rivets. Assorted lengths. We do not break packages.
No. 9K58930 Price, 3 packages for **8c**
Per dozen packages..........**26c**

29c PER POUND ASSORTED LENGTHS, No. 8 COPPER RIVETS AND BURRS.

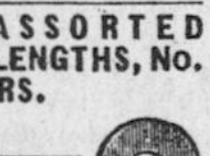

Made of the very best Michigan copper, absolutely pure. They are manufactured by improved machinery, which guarantees a perfect fit of every burr to the rivet. We carry these rivets in all desirable lengths and sizes, as per list below. Please mention size, number and length.

No. 9K58932 Size 8.

					Assorted.
Length, inches	⅜	½	⅝	¾	⅜ to ¾
Per 1 pound	28c	28c	28c	28c	29c

No. 9K58934 Size 9.

					Assorted.
Length, inches	⅜	½	⅝	¾	⅜ to ¾
Per 1 pound	29c	29c	29c	29c	30c

No. 9K58936 Size 10.

					Assorted.
Length, inches	⅜	½	⅝	¾	⅜ to ¾
Per 1 pound	31c	31c	31c	31c	32c

No. 9K58938 Size 12.

					Assorted.
Length, inches	⅜	½	⅝	¾	⅜ to ¾
Per 1 pound	33c	33c	33c	33c	34c

71c DOZEN PACKAGES
COPPERED IRON RIVETS AND BURRS.

Made of soft iron heavily coppered. Put up in ½-pound packages containing about 60 rivets and burrs. Size No. 8, assorted lengths.
No. 9K58940 Price, per package..........**7c**
Per dozen packages..........**71c**

9c STEEL RIVET SETS FOR SETTING BURRS ON HARNESS RIVETS.

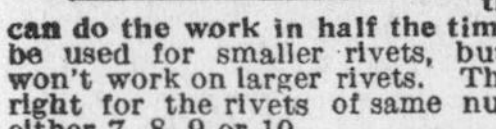

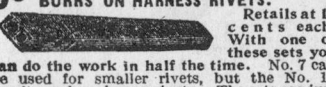

Retails at 15 cents each. With one of these sets you can do the work in half the time. No. 7 can be used for smaller rivets, but the No. 10 won't work on larger rivets. The sets are just right for the rivets of same number. Sizes, either 7, 8, 9 or 10.
No. 9K58944 Price..........**9c**

7c BEST TOOL STEEL SADDLERS' HOLLOW DRIVE PUNCH.

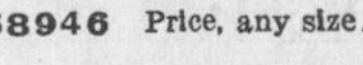

Ends are highly tempered. Sizes, 2, 4, 6, 8 or 10.
No. 9K58946 Price, any size.....**7c**

FIRST QUALITY SAND PAPER
NOT THE CHEAP, FLIMSY KIND SOLD BY OTHERS.

The paper which forms the back is extra heavy, very tough and not easily torn. Only the best quality, sharp, flint sand is used, and this is applied with superior glue. We guarantee our sand paper to be equal to any and superior to most on the market. Nos. 1 and 1½ are commonly used; No. 00 is the finest and No. 3 the coarsest. State numbers wanted when ordering. 24 sheets to the quire. If a quire is made up of assorted numbers we charge the sheet price. Quire price is not good for less than a quire of one number.

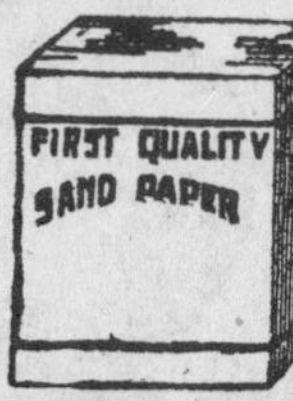

No. 9K58860

Number	00	0	½	1	1½	2	3
6 sheets for	5c	5c	5c	6c	6c	7c	7c
Per quire	13c	13c	14c	15c	16c	18c	19c

FIRST QUALITY EMERY CLOTH.

No. 9K58862 **Made of best Turkish emery,** on heavy, tough, cloth back. Well made and will wear a long time.

Number	00	0	½	1	1½	2
3 sheets for	9c	9c	9c	10c	11c	12c
Per quire	55c	57c	59c	61c	64c	69c

STEEL WOOL AND SHAVINGS

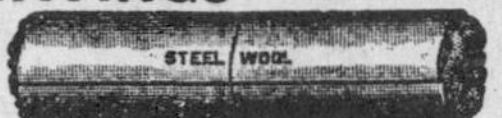

Steel Wool is a mass of fine fibers of steel, resembling curled hair, which, while sharp, does not scratch, but will cut as smoothly as the finest sand paper, emery or pumice stone. For many purposes it is superior to sand paper, etc. Used for rubbing down fillers and varnishes; in fact, it takes the place of sand paper or pumice stone, and will be found a much better article to use. Steel shavings is a coarse grade and is used for removing rust from iron preparatory to painting, also for cleaning floors or any surface of old varnish.

No. 30K2670

No. 0. Very fine, per pound..........45c	No. 3. Fine, per pound..........30c
No. 1. Fine, per pound..........35c	Steel Shavings. Per pound..........25c

BALL BEARING COMBINATION RIP, CUT OFF AND BAND SAW MACHINE.

A Marvel of Ingenuity. The Lightest Running, Fastest Cutting, Strongest Made and Lowest Priced Saw Machine in the World. Designed Especially for Carpenters, Cabinet Makers, Picture Frame Makers, Box Manufacturers, Wagon Builders and Wood Workers in General.

$58.71

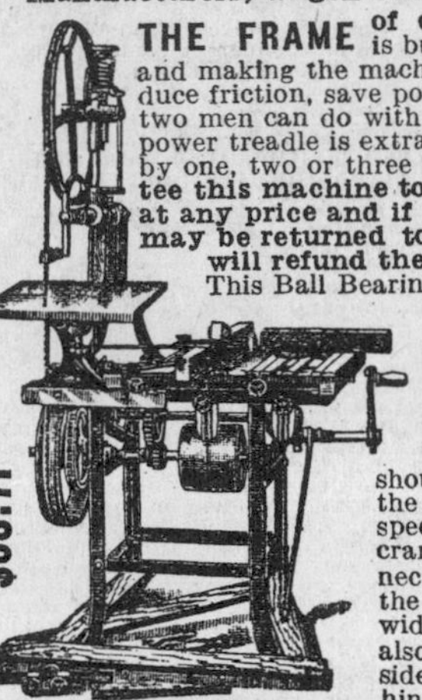

No. 9K54211

THE FRAME of our Improved Ball Bearing Saw Machine is built of angle steel, giving the greatest rigidity and making the machine strong and durable. The ball bearings reduce friction, save power and enable one man to do more work than two men can do with any other machine on the market. The foot power treadle is extra long and on heavy work power can be applied by one, two or three men. **Without regard to price we guarantee this machine to be the best machine made, unmatchable at any price and if not satisfactory after thirty days' use it may be returned to us according to our instructions and we will refund the full price paid, including transportation.** This Ball Bearing Saw Machine may be run either by foot, hand or belt power. The machine is especially adapted for ripping, cross cutting, grooving and dadoing as well as band sawing. With drive wheel on lower mandrel as shown in illustration and power applied by sprocket chain, the saw has a speed of nine revolutions to each turn of the crank. For heavy ripping the drive wheel should be fitted to the upper mandrel and with the lower mandrel thrown in gear the saw has a speed of three revolutions to each turn of the crank. The hand crank and foot treadle are connected with each other and both may be used at the same time. The rip guide is adjustable any width up to 24 inches. The cross cut guide is also adjustable and slides in iron grooves on either side of the saw. The saw table is 3 feet long, hinged in back to raise and lower, giving an adjustment of 3 inches in depth of cut on the machine. The saw table proper is made of iron and the machine measures 2 feet 9½ inches high and covers a floor space of 3 feet 6 inches by 4 feet. The driving wheel is 18 inches in diameter and weighs 40 pounds. Any size circular saw with ⅞-inch mandrel hole and up to 10 inches in diameter may be used. Tight and loose belt pulleys are 8 inches in diameter and when used should make 400 revolutions per minute, giving a speed on the saw of 1,200 revolutions per minute. Horse power required, 1½. The band saw cuts to the center of a 40-inch circle and the upper wheel has a tilting adjustment to lead the saw as desired and also for lining it up. Both band wheels have rubber bands for the saw to run on, and the machine will take band saws from ⅛ to ¾ inch wide and from 11 feet 2 inches to 12 feet long. The band saw table is made of iron planed perfectly true; measures 14¼x17½ inches and can be tilted at an angle for sawing a bevel. The distance from circular saw to band saw frame is 16 inches, but if necessary band saw can be set off entirely to clear the circular saw table for long cross cutting. With a helper to operate the machine remarkably heavy sawing can be perfectly done. Shipping weight, securely crated, about 325 pounds. Shipped only from factory in Southern Ohio.

No. 9K54211 **Combined Rip, Cross Cut and Band Saw,** complete, as illustrated, with five ball bearing journals, foot and hand power attachment, one rip guide, one angle adjustable cross cut guide with adjustable stop, 10-inch rip saw, 8-inch cross cut saw, ⅜-inch band saw 12 feet long, belt shifter, tight and loose belt pulleys, 8-inch diameter and 3-inch face. Price..........**$58.71**

No. 9K54204 **Machine, without band saw and band saw attachment,** otherwise exactly as illustrated above. Shipping weight, crated, about 285 pounds. Price....**$38.86**

No. 9K54330 **Band Saw Attachment alone without machine,** with upper and lower wheel and ⅜-inch band saw 12 feet long. Price..........**$19.89**

Jointer Attachment.

$7.31

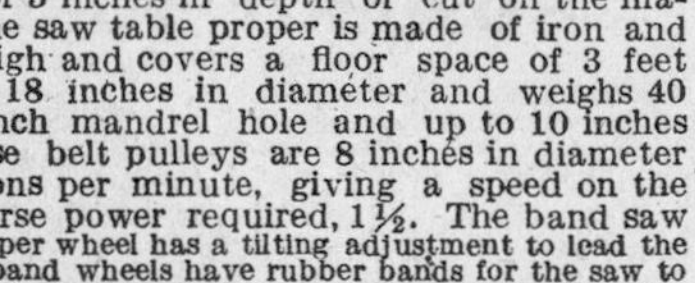

This attachment is used for chamfering, beveling or squaring an edge. Made of two steel plates adjustably set in front and back of cutter head. Plates are lined up with the top of table by four screws with lock nuts. The plate in back of cutter head can be raised equal to the depth of cut made by the knives so the material will have a support to pass on the level. Jointer attachment is made in two sizes.

No. 9K54216 **Jointer Attachment,** complete with head to cut 1¾ inches wide. Plates, 2 inches by 2 feet. Price, complete with screws, ready to attach to machine....**$7.31**

No. 9K54217 **Jointer Attachment,** complete with head to cut 3 inches wide. Plates, 3½ inches by 2 feet. Price, complete with screws, ready to attach to machine......**$9.29**

Cutter Heads for Jointing, Tenoning, Gaining, Moulding, Etc.

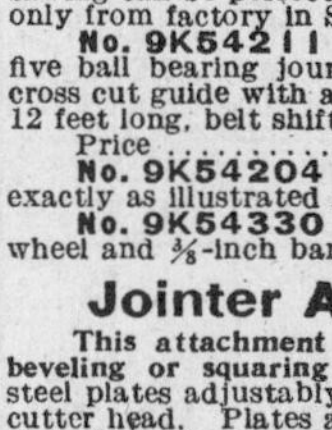

A thoroughly practical and useful attachment. Bits are securely held in place and head can be safely run at high speed. Bits may be set in head slanting or at right angles as desired. Spur or side cutters can be used on both sides. Adjustable in cut, ½ inch to 3 inches by using proper size bit. Diameter of head, 4 inches. Cutting edge circles 5½ inches. Depth of cut adjustable up to ¾ inch. We furnish straight bits only, but they can be shaped up to make any moulding desired.

No. 9K54275 **Head to fit ⅞-inch mandrel,** with straight bits 1¾ inches wide, for jointing, chamfering, etc. Price..........**$1.93**

No. 9K54276 **Head to fit ⅞-inch mandrel,** with bits 3 inches wide. Price..........**$2.62**

No. 9K54277 **Side Cutters,** for tenoning or gaining. Price..........**.35**

Adjustable Dado and Grooving Head.

No. 9K54260 **Adjustable Groover,** 7 inches in diameter, with ⅞-inch mandrel hole, cuts ⅛ to 1½ inches wide. Price..........**$4.91**

No. 9K54261 **Adjustable Groover,** 9 inches in diameter, ⅞-inch mandrel hole, cuts ⅛ to 1¾ inches wide. Price..........**$5.86**

16c FOR A FULL SIZE CAST STEEL HOLLOW SPRING PUNCH.

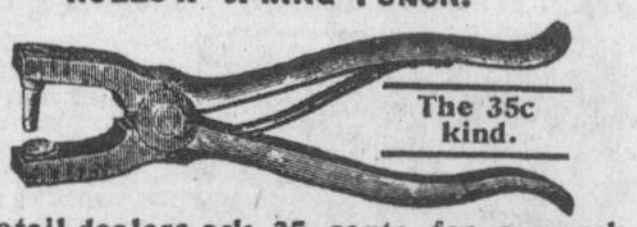

Retail dealers ask 35 cents for a punch not as good. Length, 7½ inches. Tube sizes are 4, 6, 8 and 10. State size wanted.
No. 9K58950 Price..........**16c**

36c REVOLVING SPRING PUNCH WITH FOUR DIFFERENT SIZE TUBES.

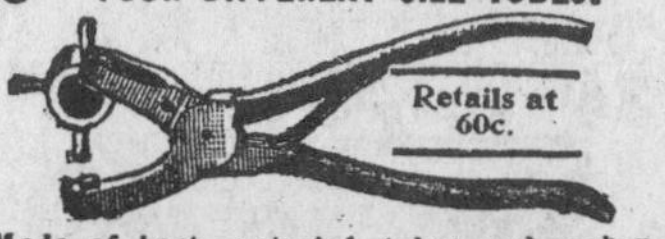

Made of best material, tubes and spring highly tempered. Usually retail at 60 cents.
No. 9K58952 Price..........**36c**
Same as above, except has six tubes of different sizes.
No. 9K58954 Price..........**45c**

$1.57 LATEST IMPROVED MITRE BOX AND SAW GUIDE COMPLETE.

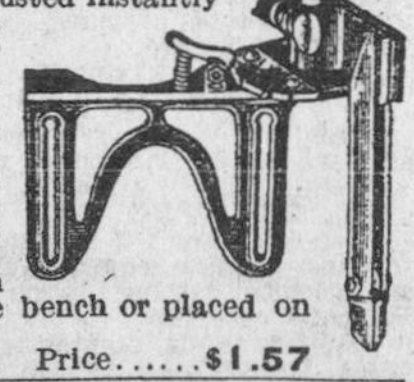

Light, strong, simple and accurate. Can be adjusted instantly to cut square or at angles of 25, 30 and 45 degrees. Any panel or hand saw may be used. Just the thing for clapboarding and general house finishing. Will cut mouldings of any width or depth. Can be fastened to the bench or placed on top of the work.
No. 9K58982 Price.....**$1.57**

$2.78 PERFECTION PATTERN MITRE BOX, STRONG AND ACCURATE.

Regular price, $5.00.

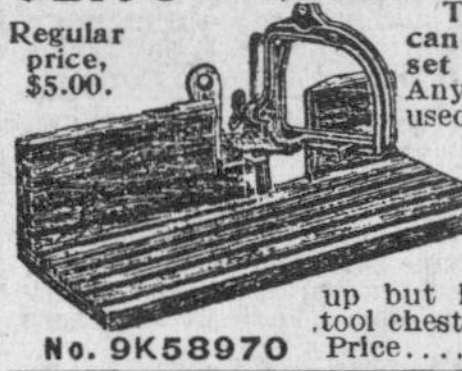

The saw guide can be instantly set at any angle. Any saw may be used, back saw, panel or hand. For cutting to exact depths use a back saw. Takes up but little space in tool chest.
No. 9K58970 Price..........**$2.78**

$8.72 FOR A LANGDON ACME MITRE BOX, COMPLETE WITH SAW.

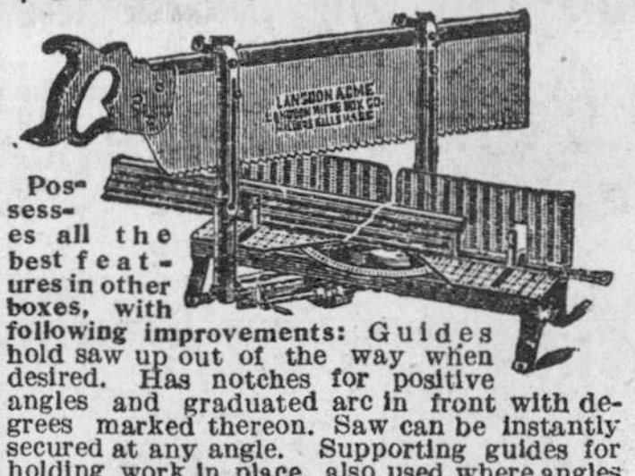

Possesses all the best features in other boxes, with following improvements: Guides hold saw up out of the way when desired. Has notches for positive angles and graduated arc in front with degrees marked thereon. Saw can be instantly secured at any angle. Supporting guides for holding work in place, also used where angles more acute than 45 degrees are desired. An appliance for quicker adjustment of extension lever. A length gauge for duplicate lengths. Steel bottom boards roughened to prevent work from slipping. A metallic index plate with degrees marked thereon. Size 1 provided with solid swinging lever, which cannot be extended. Sizes 2 and 2½ provided with extension levers by which front post can be extended to give greater width. Price includes high grade back saw.

No.	Size	Size of Saw, in.	Capacity at Right Angles, in.	Capacity at Mitre, in.	Price, with Saw
9K58972	1	24x4	7½	5	8.72
9K58974	2	26x4	10¼	7	10.44
9K58976	2½	28x5	10¼	7	12.13
9K58978	2½	30x5	10¼	7	12.62

$10.43 IMPROVED WOOD TRIMMER FOR CUTTING JOINTS AND ANGLES.

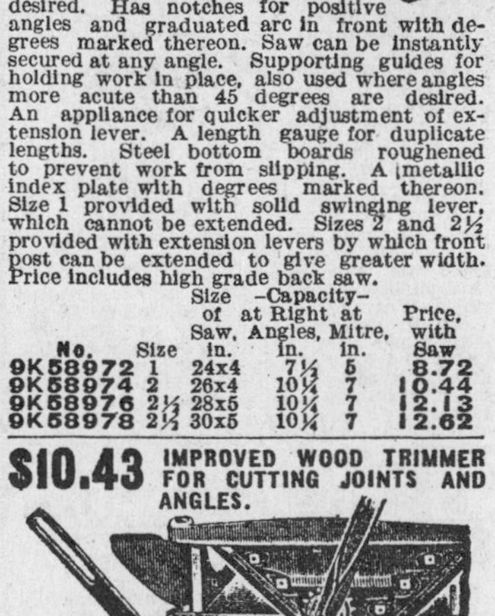

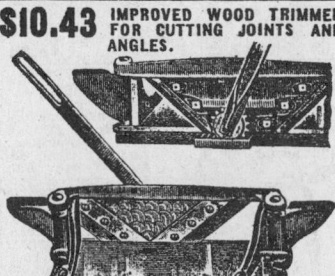

Unexcelled for cutting joints square, bevel, or at any angle, leaving a smooth and accurate finish. It cuts up to 4 inches high and 7 inches wide. For cutting off the ends of siding, flooring, mouldings, etc., will pay for itself on one job. Sold with the understanding that if it does not work entirely to your satisfaction, we will refund the amount you paid us. Shipping weight, 34 pounds.
No. 9K58994 Price..........**$10.43**
No. 9K58996 **Extra Knives for above machine.** Price, per pair..........**$2.90**

FULTON GUARANTEED SAWS

Fulton Saws are made of the finest materials by skilled American workmen. Fulton Saws are made strictly on honor, sold on merit; no extra charge for reputation. Fulton Saws are made in our own immense factory, entirely independent of all trusts. Fulton Saws are sold direct from manufacturer to consumer with no middlemen's profits added. Fulton Saws are fully warranted—you take no risk whatever. We guarantee every Fulton Saw we sell to be perfect in material and workmanship; to do everything we claim for it and to give entire satisfaction in every respect, or it may be returned to us within thirty days from date of purchase and your money will be refunded.

BECAUSE we manufacture Fulton Saws ourselves; because we are entirely independent of any combination or trust; because we are not pledged to "maintain" high prices; because we have no drummers to pay, no jobbers to protect; because we add only one small profit to the actual cost of material and labor, we are enabled to quote these remarkably low prices on Fulton Guaranteed Hand Saws.

OUR FULTON GUARANTEED HAND SAWS.

Guaranteed the Best Saw in the World or your money back.

$1.27

FOR A
26-INCH
FULTON
HAND MADE
HAND SAW.

A STRICTLY HAND MADE SAW.
Hand smithed, hand blocked, hand filed and hand set. The material in the Fulton Hand Saw is a special formula crucible steel, the very finest that can be produced. The blade is ground extra thin back, four gauges thinner than the toothed edge. This allows the Fulton Saw to run freely with very little set. Fulton Saws are smithed and blocked by hand. Very few trust made saws are properly smithed and blocked, because these operations are expensive and do not show while the saw is new. When the smithing and blocking is correctly done, a saw will work right as long as it lasts. Fulton Saws will give perfect service until the blade is actually worn away. As long as there is any of it left it will be a good saw. The blade is given a beautiful finish, not equaled by any other saw at any price. The handle is a plain pattern that just fits the hand, put on with four improved screws, and the neatest you ever saw. Fulton Hand Saws balance right and have the proper "feel." The price we put on a 26-inch Fulton Hand Made Hand Saw is $1.27, and this is the guarantee we give you with it: "Buy a Fulton Hand Saw, any size and use it thirty days. If at the end of that time you think you ever used a better saw, or that you can buy any other saw at $1.75 to $2.25 each that is better than the one you got from us, send the Fulton Saw back to us and we will refund your money."

are full bevel, hand filed and hand set. The blade is given a beautiful finish, not equaled by any other saw at any price. The teeth on a Fulton Saw are tempered to cut and hold an edge, and

No. 9K59020 The Fulton Panel or Hand Saws.

Length	Points to the inch	Price
18-inch Panel	9, 10, 11 or 12	$0.91
20-inch Panel	9, 10, 11 or 12	1.01
22-inch Panel	9, 10, 11 or 12	1.11
24-inch Hand	7, 8, 9, 10, 11 or 12	1.18
26-inch Hand	6, 7, 8, 9, 10, 11 or 12	1.27
28-inch Hand	6, 7 or 8	1.42
30-inch Hand	6, 7 or 8	1.64

No. 9K59022 The Fulton Rip Saws.

Length	Points to the inch	Price
24-inch Rip	5, 5½, 6 or 6½	$1.22
26-inch Rip	5, 5½ or 6	1.29
28-inch Rip	4, 4½, 5, 5½ or 6	1.43
30-inch Rip	4½ or 5	1.66

WE CANNOT FURNISH THESE SAWS IN POINTS OTHER THAN LISTED ABOVE.
Be sure to state length wanted and number of points when ordering hand saws.

14C FOR A JAPANNED ADJUSTABLE HACK SAW FRAME WITH 8-INCH BLADE. 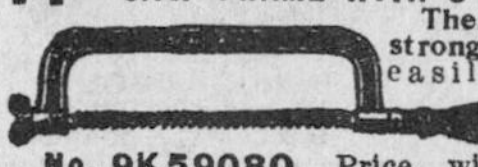
These Frames are strong, durable, and easily adjusted to four angles.
No. 9K59080 Price, with one 8-inch blade.....14c

44C NICKEL PLATED ADJUSTABLE EXTENSION HACK SAW FRAME. 
Better value than you can get elsewhere for less than 75 cents to $1.00. These frames are strong and durable, adjustable to four angles, or any length from 8 to 12 inches. Price includes one 8-inch blade.
No. 9K59084 Price.....44c

83C "STIFF AND RIGID" NICKEL PLATED EXTENSION HACK SAW FRAME. 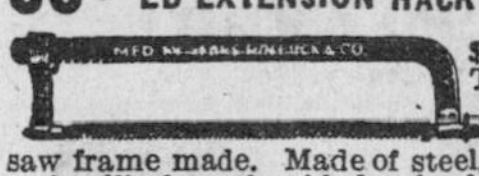
The regular $1.25 kind. This is the stiffest hack saw frame made. Made of steel, nickel plated, and will face the blades in four directions. Will hold all blades from 6 to 12 inches. Price includes one 10-inch blade.
No. 9K59086 Price.....83c

47C PER DOZ. FULTON SPECIAL 8-INCH HACK SAW BLADES.

FLINT EDGE FULTON SPECIAL

The fastest cutting hack saw blade made and the only one that will cut tool steel, steel rails, phosphor bronze and other hard metals. Flint Edge Fulton Special Blades are not intended to be filed, but are tempered so hard that they will last four times as long as an ordinary blade filed as they come from the factory. Order a lot of Fulton Special Blades, give them a fair trial and if they are not the finest blades you ever used, return them to us and we will refund your money.
No. 9K59094

Length, inches	6	8	9	10	12
Price, per doz.	41c	47c	51c	59c	69c

Fulton Hack Saw Blades, made from the best clock steel, soft on the back with highly tempered teeth. They are unbreakable, and are preferred by many. Have 14 points to the inch.
No. 9K59090

Length, inches	7	8	9	10	12
Price, per doz.	31c	34c	39c	47c	53c

Fulton Hack Saw Blades, 24 points to the inch, for cutting brass, drill rods, black pipe, tubing and similar work. Soft on the back with highly tempered teeth.
No. 9K59092

Length, inches	8	9	10	12
Price, per dozen	35c	40c	47c	53c

82C ADJUSTABLE TENSION TURNING SAW. COMPLETE WITH BLADE. 
The frame is made of birchwood, with ebonized handles. The tension is regulated by screws. Price includes one blade.

82c

No. 9K59062 Price.....82c
Extra Blades for Turning Saws, 18 inches.
No. 9K59064 Price each.....14c

83C FOR THE FINEST HAND BRACKET SAW OUTFIT MADE. 
Saw is nickel plated, has rosewood handle; frame, 5x12 inches; with 19 designs, 6 saw blades, 1 awl, 1 sheet impression paper, and directions packed in pasteboard box. Weight, 1¼ pounds.

83c

No. 9K59066 Price for outfit.....83c

Bracket Saw Blades.
Tempered Steel, 5 inches long. We do not sell less than a dozen of any one size. State size.
No. 9K59070

Size	00	0	1	2	3	4
Per dozen	5c	5c	5c	5c	5c	5c
Gross	50c	50c	50c	50c	50c	50c
Size		5	6	7	8	
Per dozen		6c	6c	6c	7c	
Gross		50c	50c	55c	60c	65c	70c

The above blades fit saws Nos. 9K59066, 9K59580, 9K59584 and 9K59604.

SPRINGFIELD HAND SAWS.

97C 26-inch size.

Manufactured by us but not as nicely finished or as highly polished as our Fulton Hand Saw described above. It is ground nearly three gauges thinner on back, carefully smithed and blocked, maple handle, four improved screws, hollow back, full bevel, hand filed, hand set and warranted as follows: "If this saw does not prove satisfactory and equal to saws made by other manufacturers that sell at 40 per cent more money, return it to us, within thirty days, and we will refund the price paid for it." If you have been accustomed to paying $1.40 to $1.65 for a 26-inch hand saw, we will be pleased to have you order a Springfield Saw at 97c, with the understanding that if you do not consider it equal to saws that sell at $1.40 and upward, you may return it to us within thirty days and we will refund your money.

No. 9K59002 The Springfield Panel or Hand Saws.

Length	Points to the inch	Price
18-inch Panel, 9, 10, 11 and 12		79c
20-inch Panel, 9, 10, 11 and 12		84c
22-inch Panel, 9, 10, 11 and 12		90c
24-inch Hand, 7, 8, 9, 10, 11 and 12		95c
26-inch Hand, 6, 7, 8, 9, 10, 11 and 12		97c

No. 9K59004 The Springfield Rip Saws.

Length	Points to the inch	Price
26-inch Rip, 5, 5½ and 6		$0.99
28-inch Rip, 5, 5½ and 6		1.12

Be sure to state length and number of points wanted.
We cannot furnish these saws in points other than as listed above.

ODD JOBS HAND SAWS.

68C 26-INCH SIZE.

This Odd Jobs Saw is warranted, but it is not ground thin on the back and it is not smithed or blocked or filed as carefully as our Fulton or Springfield Saws. It is set and sharpened and will give satisfaction to anyone who wants a saw only for odd jobs. It is as good as saws commonly retailed at $1.25 (for 26-inch size) and better than any saw sold by retail dealers for $1.00, but if you really want the best saw made, a saw that will outcut and outlast any saw made, in your own interest we urge you to buy our Fulton Special described above, but you need not hesitate to buy this saw for odd jobs.

No. 9K59008 The Odd Jobs Panel or Hand Saws.

Length	Points to the inch	Price
20-inch Panel, 9, 10 or 12		61c
24-inch Hand, 7, 8, 9 or 10		66c
26-inch Hand, 7, 8, 9 or 10		68c

No. 9K59010 The Odd Jobs Rip Saws.

Length	Points to the inch	Price
26-inch Rip, 5, 5½ or 6		73c
28-inch Rip, 5, 5½ or 6		78c

We cannot furnish these saws in points other than as listed above.
Be sure to state length and number of points wanted.

$1.43 JENNINGS' NAIL CUTTING SAW.

No carpenter who is ever called to do repair work or house wrecking should be without one of these saws in his kit. It will save him enough in one job to pay for itself. It saws wood, nails, sheet metal and gas pipe without injuring the saw. Can be filed, but does not require set, being taper concave ground. Length of blade, 18 inches.
No. 9K59036 Price.....$1.43

15C NICKEL PLATED ADJUSTABLE FRAME COPING SAW WITH 12 BLADES. 
Retailers charge 25 cents to 35 cents for this saw. All wire, 6-inch bent end blades. Depth of cut, 4 inches. Complete, with 1 dozen extra blades.

15c

No. 9K59072 Price.....15c

89C NICKEL PLATED HOLLOW BACK ADJUSTABLE COPING SAW. 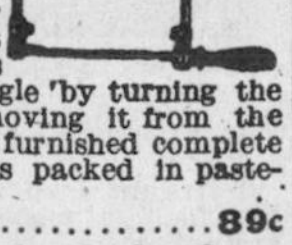 
Constructed with a hollow tubular back, through which runs a string or cable connecting both ends of saw frame, which causes the blade to run to any angle by turning the handle only, without removing it from the work. Nickel plated and furnished complete with one-half dozen blades packed in pasteboard box.
No. 9K59074 Price.....89c
Tempered Steel Blades for Coping Saws. Six inches long with bent ends.
No. 9K59076 Price, per dozen.....9c

85C FOR A 10-INCH FULTON GUARANTEED BACK SAW. 
The heavy steel back gives weight and insures a steady cut. Made from extra spring steel. Hand hammered, hand filed and ready for use. Has maple handle. Fully warranted.
No. 9K59040

Size, inches	10	12	14	16
Price	85c	$1.02	$1.14	$1.25

$1.60 FOR A 22-INCH FULTON SPECIAL MITER BOX BACK SAW.
Made especially for use with miter boxes. Measures 4 inches under the back. Length of saw is entire length of blade, the toothed edge being about 2 inches shorter.
No. 9K59042

Length, inches	22	24	28
Price	$1.60	$1.80	$2.05

7C BEST BEECHWOOD SAW HANDLES WITH VARNISHED EDGES. 
Well made of selected stock and superior to those usually offered.
No. 9K59100 Price.....7c
Panel Saw Handles.
No. 9K59102 Price.....7c

17C FOR 12 SOLID BRASS SAW HANDLE SCREWS.
These screws are made on an improved pattern, are strong and will hold securely. 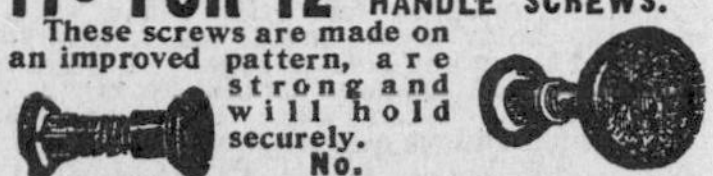
No. 21. **9K59108** No. 23.

	Size 21	Size 23
Price, per doz.	17c; 3 for.....6c	28c; 2 for.....6c

20C FOR A FULTON INTERCHANGEABLE COMPASS SAW, COMPLETE. 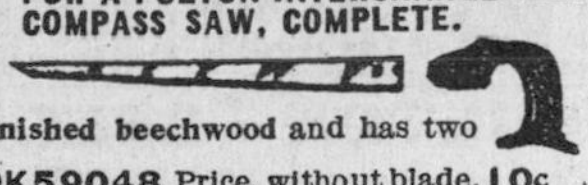
Made of selected, well finished beechwood and has two screws.
No. 9K59048 Price, without blade.....10c
Fulton Blades for above handle.
No. 9K59050

Length, inches	10	12	14	16
Price	10c	11c	12c	13c

23C FOR A 12-INCH FULTON THIN BACK COMPASS SAW. 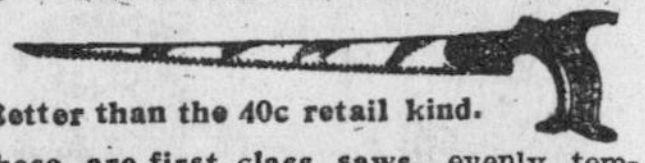
Better than the 40c retail kind.
These are first class saws, evenly tempered from butt to point, full bevel, hand filed and set ready for use. Extra finished handle, two improved screws.
No. 9K59052

Length, inches	10	12	14	16
Price	20c	23c	25c	28c

63C COMBINED KEYHOLE, COMPASS AND PANEL SAW, COMPLETE. 
Superior Nest of Saws, consisting of one handle, one keyhole blade, one compass blade, one panel or pruning blade, all interchangeable in the handle.
No. 9K59054 Price.....63c

13C FOR A MODEL KEYHOLE SAW WITH ADJUSTABLE IRON HANDLE. 
The saw blade passes through a slot in the center of the brass bolt in the front of the handle. Has 7-inch blade, thin back, filed and set.
No. 9K59056 Price.....13c
Extra Blades for above pad, 7 inches long, thin back filed and set.
No. 9K59058 Price.....10c

66C FOR A FULTON SPECIAL BUCK SAW, WITH SPRING STEEL BLADE.

RETAIL PRICE IS **$1.25**

66c

FULLY GUARANTEED.

Better than any saw you can buy elsewhere for $1.25. Frame is selected hardwood, varnish finish, heavy tinned rod with japanned turn. Threads will not strip. The blade is made of the best clock spring tempered steel with round breast. It is taper ground, extra thin on the back, hand filed and set ready for use. The peculiar shape of the tooth, the extra thin back, the expert hand filing, the high grade steel used and the extreme care exercised in its manufacture, make the Fulton Special the fastest and the easiest cutting buck saw in the world. If you cannot saw a cord of wood faster and easier with the Fulton Special Buck Saw than with any buck saw you have ever used you may return it to us within thirty days and we will refund the price paid and stand the cost of transportation both ways.
No. 9K59120 Price.....66c
Extra Fulton Special Blades.
No. 9K59124 Price, each.....34c

FULTON GUARANTEED AXES

FULTON AXES ARE MADE IN OUR OWN IMMENSE FACTORY AND SOLD ONLY BY US. FULTON AXES ARE NOT MADE BY A TRUST, HENCE OUR EXTREMELY LOW PRICES. FULTON AXES, "DIRECT FROM MAKER TO USER;" YOU PAY BUT ONE PROFIT. FULTON AXES, FULLY WARRANTED; YOU TAKE NO RISK, READ OUR GUARANTEE. FULTON AXES, THE LOWEST PRICED, HIGHEST GRADE GUARANTEED AXES MADE.

WE GUARANTEE EVERY FULTON AXE we sell to be perfect in material and workmanship, to be correctly proportioned, properly tempered, accurately ground, and entirely satisfactory in every respect or it may be returned to us and your money will be promptly refunded. We also guarantee that our axes at 64 cents to 69 cents each are better than any $1.25 axe on the market under any other brand. Our sales of over 100,000 axes last season are the best proof of this statement. PRICES THIS SEASON ARE STILL FURTHER REDUCED.

FULTON VILLAGE FORGE HAND MADE AXES.

Lumbermen, Woodchoppers, Millmen, Farmers—don't pay retail prices for inferior axes when you can get Fulton Village Forge Hand Made Axes from us at wholesale. Read all we say about the quality of these axes. Read our guarantee—send us your order. We sold more Fulton Village Forge Hand Made Axes last year than were sold under any two brands of other make. Prices this year are still further reduced for larger sales this season. Remember, we positively guarantee Fulton Village Forge Axes at 64 to 69 cents each better than any $1.25 axe on the market.

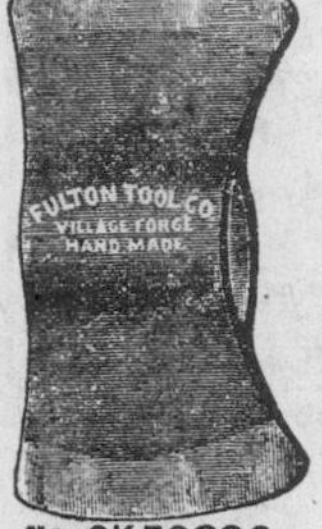

No. 9K59826
Michigan Pattern
91 cents, 4 pounds

FULTON VILLAGE FORGE AXES ARE MADE OF BEST MATERIAL.

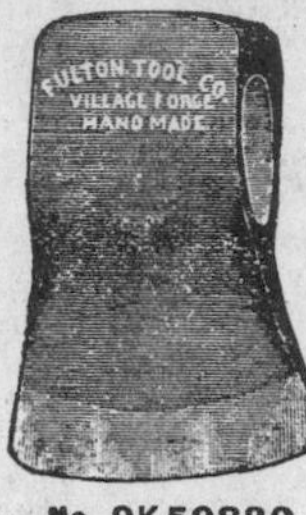

No. 9K59820
Michigan Pattern
65 cents, 3½ pounds

FULTON VILLAGE FORGE AXES ARE PROPERLY SHAPED.

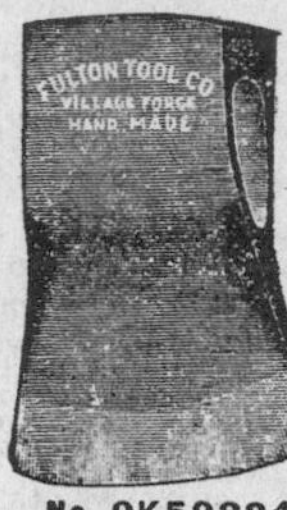

No. 9K59824
Dayton Pattern
67 cents, 4 pounds

FULTON VILLAGE FORGE AXES ARE CORRECTLY TEMPERED.

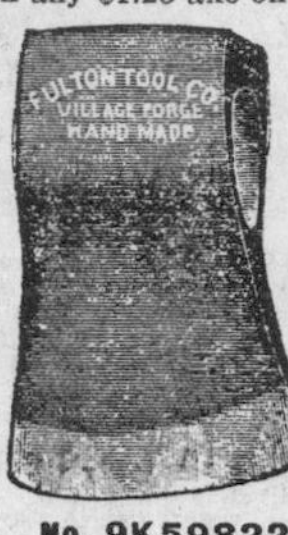

No. 9K59822
Wisconsin Pattern
68 cents, 4½ pounds

FULTON VILLAGE FORGE AXES ARE ACCURATELY GROUND.

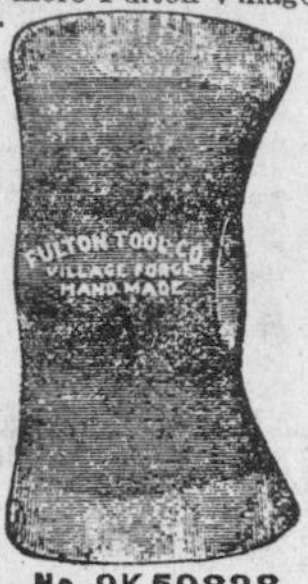

No. 9K59828
Wisconsin Pattern
93 cents, 5 pounds

FULTON VILLAGE FORGE AXES ARE HAND MADE by the old process, of the finest material money will buy and every axe is as perfect as a good workman can make it. Fulton Village Forge Axes represent full money value in each axe for every penny of the price you pay for it. The black axes come to you just as they are finished by the workmen. They are hand hammered and show the hammer marks, being ground only on the cutting edge. Fulton Village Forge Axes have inserted cutting bits of the highest grade crucible cast steel. They are hardened in brine without addition of chemicals, and are tempered one at a time over an open fire, each axe being given careful inspection by an expert workman so that they run absolutely even in temper—every one the same. They contain neither hard nor soft spots. They are tempered to cut and hold an edge. They are correctly proportioned and balance just right. **Compare them with any other axe you please,** even as high in price as $1.25 to $2.00 each, and see for yourself that they are the best axe made. If you do not think so and are not entirely pleased with your purchase from us, return the goods and we will refund your money. We own the factory making Fulton Village Forge Hand Made Axes, and guarantee every one of them to please our customers. Our prices are based on actual manufacturing cost with only our one small profit added and we can save you money in this line besides giving you only the very highest grade of goods.

THESE PRICES ARE FOR AXES ALONE, AND DO NOT INCLUDE HANDLES. BE SURE TO SPECIFY WEIGHT WHEN ORDERING AXES.

Low prices in our last catalogue still further reduced on over 3,000 Hardware Items.

Weight, pounds		3	3½	3¾	4	4½	5	5½
No. 9K59820	Michigan Pattern, Black, Single Bit. Price	64c	65c	66c	67c	68c	69c	....
No. 9K59822	Wisconsin Pattern, Black, Single Bit. Price	64c	65c	66c	67c	68c	69c	....
No. 9K59824	Dayton Pattern, Black, Single Bit. Price	64c	65c	66c	67c	68c	69c	....
No. 9K59826	Michigan Pattern, Black, Double Bit. Price		89c	90c	91c	92c	93c	94c
No. 9K59828	Wisconsin Pattern, Black, Double Bit. Price		89c	90c	91c	92c	93c	94c

Wisconsin pattern is the same as Western pattern, which it is sometimes called. Be sure to specify weight when ordering axes.

Hardware Prices reduced in this book make your saving greater than ever.

FULTON SPECIAL FULL POLISHED GUARANTEED AXES.

TEMPER EXACTLY RIGHT, NO GUESSWORK ABOUT IT.

FULTON SPECIAL AXES, FULL POLISH FINISH.

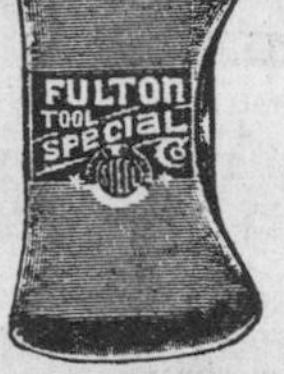

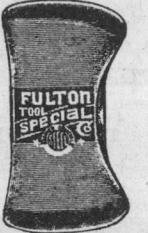

No. 9K59854
Michigan Pattern

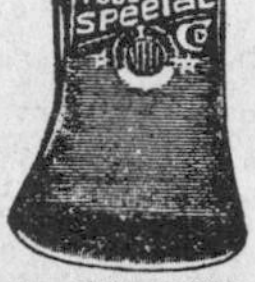

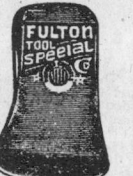

No. 9K59850
Michigan Pattern

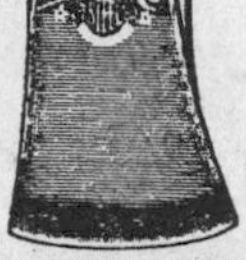

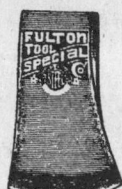

No. 9K59852
Wisconsin Pattern

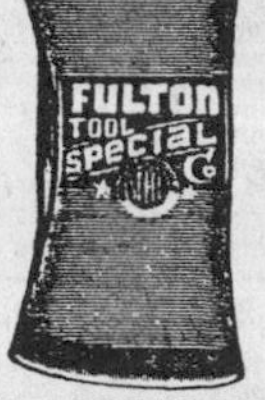

No. 9K59856
Wisconsin Pattern

FULTON SPECIAL AXES ARE MADE by the modern process with the most improved machinery, in the biggest axe factory in existence and are, next to our Village Forge Hand Made Axes, the best axes in the world. Machine made axes have overlaid instead of inserted steel bit. The cutting bits are best double refined crucible steel and every axe is warranted perfect by us. We sell thousands of dozens of these axes every year and guarantee that they are not equaled by any other axe made, except our Fulton Village Forge Hand Made goods. We make the positive statement that as good axes cannot be bought in retail stores for $1.00 to $1.25 each. Fulton Special Axes are full polished, making without doubt the handsomest axe on the market. We carry Fulton Special Axes in Michigan and Wisconsin or Western pattern, single and double bit. Order by number from price list below and give weight.

These prices are for axes alone and do not include handles. Be sure to specify weight when ordering axes.

Weight, pounds		3	3½	3¾	4	4½	5	5½
No. 9K59850	Mich. Pat., Single Bit	65c	66c	67c	68c	69c	70c	....
No. 9K59852	Wis. Pat., Single Bit	65c	66c	67c	68c	69c	70c	....
No. 9K59854	Mich. Pat., Double Bit		90c	91c	92c	93c	94c	95c
No. 9K59856	Wis. Pat., Double Bit		90c	91c	92c	93c	94c	95c

Wisconsin pattern is the same as Western pattern, which it is sometimes called. Be sure to specify weight when ordering axes.

FULTON GUARANTEED BROADAXES.

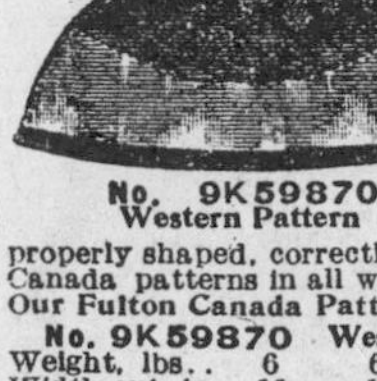

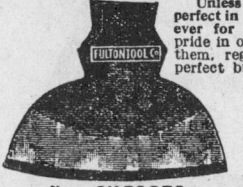

No. 9K59870
Western Pattern

Unless a broadaxe is absolutely true and perfect in manufacture, it is of no value whatever for practical use. We take particular pride in our Fulton Broadaxes and guarantee them, regardless of price, to be the most perfect broadaxes on the market. Compare them with any broadaxe you ever saw or used, even as high in price as $3.00 to $4.00, and if not found superior we will take them back and refund your money.

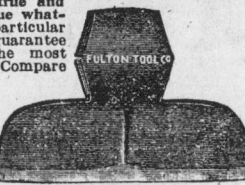

Fulton Broadaxes are made of the finest material, with best double refined crucible steel bits, properly shaped, correctly tempered and beautifully finished. We carry both Western and Canada patterns in all weights from 6 to 9 pounds. Order by number and give weight.

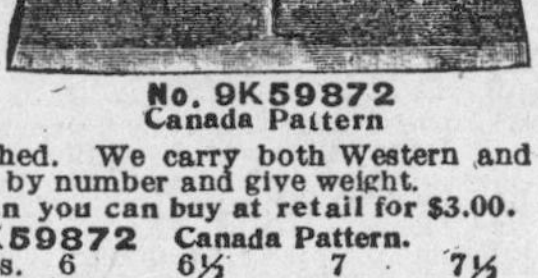

No. 9K59872
Canada Pattern

Our Fulton Canada Pattern Broadaxe is a better axe than you can buy at retail for $3.00.

No. 9K59870 Western Pattern.

Weight, lbs.	6	6½	7	7½
Width cut, in.	11	11½	12	12½
Price	$1.56	$1.58	$1.60	$1.62
Weight, lbs.		8	8½	9
Width cut, inches		13	13½	14
Price		$1.64	$1.66	$1.68

No. 9K59872 Canada Pattern.

Weight, lbs.	6	6½	7	7½
Width cut, in.	10½	11	11½	12
Price	$1.80	$1.90	$2.00	$2.10
Weight, lbs.		8	8½	9
Width cut, inches		12½	13	13½
Price		$2.20	$2.30	$2.40

We have always sold GOOD HARDWARE at lower prices than any other house. On over 3,000 Hardware items prices are STILL FURTHER REDUCED in this Catalogue.

FULTON LUMBER JACK AXES.

A fully guaranteed axe for 49 cents. Regular 90-cent value.

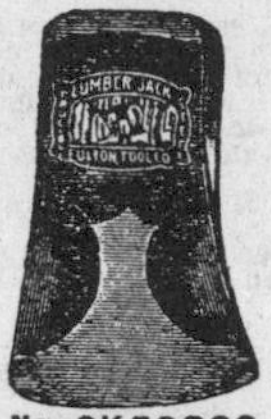

No. 9K59860
Michigan Pattern

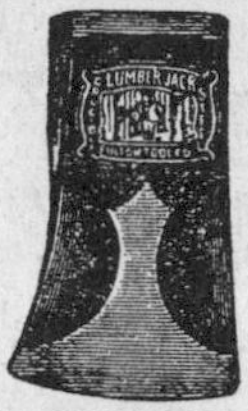

No. 9K59862
Yankee Pattern

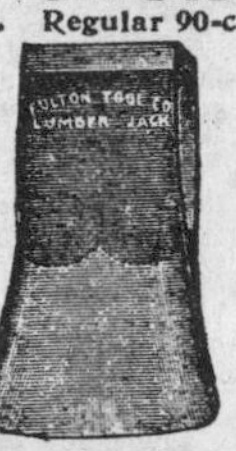

No. 9K59864
Wisconsin Pattern

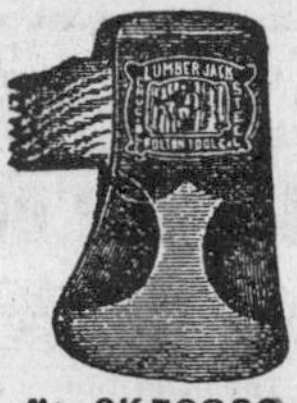

No. 9K59866
Michigan Pattern

Fulton Lumber Jack Axes at 49 to 69 cents each are the best axes ever produced for the money, and will compare in every way with axes sold by retail hardware stores at 75 to 95 cents each. Fulton Lumber Jack Axes are made in the same factory as our more expensive machine made axes, by the same workmen, are well finished and strictly first quality with overlaid cast steel cutting bit. The Michigan and Yankee patterns have Phantom beveled blades, as illustrated, while the Wisconsin pattern is made plain, as shown. We also carry the Michigan pattern with good hickory handle, properly put in. For all ordinary work Fulton Lumber Jack Axes will give entire satisfaction. Every axe warranted perfect. Fulton Lumber Jack Axes are not made in double bit. Be sure to specify weight when ordering.

Weight, pounds		3	3½	3¾	4	4½	5
No. 9K59860	Michigan Pattern, Single Bit	49c	50c	51c	52c	53c	54c
No. 9K59862	Yankee Pattern, Single Bit	49c	50c	51c	52c	53c	54c
No. 9K59864	Wisconsin Pattern, Single Bit	49c	50c	51c	52c	53c	54c
No. 9K59866	Michigan Pattern, Handled Single Bit	64c	65c	66c	67c	68c	69c

49c FOR A GENUINE FULTON GUARANTEED BOYS' HANDLED AXE.

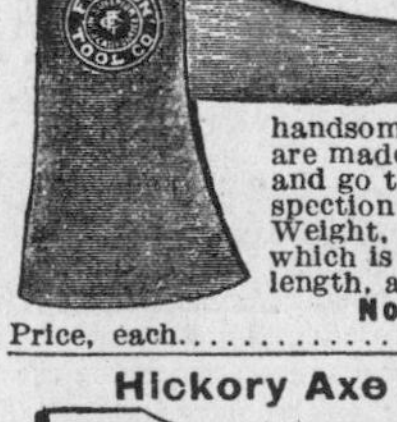

The best light axe made. Just the right weight for boys' use, splitting kindling, etc. Best steel bit, handsomely finished. They are made with the same care and go through the same inspection as our men's axes. Weight, including handle, which is about 28 inches in length, about 3¼ pounds.

No. 9K59880
Price, each.......49c

38c FOR A GENUINE FULTON GUARANTEED HUNTERS' HATCHET.

Retails at 75 cents.

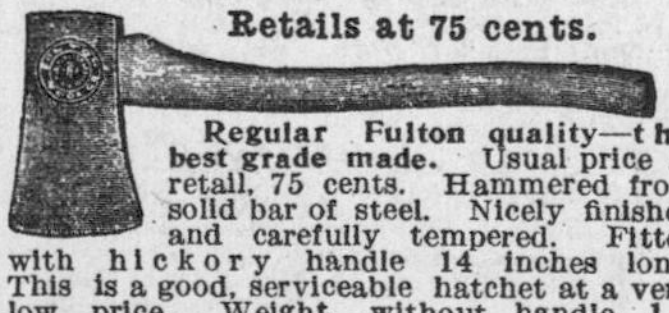

Regular Fulton quality—the best grade made. Usual price at retail, 75 cents. Hammered from solid bar of steel. Nicely finished and carefully tempered. Fitted with hickory handle 14 inches long. This is a good, serviceable hatchet at a very low price. Weight, without handle, 1½ pounds.

No. 9K59882 Price..........38c

Hickory Axe Handles.

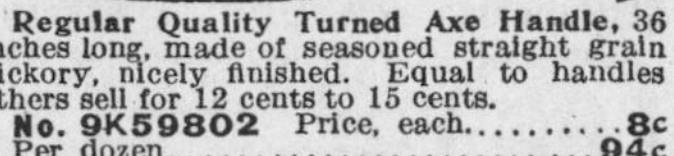

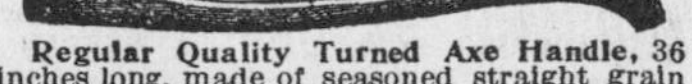

Regular Quality Turned Axe Handle, 36 inches long, made of seasoned straight grain hickory, nicely finished. Equal to handles others sell for 12 cents to 15 cents.

No. 9K59802 Price, each..........8c
Per dozen..........94c

Standard Quality Turned Axe Handle, 36 inches long, made of selected seasoned hickory, all white, sandpapered and polished.

No. 9K59804 Price, each......$0.11
Per dozen..........1.28

Boys' Standard Quality Turned Axe Handle, 28 inches long, same grade and finish as Standard Quality Handle described above.

No. 9K59806 Price..........12c

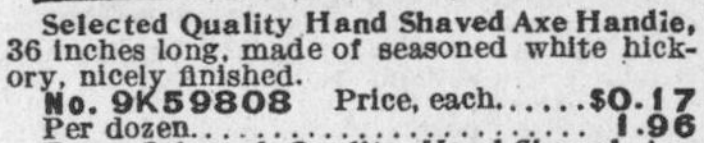

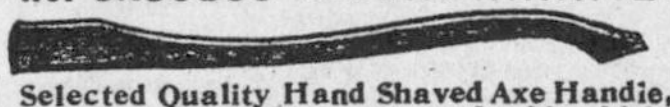

Selected Quality Hand Shaved Axe Handle, 36 inches long, made of seasoned white hickory, nicely finished.

No. 9K59808 Price, each......$0.17
Per dozen..........1.96

Extra Selected Quality Hand Shaved Axe Handle, 36 inches long, made of straight grained white hickory, extra heavy.

No. 9K59810 Price, each......$0.22
Per dozen..........2.56

14c EXTRA SELECTED QUALITY DOUBLE BIT AXE HANDLE.

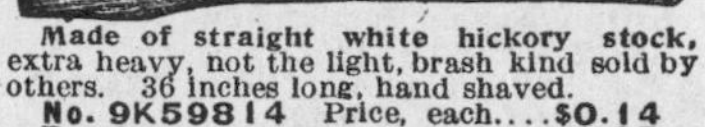

Made of straight white hickory stock, extra heavy, not the light, brash kind sold by others. 36 inches long, hand shaved.

No. 9K59814 Price, each....$0.14
Per dozen..........1.65

18c EXTRA SELECTED QUALITY BROADAXE HANDLE.

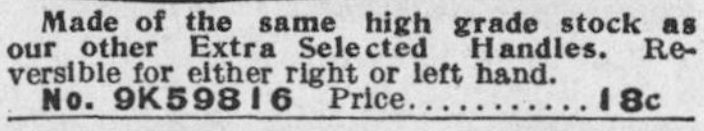

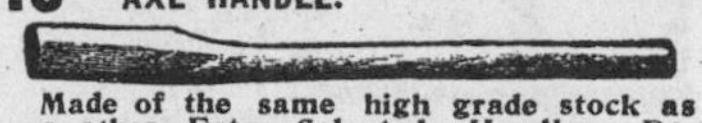

Made of the same high grade stock as our other Extra Selected Handles. Reversible for either right or left hand.

No. 9K59816 Price..........18c

16c PER DOZ. MALLEABLE AXE WEDGES.

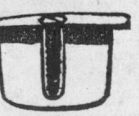

Made of best malleable iron, with iron screw, impossible for handle to pull out when this wedge is used. Weight, 2 ounces.

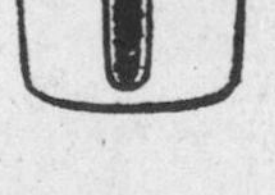

No. 9K59818
Price, each..........2c
Per dozen..........16c

YOUR SAVING IS GREATER.

GENERAL REDUCTIONS ON HARDWARE IN THIS BOOK MAKE OUR ALREADY LOW PRICES STILL MORE ATTRACTIVE.

95c MALLEABLE IRON PIPE VISE WITH TOOL STEEL JAWS.

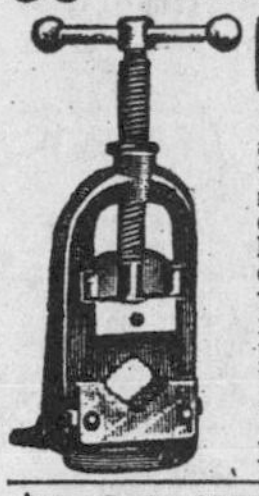

YOU PAY MORE ELSEWHERE.

Steamfitters, plumbers and gasfitters will find this the handiest vise on the market. The jaws are made of the best tool steel, accurately machined. Frame is made of malleable iron, is strong, well proportioned and nicely finished. Weighs only 7 pounds. Can be carried in tool chest. Takes pipe from 1/8 to 2 inches.

No. 9K35968
Price....95c

$1.23 OPEN HINGE MALLEABLE IRON PIPE VISE, SIZE No. 1.

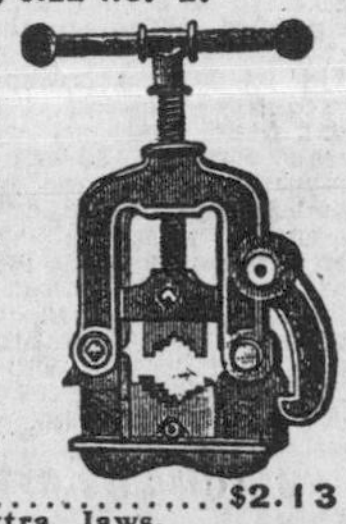

Has interchangeable cut steel jaws and self locking latch, and is constructed to do the heaviest work. Great care has been taken in manufacturing the various parts, putting the strength where most needed. Jaws are warranted.

No. 9K35970
No. 1, holds pipe from 1/4 to 2 inches. Weight, 11 1/2 pounds.
Price....$1.23
No. 2, holds pipe from 1/4 to 3 inches. Weight, 15 pounds. Price....$2.13

No. 9K35971 Extra Jaws.
For No. 1....$0.74
For No. 2....1.14

$4.59 GENUINE SMITH COMBINATION PIPE VISE, SIZE No. 1.

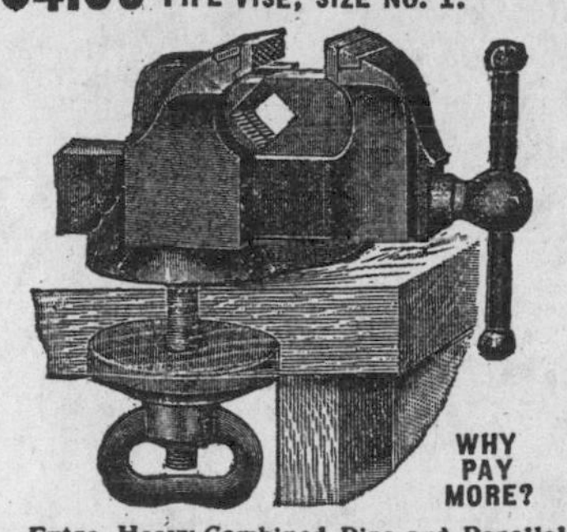

WHY PAY MORE?

Extra Heavy Combined Pipe and Parallel Vise, can be used as a swivel or stationary bottom. Has heavy steel slide bar and steel removable jaws. Material and workmanship A1. Best vise for the money sold by anyone.

No. 9K35976 Size 1, weight, 45 pounds; takes pipe 1/8 to 2 inches.
Price....$4.59
Size 2, weight, 72 pounds; takes pipe 1/4 to 3 inches. Price....$5.67

80c INVINCIBLE ONE-WHEEL PIPE CUTTER, SIZE No. 1.

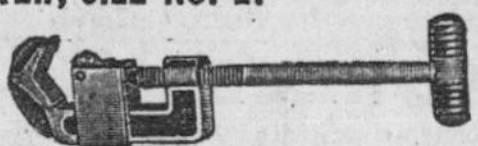

Made of malleable iron, with steel rod and tool steel cutter; lighter and stronger than any other one-wheel cutter made.

No. 9K35985	No. 1	No. 2	No. 3
Cuts pipe from	1/8 to 1 in.	3/4 to 2 in	1 1/4 to 3 in.
Price....	80c	$1.20	$3.65
Extra wheels...	6c	.09	.13

99c FOR A BARNES' THREE-WHEEL PIPE CUTTER, SIZE No. 1.

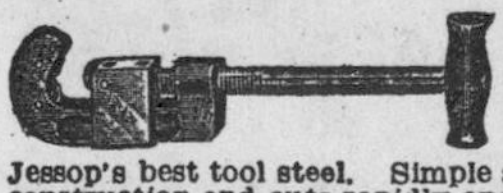

Made of malleable and wrought iron with steel pins and wheels of Jessop's best tool steel. Simple and strong in construction and cuts rapidly and easily.

No. 9K35987	No. 1	No. 2	No. 3
Cuts pipe from..	1/8 to 1 in.	1/2 to 2 in.	1 1/2 to 3 in.
Price....	99c	$1.32	$2.20
Extra wheels...	6c	.08	.09

83c SAUNDERS' PATTERN IMPROVED PIPE CUTTER, SIZE No. 1.

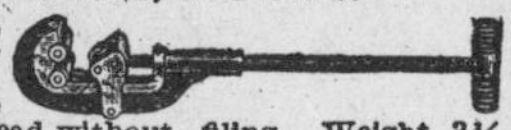

Cuts square end every time. Leaves pipe ready to thread without filing. Weight, 3 3/4 to 6 3/4 pounds.

No. 9K35996	No. 1	No. 2	No. 3
Cuts pipe from	1/8 to 1 in.	1/2 to 2 in.	2 to 3 in.
Price, complete.....	83c	$1.26	$2.90
Extra wheels.....	7c	.09	.17

58c BROWN'S ADJUSTABLE PIPE TONGS, SIZE No. 1.

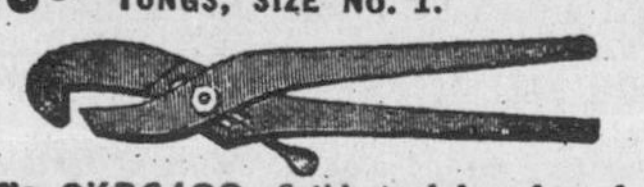

No. 9K36122 Solid steel drop forged.

Number...	1	1 1/2	2	3	4
Takes pipe from in...	1/8 to 3/4	3/8 to 1	1/2 to 1 1/4	1 to 2	1 1/4 to 3
Price......	58c	74c	85c	$1.20	$2.60

$1.99 ECONOMY PIPE STOCK AND DIES WITH STEEL CUTTERS.

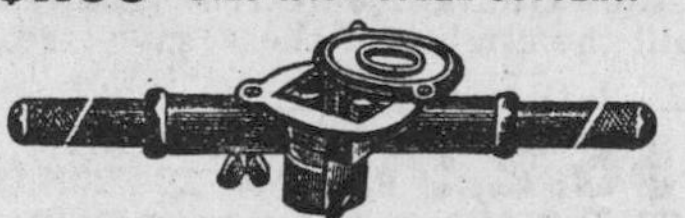

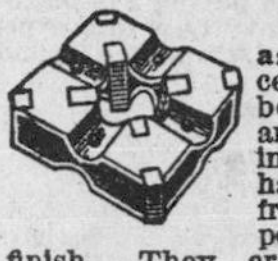

Built for strength as well as economy in price. The center part is made of the best malleable iron, handles are made of steel pipe screwed into stock. The knurled handles prevent the hands from slipping; handle finely polished, center part dark finish. They are true to size, light and fully guaranteed.

The dies are made of four cutters of the best steel. Interlocked with two homogeneous steel plates. Stock, dies and bushings in sets.

Catalogue No.	No.	Cuts Pipe, inches	Dimension of Dies	Price
9K36006	0	1/8, 1/4, 3/8, 1/2	2x2x1/2	$1.99
9K36007	1	1/4, 3/8, 1/2, 3/4, 1	2 1/2x2 1/2x3/4	3.18
9K36008	1 1/2	3/4, 1, 1 1/4	3x3x3/4	2.88
9K36009	2	1 1/4, 1 1/2, 2	4x4x7/8	4.25
9K36011	1A	1/2, 3/4, 1,	2 1/2x2 1/2x3/4	2.25
9K36012	1 1/2	B, 1/4, 3/8, 1/2, 3/4, 1, 1 1/4	3x3x3/4	4.48
9K36013	1 1/4	B, 1/2, 3/4, 1, 1 1/4, 1 1/2	3x3x3/4	4.05

No. 9K36010 Extra Dies.

Cuts Pipe, inches	Dimension of Dies	Fit Stock No.	Price
1/8, 1/4, 3/8, 1/2	2x2x1/2	0	31c
1/8, 1/4, 3/8, 1/2, 3/4, 1	2 1/2x2 1/2x3/4	1	41c
3/4, 1, 1 1/4	3x3x3/4	1 1/2 & 1 1/4	52c
1 1/4, 1 1/2, 2	4x4x7/8	2	70c

$2.23 MALLEABLE IRON PIPE STOCK WITH SOLID STEEL DIES.

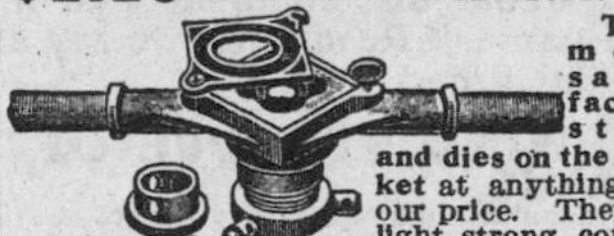

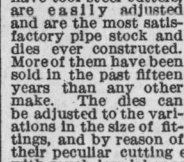

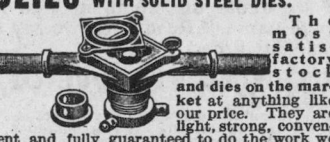

The most satisfactory stock and dies on the market at anything like our price. They are light, strong, convenient and fully guaranteed to do the work we claim for them. Nos. 2 and 3 furnished with leader screw as shown in illustration. We do not furnish leader screws with other sizes. We do not furnish taps with these sets. See No. 9K36060 for taps.

No.	9K36000	9K36001	9K36002
Pipe size	No. 0	No. 1	No. 1 1/2
of dies........	1/8, 1/4, 3/8, 1/2	1/4, 3/8, 1/2, 3/4, 1	3/4, 1, 1 1/4
Dimension of dies..........	2x1/2	2 1/2x3/4	3x3/4
Complete with dies..........	$2.23	$2.83	$2.58
Extra dies, each....	.33	.42	.65
Extra guides, each..	.07	.08	.10
No.	9K36003	9K36004	9K36005
Pipe size	No. 1 1/4	No. 2	No. 3
of dies........	1, 1 1/4, 1 1/2	1 1/4, 1 1/2, 2	2 1/2, 3
Dimension of dies........	3x3/4	4x7/8	5x1 1/4
Complete with dies........	$2.60	$3.80	$11.70
Extra dies, each ..	.65	.83	2.50
Extra guides, each.	.08	.09	.28

$2.13 LIGHTNING PUMP REPAIRERS' DIES AND STOCK.

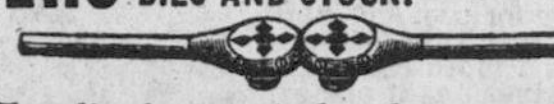

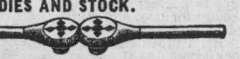

Two dies in one stock, always ready for use without changing dies. Made of the very best materials and fully warranted. Will cut a full thread. Size dies, 5/8 and 7-16 inch.

No. 9K36095 Price....$2.13

$3.49 ARMSTRONG PATTERN No. 2 ADJUSTABLE STOCK AND DIES FOR THREADING PIPE.

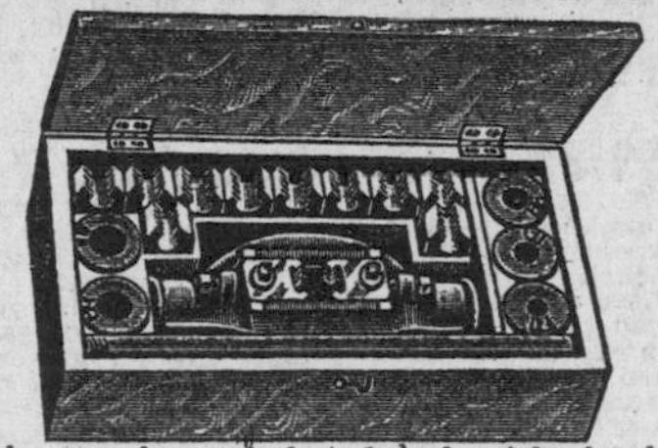

The best known pipe cutting tool on the mark t. They are made of highest grade material throughout, have tool steel cutters, are easily adjusted and are the most satisfactory pipe stock and dies ever constructed. More of them have been sold in the past fifteen years than any other make. The dies can be adjusted to the variations in the size of fittings, and by reason of their peculiar cutting edge can be worked with much less labor and accomplish the desired results in less time than with other dies. The dies have a double taper; that is, the taper at the entrance for the first few threads is greater in degree than the standard taper which forms a lead to the dies, causing them to start on the pipe without filing, even when there is a swell or burr, and requiring no pressure to start dies on the pipe. Cut five sizes, 1/4 inch to 1 inch, right hand. Complete in hardwood box. Weight, 17 pounds.

No. 9K36014 Size No. 2. Price, per set....$3.49
Extra pipe dies, each size, 2 pieces....52

$3.55 ARMSTRONG PATTERN No. 2 1/2 ADJUSTABLE STOCK AND DIES FOR THREADING PIPE.

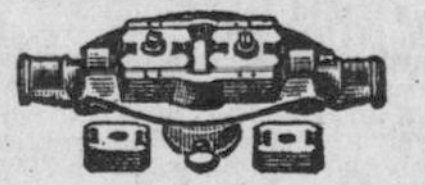

Made of the same high grade material and in the same careful manner as our No. 9K36014, described above. No. 2 1/2 Pipe Stock, complete with four dies cutting 1/2, 3/4, 1 and 1 1/4 inches, right hand. Illustration shows head only. Furnished with handles, dies and guides, complete in hardwood case.

No. 9K36015 Size No. 2 1/2. Price, per set....$3.55
Extra pipe dies, each size, 2 pieces....1.15

$5.82 ARMSTRONG PATTERN No. 3 ADJUSTABLE STOCK AND DIES FOR THREADING PIPE.

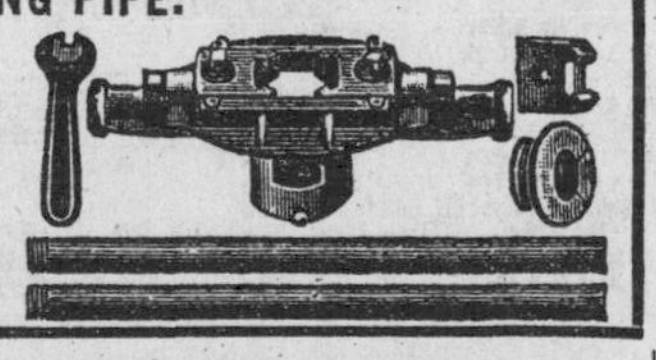

Made of the same material and in the same manner as the other Armstrong pattern pipe sets shown above. No. 3 Pipe Stock, complete with three sizes of dies cutting 1 1/4 to 2 inches. Right hand; furnished with handle, dies and guides, complete in hardwood case.

No. 9K36016 Size No. 3. Price, per set....$5.82
Extra pipe dies, each size, 2 pieces.....1.40

16c HIGH GRADE PIPE TAPS AND PIPE REAMERS, SIZE 1/8 INCH.

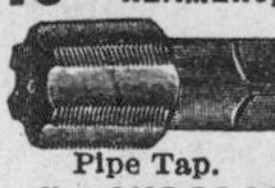

Pipe Tap.

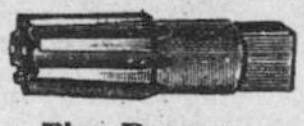

Pipe Reamer.

No. 9K36060 Pipe Tap.
No. 9K36062 Pipe Reamer.

Size, inch	1/8	1/4	3/8	1/2	3/4
Price.......	16c	19c	22c	28c	37c
Size, inches	1	1 1/4	1 1/2	2	
Price........	46c	55c	68c	92c	

69c HIGH GRADE TOOL STEEL LIGHTNING BURRING REAMER.

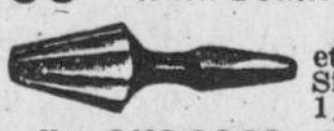

Used for reaming pipe, etc., also countersinking. Size at point, 7-16 by 1 1/4 inches at base.

No. 9K36063 Price....69c

29c FOR AN 8-INCH SOLID DROP FORGED STEEL GAS PLIER.

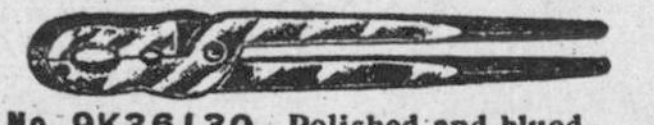

No. 9K36130 Polished and blued.

Length, inches....	8	10
Price....	29c	39c

35c COMBINATION DROP FORGED EXTRA TOOL STEEL GAS PLIER.

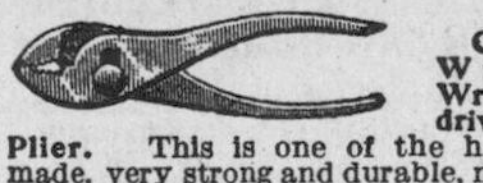

Combination Wire Cutter, Wrench, Screwdriver and Gas Plier. This is one of the handiest pliers made, very strong and durable, nicely finished. Six-inch pliers take up to 3/4-inch pipe; 8-inch and 10-inch take up to 1-inch pipe.

No. 9K36136 Black Finish.

Size, inches......	6	8	10
Price....	35c	41c	44c

No. 9K36137 Nickel Plated.

Size, inches......	6	8	10
Price....	44c	55c	60c

59c FOR AN 8-INCH ACME LIGHTNING COMBINATION WRENCH AND PLIER.

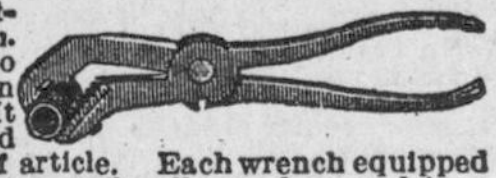

Acme Lightning Wrench. The most up to date tool on the market. It fits any and every shape of article. Each wrench equipped with wire cutter, nail puller and screwdriver. Made of the finest grade of drop forged steel, oil tempered. 6-inch are nickel plated; 8-inch and 12-inch polished. Cheap in price only.

No. 9K36139
Size, 6-inch. Price....46c
Size, 8-inch. Price....59c
Size, 12-inch. Price....68c

19c A PAIR YANKEE ADJUSTABLE PIPE WRENCH JAWS, SIZE 1.

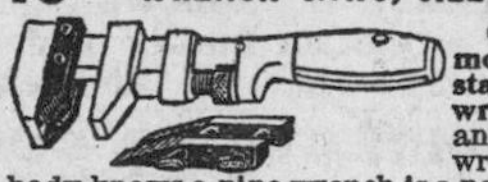

Change a common wrench instantly to a pipe wrench. Will fit any size monkey wrench. Everybody knows a pipe wrench is a necessary tool to have, but is expensive; now everybody can have one. It can be adjusted to fit pipe or bolts from 1/8 to 3 inches. Made of high grade steel. Will last a lifetime. Prices are for jaws only. You pay 35 cents at retail stores.

No. 9K36140 No. 1, fits wrench 6 inches to 10 inches in size. Price....19c
No. 2, fits wrench 10 inches to 24 inches in size. Price....23c

9c DROP FORGED ALLIGATOR PIPE WRENCH, 5 3/4 INCHES LONG.

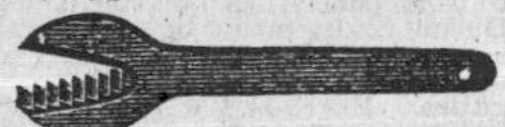

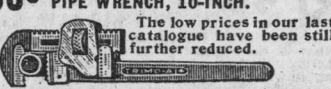

Made of a high grade tool steel, nicely finished.

No. 9K36145

Length, in.	5 3/4	9	16	22	27
Takes pipe	1/8 to 3/8	3/8 to 3/4	1/2 to 1 1/4	1 1/4 to 2	2 to 3
Price....	9c	24c	48c	72c	$1.10

68c FOR A GENUINE TRIMO TOOL STEEL PIPE WRENCH, 10-INCH.

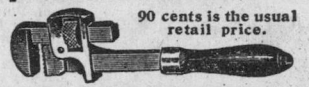

The low prices in our last catalogue have been still further reduced.

This wrench is drop forged from bar steel, is interchangeable in all its parts, does not lock upon the pipe, but releases its hold readily; grips the pipe firmly without lost motion; does not crush the pipe or slip. The movable jaw and the nut are made with a round top and bottom thread, guaranteed not to strip or burr. An inserted jaw is placed in the handle, which can be renewed for little expense when dull or worn.

No. 9K36147

Length, open, in.	10	14	18	24
Takes pipe..	1/8 to 1	1/4 to 1 1/2	1/4 to 2	1/4 to 2 1/2
Price....	68c	89c	$1.19	$1.79

64c FOR AN EXTRA HEAVY WARRANTED STILLSON PIPE WRENCH, 10-INCH.

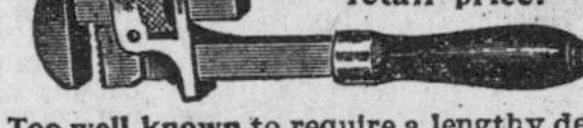

90 cents is the usual retail price.

Too well known to require a lengthy description. They are made of the best imported steel, finely finished and will give satisfaction.

No. 9K36149

Length, open, inches..	6	8	10
Takes pipe from........	1/8 to 1/2	1/8 to 3/4	1/8 to 1
Price....	57c	59c	64c
Length, open, inches.	14	18	24
Takes pipe from....	1/4 to 1 1/2	1/4 to 2	1/4 to 2 1/2
Price....	89c	$1.18	$1.78

$1.18 BEMIS & CALL'S COMBINATION NUT AND PIPE WRENCH, 10-IN.

Others ask $1.75

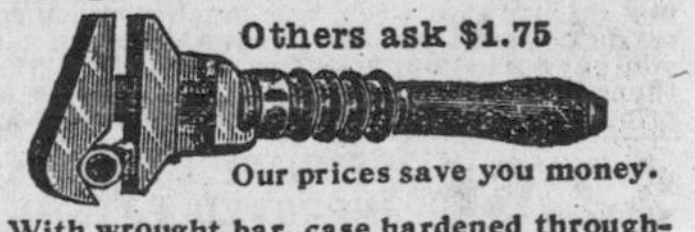

Our prices save you money.

With wrought bar, case hardened throughout, parts interchangeable; furnished with long nut, every wrench guaranteed.

No. 9K36164 10-inch, takes pipe 1/8 to 1 inch in diameter. Price....$1.18
12-inch, takes pipe 1/2 to 1 3/4 inches in diameter. Price....$1.34
15-inch, takes pipe 1/2 to 2 1/4 inches in diameter. Price....$1.89

$1.58 BROCK'S TOOL STEEL YANKEE PIPE WRENCH, SIZE 1.

DROP FORGED FROM STEEL BAR

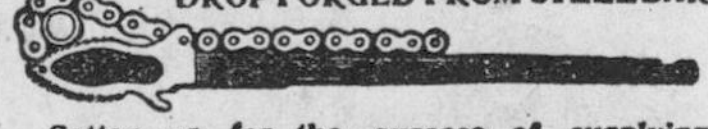

Gotten up for the purpose of supplying a first class wrench at a reasonable price. It is forged out of bar steel in one piece. The teeth are milled and tempered. The chain is made of special steel. The handle is made oblong shape and has greater resisting power against a bending strain than wrenches with handles made of round or hexagon steel. By swinging the chain from one side to the other this wrench will take more intermediate sizes of pipe than any other wrench made. We guarantee every wrench against defects and to be as good a wrench as you have ever used, or money refunded.

No. 9K36167 Size No. 1, capacity, 1/4 to 2 inches; length, 20 inches. Price, $1.58
Size No. 2, capacity, 1/4 to 3 inches; length, 27 inches. Price....$2.34
Size No. 3, capacity, 3/4 to 6 inches; length, 37 inches. Price....$3.23

WE SAVE YOU MONEY.

Low prices in our last catalogue still further reduced in this book on over 3,000 hardware items.

CIRCULAR SAW DEPARTMENT

On this and the following page we quote our complete line of Fulton Guaranteed Circular Saws at prices very much lower than it is possible for any other maker or dealer to name. Read what we say about the quality of these saws; read our binding guarantee; note that you take no risk whatever, and send us your order.

A FEW DIRECTIONS CONCERNING THE USE OF CIRCULAR SAWS.

FULTON CIRCULAR SAWS are perfect in manufacture and will give perfect service if they are handled correctly. In this connection, we call the attention of users of Fulton Circular Saws to the following points: The point of the saw tooth is the only part of the saw which should come in contact with the lumber. The points of the teeth must be kept sharp to do good work. The teeth should have just enough set to clear the blade of the saw. If too much set is given the tooth it requires more power to run and puts an unnecessary strain upon the saw. Running a saw when it is dull or with an unnecessary strain upon it may cause it to crack, this through no fault of the saw itself. Both before and after the collars are tightened a saw should be tried to see if it hangs true. If it does not hang true an attempt to run it is liable to spoil it entirely. To do good work a circular saw must be perfectly round. If one tooth is too long it brings more strain on that portion of the blade which may cause a crack at the gullet and will certainly cause the saw to work poorly. No matter how good the steel, any saw is easily broken if used when frosted. During cold weather be sure to take the frost out of the saw before attempting to set the teeth or use it. Do not use too light a mandrel. Be sure that it is heavy enough so that it will not spring and that the collars on the mandrel are true. Never file a square corner in the gullet. More saws are ruined by this one thing than from all other causes. If you file a square corner in the gullet of your saw, it will certainly crack and cannot be replaced. Never bevel any portion of the teeth except the points. The body of the teeth and the gullets should be filed straight across. The heavier the cutting to be done, the less the bevel that should be filed on front edge of point. Proper attention to points noted above will save all trouble on Fulton Circular Saws. Every saw we send out is filed and set ready for use. and if kept in the same condition as when received we guarantee it will give perfect service.

$1.22 FOR THIS 10-INCH FULTON CIRCULAR CUT OFF SAW. 10-INCH RIP SAW, $1.19.

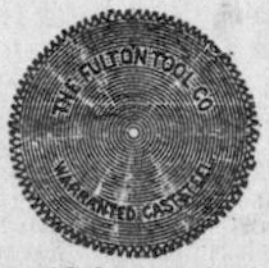

Like all other Fulton saws, this 10-inch saw is fully guaranteed. It is made of the highest grade steel that money will buy; is perfect in manufacture; hand set and hand filed; sent out sharp and ready for use, and warranted without a flaw. 10-inch saws are largely used in furniture factories and cabinet making plants. This size saw is made with a tooth especially adapted for smooth cutting and which leaves the work almost as if planed. Our Fulton 10-inch Circular Saw is made of 16-gauge steel with 1-inch mandrel hole, and runs at a speed of about 3,900 revolutions per minute. The horse power required to drive this saw varies from ½ to ¾, according to the nature of the work. 10-inch Fulton Cut Off Saws have from 100 to 120 teeth and Rip Saws from 38 to 40 teeth. This 10-inch size is our little world beater and a wonder at the low price we name of $1.22 for the cut off and $1.19 for the rip saw. We sell all other sizes in proportion and can furnish saws from 4 inches to 76 inches in diameter. See next page for price list of all sizes. Send us an order for a 10-inch Fulton Saw (or any other size), use it for thirty days, giving it a fair test in your own shop or factory and then if you do not think it is the best saw you ever used return it to us and we will at once refund your money.

$3.32 BUYS THIS 20-INCH CUT OFF SAW. $3.24 FOR THE SAME SIZE RIP SAW.

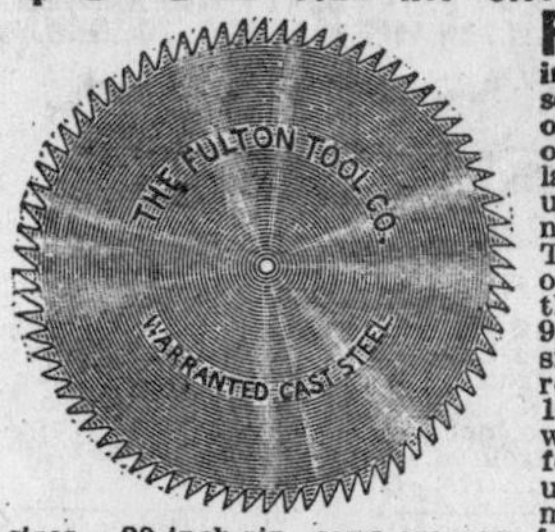

FOR THE LOW PRICE OF $3.32 we deliver this 20-inch Fulton Circular Cut Off Saw, our No. 9K59402, hand set and hand filed, sharp and ready for use, securely crated, on board cars Chicago. 20-inch Rip Saw, our No. 9K59404, only $3.24. The prices we name on 20-inch Fulton Circular Saws are wonderfully low in comparison with the prices usually asked by dealers for trust made saws that will not compare in quality with our high grade Fulton saws. These 20-inch Fulton saws as furnished by us are made of 13-gauge double refined steel, the very finest saw steel that can be produced. The cut off saws have from 80 to 90 teeth, and the rip saws from 34 to 36 teeth. The size of mandrel hole is 1 5-16 inch. Speed about 2,000 revolutions per minute, to maintain which in use, requires 1 to 1½-horse power, depending on the character of the work. 20-inch saws are in general use as stock saws, or for cutting material to estimated length. They are also used in furniture factories for large work, and for trimming in large saw mills this is one of the most popular sizes. 20-inch rip saws are very frequently used for splitting large timber to dimension, and are a favorite in many wagon factories. We ask you to compare our prices on 20-inch Fulton Circular Saws of $3.32 for cut off, and $3.24 for rip, with the prices on any other first quality saw. See how much you can save in price by buying Fulton saws, and then if we do not send you better saws than you can get elsewhere, no matter what the price, after you have tried our saws for thirty days if you are not satisfied in every way, we will take them back and refund your money. We sell other sizes in proportion. See next page for price list of all sizes of Fulton Circular Saws.

$2.66 GENUINE MIXTER'S PATENT DUPLEX SAW SWAGE, WITH IMPROVED PATENT GUIDES.

YOU PAY MORE ELSEWHERE.

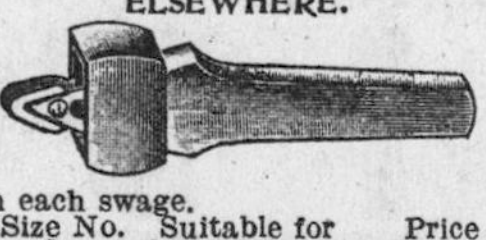

The most satisfactory and reliable swage ever made. The spreading recess acts upon the teeth of a saw back from the cutting edge and spreads them to the required width without materially reducing their lengths. It makes strong and substantial shoulders to the teeth when necessary, which will stand hard work and frozen timber, and it spreads them more on the underside, which causes the saw to cut easily, clear well and steadies it in the cut. Full directions sent with each swage.

Cat. No.	Size No.	Suitable for	Price	Cat. No.	Size No.	Suitable for	Price
9K59466	0	small thin saws	$2.66	9K59462	2	8 to 12-gauge	$3.96
9K59464	1	10-gauge and thinner	3.32	9K59460	3	5 to 10-gauge	4.66

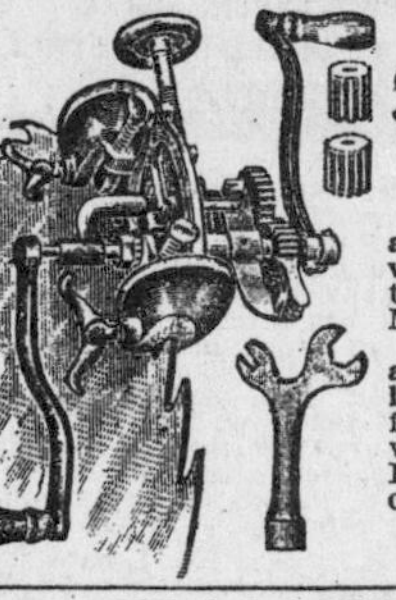

$18.69 MIXTER'S CELEBRATED PATENT AUTOMATIC SELF FEEDING CHAMPION SAW GUMMER.

Imitations of the genuine Mixter Gummer should be avoided on account of inferior quality and workmanship, which make them dear at any price. You can buy an imitation for $15.00 or less, but in comparison with the genuine Mixter Gummer they are not worth $5.00.

Self acting, throwing itself out of gear when the teeth are cut to the required depth, making them of uniform length. The line of the teeth can be cut at any angle desired, from horizontal to perpendicular. It cuts very rapidly and with no risk of bending, breaking or case hardening the saw. Full directions sent with each machine. Price includes three cutters, size, ¾, ⅞ and 1 inch, grinder and wrench.

No. 9K59470 Price........................$18.69

44c FOR A 3-8-INCH GENUINE MIXTER'S TOOL STEEL GUMMER CUTTER.

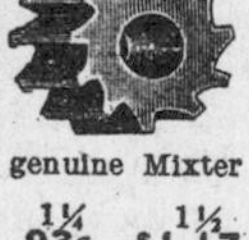

Will do as much work as six ordinary ones. No cutter genuine unless stamped "Mixter's XX." Cutters ⅜, ½ and ⅝-inch have 3-16-inch holes. Cutters ½, ⅝ and ¾-inch have 5-16-inch holes. Cutters ¾, ⅞, 1, 1⅛, 1¼ and 1½-inch have ½-inch holes, the standard size for regular arbor in the Champion gummer. You can buy imitation cutters as low as 20 cents each, but they are worthless and would be dear at 10 cents. In ordering, give size of hole as well as size of cutter, or you can send us an impression of one end of cutter on paper; state size gummer they are to be used in. We furnish cutters for Mixter's gummers only. We do not sell cheap imitations of the genuine Mixter goods.

No. 9K59476

Size, inches	⅜	½	⅝	¾	⅞	1	1⅛	1¼	1½
Price	44c	46c	47c	57c	65c	74c	84c	93c	$1.17

No. 9K59478 Extra Arbors for cutters with 5-16-inch holes. Price............ 1.98
No. 9K59480 Extra Arbors for cutters with 3-16-inch holes. Price............ 1.95

$6.22 FOR THIS 28-INCH FULTON CIRCULAR CUT OFF SAW. RIP SAW, 28-INCH, $6.12.

THE MAN who has been paying $10.00 to $12.00 for 28-inch Circular Saws that will not compare in quality with our perfect Fulton Saws will appreciate the wonderful value we offer in this popular size saw. 28-inch cut off saws are a favorite with pole sawyers and are largely used for that purpose. One of the greatest troubles with pole saws in general is caused by their tendency to crack. We equip our 28-inch Fulton saws with special round gullet teeth which entirely do away with this trouble. We sell thousands of these saws every year and have never known them to crack. Our Fulton 28-inch saws are made of finest steel, 10-gauge in thickness, with 1⅜ or 1½-inch mandrel hole and have from 72 to 80 teeth on cut off saws and 32 to 34 teeth on rip saws. The speed should be about 1,400 revolutions per minute and it requires from 1½ to 2-horse power to develop the full capacity of the saw. These saws are hand set and hand filed and are sent out sharp and ready for use. 28-inch rip saws are a great favorite in small and medium size saw mills and for ripping timber of small dimensions in quantity this size saw cannot be excelled. Remember that though we save you money in the price of Fulton saws, they are positively unequaled in quality and every saw we send out is guaranteed to please you or we will take it back and refund your money. For prices of all sizes of Fulton circular saws see list on next page.

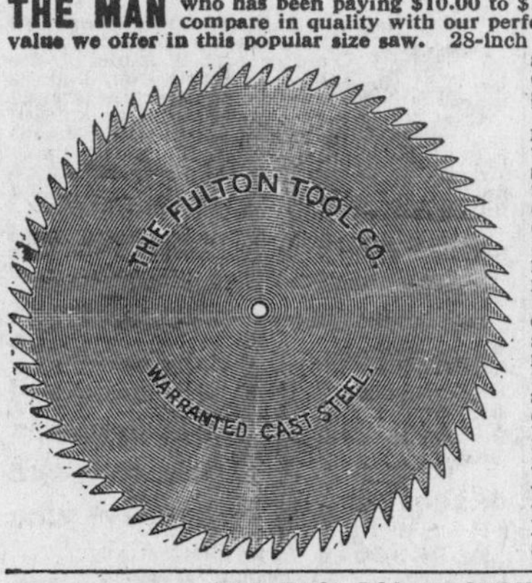

$10.18 FOR THIS BIG 36-INCH FULTON CUT OFF SAW. $10.08 FOR THE SAME SIZE RIP SAW.

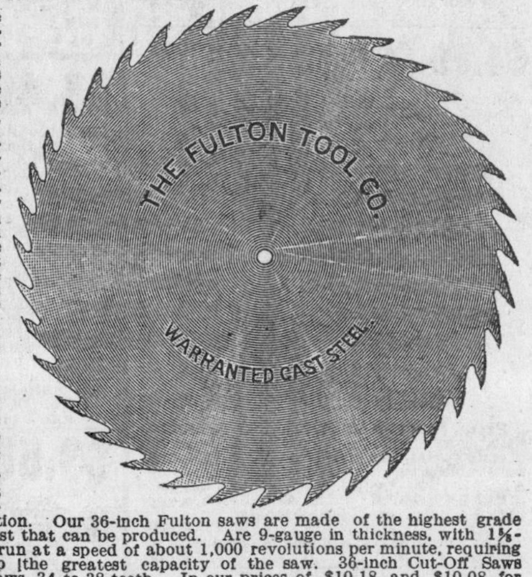

$10.18 is the low price we put on this big 36-inch Fulton Cut Off Saw, our No. 9K59402, but a price which does not begin to represent its actual value, gauged by the price of any other high grade saw on the market. Rip saw, 36 inches, $10.08, our No. 9K59404. If you can buy for $18.00 any other 36-inch saw that will compare in quality or capacity with our 36-inch Fulton saw, you can try the latter for thirty days in your own mill, making any test you find necessary and using them side by side, if you will, to find out which is the best. If at the end of thirty days you do not think the Fulton saw is the best saw you ever used, we will take it back and refund your money. 36-inch saws are a favorite size in medium and large mills, and as a general purpose saw cannot be excelled. In cutting capacity and power saving our Fulton saws are positively guaranteed the best in the world. Every Fulton saw is hand set and hand filed, sent out sharp and ready for use and so securely crated that it will reach you in perfect condition, ready to put into operation. Our 36-inch Fulton saws are made of the highest grade double refined saw steel, the best that can be produced. Are 9-gauge in thickness, with 1⅝-inch mandrel holes and should run at a speed of about 1,000 revolutions per minute, requiring 3 to 5-horse power to develop the greatest capacity of the saw. 36-inch Cut-Off Saws have 80 to 90 teeth and Rip Saws, 34 to 38 teeth. In our prices of $10.18 and $10.08 for 36-inch Fulton Cut Off and Rip Saws we save you big money and if we do not send you the best saw you ever had and one that is perfectly satisfactory, we will take it back and refund the price. Send us your order today. See price list on next page for all sizes of Fulton Circular Saws.

SAW MANDRELS.

OUR SAW MANDRELS are made by expert machinists, men who have spent years at the trade and know just what is required of a mandrel. We do not attempt to reduce the cost of machines by employing green or unskilled labor or by using inferior material. Only the highest quality of iron and steel goes into our saw mandrels. The boxes and pillows are soft gray iron. Pulleys and flanges are accurately turned. Shaft is high grade cold rolled steel, and the babbitt metal we use in the bearings is the highest quality we are able to procure. You can buy saw mandrels for less than our prices, but you take your life in your hands when you do it. A cheap, poorly made saw mandrel is dangerous to life and property, and we will not sell that kind.

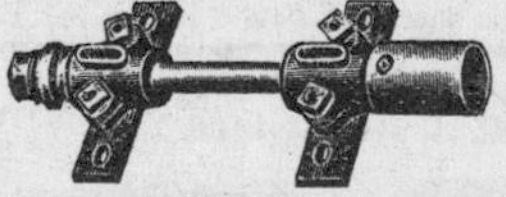

THE SAFE KIND TO BUY AND SAVES YOU MONEY.

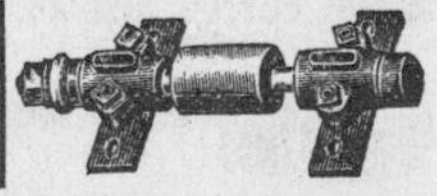

No. 9K59450 Circular Saw Mandrel with pulley on right hand side when saw is running toward you. With left hand thread. Order by number. Price as per list below.

No. 9K59452 Circular Saw Mandrel with pulley in center. Order by number and give size. Sizes and prices as per list below.

No.	Diam. of Pulley, inches	Face of Pulley, inches	Diam. of Flange, inches	Weight, lbs.	Length of Shaft, inches	Diam. of Shaft, inches	Size of hole in Saw, ins.	Price, either style
1	2½	3½	2½	18½	16½	1 1/16	1	$3.57
2	3	4	3	22½	19	1 3/16	1⅛	3.86
3	3½	4½	3½	32	21½	1 5/16	1¼	4.32
4	4	5	4	38	24	1 7/16	1 5/16	4.87
5	4½	5½	4½	44½	26	1 7/16	1 5/16	5.41
6	5	6	5	46	28	1 7/16	1⅜	5.86
7	5½	6½	5½	49	30½	1 7/16	1⅜	6.65
8	6	7	6	59	32½	1 9/16	1½	8.59
9	7	8	6	75	37	1 11/16	1⅝	9.89
10	8	9	6	80	41	1 13/16	1⅝	11.28
11	9	10	6	90	48	2 3/16	2	15.52

Mandrel will not safely run larger saws than those having same size hole in our price list of circular saws. To illustrate: The first mandrel will not safely carry a larger saw than 12 inches in diameter, and the next to the last mandrel will not run a larger saw than 36 inches in diameter.

81c FOR A LARGE SIZE SIDE FILER COMPLETE WITH FILE.

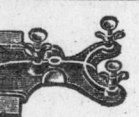

This Filer is used for dressing the sides of the points of teeth of circular saws to make them true. The most perfect device for the purpose ever invented.

No. 9K59482 Price, with file, complete..............81c
No. 9K59484 Extra Files only, for Side Filer. Good ones, not the cheap 30-cent kind. Price..................37c

FULTON CIRCULAR SAWS MADE IN OUR OWN FACTORY

ARE THE MOST WONDERFUL SAW VALUES EVER OFFERED BY ANY HOUSE.

FULTON SOLID TOOTH CIRCULAR SAW.

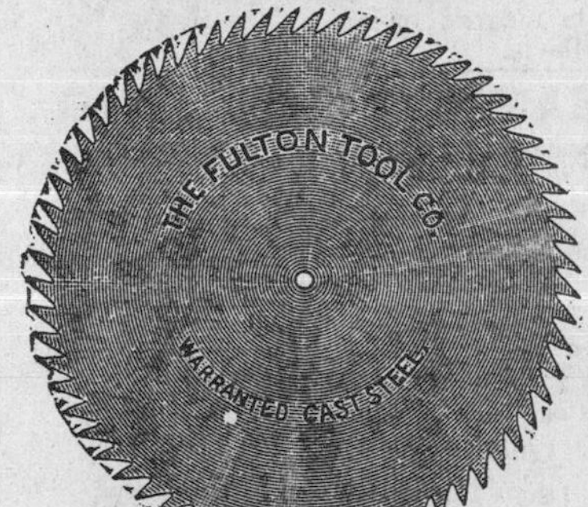
THE FULTON TOOL CO.
WARRANTED CAST STEEL

FULTON CIRCULAR SAWS are made of the finest crucible steel, tempered by our own improved process, and will cut faster and run longer without filing than any other saws made. They are smithed and blocked by the old hand process, only skilled workmen being employed for this important work. Fulton Circular Saws are carefully balanced and tested before leaving the factory, and we guarantee them to run true. Fulton Saws are hand filed and hand set, sent out sharpened and ready for use. They are finely and evenly polished, run smoother and use less power to accomplish the same amount of work than any saws made.

FULTON CIRCULAR SAWS ARE SOLD ONLY BY US, and are offered at prices very much lower than it is possible for any other dealer or maker to name. We buy raw material in immense quantities, manufacture saws in great numbers and sell them direct to the user, adding only one small profit to the actual cost of material and labor. We have no high prices to maintain, no jobbers to protect, no salesmen to pay, no big advertising bills to meet, and though Fulton Circular Saws are well and favorably known to millmen all over the United States, you pay no premium for this good reputation.

FULTON CIRCULAR SAWS ARE GUARANTEED ABSOLUTELY PERFECT in material, workmanship and finish; to run true and to outcut and outlast any saws made at even double our price. In order that you may test for yourself the strong claims we make for the superiority of Fulton Saws over any other make, we accept your order under a binding guarantee to **take back any saw that you may buy from us within thirty days** after you receive same, if you do not find it equal to or better than any saw you ever used. We could not afford to make this offer unless we knew that Fulton Saws would stand every test and prove superior in every way.

FULTON INSERTED TOOTH CIRCULAR SAW.

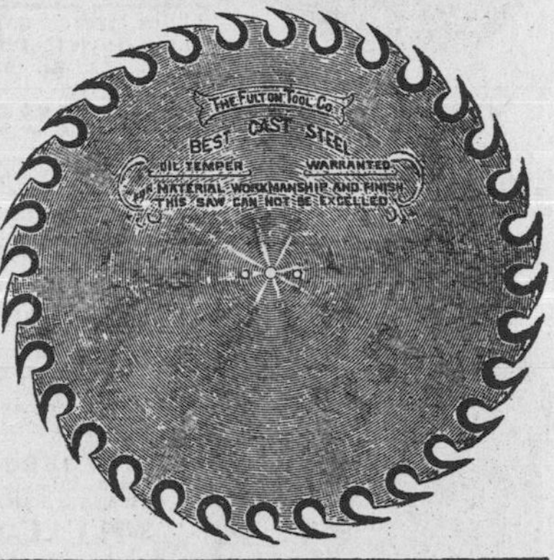
THE FULTON TOOL CO.
BEST CAST STEEL
OIL TEMPER
WARRANTED
MATERIAL, WORKMANSHIP AND FINISH
THIS SAW CAN NOT BE EXCELLED

FULTON SOLID TOOTH CIRCULAR SAWS are made of the highest grade crucible saw steel, tempered by our superior process, perfectly ground by special machinery and are exactly the same thickness all the way around at any given distance from the center. Fulton Solid Tooth Saws are carefully balanced, will not cause the arbor to tremble, cut unevenly or give you trouble in any way whatever.

EVERY FULTON SOLID TOOTH CIRCULAR SAW we send out has been carefully tested at the factory on a special machine, run at its full and highest speed to make sure that it is in proper tension, and hammered as it should be. Besides being smithed and blocked by hand, every Fulton Circular Saw we sell is **hand filed and hand set**, as this is the only proper way to do this work.

OUR FULTON SOLID TOOTH SAWS are shipped ready for use; all you have to do is to put them into immediate operation. Remember that you take no risk whatever in buying a saw from us, that it must be entirely satisfactory and you are at perfect liberty to return it to us if it does not please you. Read our guarantee at the top of this page. send us your order and let us save you money.

Price List of Fulton Solid Tooth Circular Saws.

No. 9K59402 The Fulton Cut Off Saw. Warranted.

No. 9K59404 The Fulton Rip Saw. Warranted. Circular Saws 42 inches in diameter and larger beveled, two gauges (if so ordered) without extra charge.

Diameter, inches	Thickness, gauge	Size of Hole, inches	Price, each, Cut Off Saw	Price, each, Rip Saw
4	10	½	$0.42	$0.40
6	18	¾	.58	.56
8	18	⅞	.82	.80
10	16	1	1.22	1.19
12	15	1	1.55	1.50
14	15	1⅛	1.85	1.80
16	14	1⅛	2.21	2.16
18	13	1¼	2.75	2.70
20	13	1 5-16	3.32	3.24
22	12	1 5-16	4.06	3.96
24	11	1⅜	4.78	4.68
26	11	1⅜	5.50	5.40
28	10	1⅜ or 1½	6.22	6.12
30	10	1⅜ or 1½	6.94	6.84
32	10	1⅜	8.02	7.92
34	9	1⅜	9.10	9.00
36	9	1⅜	10.18	10.08
38	9	1⅜	11.28	11.03
40	9	2	13.03	12.78
42	8	2	14.73	14.45
44	8	2	17.45	17.20
46	8	2	20.91	20.66
48	8	2	25.35	24.06
50	7	2	28.85	27.46
52	7	2	32.42	30.92
54	7	2	35.92	34.32
56	7	2	41.12	39.42
58	7	2	46.43	44.63
60	6	2	51.63	49.73
62	6	2	61.00	57.60
64	6	2	68.57	64.80
66	6	2	75.88	72.00
68	5	2	84.99	82.50
70	5	2	95.90	93.30
72	5	2	108.60	105.90

FULTON INSERTED TOOTH CIRCULAR SAWS are designed on strictly practical lines and are guaranteed positively the best inserted tooth saws on the market regardless of price. Every Fulton Inserted Tooth Circular Saw we have sent out has given perfect satisfaction and so far as we know, we have never had a dissatisfied customer on one of these saws. The steel that goes into our Inserted Tooth Circular Saws is the very best that money will buy. The points are all drop forged from a very high grade special steel made for this particular purpose, and by our process of tempering, these points are left very hard, strong and tough, enabling them to stand, without giving any trouble, the extremely hard strain and severe usage to which they are subjected. Special attention is called to the recess for holding the teeth on our inserted tooth saws. These recesses are milled out on a special machine designed and manufactured in our own factory. The use of this machine enables us to have each and every tooth in any saw exactly the same distance from the center of the saw to the point of the tooth. This is a feature rarely found in inserted tooth saws of other makes and goes far toward insuring the superiority of our Fulton Inserted Tooth Saws over any other brand or make.

READ OUR GUARANTEE at the top of this page. Note that if our Fulton Saws do not please you in every way, you are at perfect liberty to return them and your money will be promptly refunded.

Price List of Fulton Inserted Tooth Circular Saws.

Gauge given in price list regularly furnished, but any size saw will be furnished one gauge lighter or heavier as desired without extra charge. Be sure to specify on your order if you want other than regular guage.

No. 9K59412 Fulton Inserted Tooth Circular Saw.

Diameter, inches	Regular Gauge	No. of Teeth in Saw	Price, with No. 2, 3 or 4 Teeth
16	11	12	$11.10
18	11	14	12.50
20	11	16	14.35
22	11	18	16.20
24	11	20	18.05
26	10	22	19.90
28	10	24	21.75
30	10	24	24.08
32	9	28	26.40
34	9	28	28.70
36	8	30	31.50
38	8	32	33.80
40	8	34	37.00
42	8	34	39.80
44	7 or 8	36	44.00
46	7 or 8	36	47.70
48	7 or 8	24 to 40	52.30
50	7 or 8	24 to 42	58.80
52	7 or 8	24 to 44	68.50
54	7 or 8	24 to 46	76.40
56	7 or 8	30 to 48	88.00
58	7 or 8	30 to 50	97.25
60	6 or 7	30 to 52	106.50
62	6 or 7	30 to 52	115.75
64	5 or 6	30 to 54	127.35
66	5 or 6	30 to 56	138.90
68	5 or 6	30 to 56	150.50
70	4 or 5	30 to 58	164.40
72	4 or 5	30 to 60	180.60

WE CARRY IN STOCK AT ALL TIMES, ready for prompt shipment all sizes of circular saws, both cut off and rip, up to 36 inches in diameter, with holes as listed and number of teeth ordinarily used, but can ship saws with odd size holes or made to order with less delay than any other saw maker. If a saw is wanted with pin holes, send a paper pattern giving exact location. Order blanks for ordering saws will be furnished on request.

Please note that above prices are for saws set and filed; also note that prices for saws larger than 36 inches are for saws delivered on board cars at factory in Southeastern Michigan, from which point customer pays freight.

We are prepared to furnish circular saws up to 76 inches in diameter. Prices quoted on application.

We carry the plates for the following saws at our factory unfinished. All have 2-inch mandrel holes with ⅝-inch pin holes spaced 3 inches center to center. After an order is received these saws must be toothed, ground, hammered, polished, swaged and filed. Our facilities for doing this work are such that we are able to ship in much less time than is usually required by other factories. Price as per above list.

Diameter, inches	Gauge at Hole	Gauge at Rim	Teeth
42	9	10	32
44	9	10	32
46	9	10	34
48	9	10	34
50	9	10	36
52	8	9	36
54	8	9	36
56	8	9	38
58	8	9	38
60	8	9	38
62	8	9	40
64	8	9	40
66	7	8	40

On orders for saws larger than 36 inches, in order to fill same, it is necessary we should have the following specifications: Size of mandrel hole, number of teeth wanted in saw, size of pin holes, distance of pin holes from center to center, gauge at center, gauge at rim, spring or swage set, temper, speed, feed, to cut hard or soft wood, right or left hand.

Blanks for ordering circular saws sent free on request. We require from five to thirty days to fill orders for circular saws which are not regular or which are not carried in stock.

On orders for special saws, we cannot accept cancellation after order is received by us.

Fulton Narrow Band Saws.

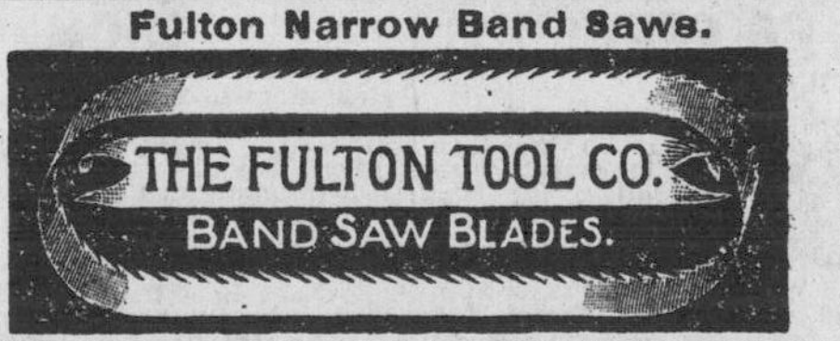
THE FULTON TOOL CO.
BAND SAW BLADES.

Made from a special brand of steel, carefully hardened and tempered by our improved process. Sufficiently hard to stand severe usage but still tough and flexible. Fully guaranteed. Saws set and sharpened. Order by number and give exact length wanted. **Be sure to specify gauge and number of teeth to the inch desired.**

No. 9K59432 Fulton Band Saws. Brazed.

Band saws brazed or with ends joined are shipped direct from factory only, customers paying transportation charges.

Add for postage as follows: Widths, ⅛, 3-16 or ¼ inch, ½c per foot; widths, 5-16, ⅜ or ½ inch, 1c per foot; widths, ⅝ or ¾ inch, 1½c per foot; widths, ⅞ or 1 inch, 2c per foot; widths, 1¼ or 1½ inch, 3c per foot; width, 1¾ in., 4c per ft.

Width, inches	Gauge No.	Length, feet 10	12	14	16	18	20
⅛, 3/16 or ¼	21 or 22	$0.49	$0.52	$0.57	$0.66	$0.73	$0.80
5/16	21 or 20	.56	.60	.65	.71	.78	.85
⅜	21 or 20	.67	.72	.76	.81	.86	.91
½	21 or 20	.73	.78	.83	.88	.94	1.02
⅝	21 or 20	.98	1.04	1.11	1.17	1.24	1.33
¾	21 or 20	1.06	1.12	1.18	1.24	1.33	1.47
⅞	20 or 19	1.19	1.24	1.31	1.38	1.47	1.58
1	20 or 19	1.34	1.41	1.49	1.56	1.67	1.78
1¼	20 or 19	1.56	1.63	1.71	1.82	1.94	2.06
1½	20 or 19	1.89	1.97	2.04	2.19	2.36	2.58
1¾	20 or 19	2.29	2.41	2.56	2.73	2.94	3.16

Saws between lengths as above listed take same price as next longer length.

No. 9K59430 Fulton Band Saws. Not brazed. Carried in stock and can be shipped with other goods from Chicago.

Width, inch	⅛, 3/16 or ¼	5/16 or ⅜	½	⅝
Price, per foot	3½c	4c	5c	6c

Width, inches	¾	⅞	1	1¼	1½	1¾
Price, per foot	7c	8c	9c	10c	13c	16c

No. 9K59440 Silver Solder for Brazing Band Saws. We do not sell less than one ounce. Price, per ounce..........82c

ON ALL ORDERS FOR INSERTED TOOTH SAWS it is necessary for us to have the following specifications: Size of saw, size of mandrel hole, number of teeth wanted in saw, style of tooth, size of pin holes, distance of pin holes from center to center, gauge of saw at center, gauge at rim, speed, feed, whether to cut hard or soft wood, and right or left hand. If desired, blanks for ordering circular saws will be sent free on request.

For saws fitted with No. 1 teeth add 10 per cent to prices above.

Prices on all sizes of Inserted Tooth Saws are for saws delivered on board cars at factory, in Southeastern Michigan, from which point customer pays the freight.

The above list gives the standard number of teeth for different sizes of saws. Saws can be furnished with less teeth if desired. For price of extra teeth only see following item.

One wrench, two extra shanks and 100 points furnished with each saw 46 inches in diameter and less.

One wrench, 6 extra shanks and 200 extra points furnished with each saw 48 inches in diameter or over.

Chisel Teeth for Fulton Inserted Tooth Circular Rip Saws.

Shipped direct from factory in Southeastern Michigan only. Customers must pay transportation charges.

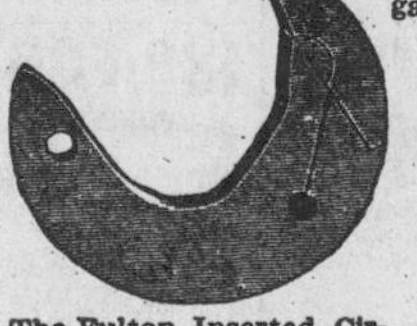

The Fulton Inserted Circular Rip Saw Tooth.

No. 9K59414 Our No. 1 Chisel Tooth for the Fulton Inserted Tooth Saw is most adapted for bolting and gang edging saws.

Price of points, each....$0.03
Per 100 .... 2.65
Price of holders, each. ... .24
Per 100 .... 21.90

No. 9K59416 Our No. 2 Chisel Tooth for the Fulton Inserted Tooth Saw is designed for heavy feeds.

Price of points, each.....$0.03
Per 100.............. 2.65
Price of holders, each.... .24
Per 100.............. 21.90

No. 9K59418 Our No. 3 Chisel Tooth for the Fulton Inserted Tooth Saw is mostly used in hard woods and is a good tooth where both hard and soft wood is cut.

Price of points, per 100........$ 2.65; each...... 3c
Price of holders, per 100...... 26.25; each 28c

No. 9K59420 Our No. 4 Chisel Tooth for the Fulton Inserted Tooth Saw is adapted to soft, pitchy lumber or where a large amount of throat room is desired.

Price of points, per 100.......$ 3.06; each...... 3½c
Price of holders, per 100...... 33.25; each...... 35c

When ordering points or holders state gauge of saw for which they are wanted. We do not handle teeth for saws of other manufacturers.

BELTING AND MILL SUPPLIES

OUR IMMENSE BUSINESS IN BELTING OF ALL KINDS enables us to place enormous contracts direct with the largest manufacturers and get the lowest prices for the best grades of goods. We save you at least 33⅓ per cent on belting and general mill supplies. Compare our prices with others and remember that **we guarantee** to satisfy you. We handle only the dependable kind of merchandise; none of the inferior qualities whatever.

ABOUT ENDLESS BELTS. With the exception of canvas belts for use on portable outfits, we do not advise the making of a belt endless as it is better to have a laced joint where stretch can be taken up when occasion requires. If belts are ordered made endless it requires from four to six days to make them ready and they must be shipped separately on account of the delay in making to order. On all endless belts allow the price of 3 feet of belt extra for the lap and the labor of making.

GUARANTEED RUBBER BELTING

Our Rubber Belting is composed of best quality cotton duck and pure Para rubber, made right, in the best manner possible, and guaranteed to stretch less than any other rubber belting on the market. Because of the belt not stretching the friction remains the same and the belt delivers full power. We do not recommend rubber belts for use on threshers as canvas belting is superior for such use. Be careful in making orders for belt, for if it is sent as ordered, it cannot be taken back or exchanged. Endless belts are made to order only as noted above.

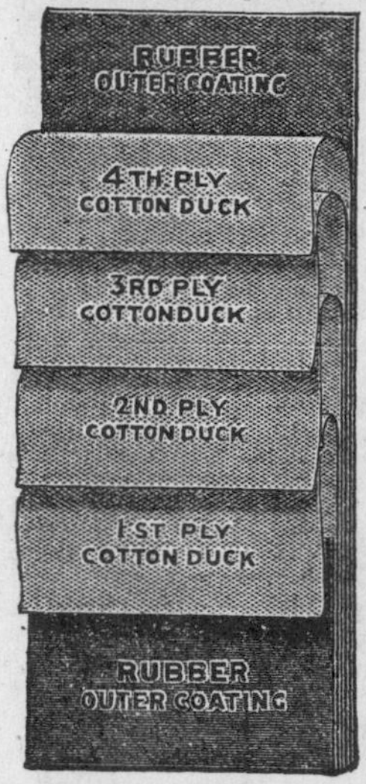

2-PLY BANNER BRAND RUBBER BELTING.

Made with rubber outer coatings as shown in illustration and with two cotton duck plies. Banner Belting is the best two-ply belting sold by anyone. Recommended for light work, hand power machines, farm machinery, etc. Equal to belting offered by others at 25 to 50 per cent more than our prices.

No. 9K38902 Banner 2-ply Rubber Belting.

Width, inches...	1	1½	1¾	2	2½	3
Price, per foot...	2½c	3½c	4½c	6c	7c	8c

3-PLY LEADER BRAND RUBBER BELTING.

Made with rubber outer coatings as shown in illustration and with three cotton duck plies, which makes it 50 per cent stronger than Banner brand quoted above. Our Leader Three-Ply Belting is the largest selling brand of rubber belting in the United States. It is an excellent belt, fully capable of hard service and guaranteed to do the work.

No. 9K38903 Leader 3-ply Rubber Belting.

Width, inches..	1½	2	2½	3	3½	4	4½	5	6
Price, per ft..	5c	7c	9c	11c	13c	15c	17c	19c	22c

4-PLY DEFIANCE BRAND RUBBER BELTING.

Made with rubber outer coatings and four heavy cotton duck plies as shown in illustration. Defiance Rubber Belting is the best belting made, bar none, strong enough and heavy enough to pull any load. Used extensively in saw mills, stone quarries and places where the service is severe. It is firm and tough, guaranteed to run true and not to separate the plies.

No. 9K38904 Defiance 4-ply Rubber Belting.

Width, inches	3	4	5	6	7	8	10	12
Price, per ft..	15c	20c	25c	30c	35c	40c	50c	65c

GUARANTEED LEATHER BELTING

We handle only reliable leather belting made from carefully selected oak tanned hides, the different grades being according to the weight of the leather, the length of the lap and the part of the hide the leather is taken from. All our leather belting has been carefully stretched on improved machinery, just enough to take out the "give," but not enough to take the life out of the leather. Don't use cheap, inferior leather belting; if you must buy cheap belting, get rubber belting. Remember, leather belting is not suitable for outdoor use or where it will get wet.

AGRICULTURAL LEATHER BELTING.

Made up to 4 inches wide, of light oak tanned leather, suitable for hand power machines, farm machinery or any light service. Not recommended for regular factory or heavy work.

No. 9K38910 Agricultural Leather Belting.

Width, inches..	1	1¼	1½	1¾	2½
Price, per foot..	5c	6c	8c	9c	10c	12c
Width, inches..			3	3½	4
Price, per foot..	13c	14c	15c	18c	20c

STANDARD LEATHER BELTING.

Made up to 6 inches in width of regular standard oak tanned stock, suitable for mill and factory use. The best general purpose belting made. Will stand severe service and any but the heaviest loads. Fully equal to the best grades offered by other concerns.

No. 9K38911 Standard Leather Belting.

Width, inches..	1	1¼	1½	1¾	2	2¼	2½	2¾
Price, per foot..	7c	8c	10c	12c	14c	16c	18c	20c
Width, inches..	3	3½	4	4½	5	5½	6	
Price, per foot..	22c	25c	28c	31c	34c	37c	40c	

ACME SPECIAL LEATHER BELTING.

Made entirely of heavy selected oak tanned leather, cut in short laps from only the solid part of the hide, thoroughly stretched, made of even thickness stock and guaranteed the most perfect belt made. We recommend this Acme Special Belting for any purpose that leather belting can be used. Especially desirable for main drive belts, heavy loads, etc. Made in widths as given, from 7 to 14 inches only.

No. 9K38912 Acme Special Leather Belting.

Width, inches..	7	8	9	10
Price, per foot..	60c	68c	76c	84c
Width, inches..	11	12	13	14
Price, per foot..	93c	$1.04	$1.16	$1.25

STITCHED CANVAS BELTING.

Ours is the strongest Stitched Canvas Belting manufactured. It is made of heavy, long fiber cotton duck or canvas, woven very hard and has rows of stitching so close together that the plies cannot separate. It is painted a red color with a special composition which gives it an excellent friction and makes it thoroughly waterproof. Proof against steam, oil, gases, etc., not affected by heat or cold, flexible under all conditions. Especially recommended for threshers, saw mills, quarries, brick yards or other heavy work. Our stitched canvas belting is thoroughly stretched before leaving the factory. Use an awl in making holes for lacing canvas belting. Never use a belt punch as it cuts the threads.

No. 9K38938 4-Ply Stitched Canvas Belt.

Width, inches..	1½	2	2½	3	3½	4	4½	5	6	7	8	9	10	12
Price, per foot..	4¾c	6¼c	7½c	9½c	11c	12½c	14½c	15¾c	19c	22c	25c	28c	31½c	37¾c

No. 9K38939 6-Ply Stitched Canvas Belt.

Width, inches..	3	4	5	6	7	8	9	10	12	14
Price, per foot..	13½c	18¼c	23c	27½c	32c	36c	41¼c	45½c	54½c	67c

ENDLESS CANVAS BELTING.

Far superior to all other canvas thresher belting on account of the process of its manufacture. The splice is made in such a manner that the belt is no thicker at this point, and is just as strong and flexible as any other part of the belt. It is painted with a composition of a reddish color, is thoroughly waterproof, and is not affected by oil or any change of temperature. It is sewed with rows of stitches throughout its entire length, which makes it practically impossible for the plies to separate. Can also be used on other machinery besides threshers. We carry the following lengths of these four-ply belts in stock and can ship promptly. The actual lengths of these belts is 3 feet less than stated, as it requires the price of 3 feet for lap and labor in making belt endless.

No. 9K38942 4-Ply Endless Belt.

Length, ft.	6 in. 4-ply	7 in. 4-ply	8 in. 4-ply	Length, ft.	6 in. 4-ply	7 in. 4-ply	8 in. 4-ply
80	$13.29	$15.68	$17.06	140	$23.22	$27.42	$31.62
100	16.58	19.59	22.56	150	24.87	29.41	33.84
120	19.87	23.48	27.07	160	26.58	31.34	36.13
130	21.59	25.47	29.37				

REDUCED HARDWARE PRICES IN THIS BOOK MAKE YOUR SAVING GREATER THAN EVER

12c PER STICK HERCULES BELT DRESSING.

The most convenient and economical dressing made. Contains nothing injurious to belts, prolongs their life and positively prevents slipping. Put up in 1-pound sticks.
No. 9K38945 Price, per stick..12c

23c PER SQUARE FOOT BEST RAWHIDE LACE LEATHER.

We sell only the best grade of tough Rawhide Lace Leather in sides of from 5 to 15 square feet. (We do not cut sides.)
No. 9K38954 Price, per square foot..23c

64c PER 100 FEET CUT RAWHIDE LACING, ¼-INCH.

Cut from selected hides by improved machinery, insuring uniformity. Comes in bunches of 100 feet. Will sell half a bunch at one-half the price of full bunch.
No. 9K38955

Width	Price, per 100 feet	Width	Price, per 100 feet
¼ inch	64c	½ inch	$1.27
5-16 inch	75c	¾ inch	1.75
⅜ inch	98c	1 inch	2.08

24c FOR THIS ADJUSTABLE LACE LEATHER CUTTER.

The best tool in use for the purpose. Adjustable to cut various widths.
No. 9K38957 Price..24c

28c FOR 50 FEET COMPOSITION WIRE BELT LACING.

There is no friction or wear on the lace while in contact with the pulley, as the strands lie flush with the face of the belt. For all work where the belts are speeded or run with idlers, or at a severe strain. 50 feet on each spool and each spool in a box. No. 1—For all single belts 6 inches wide and under. No. 2—For all belts 6 to 20 inches wide. State number.
No. 9K38962 Price, per spool....28c

7c PER DOZ. BLAKE'S PATTERN BELT STUDS, No. 1.

Save time, trouble and lace leather. The best belt fastener made. **No. 9K38964**

No..........	00	0	1	2	3
Length between shoulders....	½	1 1-16	¾	⅝	9-16
Per dozen....	10c	8c	7c	6c	4c
Per 100	78c	62c	52c	39c	28c

13c FOR 250 OVAL POINTED BELT HOOKS.

Made of Norway wire with oval points. Prices given are per box of 250 hooks.
No. 9K38959

No.	Length	Price, per box	No.	Length	Price, per box
12	25-32 inch	13c	8	1¼ inches	26c
11	29-32 inch	15c	7	1 18-32 inches	32c
10	1 1-32 inch	18c	6	1¾ inches	46c
9	1¼ inch	21c			

HIGH GRADE BABBITT METAL.

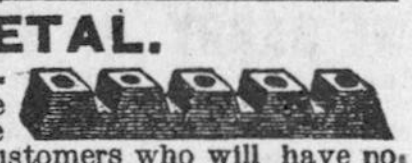

All our Babbitt Metal is made from new high grade anti-friction metals, thoroughly refined and properly mixed to meet the requirements of speed and weight. We have been handling the same high grade line for several years and have thousands of customers who will have no other. All of it is entirely dependable and will give good service for the purposes for which it is recommended by us.

No. 4 Babbitt Metal. A standard quality metal suitable for use on mowers, horse powers, pulleys, separators and farm machinery generally.
No. 9K36450 Price, per pound 7c

No. 1 Babbitt Metal. This is a good general purpose metal, of a grade higher than the preceding number and can be safely used on machinery running at average speed.
No. 9K36454 Price, per pound.........

Lubricating grade Babbitt Metal. A high grade copper mixed metal suitable for use on engines and fine machinery running at high speed and requiring perfect bearings.
No. 9K36456 Price, per pound..........16c

55c PER BAR OLD HICKORY, THE HIGHEST GRADE BABBITT METAL MADE.

Can be used on any journal, but is especially recommended for high speed machinery. It is made in round bars of about 2½ lbs. each, one side cone shaped, which fits the bottom of the melting ladle evenly, thus all parts of metal melt at once. We do not sell less than a 2½-pound bar.
No. 9K36461 Price, per bar......55c

48c PER BAR STRICTLY PURE BLOCK TIN.

Guaranteed absolutely pure. Comes in bars of about 1 pound each. We do not sell less than one bar.
No. 9K36467 Price, per bar.......48c

26c FOR A No. 1 GRAPHITE OR PLUMBAGO CRUCIBLE.

Made of the best materials, will not flake or crack.
No. 9K38470

	Height	Diameter	Price
No. 1..	3¼ inches.	2¾ inches.	26c
No. 3..	4½ inches.	3¼ inches.	39c
No. 5..	6 inches.	4 inches.	49c
No. 8..	7 inches.	4⅝ inches.	66c
No. 10..	7¾ inches.	5 inches.	79c

48c FOR OUR HEALTH SAVING, LUNG PROTECTING ACME RESPIRATOR.

The finest and most complete article ever offered for protecting the throat and lungs from dust, poisonous gases and all other impurities in places where persons are exposed and where many times life is endangered. No foundryman, thresherman, tobacco worker or farmer who is exposed to dust, smoke, etc., should be without one. Guaranteed satisfactory. Made of high grade pure white rubber. Complete with sponge and elastic band to hold it on. Weight, 6 ounces.
No. 9K36205 Price.........48c

14c FOR 200 ACME BELT HOOKS.

Simplest and most durable made. Will stand more strain than any lacing; can be used on any diameter pulley; will not cut out of belt or become loose. As good for rubber and canvas as for leather belting. Made from very best annealed coppered steel wire. Will not rust and points will not break. Put up in boxes of 200 hooks, assorted No. 0 to No. 3 or all one size, as desired. State size wanted.

No. 0..........	⅝ inch wide.	No. 2..........	¾ inch wide.
No. 1..........	½ inch wide.	No. 3..........	1 inch wide.

No. 9K38960 Price, per box, any size 14c

WE SOLD OVER SIX HUNDRED THOUSAND FEET OF RUBBER GARDEN HOSE LAST YEAR

AT LOWER PRICES THAN ANY CONCERN IN THE UNITED STATES. PRICES THIS YEAR STILL FURTHER REDUCED.

WE PLACE OUR YEARLY CONTRACT for rubber hose with the largest manufacturer of rubber goods in this country. Contracting for such immense quantities at once we are able to purchase hose at prices much lower than jobbers pay for goods that will not compare in quality with ours. Our different brands are made for us only according to our own specifications and we inspect every piece of hose that comes into our house. **All our hose is made of rubber,** no "junk" being allowed to enter into its construction. The plies are made of selected long fiber cotton duck, woven very hard. The cotton duck is treated with a solution of pure rubber gum and applied under heavy pressure. The couplings are put on in a first class manner and are absolutely watertight. **Our complete line of rubber hose** includes all plies and weights, from the best that can be produced to our "Competition," which is the cheapest that is practical. We always recommend the purchase of the heavier grades as experience has taught us that 5 or 6-ply hose will outlast several pieces of the lighter weight kind. With the exception of the "Competition" hose, our entire line is made up of the same high grade material exactly, the difference in price being on account of the increased number of plies and the pure rubber inner tube which is made heavier on the higher priced hose. **Our "Competition" hose is a reliable piece of goods,** far better than you can buy elsewhere from 8 to 9 cents per foot, but it is not made to withstand heavy pressure. In your own interest, therefore, we advise the purchase of one of our higher grades of hose that will stand high pressure, and that will last and give satisfaction for years. **We sell hose all the time,** receive fresh stocks direct from the factory every month, and send out nothing but new, perfect goods. Rubber loses its quality with age and when you buy from the average retailer the chances are you get hose that has been made a long time and is often worthless. **Our hose is covered by our usual guarantee of entire satisfaction or your money back.** We list ½-inch and 1-inch hose, but most connections are made to fit ¾-inch couplings and ¾-inch hose (inside measurement) is considered the standard size. **You should purchase a reel** to come with your hose to keep it on, as this is the most satisfactory way of handling hose and makes it last much longer by allowing the hose to be thoroughly drained after using.

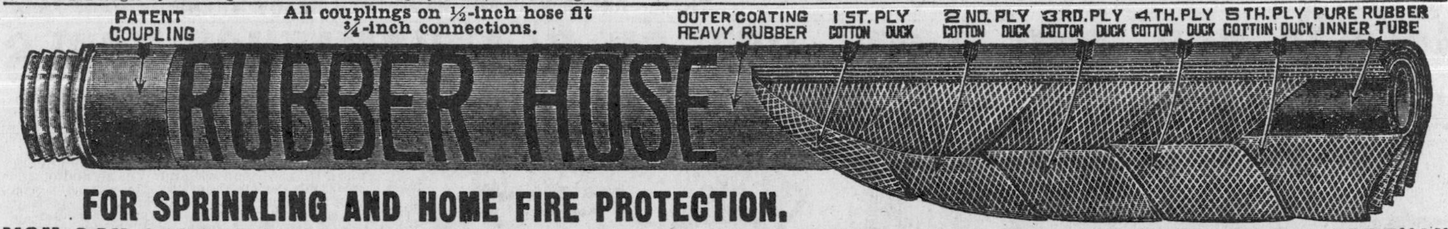

FOR SPRINKLING AND HOME FIRE PROTECTION.

YOU CAN SAVE 25 TO 50 PER CENT BY ORDERING YOUR RUBBER HOSE FROM US. **AT 8c PER FOOT** WE OFFER A BETTER GRADE OF HOSE THAN YOU CAN BUY IN YOUR HOME TOWN FOR 12c. **AT 10c PER FOOT** WE OFFER A BETTER GRADE OF HOSE THAN YOU CAN BUY IN YOUR HOME TOWN AT 15 CENTS. **AT 12 AND 14c PER FOOT** we offer absolutely the best hose made.

$2.97 3-PLY COMPETITION HOSE, ¾ INCH. 50 FEET, COMPLETE.

LESS THAN 6 CENTS PER FOOT.

The grade of hose usually offered by others at 8 to 9 cents per foot. Recommended for low pressures or country use and will give good satisfaction where pressure is not over 25 pounds. If you have higher pressure, we urge you to order our "Leader," "Defiance" or "Hercules" brands. **Carried in 50-foot lengths only,** complete with couplings put on. Size, inside diameter, ¾ inch.

No. 9K38975 Price, 50 feet, complete..........**$2.97**

8c PER FOOT 3-PLY BANNER HOSE, ¾ INCH, IN 50-FOOT LENGTHS.

Cannot be duplicated for less than 12 cents per foot. Pure rubber inner tube, 3 cotton duck plies, heavy rubber outer coating. The same high grade material as our heavier brands. Recommended for use on ordinary pressure. **We positively cannot furnish this hose except in 25 or 50-foot lengths.** Coupled complete. All couplings on ½-inch hose fit ¾-inch connections. **State size.**

No. 9K38976 Size, inside diameter	½ in.	¾ in.
Price, 25 feet, complete with couplings	$1.85	$2.10
Price, 50 feet, complete with couplings	3.50	4.00

10c PER FOOT 4-PLY LEADER GUARANTEED HOSE. SIZE, ¾ INCH, IN 50-FOOT LENGTHS.

For ordinary pressure this is the hose to buy.

A better grade of hose than you can buy at home for 15 cents per foot. Has heavy pure rubber inner tube, four long fiber, closely woven friction cotton duck thicknesses or plies, and heavy rubber outer coating. This is a high quality hose, strong and durable, **will stand any ordinary water pressure,** does not kink or bend easily, will last long and give excellent satisfaction. This Leader Hose has been our best selling quality for a number of years and we make it heavier and better than ever this year. **We positively cannot furnish this hose except in 25 or 50-foot lengths.** Coupled complete. All couplings on ½-inch hose fit ¾-inch connection. State size wanted.

No. 9K38979

Size, inside diameter	½ inch	¾ inch	1 inch
Price, 25 feet, complete with couplings	$2.09	$2.60	$3.45
Price, 50 feet, complete with couplings	3.98	5.00	6.50

12c PER FOOT 5-PLY DEFIANCE HOSE, ¾ INCH, IN 50-FOOT LENGTHS.

A better grade than retailers ever carry in stock. An extra high grade hose for heavy water pressure. This is the grade hose we illustrate. Made with pure rubber inner tube, five plies of frictioned cotton duck, and rubber outer coating. A heavier hose than the Leader, with one extra ply. Will stand the pressure and last for years. **We positively cannot furnish this hose except in 25 or 50-foot lengths, coupled complete.**

No. 9K38983 Size, inside diameter, ¾ inch.
Price, 25 feet, complete with couplings..........**$3.10**
Price, 50 feet, complete with couplings..........**6.00**

14c PER FOOT 6-PLY HERCULES HOSE ¾ INCH, IN 50-FOOT LENGTHS

The best hose made. Guaranteed to stand the heaviest water works pressure. Has an extra heavy inner tube of pure Para rubber, six plies of frictioned cotton duck, and a heavy outer coating of pure rubber. This hose will outwear and outlast any hose made and is fully guaranteed. **We positively cannot furnish this hose except in 25 or 50-foot lengths, coupled complete.**

No. 9K38985 Size, inside diameter, ¾ inch.
Price, 25 feet, complete with couplings..........**$3.60**
Price, 50 feet, complete with couplings..........**7.00**

24c PER FOOT STANDARD GRADE WIRE LINED TANK HOSE. SIZE, 2 INCHES.

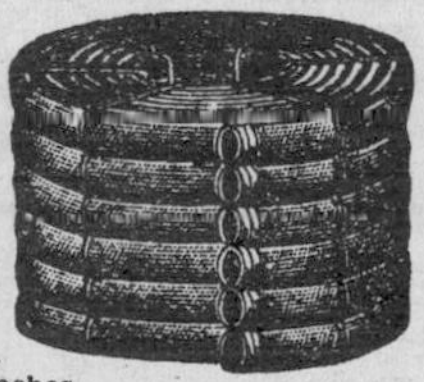

Made with smooth bore to reduce friction. The wire lining prevents the hose from collapsing and makes it extra strong. Sold in 10, 15, 20 and 25-foot pieces only. This is the hose to use in connection with our No. 42K5386 Tank Pumps. Size, 2 inches.

No. 9K35391 Price, per foot.....**24c**

36c PER FOOT ACME COTTON COVERED 2-INCH TANK HOSE.

Wire Lined, Cotton Covered Tank Hose, has a woven cotton jacket. Sold in 10, 15, 20 or 25-foot lengths only. Will outwear any hose made. Size, 2 inches.

No. 9K35390 Price, per foot....**36c**

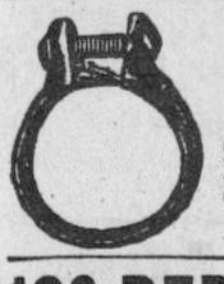

10c FOR A 2¼-INCH PATENT HOSE CLAMP FOR ABOVE HOSE.

Has nut to tighten or release clamp. Extra strong and heavy. The best tank hose clamp made.

No. 9K35393 Price..**10c**

18c PER FOOT HARD RUBBER SMOOTH BORE SUCTION HOSE, ¾ INCH.

This hose is made with extra thick walls to prevent collapsing when in use. Sold in multiples of 5 feet only, as 5, 10, 15 or 20-foot pieces and up to and including 50 feet in one piece. Couplings and clamps cost extra. See Nos. 9K39000 and 9K38998.

No. 9K35394
Size, ¾ inch. Price, per foot.....**18c**
Size, 1 inch. Price, per foot.....**21c**
Size, 1¼ inches. Price, per foot.....**25c**
Size, 1½ inches. Price, per foot.....**28c**

33c CAST STRAINER FOR ABOVE SUCTION HOSE, 2 INCHES.

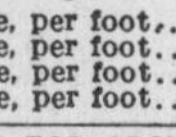

Prevents trash, etc., from entering pump. 5 inches long with 2-inch neck. Weight, 2 lbs.

No. 9K35396 Price..............**33c**

14c FOR A ¾ INCH SIZE SOLID BRASS HOSE NIPPLE.

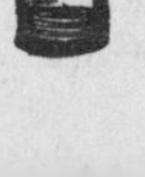

Has well cut threads, strong and durable. To be used in connecting hose to iron pipe.

No. 9K38996

Size, inch	½	¾	1
Price	12c	14c	16c

8c PER FOOT BRAIDED COTTON COVERED GARDEN HOSE, ¾ INCH, IN 50-FOOT LENGTHS.

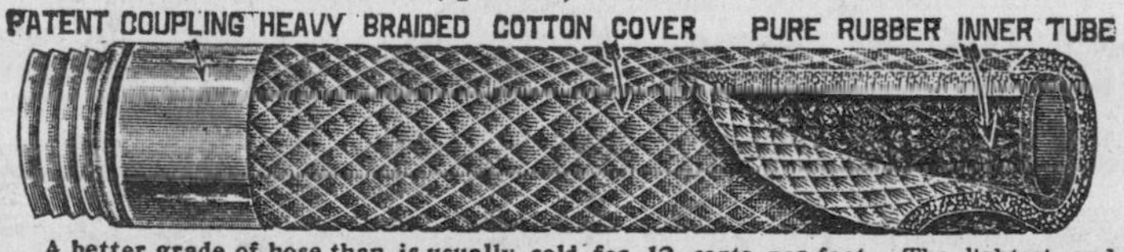

A better grade of hose than is usually sold for 12 cents per foot. The lightest and strongest hose made. The fabric is made of specially selected long fiber cotton and is perfect in construction. The inner tube is of pure rubber of good thickness. The color is pure white, which makes a very attractive appearance on the lawn. This is strictly a high grade lawn hose, with one pair couplings put on ready for use for which we make no extra charge. **We positively cannot furnish this hose except in 25 or 50-foot lengths, coupled complete.** No. 9K38980 is a good quality. No. 9K38981 is strictly a high grade; nothing better made.

Size, inside diameter, ¾ inch	No. 9K38980	No. 9K38981
Price, 25 feet, complete with couplings	$2.11	$2.59
Price, 50 feet, complete with couplings	4.00	4.99

28c PER FOOT STRICTLY STANDARD MADE STEAM HOSE. SIZE, ¾ INCH.

This is a quality of Steam Hose better than the ordinary and which we have sold for years with universal satisfaction. For ordinary steam pressure it may be depended upon to answer every requirement.

No. 9K38982

Inside Diameter	Ply	Pressure, pounds	Price, per foot	Inside Diameter	Ply	Pressure, pounds	Price, per foot
½ in.	3	40	18c	1¼-in.	5	32	54c
¾ in.	4	53.3	28c	1½-in.	5	26.7	58c
1 in.	4	40	35c				

18c PER FOOT SEAMLESS RUBBER LINED COTTON COVERED MILL HOSE. SIZE, 1½ INCHES.

For fire protection, adapted for hand engines, factories, warehouses, hotels, steamboats, public institutions, and wherever a light, durable and reliable hose for fire protection is required. It is full weight, made in the most careful manner, every section being mildew proof and guaranteed to stand water pressure of 250 pounds. Sold only in 25 or 50-foot pieces. We cannot sell less. Seamless, rubber lined.

No. 9K38984 Diameter, inches	1½	2
Price, per foot	18c	23c

YOU SAVE STILL MORE

Over 3,000 hardware items in this book still further reduced from the low prices in our last catalogue.

24c IMPROVED SOLID BRASS GEM HOSE NOZZLE, FOR ¾-INCH HOSE.

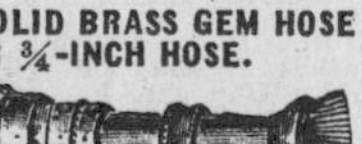

Will throw a solid stream or spray. Regulated by turning the sleeve. By far the best combination nozzle made.

No. 9K39007 Price.............**24c**

27c ADJUSTABLE STREAM SOLID BRASS HOSE NOZZLE. SIZE, ¾ INCH.

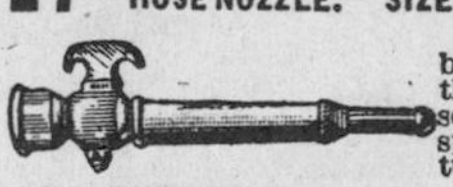

This Nozzle can be regulated to throw either a solid stream or a spray by simply turning the cock.

No. 9K39009 ¾ inch. Price....**27c**
No. 9K39010 1 inch. Price....**54c**

22c PER DOZEN HOSE SPLICER, FOR MENDING HOSE, ¾ INCH.

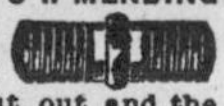

Made of malleable iron. Where hose is broken or worn, the defective place may be cut out and the two ends joined together with the splicers.

No. 9K38993 Size, inch	½	¾	1
Price, each	2c	3c	4c
Per dozen	16c	22c	32c

8c PER PAIR SOLID BRASS HOSE COUPLINGS, ¾ INCH.

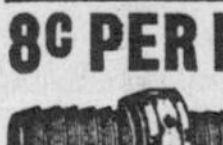

Strong and well made. Will stand any pressure that hose will. Order couplings as below the same size as the inside diameter of hose and they will fit.

No. 9K38998

Size, inches	½	¾	1	1¼	1½	2
Price, per pair	7c	8c	15c	30c	42c	78c

3c WROUGHT STEEL SURE GRIP HOSE CLAMP, ¾ INCH.

Made of wrought steel, which is guaranteed to be stronger and lighter and more pliable than any cast clamp.

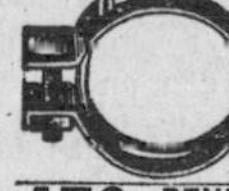

No. 9K39000
Size, ¼ inch. Price, 2c
Size, ¾ inch. Price, 3c
Size, 1 inch. Price, 4c
Size, 1¼ inches. Price, 6c
Size, 1½ inches. Price, 8c
Size, 2 inches. Price, 10c

47c REVERSIBLE LAWN SPRINKLER, FOR HIGH OR LOW PRESSURE.

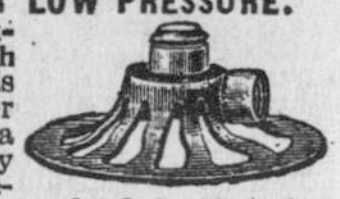

The best Lawn Sprinkler ever offered at such a low price. The cap is reversible, and a high or low spray, covering a wide area of ground, may be secured by simply reversing the cap. The standard is threaded to fit ¾-inch hose connection and is provided with an internal rubber packing. It will not clog, there being no small holes to fill up and thus retard the spray.

No. 9K39022 Price..........**47c**

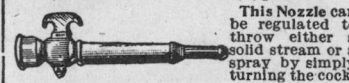

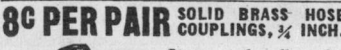

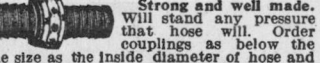

$2.38 TURBINE REVOLVING LAWN SPRINKLER FOR ¾-INCH HOSE.

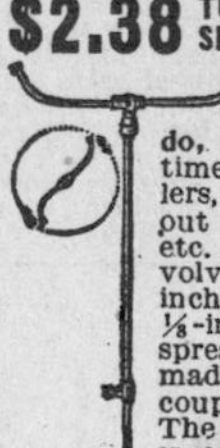

Will do the work that a lawn sprinkler is intended to do, do it right, and will last a lifetime without repairs. Lawn sprinklers, as a rule, are mere toys, get out of order, are easily broken, etc. The arms in our Turbine Revolving Sprinkler are made of ½-inch 18-gauge brass tubing with five ⅛-inch holes in each end. The spread is 22 inches. Standard is made of ½-inch steel pipe, with coupling to attach to ¾-inch hose. The swivel is made of cast brass and is constructed in such a manner that the bearings simply ride upon the stream of water when sprinkler is in operation. Five pounds pressure will operate it. It stands 2½ feet high and weighs 4½ pounds. With 15 pounds pressure it will cover 30 feet of ground. With 30 to 40 pounds pressure it will cover 50 feet of ground. Sold with a guarantee of being the best lawn sprinkler made or money refunded.

No. 9K39026 Price........**$2.38**

57c HARDWOOD HOSE REEL WITH IRON WHEELS.

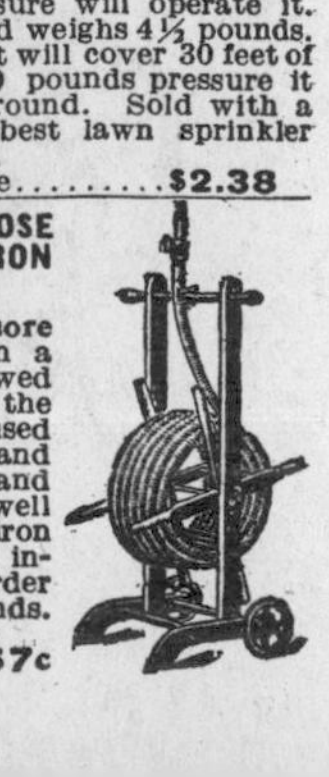

The life of hose is more than doubled if kept on a reel and the water is allowed to drain out. Saves the wear and tear on hose caused by dragging it around and prevents soiling hands and clothes. Strong and well made of hardwood, with iron wheels. Don't fail to include a reel in your order for hose. Weight, 11 pounds.

No. 9K39028
Price (no hose included).**57c**

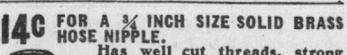

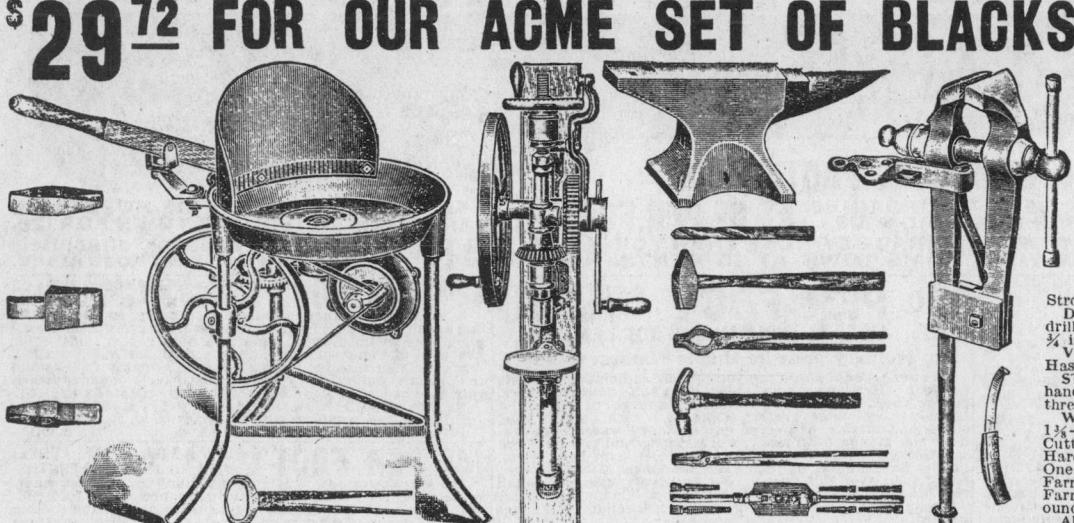
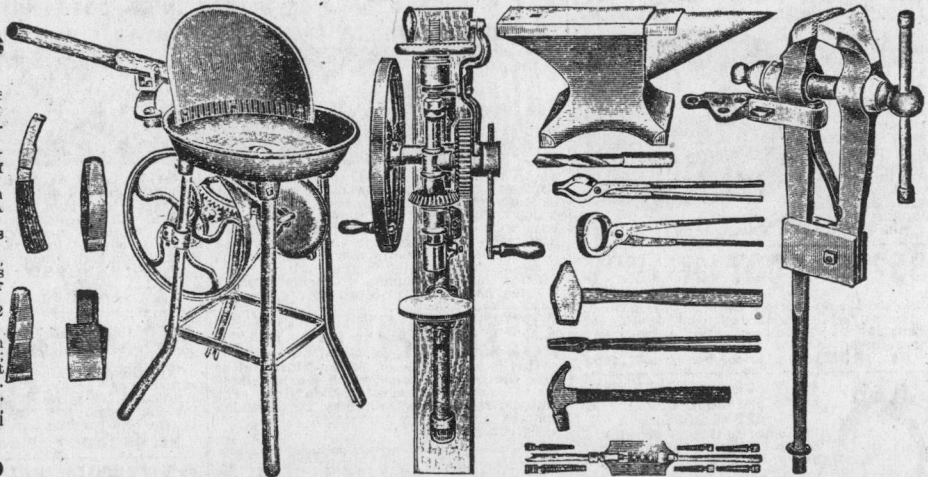
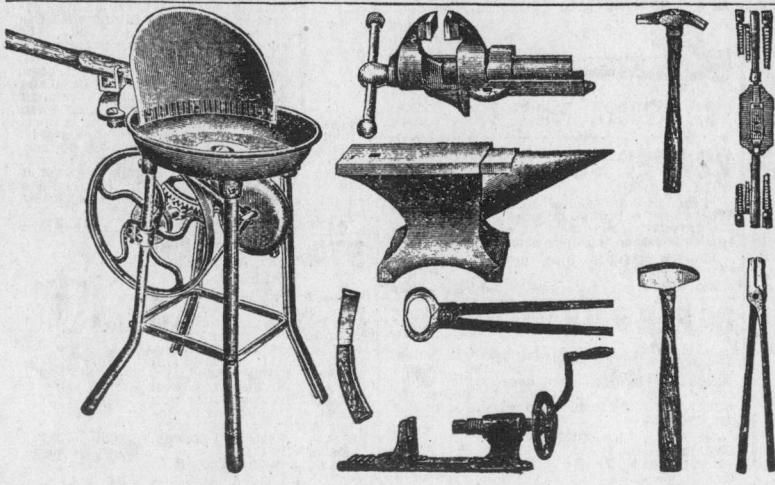

YOUR MONEY WILL BE IMMEDIATELY RETURNED TO YOU FOR ANY GOODS NOT PERFECTLY SATISFACTORY.

317

THE VULCAN SET OF BLACKSMITHS' TOOLS

SEVENTEEN HIGH GRADE TOOLS $46.53 **EIGHT GUARANTEED DRILL BITS INCLUDED WITH THIS OUTFIT.**

Each tool in this outfit is first class in every respect, and is warranted perfect in both workmanship and material. You will make no mistake in sending us your order for the Vulcan Outfit. This set is suitable for any blacksmith shop, and will give long and satisfactory service.

No. 9K31002

ANVIL—We furnish our 100-pound American Solid Wrought Anvil, forged in two pieces, welded at waist and warranted not to come loose. Face is one solid piece of tool steel, has long, perfectly shaped horn and long heel. Edges are highly tempered and will not chip.

FORGE—We furnish a Lever Forge with half hood. Has 12-inch fan, 25x36-inch hearth, is 30 inches high and weighs about 180 pounds. A forge of our own design; has perfect anti-clinker tuyere and will furnish blast enough to produce a welding heat on 3-inch iron in five minutes.

DRILL—We furnish a self feed, ball bearing, 110-pound Post Drill. Drills up to 1¼-inch holes, has 3½-inch run of spindle; takes ½-inch round shank bits and drills to center of 15-inch circle. Shafts and spindle made of best grade steel, has double gearing, double journal boxes and two speeds. The best drill ever offered in a blacksmith's outfit.

DRILL BITS—Eight ½-inch round shank Drill Bits to fit drill described above. Sizes, ⅛, 3-16, ¼, 5-16, ⅜, ½, ⅝ and ¾-inch. These bits are made of highest grade steel.

SCREW PLATE—Our Invincible Screw Plate with five taps and five pairs of dies, cutting ¼, ⅜, ½, ⅝ and ¾-inch, complete with guides and stocks, in hardwood box. Dies are easily adjusted and cut clean perfect threads. Set has two stocks, 14 and 26 inches long, and a strong, adjustable tap wrench.

VISE—We furnish a 50-pound wrought Blacksmith's Vise with solid box and steel jaws. Every vise warranted perfect. A strong, durable tool that will stand the greatest amount of wear.

APRON—Our regular split leather apron, extra large size, complete with straps; made of good tough stock, and a sure protection to one's clothes. **FARRIERS' KNIFE**—IXL Wostenholm with genuine stag handle, no better knife made. **CUTTING NIPPERS**—14-inch, made of one solid piece of steel, no welds, and have highly tempered cutting edges. **HARDIE**—Is made of cast steel, is 1-inch and fits the anvil. **HAND HAMMER**—Made of best crucible steel, weighs 3 pounds and has hickory handle. **FARRIERS' PINCERS**—14-inch, are made of one piece best tempered steel. **FARRIERS' HAMMER**—16 ounces, forged from crucible steel, has selected hickory handle. **FLAT LIP TONGS**—22 inches long, made of steel, highly tempered. **BOLT TONGS**—Will hold bolts or round iron 5-16 to ½ inch in diameter, are drop forged, strong and durable. **HORSE RASP**—14 inches long, double faced, hand cut, none better to be had. **HOT AND COLD CHISELS**—1⅛-inch cut, forged from crucible cast steel. Weight, 2¼ pounds each.

No. 9K31002 Price for complete outfit, as illustrated and described................ **$46.53**

COMPLETE OUTFITS FOR BLACKSMITHS

THE MOST REMARKABLE VALUES EVER OFFERED. Every tool warranted. Send us your order for one of these sets and save 50 per cent on cost from other houses. Not the cheap, low class tools usually worked off in outfits, but especially constructed for everyday shop use. The sets illustrated on this page are made up of our best tools such as are in general use in the largest shops throughout the country. We guarantee each item to be perfect and will replace free of charge any tool found to be defective. ARE YOU THINKING OF BUYING A SET OF BLACKSMITH'S TOOLS? Don't try to save a few dollars at the expense of quality. Pay a little more and get one of the outfits shown on this page and you will be properly equipped to do any work that may come to your shop. These sets include every tool you'll need, each one heavy enough for your requirements and each one of the highest quality.

YOU CAN SAVE MONEY BY BUYING A FULL SET. The tools included in the sets shown on this page would cost you a great deal more if bought singly. By selling them in sets, a large number at once, the transaction can be handled at less expense than if we made a separate shipment of each item. You save freight charges and have the satisfaction of starting with an entirely new set of tools. Any mechanic can do better work if he has good new tools, such as we furnish with these sets, and no mechanic can do good work with old worn out tools.

OPEN A BLACKSMITH SHOP OF YOUR OWN, ORDER A SET OF THE TOOLS SHOWN ON THIS PAGE AND YOU WILL BE COMPLETELY EQUIPPED FOR BUSINESS.

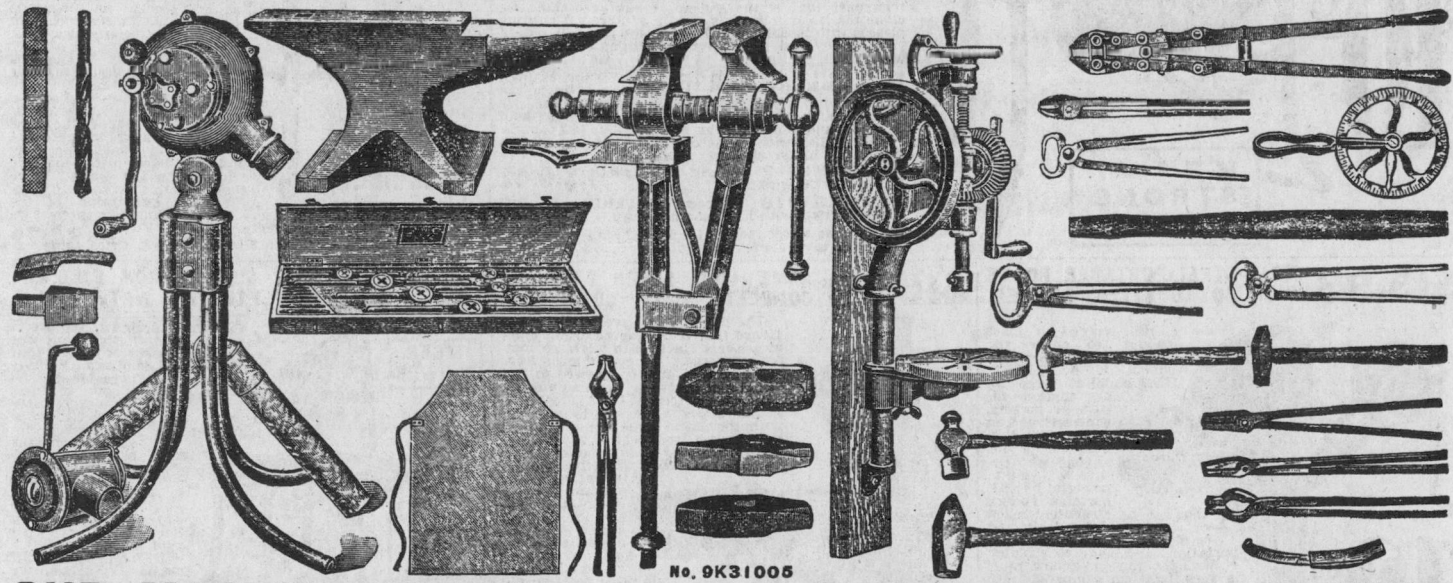

No. 9K31005

OUR MASTERWORKMAN $60.94 BLACKSMITHS' OUTFIT

TWENTY-SEVEN SUPERIOR TOOLS, TEN DRILL BITS, STRONG, HEAVY, DURABLE, GUARANTEED PERFECT.

The tools in our Masterworkman Blacksmith's Outfit would cost you at least $100.00 if bought elsewhere. All the tools needed by a blacksmith or horseshoer, and of the best quality possible to make. This outfit will take care of the heaviest work. We got it up especially for high class ironworkers, men who demand the best, and who will take nothing less. It is a heavier, stronger outfit than our Vulcan and well worth the difference in price.

ANVIL—We furnish our 125-pound American wrought Anvil with this outfit. Made entirely of wrought iron, solid forged, with tool steel face. Long, perfectly shaped horn and long heel. Anvil face is highly tempered, edges will not chip and it "rings like a bell."

BLOWER—Complete with piping and tuyere. Has flat, straight cut gears; no belts, clutches or ratchets to get out of order. Has steel shafts, composition bearings, turns easy and is almost noiseless. Has 10½-inch fan; 13-inch fan case; height, over all, 45 inches; weight, 90 pounds. Will furnish a blast equal to a 48-inch bellows and with half the labor required to work a bellows.

DRILL—We furnish an automatic feed two-speed Drill; weight, 115 pounds. Drills holes up to 1¼ inches, to center of 15-inch circle, takes ½-inch round shank drill bits, and has 3-inch run of spindle. Bearings are long, well babbitted and cannot spring or get out of line.

DRILL BITS—We furnish ten ½-inch round shank Drill Bits to fit above drill. Sizes, 3-16, ¼, 5-16, ⅜, 7-16, ½, ⅝, ¾, ⅞ and 1-inch, all of the best quality steel.

SCREW PLATE—We furnish our Invincible full mounted Screw Plate, which has a stock with each die. Complete with tap wrench, etc., in hardwood box. One of the handiest and most complete sets ever offered.

VISE—Our 60-pound solid box wrought Blacksmith's Vise with tempered steel jaws.

BOLT CLIPPERS—One pair easy Bolt Clippers, will cut up to ½-inch bolts. Adjustable to take up wear and have rubber bumpers. Bolt Clippers soon pay for themselves in time saved.

TIRE MEASURING WHEEL—We furnish a drop forged steel Tire Measuring Wheel, 24 inches around. Has raised figures and index hand. Convenient and accurate.

We also furnish with our Masterworkman Outfit:

1 pair Maude S Farriers' Pincers, 14-inch.
1 pair Nail Cutting Nippers, 12-inch.
1 pair Hoof Parers, 14-inch.
1 Wostenholm's IXL Farrier's Knife.
1 Horse Rasp, 14-inch.
1 Toe Knife, solid steel.
1 Blacksmith's Apron, large size.
1 Farrier's Hammer, 14 to 18 ounces.
1 Hot and 1 Cold Chisel, 1¼-inch cut, weight, about 2¼ pounds each.

1 Hardie to fit hardie hole in anvil.
1 pair Farrier's Tongs, 14-inch.
2 pairs Flat Tongs, 20 and 22-inch.
2 pairs Bolt Tongs holds 5-16 to ½ and ½ to ¾.
1 Blacksmith's 10-pound Steel Sledge and Handle.
1 Blacksmith's Hand Hammer, weight 3 pounds.
1 Blacksmith's Ball Pein Hammer, 2 pounds.
1 Riveting Hammer, 9 ounces.

All the above are of the very best quality, each tool guaranteed perfect and will be replaced if defective. No better tools can be made and any blacksmith ought to be proud to own them.

No. 9K31005 Price for complete outfit, as illustrated and described............ **$60.94**

OUR WHIRLWIND PORTABLE FORGE $5.19

THE FORGE WITH THE WHIRLWIND BLAST

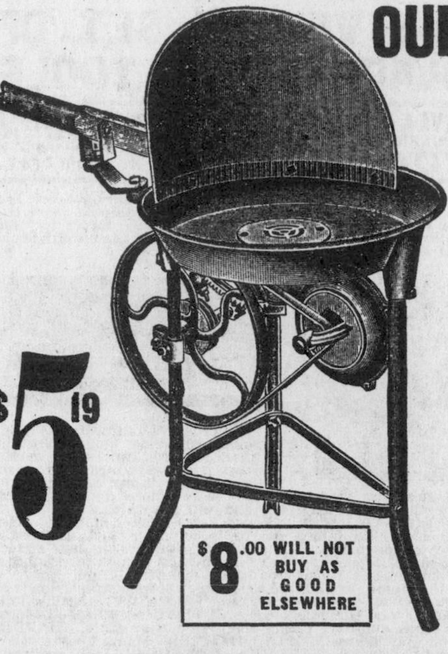

$5.19

$8.00 WILL NOT BUY AS GOOD ELSEWHERE

THE BEST LOW PRICED FORGE EVER SOLD. **In our WHIRLWIND we have a general purpose forge of such high quality that we can recommend it to blacksmiths, mechanics, farmers and others who have occasion to use a portable forge,** and at the same time have kept the price so low that it is within the reach of all. There are cheaper forges offered, some of which look very much like the Whirlwind, but if you will compare the weights and dimensions of these cheap forges with the weights and dimensions of our forge, you will find the difference all in favor of the Whirlwind. As good a forge as our Whirlwind, if purchased from your local dealer, would cost you $8.00 to $10.00. We are enabled to name the extremely low price of $5.19 because of the fact that we buy these forges in enormous quantities direct from the manufacturer, secure them at lower prices than the largest wholesalers can purchase them for, and offer them to you with only our one small profit added to the original cost of construction. Our manufacturer is headquarters for the highest grade blowers and forges on the market and every forge that we send out is guaranteed to be absolutely perfect in construction.

THE WHIRLWIND IS MOUNTED ON THREE LEGS, STRONGLY BRACED, **making it convenient to use on uneven foundations.** These legs are very stiff and rigid and have spread enough to prevent tipping. The lever is extremely simple, has a self acting ratchet, no springs or anything to get out of order. All the working parts are made from high grade tool steel, specially tempered. Forge has nicely finished hardwood handle and oak tanned leather belt. The greatest care is taken in the assembling and erecting of these machines, which results in all the parts being brought into the closest contact with each other, where they are secured by the most approved methods.

ALL THE DETAILS OF CONSTRUCTION **add to the original cost of the Whirlwind Forge,** but we think nothing is too good for our customers and we go to this extra expense in order to make the low priced Whirlwind better value than any forge offered by any other house. With a slight movement of the lever you get a strong, steady blast, amply sufficient for ordinary welding. The height of the forge is 30 inches, hearth is 22 inches in diameter, fan case 8½ inches in diameter. Weight, crated, about 92 pounds.

THIS IS THE LARGEST AND BEST CONSTRUCTED FORGE EVER OFFERED AT ANYTHING LIKE THE PRICE

and we ask you to compare the size of hearth, the weight of the forge, and the size of the fan with other forges at even double our price and draw your own conclusions.

WE ESPECIALLY RECOMMEND THIS WHIRLWIND FORGE TO FARMERS, **as it can be made to pay for itself several times over during the year.** Think of the tools and implements that are cast aside each season, not worth paying a high price to have them repaired, yet you could, on a rainy day, fix them up yourself if you had this Whirlwind Forge.

WHILE THE WHIRLWIND IS A FAR BETTER FORGE **than has ever before been offered at the low price of $5.19,** for a strictly high grade A1 forge, heavy enough for any blacksmith shop, and one that will produce a welding heat on 3-inch iron in five minutes, we refer you to our Vulcan Forge shown below. Read carefully the description of the Vulcan and if you need a heavy forge we think you will prefer to pay the slight difference and get one that will do your work quicker than any small forge can do. Understand, we do not mean to imply that the Whirlwind Forge will not do good work, for it will; but if you have a great deal of heavy work to do you will save valuable time by getting a larger, stronger forge such as the Vulcan, described below.

No. 9K31008 Whirlwind Portable Forge. Price.................... **$5.19**

IMPROVED VULCAN FORGE

ONLY $11.39 FOR THIS HIGH GRADE GUARANTEED EXTRA HEAVY BLACKSMITH FORGE.

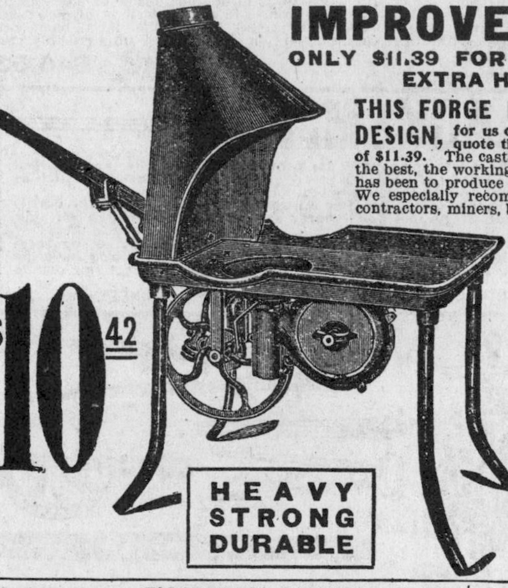

$10.42

HEAVY STRONG DURABLE

THIS FORGE IS MANUFACTURED AFTER OUR OWN DESIGN, **for us only, and in such large quantities that we are enabled to quote this first class 180-pound forge at the extremely low price of $11.39.** The castings are extra heavy and nicely finished, the workmanship the best, the working parts are tempered steel, and throughout, the one idea has been to produce the best forge on the market to sell for a popular price. We especially recommend this forge for boiler makers, machinists, railroad contractors, miners, blacksmiths and iron bridge and ship builders. A similar forge would cost you $16.00 to $18.00 if you bought from your local dealer, and even at that price it would not be finished as well as ours. We have thousands of Vulcan Forges made on a single contract, which accounts to a certain extent for our low price. Notice the size, construction and good points of the Vulcan Forge. Compare it with forges sold by other concerns for more money. Send us your order and remember that if the Vulcan is not everything we claim for it, or if for any reason you are not entirely pleased with it, ship it back to us and we will refund your money and pay the transportation charges both ways.

THE VULCAN FORGE **stands 30 inches high and has 12-inch fan case.** It has a perfect anti-clinker tuyere. The size of the hearth is 36x25 inches, large enough to hold both coal and tools. Weight, crated, about 180 pounds. It will produce with slight exertion a welding heat on 3-inch iron in five minutes.

No. 9K31017 Vulcan Portable Forge. Price, with shield.............. **$10.42**

No. 9K31018 Vulcan Portable Forge. Price, with half hood as shown..... **11.39**

Extra for water tank, to fit either of the above forges.................................. **90c**

$4.72 OUR HIGH GRADE, LOW PRICE BLACKSMITH'S PORTABLE FORGE.

TO SUPPLY THE DEMAND

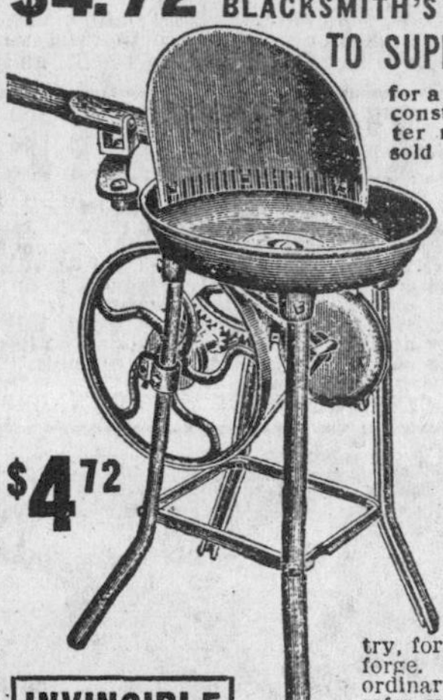

$4.72

INVINCIBLE

for a forge of this style, better constructed and made of better material than has been sold heretofore for as low a price, we have put this Invincible Forge on the market. The Invincible has lever motion and well braced legs; castings are heavy and gears are well cut; has steel ratchet, heavy shield, hickory handle and oak tanned leather belt. Forge stands 30 inches high, with fire pan 18 inches in diameter, fan case 8 inches in diameter and weighs, crated, about 82 pounds. While this is the best forge ever sold at anything like the price, and will do light work as well as any forge in the country, for a strictly high grade A1 forge, heavy enough for any ordinary blacksmith shop, we refer you to the Vulcan Forge shown on this page. Read carefully the description of the Vulcan and if you need a heavy forge, in your own interest we advise you to pay the difference and buy a Vulcan.

No. 9K31006 Invincible Portable Forge. Price, **$4.72**

$13.93 TIGER STEEL PORTABLE FORGE WITH ROYAL STYLE BLOWER.

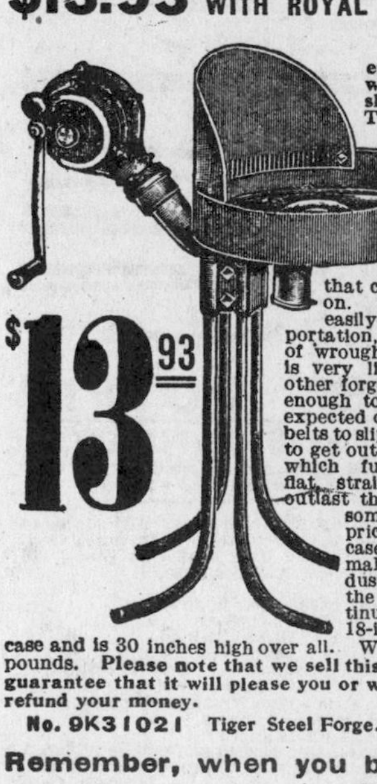

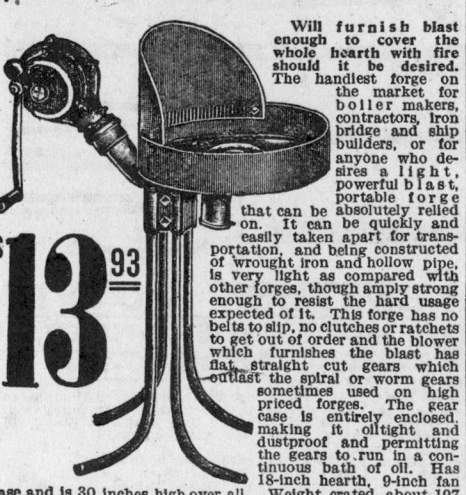

$13.93

Will furnish blast enough to cover the whole hearth with fire should it be desired. The handiest forge on the market for boiler makers, contractors, iron bridge and ship builders, or for anyone who desires a light, powerful blast, portable forge that can be absolutely relied on. It can be quickly and easily taken apart for transportation, and being constructed of wrought iron and hollow pipe, is very light as compared with other forges, though amply strong enough to resist the hard usage expected of it. This forge has no belts to slip, no clutches or ratchets to get out of order and the blower which furnishes the blast has flat, straight cut gears which outlast the spiral or worm gears sometimes used on high priced forges. The gear case is entirely enclosed, making it oiltight and dustproof and permitting the gears to run in a continuous bath of oil. Has 18-inch hearth, 9-inch fan case and is 30 inches high over all. Weight, crated, about 107 pounds. **Please note that we sell this forge under a positive guarantee that it will please you or we will take it back and refund your money.**

No. 9K31021 Tiger Steel Forge. Price..... **$13.93**

$16.58 ACME COAL SAVER FORGE, COMPLETE WITH COAL BOX.

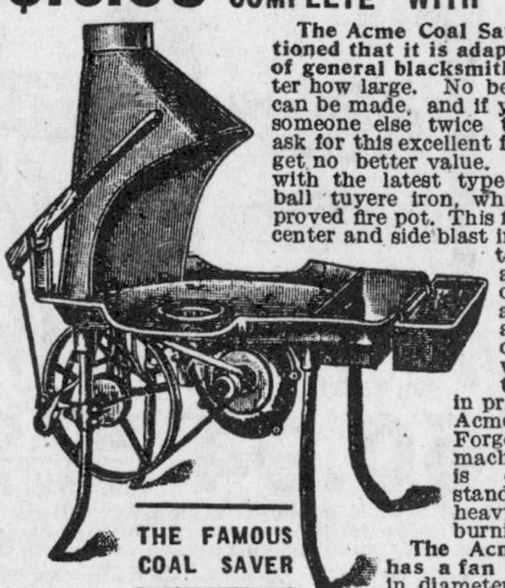

THE FAMOUS COAL SAVER

The Acme Coal Saver is so proportioned that it is adapted to any class of general blacksmith work, no matter how large. No better lever forge can be made, and if you were to pay someone else twice the amount we ask for this excellent forge you would get no better value. It is equipped with the latest type of anti-clinker ball tuyere iron, which has an improved fire pot. This fire pot combines center and side blast in such a way as to get the greatest amount of heat out of the least amount of coal and in the cost of coal alone you will soon save the difference in price between our Acme Coal Saver Forge and a cheaper machine. This fire pot is constructed to stand continuous heavy work without burning out.

The Acme Coal Saver has a fan case 14½ inches in diameter, and stands 30 inches high. Has hearth 45½x31½ inches, is 53 inches over all and weighs crated, about 325 pounds. The slope bottom coal box makes it easy to keep part of the coal wet. Every Acme Coal Saver Forge we send out is equipped with half hood, as shown. Don't forget that the Acme Coal Saver Forge will soon save in reduced coal bills alone the small difference in price over the cheap line of forges generally offered.

No. 9K31020 Price, with coal box.......... **$16.58**

No. 9K31023 Price, with coal box and water tank.................................. **18.72**

$18.12 ACME COMBINATION FORGE, COMPLETE WITH WATER TANK.

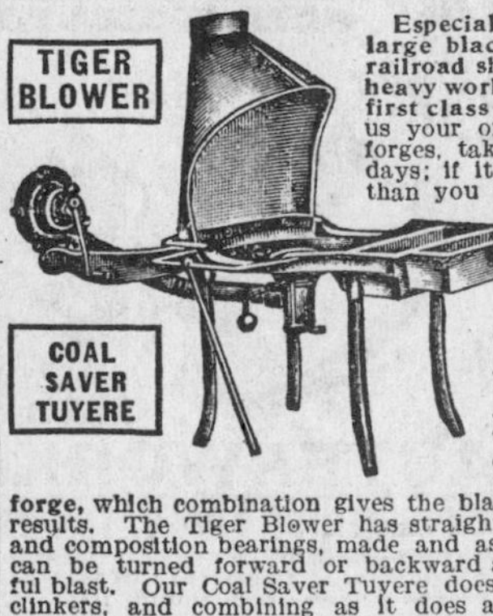

TIGER BLOWER

COAL SAVER TUYERE

Especially designed for use in large blacksmith shops, plow or railroad shops, or anywhere that heavy work is done and a strictly first class forge is required. Send us your order for one of these forges, take it and use it thirty days; if it is not a better forge than you can get elsewhere for anything like the price, or if for any reason it is not entirely satisfactory, ship it back to us at our expense and we will immediately refund your money.

IN THIS MACHINE we have combined our Tiger Steel Blower and our Coal Saver Tuyere with a high grade cast forge, which combination gives the blacksmith the very best results. The Tiger Blower has straight cut gears, steel shafts and composition bearings, made and assembled perfectly. It can be turned forward or backward and produces a powerful blast. Our Coal Saver Tuyere does not get clogged with clinkers, and combining as it does a center and side blast will get more heat out of the coal than any other, and save in cost of coal alone, in a short time, the difference in price between this high grade forge and a cheaper one. The forge is made of best grade cast iron, and will last a lifetime. The blower is extra large and the blast is direct from fan to fire, easy to operate, and the afterblast is strong and lasting. Size of hearth, 45½x31½ inches; diameter of fan case, 11½ inches; height, 30 inches; length over all, 53 inches; weight, crated, about 297 pounds.

No. 9K31024 Acme Combination Crank Forge. Price, with either coal box or water tank....... **$18.12**

No. 9K31025 Acme Combination Crank Forge. Price, with both coal box and water tank...... **$20.31**

Remember, when you buy a forge from us, all sizes, weights, etc., will correspond with catalogue description. We guarantee weights and sizes to be just as represented or money refunded.

$11.08 FOR THIS HANDSOME, STRONG AND DURABLE IMPROVED TIGER CRANK BLOWER, WITH PIPE AND TUYERE.

The best blower ever offered at anything like our price. Cannot be compared with blowers that sell elsewhere at less than $15.00 to $16.00.

Buy from us at lowest wholesale prices, save money and get the highest quality goods.

By contracting for immense quantities we secure extremely low prices; we sell for cash, have no selling expense other than our catalogue, and are thus enabled to offer you this Improved Tiger Blower at a lower price than your local dealer can buy it from his jobber. Our Tiger Blower is made of the best materials by the most skilled workmen in one of the largest and best equipped factories in the world. Has flat straight cut gears, steel shafts and composition bearings, properly assembled and geared up so that a powerful blast is furnished with very little labor and almost no noise. The gear case is offtight and dustproof, permitting gears to run in a continuous bath of oil. The blower case turns in any direction and can be pointed toward the fire, saving an extra elbow and about 10 per cent of blast force. Crank turns either way as may best suit the operator. Blower has no belts, clutches or ratchets to get out of order, stands on four legs and has a heavy base. Has 9½-inch fan, 12-inch fan case, is 45 inches high and weighs, crated, about 115 pounds. It is handsome, strong and durable; furnishes blast enough for any ordinary fire and is as steady and positive as a power blower. The after blast is strong and lasting.

Price, includes piping and heavy anti-clinker tuyere.

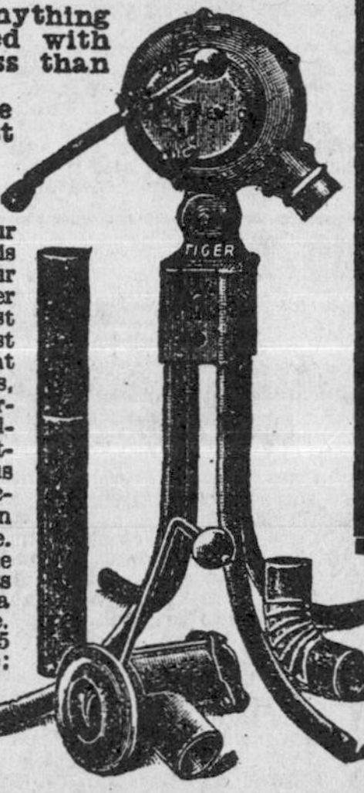

No. 9K3926 Price, complete, as illustrated and described, $11.08

WE GUARANTEE THESE TWO BLOWERS

to be first class in material and workmanship, to furnish ample blast for any ordinary fire with but little labor, and to prove entirely satisfactory in every way.

30 DAYS' FREE USE

in order that you may have the opportunity to test one of these blowers in your own shop and prove it to be all we claim for it. We sell every one of our Tiger and New Niagara Blowers with the full understanding that it may be returned to us within 30 days after you receive same if you do not find it to be the easiest running, most powerful blower you ever used and superior to any you ever saw. All we ask is a fair trial, and if it is not exactly what we claim it to be return it to us at our expense and we will immediately refund the price you paid us.

YOU SAVE MONEY.

Still lower prices in this book make your saving greater than ever.

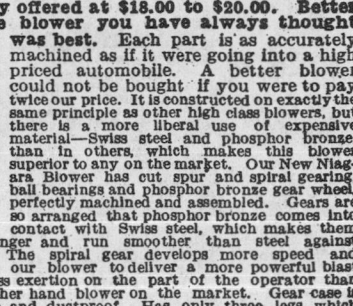

$16.64 ACME NEW NIAGARA SPIRAL GEARED, BALL BEARING BLACKSMITHS' BLOWER, COMPLETE.

Usually offered at $18.00 to $20.00. Better than the blower you have always thought was best. Each part is as accurately machined as if it were going into a high priced automobile. A better blower could not be bought if you were to pay twice our price. It is constructed on exactly the same principle as other high class blowers, but there is a more liberal use of expensive material—Swiss steel and phosphor bronze, than in others, which makes this blower superior to any on the market. Our New Niagara Blower has cut spur and spiral gearing, ball bearings and phosphor bronze gear wheel, perfectly machined and assembled. Gears are so arranged that phosphor bronze comes into contact with Swiss steel, which makes them last longer and run smoother than steel against steel. The spiral gear develops more speed and enables our blower to deliver a more powerful blast with less exertion on the part of the operator than any other hand blower on the market. Gear case is airtight and dustproof. Has only three legs which makes it very convenient for use on uneven foundations. The shafts, ball bearings and gears run in a continuous bath of oil. The fan case is on a swivel base, can be raised, lowered, or pointed in any direction, thus saving an extra elbow and at least 10 per cent of blast force. Crank can be turned either to the right or left hand as may best suit the operator. Price includes large anti-clinker coal saving tuyere and all necessary piping. Size, 11½x9x4 inches (inside measurement). Blower has 13-inch fan case, is 46 inches high and weighs, crated, about 137 pounds.

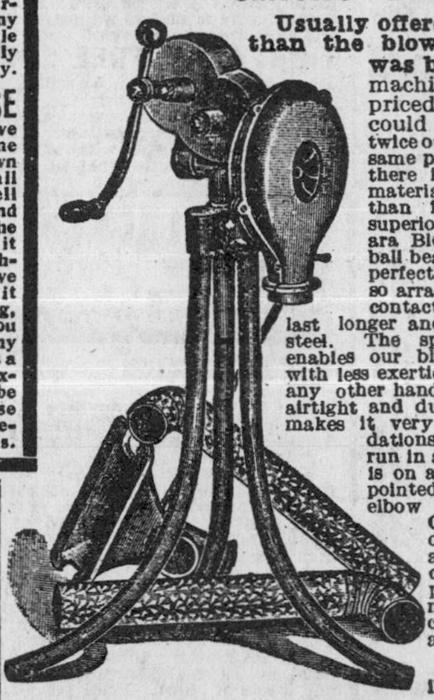

No. 9K3935 Price, complete, as illustrated and described...$16.64

$11.22 WESTERN ACME STEEL FRAME BLACKSMITHS' LEVER BLOWER.

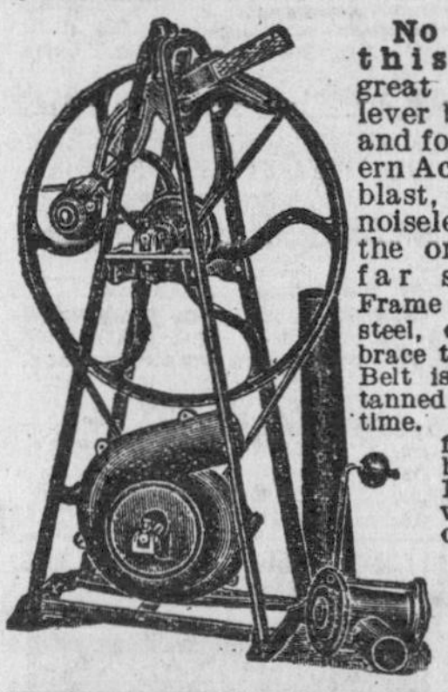

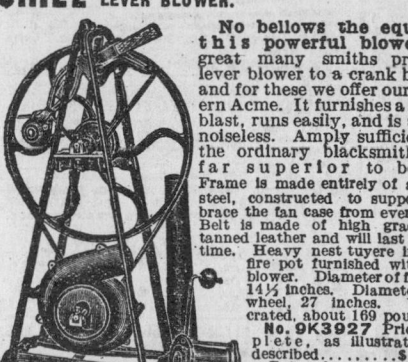

No bellows the equal of this powerful blower. A great many smiths prefer a lever blower to a crank blower, and for these we offer our Western Acme. It furnishes a steady blast, runs easily, and is almost noiseless. Amply sufficient for the ordinary blacksmith, and far superior to bellows. Frame is made entirely of angle T steel, constructed to support and brace the fan case from every side. Belt is made of high grade oak tanned leather and will last a long time. Heavy nest tuyere iron and fire pot furnished with each blower. Diameter of fan case, 14½ inches. Diameter of fly wheel, 27 inches. Weight, crated, about 169 pounds.

No. 9K3927 Price, complete, as illustrated and described..........$11.22

Extra for power attachment, pulleys, 7½x1¾ inches..........$1.98

46c SINGLE DUCK NEST TUYERE IRON, NICELY FINISHED.

Well made and substantial.
Weight, 12 pounds.
No. 9K31089 Price....46c

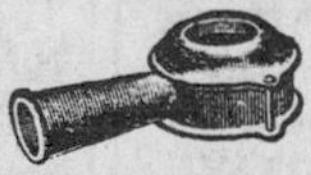

$7.41 FOR THIS ENCLOSED HOOD, HIGH GRADE LEVER FORGE.

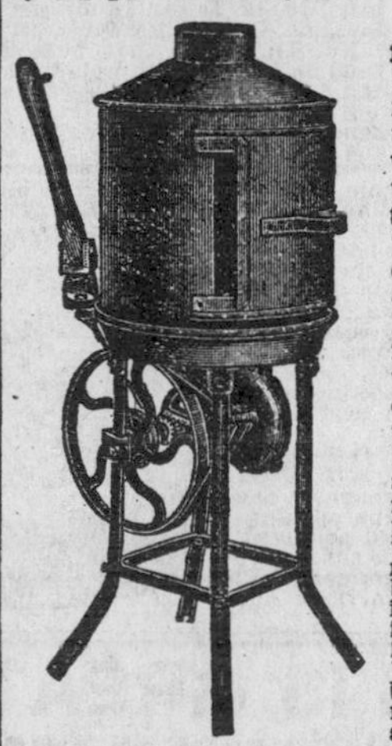

The best full hooded forge ever offered at a price so low. A hooded forge is a necessity where there is danger of fire or where smoke and gases would cause bright metal to tarnish. By running a pipe from top of forge to chimney all smoke, fumes, etc., are carried away. Makes an excellent forge for gunsmiths and others who have fine work to do, or who must work where there is danger of fire. It is built with the same care and of the same high grade material as forges at double the price. It will give satisfaction to those who require a light, rigid, high grade forge that can be depended on. It stands 30 inches high, has a fire pan 18 inches in diameter and an 8-inch fan case. Legs are made of U-shaped steel with ¼-inch braces, which makes them very rigid and stiff. Weight, crated, about 90 pounds.

No. 9K31013 Price..................$7.41

$6.77 WESTERN ACME STEADY BLAST POWER BLOWER, 10 INCHES HIGH.

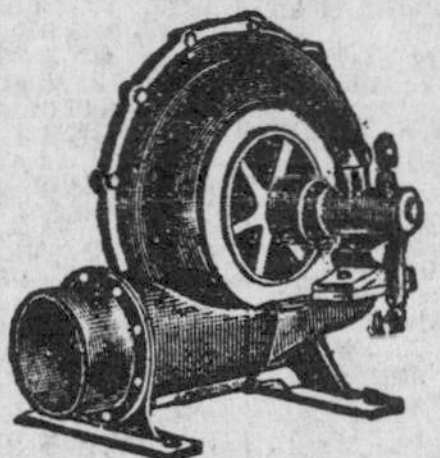

For forges, furnaces, ventilating, drying and cooling. Well made, nicely finished and will furnish a steady powerful blast. No. 9K3906 and No. 9K3907 have grease cups in addition to oil cups, so that should oil cups run dry, the grease cups will continue to lubricate and prevent heating.

	No. 9K3905	No. 9K3906	No. 9K3907
Height in inches	10	17	22
Diameter of inlet	3⅛	5½	7
Diameter of outlet	2¾	4½	7½
Face of pulley	1¼	2	3¼
Revolutions per minute, 2-oz. blast, for boiler fires	3,675	2,000	1,928
Revolutions per minute, 2-oz. blast, for forge fires	4,040	3,600	2,680
Number of forge fires	1	4	7
Square feet boiler grate surface supplied by blower	2	6	10
Weight, crated, pounds	18	58	123
Price, complete, as illustrated	$6.77	$11.40	$18.81

$1.03 CLARK'S TUYERE IRON WITH PATENT DUMP AND SHAKER.

Best quality cast iron.

No. 9K31092 Weight, 22½ pounds. Price..........$1.03

No. 9K31093 Weight, 27½ pounds. Price..........$1.24

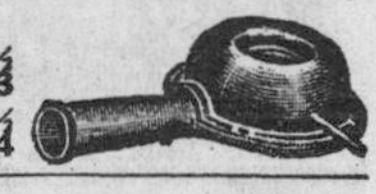

GOOD HARDWARE IS PRICED STILL LOWER IN THIS BOOK THAN IN OUR LAST CATALOGUE.

$1.28 NORTON'S PATENT ADJUSTABLE BLAST COAL SAVING TUYERE IRON.

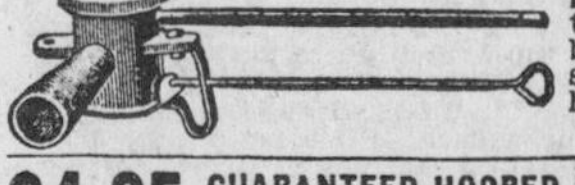

One of the best and most convenient tuyeres on the market. Cinders and ashes may be removed by pulling the small rod which opens the slide. The blast can be regulated by turning the large rod. Levers and spring can be changed to either side for right or left hand use. Weight, about 27 pounds.

No. 9K31104 Price..................$1.28

$4.05 GUARANTEED HOOPED BLACKSMITHS' 24-INCH BELLOWS.

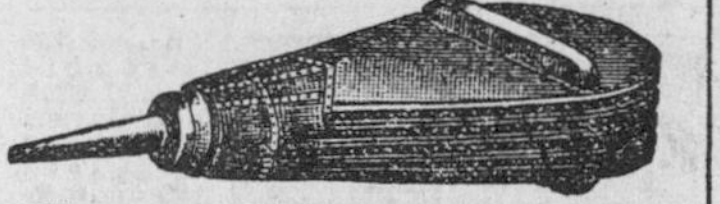

We use none but the best specially prepared cowhide leather in making our bellows. We use whitewood, basswood and pine, thoroughly seasoned so that it will not be affected by climatic changes. We guarantee our bellows equal to any on the market and superior to those generally offered, while the volume of our sales makes it possible for us to name prices below much lower than the usual prices for standard goods.

No. 9K31080 Standard Pattern, hooped.

Width, inches	Weight, pounds	Price
24	30	$ 4.05
26	35	4.83
28	40	5.26
30	45	5.71
32	50	6.14
34	60	7.02
36	68	7.91
38	78	8.78
40	100	9.65

No. 9K31084 Extra Long Pattern.

Width, inches	Weight, pounds	Price
34	73	$ 8.34
36	87	9.22
38	105	10.54
40	125	12.29

$6.67 STODDARD TIRE SHRINKER, POWERFUL AND SUBSTANTIAL.

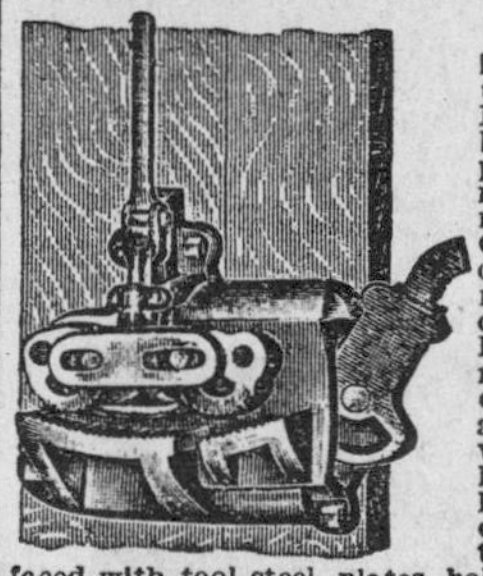

Oldest and best known on the market. Has only to be bolted to a plank fixed upright and it is ready for use. Can be easily operated by one man and requires no anti-kink attachment, as the clamp head has a wide bearing which prevents light tires from kinking. The dogs that grip the tire are faced with tool steel plates, hold the tire securely, wear a long time, can be sharpened by the user and finally replaced at small expense. These are well made, powerful machines and we guarantee them to shrink tires to their capacity.

No. 9K3755 Size 1, shrinks up to 2-inch tire. Weight, about 114 pounds. Price, $6.67

No. 9K3756 Size 2, shrinks up to 4-inch tire. Weight, about 244 pounds. Price..........$10.05

No. 9K3757 Size 3, Special, extra heavy, shrinks tire up to 4 inches and has extra jaws for setting axles up to 1¾ inches. Weight, about 310 pounds. Price..........$12.15

$5.25 IMPROVED MOLE TIRE SHRINKER, SIMPLE AND EFFECTIVE.

Others ask $8.75 for this Shrinker

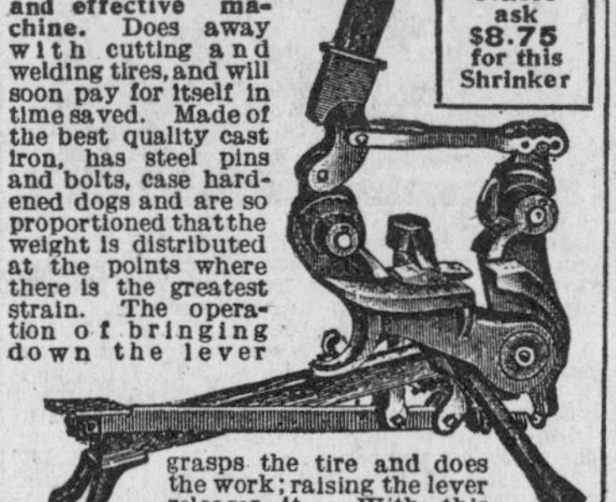

A very powerful and effective machine. Does away with cutting and welding tires, and will soon pay for itself in time saved. Made of the best quality cast iron, has steel pins and bolts, case hardened dogs and are so proportioned that the weight is distributed at the points where there is the greatest strain. The operation of bringing down the lever grasps the tire and does the work; raising the lever releases it. With this shrinker it is not necessary to remove the tire until it is upset as much as required. Can be successfully operated by one man. The anti-kink attachment holds the tire down, not allowing it to kink up, but allowing it to be shrunk as the pressure is regulated by the foot lever shown in the illustration. Sizes 2 and 3 furnished with anti-kink; size 1, without. Each size furnished with hardwood lever handle.

No. 9K3770 Size 1, for upsetting tires up to and including 2½ inches. Weight, about 127 pounds.
Price..........................$5.25

No. 9K3773 Size 2, for upsetting tires up to and including 3 inches. Weight, about 200 pounds.
Price..........................$8.20

No. 9K3778 Size 3, for upsetting tires up to and including 4 inches. Weight, about 275 pounds.
Price..........................$11.60

$6.05 ACME GEARED TIRE BENDER. BENDS A PERFECT CIRCLE.

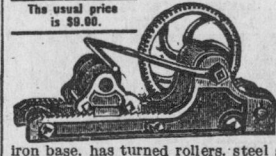

The usual price is $9.00.

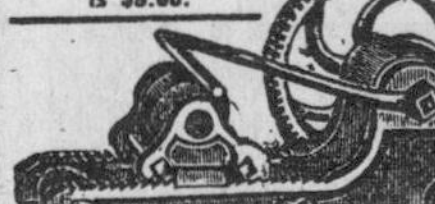

Saves labor and worry, and will soon pay for itself in time saved. This bender is made on heavy iron base, has turned rollers, steel shafts, gear and pinion and will bend tires to its capacity.

No. 9K3784 Will bend tires 3½ inches and smaller to a circle 24 inches in diameter and larger. Weight, about 90 pounds.
Price..........................$6.05

No. 9K3786 Will bend tires 6 inches and smaller to a circle 24 inches in diameter and larger. Weight, about 116 pounds.
Price..........................$6.97

$7.98 DOUBLE GEARED ADJUSTABLE CINCINNATI TIRE BENDER.

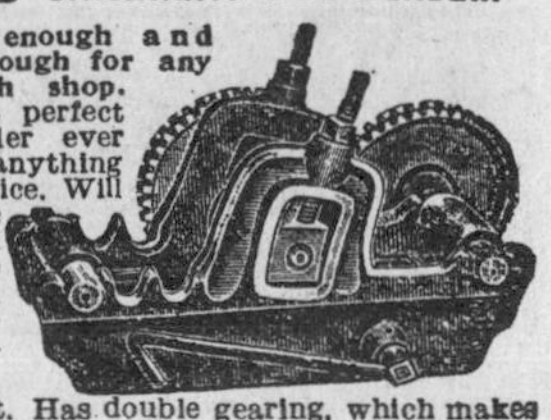

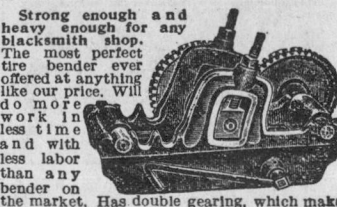

Strong enough and heavy enough for any blacksmith shop. The most perfect tire bender ever offered at anything like our price. Will do more work in less time and with less labor than any bender on the market. Has double gearing, which makes it easy to operate; patent adjustment for different thickness tires; turned rollers on steel shafts; and it will bend a perfect circle every time. Length, 24 inches; diameter of rolls, 2½ inches. Bends any size tire up to and including 5 inches. Weight, about 156 pounds.

No. 9K3790 Price..........$7.98

11c BLACKSMITHS' PLUG OR TAPER TAP. SIZE, 3-16 INCH.

TAPER TAP.

No. 9K3584   Right Hand Taper Tap.
No. 9K3586   Left Hand Taper Tap.

PLUG TAP.

No. 9K3580   Right Hand Plug Tap.
No. 9K3582   Left Hand Plug Tap.

We carry a full stock at all times and can fill orders promptly. Our taps are made of highest grade tool steel, each one warranted perfect. Give catalogue number, size and number of threads when ordering.

Size inches	Hand	No. Threads to the inch	Price each
⅛	Right	30 or 32	$0.11
3-16	Right	24 or 26	.11
¼	Right	18, 20, 22, 24 or 26	.12
5-16	Right	16, 18, 20 or 22	.12
⅜	Right	12, 14, 16 or 18	.13
7-16	Left	14	.15
7-16	Right	12, 14, 16 or 18	.15
½	Left	12 or 14	.19
½	Right	12, 14, 16 or 18	.19
9-16	Right	10, 12 or 14	.19
⅝	Left	10 or 12	.20
⅝	Right	10, 11, 12 or 14	.20
¾	Left	10 or 12	.26
¾	Left	8, 9, 10 or 12	.26
⅞	Left	9	.36
⅞	Left	8, 9 or 10	.36
1	Left	8 or 9	.49
1	Right	7, 8, 9 or 10	.49
1¼	Left	8 or 9	.69
1¼	Right	6, 7, 8 or 9	.69
1½	Left	6, 7 or 8	1.19
1½	Right	6, 7 or 8	1.19

14c TOOL STEEL REAMERS FOR WOOD OR IRON. SIZE, 1-4 INCH.

No. 9K3600 These Reamers are made of the finest English tool steel. Every one warranted to cut a smooth, clean hole. To be used in bit brace.

Size, In.	¼	5-16	⅜	7-16	½	9-16	⅝	11-16	¾
Price	14c	18c	21c	25c	28c	35c	42c	49c	56c

$7.37 GENUINE GREEN RIVER SCREW PLATE WITH ADJUSTABLE DIES.

They do the work at a single cut and will not strip threads. The dies are adjustable for wear, and to make bolts or nuts fit tightly or loosely as desired. All Green River sets sent 1-32 inch over size V thread which fits regular carriage and machine bolts.

No. 9K3724 Cuts five sizes, ¼ to ¾ inch, as follows: ¼, ⅜, ½, ⅝, ¾ inch. Complete with taps, dies and guides in hardwood case. Price $7.37
No. 9K3725 Cuts from ¼ to ¾ inch; stock, 22 inches long; 7 sizes, ¼, 5-16, 7-16, ½, ⅝, ¾ inch; taps, dies and guides complete in hardwood case. Price, per set.....$9.08

No. 9K3727 Cuts from ¼ to 1 inch; stock, 29 inches long; 9 sizes, ¼, 5-16, ⅜, ½, ⅝, ¾, ⅞ and 1 inch; taps, dies and guides complete in hardwood case. Per set, $17.80

$18.14 WILEY & RUSSELL'S LIGHTNING SCREW PLATE. CUTS 1-4 TO 1 INCH.

Makes perfect screws at a single cut. Nuts and bolts threaded with these sets always correspond. Cuts 1-32 inch over size V thread which fits regular carriage and machine bolts. Cuts from ¼ to 1 inch; stock is 29 inches long; cuts ¼, 5-16, ⅜, 7-16, ½, ⅝, ¾, ⅞ and 1 inch. Complete in hardwood case.
No. 9K3730 Price, per set.....$18.14

$18.42 WILEY & RUSSELL'S NEW LIGHTNING FULL MOUNTED SCREW PLATE.

Has a stock for each die, which does away with changing dies to cut a different size thread; all the dies may be used at once. Cuts 1-32 inch over size V thread which fits regular carriage and machine bolts. Cuts 9 sizes, ¼, 5-16, ⅜, 7-16, ½, ⅝, ¾ and 1 inch; complete with taps and dies of the above sizes, and a stock for each die. Put up in hardwood case.
No. 9K3732 Price, per set....$18.42

SCREW PLATES, STOCKS AND DIES

WE SELL MORE SCREW PLATES, STOCKS AND DIES than any other house in the United States. We handle nothing but the best goods and sell them so low you can't afford to buy elsewhere. All our stocks, dies and screw plates are made by the most reliable manufacturers, and as we handle several different makes you can order the kind you prefer and save money on any of them.

THIRTY-DAY FREE TRIAL OFFER. In order that you may test these goods in your own shop and prove them to be all we claim for them, we will take back at our own expense any set of stocks, dies or screw plates that you buy from us, within thirty days after you receive same, if you do not find them perfect in every respect, or if for any reason you are not entirely satisfied with your purchase. This unparalleled offer gives you the unusual privilege of testing our stocks, dies and screw plates without any risk on your part. All we ask is a fair trial, and if the goods are not exactly what we claim them to be, return them to us and we will immediately, without argument, refund your money.

BLACKSMITHS' STOCKS AND DIES.

No. 9K3460 Cuts 5-16 to 1-16 inch, right hand, 18, 24 and 32 threads to the inch, 4 taps and 3 sets of dies, complete. Price, per set $1.33
No. 9K3462 Cuts 5-16 to 1-16 inch, right hand, 16, 20, 24 and 32 threads to the inch, 4 taps and 4 sets of dies. Per set, $1.48
No. 9K3464 Cuts 5-16 to 1-16 inch, right hand, 18, 20, 24 and 32 threads to the inch, 4 taps and 4 sets of dies. Price, per set........$1.49
No. 9K3466 Cuts ¼ to 3-16 inch, right hand, 14 and 20 threads to the inch, and ½ to 5-16 left hand, 14 threads to the inch, 6 taps and 3 sets of dies. Price, per set....$1.88
No. 9K3468 Cuts ½ to ⅛ inch, right hand, 16, 20 and 26 threads to the inch, 6 taps and 3 sets of dies. Price, per set....$1.79
No. 9K3470 Cuts ½ to 3-16 inch, right hand, 12, 14 and 16 threads to the inch, 6 taps and 3 sets of dies. Price, per set....$1.80
No. 9K3472 Cuts ½ to 3-16 inch, right hand, 12, 16 and 20 threads to the inch, 6 taps and 3 sets of dies. Price, per set....$1.81
No. 9K3474 Cuts ½ to 3-16 inch, right hand, 12, 14 and 18 threads to the inch, 6 taps and 3 sets of dies. Price, per set....$1.82
No. 9K3476 Cuts ⅝ to 3-16 inch, right hand, 14, 18 and 22 threads to the inch, 6 taps and 3 sets of dies. Price, per set....$2.32

No. 9K3478 Cuts ⅝ to 3-16 inch, right hand, 12, 14 and 16 threads to the inch, 6 taps and 3 sets of dies. Price, per set.....$2.34
No. 9K3480 Cuts ⅝ to ¼ inch, right hand, 11, 12 and 16 threads to the inch, 6 taps and 3 sets of dies. Price, per set....$2.36
No. 9K3482 Cuts ¾ to ⅜ inch, right hand, 10, 11 and 12 threads to the inch, 3 taps and 3 sets of dies. Price, per set....$2.48
No. 9K3484 Cuts ¾ to 5-16 inch, right hand, 12, 14 and 16 threads to the inch, 3 taps and 3 sets of dies. Price, per set....$2.49
No. 9K3486 Cuts ¾ to 5-16 inch, right hand, 10, 12 and 14 threads to the inch, 3 taps and 3 sets of dies. Price, per set....$2.51
No. 9K3488 Cuts ¾ to 5-16 inch, right hand, 10, 12 and 14 threads to the inch, 3 taps and 3 sets of dies. Price, per set....$2.52
No. 9K3490 Cuts ¾ to 5-16 inch, right hand, 10, 11, 12 and 14 threads to the inch, 4 taps and 4 sets of dies. Price, per set....$2.73
No. 9K3492 Cuts ¾ to ¼ inch, right hand, 10, 12, 14 and 16 threads to the inch, 4 taps, and 4 sets of dies. Price, per set....$2.74
No. 9K3494 Cuts 1 to ⅜ inch, right hand, 9, 10 and 14 threads to the inch, 3 taps and 3 sets of dies. Price, per set....$2.76
No. 9K3496 Cuts 1 to ⅜ inch, right hand, 8, 10 and 12 threads to the inch, 3 taps and 3 sets of dies. Price, per set....$2.77

OUR INVINCIBLE LINE.

It is impossible to produce better screw plates than our Invincible line. They are made for us by one of the best known manufacturers of screw cutting machinery in the United States, a manufacturer who has been making the highest grade screw plates, stocks and dies so long that his name stands for all that is best in their manufacture. On account of the high price his goods sell for and the extremely low prices we quote, we are not allowed to use his name. If we sold these screw plates under the maker's name they would cost you far more than we ask for them. Our contract, however, stipulates that the quality shall be absolutely the best, and our Invincible Screw Plates are made up as good as the finest line this manufacturer sends out.

THE DIES ARE THE SIMPLEST ON THE MARKET.

They are not solid, but cut through on one side and a screw inserted in the opening. By simply turning this screw, the die is opened or closed. They cannot twist, do not get out of order and do not require a mechanic to adjust them. All invincible sets sent 1-32 inch over size V thread which fits regular carriage and machine bolts.

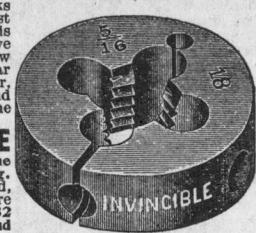

INVINCIBLE

YOUR SAVING IS GREATER

GENERAL REDUCTIONS ON HARDWARE IN THIS BOOK MAKE OUR ALREADY LOW PRICES STILL MORE ATTRACTIVE.

$7.17 PER SET INVINCIBLE ADJUSTABLE DIE SCREW PLATE, CUTS FIVE SIZES.

No. 9K3675 With five taps and five pairs dies, cutting ¼, ⅜, ½, ⅝ and ¾ inch, complete with taps, dies, guides and stocks; stocks are 14 and 26 inches long, with 16-inch tap wrench. Put up in handsome case. Price, per set..........$7.17
No. 9K3677 With seven taps and seven pairs dies, cutting ¼, 5-16, ⅜, 7-16, ½, ⅝ and ¾ inch, complete with taps, dies, guides and stocks; stocks are 14 and 26 inches long, with 16-inch tap wrench. Put up in handsome case. Price, per set $8.36
No. 9K3679 With six taps and six pairs dies, cutting ¼, ½, ⅜, ⅝ and 1 inch, complete with taps, dies, guides and stocks; stocks are 14 and 26 inches long; with 16-inch tap wrench. Put up in handsome case. Price, per set..........$10.34
No. 9K3680 Extra Dies and Collets, for above plates. Sizes, ¼, 5-16, ⅜ or 7-16. Price, each, $0.89
Size, ½ inch. Price, each.........1.24
Size, ⅝ inch. Price, each.........1.49
Size, ¾ inch. Price, each.........1.59
Size, ⅞ inch. Price, each.........1.89
Size, 1 inch. Price, each.........2.03
Above prices are for one die and one collet.

$1.48 ADJUSTABLE TAP AND REAMER WRENCH, 10-INCH.

Can be used in our Invincible Screw Plates.

Nicely finished. Jaws are made of the finest tool steel.
No. 9K3616 Price, 10-inch, holds taps ⅛ to ½ inch..........$1.48
No. 9K3617 Price, 16-inch, holds taps ½ to ¾ inch..........$1.78

$10.71 PER SET INVINCIBLE ADJUSTABLE DIE SCREW PLATE, CUTS SEVEN SIZES.

No. 9K3683 With seven taps and seven pairs dies, cutting ¼, 7-16, ½, ⅝, ¾ and 1 inch; complete with taps, dies, guides and stocks; stocks are 14 and 26 inches long. Price, per set..........$10.71
No. 9K3681 With nine taps and nine pairs dies, cutting ¼, 5-16, ⅜, 7-16, ½, ⅝, ¾, ⅞ and 1 inch; complete with taps, dies, guides and stocks; stocks are 14 and 26 inches long; put up in handsome case. Price, per set..........$12.59

$11.03 FULL MOUNTED INVINCIBLE SCREW PLATE, CUTS 7 SIZES.

FULL MOUNTED INVINCIBLE SCREW PLATE

We furnish a complete stock with each die, which does away with changing every time you wish to cut a different size thread.
No. 9K3695 Cuts seven sizes, ¼, 5-16, ⅜, 7-16, ½, ⅝, ¾ inch; complete with seven taps to match dies, and one 15-inch tap wrench, in handsome case. Price, per set..........$11.03
No. 9K3699 Cuts nine sizes, ¼, 5-16, ⅜, 7-16, ½, ⅝, ¾, ⅞, 1 inch; complete with nine taps to match dies, and two adjustable tap wrenches, 12 and 20 inches long, in handsome case. Price, per set..........$17.98

$2.17 SEPARATE PLATE BLACKSMITHS' STOCKS AND DIES.

Warranted to cut a perfect thread, to be free from flaws and of perfect workmanship.
No. 9K3525 Cuts ½ to 5-16 inch, right hand, 12, 14 and 16 threads to the inch, 3 taps and 3 pairs of dies. Price, per set..$2.17
No. 9K3527 Cuts ½ to 3-16 inch, right hand, 12, 14, 16 and 18 threads to the inch, 4 taps and 4 pairs of dies. Price, per set..$2.48
No. 9K3529 Cuts ¾ to 3-16 inch, right hand, 10, 12, 14 and 18 threads to the inch, 4 taps and 4 pairs of dies. Price, per set..$3.57
No. 9K3531 Cuts ¾ to ⅜ inch, right hand, 10, 12 and 16 threads to the inch, 3 taps and 3 pairs of dies. Price, per set..$3.61
No. 9K3533 Cuts ½ to 5-16 inch, right hand, 10, 11, 12, 14 and 16 threads to the inch, 5 taps and 5 pairs of dies. Price, per set..$4.08
No. 9K3535 Cuts ¾ to ¼ inch, right hand, 10, 12, 14, 16 and 18 threads to the inch, 6 taps and 6 pairs of dies. Price, per set..........$4.62
No. 9K3537 Cuts ¾ to ⅜ inch, right hand, 10, 11, 12, 14, 16, 18 and 20 threads to the inch, 7 taps and 7 pairs of dies. Price, per set..........$5.07
No. 9K3539 Cuts ¾ to ¼ inch, right hand, 10, 11 and 12 threads to the inch, 6 taps and 3 pairs of dies. Price, per set..$3.58
No. 9K3541 Cuts 1 to ½ inch, right hand, 8, 9, 10 and 11 threads to the inch, 4 taps and 4 pairs of dies. Price, per set..$4.86
No. 9K3543 Cuts 1 to 7-16 inch, right hand, 8, 9, 10, 11 and 12 threads to the inch, 5 taps and 5 pairs of dies. Price, per set..$5.71

89c IRON HANDLE GUNSMITHS' SCREW PLATE, CUTS 14 SIZES.

Will cut 14 different sizes, from 3-32 to 3-16 inch; intended for gunsmiths', jewelers' or model makers' use. Cuts exact sizes.
No. 9K3739 Weight, 10 oz. Price, 89c

$1.63 GUNSMITHS' AND JEWELERS' TOOL STEEL STOCKS AND DIES.

The best quality it is possible to produce. Made of finest tempered tool steel, nicely finished, and warranted perfect. These stocks and dies cut exact sizes.

No.	Weight	Cuts Thirty-Seconds	Number Taps and Dies	Price
9K3745	2½ oz.	2½ to 5	4	$1.63
9K3746	6 oz.	4 to 6	4	1.83
9K3747	9 oz.	5 to 8	5	1.98
9K3748	13 oz.	8 to 10	5	2.17

$2.97 LITTLE GIANT ADJUSTABLE DIE SCREW PLATES.

Round Adjustable Dies, 13-16 inch diameter. Each has adjustable tap wrench made of highest grade tool steel properly tempered. These plates are furnished in neat cases, with plush lined tops. These plates cut exact sizes.

LITTLE GIANT

No. 9K3621 Cutting 4³⁶, 3³⁶, 5²⁴, ⁷⁄₃₂²⁴ and ¼²⁰, 5 taps and 5 dies, stock and adjustable tap wrench. Price, per set..$2.97
No. 9K3622 Cutting 4³⁶, 6³², 8³², 10²⁴, 12²⁴, 5 taps, 5 dies, stock and adjustable tap wrench. Price, per set....$3.03
No. 9K3623 Cutting 4³⁶, 6³², 8³², 10²⁴, 12²⁴, 14²⁰, 6 taps, 6 dies, stock and adjustable tap wrench. Price, per set..$3.44
No. 9K3624 Cutting ¼⁴⁰, ³⁄₃₂³⁶, ⅛³², ⁵⁄₃₂²⁴, ³⁄₁₆²⁰, 6 taps, 6 dies, stock and adjustable tap wrench. Price, per set..$3.47
No. 9K3626 Cutting 2³⁶, 3⁴⁸, 4³⁶, 5³², 6³², 8³², 10³², 10²⁴, 12²⁴, 14²⁰, 10 taps, 10 dies, stock and tap wrench. Per set....$5.26

LITTLE GIANT

Round Adjustable Dies, 1 inch in diameter; furnished complete with adjustable wrench, etc. Nothing better. Cutting ¼⁴⁰, ⁹⁄₃₂³², ⁵⁄₁₆²⁴, ³⁄₈²⁰, ⁷⁄₁₆¹⁴. Stock, 9 inches long; 6 dies, 6 taps and adjustable tap wrench. Cuts exact sizes.
No. 9K3636 Price, per set....$4.77

$3.81 GREEN RIVER SCREW PLATE, CUTS 1-8 TO 1-4 INCH.

Screw Plate Stock, Tap Wrench and five sizes taps and guides, cuts ⅛, 5-32, 3-16, 7-32, and ¼ inch. Stock 6 inches long. V-shape thread sent unless otherwise ordered. Complete in hardwood case. Cuts exact sizes.

| ⅛ | 5/32 | 3/16 | 7/32 | ¼ |

No. 9K3720 Price, per set....$3.81

$3.63 BLACKSMITHS' UPRIGHT EASY RUNNING POST DRILL.

Can you afford to do without a drill when you can get one so cheap? If this drill saved you but one cent each day it would pay for itself in a year. If you have drilling to do, and have been using a brace or a horizontal bench drill, it will save far more than its cost the first year. You cannot afford to drill holes in the old way when you can buy a good, substantial post drill at a price as low as we quote this one. This drill is the same grade usually sold at $5.00 to $6.00, and cannot be duplicated elsewhere at anything like our price. While this is a first class drill, better than you can buy elsewhere at $5.00 to $6.00, in your own interest we suggest that you send us your order for our Acme Ball Bearing Self Feed Drill, shown on this page, as we consider it the best hand power drill on the market and worth twice the slight difference in price. Read all we say about our Acme Ball Bearing Third Gear Drill, note the improved third gear, the self feed attachment, and remember that ball bearings make a drill run easier, do more work and last longer.

This $3.63 Upright Post Drill has hand feed, is single geared and has long heavy bearings which insure easy running and prevent springing. It drills holes up to ¾ inch and to center of 12-inch circle; drill spindle is made of 1-inch steel, bored for ½-inch round shank drill bits and has up and down run of 3 inches. Upright column and feed screw are of steel. Drill table can be removed and fork used for holding wheels. Weight, crated, 58 pounds.

No. 9K3806 Price...........$3.63

$6.59 ACME SPECIAL BLACKSMITHS' SELF FEED POST DRILL.

The largest high class drill ever offered at anything like our price. It is adapted to a wide range of usefulness, and will meet the requirements of any ordinary blacksmith. It is heavy, strong and durable; one of the most convenient drills ever offered, and we guarantee it absolutely perfect in material and workmanship. This drill has four very long, perfectly straight bearings, that cannot spring or get out of line. It has our automatic self feeding device, located behind the spindle and out of the way of the operator. Feed is almost continuous, thus avoiding jamming the bit into the work. Has fast or slow speed, instantly obtained by changing crank from one shaft to the other on the same side of the drill. Drill spindle has run of 3 inches and is bored to take ½-inch round shank drills. The upright column, drill spindle and feed screw are of best steel. Drills up to 1¼-inch holes and to center of 15-inch circle. Weight, crated, 120 pounds.

$6.59

No. 9K3816 Price...........$6.59

$8.73 ACME SPECIAL BLACKSMITHS' POWER OR HAND DRILL.

This is the same as our No. 9K3816 Self Feed Post Drill, but equipped with tight and loose pulleys. It possesses all the good features of the drill described above and is an ideal tool for all kinds of work in shops provided with power. Has fly wheel and crank and can be run by hand or power as desired. It will be found very convenient to use the crank when only a few holes are to be drilled and the machinery is not running. This drill is strong, well made, nicely finished and will give entire satisfaction in shops equipped with power. Weight, crated, 132 pounds.

$8.73

No. 9K3821 Price...........$8.73

Same as above, but without fly wheel. For power use only. Weight, crated, 112 pounds.
No. 9K3820 Price...........$8.06

BLACKSMITHS' DRILLS

WE SELL MORE BLACKSMITHS' DRILLS THAN ANY CONCERN IN THE UNITED STATES. QUALITY AND PRICE HAVE DONE THE BUSINESS.

We invite comparison of our prices with the prices quoted by others. Quality for quality and size for size, our prices are 25 to 50 per cent lower than those quoted by anyone else. We are enabled to quote these extremely low prices because we sell the entire output of a large factory and we offer drills direct from factory to you with only one small profit added. We guarantee every drill we sell to be entirely satisfactory. Take it and try it and if you are not pleased with it in every way, if it is not a better drill than you can get elsewhere at anything like our price, send it back to us and we will refund the full amount you paid, including freight charges.

$7.28 ACME BALL BEARING SELF FEED THIRD GEAR BLACKSMITHS' DRILL.

$10.00 ELSEWHERE

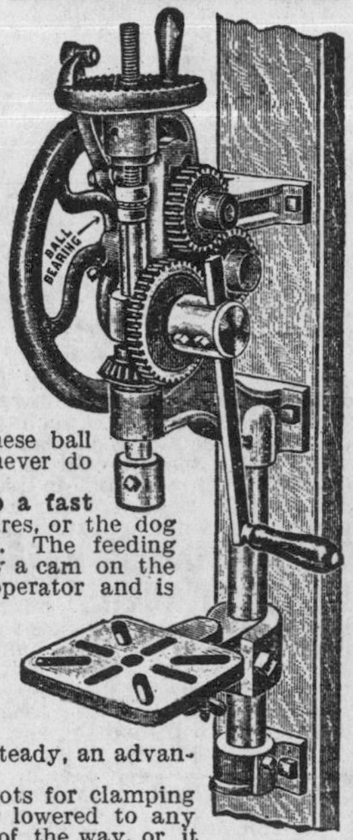

THE GREATEST BARGAIN EVER OFFERED IN A BLACKSMITHS' UPRIGHT DRILL. Quality for quality and size for size, it cannot be duplicated elsewhere for less than $10.00. It is made of the highest grade material throughout and constructed with the idea of producing the best drill on the market to sell at a popular price. It is built after our own design, made extra heavy at the points of greatest strain and combines all the good features of the different drills now being sold, together with **our improved third gear,** and other points which no other drills possess.

BALL BEARINGS are made of the finest die steel, hardened and polished, set in a cup or cone, which is also made of the finest steel. This cup being placed midway between the chuck and headpiece of drill spindle, the balls receive all the pressure and reduce the friction to almost nothing. The running of the drill is greatly improved and its life is more than doubled by these ball bearings, and, once used, a blacksmith would never do without a ball bearing drill.

SELF FEED ATTACHMENT can be set to a fast or slow speed, as the nature of the work requires, or the dog can be thrown back and the drill fed by hand. The feeding device is simple and effective. It is worked by a cam on the inside of main gear wheel out of the way of the operator and is so constructed as to give almost a continuous feed preventing the drill from jamming into the work.

OUR IMPROVED THIRD GEAR enables the operator to change from fast to slow speed by simply changing the crank from one shaft to the other. No left handed turning, as is the case when handle is put on fly wheel. The third gear also makes the drill run smooth and steady, an advantage when fine work is being done.

THE DRILL TABLE is extra heavy, has slots for clamping down any article to be drilled, can be raised or lowered to any height, and when not in use swung around out of the way, or it can be removed entirely and fork used as a wheel holder.

Has strong crank made of steel, adjustable to short or long turn as the nature of the work requires. Shaft and spindle are made of best grade tool steel, are double geared and have double journal bearings. The frame is bored, reamed and polished, insuring ease of operation. Spindle turns 1½ times to each turn of crank on fast speed; crank turns 1½ times to each turn of spindle on slow speed. Drills up to 1¼-inch holes and to center of 15-inch circle. Spindle has up and down run of 3½ inches, and is bored for ½-inch round shank drills. Weight, crated, 113 pounds.

No. 9K3812 Price...........$7.28

$1.86 FOR A HIGH GRADE COMBINATION CLAMP AND DRILL, COMPLETE WITH FIVE DRILL BITS. THE $2.75 KIND.

One of the most practical low priced combination tools on the market. Made of best materials throughout and will give good service. Has wrought iron feed screw with lathe cut threads, extra heavy malleable frame, malleable sliding clamp, and brass chuck. Length, 17 inches; height, 7 inches; weight, 6½ pounds.
No. 9K3792 Complete with five Diamond Pointed Drills, one each, 3-16, ¼, 5-16, ⅜ and ½ inch...$1.86
No. 9K3793 Complete with five Syracuse Twist Drills, one ea., 3-16, ¼, 5-16, ⅜ and ½ in...$2.50
No. 9K3794 Extra Drills for No. 9K3792. Price, per set of five............45
No. 9K3795 Extra Drills for No. 9K3793. Price, per set of five............1.10

$3.33 HIGH GRADE PERFECT COMBINED DRILL, VISE, ANVIL AND HARDIE. JAWS FACED WITH STEEL.

THE USUAL PRICE IS $5.00

THE SAVING IS IN THE PRICE $3.33

Not a toy, but a high grade tool; will save farmers, threshermen, millers and others who have odd jobs to do, several times its cost in a short time. It is so arranged that it can be converted from drill to vise instantly by merely removing the drill bit. The strongest and most practical combination ever built and is sold under our absolute guarantee to replace, free of charge, any piece that may break from practical use within one year. It is strong, durable, nicely finished, and for all ordinary work will answer the purpose of half a dozen high priced tools. A steel T rail is used for the slide or draw bar; jaws are faced with tool steel and polished; top of anvil is case hardened and polished. The drill chuck is bored to take ½-inch round shank drill bits. Drills ½-inch holes easily and is capable of drilling much larger holes. Anvil is provided with good steel cut off or hardie. Weight, complete, boxed for shipment, 64 pounds. This combination tool is not to be compared with the ordinary cast iron light weight combinations usually offered which are so cheaply constructed that they frequently break the first time heavy work is attempted with them. Our Perfect Tool Combination will stand any amount of hard service, and has a wider range of usefulness than any other combination ever sold.
No. 9K3360 Price, complete, without drill bit...........$3.33
NOTICE—For drill bits to fit the above, see No. 9K3860, this page.

$5.49 ACME SELF FEED, TWO-SPEED BLACKSMITHS' POST DRILL.

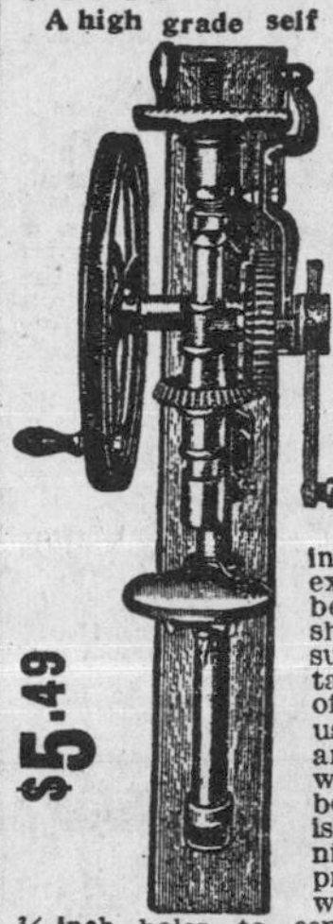

A high grade self feed drill at a lower price than others ask for hand feed drills; cannot be duplicated elsewhere for less than $7.50. It is neat, strong and durable, only the best material enters in its construction, has steel mandrel, shafts and feed screws. Self feed attachment can be set to fast or slow feed as desired, or thrown out entirely and drill changed to hand feed. The second or slow speed is obtained by use of handle on fly wheel, as shown in the illustration. Has extension crank which can be adjusted to a long or short turn as may best suit your work. The drill table can be turned out of the way when not in use, or it can be removed and the fork used as a wheel holder. Frame is bored, reamed and polished; all the gears are nicely adjusted and with proper attention this drill will last for years. Drills ¾-inch holes to center of 12-inch circle. Spindle has run of 3 inches and is bored for ½-inch round shank drills. Weight, crated, 81 pounds. While this is a good light running drill and far better than most of the drills in the blacksmith shops throughout the country, ball bearings make a drill run so much easier and last so much longer, we refer you to our Acme Ball Bearing Third Gear Drill, shown on this page. Read the description carefully, note that the difference in price is very slight, and send us your order for one of these guaranteed light running ball bearing machines.

$5.49

No. 9K3807 Price...........$5.49

$1.49 HORIZONTAL SCREW FEED STEEL SPINDLE BENCH DRILL.

While this is a good, substantial tool, made of first class material and fully capable of doing light work, at the same time, an upright post drill is so much better and more convenient than

$1.49

this old style drill, we recommend the purchase of a post drill. Our horizontal drill has steel drill spindle bored for ½-inch round shank drills. Length, 20 inches; weight, 29 pounds.
No. 9K3800 Price...........$1.49

$1.64 IMPROVED ECONOMICAL DRILL CHUCK, STRONG AND ACCURATE.

This Chuck will pay for itself in a short time, as with it straight shank drill bits can be used in drills bored for ½-inch shank bits. Well finished, strong and accurate. Furnished with ½-inch straight shank.
No. 9K3850 Holds drills ⅜-inch and smaller. Price...........$1.64
No. 9K3851 Holds drills ½-inch and smaller. Price...........$2.23

14c FOR A HALF-INCH ROUND SHANK TWIST DRILL, SIZE, ⅛ INCH.

Fits any of our blacksmiths' upright or bench drills. Will drill metal or wood. Made of highest grade steel by standard manufacturers and are guaranteed accurate. Each one is carefully inspected before it is sent out, and we will replace free of charge any drill found defective. Have ½-inch round shanks. Be sure to state size wanted.

No. 9K3860

Size		Price		Size		Price
⅛	5-32	3-16	7-32	¼	9-32	
Price....	14c	15c	15c	18c	19c	21c
Size....	5-16	11-32	⅜	13-32	7-16	15-32
Price....	22c	23c	24c	25c	26c	27c
Size....	½	17-32	9-16	19-32	⅝	21-32
Price....	27c	28c	29c	30c	34c	35c
Size....	11-16	23-32	¾	25-32	13-16	27-32
Price....	37c	38c	39c	42c	44c	45c
Size....	⅞	29-32	15-16	31-32	1 inch	
Price....	46c	49c	50c	55c	57c	

70c FOR 8 "VULCAN SPECIAL" DIAMOND POINTED BLACKSMITH'S DRILL BITS.

Forged from solid steel, hardened and tempered. Will fit any bit brace. A favorite with blacksmiths and metal workers.

No. 9K56752

| Size, in.. | ⅛ | ⅜ | ¼ | 5-16 | ⅜ | 7-16 | ½ | 9-16 | ⅝ |
| Price, ea. | 6c | 7c | 8c | 9c | 10c | 11c | 12c | 13c |

No. 9K56754 Price per set of 8 (1 each size)...........70c

30c TOOL STEEL ½-INCH ROUND SHANK COUNTERSINK, SIZE, ⅝ INCH.

Made of highest grade tool steel accurately cut. Will fit any of our drills. State size wanted.
No. 9K3857
Size, ⅝-inch with ½-inch shank. Price, 30c
Size, ¾-inch with ½-inch shank. Price, 44c

HARDWARE PRICE REDUCTIONS IN THIS BOOK MAKE YOUR SAVING GREATER THAN EVER.

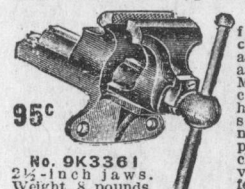

95c HIGH GRADE PARALLEL BENCH VISE WITH 2½-INCH JAWS.

95c

Fills the need for a good, cheap, light vise, adapted to metal or wood work. Made of first class material, has steel jaws and screws and is not to be compared with the cheap cast iron vises usually offered.

No. 9K3361 2½-inch jaws. Weight, 8 pounds. Price.. 95c
No. 9K3362 3-inch jaws. Weight, 12 pounds. Price..........$1.18
No. 9K3363 4-inch jaws. Weight, 30 pounds. Price..........$2.15

$1.73 CYLINDRICAL SLIDE ANCHOR BENCH VISE, 2½-INCH JAWS.

The Usual Price is $3.00

Made on the right principle. Has large wrought steel cylinder for slide. Screw is inside the cylinder and protected from dust, dirt and filings. Best quality steel jaws, nicely finished. Can be used as either a stationary or swivel bottom vise.

Our Price $1.73

No.	Width, Jaws	Opens	Weight	Price
9K3372	2½ in.	4 in.	8½ lbs.	$1.73
9K3373	3 in.	4 in.	15 lbs.	2.37
9K3374	3½ in.	5½ in.	21 lbs.	3.18

$3.18 ACME STEEL BLACKSMITHS' BENCH VISE WITH 3½-IN. JAWS.

$3.18

Made of best quality steel, nicely finished, and strong enough for all ordinary purposes. Especially recommended for blacksmiths, repairmen and others who require a good, substantial vise.

No.	Width, Jaws	Opens	Weight	Price
9K3376	3½ in.	5½ in.	28 lbs.	$3.18
9K3377	4 in.	8½ in.	42 lbs.	3.71
9K3378	4½ in.	9½ in.	55 lbs.	4.49
9K3379	5 in.	10½ in.	81 lbs.	5.27

$5.06 SWIVEL BASE VISE WITH 3½-INCH SWIVEL JAWS.

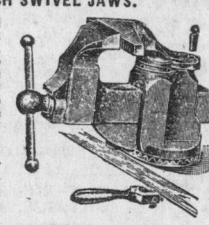

The swivel base makes it very convenient, as work can be instantly turned to right or left as may suit the workman. The back jaw is self adjusting and automatically conforms to any angle. By inserting the pin shown in the illustration the jaw becomes fixed.

No.	Width, Jaws	Opens	Weight	Price
9K3395	3½ in.	5¼ in.	34 lbs.	$5.06
9K3396	4 in.	6¼ in.	57 lbs.	6.72

$1.33 SHEPARD SWIVEL BASE BENCH VISE WITH 2½-INCH JAWS.

Made of the same high class material and finished with the same care as our heavier, higher priced vises. Especially recommended to jewelers, dentists, locksmiths and others who need a light, strong vise, made of the highest grade material. Can be used as either a stationary or swivel bottom vise. Has steel sliding bar, screw, lever and jaws. The anvil is full polished.

$1.33

No.	Width, Jaws	Opens	Weight	Price
9K3424	2½ in.	3¼ in.	10 lbs.	$1.33
9K3425	3⅜ in.	4 in.	16 lbs.	1.83
9K3426	4 in.	6 in.	25 lbs.	2.67

$1.49 ACME SWIVEL BASE BULLDOG BENCH VISE, 2½-INCH JAWS.

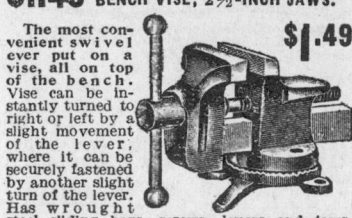

$1.49

The most convenient swivel ever put on a vise, all on top of the bench. Vise can be instantly turned to right or left by a slight movement of the lever, where it can be securely fastened by another slight turn of the lever. Has wrought steel sliding bars, screws, levers and jaws. Vise is nicely finished and anvil is full polished.

No.	Width, Jaws	Opens	Weight	Price
9K3431	2½ in.	3½ in.	11 lbs.	$1.49
9K3432	3⅜ in.	4 in.	16 lbs.	1.83
9K3433	4 in.	6 in.	28 lbs.	2.97

ACME AMERICAN WROUGHT ANVILS

THEY RING LIKE A BELL. No anvil made, English or American, surpasses our Acme in shape, material or finish. It is solid forged of two pieces of best wrought iron, welded at waist; face is made of one piece of tool steel, electrically welded to the body and warranted not to come loose. Base has sufficient spread to insure stability and prevent tipping; has long perfectly shaped horn and heel; face is trued and shaped by a special machine so that there are no hollow or uneven places; edges are perfectly tempered and will not chip. Hardie holes are straight and true, so you will have no trouble on account of anvil tools sticking or not setting level.

WE HAVE THE EXCLUSIVE SALE OF THE ACME. We take the entire output of the factory that makes them, and get them so cheap we are enabled to sell them at a lower price than others pay for anvils not as good. We sell more anvils than any concern in the United States. We could not sell so many unless they were everything we claim for them.

ACME GUARANTEED

ONLY 9½c POUND.

Usual Price is 15c

You Save More Money
The low prices on hardware in our last catalogue are lower still in this book. Over 3,000 hardware items reduced.

DON'T BE MISLED by anyone who quotes wrought anvils at a lower price than we do. They are probably made of cast iron with a wrought face or of scrap iron imperfectly welded. Read our guarantee and then read his; see if he sells them on the same liberal terms we do. No one can offer as good an anvil as ours at a price lower than we do, and when an anvil is quoted at a lower price, you may rest assured it is not as good as ours. Our anvils are unequaled for superior shape, graceful design and, what is dear to every good smith, they ring like a bell.

THIRTY DAYS' FREE USE OF OUR ACME AMERICAN WROUGHT ANVIL. To prove that our Acme is the best anvil ever offered, we sell it under our binding guarantee to take it back at our expense within thirty days after you receive same if it is not equal to or better than any anvil you ever used or if for any reason you are not perfectly satisfied with it. All we ask for it is a fair trial, and if it is not all we claim for it, return it to us and we will immediately refund the full price, together with the freight you paid. We cannot always send exact weights but will send the nearest we have to size wanted.

No. 9K3988

BETTER THAN ANY OTHER ANVIL.

Weight, 120 pounds and over. Price, per pound......	9½c
Weight, 80 to 119 pounds. Price, per pound.....	10c
Weight, 70 to 79 pounds. Price, per pound.....	10½c
Weight, 60 to 69 pounds. Price, per pound.....	11c
Weight, 50 to 59 pounds. Price, per pound.....	12½c

$2.65 STEEL FACE CAST ANVILS.

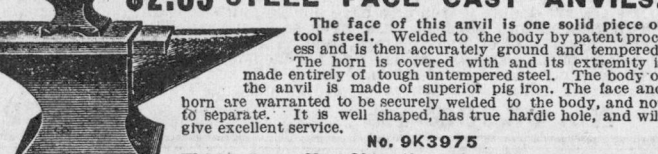

The face of this anvil is one solid piece of tool steel. Welded to the body by patent process and is then accurately ground and tempered. The horn is covered with and its extremity is made entirely of tough untempered steel. The body of the anvil is made of superior pig iron. The face and horn are warranted to be securely welded to the body, and not to separate. It is well shaped, has true hardie hole, and will give excellent service.

No. 9K3975

Weight, lbs..	20	30	40	50	60	70	80	90
Price......	$2.65	$3.10	$3.62	$4.12	$4.66	$5.30	$5.50	$6.85

$1.98 CHILLED FACE CAST IRON ANVILS.

Makes an ideal farmers' anvil. These anvils are made the same as our No. 9K3975, but without the steel face. The face on this anvil being chilled it will not chip or crack. It has the shape and finish of an all wrought anvil.

No. 9K3976

Weight, pounds..............	50	70	100
Price........................	$1.98	$2.85	$4.05

$4.72 WROUGHT BLACKSMITHS' SOLID BOX VISE, WEIGHT, 35 LBS.

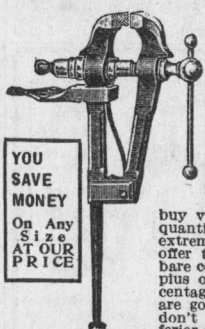

YOU SAVE MONEY On Any Size AT OUR PRICE

It is impossible to make better vises than these. They have highly tempered steel jaws; accurately cut threads and heavy screws. Made throughout of the best materials, are strong and substantial and are warranted perfect in material and workmanship. We buy vises in immense quantities, get them at extremely low prices and offer them to you at the bare cost of manufacture, plus our one small percentage of profit. If you are going to buy a vise, don't risk getting an inferior article by purchasing elsewhere. Send us your order; when the vise comes, set it up and use it thirty days; if it is not entirely satisfactory or if it is not a better vise than you can get elsewhere for anything like our price, send it back and we will refund your money, together with all transportation charges paid by you.

No. 9K3880

Weight	Width, Jaw	Price
35 pounds	3¾ inches	$ 4.72
40 pounds	4 inches	4.91
45 pounds	4⅛ inches	5.17
50 pounds	4½ inches	5.42
60 pounds	5 inches	6.01
70 pounds	5¼ inches	7.06
80 pounds	5½ inches	8.14
100 pounds	6 inches	10.29

$2.82 BLACKSMITHS' VISE BOX AND SCREW, SIZE, 1 INCH.

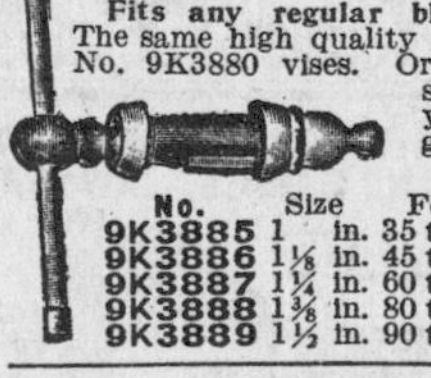

Fits any regular blacksmiths' vise. The same high quality we furnish in our No. 9K3880 vises. Order one of these screws and repair your old vise as good as new.

No.	Size	For Vises	Price
9K3885	1 in.	35 to 40 lbs.	$2.82
9K3886	1⅛ in.	45 to 50 lbs.	3.18
9K3887	1¼ in.	60 to 70 lbs.	3.23
9K3888	1⅜ in.	80 to 90 lbs.	3.57
9K3889	1½ in.	90 to 130 lbs.	5.21

$10.83 GREEN RIVER SHOEING VISE AND BOLT HEADER.

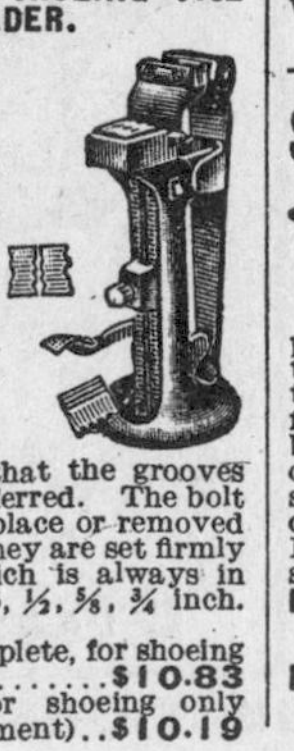

With one of these machines a blacksmith can form any shape calk he desires on a shoe in less than half the time usually required. The vise drops open when not in use, forms both sharp and straight calks, the forming die being of tool steel of proper shape. This die may be turned over for summer work, giving a straight surface for whole work. The swaging plate for sharp calks is furnished with a full number of grooves for large and small calks. It can be placed so that the grooves run either way as may be preferred. The bolt heading dies are dropped in place or removed instantly without trouble. They are set firmly by drawing a taper key which is always in place. Sizes, ¼, 5-16, ⅜, 7-16, ½, ⅝, ¾ inch. Any length up to 24 inches.

No. 9K31045 Price, complete, for shoeing and bolt heading..................$10.83
No. 9K31046 Price, for shoeing only (without bolt heading attachment)..$10.19

$4.79 EXTRA HEAVY SWIVEL BOTTOM WOODWORKERS' VISE.

$4.79

This high class vise is heavy enough for regular shop work, and the price is in reach of every coach maker, wheelwright, cabinet maker or other woodworker in the country. Usually sold for $6.00 or $7.00. Has patent swivel bottom which allows the vise to be turned to any position where a slight movement of the lever fastens it securely. Has extra heavy slide and screw made of tempered steel. Jaws are made of steel and have long taper, which makes it an especially convenient vise for woodworkers, though it can be used just as well for holding iron. Vise is handsomely finished, all bright parts including anvil being full polished. If you need a good woodworkers' vise, you will make no mistake in ordering this one. Width of jaws, 4½ inches; opens 10 inches. Weight, 44 pounds.

No. 9K3440 Price..........$4.79

$2.91 QUICK ACTING WOODWORKERS' VISE, OPENS 9 INCHES.

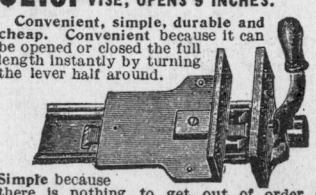

Convenient, simple, durable and cheap. Convenient because it can be opened or closed the full length instantly by turning the lever half around.

Simple because there is nothing to get out of order and there are very few parts to it; **durable** because each part is heavy and strong, made of the best material and will last a lifetime, and **cheap** because compared to other vises it is easy to make, and we buy them in such large quantities we get them at the lowest possible price. We have sold thousands of these vises to woodworkers and manual training schools and they are gaining in popularity every day.

No.	Size	Opens	Wgt.	
9K3443	3 x7½ in.	9 in.	26	$2.91
9K3444	3½x8 in.	12 in.	35	3.76

$1.06 COMBINATION VISE, ANVIL AND PIPE VISE, 3-INCH JAWS.

Has chilled face and jaws. Made of steel, malleable and cast iron. Jaws, 3 inches wide, opens 5 inches. Weight, 26 pounds.

No. 9K3370 Price..........$1.06

54c ECONOMICAL, SUBSTANTIAL CAST IRON OIL TROUGH.

Cast Iron Oil Trough, for oiling wheels with tires as wide as 4 inches. Everyone who owns a wagon should have one of these wheel oilers; prevents tires becoming loose and saves the expense of having them reset. Order one of these troughs and oil your wheels. Weight, 15 pounds.

No. 9K31378 Price..........54c

99c SELF HEATING OIL TROUGH, COMPLETE WITH MINERAL WOOL BURNER.

With one of these troughs you can oil your wheels with boiling oil, which is a much better way than applying it cold. All you have to do is to saturate the mineral wool with coal oil or gasoline, place it under the trough and apply a match; when the linseed oil gets to boiling, revolve the wheel slowly in the trough until the felloe is thoroughly saturated. This is a practical, convenient and satisfactory way of applying boiling oil to wheels. For wheels with tires up to 4 inches wide, complete, with mineral wool.

No. 9K31381 Price..........99c

$1.11 CAST STEEL LIGHTNING PLOW SHARE, 12-INCH CUT.

Lightning Plow Share, fully welded and point finished. Perfected to meet the demand for a fully welded plow share that can be quickly and easily fitted to the different makes of plows, thus saving the hard work of welding on the landside and finishing the point. The Lightning Share can be fitted to the angle of more plows than any other welded share on the market. The landside extends at the heel and is long enough to cut to fit any plow. Either right or left hand. Be sure to state which is wanted; also state size. Average weight, 13 pounds.

No. 9K31033 Made of crucible cast steel.

Size, inches.	12	14	16
Price, each..	$1.11	$1.26	$1.33

No. 9K31034 Made of soft center steel.

Size, inches.	12	14	16
Price, each..	$1.59	$1.72	$1.91

CRUCIBLE CAST STEEL ANVIL TOOLS.

Made of the best materials by skilled workmen, and each tool is fully warranted. Our anvil tools are not the cheap, light weight kind usually offered, but are heavy and strong enough for hard usage. We guarantee every anvil tool we send out to be made of best steel, to be properly tempered and to be satisfactory in every respect. Good anvil tools are just as important as a good anvil. Order some of these and get the best.

26c BLACKSMITHS' CRUCIBLE CAST STEEL HOT CUTTER.
No handle is furnished. 1¾-inch cut. Weight, 2 pounds 2 ounces.
No. 9K3192 Price................26c

27c BLACKSMITHS' CRUCIBLE CAST STEEL COLD CUTTER.
Handle is not furnished. 1¾-inch cut. Weight, 2 pounds 4 ounces. 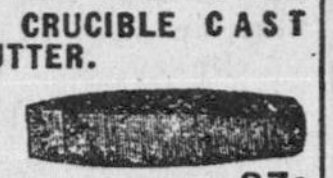
No. 9K3195 Price................27c

6c BLACKSMITHS' CRUCIBLE CAST STEEL HARDIE, SIZE, ½-INCH.
Size given is size of shank, which fits hole in anvil.
No. 9K3198

Size, inch..	½	⅝	¾	1	1¼	1½
Weight..	7 oz.	12 oz.	1 lb.	1¼ lbs.	1½ lbs.
Price....	6c	9c	12c	15c	18c

29c BLACKSMITHS' CRUCIBLE CAST STEEL FLATTER, 2-IN. SQUARE.
No. 9K3200 Without handles.

Size of face, inches	2	2¼	2½
Weight, pounds	2¾	2¾	3¾
Price	29c	33c	41c
Size of face, inches	2¾	3	
Weight, pounds	3¾	4½	
Price	45c	54c	

23c BLACKSMITHS' CRUCIBLE CAST STEEL TOP SWAGE, SIZE, ¼-INCH.
No. 9K3202 Without handles.

Size, inch.	¼	⅜
Weight, pounds	2¼	2¼
Price	23c	26c
Size, inch	½	⅝
Weight, pounds	2½	2¾
Price	27c	32c	33c
Size, inches	1	1¼	1½
Weight, pounds	2¾	2½	3½
Price	34c	36c	44c

12c BLACKSMITHS' CRUCIBLE CAST STEEL ROUND HAND PUNCHES.
Made of ⅝-inch octagonal steel, 10 inches long. Sizes, ¼, ⅜ or ½. State size wanted. Weight, about 1 pound.
No. 9K3212 Price................12c

48c CAST STEEL BLACKSMITHS' SLEDGE, WEIGHT, 8 POUNDS.
Oil finished, with polished faces. Every sledge guaranteed against defects in material and workmanship. Price does not include handles.
No. 9K3174

| Weight, lbs. | 8 | 10 | 12 | 14 | 16 |
| Price | 48c | 60c | 72c | 84c | 96c |

12c HAND SHAVED HICKORY SLEDGE HANDLES FOR ABOVE.
No. 9K3176 36 inches long.
Price................12c

48c BLACKSMITHS' HAND HAMMER, WARRANTED, WEIGHT, 2 POUNDS.
Extra quality steel, made complete with handles. Handle not included in weight.
No. 9K3122

| Weight | 2 lbs. | 2 lbs. 10 oz. | 3 lbs. | 3½ lbs. |
| Prices | 48c | 51c | 55c | 58c |

12c FOR 3 BLACKSMITHS' HAND HAMMER HANDLES.
Straight grain selected hickory. Length, 16 inches.
No. 9K3130 Price for 3 handles....12c

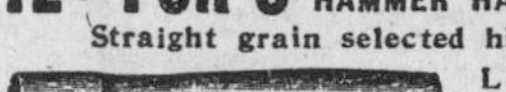

34c STANDARD PATTERN MACHINISTS' BALL PEIN HAMMER, WEIGHT, 12 OZ.
Half polished, solid cast steel, complete with hickory handles. Handles not included in weight. 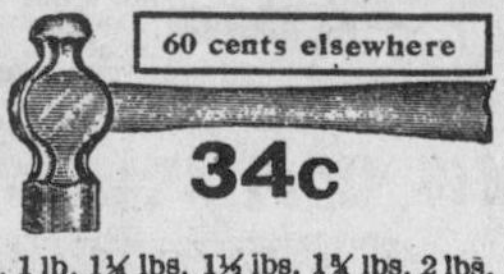
60 cents elsewhere
No. 9K3132

| Weight. | 12 oz. | 1 lb. | 1¼ lbs. | 1½ lbs. | 1¾ lbs. | 2 lbs. |
| Price | 34c | 39c | 41c | 43c | 49c | 51c |

12c FOR 3 MACHINISTS' BALL PEIN HAMMER HANDLES.
Straight grain selected hickory. Length, 16 inches.
No. 9K3135 Price for 3 handles....12c

26c BLACKSMITHS' CRUCIBLE CAST STEEL BOTTOM SWAGE, ¼-INCH.
No. 9K3204 Shanks are from ⅞ to 1¼ inches.

Size, inch.....	¼	⅜
Weight, lbs...	2¼	2½
Price.........	26c	27c
Size, inch...	½	⅝	¾
Weight, lbs..	2⅜	2⅜	2½
Price.........	29c	29c	33c
Size, inches,	1	1¼	1½
Weight, lbs..	2⅜	3	3½
Price.........	35c	36c	42c

29c BLACKSMITHS' CRUCIBLE CAST STEEL TOP FULLER, ⅜-INCH.
No. 9K3206 Oil finished, polished face. Price does not include handle.

		Price
Size, ⅜ in.; wt., 2¼ lbs..	29c
Size, ½ in.; wt., 2¼ lbs..	30c
Size, ⅝ in.; wt., 2¼ lbs..	31c
Size, ¾ in.; wt., 2⅞ lbs..	35c
Size, 1 in.; wt., 3½ lbs..	41c
Size, 1¼ in.; wt., 3½ lbs..	42c
Size, 1½ in.; wt., 3½ lbs..	45c

26c BLACKSMITHS' CRUCIBLE CAST STEEL BOTTOM FULLER, ⅜-INCH.
No. 9K3207 Shanks are from ⅞ to 1¼ inches. Oil finished, polished face.

	Price
Size, ⅜ in.; wt., 2¼ lbs..	26c
Size, ½ in.; wt., 2¼ lbs..	27c
Size, ⅝ in.; wt., 2¼ lbs..	28c
Size, ¾ in.; wt., 2⅞ lbs..	35c
Size, 1 in.; wt., 3 lbs..	36c
Size, 1¼ in.; wt., 3 lbs..	37c
Size, 1½ in.; wt., 3⅜ lbs..	41c

26c BLACKSMITHS' CRUCIBLE CAST STEEL SET HAMMER, 1¼-INCH.
No. 9K3234 Oil finished, polished face. Without handles.

Sizes of square face, inches	1¼	1½	1¾
Weight, pounds....	2¼	3¼	4¼
Price	26c	38c	56c

GENERAL REDUCTIONS IN PRICE OF HARDWARE ON THIS PAGE MAKE YOUR SAVING GREATER THAN EVER.

37c CAST STEEL PLOW OR ENGINEERS' HAMMER, WEIGHT, 18 OUNCES.
37c Finely polished; complete with handle.
Others ask 65 cents
No. 9K3120

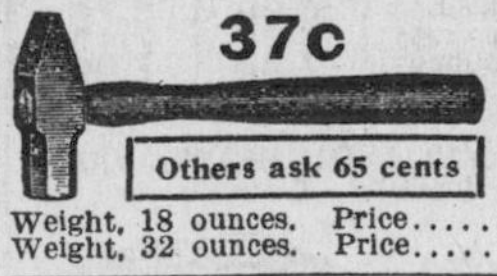

| Weight, 18 ounces | Price......... | 37c |
| Weight, 32 ounces | Price......... | 46c |

25c STANDARD PATTERN RIVETING HAMMER, WEIGHT, 7 OUNCES.
Complete with hickory handle. Polished, extra cast steel. Handle not included in weight. 
50 CENTS IS THE RETAIL PRICE.
25c
No. 9K3100

| Weight...... | 7 oz. | 9 oz. | 12 oz. | 18 oz. |
| Price....... | 25c | 26c | 27c | 31c |

12c FOR 3 HICKORY RIVETING HAMMER HANDLES.
Length, 14 inches.
No. 9K3105
Price for 3 handles................12c

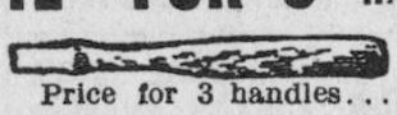

56c FOR 5 POUNDS CHERRY HEAT WELDING COMPOUND.
Every weld with Cherry Heat Welding Compound is stronger than it would be possible to make at any heat without borax. It is a perfect protection to steel from any degree of heat obtainable in a smith's forge. It will perfectly restore burnt steel. Broken castings can be reunited at a low heat with the compound, and cast iron firmly united to either wrought iron or steel. A woman might as well try to keep house without soap as for a blacksmith to try to make a weld without Cherry Heat Welding Compound.
Cherry Heat Welding COMPOUND TRADE MARK REGISTERED AUG. 22 1905
No. 9K3115
1-pound tin can. Price, per can....12c
5-pound boxes. Price, per box.....56c

YOU PAY TWICE OUR PRICE AT RETAIL
On over 3,000 hardware items low prices in our last catalogue are lower still in this book.

39c FOR 5 POUNDS E-Z WELDING COMPOUND.
A compound entirely without borax. Will make a clean, firm weld. Can be used with a very low heat which makes a better weld. There is no sloughing or boiling off and no scale. Put up in 5-pound packages.
No. 9K31116 Price, per 5-lb. pkg.. 39c

$1.43 FULL SIZE, OAK TANNED LEATHER BLACKSMITHS' APRON.
Split Leather Apron with bib and strings. Our own special brand, made of selected hides, are soft and pliable and will wear well. Strings are put on with copper rivets, reinforced with extra piece of leather and flat on both sides. Size, 28x38 inches.
No. 9K31052 Price................$1.43

$1.49 IMPROVED EASY B LT CLIPPER. CUTS UP TO 5-16 INCH.
They have all the latest improvements and are made of the best material throughout. Jaws are high grade steel, properly tempered, and can be adjusted to take up the wear of the joints and cutting edges. Each pair is fitted with rubber bumpers between the handles to avoid jars on hands or wrists. Every clipper fully warranted. Don't use small clippers on large work, you may break them; or large ones on small work, they are heavy and unhandy.
No. 9K3300 No. 0. For cutting bolts 5-16-inch or less; weight, 3 lbs. Price....$1.49
No. 1. For cutting bolts ⅜-inch or less; weight, 4½ pounds. Price........$1.97
No. 2. For cutting bolts ½-inch or less; weight, 7½ pounds. Price........$2.73
No. 3. For cutting bolts ⅝-inch or less; weight, 12½ pounds. Price........$3.92

Tire and Iron Work Bolts.
Have perfect threads in nuts and on bolts, are made of good tough material. State size and length wanted.
No. 9K31218 Diameter, 3-16 inch.

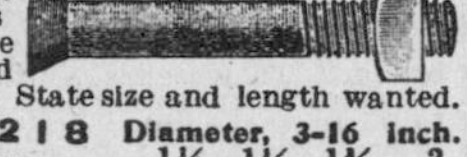

Length, inches	1¼	1½	1¾	2
Price, per 100	14c	14c	15c	16c
Length, inches	2¼	2½	2¾	3
Price, per 100	17c	18c	19c	21c

No. 9K31219 Diameter, ¼ inch.

Length, inches	1¼	1½	1¾	2
Price, per 100	22c	22c	23c	24c
Length, inches	2¼	2½	2¾	3
Price, per 100	25c	26c	27c	29c

Wrought Iron Washers.
The various sizes are large enough to easily slip over the size bolt given. State size wanted.
No. 9K31236

For bolt, inch 3-16	¼	5-16	⅜	½
No. in pound, 440	139	113	55	20
Per pound	11c	8c	7c	6c	5c
For bolt, inch	⅝	¾	⅞	1
No. in pound	13	9	10	8
Per pound	4c	4c	4c	4c

Blank and Threaded Hot Pressed Square Nuts.
Our nuts are made of first class stock and are nicely finished. We sell any quantity. The number of nuts to the pound is approximated. State size wanted.
No. 9K31250 Blank Nuts.

For bolts, inch..	¼	5-16	⅜	7-16
No. in pound....	74	39	21	13	12
Blank, price, lb.	10c	9c	7c	6c	5c
For bolts, inch..	9-16	⅝	¾	⅞	1
No. in pound....	7	6	3	2	2
Blank, price, lb.	5c	5c	5c	4c	4c

No. 9K31252 Threaded Nuts.

For bolts, inch..	¼	5-16	⅜	7-16
No. in pound....	74	39	21	13	12
Threaded, per lb.	13c	11c	9c	7c	6c
For bolts, inch..	9-16	⅝	¾	⅞	1
No. in pound....	7	6	3	2	2
Threaded, per lb.	6c	6c	5c	5c	4c

Flat and Oval Head Rivets.
Be sure to give size when ordering.
Flat head. The number of rivets to the pound is approximated. ¼ inch in diameter, any length.
No. 9K31270

Length, inches	1	1¼	1½	1¾
No. rivets to pound	58	54	50	46
Length, inches	2	2¼	2½	2¾
No. rivets to pound	42	38	34	30

Price, per pound................5c

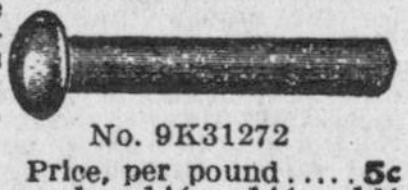

Oval head. The number of rivets to the pound is approximated. ¼ inch in diameter, any length.
No. 9K31272 Price, per pound........5c

Length, inches	1	1¼	1½	1¾
No. rivets to pound	55	52	48	44
Length, inches	2	2¼	2½	2¾
No. rivets to pound	37	33	28	23

Carriage Bolts.
Oval Head Carriage Bolts, forged nuts, full size square shoulder, well cut thread in nut and on bolt, made from soft iron, which will not break easily. We handle millions of bolts each year, buy in large quantities and get them so cheap we offer them to you at wholesale prices.

No. 9K31175 Carriage Bolts, ¼ inch in diameter. State length wanted.

Length inches	Per Doz.	Per 100	Length inches	Per Doz.	Per 100
1	$0.05	$0.28	3¾	$0.08	$0.38
1¼	.05	.28	4	.08	.39
1½	.05	.28	4½	.09	.40
1¾	.05	.29	5	.09	.43
2	.06	.30	5½	.10	.46
2¼	.06	.31	6	.10	.48
2¾	.06	.33	6½	.12	.72
3	.07	.36	7	.12	.76
3½	.07	.37	8	.14	.82

No. 9K31177 Carriage Bolts, 5-16 inch in diameter. State length wanted.

Length inches	Per Doz.	Per 100	Length inches	Per Doz.	Per 100
1¼	$0.05	$0.32	4½	$0.08	$0.49
1½	.05	.35	5	.09	.53
1¾	.05	.36	5½	.09	.56
2	.06	.38	6	.10	.58
2½	.06	.39	6½	.12	.88
2¾	.07	.40	7	.12	.92
3	.07	.42	7½	.14	.96
3½	.07	.43	8	.15	1.00
3¾	.08	.44	9	.16	1.08
4	.08	.47	10	.17	1.16

No. 9K31179 Carriage Bolts, ⅜ inch in diameter. State length wanted.

Length inches	Per Doz.	Per 100	Length inches	Per Doz.	Per 100
1¼	$0.07	$0.44	4¾	$0.12	$0.73
1½	.07	.44	5	.12	.76
1¾	.07	.47	5½	.13	.80
2	.08	.49	6	.14	.84
2½	.08	.51	6½	.16	1.28
2¾	.08	.53	7	.19	1.35
3	.09	.56	7½	.21	1.41
3¼	.09	.58	8	.23	1.47
3½	.10	.60	9	.24	1.60
3¾	.10	.62	10	.26	1.73
4	.10	.67	11	.28	1.96
4½	.11	.69	12	.29	1.99
4½	.11	.71			

No. 9K31180 Carriage Bolts, ½ inch in diameter. State length wanted.

Length inches	Per Doz.	Per 100	Length inches	Per Doz.	Per 100
1½	$0.17	$1.14	7½	$0.29	$2.08
2	.18	1.15	8	.30	2.17
2½	.19	1.16	8½	.32	2.26
2¾	.19	1.17	9	.34	2.35
3	.20	1.22	9½	.35	2.44
3½	.20	1.31	10	.37	2.52
4	.21	1.40	10½	.39	2.65
4½	.22	1.47	11	.40	2.70
5	.22	1.56	11½	.41	2.75
5½	.23	1.64	12	.42	2.88
6	.23	1.72	13	.44	3.05
6½	.25	1.90	14	.46	3.23
7	.27	1.98	15	.48	3.40

Machine Bolts.
Machine Bolts have square heads and nuts, and are round up to the head. Our machine bolts are made of the same high class material as our carriage bolts.

No. 9K31189 Diameter, ¼ inch.

Length inches	Per Doz.	Per 100	Length inches	Per Doz.	Per 100
1½	$0.07	$0.47	4½	$0.11	$0.61
2	.07	.49	5	.11	.63
2¼	.08	.52	5½	.12	.65
2½	.08	.53	6	.13	.67
3	.09	.54	6½	.15	.93
3½	.09	.56	7	.16	.95
4	.09	.58			

Be sure to give length when ordering.

No. 9K31190 Diameter, 5-16 inch.

Length inches	Per Doz.	Per 100	Length inches	Per Doz.	Per 100
1½	$0.09	$0.56	4½	$0.14	$0.76
2	.09	.59	5	.14	.79
2¼	.10	.62	5½	.16	.82
2½	.10	.65	6	.18	1.19
3	.11	.67	6½	.20	1.19
3½	.12	.72	7	.22	1.23

No. 9K31191 Diameter, ⅜ inch.

Length inches	Per Doz.	Per 100	Length inches	Per Doz.	Per 100
1½	$0.09	$0.67	5	$0.17	$0.98
2	.10	.72	5½	.19	1.02
2½	.11	.76	6	.21	1.07
3	.12	.80	6½	.24	1.48
3½	.13	.84	7	.26	1.54
4	.14	.89	7½	.27	1.60
4½	.15	.96	8	.29	1.65

Be sure to give length when ordering.

No. 9K31192 Diameter, ½ inch.

Length inches	Per Doz.	Per 100	Length inches	Per Doz.	Per 100
1½	$0.21	$1.37	7	$0.38	$2.62
2	.22	1.47	8	.40	2.83
2½	.23	1.56	9	.42	3.03
3	.25	1.67	10	.44	3.15
3½	.26	1.75	11	.48	3.42
4	.27	1.86	12	.49	3.63
4½	.29	1.94	14	.52	4.05
5	.30	2.06	16	.58	4.45
5½	.32	2.13	18	.67	4.87
6	.34	2.25	20	.81	5.20
6½	.36	2.30			

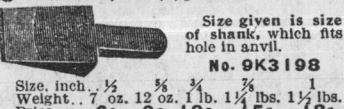

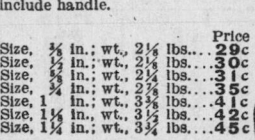

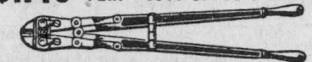

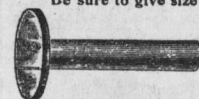

76c FOR A THREE-LEAF, 34-INCH ELLIPTIC BUGGY OR CARRIAGE SPRING.

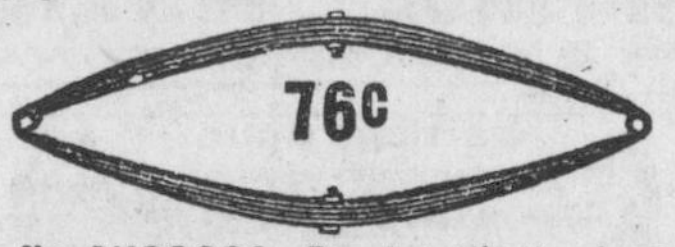

No. 9K33980 Regular elliptic shape, oil tempered, half bright. Made of the best full size spring steel, carefully tempered and guaranteed against defects of any kind. Be sure to give catalogue number and do not fail to state size and price of spring wanted.

Width, inches	No. of Leaves	Length, inches	Av. Weight for Single Spring, pounds	Price, each
1¼	3	34	15	$0.76
1¼	3	36	15	.84
1¼	4	34	19	.87
1¼	4	36	19	.94
1⅜	4	34	20	.95
1⅜	4	36	21	1.04
1½	4	36	23	1.13
1½	5	36	28	1.28
1¾	5	36	33	1.58
1¾	6	36	38	1.83

47c PER PAIR TWO-LEAF SEAT SPRINGS.

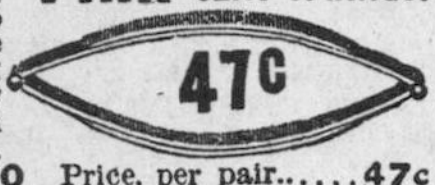

Two-leaf, 1½x26 inches. Made of best spring steel properly tempered, and are easy to put on.
No. 9K33990 Price, per pair......47c
Three-leaf, 1½x28 inches.
No. 9K33992 Price, per pair.....79c

34c FOR THE BARTEN ADJUSTABLE MALLEABLE BOLSTER STAKE.

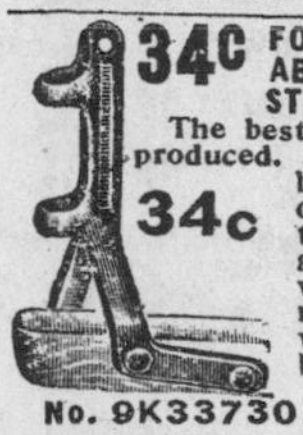

The best and cheapest stake ever produced. Mortises and numerous bolt and rivet holes which cause the ends of the bolster to split, break or decay, are no longer needed. It will fit bolsters of any thickness. It is adjustable for wide or narrow wagon boxes.
No. 9K33730 Price, each........34c

$1.09 SPIRAL TONGUE SUPPORT. STRONG, SIMPLE AND DURABLE.

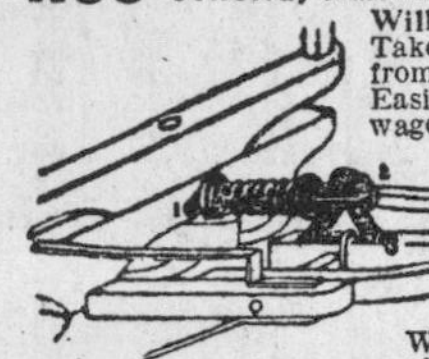

Will fit any wagon. Takes all the weight from horses' necks. Easily attached to wagon tongue.

We sell thousands of them every year and they are giving universal satisfaction.
No. 9K33776 Price, for heavy wagon $1.09

$1.67 LINDQUIST'S TONGUE SUPPORT. HOLDS THE TONGUE STRAIGHT.

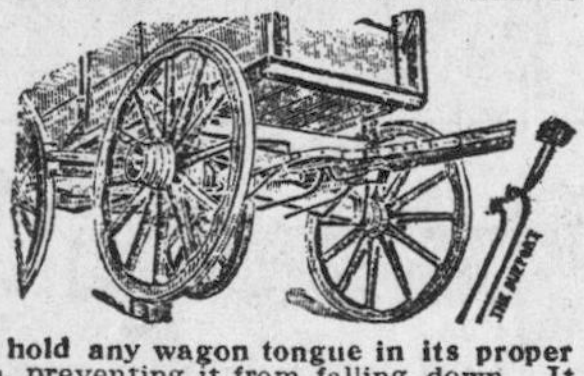

Will hold any wagon tongue in its proper position, preventing it from falling down. It relieves the necks of the horses from the weight of the tongue, thereby giving them greater ease and comfort. Can be applied in one minute. Will keep the tongue straight under any and all circumstances.
No. 9K33780 Price, ¾ inch for heavy wagons.................................$1.67

7c FOR A 6¼-INCH DROP FORGED STEEL GENERAL PURPOSE WRENCH.

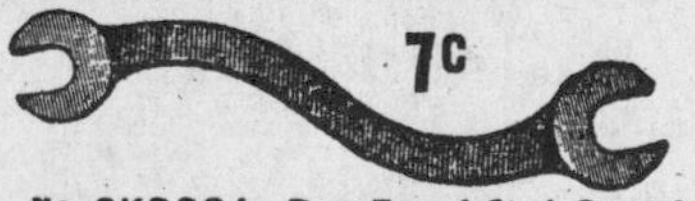

No. 9K3321 Drop Forged Steel General Purpose Wrenches. You can't afford to be without a set of these wrenches and the price brings them within the reach of all.

Size of openings	Length	Price
⅜ and ½ inch	6¼ inches	7c
½ and ⅝ inch	7⅛ inches	11c
⅝ and ¾ inch	8¼ inches	14c
¾ and ⅞ inch	9¼ inches	17c
⅞ and 1 inch	10⅜ inches	21c

Price, per set of five wrenches 66c

8c SUPERIOR CRUCIBLE CAST STEEL ALLIGATOR WRENCH, 5¼ INCHES.

Capacity, ¼ to ¾ inch, for holding or turning round or square bolts or nuts.
No. 9K3322 Price..................8c

17c NICKEL PLATED DOUBLE HEAD, ALWAYS READY WRENCH, No. 1.

No. 9K3323
Drop forged from steel of superior quality; oil tempered. Retails for 25 cents.

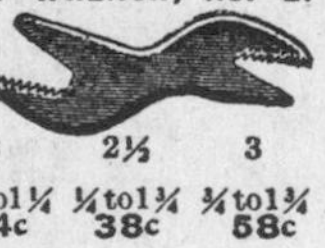

Numbers....	1	2	2½	3
Holds nuts or pipe, inches	¼ to ¾	¼ to 1¼	¼ to 1¾	¾ to 1¾
Price	17c	24c	38c	58c

HARDWARE PRICES REDUCED IN THIS BOOK ON OVER 3,000 ITEMS MAKE YOUR SAVING GREATER THAN EVER.

$1.52 PER SET FOUR AXLES, HALF PATENT, SHORT BED, ⅞ X 6½ INCHES.

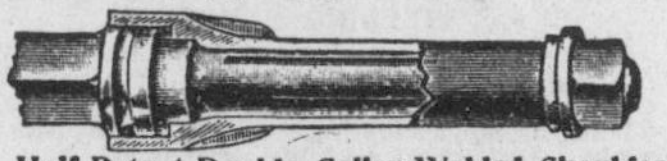

Half Patent Double Collar Welded Shoulder Steel Axles complete with boxes. These axles have an oil retaining groove which makes frequent oiling unnecessary. They are made of the best materials, carefully machined, far superior to the light weight competition goods generally offered. They are cheap in price only. Our extremely low prices are made possible because we buy in immense quantities direct from the manufacturer, and offer them to you with only one small profit added.

Size	No. 9K33900 No. 1 Short Bed. Price, per set of 4 axles	No. 9K33902 No. 2 Long Bed. Price, per set of 4 axles
⅞x6½	$1.52	$1.81
1 x6½	1.64	1.97
1⅛x6½	1.88	2.30
1⅛x7	1.89	2.31
1⅛x7½	1.90	2.32
1¼x6½	2.30	2.80
1¼x7	2.31	2.81
1¼x7½	2.32	2.82
1½x8	4.13	4.95

$1.72 PER SET LONG DISTANCE SHORT BED AXLES, ⅞ X 6½ INCHES.

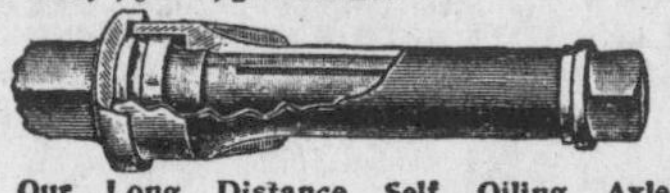

Our Long Distance Self Oiling Axle is made with an improved oil retaining groove, which holds the oil much longer than any other self oiling axle. Also the Collinge collar prevents dirt from working into the box and is acknowledged to be the easiest running axle made. Only the best grade steel used in their construction. Every axle carefully inspected before being sent out. Order a set of these Long Distance Collinge Collar Axles and make your old vehicle run like a new one.

Size	No. 9K33910 No. 1 Short Bed. Price, per set of 4 axles	No. 9K33912 No. 2 Long Bed. Price, per set of 4 axles
⅞x6½	$1.72	$2.15
1 x6½	1.87	2.22
1⅛x6½	2.24	2.64
1⅛x7	2.25	2.65
1⅛x7½	2.26	2.66
1¼x6½	2.77	3.29
1¼x7	2.78	3.30
1¼x7½	2.79	3.31

NOTE.—We cannot furnish boxes only, nor axles without boxes. A set of short bed axles (commonly called axle stubs) consists of four axles with short bed, which are intended to be welded to old axles. A set of long bed axles consists of four axles with bed long enough to make axle complete by welding in the center. We sell one-half set at one-half the price of a full set, and one-quarter set at one-qu. rter the price of full set. We cannot weld axles or set boxes. In ordering parts of sets be sure to state whether right or left hand is wanted.

$4.35 FOR A WELL MADE HIGH GRADE PIANO BOX BUGGY BODY IN THE WHITE, COMPLETE WITH SEAT.

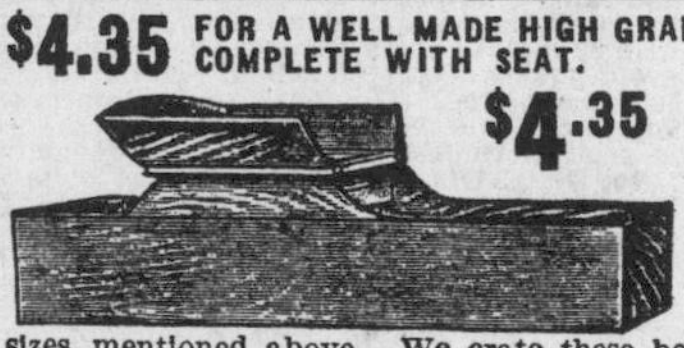

The nicest finished Buggy Body offered by anyone. Complete as shown, not ironed or painted, in the following sizes: 24x50, 24x52, 25x50 or 25x52; panels 8 inches deep. Weight, about 50 pounds. Made of the best seasoned material. The panels are well glued, clamped and screwed to frame, which make them stand the hard usage to which they are put. Dimensions given above are on bottom, outside to outside. We can furnish these bodies only in sizes mentioned above. We crate these bodies securely. Be sure to state size wanted.
No. 9K35065 Price..$4.35

$3.85 PER SET ACME ELLIPTIC BOLSTER SPRINGS. CAPACITY, 1,000 POUNDS.

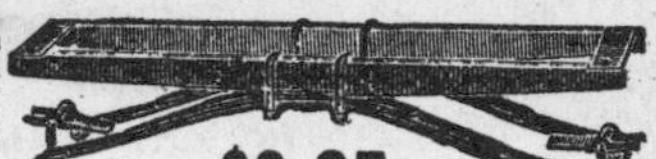

So constructed that they will not strike the bolster. They are made on the same principle as an elliptic carriage spring. Every set warranted to carry the number of pounds represented or money refunded. A set consists of two complete springs ready for use. We carry in stock and can ship immediately any of the sizes listed below, either 38 or 42 inches long, which are the regular standard lengths. 38-inch always sent unless otherwise ordered.

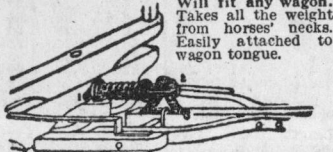

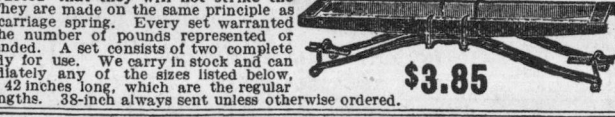

No.	Width of Steel	Number of Leaves	Springs will Carry	Weight, per Set	Price, per Set: 38 inches long	Price, per Set: 42 inches long
9K34150	1½ inches	3	1,000 pounds	66 pounds	$3.85	$4.20
9K34151	1½ inches	4	1,500 pounds	75 pounds	4.20	4.80
9K34152	1¾ inches	4	2,000 pounds	90 pounds	4.95	5.50
9K34153	1¾ inches	5	2,500 pounds	105 pounds	5.55	6.15
9K34154	2 inches	5	3,000 pounds	120 pounds	6.20	6.75
9K34155	2 inches	6	4,000 pounds	135 pounds	6.80	7.40
9K34156	2 inches	7	5,000 pounds	150 pounds	7.20	7.80
9K34157	2½ inches	6	6,000 pounds	170 pounds	8.95	9.65

19c FOR A 6-INCH DROP FORGED TOOL STEEL MONKEY WRENCH.

The kind that retails for 35 cts.

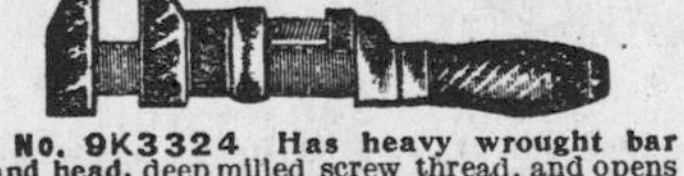

No. 9K3324 Has heavy wrought bar and head, deep milled screw thread, and opens full. This wrench is not to be compared with the common light weight kind usually sold. The 10-inch size is the best for general purposes.

Size, inches	6	8	10	12	15
Price......	19c	23c	28c	36c	48c

29c GENUINE L. COE'S IMPROVED KNIFE HANDLE MONKEY WRENCH, 6-INCH.

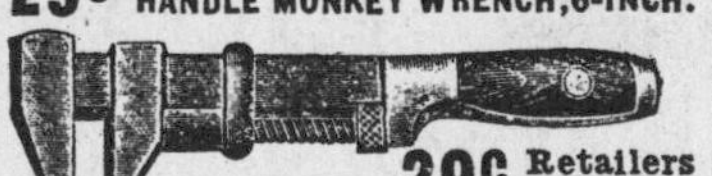

29c Retailers ask 40c.

No. 9K3325 Made of the very best materials, thoroughly case hardened, and every wrench warranted.

Size, inches	6	8	10	12	15	18	21
Will open..	⅞	1¼	1¾	2⅛	2⅝	3	4⅛
Price......	29c	42c	54c	63c	$1.06	$1.34	$1.62

36c FOR AN 8-INCH QUICK ACTING DROP FORGED MONKEY WRENCH.

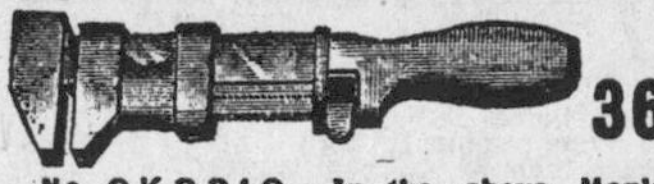

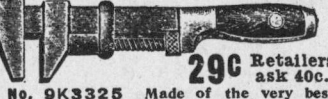

No. 9K3319 In the above Monkey Wrench we have a tool which is better value for the money than any wrench ever sold. It is made of the best grade drop forgings and steel castings; case hardened throughout. The handle is cast steel, cannot become loose. By turning the lever with the thumb the jaw may be moved up or down the bar, and can be adjusted to any size nut instantly. The best quick acting wrench on the market, with the prices as low as an ordinary wrench.

Size, length,	8 in.	10 in.	12 in.
Price........	36c	43c	49c

33c IMPROVED EXTRA HEAVY ADJUSTABLE WRENCH, 6-INCH.

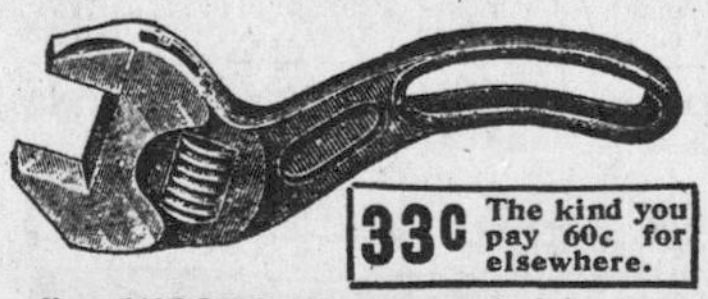

33c The kind you pay 60c for elsewhere.

No. 9K3326 Handle and frame are malleable iron. Jaws high grade tool steel. Can be used in a thousand and one places where an ordinary wrench will not go. It is constructed to stand the severest strains, and is one of the most satisfactory general purpose wrenches ever sold.

Size, inches.	6	8	10	12	14
Opens, inches	¾	1	1⅜	1⅝	2
Price	33c	43c	58c	73c	$1.01

34c ACME DROP FORGED TOOL STEEL WRENCH AND THREAD CUTTER.

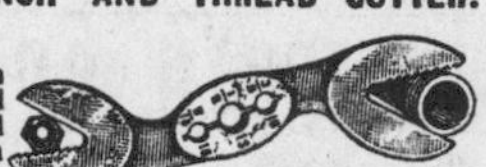

Acme Wrench and Thread Cutter. Will pay for itself in one week's time. This tool has more uses than any similar wrench on the market. Cuts three sizes of threads, 5-16, ⅜ and ½ inch. Length, 8¼ inches. Grips from ¼ to 1 inch diameter. Works equally well on pipe, fittings or nuts. The handiest wrench on the market, bar none.
No. 9K3328 Price...........................34c

39c ACME DOUBLE HEAD RATCHET TIRE BOLT WRENCH, QUICK AND EASY.

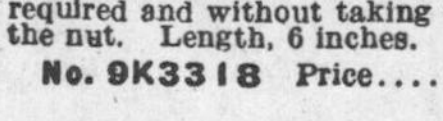

One end for 3-16-inch bolts, the other for ¼-inch. By its use the nut may be set or removed in half the time usually required and without taking the wrench from the nut. Length, 6 inches.
No. 9K3318 Price..............................39c

49c OLIVER IMPROVED MALLEABLE ADJUSTABLE WAGON JACK.

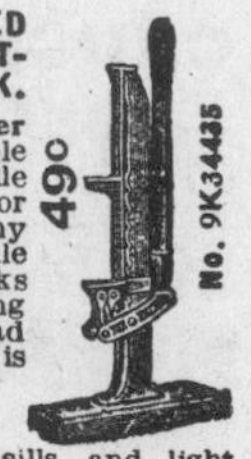

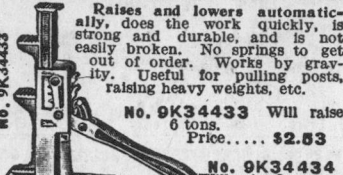

Can be handled with either hand. It is easily adjustable to any height by grasping handle and sliding the bracket up or down, catching the rivet in any notch. Pulling down the handle will raise 2½ inches and locks by passing the center. Raising the handle will lower the load easily without a jar. One raise is sufficient to remove the wheel. Can also be used to set up machinery, pull posts, replace bottom fence rails, raising sills and light frame buildings. Lifting range, 18 inches.

No.	Will Raise	Price
9K34435	1 ton	$0.49
9K34436	2 tons	.78
9K34437	3 tons	1.19

$2.53 SAMPSON MALLEABLE IRON AUTOMATIC WAGON JACK.

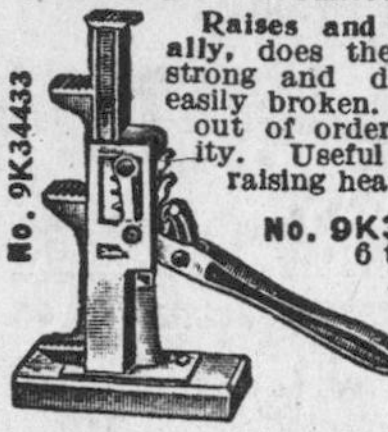

Raises and lowers automatically, does the work quickly, is strong and durable, and is not easily broken. No springs to get out of order. Works by gravity. Useful for pulling posts, raising heavy weights, etc.
No. 9K34433 Will raise 6 tons. Price..... $2.53
No. 9K34434 Will raise 8 tons. Price.. $3.52

$8.42 PEACE'S SPOKE TENON MACHINE SAVES TIME AND LABOR.

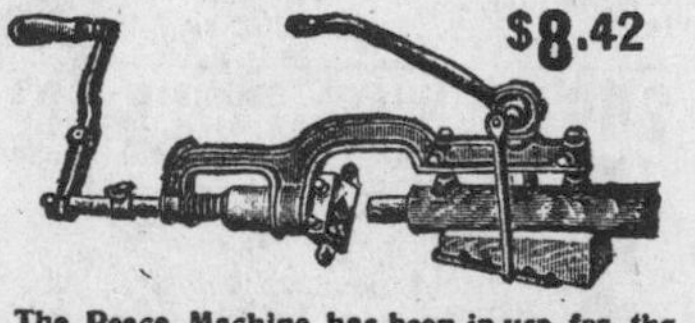

The Peace Machine has been in use for the last ten years with general satisfaction. It is made in the most workmanlike manner, all castings being malleable iron and the auger head made extra heavy. Spokes do not have to be pointed as the knife starts on the blank end and centers perfectly. The auger is kept cutting by force of the spring. Can be used on any size spoke. Cuts tenons from ¼ to 1¼ inches. These machines are great time and labor savers. Work can be done in less than half the time required by the old way. The felloe boring attachment is very convenient. The chuck to hold felloe boring bits is adjusted without removing the cutter head.
No. 9K31060 Price, without felloe attachment.................................$8.42
No. 9K31061 Price, with felloe attachment....................................$9.06

47c BONNEY PATTERN ADJUSTABLE STOP HOLLOW AUGER.

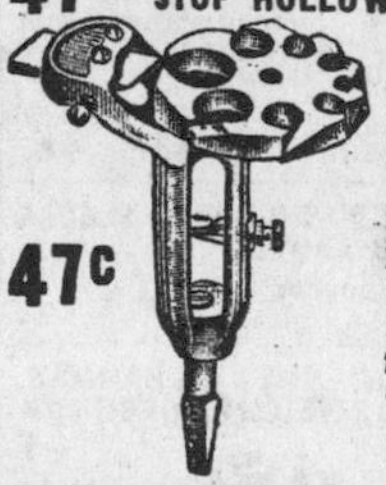

The best Hollow Auger ever offered for the price. Has adjustable stop to regulate length of tenons, cuts eight sizes from ⅜ to 1 inch, is made of malleable iron, has tempered steel cutter and hardened steel screws. Nicely finished in baked japan and nickel.
No. 9K3335 Price.............47c

$1.93 FOR THE ACME, THE BEST HOLLOW AUGER EVER MADE.

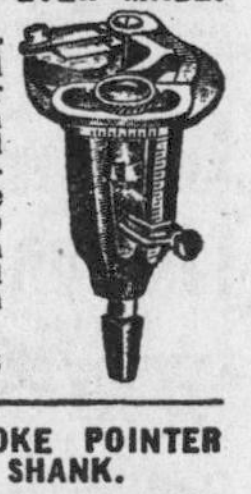

Our Acme is made throughout of the best material and is the finest hollow auger ever sold. Cuts any size tenon from ¼ to 1¼ inches; the pivoted jaws are provided with a graduated scale by which the size of the tenon is regulated. To secure required length of tenon a movable stop is operated upon a graduated scale, with rulings to sixteenths.
No. 9K3339 Price.$1.93

34c FOR A PATENT SPOKE POINTER WITH ADJUSTABLE SHANK.

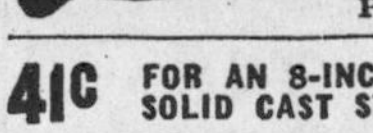

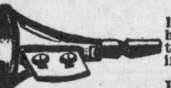

Does the work quickly, neatly and requires but little labor. Will take spokes up to 1⅜ inches in diameter.
No. 9K3346 Price............34c

41c FOR AN 8-INCH COACH MAKERS' SOLID CAST STEEL DRAWKNIFE.

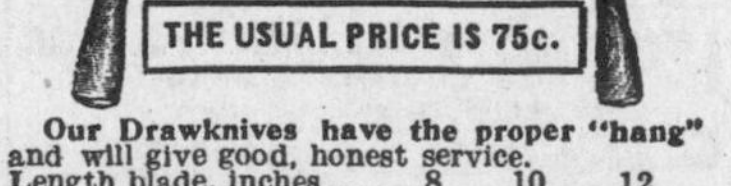

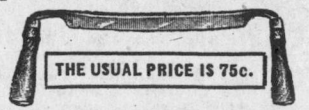

THE USUAL PRICE IS 75c.

Our Drawknives have the proper "hang" and will give good, honest service.

Length blade, inches....	8	10	12
No. 9K3348 Price.	41c	49c	53c

$7.65 PER SET

BUGGY AND WAGON WHEELS

$7.65 PER SET

OVER 60,000 SETS WERE SOLD BY US LAST SEASON

WHEELWRIGHTS, CARRIAGE MAKERS, BLACKSMITHS, LIVERYMEN, FARMERS: DON'T PAY RETAIL PRICES FOR WHEELS WHEN YOU CAN GET THEM FROM US AT WHOLESALE. READ WHAT WE SAY ABOUT THE QUALITY OF OUR WHEELS, NOTE OUR EXTREMELY LOW PRICES, REMEMBER THAT WE GUARANTEE EVERY WHEEL WE SEND OUT TO BE SATISFACTORY, AND YOU WILL READILY UNDERSTAND WHY OUR WHEEL BUSINESS HAS GROWN AS IT HAS

OUR WHEEL DEPARTMENT in connection with our large Vehicle Factory and Buggy Department sold a total of over 60,000 sets of wheels during 1907. We are leaders in the wheel business, we use more wheels each season than any other five catalogue houses combined, we control the supply of our own wheel factory, we sell wheels in such large quantities that we are able to market them through this catalogue at the very closest margin of profit; in fact, we can sell a set of wheels at actual factory cost of material and labor, with our one small margin of profit added. We buy our material in large quantities, we turn out of our wheel factory three times as many wheels as an ordinary wheel factory, our wheel business is a very small branch of our entire business; we can therefore be satisfied with about one-fourth the margin of profit on a set of wheels that an ordinary wheel manufacturer would ask. There is no doubt but that we can produce wheels in our factory at nearly one-half the cost that they can be produced in a smaller factory where about one-third of the quantity of wheels are turned out each year.

DON'T BUY A CHEAP WHEEL. By all means invest a little more and get the best. Inasmuch as a good many of our customers require a wheel at a lower price than our Selected High Grade Wheels can be made up for, we quote on this page what is called at our wheel factory Standard Wheels. While we quote a complete set of these Standard Grade Buggy Wheels with tires as low as $7.65, and while this set of wheels at $7.65 is a better wheel than you can purchase elsewhere at anything like that price, it is not in our opinion an entirely satisfactory article. This class of wheels is suitable for repair work, and is far superior to the grade usually offered by blacksmiths' supply houses. These Standard Wheels are made of a grade of material we cannot use in the manufacture of buggies—we would not use a set of these wheels as we could not guarantee them to be A1; however, for those customers who sometimes want a set of these Standard Wheels, we list them in a few sizes. In your own interest, however, if you want wheels that will give you the very best of service, that will stand the wear and tear and be absolutely satisfactory in every way, we urge you to order from our Selected High Grade line of wheels the size you require at the price quoted and we guarantee to send you a better wheel than you can buy elsewhere at even 50 per cent more than the price you pay us.

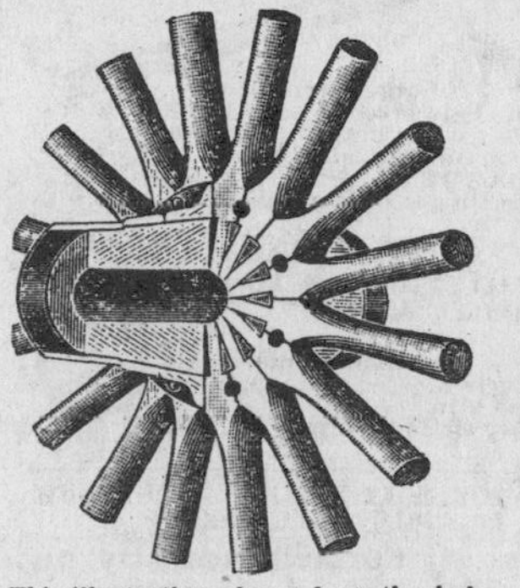

This illustration shows how the hub of a Sarven's patent wheel is made.

Why We Offer a Sarven's Patent Style Wheel.

Experience in the buggy manufacturing business has taught us that a Sarven's patent wheel will outlast two wheels of any other style; it will give better satisfaction, it is better constructed, more durable and stronger than any other wheel made. Over the wood hub of the wheel is pressed on each side of the spokes a large malleable iron shell with a flaring flange end. These are put on under hydraulic pressure, they are then drilled and riveted together, the rivets passing through the spokes. This large flange gives a bearing surface not found in other wheels, which makes a hub that is not affected by climatic changes. The spokes will not come loose in the hubs in either wet or dry weather. We know from the experience we have had that a set of Sarven's patent style wheels will outwear two sets of any other style wheels, and will not need nearly as much repairing.

Selected High Grade Buggy and Wagon Wheels.

These wheels, the kind we use in the manufacture of our best buggies, will give good service and satisfaction; they are Sarven's patent style, the hubs are made of the toughest kind of rock elm; spokes are selected graded hickory, they are perfectly shaped, dipped in glue and driven into the hubs; the whole hub is then covered with a heavy malleable iron shell with a large flange; the flanges on either side of the spokes are then riveted together at the spokes, making a serviceable, strong, never-wear-out construction. The rims are made of selected bent hickory, fitted in a workmanlike manner; the tires are put on by the old hot process, that is, the tires when welded are put in an oven and heated, so they will expand; they are then set over the rim of the wheel, the tire is run through water, making it contract; the wheel is given the proper dish; a hole is then drilled through the tire and rim between each spoke and fastened securely with a tire bolt; in fact, the tires are put on in the best possible manner, and the wheels will run twice as long as an ordinary wheel without having the tires reset. The tires are steel with round edges which project out over the rims, affording great protection to the felloes. Order a set of these wheels; if you do not find they are a better wheel than you could secure elsewere unless you paid at least 50 per cent more than our price, return them to us and we will refund your money and pay transportation charges both ways.

SELECTED GRADE

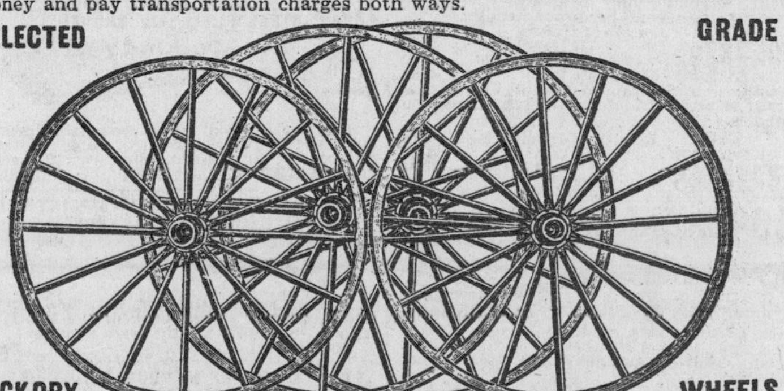

HICKORY WHEELS

Wheels are carried in stock in the following heights, namely: 38 inches, 40 inches, 42 inches, 44 inches, 46 inches and 48 inches. **Be sure to state heights wanted.**

SELECTED HIGH GRADE WHEELS IN THE WHITE, WITH TIRES.

Catalogue Number	Size of Spoke at Hub	Length of Hub where box goes in	Width of Rim	Thickness of Tire	Weight, per Set of 4 Wheels	Price, per Set of 4 Wheels, Selected Grade
	Inches	Inches	Inches	Inch	Pounds	
9K344162	1 1-16	6½	⅞	3-16	90	$ 8.95
9K344182	1⅛	6½	1	¼	100	9.35
9K344202	1¼	7	1⅛	5-16	125	11.40
9K344222	1⅜	7½	1¼	⅜	160	13.60
9K344242	1½	8	1½	½	240	19.85

Our Standard Buggy Wheels, $7.65.

These wheels we guarantee to be better quality than you can possibly secure elsewhere for considerably more than the price we ask. We can save you money on this kind of a wheel if you desire it, and we have some customers who order this grade of wheel, but we urge anyone wanting a good serviceable set of wheels that we can recommend and that we know will give satisfaction, to order our Selected High Grade Wheels. Our margin of profit is the same on the low priced wheels as it is on the High Grade Wheels; it really makes no difference to us whether you order the lower price or the higher price wheels, only that there is a satisfaction in selling to our customers a wheel that we can recommend, a wheel that will give the best service. In your own interest we urge you if you want a set of wheels, to invest a little more and order our Selected High Grade Wheels, as quoted on this page.

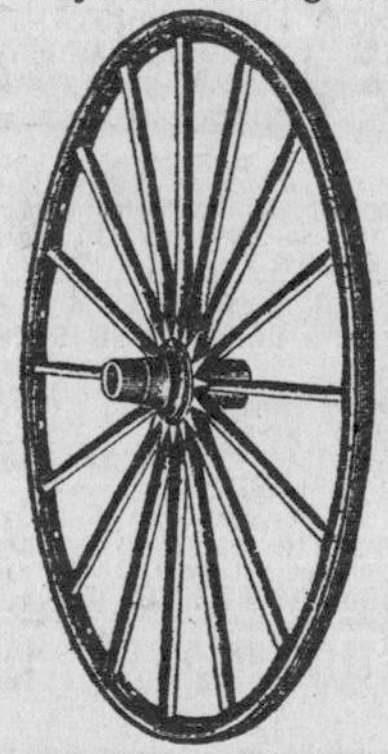

STANDARD WHEELS IN THE WHITE, WITH TIRES.

Catalogue Number	Size of Spoke at Hub	Length of Hub where box goes in	Width of Rim	Thickness of Tire	Weight, per Set of 4 Wheels	Price, per Set of 4 Wheels
	Inches	Inches	Inches	Inch	Pounds	
9K34416	1 1-16	6½	⅞	3-16	90	$7.65
9K34418	1⅛	6½	1	¼	100	8.15
9K34420	1¼	7	1⅛	5-16	125	9.95

Furnished in the following heights: 38 inches, 40 inches, 42 inches, 44 inches, 46 inches and 48 inches. **Be sure to state heights wanted.**

$2.95 TRAVELER'S BIG COMPLETE REPAIR OUTFIT.

A practical, low priced combination for travelers who are liable to meet with breakdowns or other accidents to their vehicles or harness. With this outfit repairs can be instantly made, either permanently or until repair shop can be reached. This outfit is priced so low that it will pay for itself in one case of need.

EACH OUTFIT includes: 1 Giant riveting machine; 1 solid steel spring punch; 1 set 3-inch clamps; 1 6-inch Fulton file; 1 forged steel nail hammer; 1 combination plier; wire cutter, screwdriver and reamer; 100 assorted tubular steel rivets; 1 standard 6-inch monkey wrench; 1 ebonized hollow handle set consisting of an assortment of awls, needles and spool of waxed linen thread; 4 dozen assorted length tire bolts; 4 dozen washers, assorted sizes 3/16 to ½ inch; 3 dozen threaded nuts, assorted ¼ to ½ inch; 1 box of assorted adjustable leather washers, ⅞ to 1⅛ inches; 1 gross assorted bright iron wood screws, ½ to 1½ inches; 1 pound assorted size upholstering tacks; 1 spool annealed wire and 1 assortment of wire nails and brads from ¾ to 1½ inches.

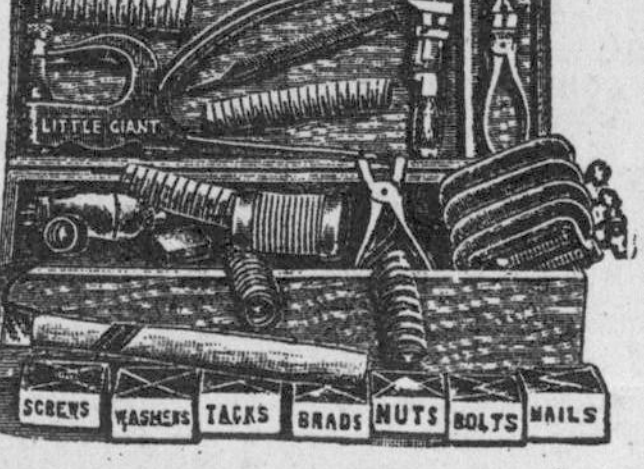

THIS OUTFIT packed in a neat hardwood box fitted with hinges and hook, may be conveniently placed under the seat of any vehicle ready for instant use when needed. Also a handy outfit to have about the house or barn.

No. 9K55033 Price, complete outfit............ **$2.95**

HOW TO ORDER.

Give us catalogue number and height of the wheels you want. Remember, the two front wheels are always lower than the two rear wheels on any kind of a vehicle. If you want wheels for a regular top buggy or runabout, there should be 4 inches difference between the two front wheels and the two rear wheels. The standard and popular size for top buggies and runabouts is 40-inch front wheels and 44-inch rear wheels, although some customers order 38-inch front and 42-inch rear wheels. On straight sill surreys there should be 4 inches difference between front and rear wheels. On cut under surreys, that is, where wheels turn under body, and on phaetons there should be 8 inches difference between the height of the front and rear wheels.

OUR ADVICE WHEN ORDERING.

If you are ordering wheels for a top buggy or runabout, order catalogue No. 9K344182 which have a 1-inch rim, and specify 40-inch front and 44-inch rear wheels. If you want a little lighter wheel on your buggy, order No. 9K344162, which has a ⅞-inch rim. If you want wheels for a surrey, order No. 9K344182, which have a 1-inch rim and specify 38 inches front and 42 inches rear; or if you want a heavier wheel, order No. 9K344202, which has a 1⅛-inch rim.

PRICES FOR PART SETS.

The quotations above are for wheels in sets of four; if you want two wheels the price will be one-half, if you want one wheel it will be one-fourth of the price quoted above.

NOTICE—If you fail to specify height of wheels desired in ordering a set, we will send 40 inches front and 44 inches rear wheels, which are the popular heights.

NOTICE—We cannot paint wheels, furnish or set boxes. Prices quoted are for wheels in the white covered with one coat of boiled oil, with tires fitted and hubs ready to be bored for the boxings.

SPECIAL CARE SHOULD BE USED IN SELECTING A WHEEL THAT IS BEST SUITED FOR THE AXLE YOU INTEND USING ON YOUR JOB. THE FOLLOWING TABLE IS TO GUIDE YOU IN ORDERING:

If you intend using ⅞x6½-inch or 1x6½inch axles, order No. 9K344162 or No 9K344182.
If you intend using 1⅛ x7-inch or 1¼x7- inch axles, order No. 9K344202.
If you intend using 1¼x7½-inch axles, order No. 9K344222.
If you intend using 1½x8-inch axles, order No. 9K344242.

Remember, steel axles must be used; thimble skeins will not fit Sarven's patent wheels.

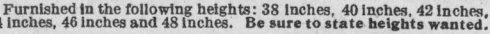

AGRICULTURAL IMPLEMENTS

OUR GOODS CANNOT BE EQUALED AT DOUBLE OUR PRICES. We take the entire output of a large independent factory and sell high grade farm and garden tools at less than half the price others ask for trust made goods. We handle no seconds. Every tool we sell is first class and will compare favorably with any on the market.

WE GUARANTEE EVERY ARTICLE WE SEND OUT TO BE PERFECT, and if you are not entirely satisfied with it, ship it back at our expense, and your money will be promptly refunded. The strongest proof of the superiority of our farm and garden tools over all others is in the enormous quantities that we sell. No other concern in the United States sells as many farm and garden tools as we do. Highest grade goods at one profit prices.

FARM AND GARDEN TOOLS TAKE A LOW FREIGHT RATE. Send us an order for these goods and you will save enough on the purchase price to pay the freight several times over. We guarantee the goods to reach you in good order and to be the highest possible grade and finish.

Reduced Prices on over 3,000 Hardware Items Make Your Saving Greater Than Ever.

$1.29 SOLID STEEL POTATO AND BEET SCOOP FORK WITH 8 TINES.

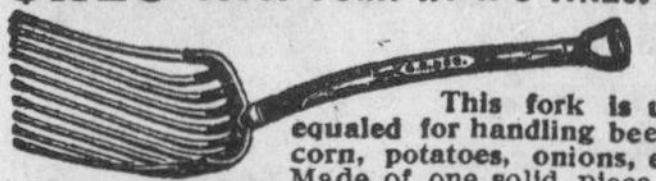

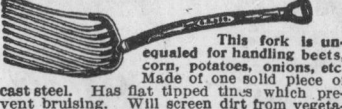

This fork is unequaled for handling beets, corn, potatoes, onions, etc. Made of one solid piece of cast steel. Has flat tipped tines which prevent bruising. Will screen dirt from vegetables; handle corn without sticking in the cobs; pitch fine manure better than any fork or shovel made. Made in three sizes, as follows:

No. 9K39169 Eight tines, 11 inches wide and 14 inches long. Price......$1.29
No. 9K39171 Ten tines, 14 inches wide and 15 inches long. Price......$1.55
No. 9K39172 Twelve tines, 18 inches wide and 16 inches long. Price......$1.82

36c REGULAR SIZE 4-FOOT 3-TINE SOLID STEEL HAY FORK.

This illustration shows the strapped ferrule.

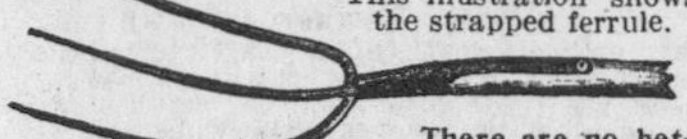

There are no better hay forks made than these. They have Plain Capped Ferrule, three oval tines, standard size and lengths; selected straight grain bent hardwood handles.

No.	Length of Handle	Price
9K39232	4 feet	36c
9K39233	4½ feet	37c
9K39234	5 feet	38c
9K39236	6 feet	42c

Capped and Strapped Ferrule, three oval tines, standard size and length; selected straight grain bent hardwood handles.

No.	Length of Handle	Price
9K39238	4 feet	42c
9K39239	4½ feet	43c
9K39240	5 feet	44c
9K39242	6 feet	47c

39c BUYS A FULL SIZE 4½-FOOT 4-TINE SOLID STEEL HAY FORK.

This illustration shows strapped handle.

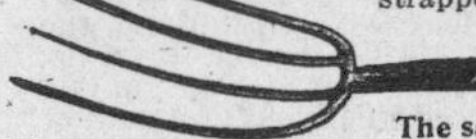

The same high grade as those described above. Have capped and plain ferrule; four oval tines; selected straight grain bent hardwood handles.

No.	Length of Handle	Price
9K39244	4½ feet	39c
9K39245	5 feet	41c
9K39246	5½ feet	45c

Capped and Strapped Ferrules, four oval tines; selected straight grain bent hardwood handles.

No.	Length of Handle	Price
9K39248	4½ feet	45c
9K39249	5 feet	47c
9K39250	5½ feet	49c

46c D HANDLE PLAIN FERRULE 4-TINE CRUCIBLE STEEL MANURE FORK.

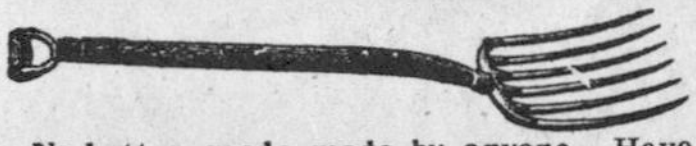

No better goods made by anyone. Have oval steel tines, 12 inches long; gold bronze finish; selected straight grain steam bent handles.

No. 9K39260 Four tines. Price..46c
No. 9K39261 Five tines. Price..61c
No. 9K39262 Six tines. Price..71c

D Handle, Capped and Strapped Ferrule Manure Forks. Oval tines, 12 inches long.

No. 9K39265 Four tines. Price..51c
No. 9K39266 Five tines. Price..66c
No. 9K39267 Six tines. Price..76c

41c LONG HANDLE PLAIN FERRULE CRUCIBLE STEEL MANURE FORK.

We are not in the farming tool trust which accounts for our low prices. These goods are cheap in price only. Capped; oval tines, 12 inches long; 4½-foot handles.

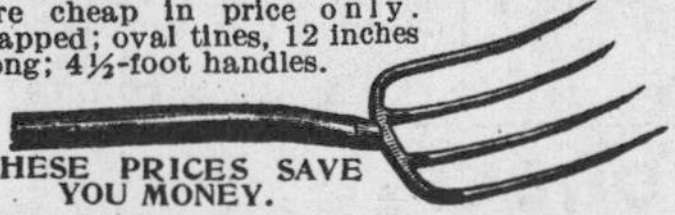

THESE PRICES SAVE YOU MONEY.

No. 9K39270 Four tines. Price..41c
No. 9K39271 Five tines. Price..59c
No. 9K39272 Six tines. Price..67c

Capped and Strapped Ferrule Manure Forks. Oval tines, 12 inches long; 4½-foot selected handles.

No. 9K39273 Four tines. Price..48c
No. 9K39274 Five tines. Price..64c
No. 9K39275 Six tines. Price..71c

73c STRAPPED FERRULE LONG HANDLE STEEL BARLEY FORK.

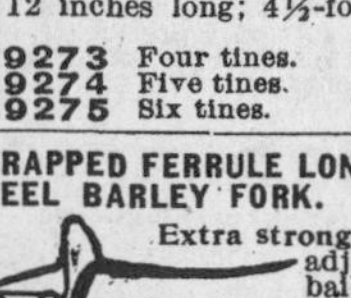

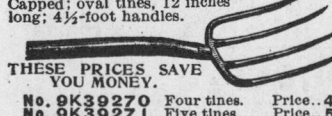

73c

Extra strong strap with adjustable wire bail and brace; four tines, 18 inches long; selected straight grain handle.

No. 9K39277 Price............73c

71c SPECIAL LONG TINE ALFALFA FORK WITH LONG HANDLE.

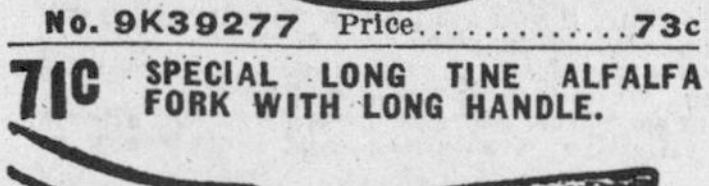

Better than the forks you have been paying $1.00 to $1.25 for. Length of tines, 16 inches; spread at points, 11½ inches; strapped ferrule; 5½-foot selected handle.

No. 9K39282 Price............71c

SILVER KING SOLID STEEL SHOVELS AND SPADES.

ABSOLUTELY THE FINEST LINE OF SHOVELS AND SPADES EVER MADE. Forged from one solid piece of highest grade crucible steel; have solid steel sockets, are full polished and have selected straight grain hardwood handles. One of these shovels or spades will outlast three or four of the ordinary kind. Because our prices are lower than you have been paying for the shovel you always thought was the best, don't think the quality of our goods is inferior. The Silver King is without a peer; the finest shovel ever made at any price.

93c SILVER KING SOLID STEEL D HANDLE ROUND POINT SHOVEL.

$1.25 elsewhere

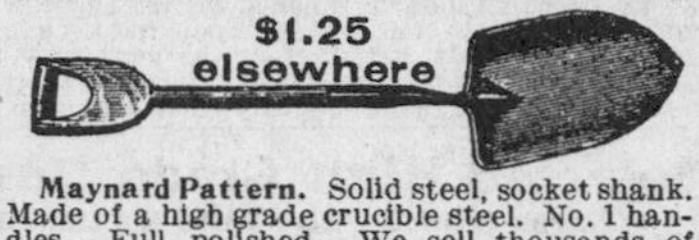

Maynard Pattern. Solid steel, socket shank. Made of a high grade crucible steel. No. 1 handles. Full polished. We sell thousands of these each month, which partly accounts for our low prices.

No. 9K39141 Price............93c

93c SILVER KING SOLID STEEL LONG HANDLE ROUND POINT SHOVEL.

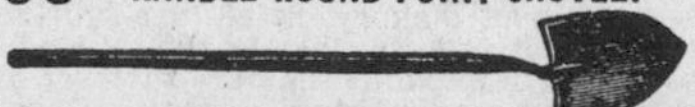

Maynard Pattern. Solid steel socket shank. Made of a high grade crucible steel. No. 1 handles. Full polished. We control the factory that makes these shovels and add but one small profit to the first cost.

No. 9K39146 Price............93c

92c SILVER KING SOLID STEEL D HANDLE SPADE, MAYNARD PATTERN.

Retailers ask $1.25

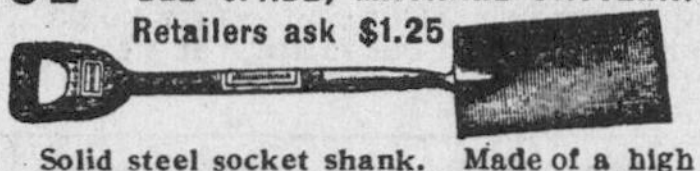

Solid steel socket shank. Made of a high grade crucible steel. No. 1 handles. Full polished. The factory that makes these goods is independent of trusts and combinations.

No. 9K39118 Price............92c

92c SILVER KING SOLID STEEL D HANDLE SQUARE POINT SHOVEL.

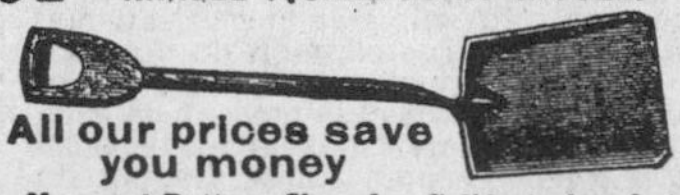

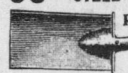

All our prices save you money

Maynard Pattern Shovels. Solid steel socket shank. Made of a high grade crucible steel. No. 1 handles. Finely polished. There are no retailers' and jobbers' profits added to the price we ask you to pay for this shovel.

No. 9K39130 Price............92c

58c D HANDLE ROUND POINT SOLID STEEL FULL SIZE SHOVEL.

The 90c kind

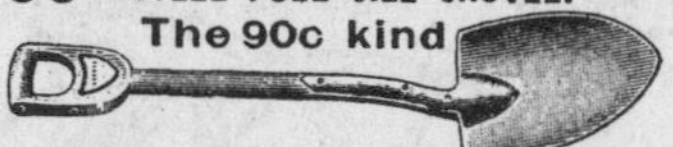

A first class tool at a reasonable price. Back and front straps riveted. Made of steel, not iron. Full polished. Size, 9⅜x12½ inch.

No. 9K39140 Price............58c

58c LONG HANDLE ROUND POINT FULL SIZE SOLID STEEL SHOVEL.

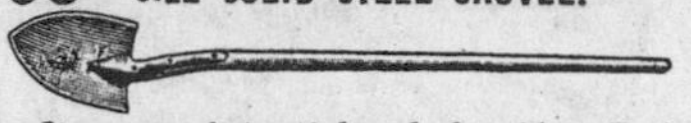

Strong, substantial and durable. Front and back strap. Full polished. Size, 9¼x11¾ inches. Selected straight grain handles.

No. 9K39145 Price............58c

48c D HANDLE NARROW MOUTH LARGE SIZE STEEL FURNACE SCOOP.

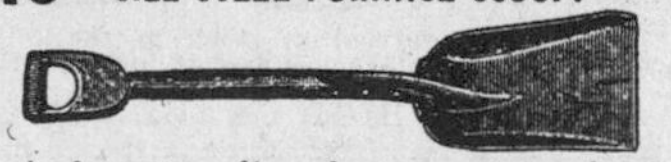

An honest, well made scoop at a price in reach of everyone. Length of blade, 13 inches; width at point, 8½ inches. A1 handles. Made in one size only.

No. 9K39161 Price............48c

53c CLEVELAND PATTERN D HANDLE EXTRA STEEL COAL SHOVEL.

YOU PAY MORE ELSEWHERE

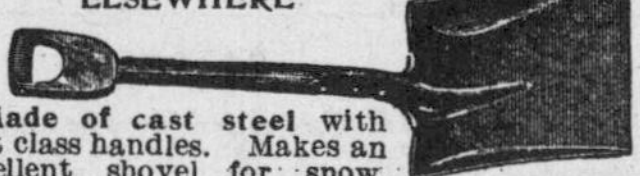

Made of cast steel with first class handles. Makes an excellent shovel for snow, grain or sawdust. Be sure to state size wanted. Made in three sizes, as follows:

No.	Size of blade	Price
9K39157	13½x14 inches	53c
9K39158	14¼x14¾ inches	56c
9K39159	14¾x15½ inches	59c

62c FOR A No. 6 CHISHOLM'S PATTERN GRAIN SCOOP SHOVEL.

Others ask $1.25

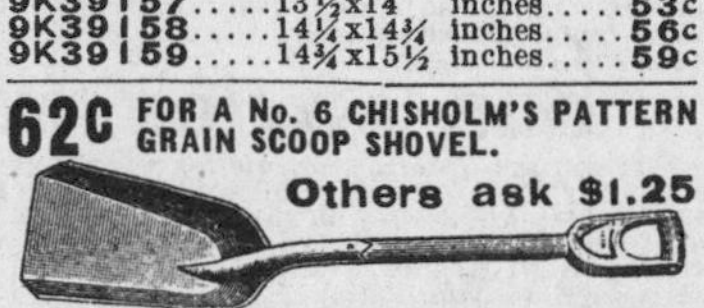

No. 9K39156 Wide mouth. A first class farmers' scoop. For handling grain, sawdust, cottonseed, snow, etc. Full polished. Be sure to state width wanted.

	No. 6	No. 7	No. 8	No. 9	No. 10
Width	13½in.	13⅞in.	14¼in.	14¼in.	14½in.
Price	62c	66c	69c	72c	75c

37c HOLLOW BACK SQUARE POINT LONG HANDLE STEEL SNOW SHOVEL

Made of one solid piece of specially refined steel. Light, strong and durable; will outwear a dozen wood shovels. Also makes a good furnace or barn shovel. Only select quality of handles used.

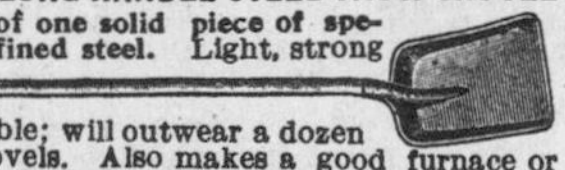

No. 9K39168 Price, with long handle 37c

58c D HANDLE SQUARE POINT SOLID STEEL REGULAR SIZE SPADE.

RETAILS FOR 90c

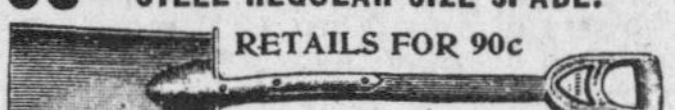

Exceptionally good value. Back and front strap. Full polished. Size, 7¼x11¾ inch, which is full regular size. Selected straight grain handles. Every spade warranted.

No. 9K39117 Price............58c

58c LONG HANDLE SQUARE POINT SOLID STEEL SPADE, FULL SIZE.

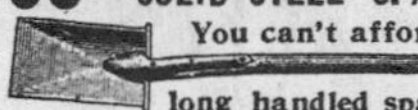

You can't afford to do without a long handled spade when you can get a good one so cheap. Back and front strap. Size, 7⅛x11⅝ inch. Full polished. Warranted selected straight grain handle.

No. 9K39124 Price............58c

58c D HANDLE SQUARE POINT PLAIN BACK SOLID STEEL SHOVEL.

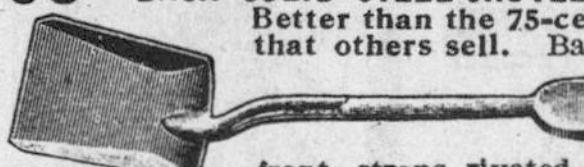

Better than the 75-cent kind that others sell. Back and front straps riveted. Size, 9¾x12 inches. Full regular size. Made of the best selected steel. Warranted A1 handles.

No. 9K39128 Price............58c

58c FOR A LONG HANDLE SQUARE POINT SOLID STEEL SHOVEL.

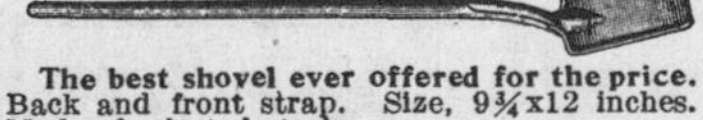

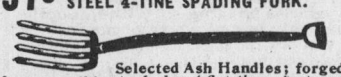

The best shovel ever offered for the price. Back and front strap. Size, 9¾x12 inches. Made of selected steel.

No. 9K39136 Price............58c

57c D HANDLE CAPPED FERRULE SOLID STEEL 4-TINE SPADING FORK.

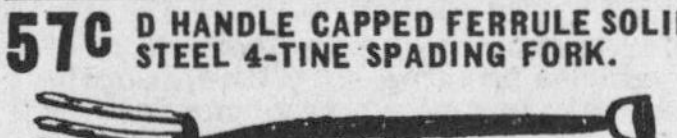

Selected Ash Handles; forged from crucible steel; has 4 flat tines; is strong and durable.

No. 9K39198 Price............57c

D Handle, Strap Ferrule Spading Fork, 4 steel tines. The strongest spading fork made.

No. 9K39199 Price............60c

94c SOLID STEEL ROUND POINT D HANDLE DRAIN SPADE.

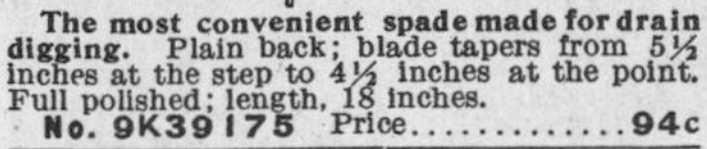

The most convenient spade made for drain digging. Plain back; blade tapers from 5½ inches at the step to 4½ inches at the point. Full polished; length, 18 inches.

No. 9K39175 Price............94c

94c SOLID STEEL SQUARE POINT D HANDLE POST SPADE.

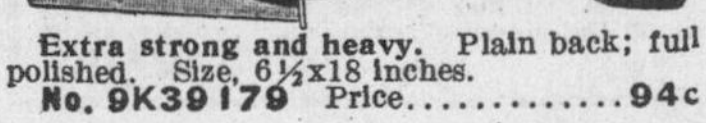

Extra strong and heavy. Plain back; full polished. Size, 6½x18 inches.

No. 9K39179 Price............94c

$1.36 FOR A 10-TINE CRUCIBLE STEEL D HANDLE COKE FORK.

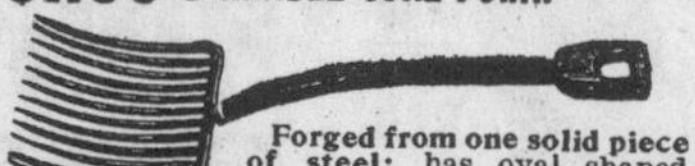

Forged from one solid piece of steel; has oval shaped tines; XXX wood D handle, strapped ferrule, and is first class throughout.

No. 9K39205 10 tines. Price, $1.36
No. 9K39206 12 tines. Price, 1.58

44c FOR A FULL SIZE CRUCIBLE STEEL 4-TINE MANURE HOOK.

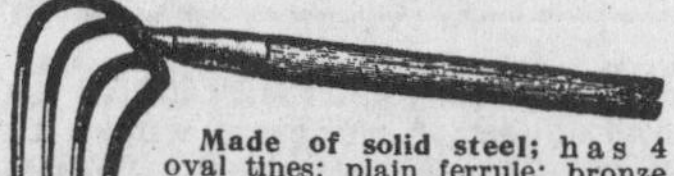

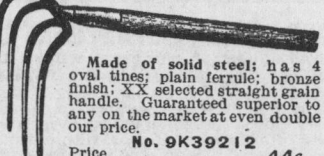

Made of solid steel; has 4 oval tines; plain ferrule; bronze finish; XX selected straight grain handle. Guaranteed superior to any on the market at even double our price.

No. 9K39212
Price............44c

34c FOR A HIGH GRADE POTATO HOOK WITH 4 ROUND TINES.

The kind that retails for 60c

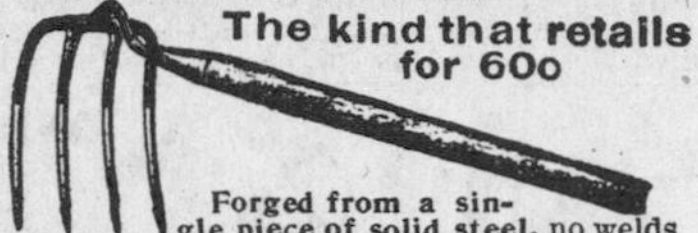

Forged from a single piece of solid steel, no welds will outlast half a dozen of the ordinary malleable iron rakes usually offered.

No. 9K39214 Price..........34c

Potato Digger. Same as above, but with four flat tines.

No. 9K39215 Price..........42c

6c MALLEABLE D HEAD FOR FORK OR SHOVEL HANDLE.

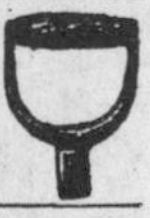

Made of best quality malleable iron; nicely finished, with polished hardwood grip.

No. 9K39217 Price.....6c

43c FOR A 12-TOOTH DIAMOND BOW CRUCIBLE STEEL RAKE.

60c will not buy as good elsewhere

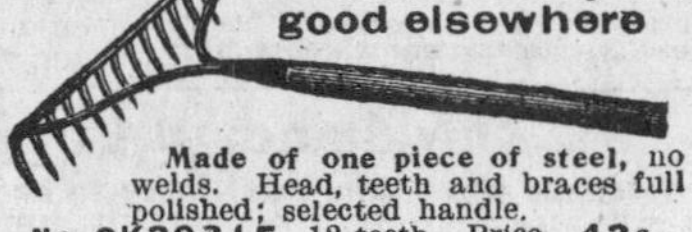

Made of one piece of steel, no welds. Head, teeth and braces full polished; selected handle.

No. 9K39315 12 teeth. Price..43c
No. 9K39316 14 teeth. Price..46c

26c FOR THIS GIBBS LAWN RAKE WITH 24 STEEL WIRE TEETH

Sharp on one side, blunt on the other; egg shaped steel tube frame; tinned steel wire teeth.

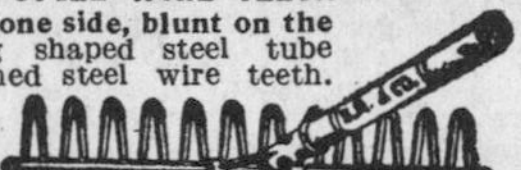

No. 9K39332
Price .26c

19c FOR A 6-TOOTH COMBINED WEEDING HOE AND RAKE.

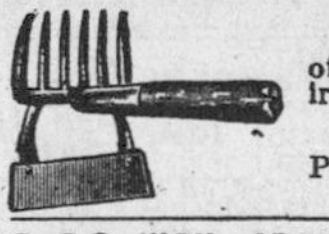

Answers the purpose of two tools. Malleable iron; cast steel blade.

No. 9K39302
Price..........19c

34c HIGH GRADE STEEL "PUSH OR PULL" RAPID EASY WEEDER.

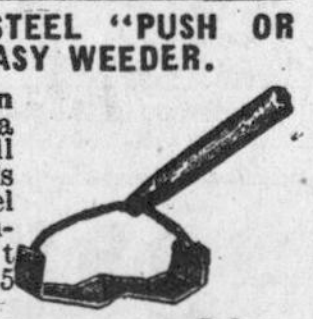

Far ahead of a common hoe. Works as easy as a garden rake. Push or pull it cuts the same. Blade is made of high grade steel and is 8 inches wide. Handle of selected straight grain hardwood and is 5 feet long.

No. 9K39305 Price..........34c

58c DIAMOND POINTED 6-TINE INVINCIBLE HAND CULTIVATOR.

90c is the regular price

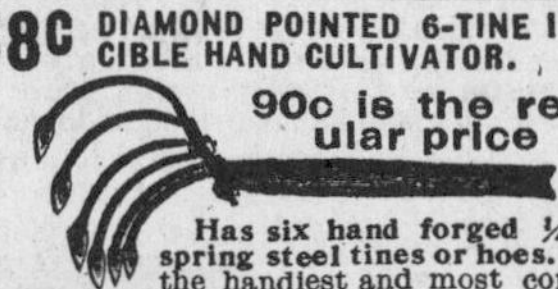

Has six hand forged ¼-inch spring steel tines or hoes. It is the handiest and most complete tool of its kind on the market. A practical, durable cultivator or hoe at a low price.

No. 9K39308 Price..........58c

58c EXTRA STRONG ADJUSTABLE SHOVEL STEEL DRAIN CLEANER.

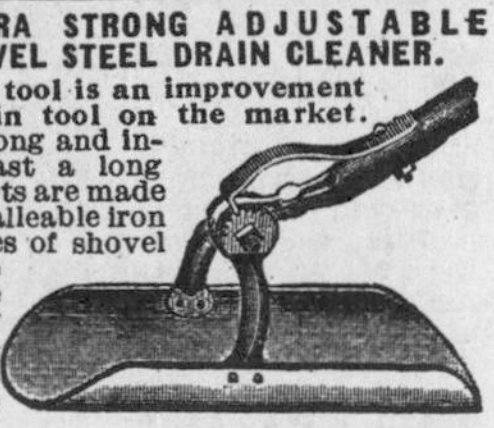

This drain tool is an improvement over any drain tool on the market. It is very strong and intended to last a long time. The parts are made of the best malleable iron and the blades of shovel steel. The handle can be set at any angle by raising the spring. When the spring is in position the blade is locked tightly and will not move or have a side motion.

No.	Size	Price
9K39190	4x15 inches	58c
9K39191	5x15 inches	59c

27c SELECTED HANDLE 7½-INCH STEEL BLADE GARDEN HOE.

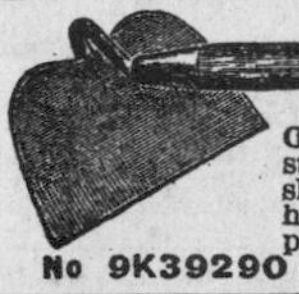

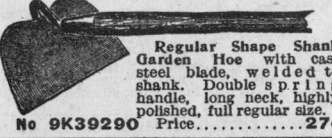

Regular Shape Shank Garden Hoe with cast steel blade, welded to shank. Double spring handle, long neck, highly polished, full regular size.
No 9K39290 Price............27c

31c SELECTED HANDLE 7½-INCH STEEL BLADE GARDEN HOE.

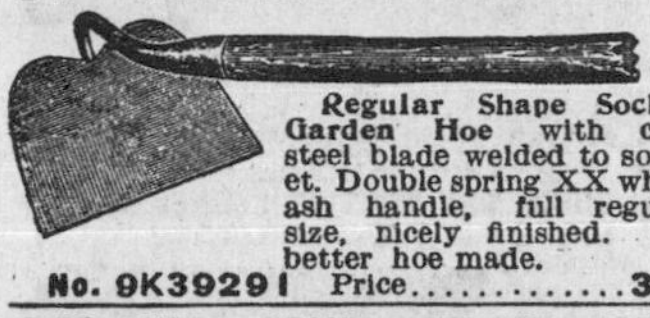

Regular Shape Socket Garden Hoe with cast steel blade welded to socket. Double spring XX white ash handle, full regular size, nicely finished. No better hoe made.
No. 9K39291 Price............31c

61c EXTRA HEAVY MORTAR MIXER AND IRRIGATION DITCH HOE.

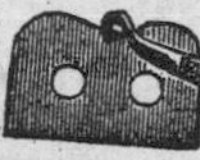

Solid shank. Finest hoe made for mixing mortar. Also an excellent hoe for cleaning irrigating ditches, as it allows the water to pass through the holes while the mud and refuse is drawn out. Blade 10 inches wide.
No. 9K39294 Price............61c

5c FOR A STEEL GARDEN TROWEL WITH 6-INCH STEEL BLADE.

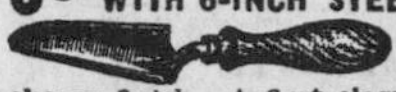

Steel shank, hardwood handle, cherry finish. A first class tool for the price.
No. 9K39334 Price............5c

15c HIGHGRADE CRUCIBLE STEEL HARDWOOD HANDLE GARDEN TROWEL.

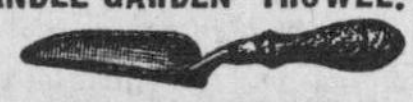

Made from one piece of steel without a weld, a better trowel than generally carried by the retail trade, varnished hardwood handle. Size, 6 inches.
No. 9K39335 Price............15c

13c FOR A LANG'S HAND WEEDER, THE HANDIEST TOOL ON EARTH.

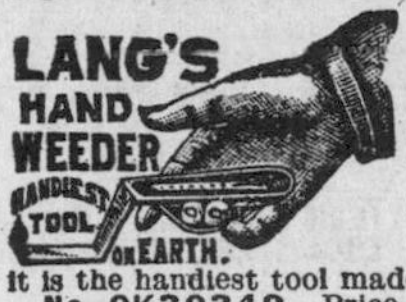

One of these weeders should be owned by all who do gardening or raise flowers. It has an elegant steel blade, sharpened to cut both ways. For getting around plants and flowers. it is the handiest tool made.
No. 9K39342 Price............13c
If by mail, postage extra, 4 cents.

19c MARVEL 3-PIECE GARDEN SET. LIGHT, STRONG AND CONVENIENT.

REGULAR 40-CENT VALUE. 19c

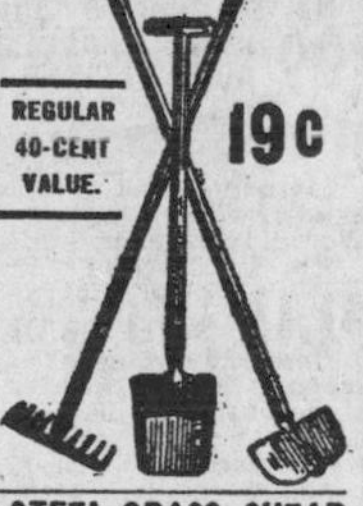

Strong enough for a man, light enough for a woman. Consists of three pieces as follows: Spade, polished steel blade 5½x4 inches, handle 24 inches long; hoe, polished steel blade 5¼x3¼ inches, handle 30 inches long; rake, malleable iron turned, 5¾ inches broad, handle 30 inches long. All handles of hardwood, varnished.
No. 9K39345
Price, per set of three pieces............19c

10c FOR A SOLID STEEL GRASS SHEAR WITH BENT HANDLE.

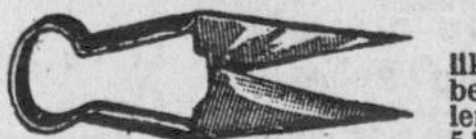

Grass Shears, like illustration; bent handles; length of blade, 5½ inches. Not recommended for shearing sheep.
No. 9K39354 Price............10c
Extra Grade Grass Shears. Solid steel blades. The best grass shears made. Will outlast and outcut three or four ordinary shears.
No. 9K39355 Price............20c

74c ACME FRUIT GATHERER, SAVES FRUIT, TIME, CLOTHES AND MONEY.

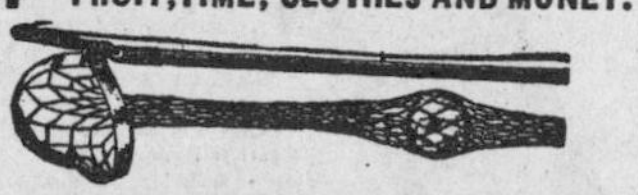

A device for gathering fruit. It will pick apples, pears, plums and similar fruit from otherwise inaccessible places and deliver it into your basket without bruise or injury of any kind. The most practical fruit gatherer ever invented. Will last indefinitely, has nothing to get out of order, is light, strong and durable.
No. 9K39367 Price............74c

36c PER POUND TOOL STEEL MILL PICKS.

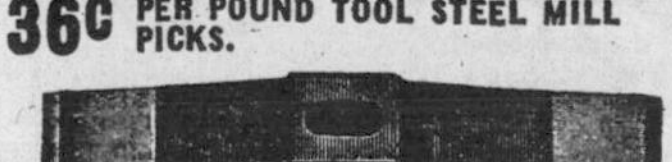

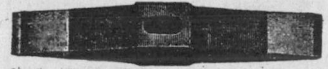

Made of special tool steel. Tempered by a secret process which insures an even temper; well finished, ready for use. Weights, 1½, 2, 2½ and 3 pounds.
No. 9K39401 Price, per pound...36c

19c MALLEABLE HANDLE PRUNING SHEAR WITH STEEL BLADES.

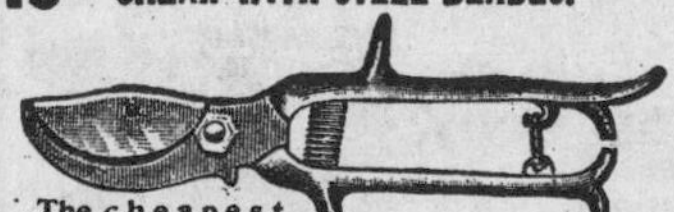

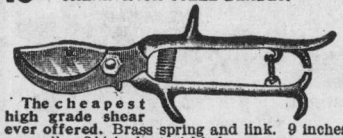

The cheapest high grade shear ever offered. Brass spring and link. 9 inches over all. 2¼-inch steel blade.
No. 9K39357 Price............19c

26c HEAVY PATTERN PRUNING SHEAR WITH TOOL STEEL BLADES.

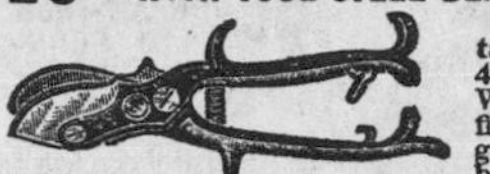

The kind retailers sell for 40 to 50 cents. Well made and finished, high grade steel blades, warranted, volute springs.
No. 9K39358 Price............26c

31c CALIFORNIA PATTERN PRUNING SHEAR. BEST STEEL CUTTERS.

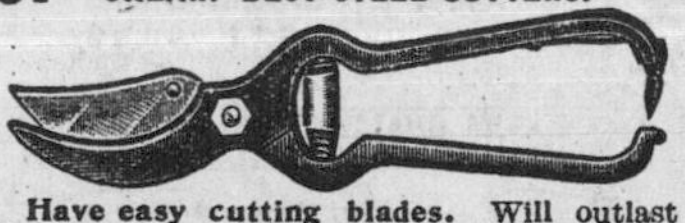

Have easy cutting blades. Will outlast three or four ordinary pruners. Made of the best material, steel blades, volute springs.
No. 9K39359 Price............31c
Extra high grade Pruning Shears. 9-inch, full nickel plated. The kind professionals prefer. Large size, extra strong and will not rust.
No. 9K39360 Price............54c

29c LOOP HANDLE PRUNING SHEAR WITH TEMPERED STEEL BLADES.

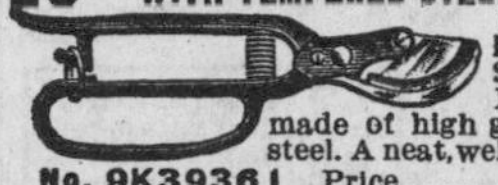

Loop Handle Pruning Shears. Blades are made of high grade English steel. A neat, well made shear.
No. 9K39361 Price............29c

54c BUCKEYE PRUNING SHEAR, ASH HANDLES, 22 IN. LONG.

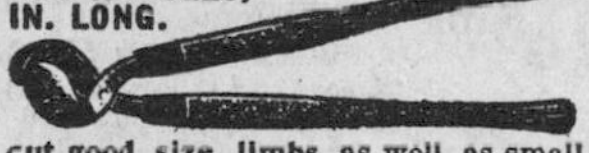

Will cut good size limbs as well as small twigs. Compound leaverage makes it so easy a child can operate it. Equipped with ash handles 22 inches long, 2-inch cast steel cutter.
No. 9K39363 Price............54c

74c EXTRA STRONG TELEGRAPH TREE PRUNER WITH STEEL BLADES.

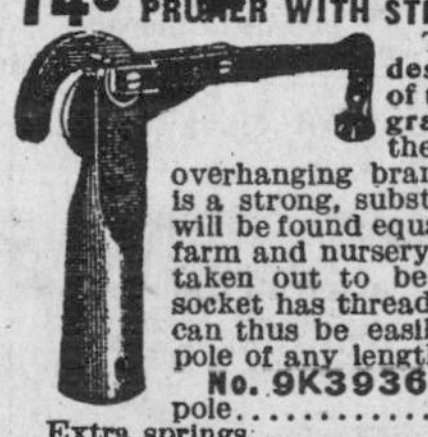

This pruner was designed for the use of telephone and telegraph men in keeping the wires free from overhanging branches of trees. It is a strong, substantial pruner and will be found equally convenient for farm and nursery use. Blade can be taken out to be sharpened. The socket has threads on the inside and can thus be easily screwed onto a pole of any length.
No. 9K39368 Price, without pole............74c
Extra springs............8c
Extra blades............8c

52c LATEST IMPROVED WATERS' TREE PRUNER, WITH 8-FOOT HANDLE.

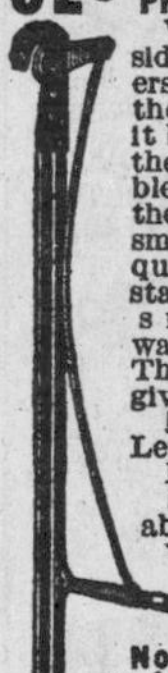

With latest improvements, is considered by fruit growers and gardeners the best on the market. Although the cutting blade is very thin, it being supported on both sides by the hook makes it strong and durable. It will cut off the largest bough the hook will admit, and also clip the smallest twig. No ladders are required, as pruning can be done while standing on the ground. Cutting blade s made of best tempered tool steel, warranted against flaws and defects. This is a first class pruner and will give satisfaction.
No. 9K39370

Length, feet....	8	10	12
Price............	52c	53c	57c

No. 9K39371 Extra knives for above pruners............9c

84c POLISHED STEEL BLADE HEDGE SHEAR, 8 INCHES.

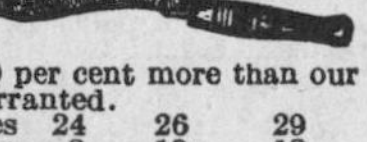

No. 9K39373 Highest grade steel blades with notch for cutting twigs; hardwood handles. Same as retailers sell for 50 per cent more than our price. Every pair warranted.

Length over all, inches	24	26	29
Length of blade, inches	8	10	12
Price............	84c	$1.20	$1.82

$1.48 HEAVY DUCK WATERPROOF MASON'S TOOL BAG, 18-INCH.

THE REGULAR $2.50 KIND.

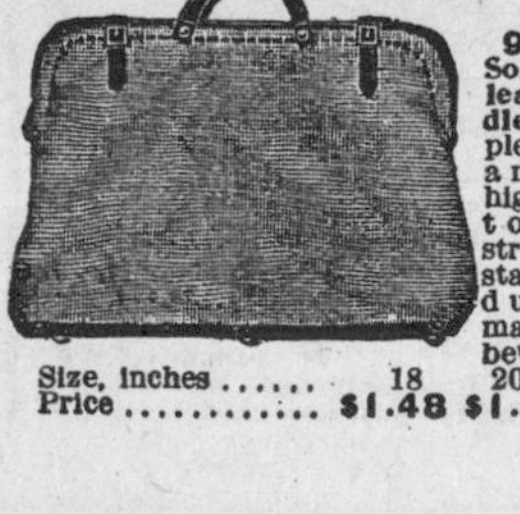

No. 9K39392 Solid frame, leather handles; complete with lock and key; a high grade tool bag, strong, substantial and durable. No mason should be without one.

Size, inches............	18	20	24
Price............	$1.48	$1.67	$1.93

35c PHILADELPHIA PATTERN 10-INCH MASON'S BRICK TROWEL.

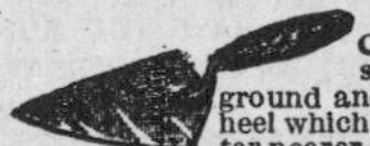

No. 9K39365 Crucible tempered steel, accurately ground and shaped, has square heel which brings weight of mortar nearer the hand. Warranted.

Size, inches............	10	10½	11
Price............	35c	37c	39c

No. 9K39366 Mason's Pointing Trowel, same quality and shape as No. 9K39365 trowel, only smaller. Warranted.

Size, inches............	4	5	6
Price............	15c	18c	20c

32c FOR A 10-INCH FORGED STEEL PLASTERING TROWEL.

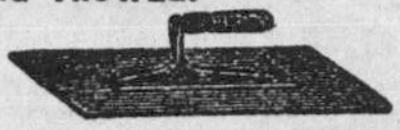

No. 9K39369 Best of steel, accurately ground and tempered and finely finished.

Size, inches.....	10	10½	11	12
Price............	32c	37c	42c	48c

35c FOR A 6-INCH FORGED STEEL CORNER TROWEL.

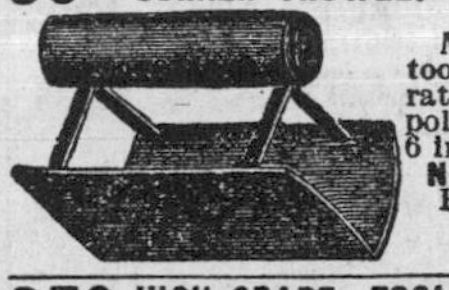

Made of best tool steel, accurately ground and polished. Length, 6 inches.
No. 9K39377 Price.....35c

35c HIGH GRADE TOOL STEEL TUCK POINTING TOOL.

Saves time and labor. Furnished in the following sizes: 3-16, ¼, 5-16, ⅜ and ½ inch.
No. 9K39378 Price............35c

27c FOR A SELECTED PLASTERERS' CORK FLOAT, SIZE, 12x4x1 INCH.

No. 9K39387 Plasterers' Cork Floats, made from one thickness of cork smoothed on both sides.
Size, 12x4x1 inch thick. Price.........27c
Size, 12x5x1¼ inches thick. Price.......45c

47c CRUCIBLE CAST STEEL STONE SLEDGE, WEIGHT, 8 POUNDS.

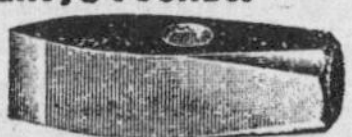

No. 9K39403 Oil finished, polished face. Without handles.

Weight, pounds..	8	10	12
Price............	47c	59c	71c
Weight, pounds..		14	16
Price............		83c	95c

32c CRUCIBLE CAST STEEL DRILLING OR STRIKING HAMMER, 3½ LBS.

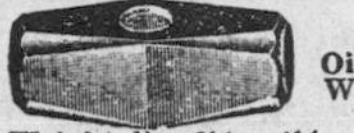

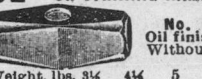

No. 9K39405 Oil finish, polished faces. Without handles.

Weight, lbs.	3½	4½	5	6	8	9
Price.....	32c	42c	44c	46c	50c	54c

44c CRUCIBLE CAST STEEL STONEMASON'S HAMMER, 3½ POUNDS.

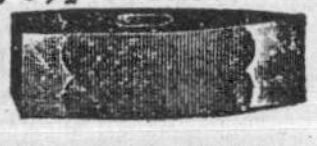

No. 9K39406 Bronzed axe finish, polished faces. Nothing better made. Handles not included.

Weight, pounds.....	3½	4	4½
Price............	44c	49c	54c

39c CRUCIBLE CAST STEEL SINGLE FACE SPALLING HAMMER, 3½ POUNDS.

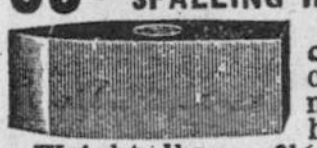

No. 9K39409 Solid cast steel, polished face, oil finish. The best hammer made. Without handles.

Weight, lbs..	3½	4	4½	5
Price............	39c	45c	50c	53c
Weight, lbs..	6		8	10
Price............	56c		74c	93c

38c CRUCIBLE CAST STEEL DOUBLE FACE SPALLING HAMMER, 3½ LBS.

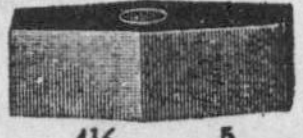

No. 9K39411 Solid cast steel, polished face, oil finish. Same grade as above. Without handles.

Weight, lbs.	3½	4	4½	5
Price.........	38c	45c	50c	53c
Weight, lbs.	6		8	10
Price.........	56c		74c	93c

Reduced Hardware Prices in this book make your saving greater than ever.

CEMENT WORKERS' TOOLS.

Wearing qualities considered, cement is the cheapest building material in the world. Thousands of people are using it. To meet the demand for high grade tools with which cement can be properly worked and finished, we quote below the finest line ever made at prices so cheap you can't afford to buy elsewhere. While we quote a line of iron and steel cement workers' tools and though they are nickel plated and as nearly rustproof as iron and steel can be made, our bronze metal tools are the finest in the world, absolutely rustproof, harder than steel and will last a lifetime.

34c NICKEL PLATED IRON CEMENT SIDEWALK EDGER, ⅜-INCH.

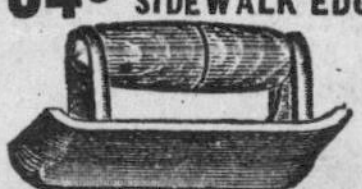

No. 9K39754 This tool is used for finishing the edge of sidewalks. Accurately shaped, smooth finish.

Size, radius, inches......	⅜	¾
Price............	34c	36c

Solid Bronze Metal Cement Edger will outwear a half dozen cast edgers. Finely finished and polished. 6 inches long, 3 inches wide, ⅜-inch radius.
No. 9K39756 Price............74c

36c NICKEL PLATED IRON CEMENT SIDEWALK GROOVER OR JOINTER.

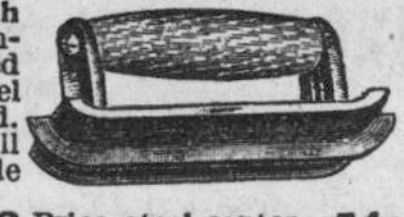

Curved at both ends, smoothly finished. Furnished all cast or steel center, as desired. Steel center will outlast two made of cast iron.
No. 9K39758 Price, steel center..54c
No. 9K39760 Price, all cast......36c
Solid Bronze Double Round End Cement Groovers, will outwear a half dozen cast groovers. Finely finished and polished, 6 inches long, 2⅞ inches wide.
No. 9K39762 Price............73c

34c NICKEL PLATED IRON CEMENT SIDEWALK CENTER.

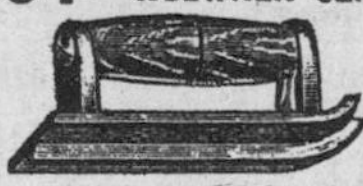

Curved at one end, square at the other. Furnished all cast or steel center, as desired.
No. 9K39764 Price, steel center 54c
No. 9K39766 Price, all cast....34c
Solid Bronze Cement Center, will outwear a half dozen cast tools. Finely finished. Length, 6 inches; width, 3 inches.
No. 9K39768 Price............74c

43c NICKEL PLATED IRON DRIVEWAY GROOVER, DOUBLE END.

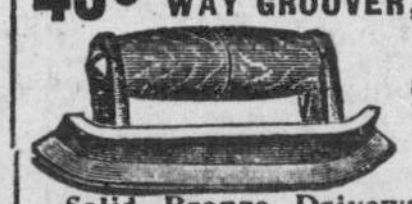

All cast, curved at both ends, smooth finish, hardwood handle.
No. 9K39770 Price......43c
Solid Bronze Driveway Groovers, will outlast a dozen common cast groovers. Finely finished and polished. Cuts heavy groove ½ inch deep.
No. 9K39772 Price............75c

$6.23 IMPROVED BRONZE SIDEWALK ROLLER WITH STEEL BEARINGS.

REGULAR RETAIL PRICE, $10.00

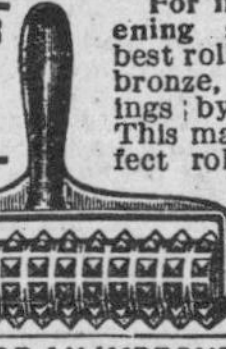

For indenting or roughening sidewalks. The best roller made. Made of bronze, cast on steel bearings; by a special process. This makes a heavy, perfect roller for a little money. Size, 3 inches diameter by 9¼ inches long.
No. 9K39774 Price..$6.23

62c FOR AN IMPROVED STEEL TAMPER, SIZE, 8 INCHES SQUARE.

OTHERS ASK $1.25 FOR THIS TAMPER.

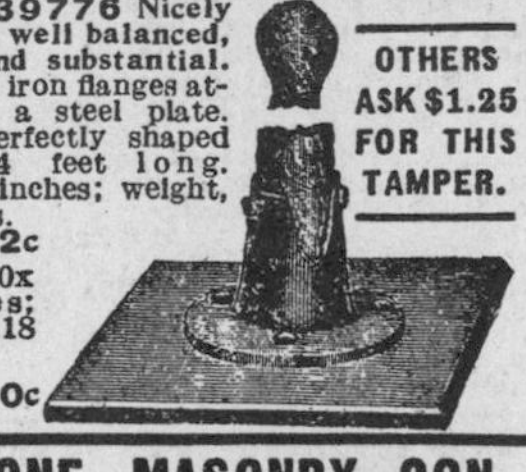

No. 9K39776 Nicely finished, well balanced, strong and substantial. Malleable iron flanges attached to a steel plate. Has a perfectly shaped handle 4 feet long. Size, 8x8 inches; weight, 14 pounds.
Price, 62c
Size, 10x10 inches; weight, 18 pounds.
Price, 80c

CYCLOPEDIA OF BRICKLAYING, STONE MASONRY, CONCRETES, STUCCOS AND PLASTERS.

By FRED T. HODGSON.

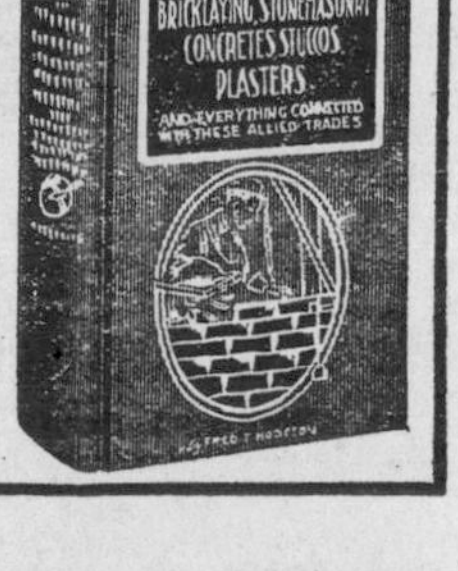

This great, new work made exclusively for us explains and instructs in a thoroughly practical way, the newest and latest methods, devices, processes and details of the new and improved methods in the use of stone, brick, stuccos, plasters and cement or concrete.

BRICKLAYING AND STONE MASONRY. Explains exactly how to lay out any kind of brick or stone work.

CONCRETES AND CEMENTS are fully treated, including reinforced concrete and hollow cement building blocks; how to construct concrete stairs, floors, ceilings, etc.

MORTARS, PLASTER AND STUCCO WORK are covered in detail. There are nearly 1,000 illustrations and diagrams, including folding plates. Most of them are reproductions from actual working drawings. Cloth, 840 pages. Size, 5¾x7¾ inches. For full description of this book, covering everything connected with these allied trades see Book Department.

No. 3K9130 Cyclopedia of Bricklaying, Stone Masonry, Concretes, Stuccos and Plasters. Price... $1.62
If by mail, postage extra, 18 cents.

28c HAMMERED STEEL, TEMPERED POINT HANDY PINCH BAR.

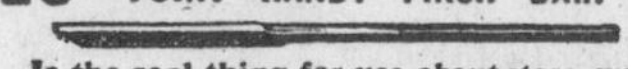

Is the real thing for use about store, warehouse, factory, barn, on truck (teaming), or about house or farm. You can move almost anything with one of them. Handy everywhere, and a single use when you need it will save many times the trifling cost. It is hammered steel, ¾ inch in the square, 3 feet long, with tempered point. Weight, 3¾ pounds.
No. 9K39445 Price, black.......28c

41c WEDGE OR PINCH POINT SOLID STEEL CROWBAR, 12-POUND.

The top illustration shows wedge point; bottom, pinch point. These are nicely finished, well proportioned, strong and substantial.

No. 9K39447 Wedge Point.			
No. 9K39448 Pinch Point.			
Weight........	12 lbs.	16 lbs.	20 lbs.
Price........	41c	55c	69c

$3.68 SAMSON RAILWAY CAR MOVER. PRACTICAL AND POWERFUL.

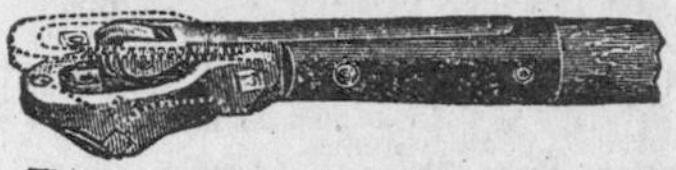

The most practical, positive and powerful device ever invented for handling railroad cars by hand, and we sell it under that guarantee. Buy a Samson and have a little switch engine of your own. Weight, 17 lbs.
No. 9K39450 Price.........$3.68

$1.60 RYAN'S PATENT POSTHOLE DIGGER, CRUCIBLE CAST STEEL BLADES.

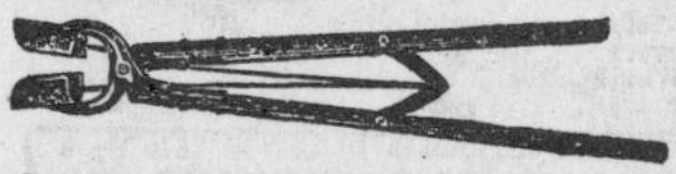

Beware of worthless imitations of this Digger sold at lower prices. The genuine Ryan Digger is warranted to work perfectly in any soil, from sticky mud to dry sand. The load is cut free from the blades and forced out by simply spreading the handles. All castings are malleable iron; blades best crucible cast steel; cleaner rods, spring steel, and handles second to none. Sold strictly on its merits. Weight, about 11 pounds.
No. 9K39457 Price..........$1.60

$1.34 ACME ADJUSTABLE POSTHOLE AUGER, QUICK AND EASY.

YOUR SAVING IS GREATER THAN EVER.

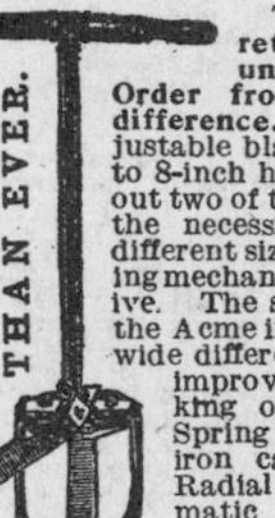

The same auger your retailer sells for $2.00 under another brand. Order from us and save the difference. It has readily adjustable blades to bore from 6½ to 8-inch holes by simply setting out two of the blades; this obviates the necessity of having several different sized augers. The dumping mechanism is simple and effective. The superior advantages of the Acme in general utility, speed, wide difference of operation with improved results, make it the king of posthole augers. Spring steel blades, malleable iron castings nicely finished. Radial adjustment, automatic downward feed, earth packs hard against disc. Weight, 11 pounds.
No. 9K39456 Price..........$1.34

60c VAUGHAN'S SOLID CAST STEEL POSTHOLE AUGER, 6-INCH.

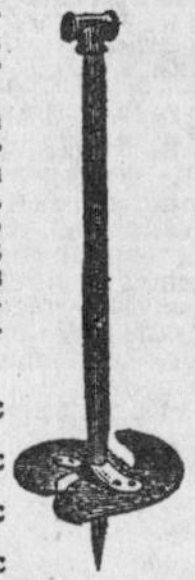

These are the well known Vaughan's pattern, the cheapest high class posthole augers on the market. If bought from a retailer would cost you $1.00 to $1.25. Blades are of solid cast steel, spring tempered. The tube is hollow. Wood handles not furnished. They are made in the following sizes. Weight, about 6 lbs.
No. 9K39460 6-inch. Price.......60c
No. 9K39461 7-inch. Price.......61c
No. 9K39462 8-inch. Price.......62c
No. 9K39463 9-inch. Price.......63c

$1.24 IMPROVED EASY POSTHOLE AUGER, SIZE, 8 INCHES.

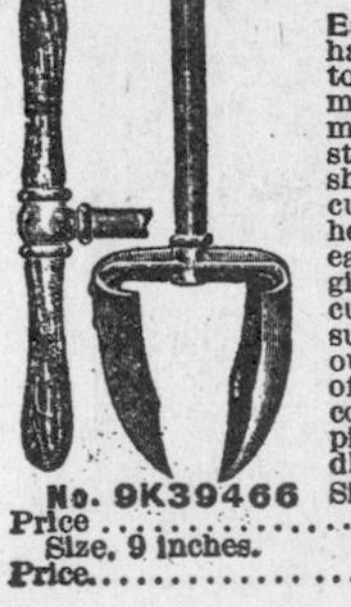

In our new Improved Easy Posthole Auger we have the easiest working tool of its kind on the market. The blades are made of high grade tool steel, highly tempered, shaped similar to a double cut auger bit. It has a heavy lip or projection on each side which, while giving a much greater cutting power, also insures a straight hole without any special attention of the operator. Comes complete with 3-foot iron pipe and hardwood handle. Weight, 10 pounds. Size, 8 inches.
No. 9K39466
Price..............................$1.24
Size, 9 inches.
Price..............................1.29

84c EXTRA HEAVY DROP FORGED TOOL STEEL SEAMLESS SIMPLEX POSTHOLE DIGGER. FASTEST AND BEST.
OUR PRICES SAVE YOU MONEY.

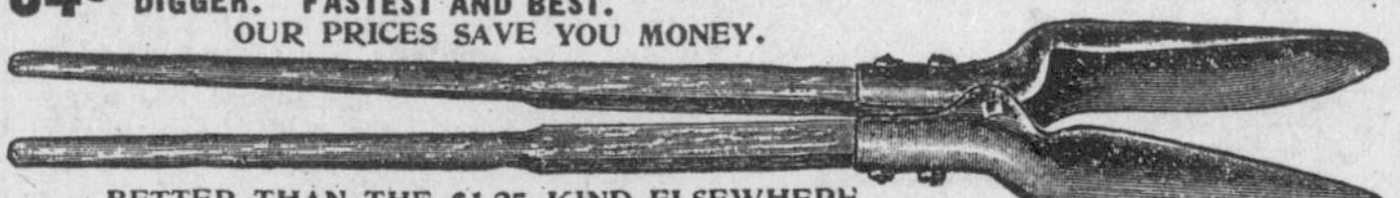

BETTER THAN THE $1.25 KIND ELSEWHERE.

Anyone can dig holes with the Simplex Digger. Easy to operate, nothing to get out of order, and more holes can be dug with it in a day than with any other digger made. Blades are drop forged from a single piece of tool steel. No welds or malleable parts to break or become loose. Handles made of ha' 'wood. Weight, 10 pounds.
No. 9K39455 Price..............................84c

25c SOLID CAST IRON POST MAUL WITH HANDLE, WEIGHT, 10 POUNDS.

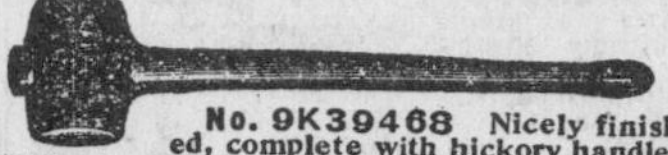

No. 9K39468 Nicely finished, complete with hickory handles.

Weight, pounds	10	13	16	18	20
Price	25c	31c	37c	41c	45c

8c SELECTED QUALITY POST MAUL HANDLE, 36 INCHES LONG.

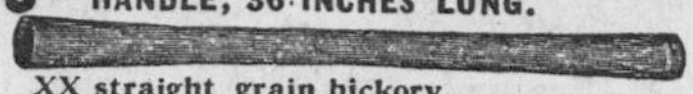

XX straight grain hickory.
No. 9K39469 Price..............8c

31c FULL WEIGHT ADZE EYE CAST STEEL RAILROAD PICK.

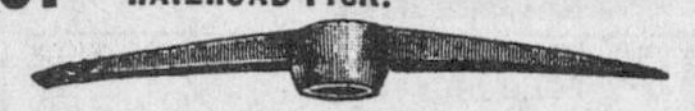

Nicely finished. Weight, 5 to 6 pounds.
No. 9K39474 Without handle.
Price..............................31c

9c SELECTED RAILROAD PICK OR MATTOCK HANDLE, 36 INCHES LONG.

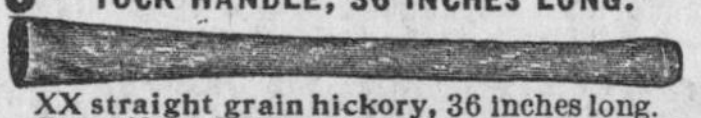

XX straight grain hickory, 36 inches long.
No. 9K39476 Price..............9c

36c ADZE EYE OIL FINISH DRIFTING PICK, WEIGHT, 4 POUNDS.

Made of best tempered cast steel.
No. 9K39480 Price does not include handle.

Weight, pounds........	4	4½	5
Price..............	36c	39c	41c

14c SELECTED QUALITY DRIFTING PICK HANDLES, 34 INCHES LONG.

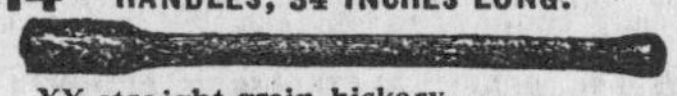

XX straight grain hickory.
No. 9K39481 Price..............14c

45c EXTRA TOOL STEEL PICK AND MATTOCK COMBINED, AXE FINISH.

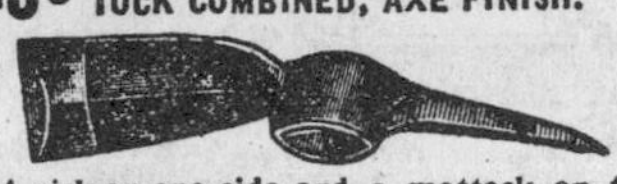

A pick on one side and a mattock on the other, as shown in illustration. Adze eye, extra tool steel. Weight, 5 pounds.
No. 9K39507 Price, without handle..............................45c
No. 9K39508 Handles for above. Hickory, 36 inches long. Price..........9c

42c EXTRA TOOL STEEL ADZE EYE LONG CUTTER MATTOCK.

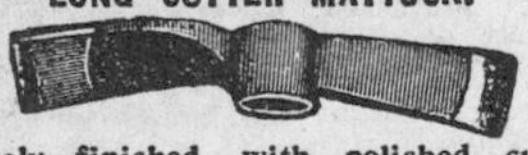

Nicely finished, with polished cutting edges, warranted. Weight, 5 to 6 pounds.
No. 9K39510 Price, without handle..............................42c
Mattock. Short cutter, same as above. Weight, 4½ pounds.
No. 9K39511 Price, without handle..............................41c
Handles for above. Hickory, 36 inches long.
No. 9K39512 Price..............12c

32c FOR A 3½-POUND CAST STEEL ADZE EYE GRUB HOE.

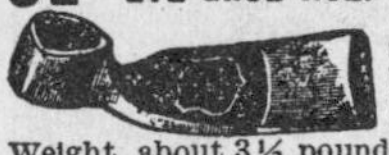

The best grade made. Cheap in price only. Axe finish, blade is about 4 inches wide. Weight, about 3½ pounds.
No. 9K39514 Price, each........32c

13c SELECTED QUALITY GRUB HOE HANDLE, 36 INCHES LONG.

Made of good quality hickory.
No. 9K39515 Price..............13c

39c EXTRA CAST STEEL ADZE EYE AXE FINISH HAZEL HOE.

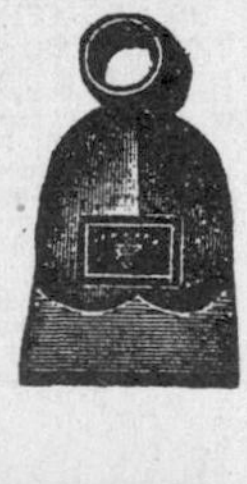

Only by selling thousands of them are we able to name this extremely low price. Size, about 6-inch cut. 10 inches long, and weighs about 3 pounds. Handles not included.
No. 9K39517
Price..................39c
Handles for above. Best selected hardwood.
No. 9K39518
Price..................14c

19c FOR A 7-INCH SOLID FORGED STEEL PLANTERS' EYE HOE.

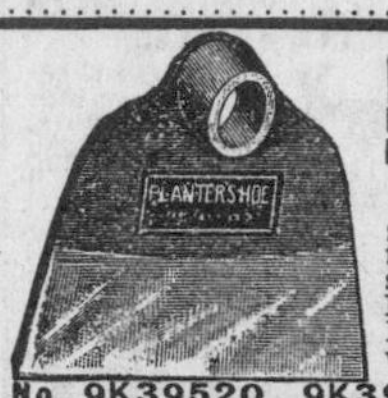

The same high grade as our other farming tools. We sell none but the best. Half polished blade. Price is for blade only, without handle.

No.	9K39520	9K39521	9K39522
Size..	7 inches	7½ inches	8 inches
Price..	19c	20c	21c

52c EXTRA QUALITY TOOL STEEL BUSH HOOK WITH SELECTED HANDLE.

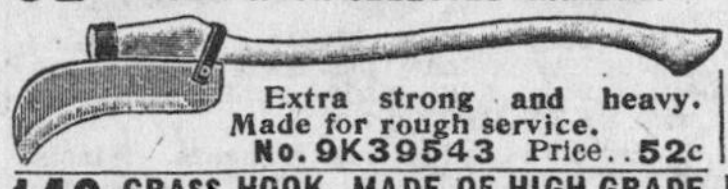

Extra strong and heavy. Made for rough service.
No. 9K39543 Price..52c

14c GRASS HOOK, MADE OF HIGH GRADE STEEL, TEMPERED IN OIL.

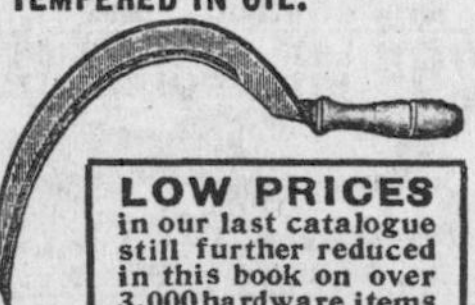

Light, strong and durable. Have the proper hang; with one of these hooks you can do twice the amount of work you can with the ordinary hind.

LOW PRICES in our last catalogue still further reduced in this book on over 3,000 hardware items

No. 9K39545 Price..............14c

23c THE GEM CRUCIBLE STEEL SCYTHE GRASS HOOK AND LAWN TRIMMER.

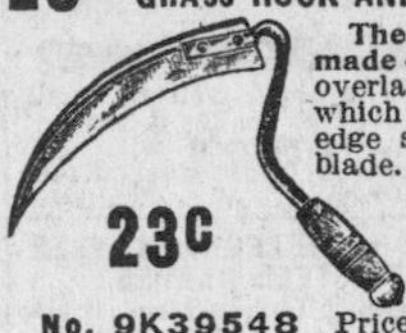

23c

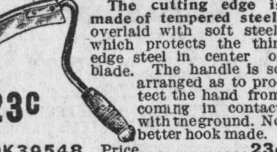

The cutting edge is made of tempered steel, overlaid with soft steel, which protects the thin edge steel in center of blade. The handle is so arranged as to protect the hand from coming in contact with the ground. No better hook made.
No. 9K39548 Price..............23c

$2.23 MORGAN PATTERN GRAIN CRADLE WITH SILVER STEEL SCYTHE.

YOUR SAVING IS GREATER THAN EVER AT OUR STILL FURTHER REDUCED PRICES.

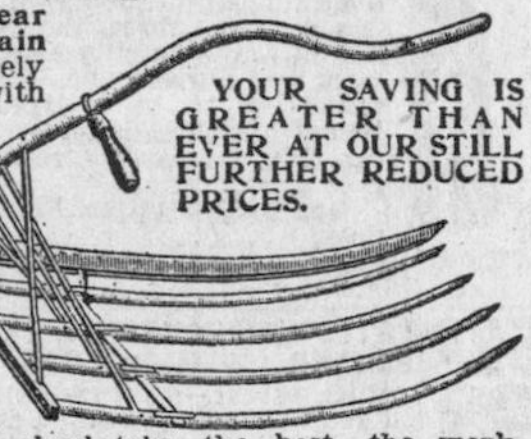

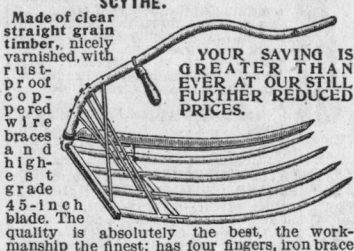

Made of clear straight grain timber, nicely varnished, with rust-proof coppered wire braces and highest grade 45-inch blade. The quality is absolutely the best, the workmanship the finest; has four fingers, iron brace and ring fastening.
No. 9K39560 Price..........$2.23

64c FOR A STANDARD WESTERN DUTCHMAN ALL STEEL GRASS SCYTHE.

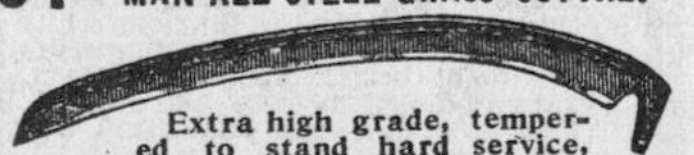

Extra high grade, tempered to stand hard service, extra wide heel. Nothing better, make, price and quality considered. Packed so that it will not be damaged on the road. Comes in lengths of 28 to 32 inches. State length.
No. 9K39562 Price..............64c

74c DOUBLE RIB EXTRA GRADE ALL STEEL GRASS SCYTHE.

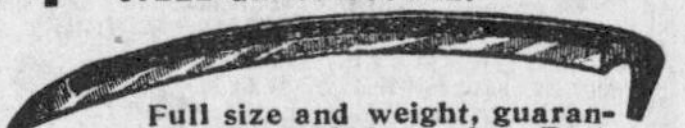

Full size and weight, guaranteed the best blade made. Both back and web polished. Heavy rib gives greater strength and rigidness. We furnish this scythe in the Clipper pattern as illustrated. Length, 28 to 32 inches.
No. 9K39563 Price..............74c

64c FOR A HIGH GRADE EXTRA CAST STEEL WEED SCYTHE.

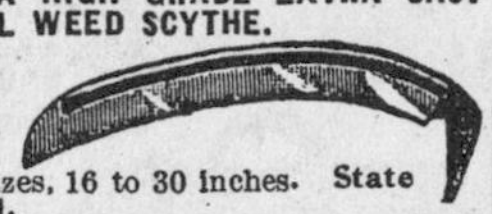

Will positively cut the thickest weeds. Rib insures strength. Sizes, 16 to 30 inches. State length wanted.
No. 9K39567 Price..............64c

65c HIGHEST GRADE EXTRA HEAVY CAST STEEL BUSH SCYTHE.

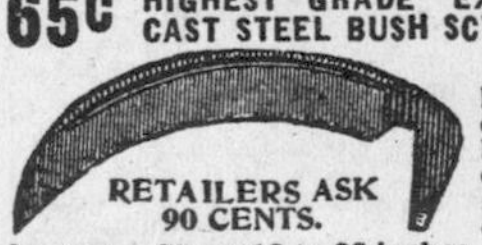

RETAILERS ASK 90 CENTS.

The same high grade as our other blades, made of the finest steel, sharpened ready for use. Sizes, 18 to 22 inches. State length.
No. 9K39568 Price..............65c

51c SELECTED STRAIGHT GRAIN GRASS SNATH WITH PATENT LOOP.

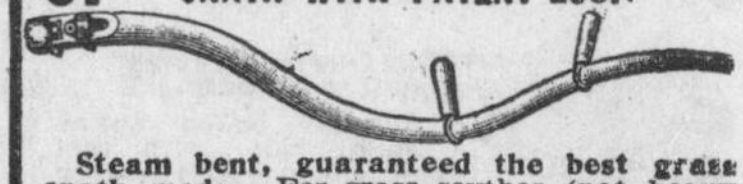

Steam bent, guaranteed the best grass snath made. For grass scythes (not heavy enough for bush scythes), complete with wrench.
No. 9K39570 Price..........51c

53c SELECTED STRAIGHT GRAIN BUSH SNATH, EXTRA HEAVY.

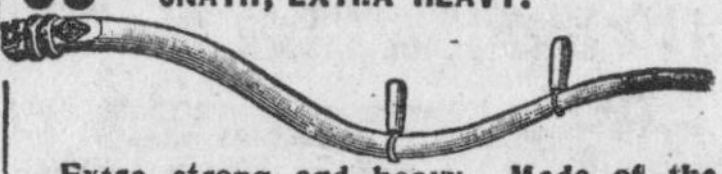

Extra strong and heavy. Made of the finest straight grain stock, steam bent.
No. 9K39572 Price..........53c

7c QUICK CUT SCYTHE STONE. FINEST STONE ON THE MARKET.

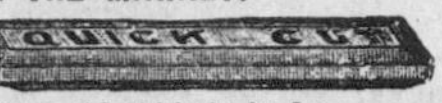

The standard for the past ten years. Others charge 15 cents for it. Size, 10x1¼x½ inches.
No. 9K39584 Price..............7c

49c SEARS' NEW IMPROVED SAW CUT TOOL STEEL HAY KNIFE.
THE 75-CENT KIND.

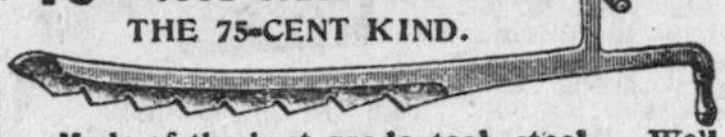

Made of the best grade tool steel. Well finished, finely tempered.
No. 9K39592 Price..............49c

61c GENUINE HIRAM HOLT LIGHTNING SAW CUT HAY KNIFE.

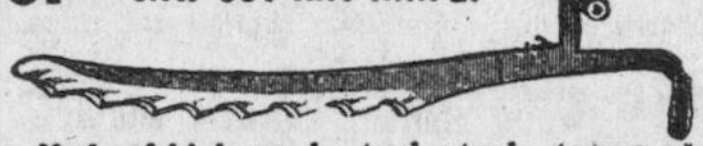

Made of high grade tool steel, tempered and hardened like a scythe. Best saw cut hay knife made. No equal for rapid work.
No. 9K39593 Price..............61c

74c FULTON TOOL STEEL SPEAR POINT HAY KNIFE.

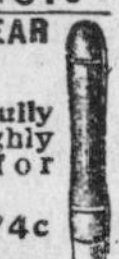

Oldest and best. Blade is carefully made of the finest tool steel, highly tempered and sharpened ready for use.
No. 9K39594 Price.........74c

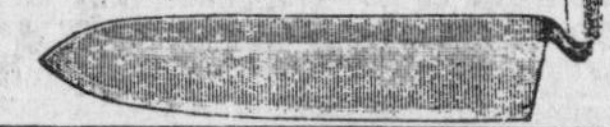

64c HEATH PATTERN UPRIGHT HAY KNIFE WITH TOOL STEEL SECTIONS.

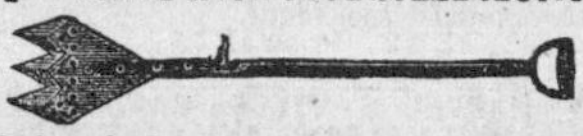

Made of the best material. Cast steel sections, same as on a mowing machine.
No. 9K39596 Price..............64c

19c HAND FORGED CUTLERY STEEL ACME CLIPPER CORN KNIFE.

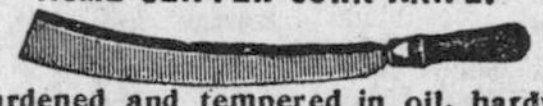

Hardened and tempered in oil, hardwood handle, which prevents turning in the hand. We will replace any knife found defective.
No. 9K39601 Price..............19c

$1.11 FOR A HALF BUSHEL SIZE ACME STEEL GRAIN SCOOP.

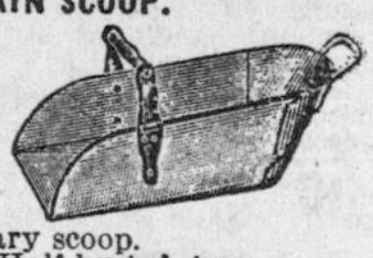

Best and strongest scoop in the market. Made of fine planished sheet steel and will outwear a dozen common scoops. Enables a man to do double the work he can do with an ordinary scoop.
No. 9K39615 Half bushel size. Price..............$1.11
No. 9K39616 Bushel size. Price..............$1.34

$2.58 LARGE SIZE WAREHOUSE TRUCK WITH STEEL NOSE AND STRAPS.

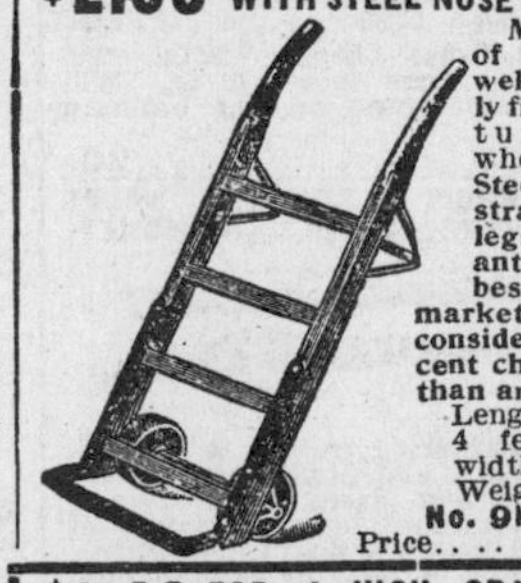

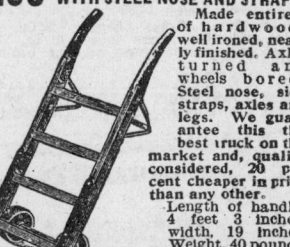

Made entirely of hardwood, well ironed, neatly finished. Axles turned and wheels bored. Steel nose, side straps, axles and legs. We guarantee this the best truck on the market and, quality considered, 20 per cent cheaper in price than any other. Length of handles 4 feet 3 inches; width, 19 inches. Weight, 40 pounds.
No. 9K39682
Price..............$2.58

$1.40 FOR A HIGH GRADE, WELL MADE FARMERS' HANDY TRUCK.

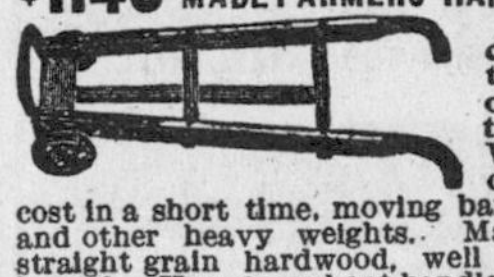

No farmer can afford to do without one of these trucks. Will save double its cost in a short time, moving barrels, boxes, and other heavy weights. Made of select straight grain hardwood, well ironed and braced. Has steam bent handles; length, 46 inches; width at upper cross bar, 18 inches. Weight, 25 pounds.
No. 9K39690 Price..........$1.40

$2.45 ENCLOSED GEAR, EASY RUNNING SUNRISE LAWN MOWER.

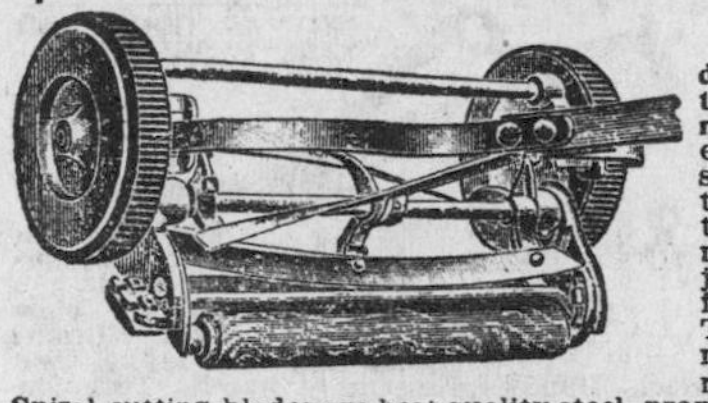

Designed to meet the demand for a low priced, thoroughly efficient mower. Sunrise Mowers are simple in construction, every part interchangeable and made throughout of the best material. Can be adjusted to cut grass different heights, as desired. The reel knife shaft is made of solid steel and runs in split bushings. Spiral cutting blades are best quality steel, properly tempered and accurately ground. The gearings are encased, preventing grass, dust, etc., from working in. The bed knife is made of crucible cast steel, highly tempered, finely ground and is self sharpening. This Sunrise Mower has adjustable handle, seasoned hardwood roller, self acting and positive pawls, and makes very little noise. Drive wheels are 8¼ inches high. Cylinder revolves when turning corners either way, as there is a ratchet in each wheel. An excellent mower for lawns too small to justify a higher priced machine. If you have a large lawn, or want the easiest running, longest wearing, highest grade mower made, we recommend our Acme Ball Bearing, shown below.

No.	9K66022	9K66024	9K66026	9K66028
Size	12-inch	14-inch	16-inch	18-inch
Shipping weight	35 lbs.	40 lbs.	42 lbs.	45 lbs.
Price	$2.45	$2.50	$2.55	$2.75

$3.67 PHOSPHOR BRONZE BEARING, FOUR-CUTTER ACME LAWN MOWER.

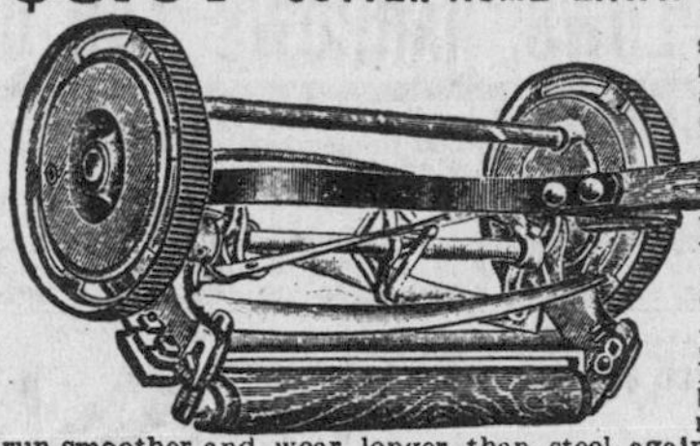

An excellent, substantial, high grade mower, strengthened and improved for this season. The drive wheels are open for one inch below the tread, thus elevating the working parts so that grit, dust, etc., cannot work in. All working parts are completely enclosed. Has phosphor bronze bearings, which in connection with steel axles, run smoother and wear longer than steel against steel. Acme Lawn Mowers run easier than others. The reel knife shaft is a bar of tempered steel, the spiral knives are spring steel, accurately ground, the bed knife is best lawn mower cast steel, highly tempered, finely ground and is self sharpening. This mower has our patent micrometer adjustment, which takes up all wear; continuous cut, self acting pawls and noiseless ratchets. The Acme Mower is fitted with hardwood roller and handle and is adjustable to cut any height. **Diameter of wheels, 9¼ inches; diameter of reel, 6 inches.** Price includes two wrenches and full directions for operating and adjusting. The 16-inch size is the most popular.

No.	9K66014	9K66016	9K66018	9K66020
Size	14-inch	16-inch	18-inch	20-inch
Shipping weight	47 lbs.	49 lbs.	51 lbs.	57 lbs.
Price	$3.67	$3.96	$4.32	$4.77

$5.72 GUARANTEED, ADJUSTABLE, NOISELESS, EASY RUNNING, BALL BEARING ACME LAWN MOWER.

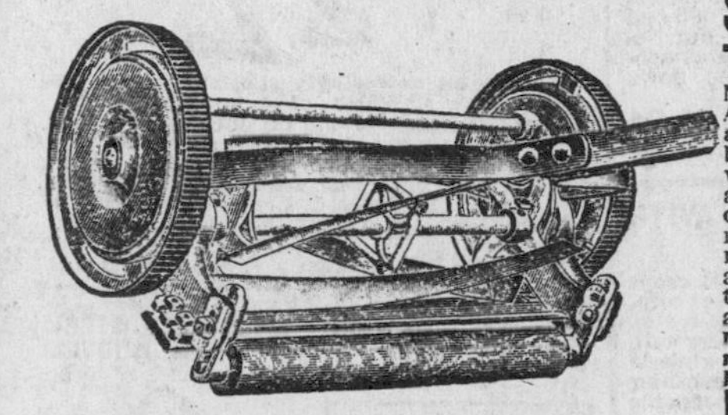

$9.50 WILL NOT BUY AS GOOD A MOWER ELSEWHERE.

THE ACME OF QUALITY. THE BEST MOWER MADE.

No matter what price you pay elsewhere, you will not get better value. The Acme Ball Bearing Lawn Mower is superior to any mower offered anywhere else at any price. Because of its accurate adjustment it is practically noiseless in operation; because of its perfect ball bearings it runs very easy and will accomplish more work with less labor than any other mower made. The Acme Ball Bearing Mower is adjustable throughout so that any wear may be taken up, thus keeping it in perfect condition season after season. The Acme Ball Bearing Mower is a heavy, well made mower, with each part of the machine strong enough to stand severe service and the material in every part is the very best to be had. None of the parts of this mower are skimped in size or weight. The wheels could be made ¼ or ½ inch lower; they could be ⅛ or ¼ inch narrower on the tread; the knife bars could be narrower and thinner and, throughout the whole machine, we could increase our profit by reducing the quality, **but we believe our customers appreciate the high quality of the mower we offer and our enormous lawn mower business (the largest in the world) has been built up by one mower selling a great many others in the same community.**

DETAILS OF CONSTRUCTION. In the Acme Ball Bearing Mower the bed knife is adjustable to cut grass any height desired. The cones and cups in the bearings are turned from solid tool steel, then case hardened; no pressed cups are used in this machine. The bearings are ground perfectly and only the best steel balls are used. The cups, cones and balls are fitted dustproof and the bearings are as accurate as those in a high grade bicycle.

THE DRIVE WHEELS ARE 9¼ INCHES IN DIAMETER and the mower has a four-bladed revolving cutter. Cutter is 6 inches in diameter and the blades are so arranged that they give a continuous cut. The blades are made of best refined steel, finely ground and accurately set. The bed knife has a spring adjustment and is at all times in cutting position. The high drive wheels, the ball bearings and the set of the handle make this the easiest running mower offered. Rollers and handle made of selected hardwood and the machine has every practical improvement in lawn mower construction.

BECAUSE SOMEONE ASKS YOU TWICE AS MUCH MONEY for a lawn mower do not think our mower must be of inferior quality. Order one of our mowers, test it side by side with any mower at double the price, and if you do not find that our mower is superior, box it up and return it to us and we will refund the price paid. We carry a large stock on hand at all seasons of the year. Price includes two wrenches and full directions for operating and adjusting. We recommend the 16-inch size for general use.

We have always sold GOOD HARDWARE at lower prices than any other house. On over 3,000 hardware items prices are STILL FURTHER REDUCED in this catalogue.

No.	9K66035	9K66036	9K66037	9K66038
Size	14-inch	16-inch	18-inch	20-inch
Weight	48 pounds	50 pounds	57 pounds	68 pounds
Price	$5.72	$5.96	$6.32	$6.93

53c ADJUSTABLE STRIPED CANVAS GRASS CATCHER. FITS ANY LAWN MOWER AND SAVES RAKING.

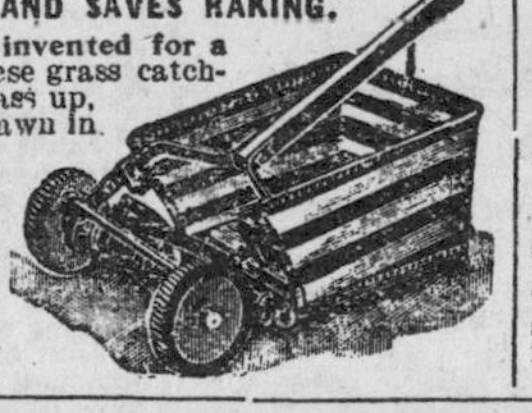

The most useful attachment ever invented for a lawn mower. When using one of these grass catchers it is not necessary to rake the grass up, which cuts the work of mowing a lawn in half. Made of heavy fancy striped canvas on an adjustable galvanized steel frame. They are made deep to prevent grass being thrown over sides or rear. Adjustable in height and width to fit any of our lawn mowers.

No. 9K66045 Price, without mower **53c**

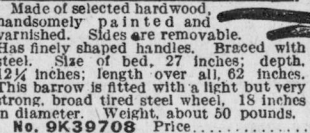

$2.35 STEEL WHEEL, HARDWOOD GARDEN WHEELBARROW, PAINTED AND VARNISHED.

The regular $3.50 good value kind and the best barrow to buy.

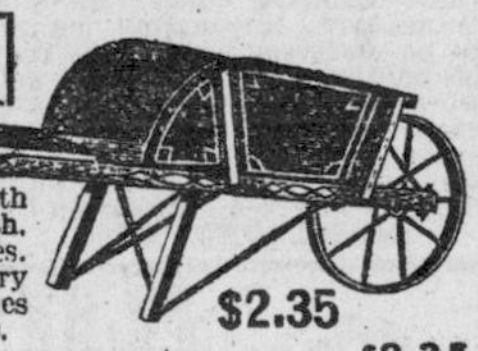

$2.35

Made of selected hardwood, handsomely painted and varnished. Sides are removable. Has finely shaped handles. Braced with steel. Size of bed, 27 inches; depth, 12¼ inches; length over all, 62 inches. This barrow is fitted with a light but very strong, broad tired steel wheel, 18 inches in diameter. Weight, about 50 pounds.

No. 9K39708 Price **$2.35**

MOWER AND BINDER SUNDRIES

WE CARRY A COMPLETE STOCK OF MOWER AND BINDER SECTIONS, GUARD PLATES, GUARDS, KNIVES AND KNIFE HEADS TO FIT THE LEADING MAKES OF MOWERS AND BINDERS.

Smooth Section. Rough Section. Guard Plate. Mower Knife or Binder Sickle. Guard. Knife Head.

THE QUALITY OF THESE GOODS is absolutely the best. If you will compare our prices on these parts with the prices dealers, agents and manufacturers ask you for the same articles you will be surprised at the amount of money you can save by sending us your orders. We cannot furnish other parts for mowers and binders than those illustrated above. Be sure to observe our directions for ordering.

DIRECTIONS FOR ORDERING.

WHEN ORDERING SECTIONS give us our catalogue number, the name and kind of machine for which sections are wanted and put down on your order how many boxes of sections you need. Take an old section from your machine, lay it on a piece of paper and with a sharp pencil mark around the outside of the section and also mark the exact size and position of the rivet holes. Then send the paper pattern to us with your order and there will be no chance for your not getting the section you need to fit your machine. Remember that smooth sections have smooth cutting edges and are used on mowing and flax machines. Rough sections have rough cutting edges and are the kind used in binders and reapers.

WHEN ORDERING GUARD PLATES tell us the name of the mower, binder or reaper for which they are wanted, give us the numbers or letters that appear on the guard the plates are to fit and also send us a paper pattern showing size and shape of the old plate and the exact position of rivet holes.

WHEN ORDERING GUARDS tell us the name of the mower, binder or reaper for which they are wanted and give us the numbers or letters which appear on the old guard.

WHEN ORDERING MOWER KNIVES OR BINDER SICKLES, be sure to tell us whether knife or sickle is wanted, give us the name of the machine, how many cutting sections are on the old knife or sickle and also give us the figures or letters on the old knife head and on the guards of the machine.

WHEN ORDERING KNIFE HEADS give us the figures or letters which appear on the old knife head, or if there are no marks on the old head, send us a sketch of the old part, showing exact shape and size of the knife head and the location of the rivet holes.

PLEASE NOTE. We sell sections and guard plates only in boxes containing twenty sections or plates, packed complete with rivets. We do not break boxes. Remember that we cannot furnish any parts for mowers or binders except those listed below and we must have full information as to the make of the machine and the size and description of parts wanted to enable us to fill your order correctly.

No. 9K71072	Box of 20 Smooth Sections. Weight, 3 pounds. Price	(If by mail, postage extra, 50 cents)	$0.73
No. 9K71097	Box of 20 Rough Sections. Weight, 2 pounds. Price	(If by mail, postage extra, 35 cents)	.75
No. 9K71103	Box of 20 Guard Plates. Weight, 1¾ pounds. Price	(If by mail, postage extra, 30 cents)	.59
No. 9K71104	Guards. Weight, 1 pound. Price, each	(If by mail, postage extra, 20 cents)	.20
No. 9K71105	4½-Foot Knife or Sickle, with 18 cutting sections or less. Weight, 9 pounds. Price		1.95
No. 9K71106	5-Foot Knife or Sickle, with 19 or 20 cutting sections. Weight, 10 pounds. Price		2.11
No. 9K71107	6-Foot Knife or Sickle, with 21, 22, 23 or 24 cutting sections. Weight, 12 pounds. Price		2.38
No. 9K71109	Knife Head. Weight, 1¾ pounds. Price	(If by mail, postage extra, 40 cents)	.23

YOUR SAVING IS EVEN MORE. Low prices in our last catalogue still further reduced on over 3,000 Hardware Items in this book.

57c FOR A SELF ADJUSTING EASY RUNNING HUSTLER CORN SHELLER.

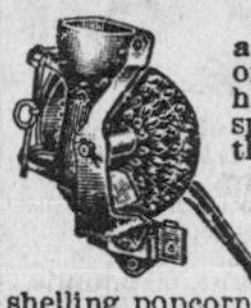

You pay $1.25 elsewhere for a sheller not as good. Made of best quality material, has hardened teeth, adjustable spring tension regulated by thumbscrew, will take any size ear, shells clean from butt to tip and does not crack the grains. Our Hustler sheller is fitted with attachment for shelling popcorn. Can be attached to any box or board. Weight, 15 pounds. Shipped from Chicago.

No. 9K72227 Price **57c**

$1.31 IMPROVED FULTON GUARANTEED ADJUSTABLE CORN SHELLER.

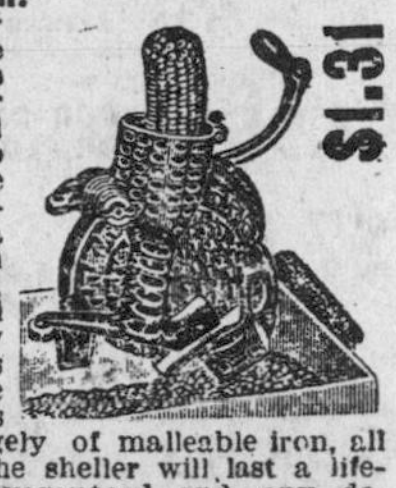

No sheller ever sold at anything like our price will do as good work. Better than shellers that sell as high as $2.50 to $3.00 each. The Fulton is a big improvement over a similar sheller which we formerly sold, having all its good points and some very important features not possessed by the other. Our price tells the rest. Made largely of malleable iron, all bearings chilled. The sheller will last a lifetime. Absolutely guaranteed and any defective parts will be replaced free. Will shell all sizes of field corn easily and rapidly. Adjustable spring tension. Positive lock adjustments. Has cob guide and picker wheel guard. Sheller can be instantly clamped to any box or plank (no holes to bore). Shipped from Chicago. Weight, 20 pounds.

No. 9K72229 Price **$1.31**

No. 9K72230 Improved Fulton Adjustable Corn Sheller with malleable butting and tipping attachment. For shelling seed corn. Price **$1.49**

For One and Two-Hole Corn Shellers, see page 546.

$1.96 HUSTLER HAND GRIST MILL WITH FLY WHEEL.

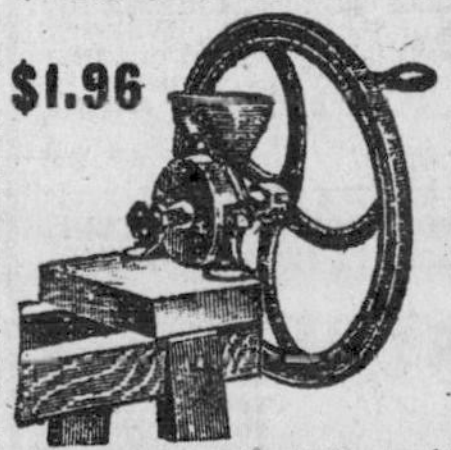

This is the mill you ought to have. It is a perfect mill with removable iron burrs and for rough, coarse grinding cannot be equaled. It will grind salt, peas, corn, wheat, rye and other grains, and is specially recommended for grinding chicken feed, hominy, etc., on account of its rapid action. Extra heavy fly wheel makes it run very easy. Will grind from ¾ to 1¼ bushels per hour, depending upon the fineness of the grinding. Constructed throughout of the finest materials, nicely finished and properly assembled. We guarantee this mill and will replace any one of them that is not entirely satisfactory. Shipped from Chicago. Weight, 30 pounds.

No. 9K72100 Price **$1.96**

Pair of Extra Burrs. Weight, 1½ pounds.

No. 9K72101 Price **39c**

$1.68 FOR A No. 1 ACME ADJUSTABLE HAND GRIST MILL.

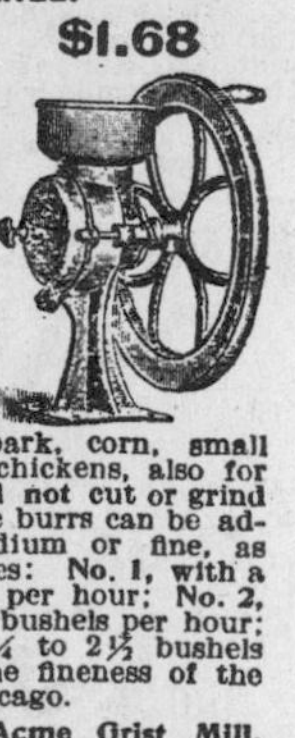

This is the handsomest, most durable, most rapid and most easily regulated hand grist mill made. It is constructed throughout of iron except the shaft, which is steel, and the burrs, which are steel alloy. These burrs will outlast three sets of ordinary gray iron burrs, and are easily and cheaply renewed. Ground dry bones and shells, cracked corn, etc., make excellent poultry foods. This mill is especially adapted to grinding dried bones and shells, roots, bark, corn, small grains, salt and feed for chickens, also for making table meal. It will not cut or grind green bones or shells. The burrs can be adjusted to grind coarse, medium or fine, as desired. Made in three sizes: No. 1, with a capacity of ½ to 1 bushel per hour; No. 2, with a capacity of ¾ to 1½ bushels per hour; No. 3 with a capacity of 1¼ to 2½ bushels per hour, depending upon the fineness of the grinding. Shipped from Chicago.

No. 9K72115 No. 1 Acme Grist Mill. Weight, 18 pounds. Price **$1.68**

No. 9K72116 No. 2 Acme Grist Mill. Weight, 36 pounds. Price **$3.24**

No. 9K72117 No. 3 Acme Grist Mill. Weight, 60 pounds. Price **$4.92**

No. 9K72125 Pair of No. 1 Extra Burrs. Weight, 2 pounds. Price **32c**

No. 9K72126 Pair of No. 2 Extra Burrs. Weight, 4 pounds. Price **77c**

No. 9K72127 Pair of No. 3 Extra Burrs. Weight, 9 pounds. Price **$1.16**

For Grinding Mills, Feed Grinders, and Corn and Cob Mills, see pages 547 and 548.

Reduced Hardware Prices in This Book Make Your Saving Greater Than Ever.

KENWOOD PLOWS, HARROWS AND CULTIVATORS

THE HIGHEST GRADE and best designed farming implements ever produced. Kenwood implements are all made in one of the largest and best equipped factories, of the finest materials and by skilled workmen. Every plow, harrow or cultivator that we sell must pass a careful inspection, both as to material and workmanship before we allow it to be shipped.

WE GUARANTEE every article quoted on this page to be perfect in material and workmanship, to be adapted to the work we recommend it for and to be entirely satisfactory, or it may be returned to us and your money will be refunded.

$3.29 KENWOOD 7-INCH STEEL BEAM RIGHT HAND PONY PLOW.

Better than you can buy at home for $5.00.

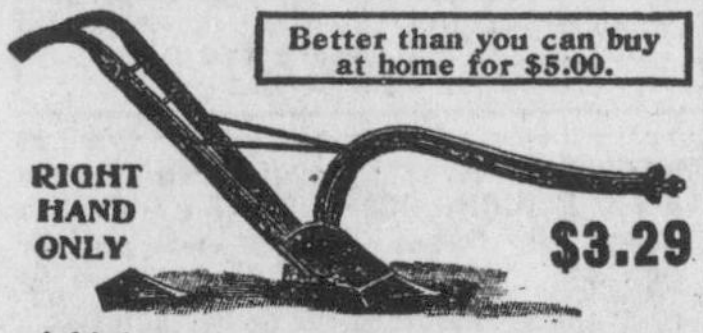

A high grade, well made, steel beam pony plow, put together with two solid steel saddles, has adjustable slip heel, extra high arch beam and is adapted to both sod and stubble plowing. Especially recommended for cotton and corn land, gardening, trucking, etc.

No. 9K7121 7-inch. Weight, 60 pounds. Price.....$3.29
No. 9K7123 9-inch. Weight, 68 pounds. Price.....$3.95
No. 9K7125 11-inch. Weight, 89 pounds. Price.....$5.45
No. 9K7131 7-inch Extra Share. Weight, 2¼ pounds. Price.....24c
No. 9K7133 9-inch Extra Share. Weight, 3¾ pounds. Price.....37c
No. 9K7135 11-inch Extra Share. Weight, 5¼ pounds. Price.....54c

$7.96 KENWOOD DRILL SEEDER, CULTIVATOR, PLOW, HOE AND RAKE.

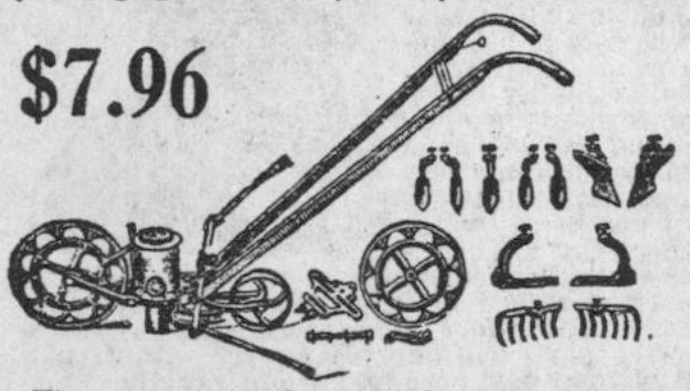

The most convenient and desirable full combination garden tool outfit on the market and the best tool made for home gardening. This combination furnishes every tool which you would be likely to need in the planting and cultivation of your garden. Can be used either as a one or two-wheel tool. Outfit consists of the drill complete, one cultivator frame, one pair of hoes, one pair of small plows, one pair of rakes, one pair of narrow cultivator teeth, one pair of wide cultivator teeth, one center cultivator tooth and one pair of improved markers. The drill has a large hopper, an agitator force feed, a steel furrow opener, drags to cover the seed, a concave rear wheel to press and compact the soil which covers the seed, and a patent indicator bearing the names of the different kinds of seed conveniently located at the side of the hopper. Will drill any kind of small seed in any desired quantity at any uniform depth and covers perfectly. Shipped knocked down from Chicago. Weight, 73 pounds.

No. 9K7903 Price.....$7.96

$4.96 KENWOOD DOUBLE WHEEL CULTIVATOR, PLOW AND RAKE.

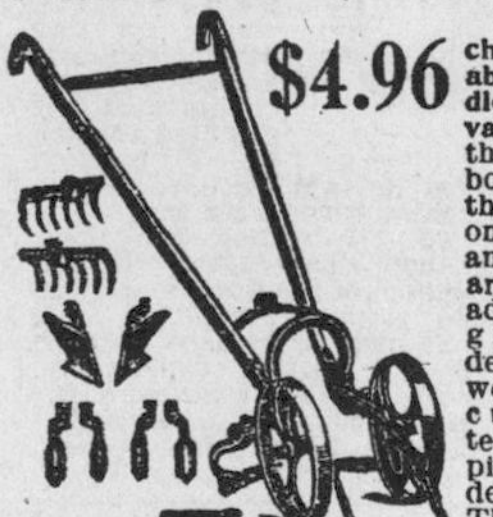

This machine is suitable for straddle row cultivation. Does the work on both sides of the row at once. It has an adjustable arch with nine adjustments to gauge the depth of the work. The cultivator teeth can be pitched to any desired angle. The outfit consists of the frame, complete with one pair of vine guards, one pair of hoes, one pair of small plows, one pair of rakes, one pair of narrow cultivator teeth and one pair of wide cultivator teeth. The best double wheel hoe outfit on the market. Shipped knocked down from Chicago. Weight, 42 pounds.

No. 9K7911 Price.....$4.96

$1.96 KENWOOD "EASY" CULTIVATOR, PLOW, HOE AND RAKE.

YOU SAVE MONEY when you buy of us at our LOW PRICES.

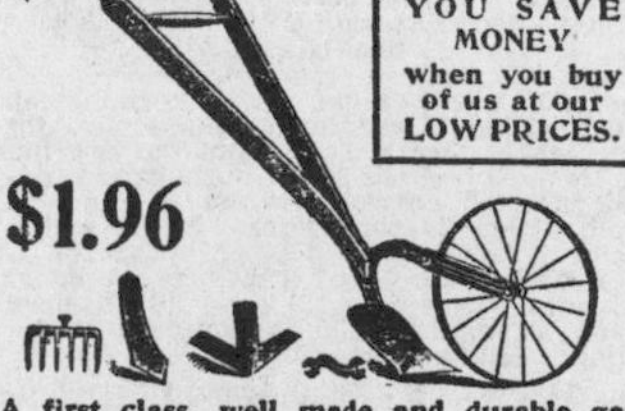

A first class, well made and durable gardeners' tool. Light, strong and easy to operate. Just right for small gardeners. By using one of these outfits a garden can be cultivated without having a clumsy horse trample on the vegetables. Requires but little force to operate. Wheel is 18 inches high. The outfit consists of the frame complete with one moldboard plow, one double end cultivator tooth, one cultivator sweep and one rake. Others ask double our price for this same style of tool. Shipped knocked down from Chicago. Weight, 22 pounds.

No. 9K7922 Price.....$1.96

$2.69 KENWOOD REVERSIBLE CULTIVATOR, PLOW, HOE AND RAKE.

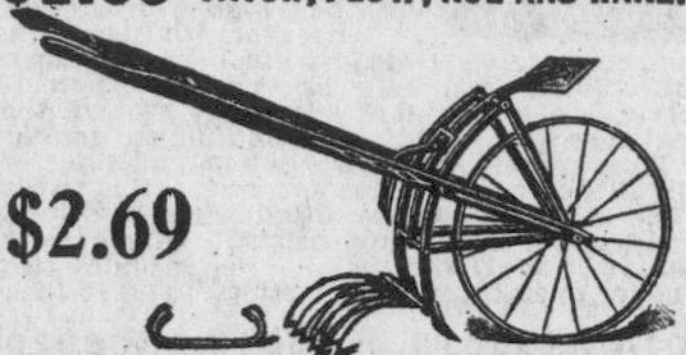

This is one of the most desirable hand cultivators on the market. It is made with attachments on both sides of the frame so that any of its various kinds of work can be done by turning the handles over the wheel. The turning blade is attached to one side of the frame. The other side carries three reversible cultivator teeth and the center tooth is movable so that it can be raised out of the way if you desire to use only two teeth. The hoe and the rake attach to the cultivator tooth side of the frame. You can use the center cultivator tooth alone, the two side teeth alone or all three teeth together, thus adapting the cultivator for all classes of work. Shipped knocked down from Chicago. Weight, 25 pounds.

No. 9K7926 Price.....$2.69

$3.06 KENWOOD ONE-HORSE STEEL FRAME HARROW WITH 14 TEETH AND LEVER EXPANDER.

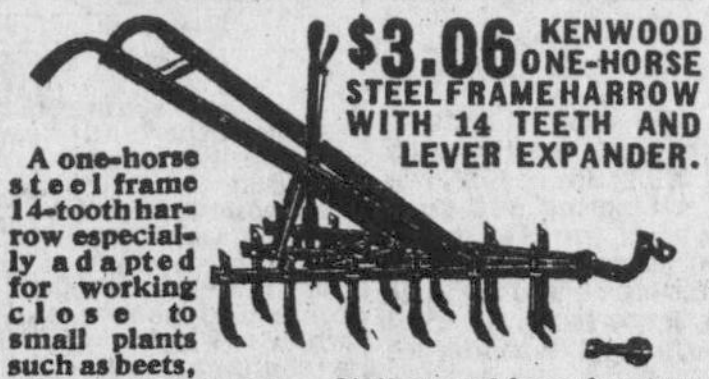

A one-horse steel frame 14-tooth harrow especially adapted for working close to small plants such as beets, tobacco, cotton, etc. It thoroughly pulverizes but throws no dirt on plants. It is fitted with compound lever expander, with which you can adjust the harrow while in motion, from 11 to 33 inches in width. Teeth can be reversed or turned as desired, presenting four different points. Can be used as a straight diamond tooth harrow, also as a smoother with sharp points down. The compound lever harrow is much more convenient than harrows with ordinary lever expander or without lever expander and well worth double the difference in price. Our side handle braces No. 9K7985 and front wheel No. 9K7983 listed with our No. 9K7976 cultivator, are very desirable attachments for this tool. Shipped knocked down from Chicago. Weight, 58 pounds.

No. 9K7972 Price.....$3.06
No. 9K7973 Extra Teeth. Weight, 1 pound. Price, each.....5c

$2.86 KENWOOD ADJUSTABLE STEEL CULTIVATOR WITH COMPOUND LEVER EXPANDER COMPLETE.

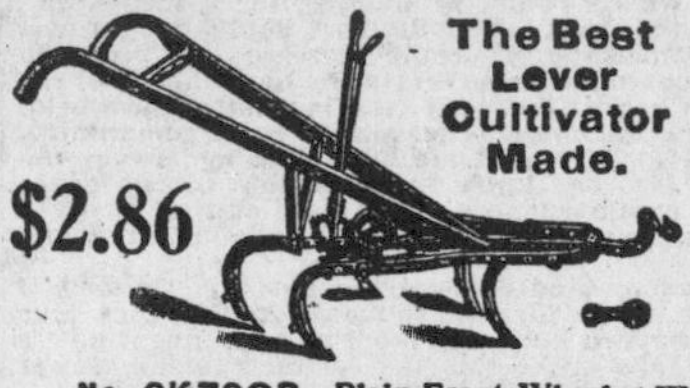

The Best Lever Cultivator Made.

It is adapted for the cultivation of all crops which are planted in rows or hills, such as corn, beets, cotton, tobacco, vegetables of all kinds, etc., and is fitted with a compound lever expander with which the cultivator can be adjusted while in motion, from 10 to 26 inches in width from center to center of teeth. Has five 3-inch reversible teeth which can be adjusted to suit all kinds of soil. Outside handle braces No. 9K7985, front wheel No. 9K7983, cultivator teeth No. 9K7993, cultivator sweeps No. 9K7995, are attachments which can be used on this cultivator and all are very desirable. Shipped knocked down from Chicago. Weight, 55 pounds.

No. 9K7976 Price.....$2.86
No. 9K7983 Plain Front Wheel. Weight, 5 pounds. Price.....30
No. 9K7985 Pair of Outside Handle Braces. Weight, 2½ pounds. Price.....15
No. 9K7993 3-inch Cultivator Teeth. Weight, 14 ounces. Price, each.....08
No. 9K7995 10-inch Cultivator Sweeps. Weight, 1¼ pounds. Price, each.....16

$4.89 KENWOOD ONE-HORSE STEEL CULTIVATOR OUTFIT WITH LEVER EXPANDER AND DEPTH REGULATOR.

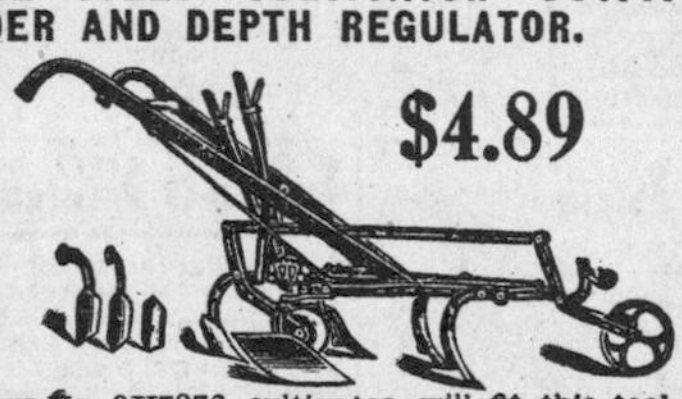

Is exactly the same as our No. 9K7976, provided with the same lever adjustment, but in addition the cultivator is fitted with front and rear depth regulating wheels adjusted by a second lever, one set of best horse hoe attachments and a pair of outside handle braces. This combination fits the tool for the cultivation of almost any crop. Broomcorn, cotton, and many other crops have to be hoed very carefully by the ordinary method of culture but either can be almost entirely worked by this cultivator. It is adapted to the cultivation of corn, potatoes, cotton, tobacco, sugar beets, etc. Cultivator teeth No. 9K7993 and cultivator sweeps No. 9K7995, listed with our No. 9K7976 cultivator, will fit this tool. Shipped knocked down from Chicago. Weight, 90 pounds.

No. 9K7977 Price.....$4.89

$2.83 KENWOOD TWO-WHEEL CULTIVATOR, PLOW, HOE AND RAKE.

$4.00 Elsewhere.

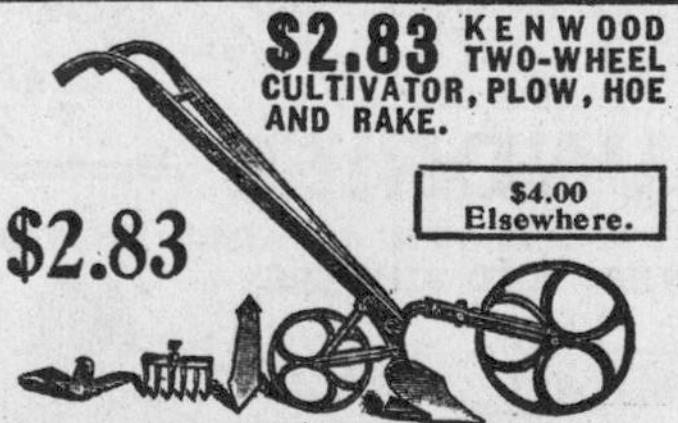

One of the best and most desirable wheel garden tools made. The rear wheel is 10 inches in diameter and runs level with the bottom of the plow. The front wheel is 16 inches in diameter and is adjustable so that you can gauge the depth of plowing or cultivation. The outfit consists of the frame complete with one moldboard plow having a landside, one double end cultivator tooth, one hoe and one rake. This tool operates very easily and runs steadily. Shipped knocked down from Chicago. Weight, 39 pounds.

No. 9K7928 Price.....$2.83

$1.31 KENWOOD AUTOMATIC STOCK WATERER, RUSTPROOF VALVE.

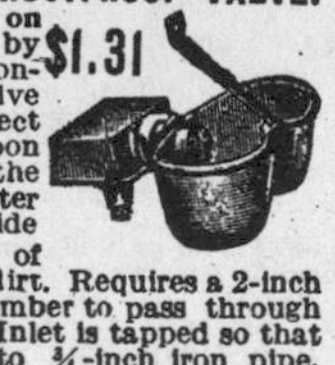

The best StockWaterer on the market. Operated by an automatic float, connected by a rustproof valve which closes on a perfect fitting valve seat. As soon as pan fills up to near the top the float shuts the water off. Float chamber is inside the barrel or tank, out of the way of all mud and dirt. Requires a 2-inch hole for stem of float chamber to pass through and is easily attached. Inlet is tapped so that it can be connected to ¾-inch iron pipe. Holds about 1½ gallons. Length, 10½ inches; width, 5¼ inches; depth, 4½ inches inside. Shipped from Chicago. Weight, 11 pounds.

No. 9K71777 Price.....$1.31

$2.47 KENWOOD PUSH BAR CULTIVATOR, HOE AND PLOW.

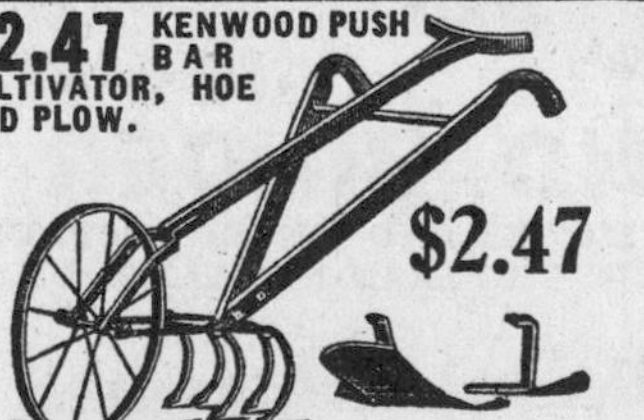

This cultivator is the easiest to operate of any of the numerous garden cultivators on the market. The operator pushes the weight of his body against the push bar which furnishes sufficient power to propel the cultivator, thus leaving the hands free to shift it in any direction. This allows the cultivator to be shifted to right or left without affecting the course of the wheel and without side draft. The wheel is 18 inches in diameter. The tools furnished are five cultivator teeth, one right hand moldboard plow and one right hand hoe. Shipped knocked down from Chicago. Weight, 23 pounds.

No. 9K7929 Price.....$2.47

$2.57 KENWOOD DISC SHARPENER WITH TOOL STEEL KNIFE.

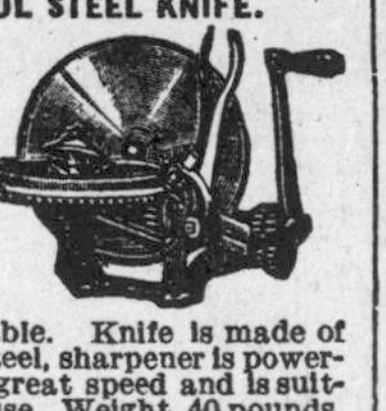

To do good work with a harrow, discs must be kept sharp. The Kenwood sharpens any size discs, from 13 to 20 inches in diameter, does the work quickly, with little labor and does not chatter. It centers perfectly, is well made, strong and durable. Knife is made of highly tempered tool steel, sharpener is powerfully geared, develops great speed and is suitable for farm or shop use. Weight, 40 pounds.

No. 9K7405 Price.....$2.57

$1.54 KENWOOD ONE-HORSE STEEL BEAM SINGLE SHOVEL PLOW

NOT AS GOOD FOR $2.25 ELSEWHERE.

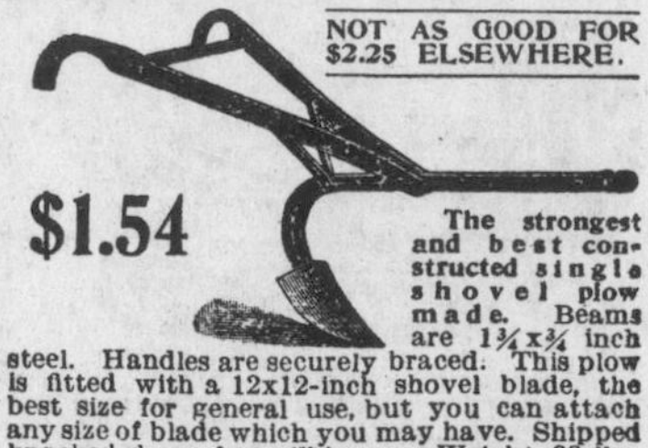

The strongest and best constructed single shovel plow made. Beams are 1¾x¾ inch steel. Handles are securely braced. This plow is fitted with a 12x12-inch shovel blade, the best size for general use, but you can attach any size of blade which you may have. Shipped knocked down from Chicago. Weight, 33 lbs.

No. 9K7941 Price.....$1.54

$2.16 KENWOOD ONE-HORSE STEEL BEAM DOUBLE SHOVEL PLOW.

Low prices in our last catalogue still further reduced in this book. The saving is yours.

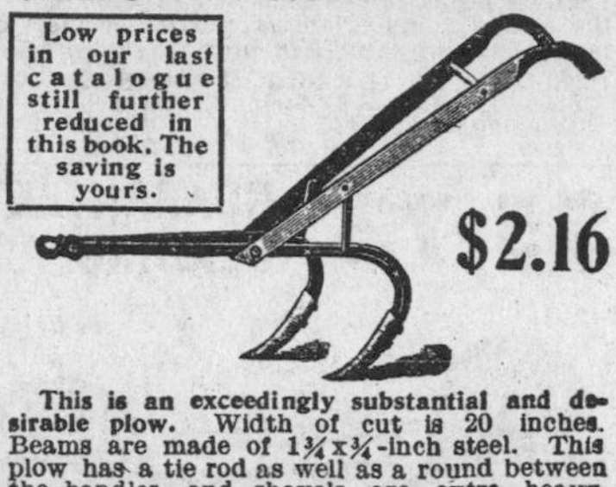

This is an exceedingly substantial and desirable plow. Width of cut is 20 inches. Beams are made of 1¾x¾-inch steel. This plow has a tie rod as well as a round between the handles, and shovels are extra heavy. Shovels are 6 inches wide, 11 inches long and have two holes. Clevis is adjustable. Shipped knocked down from Chicago. Weight, 46 pounds.

No. 9K7950 Price.....$2.16

$1.91 KENWOOD ADJUSTABLE STEEL WING WOOD BEAM SHOVEL PLOW.

On many Hardware items you pay twice our price at retail.

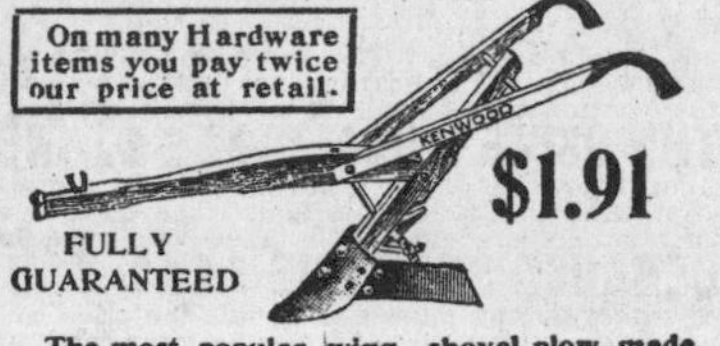

The most popular wing shovel plow made. Has extra strong wood beam and standard. Handles are well set and braced. Fitted with steel shovel blade, having adjustable steel wings which can be set at any angle and held in position by means of spread rods. Especially adapted for hilling and digging potatoes. Shipped knocked down from Chicago. Weight, 33 pounds.

No. 9K7958 Price.....$1.91

$2.73 KENWOOD COMBINED SICKLE AND TOOL GRINDER.

Fitted with Alundum Wheels.

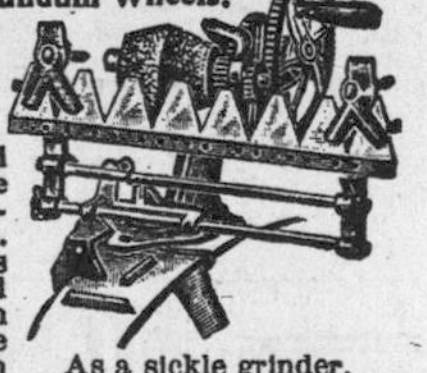

As a sickle grinder.

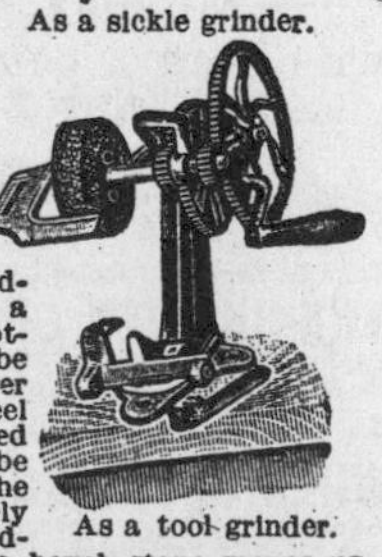

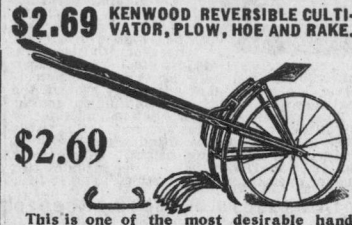

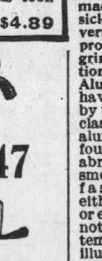

As a tool grinder.

This is absolutely THE BEST sickle and tool grinder made. Holds the sickle knife in a vertical position and provides for the grinding of four sections at one setting. Alundum wheels have been adopted by us for this high class tool because alundum has been found to be a better abrasive and to do smoother, better and faster work than either carborundum or emery, and it will not heat or draw the temper. The upper illustration shows the machine fitted for grinding sickles and with a wheel clamp on the bottom so that it can be attached to a mower wheel, but the wheel clamp can be removed and the grinder can be bolted to a bench. The sickle grinder is entirely automatic in its grinding movements. The bevel stone moves up and down against the sections and does not grind at any one point long enough to heat the sections or draw the temper. It can be adjusted to grind from point to heel or grind only down to the knife head. One side of the section can be ground alone or both can be ground evenly. The knife clamp is adjustable in every way and is arranged so that you can tip it forward and see exactly how you are grinding. When used as a tool grinder, as shown in the lower illustration, the arm which holds the arbor is raised to a horizontal position where it is held firmly and the tool rest enables you to do perfect grinding. Price is for the machine complete with one bevel sickle stone, one tool stone, one tool rest, one wheel clamp and one wrench. The arbor for the tool stone is arranged so that you can use it on any stone not over 4½ inches diameter or 1¼-inch face, with ¾-inch hole. Shipped knocked down from Chicago. Weight, 28 pounds.

No. 9K71136 Price.....$2.73

FOR HEAVY PLOWS, CULTIVATORS AND OTHER AGRICULTURAL IMPLEMENTS, SEE PAGES 536 TO 551.

A FEW OF OUR HUNDREDS

COMPARE THESE PRICES WITH WHAT YOU PAY AT YOUR HOME GROCERY FOR SUCH GOODS, always remembering that we goods to be absolutely the best grades on the market, and see for yourself what a substantial saving you can make by buying all your groceries from us. **WON'T YOU MAKE UP AN ORDER FOR GROCERIES FROM THIS AND THE OPPOSITE PAGE?** We give you variety enough here to make groceries and the values we offer. Include a number of these items with your order for other goods if you will. In making up a freight shipment of up to 100 pounds, you will not add a single cent to the freight charges if you include some of these items.

——— SEE OUR GREAT FREE GROCERY PRICE LIST OFFER ON PAGE 534 ———

1-lb. can **21c** 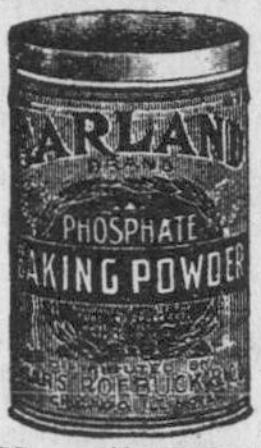
No. 7K4265

12,000 matches **58c** 
No. 7K79017

6 cans **69c** 
No. 7K52416

30-bar box **$1.02**
No. 7K74007

6 No. 1 cans **59c** 
No. 7K52796

6-lb. box **35c** 
No. 7K6705

Both for **75c** 
No. 7K4399

3 pkgs. **36c**
No. 7K76283

3 No. 1 tins for **49c** 
No. 7K53053

3 No. 1 tins **71c** 
No. 7K53083

15-lb. pail **$1.00**
No. 7K55207

6 cans **$1.04**
No. 7K52506

6 cans **47c** 
No. 7K50566

20-lb. box **$1.14**
No. 7K69557

3 1-lb. pkgs. **15c** 
No. 7K67113

5-lb. pkg. **49c** 
No. 7K4770

6 cans **41c** 
No. 7K50916

6 cans **45c** 
No. 7K5300

65c
No. 7K6635

5-lb. pkg. **44c** 
No. 7K4652

3 1-lb. pkgs. **12c** 
No. 7K42923

1-lb. can **35c** 
No. 7K4258

4 pkgs. **14c** 
No. 7K43004

1-lb. pkg. **20c**
No. 7K4595

3 No. 1 tins for **43c** 
No. 7K53153

2½-lb. box **31c** 
No. 7K7355

12 bars for **42c** 
No. 7K7411

2½ gal. can **$1.02**
No. 7K68917

15-lb. pail **$1.24**
No. 7K55817

6 cans **$1.00**
No. 7K52486

PRICE LIST OF ARTICLES ON THIS PAGE

No. 7K4258	One 1-pound can Iris Brand Baking Powder, for	$0.35
No. 7K4265	One 1-pound can Garland Brand Baking Powder, for	.21
No. 7K4399	Two 8-ounce bottles Iris Brand Flavoring Extracts, one Vanilla, one Lemon for	.75
No. 7K4595	One 1-pound package Garland Brand Shredded Cocoanut, for	.20
No. 7K4652	One 5-pound package Thompson Seedless Raisins, for	.44
No. 7K4770	One 5-pound package Casalina Brand Currants, for	.49
No. 7K5300	Six cans Iris Brand Soups, Assorted, for	.45
No. 7K6635	One 10-pound sack Matoma Brand Rice, for	.65
No. 7K6705	One 6-pound box Garland Brand Gloss Starch, for	.35
No. 7K7411	Twelve 6-ounce bars Garland Brand White Floating Soap, for	.42
No. 7K7355	One 2½-pound box Italian Cream Candy, for	.31
No. 7K42923	Three 1-pound packages Garland Brand Soda or Saleratus, for	.12
No. 7K43004	Four packages Garland Brand Yeast Cakes, for	.14
No. 7K50566	Six No. 2 cans Red Kidney Beans, for	.47
No. 7K50916	Six No. 2 cans Standard Sugar Corn, for	.41
No. 7K53153	Six No. 1 cans Medium Red Salmon, for	.69
No. 7K52486	Six No. 1 cans Fancy Salmon, for	1.00
No. 7K52506	Six No. 1 cans Fancy Chinook Salmon, for	1.04
No. 7K52796	Six No. 1 cans Shrimp, for	.59
No. 7K53053	Three tins Kippered Herring, for	.49
No. 7K53083	Three tins Mackerel with Tomato Sauce, for	.71
No. 7K53153	Three tins Smoked Haddock, for	.43
No. 7K55817	One 15-pound pail Columbia River Salmon, for	1.00
No. 7K55207	One 15-pound pail Norway KKK Herring, for	1.00
No. 7K67113	Three 1-pound packages Garland Brand Corn Starch, for	.15
No. 7K68917	One 2½-gallon can Doris Brand New Orleans Molasses, for	1.02
No. 7K69557	One 20-pound box Garland Brand Soda Crackers, for	1.14
No. 7K74007	One box (thirty 12-ounce bars) Garland Family Soap, for	1.02
No. 7K76283	Three 3-pound packages Garland Brand Washing Powder, for	.36
No. 7K79017	One box (12,000) Red Band Matches, for	.58

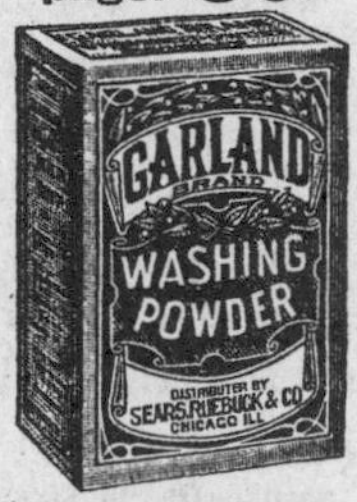

SEE OUR GREAT TEA AND COFFEE OFFER ON PAGE 534.

OF VALUES IN GROCERIES

WON'T YOU INCLUDE SOME OF THESE ITEMS WITH YOUR ORDER FOR OTHER GOODS? Remember, in a freight shipment up to 100 pounds it will not add a single cent to the cost of your freight charges, and the saving you make, therefore, on these items will be absolutely clear; besides you will get a test of the values we offer in groceries; something that you owe to yourself to make if you have not as yet tried our grocery department. We want to save you one-third on your groceries. We know we can, and remember, we guarantee to furnish the best grades on the market. If you are disappointed in the least, all you have to do is to return the goods to us at our expense and we will refund your money. REMEMBER, WE ARE QUOTING LOWEST CHICAGO WHOLESALE PRICES ON GROCERIES. THAT IS WHY OUR PRICES ARE SO LOW.

SEE OUR GREAT FREE GROCERY PRICE LIST OFFER ON PAGE 534

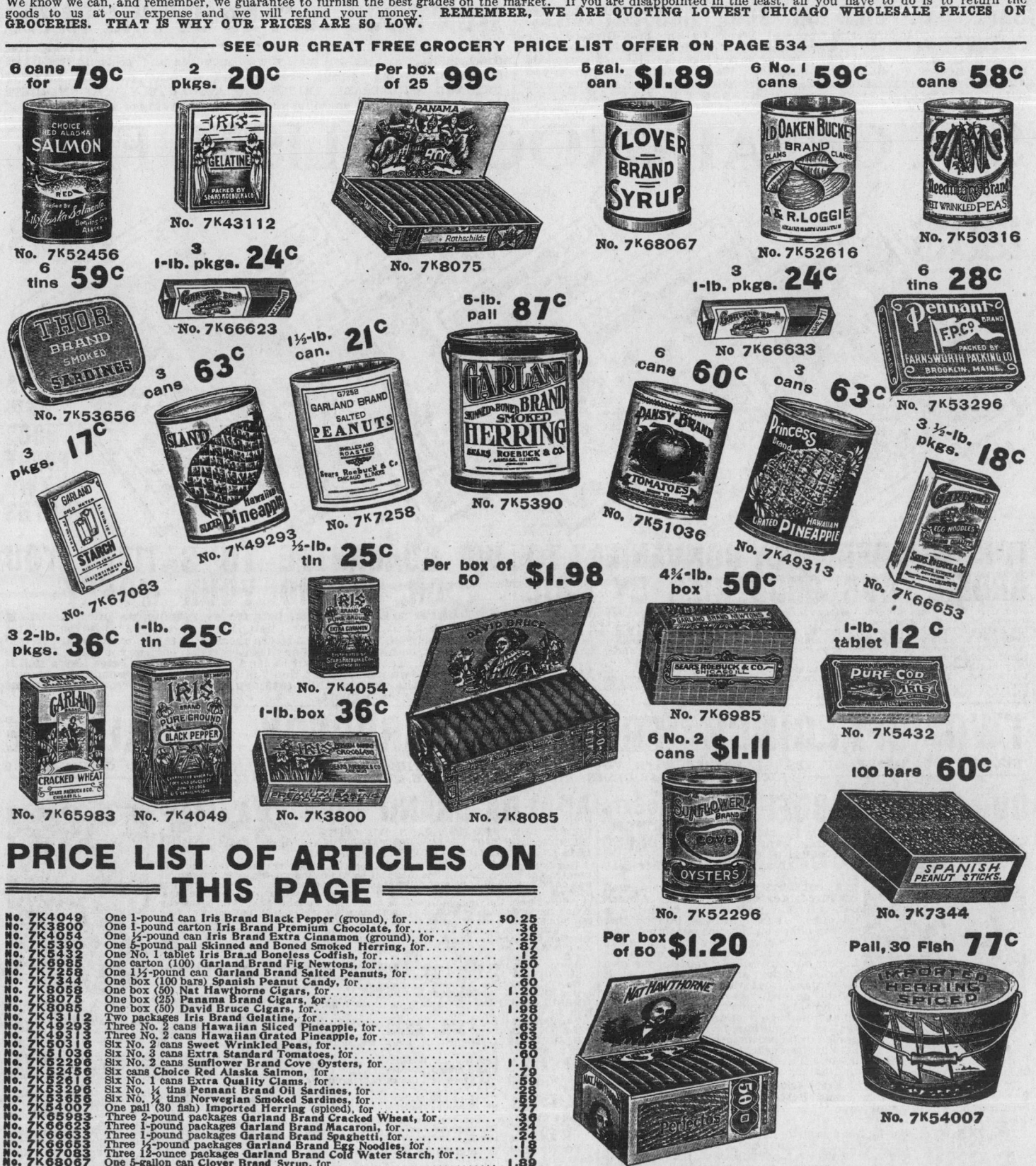

PRICE LIST OF ARTICLES ON THIS PAGE

No. 7K4049 One 1-pound can Iris Brand Black Pepper (ground), for............$0.25
No. 7K3800 One 1-pound carton Iris Brand Premium Chocolate, for.............. .36
No. 7K4054 One ½-pound can Iris Brand Extra Cinnamon (ground), for.......... .25
No. 7K5390 One 5-pound pail Skinned and Boned Smoked Herring, for.......... .87
No. 7K5432 One No. 1 tablet Iris Brand Boneless Codfish, for................. .12
No. 7K6985 One carton (100) Garland Brand Fig Newtons, for................. .50
No. 7K7258 One 1½-pound can Garland Brand Salted Peanuts, for............. .21
No. 7K7344 One box (100 bars) Spanish Peanut Candy, for.................. .60
No. 7K8058 One box (50) Nat Hawthorne Cigars, for.................. 1.20
No. 7K8075 One box (25) Panama Brand Cigars, for.................. .99
No. 7K8085 One box (50) David Bruce Cigars, for.................. 1.98
No. 7K43112 Two packages Iris Brand Gelatine, for.................. .20
No. 7K49293 Three No. 2 cans Hawaiian Sliced Pineapple, for.................. .63
No. 7K49313 Three No. 2 cans Hawaiian Grated Pineapple, for.................. .63
No. 7K50316 Six No. 2 cans Sweet Wrinkled Peas, for.................. .58
No. 7K51036 Six No. 3 cans Extra Standard Tomatoes, for.................. 1.11
No. 7K52296 Six No. 2 cans Sunflower Brand Cove Oysters, for.................. 1.11
No. 7K52456 Six cans Choice Red Alaska Salmon, for.................. .79
No. 7K52616 Six No. 1 cans Extra Quality Clams, for.................. .59
No. 7K53296 Six No. ¼ tins Pennant Brand Oil Sardines, for.................. .28
No. 7K53656 Six No. ¼ tins Norwegian Smoked Sardines, for.................. .59
No. 7K54007 One pail (30 fish) Imported Herring (spiced), for.................. .77
No. 7K65983 Three 2-pound packages Garland Brand Cracked Wheat, for.......... .36
No. 7K66623 Three 1-pound packages Garland Brand Macaroni, for.................. .24
No. 7K66633 Three 1-pound packages Garland Brand Spaghetti, for.................. .24
No. 7K66653 Three ½-pound packages Garland Brand Egg Noodles, for.................. .18
No. 7K67083 Three 12-ounce packages Garland Brand Cold Water Starch, for.......... .17
No. 7K68067 One 5-gallon can Clover Brand Syrup, for.................. 1.89

SEE OUR GREAT TEA AND COFFEE OFFER ON PAGE 534.

HIGHEST GRADE GROCERIES
AT LOWEST CHICAGO WHOLESALE PRICES

SAVE ONE-THIRD ON YOUR GROCERY BILLS

by buying all your groceries from us. Write for our Free Grocery Price List today. We have the largest grocery store in the world, the sales amounting to more than the sales of several of the largest wholesale grocery houses in Chicago combined. We guarantee to furnish you absolutely the best and highest grade groceries obtainable, and guarantee our prices to be the lowest ever named. DON'T PAY RETAIL PRICES FOR GROCERIES.

WON'T YOU JUST DO US THIS FAVOR

Write us a postal card or letter and say, "Please send me your big Free Grocery List," and we will mail you at once free and postpaid the latest edition of our big 64-page Grocery List, quoting you THE LOWEST CHICAGO WHOLESALE PRICES ON ABSOLUTELY THE HIGHEST GRADE GROCERIES, enabling you to make a saving of one-third.

SIX GREAT GROCERY LISTS FREE
FOR 1908   FOR 1908

A NEW BOOK EVERY TWO MONTHS

IT IS WONDERFULLY CONVENIENT TO ORDER YOUR GROCERIES BY MAIL

from us. We offer a greater variety than you can get in any local grocery store. Every item is absolutely guaranteed by us to be strictly high grade, thoroughly in accordance with the National Pure Food Law of June 30, 1906. You can make up your grocery order very easily, we provide you an order blank which explains itself. You can make up an order at your convenience and enclose our price in the form of a Postoffice or Express Money Order, Bank Draft or currency in a Registered Letter; mail it to us and we will ship you the goods very neatly and carefully packed, guaranteeing to furnish you fresh, high grade goods throughout. In a short time your shipment will be at the depot and you can get it just as readily as you would by buying your groceries at a retail grocery store, and then, THINK OF THE SAVING WE MAKE FOR YOU!

WE GUARANTEE TO SATISFY YOU OR REFUND YOUR MONEY

You take no risk whatever, because everything we offer is strictly guaranteed by us, and if you are disappointed in any way with any of the goods we send you, we ask you to return them to us at our expense and we will pay you back both the price and any transportation charges you paid. You will not be out one penny. Don't fail to send for our Grocery Price List which is issued every two months, and don't fail to observe the wonderful grocery offers we make you in this catalogue which show you some of the values we are able to quote.

TWO OFFERINGS FROM OUR GROCERY CATALOGUE

INCLUDE A CANISTER OF TEA OR COFFEE WITH YOUR ORDER AND TEST THE QUALITY OF THESE GOODS AND COMPARE THE PRICES WITH THOSE ORDINARILY PAID FOR SUCH QUALITIES AT RETAIL

OUR MALDEN COFFEE   19 CENTS PER POUND

Put up in airtight 5-pound canisters. The equal of coffee sold as high as 30 cents by other dealers.

A combination of choice old, well matured Mexican and South American coffees, especially rich in their cup qualities. It really isn't so strange that we can offer you this rich, smooth flavory coffee at the marvelously low price of 19 cents, when you consider the fact that we import our own coffees, and do our own roasting, mixing and blending. And it isn't strange that we can offer you so excellent a quality, a quality the equal of which cannot be purchased for less than almost double our price, when you realize that we buy nothing but the very finest grades to be procured in the coffee markets of the world. We employ experts to test the coffees, experts who buy direct from the producer, after having been on the ground and having seen and tested the article.

If you have been buying a 15-cent grade of coffee you will find our 19-cent Malden Blend better and actually cheaper, because you will get more cups of the same strength from the same quantity.

No. 7K500	Per 5-pound canister	$0.95
No. 7K5017	Per case of six 5-pound canisters	5.70
No. 7K5027	Per case of twelve 5-pound canisters	11.40
No. 7K5037	Per case of twenty 5-pound canisters	19.00

We do not sell less than a 5-pound canister of Malden Coffee.

APALDA BRAND TEAS   39 CENTS PER POUND

UNDER OUR APALDA BRAND WE OFFER A SELECTION OF THE FOLLOWING VARIETIES OF TEAS IN AN AIRTIGHT MOISTUREPROOF CAN.

This is a special selection of early crop teas from the best tea growing countries of the world. A line of teas if bought of the wholesaler in the regular way could not possibly be sold at less than 60 cents per pound. This variety is selected with special reference to its cup qualities. We import our own teas, buy direct from the resident agents in the several tea growing countries, thereby saving the profit usually paid the importer and the jobber, which explains why we can furnish this grade of tea at the remarkably low price of 39 cents per pound.

We ask you to include in your next order a canister of this tea, making your selection from the list below, and we feel sure that you will agree with us that the quality of the tea we send you is superior to the teas you have been purchasing at from 60 to 70 cents.

Apalda Brand we offer a special selection of the following varieties of teas:

SUN DRIED JAPAN. A green tea, draws beautiful light liquor.

| No. 7K200 | Per 1-pound canister | $0.39 |
| No. 7K201 | Per 3-pound canister | 1.14 |

REGULAR JAPAN. A green tea, draws fragrant light liquor.

| No. 7K202 | Per 1-pound canister | $0.39 |
| No. 7K203 | Per 3-pound canister | 1.14 |

BASKET FIRED JAPAN. A black tea, draws a very pale liquor.

| No. 7K204 | Per 1-pound canister | $0.39 |
| No. 7K205 | Per 3-pound canister | 1.14 |

GUNPOWDER. A green tea, draws light aromatic liquor.

| No. 7K206 | Per 1-pound canister | $0.39 |
| No. 7K208 | Per 3-pound canister | 1.14 |

IMPERIAL. A green tea, draws fine, pale liquor.

| No. 7K209 | Per 1-pound canister | $0.39 |
| No. 7K210 | Per 3-pound canister | 1.14 |

YOUNG HYSON. A green tea, draws medium light liquor.

| No. 7K211 | Per 1-pound canister | $0.39 |
| No. 7K212 | Per 3-pound canister | 1.14 |

ENGLISH BREAKFAST. A black tea, draws fine amber liquor.

| No. 7K213 | Per 1-pound canister | $0.39 |
| No. 7K214 | Per 3-pound canister | 1.14 |

OOLONG. A black tea, draws medium amber colored liquor.

| No. 7K215 | Per 1-pound canister | $0.39 |
| No. 7K216 | Per 3-pound canister | 1.14 |

INDIA-CEYLON. A black tea, draws dark amber colored liquor.

| No. 7K218 | Per 1-pound canister | $0.39 |
| No. 7K219 | Per 3-pound canister | 1.14 |

GREEN AND BLACK MIXED. A blended tea, draws medium amber colored liquor.

| No. 7K220 | Per 1-pound canister | $0.39 |
| No. 7K221 | Per 3-pound canister | 1.14 |

SPECIAL BREAKFAST. A blended tea, draws medium dark, very fragrant liquor.

| No. 7K222 | Per 1-pound canister | $0.39 |
| No. 7K223 | Per 3-pound canister | 1.14 |

MOVING PICTURES

WE FURNISH COMPLETE OUTFITS

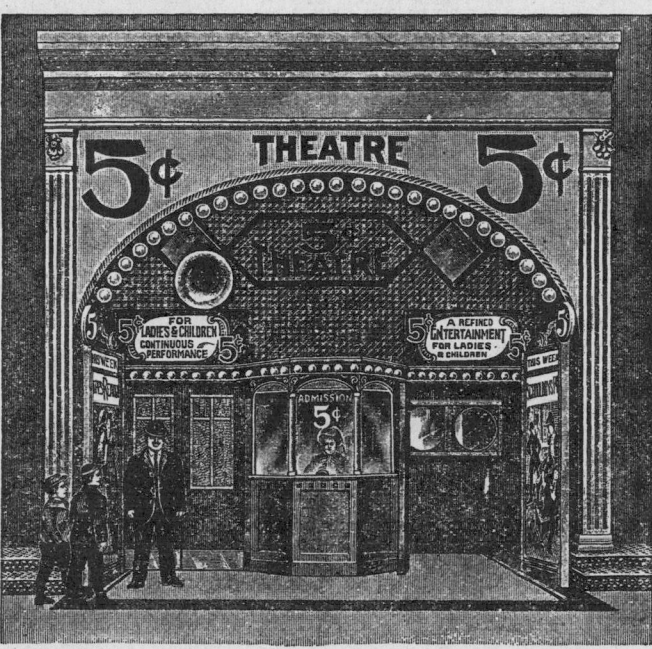

SEND FOR OUR 160-PAGE SPECIAL CATALOGUE

FOR
5-CENT THEATERS
TRAVELING EXHIBITORS
STREET ADVERTISING
LODGE WORK
CHURCH ENTERTAIN-MENTS
PUBLIC SCHOOLS

AT THE
VERY LOWEST PRICES

OF
MOVING PICTURE MACHINES
STEREOPTICONS
GAS MAKING OUTFITS
ILLUSTRATED SONG SLIDES
LECTURE SETS OF VIEWS
MOTION PICTURE FILM

AND
FULL LINE OF SUPPLIES

THE NEW 1908 MODEL MOTIOGRAPH

THE NEW "MOTIOGRAPH" MOTION PICTURE MACHINE is the greatest machine ever made for 5-cent theater work. The "Motiograph" is the most powerful, the most strongly and substantially constructed motion picture machine on the market. It is a machine that will stand the hard wear and tear of continuous service that is demanded in 5-cent theater work. In the sharpness and clearness of the pictures, freedom from flicker, ease and convenience of operation, strength and durability, it surpasses any machine yet constructed. It is made with fireproof magazines, and automatic safety fire shutter. It complies with all fire ordinances and all rules of the board of underwriters. It is the latest, most practical, and the best motion picture machine made, not only for 5-cent theatre work, which is the hardest test to which a motion picture machine can be put, but for any class of moving picture work. For complete description, full specifications, and prices, send for our big catalogue of stereopticons and motion picture apparatus which will be mailed to you free of charge.

THE MOVING PICTURE BUSINESS has grown to immense proportions, developing into a world wide enterprise, involving an invested capital of millions of dollars. Like the advent of the telephone or the graphophone, the moving picture machine was at first regarded as more or less of a curiosity, but when the possibilities of this new field became better known it grew more and more into favor with the public and recently has sprung into such popular favor that there is scarcely a city of any size in this country which does not contain a moving picture theater with an ever increasing number of regular patrons.

TRAVELING EXHIBITION WORK is today more popular than ever. An excellent plan is to map out a route which will take about a half year to cover, arranging your bookings several weeks or months in advance. Your advertising matter is sent on in advance so that when you reach each city you have only to give your exhibition, collect the receipts for the evening, and then pass to the next city. When you have finished your route, it will then be time to start and go over the same ground again with a new lecture and, if your previous exhibition has been one to deserve appreciation, you will rapidly develop a steady patronage which will be worth many dollars to you in future years.

STREET ADVERTISING is a comparatively new but extremely interesting branch of exhibition work. For this business it is only necessary to have a good stereopticon outfit, such as those described in our special catalogue of these goods. You will also require a number of stereopticon views and a considerable quantity of attractive advertising slides. You then arrange with the merchants of your city to show their advertisements for a certain amount each night, and by stretching a screen on the side of a building and placing your machine across the street, you can project your views and slides upon the screen. The novelty of this exhibition will attract many people, and you will be surprised to find how many will stop and remain for hours to watch these pictures. The merchants also feel the effects in increased business. This work can be done in your own city during the evening, as it does not in any way require all of your time.

CHURCHES, LODGES, AND SCHOOLS. Many of the largest churches are now using the stereopticon and find that it not only increases their attendance but creates a real interest in the subject of the day. Various organizations of the church will find the stereopticon a most profitable matter for their consideration. Lodge work is made far more interesting by the use of the stereopticon, and we furnish any secret society slides needed, a list of which is given in our special stereopticon catalogue. Schools and colleges are installing the stereopticon in many of their lecture rooms with most excellent results. These features and many other valuable and important facts regarding the stereopticon and moving picture business are fully described in our big 160-page Special Catalogue, which will be sent free, to any address, upon request.

THE 5-CENT THEATER IS HERE TO STAY. It fills a want that has existed in every community for a moderate priced form of clean, up to date amusement. This business offers attractive inducements to anyone with small capital who wishes to establish himself in a profitable and permanent business of his own. Almost any vacant store room can be made into a five-cent theater by removing the glass front and replacing it with a regular theater front similar to the illustration shown on this page. A show of about twenty minutes is given, and the low price of admission is an inducement which many people cannot resist.

SEND FOR OUR BIG 160-PAGE FREE CATALOGUE OF MOVING PICTURE MACHINES.

THIS IS THE LARGEST CATALOGUE of moving picture machines, stereopticons and exhibition supplies that has ever been published. This big catalogue fully illustrates and describes all of the apparatus used in public exhibition work, such as moving picture machines, stereopticons, gas making outfits, illustrated songs, moving picture film, etc., etc. It shows exactly what is needed for a complete outfit, tells how to select the best machine, gives valuable hints and suggestions for the beginner, and will prove an invaluable guide to anyone who is interested in exhibition work of any kind.

EVERY MACHINE FULLY GUARANTEED. Every moving picture machine, stereopticon, gas making outfit, or apparatus of any kind that is described in our special moving picture catalogue, is sold under the terms of our binding guarantee to be entirely satisfactory to the purchaser, or it may be returned to us at once, and the entire amount of money will be promptly refunded, including also the transportation charges on the shipment. No other machine on the market is sold under such a broad and liberal guarantee, a fact which is worthy of your careful consideration and which speaks volumes for the quality of our merchandise.

Don't fail to send for this BIG SPECIAL CATALOGUE.   It will be mailed to you ABSOLUTELY FREE.

YOU CANNOT AFFORD TO OVERLOOK THE

WONDER VALUES ON THIS PAGE

OUR WONDER VALUE DISC HARROWS.

ALL STEEL FRAME AND WEIGHT BOXES.

$14.55

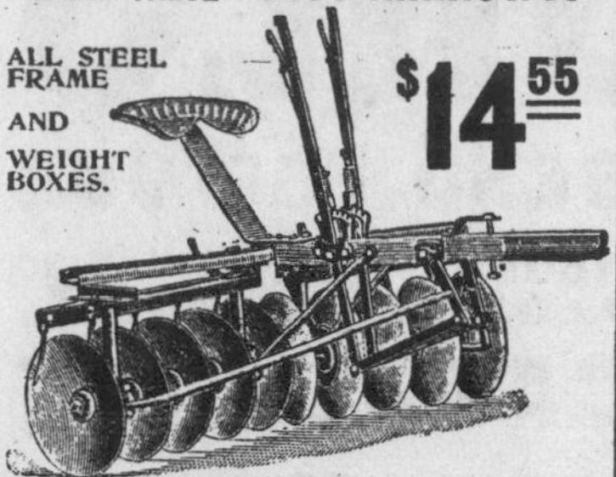

We offer these high grade up to date Double Lever Disc Harrows at prices lower than have ever been attempted upon discs of even most inferior quality. There are no more durable or perfect working disc harrows on the market and at our prices they are value which no other house can duplicate.

No. 32K435 8-16-Inch Disc Harrow. Wt., 460 lbs. Price....$14.55
No. 32K436 10-16-Inch Disc Harrow. Wt., 480 lbs. Price....$15.95
No. 32K437 12-16-Inch Disc Harrow. Wt., 500 lbs. Price....$17.35
No. 32K438 14-16-Inch Disc Harrow. Wt., 515 lbs. Price....$18.95
No. 32K439 16-16-Inch Disc Harrow. Wt., 530 lbs. Price....$20.65

OUR WONDER VALUE PONY GANG PLOWS

$12.87

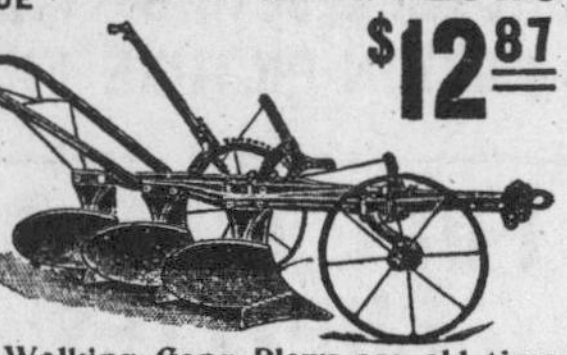

These Walking Gang Plows are old time favorites. Perfectly adapted for all kinds of shallow plowing and especially desirable for orchard cultivation. Each plow bottom is 9 inches wide and the entire width of cut of the plow is 27 inches. Price is for the plow complete, as shown in the illustration. Plows with chilled or combination bottoms furnished with three extra chilled shares, but no extra shares are furnished with No. 32K432.

No. 32K430 Chilled Pony Gang Plow. Wt., 295 lbs. Price....$12.87
No. 32K431 Combination Pony Gang Plow. Wt., 295 lbs. Price....$14.55
No. 32K432 Steel Pony Gang Plow. Wt., 295 lbs. Price....$17.85

OUR WONDER VALUE BRUSH AND GENERAL PURPOSE PLOWS.

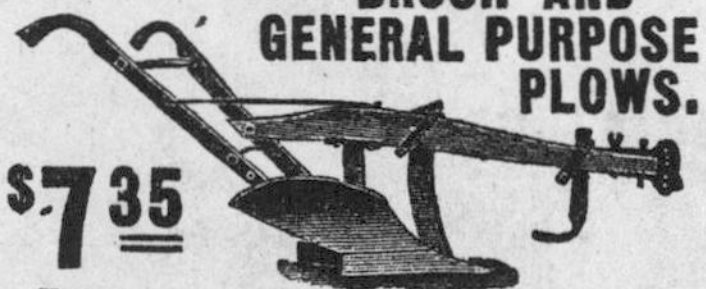

$7.35

This is one of the most popular styles of plows on the market, as it serves the purpose of a brush plow and its shape also makes it possible to use it for tame sod or stubble plowing. Moldboard, landside and share are of solid steel. This is a strong, serviceable plow and one for which every farmer has need. Price is for the plow complete, as shown in the illustration.

No. 32K415 12-Inch Brush Plow. Wt., 85 lbs. Price....$7.35
No. 32K416 14-Inch Brush Plow. Wt., 90 lbs. Price....$7.70

OUR WONDER VALUE ROD BREAKING PLOWS.

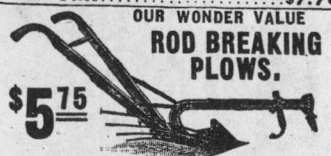

$5.75

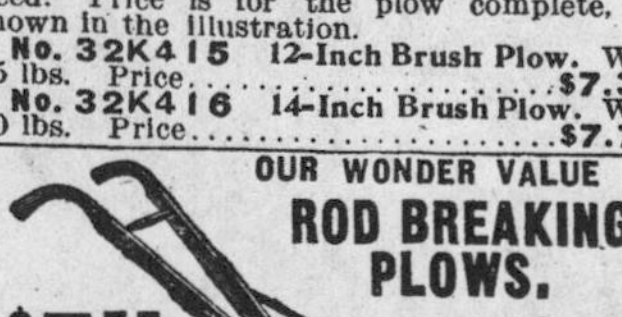

These are the highest grade and best built plows of their type. Have solid steel beam and are well braced throughout. Adjustable steel rods take the place of a moldboard. Share and fin cutter are of solid steel. Price is for plow complete, as shown in the illustration, and one extra share.

No. 32K420 12-Inch Rod Breaking Plow. Wt., 63 lbs. Price....$5.75
No. 32K421 14-Inch Rod Breaking Plow. Wt., 64 lbs. Price....$5.95
No. 32K422 16-Inch Rod Breaking Plow. Wt., 67 lbs. Price....$6.15

NOW IS THE TIME FOR YOU TO BUY.

We can save you big money on farm implements and machinery of all kinds. The articles shown on this page are selected from our regular stock and are but examples of the astonishing value represented by every farm implement and machine shown in this catalogue.

WHILE OUR PRICES ARE ABOUT ONE-HALF WHAT OTHERS ASK, no one can furnish you with a superior quality of goods. If extra fine quality, absolutely perfect and up to date goods at a saving of nearly one-half to you will bring your order, we are entitled to all of your business on farm machinery. Our guarantee to please you in every way or return your money (an offer which is made by no other house in the world) is so very liberal that our farm machinery for our own protection must be right.

WE GUARANTEE TO SATISFY YOU or you get every cent of your money back and freight charges both ways, and we repeat, if you are not satisfied in every way with any piece of farm machinery purchased from us, return it at our expense and we will refund your money along with any freight charges you may have paid out.

You will always find our quality the highest and our prices the lowest.

OUR WONDER VALUE STEEL WALKING PLOWS

OTHERS ASK $12.00 TO $15.00 FOR NO BETTER.

$7.73

SHARE, MOLDBOARD AND LANDSIDE MADE OF SOFT CENTER STEEL.

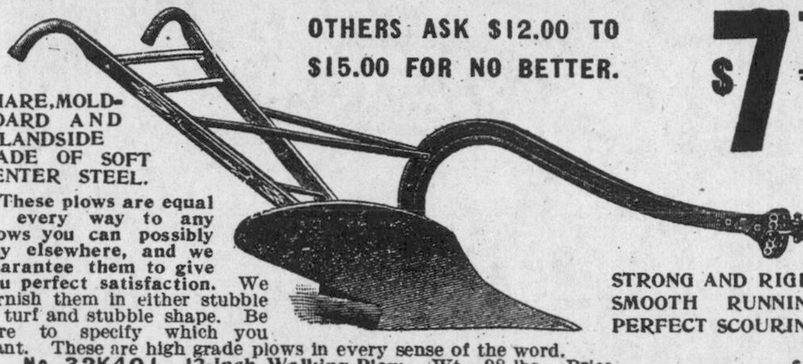

STRONG AND RIGID, SMOOTH RUNNING, PERFECT SCOURING.

These plows are equal in every way to any plows you can possibly buy elsewhere, and we guarantee them to give you perfect satisfaction. We furnish them in either stubble or turf and stubble shape. Be sure to specify which you want. These are high grade plows in every sense of the word.

No. 32K401 12-Inch Walking Plow. Wt., 98 lbs. Price....$7.73
No. 32K402 14-Inch Walking Plow. Wt., 103 lbs. Price....8.44
No. 32K403 16-Inch Walking Plow. Wt., 107 lbs. Price....9.42

OUR WONDER VALUE STEEL SULKY PLOWS

$24.75

OUR PRICE MEANS A SAVING TO YOU OF FROM $10.00 TO $15.00.

HIGH LIFT

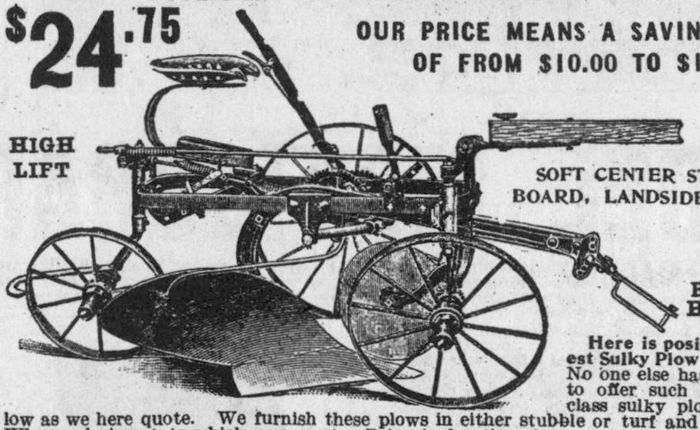

SOFT CENTER STEEL MOLDBOARD, LANDSIDE AND SHARE.

BEAM HITCH

Here is positively the greatest Sulky Plow offer ever made. No one else has ever been able to offer such high grade, first class sulky plows for prices so low as we here quote. We furnish these plows in either stubble or turf and stubble bottom. When ordering state which you want. Price is for the plow complete with pole, neckyoke, three-horse evener, weed hook and rolling coulter.

No. 32K405 14-Inch Sulky Plow. Wt., 455 lbs. Price....$24.75
No. 32K406 16-Inch Sulky Plow. Wt., 460 lbs. Price....25.65

OUR WONDER VALUE STEEL GANG PLOWS

$39.95

EQUAL IN EVERY WAY TO GANG PLOWS WHICH OTHERS SELL FOR FROM $50.00 TO $60.00

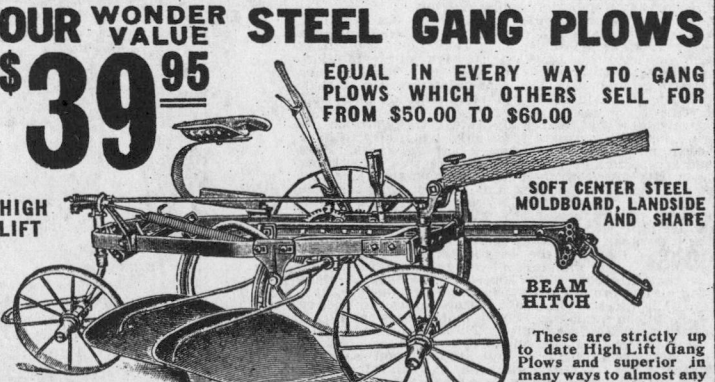

HIGH LIFT

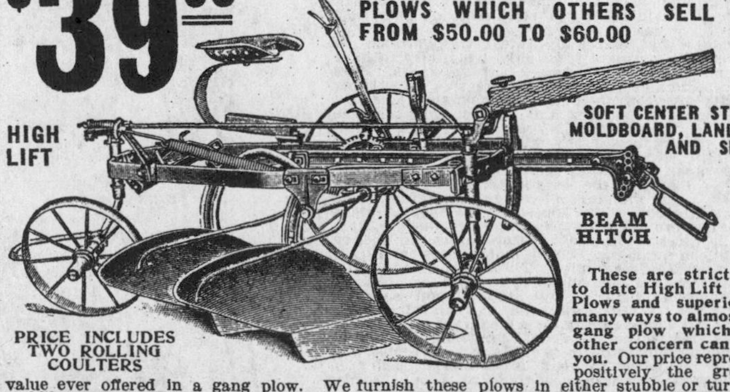

SOFT CENTER STEEL MOLDBOARD, LANDSIDE AND SHARE

BEAM HITCH

PRICE INCLUDES TWO ROLLING COULTERS

These are strictly up to date High Lift Gang Plows and superior in many ways to almost any gang plow which any other concern can offer you. Our price represents positively the greatest value ever offered in a gang plow. We furnish these plows in either stubble or turf and stubble shape. When ordering specify which you want. Furnished complete with pole, neckyoke, weed hooks, two rolling coulters and four-horse evener.

No. 32K410 12-Inch Gang Plow. Wt., 675 lbs. Price....$39.95
No. 32K411 14-Inch Gang Plow. Wt., 680 lbs. Price....40.85

OUR WONDER VALUE CULTIVATORS.

$17.65

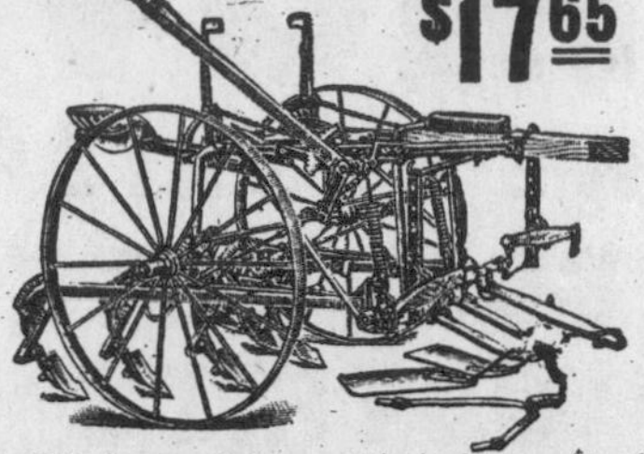

This is one of the most desirable combined Riding and Walking Cultivators on the market. All steel, excepting the pole and hitches. Wheels have wide tires and dustproof, oil-tight long distance bearings, and can be adjusted from 4 to 5 feet wide.

No. 32K450 4-Shovel Break Pin Cultivator. Wt., 410 lbs. Price....$17.65
No. 32K451 6-Shovel Break Pin Cultivator. Wt., 425 lbs. Price....$18.15
No. 32K452 8-Shovel Break Pin Cultivator. Wt., 435 lbs. Price....$18.70
No. 32K453 4-Shovel Spring Trip Cultivator. Wt., 435 lbs. Price....$19.25
No. 32K454 6-Shovel Spring Trip Cultivator. Wt., 465 lbs. Price....$20.65

$3.43 OUR WONDER VALUE ANGLE BAR HARROWS

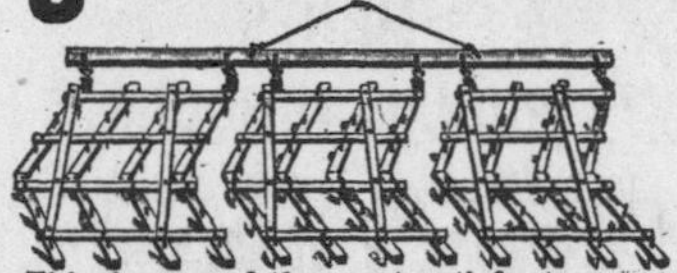

This is one of the most satisfactory wood frame harrows made. Will harrow lengthwise of sod and not track. Frame of seasoned oak, strongly riveted at each tooth and firmly braced. Teeth are ½ inch square. Price includes draw bar.

No. 32K440 48-Tooth Angle Bar Harrow. Wt., 125 lbs. Price....$3.43
No. 32K441 60-Tooth Angle Bar Harrow. Wt., 150 lbs. Price....$4.29
No. 32K442 72-Tooth Angle Bar Harrow. Wt., 190 lbs. Price....$5.15
No. 32K443 90-Tooth Angle Bar Harrow. Wt., 210 lbs. Price....$6.43

OUR WONDER VALUE SPRING TOOTH HARROWS

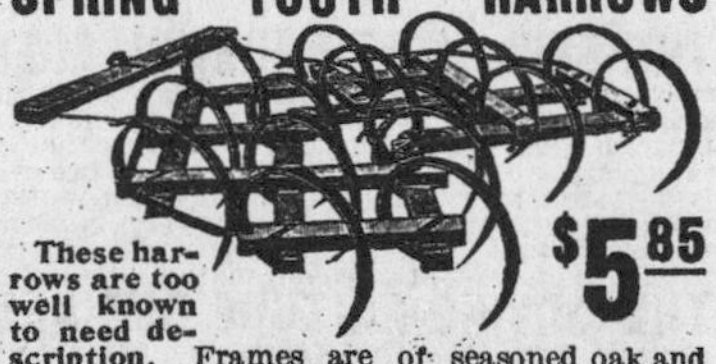

$5.85

These harrows are too well known to need description. Frames are of seasoned oak and fitted with stump guards around the sides and front. Teeth are standard size, made of high quality tempered spring steel and are firmly secured. Price includes draw bar.

No. 32K445 16-Tooth Harrow. Wt., 160 lbs. Price....$5.85
No. 32K446 18-Tooth Harrow. Wt., 170 lbs. Price....$6.65
No. 32K447 20-Tooth Harrow. Wt., 180 lbs. Price....$7.45

OUR WONDER VALUE COMBINED FEED CUTTER AND SHREDDER.

$18.95

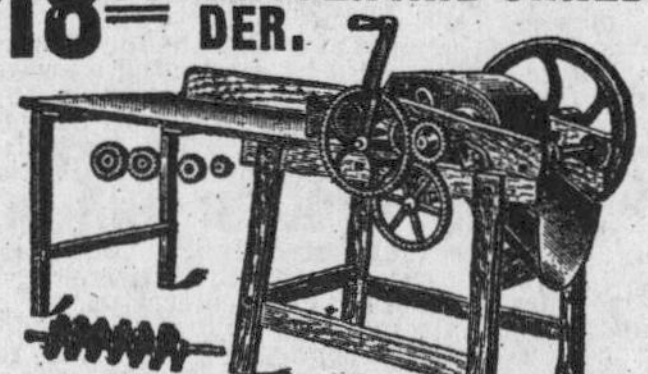

You cannot buy the equal of this machine elsewhere for less than $30.00. It cuts the fodder into short lengths and at the same time shreds each piece into small parts. Can be run by either hand or power. Requires from one to two-horse power to run it. Has 11-inch cylinder head, with thirty-eight knives. Price includes crank and pulley.

No. 32K460 Feed Cutter and Shredder. Wt., 325 lbs. Price....$18.95

OUR WONDER VALUE PRAIRIE BREAKING PLOWS.

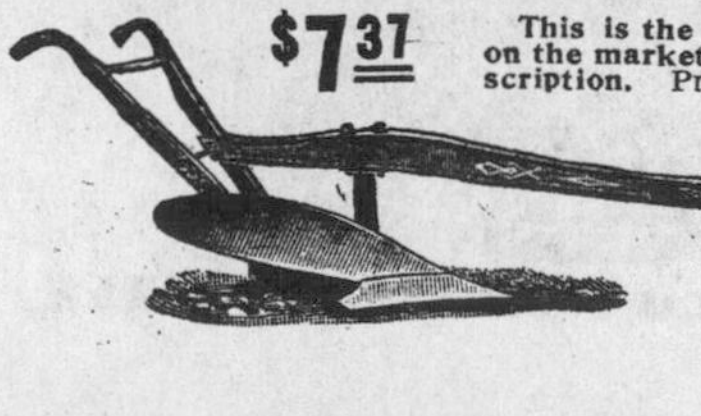

$7.37

This is the most popular style of Prairie Breaking Plow on the market and is too well known to need further description. Price is for the plow complete, as shown in the illustration and with one extra share. We will furnish plow with gauge wheel and rolling coulter for $1.85 extra.

No. 32K425 12-Inch Prairie Breaking Plow. Wt., 135 lbs. Price....$7.37
No. 32K426 14-Inch Prairie Breaking Plow. Wt., 137 lbs. Price....$7.65
No. 32K427 16-Inch Prairie Breaking Plow. Wt., 140 lbs. Price....$7.85

OUR WONDER VALUE SWEEP HORSE POWERS.

These powers are of standard design, strongly constructed, and will give splendid service and continued satisfaction. Shafts are steel and boxes babbitted; have high and low speed shafts. Illustration shows a two and four-horse power. Six-horse powers have four sweeps. Price includes about 20 feet of tumbling rod, three couplings, rod block, platform, and spring hitch for each sweep. Lead poles are furnished with two and four-horse powers.

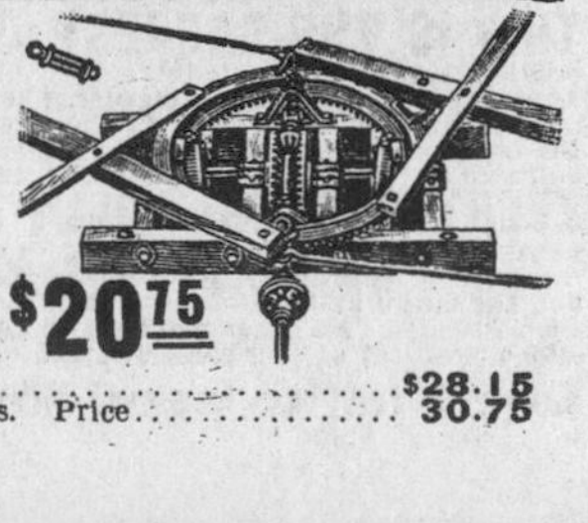

$20.75

No. 32K465 Two-Horse Power. Wt., 725 lbs. Price....$20.75
No. 32K466 Four-Horse Power. Wt., 1,015 lbs. Price....$28.15
No. 32K467 Six-Horse Power. Wt., 1,050 lbs. Price....30.75

KENWOOD STEEL WALKING PLOWS $8 62 AND UP

Made in STUBBLE and TURF AND STUBBLE Shapes

YOU CANNOT BUY A BETTER PLOW NO MATTER WHAT PRICE YOU PAY

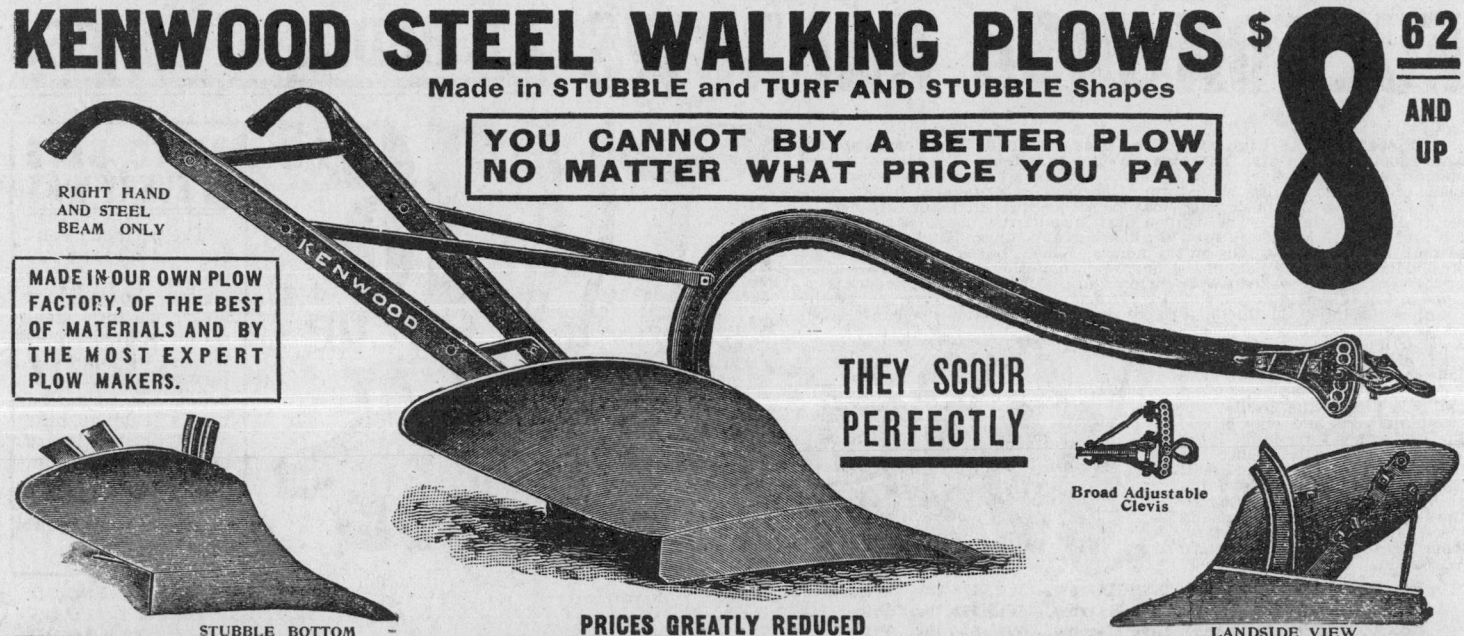

RIGHT HAND AND STEEL BEAM ONLY

MADE IN OUR OWN PLOW FACTORY, OF THE BEST OF MATERIALS AND BY THE MOST EXPERT PLOW MAKERS.

THEY SCOUR PERFECTLY

Broad Adjustable Clevis

STUBBLE BOTTOM

LANDSIDE VIEW

PRICES GREATLY REDUCED

WE WILL STAKE OUR REPUTATION ON THESE PLOWS for we know

them to be positively the best plows it is possible for anyone to produce. We make every part of them in our own perfectly equipped plow factory, under the personal supervision of one of the most expert plow makers in the country, a man with years of experience in this line of work, and one to whom any of the well known plow manufacturers would be glad to intrust their plow making. We use only the highest quality of materials, every ounce of which is subjected to most critical inspection before it is permitted to enter into the construction of the plow, and every plow after completion is inspected to insure its being absolutely perfect before it is sent to our customers. **We have confidence in these plows** because we know of what kind of material they are made and how they are made. **We are proud of them** because we feel that their splendid quality, perfect construction and superb finish are all due to our own efforts. We want every farmer in the United States to try our plows, and use them in comparison with any other make, for we know that their high quality will do much to convince one of the superior quality and value of our entire line of farm implements and induce them to order from us. For this reason we have exerted particular effort to produce

these plows in a manner which will enable us to offer them at a price so much lower than even large dealers are compelled to pay for the standard makes of plows, that no one in justice to himself can afford to buy a plow of other make until after he has given us an opportunity to demonstrate to his complete satisfaction the superior merit and value of our Kenwood plows. To make these low prices it has been necessary for us to exercise every possible economy by buying our materials in large lots and by manufacturing our plows in large quantities; this we have done, and owing to the fact that **we sell direct from our factory to you**, there is but one small profit added to the actual cost, and we are enabled to offer these plows, the best that can possibly be produced by anyone, for a price so low that we know it is an impossibility for any concern to offer plows of equal grade for less than from one-fourth to one-half more than our price. Order a Kenwood plow subject to the terms of our Free Trial Offer on page 536 of this catalogue, and if after using our plow you are not satisfied that it is the equal of any plow you can buy at any price, and a much better plow than you can buy for anything like our price, send it back to us at our expense and let us refund your money and freight charges, and you will not be out one cent. Surely you cannot ask for a more liberal proposition than this.

GENERAL DESCRIPTION. For long lived, easy running and perfect

scouring qualities these plows cannot be excelled. They are built on lines which insure the greatest possible strength and wearing qualities at every required point. Bottoms are strongly constructed and braced and have malleable frog. Shares and moldboards are made of special soft center plow steel, and each consists of practically three layers of steel; the outer layers are hard tempered, making them capable of high polish, and possessed of great wear resisting qualities. The inside or center layer is of a different quality of steel and is soft and tough; this to strengthen the part so it will withstand the hard usage to which a plow is subjected. Shares and mold boards are double shinned and shares have reinforced points, thus protecting the places at which the wear is greatest, and one will readily appreciate how much longer a share and moldboard so reinforced will last than when not so constructed. The adjustable slip heel is a most convenient and reliable means of regulating the depth of furrow. Beams are extra strong, double ribbed forged steel, with high curve to prevent fouling in trashy land. Clevis is heavy malleable iron throughout and has ample adjustment for depth of land. Each clevis jaw has a hook at the end to which the crosshead brace can be instantly attached without means of bolt when it is desired to shift the crossheads from one side to the other. Handles are heavy and made of first quality oak, perfectly formed and highly finished, they are set wide apart and have beam and set braces of flat bar steel; rounds are reinforced with steel stay rods. **These plows are perfect scouring and easy running** because, in addition to the above qualities, the shares and moldboards are of proper shape and fitted and ground with absolute accuracy. The entire plow is perfectly balanced, correctly proportioned, rigidly braced and designed with a view to combining every known improvement in walking plow construction, with the highest possible quality of workmanship and materials. The finish of our plows throughout is neat, attractive and of a very high order. You will be as well pleased with their appearance as with their many other splendid qualities. We furnish these plows in both stubble and turf and stubble shapes.

FOR PONY PLOWS AND SHOVEL PLOWS, SEE PAGE 524.

YOU NEVER SAW A MORE STRONGLY BRACED PLOW

PERFECTLY BALANCED — RIGID AT EVERY POINT

REAR VIEW

KENWOOD STEEL TURF AND STUBBLE PLOWS are of the shape and design

shown in the large illustration. They are also known as general purpose or Scotch Clipper plows. This shape of plow is without question the most popular in almost every section of the country and more of them are sold than all other shapes combined. The moldboard has a long easy turn, adapting the plows especially for tame sod plowing, the shape of the moldboard being such that the turf is turned completely under and trash and weeds are well covered. They are especially desirable for turning under clover, timothy or alfalfa sod and heavy stubble, also in old pasture land, adobe and clay soils and for deep plowing, and they are excellent pulverizers. They are the best plows for use on farms where crops are rotated and for general purpose work; in fact they have a greater range of usefulness than any other style of plow you can buy, and are as well adapted for old ground as they are for sod. Made with steel beam and in right hand shapes only.

KENWOOD STEEL STUBBLE PLOWS are of the exact

same construction and equipment as our turf and stubble plows, with the exception of the shape of the moldboard which is like that shown in the illustration of the stubble bottom. This shape of plow is a very popular one and with the exception of the turf and stubble shape more stubble shape plows are used than all other shapes combined. The moldboard is long and high, but with not so long a sweep as the turf and stubble moldboard; it will scour perfectly in the most difficult soil. They are especially adapted for use in stubble, old ground and light soils. They are excellent pulverizers and will always leave the soil in prime condition. Made with steel beam and in right hand shapes only.

WE CAN ALWAYS FURNISH REPAIRS AND EXTRAS for these

plows, and, as we make them ourselves, at the lowest factory cost. Never let the repair question influence you against ordering from us. We list extra shares in connection with the plows so that you can order them with your plow and save freight.

NO PLOW CAN BE MORE STRONGLY MADE

BOTTOM CONSTRUCTION

COMPARE OUR PLOWS WITH ANY OTHER PLOWS MADE

WE know that the more you see of other plows, the more convinced you will be that our plows are the best value you can buy anywhere.

PRICES are for plows complete as shown in the large illustration and fitted with one steel share only. Cast shares may be used if desired, and we are prepared to furnish them as well as extra steel shares at prices quoted below. We recommend that you order extra shares when ordering your plow so that they may be shipped with the plow and save you in freight charges. Shipped knocked down from factory in Southeastern Wisconsin.

ALL PARTS REINFORCED AT EVERY WEARING POINT

LANDSIDE   FROG

SHARE   SLIP HEEL   MOLD-BOARD

Steel Fin Cutter

No. 32K502	12-inch Stubble Plow.	Wt., 100 lbs.	Price............$ 8.62
No. 32K503	14-inch Stubble Plow.	Wt., 105 lbs.	Price................ 9.37
No. 32K504	16-inch Stubble Plow.	Wt., 110 lbs.	Price................ 10.12
No. 32K517	12-inch Turf and Stubble Plow.	Wt., 105 lbs.	Price................ 8.82
No. 32K518	14-inch Turf and Stubble Plow.	Wt., 110 lbs.	Price........ 9.67
No. 32K519	16-inch Turf and Stubble Plow.	Wt., 115 lbs.	Price........ 10.52
No. 32K523	12-inch Extra Steel Share.	Wt., 11 lbs.	Price................ 1.93
No. 32K524	14-inch Extra Steel Share.	Wt., 12 lbs.	Price................ 2.13
No. 32K525	16-inch Extra Steel Share.	Wt., 13 lbs.	Price................$2.33
No. 32K530	12-inch Chilled Share.	Wt., 11 lbs.	Price................ .40
No. 32K531	14-inch Chilled Share.	Wt., 12 lbs.	Price................ .45
No. 32K532	16-inch Chilled Share.	Wt., 13 lbs.	Price................ .50
No. 32K535	Steel Fin Cutter	Wt., 4 lbs.	Price................ .50
No. 32K536	Gauge Wheel	Wt., 12 lbs.	Price................ .60
No. 32K537	Rolling Coulter	Wt., 16 lbs.	Price................ 1.75

FULTON DISC HARROWS AT REDUCED PRICES

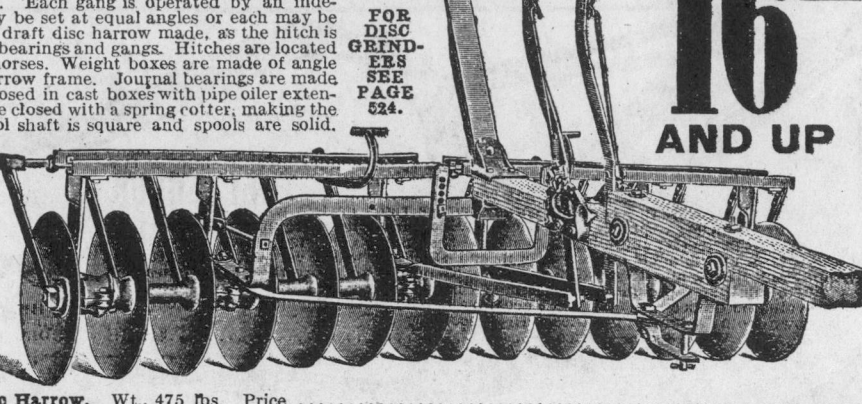

$16.75 AND UP

FOR DISC GRINDERS SEE PAGE 524.

UP TO DATE IN EVERY WAY

The perfectly constructed all steel frame, angle steel weight boxes, foot lever, spring steel scrapers, highly polished, correctly formed discs, dustproof oil soaked maple bearings, pipe oilers, double levers and low down hitch, all combine to make the Fulton the best disc harrow that money can buy.

These are the highest grade, best designed, best constructed, and most durable disc harrows on the market. They are made of steel throughout except the tongue and hitches, which are very heavy and made of the best quality of material. Each gang is operated by an independent lever so that both gangs may be set at equal angles or each may be set at different angles. The lightest draft disc harrow made, as the hitch is low and the pull is directly from the bearings and gangs. Hitches are located so that no neck weight falls on the horses. Weight boxes are made of angle steel bars and form a part of the harrow frame. Journal bearings are made of the very best oil soaked maple enclosed in cast boxes with pipe oiler extensions to top of weight boxes, which are closed with a spring cotter, making the bearings absolutely dustproof. Spool shaft is square and spools are solid. Fitted with steel scrapers. Scraper levers are within easy reach of the feet. Discs are carefully ground and tempered. The 8-disc harrow has two-horse hitch and cuts 4 feet; the 10-disc has two-horse hitch and cuts 5 feet; the 12-disc has three-horse hitch and cuts 6 feet; the 14-disc has four-horse hitch and cuts 7 feet; the 16-disc has four-horse hitch and cuts 8 feet. Better disc harrows cannot be obtained at any price. Shipped knocked down from factory in Southeastern Wisconsin.

No. 32K800	8 16-inch Disc Harrow.	Wt., 475 lbs.	Price	$16.75
No. 32K801	10 16-inch Disc Harrow.	Wt., 495 lbs.	Price	18.55
No. 32K802	12 16-inch Disc Harrow.	Wt., 515 lbs.	Price	19.90
No. 32K803	14 16-inch Disc Harrow.	Wt., 530 lbs.	Price	21.20
No. 32K804	16 16-inch Disc Harrow.	Wt., 545 lbs.	Price	23.85

KENWOOD REVERSIBLE DISC HARROWS.

$15.32

ONE OF THE MOST POPULAR IMPLEMENTS WE EVER PRODUCED.

A FIRST CLASS DISC HARROW AND DISC CULTIVATOR COMBINED IN ONE MACHINE.

This machine is growing in popularity every year and although it is designed especially for gardeners and small farmers, it is adapted to a great range of work and will be found exceedingly useful on even very large farms. Can be used either as a disc harrow or as a disc cultivator. Discs can be set at any desired angle and can be reversed to throw the dirt in or out. They can be set close together for harrowing or can be separated to 14½ inches apart for cultivating corn or small grain, so as to straddle the row. When discs are close together, the 6-disc machine cuts about 2½ feet, and the 8-disc machine about 3½ feet. Can be used for cultivating grain, hilling potatoes, cultivating tobacco, etc. Fruit growers and nurserymen use this implement to most excellent advantage by setting the gangs together and running it between rows of blackberries, grapes, etc., for which work an ordinary disc harrow would be too large and too wide. Discs can be tilted at either end to run on an incline, so as to hill or trench. Discs are carefully ground and tempered and fitted with scrapers. Neckyoke and two-horse hitch furnished with each machine. Shipped knocked down from factory in Southwestern Ohio.

No. 32K830 6 16-inch Reversible Disc Harrow. Wt., 260 lbs.
Price $15.32

No. 32K831 8 16-inch Reversible Disc Harrow. Wt., 275 lbs.
Price 16.58

KENWOOD ADJUSTABLE TONGUE TRUCK.

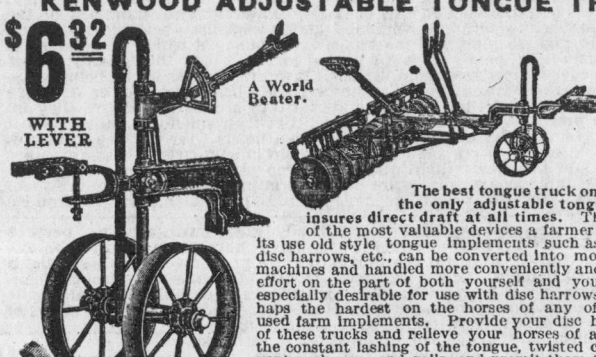

$6.32 WITH LEVER

A World Beater.

$4.98 Without Lever

The best tongue truck on the market and the only adjustable tongue truck which insures direct draft at all times. This truck is one of the most valuable devices a farmer can own, for by its use old style tongue implements such as mowers, drills, disc harrows, etc., can be converted into modern tongueless machines and handled more conveniently and with much less effort on the part of both yourself and your horses. It is especially desirable for use with disc harrows, which are perhaps the hardest on the horses of any of the commonly used farm implements. Provide your disc harrow with one of these trucks and relieve your horses of all neck weight, the constant lashing of the tongue, twisted collars, etc., prevent neck sores and galls, and permit them to work free and easy, without irritation and fret. Your horses will do more work and do it easier and better than it was ever done before, and your harrow will also accomplish much better work, for the truck will enable you to fix the tongue at the proper height to give the discs the desired suction and make them cut the same depth all the way across. This truck is made entirely of malleable iron and steel and will last a lifetime, for there is nothing about it to break or get out of order. Hitch and tongue castings can be adjusted to any point on the upright arch so as to accommodate hitches of almost any height, and both hitch and tongue will at all times retain perfectly direct draft and allow the wheels of the truck to turn square under the tongue casting, permitting your machine to be turned in its own tracks without strain. We furnish strap irons so that a forward pole can be attached if desired. The pole will carry no weight and only serve to prevent the horses from backing onto the machine. We furnish truck with lever as shown in the larger illustration, and without lever as shown in the smaller illustration, but recommend that you purchase truck with lever. This feature is one of great convenience, as it enables you to raise the hitch without stopping your team; a great advantage when working a field having hard and soft soil. Height of truck without lever is 35½ inches and of truck with lever, 38½ inches. Wheels are steel, 16 inches in diameter with 3-inch concave tires and dust caps. They are set wide enough apart to straddle rows. All parts are well finished and handsomely painted. Truck can be easily and quickly attached to any machine by simply sawing off all but about 4 feet of the tongue and bolting the tongue casting to the stub tongue as shown in smaller illustration. Bolts for attaching are furnished with truck. Shipped from factory in Central Iowa.

| No. 32K835 | Tongue Truck, without lever. | Wt., 70 lbs. | Price | $4.98 |
| No. 32K836 | Tongue Truck, with lever. | Wt., 80 lbs. | Price | 6.32 |

FOR SMALL ONE-HORSE HARROWS SEE PAGE 524.

KENWOOD "U" BAR STEEL LEVER HARROWS.

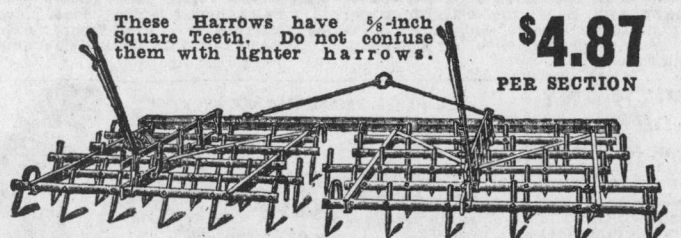

These Harrows have ⅝-inch Square Teeth. Do not confuse them with lighter harrows.

$4.87 PER SECTION

The best designed and best constructed "U" bar harrows made. Frames are made of steel throughout and are braced with diagonal cross braces. Teeth can be set at any angle by adjusting the ratchet levers, or harrow can be tilted to run on the runners. The teeth are ⅝ inch square and are firmly secured by perfect fastenings. Made in sections, each section having 30 teeth and cutting about 5 feet wide. Each corner of each section is provided with runners. Illustration shows a 60-tooth harrow. Don't expect a two-section harrow when you order No. 32K840, it consists of one section only. Drawbar is furnished with two, three or four-section harrows. When comparing prices don't overlook the fact that the teeth of these harrows are ⅝ inch square. ½-inch teeth are too light for this style of harrow. Shipped knocked down from factory in Southwestern Ohio.

No. 32K840	30-Tooth, One-Section Lever Harrow.	Wt., 130 lbs.	Price	$4.87
No. 32K841	60-Tooth, Two-Section Lever Harrow.	Wt., 250 lbs.	Price	9.74
No. 32K842	90-Tooth, Three-Section Lever Harrow.	Wt., 395 lbs.	Price	14.60
No. 32K843	120-Tooth, Four-Section Lever Harrow.	Wt., 535 lbs.	Price	19.45

KENWOOD BOSS HARROWS.

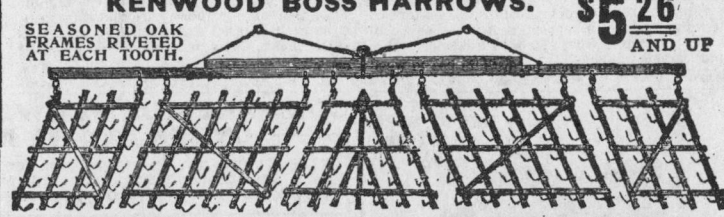

SEASONED OAK FRAMES RIVETED AT EACH TOOTH.

$5.26 AND UP

We guarantee these to be the best boss harrows made. The frames of our harrows are made of best quality seasoned oak, strongly riveted at each tooth and firmly braced. To compete with our wonderfully low prices, others are offering harrows made of cheap grades of hardwood and in many other ways inferior to ours. Do not be misled; insist upon getting a harrow of quality equal to ours and made of the best quality of oak timber. Teeth are ½ inch square. Sections are independently connected to drawbar with drop link clevises, allowing flexibility. The 60-tooth harrow cuts 10½ feet, has one center and one side section and a two-horse drawbar. The 78-tooth harrow cuts 13 feet, has one center and two narrow side sections, and a two-horse drawbar. The 102-tooth harrow cuts 16½ feet, has one center and two wide side sections, and a three-horse drawbar. The 150-tooth harrow cuts 26 feet, has one center, two wide and two narrow side sections, and a four-horse drawbar which is fitted with a sheave pulley and roller chain draft equalizer. If you purchase a 150-tooth harrow you can use it as a 78-tooth or as a 102-tooth harrow, by separating the sections and using a shorter drawbar. Shipped knocked down from factory in Southeastern Wisconsin.

No. 32K852	60-Tooth,	Two-Section Boss Harrow.	Wt., 155 lbs.	Price	$5.26
No. 32K853	78-Tooth,	Three-Section Boss Harrow.	Wt., 190 lbs.	Price	6.74
No. 32K854	102-Tooth,	Three-Section Boss Harrow.	Wt., 240 lbs.	Price	8.87
No. 32K855	150-Tooth,	Five-Section Boss Harrow.	Wt., 390 lbs.	Price	13.12

KENWOOD WOOD FRAME, STEEL LINED SPRING TOOTH HARROWS.

SEASONED OAK FRAMES.

STEEL LINED.

$7¹²

ANOTHER REDUCTION IN PRICE.

Especially adapted for use in timber country. Made in two sections, hinged and flexible at center. Frames are well seasoned oak and fitted with stump guard around the sides and front and **lined with steel on the bottoms.** Teeth are standard weight, length and size, made of the best quality of spring steel, finely tempered in oil, and firmly secured to the bars. The 16-tooth harrow cuts 5 feet; 18-tooth, 6 feet, and 20-tooth, 7 feet wide. Price includes drawbar. Don't buy an unlined harrow; it would cost you nearly as much as a lined harrow and wear out in a very short time. Shipped knocked down from factory in Southeastern Wisconsin.

No. 32K864	16-Tooth Lined Harrow.	Wt., 170 lbs.	Price	$7.12
No. 32K865	18-Tooth Lined Harrow.	Wt., 188 lbs.	Price	7.88
No. 32K866	20-Tooth Lined Harrow.	Wt., 194 lbs.	Price	8.76
No. 32K867	Extra Harrow Teeth.	Wt., 5 lbs.	Price, each	.22

KENWOOD SPRING TOOTH STEEL LEVER HARROWS.

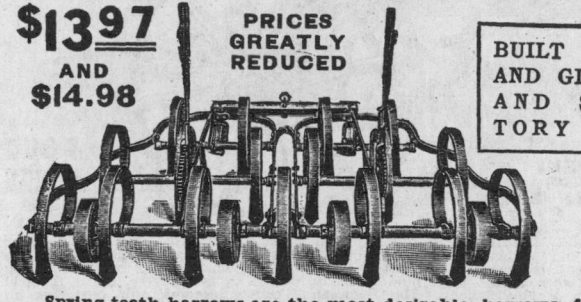

$13⁹⁷
AND
$14.98

PRICES GREATLY REDUCED

BUILT TO LAST AND GIVE LONG AND SATISFACTORY SERVICE

Spring tooth harrows are the most desirable harrows for use in timber country, and our spring tooth lever harrows are the very best harrows made of this description. They are constructed of steel and iron throughout and furnished with special design standard weight length and size teeth. The levers give the teeth any desired angle and depth. The illustration shows a wheel harrow, but we can furnish either on wheels or on shoes. Harrow has 17 teeth, cuts about 6 feet wide, is made in two section and is hinged and flexible at center. Price includes drawbar. Shipped knocked down from factory in Southeastern Wisconsin.

No. 32K875	Spring Tooth Harrow, on wheels.	Wt., 300 lbs.	Price	$14.98
No. 32K876	Spring Tooth Harrow, on shoes.	Wt., 300 lbs.	Price	13.97
No. 32K977	Extra Spring Teeth.	Wt., 5 lbs.	Price, each	.27

FOR SMALL ONE-HORSE HARROWS SEE PAGE 524.

KENWOOD SCOTCH HARROWS.

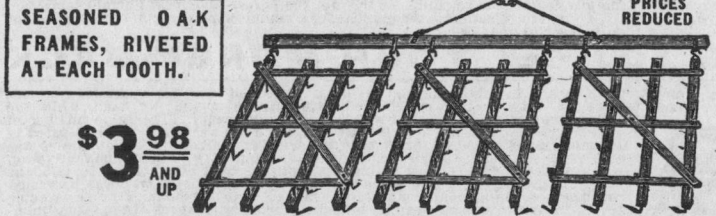

SEASONED OAK FRAMES, RIVETED AT EACH TOOTH.

PRICES REDUCED

$3⁹⁸
AND UP

This style of harrow is so popular and well known that it needs no description. Our Scotch harrows are made with seasoned oak frames, riveted at each tooth and strongly braced. Teeth are ½-inch square. Made in sections and cuts about 2 feet wide for each twelve teeth. Price includes drawbar. Shipped knocked down from factory in Southeastern Wisconsin.

No. 32K881	48-Tooth, Two-Section Scotch Harrow.	Wt., 115 lbs.	Price	$3.98
No. 32K882	60-Tooth, Two-Section Scotch Harrow.	Wt., 135 lbs.	Price	5.10
No. 32K883	72-Tooth, Three-Section Scotch Harrow.	Wt., 175 lbs.	Price	6.08
No. 32K884	90-Tooth, Three-Section Scotch Harrow.	Wt., 195 lbs.	Price	7.60

KENWOOD WOOD FRAME LEVER HARROWS.

REDUCED IN PRICE

SEASONED OAK FRAMES, RIVETED AT EACH TOOTH.

$4⁵²
AND UP

Very strong and durable, lighter than steel. Frame is made of seasoned oak, strongly riveted at each tooth, and connected by iron and steel pivot plates and cross pieces. Made in sections, each section having thirty-five ⅓-inch square teeth and cutting about 5 feet wide. The teeth can be set at any angle by adjusting the ratchet levers, or harrow can be tilted to run on the runners. Price includes drawbar. Shipped knocked down from factory in Southeastern Wisconsin.

No. 32K890	35-Tooth, One-Section Lever Harrow.	Wt., 100 lbs.	Price	$4.52
No. 32K891	70-Tooth, Two-Section Lever Harrow.	Wt., 195 lbs.	Price	8.92
No. 32K892	105-Tooth, Three-Section Lever Harrow.	Wt., 290 lbs.	Price	13.42
No. 32K893	140-Tooth, Four-Section Lever Harrow.	Wt., 385 lbs.	Price	17.87

$4⁹⁸ KENWOOD HARROW CART.
LOWER IN PRICE THAN EVER BEFORE.

ACKNOWLEDGED TO BE THE BEST HARROW CART ON THE MARKET.

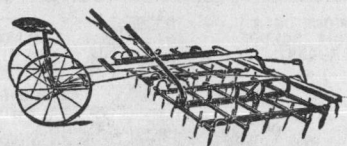

A harrow cart helps to make farming easy and profitable. Our harrow cart is a wonderfully easy rider, is remarkably low in price, and is guaranteed to be the best harrow cart made. It has essential and valuable features which will not be found in any other cart. Is strongly built and simple in construction. In operation the driver is always in line with and facing his team. The cart moves smoothly and steadily behind the harrow, riding easily with no wabbling or jolting. Made entirely of steel and iron except the connecting bar which is made of wood to give a better connection between the harrow and the cart. This bar attaches to the center of the harrow drawbar and in addition there are two iron rods with adjusting links which connect diagonally from the cart under the connecting bar and onto the drawbar, providing a better hitch than will be found on any other cart. The wheels are 24 inches in diameter with 3-inch convex tires. The bearings swivel at inner ends of axle and each wheel turns independent of the other. Turns corners perfectly. No loose nuts to lose and no rickety parts. Can be made into a first class tongue cart by bolting a tongue onto the cart in place of the connecting bar and attaching a draw iron onto the rear end of the tongue. Shipped knocked down from factory in Southeastern Wisconsin.

No. 32K898	Harrow Cart.	Wt., 85 lbs.	Price	$4.98

KENWOOD STEEL LAND ROLLERS.

$17⁴⁵
AND UP

PRICES REDUCED

PRESSED STEEL HEADS. REVERSIBLE CHILLED BEARINGS

THE EASIEST RUNNING AND MOST DURABLE LAND ROLLERS MADE.

YOU CANNOT BUY ROLLERS OF EQUAL QUALITY FOR ANYTHING LIKE OUR PRICES.

These are first class, well made and durable machines. The drums are 24 inches in diameter, made of heavy high carbon steel plates, well riveted to heavy pressed steel heads. The heavy steel shaft runs in reversible chilled iron bearings. Each drum turns independently of the other on the shaft and the shaft turns in the bearings. Seat is mounted on a steel standard. The side bars of the platform are heavy angle steel, firmly bolted to the end brackets. The draft is light, the hitch being made directly under the tongue. Frame is arranged so that a bottom board can be placed in it and weight can be placed on the roller as desired. Don't overlook the fact that our land rollers are made with pressed steel heads, like a steam boiler. They are at least one-half better and stronger than rollers with cast iron heads and are of proportionately greater value. In weight these rollers are much lighter, though stronger than rollers with cast iron ends. This saves you considerable in freight charges and you can weight the roller as heavy as you wish by loading into the platform frame. Shipped knocked down from factory in Southwestern Ohio.

No. 32K925	6-Foot Two-Section Land Roller.	Wt., 400 lbs.	Price	$17.45
No. 32K927	7-Foot Three-Section Land Roller.	Wt., 465 lbs.	Price	19.92
No. 32K928	8-Foot Three-Section Land Roller.	Wt., 485 lbs.	Price	21.20

KENWOOD SINGLE ROW STALK CUTTER.

$18⁹⁸

ALL STEEL FRAME AND WHEELS, SIX TOOL STEEL KNIVES, TEMPERED AND GROUND, CHOP STROKE, PERFECT BALANCE, LIGHT DRAFT, DUSTPROOF BEARINGS.

POSITIVELY THE MOST PERFECT WORKING AND SERVICEABLE STALK CUTTER ON THE MARKET OUTWEARS TWO OF THE ORDINARY KIND.

Price Reduced

An indispensable tool for cutting up corn stalks, cotton, etc., in the field, to prepare the field for plowing. Well made in every respect and of the best materials. Frame and wheels are steel. Wheels are high and machine is perfectly balanced, making light draft. Knives are best tool steel carefully tempered and ground. Has a chop stroke which cuts successfully and a draft equalizing spring to offset motion of the cylinder. The stalk hooks or gatherers are steel and raise automatically with the cylinder. Boxes are adjustable and all bearings are protected from dirt and dust. We take great pride in this machine, the thousands of them we have sold have given our customers such splendid satisfaction that we regard it as one of the most successful implements it has ever been our pleasure to offer. Shipped knocked down from factory in Southeastern Wisconsin.

No. 32K950	Single Row Stalk Cutter.	Wt., 475 lbs.	Price	$18.98

$49 85 THE BONANZA WAGON BOX MANURE SPREADER

GREATEST VALUE EVER OFFERED

PRICE DOES NOT INCLUDE TRUCKS.

THE HIGHEST GRADE, THE MOST THOROUGHLY UP TO DATE, AND IN EVERY WAY THE MOST SUCCESSFUL MANURE SPREADER EVER PRODUCED, OFFERED BY US AT A PRICE WHICH IS ENTIRELY BEYOND COMPETITION AND MAKES IT POSSIBLE FOR YOU TO POSSESS ONE OF THE MOST PROFITABLE OF FARM IMPLEMENTS AS WELL AS ONE OF THE GREATEST LABOR SAVING INVENTIONS OF THE AGE WITH EVERY ASSURANCE THAT THE MACHINE WILL MORE THAN PAY FOR ITSELF IN ONE SEASON'S USE ON EVEN A VERY SMALL FARM.

30 DAYS' FREE TRIAL

ENDLESS STEEL APRON

WE GUARANTEE SAFE DELIVERY

SO SIMPLE A BOY CAN RUN IT.

SO STRONG NO LOAD CAN BREAK IT.

DO NOT TIE YOUR MONEY UP IN EXPENSIVE RUNNING GEARS. THE BONANZA CAN BE USED ON ANY ORDINARY FARM WAGON TRUCK.

FOUR FEEDS

A FIRST CLASS MANURE SPREADER is one of the most profitable implements on the farm, it is a wonderful labor saver and a great money maker. It enables the farmer to utilize to the greatest possible extent, and with the least possible amount of labor, the full value of his barnyard manure, and thereby enrich his lands, increase his crops and add to his bank account. Scientific experiments have demonstrated that common barnyard manure is the most valuable of all fertilizers, but it is a well known fact that if manure is allowed to stand in the pile, the exposure to which it will be subjected will gradually result in a loss of from one-third to one-half of its valuable fertilizing properties. For this reason, in order to derive the fullest possible benefit, the manure should be spread while it is comparatively fresh so that valuable qualities, which would otherwise be lost in the barnyard, will enter into the soil which is to produce the crops. The work of spreading manure by hand is slow and costly, to say nothing of its disagreeable features. It is hard work and one of the most dreaded jobs on the farm, and for this reason most farmers delay the spreading of manure until the best part of its fertilizing qualities are wasted, and, even then, when spread by the old dung fork method, the work is not performed in such a way as to insure every part of the field receiving its share of nourishment. The Bonanza Manure Spreader will overcome all difficulties for you. It will make manure spreading such an easy task that you will find it possible to load the machine every day or so with fresh manure and haul it to your field and spread it when it will do the most good. The machine is so light of draft that an ordinary team can pull it with ease; it is so simple to handle and operate that one of your boys can run it and leave you and your farm hands free to do other work. It is so positive in its action and so reliable in its operation that you can always rest assured that the machine will do the work properly and spread the manure evenly and in such quantities as may be required, and above all, you will always know that you are realizing every cent the manure pile is capable of producing and that the Bonanza is saving money and making money for you every day.

OUR MOST LIBERAL 30 DAYS' FREE TRIAL OFFER

TO GIVE EVERYONE AN OPPORTUNITY TO TRY, test and compare our Bonanza Wagon Box Manure Spreader with any or all manure spreaders of other make and to demonstrate to your complete satisfaction that the machine is all that we claim for it, every Bonanza Wagon Box Manure Spreader we sell is shipped with the distinct understanding and agreement that you are to have thirty days from the time you receive the shipment in which to examine, try, test and operate our machine and to compare its quality, construction and efficiency with manure spreaders of other make, and if at any time within that period you find reason to feel dissatisfied with our machine and are not convinced that it represents the greatest manure spreader value ever offered; that it is the most satisfactory working manure spreader you ever saw, that it is the most simple and most economical manure spreader to handle and operate and in every way the most desirable machine of its kind you can buy, or, to make matters short, if you are not entirely satisfied that the machine is everything we claim for it and a better machine than you can possibly purchase elsewhere for anything like our price, you can return it to us and we will gladly refund your money, together with any freight charges you may have paid. Is this not the fairest and most liberal proposition you ever read? If you are considering the purchase of a manure spreader, you certainly cannot do better than to send us your order.

THE BONANZA MUST PLEASE YOU OR YOU GET YOUR MONEY BACK

THE GREATEST VALUE EVER OFFERED in the history of the manure spreader business, and one of the most astonishing values that even we, in all of our years of business experience have ever had the pleasure to offer our customers is represented by the Bonanza Wagon Box Manure Spreader. Compare our price with what others ask for imitation machines of this type which are not half so well made and do not possess the superior features which go to make the Bonanza the wonderfully successful machine it is. Compare our price with what others will ask you for out of date, cumbersome and complicated manure spreaders which require the services of an expert to operate them and a fat purse to keep them in repair. Read carefully every claim we make for our machine, bear in mind that everything we say is true; read what the other fellows say, or better still, if possible, go and watch the operation of their machines. When you have done this you should be convinced that our machine will do anything that any other machine will do, and some things which no other machine can do. We know that you will be convinced that if our machine is all that we claim for it, that you cannot afford to buy any other, because at our price we can easily save you from one-third to one-half on the transaction. Put us to the test; let us demonstrate to your complete satisfaction that our machine is the wonderful value we say it is; send us your order and when you receive the machine, put it in work for thirty days; work it day in and day out in all kinds of weather, on all kinds of ground, with as big a load as you can possibly get on it and try it on any kind of manure you wish; do not treat it gently but give it the most severe test you can possibly impose upon it; set it in motion with your horses on a walk or on a trot; change the feed at any time and as often as you wish; place the machine in competition with any other manure spreader made, no matter what price; try them side by side on the same kind of work, in fact, put it to any reasonable test you or your neighbors can devise and if at the expiration of the thirty days' trial period you are not satisfied that our machine is the most perfect working, the most economical to operate, the most convenient to handle, and in many ways the most desirable manure spreader you ever saw, and that at our price it represents the best value you can obtain anywhere, send it back to us at our expense and let us return your money, together with all freight charges you may have paid. You cannot ask for a more liberal proposition than this; we accept the full responsibility of satisfying you or you will not be out one cent.

THE BONANZA WILL MORE THAN PAY FOR ITSELF IN ONE SEASON. This is being demonstrated every day on thousands of farms. No better illustration of the superior value of machine spread manure over that spread by the old hand and fork method, and no stronger proof of the ability of the Bonanza Manure Spreader to make good all promises we make for it, can be shown than the result of a test conducted by an up to date and practical farmer with a view to determining just how much machine spread manure would increase his crops and how much money a manure spreader would make for him on one crop of corn. In this instance ten acres of ground were set apart for the test and one-half of this tract was covered with manure spread by hand, while the remaining five acres were spread with a manure spreader. The same number of loads per acre were spread on each tract; all of the soil was worked and prepared in the same manner and at practically the same time. Planting of both tracts was uniform as to time, method and quality and quantity of seed, and cultivation was conducted with a view to insuring both an equal advantage. In fact, the test from the time the manure was hauled to the field until the crop was harvested was conducted in a manner absolutely fair to both methods. The remarkable result of this test can be best described in the words of the farmer himself, who says: "From the time the crop first made its appearance it was plain to me and my neighbors who saw it that there was a much better stand of corn on the portion of the field spread by machine; the seed seemed to sprout quicker and the growth was more uniform both as to the quality of it and the number of stalks in the hill. As the crops progressed we could see that the machine spread portion of the field was better developed and gave better promise both for ear and fodder. We could plainly see that the advantage was going to be in favor of the spreader but we never dreamed that it would be anywhere near so great as it proved to be. We first harvested the five acres on which the machine was used and secured 376 bushels of as fine corn as was ever seen in this part of the country; the other five acres produced 273 bushels of corn of average grade. When marketed, we received the highest market price of 43 cents for the 376-bushel yield, while the 273-bushel yield brought 40 cents per bushel. If you figure this out you will see that the machine, on this little five-acre patch, has made us $52.48. My neighbors, as well as myself, are all surprised at what the machine has done, and I know that many manure spreaders will be sold in this section of the country." There is the story of what one farmer has done. Let us figure out just how much the manure spreader made for him. His yield from the soil spread by machine was 376 bushels or 75 1-5 bushels per acre, his crop on the other five acres which were spread by hand was 273 bushels, or 54 3-5 bushels per acre, a total yield of 103 bushels more on the machine spread tract and an average of 21 bushels more per acre. He received the top price of 43 cents per bushel for the 376-bushel yield, or $161.68, and the medium or average price of 40 cents per bushel for the 273-bushel yield, or $109.20, a clear profit of $52.48 more than he would have made had he not used the manure spreader. An increase in profit of $10.50 for every acre on which the machine was worked. Figure out for yourself how much he would have made on 50 or 100 acres. Here in one season on a small five-acre field of corn the machine produced in increased profit, $2.63 more than the price we ask for the 50-Bushel Bonanza Manure Spreader, to say nothing about the saving in labor. Do you wonder why we say it is the most profitable implement a farmer can own? No other machine can show greater returns for the money invested. You cannot afford to do without it; it will save you money and make you money on any kind of crop, and no matter whether your farm is large or small.

REAR VIEW
Note the Shear Pointed Beater Teeth. No Two Travel in a Line.

OUR ASTONISHINGLY LOW PRICE will cause some to wonder how it is possible for us to offer a machine of such extremely high quality and superior value at a price so much lower than all other manufacturers, dealers and catalogue houses ask for manure spreaders of even most inferior quality. To those who are familiar with our up to date and advanced methods of merchandising, the reason is plain, and no explanation on our part would be necessary, but for the benefit of those who have not had the opportunity to acquaint themselves with the methods and policy which have built up our institution and made us the leaders in the commercial world we are, we will give a brief history of what has proved to be one of the most startling offers the implement world has ever known. Long ago we recognized in the manure spreader a machine of wonderful possibilities, for its great value to the farmer assured it a permanent place among the most valued and indispensable of agricultural implements. In keeping with our progressive methods we immediately set our experts to work to produce a machine of this kind to which we could apply our famous low price policy and at the same time a machine which we could offer our customers with every assurance that it would give them the best of service and possess all of the requirements essential to an implement of so great importance. It was not a hard matter for us to find a manure spreader; the country was full of them, some of them very good, some of them almost worthless, but we did find it a difficult matter for us to find a machine which we thought good enough for our customers and one which we could offer with safety on our broad and liberal proposition of "satisfaction guaranteed or money refunded." In the course of our investigation, experiments and tests, we discovered

LEFT HAND SIDE OF SPREADER
Showing Lever which Throws Machine In and Out of Gear.

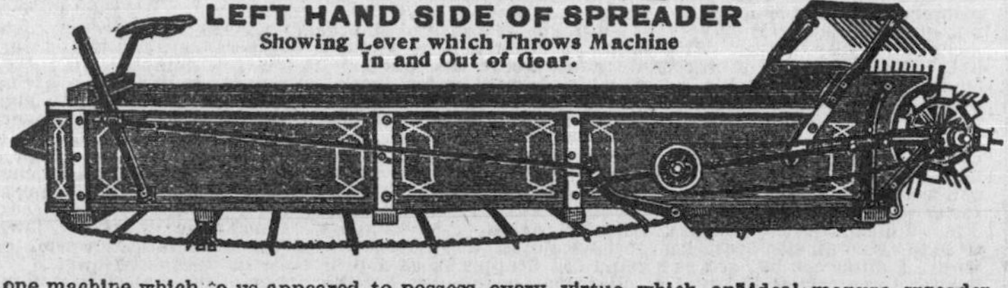

one machine which to us appeared to possess every virtue which an ideal manure spreader should possess. It was free from freak ideas and complicated and expensive mechanism, gears, cogs, etc., which are easy to break and expensive to repair. In fact, it seemed to be a perfect machine and one which would do the best of work and give long service and continued satisfaction. One feature in particular which appealed to us was that, unlike the ordinary spreader, it did not require the use of a heavy and expensively constructed truck; the machine could be set upon any ordinary farm wagon truck and two horses could easily handle it. We knew that almost every farmer had an abundance of trucks on his place and that a machine which would not require him to invest in something which he already had, would certainly appeal to him. Numerous other features of this machine impressed us most favorably, and we were convinced that providing it would do the work, **here was the machine for our customers.** To satisfy ourselves we put it to work alongside of some of the highest priced machines in the country. We worked it day in and day out; we subjected it to every test we could think of, and we found that in every way it fulfilled all claims and promises made for it; it did everything the higher priced machines could do, and it did many things they could not do. In every way it proved its superiority and convinced us that we had found the machine we wanted. We knew every farmer had need for a manure spreader; we knew that with our great selling power we could dispose of every one of these machines the manufacturer could produce; we knew that by manufacturing in such large quantities the machine could be produced at a price which would make it possible for every farmer to buy. So we went to the manufacturers with our large quantity proposition. We showed them where we could handle their entire output; where they could do away with heavy selling expense, such as traveling men's salaries and expenses, advertising expense, losses through bad accounts, etc. We showed them where by producing in the large quantities we required, they could practice greatest economy in every department of manufacture, as well as obtain bed rock prices on every pound of materials they used. We showed them in many other ways where they could produce for us at a price lower than they had ever dreamed of and at the same time make a more satisfactory profit on their business than they had ever done before. They were up to date business men, they saw the logic of our proposition, they had the machine, they had the facilities for manufacturing. We had the money to buy and the ability to sell. They accepted, and as a result closed with us the largest contract ever placed in the history of the manure spreader business. This is the story in a nutshell, it is a simple proposition; our unequaled selling power and our great purchasing power combined, with the manufacturer's producing power, have all united to make possible the production of the Bonanza Endless Steel Apron Wagon Box Manure Spreader, a wonderful machine, the best and most desirable manure spreader in the world, at a price within the means of every farmer and a price so low that no other house in the country can even hope to compete with it.

THE BONANZA IS NOT AN EXPERIMENT, it is a demonstrated success. It is produced for us by one of the oldest and best known spreader manufacturers in the country, a concern who are known as the originators of the endless steel apron wagon box manure spreader, and who have devoted years to the manufacture of this machine, which, as it stands today, is their perfected product, the best that this concern, with their years of experience, skilled labor and matchless facilities can turn out, and as good a machine as it is possible for anyone to produce. Thousands of these machines are being used throughout the country; they are giving unqualified satisfaction, and even at the high prices which dealers have asked for them, they have always been considered to be of most exceptional value. You take no risk in buying the Bonanza; you get the most up to date manure spreader on the market, a machine which has stood the test of years, the best machine that the most expert and reputable manufacturers in the world can produce, and above all, you have the protection of our broad and liberal guarantee and our thirty days' free trial offer; the most liberal proposition ever made by anyone. You cannot afford to buy a manure spreader until you have permitted us to demonstrate that the Bonanza is just the machine you want and the best built and most satisfactory manure spreader in existence. Give us the opportunity; if we cannot please you we alone are the losers.

YOUR LAND WILL INCREASE IN VALUE if you keep it well fertilized. The best fertilizer you can find will be supplied by your manure pile, and the best and most economical method of applying it will be found in a Bonanza Manure Spreader. It is a common sight to see two farms side by side, one selling for from $10.00 to $25.00 per acre more than the other. The reason for this is that the owner of one farm has permitted his land to run out, while the other has supplied the necessary nourishment to keep it fertile and always capable of producing good crops. The use of the Bonanza Manure Spreader will insure your land always being kept in the best possible condition so as to command the highest price, and in this way alone, the machine will pay for itself time and again, to say nothing of the profits it will yield in the meanwhile by increasing your crops.

VIEW WITH ONE SIDEBOARD REMOVED SHOWING ENDLESS STEEL APRON, ALSO HOW THE FORCE FEED ATTACHMENT WORKS.

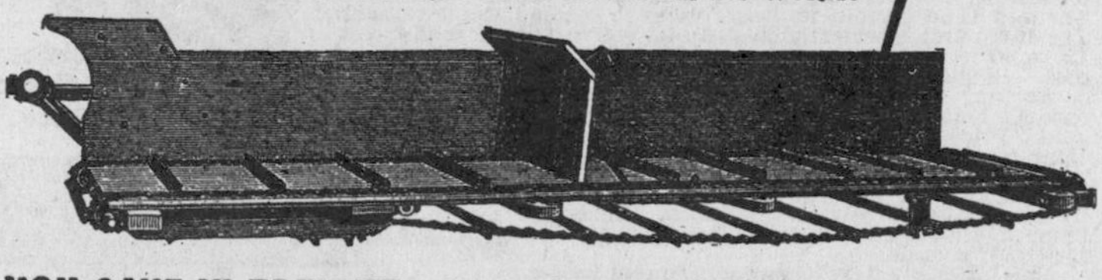

YOU SAVE IN FREIGHT when you buy the Bonanza Manure Spreader; this is another way in which we save you money. Other styles of manure spreaders weigh from two to four times as much as the Bonanza, and consequently will cost you from two to four times as much for freight charges. This extra weight does not benefit you in any way, because no machine can be stronger than the Bonanza, and again, a heavy machine requires more horses to pull it and cannot be successfully used on soft ground. The Bonanza Manure Spreader is shipped knocked down, insuring the lowest possible rate of freight and all parts are well bundled so as to provide against loss or damage in transit. WE GUARANTEE SAFE DELIVERY and should any part or parts become lost or broken in transit we will make good such loss or damage by furnishing new parts free of all charge, transportation charges prepaid.

DESCRIPTION. The Bonanza Wagon Box Manure Spreader is built in a strictly first class and workmanlike manner; all parts are made of the best materials the market affords, which are selected with a view to providing materials best suited to the requirements of each individual part. There is no machine on the market which is more honestly built or one in which its makers can take greater pride. We furnish this machine in two sizes, the 50-bushel size for use on narrow track standard gears measuring 38 inches between bolster stakes and the 60-bushel size to fit wide track standard gears measuring 42 inches between bolster stakes. THE WAGON BOX of both the 50-bushel and 60-bushel machines is 10 feet long and 15 inches deep, inside, the width inside of the 50-bushel box is 36 inches, and of the 60-bushel box, 40 inches; the bottom is made of matched lumber and is strongly braced and securely nailed, it is practically watertight so that manure juice will not leak out when machine is on the way to the field; sides are smooth dressed and made of a wood which best resists moisture and is least liable to warp. Seat is large and comfortable, strongly made from pressed steel and mounted on a spring standard possessed of great rigidity and yet of sufficient elasticity to insure comfort to the rider. The footboard is strong and is conveniently placed. FINISH—The Bonanza is finished in a manner entirely becoming to the high grade machine it is, the wagon box is well painted in a handsome wagon makers' red, the sideboards are neatly striped in black and then given a thorough coat of high grade varnish. The beater bars are painted to match the box. All iron and steel parts are painted black, which contrasts handsomely with the bright red of the box and adds greatly to the already attractive appearance of the machine.

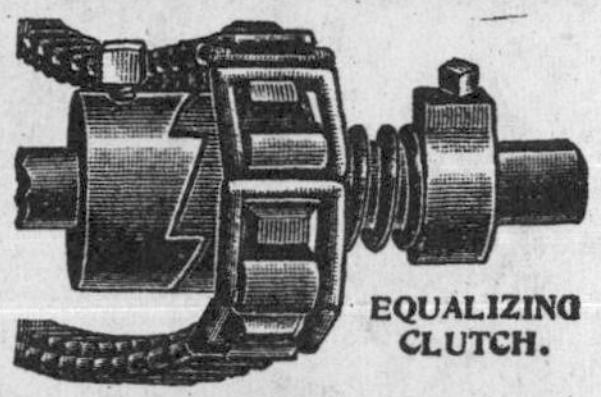

EQUALIZING CLUTCH.

THE ENDLESS STEEL APRON or conveyor is strongly made with heavy angle steel bars placed about 12 inches apart and securely riveted at each end to heavy malleable link chain belts which travel over four sprockets, two at each end of the spreader; these sprockets are mounted on heavy cold rolled steel shafts which extend under the box the full width of the machine. This insures perfect alignment at all times and makes it impossible for the apron to bind. The adjustment of the apron is made by means of heavy set screws or bolts at the front end, this device is most simple and enables you to easily keep the apron at proper tension at all times. The advantages of this steel apron over the old style wooden conveyor are many, it is much lighter and consequently light of draft, but at the same time it is far stronger, will not become foul, and cannot possibly rot or warp. THE BEATER WHEEL is strong and rigidly constructed with heavy cast heads to which the beater bars are securely bolted. These bars, seven in number, are made of carefully selected best quality hardwood and are cross riveted at intervals of about every 9 inches, so that it is impossible for them to warp or split. The teeth are ⅜-inch round solid high carbon steel and will not bend; they are securely fastened in the beater bar so that they cannot possibly become loose, they are arranged so that no two teeth travel in the same line, and when in motion throw the manure outward and away from the center. Teeth are sharpened, having a shear point, which cuts and tears the chunks of manure into fine particles or shreds, this not only insures even and uniform spreading, but also decreases the draft. THE EQUALIZING CLUTCH is one of the many valuable features found in the Bonanza Manure Spreader, which go to show the extreme care the manufacturers have exercised to insure its operation being absolutely perfect under all conditions. This clutch is provided at both ends of the beater shaft and is automatic in its action. Its purpose is to overcome all variation in the speed of the rear wagon wheels when making turns or when working on other than a straight pull, and thus always insures uniform speed at both ends of the beater wheel and driving mechanism, no matter whether the machine is driven straight ahead or turned in either direction. This is why the Bonanza always does its work in a uniform manner and never slights any part of the field.

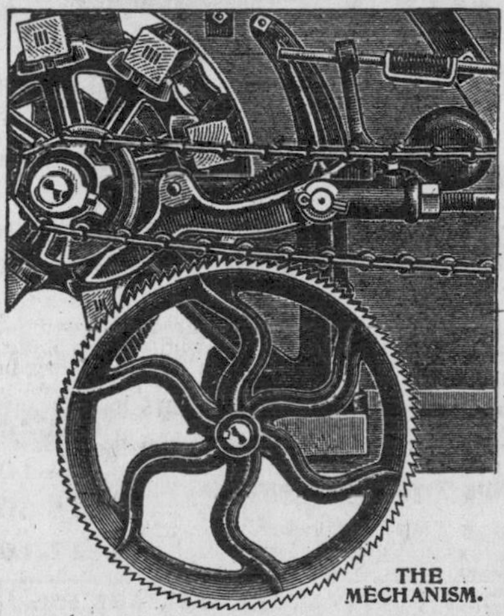

THE MECHANISM.

THE MECHANISM is simplicity itself, all working parts are iron and steel and every part designed to insure perfect and positive action and long service. Two large and perfectly formed sprockets are provided to attach to the wagon wheels by means of strong U bolts and clamp blocks. By referring to the large illustration you will note the heavy link chain belt which runs from the sprocket on the beater shaft and above the rear wheel; you will also note the lever conveniently placed to the left of the seat. The simple operation of moving this lever forward forces the idler sheaves downward until the drive chains on both sides of the machine engage with the top teeth of the sprocket wheels and then the machine is in gear. To throw the machine out of gear it is only necessary to move this lever backward and the drive chains are raised from the sprocket teeth and the conveyor and beater wheel will remain stationary and no manure will be spread until the lever is again reversed and the mechanism set in motion. The amount of manure to be spread per acre is governed by the lever to right of the seat which regulates the action of the dog on the large ratchet wheel, and thereby the speed at which the conveyor will travel and makes the machine feed at **any one of its four feeds** and spread the manure in quantities ranging from 5 to 30 loads per acre depending upon the height of your wagon wheels, this enables you to spread as thickly or as sparingly as you wish. The machine can be set in motion or thrown out of gear without stopping the horses. You can also change the feed under the same conditions thus enabling you to favor certain portions of the field or skip it entirely if desired without slowing up or stopping the team. We call attention to the shelf or guard projecting from the rear of the right hand side of the box out over the mechanism; this serves to prevent the manure from falling into the working parts and obviates all danger of these parts becoming clogged. Truly, no other manure spreader in existence is so simple and so complete and perfect in operation as the Bonanza. OUR PATENT IDLER SHEAVES constitute one of the most desirable features ever placed on a chain driven machine. They make it impossible for the chains to jump the sprockets even should they be considerably out of line. This device consists of two large iron sheave wheels over which the drive chains travel; when the machine is set in gear these sheaves are automatically forced down until the chains are engaged by the top teeth of the drive sprockets and remain there, holding the chains in place and making them run steadily and at a uniform tension. Other manufacturers have attempted to produce devices to serve this purpose but none of them are so positive and reliable in operation. The manufacturers of our machine, own and control the patents on this device and when you see it used on another machine you can rest assured, regardless of statements to the contrary, that our manufacturers are being paid a good round sum as royalty for the privilege of its use which adds to the cost of the other machine and is one more reason why they cannot be produced at a figure which will enable them to be sold at a price anywhere near so low as ours. GREAT ADJUSTABILITY is one of the strong points of this machine. It can be adjusted to meet the requirements of any width of farm wagon gear and to accommodate the variation in the dish of different styles of wagon wheels. This is accomplished by merely adjusting the small sprockets on the beater wheel shaft and the movable axle or stud upon which the idler sheaves revolve. The adjustment is easily and quickly made and enables one to line up the drive chains with the large sprockets so that the teeth will properly engage the chain and run true at all times. No chain driven machine can be successful unless this is assured. THE FORCE FEED—This most valuable and superior device consists of a detachable push board which when set at the head of the machine, engages itself with the cross bars of the apron and when the apron is in motion follows the load, forcing all of the manure before it in a steady stream and clearing the box of every atom. When it reaches the beater wheel it automatically engages itself with the raised end of the wagon box; trips itself and permits the apron to travel free of it. When reloading, it can be again set at the head of the load without disturbing the conveyor. This attachment will also be found very desirable when the machine is used for distributing powdered fertilizer, potash, lime, sand, gravel, etc. **This attachment is not part of the regular equipment of the spreader** but is furnished only as an extra at the additional price quoted under catalogue No. 32K977. Mud Lugs are desirable when the machine is used in ground that is muddy or covered with snow or ice. Under ordinary conditions these are not required but they will undoubtedly be found useful at some time or other. We furnish them as an extra in sets of eighteen, nine for each wheel, at price quoted under catalogue No. 32K978. These lugs are strong and positive in action. The large illustration on previous page shows how they are attached to the wagon wheel.

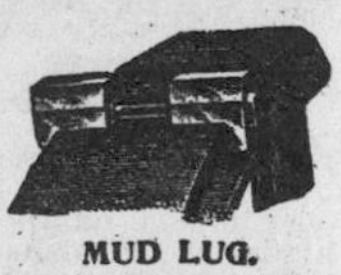

MUD LUG.

PRICE is for the complete wagon box manure spreader, consisting of the wagon box, mechanism, drive chains and the two large sprocket wheels with U bolts and clamps for attaching them, in fact everything we show in the large illustration **excepting the trucks which we do not furnish.** Mud Lugs and Force Feed Attachment are extra and furnished only when ordered and proper price allowed. **Complete instructions for putting together and operating accompany each machine.** Shipped knocked down from factory in Central Iowa.

No. 32K975 50-Bushel Bonanza Manure Spreader for use on narrow track standard gears, measuring 38 inches between bolster stakes. Wt., 650 lbs. Price $49.85

No. 32K976 60-Bushel Bonanza Manure Spreader for use on wide track standard gears, measuring 42 inches between bolster stakes. Wt., 730 lbs. Price 54.85

No. 32K977 Force Feed Attachment. Wt., 20 lbs. Price 2.75

No. 32K978 Set of eighteen Mud Lugs. Wt., 9 lbs. Price 1.65

KENWOOD RIDING AND WALKING CULTIVATORS.

$19.95 AND UP

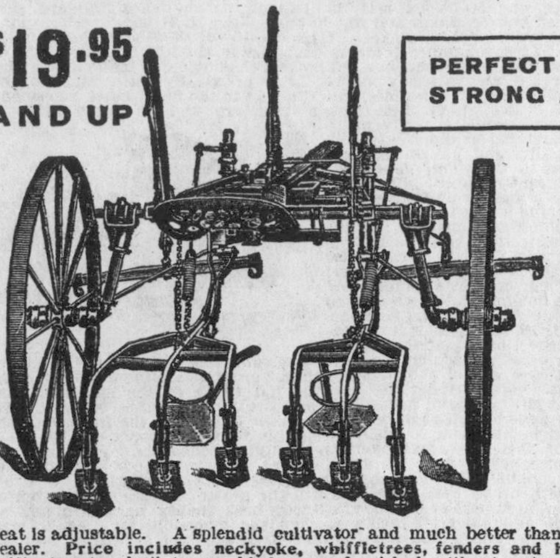

PERFECT IN OPERATION STRONG AND DURABLE

These cultivators are first class in every respect, and are the best known and most commonly used cultivators in many sections of the country. Are suitable for any soil and for any class of work. Wheels can be adjusted from 4 to 5 feet in width. Team is hitched close to the work and practically direct to the shovel beams. Hitch is low down and adjustable. Balance lever is directly in front of the driver and cultivator can be balanced perfectly whether walking or riding. Entire cultivator handles very easily and is of light draft. Lifting springs to counterbalance gangs are adjustable and can be made non-acting when at work. Seat is adjustable. A splendid cultivator and much better than is handled by the average dealer. Price includes neckyoke, whiffletrees, fenders and handles. With four-shovel cultivators two bull tongue blades are furnished without extra charge. Shipped knocked down from factory in Southwestern Ohio.

No. 32K1005	4-Shovel Break Pin Cultivator.	Wt., 350 lbs.	Price..........$19.95
No. 32K1006	6-Shovel Break Pin Cultivator.	Wt., 355 lbs.	Price..........20.70
No. 32K1008	4-Shovel Spring Trip Cultivator.	Wt., 355 lbs.	Price..........22.25
No. 32K1009	6-Shovel Spring Trip Cultivator.	Wt., 360 lbs.	Price..........24.15

KENWOOD WALKING CULTIVATORS.

$13.48 AND UP.

THE BEST OF THEIR TYPE

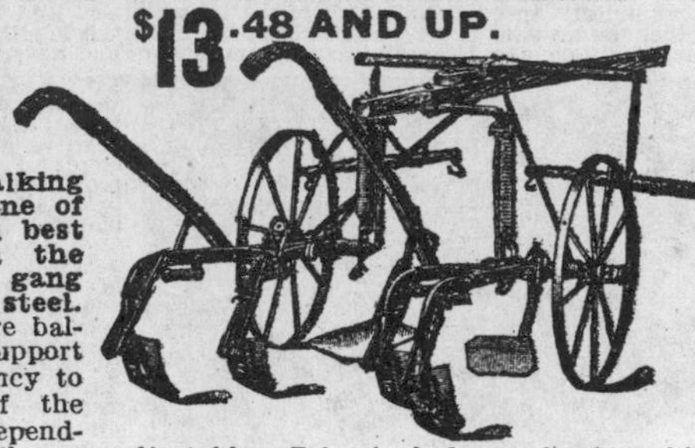

The best tongue walking cultivator made and one of the most popular and best known cultivators on the market. The frame, gang beams and wheels are steel. Gangs are pivoted and are balanced by springs, which support them but have no tendency to hold the shovels out of the ground. Each gang is independent and adjustable. Handles are adjustable. Price includes neckyoke, whiffletrees, handles and fenders. With four-shovel cultivators two bull tongue blades are furnished without extra charge. Shipped knocked down from factory in Southwestern Ohio.

No. 32K1010 4-Shovel Break Pin Cultivator. Wt., 215 lbs. Price..........$13.48
No. 32K1011 6-Shovel Break Pin Cultivator. Wt., 220 lbs. Price..........14.10
No. 32K1013 4-Shovel Spring Trip Cultivator. Wt., 220 lbs. Price..........15.50
No. 32K1014 6-Shovel Spring Trip Cultivator. Wt., 225 lbs. Price..........17.10

FOR ONE-HORSE AND GARDEN CULTIVATORS SEE PAGE 524.

KENWOOD TONGUELESS CULTIVATORS.

$11.95

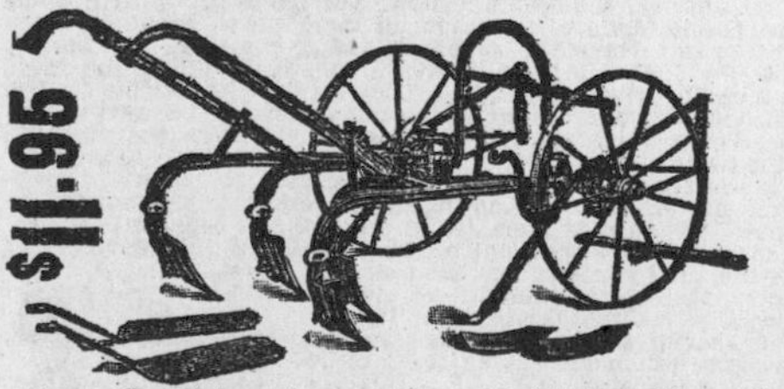

A UNIVERSAL FAVORITE

Strictly modern and up to date in every respect. Entire cultivator is made of iron and steel, except handles and whiffletrees. Both wheels and gangs are pivoted, consequently always in line, and each horse pulls its own plow. Draft bars have adjustable hitch. Gangs are adjustable. Frame is provided with gang rests and handles of gangs are adjustable. Price includes whiffletrees, handles and fenders. With four-shovel cultivators two bull tongue blades are furnished without extra charge. Shipped knocked down from factory in Southwestern Ohio.

No. 32K1032	4-Shovel Break Pin Cultivator.	Wt., 170 lbs.	Price..........$11.95
No. 32K1033	6-Shovel Break Pin Cultivator.	Wt., 175 lbs.	Price..........12.67
No. 32K1035	4-Shovel Spring Trip Cultivator.	Wt., 175 lbs.	Price..........14.45
No. 32K1036	6-Shovel Spring Trip Cultivator.	Wt., 180 lbs.	Price..........15.36

KENWOOD WOOD FRAME CULTIVATOR AND WING SHOVEL PLOW.

A Splendid Combination Tool at a Remarkably Low Price.

$3.87 **PRICE REDUCED**

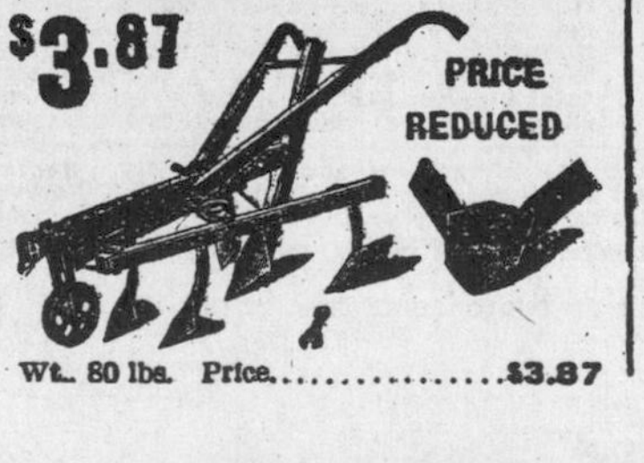

This is a one-horse tool especially adapted for cultivating corn, potatoes and other heavy work. When cultivating, the teeth can all be set to act as cultivator teeth or the rear teeth can be adjusted to act as hoes. By taking out two bolts you can remove the cultivator parts and put on the adjustable wing shovel blade in place of the rear center tooth, making one of the best wing shovel plows on the market. Cultivator is adjustable from 8 to 40 inches in width. A splendid tool for heavy one-horse work and one for which there is use on every farm. Shipped knocked down from factory in Southeastern Wisconsin.

No. 32K1045 Wood Frame Cultivator. Wt., 80 lbs. Price..........$3.87

KENWOOD TWO-HORSE CORN PLANTER.

$22.25 and up

PRICES Greatly Reduced.

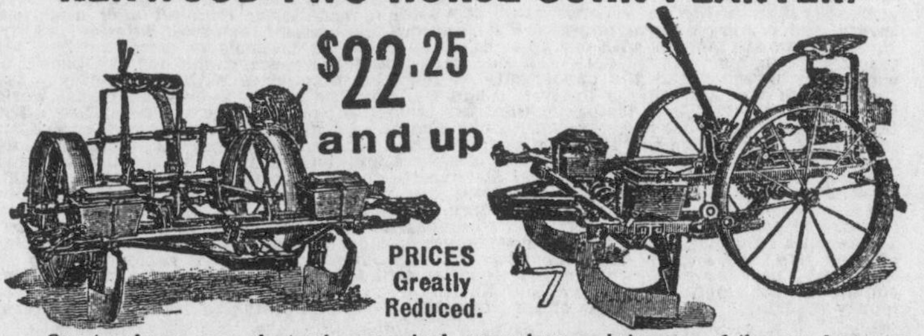

Our two-horse corn planter is recognized everywhere as being one of the very best corn planters made in this country. Its special features have been copied by many different makers but our manufacturers have kept this machine ahead of all others by making decided improvements from year to year. It is simple in construction, accurate in operation, strong and durable. Made of steel and iron throughout except the tongue. It is a full combination rotary feed planter with a double cut-off which insures perfect work. Frame is coupled close, giving driver full and easy control. Tongue is adjustable for height. Wheels are 30 inches high with 6-inch concave tires and can be run either over or off the seed row. Depth of runners can be regulated independently. **As regularly furnished, planter is standard width; that is, it can be adjusted to plant either 3 feet 6 inches or 3 feet 8 inches apart,** and checkrower wire will have buttons 3 feet 6 inches apart, but we can furnish narrow frame to plant either 3 feet 4 inches or 3 feet 6 inches, or wide frame to plant either 3 feet 8 inches or 3 feet 10 inches apart, and checkrower wire can be furnished with buttons spaced either 3 feet, 3 feet 2 inches, 3 feet 4 inches, 3 feet 6 inches, 3 feet 8 inches, 3 feet 10 inches or 4 feet apart. Checkrower is set low down so as to avoid all side draft, has positive clutch, will not miss and has automatic throw-off for wire. Planter can be used as a hand hill dropper or as a drill or with the checkrower. We furnish three sets of hill plates, adapting the planter for the average different sizes of corn, three sets of drill plates, and one set of blank plates. The drill plates, in connection with the feed sprocket wheels, can be arranged to drop one kernel of corn either 12, 16, 20, 23 or 26 inches apart. Price of No. 32K1100 is for the corn planter fitted for drilling and hand hill dropping and includes dropper seat and marker, but does not include a checkrower. Price of No. 32K1101 is for the corn planter fitted for drilling, hand hill dropping and with checkrower and 80 rods of wire and includes dropper seat, marker and stake irons. We can furnish a fertilizer attachment, which will drill or hill any quantity from 20 to 300 pounds per acre, and a pick feed cotton planting attachment which will transform the planter into a two-row cotton planter. But if wanted, they must be ordered with the corn planter, so that they can be fitted at the factory. For $29.20 we will furnish the No. 32K1101 planter with an automatic reel, as shown in the illustration at the left. Shipped knocked down from factory in Southwestern Ohio.

No. 32K1100 Hill and Drill Corn Planter. Wt., 400 lbs. Price..........$22.25
No. 32K1101 Hill, Drill and Checkrower Corn Planter. Wt., 530 lbs. Price, without automatic reel..........28.25
Price, with automatic reel..........29.20
No. 32K1102 Fertilizer Attachment. Wt., 50 lbs. Price..........10.58
No. 32K1103 Extra Wire. Wt., ½ lb. Price, per rod..........$.03¾$
No. 32K1104 Cotton Planting Attachment. Wt., 45 lbs. Price..........6.47

KENWOOD ONE-HORSE CORN DRILL.

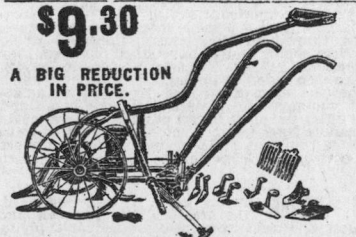

$8.40 FOR DRILL ONLY.

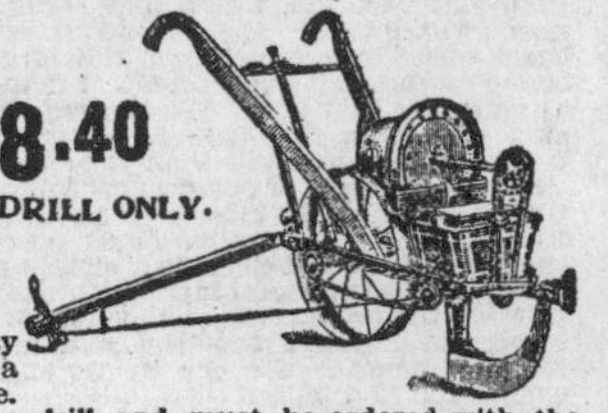

This is one of the best one-horse corn drills made. It is adapted for drilling corn, peas, beans or other small seeds. Very substantial in construction, very positive in its work and can be used to plant small seeds in almost any desired quantity. It is made of iron and steel throughout, except the handles and marker pole. The combination of seed plates and feed sprockets regularly furnished will enable you to drop one grain of corn either 6, 8, 10, 12, 13, 15, 16, 18, 19, 22, 25, 28, 40, 45 or 50 inches apart. The illustration shows the drill fitted with a fertilizer attachment, which attachment will sow continuously any quantity from 20 to 300 pounds per acre. We can also furnish a pick feed cotton planting attachment for this machine. **These attachments are not included in the price of the drill and must be ordered with the drill if wanted so that they can be fitted at the factory.** Price includes seven plates, marker and wire to connect marker. Shipped set up from factory in Southwestern Ohio.

No. 32K1115 One-Horse Corn Drill. Wt., 100 lbs. Price..........$8.40
No. 32K1116 Fertilizer Attachment. Wt., 25 lbs. Price..........2.67
No. 32K1117 Cotton Planting Attachment. Wt., 20 lbs. Price..........2.70

Genuine Manweight Garden Seeder, Cultivator, Plow, Hoe and Rake.

$9.30 A BIG REDUCTION IN PRICE.

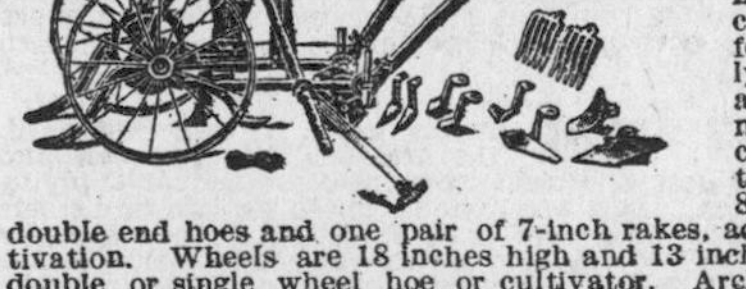

This is not a cheap imitation of or infringement on the celebrated patent Manweight Garden Tool, but is the genuine article and worth double the price of any imitation of this tool. As a seeder it will drop seed in hills from 3 to 48 inches apart or will sow continuously in drills. Has an agitator force feed. Will sow any desired quantity accurately at any depth from ¼ to 4 inches. Sows and covers the seed, presses the ground and marks the next row all at one operation. Machine is fitted with one pair of 2-inch cultivator teeth, one pair of small plows, one pair of 8-inch single end hoes, one pair of 4-inch double end hoes and one pair of 7-inch rakes, adapting the tool for all classes of garden cultivation. Wheels are 18 inches high and 13 inches apart. Machine can be used either as a double or single wheel hoe or cultivator. Arch is high enough to pass over crops 30 inches high. Machine is propelled by operator leaning the weight of his body against the push bar, leaving the hands free to guide the tool around the plants. Shipped knocked down from factory in Central Indiana.

No. 32K1135 Manweight Seeder. Wt., 80 lbs. Price..........$9.30

KENWOOD ENDGATE BROADCAST SEEDER.

$5.72 Note our Reduced Price.

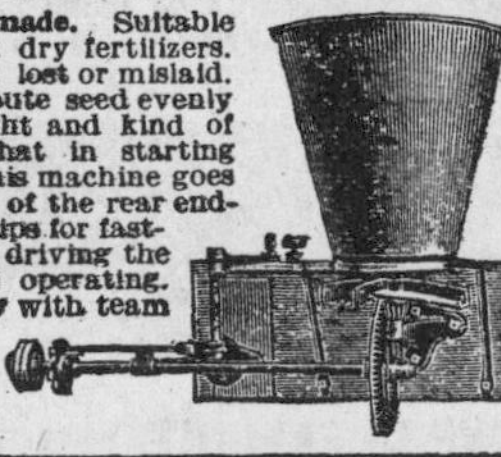

The best agitator endgate broadcast seeder made. Suitable for sowing broadcast all kinds of small seeds and dry fertilizers. The feed is adjustable, no loose plates to become lost or mislaid. The distributor is perfectly shaped and will distribute seed evenly 12 to 40 feet in width, depending upon the weight and kind of seed. Seeder is fitted with a spring clutch so that in starting or stopping there is no sudden jar or strain. This machine goes onto the rear end of the wagon, taking the place of the rear endgate. Price includes large sprocket wheel and clips for fastening it onto the wagon wheel, also chain for driving the machine, and full directions for attaching and operating. The machine will sow 100 acres of wheat per day with team traveling at the rate of 2½ miles per hour. Shipped knocked down from factory in Southeastern Wisconsin.

No. 32K1150 Kenwood Endgate Seeder. Wt., 95 lbs. Price..........$5.72

FOR GARDEN SEEDERS SEE PAGE 524.

KENWOOD STEEL FRAME WEEDER.

ANOTHER REDUCTION IN PRICE. **$6.12**

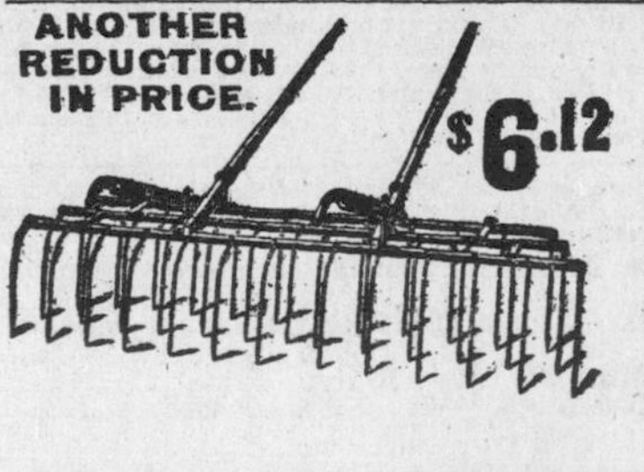

One of the best made and most desirable steel frame weeders on the market. The frame is made of heavy angle steel and is strongly braced. Weeder is 7½ feet wide, has 38 teeth which are made of square spring steel and pointed and the machine is adapted for use in any soil. A desirable tool in every way. Shipped knocked down from factory in Southern Pennsylvania.

No. 32K1175 Steel Frame Weeder. Wt., 85 lbs. Price..........$6.12

$8.37

LITTLE WONDER GRINDING MILL.

A WONDER IN WORK AS WELL AS IN PRICE

Price Reduced

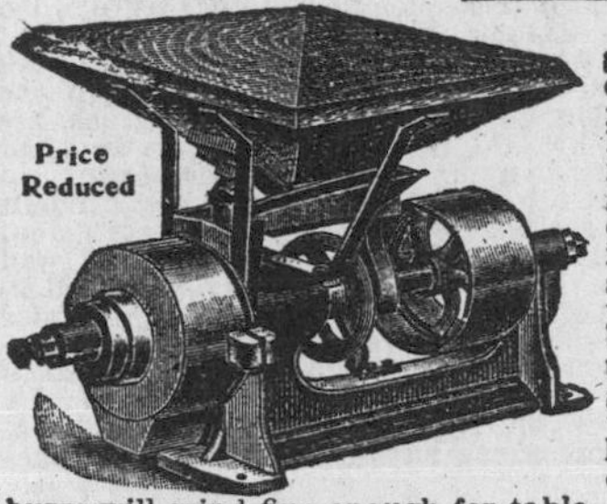

One of the most perfectly constructed grinding mills on the market. Especially adapted for use with power windmills, small gasoline engines and other light motive powers. Burrs are 5½ inches diameter and can be adjusted for grinding coarse or fine. Will grind all kinds of small grains, coffee, etc. Driving pulley is 7 inches in diameter with 4-inch face, and should make from 700 to 1,300 revolutions per minute. Capacity is from 5 to 15 bushels of mixed feed per hour, depending upon the speed of grinder and fineness of grinding. Requires from 1 to 3-horse power to run it. Burrs cannot run together when hopper is empty. Is furnished with one set of coarse and one set of fine burrs. Fine burrs will grind fine enough for table meal. When ordering extra burrs, state whether coarse or fine burrs are wanted. Shipped set up from factory in Southeastern Wisconsin.

No. 32K1650 Little Wonder Grinding Mill. Wt., 90 lbs. Price..$8.37
No. 32K1651 Pair of Extra Burrs. Wt., 4 lbs. Price.......... .62

ACME POWER FEED GRINDER.

$12.42

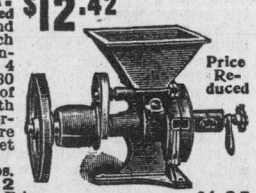

This mill is for grinding small grains and shelled corn for feed only. Can be adjusted for either coarse or fine grinding and has large capacity. Pulley is 5 inches in diameter, with 5-inch face and should run from 1,200 to 1,800 revolutions per minute. Burrs are 9 inches in diameter. Grinder requires from 4 to 8-horse power to run it, and its capacity is from 15 to 30 bushels of mixed feed per hour, depending upon the speed of the grinder and the fineness of the grinding. Is furnished with one set of coarse burrs and one set of fine burrs. When ordering extra burrs state whether coarse or fine burrs are wanted. Not intended for grinding table meal. Shipped set up from factory in Southeastern Wisconsin.

Price Reduced

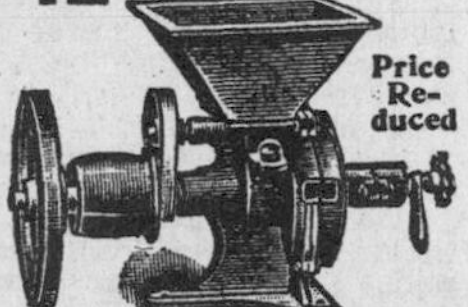

No. 32K1660 Acme Power Feed Grinder. Wt., 200 lbs. Price..........$12.42
No. 32K1661 Pair of Extra Burrs. Wt., 11 lbs. Price..........$1.05

FOR SMALL HAND GRIST OR GRINDING MILLS, SEE PAGE 523.

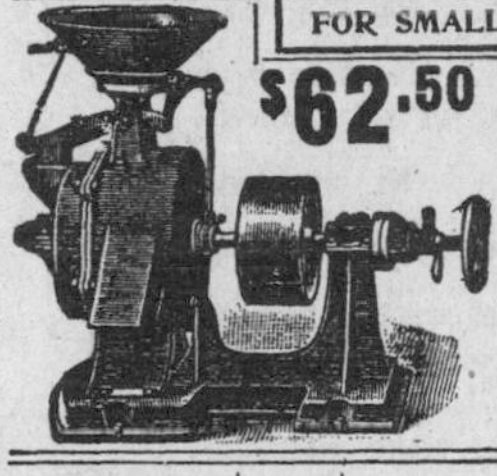

$62.50

GENUINE FRENCH BUHR MILLS.

These mills are designed for custom mill use where quantity as well as quality of grinding is desired. They will grind cool, rapidly and evenly. Spindles are extra heavy steel, accurately fitted to the runner stones, and run in long anti-friction metal bearings. Housings are lathe turned and fit perfectly tight. Stones are accurately fitted and trammed, and runner stone is balanced on the spindle. These mills can be run by any kind of belt power, can be belted from any direction, will not choke and can be run empty without injury. The 12-inch and 16-inch mills should be run about 1,100 revolutions, the 18-inch and 20-inch mills should be run about 1,000 revolutions per minute. Shipped set up from factory in Southwestern Ohio.

Catalogue No.	Size of Buhrs	Bushels per Hour	Horse Power Required	Size of Pulley, inches	Weight, pounds	Price
32K1672	12	4 to 8	2 to 4	7 x 4	500	$ 62.50
32K1673	16	8 to 16	4 to 8	10 x 6	600	89.50
32K1674	18	12 to 20	6 to 10	12 x 7	850	99.50
32K1675	20	15 to 30	8 to 12	12 x 8	1,100	124.50

STERLING No. 2 GRAIN AND SEED CLEANER AND SEPARATOR.

For Hand or Power

Price reduced to $11.75 without Sacking Elevator.

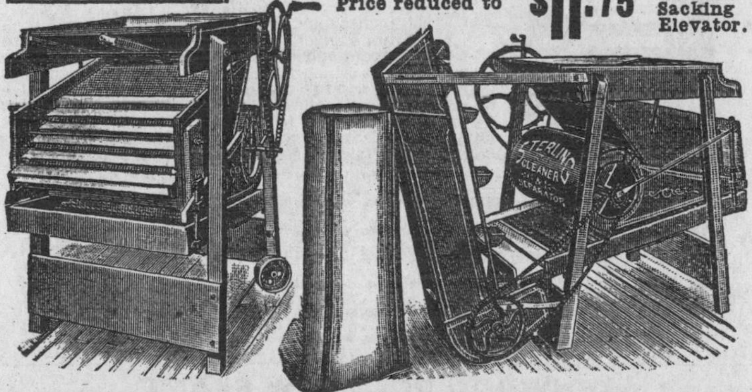

The Sterling is a strictly high class, modern, improved grain and seed cleaner and separator. It is much different from an ordinary fanning mill in principle, design and quality of work. Shoes are operated at end by shaker arm, hinged to give a straight forward and backward reciprocating motion. The grain or seed flows evenly on the sieves and screens, without any tendency to crawl to one side. Shaker arm has adjustments for a short, medium or long stroke. One stroke of the feed gate lever cuts off the feed instantly, or by an opposite stroke the gate may be opened to feed as much or as little grain or seed to the sieves as desired. The grain or seed is distributed evenly over entire width of sieves, which is necessary for perfect work. Our wheat gang has seven zinc sieves and does perfect work on wheat, rye and SUCCOTASH. The Sterling Cleaner separates wheat from tame oats or wheat from wild oats in a perfect manner. Barley gang furnished with cleaner has two zinc sieves. Sieves are 23½ inches wide. Screens for lower shoe are all wire and are 41 inches long. They are kept clean automatically by an improved screen cleaner rack. Fan is in a sheet steel drum and is driven by sprockets and chain. Main sprocket wheel has slotted stud bearing to tighten chain. Fan shaft is extended so that the 6 x 2-inch pulley we furnish may be substituted for the small sprocket wheel on the shaft when desired to operate cleaner with power. We ship the Sterling Cleaner all set up ready for work, and the advantage of receiving cleaner all complete ready to use is a desirable feature which will more than offset the little extra freight charge. **Equipment: Each Sterling Cleaner is furnished regularly with a grain outfit consisting of one 7-sieve zinc gang for wheat, rye and succotash, one 2-sieve zinc barley gang, one wire sieve for oats and corn, one long mesh wire screen (2x11) for taking tame and wild oats and cheat out of wheat and for taking oats out of barley, one coarse wire screen (8x8) for cockle and small wheat, one fine wire screen (10x10) for use when cleaning for market.** Note carefully that the equipment regularly furnished provides fully for separating SUCCOTASH without extra charge. Attachments for cleaning and separating flax, clover, millet, Hungarian, timothy and alfalfa seed can be furnished at extra cost. Special gangs for Durum wheat or Macaroni wheat can be furnished when so ordered in place of wheat gang regularly furnished, or either may be ordered as an extra if price is allowed for same. Each cleaner is equipped with a wheat gang especially adapted for the kind of wheat generally grown in the locality into which the cleaner is shipped, but if you wish to clean both small and large wheat it will require an extra wheat gang, which you must order and allow price for. Sacking elevator is driven by sprocket chain. Elevator is furnished only as an extra, and when ordered price must be allowed. Price does not include sack. Capacity depends entirely upon the kind and condition of the grain or seed being cleaned and quality of work desired. Shipped set up from factory in Southern Minnesota.

No. 32K1700 No. 2 Cleaner and Separator. Wt., 125 lbs. Price..........$11.75
No. 32K1701 Sacking Elevator. Wt., 25 lbs. Price.......... 4.46
No. 32K1702 Flax Attachment. Wt., 13 lbs. Price.......... 1.24
No. 32K1703 Clover, Millet and Hungarian Attachment. Wt., 7 lbs. Price.. .96
No. 32K1704 Timothy and Alfalfa Attachment. Wt., 7 lbs. Price.......... .98
No. 32K1705 Extra Wheat Gang. Wt., 16 lbs. Price.......... 2.95

KENWOOD AGRICULTURAL BOILERS.

Big Reduction in Prices

$7.88

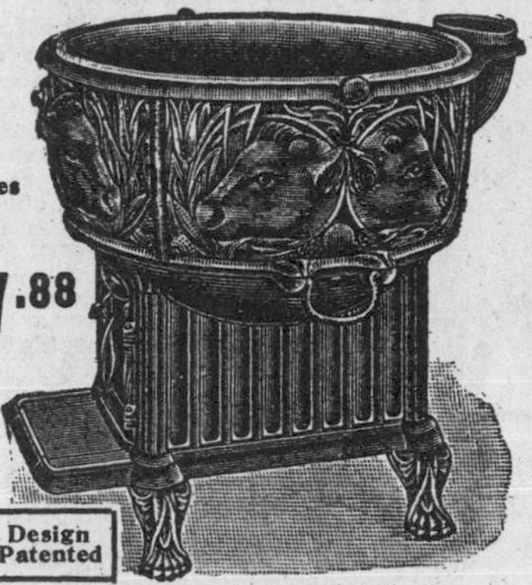

Design Patented

We guarantee these boilers to hold their full stated capacity.

The highest grade and best made as well as the most handsome and attractively designed furnaces and caldrons on the market. Exceedingly popular among both farmers and butchers. Can be used for any purpose where a fine smooth kettle is required such as rendering lard, cooking food for stock, boiling sap, melting lead, etc. **Caldrons are made of the finest charcoal iron, very smooth, with black lead finish inside and we guarantee them to be full capacity.** Furnaces are cast iron throughout, put together as well as any stove made, and are so pleasing in design that they are a decided ornament to any surroundings. Price is for furnace and caldron complete with elbow, but does not include pipe. The 15-gallon size takes 5-inch pipe; the 22-gallon and the 30-gallon, 6-inch pipe; the 45-gallon and the 60-gallon size, 7-inch pipe, and the 75-gallon size, 8-inch pipe. The furnaces for coal have iron grate and heavy fire brick lining which can be taken out and replaced through the door; they will burn wood as well as coal. Shipped set up from factory in Central Ohio.

No. 32K1900 15-Gallon Boiler, for wood. Wt., 170 lbs. Price..........$ 7.88
No. 32K1901 22-Gallon Boiler, for wood. Wt., 207 lbs. Price.......... 9.72
No. 32K1902 30-Gallon Boiler, for wood. Wt., 272 lbs. Price.......... 11.98
No. 32K1903 45-Gallon Boiler, for wood. Wt., 327 lbs. Price.......... 14.62
No. 32K1904 60-Gallon Boiler, for wood. Wt., 491 lbs. Price.......... 19.25
No. 32K1905 75-Gallon Boiler, for wood. Wt., 561 lbs. Price.......... 21.75
No. 32K1907 15-Gallon Boiler, for coal. Wt., 193 lbs. Price.......... 8.98
No. 32K1908 22-Gallon Boiler, for coal. Wt., 221 lbs. Price.......... 10.67
No. 32K1909 30-Gallon Boiler, for coal. Wt., 295 lbs. Price.......... 13.62
No. 32K1910 45-Gallon Boiler, for coal. Wt., 350 lbs. Price.......... 16.90
No. 32K1911 60-Gallon Boiler, for coal. Wt., 528 lbs. Price.......... 20.85
No. 32K1912 75-Gallon Boiler, for coal. Wt., 598 lbs. Price.......... 23.25

For $2.00 to $5.00 less, depending on size, we could sell boilers with furnaces having steel jacket above the fire box and iron linings for coal. We do not consider them good in quality or value, therefore do not handle them.

FARMERS' FRIEND FOOD COOKERS.

AT GREATLY REDUCED PRICES.

$4.46

WE GUARANTEE THEM TO HOLD THEIR FULL STATED CAPACITY

These cookers are constructed to give the best possible results from the very smallest amount of fuel. The jacket is heavy cold rolled steel plate, supported at the bottom by heavy wrought iron bands. **Kettles are made of fine grained iron with black lead finish inside, and we guarantee them to be full capacity.** The rim of the kettle rests on top of the jacket and the kettle can be easily removed. There are no legs and no bottom to this cooker. It is intended to set on the ground. For indoor use, should be set on a base made of brick and sand. Can be used for cooking food, rendering lard, or for any other purpose where an ordinary kettle can be used. Prices are for the cooker for burning wood, complete with elbow, damper, and one joint of 6-inch pipe. Coal grates and covers are extra. Shipped set up from factory in Central Ohio.

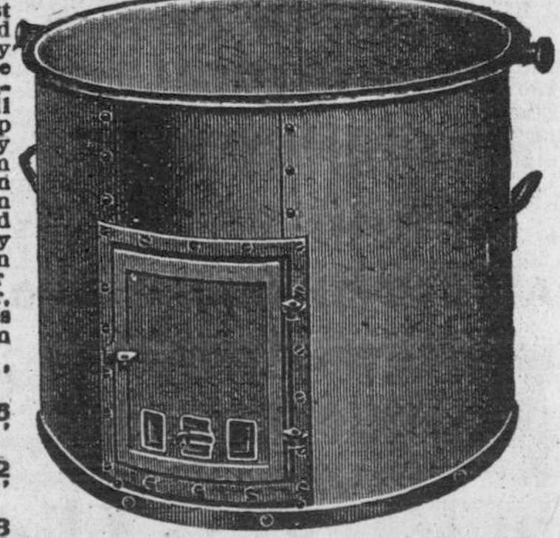

No. 32K1930 15-Gallon Farmers' Friend Cooker. Wt., 105 lbs. Price..........$4.46
No. 32K1931 22-Gallon Farmers' Friend Cooker. Wt., 125 lbs. Price..........$5.72
No. 32K1932 30-Gallon Farmers' Friend Cooker. Wt., 157 lbs. Price..........$6.78
No. 32K1933 45-Gallon Farmers' Friend Cooker. Wt., 198 lbs. Price...$ 8.35
No. 32K1934 60-Gallon Farmers' Friend Cooker. Wt., 261 lbs. Price... 10.30
No. 32K1935 75-Gallon Farmers' Friend Cooker. Wt., 310 lbs. Price... 11.95
No. 32K1937 Coal Grate for 15 and 22-gallon Cookers. Wt., 28 lbs. Price.......... 1.62
No. 32K1938 Coal Grate for 30, 45, 60 and 75-gallon Cookers. Wt., 55 lbs. Price.......... 2.32
No. 32K1940 Wood Hinged Cover for 15 and 22-gallon Cookers. Wt., 15 lbs. Price.......... .45
No. 32K1941 Wood Hinged Cover for 30, 45, 60 and 75-gallon Cookers. Wt., 30 lbs. Price.......... .55

$1.98

CALDRON KETTLES.

AT REDUCED PRICES.

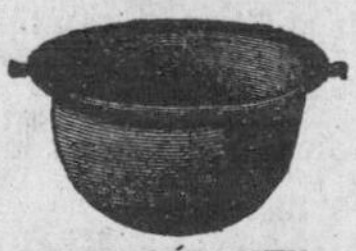

FULL CAPACITY

These kettles are exactly the same as are used in our Farmers' Friend Food Cookers. They can be used for cooking food, rendering lard, boiling syrup, etc. Shipped from factory in Central Ohio.

No. 32K1950 15-Gallon Kettle. Wt., 53 lbs. Price.$1.98
No. 32K1951 22-Gallon Kettle. Wt., 70 lbs. Price. 2.45
No. 32K1952 30-Gallon Kettle. Wt., 84 lbs. Price. 3.32
No. 32K1953 45-Gallon Kettle. Wt., 120 lbs. Price. 4.36
No. 32K1954 60-Gallon Kettle. Wt., 173 lbs. Price. 5.96
No. 32K1955 75-Gallon Kettle. Wt., 228 lbs. Price. 7.82

KENWOOD FOOD COOKERS.

$3.95

ONE OF THE MOST POPULAR COOKERS ON THE MARKET

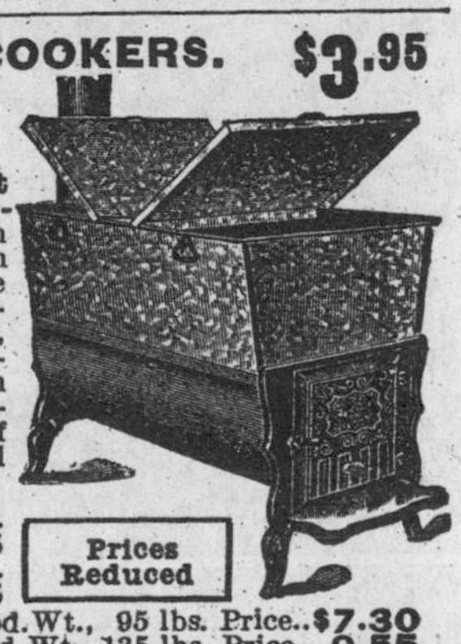

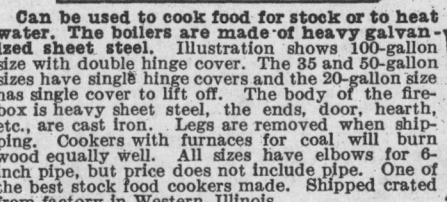

Prices Reduced

Can be used to cook food for stock or to heat water. The boilers are made of heavy galvanized sheet steel. Illustration shows 100-gallon size with double hinge cover. The 35 and 50-gallon sizes have single hinge covers and the 20-gallon size has single cover to lift off. The body of the firebox is heavy sheet steel, the ends, door, hearth, etc., are cast iron. Legs are removed when shipping. Cookers with furnaces for coal will burn wood equally well. All sizes have elbows for 6-inch pipe, but price does not include pipe. One of the best stock food cookers made. Shipped crated from factory in Western Illinois.

No. 32K1962 20-gallon Cooker, for wood. Wt., 60 lbs. Price..........$3.95
No. 32K1963 35-gallon Cooker, for wood. Wt., 70 lbs. Price..........$4.95
No. 32K1964 50-gallon Cooker, for wood. Wt., 95 lbs. Price..$7.30
No. 32K1965 100-gallon Cooker, for wood. Wt., 135 lbs. Price.. 9.55
No. 32K1967 35-gallon Cooker, for coal. Wt., 120 lbs. Price.. 7.25
No. 32K1968 50-gallon Cooker, for coal. Wt., 130 lbs. Price.. 9.25
No. 32K1969 100-gallon Cooker, for coal. Wt., 170 lbs. Price. 11.50

$9.94 HANDY FOOD COOKERS.

THE BEST OF THEIR KIND.

These cookers have cast iron fire boxes and flues and should not be confused with cookers of other make having sheet steel fire boxes which cost far less to make and therefore can be sold at lower prices. Our cookers will outlast two of the other kind and consequently are worth twice as much, although our prices are but little more than others ask for the inferior kind. They are the most convenient and desirable steel boiler food cookers made. The boiler is made entirely of heavy galvanized sheet steel, strongly bound at top and bottom and has a close fitting hinged cover. The fire box, fire flue and grate are cast iron and will keep their form and last indefinitely; others use a steel fire box. These cookers will burn wood, coal or cobs. The fire flue is 4 inches deep, extends entire length of boiler, and has a partition in center which directs the heat from fire box to opposite end, then back to smoke pipe. Can be used for cooking feed, boiling water and for many other purposes. Prices are for cooker complete with elbow and one joint of 6-inch pipe. Shipped knocked down from factory in Southwestern Michigan.

No. 32K1981 60-Gallon Handy Cooker. Wt., 200 lbs. Price..$ 9.94
No. 32K1982 90-Gallon Handy Cooker. Wt., 215 lbs. Price.. 10.95
No. 32K1983 115-Gallon Handy Cooker. Wt., 250 lbs. Price.. 12.45
No. 32K1984 160-Gallon Handy Cooker. Wt., 300 lbs. Price.. 13.95

HERCULES BOILERS and STEAM FOOD COOKERS

AT REDUCED PRICES.

The best food cooking or steaming boilers on the market. Made of boiler plate steel, which has a tensile strength of 60,000 pounds, hand riveted and tested to 100 pounds water pressure. Has regular 2-inch lap welded boiler flues which pass through the water and give large heating surface. The fire door is large and the grate will burn any kind of short or chunk fuel. Can be used for cooking or steaming any kind of food for stock, in a barrel or vat, and for many other purposes. Both sizes are 19 inches in diameter. No. 1 is 54 inches high and has 9 flues; No. 2 is 58 inches high and has 13 flues. Price is for boiler complete with hand pump, safety valve, two gauge cocks, also two valves, 2 feet of hose and with regular amount of iron pipe and fittings. Both sides are fitted for 8-inch smoke stack. Shipped knocked down from factory in Southwestern Michigan.

$23.70

No. 32K1990 No. 1 Hercules Boiler. Wt., 360 lbs. Price..$23.70
No. 32K1991 No. 2 Hercules Boiler. Wt., 430 lbs. Price.. 25.50

ADJUSTABLE SWINGING CATTLE STANCHIONS.

Price Lower Than Ever Before.

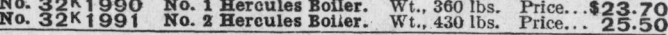

These Stanchions are much superior to any others on the market, and they are practically the only adjustable stanchions made. They can be easily and quickly adjusted so as to set the upright bars either 5, 5½, 6, 6½, 7, 7½, or 8 inches apart, adapting them for use with any animal from a small calf to a large bull. The illustration to the left shows two stanchions set in the stable framework. One shows closed and locked. When in this position it turns or swings freely on its pivots, allows the animal to take easy and natural positions whether standing or lying down, and is securely locked so that the animal cannot open it. The other shows open, and when it is in this position it is held squarely so that the animal cannot turn it and has no trouble when putting its head into the stanchion. The illustration to the right shows how the stanchions can be adjusted to different widths. The stanchions are 4 feet high. Both top and bottom are made of steel and iron, and the pivots are iron. **Sold only in lots of one-half dozen or more.** Shipped crated from factory in Southeastern Wisconsin.

ADJUSTABLE TO SEVEN WIDTHS.

No. 32K2200 Cattle Stanchions. Wt., each, 16 lbs.
Price, per half dozen..$5.88

$3.05 KENWOOD STEEL FRAME BARREL CART.

PRICE REDUCED.

Will outlast several wood frame carts. Made entirely of steel and iron. The steel wheels are 36 inches high, with 1¼ x ¼-inch tires. The frame is bolted solidly to the axle castings and these castings are made to fit the side of a barrel to which they are to be bolted. A kerosene, molasses or vinegar barrel can be used. Price includes bolts to attach to barrel and one iron bracket or rest for bottom of barrel. Shipped knocked down from factory in Southeastern Wisconsin.

No. 32K2225 Barrel Cart. Wt., 55 lbs.
Price...$3.05

$4.45 KENWOOD HAND CART.

REDUCED IN PRICE.

This is a very strongly constructed and high grade hand cart, without springs. It is especially adapted to farm and other rough usage and has an extra large and deep box, a heavy axle and very strong wheels. The box is 36 inches long, 21 inches wide and 9½ inches deep inside. The axle is 1-inch round steel. The steel wheels are 36 inches high with 1¼ x ¼-inch tires. End boards are held in place by steel rods. Both ends and sides can be removed, leaving bottom flat. Shipped knocked down from factory in Southeastern Wisconsin.
No. 32K2227 Kenwood Hand Cart. Wt., 90 lbs. Price.....$4.45

KENWOOD WOOD AND POLE SAW FRAMES.

Our line of wood and pole saw frames is the best and most complete in the United States. The construction of these machines cannot be excelled nor can an equal quality of saw frames be purchased elsewhere at such extremely low prices as we quote on these machines. All our wood and pole saw frames are knocked down and crated in the manner shown in this illustration, so that the freight charges are only about one-half what they would be were the frames knocked down and shipped in the ordinary manner. Directions for setting up accompany each frame. The cut-off saw blades which we furnish are especially made for use on our wood and pole saw frames. They are filed and set ready for use, and are fully guaranteed, and if kept properly filed and set, and run at the proper speed, they will do perfect work and give perfect satisfaction. 20 or 22-inch saw blades should be run from 900 to 1,400 revolutions per minute and require 2 to 3-horse power; 24 or 26-inch saw blades must be run from 800 to 1,200 revolutions per minute and require 4-horse power. 28 or 30-inch saw blades should be run from 700 to 1,000 revolutions per minute and require 6-horse power. **Rip saws cannot be used on these saw frames** and 30 inches is the largest cut-off saw that can be used.

KENWOOD EXTENSION TABLE WOOD SAW FRAME.

GREAT REDUCTION IN PRICES.

$11.98

For sawing poles or regular 4-foot cord wood. The table can be set at the side for sawing long poles, as shown in the illustration, or it can be set in front of the saw frame in the usual manner for sawing cord wood. The shaft is 4 feet 5 inches long with 1⅜-inch arbor and 5-inch arbor flanges. It has grooves in the boxes to prevent end play. The boxes are connected together by an iron frame which keeps them in perfect alignment. Driving pulley is 5 inches in diameter with 6-inch face. Balance wheel weighs 100 pounds. The cast iron saw guard is adjustable to fit saws from 20 inches to 30 inches in diameter. Can furnish right or left hand frame, but **we always ship right hand frame,** unless left hand frame is ordered. Shipped knocked down from factory in Southeastern Wisconsin.

No. 32K2110 Extension Table Saw Frame, without saw.
Wt., 365 lbs. Price.......................................$11.98
No. 32K2111 Extension Table Saw Frame, with 20-inch
saw. Wt., 376 lbs. Price................................ 15.52
No. 32K2112 Extension Table Saw Frame, with 22-inch
saw. Wt., 379 lbs. Price................................ 16.30
No. 32K2113 Extension Table Saw Frame, with 24-inch
saw. Wt., 382 lbs. Price................................ 17.07
No. 32K2114 Extension Table Saw Frame, with 26-inch
saw. Wt., 385 lbs. Price................................ 17.85
No. 32K2115 Extension Table Saw Frame, with 28-inch
saw. Wt., 391 lbs. Price................................ 18.63
No. 32K2116 Extension Table Saw Frame, with 30-inch
saw. Wt., 394 lbs. Price................................ 19.42

KENWOOD SLIDING TABLE WOOD SAW FRAME.

$12.98

BIG REDUCTION IN PRICES.

For sawing regular 4-foot cord wood. The table is run on two iron ways which form a part of the frame, and slides on rollers, thus being very easy to operate. The shaft is 4 feet 5 inches long, with 1⅜-inch arbor, and 5-inch arbor flanges. It has grooves in the boxes to prevent end play. Driving pulley is 5 inches diameter, with 6-inch face. Balance wheel weighs 100 pounds. The hood is made to accommodate any size of saw from 20 inches to 30 inches in diameter. Can furnish either right or left hand frame, but **we always ship right hand frame** unless left hand frame is ordered. Shipped knocked down from factory in Southeastern Wisconsin.

No. 32K2125 Sliding Table Saw Frame, without saw. Wt., 370 lbs.
Price...$12.98
No. 32K2126 Sliding Table Saw Frame, with 20-inch saw. Wt., 381 lbs.
Price... 16.52
No. 32K2127 Sliding Table Saw Frame, with 22-inch saw. Wt., 384 lbs.
Price... 17.30
No. 32K2128 Sliding Table Saw Frame, with 24-inch saw. Wt., 387 lbs.
Price... 18.07
No. 32K2129 Sliding Table Saw Frame, with 26-inch saw. Wt., 390 lbs.
Price... 18.85
No. 32K2130 Sliding Table Saw Frame, with 28-inch saw. Wt., 396 lbs.
Price... 19.63
No. 32K2131 Sliding Table Saw Frame, with 30-inch saw. Wt., 399 lbs.
Price... 20.42

KENWOOD POLE SAW FRAME.

PRICES GREATLY REDUCED.

$13.98

The strongest, best constructed and most popular Saw Frame made in the United States. Suitable for sawing cord wood and long poles of every description. The mandrel shaft is 4 feet 1 inch long with 1⅜-inch saw arbor and 5-inch arbor flanges. It has grooves in boxes to prevent end play. The mandrel shaft boxes are connected together with an iron frame which keeps them in perfect alignment. The center tightening pulley is hung on a heavy cast iron bracket with heavy steel shaft, and is so strongly built that it cannot get out of line. All pulleys are 5 inches diameter and 6-inch face. Balance wheel weighs 100 pounds. The cast iron saw guard is adjustable to fit saws from 20 inches to 30 inches in diameter. Can furnish either right or left hand frame but **we always ship right hand frame** unless left hand frame is ordered. Shipped knocked down from factory in Southeastern Wisconsin.

No. 32K2135 Pole Saw Frame, without saw. Wt., 415 lbs. Price..$13.98
No. 32K2136 Pole Saw Frame, with 20-inch saw. Wt., 426 lbs. Price.. 17.58
No. 32K2137 Pole Saw Frame, with 22-inch saw. Wt., 429 lbs. Price.. 18.38
No. 32K2138 Pole Saw Frame, with 24-inch saw. Wt., 432 lbs. Price.. 19.16
No. 32K2139 Pole Saw Frame, with 26-inch saw. Wt., 435 lbs. Price.. 19.98
No. 32K2140 Pole Saw Frame, with 28-inch saw. Wt., 441 lbs. Price.. 20.68
No. 32K2141 Pole Saw Frame, with 30-inch saw. Wt., 444 lbs. Price.. 21.58

NOTE OUR BIG PRICE REDUCTIONS

KENWOOD CANE MILLS.

FOR SORGHUM OR SUGAR CANE.

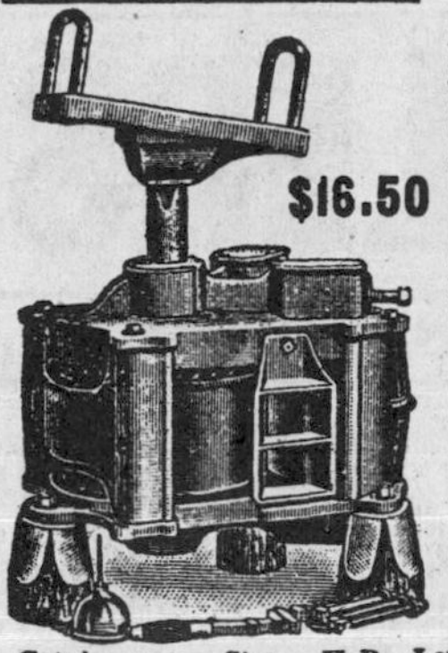

$16.50

These are extra heavy vertical three-roll mills, possessing all the good qualities of the original Great Western pattern and all the strength of the solid gear models, but without the defects of either. In fact, they are strictly up to date cane mills of the highest quality, containing all late improvements and suitable for the heaviest work. They have a bolt at each corner of the frame and are made rigid by a panel at the end. The gears are very heavy and are separate from the rolls and connected by two clutches on each gear. Both top and bottom journals run in brass boxes, are oiled from the top and constructed so that oil cannot get into the juice. All shafts are steel with turned bearings. The rollers are turned with serrated surfaces. The main rollers are flanged at top and bottom which prevents the cane from passing either up or down, and the feed guide is made so that the full length of the roll can be used. The gearing is encased. The capacity of these mills is greater than others of corresponding size, because our mills are heavier and much stronger and they press the cane dry. It is impossible to state the exact number of gallons of juice any cane mill will make, because this depends upon the richness of the cane, therefore, we state capacities in tons of cane per twelve hours. The regular sweep cap is single pitch, as shown in the illustration, but we can furnish double pitch cap, or level top cap if so ordered. Price includes sweep cap, bolts, oil can and wrench. Shipped from factory in Southwestern Ohio.

Catalogue No.	Size No.	H.P. Required	Length of Rolls, in.	Diam. of Rolls, in. Large	Diam. of Rolls, in. Small	Capacity in Tons	Wt. Lbs.	Price
32K2301	0	1	5½	10⅛	6⅛	2 to 3	440	$16.50
32K2302	1	1	6¼	11⅜	6¾	3 to 4	540	22.20
32K2303	2	2	7½	13½	7⅛	4 to 5	755	30.75
32K2304	3	2	9¾	14¾	8	6 to 7	1000	41.00
32K2305	4	2	12	16	9¼	8 to 10	1375	52.50

COOK'S EVAPORATOR PANS.

FOR SORGHUM AND SUGAR CANE.

$4.42

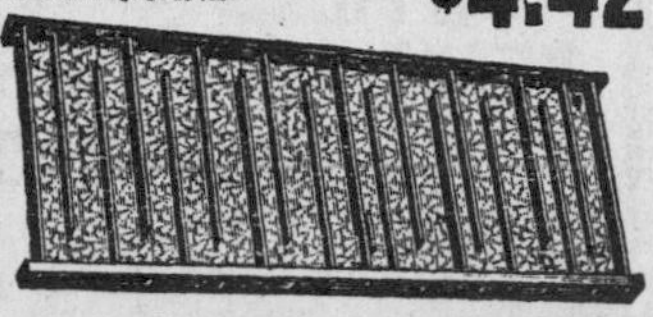

These pans are for evaporating sorghum, sugar cane and other thick juices. They are not suitable for maple sap or thin juices of any kind. They are strongly made with wood sides, heavily bound, riveted and soldered, with no seams exposed to the fire. Pans are 4 inches deep with division bars 6 inches apart. Galvanized pans are made of No. 24-gauge sheet steel. Copper pans are made of 16-ounce cold rolled copper. Syrup is drawn off through small spout in corner of pan. Price includes two skimmers. Pans can be set on brick arch or mounted on rocker furnace. All pans are 44 inches wide. Capacity for twelve hours is about as follows: 66-inch pan, 20 to 30 gallons; 72-inch pan, 30 to 40 gallons; 90-inch pan, 40 to 50 gallons; 108-inch pan, 50 to 80 gallons; 126-inch pan, 75 to 120 gallons of syrup, depending upon richness of juice. Shipped from factory in Southwestern Ohio.

No. 32K2311 66-inch Cook's Galvanized Pan. Wt., 72 lbs. Price......$ 4.42
No. 32K2312 72-inch Cook's Galvanized Pan. Wt., 84 lbs. Price..... 4.88
No. 32K2313 90-inch Cook's Galvanized Pan. Wt., 101 lbs. Price..... 6.07
No. 32K2314 108-inch Cook's Galvanized Pan. Wt., 119 lbs. Price..... 7.32
No. 32K2315 126-inch Cook's Galvanized Pan. Wt., 137 lbs. Price..... 8.48
No. 32K2321 66-inch Cook's Copper Pan. Wt., 97 lbs. Price..... 15.75
No. 32K2322 72-inch Cook's Copper Pan. Wt., 110 lbs. Price..... 17.20
No. 32K2323 90-inch Cook's Copper Pan. Wt., 135 lbs. Price..... 21.45
No. 32K2324 108-inch Cook's Copper Pan. Wt., 150 lbs. Price..... 25.85
No. 32K2325 126-inch Cook's Copper Pan. Wt., 165 lbs. Price..... 30.10

BUCKEYE EVAPORATOR PANS.

$5.82

FOR MAPLE SYRUP, SORGHUM OR SUGAR CANE.

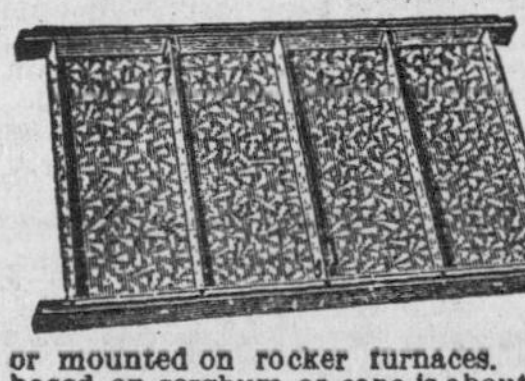

Especially adapted for making maple syrup or evaporating other thin juices, but equally as good for sorghum and sugar cane. Strongly made with wood sides and heavily bound, riveted and soldered, but the sides of the pan are turned up square so that the juice does not touch the wood. Each section is made of a single sheet, without seams, and forms a pan of itself. No seams exposed to the fire. Pans are 4 inches deep with division bars 15½ inches apart. Galvanized pans are made of No. 24-gauge sheet steel. Copper pans are made of 16-ounce cold rolled copper. Syrup is drawn off through small spout in corner of pan. Price includes two skimmers. Pans can be set on brick arch or mounted on rocker furnaces. All pans are 42 inches wide. Capacity per twelve hours based on sorghum or cane is about as follows: 63-inch pan, 30 to 40 gallons; 80-inch pan, 40 to 60 gallons; 96-inch pan, 60 to 80 gallons; 112-inch pan, 80 to 100 gallons; 128-inch pan, 100 to 120 gallons of syrup, depending upon richness of juice. On maple syrup the capacity will be much less, because it takes about 40 gallons of sap to make 1 gallon of syrup, though it evaporates quicker. Shipped from factory in Southwestern Ohio.

No. 32K2331 63-inch Buckeye Galvanized Pan. Wt., 85 lbs. Price.....$ 5.82
No. 32K2332 80-inch Buckeye Galvanized Pan. Wt., 95 lbs. Price..... 7.36
No. 32K2333 96-inch Buckeye Galvanized Pan. Wt., 105 lbs. Price..... 8.87
No. 32K2334 112-inch Buckeye Galvanized Pan. Wt., 125 lbs. Price..... 10.48
No. 32K2335 128-inch Buckeye Galvanized Pan. Wt., 145 lbs. Price..... 13.18
No. 32K2341 63-inch Buckeye Copper Pan. Wt., 100 lbs. Price..... 16.98
No. 32K2342 80-inch Buckeye Copper Pan. Wt., 110 lbs. Price..... 21.55
No. 32K2343 96-inch Buckeye Copper Pan. Wt., 125 lbs. Price..... 25.90
No. 32K2344 112-inch Buckeye Copper Pan. Wt., 140 lbs. Price..... 31.30
No. 32K2345 128-inch Buckeye Copper Pan. Wt., 160 lbs. Price..... 34.50

FURNACE FRONTS WITH GRATES, $3.48. PRICES REDUCED.

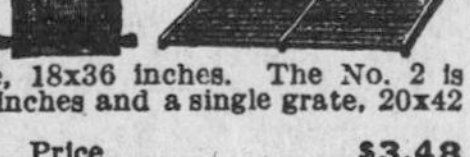

Evaporator pans are frequently mounted on a brick arch. This requires a furnace front and grate. These fronts with grates consist of door frame, door, anchor rods and grate complete. The No. 1 is suitable for use with 63 to 96-inch pans. It has a single door, 12x12 inches, and a single grate, 18x36 inches. The No. 2 is suitable for use with 90 to 108-inch pans. It has a door 13x16 inches and a single grate, 20x42 inches. Shipped from factory in Southwestern Ohio.

No. 32K2351 No. 1 Furnace Front. Weight, 85 lbs. Price..............$3.48
No. 32K2353 No. 2 Furnace Front. Weight, 140 lbs. Price.............. 6.92

ROCKER FURNACES.

$8.38

These furnaces are made to fit our Cook's or Buckeye Evaporator Pans, but when ordering you must state the length and name of the pan you want the furnace to fit. A rocker furnace and a pan together make a complete portable evaporator which can be set up and used anywhere. Furnaces are mounted on angle steel rockers and price is for furnace complete with fire door, grates and chimney, but does not include an evaporator pan. Shipped from factory in Southwestern Ohio.

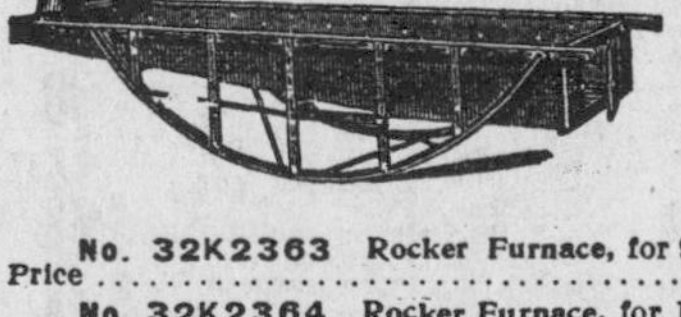

No. 32K2361 Rocker Furnace, for 63-inch or 66-inch pans. Wt., 180 lbs. Price..............$8.38
No. 32K2362 Rocker Furnace, for 72-inch or 80-inch pans. Wt., 200 lbs. Price..............$ 9.20
No. 32K2363 Rocker Furnace, for 90-inch or 96-inch pans. Wt., 215 lbs. Price.............. 10.48
No. 32K2364 Rocker Furnace, for 108-inch or 112-inch pans. Wt., 230 lbs. Price..........$11.95
No. 32K2365 Rocker Furnace, for 126-inch or 128-inch pans. Wt., 250 lbs. Price..........$13.40

DOAN DITCHING SCRAPER.

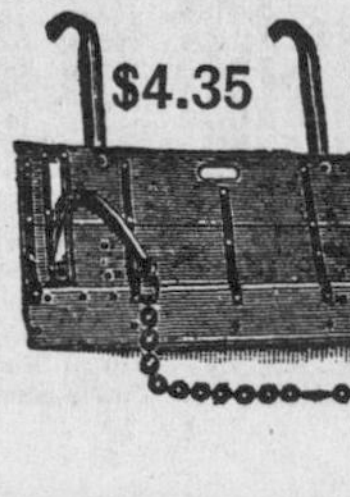

$4.35

Another Reduction in Price.

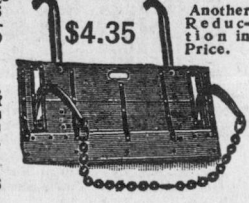

An excellent scraper for cleaning out and filling ditches, and for leveling roads and uneven places. Is well made of seasoned hardwood. Steel bit is 48 inches long, 7 inches wide and ¼ inch thick. This scraper is well ironed, has 1¾ by ⅜-inch steel hounds, with ⅜-inch cable chain. Shipped from factory in Western Ohio.

No. 32K2525 Ditching Scraper. Wt., 75 lbs. Price..............$4.35

$6.45 SELF FEED CIDER MILL.

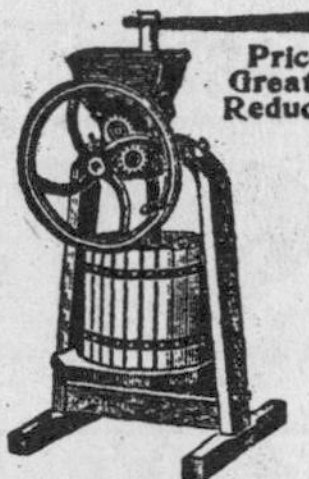

Price Greatly Reduced

This is a thoroughly desirable and first class single tub cider mill and press, which will grind apples to the perfect satisfaction of the user. It is a geared cylinder mill, grinds very rapidly and turns very easily. It is strongly constructed, is made of the best materials and nicely finished in natural wood. It is adapted to a greater range of work than any other single tub cider mill made, and is worth three of the ordinary Hutchinson pattern mill. It will grind any size of apple and has a capacity of one to two barrels of cider per day. Tub is 12 inches high and 13½ inches outside diameter. Every owner of one or more apple trees should have one of these mills, and we guarantee that the mill will give perfect satisfaction. Shipped from factory in Southern Pennsylvania.

No. 32K2385 Self Feed Cider Mill. Wt., 160 lbs. Price, $6.45

JUNIOR AND MEDIUM STANDARD CIDER MILLS

AT REDUCED PRICES.

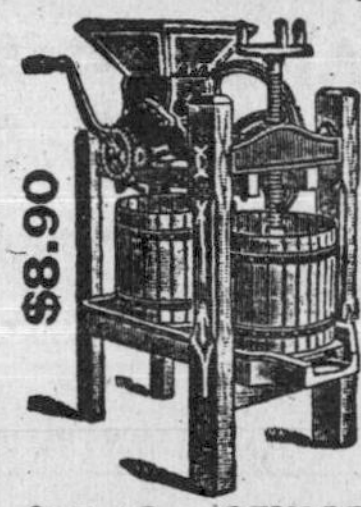

$8.90

These are the most popular sizes of Standard Cider Mills. They are strictly high grade in every particular and will give perfect satisfaction; in fact, they are the best cider mills made. The frames are heavy hardwood and are bolted together. The mill parts are cast iron and steel. The cross head for the press screw is heavy cast iron. The press screw is steel. These mills will grind large as well as small apples. The rolls are the same diameter in each size of mill, but are of different lengths. The Junior mill has a capacity of two to four barrels of cider per day and has two tubs, each 10 inches high by 12 inches outside diameter. The Medium mill has a capacity of three to six barrels of cider per day and has two tubs, each 12 inches high and 13½ inches outside diameter. Each size is back geared, has a heavy balance wheel, is operated by a single crank, has a large hopper and a force feed. Shipped from factory in Southern Pennsylvania.

No. 32K2387 Junior Cider Mill. Wt., 190 lbs. Price..$ 8.90
No. 32K2388 Medium Cider Mill. Wt., 240 lbs. Price.. 11.70

$15.40 SENIOR STANDARD CIDER MILL.

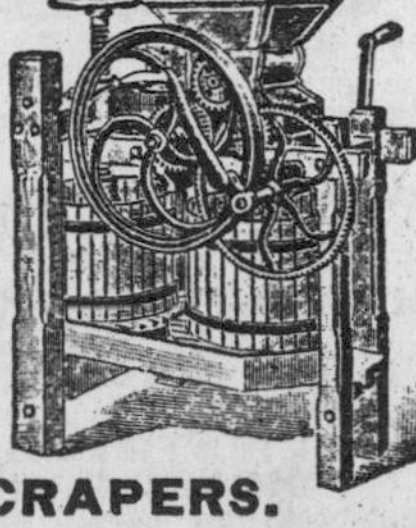

This is the largest size of our standard cider mills. It is the best designed, best built and most desirable senior size cider mill made. The frame is of heavy hardwood, strongly bolted together. The mill parts are iron and steel, the cross head for the press screw is heavy cast iron. The press screw is steel and of large diameter. The rolls are of good form and of ample size and length. This mill is double back geared, has a heavy balance wheel, a large hopper with force feed and is fitted with two cranks. It will grind large or small apples rapidly, has a capacity of six to twelve barrels of cider per day and has two tubs, each 14 inches high by 17 inches outside diameter. Shipped from factory in Southern Pennsylvania.

No. 32K2389 Senior Cider Mill. Wt., 420 lbs. Price..............$15.40

KENWOOD STEEL ROAD SCRAPERS.

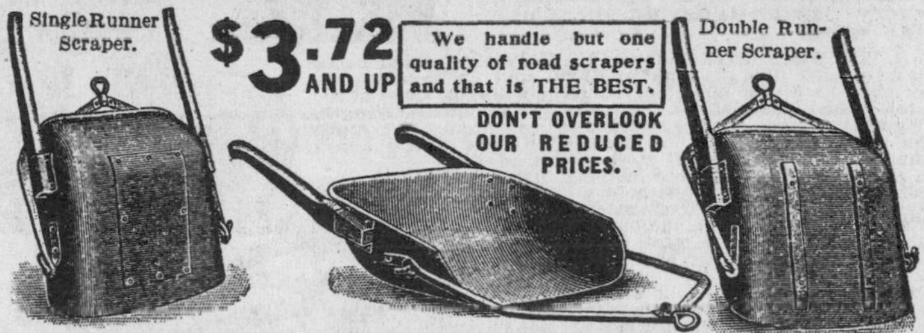

$3.72 AND UP

We handle but one quality of road scrapers and that is THE BEST.

DON'T OVERLOOK OUR REDUCED PRICES.

These are the highest grade steel road scrapers made. Do not confuse them with low quality tank steel scrapers offered by others in order to compete with our astonishingly low prices. These scrapers are made for us by old and reputable manufacturers who are acknowledged to be producers of the highest grade and most up to date road machinery in the world, they confine their efforts to the production of nothing but goods of the highest quality and on account of their matchless facilities and enormous output they are enabled to produce for us goods of the highest possible grade at a cost which enables us to offer them to you at about the same price others ask for scrapers of much inferior quality. Take our word for it, you cannot possibly buy better scrapers than these, no matter what price you pay. Send us your order and compare our scrapers with any others you can buy anywhere, and at any price, and if you are not satisfied that our scrapers are equal to, if not better than any others you can buy, and that at our price they are the best value you ever saw, send them back to us and we will gladly refund your money and pay all freight charges. The bowl of these scrapers is pressed from a single sheet of heavy specially hardened steel plate, making a round cornered and perfectly formed bowl which scours and cleans easily. The nose is rounded and enters the ground freely. Have heavy steel bail, swivel hitch and hardwood handles. Made of the highest grade 40 to 45-point carbon low sulphur scraper steel and guaranteed to be absolutely the best and most substantial steel road scraper on the market. Smooth bottom scrapers do not have runners on the bottom. Double runner scrapers are the favorite and have two steel runners, each about 1½ inches wide and ¾ inch thick. Single runner scrapers have a broad single runner made of a single heavy steel plate. Made in three sizes. No. 3 holds 3½ cubic feet and weighs 80 pounds. No. 2 holds 5 cubic feet and weighs 90 pounds. No. 1 holds 7 cubic feet and weighs 100 pounds. Shipped from factory in Western Ohio.

No. 32K2500 No. 3 Smooth Bottom Scraper. Price..............$3.72
No. 32K2501 No. 2 Smooth Bottom Scraper. Price.............. 3.97
No. 32K2502 No. 1 Smooth Bottom Scraper. Price.............. 4.27
No. 32K2503 No. 3 Double Runner Scraper. Price.............. 3.98
No. 32K2504 No. 2 Double Runner Scraper. Price.............. 4.23
No. 32K2505 No. 1 Double Runner Scraper. Price.............. 4.53
No. 32K2506 No. 3 Single Runner Scraper. Price.............. 4.50
No. 32K2507 No. 2 Single Runner Scraper. Price.............. 4.80
No. 32K2508 No. 1 Single Runner Scraper. Price.............. 5.15

For $2.50 we could sell you a tank steel scraper, such as others offer, but we consider such scrapers dear at any price and we do not handle them.

$4.63 KENWOOD TONGUE SCRAPER AND DITCHER.

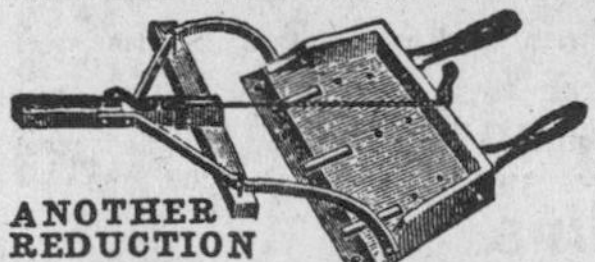

ANOTHER REDUCTION IN PRICE.

Adapted for cutting and cleaning out ditches and moving large quantities of earth quickly. The draw bars and bit are made of the best quality of steel. Body, tongue, cross bar and handles are made of well seasoned hardwood lumber, well ironed and bolted. Width, 48 inches. Shipped from factory in Western Ohio.

No. 32K2520 Tongue Scraper. Wt., 135 lbs. Price..............$4.63

KENWOOD WHEEL SCRAPERS.

The bowl is made from a single sheet of the highest grade 45 to 50-point carbon low sulphur scraper steel 3-16 inch thick, and is shaped so as to give the greatest amount of strength and carrying capacity. Cannot sag under the most severe strain. Hound hooks are stationary, very heavy, well braced and strongly riveted and carry the bowl high up from the ground. Axle is high, made from the best quality square steel. Spindles are turned and polished and fully protected by close fitting sand bands. Made in three sizes. No. 1, with 9 cubic feet capacity, has 36-inch wheels, 3x¼-inch tires and 1½-inch axle. No. 2, with 13 cubic feet capacity and 40-inch wheels, and No. 3 with 17 cubic feet capacity and 44-inch wheels, both having 3x5-16-inch tires and 1¾-inch axles. Price does not include doubletrees and neckyoke. Will furnish with Sarven hub wheels for $1.20 extra. Shipped knocked down from factory in Western Ohio.

$28.95

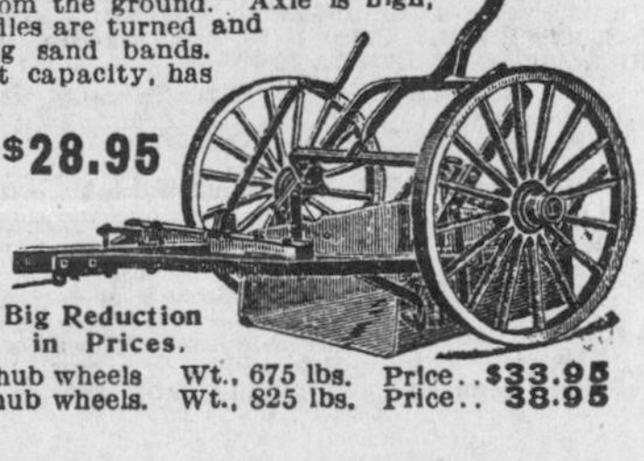

Big Reduction in Prices.

No. 32K2530 No. 1 Scraper, with wood hub wheels. Wt., 525 lbs. Price...$28.95
No. 32K2531 No. 2 Scraper, with wood hub wheels. Wt., 675 lbs. Price..$33.95
No. 32K2532 No. 3 Scraper, with wood hub wheels. Wt., 825 lbs. Price.. 38.95

PRICES GREATLY REDUCED

KENWOOD STUMP PULLERS

PRICES GREATLY REDUCED

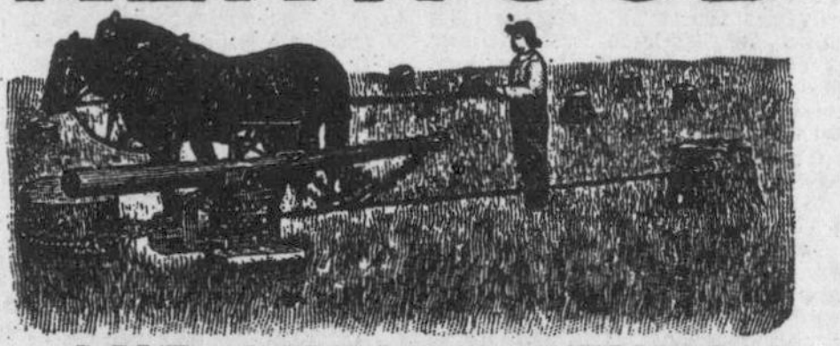

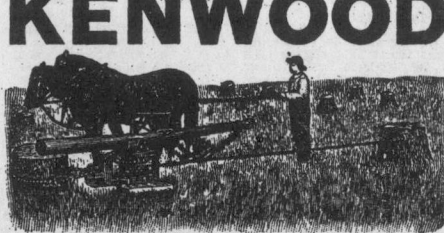

SAFE AND SIMPLE

STRONG AND DURABLE

AND ATTACHMENTS

BUILT TO DO THE WORK, AND TO DO IT SAFELY, SATISFACTORILY AND ECONOMICALLY.

DO NOT CONFOUND THEM WITH THE MANY CHEAPLY CONSTRUCTED SO CALLED STUMP PULLERS ON THE MARKET, WHICH ARE BUILT ONLY TO SELL AND WITHOUT REGARD FOR THE SAFETY OR CONVENIENCE OF THE OPERATOR. WHEN YOU BUY A KENWOOD YOU GET A GENUINE STUMP PULLER; A MACHINE OF WONDERFUL EFFICIENCY, ONE THAT WILL DO EVERYTHING WE CLAIM FOR IT (WHICH IS MORE THAN ANY OTHER STUMP PULLER MADE CAN DO) AND DO IT SAFELY AND TO YOUR ENTIRE SATISFACTION. NOTE THE RIGID CONSTRUCTION OF OUR MACHINES, THEIR WONDERFUL SIMPLICITY AND SUPERIOR DESIGN, WHICH, TOGETHER WITH THE EXTREMELY HIGH QUALITY OF ALL MATERIALS USED IN THEIR CONSTRUCTION, MAKE THEM POSITIVELY THE BEST AND MOST SUCCESSFUL STUMP PULLERS IN THE WORLD.

A FIRST CLASS STUMP PULLER IS NOT AN EXPENSE. IT IS SIMPLY AN INVESTMENT WHICH IS MADE IN ORDER THAT ITS OWNER MAY RECLAIM GOOD LANDS AND THUS GREATLY INCREASE HIS INCOME.

THE SOLID ONE-PIECE FRAME has no bolts to loosen, bend or break.

THE LONG ANCHOR NOSE keeps machine always level, cannot rear up or tip over.

THE POSITIVE WORKING RATCHET holds every inch your team can pull.

THE SCIENTIFICALLY DESIGNED DRUM preserves the cable by making every strand do its share of the work.

$17.25 AND UP

BIG PRICE REDUCTIONS

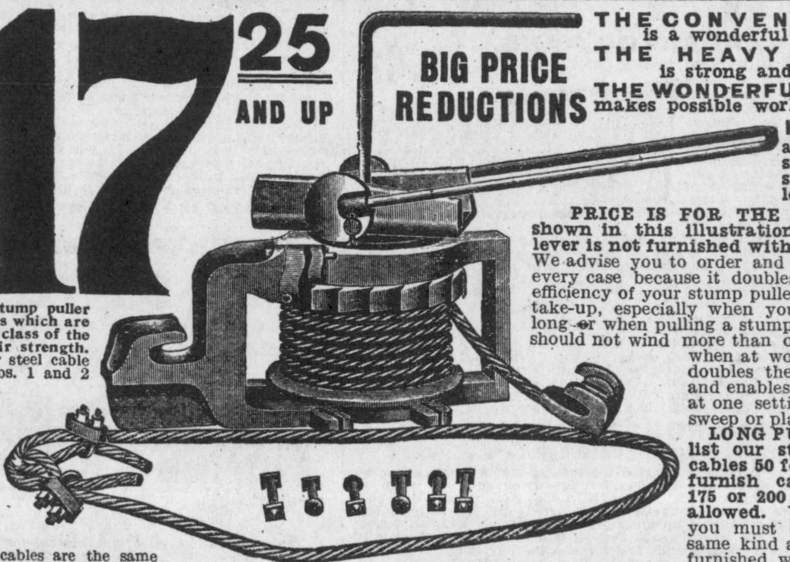

THE CONVENIENT HAND LEVER is a wonderful time and labor saver.

THE HEAVY SWEEP CASTING is strong and perfect in operation.

THE WONDERFUL DOUBLE ECCENTRIC makes possible work no other machine can do.

HIGHEST GRADE CABLE and perfectly formed cast steel hooks insure full strength, rapid hitches and long lived cables.

THE STRENGTH AND EFFICIENCY of a stump puller is no greater than the strength of the steel cables which are furnished with the machine, and the quality and class of the steel cables, as well as their size, govern their strength. We use a different size or strength of hemp center steel cable for each different size of machine. On our Nos. 1 and 2 machines we use a special steel cable made from a special grade of steel, combining high tensile strength with flexibility without any tendency to brittleness. On our larger machines we use an English steel cable, the highest grade, the strongest, the toughest and the most flexible steel cable which can be made. These cables cost a great deal more than the crcuible steel or plow steel cables, but they make our stump pullers many times more valuable than other machines, because crucible steel or plow steel cables are not suitable for this class of work. Aside from this, the design and construction of our machines are greatly superior to other makes. Anchor loop cables are the same size and grade as pulling cables and are fitted complete with cable clips.

PRICE IS FOR THE MACHINE COMPLETE, as shown in this illustration, excepting that the hand lever is not furnished with the Nos. 1 and 2 machines. We advise you to order and use a double power pulley in every case because it doubles the power and increases the efficiency of your stump puller. We also advise you to use a take-up, especially when your pulling cable is over 50 feet long or when pulling a stump on a short hitch, because you should not wind more than one layer of cable on the drum when at work, and the take-up practically doubles the amount of work you can do and enables you to pull a number of stumps at one setting. We do not furnish wood sweep or platform plank.

LONG PULLING CABLES. While we list our stump pullers with pulling cables 50 feet and 75 feet long, we can furnish cables 50, 75, 100, 125, 150, 175 or 200 feet long, if proper price is allowed. When ordering extra long cable, you must order and allow price of the same kind and size of cable as is regularly furnished with the machine.

The main frame of our stump pullers is very solid, strong and heavy. The heavy anchor hook on the front arch is long, providing a good distance between the center of the spool and the hook, thus preventing the machines from tipping. The drum is of large diameter and grooved so that the cable will wind properly from bottom to top, placing an equal strain on each strand of the cable. The sweep casting has an eccentric on each side and the machine can be put in or out of gear easily while under the heaviest strain. The ratchet holds at any point and the team can pass over the pulling cable with loose tugs or you can work the machine in corners or in close quarters. All but the Nos. 1 and 2 machines are provided with a hand lever with which you can easily wind up slack cable. On all sizes the drum can be set free to pay out the cable.

EXTRA CABLES. **We can furnish extra pulling cables or anchor cables** in 25, 50, 75, 100, 125, 175 and 200-foot lengths. For each extra cable you want, order and allow the price of the required number of feet and kind of cable wanted, one cable hook, and as many cable clips as the size of the cable requires.

We guarantee the machine part of every Kenwood Stump Puller we sell for one year from date of shipment, and will replace free any defective or broken part during that time, and we will replace any of our cable which breaks during that time, provided that the cable does not show that it has been broken by a short bend or by misuse. Order a Kenwood Stump Puller, and if it is not a better machine than you can obtain elsewhere at any price, return it at our expense and we will refund your money. Shipped from factory in Eastern Iowa.

No. 32K2601 No. 1 **Stump Puller,** suitable for use by hand or for one horse on an 8-foot sweep. Furnished with a 6-foot anchor loop and 50 feet of 5/8-inch Special steel pulling cable. Guaranteed to stand a strain of 45,000 pounds when a double power pulley is used. Weight, 300 pounds. Price........ **$17.25**

No. 32K2602 No. 2 **Stump Puller,** suitable for use with one horse on a 10-foot sweep. Furnished with an 8-foot anchor loop and 50 feet of 3/4-inch Special steel pulling cable. Guaranteed to stand a strain of 70,000 pounds when a double power pulley is used. Weight, 400 pounds. Price........ **$23.50**

No. 32K2603 No. 3 **Stump Puller,** suitable for use with two horses on a 12-foot sweep. Furnished with a 10-foot anchor loop and 50 feet of 3/4-inch highest grade English steel pulling cable. Guaranteed to stand a strain of 100,000 pounds when a double power pulley is used. Weight, 600 pounds. Price........ **$43.35**

No. 32K2604 No. 4 **Stump Puller,** suitable for use with two horses on a 14-foot sweep. Furnished with a 12-foot anchor loop and 75 feet of 7/8-inch highest grade English steel pulling cable. Guaranteed to stand a strain of 140,000 pounds when a double power pulley is used. Weight, 900 pounds. Price........ **$60.85**

No. 32K2605 No. 5 **Stump Puller,** suitable for use with two horses on a 16-foot sweep. Furnished with a 12-foot anchor loop and 75 feet of 1-inch highest grade English steel pulling cable. Guaranteed to stand a strain of 180,000 pounds when a double power pulley is used. Weight, 1,000 pounds. Price........ **$69.50**

PRICES REDUCED.

DOUBLE POWER PULLEYS.

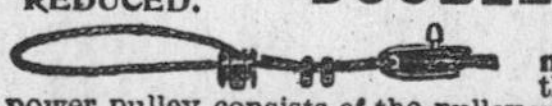

We recommend that you include one of these attachments in your order for a stump puller, as it will double the efficiency and capacity of your machine. A double power pulley consists of the pulley with the cable, a hook and the clips. The number indicates the size of machine with which they are to be used. Shipped from factory in Eastern Iowa.

No. 32K2611 No. 1 **Double Power Pulley,** with 8 feet of 5/8-inch Special steel cable. Wt., 75 lbs. Price........ **$6.42**

No. 32K2612 No. 2 **Double Power Pulley,** with 10 feet of 1-inch Special steel cable. Wt., 81 lbs. Price........ **$7.98**

No. 32K2613 No. 3 **Double Power Pulley,** with 12 feet of 1-inch English steel cable. Wt., 101 lbs. Price........ **$12.80**

No. 32K2614 No. 4 **Double Power Pulley,** with 15 feet of 1 1/8-inch English steel cable. Wt., 120 lbs. Price........ **$16.00**

No. 32K2615 No. 5 **Double Power Pulley,** with 15 feet of 1 1/4-inch English steel cable. Wt., 125 lbs. Price........ **$17.10**

CAM TAKE-UPS.

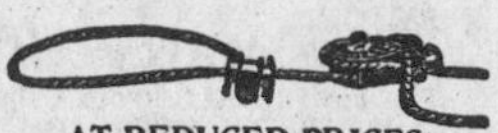

AT REDUCED PRICES.

Our Cam Take-Up is the most satisfactory take-up ever produced. It holds the cable between a grooved block and cam without injuring the cable. By using this attachment you will more than double the capacity of your stump puller, as it enables you to make hitches much more rapidly. It can be used with or without double power pulley, and at any point between the stump puller and the stump. The No. 1 is for use with our Nos. 1, 2 and 3 Stump Puller; No. 2 is for use with our No. 4 Stump Puller; and No. 3 is for use with our No. 5 Stump Puller. Price is for cam take-up complete, with hitch cable and hook. Shipped from factory in Eastern Iowa.

No. 32K2621 No. 1 **Cam Take-Up,** with 10 feet of 3/4-inch English steel cable. Wt., 48 lbs. Price........ **$8.80**

No. 32K2622 No. 2 **Cam Take-Up,** with 10 feet of 7/8-inch English steel cable. Wt., 60 lbs. Price........ **$12.85**

No. 32K2623 No. 3 **Cam Take-Up,** with 12 feet of 1-inch English steel cable. Wt., 75 lbs. Price........ **$16.10**

STUMP PULLER CABLE, HOOKS AND CLIPS.

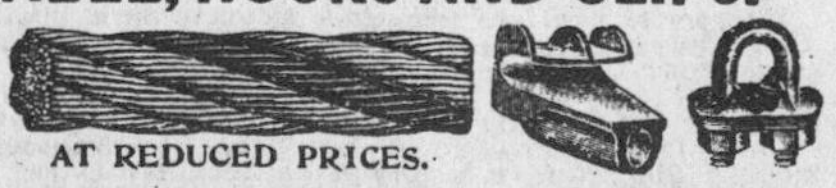

AT REDUCED PRICES.

Special Steel Cable is used with our Nos. 1 and 2 Stump Pullers and with our Nos. 1 and 2 Double Power Pulleys. English steel cable is used with our Nos. 3, 4 and 5 Stump Pullers and with our Nos. 3, 4 and 5 Double Power Pulleys, and Nos. 1, 2 and 3 Cam Take-Ups. When ordering long pulling cables or extra cable for either machines or attachments, be sure to order the same size and kind of cable regularly supplied with the machines or attachments. When ordering extra cables, always order one hook for each extra cable, and two clips for each extra cable 7/8 inch or less in diameter and three clips for each extra cable 1 inch or more in diameter. Our rope hooks are made of cast steel, others make theirs of common cast or malleable iron. This explains why our hooks may be higher in price than some others, but they are much stronger and really worth much more than the small difference in price represents. Shipped from factory in Eastern Iowa.

No. 32K2640	5/8-inch Special Steel Cable.	Wt., 3/4 lb.	Price, per foot...	$0.14
No. 32K2641	3/4-inch Special Steel Cable.	Wt., 1 lb.	Price, per foot...	.18
No. 32K2642	7/8-inch Special Steel Cable.	Wt., 1 1/4 lbs.	Price, per foot...	.24
No. 32K2643	1-inch Special Steel Cable.	Wt., 1 3/4 lbs.	Price, per foot...	.31
No. 32K2647	3/4-inch English Steel Cable.	Wt., 1 lb.	Price, per foot...	.30
No. 32K2648	7/8-inch English Steel Cable.	Wt., 1 1/4 lbs.	Price, per foot...	.33
No. 32K2649	1-inch English Steel Cable.	Wt., 1 3/4 lbs.	Price, per foot...	.47
No. 32K2650	1 1/8-inch English Steel Cable.	Wt., 2 lbs.	Price, per foot...	.57
No. 32K2651	1 1/4-inch English Steel Cable.	Wt., 2 1/2 lbs.	Price, per foot...	.72
No. 32K2653	Hook for 5/8-inch Cable.	Wt., 7 lbs.	Price, each......	1.30
No. 32K2654	Hook for 3/4-inch Cable.	Wt., 9 lbs.	Price, each......	1.65
No. 32K2655	Hook for 7/8-inch Cable.	Wt., 12 lbs.	Price, each......	1.95
No. 32K2656	Hook for 1-inch Cable.	Wt., 14 lbs.	Price, each......	2.30
No. 32K2657	Hook for 1 1/8-inch Cable.	Wt., 17 lbs.	Price, each......	2.95
No. 32K2658	Hook for 1 1/4-inch Cable.	Wt., 19 lbs.	Price, each......	3.30
No. 32K2660	Clip for 5/8-inch Cable.	Wt., 3/4 lb.	Price, each......	.15
No. 32K2661	Clip for 3/4-inch Cable.	Wt., 1 1/4 lbs.	Price, each......	.19
No. 32K2662	Clip for 7/8-inch Cable.	Wt., 2 lbs.	Price, each......	.24
No. 32K2663	Clip for 1-inch Cable.	Wt., 2 1/4 lbs.	Price, each......	.29
No. 32K2664	Clip for 1 1/8-inch Cable.	Wt., 2 1/2 lbs.	Price, each......	.34
No. 32K2665	Clip for 1 1/4-inch Cable.	Wt., 3 1/2 lbs.	Price, each......	.39

FORGED STEEL STUMP HOOKS.

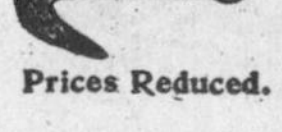

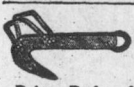

Prices Reduced.

Our stump or root hooks are extra heavy and are made of the very best forged steel. Most hooks of other manufacture are made of cast steel or malleable iron. These hooks are intended to be used for pulling mesquite brush, or where stumps are too low or so badly decayed that the pulling cable cannot be hitched around them. They are made very deep in the throat. No. 1 Stump Hook is for use with our Nos. 1 and 2 Stump Pullers; No. 2 is for use with our Nos. 3 and 4 Stump Pullers, and No. 3 is for use with our Nos. 4 and 5 Stump Pullers. Shipped from factory in Eastern Iowa.

No. 32K2626 No. 1 Steel Stump Hook. Wt., 50 lbs. Price........ **$7.95**

No. 32K2627 No. 2 Steel Stump Hook. Wt., 65 lbs. Price........ **9.60**

No. 32K2628 No. 3 Steel Stump Hook. Wt., 75 lbs. Price........ **11.20**

MARINE GASOLINE ENGINES

The successful operation of motor driven boats or launches and the full enjoyment of their ownership depends as much or more upon the engine as it does upon the hull itself. You must have a perfectly designed, correctly built and reliable engine, else your enjoyment of your motor boat will be continually interrupted, and that which should be an ideal sport will become a continued source of annoyance. Kenwood and Harvard Marine Gasoline Engines are the best engines of their respective types made and they will give you perfect satisfaction.

OUR WONDERFUL FREE TRIAL OFFER. **To give every purchaser an opportunity to thoroughly examine, test and try our Marine Gasoline Engines** and to compare the design, quality, workmanship, efficiency, durability and money value beside any other engine at any price, every engine is shipped on the understanding and agreement that after receiving the engine you are to have **thirty days** in which to give it a thorough trial and comparison. Under this offer you take no chance of loss because, if our engine does not stand the test to your perfect satisfaction, you to be the sole judge, you can return the engine at our expense and we will promptly return your money together with the freight charges you may have paid.

KENWOOD FOUR-CYCLE MARINE GASOLINE ENGINES

1½, 3 and 5-Horse Power Engines.

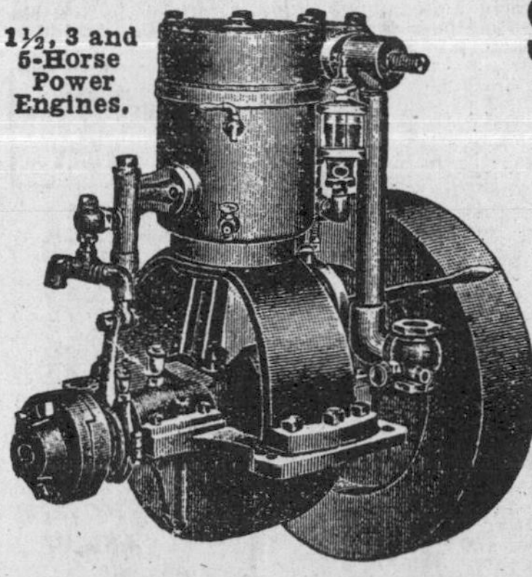

$93.25 AND UP

COMPLETE WITH BOAT OUTFIT, INCLUDING A GENUINE BRONZE REVERSIBLE PROPELLER WHEEL

YOU CANNOT BUY A BETTER ENGINE AT ANY PRICE

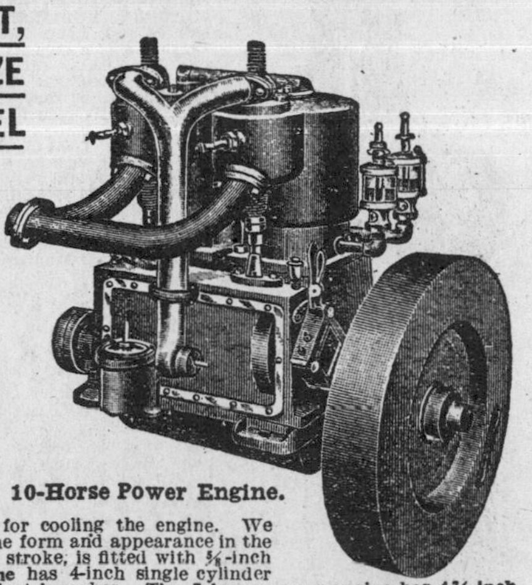

10-Horse Power Engine.

KENWOOD FOUR-CYCLE MARINE GASOLINE ENGINES **are of the highest possible grade and represent the most approved type of Marine Gasoline Engine construction.** They are the perfected product of manufacturers whose engines are everywhere recognized as standard, and to those who have a preference for an engine of the four-cycle type, they will at our exceptionally low prices prove to be value which cannot possibly be duplicated by others. These engines are of the four-cycle automobile type, perfectly balanced, simple, practical, durable, easily operated and capable of the best of results under all conditions. They are built very low and compact and set firmly in the boat, overcoming vibration and making the boat run very smoothly. **They are capable of great range of speed;** being equipped with jump spark electric igniter with timing lever, which makes the spark early or late, and thus regulates and controls the speed. The speed of the 1½, 3 and 5-horse power engines can be varied from 150 to 700 revolutions per minute, and of the 10-horse power engine from 150 to 800 revolutions per minute, or from a slow trolling gait to full speed. All sizes will, when installed in a boat of proper size and construction, drive the boat at from 6 to 8 miles per hour. The gasoline feed is by gravity from a tank which you must provide and place in the bow of the boat. The water circulation is obtained by a brass pump which provides a steady flow of water for cooling the engine. We furnish the best bronze reversible propeller wheels with these engines, they are built on the lines of a perfect solid wheel, having the same form and appearance in the forward pitch as a solid wheel, with the advantage of reversing. **The 1½-horse power engine** has 3¼-inch single cylinder with 3½-inch stroke, is fitted with ⅝-inch diameter propeller shaft and 12-inch diameter propeller wheel and is suitable for 14 to 18-foot launches. **The 3-horse power engine** has 4-inch single cylinder with 4½-inch stroke, is fitted with ¾-inch diameter propeller shaft and 14-inch diameter propeller wheel and is suitable for 16 to 20-foot launches. **The 5-horse power engine has 4⅞-inch** single cylinder with 5-inch stroke; is fitted with 1-inch diameter propeller shaft and 18-inch diameter propeller wheel and is suitable for 18 to 25-foot launches. **The 10-horse power engine** has 5-inch double cylinders with 5-inch stroke; is fitted with 1¼-inch diameter propeller shaft and 22-inch diameter propeller wheel and is suitable for 25 to 40-foot launches. While we rate this engine at only 10-horse power it will actually develop as much power and drive a boat just as fast if not faster than engines which others rate at 15-horse power. All fittings and trimmings furnished with these engines are of the very best quality. Prices are for the engines complete, with spark coil, spark plug, batteries, switch, wire, carbureter, muffler, pump, lubricators, oil cups, wrench, starting crank, sample can of gasoline engine oil, a 6-foot propeller shaft with coupling, 5 feet of brass tubing, the **bronze** propeller wheel, stuffing box, lag bolts, etc., **and full instructions for operating the engine;** in all the best and most complete four-cycle marine gasoline engine outfit ever offered. These engines are handsomely finished in green enamel; crated in a substantial manner and delivered free on board cars at the factory in Southern Michigan, from which point you must pay the freight.

No. 32K4725	1½-Horse Power Kenwood Marine Gasoline Engine, with boat fittings for fresh water.	Weight, 145 pounds.	Price......$ 93.25
No. 32K4726	1½-Horse Power Kenwood Marine Gasoline Engine, with boat fittings for salt water.	Weight, 145 pounds.	Price...... 97.15
No. 32K4730	3-Horse Power Kenwood Marine Gasoline Engine, with boat fittings for fresh water.	Weight, 235 pounds.	Price...... 114.25
No. 32K4731	3-Horse Power Kenwood Marine Gasoline Engine, with boat fittings for salt water.	Weight, 235 pounds.	Price...... 119.00
No. 32K4735	5-Horse Power Kenwood Marine Gasoline Engine, with boat fittings for fresh water.	Weight, 450 pounds.	Price...... 164.75
No. 32K4736	5 Horse Power Kenwood Marine Gasoline Engine, with boat fittings for salt water.	Weight, 450 pounds.	Price...... 172.25
No. 32K4740	10-Horse Power Kenwood Marine Gasoline Engine, with boat fittings for fresh water.	Weight, 625 pounds.	Price...... 306.65
No. 32K4741	10-Horse Power Kenwood Marine Gasoline Engine, with boat fittings for salt water.	Weight, 625 pounds.	Price...... 318.50

HARVARD TWO-CYCLE MARINE GASOLINE ENGINES

2, 3 and 5-Horse Power Engines.

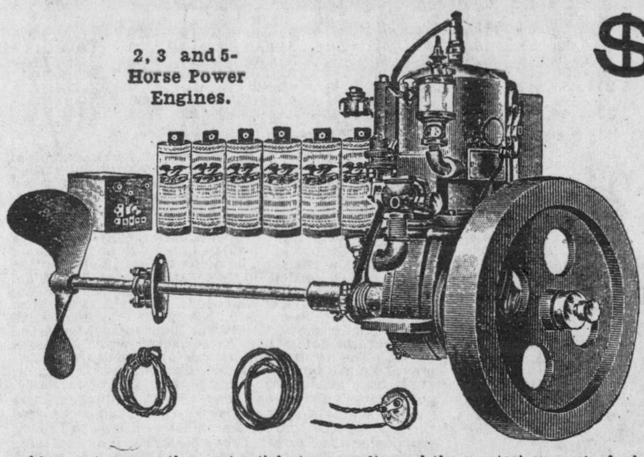

$54.60 AND UP

WITH COMPLETE BOAT OUTFIT, AS SHOWN IN THE ILLUSTRATION AT THE LEFT. EVERYTHING BUT GASOLINE TANK AND PIPING

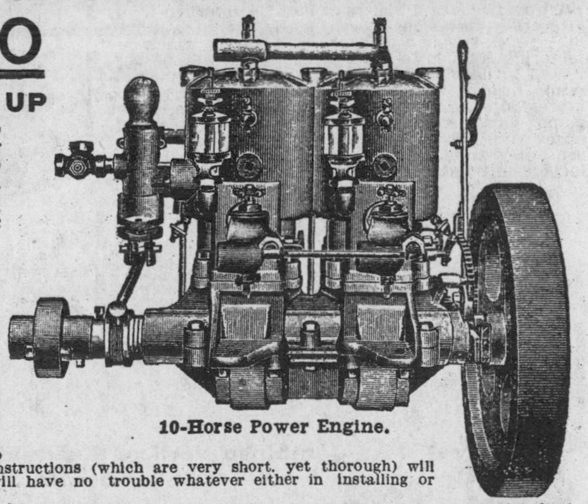

10-Horse Power Engine.

HARVARD TWO-CYCLE MARINE GASOLINE ENGINES **are so simple that a boy or girl can operate them even under the most adverse circumstances.** They have no valves, no cams, no gears and no springs, and undoubtedly have the fewest number of parts possible and still be provided with all the latest improvements. You need no extensive knowledge or practical experience with gasoline engines to enable you to secure the most satisfactory results, and the greatest amount of pleasure. Just a little study of our instructions (which are very short, yet thorough) will enable you to install the engine correctly in your boat and to learn all about the engine and its parts, so that you will have no trouble whatever either in installing or operating your engine. Their extreme simplicity is one of the strong features which make these engines so popular.

THE IMPORTANT DIMENSIONS **and adaptability of the engines are as follows:** THE 2-HORSE POWER ENGINE has 3-inch bore with 3½-inch stroke, is fitted with ¾-inch diameter propeller shaft and 11-inch diameter propeller wheel and is suitable for 14 to 18-foot launches. Its net weight is 105 pounds; shipping weight, about 130 pounds. THE 3-HORSE POWER ENGINE has 3¾-inch bore with 3½-inch stroke, is fitted with ¾-inch diameter propeller shaft and 13-inch diameter propeller wheel and is suitable for 16 to 20-foot launches. Its net weight is 120 pounds; shipping weight, about 150 pounds. THE 5-HORSE POWER ENGINE has 4½-inch bore with 4-inch stroke, is fitted with 1-inch diameter propeller shaft and 17-inch diameter propeller wheel and is suitable for 18 to 25-foot launches. Its net weight is 160 pounds; shipping weight, about 200 pounds. THE DOUBLE CYLINDER 10-HORSE POWER ENGINE has 4½-inch bore with 4-inch stroke, is fitted with 1⅛-inch diameter propeller shaft and 17-inch diameter propeller wheel and is suitable for 25 to 40-footers. Its net weight is 350 pounds; shipping weight, about 410 pounds.

AS LISTED BELOW. **Harvard Two-Cycle Marine Gasoline Engines with complete boat outfit** consist of the engine complete with equipment, which is as follows: Engine, power water circulating pump, commutator with speed and reversing lever, necessary lubricators, carbureter, necessary grease cups, air and drain cocks, one spark coil for each cylinder, six dry batteries for each cylinder, one switch for each cylinder, one spark plug for each cylinder, one box for each set of dry battery cells, the necessary amount of rubber covered wire and electric wire cord and staples for same, one muffler, one package of wood screws, one oil can, one "S" wrench, one can of cylinder lubricating oil, the propeller shaft coupling, the propeller shaft, the propeller wheel, the stuffing box, the lag screws for the stuffing box, and a complete set of instructions showing you how to install the engine in your boat and how to successfully operate the engine; in other words, the most complete **two-cycle** marine gasoline engine outfit ever offered. The engines are handsomely finished in green enamel. The engine is crated in a substantial manner and delivered free on board the cars at the factory in Southeastern Michigan, from which point you must pay the freight.

No. 32K4700	2-Horse Power Harvard Marine Gasoline Engine, with boat fittings for fresh water.	Price......$ 54.60
No. 32K4701	2-Horse Power Harvard Marine Gasoline Engine, with boat fittings for salt water.	Price...... 61.85
No. 32K4702	3-Horse Power Harvard Marine Gasoline Engine, with boat fittings for fresh water.	Price...... 64.15
No. 32K4703	3-Horse Power Harvard Marine Gasoline Engine, with boat fittings for salt water.	Price...... 71.00
No. 32K4704	5-Horse Power Harvard Marine Gasoline Engine, with boat fittings for fresh water.	Price...... 85.25
No. 32K4705	5-Horse Power Harvard Marine Gasoline Engine, with boat fittings for salt water.	Price...... 96.50
No. 32K4708	10-Horse Power Harvard Marine Gasoline Engine, with boat fittings for fresh water.	Price...... 213.75
No. 32K4709	10-Horse Power Harvard Marine Gasoline Engine, with boat fittings for salt water.	Price...... 229.50

YOU NEED NOT TAKE OUR WORD; READ THIS.

Sears, Roebuck & Co., Chicago, Ill. Slidell, Louisiana.

Gentlemen:—I received engine and propeller wheel all O. K. I set engine in boat and made all wire connections myself. I then put engine to the most severe test it has ever been my misfortune to make. I ran boat out of Bayou across Lake Pontchartrain and up Pearl River to my landing, a distance of 35 miles, through one of the worst storms it has ever been my lot to get caught in, and I will say in conclusion that engine behaved perfectly in every particular and to base my opinion on said test your engine has proven far superior to any that I have ever seen,

Very truly yours,
R. J. TAYLOR.

NOTE:—After seeing Mr. Taylor's engine work, several of his neighbors have purchased marine engines from us, and all are highly satisfied. Our engines speak for themselves and where we sell one of them we invariably sell others in the same locality.

STEAM ENGINES AND BOILERS

SPECIAL NOTE WHEN YOU ORDER A VERTICAL ENGINE AND A BOILER TOGETHER THEY WILL BE MOUNTED ON SEPARATE BASES UNLESS YOU TELL US THAT YOU WANT THEM MOUNTED ON A COMBINED BASE.

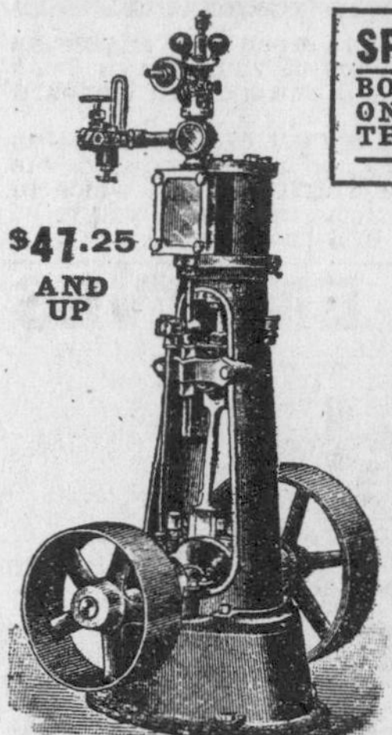

$47.25 AND UP

Kenwood Vertical Steam Engines.

These engines are of the center crank type with throttling governor, perfect in design, thoroughly well built and of the best of materials. They are low and compact, combining great strength and rigidity, are nicely finished and handsomely painted. Every point which could add to the strength and durability of the engine has been carefully considered and adopted. They are the best plain side valve vertical steam engines which can be built, are up to date in every particular and give perfect satisfaction to every user. We guarantee that they will give you equally as perfect satisfaction, or they can be returned at our expense, and we will promptly return your money. These engines are sold under our regular free trial terms, excepting that we allow thirty days' trial on them instead of ten days. Each engine is furnished with governor, governor belt, governor pulley, oil cups, throttle valve, cylinder lubricator, belt pulley and fly wheel, and is complete, ready to start. Steam and exhaust pipe is not furnished unless a boiler is ordered with the engine, and foundation bolts or rods are not furnished by us under any circumstances. Shipped from factory in Southwestern Michigan.

NOTE OUR REDUCED PRICES

Catalogue Number	Horse Power	Size of Cylinder, inches	Diameter of Shaft, inches	Size of Fly Wheel, inches	Size of Belt Pulley, inches	Steam Pipe, inches	Exhaust Pipe, inches	Revolutions, Per Minute	Weight in Pounds	Price
32K4801	1½	2½x3½	1⅛	13x3½	6x3½	⅜	½	400	250	$ 47.25
32K4802	2	3 x4½	1½	16x4½	10x4½	½	¾	350	325	59.50
32K4803	3	3½x4½	1½	16x4½	10x4½	½	¾	350	350	65.75
32K4804	4	4 x5	1½	17x4½	12x4½	¾	1	325	500	75.90
32K4806	6	5 x6½	2	20x6	14x6½	1	1¼	250	750	99.50
32K4808	8	6 x8	2½	24x6	16x7	1¼	1½	200	1250	116.75
32K4810	10	7 x8	2½	26x6¾	18x8	1½	2	200	1500	138.00

Kenwood Vertical Steam Boilers.

Our Vertical Steam Boilers are made with flange steel, heads and shell having a tensile strength of 60,000 pounds to the square inch. Lap welded tubes are used throughout. No second hand locomotive tubes or cast iron heads or cast iron water legs are used in these boilers, such as are used in many of the cheaply constructed vertical boilers now on the market. Each boiler has a handhole in the water leg on each side of the boiler, and one at the front and back above the crown sheet, making them easy to clean. They are subjected to a thorough test under 150 pounds hydrostatic pressure, and are guaranteed to carry 125 pounds steam pressure with perfect safety. All boilers above 26 inches diameter have double riveted vertical seams. **These boilers are not suitable for house heating purposes.** Steam boilers cannot be returned to us after they have once been used, but in a thirty days' trial, should a boiler show a defect which our factory has failed to detect, the defect will be corrected without charge by us. The fixtures and trimmings furnished are as follows: Base, hood, doors, grates, injector fitted to boiler, steam gauge, water gauge, gauge cocks, pop safety valve and blow off, check and stop valves. Whistle, stack and piping are not included in price of boiler. Shipped from factory in Southwestern Michigan.

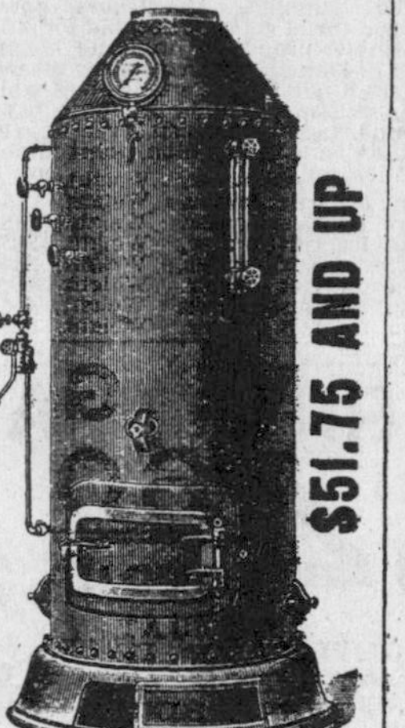

$51.75 AND UP

DON'T OVERLOOK THESE REDUCED PRICES

Catalogue Number	Horse Power	Diameter of Boiler, inches	Total Height, inches	Diameter of Furnace, inches	Height of Furnace, inches	Thickness of Shell, inches	Thickness of Heads, inches	Thickness of Fire Box, in.	Length of Tubes, inches	Number of 2-inch Tubes	Size of Stack Required, in.	Weight in Pounds	Price
32K4822	1¾	20	50	16	18	3-16	¼	¼	18	19	8	475	$ 51.75
32K4823	3	20	60	16	18	¼	5-16	¼	32	19	8	620	68.75
32K4824	4	24	66	20	18	¼	5-16	¼	32	31	10	890	83.25
32K4826	6	26	76	22	22	¼	5-16	¼	38	37	10	1300	99.75
32K4828	8	30	76	26	24	¼	5-16	¼	36	43	10	1550	118.25
32K4830	10	30	94	26	26	¼	⅜	¼	48	43	10	1650	130.00
32K4832	12	36	98	31	26	¼	⅜	5-16	48	55	16	2350	158.50

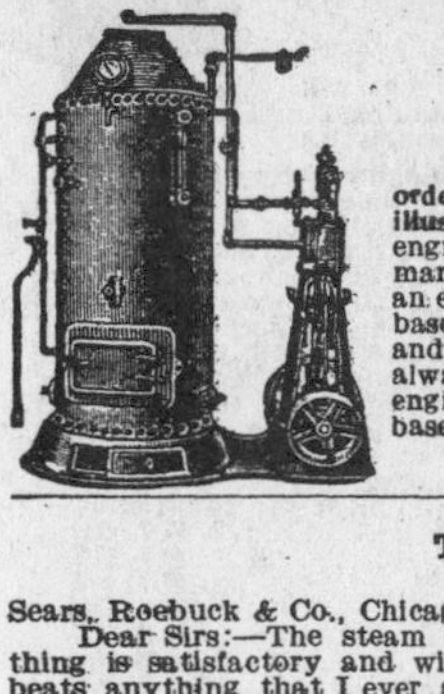

Combined Vertical Steam Engine and Boiler Outfits.

Our Vertical Steam Engines and Vertical Steam Boilers, when ordered together, can be mounted on a combined base as shown in this illustration, and when you specify in your order that you want the engine and boiler on a combined base, they will be mounted in this manner and will be furnished with both steam and exhaust pipe. If an engine and boiler are ordered together, but are wanted on separate bases, we will furnish sufficient steam and exhaust pipe to set the engine and boiler 5 feet apart, measuring from center to center. You should always select a boiler with as much or greater horse power than the engine. Vertical engines and boilers will be shipped on separate bases unless ordered on combined bases.

THIS IS WORTH READING.

Witoka, Minn.

Sears, Roebuck & Co., Chicago, Ill.

Dear Sirs:—The steam engine which I got from you is all right in every way. Everything is satisfactory and without a fault. The Little Giant Grinding Mill is a corker and beats anything that I ever saw for a 6-inch burr to grind feed. I think that I can grind a good deal more in an hour than you state in your catalogue.

Yours for more trade, AUG. LEDEBUHR.

SAVED AT LEAST $50.00.

Sears, Roebuck & Co., Chicago, Illinois. Caldwell, Ohio.

Gentlemen:—I want to write and tell you that I am well pleased with the boiler and engine I bought of you last spring. I am using them on a drilling machine for drilling water wells. They furnish plenty of power and are satisfactory in every respect. I saved $50.00 at least on them by buying them of you. I remain, Very truly yours, W. S. McBRIDE.

Kenwood Horizontal Steam Engines.

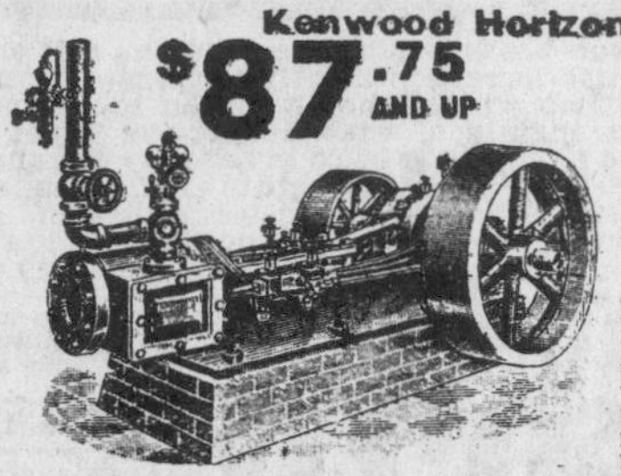

$87.75 AND UP

These are strictly high grade engines of the center crank single slide valve type. Every part has been carefully designed with a view to making the engines perfect in every respect. The valve is the regular "D" pattern, accurately balanced by a circular plate on the back, in which is a floating ring, which is kept in place by the pressure of the steam. The ports are long and narrow, which reduces the travel of the valve and allows both valve and seat to wear straight. The fittings and trimmings furnished with these engines are of the very best quality. Price is for the engine complete with governor, governor pulley, fly wheel, belt pulley, a set of nickel plated glass oilers, sight feed lubricator, throttle valve and two cylinder cocks. Price does not include steam and exhaust pipe or foundation rods; these we do not furnish. Shipped from factory in Southwestern Michigan.

A BIG REDUCTION IN PRICES

Catalogue Number	Horse Power	Size of Cylinder, inches	Diam. of Shaft, inches	Size of Fly Wheel, inches	Size of Belt Pulley, inches	Steam Pipe inches	Exhaust Pipe, inches	Revolutions per Minute	Weight in Pounds	Price
32K5180	4	4 x 5	1½	17x 4½	12x 4½	¾	1	325	625	$ 87.75
32K5181	5	4½x 5	1½	17x 4½	12x 4½	¾	1	325	675	98.50
32K5182	6	5 x 6½	2	20x 6	14x 6½	1	1¼	250	750	107.00
32K5183	7	5½x 6½	2	24x 6	14x 6½	1	1¼	250	875	113.25
32K5184	8	6 x 8	2½	24x 6	16x 6½	1¼	1½	200	1100	124.75
32K5185	10	7 x 8	2½	26x 6¾	16x 6½	1½	2	200	1350	149.25
32K5186	12	8 x 8	2½	30x 6¾	18x 8	1½	2	175	1450	162.00
32K5187	15	7½x10	3⅛	30x 6¾	20x 8	1½	2	175	1550	178.75
32K5188	20	9½x10	3⅛	35x 6¾	24x10	2½	3	165	2400	213.75
32K5189	25	9½x12	3⅝	40x10½	24x10	2½	3	165	3200	252.00
32K5190	30	10 x12	3⅝	40x10½	24x12	2½	3½	165	3500	294.00

Kenwood Horizontal Tubular Steam Boilers.

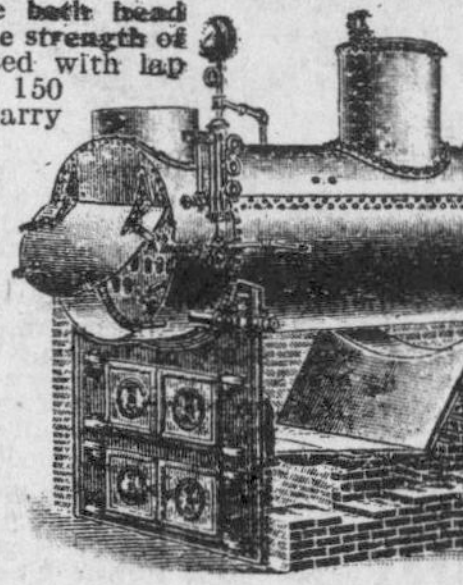

$149.75 AND UP

Our Horizontal Tubular Steam Boilers have **both head and shell made from flange steel having a tensile strength of 60,000 pounds to the square inch.** They are fitted with lap welded tubes, subjected to a thorough test under 150 pounds hydrostatic pressure and guaranteed to carry 125 pounds steam pressure with perfect safety. They have a manhole over the tubes and a handhole below the tubes, the handhole being in the front end. **These boilers are not suitable for house heating purposes.** Steam boilers cannot be returned to us after they have once been used, but in a thirty days' trial, should the boiler show a defect which our factory has failed to detect, the defect will be corrected without charge by us. The fixtures furnished are as follows: Half arch front complete with all castings, grates, stack and guys, combination water column with steam and water gauges and three gauge cocks, pop safety valve, blow off valve and an injector complete with pipes and valves fitted. Price does not include brickwork, neither does it include steam or exhaust pipe; these we do not furnish. Shipped from factory in Southwestern Michigan.

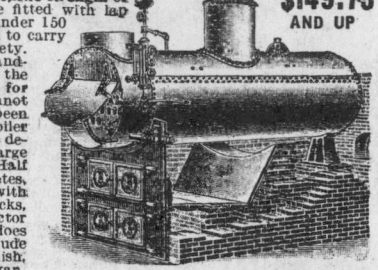

PRICES GREATLY REDUCED

Catalogue Number	Horse Power	Diameter of Boiler, inches	Length of Boiler, feet	Heating Surface, square feet	Number of 3-inch tubes	Thickness of Shell, inches	Thickness of Heads, inches	Grate Surface, inches	Length of Stack, feet	Diameter of Stack, inches	Weight Complete, Pounds, About	Price
32K5200	8	30	5	120	20	¼	5-16	30x30	24	14	2800	$149.75
32K5201	10	30	7	150	20	¼	5-16	34x30	24	14	3250	163.50
32K5202	12	30	8	180	20	¼	5-16	34x30	24	14	3600	180.00
32K5203	15	36	8	226	26	¼	⅜	36x36	24	16	4000	225.75
32K5204	20	36	10	300	28	¼	⅜	42x36	24	16	4750	255.50
32K5205	25	36	12	375	30	9-32	⅜	42x42	35	20	6050	306.00
32K5206	30	42	10	446	40	5-16	⅜	42x44	35	22	7000	391.50
32K5207	35	44	10	530	44	5-16	⅜	48x44	40	22	7250	419.75

Kenwood Economy Steam Boilers.

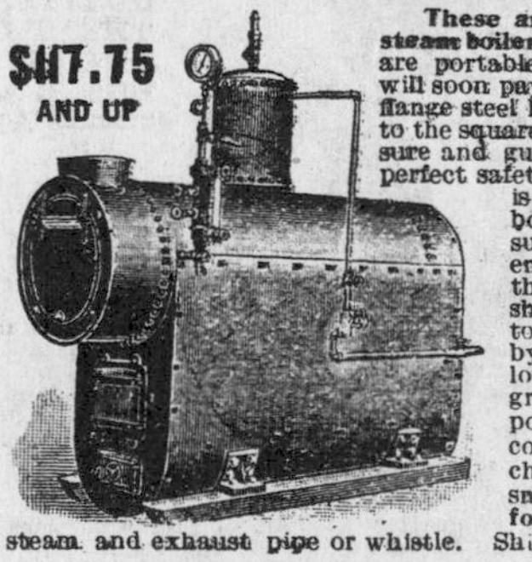

$117.75 AND UP

These are considered the most convenient and economical steam boilers made. They are self contained, require no setting, are portable and are quick and ready steamers. The fuel saved will soon pay for the boiler. Our Economy boilers are made with flange steel heads and shell, having 60,000 pounds tensile strength to the square inch, are tested under 150 pounds hydrostatic pressure and guaranteed to carry 125 pounds steam pressure with perfect safety. The fire box is lined with fire brick and the boiler is mounted on skids. The dome is detachable and the boilers can be loaded in box cars. These boilers are suitable for use with either vertical or horizontal steam engines. Steam boilers cannot be returned to us after they have once been used, but in a thirty days' trial, should a boiler show a defect which our factory has failed to detect, the defect will be corrected without charge by us. The fixtures and fittings furnished are as follows: Smoke box extension, door and stack saddle, grate bars, bearing bars, bridge wall, fire brick lining, pop safety valve, steam gauge and syphon, water column with glass water gauge, two gauge cocks, feed check and blow off valves, injector fitted to boiler, smoke stack and guys. **These boilers are not suitable for house heating purposes.** Price does not include steam and exhaust pipe or whistle. Shipped from factory in Southwestern Michigan.

SEE THESE REDUCED PRICES

Catalogue Number	Horse Power	Diam. of Boiler, inches	Length of Tubes, feet	Number of 3-inch Tubes	Thickness of Shell, inches	Thickness of Heads, inches	Grate Surface, inches	Length of Stack, feet	Diameter of Stack, inches	Weight Complete, Pounds, About	Price
32K5230	4	26	3	15	¼	5-16	24x20	20	12	2400	$117.75
32K5231	5	26	4	15	¼	5-16	24x20	20	12	2800	135.50
32K5232	6	26	5	15	¼	5-16	24x20	20	12	3300	156.00
32K5233	7	30	5	22	¼	5-16	24x24	24	14	3700	171.25
32K5234	8	30	6	22	¼	5-16	30x24	24	14	4200	195.50
32K5235	10	30	7	22	¼	5-16	30x24	24	14	4700	217.25
32K5236	12	30	8	22	¼	5-16	30x24	24	14	5300	229.50

Smoke Stack and Whistles For Steam Boilers.

Our smoke stack is made in standard lengths and of standard thickness of material. Elbows for stack will be furnished at price of 8 feet of stack. Price does not include guys. Whistles are complete with valves and are fitted to the boiler. If you want a whistle fitted to the boiler you must order from this list. Shipped from factory in Southwestern Michigan.

No. 32K5240	8-inch Stack, per foot.	Wt., 5 lbs.	Price $0.54
No. 32K5241	10-inch Stack, per foot.	Wt., 8 lbs.	Price .... .72
No. 32K5251	12-inch Stack, per foot.	Wt., 9 lbs.	Price .... .88
No. 32K5243	14-inch Stack, per foot.	Wt., 11 lbs.	Price 1.03
No. 32K5245	16-inch Stack, per foot.	Wt., 13 lbs.	Price 1.18
No. 32K5248	20-inch Stack, per foot.	Wt., 19 lbs.	Price 1.41
No. 32K5249	22-inch Stack, per foot.	Wt., 21 lbs.	Price 1.56
No. 32K5260	1-inch Whistle.		Price 2.03
No. 32K5262	1½-inch Whistle.		Price 2.74
No. 32K5263	2-inch Whistle.		Price 3.53

BEEHIVES AND BEE KEEPERS' SUPPLIES

ASTONISHING REDUCTION IN PRICES

Our Goods are the Best | **Our Prices are the Lowest**

IT NEEDS BUT A COMPARISON OF OUR PRICES WITH THOSE OF OTHERS TO CONVINCE YOU OF THE BIG SAVING YOU CAN MAKE BY BUYING YOUR BEEHIVES AND SUPPLIES FROM US.

BIG PRICE REDUCTIONS.

$6.82 FOR FIVE EXTRACTING HIVES. Shipped Knocked Down.

$7.68 FOR FIVE STANDARD HIVES. Shipped Knocked Down.

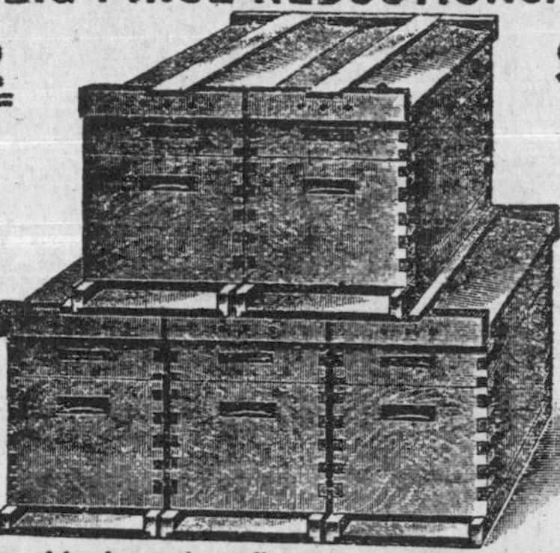

BEST MADE | **HIGHEST GRADE**

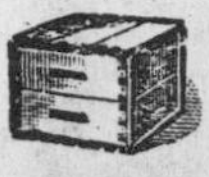

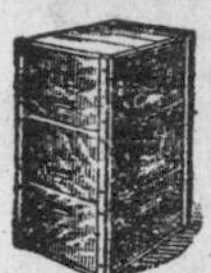

Our line of bee keepers' supplies is comprised of the best, most modern and most desirable hives, etc., on the market, and you can make your selection of any articles listed on this page with every assurance that the goods you receive will be of first class A No. 1 quality, for we handle but one grade of these goods and that is the best. They are made by a manufacturer who has been in this line of business for over forty years and who understands every requirement of the up to date bee keeper. Beehives are generally used $1\frac{1}{2}$ stories high, that is, with brood or bottom hive and one hive superior top hive, but you can make two-story hives by ordering extra hive supers. They are always shipped partly knocked down and are not painted. The small top illustration at the left shows a crate of five hive supers; the one below it shows a crate of five brood hives; together they make five $1\frac{1}{2}$-story hives. Our brood hives are standard size, with Langstroth frames, and are $18\frac{1}{4}$ inches long by $12\frac{1}{4}$ inches wide inside. They have invertible bottom and rainproof top. Brood hives are $9\frac{1}{2}$ inches deep and are complete with eight self spacing frames, one follower, one bottom and one cover. Beehives are generally sold in lots of 5, 10, etc., but we list single hives so that our customers may order any quantity consisting of five or more. All bee keepers' supplies are shipped from the same factory and you should always order enough of these goods so that the shipping will weigh 100 pounds or more. All beehives and bee keepers' supplies are shipped from the factory in Western Iowa.

STANDARD DOVETAILED HIVES.

Big Reduction in Price.

$7.68 FOR FIVE.

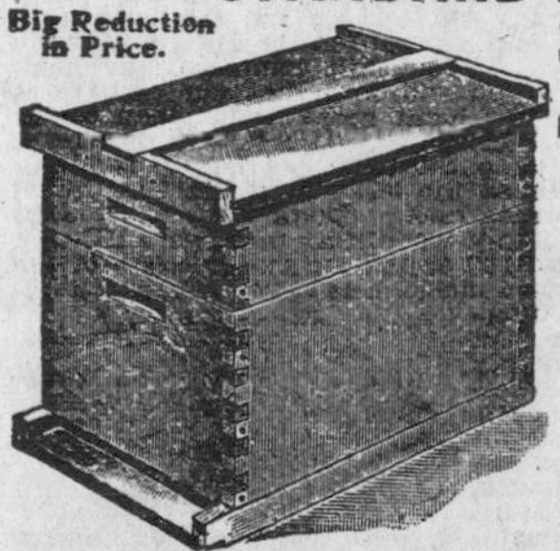

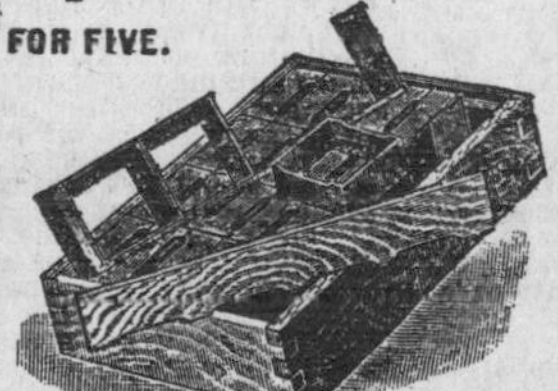

These are standard dovetailed hives and are fitted with supers and sections for comb honey. The illustration at the left shows a complete $1\frac{1}{2}$-story hive. The illustration at the right shows the hive super, which is $4\frac{3}{4}$ inches deep and fitted with six scalloped section holders, five separators, one adjustable follow board, twenty-four $4\frac{1}{4}$x$4\frac{1}{4}$x$1\frac{7}{8}$-inch scalloped sections and twenty-four foundation starters. Extracting frames cannot be used in these supers. Brood hives are standard size.

No. 32K3500	Crate of five $1\frac{1}{2}$-story Standard Hives Wt., 130 lbs. Price	$7.68
No. 32K3502	Crate of five extra Standard Hive Supers. Wt., 38 lbs. Price	2.86
No. 32K3503	Single $1\frac{1}{2}$-story Standard Hive. Wt., 27 lbs. Price	1.86

EXTRACTING DOVETAILED HIVES.

Greatly Reduced in Price.

$6.82 FOR FIVE.

These hives are especially designed for honey that is to be extracted from the comb. The illustration at the left shows a complete $1\frac{1}{2}$-story hive. The illustration at the right shows the hive super, which is $5\frac{3}{4}$ inches deep and fitted with eight $5\frac{3}{8}$-inch shallow Hoffman frames. Sections cannot be used in these supers. The brood hive is the same as is used with our Standard hive.

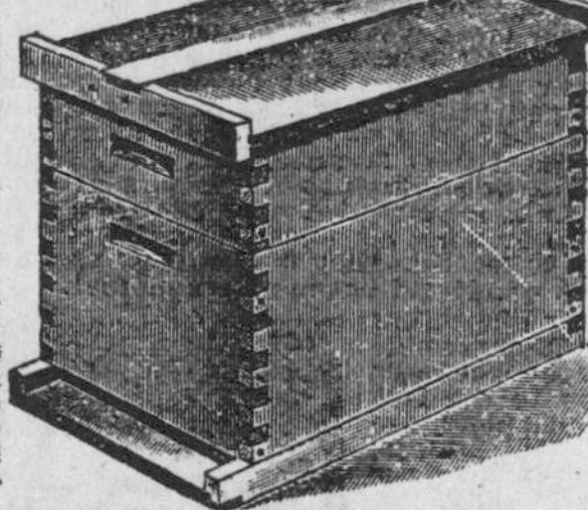

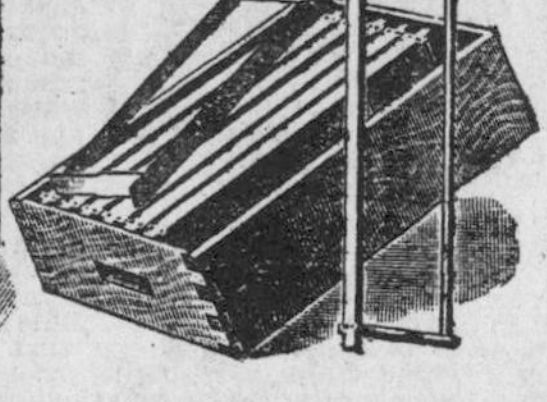

No. 32K3510	Crate of five $1\frac{1}{2}$-story Extracting Hives. Wt., 127 lbs. Price	$6.82
No. 32K3512	Crate of five extra Extracting Hive Supers. Wt., 35 lbs. Price	$1.94
No. 32K3513	Single $1\frac{1}{2}$-story Extracting Hive. Wt., 27 lbs. Price	$1.68

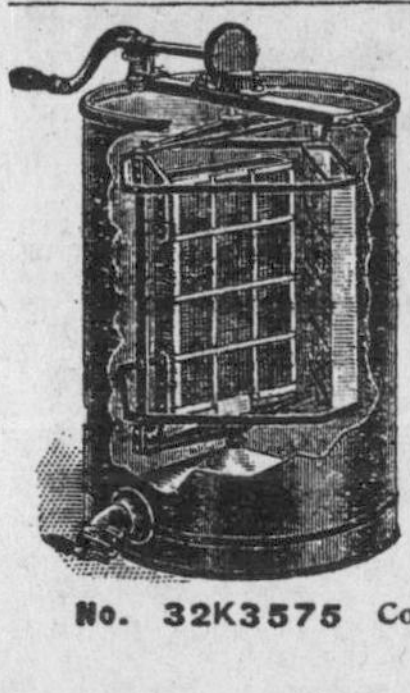

$9.98 NO. 15 COWAN HONEY EXTRACTOR, REDUCED FROM $11.25.

THE MOST SUCCESSFUL EXTRACTOR MADE.

The highest grade extractor on the market. Strongly made of galvanized steel, with conical bottom and supplied with anchor rods. The comb pockets are hinged like a door inside of a pair of hoops; the combs are put into these pockets (after uncapping), the honey extracted from one side by a few turns of the crank, and then without touching the comb, the pocket is swung around and a few more turns of the crank extracts the honey from the other side. Intended for extracting from frames, but pockets are $2\frac{1}{4}$ inches wide, so that honey can be extracted from partly filled sections by placing them in a wide frame. Comb pockets are $9\frac{3}{4}$ inches, can is 20 inches in diameter and 28 inches high. The very best extractor made and suitable for general work.

No. 32K3575 Cowan Honey Extractor. Wt., 70 lbs. Price $9.98

ORDER YOUR BEE SUPPLIES WITH YOUR BEEHIVES.

Nearly all orders for these goods are for five or more $1\frac{1}{2}$-story hives, with perhaps one or more crates of five extra hive supers and such quantity of section boxes, wax foundation and other small supplies as the purchaser may require. The crates of five $1\frac{1}{2}$-story hives, as well as the honey extractor, are heavy enough to make a freight shipment alone which will be profitable to the purchaser, but we list the small and light weight supplies only for the accommodation of our customers and with the recommendation that you be **sure to order such of these small supplies as you want at the same time that you order your hives,** then the small supplies will be shipped with the hives with very little if any extra cost for freight. We reserve the right to return your money on orders for bee supplies when the bee supplies ordered do not make a total weight of about 100 pounds. **All Beehives and Bee Supplies are shipped from the factory in Western Iowa.**

Hoffman Self Spacing Frames.

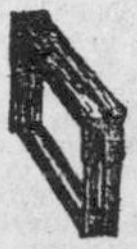

The deep frame is the same size as the Langstroth frames used in all of our brood hives. It is $17\frac{5}{8}$ inches long by $9\frac{1}{8}$ inches deep, with 19-inch top piece. The shallow frame is the same as is used in our extracting hive supers. It is $17\frac{5}{8}$ inches long, $5\frac{3}{8}$ inches deep and has 19-inch top piece. Sold only in full crates. Shipped knocked down.

No. 32K3520 Crate of 100 Shallow Hoffman Frames. Wt., 26 lbs., Price, $1.72

No. 32K3521 Crate of 100 Deep Hoffman Frames. Wt., 45 lbs. Price $2.52

Section Honey Boxes.

At Reduced Prices.

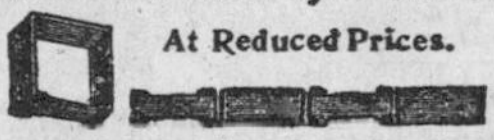

Our one-piece scalloped sections are made of clear basswood, perfect in finish and free from defects. They are No. 1 grade and the very best sections made. Size is $4\frac{1}{4}$x$4\frac{1}{4}$x$1\frac{7}{8}$ inches. Sold only in full crates. Shipped knocked down.

No. 32K3524 Crate of 250 Sections. Wt., 18 lbs. Price $1.39

No. 32K3525 Crate of 500 Sections. Wt., 36 lbs. Price $2.48

Wax Comb Foundation.

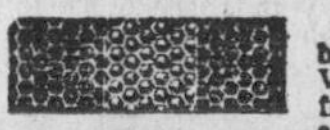

Made of strictly pure, bright yellow bees' wax. Very tough, perfectly free from grit and dirt and easily worked by the bees. Brood foundation sheets are 8x$16\frac{1}{2}$ inches and run about 7 sheets to the pound. Super foundation sheets are $3\frac{5}{8}$x$16\frac{1}{2}$ inches and run about 25 sheets to the pound. Sold only in even pounds.

No. 32K3528 Medium Brood Foundation. Price, per lb. 55c

No. 32K3529 Thin Super Foundation. Price, per lb 62c

Parker Foundation Fastener.

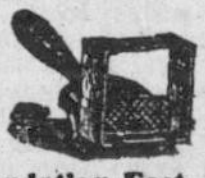

A splendid tool for fastening comb foundation into section boxes. Made only for $4\frac{1}{4}$x$4\frac{1}{4}$-inch sections.

No. 32K3532 Parker Foundation Fastener. Wt., $\frac{3}{4}$ lb. Price 24c

Hand Section Press.

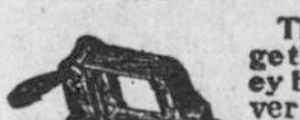

This press is for putting together one-piece section honey boxes. One sweep of the lever presses the dovetailed ends together squarely, without breaking the corners. Made only for $4\frac{1}{4}$x$4\frac{1}{4}$-inch sections.

No. 32K3538 Hand Section Press. Wt., $1\frac{1}{4}$ lbs. Price 48c

Champion Bee Smoker.

Reduced to 74 Cents.

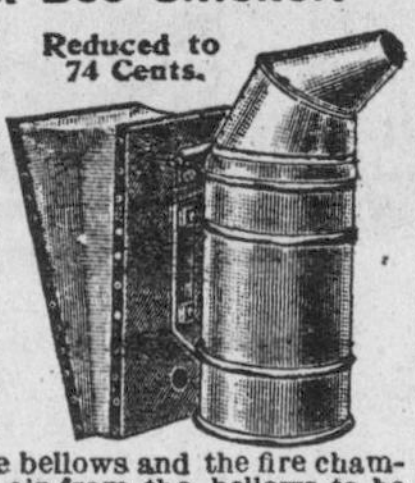

The best smoker on the market, convenient, well made and very serviceable. Has $3\frac{1}{2}$-inch lined fire chamber made of heavy tin, beaded. The metal parts which attach the fire chamber to the bellows are firmly secured to both fire chamber and bellows. Nozzle is hinged to top of bellows. The air passage between the bellows and the fire chamber compels all the air from the bellows to be forced through the fuel. Its strength of blast is surprising.

No. 32K3541 Champion Bee Smoker. Wt., $1\frac{3}{4}$ lbs. Price 74c

Globe Bee Veil.

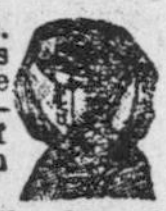

The best protection against bees. Has five light spring steel bars which keep the veil away from the face and neck. These bars are buttoned to studs on the neckband of the veil. Made of French cotton tulle with silk face piece.

No. 32K3544 Globe Bee Veil. Wt., 5 ounces. Price 93c

Drone Trap and Swarm Guard

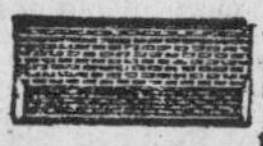

For exterminating drones when too numerous and to prevent loss of swarms. Front and back are covered with perforated zinc through which the workers can pass, but with holes too small for drones and fertile queens. In the act of swarming, the queen enters the upper compartment and the workers cluster on the trap ready to be hived.

No. 32K3547 Drone Trap. Wt., $\frac{1}{2}$ lb. Price 42c

Wood Slat Zinc Honey Board.

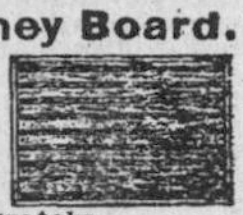

Made for 8-frame hives. Has thin slats within the rim, with strips of zinc having two rows of holes between each two slats. Stiffer and stronger than other forms, and preserves the bee space more accurately.

No. 32K3550 Wood Slat Zinc Honey Board. Wt., $1\frac{1}{2}$ lbs. Price 24c

La Reese Bee Escape.

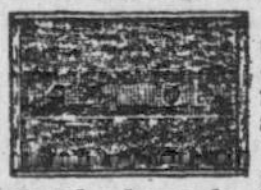

This escape can be placed under hive supers which are crowded with bees, without fear of smothering the bees and it cannot become clogged. The hum of the bees below induces the upper bees to descend through the wire cones in less time than with any other escape.

No. 32K3553 La Reese Bee Escape. Wt., $1\frac{1}{2}$lbs. Price 33c

Division Board Bee Feeder.

This is the most satisfactory feeder made. It sets into the brood hive in place of a brood frame or the division board. It can be used for stimulating as well as feeding in the winter. Bees can be fed without exposing the cluster and without smoking. Holds three pints, is nailed together and inside is coated with paraffine wax.

No. 32K3556 Division Board Bee Feeder. Wt., $\frac{3}{4}$ lb. Price 26c

Porter Bee Escape.

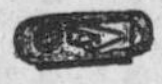

This device is to be placed in the center of a honey board and saves a great deal of work and worry, such as smoking and brushing bees out of hive supers. We furnish this bee escape without board. Just place the escape in a board of proper size and slip the escape with board between super and hive and the next morning your bees are all out of the super.

No. 32K3558 Porter Bee Escape. Wt., 2 ounces. Price 19c

Bee Brush.

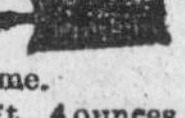

A strongly made and very durable brush with soft and pliable fibers, secured in a strong wood handle, long enough to reach across an ordinary Langstroth frame.

No. 32K3565 Bee Brush. Wt., 4 ounces. Price 17c

Swarm Catcher.

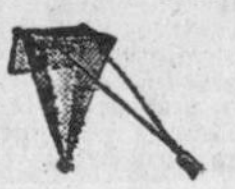

This is a very simple catcher but is the best made. It is a conical wire basket with four sides and a cover and is to be attached to a long pole or handle. Pole is not included in price, as any long pole will answer.

No. 32K3570 Swarm Catcher. Wt., 4 lbs. Price 79c

ALL BEE KEEPERS' SUPPLIES AND BEEHIVES ARE SHIPPED FROM THE FACTORY IN WESTERN IOWA.

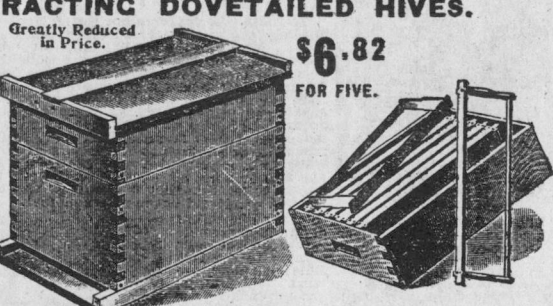

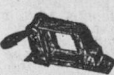

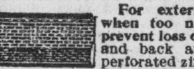

$7.72 AND UP IMPERIAL INCUBATORS

THEY CHALLENGE THE WORLD ON QUALITY, EFFICIENCY, SIMPLICITY, CAPACITY AND VALUE

MADE EXPRESSLY FOR US BY THE BEST AND MOST FAVORABLY KNOWN INCUBATOR FACTORY IN THE WORLD.

SIXTY DAYS FREE TRIAL

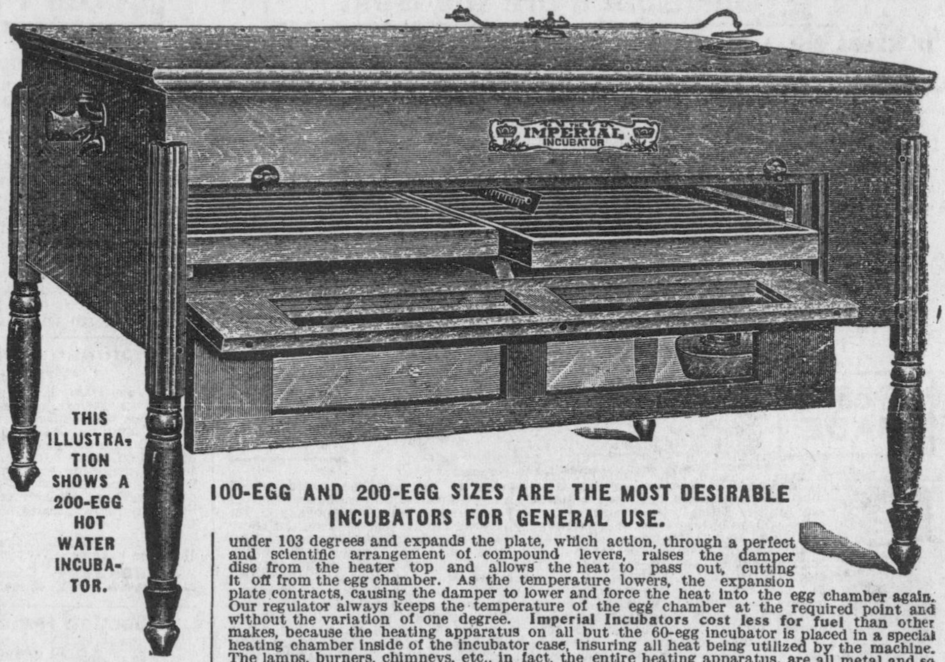

THIS ILLUSTRATION SHOWS A 200-EGG HOT WATER INCUBATOR.

100-EGG AND 200-EGG SIZES ARE THE MOST DESIRABLE INCUBATORS FOR GENERAL USE.

IMPERIAL INCUBATORS **are the best made, the most highly perfected and above all the most successful incubators that have ever been produced by any manufacturer.** They are made expressly for us by the leading incubator manufacturers of this country, who have devoted more than twenty-five years to the production and perfection of these machines, which have always been acknowledged to be the highest grade and most perfect working incubators made, and which have been improved from year to year until now in their present highly perfected form they are the best hatching machines it is possible for the most expert and successful incubator manufacturers in the world to produce, and the perfected result of more than twenty-five years of conscientious labor, careful study and costly experiments by men who possess a more thorough knowledge of the requirements of a successful incubator than do any other manufacturers. During our many years in the incubator business we have sold more incubators and brooders than any other one concern in the United States, our sales for a single year running as high as 25,000 machines, and more of our machines are today in successful and satisfactory use than any others made. This wonderful success is due entirely to our efforts to always give our customers the best value in these goods it was possible to give, and with the Imperial Incubators, our improved and perfected machines, we feel assured of greater success than ever before, because we know that with their improved construction and their many highly perfected features which make them capable of producing still better and more profitable results, with greater convenience and economy than ever before, **they represent the greatest incubator values ever offered.** We want every farmer and poultry raiser in the country to let the Imperial Incubators and Brooders demonstrate to them their superior value. We are proud of these machines and know that you cannot help but be pleased with them and highly satisfied with the splendid results you will obtain; and in order that everyone everywhere may have an opportunity to see, try, test, compare and operate our machines, we offer them on the most favorable terms anyone can ask, those named in our **liberal sixty days' free trial offer.** We cannot say enough in favor of these incubators and brooders; we want to send the machines to you and let them speak for themselves; we want you to run and test them for sixty days after receiving them, which allows you more than enough time to bring off two hatches, and we are sure that after you have done this you will be so well pleased with their quality, efficiency and superiority that you, too, will become one of the thousands of highly satisfied owners of our incubators and brooders, and will use them in preference to all others.

OUR LIBERAL SIXTY DAYS' FREE TRIAL OFFER. **Imperial and Wyandotte Incubators and Brooders** are shipped on the understanding and agreement that after receiving them you are to have sixty days in which to give them a thorough trial and to compare them with incubators and brooders of any other make, and if you do not find our machines to be better in every way than any others you can buy, no matter what price you pay, and if during the trial period you find any reason to be dissatisfied either with the quality, utility or value of our machines you can return them at our expense and we will promptly return your money, together with the freight charges you paid. You take no risk whatever in ordering incubators and brooders from us. **They must satisfy you or you get your money back.**

IMPERIAL INCUBATORS **are made in both hot air and hot water types,** which, outside of the heating apparatus, are identical in construction and quality and either type, when properly operated, will give equal satisfaction. **The incubator cases are made of best quality, thoroughly seasoned, bone dry cypress lumber,** the wood which best resists the action of moisture and changes in climate and atmospheric conditions, and will not warp or crack. **They have double walls** with dead air space between. This space is filled with the best non-heat conducting materials known; the top is thoroughly insulated with several layers of sheet fiber and wool closely packed, thus making the case capable of holding the heat and impervious to changes in the outside temperature. **Doors are double,** one inside of the other, both closing against jambs and independent of the other, sealing the case so that cold air cannot possibly enter from this source. Doors have glass fronts so that you can see all parts of the egg chamber without opening. **Egg trays are supplied with our patent turning rack,** a great time and labor saver which enables you to turn all of the eggs at once. **Nursery space is provided under egg trays** to which young chicks as hatched can retreat from the heat and out of the way of hatching chicks. This makes it unnecessary to open the doors while the hatch is on and prevents loss on account of chilling. **The regulator is the most accurate and reliable** that has ever been devised. It consists of a corrugated expansion plate filled with fluid, which boils and forms steam at a temperature just under 103 degrees and expands the plate, which action, through a perfect and scientific arrangement of compound levers, raises the damper disc from the heater top and allows the heat to pass out, cutting it off from the egg chamber. As the temperature lowers, the expansion plate contracts, causing the damper to lower and force the heat into the egg chamber again. Our regulator always keeps the temperature of the egg chamber at the required point and without the variation of one degree. **Imperial Incubators cost less for fuel** than other makes, because the heating apparatus on all but the 60-egg incubator is placed in a special heating chamber inside of the incubator case, insuring all heat being utilized by the machine. The lamps, burners, chimneys, etc., in fact, the entire heating apparatus, are all metal and so constructed as to make it **impossible for lamps to explode** or for the machines to catch fire. **Thermometers are of highest quality.** We use only the highest priced and most reliable thermometers made, and every thermometer is tested by the U. S. standard after being seasoned for from six months to one year, thus insuring an absolutely perfect registering thermometer in every incubator we sell.

GREATER CAPACITY **will be found in Imperial Incubators than in corresponding sizes of other makes.** In this feature as well as many others we can convince you that our machines are of greater value and are more honestly built than any other incubators made. Our incubators **when used without the patent turning rack** will hold the full number of eggs at which we rate them and our capacities are based upon average size hens' eggs. If you will compare our incubators with other makes, you will find that our egg trays **will hold from 10 to 25 per cent more eggs** than other incubators of same rated capacity. The illustrations here shown are made from actual photographs of one of our 100-egg trays. The illustration at the left shows the tray filled with eggs, without the turning rack. There are exactly **120 average size hens' eggs** in this tray, which is the size of tray we furnish with every 100-egg incubator we sell; other manufacturers would list this as a 130 or 140-egg machine, so you see that when you buy our 100-egg incubator you get as large a machine as if you bought a 140-egg machine of some other make. The trays of all the different sizes of our machines will invariably hold more eggs than we say they will. The other illustration shows this same tray filled with eggs, when the turning rack is used. This necessarily decreases the capacity and this tray now holds 80 eggs. This is about the regular capacity of the average 100-egg incubator of other make, so you see that even when the patent turning rack is used our machines are of as great capacity as machines which do not possess this desirable feature. Turning rack can be easily removed from the egg tray, enabling you to use the machine with or without this attachment. **All sizes are rigidly mounted** on nicely turned legs, secured with screws. Machines are handsomely finished in the natural color; the top and sides are smooth dressed and thoroughly primed with the best wood filler and then given two coats of best varnish, the last coat being applied after the first has dried, insuring a high finish.

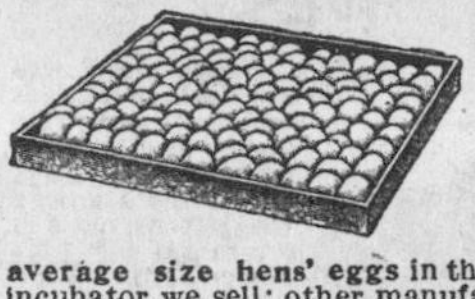

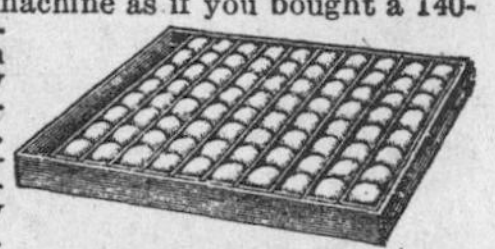

IMPERIAL HOT AIR INCUBATORS.

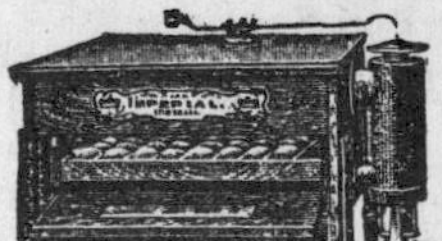

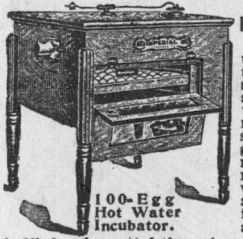

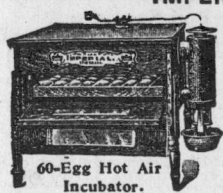

60-Egg Hot Air Incubator.

On account of their simplicity and the ease with which they can be operated, these machines are more generally used than hot water incubators and to those who do not have a preference for a hot water incubator we recommend the selection of a hot air machine. The general construction of these machines is as described above, and with the exception of the heating apparatus they are exactly the same as our hot water machines, and when properly operated they will prove just as desirable and capable of the best results it is possible to obtain. They are heated by hot air exclusively and are provided with **our superior double heating system,** which supplies heat both above and below the egg tray. With the exception of the 60-egg incubator, the heater is enclosed in the incubator case. All parts of the heating apparatus are steel, the lamp bowls are strongly made of pressed steel and galvanized after completion, which makes it impossible for them to leak. The capacity at which we list these machines is the number of average size hens' eggs the machines will hold when used without the patent turning rack. When turning rack is used capacity will be reduced about one-third. Price includes patent turning rack, a high grade thoroughly tested thermometer, an egg tester **and a complete instruction book, which contains much valuable and practical information on poultry raising.** Shipped from factory in Western Illinois.

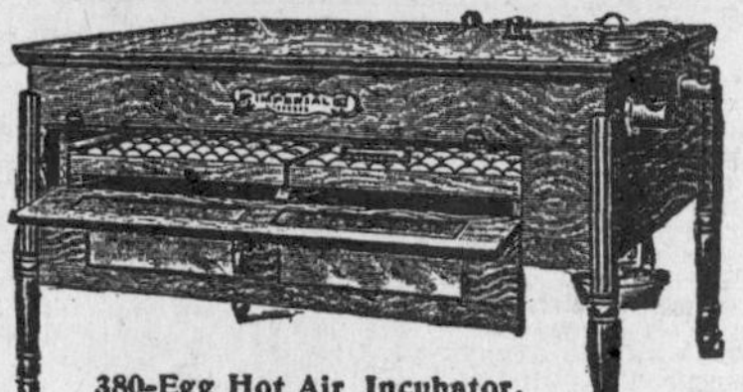

380-Egg Hot Air Incubator.

No. 32K3020 60-Egg Imperial Hot Air Incubator. Size No. 149.
Wt., 51 lbs. Price .... **$ 7.72**

No. 32K3022 100-Egg Imperial Hot Air Incubator. Size No. 151.
Wt., 130 lbs. Price **10.88**

No. 32K3024 200-Egg Imperial Hot Air Incubator. Size No. 153.
Wt., 174 lbs. Price **15.10**

No. 32K3026 280-Egg Imperial Hot Air Incubator. Size No. 155.
Wt., 225 lbs. Price **19.55**

No. 32K3028 380-Egg Imperial Hot Air Incubator. Size No. 157.
Wt., 265 lbs. Price **24.35**

IMPERIAL HOT WATER INCUBATORS.

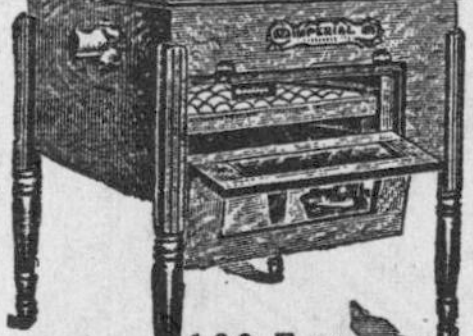

100-Egg Hot Water Incubator.

To those who prefer a hot water incubator we recommend these as the most superior and successful machines of this type. Outside of the heating apparatus they are exactly the same as our hot air incubators and while they are perhaps not so simple or convenient to operate as our hot air machines, the fact that the heat is supplied by a tank of hot water which naturally retains the heat for some considerable time, even should you chance to neglect filling your lamp and permit it to go out, and in this way sometimes prevents the loss of a hatch, makes them great favorites with many poultry raisers. These machines, in addition to the heat generated through the hot water tank, are supplied with heat from a hot air tank above and also by a hot air inlet below the egg tray. From this it is easy to see that they utilize all of the heat from the lamp and are **wonderful economizers of fuel.** The hot water tank is filled and emptied through a pipe and faucet at the end of the machine, which makes it impossible for water to be spilled or boil over on the incubator case. We direct particular attention to the fact that the hot water tanks of these machines are **made of 14-ounce copper,** so that they will be durable and will not rust out. Some makers use steel for hot water tanks, coat them with aluminum paint and call them aluminum. This kind of a tank is worthless for hot water and will rust out in the first season, while copper tanks will last indefinitely. Excepting on the 60-egg incubator the heaters are inclosed in the incubator case. All heater parts are of steel and lamp bowls are made from pressed steel and galvanized after completion, which makes it impossible for them to leak. The capacity at which we list these machines is the number of average size hens' eggs they will hold when used without the patent turning rack. When turning rack is used, capacity will be reduced about one-third. Price includes patent turning rack, a high grade thoroughly tested thermometer, an egg tester, a funnel and a **complete instruction book, which contains much valuable and practical information on poultry raising.** Shipped from factory in Western Illinois.

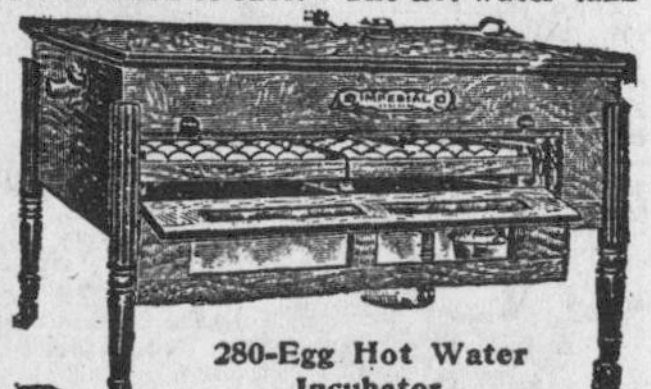

280-Egg Hot Water Incubator.

No. 32K3021 60-Egg Imperial Hot Water Incubator. Size No. 150.
Wt., 55 lbs. Price .... **$ 9.12**

No. 32K3023 100-Egg Imperial Hot Water Incubator. Size No. 152.
Wt., 158 lbs. Price **12.68**

No. 32K3025 200-Egg Imperial Hot Water Incubator. Size No. 154.
Wt., 187 lbs. Price **18.90**

No. 32K3027 280-Egg Imperial Hot Water Incubator. Size No. 156.
Wt., 236 lbs. Price **23.95**

No. 32K3029 380-Egg Imperial Hot Water Incubator. Size No. 158.
Wt., 280 lbs. Price **29.95**

$4.68 WYANDOTTE INCUBATOR.
The Best Single Wall Incubator Made.

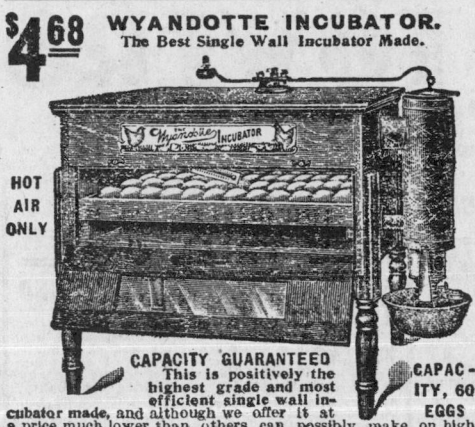

HOT AIR ONLY

CAPACITY GUARANTEED
CAPACITY, 60 EGGS

This is positively the highest grade and most efficient single wall incubator made, and although we offer it at a price much lower than others can possibly make on high grade machines, it should not be confused with the many cheaply constructed incubators on the market which are made only to sell and cannot possibly give satisfaction. The Wyandotte Incubator is a high grade and perfect working incubator in every sense of the word. It differs from our Imperial Incubators only in the fact that it is made only as a hot air machine, does not have our patent turning rack, and is a single wall incubator intended for use in a room where the external temperature is practically even at all times, and when properly operated will hatch just as large a percentage of well fertilized eggs as any incubator made. This machine is designed especially for beginners and small poultry raisers, and is made in one size only; its capacity is 60 average size hens' eggs; we guarantee this capacity and we will be glad to have you compare the size of this machine with so called 60-egg incubators of other makes; you will be surprised to see how many more eggs our machine will hold. The construction of this incubator cannot be excelled by any single wall machine on the market. Materials, workmanship and finish are of high quality. The case is made of thoroughly seasoned, bone dry cypress lumber, which will not warp or crack, and is smooth dressed, well varnished and finished in natural wood color. It is mounted on nicely turned legs, fastened to the case with screws. The case has double bottom and the top is insulated with the best non-heat conducting packing. Door is single, has double glass and closes against felt jambs. Egg tray is well made and has screen bottom. There is a nursery space below it to accommodate young chicks as they are hatched. Regulator is exactly the same as that used on our Imperial Incubators. Heater jacket and lamp bowl are heavy galvanized steel. Heater pipes are steel. From the above you will see that this machine is first class throughout, and we wish to impress upon you once more that it is a strictly high grade incubator and not in the same class with the low priced incubators many others offer. We could offer and sell a 60-egg incubator at $2.75 to $3.85 but experience has taught us that such incubators are dear at any price; they cannot possibly give satisfaction or reflect credit upon their manufacturer or the concern who sells them. Do not risk wasting time and money by entrusting valuable eggs to the care of such inferior machines. You run the risk of losing more in the price of one setting of eggs than the small difference in the price of one of these unreliable and cheaply constructed affairs and a genuine incubator like the Wyandotte. Price includes a high grade thoroughly tested thermometer, an egg tester, and a complete instruction book with valuable information on poultry raising. Shipped from factory in Western Illinois.
No. 32K3035   Wyandotte Hot Air Incubator.   Size No. 181.   Wt., 44 lbs.   Price $4.68

WYANDOTTE BROODERS, $2.72
FOR INDOOR USE.

SUPERIOR TO ALL OTHER INDOOR BROODERS.

These brooders are intended for use within a building but in mild weather they may be used out of doors if protected by a shed roof. They are built on the "mother hen" plan, that is, the heating apparatus is in the top, as it should be. These brooders are divided into two compartments by a curtain of heavy woolen cloth; one compartment is about fifteen degrees warmer than the other, and the chicks can go to or from the heat at will. The pure air circulation is perfect and the brooders maintain an even temperature at all times. The hot air and hot water tanks are identical in construction, except that the hot air tanks are steel while the hot water tanks and reservoir are made of copper. The heating arrangement of these machines is such that the fumes from the lamp cannot enter the brooding chamber, and the lamps are placed and protected so that they are absolutely safe under all conditions. Lamp bowl and exposed parts of heater are heavy galvanized steel. These brooders have a single door with a glass panel, are easy to clean and furnish plenty of light as well as heat for the young chicks. While these machines will give perfect satisfaction when used indoors, we recommend that you select an outdoor brooder because it can be used with equal success indoors and also out of doors under reasonable weather conditions. Every poultry raiser should have one or more brooders. They are absolutely necessary in order to experience the best of success. You cannot always entrust your chicks to the care of a hen with safety, for she is apt to abandon and neglect them and the increased number of chicks you will raise by using a brooder will more than pay for the machine. The most successful poultry raisers in the country use our brooders, which not only speaks well for our machines but proves conclusively that the brooder method is the only successful and profitable way in which to raise young chicks. Price includes a high grade thermometer, a runway, an instruction book and all attachments. Shipped from factory in Western Illinois.

No. 32K3075	50-Chick Wyandotte Hot Air Brooder. Size No. 133. Wt., 35 lbs.				$2.72
No. 32K3076	50-Chick Wyandotte Hot Water Brooder. Size No. 122. Wt., 37 lbs.				$4.12
No. 32K3077	100-Chick Wyandotte Hot Air Brooder. Size No. 135. Wt., 50 lbs.				$4.82
No. 32K3078	100-Chick Wyandotte Hot Water Brooder. Size No. 124. Wt., 53 lbs.				$6.42
No. 32K3079	200-Chick Wyandotte Hot Air Brooder. Size No. 137. Wt., 57 lbs.				$6.62
No. 32K3080	200-Chick Wyandotte Hot Water Brooder. Size No. 126. Wt., 60 lbs.				$8.68

IMPERIAL BROODERS, $6.72
FOR INDOOR AND OUTDOOR USE.

POSITIVELY THE BEST AND MOST SUCCESSFUL BROODERS MADE.

Without Question the Most Popular as Well as the Most Desirable Brooders on the Market.

These brooders combine more good points than any other make or style of brooder. While they are constructed especially for outdoor use, they can be used indoors just as successfully. They are warmed by top heat exclusively, on the "mother hen" plan. These brooders have a center compartment partitioned off from the outer compartments by heavy woolen cloth curtains, the temperature of the center compartment is about fifteen degrees warmer than the outer ones, and the chicks can go to or from the heat at will. The open door in the illustration shows the heating lamp, which is placed within a metal lined chamber, thoroughly protected from wind and weather, easy to get at and arranged so that the fumes from the lamp cannot enter the brooding chamber. The pure air circulation is perfect and the brooders will maintain an even temperature at all times. The roof and doors are covered with heavy sheet steel, and the entire machine is nicely painted. The glass in the front affords abundance of light for the young chicks, and the doors are arranged so that every part of the brooder can be easily cleaned, and either door may be opened in warm weather to let in any desired amount of sunlight and fresh air. The tanks of the hot air machines are made of steel, but the hot water tanks and reservoirs of the hot water machines are made of copper. The lamp bowl, heater jacket and lining of the lamp chamber are made of heavy galvanized steel. In order to experience the best of success every poultry raiser should have one or more brooders. You cannot depend upon the hen to safely rear the chicks entrusted to her care. She is apt to abandon and neglect them, and the chicks you lose would easily pay for a brooder. The most successful poultry raisers everywhere have abandoned the old hen method and now use brooders exclusively, and with most profitable results. The fact that more of our brooders are used than perhaps all other makes and styles combined proves conclusively that they are recognized as the best. Price includes a high grade thermometer, a runway, an instruction book and all attachments. Shipped from factory in Western Illinois.

No. 32K3085	100-Chick Imperial Hot Air Brooder. Size No. 145. Wt., 65 lbs.	$6.72
No. 32K3086	100-Chick Imperial Hot Water Brooder. Size No. 134. Wt., 70 lbs.	8.48
No. 32K3087	200-Chick Imperial Hot Air Brooder. Size No. 147. Wt., 84 lbs.	9.62
No. 32K3088	200-Chick Imperial Hot Water Brooder. Size No. 136. Wt., 86 lbs.	11.52
No. 32K3089	300-Chick Imperial Hot Air Brooder. Size No. 175. Wt., 152 lbs.	12.62
No. 32K3090	300-Chick Imperial Hot Water Brooder. Size No. 174. Wt., 161 lbs.	15.12

$6.92 ACME No. OB GREEN BONE CUTTER.
JUST THE MACHINE FOR THE SMALL POULTRY RAISER.

PRICE REDUCED.

This machine is back geared, is operated by a handle on the rim of a large balance wheel, and is suitable for a flock of 50 to 75 fowls. It is made with a standard and is to be fastened to a bench. The bone box is 3¼x4⅝x6 inches inside. The machine is fed by a hand feed screw which has a split nut that swings entirely out of the way when you are filling the bone box. This cutter has one straight and two corrugated knives. We guarantee this machine to give better satisfaction than any other green bone cutter of similar size or price. Shipped from factory in Western Pennsylvania.
No. 32K3200   No. OB Bone Cutter.   Wt., 75 lbs.
Price $6.92

ACME No. 13 GREEN BONE CUTTERS.

A combined geared hand and power machine, which, when run by power, is suitable for a flock of 1,500 fowls. When run by hand, being geared 4 to 1, it turns very easily and is suitable for a flock of 400 fowls. Has a bone box 4x4x20 inches inside, has three corrugated knives and one straight knife, has a split nut and an adjustable automatic feed. This machine is also provided with a safety device which stops the feed instantly in case a piece of iron or other metal gets into the bone box. No. 13H has balance wheel and handle, and is for hand only. No. 13HP has balance wheel and handle and a 12-inch by 4-inch pulley and is for hand or power. No. 13P has no balance wheel or handle, but has 12-inch by 4-inch tight and loose pulleys and is for power only. Shipped from factory in Western Pennsylvania.

$17.50 and up

Prices Reduced.

No. 32K3240	No. 13H Bone Cutter.	Wt., 165 lbs.	$17.50
No. 32K3241	No. 13HP Bone Cutter.	Wt., 170 lbs.	19.25
No. 32K3242	No. 13P Bone Cutter.	Wt., 175 lbs.	21.95

ACME Nos. 9, 10, 11 AND 12 GREEN BONE CUTTERS AT REDUCED PRICES.

$8.87 AND UP

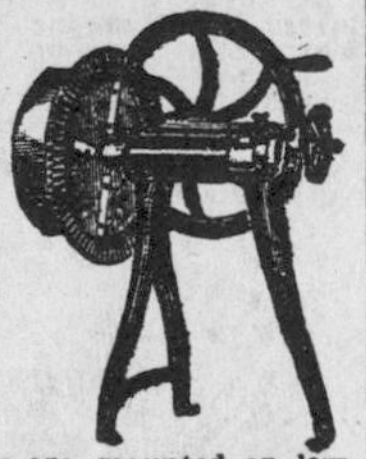

These back geared cutters are the popular sizes for general use. We guarantee them to be the very best, most durable, easiest running and most satisfactory green bone cutters made, and that with the same amount of manual labor or power applied they will cut more green bone than any other machine made for this purpose. They will cut dry or green bones with the meat on them just as they come from the butcher shop, without clogging, and fine enough for chicks four days old. The machines have three solid tool steel knives. Two of the knives are corrugated and these cut grooves into the end of the bone as it is fed to them. A straight knife follows, which makes a clean, smooth cut through all the meat and gristle, obviating the stringy texture of the cut bone, which other cutters produce. They are mounted on low legs, as shown in the illustration at the left, or on high legs, as shown at the right. In the price lines LL stands for low legs and HL for high legs. The feed is automatic and adjustable. Nos. 9 and 11 have a solid nut on the feed screw and the feed screw must be turned back when filling the bone box, but Nos. 10 and 12 have a split nut which allows the feed screw to be pulled back instantly. The balance wheels are very heavy and the cutters operate easily. The Nos. 9 and 10 cutters have a bone box which is 3½x3x11 inches inside and are suitable for a flock of from 100 to 150 fowls. The Nos. 11 and 12 cutters have a bone box which is 4x3x13 inches inside and are suitable for a flock of from 200 to 250 fowls. By ordering a driving pulley with either of these machines they can be run by power and the capacity will be fully double what it is by hand. Shipped from factory in Western Pennsylvania.

No. 32K3225	No. 9LL Bone Cutter.	Wt., 107 lbs.	$8.87
No. 32K3226	No. 9HL Bone Cutter.	Wt., 125 lbs.	10.62
No. 32K3227	No. 11LL Bone Cutter.	Wt., 120 lbs.	11.52
No. 32K3228	No. 11HL Bone Cutter.	Wt., 138 lbs.	13.32
No. 32K3229	No. 10LL Bone Cutter.	Wt., 108 lbs.	10.72
No. 32K3230	No. 10HL Bone Cutter.	Wt., 126 lbs.	12.42
No. 32K3231	No. 12LL Bone Cutter.	Wt., 121 lbs.	13.38
No. 32K3232	No. 12HL Bone Cutter.	Wt., 139 lbs.	15.15
No. 32K3233	12x4-inch Pulley.	Wt., 18 lbs.	1.36

$5.37 IDEAL SANITARY PEST PROOF COOP.

Will protect your chicks against disease, vermin, pests and drowning and will save you more than their cost in one season.

COVERED RUNYARD $1.58

No question more seriously concerns every poultry raiser than that of caring for chicks from the time they are hatched until they are of a marketable or self dependent age. Every farmer or poultry raiser has suffered loss from such common pests as rats, minks, weasels, skunks, hawks, etc. and from various diseases which were caused entirely by unsanitary and poorly ventilated coops. The Ideal Sanitary Pest Proof Brood Coop was designed by a practical poultry raiser who had suffered from such losses as these, and who was determined to turn these losses into profits. His success was so pronounced that he decided to give the benefit of his experience to other poultry raisers, and now these coops are used by thousands of farmers and poultry raisers who consider them indispensable.

Coop is made entirely of galvanized sheet metal and will last a lifetime. Disease germs and vermin will not inhabit metal, and for this reason the coop, if kept reasonably clean, is lice and disease proof. Made in sections and can be easily set up and taken apart without tools of any kind; no screws, bolts or other fastenings required. Has sheet metal floor from which the coop can be lifted and easily scrubbed and cleaned. Ends are open and have removable upright bars and swinging ventilated doors which, when closed, fasten securely on the inside. It is impossible for any animal to enter, or for chicks to escape when doors are closed. Screened ventilator at top insures plenty of fresh air and makes it impossible for chicks to smother; the coop also affords ample protection during rain storms so that chicks cannot drown. These coops will pay for themselves in one season in the increased number of chicks you will be enabled to raise. They are a handsome addition to any poultry yard or farm. Coop will easily accommodate 60 chicks with one hen. We can furnish screen covered runyards, as shown in illustration. These can be set at either or both ends of the coop and afford protection during the day with ample room for exercise. They are made in sections, consist of three side panels and one screened top panel, and can be set up and arranged in almost any manner desired. Coop is 27 inches high, 26 inches long and 36 inches wide. Runyards are 12 inches high and 28 inches square. Complete instructions for setting up accompany each coop. Shipped knocked down and crated from factory near Chicago.
No. 32K3150   Ideal Sanitary Pest Proof Coop.   Wt., 45 lbs.   Price.... $5.37
No. 32K3151   Screen Covered Runyard.   Wt., 12 lbs.   Price 1.58

WINDMILLS AND TOWERS

AT GREATLY REDUCED PRICES

OUR BROAD AND LIBERAL GUARANTEE

WE GUARANTEE that every Kenwood Windmill, when properly put together, erected and cared for according to the instructions which we furnish, will run in lighter winds, endure as hard service, be as durable and accomplish as much work as any other windmill made, of corresponding size and style. Also that our towers, when properly put together, erected and anchored according to the instructions which we furnish, will stand without damage all winds which do not blow down substantial buildings or live trees in the immediate neighborhood. This guarantee to be in full force and effect for one year from the date you receive the windmill or tower. It is a guarantee which cannot be safely duplicated by other windmill manufacturers or dealers, but one which we know that we can make with perfect safety, because of the stanch and perfect construction of the KENWOOD WINDMILLS AND TOWERS.

IF THERE IS ANY ONE LINE OF MERCHANDISE SOLD BY US

in which we take particular and pardonable pride it is our line of Kenwood Windmills and Towers. We have long been acknowledged leaders in the windmill business, and the extremely high quality and wonderful value of our windmill goods have gained for them a reputation for excellence equaled by no other make of windmills and towers. When we first started in the windmill business we determined to furnish our customers with the best windmills and towers which could possibly be made, at prices which manufacturers of even the most cheaply constructed and unreliable goods of this character could not possibly duplicate. The fact that our continually growing windmill business is today larger than that of all other catalogue houses combined, and with possibly one or two exceptions larger than the total output of any one other manufacturer, proves conclusively that we have succeeded and that our customers fully appreciate the wonderful value we are giving them. You will find hundreds of Kenwood Windmills and Towers in use in almost every section of the country. Ask any owner of a Kenwood Windmill outfit what he thinks of it; we know that his answer will convince you that you cannot do better than to send us your order. While our windmills and towers have always been splendid windmills and towers, we have constantly been striving to make them better, both in quality and efficiency, and we know positively and thousands of our highly satisfied customers will testify that Kenwood Windmills and Towers are the best windmills and towers that have ever been produced by any manufacturer and that they possess more up to date and desirable features and improvements than any other windmills and towers made. Kenwood Windmills and Towers are manufactured complete in the most perfectly equipped and up to date windmill factory in the country, every part is designed and produced under the direct supervision of men who have made the construction of high grade windmills and towers a life long study and who are acknowledged to be the most expert in the business, every ounce of material used is the best the market affords and nothing but the highest class of workmanship is employed. In addition to this every part is subjected to the most rigid inspection, and only those which are absolutely perfect, both in workmanship and material, are permitted to enter into the construction of the windmill or tower. Such inspection as this would suffice with any ordinary manufacturer, but not with us, for when our windmills and towers are completed they are again submitted to another most careful examination before shipping to see that they are in complete and perfect condition and ready to go together easily and properly so that our customers may be subjected to no delay or inconvenience whatever when erecting and operating their outfits. Order a windmill and tower from us and you will be satisfied not only that all we say is true but that you have an outfit superior to any you have ever seen; and you will also understand why thousands of our customers as well as ourselves are so enthusiastic over the merits of Kenwood Windmills and Towers.

OUR UNEQUALED 60 DAYS' FREE TRIAL OFFER

EVERY KENWOOD WINDMILL AND TOWER we sell is shipped on the understanding and agreement that, after receiving, you are to have SIXTY DAYS in which to give them a thorough trial and to compare them with windmills and towers of any other make, and if during the trial period you find any reason to be dissatisfied either with the quality, utility or value of our windmills and towers and if you are not convinced that our windmills and towers are better than you can buy elsewhere at any price, you can return them to us at our expense and we will promptly return your money, including freight charges you may have paid. You take no risk whatever in ordering windmill goods from us. They must satisfy and please you or you get your money back.

REMEMBER, our line of windmill goods is the most complete in the country, and if you want a windmill, tower or a complete pumping windmill outfit different from those we here list, or a power windmill outfit, or, in fact, windmill goods of any description, **write us**; we will save you money and furnish you the best windmill goods on earth. In order to insure your letter receiving our most prompt and careful attention address: WINDMILL EXPERT, care Sears, Roebuck & Co., Chicago, Ill.

KENWOOD BALL BEARING BACK GEARED STEEL WINDMILLS $13.75

NO TROUBLE TO ERECT OUR WINDMILLS. THE SIMPLE DIRECTIONS WE FURNISH MAKE IT EASY FOR ANYONE. READ THIS:

Sears, Roebuck & Co., Chicago, Ill. Colusa, Kans.

Dear Sirs:—The windmill I recently bought of you gives entire satisfaction. With the instructions you sent I had no trouble at all in putting it together, the wheel lined perfectly and the mill works to perfection. I would not trade it for any mill I ever saw.

Yours truly, C. W. ROBERTSON.

SCORES OF TESTIMONIALS JUST AS GOOD AS THE ABOVE ARE PRINTED IN OUR SPECIAL WINDMILL CATALOGUE.

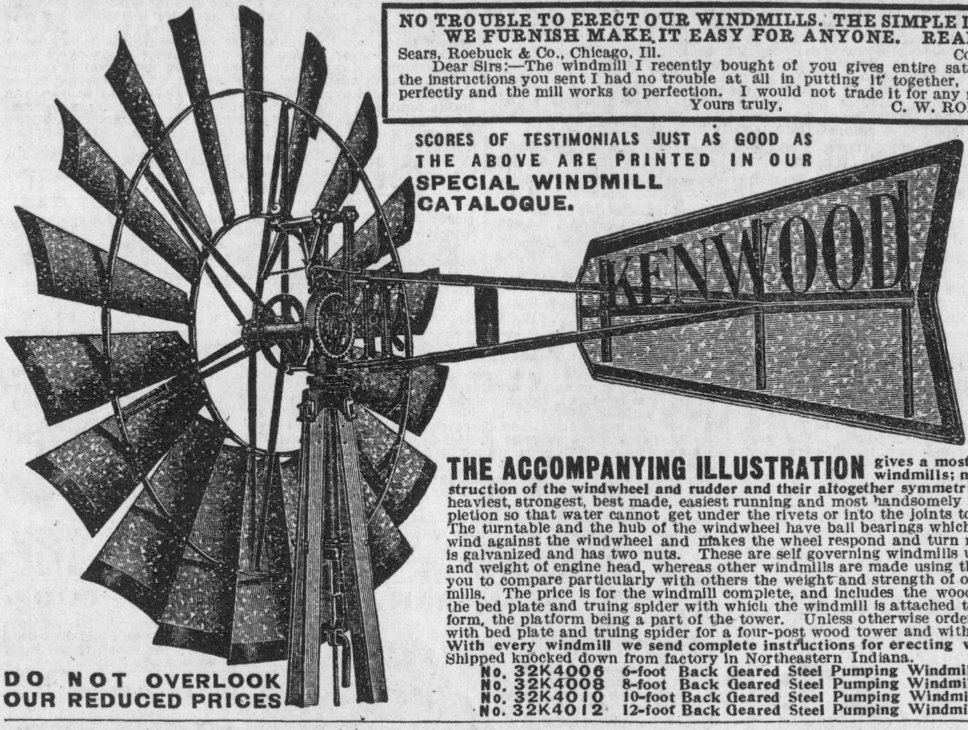

ORDER A KENWOOD WINDMILL. If you do not find it to be the most handsome, the easiest running, the most perfectly constructed, the most durable and in every way the best windmill you have ever seen and a better windmill than you can buy elsewhere at any price, return it to us and get your money back, including the freight charges you may have paid. Put us to the test; we must satisfy you or you will not be out one cent.

YOUR NAME ON THE WINDMILL RUDDER FREE. Our windmills are tipped with red on the ends of the windwheel sails and around the rudder sheet and are the most handsomely finished windmills made. The name KENWOOD is stenciled on both sides of the rudder. When you place your order, if you will CAREFULLY PRINT thereon your initials and last name, and state that you want your name put on the rudder, we will stencil it on both sides without charge, but we cannot put on more than your initials and last name, but if you so instruct, we will send the windmill with a plain rudder, or leave off the brand Kenwood and stencil your name or your firm name and the name of your town on both sides of the rudder. This is especially important to DEALERS who wish to sell and erect our windmills.

THE ACCOMPANYING ILLUSTRATION gives a most excellent idea of the superior construction of our back geared windmills; note the wonderful simplicity of their mechanism, the rigid construction of the windwheel and rudder and their altogether symmetrical and handsome appearance. These are without question the heaviest, strongest, best made, easiest running and most handsomely finished windmills on the market. They are galvanized after completion so that water cannot get under the rivets or into the joints to rust them away. The engine head is simple, strong and durable. The turntable and the hub of the windwheel have ball bearings which reduces the end thrust friction caused by the pressure of the wind against the windwheel and makes the wheel respond and turn more quickly when the wind changes its direction. Every bolt is galvanized and has two nuts. These are self governing windmills under all conditions. Each size of windmill has a different size and weight of engine head, whereas other windmills are made using the same engine head for different sizes. In this respect we ask you to compare particularly with others the weight and strength of our 10-foot windmills, one of the most important sizes of windmills. The price is for the windmill complete, and includes the wood pump pole, the pull-out wire, a first class reefing gear, and the bed plate and truing spider with which the windmill is attached to the tower or mast, but price does not include a tower or a platform, the platform being a part of the tower. Unless otherwise ordered, when a windmill is ordered without a tower, we will ship it with bed plate and truing spider for a four-post wood tower and with sufficient pump pole and pull-out wire for a tower 40 feet high. With every windmill we send complete instructions for erecting windmills and towers and for building four-post wood towers. Shipped knocked down from factory in Northeastern Indiana.

DO NOT OVERLOOK OUR REDUCED PRICES

No. 32K4006	6-foot Back Geared Steel Pumping Windmill.	Wt., 290 lbs.	Price......$13.75
No. 32K4008	8-foot Back Geared Steel Pumping Windmill.	Wt., 425 lbs.	Price...... 18.32
No. 32K4010	10-foot Back Geared Steel Pumping Windmill.	Wt., 630 lbs.	Price...... 24.90
No. 32K4012	12-foot Back Geared Steel Pumping Windmill.	Wt., 970 lbs.	Price...... 42.40

$18.15 Kenwood Direct Stroke Steel Pumping Windmills.

PRICES GREATLY REDUCED.

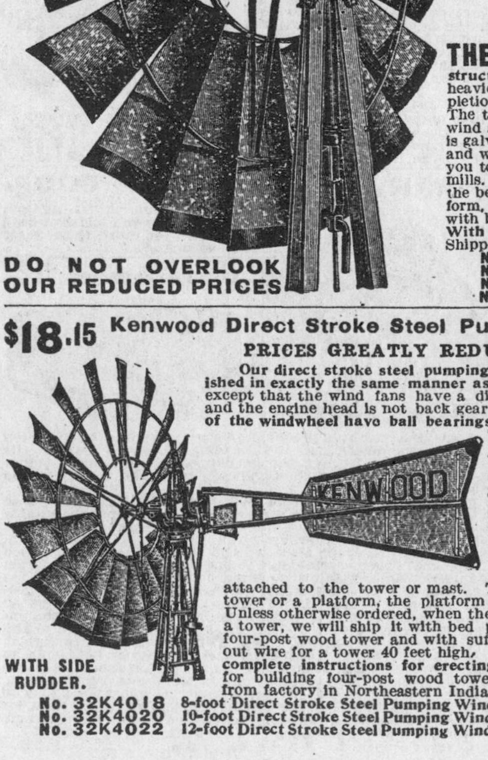

WITH SIDE RUDDER.

Our direct stroke steel pumping windmills are built and finished in exactly the same manner as our back geared windmills, except that the wind fans have a different angle and curvature and the engine head is not back geared. **The turntable and hub of the windwheel have ball bearings.** Every bolt has two nuts. These windmills will govern perfectly under all conditions. **They are furnished with side rudders or air governors, as shown in the illustration.** The price is for the windmill complete, with side rudder, and includes the wood pump pole, the pull-out wire, a first class reefing gear, and the bed plate and truing spider with which the windmill is attached to the tower or mast. The price does not include a tower or a platform, the platform being a part of the tower. Unless otherwise ordered, when the windmill is ordered without a tower, we will ship it with bed plate and truing spider for a four-post wood tower and with sufficient pump pole and pull-out wire for a tower 40 feet high. **With every windmill we send complete instructions for erecting windmills and towers, and for building four-post wood towers.** Shipped knocked down from factory in Northeastern Indiana.

			Price
No. 32K4018	8-foot Direct Stroke Steel Pumping Windmill.	Wt., 400 lbs.	$18.15
No. 32K4020	10-foot Direct Stroke Steel Pumping Windmill.	Wt., 565 lbs.	24.70
No. 32K4022	12-foot Direct Stroke Steel Pumping Windmill.	Wt., 825 lbs.	41.75

$17.50 Kenwood Direct Stroke Wood Pumping Windmills.

BIG REDUCTION IN PRICES.

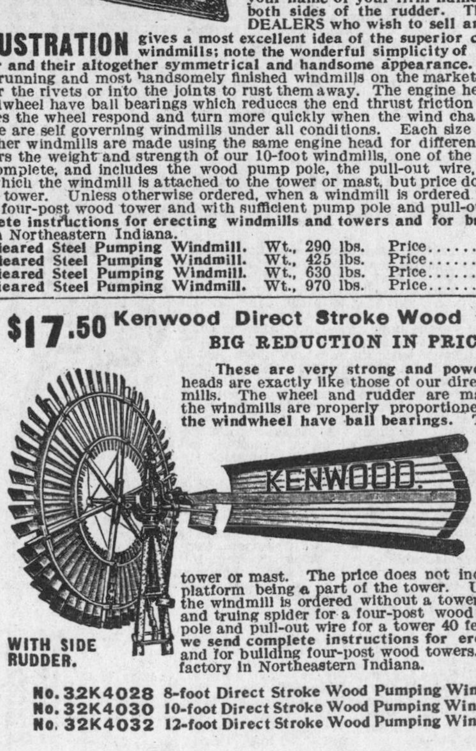

WITH SIDE RUDDER.

These are very strong and powerful windmills. The engine heads are exactly like those of our direct stroke steel pumping windmills. The wheel and rudder are made of wood and all parts of the windmills are properly proportioned. **The turntable and hub of the windwheel have ball bearings.** These windmills will govern perfectly under all conditions. **They are furnished with side rudders or air governors, as shown in the illustration.** The price is for the windmill complete with side rudder and includes the wood pump pole, the pull-out wire, a first class reefing gear and the bed plate and truing spider with which the windmill is attached to the tower or mast. The price does not include a tower or platform, the platform being a part of the tower. Unless otherwise ordered, when the windmill is ordered without a tower, we will ship it with bed plate and truing spider for a four-post wood tower and with sufficient pump pole and pull-out wire for a tower 40 feet high. **With every windmill we send complete instructions for erecting windmills and towers, and for building four-post wood towers.** Shipped knocked down from factory in Northeastern Indiana.

			Price
No. 32K4028	8-foot Direct Stroke Wood Pumping Windmill.	Wt., 390 lbs.,	$17.50
No. 32K4030	10-foot Direct Stroke Wood Pumping Windmill.	Wt., 485 lbs.,	22.90
No. 32K4032	12-foot Direct Stroke Wood Pumping Windmill.	Wt., 650 lbs.,	34.90

COMPLETE WINDMILL WATER SUPPLY OUTFITS $35.45 AND UP

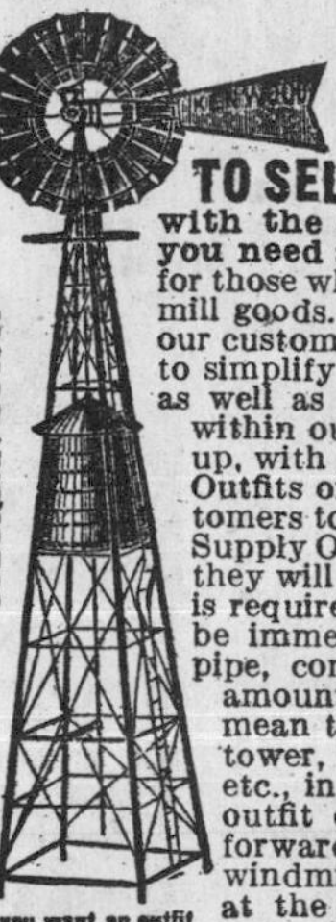

SUBURBAN OUTFIT

If you want an outfit like this WRITE US.

TO SELECT A COMPLETE WINDMILL OUTFIT, with the assurance that you have ordered just what you need and everything you need, is sometimes difficult for those who have not had more or less experience with windmill goods. Realizing this fact and with a desire to afford our customers every possible convenience when ordering and to simplify both the ordering and erecting of their outfits, as well as effect for them every saving in labor and money within our power, we have had our windmill expert make up, with extreme care, complete Windmill Water Supply Outfits of every description, making it possible for our customers to purchase from us any kind of a Windmill Water Supply Outfit they may require, and when they receive it they will find it to be complete in every way and exactly what is required and every part will be fitted so that the outfit may be immediately erected, and as all threads will be cut, every pipe, connection, etc., will go together with the least possible amount of labor on their part. When we say **complete** we mean the outfit will consist of not only the windmill and tower, but will also include the pump, rod, pipe, cylinder, etc., in fact, everything needed to make up the kind of an outfit ordered; and furthermore the complete outfit will be forwarded at the same time and in one shipment from our windmill factory, so that all parts of the outfit will reach you at the same time, protecting you against delay and insuring you the lowest possible amount of freight.

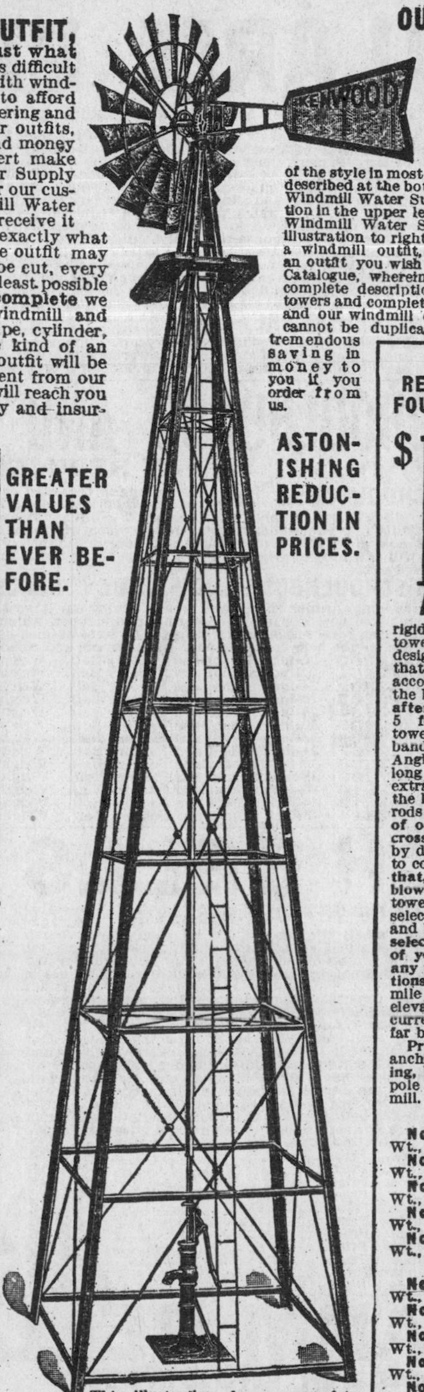

This illustration shows a complete Regular Windmill Water Supply Outfit, such as we list below, under Catalogue No. 32K4224.

OUR REGULAR WINDMILL Water Supply Outfits, the kind shown in the large illustration, are the only ones we list in this catalogue. Our reason for this is that, in order for us to properly describe the many sizes and styles of outfits we are in a position to furnish, they would require much more space than it is possible for us to devote to them in this big book. "Regular" Windmill Water Supply Outfits are of the style in most general use, and you will find them priced and described at the bottom of this page, but if you wish a Suburban Windmill Water Supply Outfit, such as shown in the small illustration in the upper left hand corner of this page, or a Combination Windmill Water Supply Outfit, such as shown in the small illustration to right of this paragraph, or in fact any kind of a windmill outfit, write us, telling us exactly what kind of an outfit you wish and we will send you our Special Windmill Catalogue, wherein you will find handsome illustrations and complete descriptions of the many different styles of windmills, towers and complete Windmill Water Supply Outfits we furnish, and our windmill expert will quote you prices which we know cannot be duplicated by any other concern and will mean a tremendous saving in money to you if you order from us.

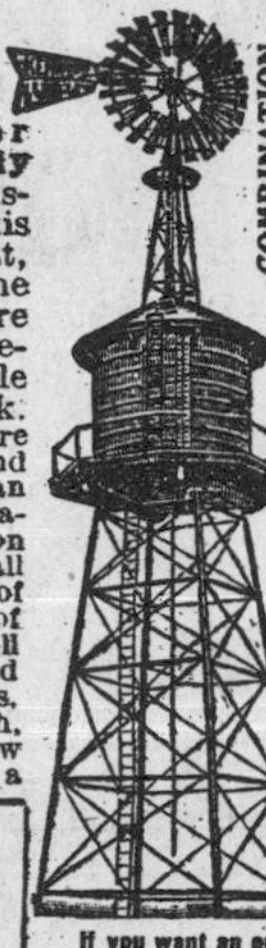

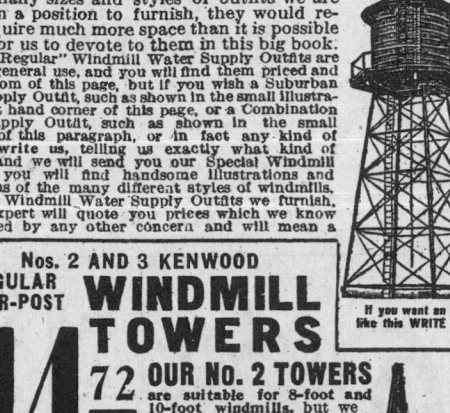

COMBINATION OUTFIT

If you want an outfit like this WRITE US.

GREATER VALUES THAN EVER BEFORE.

ASTONISHING REDUCTION IN PRICES.

No. 1 KENWOOD REGULAR FOUR-POST WINDMILL TOWERS $12.92 AND UP

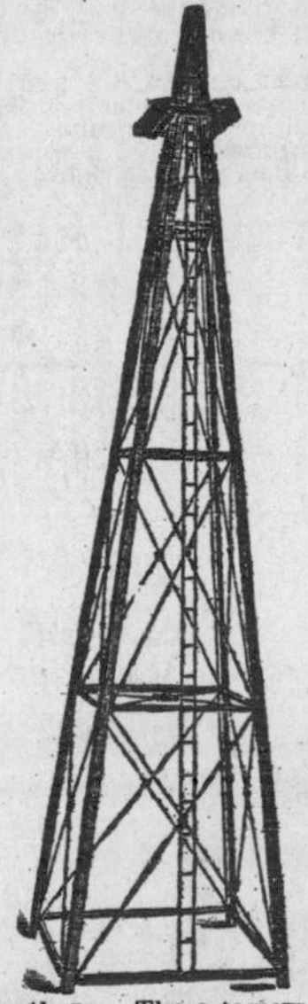

THESE TOWERS ARE SUITABLE for use with 6-foot and 8-foot windmills but, in view of the small difference in price, we recommend that a No. 2 tower be used with an 8-foot windmill. These towers are of more rigid construction and are stronger than any other towers made for these sizes of windmills. They are made of the best of materials and are properly proportioned and braced in every way. Corner posts are 10 feet 6 inches long, from which you will see that **our towers are full height**, the extra 6 inches on each corner post being allowed for the lap of one corner post over the one below it. This feature, in addition to making a stronger and better finished tower, also serves as a rainshed and prevents water from gathering in the corner post joints. Every corner post, brace, band, girt, bolt and nut of our towers is **galvanized after completion, that is, after all cutting, punching and other machine work is done, after all rivets are set and after all threads are cut.** This is a most important feature because it insures every part of the steel being covered with a non-rusting metal and makes our towers more rustproof than others. These towers have one set of bands for each 10 feet of their height, also a band at the platform and two bands above the platform which serve as steps. They are braced both lengthwise and crosswise at every corner post joint by diagonal cross rods having tension adjustment and which run from corner post to corner post, making them so rigid that when properly anchored they cannot be blown down. Always select a tower which will elevate the bottom of your windmill from 10 to 20 feet above any trees, buildings or other wind obstructions which are within a quarter of a mile of the windmill; if conditions are such that the extreme height of No. 1 tower will not make this possible you should order a No. 2 tower of proper height. Price is for the tower complete with platform, ladder, rod guides, anchor posts and anchor plates, and complete instructions for erecting, but does not include windmill bed plate, truing spider, pump pole, pull-out wire or reefing gear, these being parts of the windmill. Shipped knocked down from factory in Northeastern Indiana.

No. 32K4112 20-foot No. 1 Regular Windmill Tower. Wt., 340 lbs. Price........$12.92
No. 32K4113 30-foot No. 1 Regular Windmill Tower. Wt., 480 lbs. Price........$19.62
No. 32K4114 40-foot No. 1 Regular Windmill Tower. Wt., 650 lbs. Price........$26.62

Nos. 2 AND 3 KENWOOD REGULAR FOUR-POST WINDMILL TOWERS $14.72 AND UP

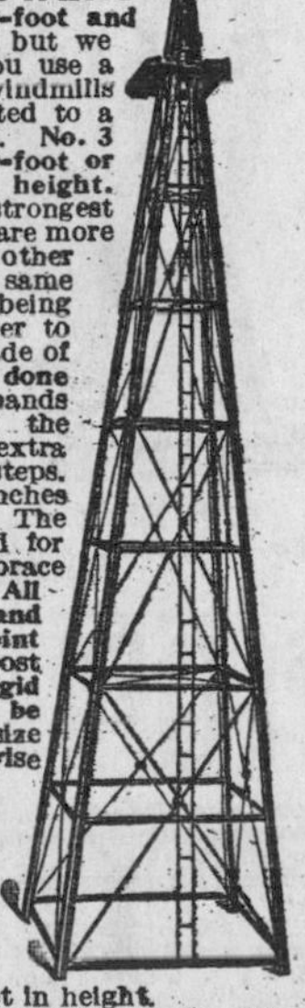

OUR No. 2 TOWERS are suitable for 8-foot and 10-foot windmills, but we recommend that you use a No. 3 tower for 10-foot windmills when they are to be elevated to a height greater than 40 feet. No. 3 towers are suitable for 10-foot or 12-foot windmills at any height. These towers are of the strongest possible construction, they are more rigidly braced and better made than any other towers on the market. Both styles are of the same design and construction, the only difference being that the No. 3 tower is made heavier in order to accommodate larger windmills. They are made of the best of materials and **all galvanizing is done after completion.** These towers have bands 5 feet apart for the entire height of the tower, also a band at the platform and two extra bands above the platform, which also serve as steps. Angle steel corner posts are made 10 feet 6 inches long and lap outside to make a rain shed. The extra 6 inches on each corner post is allowed for the lap, making **our towers full height. The brace rods are provided with tension adjustment. All of our towers are braced both lengthwise and crosswise at every corner post or section joint** by diagonal cross rods running from corner post to corner post, and **they are so strong and rigid that, when properly anchored, they cannot be blown down.** The selection of the largest size tower which is suitable for the windmill is a wise selection and will add greatly to the value and beauty of your windmill outfit. **Always select a tower which will elevate the bottom of your windmill from 10 to 20 feet above any trees, buildings or other wind obstructions,** which are within a quarter of a mile of the windmill. Low towers do not elevate the windmill into the steady air currents and a windmill is safer and gives far better results on towers from 30 to 60 feet in height.

Price is for the tower complete with platform, ladder, rod guides, anchor posts and anchor plates, **and complete instructions for erecting,** but does not include windmill bed plate, truing spider, pump pole pull-out wire, or reefing gear, these being parts of the windmill. Shipped knocked down from factory in Northeastern Indiana.

No. 2 Regular Windmill Towers.

No. 32K4122 20-foot No. 2 Regular Windmill Tower. Wt., 395 lbs. Price........$14.72
No. 32K4123 30-foot No. 2 Regular Windmill Tower. Wt., 565 lbs. Price........$22.20
No. 32K4124 40-foot No. 2 Regular Windmill Tower. Wt., 735 lbs. Price........$29.87
No. 32K4125 50-foot No. 2 Regular Windmill Tower. Wt., 1,065 lbs. Price........$39.85
No. 32K4126 60-foot No. 2 Regular Windmill Tower. Wt., 1,385 lbs. Price........$48.65

No. 3 Regular Windmill Towers.

No. 32K4132 20-foot No. 3 Regular Windmill Tower. Wt., 445 lbs. Price........$18.40
No. 32K4133 30-foot No. 3 Regular Windmill Tower. Wt., 635 lbs. Price........$27.60
No. 32K4134 40-foot No. 3 Regular Windmill Tower. Wt., 900 lbs. Price........$39.20
No. 32K4135 50-foot No. 3 Regular Windmill Tower. Wt., 1,265 lbs. Price........$52.45
No. 32K4136 60-foot No. 3 Regular Windmill Tower. Wt., 1,640 lbs. Price........$63.70

"REGULAR" WINDMILL WATER SUPPLY OUTFITS. BIG REDUCTION IN PRICES.

A "REGULAR" WINDMILL WATER SUPPLY OUTFIT consists of one windmill, one Regular windmill tower, **one windmill lift pump, and one outside capped iron cylinder with galvanized iron suction pipe and steel pump rod to connect it with the pump, and instructions for erecting the windmill and tower.** Regular outfits with 6-foot windmills will have a 2½x12-inch cylinder for wells of 25 feet or less in depth and a 2x12-inch cylinder for wells of from 30 to 50 feet in depth. With 8-foot windmills the cylinder will be 3x12 inches for wells of 50 feet or less in depth, 2½x12 inches for wells of from 55 to 85 feet in depth, and 2x12 inches for wells of from 90 to 125 feet in depth. With 10-foot windmills the cylinder will be 3x14 inches for wells of 85 feet or less in depth and 2½x14 inches for wells of from 90 to 125 feet in depth. By depth of well we mean the distance from the pump platform to the bottom of the cylinder. Don't forget to tell us how far you want the bottom of the cylinder below the pump platform and remember that the cylinder should always be in the water and at least 2 feet above the bottom of the well. **At the prices shown below the cylinder will not be placed over 25 feet below the pump platform,** nor will any deduction be made for placing it less than 25 feet; however, we will place the cylinder at any depth you specify, not exceeding 50 feet for 6-foot windmills, or 125 feet for 8-foot or 10-foot windmills but for a depth of well greater than 25 feet you must allow and add to the price of the outfit **16 cents** for each additional foot in depth, this to pay for the extra pipe and pump rod required and the labor of fitting same. We can furnish an outside capped brass body cylinder in place of the iron cylinder for **$1.35** extra, or we can furnish a cockspout force pump, in place of the lift pump, for **$2.30** extra, or a three-way force pump, in place of the lift pump, for **$3.45** extra, but should you wish to make either of these changes you must be careful to state them plainly in your order and to add the correct amounts to the price of the outfit which you order. The prices we name below are based upon a back geared steel windmill being used with the outfit, but if you want the same size of direct stroke steel windmill or direct stroke wood windmill in place of the back geared mill, deduct the price of the back geared windmill we list with the outfit and add the price of the direct stroke windmill which you want. The 6-foot windmill is made only in the back geared pattern. Shipped knocked down from factory in Northeastern Indiana.

No. 32K4202	Regular Windmill Outfit, with 6-foot back geared steel windmill and 20-foot No. 1 tower.	Wt., 790 lbs.	Price........	$35.45
No. 32K4203	Regular Windmill Outfit, with 6-foot back geared steel windmill and 30-foot No. 1 tower.	Wt., 930 lbs.	Price........	42.25
No. 32K4204	Regular Windmill Outfit, with 6-foot back geared steel windmill and 40-foot No. 1 tower.	Wt., 1,100 lbs.	Price........	49.25
No. 32K4222	Regular Windmill Outfit, with 8-foot back geared steel windmill and 20-foot No. 2 tower.	Wt., 980 lbs.	Price........	41.85
No. 32K4223	Regular Windmill Outfit, with 8-foot back geared steel windmill and 30-foot No. 2 tower.	Wt., 1,150 lbs.	Price........	49.40
No. 32K4224	Regular Windmill Outfit, with 8-foot back geared steel windmill and 40-foot No. 2 tower.	Wt., 1,320 lbs.	Price........	57.00
No. 32K4225	Regular Windmill Outfit, with 8-foot back geared steel windmill and 50-foot No. 2 tower.	Wt., 1,650 lbs.	Price........	66.95
No. 32K4226	Regular Windmill Outfit, with 8-foot back geared steel windmill and 60-foot No. 2 tower.	Wt., 1,970 lbs.	Price........	75.80
No. 32K4232	Regular Windmill Outfit, with 10-foot back geared steel windmill and 20-foot No. 3 tower.	Wt., 1,235 lbs.	Price........	52.10
No. 32K4233	Regular Windmill Outfit, with 10-foot back geared steel windmill and 30-foot No. 3 tower.	Wt., 1,425 lbs.	Price........	61.30
No. 32K4234	Regular Windmill Outfit, with 10-foot back geared steel windmill and 40-foot No. 3 tower.	Wt., 1,690 lbs.	Price........	72.90
No. 32K4235	Regular Windmill Outfit, with 10-foot back geared steel windmill and 50-foot No. 3 tower.	Wt., 2,055 lbs.	Price........	86.15
No. 32K4236	Regular Windmill Outfit, with 10-foot back geared steel windmill and 60-foot No. 3 tower.	Wt., 2,430 lbs.	Price........	97.40

SCHOOLHOUSE, FACTORY, CHURCH AND FIRE ALARM BELLS

MADE OF OUR FAMOUS CRYSTALLINE BELL METAL.

BEWARE OF BELLS NAMED IN IMITATION OF OUR FAMOUS CRYSTALLINE METAL BELLS.

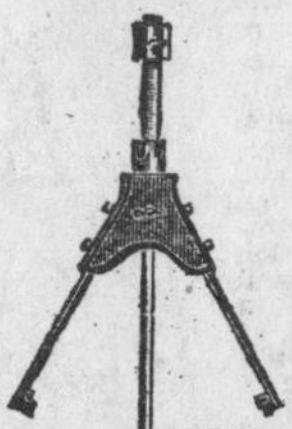

The Improved Springs and Clapper used on our School, Factory and Church Bells.

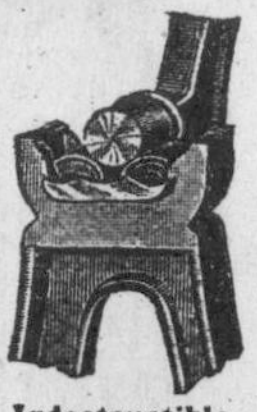

Indestructible Roller Bearings used on our 44 and 48-inch School, Factory and Church Bells.

OUR BELLS ARE CELEBRATED for their volume of sound and for their loud, clear, round and sweet tone. They are high grade composition bells, being made from our wonderful Crystalline bell metal, a most superior composition metal of high quality which makes our bells worth many times as much as any of the so called alloy and cast iron bells which others offer. Our Crystalline Metal Bells are almost as good as the best copper and tin bells made, which, of course, sell for much higher prices, and if you will invest the same amount of money in one of our bells that you would in a copper and tin bell, you will secure a bell with a greater volume of sound, more far reaching and with a more satisfactory tone than any copper and tin bell you can buy for anywhere near the same money. **Our line of bells is most complete and embraces an assortment of styles and sizes which will meet the requirements of almost everyone. You will find our prices exceedingly low,** in fact, much lower than others ask for greatly inferior bells which cannot compare with ours in any way. We solicit your order on the terms **of our sixty days' free trial offer** backed by **our five-year guarantee.** We will save you fully from one-fourth to one-half in price and give you greater value than you can obtain elsewhere and our bells must please and satisfy you in every way or you get all your money and freight charges back.

SIXTY DAYS' FREE TRIAL. **Every bell we sell is shipped with the understanding and agreement that after receiving it you are to have sixty days in which to give it a thorough trial** and to compare it in tone, volume and quality with composition bells of any other make, and if, during the trial period, you find any reason to be dissatisfied, you can return the bell to us at our expense and we will promptly return your money, together with the freight charges you paid when you received the bell.

OUR FIVE-YEAR GUARANTEE AGAINST BREAKAGE. **As a guarantee that the bells we sell are the highest grade bells cast, as a positive guarantee against breakage,** and for the absolute protection of the purchaser, we guarantee each and every bell we sell against breakage for five years. Should any piece or part of our famous Crystalline Metal Church, Schoolhouse, Factory or Fire Alarm Bells break through defect in material or workmanship with ordinary use at any time within five years from the date of shipment we will furnish a new piece or part to take the place of the broken part, or if necessary we will furnish an entirely new bell, free of charge.

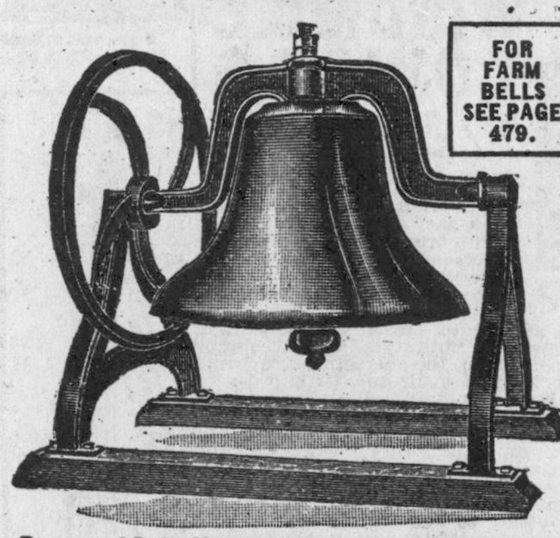

FOR FARM BELLS SEE PAGE 479.

Beware of Bells Named in Imitation of our Famous Crystalline Metal Bells.

SCHOOLHOUSE AND FACTORY BELLS $6.12

AT REDUCED PRICES

A SCHOOLHOUSE BELL **is no longer regarded as a luxury, but as a prime necessity,** for it not only serves the purpose of a neighborhood clock, by summoning the children to school at a uniform time, so that tardy, pupils will not be continually straggling in to interrupt and delay the duties of the day, but it does much to instill the habits of punctuality into your children, the value of which will be more appreciated by them the older they grow. **Factories will also find a bell a most profitable investment,** for in addition to the saving of time, lost through tardy workers who depend on their own clocks a bell will add tone to their plant and, as the entire community will learn to measure their time by it, it will become an everlasting advertisement.

OUR SCHOOLHOUSE AND FACTORY BELLS **are all of the same general design,** they differ only in size and in the fact that our 44 and 48-inch bells are mounted on **indestructible roller bearings,** which enable one person to ring our largest bells with as great ease and regularity as a small bell can be rung. All sizes are fitted with our improved springs and clapper, which insures a full stroke of the clapper without the possibility of a second stroke. Iron rope wheels are furnished with 20 to 36-inch bells and sectional wood rope wheels with 38 to 48-inch bells. Weights and prices are for the bells complete with frame, wheel and wood sills. Shipped from factory in Central Ohio.

No. 32K2800	20-inch School and Factory Bell.	Weight, 165 pounds.	Price....$ 6.12
No. 32K2801	22-inch School and Factory Bell.	Weight, 205 pounds.	Price.... 7.52
No. 32K2802	24-inch School and Factory Bell.	Weight, 250 pounds.	Price.... 9.52
No. 32K2803	26-inch School and Factory Bell.	Weight, 350 pounds.	Price.... 13.32
No. 32K2804	28-inch School and Factory Bell.	Weight, 450 pounds.	Price.... 18.40
No. 32K2805	30-inch School and Factory Bell.	Weight, 570 pounds.	Price.... 22.10
No. 32K2806	32-inch School and Factory Bell.	Weight, 640 pounds.	Price.... 23.65
No. 32K2807	34-inch School and Factory Bell.	Weight, 765 pounds.	Price.... 28.30
No. 32K2808	36-inch School and Factory Bell.	Weight, 950 pounds.	Price.... 36.10
No. 32K2809	38-inch School and Factory Bell.	Weight, 1,010 pounds.	Price.... 43.95
No. 32K2810	40-inch School and Factory Bell.	Weight, 1,300 pounds.	Price.... 50.55
No. 32K2812	44-inch School and Factory Bell.	Weight, 1,790 pounds.	Price.... 77.15
No. 32K2814	48-inch School and Factory Bell.	Weight, 2,280 pounds.	Price.... 97.00

$10.94 CHURCH BELLS

NO CHURCH CAN AFFORD TO DO WITHOUT A BELL

and invariably the congregations who feel that they cannot afford it are the ones who need a bell the most. To be complete, a church demands a bell; in fact, in order for a church to fully serve its purpose a bell is a necessity, for it marks the hour set for prayer and service, it invites the stranger to attend, reminds the careless of the sanctity of the Sabbath Day and awakens all to a sense of duty. If your church is without a bell and is not prospering, our advice would be, **buy a bell.** It will do more to awaken interest and increase attendance and the amount of collections, than any other investment you can make. The low prices at which we offer our Crystalline Metal Church Bells make it possible for even the poorest of churches to afford one. Of course, better satisfaction will be experienced with a large bell than with a small one, as the larger the bell the greater the volume of sound and mellowness of tone, but our smaller bells will give splendid satisfaction and answer the purpose well until you can afford a larger one. Our church bells are all of the same general design; they differ only in size and in the fact that the standards of the 44 and 48-inch bells are fitted with our **indestructible roller bearings,** which make it possible to ring our largest bells with as much ease and regularity as a small bell can be rung. All sizes have tolling hammer and are fitted with our improved springs and clapper, which insures a full stroke of the clapper without the possibility of a second stroke. Iron rope wheels are furnished with 24 to 36-inch bells and sectional wood rope wheels with 38 to 48-inch bells. We will place inscriptions of less than ten words on our church bells for $4.00 extra and inscriptions of from ten to twenty words for $7.00 extra, but **bells with inscriptions are not returnable.** Weights and prices are for the bells complete with frame, wheel and wood sills. Shipped from factory in Central Ohio.

No. 32K2822	24-inch Church Bell.	Weight, 258 pounds.	Price....$10.94
No. 32K2823	26-inch Church Bell.	Weight, 358 pounds.	Price.... 14.68
No. 32K2824	28-inch Church Bell.	Weight, 465 pounds.	Price.... 19.85
No. 32K2825	30-inch Church Bell.	Weight, 585 pounds.	Price.... 24.10
No. 32K2826	32-inch Church Bell.	Weight, 655 pounds.	Price.... 25.55
No. 32K2827	34-inch Church Bell.	Weight, 780 pounds.	Price.... 30.30
No. 32K2828	36-inch Church Bell.	Weight, 967 pounds.	Price.... 38.45
No. 32K2829	38-inch Church Bell.	Weight, 1,027 pounds.	Price.... 46.30
No. 32K2830	40-inch Church Bell.	Weight, 1,317 pounds.	Price.... 52.90
No. 32K2832	44-inch Church Bell.	Weight, 1,824 pounds.	Price.... 79.35
No. 32K2834	48-inch Church Bell.	Weight, 2,314 pounds.	Price.... 99.40

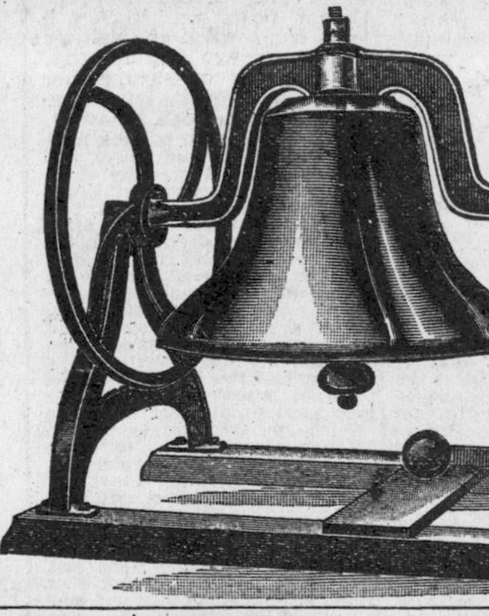

BIG REDUCTION IN PRICES.

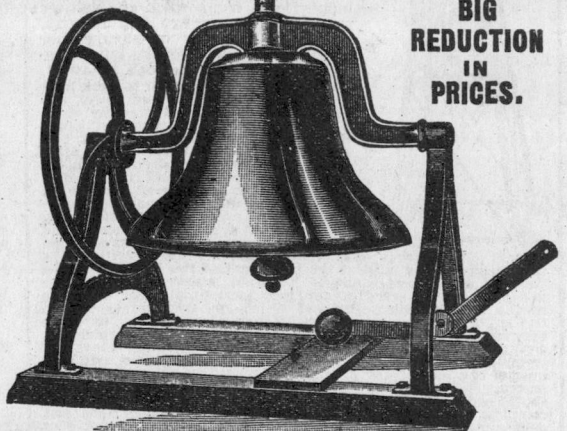

$14.80 FIRE ALARM BELLS $18.55

MADE IN TWO STYLES.

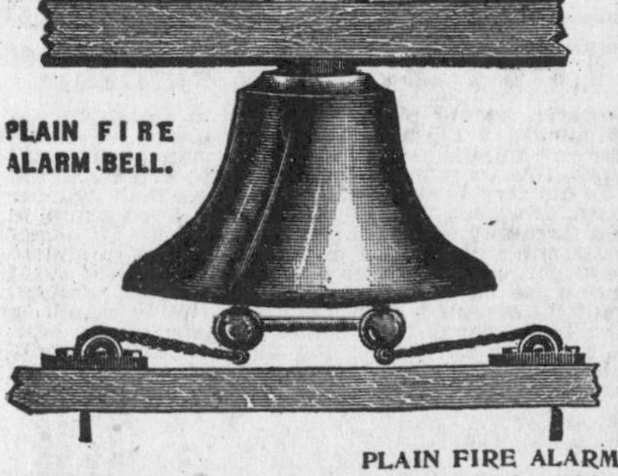

PLAIN FIRE ALARM BELL.

THE GREAT PROTECTION **afforded by a first class fire alarm bell is something which no town, village or community, no matter how small, can afford to do without.** In our Crystalline Metal Fire Alarm Bells we offer the opportunity to supply this protection at a cost so small that it is hardly worth considering when one thinks of the lives and property the bell may save. Our fire alarm bells are made in two styles or patterns. Our Plain Fire Alarm Bells on account of their simple construction are the least expensive to buy, and consist of the plain bells and fittings and are intended to be mounted on timbers, as shown in the illustration. Our Mounted Fire Alarm Bells are more desirable as they are complete in themselves and are more easily set up. They consist of the complete bells with iron frames and wood sills. Both styles have double clapper, which enables one person to ring any size of bell with ease, as the pull of the rope is much shorter than when a single clapper is used. **We advise the selection of as large a bell as possible,** for the larger the bell, the greater the volume of sound and the farther it can be heard. To be a success at all times, an alarm bell must be capable of being heard at any time and for a considerable distance, and large bells are the ones to insure this. Price of our Plain Fire Alarm Bells includes the bell complete with bolt and washers for securing to timbers and two rope wheels but does not include timbers or rope. Price of our Mounted Fire Alarm Bells includes the bell complete with frame and sills, as shown in the illustration, excepting that we do not furnish the rope. Our fire alarm bells are made from Crystalline Metal of special hardness in order for them to best suit their purpose and for this reason there will usually be about 10 days' delay in shipping. Shipped from factory in Central Ohio.

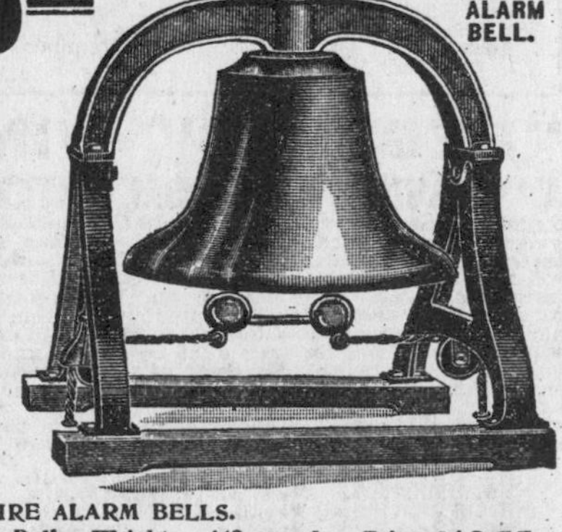

MOUNTED FIRE ALARM BELL.

PLAIN FIRE ALARM BELLS.

No. 32K2844	28-inch Plain Alarm Bell.	Weight, 357 pounds.	Price....$14.80
No. 32K2845	30-inch Plain Alarm Bell.	Weight, 404 pounds.	Price.... 18.50
No. 32K2846	32-inch Plain Alarm Bell.	Weight, 444 pounds.	Price.... 21.40
No. 32K2847	34-inch Plain Alarm Bell.	Weight, 502 pounds.	Price.... 23.60
No. 32K2848	36-inch Plain Alarm Bell.	Weight, 663 pounds.	Price.... 31.00
No. 32K2849	38-inch Plain Alarm Bell.	Weight, 771 pounds.	Price.... 35.20
No. 32K2850	40-inch Plain Alarm Bell.	Weight, 890 pounds.	Price.... 40.15
No. 32K2852	44-inch Plain Alarm Bell.	Weight, 1,258 pounds.	Price.... 54.90
No. 32K2854	48-inch Plain Alarm Bell.	Weight, 1,707 pounds.	Price.... 77.95

MOUNTED FIRE ALARM BELLS.

No. 32K2864	28-inch Mounted Alarm Bell.	Weight, 443 pounds.	Price. $18.55
No. 32K2865	30-inch Mounted Alarm Bell.	Weight, 516 pounds.	Price. 23.85
No. 32K2866	32-inch Mounted Alarm Bell.	Weight, 556 pounds.	Price. 26.95
No. 32K2867	34-inch Mounted Alarm Bell.	Weight, 658 pounds.	Price. 31.15
No. 32K2868	36-inch Mounted Alarm Bell.	Weight, 854 pounds.	Price. 38.55
No. 32K2869	38-inch Mounted Alarm Bell.	Weight, 985 pounds.	Price. 45.20
No. 32K2870	40-inch Mounted Alarm Bell.	Weight, 1,140 pounds.	Price. 52.25
No. 32K2872	44-inch Mounted Alarm Bell.	Weight, 1,647 pounds.	Price. 77.65
No. 32K2874	48-inch Mounted Alarm Bell.	Weight, 2,137 pounds.	Price. 98.25

U. S. STANDARD PLATFORM AND WAGON SCALES

EXTRA QUALITY GRADE AND "STANDARD" GRADE PORTABLE PLATFORM SCALES, PIT WAGON SCALES AND PITLESS WAGON SCALES, DIRECT FROM FACTORY TO USER, WITHOUT THE JOBBER'S AND DEALER'S PROFITS, SAVING OUR CUSTOMERS FULLY ONE-HALF IN PRICE.

OUR SCALES ARE SCIENTIFIC AND ACCURATE weighing machines, built upon honor and built to give perfect satisfaction to our customers, and this we guarantee they will do. We sell these built on honor scales at about one-half the price which others ask for scales no better, if as good as ours; we give our customers an opportunity to try and test our scales in comparison with scales of any or all other makes, we guarantee them for a long term of years and we ship the scales on the understanding and agreement that if for any reason they do not prove perfectly satisfactory you can return them at our expense and we will return your money and reimburse you for all freight charges paid by you. Under these conditions you cannot make a mistake in sending your order to us, because if our scales do not prove as good as we represent them to be, you will lose absolutely nothing, the scales can be returned to us and you will not be out one penny either for the scales or the freight on them.

WE CONFINE OUR EFFORTS to the production and sale of Extra Quality Grade and "Standard" Grade Scales, the very best scales which skilled mechanics can make from the highest quality of materials obtainable. We do not make, offer or sell low grade, price competition scales; such scales are, dear at any price, are not good weighing machines, and cannot give satisfaction to the purchaser. If you are in need of a scale, you want a good scale, a scale which will weigh correctly, one that you can depend upon and swear by, not swear at. Buy the best scale you can afford to buy, and you will find that it will give you the greatest degree of satisfaction and prove to be the cheapest in the end.

OUR ATLAS BRAND EXTRA QUALITY SCALES are the best and highest grade scales made, and are the scales which we advise our customers to purchase. They are made of the best materials obtainable, by the highest class of mechanics it is possible to employ in this line of work, inspected and tested in every detail, perfectly sealed and guaranteed to weigh accurately from the smallest division on the beam to the full capacity of the scale. They are, in fact, perfect weighing machines, upon which you can place absolute dependence, the accuracy of which no one can question. We sell our Extra Quality Grade Atlas Scales at lower prices than others ask for their standard and medium grade scale.

OUR NEW CENTURY BRAND SCALES are our "standard" grade scales, but they are very much better and of higher quality than the scales which many others list as their highest grade scales. We build and sell this standard grade of scales because we recognize the fact that there are many who through lack of means or through infrequent use of their scales, do not feel that they can afford the best, yet who do require a scale and who must have one upon which they can depend for accuracy and reliability. Our New Century Scales are not quite as strongly built as are our Atlas Scales, and are not quite as perfect in detail, but they are built correctly, they will weigh accurately and they will give good satisfaction under the conditions mentioned. We sell our Standard Grade New Century Scales at prices nearly if not fully as low as others ask for low grade, price competition scales.

OUR PRICES ON SCALES ARE WONDERFULLY LOW, so low in fact that one not knowing all about our manner of doing business, the tremendous volume of business which we transact annually and our consequent economical methods of manufacturing and handling merchandise of all kinds, could hardly believe it possible for us to sell perfect and high quality scales at such extremely low prices, but with a thorough understanding of our great financial resources which enable us to buy either raw materials or manufactured products in extremely large quantities and for spot cash, and with a knowledge of our perfect and economical methods of doing business, you can at once realize that we can afford to transact business on a very much smaller margin of profit over the actual cost to manufacture, than would be required to meet even a small part of the expenses of concerns selling merchandise by the old time methods or of concerns whose volume of business is not one-half so great as ours.

WHY WE CAN SELL OUR SCALES AT LOW PRICES. We have our scales made for us under special contract in very large quantities in one of the best equipped scale factories in the United States. There are no expenses in the manufacture of them other than the cost of the raw materials, which are bought in very large quantities, and often lower than the lowest market prices, and the actual cost of the labor which enters into the construction of the scales. There is no cost to the factory in selling because our contract is continuous, and we take the entire output of the factory; no losses to make up because we pay spot cash for everything. The shop cost is reduced to the lowest possible amount by the aid of every known improvement in up to date and automatic scale making machinery, and the cost of handling is reduced to a minimum as the raw materials are unloaded direct from the cars into the factory and the finished scales are loaded direct from the factory and shipped direct to our customers without any cartage or other avoidable expense. To the actual cost of the raw materials and labor we add but one profit and our profit on each scale sold is very small indeed, but with our enormous volume of business, turning our money many times each year, this small margin of profit on each article we sell makes for us a very satisfactory profit at the end of the year and enables us to sell our scales at almost the exact first or manufacturing cost. No other concern in the United States is in position to do this, simply because no other general merchandise house has a volume of business approximating as much as ours by nearly one-half, and it's the volume that counts and makes for low prices.

OUR SCALES ARE U. S. STANDARD.

THEY ARE SEALED TO U. S. STANDARD WEIGHTS. This means that each sliding poise weight and each loose weight is tested and corrected to correspond exactly with weights the accuracy of which are established by the U. S. Government, and each beam and balance poise is tested and corrected in the same manner, that each pivot and lever is tested and corrected until by actual test with the U. S. standard weights the scale weighs accurately and proves sensitive, the testing and sealing weights being placed at different periods of the process at each corner and in the center of the scale platform, proving and testing the scale at every point, and no scale is allowed to pass inspection until it is proven absolutely accurate and sensitive at every point and is so sealed. Using, as we do, the very best materials which can be put into scales, employing, as we do, the highest class of scale mechanics which can be employed, testing and sealing our scales, as we do, to U. S. standard weights, insures to you and to all our customers the highest grade of scales which can be made, and we sell our scales at prices which enable you to save a great deal of money and to secure far greater value than you could obtain elsewhere.

NO TROUBLE TO ERECT OUR SCALES.

ANYONE CAN SET THEM UP EASILY, quickly and correctly. We send plain, simple instructions with every scale and plans and specifications with each wagon scale.

EVERY FARMER, EVERY MERCHANT, EVERY COAL OR GRAIN DEALER, in fact everyone who buys or sells goods, produce, coal, grain, stock, etc., should own a set of scales. The saving made and the satisfaction of knowing that you are not being compelled to pay for more than the actual weight you receive, and the fact that you know positively that you are being paid for the full weight you have to sell, will warrant you in buying the best scales obtainable. You will save the price of the best platform scale made in less than six months and in the same time the best wagon or stock scales made will more than pay for themselves. A hundred pounds more or less in the weight of one steer or a half dozen head of sheep or hogs, cannot be detected except upon the scales, yet at 5 cents a pound its loss would cost you $5.00. With corn at 50 cents a bushel the loss of a couple of bushels per load on twenty-five or thirty loads means the price of a good wagon scale. The same relative loss on wheat at 80 or 90 cents per bushel means a great deal more than the price of the scale, and so it is with everything which is bought or sold by weight. You cannot afford to buy and sell by guess, to run the risk of being cheated, to take whatever is given you for your produce, or to have the results of your own hard labor go for naught while others thrive at your expense. It would be foolish and expensive for you to do so. A good wagon scale is a money making as well as a money saving investment, and at our prices the investment is very small when compared to the amount of money it will make and save for you.

OUR GREAT SIX MONTHS' FREE TRIAL AND TEST OFFER. To permit you to prove to your own satisfaction that our platform and wagon scales are all that we claim for them, that they are the equal of any scale on the market, that they are much better value at our prices than can possibly be obtained elsewhere, should you purchase one of our Atlas Brand Platform or Wagon Scales, we will allow you **six months** from the time the scale is received by you in which to examine, test and use it, and to compare it with any other make of scales in your neighborhood or which can be bought at double our price. If at any time during this period you are not fully satisfied that our scale is all that we claim for it, that it is high grade in workmanship and material, that it is accurate and true in weighing, that it is strong and durable and will meet your requirements in every way, and that it is a much better scale than you could purchase elsewhere at anything like our price, or if you are not satisfied that you have saved money by purchasing our scale, you can return it to us at our expense and we will cheerfully return the money you paid for it and reimburse you for the freight you paid on the scale when you received it. **On our New Century brand of scales the trial period is thirty days instead of six months.** You run no risk in ordering a scale from us; it must please and satisfy you or you get your money back.

OUR TEN TO THIRTY YEARS' GUARANTEE: We guarantee all of our portable platform and wagon scales against all defects in material or workmanship for a long term of years, by which guarantee we agree that should any piece or part give out or break by reason of defect in material or workmanship during the term of the guarantee, we will make it good by furnishing free new parts to take the place of the defective parts. Our Atlas Platform Scales are guaranteed for twenty years, **our Atlas Wagon Scales are guaranteed for thirty years,** our New Century Platform Scales are guaranteed for ten years, and our New Century Wagon Scales are guaranteed for fifteen years. A guarantee like this is absolute protection to you and it could not and would not be made did we not know that our scales are the best scales which can be made.

WE GUARANTEE SAFE DELIVERY. Our scales are shipped knocked down and strongly boxed in well made cases. Breakage or loss of parts in transit is very rare, but if you buy a scale from us, should any part or parts of the scale be damaged, broken or lost while in transit, we will promptly send you such parts as are necessary to replace the damaged, broken or lost parts, free of charge, and will prepay the transportation charges so that you will not lose a penny.

ABOUT THE FREIGHT CHARGES. Our wagon and platform scales are shipped direct from the factory in Southeastern Michigan. Wagon scales take a very low rate of freight, only about 25c per 100 pounds for 200 miles, about 45c per 100 pounds for 500 miles and about 70c per 100 pounds for 800 miles. The freight charges on an Atlas 5-Ton Pitless Wagon Scale to Ft. Wayne, Ind., would be about $2.70, or to Rochester, N. Y., about $3.45. On an Atlas 5-Ton Pit Wagon Scale to Rochester, N. Y., the freight charges would be about $1.98, or to Grinnell, Iowa, about $3.82. On an Atlas 1200-Pound Platform Scale to Ft. Wayne, Ind., the freight charges would be about 99 cents, or to Grinnell, Iowa, about $1.78. The freight charges which you must pay are, as you will note, very small, almost nothing compared to the saving you will make by buying your scales from us.

BUY A GUARANTEED WAGON SCALE from us and compare it with scales used in your vincinity which cost from two to three times our price. We want you to do this because otherwise you would not realize what a great difference there is in favor of our scales, what a great improvement our non-breakable trussed steel levers are over the ordinary steel levers or over the more commonly used breakable cast iron levers. We want you to see for yourself how accurate and sensitive our scales are, and what a grand, good scale we can furnish at our wonderfully low prices.

NEW CENTURY "STANDARD" PORTABLE PLATFORM SCALES

GUARANTEED FOR TEN YEARS.

AT $7.56 TO $8.92, ACCORDING TO CAPACITY, WE OFFER OUR NEW CENTURY PLATFORM SCALES AS SUPERIOR TO SCALES REGULARLY SOLD BY MANUFACTURERS, JOBBERS, SCALE DEALERS AND OTHERS AT $12.00 TO $15.00.

THESE ARE FIRST CLASS "STANDARD" GRADE SCALES made especially to meet the requirements of those who, through infrequent use of their scales, do not feel that they can afford or require the best, yet who do require a scale upon which they can depend for accuracy and reliability. They are mighty good scales, well made in every particular, made of high grade materials, sealed to U. S. standard weights, fitted with a solid brass single beam which is milled and polished and with a square brass sliding poise weight which is also milled and polished; in fact, although we call them standard grade scales, they are far better than many others sell as their highest grade scales and for which they ask nearly double our prices. In weighing qualities and in the materials and finish of the essential parts, such as the beam, the sliding poise, the tool steel knife edge pivots, etc., there are no better scales made, but they are not as strong, as heavy, or as well finished in many of the details as are our Atlas Extra Quality Grade Heavy Platform Scales, and if you have any considerable amount of weighing to do or are not limited in the price you pay, we strongly advise you to select and order our Atlas Extra Quality Grade Heavy Platform Scales, because we know you will find the highest grade scales, the most satisfactory and the cheapest in the end. In our New Century Platform Scales the main frame, the platform and the levers are made of smooth gray iron, the wheels are secured by nuts on solid steel axles (not cast iron pins) which extend from side to side through and under the frame; all knife edge lever pivots and beam pivots are made of tool steel, carefully hardened and tempered; the pivot loops are also carefully hardened. There is no binding or friction, everything works with free and easy action insuring accurate and sensitive weighing qualities. The platform center, the pillar and the pillar cap are made of clear hard maple, finished with two coats of Prussian blue lead paint and a coat of varnish. The pillar is secured to the main frame by two ⅜-inch steel rods which hold the pillar firm and solid. The beam is connected to the long platform lever by a two-piece steelyard rod which has a hardened hook where it comes in contact with the bottom pivot and which hooks into the pivot loop of the scale beam. The exterior of the iron parts is finished in black japan and the entire scale presents a very attractive appearance. Platform sizes are: 600-pound scale, 16½x24 inches; 800-pound scale, 17x24½ inches; 1000-pound scale, 17½x25 inches. The beams of these scales are graduated on both sides by ¼-pound marks to 50 pounds. Each scale is provided with loose weights equal to the balance of the scale capacity and varying in sizes so that you can weigh anything from the smallest graduation on the beam to the full capacity of the scale. While we recommend the selection of our Atlas Extra Quality Grade Heavy Platform Scales as being the most desirable platform scales you can buy, we wish to assure you that our New Century Standard Grade Platform Scales are accurate and reliable weighing machines and that they are far better value than you can obtain elsewhere at any price. **We guarantee them for ten years against all defects in materials or workmanship and for that period of time we will furnish free new parts to take the place of any parts which may break by reason of defect, and we allow you thirty days' trial from the time you receive the scale in which to set it up and test it and prove for yourself whether or not it is satisfactory to you.** These scales are shipped knocked down and securely boxed from the factory in Southeastern Michigan, from which point the purchaser must pay the freight. **Plain, simple directions for setting up are sent with each scale.**

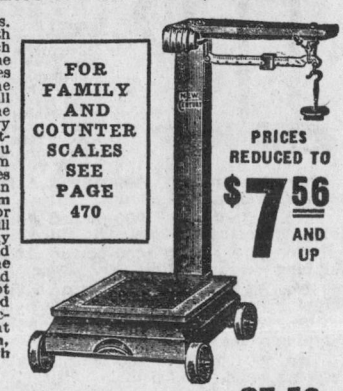

FOR FAMILY AND COUNTER SCALES SEE PAGE 470

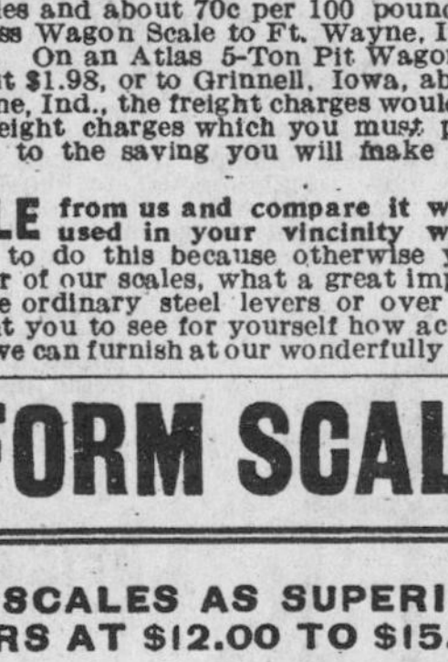

PRICES REDUCED TO $7.56 AND UP

No. 32K7010	600-pound New Century Platform Scale.	Shipping weight, 146 pounds.	Price........$7.56
No. 32K7011	800-pound New Century Platform Scale.	Shipping weight, 153 pounds.	Price........8.33
No. 32K7012	1000-pound New Century Platform Scale.	Shipping weight, 158 pounds.	Price........8.92

ATLAS EXTRA QUALITY HEAVY PORTABLE PLATFORM SCALES

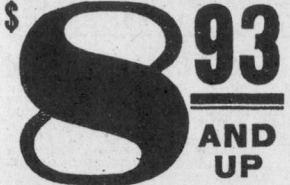

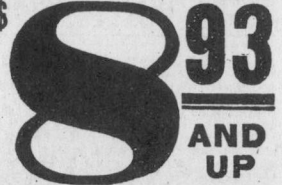

$8.93 AND UP — THE BEST AND HIGHEST GRADE SCALES MADE — GUARANTEED FOR TWENTY YEARS — $8.93 AND UP

THE GREATEST SCALE VALUE EVER OFFERED. THE VERY BEST AND HIGHEST GRADE PLATFORM SCALES IT IS POSSIBLE TO MANUFACTURE. NOTHING SHOWN IN OTHER CATALOGUES TO COMPARE WITH THEM. EQUAL TO SCALES FOR WHICH THE BEST KNOWN SCALE MANUFACTURERS ASK FROM $20.00 TO $50.00.

ATLAS EXTRA QUALITY HEAVY PLATFORM SCALES are as good as platform scales can be made. They are made extra strong and heavy, of the very best materials obtainable, by the best mechanics employed in scale manufacturing; every part entering into their construction is perfectly made, fitted and inspected and they are very handsomely finished and sealed to U. S. standard weights. They are built to withstand hard usage day in and day out, and to weigh accurately under all conditions. In fact, there are no better scales made and none better could be bought at any price. They are the BEST and HIGHEST GRADE scales made, and are the scales we would especially recommend you to select and order if you wish to use a scale constantly, day after day. They will give you perfect satisfaction and you will find them sensitive, accurate, reliable and durable under any and all conditions.

OUR SIX MONTHS' FREE TRIAL OFFER. Every Atlas Platform Scale is sold with the distinct understanding and agreement that its purchaser is to have six months' trial from the date the scale is received, in which to test and try the scale under any and all conditions, to compare it with any or all other makes of scales, and to prove to his own satisfaction that the scales are all that we represent them to be. In other words, if you purchase an Atlas Platform Scale you are to have six months in which to satisfy yourself that the scales are in every way the high grade scales we represent them to be, that they are as good as any scales you could buy at from two to three times our price, consequently the greatest scale value ever offered, and that you have saved considerable money by purchasing from us. If at any time during this period you are not perfectly satisfied with the scale, you will be at liberty to return it to us at our expense and we will cheerfully return the money you paid for it and reimburse you for the freight you paid on the scale when you received it.

ATLAS PLATFORM SCALES ARE GUARANTEED FOR TWENTY YEARS. We guarantee our Atlas Platform Scales against all defects in material or workmanship for twenty years from date of shipment, by which guarantee we agree that should any piece or part give out or break by reason of defect in material or workmanship, we will make it good by furnishing, free, new parts to take the place of the defective parts. When you buy your scales from us you are protected against unjust repair charges.

THIS LARGE ILLUSTRATION is an exact photographic reproduction of the Atlas 600-pound Platform Scale. It shows the scale in its design and proportions precisely as it would appear if it were placed before you, except that we cannot show you in this picture how nicely the scale is finished or what a pleasing appearance it has. The sectional illustration at the right side of this page shows the substantial construction of the scale throughout, the arrangement of the levers, the knife edge pivot bearings, the pivot loops, the two-piece steelyard connection, the large and well proportioned wheels and the manner in which they are secured to the large full length steel axles. All Atlas Platform Scales are constructed in the same way, except that the larger sizes are built heavier and stronger in proportion to their size and capacity. In fact, Atlas Platform Scales are built as good as it is possible to build a scale and they will give perfect satisfaction to the most critical user.

THESE SCALES ARE MADE WITH SINGLE AND DOUBLE BEAMS. The single beam is shown in the main illustration and the double beam is shown separately. On the 600, 800 and 1000-pound scales the beams are graduated on both sides by ¼-pound marks to 50 pounds, and on the larger sizes they are graduated on both sides by ½-pound marks to 100 pounds. The lower bar of the double beam is graduated the same as the upper bar. The beams are solid brass, milled and polished, and are fitted with square brass sliding poise weights, which are also milled and polished. The sliding poise weights of the double beam scales have knurled head brass set screws so that either bar may be used for tare weight. Each scale is provided with loose weights equal to the balance of the scale capacity and varying in size so that you can weigh anything from the smallest graduation on the beam to the full capacity of the scale.

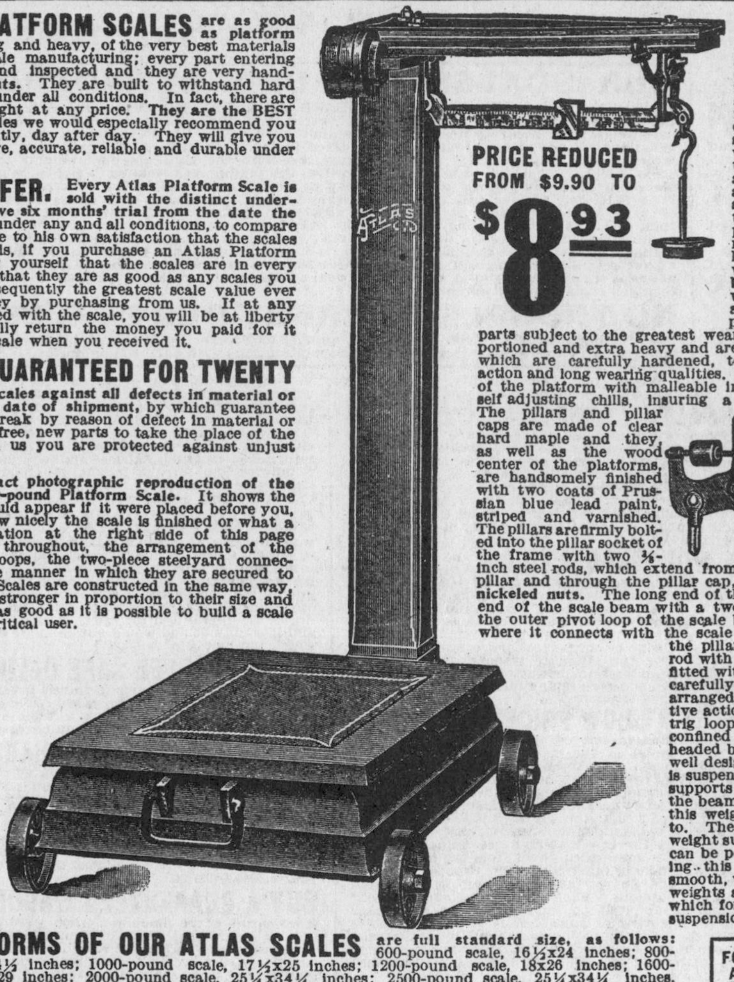

PRICE REDUCED FROM $9.90 TO $8.93

ATLAS PLATFORM SCALES ARE PERFECT IN CONSTRUCTION. All iron parts are made of high grade smooth gray iron with exterior parts finished in black japan. The frames are extra heavy and are supported by heavy solid steel full length axles, with large wheels, which are held in place with threads and nuts. These full length steel axles, with wheels held in place by nuts, are superior in every way to the cast iron stub end axles commonly used, on which the wheels are generally secured with cotter pins. The platforms are of ample size, made very strong and heavy and with hardwood centers. They are provided with check pins at front and back, and the bearing feet are faced with tool steel, which is hardened and tempered, insuring a perfect bearing the full length of the pivots and accuracy and long life to the parts subject to the greatest wear and strain. The levers are well proportioned and extra heavy and are fitted with tool steel knife edge pivots, which are carefully hardened, tempered and ground, insuring sensitive action and long wearing qualities. They are suspended from the four corners of the platform with malleable iron corner loops, which are fitted with self adjusting chills, insuring a perfect bearing, free of all friction. The pillars and pillar caps are made of clear hard maple and they, as well as the wood center of the platforms, are handsomely finished with two coats of Prussian blue lead paint, striped and varnished. The pillars are firmly bolted into the pillar socket of the frame with two ⅜-inch steel rods, which extend from the frame up through the length of the pillar and through the pillar cap, where they are secured by acorn shaped nickeled nuts. The long end of the scale levers is connected to the short end of the scale beam with a two-piece steelyard rod, which hooks onto the outer pivot loop of the scale beam and is fitted with a hardened loop where it connects with the scale lever. The beams are suspended from the pillar cap and connected to the steelyard rod with perfectly hardened pivot loops and are fitted with tool steel knife edge pivots, which are carefully hardened, tempered and ground, all being arranged so that friction is eliminated and sensitive action and accurate weighing is assured. The trig loop in which the outer end of the beam is confined is secured to the pillar cap with a nickel headed bolt and is provided with a suitable and well designed beam lock. The poise weight which is suspended from the end of the beam and which supports the loose weights is the weight by which the beam is sealed and the shot or lead within this weight should never be taken out or added to. The beams are provided with a balance ball weight supported by a threaded rod and the scales can be perfectly balanced at any time by adjusting this ball weight. The loose weights are smooth, well proportioned, sealed to U. S. standard weights and are carried on an iron weight rack, which forms the top of the pillar and provides a suspension point for the scale beam.

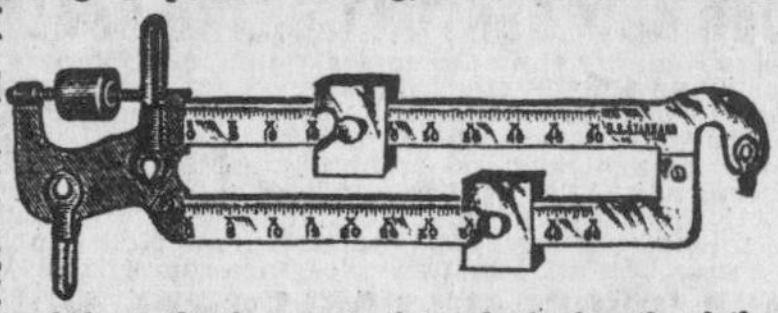

FOR FAMILY AND COUNTER SCALES SEE PAGE 470.

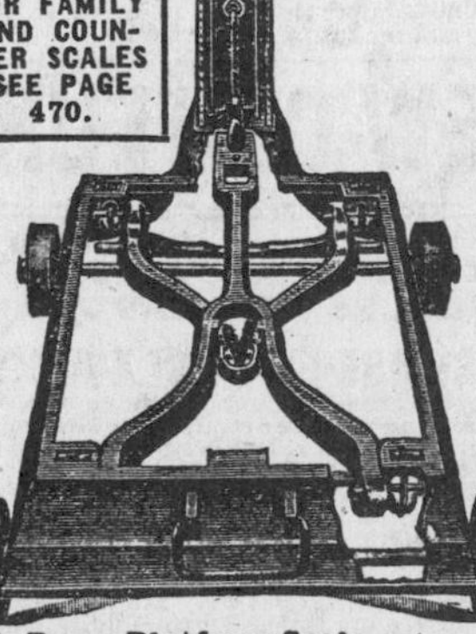

THE PLATFORMS OF OUR ATLAS SCALES are full standard size, as follows: 600-pound scale, 16½x24 inches; 800-pound scale, 17x24½ inches; 1000-pound scale, 17½x25 inches; 1200-pound scale, 18x26 inches; 1600-pound scale, 20x29 inches; 2000-pound scale, 25¼x34¼ inches; 2500-pound scale, 25¼x34¼ inches. Some manufacturers and dealers add extra weights to increase the capacity of the scales they sell. A 400-pound scale with weights for 600 pounds is not a 600-pound scale. The entire scale must be constructed for the weight capacity it is to carry, and the platform as well as all other parts of the scale must be properly proportioned. Our scales are so proportioned and constructed, and when you order a 600-pound capacity scale from us you get a scale which is properly built to weigh 600 pounds.

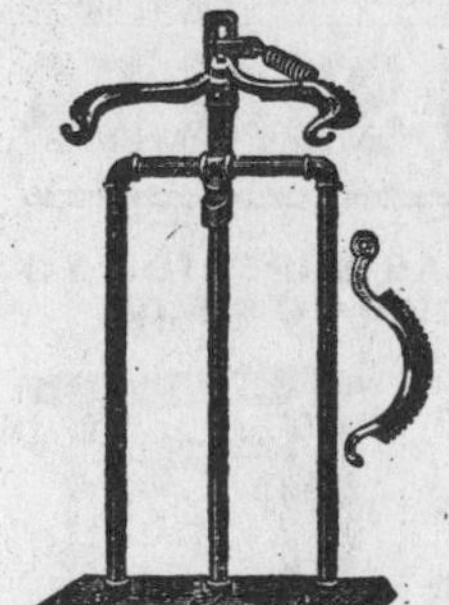

BAG RACK ATTACHMENT

IT IS OFTEN VERY CONVENIENT TO HAVE A BAG RACK ATTACHMENT on your platform scale, especially if you have any considerable amount of grain to be put up in bags or sacks, because such an attachment enables one man to do the work which would otherwise require two men. We can furnish the bag rack attachment, shown in the illustration at the left of this page, and fit it onto the platform of any size of Atlas or New Century Platform Scales, provided the attachment is ordered with the scale and extra price allowed. The attachment consists of a three-post iron pipe frame with brackets to bolt onto the scale platform, a slotted standard providing adjustment for height, two curved arms or jaws with serrated edges for holding the bag or sack, and a coil spring to hold the jaws open to the full size of the bag. If you have use for it, this attachment will be found exceedingly desirable. This bag rack attachment is listed below, under Catalogue No. 32K7053, and is furnished only when ordered with a scale and proper price allowed.

PLAIN, SIMPLE DIRECTIONS for setting up are sent with all Atlas Platform Scales. The scales are shipped knocked down and securely boxed, from the factory in Southeastern Michigan, from which point the purchaser must pay the freight. Order an Atlas High Grade Extra Heavy Platform Scale at our extremely low prices; you will find the freight will be but very little and you will be surprised at the wonderful value in these scales and the perfect satisfaction they will give you.

No. 32K7030 600-pound Atlas Single Beam Platform Scale. Shipping weight, 159 pounds. Price....$ 8.93
No. 32K7031 800-pound Atlas Single Beam Platform Scale. Shipping weight, 167 pounds. Price.... 9.86
No. 32K7032 1000-pound Atlas Single Beam Platform Scale. Shipping weight, 173 pounds. Price.... 10.22
No. 32K7033 1200-pound Atlas Single Beam Platform Scale. Shipping weight, 245 pounds. Price.... 12.38
No. 32K7034 1600-pound Atlas Single Beam Platform Scale. Shipping weight, 272 pounds. Price.... 13.62
No. 32K7035 2000-pound Atlas Single Beam Platform Scale. Shipping weight, 369 pounds. Price.... 16.88
No. 32K7036 2500-pound Atlas Single Beam Platform Scale. Shipping weight, 375 pounds. Price.... 18.48

No. 32K7045 600-pound Atlas Double Beam Platform Scale. Shipping weight, 161 pounds. Price....$ 9.96
No. 32K7046 800-pound Atlas Double Beam Platform Scale. Shipping weight, 169 pounds. Price.... 10.89
No. 32K7047 1000-pound Atlas Double Beam Platform Scale. Shipping weight, 175 pounds. Price.... 11.42
No. 32K7048 1200-pound Atlas Double Beam Platform Scale. Shipping weight, 247 pounds. Price.... 13.98
No. 32K7049 1600-pound Atlas Double Beam Platform Scale. Shipping weight, 274 pounds. Price.... 15.22
No. 32K7050 2000-pound Atlas Double Beam Platform Scale. Shipping weight, 371 pounds. Price.... 18.48
No. 32K7051 2500-pound Atlas Double Beam Platform Scale. Shipping weight, 377 pounds. Price.... 20.28

No. 32K7053 Bag Rack Attachment. Weight, 13 pounds. Price....$1.98

THE BEAM BOXES AND BEAMS OF OUR WAGON SCALES

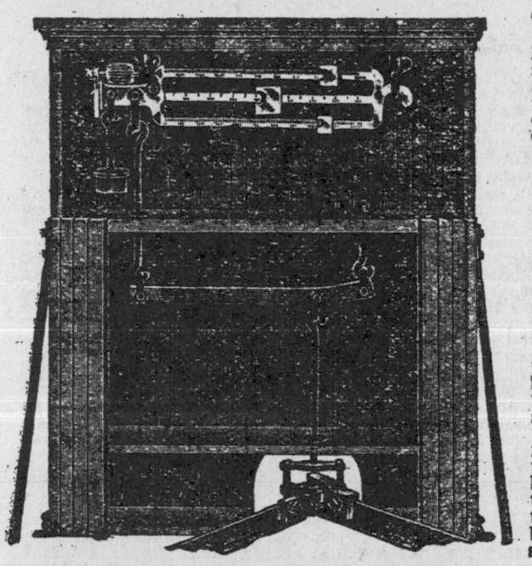

THE BEAM BOXES of our Atlas Pit and Atlas Pitless Wagon Scales are larger, roomier, better designed, better made and better finished than the beam boxes furnished with the highest priced scales on the market; in fact, the beam boxes of the Atlas Wagon Scales, like the scales themselves, are as good as it is possible to make them. They are made of the best of lumber and finished with the best lead and oil paint. The opening to the shelf lever is through a panel (not several separate strips) made of matched lumber, cleated on the inside and held in place by two screws. The beam drop door is made of matched lumber, cleated on the inside for strength and on the ends for finish. This door is fitted with a flat key multiple tumbler lock so that meddlesome people cannot pick it and tamper with the scale beam or its sealing. The beam boxes of the New Century Scales are not as large and roomy as are those for the Atlas Scales, but they are made of the best of materials, finished with the best of paint and are the equal in every respect of the beam boxes generally furnished by others with their highest grade scales. The illustration shows the Atlas beam box with the braces which are used on the pitless scales.

THE BEAMS ARE SOLID BRASS. Our Atlas and our New Century Wagon Scales are all furnished with solid brass full capacity beams, which are milled and polished and fitted with brass sliding poise weights which are also milled and polished. Very few other scales, even of those selling at two to three times our prices, are fitted with solid brass beams, most of them simply having a thin brass face on iron beams and many of them being fitted with iron sliding poise weights. Brass is the best material for scale beams, therefore we use it. No loose weights are required on any of our wagon scales except on the 6 and 8-ton pit scales, each of which requires a jug weight when weighing over 5 tons.

NEW CENTURY FULL CAPACITY, SOLID BRASS, TWO-BAR BEAM.

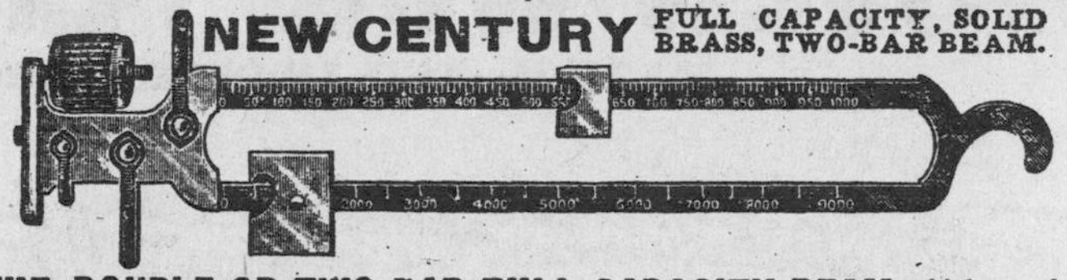

THE DOUBLE OR TWO-BAR FULL CAPACITY BEAM which we furnish on our New Century Wagon Scales is graduated on the upper bar to 1,000 pounds by 5-pound marks and the lower bar is graduated by 500-pound notches to the balance of the capacity of the scale. This beam is much more convenient than a compound beam or a beam requiring loose weights.

ATLAS FULL CAPACITY, SOLID BRASS, THREE-BAR BEAM.

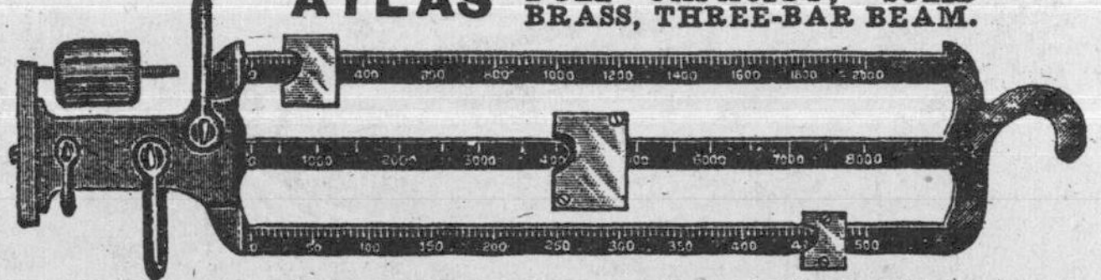

THE TRIPLE OR THREE-BAR FULL CAPACITY BEAM furnished on all of our Atlas Wagon Scales is the most convenient and most desirable scale beam made. With it you can obtain the net, tare and gross weights of anything within the capacity of the scale, and all weights are easily and quickly read. The upper bar is graduated to 2,000 pounds by 10-pound marks, the lower bar is graduated to 500 pounds by 2½-pound marks, and on scales of 5 tons capacity or less the middle bar is graduated by 500-pound notches to the balance of the capacity of the scale. On 6 and 8-ton scales the middle bar is graduated to 8,000 pounds by 500-pound notches, the balance of the capacity being obtained by a loose jug weight. The sliding poise weight of the upper bar is provided with a knurled head brass set screw so that it can be fastened at any place on the beam, the weight of the empty wagon or tare weight being generally obtained on this bar.

NEW CENTURY STANDARD PIT WAGON SCALES

$31.25 AND UP

3, 4 AND 5 TON CAPACITIES.

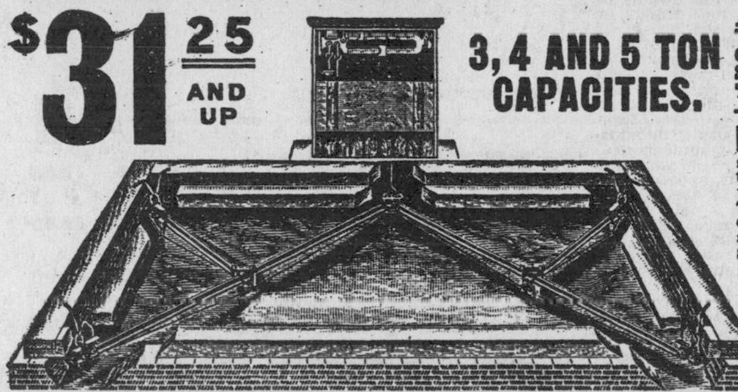

GUARANTEED FOR 15 YEARS

ONLY $31.25 TO $33.70, ACCORDING TO CAPACITY, FOR OUR NEW CENTURY STANDARD GRADE PIT WAGON SCALES. BETTER PIT WAGON SCALES THAN THOSE REGULARLY SOLD BY MANUFACTURERS, JOBBERS, SCALE DEALERS AND OTHERS AT $45.00 TO $55.00

NEW CENTURY PIT WAGON SCALES are first class standard grade scales, as good if not better than pit wagon scales which others sell as their highest grade scales. They are well made in every particular, made of high grade materials throughout, sealed to U. S. standard weights, furnished with full capacity, double bar, solid brass beams, which are milled and polished and fitted with brass sliding poise weights, which are also milled and polished. They are scales upon which you can absolutely depend for accuracy and reliability and which will give most excellent service in ordinary use, but they are not as substantial or as well finished in many of the details as are our Atlas Extra Quality Grade Pit Wagon Scales, and if you want a pit wagon scale of the very best grade, one which will prove durable and satisfactory under any and all conditions and under continuous and hard usage, we recommend that you select and order our Atlas Extra Quality Grade Pit Wagon Scales, because with a wagon scale there is no question but what the highest grade scale made will prove the cheapest and most satisfactory scale you can buy. In our New Century Pit Wagon Scales the levers are made of T shaped steel bars and the long levers are reinforced by steel truss rods, making them perfectly rigid and unbreakable. The parts of the scales upon which much of their sensitiveness and accuracy depend, that is, the connections between the long and short levers, the lever heads, the platform bearings, the corner irons, the connection between the scale levers and the scale beam, the tool steel knife edge pivots and the pivot loops, are all practically the same as on the Atlas scales, made of the same high grade materials and made just as carefully. The two-bar, solid brass, full capacity beam used on these scales is fully described at the top of this page. The beam box is well made of good materials, full standard size, fitted with a lock and key and finished with the best quality of lead and oil paint. All sizes of these scales are made for an 8-foot by 14-foot platform. They can be set on either wood or masonry foundations, and require a very shallow lever pit, only 16 inches to bottom of sills, or 22 inches to top of platform. We do not furnish any of the woodwork for the frame or platform, but we do furnish plain, simple instructions for setting up, with plans showing the exact size and shape of every piece of timber in the frame and platform. We recommend our Atlas Extra Quality Pit Wagon Scales as being the best selection you can make and the best pit wagon scales you can buy, but we assure you that our New Century Standard Pit Wagon Scales are accurate and reliable weighing machines, fully equal to scales which others sell as their highest grade scales and for which they ask from one and one-half to two times our prices. We guarantee them for fifteen years against all defects in material or workmanship and for that period of time we will furnish free new parts to take the place of any parts which may break by reason of defect, and we allow you thirty days' trial from the time you receive the scale in which to set it up and test it and prove for yourself whether or not it is satisfactory to you. These scales are shipped knocked down from the factory in Southeastern Michigan, from which point the purchaser must pay the freight. All small parts are securely boxed and the beam box is crated. Complete and simple directions for setting up are sent with each scale.

No. 32K7083 3-Ton New Century Pit Wagon Scale. Shipping weight, 525 pounds. Price........$31.25

No. 32K7084 4-Ton New Century Pit Wagon Scale. Shipping weight, 545 pounds. Price........$32.50

No. 32K7085 5-Ton New Century Pit Wagon Scale. Shipping weight, 565 pounds. Price........$33.70

NEW CENTURY STANDARD PITLESS WAGON SCALE

AT $39.85 WE OFFER OUR 5-TON NEW CENTURY STANDARD GRADE PITLESS WAGON SCALE, WITH FULL CAPACITY SOLID BRASS BEAM. A SCALE FULLY EQUAL TO THOSE FOR WHICH OTHERS ASK $55.00 TO $65.00.

5-TON CAPACITY

PATENTS PENDING

$39.85

GUARANTEED FOR 15 YEARS

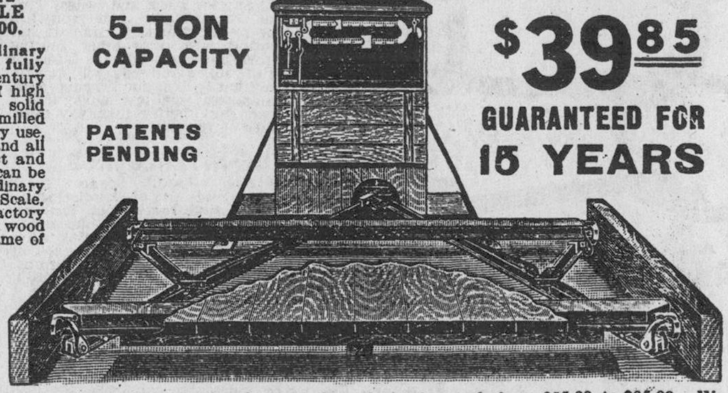

AN ACCURATE AND RELIABLE PITLESS WAGON SCALE, suitable for ordinary farm use, and fully equal in quality to those which others sell as their highest grade pitless scale. Our New Century Pitless Wagon Scale is a first class standard grade scale, well made in every particular, made of high grade materials, sealed to U. S. standard weights, furnished with a full capacity, double bar, solid brass beam, which is milled and polished and fitted with brass sliding poise weights, which are also milled and polished; in fact, it is a scale of exceptionally good value and a most excellent scale for ordinary use, but if you want a pitless wagon scale which will prove durable and satisfactory under any and all conditions of service for which a pitless scale should be used, then we strongly advise you to select and order an Atlas All Steel Extra Quality Pitless Wagon Scale, the very best pitless wagon scale which can be made, because, while the New Century Scale is accurate and reliable and is serviceable under ordinary conditions, it is not as substantial or as well finished in many of its details as is the Atlas All Steel Scale, and if you have any considerable use for a scale we know you will find the best scale the most satisfactory and the cheapest in the end. Our New Century Pitless Wagon Scale is made to be used with 3x12-inch wood end sills, these sills being firmly secured to the iron pipe frame tie rods and forming part of the frame of the scale. The levers are made of heavy T shaped steel bars and the long levers are strongly reinforced with heavy trusses made of flat steel bars which are turned edgewise. The platform sill, which is next to the beam box, is made from a heavy I shaped steel beam, but the outer sill is to be made of timber. All knife edge pivots are made of heavy tool steel, carefully hardened, ground and tempered. The corner loops, from which the levers are suspended, are very heavy and have hardened bearings for the pivots. The connections between the long and short levers, the lever heads, the platform bearings and the connection between the scale levers and the scale beam, parts upon which much of the sensitiveness and accuracy of the scale depend, are all practically the same as on the Atlas scale, made of the same high grade materials and made just as carefully. The beam box is full standard size, well made of good materials, fitted with a lock and key and finished with the best quality of lead and oil paint. The beam furnished on this scale is the two-bar, solid brass, full capacity beam, which is fully described at the top of this page. The scale is made for an 8-foot by 14-foot platform. When set up the measurement from the ground to the top of the platform is only 12 inches. We do not furnish any of the woodwork for the platform or the sills, but we do furnish plain, simple instructions for setting up, with plans showing the exact size and shape of the sills and of the lumber for the platform, and also showing how to build a foundation for the scale, so that should you wish to set the scale on a foundation you can do so. We recommend and advise you to select and order the Atlas Extra Quality Pitless Wagon Scale because the Atlas is unquestionably the best and most satisfactory pitless wagon scale which can be bought at any price, but we assure you that our New Century Standard Pitless Wagon Scale is an accurate and reliable weighing machine, which you will find fully as good if not better than pitless scales which others sell as their very best scales and for which they ask from $55.00 to $65.00. We guarantee the New Century Pitless Wagon Scales for fifteen years against all defects in material or workmanship, and for that period of time we will furnish free new parts to take the place of any parts which may break by reason of defect, and we allow you thirty days' trial from the time you receive the scale in which to set it up and test it and prove for yourself whether or not it is satisfactory to you. This scale is shipped knocked down from the factory in Southeastern Michigan, from which point the purchaser must pay the freight. All small parts are securely boxed and the beam box is crated. Plain, simple instructions for setting up are sent with the scale.

No. 32K7095 5-Ton New Century Pitless Wagon Scale. Shipping weight, 675 pounds. Price........$39.85

SEE PAGES 566 AND 567 FOR THE BEST MADE EXTRA QUALITY WAGON SCALES.

WOVEN WIRE FENCING

THE BEST FENCING WHICH CAN BE MADE. OFFERED BY US AT ABOUT ONE-HALF THE PRICES OTHERS ASK

MADE IN AND SHIPPED DIRECT FROM OUR OWN FACTORY.

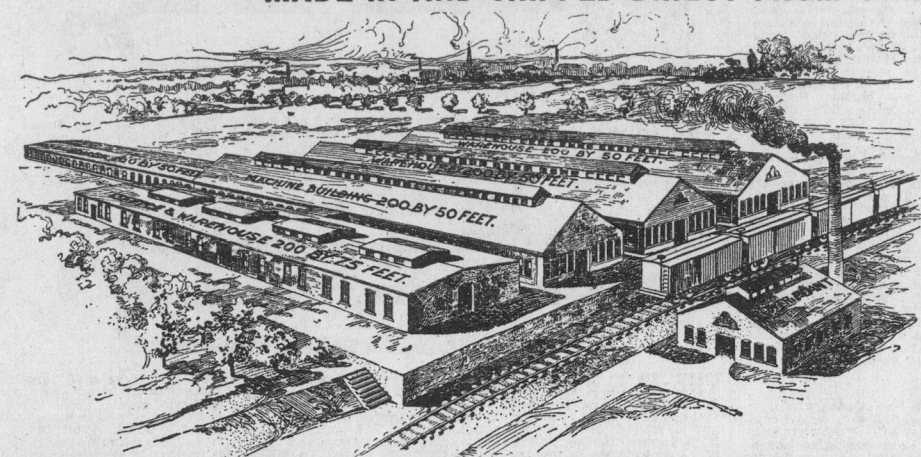

OUR FENCING FACTORY AT KNIGHTSTOWN, IND., ONE OF THE LARGEST FENCING FACTORIES IN THE WORLD.

OUR WOVEN WIRE FENCING is made in our own modern, up to date fencing factory at Knightstown, Ind., the best equipped, the best arranged for rapid and economical work, and one of the largest fencing factories in the world, consisting of the several large buildings shown in the accompanying illustration and providing more than 50,000 square feet of available floor space. The machine room of this factory is equipped with twenty modern looms of special design, together with spoolers and other machinery, having a combined capacity of about 4,000,000 rods of woven wire fencing per year when working on regular time, or nearly 8,000,000 rods per year when working double time. A tremendous capacity, but our fencing has become so popular and, at our low prices, our fencing business has grown so rapidly that we found it necessary to enlarge our factory to this enormous capacity in order that we might be able to give the prompt service which we always endeavor to give. During the past spring, before the enlargement of our factory, we were compelled to refund to our customers money for well nigh a million rods of fencing for which we had received actual orders, but now we are in position to accept all fencing orders which may be sent to us and to fill them promptly.

THE WEAVE of our Square Mesh Fencing is shown in the accompanying illustration, which is a picture of our 26-inch 7-line wire Standard X-L-ALL Fencing, with interlocked stay wires 6 inches apart. The picture is reduced in the height of the fencing and in the width and height of the meshes, but it shows the exact weave and the wires are shown in their exact sizes, namely heavy No. 9 hard galvanized steel top and bottom line wires and No. 12 galvanized steel interlocked stay wires and intermediate line wires. From this illustration you will readily understand that our interlocked stays make ours the best, strongest, neatest, handsomest and lightest woven wire fencing which can be made. By comparison with one of the leading fences now on the market and which is made with short stays tied at every line wire, you will quickly realize why our fencing, though made of wires of equal sizes, does not weigh as many pounds per rod as other fencing, yet can be produced and sold for less money and is just as strong if not stronger. In our fencing there are no knots or ties requiring a waste of wire as there are in other fencings, and because of this in a ten-line wire fencing we save no less than 825 inches of wire per rod of fencing, which means that when you buy your fencing from us you not only do not pay for waste and useless wire, but the freight costs you less per rod of fencing. Compare our fencing with any other fencing either on your neighbor's farms or at the stores and you will quickly see that while our fencing costs you a great deal less money it is a great deal better than any other make of fencing.

THE INTERLOCKED stay wires of our X-L-ALL Square Mesh Fencing are one of the distinctive strong features of our fencing. You will note in the illustration that the lock on these stay wires runs in alternate directions. This makes the fencing very strong, makes it keep its shape, makes it go up stiff and straight like a board and when our fencing is

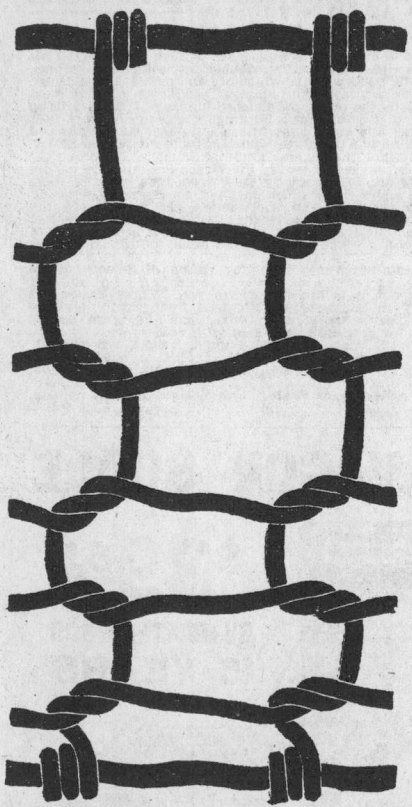

properly put up and evenly stretched it is the handsomest as well as the most durable woven wire fencing on the market.

OUR FENCING IS HEAVILY CRIMPED, making it very elastic, providing amply for expansion and contraction caused by changes in temperature and allowing our fencing to be stretched perfectly flat and smooth without straining it in any way. Too much care cannot be exercised when erecting woven wire fencing, to see that the fencing is properly stretched, but the crimping in our fencing makes it very easy to erect and stretch properly.

THE WIRE IN OUR FENCING is identical in every way with that which is woven into nearly every well known fencing. It is made by the same mills, of the same grade of steel and galvanized just as heavily and in the same way. Don't let anyone make you believe that their fencing is made of better wire or that it is galvanized better, because it is not so. Very few fencing manufacturers draw their own wire and those who do cannot and do not produce better wire than is used in our and other well known fencing. The only difference in woven wire fencing of different makes is in the size of the wires used, the method and style of weaving the fencing and the quality of the workmanship as it appears in the finished fencing. We tell you the exact size of the wires we use in our different fencings. We claim that the method and style of our weaving and the workmanship as shown in our finished fencing is the best which can be produced and we back our claims by a very broad guarantee.

OUR PRICES ARE BELOW ALL COMPETITION and there are many reasons why we are able to make these low prices. The great saving of wire just mentioned is one reason. Our factory is carefully laid out so as to avoid all cartage and all other unnecessary handling expense and so that we may manufacture our fencing at the very smallest possible shop cost. A receiving and shipping platform of large proportion extends past the entire frontage of the factory alongside of our own switching tracks. All of our wire and raw material comes to us in carloads and is unloaded directly into our big warehouse. From this warehouse the wire is taken into the machine building as required. Our twenty big special looms, some of which are double headers, are exceptionally rapid machines, in fact, they will weave more rods of high grade fencing per day than any other machines we have ever seen or heard of. The woven wire leaves the looms in finished bales ready for shipment and is taken into the warehouse beyond the machine room. When our fencing is shipped to our customers it is loaded directly into the cars, so that there is no hauling, cartage or teaming either in the receiving, manufacturing or shipping. When you consider the tremendous tonnage which our fencing business amounts to annually, you can easily appreciate the great saving even this item effects in our costs and consequently in our selling prices, because every saving which we can effect is given to our customers in the way of reduced prices. We sell our fencing at prices which are actually lower than it costs many manufacturers to make their fencing.

THE MONEY YOU SAVE when you buy fencing from us is well worth considering. Our big fencing factory with its splendid arrangement for making and handling fencing at the lowest possible first cost and with its equipment of wonderfully perfect and rapid looms which weave the fencing about twice as fast as fencing can be made on other machines, is a big factor in the making of our prices. We produce our fencing at a lower cost than anyone else and to this first cost, which is the cost of the wire and the making of the fencing, we add but one profit, a profit which is so small that it would not pay the expenses of even one of the middlemen who enter into the transaction through the ordinary method of selling fencing. We furnish you the best, the strongest and the most desirable woven wire fencing which can be made and ship it to you direct from our factory with but our one small profit added to our manufacturing cost.

OTHER FENCING MANUFACTURERS employ traveling salesmen at large expenses, selling their fencing to jobbers or wholesalers. The jobbers or wholesalers sell to the dealers or agents and the dealers or agents sell to the farmer or user. Each of these middlemen must make a profit and they must also make enough to pay their expenses and losses in addition to their profits. If you buy from the dealer or agent, in addition to the manufacturers' profit and expenses you must pay the profits, expenses and losses of each of the middlemen, and this is only a part of what you save when you buy your fencing from us. Send us your order and save these extra profits and money for yourself.

WHEN COMPARING PRICES look carefully to the size of wire used. There is a big difference in the value and durability of fencing, depending upon the size of wires of which the fencing is made. Even one-half gauge in size is very important. Where we use No. 9 wire for top and bottom line wires you will find others using No. 0½. Where we use No. 12 wire for stay wires and intermediate line wires you will find others using No. 12½ or even as light as No. 13. This difference in gauge of wire, while very little in figures, is very large when the value and durability of the fencing is considered. Our prices are much lower than anyone else can afford to make, yet at our prices we furnish you fencing made of full standard gauge wire, better fencing than you can buy elsewhere at much higher prices and greater value than anyone else can give you. We tell you the exact gauge of the wires used in each of our different fencings and wherever we use light gauge wires our prices will be found correspondingly lower.

WE GUARANTEE OUR FENCING to be made of as good and as well galvanized wire as is in any woven wire fencing on the market. We guarantee it to be made of the sizes of wires stated in this catalogue. We guarantee that it is exactly as represented by us and that any fencing which you order from us will be perfectly satisfactory to you, or if it is not you can return it to us and we will not only return your money but will reimburse you for the freight you paid when you received the fencing. We also guarantee that any fencing which we ship to you will reach your station in good condition. You run no risk when ordering fencing from us, because when you receive the fencing if it does not please and satisfy you or if you decide that you would rather have another make, you can return our fencing and get your money back.

EVERY ORDER WILL BE FILLED PROMPTLY. No matter whether you send us an order for a small or a large amount of fencing, or if the order be a club order made up among neighbors, for various amounts and kinds of fencing to be shipped in one car, every order will receive our prompt and careful attention and we will ship the fencing as quickly as the order can be handled. We have now and will always keep on hand thousands of tons of wire ready to be woven into fencing. Our factory is running continuously on full time, we are keeping our warehouses full of fencing ready for immediate shipment and rather than allow any delay in shipping we will put the factory on double time. You can send us your fencing orders with every assurance that you will save money, that the fencing you receive will be the best that can be made and that your orders will be filled promptly.

Size and Strength of Wire Used in Our Woven Wire Fencing.

EXACT SIZES OF WIRE	Size Number	Number of feet in one pound	Breaking strength in pounds
	9	17.24	1560
	10	20.70	1280
	11	26.07	1000
	12	34.24	800
	13	44.64	568
	14	59.07	456
	15	72.90	352

24 8/10 CENTS A ROD AND UP STANDARD X-L-ALL SQUARE MESH FENCING 24 8/10 C
INTERLOCKED STAYS, SPACED 6 INCHES APART

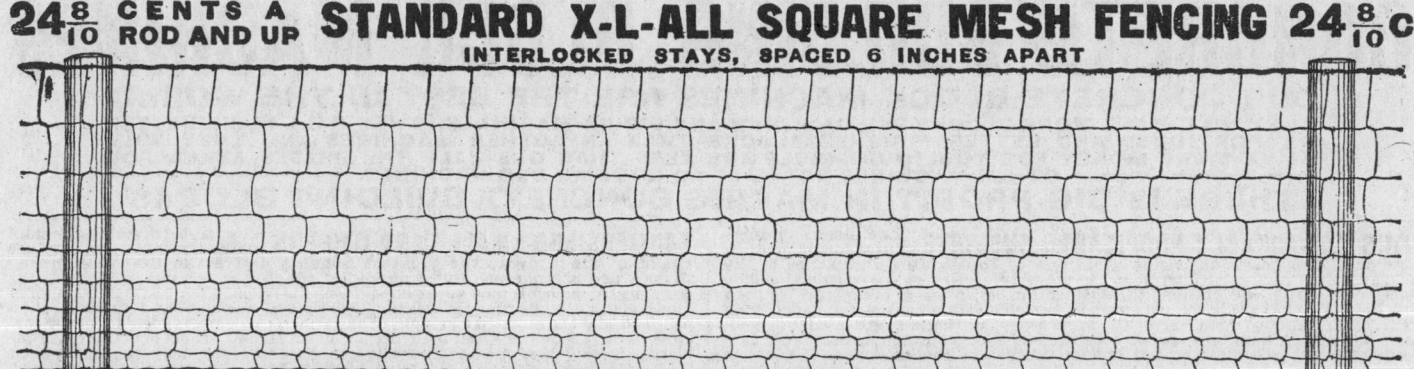

OUR STANDARD X-L-ALL FENCING
is the best fencing which we make, and we guarantee it to be the best fencing made in the United States. The interlocked stay wires in this fencing are spaced six inches apart. The top and bottom line wires are made of No. 9 hard galvanized steel wire. These single No. 9 wires are each as strong as a cable made of two No. 12 wires, such as is frequently used, and they will resist rust about four times as long as the cables, making the Standard X-L-ALL Fencing exceptionally durable, because the durability of fencing depends greatly upon the top and bottom line wire. The intermediate line wires and the interlocked stay wires are made of No. 12 galvanized steel wire. In weaving, the lock puts a crimp in both line and stay wires, making practically a spiral spring which operates both horizontally and vertically. In addition to this the woven fabric is heavily crimped, making the Standard X-L-ALL Fencing one of the most elastic fencings on the market. With our interlocked stays, should one of the line wires or one of the stay wires break by accident or otherwise, it can be easily repaired, because, being interlocked, it does not loosen up beyond the second wire. Use a fence stretcher (not a wire stretcher) when you erect your fence, and you will find the Standard X-L-ALL not only the best but the handsomest fencing on the market.

IF YOU ARE IN DOUBT
as to what fencing to buy, you will make no mistake in selecting our Standard X-L-ALL Fencing. There is nothing better made and you will never wish that you had ordered something cheaper. Do not pay a big penalty, an extra price, for the sake of buying fencing on time. We sell for cash only, but anyone who owns the land which he wishes to fence can easily borrow the money with which to pay for the fencing, if this be necessary, and the interest he would have to pay would be very little as compared to the saving he would make by buying the fencing from us at our direct from factory to user one profit low prices.

THE FREIGHT ON FENCING is a very small item. At our prices we deliver our fencing, on board the cars at Knightstown, Ind., from which point the purchaser pays the freight, but the freight charges are very low and amount to very little when compared with the amount we save you in the cost of the fencing. Order your fencing from us and you will find that after paying the freight you will have made a big money saving, and remember that we guarantee that our fencing will please you and satisfy you or you can return it and we will not only return your money but reimburse you for the freight you paid when you received the fencing.

26-Inch Standard X-L-ALL Fencing, 24 8-10 Cents per Rod.

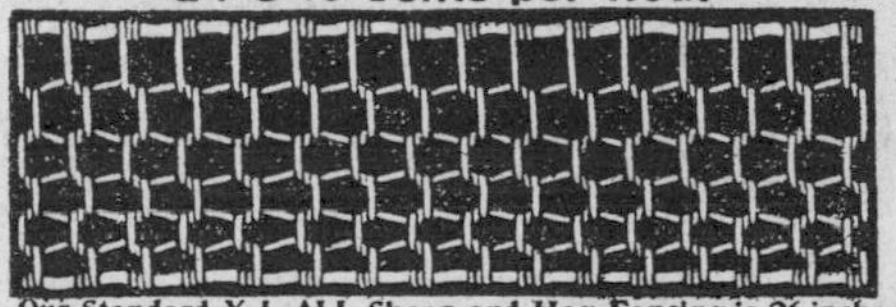

Our Standard X-L-ALL Sheep and Hog Fencing is 26 inches high and has 7 line wires. The spaces between the line wires, commencing at the bottom, are 3, 3½, 4, 4½, 5 and 6 inches respectively. The interlocked stay wires are spaced 6 inches apart. The top and bottom line wires are made of No. 9 hard galvanized steel wire and the stay wires and intermediate wires are made of No. 12 galvanized steel wire. This height of fencing is commonly used with three lines of barbed wire above it and frequently with a line of barbed wire at the bottom, making a fence four feet or more in height. We make this fencing in bales containing 5, 10, 20 and 40 rods, and do not cut bales. Weight, per 100 rods, 708 pounds. Shipped from factory in Knightstown, Indiana.

No. 32K5205 26-inch Standard X-L-ALL Fencing.			
Rods in bale	5	10	20	40
Price, per bale	$1.24	$2.48	$4.96	$9.92

33-Inch Standard X-L-ALL Fencing, 28 Cents per Rod.

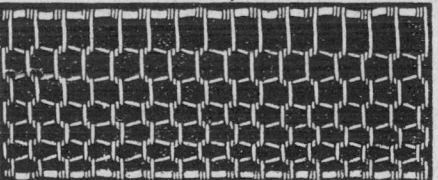

Our Standard X-L-ALL Low Stock Fencing is 33 inches high and has 8 line wires. The spaces between the line wires, commencing at the bottom, are 3, 3½, 4, 4½, 5, 6 and 7 inches respectively. The interlocked stay wires are spaced 6 inches apart. The top and bottom line wires are made of No. 9 hard galvanized steel wire, and the stay wires and intermediate line wires are made of No. 12 galvanized steel wire. This height of fencing is commonly used with two lines of barbed wire above it, and often with a line of barbed wire at the bottom, making an exceptionally strong fence four feet or more in height. We make this fencing in bales containing 5, 10, 20 and 40 rods, and do not cut bales. Weight, per 100 rods, 808 pounds. Shipped from factory in Knightstown, Indiana.

No. 32K5207 33-inch Standard X-L-ALL Fencing.			
Rods in bale	5	10	20	40
Price, per bale	$1.40	$2.80	$5.60	$11.20

41-Inch Standard X-L-ALL Fencing, 31 2-10 Cents per Rod.

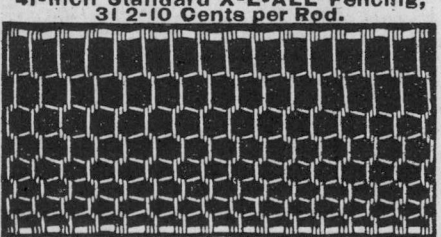

Our Standard X-L-ALL High Stock Fencing is 41 inches high and has 9 line wires. The spaces between the line wires, commencing at the bottom, are 3, 3½, 4, 4½, 5, 6, 7 and 8 inches respectively. The interlocked stay wires are spaced 6 inches apart. The top and bottom line wires are made of No. 9 hard galvanized steel wire and the stay wires and intermediate line wires are made of No. 12 galvanized steel wire. This height of fencing is commonly used with one line of barbed wire above it and sometimes with a line of barbed wire at the bottom, making a fence four feet or more in height. We make this fencing in bales containing 5, 10, 20 and 40 rods, and do not cut bales. Weight, per 100 rods, 904 pounds. Shipped from factory in Knightstown, Indiana.

No. 32K5209 41-inch Standard X-L-ALL Fencing.			
Rods in bale	5	10	20	40
Price, per bale	$1.56	$3.12	$6.24	$12.48

50-Inch Standard X-L-ALL Fencing, 36 2-10 Cents per Rod.

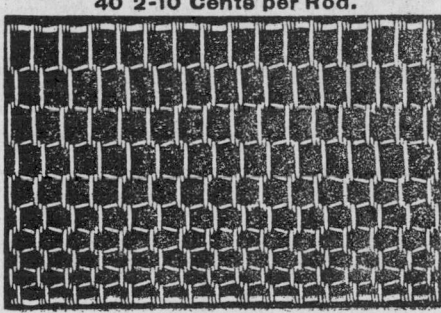

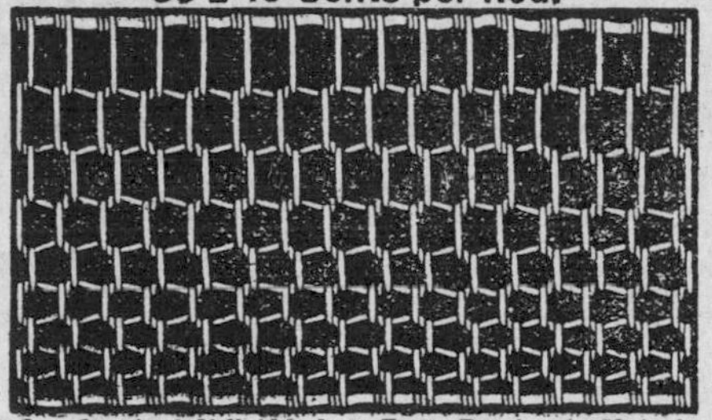

Our Standard X-L-ALL Low Farm Fencing is 50 inches high and has 10 line wires. The spaces between the line wires, commencing at the bottom, are 3, 3½, 4, 4½, 5, 6, 7, 8 and 9 inches respectively. The interlocked stay wires are spaced 6 inches apart. The top and bottom line wires are made of No. 9 hard galvanized steel wire and the stay wires and intermediate line wires are made of No. 12 galvanized steel wire. This height of fencing will turn all kinds of stock even without barbed wires above it, but lines of barbed wire may be placed above and below it, making a fence 60 inches or more in height. It is the most popular height of fencing made for general farm fencing, and if you have a piece of land or a farm which you wish to fence you will make no mistake in selecting this height and style of fencing. We make this fencing in bales containing 5, 10, 20 and 40 rods, and do not cut bales. Weight, per 100 rods, 1,058 pounds. Shipped from factory in Knightstown, Indiana.

No. 32K5211 50-inch Standard X-L-ALL Fencing.			
Rods in bale	5	10	20	40
Price, per bale	$1.81	$3.62	$7.24	$14.48

60-Inch Standard X-L-ALL Fencing, 40 2-10 Cents per Rod.

Our Standard X-L-ALL High Farm Fencing is 60 inches high and has 11 line wires. The spaces between the line wires, commencing at the bottom, are 3, 3½, 4, 4½, 5, 6, 7, 8, 9 and 10 inches respectively. The interlocked stay wires are spaced 6 inches apart. The top and bottom line wires are made of No. 9 hard galvanized steel wire and intermediate line wires are made of No. 12 galvanized steel wire. This makes an ideal farm fence and, while lines of barbed wire may be stretched above or below it, this fencing is high enough to stop any kind of stock without the use of barbed wire. We make this fencing in bales containing 5, 10, 20 and 40 rods, and do not cut bales. Weight, per 100 rods, 1,186 pounds. Shipped from factory in Knightstown, Indiana.

No. 32K5213 60-inch Standard X-L-ALL Fencing.			
Rods in bale	5	10	20	40
Price, per bale	$2.01	$4.02	$8.04	$16.08

$4.48 WOVEN WIRE FENCE STRETCHER AND SAFETY HOIST

THIS IS A COMBINED WOVEN WIRE FENCE STRETCHER AND SELF-LOCKING TACKLE BLOCK OR SAFETY HOIST. IT CAN BE USED BY HAND OR POWER AND ADJUSTED SO AS TO PUT ANY DESIRED TENSION ON EITHER TOP OR BOTTOM LINE WIRES OR AN EQUAL TENSION ON BOTH WIRES.

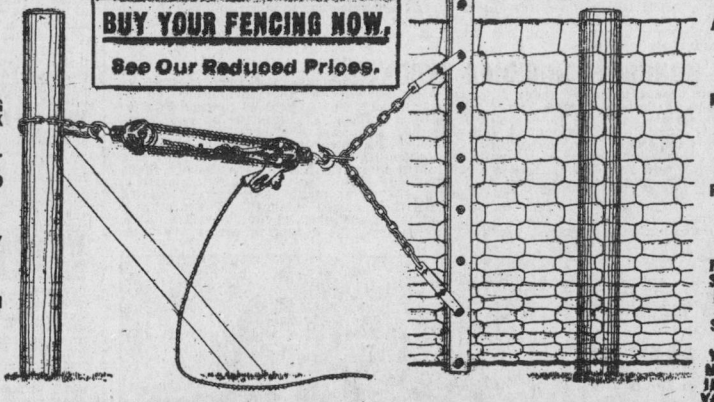

BUY YOUR FENCING NOW. See Our Reduced Prices.

IT WILL HOLD AT ANY POINT WITHOUT SLIPPING. EVERY POUND PULLED ON THE ROPE IS EQUAL TO FOUR POUNDS ON THE PULL WIRE. DO NOT SPOIL A GOOD FENCE BY FAILING TO STRETCH IT PROPERLY. BUY THIS STRETCHER AND YOU WILL HAVE NO TROUBLE IN ERECTING YOUR FENCE.

IT IS EASY TO ERECT WOVEN WIRE FENCING
and when woven wire fencing is properly erected it makes the handsomest, the most durable and the most satisfactory fence in the world, but any woven wire fencing must be evenly stretched else its meshes will be drawn out of shape and the fence will present an unsightly appearance and its value and durability will be depreciated. You cannot stretch woven wire fencing and erect it properly by attaching ordinary wire stretchers to the top and bottom line wires. The entire width of the fencing must be firmly and squarely clamped within some device which will hold and stretch every line wire evenly, then you will find it easy to stretch and erect the fencing properly. Our tackle block fence stretcher is the best device on the market for stretching woven wire fencing. It consists of two heavy hardwood clamps with bolts for attaching the clamps securely across the entire width of the fencing, a pair of broad steel clevises with chains to connect with the tackle blocks, and a pair of double sheave tackle blocks one of which is fitted with a safety device which grips the rope and holds it wherever the pull is stopped. The blocks are made for use with ¾-inch manila or sisal rope and aside from their use in the fence stretcher they can be used either as ordinary tackle blocks or as a safety hoist, and when used as a safety hoist with ¾-inch manila rope one man can easily raise 600 pounds, or with a team they have a capacity of 2½ tons and they will hold the load wherever it is stopped. It is not necessary that you purchase a special fence stretcher, but you will find our stretcher very convenient and well worth its price, because its blocks can be used for so many different purposes. If you don't wish to invest in a fence stretcher you can make your own clamps and use any tackle blocks which you have or can borrow, but in any case you should stretch your woven wire fencing carefully and properly. The price does not include rope or whiffletrees. These are shown in the illustration so that you may see how the stretcher is to be used. Any length of rope 30 feet or longer, can be used. Shipped from factory in Knightstown, Indiana.

No. 32K5385 Woven Wire Fence Stretcher. Weight, 48 pounds. Price $4.48

CONCRETE BUILDING BLOCK MACHINES

OUR CONCRETE BLOCK MACHINES ARE THE BEST IN THE WORLD.

THEY WILL MAKE MORE BLOCKS PER DAY THAN ANY OTHER MACHINES, THEY WILL MAKE BETTER PROPORTIONED AND BETTER FINISHED BLOCKS THAN ANY OTHER MACHINES AND THEY WILL MAKE MORE MONEY FOR YOU. OUR PRICES ARE LESS THAN ONE-HALF THE PRICES ASKED FOR OTHER MACHINES NOT HALF SO GOOD AS OUR MACHINES.

THERE IS BIG PROFIT IN MAKING CONCRETE BUILDING BLOCKS.

THIS REMARKABLY PROFITABLE BUSINESS **has been wonderfully developed in the past few years until now it is one of the leading industries of the country.** It is of great interest to the property owner because concrete building blocks are better and cheaper than either lumber, brick or stone, and by their use his buildings can be erected cheaper, better and more artistic in design than with other building materials, at the same time insuring warmth in winter, coolness in summer, more substantial construction and protection against fire. It is beneficial to the contractor and builder because of the cheapness of concrete building blocks compared with other building materials and because of its adaptability to all building purposes. It is a boon to the village lumber and building material dealer because it enables him to build up his business by adding concrete products to his line with most satisfactory profits to himself and with still greater profits if he makes blocks to sell in his own yards. He can purchase either a simple or a very complete outfit from us at wonderfully low prices.

FARMERS AND SMALL LAND OWNERS **who have gravel pits or sand banks on their property are the ones who can reap the greatest benefits and make the most money in the use of concrete building block machines,** because, aside from the cement used, which is only about one-fifth of the whole, their material costs absolutely nothing, while they can sell the blocks for as much as the man who is compelled to buy his sand and gravel. The farmer can employ men to make concrete blocks all the time and with big profit to himself, or his help can make the blocks on rainy days and at other idle periods, or he can make the blocks alone if he employs no help. He can build his own house, his barns and other farm buildings all with material of his own making, and he can sell his surplus products at a large profit. A modest concrete block making outfit of our make costs but very little and every farmer who can use one to advantage should not hesitate in making the investment. The saving you would make on one building alone would more than pay for a good outfit, aside from the profit you would make by selling the blocks.

WE PUBLISH A SPECIAL CONCRETE BUILDING BLOCK MACHINERY CATALOGUE

which will be sent free to anyone who will write and ask for it. This valuable book contains large and handsome illustrations of our complete line of concrete building block machinery, the highest grade and very best concrete block machines ever produced. It shows the machine complete and in parts, giving full and complete descriptions of everything. It explains to you why our machines are better, faster and more perfect than any other machines and quotes the machines at prices below all competition. **This big free book** gives a world of information about the concrete industry and the past and present uses of concrete in its various forms. It contains illustrations of the products which can be made with our machinery as well as pictures of beautiful cottages, homes, etc., which can be built from these products. It gives many reasons why concrete is superior to all other building materials, and treats at length upon the concrete building block branch of industry, in which the farmer, the village building material dealer, the small contractor or builder, and the ordinary property owner is most interested. It tells you what cement is made of, what kind of cement and other material to use for different purposes, how to proportion and mix the cement and other material for successful concrete block work, how to make the blocks, how to color the face of the blocks, what kind and how much coloring to use, how to mix and use the coloring, how to mix the mortar for laying the blocks, how to lay the blocks, how and when to plaster directly on the blocks, how to apply pebble dash or any other finish and how to waterproof the blocks. In fact, this free book tells you all about concrete block making, and how to secure the best results and the biggest profits by using our **low priced, high grade, up to the minute concrete block machines.**

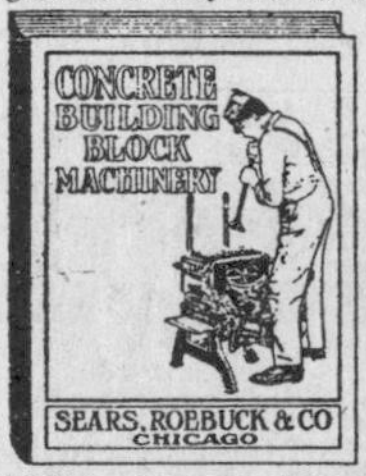

CONCRETE IS A BUILDING MATERIAL

made of cement, mixed in varied proportions with coarse materials called aggregates, and dampened with water. The aggregates may consist of either sand, gravel or crushed stone, or all of these combined, the proportions of the cement and the aggregates and the amount of water used being regulated by the required strength of the concrete product, the method by which the mixture is made into form, and the manner in which it is to be used. There are two methods of making concrete. One is known as the wet process, in which the mixture is made wet enough so that it can be poured into a specially prepared mould, in which it remains until it has set and hardened. The other is known as the dry process, in which the mixture is dampened only enough to cause the cement and the aggregates to adhere or cling together under slight pressure so that when the mixture is tamped into a machine mould or flask it can be removed as soon as it is made into the desired form and set to one side to dry and harden.

GROUTING, WHICH IS THE WET PROCESS MIXTURE,

has been in use for thousands of years. It has been determined that the pyramids of Egypt were made by this process. There are concrete buildings in Rome which have been in use for over 1,400 years; in England and Ireland there are castles and towers which were built of this material hundreds of years ago, proving conclusively that concrete is the most durable of all building materials. The United States Government has adopted this material for building extensive public improvements, such as harbor walls, breakwaters, etc., and the great railroad companies, contractors and public corporations use it in building bridge piers, culverts and foundations for buildings of every description. The wet process is not generally used except in extensive building operations because the form or mould must be built especially for every part of the constructive work, but the invention of machines for making building blocks places the farmer, the material dealer, the small builder and the ordinary property owner in position to make use of this wonderful building material and at a cost far below that of any of the other materials now in use.

HOLLOW CONCRETE BUILDING BLOCKS

are made by the dry mixture process, the only process by which concrete products can be made in a machine allowing the formed block to be removed immediately from the mould or flask and the machine to be used continuously for making additional blocks. Any form, shape or design of block may be made by machinery, depending only upon the equipment of the machines, and anyone either with or without skill or previous experience can make perfect blocks with our concrete building block machines, because our machines are both simple and perfect and the instructions which we provide are so simple and complete that no one can fail to obtain satisfactory results with them. Concrete blocks for building purposes are generally made hollow, to permit air circulation in the walls of the building while still allowing the blocks to be made of the correct size and with the smallest amount of material consistent with the required strength. The mixture is tamped into the mould or flask of the machine and when the block is completed it is taken out of the machine on its pallet and set away to undergo the curing process, which takes from ten to twenty days. During the curing the block crystallizes until it becomes hard enough to be laid in the wall, and this crystallization continues from year to year until the block finally becomes almost like flint in hardness and durability.

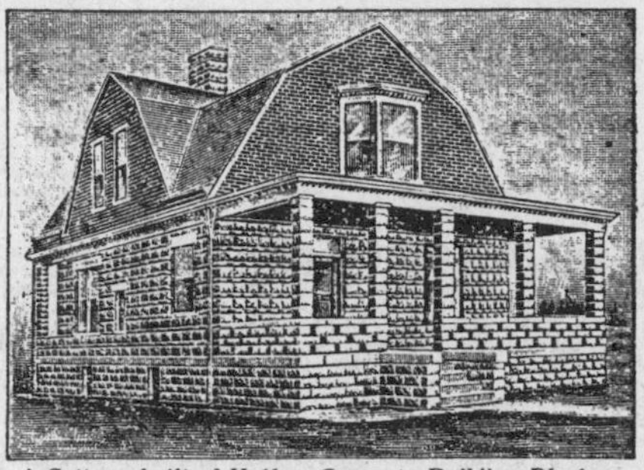
A Cottage built of Hollow Concrete Building Blocks.

ANYONE, ANYWHERE, CAN MAKE MONEY

and lots of it by engaging in this new and attractive business. There is a big demand for concrete building blocks and this demand is increasing with wonderful strides. Concrete blocks are now being universally used for buildings on the farm, in the villages and in cities. The material for making the blocks aside from the cement, that is, sand and gravel, can be found anywhere and costs almost nothing, and the cement can be bought very cheaply. No experience is necessary because the work is simple and our instructions are thorough, and at our extremely low prices you can purchase a very complete concrete building block machine and outfit for a very small amount of money. No matter whether you engage in the business extensively or only to fill in on rainy days and idle hours, you will find it profitable, and if you are a farmer the blocks, you would use in your own buildings will more than save you the price of a good machine.

OUR CONCRETE BUILDING BLOCK MACHINES

and the special concrete block moulds, concrete brick machines, concrete mixers, etc., which are shown on the following pages, are the very highest type and highest grade of concrete working machines which it is possible to manufacture. This is particularly true in relation to our Wizard Concrete Building Block Machines, which are the best designed and best made building block machines on the market. They are the only strictly automatic concrete block machines made, so far as we know, and they will turn out better proportioned, better made and better finished blocks than any other machines and at about twice the speed of the average machines. This perfection has been reached through the efforts of our manufacturers, who are thoroughly practical concrete machine designers and builders employing the highest class of mechanics and the most up to date methods of manufacture combined with the practical and theoretical knowledge of the expert whom we employ continuously for the sole purpose of improving our concrete machinery and keeping it in the lead of all other machines.

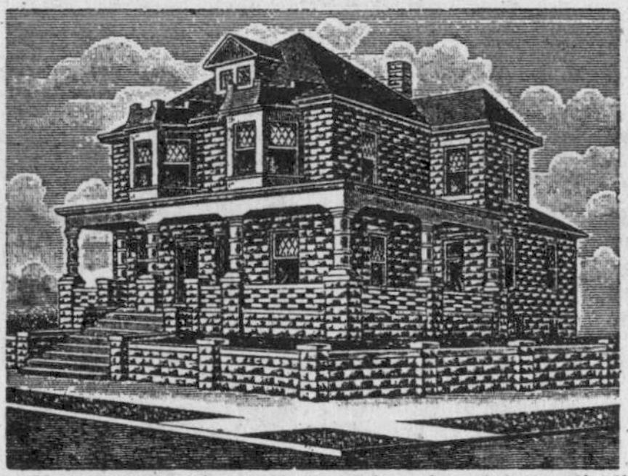
House, porch columns, balustrade and retaining wall all built of Hollow Concrete Building Blocks.

OUR PRICES ARE EXTREMELY LOW.

While the quality and efficiency of our concrete working machinery is as high as the highest, our prices are very much lower than others ask for machines of inferior grade and only about one-half the prices you would be compelled to pay for machines which would anywhere near approach ours in quality, and we honestly believe that you cannot buy elsewhere at any price machines as efficient and satisfactory as ours. We can afford to make low prices because we have our machines manufactured in very large quantities under special contracts. The manufacturers have no selling or collection expenses, as we take their output and pay them spot cash for everything. Our method of selling direct to the user is far more economical than that of the ordinary dealer; there are no jobbers', wholesalers', agents' or middlemen's profits of any kind to pay; our prices are based on the actual cost of the material and labor with but our one small profit added, allowing us to sell to our customers at prices which are really as low or lower than the biggest jobbers would have to pay for the same class of goods. We furnish you the best concrete working machinery which can be made, and we effect a big money saving for you in our wonderfully low prices.

OUR THIRTY DAYS' FREE TRIAL AND TEST OFFER

While the statements which we make in relation to our concrete machinery, as well as all other goods we sell, are absolutely true and not exaggerated in any way, you need not depend upon these statements alone. If you order your concrete machinery from us we allow you thirty days' free trial. For instance, should you order a Wizard Concrete Building Block Machine from us, you would have thirty days from the time you received the machine in which to examine, test and use it and to compare it in value, efficiency, speed and perfection of product with any or all other machines, no matter what the price of the other machines may be, then if you do not find that the Wizard is all that we claim for it, that it is high grade in every way, that it is strong and durable, that it does better and faster work and gives you better satisfaction than any other machine you could buy, or if you are not satisfied that you have saved money by purchasing from us, you can return the machine at our expense and we will cheerfully return your money and reimburse you for the freight you paid when you received the machine. You are the sole and only judge of the quality, efficiency and value of our machines. They must please and satisfy you or you get your money back.

WE GUARANTEE OUR CONCRETE MACHINERY

against all defects in material and workmanship for one year from date of shipment, by which guarantee we agree that should any piece or part give out or break by reason of defect in material or workmanship during the term of the guarantee we will make it good by furnishing free new parts to take the place of the defective parts.

WE GUARANTEE SAFE DELIVERY.

Our concrete machines are prepared and protected for shipment in the best possible manner. Breakage or loss of parts in transit is very rare but, should any part be damaged, broken or lost while in transit, we will promptly send you such parts as are necessary to replace the damaged, broken or lost parts, free of charge, and will prepay the transportation charges so that you will not lose one penny.

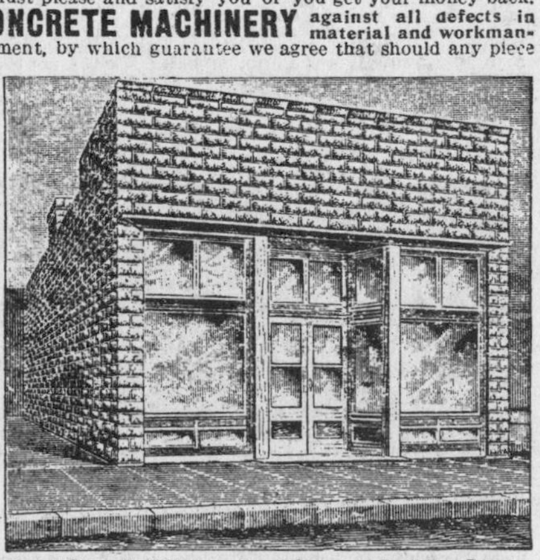
A Small Store Building made of Concrete Building Blocks.

ABOUT THE FREIGHT CHARGES.

Our concrete working machines are shipped direct from the factory and take a very low rate of freight, only about 40 cents per 100 pounds for 200 miles, about 75 cents per 100 pounds for 500 miles and about $1.20 per 100 pounds for 800 miles. The freight charges on the Wizard Concrete Building Block machine with full outfit, weighing about 520 pounds, to Auburn, Indiana, would be about $1.72, or to Lewiston, Maine, about $2.96, or to Manhattan, Kansas, about $6.60. The freight charges which you must pay are, as you will note, very small, almost nothing compared with the saving you will make by sending your order to us. Don't let the freight question worry you; we will save you money no matter where you live.

THE WIZARD CONCRETE BUILDING BLOCK MACHINES

AUTOMATIC IN THE REAL SENSE OF THE WORD

THE RAPID BLOCK PRODUCERS—THE BIG MONEY MAKERS

OUR WIZARD CONCRETE BUILDING BLOCK MACHINES which are illustrated, described and priced on the following three pages represent the very highest type of development in concrete building block machinery, and so far as we know they are the only strictly **automatic** block machines on the market at the present time. They are **automatic** in opening and closing, they are locked **automatically**, the cores are drawn **automatically** and just the pressure of the foot against a foot lever causes the cores to enter and take their places instantly. These machines produce a perfect block because they square up perfectly, lock rigidly and open without jarring, and because the shape of the cores is such that no tamping is required before the cores are entered into the mould, consequently there is no hard tamped parting line below the cores to cause the block to crack, as there is in blocks made in other machines. It is the hard tamped parting line and the jarring of the machine when turning and opening the mould which breaks the blocks and causes the greatest trouble for the block maker who uses the usual type of machine. There is none of this trouble in the Wizard.

THE WIZARD BLOCK MACHINE is made in various sizes, to meet all requirements. In the standard length of block, namely 16 inches long, we can furnish separate machines for making blocks 8 inches high by either 8 inches, 9 inches, 10 inches or 12 inches wide, and in the 24-inch length of block we can furnish separate machines for making blocks 8 inches high by either 9 inches or 12 inches wide. You can purchase a separate machine for each size of block, or you can purchase one or more separate machines and as many of the different interchangeable moulds as you wish, depending upon the completeness of the outfit you want, because all of the different sizes of moulds fit onto the same frame or stand and each is complete with all the parts necessary to make the change, which change can be made easily and quickly. In height and in length blocks made with our concrete building block machines are ¼ inch less than the measures given. This is to allow for the mortar joint.

THE WIZARD IS THE MOST RAPID BLOCK MAKER on the market and it is strictly a one-man machine; that is, one man can operate it as easily and we believe as rapidly as two men can operate an ordinary machine costing twice as much as we ask for the Wizard. This is what the **automatic features** accomplish for you; in other words, we furnish you a machine at about one-half the price others ask, with which you can make blocks about twice as fast as on other machines.

THE FOLLOWING ILLUSTRATIONS show fourteen different designs of blocks which can be made on either size of the Wizard Building Block Machines, with the face plates and end doors for which we now have patterns, and whenever a new design becomes popular we shall add it to our line. These illustrations show blocks with two cores, as made on the 16-inch machines. The blocks made on the 24-inch machines have three cores, otherwise their general appearance is the same as in these illustrations. Blocks made on the Wizard machines have about 33⅓ per cent of air or core space and 66⅔ per cent concrete material, this being the standard of proportions recognized as requisite for proper strength in the block and economy in materials. Face plates for making one half block and two quarter blocks at the same time, as shown in the last of these fifteen illustrations, can be furnished for either size of machine in any of the different designs. The regular outfit with each machine includes a set of face plates and end doors for making standard plain face blocks and a set of face plates and end doors for making standard rock face blocks, there being a face plate for whole blocks and a face plate for halves and quarters in each set. You can order your machine fitted with sets of face plates and end doors for any two of the different designs in place of the two standard designs without extra charge, and you can order as many sets of face plates and end doors of the other designs as you wish, allowing our catalogue price for each additional set ordered.

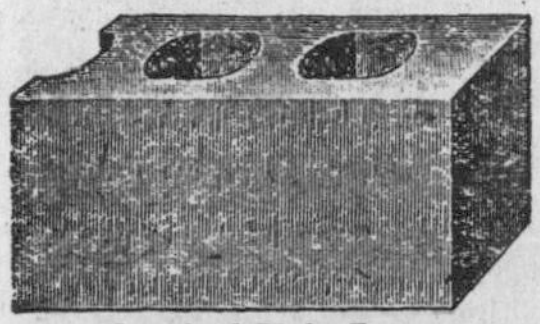
Standard Plain Face.

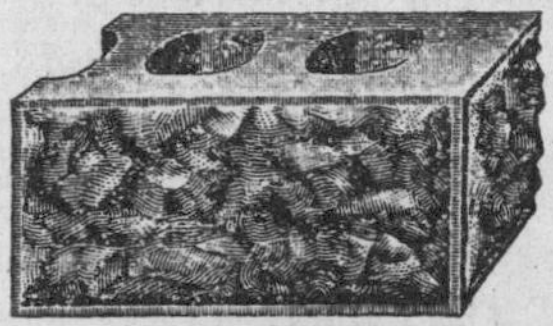
Standard Rock Face.

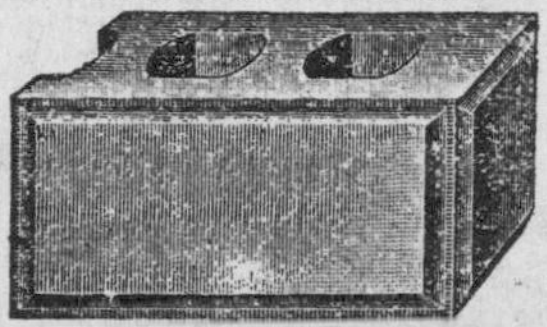
Panel Face.

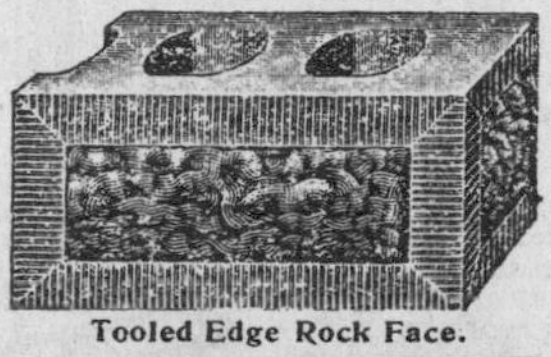
Tooled Edge Rock Face.

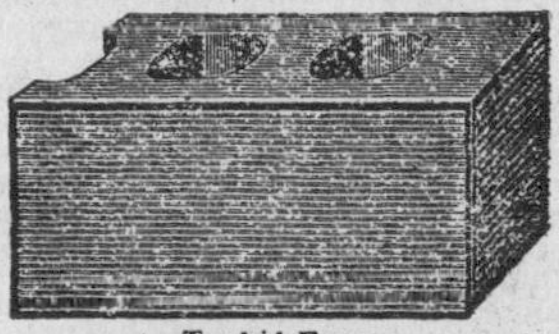
Tooled Face.

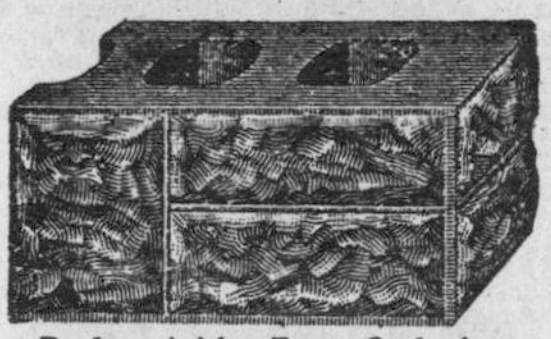
Broken Ashler Face, Style A.

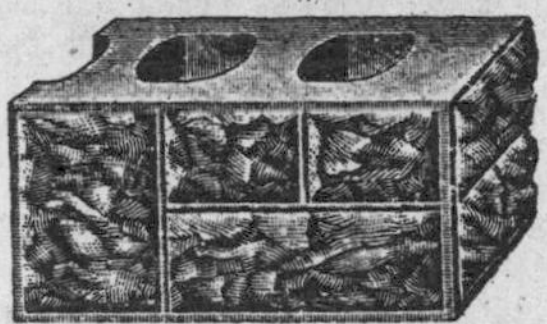
Broken Ashler Face, Style B.

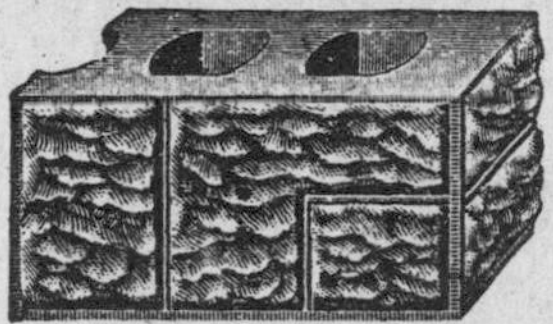
Broken Ashler Face, Style C

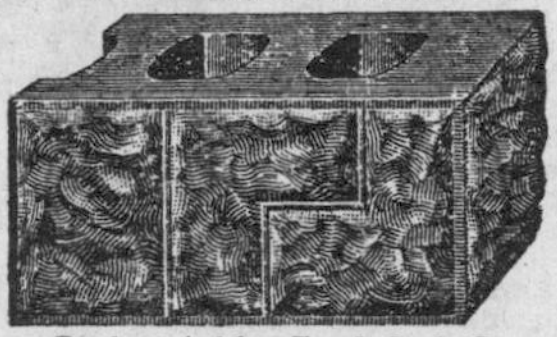
Broken Ashler Face, Style D.

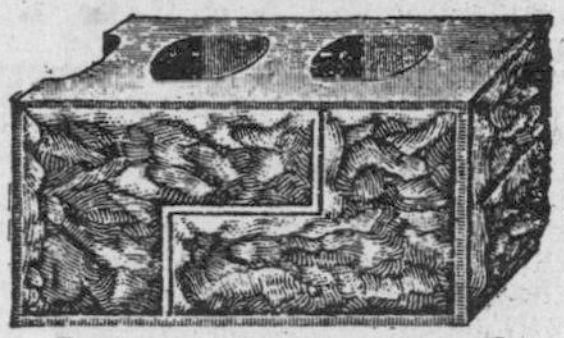
Broken Ashler Face, Style B.

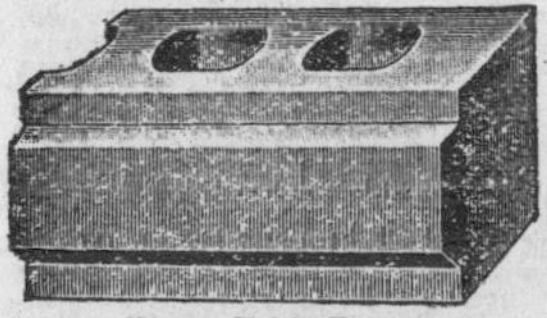
Water Table Face.

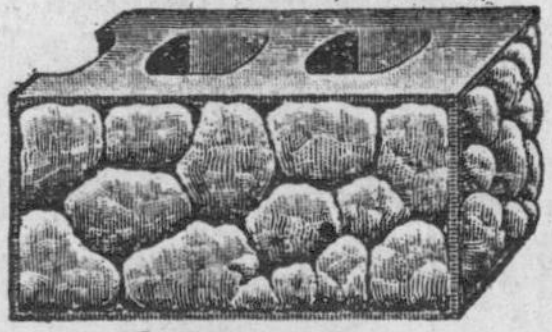
Cobblestone Face.

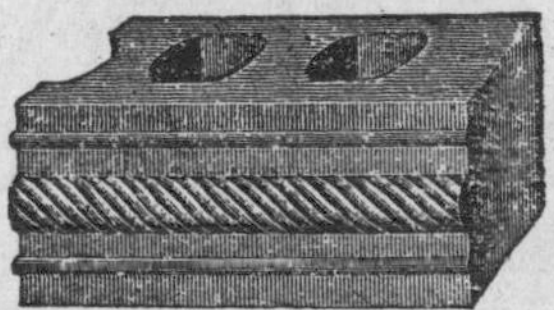
Rope Face.

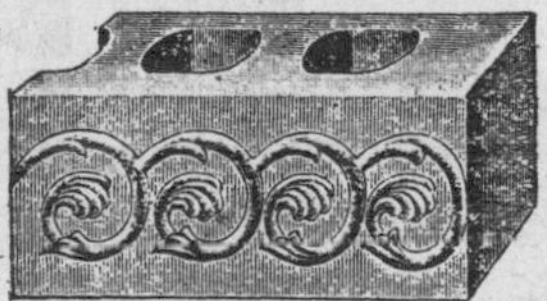
Scroll Face.

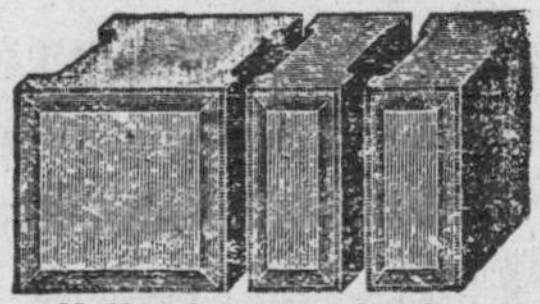
Half and Quarter Blocks.

OUR MACHINES MAKE THE BLOCKS FACE DOWN. This is the only way in which a perfect block can be made, using fine material for the face and coarse material for the body of the block. You can make the face mixture as rich as you wish and the body mixture with the smallest amount of cement allowable, thus producing a high class beautifully faced block at the least possible cost. You can make blocks of any desired color in the face mixture without wasting coloring matter in the body of the block; and with as perfect a machine as the Wizard is, using a correct mixture and tamping it properly, you are assured of a perfectly made and perfectly finished block every time.

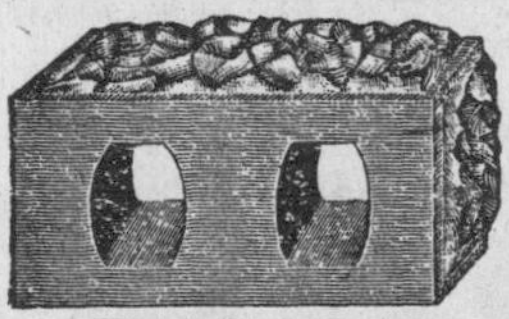
Wizard Block Cores.

THE SHAPE OF THE CORES in blocks made with the Wizard Block Machines, as shown in this illustration, is radically different from that in general use. Most machines make blocks with square cornered cores, compelling the operator to tamp the mixture next to the face of the block before the cores are inserted in the mould, thus leaving a hard tamped parting near the core line of the block which makes it weak and liable to crack or separate. This parting line and the square core corners are the causes which result in cracked blocks and only a very slight jar is required to crack the blocks under these circumstances. The cores of the Wizard blocks are elliptical. This allows you to lay the face material, insert the cores and fill the mould with coarse material before starting to tamp, because in the tamping the tamper follows the core sides and the mixture is tamped in the face of the block and under the cores just as hard as in any other part of the block and without any tamped parting lines. There are no square corners to start cracks and the arched form of the core sides adds greatly to the strength of the block. If your mixture is right, and it is very easy to secure the proper mixture, every block made in the Wizard machine will be a perfect block.

THE REGULAR OUTFIT furnished with our Wizard Building Block Machines enables you to make standard plain face and standard rock face blocks (or any other two designs you select instead of these) in whole, half and quarter blocks, with core ends and return ends, whole blocks for return or inside corners, joist blocks and gable blocks. We make attachments and extras for these machines, which are not included in the price of the machines, but which can be ordered at the time the machine is ordered or at any other time, at the prices shown in our catalogue. These attachments and extras are as follows:

BAY WINDOW BLOCK ATTACHMENTS. Bay windows are generally made at an angle of 45 degrees but they can be made at any angle desired. This illustration shows how to lay up bay window blocks so as to break joints and make the bay as large or as small as you wish. We can furnish with either Wizard or Buckeye building block machines adjustable bay window block attachments which will make both inside and outside angle blocks. A bay window block attachment consists of a face plate having an adjustable end piece for forming the angle end of the block and, aside from making bay window blocks, the attachment can be used for making three-quarter blocks with square ends which will often be found very convenient. These attachments can be furnished only for blocks of the following designs: Plain face, rock face, panel face, tooled edge rock face, tooled face and cobblestone face. When ordering you must be careful to tell us which design of face you want and to allow our catalogue price for the attachment.

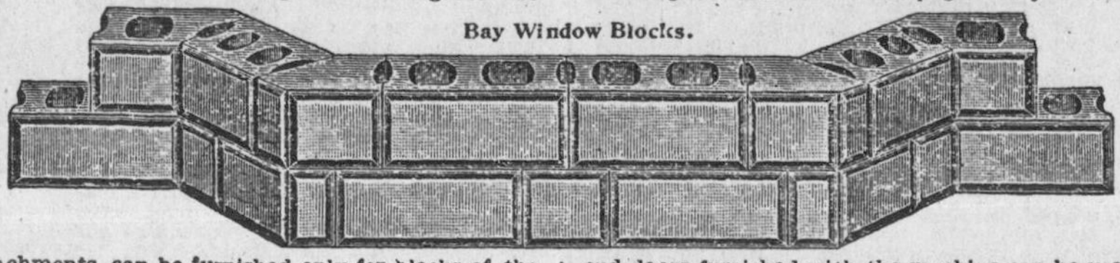
Bay Window Blocks.

FOUR-INCH COURSE BLOCK ATTACHMENTS. While any of the different face designs in full height blocks (8 inches) can be used for belt courses and while the water table face is most generally used for this purpose, it is frequently desirable to use blocks only 4 inches in height for belt and trimming courses. These 4-inch blocks can also be used in connection with 8-inch blocks to obtain a broken ashler effect in the wall. We can furnish 4-inch course block attachments with either Wizard or Buckeye building block machines. A 4-inch course block attachment consists of a face plate for making two whole blocks, a face plate for making two half and four quarter blocks, a pair of return end doors, four dividing plates for making the half and quarter blocks, and two dividing pallets for the length of the blocks. As you will note we only furnish two dividing pallets with the attachment, but you will require as many dividing pallets as you wish to make moulds per day, and these should be ordered when you order the attachment; however, the same dividing pallets can be used with attachments for different designs of blocks. These attachments can be furnished only for blocks of the following designs: Plain face, rock face, panel face and tooled face. When ordering you must be careful to tell us which design of face you want and to allow our catalogue price for the attachment and for such extra dividing pallets as you see fit to order.

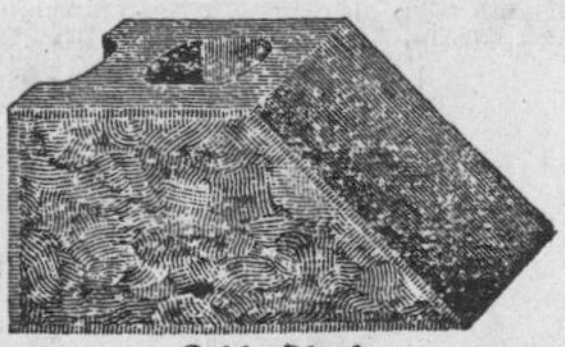
Gable Block.

CIRCLE BLOCK ATTACHMENTS. Circular bay windows, or swell fronts or circular corners, require blocks having convex or circular faces. We can furnish with either Wizard or Buckeye building block machines 8-foot radius, 10-foot radius and 12-foot radius circle block attachments in the two standard face designs, that is, plain face and rock face, and in the water table design, but it requires a separate attachment for each different radius and face design. A circle block attachment consists of a face plate for making whole blocks and a pair of core end doors with dividing plates for the fractional blocks. When ordering be careful to tell us which design of face and which radius you want and to allow our catalogue price for the outfit.

SPECIAL FACE DESIGNS. The regular outfit of our Wizard Building Block Machines includes the face plates and end doors for making whole, half and quarter blocks, with plain ends, core ends and return ends, in the standard plain face and standard (medium) rock face designs, or your choice of any two of the designs illustrated on this page. If you wish any of the other designs or a shallow rock face or a heavy rock face be sure to state which design you want and to allow our catalogue price for the extras which you order. We list the face plates for making whole blocks, the face plates for making fractional blocks, and the right hand and left hand doors separately, so that you need order only such face plates and end doors as you wish; but for a complete set of face plates and end doors for any one design you would require one face plate for whole blocks, one face plate for half and quarter blocks, one right hand and one left hand end door. The plain end doors and core end doors furnished with the machine can be used in making blocks of any face design.

GABLE BLOCKS, such as illustrated above, can be made in any of the face designs which you have with your machine, the dividing plate for this work being furnished with the machine.

FOR DESCRIPTION OF WIZARD MACHINES AND PRICES OF MACHINES AND ATTACHMENTS SEE PAGES 576 AND 577.

$42⁵⁰ WIZARD CONCRETE BUILDING BLOCK MACHINE

THE WIZARD IS THE BEST

CONCRETE BUILDING BLOCK MACHINE MADE

It contains all up to date scientific improvements known to this class of machinery. In offering you this high grade machine, we claim it has no equal and that it is superior to concrete block machines which are sold as high as from $100.00 to $200.00.

THIS ILLUSTRATION shows a Wizard Concrete Building Block Machine closed and ready to receive the concrete material for making the block. Observe its compact construction and note that every part is mechanical in detail; that is, it will automatically accomplish the work itself with but little assistance from the operator. These machines should not be confused with many concrete block machines of other makes, which are no more than mould boxes, flasks and forms. The **Wizard** is made to perform practically all the work and not you, and such a valuable consideration, together with many other superior qualities, places the Wizard in a higher class than so called concrete block machines which are only mere contrivances made to assist hand-labor. We give you a machine which will do the work in greater proportion and much faster than it can be accomplished by any other method.

THE FRAME is well proportioned and supported with ribs and braces which prevent the flask or mould from jarring, sagging or shifting when the block is being made. A large percentage of blocks are broken during the process of their making in other machines because the frame or stand of the machine they are made on is too weak to prevent the jarring of the flask. A mere glance at the Wizard will show the substantial construction of the frame of our machine, which eliminates all possibility of blocks becoming cracked or broken by jarring of the flask or mould.

THE FLASK OR MOULD is constructed according to the face down principle. All parts of the flask or mould swing from perfect centers which gives the mould a perfectly square shape when it is closed and completely releases the block when the mould is opened. The face down feature of the mould gives the block a sharp and compact face, enables you to obtain a better proportioned mixture and makes it necessary to use coloring only for the face of the block. It also makes it possible to use a fine quality of mixture for the face of the block and a coarser mixture for the body of the block. The mould is proportioned so as to permit the proper percentages of air space and bearing area, making them about 33⅓ per cent air space or cores and 66⅔ per cent bearing surface. All parts of the mould which are put into action during the process of making a block, work automatically in opening and closing the form; this is produced by their connection to levers which are moved by the operator.

THE LEVERS are two in number and are used by the operator in turning the mould forward in the course of releasing the block. The end doors are separated from the block when the levers are spread and the face plate is withdrawn by a straight away release when the levers are lifted; also the entire mould is swung back and away from the block with the same operation which is used in withdrawing the face plate. These three actions completely release the block so that it can be carried away on its pallet. In closing the mould the same levers are used and the same number of operations are required. The time required for all operations both in releasing and in closing the mould is only a small fraction of a minute and the work is all performed by the two levers and does not require the handling of any other part of the machine. This is one of the automatic features of our Wizard machine.

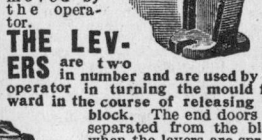

THE CORES ARE TWO IN NUMBER on the 16-inch machine and three of them are used on the 24-inch machine. They are shaped in such a manner as to allow the concrete while being tamped ample opportunity to follow the surface of the cores to a point directly under the center of the cores. This shape of core is very superior to all others because it gives the block firmness directly under the cores and sufficient strength to the tie pieces, which eliminates all liability of the blocks cracking or breaking while being removed from the machine. The cores are attached to the automatic core extractor by a steel rod which swings between a yoke. This prevents binding when they are being withdrawn by the extractor.

8x8x16 INCHES

COMPLETE WITH BIG OUTFIT

As listed and described on page 577.

OUR AUTOMATIC CORE EXTRACTOR

is a wonderful improvement on modern concrete block machinery. The old way of extracting the cores by hand, weights and levers has been overcome by this our modern method. It takes a great deal of time to insert and extract the cores by hand and it is hard work, considering the way the concrete material is tamped around the cores. **OUR WIZARD CONCRETE BLOCK MACHINE** is provided with this automatic core extractor which extracts the cores automatically when the flask is turned over to release the stone and the simple act of stepping on the foot treadle inserts the cores when the mould is turned back for the tamping of the concrete mixture for a new block.

THE REGULAR OUTFIT we furnish with this machine is such as is most generally used in making a standard variety of blocks. Special attachments, such as Bay Window, Circle Block and 4-Inch Course Block Attachments, are extra and are furnished only when ordered and proper price allowed. The regular outfits furnished with the machines are illustrated and described on the following page.

THE SHELF adds a valuable feature to our Wizard machine. The operator in making a block can use only one tool at a time and the shelf is a most convenient place upon which to place the remaining tools and keep them within easy reach when he wants to use them, otherwise they would be thrown on the floor and kicked about, making it necessary to look for them when they are wanted. All of this takes time and you can easily see the great amount of time and stooping that is saved by this shelf.

THE PALLET is an important part of a concrete block machine because so much depends upon it. Weak and uneven pallets will crack the blocks. Wood pallets will warp and twist out of shape and they become too flexible. We have provided our Wizard machine with cast iron pallets of proportionate weight and strength. These pallets have handles on them so that the operator needs no carrying device to lift the block out of the machine and carry it away. Twenty-five pallets are furnished with each machine, but you should have as many pallets as you wish to make blocks per day.

THE WIZARD HAS NO COMPLICATED ADJUSTMENTS such as are found on concrete block machines of other makes. There are no gears, sprockets, ratchets, springs, screws or slides to get out of order or clog up with concrete mixture when you are at work. In order to obtain the full capacity from any concrete block machine, it is necessary that the machine shall work smoothly and without a hitch, for should you have to stop in the midst of your work to adjust complicated parts and clean gears, ratchets or slides which become clogged up with concrete mixture that spills over the edge of the mould during the tamping of the block, you cannot receive the full capacity of the machine. It is well to consider that your profit depends upon the quality and number of blocks your machine makes in a fair day's work and when you own a Wizard Concrete Building Block Machine you receive the full benefit from your investment and labor and greater value than is given by any other concrete block machine in the world.

YOU SAVE ENOUGH IN LABOR on our Wizard Concrete Block Machine to pay for the machine in sixty days. One man can make blocks on our Wizard machine about as fast as two men can make them on any other concrete block machine. All concrete block machines make blocks, but few aside from the Wizard make perfect blocks and no other machine will make them so rapidly and with as little exertion and expense on the part of the operator as the Wizard. We know of several instances where one man has made a perfect block on the Wizard in one minute's time. We do not mean to say that everyone under all conditions can make a block for every minute of the working day, but we simply mean to illustrate the speed of which the machine is capable and the great amount of work it is possible for you to do alone on this machine. If it takes two men to operate other makes of concrete block machines in order to get a fair product for one day's work and the cost of labor to do the work is approximately $2.00 per day for each man, add $2.00 a day for every day you use a man to assist you to the price of the machine and you will find that it will make the machine an expensive one. You buy our Wizard Concrete Block Machine and you operate it alone and you can make a better block and about as many blocks as two men could make on the other machine. You save that $2.00 a day that you would have to pay for the extra man had you the other machine; deduct that $2.00 saved every day from the price paid for the Wizard and you will find that this saving of $2.00 a day will in a very short time pay for your Wizard machine and all over that can be applied to your net profits. Should you choose to operate the Wizard Concrete Block Machine with two men you can do so and by so doing you will double its capacity.

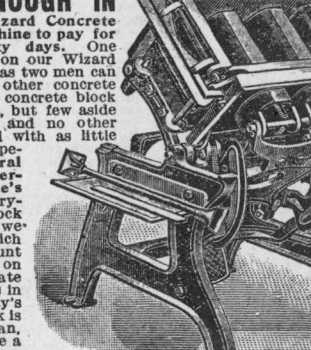

UNIQUE PORCH COLUMN, PIER, RAIL AND BALUSTER MOULDS

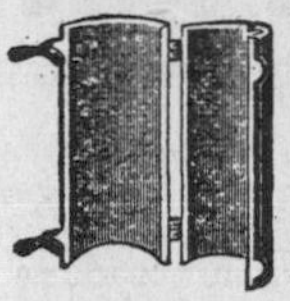
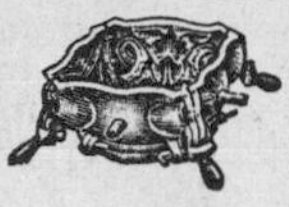

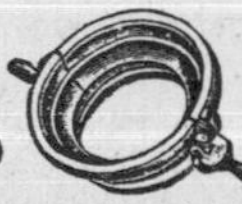

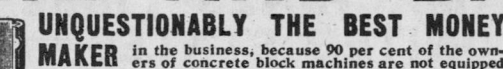

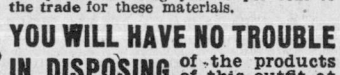

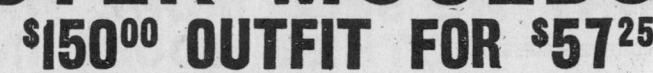

UNQUESTIONABLY THE BEST MONEY MAKER in the business, because 90 per cent of the owners of concrete block machines are not equipped with an outfit for making porch materials, and the demand for such materials for use with concrete block houses and frame buildings is becoming greater every day. Porch materials command big prices on account of their scarcity and it depends upon the design of the materials as to the price you receive. We believe that an outfit, such as we describe and illustrate on this page, will not only bring you the best prices but bring you 95 per cent of the trade for these materials.

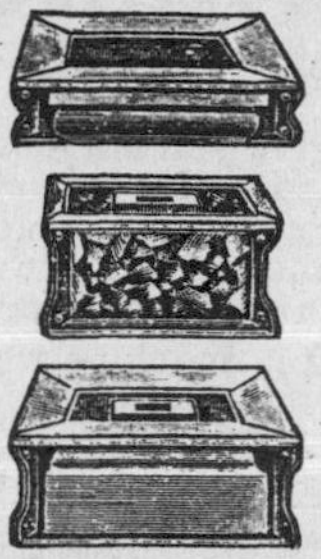

YOU WILL HAVE NO TROUBLE IN DISPOSING of the products of this outfit at enormously large profits, because of the artistic designs and the complete form in which they are made, and their comparatively small cost will attract the attention of every builder. No residence is complete without a porch, and no concrete block plant is complete without our Unique Porch Mould Outfit. Why not be up to date if you are a concrete block manufacturer and complete your line by adding this big profit making outfit to your list? You will have to show the customer what you make before he buys from you. Perhaps he thinks that such a complete and artistic line of porch materials cannot be made of concrete? If so, it is up to you to show him that it can be made, and the only way to do so is to convince yourself first by purchasing an outfit from us at our astonishingly low prices.

$150.00 OUTFIT FOR $57.25

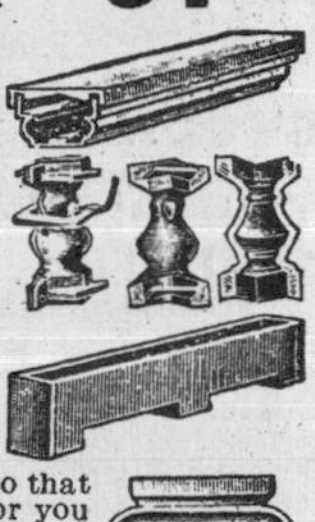

WE ARE OFFERING our Unique Porch Column, Pier, Rail and Baluster Mould Outfit complete in either of two designs for about one-third what others ask for an outfit not half as complete as this one. The outfit consists of 1 2-foot Plain Column Mould with fluted attachment for making plain and fluted columns; 1 Ornamental Column Capital in either Ionic or Gothic design; 1 O. G. Round Column Base Mould; 1 O. G. Square Pier Base Mould; 1 Pier Body Mould in choice of design; 1 Pier Cap Mould in either Plain or Egg and Dart design; 1 Plain Bottom Rail Mould; 1 Set of Four Half Baluster Moulds; and 1 Top Rail Mould in either Plain or Egg and Dart design. The ten small illustrations on this page show the complete outfit of moulds and the two column and rail illustrations on each side of this page show the products which can be made with the moulds. Every column mould is complete for making plain or fluted columns, so that it makes no difference how you order this part, because it is furnished complete, so that you can make a plain column with or without ornamental pier or rail, or you can make a fluted column with or without ornamental pier or rail. Be sure to state the size column wanted, and design of capital, pier and rail wanted.

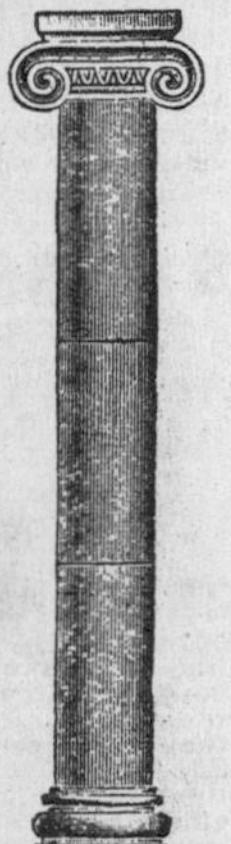

THE VARIOUS DESIGNS of moulds for the Pier Body are as follows: Rock Face, Panel Face, Tooled Face, Tooled Margin Rock Face, and Bush Hammer Face designs. The design of Pier Cap is Plain and Egg and Dart Moulding. The design of Top Rail is Plain and Egg and Dart Moulding. The design of Column Capitals are Gothic and Ionic. In ordering your outfit or separate moulds, state the size of column wanted and the design of various moulds wanted.

WE GUARANTEE EVERY OUTFIT or mould to be perfect in construction and material and, if not found satisfactory after ten days' trial, you may return the same at our expense and we will refund all money paid, together with freight charges.

PRICE LIST OF UNIQUE OUTFITS AND SEPARATE MOULDS. SHIPPED FROM FACTORY IN CENTRAL WISCONSIN.

No. 32K5830 10-inch Unique Porch Column, Pier Rail and Baluster Mould Outfit, complete. State design wanted. Shipping weight, 632 pounds. Price $57.25

No. 32K5831 12-inch Unique Porch Column, Pier Rail and Baluster Mould Outfit, complete. State design wanted. Shipping weight, 757 pounds. Price $65.50

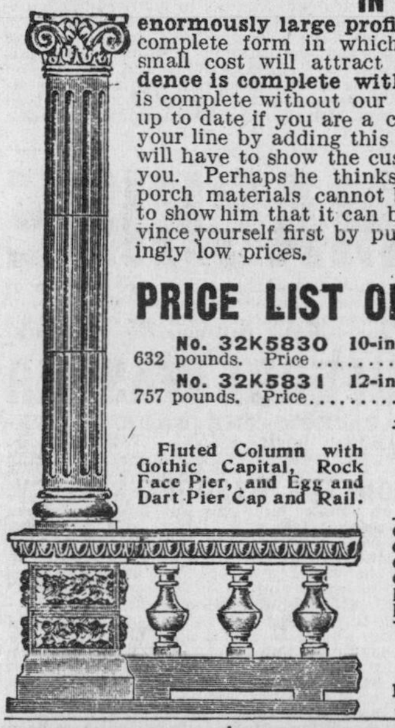

Fluted Column with Gothic Capital, Rock Face Pier, and Egg and Dart Pier Cap and Rail.

SEPARATE MOULDS	FOR 10-INCH COLUMN			FOR 12-INCH COLUMN		
	Catalogue No.	Wt. lbs.	Price	Catalogue No.	Wt. lbs.	Price
O. G. Round Column Base Mould	32K5834	40	$ 4.32	32K5844	60	$ 5.18
Combination Plain and Fluted Column Mould	32K5835	130	11.25	32K5845	155	13.40
Ornamental Cap Mould (Gothic or Ionic)	32K5836	80	8.62	32K5846	100	10.35
O. G. Pier Base Mould	32K5837	70	6.92	32K5847	95	8.30
Pier Body Mould, (State design wanted)	32K5838	65	5.62	32K5848	85	6.22
Pier Cap Mould (Plain or Egg and Dart)	32K5839	60	8.25	32K5849	75	9.45

No. 32K5854 Porch Bottom Rail Mould. Shipping weight, 65 pounds. Price $5.22
No. 32K5855 Baluster Half Mould. Shipping weight, 13 pounds. Price 1.04
No. 32K5856 Porch Top Rail Mould. (Plain or Egg and Dart.) Shipping weight, 70 pounds. Price 6.05

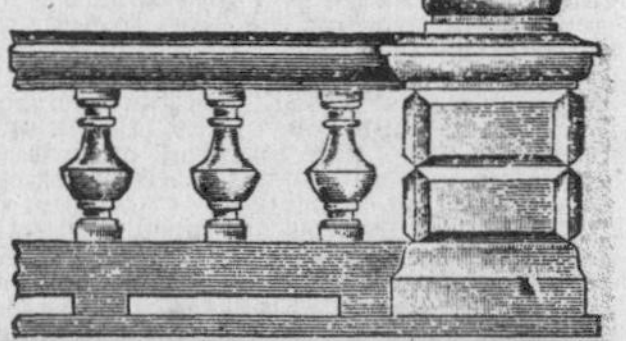

Plain Column with Ionic Capital, Panel Pier, and Plain Pier Cap and Rail.

OUR $57.25 HANDY TWO-WAY TEN-BRICK SIZE BRICK MACHINE

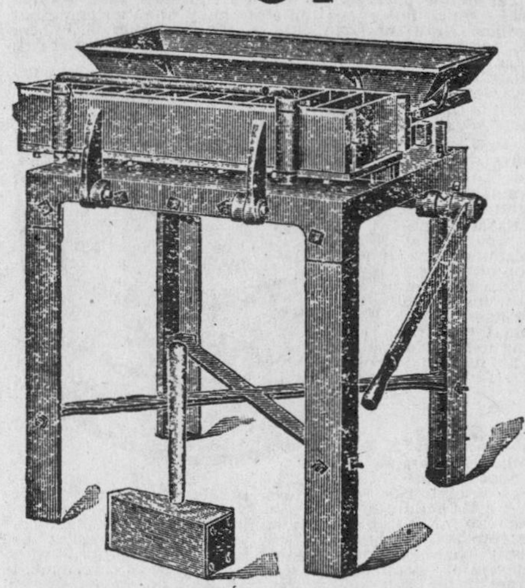

IT IS THE ONLY TWO-WAY BRICK MACHINE MADE THAT WILL MAKE PRESSED BRICK FACE DOWN AND ROUGH WALL BRICK FACE UP. ONE MAN CAN MAKE 3,000 PERFECT CONCRETE BRICK IN ONE DAY.

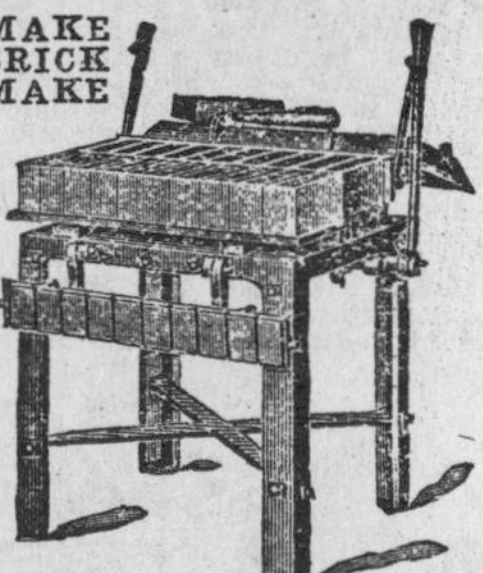

CONCRETE BRICK IS JUSTLY POPULAR because it replaces the common clay brick and is just as nicely finished and more durable than the clay brick. Concrete brick possess the same qualities as do concrete blocks. They become harder by age and cannot be destroyed by fire. Concrete brick buildings, together with concrete block and grout buildings, have lived through severe fires, such as the Baltimore and San Francisco fires, in which buildings of clay brick and stone have been totally destroyed.

NO CONCRETE BLOCK PLANT IS COMPLETE without our Handy Two-Way Ten-Brick Size Machine, because, if you are in the concrete building material business, you are sure to have frequent calls for concrete brick by people who want concrete building material other than concrete blocks. This has been the experience of many of our customers who did not possess a good concrete brick machine, and as they had no facilities for making concrete brick they lost some large and profitable orders for concrete brick. We recommend that you be prepared for such emergencies by possessing one of our Handy Two-Way Ten-Brick Size Machines.

THE COST OF CONCRETE BRICK is about 30 per cent less than common clay brick and about 65 per cent less than pressed clay brick. It takes about $4.50 worth of material to make 1,000 concrete brick, and if the cost of labor on our Handy Two-Way Ten-Brick Size Machine is $1.20 per 1,000 brick, the cost of 1,000 concrete brick made on the Handy machine, including material and labor, would be $5.70. The average cost of common clay brick is $8.00 per 1,000 and the average cost of pressed clay brick is $17.00 per 1,000. These figures, which are taken as an average cost in different localities, would make the cost of concrete brick $2.30 per 1,000 less than common clay brick and $11.30 per 1,000 less than pressed clay brick.

YOU RECEIVE TWO MACHINES IN ONE when you buy our Handy Two-Way Ten-Brick Size Machine, that is, a machine that will make bricks on either the face down or face up principle. Brick machines which are sold by others make brick only one way, either on the face down principle or face up principle, and even then they ask over twice the price we ask for our Handy Two-Way Ten-Brick Size Machine.

A PERFECT IMITATION OF THE FINEST PRESSED BRICK can be made on our Handy Two-Way Ten-Brick Size Machine, because you can use a colored and better quality facing on this machine when the bricks are made on the face down principle, the same as concrete blocks are made on our Wizard Concrete Block Machine, and almost any style ornamental design brick can be made on this machine, because it is on the face down principle. You can make a common concrete brick that is not finished on our Handy Two-Way Ten-Brick Size Machine also. Bricks of this character are used for filling in purposes or the building of back walls, or walls which do not require a finished pressed face brick. This style of brick is made on the face up principle and they are made directly on the pallet. This method of making the brick increases the output about 1,000 brick a day more than the face down principle way, because it is less work than the face down method and does not require the turning of the machine over to relieve the brick, as is required when the machine is operated on the face down principle.

YOU DO NOT WANT TO FILL AN ORDER with faced brick when it calls for common brick and when you have only been paid the price for common brick and your customer would not feel satisfied if you filled his order with common brick when he ordered faced brick and he paid you for faced brick quality. Well, that is what you would have to do if you possessed the brick machines sold by some others, because it would be one of the two principles, either face down or face up or you would have to own two different machines at an investment equal to the price of four of our Handy Two-Way Ten-Brick Size Machines. With our Handy Two-Way Ten-Brick Size Machine, you can fill an order for any quality, faced or common brick and ornamental design brick also, and your investment will be in but one machine which will cost you less than one-half the price asked by the others for one way principle machines.

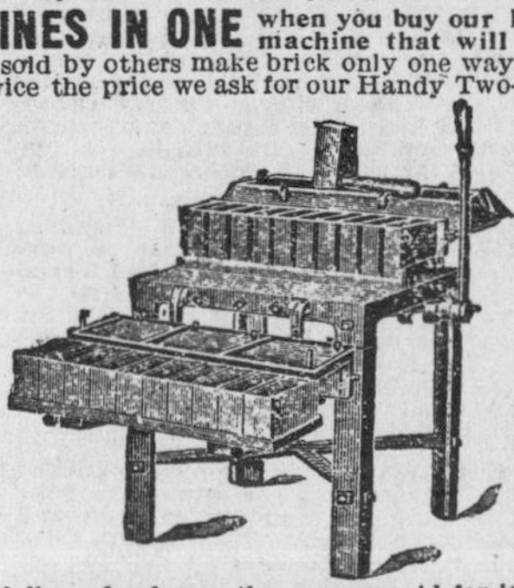

THE QUALITY AND FINISH of our Handy Two-Way Ten-Brick Size Machine is of the very best. Every part that comes in contact with the forming of the brick is machine planed and milled; every piece of steel used for the division plates and ends are of the best quality steel known, and they are ground by high speed grinders to exact dimensions and are polished to a high finish, so that they deliver the brick smoothly and with a finish like that of pressed brick. Our Handy Two-Way Ten-Brick Size Machine is put together by the best mechanics obtainable, and every partition and form that goes to shape a brick is exact in dimensions, so that when the ten concrete bricks are delivered from the machine they are all of uniform and standard size and the edges are sharp and solid.

THE SAME GUARANTEE is given with every one of our Handy Two-Way Ten-Brick Size Machines as is given with our concrete block machine. If it is not as described by us and you are not satisfied after ten days' trial, you may return it to us and we will cheerfully refund you the money paid for it, together with the transportation charges.

THE OUTFIT CONSISTS of one of our Handy Two-Way Ten-Brick Size Machines, one hopper, one mallet, one float, one steel striker and two sample wood pallets. Shipped from the factory in Central Wisconsin.

No. 32K5890 Handy Brick Machine, complete with regular outfit. Shipping weight, 440 pounds. Price $57.25

No. 32K5891 Special Ornamental Face Plates. Weight, 2 pounds. Price, each, per brick .... .45

WASHING MACHINES

WHY WE SELL MORE WASHING MACHINES THAN ANY OTHER HOUSE IN THE UNITED STATES

FIRST: Every machine we offer is sold on its merits. We give you six months' free trial to test what our machines will do for you. We have improved the quality from time to time and have done more to perfect washing machines than any other concern in the country.

SECOND: We sell our machines for just actual manufacturer's cost, plus our one small percentage of profit, saving you all the handling expenses and profits of agents and dealers. We save you from one-third to one-half the price and guarantee to furnish the best machines made.

THIRD: We offer you a large line to select from at a wide range of prices meeting the requirements of everybody.

FOURTH: We guarantee to satisfy you in every way with any machine we sell you, or you may return it to us and we will refund to you both the price and any transportation charges you paid.

WE GIVE A FIVE-YEAR GUARANTEE **on our Mississippi, our Superba, our Wizard and our Royal Washing Machines.** On all the other washing machines we sell we give a guarantee of **one year.** By the terms of this guarantee we will **replace, free of charge,** any piece or part of our Mississippi, Superba, Wizard or Royal Washing Machines that gives out by reason of any defect in material or workmanship within a period of five years from date of purchase; or, in the case of our other washing machines, we will replace any piece or part that gives out by reason of any defect in material or workmanship within a period of one year from date of purchase. Our system of rigid inspection at the factory prevents imperfect material or workmanship from getting into our machines, and they are of such high grade throughout that they will, with ordinary care, last a lifetime.

YOU GET SIX MONTHS' FREE TRIAL **to test our washing machines.** Whether you mention it in your order or not, we will ship you the washing machine you select from our catalogue with the understanding that you are to have six months' free trial. By this liberal plan you may select any washing machine we offer, write down the catalogue number in your order, enclose our price, send us your order, and we will ship the machine with the understanding that you may take it home, test it and try it out, and compare it with any other machine on the market, and if within six months you should conclude that you have not gotten by all means the best machine for quality, material and value that you could possibly get, and if you don't think you have made the best investment possible as compared with any other investment you could make in washing machines of other makes, you are at perfect liberty to return the machine at our expense and we will refund to you both the price and any transportation charges you paid.

$6.38 OUR SUPERBA BALL BEARING WASHING MACHINE

If you want the very best and the highest grade reciprocating or swing washing machine made in the world, a machine which combines every good feature of all other swing washing machines with many special patented features owned and controlled by us and not to be found on any other washing machine made, if you want a swing washing machine that will do a big washing quicker and better than any other swing washing machine no matter what its name, make or price, and a machine which runs so easily as to require almost no effort at all, by all means send us $6.38 and order our Superba Ball Bearing Machine as illustrated and described on this and on opposite page.

THIS IS ABSOLUTELY THE BEST MACHINE

of the reciprocating or swing washing machine type that we have ever offered you. While those who have **bought our machines heretofore are perfectly satisfied with them and claim that we have sold them the best machines they have ever seen for the money,** while our Mississippi and Superba Machines and others we have offered in the past were the best machines in quality, material and workmanship and efficiency that were ever put upon the market, and while one would think it would be hard to find any room for improvement in the machines we have been selling, yet we were not satisfied to let it rest at that, but we have been constantly seeking to **make still further improvements.** We have made many improvements by testing and trying new features, and have been able to bring our washing machines for this season up to a still higher grade of efficiency than ever before. Every machine in this line is the best of its kind that we or any manufacturer has produced, but **our Superba Ball Bearing, our easy running wonder, described on this and the opposite page, represents the perfection of washing machine manufacturing in this type of machines.** Nothing would please us more than to have you compare our Superba Ball Bearing, easy running wonder with the highest class machines of this type made by others at any price, and we know that your judgment will be in our favor. **Don't pay $12.00 to $15.00 for a washing machine. You simply throw money away if you do. $6.38 is all you need to pay for the best swing washing machine made.**

OUR PATENTED FEATURES **make it possible for you to wash anything in the Superba which can be washed in any washer, a claim which cannot be made for any other reciprocating washing machine offered by others even at $12.00 to $15.00.** Heavy blankets, rugs, comforters, carpets, mechanics' blouses and overalls, men's working clothes of all kinds pass through this machine with ease, and yet the Ball Bearing Superba is so scientific in construction that the most delicate fabrics, even rare laces and delicate curtains are thoroughly cleansed without the slightest injury to the materials.

SEE THE ILLUSTRATION **showing the interior construction. On the bottom of both the tub and the rubber are secured hardwood cleats which radiate from the center.** The rubber is perforated to permit free circulation of the hot soapy water. The clothes are thrown into the machine and the rubber set down over them. As you swing the tub in one direction the rubber revolves in the opposite direction and gently agitates the clothes, so that every thread of them is subjected to the powerful currents of boiling water created by the peculiar motion of the tub and the agitator. Back and forth the tub swings. At every swing these great boiling currents are forced through the clothes again and again, hundreds of times. The centrifugal force, generated by the rotary motion of the machine, throws the cleansing currents of boiling water to the outside, and when the reverse movement occurs it is thrown back to the center on the top of the agitator whence it is drawn down through the holes and forced through and through the clothes, carrying all the dirt with it. In five to eight minutes the tubful of clothes is washed to snowy cleanliness.

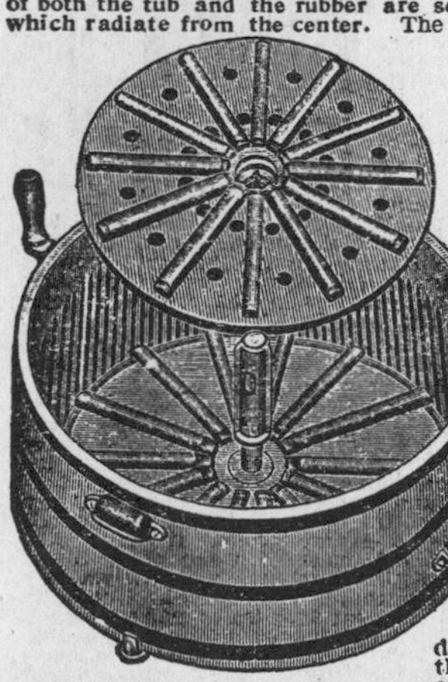

SIX MONTHS' FREE TRIAL. **Send us your order enclosing our $6.38 price and we will send the Superba Ball Bearing Machine** to you with the understanding that you may use it a full six months if you wish before deciding whether or not you will keep it. Use it once or twice a week, or every day if you wish, use it for washing everything and anything that you find necessary to send through the laundry, and after you have used it six months, after you have subjected it to every trial and test that you wish, if you then feel that you are willing to return to the old way of washing clothes by hand, or if you feel after this six months' use of the Superba that you would rather have any other washing machine you ever saw, or that the Superba is not all we represent it to be, just return the machine to us at our expense, and we will refund your money and pay the transportation charges both ways. Thousands of these machines have been sold under these conditions, thousands of pleased customers testify to their high quality and their wonderful value as the best reciprocating washing machine in the world.

WE WANT YOU TO FEEL **absolutely free to take advantage of this free trial offer.** You need not have the slightest hesitancy, because, whether or not you say in your order that you want to try it, you have this privilege. We make this **Free Trial Proposition** in good faith and if for any reason you are dissatisfied after six months' use of the machine simply send it back and get your money.

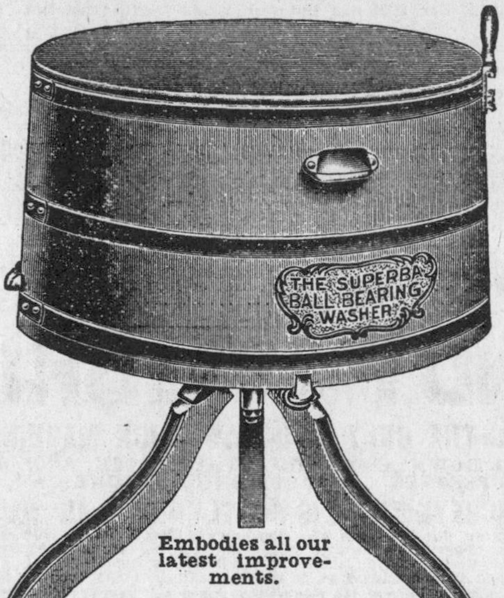

Embodies all our latest improvements.

PATENTED.

THE EASY RUNNING WONDER.

BUY A SUPERBA WASHER

AND GET AWAY FROM THE BACK BREAKING AND SPIRIT BREAKING WASHDAY.

GET AWAY FROM THE WASHDAY SLAVERY. **Do your washing in an hour or so in the morning and have the rest of the day to devote to other things.** Make Monday the easiest day of the week, instead of the hardest. Remember that the Superba Washer will pay for itself in a few months in the wear and tear of the washboard rubbing it saves. It does not rub the clothes to pieces as you do on the washboard. It does not drag the clothes through the water; it cleanses by forcing the boiling water through the clothes and not by dragging the clothes through the water. It is built upon an entirely new principle and is the best thing you ever saw for washing clothes. We want you to order a washing machine today, we want you to give it six months' trial, to compare it with any washing machine you have used or is used by anyone in your neighborhood, and if at the end of that time you are not convinced that it is the greatest boon for womankind that has ever been put on the market, you can return it to us at our expense and we will refund your money. Shipped from the factory in Southern Michigan.

THE BOTTOM VIEW OF THE TUB, **shows the gearing, the steel motor springs, the anti-friction ball bearings and the brake which holds the tub stationary when wringing out the clothes.** Note the simplicity of the construction. There are no heavy fly wheels. No complicated gearing in which to catch and mutilate the fingers. Nothing to get out of order. The tub is carried on a steel pivot and rests on anti-friction ball bearings, making the strongest and simplest washing machine movement ever manufactured. The top of the tub is so constructed that a wringer can be attached at any point. The tub is steam tight. There are no foul, steamy odors from the soiled clothes to endanger the health of the user. No sloppy floors nor wet garments. The heat and steam are retained in the tub, as they should be and are not permitted to escape.

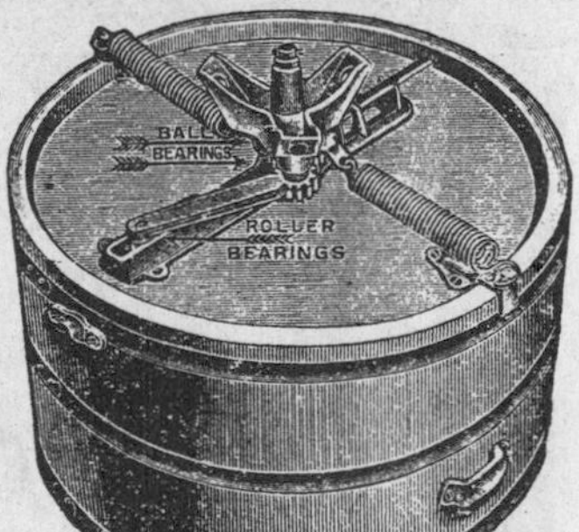

HARDENED STEEL BALL BEARINGS **running in tempered steel cones, support the entire weight of our Superba tub and its contents. These ball bearings are almost frictionless, and our Superba Washer revolves with the slightest touch.** A little child can run it just as well as a strong woman, and do the washing just as well. You can run it just as easily setting in a chair as standing. You can run it fast or slow, just as you like. No matter how you run it, it washes the clothes more quickly, more perfectly than any other machine. It is equipped with two powerful steel motor springs. These are mounted underneath the tub, out of the way, and do almost all the work of swinging the tub, requiring just a little help from you at each swing. You swing the tub on its ball bearings about one-third of a revolution and the steel motor springs underneath reverse the movement and swing the tub in an opposite direction. Back and forth the tub swings on its ball bearings with just a little help from you at each swing, and the washing is done almost before you know it. These motor springs are made from the finest tempered spring steel, and we guarantee that they will never weaken and never break.

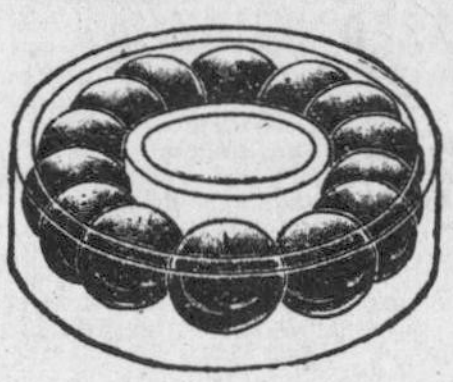

THE MEASUREMENTS **of the Superba Washing Machine are as follows:** The height from the floor to the top of the tub is 31 inches. The tub staves are 14½ inches long and guaranteed to be not less than 13-16 inches thick. The outside diameter of the tub at the top is 23¼ inches and at the bottom it is 25¼ inches. Formerly we made this machine with the large end of the tub up, but we have changed the construction and are now building the machine with the large end of the tub down so as to give greater water capacity and make the machine more efficient. On our Superba as well as on all our other round tub washing machines, we furnish larger and better made tubs, tubs with thicker staves and of better quality throughout than will be found on washing machines of other makes.

CONTINUED ON OPPOSITE PAGE.

$6⁻³⁸ OUR SUPERBA BALL BEARING WASHING MACHINE

THE EASY RUNNING WONDER

IF YOU WANT THE EASIEST RUNNING WASHING MACHINE ON THE MARKET; if you want the best made swing washing machine to be found anywhere; if you want a machine that will do more work and do it quicker and with less labor on your part than any other swing washing machine made, you have all your desires fulfilled in our SUPERBA BALL BEARING WASHING MACHINE, fully illustrated and described on this and on the opposite page.

A THOROUGH CLEANSING WASHER

A GREAT CLOTHES and LABOR SAVER.
EVEN A CHILD CAN RUN IT.
GUARANTEED FOR FIVE YEARS AGAINST DEFECTS.

YOU HAVE SIX MONTHS' FREE TRIAL

to test its qualities, and if it does not do exactly as we claim, you may return it and we will refund both the price and any transportation charges you paid.

SEND US YOUR ORDER TODAY.

OUR PRICE REDUCED. BETTER THAN EVER BECAUSE OF IMPROVEMENTS.

Mother goes right on with her regular work while her little helper finds it so easy to swing the Superba to and fro that she is glad to do it. The washing is all done quickly and easily, and washday is no harder day for the family than any other day of the week.

DON'T PAY FROM $12.00 TO $15.00 FOR A WASHING MACHINE

somewhat similar in appearance to our Superba. There are a few reciprocating washing machines which look somewhat like our Superba and which are offered in newspaper and magazine advertisements at prices ranging as high as $15.00, a price which many manufacturers are obtaining for machines which do not begin to compare in any way whatsoever with our Superba Ball Bearing Machine. These similar appearing machines are wholly lacking in the splendid features which are to be found in the Superba; features which make it run easily, do its work more thoroughly and much quicker than others, patented features which are owned and controlled exclusively by us. For instance, no other reciprocating washing machine sold by other makers has the double springs to reverse the motion of the tub and the agitator, or the special ball bearings which make the operation of the machine so easy—all these patented improvements owned by us and to be found only in the Superba Ball Bearing Washer.

OUR GUARANTEE ON THE SUPERBA

IN ADDITION TO GIVING YOU SIX MONTHS' FREE TRIAL,
a full six months in which to use the Superba Ball Bearing Washing Machine to decide whether or not you will keep it; remember, we guarantee this machine not only to wash more clothes and wash them cleaner and wash them in less time than any other reciprocating washing machine made, but

See illustrations and description on opposite page, showing construction of our Superba Easy Running Wonder Washing Machine, showing why it is absolutely the best made and easiest running washing machine on the market, regardless of name, make or price of other machines.

we also guarantee it for five years against all defects in material and workmanship. We give this long term guarantee to protect you against any hidden defect or flaw which may not appear within the six months' trial period and which defect or flaw was not discovered by our factory inspectors, and under the term of this five years' guarantee should any part break because of defect in material or workmanship, we will furnish a new part to take the place of the defective part, absolutely free of charge, at any time within this five-year period.

OUR SIX MONTHS' TRIAL, our liberal guarantee surely ought to convince you of our high opinion of this splendid washing machine, and under these liberal conditions surely you can well afford to send us an order at our $6.38 price. Remember, you do not take the slightest risk, you cannot lose a penny by the transaction if you order the Superba, because it is your privilege to return the machine to us and get your money back if you are dissatisfied after six months' trial, and every defect in material or workmanship developing within five years is protected by our binding guarantee. Just think what it would mean to you if you have never owned a washing machine, or if you have owned one of the old style, hard running, slow cleansing, unsatisfactory washing machines manufactured by others, to own a high grade machine, a Superba Ball Bearing Washer which will easily wash a tubful of dirty clothing in from five to eight minutes if our simple directions are followed. The Superba makes washday so easy that you will regret that you did not take advantage of our free trial offer and liberal terms long ago. If you have been accustomed to spending an entire day in back breaking labor over the washtub, you will find that our Superba Washer will do the same washing in a couple of hours and do it much easier and much better than you could do it in the old way and that after having used this machine once, you would never be satisfied to do without it.

No. 32K7510 Superba Washing Machine. Shipping weight, 75 pounds. Price........ **$6.38**

$7⁻⁶⁸ SUPERBA BALL BEARING COMBINATION WASHING MACHINE

Our Superba Ball Bearing Washer, our Easy Running Wonder combined with basket or tub stand and wringer board is the latest and best. It saves a separate wash bench. Saves taking off and replacing the wringer. It is complete in itself and yet takes up no more room than an ordinary washing machine.

REDUCE YOUR WASHDAY TO HALF or three-quarters of an hour once a week by using the Superba Ball Bearing Combination Washer. It is built the same as our regular Superba Washer, with the same powerful motor springs that do the work for you. The same anti-friction ball bearings which make running the washer a pleasure, it is so easy. The same patented features which wash the clothes with such quickness and to snowy whiteness. All the features which have made our Superba Ball Bearing Washer the biggest selling and most popular washing machine ever put on the market. In addition to this, our Superba Combination Washer is equipped with a folding hardwood bench braced with steel braces making it perfectly rigid and strong. It furnishes a convenient stand for the clothes basket or rinsing tub, and a strong and solid support for the wringer. The stand is made of selected materials, it is very substantial in construction, thoroughly braced and handsomely finished. This Combination Washing Machine is shipped from the factory in Southern Michigan.

No. 32K7515 Superba Combination Washing Machine. Shipping weight, 105 pounds. Price **$7.68**

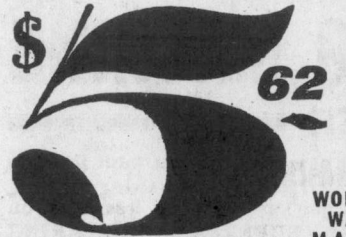

$5.62 GENUINE MISSISSIPPI WASHING MACHINE

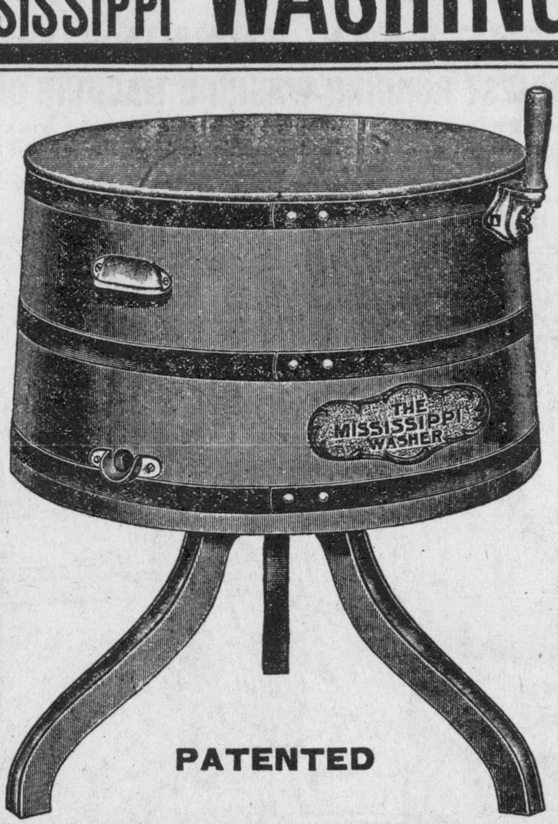

PATENTED

THIS WONDERFUL WASHING MACHINE, sold at a price but little more than the old style washtub and washboard cost, will be a revelation to any other woman. It washes anything and does it better than any reciprocating washing machine ever invented with the single exception of our Superba described on the next page. Delicate lace, heavy carpets, rugs, horse blankets, bed clothing, all go through this machine, and are cleansed as thoroughly as ordinary wearing apparel. No matter what may be in the tub, or whether the quantity be large or small, it makes no difference, it does not affect the easy work of the operator. The Mississippi washer cleanses by really forcing the cleansing currents of hot, soapy water through every thread and fiber of the clothes by constantly and gently stirring them with an easy rolling motion, so that every garment is subjected to a perfect cataract of boiling water. The Mississippi does not drag the clothes, but instead, it gently stirs them and forces the powerful cleansing currents back and forth and through every fiber with every swing of the tub. In the Mississippi the water does the washing, there being no dragging or pulling about. The tub swings on a steel pivot, running in oil on a hardened bearing. The marvelous motor spring does nine-tenths of the work, and so easily and so simply is it operated, whether it be empty or full of clothes, that a child can start it by grasping the operating handle and drawing it to one side. As the tub swings around about one-third of a revolution, the heavy steel motor spring underneath reverses the movement and swings the tub in the opposite direction. Back and forth the tub swings on its steel bearing, with just a little help from you at each swing, and so easily is it operated, that you can sit in a chair and do the washing as easily as if you were standing.

THE MISSISSIPPI is a triple motion, reciprocating and oscillating washing machine. The hardened steel pivot on which the tub is mounted, is a little to one side of the center, which gives the tub an oscillating movement in addition to the reciprocating action. A steel roller, operating in a slot, conveys the motion to the agitator which moves in the opposite direction inside the tub, giving the machine three separate and distinct motions. As the tub swings one way, the agitator inside the tub turns in the opposite direction, and this compound motion, in combination with the oscillating motion of the tub and the quick reverse movement, creates powerful cleansing currents of boiling water which, by centrifugal force and suction, are forced through and through every thread and fiber of the clothes at each swing of the tub, cleansing them with three times the rapidity, cleansing them with one-third of the labor of the old way of washing, cleansing them more thoroughly than any other way, and doing it with almost no labor at all. The Mississippi will wash a big tubful of dirty clothes in from five to ten minutes easily and do it better than could be done by hand. It does not pull off buttons, nor tear any clothes; it does not wear them out by rubbing them over hard, rough surfaces, but it simply washes the dirt out of them quicker and more thoroughly than they can be washed by any other known method.

NO LABOR SAVING DEVICE KNOWN that is offered the housewife can compare with the Mississippi Washer in labor saving, time saving and clothes saving. If you buy the Mississippi Washer in accordance with our liberal free trial offer, it will end the drudgery of washday, it will simplify the labor of housekeeping, it will so economize your time that hours which you now devote to washing may be more profitably and more pleasantly employed. The Mississippi will make you a free woman.

GUARANTEED FIVE YEARS. We guarantee every Mississippi Washing Machine for five years, guaranteeing every piece and part that enters into the construction, guaranteeing its action and operation, guaranteeing everything about it absolutely perfect for five years with our binding guarantee, and if any piece or part gives out within five years by reason of defect in materials or workmanship, we will replace it free of charge; the longest, strongest, most binding guarantee ever given on a washing machine and shows the confidence we have in the Mississippi and what a wonderful washer, what a marvelous money saving, time saving and labor saving machine it really is.

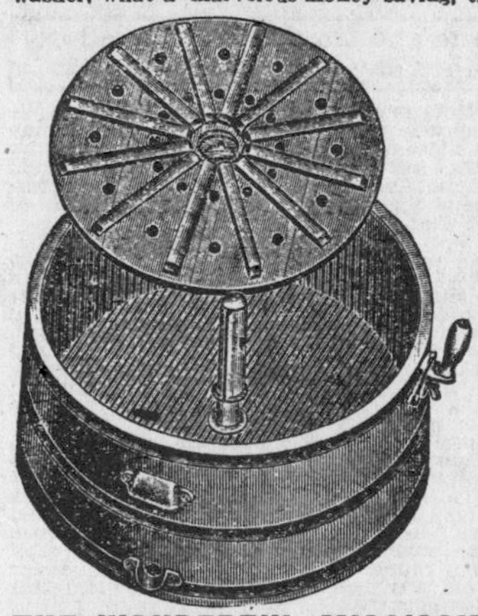

BUSY HOUSEWIFE, DON'T TOIL and sweat any more over the washtub. Don't give up all of Monday morning to the weekly washing, don't worry along with any of the out of date washing machines, don't wear yourself out bending over the old style washboard and rubbing the clothes until you almost wear them out also, don't spend two hours over a hot, steaming, unhealthful tub, when with the Mississippi you can do the whole washing in fifteen minutes; with the Mississippi you can do it better than ever before, in less than one-tenth the time, with almost no work at all. No other washing machine will do for you what the Mississippi will.

LET THE MISSISSIPPI DO YOUR WORK. Why worry along in the old way when the Mississippi will do the work, with no wear on the clothes, so much time saved and at such small expense? Figure it out for yourself. $5.62 is our low price for the Mississippi, a price that barely covers cost of material and labor with our one small profit added. The machine will wear for many years (we guarantee it perfect for five years). Suppose it costs you $5.62 for five years, 260 weekly washings. About 2 cents a week is all it costs, and just consider the convenience, the saving in time, labor and money—all at a cost of 2 cents a week!

THE WONDERFUL MISSISSIPPI WASHER is the new, easy way of washing clothes. This wonderful invention makes blue Monday a thing of the past, turns the sighs and groans of washday into smiles of delight and pleasure. It makes washday easy, washes a whole tubful of clothes in about the same time that a single garment can be washed on a washboard in the old way and with almost no work at all. It runs so easy that a little girl, eight or nine years old, can run it as easily as a grown person. In fact, it almost runs itself. Best of all, it washes the clothes to snowy whiteness without rubbing or wearing. It doesn't tear off buttons, doesn't fray the edges. Washes heavy rugs and blankets just as easily as handkerchiefs and napkins. It doesn't let the foul steam escape and doesn't slop the floor. It is an entirely new invention and operates on a new principle, washing clothes, not by dragging them back and forth through the water, but by forcing the boiling suds through and through every mesh and fiber of the clothes in a perfect cataract. By doing away with all the wear and tear of hand rubbing and of dragging back and forth through the water, it makes the clothes last more than twice as long, as they get more wear in one washing in the old hard way than in several weeks' use. Our Mississippi is so much easier to operate than any other washer offered by others, so much easier than using a washboard, washes so clean and does it so quickly that it makes washday a day to look forward to with pleasure.

OUR VERY LIBERAL TERMS

The Mississippi Washing Machine is such a remarkable value at our $5.62 price, it is so far in advance of any other washing machine offered by any other firm or individual, that we are perfectly willing to send it to you on the most liberal conditions. Send us your order, inclosing our $5.62 price, and we will immediately ship this washing machine to you with the distinct understanding and agreement that it must prove absolutely satisfactory to you in every way, it must be just as represented and such a washing machine as will give you absolute satisfaction in every respect. If, however, for any reason you are not satisfied that it is wonderful value at our price, and a better machine than you can get from others even at a much higher price, you may return the machine to us at our expense at any time within six months, and we will immediately refund your money.

YOU HAVE A FULL SIX MONTHS' TRIAL, during which time you can put the Mississippi to any test, compare it with any $10.00 to $15.00 washer sold by any other concern, and if the Mississippi does not wash the clothes cleaner with less wear and tear and do it in one-half the time and with almost no work at all, you can return it to us at our expense at any time during the six months and we will immediately refund your money.

THE MISSISSIPPI is worth five times as much as machines that are being sold at double our special $5.62 price. It is a wonderful and thoroughly well made machine. The tub is generously large, built with large end down, so you have the most room just where you need it, built throughout of selected Louisiana cypress, which grows in the southern swamps, and which will resist the action of water, acids and chemicals better than any other wood known to man. The tub of the Mississippi Washer is steamtight and watertight, and permits no foul, steamy odors to escape to endanger the health of the housewife. There are no sloppy floors or wet garments, the heat and steam are retained in the tub as they should be, and are not permitted to contaminate the atmosphere as do open washers and tubs. The tub is corrugated on both the sides and the bottom inside, very much like a washboard. These corrugations help to clean the clothes that come in contact with them by gently rubbing them. This rubbing is not the hard, violent kind that they usually get on the washboard, as the clothes are swimming in the boiling water and are only gently stirred by the motion of the agitator and tub. The boiling currents forced through the clothes do practically all the cleaning. A heavy iron brace is fastened securely to the bottom of the tub on the outside, which prevents any tendency of the bottom of the tub to warp. Into this brace is screwed the socket in which the agitator post runs, and as the top is above the water line, a perfect watertight joint is secured. The machine rests upon three heavy hardwood legs securely bolted to heavy iron sockets, and will stand steady on any floor, no matter how uneven.

IT IS FINISHED throughout in a handsome manner. All screws, nails and iron parts inside the tub are heavily galvanized or tinned, making rust spots on the clothes impossible. The agitator or rubber sets down upon the center post which passes up through the bottom of the tub and adjusts itself automatically to any quantity of clothes, from a few pieces to a tubful. The motor spring is made from the finest spring steel and carefully tempered. It is just the right weight and strength to reverse the motion of the tub and bring it back quickly without offering too much resistence to the swing of the operator; it gives the tub its full sweep, but does not permit it to lag. Thus the spring really does the work. By the ingenious construction of the Mississippi we have a washing machine with double the capacity of other washing machines operated similarly, and four times the capacity of the average washing machine.

THE MEASUREMENTS of the Mississippi Washing Machine are as follows: The height from the floor to the top of the tub is 31 inches. The tub staves are 14½ inches long, and guaranteed to be not less than 13-16 inch thick. The outside diameter of the tub at the top is 23¼ inches, and at the bottom it is 25¼ inches. No other washing machine has a larger, stronger or better made tub, and very few are made with staves as thick as we use. The top of the tub is so constructed that a wringer can be attached at any point, and there is a locking device under the tub which holds the tub stationary.

IT IS A MACHINE THAT MUST BE SEEN, examined and compared with other washing machines to appreciate its real value. It is the most economical machine made in the consumption of soap, and it will save our special price, $5.62, in the consumption of soap alone in two years. It is the greatest labor saver ever invented, and will save our special price, $5.62, in the amount of labor required in just a few weeks. It does better washing than any other machine made, and will save the price, $5.62 in the better appearance of the work done in a very short time. It wears clothes the least of any machine made, and will save our special $5.62 price in a few months in saving of wear on clothing. It is the most wonderful washing machine invention on the market, the only machine with our new patent double reciprocating cross current action that makes washing easy, simple, quick, thorough, double the capacity of any other machine made, and with our spring motor—a spring doing almost all of the labor—a child can operate it easily—in short, a machine which outclasses any other reciprocating washer made, with the single exception of the Superba illustrated and described on the next page.

SEE THE ILLUSTRATION, which shows you all the gearing there is to the Mississippi. Notice that there are no complicated cog wheels, no heavy fly wheels (the tub itself is the fly wheel), notice the heavy iron brace that strengthens the bottom and prevents it warping, and at the same time forms a strong solid foundation for the center post. The powerful steel spring, which is one of the main features of the Mississippi, is also shown. We guarantee it never to break or weaken. This motor spring really does almost all the work of swinging the tub and requires just a little help from you at each swing.

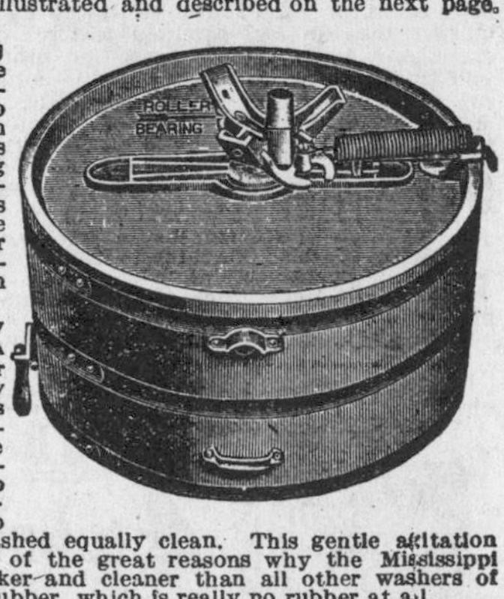

NOTE THE SIMPLE CRANK, with its steel roller bearing at the only point where there is any friction, operating in a slot in the frame, giving the reverse movement to the rubber that gently stirs the clothes, so that all parts are washed equally clean. This gentle agitation of the clothes is one of the great reasons why the Mississippi washes so much quicker and cleaner than all other washers of this pattern, which are made with a stationary rubber, which is really no rubber at all.

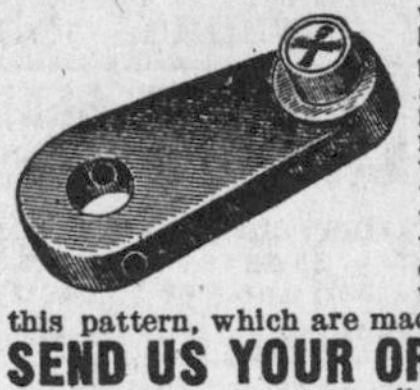

SEND US YOUR ORDER TODAY and let us send you this fine machine. We guarantee every Mississippi Washing Machine for five years against all defects in material and workmanship, and guarantee that it will reach you safely. The Mississippi has pleased and delighted thousands of others and it will surely satisfy you. Shipped from the factories in Western New York and Southern Michigan.

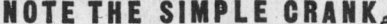

No. 32K7505 Mississippi Washing Machine. Shipping weight, 70 pounds. Price....**$5.62**

$2.98 NEW ELECTRIC WASHING MACHINE

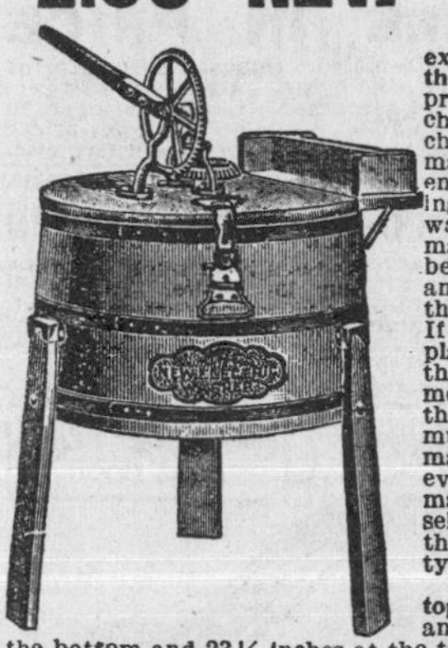

The round tub lever rotary washing machine has been extremely popular for many years and thousands upon thousands of them have been sold. It was with a view to improving the design and quality of this style of washing machine that we have produced this New Electric Washing Machine which we offer at $2.98. It is somewhat similar to the machine we have heretofore sold as the "American," but it is entirely different in construction from any lever rotary washing machine we have sold in the past, or from any lever rotary washing machine that is sold by any other dealer, whether mail order house or local retailer. The only similarity between this machine and others of this type is in the lever and gearing mechanism by which the machine is operated, the brackets for the gearing and the dolly within the tub. If you could see this New Electric Washing Machine and place it beside others of this type which have been sold in the past, and which are now offered by other dealers at much more that our $2.98 price, you would see at a glance that there is no comparison between them because ours is of so much better proportions, it is built of so much better materials with better finish, better fitted, it shows every evidence of superior workmanship and the highest class materials are used in its construction; so that even were we to sell this improved New Electric Washing Machine at double the price asked by others for inferior machines of this type, you would gladly pay our price and take our machine.

The New Electric stands 29 inches from the floor to the top of the tub, the staves of the tub are 14½ inches long and 13-16-inch thick, the tub is 25¼ inches in diameter at the bottom and 23¼ inches at the top. The inside of the tub is finished corrugated, as is the interior of the tubs of the Empress and Wizard described elsewhere in these pages. We use heavy legs on this machine. They are 3½ inches wide, supported at the upper edge by an iron bracket and bolted to the tub at the lower end of the staves. The tub handles, the top hasps, the hinges for the top, and the braces for the wringer board are all manufactured from pressed steel. The tub is handsomely painted in brilliant carmine, with black hoops, all given a coat of high quality varnish and it presents a very handsome appearance. The top of the machine, the wringer board and the legs are finished in the natural wood with a coat of good varnish. The leg brackets, the gearing and all iron trimmings are finished in aluminum bronze.

At our $2.98 price we put more value in this machine than any other manufacturer or dealer can possibly offer in a machine of this type, and if you want the best washing machine of the lever rotary type with round tub, a machine which we guarantee to give satisfaction and which, because of its thorough construction and high class materials, will give most satisfactory service, by all means send us your order for this, our New Electric. Shipped from the factory in Southern Michigan.

No. 32K7528 New Electric Washing Machine. Shipping weight, 65 pounds. Price........ **$2.98**

$3.12 SCOTT'S WESTERN WASHING MACHINE

No. 3 Size. Extra Large.

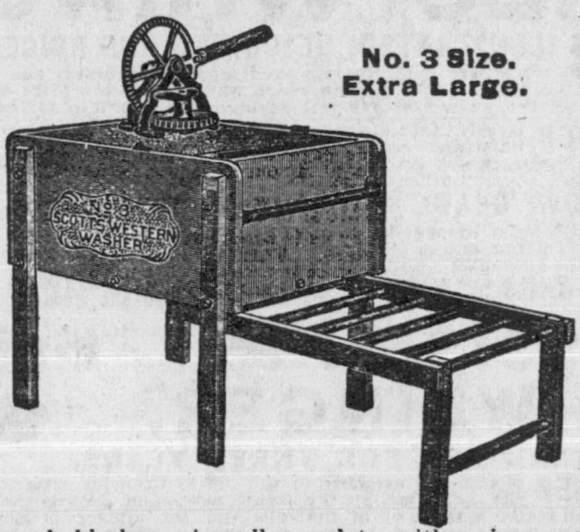

This is the standard square tub, lever washing machine extremely well known and very much in demand, especially in the southern states. This machine is manufactured expressly for us in our big factory which is equipped with the very highest grade special machinery for the production of washing machine parts and the construction of the highest grade washing machines of the several styles illustrated and described in these pages, and we can say without fear of successful contradiction that in this machine which we offer at $3.12 we are giving you greater value than has ever been offered in a washer of this style. We build it in the one size, the No. 3 size, which is extra large, and we send it to you at this remarkably low price, all complete with wringer compartment and basket or tub stand just as shown in the illustration. This machine stands 29 inches from the floor to the top of the tub; the tub sides are 13 inches high 13-16-inch thick, and the tub measures 20½ inches wide, and 26 inches long outside. All the gearing and gear brackets are finished in aluminum bronze, and the entire machine is tastefully painted, ornamented and varnished. If you desire a washing machine of this type and the very best value you can get for the money, a machine exceptionally well built from the very best materials, a machine which has been inspected at the factory and which goes to you as a guaranteed washer, by all means send us your order, enclosing our $3.12 price, and we will send it to you from the factory in Southern Michigan, guaranteeing that it will please you.

No. 32K7529 Scott's Western Washing Machine. Shipping weight, 75 pounds. Price........ **$3.12**

$1.93 QUICK AND EASY WASHING MACHINE

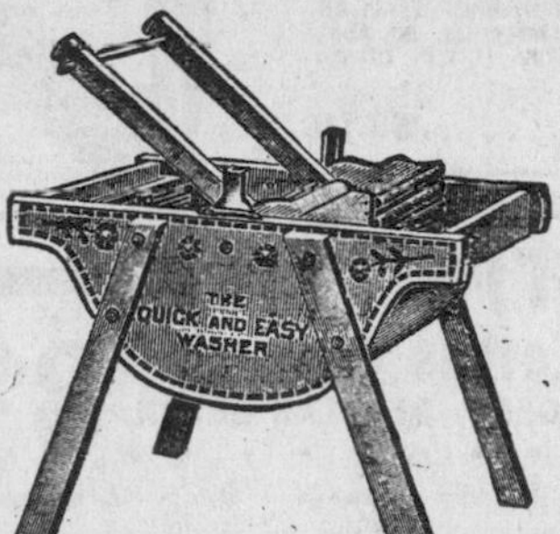

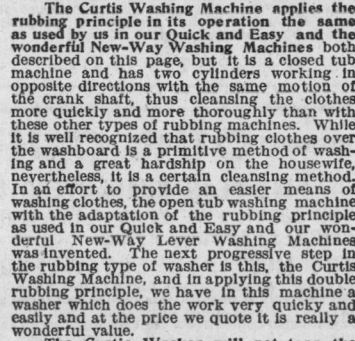

Our ability to give exceptional value in washing machines, to supply your wants in any style washing machine which have proven satisfactory in the hands of the user, could not be better proven than in this Quick and Easy Washing Machine which we offer you at $1.93. The Quick and Easy Washing Machine is a very high class, open tub washer, a much better machine, made from better materials than the machine of this type sold by anyone else. Its wood sides and ends are 13-16-inch thick and it has a galvanized sheet steel bottom. It has a better bottom rub board and a better made rubber than will be found in other machines of this type and it is finished throughout in an attractive manner. The cleats on the bottom rub board and on the swinging rubber are carefully rounded and are guaranteed not to injure any fabric washed in this machine. It stands 24 inches high from the floor to the top of the tub, and the tub measures 13 inches deep in the center, 20 inches wide outside and 31 inches long outside the end pieces, and it is provided with a wringer compartment. The machine is handsomely painted, ornamented and varnished, the legs being finished in natural wood.

For a very low cost washer and yet one which washes the clothes by the recognized principle of rubbing them, a machine which will handle the very dirtiest garments and cleanse them perfectly, we can recommend this machine; but before you order we would like to call your attention to our wonderful "NEW-WAY" Lever Washing Machine, illustrated and described on this page, in which the same principle is applied, though its method of operation has been improved upon, making it easier to operate and a much more convenient machine. However, if the Quick and Easy machine will serve your purpose, if you want an open tub washer of strictly first class construction, and better than any machine of this type offered by any other firm or individual at home or elsewhere and sold at a very low price, by all means order the Quick and Easy Washer at our $1.93 price. It is shipped from the factory in Southern Michigan.

No. 32K7530 Quick and Easy Washing Machine. Shipping weight, 45 pounds. Price........ **$1.93**

$4.93 IMPROVED CURTIS WASHING MACHINE

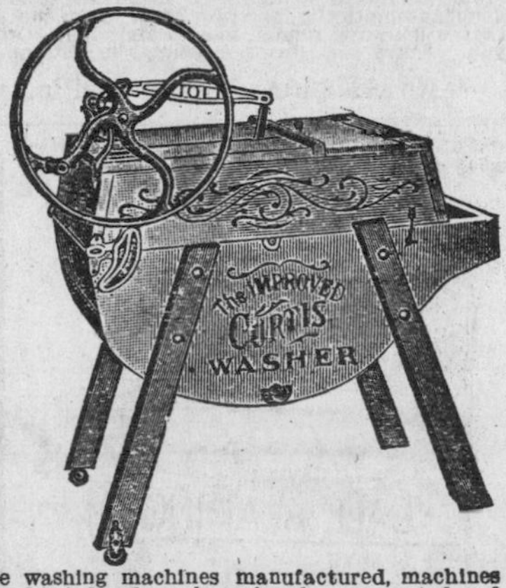

The Curtis Washing Machine applies the rubbing principle in its operation the same as used by us in our Quick and Easy and the wonderful New-Way Washing Machines both described on this page, but it is a closed tub machine and has two cylinders working in opposite directions with the same motion of the crank shaft, thus cleansing the clothes more quickly and more thoroughly than with these other types of rubbing machines. While it is well recognized that rubbing clothes over the washboard is a primitive method of washing and a great hardship on the housewife, nevertheless, it is a certain cleansing method. In an effort to provide an easier means of washing clothes, the open tub washing machine with the adaptation of the rubbing principle as used in our Quick and Easy and our wonderful New-Way Lever Washing Machines was invented. The next progressive step in the rubbing type of washer is this, the Curtis Washing Machine, and in applying this double rubbing principle, we have in this machine a washer which does the work very quicky and easily and at the price we quote it is really a wonderful value.

The Curtis Washer will not tear the clothes, and on account of the balance wheel, the machine will work so easily that a child can operate it. This machine is made of selected Louisiana cypress, the exact same materials as are used in the very highest grade washing machines manufactured, machines which sell at $10.00 to $15.00 and $20.00; and it is handsomely painted, ornamented and varnished. The balance wheel is painted, and all iron work and trimmings throughout are finished in gold bronze. This machine stands 33 inches high from the floor to the top of the tub cover, it measures 19½ inches wide outside, 29 inches from the back of the machine to the wringer compartment, and including the wringer compartment is 34 inches long. The tub is 13½ inches deep at the center and the top has a depth of 7 inches. The bottom is made of heavy, non-rusting, galvanized iron, and all the iron parts coming in contact with the water are heavily tinned or galvanized to prevent rusting.

This is the highest type of rubbing machine now on the market, and we will be very glad to receive your order and ship the machine to you with the understanding and agreement that it must prove entirely satisfactory to you, must be better value than you can secure anywhere else in a machine of this type or it may be returned to us at our expense of transportation charges both ways and we will refund your money. This machine is shipped from factories in Western New York and Southern Michigan.

No. 32K7535 Improved Curtis Washing Machine. Shipping weight, 100 pounds. Price........ **$4.93**

$3.48 WONDERFUL "NEW-WAY" LEVER WASHING MACHINE

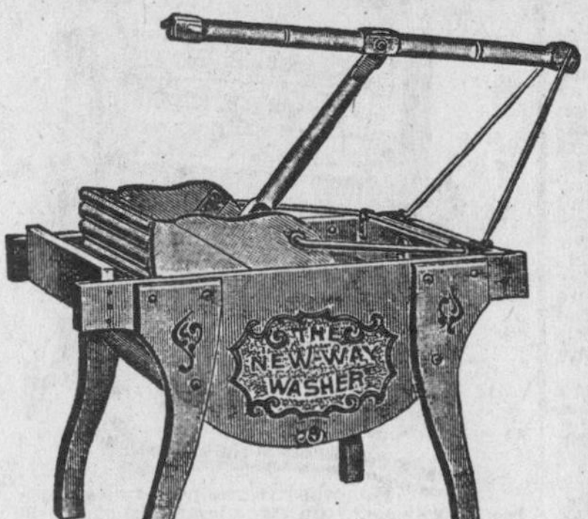

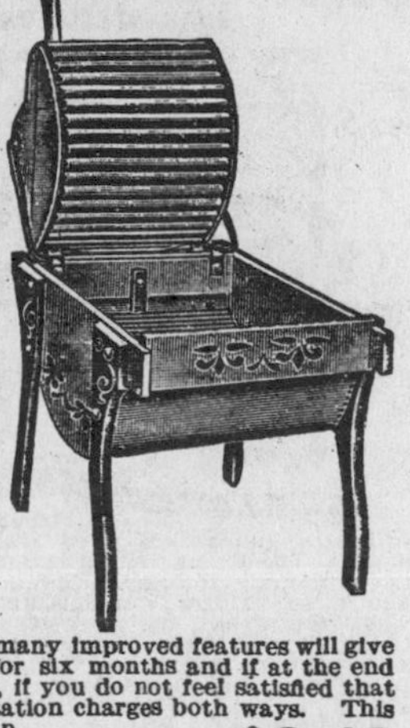

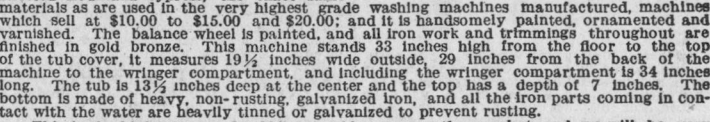

This wonderful New-Way Lever Washing Machine is a vast improvement over the ordinary open tub washing machine, and though it is somewhat similar in general appearance and washes on the same principle as our Quick and Easy machine described above, it has many improved features which make it the very highest grade and most efficient open tub washing machine built on the rub board principle. In the ordinary style of open tub washing machine the weight of the rubber alone, in addition to the rocking motion, must be depended upon to cleanse the clothes. Where very heavy and very dirty garments are placed in the tub it requires much more work and more time and exertion to complete the washing in the ordinary open tub style machine than it does in this new, improved New-Way Lever Washing Machine, and if you will glance at the illustrations you will notice that by an ingenious arrangement of levers it is possible to obtain wonderful power, and the heaviest and dirtiest garments may be sent through this machine with ease. The rubber is operated by a lever which is hinged by a bale connection to one end of the tub and connected at its center with the center post of the swinging rubber (please see the illustration to the left). The weight of the rubber and lever connections is sufficient in the washing of light clothes, laces, etc., but the instant heavy clothes are put into the tub requiring more pressure, the adaptation of the lever principle in this washing machine enables the operator with very little exertion to bring almost any pressure to bear which may be necessary in the washing of blankets, heavy work clothing, etc. By the arrangement of bale and levers, when the washing is completed, the rubber may be quickly lifted up and back out of the way, giving easy access to the tub, and when it is in this position (as shown in the illustration to the right) the drippings fall directly back into the tub so that when you use the New-Way Lever Washing Machine there is no need of having wet and sloppy floors. The corrugated bottom of the tub and the corresponding corrugations on the rocking rubber are carefully rounded and will not injure the finest garment. The machine stands 24 inches high from the floor to the top of the tub; the tub sides and ends are made of 13-16-inch lumber, and the tub bottom is made of heavily galvanized sheet steel. The tub measures 20 inches wide, and is 31 inches long outside the end pieces, and is provided with a wringer compartment. The machine is very handsomely painted, ornamented and varnished; all iron work being heavily galvanized or coated with aluminum bronze.

You can have a six months' free trial of this washing machine and if you want the best open tub style washing machine, one that is very carefully built, with first class materials used throughout, send us $3.48 and let us ship you this wonderful New-Way Lever Washing Machine according to our liberal terms as explained on page 582. This is a machine which we can recommend to our customers who desire the open tub style of washer, and while it costs more than the ordinary open tub washer, if you have a medium or large washing to do each week, and if you have heavy garments to wash, you will find this New-Way Lever Washing Machine with its many improved features will give you such ample satisfaction that you can well afford to pay the slightly higher price. If you send us your order at our $3.48 price you can use the machine for six months and if at the end of that period you are not fully satisfied to keep the machine as the very best open tub rub board style washer that you can get, no matter what the price, if you do not feel satisfied that it is strictly the highest grade machine of this type you know of, you may return it to us at our expense and we will refund your money and pay the transportation charges both ways. This machine is securely crated, with legs placed within the tub and handle detached and folded on top, and is shipped direct from the factory in Southern Michigan.

No. 32K7540 New Way Lever Washing Machine. Shipping weight, 55 pounds. Price........ **$3.48**

CLOTHES WRINGERS

UNEXCELLED IN QUALITY UNMATCHABLE IN PRICE

THE CLOTHES WRINGERS ILLUSTRATED, DESCRIBED AND PRICED on this page make up the finest line and best values ever assembled. Only standard patterns of clothes wringers which we can FULLY GUARANTEE are sold by us. All of our wringers are made in the largest factory in the world, are made by improved modern machinery and skilled workmen, insuring a finished wringer which cannot be surpassed. Clothes wringers of the same pattern as our Protection Ball Bearing Wringer, on which we name the low price of $3.28, are never sold by hardware stores for less than $5.00 to $6.00, while on our lower priced wringers we give you the advantage of the same proportionate saving in price, and in addition guarantee to give you better made and more durable goods than you can get anywhere else.

THE LIFE OF A WRINGER largely depends upon the rolls. Every wringer illustrated on this page is fitted with pure white rubber rolls, immovably fastened to the shaft, and grade for grade our rolls will be found far better and more durable than those sold by any other concern.

WE DO NOT HANDLE LOW GRADE COMPETITION WRINGERS. With the exception of our No. 9K2208, every wringer sold by us is fitted with rolls which are guaranteed by us in ordinary use to last from one to five years. This guarantee means that if a roll gives out within the life of the guarantee we will replace it without cost to you.

OUR WOOD FRAME WRINGERS are made of selected hard maple, heavily coated with waterproof varnish to insure the greatest durability. In our metal frame wringers the frames are made of the best quality materials, thoroughly protected from rust by heavy galvanizing.

WE ARE THE LARGEST DEALERS IN CLOTHES WRINGERS IN THE WORLD. Our immense business on clothes wringers has been built solely on the high quality of our goods in connection with our low prices. We sell absolutely no seconds or inferior grade wringers and we guarantee every wringer we send out, even our cheapest and lowest priced one, to be entirely satisfactory when received. If it is not satisfactory it may be returned to us at our expense and we will return the full purchase price.

All clothes wringers are shipped promptly from stock in Chicago.

THE MISSISSIPPI CLOTHES WRINGER, $3.16

NOTHING ELSE IS AS GOOD.

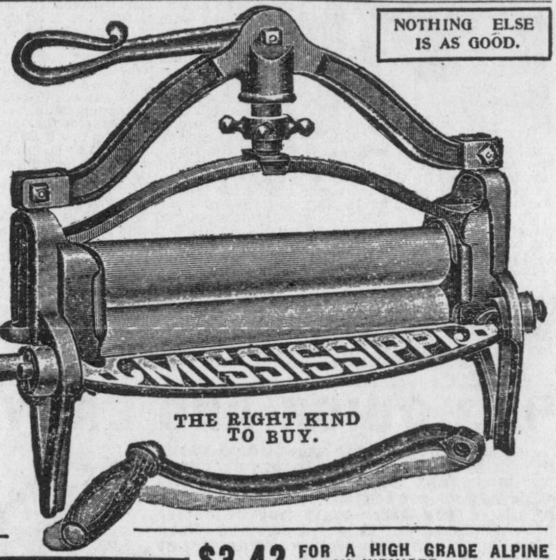

THE RIGHT KIND TO BUY.

GUARANTEED FOR THREE YEARS.

THE MISSISSIPPI WRINGER is instantly attached to the tub by throwing over the top lever, which, at the same time, by the same movement, adjusts the pressure on the rolls. By throwing the lever to one side all strain is taken off of the rolls and the wringer is loosened from the tub in an instant. Reverse the lever and the tub is grasped by the tub clamps, firmly and immovably, at the same time the pressure on the rolls is automatically adjusted. By turning the set screw near the top of the frame it can be adjusted to any pressure on the rolls so as to wring the clothes just as dry as you like them and to any pressure on the tub clamps. Once adjusted it requires no further attention. It is instantly attached and instantly removed.

OUR MISSISSIPPI is the greatest improvement ever made in the manufacture of wringers and has always sold heretofore for $9.00. Our price is $3.16 for this great wringer with all its improvements. The frame is made throughout of the finest annealed malleable iron, and will not break should you drop it on the floor or in any other way misuse it. It is heavily galvanized and will never rust, even after years of use. The pressure spring is of the finest tempered crucible steel and adjusts itself to any unevenness, so that you can wring out goods that are thick at one end and thin at the other and both ends will be equally dry. The cog wheels are enclosed and cannot crush the fingers. The rolls, which are the most important part of a wringer, are made of fine Para rubber; they are soft and elastic, and are fully guaranteed for three years; they are vulcanized immovably onto the shaft and will never twist or become loose. We guarantee these rolls for three years, as should there be any hidden flaw in the rubber it will surely appear within that time, and if it does not you can rest assured that they will last for at least ten or fifteen years in ordinary family use.

OUR MISSISSIPPI WRINGER is extra large family size, with rolls 11x1¾ inches in size. While it is especially adapted for use with our Mississippi Washer, it can be used with any washing machine or with any tub, as the tub clamps are quickly adjusted for any thickness. THE MISSISSIPPI WRINGER WILL BE SURE TO PLEASE YOU. There are no clamps to be tightened in putting it on the tub, no set screws to adjust the pressure on the rolls. It is all done automatically, and best of all, when you are not using the wringer there is no pressure on the rolls, so that they will always remain smooth and round. Order the Mississippi Wringer and we will guarantee that it will please you. Every one is packed securely in a strong wooden box. Shipping weight, 27 pounds.

No. 9K2207 Regular selling price, $9.00; our price....................$3.16

$3.28 PROTECTION BALL BEARING ENCLOSED GEAR WRINGER, GUARANTEED FOR THREE YEARS.

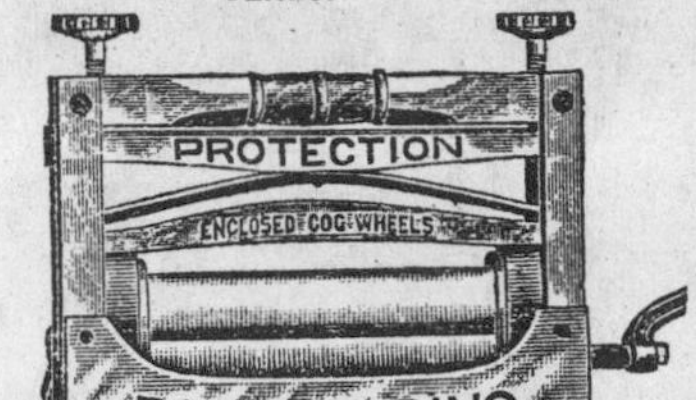

An extra high grade wringer. The rolls are warranted by us for three years and in ordinary household use should last ten years. The enclosed gear wheels are a valuable feature, not only preventing children and others catching and crushing their fingers in the gearing, but also protecting the gear wheels from dirt and wear. Has selected hard maple frame, natural finish, with steel equalizing pressure spring; wheel top screws, combination clamps that fit any wood, galvanized iron or fiber tub. Equipped with our improved ball bearings that make the Protection turn twice as easy as an ordinary wringer. Size of rolls, 10x1¾ inches. Weight, boxed, 26 pounds.

No. 9K2220 Price...........$3.28

$2.37 FOR THIS IMPROVED KEENE WOOD FRAME WRINGER, GUARANTEED FOR ONE YEAR.

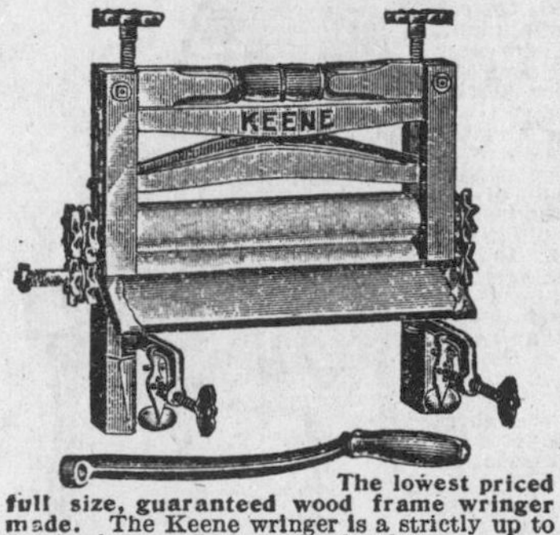

The lowest priced full size, guaranteed wood frame wringer made. The Keene wringer is a strictly up to date wringer. It has all the improvements known to wringer manufacturers. It has wheel top screws, tub screws that will fasten to galvanized iron, fiber or wooden tubs, steel pressure springs and double cog wheels. It is guaranteed for one year. Size of rolls, 10x1¾ inches. Weight, boxed, 24 pounds.

No. 9K2210 Price...........$2.37

OUR CURTIS LINE

OF FIVE-YEAR GUARANTEED CLOTHES WRINGERS. $3.67

THE CURTIS FIVE-YEAR CLAMP WRINGER. REGULAR RETAIL PRICE, $7.00; OUR PRICE - - - - - - - - - - -

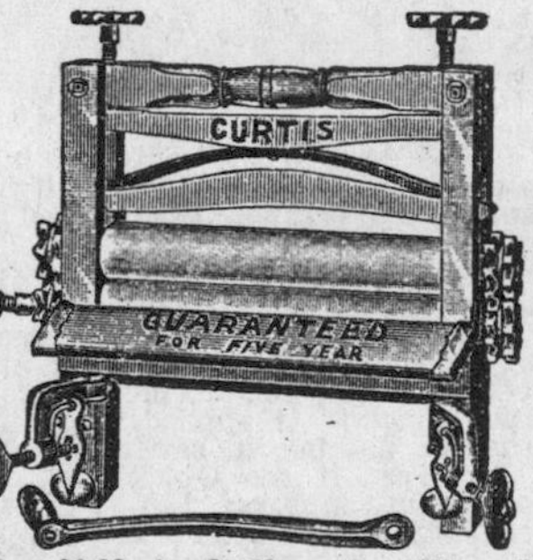

THE MOST PERFECT WRINGER MADE. Money cannot buy a better wringer, as it is not possible to make a higher grade article. Every piece of material used in making this wringer is positively the best quality. The rolls measure 11x1¾ inches and are made of pure elastic Para rubber, which will wring drier and last longer than any other. Every roll is guaranteed for five years and if one proves defective within that time we will replace it free of all expense. The steel spring in the Genuine Curtis Wringer gives an even and elastic pressure and the improved guide board spreads the clothes as they pass between the rolls, causing them to wear evenly and adds to the life of both the wringer and the clothes.

REMEMBER THAT YOU CANNOT BUY AT ANY PRICE A BETTER WRINGER THAN THE GENUINE CURTIS, as it is not possible to produce a better article. We take the entire output of the factory on the Genuine Curtis, highest grade five-year guarantee wringer and it can only be bought from us. Remember that while our price for this finest quality wringer is only $3.67, imitations of it, with inferior quality rolls, are regularly sold by local dealers for $6.00 to $7.50 each. We sell thousands of the Genuine Curtis wringers every year and have never known one to fail to please. Shipping weight of the Genuine Curtis Five-Year Guaranteed Wringer, 25 pounds.

No. 9K2223 Price.......................................$3.67

CURTIS FIVE-YEAR GUARANTEED BENCH WRINGER. REGULAR RETAIL PRICE, $7.50; OUR PRICE - - - - - - - $4.71

Guaranteed for five years.

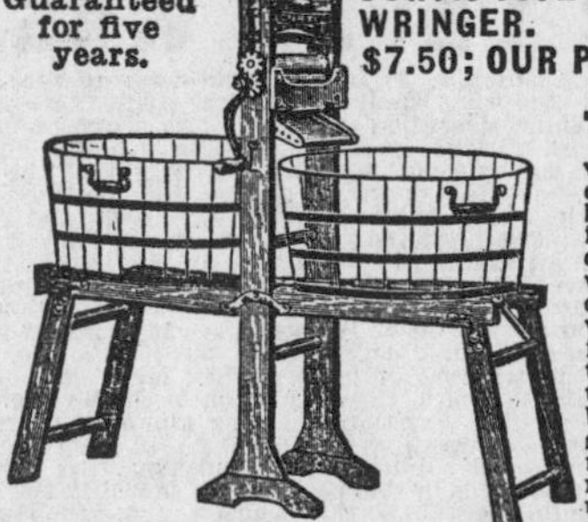

THE KING OF WRINGERS. Exactly the same wringer as the Curtis Clamp Wringer described above, but with folding bench, which holds two tubs, as shown in illustration. Nothing better has ever been produced. Has pure elastic Para rubber rolls, size, 11x1¾ inches, which will wring drier and last longer than any other. We warrant these rolls for five years, and with ordinary care they should last fifteen years in family use. The folding bench, holding two tubs, has an oscillating dripboard which conducts the water into either tub. Has best lignum vitae bearings; improved guide board, steel pressure spring; is constructed in the most substantial manner, and when folded will occupy but little more floor space than an ordinary wringer. Shipping weight, 46 pounds.

No. 9K2236 Price (not including tubs) $4.71

$2.38 FOR THE ACME STAR, GUARANTEED FOR ONE YEAR. THE LOWEST PRICED GUARANTEED WRINGER EVER OFFERED.

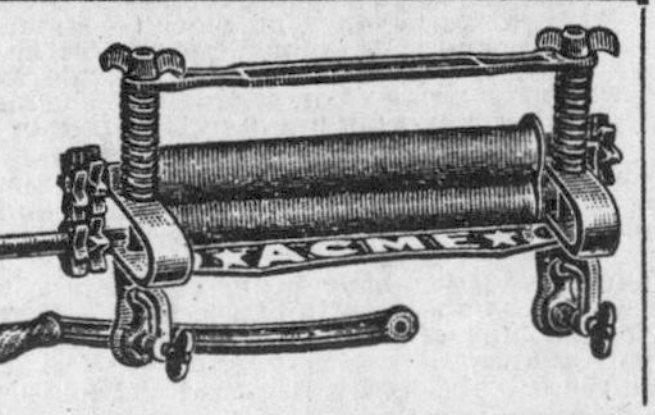

Special features of merit in the Acme Star iron frame wringer is that it has steel spiral pressure springs and thumb nuts, by which the pressure can be adjusted the same as any wood frame wringer. It is furnished with high grade rolls, size, 10x1¾ inches, guaranteed for one year. The Acme Star has double cog wheels, is galvanized, rustproof and the best value ever offered for the price. Weight boxed, 21 pounds.

No. 9K2205 Price.............$2.38

$3.42 FOR A HIGH GRADE ALPINE BENCH WRINGER.

Guaranteed for one year.

$3.42

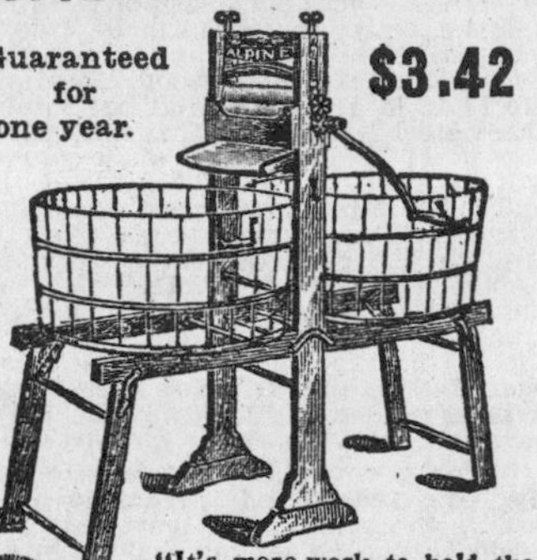

"It's more work to hold the tub than to turn the wringer." Use a bench wringer and you don't have to hold the tub. The bench is strong and durable, large enough to accommodate two large tubs. When not in use bench folds up, taking but little more room than an ordinary wringer. Clothes can be put in from either side. The wringer is well made. Size of rolls, 10x1¾ inches. Weight, 45 pounds.

No. 9K2234 Price (not including tubs)...........................$3.42

$1.69 FOR A FULL SIZE FOWLER CLOTHES WRINGER.

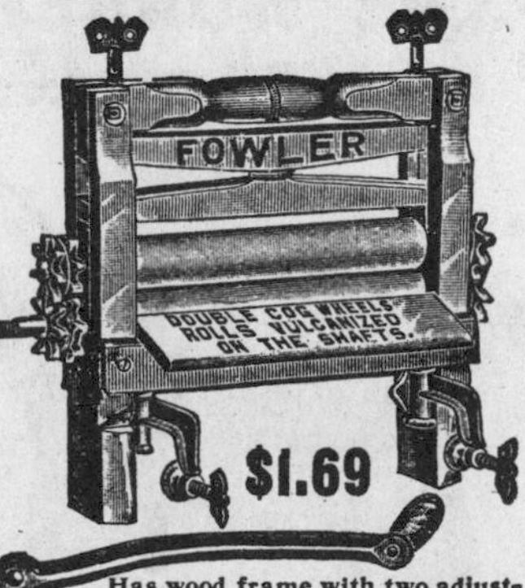

Has wood frame with two adjusting screws and iron tub clamps, as shown in illustration. The rolls are ordinary grade, not warranted, but are the best ever offered at the price and will give good service and satisfaction in use. While we recommend our five-year guaranteed Curtis wringer, we offer the Fowler as the best cheap wringer made and the one to buy when a low priced wringer is wanted. Rolls, 10x1¾ inches. Weight, boxed, 22 pounds.

No. 9K2208 Price..........$1.69

HARDWARE PRICES LOW IN OUR LAST CATALOGUE STILL FURTHER REDUCED IN THIS BOOK.

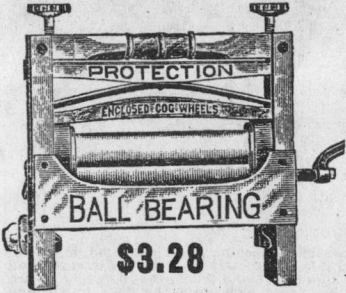

STEEL ROOFING.

THE CHIEF MERITS OF STEEL ROOFING are its cheapness, durability, ease of application and protection against fire. Our painted roofing is coated on both sides with iron oxide, reground in pure boiled linseed oil, applied with brushes. **A layer of roofing felt should invariably be laid under all metal roofing,** where gas or steam is used in the building, or where there is heat next to the roof. It will prevent dripping or sweating from condensation in cold weather, protect the paint on the under side of roof and serve as nonconductor of heat and cold. **While our roofing is of the finest quality it will rust if not protected with paint.** As soon as applied on a building, we recommend that the roofing be well coated with the best iron oxide or graphite paint. After a period of a year another coat should be applied and then at intervals of three or four years, as may be found necessary.

Painted roofing weighs about 70 pounds per 100 square feet. Galvanized roofing weighs about 90 pounds per 100 square feet. All steel roofing and sheet metals will be shipped direct from our factory in Ohio, from which point customer pays freight.

V-Crimped Roofing.

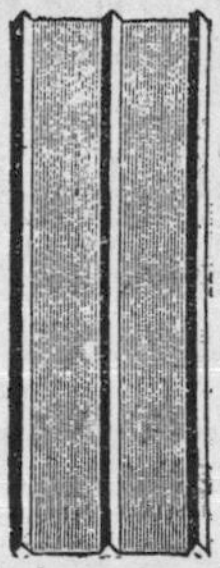

This is the cheapest of all roofing offered and costs less to put on the roof. Any person can apply it who can drive a nail. It is put down with an end lap only, or with end locks; the latter being the better method. When end locks are turned, a cleat should be used in the middle of the end lock, which prevents the sheet from rattling. It is made in two ways, namely, with side crimps only, or 2-V crimp, as illustrated, and with side and center crimps or 3-V crimp, having a crimp in center of sheet. 1 pound 1¾-inch No. 10 barbed wire nails, 1 pound dry mineral paint, 50 feet V sticks are required to lay a square of this roofing. 100 feet V sticks required for 3-V crimp roofing.

V-Crimped Roofing 2-V crimp, 28-gauge steel. Sheets will lay 24 inches from center to center of crimps. The ends of sheets should be lapped not less than 3 inches. May be laid over sheathing, shingles, lath or direct to rafters placed 24 inches from center, on any roof having a pitch of more than 2 inches to the foot. The ends of sheets can either be lapped 3 inches or more, or put together with lock joint.

To lay direct to rafters without sheathing: Set rafters 24 inches from center to center, and nail V wood strips on top surface of rafters. Place cross piece between rafters, level with the top of rafters, to support and nail the end of sheet. Begin at left hand corner of eaves, and end of building, and lay sheets from eaves to ridge, allowing 3 inches for end lap and one crimp for side lap. Nail through the crimp about every 8 inches. At end lap use four nails to the lap. When laid without end locks no special tools are required. When end locks are made a joiner, snips and mallet will be required.

No. 63K3077 2-V Crimp Roofing, painted both sides.

Length of sheet, feet	5	6	7	8	9	10
Price, per sheet	22c	26c	31c	35c	39c	44c

No. 63K3078 2-V Crimp Galvanized Roofing.

Length of sheet, feet	5	6	7	8	9	10
Price, per sheet	39c	47c	55c	63c	71c	79c

The above price is for roofing only and does not include sticks, nails or paint.

No. 63K3085 3-V Crimp Roofing, painted both sides. Lays 23½ inches from center to center of outside crimps.

Length of sheet, feet	5	6	7	8	9	10
Price, per sheet	23c	28c	32c	37c	42c	46c

No. 63K3086 3-V Crimp Roofing, galvanized.

Length of sheet, feet	5	6	7	8	9	10
Price, per sheet	41c	48c	57c	65c	73c	81c

No. 63K3081 V Sticks for V Crimp Roofing. Sold in any quantity (50 feet required for each square of 2-V roofing and 100 feet for 3-V roofing). Price, per 100 feet....20c

No. 63K3087 Dry Red Mineral Paint. (One pound required for each square of roofing.) Price, per pound....2c

No. 63K3088 Barbed Wire Roofing Nails, 1¾ inches long. (One pound required for each square of roofing.) Price, per pound....4c

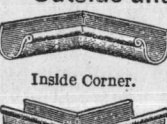

Plain Roll and Cap Roofing.

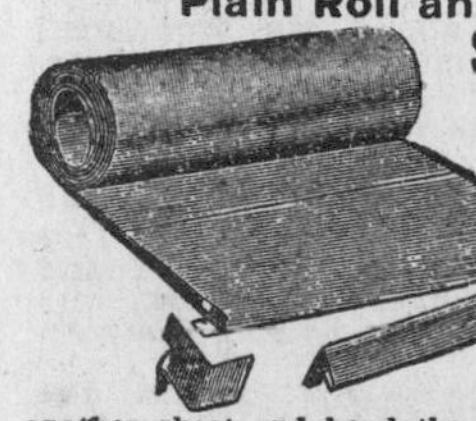

$2.60 PER ROLL

Used on all kinds of buildings with entire satisfaction and is easily applied. The only tools needed are a pair of edging tongs, a pair of squeezing tongs, a wooden mallet or hammer, and a pair of snips. Turn up the edge with your edging tongs, then cut into desired length; place one sheet on the roof, fasten with the cleat, then lay another sheet and bend the top of the cleat over the standing seam of the two edges, place the long caps over the seam and tighten the cap with the squeezing tongs or mallet and hammer. See price and description of tools below. These tools are sold at a price that barely represents the cost to us, and are furnished for your convenience. A roll is 26¼ inches wide and contains 50 lineal feet, which covers one square or 100 square feet. With each roll we furnish 50 side cleats and 51 lineal feet of caps. Sold only in full rolls.

No. 63K3070 Plain Roll and Cap Roofing, made of 28-gauge steel, painted both sides. Weight, per square, about 74 pounds. Price, per square, as described above, painted, $2.60

No. 63K3071 Price, per square, galvanized, (weight, 91 pounds)....4.60

Pressed Standing Seam Roofing, or Double Cap Steel Roofing.

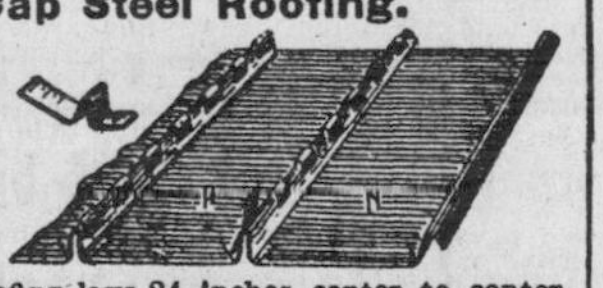

It is used on all kinds of buildings. Rapidly layed, no skill required. Sheets are made from metal 28 inches wide which are formed with a continuous cleat and can be firmly nailed to the roof boards rendering it storm proof. This roofing lays 24 inches center to center. We furnish sufficient cleats to lay the roofing. For paint and nails see No. 63K3087 and No. 63K3088. One-half pound nails and one pound paint required for each square 50 lineal feet.

No. 63K3075 Pressed Standing Seam Roofing, made of 28-gauge sheet steel, painted both sides. Weight, per square, 100 square feet, about 71 pounds. Width of sheets 24 inches.

L'gth of sheet, ft.	5	6	7	8	9	10
Per sheet	24c	29c	33c	38c	43c	48c

No. 63K3076 Pressed Standing Seam Roofing, made of 28-gauge steel, galvanized. Width of sheets 24 inches.

L'gth of sheet, ft.	5	6	7	8	9	10
Per sheet	41c	49c	57c	65c	73c	81c

The following tools are required to lay this roofing: 1 pair squeezing tongs, 1 jointer, 1 pair snips and 1 mallet. A square is 10 feet each way, or 100 square feet.

Edging Tongs.

No. 63K3090 Edging Tongs; used in turning up the standing seam in roll cap roofing. Price, 35c

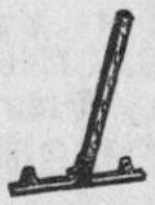

Tinner Snips.

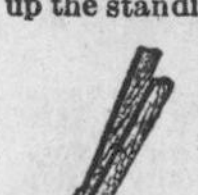

No. 63K3091 A pair of good hand forged Tinner Snips. Length, 9 inches, 2¼-inch cut, fully warranted. Price....68c

Squeezing Tongs.

No. 63K3093 Squeezing Tongs; used in squeezing the seams on roll cap and pressed standing seam, or double cap roofing. Price....40c

Jointers.

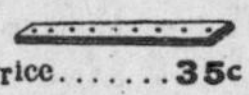

No. 63K3095 Jointer or End Locker; used in making the end locks on V crimp and pressed standing seam, and other roofings. Price....35c

Steel Brick Siding.

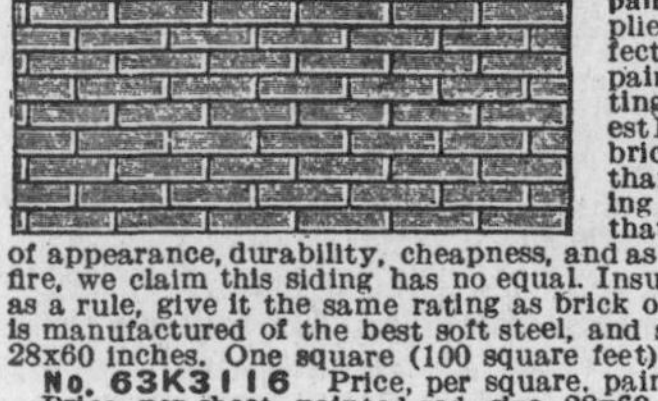

Steel Brick Siding, painted both sides. Applied easily, lays perfectly smooth and, after painting, cannot be distinguished from the finest Philadelphia pressed brick. It costs no more than the best wood siding and about one-fifth that of brick. In beauty of appearance, durability, cheapness, and as a protection against fire, we claim this siding has no equal. Insurance underwriters, as a rule, give it the same rating as brick or stone. This siding is manufactured of the best soft steel, and shipped in sheets of 28x60 inches. One square (100 square feet) equals 8 4-7 sheets.

No. 63K3116 Price, per square, painted....$2.30
Price, per sheet, painted red, size, 28x60 inches....27

No. 63K3117 Galvanized Brick Siding. Per square 4.00
Price, per sheet, size, 28x60 inches....47

No. 63K3139 Steel Rock Face Brick Siding. Size of single brick, 2 4-5x8¼ inches. Size of sheet, 28x60 inches. Painted red. Price, per sheet....29c

No. 63K3141 Steel Rock Face Brick Siding. Same as preceding, except is galvanized. Price, per sheet....48c

Pressed Corrugated Sheets for Siding, Ceiling, Fireproof Partitions, Etc.

The strongest sheet metal known to the trade. For structures of moderate cost or light, inexpensive framings that are intended to be fireproof, no better material can be had. The rigidity imparted to comparatively light sheets by corrugating makes them self supporting. For siding, 1-inch end laps will do. If used for roofing, the roof should have a pitch of not less than 3 inches to the foot. Sheets should have 3 to 6 inches end lap and one and one-half, or two corrugations side lap.

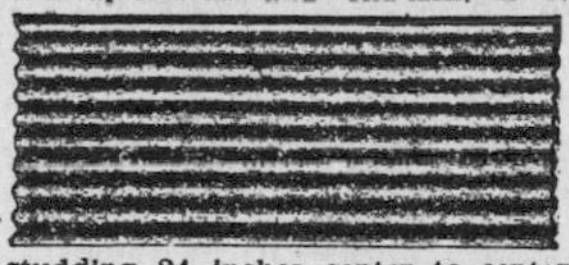

Corrugated Sheets, 28-gauge with 2½-inch corrugations. Sheets are 26¼ inches wide. Allowing one corrugation for lap on each side, it leaves a covering surface 24 inches wide, which lays to advantage on rafters or studding 24 inches center to center. The end lap should be from 1 to 6 inches. Sheets are 5, 6, 7, 8, 9 and 10 feet long.

No. 63K3105 Corrugated Sheets. 28-gauge, 2½-inch corrugations. Painted both sides.

Length of sheet, ft.	5	6	7	8	9	10
Per sheet	24c	28c	33c	38c	43c	48c

No. 63K3106 Corrugated Sheets. 28-gauge, 2½-inch corrugations. Galvanized.

Length of sheet, ft.	5	6	7	8	9	10
Per sheet	41c	49c	57c	65c	74c	82c

Above prices do not include paint or nails.

No. 63K3107 Corrugated Sheets with 1¼-inch corrugations. Allowing one corrugation for side lap, it lays 24 inches wide, 28-gauge, painted both sides.

Length of sheet, ft.	5	6	7	8	9	10
Per sheet	25c	29c	35c	40c	46c	50c

No. 63K3108 Corrugated Sheets with 1¼-inch corrugations, 28-gauge, galvanized.

Length of sheet, ft.	5	6	7	8	9	10
Per sheet	43c	52c	61c	69c	78c	88c

For paint and nails see Nos. 63K3087 and 63K3088.

Beaded Steel Siding and Ceiling.

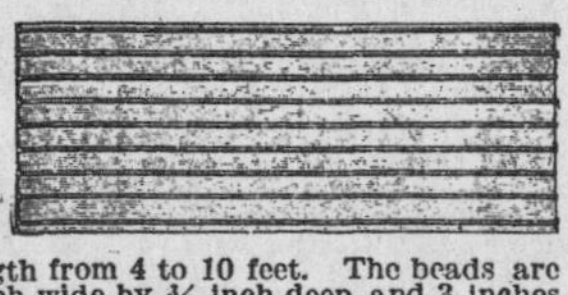

Made from the best quality box annealed steel, painted on both sides with the best iron oxide paint, ground in pure linseed oil. Sheets, when beaded, cover 24 inches from center to center of outside beads, and can be furnished any length from 4 to 10 feet. The beads are small corrugations, ⅜ inch wide by ⅜ inch deep and 3 inches from center to center. In applying, no special tools are required. The sheets should be lapped 1 or 2 inches at ends, and over one crimp at side. They can be applied perpendicularly or horizontally (as desired) to boards, studding or joists placed the proper distance apart, or put on over old plaster.

No. 63K3115 Beaded Siding or Ceiling. Painted.

Length, feet	4	5	6	7	8	9	10
Per sheet	20c	24c	29c	34c	39c	44c	49c

Roll Ridge Caps.

No. 63K3145 Round Ridge Roll. Makes a neat waterproof cap for the ridge of roofs. It is made in 8-foot lengths. We do not furnish cut lengths. Diameter of roll, 2 inches; width of apron, 2½ inches; girth, 10 inches. Per length, painted. 28c

No. 63K3144 Round Ridge Roll, galvanized. Diameter of roll, 2 inches; width of apron, 2½ inches; girth, 10 inches. Price, per length, 8 feet long, galvanized....31c

Valley Tin.

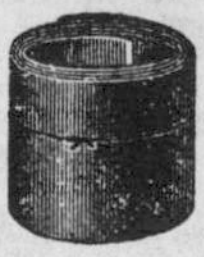

No. 63K3198 Made of a good grade of tin plate in a continuous strip, locked and soldered and painted one side. Full lengths are 50 feet, but we can furnish any quantity

Width, inches	14	20	28
Price, per lineal foot	$0.05	$0.06½	$0.09½
Per 50-foot lengths	1.75	2.33	3.25

No. 63K3197 Galvanized Valley in Rolls. Made of 28-gauge steel, 14 inches wide.

Length of roll, feet	25	50
Price, per roll	$1.25	$2.45

Continuous Tin Roofing.

No. 63K3200 Made of IC tin plate, locked and soldered together by hand. Put up in rolls containing 120 lineal feet, 20 inches wide, containing 200 square feet. The strips are perfectly straight and ready to lay on the roof. Considered the best and most convenient form of roofing tin ever placed on the market. Painted on under side. Weight, per roll, 105 pounds. We cannot sell less than a full roll. Price, per roll....$6.40

Patent Slip Joint Eaves Trough.

Can Be Put Together Without Soldering Iron.

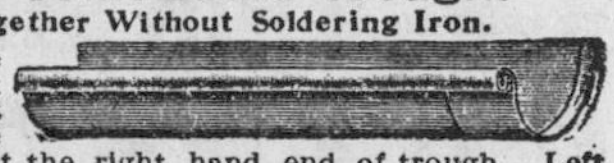

When ordering state whether right or left hand is wanted. Right hand means that the water is to discharge at the right hand end of trough. Left hand that the water is to discharge at the left hand end. The above picture shows a right hand. The same rule also applies to corners, etc.

No. 63K3148 Slip Joint Eaves Trough. Right hand.
No. 63K3149 Slip Joint Eaves Trough. Left hand.

Galvanized Slip Joint Eaves Trough. Made of 28-gauge steel. Made in 10-foot lengths. We do not furnish cut lengths. Size is taken inside of bead. Price includes one slip joint with each length of trough.

Size, inches	3½	4	4½	5	6
Weight, per length, lbs.	5½	6	6½	7½	8½
Price, per length	30c	34c	39c	40c	48c

Outside and Inside Corner Mitre.

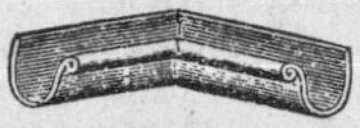

Inside Corner.

Outside Corner.

These mitres are made complete, ready for use, for both inside and outside bead. Be sure to state if right or left hand is wanted.

No. 63K3158 Inside Corner, slip joint. Right hand.
No. 63K3159 Inside Corner, slip joint. Left hand.
No. 63K3162 Outside Corner, slip joint. Right hand.
No. 63K3163 Outside Corner, slip joint. Left hand.

Size, inches	3½	4	4½	5	6
Price, slip joint, each	$0.16	$0.17	$0.18	$0.19	$0.21
Per dozen	1.75	1.90	2.00	2.10	2.25

Adjustable Outlet and End Cap.

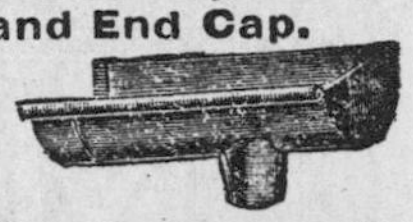

The illustration represents outlet in position, with end of trough closed with slip joint end cap. Anyone can put this on. No soldering needed. Prices do not include end cap as shown in illustration. For prices of end cap see No. 63K3161.

No. 63K3160 Adjustable Outlet. To fit eaves trough

Size, inches	3½	4	4½	5	7
Fitted for conductor, Size, inches	2	2	3	3	4
Price, each	$0.09	$0.10	$0.11	$0.11	$0.13
Per dozen	1.00	1.08	1.19	1.22	1.46

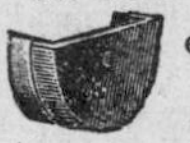

No. 63K3161 End Cap Slip Joint To fit eaves trough.

Size, inches	3½	4	4½	5	6
Price, each	5c	5c	6c	6c	7c
Per dozen	50c	55c	60c	70c	80c

Wire Eaves Trough Hangers.

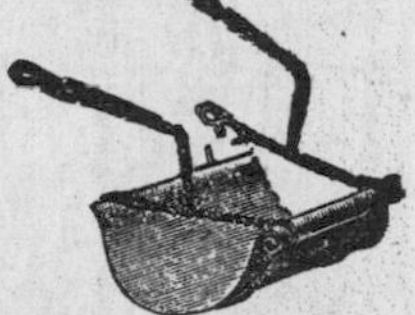

No. 63K3170 Wire Eaves Trough Hangers, made of 11-gauge steel wire galvanized. While there are cheaper grades of wire hangers on the market we believe that our customers will get better value for their money by buying our patent wire eaves trough hanger, as it is the very best made.

Size, inches	3½	4	4½	5	6
Price, per dozen	$0.11	$0.12	$0.13	$0.14	$0.16
Per gross	1.08	1.20	1.32	1.44	1.58

Conductor Pipe.

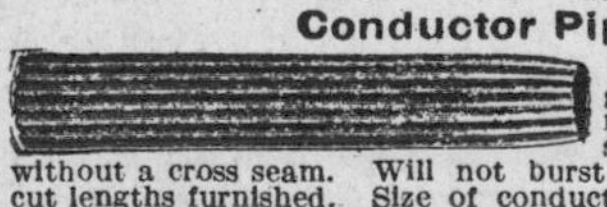

Galvanized Corrugated Conductor is made of No. 28-gauge steel in 10-foot lengths, without a cross seam. Will not burst when full of ice. No cut lengths furnished. Size of conductors suitable for eaves trough.

Size of eaves trough, inches	3½	4	4½	5	6	7
Size of conductor, inches	2	2	3	3	4	5

No. 63K3180 Round Galvanized Corrugated Conductor.

Size, inches	2	3	4	5
Price, per length	33c	38c	50c	63c

Elbows and Shoes.

Corrugated, Galvanized, Expanding. When ordering, always specify by number the angle desired, as shown here.

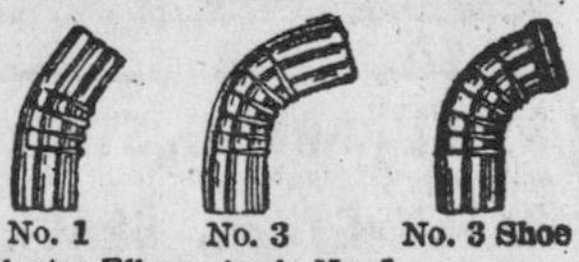

No. 1 No. 3 No. 3 Shoe

No. 63K3181 Conductor Elbow, Angle No. 1.
No. 63K3183 Conductor Elbow, Angle No. 3.

Size, inches	2	3	4	5
Price, each	$0.07	$0.08	$0.09	$0.15
Per dozen	.60	.75	.95	1.75

No. 63K3184 Round Galvanized Corrugated Shoes.

Size, inches	2	3	4	5
Price	8c	9c	10c	18c

Conductor Funnel.

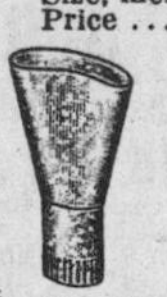

No. 63K3187 Conductor Funnel, for running two conductors into one; size indicates size of lower spout.

Size, inches	2	3	4	5
Price, each	16c	20c	27c	34c

Rain Water Cut Off.

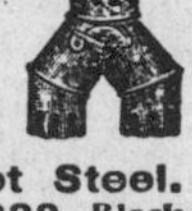

No. 63K3193 For Corrugated Conductor.

Size, inches	2	3	4
Each	$0.14	$0.16	$0.21
Per dozen	1.50	1.73	2.27

Black Sheet Steel.

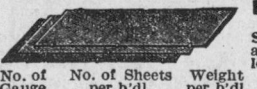

No. 63K3222 Black Sheet Steel, standard grade, absolutely flat, free of buckles. Size of sheets, 28x96 ins.

No. of Gauge	No. of Sheets per b'dl.	Weight per b'dl.	Price, per sheet	Price, per bundle
24	7	131 lbs.	55c	$3.69
26	8	112 lbs.	44c	3.23
27	9	114 lbs.	41c	3.41
28	10	117 lbs.	39c	3.59

Galvanized Sheet Steel.

No. 63K3225 Galvanized Sheet Steel, standard grade, absolutely flat, free of buckles. Size of sheet, 28x96 inches.

No. of Gauge	No. of Sheets per b'dl.	Weight, per b'dl.	Price, per sheet	Price, per bundle
24	7	151 lbs.	84c	$5.48
26	8	135 lbs.	71c	5.25
27	9	142 lbs.	69c	5.86
28	10	146 lbs.	68c	6.38

NOTICE—Prices on galvanized and black sheet steel are subject to fluctuations of the market. In event of decline, we will give our customers the benefit of any reduction and return the difference in price.

BUILDING PLANS, MATERIALS, AND APPLIANCES

ETC., REPRESENT ONLY A FEW OF THE ITEMS SHOWN IN OUR SPECIAL MILL WORK CATALOGUE.
SAVE FROM 25 TO 50 PER CENT BY SENDING FOR OUR GREAT MILL WORK PRICE MAKER TODAY

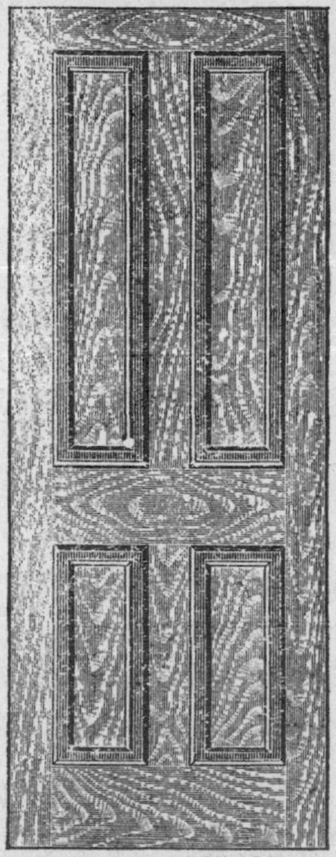

69c No. 63K6877 2x6 feet ⅞ 4-Panel, B Grade, Solid Yellow Pine. Well made and suitable for inside use.

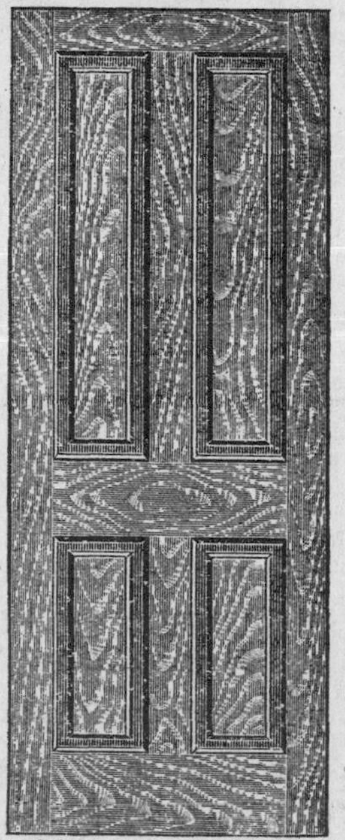

$1.03 No. 63K6945 2x6 feet ⅞ 4-Panel Painted and Grained Imitation Quarter Sawed Oak. Finest grained door made.

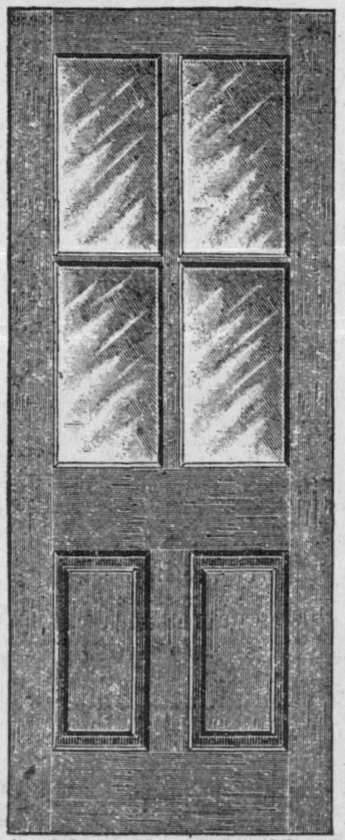

$1.90 No. 63K6762 2 feet 6 inches by 6 feet 6 inches 1⅜ Painted and Glazed Single Strength Glass.

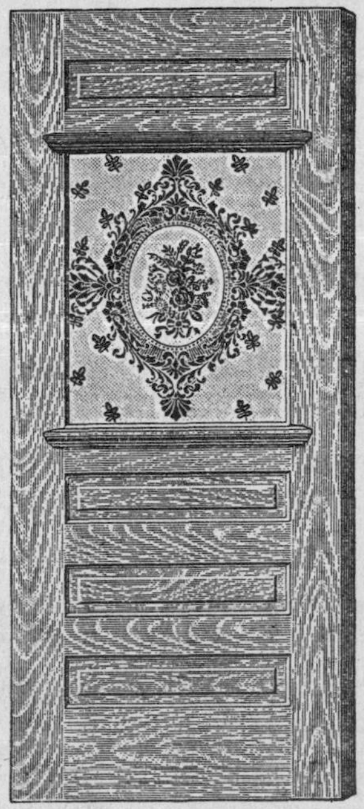

$2.80 No. 63K777½ Metropole Door. Pine. B grade, glazed as illustrated. Size, 2 feet 6 inches by 6 feet 6 inches, 1⅜ inches thick.

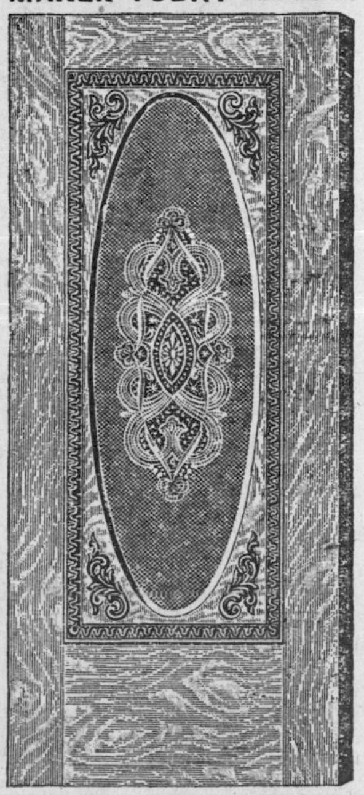

$9.45 No. 63K98 Superba Design Veneered Birch, glazed beautiful lace design, as illustrated, 1¾ inch thick. Size, 2 feet 8 inches by 6 feet 8 inches.

MOULDINGS IN ENDLESS VARIETY

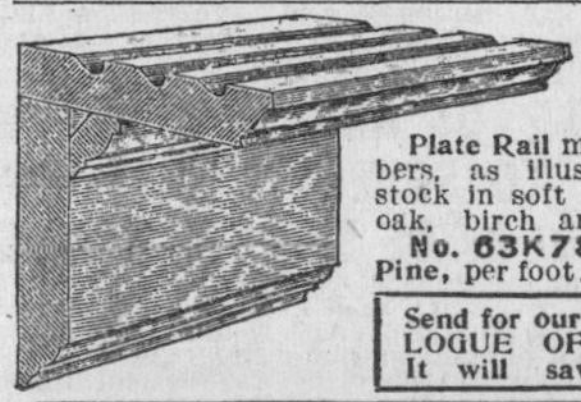

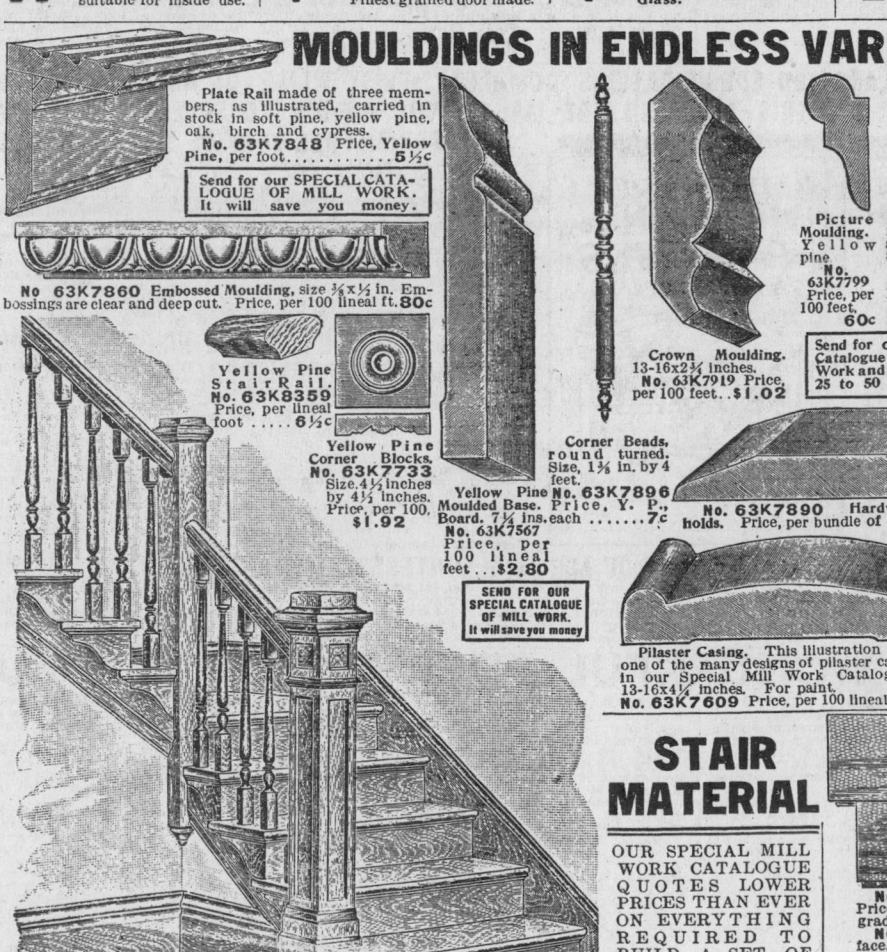

Plate Rail made of three members, as illustrated, carried in stock in soft pine, yellow pine, oak, birch and cypress.
No. 63K7848 Price, Yellow Pine, per foot..............5½c

Send for our SPECIAL CATALOGUE OF MILL WORK. It will save you money.

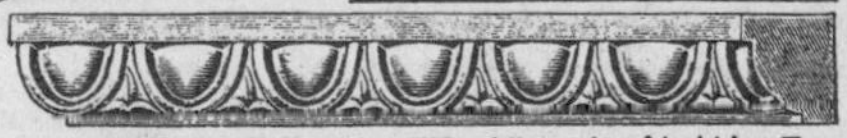

No 63K7860 Embossed Moulding, size ⅜x½ in. Embossings are clear and deep cut. Price, per 100 lineal ft. **80c**

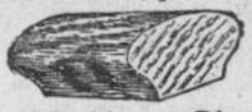

Yellow Pine Stair Rail. No. 63K8359 Price, per lineal foot 6½c

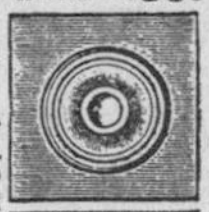

Yellow Pine Corner Blocks. No. 63K7733 Size, 4½ inches by 4½ inches. Price, per 100, **$1.92**

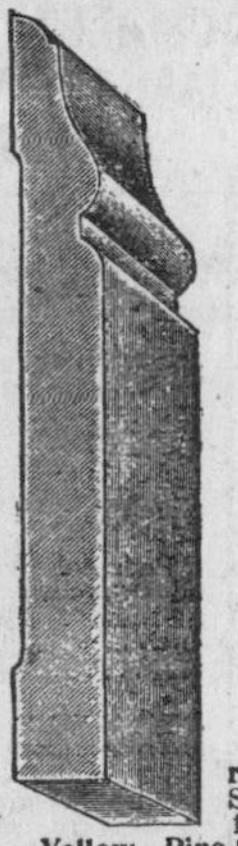

Yellow Pine Moulded Base. Board. 7¼ ins. No. 63K7567 Price, per 100 lineal feet...**$2.80**

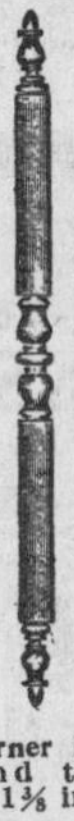

Corner Beads, round turned. Size, 1⅜ in. by 4 feet. No. 63K7896 Price, Y. P., each 7c

SEND FOR OUR SPECIAL CATALOGUE OF MILL WORK. It will save you money

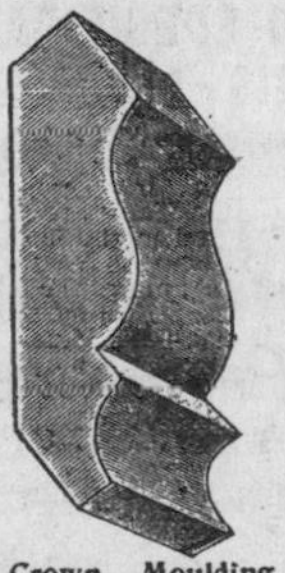

Crown Moulding. 13-16x2¾ inches. No. 63K7919 Price, per 100 feet..**$1.02**

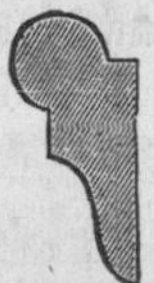

Picture Moulding. Yellow pine. No. 63K7799 Price, per 100 feet, **60c**

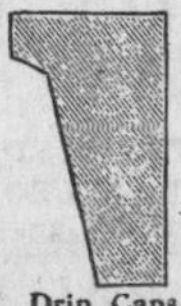

Drip Caps for windows and doors. Size, 1⅛x1⅜ inches. No. 63K7930 Price, per 100 lineal feet, **$1.14**

Send for our Special Catalogue of Mill Work and save from 25 to 50 per cent.

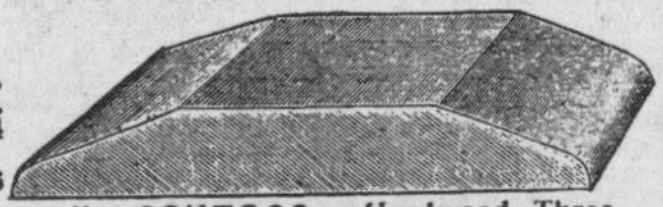

No. 63K7890 Hardwood Thresholds. Price, per bundle of 10 ....**39c**

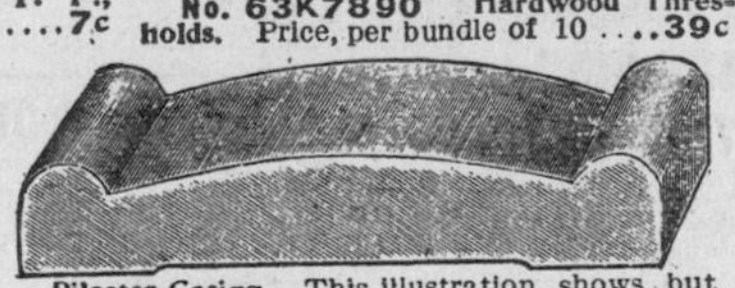

Pilaster Casing. This illustration shows but one of the many designs of pilaster casing shown in our Special Mill Work Catalogue. Size, 13-16x4¼ inches. For paint.
No. 63K7609 Price, per 100 lineal ft., **$1.54**

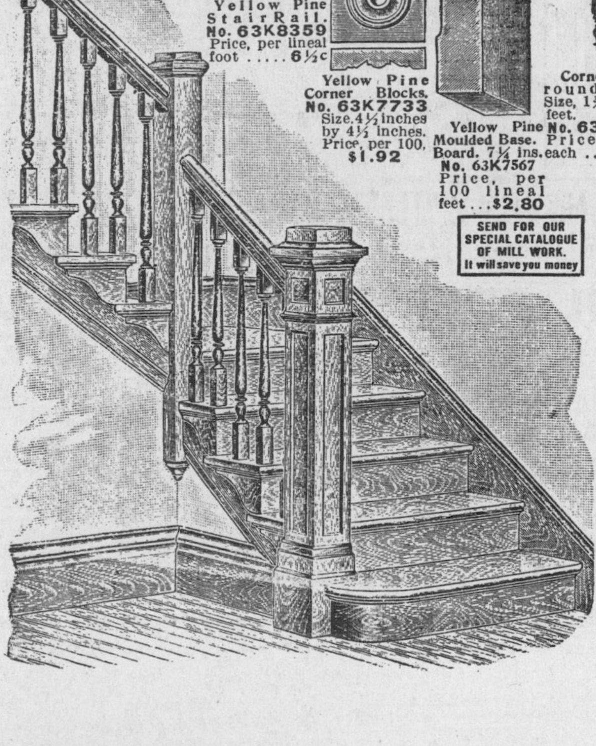

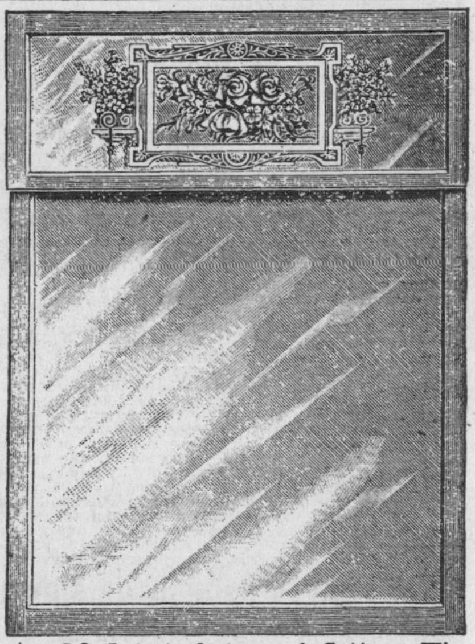

$3.28 Latest designs of Cottage Windows always on hand. A large assortment to select from. Top light, 40 inches by 14 inches. Bottom light, 40 inches by 40 inches.
No. 63K7124 Price..................**$3.28**

STAIR MATERIAL

OUR SPECIAL MILL WORK CATALOGUE QUOTES LOWER PRICES THAN EVER ON EVERYTHING REQUIRED TO BUILD A SET OF STAIRS.

OUR PRICES ARE THE LOWEST.

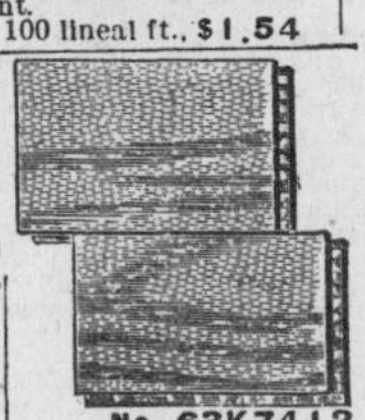

FLOORING AND CEILING.

The limited space permits us to offer only a few items in Soft and Hardwood Flooring. We request all customers interested in flooring and ceiling to send for our Special Mill Work Catalogue, which shows a variety of 18 different kinds and sizes. The descriptions below simply give you an idea of the very low prices we quote.

No. 63K7412 Beaded Red Gum Ceiling. ⅜-inch by 3¼-inch face. Price per 1,000 feet surface measure (figured 4 inches wide) select grade..........**$16.25**

No. 63K7396 Red Gum Flooring. 13-16 inch thick, 2¼-inch face. Price, per 1,000 feet, surface measure (figured 3 inches wide), select grade..........**$26.25**

No. 63K7441 Royal Acme Polished Maple Flooring. ⅞x2-inch face, select. Price, per 1,000 feet, surface measure (figured ½ inch wider than face measure), select grade end matched..........**$21.58**

No. 63K7434 Royal Acme Polished Oak Flooring. 13-16 inch thick by 2¼-inch face. Price, per 1,000 feet, surface measure (figured ¾ inch wider than face measure), select grade end matched..........**$43.20**

$100.00 SET OF BUILDING PLANS COMPLETE WITH SPECIFICATIONS FREE

LET US BE YOUR ARCHITECT WITHOUT COST TO YOU, let us save you one-fourth to one-third of the cost of your next building, whether it be a modest little cottage or a mansion, let us show you how to build a better constructed, a more conveniently arranged and more up to date house than it would be possible for you to build by depending upon your local builder or architect, who would charge you for drawings and specifications a price ranging all the way from $50.00 to $200.00, depending upon the size and kind of house you propose to build. We are furnishing the plans and specifications used by some of the most critical builders in the country. The many who have used our plans and specifications tell us that we have made a wonderful saving in cost of material and architects' fees, they tell us the houses erected from our plans are the most conveniently arranged and the best in their community, and they have advised their friends who contemplate building to use our plans and specifications and to secure our great free book of Mill Work and Building Material.

EVERY FREE HOUSE PLAN WE OFFER represents the most careful study of the best known licensed architects in this country who were especially engaged by us for this service. Before making these plans our architects carefully canvassed the requirements of people in all parts of the United States, embodying the very latest ideas in these plans and giving us houses suited for the city, the town and the farm home. These complete building plans which we give free bring out the ideas of the best posted contractors and builders in this country, as well as the very best architects, and give you ideas and suggestions which it would be impossible for you to secure from any other concern at any price.

OUR COMPLETE SET OF PLANS AND SPECIFICATIONS which we furnish you free of charge, as explained further on, portrays the house or building so simply, so plainly that even those absolutely unfamiliar with building can get at a glance an exact idea of just what the building is, how it is laid out and how it will look when completed. Our plans show the following:

1. A perspective view of the completed building, showing the house as finished by the builder, giving you an exact understanding of what the house will look like when it is ready for occupancy.
2. Complete floor plans, including foundation or cellar, first and second floors, showing the exact size and arrangement of the rooms, the location of doors, windows, stairs, plumbing, heating, lighting, etc. In fact, showing everything as plainly as though you were inspecting a completed house.
3. A complete set of working drawings, regular architect's blue prints, with all details and dimensions plainly marked. These working drawings are to a scale of one-fourth inch to the foot, the most convenient scale to work from, and they are so accurately drawn and are so complete that any mechanic will understand them and can follow them successfully. The set of working drawings consists of the following:
   Front elevation, showing the front view of the house.
   Right side elevation, showing the right side view of the house.
   Left side elevation, showing the left side view of the house.
   Rear elevation, giving a back view of the house.
   Foundation plans, giving information with reference to excavation, thickness of foundation walls, depth of foundation walls, etc.
   First Floor Plans with sizes of rooms, partitions, doorways, windows, etc., given in detail.
   Second Floor Plans (if a two-story structure) giving size of rooms, partitions, location of windows, doors, etc., in detail.
   Detailed drawings of materials, showing style of window trimming, stair finish, balusters, hardware, porch finish, cornice finish, and all the material necessary to give style and character to the structure inside and out.
4. Complete specifications of material and labor required, outlining all the conditions under which a contract is let, providing the building be erected by contract.

COMPLETE BILL OF MATERIALS AND LABOR explaining the digging of cellar or basement, the carpenter work, the mason work, the lathing and plastering, quantity and dimensions of timbers required, also the quantity and kind of exterior finishing lumber, porch work, roofing, flooring, window and door frames, doors and windows, inside finishing lumber including all moulding, stair work, etc.; building hardware, such as door locks, hinges, cupboard catches, drawer pulls, sash locks, gutters and eavestrough, glass, paints, varnishes and fillers for outside and inside painting.

ALL THIS DETAILED INFORMATION will be given to you so definitely that you can estimate almost to a dollar what the building when completed will cost you; and we also show you how to get these materials at such wonderfully low prices that you can save hundreds of dollars on any new home you contemplate building. In addition to all these details, all this information, we will furnish you on request absolutely free of charge the following:

A COMPLETE SET OF PLUMBING PLANS FREE with specifications for piping, waste pipes, hot water boiler connections, bath tub, water closet, pumps, wash bowl, etc. Please remember that we are able to show you wonderful savings on your plumbing: we are able to supply you with the very finest goods at prices about half those usually charged because we are absolutely independent of the plumbing goods trust, and we will give you such full and complete information as will enable you to have all these desirable conveniences in your home at a wonderful saving in cost.

A COMPLETE SET OF GAS FITTING PLANS and specifications free, which plans and specifications include detailed information with reference to piping, gas fixtures, gas stove connections, etc.

A COMPLETE SET OF HEATING PLANS FREE. These plans will give you definite information with reference to heating your home with either a hot air furnace, a hot water boiler or a steam heating boiler. These plans and specifications will show you where to place hot air registers, hot water or steam radiators, just how much tin piping and how many registers will be necessary for hot air furnace heating, together with the cost of the same, or just the size of hot water or steam boiler required, amount of piping and the number of radiators necessary and the exact cost.

ALL OF THESE PLANS WHICH WE GIVE YOU FREE under our easy conditions are so simple and plain that any average mechanic can follow our instructions with the aid of our working drawings. Indeed, thousands of our customers who have been buying heating plants and plumbing materials from us in recent years have installed this material themselves, thus saving the large labor bills often paid for this kind of work.

TO GET ANY OF OUR $100.00 BUILDING PLANS AND SPECIFICATIONS COMPLETE, FIRST WRITE US AND SAY, "SEND ME YOUR BOOK OF MODERN HOMES," AND THIS BOOK WILL BE MAILED YOU FREE TO SELECT FROM.

IT IS NECESSARY TO SEND FOR THIS BEAUTIFUL BOOK OF MODERN HOMES FROM WHICH TO SELECT YOUR HOUSE BEFORE ORDERING YOUR PLANS.

SEND TODAY IF YOU INTEND TO BUILD and get a free copy of this great book at once and save all the way from $250.00 to $1,000.00 on your future home. When you receive this free Book of Modern Homes, examine it carefully and we are sure that you will find a house well suited to your requirements. Select the house you feel is the one you would like to know all about, the one that you think would please you, and when you have decided, write us as explained in the Book of Modern Homes and we will immediately send you a complete set of plans and specifications, everything just as we have described above. Examine the plans and specifications very carefully, note the kind and quality of all the materials we have specified, the kind of mill work, its splendid quality, its beautiful design; note the class of hardware specified, the plumbing goods, the heating plant; please note everything specified by us and which we are able to sell you, then compare the qualities we offer you with the qualities you can secure at home or elsewhere, and then, above all, compare the prices we name on the articles specified with the prices you would be compelled to pay any other firm or individual at home or elsewhere. We are anxious to have you make this comparison very carefully because we know when you do so, you will find that our prices are so very much lower than the prices quoted by anyone else, our qualities are better, in fact, our goods are absolutely guaranteed or your money will be sent back to you, together with the transportation charges, that you will see how greatly to your advantage it will be to send us your order for building material.

DO NOT BREAK GROUND OR SIGN A BUILDING CONTRACT WITHOUT GETTING A COPY of this book. It may result in saving you one-half the cost of your future home. It will enable you to get better services free of charge than you would be able to get for one hundred dollars from your local architect. This book will explain all about the wonderful hundred dollar set of building plans we offer you free of charge, it will tell you everything you could want to know about home building.

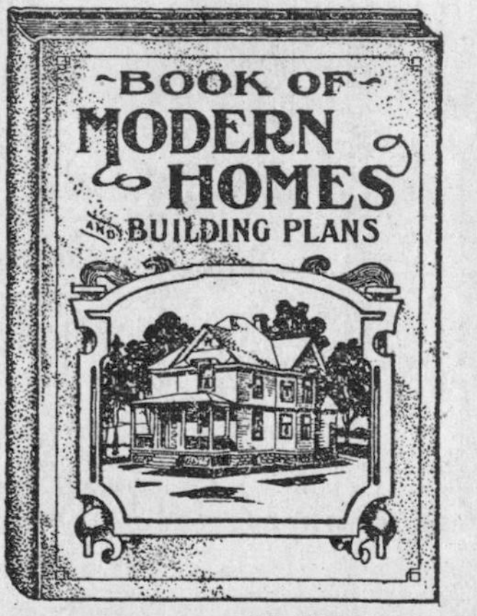

OUR SPECIAL FREE BOOK OF MODERN HOMES shows a large variety of completed houses, together with the floor plans of each, as shown on the next two pages of this book. These houses range in price from $700.00 to $4,000.00, and these prices represent houses which could not be built for many hundreds of dollars more than these prices, except under our plans and specifications. Please do not overlook the fact that this Book of Modern Homes means a wonderful saving to you. Every house we show is plainly marked with a price, the lowest price that has ever been named for a good substantial house built in recent years, and this price is guaranteed by our specifications and quotations. This special Book of Modern Homes, which we will send you free, shows you how much better and how much bigger a house you can build for your money than it would be possible for you to build by using any other plans.

THIS ELEGANT BOOK, THE FINEST BOOK OF ITS KIND EVER PUBLISHED, illustrates and describes a vast number of beautiful completed houses. Every illustration within this book is made with the finest half-tone cuts, printed on best grade of enameled paper. Every illustration used in this book was reproduced from washed drawings made by some of the foremost architects in this country. This book will convey more ideas to you in five minutes than an architect would in a year, as it shows each one of these houses as it stands on the lot, giving you an exceptionally fine perspective view of the exterior, and directly below this picture we show the drawn floor plans which are drawn on a scale 1-16 of an inch to the foot. All rooms are plainly marked with the sizes. The plans also give you the exact locations of all the windows, doors, stairs, porches, etc., in fact it is so plainly put before you that you could receive no better idea if you were to personally visit one of the completed houses built from these plans.

IF YOU ARE AT ALL INTERESTED IN BUILDING, send for this book today. Simply write us and say, "Send me your Book of Modern Homes", and the book, as illustrated, will be sent you immediately, free and postpaid. Then, after you have received this beautiful Book of Modern Homes you can study it carefully, decide on the kind of building you would like, and get the complete set of detailed plans and all specifications, as explained above, and as more fully explained in this free Book of Modern Homes.

WHY WE MAKE THIS WONDERFUL FREE OFFER TO YOU

WE WANT TO EXPLAIN why we are giving away free of charge a $100.00 set of building plans and specifications complete. First of all, we want to supply you with all the material which will enter into your new home with the single exception of the rough lumber, but we realize that we cannot secure your patronage unless we are able to show you that it is very decidedly to your advantage in dollars and cents to purchase this material from us. We do the largest mill work business in the world, we own our own plumbing goods factory, we manufacture hot air furnaces, steam and hot water boilers, radiators, and all the materials which enter into plumbing, steam, hot water and gas fitting. We handle more builders' hardware than any retail concern in the world, and our business in all these lines is so enormous and our policy of selling at the mere cost of material, which in this case means manufacturing cost, with just one small margin of profit added, that the prices we name on everything which enters into the construction of a building are so much lower than the prices asked by local dealers who sell you goods which have passed through manufacturers', jobbers' and retailers' hands and therefore paid a profit to several individuals, that we can show you a very large saving. We are the only concern in the world which can furnish you all the articles you need in the construction of a house or barn in the finest quality of goods at such wonderfully low prices, and we know that if we can just have opportunity to prove to you in dollars and cents what we can do for you, that entirely in your own interest you would be glad to send us your order when you build. Therefore, we offer these plans and specifications, complete in every respect, absolutely free of charge. We decided to employ the most skillful architects in this country to prepare a large variety of plans and specifications for us, covering a range of buildings from the modest cottage to the more pretentious mansion. We have issued a Book of Modern Homes, showing a large variety of completed houses with the floor plans of each. Among these plans surely you will find one which will meet your requirements, and when we show you in dollars and cents how much we can save you, then you will be glad to use these building plans which we will give you without charging you one penny for them, saving you from $50.00 to $100.00 on the plans and several hundred dollars on the house, and you will immediately give our complete lines of building materials your careful consideration, and as a result of our extremely low prices we will receive a liberal share of your orders for mill work and other building materials.

THIS IS THE MOST LIBERAL OFFER ever made by any concern. If you intend to build, if your neighbor intends to build, or if a friend intends to build, no matter how low in cost or how expensive the proposed house may be, neither you nor your neighbor nor your friends can afford to overlook this great free offer.

OUR PLANS SPECIFY in a plain, concise manner every item of material which will be required in the new building, including mill work, windows, doors, flooring, lumber, lathing, plaster, foundation material, chimney material, hardware, glass, piping, heating, in fact, every item which goes to make up a complete home with every modern convenience. These plans save you the trouble of figuring the material, because they are so carefully worked out that every piece of lumber will cut to the best advantage with the least waste. Every item of expense is figured much closer than it would be possible to figure it in any other way. If it were not for the fact that we build over a thousand homes from a single one of these plans we could not possibly afford to give the great amount of attention that is necessary to make these plans so complete, nor could we afford to employ the most skillful licensed architects in this country to prepare these plans for us.

OUR PLANS ARE VERY EASY TO UNDERSTAND, any carpenter, any person familiar with carpentering or anyone with a little experience in building can construct any one of our buildings in a rapid and intelligent manner by the use of these plans and specifications. They are so complete in every detail that they enable the carpenter to accomplish more in less time than it would be possible for you to accomplish by the average plans and working drawings.

$725.00 AND OUR FREE BUILDING PLANS
WILL BUILD, PAINT AND COMPLETE READY FOR OCCUPANCY
THIS $1,100.00 SIX-ROOM COTTAGE

PLANS FOR THIS $725.00 HOUSE, OR ANY ONE OF THE MANY HOUSES WE OFFER, ARE FREE, AS FULLY EXPLAINED ON PAGE 594.

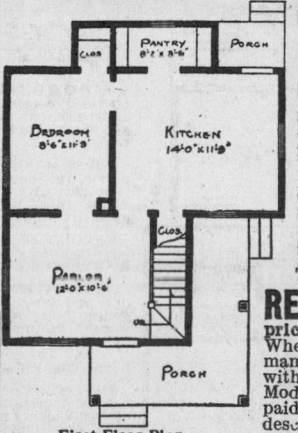

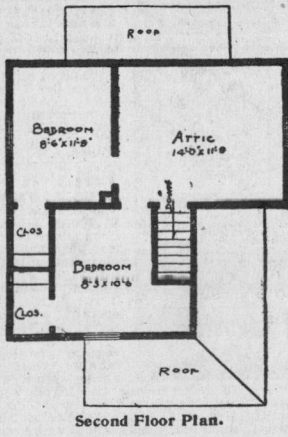

First Floor Plan.

Second Floor Plan.

COMPARE THIS, OUR $725.00 HOUSE,
with a house which would cost in your locality from $1,100.00 to $1,400.00. If in doubt send for the plans for this building and compare the exterior, the size, the foundation, the porch work and all outer trimmings of this building, then compare the interior finish, the doors, the windows and trim, hardware, in fact all materials that we specify in these special plans and specifications, and you will be immediately convinced beyond doubt that we can save you all we claim. This $725.00 house which we show on this page represents but one of the many wonderful values we show in our beautiful book of Modern Homes. We guarantee to show you a saving in the same proportion on all the houses we furnish plans and material for, which will range from $725.00 to $4,000.00. With our plans you can build an $1,800.00 house for $1,200.00, a $2,000.00 house for $1,500.00, a $2,400.00 house for $1,750.00, etc. This wonderful saving in cost by using our plans and specifications is so great that many persons wonder how such extraordinary values are possible, and to such people we wish to say that the enormous saving is only made possible by our selling mill work, hardware and other kinds of material we furnish to you at manufacturers' cost plus one small percentage of profit. We save you a large chain of profits, profits which go to the manufacturer, the jobber, the retail lumbermen, architects; we plan our houses with a view of the strictest economy by making lumber cut to the very best advantage, which in itself represents a saving from 10 to 20 per cent in this commodity alone.

IF YOU ARE INTERESTED IN BUILDING,
no matter how small or how large a house, do not overlook our wonderful offers. Our building plans and specifications, which are so plainly outlined and described in our special book of Modern Homes, have saved many of our customers hundreds of dollars. You cannot afford to overlook this wonderful opportunity.

THE PLANS FOR THIS HOUSE OR ANY
OTHER HOUSE will be sent you the same day we receive your order. The plans we send you are regular blue prints, plans which are drawn ¼-inch to the foot and are positively accurate in every detail, showing the front and side elevation, floor plans, the interior details, etc. All our plans are printed by electric blue print process on the finest grade of paper, showing every line and figure perfect and distinct.

OUR SPECIFICATIONS ARE TYPEWRITTEN
on the finest grade of linen paper and bound in a very artistic manner with an attractive heavy linen cover. These specifications consist of from fifteen to twenty pages of closely typewritten matter which gives full instructions for carrying out the work, everything is explained in a clear and explicit manner. Our plans and specifications are so carefully drawn up that they can be made a basis of contract between yourself and the contractor, as it fully explains how a contract should be let. The plans define what work must be performed by the contractor, what work must be performed by the carpenter, specifies what kind or grade of material must be used; in fact, it would represent a more definite contract than it would be possible for your home architect to draw up, as it is the result of many years practice of some of the best architects in this country.

GOOD MATERIALS MAKE GOOD HOUSES.
When planning our houses it is a question of how good, not how cheap. This statement is easily proven by referring to some of the materials we illustrate and describe here below. In using our plans you take no risk of getting poor materials, such as might occur if the work was done by some unscrupulous contractor. The mill work specified is the best in their respective grades. You take no risk when building from our plans, as we positively guarantee every piece of material we specify and, providing same is not entirely satisfactory, it may be returned and your money will be refunded together with all transportation charges.

OUR $725.00 HOUSE, ILLUSTRATED ABOVE, CONSISTS OF SIX FAIR SIZED ROOMS
arranged in such a manner that it can be most economically heated. First floor, large kitchen, 14 by 11 feet 9 inches; bedroom, 8 feet 6 inches by 11 feet 9 inches; parlor, 12 feet by 10 feet 6 inches. Second floor, front bedroom, 8 feet 3 inches by 10 feet 6 inches; rear bedroom, 8 feet 6 inches by 11 feet 9 inches. One large attic, 14 feet by 11 feet 9 inches. The bedrooms have large roomy closets.

REMEMBER,
we can furnish plans for houses ranging in price from $725.00 to $4,000.00 free. Whether it be a modest little home or a mansion, be sure and do not consider building without first sending for our beautiful book of Modern Homes, which will be sent free, postpaid. This special book is illustrated and described on page 594.

$100.00 FREE
BUILDING PLAN OFFER FULLY EXPLAINED ON PAGE 594. BE SURE TO READ EVERY WORD OF THIS GREAT FREE OFFER.

THE FRONT DOOR
furnished with our $725.00 house is covered with two coats of paint and handsomely grained to imitate oil finished Red Oak and finished with a heavy coat of varnish, size, 2 feet 8 inches by 6 feet 8 inches, glazed with a sand blast design like illustration. Doors of this quality, as a rule, are only to be found in a much higher priced house. Inside doors, as illustrated to the right, are fine Yellow Pine and will take an elegant oil finish.

THIS HANDSOME COTTAGE WINDOW
is furnished in our $725.00 house. The top sash, size 14x40 inches, is glazed with beautiful sand blast design exactly like illustration. The bottom sash, size 40x46 inches, is glazed with best AA quality double strength glass.

SEE THE EXCELLENT HARDWARE
we specify in the construction of our $725.00 house. These locks have genuine cast bronze front, bolts and strike, heavy wrought bronze knobs and 2¼ x 7½-inch outside escutcheons. The raised surface is shown by white lines and the background is in black. Compare these locks with houses in your neighborhood and you will be convinced that the hardware we specify is better in our $725.00 house than that which is usually furnished in a $1,200.00 house.

All mill work material specified in our houses is made under our own supervision in our own factories. We can guarantee our customers that any mill work material we specify is the best in the market.

WONDERFUL VALUES IN HOT AIR FURNACES
QUICK, POWERFUL, FRESH AIR VENTILATING AND HEATING.

FOR $53.94 extra we will ventilate and heat this house to an average of 70 degrees and in the coldest climate during the coldest weather, with our famous Acme Hummer Soft Coal Furnace.

FOR $56.49 we will heat it with our Acme Tropic Anthracite Coal Furnace, all completely equipped with all hot air pipes and registers.

WRITE FOR OUR BIG FURNACE BOOK
where we tell you all about these wonderful ventilating and heating furnaces, and how to send us a rough sketch of the ground plan of your house. If you are building a new house or rebuilding an old one, you cannot afford to be without our prices. Get our estimates now and order early.

GREAT WOOD MANTEL OFFER.

$10.53

Mantel No. 248

$10.53 for this beautiful, solid oak Mantel. For $10.53 extra we will supply this house with this splendid cabinet mantel.

$4.00 extra for beautiful colored enamel tile facing and hearth.

$2.93 extra for oxidized copper finish coal grate outfit with summer front.

Send for our big, free, beautifully illustrated Mantel Catalogue, fully described on page 159.

$1700.00 AND OUR FREE BUILDING PLANS

WILL BUILD, PAINT AND COMPLETE READY FOR OCCUPANCY, THIS $2,500.00 EIGHT-ROOM HOUSE

READ OUR WONDERFUL FREE BUILDING PLAN OFFER FULLY EXPLAINED ON PAGE 594.

TO SAVE ONE-THIRD the cost of your next building, to get the best, a modern and conveniently arranged house made of the best materials, to get valuable advice on how to save on cost of construction, read every word of our wonderful FREE BUILDING PLAN OFFER ($50.00 or $100.00 saved alone on architect fees), then read how we can save you from 25 to 33 per cent besides for materials, including mill work, hardware, plumbing and heating. Read how we can build you a bigger and better house for less money than any other concern on earth. All this valuable information is fully explained on page 594.

WE SPECIFY ONLY GOOD SUBSTANTIAL MATERIAL in all our houses, believing that a cheap or poorly constructed house is expensive at any price. We offer a few examples of the material used in our $1,700.00 eight-room house. Such material, as a rule, is used only in houses costing $2,500.00 and upward.

THIS ARTISTIC FRONT WINDOW, bottom sash, size, 40x46, glazed with best quality double strength glass. Top sash, size, 40x14, glazed with beautiful leaded art glass, as shown in illustration.

WE SPECIFY the best A quality Nona River soft pine doors, in five-panel style, finely selected and are suitable for natural oil finishes.

THE FRONT DOOR specified for this house is exactly like illustration. It is made of the finest quality Nona River pine with genuine wood carvings and massive cap and apron trimmings. Size, 2 feet 8 inches by 6 feet 8 inches, 1⅜ inches thick, glazed with etched art glass, as shown in this illustration. Get our plans and specifications and see how good all the material is that we specify in our houses.

THIS ILLUSTRATION AT THE RIGHT shows the kind of hardware used in our $1,700.00 house. Front door lock in the beautiful colonial pattern is furnished in antique copper or polished bronze finish. We specify all material we furnish by giving it our regular catalogue number, thus enabling our customers to refer to our catalogue, which gives very complete descriptions as to quality, size, etc. Every article furnished by us in all of our houses is sold under our liberal guarantee, providing that if goods are not exactly as represented same may be returned and your money will be refunded.

$57.25 FOR OUR EVER READY PNEUMATIC WATER SUPPLY OUTFIT

with hand force pump, which is illustrated here, can be installed in this our $1,700.00 or any of our houses. With this $57.25 outfit it is possible to have an abundant supply of cool, fresh water always ready for use. With this system water does not become stagnant or warm in summer and ice cold in winter as is the case with overhead tanks. This pneumatic tank can be set vertically or horizontally. In the basement or underneath the ground below the frost line. The system shown in the illustration is our No. 42C2044 fully illustrated and described in our Special Hot Water Heating Catalogue. We will send a copy FREE immediately upon receipt of request. A postal will bring one by return mail. With this system you can enjoy the same conveniences as though you were located in the city which has the regular water supply. With these outfits we furnish a blue print diagram showing how the connections between the tank and pump are made and also send full instructions for setting up and operating.

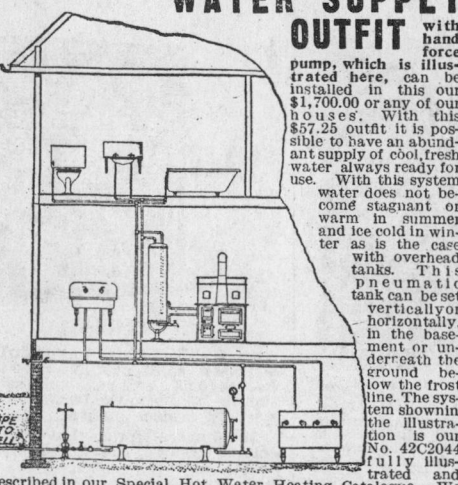

A GOOD, SUBSTANTIAL HOUSE, consisting of two floors and basement with siding exterior and shingle roof and stone foundation.

FIRST FLOOR contains large parlor, vestibule hall, sitting room, bedroom with closet, bathroom, dining room with china closet, a good size kitchen and pantry.

SECOND FLOOR contains three large bedrooms, large clothes closets, linen closet and hall.

THE INTERIOR finish in the first and second floors is made of yellow pine, which will make an elegant natural finish, giving an appearance equal, if not superior, to oak. The kitchen and pantry have a maple floor.

BASEMENT. Large and roomy basement; size, 27 feet 6 inches by 33 feet 4 inches and 6 feet 3 inches high, well lighted and ventilated. Width of house, 27 feet 6 inches; length of house, 47 feet 3 inches; height of first story, 9 feet; height of second story, 8 feet.

Every plan we offer has the seal of a licensed architect affixed, which is a guarantee that the specifications are in accordance with the building laws and will stand the closest inspection by city or country building inspectors.

FIRST FLOOR PLAN.

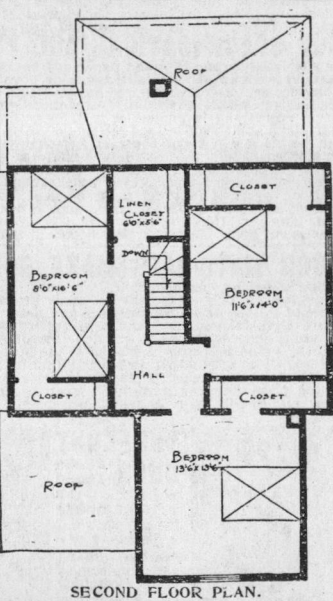

SECOND FLOOR PLAN.

WE HEAT AND VENTILATE IT

WONDERFUL OFFER IN HOUSE HEATING AND VENTILATING FURNACES.

FOR $79.52 EXTRA, we will heat this big house to an average of 70 degrees in the coldest climate, during the coldest weather, with our famous Acme Hummer Soft Coal Furnace.

FOR $81.95 we will heat it with our Acme Tropic Anthracite Coal Furnace. All completely equipped with all hot air pipes and registers. Our Big Furnace Book free for the asking. If you are building a new house or remodeling an old one, you cannot afford to be without this Big Furnace Book. Get our estimate now and order early.

SEE OUR WONDERFUL WOOD MANTEL OFFER ON PAGES 159 AND 595.

$1995.00 AND OUR FREE BUILDING PLANS

WILL BUILD, PAINT AND COMPLETE, READY FOR OCCUPANCY, THIS $3,000.00 HOUSE

READ ALL ABOUT OUR GRAND FREE OFFER, FULLY EXPLAINED ON PAGE 594.

THIS HANDSOME NINE-ROOM CONCRETE RESIDENCE, a structure which could not be duplicated for less than $3,000.00 if built in the old fashioned way with natural finished stone, can be built according to our free plans and specifications for $1,995.00. This elegant house is constructed with 8-inch by 16-inch concrete blocks, a material which is identical with hand finished stone, but which will outwear, give better satisfaction, is more sanitary, perfectly dry at all seasons of the year, cool in summer, warm in winter. Concrete construction is no longer in the experimental stage. Some of the most costly and largest residences and office buildings erected during the last ten years have been made of concrete construction and have proven to be superior to frame or stone buildings in every respect.

CONCRETE HOUSES can be erected at one-third less than any other kind of stone structures. They can be built in less time and with much lower priced labor than other kind of structures. With one of our Wizard or Buckeye Concrete Block Machines, fully described on pages 574 to 579, anyone can make a sufficient number of blocks at leisure moments during the dull season of the year to erect his buildings and thus save the cost of labor. Our $1,995.00 price includes the cost of hired labor.

WE FURNISH FREE BUILDING PLANS AND SPECIFICATIONS for a large variety of concrete block and frame houses. This grand free offer is fully explained on page 594. These plans are made by some of the best licensed architects in this country who have carefully studied the requirements of our trade, and every plan we offer is so carefully and accurately laid out that all unnecessary waste of material and labor is entirely eliminated.

IF YOU ARE INTERESTED IN BUILDING, if you want to save one-third to one-half of the entire cost on your future home read all about our free offer on page 594, which fully explains the greatest building proposition ever made. When you have read all we have to tell you on page 594, send for our special Book of Modern Homes from which you may select the house which meets your requirements in every particular; tell us the number of the house you want to know more about and we will send you a complete set of our free plans and specifications which will itemize every piece of material, which will give you an approximate cost of the labor, in fact will give you all and more information than you would be able to get from an architect in your home town, who would charge you from $50.00 to $100.00 or more for his expert advice.

BESIDES SAVING YOU THE ENTIRE COST OF ARCHITECT FEES for plans and specifications, we save you one-third the cost of your mill work, including windows, doors, mouldings, casings, stairwork, grilles, flooring. We also save you from 25 to 50 per cent on the cost of your plumbing materials, furnaces and hot water systems, water supply outfits, paints and varnishes, building hardware, in fact we can save you on every item which enters the construction of any house, dimension timber excepted. Remember, we supply only first quality material, in fact, better material than many architects specify. To illustrate, for an example, the kind of material we specify in the house illustrated on this page, we show and describe a few of the many items we furnish. You'll find they are equal in every respect to material usually specified in houses ranging from $3,000.00 to $4,500.00.

MASSIVE FRONT DOOR exactly like illustration to the left. Made of the finest selected pine in plain design. Glazed with the finest beveled French plate glass. Size, 3x7 feet, 1¾ inches thick.

REAR DOOR made of the finest selected A quality Nona River soft pine; beautiful raised panel design, glazed with artistic etched glass design, finished in natural finish. Size, 3x7 feet, 1⅜ inches thick. REMEMBER, OUR PLANS ARE FREE.

LARGE ARTISTIC FRONT WINDOW furnished with this

house is exactly like illustration to the right. Top sash 40x16 inches, glazed with art leaded sheet glass. Bottom sash 40x40 inches, glazed with heavy double strength AA quality glass.

FIVE CROSS PANEL INTERIOR DOORS made of the finest quality Nona River soft pine, yellow pine panels, perfectly adapted for oil finish, size, 2 ft. 6 in. by 6 ft. 6 in.

OUR CONCRETE BUILDING BLOCK MACHINES, the lowest priced, the highest grade, the most perfect and most rapid concrete block machines made, are illustrated, described and priced on pages 574 to 581. With our machines you can make all the concrete blocks, columns, porch rails, etc., for this house or any other style of concrete block buildings. Our machines are perfect and our low prices will surprise you.

Our $1,995.00 House

illustrated above, consists of nine good sized rooms and bath room, as shown in these floor plans.

FIRST FLOOR, kitchen, 13x10 feet, and pantry; dining room, 14x12 feet; living room, 14x16 feet 6 inches; reception hall, 11 feet 6 inches by 11 feet; bedroom, 11 feet 6 inches by 14 feet.

SECOND FLOOR, bedroom, 12x12 feet; bedroom, 9 feet 6 inches by 12 feet; bedroom, 10 feet 6 inches by 12 feet 6 inches; bedroom, 11 feet 6 inches by 7 feet; bathroom, 7 feet by 5 feet 9 inches; linen closet and hall. Bedrooms have large closets.

The arrangement of our houses is such that they can be well heated with very little expense. Our $1,995.00 house is but one of the many frame or concrete houses for which we are able to furnish our free building plans and specifications. No matter what price house you may want to build, remember we can save you from 25 to 50 per cent. Be sure to read all about our wonderful free plan offer, which is fully explained on page 594.

DESIGN #1152 FIRST FLOOR

DESIGN #1152 SECOND FLOOR

INSTALL THIS $300.00 HOT WATER HEATING PLANT IN THIS HOUSE FOR $209.14

HOT WATER HEATING is the most satisfactory means of heating. While its first cost is a trifle higher than furnace or steam systems, it is much cheaper in the long run, as it will save many times its first cost in economy of fuel. Unlike any other system, it can be regulated to maintain an even temperature at all times.

THIS PLANT CONSISTS of our 127 sectional water boiler, seven 38-inch three-column hot water radiators, all necessary valves, union elbows, air valves, pipe and fittings, as shown in the illustration to the right. This hot water plant, although moderate in price, will comfortably heat this house with the exposures on four sides, during the coldest winter weather and will maintain a uniform temperature at 70 degrees when the outside temperature is 10 degrees below zero. This plant will be found suitable for this house in any part of the United States.

WHETHER YOU ARE BUILDING a new house or whether you intend to install some means of heating in your home, do not fail to read all about our hot water and steam heating plants, fully described on page 613.

ON REQUEST, we will furnish an estimate for plant in this or any other house based on any special conditions. With each order for one of these plants we will furnish working drawings and complete instructions for setting up. The illustration to the right shows this heating plant set up.

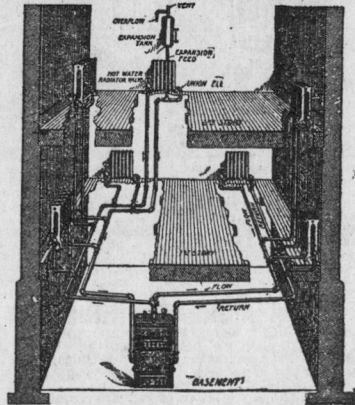

SEE OUR GREAT OFFER IN WOOD MANTELS ON PAGES 159 AND 595.

PLUMBING GOODS SUPPLIES
AT REDUCED PRICES

Our sales on this line of material has increased to such an extent during the past year that our factory has been able to materially reduce the cost of production on account of the increased volume of business. As it has always been our custom to add but one small margin of profit to our actual cost on all merchandise, we are glad to give our customers the benefit of this reduction, and it will no doubt be very apparent to you, by studying the following pages of this catalogue, THAT THESE PRICES HAVE BEEN MATERIALLY REDUCED.

WE SHOW on this and the following pages of this catalogue a complete line of plumbing material at prices, quality considered, which defy competition. This line of goods has heretofore been controlled by the Plumbing Trust, and in order to offer to our customers the values in this line which we have in others listed in our catalogue, we have erected our own Plumbing Goods Factory, and we now own these goods at the right prices, and are absolutely independent of any trust or combination of any sort.

IN THIS FACTORY we manufacture none but the highest grade of plumbing material, material which would stand our guarantee, allowing you to return any goods not thoroughly satisfactory to you and we will refund your money and pay the transportation charges both ways. Knowing from a careful comparison of our

goods with those turned out by other manufacturers, we feel confident in saying that we can save you about one-third on this line of material.

WE SHOW ON THIS PAGE for the convenience of our customers, complete bathroom outfits with bath tubs, lavatories and closets all complete, with supply and waste pipes, in combinations, including all fittings above the floor.

SHOULD YOU, HOWEVER, not desire to purchase these outfits, complete, in this way, you will find the different articles listed separately on the following pages, from which you may select any pieces which will suit you.

OUR PERFECTION BATHROOM OUTFIT $43.80
REDUCED FROM $46.78

WE ILLUSTRATE IN OUR PERFECTION BATHROOM OUTFIT A COMBINATION WHICH IS STRICTLY HIGH GRADE, AND ONE WHICH HAS GIVEN OUR CUSTOMERS UNIVERSAL SATISFACTION. WE HAVE SENT OUT THOUSANDS OF THESE OUTFITS, AND HAVE YET TO HEAR FROM OUR FIRST DISSATISFIED CUSTOMER ON THIS COMBINATION.

THE CLOSET furnished with this outfit is a low down pattern, is thoroughly sanitary, and one that will pass the most rigid inspection. The tank of this outfit is made of golden oak, thoroughly seasoned and highly polished. It has a capacity of 6½ gallons, which is sufficient to cause a positive and powerful flush. It is lined with copper, all fittings and trimmings are made of heavy brass, and it is furnished with a Douglas valve, which is one of the best valves on the market on account of its simplicity. The water is shut off by a rubber ball setting into the seat of the flush valve, and should it become necessary at any time to repair this valve, all that is necessary is to unscrew this rubber ball from the rod and screw in a new ball, an operation which any child would have no difficulty in performing. It is also furnished with a china push button at the front of the tank, which adds considerably to the appearance of the tank. The seat furnished with this outfit is a golden oak. Closet seat, which is highly polished, is furnished with cover. It is also furnished with offset nickel plated heavy brass hinges. The bowl furnished with this closet is a syphonic action bowl made of the highest grade English vitreous earthenware, and is the equal to any pottery on the market, regardless of price. We furnish this closet complete with tank, seat, bowl, supply pipes and nickel plated closet screws to fasten bowl to floor.

THE LAVATORY furnished with this outfit is a cast iron porcelain enameled lavatory 18x21 inches in size, an 8-inch back and a 4-inch roll rim. We consider this lavatory one of the neatest and most efficient lavatories ever placed on the market. It is furnished complete with a sanitary soap tray, 1¼-inch heavy nickel plated S trap, with vent to wall and waste to floor, two nickel plated low down compression basin cocks with china tops marked "Hot" and "Cold," two nickel plated supply pipes from basin to floor.

THE BATH TUB furnished with this outfit is a 5-foot cast iron roll rim bath tub. It is manufactured from the highest grade gray cast iron, is graceful in appearance and is equal to any bath tub on the market. We furnish this bath tub complete with a No. 4½ Fuller bath cock made of brass, highly nickel plated and connected with brass nickel plated waste and overflow pipes, and two heavy brass nickel plated supply pipes.

WE APPRECIATE that other concerns are advertising plumbing goods, which in appearance are cheaper than this outfit, but when you take into consideration that we furnish nothing but the highest grade material, all of which we guarantee to be strictly perfect, all fittings made of brass, heavily nickel plated, we believe we have the cheapest outfit on the market today. The closet in this outfit is shipped from Chicago, the bath tub and lavatory from our factory in Southeastern Wisconsin. Shipping weight, about 480 pounds.
No. 42K214   Price...................... **$43.80**

For the convenience of our customers, we can furnish the above outfit with all fittings threaded for iron pipe connection at an extra charge of $1.50.

OUR LEADER BATHROOM OUTFIT, $33.90
REDUCED FROM $34.95.

We illustrate in our Leader Bathroom Outfit one of the best medium priced bathroom outfits, quality considered, that was ever offered by anyone.

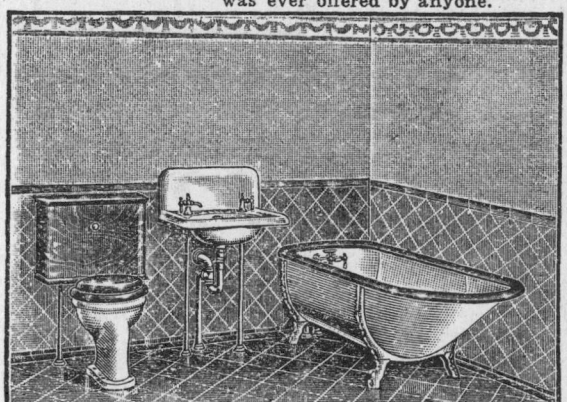

THE CLOSET furnished with this outfit is a lowdown pattern with tank of golden oak, nicely polished. It is lined with heavy copper and is furnished with a positive flush valve and with a china push button, a slight touch of which will empty the tank completely. The closet bowl is made of the highest grade of English vitreous earthenware and has a syphonic action.

THE BATH TUB furnished with this outfit is a 5-foot heavy roll rim, cast iron, enameled inside with a heavy coat of white enamel put on by a special process, which we guarantee will not flake or peel. The outside is handsomely painted and the legs are trimmed with gold bronze. The rim is made of oak, is 3 inches wide and 1½ inches thick. The overflow and waste are made of brass and are heavily nickel plated. The tub is furnished complete with nickel plated brass supply pipes and No. 4½ Fuller bath cock.

THE LAVATORY furnished with this outfit is an enameled iron lavatory, size 18x24 inches, with a 10-inch back. The slab and back all being in one piece makes a thoroughly sanitary article, and it is furnished with a sanitary soap tray, nickel plated chain and chain stay, improved wall brackets, nickel plated brass Fuller basin cocks, nickel plated brass S trap with waste to floor and vent to wall and nickel plated brass supply pipes to floor.

IT IS NOT A CHEAP, SHODDY OUTFIT, but is made up of No. 1 material, and while it is not as pretty or substantial an outfit as our Perfection Outfit, nevertheless it is a bargain, and for a person wanting a cheap outfit we believe that this one, at the price we ask for it, has no equal. The closet on this outfit is shipped from Chicago. The lavatory and bath tub from our factory in Southeastern Wisconsin. Shipping weight, about 280 pounds.
No. 42K204   Price.................... **$33.90**
For the convenience of our customers we can furnish this outfit with all fittings threaded for iron pipe connections at an extra charge of $1.35.

OUR GEM BATHROOM OUTFIT, $51.10
REDUCED FROM $55.95.

IN OUR GEM BATHROOM OUTFIT WE ARE OFFERING TO OUR CUSTOMERS a strictly high grade bathroom outfit, and one that is suitable for any bathroom. We have gotten up this outfit in order that our customers may have an opportunity of equipping their homes with an outfit equal to anything on the market, regardless of price.

THE TUB furnished with this outfit is a 5-foot heavy roll rim, cast iron, highly enameled bath tub with claw pattern feet, and is furnished complete with our No. 4½ brass nickel plated bath cock, nickel plated heavy brass supply pipes, and nickel plated brass connected waste and overflow.

THE LAVATORY furnished is an 18x24-inch lavatory with a 10-inch back, made of high grade cast iron, heavily enameled by a special process which we guarantee will not flake, craze or peel off. It has a large apron as shown in illustration, and is furnished complete with our bell trap, nickel plated air chamber supply pipes and nickel plated brass faucets.

THE CLOSET furnished in this outfit is a syphon jet bowl with a low down tank and seat. The tank is a highly polished tank fitted with heavy brass trimmings, has a china push button in front of tank, a slight touch of which releases the valve and causes a positive flush. It is furnished with a heavy brass nickel plated supply pipe from tank to the floor. The seat is made of highly polished oak and has heavy brass nickel plated offset hinges. The bowl furnished with this closet is made of the very highest grade of English vitreous earthenware.

WE FEEL POSITIVE any person purchasing this outfit from us will be more than satisfied with the quality of the goods and the appearance of the outfit, as it is impossible for us to do justice to this outfit by anything which we might say of it. The closet in this outfit is shipped from Chicago. The bath tub and lavatory from our factory in Southeastern Wisconsin. Shipping weight, about 550 pounds.
No. 42K215   Price.................... **$51.10**
For the convenience of our customers we can furnish the above outfit with all fittings threaded for iron pipe connections at an extra charge of $1.50.

HOW TO INSTALL WATER CLOSETS.

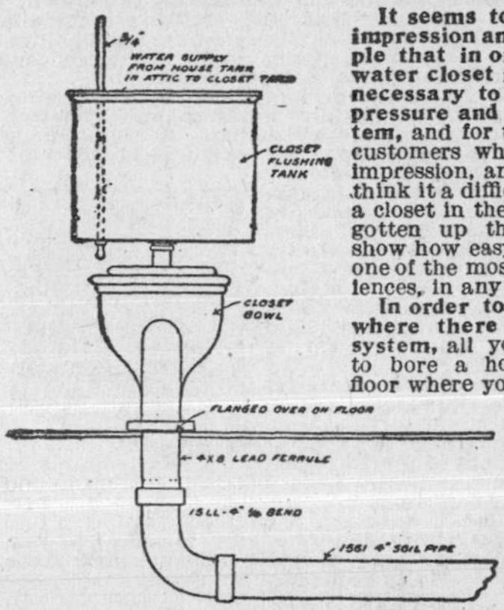

It seems to be the general impression among country people that in order to install a water closet in a home it is necessary to have city water pressure and a sewerage system, and for the benefit of our customers who are under this impression, and for those who think it a difficult task to install a closet in their home, we have gotten up this illustration to show how easy it is to put this, one of the most modern conveniences, in any home.

In order to install a closet where there is no sewerage system, all you have to do is to bore a hole through your floor where you want to place your closet, large enough to place one of our No. 42K1460 4 x 8 lead ferrules into, bend the end of this ferrule over the hole, then putty around the edge of the hole, then place the hole in the closet bowl into this ferrule and screw the bowl to floor with the closet screws which we furnish. Then place one of our No. 42K1566 4-inch quarter bends onto the other end of this ferrule, which you can calk onto the ferrule by using our No. 42K1866 oakum and enough 4-inch soil pipe to run from closet to cesspool, which you can dig yourself in any part of the yard. In connecting these joints we would recommend that you use our No. 42K1866 oakum, allowing about one pound for each joint you wish to connect.

All that is necessary for you to have in order to have one of these closets in your home is a tank on top of your house or in your attic, connect this tank with the closet tank, to allow the water to fill the closet tank. We would also recommend that you place one of our No. 42K5870 ½-inch stops somewhere between the closet tank and the tank in the attic, as you can then shut off the water from the tank at any time you desire, should your closet tank get out of order, so that you may make repairs.

OUR SPECIAL LOW DOWN OUTFIT, REDUCED TO - - - - $12.96

No. 42K111 We show in our Special Low Down Outfit a closet which we believe is one of the best bargains ever offered by anyone, and the only reason that it is possible for us to offer an outfit such as this at the abovenamed price is on account of the quantities in which we purchase them. The tank furnished with this outfit is a 6½-gallon tank and is lined with heavy copper from the bottom of the tank to the height in which the water stands in the tank. From this part to the top of the tank is placed a very heavy galvanized iron strip which prevents the moisture from eating through the wood, often the case with the majority of the low cost closets on the market today. This tank is fitted with a Douglas valve, which is one of the simplest and best valves on the market. It is operated by a rubber ball setting into the seat of the brass flush valve, and should it at any time become necessary to repair this closet through the valve wearing out, all that is necessary for you to do is to purchase a new rubber ball, unscrew the old ball from the rod of the closet and screw the new ball into place, an operation which any child can perform without any difficulty; no calling of plumbers when the tank leaks, as this valve is so simple that any person would have no difficulty in repairing it. The tank is made of golden oak which is well seasoned and highly polished, and is furnished with a china push button, a slight touch of which raises the Douglas ball, releases the water and causes a positive flush of the closet bowl. The seat furnished with this outfit is also of golden oak, made of well seasoned oak highly polished. It is furnished with nickel plated offset hinges, which are made of heavy brass, which will practically wear a lifetime. The seat is furnished with rubber bumpers where they are necessary. The bowl furnished with this outfit is a syphonic action closet bowl. It is made of the highest grade of English vitreous earthenware, is nicely glazed and polished, and the equal of pottery sold by anyone, regardless of price. We furnish nickel plated closet screws with this outfit to fasten bowl to floor. We also furnish a heavy brass nickel plated supply pipe reaching from tank to the floor. The connection furnished with this outfit to attach the bowl to the tank is a heavy brass nickel plated elbow. The closet roughs in at 12 inches from the wall. Weight, 100 pounds.

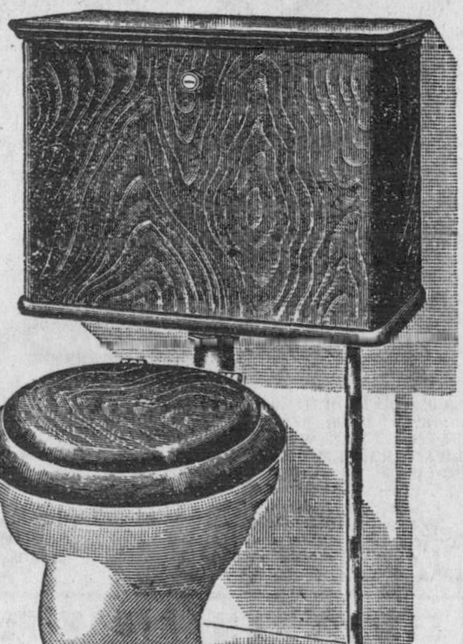

$12.96

Price, complete as described, with plain bowl......**$12.96**

If bowl is wanted with local vent, add 25 cents to above price.

We can furnish this style of bowl only, without tank or seat, for $4.75.

SYPHONIC ACTION, LOW TANK, WASH DOWN COMBINATION CLOSET $11.96

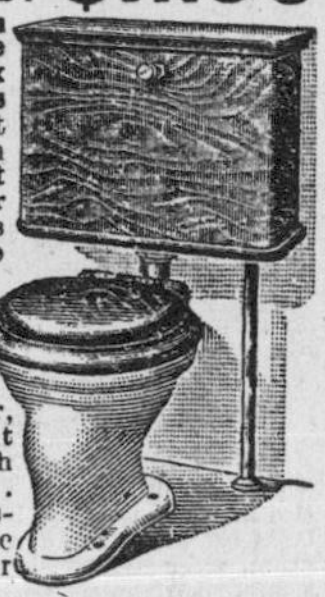

No. 42K110 Our Low Tank, Wash Down Combination is the most up to date closet sold by anyone at the price we ask for it and is lower than a closet of this kind was ever sold at before. And while it is not as well constructed or as sanitary an outfit as our No. 42K111, we guarantee it to be the equal of any wash down closet ever put on the market at anywhere near this price. The tank, seat and cover are made of solid oak, golden oak finish, tank is a 6½ gallon tank, is copper lined; has copper floats, solid brass, valve, improved flushing valve. All trimmings, hinges, etc., made of cast brass, heavily nickel plated. Supply pipe is ⅝ inch in diameter, made of brass also nickel plated. A slight pressure of the valve button gives a flush that empties the tank completely. Furnshed complete, as shown in the illustration. Weight, 100 pounds. Before ordering this closet read description of our No. 42K111 closet on this page.

Price, complete, with plain bowl......................**$11.96**

If wanted with local vent, add 25 cents to the above price.

We can furnish this style bowl only, without seat or tank, for $4.75.

PIANO POLISH QUARTER SAWED OAK, LOW DOWN CLOSET, REDUCED TO - - - - - - $14.15

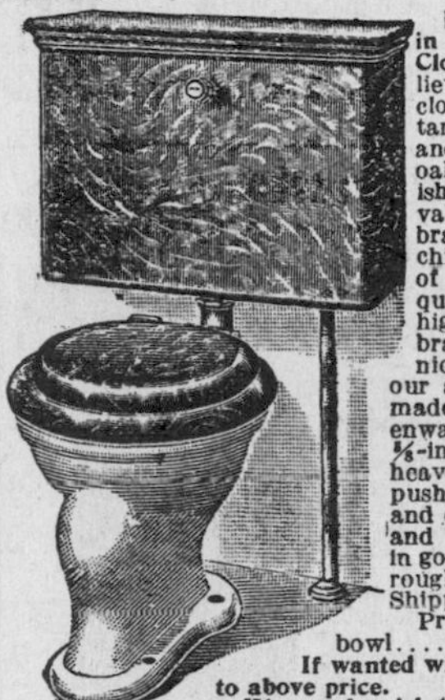

No. 42K116 We have in our Quarter Sawed Oak Closet Combination, we believe, the best syphon action closet on the market. The tank is a 6½-gallon tank, and is made of quarter sawed oak with a high piano polish, is lined with copper; all valves and fittings are heavy brass and are equipped with a china push button in front of tank. The seat is made of quarter sawed oak with a high piano polish, has heavy brass offset hinges, highly nickel plated. The bowl is our syphon action bowl and is made of vitreous English earthenware. Supply pipe is made of ⅝-inch heavy brass tubing, heavily nickel plated. A slight push of the button opens valve and causes an instant, noiseless and positive flush. Furnished in golden oak finish. This closet roughs in at 12 inches from wall. Shipping weight, 100 pounds.

Price, with plain bowl..................**$14.15**

If wanted with local vent, add 25 cents to above price.

We can furnish this style bowl only, without tank or seat, for $4.75.

ENAMELED IRON HOPPER CLOSET - $10.75

REDUCED FROM $11.05.

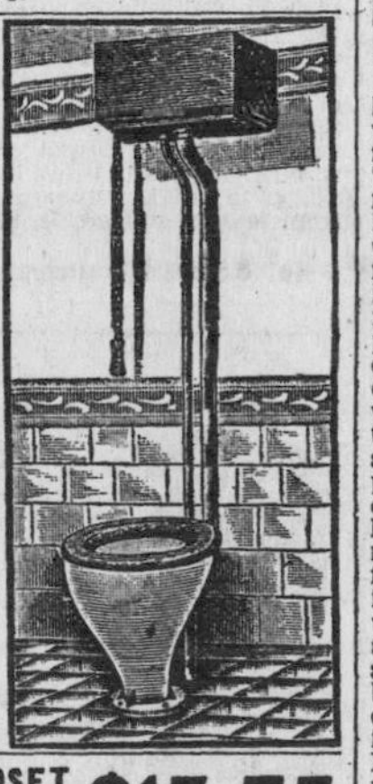

No. 42K131 In our Enameled Hopper Closet we are able to offer our customers a very serviceable closet for basements or any place where a closet will be subject to rough and careless use. The bowl is made of iron, enameled white on the inside and painted on the outside. The tank is a golden oak closet tank and is lined with heavy copper; has loose board back to attach tank to wall. The trimmings are made of heavy brass. Furnished complete, with bowl, tank, seat and nickel plated brass flush and supply pipes. This seat cannot be raised as in our other outfits, but is screwed stationary onto bowl. Weight, about 100 pounds.

Price, complete........**$10.75**

LOW TANK COMBINATION CLOSET WITH SYPHON JET BOWL, REDUCED FROM $16.25. $15.75

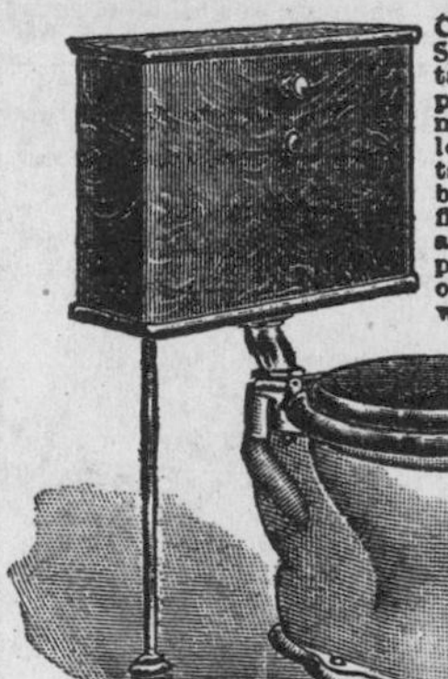

No. 42K120 Low Tank Combination Closet, with Syphon Jet Bowl. The low tank closet is by far the most popular closet now on the market. It does away with the long supply pipes and high tank. Has a 2-inch opening in bowl, which insures a positive flush every time; is noiseless and neat in appearance. Can be placed in an out of the way place or under stairs where high tank will not go. The tank is made of solid oak, golden oak finish, is lined with heavy sheet copper, has copper float, brass valve, etc. The valve is our improved positive flush valve, cannot get out of order. A slight pressure of the valve lever or button empties the tank completely. The seat and cover are made of oak, with heavy brass offset hinges, heavy nickel plated; supply pipe is ⅝ inch in diameter, nickel plated; furnished complete ready to set up with a heavy brass nickel plated connection from tank to bowl. The bowl is high grade vitreous English earthenware—syphon jet style—roughs in at 14 inches from wall and is by far the best pottery made. Shipping weight, about 115 pounds.

Price, complete, with plain earthenware bowl......**$15.75**

If wanted with local vent, add 25 cents to above price.

We can furnish this style bowl only, without tank or seat, for $9.20.

PIANO POLISH QUARTER SAWED OAK OUTFIT WITH SYPHON JET BOWL, COMPLETE, REDUCED TO - - - $17.25

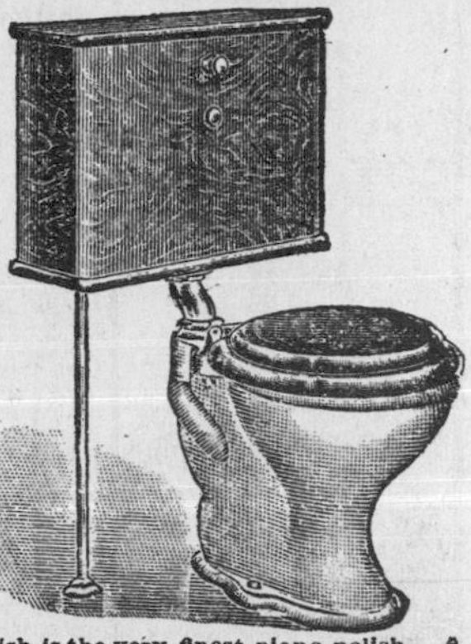

No. 42K125 Low Down Tank, Syphon Jet Combination Closet. Has a round cornered quarter sawed oak tank with heavy moulding attached to cover. Piano finish and extra heavy trimmings. Tank is lined with copper, has copper float, brass valves, etc. Seat is quarter sawed oak with heavy offset brass hinges, heavily nickel plated; supply pipe is ⅝-inch, made of brass, nickel plated with china push button flush in front of tank; a slight pressure empties the tank completely. The bowl is a genuine syphon jet high grade vitreous English earthenware. Nothing better made. It is similar to our No. 42K120, but made of much better material. All trimmings are heavier and finish is the very finest piano polish. A high class closet in every respect. Furnished complete with heavy brass nickel plated connection to connect tank to bowl. This closet roughs in at 14 inches from wall. Shipping weight, about 115 pounds.

Price, complete, with plain bowl...............**$17.25**

If wanted with local vent add 25 cents to above price.

We can furnish this style bowl only, without tank or seat, for $9.20.

IMPROVED PATTERN ENAMEL IRON HOPPER CLOSET, REDUCED TO - $4.76

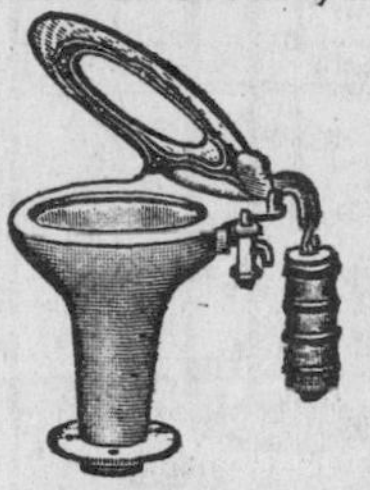

No. 42K100 This is our latest Improved Hopper Closet, complete with brass valve, heavy round seat and iron weight. This closet is intended to be connected to water supply. When seat is lowered it opens valve and when seat raises, which it does automatically, it shuts off the valve and water. It can be connected with ¾ or 1-inch lead pipe. No waste or supply pipes or tank furnished in this outfit. Weight, 50 pounds.

Price, complete, as shown in illustration....................**$4.76**

We can furnish the above closet, tapped for ½-inch iron pipe, for an additional charge of 50 cents over prices quoted.

IMPROVED ENAMEL FROSTPROOF CLOSET, COMPLETE, REDUCED TO $9.89

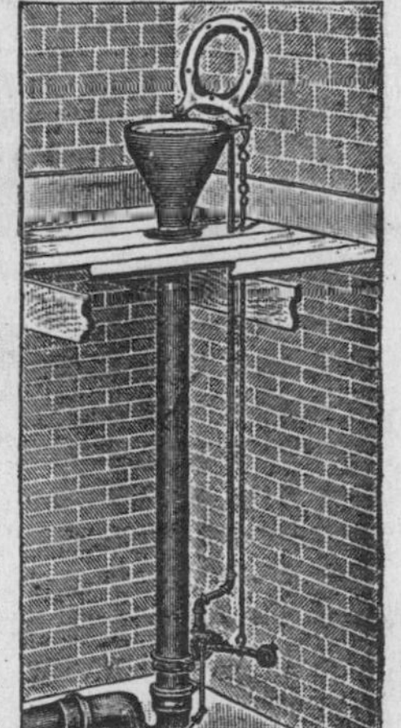

No. 42K105 In our New Frostproof Closet we believe we have one of the best frostproof closets on the market. The heavy brass valve which we furnish is placed below the frost line and is connected to hopper with a heavy coppered chain, fastened to seat. When seat is lowered, the valve opens automatically and flushes the hopper. When seat is raised, it closes the valve and opens the drain pipe, which allows all water left in pipes to drain into trap, which leaves pipes at all times free from water. The price we ask for this outfit is complete with cast iron hopper, heavily enameled inside, heavy round wood seat, heavy brass frostproof valve, 5 feet cast iron soil pipe, cast iron P trap, wrought iron supply pipe, chain and lever and combination lead and iron ferrule. This is the best outfit to use in cold or exposed places, because water is always below frost line. No closet tank is furnished or needed with this outfit. Weight, 110 pounds.

Price, complete......**$9.89**

PEERLESS WASHOUT WATER CLOSET, WITH LOOSE BOARD TANK, REDUCED FROM $12.15 TO - - - - $11.75

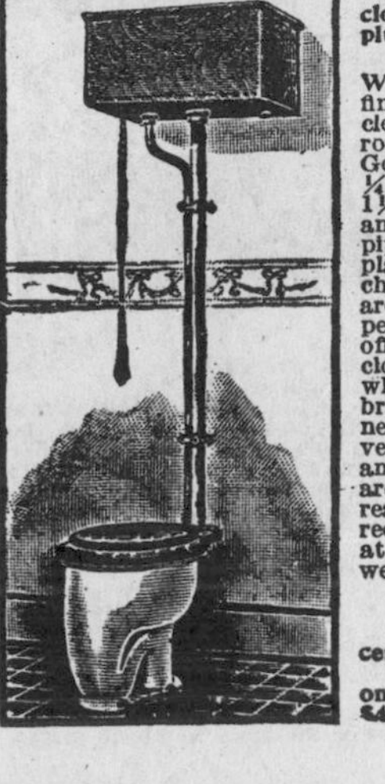

At $11.75 we offer this water closet as the equal of closets that plumbers sell at $16.00 to $20.00.

No. 42K130 Our Peerless Water Closet is by far the best finished and most up to date closet on the market. It has a round cornered oak syphon tank, Golden oak finish, with double ¼-inch sawed oak attached seat, 1¼-inch nickel plated flush pipe and ½-inch nickel plated supply pipe, with No. 3 front washout plain earthenware bowl. The chain and pull and all fixtures are nickel plated. Tank is copper lined, has patent float cut-off, with chain and pull to flush closet, and with loose back, which does away with iron brackets and makes a much neater job. It is made of the very best materials throughout and the workmanship and finish are perfect. Furnished complete, ready for use, no fitting or extras required. This closet roughs in at 10 inches from wall. Shipping weight, about 90 pounds.

Price, with plain bowl..........**$11.75**

If wanted with vent, add 25 cents to above price.

We can furnish this style bowl only, without tank or seat, for $4.10.

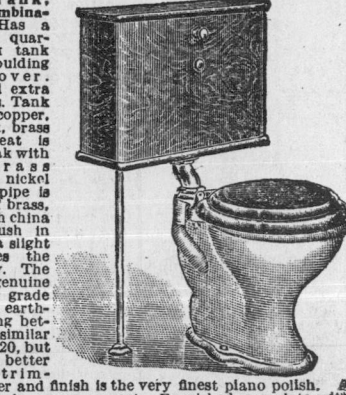

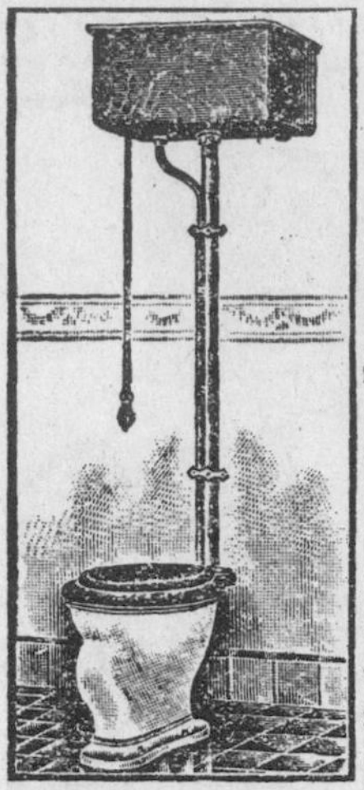

PEERLESS COMBINATION HOPPER AND TRAP CLOSET, WITH LOOSE BOARD TANK - $12.90

REDUCED FROM $13.22.

No. 42K136 Combination Hopper and Trap or Wash Down Closet. This makes one of the best low priced outfits we carry. The tank is made of oak, golden oak finish. The pipe and fittings are the same as described in our No. 42K130 closet. Everything is first class. Could not work better nor last longer at any price. A great many prefer this combination hopper to the regular No. 3 front washout, as shown in No. 42K130, as it gives a more positive flush, has greater force, etc. The tanks are fitted with a loose board back, which makes a much neater and better job than tanks furnished with brackets. This closet roughs in 9 inches from wall. Shipping weight, 95 pounds.

Price, complete, ready to set up.............$12.90

If wanted with local vent, add 25 cents to above price.

We can furnish this style bowl only, without tank, seat or supply pipes, for $4.70.

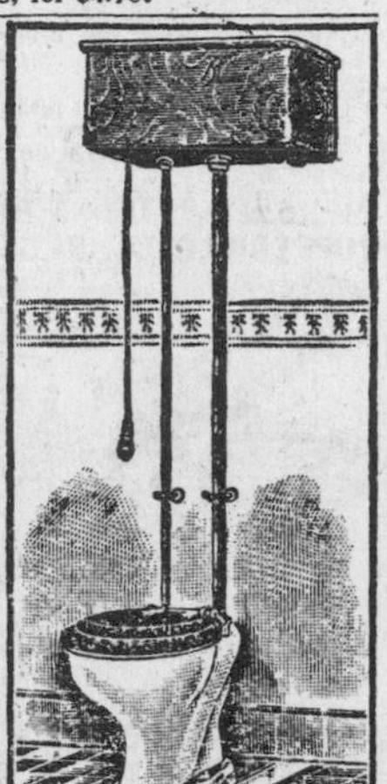

PEERLESS SYPHON JET WATER CLOSET, WITH LOOSE BOARD TANK, REDUCED FROM $18.36 $16.75

No. 42K141 Water Closet, complete as shown in illustration. Tank is copper lined; outside made of quarter sawed oak, golden oak finish; has syphon jet; 1¼-inch nickel plated flush pipe; ⅜-inch nickel plated supply pipe. Has heavy oak seat and cover attached to bowl; chain and pull, nickel plated. Furnished complete, with chain, pull, straps and floor bolts. The tanks are furnished with loose backs, which make a neater and better job. A very neat and substantial closet at a moderate price. This closet roughs in 11 inches from wall. Shipping weight, 105 pounds.

Price, with plain bowl $16.75

If wanted with local vent, add 25 cents to above price.

We can furnish this style bowl only, without tank, seat or supply pipes, for $9.15.

HIGH GRADE ROLL RIM PORCELAIN ENAMELED IRON BATH TUB, REDUCED TO - - $14.60

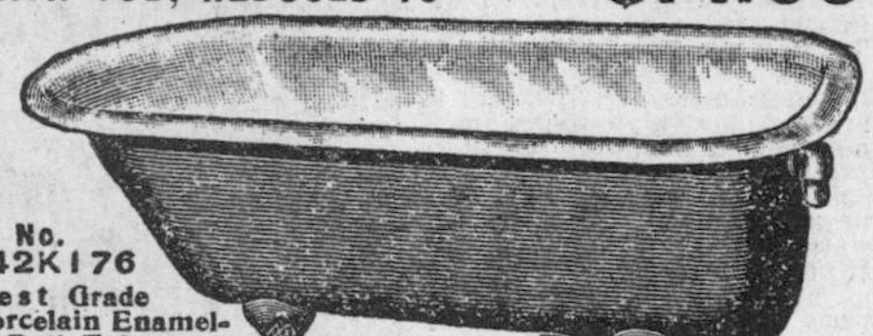

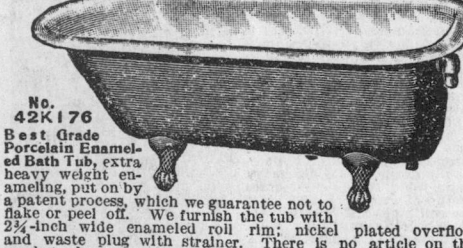

No. 42K176 Best Grade Porcelain Enameled Bath Tub, extra heavy weight enameling, put on by a patent process, which we guarantee not to flake or peel off. We furnish the tub with 2¾-inch wide enameled roll rim; nickel plated overflow and waste plug with strainer. There is no article on the market where more second hand goods are disposed of than bath tubs. We guarantee all our tubs to be strictly A Grade goods, remember this when comparing prices. Enameled inside, painted one coat outside. Height on legs, 23 inches; width over all, 30 inches; depth inside, 17 inches. Shipped from our factory in Southeastern Wisconsin.

Size of tub	4½ feet	5 feet	5½ feet
Weight, about......	250 lbs.	300 lbs.	350 lbs.
Price............	$14.60	$15.92	$18.13

NOTICE—For No. 4½ Fuller Hot and Cold Combination Cock, add $2.08 to prices given above.

HIGH GRADE ROLL RIM WHITE PORCELAIN ENAMELED BATH TUB $18.85

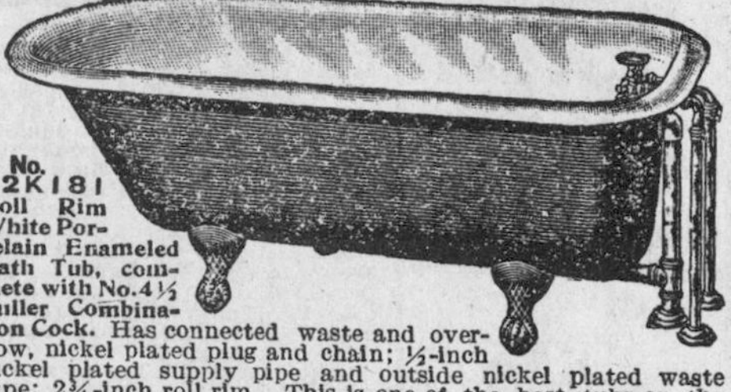

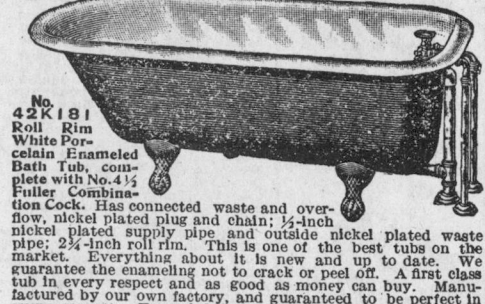

No. 42K181 Roll Rim White Porcelain Enameled Bath Tub, complete with No. 4½ Fuller Combination Cock. Has connected waste and overflow, nickel plated plug and chain; ½-inch nickel plated supply pipe and outside nickel plated waste pipe; 2¾-inch roll rim. This is one of the best tubs on the market. Everything about it is new and up to date. We guarantee the enameling not to crack or peel off. A first class tub in every respect and as good as money can buy. Manufactured by our own factory, and guaranteed to be perfect in every respect. Enameled inside, painted one coat outside. Price includes everything complete, ready for use. Height on legs, 23 inches; width over all, 30 inches; depth inside, 17 inches. Shipped from our factory in Southeastern Wisconsin.

Size of tub	4½ feet	5 feet	5½ feet
Weight, about......	250 lbs.	300 lbs.	350 lbs.
Price............	$18.85	$19.77	$21.82

Can furnish above tubs with compression bath cocks if desired at same price.

We can furnish the above tubs with all connections threaded for iron pipe at an additional cost of 50 cents to above prices.

OUR NEW MODEL STEEL BATH TUB, REDUCED TO - - - - - $5.95

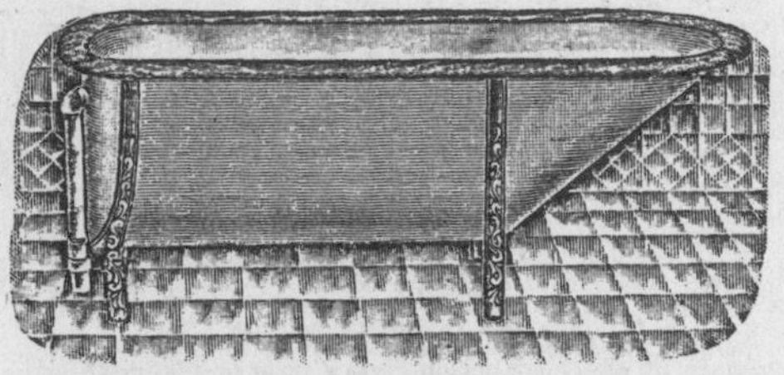

Our New Model Steel Bath Tub is the height of perfection in steel tubs, embodying all the good points of all steel tubs on the market. Made of heavy gauge galvanized sheet steel, over which a heavy coat of white enamel is put on by a special process, which we guarantee will not flake or peel off. The rim is of 3-inch highly polished oak, 1½ inches thick. The outside of tub is highly painted, the legs are highly painted and tinted in bronze, which gives the tub a handsome appearance. The overflow and waste are made of heavy brass tubing, nickel plated, and are threaded so that they may be attached to either lead or iron piping. Furnished with plug and chain, fitted for our No. 4½ Fuller Bath Cock. Shipping weight, about 90 pounds. Shipped from factory at Detroit, Mich.

No. 42K160 Size, 4 feet 6 inches. Price.......$5.95
No. 42K161 Size, 5 feet. Price 6.42
No. 42K162 Size, 5 feet 6 inches. Price 6.74
No. 42K163 Size, 6 feet. Price 7.54

NOTICE—For No. 4½ Fuller Bath Cock, add $2.08 to prices given above.

OUR MODEL NICKEL PLATED GASOLINE HEATER - - - $12.15

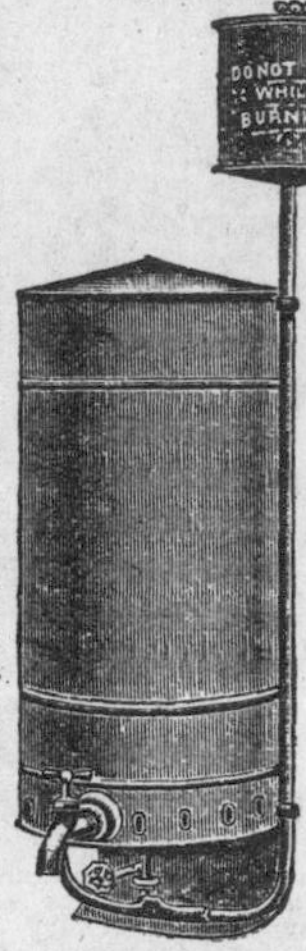

We show in our Model Gasoline Heater one of the best gasoline heaters on the market. It is made of 24-gauge galvanized iron incased in a nickel plated white metal and is an ornament to any bathroom. It is 28 inches high and 12 inches in diameter and will hold 13¾ gallons of water. The bottom of the heater is made of heavy copper and the coil for the heater is placed under the copper bottom. It is also made so that the tank can never become empty, which is the fault with other heaters, and prevents bottom of heater from burning out. The circulation is created by a ⅜-inch copper coil 6 inches in length, extending from recepticle up into the heater, which insures circulation and rapid heating qualities. The fire coming in contact with the copper bottom and the faucet so arranged that all the water drawn from the tank passes through the recepticle, enabling one to get hot water almost instantaneously. Small quantities of water heated in two minutes, and will also heat the water ready for bathing in 20 minutes. Shipping weight, 40 pounds. Shipped from factory in Detroit, Mich.

No. 42K217 Price....$12.15

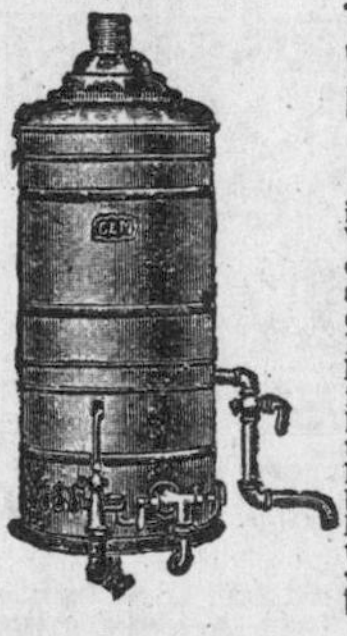

THE GEM INSTANTANEOUS WATER HEATER - $17.48

REDUCED FROM $19.85.

No. 42K224 We have secured in our Gem Instantaneous Water Heater a heater which has been on the market a great number of years and one which we can guarantee to our customers to give excellent satisfaction. It is made entirely of heavy copper, highly nickel plated. It is 11 inches in diameter, 28 inches high, and will heat 2 to 3 gallons of water per minute to a temperature of 100 degrees Fahrenheit. No waiting to heat water for a bath. All that is necessary to obtain hot water is to turn on the water, light the gas, and in less than one minute you have hot water running in your bath tub. Shipping weight, 65 pounds.

Price $17.48

OPEN PLUMBING MARBLE LAVATORIES - - - - - - - $9.05

Italian Marble Slab, 20x24 inches, 1¼ inches thick, 8-inch back, 14-inch round patent overflow basin, nickel plated metal plug with rubber stopper, nickel plated S trap; No. 1 Fuller basin cocks, chain and stays, and nickel plated brackets. Shipping weight about 70 pounds.

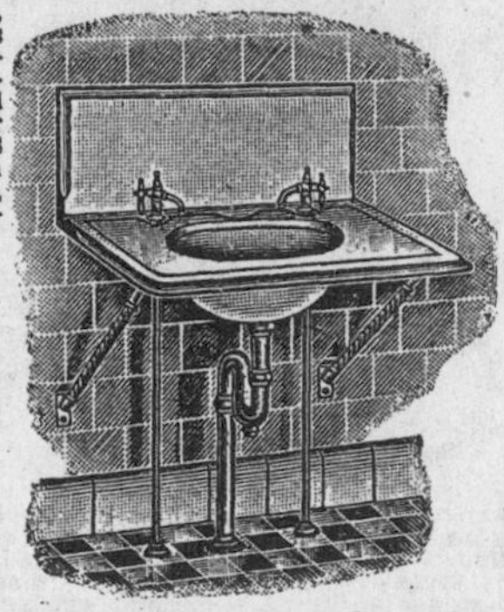

No. 42K239 Tennessee Marble.

Price, with 14-inch round bowl.....$9.05

Price, with 14x17-inch oval bowl.......$9.98

No. 42K240 Italian Marble.

Price, with 14-inch round bowl......$9.83

Price, with 14x17-inch oval bowl.....$10.72

We can furnish any of the above lavatories fitted with nickel plated brass air chamber supply pipe at an additional cost of $2.60.

We can furnish the above lavatories with all connections threaded for iron pipe if wanted, at an extra cost of 75 cents.

PORCELAIN ENAMELED IRON WARE. AT REDUCED PRICES.

In buying Enameled Sinks, Lavatories, Tubs, etc., from us, remember you get first quality goods—no seconds, and any piece found imperfect in any way can be returned to us at our expense. Our low prices may lead you to believe there is something wrong in the quality. All we ask is a trial order. There is no better ware made, quality, style and finish considered, than the following line of enameled ware.

It is made in one of the most modern and complete foundry and enameling plants. Only skilled workmen employed who have had years of experience in enameling. We have made our prices low, as we intend to sell more goods of this kind than any jobber in the United States.

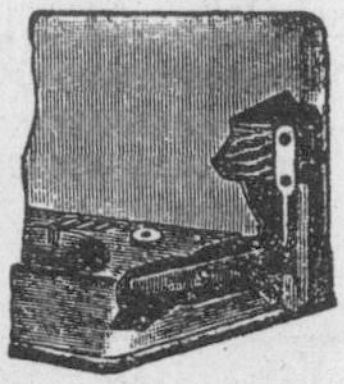

All the following Enameled Cast Lavatories requiring brackets are furnished with our Improved Acme Bracket, unless otherwise ordered. This bracket always insures a rigid, firm lavatory, as a thin board can be nailed onto studding, when the bracket can be screwed onto the board. It is not always possible to strike a studding when bracket is screwed to the wall.

Our sales on this line of material have increased to such an extent during the past year that our factory has been able to materially reduce the cost of production on account of the increased volume of business. As it has always been our custom to add but one small margin of profit to our actual cost on all merchandise, we are glad to give our customers the benefit of this reduction, and it will no doubt be very apparent to you, by studying the following pages of this catalogue, that these prices have been materially reduced.

WHITE PORCELAIN ONE-PIECE LAVATORY, REDUCED TO - - $4.98

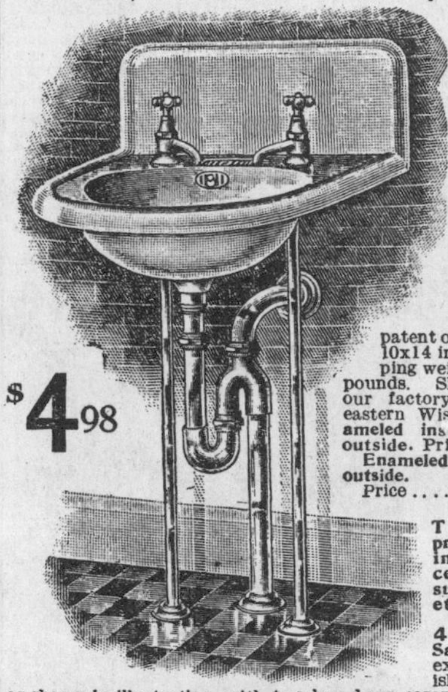

$4.98

No. 42K2865 Porcelain One-Piece Half Circle Lavatory, with patent brackets, sanitary soap tray, waste plug and coupling, nickel plated chain stay and chain. Size of slab, 18x21 inches; height of back, 8 inches; size of patent overflow bowl, 10x14 inches. Shipping weight about 69 pounds. Shipped from our factory in Southeastern Wisconsin. Enameled inside, bronzed outside. Price, $4.98

Enameled inside and outside. Price.......$6.25

NOTICE—The above prices do not include faucets, traps or supply pipes, etc.

No. 42K2815 Same as above, except furnished complete as shown in illustration, with two low down compression basin cocks with cross handles and china tops, one 1¼-inch nickel plated S trap with waste to floor and vent to wall, and two nickel plated supply pipes to floor with flanges. Everything complete, as shown in illustration.

Enameled inside and bronzed outside. Price..... $9.50

Enameled inside and outside. Price........... 10.57

We can furnish these lavatories, with all connections threaded for iron pipe, at an extra cost of 75 cents over prices quoted.

If above lavatory is wanted without revent on trap, deduct 15 cents from prices quoted.

STANDARD AMERICAN PLUMBING.

HOT AIR AND HOT WATER HEATING, STEAM AND GAS FITTING.

BY CLOW AND DONALDSON.

Two Volumes in One. Over 600 Pages. Fully Illustrated.

CONTAINS:

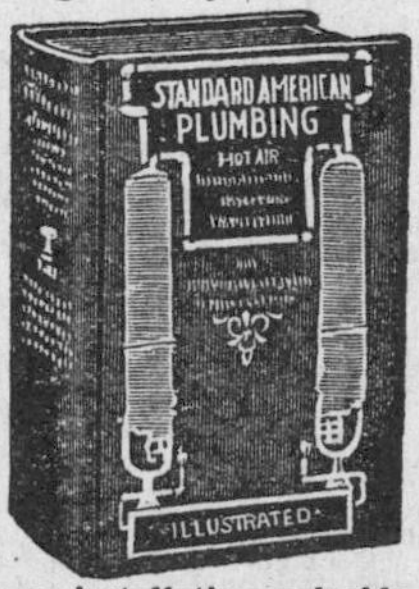

Practical Up to Date Plumbing, by Geo. B. Clow. Retail price, $1.50. Hot Water Heating, Steam and Gas Fitting, by William Donaldson. Retail price, $1.50.

SANITARY PLUMBING. Covering details regarding the installation of hot and cold water drainage systems, modern bath rooms, fittings and devices, including closets, urinals, tubs, wash basins, etc.

MODERN HOT WATER, HOT AIR AND STEAM HEATING. Heating systems, steam boilers, piping and fittings, installation, valuable tables, etc. Furnace heating, furnaces, pipes, general instructions, etc.

STEAM AND GAS FITTING, describing methods of piping, fittings, meters, burners, etc., together with useful pointers and tables.

WORKING DRAWINGS. Fifty actual productions of the boss plumbers' working blue prints. They are diagrams and sketches of practical layout of pipe connections and fittings for residences, flats, stores, etc. In addition, there are over 250 illustrations, relative to modern sanitary plumbing, hot air and hot water heating, steam and gas fitting, etc. Bound in silk cloth. Size of book, 5½x7¾ inches. For full description of this splendid work see Book Department.

No. 3K9180 Standard American Plumbing. Hot Air and Hot Water Heating, Steam and Gas Fitting. Price....(If by mail, postage extra, 18 cents.)..$1.62

OUR LEADER HALF-CIRCLE ENAMELED IRON APRON LAVATORY — $6.68

REDUCED TO $6.68

We show in our Leader Lavatory, one of the neatest, most compact and serviceable lavatories on the market today. This lavatory is 18x21 inches with an 8-inch back, is furnished with a patent overflow basin 10x14 inches, and is made in one piece, which guarantees it to be thoroughly sanitary. We have sold a great number of these lavatories during the past year, and we have yet to hear of the first complaint on them. This lavatory is made of the highest grade of gray cast iron, and is enameled by a process which we will guarantee not to flake or peel off. Shipped from our factory in Southeastern Wisconsin.

No. 42K3456 Enameled Iron Lavatory, with sanitary soap tray, waste plug and coupling, rubber stopper, chain stay, and nickel plated brass overflow, strainer and brackets. Shipping weight, 80 pounds. Enameled inside. Price...$6.68
Enameled inside and outside. Price............. 7.98
NOTICE.—The above price does not include faucets, traps or supply pipes.

No. 42K3506 Same as above, except furnished with two lowdown compression cocks with china tops, one 1¼-inch nickel plated S trap with waste to floor and vent to wall, two nickel plated brass straight supply pipes to floor, everything complete as shown in illustration.
Enameled inside, bronzed outside........$11.27
Enameled inside and outside. Price 12.60
We can furnish these lavatories with all connections and threaded for iron pipe at an extra cost of 75 cents over prices quoted. If lavatory is wanted without revent on trap, deduct 15 cents from prices quoted.

ONE-PIECE SQUARE PORCELAIN LAVATORY, REDUCED TO — $7.35

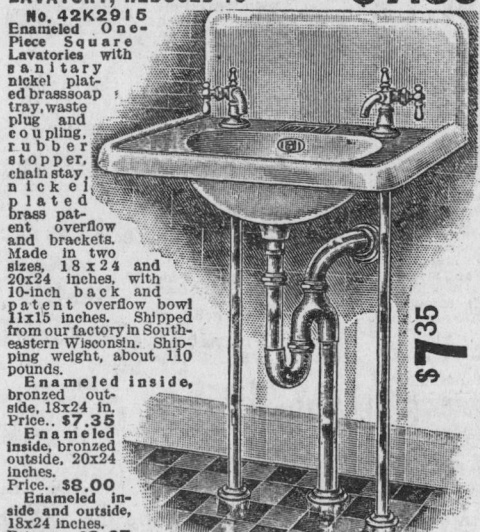

$7.35

No. 42K2915 Enameled One-Piece Square Lavatories with sanitary nickel plated brass soap tray, waste plug and coupling, rubber stopper, chain stay, nickel plated brass patent overflow and brackets. Made in two sizes, 18x24 and 20x24 inches, with 10-inch back and patent overflow bowl 11x15 inches. Shipped from our factory in Southeastern Wisconsin. Shipping weight, about 110 pounds.
Enameled inside, bronzed outside, 18x24 in. Price...$7.35
Enameled inside, bronzed outside, 20x24 inches. Price..$8.00
Enameled inside and outside, 18x24 inches. Price....$8.67
Enameled inside and outside, 20x24 inches. Price..$9.00
NOTICE—The above prices do not include faucets, traps or supply pipes, etc.

No. 42K2965 Same as above, except furnished complete with two nickel plated Fuller basin cocks, one 1¼-inch nickel plated S trap with waste to floor and vent to wall, and two straight supply pipes to floor with flanges. Everything complete, as shown in illustration.
Enameled inside, bronzed outside, 18x24 in. Price.$11.95
Enameled inside, bronzed outside, 20x24 in. Price..12.60
Enameled inside and outside, 18x24 inches. Price..13.27
Enameled inside and outside, 20x24 inches. Price..13.60
We can furnish these lavatories, with all connections threaded for iron pipe at an extra cost of 75 cents over prices quoted. If above lavatory is wanted without revent on trap, deduct 15 cents from prices quoted.

ENAMELED IRON ONE-PIECE CORNER LAVATORY, REDUCED TO — $4.64

$4.64

No. 42K3115 Enameled Iron One-Piece Corner Lavatories, with sanitary nickel plated brass soap dish, waste plug and coupling, rubber stopper, chain stay, nickel plated overflow strainer and wall brackets. Length, on sides, 16½ inches; back, 6 inches high. Size of patent overflow bowl, 10x14 inches. Shipped from our factory in Southeastern Wisconsin. Shipping weight, about 60 pounds.
Enameled inside, bronzed outside. Price...........$4.64
Enameled inside and outside. Price..............5.64
NOTICE—The above prices do not include faucets, traps or supply pipes.

No. 42K3165 Same as above, except furnished complete with two brass nickel plated compression basin cocks, 1¼-inch nickel plated trap with waste to floor and vent to wall, two brass nickel plated supply pipes to floor with flanges. Everything complete, as shown in illustration.
Enameled inside, bronzed outside. Price.........$8.76
Enameled inside and outside. Price.............9.90
We can furnish these lavatories, with all connections threaded for iron pipe at an extra cost of 75 cents over prices quoted.
If above lavatory is wanted without revent on trap, deduct 15 cents from prices quoted.

ENAMELED ONE-PIECE CORNER LAVATORY, REDUCED TO — $5.25

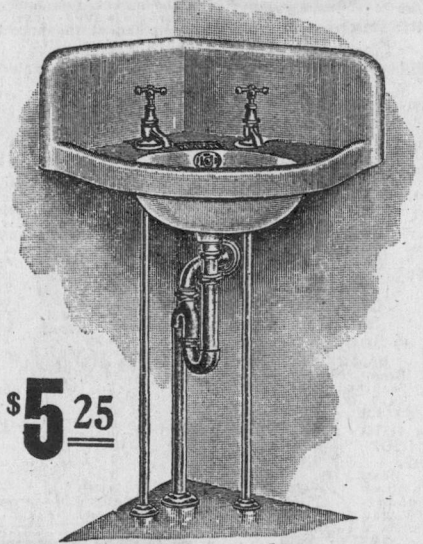

$5.25

No. 42K317 Enameled One-Piece Corner Lavatories with sanitary soap tray, waste plug and coupling, rubber stopper, chain stay, nickel plated overflow strainer and wall brackets. Length on sides, 18½ inches; height of back, 6 and 8 inches. Size of bowl, 10x14 inches. Shipped from our factory in Southeastern Wisconsin. Shipping weight, about 90 pounds.
Enameled inside, bronzed outside, 6-inch back. Price. $5.25
Enameled inside, bronzed outside, 8-inch back. Price. 5.60
Enameled inside and outside, 6-inch back. Price.... 6.65
Enameled inside and outside, 8-inch back. Price.... 7.80
NOTICE—The above prices do not include faucets, traps or supply pipes.

No. 42K318 Same as above, except complete with nickel plated S trap with waste to floor and vent to wall. Nickel plated straight supply pipes to floor and two low down compression nickel plated brass faucets. Everything complete as shown in illustration.
Enameled inside, bronzed outside, 6-in. back. Price.$10.07
Enameled inside, bronzed outside, 8-in. back. Price. 10.27
Enameled inside and outside, 6-in. back. Price.. 11.60
Enameled inside and outside, 8-in. back. Price...11.95
We can furnish these lavatories with all connections threaded for iron pipe at an extra cost of 75 cents over prices quoted.
If above lavatory is wanted without revent on trap, deduct 15 cents from prices quoted.

ENAMELED CORNER ONE-PIECE APRON LAVATORY — $7.98

$7.98

No. 42K3215 Enameled Iron One-Piece Corner Apron Lavatories, with sanitary nickel plated brass soap tray, waste plug and coupling, rubber stopper, nickel plated chain stay, nickel plated overflow strainer and wall brackets. Length on sides, 20 inches; height of back, 8 inches; patent overflow basin, 10x14 inches. Shipped from our factory in Southeastern Wisconsin. Shipping weight, about 90 pounds.
Enameled inside, bronzed outside. Price..........$7.98
Enameled inside and outside. Price..............9.25
NOTICE—The above prices do not include faucets, trap or supply pipes.

No. 42K3265 Same as above, except furnished with two low down compression basin cocks with china tops, one 1¼-inch nickel plated S trap with waste to floor and vent to wall, two nickel plated offset air chamber supply pipes with flanges to floor. Everything complete as shown in illustration.
Enameled inside, bronzed outside. Price.......$14.07
Enameled inside and outside. Price.........15.07
We can furnish these lavatories with all connections threaded for iron pipe at an extra cost of 75 cents over prices quoted.
If above lavatory is wanted without revent on trap, deduct 15 cents from prices quoted.

ENAMELED IRON ONE-PIECE APRON LAVATORY, REDUCED TO — $9.55

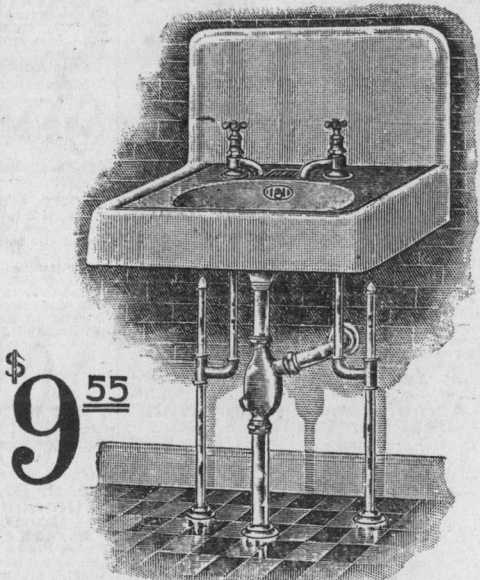

$9.55

No. 42K3705 White Enameled Iron One-Piece Apron Lavatories, with sanitary nickel plated soap tray with waste plug and coupling rubber stopper, chain stay, nickel plated overflow strainer and wall brackets. Made in two sizes, 18x24 inches with 10-inch back, and 20x24 inches with 12-inch back; size of patent overflow bowl 11x15 inches. Shipped from our factory in Southeastern Wisconsin. Shipping weight, about 140 pounds.
                                                    Price
Enameled inside, bronzed outside. Size, 18x24 in..$ 9.55
Enameled inside, bronzed outside. Size, 20x24 in.. 10.60
Enameled inside and outside. Size, 18x24 inches.. 11.55
Enameled inside and outside. Size, 20x24 inches.. 12.60
NOTICE—The above prices do not include faucets, trap or supply pipes.

No. 42K3655 Same as above, except furnished with two low down cross handle brass nickel plated compression cocks, with china tops, one nickel plated bottle trap, with waste to floor and vent to wall, two nickel plated offset air chamber supply pipes to floor. Everything complete as shown in illustration.
Enameled inside, bronzed outside. Size, 18x24 in.$15.64
Enameled inside, bronzed outside. Size, 20x24 in.. 16.67
Enameled inside and outside. Size, 18x24 inches. 17.40
Enameled inside and outside. Size, 20x24 inches. 18.47
We can furnish these lavatories with all connections threaded for iron pipe at an extra cost of 75 cents over prices quoted. If above lavatory is wanted without revent on trap, deduct 15 cents from prices quoted.

Heavy, Full Riveted, Galvanized Range Boilers.

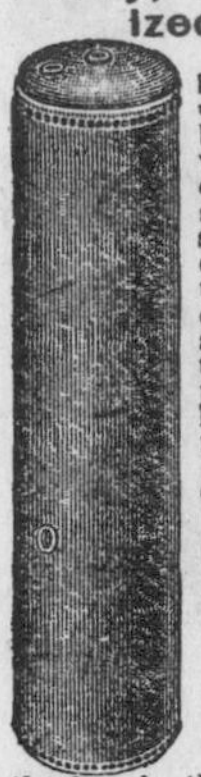

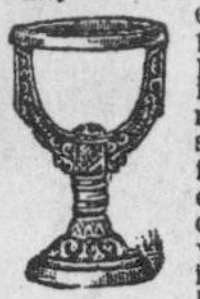

Range boilers can only be used in homes where there is a constant water pressure, which can only be obtained in cities having water works or homes equipped with elevated tanks or with our water supply outfits. Where you have such pressure, these tanks can be connected with lead or iron pipes to a water front in a cook stove or to a coil in a hot air furnace and hot water can be drawn from the faucets without any extra expense. Our boilers are made of a heavy gauge of galvanized iron fully riveted with galvanized rivets and tested to a pressure of 200 pounds before leaving our house. Furnished complete with stand, galvanized, inside tubes and extra heavy brass couplings. The galvanized boiler tube is screwed into the boiler coupling with the female thread on the inside of coupling, and then dropped through one of the openings on the top of the boiler. This tube is for the cold water going into the boiler, and the other coupling is for the hot water coming out of the boiler. The bottom opening of boiler is used to drain the boiler and to connect to the lowest connection on the stove or furnace, and the side opening is used to connect with the top connection of stove or furnace in order to create a circulation.

30-gallon boilers are used in a small residence to supply hot water for kitchen and bathroom.

40-gallon boilers are used in a home to supply hot water for a kitchen, bathroom, sink and laundry tub in basement.

52-gallon boilers are used to supply hot water for two or three flats with bath room and kitchen.

	Gallons	Height, inches	Weig't, pounds	Price
No. 42K1081	30	60	72	$6 14
No. 42K1083	40	60	85	7.55
No. 42K1084	52	60	120	13.59

The above prices are for boilers fitted for lead pipe connection; if wanted for iron pipe connection add 30 cents to above prices.

Brass Boiler Couplings.

Heavy Brass Boiler Couplings for above boilers, made for either lead or iron pipe connections.

No. 42K1091 Lead Pipe Connection. Price, per set of 4 pieces............$0.98

No. 42K1092 Iron Pipe Connection. Price, per set of 4 pieces............$1.28

Peerless Water Heater. $6.38

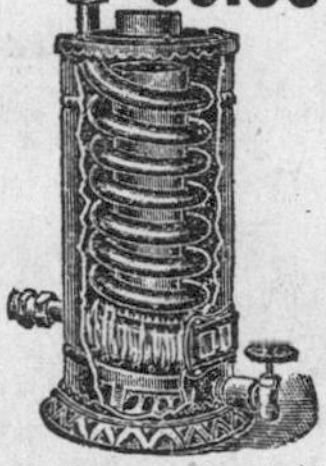

In our Peerless Water Heater we have a moderate priced copper coil heater and one which we are sure will give good results. It has a coil of best seamless drawn copper tubing, which provides ample heating surface and possesses many advantages over cast iron devices, iron pipes, etc., being not only a better heat conductor, but reducing the number of joints to a minimum. It can be connected readily to any range boiler without using special connections or fittings. Each heater is fitted with ground-joint brass unions. The conical deflector forces the flame and heated air to circulate close to the coil, and prevents downdraft. The jacket is lined with asbestos, which prevents the escape of heat into the surrounding air. It is 8-inch diameter, 15 inches high, ¾-inch tube. Usually connected with 30 or 40-gallon boiler to supply hot water to sink, bath room and lavatory. Weight, 25 pounds.

No. 42K1080 Price, with Russia Iron Jacket............$6.38

Acme Water Heater With Cast Iron Casing, $5.90.

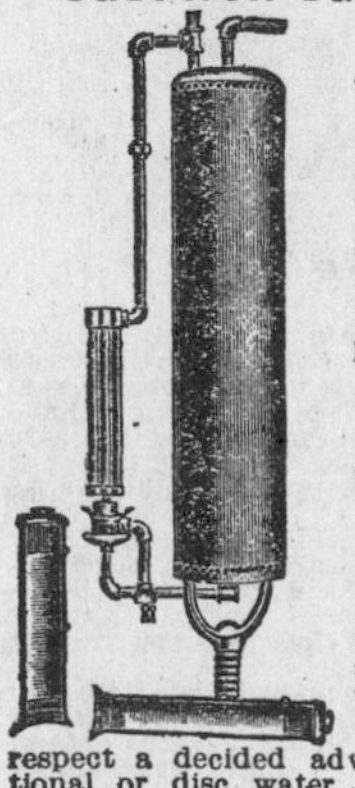

In our Acme Water Heater, with cast iron jacket, we believe we have the best range boiler water heater on the market regardless of price. The casing, or jacket is made of cast iron, which is more durable and will last longer than the sheet steel, in two sections, each section lined with asbestos, which prevents the heat escaping. The two sections are bolted together when on the heater, through lugs on the outside of the casing. These casings can always be removed with comparative ease and without disconnecting the gas or water. All Acme round water heater coils can be taken apart and cleaned, having in this respect a decided advantage over the sectional or disc water heaters. Weight, 56 pounds.

No. 42K1077 Cold water supply pipe, ¾ inch; hot water outlet, ¾ inch; capacity, 30 to 40-gallon boiler. Price........$5.90

No. 42K1078 Cold water supply pipe, 1 inch; hot water outlet, 1 inch; capacity, 50 to 60-gallon boiler. Price..........$8.20

The above prices are for heater only and do not include boiler.

BATHROOM AND LAVATORY FURNISHINGS

AT REDUCED PRICES.

We have secured an exceptionally fine line of bathroom fixtures, and at prices we believe your saving will average nearly 50 per cent. They are made of brass, heavily nickel plated, and with ordinary care will last a lifetime. Do not compare these prices with the shoddy bathroom fixtures sold by other concerns.

BATHROOM TRIMMING OUTFIT - - - - $1.98

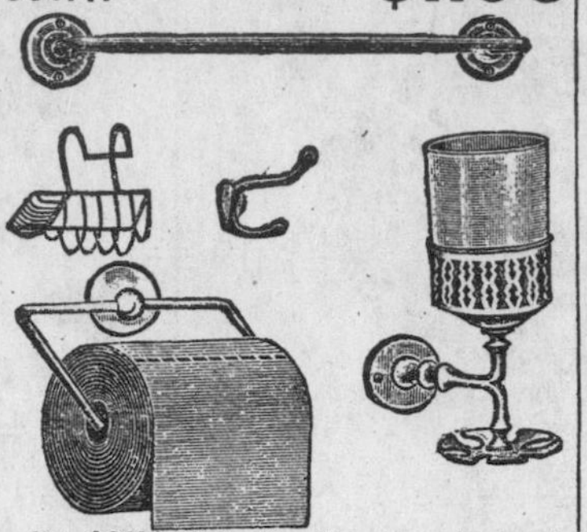

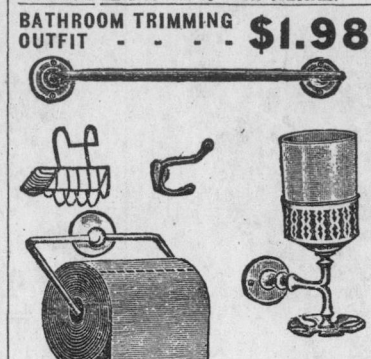

No. 42K1109 For the convenience of our customers we have gotten up this set, which consists of the most necessary bathroom trimmings, namely, an 18-inch towel bar, combination sponge and soap holder, towel hook, paper holder and combination toothbrush and tumbler holder. Each of the above articles is made of brass, highly nickel plated, and we know that anyone of our customers purchasing one of these outfits will be highly pleased with it. The tumbler or toilet paper is not included in price quoted below. Weight, about 3¼ pounds.

Price..................$1.98

Single Robe Hooks.

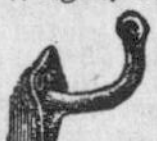

No. 42K1110 Brass Nickel Plated Single Robe Hooks. Come complete with screws. Weight, 1½ ounces.

Price, per dozen, $1.05; each........9c

Double Robe Hooks.

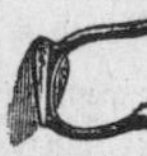

No. 42K1115 Brass Nickel Plated Double Robe Hooks. Medium size. Complete with screws. Weight, 2 ounces.

Price, each, reduced to $0.11
Per dozen, reduced to 1.20

Coat and Hat Hooks.

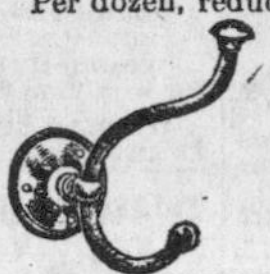

No. 42K1120 Heavy Brass Nickel Plated Coat and Hat Hooks. Finest hook made. 7 inches long. Weight, 4 ounces.

Price reduced to....31c

Wall Soap Cup.

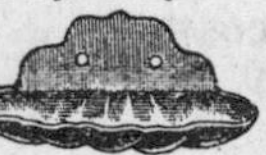

No. 42K1130 Brass Nickel Plated Wall Soap Cup, 3¾ inches wide by 4½ inches long. Weight, 4 ounces.

Price reduced to..12c

Soap Dish.

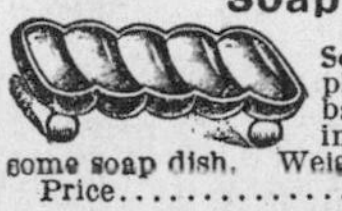

No. 42K1134 Brass Soap Dish. Heavily nickel plated, with heavy brass ball feet. Size, 3x4½ inches. A very handsome soap dish. Weight, 10 ounces.

Price..................24c

Soap Cups.

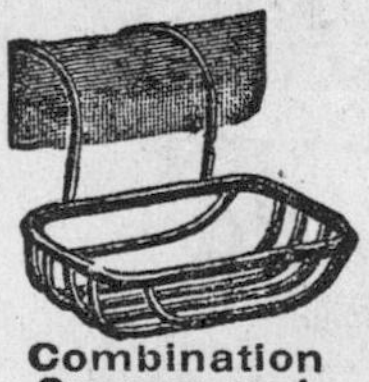

No. 42K1140 Soap Cups for the rim of the bath, solid brass, nickel plated, finely finished. Hanging rods can be adjusted so as to fit any tub. Size, 6x3½ inches. Weight, 10 ounces.

Price reduced to 46c

Combination Sponge and Soap Holder.

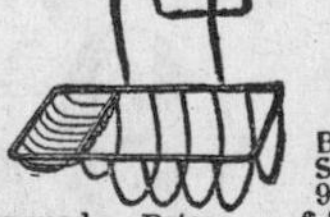

No. 42K1151 Heavy Brass Nickel Plated Soap and Sponge Holder, 9x10 inches. Weight, 1 pound. Price......$1.12

Tooth Brush and Tumbler Holder Combined.

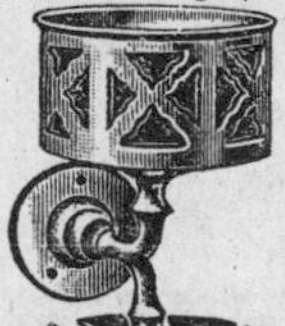

No. 42K1160 Brass Nickel Plated Tooth Brush and Tumbler Holder. Height, 4½ inches. Weight, 7 ounces. Price reduced to..............44c

Combination Tumbler and Soap Holder.

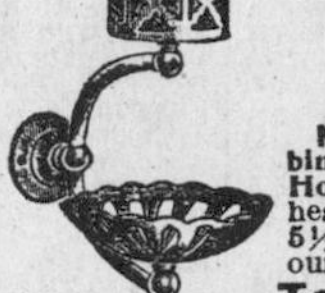

No. 42K1165 Combination Tumbler and Soap Holder. Made of brass, heavily nickel plated. Size, 5½x8 inches. Weight, 12 ounces. Price.......83c

Towel Rack.

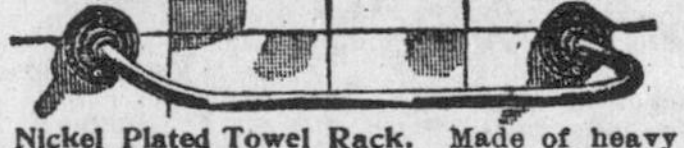

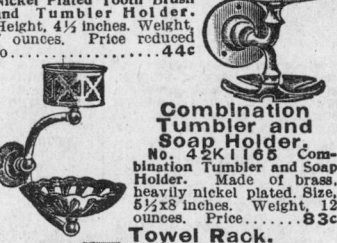

Nickel Plated Towel Rack. Made of heavy brass, heavily nickel plated. Strong and durable; finely finished bar is ½ inch in diameter; projects 2¼ inches from wall. Average wt..8 oz.

No. 42K1180 Length, 15 in. Price..27c
No. 42K1181 Length, 18 in. Price..30c
No. 42K1182 Length, 24 in. Price..33c

Extra Heavy Towel Rack.

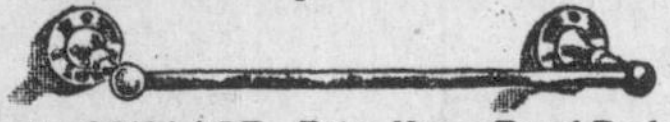

No. 42K1187 Extra Heavy Towel Rack. Made of brass, nickel plated, with cast brass posts. Diameter of bar, ½ inch; width from wall, 3 inches. Weight, about 8 ounces.

Length, 15 inches. Price reduced to.....47c
Length, 18 inches. Price reduced to.....48c
Length, 24 inches. Price reduced to.....52c

Two-Arm Towel Rack.

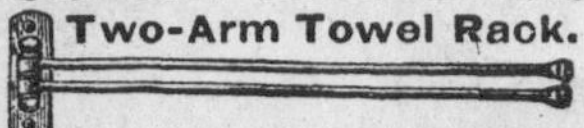

No. 42K1192 Nickel Plated Towel Rack. Two-arm; diameter of bars, ½ inch. Brass heavily nickel plated. Length, 12½ inches. Weight, 1½ pounds.

Price reduced to..........................44c

Bath Spray.

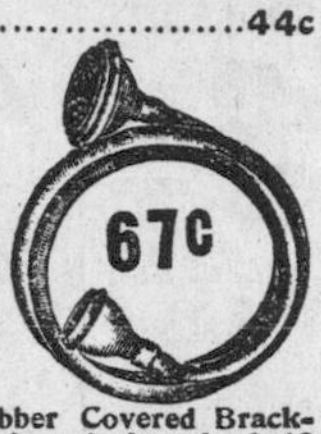

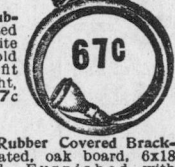

No. 42K1217 Rubber bound, nickel plated spray with 5 feet of white rubber hose and hold fast rubber bulb, will fit over any faucet. Weight, 12 ounces. Price..67c

67c

Bath Tub Seat.

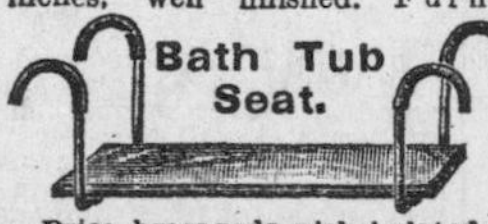

No. 42K1222 Rubber Covered Brackets. heavily nickel plated, oak board, 6x18 inches, well finished. Furnished with either steel or brass rods. Weig't 3½ pounds. Price, steel rods, nickel plated....47c

Price, brass rods, nickel plated..........72c

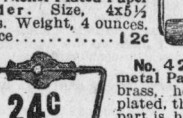

Toilet Paper Holders.

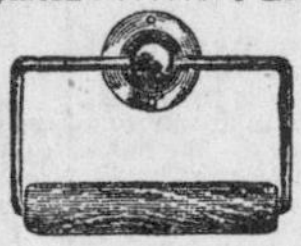

No. 42K1227 Stamped Brass Nickel Plated Paper Holder. Size, 4x5½ inches. Weight, 4 ounces.

Price............12c

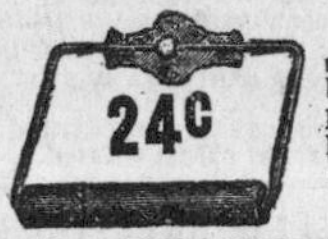

24c

No. 42K1228 All metal Parts made of cast brass, heavily nickel plated, the roller or wood part is highly enameled. Weight, 6 ounces.

Price............24c

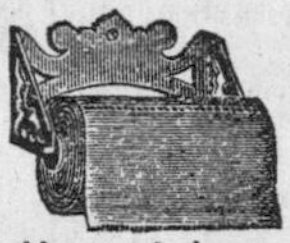

No. 42K1233 This is one of the neatest and best Toilet Paper Holders on the market. It is made of brass, heavily nickel plated, and at the price we ask for it is a bargain. It must be seen to be appreciated. For people wanting a high grade holder we feel confident this one will give satisfaction. Weight, 9 ounces. Price..........62c

SHOWER BATH YOKE, WITH 6 FEET OF HOSE $1.12

No. 42K1247 A lady can use it without wetting her head. Each limb can be showered separately, placing the arm or leg through the yoke. There is no splashing of walls or floor, as the sprays or jets of water are directed inwardly and flow over all parts of the body. This yoke is made of brass, highly nickel plated, and will last a lifetime. Weight, 12 ounces.

Price...........$1.12

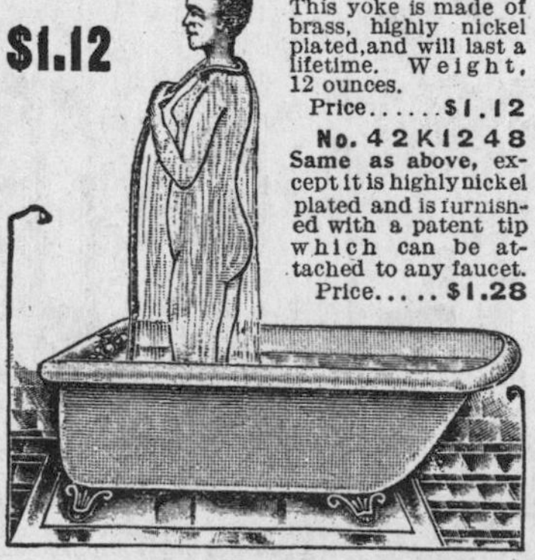

$1.12

No. 42K1248 Same as above, except it is highly nickel plated and is furnished with a patent tip which can be attached to any faucet.

Price.....$1.28

Compression Basin Cocks.

At Reduced Prices.

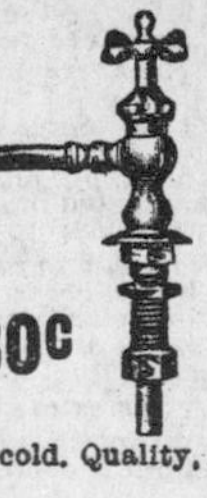

80c

No. 42K1267 Compression Basin Cocks, T handle. Made of brass. Heavily nickel plated. Weight, 1 pound.

Price reduced to......60c

Nickel Plated Basin Cocks.

No. 42K1272 Low Down Nickel Plated Basin Cocks, with cross handles and china tops, indexed hot and cold. Quality, A1. Weight, 1 lb. Price..80c

Fuller Basin Cocks.

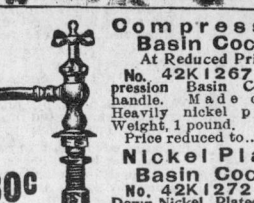

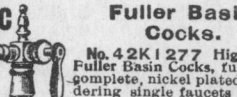

80c

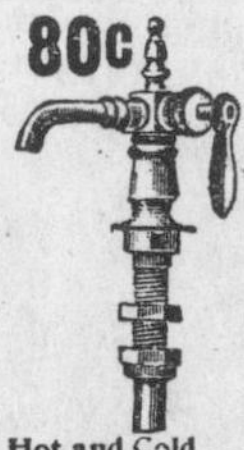

No. 42K1277 High Grade Fuller Basin Cocks, furnished complete, nickel plated. In ordering single faucets be sure to state whether left or right hand is wanted. Wt. 1¼ lbs.

Price reduced to.....80c

Combination Bath Cocks. $1.98

No. 42K1302 No. 4½ Fuller Cast Brass Combination Hot and Cold Bath Cocks. Nickel plated, complete, ready for use. One of the heaviest and best finished cocks on the market; nothing cheap about it but the price. Weight, 4 pounds. Price reduced to $1.98

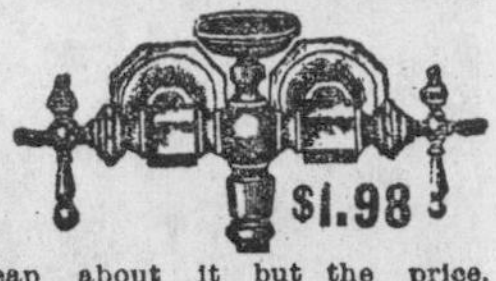

$1.98

Compression Bath Cocks.

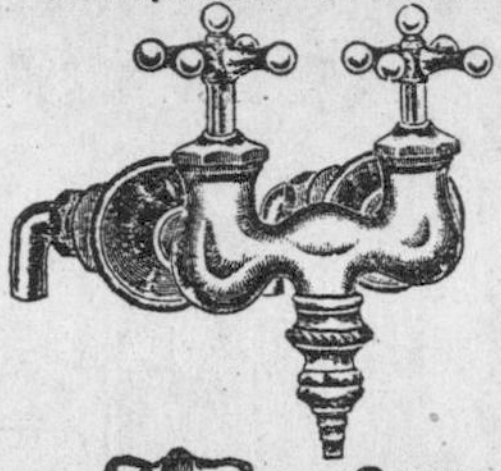

No. 42K1307 Brass Nickel Plated Compression Bath Cocks. Combination hot and cold. A heavy well made cock. Complete as shown in illustration. Price...$1.95

Compression Plain Bibbs, with Flange.

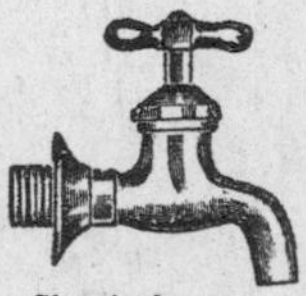

No. 42K1325 Plain Compression Bibbs, with flange, screwed for iron pipe. Made of brass, finely finished.

Size, inch	½	¾	1
Weight	1 lb.	1½ lbs.	2¼ lbs.
Price reduced to	46c	55c	$1.30

Compression Hose Bibbs, with Flange. 52c

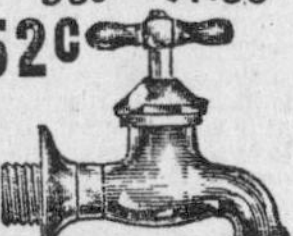

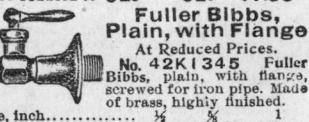

No. 42K1330 Compression Hose Bibbs, with flange, screwed for iron pipe. Made of brass, finely finished.

Size, inch	½	¾	1
Weight	1⅛ lbs.	1¼ lbs.	2¾ lbs.
Price reduced to	52c	62c	$1.50

Fuller Bibbs, Plain, with Flange

At Reduced Prices.

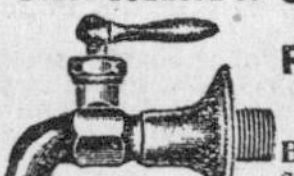

No. 42K1345 Fuller Bibbs, plain, with flange, screwed for iron pipe. Made of brass, highly finished.

Size, inch	½	⅝	1
Weight	14 oz.	1⅛ lbs.	2 lbs.
Price, brass finished	54c	59c	$1.40
Price, nickel plated	60c	67c	1.65

Fuller Hose Bibbs, with Flange. 60c

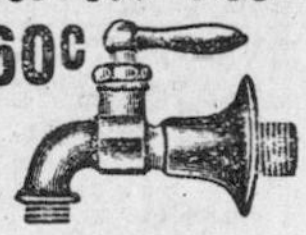

No. 42K1350 Fuller Hose Bibbs, with flange, screwed for iron pipe. Made of brass, highly finished.

Size, inch	½	⅝	1
Weight	15 oz.	1 lb.	2 lbs.
Price, brass finished	60c	67c	$1.40
Price, nickel plated	67c	75c	1.60

Fuller Bibbs, Plain.

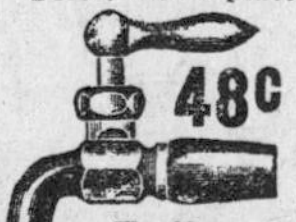

48c

No. 42K1365 Plain Fuller Bibbs, for lead pipe connection, made of brass, highly polished.

Size, in.	⅜	⅝	1
Wt.	12oz.	1¼ lbs.	2 lbs.
Price	48c	51c	$1.05

Fuller Hose Bibbs.

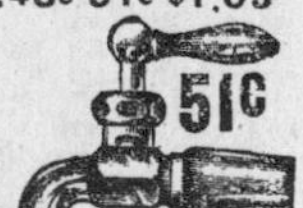

51c

No. 42K1370 Fuller Hose Bibbs, for lead pipe connections. Made of brass, highly polished.

Size, in.	⅜	⅝	1
Wght.	12 oz.	1¼ lbs.	2 lbs.
Price...	51c	55c	$1.10

Bibbs.

52c

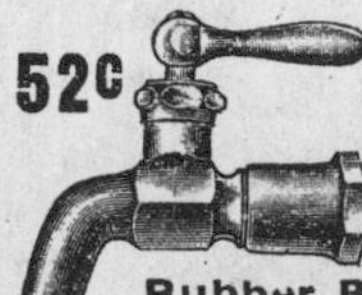

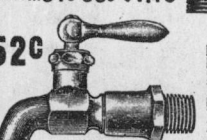

No. 42K1375 Fuller Pattern Plain Bibbs, for iron pipe, finished brass.

Size, in.	½	⅝
Weight,	11oz.	1lb.
Price..	52c	56c

Rubber Balls for Fuller Bibbs.

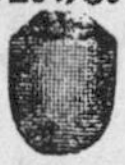

No. 42K1380 Size for bibbs, ⅜ inch, 5c; ⅝ inch, 5c; 1 inch.........6c

Fuller Pattern Hose-Bibbs.

56c

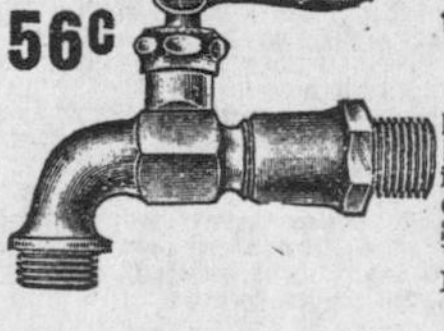

No. 42K1382 Fuller Pattern Hose Bibbs, for iron pipe, finished brass.

Size, in.	½	⅝
Wgt..	13 oz.	1lb.
Price..	56c	60c

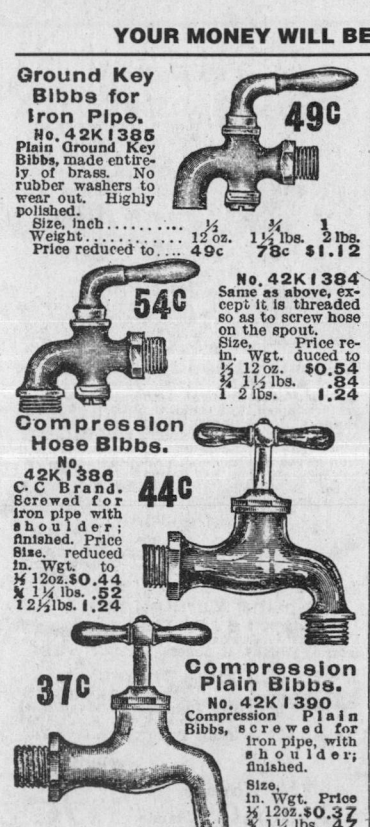

Ground Key Bibbs for Iron Pipe.

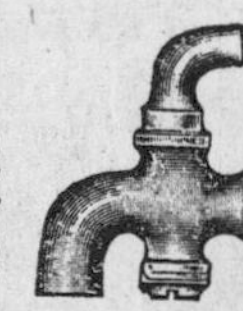

49c

No. 42K1385 Plain Ground Key Bibbs, made entirely of brass. No rubber washers to wear out. Highly polished.

Size, inch	½	¾	1
Weight	12 oz.	1½ lbs.	2 lbs.
Price reduced to	49c	78c	$1.12

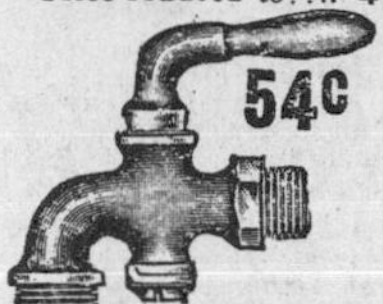

54c

No. 42K1384 Same as above, except it is threaded so as to screw hose on the spout.

Size, in.	Wgt.	Price reduced to
½	12 oz.	$0.54
¾	1½ lbs.	.84
1	2 lbs.	1.24

Compression Hose Bibbs.

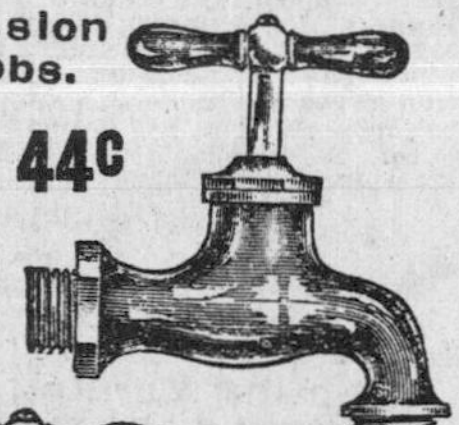

44c

No. 42K1386 C. C Brand. Screwed for iron pipe with shoulder; finished.

Size in.	Wgt.	Price reduced to
½	12oz.	$0.44
¾	1¼ lbs.	.52
1	2½lbs.	1.24

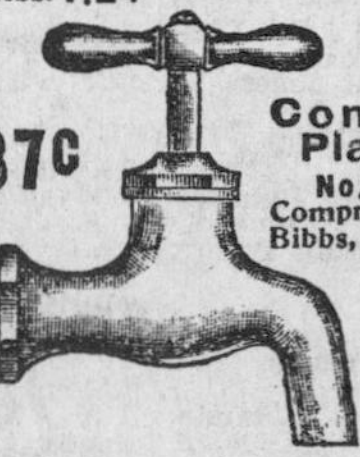

37c

Compression Plain Bibbs.

No. 42K1390 Compression Plain Bibbs, screwed for iron pipe, with shoulder; finished.

Size, in.	Wgt.	Price
½	12oz.	$0.37
¾	1¼ lbs.	.47
1	2½lbs.	1.17

Compression Sill Cocks.

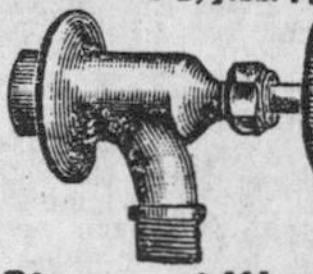

No. 42K1402 Compression Sill Cocks, finished ready for use. Size, ¾ inch. Weight, 1 pound. Price........64c

Lever Handle Stop and Waste for Iron Pipe.

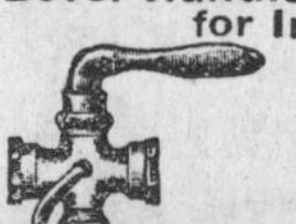

No. 42K1410 Lever Handle Stop and Waste, for iron pipe, finished and polished.

Size, inch	½	⅜
Weight	12 oz.	1 lb.
Price	65c	84c

Male Soldering Nipples.

No. 42K1435 Male Straight Soldering Nipple, screwed for iron pipe outside.

Size, inches	½	¾	1	1¼	1½	2
Weight	3 oz.	4 oz.	6 oz.	8 oz.	9 oz.	12 oz.
Price	9c	10c	12c	21c	26c	33c

Brass Soldering Unions.

No. 42K1445 Brass Soldering Unions.

Size, inches	½	¾	1	1¼	1½
Weight	2 oz.	3 oz.	5 oz.	7 oz.	8 oz.
Price	11c	14c	17c	27c	33c

Iron Body, Brass Screw, Trap Screw Ferrule.

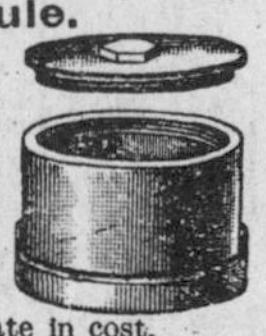

No. 42K1450 The body is cast iron in regular pipe sizes, fitting the hub neatly and making a good wall to calk against. The projections on side prevent ferrule turning after being calked. The cover being of brass cannot unite with the iron, and the threads are thereby made proof against rust. It is the best ferrule made and moderate in cost.

Size, inches	2	3	4
Weight	1¼ lbs.	2 lbs.	2½ lbs.
Price	16c	21c	27c

Brass Ferrules.

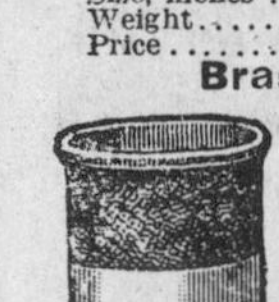

No. 42K1455 Brass Ferrules to be used in connecting closet waste pipe to soil pipe.

Size, 2x4 inches. Weight, 14 ounces. Price........15c

Size, 4x4 inches. Weight, 1½ pounds. Price........30c

No. 42K1460 Lead Ferrules.

Size, inches	2x4	4x4	4x6	4x8	4x12
Weight, lbs.	1½	3½	4½	5¼	7½
Price	17c	31c	52c	62c	84c

Soft Metal Iron Couplings.

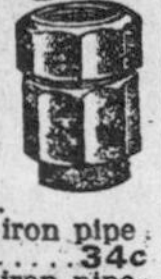

No. 42K1465 With our Acme Coupling any ordinary mechanic can make a perfect joint without the aid of a plumber. Lead and iron pipe can be connected in a few minutes. No wiping joints. Guaranteed to make a perfect joint. Average weight, 8 ounces.

Size, ½-inch lead pipe to ½-inch iron pipe. Price........34c

Size, ¾-inch lead pipe to ¾-inch iron pipe. Price........48c

Size, 1-inch lead pipe to 1-inch iron pipe. Price........62c

Size, 1¼-inch lead pipe to 1¼-inch iron pipe. Price........72c

Lead to Lead Coupling.

No. 42K1470 Acme Coupling for connecting lead pipe to lead pipe, no wiping or soldering joints. Can be easily taken apart in case of stoppage in the pipe. Average weight, 8 ounces.

Size, inches	½	¾	1	1¼
Price	35c	50c	62c	72c

Acme Water Filters.

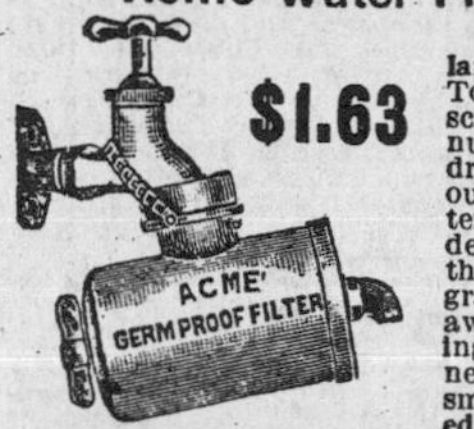

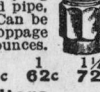

$1.63

Fits any spigot, large or small. To clean, unscrew thumb nut on end and draw the stone out. These filters will last indefinitely, except the stone, which gradually wears away from cleaning. Can be renewed at a very small cost. Cleaned in one minute. Capacities vary with pressure and condition of water. Weight, 3½ pounds.

No. 42K1485 No. 1, capacity 5 gallons per hour, galvanized. Price........$1.63

No. 42K1486 No. 1, capacity 5 gallons per hour, nickel plated. Price........$2.02

No. 42K1487 Extra stones for above filter. Price........48c

Drawn Lead Traps.

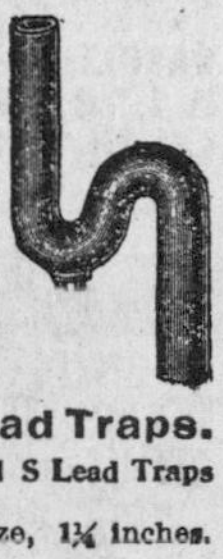

Full S Standard Heavy Drawn Lead Traps for Sinks, Basins, etc.

No. 42K1490 Size, 1¼ inches. Weight, 2⅜ pounds. Price........28c

No. 42K1491 Size, 1½ inches. Weight, 4 pounds. Price........44c

No. 42K1492 Size, 4 inches. Weight, 16½ pounds. Price........$1.56

Extra Long S Lead Traps.

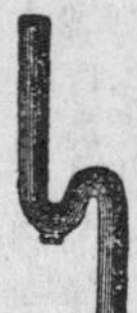

Extra Long Standard S Lead Traps for Sinks, Basins, etc.

No. 42K1497 Size, 1¼ inches. Weight, 4 pounds. Price........45c

No. 42K1498 Size, 1½ inches. Weight, 6 pounds. Price........66c

Long S Lead Trap, Vented.

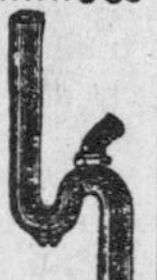

Long S Lead Trap, Vented, as per illustration.

No. 42K1502 Size, 1¼ inches. Wt., 4½ lbs. Price........83c

No. 42K1503 Size, 1½ inches. Wt., 7 lbs. Price........$1.12

Half S Lead Traps.

Standard Heavy Half S Lead Traps, to be used in connection with sinks, basins, etc.

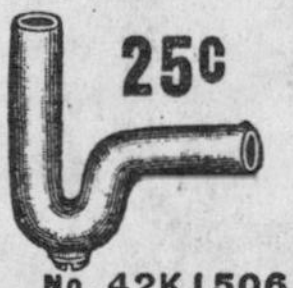

25c

No. 42K1504 Size, 1¼ inches. Weight, 4½ pounds. Price........25c

No. 42K1505 Size, 1½ inches. Weight, 7 pounds. Price........36c

No. 42K1506 Size, 4 inches. Weight, 12 pounds. Price........$1.20

Three-Quarter S Lead Traps.

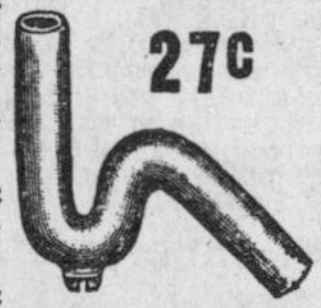

27c

Standard Three-Quarter S Lead Traps, to be used in connection with sinks, basins, etc.

No. 42K1508 Size, 1¼ inches. Weight, 1¾ pounds. Price........27c

No. 42K1509 Size, 1½ inches. Weight, 3⅛ pounds. Price........39c

Combination Lead Bends and Ferrules.

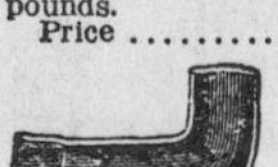

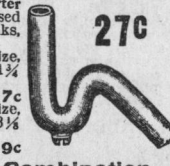

No. 42K1514 Combination lead bends and ferrules, to be used in connecting soil pipe with closet bowl.

Size, inches	4x12	4x14	4x18
Weight	9⅛ lbs.	10¾ lbs.	12 lbs.
Price	$1.05	$1.18	$1.35

Short Bends.

Lead Short Bends, standard grade and sizes.

Cat. No.	Size	Weight	Price
42K1522	2 in.	2⅜ lbs.	28c
42K1524	4 in.	7½ lbs.	78c

Lead Drum Traps.

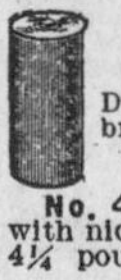

No. 42K1530 Lead Drum Traps. Diameter, 4 inches; length 9 inches, with brass screw. Weight, 4½ pounds. Price........96c

No. 42K1536 Same as above, except with nickel plated top and screw. Weight, 4¼ pounds. Price........$1.07

No. 42K1535 Lead Drum Traps, with connection and brass screws. Weight, 4¼ lbs. Price.$1.31

Long Bends.

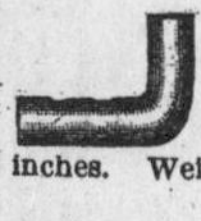

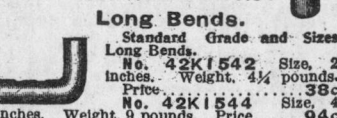

Standard Grade and Sizes Long Bends.

No. 42K1542 Size, 2 inches. Weight, 4¼ pounds. Price........38c

No. 42K1544 Size, 4 inches. Weight, 9 pounds. Price........94c

Cast Iron Soil Pipe.

At Greatly Reduced Prices.

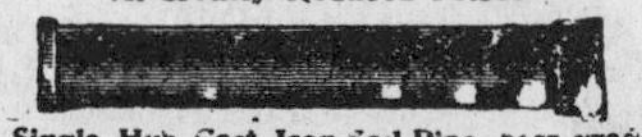

Single Hub Cast Iron Soil Pipe, best grade; comes in 5-foot pieces only.

Our No. 42K1550 to No. 42K1552 2-inch soil pipe is used for the waste pipe for sink and laundry tubs to run from sewer to the roof of house.

Our No. 42K1551 to No. 42K1553 4-inch soil pipe is used for waste pipe for closet and to run from closet to sewer, or from sewer to roof.

No. 42K1550 Standard, 2-inch size. Price, per foot........10½c

No. 42K1551 Standard, 4-inch size. Price, per foot........16½c

No. 42K1552 Extra heavy, 2-inch size. Price, per foot........12c

No. 42K1553 Extra heavy, 4-inch size. Price, per foot........25½c

2-inch standard pipe weighs 17½ pounds per 5-foot length.

4-inch standard pipe weighs 32½ pounds per 5-foot length.

2-inch extra heavy pipe weighs 27½ pounds per 5-foot length.

4-inch extra heavy pipe weighs 65 pounds per 5-foot length.

Double Hub Soil Pipe.

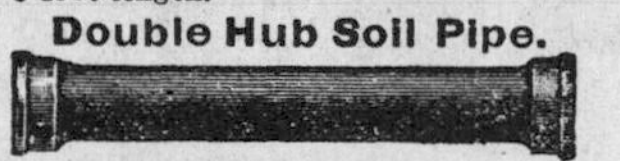

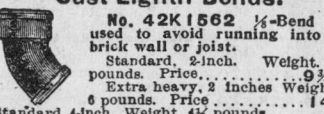

No. 42K1558 Double Hub Soil Pipe. Best grade. Sold in 5-foot pieces only.

Our No. 42K1558 2-inch and 4-inch soil pipe has a hub on both ends, and is used because it can be cut any length you desire and not waste any pipe.

Standard, 2-inch. Price, per foot........12¾c

Extra heavy, 2-inch. Price, per foot........14½c

Standard, 4-inch. Price, per foot........19c

Extra heavy, 4-inch. Price, per foot........28c

2-in. standard weighs 17½ lbs. per 5-ft. lengths.

4-in. standard weighs 32½ lbs. per 5-ft. lengths.

2-in., extra heavy, 27½ lbs. per 5-ft. lengths.

4-in., extra heavy, 65 lbs. per 5-ft. lengths.

SOIL PIPE FITTINGS.

At Reduced Prices.

Cast Eighth Bends.

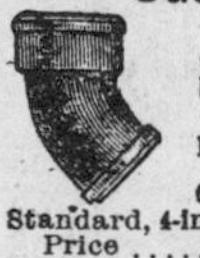

No. 42K1562 ⅛-Bend is used to avoid running into a brick wall or joist.

Standard, 2-inch. Weight, 3 pounds. Price........9¾c

Extra heavy, 2 inches Weight, 6 pounds. Price........14c

Standard, 4-inch. Weight, 4¾ pounds. Price........21¾c

Extra heavy, 4-inch. Weight, 6½ pounds. Price........28c

Cast Quarter Bends.

Cast Quarter Bends for Soil Pipe are used at the bottom of soil pipe running to the roof, to connect to the sewer on the outside.

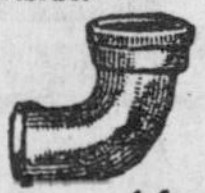

No. 42K1565 Standard, 2-inch. Weight, 4 pounds. Price........9¾c

No. 42K1566 Standard, 4-inch. Weight, 8 pounds. Price........21¾c

No. 42K1567 Extra heavy, 2-inch. Weight, 6 pounds. Price........14c

No. 42K1568 Extra heavy, 4-inch. Weight, 12 pounds. Price........28c

Tapped Cross.

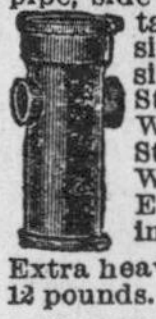

No. 42K1572 Cast Iron Cross for soil pipe, side opening, tapped for iron pipe. Our tapped crosses are used to connect sinks or lavatories to one on each side of partition.

Standard, 4x1½ inches opening. Weight, 9 pounds. Price........74c

Standard, 4x2 inches opening. Weight, 9 pounds. Price........75c

Extra heavy, 4x1½ inches opening. Weight, 12 pounds. Price........95c

Extra heavy, 4x2 inches opening. Wt., 12 pounds. Price........96c

Cast Sanitary Cross.

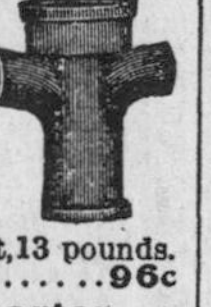

No. 42K1573 Cast Sanitary Cross for soil pipe, side opening, tapped for 1½ and 2-inch iron pipe.

Standard, 4x1½ inches. Weight, 10 lbs. Price........74c

Extra heavy, 4x1½ in. Weight, 13 lbs. Price........95c

Standard, 4x2 inches. Weight, 10 lbs. Price........75c

Extra heavy, 4x2 inches. Weight, 13 pounds. Price........96c

Cast Quarter Bends.

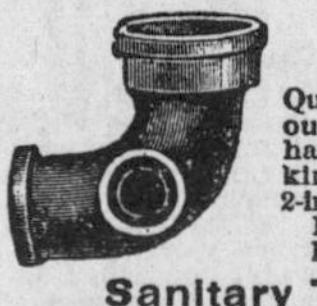

No. 42K1576 Cast Quarter Bends, with side outlet. Either right or left hand. Be sure to state kind wanted. Size, 4 in. with 2-in. side outlet. Wt. 12 lbs.

Price, standard........44c

Price, extra heavy........50c

Sanitary T Branches.

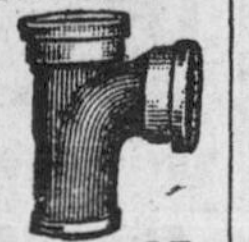

Cast Sanitary T Branches for Soil Pipe are used in connection with soil pipe to connect the waste of lavatories, sinks and closets.

No. 42K1580 Standard, 2x2 inches. Weight, 4 lbs. Price. per foot........15c

No. 42K1581 Standard, 4x4 inches. Weight, 10 lbs. Price........37c

No. 42K1582 Extra heavy, 2x2 inches. Weight, 7 pounds. Price, per foot........21½c

No. 42K1583 Extra heavy, 4x4 inches. Weight, 14 pounds. Price, per foot........52c

No. 42K1584 Standard, 4x2 inches. Weight, 8 pounds. Price, per foot........37c

No. 42K1585 Extra heavy, 4x2 inches. Weight, 20 pounds. Price, per foot........52c

Sanitary T Branches.

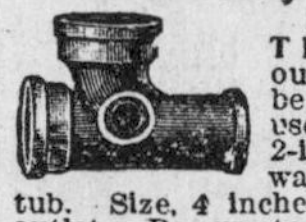

No. 42K1590 Sanitary T Branches, with 2-inch side outlet. Made of cast iron, to be used with soil pipe. Is used for waste of closet, and 2-inch side opening is for waste of lavatory and bath tub. Size, 4 inches, either right or left side outlet. Be sure to state which is wanted.

Standard. Weight, 12 pounds. Price.59c

Extra heavy. Weight, 22 lbs. Price.74c

T Branches.

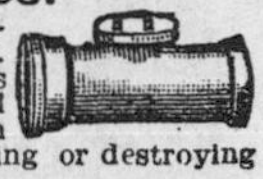

Cast T Branches, with clean-out cap; standard quality. T branches with cleanouts are used on any length of soil pipe, so as to be able to clean out the pipe without breaking or destroying any pipe.

No. 42K1594 Size, 2 inches, with 2-inch screw. Weight, 3½ pounds. Price........31c

No. 42K1595 Size, 4 inches, with 4-inch screw. Weight, 6½ pounds. Price........54c

Tapped Increasers.

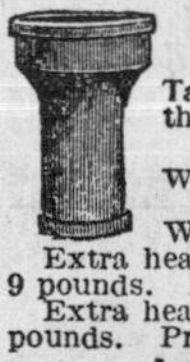

No. 42K1601 Cast Iron Tapped Increasers. Small opening, threaded for iron pipe.

Standard. Size, 4x1½ inches. Weight, 7 pounds. Price........30c

Standard. Size, 4x2 inches. Weight, 7 pounds. Price........32c

Extra heavy. Size, 4x1½ inches. Weight, 9 pounds. Price........37c

Extra heavy. Size, 4x2 inches. Weight, 9 pounds. Price........40c

Long Increasers.

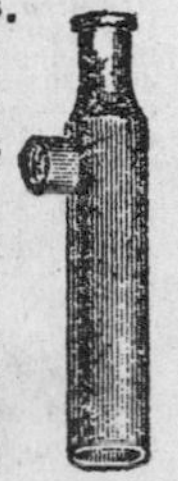

Cast Iron Long Increasers, for soil pipe, for calking; tapped on side. Our increasers are used at the top of soil pipe going through the roof, in order to let the air get a better chance to carry away any sewer gas or other foul odors.

No. 42K1605 Standard. Size, 2 to 4x24 inches. Weight, 13 pounds. Price........80c

No. 42K1606 Extra heavy. Weight, 22 pounds. Price........90c

No. 42K1607 Standard. Size, 4 to 5x30 inches. Weight, 33 pounds. Price........93c

No. 42K1608 Extra heavy. Weight, 40 pounds. Price........$1.10

Cast Double Hubs.

No. 42K1612 Cast Double Hubs for Soil Pipe.

Standard. Size, 2 inches. Weight, 3 pounds. Price.7½c

Extra heavy. Size, 2 inches. Weight, 4½ pounds. Price11c

Standard. Size, 4 inches. Weight, 6 pounds. Price........16½c

Extra heavy. Size, 4 inches. Weight, 8 pounds. Price........20½c

Cast Reducers.

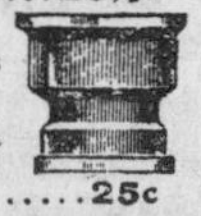

No. 42K1616 Cast Reducers for Soil Pipe.

Standard. Size, 4x2 inches. Weight, 4 pounds. Price. 19½c

Extra heavy. Size, 4x2 inches. Weight, 6 pounds. Price........25c

Pipe Hooks.

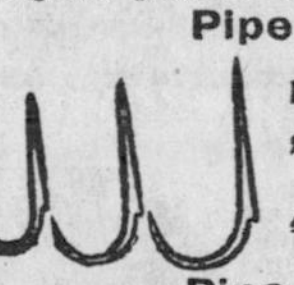

Pipe Hooks for Soil Pipe.

No. 42K1620 Size, 2 inches. Weight, 6 ounces. Price........4c

No. 42K1621 Size, 4 inches. Weight, 6 ounces. Price........5½c

Pipe Rests.

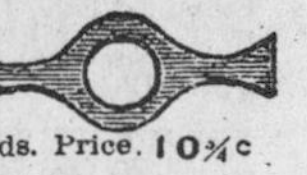

No. 42K1625 Pipe Rests for Soil Pipe. Standard grade.

Size, 2 inches. Weight, 2 pounds. Price........9c

Size, 4 inches. Weight, 4 pounds. Price. 10¾c

Cast S Traps.

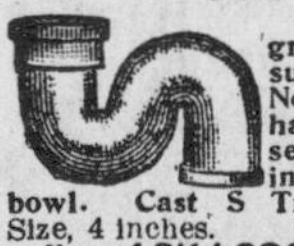

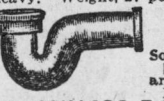

Our traps are used in the ground and on top for closets, such as No. 42K924 and No. 42K100 closets, which have no traps to prevent sewer gas and stench coming up through the closet bowl. Cast S Traps for Soil Pipe. Plain. Size, 4 inches.

No. 42K1630 Standard. Weight, 19 pounds. Price........44c

No. 42K1631 Extra heavy. Weight, 28 pounds. Price........69c

Cast Three-Quarter S Traps.

Cast Three-Quarter S Traps. Plain. Size, 4 inches.

No. 42K1632 Standard. Weight, 18 pounds. Price........44c

No. 42K1633 Extra heavy. Weight, 27 pounds. Price........69c

Cast Half S Traps.

Cast Half S Traps, for Soil Pipe. Size, 4 inches.

No. 42K1635 Standard. Weight, 18 pounds. Price........44c

No. 42K1636 Extra heavy. Weight, 27 pounds. Price........69c

Half S Trap with Vent.

No. 42K1640 Half S or P Trap with vent. Made of cast iron. Size, 4 inches, with 2-inch vent. Standard. Weight, 20 pounds. Price........65c

Extra heavy. Weight, 29 pounds. Price. 87c

Three-Quarter S Trap with Vent.

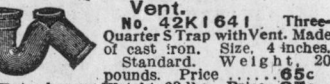

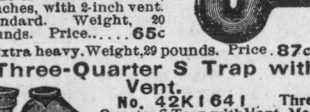

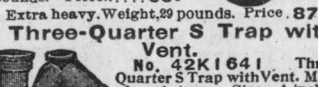

No. 42K1641 Three-Quarter S Trap with Vent. Made of cast iron. Size, 4 inches, Standard. Weight, 20 pounds. Price........65c

Extra heavy. Weight, 29 lbs. Price........87c

Cast S Trap with Vent.

No. 42K1645 Cast S Trap with Vent. Size, 4 inches with 2-inch vent. Standard. Weight, 21 pounds. Price.........65c Extra heavy. Weight, 30 pounds. Price.......87c

Cast Sanitary T Branches Tapped for Iron Pipe.

No. 42K1650 Cast Sanitary T Branches, tapped for iron pipe. Standard. Size, 4x1½ inches. Weight, 7 pounds. Price....48c Standard. Size, 4x2 inches. Weight, 7 pounds. Price..........49c Extra heavy. Size, 4x1½ inches. Weight, 14 pounds. Price..........64c Extra heavy. Size, 4x2 inches. Weight, 14 pounds. Price..........65c

Ventilating Branches.

No. 42K1655 Cast Iron Ventilating Branches, with side outlets for soil pipe. Standard, 4x2-inch outlet. Weight, 9 pounds. Price..43c Extra heavy, 4x2-inch outlet. Weight, 18 pounds. Price..54c

Ventilating Caps.

No. 42K1660 Cast Iron Ventilating Caps, for soil pipe. Our ventilating caps are used in connection with our No. 42K1701 trap, which is run outside the house in the ground and up to the top of the ground with the vent cap. Standard. Size, 4x6 inches long. Weight, 7 pounds. Price..........26c Extra heavy. Size, 4x6 inches long. Weight, 15 pounds. Price..........37c

Roof Plates.

No. 42K1665 Cast Roof Plate, for soil pipe. Size, 4 inches. Standard. Weight, 4 pounds. Price..........12c Extra heavy. Weight, 8 pounds. Price..18c

Roof Flashing.

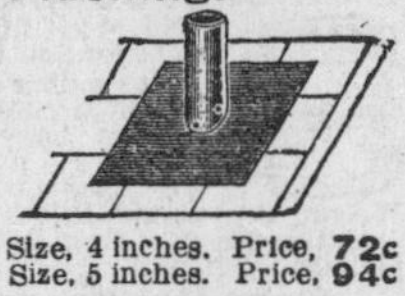

Galvanized Roof Flashing, to be connected to soil pipe on top of roof. Furnished in two sizes, 4 and 5 inches. Weight, about 12 pounds.

No. 42K1666 Size, 4 inches. Price, 72c
No. 42K1667 Size, 5 inches. Price, 94c

Cast T Branches, Tapped for Iron Pipe.

No. 42K1670 Cast T Branches, tapped for iron pipe. Standard, weight, 7 pounds. Extra heavy, weight, 14 pounds.

	Standard	Extra heavy
Size, 4x1½ inches. Price....	48c	63c
Size, 4x2 inches. Price....	49c	64c

Y Branches.

No. 42K1680 Cast Y Branches, for soil pipe, are used for connecting the waste of lavatories, tubs, sinks and closets to soil pipe. Standard. Size, 2x2 inches. Weight, 5 lbs. Price.....15c Standard. Size, 4x2 inches. Weight, 12 lbs. Price....37c

	Weight, lbs.	Price
Standard. Size, 4x4 inches.	13	37c
Extra heavy. Size, 2x2 inches.	10	22c
Extra heavy. Size, 4x2 inches.	23	52c
Extra heavy. Size, 4x4 inches.	25	53c

Sanitary Crosses.

No. 42K1685 Cast Sanitary Cross, for soil pipe, are used to connect two closets, lavatories, sinks or tubs on the same floor opposite each other to the same soil pipe. Standard. Size, 2x2 in. Weight, 5 lbs. Price..30c Extra heavy. Size, 2x2 inches. Weight 10 lbs. Price..........44c

	Wt. lbs.	Price
Standard. Size, 4x2 inches.	10	55c
Standard. Size, 4x4 inches.	12	56c
Extra heavy. Size, 4x2 inches.	21	67c
Extra heavy. Size, 4x4 inches.	24	68c

Half S Trap with Hand Hole and Cover.

No. 42K1686 Half S Trap with hand hole and cover. Size, 4 inches. Standard. Weight, 20 lbs. Price..........65c Extra heavy. Weight, 29 lbs. Price...87c

Three-Quarter S Trap with Hand Hole and Cover.

No. 42K1687 Three-Quarter S Trap with hand hole and cover. Size, 4 inches. Standard. Wt., 21 lbs. Price.........65c Extra heavy. Weight, 30 lbs. Price.....87c

Full S Trap with Hand Hole and Cover.

No. 42K1688 Full S Trap with hand hole and cover. Size, 4 inches. Standard. Weight, 21 lbs. Price..........65c Extra heavy. Weight, 30 lbs. Price...87c

Offsets.

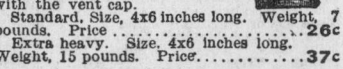

No. 42K1690 Cast Offsets for soil pipe, are used to run the soil pipe over any distance to avoid any obstructing article.

	Standard Price.	Extra Heavy
Size, 2x 4 inches.	16c	30c
Size, 2x 6 inches.	20c	33c
Size, 2x12 inches.	30c	43c
Size, 4x 4 inches.	33c	46c
Size, 4x 6 inches.	39c	53c
Size, 4x12 inches.	54c	76c

Quarter Bends with Heel Outlet.

No. 42K1695 Cast Quarter Bends, with heel outlet, for soil pipe.

	Wt. lbs.	Price
Standard. Size, 2x2 inches.	5	31c
Standard. Size, 4x2 inches.	7	43c
Extra heavy. Size, 2x2 inches.	6	33c
Extra heavy. Size, 4x2 inches.	11	50c

Running Trap.

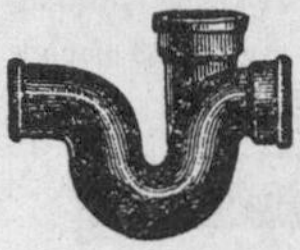

Cast Iron Running Trap for soil pipe.
No. 42K1700 Standard. Size, 2 inches with 2-inch vent. Weight, 6 lbs. Price, 41c Extra heavy. Weight, 9 pounds. Price......50c
No. 42K1701 Standard. Size, 4 inches with 4-inch vent. Weight, 15 lbs. Price...75c Extra heavy. Weight, 28 lbs. Price...98c

Running Trap with Hand Hole and Cover.

No. 42K1702 Running Trap with hand hole and cover. Standard. Size, 4 inches. Weight, 15 pounds. Price......59c Extra heavy. Weight, 30 lbs. Price..81c

Clean Out Y with Brass Screw Cover.

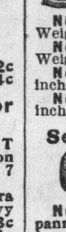

For Standard and Extra Heavy Pipe, to be placed in vent pipe, so that soil pipe may be cleaned out at any time without destroying soil pipe.

No. 42K1703 Standard. Size, 2 inches. Weight, 10 pounds. Price...........55c
No. 42K1703 Standard. Size, 4 inches. Weight, 13 pounds. Price..........88c
No. 42K1704 Extra heavy. Size, 2 inches. Weight, 23 pounds. Price.......58c
No. 42K1704 Extra heavy. Size, 4 inches. Weight, 25 pounds. Price......92c

Service or Stop Cock Boxes.

No. 42K1706 Made of cast iron, japanned. Size, 3 inches in diameter, extends from 34 to 58 inches. Weight, 18 pounds. Price..........$1.06

Cast Cesspools.

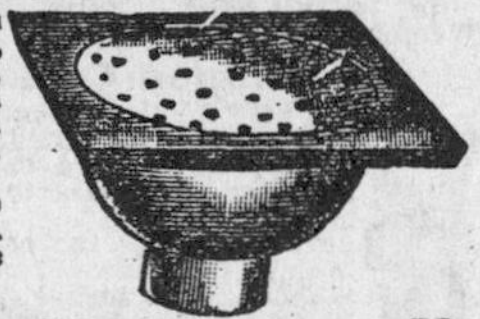

Cast Iron Cesspools, with bell trap, to be used in connection with soil pipe.
No. 42K1710 Size, 6x6 inches. Price......41c
No. 42K1711 Size, 9x9 inches. Price..........52c
No. 42K1712 Size, 13x13 inches. Price..........78c

Pipe Hydrants.

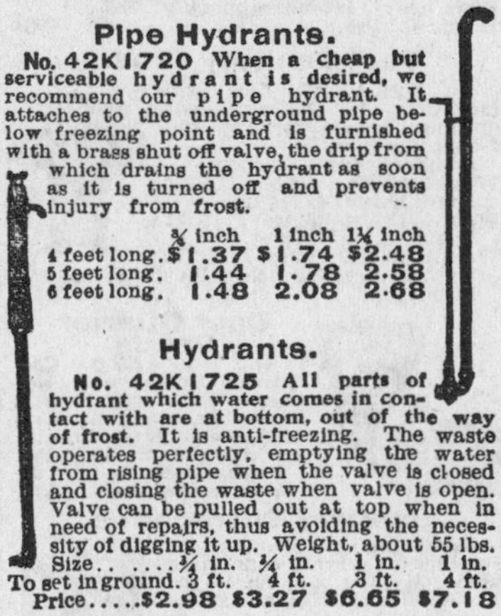

No. 42K1720 When a cheap but serviceable hydrant is desired, we recommend our pipe hydrant. It attaches to the underground pipe below freezing point and is furnished with a brass shut off valve, the drip from which drains the hydrant as soon as it is turned off and prevents injury from frost.

	¾ inch	1 inch	1¼ inch
4 feet long.	$1.37	$1.74	$2.48
5 feet long.	1.44	1.78	2.58
6 feet long.	1.48	2.08	2.68

Hydrants.

No. 42K1725 All parts of hydrant where water comes in contact with are at bottom, out of the way of frost. It is anti-freezing. The waste operates perfectly, emptying the water from rising pipe when the valve is closed and closing the waste when valve is open. Valve can be pulled out at top when in need of repairs, thus avoiding the necessity of digging it up. Weight, about 55 lbs.

	½ in.	¾ in.	1 in.	1 in.
Size.	¾ ft.	4 ft.	3 ft.	4 ft.
To set in ground. 3 ft.	$2.98	$3.27	$6.65	$7.18

Spring Gauge Proving Outfits.

No. 42K1750 Spring Gauge Proving Outfits, for testing gas pipes. Complete as shown in illustration. Weight, 6 pounds. Price, per set..........$6.85

Handy Force Pump, with Valve, 36c.

No. 42K1880 The Handy Force Pump is used for forcing stoppages and cleaning waste pipes, closets and sinks, wash bowls, bath tubs, etc. No plumber, janitor, hotel, restaurant or residence should be without one. One stoppage of your pipes will pay for it. Thousands of them sold with the best results. It is made with a heavy rubber cup on the end of a 3-foot wooden handle, furnished with valve. Weight, 12 ounces. Price, with valve..........36c

ACME GASOLINE BULB BLAST FURNACE $2.98

No. 42K1770 Acme Bulb Furnace with improved coils, which will produce a blue and hot flame and which is equal to any furnace on the market in melting metals. Furnished complete with shield to hold melting pot and cast iron melting pot. Weight, 17 pounds. Price, reduced to...$2.98

GASOLINE BLOW TORCHES WITH IMPROVED LEVER HANDLE $2.98

$2.98

No. 42K1771 Gasoline Torch, is made for general utility, especially adapted for heating soldering coppers, melting, paint burning and suitable for light brazing. Tanks are constructed of heavy seamless drawn brass, having strong, corrugated, concave brass seamed bottom, with bottom filler plug—the bottom serving as a funnel for filling. It is fitted with our burner and pump with strong connections and simple and accessible valves. Connections reinforced with locknuts on inside of tank. Is a powerful heater at full flame. Capacity of tank, 1 quart. Weight, packed for shipment, 4¼ pounds. Price..........$2.98

$2.73

No. 42K1772 Gasoline Torch, has smaller burner than the one described under preceding number and the tank is smaller, having capacity of 1 pint. Tanks are constructed of heavy, seamless drawn brass having strong corrugated bottom with bottom filler plug—the bottom serves as a funnel in filling the torch. It is fitted with burner and pump with strong connections and simple and accessible valves. This size torch is commonly preferred by painters as it is so much lighter when filled with gasoline. The price does not include soldering copper. Shipping weight, about 4 pounds. Price..........$2.73

Plumbers' or Melting Ladles.

No. 42K1780 Steel bowl with wrought iron handle.

Size across bowl, inches.	3	4	5
Weight.	12 oz.	1 lb.	1½ lbs.
Price.	11c	13c	17c

GEM BIB SEAT DRESSER - - - $1.10

No. 42K1790 The Gem Bib Seat Dresser is the most practical tool of its kind on the market. Cutters are rose pattern and the inside of bell is threaded for the purpose of screwing in top of bib. Cannot grind crooked. Weight, 9 ounces. Price..........$1.10

Pipe Bender.

Pipe Bender to be placed inside lead pipe when bending to avoid kinks in pipe. Made of a high grade spring steel.
No. 42K1795 Size, 1¼ inches. Weight, 2¼ pounds. Price..........28c
No. 42K1796 Size, 1½ inches. Weight, 3¼ pounds. Price..........33c

Boxwood Dresser.

No. 42K1800 Plumbers' Boxwood Dressers. Weight, 1 lb. Price..........45c

Oval Shave Hook.

No. 42K1805 Plumbers' Oval Shave Hooks. Steel blade. Weight, 4 ounces. Price..........17½c

Turning Pins.

No. 42K1810 Plumbers' Turning Pin.
No. 1. Weight, 2 ounces. Price..........17½c
No. 2. Weight, 3 ounces. Price..........18½c
No. 3. Weight, 4 ounces. Price..........19½c

Drift Plugs.

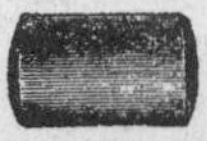

No. 42K1811 Boxwood Drift Plugs. Weight, about 1 oz. Sizes, inches 1 1¼ 1½ Price....9c 11c 13c

Asbestos Lead Joint Runners.

No. 42K1815 Asbestos, being unaffected by heat, is admirably adapted for making joint runners, for running lead or molten metal in soil, water or gas pipe. The accompanying illustration shows the runners as applied to pipe. Weight, 1½ pounds. No. 2, ¾-inch. Round, for 4, 5 and 6-inch pipe, each..........$1.29

Bending Pins.

No. 42K1820 Plumbers' Bending Pins. Weight, 1 lb. Price..........14½c

Spring Yarning Irons.

No. 42K1825 Plumbers' Yarning Irons. Weight, 10 ounces. Price.....29c

Calking Chisel.

No. 42K1831 Plumbers' Calking Chisel. Made of high grade steel. Weight, 1¼ pounds. Price.....17c

Tap Borers.

No. 42K1835 Plumbers' Tap Borers. Made of high grade English steel. Weight, 5 oz. Price.....21c

Wiping Cloths.

No. 42K1845 Plumbers' Wiping Cloths. Neat and compact, made of the very best ticking. Weight, 1 ounce. Price..........5½c

Alcohol Lamps.

Gasfitters' Alcohol Lamps. Made of tin, finely finished. Weight, about 10 ounces. **No. 42K1855** Tin. Price..........39c

Spun Oakum.

No. 42K1866 Oakum, for calking iron pipe, soil pipe and fittings. Price, per lb..$0.05½ Price, per 50-pound bale......2.40

Lead Pipe.

No. 42K1870 Lead Pipe. Prices subject to change without notice.

		Price, per foot
Lead Pipe, ⅜ in. in diam., 10 oz. to foot.	4½c
Lead Pipe, ¾ in. in diam., 1 lb. to ft.	7c
Lead Pipe, 1 in. in diam., 1½ lbs. to ft.	10½c
Lead Pipe, 1¼ in. in diam., 2 lbs. to ft.	14c
Lead Pipe, 1½ in. in diam., 3 lbs. to ft.	21c
Lead Pipe, 2 in. in diam., 3 lbs. to ft.	22c

Strong Lead Pipe.

No. 42K1875

	Price, per foot
Lead Pipe, ½-in. diam., 1¼ lbs. to foot.	8½c
Lead Pipe, ¾-in. diam., 2 lbs. to foot.	13c
Lead Pipe, ¾-in. diam., 3¼ lbs. to foot.	15c
Lead Pipe, 1-in. diam., 3¼ lbs. to foot.	21½c

Sheet Lead.

No. 42K1885 Sheet Lead furnished in two sizes. Thickness, 1-32 and 1-16-inch. 1-32-inch weighs 2 pounds to the square foot; 1-16-inch weighs 4 pounds to the square foot. Always state thickness wanted. Price, either thickness, per pound.. 8½c

Plumbers' Solder.

No. 42K1900 High Grade Plumbers' Refined Metal Solder. Comes in bars of about 1½ pounds each. We do not sell less than a bar. Our solder is so rich in tin that one pound of our composition will do the same work as two pounds of most of the refined and wiping solder on the market, consequently it is the cheapest solder you can buy. Price, per pound..........21c

Pig Lead.

No. 42K1905 Genuine Pig Lead. Comes in pigs of about 80 pounds each and ingots 7 pounds each. Price, per pound, in 80-pound pigs.... 6c Price, per pound, in 7-pound ingots..6½c

STEAM AND HOT WATER HEATING PLANTS

OUR 1908 LINE OF HERCULES BOILERS IS SUPERIOR TO ANY LINE OF HEATERS, EITHER ROUND OR SECTIONAL THAT ARE ON THE MARKET TODAY.

THE HERCULES STEAM AND HOT WATER BOILERS, shown on this page, are of the vertical sectional type and have all the advantages of the round boiler, such as compact fire pot and simplicity of construction, while they also have the superior advantages of the sectional boiler such as long fire travel, increased heating surface and the correct proportions between the grate and the heating surface. The fire pot is deep and return flues ample, so it will do its work economically and with the least attention. It will carry coal enough to maintain perfect combustion for twelve hours with ordinary care and attention. For hot water heating this heater is superior to any small heater on the market as it has a perfect interior circulation, and this is also especially advantageous for steam, as the steam is more easily generated and is quickly separated from the water, so that the water is not carried up into the pipes with the steam. The heater is thoroughly tested before leaving the works and is made up and shipped in two parts, base and grates in one, and the sections in the other, which makes it easy to erect. Its compact form enables it to be carried into a building as easily as a radiator.

The steam boiler is furnished complete with all steam trimmings, such as steam gauge, water gauge, water column and damper regulator, and safety valve. These are not necessary with a hot water boiler. All boilers are furnished complete with firing tools, such as poker, hoe and flue brush.

Hercules Steam and Hot Water Boilers.
Shipped from Factory in Western Pennsylvania.

WRITE FOR THIS FREE SPECIAL HEATING CATALOGUE

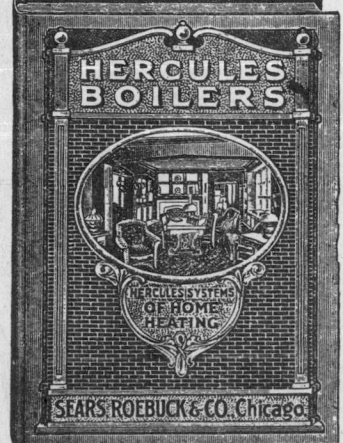

TO GIVE YOU AN IDEA as to the wonderful values we are offering in heating material, we list, on this page, a few items which will show you how much money you can save by ordering your heating apparatus from us. However, if you are desirous of purchasing a complete heating plant, we would ask you to send for our free Special Catalogue on "Hercules Systems of Home Heating," and a copy of it will be forwarded to you at once, free. This catalogue shows a most complete line of steam and hot water heating boilers, radiators, valves, pipe, fittings, etc., in fact, everything necessary for the complete installation of steam and hot water heating plants. When we send you the free Special Catalogue we will also send you a printed diagram sheet which you can fill out showing the style and size of your house and what rooms you want radiators in and upon receipt of this plan we will furnish you an estimate of the entire plant, just what is required and what it will cost you.

ALL THIS IS FREE. We make no charge for our estimate. Then, if you find our price satisfactory and send us your order, we will gladly go ahead and make up the complete working drawing. If you desire, we will send the working drawings to you for your final inspection and revision before making shipment.

No.	Size of Fire Pot, inches	Size of Smoke Pipe, in.	Height, inches	Floor Space, including Smoke Box	Flow and Return	Rating Water	Rating Steam	Price, Water	Price, Steam
124	12x11	7	47	22x24 in.	2-2	250	125	$30.25	$40.50
125	12x14	7	47	22x28 in.	2-2	350	200	42.25	53.00
126	12x17	7	47	22x32 in.	2-2	450	275	54.00	62.00
127	12x20	7	47	22x36 in.	3-2	575	350	68.00	76.00

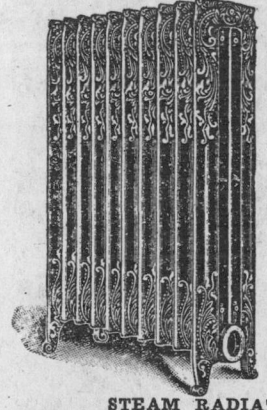

ACME STEAM OR HOT WATER THREE-COLUMN RADIATORS.

Shipped from Factory in Western Pennsylvania.

OUR RADIATORS are of the latest approved design and the ornamentation cannot fail to be acceptable to any of our customers as it is pleasing and harmonious. Our radiators are constructed to hold a pint of water to a foot of radiating surface. This enables us to have a wider space between the sections for the circulation of the air and enables the radiators to do more effective work in giving off heat, both by radiation and contact with the air.

THE CASTINGS are made of the finest grade of gray iron of uniform thickness, with corrugated heating surface and are free from all flaws and pinholes. The radiators are tested to 70 pounds' pressure before leaving our factory. We can furnish radiators in any number of sections desired.

When ordering be sure to state whether you want radiators for steam or hot water.

STEAM RADIATORS ARE TAPPED AS FOLLOWS:

Up to 24 feet	1-inch supply
24 feet to 50 feet	1¼-inch supply
50 feet to 100 feet	1½-inch supply
Over 100 feet	2-inch supply

HOT WATER RADIATORS ARE TAPPED AS FOLLOWS:

Up to 50 feet	1-inch feed and return
50 feet to 75 feet	1¼-inch feed and return
Over 75 feet	1½-inch feed and return

No. 42K2055 LIST OF SIZES, THREE-COLUMN RADIATORS.

No. of Sections	Length, inches	45-inch Height, 6 sq. ft. per Section	38-inch Height, 5 sq. ft. per Section	32-inch Height, 4½ sq. ft. per Section	26-inch Height, 3¾ sq. ft. per Section	20-inch Height, 3 sq. ft. per Section
		HEATING SURFACE—SQUARE FEET				
2	5	12	10	9	7½	6
3	7½	18	15	13½	11¼	9
4	10	24	20	18	15	12
5	12½	30	25	22½	18¾	15
6	15	36	30	27	22½	18
7	17½	42	35	31½	26¼	21
8	20	48	40	36	30	24
9	22½	54	45	40½	33¾	27
10	25	60	50	45	37½	30
11	27½	66	55	49½	41¼	33
12	30	72	60	54	45	36
Price, per sq. ft., steam		20c	20c	22½c	24c	27c
Price, per sq. ft., hot water		20½c	21c	23c	25c	28c

Quick Opening Hot Water Radiator Valves with Unions.

No. 42K2085 Quick Opening Hot Water Radiator Valves. Made of solid brass, nickel plated, with union, one-half turn opens valve to full capacity.

Size, inches.	¾	1	1¼
Price	62c	80c	$1.10
Size, inches.	1½	2	
Price	$1.57	2.42	

Radiator Valves with Unions.

No. 42K2090 Radiator Valves, full nickel plated, for steam. Made of solid brass, finely finished, with union, as shown in illustration.

Size, ¾ inch.	Price $0.83
Size, 1 inch.	Price 1.05
Size, 1¼ inches.	Price 1.41
Size, 1½ inches.	Price 1.78
Size, 2 inches.	Price 2.89

Union Elbows for Hot Water Radiators with Unions.

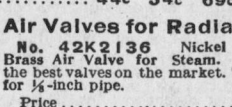

No. 42K2140 Brass Nickel Plated Unions for hot water radiators.

Size, inches.	¾	1	1¼	1½
Price	44c	54c	69c	86c

Air Valves for Radiators.

No. 42K2136 Nickel Plated Brass Air Valve for Steam. One of the best valves on the market. Tapped for ⅛-inch pipe.

Price 42c

Cast Iron Steam and Gas Fittings.

Malleable Iron Fittings cannot be used for this purpose.

No. 42K2095 Cast Iron Steam or Gas Elbows.

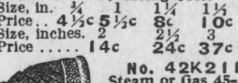

Size, in.	¾	1	1¼	1½	2	2½	3
Price	3c	3½c	6c	7c	9c	17c	26c

No. 42K2100 Cast Iron Steam or Gas Tees.

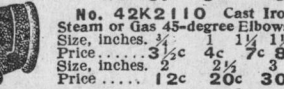

Size, inches.	¾	1	1¼	1½
Price	4½c	5½c	8c	10c
Size, inches.	2	2½	3	
Price	14c	24c	37c	

No. 42K2105 Cast Iron Steam or Gas Reducing Tees.

Size, inches.	¾	1	1¼	1½
Price	4½c	5½c	8c	10c
Size, inches.	2	2½	3	
Price	14c	24c	37c	

No. 42K2110 Cast Iron Steam or Gas 45-degree Elbows.

Size, inches.	¾	1	1¼	1½
Price	3½c	4c	7c	8c
Size, inches.	2	2½	3	
Price	12c	20c	30c	

No. 42K2115 Cast Iron Steam or Gas Reducing Elbows.

Size, inches.	¾	1	1¼	1½
Price	3c	4c	6½c	8c
Size, inches.	2	2½	3	
Price	11c	20c	30c	

Compression Air Valve With Key.

No. 42K2131 Compression Air Valve. With lock and shield, made of solid brass, finely nickeled. These valves are always used on hot water radiators as the automatic air valves for hot water radiators are not practical. We recommend the loose key valves as the key may be removed after valves are turned on or off, and thus prevent anyone from meddling with the valves.

Size, ⅛ inch. Price, each ... 11c

Keys extra. Price, each 5c

EVERY FARMER HIS OWN PUMP MAN

We illustrate on this and the following pages of this catalogue, one of the most complete lines of pumps of all styles and sizes at prices (quality considered) lower than ever shown by any manufacturer or dealer. The line of pumps shown on this and the following pages has been selected after a great deal of study, and the claims we make for our pumps are not merely talk but the facts as shown by actual tests. Our pump business has grown steadily and we feel the reason for this is that we ship only such pumps as we know will give our customers the best of satisfaction. We show on these pages, for the convenience of our customers, complete pump outfits for different depth wells. The prices quoted include pump, piping, cylinders, cylinder rods, everything cut and threaded complete, so that all you have to do when you receive the pump is to screw the pipes together, lay a few boards over your well for a platform, nail or bolt your pump to this platform, and the equipment is complete, ready to pump water.

Our sales on pumps during the past year has increased to such a proportion that it has enabled us to purchase these goods at lower prices than ever before, and following our usual custom of adding but one small percentage of profit, we are pleased to give our customers the benefit of this reduction, and it no doubt will be apparent to you by studying these pages that these prices have been materially reduced.

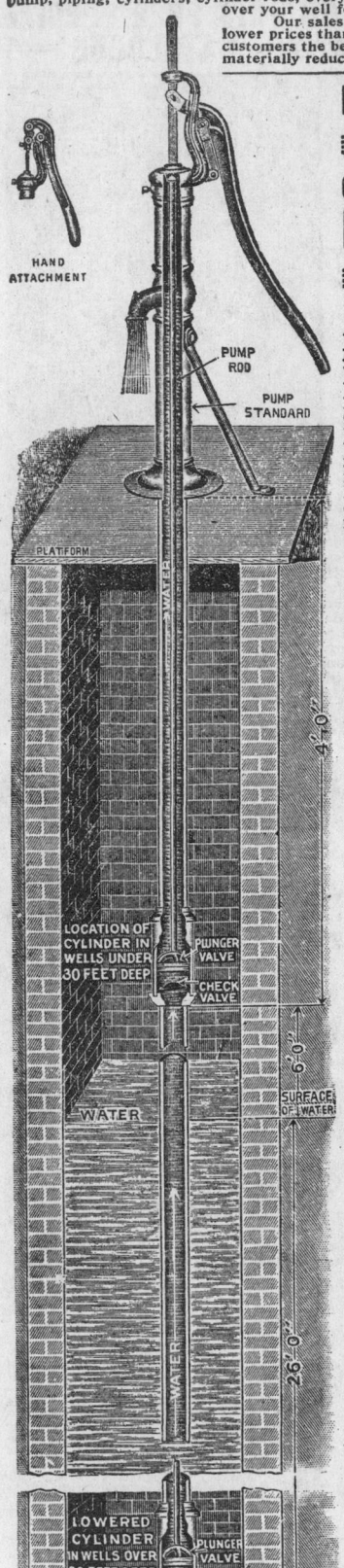

EUREKA ANTI-FREEZING LIFT PUMP

COMPLETE WITH GALVANIZED PIPE

FOR DUG OR OPEN WELLS

$4.92
REDUCED FROM $5.24

In our EUREKA WINDMILL LIFT PUMP, as shown in this illustration, we offer you a pump suitable for dug or open wells with a heavy three joint revolving cap. All bearings are fitted with large, heavy turn pins, which will outwear a dozen ordinary bolts used in other makes of this style pump. It is fitted with a close top cap which prevents dirt, sticks, or gravel falling into the top or working valves of this pump. The set length screws into the pump at spout which leaves an air space between pipe and pump and prevents water freezing in winter time. The prices quoted below on these pumps are for pumps fitted with iron cylinder, but where well is over 30 feet deep we recommend the use of our brass body cylinder. This is a heavy, substantial pump, and we guarantee it to give good satisfaction in wells up to 80 feet deep when the cylinder is lowered for deep wells as shown in illustration. This pump is equipped with a swinging fulcrum which gives a much freer action when used by hand, and prevents cramping or binding when used in connection with the windmill. We furnish this pump with a heavy cast handle, a good substantial brace, and with 1¼-inch galvanized pipe. It is nicely painted in green and tinted in bronze. This pump is intended for use in dug or open wells and is intended to lift and not to force water. For such a well we can guarantee this pump to be equal to any pump on the market, and we know that anyone of our customers purchasing one of these outfits will be highly pleased with it. Do not hesitate to order this pump through fear you cannot set it in the well. We cut and thread the pipes and rods, and all you have to do is to screw the pipes and rods together, set it on your platform, and you are ready to pump water. We furnish this pump with a combination head and it can be used either to attach to a windmill or pumping by hand. If, however, you desire to purchase this pump for hand use only, with a top such as shown in the small illustration on this page, we can furnish it in this way, and if you desire your pump fitted in this manner, you can deduct 50 cents from the prices quoted below.

THE PRICES quoted below are for complete outfits, pump, galvanized pipe, cylinder and rod all cut and threaded to the proper lengths, complete with a 3x10-inch iron cylinder, which is most commonly used. If, however, you desire a large quantity of water, we can furnish a 3½-inch cylinder at 50 cents over prices quoted below.

No. 42K5100 Pump and outfit complete for 10-foot well. Wt., 90 lbs.	**$4.92**	
No. 42K5101 Pump and outfit complete for 15-foot well. Wt., 102 lbs.	5.47	
No. 42K5102 Pump and outfit complete for 20-foot well. Wt., 114 lbs.	6.02	
No. 42K5103 Pump and outfit complete for 25-foot well. Wt., 126 lbs.	6.57	
No. 42K5104 Pump and outfit complete for 30-foot well. Wt., 138 lbs.	7.87	
No. 42K5105 Pump and outfit complete for 40-foot well. Wt., 174 lbs.	10.47	
No. 42K5106 Pump and outfit complete for 50-foot well. Wt., 200 lbs.	13.57	

If pump is wanted for wells over 50 feet deep, just state how deep the well is in which you desire to use this pump and allow 16 cents for each foot over the price quoted for the 50-foot well. For example: If your well is 75 feet deep, the price of the outfit would be as follows: Cost of 50-foot well, $13.57; 25 feet extra at 16 cents a foot, $4.00; or a total of $17.57. The above prices are for pumps fitted with iron cylinders. We recommend the use of a brass body cylinder. If wanted with 3x10-inch brass body cylinder instead of the iron, add $1.50 to above prices.

EUREKA ANTI-FREEZING DRIVE WELL OUTFIT

COMPLETE WITH GALVANIZED PIPES

$5.95
REDUCED FROM $6.78

In our EUREKA DRIVE WELL OUTFIT, we are able to offer our customers an outfit which for simplicity has no equal. The pumps are intended to be used in places where water is reached within 25 feet from the surface of the earth and in ground in which there is no rock.

WE FURNISH THIS OUTFIT in such a way that any person, whether or not he has ever seen a pump, can readily put it in with absolutely no chance for failure. In order to install a drive well, all that is necessary to do is to dig a hole from three to four feet square and about four feet deep, so that the cylinder of the pump may be placed in same to avoid the pump freezing in winter time. After your hole is dug, screw the drive well point onto one of the pieces of pipe, which we furnish, with a coupling, then screw the driving cap, which we furnish, on top of this pipe and drive this into the ground with a post maul, which you will find listed on page 522 of this catalogue as No. 9K39468. When the first length of pipe is driven down remove the cap, screw another piece of pipe into the coupling you attach to the one already driven into the ground, and drive this into the ground. Repeat the operation as often as necessary until you have your pipe driven down into the water. Then screw the pipe onto the cylinder of the pump, place some manure around the cylinder of the pump in the hole which you have dug, to prevent cylinder from freezing, and you have your outfit ready for pumping. After you have your pump screwed together, all that is necessary for you to do is to lay three or four pieces of plank or board over the top of your well to answer the purpose of a platform.

THE PUMP furnished with this outfit is our Eureka Close Top Windmill Pump, and is a pump which we can guarantee to be the equal of any pump in the market for this style work. It has a revolving cap, is furnished with large heavy turn pins, which will outwear a dozen ordinary bolts such as are furnished with other makes of this style pump. It is furnished with a swinging fulcrum, which gives the pump a much freer action and prevents binding or cramping when the pump is used for hand pumping. The cylinder furnished with this pump is made of the best grade of material by skilled mechanics, and is truly and mechanically bored and polished. The pipe furnished is all galvanized pipe, and it will not rust. We furnish this pipe fitted with a combination top suitable for hand or windmill pumping, and even though you have no windmill at the present time, we recommend that you purchase the pump in this way, as you may at a later date decide to attach a windmill to it; but should you prefer to buy this outfit for hand pumping, with a top such as shown in the small illustration, you can order it in this way and deduct 50 cents from prices quoted below.

WHILE THIS PUMP can be used for any depth well, providing you dig the hole to within 25 feet of the water, we do not recommend it for wells over 25 feet deep, nor in stony ground, but in places where the water is not more than 25 feet from the surface we can guarantee this outfit to give excellent satisfaction. The way to ascertain as to when you strike water, all that is necessary to do is to procure a strong cord, attach a small piece of iron or lead to the end of this string, and after you have driven each piece of pipe into the ground, just drop this string into the piping, and you can then readily see after pulling the string out as to whether or not you have struck water.

DO NOT ALLOW ANYONE to lead you to believe that you will not be able to put in these pumps yourself after you have received them. By studying the illustration of drive well pumps on this page, and by following our instructions as to how to drive this well, we are positive that you will have absolutely no trouble in installing it; and, furthermore, after you have received the pump and pipe, if it is not thoroughly satisfactory to you you are at no loss whatsoever, as you can return the pump and pipe to us and we will refund your money together with transportation charges both ways.

BEFORE ORDERING THIS PUMP, all you have to do is to ask your neighbor, who now has a pump, how deep he was compelled to dig or drive his well before he struck water, and you can order an outfit accordingly.

The following prices are for pump outfits complete with 1¼x30-inch sixty gauze cast head well point, 3x10-inch iron cylinder, 1¼-inch driving cap, and enough 1¼-inch galvanized pipe to complete wells for the depths specified below.

No. 42K5110 Pump and outfit complete for 10-foot well. Wt., 96 lbs.	**$5.95**	
No. 42K5111 Pump and outfit complete for 15-foot well. Wt., 108 lbs.	6.50	
No. 42K5112 Pump and outfit complete for 20-foot well. Wt., 120 lbs.	7.05	
No. 42K5113 Pump and outfit complete for 25-foot well. Wt., 130 lbs.	7.55	

The above prices are for pumps furnished with iron cylinders. We recommend the use of brass body cylinders, which we furnish. If wanted, add $1.50 to the above prices.

EUREKA DOUBLE ACTING DRILLED WELL FORCE PUMP AND COMPLETE OUTFIT, $13.50

REDUCED FROM $15.12

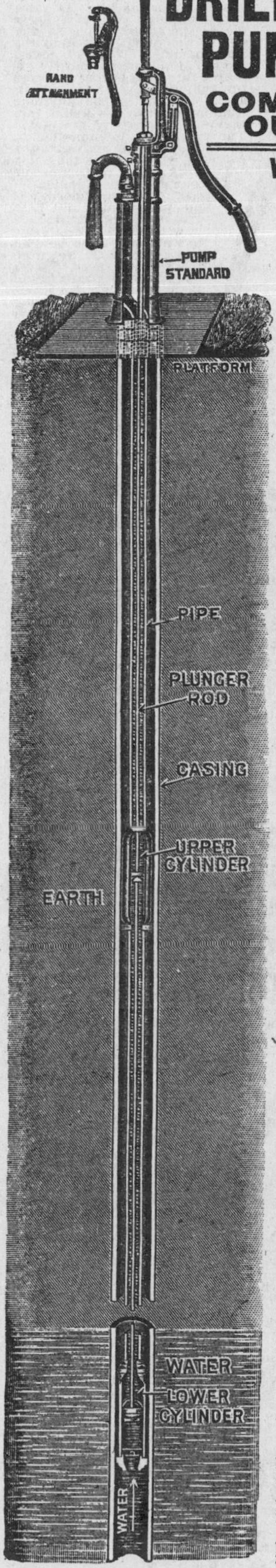

WE SHOW IN THIS ILLUSTRATION our Double Acting Deep Drilled Well Force Pump and Outfit as it appears when placed in a well. This is a very popular pump where it is necessary to bore or drill a well, and it is also used very extensively and with the best of satisfaction in open or dug wells in depths of from 75 to 150 or 200 feet. This is the outfit which is used in places where the strata of the earth is composed of hard substance, and where it is necessary to drill or bore to the water instead of digging a well. These pumps are made with a windmill head to be attached to windmills, and are made so that all the parts below the platform will enter and pass into the well casing when used in drilled hole. To fit a drilled well with this pump it is not necessary to cut off the casing as in this style pump of other makes, and therefore the casing may be carried up close to the platform, thus keeping out surface water and other impurities.

IN ORDER TO INSTALL A DRILLED OR BORED WELL, we would recommend that you employ a well driller or borer in your local town to bore this hole for you, and also put in your casing, if you desire your well to be cased, and after this is done, all that is necessary for you to do in order to be insured of a perfect working pump is to refer to the table below, order the outfit for the depth well which you have, and we will ship this pump to you complete with piping and rods cut and threaded complete with all the necessary fittings which you will need to connect the pump, and all that will be necessary for you to do will be to screw the different pipes and rods together, which any boy or man can do, set it into your well, and you are ready for pumping. This pump, as you will see by the illustration, is furnished with two cylinders which makes it a double acting pump. This pump has a very free movement as with upward stroke of the handle only half of the water pumped is discharged, the other half being retained by the smaller or upper cylinder, and is discharged by the downward movement of the handle. This causes a continuous flow of water and does away with all lost motion and there are no jars or jolts when this pump is working. The upper cylinder of this pump is placed about 5 feet below the base of the pump, and the bottom cylinder is extended to the required distance to reach the water. This, however, is all taken care of by our expert pump men, and as before stated, everything will be cut and threaded so that any person whether or not they have ever seen a pump, will find no trouble whatever in screwing it together and setting it in a well. While we recommend this pump as the best pump for drilled or bored wells, it is one of the best outfits which we have or can furnish for deep, open, or dug wells or in a well where a large amount of water is required. We furnish this pump complete with a strainer at the bottom of pipe which prevents any dirt, sticks or sediment from getting into the valves of the pump, also with hose attachment for spout, as this is a force pump and can be used very satisfactorily for sprinkling purposes; pump rods, and couplings all threaded and cut and enough galvanized pipe to fit the well as per the specified depths below. In ordering this pump, all that is necessary for you to do is to find the depth of the well in which you intend to place your pump, and order an outfit as per the table below to fit it, and this pump will come to you all ready to be screwed together and put into the well. We furnish this pump with a brass lined upper cylinder, and a brass lower cylinder both of which are 2½x12 inches.

No. 42K5120 Pump and complete outfit for 30-foot well. Weight, 172 pounds **$13.50**

No. 42K5121 Pump and complete outfit for 40-foot well. Weight, 200 pounds **15.10**

No. 42K5122 Pump and complete outfit for 50-foot well. Weight, 230 pounds **16.70**

No. 42K5123 Pump and complete outfit for 60-foot well. Weight, 260 pounds **18.30**

No. 42K5124 Pump and complete outfit for 75-foot well. Weight, 300 pounds **20.70**

The above outfits are for wells specified in the above table, but should you desire to place one of these pumps in a well deeper than 75 feet we make an additional charge of 16 cents per foot for each foot deeper than 75 feet. For example: If your well is 100 feet deep, an outfit for a 75-foot well would cost you $20.70, and you would add 25 feet at 16 cents per foot which would be $4.00, plus $20.70. Total for 100-foot well, $24.70.

PERFECT IMPROVED PURIFYING PUMP, $4.48.

This is the pump advertised by some concerns as their greatest bargain in pumps and the prices they ask are much higher than those we quote for it. While it is an excellent pump for the money, we ask you to note our full line of pumps of all kinds of value equally as great as this one. We sell more pumps than all the other catalogue houses put together and our large sales enable us to buy in such great quantities that we get very close prices. Our qualities and prices have built up this enormous pump business.

Our Perfect Purifying Pump is of the simplest pump construction in the world for raising water and at the same time purifying it. It is adjustable to any well or cistern. It is of very durable construction and materials; operates with an endless chain made from the best of galvanized wire manufactured and tempered expressly for these pumps, to which water buckets of the best grade of galvanized iron are attached. These pumps are adapted to wells or cisterns not over 40 feet in depth, but we do not recommend them for use in wells or cisterns beyond 30 feet deep. For wells of greater depth, we urge you to purchase one of our iron pumps as described on pages 614 to 617 of this catalogue. **You will note by the illustration that buckets and chains run through a bearing which hangs in the water at the bottom of the well and in ordering this pump you should order equipment which will reach within 2 feet of the bottom. This pump always furnishes the water from the bottom, as no water enters cups until after they have passed over the bearing at the bottom and begun the upward movement, when the air escapes and they are filled with the best and the coldest water. This pump is so constructed that none of the objections common to other pumps of somewhat similar construction can be urged against it. There are neither suckers nor valves, no wooden tubing to rot out or rusty iron to come in contact with the water, so that your water supply is always pure, sweet and wholesome. The pump comes complete with chain, cups, lower bearing, ready to be placed in wells of different depths, as indicated in price list below. Average weight, about 75 pounds.**

No. 42K5442	Complete for 10-foot well. Price	$ 4.48
No. 42K5443	Complete for 15-foot well. Price	5.44
No. 42K5444	Complete for 20-foot well. Price	6.29
No. 42K5460	Complete for 25-foot well. Price	7.19
No. 42K5461	Complete for 30-foot well. Price	8.09
No. 42K5462	Complete for 35-foot well. Price	9.24
No. 42K5463	Complete for 40-foot well. Price	10.25
No. 42K5445	Extra Galvanized Buckets and Chain. Price, per foot	.08¾

OUR IMPROVED WOOD CURB RUBBER BUCKET CHAIN PUMP AND EQUIPMENT, $2.84.

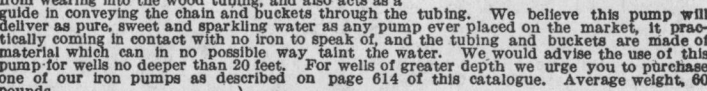

This illustrates our Improved Wood Rubber Bucket Curb Pump showing the inside workings as to how water is drawn with it, and also showing how tubing is placed in the well, and also how rubber buckets are attached to chain. This is one of the best pumps in this line for efficiency, workmanship, material and appearance. The curb is made of No. 1 select white wood with two heavy coats of paint. It is put together with special cement coated nails which will not rust and will not pull out. It has a detachable top which can be easily removed, exposing all the working parts of the pump for renewals or repairs without moving pump. It is furnished with a well made, large sized sprocket wheel, nicely painted, heavy shafting, substantial shaft boxes, ratchet and dog, iron handle with wood grip, all of which are neatly painted. The castings on these pumps are all lettered with casting numbers so repairs or duplicate parts can be ordered by anybody without any possibility of errors or mistakes. The chain furnished with these pumps is made of a special grade iron manufactured especially for this purpose, of a heavy gauge and galvanized by a special process which we can guarantee not to rust. The buckets furnished with this pump are made of pure gum rubber with large inside flanges and links of galvanized steel which makes it practically impossible for rubbers to shift or become loose. Each bucket is notched so as to allow water to drain from tubing into cistern when pump is not in operation so as to prevent freezing in cold weather. The tubing furnished with this pump is made of select poplar which will not taint the water and is almost indestructible with ordinary care. The ends of tubing are made with tongue and socket, no coupling required to connect tubing together. We furnish a cast iron shoe or guide to be placed at the bottom of the tubing of each pump which prevents the chain from wearing into the wood tubing, and also acts as a guide in conveying the chain and buckets through the tubing. We believe this pump will deliver as pure, sweet and sparkling water as any pump ever placed on the market, it practically coming in contact with no iron to speak of, and the tubing and buckets are made of material which can in no possible way taint the water. We would advise the use of this pump for wells no deeper than 20 feet. For wells of greater depth we urge you to purchase one of our iron pumps as described on page 614 of this catalogue. Average weight, 60 pounds.

No. 42K5472 Rubber Bucket Chain Pump with complete equipment for wells 10 feet deep. Price $2.84

No. 42K5473	Pump and complete equipment for 13-foot wells. Price....	3.07
No. 42K5474	Pump and complete equipment for 15-foot wells. Price....	3.38
No. 42K5475	Pump and complete equipment for 18-foot wells. Price....	3.80
No. 42K5476	Pump and complete equipment for 20-foot wells. Price....	3.96

WOOD FARM PUMPS.

Our Wood Pumps are made from the best selected stock. They are thoroughly painted, striped and varnished. These pumps are furnished with iron handle brackets and iron spouts. The plunger, which is the vital part of a suction pump, is of the very latest improved pattern. Our wood pumps are adapted for wells not more than 30 feet deep. If well is of greater depth, we recommend that you select one of our iron pumps as described on pages 614 and 615 of this catalogue. **To select a wood pump**—For wells 20 feet or less in depth, order 6-foot pump. For wells 20 to 25 feet deep, order 7-foot pump. For wells 25 to 30 feet deep, order 8-foot pump. Besides the pump, order enough tubing of size to match pump to reach from the bottom of pump to bottom of well. Tubing comes in lengths of 12 feet or less. When more than 12 feet of tubing will be required to reach to the bottom of the well, order coupling for each joint to connect the tubing.

GENERAL PURPOSE WOOD PUMP, $2.54.

This General Purpose Wood Pump is 6 inches square, has 3½-inch bore and 9-inch stroke. It has a capacity of 60 gallons of water per minute. While this pump throws an ample supply of water, it operates very easily and ladies and children can work it with ease. Average weight of these pumps, about 47 pounds. Outside measure, 6x6 inches.

	Length	Price, Plain Pump	Price, with Porcelain Lined Cylinder.
No. 42K5412.....	6 feet	$2.54	$3.25
No. 42K5413.....	7 feet	2.78	3.45
No. 42K5414.....	8 feet	3.04	3.70

No. 42K5415 Tubing to fit above pump, 4 inches square, with 1¼-inch bore. Price, per foot 9¾c

No. 42K5416 Couplings for tubing. Price, each 24½c

CHALLENGE WATER ELEVATOR AND PURIFYING PUMP - - - $6.53

Our Challenge Water Elevator is exactly the same in construction as our No. 42K5442, as explained on previous page. It operates with a chain composed of galvanized wire links to which are attached galvanized cups, the only difference being that this pump has a galvanized steel curb instead of wood. This makes a much better pump in every way. It will last longer, will not rust or decay. All castings and fittings are extra heavy.

This pump is not adapted for wells over 40 feet deep and we do not advise its use in wells over 30 feet deep. If well is beyond the depth of 30 feet, we suggest you order one of our iron pumps, as described on pages 614 and 615 of this catalogue.

In ordering, order the equipment which will reach to within 2 feet of the bottom of the well. The pump comes complete with curb, chains, buckets and lower bearings ready to place in wells of various depths, as indicated in price list below. Average weight, 75 pounds.

No. 42K5446 Complete with buckets for 10-foot well. Price........$6.53
No. 42K5447 Complete with buckets for 15-foot well. Price........$7.50
No. 42K5448 Complete with buckets for 20-foot well. Price........$8.32
No. 42K5449 Complete with buckets for 25-foot well. Price........$9.28
No. 42K5450 Complete with buckets for 30-foot well. Price........$10.20
No. 42K5453 Extra Galvanized Buckets. Price, per foot........8¾c

INVINCIBLE ALL GALVANIZED STEEL CHAIN PUMP CURB, WITH GALVANIZED STEEL TUBING - - - - $3.93

The Invincible Patent Galvanized Steel Curbs, illustrated herewith, made on the same principle as our No. 42K5472 pump, except the pump is made of 24-gauge galvanized steel instead of wood, and is furnished with steel tubing instead of wood. They are fitted with a heavy cast iron base at the bottom to support the curb which allows the body of the curb to project down and into the opening in the well or cistern cover. This, together with the special feature of the fixtures being below the top line of the curb, prevents any water leaking out on top of the well or cistern cover, and when top of curb is off, the fixtures are fully protected by the sides of the curb. These curbs are fitted with our latest improved noiseless roller bearing fixtures and this, together with construction of the highest grade materials and workmanship, makes it the most complete chain pump curb on the market and one that we fully recommend to our customers. The tubing is made of the best grade No. 24 galvanized steel. It is formed perfectly round with the seam air and watertight. This pump is adapted for wells up to 30 feet in depth, but we do not recommend their use in wells over 20 feet in depth. If your well is of greater depth, we recommend our iron pumps, as described on pages 614 and 615 of this catalogue.

Prices quoted below include curb, galvanized tubing, chain and buckets complete, ready to set in wells of various depths, as indicated below. Dimensions of curb, 18x8 inches. Average weight, 75 pounds.

No. 42K5455 Complete equipment for 10-foot well. Price........$3.93
No. 42K5456 Complete equipment for 12-foot well. Price........$4.30
No. 42K5457 Complete equipment for 15-foot well. Price........$4.45
No. 42K5458 Complete equipment for 18-foot well. Price........$5.03
No. 42K5459 Complete equipment for 20-foot well. Price........$5.58

Remember, in reducing our prices on this line that we still maintain the standard quality of our goods.

Chain Pump Buckets, 4¾ Cents.

No. 42K5477 Rubber Buckets, for chain pump. Price, each........4¾c
Per dozen........48c

Galvanized Pump Chain, 2¾ Cents.

No. 42K5478 Extra Chain for above pumps.
Price, per foot........2¾c

Chain Pump Tubing, 5¾ Cents.

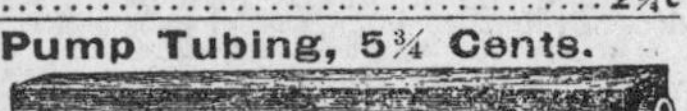

No. 42K5483 Our Chain Pump Tubing, as shown in the illustration, comes in 8, 10 and 12-foot pieces and is made of high grade wood with bore of 1⅝ inches. It is designed for use in connection with our wood and chain pumps and is offered you at a very low price. Weight, about 2 pounds per foot.
Price, per foot, extra chain pump tubing........5¾c

Galvanized Steel Tubing, 6¾ Cents.

No. 42K5486 Galvanized Steel Tubing to be used in connection with our No. 42K5455 to No. 42K5459 chain pumps. Furnished in 5-foot, 6-foot, 7-foot, 8-foot lengths. Reservoir tubing is used in connection with the pump curb. Funnel tubing goes at bottom of pump, and plain tubing is used for connecting the reservoir and funnel tubing where the two above pieces are not sufficient for the depth of the well. Either style, same price. Be sure to state style wanted.
Price, per foot........6¾c

REVOLVING TOP PITCHER SPOUT PUMP - - - - - - - - 79c

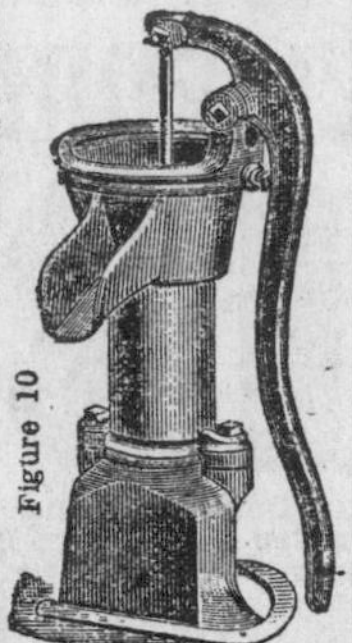
Figure 10

This illustration shows our Closed Top Pitcher Spout Pump. These pumps are adapted for use in cisterns or wells where the surface of the water is not more than 20 feet below the place where they are to be set. The cylinder is placed in the body of the pump, is truly bored, and made for lifting water and not for forcing it. It is made with trip valves, thus enabling the water to run back into the well by simply raising the handle. This prevents the water from standing in the pipe and does away with all danger of its freezing in cold weather. These pumps are used mostly in kitchens and are generally placed on the kitchen sink. The piping is run from pump down into the well if well is directly under sink. If your well is out in the yard pipe may be run from pump down under the floor, then out and down into the well. The handle of the pump may be swung in any direction, as the top is revolving. To make an outfit for your well order this kind of pump with either brass or iron lined cylinder, and enough pipe to reach into water of well. We advise purchasing brass lined cylinder pumps, as they last much longer and work easier and better. For pipe see No. 42K5710 and No. 42K5711 on another page of this catalogue. Our No. 42K5207 is the one we recommend except where a large amount of water is wanted, and in such cases we advise purchasing No. 42K5209. The average weight of these pumps is 28 pounds.

No. 42K5206 No. 1, 2½-inch cylinder for 1¼-inch pipe. Price, iron........$0.79
Price, brass lined........1.73
No. 42K5207 No. 2, 3-inch cylinder for 1¼-inch pipe. Price, iron........$1.10
Price, brass lined........1.83
No. 42K5209 No. 4, 4-inch cylinder for 1½-inch pipe. Price, iron........$1.45
Price, brass lined........2.46

OUR PERFECT CISTERN FORCE PUMP - - - - $4.63

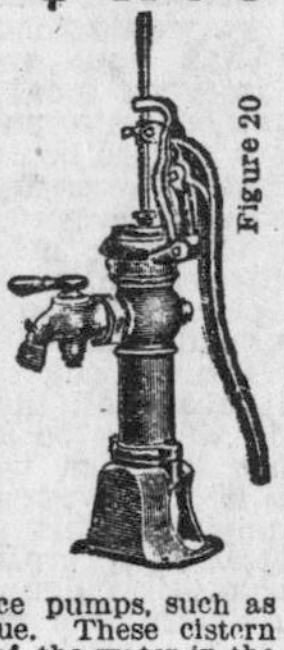
Figure 20

In this illustration we show a pump which has all the fine points of our pitcher spout pump, together with a power to force water. These pumps are all tapped in the back, so that 1-inch pipe may be screwed into pump, and by turning the lever of cock at spout the water is stopped from going through spout and is forced through back of pump to a tank or reservoir. We furnish this pump in two styles. The Nos. 42K5214 and 42K5215 are furnished with a cock and spout, as shown in illustration, to which 1-inch hose may be attached when it is desired to be used for sprinkling purposes. The Nos. 42K5221 and 42K5222 have a common round spout with which we furnish a shutoff clevis and a hose clevis instead of the cock at spout. We highly recommend these pumps where a small amount of water is wanted, but for a barnyard or outside pump we advise purchasing one of our heavy set length force pumps, such as our No. 42K312, as shown in this catalogue. These cistern pumps cannot be used where the surface of the water in the well or cistern is more than 25 feet below the place where they are to be set. We recommend as a pump for general use our No. 42K5215, as it is brass lined, and with ordinary care will last almost indefinitely. All of these pumps are tapped in the base to admit 1¼-inch pipe, and we cannot furnish them to take pipe of any other size. For pipe see Nos. 42K5710 and 42K5711, page 619, of this catalogue. Average weight of these pumps is 35 pounds.

No. 42K5214 3-inch iron body. Price........$4.63
No. 42K5215 3-inch brass lined body. Price........5.68
No. 42K5221 3-inch iron body. Price........4.02
No. 42K5222 3-inch brass lined body. Price........4.87

OUR ANTI-FREEZING LIFT PUMP - - - $3.10

We show herewith a lift pump with 6-inch stroke, which is adapted for wells not over 30 feet deep. The pump has a revolving top, so that handle may be turned to any side while pumping. The 4-foot piece of pipe which connects the cylinder to pump screws into the pump at spout, thus creating an air space between pump and cylinder, which prevents water from freezing in cold weather. The cylinder is made of iron, truly bored and polished, 10 inches long and tapped to take 1¼-inch pipe. We show these pumps with three sizes of cylinders, 3, 3½ and 4 inches in diameter. For ordinary use and the one most commonly sold, we recommend our No. 4 pump, which has a 3-inch cylinder. In case a large amount of water is desired, or where pump is to be used in a shallow well, we advise purchasing our No. 6 or No. 8 pump. While this is an excellent pump and gives entire satisfaction for wells up to 30 feet in depth, we believe, for the small difference in cost, our customers will obtain a much better bargain by procuring our No. 42K264 or No. 42K266. When ordering this pump remember we furnish 4 feet of pipe, as shown in illustration, to reach from platform to cylinder, so if your well is 25 feet deep, you need only order 21 feet of pipe to complete your outfit. We list pipe on page 619 of this catalogue under Nos. 42K5710 and 42K5711. The No. 4 pump will lift 9 gallons of water per minute, the No. 6 will lift 12 gallons, and the No. 8 16 gallons. Average weight is 62 pounds.

No. 42K5256
No. 4, 3-inch cylinder. Price........$3.10
No. 6, 3½-inch cylinder. Price........3.40
No. 8, 4-inch cylinder. Price........4.05

AT THE PRICES SHOWN ON THESE GOODS YOUR SAVINGS ARE GREATER THAN EVER BEFORE. OUR CONSTANT AIM IS TO INCREASE THE QUALITY OF OUR GOODS, AND NONE IS SOLD BY US WHICH IS NOT UP TO STANDARD.

TRIUMPH HAND ANTI-FREEZING LIFT PUMP, REDUCED FROM $4.20 TO - - - - - - - $3.74

Oscillating Link.

We know that in this pump we have the best 6-inch stroke lift pump on the market. It has a heavy revolving cap which allows the handle to be swung to any side of the pump desired by the one pumping. This cap covers the top of the pump entirely except where the piston rod goes through, thereby preventing sticks, dirt, or, in fact, anything from falling into the well or into the working parts of the pump. The piston rod is connected to the handle with an oscillating coupling, which makes the pump work easy and prevents cramping and binding of rod. We recommend this pump and guarantee it to give excellent satisfaction in wells up to 80 feet deep, but where it is to be used in wells over 30 feet deep the cylinder must be extended to within 10 feet of the water. We also advise using a brass body cylinder in place of the iron cylinder when used in wells over 30 feet deep, as they last longer and work easier, for which we charge $1.50 in addition to the prices quoted below. We charge 5 cents per foot for the rod and couplings which are needed to extend the cylinder, and all you need in addition to this is enough 1¼-inch pipe to reach to the bottom of well. The pump is furnished complete with 4 feet of pipe and rod and a 10-inch cylinder, either 3 or 3½ inches in diameter, at prices stated below. This pump is nicely painted in green and tinted in bronze. Our No. 42K264 is the one most used, but in shallow wells where a large amount of water is desired our No. 42K266 is better. For prices on pipe see Nos. 42K5710 and 42K5711 on page 619 of this catalogue. The No. 42K264 pump will lift 9 gallons of water per minute, and the No. 42K266 will lift 12 gallons of water per minute. Average weight of these pumps is 70 pounds.

No. 42K264 No. 4, 3-inch cylinder Price reduced to........$3.74
No. 42K266 No. 6, 3½-inch cylinder. Price reduced to........$3.98

We give herewith an example showing how to order pipe, rod, etc., for a well 50 feet deep, so if your well is deeper all you have to do is to order more pipe and rod in proportion, and if it is not so deep, order less.

EXAMPLE.		Price
No. 42K264	1 Pump No. 4, with 3-inch cylinder..	$3.74
No. 42K5711	46 feet 1¼-inch galvanized pipe at 11 cents per foot........	5.06
Special.	36 feet extending cylinder at 5 cents a foot........	1.80

TRIUMPH WINDMILL ANTI-FREEZING LIFT PUMP - - - $3.90

We show in this illustration a windmill pump with 6-inch stroke, which when cylinder is extended into well, as explained under No. 42K264 pump on this page, will give excellent results in wells up to 100 feet deep. This is a pump we guarantee to be the equal of pumps sold for double the price by other concerns. Do not let the exceptionally low price at which we sell it lead you to believe that it is a cheap, shoddy pump such as other concerns offer as a leader. We know that this pump has no superior at any price for the purpose we recommend it. The piston rod works through a double fulcrum, which guides and steadies the stroke of the pump. This pump has a closed top which prevents sticks and dirt or, in fact, anything from falling into the working parts of the pump. Although this pump is especially designed to be operated by a windmill, it is also an easy working hand pump, and as the handle is furnished just as shown in the picture, it is easily seen what a splendid combination it is. We furnish pump complete with a 4-foot set length and 10-inch iron cylinder, but when it is to be used in wells over 30 feet deep, we advise our customers to order it with brass body cylinder, for which we make an extra charge of $1.50 over prices given below. It is necessary to have this cylinder extended when used in wells over 30 feet deep, as explained under No. 42K264 on this page. We furnish this pump with either 3 or 3½x1-inch iron cylinder. The 3-inch cylinder is the size most used and the one we recommend for ordinary use, but where you have a shallow well and desire a large amount of water, we advise the 3½-inch cylinder pump. Average weight is about 75 pounds. The No. 42K276 No. 4, 3-inch cylinder pump will lift 9 gallons of water per minute, and the No. 42K278 No. 6, 3½-inch cylinder pump will lift 12 gallons per minute.

No. 42K276 No. 4, 3-inch cylinder. Price........$3.90

No. 42K278 No. 6, 3½-inch cylinder. Price........$4.35

WE RECOMMEND THE USE OF BRASS BODY OR BRASS LINED CYLINDERS ON ALL OUR PUMPS, AS THEY ARE ALMOST INDESTRUCTIBLE AND WILL OUTWEAR SEVERAL OF THE COMMON IRON KIND.

OUR IMPROVED EXTRA HEAVY LIFT PUMPS FOR FEED YARDS AND HEAVY WORK - - - - $4.45

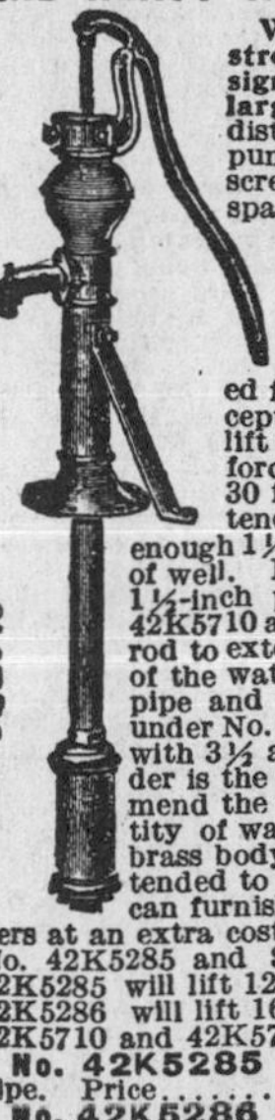

Figure 78

We show here our extra heavy 6-inch stroke hand lift pump, which is especially designed for stock and feeding yards where large quantities of water are needed. The distance from bottom of cylinder to flange on pump is 4 feet. The 1¼-inch set length is screwed into pump at spout, creating an air space between cylinder and pump, which prevents the water from freezing in the pump in cold weather. The pump is made throughout of heavy material. The cylinder is heavy and strong and capable of lifting large quantities of water. Remember, we guarantee this pump to be adapted for general purposes, and one which is exceptionally powerful in deep wells. This is a lift pump, however, and cannot be used for forcing water. For wells up to and including 30 feet in depth, the cylinder need not be extended. All that is necessary to do is to order enough 1½-inch pipe to reach from cylinder to bottom of well. If well is over 30 feet deep, order sufficient 1½-inch pipe to reach to the bottom, see Nos. 42K5710 and 42K5711 for price; also allow for enough rod to extend cylinder to within 10 feet of the surface of the water, at 5 cents per foot. See how to order pipe and rod in cases of this kind as explained under No. 42K264. We furnish this pump in two sizes, with 3½ and 4-inch cylinders. The 3½-inch cylinder is the one most commonly used, but we recommend the 4-inch cylinder for use when a great quantity of water is required. We advise the use of brass body cylinders instead of iron when it is intended to place pump in wells over 30 feet deep, and can furnish these pumps fitted with brass body cylinders at an extra cost over prices given below of $1.50 on the No. 42K5285 and $1.80 on the No. 42K5286. The No. 42K5285 will lift 12 gallons of water per minute and the No. 42K5286 will lift 16 gallons per minute. For pipe see Nos. 42K5710 and 42K5711. Average weight about 80 pounds.

No. 42K5285 3½-inch cylinder, fitted for 1½-inch pipe. Price $4.45

No. 42K5286 4-inch cylinder, fitted for 1½-inch pipe. Price $4.60

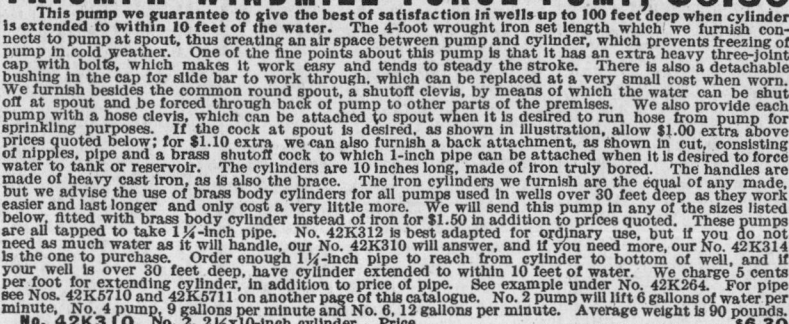

ACME DOUBLE ACTING, DRILLED WELL, HAND FORCE PUMP WITH BRASS LINED UPPER CYLINDER AND BRASS LOWER CYLINDER. $9.63

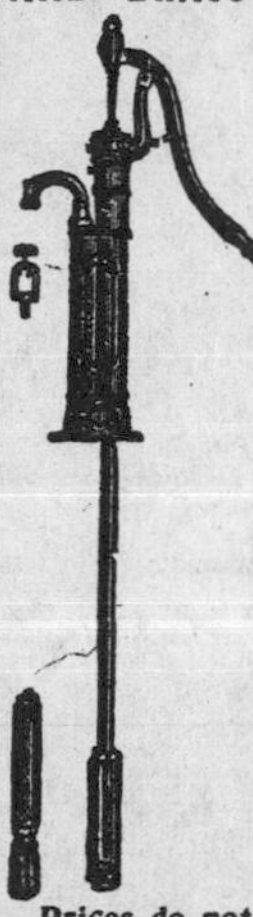

This illustration shows our Acme Double Acting, Drilled Well Hand Force Pump, adapted for drilled wells of small bore of any depth. This pump is equipped with double cylinders and has very free movement, as with the upward stroke of the handle only one-half of the water is discharged, the other half being retained by the smaller or upper cylinder and is discharged with the downward movement of the handle. This gives a continuous flow of water and does away with all lost motion and prevents jars and jolts when the pump is being operated. It makes it particularly easy to operate by hand.

This pump is so constructed that the cylinders and all its parts below the platform will enter and pass into the casing or drilled hole. To use this pump it is not necessary to cut off casing, as with many other styles of pumps, and casing may, therefore, be carried up to the platform, thus keeping out surface water and other impurities. Although the pump is especially adapted for drilled wells, it has no superior for dug or open wells. Upper cylinder is brass lined and lower cylinder is brass with brass seat valves. Pump is furnished with a strainer and hose attachment without additional charge. This is a strictly first class, desirable, dependable pump in every respect, and is guaranteed to give perfect satisfaction. This is a hand pump only and cannot be used with windmill.

Prices do not include pipe or pump rod. If to be used in wells more than 25 feet deep, lower cylinder should be dropped to within 10 feet of the bottom of well, and you should order pipe enough to reach to within two feet of the bottom. For pipe, see Nos. 42K5710 and 42K5711. See outfit on page 614 of this catalogue for complete outfits of this style pump.

No. 42K5327 Size 2, has 2½-inch cylinder for 1¼-inch pipe. Will go into 3-inch cased well. Price........ $9.63

No. 42K5328 Size 4, has 3-inch cylinder for 1¼-inch pipe. Will go into 3½-inch cased well. Price........ $9.73

No. 42K5329 Size 6, has 3½-inch cylinder for 1½-inch pipe. Will go into 4-inch cased well. Price........ $10.40

If wanted with brass lined lower cylinder in place of all brass, deduct 50 cents from above prices.

OUR HIGH GRADE HEAVY ACME IMPROVED WINDMILL FORCE PUMP STANDARDS - - - - $4.12

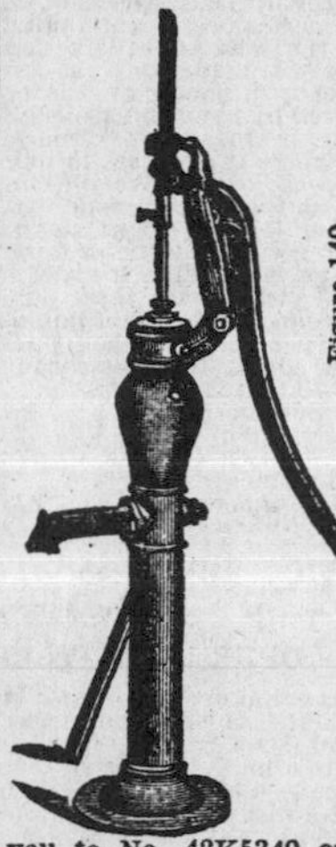

Figure 140

This shows our Improved Acme Windmill Force Pump or Standard. No cylinder or pipe is furnished with this pump at prices given. The Acme Pump Standard is equipped with a brass stuffing box and the piston rod works through a special bushing which prevents it from wearing out easily. There is a threaded outlet directly back of spout on the barrel of the pump into which 1-inch pipe may be screwed. This 1-inch pipe may be run to a tank or reservoir and water forced through it to same. We furnish a shutoff for the spout, by the use of which water is stopped from running out the spout and made to run out the opening at the back of the pump. This is a very much heavier standard than the ordinary pump is equipped with and is especially designed for deep wells. **Prices quoted are for standard alone and do not include pipe, cylinder or rod, and it cannot be used without these parts.** For pipe see catalogue Nos. 42K5710 and 42K5711; for cylinders see catalogue Nos. 42K5528 to 42K5592; and for pump rods to be used in extending cylinder see No. 42K5630. For an example as to how to order an outfit of this kind, we refer you to No. 42K5349 on this page. Average weight of this pump is 80 pounds.

No. 42K5347 Size 1, 6-inch stroke for 1¼-inch pipe. Price........ $4.12

No. 42K5351 Size 2, 10-inch stroke for 2-inch pipe. Price........ $4.52

EXTRAS—If a back attachment is wanted, such as is shown and described under No. 42K310, allow $1.10 in addition to prices given above, and if a shutoff cock at spout is desired, allow $1.00 in addition to prices above.

TRIUMPH HEAVY HAND FORCE PUMP - - - - - - - - $5.45

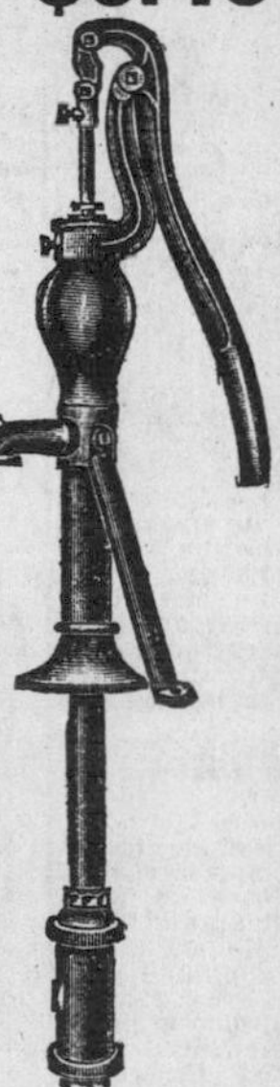

In this pump we offer our customers a 6-inch stroke heavy hand force pump, and one that we guarantee to give excellent satisfaction under the most difficult conditions. The bearer or fulcrum is extra heavy and can be swung so as to place handle on any side of pump desired. It is equipped with an oscillating link, which connects handle to piston rod, and has the effect of making pump work easy. The piston rod is made of polished steel and works through a heavy brass bushing, which is screwed into a stuffing box of ample size to allow plenty of packing. This offsets the wear and tear that the rod of an ordinary pump is subjected to. This pump is complete with a 4-foot set length of wrought iron pipe, which is screwed into it at spout, thus making an air space which prevents water freezing in it in cold weather, and a 10-inch iron cylinder truly bored and polished. The spout is a plain round one furnished with a shutoff clevis attached to it, so that the water may be shut off at spout and forced through the back of the pump to tank or other places on the premises. We also furnish a hose clevis, so that ¾-inch hose may be attached to spout for sprinkling purposes. We can furnish with this pump a cock at spout, which can be turned off or on by turning a lever at spout, for $1.00 in addition to prices quoted below. The shutoff cock is also threaded at spout, to which ¾-inch hose may be attached for sprinkling, washing buggies, etc. We can also furnish it with back attachments, see illustration No. 42K310 on this page, consisting of nipples, pipe and brass lever shutoff cock for $1.10 extra. This pump will work successfully in wells 80 feet deep when cylinder is lowered to within 10 feet of the water. It is furnished complete with a heavy cast handle, a good substantial brace, is neatly painted in green and tinted in bronze. We can furnish these pumps in three sizes, with 2½, 3 or 3½-inch cylinder. The one with 3-inch cylinder is most commonly used and is the one we recommend for ordinary purposes. We show below, however, the capacity of the different sizes, and if more or less water is needed, order one of the others. The pump just as shown in illustration is suitable for pumping water if well is 30 feet deep or under, and all that is needed in addition to pump is enough 1¼-inch pipe to reach from cylinder to bottom of well, but if well is over 30 feet deep, order cylinder extended and pipe as explained under No. 42K264. No. 2 will lift 6 gallons of water per minute. No 4 will lift 9 gallons of water per minute. No. 6 will lift 12 gallons of water per minute. Average weight is about 80 pounds.

No. 42K301 No. 2—2½-inch cylinder. Price........ $5.45

No. 42K302 No. 4—3 -inch cylinder. Price........ 5.55

No. 42K303 No. 6—3½-inch cylinder. Price........ 5.65

DOUBLE ACTING FORCE PUMPS WITH BRASS LINED CYLINDER AND THREE-WAY COCK - - $9.98

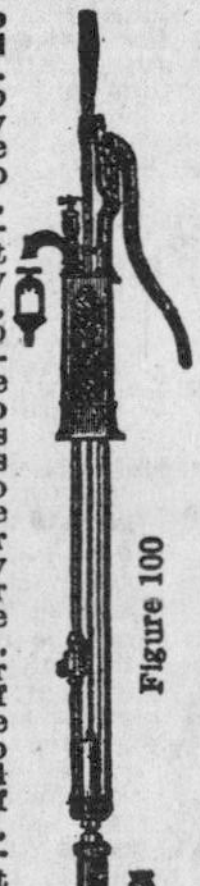

Figure 100

This is the best Double Acting Force Pump made regardless of price. It has a windmill head and can be used with windmill or by hand. The spout may be revolved to any side of pump desired. The upper cylinder is made of heavy seamless brass tubing; the lower cylinder is made with brass valve seats. We furnish this pump with malleable iron hose attachment for spout, so hose may be run from pump for sprinkling purposes. There is a vertical three-way cock 3 feet below the platform, by means of which water may be forced underground to tanks, reservoirs, etc., by simply running 1-inch pipe from this cock to place desired. The shutoff rod of the three-way cock is operated by a rod that reaches to the top of spout on pump. The fact that this pump has two cylinders equalizes the strain and makes the pump work easily, doing away with all jars or jolts, and as this pump is furnished with two cylinders, the downward stroke of the handle causes only one-half of the water in the cylinder to discharge, the other half being discharged by the upward stroke, creating a steady flow of water from the spout. This pump we guarantee to give perfect satisfaction in wells up to 150 feet deep, but in wells more than 30 feet in depth the lower cylinder must be extended to within 10 feet of the water. We charge 5 cents per foot for the rod complete with couplings, which is used to extend cylinder, and all you need besides the rod is enough 1¼-inch pipe to reach to the bottom of well. This pump is furnished in three sizes, namely, 2½, 3 or 3½-inch cylinders. For ordinary use we recommend the 3-inch cylinder, but in wells over 100 feet deep we advise purchasing our 2½-inch cylinder, as it lifts less water at each stroke and therefore works easier in deep wells. The pump with 3½-inch cylinder is best adapted for use in wells from 30 to 50 feet deep where a great quantity of water is required. For pipe see Nos. 42K5710 and 42K5711. These pumps are all fitted for 1¼-inch pipe. Pump with 2½-inch cylinder will lift six gallons of water per minute; 3-inch cylinder will lift nine gallons of water per minute, and 3½-inch cylinder will lift twelve gallons of water per minute. For further information in regard to ordering pumps with cylinder extended, see example under No. 42K264. Average weight of these pumps is 105 pounds.

No. 42K5323 With 2½-inch cylinder. Price.. $9.98

No. 42K5324 With 3-inch cylinder. Price.. 10.80

No. 42K5325 With 3½-inch cylinder. Price.. 11.50

EXTRA HEAVY WINDMILL LIFT PUMP STANDARD - - - $3.49

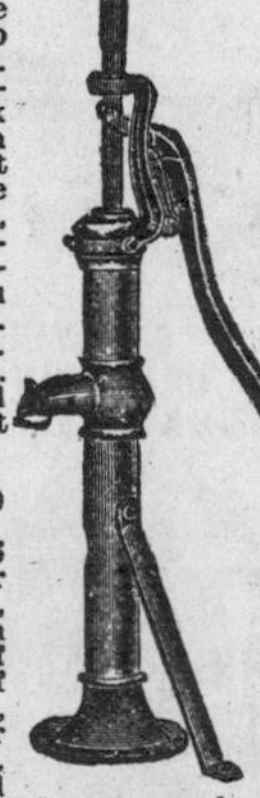

Figure 145

This illustration shows our extra heavy Windmill Lift Pump Standard. This is a lift pump only and cannot be used for forcing water. If a force pump is wanted, order No. 42K5347 or No. 42K5351. This standard is very satisfactory if used in pumping water for stock or feed yards. It is much heavier than our common windmill pump and the spout is higher from the platform. The size pipe ordinarily used with it is 2 inches, but we can furnish it for 1½-inch or 1¼-inch pipe. Prices given below do not include pipe, cylinder or rod, which you must have to make a complete outfit. For pipe, see No. 42K5710 and No. 42K5711, and for cylinders see Nos. 42K5528 to 42K5592. The rod is listed under No. 42K5630. The average weight of these pumps is 75 pounds.

No. 42K5349 6-inch stroke. Price........ $3.49

No. 42K5350 10-inch stroke. Price........ 4.05

EXAMPLE—If you desire an outfit for a 40-foot well, select the pump you want, either No. 42K5349 or No. 42K5350, then include with this 40 feet of 2-inch pipe if you wish to use a 4-inch, or 40 feet of 1½-inch pipe with the 3½-inch cylinder, or 40 feet of 1¼-inch pipe if any smaller size cylinder than 3½ inches is to be used. Select the kind of cylinder wanted and allow for extending the cylinder 30 feet, at 5 cents per foot, or $1.50. For prices on pipes see Nos. 42K5710 and 42K5711 on page 619 of this catalogue.

UNDERGROUND VALVE FORCE PUMPS - - - - $9.23

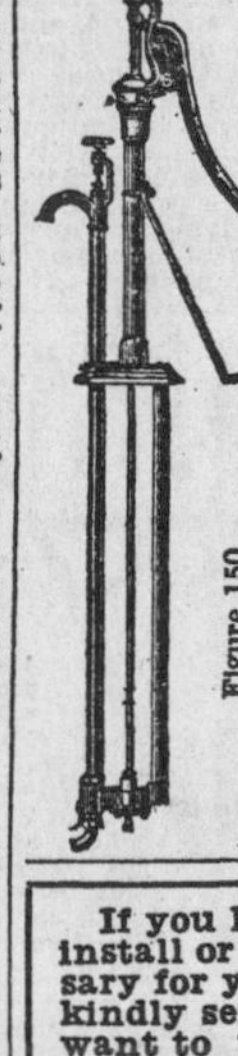

Figure 150

This pump is especially designed for 2-inch tubular wells, but can be used in open or drilled wells with 1¼-inch pipe. By use of the wheel in the top of the spout, the water can be discharged either through the spout or through an underground pipe, which may be attached at valve on bottom of pump. It differs from and is superior to other three-way valve pumps, because the operating screw, which is brass, is below near the valve and not at the gooseneck, consequently, there is no possibility of the pump freezing up in cold weather. The pipe on the right forms the air chamber. When this pump is used for tubular wells, it is made with a cap at the stuffing box, which when unscrewed leaves an opening large enough to pull the plunger up through without disconnecting the pipe or moving the pump. The pump is threaded to take 2-inch pipe, but may be bushed to take as small as 1 inch. The discharge is fitted for 1-inch pipe and the gooseneck is fitted with a clevis for ¾-inch hose. Prices stated below are for pump only and do not include any pipe, cylinder or rod. For pipe see No. 42K5710 and No. 42K5711, and for rod see No. 42K5630. Cylinders are listed under No. 42K5528 to No. 42K5592. Average weight is 120 pounds.

No. 42K5352 6-inch stroke. Price........ $9.23

No. 42K5353 10-inch stroke. Price........ 9.65

TRIUMPH WINDMILL FORCE PUMP, $6.30

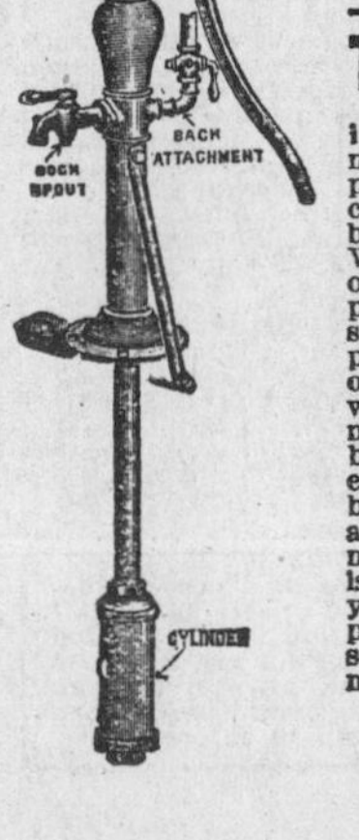

This pump we guarantee to give the best of satisfaction in wells up to 100 feet deep when cylinder is extended to within 10 feet of the water. The 4-foot wrought iron set length which we furnish connects to pump at spout, thus creating an air space between pump and cylinder, which prevents freezing of pump in cold weather. One of the fine points about this pump is that it has an extra heavy three-joint cap with bolts, which makes it work easy and tends to steady the stroke. There is also a detachable bushing in the cap for slide bar to work through, which can be replaced at a very small cost when worn. We furnish besides the common round spout, a shutoff clevis, by means of which the water can be shut off at spout and be forced through back of pump to other parts of the premises. We also provide each pump with a hose clevis, which can be attached to spout when it is desired to run hose from pump for sprinkling purposes. If the cock at spout is desired, as shown in illustration, allow $1.00 extra above prices quoted below; for $1.10 extra we can also furnish a back attachment, as shown in cut, consisting of nipples, pipe and a brass shutoff cock to which 1-inch pipe can be attached when it is desired to force water to tank or reservoir. The cylinders are 10 inches long, made of iron truly bored. The handles are made of heavy cast iron, as is also the brace. The iron cylinders we furnish are the equal of any made, but we advise the use of brass body cylinders for all pumps used in wells over 30 feet deep as they work easier and last longer and only cost a very little more. We will send this pump in any of the sizes listed below, fitted with brass body cylinder instead of iron for $1.50 in addition to prices quoted. These pumps are all tapped to take 1¼-inch pipe. No. 42K312 is best adapted for ordinary use, but if you do not need as much water as it will handle, our No. 42K310 will answer, and if you need more, our No. 42K314 is the one to purchase. Order enough 1¼-inch pipe to reach from cylinder to bottom of well, and if your well is over 30 feet deep, have cylinder extended to within 10 feet of water. We charge 5 cents per foot for extending cylinder, in addition to price of pipe. See example under No. 42K264. For pipe see Nos. 42K5710 and 42K5711 on another page of this catalogue. No. 2 pump will lift 6 gallons of water per minute, No. 4 pump, 9 gallons per minute and No. 6, 12 gallons per minute. Average weight is 90 pounds.

No. 42K310 No. 2, 2½x10-inch cylinder. Price........ $6.30

No. 42K312 No. 4, 3 x10-inch cylinder. Price........ 6.35

No. 42K314 No. 6, 3½x10-inch cylinder. Price........ 6.40

If you have any doubt about being able to install or to figure out what material is necessary for you to install one of these pumps, kindly send us a rough sketch of where you want to use it, how deep the well is and where you want to convey water, and we will furnish you an estimate on the exact cost of the outfit which you need without any expense to you whatsoever and without placing yourself under any obligation to us.

ACME ROTARY POWER FORCE PUMP - - - - - - $7.70

Figure 180

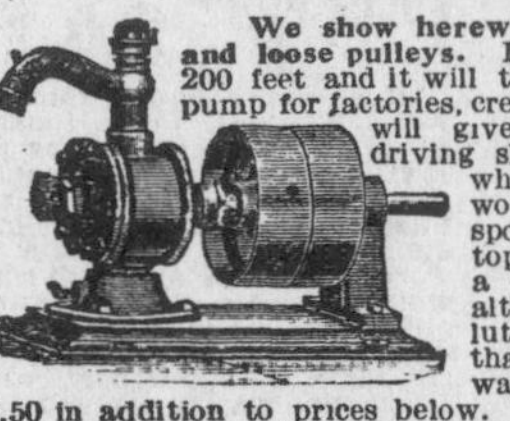

We show herewith our Acme Rotary Force Pump complete with tight and loose pulleys. It is a fine protection in case of fire, as it will force water 200 feet and it will throw a solid stream of water 30 feet. It is an excellent pump for factories, creameries or for any building where power can be had. It will give the best of satisfaction for irrigating purposes. The driving shaft is made long enough to allow the use of a balance wheel with handle on the end of it, so that pump may be worked by hand in case engine should be out of order. The spout is threaded for iron pipe at the end and also at the top where it connects to pump. These pumps can be run at a speed of 200 revolutions per minute without injury, although we recommend running them at about 100 revolutions. A pump of this kind should not be placed more than 20 feet from the water to work successfully. If wanted with balance wheel and handle for hand power, allow $2.50 in addition to prices below. We guarantee these pumps to do just what we say they will do but cannot advise them for pumping acids or hot liquids. The second column of figures in the table below gives the capacity per minute when pump is running at a speed of 100 revolutions. Pump comes complete as illustrated, but without pipe or belting. For pipe see Nos. 42K5710 and 42K5711. Weight, 75 to 150 pounds.

Cat. No.	Gallons	Size Suction Pipe	Size Pulleys	Price
42K5370	13	1 inch	7x2½ inches	$ 7.70
42K5371	14	1 inch	7x2½ inches	10.78
42K5372	17	1¼ inches	7x2½ inches	12.77
42K5373	27	1½ inches	11x3 inches	18.48
42K5374	36	2 inches	11x3 inches	23.10

OUR WONDERFUL AUTOMATIC PUMP, REDUCED FROM $5.69 TO - - - $4.80

NO POWER REQUIRED. OPERATES ITSELF.

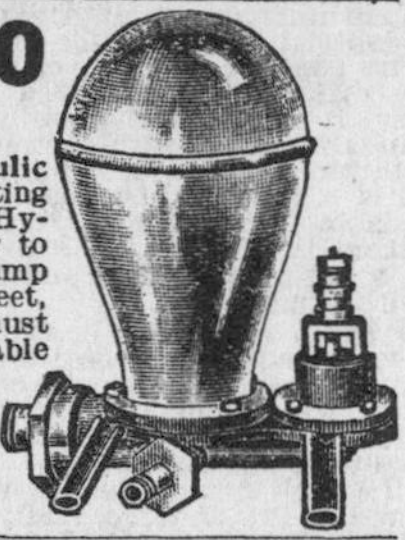

THIS ILLUSTRATION shows our Acme Automatic Hydraulic Ram, the most wonderful self acting pump ever put on the market. HOW TO USE IT. The Acme Hydraulic Ram is used to elevate water to a high tank or reservoir, or to force water a long distance from the source of supply. Set this pump below a spring or stream of water at a distance of from 25 to 50 feet, for each 10 feet that you wish to elevate the water, the pump must be placed 1 foot lower than spring. Determine by means of the table below what size pump you need. Order enough pipe to answer your purpose, prices of which you will find on page 619 of this catalogue, under Nos. 42K5710 and 42K5711. All you have to do is to connect feed or supply pipe to pump and discharge pipe to tank to which you wish to elevate water. The water from your spring flowing into the pump is all the power needed.

Catalogue Number	Gallons of Water per Minute necessary to Operate Ram	Size of Supply Pipe	Size of Pipe Discharge	Weight, Pounds	Price
42K5397	No. 2, ½ to 2	¾ in.	⅜ in.	25	$ 4.80
42K5398	No. 3, 1¼ to 4	1 in.	½ in.	35	5.88
42K5399	No. 4, 3 to 7	1¼ in.	½ in.	40	7.50
42K5400	No. 5, 6 to 14	2 in.	¾ in.	70	11.75
42K5401	No. 6, 12 to 25	2½ in.	1 in.	85	21.35

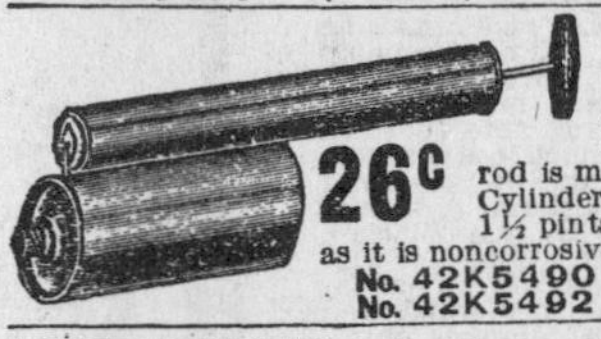

Acme Sprayer or Lightning Bug Exterminator.

26c

We have improved our Acme Sprayer for this season, and have now the best low priced sprayer sold by anyone. It is made of heavy IX tin or brass; piston rod is made of heavy steel rod, with a hardwood stuffing box. Cylinder is 1¾x15 inches. Weight, about 2 pounds. Capacity, 1½ pints. We recommend the use of the brass tank sprayer as it is noncorrosive and will outwear several tin ones.

No. 42K5490 Price, IX tin 26c
No. 42K5492 Price brass tank with brass tube 54c

ACME SPRAYER. A SELF OPERATING OR AUTOMATIC SPRAYER $3.32

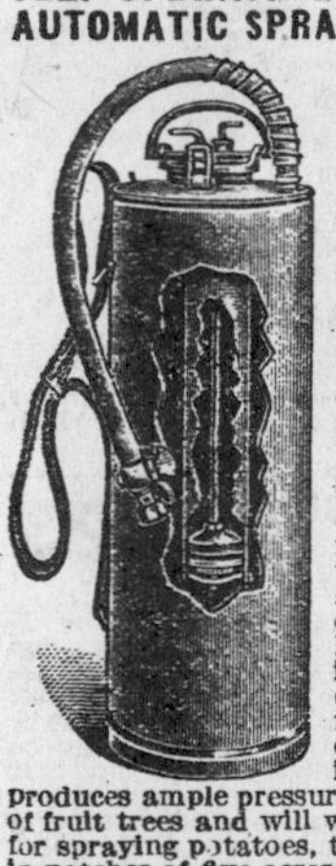

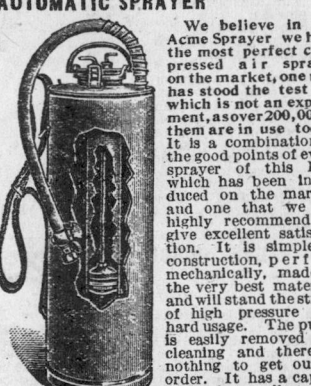

We believe in our Acme Sprayer we have the most perfect compressed air sprayer on the market, one that has stood the test and which is not an experiment, as over 200,000 of them are in use today. It is a combination of the good points of every sprayer of this kind which has been introduced on the market, and one that we can highly recommend to give excellent satisfaction. It is simple in construction, perfect mechanically, made of the very best material, and will stand the strain of high pressure and hard usage. The pump is easily removed for cleaning and there is nothing to get out of order. It has a capacity of four gallons and produces ample pressure for spraying all kinds of fruit trees and will work very satisfactorily for spraying potatoes, tobacco, tomatoes, etc., in patches of five acres or less. Enough compression is obtained with eight or ten strokes of the piston to spray for several minutes a mist like spray, or a solid stream. It is indispensible for spraying green houses and poultry houses with whitewash or for spraying any kind of insecticides or disinfectants. We furnish this sprayer in either galvanized iron or brass with two feet of hose, and with common cock as shown in illustration, or with automatic cock which will work much more satisfactorily, as all that is necessary to do when the sprayer is fitted in this way, is to merely press the handle to turn on the spray, and by releasing the handle, it shuts off automatically. We advise our customers to purchase the brass sprayer as it is non-corrosive and will practically wear a life time, and while the price on our brass sprayers is a little higher than the galvanized, nevertheless, we believe it is a cheaper sprayer to buy in the end. We list this sprayer with common cock and automatic cock, but would recommend the use of the sprayer with the automatic cock. We can also furnish extension pipes which can be screwed on to the nozzle and extended to any length desired. We show the prices of these extensions below. Weight, 7 pounds; capacity, 4 gallons.

No. 42K5501 Galvanized Sprayer with common cock. Price $3.32
No. 42K5501 Galvanized Sprayer with automatic cock. Price $3.90
No. 42K5502 Brass Sprayer with common cock. Price $4.98
No. 42K5502 Brass Sprayer with automatic cock. Price $5.55
2-foot extension pipe, galvanized. Price, .19
2-foot extension pipe, brass. Price .... .26

ACME IMPROVED SPRAYER - - - - $8.75

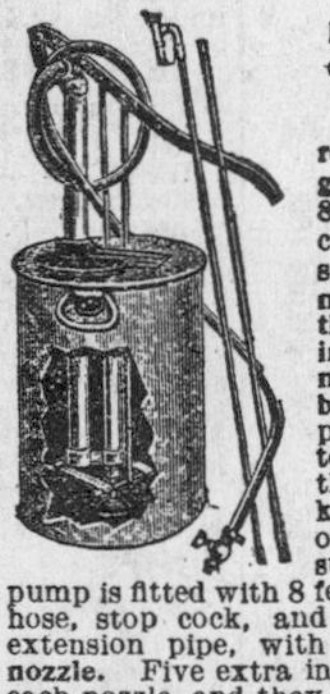

For Whitewashing and General Spray Purposes.

No. 42K5503 The reservoir is made of heavy galvanized iron and holds 8 gallons of mixture. The cover is reinforced and so designed that the pump may be instantly removed, thus exposing all working parts. The pump is made entirely of heavy brass except the handle parts. There is an agitator which is operated by the handle and which keeps the solution thoroughly mixed about the suction opening. This pump is fitted with 8 feet of three-ply discharge hose, stop cock, and two 4-foot lengths of extension pipe, with latest pattern Vermorel nozzle. Five extra inserts are furnished with each nozzle, and they can be replaced as often as necessary to keep the spray of uniform size. The Acme No. 3 Sprayer is perfectly practical and convenient for spraying large trees or whitewashing and painting large factories as well as poultry houses and other buildings. The machine loaded is easily carried from place to place, and has a decided advantage over sprayers that are mounted upon barrels or other large reservoirs. Weight, 30 pounds. Price $8.75

IMPROVED SPRAY AND FORCE PUMP. 68c

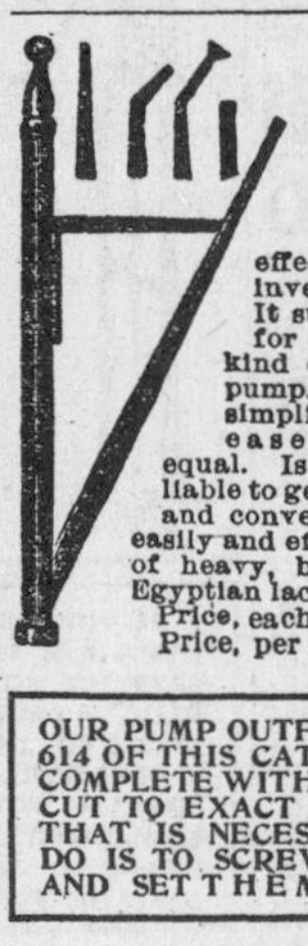

No. 42K5518 Improved Spray and Force Pump. It is beyond question the most perfect and effective hand apparatus ever invented for throwing water. It supplies a universal want, for every family needs some kind of a force sprinkler and pump. In variety of service, simplicity of construction and ease of operation, it has no equal. Is always ready for use, not liable to get out of order, and so light and convenient that it can be used easily and effectively by anyone. Made of heavy, bright tin coated with Egyptian lacquer. Weight, 2¼ pounds.
Price, each $0.68
Price, per dozen 7.30

OUR PUMP OUTFITS LISTED ON PAGE 614 OF THIS CATALOGUE GO TO YOU COMPLETE WITH ALL PIPE, ROD, Etc., CUT TO EXACT LENGTHS, AND ALL THAT IS NECESSARY FOR YOU TO DO IS TO SCREW THEM TOGETHER AND SET THEM IN YOUR WELL.

OUR NEW ACME TANK PUMP - - - - - - - $5.63

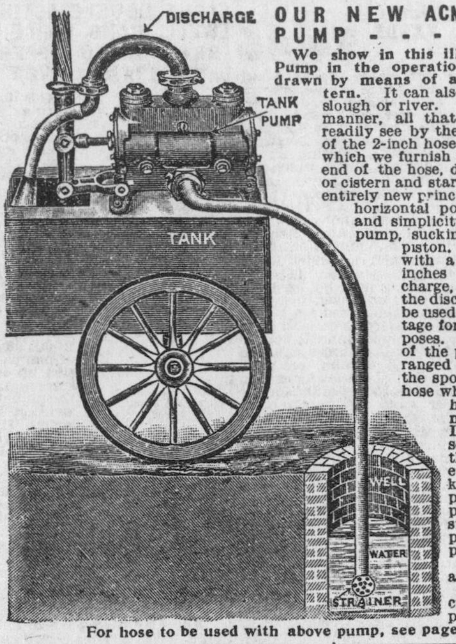

We show in this illustration our New Acme Tank Pump in the operation of filling a tank with water drawn by means of a 2-inch hose from a well or cistern. It can also be used in drawing water from a slough or river. In order to use this pump in this manner, all that is necessary to do, as you can readily see by the illustration, is to attach one end of the 2-inch hose to pump, place the 2-inch strainer, which we furnish free with the pump, on the other end of the hose, drop this into the water in the well or cistern and start pumping. This pump is made on entirely new principles, the cylinder being placed in a horizontal position, which gives great strength and simplicity. It is strictly a double acting pump, sucking water at each stroke of the piston. Cylinders 5 inches in diameter, with a 5-inch stroke. Openings are 2 inches in size for both suction and discharge, and has an extra connection for the discharge pipe, so that 1-inch hose may be used if desired, which is of great advantage for sprinkling or fire protection purposes. The spout is attached to the top of the pump and is reversible and so arranged that the largest pail will fit under the spout, thus avoiding the use of lead hose when a pail of water is wanted. It has a capacity of two barrels per minute, and will force water 60 feet. It is equipped with brass valve seats, and we can guarantee it to be the equal of any pump of this style ever placed on the market. We know that there are other tank pumps on the market sold at lower prices than ours, but, quality considered, this is by far the cheapest pump to buy. Weight, about 95 pounds.

No. 42K5386 Price, complete, as shown in illustration .. $5.63
No. 42K5386½ 5-inch crimped plunger leathers for above pump. Price, each 28c

For hose to be used with above pump, see page 505 of this catalogue.

ACME HIGH GRADE BARREL SPRAYING PUMP - - - - $6.12

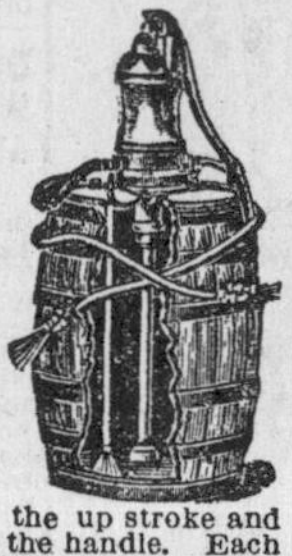

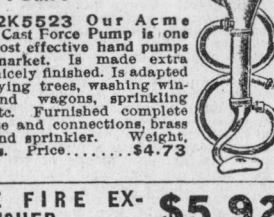

Acme New Improved Barrel Spray Pump with brass upper and brass lined lower cylinders, brass plunger, brass check valve and brass valve seats. All working parts coming in contact with the liquid are brass. The body of the pump is a large air chamber, and after the pump is under pressure it will discharge a steady spray lasting two minutes or more with one stroke of the handle, thus making it easy to operate. It is double acting, discharging half the water on the up stroke and half on the down stroke of the handle. Each pump is fitted with a jet agitator or can be furnished with a paddle agitator, if preferred, at an extra charge. It can be used for many other purposes besides spraying, such as washing windows, buggies, extinguishing fires, sprinkling lawns, flowers, etc. Prices do not include the barrel.

No. 42K5513 Includes pump, jet agitator, suction pipe and brass strainer (no hose). Weight, 69 pounds. Price .. $6.12
No. 42K5514 Includes pump and trimmings complete with one lead ½-inch three-ply discharge hose, 5 feet long and Vermorel nozzle. Weight, 70 pounds. Price .. $7.43
No. 42K5515 Includes pump and trimmings complete with two leads ½-inch three-ply discharge hose, each 5 feet long, and Vermorel nozzle. Weight, 76 pounds. Price, $8.45
Bordeaux nozzles will be furnished in place of Vermorel, if preferred, at same price.
No. 42K5516 Galvanized Extension Tubes, 8 feet long. Weight, 3½ lbs. Price, 54c

SPRAYING PUMP - $2.03

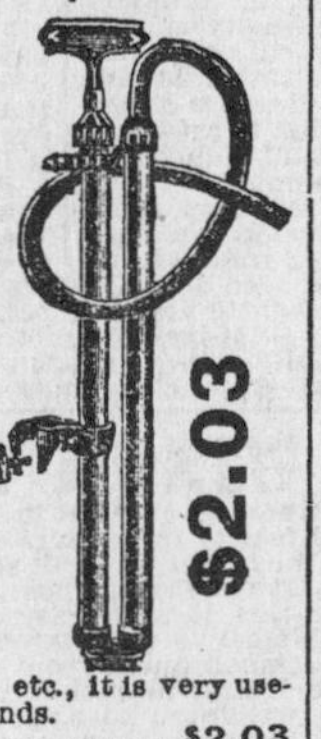

No. 42K5520 The construction of the pump requires the pressure on the handle to be all done on the down stroke, the pressure on the cylinder acting as a cushion, and partly forcing the handle up again, thus making it very easy of operation, requiring no foot rest or other device to steady it. The hose can be detached at top of pump and a nozzle attached in its place, either for spraying, sprinkling, or throwing a solid stream. It is also arranged so that a small stream is discharged with great force from the bottom of the pump into the bucket or barrel, serving to thoroughly agitate the mixture at all times when the pump is in use. For washing buggies, windows, etc., it is very useful. Weight, about 5 pounds.
Price $2.03

REMEMBER, THAT SHOULD YOU PURCHASE ANY OF THESE GOODS FROM US, AND AFTER RECEIVING THEM, YOU CANNOT SET THEM UP, YOU ARE AT ABSOLUTELY NO LOSS WHATEVER, AS WE WILL REFUND YOUR MONEY AND PAY THE TRANSPORTATION BOTH WAYS ON ANY MATERIAL WHICH YOU DESIRE TO RETURN.

ACME PORTABLE CAST FORCE PUMP. $4.73

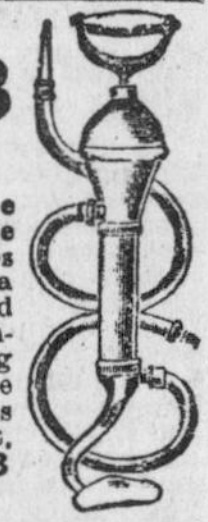

No. 42K5523 Our Acme Portable Cast Force Pump is one of the most effective hand pumps on the market. Is made extra strong; nicely finished. Is adapted for spraying trees, washing windows and wagons, sprinkling lawns, etc. Furnished complete with hose and connections, brass nozzle and sprinkler. Weight, 11 pounds. Price $4.73

ACME FIRE EXTINGUISHER - - $5.92

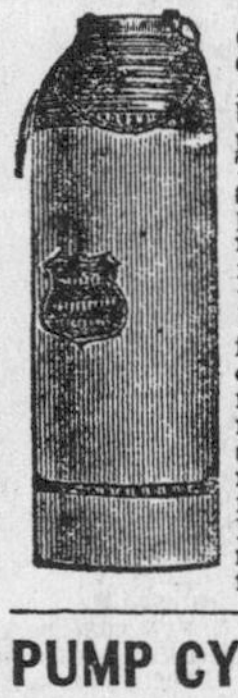

No. 42K5525 A device that every store, factory and residence should be equipped with. Absolute protection against loss by fire can now be assured to property owners at a small cost. The Acme Chemical Fire Extinguisher is the simplest and most powerful machine made. It is made of heavy copper securely riveted and soldered and highly polished. Holds three gallons and throws a stream 40 feet when in action. The solution used contains no acids to destroy fabrics, etc., although it is the most powerful fire extinguisher solution known. Solution for recharging can be obtained from any druggist for 15 cents. Full directions sent with each machine. Weight, when ready for use, 12 lbs. Price .$5.92

PUMP CYLINDERS - 75c

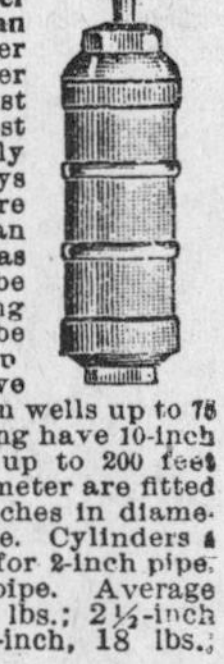

By means of the cylinder water is raised, and unless the cylinder is well made no good results can be obtained. A good cylinder must be bored true and plunger must fit accurately. Valves must be simple and durable. The cost of repairing a cylinder is usually more than its first cost, so it pays to get the best. Our cylinders are the best that skilled workmen can produce and our prices as low as equally well made goods can be sold for. Cylinders 10 inches long have 6-inch stroke and can be used in wells up to 35 feet deep. Cylinders 12 inches long have 6-inch stroke and can be used in wells up to 75 feet deep. Cylinders 16 inches long have 10-inch stroke and can be used in wells up to 200 feet deep. Cylinders 2 inches in diameter are fitted for 1-inch pipe. Cylinders 3½ inches in diameter are fitted for 1½-inch pipe. Cylinders 4 inches in diameter are fitted for 2-inch pipe. All others fitted for 1¼-inch pipe. Average weight of cylinder, 2-inch, 10 lbs.; 2½-inch 11 lbs.; 3-inch, 14 lbs.; 3½-inch, 18 lbs.; 4-inch, 26 lbs.

Iron Body Cylinders.

No.	Diam., inch.	10 in. long	12 in. long	16 in. long
42K5528	2	$0.75	$1 10	$1.20
42K5530	2½	.87	1.20	1.40
42K5532	3	1.00	1.40	1.60
42K5534	3½	1.40	1.80	2.25
42K5535	4	1.80	2.30	2.90

Do not let anyone lead you to believe that you will be unable to install a pump outfit after you have procured it, as everything is all cut and threaded to exact lengths, and any boy or man can put it together, even though they have never seen a pump before.

ACME SIGHT FEED CYLINDER LUBRICATOR - - $2.32

For Portable Engines, Steam Pumps, etc. Without Gauge Glass.

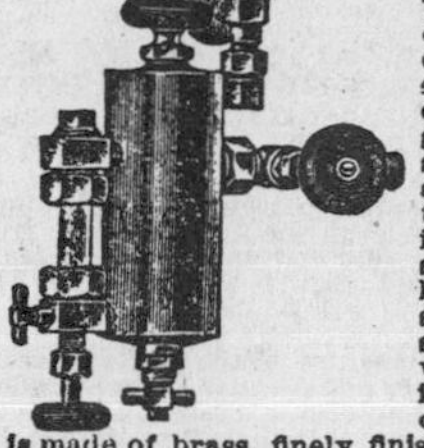

No. 42K6253 This Lubricator is of the same high class as our No. 42K6251 with the exception of the gauge glass for showing the amount of oil in the reservoir, making it a very substantial and cheap lubricator where such a cup is desired. It is sold with the same binding guarantee as our No. 42K6251, and is made of brass, finely finished.

Size	Weight, lbs.	Pipe Thread on Support Arm	Price
⅓ pint	5½	⅜ inch	$2.32
½ pint	7	⅜ inch	2.73
1 pint	8	½ inch	3.84
1½ pints	8½	½ inch	4.38
1 quart	9½	½ inch	4.90

ACME SINGLE CONNECTION LUBRICATOR - - $2.48

For Stationary, Traction and Portable Engines, Steam Pumps, etc.

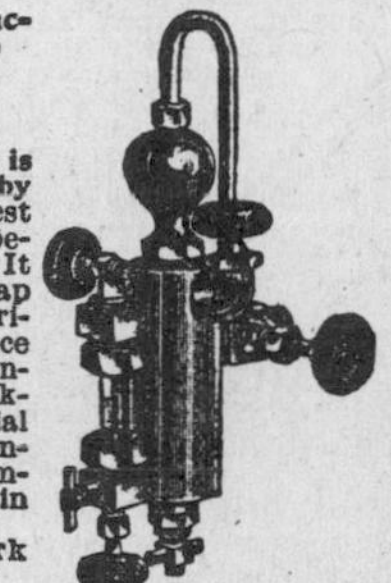

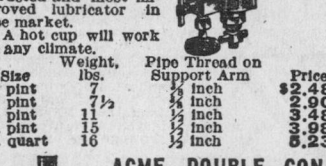

No. 42K6255 This Lubricator is strictly in a class by itself, being the best that money and experience can produce. It is not an ordinary cheap single connection lubricator, but is a device made on scientific principles; first class workmanship and material and is the best constructed and most improved lubricator in the market.

A hot cup will work in any climate.

Size	Weight, lbs.	Pipe Thread on Support Arm	Price
¼ pint	7	⅜ inch	$2.48
½ pint	7½	⅜ inch	2.90
½ pint	11	½ inch	3.48
1 pint	15	½ inch	3.98
1 quart	16	½ inch	5.23

ACME DOUBLE CONNECTION LUBRICATOR

$2.12

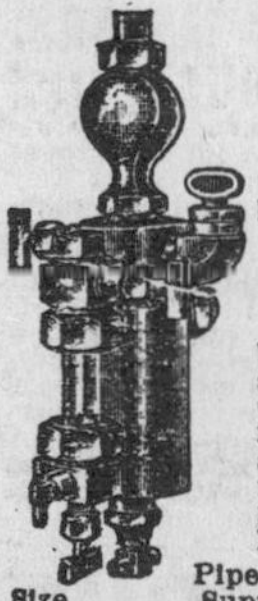

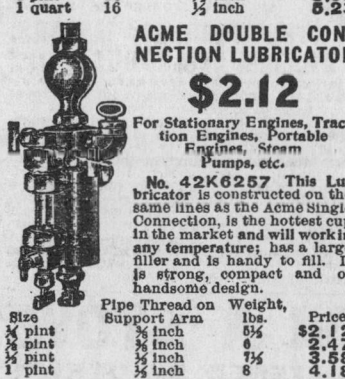

For Stationary Engines, Traction Engines, Portable Engines, Steam Pumps, etc.

No. 42K6257 This Lubricator is constructed on the same lines as the Acme Single Connection, is the hottest cup in the market and will work in any temperature; has a large filler and is handy to fill. It is strong, compact and of handsome design.

Size	Pipe Thread on Support Arm	Weight, lbs.	Price
¼ pint	⅜ inch	5½	$2.12
⅜ pint	⅜ inch	6	2.47
½ pint	½ inch	7½	3.58
1 pint	½ inch	8	4.18

ACME JUNIOR DOUBLE CONNECTION LUBRICATOR,

$1.87

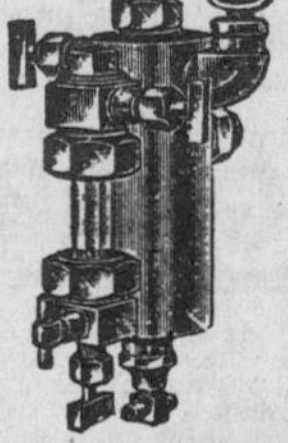

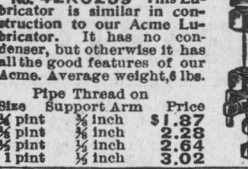

No. 42K6259 This Lubricator is similar in construction to our Acme Lubricator. It has no condenser, but otherwise it has all the good features of our Acme. Average weight, 6 lbs.

Size	Pipe Thread on Support Arm	Price
¼ pint	⅜ inch	$1.87
⅜ pint	⅜ inch	2.28
½ pint	½ inch	2.64
1 pint	½ inch	3.02

Model X Automatic Injectors.

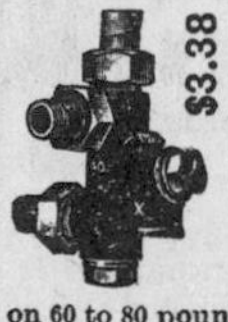

Every Model X Injector is carefully tested before leaving the factory, and no machine is allowed to go out that will not work on the following points (while nearly all of them will do much better). Start low, 18 to 22 pounds steam on 4-foot lift; work high, 152 to 160 pounds steam on 4-foot lift; lift water 20 to 22 feet on 60 to 80 pounds steam; handle hot water, 120 to 125 degrees at 60 to 80 pounds steam; handle hot water, 112 to 115 degrees at 100 pounds steam; handle hot water, 85 to 100 degrees at 125 pounds steam. The Model X Injector is one of the most reliable injectors on the market and will interchange with Penberthy and other injectors and is thoroughly guaranteed by us.

No. 42K6296

Size	All Pipe Connections	Capacity 65 to 90 lbs., 2 ft. lift, gals. per hour	Horse Power for ordinary type boiler	Horse Power on a basis of 30 lbs. evaporation per H. P. per hour	Price
	Inches				
20	⅜	60	2 to 6	4 to 8	$3.38
30	⅜	80	4 to 8	6 to 12	3.60
35	½	140	8 to 16	12 to 20	4.05
40	½	190	16 to 23	20 to 30	4.50
50	¾	270	23 to 30	30 to 45	5.63
60	¾	370	30 to 45	45 to 60	6.75
70	1	490	45 to 65	60 to 80	9.00
80	1	620	65 to 80	80 to 110	10.13

The above capacities are based on actual tests and are guaranteed. As will be seen from above, any size Model X will deliver more water than the corresponding size of any other make, while the capacity can be cut down about one-half by simply throttling water supply valve.

THE HANCOCK INSPIRATOR, STATIONARY TYPE - $4.80

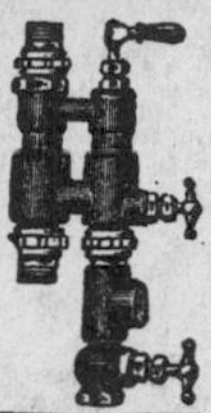

No. 42K6300 The Hancock Inspirator, Stationary Type, for Feeding Stationary, Marine and Portable Boilers. It works with low or high steam pressure on all lifts up to 25 feet. Water can be elevated above the Hancock Inspirator about 2½ feet for each pound of steam pressure. With 45 pounds steam pressure, water can be lifted 25 feet and elevated 112½ feet above the inspirator, a total elevation of 137½ feet.

Size	Pipe Connections: Steam	Pipe Connections: Suction and Delivery	Pipe Connections: Overflow	Capacity per hour with 60 lbs. steam pressure, gallons	Horse Power: For the ordinary type of Boiler and Engine	Horse Power: On a basis of 30 lbs. Evaporation per H. P. per hour	Prices Stationary type
7½	⅜	⅜	¼	60	4 to 6	5 to 8	$4.80
8¾	⅜	½	⅜	90	6 to 8	8 to 15	5.40
10	⅜	½	⅜	120	8 to 15	15 to 25	6.00
12½	½	¾	½	220	15 to 30	25 to 35	7.50
15	½	¾	½	300	30 to 40	35 to 60	9.00
7½	¾	1	¾	420	40 to 60	60 to 75	12.00

The H-D Ejector or Jet Pump.

Made with Independent Coupling and Tubes.

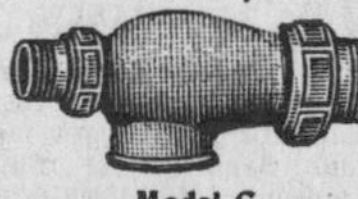

Model C.

No. 42K6312 They are used for lifting and conveying water and other liquids from one level to another in mines, pits or wells. The H-D Ejector will lift 24 feet. When it is desired to raise the liquid to a greater distance, place the Ejector near the liquid and elevate it. With a steam pressure of 65 pounds it will elevate 50 to 60 feet, and with 100 pounds steam up 70 to 80 feet.

Size, No.	Pipe Connections: Steam	Pipe Connections: Suction and Delivery	Capacity per Hour	Price
1 Brass	⅜	½	250 gals.	$1.80
2 Brass	⅜	¾	500 gals.	2.25
3 Brass	¾	1	960 gals.	3.38
4 Brass	1	1¼	1300 gals.	4.50

Farm Engine and Yacht Pop Valve.

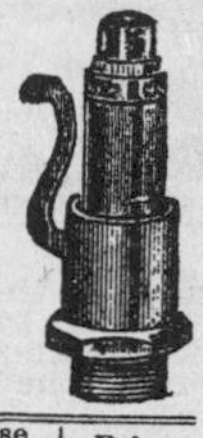

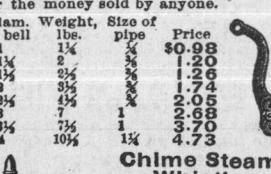

No. 42K6330 Made of brass, finely finished, full relieving capacity and very sensitive. Connect valve onto top of boiler when possible. When pipe connections are used, have them full diameter of valve or larger, and as short and free from bends as possible. In ordering, state horse power, size of boiler and highest working pressure.

Size	Size Steam connection	Wt., lbs.	Horse power	Price
¾-in.	¾-inch	1½	8	$1.63
1-in.	1-inch	2½	12	1.96
1¼-in.	1¼-inch	3½	18	2.31
1½-in.	1½-inch	4½	20	3.25
2-in.	2-inch	6½	30	4.88

We handle a complete line of everything needed by the plumber and steamfitter, both in tools and fittings. We sell at prices way under the trust prices.

Eclipse Governors.

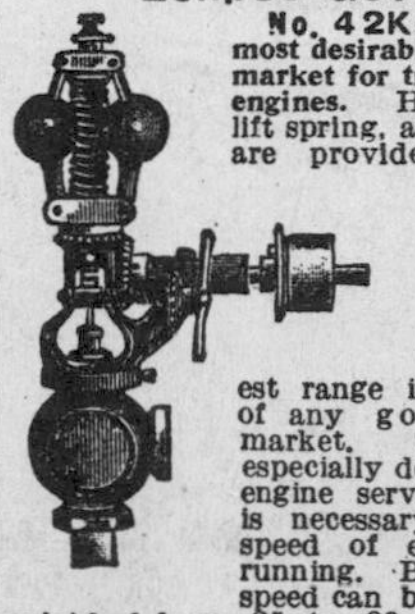

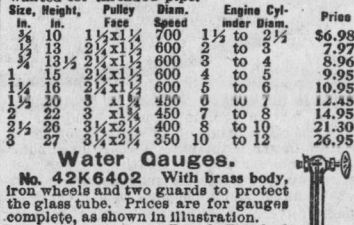

No. 42K6398 This is the most desirable Governor in the market for traction and sawmill engines. Has lever without lift spring, and adjustable steps are provided on all sizes, whereby the valve may be raised or lowered and the speed materially changed. This, together with change of spring tension, gives it the broadest range in change of speed of any governor in the market. This governor is especially designed for traction engine service and where it is necessary to change the speed of engine while it is running. By this device the speed can be increased or diminished from 25 to 30 per cent without changing the tension of spring. Also with this improvement the engineer can give the engine sufficient speed for any kind of road service, and immediately change it to the proper speed for threshing or other purposes without stopping. This governor is otherwise constructed so the jolting of the engine over rough and uneven ground or roads has but slight effect on the regulation. In ordering it is always best to give the make of engine; how fast you intend to run it; diameter of pulley on engine; shaft to drive the governor; diameter of base flange and if wanted for threaded pipe.

Size, In.	Height, In.	Pulley Face	Diam. Speed	Engine Cylinder Diam.	Price
⅜	10	1½x1¼	700	1½ to 2½	$6.98
½	13	2¼x1½	600	2 to 3	7.97
¾	13½	2¼x1½	600	3 to 4	8.96
1	15	2¼x1½	600	4 to 5	9.95
1¼	16	2¼x1½	600	5 to 6	10.95
1½	20	3 x1¾	450	6 to 7	12.45
2	22	3 x1¾	450	7 to 8	14.95
2½	26	3¼x2¼	400	8 to 10	21.30
3	27	3¼x2¼	350	10 to 12	26.95

Water Gauges.

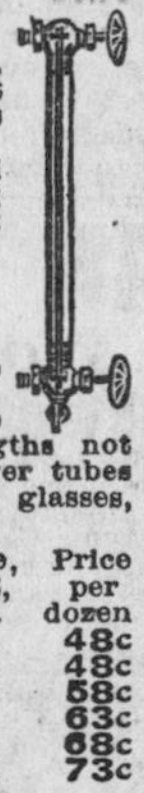

No. 42K6402 With brass body, iron wheels and two guards to protect the glass tube. Prices are for gauges complete, as shown in illustration.

Size		Rough	Finished
Pipe ⅜, Glass ⅝x10.	Price,	87c	$1.22
Pipe ½, Glass ⅝x12.	Price,	88c	1.23

Genuine Scotch Glass Tubes.

For Water Gauges.

No. 42K6406 These gauge glasses are imported by us direct, size labeled on end of each, and we warrant them equal to any. Lengths not regular, charged price of next longer tubes of same diameter. Average weight, 6 glasses, 2 pounds.

Lgth. ins.	Price, for 6 ½ in.	Price, per dozen	Price, for 6, ⅝ in.	Price, per dozen	Price, for 6, ¾ in.	Price per dozen
10	20c	39c	24c	39c	28c	48c
11	22c	43c	25c	43c	28c	48c
12	24c	46c	26c	45c	32c	58c
13	28c	54c	28c	53c	38c	63c
14	28c	55c	29c	54c	38c	68c
15	30c	58c	30c	57c	42c	73c

We do not sell less than 6 glasses.

AT THE REDUCED PRICES SHOWN IN THIS CATALOGUE YOUR SAVINGS ARE LARGER THAN EVER.

Float Valves.

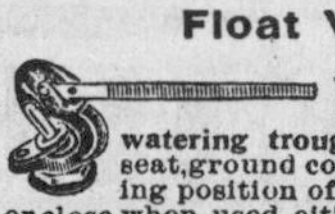

No. 42K6475 This Valve is used to regulate the supply of water in a watering trough. It has brass valve seat, ground connections, etc. By changing position of lever it will either open or close when used either on bottom or side of tank, or when two levers are used it can be used to open or close.

Size, inches	¾	1	1¼	1½	2	2½
Weight, lbs.	2	2½	3¼	4	9½	12
Price, valve only	78c	91c	$1.04	$1.92	$3.05	$4.75

STEAM WHISTLE WITH VALVE AT REDUCED PRICES - - 98c

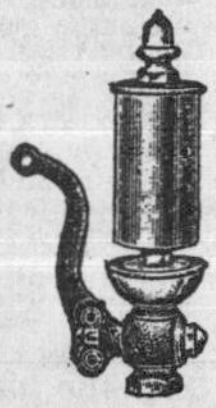

No. 42K6350 The bell is made of brass; valve, etc., of steam metal. The best whistle for the money sold by anyone.

Diam. of bell	Weight, lbs.	Size of pipe	Price
1	1¼	¼	$0.98
1¼	2	⅜	1.20
1½	2½	⅜	1.26
2	3½	¾	1.74
2½	4½	¾	2.05
3	7	1	2.68
3½	7½	1	3.70
4	10½	1¼	4.73

Chime Steam Whistles.

At Reduced Prices.

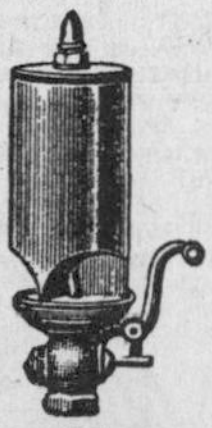

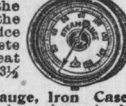

No. 42K6354 Single Bell Chime Whistle, made of highly polished brass. Gives three distinct tones. Very simple in construction.

Diameter of bell	Wt., lbs.	Size of pipe	Price
2	3	½	$3.56
3	5½	¾	6.21
4	10½	1	8.87
5	20	1¼	15.54
6	31	1½	21.16

Steam Gauges.

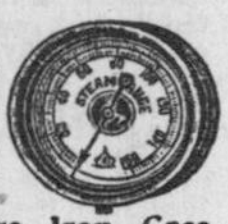

Our Steam Gauges are the best made and worth two of the many cheaper ones. Our price of $1.19 and upward, complete with cock, will mean a great saving for you. Weight, 3½ pounds.

No. 42K6362 Steam Gauge, Iron Case, japanned, to register 200 pounds or less, single spring. Weight, about 3½ pounds.

Size, inches	3½	4½	5
Price	$1.19	$1.22	$1.30

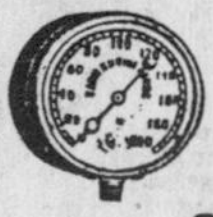

No. 42K6364 Steam Gauges, Iron Case, with auxiliary spring for steamboats, portable and traction engines. Size, 4½ inches. Graduated 300 pounds. Weight, 3½ pounds. Price...... $1.85

Safety Valves.

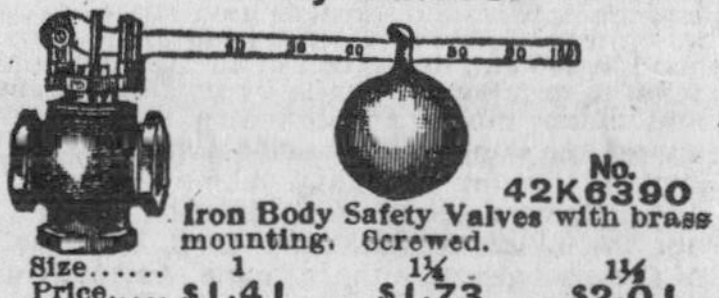

No. 42K6390 Iron Body Safety Valves with brass mounting. Screwed.

Size	1	1¼	1½
Price	$1.41	$1.73	$2.01
Size	2	2½	3
Price	2.73	4.62	6.00

Copper Tank Float.

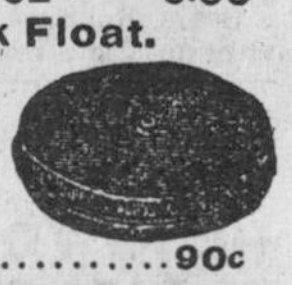

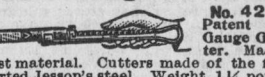

No. 42K6478 To be used in connection with No. 42K6475 Valve. When fastened to lever will open and shut automatically. Size, 9½x2¾ inches. Weight, 1 pound. Price...... 90c

Water Gauge Glass Cutter.

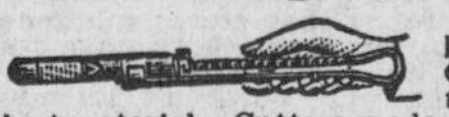

No. 42K6410 Patent Water Gauge Glass Cutter. Made of the best material. Cutters made of the finest imported Jessop's steel. Weight, 1¼ pounds. Price...... 34c

OUR LUBRICATORS, Whistles and Steam Trimmings in general are all tested before leaving our factory and we can guarantee them to give perfect satisfaction.

THE KEEPING OF GASOLINE NO LONGER A MENACE TO YOUR BUILDING

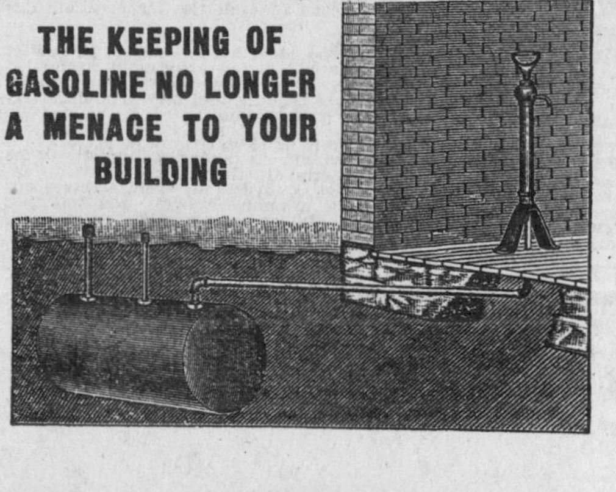

GASOLINE PUMP OUTFIT

THE UNDERGROUND OUTFIT SHOWN HERE IS INTENDED TO BE PRACTICABLE RATHER THAN ELABORATE.

THE TANK IS A SIXTY-GALLON GALVANIZED HEAVY STEEL TANK, and is covered with a coat of asphaltum to prevent rusting in the ground. The pump is made of heavy brass and iron; all the wearing parts are made of brass and have no leather or rubber packing or washers to wear out. It is a plain lift pump and is intended for use only where gasoline does not have to be lifted over 8 feet from bottom of tank to spout of pump, and the horizontal pipe not over 30 feet. This tank should be buried from 12 to 24 inches in the ground, according to climatic conditions. All joints must be screwed tight; white lead should be put on threads before screwing together, and pump should be screwed to floor, so it will be rigid. We recommend placing a wooden box in the ground in which to place tank, as this will prevent tank absorbing moisture. This outfit is furnished complete with tank, pump, 3 feet of 1½-inch filler pipe, 3 feet of ¼-inch vent pipe, 20 feet of ¾-inch pipe, and two ¾-inch elbows.

No. 42K5521 Price, complete **$21.25**

WEHRLE STOVES AND RANGES

DIRECT from the largest stove foundry in the world, our own foundry at Newark, Ohio, the foundry we own and control, operated for us by the Wehrle Brothers, the best stove makers in the country, we offer the highest grade stoves and ranges it is possible to manufacture. We offer you these stoves at prices only a little above our foundry cost, less than retailers pay at wholesale, even less than the small manufacturers' cost. You can save $10.00 to $30.00 on any one of our high grade stoves against the lowest price named by any retail dealer.

"WEHRLE" IS THE NAME we are now putting on all our new models of stoves. "Wehrle" is the brand or trade mark that henceforth will be found on all the new style stoves we are bringing out, and hereafter the name plate "Wehrle Model" will be the standard in the stove business; it will stand for the best and highest grade stove of this particular style, nothing better at any price, nothing to compare with it in stove value for the money.

THE WEHRLES, WILLIAM AND AUGUST, two brothers, brought up in the stove business, the best known stove men in the trade among stove manufacturers, admitted by everyone connected with stove manufacturing to be the greatest authorities in the country on stove construction, have complete charge of this mammoth stove foundry for us; they have always had charge of it since its beginning ten years ago, and it is due to this fact, their able management and their expert knowledge of stove making, as well as our low price policy, that has enabled our stove department to grow by leaps and bounds, compelled us to enlarge the foundry year by year until now we run eight cupolas, melting 25,000 tons of pig iron a year and producing 200,000 stoves a year, each and every stove sold through our catalogue, sold direct to the user at foundry cost with but our one small percentage of profit added.

THESE EXPERT STOVE MAKERS and foundry men, the Wehrle Brothers, Messrs. William and August Wehrle, who superintend most closely every detail of the manufacturing, stand for the very best in stove making and it is partly for this reason that we are bringing the name "Wehrle," to the front so prominently, but there is still another reason, and the explanation of this reason forms a most interesting story that every one of our customers will read and appreciate.

WHY WE FROM NOW ON WILL USE THE TRADE MARK "WEHRLE" ON ALL OUR BEST STOVES AND RANGES

What we have been compelled to do to safeguard our interests, to prevent unscrupulous and dishonest dealers and manufacturers from deceiving the buying public, and especially to protect our customers.

OUR STOVE BUSINESS is the wonder of the trade. It is the unit for comparison with every other manufacturer, wholesaler, jobber or retailer. It is the target for everyone in the trade to shoot at. Our stove orders have increased year by year, the foundry has expanded and manufacturers and dealers alike have observed the marvelous growth of our Stove Department; they have particularly noted the high quality of our stoves and the wonderful reputation we were building up, especially on certain of our highest grade stoves and ranges.

WHAT DID THEY DO?
Unable to compete with us, prohibited by their methods of doing business from meeting our low prices, debarred through lack of equal ability (the Wehrles') and organization (our immense foundry) from matching us in quality, unable to show the stove buyers of the country the saving we offer them, forced, therefore, to see our stove business greatly increase season after season, what did they do? We regret to say it, but they were dishonest.

HOW? Our Acme Triumph, the world's finest steel range is our most popular stove, our best seller, it is the steel range standard of the country, the range that is winning its way into every community. The manufacturers and dealers have tried to take advantage of this fact, have tried to trade on the good name and reputation of the Acme Triumph, have tried to deceive the public by putting out cheap, imitation and inferior ranges and branding them exactly the same or almost the same as our "Acme Triumph." Throughout the country we hear of "Triumph" ranges, "Trump" ranges, "Akme Triumph" ranges, "Acme Triump" ranges; hundreds of our customers have written like this: "I see a 'Triumph' range in one of the store windows of our town, marked $28.00. Is it the same as your 'Acme Triump'?" Of course, none of these ranges were the genuine Acme Triumph made in our foundry by the Wehrles and sold only by us through our catalogue. Yet many unscrupulous manufacturers and equally unscrupulous dealers, intended that the stove buyer should believe such range was a Sears, Roebuck Acme Triumph Range and many buyers would purchase, thinking they were getting a real genuine Acme Triumph only to learn later of the deception.

LARGEST IN THE WORLD

OUR STOVE FOUNDRY AT NEWARK, OHIO.

DESCRIPTIVE NAMES like Triumph, Charm, Sunburst, etc., cannot be copyrighted; absolute protection is not accorded the concern adopting such names; yet these special stoves of ours have earned such reputation throughout the country, that we could not afford to confuse our customers, by naming those particular stoves with new names. But now that we are bringing out some new and wonderfully high grade stoves, new models offered by us for the first time, stoves that are far in advance of anything on the market, we have the opportunity of naming and branding them in a way that will distinguish them forever, prevent deception by imitators, connect them closely with our foundry and the makers, and protect our stove customers, their friends, and their friends' friends, who form a constantly widening chain of customers for us. We have decided to use the name of "Wehrle," a proper name; it can't be counterfeited, imitated, duplicated or copied, and hereafter "Wehrle" will be the name (identified by model number) that goes on every new style stove or range we bring out.

THE WEHRLES, MESSRS. WILLIAM AND AUGUST, have a great reputation to uphold; they have already established a standard of excellence in our best stoves that is not easy to surpass. In steel range making they created a model, the Acme Triumph, that has been the highest notch in steel ranges for a long time; yet in the new ranges, the Wehrle Models, there are many improvements and new features over the Acme Triumph, the result of study and experience. In the Acme Charm, the steel range on legs, the Wehrles built for us a range that jumped into quick popularity justified by its great merit; still in the Wehrle Model No. 22 the Wehrles have gone a step further and made a range on legs, one that is beyond comparison with anything on the market. In cast iron ranges our Acme Liberty-Kenwood has stood for the highest grade in the world; but the new cast iron range, our Wehrle Model No. 30, embodies more improvements, more features, is strengthened, perfected in many ways and thus we keep far in advance of all others on stove quality.

From the foregoing you will understand why our new style stoves will all carry the registered trade mark or brand "Wehrle," and why "Wehrle" is so much better in quality and so much lower in price than any other stove manufactured today.

HOW YOU CAN SAVE ABOUT $20.00 ON A STOVE

HOW YOU CAN GET A STOVE BETTER IN QUALITY THAN ANYTHING OFFERED BY OTHERS

TO SAVE THE LARGEST AMOUNT OF MONEY on a purchase of a stove very much better than stoves sold generally in hardware stores, just a little better than the best stoves sold by the specialty stove dealers, place your order with us for one of our new Wehrle Models. While you can save money on any stove you order from us, from the lowest price to the finest, while our Acme Triumph, Acme Charm, Acme Liberty-Kenwood, Acme Sunburst are wonderful values compared to what you can buy elsewhere, yet for the greatest stove value for your money, for the greatest possible value, we must refer you to the Wehrle Models, you get the very best and highest grade possible, better than the stoves widely advertised and sold at the very highest prices. Let us induce you to order a Wehrle Model. For value, for satisfaction, for quality, for perfection in very detail, a Wehrle Model stove admits of no comparison. Send us your order, enclosing our price for a Wehrle stove and if it is not exactly as represented, the very best stove you ever saw, highly satisfactory, and if you have not made a big saving in cost, then send it back and get your money back including any freight charges you paid.

OUR BINDING GUARANTEE

OUR WRITTEN BINDING GUARANTEE is sent with every stove sold by us. Note the very broad scope of this guarantee as shown in the facsimile opposite. We will correct, without any expense to you, any defect of any nature whatsoever, which by any accident may have escaped the rigid inspection at the foundry, and which develops when the stove is put in use. No other stove manufacturer stands behind his product as we do. Please remember that a guarantee is no better than the concern that makes it, and that when we give a guarantee on any merchandise it means that all the resources of this responsible mercantile institution are behind it.

WE GUARANTEE every piece and part that enters into the stove we sell you to be perfect in material, perfect in manufacture, perfect in operation, and unequaled by any other stove or range of its class in durability and beauty, in economy in the consumption of fuel, and if you do not find it so, you may return it to us at our expense, and we will immediately return your money, together with all the transportation charges paid by you.

WE FURTHER GUARANTEE every stove you order from us to reach you in perfect condition. We are very careful in preparing our stoves for shipment, they are very securely crated, every loose part is properly attached to the stove or enclosed, and we know that it will reach you in the same perfect condition in which it leaves our hands. If, however, when the stove reaches your station and is examined by you, you find that any piece or part is cracked, broken, or damaged in any way whatsoever, remember that we will replace or repair such cracked, broken, damaged or missing part free of any cost to you.

DOUBLE THE VALUE OF YOUR DOLLAR
BY PURCHASING NEEDED ARTICLES FROM US AT OUR GREATLY REDUCED PRICES.

THE UTMOST CARE is taken in selecting, grading, and testing raw materials which enter into the manufacture of our entire line of stoves and ranges. Take the item of iron, for instance. We are sure it will interest you to know that every particle of pig iron we use is subjected to a most careful analysis by our chemist before it is put into the cupola to be melted. The several grades required for the different lines of castings are each carefully weighed and mixed in proportion to the different chemicals contained therein, such as silicon, sulphur, carbon, etc., as for covers, centers and top sections. A different mixture or composition is required for linings, grates, etc. After the mixture has been melted, a batch of molten iron is run from the cupola, is chemically analyzed, and tested to make sure of a long lasting, fire resisting mixture, and if, perchance, it does not stand the test to which it is subjected, it is again mixed, melted, analyzed and tested until the proper strength is obtained, which can be relied upon to a certainty.

WE KNOW THAT EVERY CASTING IS RIGHT, and, furthermore, you cannot name another stove manufacturer that takes this precaution and exercises the same painstaking care.

CAREFUL INSPECTION. Every stove and range we make is set up complete, all parts carefully fitted and critically inspected, thus avoiding the possibility of any one being shipped that is not absolutely perfect in every way.

THE WAY WE CRATE THEM

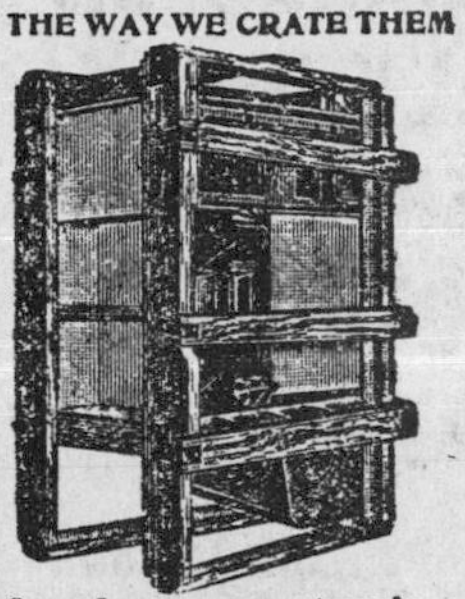

One of our ranges strongly crated for a short or long journey.

IT IS OUR AIM to build the highest grade stoves it is possible to create, the most modern, the best heaters, the best bakers, the most economical users of fuel stoves that others are striving to equal, stoves when sold to you and used by you will be found to be so much better than you have hoped for, so satisfactory from every standpoint that we will secure your lasting good will and patronage. No concern in the world can succeed in business on first orders alone, and it has been our purpose to so excel all the manufacturers of stoves and ranges that not a single customer shall ever have occasion to criticise the merchandise we send him or find fault with the manner in which we deal with him, and our six million satisfied customers throughout the United States is proof of our ability to give the highest qualities and the best values of any supply house in existence.

SO SURE ARE WE that the stoves we sell are unapproached by those manufactured by any other stove concern in the world, so sure are we that it is impossible to produce better stoves and ranges than those we offer, so positive are we that in price and quality comparison we stand absolutely alone as stove manufacturers and dealers, that we are willing to have our product stand side by side with the product of any other stove manufacturer or dealer and have you submit them to every test, to have you judge of their merits in practical operation, to have you say whether all our claims and more are not absolutely proven and established by a thorough test in your own home.

UNDER THESE LIBERAL TERMS, and in view of our binding guarantee of quality, our guarantee of satisfaction, our free trial offers, certainly you cannot afford to send to any other manufacturer or dealer for a stove or range until you have first sent for one of the high class stoves or ranges manufactured by us in the largest and best equipped stove foundry in the world.

THE QUESTION OF QUICK DELIVERY, SHIPMENT FROM A WAREHOUSE NEAR YOU AND HOW WE MAKE THE FREIGHT CHARGES VERY LOW, FULLY EXPLAINED ON NEXT PAGE.

INSTRUCTIONS ON HOW TO ORDER STOVES AND RANGES

ALL COOK STOVES AND RANGES are variously numbered as follows: 7-17, 8-18 and 9-21, etc. The first number given denoting the size of griddle covers or lids and the last two figures the width of the oven in inches. Do not order a No. 9 stove if your cooking utensils are No. 8, as they will not fit.

BE SURE YOU SELECT A STOVE LARGE ENOUGH for your requirements. Measure the oven and the top of your old stove or one of your neighbor's stoves, if it is about the size you want, and then compare it with the measurements given in our catalogue.

IF YOU USE WOOD ONLY AS FUEL, always select a stove from among those offered for wood, thus obtaining a larger fire box than is furnished with a combination wood and coal burner. If steel range is wanted be sure to state whether for coal or wood. If you use coal as fuel do not make the mistake of selecting a stove which is offered to burn wood only, or of ordering a heating stove for soft coal when we offer it as a hard coal burner only.

WE CAN ONLY FURNISH OUR STOVES as illustrated and described in catalogue. Do not ask us to send you a range with fire box on the opposite end from that shown in illustration or to leave off or put on more nickel, as we cannot do it. We do not furnish stove pipe or cooking utensils with our stoves at prices quoted. Neither does your dealer, unless he charges you enough for the stove to allow him to include them free.

IF AFTER READING DESCRIPTIONS CAREFULLY you still desire information regarding any of our stoves it will be promptly and cheerfully furnished upon receipt of your inquiry.

DON'T ORDER THE CHEAPEST STOVE we list and expect it to be the equal of the highest priced stove your dealer has. We can save you from 25 to 50 per cent of the purchase price, size for size and style for style, over the price your dealer asks for the stove he offers you.

AFTER WRITING YOUR ORDER, check it over closely to see that you have written down correctly catalogue number, fuel used, name and size of stove wanted and correct price.

YOUR MONEY BACK IF YOU ARE NOT SATISFIED

YOU TAKE NO RISK whatever in sending us your order. If the stove we send you doesn't prove perfectly satisfactory in every way and the greatest bargain in this line you ever saw or heard of, you can return it to us at our expense and we will promptly return your money, including what you paid for freight charges. Remember also, you have thirty days' trial, during which time you can assure yourself that you have obtained from us the greatest possible value for your money. If you feel dissatisfied at any time during the thirty days you can return the stove and your money will be promptly refunded.

IN ORDERING, please note what we say above about how to select the stove you need. Write your order on one of our regular order blanks or any plain sheet of paper. Be sure to state the catalogue number and enclose our price. You can send us a postoffice money order, an express money order, a bank draft, or send the money in a registered letter. State the amount of money you enclose and in what form. Be sure to sign your name, address and give us shipping instructions and the stove will go to you promptly and, as before stated, under our guarantee of "Your money back if you are not satisfied," and with the additional privilege of thirty days' free trial.

COOKING UTENSILS ARE EXTRA

WHEN YOU ORDER STOVES at the prices quoted in this catalogue, please understand that we furnish only the stove as illustrated and described, and no stove pipe and no cooking utensils are furnished with it. If you desire any stove furniture or cooking utensils, they should be selected from either this Big Catalogue or our Tinware Catalogue. The stove furniture will be shipped from our stock in Chicago, while the stove will be sent to you direct from our foundry at Newark, Ohio, or from warehouse nearest you, thus making two shipments, one from the foundry or warehouse and one from our store. For this reason we specially urge you to make your order for cooking utensils large enough to make the purchase profitable to you, remembering that 50 to 100 pounds will, as a rule, go by freight from Chicago for as little freight charge as would 10 pounds. By consulting the pages of this catalogue you will quickly discover that every sort of stove and kitchen utensil is carried in stock by us, and our quality and price inducements are the best offered by any firm or dealer or individual, and we suggest that you turn to these pages now and note what an elegant line of iron, steel and enameled ware we handle, and see the generous equipment a few dollars will purchase from these pages.

OUR 30 DAYS' FREE TRIAL OFFER

TO PROVE TO YOU that we will furnish you with a handsomer, a better, a stronger made and better finished and more lasting and more economical fuel consuming stove than you could buy anywhere else, and at a big saving in cost to you, we make you this most liberal thirty days' free trial offer, an offer which enables you to find out, without expense to you, just what we mean when we say that we are selling the world's leaders in stoves and ranges.

SELECT ANY ONE OF OUR STOVES as illustrated, described and priced in the pages of this catalogue, send us the price of the stove which you would like to test, and we will send it to you with the understanding and agreement that you may use the stove in your own home for thirty days, during which time you may put it to every possible test that may be devised. You may compare it with any other stove you have used, and the stoves used by your friends and neighbors, and the stoves that other dealers are anxious to sell you and if you do not find after this thirty days' trial that it is in every way better than any stove you can buy from your dealer at home or elsewhere, if you are not absolutely convinced that you have made a big saving in cost, and that you have received just the sort of a stove that you have been anxious to secure, you may return the stove to us at our expense, and we will immediately return your money, together with all the transportation charges paid by you.

NO FAIRER OFFER COULD BE MADE by any firm or individual than this thirty days' free trial offer; it gives you every opportunity that could be asked to investigate the merits of our stoves and we are able to make an extremely liberal offer because we know our stoves so well, because we know that the stoves we sell are themselves the best argument that could possibly be made for them. They really sell themselves, and when we have secured an order in a town or locality it is no uncommon thing to receive innumerable additional orders from the same town or locality as a result of the splendid advertising this stove does for us.

IMMEDIATE SHIPMENT. We carry in stock, crated and ready for immediate shipment, an enormous quantity of all the stoves and ranges described and illustrated in this catalogue, on which we can make an immediate shipment. There will be no delay whatever in filling your order.

EVERY STOVE AND RANGE WE MAKE is set up and thoroughly inspected before being crated ready for shipment, which insures the perfect fitting of all parts.

HOW TO GET REPAIRS FOR OUR STOVES

WEHRLE MODELS AND ACMES SELDOM NEED REPAIRS. Our stoves do not often need repairs but when breakage occurs or parts wear out, and repairs are needed, they always fit. The fact that today we are able to furnish repairs for every stove we have ever sold, makes our guarantee doubly valuable. We handle repairs on an entirely different basis from that of other dealers, because we supply you with the needed part at foundry cost, a mere fraction of what is usually charged by others for such repairs.

WHEN YOU BUY A STOVE FROM US we send you a repair list to make it easy for you to order any piece or part you may need in the years to come. For example, if in the course of the next five or ten years a piece or part should break by accident or otherwise, by referring to the little repair book we send you, you may instantly tell by number just what piece or part you need. Order this part from us by number taken from the booklet; the booklet we send you gives the prices, which is a mere fraction of what others would charge for similar parts, and we will get the needed part to you immediately.

ANOTHER IMPORTANT FEATURE of our stove repairs and parts lies in the fact that all of them are made interchangeable and it will be no trouble at all for you to make the repairs in your own home without the assistance of anyone else. You will find that no grinding or filing will be necessary to get the new part in place. In short, we take the best possible care of our customers that we know how to take, and when you buy a stove from us, you may do so with the assurance that our interest in you and the article we sell does not end when we have received your money and the stove has been delivered to you.

IN ORDERING REPAIRS FOR STOVES, it is very important to give your purchase invoice number or the most complete and explicit information possible. By strictly adhering to the following rules, a great deal of annoyance, expense and delay may be averted: 1st. State whether stove is for coal only, for wood only, or a combined wood and coal burning construction. 2d. If cook stove or range, say if square top or with reservoir. 3d. The back of the stove is at the pipe collar. Stand facing the hearth on a cook stove or facing the oven door of a range. 4th. Give full number, shown on outside of main top. In many instances the same size of griddle holes are placed on different stove bodies, namely, 7-18, 8-18 8-20, 9-20, etc., and the single No. 7, 8 or 9 in this instance would be no indication of the correct size of the stove. 5th. Be particular to furnish all dates of patents. 6th. When legs are desired, say if stove is supplied with legs only or on leg base. 7th. Give name of stove in full. A strict observance of these directions will be mutually advantageous.

ABOUT THE FREIGHT CHARGES

THE PRICES QUOTED in this catalogue are for the stoves delivered on board the cars at our foundry in Newark, Ohio, or from a special warehouse from which point you must pay the freight charges. Stoves are accepted by the railroad companies at a very low freight rate (third class) and you will find the freight charges amount to next to nothing in comparison to what you will save in price. We have shipped stoves as far as California, and have received letters from our customers declaring that when the freight charges were paid by them for this long haul they even then saved as much as $25.00 on a high class steel range. You must remember that you have to pay the freight charges just the same when you buy from the home dealer, because he adds it to the cost price of the stove to him, and in many instances the dealer having purchased his stock through jobbers or wholesalers, the freight charges which you pay when you buy from him are several times what they would be if you bought your stove from us and paid the freight charges from Newark, Ohio.

TAKE, FOR EXAMPLE, our very largest Wehrle Model No. 20, weighing 556 pounds, or our largest Acme Sunburst hard coal base burner, weighing 465 pounds. Either of these stoves could be shipped from 100 to 500 miles for a freight charge amounting to from 50 cents to $1.50, according to the distance. Our lighter weight stoves would be proportionately lower, so that you can very readily see that the freight charges are next to nothing.

HOT WATER FRONTS

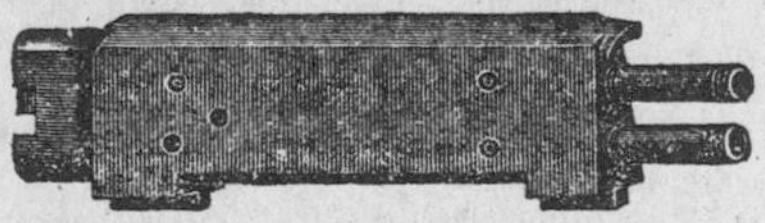

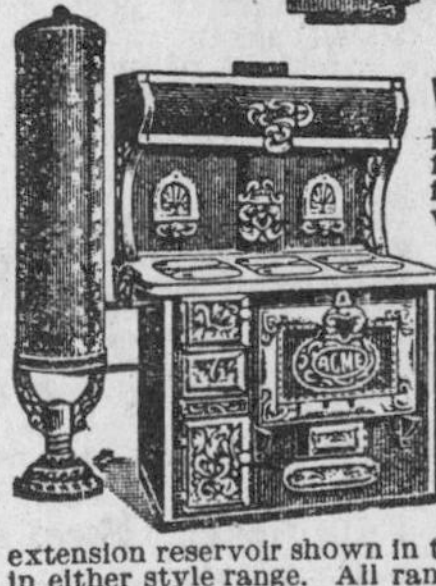

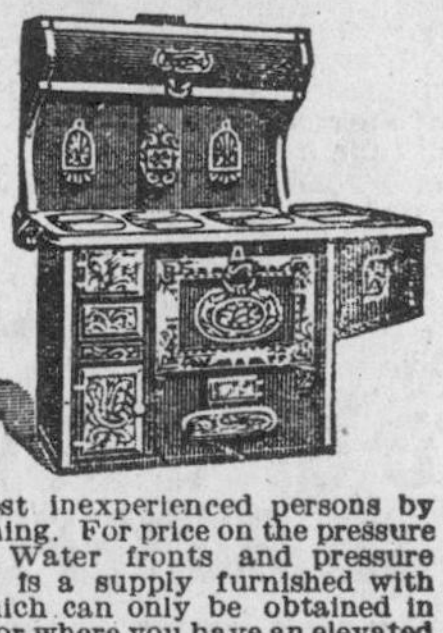

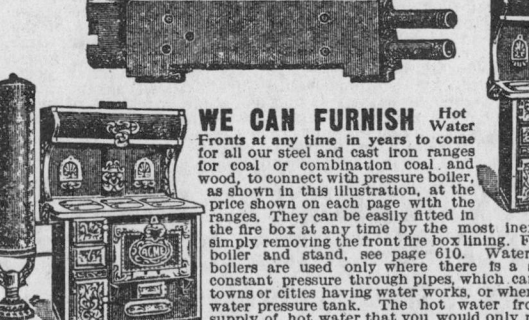

WE CAN FURNISH Hot Water Fronts at any time in years to come for all our steel and cast iron ranges for coal or combination coal and wood, to connect with pressure boiler, as shown in this illustration, at the price shown on each page with the ranges. They can be easily fitted in the fire box at any time by the most inexperienced persons by simply removing the front fire box lining. For price on the pressure boiler and stand, see page 610. Water fronts and pressure boilers are used only where there is a supply furnished with constant pressure through pipes, which can only be obtained in towns or cities having water works, or where you have an elevated water pressure tank. The hot water front gives such ample supply of hot water that you would only require a square range, as shown in the illustration on the left, instead of one with the extension reservoir shown in the illustration on the right. However, water fronts can be fitted in either style range. All ranges ordered with hot water fronts will in all cases be fitted in the range before leaving our foundry, unless otherwise ordered. Please understand we make no charge for this work, and therefore advise all our customers to allow us to do it for them and save them time and money.

READ THE NEXT PAGE OVER CAREFULLY AND LEARN WHAT WE ARE DOING TO MAKE WONDERFULLY QUICK DELIVERY FROM A WAREHOUSE VERY NEAR YOU AND GIVE YOU THE BENEFIT OF OUR CARLOAD SHIPPING RATE ON SIX OF OUR HIGHEST GRADE RANGES AND WORLD WONDER BASE BURNERS.

A QUESTION OF QUICK DELIVERY

When we tell you that we have thirteen warehouses full of our the highest grade ranges and base burners, warehouses in all the principal shipping points in the United States, what does that mean to the prospective stove buyer?

NOW LISTEN TO THIS PROPOSITION:

IF YOU HAVE ANY USE FOR ONE OF THESE STOVES, if you contemplate buying a stove, if you **wish to take advantage of this most extraordinary offer,** if you wish to save from $25.00 to $30.00 in the cost of the highest grade stove possible to build, please get your order to us at once for one of these six special stoves, for we have these six stoves in different sizes on hand in a warehouse right near you, securely crated, ready for immediate shipment, and in perfect condition. You will get the stove in wonderfully quick time and you will save something on the freight charges.

HOW WE MAKE THE FREIGHT CHARGES VERY LOW.

WE FIRST SHIP THESE STOVES to the various points named in solid carload lots, receiving from the railroad company the very lowest carload freight rate, so that when we receive your order here in Chicago for one of these stoves we immediately send your order by special delivery mail to our stove warehouse, the one nearest to you, and order the stove shipped to your railroad station on your order, without any delay and at once. We know it leaves the warehouse near you in perfect condition; we know it will reach you from a few hours to a day or two at the most from the time it leaves the warehouse, and when you do get it you will have to pay only the carload shipping rate from our Newark (Ohio) foundry to the warehouse nearest you.

THIS CARLOAD RATE is considerably less than the expense of shipping a single stove by freight. Now, in addition to this very low carload shipping rate from our foundry at Newark, Ohio, to the warehouse near you, you will also have to pay the very small freight charges for the short haul from this warehouse to your railroad station, but the sum total freight you will have to pay when you receive the stove (which will be the carload shipping rate from our foundry at Newark, Ohio, to the warehouse nearest you, together with the small local rate for the short haul from this warehouse to your railroad station) will, as a rule, amount to much less than the freight charges you would have to pay if the stove were shipped to you singly as one shipment from the foundry at Newark, Ohio, to your railroad station.

NOT ONLY WILL THIS SYSTEM OF SHIPPING these wonderful stoves from warehouses make the freight charges very low, but you will be surprised with our wonderfully quick delivery. These six stoves we carry in stock in these different warehouses, from which we can get to almost any station east of the Rocky Mountains or any station in New York State or any of the New England States in just a day or two; and they are the six highest grade stoves we make and the six highest grade stoves in the world; and by this method you will be surprised how little the freight charges will amount to and how quickly we get any of these stoves to you. And further, under this system, there is practically no chance for the stove to reach you in any way damaged, no chance for any disappointment. Therefore, if you want to get the **greatest value** that we can possibly give you in a stove, one of the very best stoves we make, one of the best stoves made in the world; if you want to get it in the shortest possible time and take advantage of the very low carload freight rate that this system gives, then **by all means** go to your R. F. D. carrier, express agent, banker, or postmaster and get a money order, express order, or bank draft drawn in our favor. Select one of these stoves, giving the catalogue number, name, and size of stove wanted, enclose the amount in a letter addressed to **Sears, Roebuck & Co.,** Chicago, Ill., and tell us to send you one of our highest grade stoves, either one of the stoves above mentioned, and we will surprise you in the promptness of delivery, the low freight charge and the most extraordinary value.

JUST THIS!

TO GET ONE OF OUR BEST STOVES to you in just a day or two or, at the farthest, a few days from the date we receive your order, to make sure that the stove reaches you in perfect order, to remove any chance for breakage or damage, to insure your having very little freight charges to pay, we have arranged with the railroad companies to take these six highest grade ranges and base burners in all their different sizes through in solid cars from our foundry at Newark, Ohio, to our many warehouses throughout the United States at the lowest possible freight rate.

Our **WEHRLE MODEL** No. 20, Six-Hole Steel Range, illustrated and described on page 629.

Our **WEHRLE MODEL** No. 22, Six-Hole Steel Range on legs, as illustrated and described on page 634.

Our Reliable Well Known **ACME TRIUMPH** Six-Hole Steel Range, as illustrated and described on page 636.

Our **ACME CHARM** Six-Hole Steel Range on legs, as illustrated and described on page 638.

Our **WEHRLE MODEL** No. 30, New, Elegant, Big Six-Hole Cast Range, as illustrated and described on page 642.

Our World Wonder **ACME SUNBURST** Base Burner, as illustrated and described on page 650.

THESE SIX WONDERFUL STOVES,

THE GREATEST AND BEST MADE in the world, are carried in stock in warehouses in various parts of the United States, securely crated and ready for immediate shipment; so no matter where you live we can ship one of these six stoves from the point nearest you and thus get it to you in a very short time, with very little freight charges for you to pay. These six stoves we carry in stock and can ship to you at a moment's notice from the following points:

FARGO, N. DAK.
SIOUX FALLS, S. DAK.
ST. PAUL, MINN.
WATERLOO, IOWA.
DAVENPORT, IOWA.
MILWAUKEE, WIS.
ST. LOUIS, MO.
KANSAS CITY, MO.
OMAHA, NEB.
WICHITA, KANS.
NEWARK, OHIO.
HARRISBURG, PA.
ALBANY, N. Y.

HOW WE MAKE WONDERFULLY QUICK SHIPMENTS ON OUR OTHER STOVES

FROM OUR NEWARK, OHIO, FOUNDRY. Do not let the question of distance prevent you from ordering a stove or range from us. By reason of our owning and operating in Newark, Ohio, the largest stove foundry in the world, we have arranged with the railroad companies, because of the vast volume of business we give them, to ship every day throughout the year in solid carload lots to junction points. These solid carload lots go through by fast freight to junction points, from which individual shipments are promptly forwarded. At all these junction points there is a trained force of men and a system to dispatch the individual stove shipments promptly, and there will be no delay in getting the stove you order to you.

PLEASE REMEMBER that the only stoves we have stored in the different warehouses are named on this page and the only freight that you will have to pay is the carload shipping expense from our foundry at Newark, Ohio, to the warehouse nearest you, which is considerably less than the freight charges one has to pay when shipping one stove alone by freight, and, **in addition to this carload shipping expense,** you will also have to pay the small freight charge for the short haul from this warehouse to your nearest railroad station, and when you receive the stove you will find that the sum total freight charges will amount to considerably less than if the stove were shipped to you singly as one shipment from the foundry at Newark, Ohio.

Our **WEHRLE** MODEL No. 20, complete with reservoir and high closet, at $29.75 to $32.89, according to size.

Our **WEHRLE** MODEL No. 22, Six-Hole Steel Range on Legs, complete with reservoir and warming closet, at $29.87 to $32.92, according to size.

Our **ACME TRIUMPH** Six-Hole Steel Range, complete with reservoir and high closet, from $24.95 to $29.48, according to size.

Our **ACME CHARM** Six-Hole Steel Range, complete with reservoir and high closet, one size only, at $20.95.

Our **WEHRLE** MODEL No. 30, Big, Six-Hole, Full Nickeled, Cast Range on Legs, at $33.95 to $37.40, according to size.

Our World Wonder **ACME SUNBURST** Base Burner, at $23.95 to $30.68, according to size.

TO GIVE OUR CUSTOMERS AND FRIENDS LIVING SOUTH OF THE OHIO RIVER THE BENEFIT OF QUICK DELIVERY AND OUR VERY LOW FREIGHT RATE

WE HAVE ARRANGED TO SHIP DAILY IN CARLOAD LOTS to the leading gateways or junction points in the South our five highest grade ranges, the best ranges in the world.

Our **WEHRLE MODEL** No. 20, Six-Hole Full Nickeled Steel Range, as illustrated and described on page 629.
Our **WEHRLE MODEL** No. 22, Six-Hole Steel Range on Legs, as illustrated and described on page 634.
Our Reliable Well Known **ACME TRIUMPH** Six-Hole Steel Range, as illustrated and described on page 636.
Our **ACME CHARM** Six-Hole Steel Range on Legs, as illustrated and described on page 638.
Our **WEHRLE MODEL** No. 30, New, Elegant, Big Six-Hole Cast Range, as illustrated and described on page 642.

THESE SOLID CARLOAD LOTS of our highest grade ranges leave our foundry daily, and immediately upon arrival of these solid cars at the various gateways or junction points, the ranges are unloaded and handled by experienced freight men, and immediately dispatched to the

UNEQUALED IN MECHANICAL PERFECTION

WEHRLE MODEL No. 20

SIX-HOLE FULL NICKELED BLUE POLISHED STEEL RANGE,

$29.75 AND UP

THE HIGHEST GRADE — STEEL RANGE — MADE IN THE WORLD

BURNS ANY KIND OF FUEL, HARD OR SOFT COAL, WOOD, COKE OR CORN COBS.

CAST IRON LEFT END, GUARANTEED NOT TO WARP, BUCKLE OR BURN OUT.

GUARANTEED RUSTPROOF CAST IRON RESERVOIR CASING.

HOW WE CAME TO BUILD A STEEL RANGE TO SELL AS HIGH AS $29.75 AND UPWARD, according to size, and how it is possible to build a range so good and so perfect as to make it cost the customer $4.80 more than our now famous Acme Triumph Blue Polished Steel Range, heretofore the highest grade steel range made in America, to which hundreds of thousands of our satisfied customers who are now using our Acme Triumph Steel Range, illustrated and described on page 636, will cheerfully attest.

(Continued on next page.)

PRICES OF THE WEHRLE MODEL No. 20 SIX-HOLE STEEL RANGE, WITH HIGH WARMING CLOSET AND RESERVOIR.

Securely crated, delivered on cars at our foundry at Newark, Ohio, or from our warehouse very near you.   Prices do not include pipe or cooking utensils.   For cooking utensils see pages 461 to 466.   Made in six sizes as listed herewith.   See next page for Wehrle Model No. 20 Steel Range without reservoir and without warming closet.

Catalogue No.	Range No.	Size of Lids	Size of Oven, inches	Main Top Including Reservoir, inches	Height to Main Top, inches	Height of Warming Closet, in.	Size Pipe to Fit Collar, inches	Capacity of Reservoir, qts.	Shipping Weight, pounds	PRICE
22K10	7-16	7	16x21x14	45x28½	31	27	7	13½	520	$29.75
22K11	8-16	8	16x21x14	45x28½	31	27	7	13½	520	30.05
22K12	8-18	8	18x21x14	47x28½	31	27	7	17	535	31.27
22K13	9-18	9	18x21x14	47x28½	31	27	7	17	535	31.52
22K14	8-20	8	20x21x14	49x28½	31	27	7	22	555	32.60
22K15	9-20	9	20x21x14	49x28½	31	27	7	22	555	32.89

On all the above sizes the fire box is 8¾ inches wide, 8½ inches deep.   Its length for coal is 18 inches and for wood 26 inches.

READ THE NEXT FOUR PAGES CAREFULLY AND LEARN MORE ABOUT OUR WEHRLE MODEL No. 20 SIX-HOLE BLUE POLISHED STEEL RANGE.

REASONS WHY OUR ENTIRELY NEW WEHRLE MODEL No. 20 SIX-HOLE FULL NICKELED BLUE POLISHED STEEL RANGE HAS MORE EXCLUSIVE FEATURES AND IS THE HIGHEST GRADE STEEL RANGE MADE IN THE WORLD

$29 75 AND UPWARD

DETERMINED THAT THERE SHOULD ALWAYS COME FROM OUR STOVE FACTORY AT NEWARK, OHIO (The Wehrle Co.), the highest grade steel ranges and cast iron stoves it is possible to build, we asked ourselves the question, "Would it be possible to in any way improve the famous $24.95 Acme Triumph Steel Range?" Not only did we ask ourselves, but we put the question up to the highest stove authorities known to stove making, inventors, designers, moulders, pattern makers, etc., and without a single exception there came the response, "You are already making and selling in the Acme Triumph Steel Range the highest grade steel range made. Why attempt to make anything better?" Our reply in every instance has been, "Nothing is good enough if there is any possibility of improving it," and they came back with the question, "Is it possible to improve your Acme Triumph Range?" More than a year was spent at this work, looking for ways to improve our Acme Triumph, and while excepting only this, the Wehrle Model No. 20, which is offered at $29.75 and upward, with full equipment, the Acme Triumph, shown on page 636, is positively the highest grade steel range made in America; nevertheless, we have in this Wehrle Model No. 20, offered at $29.75 and upward, with full equipments, made some marked improvement over the world wide highest grade range made in America, the Acme Triumph.

WE HAVE GREATLY IMPROVED OUR ACME TRIUMPH in that we have brought out several new and valuable features in stove making. We have in this magnificent **WEHRLE MODEL No. 20** improved the design, shape, model and beauty over anything ever made. We have succeeded in getting a higher grade of sheet steel than has ever been used in steel range making. We have succeeded in having made for us a higher grade, thicker, heavier, and by far better asbestos lining, which insures better heat control, and for the purpose of

making parts that would in time wear out under ordinary conditions become practically everlasting. We have succeeded in introducing a special design **cast iron oven bottom**, which insures safe, even and quick baking and has proven the most valuable feature ever introduced in steel ranges and does away with every possibility of warping. While this feature is very well covered in our Acme Triumph Steel Range by our new special system of reinforcing, bolting and bracing with heavy cast cross section braces, which guarantees the oven bottom to remain level and not buckle, warp or sag—a point that in steel ranges of other makes has given some trouble; in short, we have studied all the methods of securing more heat and better baking at much less cost; we experimented with all the new arrangements of flues, dampers, grates, linings to direct the heat and selected the points just where we could get the best results, and in this new **WEHRLE MODEL No. 20** we can say without fear of contradiction that we have embodied more new and practical features than have ever been known in steel range construction.

A VERY VALUABLE FEATURE.

BY MEANS OF A SILVER NICKELED LIFTER as illustrated on page 631, the top or anchor plate directly over the fire can be easily raised and held in place by ratchets at three different heights. This exclusive feature, which has entirely done away with having to lay the fire by removing the lids and sliding them over the top, and which will be found most convenient and serve admirably for broiling steaks or chops or toasting bread, and is often used in place of the pouch feed for the purpose of evenly filling the fire box with coal or wood—this feature alone is worth everything to the party who uses the stove.

OTHER THINGS WE HAVE DONE TO MAKE THE WEHRLE MODEL THE FINEST RANGE IN THE WORLD.

WE HAVE GOTTEN OUT A SPECIAL THERMOMETER which is entirely out of the ordinary.

WE HAVE DEVELOPED A NEW SYSTEM for enameling our reservoir tanks and constructing our reservoir casing.

WE HAVE EXPERIMENTED AND FOUND THE WAY—at the expense of a most costly special automatic punching machine—to so punch and fit the heavy special steel parts as to make this stove absolutely airtight.

WE HAVE INTRODUCED a very special heavy cast iron flue back construction which can never burn or rust out.

WE HAVE INTRODUCED A DAMPER and fire control not approached in any other steel range made.

WE HAVE A SYSTEM BY WHICH THE OVEN IS HEATED EVENLY, by which the heat in the oven is controlled, which will always be indicated by our special high grade thermometer and will show, by comparison, a control of heat not approached by any other steel range made.

TO MAKE THE FREIGHT CHARGES VERY LOW and to get this WEHRLE

MODEL No. 20 Steel Range to you in just a day or two or, at the farthest, a few days after we receive your order, we have this WEHRLE MODEL No. 20 Steel Range, complete with reservoir and high closet, in all sizes as illustrated on page 629, securely crated and ready for immediate shipment from warehouses in the following cities:

FARGO, N. DAK.	ST. LOUIS, MO.
SIOUX FALLS, S. DAK.	KANSAS CITY, MO.
ST. PAUL, MINN.	OMAHA, NEB.
WATERLOO, IOWA.	WICHITA, KAN.
DAVENPORT, IOWA.	NEWARK, OHIO.
MILWAUKEE, WIS.	HARRISBURG, PENNA.
	ALBANY, N. Y.

HOW WE MAKE WONDERFULLY QUICK DELIVERY FROM A WAREHOUSE VERY NEAR YOU fully explained on page 628.

IN WORKING OUT ALL THESE IMPROVEMENTS, improvements not found in any other steel range of any other make, and following the fundamental policy of our house to place our stoves and ranges in the hands of our customers at actual cost of manufacture, plus our one small margin of profit, we deem it only right to give our customers the benefit of our facilities and advantages and offer this new **WEHRLE Model No. 20** at the heretofore unheard of price of $29.75 and upward, according to size, with full equipment as illustrated, including high warming closet and deep porcelain lined reservoir, and in asking you $29.75 for this range, only $4.80 more than our Acme Triumph Steel Range, which—excepting only this our Wehrle Model No. 20 as shown on page 629 and our Wehrle Model No. 22 as shown on page 634—is positively the highest grade steel range made in the world, we wish to explain that if you want the best steel range that money can buy, you will send us your order for this the **WEHRLE Model No. 20** and we will be only too glad to send it to you with the understanding and agreement that you can give it a **THIRTY DAYS' TRIAL,** during which time you can put it to every test and comparison, and if you do not say with us that it is by far the best steel range made, by far the best steel range you have ever seen, if you do not say that it is worth from $10.00 to $25.00 more than the range you can buy from your dealer at home or elsewhere for $50.00, you can return this **WEHRLE Model No. 20** Steel Range to us at our expense and we will immediately return your money, together with any freight charges paid by you.

WHAT IS MEANT BY A WEHRLE MODEL RANGE OR STOVE? Simply a standard of excellence imposed by Messrs. Wehrle on every range or stove built in our Newark, Ohio, foundry, and a name which means, always has meant and always will mean absolutely the best made in the world. The Wehrles' experience in stove and range making extends over a period of 40 years and they have always been looked upon as authority on stoves and ranges and commonly known among stove makers as "stove specialists." In all of these years they have never made a stove or range that they could not conscientiously recommend, and in presenting this new **WEHRLE MODEL No. 20,** made by the well known Wehrles in our foundry at Newark, Ohio (the largest stove foundry in the world), we know that we are offering our customers the handsomest and finest article of kitchen furniture ever placed before the American public.

UNEQUALED IN MECHANICAL PERFECTION.

GREATER PAINS WERE NEVER TAKEN with any range than with this **WEHRLE MODEL No. 20** to make it flawless in construction. Artists and designers with lifelong experience in designing and manufacturing stoves worked over it months and months in order that we might honestly claim that it is without an equal and positively the best made steel range in the world, and with the idea in mind to keep the quality high and the cost low, together with our unequaled facilities for making stoves in such enormous quantities, we have been enabled to reduce the manufacturing cost of this range to a point that is an agreeable surprise to us and we can offer this **new model** at the heretofore unheard of price of from $29.75 and upward, according to size.

THE ILLUSTRATION ON PRECEDING PAGE, REPRODUCED FROM AN ACTUAL PHOTOGRAPH, will give you some idea of the beauty of this range. It shows the range almost as plainly as viewing the range itself, and by carefully reading and following the general description on this and the next three pages you will learn exactly what you are going to get when you buy this range. You will learn why we are fully justified in making the statement that it is absolutely the best steel range made in the world. So sure are we that we have succeeded in making and bringing out the best made range in the world that, to protect ourselves against unscrupulous manufacturers and unscrupulous dealers who are at all times watching and awaiting an opportunity to copy and counterfeit an article of genuine merit, we have registered with the U. S. Patent Office at Washington, D. C., the designs, the patterns and the name "WEHRLE MODEL," and this name will at all times cover the best made steel range in the world and is an absolute guarantee that you get the finest, best and by far the handsomest range that it is possible to produce.

WE HAVE SEEN SOME OF OUR RANGES COPIED and photographed with the name but slightly changed, a complete steal, and presented to prospective stove buyers as a stove like the original and genuine made by us at our foundry at Newark, Ohio, and in order to protect and safeguard ourselves against such pirates and those people who are so low (both makers and sellers) that they will, in their efforts to deceive, pick the best thing in the world and make and offer their stolen and spurious counterfeit, we have copyrighted both name and design of our **WEHRLE MODEL** Stoves and Ranges.

IN THIS NEW WEHRLE MODEL No. 20,

the best made steel range in the world at $29.75 and upward, will be found the highest grade steel plate used by any other stove manufacturer. To secure the perfect and economical operation of a range it is essential that it should be airtight and this result can only be accomplished by riveting every joint in the entire construction. This is the way the WEHRLE Model No. 20 is built. Every piece of material that enters into the construction of this magnificent steel range, every process through which the various parts pass in our great foundry, is so closely inspected, so carefully designed that the WEHRLE Model No. 20 Six-Hole Blue Steel Range comes to you as a perfect steel range, a range miles and miles in advance over the average range offered at from two to three times the price we ask that there is no possible comparison between them.

FURTHERMORE, IT WILL INTEREST YOU TO KNOW that every piece of stove plate employed in the construction of this magnificent range goes through the selfsame careful and close inspection as the sheet steel, and if, perchance, a piece of casting with the slightest flaw or defect is detected, the entire piece goes to the scrap heap, and it will readily be seen that it is next to impossible for us to mount an imperfect piece of casting or stove plate in constructing our **WEHRLE Model No. 20 Six-Hole Blue Steel Range** or, in fact, any other of our ranges.

PRICES OF WEHRLE MODEL No. 20 STEEL RANGE WITHOUT RESERVOIR AND WITHOUT WARMING CLOSET.

IF WANTED WITHOUT WARMING CLOSET, deduct $3.00 from the prices listed on preceding page. When ordered without warming closet, this magnificent range is furnished with a handsomely designed tea rail, ornamented with two beautifully carved and highly polished silver nickeled swing shelves, on which to place teapot or other articles to be kept warm.

IF WANTED WITHOUT RESERVOIR, BUT WITH WARMING CLOSET, deduct $3.00 from prices listed on preceding page. When ordering without reservoir, the range is equipped with a handsome end shelf, which is easily bolted to the right end of the main top.

IF WANTED WITHOUT WARMING CLOSET AND WITHOUT RESERVOIR, deduct $6.00 from the prices listed on preceding page. When ordering without warming closet and without reservoir, the range is furnished with a handsomely designed tea rail, ornamented with two beautifully carved and highly polished silver nickeled swing shelves, on which to place teapot or other articles to be kept warm and with a handsome end shelf.

WATER FRONT for the Wehrle Model No. 20 Six-Hole Steel Range, extra, $2.50. Do not mistake water fronts for water reservoirs. These can easily be fitted into the fire box at any time by simply removing the front lining. Water fronts are only used where there is a water supply furnished with a constant pressure through pipes, which can only be obtained in towns and cities having water works or from an elevated pressure tank.

READ THIS, THE PRECEDING AND FOLLOWING PAGES VERY CAREFULLY

$29 75

AND LEARN THE MANY REASONS AND STRONG FEATURES WHICH MAKE OUR WEHRLE MODEL No. 20 SIX-HOLE BLUE POLISHED STEEL RANGE

THE BEST STEEL RANGE MADE IN THE WORLD

AND UPWARD

DETAILED DESCRIPTION OF OUR NEW WEHRLE MODEL No. 20

THE BODY of the Wehrle Model No. 20 Steel Range is made of Wellsville blue polished steel, the best to be had at any price. At one time it was called Russian iron. It is beautifully smooth and uniformly colored, and simply wiping it with a cloth serves to keep it clean. It is built strong and rigid, no seams or joints to rust out, permit leakage of ashes, or permit the escape of heat. The body is riveted with the best steel head rivets driven cold by hand, and it is constructed by skilled workmen from the world famous Wellsville polished steel, which is by far superior to a painted or enameled body such as is used by many manufacturers. A painted body has to be repainted, always looks gummy and unsanitary, turns brown, accumulates lint, dust, and can never be repaired successfully, whereas the genuine Wellsville polished blue steel as used in this, our Wehrle Model No. 20 Steel Range, is the best material obtainable, will not turn white, crack, chip or peel from the action of the fire

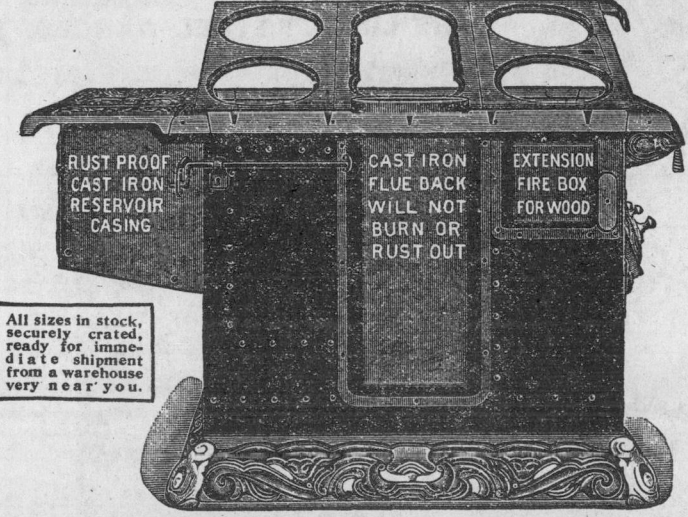

RUST PROOF CAST IRON RESERVOIR CASING

CAST IRON FLUE BACK WILL NOT BURN OR RUST OUT

EXTENSION FIRE BOX FOR WOOD

All sizes in stock, securely crated, ready for immediate shipment from a warehouse very near you.

and requires no blacking and very little attention. The sheets of steel are handled and re-handled in oil at the rolling mill at our foundry at Newark, Ohio, which preserves the beautiful color from spots and markings as it passes through the hands of the workmen. It also protects the beautiful polish from any possible damage by exposure to the weather in shipping, so that when you receive the range the blue polished steel is just as perfect as when it was first finished.

MAIN TOP, COVERS, CENTERS AND ANCHOR PLATES.

We take considerable pride in the care which we exercise in selecting raw materials which are to go into our Wehrle Model No. 20 Steel Range. In order to make these parts of the strongest iron that can be procured, each car of pig iron is tested by our expert chemist and accepted only if it meets the highest standard of quality. Since the vital parts of a range that really do the work and are exposed to the direct action of the fire are the fire box, main top, covers, centers and anchor plates, and these are the parts that must stand the test of wear and tear, exceptional effort for durability is made by us on every range we manufacture and the strictest attention to detail in workmanship is given to every part. Each of these parts is so cast that strength and rigidity is given where actual test and our long experience have shown us that strength is needed. By consulting the illustrations on this page you will readily see that from the construction of the main top, covers, centers and anchor plates it is next to impossible for them to warp, and you also observe the improved lift cover plate, which is of great convenience, and by a convenient adjustment you have the front top elevated so that you can broil, toast, poke the fire or put in coal and have the whole surface of the fire to work on without touching a lid lifter. These plates must not be compared with the cheap malleable iron main tops, covers, centers and anchor plates some manufacturers use in their so called "steel ranges." Malleable iron melts at a lower temperature than first class stove castings, and for this reason the latter (which we use on our Wehrle Model No. 20 Six-Hole Steel Range) are more durable for use where the parts come in direct contact with the fire. You will never have any trouble due to cracking or warping of these parts when you buy and use the Wehrle Model No. 20 Steel Range. Every piece of casting that we use is carefully tested. We guarantee that no mixture of any metals of any doubtful quality enters into the manufacture of our castings and that we produce only the best stove plate. In making the stove plate used in the construction of our Wehrle Model No. 20 Steel Range we make provision for the expansion and contraction of the iron which comes with the daily use of the range, and our castings retain their shape as long as the range is in use.

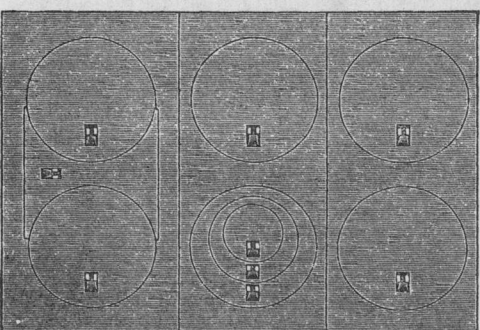

This illustration shows the smooth, perfect covers, centers and anchor plates.

THE ELEVATED TOP. By means of a silver nickeled lifter the top or anchor plate directly over the fire can be easily raised and held in place by ratchets at three different heights, as shown in illustration, a new feature which has entirely done away with having to lay the fire by removing the lids and sliding them around over the top of the range. The hinge or lift top enables the user to spread coal evenly over the fire, which means uniform heat and will be found very convenient and serves admirably for broiling steaks or chops or toasting bread. It is one of the exclusive features found only in our new 1908 Wehrle Model No. 20 Full Nickeled Steel Range.

ASBESTOS LINING. The asbestos insulation of a steel range is probably one of the most important features and to this detail we have given the most careful attention. The heavy, thick insulation extends entirely under the bottom of oven flue, preventing the heat from burning the floor and retaining the heat in the oven. When no reservoir is attached, it also extends entirely over the right end of the range and, with reservoir, the lower half only is insulated. The back and all flues are similarly insulated. We have taken particular care in doing this work. The liberal use of the asbestos lining protects and insures the steel body from either burning or rusting out. The asbestos being fireproof and a non-conductor, retains the heat, adds greatly to the life of the range, adds wonderfully to its baking qualities, makes it easy to control and an economical fuel consumer.

COAL FEED POUCH AND BROILER DOOR. Particular notice should be taken of this new invention and device of entirely new design, the pouch feed and broiler door, which is hinged on the left end of all sizes and styles of our Wehrle Model No. 20 Six-Hole Steel Range. By referring to the large illustration on page 629 you will observe that it provides a capacious coal feed pouch with an always cold lift on cover or door which gives us a combination coal feed and broiler door at the same time. Fresh fuel may be placed on the fire through the broiler or feed door without disturbing what is cooking on the top of the range. Lift the door and a broiler may be inserted through the opening and you can easily "broil to a turn." All the fumes of the broiler are carried up the smoke flue while the steak or chops broiled over the bed of red hot coals remain sweet and wholesome. This combination pouch feed and broiler door extends downward to the draft registers and is part of the same stove plate casting and is fitted with a check draft to control and regulate the fire. There is no japanning or enamel to burn off and it requires no more attention to keep it in beautiful condition than do the main top, covers and centers.

Elevated top makes broiling a pleasure.

GRADUATED LID OR NEST COVER.

Every Wehrle Model No. 20 Steel Range with the exception of size 7-16 is fitted with five solid covers and the one nest cover or graduated lid, as shown in the illustration. This is a very convenient little device, as the varying sizes of the openings in the cover will be found very useful.

THE DRAFT OR POKER DOOR.

At the left of the range and directly below the feed and broiler door will be found the draft or poker door. It is made unusually long, so that it supplies equally to all parts of the fire, has two check registers, insuring a perfect bed of fire with no dead corners. By means of a turnkey the entire door can be dropped, giving easy access to the grate and enabling the user to poke the fire through this opening if so desired.

THE WOOD FEED DOOR.

Careful examination of many of the steel ranges now offered for sale will show that most manufacturers are careless about fitting doors where they come in contact with the frames. This is, of course, an exceedingly important point, for a careless fit means a continual flow of cold air to the interior of the stove. If this occurs above the fire box it acts as a check on the fire and makes quick baking almost impossible, owing to the fact that the fire cannot be made to produce the intense heat. From the illustrations of this range you will immediately notice that each door is carefully ground and fitted perfectly tight, touching on every edge, and when closed the doors are held securely in place by latches and are very easy to operate. The door is substantially mounted with hinge pins, and is furnished with an Alaska cold wire silver nickeled knob. It swings to the left and is lined so as to prevent the ashes from piling against the inside and falling to the floor when the door is opened. From the illustrations of the range you can see that the door is of beautiful design. The nickeled panel on the outside is a separate silver nickeled casting, the process of nickeling being so perfect that discoloring by the action of the fire is impossible.

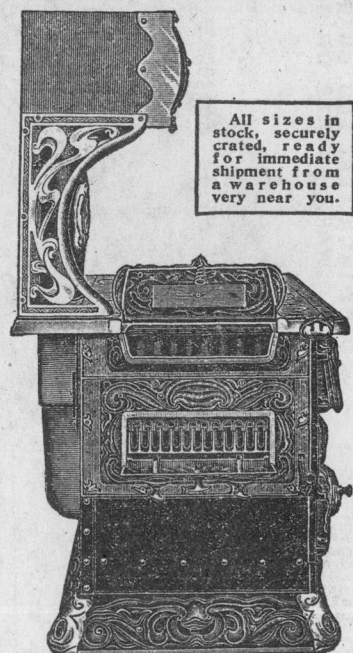

All sizes in stock, securely crated, ready for immediate shipment from a warehouse very near you.

View showing the substantial pouch feed, draft or poker door and full cast left end.

TURN TO THE NEXT PAGE AND LEARN MORE ABOUT OUR WEHRLE MODEL No. 20 RANGE

THE FINEST STEEL RANGE ON LEGS IN THE WORLD

WEHRLE MODEL No. 22

SIX-HOLE FULL NICKELED BLUE STEEL —RANGE—

$29⁸⁷
AND UP

ON LEGS. YOU CAN SWEEP UNDER IT.

IT HAS NO COMPARISONS, NO SUPERIORS, FEW EQUALS IN THE LINE OF STEEL RANGES.

BURNS ANY KIND OF FUEL, HARD OR SOFT COAL, WOOD, COKE OR CORN COBS.

CAST IRON LEFT END, GUARANTEED NOT TO WARP, BUCKLE OR BURN OUT.

GUARANTEED RUSTPROOF CAST IRON RESERVOIR CASING.

THIS MAGNIFICENT MASSIVE SIX-HOLE STEEL RANGE is another one of the new WEHRLE productions. It is their new steel range on legs—the very latest, best and finest—a steel range conceived, planned, designed, worked out, trimmed and finished as a result of our suggestion to the Wehrles to give us something entirely new and something we could offer our customers far, far in advance of anything the market has afforded. This idea the Wehrles took hold of about a year ago and months and months have been spent in the preparation of drawings, designs, pattern making, model building, trying and testing, and this Wehrle Model No. 22 Handsome Six-Hole Steel Range is the result. It is the perfection of their plans and our ideas of the very finest steel range on legs possible to produce. It is built up from the floor. You can sweep under it. It has no comparisons, no superiors, few equals in the line of steel ranges. It is such a range as has been seen in but few sections of the country and in but a few of the largest special stove stores in metropolitan cities do they show and sell steel ranges of the quality, grade or rank of this, our Wehrle Model No. 22 full nickeled blue steel range.

IF WANTED WITHOUT WARMING CLOSET, BUT WITH RESERVOIR, deduct $3.00 from prices listed. When ordered without warming closet this magnificent range is furnished with handsome designed tea rail, ornamented with two beautifully carved and highly polished silver nickeled swing shelves on which to place teapot or other articles to be kept warm.

IF WANTED WITHOUT RESERVOIR BUT WITH WARMING CLOSET, deduct $3 00 from prices listed. When ordered without reservoir, the range is equipped with a handsome end shelf which is easily bolted to the right end of

IF WANTED WITHOUT WARMING CLOSET AND WITHOUT RESERVOIR, deduct $6.00 from the prices listed. When ordered without warming closet and without reservoir the range is furnished with a handsomely designed tea rail, ornamented with two beautifully carved and highly polished silver nickeled swing shelves on which to place teapot or other articles to be kept warm, and with a handsome end shelf.

WATER FRONT FOR THE WEHRLE MODEL No. 22 STEEL RANGE, extra, $2.50. Do not mistake water fronts for water reservoirs. Water fronts can easily be fitted into the fire box at any time by simply removing the front lining. Water fronts are used only where there is a water supply furnished with a constant pressure through pipes, which can be obtained only in towns and cities having water works or from an elevated pressure tank.

PRICE LIST OF OUR WEHRLE MODEL No. 22 SIX-HOLE FULL NICKELED BLUE STEEL RANGE, with High Closet and Porcelain Lined Reservoir. Prices do not include pipe or cooking utensils. For cooking utensils see pages 461 to 466. Strongly crated, ready for shipment from a warehouse near you or from our foundry at Newark, Ohio.

Catalogue No.	Stove No.	Size of Lids, In.	Size of Oven, inches	Main Top, including Reservoir, in.	Height to Main Top	Height of Warming Closet, in.	Size of Pipe to Fit Collar	Capacity of Reservoir, qts.	Ship'g Wt. without Resv'r, lbs	Ship'g Wt. with Resv'r, lbs	PRICE
22K70	7-16	7	16x21x14	45x28½	31 in.	27	7 in.	13½	520	570	$29.87
22K71	8-16	8	16x21x14	45x28½	31 in.	27	7 in.	13½	520	570	30.17
22K72	8-18	8	18x21x14	47x28½	31 in.	27	7 in.	17	535	585	31.27
22K73	9-18	8	18x21x14	47x28½	31 in.	27	7 in.	17	535	585	31.52
22K74	8-20	9	20x21x14	49x28½	31 in.	27	7 in.	22	555	605	32.60
22K75	9-20	9	20x21x14	49x28½	31 in.	27	7 in.	22	555	605	32.92

On all the above sizes the fire box is 8¾ inches wide and 8½ inches deep. Its

REMEMBER, THIS HANDSOME STEEL RANGE, WEHRLE MODEL No. 22 IS OFFERED ON THE SAME LIBERAL TERMS THAT WE OFFER ALL OUR STOVES

WE HAVE BROUGHT OUT a better and higher priced steel range on legs than anything we have heretofore offered. Nothing is too good for our customers. Our trade includes the very finest families in the country. We number our customers in the biggest cities as well as the smallest villages. We find there is a constant demand among this class of trade and our customers for the best articles in nearly every line. While our Acme Charm, a low priced steel range on legs, gives the greatest satisfaction, we feel that our trade will appreciate, something still finer, something very fine, very much better than the ordinary, a range on newer lines, better construction, better finish, more elaborate and finer detail work, a steel range way out of the ordinary class, one in a class by itself; and this is what we have produced in the Wehrle Model No. 22 Six-Hole Steel Range. It is a steel range for our finest trade, for those who appreciate the very best, and to such we cannot recommend it too highly.

PLEASE REMEMBER we ship our WEHRLE MODEL No. 22 Blue Polished Steel Range, complete as illustrated, from a warehouse very near you. The freight charges will be very low and you will get the range in a very few days after we receive your order.

SEND US YOUR ORDER FOR THE SIZE WANTED, enclosing our price. By referring to the price list at the bottom of opposite page you will note that catalogue No. 22K70 range, No. 7-16, is the smallest WEHRLE MODEL No. 22 Steel Range we make. It has six 7-inch cooking holes and a 16-inch oven, and before making your selection BE SURE to refer to the table of sizes, and select a range large enough to answer your requirements and fit your cooking utensils. When the stove has been received, take it home, set it up and use it for thirty days; put it to all possible tests, let any judge give his opinion; and if you are not satisfied in every way that you have received a range value that cannot be duplicated at home or elsewhere even at double our price, you can return the range to us at our expense and we will promptly return your money and all the freight charges you have paid. With every range we send our written binding guarantee, protecting you against any possible defect, but we don't need to guarantee our WEHRLE MODEL No. 22 Steel Range, for it is a range that cannot possibly have any defects.

DETAILED DESCRIPTION OF WEHRLE MODEL No. 22 SIX-HOLE BLUE POLISHED STEEL RANGE

THE FINEST STEEL RANGE MADE IN THE WORLD. YOU CAN SWEEP UNDER IT

THIS WEHRLE MODEL No. 22 Steel Range is a companion stove to our other WEHRLE MODEL No. 20 Steel Range illustrated and described on page 629. We have followed the same patterns, the same idea of building, in fact, we have brought out a range built along the same lines as the WEHRLE MODEL No. 20, embodying all the strong features. We are using the same high grade blue polished steel in building the body, a higher grade than has ever been used in steel range making and by far a better grade and higher quality, thicker and heavier asbestos lining.

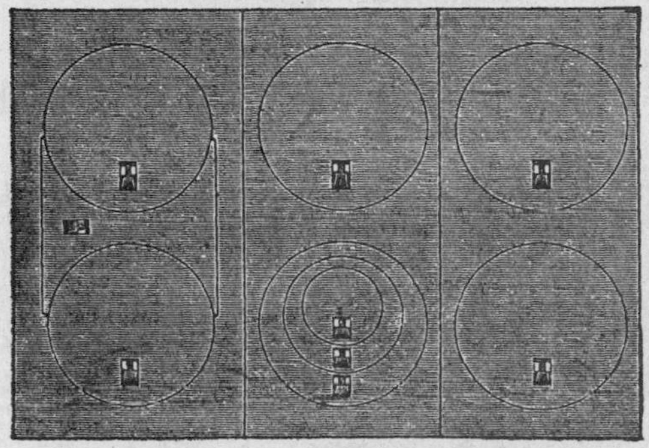

THE MAIN TOP, COVERS, CENTERS AND ANCHOR PLATES. **These castings are made from a carefully prepared mixture of the best pig iron for the purpose** known and are the best castings to resist the action of fire that it is possible to produce and are constructed in such a manner as to prevent warping and cracking. The covers and centers will outlast three or four sets that are made out of ordinary gray iron.

ASBESTOS SHEETS are used where necessary both **as a protection against overheating the exposed parts,** and also to retain heat and radiate it gradually into the oven where it is needed.

THE ELEVATED TOP. By means of a silver nickeled lifter the top or anchor plate **directly over the fire can be easily raised and held in place by ratchets at three different heights.** This will be found an ideal arrangement for laying the fire and also enables the user to spread coal evenly over the fire and serve admirably for broiling steaks or chops or toasting bread, as illustrated on page 631.

COAL FEED POUCH AND BROILER DOOR. By referring to the large illustration on **the opposite page you will observe we provide a capacious coal feed pouch, with an always cold lift on cover of door, which gives us a combination coal feed and broiler door at the same time.** Fresh fuel may be placed on the fire through the broiler or feed door without disturbing what is cooking on top of the range.

THE WOOD FEED DOOR **is extra large, swings to the left, making it very convenient for firing.** It is lined so as to prevent the ashes from piling against the inside and falling to the floor when the door is opened. The nickel panel on the outside is a separate silver nickeled casting—the process of nickeling being so perfect that discoloring by the action of the fire is impossible. The door is perfectly fitted, touching at every edge, and is securely held in place. There is no desirable feature that you will find in any other high grade range that you will not find in this.

MADE WITH A LARGE FIRE BOX, WITH ASH CHUTE BELOW **which conducts the ashes direct to the ash pan; large wire bailed ash pan; coal feed pouch or broiler door;** elevated top for feeding the fire, broiling or toasting; big wood feed door; duplex grate; large reservoir tank; an improved and by far the best oven construction; highest grade oven door thermometer; the best cast flue construction; special poker door; special cast iron reservoir casing; strongest lids, tops, covers, centers and anchor plates; **everything about this magnificent range is the very best.**

LET US INDUCE YOU TO SEND US YOUR ORDER
ENCLOSING OUR PRICE

FOR THIS OUR NEW WEHRLE MODEL NO. 22 STEEL RANGE

So that we can get it to you quickly and that you will have very low freight charges to pay, we have stored this range in all six sizes, complete with full equipment, as illustrated, in warehouses in the following cities:

FARGO, N. DAK. MILWAUKEE, WIS. WICHITA, KAN.
SIOUX FALLS, S. DAK. ST. LOUIS, MO. NEWARK, OHIO
ST. PAUL, MINN. KANSAS CITY, MO. HARRISBURG, PA.
WATERLOO, IOWA OMAHA, NEB. ALBANY, N. Y.
DAVENPORT, IOWA

JUST SELECT THE SIZE RANGE YOU WANT, enclose our price, and the day we receive your order, that day we will send a letter to our warehouse, the one nearest to you, and instruct them to ship the range to you immediately. The man at the warehouse will deliver the range at once to the railroad company at the town in which our warehouse is located and from there it will take only a day or two at the longest for the range to reach you at your nearest railroad station. There is no possible chance for delay. YOU CANNOT BE DISAPPOINTED. You will get the range in just a few days. It is sure to reach you safely and in perfect condition. We guarantee this.

WE HAVE ARRANGED WITH THE RAILROAD COMPANIES to take this range **through for us in solid carload lots from our foundry to our many warehouses all over the country at the lowest possible freight rate.** We give you the benefit of all this carload shipping rate and expense and the only additional freight you will have to pay when you receive the range is, the very small local freight charges from our warehouse to your railroad station, but the sum total of freight charges you will have to pay when you receive the range will not, as a rule, amount to more than one-half to two-thirds the freight charges you would have to pay if the range were shipped to you singly as one shipment from our foundry at Newark, Ohio, to your railroad station. After paying this freight, take the range home, set it up, start the fire and give it a thorough test; notice the amount of fuel consumed, compare it with other ranges you have ever used—the large oven, the beautiful indispensable full standard steel warming closet, the lift or hinge cover so easily elevated and adjusted for broiling, toasting, or laying the fire, the large reservoir tank, the dampers, the draft, the general heat control; in short, observe the entire construction and general appearance of the range and how, in every respect, it outclasses and outmatches any range you have ever seen; give it a thorough test for thirty days; test it out in your own way; compare it with ranges sold in your section of the country at more than double our price, and if you do not find it to be the most satisfactory range that you could get from your dealer at home or elsewhere at double our price—in short, if for any reason whatsoever you are dissatisfied, write a letter to us at Chicago and tell us that you want to return the range and we will send you instructions how to return the range and immediately refund your money, together with all the freight charges you may have paid. THE TEST WON'T COST YOU ONE CENT.

WE MAKE THIS LIBERAL 30-DAY FREE TRIAL OFFER because we want you **to convince yourself of the superiority of this magnificent WEHRLE MODEL No. 22 Six-Hole Full Nickeled Blue Polished Steel Range, through an actual test and not because of any statement that we make.** No other stove manufacturer or dealer dares to make an offer like this. We do it because we know that this WEHRLE MODEL Steel Range is the best steel range made in the world and will stand the test. If it could not stand the test, we could not afford to make this statement or send it out on thirty days' trial, because then every one would come back to us.

THE DUPLEX ANTI-CLINKER GRATE and our new, improved, perfect, easy operating grate switch or shaking device is the exact same construction as illustrated and described on page 632 and used on our WEHRLE MODEL No. 20 Six-Hole Steel Range.

THE LARGE ASH PAN. Every range is equipped **with a large steel ash pan with bail as illustrated.** It holds all the ashes that should be produced in twenty-four hours. The ash guards are so placed over the ash pan that all ashes necessarily drop into it. The ash pit door and all dampers and checks are fitted accurately, which makes the regulating of the fire an easy operation.

CAST IRON FLUE BACK. **This feature of our WEHRLE MODEL No. 22 Six-Hole Steel Range is made of cast iron and we guarantee it will not give out in twenty-five years' use.** Many ranges are made with light sheet iron or sheet steel flue backs, which will not last to exceed two or three years, for the reason that the creosote and condensation that accumulates in this flue back from the smoke pipe and chimney eats out and perforates sheet steel in a short time. Our all cast flue back, made in one piece (as shown in illustration on page 631), will never rust or rot out like steel flue backs.

THE FIRE BOX of this WEHRLE MODEL, No. 22 Steel Range **is made of the best grade of gray iron, which is the best for the purpose.** We use no scrap iron and thus can guarantee them to be the most durable made. It is the right material, the right size, right shape and right weight to give good and faithful service. The linings are heavy and corrugated and protected by an air space behind them.

CLEAN-OUT CHUTE **is located underneath the oven door.** It is good size so the space under the oven can be cleaned out thoroughly and quickly. The PANEL covering the clean-out chute is handsomely nickeled, easily removed and adjusted.

THE DAMPER. **The direct draft damper mounted on the outside of the range does not come in contact with the fire;** consequently cannot burn out or warp. It is conveniently located and is operated from the front of the stove, thus avoiding the necessity of leaning over the hot stove, as would be necessary if the damper handle were near the smoke pipe.

Quick Heating Reservoir and Damper Construction.

RESERVOIR CASING. **Every part of our reservoir casing is made of the best cast iron stove plate,** is of extremely handsome rococo design and beautifully ornamented with handsome silver nickeled medallion. We guarantee it never to rust or burn out. A depression in the bottom of the casing receives and holds all condensation until it is absorbed by the heat. Steel or sheet iron reservoir casings, used on ranges by many manufacturers, are not found to be practical, for they soon corrode and rust out from creosote and moisture.

Large Porcelain Lined Water Tank with Art Nouveau Covers.

SPECIAL AND IMPROVED RESERVOIR CONSTRUCTION.

THE RESERVOIR TANK **is of large capacity, best porcelain lined, easily kept clean and easily lifted out,** a feature that we feel sure will be appreciated by every housekeeper.

THE RESERVOIR CAPACITY **of the WEHRLE MODEL No. 22 Steel Range is from 13½ to 22 quarts, according to size.** By turning the reservoir damper, heat is thrown under the reservoir (as shown in illustration), heating the water boiling hot. The two reservoir covers are of the Art Nouveau pattern, beautiful design to harmonize with the general pattern of the range.

THE CAST IRON OVEN BOTTOM. **This is another new and original feature to be found in WEHRLE MODEL Ranges only.** Our many tests and long experience have proven the many advantages of a cast iron oven bottom. Cast iron being by far more porous than steel, has about 75 per cent greater radiating efficiency, and by using the highest grade cast stove plate for the oven bottom in this WEHRLE MODEL Steel Range, we get much more heat in the oven with by far less fuel and get it more quickly and will give an even and uniform heat in all of its parts, making it bake evenly over its entire surface. It will positively never warp or buckle.

THE OVEN DOOR. **The oven door is handsomely carved, silver nickel plated, drops flush with the oven bottom,** thus forming an extension shelf, which makes it possible to draw out and turn a roast without having to lift it. **Attention is called to the silver nickeled oven door handle,** it not only being ornamented and beautifully silver nickeled, but is extra long, making it very convenient in opening and closing the door. It is extra heavy and with our improved catch it holds the door firmly to the body of the range and is guaranteed to remain as cool and comfortable to the touch as it is beautiful to the sight.

OUR DEPENDABLE OVEN DOOR THERMOMETER **is the only absolute, positive means by which an oven can be regulated.** The exact same thermometer used in our WEHRLE MODEL No. 20 Steel Range, illustrated and described on page 632.

THE LARGE ROOMY BLUE POLISHED WARMING CLOSET WITH ROLLING FRONT. **This equipment extends along the full length of the range body and has become an almost indispensable attachment to this article of kitchen furniture.** It is just the proper height for the average person to easily reach. It has a roll front door, which rolls back like the front of a roll top desk, entirely out of the way, taking up no room and permitting the whole of the interior of the closet to be exposed, making a convenient and indispensable receptacle. Highly polished silvered nickeled bands ornament the front and sides and the warming closet door is so carefully counterbalanced that it works with ease.

TEAPOT HOLDERS. **To the right and left of the high closet pipe are handsomely silver nickeled teapot holders.**

GAS ATTACHMENT, as illustrated on page 633, can be furnished with any size of our **WEHRLE MODEL No. 22 Six-Hole Steel Range when ordered without reservoir.** This convenient attachment consists of one giant and simmering burner and one regular burner, making two distinct cooking places with excellent air mixers. The size of the top of gas attachment is 12x21 inches. Easily connected with gas supply by rubber tubing or iron pipe. If baking is desired with gas, our drop door portable steel oven illustrated and described on page 662, placed over the burners will prove very effective and economical. We can furnish sizes of this WEHRLE MODEL No. 22 Steel Range with gas attachment, the exact same but without reservoir, at the same prices listed on page 634. When ordering this attachment be sure to state whether you use natural or manufactured gas. Attachment cannot be used with gasoline or acetylene gas. **Range with gas attachment can be shipped from Newark, Ohio, only.**

IMPROVED ACME CHARM SIX-HOLE STEEL RANGE

REDUCED IN PRICE.

$15.95

IT'S ON LEGS! BUILT UP FROM THE FLOOR. BURNS ANY KIND OF FUEL, hard coal, soft coal, coke, wood or corn cobs. In the front rank. The latest and best Steel Range on legs on the market.

$15.95 IS OUR VERY LOW PRICE AND UPWARD, ACCORDING TO EQUIPMENT. for the Acme Charm Six-Hole Steel Range without reservoir and warming closet, but with our dependable oven thermometer, an equipment found to be very desirable and satisfactory to answer all requirements for those who do not care to have the convenience of a large reservoir tank or a convenient warming closet.

$20.95 is the remarkably low price for our Big ACME CHARM SIX-HOLE STEEL RANGE, complete with reservoir and warming closet and oven door thermometer, exactly as illustrated. The lowest price ever heard of for a very fine steel range on legs. Never before has such a low price been put on such a big steel range on legs that comes anywhere near the Acme Charm in quality. This style of range, the Acme Charm on legs, built up from the floor; you can sweep under and keep the floor clean (every housewife will appreciate this feature), has only been made by us and catalogued by us for the past year. It is just one year in our catalogue, and it is astonishing how popular it has become. Never before have we introduced a steel range that has proven itself such a big seller. The Acme Charm has taken hold wonderfully. A large share of all our range orders call for the Acme Charm. It has jumped in one year into the front rank of our best sellers, and the sales are increasing daily. An Acme Charm once in a household is sure to sell another. It's a constantly increasing demand, a regular endless chain of orders for our big Acme Charm Six-Hole Steel Range.

SO POPULAR has our Acme Charm Six-Hole Steel Range (complete, as illustrated) become that we have arranged to keep an enormous stock of the new, improved and latest style always on hand in different cities throughout the country, so that we can give our customers prompt service and quick delivery. We have this range complete, as illustrated, stored in warehouses in the various cities mentioned on the opposite page, and if you order an Acme Charm Steel Range complete, as illustrated, for $20.95, it will be shipped from the nearest warehouse and reach you in just a day or two.

OUR NEW ACME CHARM embodies every desirable feature and is made throughout of the very best material, exhibiting the finest workmanship; in every way the handsomest and most substantial new style "steel range on legs" ever produced, which tends to make the art of cooking a pleasure.

CAST IRON LEFT END. Guaranteed not to warp, buckle or burn out.

THIS ILLUSTRATION shows the stove with complete equipment, rustproof cast iron reservoir casing, deep porcelain lined reservoir, warming closet and dependable oven thermometer, all complete, $20.95.

Prices do not include pipe or cooking utensils.

Made with entire cast iron left end and hearth, preventing ashes from spilling when removed. Nothing to warp or burn out. Furnished with full size removable ash pan.

GUARANTEED RUSTPROOF CAST IRON RESERVOIR CASING.

A RANGE OF QUALITY.

Combined in the construction of this, our improved Acme Charm Six-Hole Steel Range, are more modern ideas, more special features, all the latest improvements of practical value to steel ranges— the best, most substantial construction throughout. The oven is a perfect baker. In short, it has more points of general merit than are found in ranges sold by others at double our price. The Body is made from Wood's cold rolled open hearth steel, the very best we can buy; the main top, covers and centers are made from the highest grade Birmingham pig iron, and are constructed to stand hard usage; the Oven Door is evenly balanced, drops flush with the oven, forming a convenient shelf; the Fire Box, Duplex Grate and Flue Construction are built for economy in the consumption of fuel; the Deep Ash Pit, the large Wire Bailed Ash Pan, large Pouch Feed Door with Alaska nickel wire handle, Cast Iron Flue Back or smoke box, securely braced Oven Bottom, High Closet with roll top door handsomely nickeled handle and ornament, Full Cast Left End guaranteed not to warp or buckle; our Genuine Oven Door Thermometer and many other strong features, all go to make it the biggest stove value you have ever seen, if it is not all and even more than we claim for it, and if you are not fully convinced that you have made a big saving of money, you can return the big range to us at our expense of freight charges both ways and we will immediately return your money.

Price, complete, with **RESERVOIR, WARMING CLOSET** and **OVEN DOOR THERMOMETER, as shown** in illustration, $20.95.

THIS STOVE IS No. 8-19. The oven is 18x20¾x12 inches; has six No. 8 cooking holes; top cooking surface, with reservoir extension, is 28¾x42¾ inches; height from floor to main top, 30 inches; distance from main top to top of warming closet is 26½ inches, total height, including closet, 56½ inches. The fire box is 8½ inches wide and 5½ inches deep. Its length for coal is 18 inches; for wood, 24 inches. Capacity of reservoir, 17 quarts. See page 627 for water fronts.

ALL OUR STEEL RANGES ARE SHIPPED. You have only to put on the pipe, when it is ready for fire, the same as if you were moving an old stove from one room to another.

Water fronts for the Acme Charm Steel Range, $2.50. complete ready to set up with all loose parts packed inside.

LET US HAVE YOUR ORDER for this big Six-Hole Acme Charm Steel Range, complete with reservoir and warming closet and oven door thermometer, at the astonishingly low price of $20.95, enclosing this amount with your order, addressed direct to Sears, Roebuck & Co., Chicago, Ill. The range will go to you direct from a warehouse very near you, or our foundry at Newark, Ohio, without any delay, with the understanding and agreement that if it is not the biggest stove value you have ever seen, if it is not all and even more than we claim for it, and if you are not fully convinced that you have made a big saving of money, you can return the big range to us at our expense of freight charges both ways and we will immediately return your money.

MADE IN ONE SIZE ONLY, AS LISTED BELOW.

		Shipping weight
No. 22K190 Price for range complete, with reservoir and warming closet. weight, 433 pounds	$20.95	
No. 22K191 Price for range with reservoir, but without warming closet. weight, 365 pounds	$18.00	
No. 22K192 Price for range with warming closet, but without reservoir. weight, 350 pounds	$19.00	
No. 22K193 Price for square top range, without reservoir or warming closet. weight, 295 pounds	$15.95	

READ THE DETAILED DESCRIPTION OF OUR
IMPROVED ACME CHARM
SIX-HOLE STEEL RANGE

IT'S ON LEGS--BUILT UP FROM THE FLOOR

$15.95

READ WHAT WE ARE DOING TO MAKE WONDERFULLY QUICK DELIVERY ON THIS

OUR IMPROVED ACME CHARM SIX-HOLE STEEL RANGE

Complete, as illustrated on the opposite page, from the following cities:

FARGO, N. DAK.	DAVENPORT, IOWA.	KANSAS CITY, MO.	NEWARK, OHIO.
SIOUX FALLS, S. DAK.	MILWAUKEE, WIS.	OMAHA, NEB.	HARRISBURG, PA.
ST. PAUL, MINN.	ST. LOUIS, MO.	WICHITA, KANS.	ALBANY, N. Y.	WATERLOO, IOWA.

AND UPWARD ACCORDING TO EQUIPMENT.

REDUCED IN PRICE

TO MAKE THE FREIGHT CHARGES VERY LOW and insure QUICK DELIVERY, we have this, our newest ACME CHARM SIX-HOLE STEEL RANGE, complete with reservoir and high closet, on hand in a warehouse in all of the cities mentioned above, securely crated and ready for immediate shipment and in perfect condition. To insure your having very little freight charges to pay, we have arranged to first ship this NEW ACME CHARM SIX-HOLE STEEL RANGE, complete with reservoir and warming closet, in solid carload lots direct to the various points named, receiving from the railway company the very lowest carload freight rate, so that you can go to your postmaster, R. F. D. carrier, express agent or banker, and get a money order drawn in your favor, enclosing $20.95 in your letter, addressed direct to SEARS, ROEBUCK & CO., Chicago, Ill., and we will immediately send your order by special delivery to our stove warehouse, the one nearest you, and order the stove shipped to your railroad station on your order at once.

WE KNOW IT LEAVES THE WAREHOUSE NEAR YOU IN PERFECT CONDITION. We know that it will reach you in from a few hours to a day or two at the most from the time it leaves the warehouse, and when you do get it, you will only have the carload rate to pay from our foundry at Newark, Ohio, to the warehouse nearest you (which is usually half the freight charges that one has to pay when but one range is shipped by freight). In addition to this very low carload rate from the foundry to the warehouse near you, you will also have to pay very small freight charges for the short haul from this warehouse to your nearest railroad station, but the total freight you have to pay when you receive the range will, as a rule, amount to much less than the freight charges you would have to pay if the stove were shipped to you singly as one shipment from the foundry at Newark, Ohio, to your railroad station.

DURABILITY. Our Big Acme Charm Six-Hole Steel Range, with full equipment of reservoir and warming closet, is extra heavy and will outweigh and outclass and outlast steel ranges sold by other dealers at double our price. Not only the steel body, but all the castings, main top, centers and fire box linings are built to last. For illustration, note the heavy cast iron flue back at the back of range, through which all products of combustion pass to chimney. Examine other makes of ranges and you will generally find this flue back of sheet steel. This material will not stand the strain and will soon rust out. The high principles of honest workmanship, the dependable high grade cast reservoir casing and the advanced and original ideas of design and art of stove building have made this range construction famous as a thoroughly dependable, powerful fuel saving range, which brings to the user every luxury and the self same pleasure enjoyed by those possessing a range at double the price we ask for our big Acme Charm, complete with reservoir and warming closet.

30 DAYS' FREE TRIAL. Send us your order, enclosing our price of $20.95 for the big Acme Charm Six-Hole Steel Range, complete with Reservoir, Warming Closet and Oven Door Thermometer, or $15.95 without the full equipment of reservoir and warming closet, but with oven thermometer, and the big range will be shipped immediately direct to your station from our warehouse nearest you, with the full understanding and agreement that you may use the big range in your own home for thirty days, during which time you may put it to every possible test that may be devised, examine it and observe its long rangy lines, cook, bake and roast on it, then you will fully appreciate why Our Big Acme Charm

Six-Hole Steel Range is without a peer among ranges selling at double the prices we ask.

THE BODY. The most important part of our steel range is the body. The body of our Acme Charm is built like a boiler and made from Wood's cold rolled open hearth steel, the very best that we can buy, strongly put together with wrought rivets and bands, reinforced at every part. The body is given a high black finish. It is constructed by skilled workmen from heavy steel, which is rigid, airtight and durable; no seams or joints to rust out, leak ashes, or permit the escape of heat. Has full cast iron left end. Guaranteed not to warp, buckle or burn out.

ASBESTOS LINING. All parts of the steel body exposed to direct action of the fire are lined with asbestos, particular care being taken in doing this work. This protects and insures the steel body from either burning or rusting out. The asbestos being fireproof and a nonconductor retains the heat, adds greatly to the life of the stove, adds wonderfully to its baking possibilities, makes it easy to control and makes an economical fuel consumer.

HIGH WARMING CLOSET. The large, commodious roll top closet and shelf are made of cold rolled sheet steel, beautifully shaped and handsomely finished. The closet and shelf have highly polished nickel handle and bands and the closet door is so carefully counterbalanced that it works very easily, the weight of the hand being sufficient to open it. It is trimmed with nickel steel bands along the front, as shown in illustration. The teapot holders to the left and right are handsomely nickeled and conveniently arranged.

MAIN TOP, COVERS AND CENTERS. The sectional main top and centers are cut and braced in exactly the same manner as our highest grade ranges, and are constructed to stand hard usage for many years and to prevent cracking from excessive heat. We furnish this range with six 8-inch lids, including one graduated or sectional lid, made from the best stove plate. Has long cut center supported by posts.

FIRE BOX. The fire box is of large size and correctly proportioned to the size of flue so as to give the best results for a minimum amount of fuel consumed, and is easily adapted for the consumption of hard or soft coal, wood, coke or corn cobs. The linings are heavy and so constructed that they will give long service, they are sectional and easily removed and protected by an air space behind them. It is furnished with an extension at the back end of the fire box which permits the use of wood 23 inches in length.

DUPLEX GRATE. This Big Acme Charm Steel Range is fitted with our special Duplex Grate, as shown in illustration, extra heavy, the most satisfactory grate made, and designed for any kind of fuel. It is simple and very easy to operate. One movement of the shaker cuts out all cinders and dead ashes. Reversing the grate forms a perfect fire box for a wood fire, and thus it will be seen that our special duplex grate can be used either for coal or wood.

THE OVEN of this range is made of the best quality of smooth cold rolled steel, securely riveted and braced to the body of the range in such a manner as to make all the joints perfectly tight. All seams and joints are carefully riveted airtight. The oven is made in one size only and measures 18x20¾x12 inches, and is furnished with steel slide oven rack which cannot be broken.

OVEN BOTTOM. The oven bottom of this handsome range is made of the highest grade, best selected sheet steel stock, so constructed, bolted, braced and reinforced that we guarantee it to always remain level and never to buckle, warp or sag. We do not use cast oven bottoms because they are subject to fire crack and the construction of our reinforced, bolted and braced steel oven bottom insures more heat in the oven for less fuel and much more satisfaction.

OVEN TOP. The oven top is properly protected by a corrugated cast plate extending back from the fire box, which makes the heat in the oven uniform.

COAL FEED POUCH AND BROILER DOOR. On the left end of the range we provide a capacious coal feed pouch with an Alaska nickel wire lift on the door, as shown in the illustration. It can be used for putting in fuel when coal is used, also for broiling purposes. This is an ideal arrangement and one which will be found very convenient.

ASH PAN. Extra large, heavy, reinforced ash pan, with wire handle, provided with guards, which make all ashes fall into the ash pan.

FLUE BACK. The flue back, which conducts the heat from the flue beneath the oven to the stove pipe, is made of the highest grade cast iron stove plate. This is a very important feature. Nearly all ranges sold for even double the price of our Acme Charm are made with a thin sheet steel flue back, which easily rots out by condensation or creosote moisture which sometimes runs down the chimney into the flue back. We guarantee our cast iron flue back never to burn or rust out.

THE RESERVOIR CASING. This is entirely new and original. Every part of the casing is handsomely carved and made of cast iron. The steel or sheet-iron reservoir casings used on ranges of other manufacturers are found not to be practical or serviceable, for they soon corrode and rust out from creosote and moisture and we do not use them. A depression in the bottom of the casing receives and holds all condensation until it is absorbed by the heat. The reservoir tank is removable, porcelain lined and holds 13½ quarts of water. By turning the reservoir damper, heat is thrown under the reservoir, heating the water boiling hot. The two covers are heavily japanned and operate on center divide hinges.

OVEN THERMOMETER. We equip our Acme Charm with a Dependable Oven Thermometer. It is mounted in the oven door and it accurately shows the temperature of the oven without the necessity of opening the door. Fully illustrated and described on page 632

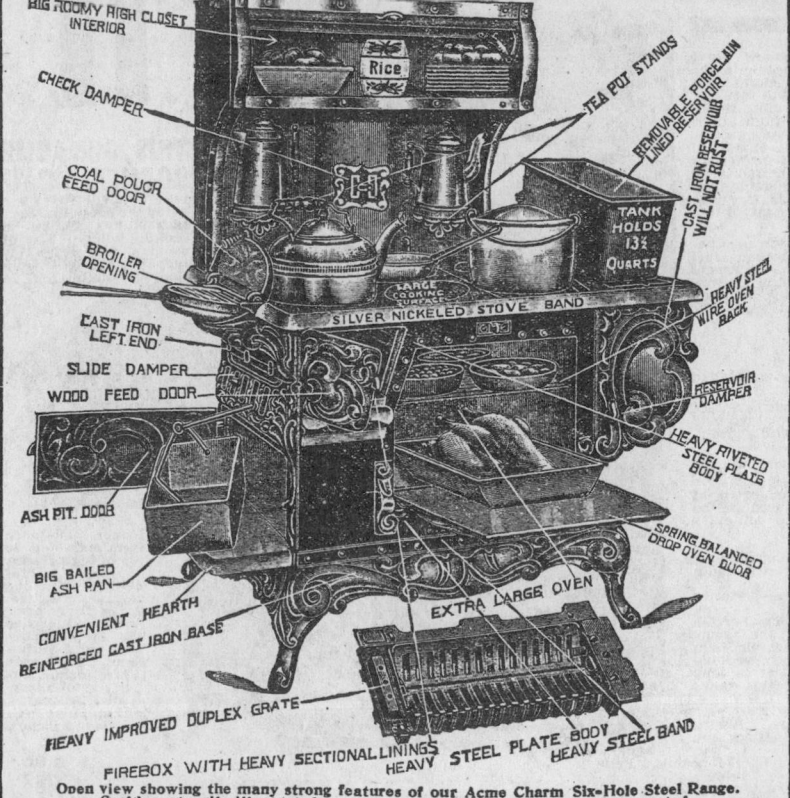

BIG ROOMY HIGH CLOSET INTERIOR
Rice
CHECK DAMPER
TEA POT STANDS
COAL POUCH FEED DOOR
REMOVABLE PORCELAIN LINED RESERVOIR
CAST IRON RESERVOIR WILL NOT RUST
TANK HOLDS 13½ QUARTS
BROILER OPENING
LARGE COOKING SPACE
SILVER NICKELED STOVE BAND
HEAVY STEEL WIRE OVEN BACK
CAST IRON LEFT END
SLIDE DAMPER
WOOD FEED DOOR
RESERVOIR DAMPER
HEAVY RIVETED STEEL BODY PLATE
ASH PIT DOOR
BIG BAILED ASH PAN
SPRING BALANCED DROP OVEN DOOR
CONVENIENT HEARTH
REINFORCED CAST IRON BASE
EXTRA LARGE OVEN
HEAVY IMPROVED DUPLEX GRATE
FIREBOX WITH HEAVY SECTIONAL LININGS
HEAVY STEEL PLATE BODY
HEAVY STEEL BAND

Oven view showing the many strong features of our Acme Charm Six-Hole Steel Range.
Cooking utensils illustrated are not furnished with range at prices quoted.

ACME HUMMER SIX-HOLE STEEL RANGE $17.52

A REDUCED PRICE

BURNS ANY KIND OF FUEL, HARD OR SOFT COAL, COKE, WOOD OR CORN COBS.

THE STANDARD OF POPULAR PRICED STEEL RANGES. GREATLY IMPROVED FOR 1908.

COMPLETE AS ILLUSTRATED. Our great and improved Acme Hummer Six-Hole Steel Range is designed and made by us to supply our customers with a very high class, full standard steel range, complete with reservoir and warming closet, at an extremely moderate price, and nowhere else in the pages of this catalogue is our ability to produce a high grade steel range at an extremely low price so thoroughly demonstrated as it is on this page. At this remarkably low price of only $17.52 we supply you with this beautiful range, improved throughout, just as illustrated, complete with high warming closet and rustproof porcelain lined reservoir, heavier, larger and handsomer than most steel ranges sold at double the price we ask.

THIS, OUR ACME HUMMER STEEL RANGE, is put up throughout in the most substantial form, the bending, punching, riveting and forming in general being accurate and the riveting close, firm and tight. Wherever in the structure the fire comes in contact with it, cast plates are worked in for protection. Other features of the range are: Extra and original dampers, the firebox construction, which is an original one and offers many conveniences and advantages; the body is manufactured from selected cold rolled steel of a heavier, stronger gauge than is used by manufacturers of similar ranges at double our prices; the fire and oven doors are ground and closely fitted; the oven door drops flush with the oven bottom, forming a convenient shelf; in short, the range is built on excellent lines throughout. By reason of our unequaled method and system we are enabled to produce this elegant range to meet the demands of those who are inclined to spend a small amount and yet get an honestly built range that has good material in all its parts and is constructed in a most satisfactory manner, and offer it at $17.52 complete, with reservoir and warming closet, under our written binding guarantee, as explained on page 626.

DETAILED DESCRIPTION.

THE BODY is manufactured from selected cold rolled sheet steel of a heavier and stronger gauge than is used in ranges that retail at much higher prices. It is thoroughly put together, riveted with wrought iron rivets, strongly reinforced and braced in every part.

HIGH CLOSET is of generous proportions. It is just at the right height and has a balanced door.

MAIN TOP, covers and centers are made of the highest grade gray iron, which stands the heat better and is less liable to crack or warp than any other material. This range is furnished with five solid lids and one sectional or nest lid, made from the best stove plate. It has long cut centers and all loose parts of top are carefully fitted with sufficient allowance for heat expansion.

THE FIRE BOX is of our well known type with famous Acme Duplex grate which is instantly converted into a coal burning grate or a wood burning grate at the will of the operator.

THE OVEN is of very generous proportions, with spring balanced drop oven door, and it is an extremely quick and even baker.

THIS STOVE IS No. 8-19. The oven is 18x20¾x12 inches. Has six No. 8 cooking holes. Top cooking surface with reservoir extension is 42½x29 inches; without reservoir, including end shelf, 39½x28½ inches. Height from floor to main top, 29½ inches. Distance from main top to top of high closet, 26½ inches. Total height, including closet, 54½ inches. Length of fire box for wood, 24 inches. Size pipe to fit collar, 7 inches. Furnished with large steel ash pan.

WE RECOMMEND the Acme Hummer to those who cannot afford our Acme Triumph or Acme Charm Steel Ranges. But, if you can add a few more dollars to the purchase price of the Acme Hummer, turn to the pages describing the Acme Triumph Steel Range, which is unapproached in any respect by the ranges offered by other manufacturers or dealers at from $60.00 to $90.00, and if you can afford to pay the few dollars additional, necessary to secure one of these highest grade ranges, we would strongly advise that you do so.

PRICES, STRONGLY CRATED AND DELIVERED ON THE CARS AT OUR FOUNDRY AT NEWARK, OHIO.

No. 22K195 Price for Square Top Range, without high closet or reservoir. Shipping weight, 291 pounds..$12.62

No. 22K196 Price for Reservoir Range, without high closet. Shipping weight, 358 pounds......15.12

No. 22K197 Price for Square Top Range, without reservoir, but with high closet. Shipping weight, 363 pounds......15.37

No. 22K198 Price for Range complete, exactly as illustrated, with high warming closet and porcelain lined reservoir. Shipping weight, 430 pounds......17.52

Water Back for Acme Hummer......2.50

(See page 627 about hot water fronts.)

REPAIR PARTS. We always carry a complete stock of repairs and repair parts, and in years to come, even ten years hence, we will be able to deliver you any piece or part to replace or repair any part which, perchance, has become defective from long usage or breakage, and this at actual cost; a mere fraction of what other dealers charge.

OUR LARGE STOCK INSURES PROMPT SHIPMENT.

Cast Iron Left End Guaranteed not to Warp, Buckle or Burn Out.

ACME BOOMER SIX-HOLE STEEL RANGE $11.98

REDUCED IN PRICE

AS A WONDERFUL ILLUSTRATION of what we can do in our Newark Stove Foundry, and as proof positive of our ability to build better stoves and ranges and sell them at lower prices than the prices asked by any other manufacturer or dealer in the world, we made this, our Acme Boomer Range, which we offer at $11.98, complete with reservoir and high warming closet. Ranges have been widely advertised by other foundries and dealers at prices ranging from $18.00 to $22.50, and in those advertisements representations have been made that the ranges are strictly high grade in every respect. To show our customers how cheaply constructed those advertised ranges are, and how much greater value we offer in the stoves and ranges made by us in our Newark foundry, we purchased samples of the ranges widely advertised at $18.00 to $22.50, and after getting these samples, we had our expert range builders make an exact duplicate of these ranges, that is to say, taking the best features of every one of them and putting them into this range to show at what price we would be able to build and sell a range in every respect the equal of the cheaply built ranges offered by others at from $18.00 to $22.50.

UNDERSTAND, WE DO NOT OFFER this Acme Boomer as a high grade range because it is not the equal of any other steel range shown in our catalogue, but we do guarantee it to be just as good as stoves and ranges offered by others at from $18.00 to $22.50. It is a very satisfactory baker, economical in the consumption of fuel, quick to heat and quick to act. In making it we have constructed the main top and covers of good stove plate. It has six cooking holes, and with ordinary care and usage the main top and covers will last for years. It has a convenient warming closet.

DETAILED DESCRIPTION.

THE BODY is manufactured from cold rolled sheet steel of a heavier and stronger gauge than is used by other foundries and dealers at prices ranging from $18.00 to $22.50.

THE MAIN TOP. In manufacturing this, our Acme Boomer Steel Range, we have constructed the main tops and covers of good stove plate. It has six cooking holes and, with ordinary care and usage, the main top and covers will last for years. All parts of the main top are carefully fitted, with sufficient allowance for heat expansion.

HIGH WARMING CLOSET is of generous proportions, is just at the right height, and will be found very convenient. The height of warming closet is 23 inches.

FIRE BOX. The fire box in our Acme Boomer Steel Range is an improved fire box, equipped with our flat dump style grate, which grate is lighter than our perfect duplex grate as used in the highest grade ranges made by us. With every range we supply we include, free of cost, an extra grate for wood, so that you can burn either hard coal, soft coal or wood.

THE ASH PAN is made of cold rolled steel with handsome draw out handle.

THE OVEN is of very generous proportions, perfectly square, is a very satisfactory, quick, even baker, and is furnished with a steel wire oven rack and convenient clean out directly under the oven door.

THE OVEN DOOR is our latest swing pattern, attractive rococo design, steel lined, perfectly square and fits snug to the body of the range, thus retaining all the heat in the oven.

THE RESERVOIR is made of galvanized iron and heats by direct contact with the end of the range. It can be adjusted to either end and, if so desired, can also be used on top of the range. Being made of galvanized iron, it will not rust or corrode and is by far a better reservoir than that on ranges offered for $18.00 to $22.50 by other dealers. This is the only steel range we build without cast iron reservoir casing. It is simply made of galvanized iron and will not last as long as the cast reservoir casing which is used by us on all our other ranges. In shipping this range we pack the reservoir inside the oven. It is easily attached to the right or left end of the range.

THE FLUE BACK which conducts the heat from the flue beneath the oven to the stove pipe is made of the highest grade cast iron stove plate. This is a very important feature. Nearly all steel ranges sold for more than double the price we ask for this, our Acme Boomer Range, are made with a thin sheet steel flue back, which easily rots out.

THIS, OUR ACME BOOMER, IS MADE IN ONE SIZE ONLY. This stove is 8-16; the oven 16x18x11 inches, has six No. 8 cooking holes. Size of cooking top, 30½x21½ inches. Height from floor to main top 26 inches. Distance from main top to top of high closet, 23 inches. Total height, including closet, 49 inches. On the Acme Boomer the fire box is 7 inches wide and 5 inches deep. Its length is 17½ inches. Capacity of reservoir, 21 quarts. Size of pipe to fit collar, 6 inches.

No. 22K200	Square top range, without high closet or reservoir, shipping weight, 174 pounds. Price	$ 9.60
No. 22K201	Reservoir range, without high closet, shipping weight, 180 pounds. Price	10.35
No. 22K202	Square top range, without reservoir, but with high closet, shipping weight, 202 pounds. Price	11.62
No. 22K203	Steel range complete, just as illustrated, with high closet and reservoir, shipping weight, 208 pounds. Price	11.98

THESE PRICES DO NOT INCLUDE PIPE OR COOKING UTENSILS. WE DO NOT FURNISH WATER FRONT FOR THE ACME BOOMER RANGE.

$15 58 FOR OUR NEW 1908 ACME PROGRESS FOUR-HOLE STEEL COOK STOVE

BURNS ANY KIND OF FUEL, HARD OR SOFT COAL, WOOD, COKE OR CORN COBS.

A REDUCED PRICE.
We offer this wonderful new 1908 pattern Acme Progress Steel Cook Stove as the very latest and very highest grade steel cook stove offered on the market, the equal of any steel cook stove you can buy at double our price. It will burn hard or soft coal, coke, wood, or any other fuel; it will be found to be the most adaptable steel cook stove you can buy, and

IT IS SOLD TO YOU UNDER OUR POSITIVE BINDING GUARANTEE OF SATISFACTION OR YOUR MONEY BACK.

THE BODY of the Acme Progress Steel Cook Stove is made of heavier steel than is used by other makers. The heavy steel plates are accurately cut and punched for riveting and they are very carefully milled and fitted together; they are securely hand riveted, thoroughly braced, and so thoroughly are they designed and so carefully are they made that an Acme Progress Steel Cook Stove will be in better condition after five years of constant use than the ordinary light weight or cast iron cook stove would be after but one year's use.

THE MAIN TOP. The main top, cover and centers are made of the very finest cast stove plate from the purest pig iron, and should not be confused with malleable top ranges which other manufacturers sometimes call "steel" with the deliberate purpose to deceive you. No malleable iron top ever made can compare in lasting quality with the cast stove plate tops used in the manufacture of our stoves and ranges.

THE FIRE BOX is well constructed of proper depth and width to provide enough heat for the oven without waste of fuel. With the two end pieces removed and the cast iron extension attached, the fire box is easily prepared for burning wood, making the length of fire box for wood 23½ inches. We equip the Acme Progress with duplex grate, which can be used for hard or soft coal, wood, or any other fuel, as shown on page 637.

THE PERFECT OVEN of the Acme Progress Steel Cook Stove is made from extra heavy cut steel plate, hand riveted with wrought rivets, carefully reinforced throughout, and with our arrangement of flues and airtight construction it is a very quick, fine and satisfactory baker. It is of very generous proportions, being 17½x20x12 inches in size, and it has one steel spring counterbalanced drop oven door on the right side, with rococo cast frame and handsomely nickeled medallion center plate and handle. The oven bottom of our Progress Steel Cook Stove is made of the highest grade selected stock sheet steel, so constructed, bolted, braced, and reinforced that it will always remain level, and there is absolutely no possibility of it buckling, warping, or sagging. The oven top is protected with a heavy corrugated cast plate which also serves to distribute the heat to all parts of the oven. The oven door is on the right side (the left side left blank). The door opens downward the same as on our steel ranges, forming a large, commodious shelf. The oven door frame is very strong and ornamented with a beautifully nickeled medallion handle and panel.

THIS STOVE is furnished in numbers 8-20 or 9-20 sizes. Its cooking surface has four holes and the size of the top, including extension reservoir, is 42½x26 inches. The height from floor to main top is 30½ inches. Length of fire box for wood, 23½ inches; size pipe to fit collar, 7 inches. This stove is furnished complete with lifter, shaker and scraper for removing the soot from under the oven.

WOOD FEED DOOR swings to the left and is constructed to prevent ashes from piling against the inside and falling to the floor when the door is opened. THE ASH DOOR is extra large, the ash pan is made of the highest standard grade refined steel, fits the large, roomy hearth under the ash door, which prevents the ashes from spilling on the floor when being removed. The bottom edge is reinforced with heavy steel, which is run around the entire body of the stove and strongly riveted to the steel plates of the body.

THE HEAVY CAST BASE, as will be seen by referring to the illustration of our Acme Progress Four-Hole Steel Cook Stove, is fitted with a very heavy cast iron base of the very newest rococo pattern.

THE LARGE RESERVOIR TANK is made of the best grade of cast iron, white porcelain lined to prevent rusting. Easily kept clean and removable. It has a capacity of 17 quarts. DAMPERS are convenient to reach and so placed that they are easily regulated. POUCH FEED—The Progress Steel Cook Stove has a large pouch feed for feeding coal or coke and will also permit of the insertion of a broiler over the fire.

Prices, strongly crated and delivered on cars at our foundry at Newark, Ohio:

No. 22K205 Price, No. 8-20, with reservoir and 8-inch lids $15.58
On this stove the fire box is 8½ inches wide and 5½ inches deep, its length for coal is 18 inches and for wood 23½ inches. Capacity of reservoir, 17 quarts. Shipping weight, 340 pounds.
No. 22K206 Price, No. 9-20, with reservoir and 9-inch lids $15.88
Prices do not include pipe or cooking utensils. For cooking utensils, see pages 461 to 466.

IF DESIRED WITHOUT RESERVOIR BUT WITH END SHELF, DEDUCT $2.00 FROM EITHER SIZE.

ACME ROVER GENUINE STEEL FOUR-HOLE COAL AND WOOD STOVE $6 75

A REDUCED PRICE. WITH RESERVOIR MODEL OF 1908 — ONLY 6 AND UPWARD

Three sizes, direct from our foundry, offered at $6.75, $7.75 and $8.75, according to size, as listed below.

COMPARE THE PRICES with any prices you have ever seen or heard of, in either a steel or cast iron reservoir cook stove, and you will find the price we are offering on this reservoir steel cook stove less than one half what others charge, and it is positively THE GREATEST STOVE VALUE THE WORLD HAS EVER SEEN.

COMPARED WITH THE LOWEST PRICES we could possibly make you on any of our cast iron reservoir cook stoves we save you easily from $4.00 to $7.00, and compared with any other steel cook stove we could sell you we show you a saving of from $6.00 to $8.00; and compared with any price any other maker or dealer could offer you we show you a saving in cost on this, OUR ACME ROVER STEEL COOK STOVE WITH RESERVOIR, of easily $7.00 to $15.00.

THE BODY is made of the highest grade sheet steel, thoroughly bolted, braced, reinforced throughout, the very best oven construction; our new special flue, draft damper and circulating system, made to burn hard coal, soft coal, or wood. With each stove we furnish a special grate for wood. Has a cast top—the exact same grade of top that we use in our highest grade stoves and ranges; four lids, cut centers, supported by our own special system of construction. At the special price named, the stove is furnished with a detachable or removable reservoir, as shown in illustration. In shipping the stove we pack the reservoir inside of the oven, and the stove is crated in a way that there is no chance of its reaching you in bad condition—in fact the stove is unbreakable.

WE HAVE A LARGE STOCK OF these stoves on hand, ready for immediate shipment. It will just take a few days for your order to reach us and the stove to reach you. The stove being made of sheet steel is comparatively light and the freight charges will amount to next to nothing. This stove can be shipped from 100 to 500 miles at from 35 cents to 75 cents; from 500 to 1,000 miles at from 50 cents to $1.00; greater or lesser distances in proportion.

THIS ILLUSTRATION, engraved by our artist from a photograph, showing our new 1908 model Acme Rover, four-hole, reservoir, all steel cook stove, which we offer at $6.75, $7.75 and $8.75, will give you a good general idea of the appearance of this stove.

REPAIR PARTS.
We will always carry a complete stock of repairs and repair parts in years to come; even ten years hence we will be able to deliver you any piece or part to replace or repair any defective part and this at actual cost, a mere fraction of what other stove dealers charge.

DETAILED DESCRIPTION   NOTE OUR REDUCTION IN PRICE

THE BODY is built of heavy smooth steel plate, is substantially put together, riveted with wrought iron rivets, strongly reinforced and braced in every part. The heavy plates are well riveted and jointed.

THE MAIN TOP. In manufacturing this, our Acme Rover, we have constructed the main top and covers of good stove plate. It has four cooking holes and with ordinary care and usage the main top and covers will last years. All parts of the main top are carefully fitted, with sufficient allowance for heat expansion.

THE LARGE FIRE BOX. It has an extra large fire box, provided with practical cast iron linings, with shaking and dumping grate. With every stove we include, free of cost, an extra grate for wood, so you can burn hard coal, soft coal or wood.
THE FIRE DOOR is beautifully designed and swings to the left.
THE ASH PIT is large and roomy and is provided with a large ash pan.
THE DRAFT SLIDE is in front, of more than usual capacity.
THE OVEN is of very generous proportions, perfectly square, is a very satisfactory, quick and even baker, and is furnished with a steel wire oven rack.
THE OVEN DOOR is on the right side (the left side left blank). It is our latest swing pattern, attractive rococo design, steel lined, perfectly square, and fits snug to the body of the stove, thus retaining all the heat in the oven.

THE FLUES are ample and provided with cleanout in rear of ash pit, which is reached from the front of the stove.
THE RESERVOIR is made of galvanized iron, heats by direct contact with the side of the stove, is removable and can be used on either end or rear side at pleasure, or can be used on top of stove as occasion requires.
GOOD SERVICE. The long looked for steel cook stove for practical people, neat, compact, serviceable and cheap. No such value in a cook stove ever offered before. This, our Acme Rover Steel Cook Stove, is shipped ready to set up, the four legs and all other loose parts packed inside. When received you have only to put on the legs, pipe and other loose parts, when it is ready for fire, the same as if you were moving an old stove from one room to another.

PRICES FOR OUR ACME ROVER STEEL COOK STOVE, FOR COAL AND WOOD, WITH RESERVOIR, FOUR COOKING HOLES, DUMPING GRATE, LARGE ASH PAN, STEEL OVEN RACK, GALVANIZED RESERVOIR ADJUSTABLE TO EITHER END, SIDE OR BACK.

Catalogue Number	Range Number	Size of Lids	Size of Oven, inches	Main Top, including Reservoir	Height of Main Top, inches	Size of Pipe to Fit Collar, inches	Size of Fire Box, inches			Capacity of Reservoir	Weight, Pounds	Price
							Length	Width	Depth			
22K210	7-12	No. 7	12x16x10	35 x19 inches	25	6	16½	6½	4	14 quarts	127	$6.75
22K211	8-14	No. 8	14x18x10½	37½x21 inches	25½	6	17	6½	4½	18 quarts	147	7.75
22K212	8-16	No. 8	16x18x11	40½x21½ inches	26½	6	17½	7	5	21 quarts	163	8.75

$23.95

REDUCED IN PRICE

THREE TONS OF HARD COAL and an Acme Sunburst will keep your big house more comfortable than any other base burner will keep it with five tons of coal, and so economical is this our Acme Sunburst Base Burner in the consumption of coal in comparison with any of the base burners on the market it will save you from 25 to 50 per cent on your coal bills. DON'T FAIL TO READ THE FOLLOWING PAGE TO LEARN MORE ABOUT OUR ACME SUNBURST BASE BURNER.

—QUICK— DELIVERY.

This beautiful Acme Sunburst Base Burner is stored in our various warehouses, securely crated and ready for immediate shipment from any of the following cities: Fargo, N. Dak., Sioux Falls, S. Dak., Minneapolis, Minn., Davenport, Ia., Waterloo, Ia., Milwaukee, Wis., St. Louis, Mo., Kansas City, Mo., Omaha, Neb., Wichita, Kansas, Newark, O., Harrisburg, Penna., Albany, N. Y.

HOW WE CAN MAKE WONDERFULLY QUICK DELIVERY FULLY EXPLAINED ON PAGE 628.

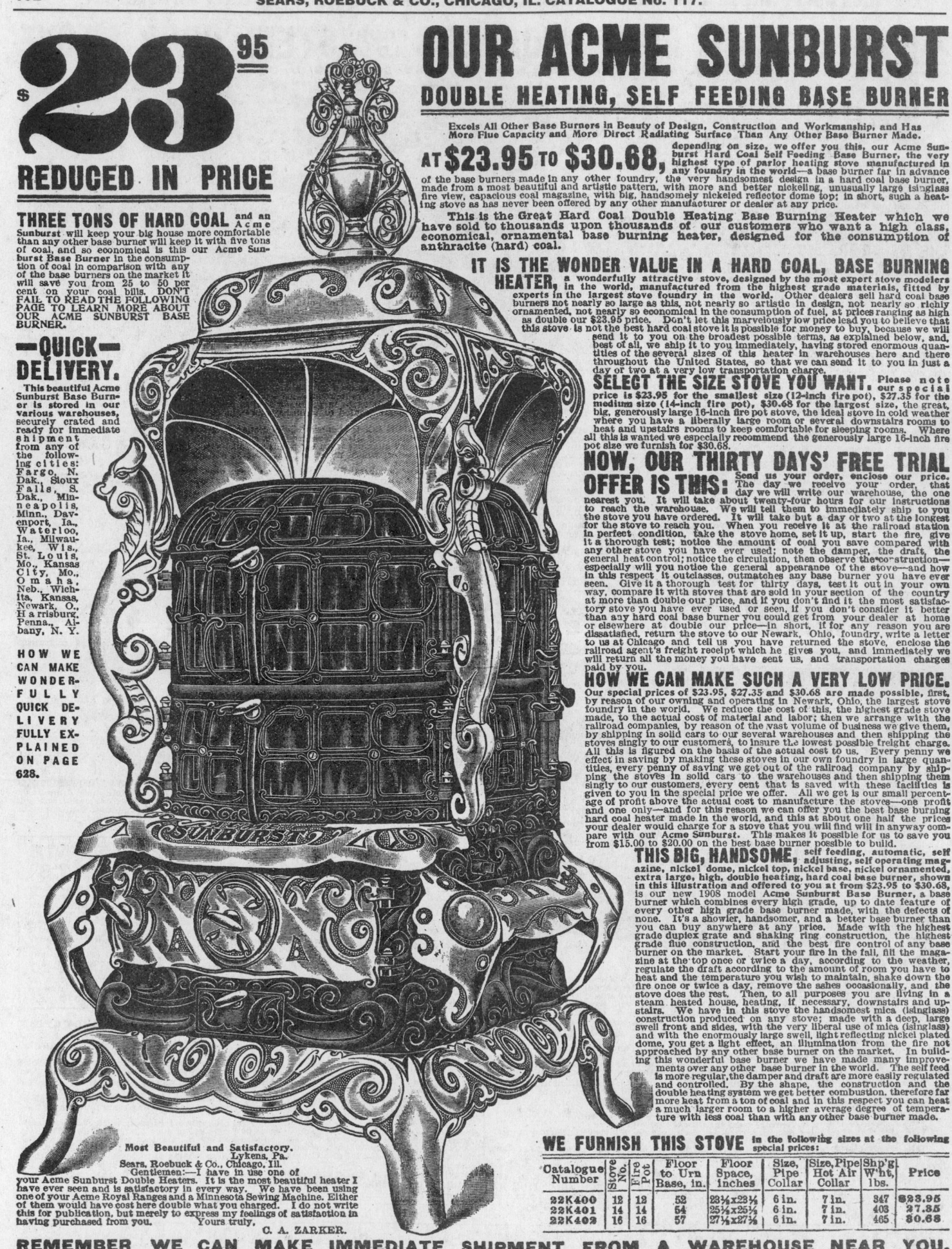

Most Beautiful and Satisfactory.
Lykens, Pa.
Sears, Roebuck & Co., Chicago, Ill.
Gentlemen:—I have in use one of your Acme Sunburst Double Heaters. It is the most beautiful heater I have ever seen and is satisfactory in every way. We have been using one of your Acme Royal Ranges and a Minnesota Sewing Machine. Either of them would have cost here double what you charged. I do not write this for publication, but merely to express my feelings of satisfaction in having purchased from you.
Yours truly,
C. A. ZARKER.

OUR ACME SUNBURST
DOUBLE HEATING, SELF FEEDING BASE BURNER

Excels All Other Base Burners in Beauty of Design, Construction and Workmanship, and Has More Flue Capacity and More Direct Radiating Surface Than Any Other Base Burner Made.

AT $23.95 TO $30.68, depending on size, we offer you this, our Acme Sunburst Hard Coal Self Feeding Base Burner, the very highest type of parlor heating stove manufactured in any foundry in the world—a base burner far in advance of the base burners made in any other foundry, the very handsomest design in a hard coal base burner, made from a most beautiful and artistic pattern, with more and better nickeling, unusually large isinglass fire view, capacious coal magazine, with big, handsomely nickeled reflector dome top; in short, such a heating stove as has never been offered by any other manufacturer or dealer at any price.

This is the Great Hard Coal Double Heating Base Burning Heater which we have sold to thousands upon thousands of our customers who want a high class, economical, ornamental base burning heater, designed for the consumption of anthracite (hard) coal.

IT IS THE WONDER VALUE IN A HARD COAL, BASE BURNING HEATER, a wonderfully attractive stove, designed by the most expert stove modelers in the world, manufactured from the highest grade materials, fitted by experts in the largest stove foundry in the world. Other dealers sell hard coal base burners not nearly so large as this, not nearly so artistic in design, not nearly so richly ornamented, not nearly so economical in the consumption of fuel, at prices ranging as high as double our $23.95 price. Don't let this marvelously low price lead you to believe that this stove is not the best hard coal stove it is possible for money to buy, because we will send it to you on the broadest possible terms, as explained below, and, best of all, we ship it to you immediately, having stored enormous quantities of the several sizes of this heater in warehouses here and there throughout the United States, so that we can send it to you in just a day or two at a very low transportation charge.

SELECT THE SIZE STOVE YOU WANT. Please note our special price is $23.95 for the smallest size (12-inch fire pot), $27.35 for the medium size (14-inch fire pot), $30.68 for the largest size, the great, big, generously large 16-inch fire pot stove, the ideal stove in cold weather where you have a liberally large room or several downstairs rooms to heat and upstairs rooms to keep comfortable for sleeping rooms. Where all this is wanted we especially recommend the generously large 16-inch fire pot size we furnish for $30.68.

NOW, OUR THIRTY DAYS' FREE TRIAL
OFFER IS THIS: Send us your order, enclose our price. The day we receive your order, that day we will write our warehouse, the one nearest you. It will take about twenty-four hours for our instructions to reach the warehouse. We will tell them to immediately ship to you the stove you have ordered. It will take but a day or two at the longest for the stove to reach you. When you receive it at the railroad station in perfect condition, take the stove home, set it up, start the fire, give it a thorough test; notice the amount of coal you save compared with any other stove you have ever used; note the damper, the draft, the general heat control; notice the circulation, then observe the construction—especially will you notice the general appearance of the stove—and how in this respect it outclasses, outmatches any base burner you have ever seen. Give it a thorough test for thirty days, test it out in your own way, compare it with stoves that are sold in your section of the country at more than double our price, and if you don't find it the most satisfactory stove you have ever used or seen, if you don't consider it better than any hard coal base burner you could get from your dealer at home or elsewhere at double our price—in short, if for any reason you are dissatisfied, return the stove to our Newark, Ohio, foundry, write a letter to us at Chicago and tell us you have returned the stove, enclose the railroad agent's freight receipt which he gives you, and immediately we will return all the money you have sent us, and transportation charges paid by you.

HOW WE CAN MAKE SUCH A VERY LOW PRICE.
Our special prices of $23.95, $27.35 and $30.68 are made possible, first, by reason of our owning and operating in Newark, Ohio, the largest stove foundry in the world. We reduce the cost of this, the highest grade stove made, to the actual cost of material and labor; then we arrange with the railroad companies, by reason of the vast volume of business we give them, by shipping in solid cars to our several warehouses and then shipping the stoves singly to our customers, to insure the lowest possible freight charge. All this is figured on the basis of the actual cost to us. Every penny we effect in saving by making these stoves in our own foundry in large quantities, every penny of saving we get out of the railroad company by shipping the stoves in solid cars to the warehouses and then shipping them singly to our customers, every cent that is saved with these facilities is given to you in the special price we offer. All we get is our small percentage of profit above the actual cost to manufacture the stoves—one profit and one only—and for this reason we can offer you the best base burning hard coal heater made in the world, and this at about one half the prices your dealer would charge for a stove that you will find will in anyway compare with our Acme Sunburst. This makes it possible for us to save you from $15.00 to $20.00 on the best base burner possible to build.

THIS BIG, HANDSOME, self feeding, automatic, self adjusting, self operating magazine, nickel dome, nickel top, nickel base, nickel ornamented, extra large, high, double heating, hard coal base burner, shown in this illustration and offered to you at from $23.95 to $30.68, is our new 1908 model Acme Sunburst Base Burner, a base burner which combines every high grade, up to date feature of every other high grade base burner made, with the defects of none. It's a showier, handsomer, and a better base burner than you can buy anywhere at any price. Made with the highest grade duplex grate and shaking ring construction, the highest grade flue construction, and the best fire control of any base burner on the market. Start your fire in the fall, fill the magazine at the top once or twice a day, according to the weather, regulate the draft according to the amount of room you have to heat and the temperature you wish to maintain, shake down the fire once or twice a day, remove the ashes occasionally, and the stove does the rest. Then, to all purposes you are living in a steam heated house, heating, if necessary, downstairs and upstairs. We have in this stove the handsomest mica (isinglass) construction produced on any stove; made with a deep, large swell front and sides, with the very liberal use of mica (isinglass) and with the enormously large swell, light reflecting nickel plated dome, you get a light effect, an illumination from the fire not approached by any other base burner on the market. In building this wonderful base burner we have made many improvements over any other base burner in the world. The self feed is more regular, the damper and draft are more easily regulated and controlled. By the shape, the construction and the double heating system we get better combustion, therefore far more heat from a ton of coal and in this respect you can heat a much larger room to a higher average degree of temperature with less coal than with any other base burner made.

WE FURNISH THIS STOVE in the following sizes at the following special prices:

Catalogue Number	Stove No.	Fire Pot	Floor to Urn Base, in.	Floor Space, inches	Size, Pipe Collar	Size, Pipe Hot Air Collar	Shp'g W'ht, lbs.	Price
22K400	12	12	52	23½x23½	6 in.	7 in.	347	$23.95
22K401	14	14	54	25½x25½	6 in.	7 in.	403	27.35
22K402	16	16	57	27½x27½	6 in.	7 in.	465	30.68

REMEMBER WE CAN MAKE IMMEDIATE SHIPMENT FROM A WAREHOUSE NEAR YOU.

$20 95

PRICE REDUCED

IMMEDIATE SHIPMENT

We have stored at Newark, Ohio foundry, strongly crated and ready for immediate shipment; enormous stocks of this, our Acme Corona Base Burner and can make an immediate shipment.

QUICK DELIVERY. Please remember our World Wonder Acme Sunburst Base Burner illustrated and described on opposite page is stored in our various warehouses, securely crated, ready for immediate shipment from the following points: Fargo, No. Dak.; Sioux Falls, So. Dak., Minneapolis, Minn., Waterloo, Iowa, Davenport, Iowa, Milwaukee, Wis., St. Louis, Mo., Kansas City, Mo., Omaha, Nebr., Wichita, Kan., Harrisburg, Penna., Newark, Ohio and Albany, N. Y.

CORONA BASE BURNER

A THOROUGHLY GOOD SELF FEEDING, DOUBLE HEATING, RETURN FLUE HARD COAL BASE BURNER.

In calling attention to this, our Acme Corona Automatic Self Feeding, Double Heating, Return Flue, Hard Coal Base Burner, we believe we have the most perfect hard coal parlor heater—a heating stove which is brought right up to date and carrying all the patented and exclusive features for which our stoves are famous, and we offer this magnificent heater at $20.95, $23.75 and $26.62, according to size.

WE EXCEL IN THE MANUFACTURE OF BASE BURNERS and it is a recognized fact that more heat and satisfactory temperature can be obtained from the use of a hard coal base burner than from any other kind of heating stove. With a first class base burner, such as our Acme Sunburst, as illustrated and described on the preceding page, and our Acme Corona base burner herewith illustrated, your home can be heated to a satisfactory temperature and, with little attention, kept there during the entire winter months, and in order to obtain such results it is absolutely necessary to get a stove that is properly fitted and adjusted. This, our Acme Corona Base Burner, offered at the prices $20.95, $23.75 and $26.62 is made from an entirely new pattern, a pattern designed by our own high class stove artist, and if you will just glance at this illustration you will immediately decide that it is a wonderfully attractive stove and an ornament to any home. It is built along identically the same lines followed by us in manufacturing our Acme Sunburst. It has all the special features which distinguish the Sunburst from all other base burners—the only difference between the two stoves being the amount of silver nickeling with which they are ornamented—and we guarantee it to be in heating power, in simplicity of operation, in quality of materials and workmanship, the equal of any hard coal base burner ever produced in any foundry, no matter what its name, make or price, and if you do not feel that you can pay the few dollars extra to secure our beautiful silver nickel plated, handsome Acme Sunburst, as described on opposite page, then take the next best stove, the exact same stove with less nickeling, this, our Acme Corona, at our special prices of $20.95, $23.75 and $26.62, according to size.

A CAREFUL INSPECTION OF THIS STOVE will prove that we have not spared any expense in designing this handsome base burner, as the illustration will give you a very good idea of the attractive pattern and delicate tracery of the silver nickeled ornamented parts and dome, corner ornaments, name plate, draft register, foot rails and leg base are all beautifully nickel plated by our silver nickeling process, polished to the highest degree, and this beautiful finish, with only ordinary care, is practically indestructible. The reflectors above the fire view doors with mirror polished surfaces, double and treble the glow of the coals within and flood the room with light.

THE FIRE POT AND MAGAZINE which are exposed to the most intense heat are made extra heavy. They can be easily removed through the front door of the stove. Our Duplex Grate is of the same type of construction as used in our Acme Sunburst, our famous shaker ring and duplex dumping grate, and all dead ashes, cinders and clinkers are quickly and easily cut out and dropped to the ash pan below without disturbing the fire above. In conjunction with our new screw draft register, which may be regulated to a fraction of a degree, this patented fire pot and grate enables you to so control the fire in this popular self feeding hard coal base burner that, for evenness of heat, economy in the consumption of fuel, it is unsurpassed by any stove produced.

THE DOUBLE HEATING FLUE, of the same design identically as that used on our highest grade base burner, our Acme Sunburst, gives this stove its wonderful heating power. The cold air is drawn from the floor at the bottom of the stove, is circulated around the hot surfaces of the stove, and discharged through the hot air flue at the top. The air circulates so rapidly and so positively that your home will be free from cold corners, and by actual test this heating process is so rapid and the circulation so perfect that the temperature of the room heated with this, our Acme Corona will only vary three or four degrees between the floor and ceiling. No other hard coal base burner, except our Acme Sunburst, will yield such results and it is this exclusive double heating feature with which our base burners are equipped which enables us to heat a great big house so evenly and so satisfactorily at a lower expense for fuel than can be shown by any other hard coal base burner selling for twice the prices we ask.

A PIPE MAY BE ATTACHED to the top of the hot air flue and carried to a register in the floor above, so that a portion of the heat developed by this, our Acme Corona, will pass to the floors above and heat one or more rooms as comfortably as the floors below with no additional consumption of fuel.

THE SILVER NICKELED DOME TOP surmounting the fire chamber of this handsome base burner is large and handsomely designed; its beautiful, massive outlines are clearly shown in the illustration, which is made direct from a photograph, and we know that if you order this, our Acme Corona, at our special prices of $20.95, $23.75 and $26.62, according to size, you will be delighted with your purchase, as thousands of our customers have been before you.

THE WORKMANSHIP AND FINISH are as nearly perfect as the most skilled and experienced mechanics could make them. Every Corona base burner is rigidly inspected and reinspected before it leaves our foundry. The mounting is done in such a manner that no uneven surfaces are visible or unnecessary openings exposed where the castings are drawn together. This department is in the hands of men who have had years of experience in this kind of work, and which enables them to produce an absolute perfect fitting stove.

THIS STOVE IS WELL ADAPTED to any home and it will heat almost any size room or house. It comes in three sizes, the fire chamber measuring 13, 15 and 17 inches, and it really represents such value as has never before been put in any hard coal base burner on the market. It has the latest tea kettle attachment; it has the latest and best heating flue construction; it has the latest ash pit and pan of large size; it has our highest grade interior construction, and it is altogether one of the very best, longest lived, and most satisfactory hard coal self-feeding base burning stoves on the market.

OUR BINDING GUARANTEE of quality, our thirty days free trial and refund proposition such as we offer, also applies to this, our Acme Corona, and we will send it to you with the distinct understanding and agreement that you may use it thirty days in your own home, and if you do not decide that it is in every way all that you could expect or ask for in a high grade, perfectly constructed, hard coal base burner, the very best value that you can secure at home or elsewhere—a stove consuming less fuel than any other base burner and sold to you at a big saving in cost—it may be returned to us at our expense of transportation charges and we will refund your money.

A WORD ABOUT FREIGHT CHARGES. The freight charges on any one of our Acme Stoves and Ranges will amount to next to nothing in comparison to what you save in price.

Prices of Acme Corona Base Burner, strongly crated and delivered on the cars at our Newark, Ohio, foundry.

Catalogue Number	Stove Number	Size of Fire Pot	Floor to Base of Urn	Floor Space, inches	Size Smoke Pipe Collar, inches	Size Pipe Hot Air Collar, inches	Shipping Weight, pounds	Price
22 K405	13	13 inches	52 inches	23½ x 23½	6	7	331	$20.95
22 K406	15	15 inches	54 inches	25½ x 25½	6	7	375	23.75
22 K407	17	17 inches	57 inches	27½ x 27½	6	7	431	26.62

SAVED $22.00. ARRIVED O. K. AND NOBODY CAN BEAT IT.

Sears, Roebuck & Co.

Bloomington, Ill.

Dear Sirs:— I am very well pleased with our Acme Corona Base Heater. It is a fine stove. It came here O. K. in every respect, and everybody that looks at it says it is a beauty. I will say that I have saved $22.00 on the stove, and have just as good a stove as anybody. There is no doubt but that you will sell more stoves in Bloomington. I know that nobody can beat it for quality. It draws well and heats well in every respect.

Yours truly,

J. LE BANDI, 1308 N. Mason Street.

In writing to above party please enclose a 2-cent stamp for reply.

ACME WILDWOOD RETURN FLUE TODD STOVE.

$9.55 AND UP

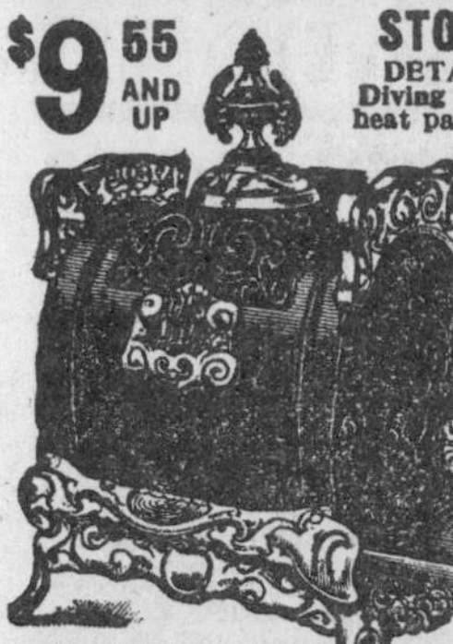

REDUCED IN PRICE

DETAILED DESCRIPTION. The Diving Return Flue. The flame and heat pass down the front, around the oval bottom and up toward the pipe at the back. This diving return flue and up flue are the full length of the stove and take advantage of all radiating surface around the oval. **Main Body.** The body is made of blue polished steel and the cast ends are of heavy rococo modeling, as shown in illustration. They are trimmed at the top with massive nickeled end ornaments, nickeled with our unapproachable silver nickeling process and polished to a mirror finish. **Swing Top.** This openwork but highly polished silver nickeled swing top turns to the left, giving access to one cooking hole in the main top. **Main Top.** This heavy rococo model main top extends back to the smoke collar, and this smoke collar is for vertical pipe, as indicated in the illustration, but can be unbolted and reversed to accommodate horizontal pipe, entering the chimney directly back of the stove, when so desired. **Nickel Trimmings.** The other nickel finish not described above consists of the handsome medallion name plate, large and massive foot rail, broad, sweeping leg frame and feet, and a nickeled screw draft register in the fire door. The fire door comes in contact with the rolling damper handle when the door is open, allowing the smoke to go directly up the pipe while placing fuel in the fire chamber. This prevents smoke creeping out of the top of the door; and, as an additional protection, we have a drop smoke plate immediately inside the upper front of the fire door. **Linings.** The inner lining is very heavy cast stove plate and the oval of the bottom inside is below the hearth line and connecting directly with the ash pit in the hearth.

We offer this, our Acme Wildwood Diving Return Flue Todd Stove, at the following prices, delivered on board cars at our factory in Newark, Ohio:

Catalogue Number	Stove No.	Length Fire Box, inches	Size of Door Opening, inches	Floor to Urn Base, inches	Floor Space, inches	Pipe Collar, inches	Weight, Pounds	Price
22K465	26	25	13x10	30	26x19	6	175	$ 9.55
22K466	28	27	13x10	30	28x19	6	181	10.12
22K467	30	29	15x11	32	30x19	6	202	11.52
22K468	32	31	15x11	32	32x19	6	212	13.22

THE ACME BUCKEYE.

WOOD BURNER.

Burns Wood, Straw, Hay, Cobs, Corn, Peat, Trash or Anything Used for Fuel, Excepting Coal.

$4.50

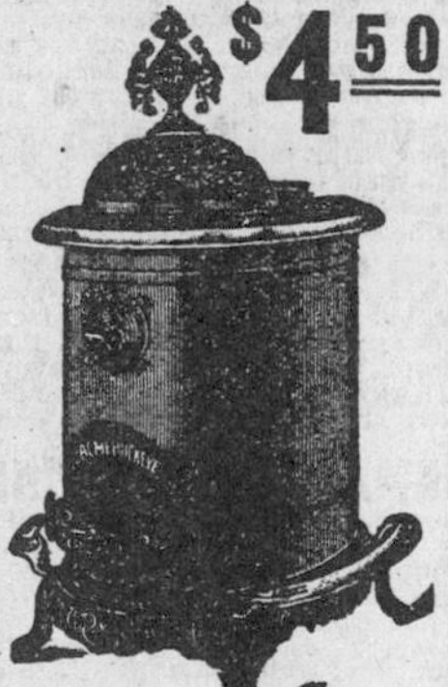

The Acme Buckeye Airtight Hot Air Circulator at $4.50 and $5.10. The Acme Buckeye has all the features of the Acme Wildwood shown above, excepting it is made in smaller sizes, and is of different ornamentation. It has the same hot blast draft and circulating system, and burns anything excepting coal. The screw drafts are the same, making it airtight when keeping fire. Has nickeled top band and foot rails. We claim further for these hot air heaters that one of our stoves will be found in perfect condition after the ordinary thin, lightly constructed airtight heater has been worn and burned out. We build these heaters from the best material that money can buy, use only thé highest grade sheet steel, and a thicker steel than is used by other makers. We use stronger, heavier, better fitting and better finished castings, we put on more nickeling and trimming, and we guarantee to furnish you a better airtight heater than you could get elsewhere, and that at a little more than one-half the price charged by others. Every stove is put out under our binding guarantee, and after giving it ten days' thorough trial, if you are not convinced that you have received a better stove in every particular than you could have purchased elsewhere of the same size and style, you can return it to us at our expense, and we will immediately return your money. **Size of pipe to fit collar is 6-inch on both sizes.**

Price list of the Acme Buckeye, with hot air blast draft and hot air circulating system, strongly crated and delivered on board cars at our Newark, Ohio, foundry.

Catalogue Number	Stove Number	Length Inside, inches	Width Inside, inches	Top Feed Opening, inches	Shipping Weight, pounds	Price
22K502	19	19½	13	9¾	105	$4.50
22K503	22	22	15	11¾	130	5.10

All stoves illustrated in this catalogue are sold under our written binding guarantee and if not entirely satisfactory can be returned to us at our expense, and we will refund your money and freight charges.

ACME GIANT

BURNS ANY THING

$4.95

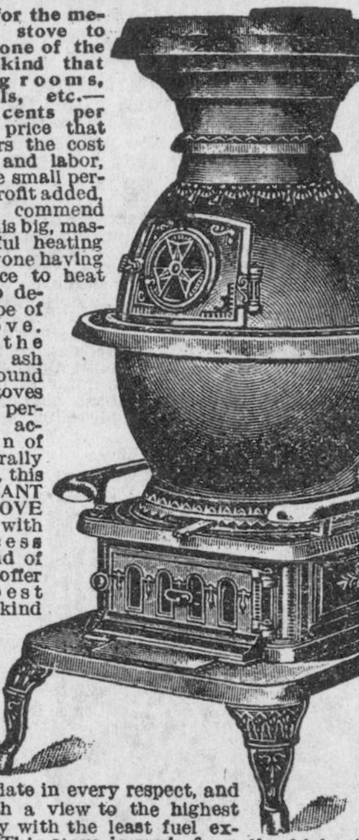

PRICE REDUCED

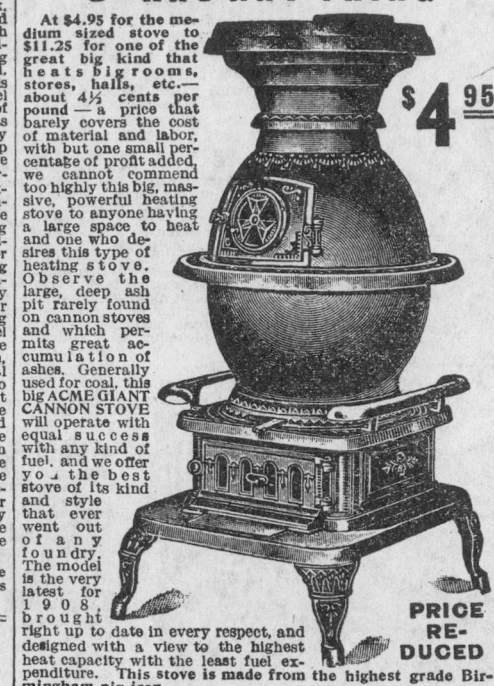

At $4.95 for the medium sized stove to $11.25 for one of the great big kind that heats big rooms, stores, halls, etc.—about 4½ cents per pound—a price that barely covers the cost of material and labor, with but one small percentage of profit added, we cannot commend too highly this big, massive, powerful heating stove to anyone having a large space to heat and one who desires this type of heating stove. Observe the large, deep ash pit rarely found on cannon stoves and which permits great accumulation of ashes. Generally used for coal, this big ACME GIANT CANNON STOVE will operate with equal success with any kind of fuel, and we offer you the best stove of its kind and style that ever went out of any foundry. The model is the very latest for 1908, brought right up to date in every respect, and designed with a view to the highest heat capacity with the least fuel expenditure. This stove is made from the highest grade Birmingham pig iron.

THE INTERIOR CONSTRUCTION is perfected to give absolute fire control, all parts being carefully fitted, braced, stayed and reinforced by our own special process, resulting in the production of the strongest cannon stove on the market, proven best by test. It is made extra heavy throughout, and has a swing feed door, large ash pit door, large ash pit, cast foot rails, draw center and shaking grate; has special heavy fire pot. The top is so arranged that a drum can be attached at any time. 25 cents to $2.00 will pay the freight to any point within 100 to 1,000 miles from our Newark, Ohio, foundry, according to distance and size of the stove selected.

PRICES DELIVERED ON THE CARS AT OUR NEWARK, OHIO, FOUNDRY.

Catalogue Number	Stove Number	Diameter of Fire Pot Inches	Height, inches	Size Pipe to Fit Collar, inches	Floor Space, inches	Weight, pounds	Price
22K475	13	13	40	6	18 x20	134	$ 4.95
22K476	15	15	45½	6	20½x23½	172	6.13
22K477	17	17	47	7	22 x25½	233	8.37
22K478	20	20	56	7	25 x28	319	11.25

THE ACME HICKORY AIRTIGHT AT $4.95 AND $5.62.

$4.95

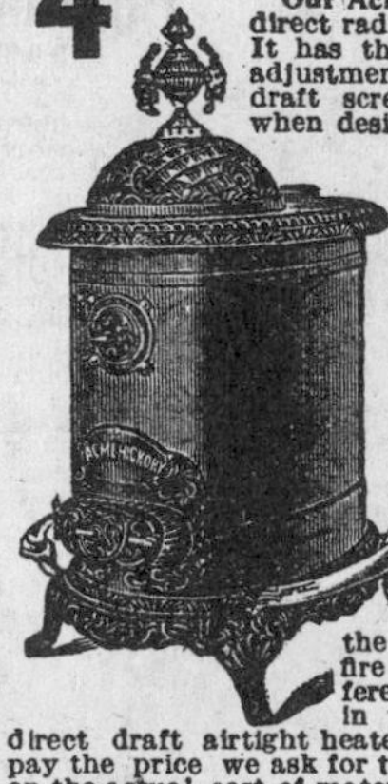

Our Acme Hickory at $4.95 and $5.62 is a direct radiator, instead of a hot air circulator. It has the hot blast down draft with screw adjustment, the large ash opening with direct draft screw adjustment, making it airtight when desired to keep fire. The urn and foot rails are handsomely nickeled. We guarantee this positively the highest grade, best made, most economical in the consumption of fuel and the best distributer of heat of any direct draft, sheet steel airtight stove made, and for the trifling difference in cost between this, our special direct down draft, fancy trimmed airtight, and the more common sheet steel airtight heater, we would especially recommend that you select this stove. This direct draft airtight heater differs from most all other direct draft airtight heaters in that it has a hot blast down draft with the latest screw attachment, making it more economical in the consumption of fuel, more even in the distribution of heat, holding your fire more easily under control. The difference in the cost of the fuel consumed in this stove as against the ordinary direct draft airtight heater will in one winter far more than pay the price we ask for the stove. Our special price is based on the actual cost of material and labor in our own foundry, the largest stove foundry in the world, with but our one small percentage of profit added. These prices are lower than dealers can buy elsewhere in carload lots. Size of pipe to fit collar is 6 inches on both sizes. We can always furnish repairs for Acmes if needed in future years.

Price list of the Acme Hickory with hot blast draft, strongly crated and delivered on the cars at our foundry in Newark, Ohio.

Catalogue Number	Stove No.	Length Inside, inches	Width Inside, inches	Top Feed Opening, inches	Shipping Weight, pounds	Price
22K504	21	21	15	9¾	95	$4.95
22K505	24	24	17	11¾	120	5.62

NEW IMPROVED ACME CANNON

$1.82

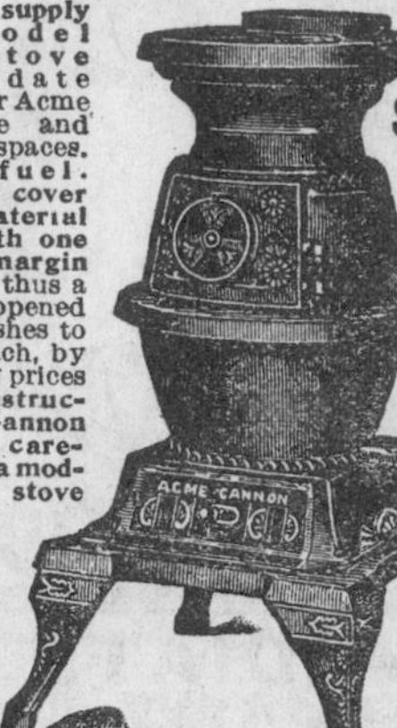

At $1.82 and up we supply this new 1908 model Cannon Heating Stove of approved up to date design, smaller than our Acme Giant Cannon Stove and made for use in smaller spaces. Burns any kind of fuel. Special prices named cover only the cost of material and workmanship with one small conscientious margin of profit added, and thus a great opportunity is opened for the dealer who wishes to buy to sell again, which, by reason of these very low prices he can readily do. Construction of this Acme Cannon Stove is the result of careful experiment and as a moderate priced cannon stove for use in small rooms we guarantee the highest grade in the world. It follows the general lines of the original style cannon heating stove but is the perfected result of careful experiment, embodying modern, up to date features not contained in any cannon stove offer by any other manufacturer in the country.

Catalogue No.	Stove No.	Diameter of Fire Pot	Height	Size of Pipe to Fit Collar	Actual Weight, pounds	Price
22K480	6	9 in.	23½ in.	5 in.	48	$1 82
22K481	7	10 in.	27½ in.	5 in.	54	2.37
22K482	8	11 in.	29½ in.	6 in.	65	2.71
22K483	9	12 in.	32 in.	6 in.	76	3.11

HOT BLAST SHEET STEEL AIRTIGHTS AT $1.69 AND UP WITHOUT FOOT RAILS; $2.23 AND UP WITH FOOT RAILS, AS ILLUSTRATED.

$1.69

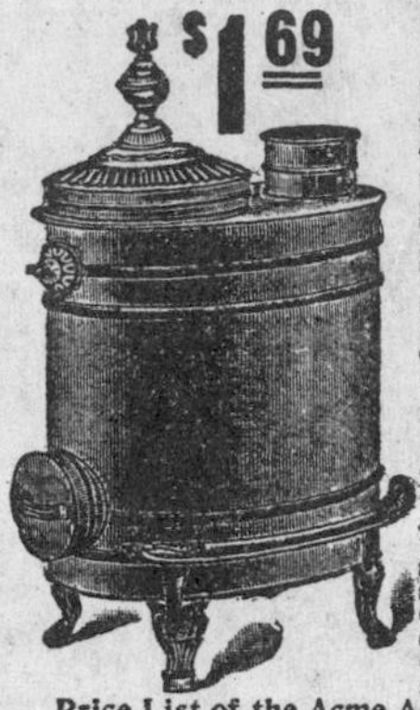

This illustration shows our better grade with hot blast down draft. A better stove than those quoted below for the following reasons: The hot blast draft heats the air before it reaches the fuel, thus producing perfect combustion. The double lining extends up 12 inches from the bottom. The body is made of 26-gauge smooth steel, the lining is 20-gauge. Has fine nickel urn. It will burn chunks, knots, chips, straw, cobs, hay or trash, or anything used for fuel, except coal. The pipe should be provided with a damper. Put two or three inches of ashes in bottom of stove before building fire, and always leave about this quantity when cleaning the stove. In setting up this stove, put the crimped end of stove pipe down. All sizes take 6-inch stove pipe. It has a check draft in the stove top. Strongly crated and delivered on the cars at our foundry in Newark, Ohio.

Price List of the Acme Airtight Smooth Steel Heater.

Catalogue Number	Stove No.	Floor to Urn Top, inches	Length, inches	Width, inches	Height of Body, ins.	Size of Feed Opening, ins.	Size of Ash Opening, ins.	Shipping Weight, lbs.	Price, Smooth Steel Without Foot Rails	Price, Smooth Steel With Foot Rails
22K510	220	34	20½	16½	19¾	10½	6½	40	$1.69	$2.23
22K511	224	38⅝	23¾	17	23¾	12½	6½	45	1.95	2.55
22K512	230	38⅝	29½	17	23¾	12½	6½	50	2.41	3.16

Price List of the Acme Airtight Polished Steel Heater: Body of this stove is made of polished steel and does not require blacking.

Catalogue Number	Stove No.	Floor to Urn Top, ins.	Length, inches	Width, inches	Height of Body, ins.	Size of Feed Opening, ins.	Size of Ash Opening, ins.	Shipping Weight, lbs.	Price, Polished Steel without Foot Rails	Price, Polished Steel with Foot Rails
22K513	320	34	20½	16½	19¾	10½	6½	40	$2.10	$2.69
22K514	324	38⅝	23¾	17	23¾	12½	6½	45	2.47	3.08
25K515	330	38⅝	29½	17	23¾	12½	6½	50	3.01	3.72

SHEET STEEL AIRTIGHT HEATING STOVES, 83 CENTS AND UPWARD.

Delivered on the Cars at Our Foundry in Newark, Ohio.

83c

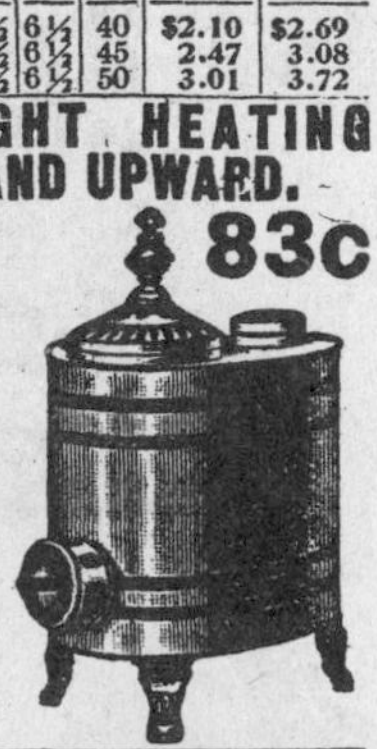

Our line of Sheet Metal Airtight Heaters gives an assortment of styles and sizes not offered by any other makers in the country, and includes the smallest direct draft airtight to the largest down draft hot blast blue polished steel airtight. OUR DOT AIRTIGHT HEATER FOR WOOD. While it is small it is good and suitable for small rooms. It is a direct draft stove, taking in the draft at the ash opening. Has oval sheet body 18, 20 and 24 inches long, and is not lined on the inside like our better airtights. The small size has but three legs, equal distances apart, to support it. The two other sizes have four legs or feet, as shown in the illustration.

Catalogue Number	Stove No.	Floor to Urn Top, inches	Length, inches	Width, inches	Height, inches	Pipe Collar, inches	Shipping Weight, lbs.	Price
22K506	18	28½	17¾	14½	13¾	5	30	$0.83
22K507	21	34	20½	16⅝	19¾	6	35	1.38
22K508	25	38⅝	33¾	17	23¾	6	40	1.68

ACME CHAMPION

THE BEST BOX STOVE MADE.

At $2.49 to $7.25 this is a handsome and well made box heating stove. The top on our box stove swings to one side and the largest chunks of wood may be fed from the top as well as the front. This big top plate swings and is supplied with lids and centers. Size 18 has one 6-inch cover, while size 22 has a 7-inch cover; size 25 is supplied with two 7-inch covers; sizes 28 and 30 have 8-inch covers and one short center; sizes 34 and 36 are provided with two 9-inch covers and a short center. The large sized stoves are invaluable as combination big wood heater and cook stoves, and are so used by thousands of our customers in the cold winter when breakfast may be gotten on the box stove without firing up the cook stove in the kitchen.

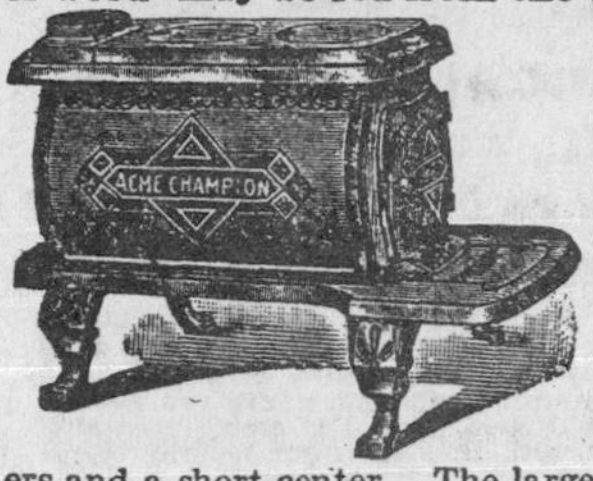

The front end of the stove has a large swing door with a tight fitting slide damper. Every feature that tends to make an up to date 1908 model box stove enters into the construction of our Champion Box. Prices, according to size, quoted below:

Catalogue No.	Stove No.	Height, inches	Size of Door Opening, inches	Size Opening in Main Top, inches	Length Inside, inches	Size Pipe to fit Collar	Actual Weight, lbs.	Price
22K490	18	19½	5½x 7½	6¾x10	19	5 in.	63	$2.49
22K491	22	21½	7½x 8¾	9 x14	23	6 in.	87	3.40
22K492	25	23	8¾x10	10 x18	25½	6 in.	109	4.20
22K493	28	26	9¾x10	10¾x20¾	28	6 in.	132	5.20
22K494	30	26	9¾x10½	10¾x20¾	30½	6 in.	137	5.40
22K495	34	29½	12½x13½	12¾x25	35	6 in.	188	7.00
22K496	36	29½	12½x13½	12¾x25	37	6 in.	190	7.25

$1.98 TO $3.44 ACME PET

HARD OR SOFT COAL LAUNDRY STOVE.

This, our Acme Pet Coal Burning Laundry Stove, has every improvement, including our own dumping grate and is made with two cooking holes. It has a large front pouch feed for putting in coal, has a large size top to take on a big wash boiler, and is made to take 6-inch stove pipe.

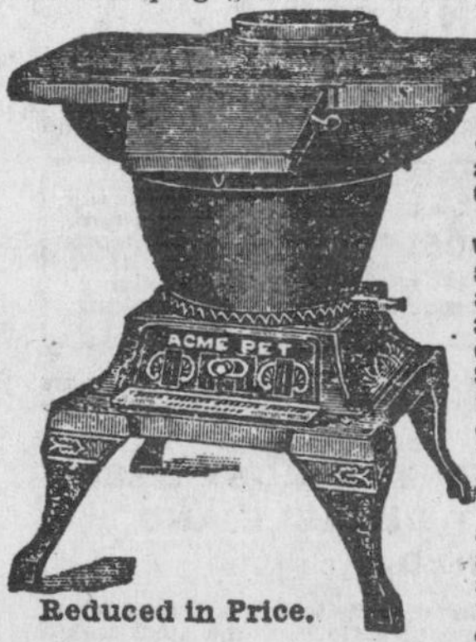

Reduced in Price.

If you have any use for a laundry stove to burn coal, and do not require a stove as large as our Acme Moose at $3.98, illustrated on this page, you will certainly make no mistake in ordering this our **Acme Pet Laundry Stove** in any of the four sizes, at $1.98, $3.11, $3.17 and $3.44, according to size. The freight charges on this laundry stove will amount to practically nothing at all compared with our saving to you in price, as 25 to 75 cents will pay the freight on this stove to any point from 100 to 1,000 miles from our foundry at Newark, Ohio.

We furnish this stove under our binding guarantee, all complete, delivered on board cars at Newark, Ohio, at the different prices as listed below:

Catalogue No.	Size	Size of Covers	Top Surface, in.	Diameter of Fire Pot	Height, inches	Weight, pounds	Price
22K520	50	7½ in.	15x18	9 in.	18	57	$1.98
22K521	7	7 in.	14x19½	11 in.	22½	73	3.11
22K522	88	8 in.	14x19½	11 in.	22½	73	3.17
22K523	8	8 in.	14x21	12½ in.	23½	84	3.44

Turn to page 628 and learn what we are doing to make wonderfully quick delivery on our highest grade steel ranges from a warehouse very near you.

ASK YOUR NEIGHBORS who have bought stoves from us how we have pleased them and how much money we have saved them. Don't buy a range or stove of any kind until you first give us the opportunity of placing one of our ranges or stoves in your home on our 30 days' trial plan. Don't think the freight charges will be too much, don't think you will be delayed in getting the stove, don't think you will have any trouble in setting it up and working it, don't think there will be any trouble about getting repairs in the years to come. We guarantee you against all this, and after you have given the stove 30 days' trial if you are not perfectly satisfied with it, send it back at our expense and we will immediately return your money.

$3.98 FOR OUR ACME MOOSE LAUNDRY STOVE.

$3.98

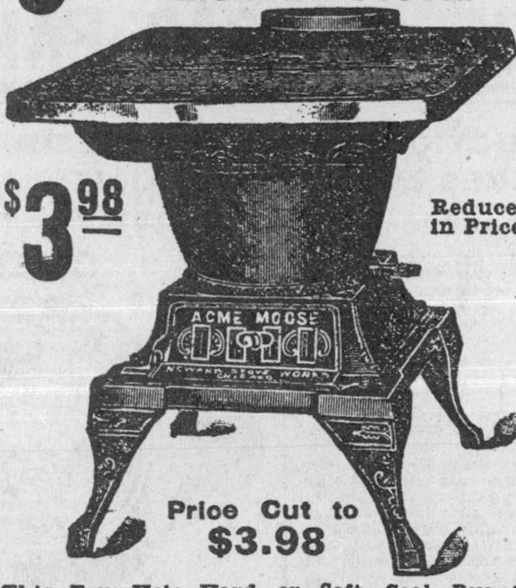

Reduced in Price.

Price Cut to $3.98

This Four-Hole Hard or Soft Coal Burning Laundry Stove is the very best coal laundry stove manufactured in any stove foundry in the world. It far outclasses any other laundry stove on the market in every respect, regardless of name, make or price. There is no laundry stove that compares with it either in quality of materials, size, attractiveness of design, special grate features, etc., and as a big, well made, perfect laundry stove we guarantee it to give you absolute satisfaction.

At our $3.98 price it is really the most wonderful value; it has a very large top, carrying four covers, each fitting in a No. 8 cooking hole, and top measurement over all is 21x22 inches—big enough to accommodate a great big wash boiler and cooking utensils at the same time. It will also take the new style steel or galvanized iron tubs now in common use and its arrangement of the fire pot and construction of main top is such that the heat is evenly distributed and it is a quick heater, economical in the use of fuel, and a splendid up to date laundry stove, with all the good features of every laundry stove on the market and the defects of none.

We furnish our Acme Drum Oven at $1.98 extra, as illustrated and described below, and which, in connection with this laundry stove, makes a complete cooking stove. This stove weighs 105 pounds, has four cooking holes. Diameter of fire pot, 12½ inches. Top cooking surface, 21x22 inches. Height, 23½ inches.

Immediate Shipment. We have a large stock stored ready for immediate shipment.

No. 22K530 Price....................$3.98

OUR NEW IMPROVED

1908 MODEL ACME DRUM OVEN, NOW ONLY - - $1.98

Reduced in Price.

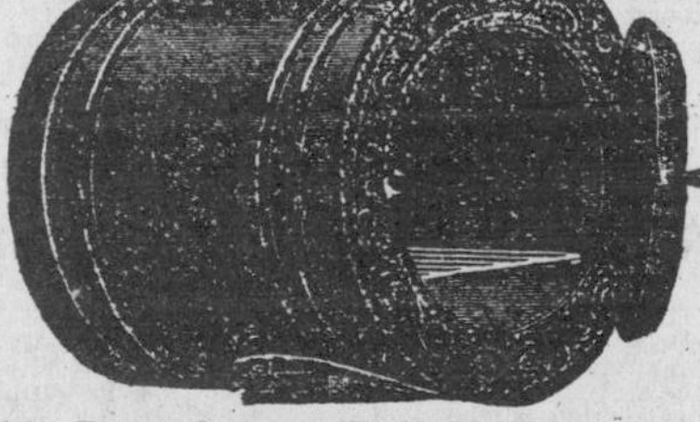

This Drum Oven will make a good cooking stove out of any heater or laundry stove. Attach this oven to any 6-inch stove pipe and to any laundry stove or to any heating stove and you will have an ideal cooking stove and heater or laundry stove combined in one. The body is substantially constructed of cold rolled steel, cast front and back, cast collar top and bottom to fit 6-inch pipe. Is fitted with removable steel rack. Oven measures 10 inches wide, will easily accommodate a large 9-inch pie plate or a 9x18-inch baking or roasting pan. It is so constructed to give a circulation of heat that the oven will heat evenly and thoroughly, making it a first class baker. We would especially recommend that in ordering a laundry stove or a small heating stove that you order one of our **Acme Drum Ovens.** Even though you have a cook stove or a range in your kitchen, you will find this, our **Acme Drum Oven,** almost indispensable, attached to your laundry stove or heater, for oftentimes you will find it convenient, on washday, to get your lunch or dinner on the laundry stove in connection with the Acme Drum or in the evening a quick luncheon or small supper or dinner can be conveniently prepared on one of our heating stoves in combination with this new 1908 **Model Acme Drum Oven,** which we furnish for only $1.98. The outside measurement of the drum is 20x15 inches. Shipping weight, 40 pounds. It's a wonderfully quick baker, saves the waste of heat passing up the pipe; tends, in connection with the heating stove, to give more radiation, therefore more heat, out of a given amount of fuel and is especially efficient when used in connection with a laundry or heating stove.

No. 22K531 Price....................$1.98

$2.98 TO $3.64 ACME PRIDE

SPECIAL HARD OR SOFT COAL BURNING LAUNDRY STOVE.

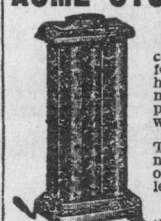

This is our new model 1908 improved special coal burning laundry stove, our Acme Pride, which we offer at only $2.98 and up, a price representing the mere cost of materials and labor in our own stove foundry at Newark, Ohio, where manufacturing costs are lower than in any other stove foundry in the world, and to this very low manufacturing cost we add only one small margin of profit, so that this stove, when sent to you at our $2.98 to $3.64 price, represents better value and it is in every way a better laundry stove than you could secure at a much higher price.

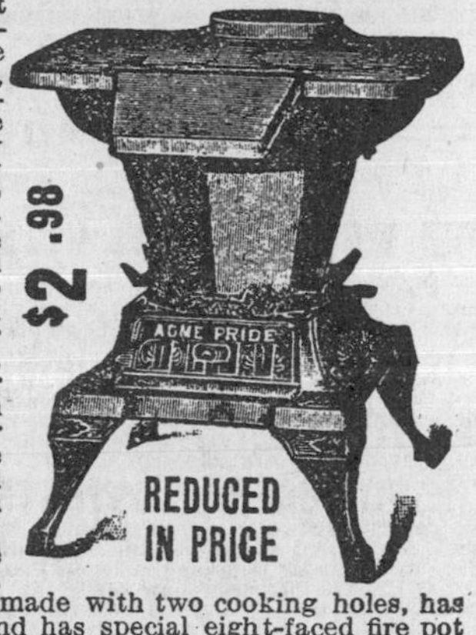

REDUCED IN PRICE

This, our Acme Pride Improved Laundry Stove, is made with two cooking holes, has a very liberal top and has special eight-faced fire pot equipped with special holders, so that you may heat eight sad irons at one time. **These special features make it an ideal laundry stove,** and as it is a splendid heater and the irons lie close to the fire, they heat quickly while you may be using the top of the stove for cooking or some other purpose. It has large special pouch feed for coal and our special dumping grate.

Immediate Shipment. We have a large stock stored ready for immediate shipment.

Acme Pride, made in three sizes as listed below, and delivered on cars at Newark, Ohio.

Catalogue No.	Stove No.	Size of Covers	Top Surface, inches	Size of Pipe to fit Collar	Diameter of Fire Pot, in.	Height, inches	Weight, pounds	Price
22K525	7	7 in.	13½x19½	6 in.	11½	25	78	$2.98
22K526	88	8 in.	13½x19½	6 in.	11½	25	78	3.40
22K527	8	8 in.	14 x21	6 in.	12½	25	93	3.64

ACME STOVE PIPE RADIATORS.

Square Style.

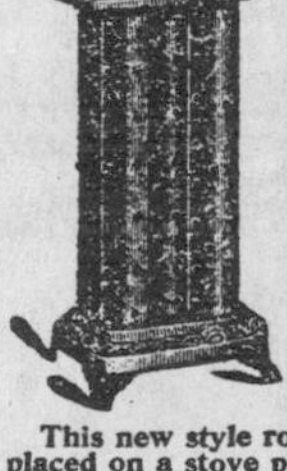

For use with stoves burning anthracite coal or wood. This style is adapted only for floors above the stove. They are very handsome in design, and are bought by many who would not otherwise run a stove pipe through their house. Cannot be used with soft coal.

No. 22K537 For 6-inch stove pipe. Tubes made of Woods' refined iron. Aluminum finished, cast iron top and base. Size of base, 17½x13¾ inches; height, with legs, 37 inches. Weight, crated, 60 pounds. Price....................$4.25

No 22K538 Same as above, except the body is made of Woods' patent planished iron. Price....................$4.98

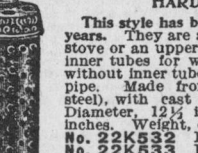

This new style round Acme Radiator can be placed on a stove pipe in the same room with a stove, or it can be placed in an upstairs room on a stove pipe by running through from any kind of a stove below and will heat the upper room without the expenditure of a single extra cent for fuel. When used in the same room with the stove the feet for the radiator are not required, but when you attach it to the stove pipe in the upper room it has a set of feet to support it at the floor. For use with stoves burning anthracite coal or wood. Weight, crated, 30 pounds.

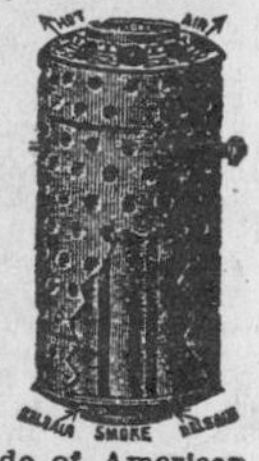

No. 22K539 For 6-inch stove pipe, made of smooth cold rolled steel. Diameter, 12 inches. Height, with feet, 30½ inches. Price....................$2.65

No. 22K540 For 6-inch stove pipe, made of American patent planished iron. Diameter, 12 inches. Height, with feet, 30½ inches. Price....................$3.25

The Original Round Style Radiator.

HARD OR SOFT COAL.

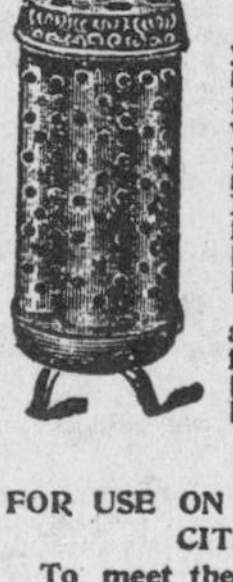

This style has been successfully sold for many years. They are adapted either for the back of stove or an upper room or hall. Furnished with inner tubes for wood and anthracite coal and without inner tubes for soft coal, for 6-inch stove pipe. Made from Woods' refined iron (sheet steel), with cast iron ends. Aluminum finish. Diameter, 12½ inches; height, with legs, 38 inches. Weight, crated, 50 pounds.

No. 22K532 For soft coal.......$3.80
No. 22K533 For hard coal or wood. 3.85

No. 22K534 and No. 22K535 are the same as above, except made of Woods' patent planished iron.

No. 22K534 For hard coal or wood. $4.84
No. 22K535 For soft coal........ 4.80

Round Pipe Style.

FOR USE ON STOVES BURNING ANTHRACITE COAL OR WOOD.

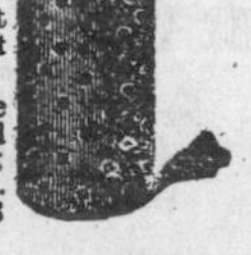

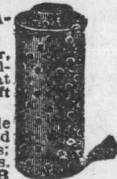

To meet the demand for a cheap radiator, this style is added. It is small but very efficient, either on the back of a stove or to heat small upper rooms. Cannot be used with soft coal.

No. 22K536 For 6-inch stove pipe. Made of Woods' refined iron, with aluminum finished cast iron top and base. Diameter, 10 inches; height, 28 inches. Weight, crated, 27 pounds. Price....................$1.98

SPECIAL VALUES IN WEHRLE MODEL No. 80 NEWEST COLONIAL DESIGN GAS RANGES $11.08 TO $20.06

ABSOLUTELY PERFECT IN CONSTRUCTION. THE MOST DESIRABLE, ECONOMICAL AND SATISFACTORY GAS RANGES MADE. SAVE TIME, LABOR AND FUEL.

READ THIS PAGE CAREFULLY AND LEARN THE MANY ADVANTAGES OF COOKING WITH GAS.

OUR WEHRLE MODEL No. 80 GAS RANGES make gas, beyond question, the most satisfactory of all fuels. Our valves, our burners, our ovens, our flue system, in short, our entire construction make our Wehrle Model No. 80 Gas Ranges absolutely perfect in operation, embodying the following strong features: Strength, Durability, Economy, Cleanliness, Quickness, Convenience, Attractiveness, Simplicity and Reliability.

THEY ARE BUILT IN OUR NEWARK, OHIO, Stove and Range Foundry—the largest in the world. We own our own natural gas wells in Newark and use natural gas in our works and our offices. Our superintendent and workmen use it in their homes, giving us the advantage—in being located in a natural gas town—of building natural gas ranges where we can test every range we build before shipping.

THE PICTURES ILLUSTRATE our latest original designs sold direct to the customer at actual foundry cost with but our one small percentage of profit added, thereby eliminating all dealers', jobbers' and middlemen's profits and sold to you under our binding guarantee, that if they are not all or even more than we claim for them and, after a thorough test, if you do not find our Wehrle Model No. 80 Gas Ranges the best constructed, the best bakers, the quickest way, the safest way, the cheapest way and, by far, the cleanest way of cooking, and if the gas range that we send you is not satisfactory in every way and the greatest bargain you have ever heard of, you can return it to us at our expense and we will promptly refund your money, including what you paid for freight charges.

WHEN YOU HAVE BOUGHT A WEHRLE MODEL No. 80 GAS RANGE you can feel satisfied you have bought the very best that money can buy. In the construction you will get the benefit of our number of years' experience in building stoves and ranges. We employ only the most skilled labor and, operating as we do the largest stove and range plant in the world, running steadily every working day in the year and by the introduction of the very latest, new and modern gas range making machinery, we have been able to turn out these ranges at a minimum of cost.

THE OVEN DOOR is equipped with our Special Oven Door Thermometer, as illustrated, which measures heat just as a clock measures time, or a steam gauge measures steam pressure. Tells you when your oven has reached the degree of heat desired, makes it easy to maintain a uniform temperature and makes good baking easy to the most inexperienced. This magnificent range and dependable thermometer do away with "bad luck" when baking, which is more often due to improper heat in the oven than any other cause.

OVEN THERMOMETER.

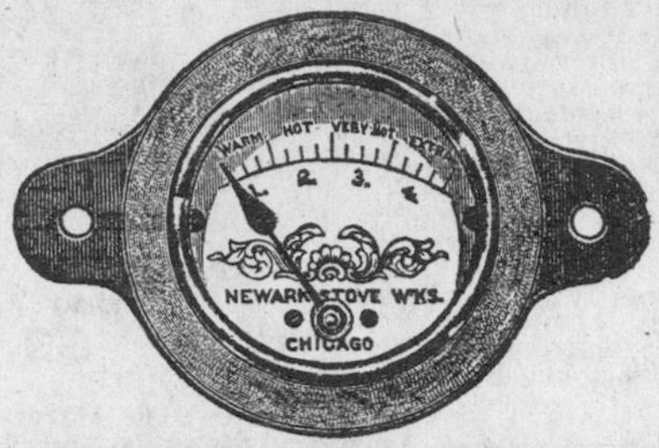

WARM HOT VERY HOT EXTRA
1. 2. 3. 4.
NEWARK STOVE W'KS.
CHICAGO

EVERY HOUSEKEEPER will immediately appreciate the advantages of our Oven Thermometer, which we furnish free with our Wehrle Model Gas Ranges, and will find it one of the most necessary and valuable parts. It is accurate in registration and as near perfection as it is possible to attain. Tells you how to manage your fire, how to reach the proper degree of heat for baking, how to save gas bills. It shows accurately the temperature of the oven without the necessity of opening the door, which allows the accumulated heat to escape. In short and unquestionably our dependable oven door thermometer is the greatest convenience and the greatest gas saver ever brought to the housekeeper's aid.

YOUR GAS COMPANY will connect any of our Wehrle Model Gas Ranges for you at the same small charge they always make and they will not ask you any more because the stove is not bought from them. Gas companies are always glad to connect our ranges, as they are desirous of selling their product of gas and are not anxious to be dealers in gas stoves. They were compelled to go into the gas stove business because the stove and hardware dealers asked such high prices that the people would not buy a gas stove. In this way the use of gas was greatly restricted, but our prices on gas stoves are so low and we sell so many gas stoves and ranges that the gas companies are very friendly to us and connect the stoves for our customers for the same small fee they charge when they sell a stove or range and you will find the gas companies recommend our stoves and ranges everywhere as the most economical, durable and efficient stoves and ranges to be found.

REMEMBER ALSO, you have thirty days' trial, during which time you can assure yourself that you have obtained from us the greatest possible value for your money. If you feel dissatisfied at any time during the thirty days' trial you can return the range to us and your money will be promptly refunded.

DETAILED DESCRIPTION WEHRLE MODEL No. 80 GAS RANGES AT $11.08 TO $20.06

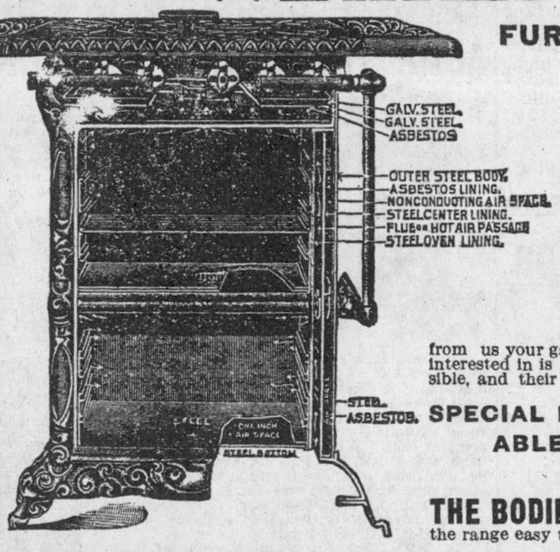

GALV. STEEL
GALV. STEEL
ASBESTOS
OUTER STEEL BODY
ASBESTOS LINING
NONCONDUCTING AIR SPACE
STEEL CENTER LINING
FLUE OR HOT AIR PASSAGE
STEEL OVEN LINING
STEEL
CH. INCH AIR SPACE
STEEL BOTTOM
STEEL
ASBESTOS

The same cooking utensils used on your coal and wood burning stove can be used on any of our gas stoves with equally good results.

FURNISHED FOR EITHER NATURAL OR MANUFACTURED GAS AND FOR ANY PRESSURE DESIRED. CANNOT BE USED WITH GASOLINE OR ACETYLENE GAS.

THESE ARE THE VERY HIGHEST GRADE GAS RANGES, the best on the market, made of the highest grade of polished steel of beautiful color, not requiring blacking or japan. Every range is guaranteed to be perfect in operation and workmanship. The ranges must be seen to be appreciated. The illustrations do not do them justice. We guarantee our gas ranges to be the very best and most improved construction, most desirable, most economical, most durable and by far the handsomest gas ranges made in the world. They are built especially with a view to economy in the use of fuel. **We guarantee our gas ranges will do more work, using less gas, than any other ranges on the market.** They can be set near the open door without being affected by the drafts, as the sides are closed all around. We offer these splendid ranges on the same basis as we offer our other goods, namely, the manufacturing cost with just our one small percentage of profit added. If you buy a gas stove or range from us your gas company will connect it for you for the same small charge they make when they furnish the range. All they are interested in is getting you to burn their gas and they will gladly make it just as much to your advantage to use a gas stove as possible, and their charge for connecting it will be very little.

> **THESE RANGES** bake cakes, pies, bread and broil with same fire. Heat water and cook with same fire. Have special burners for slow cooking. Have special burners for fast cooking.

SPECIAL FEATURES WHICH MAKE OUR LINE OF GAS RANGES THE MOST DESIRABLE BEST CONSTRUCTED MOST ECONOMICAL, MOST DURABLE AND HANDSOMEST GAS RANGES IN THE WORLD.

THE BODIES are constructed of Wellsville polished steel. Double protected asbestos lined oven walls to keep the heat where it belongs. No japan or other paint used on the bodies to burn off, and the smooth surface of the steel makes the range easy to keep clean.

THE OVEN insulation is perfect and consists of an outer steel body, asbestos lining and air space, an inner steel lining and a hot air flue (see sectional view). This construction prevents any loss of heat by radiation through the sides of the stove into the room. The oven top is of heavy sheet steel, lined with asbestos. The construction of the oven flues is such that the oven is evenly heated and the burning of foods at the bottom is prevented. The oven rack is of wire, insuring cleanliness.

OVEN BOTTOM is made of cast iron stove plate. We call special attention to this original feature in our entire line of Wehrle Model Gas Ranges as being far superior to steel. The cast iron bottom always remains level and will not buckle or warp as a steel bottom is sure to do when it comes in direct contact with the gas flame and also has the advantage of retaining 80 per cent more heat than steel oven bottoms found in other gas ranges.

THE CAST OVEN BOTTOM is fitted with a 7-inch cooking lid and extra grate, providing an extra cooking hole when the oven is not in use for baking purposes. This is one of the many useful, strong, exclusive features of our Wehrle Model Gas Range.

MATCH SCRATCHER on the main front will be found very convenient and satisfactory. Does away with the necessity of defacing your walls, range or floor when ready to light burners for cooking.

THE OVEN FLUES force the heat to travel a greater distance and cover more surface than is possible with any other gas range made, so that every unit of heat is utilized and the oven evenly heated without dead corners, on a small amount of gas, and will "bake even," top and bottom, the most delicate cake or pastry on either the upper or lower rack, or both at the same time.

OVEN DOORS are made double with lining of asbestos, are carefully spring poised so that they may be opened or closed without jarring the range, thus protecting it. When open, the door forms a most convenient shelf flush with the oven bottom. The oven door balancing spring is very simple and effective.

THE LOWER OR BROILING OVEN has pressed steel drip pan with strong wire rack open at one corner to baste meat with spoon. The bottoms are double, with circulating air space, and prevent excessive heat near the floor.

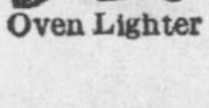

Oven Lighter

OVEN AND BROILER BURNERS are very powerful and give four lines of flame. They are provided with a pilot oven lighter as illustrated.

TOP BURNERS. All of these ranges are equipped with four top burners made from the finest gray iron, acknowledged to be the only material standing continued hard use in burning gas. Three of these burners are single burners, as illustrated, and produce 40 jets of hot flame. One of the burners is a giant burner of triple capacity, with simmering burner in the center as illustrated, and produces 80 jets of hot flame. The giant burner produces quick heat; the simmering burner produces slow heat. Each burner has nickel plated adjustable air mixers, which economically provide for the mixture of air and gas in the ratio of 80% air to 20% gas. These burners lift out without loosening a bolt, leaving the top open and clear for cleaning. These burners are guaranteed non-leaking, easy to regulate and easy to keep clean.

Single Burner.

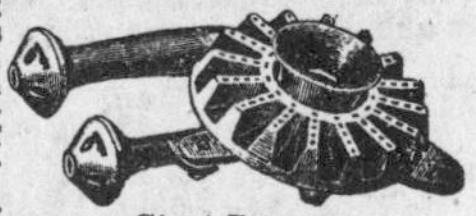

Giant Burner.

THE OVEN AND BROILER BURNERS on the entire line of Wehrle Model Gas Ranges are made of cast iron, cored and in one piece. Ordinary gas range burners are often made in two pieces, causing leaks and wasting gas, and we can only caution you to beware of such cheap construction.

BURNER VALVES. All burners are fitted with heat resisting wood handled lever valves as illustrated. These are positive in action, non-leaking and absolutely safe in operation and have been proven by experience to be the only valves which will not get out of order.

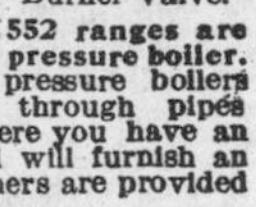

Burner Valve.

WATER HEATERS. Our Nos. 22K547, 22K548, 22K551 and 22K552 ranges are furnished with a water heater to connect with a pressure boiler. For price on the pressure boiler see page 610. Water heaters and pressure boilers are used only where there is a supply furnishing constant pressure through pipes which can only be obtained in towns and cities having water works or where you have an elevated water pressure tank. The water heater is of large capacity and will furnish an abundance of hot water at a minimum cost of fuel. The water heater burners are provided with a lighter. Two cooking holes with lids are provided over water heaters.

CAREFUL INSPECTION. Every gas range and gas heater we build is set up complete and thoroughly inspected and tested before being crated for shipment, thus insuring perfect operation and accurate fitting of all parts.

Better ranges for the money could not be made, and more satisfactory ranges to use cannot be found. They are guaranteed the greatest values ever offered in gas ranges.

WEHRLE MODEL No. 80 Single Oven GAS RANGE.

WITH COUNTERBALANCED DROP OVEN DOOR.

AT $11.08 TO $12.88 we offer this famous single oven gas range at prices lower than the lowest, lower than anyone can offer them, lower than any gas company cares to sell them, so low that gas companies are buying them from us and are proud to connect them for you at a small fee, and so low that it relieves them of the expense and trouble of trying to sell gas ranges, for we are selling them so fast they are kept busy increasing their facilities and capacity for supplying gas. Handsomely designed removable cast end shelves. Closely fitted and even baking oven, fitted with our dependable oven door thermometer which accurately indicates the proper heat for baking and saves gas bills. Handsomely carved oven door frame with genuine silver nickel plated oven door handle and name plate, and silver nickeled valve line. Note the full description on preceding page. Has three standard star burners, one triple capacity giant burner with simmering burner in center and lighting separately. Four-line burner for oven and oven lighter. The illustration shows it ready for natural gas. When ordered for artificial gas we furnish it with open top grates. We can always furnish repairs for our gas ranges.

CAREFUL INSPECTION. Every gas range and gas heater we build is set up complete and thoroughly inspected and tested before being crated for shipment, thus insuring perfect operation and accurate fitting of all parts.

PRICE LIST SINGLE OVEN GAS RANGE. Do not fail to state whether you use manufactured gas or natural gas. The ranges cannot be used with gasoline or acetylene gas.

Catalogue No.	Stove No.	Size of Top, Including End Shelves, inches	Size of Oven, inches	Height from Floor, inches	Shipping Weight, pounds	Price for Manufactured Gas	Price for Natural Gas
22K545	16P	35½x22¼	16x16¼x11	30	162	$11.08	$11.58
22K546	18P	37½x22¼	18x16¼x11	30	170	12.33	12.88

WEHRLE MODEL No. 80 GAS RANGE.

WITH LOW BROILING OVEN. IMPROVED NEW DESIGN.

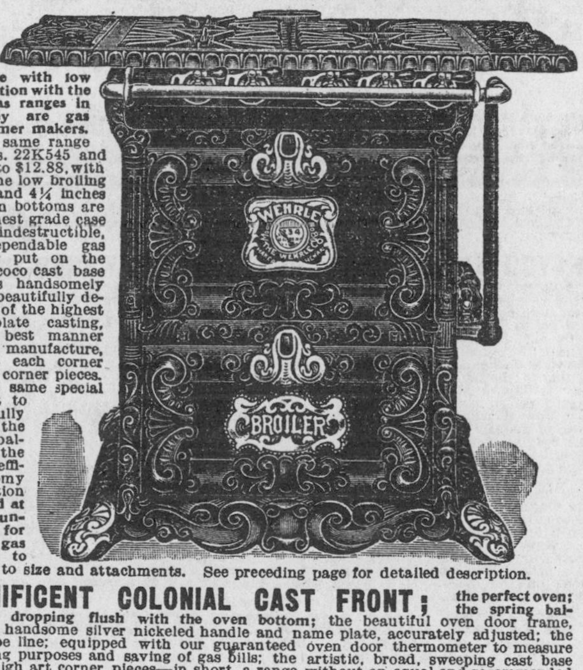

AT $13.93 TO $15.93 we offer this Drop Door Gas Range with low broiler in competition with the highest priced gas ranges in the world. They are gas savers and customer makers. This is the exact same range as Catalogue Nos. 22K545 and 22K546 at $11.08 to $12.88, with the addition of the low broiling oven, and is 3¼ and 4¼ inches higher. The oven bottoms are made of the highest grade case iron, practically indestructible, and a more dependable gas range was never put on the market. The rococo cast base or foundation is handsomely ornamented and beautifully designed; is made of the highest quality stove plate casting, finished in the best manner known to stove manufacture, and trimmed at each corner with swell nickel corner pieces. It has the exact same special points of interest to the user, as carefully described above, the same counterbalanced oven door, the guarantee of efficiency and economy in the consumption of gas, and is sold at the heretofore unheard of price for such an elegant gas range of $13.93 to $15.93, according to size and attachments. See preceding page for detailed description.

THE MAGNIFICENT COLONIAL CAST FRONT; the perfect oven; the spring balanced oven door dropping flush with the oven bottom; the beautiful oven door frame, ornamented with handsome silver nickeled handle and name plate, accurately adjusted; the silver nickeled pipe line; equipped with our guaranteed oven door thermometer to measure the heat for baking purposes and saving of gas bills; the artistic, broad, sweeping cast base with its ornate high art corner pieces—in short, a range without an equal and recommended to the wide awake housekeeper for economy in doing any kind of cooking.

The illustration shows it ready for manufactured gas. When ordered for natural gas, we furnish this range with closed lids or griddle covers. One of these lids is made in two sections to accommodate different size utensils.

PRICE LIST WEHRLE RANGE WITH LOW BROILING OVEN. Do not fail to state whether you use manufactured gas or natural gas. These ranges cannot be used with gasoline or acetylene gas.

Catalogue No.	Stove No.	Size of Top, Including End Shelves, inches	Baking Oven, inches	Broiling Oven, inches	Height from Floor, inches	Shipping Weight, pounds	Price for Manufactured Gas	Price for Natural Gas
22K549	26P	35½x22¼	16x16¼x11	16x16¼x9¼	32½	181	$13.93	$14.43
22K550	28P	37½x22¼	18x16¼x11	18x16¼x9¼	33½	193	15.43	15.93

30 DAYS' TRIAL.

REMEMBER, we have a large stock on hand, all crated and ready for immediate shipment, and accept your order for one of our very highest grade Wehrle Model Gas Ranges, with the understanding and agreement that you can give it thirty days' trial, and if, during that time, you have any reason to feel dissatisfied, if it does not operate perfectly, if you find it is not by far the most wonderful labor saving and fuel saving stove you have ever used, and if you find you have not made an immense saving in every way, and that we have furnished you one of our Wehrle Model Gas Ranges at just half the price such a stove would cost you from any other dealer, you are at perfect liberty to return the stove to us at our expense, and we will immediately refund your money, including the transportation charges you have paid.

WEHRLE MODEL No. 80 Single Oven GAS RANGE.

With Water Heater Extension, Containing Water Coil to be Connected to a Range Boiler Having City Water Pressure.

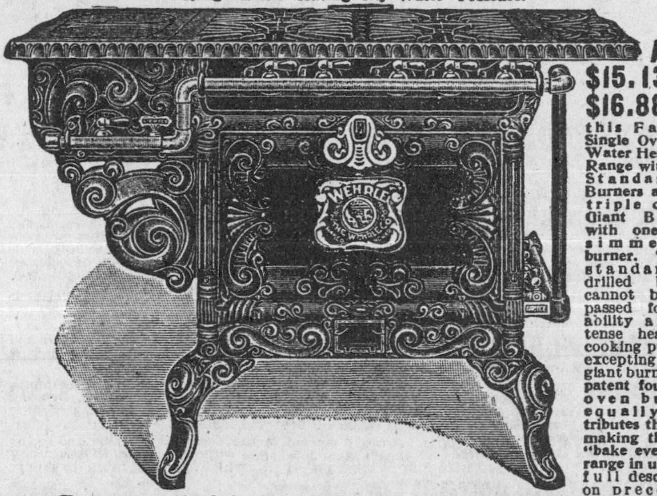

AT $15.13 TO $16.88 we offer this Famous Single Oven and Water Heater Gas Range with three Standard Star Burners and one triple capacity Giant Burner with one small simmering burner. These standard star drilled burners cannot be surpassed for durability and intense heat for cooking purposes excepting by our giant burner. Our patent four-line oven burner equally distributes the heat, making the only "bake even" gas range in use. See full description on preceding page. Has a gorgeously designed cast front (Colonial design). Perfect spring balanced oven door, drops flush with the oven bottom. Perfect baking oven. Artistic oven door and frame, with silver nickeled oven door handle and name plate. Large and efficient water heater attachment; will heat a 30-gallon range boiler at a minimum cost for gas; pilot light for oven and water heater burners. Accurately adjusted silver nickeled pipe line. Equipped with our guaranteed oven door thermometer to measure the heat for baking and saves gas bills. Illustration shows range with open top grates for artificial gas. When ordered for natural gas we furnish the range with closed lids or griddle covers. One of these lids is made in two sections to accommodate different size utensils. Gas cocks are nickeled on brass and provided with non-conducting maple wood handles.

PRICE LIST WEHRLE SINGLE OVEN GAS RANGE. Including water heater extension and water coil. Do not fail to state whether you use manufactured gas or natural gas. These ranges cannot be used with gasoline or acetylene gas.

Catalogue No.	Stove No.	Size of Top, Including Water Heater and End Shelf, inches	Size of Oven, inches	Height from Floor, inches	Shipping Weight, pounds	Price for Manufactured Gas	Price for Natural Gas
22K547	16W	39½x22¼	16x16¼x11	30	170	$15.13	$15.63
22K548	18W	41½x22¼	18x16¼x11	30	185	16.38	16.88

WEHRLE MODEL No. 80 GAS RANGE.

With Convenient, Large, Roomy, Low Broiling Oven, With Powerful Water Heater Extension, Containing Water Coil to be Connected to a Range Boiler Having City Water Pressure.

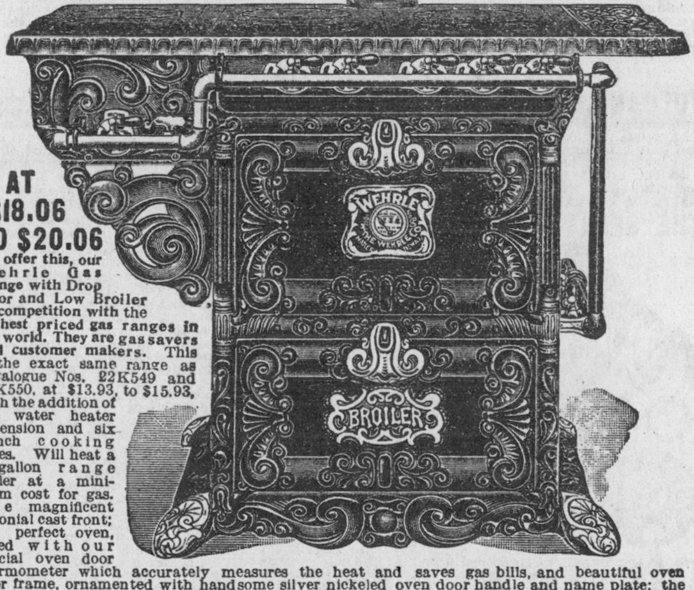

AT $18.06 TO $20.06 we offer this, our Wehrle Gas Range with Drop Door and Low Broiler in competition with the highest priced gas ranges in the world. They are gas savers and customer makers. This is the exact same range as Catalogue Nos. 22K549 and 22K550, at $13.93, to $15.93, with the addition of the water heater extension and six 7-inch cooking holes. Will heat a 30-gallon range boiler at a minimum cost for gas. The magnificent Colonial cast front; the perfect oven, fitted with our special oven door thermometer which accurately measures the heat and saves gas bills, and beautiful oven door frame, ornamented with handsome silver nickeled oven door handle and name plate; the powerful water heater and artistic, broad sweeping cast base, with its ornate high art nickeled corner pieces—in short, embodying all the strong and up to date features of every other high grade gas range, with the defects of none, and our untiring labor and strong efforts to produce absolutely the best, stamps our entire line of Wehrle Model Gas Ranges without an equal and recommends them to the wide awake housekeeper for economy, simplicity, durability and reliability. See preceding page for detailed description.

The illustration shows it ready for natural gas. When ordered for artificial gas we furnish this range with open top grates.

PRICE LIST WEHRLE LOW BROILING GAS RANGE, INCLUDING WATER HEATER EXTENSION AND WATER COIL. Do not fail to state whether you use manufactured gas or natural gas. These ranges cannot be used with gasoline or acetylene gas.

Catalogue No.	Stove No.	Size of Top, Including Water Heater and End Shelf, ins.	Baking Oven, inches	Broiling Oven, inches	Height from Floor, inches	Shipping Weight, pounds	Price for Manufactured Gas	Price for Natural Gas
22K551	26W	39½x22¼	16x16¼x11	16x16¼x9¼	32½	205	$18.06	$18.56
22K552	28W	41½x22¼	18x16¼x11	18x16¼x9¼	33½	225	19.56	20.06

Every stove is thoroughly inspected and tested before shipment.

PROMPT SHIPMENT. We have a large stock on hand, crated, ready for immediate shipment, and when you decide to send us your order, enclose our price and the stove will be sent direct to you without any delay whatever.

A WORD ABOUT FREIGHT CHARGES. The freight charges on one of our Wehrle Gas Ranges will amount to next to nothing in comparison to what you save in price. Any one of them can be shipped to almost any point in Ohio, Indiana, West Virginia or Kansas for from 50 cents to $2.00; other states in proportion, according to distance.

CAREFUL INSPECTION. Every gas range and gas heater we build is set up complete and thoroughly inspected and tested before being crated for shipment, thus insuring perfect operation and accurate fitting of all parts.

SAFES

SOLD DIRECT FROM OUR FACTORY AT NEWARK, OHIO.

The Vulcan Safe is the only safe you can buy at a fair margin of profit over factory cost; the only safe sold on a long free trial, and the only safe that is covered by a written long term guarantee. The Vulcan Safes are built to last a lifetime. The fireproof qualities are permanent. The Vulcan Safe will be just as fireproof in ten, twenty or fifty years from now as it is today.

THE VULCAN CONSTRUCTION.

ALL VULCAN SAFES are built with one piece of tough wrought steel forming the sides, top and bottom. This is strongly riveted with heavy boiler rivets to the wrought steel front and back frames which are each made from one continuous angle of bar steel passing entirely around the body of the safe. The bottom is made double to secure greater strength and rigidity. The back is a single plate of selected wrought steel. The front of the door is also a solid plate of heavy hammered wrought steel.

THE BODY OF THE SAFE is riveted and braced in a way which insures enormous strength and avoids the danger of breaking open by falling from great heights or being crushed by heavy timbers or falling walls.

THE BOLT WORK AND LOCKS are fitted on the inner edge of the doors and the inner steel door plate is removable, making them easy of access for oiling or changing the combination.

THE DOORS are secured by heavy round bolts projecting from both sides into the jambs of the safe (on the larger sizes from the top and bottom also), insuring perfect security. The doors are provided with from three to seven flanges or rebates according to the size, which serve to prevent the entrance of heat and insure a perfectly tight joint.

WE USE OUTSIDE HINGES strongly riveted to the steel angle frame and to the heavy steel door plate without cutting, thus insuring great strength. They are fitted with finely nickel plated tips which are removable for oiling.

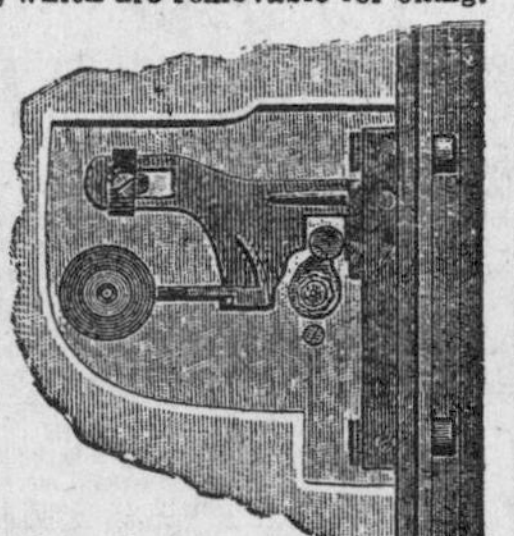

OUR SPECIAL VULCAN BOLT WORK is very strong but simple in design, is easily operated and never gets out of order. All bolts are turned, polished and nickel plated. No part of the bolt work is in any way connected with the lock plate but is operated independently by a cold rolled steel handle to the left of the lock dial.

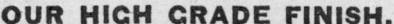

OUR FIREPROOF CEMENT is an absolutely fireproof steam generating preparation which is introduced between the interior and outer walls of our safes in a semiliquid state, filling every crevice and adhering firmly to the steel body. In a short time it becomes perfectly dry and hard as granite, adding greatly to the strength of the safe. Our steam generating cement is the best and most costly that can be procured and is mixed by experts. There is nothing better to be had. It insures perfect safety to the contents of the safe in the hottest and fiercest fires. The chemical change which it undergoes when subjected to great heat develops a vast quantity of vapor which fills every pore of the filling and forms a cool moist wall entirely surrounding and protecting the contents of the safe. The doors are protected in the same manner. A heavy wall of our fireproof cement between the lock case and the front of the door makes it just as fireproof as the body of the safe. Our fireproof filling will remain unchanged and retain its fire resisting properties for centuries. Vulcan Safes never wear out and never lose their fireproof qualities.

THE CABINET WORK is handsomely finished in imitation cherry and varnished. In the larger safes the front is decorated with fancy beaded moulding. The fronts of the drawers are finished in costly decorative woods, such as birdseye maple, and quarter sawed oak. The cabinets are all nicely carpeted, equipped with subtreasury, with high grade lock, with two flat keys, also with pigeonholes, drawers and book spaces as described and illustrated.

OUR HIGH GRADE FINISH.

VULCAN SAFES ARE FINISHED IN BLACK, beautifully ornamented with gold stripings and decorated with original and artistic marine views and finished with the best varnish. Our decorators are real artists in their line and take pride in the beauty of their work. Dial knob, hinge tips and bolt handles are nickel plated and highly polished. The designs are not all the same but vary according to the taste of the artist. The glossy black finish of the safe contrasting with the bright colors used in decorating and striping and in the marine views gives a beautiful effect which it is impossible to do justice to in a photograph. Our high grade finish makes the Vulcan Safe an ornament to the most elegantly furnished office or storeroom.

THE GREAT EAGLE COMBINATION LOCK, used on our line of safes listed on this and the following page, is made by the Eagle Lock Co., of Terryville, Conn., a concern with a world wide reputation as manufacturers of locks of the highest quality. This Combination Lock is a model of strength and simplicity. It cannot be picked by the most expert and yet is so simple that the combination can be changed by the owner in a few minutes at any time by simply removing the inner steel door plate and following the simple directions which accompany the safe. It is susceptible to thousands of changes in combination and is absolutely positive in action. It always opens on the correct combination and there is no possibility of opening it on any other. It never slips and never fails. It is constructed throughout of solid brass and cold rolled steel and will never wear out in use. The dial knob is extra large and handsomely nickel plated and is connected with a series of three tumblers by a rolled steel shaft passing through a heavy metal tube. The lock is arranged so that the door can be closed, the bolts thrown and the dial turned five or ten numbers (practically locking the safe) without throwing the combination. This is a great convenience, especially if the owner wishes to leave the office for a few minutes and at the same time have the safe locked. Upon his return he simply reverses the dial to the last number on which the combination is set and he can open the safe. This superior Combination Lock is especially designed for the Vulcan Safe. It is stronger and better in every way than locks furnished by safe makers who make their own locks, and who, making comparatively few, cannot turn out as good a lock as the celebrated Eagle Lock Co., which makes a specialty of high grade lock work exclusively.

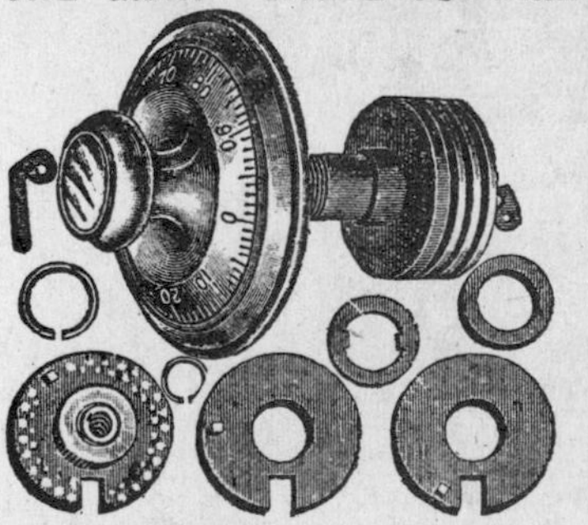

NO SAFE CAN POSSIBLY BE MORE FIREPROOF THAN THE VULCAN. Do not be misled by vague talk about cast iron safes. The facts are these: The flanges on the door, the door frame, the legs and the wheels of the Vulcan Safe, and on every other safe no matter whom it is made by, are made of cast iron, because this is the best and only suitable material for this purpose. The balance of the frame of the Vulcan Safe and of all other first class safes is made of steel. Having our own iron foundry, we have an advantage over other makers as we can and do control the quality of the iron so as to secure the greatest strength and toughness. Any part which fails to pass inspection is broken up and remoulded, so there is practically no waste. Nine-tenths of the other safe makers buy their castings where they can get them the cheapest and frequently use castings which are brittle or contain flaws, rather than stand the loss it would entail if they were not used.

BETTER AND MORE FIREPROOF SAFES than the Vulcan are not made and should you pay an agent or dealer more than our price, the difference is not in the quality of the safe, but solely in the handling expenses and in the middleman's profit.

DIMENSIONS. Please note that in stating the dimensions we give, first, the height, second, the width, and third, the depth in inches.

WEIGHTS. We give the estimated weight of each safe in the descriptions as an aid in calculating freight charges. The exact weight of each safe cannot be given, as safes of the same size will vary considerably, owing to the nature of the fireproof filling. When seasoning, a safe will lose from 50 to 200 pounds according to the size. The more porous the filling, the more fireproof it is and the lighter the weight of the safe.

WE LETTER THE NAME OF THE PURCHASER in gold over the door, free of charge, when so ordered, but not otherwise. If no lettering is desired please so state in your order. A printed copy of the name should be supplied if desired on safe. The name of the manufacturers, the Vulcan Safe and Lock Company, is lettered on the inside of the door unless otherwise desired. OUR NAME DOES NOT APPEAR ON THE SAFE.

REGARDING FREIGHT CHARGES. Our safes are all shipped from our factory at Newark, Ohio, and take third class rate of freight. The freight charges amount to almost nothing compared to your saving in price. For example: Third class freight will be for 200 miles, 15 to 20 cents per hundred pounds; 400 miles, 30 to 40 cents per hundred pounds; 700 miles, 40 to 50 cents per hundred pounds; and 1,000 miles, 60 to 70 cents per hundred pounds, from which you can calculate very closely what the freight will amount to. You will note that it is a very small item indeed, compared to your saving in price, and to reassure you on this point we will guarantee that after having paid the freight charges in addition to our price, your Vulcan Safe will cost you less than one-half what you can procure a safe of the same size and grade for in your home town.

WE CAN MAKE CHANGES IN THE CABINET WORK IF DESIRED.

WE CAN BUILD ANY OF OUR SAFES TO ORDER with the cabinet work arranged in any way desired and any additional drawers or pigeonholes put in, charging only the extra cost of making the change. Complete change of cabinet work usually causes a delay of two or three weeks in making shipments as it necessitates building the safe to order. Send us a diagram of what is wanted and we will advise you what the additional cost will be, if any. While we cannot alter the height and width of our safes, we can build safes to order of any desired depth. This will usually require about a month's time and will add somewhat to the cost. If you cannot use any of the safes listed in this catalogue write us and tell us just what you need and we can furnish it much cheaper than you could buy it elsewhere.

IF YOU ARE THINKING OF BUYING ANY KIND OF A SAFE and do not find it illustrated on these pages, write us a postal card and simply say, "Send me your latest big Special Safe Catalogue" and it will go to you by return mail, postpaid, free, with our compliments. Our entire line of Vulcan Fireproof Safes, only part of which are shown in this catalogue, are shown most completely in the big free Safe Catalogue. Every safe is illustrated with a handsome engraving reproduced from a photograph, which shows you just how it will look; will give you as good an idea of the safe as if it were before you. In our Special Safe Catalogue we go into details, describe the process of building Vulcan Safes from the first operation to the last; tell how our fireproof filling is mixed and explain why it will last and retain its fire resisting qualities for centuries. It tells of our improved method of construction, which enables us to build Vulcan Safes so accurately and at such a low cost; explains more fully our simple selling system and why our prices are only about one-half what other safe dealers ask. In fact, it is the most comprehensive safe catalogue ever issued and contains information which every buyer of a safe should know; gives hints on the care of safes; tells you how to change combinations on the locks. It explains why a fireproof safe is a necessity in every home and to every business man.

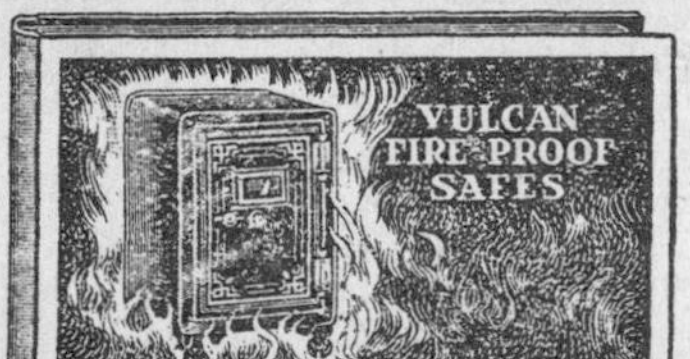

FOR LARGER SIZES AND OTHER STYLES OF SAFES, write us a letter or postal card and say, "Send me your latest big Special Safe Catalogue" and we will send it free, with complete illustrations and descriptions of our entire line of safes.

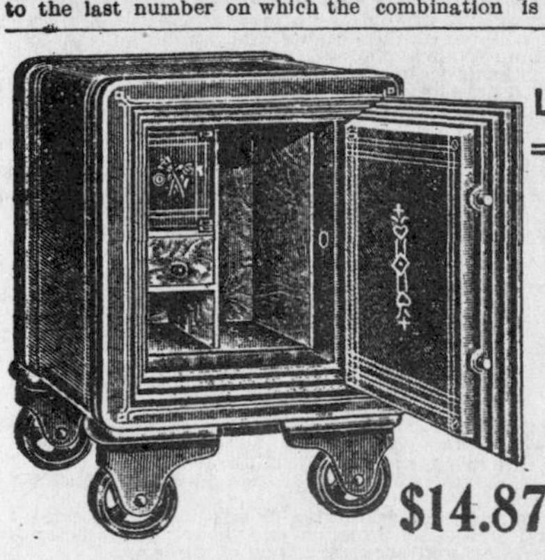

$14.87

OUR LITTLE JEWEL FIREPROOF SAFE AT ONLY $14.87

ONLY $14.87 for our Little Jewel Safe. A perfect high grade safe with solid fireproof walls, steel body and steel angles, equipped with the Eagle Combination Lock at only $14.87. At $14.87 our Jewel Safe is wonderful value. It is just as well finished and just as well constructed as our larger safes and affords perfect protection against the hottest fire. You cannot afford to be without our Jewel Safe or a larger one for even a single day. It will protect you against tramps, sneak thieves and unwelcome intruders. It will preserve your notes, mortgages, leases, deeds and other valuable papers, your money, jewelry and postage stamps, so that you can leave your home for days with a feeling of security as you know they cannot be tampered with. We use the same grade of steel in the walls, the same steam generating fireproof cement in our Jewel Safe as in our larger safes. It is a little jewel in its way and the interior capacity is ample for protecting papers and valuables in the home. Are your insurance policies and valuables in a safe place now? Are they protected from the ravages of fire and marauders? If not, order a Jewel Safe today and be secure. It will protect your valuables and guard your interests for more than a lifetime. Our Jewel Safe weighs 300 pounds. It is mounted on wheels and can be easily moved from room to room yet is sufficiently heavy so that it cannot be carried off without attracting attention. It is splendid value and we fully guarantee it to please you.

DIMENSIONS.

Outside Measure.	Inside Measure.
Height, 24 inches.	Height, 12 inches.
Width, 14⅝ inches.	Width, 8⅛ inches.
Depth, 16⅝ inches.	Depth, 9 inches.

Arrangement of Cabinet Work.

One 5x4-inch iron cash box with duplicate flat key lock.
One 3x4-inch drawer with knob.
One 3½x4-inch pigeonhole.
One 12x3½-inch book space.

No. 22K700 Our Jewel Guaranteed Fireproof Safe. Price.......$14.87
Shipping weight, about 300 pounds. Securely wrapped, packed and padded to avoid being marred or damaged in transit, and delivered on the cars at our foundry in Newark, Ohio. **Our Jewel Safe is not made with inner door.**

OUR WONDER FIREPROOF SAFE $16.27

ONLY $16.27 FOR OUR WONDER GUARANTEED FIREPROOF SAFE. The size suitable for the home, for clergymen, doctors and others, whose papers, although not bulky, are valuable. At $16.27 our Wonder Safe is the cheapest insurance you ever bought. You pay but one premium and that is the first cost and it will last for more than a lifetime. Our Wonder Safe at $16.27 is equipped with the genuine Eagle three-tumbler combination lock, susceptible to thousands of changes in combination and unpickable by the most expert cracksman. It is perfectly high grade, strictly fireproof in every way, finished and decorated in the most elegant manner, equipped with iron subtreasury in which money and valuables are absolutely secure and an additional drawer for small articles or papers. It is built so strongly and substantially that there is no wear out to it. Constructed of the same materials and in the same careful manner as safes costing ten times as much. Regular safe dealers will ask you not less than $35.00 for a safe that cannot in any way compare with our Wonder. This is one of our leading household safes and on this size our usual small margin of profit is cut closer than ever. Our $16.27 price is almost the cost of the material and labor which enters into the construction of this safe. We can furnish our Wonder Safe, as well as the larger sizes, with an additional wrought steel inside door, secured with a high grade key lock, with two flat keys, for $17.77. This is not only an additional protection but a great convenience as well, as should the large fireproof door be permitted to remain open during the daytime the inner steel door can be kept locked and

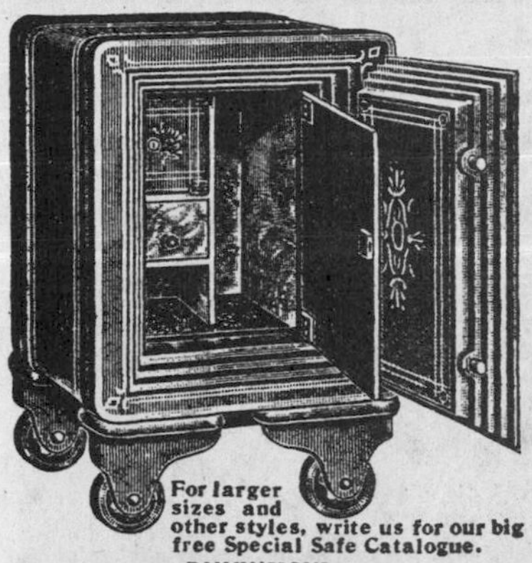

For larger sizes and other styles, write us for our big free Special Safe Catalogue.

DIMENSIONS.

Outside Measure.	Inside Measure.
Height, 25½ inches.	Height, 13⅜ inches.
Width, 17 inches.	Width, 10¼ inches.
Depth, 17½ inches.	Depth, 10 inches.

Arrangement of Cabinet Work.

One 6x4¾-inch cash box with duplicate flat key lock.
One 3x4¾-inch drawer with knob.
One 3¼x4¾-inch pigeonhole.
One 13x4⅞-inch book space.

only opened when occasion requires. Order a Wonder Safe at $16.27 for single door, or $17.77 for extra inner steel door today, subject to a full month's trial, and if you are not more than satisfied and delighted with it, in every way, remember, that you can return it to us and we will refund all your money and pay all the transportation charges both ways. If your valuables are not already protected in a safe, do not think of leaving them exposed for a single day longer. Their loss may cause you untold trouble and perhaps the results of a lifetime of saving will be swept away in a few minutes. Order a fireproof safe today. Securely wrapped, packed and padded to avoid being marred or damaged in transit, and delivered on the cars at our factory in Newark, Ohio.

No. 22K702 Wonder Guaranteed Fireproof Safe. Price **$16.27**
Shipping weight, about 350 pounds.

No. 22K703 Wonder Guaranteed Fireproof Safe, equipped with extra inner door, with Yale pattern lock, with two flat keys. Price **$17.77**

Remember, we letter your name in handsome gold letters free of charge when plainly ordered, but not otherwise. Please state whether you wish your safe lettered or not.

OUR BIG 600-POUND STEEL FIREKING $20.47

$20.47 FOR THE HIGH GRADE 600-POUND STEEL FIREKING SAFE. At only three cents a pound, hardly more than the bare cost of the raw material, our Fireking Safe, as you must see, is wonderfully cheap. Consider the cost of the brass and of the steel, the cost of the fireproof steam generating cement, the cost of the cabinet work, the locks and of the finishing, and you will realize what a wonderful bargain you will receive in our Steel Fireking Safe. No dealer would think of selling a safe like this for less than $50.00. Order a Steel Fireking Safe at $20.47, the price for single door, or $21.97, our price with extra inner wrought steel door, and give it a full month's trial in your own office and satisfy yourself that every word we say about it is true. Assure yourself that it is a wonderful bargain and that you have saved at least $30.00 by buying it from us. Remember, that we guarantee our Steel Fireking to be absolutely fireproof, guarantee the material, the workmanship, the strength and solidity of construction, and a written binding guarantee goes with every one. No one else can offer you a safe of anything like the same quality for anything like our price. The size is exactly suited for country merchants, doctors, lawyers or farmers. The interior contains ample space for a small set of books, and is divided in the most convenient manner with pigeonholes, drawer and iron subtreasury, with high grade Yale pattern key lock. Securely wrapped, packed and padded to avoid being marred or damaged in transit, and delivered on the cars at our factory in Newark, Ohio.

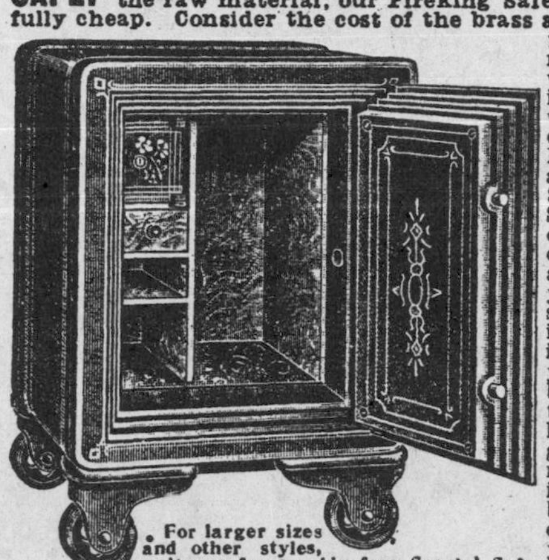

For larger sizes and other styles, write us for our big free Special Safe Catalogue.

DIMENSIONS.

Outside Measure.	Inside Measure.
Height, 31⅞ inches.	Height, 17½ inches.
Width, 20⅛ inches.	Width, 12 inches.
Depth, 20⅜ inches.	Depth, 12 inches.

Arrangement of Cabinet Work.

One 6x4¾-inch iron cash box with duplicate flat key lock.
One 3x4¾-inch drawer with knob.
One 3x4¾-inch pigeonhole.
One 4½x4¾-inch pigeonhole.
One 17½x6⅞-inch book space.

No. 22K708 Our Steel Fireking Fireproof Safe. Price ... **$20.47**
Shipping weight, 600 pounds.

No. 22K709 Our Steel Fireking Fireproof Safe, equipped with extra inner wrought steel door, with Yale pattern key lock and two flat keys in addition to the heavy fireproof outer door with combination lock. Price, **$21.97**

$18.90 FOR OUR RELIANCE FIREPROOF SAFE

OUR RELIANCE FIREPROOF SAFE AT ONLY $18.90 is a splendid safe for **small business concerns and professional men.** The Reliance Safe will add dignity to your business and increase your standing in your community. Invest $18.90 in a Reliance Safe with single door, or $20.15 in a Reliance Safe with an extra inner wrought steel door, and it will protect your cash and valuables and, what is even more necessary, your books which contain the entire history of your business and are the only record of what is due you and what you owe. Remember, that the highest courts in the land have repeatedly decided that without proof of loss, insurance cannot be collected. Unless your books and inventory, or evidence of stock on hand are protected in a fireproof safe, they will burn with the stock. You will have no proof of your loss, nothing to show what you had at the time of the fire. The result is, your insurance policies are void. The money you have paid for premiums is gone. You cannot collect the value of your loss as you cannot prove it. Think how serious a loss of this kind would be. Can you afford to be without a fireproof safe another day? Remember, our Reliance Safe is just as fireproof as the larger sizes, built in the same careful manner and of the same material. No detail of construction, no matter how small, has been overlooked to produce the best. If you do not feel that you can afford to pay more than $18.90 for a single door, or $20.15 for the wrought steel inner door for the protection of your records, by all means purchase a Reliance Safe and you can rest contented. It will protect you absolutely. Remember, we guarantee it to be absolutely fireproof, we guarantee it to be as strong and durable as a combination of solid steel and cement of the hardness of stone can make it. It is equipped with a high grade triplex combination lock which never gets out of order, cannot be picked and yet can be opened in a few moments' time by the person acquainted with the combination—a combination which can be changed as often as desired. We letter your name in gold over the door when so ordered, free of charge. Remember, our name does not appear on any safe, only the factory name—The Vulcan Safe & Lock Co.—on the inside of the outside door in gold letters. We can leave this off also when desired. Securely wrapped, packed and padded to avoid being marred or damaged in transit, and delivered on the cars at our factory in Newark, Ohio.

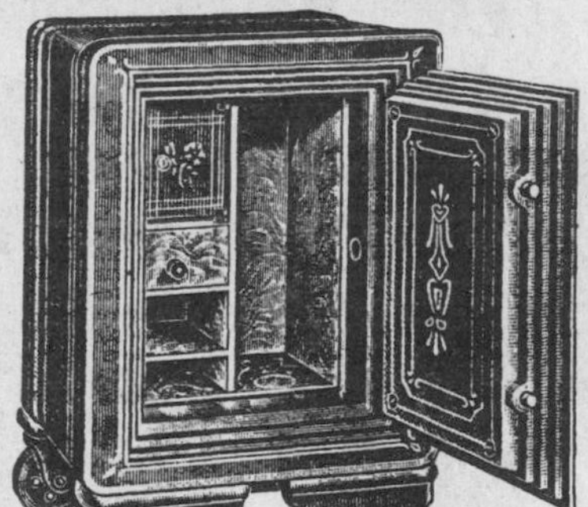

For larger sizes and other styles, write us for our big free Special Safe Catalogue.

DIMENSIONS.

Outside Measure.	Inside Measure
Height, 28½ inches.	Height, 15⅛ inches.
Width, 17 inches.	Width, 10 3-16 inches.
Depth, 18⅝ inches.	Depth, 11 inches.

Arrangement of Cabinet Work.

One 6x4¾-inch iron cash box with duplicate flat key lock.
One 3x4¾-inch drawer with knob.
One 3x4¾-inch pigeonhole.
One 2⅜x4¾-inch pigeonhole.
One 15x4⅞-inch book space.

No. 22K705 Our Reliance Fireproof Safe. Price **$18.90**
Shipping weight, about 450 pounds.

No. 22K706 Our Reliance Fireproof Safe, with extra inner wrought steel door with pattern lock, with two flat keys. The inner door is a great convenience and we especially recommend its purchase. Price **$20.15**

$23.62 FOR OUR UNION FIREPROOF SAFE

THIS BIG SOLID FIREPROOF SAFE, as strong as steel and cement can make it, weighing 750 pounds, at only $23.62. Our Union Safe is one of our most popular patterns. It is especially adapted for country merchants, lawyers and doctors, and is really a splendid safe for the money. Safe dealers who ask $65.00 for safes of this size, marvel at our $23.62 price for single door, or $24.87 price with extra wrought steel inner door. Other safe manufacturers say that such a safe cannot be produced for anything like this price, yet with our great capacity and improved facilities for manufacturing, we can actually offer our Union Safe at a price which is lower than other manufacturers must pay for the material and labor alone which enter into its construction. At $23.62 our Union Safe gives you absolute protection from fire for more than a lifetime. It is built to last a century, and will retain its fireproof qualities and be just as fireproof at the end of fifty or seventy-five years as it was the day you bought it. Our fireproof filling is the result of many years careful scientific experimenting on the part of an expert who has spent his life in perfecting this branch of business. It is not only perfect and enduring fire protection, but we can absolutely guarantee against damp and swollen safes. Remember, that every Vulcan Safe is sold subject to thirty days' trial in your own office, store, salesroom or home, and if, after careful examination, you do not find it all and even more than we claim for it, and if you have not made a big saving in price, return it at our expense of freight charges both ways and we will return your money. Our sole aim is to satisfy our customers, and we do not wish any customer to keep anything purchased from us which does not give perfect satisfaction. On this basis we have built up our great business—one of the largest in the United States. Securely wrapped, packed and padded to avoid being marred or damaged in transit, and delivered on the cars at our factory in Newark, Ohio.

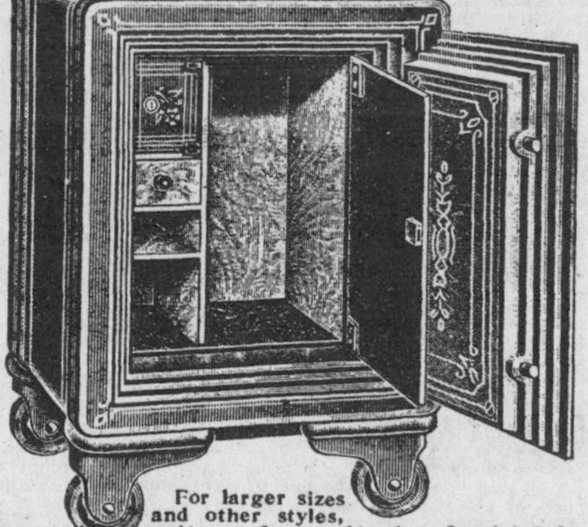

For larger sizes and other styles, write us for our big free Special Safe Catalogue.

DIMENSIONS.

Outside Measure.	Inside Measure.
Height, 34 inches.	Height, 19 inches.
Width, 22½ inches.	Width, 14 inches.
Depth, 21⅜ inches.	Depth, 12½ inches.

Arrangement of Cabinet Work.

One 6x4¾-inch iron cash box with duplicate flat key lock.
One 3x4¾-inch drawer with knob.
One 3x4¾-inch pigeonhole.
One 6x4¾-inch book space.
One 19x8⅞-inch book space.

No. 22K711 Our Union Guaranteed Fireproof Safe. Price **$23.62**
Shipping weight, 750 pounds.

No. 22K712 Our Union Guaranteed Fireproof Safe, the same as above, but equipped with an extra wrought steel inner door, with key lock in addition to the heavy outside door. Price **$24.87**

1908
PHOTOGRAPHY AND PRINTING

$13.90

GENERAL CONSTRUCTION.

The Conley Long Focus Cameras are made throughout from carefully selected Honduras mahogany, except the leather cover edreversible back which is of cherry because of its greater strength. All joints are dovetailed, and all corners are rounded. The woodwork is all finished with the highest piano polish. The covering is the very best quality of heavy bear grain leather. All metal parts are made from brass, heavily nickel plated, accurately fitted and highly polished. The illustrations on this page, all of them engraved direct from photographs of the camera, will give you some idea of the appearance of the Conley Long Focus Camera, but in order to fully appreciate the unusual value represented in this camera, it must be seen. The beautifully polished mahogany woodwork and the highly finished nickel plated brass trimmings, contrasted with the fine black bear grain morocco leather covering and the rich red leather bellows give to this camera a strikingly handsome appearance.

The Conley Long Focus Camera is made with a fine rack and pinion focus movement, accurately adjusted, positively without lost motion. The front is made with rising and falling adjustment and also sliding or shifting adjustment. The lens board is instantly detachable and just as quickly replaced. The finder is of the brilliant type of construction, extra large, made of polished mahogany and fitted with nickel plated adjustable hood. The focus scale is accurately made and adjusted with extreme care. The bed is attached to the box of the camera with a fine nickel plated piano hinge, insuring strength, rigidity and adding to the beautiful appearance of the camera.

THE SWING BACK.

The Conley Long Focus Camera is equipped with the most approved form of swing back, this important adjustment being operated and controlled entirely by two set screws, one at the base of each side arm. By simply loosening these set screws, the back of the camera can be swung either forward or backward to any desired angle and securely held by tightening the same screws, an adjustment that is quickly and easily made.

REVERSIBLE BACK.

The Conley Reversible Back, with single button release, is the most easily operated and the most convenient form of reversible back made. By pressing a single concealed button on the side of the camera this back is instantly detached as shown in the illustration, for changing from horizontal to vertical pictures, or vice versa. There are no troublesome clips or catches to cause annoyance in the manipulation of this reversible back, and the camera is instantly available for taking pictures either the short way or the long way of the plate.

BELLOWS.

We equip the Conley Long Focus Cameras with an exceptionally high class bellows, made from the best grade of red Russia leather lined with a special lightproof gossamer cloth, and in its construction only the best rubber cement is used, which insures flexibility and long life to the bellows. This bellows is made extra long thus securing results in landscape photography, portraiture, copying, etc., which are entirely beyond the capacity of ordinary short bellows cameras. This long bellows also permits the use of the single combinations of the lens when desired, the single combinations having a greater focal length than the complete lens and requiring for their use an extra long bellows.

THE AUXILIARY BED.

With every one of these cameras we furnish without extra charge our Conley all metal auxiliary bed, made with rack and pinion focus movement for using short focus or wide angle lenses. When wide angle lenses are used with cameras which are not equipped with an auxiliary bed, the main bed, by reason of the wide angle covered by the lens, is included in the picture, thus cutting off part of the view and making the negative useless. The Conley Long Focus Camera is so constructed that the main bed can be dropped down entirely out of the way and the camera front extended by means of the auxiliary bed when using a wide angle lens.

This illustration shows method of using wide angle lens with auxiliary bed.

THE CONLEY AUTOMATIC FRONT CLAMP

is the latest and best front clamp that has ever been devised. To extend the camera for use, the front is drawn out by the small lever of the automatic clamp, and the pulling of this lever forward when drawing out the camera releases the automatic clamp, permitting the camera front to move freely, either forward or backward, and when this lever is released it snaps back to its position and automatically locks or clamps the camera front at any desired point.

THE CARRYING CASE.

Every Conley Long Focus Camera is equipped with a solid sole leather carrying case with compartments for the camera and a supply of extra plate holders. The case for the 4x5 camera has space for the camera and five plate holders, and the other three sizes, the 5x7, 6½x8½ and 8x10, have room for the camera and six plate holders.

CONLEY LONG FOCUS CAMERAS

SIZE 4x5, $13.90 | SIZE 6½x8½, $28.00

SIZE 5x7, $17.95 | SIZE 8x10, $37.00

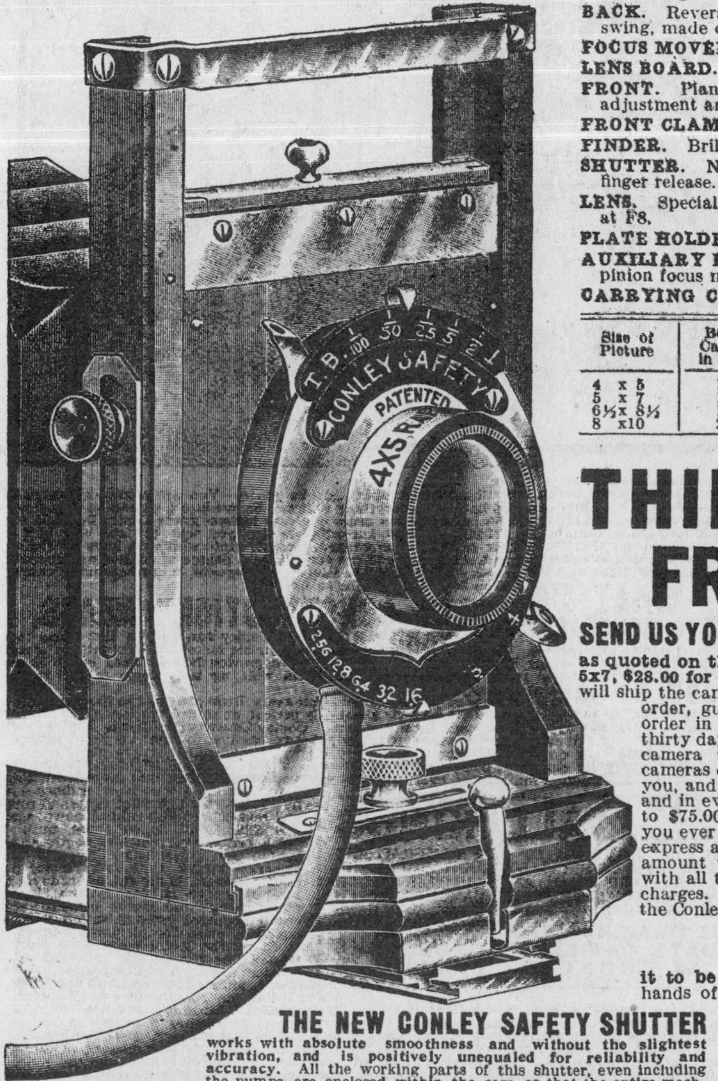

SPECIFICATIONS

WOODWORK. Solid Honduras mahogany, specially selected, with dovetailed joints and rounded corners; piano finish.

METAL PARTS. Brass and best tool steel, nickel plated and highly polished.

COVERING. Heavy bear grain morocco leather.

BELLOWS. Genuine red Russia leather, gossamer lined, extra long.

BACK. Reversible, with single button release and improved swing, made of selected cherry, leather covered.

FOCUS MOVEMENT. Rack and pinion.

LENS BOARD. Detachable; instantly removed or replaced.

FRONT. Piano polished mahogany, with rising and falling adjustment and horizontal or side shift adjustment.

FRONT CLAMP. Our new Conley Automatic.

FINDER. Brilliant; extra large with nickel plated hood.

SHUTTER. New Conley Safety, with both pneumatic and finger release.

LENS. Special high grade, Double Symmetrical, working at F8.

PLATE HOLDER. Conley Improved Flexible Valve.

AUXILIARY BED. All metal, nickel plated, with rack and pinion focus movement.

CARRYING CASE. Extra heavy solid black sole leather.

Size of Picture	Bellows Capacity in Inches	Dimensions Camera, Closed in Inches	Dimensions Carrying Case in Inches
4 x 5	11¾	3⅛ x 6¼ x 6¼	3⅝ x 6⅞ x 12
5 x 7	16¼	3¾ x 8⅝ x 8⅝	4⅜ x 9⅛ x 15½
6½ x 8½	19¾	4½ x 10¼ x 10¼	4⅞ x 10⅞ x 19
8 x 10	22¾	4¾ x 11¾ x 11¾	5½ x 12¼ x 21¾

THIRTY DAYS' FREE TRIAL

SEND US YOUR ORDER, telling us the size you want. Enclose our special price as quoted on this page, $13.90 for the 4x5, $17.95 for the 5x7, $28.00 for the 6½x8½, $37.00 for the 8x10 size. We will ship the camera to you immediately upon receipt of your order, guaranteeing that it will reach you in perfect order in just a few days time and you can try it for thirty days. During these thirty days you can put the camera to any test, you can compare it with other cameras costing two or three times the price we ask you, and if you do not find it all that we claim for it, and in every way equal to cameras costing from $50.00 to $75.00, if you do not find it the greatest bargain you ever saw or heard of, you can send it back to us by express at our expense, and we will return to you the amount which you paid us for the camera, together with all the money you have paid for transportation charges. You take no risk whatever when you order the Conley Long Focus Camera.

WE GUARANTEE

it to be simpler, to do better work, either in the hands of the beginner or the experienced operator, to be better made, longer lived and better in every way than the most expensive cameras sold by other dealers.

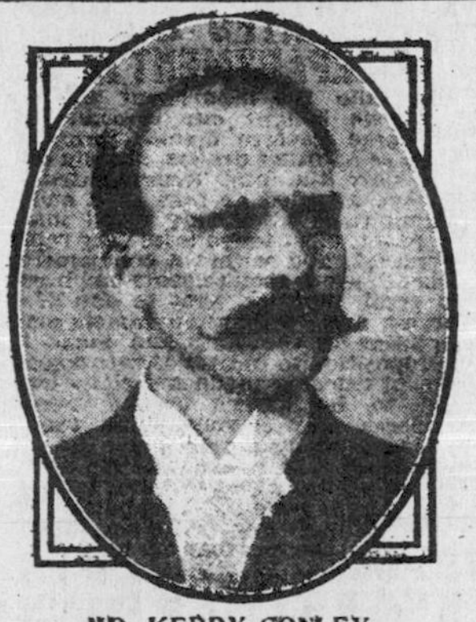

MR. KERRY CONLEY,
President Conley Camera Co.
Photograph made with Conley Long Focus Camera.

THESE PORTRAITS of Messrs. Kerry Conley and Fred Conley, makers of the Conley Cameras, are reproduced by the half-tone process direct from original photographs without retouching, made with the Conley Long Focus Camera. These portraits of the Conley brothers will give you some idea of the quality and style of work that can be done with the Conley Long Focus Camera. Of course, the fine detail and photographic perfection of the original pictures cannot be brought out on this printed page, but these pictures will serve to give you some idea of the original pictures and will help you to understand the kind and quality of work that can be done with these remarkable cameras.

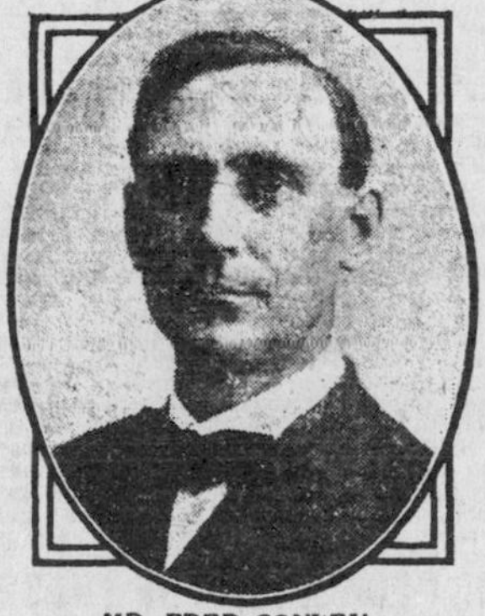

MR. FRED CONLEY,
Vice-President Conley Camera Co.
Photograph made with Conley Long Focus Camera.

THE NEW CONLEY SAFETY SHUTTER

works with absolute smoothness and without the slightest vibration, and is positively unequaled for reliability and accuracy. All the working parts of this shutter, even including the pumps, are enclosed within the case, so that the entire mechanism is perfectly protected from injury. The New Conley Safety Shutter gives, with one pressure of the bulb, instantaneous exposures of 1-25, 1-50 and 1-100 of a second, and, also with one pressure of the bulb, time exposures of 1 second, ½ second or 1-5 second. With the indicator set to B, the first pressure of the bulb opens the shutter, which remains open as long as the pressure on the bulb is held and closes when the pressure is released, a very convenient means for making short time exposures. For long time exposures or when opening the shutter for focusing, the indicator is set to T, when one pressure of the bulb opens the shutter, and it remains open until the bulb is again pressed. In exactly the same manner the shutter may also be operated by finger release instead of bulb, the finger release lever being located at the upper left hand side of the shutter. It is light and campact, graceful in design and beautifully finished and is absolutely safe, as it cannot be opened until it has been set by pressing the setting lever down, and thus there is no danger of premature exposure or accidental opening of the lens.

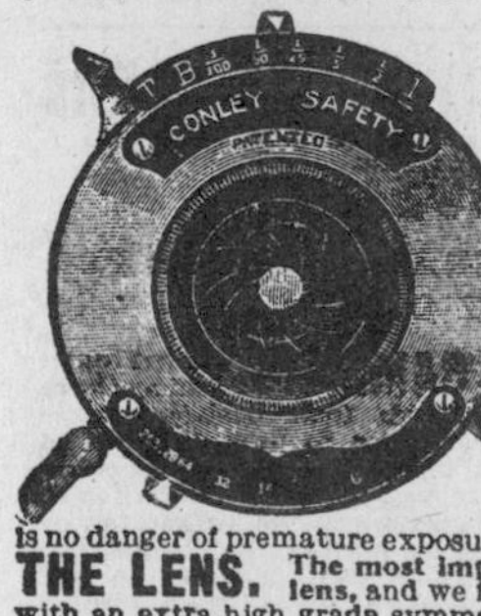

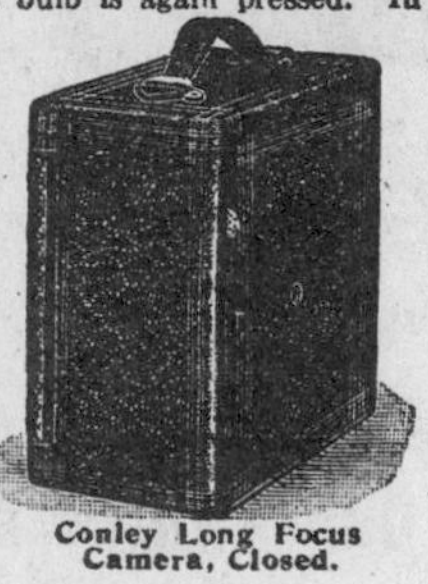

Conley Long Focus Camera, Closed.

THE LENS. The most important part of any camera is the lens, and we fit the Conley Long Focus Cameras with an extra high grade symmetrical lens, a double combination symmetrical lens manufactured expressly for use with this camera, the very highest grade symmetrical lens that we can buy. Either the front or rear combinations of this lens can be used alone when desired, the focal length of either combination being about double that of the entire lens. This greatly increases the efficiency of the camera, as results can often be obtained with the single combinations that would be impossible with the complete lens.

The following table shows the sizes and focal lengths of these lenses in inches.

Size of Picture	Diameter Across Hood	Equivalent Focus	Focus Single Combination
4 x 5	1 3/16	6¼	10¾
5 x 7	1 3/16	8	14¼
6½ x 8½	1¾	10½	18
8 x 10	2 3/16	12½	20¼

PRICES WITH REGULAR EQUIPMENT.

Double Symmetrical Lenses and Conley Safety Shutters.

No. 20K150 The Conley Long Focus Camera, 4x5. Price...$13.90
No. 20K151 The Conley Long Focus Camera, 5x7. Price... 17.95
No. 20K152 The Conley Long Focus Camera, 6½x8½. Price 28.00
No. 20K153 The Conley Long Focus Camera, 8x10. Price.. 37.00

The above prices include the camera complete, with symmetrical lens and Conley Safety Shutter, auxiliary bed for Wide Angle Lens, sole leather carrying case, one Conley Flexible Valve Double Plate Holder and "Complete Instructions in Photography."

No. 20K40 Shoulder Strap for carrying case, if desired. Price, each........25c

For Complete Developing and Printing Outfits, suitable for use with the Conley Long Focus Camera, see page 683.

PRICES WITH CONLEY SERIES V, F6.8, ANASTIGMAT LENS.

With Conley Series V Anastigmat Lens and Conley Safety Shutter.

No. 20K162 Conley Long Focus Camera, 4x5. Price..................$33.35
No. 20K163 Conley Long Focus Camera, 5x7. Price.................. 45.70
No. 20K164 Conley Long Focus Camera, 6½x8½. Price.............. 59.20
No. 20K165 Conley Long Focus Camera, 8x10. Price................ 80.85

With Conley Series V Anastigmat Lens and Bausch & Lomb Volute Shutter.

No. 20K166 Conley Long Focus Camera, 4x5. Price..................$40.85
No. 20K167 Conley Long Focus Camera, 5x7. Price.................. 51.20
No. 20K168 Conley Long Focus Camera, 6½x8½. Price.............. 65.70
No. 20K169 Conley Long Focus Camera, 8x10. Price................ 86.85

The prices quoted on Nos. 20K162 to 20K169, inclusive, are for the camera complete with Conley Series V Anastigmat Lens, shutter as specified, carrying case and one plate holder.

See page 684 for full description of the Conley Series V Anastigmat Lens.

WIDE ANGLE LENSES.

No. 20K178 Wide Angle Lens for 4x5 Long Focus Camera. Price......................$2.90
No. 20K179 Wide Angle Lens for 5x7 Long Focus Camera. Price...................... 3.70
No. 20K180 Wide Angle Lens for 6½x8½ Long Focus Camera. Price.................. 5.95
No. 20K181 Wide Angle Lens for 8x10 Long Focus Camera. Price...................... 7.80

These Wide Angle Lenses fit the shutters furnished with the regular equipment. They do not fit the shutters furnished with Anastigmat Lenses.

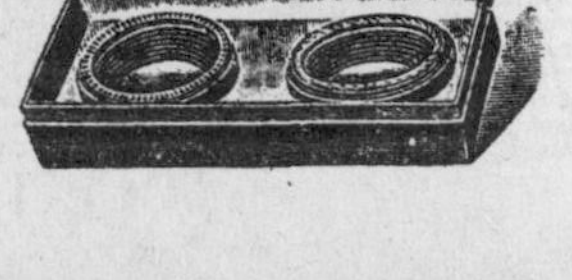

HOW WE CAME TO BUILD OUR OWN CAMERAS

WE STARTED OUR CAMERA DEPARTMENT IN 1897 and while the department was still small we bought our cameras from the large Eastern manufacturers, the same as all other dealers, but by handling only the best cameras that the market afforded at that time, and by selling them at a very small margin of profit, our camera sales very rapidly increased, and within a comparatively short time our requirements had become so great that we went to one of the largest and best known camera manufacturers in the East and made him a proposition to furnish us with a special line of cameras made especially for us, and to be known as the "Seroco" Cameras. By having these cameras made expressly for us under the name "Seroco," and by contracting for the largest quantity that had ever been purchased by any one dealer, we bought them at exceedingly low prices and we were able to sell cheaper than our competitors.

WE CONTINUED THIS ARRANGEMENT with the Eastern manufacturer for a number of years, and during this time we were always able to sell better cameras for less money than any of our competitors, and the Seroco cameras became well known throughout the entire country, and became accepted as standards of excellence in camera construction. Finally, the Camera Trust, having become more and more powerful, forced the manufacturer of the Seroco cameras to sell out, and as soon as they acquired control of this factory, together with all other camera factories, they refused to furnish us with cameras unless we would allow them to dictate to us the prices at which we should sell them.

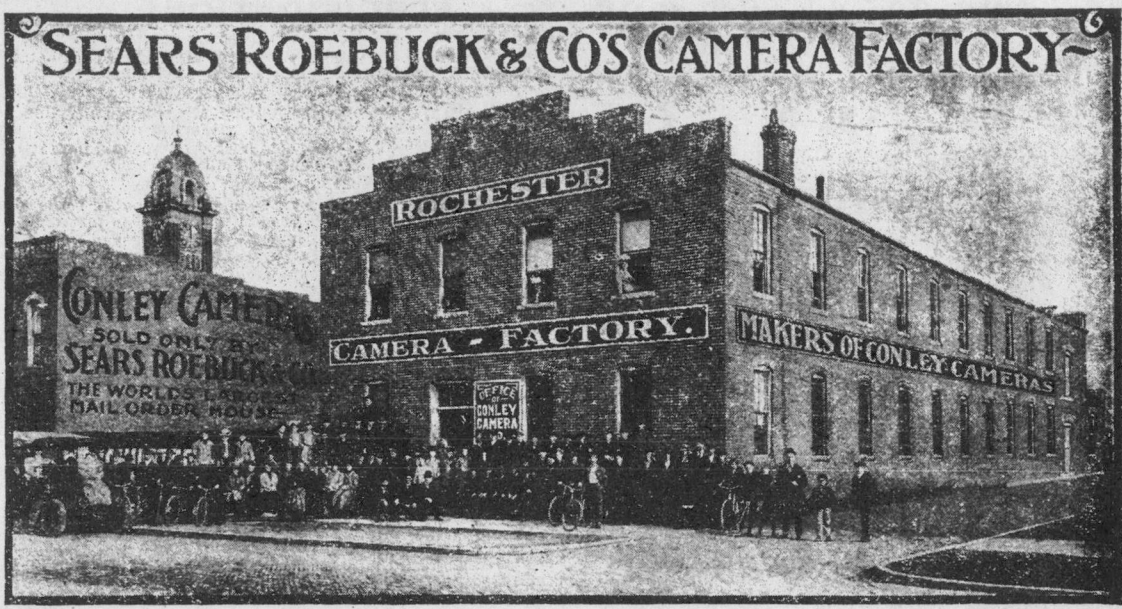

SEARS ROEBUCK & CO'S CAMERA FACTORY

AFTER HAVING SOLD SEROCO CAMERAS FOR YEARS AT LOW PRICES, and having built up a very large business on this basis, we did not feel that we could, in justice to our customers, submit to the terms dictated by the trust, which would compel us to advance all our camera prices from 50 to 100 per cent, and we therefore decided to establish our own camera factory, where we could build cameras of the highest grade and sell them at any price which we saw fit. We had had some dealings at that time with Messrs. Kerry Conley and Fred Conley of Spring Valley, Minnesota, and we knew them to be men of great ability as manufacturers—men whose knowledge of camera making was second to none, and we entered into an arrangement with these gentlemen to build and operate for us a big, modern, complete camera factory, a factory whose entire resources should be devoted to making Seroco cameras, making us absolutely independent of the trust, and enabling us to sell better cameras at lower prices than we had ever been able to do in the past—better cameras at one-half the prices that the ordinary trust dealer is compelled to charge.

BEFORE THE END OF THE FIRST YEAR, after this arrangement was entered into, the Conley Camera Co. had outgrown their quarters in Spring Valley, and it was found necessary to secure a larger and better equipped factory and a much larger force of workmen. Spring Valley is not a large town. We found it impossible to secure sufficient skilled help there to operate the factory, and after considering the advantages of various other cities and towns, it was decided that the city of Rochester, Minnesota, offered greater advantages than any other place, and we therefore purchased in the city of Rochester a large, well built, substantial factory building, a building ideally adapted to the manufacture of cameras. The new factory was soon completely equipped with new and up to date machinery, and within a short time we were turning out Seroco cameras of better quality than ever before, and of vastly better quality than the Seroco cameras which, in the past, had been made for us by Eastern manufacturers. Every year since we went into the new factory has seen improvements in the way of new and special machinery, better facilities and increased skill on the part of the various operatives throughout the factory.

THE PERFECTION OF THESE CAMERAS, the faultless construction, the beautiful designs and the perfect finish, all the various improvements that go to make them, in every sense of the word, the very finest cameras on the market today, is all due to the mechanical genius and wonderful manufacturing ability of Messrs. Kerry Conley and Fred Conley, the men who make these cameras for us, and it seems only right and fitting that these products of their skill and untiring efforts should bear the name of "Conley."

THE NAME "CONLEY" on a camera will in itself be a guarantee of quality. We will never put out a camera under the name of "Conley," either low priced or high priced, that is not the very best camera of its class that can be produced. If you order one of our Conley Sr. Box cameras at $1.95, you will

receive the very best 4x5 Box camera that can be made. You will receive a camera into which the Conley Brothers have put everything that can be put into a camera of this class to make it the best that can be built. If you order our very highest grade Conley Double Extension camera, at $21.50, $27.00, or $35.60, according to size, you will get the very best and highest grade camera that can be manufactured, a camera into which we have put the very best materials that the market affords, and the very highest degree of skilled workmanship; a camera that is equal in every respect and in many ways superior to corresponding cameras sold by the Trust at $40.00 to $65.00, according to size.

WHAT "CONLEY CONSTRUCTION" MEANS.

THE GENERAL CONSTRUCTION of the Conley cameras as they come to us from our big factory in Rochester is so much better and so different from that of cameras which we previously purchased in the Eastern market, they have so much individuality about them that we have come to refer to these distinctive features as "Conley Construction."

CONLEY CONSTRUCTION means that every little detail in the camera is as absolutely perfect as skilled workmen and thorough supervision by expert management can produce. Conley Construction means that in every camera we turn out, from the very lowest priced box camera to the very highest grade long focus and double extension styles, every corner is dovetailed, every piece of leather for covering is carefully inspected and rejected if it shows the slightest imperfection. Conley Construction means that every piece of mahogany that enters into the construction of our cameras is varnished, rubbed down by hand with oil, pumice stone and rouge, and revarnished and rubbed down again, and still again, three times, until the finish has the very highest degree of perfection and permanency. Conley Construction means that every metal part in the camera is die cut or made on the most expensive milling machines, heavily nickel plated and highly polished; not a cheap lacquered brass finish but the most beautiful, most durable finish that can be given to the metal parts of a camera. Conley Construction means that every shutter must be carefully inspected and tested, must be tried at every speed, must be tried for time exposures, bulb exposures and instantaneous exposures of all speeds,

---

IMPROVEMENTS OF ALL KINDS.

HAVE BEEN CONSTANTLY MADE IN THE DESIGN AND FINISH OF OUR CAMERAS, AND AT THE BEGINNING OF THIS SEASON WE FIND OUR CAMERAS SO MUCH BETTER IN EVERY WAY THAN EVER BEFORE, SO MUCH BETTER THAN ANY CAMERAS WHICH ARE OFFERED BY OUR COMPETITORS, SO MUCH BETTER THAN THE CAMERAS WHICH FOR YEARS WE HAVE SOLD UNDER THE NAME OF "SEROCO," THAT WE HAVE **DECIDED TO GIVE OUR CAMERAS, IN THE FUTURE, A NEW NAME.**

HEREAFTER, OUR CAMERAS, THE CAMERAS THAT WE MAKE IN OUR BIG, MODERN, UP TO DATE CAMERA FACTORY IN ROCHESTER, WILL BE KNOWN AS "CONLEY" CAMERAS.

---

and our inspectors must certify that it is absolutely perfect before it is permitted to leave the factory. Conley Construction means that every lens must be tested and proven perfect before it is put on the camera. Conley Construction means that every piece of lumber that enters into the construction of our cameras, every bit of mahogany that we use must be carefully subjected to an air drying process of seasoning for several months, then to a further process of careful kiln drying before it is used in the construction of a camera. Conley Construction, in short, means perfection in camera making. It means an attention to details that other manufacturers cannot afford to give. It means more for your money than you can possibly get from any other camera maker.

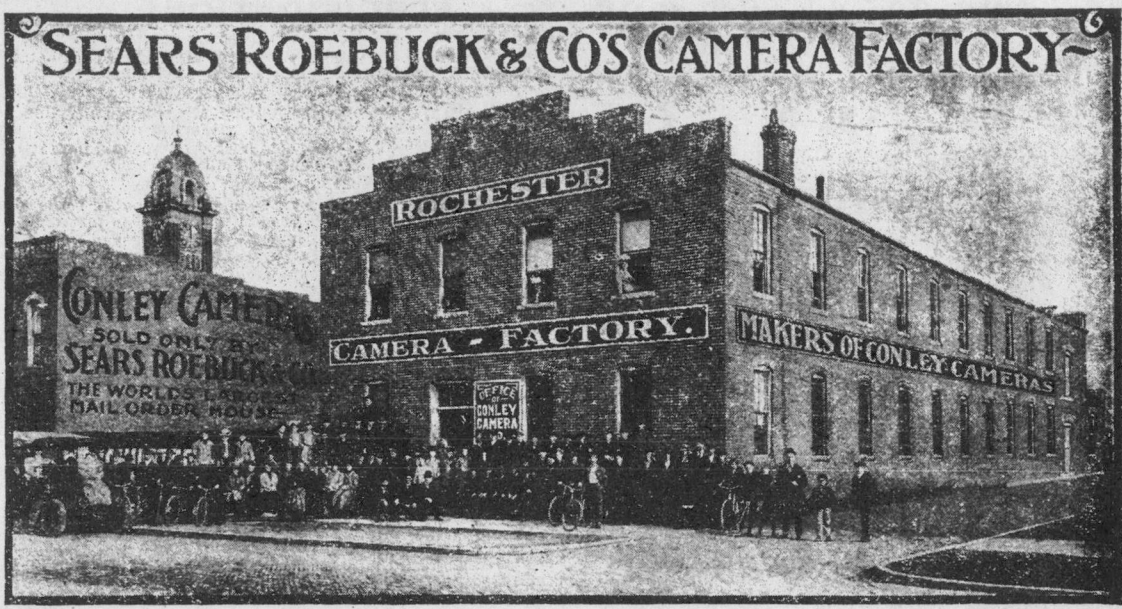

Conley Camera Company

Hereby guarantees that this Camera No___ is made of highest grade material throughout and is thoroughly inspected and adjusted and perfect in operation. We guarantee it for twenty years and will replace any part that proves defective during that period of time.

Dated at Rochester this___ day of___ 190__

Conley Camera Company

Fred Conley   Kerry Conley

WE ARE FIGHTING THE CAMERA TRUST

WITH BETTER CAMERAS AT LOWER PRICES THAN THEY CAN OFFER.

PRACTICALLY ALL CAMERAS except ours are sold by the Trust or marketed by the Trust through their dealers, and these cameras are sold at prices from two to four times the prices which we ask for Conley cameras of corresponding styles and better quality. We have been threatened with all sorts of trouble by the Trust if we refuse to join this combination of camera manufacturers in an effort to compel you to pay two or three prices for your camera, but we refuse to be intimidated, and will continue to manufacture our own cameras, in our own factory and sell them at our own prices, prices which represent but the mere cost of materials and labor, with our one small percentage of profit added.

CONLEY CAMERAS ARE GUARANTEED FOR TWENTY YEARS.

NO OTHER CAMERA on the market today carries any such guarantee as a protection to the purchaser. No other manufacturer in the United States today can afford to guarantee his cameras for twenty years. No other camera is so well made, so perfect in every detail of construction, and it is for this reason that no other manufacturer can give such a guarantee on his cameras as we give with every Conley camera—the strongest and most binding guarantee, covering the longest period of time given on any camera. Conley cameras, manufactured in our own factory at Rochester, Minn., and sold only by us, are the only cameras in the world guaranteed by their makers for twenty years, as we guarantee every Conley camera which we sell.

OUR THIRTY DAYS' FREE TRIAL COMPARISON OFFER.

SEND US AN ORDER for any style of Conley camera, enclose our price as quoted in this catalogue, and we will forward the camera which you select, with the understanding and agreement that you can try it for thirty days, during which time you can put it to every test, you can compare it with other cameras of corresponding styles sold by the Trust at three and four times the prices which we ask you for the Conley cameras, and if you don't find it satisfactory in every way, far lower in price than any corresponding camera with which you may compare it, better in quality and entirely satisfactory to you in every detail, return it to us by express, at our expense, and we will refund to you, without question, the entire purchase price and also reimburse you for any transportation charges which you may have paid out.

THE 4x5 CONLEY SENIOR BOX CAMERA

$1 95

WITH GENUINE CONLEY FLEXIBLE VALVE PLATE HOLDER
MADE AT OUR OWN FACTORY AT ROCHESTER
BETTER THAN BOX CAMERAS SOLD BY OTHER DEALERS AT FROM $4.00 TO $5.00.

THIS CAMERA USES DRY PLATES ONLY, EXACTLY THE SAME KIND OF PLATES USED BY THE BEST PROFESSIONAL PHOTOGRAPHERS.

Genuine Meniscus Achromatic Lens.
Automatic Time and Instantaneous Shutter.
Conley Flexible Valve Plate Holder.

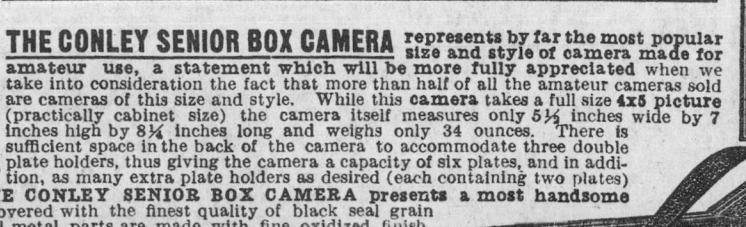

THE CONLEY SENIOR BOX CAMERA represents by far the most popular size and style of camera made for amateur use, a statement which will be more fully appreciated when we take into consideration the fact that more than half of all the amateur cameras sold are cameras of this size and style. While this camera takes a full size 4x5 picture (practically cabinet size) the camera itself measures only 5¼ inches wide by 7 inches high by 8¼ inches long and weighs only 34 ounces. There is sufficient space in the back of the camera to accommodate three double plate holders, thus giving the camera a capacity of six plates, and in addition, as many extra plate holders as desired (each containing two plates) may be carried. THE CONLEY SENIOR BOX CAMERA presents a most handsome appearance, being covered with the finest quality of black seal grain keratol leather, and all metal parts are made with fine oxidized finish.

EASY TO OPERATE. The Conley Senior Box Camera is the simplest and easiest kind of a camera to use. No previous experience is necessary, everything is simple and easy to understand, and the big book of instructions, which comes free with the camera, tells you in plain and simple language all that you need to know in order to make GOOD PICTURES.

YOU WILL BE SURPRISED to see how easy it is to take GOOD PICTURES with the Conley Senior Box Camera, and you will derive the greatest pleasure from the beautiful pictures you can make of your friends and relatives, brothers and sisters; your dogs, cats and horses; the home, both inside and out; pretty landscapes, buildings and places of interest seen while traveling; and especially pictures of the baby in all its cute and amusing positions. It will not be fully realized, until after years, what treasures have been secured in the way of pictures of friends and places or things of interest.

THE LENS is a fine single achromatic, of the Meniscus style of construction, specially ground from the finest imported Mantois optical glass, the best universal or fixed focus lens that can be made. This lens possesses great depth of focus, giving perfectly sharp detail both to objects at a distance and to those which are nearby, and is guaranteed to cover the plate fully to the extreme corners.

world unless the holders are absolutely light-tight and perfect in construction. That is why we furnish with the Conley Senior Box Camera the genuine Conley Improved Flexible Valve Plate Holder, the exact same style and quality of holder that we furnish with our very highest priced folding cameras.

THE SHUTTER is entirely automatic in action, being operated for either time or instantaneous exposures simply by pressing the lever at the side of the camera. This shutter is always set and ready for immediate action, its construction is exceedingly simple, there are no complicated parts to get out of order and of all shutters heretofore designed for use with box cameras this one is the simplest, the most effective and the most reliable.

TWO VIEW FINDERS are provided, one for use when making pictures the long way of the plate (4 inches high and 5 inches wide), and the other for use when making pictures the short way of the plate (5 inches high and 4 inches wide), thus enabling the operator to accommodate the shape and style of picture to the subject. These view finders are most carefully and accurately made and perfectly adjusted.

TWO TRIPOD SOCKETS. The Conley Senior Box Camera is made with two tripod sockets, one on the side, the other on the bottom of the camera, so that pictures may be made either the long or the short way of the plate when using a tripod.

UNDERSTAND, HOWEVER, THIS CAMERA MAY BE USED EITHER WITH OR WITHOUT A TRIPOD,

just as the user prefers. A tripod is a convenience, especially when making time exposures, but is not by any means a necessity, and the finest kind of pictures may be made without a tripod.

REMEMBER HOW SIMPLE THE CONLEY SENIOR BOX CAMERA is; the shutter is always set, you don't have to turn any buttons or push any levers before making an exposure, operations which are very apt to be forgotten or wrongly executed in the excitement of the moment; and you don't have to focus each time a picture is made, as the lens is of universal focus, always ready. With other cameras many a fine picture is lost because of the delay in setting the shutter, focusing, etc. In the meantime the subject is gone or the scene is changed, but the Conley Senior Box Camera is always ready for instant action.

CONLEY IMPROVED FLEXIBLE VALVE PLATE HOLDER. With every Conley Senior Box Camera we furnish the genuine Conley Improved Flexible Valve Double Plate Holder, made with the famous Drake Light Proof Flexible Valve, the very best plate holder on the market. It is the custom of practically all camera manufacturers to furnish cheap, poorly made plate holders with box cameras, and three-fourths of all the failures in picture making are due to faulty plate holders. As a matter of fact, the plate holder is the most important part of a camera, because good pictures cannot be made with the best camera in the

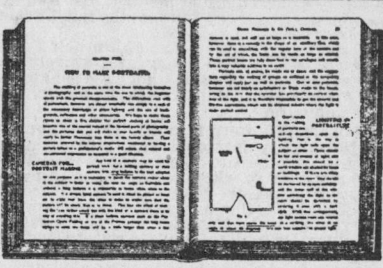

"COMPLETE INSTRUCTIONS IN PHOTOGRAPHY" **FREE**

WITH EVERY CONLEY SENIOR BOX CAMERA we include, without extra charge, our big 112-page manual, "Complete Instructions in Photography," the largest, the simplest and the most complete guide to photography ever published. This book makes everything plain, clear, simple and easy to understand, and not only insures success to the beginner in picture making but contains a fund of valuable information for the experienced photographer.

COMPLETE DEVELOPING, FINISHING AND MATERIAL OUTFIT.

The Big Outfit which we furnish with the Conley Senior Box Camera, at the prices quoted below, contains everything necessary for developing, printing, toning and mounting pictures complete. Every item that goes into this outfit is good, the plates and paper are guaranteed fresh and perfect, the chemicals full strength and of the highest purity, and all the other items strictly high class, well made and serviceable. Understand, we furnish the camera alone (with one double plate holder) for $1.95, but we especially urge that you order the Camera and Outfit, all complete, ready for use, at our special price of $3.15.

The Complete Outfit at $3.15 contains the following items:

1 4x5 Conley Senior Box Camera	1 Paste Brush	1 Package Concentrated Dry Toner (makes 8 ounces of solution)
1 4x5 Conley Improved Flexible Valve Plate Holder	1 Graduated Glass for Measuring Liquids	1 Dozen Sheets Sensitized Paper
1 Metal Dark Room Lamp	1 Dozen Card Mounts, with fancy embossed borders	1 Printing Frame
1 Tray for Developing Plates	1 Package Concentrated Dry Developer (makes 8 ounces of solution)	1 Package Hypo for fixing Negatives and Prints
1 Tray for Fixing Plates		
1 Tray for Toning Prints		1 Tube of fine Scented Photo Mounting Paste
1 Print Roller for smoothing down the mounted prints	1 Copy of "Complete Instructions in Photography"	
½ Dozen Dry Plates		

No. 20K60 The 4x5 Conley Senior Box Camera, with one Conley Improved Flexible Valve Double Plate Holder, and Complete Developing, Finishing and Material Outfit, exactly as described and illustrated on this page. Price....(Shipping weight, 10¼ pounds)........ **$3.15**

No. 20K61 The 4x5 Conley Senior Box Camera, with one Conley Improved Flexible Valve Double Plate Holder, but without Developing, Finishing and Material Outfit. Price......(Shipping weight, 4 pounds)...... **$1.95**

No. 20K652 Extra Plate Holders, for 4x5 Conley Senior Box Camera, Genuine Conley Improved Flexible Valve Plate Holders, each holder will carry two dry plates. Price, 5 for **$1.85**; each..... (If by mail, postage extra, each, 6c)....**38c**

CONLEY POCKET FOLDING CAMERA

DIMENSIONS.

	Focal Capacity, inches	Camera Closed, inches	Carrying Case, inches
3¼x4¼	6	2x4¼x5½	2½x6x8½
4x5	6¾	2x5⅛x6¼	2½x6¾x10⅓

SPECIFICATIONS. Woodwork—Solid mahogany, dovetailed corners, piano finish. **Metal parts**—Brass, nickel plated, highly polished. **Covering**—Genuine seal grain leather. **Bellows**—Best red Russia leather. **Front**—One piece, all metal, with new screw actuated clamp. **Finder**—Ground glass, reversible. **Piano Hinge**—Nickel plated. **Shutter**—Wollensak Junior, automatic, pneumatic release. **Lens**—High grade single achromatic. **Plate Holder**—Improved Conley flexible valve. **Carrying Case**—Keratol covered.

REDUCED TO $4.75 FOR 3¼x4¼ size

$4.95 FOR 4x5 size

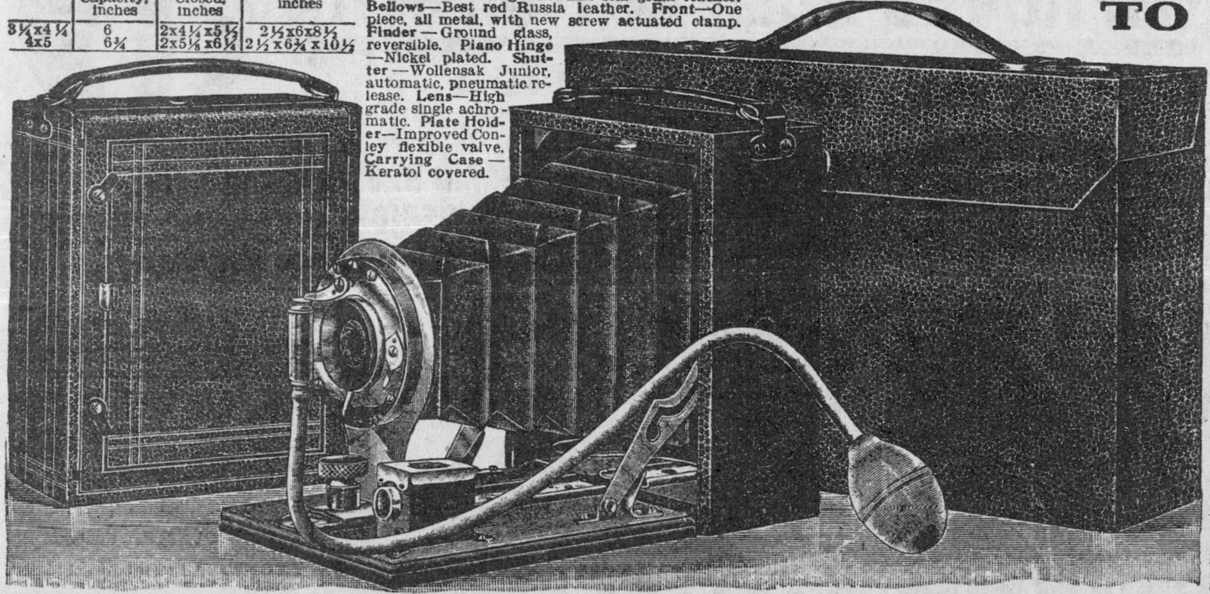

VERY COMPACT. This camera folds into such small space that it may easily be carried in the coat pocket, and is exceedingly convenient, serviceable and effective. It is well made throughout, handsomely finished, covered with genuine leather; the woodwork is beautifully polished; the metal parts are all finely finished and heavily nickel plated; in short, it is a suprisingly good camera at our special reduced prices of $4.75 for the 3¼x4¼ size, and $4.95 for the 4x5 size.

ALTHOUGH SOLD AT A WONDERFULLY LOW PRICE, these Conley Pocket Folding Cameras are strictly high class instruments in every way. While they do not possess all of the adjustments and improvements which some of our higher priced cameras have, yet they are made throughout in the best possible way. Only the best materials are used in their construction, solid Honduras mahogany, with piano finish, genuine seal grain leather covering, all metal parts of brass heavily nickel plated and highly polished, red Russia leather bellows lined with lightproof gossamer cloth, and high class workmanship in every detail of construction.

THE LENS AND SHUTTER. THE LENS with which we equip the Conley Pocket Folding Cameras is an exceedingly good single achromatic lens, ground especially for these cameras from the highest grade of imported optical glass and guaranteed to cover the plate sharply to the extreme corners. This single achromatic lens possesses unusual depth of focus and sufficient rapidity to insure fully timed negatives under good light conditions even with the fastest instantaneous exposures. THE SHUTTER is the Wollensak Junior Automatic, operated either by bulb or finger release, and arranged for time, bulb and instantaneous exposures. It is self setting or automatic, and fitted with a fine iris diaphragm.

THE CONLEY POCKET FOLDING CAMERA is fitted with reversible view finder, spring actuated ground glass focusing screen at the rear protected by hinged panel, accurately adjusted focusing scale, special ornamental side arms, strong leather handle, nickel plated piano hinge and each camera comes complete with substantial keratol covered carrying case containing space for the camera and extra plate holders.

No. 20K90 Conley Pocket Folding Camera, 3¼x4¼, complete with one Conley plate holder and carrying case. Shipping weight, 3½ pounds. Price.. **$4.75**

No. 20K91 Conley Pocket Folding Camera, 4x5, complete with one Conley plate holder and carrying case. Shipping weight, 4¼ pounds. Price.. **4.95**

CONLEY SENIOR FOLDING CAMERA

SPECIFICATIONS. Woodwork—Solid mahogany, dovetailed corners, piano finish. **Metal parts**—Brass and steel, nickel plated and highly polished. **Covering**—Genuine seal grain leather. **Bellows**—Fine red Russia leather. **Front**—Mahogany, with rising and falling adjustment. **Finder**—Ground glass, reversible. **Shutter**—Wollensak Junior, automatic. **Lens**—Double rectilinear. **Carrying Case**—Keratol covered. **Plate Holder**—Conley improved flexible valve.

REDUCED TO

$5.98 FOR 4x5 size | **$7.80 FOR 5x7 size**

DIMENSIONS.

Size, in.	Focal Capacity, inches	Camera Closed, inches.	Carrying Case inches	Capacity of Carrying Case
4x5	6¾	2½x5¼x6¼	3x6¾x11	Camera and Four Holders
5x7	8	2¾x6⅝x8½	3½x9x13½	Camera and Five Holders

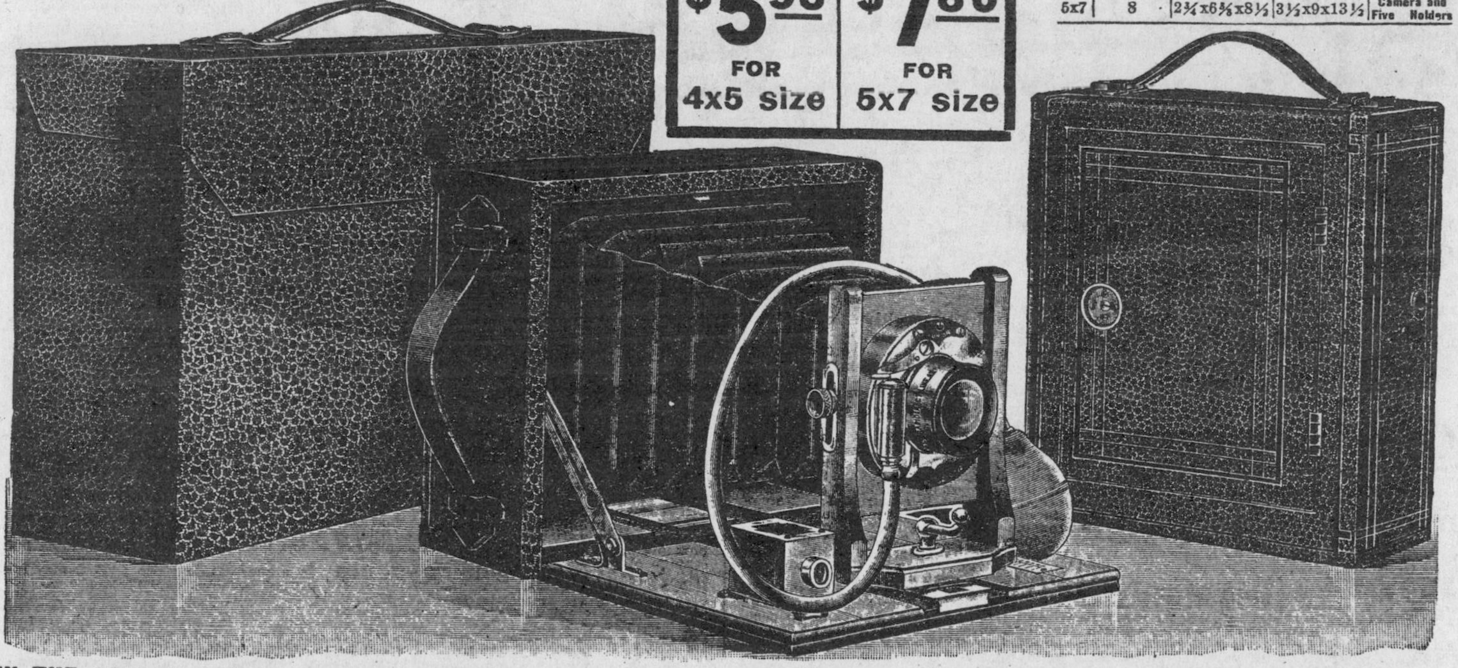

IN THE CONLEY SENIOR FOLDING CAMERA we offer an instrument embodying the most up to date features of all high grade folding cameras, but without those adjustments which serve only to increase the cost of the camera without adding to its real value as a picture taking machine. It is a good camera that can in every way be depended upon.

SOME OF THE BEST PICTURES that have been sent in to us by our customers have been made with the Conley Sr. Folding Camera. Almost every day in the year we receive samples of work which our customers have done with the various cameras listed in this catalogue, samples of the pictures which they have made with our various folding cameras, including our Long Focus and Double Extension Cameras, and **some of the very best pictures that have come to us in this way have been taken with the Conley Senior Folding Camera.**

WE PUT INTO THE CONLEY SENIOR FOLDING CAMERA the very best materials, the exact same materials that we use in the construction of our highest priced cameras. It is made throughout from the best Honduras mahogany, thoroughly seasoned and kiln dried; the covering is genuine pebble grain morocco leather; the bellows is red Russia leather, gossamer lined, and all metal parts are of brass, heavily nickel plated and highly polished.

THE DOUBLE RAPID RECTILINEAR LENS with which we equip this camera is a high class, rapid lens, the exact same style and quality of lens that is used by other camera manufacturers on cameras selling at from $15.00 to $20.00, a lens that we can absolutely guarantee in every way.

THE SHUTTER is the Wollensak Junior Automatic, an exceedingly convenient and easy shutter to operate, made throughout in the very best and most accurate manner, a shutter of handsome design and beautiful finish. It is operated either by bulb release or finger release, is arranged for making time, bulb or instantaneous exposures, and is fitted with a fine iris diaphragm.

OTHER ADJUSTMENTS. The Conley Senior Folding Camera is made with rising and falling front, reversible view finder, spring actuated ground-glass focusing screen, accurately adjusted focus scale, and comes complete with substantial keratol covered carrying case with space for the camera and extra plate holders.

No. 20K100 Conley Senior Folding Camera, 4x5, with one Conley plate holder and carrying case. Shipping weight, 4½ pounds. Price........ **$5.98**

No. 20K101 Conley Senior Folding Camera, 5x7, with one Conley plate holder and carrying case. Shipping weight, 6½ pounds. Price........ **7.80**

IMPROVED COMPACT CAMERA

THE 1908 MODEL

IS MADE WITH
DOUBLE RAPID RECTILINEAR LENS.
WOLLENSAK SENIOR AUTOMATIC SHUTTER.
RACK AND PINION FOCUS MOVEMENT.

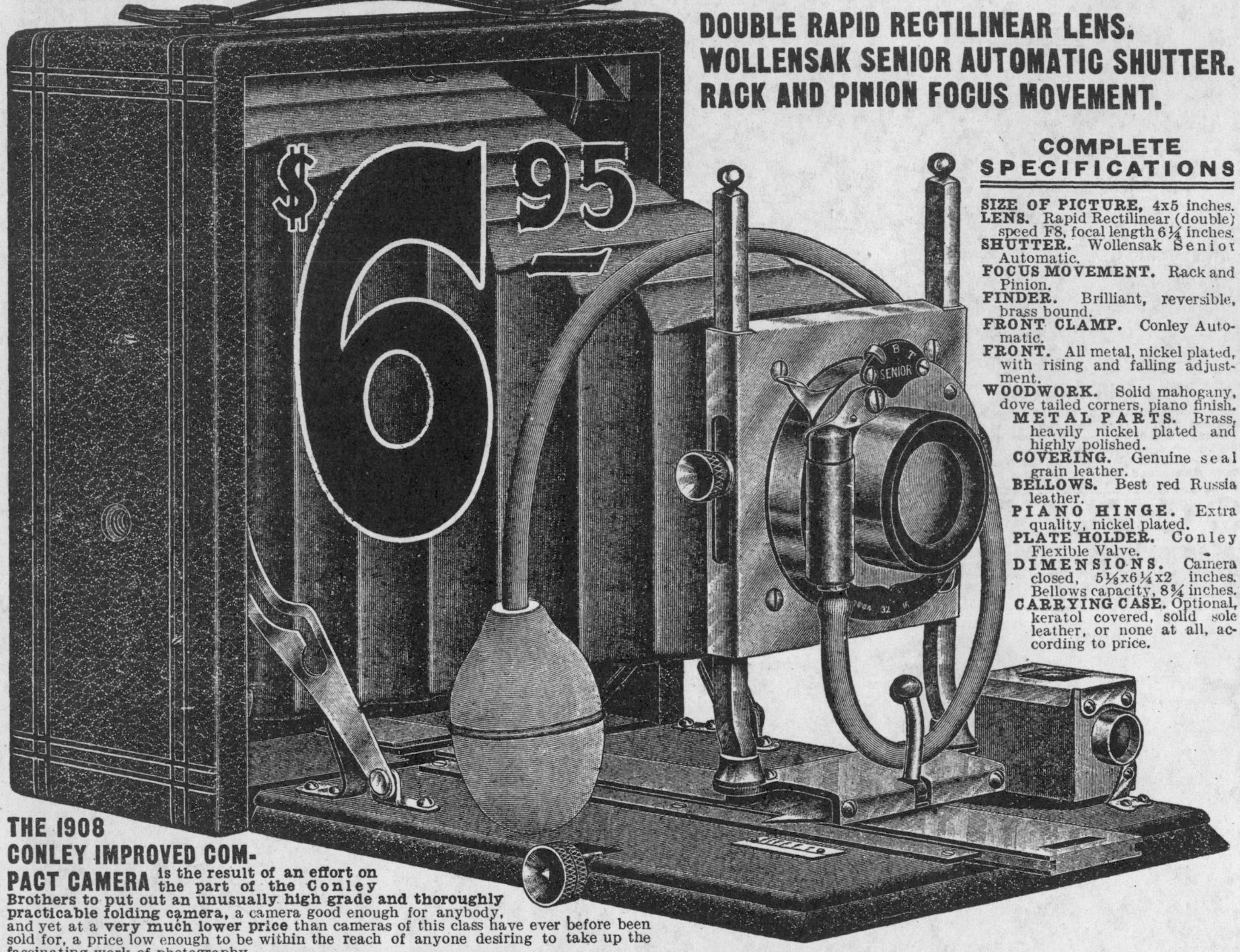

COMPLETE SPECIFICATIONS

SIZE OF PICTURE, 4x5 inches.
LENS. Rapid Rectilinear (double) speed F8, focal length 6¼ inches.
SHUTTER. Wollensak Senior Automatic.
FOCUS MOVEMENT. Rack and Pinion.
FINDER. Brilliant, reversible, brass bound.
FRONT CLAMP. Conley Automatic.
FRONT. All metal, nickel plated, with rising and falling adjustment.
WOODWORK. Solid mahogany, dove tailed corners, piano finish.
METAL PARTS. Brass, heavily nickel plated and highly polished.
COVERING. Genuine seal grain leather.
BELLOWS. Best red Russia leather.
PIANO HINGE. Extra quality, nickel plated.
PLATE HOLDER. Conley Flexible Valve.
DIMENSIONS. Camera closed, 5⅛x6¼x2 inches. Bellows capacity, 8¾ inches.
CARRYING CASE. Optional, keratol covered, solid sole leather, or none at all, according to price.

THE 1908 CONLEY IMPROVED COMPACT CAMERA is the result of an effort on the part of the Conley Brothers to put out an unusually high grade and thoroughly practicable folding camera, a camera good enough for anybody, and yet at a very much lower price than cameras of this class have ever before been sold for, a price low enough to be within the reach of anyone desiring to take up the fascinating work of photography.

SPECIAL FEATURES.

THE 1908 CONLEY IMPROVED COMPACT CAMERA is made with rack and pinion focus movement, making it very easy to quickly and accurately focus the Camera. It is equipped with the Conley automatic patent front clamp, the most convenient and satisfactory front clamp ever devised, the exact same front clamp that we use on our highest grade Long Focus and Double Extension cameras. The front of this camera is constructed entirely of brass, nickel plated and highly polished, and is made with rising and falling adjustment for regulating the relative amounts of sky and foreground. Besides the rack and pinion focus movement with all metal rising and falling front, Conley automatic front clamp and other special features, this camera is equipped with an extra quality reversible brilliant view finder, nickel plated piano hinge, highly ornamental side arms, strong leather handle and spring actuated ground glass focusing screen with mahogany back panel.

THE DOUBLE RAPID RECTILINEAR LENS which we furnish with the 1908 Conley Improved Compact Camera is exactly the same grade of rapid rectilinear lens that is used on cameras costing from three to five times the price we ask for the Conley Improved Compact Camera. It is a lens that possesses unusual depth of focus and great covering power, and it works with great rapidity, making the camera especially suited to instantaneous or snap shot exposures. This lens is guaranteed to cover the entire plate to the extreme corners and produces an unusually clear cut and snappy negative.

THE WOLLENSAK SENIOR AUTOMATIC SHUTTER with which we equip the 1908 Conley Improved Compact Camera is arranged for instantaneous exposures and bulb or time exposures of any desired length. This shutter is exceedingly easy of adjustment and works very smoothly, without the slightest vibration. It is an automatic shutter, by which

we mean that after each exposure it automatically resets itself for the next one and is thus always ready for instant use. It is not necessary to set it before an exposure can be made. This shutter can be operated either by finger release or by pneumatic bulb. It is provided with a fine iris diaphragm for regulating the size of the opening, and is in every way a high class, reliable and satisfactory shutter.

THE RACK AND PINION FOCUS MOVEMENT is a feature usually found only in cameras sold at much higher prices and it is an adjustment that contributes greatly to the ease and convenience of operation. The speed and accuracy with which the camera is focused by this rack and pinion movement adds to the efficiency of the instrument and insures a larger percentage of perfect pictures.

MATERIALS AND WORKMANSHIP. In manufacturing the 1908 Conley Improved Compact Camera we use only the very highest grade materials, the exact same style and quality of materials that we employ in our highest grade cameras. The best quality of carefully selected, thoroughly seasoned and kiln dried mahogany is used for all of the woodwork, and the covering is a high grade of seal grain morocco leather. The bellows is made from the best red Russia leather lined with lightproof, black gossamer cloth. All metal parts are of brass, nickel plated and highly polished. The workmanship in every way is thoroughly first class, these cameras being put up by the same workmen who put up our highest priced cameras. The same leather workers put on the covering; the same finishers give to this camera its beautiful piano polish; the same skilled workmen assemble the cameras, putting together the different parts as they come from the various departments of the factory, and every Conley Improved Compact Camera that leaves our store is just as carefully inspected and guaranteed to reach the purchaser in exactly the same perfect condition as the most expensive cameras that we sell.

PRICES.

No. 20K111 Conley Improved Compact Folding Camera, 4x5, with one Conley flexible valve plate holder, without carrying case, exactly as illustrated and described on this page. Shipping weight, 3½ pounds. Price.................. **$6.95**

No. 20K112 Conley Improved Compact Folding Camera, 4x5, complete with one plate holder, same as No. 20K111, but with substantial keratol covered (imitation leather) carrying case, containing space for the camera and four plate holders. Shipping weight, 4¾ pounds. Price.................. **7.45**

No. 20K113 Conley Improved Compact Folding Camera, 4x5, complete with one plate holder, same as No. 20K111, but with solid sole leather carrying case, containing space for the camera and four plate holders. Shipping weight, 4¾ pounds. Price.................. **8.40**

4x5 $9.30

5x7 $12.50

CONLEY A FOLDING CAMERA

SPECIFICATIONS.

Woodwork—Solid mahogany, dovetailed corners, piano finish. **Metal Parts**—Brass, nickel plated and highly polished. **Covering**—Genuine seal grain leather. **Bellows**—Best red Russia leather. **Back**—Non-reversible. **Front**—All metal, with rising and falling adjustment. **Front Clamp**—New Conley automatic. **Finder**—Ground glass, reversible. **Piano Hinge**—Nickel plated. **Shutter**—New Conley Safety, pneumatic release. **Lens**—Double rectilinear. **Plate Holder**—Conley improved flexible valve. **Carrying Case**—Solid sole leather.

DIMENSIONS.

	Focal Capacity inches	Camera Closed, inches	Carrying Case, inches	Capacity of Carrying Case
4x5	6¾	2⅛x5¼x6¼	3 x6¾x11	Camera and Four Holders
5x7	8	2⅜x6⅝x8⅛	3¼x8⅞x13½	Camera and Five Holders

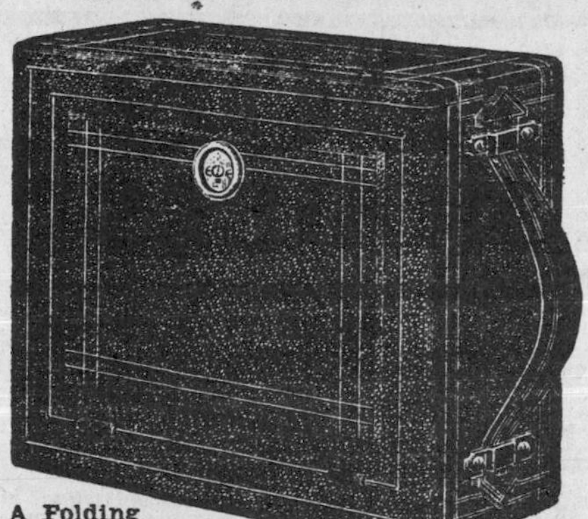

MADE AS GOOD AS WE KNOW HOW. The Conley A Folding Camera is cheap only in price. We make it just as good as we know how. We put into it the very best materials that we can buy, the best mahogany, the best leather, the exact same high grade materials that we use in our higher priced cameras. The parts of the Conley A Folding Camera are made by the same mechanics who make the parts for our highest priced cameras. They are assembled, put together, and finished by exactly the same workmen that we employ on our highest grade Long Focus and Double Extension Cameras, and throughout the factory these cameras receive exactly the same painstaking care, the same rigid inspection and the same strict attention to the smallest details of construction.

THE HIGH GRADE DOUBLE RAPID RECTILINEAR LENS with which we equip the Conley A Folding Camera is a lens that we can guarantee in every respect. It works at a speed of F 8, ample speed for making instantaneous exposures even under comparatively poor conditions of light, possesses great depth of focus, covers the plate sharply to the extreme corners, even with full aperture, yielding a sharp, clear cut, snappy negative. This lens is the exact same style and quality that is used by many of the eastern camera manufacturers in cameras that sell at from $25.00 to $30.00.

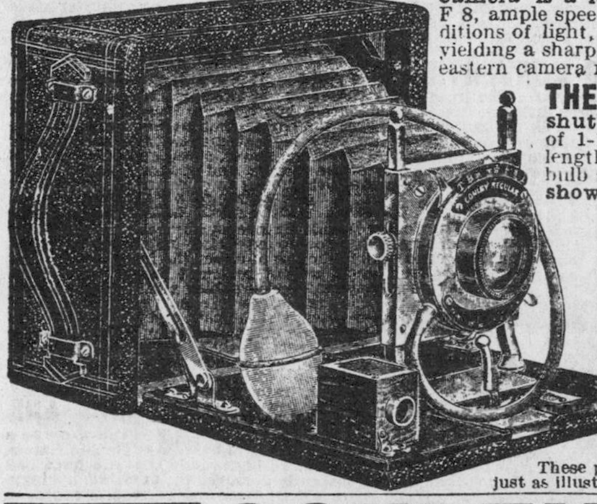

THE NEW CONLEY SAFETY SHUTTER. The 1908 Conley A Folding Camera is equipped with the new Conley Safety shutter, the exact same shutter that we use on our Conley Long Focus Camera. This shutter is arranged for making exposures of 1-100, 1-50, 1-25, 1-5, 1-2 or 1 full second with one pressure of the bulb or time exposures of any desired length with two pressures of the bulb, and short time exposures by opening the shutter with a pressure of the bulb and closing it by releasing the pressure. **On the page devoted to our Conley Long Focus Camera we show a large illustration and give a more complete description of this new Conley Safety shutter.**

SPECIAL FEATURES. The Conley A Folding Camera is made with rising and falling front for regulating the relative amount of sky and foreground, spring actuated ground glass focusing screen protected by hinged, morocco covered, mahogany back panel, accurately adjusted **focus scale**, two tripod sockets, and high grade reversible view finder. This camera is made with the new Conley **automatic front clamp**, the very best front clamp ever invented, and our new **all metal front**. The beautifully grained, highly polished mahogany with the all metal, nickel plated front and nickel plated trimmings throughout makes this camera an exceedingly attractive one in appearance.

CARRYING CASE. Every Conley A Folding Camera comes complete with fine sole leather carrying case, substantially made from heavy sole leather, fitted with patent catch and strong leather handle. These cases contain room for the camera and a number of extra plate holders.

No. 20K120 Conley A Folding Camera, 4x5. Price.. **$9.30**
Shipping weight, 5½ pounds.

No 20K121 Conley A Folding Camera, 5x7. Price. **$12.50**
Shipping weight, 8 pounds.

These prices include the camera complete with lens, shutter and sole leather carrying case, just as illustrated and described on this page, and one Conley flexible valve plate holder.

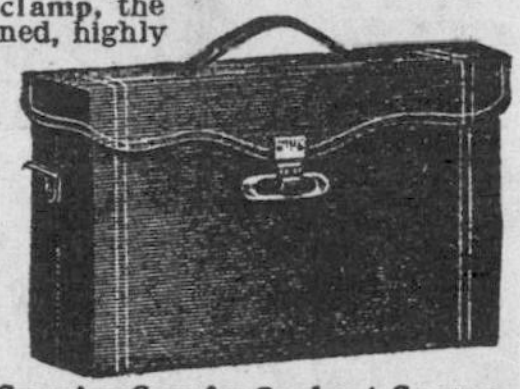

Carrying Case for Conley A Camera.

4x5 $11.50

5x7 $15.25

CONLEY C FOLDING CAMERA

SPECIFICATIONS.

Woodwork—All solid mahogany, piano finish. **Metal Parts**—All brass and steel, nickel plated and highly polished. **Covering**—High grade seal grain leather. **Bellows**—Best red Russia leather. **Back**—Reversible, with single button release and improved swing. **Focus Movement**—Rack and pinion. **Front**—All metal, new design, with rising and falling adjustment. **Front Clamp**—New Conley automatic. **Finder**—Brilliant, hooded. **Piano Hinge**—Nickel plated. **Shutter**—New Conley Safety, pneumatic release. **Lens**—High grade double symmetrical. **Plate Holder** — Conley improved flexible valve. **Carrying Case**—Solid sole leather.

DIMENSIONS.

	Focal Capacity inches	Camera Closed, inches	Carrying Case, inches	Capacity of Carrying Case
4x5	9½	3⅛x6¼x6¼	3½x7x12	Camera and Five Holders
5x7	12⅞	3⅜x8½x8⅛	4¼x9x15¾	Camera and Six Holders

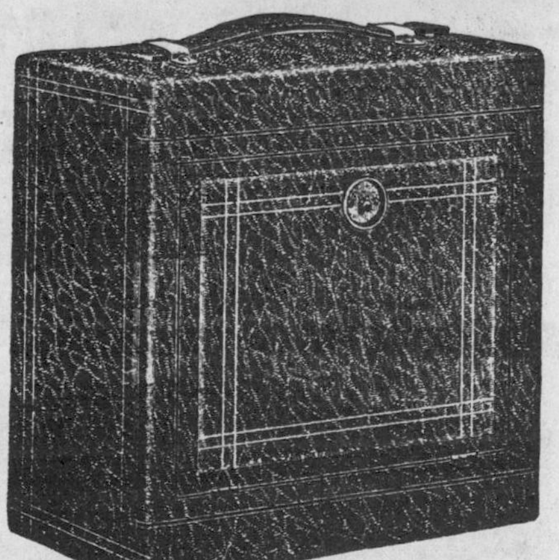

WE OFFER THE CONLEY C CAMERA as the equal in every way of any camera of its class on the market regardless of price. We offer the Conley C Camera, in sizes 4x5 and 5x7, at our special prices of $11.50 and $15.25, as equal to cameras sold by other dealers at from $20.00 to $30.00. It represents the acme of perfection in this style of a camera, embracing all of the latest improvements and attachments ever put into a camera of this design.

THE SPECIAL FEATURES OF THIS CAMERA, the features that particularly commend it to the careful and discriminating buyer, are the reversible back, the vertical swing, the rack and pinion focus movement, the new Conley Safety shutter, and the high grade double symmetrical lens. Besides these more important features, the Conley C Folding Camera is made with all metal rising and falling front, brilliant hooded finder, accurately adjusted focus scale, spring actuated ground glass focusing screen protected by hinged leather covered mahogany back panel, piano hinge, and Conley automatic front clamp.

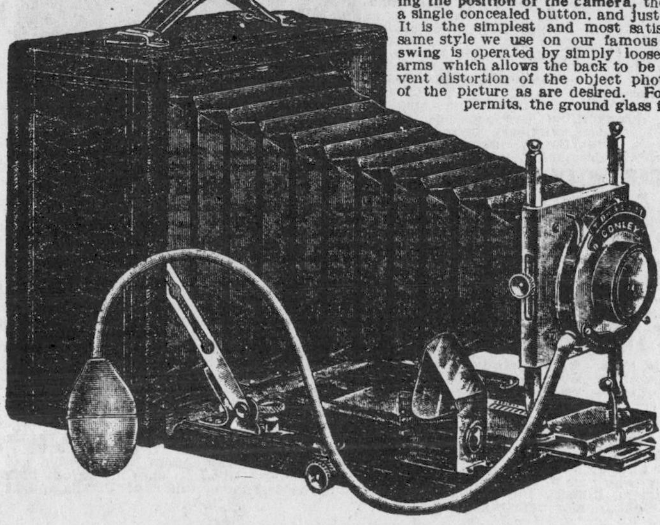

THE REVERSIBLE BACK with vertical swing enables the user of this camera to make either upright or horizontal pictures without changing the position of the camera, the back being instantly detachable by pressing a single concealed button, and just as quickly replaced in either position desired. It is the simplest and most satisfactory reversible back yet made, the exact same style we use on our famous Conley Long Focus Cameras. **The vertical swing** is operated by simply loosening two set screws at the bases of the side arms which allows the back to be swung forward or backward, in order to prevent distortion of the object photographed when it is found necessary to tilt the camera up or down in order to include such portions of the picture as are desired. **Focusing is accomplished by a fine rack and pinion movement,** using, when the nature of the work permits, the ground glass focusing screen at the rear of the camera, or the instrument may be used as a hand camera, the picture centered and located by means of the view finder and focused by the accurately adjusted focus scale conveniently located on the bed of the camera.

THE LENS. With the Conley C Folding Camera we furnish an extra high grade double symmetrical lens, the exact same style and quality of lens that we furnish with our Conley Long Focus Camera, a lens which is equal in every respect to the lenses used in cameras sold by other dealers at three times the price we ask for this camera. This lens works at a speed of F 8, has great depth of focus, a very flat field, and is guaranteed to cover the plate to the extreme corners, even when used at full aperture. **The new Conley Safety shutter** is a feature of the new 1908 model of the Conley C Folding Camera, and is a most thoroughly reliable, easily operated shutter. This shutter represents the very latest advances in shutter construction, embodying ideas that are the result of years of study, experiment, and practical experience, and is the best shutter of this type that has yet been invented. **This is exactly the same style of shutter that we furnish with our Conley Long Focus Camera, and on page 678 will be found a large illustration and more complete description of this new shutter.**

No. 20K130 Conley C Folding Camera, 4x5. Price.............. **$11.50**
Shipping weight, 6 pounds.

No. 20K131 Conley C Folding Camera, 5x7. Price.............. **$15.25**
Shipping weight, 10¾ pounds.

These prices include the camera complete with double symmetrical lens, Conley Safety shutter, one Conley Flexible Valve plate holder, and our best grade sole leather carrying case.

"COMPLETE INSTRUCTIONS IN PHOTOGRAPHY"

Our big 112 page manual sent free with every camera we sell. See page 683 for description of this valuable book.

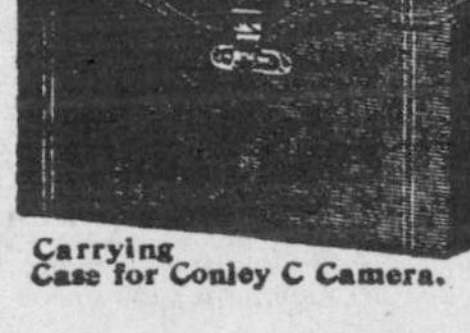

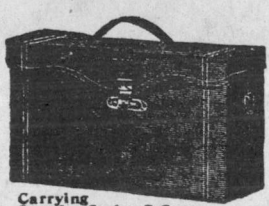

Carrying Case for Conley C Camera.

CONLEY DOUBLE EXTENSION CAMERAS

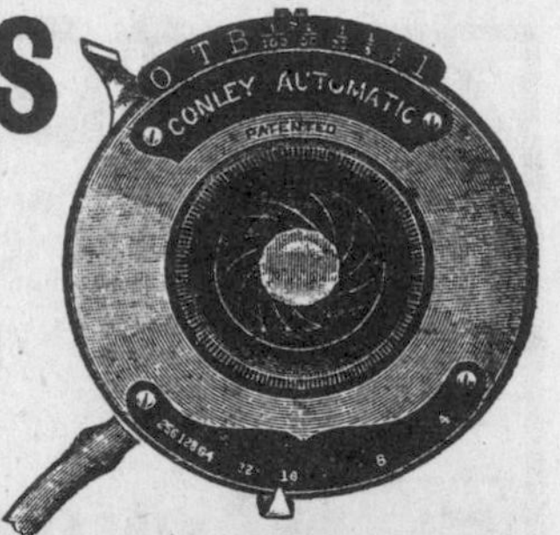

1908 MODELS — 4x5 $21.50 — 5x7 $27.00 — 6½x8½ $35.60

SPECIFICATIONS.

Camera	Focal Capacity	Size Camera, Closed	Size Carrying Case
4 x5	16¼ inches	4 x 6¼x 6⅝ inches	4½x 7¼x11¾ in.
5 x7	23 inches	4⅛x 8½x 9 inches	4⅝x 9½x15¼ in.
6½x8½	27¼ inches	4¾x10⅛x11¾ inches	5¼x11¼x18½ in.

WOODWORK—All solid mahogany, dovetailed corners, French polished.
METAL PARTS—All brass and steel, nickel plated and highly polished.
COVERING—Best quality heavy walrus grain leather.
BELLOWS—Best red Russia leather, gossamer lined, copying length.
BACK—Reversible with single button release and improved swing.
FOCUS MOVEMENT—Improved rack and pinion, with automatic pinion lock.
LENS BOARD—Detachable, instantly removed or replaced.
FRONT—Double adjusting, vertical and horizontal movements.
FRONT CLAMP—New Conley Automatic.
FINDER—Brilliant, brass bound and hooded.
CAMERA BED—Three-section, with new Conley all metal track and piano hinge.
SHUTTER—Latest Conley Automatic, pneumatic release.
LENS—High grade, rapid convertible three-focus.
PLATE HOLDER—Conley Improved Flexible Valve.
AUXILIARY BED—All metal, rack and pinion.
CARRYING CASE—Heavy sole leather, with space for the camera and six double plate holders.

SPECIAL FEATURES OF THE 1908 MODELS

THE NEW CONLEY AUTOMATIC SHUTTER is absolutely perfect in action, simple in construction, beautiful in design, convenient and easy to operate. It makes, automatically, with one pressure of the bulb, instantaneous exposures of 1-25, 1-50 or 1-100 of a second. It makes, also automatically, with one pressure of the bulb, time exposures of 1-5, 1-2 or 1 full second. It makes short time exposures with one pressure of the bulb, the shutter remaining open until the pressure is released. It makes long time exposures, exposures of any desired length, with two pressures of the bulb, the first pressure opening the shutter, the second one closing it. By moving the indicator to the letter O, the shutter is opened and remains open for focusing. **All working parts, including the valves and the pumps, are entirely enclosed within the case** where they are absolutely protected from dust or injury of any kind. Every part is made as accurately and carefully as the parts of a watch, resulting in the smoothest action, the most perfect balance and the least possible friction. This new shutter is entirely automatic, resetting itself after each exposure. There is no shutter made that is more perfect in action or more beautiful in design. It is beautifully finished in dark lacquered brass with the speed plate and diaphragm scale enameled in black with white lettering, and it is fitted with a finely made, accurately adjusted iris diaphragm.

THE SPECIAL F 8 THREE-FOCUS CONVERTIBLE LENS. This is a double lens composed of two perfectly corrected combinations, either of which can be used alone if desired. The front combination has a longer focal length than the rear combination, thus affording the choice of three different focal lengths, the front combination alone, the rear combination alone, or the complete lens. This lens is ground from the very highest grade of imported Mantois optical glass, possesses great depth of focus and flatness of field, unusual covering power, speed and fine definition. The three different focal lengths add greatly to the scope and efficiency of the camera, and makes possible results entirely beyond the capacity of cameras fitted with cheaper lenses or made with shorter focal capacities. The focal lengths of these lenses are as follows:

Equivalent Focus of Lens	Focus Rear Combination of Lens	Focus Front Combination of Lens
4 x5 ... 6¾-in.	11 inches	14 inches
5 x7 ... 8 -in.	14 inches	18 inches
6½x8½ ... 11 -in.	18 inches	22 inches

THE EXTRA LONG, COPYING LENGTH, BELLOWS. The Conley Double Extension Cameras are made with an extra long, double extension bellows, a bellows of sufficient length to permit the use of either the front or rear combinations of the lens alone, and of sufficient length to make the camera available for copying, photographing small objects at very close range, special effects in landscape work, architectural subjects, and portraiture. This bellows is made from the highest grade of red Russia leather, lined with a special lightproof gossamer cloth, and in its construction we use a special pure rubber cement, insuring long life to the bellows and keeping the leather always soft and pliable.

THE REVERSIBLE BACK AND VERTICAL SWING. The Conley Double Extension Camera is so made that the back can be instantly detached by pressing a single concealed button and as readily replaced in position for either vertical or horizontal pictures. It is the most easily operated reversible back made, having no clips or catches of any sort to adjust. This back is so constructed that it can be swung backward or forward to any desired angle simply by loosening the set screws at the bases of the side arms. This adjustment, technically known as a vertical swing and usually spoken of simply as the "swing back," is practically indispensable when photographing buildings or other objects where it is necessary to tilt up the front of the camera. Tilting a camera, either up or down results in distortion unless corrected by use of a properly constructed swing back.

GENERAL CONSTRUCTION. These cameras are made throughout from carefully selected, thoroughly seasoned, kiln dried Honduras mahogany. The corners are all rounded, and all joints are dovetailed. Special care is exercised in the finish of the woodwork, a special process of rubbing and polishing giving it an unusually beautiful appearance with high piano polish.

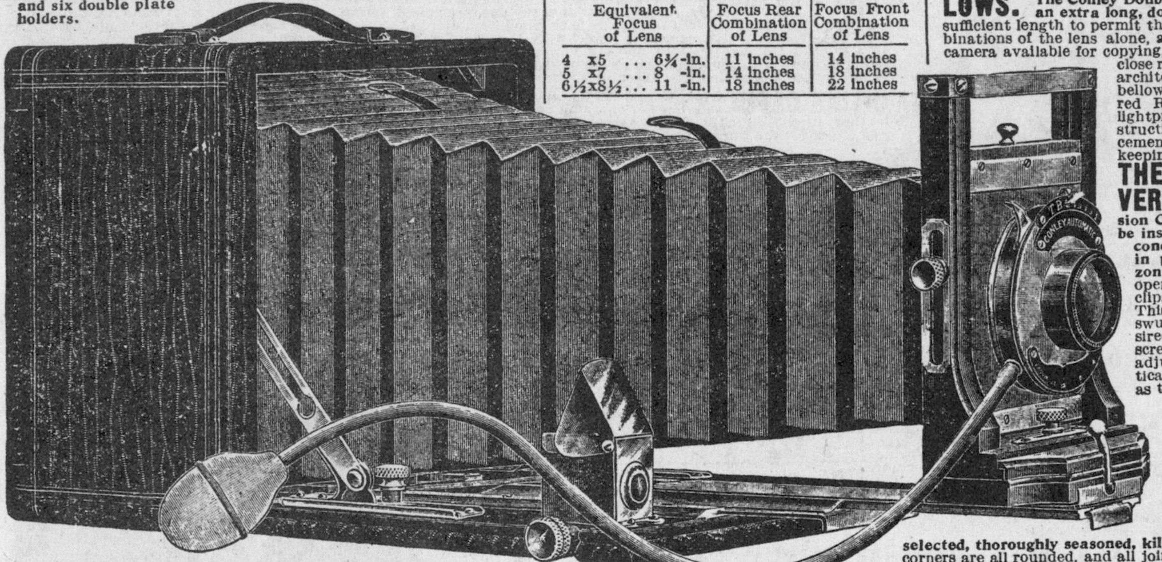

Conley Double Extension Camera, partly extended.

THE METAL PARTS are made throughout from brass, heavily nickel plated, highly polished and accurately fitted. The covering is the best grade of heavy walrus grain leather, a most handsome and durable covering. The workmanship throughout is of the highest grade, the most careful attention being given to even the smallest details and, when you order the Conley Double Extension Camera, you can expect to receive a camera that is as nearly absolutely perfect as the very best makers can possibly produce.

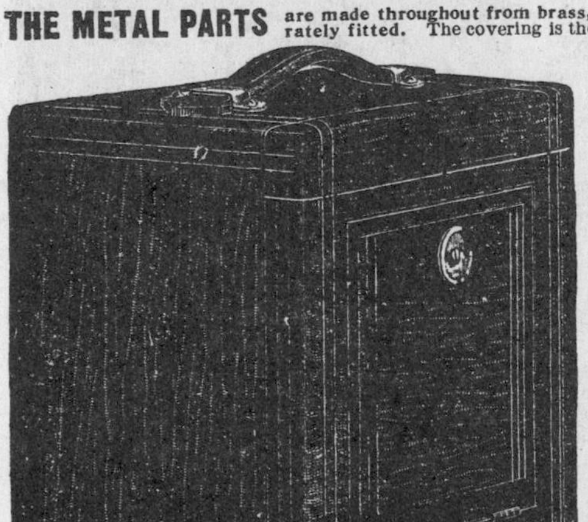

Conley Double Extension Camera, closed.

ADJUSTMENTS. The Conley Double Extension Camera is fitted with every adjustment, every convenience, and every improvement that can in any way add to its effectiveness and ease of operation. The all metal double extension triple bed, made in three sections, is so designed and constructed as to secure the greatest possible strength and rigidity, even when the bellows is fully extended. There is no other double extension camera made which works with such smoothness and perfection.

THE CONLEY AUTOMATIC FRONT CLAMP automatically locks the front of the camera at any point on the bed to which it may be drawn out, and automatically releases it when the lever is grasped to push the front back. The fine rack and pinion focus movement works very smoothly and when the camera is focused it may be securely locked by simply pressing in the pinion. The double sliding front is made with both vertical motion (rising and falling movement) and side shift. The main bed of the camera is attached to the box by a strong, smooth working and substantial piano hinge. The lens board is detachable and can be instantly removed and just as easily replaced.

WITH EACH CONLEY DOUBLE EXTENSION CAMERA we furnish our special all metal, rack and pinion auxiliary bed, by means of which a very short focus or wide angle lens can be used. The main bed drops down out of the way by detaching the side arms, and the auxiliary bed, which can be instantly adjusted, then supports the front of the camera. The manner of using this auxiliary bed is more fully explained in connection with our Conley Long Focus Camera on page 670.

PRICES WITH REGULAR EQUIPMENT.

Rapid Convertible Three-Focus Lens and Conley Automatic Shutter.

No. 20K190 Conley Double Extension Camera, 4x5. Price..............$21.50
No. 20K191 Conley Double Extension Camera, 5x7. Price..............$27.00
No. 20K192 Conley Double Extension Camera, 6½x8½. Price..........$35.60

Above prices are for the camera complete with rapid convertible three-focus lens, Conley automatic shutter, auxiliary bed for wide angle lens, one Conley improved flexible valve, plate holder and sole leather carrying case.

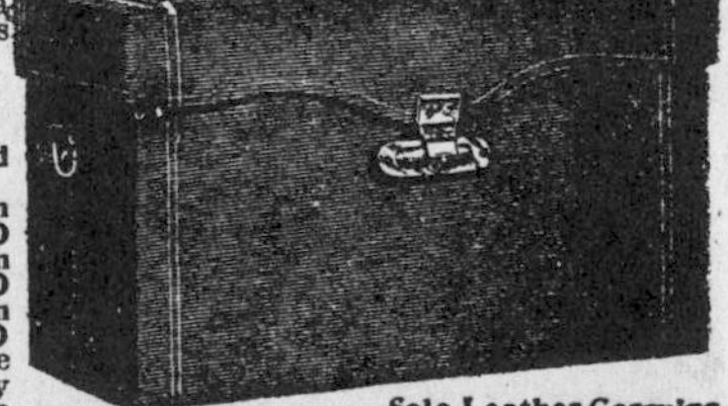

Sole Leather Carrying Case for Conley Extension Double Camera. Holds camera and six plate holders.

PRICES WITH CONLEY SERIES V, F 6.8, ANASTIGMAT LENS.

With Conley Series V Anastigmat Lens and Wollensak Automatic Shutter.

No. 20K199 Conley Double Extension Camera, 4x5. Price..................$38.45
No. 20K200 Conley Double Extension Camera, 5x7. Price.................. 51.65
No. 20K201 Conley Double Extension Camera, 6½x8½. Price.............. 64.35

With Conley Series V Anastigmat Lens and Bausch & Lomb Volute Shutter.

No. 20K202 Conley Double Extension Camera, 4x5. Price..................$46.15
No. 20K203 Conley Double Extension Camera, 5x7. Price.................. 57.15
No. 20K204 Conley Double Extension Camera, 6½x8½. Price.............. 70.85

The prices quoted on Nos. 20K199 to 20K204, inclusive, are for the camera complete with Conley Series V Anastigmat lens, shutter as specified, carrying case and one plate holder.

See page 684 for complete description of the Conley Series V Anastigmat Lens.

WIDE ANGLE LENSES, in cells to fit the Conley Automatic Shutters, and interchangeable with the regular Rapid Convertible Three-Focus Lenses.

No. 20K178 Wide Angle Lens, for 4x5 Camera. Price. $2.90
No. 20K179 Wide Angle Lens, for 5x7 Camera. Price. 3.70
No. 20K180 Wide Angle Lens, for 6½x8½ Camera. Price. 5.95

These wide angle lenses fit the shutters of the regular equipment as listed above but do not fit the shutters furnished with anastigmat lens equipment.

1906 MODEL 4x5 CONLEY DOUBLE EXTENSION CAMERA, $14.75.

No. 20K193 Conley Double Extension Camera, 4x5, 1906 model. Price......$14.75

We have a quantity of these 1906 models on hand, brand new and in perfect order, 4x5 size only, which we will close out at the price quoted above, $14.75. They are strictly high class cameras, differing from the late models only in shutters and certain minor details, and, at $14.75 each, are most remarkable bargains.

$4.95 CONLEY STEREO BOX CAMERA

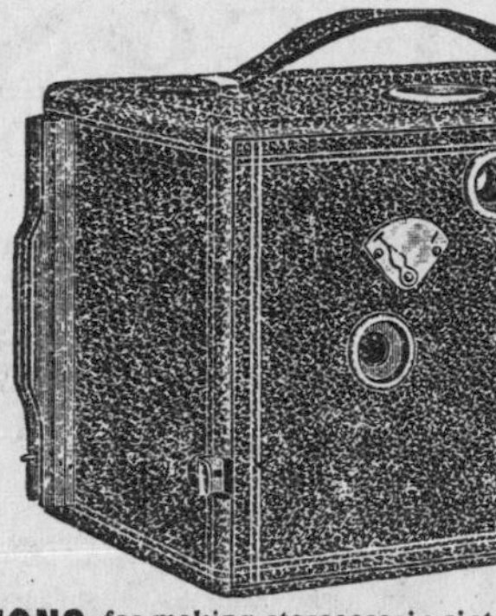

STEREOSCOPIC PHOTOGRAPHY is intensely interesting, and there is nothing more beautiful than a stereoscopic photograph, but many photographers have a mistaken idea that stereoscopic pictures are difficult to make, while as an actual matter of fact, they are just as easy to make as any other photograph, provided one is equipped with the proper apparatus. Any one who can operate a camera of any kind can operate a stereoscopic camera and can make high class stereoscopic pictures.

A STEREOSCOPIC VIEW seen through the stereoscope brings the original scene before us in a way that seems almost like magic, so wonderful is the effect of distance, depth, relief and solidity. The marvelously true to life appearance, everything seemingly full, natural life size; the wonderful detail, the perspective, the figures springing up in the foreground as distinct and real as if alive, makes the stereoscopic view a most delightful entertainer. Seen for the first time, the effect is most startling, and yet the making of these marvelously wonderful pictures is very simple.

OUR CONLEY STEREO BOX CAMERA AT $4.95, a mere fraction of the price at which stereoscopic cameras have heretofore been offered, is perfectly designed, well made and capable of making the most perfect stereoscopic views. This camera uses 4¼x6½ plates and makes full regular size stereoscopic views, the exact same style, size and quality of views that you, no doubt, have often seen offered for sale by canvassers at $2.00 or more per dozen. With this simple and inexpensive stereoscopic camera, you can make stereoscopic views of your own home, your friends, your family and objects of interest of all kinds.

THE LENSES AND SHUTTER. This camera is fitted with two perfectly matched, single achromatic, fixed focus lenses, made especially for stereoscopic work, each pair carefully and accurately matched. The shutter is the Conley Special Automatic Stereo Shutter, a shutter that is very easy to operate, very effective and reliable, and of the simplest possible construction. The shutter is always set, always ready for an exposure, and is operated simply by pressing the small lever at the side of the camera. With the indicator set to I, a single pressure of the lever makes an instantaneous exposure, simultaneously opening and closing both lenses. With the indicator set to T the shutter is ready for time exposures, the first pressure opening the shutter, which remains open until the lever is again pressed.

$4.95 IS AN UNHEARD OF PRICE for a stereoscopic camera, and yet at this price we offer in the Conley Stereo Box Camera, an instrument that we can absolutely guarantee to make high class stereoscopic pictures. It is substantially made from thoroughly seasoned and kiln dried lumber, covered with best quality of seal grain black keratol with nickel plated trimmings. It measures 5½x5⅞x8 inches, and weighs, complete, including plate holder, 33 ounces.

COMPLETE INSTRUCTIONS for making stereoscopic pictures are sent free of charge with every stereoscopic camera that we sell, and anyone with the help of these simple instructions, can easily make the most interesting and beautiful stereoscopic pictures.

No. 20K135 Conley Stereo Box Camera, exactly as illustrated and described above, with one Conley Improved Flexible Valve Plate Holder, 4¼x6½. Shipping weight, 3½ pounds. Price.......... **$4.95**

Extra plate holders are 45 cents each. See page 681.

CONLEY SPECIAL STEREOSCOPIC CAMERA

$14.90

THE CONLEY SPECIAL STEREOSCOPIC CAMERA is designed for those who want something more complete and elaborate than the box camera, and yet at a moderate price. Only the best materials are used in the construction of this camera, selected mahogany for the woodwork, genuine leather for the covering, every part made with the utmost care and the entire camera assembled and put together in the most accurate manner.

THE LENS AND SHUTTER. We equip this camera with a pair of rapid rectilinear lenses, very carefully and accurately matched for stereoscopic work, and these lenses are mounted in the Wollensak Senior Automatic Shutter.

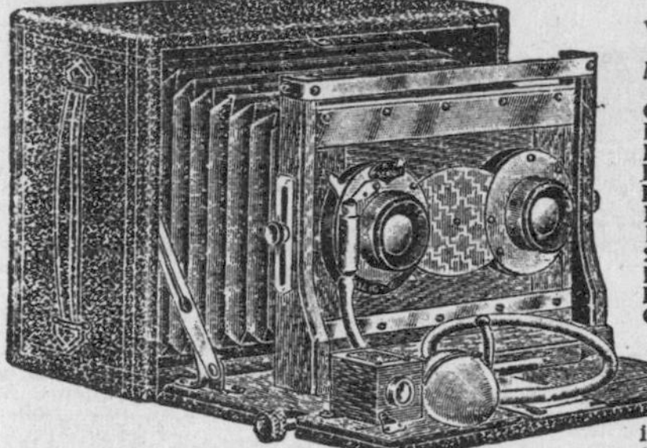

SPECIFICATIONS.

- WOODWORK—All solid mahogany, dovetailed corners, piano finish.
- METAL PARTS—Brass, heavily nickel plated, highly polished.
- COVERING—Genuine seal grain leather.
- BELLOWS—Best red Russia leather, gossamer lined.
- FOCUS MOVEMENT—Rack and pinion.
- LENS BOARD—Detachable.
- FRONT—Mahogany with rising and falling movement.
- FRONT CLAMP—Conley Automatic.
- FINDER—Ground glass, brass bound.
- SHUTTER—Wollensak Senior Automatic.
- LENS—High grade rapid rectilinear.
- PLATE HOLDER—Conley Improved Flexible Valve.
- CARRYING CASE—Keratol covered, with space for camera and five plate holders.
- DIMENSIONS—3¾x6⅝x8½ inches, closed.

No. 20K138 Conley Special Stereoscopic Camera, complete with lens and shutter as illustrated and described above, with keratol covered carrying case and one 5x7 Conley Improved Flexible Valve Plate Holder. Price...... **$14.90**

CONLEY PROFESSIONAL STEREOSCOPIC CAMERA $28.50

THE CONLEY PROFESSIONAL STEREOSCOPIC CAMERA is our highest grade stereoscopic camera, a camera that is absolutely complete in every detail, possessing every adjustment and every improvement that has in any way been found useful in stereoscopic photography. This stereoscopic camera is made with the latest improved automatic spring roller septum, which rolls up or unrolls automatically as the camera is opened or closed, double shifting front with both rising and falling movement and side shift, detachable lens board, rack and pinion focus movement, reversible back, brilliant hooded finder, ground glass focusing screen protected by hinged, leather covered, mahogany panel, genuine leather covering, nickel plated metal plated metal parts, and genuine leather bellows;

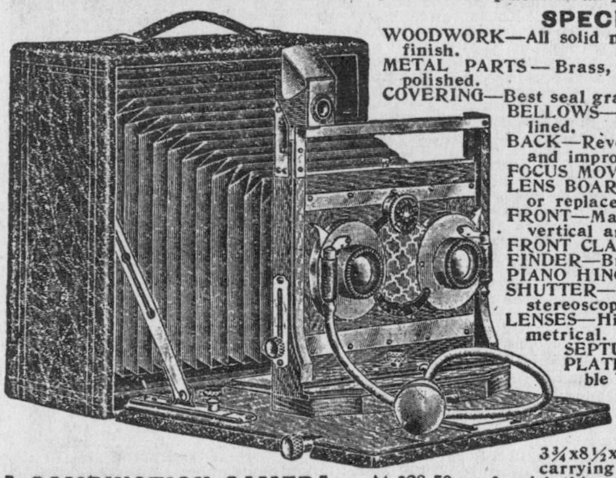

SPECIFICATIONS.

- WOODWORK—All solid mahogany, dovetailed corners, piano finish.
- METAL PARTS—Brass, heavily nickel plated and highly polished.
- COVERING—Best seal grain leather.
- BELLOWS—Best red Russia leather, gossamer lined.
- BACK—Reversible, with single button release and improved swing.
- FOCUS MOVEMENT—Rack and pinion.
- LENS BOARD—Detachable, instantly removed or replaced.
- FRONT—Mahogany, double shifting, with both vertical and horizontal movements.
- FRONT CLAMP—New Conley Automatic.
- FINDER—Brilliant, hooded.
- PIANO HINGE—Nickel plated.
- SHUTTER—Wollensak Regular, double valve stereoscopic.
- LENSES—High grade, stereoscopic, double symmetrical.
- SEPTUM—Improved spring roller curtain.
- PLATE HOLDER—Conley Improved Flexible Valve.
- CARRYING CASE — Heavy sole leather, with space for camera and six plate holders.
- DIMENSIONS — Camera closed, 3¾x8½x8¾ inches; focal capacity, 16 inches; carrying case, 4¼x9x15¼ inches.

A COMBINATION CAMERA. At $28.50 we furnish this camera equipped only for stereoscopic work, but by adding the 5x7 lens and shutter with extra front board, which we furnish for $6.30 extra, the camera may be used for either full size single 5x7 pictures or for stereoscopic views. As a 5x7 camera it possesses all of the adjustments and good qualities that are necessary for the highest grade of work, corresponding practically in its various details and adjustments to our 5x7 Long Focus Camera.

THE LENS AND SHUTTER. We equip the Conley Professional Stereoscopic Camera with a pair of extra high grade, double symmetrical lenses, especially ground for stereoscopic work and accurately matched. These lenses are mounted in the Wollensak Double Valve Regular Shutter arranged for automatic instantaneous exposures of various lengths from one second to one hundredth part of a second, and time or bulb exposures of any desired length.

No. 20K140 Conley Professional Stereoscopic Camera, complete, with double symmetrical stereoscopic lenses, Wollensak Regular Stereoscopic Shutter, one 5x7 Conley Improved Flexible Valve Plate Holder, and sole leather carrying case. Shipping weight, 16 pounds. Price.......... **$28.50**

No. 20K142 Double Symmetrical Lens, for single 5x7 pictures, with Conley Safety Shutter and extra front board to fit the Conley Professional Stereoscopic Camera. If by mail postage extra 8 cents. Price, complete with shutter, front board, bulb and tube.......... **$6.30**

No. 2 CONLEY VIEW CAMERA

SPECIFICATIONS.

- WOODWORK—Spanish cedar, mahogany finish.
- METAL PARTS—Brass, nickel plated.
- BELLOWS—Fine quality black keratol, gossamer lined.
- BACK—Reversible, with spring actuated ground glass screen.
- FOCUS MOVEMENT—Rack and pinion with diagonal rack.
- LENS BOARD—Detachable.
- FRONT—Rising and falling, operated by rack and pinion movement.
- BED—Cherry, two section with piano hinge.
- SWING—Single, operated by rack and pinion.
- PLATE HOLDER—Conley Improved Flexible Valve.
- CARRYING CASE—Canvas covered, with metal bound corners.

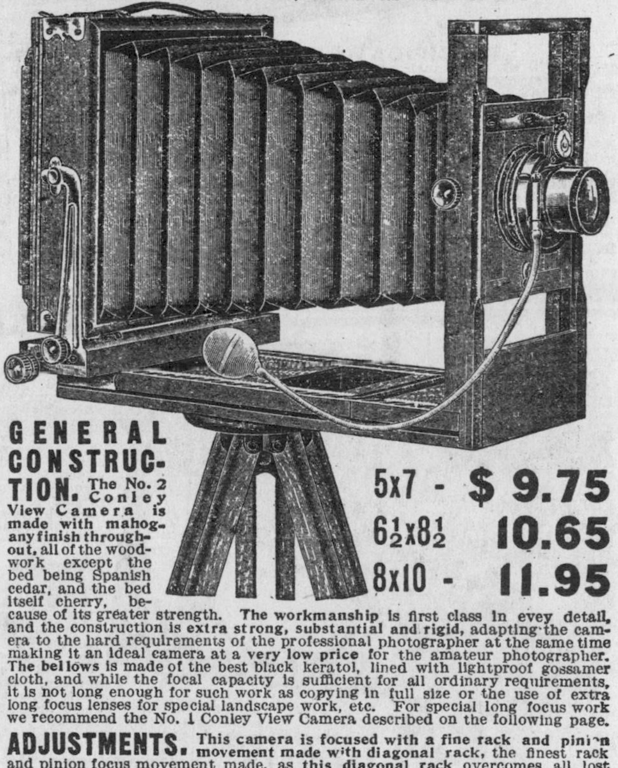

5x7 -	$ 9.75
6½x8½	10.65
8x10 -	11.95

GENERAL CONSTRUCTION. The No. 2 Conley View Camera is made with mahogany finish throughout, all of the woodwork except the bed being Spanish cedar, and the bed itself cherry, because of its greater strength. The workmanship is first class in evey detail, and the construction is extra strong, substantial and rigid, adapting the camera to the hard requirements of the professional photographer at the same time making it an ideal camera at a very low price for the amateur photographer. The bellows is made of the best black keratol, lined with lightproof gossamer cloth, and while the focal capacity is sufficient for all ordinary requirements, it is not long enough for such work as copying in full size or the use of extra long focus lenses for special landscape work, etc. For special long focus work we recommend the No. 1 Conley View Camera described on the following page.

ADJUSTMENTS. This camera is focused with a fine rack and pinion movement made with diagonal rack, the finest rack and pinion focus movement made, as this diagonal rack overcomes all lost motion and results in a very smooth, perfect action. The back is reversible and is made with a centrally pivoted vertical swing, operated by rack and pinion. The front is made with removable lens board and with rising and falling adjustment operated by a rack and pinion. The bed is made of selected cherry, in two sections with piano hinge, and is extra strong and rigid.

PRICES WITHOUT LENS OR SHUTTER.

No. 20K250 No. 2 Conley View Camera, 5x7; focal capacity 13¾ inches. Without lens or shutter. Price.......... **$9.75**

No. 20K251 No. 2 Conley View Camera, 6½x8½; focal capacity, 15¼ inches. Without lens or shutter. Price.......... **$10.65**

No. 20K252 No. 2 Conley View Camera, 8x10; focal capacity, 17 inches. Without lens or shutter. Price.......... **$11.95**

The prices quoted above on the No. 2 Conley View Camera include the camera as illustrated and described, with one Conley Plate Holder and strong canvas covered Carrying Case, with space for lenses and six plate holders. These prices do not include tripod, and we recommend our hardwood sliding tripod for use with this camera. See page 682 for prices and descriptions.

PRICES with CONLEY RAPID RECTILINEAR LENS and UNICUM SHUTTER.

No. 20K253 No. 2 Conley View Camera, 5x7, with Conley Rapid Rectilinear Lens and Unicum Shutter. Price.......... **$19.45**

No. 20K254 No. 2 Conley View Camera, 6½x8½, with Conley Rapid Rectilinear Lens and Unicum Shutter. Price.......... **$24.25**

No. 20K255 No. 2 Conley View Camera, 8x10, with Conley Rapid Rectilinear Lens and Unicum Shutter. Price.......... **$29.90**

These prices on the No. 2 Conley View Camera include the camera complete with Conley Rapid Rectilinear Lens, Unicum Shutter, one Conley Plate Holder and strong canvas covered carrying case with space for camera, lens, shutter and six plate holders. Tripod is not included, and we recommend our hardwood sliding tripod for use with this camera; See page 682 for price.

Sig. 41—1st Ed.

No. 1 CONLEY VIEW CAMERA

IMPROVED 1908 MODEL.

—THESE PRICES— INCLUDE CAMERA, CONLEY IMPROVED FLEXIBLE VALVE PLATE HOLDER, COMBINATION TRIPOD AND CARRYING CASE.

5x7.......... $14.65
6½x8½.......... 16.10
8x10.......... 18.25

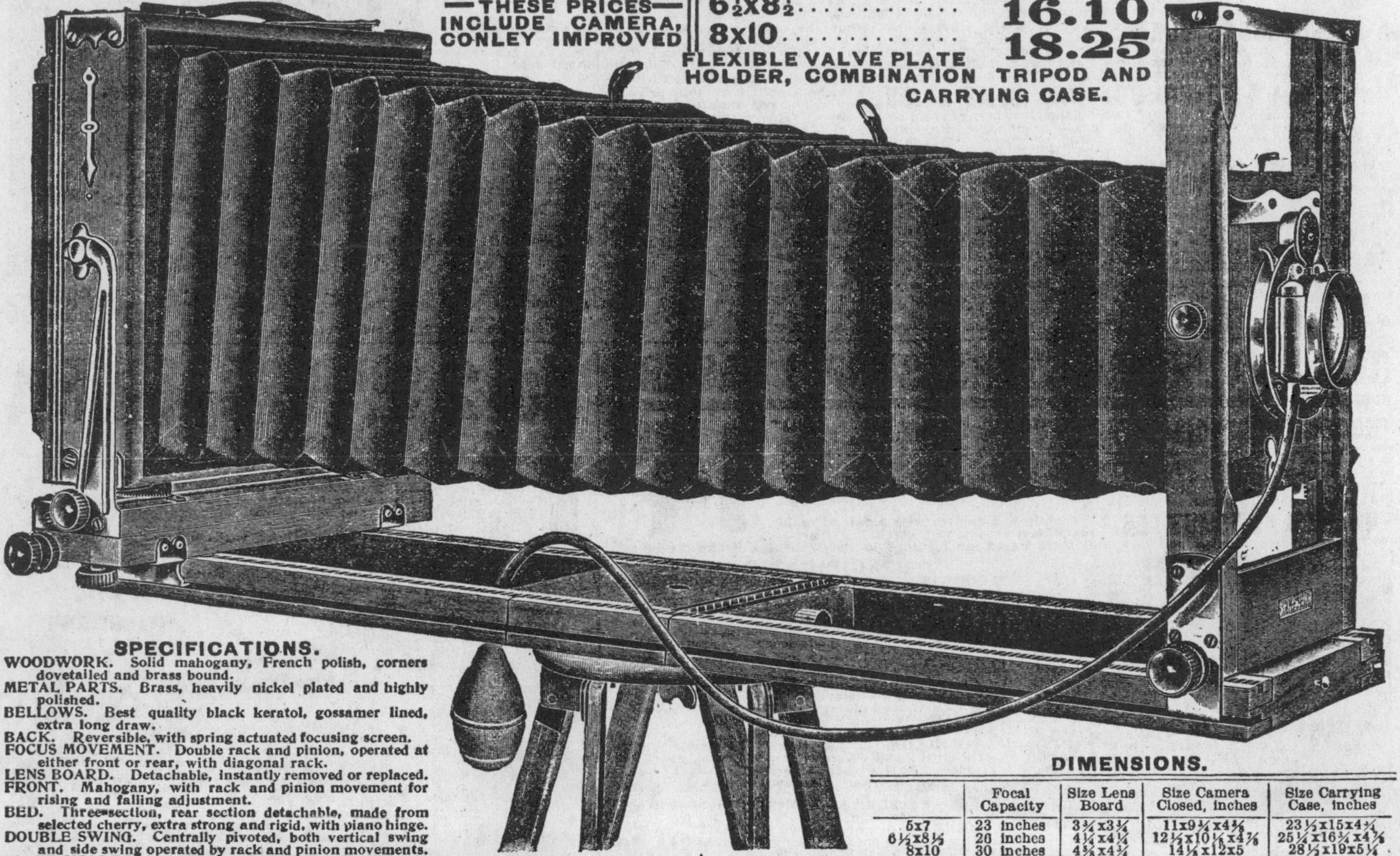

SPECIFICATIONS.

WOODWORK. Solid mahogany, French polish, corners dovetailed and brass bound.
METAL PARTS. Brass, heavily nickel plated and highly polished.
BELLOWS. Best quality black keratol, gossamer lined, extra long draw.
BACK. Reversible, with spring actuated focusing screen.
FOCUS MOVEMENT. Double rack and pinion, operated at either front or rear, with diagonal rack.
LENS BOARD. Detachable, instantly removed or replaced.
FRONT. Mahogany, with rack and pinion movement for rising and falling adjustment.
BED. Three-section, rear section detachable, made from selected cherry, extra strong and rigid, with piano hinge.
DOUBLE SWING. Centrally pivoted, both vertical swing and side swing operated by rack and pinion movements.
PLATE HOLDER. Conley Improved Flexible Val--e.
TRIPOD. Selected ash, combined folding and sliding, extra strong and rigid.
CARRYING CASE. Canvas covered, cloth lined, with brass bound corners.

DIMENSIONS.

	Focal Capacity	Size Lens Board	Size Camera Closed, inches	Size Carrying Case, inches
5x7	23 inches	3¾x3¾	11x9¾x4⅜	23½x15x4¼
6½x8½	26 inches	4¼x4¼	12½x10⅛x4⅞	25¼x16¾x4⅞
8x10	30 inches	4⅝x4¾	14⅛x12x5	28½x19x5¼

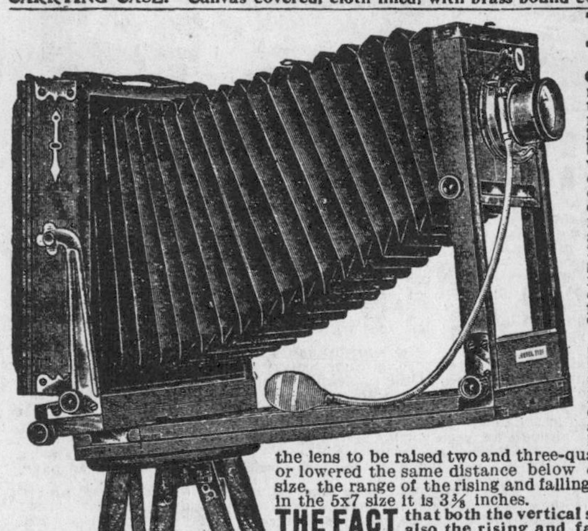

THIS ILLUSTRATION shows the No. 1 Conley View Camera with the front raised, and the camera tilted up as is frequently necessary in photographing buildings, and the back is shown swung forward to overcome the effect of tilting the camera. It should be especially noted that the rising and falling front and the swing back have, in this camera, a much greater range of movement than is usual in cameras of other manufacture.

THE RISING AND FALLING FRONT in the 8x10 size of the No. 1 Conley View Camera has a movement up and down of five and one-half inches, permitting the lens to be raised two and three-quarter inches above center, or lowered the same distance below center. In the 6½x8½ size, the range of the rising and falling front is 4⅜ inches, and in the 5x7 size it is 3⅜ inches.

THE FACT that both the vertical swing and the side swing, also the rising and falling front are operated by rack and pinion movements, adds greatly to the facility with which this camera can be handled. The side swing will be found especially advantageous on interior work where it is frequently impossible to sharply focus both sides of the picture without recourse to this useful adjustment.

FOR PROFESSIONAL PHOTOGRAPHERS the No. 1 Conley View Camera meets every possible requirement. An ideal outfit for general viewing, groups, landscapes, residences, architectural subjects; in fact, every class of work that naturally comes to the professional photographer in the course of his business, even including high class portrait work.

FOR AMATEUR PHOTOGRAPHERS, especially those who may some day take up photography as a profession, the No. 1 Conley View Camera is an ideal outfit, as it is adapted to every branch of photography. Indoor and outdoor views, landscapes, buildings and groups, instantaneous and flashlight pictures, high class portrait work either at home or in the studio, commercial work and copying, in fact, everything that can be done with any camera can be done with the No. 1 Conley View Camera.

AN EXPERTS' OPINION OF THE CONLEY VIEW CAMERA.

THE INGERSOLL VIEW CO., Home Office and Factory,
88 and 92 W. 4th Street, Ingersoll Building,
St. Paul, Minn., U. S. A.

St. Paul, Minn., Nov. 25th, 1907

Sears, Roebuck & Co.
Gentlemen:—Please note enclosed order; and I wish to say that we have discarded all other makes of 8x10 view cameras in our establishment, and now have four of your No. 1 Conley View Cameras with some fifty extra 8x10 holders, the entire outfit of lenses and holders being interchangeable, proves of greatest convenience to us, and we might add that we consider your outfits by far the best on the market in point of quality and prices. We can hardly understand how you can turn out such substantially made, perfectly adjusted, and beautifully finished goods at your prices. We really prefer them to any on the market at any price. May your output and quality never grow less.

Yours very truly, T. W. INGERSOLL.

THE GENERAL CONSTRUCTION of the No. 1 Conley View Camera combines all the good points that expert camera makers know how to put into a camera. The carefully selected mahogany, with finest high polish rubbed finish; the metal parts heavily nickel plated, carefully fitted and highly polished; the bellows of the best quality black keratol, lined with lightproof gossamer cloth; the three-section bed, extra strong and rigid, made from selected cherry, with piano hinge. These are the points that, combined with conscientious, expert workmanship, make for strength, durability and elegance of appearance.

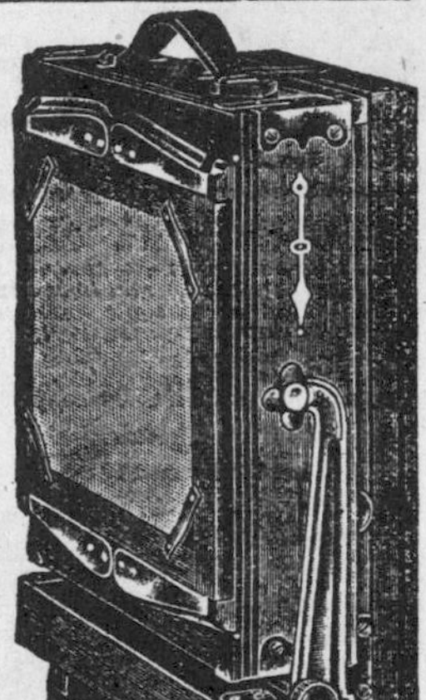

No. 1 Conley View Camera, Folded.

SPECIAL FEATURES OF THE No. 1 CONLEY VIEW CAMERA. While keeping foremost in our minds at all times the fact that a view camera must be suited to the hardest kind of practical service, strong, rigid, substantial and durable, we have at the same time incorporated into this camera all those conveniences, all those adjustments and all those improvements that help to make a camera easy to use, and that make it possible to do things which cannot be done with less perfectly equipped cameras. THE BACK is reversed instantly and easily, simply by lifting a small catch in plain sight; no concealed buttons, no clips nor other devices to get out of order and make the operation difficult. THE LENS BOARD is instantly detachable, and just as easily and quickly replaced, simply by turning a small button which automatically locks itself. THE CENTRALLY PIVOTED DOUBLE SWING is operated by two fine rack and pinion movements, one for the vertical swing and one for the side swing. THE RISING AND FALLING ADJUSTMENT of the front is also operated by a fine rack and pinion. THE BED is made in three sections, with the rear section detachable so that it may be removed when not required. THE TRIPOD which we furnish with the No. 1 Conley View Camera is an extra strong, extra heavy, extra rigid tripod, made from the best selected ash, folding so compactly that it may be carried in the same case with the camera; absolutely the best tripod that can be made. THE CARRYING CASE is made extra strong, covered with canvas, lined with cloth, reinforced with wooden partitions and brass bound corners, and fitted with a substantial leather handle.

No. 1 CONLEY VIEW CAMERA WITHOUT LENS OR SHUTTER.

No. 1 Conley View Camera, Improved 1908 Model, with one Conley Improved Flexible Valve Plate Holder, Combination Tripod and Carrying Case, **without Lens or Shutter.**

No. 20K225 No. 1 Conley View Camera, 5x7. Price..................$14.65
No. 20K226 No. 1 Conley View Camera, 6½x8½. Price.............. 16.10
No. 20K227 No. 1 Conley View Camera, 8x10. Price................ 18.25

No. 1 CONLEY VIEW CAMERA WITH RAPID RECTILINEAR LENS AND UNICUM SHUTTER.

No. 1 Conley View Camera, Improved 1908 Model, with one Conley Improved Flexible Valve Plate Holder, Combination Tripod, Carrying Case and Conley Rapid Rectilinear Lens with Unicum Shutter. See page 684 for the description of this lens.

No. 20K229 No. 1 Conley View Camera, 5x7. Price..................$24.35
No. 20K230 No. 1 Conley View Camera, 6½x8½. Price.............. 29.70
No. 20K231 No. 1 Conley View Camera, 8x10. Price................ 36.45

No. 1 Conley View Camera, with Conley Series V Anastigmat Lens and Automatic Shutter.

No. 20K237 No. 1 Conley View Camera, 5x7. Price..................$47.45
No. 20K238 No. 1 Conley View Camera, 6½x8½. Price.............. 58.30
No. 20K239 No. 1 Conley View Camera, 8x10. Price................ 75.10

No. 1 Conley View Camera, with Conley Series V Anastigmat Lens and Volute Shutter.

No. 20K241 No. 1 Conley View Camera, 5x7. Price..................$52.95
No. 20K242 No. 1 Conley View Camera, 6½x8½. Price.............. 64.80
No. 20K243 No. 1 Conley View Camera, 8x10. Price................ 81.10

See page 684 for description of this Anastigmat Lens.

THE PRICES quoted for Nos. 20K237 to 20K243, inclusive, are for the camera complete with Conley Series V Anastigmat Lens, shutter as specified, carrying case, combination tripod and one double plate holder.

DON'T FAIL to read the description of our new Conley Flexible Valve Plate Holder on page 681, and when you order the View Camera include at least five extra holders in your order.

CONLEY IMPROVED FLEXIBLE VALVE PLATE HOLDERS

MADE WITH DRAKE'S LIGHTPROOF FLEXIBLE VALVE AND SPRING BAR PLATE LOCKING DEVICE.

4x5 SIZE 40c | 5x7 SIZE 45c

OTHER SIZES IN PROPORTION

THESE PLATE HOLDERS FIT
ALL CONLEY CAMERAS — ALL SEROCO CAMERAS
ALL CENTURY CAMERAS — ALL PREMO CAMERAS
ALL SENECA CAMERAS

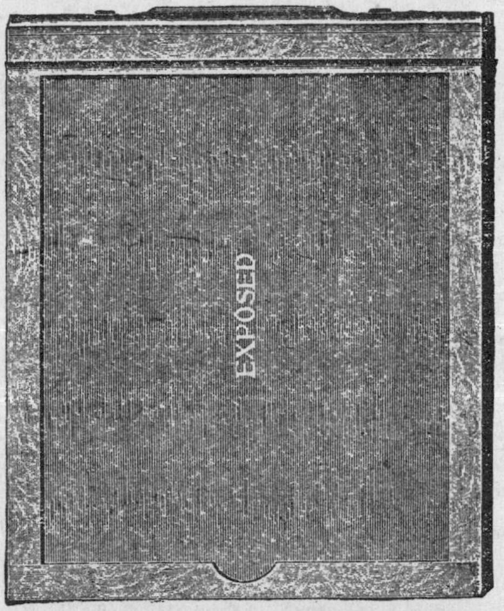

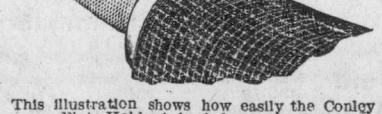

GOOD RESULTS IN PHOTOGRAPHY DEPEND UPON THE PLATE HOLDER. It is often stated that the lens is the most important part of a photographic outfit, and in a certain sense this is true. It is a fact, however, that very good pictures can be taken even with a very cheap lens—even with a lens of quite inferior quality, if it is properly used. It is a fact that excellent pictures can be taken with a very cheaply constructed camera, but it is an impossibility to take good pictures with any kind of a camera, no matter how well it is made, no matter how perfect it may be in all its details, unless the plate holders are perfect, and considering this fact that **good pictures are an impossibility without perfect plate holders,** it would seem more reasonable to consider the plate holder the most important part of the camera. If the plate holder is faulty every picture taken is faulty. A little light coming in through the valve when the slide is inserted or withdrawn will more than offset all the good qualities that the rest of the outfit may possess. Unless the plate holder is made of the best of materials, the most carefully seasoned and kiln dried lumber, unless the utmost precautions are adopted in carefully and accurately fitting the various parts of the holder together, and unless the design is absolutely perfect, it is certain the holder will sooner or later leak light, resulting in the loss of much good material and time.

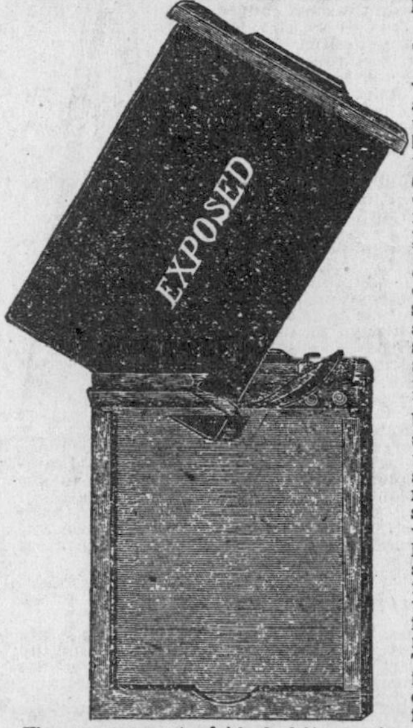

The arrangement of black felt, elastic wafer and series of coiled springs constituting the Drake Flexible Valve is indicated in this illustration.

THE DRAKE FLEXIBLE VALVE. The special feature which distinguishes the Conley Plate Holders from all other plate holders, the feature which places them in a class by themselves, is the new Drake Lightproof Flexible Valve. The illustration on this page will give you some idea of the construction of this valve, which is, beyond question, the most perfect device yet invented for excluding light from the plate holder. The Drake Flexible Valve, fully protected by patent consists of a most ingenious and clever arrangement of small coiled springs, a flexible celluloid wafer, and black felt, so arranged and constructed that it is absolutely impossible for any light to get into the plate holder at any time, either when the slide is in place or while it is being withdrawn or inserted. The slide may be inserted cornerwise, and the valve will automatically close up all around the edges of the slide, making light struck plates an impossibility. With other plate holders the valve opens clear across the end of the holder, and, of course, lets in a certain amount of light both when the slide is inserted and when it is withdrawn unless the greatest possible care is taken to insert it evenly and squarely, which is not always practicable in actual work. The advice given in every photographic instruction book regarding the extreme care necessary when inserting the slide is unnecessary if the Conley holders are used, as the Drake Flexible Valve automatically prevents the danger of light struck plates.

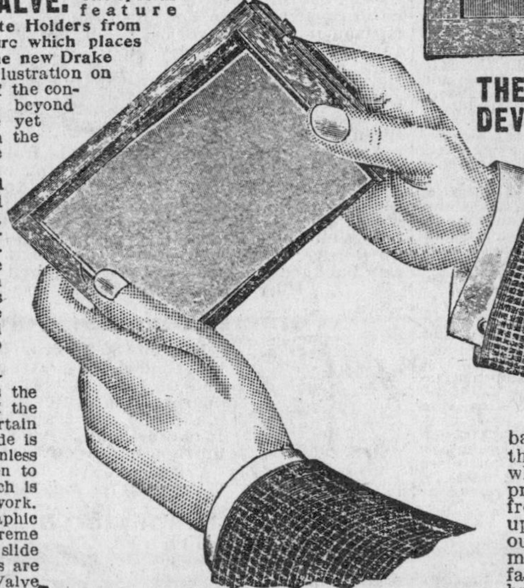

This illustration shows how easily the Conley Plate Holder is loaded or unloaded.

THE SPRING BAR PLATE LOCKING DEVICE. Every Conley Plate Holder is now made with the improved spring bar plate locking device, a bar of hardwood extending across the bottom of the holder and actuated by a concealed spring. This device locks the plate firmly in position in the holder, and distributing the pressure evenly along the entire edge of the plate prevents any possibility of breakage. This device makes the Conley Plate Holder an exceedingly easy holder to load or unload, as in placing a plate in the holder it is simply rested against the spring bar which is then pressed down with the thumb and the plate falls into position where it is held firmly by the upward pressure of the bar. To remove the plate from the holder, the pressure of the thumb upon the spring bar releases it, as shown in our illustration, and the plate is easily removed without touching the sensitive surface with the fingers and without danger of breaking either the plate or the finger nails, as so frequently happens with the old style plate holders.

GENERAL CONSTRUCTION. The Conley Plate Holders are made good all the way through; the finish, workmanship and materials being equal to any plate holder on the market and superior to most, although sold at less than half the prices which are asked today by most dealers. While the Drake Lightproof Flexible Valve and the Spring Bar Plate Locking Device are features which alone make these holders better than any holders with which they may be compared, they do not constitute the only points in which these holders excel. The general construction, the finish, the careful attention to even the smallest details, makes these holders superior to any other holder manufactured. The wood used in their construction is the very finest, carefully selected, straight grained, throughly seasoned and kiln dried cherry. Every joint is dovetailed, every part made with the utmost accuracy, and they are put together by workmen of the highest skill. Every holder is carefully inspected before it leaves the factory and rejected if it shows the slightest imperfection either in material or workmanship. Instead of an ordinary shellac finish with which most manufacturers are contented, the Conley Holders are made with a fine, hand rubbed mahogany finish, a finish that not only gives them a handsome and ornamental appearance, but facilitates the smoothness and ease with which they are placed in or removed from the camera. The Conley Plate Holder as now made represents the results of three years of the most careful study and experiment.

PRESSED BOARD OR HARD RUBBER SLIDES. We put up the Conley Plate Holders with either pressed board slides or hard rubber slides. Our pressed board slides are made from a very special quality of pressed board which is given a hand rubbed, pumice stone finish, making a very smooth working slide, closely resembling hard rubber in appearance. The hard rubber slides are glossier and present a somewhat handsomer appearance than the pressed board slides, but in our opinion the pressed board are more satisfactory because there is no danger of breakage. Hard rubber is brittle and always liable to breakage. Moreover, it is apt to become electrified, attracting to itself particles of dust, etc., which become transferred to the plate, resulting in pin holes and other imperfections. The pressed board slides have the word "Exposed" printed on one side in white letters. When the holder is loaded, the slide is placed with the blank side out, and after the exposure is made, the slide is replaced with the word "Exposed" on the outside. The surface of the hard rubber slides does not permit of the printing of the word "Exposed" and with these slides we make the handle, that is, the wooden part at the end, black on one side, leaving it the natural color of the wood on the other, thus affording a means of indicating whether the plate has been exposed or not.

Improved Conley Inside Kits.

FOR USING SMALLER SIZE PLATES.

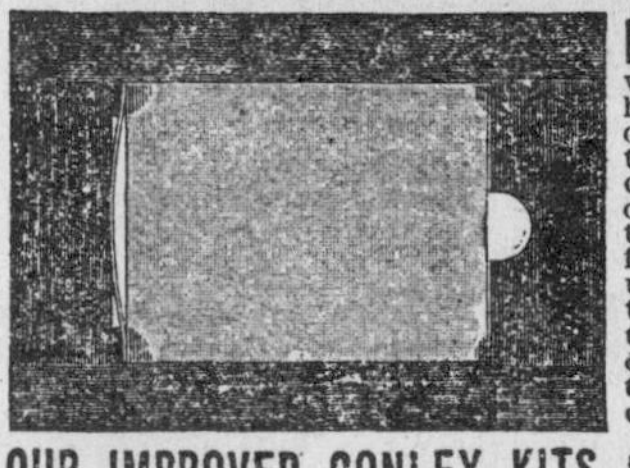

KITS are thin wooden frames which fit into a plate holder, the same as an ordinary plate, and the opening in the center holds a plate of smaller size than the holder is designed for. They are to be used when it is desired to use **smaller plates** than the regular size of the camera, and **thus save the expense of a larger plate.**

OUR IMPROVED CONLEY KITS are made with special inside corner supports and a spring across one end by which the plate is held firmly in position, a great improvement over any previous style of kit.

			Price
No. 20K675	Kit, 4 x5	to hold 3½x3½ plates	10c
No. 20K676	Kit, 4 x5	to hold 3¼x4¼ plates	10c
No. 20K678	Kit, 5 x7	to hold 3¼x4¼ plates	14c
No. 20K679	Kit, 5 x7	to hold 4 x5 plates	14c
No. 20K681	Kit, 5 x8	to hold 4 x5 plates	16c
No. 20K683	Kit, 6½x8½	to hold 4 x5 plates	20c
No. 20K684	Kit, 6½x8½	to hold 4¼x6½ plates	20c
No. 20K685	Kit, 6½x8½	to hold 5 x7 plates	20c
No. 20K686	Kit, 6½x8½	to hold 5 x8 plates	20c
No. 20K687	Kit, 8 x10	to hold 4 x5 plates	24c
No. 20K688	Kit, 8 x10	to hold 4¼x6½ plates	24c
No. 20K689	Kit, 8 x10	to hold 5 x7 plates	24c
No. 20K691	Kit, 8 x10	to hold 6½x8½ plates	24c

If by mail, postage extra, on 4x5, 2c; 5x7, 3c; 5x8, 4c; 6½x8½, 5c; 8x10, 8c.

We cannot furnish any sizes not quoted in above list.

CONLEY HOLDERS FOR BOX CAMERAS.

No. 20K650 Conley Improved Flexible Valve Plate Holders, 3½x3½, pressed board slides, fit the Perfection Jr. Camera, Seroco Jr. Box Camera and Conley Jr. Box Camera.
Price, 5 for **$1.60**: each, ...(If by mail, postage extra, each, 5 cents.).................... **33c**

No. 20K652 Conley Improved Flexible Valve Plate Holders, pressed board slides, fit the Delmar Camera, the Seroco Sr. Box Camera and the Conley Sr. Box Camera, also the Cyclone Camera. **This holder does not fit our folding cameras.**
Price, 5 for **$1.85**; each, ...(If by mail, postage extra, each, 6 cents.).................... **38c**

CONLEY HOLDERS WITH PRESSED BOARD SLIDES.

Conley Flexible Valve Plate Holders, pressed board slides, fit all Seroco and Conley Folding Cameras, Seroco and Conley View Cameras (except 6½x8½ sizes,) all Premo Cameras, all Century Cameras and all Seneca Cameras.

No. 20K655 Size, 3¼x4¼. Price, 5 for **$1.70**; each,.......(If by mail, postage extra, each, 5 cents)....... **35c**
No. 20K656 Size, 4x5. Price, 5 for **$1.95**; each,.......(If by mail, postage extra, each, 6 cents)....... **40c**
No. 20K657 Size, 4¼x6½. Price, 5 for **$2.08**; each,.......(If by mail, postage extra, each 9 cents)....... **43c**
No. 20K658 Size, 5x7. Price, 5 for **$2.18**; each,.......(If by mail, postage extra, each, 10 cents)....... **45c**
No. 20K659 Size, 6½x8½. Price, 5 for **$2.90**; each,.......(If by mail, postage extra, each, 15 cents)....... **60c**
If for View Camera, order No. 20K670.
No. 20K660 Size, 8x10. Price, 5 for **$3.65**; each,.......(If by mail, postage extra, each, 20 cents.)....... **75c**

CONLEY HOLDERS WITH HARD RUBBER SLIDES.

Conley Flexible Valve Plate Holders, with glossy hard rubber slides, fit all Seroco and Conley Folding Cameras, Seroco and Conley View Cameras (except 6½x8½ sizes), all Premo Cameras, all Century Cameras and all Seneca Cameras.

No. 20K663 Size, 4x5. Price, 5 for **$2.50**; each,.......(If by mail, postage extra, each, 6 cents)....... **$0.52**
No. 20K665 Size, 5x7. Price, 5 for **$3.08**; each,.......(If by mail, postage extra, each, 10 cents)....... **.65**
No. 20K666 Size, 6½x8½. Price, 5 for **$4.35**; each,.......(If by mail, postage extra, each, 15 cents)....... **.90**
If for View Camera, order No. 20K671.
No. 20K667 Size, 8x10. Price, 5 for **$5.60**; each,.......(If by mail, postage extra, each, 20 cents)....... **1.15**

CONLEY HOLDERS FOR 6½x8½ VIEW CAMERAS.

No. 20K670 Conley Improved Flexible Valve Plate Holder, 6½x8½, with pressed board slides, fits the 6½x8½ Seroco or Conley View Cameras. Price, 5 for **$2.90**; each.............(If by mail, postage extra, each, 16 cents.)............ **60c**

No. 20K671 Conley Improved Flexible Valve Plate Holder, 6½x8½, with hard rubber slides, fits the 6½x8½ Seroco or Conley View Cameras. Price, 5 for **$4.35**; each,.......(If by mail, postage extra, each, 16 cents.)....... **90c**

BE SURE TO STATE NAME OF CAMERA WHEN ORDERING HOLDERS.

You get one plate holder FREE with your camera, and if you order five extra holders you can take advantage of the special prices which we quote on these holders in lots of five and then have six holders, which will just hold contents of one box of dry plates.

The Expo Watch Camera.

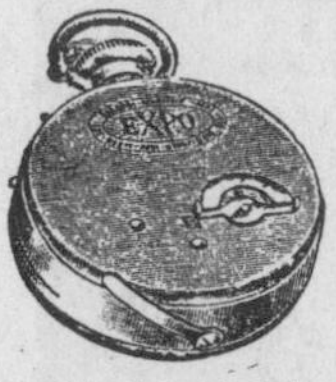

A True Vest Pocket Detective Camera. The Expo Camera is the smallest practical camera ever made, and, although it is so small that it can readily be carried in the vest pocket, it is at the same time a strictly high class practical instrument in every way. The Expo Camera is a daylight loading camera using film, and can be loaded for twenty-five exposures at a time. This camera looks exactly like a fair sized watch and pictures can be taken with it anywhere without anyone suspecting that a camera is being used. The pictures taken with the Expo Camera are ⅞ of an inch long by ⅝ of an inch wide, the exact size shown in our illustration. This camera can be used for either time or instantaneous exposures and is suitable for landscapes, street scenes, groups, portraits, etc., in fact, just exactly the same kind of work which is accomplished by larger and more expensive cameras. The Expo Camera is carefully constructed from metal throughout, nickel plated, fitted with a fine achromatic lens and is guaranteed in every respect. So perfect are the negatives made with this little vest pocket camera that the pictures can be enlarged without sacrificing the detail or other good qualities.

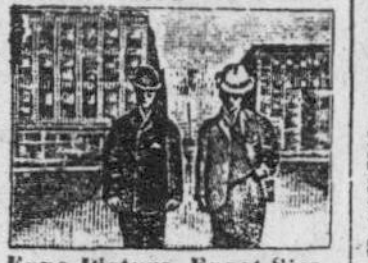

Expo Picture, Exact Size.

No. 20K375 The Expo Watch Camera. Price, complete, without film....(Postage extra, 10 cents)......$2.25

No. 20K376 View Finder, for Expo Watch Camera. Price..45c

If by mail, postage extra, 5 cents.

No. 20K377 Daylight Loading Film for Expo Camera, twenty-five exposures to the roll. Price, per roll.......18c

If by mail, postage extra, 1 cent.

Our Special Portrait Outfit.

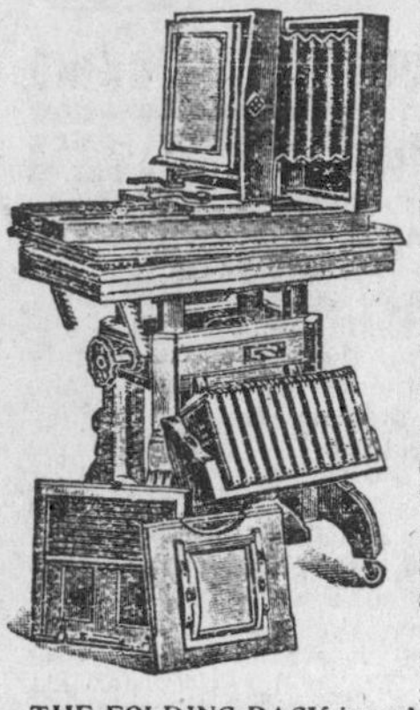

No. 20K500 THIS OUTFIT CONSISTS OF AN 8x10 CAMERA, Camera Stand and Reversible Cabinet attachment.

CAMERA IS MADE FROM BEST HARDWOOD finely finished. All adjustments are automatic and self locking. Has 30-inch bed, best India rubber bellows.

STAND IS THE WIZARD No. 7, fitted with automatic balancing device, raises and lowers with the lightest touch, can be locked in any position by lever at side. Firm and rigid, made of hardwood, finely finished. Top measures 17x32½ inches.

THE NELSON AUTOMATIC HOLDER is included, the best studio plate holder made. Plates are put in or removed without turning a button, the back does not require to be opened, no spring to press on back of plate. Takes any size of plate from 8x10 to 2x2.

THE REVERSIBLE CABINET ATTACHMENT has spring actuated ground glass, and uses modern double plate holders.

THE FOLDING RACK is made of hardwood, holds twelve double plate holders, and is attached to side of stand.

Price, complete..$36.75

No lens or shutter is included.

We recommend our No. 20K1125 Lens and the No. 20K850 Silent Shutter for use with this outfit.

Our Best Penny Picture Camera.

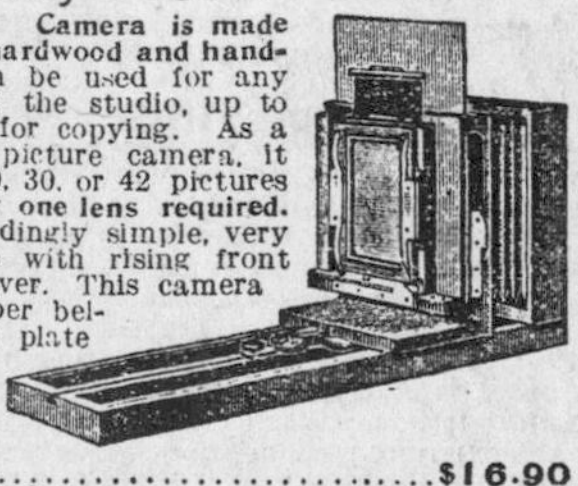

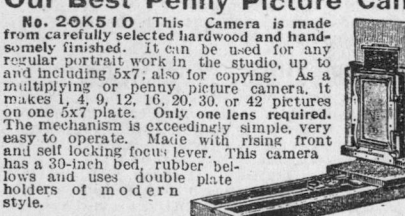

No. 20K510 This Camera is made from carefully selected hardwood and handsomely finished. It can be used for any regular portrait work in the studio, up to and including 5x7; also for copying. As a multiplying or penny picture camera, it makes 1, 4, 9, 12, 16, 20, 30, or 42 pictures on one 5x7 plate. Only one lens required. The mechanism is exceedingly simple, very easy to operate. Made with rising front and self locking focus lever. This camera has a 30-inch bed, rubber bellows and uses double plate holders of modern style.

Price, with one double plate holder..$16.90

Extra plate holders, each..65

We especially recommend our Portrait Lens No. 20K1125 for use with this camera.

No. 20K511 Camera Stand, suitable for the above Penny Picture Camera. This is the well known No. 00 stand, made with patent stop for holding adjustable central support at any height, and semi-automatic tilting attachment. Answers all ordinary requirements. Price..................$3.15

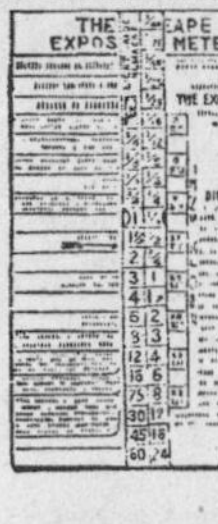

Exposure Meter.

No. 20K778 Cheape Exposure Meter. A simple and easily used device by means of which the correct exposure for any kind of picture, either indoors or outdoors, under any kind of weather conditions, may be instantly and accurately determined. The Cheape Exposure Meter is very nicely made from white celluloid, with letters and figures in blue and red. It is one of the easiest to use and the most satisfactory exposure meters on the market. Full directions with each one.

Price..25c

If by mail, postage extra, 1 cent.

Exposure Meter.

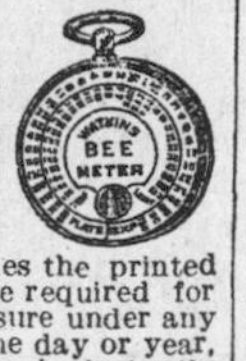

No. 20K780 The Bee Exposure Meter. A thoroughly reliable, practical and easily used exposure meter, made same size and shape as a small watch, diameter only 1¾ inches. The use of this little exposure meter does away entirely with the annoying calculations as to the time of day and weather conditions, which are a part of the process of using exposure meters of other types. With this meter a little strip of sensitized paper is exposed through a slot in the face of the instrument until its tint matches the printed tint beside the slot, and, with the length of time required for matching this tint as a factor, the correct exposure under any conditions of light or weather, at any time of the day or year, indoors or outdoors, with any brand of plates, is instantly determined.

Price, complete, with a supply of sensitized paper, full instructions and speed card..$1.10

If by mail, postage extra, 4 cents.

The Conley Silent Shutter.

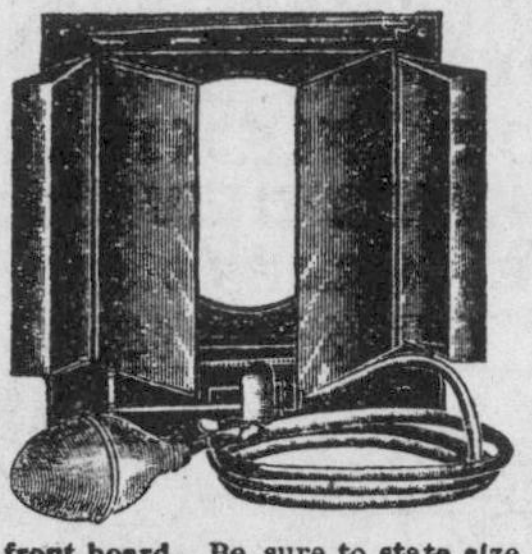

No. 20K850 The Silent Shutter, a new device absolutely noiseless in opening. The photographer who has experienced repeated failures by reason of a child subject, or a member of a group looking toward the lens at the critical moment, because he heard the "click" of the shutter will appreciate this new shutter, which opens with absolute silence. The cups at the sides form air cushions which arrest the wings as they open, thus avoiding all sound. Bulb and 6 feet of rubber hose furnished with each shutter.

This shutter is placed back of lens or inside of front board. **Be sure to state size** wanted.

Size of opening, inches	2	2½	3	3½
Size of shutter, inches	3⅞x4½	4⅜x5	5x5½	5⅜x6
Price	$4.50	$4.50	$4.50	$4.50

Size of opening, ins.	4	4½	5	5½	6
Size of shutter, ins.	6x6½	6½x7	7x7½	7½x8	8x8½
Price	$4.50	$5.40	$6.30	$7.20	$8.10

The Morrison Vignetter.

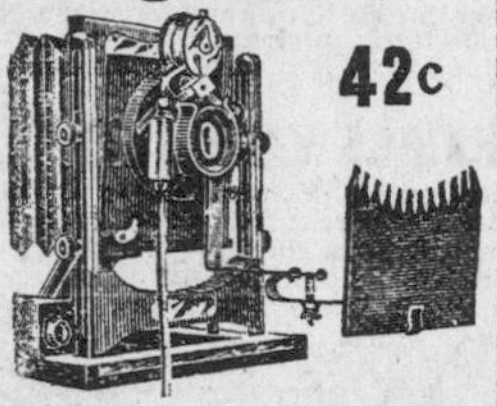

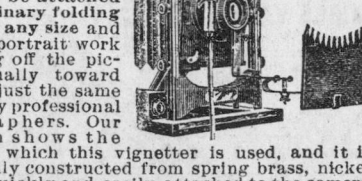

42c

No. 20K860 The Morrison Vignetter is a very ingenious device, which can be attached to any ordinary folding camera of any size and is used in portrait work for shading off the picture gradually toward the edges, just the same as is done by professional photographers. Our illustration shows the manner in which this vignetter is used, and it is substantially constructed from spring brass, nickel plated, is quickly and easily attached to the camera and should form a part of every photographic outfit. There are two vignetting cards, each with different colors on each side, making four colors in all: black, dark gray, light gray and white, so that the color of any background can be exactly matched. Price, 42c

If by mail, postage extra, 4 cents.

Camera Level, 31 Cents.

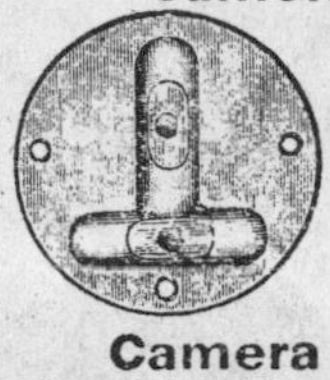

No. 20K870 This Little Level is intended to be attached to the bed of the camera, enabling the operator to quickly and easily place the camera perfectly level. It is nicely made from brass, finely finished and **accurately adjusted.**

Price..31c

If by mail, postage extra, 2 cents.

Camera Bulbs, 15c and 18c.

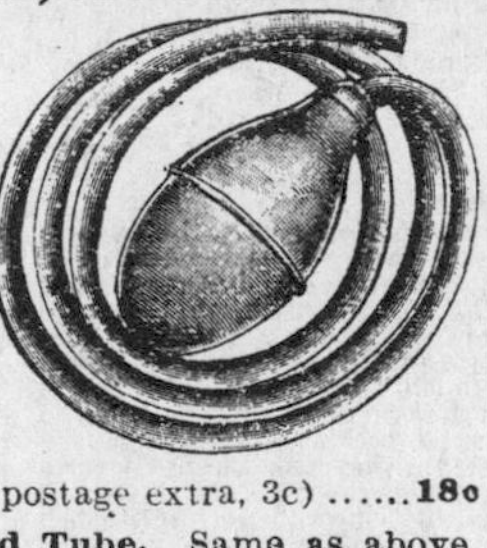

No. 20K882 Bulb and Tube for Camera. Made from the very best quality of red rubber, very elastic; tube is 14 in. long and can be fitted to any shutter. Rubber always becomes hard, brittle or rotten after a certain length of time, and if the bulb and tube you now have has become useless you can easily fit one of these to your shutter.

Price........(If by mail, postage extra, 3c)......18c

No. 20K883 Bulb and Tube. Same as above, but small size for compact folding film cameras; short tube. Price..15c

If by mail, postage extra, 3 cents.

No. 20K884 Rubber Tubing, for camera bulbs, best grade red rubber, diameter, 3/16 inch. Price, per foot......4c

If by mail, postage extra, for five feet or less, 2 cents; five to twelve feet, 3 cents.

Sliding Tripod, 45 Cents.

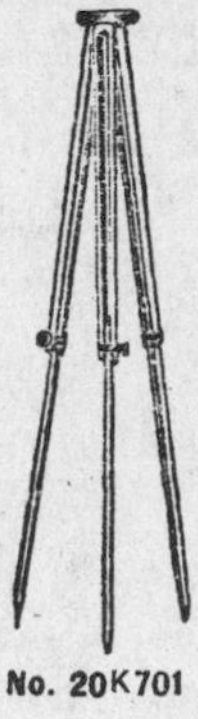

No. 20K701

No. 20K701 Sliding Tripod for 4x5 cameras. A light, well made, handsomely finished tripod, made from selected spruce, folding compactly, and adapted to any 4x5 hand camera or folding hand camera, such as the Seroco Sr. Box or other light cameras. Price...45c

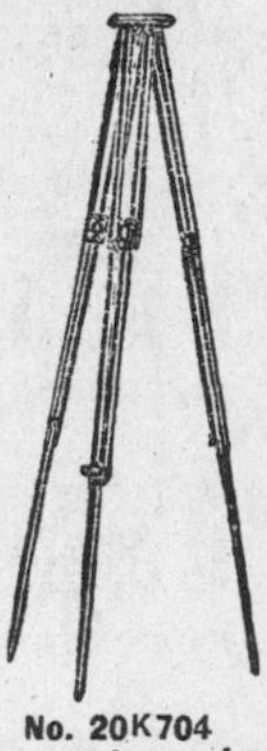

No. 20K704

Combination Tripod, $1.20.

No. 20K704 Combination Tripod for 4x5 cameras. A light, well made, combined sliding and folding tripod, with detachable head; suitable for use with any 4x5 camera, and even for 5x7, provided the camera is not very heavy. Price...$1.20

Ebony Combination Tripod, $1.50.

No. 20K706 Ebony Combination Tripod, same as No. 20K704, but with dead black ebony finish and nickel plated metal parts. A very handsome and high grade tripod.

Price..$1.50

Sliding Tripods, $1.40 to $2.10.

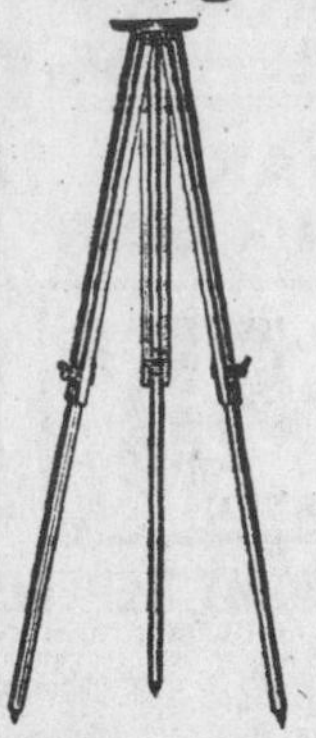

Our Best Grade Sliding Tripod is without a doubt the most perfect sliding tripod made. Constructed of best selected spruce, top of three-piece wood to prevent warping and covered with felt. A special brass binding plate, operated by set screw, clamps the legs securely at any desired height. Suitable for hand cameras, folding hand cameras or regular view cameras. Be sure to state size wanted.

No. 20K710 Sliding Tripod. For cameras from 4x5 to 6½x8½. Price..................$1.40

No. 20K711 Sliding Tripod. For cameras from 5x8 to 8x10. Price..................$1.75

No. 20K712 Sliding Tripod. For cameras from 8x10 to 11x14. Price..................$2.10

Combination Tripods, $2.10 to $3.15.

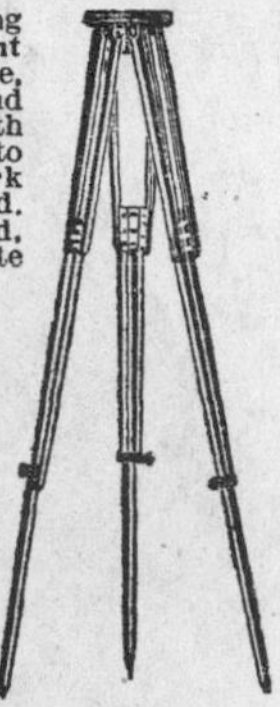

Combination Tripod. A combined sliding and folding tripod, one of the most convenient forms yet devised. Quickly set up for use, readily adjusted to any desired height and perfectly rigid. Made in three sections with detachable head; the lower section slides into the second, while the upper section folds back upon it, thus making a very compact tripod. Made from specially selected, straight grained, thoroughly seasoned ash. Be sure to state size wanted.

THE BEST TRIPOD MADE.

No. 20K717 Combination Tripod. For cameras from 4x5 to 6½x8½. Price..$2.10

No. 20K718 Combination Tripod. For cameras from 6½x8½ to 10x12. Price..$2.45

No. 20K719 Combination Tripod. For cameras from 10x12 to 14x17. Price, $3.15

NOTE—We believe it pays to use good, strong, heavy, rigid tripods. It is the practice of nearly all dealers in photographic supplies to overstate the capacity of tripods. Tripods corresponding in weight, strength and rigidity to our No. 20K717 combination are recommended by most dealers and manufacturers for 6½x8½ cameras. In our opinion a tripod of this weight is best suited to a 5x7 or 4x5 camera. Most dealers recommend a tripod corresponding to our No. 20K718 combination for 11x14 and 14x17 cameras. In our opinion a tripod of this weight is best suited to an 8x10 camera. Compared with other tripods of the same weight, strength and serviceability, our prices are lower than the prices of any dealer with whom we have compared.

Telescopic Metal Tripods.

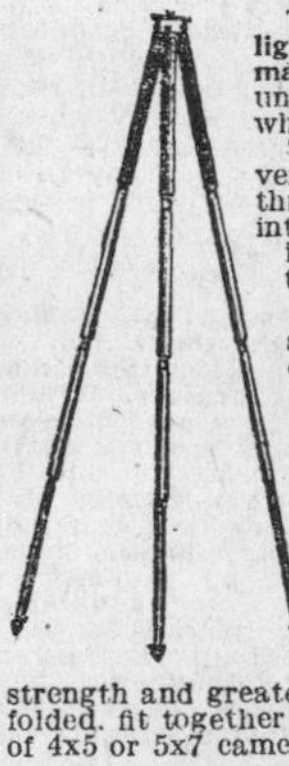

These New Telescopic Metal Tripods are the lightest and most compact tripods on the market. They are very convenient to use under all conditions and especially desirable when traveling.

They are very substantially constructed, very carefully made and finely finished throughout. Each joint telescopes, or slides into the joint above it, a spring catch holding the legs of the tripod firmly when they are fully extended.

No. 20K725 Telescopic Tripod. Three sections, adapted to light 4x5 or smaller cameras. Price..........$1.50

No. 20K727 Telescopic Tripod. Four sections, heavier tubing than No. 20K725 adapted to ordinary 4x5 cameras. Price..$1.95

No. 20K729 Telescopic Tripod. Five sections and heavier and stronger tubing, adapted to heavy 4x5 and light 5x7 cameras. Price..........$2.65

No. 20K731 Telescopic Tripod. Seven sections, extra high grade, made of heavier tubing giving additional strength and greater compactness, as the seven sections, when folded, fit together very compactly. Suitable for any style of 4x5 or 5x7 camera. Price..........$3.00

Focus Cloth, 25 Cents.

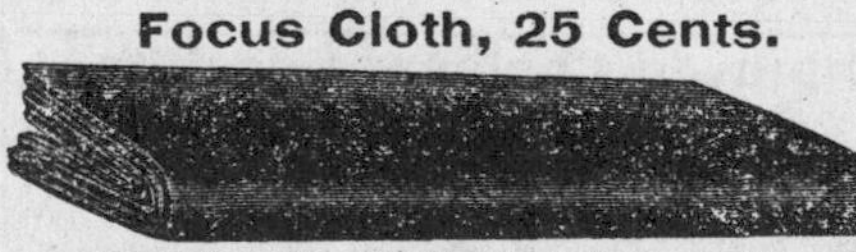

No. 20K750 Fine Quality Black Gossamar Focus Cloth 36x36 inches. Price..25c

If by mail, postage extra, 9 cents.

No. 20K751 Focus Cloth. Same as above, but double size, 36x72 inches. Price..50c

If by mail, postage extra, 17 cents.

Negative Preservers.

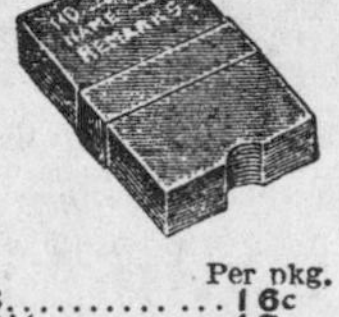

No. 20K760 Envelopes for preserving Negatives, made of strong manilla, the proper size for negatives, open at the end and have notched cut for admitting thumb and finger in removing; **printed on the face with lines for numbers, description, etc.;** put up in packages of 50 each. Be sure to state size wanted.

Size	Per pkg.	Size	Per pkg.
3½x3½	7c	5 x 8	16c
3¼x4¼	8c	6½x 8½	18c
4½x5½	11c	8 x10	23c
5 x7	14c		

Photo Beacon Exposure Card, 15c.

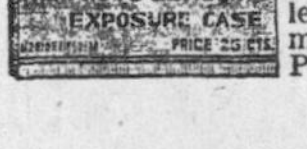

No. 20K775 A Little Book of Tables which gives you the exact exposure at any hour of the day, and any day of the year, with any brand of plates, or any speed of lens. Simple and absolutely correct. No more over exposed or under exposed plates. Price (If by mail, postage extra, 1c). 15c

COMPLETE INSTRUCTIONS IN PHOTOGRAPHY FREE

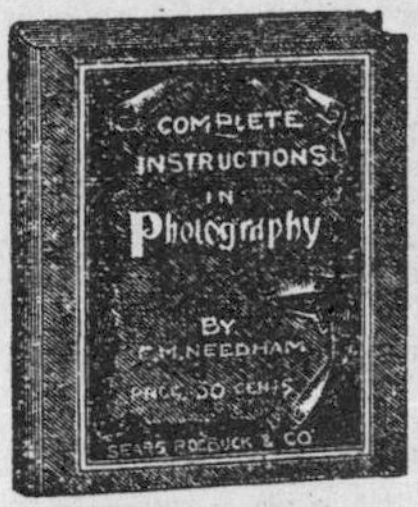

WITH EVERY CAMERA THAT WE SELL and with every complete developing outfit we include, absolutely free of charge, our big 112-page manual of photography. There is no other book like it. It was written expressly for us. It is published only by us and can be secured only from us.

WRITTEN BY AN EXPERT. The author of "Complete Instructions in Photography" is an expert photographer, a man who has spent his entire life in photographic work, in teaching photography and in selling photographic materials to both amateur and professional photographers. His knowledge of cameras, lenses and the various materials used in photography is second to none, and his ability to transmit this knowledge to others in a plain, simple and easily understood manner makes this book, especially to the beginner in photography, far more valuable than the largest and most pretentious encyclopedias of photography. The experience gained by the author of this book, not only in the actual processes of photography, but in his contact with other photographers, with amateurs and with beginners as well as with professional photographers, enables him to appreciate and understand better, perhaps than anyone else, the difficulties met with and the errors made by beginners. This experience enables him to understand just what the beginner wants to know, and enables him to make it plain and simple, so that it is easily understood and so that good results in picture making are practically certain for anyone who uses this book as a guide.

MAKES PHOTOGRAPHY EASY. "Complete Instructions in Photography" answers all your questions solves all your difficulties, anticipates all your troubles and makes photography easy. Indispensable to the beginner, invaluable to the advanced photographer. "Complete Instructions in Photography" tells secrets of the trade never before published; gives valuable information heretofore possessed only by a few professional photographers; **gives dozens of valuable formulas or recipes**; tells you how to make your own developers, your own solutions of all kinds; tells you how to determine the correct amount of exposure, how to save plates which are wrongly exposed, how to make good portraits, how to make blue paper, how to dry a negative in five minutes, **how to make money in photography**, how to avoid all the troubles sometimes met with by beginners, how to select a camera; tells all about a hundred other things which we haven't space to mention here.

"COMPLETE INSTRUCTIONS IN PHOTOGRAPHY" FREE WITH EVERY $2.50 ORDER.

Besides including "Complete Instructions in Photography" free with every camera we sell, and free with every developing outfit we send out, we will also, if requested, include it free with every order for photographic merchandise that amounts to $2.50 or more. We make this special offer in order to accommodate those who already own a camera or a developing outfit and who are purchasing additional supplies from time to time. Remember, with every order for photographic goods amounting to $2.50 or more we will include, absolutely free of charge (provided you plainly state in your order that you desire the book), one copy of "Complete Instructions in Photography." We do not send the book unless you expressly state in your order that you desire the book. Thousands of our customers already possess this book and would have no particular use for a second copy, but if your order amounts to $2.50 or more, and you plainly state that you desire a copy of the book, it will be included in the shipment and sent to you free of any expense.

98c TO $1.35 ACCORDING TO SIZE.

SERIES "A" DEVELOPING, FINISHING AND MATERIAL OUTFITS FOR EITHER PLATE CAMERAS OR FILM CAMERAS.

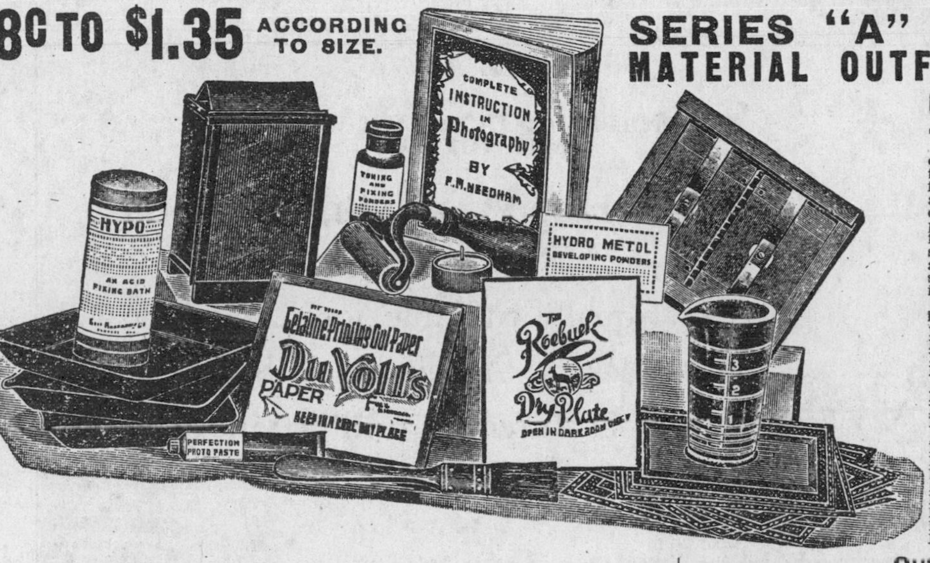

THESE SERIES "A" Developing, Finishing and Material Outfits contain everything that is necessary for developing, printing and finishing pictures. We urge everyone who orders a camera from us to include, with the camera, one of these fine outfits and thus secure, right at the start, at the lowest possible cost, everything necessary to commence work. Everything that we put into these outfits is good; plates and papers guaranteed fresh and perfect; chemicals guaranteed full weight and full strength; accessories guaranteed strictly high class, well made and serviceable. The Series "A" Outfits are put up in seven sizes and are suitable for use with any cameras of corresponding size that we sell.

Arranged for plate cameras, each outfit contains the following items:

1 Package Concentrated Dry Toner (makes 8 ounces of solution).
1 Tray for Developing Plates.
1 Tray for Fixing Plates.
1 Package Concentrated Dry Developer (makes 8 ounces of solution).
1 Metal Dark Room Lamp.
1 Tray for toning prints.
1 Print Roller for smoothing down the mounted prints.
½ Dozen Dry Plates.
1 Dozen Sheets Du Voll's Sensitized Paper.
1 Printing Frame.
1 Package Hypo for fixing Negatives and Prints.
1 Paste Brush.
1 Graduated Glass for Measuring Liquids.
1 Dozen Card Mounts, with fancy embossed borders.
1 Tube of fine scented Photo Mounting Paste.
1 Copy of "Complete Instructions in Photography."

Outfits for Plate Cameras.

No. 20K601	Series "A" Outfit for 2½x2½ plate camera. Price	$0.98
No. 20K602	Series "A" Outfit for 3½x3½ plate camera. Price	1.05
No. 20K603	Series "A" Outfit for 3¼x4¼ plate camera. Price	1.12
No. 20K604	Series "A" Outfit for 4x5 plate camera. Price	1.20

There is no Camera included with these Outfits.

Outfits for Film Cameras.

We also put up these outfits arranged especially for film cameras, the list of items being the same as included in the outfit for plate cameras, except that we put in one roll of film (six exposures) instead of the package of dry plates, and the printing frame is fitted with a glass.

No. 20K610	Series "A" Outfit for 2¼x3¼ film cameras. Price	$1.00
No. 20K611	Series "A" Outfit for 2½x4¼ film cameras. Price	1.05
No. 20K612	Series "A" Outfit for 3½x3½ film cameras. Price	1.10
No. 20K613	Series "A" Outfit for 3¼x4¼ film cameras. Price	1.15
No. 20K614	Series "A" Outfit for 4x5 film cameras. Price	1.30
No. 20K615	Series "A" Outfit for 3¼x5½ film cameras. Price	1.35

There is no Camera included with these Outfits.

SERIES "B" DEVELOPING, FINISHING AND MATERIAL OUTFITS FOR EITHER PLATE CAMERAS OR FILM CAMERAS.

$2.10 TO $4.75 ACCORDING TO SIZE.

OUR SERIES "B" Developing, Finishing and Material Outfits are the largest, the best and the most complete outfits ever offered. They are suitable for use with every 4x5, 5x7, 6½x8½ and 8x10 camera which we sell and we strongly advise everyone who buys a 4x5 or larger camera to order one of these outfits and thus secure this big assortment of necessary supplies and apparatus for less than one-half the money these same goods would cost if purchased separately from the regular dealers in photographic supplies. Every item contained in our big Series "B" Outfits is extra high grade, the best the market affords, suitable for use with our very best cameras. Not an unnecessary item is included. You will need everything contained in these outfits when you commence making pictures. Arranged for plate cameras, each outfit contains the following items.

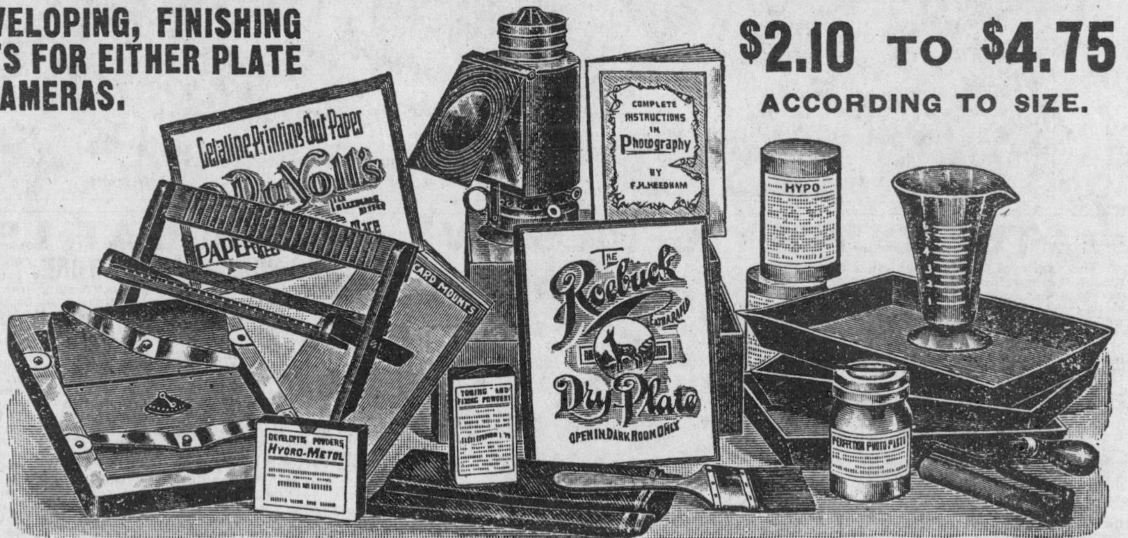

1 High Grade Metal Ruby Lamp with Oil Burner.
25 Card Mounts.
1 Compressed Fiber Tray for developing.
1 Compressed Fiber Tray for fixing.
1 Compressed Fiber Tray for toning.
1 Folding Negative Rack to hold 24 plates.
1 8-Ounce Cone Shaped Graduate.
1 Heavy Printing Frame.
1 Paste Brush.
1 Fine Gossamer Focus Cloth.
1 Dozen Extra Rapid Roebuck Dry Plates.
1 Package Toning and Fixing Powders (makes 24 ounces of toner).
1 Package Hydro-Metol Developing Powders (makes 24 ounces developer).
1 Pound Hyposulphite of Soda.
1 Print Roller.
1 Dozen Sheets Du Voll's Sensitized Paper.
1 Jar Photo Paste.
1 Copy of "Complete Instructions in Photography."

Outfits for Plate Cameras.

No. 20K630	Series "B" Outfit for 4x5 plate camera. Price	$2.25
No. 20K631	Series "B" Outfit for 5x7 plate camera. Price	3.10
No. 20K632	Series "B" Outfit for 6½x8½ plate camera. Price	3.65
No. 20K633	Series "B' Outfit for 8x10 plate camera. Price	4.75

There is no Camera included with these Outfits.

Outfits for Film Cameras.

We also put up these Series "B" Outfits arranged for film cameras, the list of items being the same as included in the outfits for plate cameras, except that we put in one roll of film (12 exposures) in place of the dry plates, a box of push pins in place of the negative rack; the focus cloth is omitted and the printing frame is provided with a glass.

No. 20K639	Series "B" Outfit for 3½x3½ film camera. Price	$2.10
No. 20K640	Series "B" Outfit for 3¼x4¼ film camera. Price	2.20
No. 20K641	Series "B" Outfit for 4x5 film camera. Price	2.35

There is no Camera included with these Outfits.

With both the 3½x3½ and 3¼x4¼ outfits for film cameras we furnish 4x5 trays and printing frame, as this size is more convenient to work with.

THE CONLEY F 8 RAPID RECTILINEAR LENS

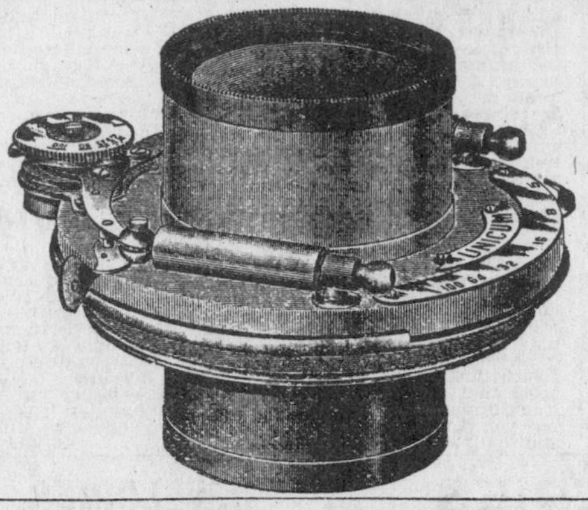

For years we have sold the Seroco Rapid Rectilinear Lens, and thousands of photographers who have purchased this lens will tell you that they never saw a better Rectilinear lens at any price. This season we offer the new Conley Rapid Rectilinear Lens, built on exactly the same principles as ever, **but made just a little better** than the old style.

This is a good lens for the professional photographer who does all around work, both indoors and outdoors. It is a good lens for the amateur photographer who wants an instrument suitable for landscape work, buildings, groups, etc., and at the same time one capable of making a good portrait. The Conley Rapid Rectilinear Lens will do all these things and do them well. **It is a good lens.**

Perfectly Rectilinear. The Conley Rapid Rectilinear Lens is perfectly rectilinear, rendering the straight lines of buildings, or other subjects, absolutely without distortion, possesses a remarkable depth of focus and flatness of field, giving the most brilliant definition and detail. **This lens is unsurpassed for landscape work,** views of buildings and other architectural subjects, flashlights, groups and instantaneous work. **It represents better value than any other lens** on the market, and is **superior in every respect to many lenses** sold at double our prices.

Construction. The Conley Rapid Rectilinear lens is composed of two perfectly corrected combinations, each combination consisting of two lenses, one of flint glass, the other of crown glass. These lenses are specially ground from the finest imported, genuine Mantois optical glass, and the entire lens is fully corrected for both chromatic and spherical aberration. **This lens is** handsomely mounted in lacquered brass and equipped with the Unicum shutter.

The Unicum Shutter. This shutter gives exposures of 1 second, ½ second, $\frac{1}{5}$ second, $\frac{1}{25}$ second or $\frac{1}{100}$ second, with one pressure of the bulb. With indicator set to "B" a pressure of the bulb opens the shutter, which remains open until the pressure is released. With indicator set to "T" the first pressure of the bulb opens the shutter, which remains open until the bulb is again pressed. Back of the shutter blades is a perfect **Iris Diaphragm,** the opening being instantly adjustable to any desired size by the index lever at lower margin of shutter. **Accuracy and entire freedom from jarring are secured by a pneumatic retarding device,** and the actuating mechanism of the shutter is fully protected from injury or dust. Made from bronze metal, with nickel plated trimmings, very handsomely finished throughout.

No. 20K1101 The Conley F 8 Rapid Rectilinear Lens with Unicum Shutter.

Size of View, inches	Equivalent Focus, inches	Diameter Image Circle, inches	Diameter Across Hood, inches	Price of Lens Complete With Unicum Shutter
4 x 5	6¾	9	1¼	$ 8.50
5 x 7	8¾	10½	1¾	9.70
5 x 8	9¼	11	1¾	10.50
6½ x 8½	12	13¼	2	13.60
8 x 10	14¾	16	2⅜	18.20

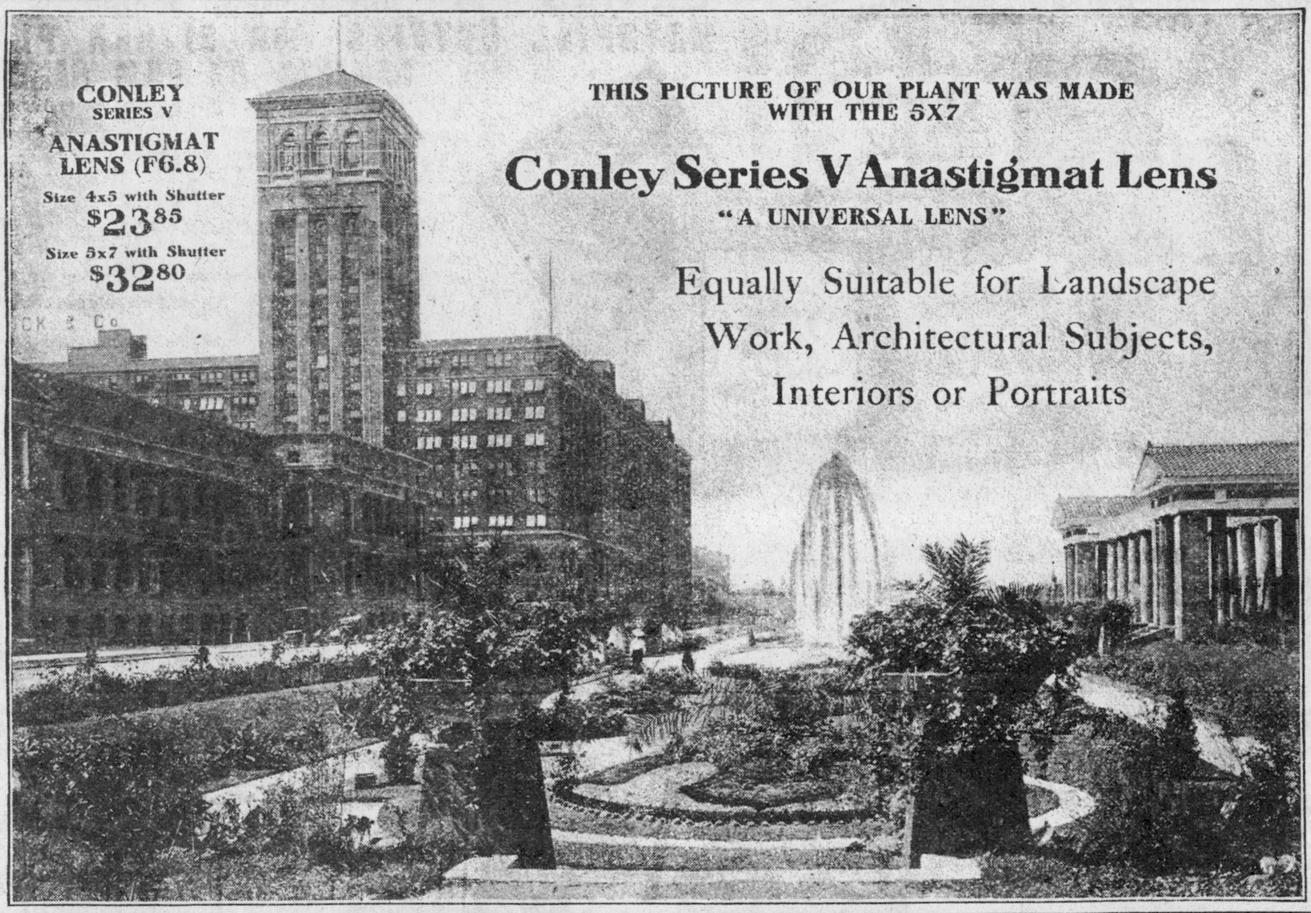
CONLEY
SERIES V
ANASTIGMAT
LENS (F6.8)
Size 4x5 with Shutter
$23.85
Size 5x7 with Shutter
$32.80
THIS PICTURE OF OUR PLANT WAS MADE
WITH THE 5X7
Conley Series V Anastigmat Lens
"A UNIVERSAL LENS"
Equally Suitable for Landscape
Work, Architectural Subjects,
Interiors or Portraits

THE CONLEY SERIES "V" ANASTIGMAT LENS, F 6.8

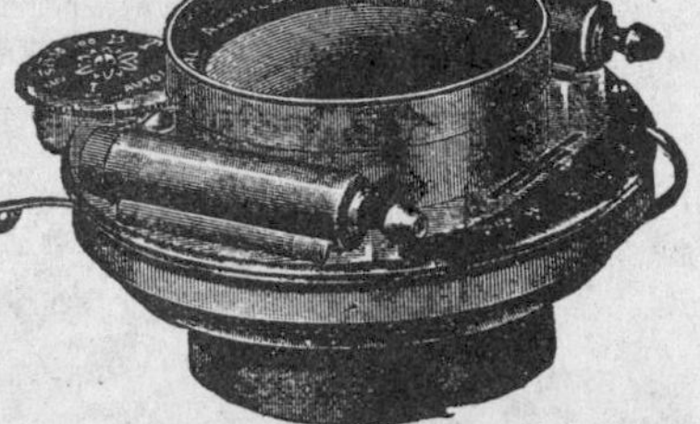

The Conley Series V Anastigmat Lens meets the requirements of the average photographer, either amateur or professional, better than any other lens that we handle, and to the purchaser who wants a lens that is suitable for any kind of work we recommend it above any other lens. It is a double anastigmat of the most perfect type, in every sense of the word a universal lens, being suitable for practically any kind of photographic work, including landscapes, architectural subjects, portraits, groups, studio use and high speed instantaneous work. **The designers of this lens** have succeeded in absolutely eliminating all traces of astigmatism and at the same time have produced a lens absolutely free from chromatic or spherical aberration.

In defining power, depth of focus, flatness of field and brilliancy of illumination the Conley Series V Anastigmat Lens is not surpassed by any anastigmat lens on the market, regardless of price.

The Conley Anastigmat Lens is of the double symmetrical type, the front and rear combinations being of the same construction. They are ground from the very highest grade Jena optical glass, made expressly for the manufacture of the highest grade anastigmat lenses.

In construction this lens is of the double anastigmat symmetrical type, composed of two systems, each system made up of four elementary lenses, cemented together in pairs. **Both the front combination and rear combination are fully corrected and may be used alone, having a focal length about twice that of the complete lens.**

The Shutter. We furnish the Conley Series V Anastigmat Lens with either the Wollensak Automatic Shutter, as shown in the illustration, or with the Bausch & Lomb Volute shutter.

The Automatic Shutter is a self setting shutter and in reliability, speed and ease of operation is undoubtedly the best automatic shutter made. With one pressure of the bulb it gives exposures of 1 second, ½ second, $\frac{1}{5}$ second, $\frac{1}{25}$ second, $\frac{1}{50}$ second or $\frac{1}{100}$ second, and with two pressures of the bulb, time or bulb exposures of any length. It is graceful in design, light in weight and perfect in action, releasing smoothly, without jar or vibration. Fitted with Iris diaphragm.

The Volute Shutter is the highest type of Iris diaphragm shutter, extra rapid, very compact, dustproof and durable. It is beautifully finished throughout; made like a watch in point of accuracy and fine workmanship.

THIS PICTURE OF OUR STORE, which was taken with the Conley Series V, F 6.8, Anastigmat Lens, will give you some **idea of what this lens can do.** Unfortunately, however, the poor quality of paper upon which this page is printed makes it impossible for us to show in this picture **the sharpness and wonderful detail that actually exists in the original picture itself.** WE HAVE SELECTED THIS PICTURE to show the work of this lens, because it is a particularly difficult picture to make; in fact, it would be practically impossible to make this photograph with an ordinary lens. The wonderful depth of focus possessed by this lens is well illustrated by this picture, as the vases in the foreground are within ten feet of the camera, while the extreme distance, clear down beyond the large building, is nearly one-half mile away, yet **both the foreground and the most distant objects are absolutely sharp in the original photograph.** The top of the tower is 240 feet above the ground, and in order to include it in the picture it was necessary to raise the camera front as high as it would go, and the wonderful covering power of the lens is shown by the fact that the top of the tower, even with the lens thus thrown some two or three inches off center, is still perfectly sharp.

FOR HOME PORTRAIT WORK the Conley Series V, F 6.8, Anastigmat Lens is a perfect instrument. For successful portrait work under the ordinary conditions existing in the home a fast lens is necessary, and this lens has speed. It is fast enough to permit exposures as short as $\frac{1}{25}$ of a second in an ordinarily well lighted living room. It is fast enough to make "snap shots" of the baby in your parlor at home, and the pictures will be better than you would get amid the distracting conditions of the professional photographer's studio. **PORTRAIT WORK is the most interesting branch of photography,** but it requires a good lens, and the Conley Series V Anastigmat is a good lens, not only for portrait work but for all kinds of photography.

No. 20K1110 The Series V, F 6.8, Conley Anastigmat Lens. Prices as follows:

Size of Plate covered at full Aperture.	Diameter of Image Circle, inches.	Equivalent Focus, inches.	Focal length, rear Combination, inches.	Diam. Measured across hood, inches.	Price with Automatic Shutter.	Price with Volute Shutter.
3¼ x 4¼	6½	5	10	1¼	$21.90	$29.60
4 x 5	8½	6	12	$1\frac{5}{16}$	23.85	31.55
5 x 7	11	7	14	1⅜	32.80	38.30
6½ x 8½	14	10	20	$1\frac{13}{16}$	42.20	48.70
8 x 10	17	13	26	2_{16}	56.85	62.85
10 x 12	20	15	30	2⅞	68.80	not made
11 x 14	24	16½	33	$3\frac{1}{16}$	88.00	not made

These prices include bulb and tube.

THIS LENS CAN BE FITTED TO ANY FOLDING OR VIEW CAMERA. Send us the front board of your camera with your order for the lens, and we will mount it without extra charge.

The Monarch Wide Angle Lens.

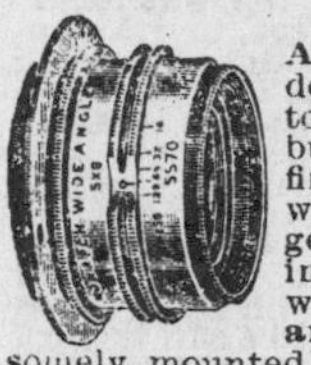

No. 20K1120 The Monarch Wide Angle Lens embraces an angle of 90 degrees, making it especially adapted to photographing the interiors of buildings, out of door views in confined situations; in fact, any work where it is difficult or impossible to get far enough away from the subject in order to get it all on the plate with an ordinary lens. **Our Monarch Wide Angle Lenses** are handsomely mounted in lacquered brass with fine Iris diaphragm. Made expressly for us by the Bausch & Lomb Optical Company, and represents the latest advances in the making of lenses of this type. **The speed of this lens is F 16.**

Size of View, inches	Equivalent Focus, inches	Diameter Across Hood, inches	Price, with Iris Diaphragm
4 x 5	3⅛	$1\frac{9}{32}$	$5.70
5 x 7	5¼	$1\frac{9}{32}$	6.80
5 x 8	5½	$1\frac{9}{32}$	7.10
6½ x 8½	6½	$1\frac{9}{32}$	9.90
8 x 10	8	$1\frac{9}{32}$	12.80

The Seroco Rapid Portrait Lens.

SERIES II. SPEED F 5.

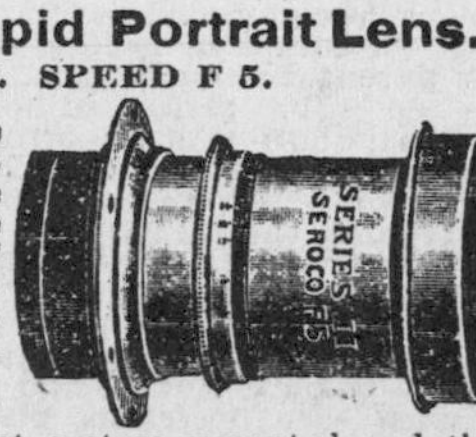

No. 20K1125 The Seroco Rapid Portrait Lens, Series II, is a true portrait lens of the most approved type of portrait lens construction. These lenses are ground from the best imported optical glass, composed of two systems of two glasses each, the front system cemented and the rear system made with an air space between the two glasses. The special formula by which these lenses are ground, combined with their large diameter, gives them a high working speed, producing brilliant negatives with plenty of detail with the shortest possible exposures.

We recommend the Series II Seroco Rapid Portrait Lens as the very best moderate priced portrait lens ever placed on the market, and for general all around work in the studio these lenses cannot be surpassed. These lenses are beautifully finished in lacquered brass with black trimmings, and fitted with a very fine Iris diaphragm.

Size of Plate Covered, inches	Diameter of Lens, inches	Equivalent focus, inches	Distance for Stand'g Cabinet, feet	Price with Iris Diaphragm
4 x 5	1⅞	7	8	$11.65
5 x 7	2¼	10	10½	13.50
6½ x 8½	2½	12	13	18.75
8 x 10	3	14	15	30.00

Ray Filters at 60 Cents.

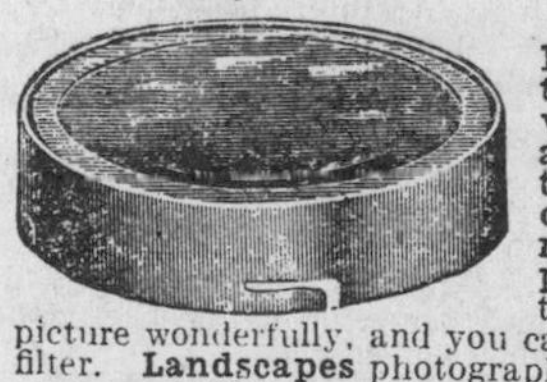

No. 20K1140 A Ray Filter absorbs the violet and ultra-violet rays of light and produces a picture in which the color values are correct. Clouds in a photograph improve the artistic value of the picture wonderfully, and you can get them with a ray filter. **Landscapes** photographed with the ray filter possess a brilliancy and contrast which it is impossible to obtain otherwise; and in the photographing of flowers, paintings or any brightly colored subjects, the ray filter is practically indispensable.

No. 1 for lenses $1\frac{5}{16}$ inches in diameter **$0.60**
No. 2 for fixed focus or box cameras .... **.60**
No. 3 for lenses $1\frac{7}{16}$ inches in diameter .... **.60**
No. 4 for lenses 1½ inches in diameter .... **.75**
No. 5 for lenses 1¾ inches in diameter .... **.90**
No. 6 for lenses 2 inches in diameter .... **.90**
No. 7 for lenses 2¼ inches in diameter **1.05**
No. 8 for lenses 2½ inches in diameter **1.20**
No. 9 for lenses 2¾ inches in diameter **1.35**

If by mail, postage extra, on Nos. 1 to 6, 4 **cents;** Nos. 7 to 10, **6 cents.**

Any of the above sizes are suitable for lenses ¼ inch less in diameter than size mentioned.

State exact diameter of lens when ordering.

Any Size Duplicator for 17 Cents.

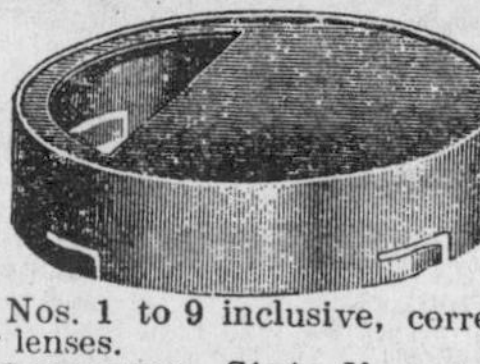

No. 20K1148 Duplicator. A device enabling one to photograph a person in two positions on the same plate. Very humorous and interesting pictures can be made in this way. Can be used with any folding camera. Made in sizes Nos. 1 to 9 inclusive, corresponding to our auxiliary lenses.

Cannot be used with box cameras. State diameter of lens. Be careful to state size wanted.

Price, each, any size **17c**

If by mail, postage extra, 3 to 5 cents.

WE ALWAYS UNDERSELL

outdistance and outclass all competition. Following our well established policy of steadily lowering prices we have still further reduced them in this catalogue.

AUXILIARY ENLARGING AND COPYING LENSES.

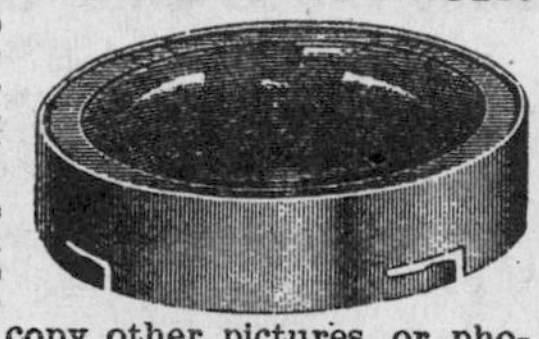

No. 20K1155 These lenses are used in connection with the regular lens of any folding camera, greatly increasing its power. By the use of these lenses, copying and enlarging may be done with any folding camera, enabling one to copy other pictures or photograph small articles to their full size or even larger. **A 4x5 photograph copied with an ordinary camera will make a picture about the size of a postage stamp, but when copied with the aid of this lens can be made full size or larger.** Many uses for this valuable discovery will readily suggest themselves to the user.

No. 1 for 4x5 camera with lens $1\frac{5}{16}$ in. in diam... **$0.90**
No. 2 for 5x7 camera with lens $1\frac{5}{16}$ in. in diam... **.90**
No. 3 for fixed focus or box cameras............ **.90**
No. 4 for 4x5 camera with lens $1\frac{7}{16}$ in. in diam... **.90**
No. 5 for 5x7 camera with lens $1\frac{7}{16}$ in. in diam... **.90**
No. 6 for 4x5 camera with lens 1½ in. in diam... **1.20**
No. 7 for 5x7 camera with lens 1½ in. in diam... **1.20**
No. 8 any size camera with lens 1¾ in. in diam... **1.35**
No. 9 any size camera with lens 2 in. in diam... **1.50**
No. 10 any size camera with lens 2¼ in. in diam... **1.65**
No. 11 any size camera with lens 2½ in. in diam... **1.80**
No. 12 any size camera with lens 2¾ in. in diam... **1.95**
No. 13 any size camera with lens 3 in. in diam... **2.10**

If by mail, postage extra, on Nos. 1 to 7, **3 cents;** Nos. 8 to 10, **6 cents;** Nos. 11 to 13, **10 cents.**

In measuring your lens, take the outside diameter, remembering that the enlarging lens slips over your regular lens same as a cap.

Any of the above sizes are suitable for lenses ¼ inch less in diameter than size mentioned.

Auxiliary Portrait Lenses.

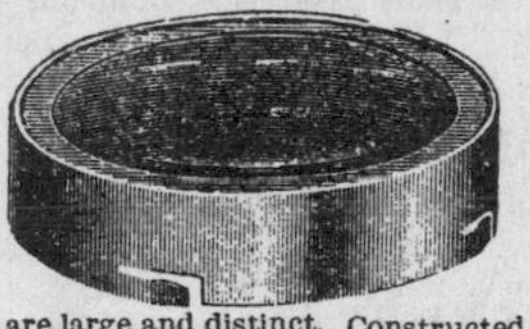

No. 20K1158 In making portraits with the ordinary folding hand camera, the great difficulty heretofore has been the small size of the faces. This portrait lens, however, entirely overcomes this difficulty and enables anyone with any kind of a folding camera to make portraits in which the faces are large and distinct. Constructed in the same style and used in same manner as the enlarging lens No. 20K1155.

No. 1 for 4x5 camera with lens $1\frac{5}{16}$ in. in diam... **$0.90**
No. 2 for 5x7 camera with lens $1\frac{5}{16}$ in. in diam... **.90**
No. 3 for fixed focus or box cameras............ **.90**
No. 4 for 4x5 camera with lens 1⅜ in. in diam... **.90**
No. 5 for 5x7 camera with lens 1⅜ in. in diam... **.90**
No. 6 for 4x5 camera with lens 1½ in. in diam... **1.20**
No. 7 for 5x7 camera with lens 1½ in. in diam... **1.20**
No. 8 any size camera with lens 1¾ in. in diam... **1.35**
No. 9 any size camera with lens 2 in. in diam... **1.50**
No. 10 any size camera with lens 2¼ in. in diam... **1.65**
No. 11 any size camera with lens 2½ in. in diam... **1.80**

If by mail, postage extra, on Nos. 1 to 7, **3 cents;** Nos. 8 to 10, **6 cents;** No. 11, **10 cents.**

In measuring your lens, take the outside diameter, remembering that the portrait lens slips over your regular lens same as a cap.

Any of the above sizes may be used on lenses ¼ inch less in diameter than size given.

Auxiliary Lens Sets, $2.55.

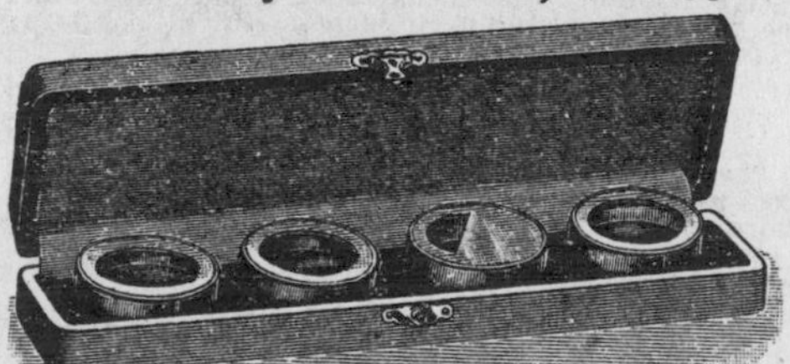

No. 20K1162 These sets contain one copying and enlarging lens, one portrait lens, one ray filter and one duplicator, **all contained in a beautiful plush lined leather case.** Be careful to mention size wanted.

Put up only in the following sizes:

Set No. 1 for 4x5 camera with lens $1\frac{5}{16}$ in. diam.. **$2.55**
Set No. 2 for 5x7 camera with lens $1\frac{5}{16}$ in. diam... **2.55**
Set No. 3 for 4x5 camera with lens $1\frac{7}{16}$ in. diam... **2.55**
Set No. 4 for 5x7 camera with lens $1\frac{7}{16}$ in. diam... **2.55**

Postage extra on any size, if sent by mail, 10 cents.

Larger sizes are not put up in cases.

Candle Ruby Lamp, 14 Cents.

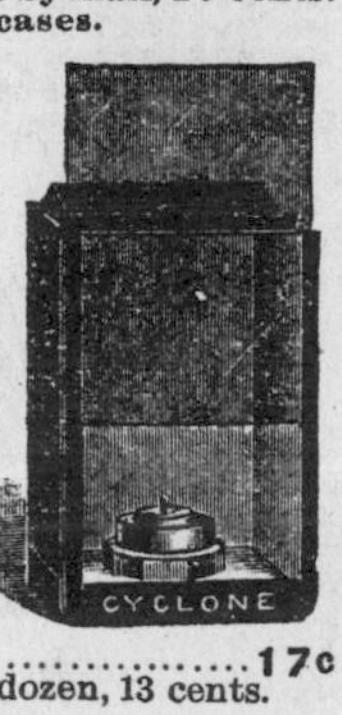

No. 20K1206 Candle Ruby Lamp, constructed of metal, has deep ruby glass, burns candle. A very convenient and satisfactory lamp at a low price. Price.................. **14c**

Not mailable.

Extra Candles.

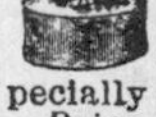

No. 20K1207 Candles to fit above lamp, small flat paraffine candles in pasteboard cups, burn two hours. Made especially for dark room lamps.

Price, per dozen........................ **17c**

If by mail, postage extra, per dozen, 13 cents.

Large Oil Ruby Lamp, 65 Cents.

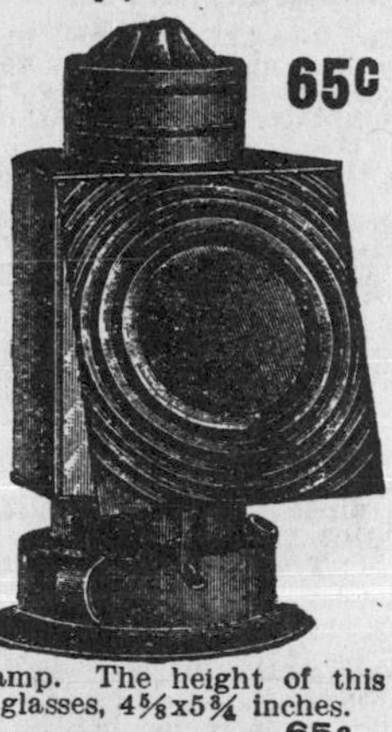

No. 20K1210 This is an extra large high class oil burning dark room lamp, made on improved and scientific plans. It is provided with a new patent burner, giving a volume of light never before secured with lamps of this style, and the general construction is such as to insure perfect combustion without smoke or odor. It is made with hinged metal front, which can be placed at any angle to regulate the volume of light and is fitted with both orange and deep ruby glass, insuring a perfectly safe or non-actinic light. The reservoir can be filled from the outside and the light can be turned up or down without opening the lamp. The height of this lamp is 10⅜ inches; size of glasses, 4⅝x5¾ inches.

Price.. **65c**

Not mailable.

Medium Size Oil Ruby Lamp, 40c.

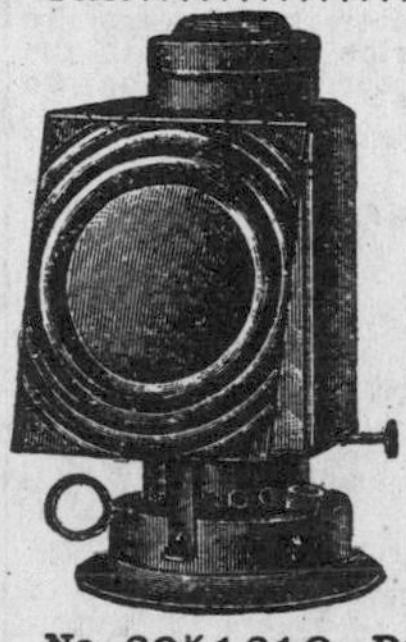

No. 20K1211 This lamp is made exactly the same as the large lamp described above, but is smaller, measuring 8⅛ inches high, with ruby and orange glasses 3⅝ x4⅝ inches.

Price...................... **40c**

Not mailable.

Ruby and Orange Glass.

No. 20K1216 Deep ruby glass for dark room use, replacing broken glass in ruby lamps, etc. Carefully selected for non-actinic qualities.

Size, inches		Price
3¼x 4⅜	Fits our candle lamp...........	**7c**
3⅝x 4⅝	Fits our medium oil lamp..........	**8c**
4 x 5	....	**8c**
4⅝x 5⅜	Fits our large oil lamp..........	**10c**
5 x 7	....	**12c**
6½x 8½	....	**16c**
8 x10	....	**20c**
10 x12	....	**30c**
11 x14	....	**45c**
16 x20	....	**85c**

No. 20K1217 Orange glass, used in combination with ruby glass for dark room lights, also very fine for working developing papers by. Sizes and prices same as quoted above for ruby glass.

Ruby Fabric, 15 Cents.

No. 20K1219 Ruby Fabric. A good substitute for ruby glass, and not liable to breakage. Size, 15x18 inches. Price, per sheet in mailing tube. **15c**

If by mail, postage extra, per sheet, 5 cents.

One Dozen Postoffice Papers, 12c.

No. 20K1220 Postoffice Paper. A yellow paper for dark room use, making ruby light, etc.

Size, 18x22 inches. Price, per dozen sheets.. **12c**

If by mail, postage extra, 15 cents.

Ground Glass.

No. 20K1230 Ground Glass for replacing broken screens in cameras, making transparencies, etc., finest quality, mud ground. State size wanted.

Size	Price	Size	Price
3¼x4¼	**6c**	6½x8½	**15c**
4 x5	**8c**	8x10	**20c**
4¼x6½	**10c**	10x12	**32c**
5 x7	**11c**	11x14	**42c**
5 x8	**13c**		

Measuring Glasses, 4 Cents.

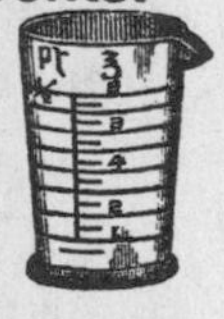

No. 20K1240 Tumbler Shaped Measuring Glasses. For liquids; graduated with ounces and drams; not quite as convenient as the regular cone shaped graduate, but preferred by many on account of the extremely low price. Be sure to state size wanted. Price, 2 ounce.... **4c**

Price, 4 ounce........................ **6c**

Price, 8 ounce........................ **9c**

Not mailable.

Pressed Line Graduates.

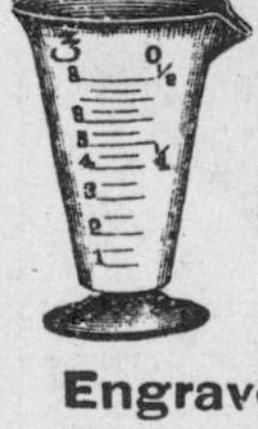

No. 20K1242 Cone Shaped Graduates. For measuring liquids; marked with scale showing ounces and drams. **Perfectly accurate.** Be sure to state size wanted. Price, 1 ounce...... **8c**

Price, 2 ounce.................... **9c**
Price, 4 ounce.................... **13c**
Price, 8 ounce.................... **19c**
Price, 16 ounce.................... **27c**

Engraved Graduates.

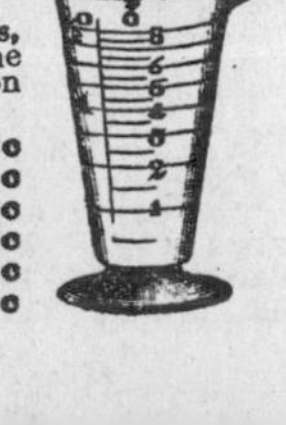

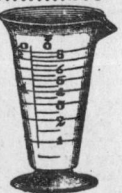

No. 20K1244 Cone Shaped Graduates, all lines and figures engraved by hand, the most carefully made and accurate graduate on the market. Be sure to state size wanted.

Price, 1 ounce.................. **12c**
Price, 2 ounce.................. **14c**
Price, 4 ounce.................. **20c**
Price, 8 ounce.................. **32c**
Price, 16 ounce.................. **50c**
Price, 32 ounce.................. **88c**

Hydrometers, 16 Cents.

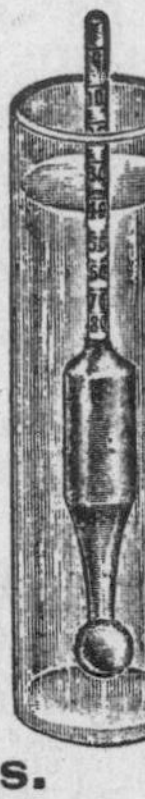

No. 20K1248 For making up solutions by hydrometer test instead of using scales and weights; very convenient. Complete, with glass jar, in wooden box. Price 16c
If by mail, postage extra, 9 cents.

Fluted Glass Funnels, 13c.

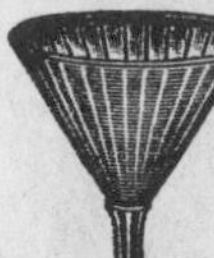

No. 20K1255 Glass Funnels, fluted, for filtering. More desirable than plain funnels, because filtering is much more rapid. Be sure to state size wanted.

Size	Price	Size	Price
¼ pint	13c	1 quart	20c
1 pint	16c	2 quart	34c

Too heavy to send by mail.

Filter Paper, 6 Cents.

No. 20K1258 Filter Paper. Round, in packages of 10 sheets. Be sure to state size wanted.

Price, 18 inches in diameter, per package, 16c
Price, 13 inches in diameter, per package..9c
Price, 10 inches in diameter, per package..7c
Price, 8 inches in diameter, per package..6c

New Style Photo Scale for 35 Cents.

35c

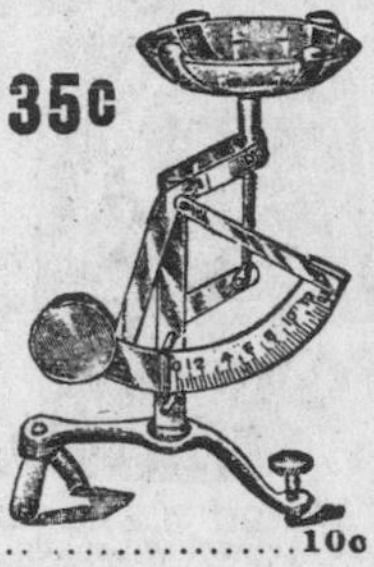

No. 20K1265 The best scale yet devised at a low price; answers all the requirements in making up solutions, etc. Simple, nothing to get out of order, accurate and convenient, no loose weights. Weighs up to 12 drams. Pan is made of glass and easily cleaned. Price 35c
If by mail, postage extra, 6 cents.

No. 20K1267 Extra Glass Pans for No. 20K1265 Scale. Price 10c

An Imported Scale for $1.20.

$1.20

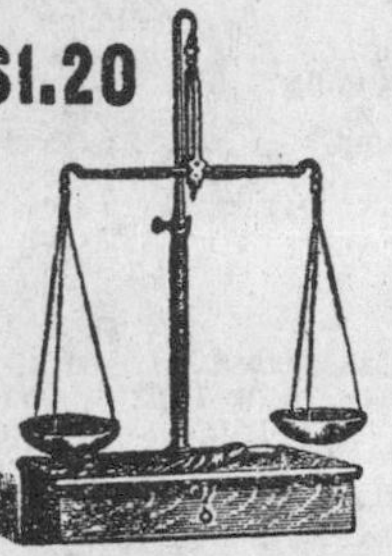

No. 20K1268 Our Imported Balance Scale, made in Germany, has 2¼-inch brass pans, brass pillar, 6-inch beam, and stands 12 inches high when set up for use. The entire scale packs away in the box on which it is set up, has complete set of weights from ½ grain to 2 drams and comes complete in oak box.
Price, complete $1.20
If by mail, postage extra, 13 cents.

Our Best Photo Scale.

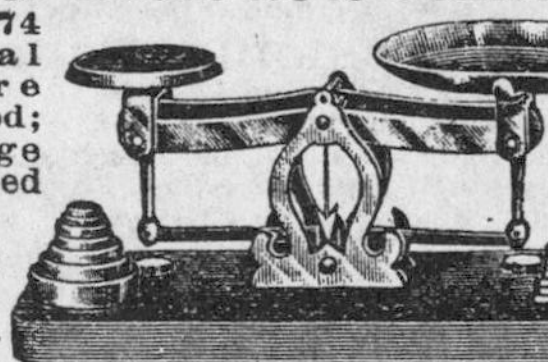

$2.10

No. 20K1274 All metal parts are nickel plated; it has large nickel plated pan, 3⅛ in. in diameter; it is very sensitive, finely finished, accurately adjusted and durable. Two complete sets of weights are included, one set of avoirdupois, $\frac{1}{16}$ of an ounce to 2 ounces, and one set of dram, scruple and grain weights.
Price, complete $2.10
If by mail, postage extra, 22 cents.

Special Composition Trays.

10c

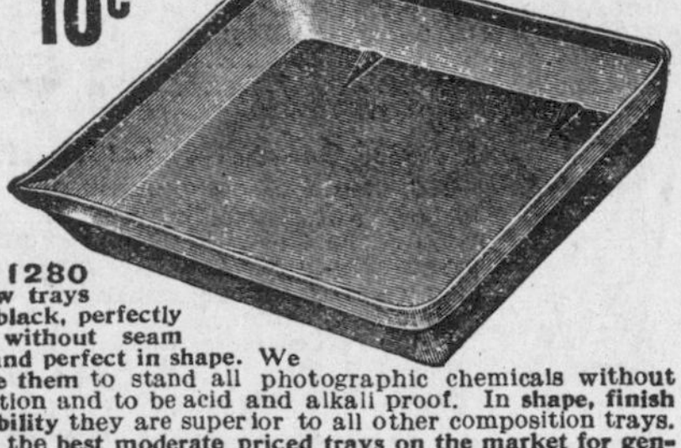

No. 20K1280 These new trays are jet black, perfectly smooth, without seam or joint and perfect in shape. We guarantee them to stand all photographic chemicals without deterioration and to be acid and alkali proof. **In shape, finish and durability** they are superior to all other composition trays. **They are the best moderate priced trays on the market for general purposes,** developing negatives, toning, washing prints, etc.

For plates 3½x3½ or 3¼x4¼. Price, each ..10c
For plates 4x5 inches. Price, each 11c
For plates 5x7 inches. Price, each 21c
For plates 5x8 inches. Price, each 23c
For plates 6½x8½ inches. Price, each 32c
For plates 8x10 inches. Price, each 47c

You can save time in the darkroom by using large trays. For example, you can develop two 4x5 plates at once in a 5x8 tray, and two 5x7 or four 4x5 plates in an 8x10 tray.

Best Grade Elite Enameled Steel Trays.

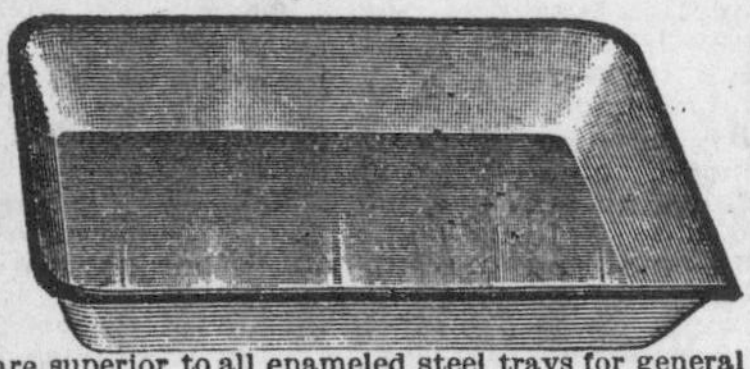

No. 20K1287 Genuine Imported Elite Steel Ware Trays for photographic use; guaranteed to be absolutely chemical proof. These trays are superior to all enameled steel trays for general all around purposes. They are equally well adapted to developing and fixing plates, toning prints and washing. **They are as easily cleaned as a porcelain tray.** They are absolutely proof against the action of all chemicals, including the most powerful acids. They are made in one solid piece, without joints or seams, and are practically unbreakable. The Elite steel trays are underglazed and quadruple coated; guaranteed to be the very finest tray that can be produced. Be sure to state size wanted.

For plates, inches	4x5	5x7	6½x8½	8x10
Price	21c	44c	65c	96c
For plates, inches	10x12	11x14	12x16	14x17
Price	$1.44	$1.92	$2.25	$3.25
For plates, inches			16x20	18x22
Price			$3.85	$5.45

The large sizes are fine for toning.

Porcelain Trays.

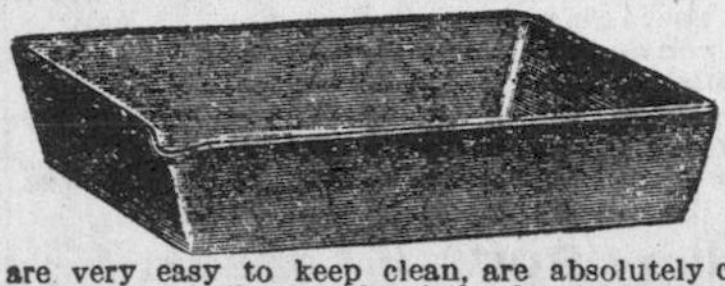

No. 20K1289 Porcelain Trays, the best grade of imported white porcelain, extra deep. These trays are very easy to keep clean, are absolutely chemical proof, and are generally considered the finest trays made for toning and other work. Be sure to state size wanted.

For plates, inches	4x5	5x7	5x8	6½x8½	8x10
Price	40c	52c	63c	68c	85c

Developing Tank for Films, 88c.

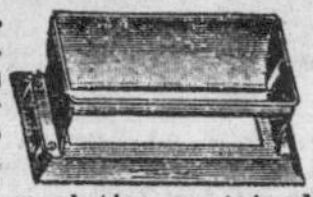

No. 20K1295 Developing Tank for developing roll films. This device consists of a tank 7 inches long by 4 inches wide, with a nickel plated metal rod extended lengthwise of the tank in such a manner that the end of a strip of film can be slipped under the roller and the film drawn up and down through the developing solution contained in the tank. This tank not only makes the developing of roll film in strips very easy and insures good results, but at the same time it is very economical, as the amount of developing solution required in a tank of this design is much less than would be used with an ordinary tray. Strongly and substantially made throughout of metal, and nickel plated.
Price 88c

Rubber Finger Tips, 9 Cents.

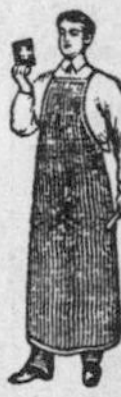

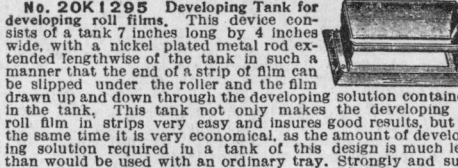

No. 20K1309 Rubber Finger Tips, made of pure rubber, put up in sets of three; prevents staining the fingers when developing, etc. Price, per set 9c
If by mail, postage extra, 1 cent.

Rubber Aprons, 39 Cents.

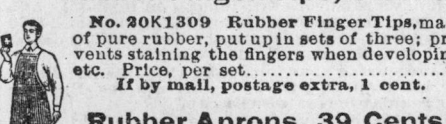

No. 20K1312 Rubber Aprons. Made especially for photographers; protect the clothing from chemical stains and dirt of all kinds. Length, 40 inches. Price 39c

Fixing Baths.

25c

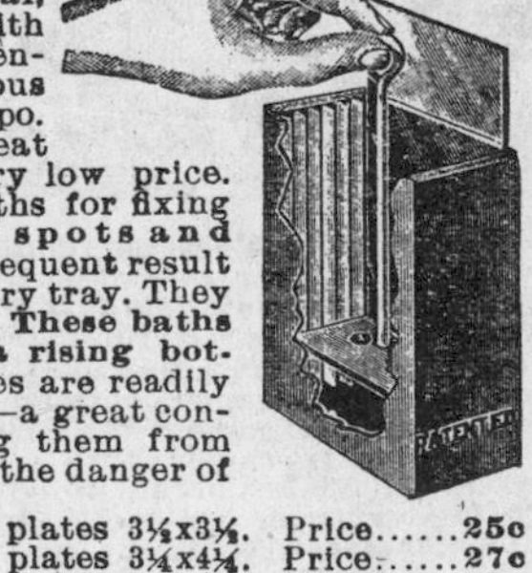

These Fixing Baths are made of metal, thoroughly coated with a preparation which renders them impervious to the action of hypo. They are a very great convenience at a very low price. The use of these baths for fixing **avoids the danger of spots and stains,** which is the frequent result of fixing in the ordinary tray. They hold six plates each. **These baths are provided with a rising bottom,** so that the plates are readily raised above the top—a great convenience in removing them from the box and avoiding the danger of scratching

No. 20K1316 For plates 3¼x3¼. Price 25c
No. 20K1317 For plates 3¼x4¼. Price 27c
No. 20K1318 For plates 4x5. Price 30c
No. 20K1319 For plates 5x7 or 5x8. Price 42c
If by mail, postage extra, 9, 9, 10 and 17 cents.

Folding Negative Rack.

12c

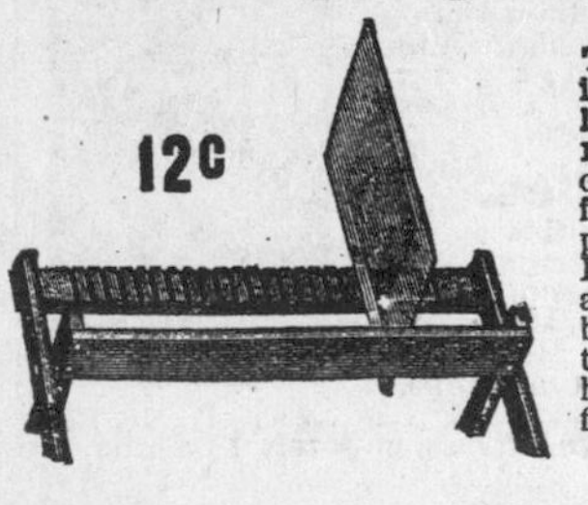

No. 20K1365 This negative drying rack is strongly and neatly made, folds up compactly and is by far the best low priced rack made. It will hold 24 negatives and is suitable for any size up to 8x10. Made of hardwood, oil finished.
Price 12c

Zinc Washing Box.

78c

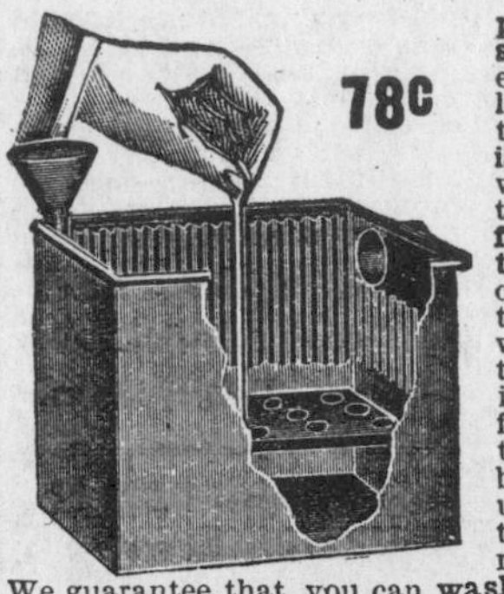

This washer is perfect in its construction. The water enters through the inlet tube and is carried to the bottom, and is circulated over the whole area of the box, thus **insuring uniform washing of the plates.** It is carried off through the outlet tube. The water can be carried to the box by attaching a rubber hose from the faucet to the inlet tube, or the box can be placed under the faucet and the water allowed to run into the funnel.

We guarantee that you can **wash twenty 4x5 negatives in fifteen minutes** in our washer.

The corrugations are extra deep and extend from the top downward, as will be seen in the illustration. One of the many good qualities and one that has greatly been the means of making our washer celebrated, is our **patent lifting bottom;** by means of the rod in the center, the perforated bottom can be lifted up as high as the bottom of the corrugations, which brings the plates above the top of the box so that they can be held by the edge, thus **removing all danger of scratching the films.**

Where running water cannot be procured, this is still the **"Ideal Washer."** It will be seen that the inlet tube enters from the top, which allows the box to remain full of water, so that by filling and emptying the box a few times and allowing several minutes between each operation, plates can be thoroughly washed.

This washer is **constructed of heavy zinc throughout.** The lifting bottom can be taken out if necessary.

No. 20K1344 For plates 3½x3½, or 3¼x3¼. Price $0.78
No. 20K1345 For plates 4x5 and 5x7. Price 83
No. 20K1346 For plates 3¼x4¼, 4¼x4¼, or 4¼x6½. Price 85
No. 20K1347 For plates 5x7 and 6½x8½. Price 1.18
No. 20K1348 For plates 6½x8½ and 8x10. Price 1.35
No. 20K1349 Rubber Hose, suitable for attaching these boxes to hydrant. Price, per foot 08

Amateur Printing Frames.

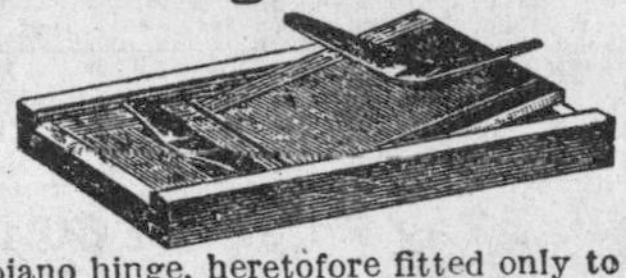

Light Weight Printing Frame. The best light weight frame made and a great improvement over the ordinary style. A special point of advantage is the piano hinge, heretofore fitted only to the highest priced frames, giving strength and durability. The finish throughout is good. Be sure to state size wanted.

No. 20K1410 Amateur Printing Frames, without glass.

Size, inches	2½x2½	3½x3½	3¼x4¼
Price	10c	11c	12c
Size, inches	4x5	3⅝x6	5x7
Price	13c	14c	17c

The 3⅝x6 frame is used for printing post cards from negatives 3¼x5½ inches or smaller.

No. 20K1411 Amateur Printing Frames, with glass.

Size, inches	2½x2½	3½x3½	3¼x4¼
Price	12c	13c	14c
Size, inches	4x5	3⅝x6	5x7
Price	16c	18c	22c

Glass in a printing frame is necessary when printing from glass negatives smaller than the frame, and in all cases when printing from film negatives. We furnish only the best imported glass.

Professional Printing Frames.

24c

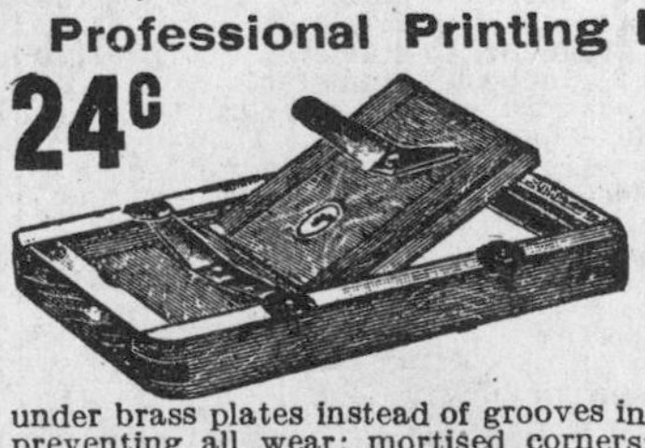

Heavy Weight Printing Frames. The finest printing frame manufactured; strongly and substantially constructed throughout, heavy brass springs sliding under brass plates instead of grooves in the wood, thus preventing all wear; mortised corners; back in three pieces to prevent warping; finished throughout in the best possible manner. **It pays to get good printing frames, and these frames are the best made.**

No. 20K1415 Professional Printing Frames, without glass.

Size, inches	3¼x4¼	4x5	4¼x6½	5x7	5x8
Price	24c	25c	28c	33c	35c
Size, inches	6½x8½	8x10	10x12	11x14	14x17
Price	40c	50c	83c	$1.20	$1.50

No. 20K1416 Professional Printing Frames, with glass.

Size, inches	3¼x4¼	4x5	4¼x6½	5x7
Price	26c	28c	32c	38c
Size, inches		5x8	6½x8½	8x10
Price		41c	48c	61c

Glass in printing frame is necessary when printing from film negatives, also when using glass negatives that are smaller than the frame. Our frames are fitted with the finest imported glass, guaranteed absolutely free from blemishes of any kind.

PRINT WASHERS

THIS PRINT WASHER is so constructed that prints are kept thoroughly separated and constantly in motion without requiring any attention whatever during the entire process of washing. The eccentric motion that is imparted to the water within the washer has the peculiar faculty of keeping the prints separate from each other all the time and keeping them in constant motion and always in contact with fresh water. This Print Washer not only saves a great deal of work, as the process of washing by the old methods is a long, tiresome and tedious one, but at the same time it insures better results. Prints that are not thoroughly washed will not be permanent, and are certain to fade and discolor within a short time. With this Print Washer the prints are always thoroughly washed, and the washing is done with the least possible trouble and labor.

No. 20K1360 For prints 4x5 or smaller, 9 inches in diameter. Price..................$1.12
No. 20K1362 For prints 5x7 or smaller, 12 inches in diameter. Price................. 1.55
No. 20K1363 For prints 6½x8½ or smaller, 16 inches in diameter. Price............... 2.70
No. 20K1364 For prints 8x10 or smaller, 20 inches in diameter. Price............... 3.85

DEVELOPING TANKS

FOR AUTOMATIC DAYLIGHT DEVELOPMENT OF GLASS PLATE NEGATIVES.

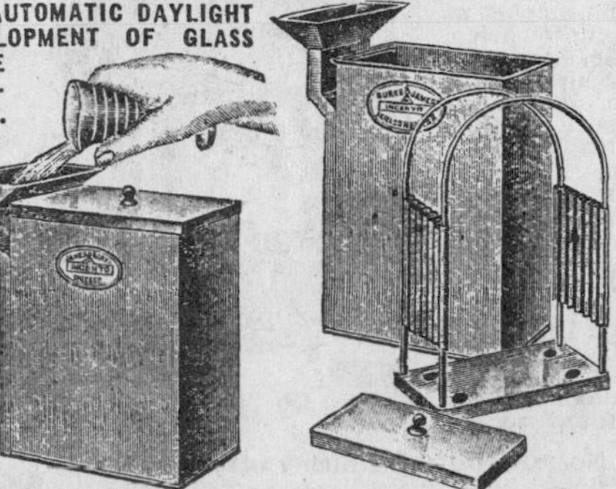

THE DEVELOPING TANK. The process of developing a plate with this tank is exceedingly simple, and the results obtained are as good, if not better than can be obtained by the old process of developing in a tray in a dark room. The exposed plates are transferred from the plate holder to the developing tank in the dark room or in a changing bag, after which the tank can be carried out into ordinary light, developer poured in through the funnel, and at the end of fifteen or twenty minutes the plates will be fully developed and can then be fixed and washed in the ordinary manner. This tank can be used only for developing, as zinc will not stand the action of hypo. The brass tank listed below can be used for both developing and fixing, as it is made of brass, heavily nickel plated, and will stand the action of any chemicals used either in developing or fixing.

No. 20K1371 Zinc Tank for plates, 3¼ x4¼ inches or lantern slides. Price.....................$0.80
No. 20K1372 Zinc Tank for plates, 4x5. Price.... .85
No. 20K1373 Zinc Tank for plates, 5x7. Price.... 1.17
No. 20K1374 Zinc Tank for plates, 6½x8½. Price.. 1.50
No. 20K1375 Zinc Tank for plates, 8x10. Price.. 1.68

NICKEL PLATED BRASS DEVELOPING TANK. This tank is made upon exactly the same principle as the zinc tank just described, but is constructed throughout from brass heavily nickel plated, therefore permitting the use of hypo in the tank as well as the developing solution. The plates are placed in this tank in the dark room or in a changing bag, if a dark room is not accessible, the developer poured in, and at the end of fifteen or twenty minutes the plates are fully developed. The developer can then be poured off, and the tank filled with Hypo solution for fixing. This tank used in connection with the changing bag listed below makes it possible to perform the entire process of developing and fixing a glass plate negative by daylight. With an equipment consisting of this Automatic Daylight Developing Tank and the Changing Bag listed below, negatives can be made at any time and in any place without using a dark room at all. Any developer can be used, but it is customary to make it a little weaker by adding more water than when developing in the ordinary manner in a tray. Full instructions are sent with each outfit so that the length of time required with any strength of developer will be accurately known, and there is thus no necessity for examining the plates during the process of development.

No. 20K1376 Brass Tank for plates, 3¼x4¼ inches or lantern slides. Price.....................$1.73
No. 20K1377 Brass Tank for plates, 4x5. Price.... 1.80
No. 20K1378 Brass Tank for plates, 5x7. Price.... 2.63
No. 20K1379 Brass Tank for plates, 6½x8½. Price 2.98
No. 20K1380 Brass Tank for plates, 8x10. Price.. 3.95

DEVELOPING POWDER

FOR AUTOMATIC TANK DEVELOPMENT, 20 CENTS.

No. 20K1381 Tank Developing Powder put up in packages of six powders, each powder sufficient to make eighteen ounces of developer, or a total for the package of one hundred and eight ounces. Price, per package (six powders sufficient for one hundred and eight ounces of developer..**20c** If by mail, postage extra, 3 cents.

CHANGING BAG

This is an exceedingly well made, perfectly light tight and easily handled Changing Bag. It is made from a fine quality of black sateen lined with the best black rubber cloth, making an absolutely light tight bag. By means of this bag plate holders can be loaded at any time in daylight, the bag being opened at the bottom, the box of plates and the plate holders placed inside, and the bag then closed up. The hands are then placed through the arm holes, and the plates can be easily removed from the box and put into the plate holders without the slightest danger of injury by light. Equipped with one of these Changing Bags and the Automatic Brass Developing Tank described above, the holders can be loaded and the plates developed without the use of a dark room at all.

Price
No. 20K1385 Suitable for plates 4x5 or smaller $1.10
No. 20K1386 Suitable for plates 5x7 or smaller.... 1.40
No. 20K1387 Suitable for plates 6½x8½ or smaller.. 1.50
No. 20K1388 Suitable for plates 8x10 or smaller.... 2.10

BACKGROUNDS

OUR BACKGROUNDS ARE ALL PAINTED IN OIL ON FINE MUSLIN, perfectly waterproof, and will not crack; practically indestructible. Do not compare our grounds with water color grounds or distemper, which are ruined if touched by water and can hardly be handled without cracking. A secret process known only to the painter who makes our backgrounds, enables him to get a perfect dull or dead finished surface in oil, making an ideal background, crackproof, waterproof and photographically correct.

CLOUDED HEADGROUNDS.

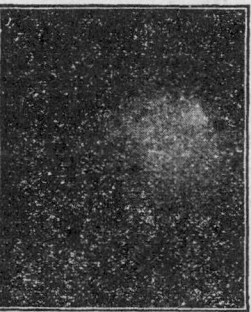
Clouded Design No. 40.

Clouded Design No. 41.

Clouded Design No. 42.

No. 20K1650 The above headgrounds, in clouded designs, Nos. 40, 41 and 42, are especially suitable for bust pictures, although the larger sizes, 5x7 and 6x8, are extensively used for full figure work and small groups. Very artistic, up to date grounds, giving the soft, shadowy effects so desirable in portrait work. Painted in oil on the best muslin. No better headgrounds are made at any price. State whether you want design No. 40, 41 or 42. These grounds are suitable for either right or left light, and several different effects can be obtained by using the ground in different positions. Be sure to state size wanted.

Size, 4x4 feet. Price.....$0.75
Size, 5x6 feet. Price.... 1.00
Size, 5x7 feet. Price.... 1.35
Size, 6x8 feet. Price.... 1.98

SPECIAL COLORED HEADGROUND.

No. 20K1655 This is a special design, made expressly for us and painted in colors; green, salmon, black and white, producing a most pleasing appearance and giving the most perfect photographic quality. This ground is painted on the best grade of muslin, perfectly waterproof and guaranteed not to crack. Made in two sizes only. Be sure to state size wanted.

Design No. 60.
Size, 5x6 feet. Price......... $1.50
Size, 6x8 feet. Price.......... 2.50

Headground No. 60.

BLACK AND BLUE-WHITE GROUNDS.

No. 20K1660 These perfectly plain, flat tinted backgrounds are the very latest and most up to date grounds for portrait work. They are suitable both for indoor and outdoor use, make splendid grounds for the use of amateur photographers and are extensively used by the most up to date professional photographers in the large cities.

The blue-white ground photographs almost white, having just enough tint in it to afford a little contrast with white draperies, and is the best color to use if the pictures are to be vignetted. The black ground is a perfect dead black and is particularly desirable when making portraits with Rembrandt lighting. Be sure to state size wanted.

Size, 5x 6 feet. Price.....................$1.00
Size, 6x 8 feet. Price..................... 2.00
Size, 8x10 feet. Price..................... 5.25
Size, 8x15 feet. With floor extension. Price. 6.90

SCENIC BACKGROUNDS.

Scenic Design No. 1.

Scenic Design No. 10.

Scenic Design No. 5.

Scenic Design No. 7.

No. 20K1665 The above illustrations show our line of scenic backgrounds, painted expressly for us, the very latest and most artistic designs, painted in oil, on the best grade of muslin, guaranteed to be waterproof, will not crack, and will stand more rough handling than any other grounds made.

Size, 6x 8 feet. Price.....................$ 3.90
Size, 8x 8 feet. Price..................... 4.60
Size, 8x10 feet. Price..................... 5.80
Size, 8x15 feet. With Floor Extension. Price.. 7.50
Size, 10x15 feet. With Floor Extension. Price.. 9.30
Size, 12x15 feet. With Floor Extension. Price.. 11.80

State size, design, and which side light falls on when ordering. If light falls on right side of sitter, when sitter is in position, it is "right light." Right light falls on left side of operator when operator faces sitter. Do not judge these backgrounds by the prices we ask for them. There are no better grounds painted at any price.

FREE REMEMBER, with every order for photographic goods amounting to $2.50 or more we will send you, without charge (if you ask for it) our big 112-page "COMPLETE INSTRUCTIONS IN PHOTOGRAPHY." See page 683 for description of this book.

Masks, 19 Cents.

Every package contains a large assortment of fancy and novel designs.

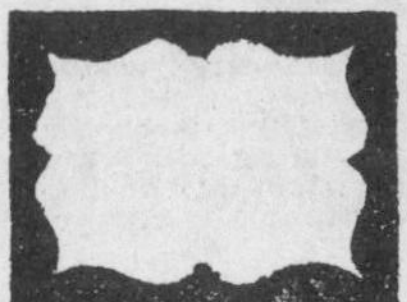

A NECESSARY ADDITION TO ANY PHOTOGRAPHIC OUTFIT.

Made from tough opaque paper, and designed to be placed between negative and sensitized paper while printing, thus producing oval, circular or various fancy shaped prints from any negative. The illustration shows only one of the many sizes of styles. Made for the following negatives: 2¼x3¼, 3½x3½, 3¼x4¼, 4¼x4¼, 4x5 and 5x7.

No. 20K1425 Masks. Assortment No. 1 contains one oval, one circle, one rectangle, one round corner rectangle, the balance being a variety of ornamental designs. Price, per package, any size....19c

No. 20K1426 Masks. Assortment No. 2 composed entirely of ornamental designs, all different from Assortment No. 1.
Price, per package, any size....19c
If by mail, postage extra, any size, 2 cents;
Be sure to state size wanted.

Print Trimmers, 14c to 19c.

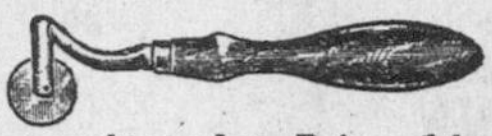

No. 20K1435 Straight Trimmers, for trimming prints; the cutting knife is a small wheel which revolves and leaves very clean edge. Price..14c
If by mail, postage extra, 3 cents.

No. 20K1436 Extra wheels, each....8c

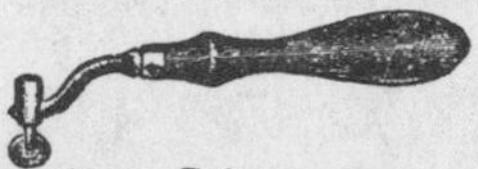

No. 20K1438 Swivel Trimmers, same as No. 20K1435, but cutting wheel is swivel mounted and can follow curved surface. Price....16c
If by mail, postage extra, 3 cents.

No. 20K1439 Extra wheels, each....8c
NOTE—Prints must be laid on a sheet of metal or piece of glass when using above trimmers or the rotary trimmer described below.

No. 20K1446 Rotary Trimmer, for trimming round, oval or square prints; ball bearing knife, easily and quickly changed; a perfect cutter; very handy; can be carried in vest pocket. Price...19c
If by mail, postage extra, 2 cents.

No. 20K1447 Extra Knives for No. 20K1446, regular style. Price...11c

No. 20K1448 Mask Knives, for above rotary trimmer, with shoulder constructed so that a white margin can be left around print. Price....15c

Trimming Forms, 14 Cents.

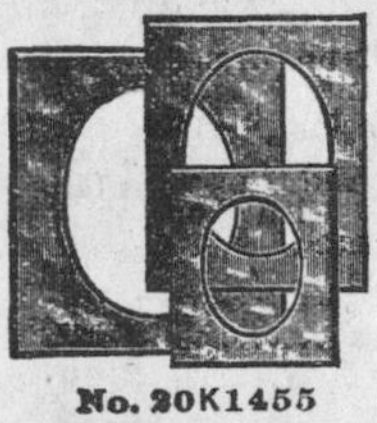

No. 20K1455

No. 20K1455 Perfectly made steel trimming forms, with copper oxidized finish. Be sure to state size wanted.

Size		Size
No. 0. Oval...1⅜x2	A.	Oval...1 7/16x2 7/16 inches
No. 1. Oval...2x2¾, ¼ Cab.	B.	Oval...1⅞x3⅛ inches
No. 2. Oval...3x4 1/16, ¾ Cab.	C.	Oval...2 9/16x5 1/16 inches
No. 3. Oval...3 7/16x4, 15/16 Cab.	D.	Oval...1⅜x2 11/16 inches
No. 4. Oval...2 5/16x3 7/16	E.	Oval...2¼x4 inches
No. 5. Oval...3¾x5¾	F.	Oval...2½x5 1/16 inches
No. 6. Oval...4¼x6	G.	Oval...2⅛x5⅝ inches
No. 9. Circle...2⅜ inches	H.	Oval...1 13/16x3 9/16 inches
No. 10. Circle...3 inches	J.	Oval...2¾x5 3/16 inches
No. 11. Circle...3¼ inches	K.	Oval...3 1/16x6⅜ inches
	L.	Oval...1⅞x2 11/16 inches
	M.	Oval...2½x3½, ½ Cab.

Price, each, any size....14c
Be sure to state size wanted.

Trimming Boards, 42 Cents.

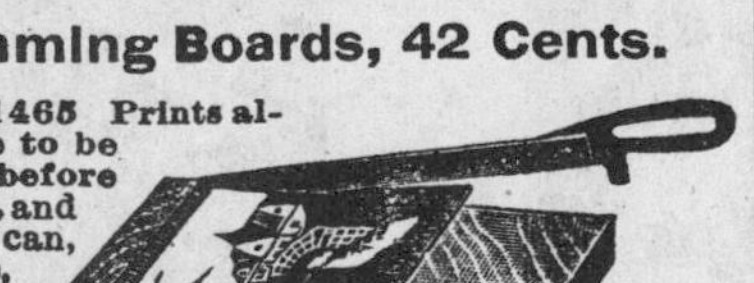

No. 20K1465 Prints always have to be trimmed before mounting, and while this can, of course, be done fairly well with scissors or knife, at the same time the advantages of a regular trimmer as here illustrated will be readily apparent. **It trims the prints quickly, easily and squarely.** The blade is made of finest tempered steel, the board of polished hardwood, has graduated measure which also serves as guide for the paper. Our illustration shows way in which this trimmer is used. Trims any size up to and including 4x5. Price....42c

No. 20K1466 Trimming Board, same as No. 20K1465, **but** larger, suitable for prints up to 5x7. Price....60c

No. 20K1467 Trimming Board, same as No. 20K1465, but with 10¼-inch blade, suitable for any size **up to and including 8x10.** Price....$1.15

ALWAYS GIVE CATALOGUE NUMBER IN FULL AND SIZE WHEN YOU WRITE YOUR ORDER.

Our Best Trimming Board.

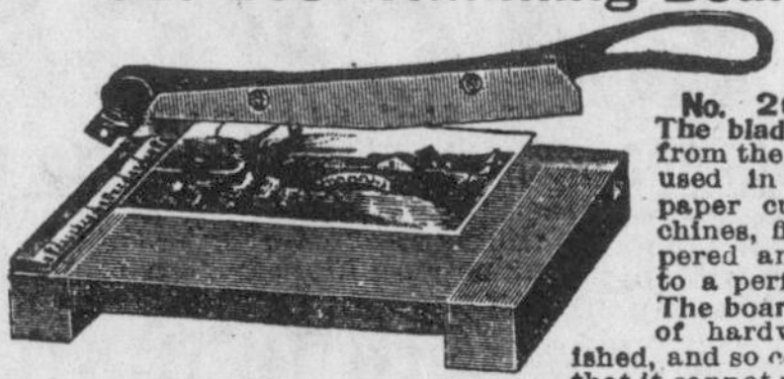

No. 20K1472 The blade is made from the same steel used in the best paper cutting machines, finely tempered and ground to a perfect edge. The board is made of hardwood, polished, and so constructed that it cannot warp. The spring joint, by which the blade is attached, allows a slight lateral motion, so that the two cutting edges are in perfect contact at every point, insuring perfect, clean cut edges to either cards or paper. The illustration shows method of trimming a print.

Length of blade, inches	6¼	8½	10½	12½
Price	95c	$1.30	$1.55	$2.10

Centering Square, 22 Cents.

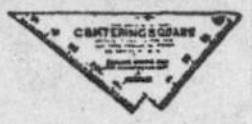

No. 20K1480 Centering Square. A novel device by means of which photographic prints can be instantly and accurately centered on the card mount. Everyone knows how difficult it is to put the pictures square on the card sometimes, and this little device overcomes all this trouble, resulting in much better looking pictures. Made of brass, nickel plated, full instructions with each one. Price...22c

Push Pins, 18 Cents.

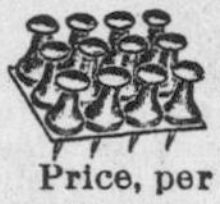

No. 20K1485 Push Pins. For hanging up films and prints to dry, strong, sharp pointed steel pins with large, substantial heads. A great convenience for any photographer.
Price, per box of 12 pins....18c

Print Rollers, 12c.

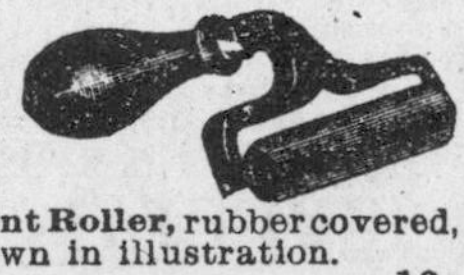

Indispensable for smoothing down prints after mounting and for squeegeeing prints on ferrotype plates.

No. 20K1490 4-inch Print Roller, rubber covered, large wood handle, as shown in illustration.
Price....12c

No. 20K1491 6-inch Print Roller, rubber covered, large wood handle, as shown in illustration.
Price....16c

Photo Paste in Jars, 9c.

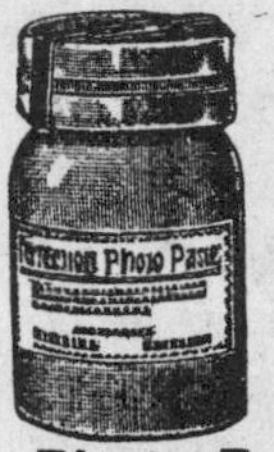

No. 20K1506 Perfection Photo Paste. The most perfect paste ever made for mounting photographs. It is always ready for use, of great adhesive power and will not mold, sour or deteriorate in any way. The Perfection Paste is a purely vegetable paste, containing no acids or other ingredients injurious to photographs.

Price, 4-ounce jar....9c
Price, 8-ounce jar....14c
Price, 16-ounce jar....28c
Price, 32-ounce jar....48c
Unmailable on account of weight.

Photo Paste in Tubes, 4 Cents.

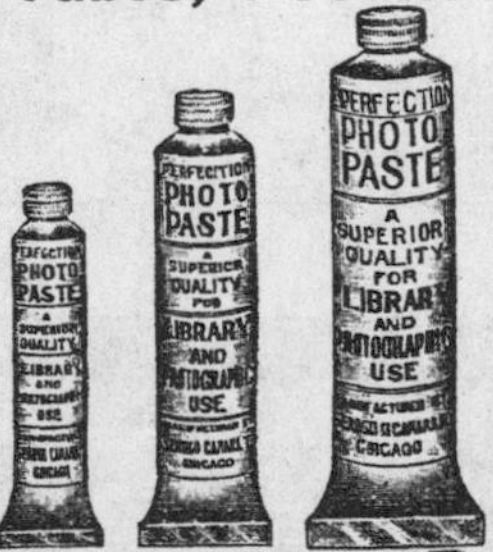

No. 20K1510 This Paste is the same as described under No. 20K1506, but is put up in collapsible soft tin tubes. Paste put up in this way never gets hard or dry and is always ready for use.
Price, 1-ounce tube..4c
If by mail, postage extra, 5 cents.
Price, 2-ounce tube..6c
If by mail, postage extra, 7 cents.
Price, 4-ounce tube..9c
Postage extra, 14c.

Brushes.

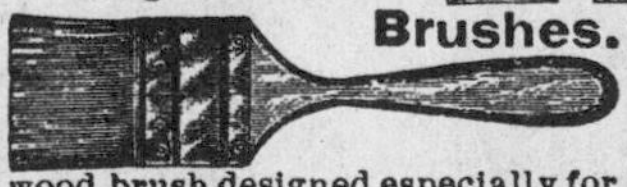

No. 20K1518 Bristle Brushes for pasting; an exceptionally well made wood brush designed especially for photographic use, handle, tin bound. Be sure to state size wanted.

1 inch wide	3c	2½ inches wide	9c
1½ inches wide	4c	3 inches wide	11c
2 inches wide	6c		

No. 20K1519 Camel's Hair Brushes, tin bound, wood handles. The very finest and softest camel's hair brushes made, guaranteed not to scratch the surface of a dry plate. Used for dusting plates before placing in holder, dusting negatives, etc. Cheaper brushes cannot be safely used on the sensitive film of a plate.

1 inch wide	14c	2½ inches wide	36c
1½ inches wide	20c	3 inches wide	46c
2 inches wide	25c		

Blotting Paper, 8c per Dozen.

No. 20K1526 Photographers' Blotting Paper, for mounting prints. Chemically pure and perfectly lintless. Be sure to state size wanted.
Price, 9x12 inches, per dozen....8c
Price, 20x24 inches, per dozen....29c
If by mail, postage extra, per dozen, 10c and 35c.

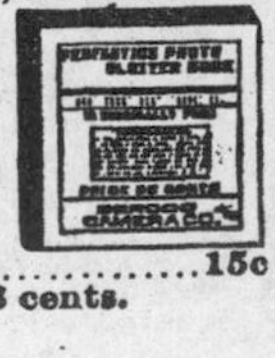

No. 20K1527 Perfection Blotter Book. A very handy device for drying prints perfectly flat. This book consists of 12 sheets of chemically pure, lintless blotting paper, 9x12 inches, interleaved with a fine quality of wax paper, bound in heavy manila, with leatherette back.
Price....15c
If by mail, postage extra, 13 cents.

Squeegee Plates, 4c.

No. 20K1546 Ferrotype Plates, extra fine quality, for squeegeeing or producing a glossy finish without burnishing. Be sure to state size wanted.
Size, 5x7 inches. Price....4c
Size, 7x10 inches. Price....7c
Size, 10x14 inches. Price....9c
If by mail, postage extra, 4, 7 and 12 cents, according to size.

Extra Heavy Squeegee Plates.

No. 20K1547 Extra Heavy Squeegee Plates, very fine quality, made in 10x14-inch size only. Price, 19c
If by mail, postage extra, 16 cents.

Burnishers.

Amateur Burnishers, the only thoroughly practical oil heating, double roller burnishers yet placed on the market at a low price. **They are thoroughly well made** in every respect, simple, clean, economical and safe. Make your outfit complete by adding one of these excellent machines. **Suitable also for regular professional use.**

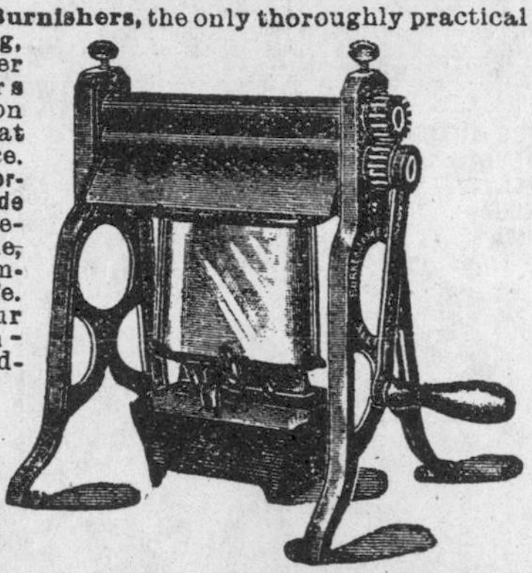

No. 20K1560 Burnisher with 6-inch roller. Price....$3.75
No. 20K1561 Burnisher with 8-inch roller. Price....4.50
No. 20K1562 Burnisher with 10-inch roller. Price....6.00
No. 20K1563 Burnisher with 12-inch roller. Price....7.50

Emboss Your Own Cards.

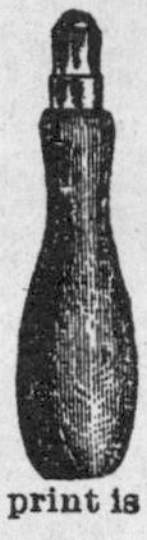

No. 20K1572 Embossing Tool, for making raised center mounts from ordinary plain cards. This tool is used in connection with above trimming forms. The card is simply laid on the form and the embosser, which consists of a very perfect steel ball, mounted in the end of a substantial handle, is run around the edge of the form with sufficient pressure to depress the cardboard. It works perfectly with any kind of plain cardboard. The card, of course, is embossed with the same form used to trim the prints, consequently oval prints of any size may be made without investing in a large assortment of embossed cards, and the print is sure to fit the embossing.
Price....65c
If by mail, postage extra, 3 cents.

Retouching Goods.

No. 20K1580 A. W. Faber's Pencils. The best pencils in the world for retouching; any degree of hardness; 3-H sent unless otherwise ordered.
Price, per dozen, 90c; each....8c

No. 20K1585 Sable Brushes. For spotting; polished cedar handles; nickel plated ferrules; Nos. 1 to 6. Price....5c

No. 20K1587 India Ink. Lion Head brand; for spotting. Price, per stick....9c

No. 20K1589 Spotting Colors. Set of three improved spotting colors on celluloid sheets, suitable for any kind of paper; very handy. Price....12c

No. 20K3326 Retouching Glass, 4 inches in diameter; highest grade manufactured; very powerful; nickel plated rim; black wood handle. Price..$1.25

No. 20K3309 Retouching Glass, 4 inches in diameter, ordinary quality, **same as the regular photo supply houses furnish.** Price....70c

No. 20K1595 Calcined Flour. A retouching medium for producing a fine matte surface on negatives so they will take the pencil readily and smoothly. **Guaranteed not to scratch.** Price, per can, 25c

No. 20K1597 Retouching Varnish or Dope. A fine retouching medium, suited to either hard or soft pencil. Price, per bottle....15c

No. 20K1599 Retouching Frame. Fitted with adjustable reflector, ground glass and drawer for pencils. **Folds compactly when not in use.** For 8x10 or smaller. Price....$2.30

No. 20K901 "Retouching Negatives and Prints." A complete guide to retouching, describing all the various methods and explaining everything very fully. Price, per copy....25c

MAKE YOUR ORDER for supplies amount to $2.50 and get free a copy of "Complete Instructions in Photography."

DU VOLL'S GELATINE PRINTING-OUT PAPER

AN IMPROVED FORM OF SEROCO PAPER ★ PRINTS BY SUNLIGHT

THE HIGHEST GRADE GELATINE PRINTING-OUT PAPER MADE

10c PER DOZEN IS OUR SPECIAL PRICE FOR THE 4x5 SIZE, OTHER SIZES IN PROPORTION.

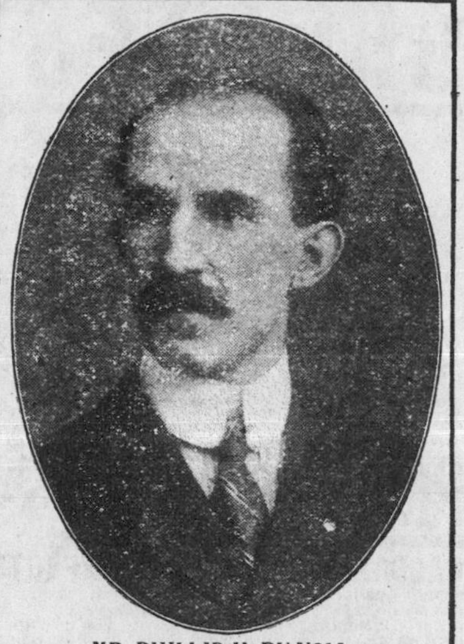

MR. PHILLIP H. DU VOLL.
Photograph made with No. 1 Conley View Camera.

"SEROCO" IS THE NAME under which we have sold our Gelatine Printing-out Paper for years and on which we have built up the largest business in printing-out paper in the world. "Seroco" paper was good paper. Apparently it possessed all of the qualities that the ideal printing-out paper should possess, but **Mr. Phillip H. Du Voll showed us how even "Seroco" paper could be improved.** When Mr. Du Voll first told us that certain slight changes in the method of manufacture would improve this paper, we were skeptical. "Seroco" was good paper. We knew it was good paper, and we very much doubted the possibility of improving it, but the more we saw of Mr. Du Voll, the more respect we came to have for his opinion, and when he demonstrated that "Seroco" paper could be improved, we "got into line."

DU VOLL'S PAPER IS AN IMPROVED "SEROCO" PAPER.

It possesses all the good qualities of the original "Seroco" paper, and in addition its keeping qualities are better. It will keep in good usable condition longer than any other gelatine printing-out paper on the market, and even if kept until it becomes a little discolored with age, it will clear up in the process of toning and fixing and yield perfect prints. **Du Voll's paper gives even more detail** than the old "Seroco" paper, and, therefore, comes just a little nearer to getting absolutely everything there is in the negative. With Du Voll's paper the shadows are just as richly transparent, deep and brilliant, the half tones just as soft and full of detail, there is that same unequaled delicacy and gradation throughout the entire print that made "Seroco" paper famous, and **the range of tone is greater.** It tones easily and without loss of richness or gradation to any color, from a warm sepia to a deep blue black.

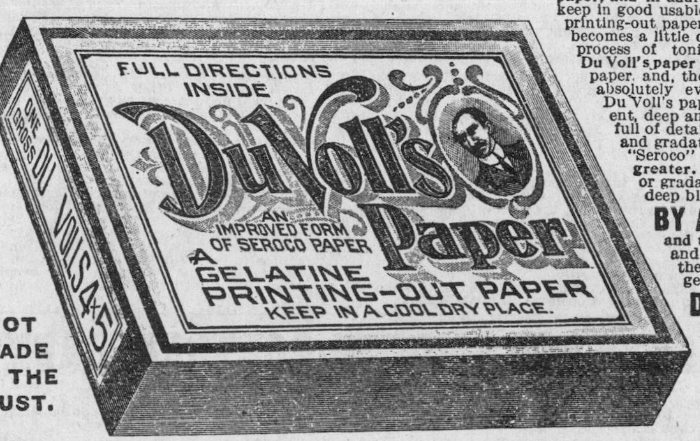
FULL DIRECTIONS INSIDE
ONE GROSS DU VOLL'S 4x5
Du Voll's Paper
AN IMPROVED FORM OF SEROCO PAPER
A GELATINE PRINTING-OUT PAPER
KEEP IN A COOL DRY PLACE.

NOT MADE BY THE TRUST.

BY A SPECIAL PROCESS the film or gelatine coating of Du Voll's paper is so thoroughly hardened and toughened that it retains its firmness throughout the operations of toning, fixing, and washing, **and yet it is not brittle.** This makes it an ideal paper for use in hot weather, as the softening of the film during manipulation, or the cracking of the film while printing, faults so common to other gelatine papers, are unknown with Du Voll's paper.

DU VOLL'S PAPER IS HANDLED JUST THE SAME AS "SEROCO" PAPER.

Remember, this new paper is simply an improved form of the old, well known proven and reliable "Seroco" paper. There are no changes whatever in the method of using this paper. If you already understand the working of "Seroco" paper, you will have nothing new to learn in using Du Voll's paper. It is printed by sunlight, toned, fixed and washed just exactly the same as "Seroco" paper.

AN EASY PAPER TO WORK. **Du Voll's paper is printed by sunlight and can be toned in an ordinary plain gold toning bath that anyone can make up without the slightest trouble.** After toning, the prints are fixed in a plain hypo bath, just a simple bath made by dissolving a little hypo in water, and after fixing, the prints are washed in plain water. This is known as the "separate toning and fixing" process, but if preferred, this paper may be worked by the "combined toning and fixing" process in which the prints are toned and fixed in one solution, this being the simplest and easiest method of working printing-out papers. The entire process of printing, toning, fixing and washing is exceedingly simple and easy. No dark room is required, and good results even in the hands of a beginner are certain. The tones which this paper will yield, even in the hands of inexperienced workers, are of unequaled brilliancy with rich transparent shadows, silky half tones, and a clearness in the high lights that is unsurpassed.

IMPORTED STOCK. **Sensitized papers are made by coating the paper itself, which is known as the raw stock, with a sensitive gelatine emulsion.** This process of coating the paper is one requiring the greatest skill, the utmost care and accuracy, and the most complete and perfect equipment in the way of special coating machines and other apparatus. Du Voll's paper is coated on the very best grade of genuine imported stock, the most expensive and highest grade stock that can be bought in Europe. In making the emulsion only the very best quality of imported gelatine, the highest grade gelatine that can be imported, a gelatine manufactured expressly for emulsion making is used, and all the other chemicals, the silver, the various salts of iodine and bromine are of the highest degree of purity, all made expressly for this paper by the best manufacturers in Germany.

RICH IN SILVER. **The most important ingredient of an emulsion for printing-out paper is the silver.** It is to silver that the paper owes its sensitiveness, and the results which a gelatine paper will yield depend in a very large measure upon the quantity and quality of silver present in the emulsion. If there is not enough silver, the prints will lack richness; they will be difficult to tone to an agreeable color, and the finished prints will lack permanency. Du Voll's paper is rich in silver, and yields prints that will surprise photographers who have been accustomed to cheaper and inferior papers.

MADE EXCLUSIVELY FOR US. **Du Voll's paper cannot be obtained from any other dealer.** It is made especially for us in one of the largest and most perfectly equipped sensitized paper factories in America, made under the supervision of one of the most expert and successful photographic paper makers in the world. This paper embodies the results of years of experience in the manufacture of sensitized products, combining the good qualities of all other gelatine printing-out papers with special qualities of its own, qualities possessed by no other gelatine printing-out paper. Du Voll's paper should not be compared with cheap, low priced printing-out papers. It is a high class product, a paper in the making of which no expense is spared. It is rich in silver. It is coated on the most expensive raw stock that can be imported, and all of the materials that enter into the emulsion are of the highest degree of purity. Imported stock, silver, extra quality gelatine and other chemically pure materials all cost money. The services of expert chemists and the thoroughly modern and up to date equipment of the factory in which this paper is coated also cost money. Du Voll's paper, as compared with other gelatine printing-out papers, is an expensive paper to produce, but our ability to handle merchandise on an exceedingly small margin of profit enables us to sell this paper, in spite of its high cost of production, at prices actually lower than other dealers are compelled to charge for papers of inferior quality.

EVERY SHEET GUARANTEED. **Du Voll's paper is carefully sorted and thoroughly examined before it is packed.** Every sheet is subjected to the most rigid scrutiny for blemishes or imperfections of any kind, and every sheet that we send out is positively perfect. We absolutely guarantee every sheet of Du Voll's paper to be first choice, first quality, carefully sorted, and every gross will yield 144 perfect prints.

PRICES.

No. 20K1702 Du Voll's Printing-Out Paper.

Size		Price per Dozen	Price per Gross
2½x 2½		$0.07	$0.68
3½x 3½		.09	.90
3¼x 4¼		.09	.90
4 x 5		.10	.97
3⅞x 5½	(Cabinet)	.11	.98
3¼x 5½	(3A Kodak)	.10	.85
3½x 6	(Stereo, diecut with arched tops)	.12	.95
4 x 6		.15	1.25
5 x 7		.23	2.12
5 x 8		.24	2.35
6 x 8		.30	2.90
6½x 8½		.33	3.10
7 x 9		.38	3.85
7½x 9½		.42	4.25
8 x10		.44	4.75
10 x12		.60	6.50
11 x14		.80	8.50
14 x17		1.20	12.75
20 x24		2.40	24.00
4 x 5	Seconds		.73
Cabinet Seconds			.80
10-foot rolls, 26 inches wide.	Price, each		1.25
10-yard rolls, 26 inches wide.	Price, each		3.20

Less than one gross is sold at dozen rate only. For example: One-half gross of 4x5 (which is 6 dozen) would cost 60 cents; (6 dozen at 10 cents per dozen), and not one-half of 97 cents. **We cannot violate this rule under any circumstances.**

AZURO BLUE PRINT PAPER.

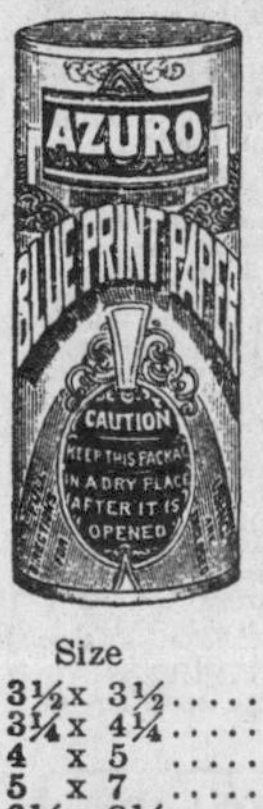
AZURO
BLUE PRINT PAPER
CAUTION
KEEP THIS PACKAGE IN A DRY PLACE AFTER IT IS OPENED

No. 20K1755 **Blue print paper affords the simplest process known for producing a photographic print.** It is exceedingly easy to manipulate, requires no toning nor fixing; in fact, no chemicals of any kind. It is printed by sunlight in the ordinary manner and then simply washed in clear water, which completes the process of making a finished blue print photograph. The prints are of a brilliant blue and white color, and the beautiful results, extreme simplicity and low cost make this paper a favorite with nearly all photographers.

Azuro Blue Print Paper is an unusually high grade blue paper, coated on the very best quality of imported stock, and prints made on this paper possess a brilliancy of tone, a depth of color, and a clearness and sharpness that is unequaled by any other blue print paper on the market.

Put up in hermetically sealed tin cans, 24 sheets to a can.

Size	Price, per can
3½x 3½	12c
3¼x 4¼	12c
4 x 5	15c
5 x 7	25c
6½x 8½	38c
8 x10	60c

BLUE PRINT SOUVENIR POSTAL CARDS.

No. 20K1757 Blue Print Postal Cards, because of their simplicity, have proven very popular, and they afford a most economical and easy method of making souvenir postal cards from your own negatives. These cards are the regulation postal card size and style, with space on one side for the address and the message, and sensitized on the other side. They are printed by sunlight, the same as any other style of blue print paper and finished by simply washing in plain water. No chemicals of any kind are required.

Put up in hermetically sealed tin cans, containing 12 cards in a can. Price, per can. **13c**
Postage extra, when sent by mail, 4 cents.

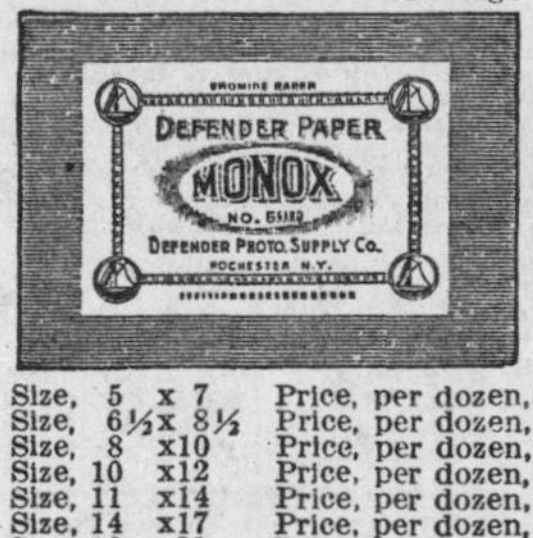
BROMIDE PAPER
DEFENDER PAPER
MONOX
DEFENDER PHOTO. SUPPLY CO.
ROCHESTER N.Y.

MONOX BROMIDE PAPER.

No. 20K1750 Monox Bromide Paper, made by the Defender Photo Supply Company, is a thoroughly reliable and uniform paper. It is noted for its soft beautiful blacks, deep, rich transparent shadows, and is unequaled in its class for detail. It is very rapid and gives a good sharp image. It has a brilliant and subtle individuality of its own that distinguishes it from all other bromide papers. There are no cold blue tones in Monox paper, no chalky whites, and no intense blacks. It is an ideal paper for making enlargements, and has been brought to such a state of perfection that it is also perfectly satisfactory for contact printing.

Size	Price, per dozen	per half gross	per gross
Size, 5 x 7	$0.22	$1.27	$2.44
Size, 6½x 8½	.41	2.18	4.12
Size, 8 x10	.53	3 10	6.00
Size, 10 x12	.82	4.80	9.00
Size, 11 x14	1.05	6.00	11.55
Size, 14 x17	1.61	9.38	18.00
Size, 16 x20	2.10	12.00	23.62
Size, 20 x24	3.15	18.75	36.00

GREATEST OF DEVELOPING PAPERS

PRINTS AT NIGHT

CARBON MATTE, ROUGH, GLOSSY AND SMOOTH PORTRAIT DARKO

PRICES ON CARBON MATTE, ROUGH, GLOSSY AND SMOOTH PORTRAIT DARKO

ORDER BY CATALOGUE NUMBER AS SHOWN ABOVE.

Size	Dozen	Half gross	Gross	Size	Dozen	Half gross	Gross	Size	Dozen	Half gross	Gross
3½ x 3½	8c	$0.46	$0.87	5 x 7	16c	$.91	$1.73	8 x 10	40c	$2.28	$4.32
3¼ x 4¼	9c	.52	.98	5 x 8	19c	1.09	2.06	3½ x 6 (Die-cut, with arched			
3¼ x 5½ (3A Kodak)	10c	.58	1.12	6 x 8	26c	1.44	2.85	tops, for stereoscopic			
4 x 5	10c	.57	1.08	6½ x 8½	29c	1.66	3.14	pictures) made in			
3⅞ x 5½ (Cabinet)	11c	.63	1.19	7 x 9	33c	1.80	3.45	glossy only	14c	.68	1.30
4 x 6	13c	.74	1.41	7½ x 9½	36c	1.95	3.75	Order by the gross; it will keep good for months.			

BRILLIANT DARKO.

CARDBOARD DARKO.

SILVERED DARKO.

SEE NEXT PAGE FOR THE NEW INDIA-TINT DARKO AND THE DARKO POSTAL CARDS

INDIA-TINT DARKO.

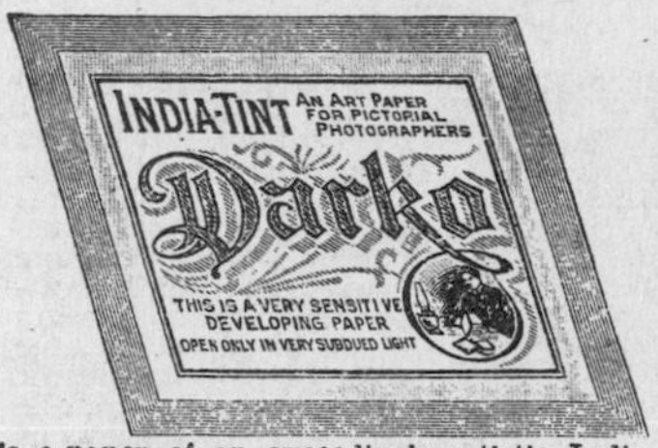

No. 20K1728 INDIA-TINT DARKO is an art paper, an entirely new idea in sensitized papers, and its unusually artistic qualities add greatly to the possibilities in real pictorial photography. India-Tint Darko is coated on a special India tint stock, that is, a paper of an exceedingly artistic India tint color. The surface is rough. It is especially suited to landscapes, interiors, figure studies and portraits. It is a paper that will meet with the approval of real artists, and is entirely different from any other sensitized paper. Prints made on India-Tint Darko resemble beautiful etchings, and there is a softness and delicacy about these prints that is not obtainable by any other photographic printing process. India-Tint Darko is worked just the same as the other varieties of Darko, printed, developed, fixed, and washed, just the same as any developing paper, is very easy to work, and the beautiful India tint color of the paper itself, contrasted with the rich blacks of the picture, is uniquely artistic and delicately beautiful.

Put up only in packages of two dozen sheets.

Size	Price, per pkg.
3½x3½ inches	20c
3¼x4¼ inches	22c
4 x5 inches	26c
3⅞x5½ inches	28c
5 x7 inches	40c
6½x8½ inches	70c
8 x10 inches	96c

There are 24 sheets to a package.

DARKO SOUVENIR POST CARDS.

15c PER DOZEN

CARBON MATT.
GLOSSY.
VELVET.

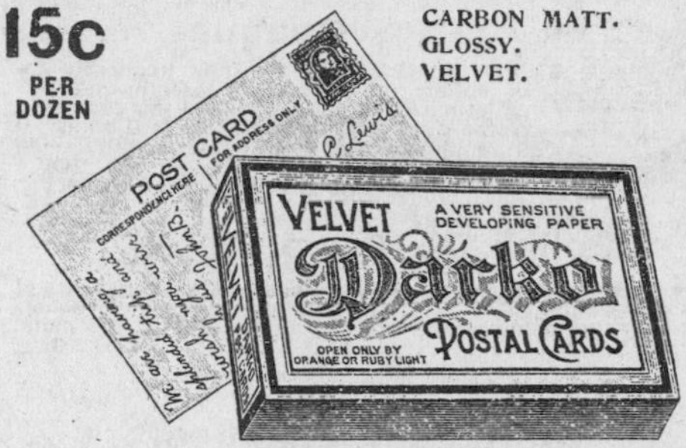

DARKO POSTAL CARDS enable you to make beautiful souvenir post cards from your own negatives. These cards are full regulation post card size, made in the latest style with space for address and message on one side and sensitized on the other side. They are just as simple and easy to work as any other style of Darko, and possess all the characteristic good qualities of Darko.

Made in Three Surfaces, Carbon Matt, Glossy and Velvet.

No. 20K1740 Carbon Matt Post Cards. This is the original matt surface card, the kind we have sold for years, and will always be popular.
Price, per half gross, **75c**; per dozen **15c**

No. 20K1741 Glossy Post Cards. This card is made with a high gloss on pure white stock, making a particularly brilliant and attractive print, with great distinctness of detail.
Price, per half gross, **75c**; per dozen **15c**

No. 20K1742 Velvet Post Cards. The surface of these cards is a semi-matt, a happy medium between the Carbon Matt and the Glossy, and makes a rich, velvety print.
Price, per half gross, **75c**; per dozen **15c**

There are NO PICTURES on these cards; they are perfectly blank and sensitized for photographers' use.

DARKO DEVELOPERS AND SEPIA TONER.

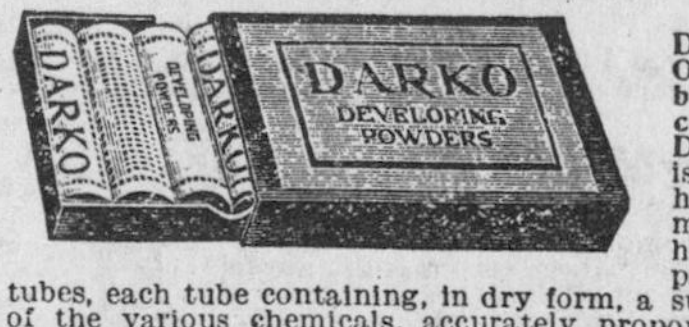

No. 20K1715 DARKO DEVELOPER is the very best developer that can be made for Darko papers. It is a combination of hydrochinon and metol, put up in hermetically sealed paraffine lined tubes, each tube containing, in dry form, a sufficient quantity of the various chemicals, accurately proportioned, to make four ounces of liquid developer when dissolved in water. Each package contains six of these tubes and, therefore, makes twenty-four ounces of developer, and this developer is suitable for working any of the various varieties of Darko Paper, including the postal cards. Price, per package **20c**
If by mail, postage extra, 5 cents.

No. 20K1717 ANTI-FRICTION DEVELOPER. This is a modified form of the regular Darko Developer put up in exactly the same way, but especially adapted to the Glossy Darko. Prints made on glossy developing papers are sometimes subject to dark lines, or markings, known as friction marks, and the use of this special Anti-Friction Developer prevents the occurrence of these marks. It is also an unusually good developer for any of the other varieties of Darko, especially for the Brilliant Darko and Velvet postal cards.
Price, per package of six tubes (makes twenty-four ounces of developer) **20c**
If by mail, postage extra, 5 cents.

No. 20K1719 DARKO SEPIA TONER. This is a special preparation put up in the same way as the regular Darko Developer, six hermetically sealed tubes in a package, and with this preparation prints made on any style of Darko Paper can be toned to a beautiful light brown or sepia color. The use of Darko Sepia Toner is very simple, the effects are very pleasing, and it can be used with any kind of Darko Paper. It gives especially pleasing results with India-Tint Darko. Price, per package (six tubes) **32c**
If by mail, postage extra, 5 cents.

THE "BLUE LABEL" ROEBUCK DRY PLATES.

NOT MADE BY THE TRUST.

4X5 36c

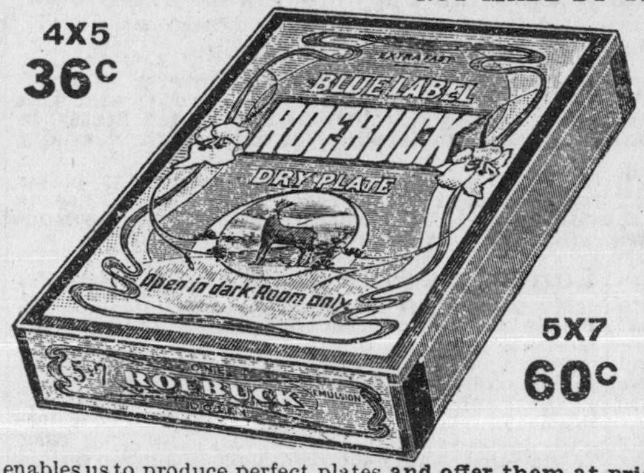

5X7 60c

No. 20K1775 We offer the new "Blue Label" Roebuck Dry Plate as the equal of any dry plate made, a plate that can be depended upon under any conditions, a plate that is suitable for any kind of work.

THE ROEBUCK DRY PLATES are coated on the finest quality of imported Belgium glass, carefully sorted and free from bubbles, scratches or other imperfections.

THE EMULSION IS RICH IN SILVER, yielding strong, vigorous negatives with a wealth of detail and no tendency whatever toward fogging. The factory in which the "Blue Label" Roebuck plates are made is one of the most perfectly equipped dry plate factories ever built, furnished with the very latest and most approved styles of coating machines, and a most complete system of ventilation and refrigeration, giving perfect control of both temperature and hygroscopic conditions. **It is this perfect equipment** combined with long experience in dry plate making and the most perfect materials, which enables us to produce perfect plates **and offer them at prices heretofore considered impossible.**

THE "BLUE LABEL" ROEBUCK PLATES ARE EXCEEDINGLY RAPID giving the finest possible results **in the studio where short exposures are so desirable. For landscapes, portraiture, interiors, flashlight work, instantaneous exposures,** in fact, any work requiring a uniformly rapid and reliable plate, the Roebuck plate is unsurpassed. In brilliancy, detail, uniformity and speed, this plate will satisfy the most exacting operator.

Size	Quantity in Case, dozen	Price, per Case	Price, per Dozen	Size	Quantity in Case, dozen	Price per Case	Price per Dozen
2 x 2	50	$6.18	$0.13	4¼x 6½	24	$11.17	$0.49
2½x 2½	50	7.60	.16	5 x 7	24	13.68	.60
2½x 4	50	9.03	.19	5 x 8	24	15.51	.68
3½x 3½	36	7.52	.22	6½x 8½	12	10.26	.90
3¼x 4¼	36	8.55	.25	8 x10	12	14.82	1.30
4¼x 4¼	30	9.40	.33	10 x12	4	8.63	2.27
4 x 5	30	10.26	.36	11 x14	3	9.24	3.24
4¼x 5½	24	9.35	.41	14 x17	3	13.85	4.86

SEE NEXT PAGE FOR LUMIERE'S PLATES.

Photographic Instruction Book.

281 PAGES. FULLY ILLUSTRATED. BOUND IN CLOTH. BY TOWNSEND D. STITH.
Publisher's price, $1.00; our price.. **40c**

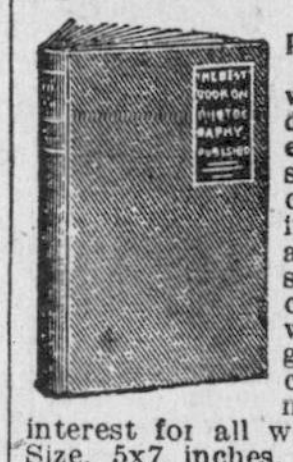

No. 20K965 A systematic course and working guide in all the processes which ordinarily take up the attention of camera workers. This is absolutely the best book on the subject published. It tells how to choose a camera, all about developing, all about printing and the different methods of toning. Tells all about the different kinds of plates and sensitized papers, how to use each and their special advantages. Explains in detail the best way to make interiors, flashlights, portrait groups, landscapes. Hints on retouching, copying, making lantern slides and enlargements, and thousands of other subjects of interest for all who would know and understand the camera. Size, 5x7 inches. 281 pages. Publisher's price, $1.00; our price....... (If by mail, postage extra, 8 cents.)....... **40c**

Hammer's Dry Plates.

MADE BY HAMMER DRY PLATE CO.
NOT IN THE TRUST.

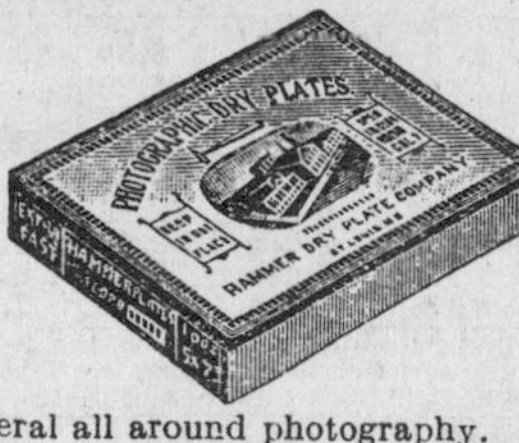

No. 20K1780 Hammer's Dry Plates, another of the well known standard brands; is considered by professional photographers to be one of the best plates made. We furnish this plate in one speed only—the extra fast — suitable for studio work or general all around photography.

Size	Quantity in Case	Price, per Case	Price, per Doz.
3½x 3½	30 doz.	$ 7.57	$0.28
3¼x 4¼	30 doz.	8.52	.31
4 x 5	30 doz.	12.30	.44
4¼x 6½	30 doz.	17.03	.62
5 x 7	20 doz.	13.90	.75
5 x 8	20 doz.	15.77	.85
6½x 8½	12 doz.	12.48	1.12
8 x10	12 doz.	18.16	1.63
10 x12	4 doz.	10.60	2.86
11 x14	4 doz.	15.14	4.08
14 x17	3 doz.	17.03	6.12

Seed's Dry Plates.

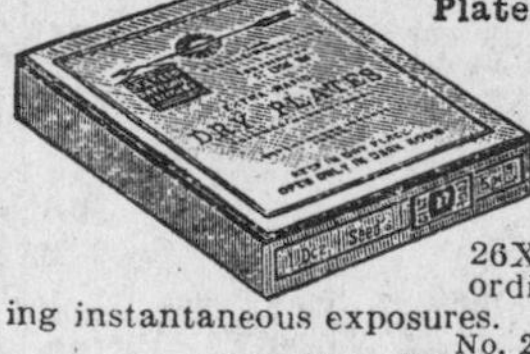

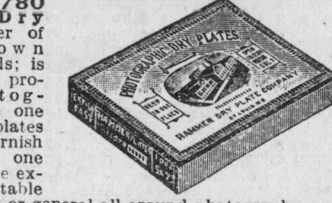

No. 20K1782 Seed's Plates have been on the market so long and are so widely known as **good plates** that comment upon their merits is almost unnecessary. The No. 27 is extremely rapid, but the No. 26X is fast enough for all ordinary work, even including instantaneous exposures.

Size	Quantity in Case	No. 26X Price, per Case	No. 26X Price, per Doz.	No. 27 Price, per Case	No. 27 Price, per Doz.
3½x 3½	30 doz.	$ 8.15	$0.29	$ 8.73	$0.31
3¼x 4¼	30 doz.	9.17	.33	9.82	.35
4 x 5	30 doz.	13.25	.47	14.19	.51
4¼x 6½	30 doz.	18.34	.66	19.65	.70
5 x 7	20 doz.	14.94	.80	16.01	.86
5 x 8	20 doz.	16.98	.91	18.20	.97
6½x 8½	12 doz.	13.45	1.20	14.41	1.28
8 x10	10 doz.	16.30	1.75	17.46	1.87
10 x12	4 doz.	11.41	3.06	12.23	3.26
11 x14	4 doz.	16.30	4.37	17.46	4.66
14 x17	3 doz.	18.34	6.55	19.65	6.99

The Book of Photography, $2.48.

744 PAGES, 1,000 ILLUSTRATIONS, 48 FULL PAGE PLATES.

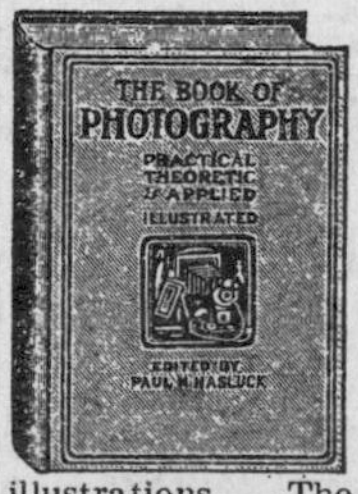

No. 20K967 "The Book of Photography," by Paul N. Hasluck, is the most comprehensive description of the art yet published. A complete photographic library in one big, handsome volume, 7x10 inches, substantially bound in cloth. Contains a vast amount of information, put in a simple and direct way. No other book approaches this in the fulness and up to date character of its information. Formulae and working methods accompany the processes with illustrations. The index, covering 24 pages, gives instantaneous reference to the contents of the work in detail. Our price **$2.48**
If by mail, postage extra, 32 cents.

The Complete Photographer, $3.15

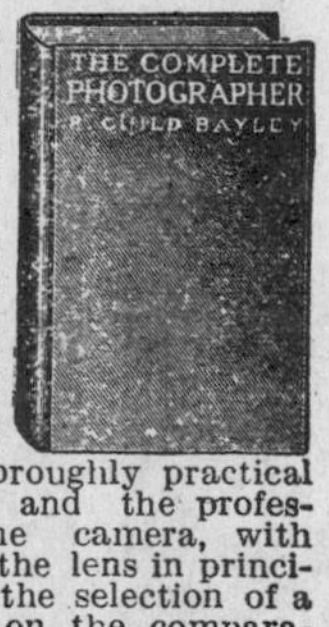

No. 20K969 "The Complete Photographer," by R. Child Bayley, is a splendid book, containing 397 pages, 59 halftone illustrations and 40 line cuts. This book includes an authoritative history of photography, its development and progress from its earliest beginnings to the present day; an exhaustive modern demonstration of every phase of photography — landscape, portraiture, pictorial, architectural, scientific; a perfect guide to the correct application of formulae to photography, which makes it a thoroughly practical working manual for the beginner and the professional; a model exposition of the camera, with valuable hints as to its handling; of the lens in principle, the lens in use, with advice on the selection of a lens; a lucid and valuable discussion on the comparative merits of plates and films, their rapidity, halation and its causes, etc. The book contains also an illuminating chapter on each of the following subjects: Exposure, development, intensification and reduction, the print, platinum printing, the drawing of a photograph, the carbon process, bromide papers, dodging and "faking", the dark room, the hand camera, pinhole photography, orthochromatic and three-color photography, enlarging, reducing, slide making, exhibitions and societies, photography and the printing press. Every camera enthusiast will find **The Complete Photographer** indispensable. Even those who do not develop or print their own pictures will want to have it for its practical field suggestions. The book will be treasured, too, for the superb series of illustrations which represent the crowning efforts of photography in every field, from the subtlest portraiture to the most ideal landscape. Our price **$3.15**
If by mail, postage extra, 17 cents.

OUR ALREADY LOWEST PRICES have been still FURTHER REDUCED in this BIG CATALOGUE. Just compare the prices in this book with the prices quoted by us in previous catalogues and note the additional savings we make for you.

LUMIERE'S DRY PLATES.

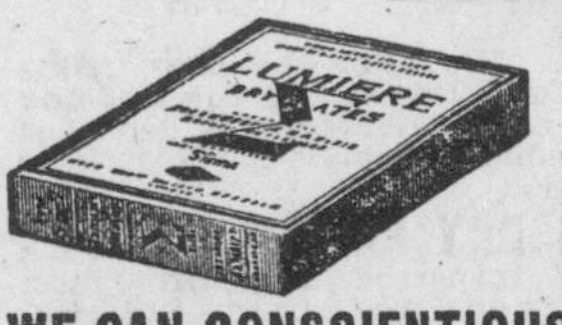

For a great many years the Lumiere Plates have been known as the best and highest grade of dry plates manufactured in Europe.

THE LUMIERE COMPANY is the largest manufacturer of sensitized products in Europe, and this famous company has now opened a factory in the United States, in which they are making their complete line of extra high class dry plates.

WE CAN CONSCIENTIOUSLY RECOMMEND the Lumiere plates to our customers as plates representing in every respect the highest degree of perfection. We carry in stock the Sigma, the Blue Label, the Panchromatic C and the Non-Halation Ortho brands of the Lumiere plates, affording a wide range of special qualities.

Lumiere's Sigma Plates.

No. 20K1785 **The Sigma brand of Lumiere dry plate is a plate of extreme rapidity, the most rapid plate on the market.** The Sigma plate produces negatives that are exceptionally fine grained and absolutely free from chemical fog. These plates are especially adapted to studio work on dark days, to flashlight work, instantaneous pictures on gloomy days, and for all classes of work where an extremely rapid plate is desirable. For general use with folding hand cameras, where most of the exposures are instantaneous, and where many of the pictures are taken under adverse conditions, these plates are unexcelled. For high speed instantaneous work, such as focal plane shutter exposures with the Reflex camera, the Sigma plate stands without an equal. See prices below.

Lumiere's Blue Label Plates.

No. 20K1787 **The Blue Label brand of the Lumiere plate is exactly the same kind of a plate as the Sigma,** possessing all the good qualities of the Sigma plate, but is not quite so rapid, requiring exposures about 50 per cent longer than the Sigma. The Blue Label Lumiere plate is adapted to general all around work, especially for portrait work in the studio. Although not possessing as great rapidity as the Sigma plate, it is at the same time sufficiently rapid for all ordinary requirements, including **quick, instantaneous exposures.** The Blue Label plate allows a little more latitude in exposure than the Sigma, owing to the fact that is a little slower, and for this reason is perhaps a somewhat easier plate to use, and is preferred by most workers for general purposes.

Size	Quantity in Case	No. 20K1787 Blue Label Price per Case	No. 20K1787 Blue Label Price per Doz.	No. 20K1785 Sigma Price per Case	No. 20K1785 Sigma Price per Doz.
3½x 3½	30 doz.	$ 8.15	$0.29	$ 8.73	$0.31
3¼x 4¼	30 doz.	9.17	.33	9.82	.35
4 x 5	30 doz.	13.25	.48	14.19	.51
5 x 7	20 doz.	14.94	.80	16.01	.86
5 x 8	20 doz.	16.98	.91	18.20	.97
6½x 8½	12 doz.	13.45	1.20	14.41	1.28
8 x10	10 doz.	16.30	1.75	17.46	1.87
10 x12	4 doz.	11.41	3.06	12.23	3.26
11 x14	4 doz.	16.30	4.37	17.46	4.66
14 x17	3 doz.	18.34	6.55	19.65	6.99

Lantern Slide Plates.

No. 20K1793 **Lumiere's Lantern Slide Plates.** An extra high grade lantern slide plate, 3¼x4 inches. Price, per case (thirty dozen), **$9.60;** per doz., **34c**

Special Lumiere Chemicals.

Lumiere plates can be worked with any of the standard developers and other chemicals in common use, but the special Lumiere chemicals are exceptionally good and we recommend them not only for the Lumiere plates, but for all other plates as well.

No. 20K1795 Dianol, a new developing agent requiring no alkali. Put up in tubes ready for use.
Price, per box of five tubes **30c**
If by mail, postage extra, 5 cents.

No. 20K1797 **Formosulphite,** a new product, used as a substitute for both preservative and alkali (sulphite of soda and carbonates) in developers. Used with pyro, hydrochinon and other developers it produces greater density and brilliancy. Other advantages are greater economy, good keeping qualities and hardening effect on the film.
Price, per pound, **45c**; per 4-ounce bottle **18c**

No. 20K1799 Lumiere's Fixing Salt, makes one quart of fixing solution for plates; very fine. Price, per package.. **10c**

Lumiere's Panchromatic C Plates.

No. 20K1789 **Lumiere's Panchromatic C Dry Plates are true orthochromatic plates,** made especially sensitive to green, yellow and red, making them particularly adapted to landscape work and general outdoor photography.

The Panchromatic C Plates are particularly desirable for photographing landscapes, flowers, paintings, portrait work, etc., as they give true color values—that is, they show a difference between certain shades or colors, which would all appear alike if photographed with an ordinary plate.

With ordinary plates we have reds that take too black, blues that take too white, and yellow or orange that takes the same as red, black or green. These Panchromatic C plates discriminate in these and other colors, making negatives in which the true values of these colors are shown.

Landscapes made with the Panchromatic C plates possess a brilliancy not to be obtained with any ordinary plate. Flowers, paintings, and other highly colored subjects cannot be successfully photographed without the use of these color sensitive plates. Portraits made with these plates are far superior to portraits made with ordinary plates.

The speed of this plate is the same as the Lumiere Blue Label. See prices below.

Lumiere's Non-Halation Ortho Plates.

No. 20K1791 Lumiere's Non-Halation Ortho Plate is a combination orthochromatic and non-halation plate of the very highest quality.

Interior views can be made with these plates directly toward bright windows or open doors. They preserve perfect detail in tree tops outlined against a bright sky, they add wonderfully to the brilliancy of white draperies in portraiture, they are indispensable for photographing snow scenes. The combined non-halation and orthochromatic properties of this plate make it an ideal plate for landscape work, yielding brilliant negatives, absolutely free from halation, and with true color values.

Halation is avoided in this plate by an entirely new process, the plate being coated, before the emulsion is put on, with a dark red dye, which absorbs all light rays penetrating the emulsion, absolutely preventing reflection from the glass and in this way overcoming all halation. After the plate is developed and fixed the red dye is removed from the plate by immersing the negative for a few moments in the Lumiere Special Non-Halation Dye Remover.

The speed of this Non-Halation Ortho Plate is the same as Lumiere's Blue Label Plate, making it suitable for general photography, including very quick, instantaneous work.

Size	Quantity in Case	No. 20K1789 Panchromatic C Price, per Case	No. 20K1789 Panchromatic C Price, per Doz.	No. 20K1791 Non-Halation Ortho Price, per Case	No. 20K1791 Non-Halation Ortho Price, per Doz.
3½x 3½	18 doz.	$ 5.59	$0.33	$ 6.29	$0.37
3¼x 4¼	18 doz.	6.29	.37	6.99	.41
4 x 5	12 doz.	6.06	.54	6.52	.58
5 x 7	12 doz.	10.25	.91	11.18	.99
6½x 8½	8 doz.	10.25	1.36	11.18	1.47
8 x 10	6 doz.	11.18	1.98	12,11	2.14
10 x 12	2 doz.	6.52	3.46	6.52	3.46
11 x 14	2 doz.	9.32	4.95	9.32	4.95
14 x 17	2 doz.	13.97	7.42	13.97	7.42

The prices quoted above on the **Non-Halation Ortho Plates** include a sufficient supply of the Dye Remover, which comes packed right with each box of plates.

BARNET FILM.

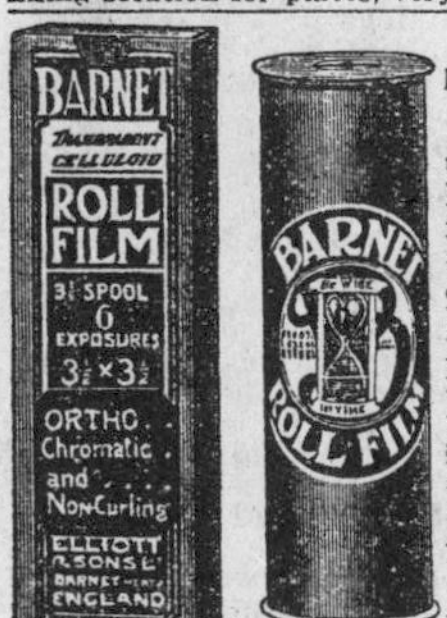

DAYLIGHT LOADING, NON CURLING AND ORTHOCHROMATIC. FOR USE IN ANY KODAK, BUCKEYE, ANSCO, HAWKEYE, OR SEROCO FILM CAMERA.

No. 20K1811 **Barnet Film is put up in regular daylight loading cartridges of six or twelve exposures** and is adapted to any modern make of daylight loading film camera, including the Eastman Kodaks and the Seroco Film Cameras. **Made in England.** Barnet film is made by Elliott & Sons, Lt'd., of Barnet, England, recognized as one of the foremost manufacturers of dry plates and films in the world. Until this season Elliott & Sons marketed their entire product in the British Islands and Europe, but this year, for the first time, this wonderfully good film is offered to American users. We have tested this film in comparison with the best film produced both in this country and Europe, and we consider it, beyond question, the best film manufactured today. The name, Elliott & Sons, is in itself a guarantee of perfect quality, and every roll of Barnet film which we sell is put out under our own binding guarantee as to quality, guaranteed to be equal to any film on the market regardless of price, and is also sent out under the guarantee of Elliott & Sons. We will replace without charge any Barnet film found defective to the slightest extent. We will replace without charge or refund the entire purchase price for any Barnet film that is not found absolutely perfect. **Barnet Film is an anti-trust film.** When you buy Barnet film, you are not only getting the best film that can be obtained anywhere in the world, but at the same time you are contributing to the support of anti-trust manufacturers and you will be helping to keep down the prices of photographic goods.

No. 20K1811 Size, 1½x2—For Pocket Kodak. Price, per 12 exposure roll.... **$0.21**

No. 20K1812 Size, 2¼x2¼—For No. 1 Brownie or No. 1 Buster Brown Camera. Price, per 6 exposure roll .... **.12**

No. 20K1813 Size, 2¼x3¼—For No. 2 Brownie, No. 2 Buster Brown, No. 3 Buster Brown and No. 1 Folding Buster Brown. Price, per 6 exposure roll... **$0.17**
Price, per 12 exposure roll .... **.21**

No. 20K1814 Size, 1⅝x2½—For No. 0 Folding Pocket Kodak. Price, per 6 exposure roll .... **.12**
Price, per 12 exposure roll .... **.21**

No. 20K1815 Size, 2¼x3¼—For No. 1 Folding Pocket Kodak. Price, per 6 exposure roll .... **.17**
Price, per 12 exposure roll .... **.34**

No. 20K1816 Size, 2½x4¼—For No. 1A Folding Pocket Kodak and Ansco Jr. Price, per 6 exposure roll, **.21**
Price, per 12 exposure roll .... **.42**

No. 20K1817 Size, 3¼x4¼—For No. 3 Folding Pocket Kodak, No. 3 Weno Hawkeye, Stereo Weno Hawkeye, No. 3 Buckeye, Nos. 2, 4 and 6 Ansco and Nos. 3, 5, 7 and Stereoscopic Seroco Film Cameras.
Price, per 6 exposure roll .... **.30**
Price, per 12 exposure roll .... **.58**

No. 20K1818 Size, 3½x3½—For No. 2 Folding Pocket Kodak, No. 2 Flexo, No. 2 Bullseye, No. 2 Bullet, No. 2 Stereo Kodak, No. 4 Panorama Kodak, Tourist Buckeye, No. 2 Weno Hawkeye, No. 3B Al Vista, No. 1 Ansco and No. 1 Seroco Film Camera.
Price, per 6 exposure roll .... **.25**
Price, per 12 exposure roll .... **.50**

No. 20K1819 Size, 3¼x5½. For No. 3A Folding Pocket Kodak and Nos. 9 and 10 Ansco.
Price, per 6 exposure roll .... **.34**
Price, per 10 exposure roll .... **.58**

No. 20K1820 Size, 4x5—For Nos. 3, 5 and 7 Ansco, No. 4 Folding Buckeye, No. 4 Weno Hawkeye, No. 4 Folding Hawkeye, No. 4 Bullseye, No. 4 Bullet, Nos. 4B and 4G Al Vista, Nos. 2, 4, 6 and 8 Seroco Film Cameras. Price, per 6 exposure roll .... **.38**
Price, per 12 exposure roll .... **.75**

No. 20K1821 Size, 4¼x3¼—For No. 3 Cartridge Kodak. Price, per 6 exposure roll .... **.30**
Price, per 12 exposure roll .... **.58**

No. 20K1822 Size, 5x4—For No. 4 Cartridge Kodak and Nos. 5B, 5D, 5F and 5C Al Vistas. Price, per 6 exposure roll .... **.38**
Price, per 12 exposure roll .... **.75**

No. 20K1823 Size, 7x5—For No. 5 Cartridge Kodak and Nos. 7D, 7E and 7F Al Vistas. Price, per 6 exposure roll .... **.67**
Price, per 12 exposure roll **1.34**

Savigny's Transparent Water Colors.

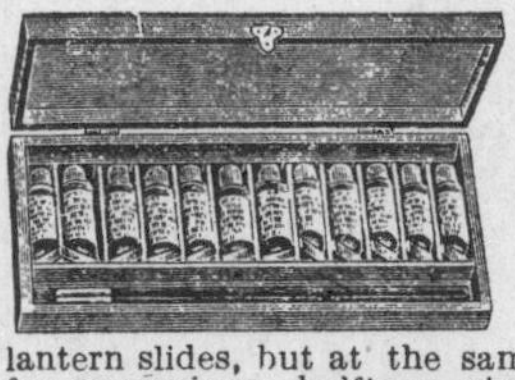

Extra high grade transparent moist colors, put up in collapsible tin tubes, the most permanent, purest and finest transparent water colors made. Savigny's transparent water colors are made especially for coloring photographs or lantern slides, but at the same time are also suitable for engravings, halftone pictures, etc. No previous experience or skill is required in using these colors, and you can add very greatly to the beautiful appearance of your photographs by coloring them with these permanent, easily applied colors.

No. 20K1900 **Size No. 0.** Eight different colors, in pasteboard box. Price **75c**
If by mail, postage extra, 8 cents.

No. 20K1901 **Size No. 1.** Twelve different colors, in polished cherry box. Price....... **$1.40**
If by mail, postage extra, 12 cents.

No. 20K1902 **Size No. 2.** Sixteen different colors, in polished cherry box. Price....... **$1.87**
If by mail, postage extra, 14 cents.

Litmus Paper.

No. 20K1912 Litmus Paper, for testing solutions to ascertain whether alkaline or acid; very useful in making toning baths. Put up in bottles containing 100 sheets. State whether red or blue is desired. Price, per bottle....... **8c**
If by mail, postage extra, 3 cents.

Opaque.

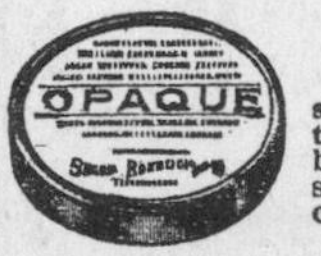

No. 20K1916 **It is frequently desirable to block out or render opaque certain parts of a negative, and this can easily be done with this preparation,** which is simply applied to the negative with a small camel's hair brush. Price, per box, **20c**
If by mail, postage extra, 3 cents.

Polish for Ferro Plates.

No. 20K1920 Ferrotype Plate Polish. A small quantity of this preparation rubbed over the ferrotype plate before squeegeeing makes it impossible for the print to stick to the plate. Price, per box **10c**
If by mail, postage extra, 2 cents.

Martin's Specialties.

A line of special photographic preparations, radically different from anything on the market and of great merit.

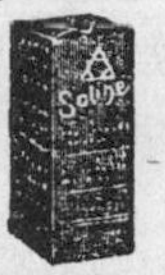

No. 20K1925 Soline, a liquid for sensitizing cloth, paper, postal cards or other materials. Prints made on cloth can be washed without injury; very useful in making sofa pillows, banners, tidies, book marks, etc. Price **30c**

No. 20K1926 Intensine, an intensifier in dry form for glass or film negatives or lantern slides. An extra good intensifier. Price.... **15c**

No. 20K1927 Platyn, a single platinum toner that gives fine platinum tones on any kind of printing-out paper, or on cloth prints made with Soline. Price, per ½-ounce bottle, sufficient for 80 ounces toning bath **39c**

Blue Print Powder.

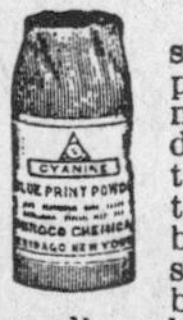

No. 20K1933 **Blue Print Powder.** A special chemical preparation for sensitizing paper, cloth, cards or other materials for making blue prints. The powder is simply dissolved in water and the solution applied to the paper or cloth, or whatever it is desired to make the picture upon, with a camel's hair brush. By using this special blue print sensitizing preparation you can make beautiful blue prints on writing paper, on cloth, on cardboard, or on almost any material that you may desire. Full directions with each package.

Price, per 1-ounce bottle, **13c**; per tube..... **9c**
If by mail, postage extra per ounce, 3c, per tube 2c

Hydro-Metol Developer.

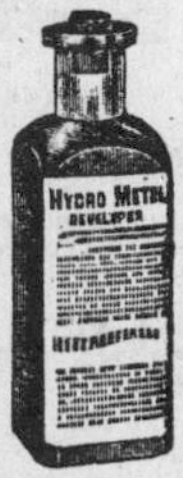

No. 20K1945 **We consider this the best liquid developer, being a combination of the well known hydrochinon and metol; works very rapidly, never fogs the plate, brings out all the details and gives a very brilliant negative.** Price, per 8-oz. bottle... **18c**
Unmailable on account of weight.

Do not order liquid developer in the winter, as it may freeze on the way to you, breaking the bottle and damaging other goods.

DEVELOPING POWDERS.

We especially recommend the purchase of developers in powder form, as they ship better, transportation charges are exceedingly small and the purchaser gets the greatest possible value for the money, as the expense of bottling, compounding, etc., is all saved.

Eikonogen Developing Powder.

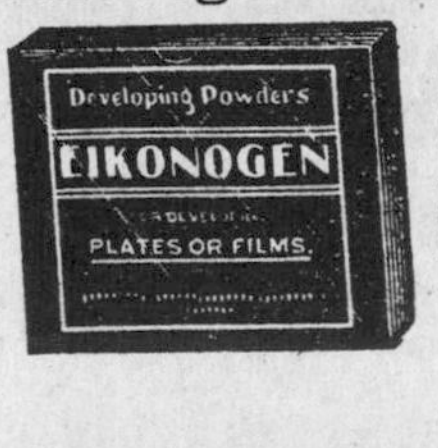

No. 20K1950 **These Powders afford a very convenient means for preparing the liquid Eikonogen developer; avoids the risk of breakage in transportation, and always insures a fresh and strong developer. Each package contains six sets of powders, which is sufficient to prepare 24 ounces of concentrated developer.**
Price, per package...... **15c**
If by mail, postage extra, 3 cents.

Hydro-Metol Developing Powders.

No. 20K1952 Our Hydro-Metol Developing Powders, a combination of hydrochinon and metol, are made from the purest chemicals, put up in the most careful and exact manner, and will be found a perfect developer in every way. Our Hydro-Metol Developing Powders work very rapidly, do not fog or stain the plate, and produce brilliant, sparkling negatives, full of detail and of the most perfect printing quality. The best developing powder made.

Price, per package containing six powders, sufficient to make 24 ounces of developer. Price...16c
If by mail, postage extra, 3 cents.

Eiko-Hydro Developing Powders.

No. 20K1954 A combination of Eikonogen and Hydrochinon, making a developer equally well suited to time exposures or instantaneous work, and one of our most popular productions. This developer works rapidly, is clean and stainless and produces a bright, snappy negative. Price, per package of six powders, sufficient for 24 ounces of developer. Price....15c
If by mail, postage extra, 3 cents.

TONERS.

No. 20K1960 Combined Toning and Fixing Solution, a high grade toning and fixing bath in one solution. For toning DuVoll's paper or any kind of gelatin printing-out paper. Our Combined Toning and Fixing Solution yields a variety of tones, and as it is rich in gold it may be used repeatedly. Price, per 16-ounce bottle, 29c; per 8-ounce bottle.....16c
Unmailable on account of weight.

Gold Toning Solution.

No. 20K1962 Many photographers prefer to work their paper in separate baths, that is, the toning and fixing being done in two separate baths; and this is certainly the most correct method, as prints made in a combined toning and fixing bath are very apt to fade or discolor in time. This gold toning solution requires only to be diluted with water, and after toning the prints are fixed in a plain solution of hypo. Concentrated. Price, per 8-oz. bottle,..27c
Unmailable on account of weight.

Toning and Fixing Powders.

No. 20K1964 Toning and Fixing Powders, for preparing the combined toning and fixing bath. The toning bath made from these powders possesses all the good points of our regular liquid toner, and for use is simply dissolved in water. These Toning and Fixing Powders are radically different from any other preparation of the kind on the market, and are the only thoroughly reliable and perfect toner and fixer in dry form ever made. Made especially for DuVoll's paper, but yield splendid results with any gelatin printing-out paper. Price, per package, sufficient for 36 ounces solution. 15c
If by mail, postage extra, 7 cents.

Platinum Toning Solution.

No. 20K1966 Platinum Toning Solution, for producing black tones on any gelatin printing-out paper, such as DuVoll's. The platinum finish is very popular and this toning bath affords an easy method of obtaining fine black platinum tones at small expense; also produces fine results with Autotone paper.
Price, per 8-ounce bottle, concentrated...................39c
Unmailable on account of weight.

Intensifying Powders.

No. 20K1970 Intensifying Powders, for strengthening weak negatives. Require only to be dissolved in water to make ready for use. One package makes 24 ounces of solution.
Price, per package.................................16c
Unmailable.

Reducing Powders.

No. 20K1972 Reducing Powders for thinning negatives which are too dense. When dissolved in water this powder forms a reducing solution ready for use. Each package makes 24 ounces of solution. Price, per package.............15c
If by mail, postage extra, 2 cents.

Neg-Dry.

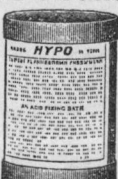

No. 20K1980 Neg-Dry is a hardener for either plates or paper and is a most remarkable preparation. One of the most annoying things in photography is the long time required for a negative to dry after washing. When treated with this preparation the negative can be dried in five minutes by artificial heat, and the film becomes so hard that it can scarcely be scratched or marred in any way. Used with Darko paper, the finished prints can be dried within a few minutes after development. Can be used over and over again. Price, per 4-ounce bottle.................................17c
Unmailable on account of weight.

Acid Hypo.

No. 20K1985 Acid Hypo is a preparation in dry form for making the acid fixing bath. Requires only the addition of water to make it ready for use. The acid fixing bath is of great advantage, both for plates and films, and for developing papers, having a clearing effect and preventing fog.
Price, per box.................................8c
If by mail, postage extra, 5 cents.

Photographic Chemicals.

We absolutely guarantee the purity of our photographic chemicals.

No. 20K2001 Pyrogallic Acid, the old reliable developer. Our Pyro is a pure, resublimed pyrogallic acid, of the very finest quality, guaranteed equal to any pyro on the market, regardless of price. Put up in tins.

| Price, per pound....$2.30 | Price, per ¼-pound....65c |
| Price, per ½-pound.... 1.25 | Price, per ounce.........20c |

No. 20K2003 Schering's Pyro, a standard make of pyro, still preferred by many photographers.

| Price, per pound....$2.30 | Price, per ¼-pound....65c |
| Price, per ½-pound.... 1.25 | Price, per ounce.........20c |

No. 20K2005 Hydrochinon, strictly chemically pure, perfectly white, the best hydrochinon we can buy.

| Price, per pound....$1.92 | Price, per ¼-pound....50c |
| Price, per ½-pound.... .98 | Price, per ounce.........16c |

No. 20K2007 Eikonogen, best grade, imported from Germany. Put up in tins.

| Price, per pound....$3.35 | Price, per ¼-pound....$1.02 |
| Price, per ½-pound.... 1.79 | Price, per ounce.........30 |

No. 20K2008 Metol, in original packages.

| Price, per pound....$8.00 | Price, per ¼-pound....$2.42 |
| Price, per ½-pound.... 4.46 | Price, per ounce.........65 |

No. 20K2009 Glycin, in original packages.

| Price, per pound....$8.00 | Price, per ¼-pound....$2.42 |
| Price, per ½-pound.... 4.46 | Price, per ounce.........65 |

No. 20K2010 Amidol, in original packages.

| Price, per pound....$8.00 | Price, per ¼-pound....$2.42 |
| Price, per ¼-pound.... 4.46 | Price, per ounce.........65 |

Defendol.

A New Developing Agent for either Plates or Paper.

No. 20K2015 Defendol, the new developing agent, offers advantages over any developer yet produced and is suitable for any paper, such as Darko, Luster, etc., or for dry plates. Defendol is not poisonous, it does not stain the fingers; plates can be left in it for hours and still remain clear; it is cheaper than other developers; it keeps indefinitely in dry form; it remains clear in solution longer than other developers. Defendol retains its working qualities to the last drop, being practically inexhaustible; it can be used over and over again, and it is the best developer known for bromide papers. No sulphite of soda is necessary in making up Defendol developer, no other chemical except dry carbonate of soda being required. Price

	Price
½-oz. package makes about 30 ozs. developer...........	$0.21
1-oz. package makes about 60 ozs. developer...........	.40
4-oz. package makes about 7½ qts. developer...........	1.50
8-oz. package makes about 7½ gals. developer...........	2.80
16-oz. package makes about 15 gals. developer...........	5.20

No. 20K2020 Acetic acid, No. 8, 1-oz. bottle, 5c; 1-lb. bottle...........20
No. 20K2022 Citric acid, crystals, 1-oz. bottle...........10
No. 20K2024 Muriatic acid (known also as hydrochloric acid), 2-oz. bottle, 18c; 1-lb. bottle...........44
No. 20K2026 Nitric acid, 1-oz. bottle, 12c; 1-lb. bottle...........36
No. 20K2028 Oxalic acid, crystals, 2-oz. bottle, 15c; 1-lb. bottle...........30
No. 20K2030 Sulphuric acid, C. P., 1-oz. bottle, 12c; 1-lb. bottle...........33
No. 20K2035 Alcohol, pure, for photographic uses, ½-pint bottle...........35
No. 20K2043 Alum, pulverized, 1-lb. package...........15
No. 20K2045 Alum, chrome, 1-lb. box...........15
No. 20K2047 Ammonia, liquid conc., U.S.P., 1-lb. bottle...........26
No. 20K2053 Ammonium bromide, 1-oz. bottle...........12
No. 20K2055 Ammonium bichromate, 1-oz. bottle, 15c; 1-lb. bottle...........1.12
No. 20K2057 Ammonium carbonate, 1-lb. bottle...........40
No. 20K2059 Ammonium chloride, 1-oz. bottle, 10c; 1-lb. bottle...........35
No. 20K2061 Ammonium sulphocyanide, 1-oz. bott...........15
No. 20K2065 Formalin, put up in 4-oz. bottles. Per bottle...........18
No. 20K2068 Glycerin, very pure, 1-oz. bottle...........08

Gold Chloride at 40 Cents.

Guaranteed Full Weight.

No. 20K2075 Gold chloride, pure, 15-gr. bottle, per dozen, $4.72; each...........40c
No. 20K2076 Gold and sodium, chloride, 15-gr. bot....35c
No. 20K2079 Iodine, resublimed, 1-oz. bottle...........33c
No. 20K2082 Iron protosulphate, 1-lb. package...........6c
No. 20K2084 Iron and ammonia, citrate, 1-oz. bot....12c
No. 20K2087 Lead nitrate, 1-oz. bottle...........12c
No. 20K2089 Lead acetate (sugar of lead), 1-oz. bot....12c
No. 20K2095 Mercury bichloride (corrosive sublimate), 1-oz. bottle...........15c
No. 20K2105 Potassium bromide, 1-oz. bottle...........15c
No. 20K2107 Potassium carbonate, 1-lb. package...........25c
No. 20K2109 Potassium cyanide, 4-oz. can, 20c; 1-lb. can...........60c
No. 20K2111 Potassium ferrocyanide (yellow prussiate of potash), 1-oz. package...........12c
No. 20K2113 Potassium ferricyanide (red prussiate of potash), 1-oz. package...........15c
No. 20K2115 Potassium iodide, 1-oz. package...........30c
No. 20K2117 Potassium oxalate, neutral, 1-lb. pkg....25c
No. 20K2120 Platinum chloride, 15-gr. bottle...........70c
No. 20K2125 Silver nitrate, 1-oz. bottle...........55c
No. 20K2130 Sodium acetate, 1-oz. bottle...........8c
No. 20K2132 Sodium bicarbonate, 1-oz. package...........5c
No. 20K2134 Sodium bisulphite (acid sulphite), pure, 1-oz. bottle...........12c
No. 20K2136 Sodium carbonate (sal soda), crystals, pure, 1-lb. package...........9c
No. 20K2138 Carbonate of soda, dry, a very high grade carbonate (sal soda), guaranteed absolutely chemically pure. Per 1-lb. bottle...........22c
No. 20K2140 Sodium citrate, 1-oz. bottle...........14c
No. 20K2142 Sodium sulphite, crystals, pure. Per 1-lb. bottle...........10c
No. 20K2144 Sulphite of soda, dry, a very high grade sulphite, guaranteed absolutely chemically pure. Per 1-lb. bottle...........32c

10 Pounds of Hypo for 35 Cents.

Hyposulphite of Sodium, or Hypo, as the photographers call it, is one of the most important chemicals used in photography, and none but the best grade should ever be used.

OUR HYPO is the best chemically pure pea crystals, free from dirt, small, perfectly formed crystals. Clean and dry. No caking, no waste.

No. 20K2150 Pea Crystal Hypo, in 1-lb. sealed cartons. Price, per lb............$0.04
If by mail, postage extra, 21 cents.

No. 20K2152 Pea Crystal Hypo, in 10-lb. sealed package. Price, per package (10 lbs.)...........35
No. 20K2155 Pea Crystal Hypo, in original keg. Price, per keg (100 lbs.)...........2.00
Our Hypo is all sold in sealed packages, clean and pure.

CARD MOUNTS

Collins' Plain Bevel Edge Melton Cards.

No. 20K2203 A perfectly plain, fine quality, round cornered, bevel edged melton surface card, suitable for almost any kind of a picture.
Colors, Scotch gray or carbon black.

Size of Card	For Photos	Price, per 100	Price, per 25
4¼x4¼	3½x3½	$0.40	11c
4½x5¼	3½x4¼	.45	12c
5¼x6½	4 x5	.68	18c
5¾x7½	3½x5½	.80	22c
7 x9	5 x7	1.28	35c

Be sure to state size and color wanted.

Collins' "Mantello" Cards.

No. 20K2207 This is a good quality card, with fancy embossed border of very handsome design, wide margin, square corners and straight edges.
Colors, sage green, ash gray or enameled white.

Size of Card	For Photos	Price, per 100	Price, per 25
2⅞x3¾	1½x2	$0.24	7c
3½x3½	2½x2½	.37	9c
4 x5	2¼x3¼	.47	12c
4 x5	3½x3½	.56	15c
4¾x5¾	3½x4¼	.58	16c
4½x6	2½x4¼	.60	17c
5½x6½	4 x5	.72	19c
5 x7	3½x5½	.74	20c
7 x9	5 x7	1.40	38c

Be sure to state size and color wanted.

Collins' "Magnifico" Cards.

No. 20K2213 A remarkably attractive card at an exceedingly low price. Square corners, plain beveled edges, white center and ash gray border with delicate ornamental design in white (not embossed). The white center gives a masked effect to the mounted photograph. Color, border, ash gray; center and design, white.

Size of Card	For Photos	Price, per 100	Price, per 25
4½x5¼	3½x4¼	$0.70	18c
4¾x5¾	3½x4¼	.72	19c
5½x6½	4 x5	.92	25c
7 x9	5 x7	1.48	39c

Be sure to state size wanted.

Collins' "Grando" Cards.

No. 20K2214 A card intended especially for landscape photographs. Color and design exactly the same as the "Magnifico" cards, but made with straight edges and somewhat lighter stock.
Color, border, ash gray; center and design, white.

Size of Card	For Photos	Price, per 100	Price, per 25
7x 9	5 x7	$1.15	30c
9x11	6½x8½	1.60	42c
10x12	8 x10	2.08	55c

Be sure to state size wanted.

"The Harvard Special" Cards.

No. 20K2218 An unusually handsome card, made especially for us by the A. M. Collins Manufacturing Co. Made from a fine quality of cardboard with extra wide border, beautifully embossed, with an entirely new and very attractive design. Plain straight edges and square corners.
Colors, Scotch gray or carbon black.

Size of Card	For Photos	Price, per 100	Price, per 25
4¼x6	2½x4¼	$0.68	18c
4½x5¼	3½x3½	.75	20c
5 x6	3½x4¼	.80	22c
5¼x7½	3½x5½	.93	25c
6 x7	4 x5	.95	26c
7 x9	5 x7	1.54	40c

Be sure to state size and color wanted.

Collins' "958" Embossed Cards.

No. 20K2223 A quietly elegant and unobtrusive card, with narrow design around center, embossed in color which adds to the appearance of the mount and assists greatly in bringing out the full value of the mounted photograph. The ash gray card is very effective for prints on Darko paper.
Colors, ash gray or carbon black.

Size of Card	For Photos	Price, per 100	Price, per 25
5½x6½	3½x3½	$0.82	22c
5 x6	3½x4¼	.90	24c
5¼x7½	3½x5½	1.00	27c
6 x7	4 x5	1.04	28c

Be sure to state size and color wanted.

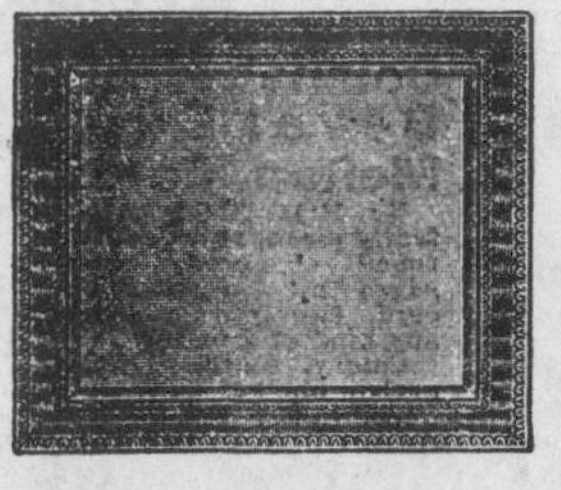

Collins' Enameled "Mantello" Cards.

No. 20K2227 This is a very pretty mount, made from fine enameled cardboard with white center and queen's gray border. The border, which is wide, is embossed in a very pleasing design. Square corners and plain edges.

Color, center white; border queen's gray.

Size of Card	For Photos.	Price, per 100	Price, per 25
5 x5	3½x3½	$0.90	24c
4¾x5¾	3¼x4¼	.94	25c
5½x6½	4 x5	1.05	27c
7 x9	5 x7	2.15	55c

Be sure to state size wanted.

Collins' "1776" Embossed Cards.

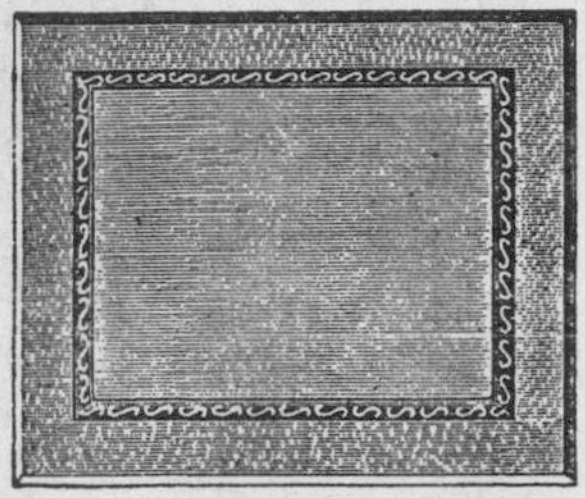

No. 20K2232 This is probably the most artistic mount at a reasonable price that has ever been offered. It is made from extra heavy, thick stock of fine quality and embossed in color with very handsome design. Made with square corners and plain beveled edges.

Colors, white or ash gray.

Size of Card	For Photos	Price, per 100	Price, per 25
6 x7	4 x5	$1.22	32c
5¼x7½	3¼x5½	1.30	34c
7 x9½	4¼x6½	1.80	47c
7 x9	5 x7	1.90	50c

Be sure to state size and color wanted.

Collins' "Whitlyn" Cards.

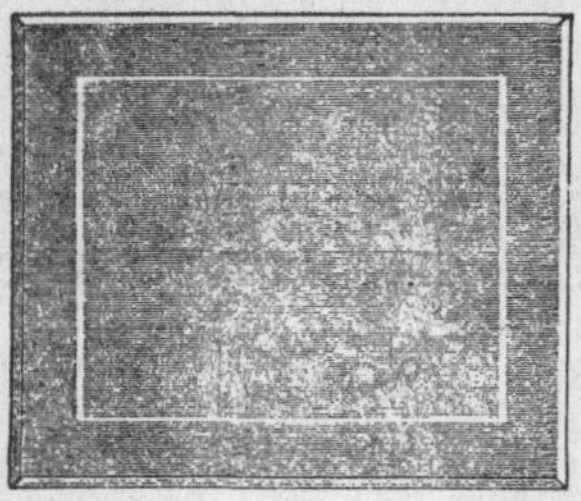

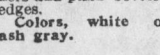

No. 20K2237 A square cornered, bevel edged, melton surface card, with narrow line engraved in white around center. An unusually fine card made from extra quality cardboard. The white engraved line surrounding the print gives to the picture a most pleasing finish.

Colors, Scotch gray or carbon black.

Size of Card	For Photos	Price, per 100	Price, per 25
5¼x5¼	3½x3½	$1.21	32c
5 x6	3¼x4¼	1.26	33c
5¼x7½	3¼x5½	1.38	36c
6 x7	4 x5	1.42	37c
7 x9	5 x7	2.10	55c

Be sure to state size and color wanted.

Collins' "Semper Paratus" Slip Cards.

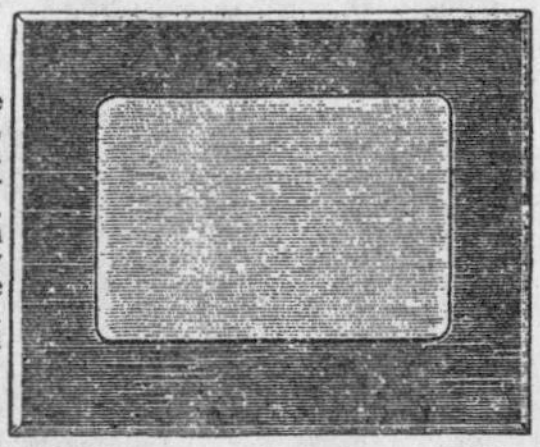

No. 20K2242 These cards require no pasting, the prints being slipped into place through the opening at the back of the card. The print is held firmly in place, but may be easily removed if desired. Made from fine quality of stock with square corners and plain beveled edges.

Color, carbon black.

Size of Card	For Photos	Shape of Opening	Price, per 100	Price, per 25
5 x5	3½x3½	square	$1.26	32c
4⅝x5⅝	3¼x4¼	square	1.18	30c
5½x6½	4 x5	square	1.52	39c
4⅞x7⅛	3¼x5½	square	1.68	43c
7 x9	5 x7	square	2.38	60c
5 x5	3½x3½	oval	1.30	33c
4⅝x5⅝	3¼x4¼	oval	1.22	31c
5½x6½	4 x5	oval	1.58	40c

Be sure to state size wanted.

Collins' "1607" Embossed Cards.

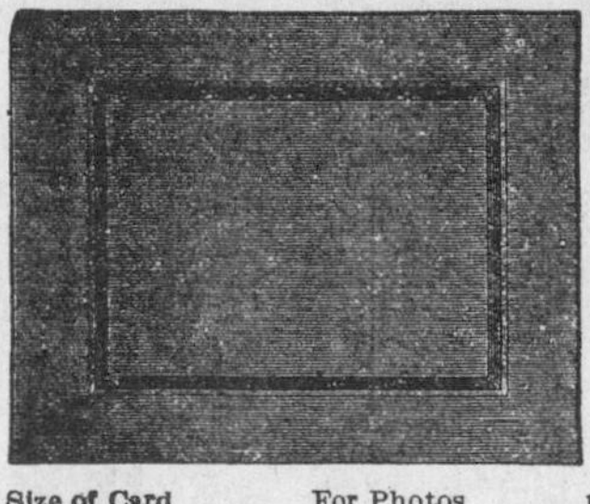

No. 20K2247 This is an unusually high grade card, made from extra heavy and thick board of extra quality, with square corners and plain beveled edges. It is made extra large, with wide border and is handsomely embossed. A card that is worthy of the best pictures.

Colors, white or ash gray.

Size of Card	For Photos	Price per 100	Price per 25
5¾x6¾	3¼x4¼	$1.20	32c
6⅞x7⅞	4 x5	1.52	40c

Be sure to state size and color wanted.

Plain White Cardboard.

No. 20K2252 Plain White Cardboard of fairly good quality, with square corners and straight edges. Enameled on one side. Put up in packages of 50.

Size of Card	Price, per 1,000	Price, per 50
4¼x 5½	$1.56	8c
5 x 7	2.33	12c
5 x 8	2.51	14c
6½x 8½	4.46	23c
8 x10	6.60	34c
10 x12	9.70	50c
11 x14	11.64	60c

Be sure to state size wanted.

Collins' Standard Mounting Board.

We furnish this high grade melton cardboard, the standard Collins' board, in three weights, 10-ply, 12-ply and 16-ply, the thickness being shown by the following lines:

10-ply.

12-ply.

16-ply.

This board is noted for its absolutely smooth surface and freedom from imperfections. It takes the print better than any other cardboard made and is used by the best photographers everywhere

Colors, carbon black or Burmese brown.

Note—Carbon black is not a dead black, and it harmonizes with almost any kind of a print. The Burmese brown cards harmonize very nicely with prints on developing papers.

Size of Card	No. 20K2257 10-ply		No. 20K2258 12-ply		No. 20K2259 16-ply	
	Price, per 100	Price, per 25	Price, per 100	Price, per 25	Price, per 100	Price, per 25
7 x 9	$0.60	16c	$0.80	21c	$1.20	$0.32
8 x 10	.72	19c	.92	24c	1.40	.37
10 x 12	1.00	27c	1.28	34c	2.00	.53
11 x 14	1.24½	33c	1.60	43c	2.48	.65
14 x 17	2.48	65c	3.20	85c	4.96	1.28

Be sure to state size and color wanted.

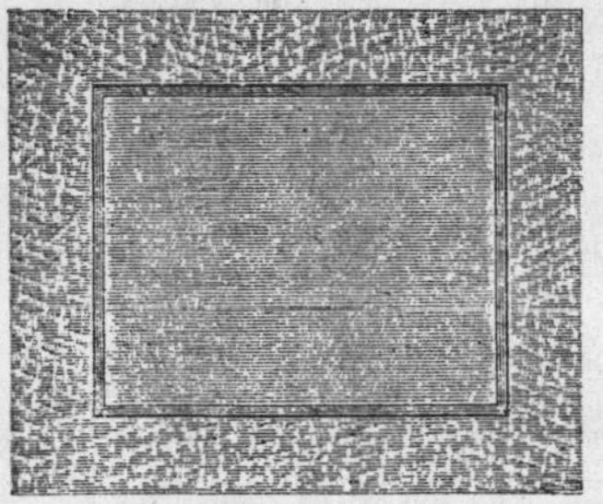

Collins' "Mantello" Mounts.

No. 20K2262 Fine quality embossed cards, made from good solid 14-ply stock, square corners and plain straight edges.

Colors, carbon black or Scotch gray.

Size of Card	For Photos	Price, per 100	Price, per 25
7 x 9	3¾ x 5½	$1.40	36c
8 x 10	5 x 7	1.87	48c
10 x 12	6½ x 8½	2.72	70c
11 x 14	8 x 10	2.98	77c

Be sure to state size and color wanted.

Collins' Penny Picture Cards.

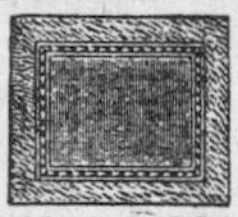

No. 20K2267 Good quality cards, for penny pictures, with handsome embossed border. Size of card, 2⅜x2¾, for photos 1¼x1½.

Colors, queen's gray, sage green or white enamel.

Price, per 1,000..... **$1.40;** per package of 250..... **38c**

Be sure to state color wanted.

Collins' "Novella" Portrait Cards.

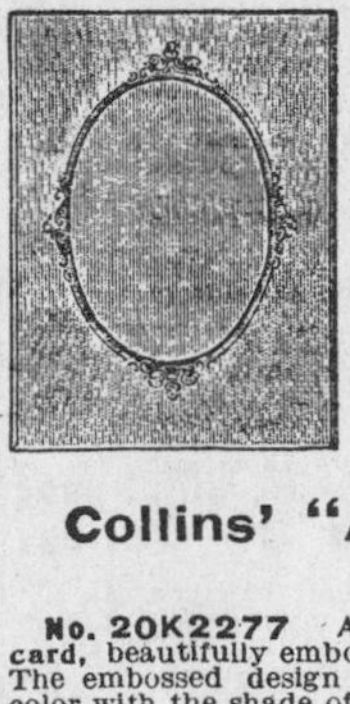

No.20K2272 A surprisingly good card at a very low price. In beauty of design and finish this strong and substantial card stands at the head of moderate priced mounts, heavy stock, square corners and plain beveled edges.

Colors, white, burmese brown or ebony black.

Size of Card	For Oval Photos	Price, per 100	Price, per 25
4¼x6	2 x2¾	$0.75	20c
5 x7	2⅝x3⅝	1.00	26c
5¼x7¼	3 x4⅛	1.02	27c
6 x8	3½x5	1.24	32c
5 x8½	2¾x5¼	1.25	33c

Be sure to state size and color wanted.

Collins' "Alexandra" Portrait Cards.

No. 20K2277 A fine portrait card, beautifully embossed in color. The embossed design harmonizes in color with the shade of the mount, is richly ornamental, but not in the least obtrusive—one of the best dark border cards made.

Colors, Burmese brown or ash gray.

Size of Card	For Oval Photos	Price, per 100	Price, per 25
4¼x6½	2 x2¾	$0.89	23c
5 x6½	2⅝x3⅝	1.04	27c
5¼x7¼	3 x4⅛	1.08	28c
6 x8	3½x5	1.27	33c
4¼x7⅛	1⅞x3⅝	1.00	26c
5 x8½	2¾x5¼	1.28	34c

Be sure to state size and color wanted.

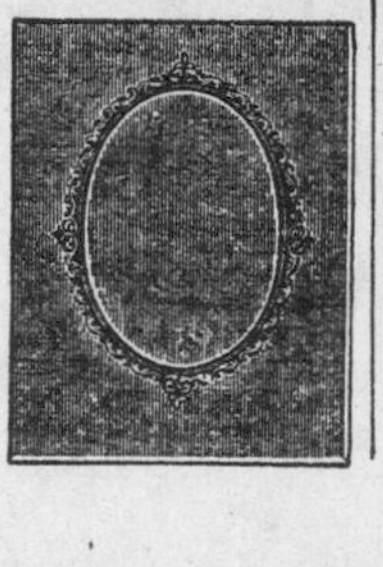

Collins' "Imperator" Portrait Cards.

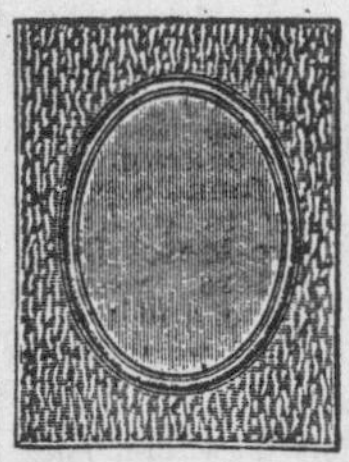

No. 20K2286 A staple mount with a wonderfully effective rough surface and wide, massive roll design, good heavy stock, square corners and plain bevel edges. Has every appearance of being a much more expensive mount.

Colors, white or ash gray.

Size of Card	For Photo	Shape of Opening	Price, per 100	Price, per 25
5¼x7¼	2¾x3⅞	square	$1.21	32c
6 x8	3⅞x5½	square	1.59	41c
5½x9	3 x5½	square	1.68	44c
5¼x7¼	2⅝x3⅝	oval	1.25	33c
5¼x7¼	3 x4⅛	oval	1.25	33c
6 x8	3½x5	oval	1.59	41c

Be sure to state size and color wanted.

Collins' "Liberty" Folder.

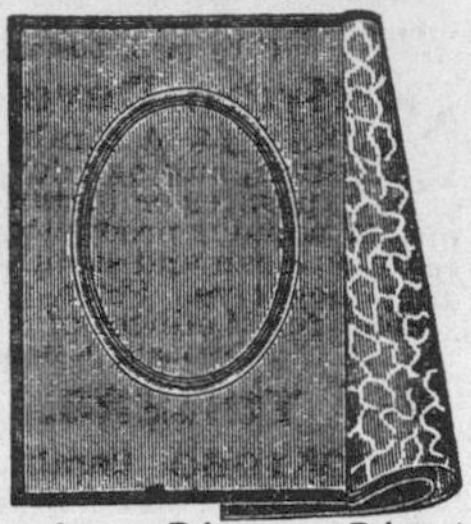

No. 30K2295 A most effective holder at a very low price. The cover is the best quality of heavy paper, the tissue a beautiful moire embossed pattern, and the enclosed mount is of fine heavy stock with handsome embossed design, square corners and plain beveled edges.

Colors, Cornwall gray and sable brown.

Size of Folder	For Photos	Shape of Opening	Price, per 100	Price, per 25
5⅜x7½	2⅝x3⅝	oval	$2.47	65c
6¼x9¼	3½x5	oval	3.19	83c
6¼x9¼	2¾x5½	oval	3.19	83c
5⅜x7½	2¾x3⅞	square	2.47	65c
6¼x9¼	3⅞x5½	square	3.19	83c
6¼x9¼	3 x5½	square	3.19	83c

Be sure to state size and color wanted.

The Little Gem Albums.

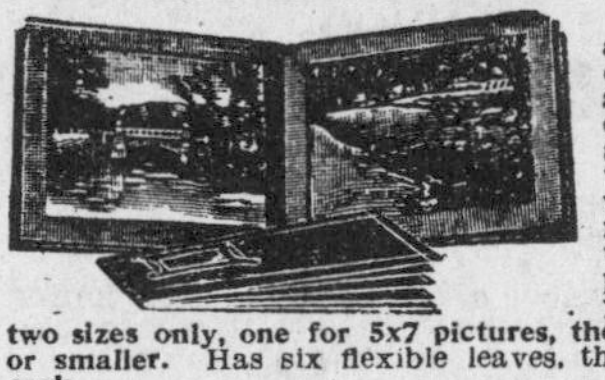

You frequently have a few pictures which are especially interesting, and which if mounted on cards are apt to get soiled or misplaced; but this neat little booklet will exactly fill your requirements, bring out the beauty of your photographs and please your friends. Made in two sizes only, one for 5x7 pictures, the other for pictures 4x5 or smaller. Has six flexible leaves, thus holding 12 pictures each.

No. 20K2401 The Little Gem Album for pictures 4x5 or smaller. Price........................ **8c**

No. 20K2402 The Little Gem Album for pictures 5x7. Price........................ **12c**

Order several, they are cheaper than card mounts.

Flexible Leaf Albums.

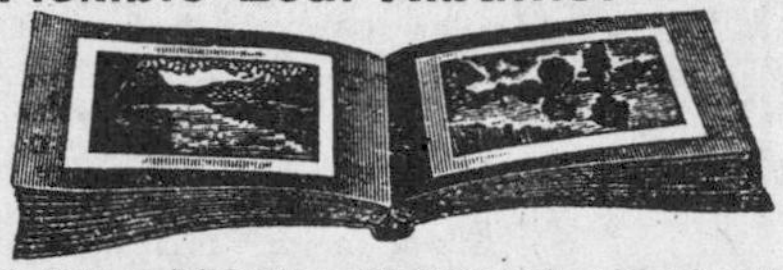

These very attractive albums are made with flexible covers and leaves, bound in best black English book cloth, or full leather with either seal grain or heavy walrus grain effect. The leaves are of the popular ash gray tint, harmonizing with almost any kind of print, and making the albums suitable either for matt surface prints on developing paper, or for glossy squeegeed prints on printing out papers. In mounting on these thin flexible leaves it is only necessary to put a little paste on each corner or along one edge of the print.

Catalogue No.	Size of Leaf, inches	Number of Leaves	Price, English Cloth	Price, Seal Grain Leather	Price, Heavy Walrus Grain Leather
20K2410	5½x 7	25	$0.20	$0.38	$0.54
20K2411	5½x 7	50	.32	.44	.60
20K2412	7 x10	25	.35	.64	.74
20K2413	7 x10	50	.44	.72	.90
20K2414	10 x12	25	.59	.96	1.28
20K2415	10 x12	50	.64	1.10	1.42
20K2416	11 x14	25	.70	1.15	1.70
20K2417	11 x14	50	.82	1.60	1.90

Pleasing effects are secured by putting several prints on a page; for example, four prints, 4x5, just fit the 11x14 leaf.

Souvenir Postal Card Albums.

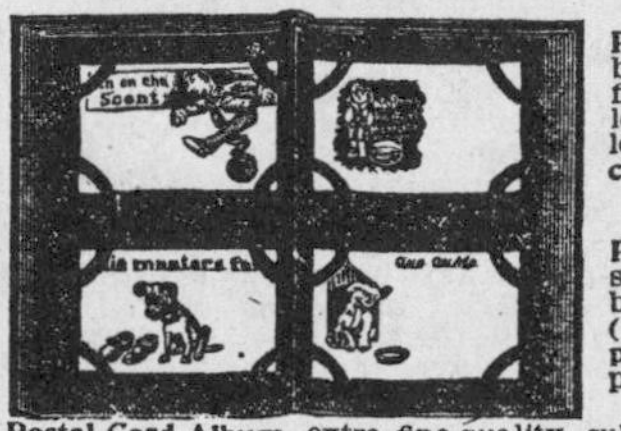

No. 20K2481 Postal Card Album, bound in cloth with fine quality melton leaves, 24 pages (12 leaves), holds 24 postal cards, one on a page. Price........ **18c**

No. 20K2482 Postal Card Album, same as No. 20K2481, but larger size, 24 pages (12 leaves), holds 48 postal cards, one on a page. Price...... **30c**

No. 20K2486 Postal Card Album, extra fine quality, substantially bound, 100 pages (50 leaves), holds 100 postal cards, one on a page.

Price, bound in fine silk finish black cloth **38c**

Price, bound in heavy extra quality black walrus grain leather................................ **69c**

No. 20K2487 Postal Card Album. Same quality as No. 20K2486 but larger size, 100 pages (50 leaves), holds 200 postal cards, two on a page.

Price, bound in fine silk finish black cloth **70c**

Price, bound in heavy, extra quality black walrus grain leather...................................... **$1.40**

No. 20K2488 Postal Card Album, same as No. 20K2486 but still larger size, 76 pages (38 leaves), holds 304 postal cards, four on a page.

Price, bound in fine silk finish black cloth.......... **$1.25**

Price, bound in heavy, extra quality black walrus grain leather **$2.70**

ABOUT THE QUALITY OF OUR DRAWING INSTRUMENTS.

OUR LOW PRICES EXPLAINED.

WE RECEIVE MANY INQUIRIES from customers, asking if we can furnish drawing sets with certain American dealers' names stamped on the instruments, and there seems to be an impression that instruments bearing these American dealers' names are in some way superior. There also seems to be a tendency among some of our customers, especially those who do not know us well, to **question the quality of our drawing sets,** because of the extremely low prices at which we sell them. We believe that **a plain statement of the facts in reference to drawing instruments** will enable our customers to understand how we are able to make these prices.

PRACTICALLY ALL THE DRAWING INSTRUMENTS sold in the United States are manufactured in Switzerland and Germany. These Swiss and German manufacturers supply the world with drawing instruments. Now, those American dealers, those dealers whose names are seen on instruments in this country, buy these instruments from the same Swiss and German manufacturers who supply us with our instruments, **they buy the exact same quality,** and the manufacturers stamp on the instruments the names of the American dealers who sell them.

SOME OF THESE AMERICAN WHOLESALE DEALERS PRETEND TO BE MANUFACTURERS but they are not. They buy their instruments from the exact same factories in Europe that we buy ours, and they buy the exact same styles and qualities of instruments. The big American wholesale dealer makes up an order every season for drawing instruments, and he gives this order to a New York importing house. The New York importing house transmits the order to a commission man in Europe and the commission man places the order with the factory, where the goods are made up and **stamped with the American wholesale dealer's name.** Now, the factory makes its profit,

the commission man makes his profit, the New York importing house makes another profit, the big American wholesale dealer makes his profit when he sells the goods to the retail dealer, and the retail dealer adds on still another good, generous profit, when he sells the goods to the user. This system of marketing drawing instruments means that there are **many profits between the factory and the user,** and the fact that the American dealer's name is stamped on the instruments means nothing at all, except a higher price to the user.

WE BUY OUR INSTRUMENTS from the exact same factories that supply the big American wholesale dealers, but our European representative places our order direct with the factories in Switzerland and Germany, and when the goods reach our store there has been only one profit made on them—namely, the manufacturer's profit. We sell the instruments direct to the user, and, therefore, between the manufacturer and the user there is just one small percentage of profit added to the cost of the goods. **That is why we can sell the same quality of instruments for less money than the retail dealer;** that is why we can absolutely guarantee that every set of instruments described on this page is equal in every way to instruments sold by the ordinary dealer at double our price.

WE ASK YOU $9.30 for our No. 20K4125 set. This exact same set, made in the same factory and identical in quality, if sold through the regular channels and stamped with some American dealer's name, would be retailed at from **$18.00 to $20.00,** and the only difference between our set at $9.30 and the American dealer's set at $20.00, lies in the fact that the American dealer's name is stamped on his set and it is not stamped on the set that we sell you. **The quality is exactly the same.** The American retail dealer asks you from $10.00 to $12.00 for a set corresponding in every way to our No. 20K4110, the exact same quality that we sell you for $5.85.

DO YOU THINK that the American dealer's name stamped on a drawing instrument is worth the price you are compelled to pay for it?

$1.15 Buys This Scholars' Set.

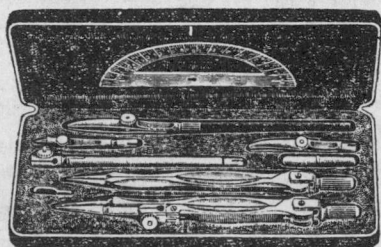

No. 20K4100 Scholars' Fine Drawing Set, consisting of 5-inch Ruling Pen, 5-inch Compass with needle, pen and pencil points, 5-inch Plain Dividers, Metal Protractor and Case of Leads.
  Price, per dozen.......$13.25
  Each..................... 1.15
  If by mail, postage extra, 8 cents.

Fine Pivot Joint Set for $3.75.

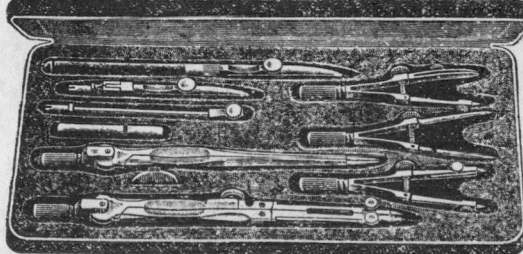

No. 20K4105 Fine Quality German Silver Drawing Set, consisting of 5½-inch Ruling Pen with spring blade 3½-inch Steel Spring Bow Dividers, 3½-inch Steel Spring Bow Pencil, 3½-inch Steel Spring Bow Pen, 5¾-inch Pivot Joint Dividers, 5-inch Pivot Joint Compass with pen and pencil points, Lengthening Bar for Compass and Box of Leads. The best set ever sold for less than $5.00.
  Price, per dozen, $43.65; each, $3.75
  If by mail, postage extra, each, 14 cents.

Big Value at $5.85.

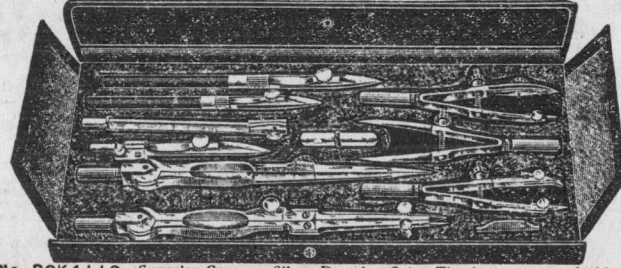

No. 20K4110 Superior German Silver Drawing Set. The instruments of this set are made from the finest grade of hard German Silver, carefully tempered and highly finished. The tongues of the joints, needle points and other steel parts are made from the best English Steel, finely tempered and hardened. Both the dividers and compasses are made with the famous pivot joint, universally accepted by draftsmen as the most desirable joint made. The following instruments are included: 4¼-inch Ruling Pen with spring blade, 5-inch Ruling Pen with spring blade, 5-inch Hair Spring Dividers with pivot joint; 5½-inch Compasses, pivot joint, with pen, pencil and needle points, Lengthening Bar for Compasses, 3½-inch Spring Bow Dividers with metal handle, 3½-inch Spring Bow Pencil with metal handle, 3½-inch Spring Bow Pen with metal handle and Box of Leads. This elegant set is contained in our new style folding pocketbook case, made of genuine seal grain morocco leather and lined with silk velvet.
  Price, per dozen, $68.10; each....................$5.85
  If by mail, postage extra, each, 14 cents.

High Grade Wrought Metal Set for $7.60.

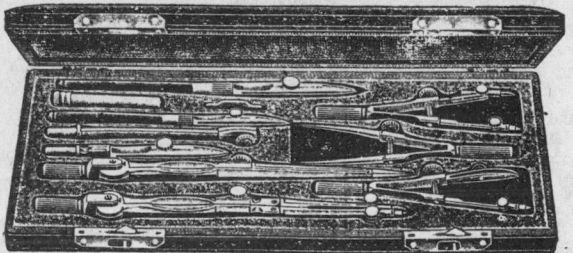

No. 20K4115 Extra High Grade German Silver Wrought Metal Drawing Set, consisting of 5-inch Ruling Pen, 4¼-inch Ruling Pen, 3½-inch Steel Spring Bow Dividers, 3½-inch Steel Spring Bow Pen, 3½-inch Steel Spring Bow Pencil, 6-inch Pivot Joint Hair Spring Dividers, 6-inch Pivot Joint Compass, pen and pencil points, Lengthening Bar for Compass and Case of Leads. We guarantee this set to equal in quality any set sold by ordinary dealers at $15.00. It is a set that will meet the requirements in the very best technical schools in this country. This set is put up in the regulation leather covered slide catch pocket case, lined with silk velvet.
  Price, per dozen, $88.46; each........... (Postage extra, each, 13c) $7.60

Our Special College Set at $8.75.

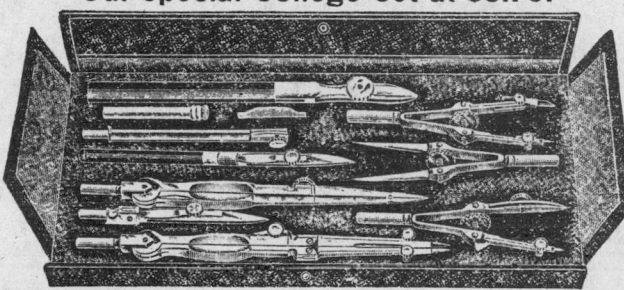

No. 20K4120 A very high grade Wrought Metal German Silver Drawing Set. Made up of 1 6-inch Swedish border line Ruling Pen, 1 4½-inch Ruling Pen, 1 6-inch Pivot Joint Compass with pen and pencil points and Lengthening Bar, 1 6-inch Pivot Joint Hair Spring Dividers, 3½ inch Center Wheel Spring Bow Pen, 3½-inch Center Wheel Spring Bow Dividers, 3½-inch Center Wheel Spring Bow Pencil and Case of Leads. This is one of the most popular and practical sets of Drawing Instruments on the market. It has been especially designed to meet the requirements of college and mechanical course students. The instruments are of the very best material throughout, finely finished, and will meet with the approval of the most exacting professors of mechanical courses. The instruments are put up in a rich silk velvet lined pocketbook case. Price, per dozen. $101.85; each.................$8.75
  If by mail, postage extra, each, 14 cents.

Our Special Wrought Metal Set at $9.30.

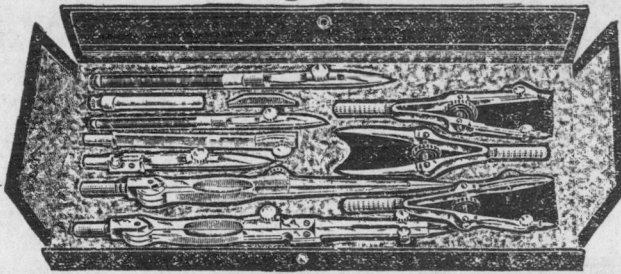

No. 20K4125 Extra High Grade German Silver Drawing Set, consisting of 5-inch Ruling Pen, 4¼-inch Ruling Pen, 3½-inch Steel Spring Bow Dividers, 3½-inch Steel Spring Bow Pen, 3½-inch Steel Spring Bow Pencil, 6-inch Pivot Joint Hair Spring Dividers, 6-inch Pivot Joint Compass, pen and pencil points, Lengthening Bar for Compass, Case of Leads. We cannot recommend this set too highly. Every instrument is made with the utmost care and guaranteed to be perfect. Workmanship and materials used throughout are the very highest grade, and we know that this set is equal in quality to any set sold regardless of price. This set is put up in the very latest style folding pocketbook case, made with the finest quality morocco leather and lined with brown chamois skin, giving the set an exceptionally rich appearance. It is a case well fitted to contain this exceptionally high grade set of instruments. Price, per dozen, $108.25; each.................$9.30
  If by mail, postage extra, each, 13 cents.

$11.90 for This Big Pivot Joint Drawing Set.

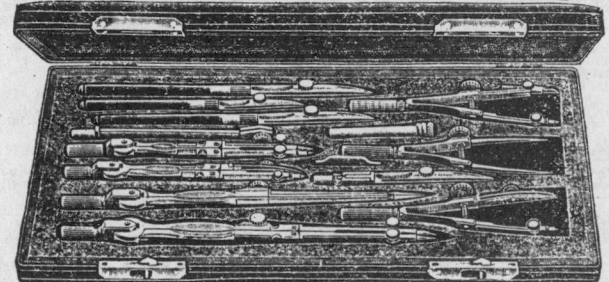

No. 20K4130 This is one of the largest and most complete sets of extra high grade pivot joint German Silver Instruments that we handle, and is designed especially to meet the requirements of those who desire not only the very highest grade of instruments, but at the same time the most complete assortment and largest number of pieces. This set consists of 5½-inch Ruling Pen, 5-inch Ruling Pen, 4¼-inch Ruling Pen, 3½-inch Steel Spring Bow Dividers, 3½-inch Steel Spring Bow Pen, 3½-inch Steel Spring Bow Pencil, 5¾-inch Pivot Joint Hair Spring Dividers, 6-inch Compass set and pen and pencil points, 4½-inch Pivot Joint Compass, pen point and needle point, 4½-inch Pivot Joint Compass, needle point and pencil point, Lengthening Bar for the 6-inch Compass, Case of Leads. The largest set of strictly high grade absolutely guaranteed instruments ever sold for less than $25.00. This set is put up in the regulation style morocco covered slide catch pocket case, lined with fine quality silk velvet.
  Price, per dozen, $138.50; each... (If by mail, postage extra, each, 23c)..... $11.90

OUR FINEST PROFESSIONAL DRAWING SET AT $15.80.

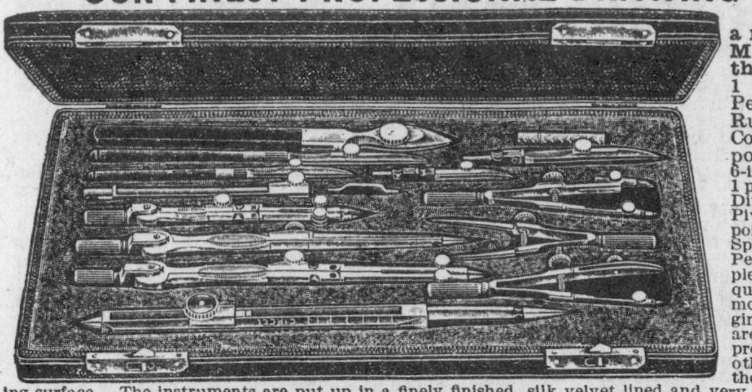

No. 20K4135 Most complete and finest quality Wrought Metal German Silver Drawing Set that can be produced. Consists of 1 6-inch Swedish border-line Ruling Pen, 1 5½-inch Ruling Pen, 1 4-inch Ruling Pen, 1 pair 6-inch Pivot Joint Compasses with pen and pencil points and Lengthening Bar, 1 pair 6-inch Pivot Joint Hair Spring Dividers, 1 pair very best grade 7½-inch Proportional Dividers for lines and circles, 1 pair 4-inch Pivot Joint Compasses, with pen and pencil points, 3½-inch Spring Bow Pen, 3½-inch Spring Bow Dividers, 3½-inch Spring Bow Pencil and case of leads. This set is complete in every respect, and unexcelled in quality. It fills the requirements of the most exacting architects, builders and engineers. All joints and working points are finished with the utmost skill and care, producing extremely accurate results. All other parts are finished and polished to the highest degree, making the finest wearing surface. The instruments are put up in a finely finished, silk velvet lined and very substantial Slide Lock Case, the very finest appearing and best wearing case made. Price, per dozen, $183.90; each.....(Postage extra, 26 cents).....$15.80

Complete Drafting Outfit, $7.75.

This big and complete Draftman's Outfit is strictly high class throughout, every item carefully selected, the very best quality that we can secure and absolutely guaranteed. An outfit that is suitable for correspondence school work, and in every way superior to the outfits usually furnished for such work. **Hawkins' Self Help Mechanical Drawing,** the complete manual of mechanical drawing included with this outfit, contains 320 pages, and 300 illustrations. It is strongly and handsomely bound in fine silk finish green cloth, with title stamped in gold, printed on the very finest white calendered paper, with full gold edges; extra large size, measuring 7x10 inches. This book covers the subject of mechanical drawing from start to finish, and is carefully arranged according to the fundamental principles of the art of drawing. It gives full information regarding drawing materials and instruments, free hand drawing, mechanical drawing, geometrical drawing, penciling, projection, inking-in drawings, lettering, etc. It gives drawing office rules, rules for patent office drawings, useful tables of all kinds; in short, the most complete, comprehensive and practical book published on mechanical drawing.

The Outfit contains the following items: 1 copy Hawkins' Self Help Mechanical Drawing for home study.

1 set of our No. 20K4105 pivot joint instruments, with three bow instruments, compasses, dividers, pen, etc.
1 16x22 Drawing Board.
1 24-inch T Square, mahogany, ebony lined.
1 4½-inch German Silver Protractor, engine divided.
1 12-inch Triangular Boxwood Scale, engine divided.
1 8-inch Transparent Celluloid Triangle, 30x60 degrees.
1 6-inch Transparent Celluloid Triangle, 45 degrees.
1 Hard Rubber Curve.
1 Dozen Brass Thumb Tacks, fine quality.
1 Venus Pencil, HHHH.
1 Bottle Higgins' Waterproof Ink.
1 Ink and Pencil Eraser.
2 Sheets 16x21 Tracing Cloth.
6 Sheets Whatman's Best Drawing Paper, 15x20.

No. 20K4150 Complete Drafting Outfit, as described above. Price, complete.....$7.75

Spring Bow Instruments.

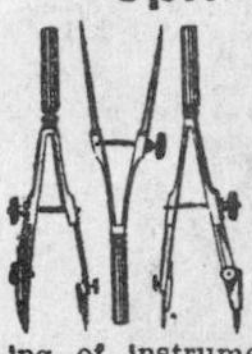

No. 20K4200 Spring Bow Dividers, finely tempered English steel, German silver handle, 3½ inches long. Price.....35c
If by mail, postage extra, 3 cents.

No. 20K4201 Spring Bow Pencil, finely tempered English steel, German silver handle; 3½ inches long. Price.....55c
If by mail, postage extra, 3 cents.

No. 20K4202 Spring Bow Pen, finely tempered English steel, German silver handle; 3½ inches long. Price.....55c
If by mail, postage extra, 3 cents.

No. 20K4203 Spring Bow Set, consisting of instruments Nos. 20K4200, 20K4201 and 20K4202 in fine morocco covered case. Price. (Postage extra, 4c.).$1.90

Ruling Pen.

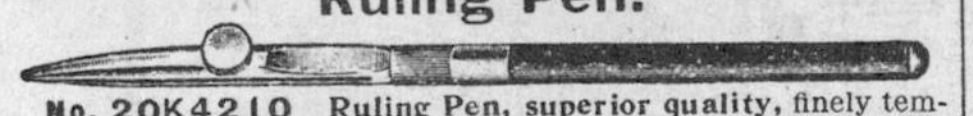

No. 20K4210 Ruling Pen, superior quality, finely tempered English steel, upper blade with spring, ebony handle. 5 inches long. Price, each....(Postage extra, 2 cents)...48c

Slide Rule, $3.55.

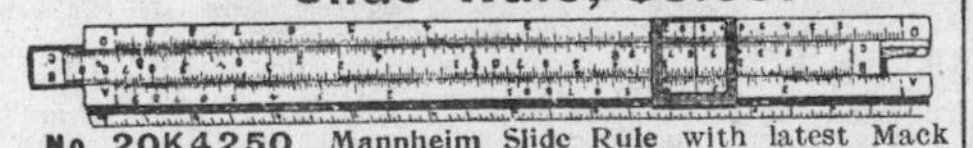

No. 20K4250 Mannheim Slide Rule with latest Mack improvement, constructed so that extremely dry or wet weather does not affect the free running of the slide. This rule is one of the very best made and is guaranteed to do all calculations that can be done with any other rule on the market.
Price, with complete instructions.....$3.55
If by mail, postage extra, 10 cents.

Protractors.

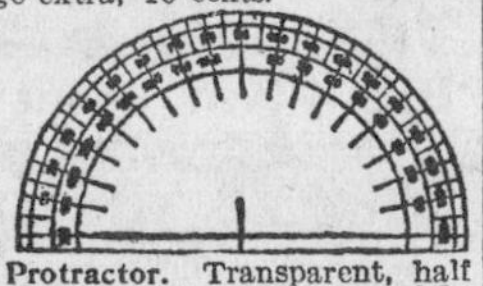

Used for dividing circles into any number of equal parts and determining angles.

No. 20K4260 Brass Protractor. Diameter 4¼-inch half circle, 1 degree graduations, a high grade instrument. Price. (Postage. ex. 2c.). 19c

No. 20K4264 Celluloid Protractor. Transparent, half circle, diameter, 6 inches, ½ degree graduations. Price...48c
If by mail, postage extra, 2 cents.

No. 20K4268 German Silver Protractor. Half circle, diameter, 5⅛ inches, ½ degree graduations. Price.......45c
If by mail, postage extra, 2 cents.

Triangular Boxwood Scales.

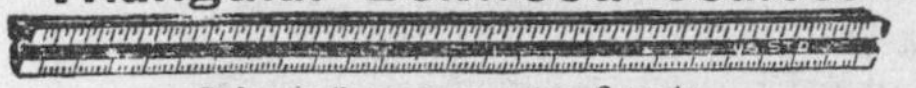

If by mail, postage extra, 6 cents.

No. 20K4275 Architects' Triangular Boxwood Scale, divided 3-32, 3-16, ⅛, ¼, ⅜, ½, ¾, 1, 1½, 3-inch to the foot, 1-16-inch. Best seasoned boxwood, engine divided, U. S. standard, 12 inches long. Price.....38c

No. 20K4277 Architects' Triangular Boxwood Scale, same as No. 20K4275, but with white edges, 12 inches long. Price.....$1.26

No. 20K4280 Engineers' Triangular Boxwood Scale, divided, 10, 20, 30, 40, 50, 60 parts to inch, best seasoned boxwood, engine divided, U. S. standard, 12 inches long. Price.....38c

No. 20K4282 Engineers' Triangular Boxwood Scale, same as No. 20K4280, but with white edges, 12 inches long. Price.....$1.26

Do not judge these scales by the price. We will refund your money if you do not find them equal to the highest priced scales offered by other dealers.

Wooden Triangles.

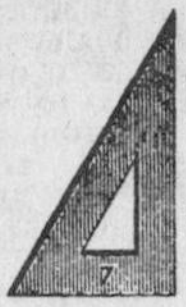

No. 20K4300 Cherry Triangles, 30 by 60 degrees, mortised joints.

Size, inches	8	10	12	14
Price	11c	13c	16c	22c
If by mail, postage extra	3c	4c	5c	6c

No. 20K4301 Cherry Triangles, 45 degrees, mortised joints.

Size, inches	6	8	10	12
Price	11c	13c	17c	22c
If by mail, postage extra	3c	4c	5c	6c

Transparent Celluloid Triangles.

These triangles allow more rapid and accurate work owing to their transparency, do not collect dust, and keep their edges almost like metal tools.

No. 20K4305 Transparent Celluloid Triangles 30 by 60 degrees, open center.

Size, inches	4	6	8	10	12	14
Price	14c	23c	38c	48c	58c	80c
If by mail, postage extra	2c	3c	4c	5c	6c	8c

No. 20K4306 Transparent Celluloid Triangles, 45 degrees, open center.

Size, inches	4	6	8	10	12	14
Price	22c	30c	40c	58c	87c	$1.10
If by mail, postage extra	2c	3c	4c	5c	6c	8c

T Squares.

No. 20K4315 T Square, with cherry blade and fixed head.

Length, inches	15	18	24	30	36	42
Price	12c	15c	17c	21c	25c	29c

Weight of 15, 18, and 24-inch, packed 11, 14 and 26 ounces. Larger sizes not mailable. (For postage rate see page 10.)

No. 20K4318 T Square, maple blade and black walnut fixed head.

Length, inches	24	30	36	42	48	54
Price	29c	33c	38c	42c	47c	60c

Weight of 24-inch, packed, 26 ounces. Larger sizes not mailable. (For postage rate see page 10.)

No. 20K4321 T Square, cherry blade and movable head, with improved clamping swivel.

Length, inches	24	30	36	42
Price	57c	68c	75c	90c

Weight of 24-inch, packed, 26 ounces. Larger sizes not mailable. (For postage rate see page 10.)

No. 20K4324 T Square, mahogany, ebony lined blade and fixed head. A very fine square.

Length, inches	24	30	36	42	48
Price	65c	79c	90c	$1.08	$1.26

Weight of 24-inch packed, 26 ounces. Larger sizes not mailable. (For postage rate see page 10.)

Drawing Boards.

No. 20K4335 Drawing Board, made of pine with two drawing surfaces and side ledges.

Size, inches	12x17	16x22	20x24½	23x31
Price	57c	70c	80c	$1.24

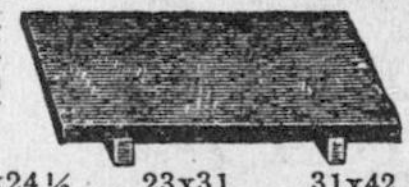

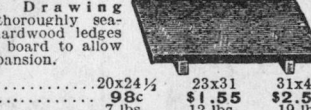

No. 20K4337 Drawing Board, made of thoroughly seasoned pine with hardwood ledges dovetailed into the board to allow contraction and expansion.

Size, inches	20x24½	23x31	31x42
Price	98c	$1.55	$2.55
Shipping weight	7 lbs.	12 lbs.	19 lbs.

Folding Stand, $5.85.

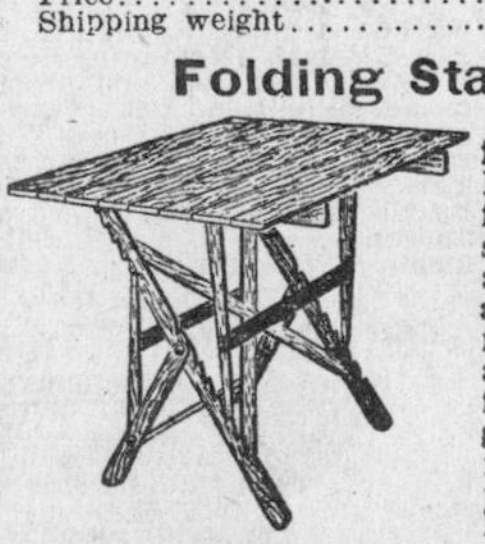

No. 20K4340 Folding Stand and Drawing Board, especially designed for architects' use. The stand is made very rigid and has a great range of adjustment. Height running from 31 to 41 inches, and the slant of board from horizontal to 45 degrees. The board is made from the finest selected pine wood and has special hardwood edges.

Price, complete, size, 31x42 inches.....$5.85
Price, complete, size, 36x55 inches.....7.35
Shipping weight, large size, 60 lbs.; small size, 50 lbs.

Thumb Tacks.

No. 20K4360 Steel Thumb Tacks, stamped from one piece of steel. An excellent tack at a very low price. Put up only in boxes of 100.

Diameter, inch	5/16	⅜	½
Price, per box of 100	24c	30c	39c

If by mail, postage extra, per box, 3, 6 and 7 cents.

Brass or German Silver Thumb Tacks.

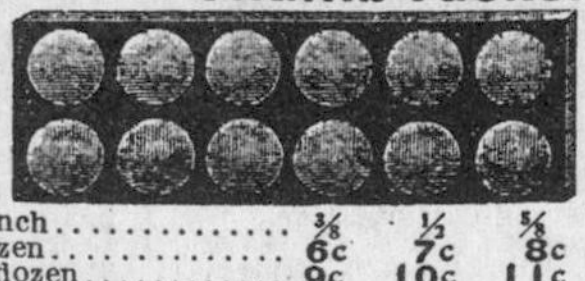

No. 20K4362 First quality Tacks made with either German silver or brass heads. Cannot push through nor pull out. Each dozen put up in cork, as shown in illustration.

Diameter, inch	⅜	½	⅝
Brass. Price, per dozen	6c	7c	8c
German silver. Per dozen	9c	10c	11c

If by mail, postage extra, per dozen, 2 cents.

Irregular Curves.

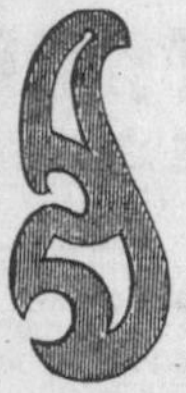

No. 20K4370 Irregular Curves, accurately made from hard rubber, and invaluable for drawing in irregular curves. Price.....(Postage extra, 3c).....27c

No. 20K4372 Irregular Curves, same as No. 20K4370, but made of transparent celluloid. Price..(Postage extra, 3c)...39c

Liquid Drawing Inks.

No. 20K4380 Higgins' Black Waterproof Ink. Put up in ¾-ounce bottles. Stopper fitted with quill for filling pen.
Price, per dozen, $2.25; per bottle.......19c
If by mail, mailing tube and postage extra, 10 cents.

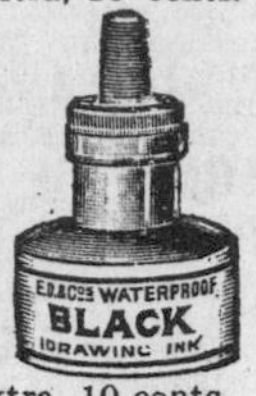

No. 20K4385 Celebrated Dietzgen Black, Waterproof Ink. This ink is guaranteed to be the acme of quality. The recipe for this ink has recently been perfected after years of careful study to obtain an ink that would fulfill the requirements of the most particular draftsmen. Put up in 1-ounce bottles with patent stopper and quill to fill pen.
Price, per bottle.....$0.20
Per dozen.....2.30
If by mail, mailing tube and postage extra, 10 cents.

No. 20K4386 Dietzgen Colored Drawing Inks, indelible, put up in same style bottles as No. 20K4385, with quill for filling pen; yellow, orange, scarlet, carmine, blue, green or brown. Be sure to state color wanted. Weight, packed, 13 ounces. Price, per bottle.....$0.20
Per dozen, assorted colors.....2.30
If by mail, postage and mailing tube extra, 10 cents.

India Ink.

No. 20K4390 Lion Head India Ink, first quality black.
Price, small size.....9c
Large size, 3 times small size..(Postage extra, 1c)...21c

Venus Drawing Pencils, 9 Cents.

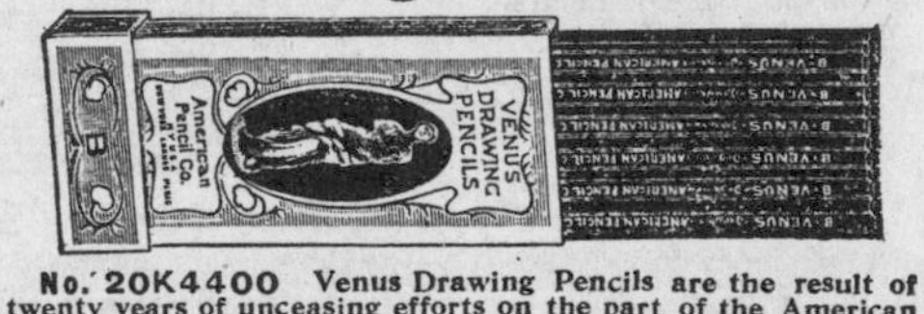

No. 20K4400 Venus Drawing Pencils are the result of twenty years of unceasing efforts on the part of the American Lead Pencil Company to produce an absolutely perfect drawing pencil, and as such, this pencil is now recognized by the most experienced draftsmen. This pencil comes in 12 different grades, as follows;
B, HB, F, H, 2H, 3H, 4H, 5H, 6H, 7H, 8H, 9H. Be sure to state degree of hardness wanted.

	Each.	Per dozen	Per gross
Price	9c	$1.00	$11.40

If by mail, postage extra, per dozen, 6 cents; each, 1 cent.

Crow Quill Pens.

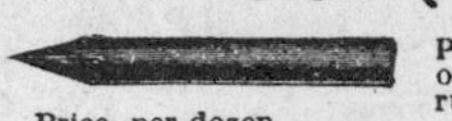

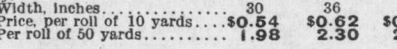

No. 20K4410 Crow Quill Pens, very fine and stiff, put up on cards of one dozen, with hard rubber holder. Genuine Gillott's.
Price, per dozen.....48c
If by mail, postage extra, 3 cents.

Sponge Rubber.

No. 20K4415 Sponge Rubber, extra fine grade, very soft and pure, with solid rubber back. Very useful in cleaning drawings and erasing pencil lines, without disturbing ink lines. Price.....24c
If by mail, postage extra, 2 cents.

Drawing Papers.

No. 20K4425 German Drawing Paper, an excellent white paper, strong, stands pencil erasing well, has slightly grained surface, suitable for work in pencil, ink or colors.
Size, 10x13½ inches. Price, per quire (24 sheets)..18c
Size, 13½x20 inches. Price, per quire (24 sheets)..35c

No. 20K4430 Whatmann's Drawing Paper, either hot or cold pressed. This paper is hand made from the finest linen stock and is universally conceded by draftsmen to be the finest drawing paper made. The hot pressed has a smooth surface, mostly used for very fine drawing. The cold pressed has a finely grained surface, used for general drawings and water color work.
Size, 13x17 inches. Price, per quire.....$0.53
Size, 15x20 inches. Price, per quire.....78
Size, 19x24 inches. Price, per quire.....1.50
Size, 22x30 inches. Price, per quire.....2.60
Size, 27x40 inches. Price, per quire.....4.65
Always state whether "hot" or "cold" pressed is desired.

No. 20K4435 Cream Drawing Paper, the best paper made for preliminary drawings and sketching. Stands erasing perfectly, and takes pencil, ink, or water color well. The cream tint is agreeable to the eye, and admits of much handling without showing soil. Does not break when folded.

Width, inches	30	36	42
Price, per yard	11c	13c	18c

Tracing Cloth.

No. 20K4440 Tracing Cloth, fine quality, one side glazed, the other side dull.

Width, inches	30	36	42
Price, per yard	$0.35	$0.40	$0.50
Per roll of 24 yards	6.18	8.88	11.90

Tracing Paper.

No. 20K4445 Tracing Paper, dull finish, very tough and transparent. Takes either pencil or ink and stands erasing. Comes only in 20-yard rolls, 42 inches wide.
Price, per roll.....$1.05

No. 20K4450 Oil Finish Tracing Paper, very thin and transparent. Specially adapted for printing blue prints from, and for making tracings from blue prints. Comes only in 20-yard rolls, 39 inches wide. Price, per roll.....95c

Blue Print Paper.

No. 20K4455 Blue Print Paper, very best quality for architect's use. This is a satin finished paper, giving a rich, deep blue color and clear whites. Furnished with regular coating during the summer months and extra rapid coating during the winter months. Furnished in 10 and 50-yard rolls only.

Width, inches	30	36	42
Price, per roll of 10 yards	$0.54	$0.62	$0.68
Per roll of 50 yards	1.98	2.30	2.57

THE GLORIA MAGIC LANTERN OUTFITS

$4.98 TO $6.85

GENUINE GLORIA MAGIC LANTERNS, Made by Ernst Plank, in Nuremberg, Germany.

THE GLORIA Magic Lanterns come from the famous factory of Ernst Plank, Nuremberg, Germany, noted as the maker of the finest magic lanterns in the world. They are strictly high-grade lanterns, made of genuine Russia sheet iron lacquered, with brass trimmings, finely finished all the way through; handsome and fine appearing, as well as thoroughly practical, strong and durable lanterns. **THE LENSES** and other special features. The Gloria Lanterns are provided with two large size condensing lenses, and a fine, specially ground projection lens which is focused by rack and pinion movement. This perfect optical construction, together with the powerful duplex lamp, results in producing on the screen, a sharp, clean cut picture of unusual brilliancy and clearness. The lamp with which the Gloria Lantern is equipped is made with double or duplex burner, giving an exceptionally white and powerful light, and perfect ventilation is secured by the ample air spaces at the bottom of the lantern and the tall Russia iron chimney. This lantern burns ordinary kerosene (coal oil) and is an exceptionally fine instrument for parlor exhibitions.

PACKED IN WOODEN CASE. The Gloria Lanterns, together with all the slides, the colored slide, the slip slide, the movable scenery slide, the chromotrope, and one extra glass chimney, comes packed in a well made hinged cover wooden case, and will certainly delight and please any boy or girl who is fortunate enough to get one.

No. 20K2831 Gloria Magic Lantern Outfit, size No. 1. Exactly as illustrated and described above, using slides 2 inches wide, producing pictures on the screen from 3 to 4 feet in diameter. Shipping weight, 9¾ pounds.
Price, for the complete outfit.......... **$4.98**

No. 20K2833 Gloria Magic Lantern Outfit, size No. 2. Exactly the same as outfit No. 20K2831, but larger size, using slides 2⅜ inches wide, and producing pictures 4 to 5 feet in diameter. Shipping weight, 11 pounds.
Price, for the complete outfit **$5.90**

No. 20K2835 Gloria Magic Lantern Outfit, size No. 3. Exactly the same as outfit No. 20K2831, but still larger, using slides 2¾ inches wide, and producing pictures from 5 to 6 feet in diameter. Shipping weight, 12¾ pounds. Price, for the complete outfit **$6.85**

EACH GLORIA MAGIC LANTERN OUTFIT CONTAINS OUR GLORIA MAGIC LANTERN,

TWELVE COLORED SLIDES with four pictures on each slide, making 48 different pictures.
ONE COMIC SLIP SLIDE producing most amusing effects.
ONE MOVABLE SCENERY SLIDE always an interesting feature to the youngsters.
ONE BRILLIANT CHROMOTROPE or artificial fire works slide.
FIFTY ADVERTISING POSTERS large size, sure to bring out a big audience.
FIFTY ADMISSION TICKETS regular full size tickets.

PLEASURE AND PROFIT. The Young People not only derive great pleasure from giving MAGIC LANTERN EXHIBITIONS, but the business training which they gain in all the various details connected with the management of an entertainment, putting up advertising posters, selling tickets, etc., gives them ideas of the rudiments of money making which starts them on the highway to business success. REMEMBER that each outfit is complete, containing a fine Magic Lantern, a splendid assortment of Colored Views, a large supply of Advertising Posters and plenty of Tickets. Interesting, instructive and profitable. You will easily make the original cost of the outfit in your first exhibition; after that it's all profit.

THE HOME MAGIC LANTERN OUTFITS.

48c to $1.89 according to size.

Our illustration gives a very exact idea of the general appearance and construction of the Home Magic Lantern. The body of this lantern is made of metal, japanned in black, handsomely decorated in gilt and mounted on wood base board. Burns ordinary kerosene or coal oil.

No. 20K2805 The Home Magic Lantern Outfit No. 1, with Home Magic Lantern as described above, using slides 1 3-16 inches wide, and magnifying pictures to about 1 foot in diameter. The complete outfit contains lantern, six colored slides, three to four pictures on each slide, twenty-five advertising posters and twenty-five admission tickets.
Price, complete. 48c
If by mail, postage extra, 24 cents.

No. 20K2808 Home Magic Lantern Outfit No. 2, same as No. 20K2805, but using slides 1 9-16 inches wide, magnifying pictures to 2 feet and including twelve colored slides instead of six.
Price, complete (If by mail, postage extra, 52c.)..........$1.25

No. 20K2811 Home Magic Lantern Outfit No. 3, same as No. 20K2805, but using slides 2 inches wide, magnifying pictures to about 3 feet in diameter.
Price, complete.. $1.89
Shipping weight, 4½ pounds.

THE BRILLIANT MAGIC LANTERN OUTFITS.

$1.90 to $3.75 according to size.

The Brilliant Magic Lanterns are very handsome instruments of the upright style, finely finished in brass, bronze, and nickel plate, with the body of the lantern enameled in bright red. They are provided with double convex condensing lens and finely ground projecting lens. In addition to the regular long glass slides, these lanterns also use a slide in the form of a round disc with six views. Each lantern contained in neat wood box with handle.

No. 20K2816 The Brilliant Magic Lantern Outfit No. 1, with Brilliant Magic Lantern as described above, using slides 1⅜ inches wide and magnifying pictures to about 2 feet in diameter. The complete outfit consists of lantern, six long glass colored slides, three to four views on each slide, three glass discs with six colored views on each disc, twenty-five advertising posters and twenty-five admission tickets. Shipping weight, 3½ pounds. Price, complete $1.90

No. 20K2819 Brilliant Magic Lantern Outfit No. 2, same as No. 20K2816, but using slides 1¾ inches wide, magnifying pictures to about 3 feet in diameter. Shipping weight, 5½ lbs.
Price, complete $2.98

No. 20K2823 Brilliant Magic Lantern Outfit No. 3, same as No. 20K2816, but using slides 2 inches wide, magnifying pictures to about 4 feet in diameter. Shipping weight, 7½ lbs.
Price, complete $3.75

Colored Slides.

Plain Colored Slides.

No. 20K2841 These slides are all highly colored and each slide has from three to four views. They are put up in packages of one dozen slides and each package contains an assortment of both comic and scenic views. **We cannot sell less than one package**, and we are unable to furnish any special subjects.

Width, inches	Price, per pkg. of 1 dozen	If by mail, postage extra	Width, inches	Price, per pkg. of 1 dozen	If by mail, postage extra
1 3/16	20c	9c	2	$0.64	23c
1⅜	30c	12c	2⅜	.85	31c
1 9/16	36c	18c	2¾	1.11	38c
1¾	51c	21c			

Comic Movable Slides.

No. 20K2843 These pictures are painted in bright colors on glass slips, which slide into metal frames, each slide containing two comic views. Very amusing effects are produced by suddenly slipping the second view into the place of the first. Put up in packages of one dozen slides each.

Width, inches	Price, per pkg. of 1 dozen	If by mail, postage extra	Width, inches	Price, per pkg. of 1 dozen	If by mail, postage extra
1⅜	60c	17c	2	$1.08	30c
1 9/16	67c	20c	2⅜	1.28	36c
1¾	92c	25c	2¾	1.48	50c

The Brilliant Slides.

No. 20K2845 Brilliant Slides, printed on celluloid and made in one size only, 2 inches wide, but can be used in any lantern using slides 2 inches or wider. If your lantern uses slides 2⅜ or 2¾ inches wide, we will include, for 8c extra, a small wooden carrier. Each series of the Brilliant Slides contains twelve slides, three pictures on each slide, making a total of thirty-six views in each series. Order by series. All the Brilliant Slides are 2 in. wide.

Series		Price
A	Noted Places Around the World	36c
B	Miscellaneous Views, mostly very comic	36c
H	Old and New Testament Bible Views	36c
I	Comic, each good for a laugh	36c
M	American and Foreign Scenery	36c

If by mail, postage extra, per set, 3 cents.

Chromotropes.

No. 20K2847 These Slides, known also as artificial fire-works, consist of two glass discs, painted in bright colors in radiating geometrical patterns, which are revolved in opposite directions by means of the small crank, producing a very brilliant effect. Several different patterns of each size can be furnished.

Width, 1 9-16 inches; price..................25c
Width, 1⅜ inches; price..................30c
Width, 2 inches; price..................33c
Width, 2⅜ inches; price..................36c
Width, 2¾ inches; price..................39c
If by mail, postage extra, on any size, 5 cents.

Genuine Photographic Slides.

Heretofore real photographic slides could be obtained only in the regular professional size, suitable only for use with the large professional stereopticons; they were made with only one view on a slide, and cost from 35 to 50 cents per view. Each set of our genuine photographic slides contains twelve slides, and there are four views on each slide, making a total of forty-eight views in every set. With every set we include a printed lecture, giving a complete description of every view.

No. 20K2849 Spanish-American War Set, photographic slides. See prices below.
No. 20K2850 Russian-Japanese War Set, photographic slides. See prices below.
No. 20K2852 St. Louis Exposition Set, photographic slides. See prices below.
No. 20K2853 San Francisco Earthquake Set, photographic slides. See prices below.
No. 20K2854 Bible Views Set, photographic slides. See prices below.

PRICES on any of the above sets of photographic slides are as follows:
Width, 1 9-16 inches; price, per set, with lecture....$1.13
Width, 2 inches; price, per set, with lecture....1.35
Width, 2⅜ inches; price, per set, with lecture....2.48
Width, 2¾ inches; price, per set, with lecture....2.93
Sold only in sets. We cannot sell less than a set.
If by mail, postage extra, for 1 9-16 inch, 20 cents; for 2 inch, 26 cents; for 2⅜ inch, 38 cents; for 2¾ inch, 44 cents.

Extra Chimneys and Wicks.

No. 20K2865 Chimney to fit any of the Home, Brilliant or Gloria Magic Lanterns. Price, each, any size......10c
If by mail, postage extra, for small sizes, 7 cents each; for large sizes to fit Gloria lanterns, 17 cents.

No. 20K2866 Wicks, to fit any of our magic lanterns. Price, six for..............................5c

NOTICE—When ordering chimneys or wicks be sure to state which lantern they are to fit.

NOTE—These photographic slides can be used with any of our Juvenile Lanterns except Nos. 20K2805 and 20K2816. Note in the description of the lanterns the size of slide used, and select the corresponding size in these photographic slides.

GUNS AND SPORTING GOODS

IN OUR OWN FIRE ARMS FACTORY at Meriden, Conn., a factory known as the Meriden Fire Arms Co., of Meriden, we make, under the direct management of Mr. A. J. Aubrey, president of our factory, a most complete line of exceptionally high grade fire arms, including hammer and hammerless single and double barrel breech loading shotguns, hammer and hammerless revolvers in various styles, all of which we sell under our famous Aubrey binding guarantee as the highest grade fire arms made in this country, and we sell them at prices based on the actual cost to produce in our own factory, plus our one small percentage of profit, prices so low that you can buy from us an Aubrey gun, made in our own factory, an arm of the highest standard of quality, at a much lower cost to you than you would have to pay for very inferior goods of other makes.

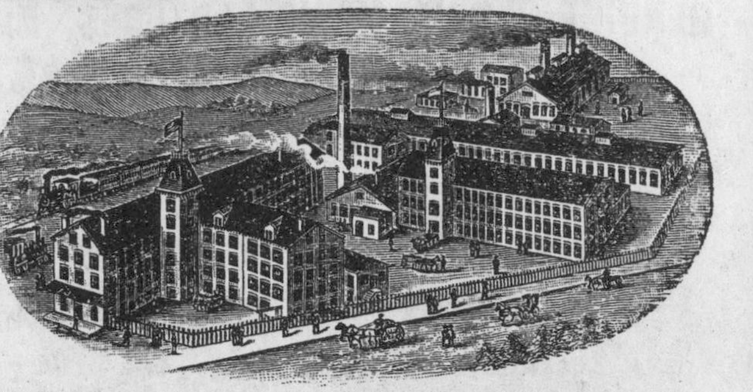

OUR GUN AND REVOLVER FACTORY AT MERIDEN, CONN.

WE SHOW YOU in a small illustration or picture a general view of our big fire arms factory at Meriden, Conn., the Meriden Fire Arms Co., a factory of which we are the sole owners and controllers, and you can get an idea of the size of this factory from the small illustration. It consists of five buildings, one three-story building 30x200 feet, one three-story building 30x70 feet, one one-story building 50x125 feet, one three-story building 30x140 feet and one four-story building 40x100 feet, and adjoining the buildings now erected there are about ten acres of vacant land belonging to us, all supplied with the best railroad side track facilities, and which ground we hope in the near future to cover in its entirety with the enormous factory we are reasonably sure of growing into as we increase our capacity and add to our line the various models we now have in process.

THIS, OUR GUN FACTORY, is located in the center of the fire arms manufacturing district, where skilled labor for this class of goods can be secured to the best advantage, and where the expenses of operating are reduced to the minimum. It is conveniently situated as regards transportation; railroad tracks are built in, onto and around our property for our special use, the factory is equipped with the highest type of gun and revolver making machinery, every machine that reduces labor and therefore expense, and we believe it is the most complete and most ideal fire arms factory in existence. Our output in this factory is already so large that we have reduced the purchase cost of the raw materials to the very minimum, and operating as we do continuously every day in the year, we are able to reduce our labor and manufacturing cost to a point not reached by any other makers in the country.

WHILE, AS BEFORE STATED, we show a very complete line of all well known standard fire arms, and we sell them at the lowest possible price based on their cost to us at the factory, to get the greatest possible value for your money, to get the benefit of our actual factory cost in our own factory, the cost of material and labor, with but our one small percentage of profit added, to get almost double the value of your money and to be secured by a written binding guarantee, we especially urge, in your own interest, that in ordering a fire arm from us you order an A. J. Aubrey gun.

OUR TEN DAYS' FREE TRIAL OFFER

IF YOU ORDER ANY FIRE ARM FROM US it must not only reach you in perfect condition, reach you promptly and prove perfectly satisfactory, but you also have the privilege of giving this fire arm ten days' thorough trial, during which time you can put it to every reasonable test, and if you use it with reasonable care, and if for any reason it doesn't prove satisfactory to you, you can return it to us at our expense any time within the ten days, and we will immediately return your money, together with any express or freight charges you may have paid. On all A. J. Aubrey guns and revolvers we give sixty days' free trial.

This is MR. A. J. AUBREY, President and General Manager of the Meriden Fire Arms Co. Mr. Aubrey is the designer of the famous A. J. Aubrey fire arms, and has a reputation as a builder of high grade fire arms which places him in the front rank among the gun manufacturers of the world. Before identifying himself with the Meriden Fire Arms Co., Mr. Aubrey was connected with several of the largest manufacturers of high class fire arms in this country. His experience extends back over a long period of years, in fact he has spent his entire life up to date in the gun business. The success he attained in the manufacture and designing of fire arms sold under different brands has been secondary only to the success attained in the manufacture of the fire arms which he has deemed worthy to bear as a brand his own name, namely, A. J Aubrey.

OUR SIXTY DAYS' FREE TRIAL OFFER AND TWENTY YEARS' BINDING GUARANTEE ON A. J. AUBREY FIRE ARMS.

IF YOU SEND US AN ORDER for an A. J. Aubrey fire arm, either a double or single barrel shotgun or revolver, it goes to you with all the privileges of any other fire arm, and the further privilege that you can have sixty days in which to put it to every test. All we ask is that you take reasonable care of the Aubrey fire arm, test it for target, for penetration, for pattern, for long, hard shooting, for strength, for appearance, for finish, put it up against any kind of a fire arm of any make, satisfy yourself in every particular, and remember, any time within sixty days, for any reason of your own, reasons you need not give us, you have the privilege of returning any Aubrey fire arm to us within sixty days, all at our expense, and we will immediately return your money, together with any freight or express charges you may have paid. With any A. J. Aubrey fire arm you have this further assurance and guarantee. As before stated, accompanying every Aubrey fire arm is our written binding twenty-year guarantee, by the terms and conditions of which if any piece or part of an A. J. Aubrey fire arm gives out within twenty years by reason of defect in material or workmanship, we will replace or repair such defective part free of any cost to you.

HOW TO ORDER.

SELECT THE GUN OR FIRE ARM YOU WANT, be sure you give the right catalogue number, the gauge (being the size of barrel or bore), be sure to give us the length of barrel wanted, enclose our price and send your order to us.

20 YEARS
Certificate of Guarantee,
This certifies that the Gun the name
& number of which has been registered is

OUR TWENTY YEARS' BINDING GUARANTEE AS APPLIED TO ALL A. J. AUBREY GOODS.

TO SHOW THE HIGH QUALITY of the A. J. Aubrey goods, fire arms made in our own gun factory at Meriden, Conn., we issue with every fire arm bearing the name of A. J. Aubrey our famous written binding twenty-year guarantee.

IF YOU BUY FROM US an A. J. Aubrey fire arm, either a double or single barrel shotgun, or an A. J. Aubrey revolver or other fire arm, when we send you the fire arm we will also send you our written binding twenty-year guarantee, such a guarantee as is given with no other fire arm made in America. By the terms and conditions of this famous twenty-year binding guarantee, applied only to A. J. Aubrey fire arms, if any piece or part of any A. J. Aubrey fire arm gives out by reason of defect in material or workmanship, at any time within twenty years, we will repair or replace such defect free of cost to the purchaser.

$13.85 THE GREAT A. J. AUBREY GUN

AT $13.85, $16.35, $19.35 AND ON UP TO $38.50, as shown in this catalogue, we at all times carry in stock a full supply of the celebrated A. J. Aubrey Hammerless Double Barrel Breech Loading Shotguns, in plain finish, also in elaborate engravings and ornamentations; in fact the higher grade guns which we show in this catalogue and which we now carry in stock and which we offer at from $26.75 to $38.50 while formerly made only to order and until this season the very highest grade Aubrey gun we carried in stock, is the one we sell at $22.35, and before this they were made only singly to order; but the demand for made to order guns has been so very great that Mr. Aubrey has advised us to put the more popular ones in stock and make them up regular in quantities, and the guns we show on page 708 at $26.75 to $38.50, which we now carry in stock and which we heretofore furnished only under special order, and then made to order, are in every way superior to any stock guns of any other make, the equal of guns that sell generally at five times the price we offer them.

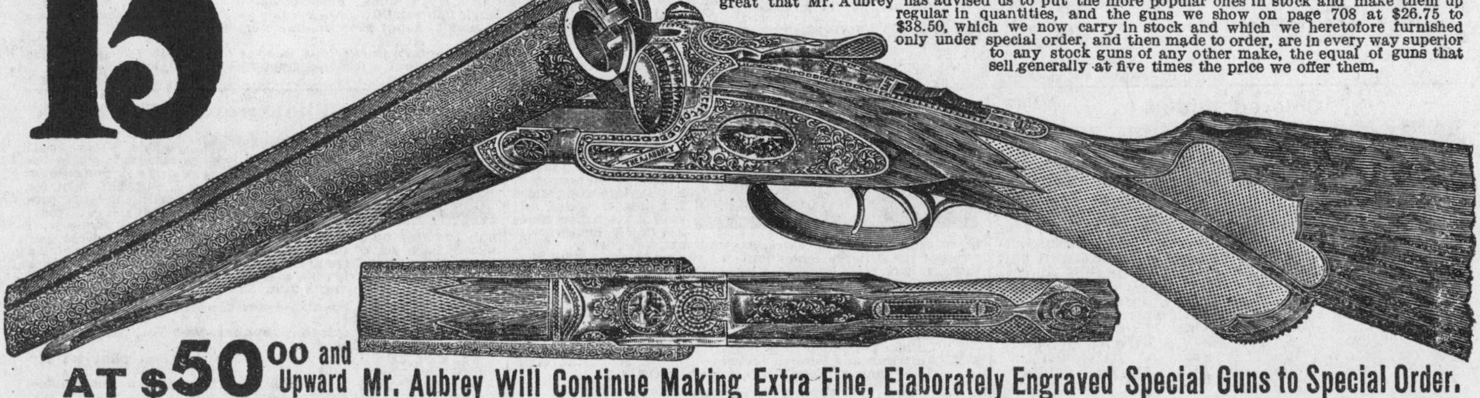

AT $50.00 and Upward Mr. Aubrey Will Continue Making Extra Fine, Elaborately Engraved Special Guns to Special Order.

FOR THE BENEFIT OF CONNOISSEURS, experts, trap and professional shooters, for the lovers of something most extraordinary in the highest grade double barrel hammerless breech loading shotguns possible to make, Mr. A. J. Aubrey, President of the Meriden Fire Arms Co., at Meriden, Conn. (our own gun factory), will make to order the most beautifully finished double barrel hammerless shotguns made in the world at prices ranging from $50.00 up.

IF YOU WANT A SPECIAL GUN, a particular style of finish, weight, shape, etc., a certain drop, or anything special, Mr. Aubrey will make you a gun to your order at a mere fraction of what others charge for fine made to order guns. You may want a certain weight, a certain drop, a special made stock as to length, shape target, style, design, color, kind of wood, etc., you may want special barrels, special boring, special finished barrels; you may want a special individual style of engraving, you may want Mr. Aubrey to put on his famous automatic shell ejector, a hand made ejector on a gun made to order, or if you want anything in this line Mr. Aubrey will do it for you as no other man in America can. If you want anything very special in an Aubrey gun, something finer than we list even in this catalogue, still finer than our $38.50 gun, then please write to Mr. Aubrey direct, addressing your letter to Mr. A. J. Aubrey, President Meriden Fire Arms Co., Meriden, Conn. Mr. Aubrey will be glad to take the matter up with you personally, referring to every little detail, and personally he will tell you all about it, and at the same time make a price so low that we are sure you will be agreeably surprised. Don't write to Mr. Aubrey about our regular standard stock guns, for these are always on hand, ready for immediate shipment, and it is unnecessary to write him about any gun other than a special made to order gun.

UNDERSTAND, all Aubrey guns are the same standard of quality, whether you buy our $13.85 Aubrey gun, as shown in this catalogue, or the higher grades which we show in this catalogue up to $38.50. They are all the highest standard of quality, all built on the same lines, all the parts of all the grades are interchangeable. When you go higher than the highest price we quote in this catalogue, namely $38.50, understand, you are going into something exceedingly special in finish or in design or shape, something specially suited to yourself, and in ordering such a gun we ask you to take the matter up with Mr. Aubrey personally. Mr. Aubrey is not authorized and could not sell you any one of the Aubrey guns we carry in stock, but he is authorized on these most extraordinary matters, very special made to order and special guns, to take the matter up personally with the purchaser, give him all the information he can, quote him our lowest price, the price that Mr. Aubrey figures the gun will cost to make, plus only our one small percentage of profit; and having corresponded with you himself and having received your order, it then becomes his duty, under his personal direction, to make this gun, and, dealing with the man who is directly the manufacturer of the gun, the gun coming under his eyes in every process of manufacture, you are absolutely sure of understanding each other, you get the best possible advice from the man who knows and who makes the gun, the man who follows it through its course of construction; therefore you are sure of getting just exactly what you want, and a service such as you could not get from any other maker or seller of guns in America.

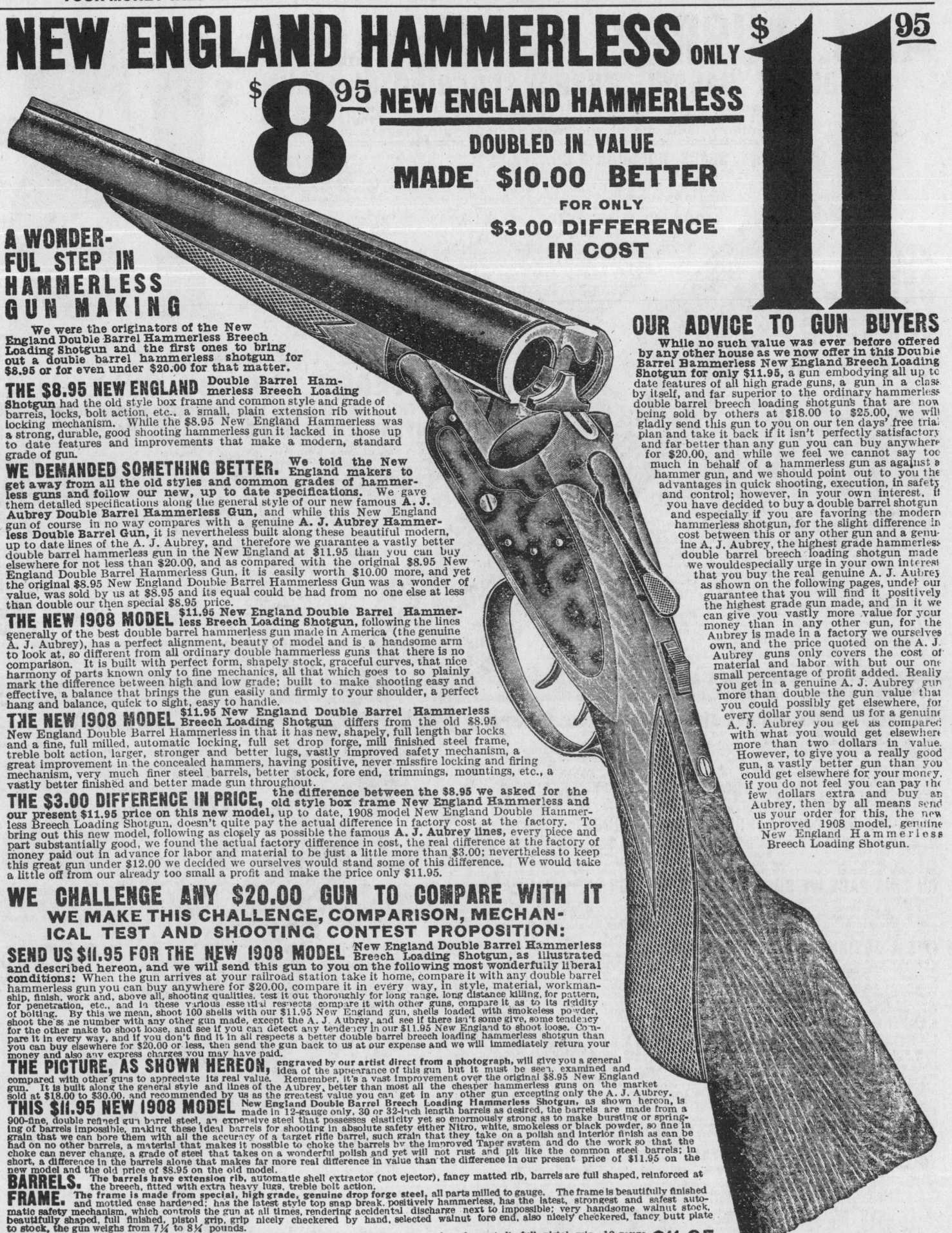

NEW ENGLAND HAMMERLESS ONLY $11⁹⁵

$8⁹⁵ NEW ENGLAND HAMMERLESS

DOUBLED IN VALUE
MADE $10.00 BETTER
FOR ONLY
$3.00 DIFFERENCE IN COST

A WONDERFUL STEP IN HAMMERLESS GUN MAKING

We were the originators of the New England Double Barrel Hammerless Breech Loading Shotgun and the first ones to bring out a double barrel hammerless shotgun for $8.95 or for even under $20.00 for that matter.

THE $8.95 NEW ENGLAND Double Barrel Hammerless Breech Loading Shotgun had the old style box frame and common style and grade of barrels, locks, bolt action, etc., a small, plain extension rib without locking mechanism. While the $8.95 New England Hammerless was a strong, durable, good shooting hammerless gun it lacked in those up to date features and improvements that make a modern, standard grade of gun.

WE DEMANDED SOMETHING BETTER. We told the New England makers to get away from all the old styles and common grades of hammerless guns and follow our new, up to date specifications. We gave them detailed specifications along the general style of our new famous A. J. Aubrey Double Barrel Hammerless Gun, and while this New England gun of course in no way compares with a genuine A. J. Aubrey Hammerless Double Barrel Gun, it is nevertheless built along these beautiful modern, up to date lines of the A. J. Aubrey, and therefore we guarantee a vastly better double barrel hammerless gun in the New England at $11.95 than you can buy elsewhere for not less than double $20.00, and as compared with the original $8.95 New England Double Barrel Hammerless Gun, it is easily worth $10.00 more, and yet the original $8.95 New England Double Barrel Hammerless Gun was a wonder of value, was sold by us at $8.95 and its equal could be had from no one else at less than double our then special $8.95 price.

THE NEW 1908 MODEL $11.95 New England Double Barrel Hammerless Breech Loading Shotgun, following the lines generally of the best double barrel hammerless gun made in America (the genuine A. J. Aubrey), has a perfect alignment, beauty of model and is a handsome arm to look at, so different from all ordinary double hammerless guns that there is no comparison. It is built with perfect form, shapely stock, graceful curves, that nice harmony of parts known only to fine mechanics, all that which goes to so plainly mark the difference between high and low grade; built to make shooting easy and effective, a balance that brings the gun easily and firmly to your shoulder, a perfect hang and balance, quick to sight, easy to handle.

THE NEW 1908 MODEL $11.95 New England Double Barrel Hammerless Breech Loading Shotgun, differs from the old $8.95 New England Double Barrel Hammerless in that it has new, shapely, full length bar locks and a fine, full milled, automatic locking, full set drop forge, mill finished steel frame, treble bolt action, larger, stronger and better lugs, vastly improved safety mechanism, a great improvement in the concealed hammers, having positive, never missfire locking and firing mechanism, very much finer steel barrels, better stock, fore end, trimmings, mountings, etc., a vastly better finished and better made gun throughout.

THE $3.00 DIFFERENCE IN PRICE, the difference between the $8.95 we asked for the old style box frame New England Hammerless and our present $11.95 price on this new, up to date, 1908 model New England Double Barrel Hammerless Breech Loading Shotgun, doesn't quite pay the actual difference in factory cost at the factory. To bring out this new model, following as closely as possible the famous A. J. Aubrey lines, every piece and part substantially good, we found the actual factory difference in cost, the real difference at the factory of money paid out in advance for labor and material to be just a little more than $3.00; nevertheless to keep this great model under $12.00 we decided we ourselves would stand some of this difference. We would take a little off from our already too small a profit and make the price only $11.95.

WE CHALLENGE ANY $20.00 GUN TO COMPARE WITH IT
WE MAKE THIS CHALLENGE, COMPARISON, MECHANICAL TEST AND SHOOTING CONTEST PROPOSITION:

SEND US $11.95 FOR THE NEW 1908 MODEL New England Double Barrel Hammerless Breech Loading Shotgun, as illustrated and described hereon, and we will send this gun to you on the following most wonderfully liberal conditions: When the gun arrives at your railroad station take it home, compare it with any double barrel hammerless gun you can buy anywhere for $20.00, compare it in every way, in style, material, workmanship, finish, work and, above all, shooting qualities, test it out thoroughly for long range, long distance killing, for pattern, for penetration, etc., and in these various essential respects compare it with other guns, compare it as to its rigidity of bolting. By this we mean, shoot 100 shells with our $11.95 New England gun, shells loaded with smokeless powder, shoot the same number with any other gun made, except the A. J. Aubrey, and see if there isn't some give, some tendency for the other make to shoot loose, and see if you can detect any tendency in our $11.95 New England to shoot loose. Compare it in every way, and if you don't find it in all respects a better double barrel breech loading hammerless shotgun than you can buy elsewhere for $20.00 or less, then send the gun back to us at our expense and we will immediately return your money and also any express charges you may have paid.

THE PICTURE, AS SHOWN HEREON, engraved by our artist direct from a photograph, will give you a general idea of the appearance of this gun but it must be seen, examined and compared with other guns to appreciate its real value. Remember, it's a vast improvement over the original $8.95 New England gun. It is built along the general style and lines of the Aubrey, better than most all the cheaper hammerless guns on the market sold at $18.00 to $30.00, and recommended by us as the greatest value you can get in any other gun excepting only the A. J. Aubrey.

THIS $11.95 NEW 1908 MODEL New England Double Barrel Breech Loading Hammerless Shotgun, as shown hereon, is made in 12-gauge only, 30 or 32-inch length barrels as desired, the barrels are made from a 900-fine, double refined gun barrel steel, an expensive steel that possesses elasticity yet so enormously strong as to make bursting or springing of barrels impossible, making these ideal barrels for shooting in absolute safety either Nitro, white, smokeless or black powder, so fine in grain that we can bore them with all the accuracy of a target rifle barrel, such grain that they take on a polish and interior finish as can be had on no other barrels, a material that makes it possible to choke the barrels by the improved Taper system and do the work so that the choke can never change, a grade of steel that takes on a wonderful polish and yet will not rust and pit like the common steel barrels; in short, a difference in the barrels alone that makes far more real difference in value than the difference in our present price of $11.95 on the new model and the old price of $8.95 on the old model.

BARRELS. The barrels have extension rib, automatic shell extractor (not ejector), fancy matted rib, barrels are full shaped, reinforced at the breech, fitted with extra heavy lugs, treble bolt action.

FRAME. The frame is made from special, high grade, genuine drop forge steel, all parts milled to gauge. The frame is beautifully finished and mottled case hardened; has the latest style top snap break, positively hammerless, has the latest, strongest and safest automatic safety mechanism, which controls the gun at all times, rendering accidental discharge next to impossible; very handsome walnut stock, beautifully shaped, full finished, pistol grip, grip nicely checkered by hand, selected walnut fore end, also nicely checkered, fancy butt plate to stock, the gun weighs from 7¼ to 8¼ pounds.

No. 6K109 Special steel barrels as described, 30 or 32 inches long (state length wanted), full pistol grip, 12-gauge only, weight, 7¼ to 8¼ pounds, as desired, our special price only..................$11.95

OUR ADVICE TO GUN BUYERS

While no such value was ever before offered by any other house as we now offer in this Double Barrel Hammerless New England Breech Loading Shotgun for only $11.95, a gun embodying all up to date features of all high grade guns, a gun in a class by itself, and far superior to the ordinary hammerless double barrel breech loading shotguns that are now being sold by others at $18.00 to $25.00, we will gladly send this gun to you on our ten days' free trial plan and take it back if it isn't perfectly satisfactory and far better than any gun you can buy anywhere for $20.00, and while we feel we cannot say too much in behalf of a hammerless gun as against a hammer gun, and we should point out to you the advantages in quick shooting, execution, in safety and control; however, in your own interest, if you have decided to buy a double barrel shotgun and especially if you are favoring the modern hammerless shotgun, for the slight difference in cost between this or any other gun and a genuine A. J. Aubrey, the highest grade hammerless double barrel breech loading shotgun made we would especially urge in your own interest that you buy the real genuine A. J. Aubrey as shown on the following pages, under our guarantee that you will find it positively the highest grade gun made, and in it we can give you vastly more value for your money than in any other gun, for the Aubrey is made in a factory we ourselves own, and the price quoted on the A. J. Aubrey guns only covers the cost of material and labor with but one small percentage of profit added. Really you get in a genuine A. J. Aubrey gun more than double the gun value that you could possibly get elsewhere, for every dollar you send us for a genuine A. J. Aubrey you get as compared with what you would get elsewhere more than two dollars in value. However, to give you a really good gun, a vastly better gun than you could get elsewhere for your money, if you do not feel you can pay the few dollars extra and buy an Aubrey, then by all means send us your order for this, the new improved 1908 model, genuine New England Hammerless Breech Loading Shotgun.

A. J. AUBREY HAMMERLESS

DOUBLE BARREL BREECH LOADING SHOTGUN

Is made by the Meriden Fire Arms Co., of Meriden, Conn., under the direct and personal supervision of Mr. A. J. Aubrey, President of the Company, and one of the most famous gun makers in America

$13.85

WE, SEARS, ROEBUCK & CO., are the owners of the Meriden Fire Arms Co., of Meriden, Conn. Every gun and revolver made in this factory is made for us and sold only by us, we being the owners and sole controllers of the situation, thus making it possible to control the quality of material, workmanship, style and finish, and to turn out of this factory, as we do, the highest grade fire arms made in America, and yet offer them to our customers on the basis of the actual cost to produce, the cost of materials and labor, with but our one small percentage of profit added.

OUR MR. R. W. SEARS, on a visit to the Meriden Fire Arms Co., at Meriden, Conn., looking over a gun case which almost covers the walls of Mr. Aubrey's office, and which contains samples of nearly all the modern style guns made in this and other countries (these guns have been before Mr. Aubrey's eyes all the time as he has been getting out this gun, that the best in everything might be segregated in this one production of his)—Mr. Sears, going to this case, observed a number of these Aubrey guns in their different finishes as shown in these several pages and herein priced at $13.85 and upward, and going over them, he remarked to Mr. Aubrey, that he, Mr. Sears, didn't think it was wise to finish any guns up specially fine for samples, as he had in the case of these several guns, that the guns in his case as specimens of our stock should be regular stock, no better than the average gun as it comes completed through the factory. Mr. Sears made this remark for the reason that these guns referred to in the case seemed to be so perfect in every imaginable detail, so beautiful in finish, in every piece and part, that they must have received some special attention in the final finish, at the hands of the most skilled operator. Mr. Aubrey replied to Mr. Sears in these words: "Mr. Sears, these are not special guns; on the contrary, they represent simply samples as taken from week to week, or time to time out of our finished stock at random, that I may know positively what the average quality of our guns is."

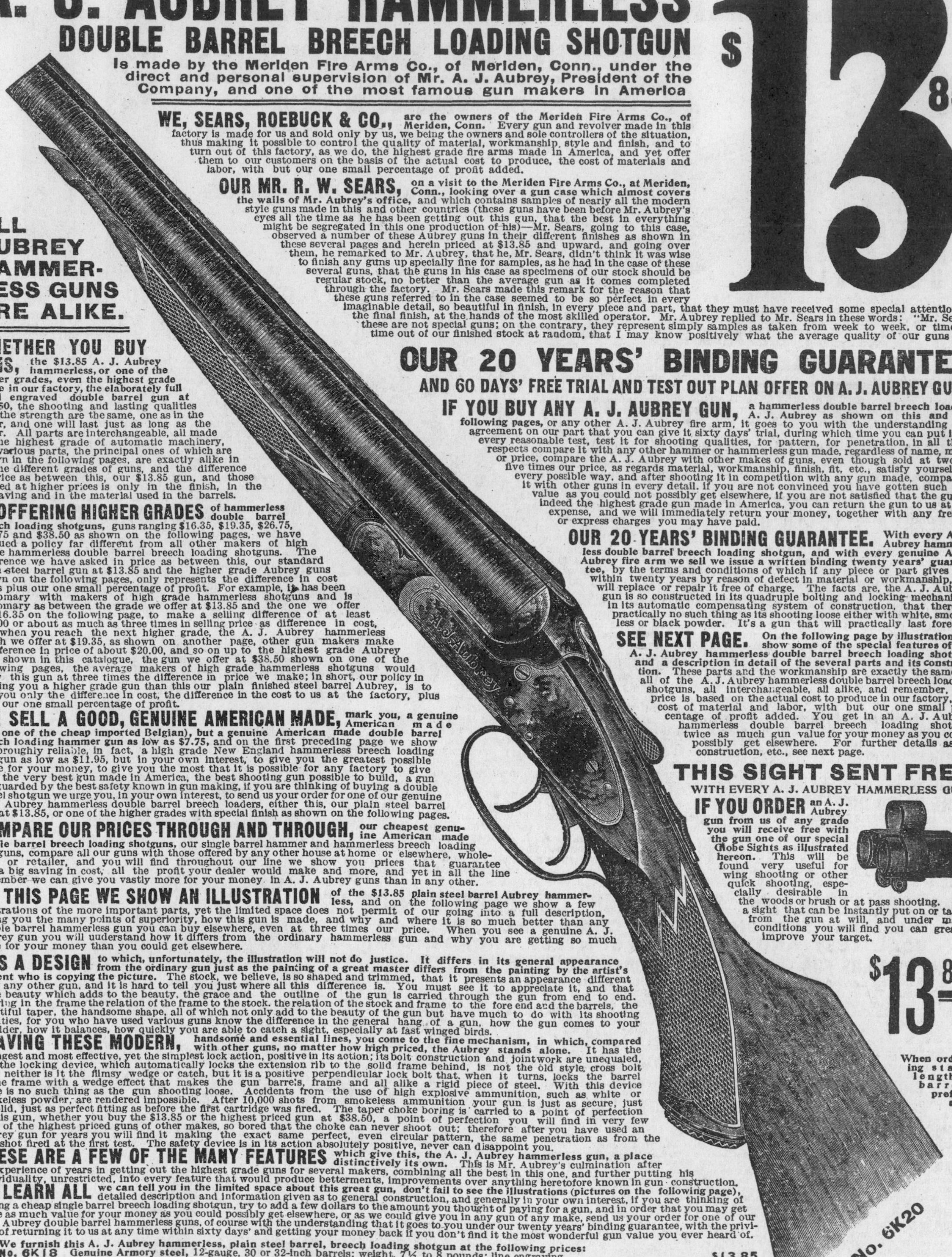

No. 6K20

ALL AUBREY HAMMERLESS GUNS ARE ALIKE.

WHETHER YOU BUY THIS, the $13.85 A. J. Aubrey hammerless, or one of the higher grades, even the highest grade made in our factory, the elaborately full hand engraved double barrel gun at $38.50, the shooting and lasting qualities and the strength are the same, one as in the other, and one will last just as long as the other. All parts are interchangeable, all made on the highest grade of automatic machinery, the various parts, the principal ones of which are shown in the following pages, are exactly alike in all the different grades of guns, and the difference in price as between this, our $13.85 gun, and those offered at higher prices is only in the finish, in the engraving and in the material used in the barrels.

IN OFFERING HIGHER GRADES of hammerless double barrel breech loading shotguns, guns ranging $16.35, $19.35, $26.75, $29.75 and $38.50 as shown on the following pages, we have pursued a policy far different from all other makers of high grade hammerless double barrel breech loading shotguns. The difference we have asked in price as between this, our standard plain steel barrel gun at $13.85 and the higher grade Aubrey guns shown on the following pages, only represents the difference in cost to us plus our one small percentage of profit. For example, it has been customary with makers of high grade hammerless shotguns and is customary as between the grade we offer at $13.85 and the one we offer at $16.35 on the following page, to make a selling difference of at least $10.00 or about as much as three times in selling price as difference in cost, and when you reach the next higher grade, the A. J. Aubrey hammerless which we offer at $19.35, as shown on another page, other gun makers make a difference in price of about $20.00, and so on up to the highest grade Aubrey gun shown in this catalogue, the gun we offer at $38.50 shown on one of the following pages, the average makers of high grade hammerless shotguns would show this gun at three times the difference in price we make; in short, our policy in offering you a higher grade gun than this our plain finished steel barrel Aubrey, is to ask you only the difference in cost, the difference in the cost to us at the factory, plus only our one small percentage of profit.

WE SELL A GOOD, GENUINE AMERICAN MADE, mark you, a genuine American made (not one of the cheap imported Belgian), but a genuine American made double barrel breech loading hammer gun as low as $7.75, and on the first preceding page we show a thoroughly reliable, in fact, a high grade New England hammerless breech loading shotgun as low as $11.95, but in your own interest, to give you the greatest possible value for your money, to give you the most that it is possible for any factory to give you, the very best gun made in America, the best shooting gun possible to build, a gun safeguarded by the best safety known in gun making, if you are thinking of buying a double barrel shotgun we urge you, in your own interest, to send us your order for one of our genuine A. J. Aubrey hammerless double barrel breech loaders, either this, our plain steel barrel gun at $13.85, or one of the higher grades with special finish as shown on the following pages.

COMPARE OUR PRICES THROUGH AND THROUGH, our cheapest genuine American made double barrel breech loading shotguns, our single barrel hammer and hammerless breech loading shotguns, compare all our guns with those offered by any other house at home or elsewhere, wholesaler or retailer, and you will find throughout our line we show you prices that guarantee you a big saving in cost, all the profit your dealer would make and more, and yet in all the line remember we can give you vastly more for your money in A. J. Aubrey guns than in any other.

ON THIS PAGE WE SHOW AN ILLUSTRATION of the $13.85 plain steel barrel Aubrey hammerless, and on the following page we show a few illustrations of the more important parts, yet the limited space does not permit of our going into a full description, telling you the many points of superiority, how this gun is made, and why and where it is so much better than any double barrel hammerless gun you can buy elsewhere, even at three times our price. When you see a genuine A. J. Aubrey gun you will understand how it differs from the ordinary hammerless gun and why you are getting so much more for your money than you could get elsewhere.

IT'S A DESIGN to which, unfortunately, the illustration will not do justice. It differs in its general appearance from the ordinary gun just as the painting of a great master differs from the painting by the artist's student who is copying the picture. The stock, we believe, is so shaped and trimmed, that it presents an appearance different from any other gun, and it is hard to tell you just where all this difference is. You must see it to appreciate it, and that same beauty which adds to the beauty, the grace and the outline of the gun is carried through the gun from end to end, showing in the frame the relation of the frame to the stock, the relation of the stock and frame to the fore end and the barrels, the beautiful taper, the handsome shape, all of which not only add to the beauty of the gun but have much to do with its shooting qualities, for you who have used various guns know the difference in the general hang of a gun, how the gun comes to your shoulder, how it balances, how quickly you are able to catch a sight, especially at fast winged birds.

LEAVING THESE MODERN, handsome and essential lines, you come to the fine mechanism, in which, compared with other guns, no matter how high priced, the Aubrey stands alone. It has the strongest and most effective, yet the simplest lock action, positive in its action; its bolt construction and jointwork are unequaled, and the locking device, which automatically locks the extension rib to the solid frame behind, is not the old style, cross bolt lock, neither is it the flimsy wedge or catch, but it is a positive perpendicular lock bolt that, when it turns, locks the barrel to the frame with a wedge effect that makes the gun barrels, frame and all alike a rigid piece of steel. With this device there is no such thing as the gun shooting loose. Accidents from the use of high explosive ammunition, such as white or smokeless powder, are rendered impossible. After 10,000 shots from smokeless ammunition your gun is just as secure, just as solid, just as perfect fitting as before the first cartridge was fired. The taper choke boring is carried to a point of perfection in this gun, whether you buy the $13.85 or the highest priced gun at $38.50, a point of perfection you will find in very few even of the highest priced guns of other makes, so bored that the choke can never shoot out; therefore after you have used an Aubrey gun for years you will find it making the exact same perfect, even circular pattern, the same penetration as from the first shot fired at the first test. The safety device is in its action absolutely positive, never can disappoint you.

THESE ARE A FEW OF THE MANY FEATURES which give this, the A. J. Aubrey hammerless gun, a place distinctively its own. This is Mr. Aubrey's culmination after an experience of years in getting out the highest grade guns for several makers, combining all the best in this one, and further putting his individuality, unrestricted, into every feature that would produce betterments, improvements over anything heretofore known in gun construction.

TO LEARN ALL we can tell you in the limited space about this great gun, don't fail to see the illustrations (pictures on the following page), detailed description and information given as to general construction, and generally in your own interest, if you are thinking of buying a cheap single barrel breech loading shotgun, try to add a few dollars to the amount you thought of paying for a gun, and in order that you may get twice as much value for your money as you could possibly get elsewhere, or as we could give you in any gun of any make, send us your order for one of our A. J. Aubrey double barrel hammerless guns, of course with the understanding that it goes to you under our twenty years' binding guarantee, with the privilege of returning it to us at any time within sixty days' and getting your money back if you don't find it the most wonderful gun value you ever heard of.

We furnish this A. J. Aubrey hammerless, plain steel barrel, breech loading shotgun at the following prices:

No. 6K18	Genuine Armory steel, 12-gauge, 30 or 32-inch barrels; weight, 7½ to 8 pounds; line engraving	$13.85
No. 6K20	Genuine imported Liege twist barrels, 12-gauge, 30 or 32-inch barrels; weight, 7½ to 8 pounds; line engraving	14.85
No. 6K22	Genuine two-blade Damascus Liege imported barrels, 12-gauge, 30 or 32-inch barrels; weight, 7½ to 8 pounds; line engraving	17.35

Weight, packed for shipment, about 14 pounds.

OUR 20 YEARS' BINDING GUARANTEE

AND 60 DAYS' FREE TRIAL AND TEST OUT PLAN OFFER ON A. J. AUBREY GUNS

IF YOU BUY ANY A. J. AUBREY GUN, a hammerless double barrel breech loading A. J. Aubrey as shown on this and the following pages, or any other A. J. Aubrey fire arm, it goes to you with the understanding and agreement on our part that you can give it sixty days' trial, during which time you can put it to every reasonable test, test it for shooting qualities, for pattern, for penetration, in all these respects compare it with any other hammer or hammerless gun made, regardless of name, make or price, compare the A. J. Aubrey with other makes of guns, even though sold at two to five times our price, as regards material, workmanship, finish, fit, etc., satisfy yourself in every possible way, and after shooting it in competition with any gun made, comparing it with other guns in every detail, if you are not convinced you have gotten such gun value as you could not possibly get elsewhere, if you are not satisfied that the gun is indeed the highest grade gun made in America, you can return the gun to us at our expense, and we will immediately return your money, together with any freight or express charges you may have paid.

OUR 20 YEARS' BINDING GUARANTEE. With every A. J. Aubrey hammerless double barrel breech loading shotgun, and with every genuine A. J. Aubrey fire arm we sell we issue a written binding twenty years' guarantee, by the terms and conditions of which if any piece or part gives out within twenty years by reason of defect in material or workmanship, we will replace or repair it free of charge. The facts are, the A. J. Aubrey gun is so constructed in its quadruple bolting and locking mechanism, in its automatic compensating system of construction, that there is practically no such thing as its shooting loose either with white, smokeless or black powder. It's a gun that will practically last forever.

SEE NEXT PAGE. On the following page by illustration we show some of the special features of the A. J. Aubrey hammerless double barrel breech loading shotgun and a description in detail of the several parts and its construction. These parts and the workmanship are exactly the same on all of the A. J. Aubrey hammerless double barrel breech loading shotguns, all interchangeable, all alike, and remember, the price is based on the actual cost to produce in our factory, the cost of material and labor, with but our one small percentage of profit added. You get in an A. J. Aubrey hammerless double barrel breech loading shotgun twice as much gun value for your money as you could possibly get elsewhere. For further details as to construction, etc., see next page.

THIS SIGHT SENT FREE

WITH EVERY A. J. AUBREY HAMMERLESS GUN.

IF YOU ORDER an A. J. Aubrey gun from us of any grade you will receive free with the gun one of our special Globe Sights as illustrated hereon. This will be found very useful for wing shooting or other quick shooting, especially desirable in the woods or brush or at pass shooting. It's a sight that can be instantly put on or taken from the gun at will, and under many conditions you will find you can greatly improve your target.

$13.85

When ordering state length of barrels preferred.

A. J. AUBREY HAMMERLESS
DOUBLE BARREL BREECH LOADING SHOTGUN

$13 85

ILLUSTRATIONS AND DESCRIPTIONS OF SOME OF THE PARTS OF THE AUBREY HAMMERLESS DOUBLE BARREL BREECH LOADING SHOTGUN

JUST A FEW FEATURES are shown hereon to give you an idea of the individuality of this gun, how all essential parts have been cared for in the matter of strength, workmanship and finish, an opportunity for you to compare the general mechanical construction and design of the Aubrey hammerless with any other hammerless gun made, a chance for you to see for yourself that the Aubrey Hammerless Double Barrel Breech Loading Shotgun is indeed the highest grade double barrel breech loading shotgun made. The limited space does not permit of our going into all the details. To know and to fully appreciate what an Aubrey Double Barrel Hammerless Breech Loading Shotgun really is, and how much better it is than an ordinary hammerless double gun, why and wherein it is better than any other double hammerless gun on the market, you must see, examine and compare the Aubrey Hammerless Double Barrel Breech Loading Shotgun with others to appreciate the value we are giving, how much it is possible for us to furnish you from our new gun factory at Meriden, Conn., when we name a price based on the actual cost of material and labor in our own factory, with but our one small percentage of profit added.

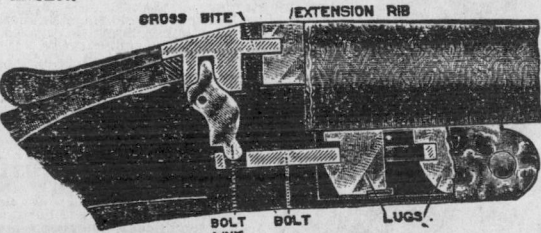
Illustration No. 1.

ILLUSTRATION No. 1 will give you a little idea of the breech construction of the double Aubrey hammerless. All Aubrey barrels are reinforced at the breech and made extra strong. They are bored by the taper system, reinforced, and are, therefore, specially adapted to white or smokeless powder as well as black powder. The Aubrey breech construction is not matched by any other gun on the market.

This illustration also shows the new extension rib used on the Aubrey Double Barrel Hammerless Guns. This rib, you will note from the illustration, is deeper, heavier and stronger than the ordinary extension rib. Note the heavy slot cut in the rib, which engages with the solid steel cross bite in the top lever, firmly locking the barrel and frame, preventing any possibility of this gun shooting loose. We have tested this extension rib lock thoroughly. In testing this extension rib lock we have taken out the bottom bolts and shot over 1,000 shells with just this extension rib lock holding the barrels to the frame. After shooting 1,000 shells we found the gun just as rigid and as strong as ever.

Bear in mind that, in addition to this extension rib cross bite locking device you also have two bolts engaging with the lugs in the bottom of the barrel, making this the strongest bolted gun on the market.

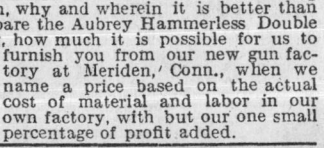

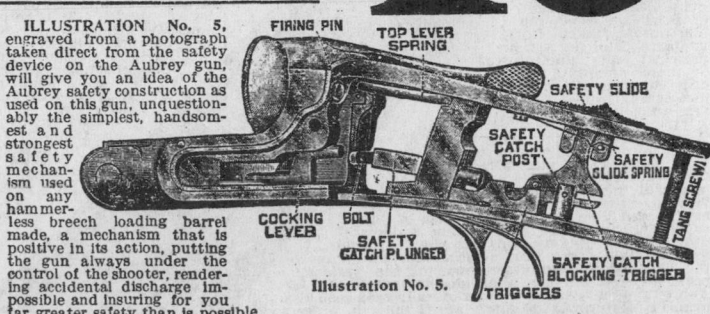
Illustration No. 5.

ILLUSTRATION No. 5, engraved from a photograph taken direct from the safety device on the Aubrey gun, will give you an idea of the Aubrey safety construction as used on this gun, unquestionably the simplest, handsomest and strongest safety mechanism used on any hammerless breech loading barrel made, a mechanism that is positive in its action, putting the gun always under the control of the shooter, rendering accidental discharge impossible and insuring for you far greater safety than is possible in a hammer gun; no triggers to slip from your fingers, an unmatchable safety construction.

Illustration No. 2.

ILLUSTRATION No. 2 of the bolt locking mechanism, which, in the frame, as the gun is closed, engages with the slot in the extension rib, will give you an idea of the locking mechanism of this gun; undoubtedly the most positive and by far the strongest mechanism furnished on any double gun made.

Illustration No. 6.

ILLUSTRATION No. 6 shows a portion of the frame construction, the flat water table, the double lock bolt, a portion of the lock construction and the cocking bolts. Little idea of the superiority brought out in this construction can be had except by a comparison of this, the Acme frame and bolt and locking action, compared with other hammerless guns.

Illustration No. 3.

ILLUSTRATION No 3 shows the style of the full taper shaped and finished matted rib which is used on all Aubrey Hammerless Double Barrel Breech Loading Shotguns. This is undoubtedly the handsomest, most shapely and truest matted rib construction made.

Illustration No. 7.

ILLUSTRATION No. 7 shows you the two heavy double steel lugs with their treble lock construction, the flat table, the reinforced barrel connection construction, the extractor and the bottom view of the slotted self locking extension rib.

Illustration No. 8.

ILLUSTRATION No. 8 will give you simply a little idea of the shapely appearance of the fore end used on the Aubrey hammerless gun. It is, of course, made of carefully selected walnut stock, nicely checkered ornamentation, is very shapely, as the illustration shows. It has the best automatic locking mechanism known, by which it locks automatically squarely to the barrel.

ILLUSTRATION No. 4, engraved from a photograph of the interior of one of the locks, will give you some idea of the simplicity, the strength and the positiveness of action of the Aubrey lock, which is a full shaped, full finished bar lock, and undoubtedly the highest grade gun lock used on any double hammerless gun made.

Illustration No. 4.

Illustration No. 9.

ILLUSTRATION No. 9 shows the bottom of the fore end. You can see the locking device, the fancy metal tip and the general scheme of fore end construction as used on the Aubrey gun.

STOCK. All Aubrey double hammerless guns have carefully selected walnut stock. The stocks are beautifully shaped, are full pistol grip, all grips capped with fancy rubber caps, fancy rubber butt plates, beautiful lines, such stocks, in fact, as you will find on very few guns, even though sold at five times this price.

BORING SYSTEM. All Aubrey double barrels are taper choke bored by the celebrated taper system, so bored that the choke can never be shot out, and even after you have shot 10,000 smokeless powder shells, either barrel will make exactly the same pattern, the same penetration as from the first shot.

QUALITY OF STEEL USED IN BARRELS. In all Aubrey guns we use the highest grade of special gun barrel steel possible to obtain. For example, in the $13.85 grade we use the finest crystal barrel steel, a steel that takes a wonderfully fine polish, a steel that does not easily rust or pit, a steel insuring the greatest possible strength, and yet a grade of steel with a resiliency or sufficient amount of spring and life, and a steel that takes on a vastly better polish and color than the ordinary grades. In our twist steel barrels we use nothing but the genuine imported Liege full twist, the highest grade of twist steel barrels obtainable. In our Damascus steel barrels we also use a genuine Liege full double bladed Damascus steel.

IN PRESENTING THE AUBREY GUN to you in the different grades, we wish it clearly understood that the quality of workmanship, the strength, the endurance, in fact, in every essential way, one gun is like the other; the $13.85 grade will last as long, shoot as well and give as good satisfaction as the highest priced Aubrey gun we offer. They differ only in the barrels and in the special finish given them. These guns are 12-gauge, they come with either 30 or 32-inch barrels, as desired (in ordering state length of barrels preferred); they weigh from 7½ to 8 pounds.

UNDERSTAND, all frames are made from the highest grade drop steel forgings, all accurately milled, cut and finished, all barrels are given a specially high finish, beautifully case hardened with a mottled finish, all parts are interchangeable.

ABOUT FURNISHING NEW PARTS OR REPAIRS

ALL PARTS BEING INTERCHANGEABLE, we can, in case you should want any part to replace another, even in the years to come, always furnish you these parts from stock, and will gladly furnish any part to any owner of an Aubrey gun at actual factory cost, plus only our one small percentage of profit, a mere fraction of what you would have to pay others for a similar part to another gun; further, if it comes within the limits of our twenty years' binding guarantee any such part will, of course, be furnished to you free of cost.

UNDERSTAND, with every gun we send a written binding twenty years' guarantee, by the terms and conditions of which, if any piece or part gives out within twenty years, by reason of defect in material or workmanship, we will replace or repair it free of charge.

No. 6K18 Genuine crystal barrels, 12-gauge; length of barrels, 30 or 32 inches (state length preferred); weight, 7½ to 8 pounds; handsome line engraving. Price, only.................. **$13.85**

No. 6K20 Genuine imported Liege steel twist barrels, 12-gauge; length of barrels, 30 or 32 inches (state length preferred); weight, 7½ to 8 pounds; beautiful line engraving. Price.................. **14.85**

No. 6K22 Genuine double blade imported Liege Damascus full finished steel barrels; 12-gauge; length of barrels, 30 or 32 inches (state length preferred); weight, 7½ to 8 pounds; beautiful line engraving. Price.................. **17.35**

A. J. AUBREY —1908 MODEL DOUBLE BARREL— HAMMERLESS SHOTGUN

$16^{35}

THIS A. J. AUBREY HAMMERLESS SHOTGUN at $16.35 for the twist barrel and $18.85 for the two-blade Damascus barrel gun, is the same gun we furnish in the plain finish at $13.85 for the plain steel barrel, or $14.85 for the twist barrel. The difference in price between this gun and the $13.85 gun is accounted for by the beautiful hand engraving on the locks and frame, the special, fine checkering, and the extra high finish placed on this higher priced gun. Otherwise, in construction and outline, this gun is the same as the lower priced guns described on a previous page. These guns are designed and manufactured to meet a large demand for a handsome engraved hammerless gun at a low price, and considering the workmanship and finish of these guns, taking note of the beautiful engraving, this gun, at $16.35, is a better gun and better value than you could obtain in any other make of American guns for double the money.

SEE PAGE 705 for illustrations and complete descriptions of the various parts of the A. J. Aubrey Double Barrel Hammerless Shotguns. On this page of parts we show you illustrations taken from photographs of the various principal parts and features of these wonderful guns in order to give you some fair idea of what wonderful value we are offering in these, our A. J. Aubrey Shotguns. Words cannot do these guns justice, and in order to give you something more tangible than mere phrases, truthful as they are, we have endeavored, by means of the illustrations shown on page 705, to convey to you more definite information and give you a clearer idea of what wonderful guns these Aubrey guns really are. Study the description of this gun as given on this page carefully, then turn to page 705 and study the illustrations and descriptions of the various parts, and you will have a fair idea of what the A. J. Aubrey gun really is, but in order to really get a good idea of this gun, in order to appreciate it fully, in order to realize what extraordinary value this gun is at our price, it is really necessary that you see this gun, handle it, note its beautiful lines, feel how nice it comes up to the shoulder, take it out and shoot it in the field or at a target, and test it in every conceivable way, for which an excellent opportunity is given you, as fully explained in our sixty-day free trial offer. We know that if you could see this $16.35 A. J. Aubrey Hammerless Gun in comparison with any $25.00 or $30.00 gun on the market, you would not hesitate more than the few moments it would take you to grasp the immense superiority of the A. J. Aubrey Gun which we sell for $16.35, to make your selection. As compared with other guns, this A. J. Aubrey Gun, which we sell for $16.35, ought to sell for at least $35.00, but as fully explained in the descriptive pages of these guns, we own and control the Meriden Fire Arms Co., the largest and most complete plant of its kind in the world, and it is our intention to furnish double barrel hammerless guns for less money, quality considered, than it is possible for anyone else to do. We are content with but one small margin of profit over the actual cost of material and labor, and we are, therefore, able to offer you these most wonderful values.

COMPARED WITH PRICES CHARGED BY OTHERS, we have some wonderful gun values in this catalogue. Take the New England Gun, shown on another page, a hammerless gun for $11.95, which you cannot match elsewhere for much less than double our price. We have some wonderful values in single guns. We show such values in American hammer and Belgian hammer breech loading guns as you can get from no other house, and, of course, if you are about to order a single gun or a hammer gun we would very much appreciate your order. We believe we own these other guns at lower cost to us than most sellers, and we know we are willing to sell you any gun you want at a smaller profit to ourselves than anyone else would ask, but when it comes down to measuring real value there is nothing we have to offer in our catalogue and which we are able to give you for your money in the gun line anything like what we can give you in an Aubrey Hammerless Double Barrel Breech Loading Shotgun.

TO HELP YOU to select an Aubrey gun we want to emphasize that while there is a difference in price between $13.85 for our plain steel barrel Aubrey gun and this and the higher priced Aubrey guns, shown on the following page, this difference represents only the exact difference in cost to us, less our one small percentage of profit, but we don't want you to think that it is necessary to pay more than $13.85 in order that you may get a stronger or better shooting gun. In strength and shooting qualities the lowest priced Aubrey gun is as good as money, material and mechanical skill can make a gun. As we go up in price from $13.85 we put it in the finer finished barrels, in the hand engraved lock, frame, trimmings, etc., and later in the most carefully selected domestic and foreign curled and fancy antique walnut woods. The difference in these guns is much like the difference in the engraving of a watch. It bears no relation to the gold on which the engraving is placed, nor does it bear any relation to the movement (the works) that the case contains. Many people, however, after having all that money can buy in the essential parts of a gun, the shooting qualities, strength, outline, etc., are fond of a little extra finish, especially when they can get it at less than one-half what others charge, and to accommodate those who wish something extra fine, we offer these hand engraved Aubrey guns, and we offer in place of the armory steel barrel guns the genuine laminated steel and two-blade Damascus steel barrels.

BEFORE THESE hammerless guns were brought out for us by Mr. Aubrey we had with Mr. Aubrey a great many interviews and at some of these interviews we had laid on the table before us samples of most of the high grade hammerless guns made in this country and also some of English make. We told Mr. Aubrey we wanted to get out the best hammerless shotgun ever made. We were willing to equip a factory with every known modern labor saving machine, and we were willing the factory should run to its full capacity every day in the year, willing to go to practically any expense that we might get the best gun made and this provided we could, under these conditions, make the gun at a cost so low that after adding our one small percentage of profit to this cost we could offer the highest grade gun made in America at a most popular and attractive price. Discussing the matter at length as we naturally did before engaging Mr. Aubrey, as to buying and building our plant and machinery, the discussions ran something like this: Picking up one of the highest grade American guns, we would say to Mr. Aubrey, "How do you like this gun?" and he would comment favorably on several points, but would then by saying, "This gun is defective here and there," pointing out the weak or objectionable spots, and so we went down the list of nearly all the American guns and some of the English guns, Mr. Aubrey pointing out the strong features, also the weak, and in nearly all of the highest grade guns he found places to comment favorably and places to criticise. Summing the whole matter up and before we made our start, we asked: "Mr. Aubrey, is it possible to bring out a gun that will include all the strong and durable features you have pointed out and a gun that will be free from any and all the objectionable features that you have pointed out, and which you have found, more or less, in every American and English gun we have shown you?" He said: "This can be done if you will give me time and money," explaining that the last double barrel hammerless gun he got out for another maker was produced and on the market in about six months' time from the starting point, but he said to us, "Gentlemen, what you exact of me will take several times six months." Nevertheless, we had confidence in Mr. Aubrey, we engaged him, we built the factory, we furnished the equipment he wanted, and instead of producing this gun in six months, as he did the last gun he made for another maker, it was nearly three years before Mr. Aubrey was ready to put it on the market. These are the reasons why we can put this gun out on our 20-year binding guarantee, why we can afford to give sixty days' free trial test and comparison privilege, and this is why we can offer this gun at this incomparably low price, for it is made in our own factory.

YOU WILL NOTE FROM THE ILLUSTRATION that this engraving is elaborate, but at the same time is neat and has not that flashy look that is so noticeable on cheap, machine engraved guns. If you are desirous of having a gun that combines maximum strength with the highest finish and artistic workmanship, a gun that you would be proud to show at a trap shoot where many well known makes of guns will be on display, a gun that presents a handsomer appearance than any gun you could buy for from $30.00 to $50.00, we would advise you to buy this gun at $16.35 for the laminated steel barrels, or $18.85 for the Damascus barrels. We know that you would be more than pleased, and that you would be satisfied that you had saved more than half of what you would have to pay for a gun of any other make that would in any way compare with this beautiful hand engraved A. J. Aubrey Gun.

DETAILED DESCRIPTION

THE DESCRIPTION OF THIS, our $16.35 and $18.85 Aubrey Gun, as illustrated hereon and as quoted below, is identical (exactly the same) with the $13.85 Aubrey gun on preceding page in every detail excepting the finish. This $16.35 and $18.85 gun differs only in that it is elaborately engraved, exactly as illustrated. The lock, bolts, frame, guard, and all the metal parts are beautifully hand engraved and, unfortunately, the illustration fails to do the gun justice in bringing out the beautiful effects produced by this hand engraving and if you want something extraordinary in the way of finish, something that you would pay extra for several times over the price we ask, then we would advise you to select this special hand engraved gun; otherwise every piece and part is interchangeable, made from the same material, exactly the same as the $13.85 Aubrey gun on preceding page.

THE DIFFERENCE BETWEEN THIS GUN AND THE LOWER PRICED AUBREY GUN described on the previous page is entirely in the additional work we have put on this gun in our efforts to combine beauty and strength. There is not a manufacturer in the country but would charge as much for this additional engraving as we do for the entire gun. This engraving is done by expert engravers, and is equal to the work done on any of the $50.00 and $60.00 guns on the market.

GLOBE SIGHT FREE.

We include with every one of these guns one of our celebrated Globe Sights, which are patented and which are manufactured and controlled exclusively by us. These sights are of great value to the shooter, and may be instantly attached or detached.

No. 6K34

$16^{35}

ORDER BY CATALOGUE NUMBER IN FULL AND STATE LENGTH OF BARRELS WANTED.

Catalogue No.	Grade	Style of Barrels	Gauge	Length of Barrels, In.	Weight, Lbs.	Finish	Price
6K30	A. L. E.	Genuine Twist or Laminated	12	30 or 32	7½ to 8	{ Leaf Style Engraving	$16.35
6K34	A. D. E.	Genuine 2-Blade Damascus	12	30 or 32	7½ to 8		18.85

Weight, packed for shipment, 14 pounds.

A. J. AUBREY HAMMERLESS DOUBLE BARREL SHOTGUN $19 35

LATEST MODEL BETTER, STRONGER AND HANDSOMER THAN EVER BEFORE

$19.35 IS OUR PRICE for this high grade A. J. Aubrey Hammerless Gun with beautiful and elaborate hand engraved locks and frame, fitted with genuine twist barrels. In this gun at $19.35 for the genuine twist barrel gun, or $22.35 for the same gun fitted with fine two-blade Damascus barrels, we offer you value which you could not duplicate for less than $30.00 or more in any other American made gun. The engraving on these guns is better than that found on any of the $50.00 or $60.00 guns on the market. The finish, the inside lock work and the close, fine checkering on the full pistol grip stock and on the finely shaped walnut fore end, are better and handsomer than those found on almost any other make of gun, regardless of price. These guns have been made to supply a demand for a high grade gun of beautiful design and finish at a popular price, a price of about one-half of what you would ordinarily have to pay for a gun of this design and quality.

WE CAN FURNISH YOU HIGHER GRADE Aubrey guns than these at $19.35 and $22.35. You will find illustrated on another page Aubrey Hammerless Guns at $26.75 and $38.50. If you want a still higher priced gun than $38.50, if you want a gun of a special design, a gun with more elaborate engraving, a gun built specially to your order, in accordance with your requirements, then we recommend that you write to Mr. A. J. Aubrey, president of the Meriden Fire Arms Co., Meriden, Conn., and he will endeavor to supply your wants, but do not write Mr. Aubrey if you do not intend to pay more than $38.50 for a gun. See the introductory page of this catalogue for full information regarding specially made guns.

THE VALUE

of the A. J. Aubrey Hammerless Gun in comparison with any other make gun, either hammer or hammerless, can hardly be estimated, as the Aubrey gun is so much better in finish, shooting qualities, alignment, choke boring, construction, so distinctive in itself, that a comparison with any other make of gun, either hammer or hammerless, would convince even the novice that, considering the price at which our guns are sold we would be justified in asking more than treble the prices we now ask for these guns.

AT PRESENT

we show a large line of all standard makes of guns, both hammer and hammerless, giving you a large assortment from which to select, but we know it is but a question of a short time when the sales of the A. J. Aubrey will so far exceed the combined sales of the other guns as to enable us to eliminate all guns but the A. J. Aubrey Guns from our catalogue.

THE MATERIAL,

design, workmanship, shooting qualities and general construction of the Aubrey guns are so far in advance of the other guns, the prices we ask for the Aubrey guns are so incomparably low that when these guns are thoroughly introduced and the value embodied in them is well known, no man will buy a gun other than the A. J. Aubrey.

WE HAVE AT MERIDEN, CONN.,

one of the largest gun factories in the world. We have surrounding this factory many acres of land to enable us to enlarge this already enormous plant to take care of the growing demand. Our output today in double hammerless guns, single guns and revolvers, is larger than that of any factory in the country, which is marvelous, when you stop to consider the few years that these guns have been on the market as compared with standard makes of guns which have been on the market for the last twenty or thirty years. To build up a business in this short space of time so as to be able to dispose of the output of the largest fire arms factory of its kind in the world, certainly speaks well of the wonderful value of these guns. Never in the history of the gun business has any line of fire arms shown the rapid growth in sales that the A. J. Aubrey goods have shown. We know that as these guns become better known, the sales will double and treble, making it necessary to keep on increasing our already enormous factory.

THE MANAGEMENT,

equipment and system of manufacturing are such that we are able to manufacture a thousand guns with the same care and attention to detail as if we were manufacturing but one hundred. The factory is so thoroughly divisionized; every step in the manufacture of these guns is under the watchful eye of a careful, trained inspector. The machine work performed by the highest grade automatic machines is so accurate to the thousandth part of an inch, the parts are so strictly interchangeable, that you will find that not the slightest detail in the construction of the guns has in any way been overlooked or neglected.

OUR LIBERAL SIXTY-DAY FREE TRIAL OFFER,

as fully given on page 702, and our binding twenty-year guarantee fully protect you in the purchase of one of these guns. If you are desirous of purchasing a gun, send us your order for an A. J. Aubrey, and if you do not find it all we claim it to be, a better gun than you could obtain elsewhere at any price, if you are not satisfied with its shooting qualities, its construction, or, in short, if you are not pleased with your purchase, return the gun to us, and we will cheerfully refund the price you paid, as well as any express charges.

THE RANGE OF PRICES

on Aubrey guns is large; the guns are graded to suit everyone who wishes to purchase a gun, the prices ranging from $13.85 for the blued steel barrel gun to $38.50 for three-blade Damascus barrel gun; and although there is a considerable range of prices, as stated, the quality in all Aubrey Guns is uniform. The $13.85 gun will shoot just as well and wear just as well as the $38.50 gun. The mechanical construction is the same, and the mechanism is identical in the cheapest gun as in the highest priced. The difference in price is accounted for entirely by the difference in the cost of the various grades of barrels and the additional work put on the guns, the checkering and engraving, and the special selected imported stocks with which the higher priced guns are fitted, and whether you buy an A. J. Aubrey Gun at $13.85 or any of the higher grades, you are assured of getting a gun that will give you absolute satisfaction, a gun that will shoot better and last longer than any other gun you could possibly buy and such value as you could not possibly obtain in the purchase of any other gun.

SEE PAGE 705

for illustrations and full descriptions of the various parts entering into the construction of the A. J. Aubrey Hammerless Gun. By studying these illustrations and descriptions carefully, you will appreciate to some small extent the wonderful construction of this great gun. We want you to know all about this gun, as the more you know about it, the more certain we are of receiving your order. We have endeavored to describe these guns carefully, have given a description in detail of each and every part. We show, as stated, illustrations on another page taken from photographs of the various parts, so that you, in making your selection, will know just what to expect, so that you will be in a position to make a selection to your best interest, and remember, you are fully protected by our most liberal and binding guarantee and 60 days' free trial offer, as fully given on page 702.

GUARANTEED 20 YEARS 60 DAYS' FREE TRIAL

THE HAND ENGRAVING

EVERY LINE OF THIS ENGRAVING is done by hand, at the bench. The locks, as illustrated, are most elaborately engraved by hand; the frame, body, top and sides, the trigger guard, the tang, the break, the whole is most beautifully finished.

IF YOU WANT A MOST EXTRAORDINARY GUN, something entirely out of the ordinary in beautiful lines and hand engraved finish, then we would especially like to receive your order for this our high grade Aubrey. Send us your order, enclose our price, $19.35, if you wish genuine laminated steel barrels; $22.35, if you wish genuine two-blade Damascus steel barrels (of course you will state whether you wish barrels 30 or 32 inches long), with it we will send our written binding 20-year guarantee, by the terms and conditions of which if any piece or part gives out by reason of defect in material or workmanship within 20 years, we will replace or repair it free of charge. We will also send the gun to you with the understanding and agreement that it must reach you promptly, must reach you in perfect order, and after you have received it you have the privilege of giving it 60 days' thorough test, and during this time you can compare it with other guns as to its shooting qualities, the penetration it will make, the target and the pattern you can get, its long range shooting qualities; compare it in any way you may like, you be the sole judge, and you need not make any explanation to us if at any time during the 60 days you decide you don't want to keep the gun, you can return it to us at any time within 60 days at our expense, without explanation or reason from you of any kind, and the day we receive the gun we will pay the express charges and immediately return to you all the money you may have sent us, including any express charges you may have paid.

BE SURE TO MENTION LENGTH OF BARREL WANTED.

$19 35

DESCRIPTION

Read the description of our $13.85 Aubrey Gun, as appearing on one of the preceding pages, and you have all the description of this, our highest grade Aubrey Gun except for the elaborate hand engraving; otherwise the guns are alike. This has the quadruple bolt, our revolving, wedging bolt construction; has the automatic locking extension rib, it is taper choke bored by the celebrated Aubreyized taper system, built on an alignment giving it such a perfect balance, such a perfect hang, such beautiful control, making it a gun that will come to the shoulder with the stock tight to the shoulder, with the barrel so balanced that you catch the top of the sight and quickly line it with the game, do it as you can do it on no other gun. Built as we say, exactly the same as the $13.85 gun, except for the hand engraved finish, put out under our binding guarantee, is the Aubrey Hammerless Double Barrel Breech Loading Shotgun, which we most earnestly advise you to consider when about to buy a gun, whether you have been thinking of buying a hammer or hammerless from us or anyone else of any make, at any price.

WE FIT THIS HIGHER GRADE OF GUN

with an extra fine English walnut stock, using great care in selecting the wood for the stock and fore end so as to use only the most beautiful grain. The stock and fore end are made additionally attractive by the beautiful hand checkering, which is of a beautiful design, if you will note the illustration. It is all done by hand with very fine tools, requiring twice the time ordinarily required to checker an ordinary gun. All in all, in this, our best grade Aubrey gun, we aim to combine beauty with strength, and to realize how successful we have been in this respect you really have to see the gun, for which an opportunity is afforded you by our liberal sixty-day free trial offer, as fully given on page 702.

WE GIVE AWAY FREE with every one of these Guns OUR SPECIAL GLOBE SIGHT

which is a big help to the shooter for wing shooting. This sight is patented and is manufactured and controlled exclusively by us. This sight can be instantly attached or detached from the gun, and the regular front sight of the gun does not in any way interfere with the use of this globe sight. Every one of these guns bears the name, A. J. Aubrey, the strongest guarantee on the highest quality material and workmanship ever embodied in a shotgun of any kind. The name "A. J. Aubrey" on this gun means more to you than the name on any other gun. It means that you are getting the highest quality and the greatest value it is possible to produce. It further means that you are fully protected for a period of twenty years against defective material or construction by a binding guarantee.

Catalogue No.	Grade	Style Barrels	Gauge	Length of Barrels	Weight, Pounds	Finish	Price
6K50	A. S. E.	Genuine Twist	12	30 or 32 in.	7¼ to 7¾	Fine Line Scroll and Game Engraving	$19.35
6K52	D. S. E.	Genuine Two-Blade Damascus	12	30 or 32 in.	7¼ to 7¾		22.35

No. 6K52

WEIGHT PACKED FOR SHIPMENT, ABOUT 14 POUNDS.

WHEN ORDERING give catalogue number, length of barrels and weight desired. We will send you a gun in accordance with your wishes, a gun that we know will please you in every particular.

$26.75 AUBREY HAMMERLESS SPECIAL

AS SHOWN ON THE INTRODUCTORY PAGE OF THIS CATALOGUE, PAGE 702, MR. AUBREY HAS BEEN AND IS MAKING SPECIAL A. J. AUBREY GUNS TO ORDER.

UNDERSTAND, YOU CAN HAVE SIXTY DAYS' FREE TRIAL

We will be glad, on receipt of the price, to send you any one of the guns shown on this page, with the understanding and agreement that you can give it sixty days' free trial, during which time you can put it to every test, and if you are not satisfied with your purchase you can return the gun to us at our expense, and we will immediately return your money.

Understand, every gun carries with it OUR WRITTEN BINDING TWENTY YEARS' GUARANTEE, by the terms and conditions of which if any piece or part gives out within twenty years, by reason of defect in material or workmanship, we will replace or repair it free of charge. Understand also, this gun is in every detail of construction exactly the same as the $13.85 Aubrey, 12-gauge only, 30 or 32-inch barrels (be sure to state length of barrels wanted), quadruple bolt action, wedge automatic self locking and bolting mechanism, which bolts the barrel through the matted extension rib to the frame, highest grade safety, the very best of everything.

AMONG THE TRAP AND FIELD SHOOTERS and especially among the professional trap shooters there are a great many gun fanciers, those who want something exceedingly fine in finish, some specially fine, very elaborate hand engraving, engraving where an artist must be employed, and where in some instances to execute some special orders, we have been compelled to employ the most skilled artist at as high as five or six dollars a day for a full week, where a very elaborate, beautiful, fine and artistic engraving design would have to be carried out, and occasionally some professional trap shooter or other customer may want something most elaborate, a special kind of grain in a fine Italian stock. He may call for a special weight, a special drop, irregular length, and to accommodate all these, as explained in the introductory, on page 702 Mr. Aubrey is always ready to figure on anything special, on a gun made to order, and those wishing to figure with him on such guns can write him direct, addressing their letters to Mr. A. J. Aubrey, President Meriden Fire Arms Company, Meriden, Connecticut.

THE PAST YEAR the demand for special guns at the prices Mr. Aubrey has been able to quote, ranging from about $30.00 to $50.00, has been so great that Mr. Aubrey decided to get out regularly and allow us to offer in our catalogue the guns shown on this page, which are higher grade in finish than we have ever before offered, and which are designed to supply the wants of many of those who heretofore have been going to Mr. Aubrey for something in this line of special finish in guns made to order. Mr. Aubrey has explained to us that by getting out these special, high grade finished styles shown on this page in large quantities, several hundred of each at a time, he can very materially reduce the cost as against getting them out singly special to order; in other words, the guns we offer you on this page at $26.75 to $38.50 if gotten out singly, special to order as heretofore, could not be furnished even by Mr. Aubrey, direct from the factory, at less than $10.00 to $15.00 more money each.

IN OFFERING THESE HIGHER GRADE, more elaborately engraved and finished guns shown on this page, which heretofore Mr. Aubrey has only made singly, special to order, Mr. Aubrey feels he would be saving at least $10.00 to $15.00 in price on a gun to those who take advantage of the guns shown on this page, which we will now carry regularly in stock, and it will give his Special Order Department an opportunity of devoting themselves to special made to order guns, to the executing of special orders for something entirely out of the ordinary at from $50.00 upward; in other words, for your information, it is the custom of several of the makers of the finest guns to make guns to order at prices ranging from $100.00 to $500.00. Mr. Aubrey hereafter, on special made to order guns, will confine himself only to these, the very finest, but instead of naming you prices as others do, ranging from $100.00 to $500.00, he will undertake to execute any special order, giving you something that will outclass any gun that you can buy elsewhere in a special order gun at one-third the price other high grade makers charge for their extra fine special made to order goods.

This is the exact same gun as all A. J. Aubrey Hammerless Guns shown on preceding pages. It differs only in its most elaborate finish.

WHILE THE BARRELS IN THIS SPECIAL GUN which we offer at $26.75 are plain steel barrels, they are made from the finest carbon gun barrel steel that money can buy, they have been given a finish that is indescribable, something you really must see to appreciate. The elaborate and beautiful finish of this gun is represented more especially in the very handsome hand engraving, the work of a famous artist, engraving that covers the locks, frame, guards, break, etc., in the beautiful imported buried walnut stock, in the elaborate checkering, beautiful decorating, the high polish and finish throughout; in short, the difference in price between this, our special Aubrey gun at $26.75 and the cheapest Aubrey gun we offer which is $13.85. The difference of $12.90 represents but little more than the actual difference in labor that has gone to make this the beautiful gun it is.

DURING THE PAST YEAR following the directions of the customers, mostly professional trap shooters, Mr. Aubrey has made singly to specific orders a large number of these guns, and almost without exception from every buyer he has received the most flattering testimonials.

HAVING MADE SO MANY OF THESE GUNS to special order, almost identical with the gun here shown, and being compelled by reason of making them singly to order to charge from $40.00 to $45.00 in order to cover the expense where made singly to order and allowing a small manufacturing profit, we decided this season to bring them out in one hundred lots, taking them through every part of the factory, otherwise in a most special way, but at the same time give our customers the benefit of all the saving by taking these guns through the factory in one hundred lots instead of one gun to order singly at a time. Figuring out this saving as carefully as we can it amounts to about $15.00 a gun, or going over the actual cost of producing this gun as shown on this page, the cost of material and labor, carefully calculated through every part of the factory, and then adding only our one small percentage of profit, we find we can offer it for $26.75.

IF YOU WANT A DOUBLE BARREL hammerless breech loading shotgun that is entirely out of the ordinary a beautiful thing to look at, as fine a shooting gun as was ever made, something that will be a joy forever, something that will be in appearance, in fact in every way handsome and better than you would be likely to find in a party of a dozen hunters, then we advise you to order one of these finest special made guns.

No. 6K55 12-gauge, 30 or 32-inch barrels of XX carbon steel. Weight, 7½ to 8 pounds **$26.75**

No. 6K56 The exact same gun, 12-gauge, 30 or 32-inch, 7½ to 8 pounds, with the very finest imported three-blade, full finished Damascus steel barrels........ **30.75**

$38.50 AUBREY DAMASCUS SPECIAL

GOING JUST A LITTLE FARTHER in the Special Gun Department, Mr. Aubrey has given us in this the finest Aubrey gun we carry in stock, the exact same gun that he has heretofore been getting out only on special order, one gun at a time, at $60.00, and we guarantee it in every way equal to any gun you can have made to order by any of the high grade makers for $150.00.

IN TAKING CARE of the Made to Order Department at Meriden, Conn., during the last twelve months, a great many of these guns have been gotten out to order following the specifications which have come mostly from professional trap shooters, and except for a little variation here and there, many of these guns have been identical with the guns we here offer you for $38.50, and in executing these orders, figuring only the actual cost of producing, where the gun is put through singly on a special order, Mr. Aubrey has been compelled, in order to get his one small manufacturing profit, to get about $60.00 for these special guns. Now we bring them out in lots of one hundred, give you all the benefit of all the saving by making them in one hundred lots instead of one at a time singly, and offer you a price of $38.50.

UNDERSTAND, this gun will shoot no better, last no longer and give no better satisfaction as a shooting arm than the $13.85 Aubrey shown on preceding page, for the machine parts are identical throughout. This, like the $13.85 Aubrey, is the best shooting gun made in the world. No gun made at any price will shoot farther, kill at longer range, give better target, better balance or safety. The only object in buying a specially fine finished gun like this, in fact, the only inducement we can offer you is, that you will have not only the best mechanical and the best shooting gun possible to build but you will also have something entirely out of the ordinary, a handsome and better gun than anyone in your neighborhood. You can match it up, if you please, with any gun made to order by any other maker, even at $100.00 or $150.00 or more. There's a world of work; days and days of hand labor at the hands of the most skilled artist have gone into this gun to make it the thing of beauty that it is. The very elaborate hand engraving on the lock plates, the frame, the break, the guards, etc.; the buried imported Italian walnut wood that has gone into the stock has been selected with great care, the beautiful three-blade imported Liege full Damascus steel barrels have been selected with great care, all parts have been very highly polished and finished; in short, this gun has been gotten out practically without regard to expense. It's Mr. Aubrey's masterpiece, by far the finest gun we carry in stock, and the price we name, $38.50, barely covers the cost of material and labor in our own factory, with but our one small percentage of profit added. It is no doubt a handsomer and better gun than many special made to order guns that are sold at $100.00 to $150.00.

READ WHAT ONE OF OUR CUSTOMERS SAYS OF THE FINEST AUBREY GUN.

Sears, Roebuck & Co. Milford, Conn.

Dear Sirs:—I take pleasure in writing a few lines to let you know that I am very much pleased with my special order A. J. Aubrey gun, which I received direct from the factory. I have given it a good, fair trial and it outshoots and outpatterns (with various sized shot ranging from No. 6 to No. 12) any other gun that I own, and I own four high priced American made guns which aggregate sixteen times as much in cost as my Aubrey, and I consider the Aubrey far superior in design and workmanship to any one of them and a finer balanced gun, also showing a higher art of scientific gun making. Several years ago I worked as a machinist and tool maker and also on gun work, so I think that my judgment ought to be good, as I have been a hard man to please in the matter of guns. I think your Mr. A. J. Aubrey one of the most competent men to provide for the special needs and fancies of trap and field shots. Wishing you every success, I remain,

Very truly yours, C. E. BACKER, V. M. D.

IF YOU WANT THE FINEST THING IN YOUR NEIGHBORHOOD, something entirely out of the ordinary, if you appreciate a really beautiful thing, a work of art, and you want to buy it at a mere fraction of what any attempt at this point of excellence has cost any other factory, then send for this gun, and we will send it to you with the understanding and agreement that you can give it sixty days' trial, during which time you can put it to every test, and if you are not satisfied with your purchase you can return it to us at our expense and we will immediately return your money. With every gun we issue our written binding twenty years' guarantee, by the terms and conditions of which if any piece or part gives out by reason of defect in material or workmanship, we will replace or repair it free of charge.

THE HAND CHECKERING, shaping, polishing, selection of materials, the engraving, everything about this gun is truly a work of art.

This gun, like all Aubrey guns, comes in 12-gauge, 30 or 32-inch barrels (be sure to state length of barrels wanted), weighs 7¼ to 7¾ pounds, and this particular gun is furnished in one of the most elaborate, carefully selected, most elaborately finished three-blade imported Liege Damascus steel barrels.

No. 6K58 Our special price for this gun **$38.50**

NEW ENGLAND WONDER

$10⁹⁵

WE CHALLENGE ANY GUN MAKER

OR GUN SELLER IN AMERICA TO PRODUCE THE EQUAL OF THIS AMERICAN GUN WITHIN $5.00 OF OUR PRICE.

PAY $25.00 FOR A GUN

YOU CAN BUY FROM YOUR DEALER AT HOME OR ELSEWHERE, AND THEN COMPARE IT WITH THIS, OUR NEW ENGLAND $10.95 GUN, AND YOU WILL FIND OURS A FAR SUPERIOR GUN IN EVERY PIECE, PART AND WAY.

TAPER CHOKE BORED

NEW ENGLAND

FOR SEVERAL YEARS we have been handling the Norwich double barrel breech loading shotgun which we have been able to offer at prices ranging from $11.72 to $16.10. The Norwich gun is a thoroughly reliable gun; so long as we handled it, far better in value than any double hammer gun we were able to buy and offer our customers, but with a view to making our hammer guns still much higher in grade, determined to give our customers still much more for their money than ever before, we arranged at our own factory (the Meriden Firearms Company of Meriden, Conn.,) to build a full line of the highest grade hammer double barrel breech loading shotguns made, the A. J. Aubrey line, and these we show on other pages in this department at prices ranging from $12.59 upward; then to get another gun that we could sell at a lower price and yet outclass in quality the Norwich guns we have sold in the past, we arranged with a New England maker, who also makes for us our $11.95 hammerless gun, to make for us a strictly high grade double barrel hammer gun, following the lines of the famous A. J. Aubrey, and as a result, we can offer you in this New England gun at $10.95, a vastly better double barrel breech loading shotgun than we have ever before been able to offer at even $15.00. It is made along the same lines as the A. J. Aubrey, and while in the making of this New England gun we do not employ the same skilled mechanics or give that rigid inspection and beautiful finish found only in the Aubrey, still we have made it in its various parts almost identical with the Aubrey, and in this New England factory employ the same grade of gun mechanics and workmen, use the same grade of machine tooling, finishing, etc., as is used in practically all gun making factories outside of the Meriden Firearms Company, so while this, our special $10.95 gun, will compare in workmanship, finish, fit, etc., with guns made by other American makers that sell even at double this price, it combines all of the high grade mechanical advantages of the A. J. Aubrey, making it a wonderful improvement over any gun on the market that you can buy elsewhere at anything like the price.

THIS $10.95 NEW ENGLAND GUN is made so good that we extend with this gun the same liberal guarantee and the same liberal free trial offer that we extend with all of the famous A. J. Aubrey guns.

IF YOU SEND US YOUR ORDER for this, our new improved 1908 model New England Wonder hammer breech loading shotgun, we will send it to you with the understanding and agreement that you can give it a free test, compare it with any gun you can buy elsewhere at double the price, and if you are not perfectly satisfied with your purchase, if you are not convinced you have gotten far more value for your money than you could have gotten elsewhere, you are at liberty to return the gun to us at our expense, and we will immediately return your money.

LIKE THE FAMOUS A. J. AUBREY DOUBLE HAMMER GUN

SHOWN ON THE FOLLOWING PAGES AT $12.59 AND UPWARD, THIS NEW ENGLAND GUN HAS THE FOLLOWING SPECIAL STRONG AND VALUABLE FEATURES:

BARRELS—The barrels are made from the very finest crystal barrel steel, highly polished and finished, and a grade of steel, that when finished, will not rust, pit or mark like the cheaper grade guns. The barrels are beautifully tapered, they are reinforced at the breech, they have extra heavy top and bottom rib, the top rib is matted, tapered, beautifully shaped and accurate in alignment. The reinforcing of the breech makes the gun an ideal gun for smokeless powder as well as black powder, and reduces the recoil or kick to the very minimum, putting the entire force of the powder into the penetration of the shot. The barrels are beautifully finished and they are accurately choke bored by the Taper system, which guarantees a pattern, target, penetration and long distance killing not effected by any of the cheaper guns.

EXTRACTOR—These barrels are fitted with the very latest shell extractor, which is positive in its action.

HEAVY BOLT ACTION—These barrels are fitted with extra heavy bolts, made very strong, thus insuring a perfect lock and strength by which the gun, even with the use of black or white powder, cannot wear loose or shaky. The bolt action of this gun cannot be in any way compared with the cheaper guns on the market.

FRAME—This gun is made with one of the heaviest, strongest and most durable drop steel forged frames made; extra strong and heavy in every part, well finished, case hardened and handsomely colored. It has the latest Norwich firing pins, handsomely shaped, perfect acting top snap break, neat low circular hammers, very strong, genuine bar locks with steel hardened interchangeable parts, perfectly finished and all points of contact are made of case hardened tool steel.

STOCK—Stock is made from carefully selected straight grained walnut, thoroughly seasoned, perfectly shaped. The stock is fitted to the frame by an automatic stock fitting machine, which insures a perfect fit, and the frame and stock are so constructed in points of contact as to insure the strongest kind of a stock where many guns are weak. This stock is full pistol grip and comes with a handsomely ornamented butt plate as illustrated.

FORE END—This, our $10.95 gun, is fitted with a self locking beautifully finished and checkered walnut fore end, strong steel tip and steel tang.

SAFE AND DURABLE—First, in considering hard, long range shooting, extra penetration, extra target, the question of strength, durability and safety has not been overlooked, and while it is not safe to use white or nitro powder in many of the cheap American made guns, this gun is built for shooting either white, black or nitro powder. It has been built extra strong of the best material, strongly locked, strongly reinforced, especially strong where many guns are weak, all with a view of giving you a gun that will be always safe, always reliable, a gun that will last for years and give the very best of satisfaction.

THE HIGH GRADE AUBREY FEATURES that are carried out in this, our $10.95 gun, are the quadruple bolt locking mechanism, the special interchangeable bar locks, the reinforcing of the barrels at the breech, the crystal barrel steel used in the barrels, the barrel finishing and the choke boring, the beautiful alignment, the hang, the shape, that perfect balance, that means when you bring the gun to your shoulder and cast your eye over the matted rib between the two barrels you catch the sight instantly, and even though it be on fast wing shooting, this sight instantly gets in line with the game, and this is all effected by the higher art of scientific gun making, which has been developed by Mr. A. J. Aubrey, and introduced and used in this $10.95 gun for the purpose of putting this gun in a class by itself. The Aubrey ideas of wonderful barrel construction, perfect milling, extra heavy, rigid, everlasting drop steel forged frame, strong at every point, a gun that will not shoot loose, a gun with none of the earmarks of cheapness, a gun that will shoot as well as any gun made, regardless of name, make or price; you will find all these features in this new improved 1908 model New England Wonder.

TAKE OUR ADVICE

IF YOU DON'T BUY a genuine A. J. Aubrey, then buy this gun, the New England make, made on the A. J. Aubrey lines, and believe us, it isn't to your advantage to buy a cheaper gun, for in this and the A. J. Aubrey guns you get so much more for your money than we or any other house can possibly offer you in any other gun made, and, remember, we send this gun to you on the same conditions with the Aubrey guns, with the understanding and agreement that you can give the gun sixty days' trial, during which time you can put it to every reasonable test, and if, at any time during the sixty days, you should become dissatisfied with your purchase, you can return the gun to us at our expense, and we will immediately return your money, together with any freight or express charges you may have paid. We also guarantee this gun under a written binding guarantee for twenty years.

IF AT ANY TIME in the years to come you should want any piece or part to repair one of these guns, we will always carry it in stock, and will supply it to you at actual factory cost, plus only our one small percentage of profit, and if it comes within the limits of our guarantee we will furnish such parts free of cost to you.

$10⁹⁵

WITH EVERY ONE OF THESE $10.95 NEW ENGLAND DOUBLE BARREL BREECH LOADING SHOTGUNS WE ISSUE A

WRITTEN BINDING

20-YEAR

GUARANTEE

BY THE TERMS AND CONDITIONS OF WHICH IF ANY PIECE OR PART GIVES OUT WITHIN 20 YEARS, BY REASON OF DEFECT IN MATERIAL OR WORKMANSHIP, WE WILL REPLACE OR REPAIR IT FREE OF CHARGE.

No. 6K81   We furnish this gun exactly as illustrated and described under our 20-year written binding guarantee, 12-gauge only, 30 or 32-inch barrels, as desired, combining every high grade feature of every gun with the defects of none, weighing 7½ to 8 pounds, complete with the very finest genuine crystal barrel steel barrels, beautifully finished throughout. Price..   **$10.95**

No. 6K81

A. J. AUBREY SPECIAL

$15.50

FOR THE BENEFIT OF THOSE WHO WISH SOMETHING OUT OF THE ORDINARY, those who wish not only the highest grade hammer double barrel breech loading shotgun made, but want the gun with specially fine finish, elaborate hand engraving, mounting, etc., Mr. Aubrey has gotten out for us in our own factory at Meriden, Conn., The Meriden Firearms Company, this specially finished, elaborately hand engraved hammer double barrel breech loading shotgun and, going over the cost calculation, first, the cost of the raw material and then the cost of labor in making and shaping the different parts, and the cost of the hand work in the engraving, ornamenting, mounting, etc., we find we are able, with our one small percentage of profit added, to offer you this gun at the astonishingly low price, exactly as illustrated and described, of only $15.50.

COMPARE THIS, OUR $15.50 A. J. AUBREY SPECIAL, with the A. J. Aubreys shown on the first two preceding pages, which we offer at $12.59, and you will note a difference in price of $2.91 Now, we wish to explain, that excepting for the hand finish in the engraving, ornamentation and extra high polish, in the fine checkering, in the special polishing of the stock, these guns are identically the same, whether you buy the Aubrey at $12.59 or the higher grade Aubrey gun at $15.50. One is just as strong as the other, all parts are exactly the same and interchangeable, one will last and shoot just as well as the other, but this difference of $2.91 in price represents the actual difference in cost to us, plus only our one small percentage of profit. The $2.91 difference in price we have paid out in hand labor.

AFTER MAKING THE REGULAR GRADE AT $12.59, the gun as shown on the first two preceding pages, we have added $2.91 in labor. This has been added in giving the barrels a very high grade finish, an extraordinary polish and in elaborately engraving by hand the locks, frame, triggers, guard, tang, snap break, etc., and by otherwise finishing this gun up in order to make it something entirely special, something out of the ordinary.

IF YOU WANT A HAMMER GUN in place of a hammerless, a double barrel breech loading hammer shotgun, made by the best maker in America, made by Mr. Aubrey, and a gun bearing his name is a guarantee forever for quality, a gun made in our own factory, the Meriden Firearms Company of Meriden, Conn., and you want it exactly on the basis of what it costs to build, the cost of material and labor, with but our one small percentage of profit added, a gun that will shoot as strong, kill at as long a range, give as good a target, penetration and pattern as any gun made, regardless of name, make or price, a gun that will practically last forever, a gun that is choke bored by a system that you are sure will shoot as well after ten years constant shooting as the day you receive it, a gun that will not shoot loose, then by all means order an A. J. Aubrey Double Barrel Breech Loading Shotgun, and for something especially fine, specially hand engraved and elaborately finished throughout, then by all means order this, our $15.50 A. J. Aubrey.

ABOUT REPAIR PARTS We guarantee to have in stock at all times a full assortment of all kinds of repairs to all Aubrey guns, which we will furnish you promptly on request in case you should need any kind of a repair part, and if it comes within the limits of our guarantee it will be furnished you free; otherwise, you will get it at exactly factory cost, a mere fraction of the price other makers ask for gun parts.

WHILE WE QUOTE double barrel breech loading shotguns, American made, reliable breech loading shotguns as low as $7.75, another at $8.95 and still another very high grade gun at $10.95, and any of these guns at the prices quoted, $7.75 to $10.95, are worth twice as many as any of the cheap Belgian guns which are usually sold at $8.00 to $15.00, nevertheless, in your own interest, in order to get the best possible value for your money, in order that you can get the best gun made in America, a gun that will shoot further, give better penetration, kill at longer range, a gun that will give you more satisfaction than any other gun, a safer gun, a gun where your dollar will go farthest, we advise you by all means to buy a genuine A. J. Aubrey.

CONSIDER THE POINTS IN WHICH IT EXCELS ALL OTHER DOUBLE BARREL GUNS MADE.

SEE THE FIRST TWO PRECEDING PAGES on which we show an illustration of the gun and the parts of the $12.59 gun, and remember the parts of this are exactly the same, and it differs from all other double barrel hammer breech loading shotguns made. It is built on the very same lines of the highest grade hammerless double barrel breech loading shotgun ever produced, the genuine A. J. Aubrey. It differs from other hammer guns in that it has the quadruple bolt action, reinforced breech, automatic wedge locking mechanism, which locks the barrels to the frame as securely as if the entire gun were one solid piece, has the strongest known flat water table, the strongest known firing pins, best possible lock construction, low circular hammers, all points of contact are of tool steel, hardened; taper choke bored by the latest and best system, beautiful alignment, perfect balance, correct hang, so contructed that when you raise this gun to your shoulder and cast your eye over the matted rib, you catch the sight instantly, and if at wing shooting instantly you get the sight and line with the bird. This question of hang, of adjustment, of easy action, means everything in gun making, and you get it all in the genuine A. J. Aubrey guns. Every A. J. Aubrey gun bears the name impressed in the lock of the gun.

IF YOU COULD COME TO OUR STORE, go into our Gun Department and there have brought before your personal inspection all American guns made, even though they sell at two to three times the price at which we offer this gun, and there also bring to your inspection and attention the various Belgian guns on the market, and you could go over them carefully and compare them in every little detail with this genuine A. J. Aubrey gun, there would be no question as to your decision, no chance of anyone getting an order from you for anything but a genuine A. J. Aubrey. Better still, if you could visit the factory at Meriden, Conn., and there see the effort we are making, how these guns are made and the material from which they are made, the kind of workmanship, the kind of machinery, tools and equipment we have for making every piece and part perfect, if you could see our system of inspection, how every piece and part must be made to gauge and how closely every piece and part is inspected, if you could follow the gun through the factory to where it is assembled and where it gets its last inspection, and see it tested for target, see all that is demanded of the gun at the factory, more especially, after that if you could go through any other gun factory in America and contrast the difference in the kind of material we use and the way we use it, the inspection we give the work and the care taken, the exactness at every point, you would then be able to appreciate something of the value we are offering in A. J. Aubrey goods; but since you cannot see the different guns in our store and make your own comparison, or you cannot visit our factory at Meriden, we only ask that before you buy any other make of gun than an A. J. Aubrey, you let us send you the Aubrey to see, examine and test under our sixty days' free trial, and if at the end of the sixty days for any reason you are not satisfied with your purchase, you can return the gun to us at our expense, and we will immediately return your money.

THIS GUN, AS BEFORE EXPLAINED, COMES IN 12-GAUGE ONLY, 30 OR 32-INCH BARRELS, reinforced at the breech, quadruple lock action, automatic wedge extension rib and frame locking mechanism, full pistol grip, checkered grip and fore end, automatic locking fore end, top snap break, low circular hammers, all points of contact made of finest, full finished tool steel, very elaborately engraved and decorated by hand, and furnished complete under our binding twenty years guarantee at the following prices:

COMPARING THIS FULL HAND ENGRAVED and hand finished double barrel hammer gun with anything we have ever been able to offer in the past when purchased from any other factory, there is no comparison whatever in the value we are giving.

UNTIL THIS SEASON Mr. Aubrey made for us in our own factory at Meriden, no double barrel hammer breech loading shotguns, the entire double barrel shotgun product being confined to the hammerless gun only, but this season, and for the reasons explained on the first two preceding pages, we have decided to offer our own gun from our own factory, built as good as the highest mechanical skill could do, with the best materials money could buy, and as a result we have in the Aubrey hammer gun, both in the gun offered on the first preceding pages at $12.59, and in this special hand engraved and hand finished gun, more than double the real intrinsic value, more than twice as much for your money as we have ever before been able to offer in any double hammer gun which we could buy from any factory.

COMPARED WITH HAND ENGRAVED GUNS we have offered before, guns made by reputable American gun makers, and guns we were compelled to sell at $15.00 to $20.00, this special Aubrey gun which we offer you in the full hand engraved finish is easily worth double.

SEE THE FIRST PRECEDING PAGE for the way this gun is constructed, the kind of parts that go to make this the highest grade gun on the market, and then in comparing this special hand engraved and hand finished gun with any gun we have ever before been able to offer, we put a worth on this not approached by any gun made or offered by any maker in any quantity, even at double our price.

IN BUYING HAND ENGRAVED and hand finished guns from other makers, we have been compelled to accept coarse engraving, and at times, poor finish and fitting, comparatively poor case hardening and finish, while in this our $15.50 Aubrey gun, we are able, in controlling our own factory, to give the gun the highest possible finish, to beautifully finish the barrels, give you a very elaborate hand engraving on the frame, locks, lock plate, tang, break, guard, etc., to give you a very different stock and pistol grip construction, in short, to give you something way out of the ordinary.

$15.50

No. 6K91

No. 6K91   Very finest genuine crystal gun barrel steel, full finished, 12-gauge, 30 or 32-inch barrel; weight, 7¼ to 7¾ pounds.   Price.......$15.50
No. 6K92   Genuine imported two-blade Liege twist barrels, 12-gauge, 30 or 32-inch barrels; weight, 7½ to 8 pounds.   Our special price....   16.50
No. 6K93   Genuine imported Liege two-blade Damascus steel barrels, 12-gauge, 30 or 32-inch barrels; weight, 7½ to 8 pounds.   Our special price   19.50
For detailed illustration showing parts and description of same, see first preceding page.

A. J. AUBREY SPECIAL $15⁵⁰

THE FOLLOWING ILLUSTRATIONS AND DESCRIPTIONS WILL GIVE YOU SOME IDEA OF THE GENERAL CONSTRUCTION OF THE AUBREY DOUBLE HAMMER BREECH LOADING SHOTGUN

THIS VERY CONSTRUCTION CARRIES THROUGH EXACTLY THE SAME ON ALL GRADES OF AUBREY HAMMER BREECH LOADING GUNS. THE HIGHER GRADE GUNS, THOSE MADE WITH SPECIALLY FINE BARRELS AND THOSE ELABORATELY HAND ENGRAVED, AS SHOWN ON THE FOLLOWING PAGES, HAVE THE EXACT SAME PARTS AS THE $12.59 GUN ILLUSTRATED ON PAGE 711. ALL PARTS ARE INTERCHANGEABLE AND ALL THE BEST THAT MECHANICAL SKILL CAN PRODUCE.

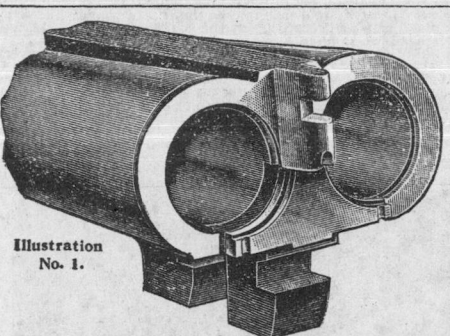

Illustration No. 1.

ILLUSTRATION No. 1 shows the extension rib construction of the Aubrey double hammer breech loader. You will note it is a deep, square extension rib with a slot at the end which engages when closed with the automatic wedge bolt locking mechanism in the frame, and we believe this is the only double hammer gun made that has any such positive lock construction, so strong and so firm that when the gun is closed it is to all purposes one solid piece or bar of steel, and whether you shoot smokeless or black powder there is no possibility of its shooting loose. This illustration also shows the heavy reinforced breech, giving this gun enormous strength. This is a portion of the automatic wedge locking mechanism found only on the Aubrey guns, the exact same construction as is used on the celebrated Aubrey hammerless, a system of wedged locking construction that makes the gun rigid, safe, prevents its shooting loose, and renders it the ideal smokeless powder gun, a feature that has much to do with eliminating the recoil or kick common to the lower grade of guns.

ILLUSTRATION No. 2 shows a section of the matted rib that goes on these guns. It's an extra strong, full taper shaped, full finished, beautifully matted rib, and the strongest barrel jointed matted rib construction made. This small illustration cannot do the beautiful extension rib justice. The matting on the rib is of a special design, does not reflect the light and greatly adds to the beautiful appearance of the gun.

Illustration No. 2.

BRIDLE
SEAR SPRING
SEAR
MAIN SPRING REBOUND TUMBLER TUMBLER

Illustration No. 3.

ILLUSTRATION No. 3 gives you some idea of the lock construction. Understand, all parts are interchangeable, and all parts with bearing are made from the finest full tempered tool steel.

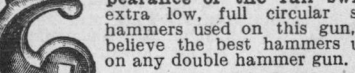

Illustration No. 4.

ILLUSTRATION No. 4 shows you the shapely appearance of the full swing, extra low, full circular steel hammers used on this gun, we believe the best hammers used on any double hammer gun.

Illustration No. 5.

ILLUSTRATION No. 5 shows the shell extractor, which is automatic and positive in its action, very strong and attached to an extra heavy steel bolt construction.

ILLUSTRATION No. 6 shows the bottom of the breech with the extra heavy double lugs and flat water table reinforced breech construction, built throughout with a view to making the use of white, smokeless or other high explosive powders perfectly safe, to give the very minimum of recoil or kick and to strengthen the gun in every possible way.

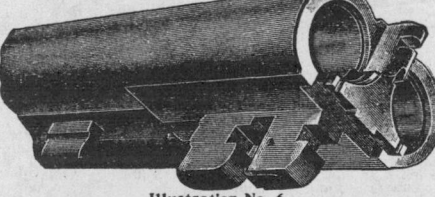

Illustration No. 6.

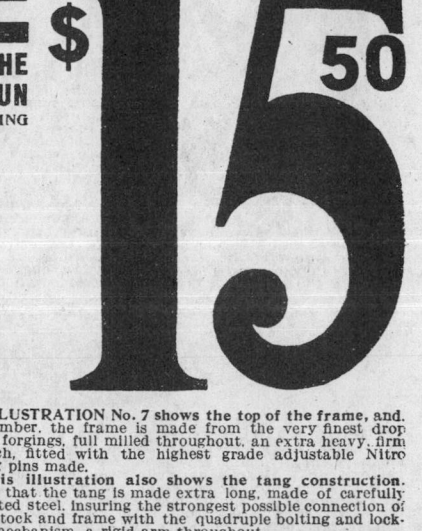

Illustration No. 7.

ILLUSTRATION No. 7 shows the top of the frame, and, remember, the frame is made from the very finest drop steel forgings, full milled throughout, an extra heavy, firm breech, fitted with the highest grade adjustable Nitro firing pins made.

This illustration also shows the tang construction. Note that the tang is made extra long, made of carefully selected steel, insuring the strongest possible connection of the stock and frame with the quadruple bolting and locking mechanism, a rigid arm throughout.

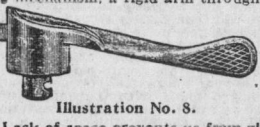

Illustration No. 8.

ILLUSTRATION No. 8 shows the top snap break, the very latest style, full finished, tool steel, matted tip, top lever break, the strongest break construction possible to produce.

Lack of space prevents us from giving you a better idea of this excellent top lever locking device. It is the strongest and most positive rib locking device ever placed on a gun. The solid steel extension which connects with the rib is firmly set in the top lever and connects directly with the slot cut in the extension rib. It is impossible for it to ever wear loose, and you will find, after you have shot a thousand shells, your gun is as tight as when you first received it. This top lever construction is found only on the A. J. Aubrey guns.

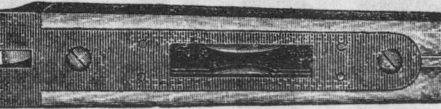

Illustration No. 9.

ILLUSTRATION No. 9 shows the locking device which automatically and rigidly locks the fore end to the barrel. There is no possibility of its shooting loose.

Illustration No. 10.

ILLUSTRATION No. 10 shows the shapely automatic self locking walnut fore end, with full finished metal tip. The fore end is beautifully shaped and, as shown in the above illustration, it has the best known automatic lock connection.

DETAILED DESCRIPTION

THESE AUBREY HAMMER DOUBLE BARREL BREECH LOADING SHOTGUNS have an alignment and a hang that insures the best possible target. As the gun is lifted to the shoulder and the eye sights over the barrels, you immediately catch sight of the game whether standing or on the wing; in fact, there is a balance and an evenness of weight, a hang which you will get on no other gun made.

THE BARRELS are made of the highest grade steel, they are all choke bored by the Taper system, so bored that the choking will never shoot out, reinforced at breech, reinforced matted top rib, reinforced bottom rib, double lugs, four-bolt construction.

GAUGE—All these guns are 12-gauge only. Barrels are 30 or 32 inches long, as desired. Be sure to state length of barrels wanted.

FRAMES—The frames are made from the very finest drop steel forgings, all perfectly milled, polished, shaped and fitted.

LOCKING CONSTRUCTION—These guns have the highest grade automatic wedge locking mechanism, locking the barrels rigidly to the frame and stock, so that they never can shoot loose.

LOCKS—The locks are all the very latest type bar locks, all parts interchangeable, full finished, every part that has a bearing is made of the finest tool steel, tempered.

STOCK CONNECTION—The stocks are all set in by carefully fitting the frame and locks to the stock, and all have extra long tang with reinforced connection throughout.

STOCK AND FORE END—Stocks are all made of carefully selected walnut, full finished shaped with perfect alignment, to which the barrels, frame, locks, pistol grip and all are in perfect harmony in alignment and shape. The stocks are full pistol grip, with fancy rubber butt plate on grip and stock. Grips are full checkered, fore ends are made from carefully selected walnut, full shaped, full checkered and equipped with the best known automatic locking device.

TRIGGERS, HAMMERS, GUARDS, etc.—Guns are equipped with the finest low circular hammers, beautifully shaped; neat, long lever triggers, beautifully shaped; neat, thin, yet strong trigger guard; latest reinforced, double acting, top snap lever.

CASE HARDENING AND FINISHING—These guns are all given an extra fine finish. The frame, locks, hammer, tang, etc., are all case hardened, with beautiful full mottled finish.

SHOOTING QUALITIES—As before explained, the shooting qualities of these guns are unequaled for long distance killing, long range shooting, for penetration, pattern or target. Both barrels are full choke bored, so firmly constructed that, unlike other guns, there is no recoil or kicking. That which in other guns goes into the recoil in the A. J. Aubrey gun goes to give greater force to the shot.

OUR 60 DAYS' FREE TRIAL OFFER

REMEMBER, with every one of these guns we give a sixty days' free trial; that is, you have the privilege of using any Aubrey gun for sixty days, during which time you can put it to every reasonable test and comparison in competition with any gun made, and if you are not satisfied you are getting better value than you could get in any other gun made you can return the gun to us at our expense, and we will immediately return your money.

REMEMBER OUR 20 YEARS' BINDING GUARANTEE

REMEMBER, every Aubrey gun is covered by our written binding twenty years' guarantee, by the terms and conditions of which if any piece or part gives out by reason of defect in material or workmanship, within twenty years, we will replace or repair it free of charge. With care it will last a lifetime.

UNDERSTAND, the various parts, the workmanship throughout, the strength, the shooting qualities and the lasting qualities of our $12.59 Aubrey gun, are exactly the same as the higher grade Aubrey guns shown on the following pages up to $18.75, the only difference in the guns being the difference in the grade of barrels used and the amount of hand engraving and hand work on the finish. For more elaborately finished Aubrey guns see following pages.

WE FURNISH THIS, the genuine A. J. Aubrey hammer double barrel breech loading shotgun, exactly as illustrated and described on these two pages, with all of the high grade up to date features of the new celebrated Aubrey hammerless gun, furnish it under our guarantee as the highest grade hammer double barrel breech loading shotgun made, at the following special prices:

No. 6K91 Very finest Crystal steel, full finished barrels, 12-gauge, length of barrels 30 or 32 inches, as desired; weight, 7½ to 8 pounds. Price....$15.50
No. 6K92 Genuine imported Liege triple-leaf twist steel barrels, 12-gauge, 30 or 32-inch barrels; weight, 7½ to 8 pounds. Price............. 16.50
No. 6K93 Genuine imported Liege double blade Damascus steel barrels, 12-gauge, 30 or 32-inch barrels; weight, 7½ to 8 pounds. Price......... 19.50

The preceding page shows an illustration of the gun, but this page shows the illustrations of the various parts, and on the next following pages you will find the exact same gun with elaborate hand engraving and hand finish, for those who wish a still finer finish, yet otherwise the exact same gun as the one shown on page 711 at $12.59.

$18.50 THE A. J. AUBREY FINEST
MILLIONAIRE'S GUN FOR THE COMMON PEOPLE

OUR MR. A. J. AUBREY, president and general manager of our gun factory, the Meriden Fire Arms Company of Meriden, Connecticut, suggested to us that in the getting out of our new genuine A. J. Aubrey hammer double barrel breech loading shotgun, we ought to do something out of the ordinary, that after making these guns better than any other guns made, giving the double hammer gun all possible features of the highest grade hammerless gun, the quadruple bolting action, reinforcing at barrels, automatic wedge extension rib and frame lock, the highest grade bar lock, special firing pins, special tool steel bearings, the highest possible grade of alignment, adjustment and all, after we had completed all this, as we have in the Aubrey hammer double barrel breech loading shotgun, which we offer at $12.59 on another page, and on which page you can see the illustrations and descriptions of the working parts, which are exactly the same in all Aubrey double hammer guns, but after doing all this we ought to get out one gun which in general finish, in the engraving, decorating, ornamentation, polish and fine outside finish would naturally outclass anything on the market, even though sold at double the price we offer, and this Mr. Aubrey has accomplished in the gun we here offer you at $18.50. Mr. Aubrey suggested that rather than making some extra high grade guns specially to order in the hammer guns, that he make a regular gun for stock, making it along the lines, with all the engraving, all the finish, all of the special ornamental features, that he ordinarily would put into a gun made to order, and yet get them out in such large numbers that he could reduce the cost of manufacture to the very minimum, so in getting out this gun he starts as a basis on his regular $12.59 gun, which is shown in detail on other pages in this department, and from this he goes to a special hand finish, using only the most skilled mechanics in the hand polishing, in the elaborate hand engraving, which covers the locks, frame, tang, break, guard, etc., in the beautiful polish put on the barrels and the fancy ornamental checkering on the full pistol grip and fore end, on the selection of the stock and the polishing of the same. All this has been done in this gun, and yet at practically no cost compared with the prices charged by others. For example, this exact same gun in every part is shown on another page at $12.59. Here in this specially finished gun, a gun that ordinarily would come under the head of made to order guns, and which other makers would charge at least $50.00 for, and from that upward, we make only the slight difference in cost of $5.91, and this $5.91 represents only the actual labor and time plus only our one small percentage of profit, this labor put on to making this the finest thing we could possibly turn out of our factory, something in the way of a high finish and ornamentation and elaborate hard engraving that you could not get on any gun of any other make excepting you made it to order, in which case you would probably have to pay from two to four times the special $18.50 price we ask.

IF YOU HAVE DECIDED to buy a double barrel breech loading shotgun, then by all means select an Aubrey If you don't select an Aubrey hammerless, select one of these Aubrey hammer guns. Understand, whether you select the lowest priced Aubrey double gun, whether it be a hammer or hammerless gun, the shooting qualities, the strength, the design and parts are exactly alike. The difference in the price of the Aubrey guns is only the difference in the barrels, and in the hand finish on the outside of the gun. You should select an Aubrey, first, because you have the privilege of giving it 60 days' trial, during any of which time you can, if you are not perfectly satisfied with your purchase, return the gun to us at our expense, and we will immediately return your money. You should select an Aubrey gun as compared with any gun made, because you get more than twice as much real value for your money as you could get in any other gun made, regardless of name, make or price, you get a gun made in our own factory at a price to you that barely covers the cost of material and labor with but our one small percentage of profit added, you get a gun covered by a written binding 20-year guarantee, you get a gun that combines the good qualities of every other high grade gun made, with the defects of none. Remember, this gun which we show you at $18.50 is exactly the same in material, workmanship and parts as the gun shown at $15.50 and $12.59 on the preceding pages, all the high grade features of the highest grade hammerless gun made; 12-gauge only, 30 or 32-inch barrels as desired, taper choke bored, extension rib, quadruple bolt locking mechanism, automatic wedge locking mechanism; which locks the extension rib squarely to the frame. low circular hammers; rebounding locks, top snap break, long tang, reinforced breech, flat water table, all points of contact made of the finest tool steel, hardened. This gun is very elaborately engraved by hand, ornamented and decorated, the very best of everything, and we furnish it in the different grades of barrels at the following special prices. **Be sure to state length of barrels wanted.**

No. 6K95 Very finest crystal barrel steel; 12-gauge; 30 or 32-inch barrels; weight, 7½ to 8 pounds. Price..**$18.50**

No. 6K96 Very finest imported double blade Liege twist steel barrels; 12-gauge; 30 or 32-inch barrels, weight, Price........................**$19.25**

No. 6K97 Very finest imported Liege two-blade Damascus steel barrels, full finished; 12-gauge; length of barrels, 30 or 32 inches; weight 7½ to 8 pounds. Price......**$22.20**

For illustrations of parts of this gun see preceding pages.

$11.75 GREENER ACTION WONDER

THIS IS A GENUINE GREENER ACTION, cross bolt, automatic self acting, self locking imported Liege double barrel hammer breech loading shotgun, which we are offering for only $11.75

THE ORIGINAL GREENER GUN, a gun made in England, and a gun made famous by its cross bolt, self acting and locking mechanism, a lock by which, when the gun is closed, a cross bolt runs clear through the frame and through a round hole in the deep extension rib, rigidly locking the barrels to the frame. This is a gun that sold and is still selling at prices ranging from $200.00 to $500.00, and the great feature in the original Greener gun which sells at $200.00 to $500.00 is this cross bolt automatic mechanism, and this has been reproduced in this genuine imported Liege gun. It has the genuine Greener cross bolt, automatic self locking, self acting mechanism, and by special arrangement with the manufacturer we are able to offer this gun at the incomparably low price of **$11.75.**

THIS GENUINE LIEGE GUN, with its Greener cross bolt, self locking, self acting mechanism, is a gun that is usually sold in this country at from $25.00 to $30.00. It is a gun that cannot be compared in any way with the ordinary Belgian guns on the market that sell generally at prices ranging from $9.00 to $15.00, for it differs from the ordinary or cheap grade guns, first, in its Greener action, with its cross bolt, self acting, self locking mechanism, it differs, too, in that it is not cylinder bored, it will not scatter the shot, but, on the contrary, both barrels are choke bored, the left barrel, a very close choke, the right barrel, a medium choke. The gun is also reinforced at the breech and also has a genuine steel frame, case hardened. With its automatic rigid locking mechanism to the Greener action you have a gun that is true, strong, a gun in which the recoil or kick is reduced to the minimum, a gun that will make an excellent target, a long range shooting arm, something thoroughly strong and safe, perfectly safe for any kind of powder used in any gun, either white, smokeless or black. You have in this gun the regular Liege full bar lock, with low circular hammers, it is neatly engraved by hand, the barrels are given a specially fine finish, in fact a genuine Damascus finish. While giving the barrels all the appearance, all the beauty of the most expensive genuine Damascus barrels, still, of course, it should be understood the barrels are not genuine Damascus. They are made of fine armory steel, beautifully finished on the inside, accurately choke bored and then given that most elaborate, full, fine Damascus finish on the outside, a Damascus outside finish that so far they have been able to produce only in Liege, and as a result, with these imported, full Damascus finished barrels, with the Greener action and the cross bolt, self locking, self acting mechanism, with the hand engraved locks, frame, guards, etc., with the fine imported walnut stock, which is nicely finished, with full pistol grip, checkered fore end and fancy butt plate, you have a gun that has all the appearance of a gun that sells generally at more then ten times the price, and you have at the same time a thoroughly strong, reliable, safe, strong shooting double barrel breech loading shotgun.

HOW WE CAN MAKE THE PRICE ONLY $11.75

UNDER A CONTRACT **with the famous Liege maker we take all the guns that this great maker makes for the American trade.** Formerly the maker who furnishes us these guns, made exclusively for the European and South African trade, and our gun buyer, visiting Liege for the purpose of making the best possible arrangement, went to all the different gun makers in this great gun making city, to find where the very best guns were made, and he found that the very best guns made in Liege were made by the maker of this gun, but none were made for the American market. He built exclusively for the European and South African trade, but we succeeded in making an arrangement with him to build for us and only us in America; therefore we are the first and the only concern in this country who are able to get guns from this famous maker, and under our contract we take all he makes for America. We have made a most favorable contract, taking advantage of the low labor cost in Liege, and the actual cost to us for these guns laid down here, plus our one small percentage of profit, is the price we make you, only $11.75, and if you were to go to your dealer at home for a gun you would pay at least double our price for any gun that would in any way compare with the gun we here offer you for only $11.75.

Small Sectional Illustration of Greener Action.

FROM THIS ILLUSTRATION, engraved by our artist direct from a photograph, you can get some idea of the Greener action, with its self acting, self locking mechanism, by which, when the gun is broke or open, it releases the barrels; when closed it automatically, with its rigid steel cross bolt, locks through the extension rib, thereby locking the barrel securely to the frame, making it an ideal gun for smokeless powder, a gun that cannot shoot loose, a gun in which there is very little recoil or kick, a gun that gives you wonderful results at long distances.

THIS GREENER ACTION GUN has an extra strong reinforced breech; the breech is made extra strong and reinforced to adapt it especially to white or smokeless powder as well as black powder, to reduce the recoil or kick to the very minimum, and to guard against any possibility of the gun shooting loose.

Small Illustration of Breech Showing the Thickness of the Breech.

WE FURNISH THIS GUN EXACTLY AS ILLUSTRATED, WITH ITS GREENER ACTION,

self acting, self locking cross bolt mechanism, beautiful Damascus finished barrels, hand engraved trimming throughout, fine imported walnut stock, full finished, full pistol grip with fancy checkered grip and fore end, fancy rubber butt plates, reinforced breech, top snap break, fine Damascus finished, choke bored, close shooting barrels; 12-gauge only; length of barrels 30 inches; weight 7½ to 8 pounds.

No. 6K101 Our special price..**$11.75**

L. C. SMITH HAMMERLESS GUNS

MADE BY THE HUNTER ARMS CO., FULTON, N. Y.

PRICES—THE MANUFACTURER FIXES THE SELLING PRICE OF THESE GUNS AND WILL NOT ALLOW US OR ANY OTHER HOUSE TO SELL THEM LOWER.

OUR BINDING GUARANTEE. EVERY GUN WHICH WE SELL IS COVERED BY OUR BINDING GUARANTEE, WHICH MEANS THAT IF ANY PIECE OR PART GIVES OUT BY REASON OF DEFECTIVE MATERIAL OR WORKMANSHIP WITHIN ONE YEAR, WE WILL REPLACE IT FREE OF CHARGE. You may order any gun of us, and if you do not find it satisfactory, or as represented, you may return it to us at our expense of transportation charges both ways and we will immediately refund your money.

GENERAL DESCRIPTION. All L. C. Smith Hammerless Guns are full choke bored, have English walnut pistol grip stock, tapered matted rib, case hardened locks and frame, rubber butt plate, compensating extension rib and fore end and patent safety slide. OUR PATENT GLOBE SIGHT is furnished free with all Smith guns.

ARMOR STEEL BARRELS.

Globe Sight free with this gun.

BORED FOR NITRO POWDER

$25.00

No. 6K126

This is the L. C. Smith No. 00 grade, the one that is fitted with armor steel barrels, full choke bored, no engraving, and fully warranted.

Be sure to state length of barrels wanted.

Catalogue Number	Grade	Style of Barrels	Gauge	Length of Barrels	Weight	Price
6K126	No. 00	Armor Steel	12	30 or 32 inches	7½ to 8 lbs.	$25.00

Weight, packed for shipment, about 14 pounds.

NOTICE. All our guns are tested with heavy loads and cannot burst except by carelessness, obstruction in the barrel or improper home loaded shells with nitro or dense powder. We are not responsible for burst gun barrels.

DAMASCUS BARRELS.

GLOBE SIGHT free with this gun.

BORED FOR NITRO POWDER.

$32.90

No. 6K140

The No. 0, No. 1 and No. 2 grades are all fitted with Damascus barrels of three qualities. All of them are very good, but the figure varies in size; for example, the figure of the three-blade is much finer than in the plain Damascus. The No. 0 is plain finished, the No. 1 has line engraving and the No. 2 has fine scroll and game engraving on the lock plates. All are choke bored for black or nitro powder and fully warranted by the factory. **Be sure to state length of barrels wanted.**

Catalogue Number	Grade	Style of Barrels	Finish	Gauge	Length of Barrels	Weight, Lbs.	Price
6K132	No. 0	Damascus	Plain	12	30 or 32 in.	7½ to 8	$32.90
6K136	No. 1	2-Blade Damascus	Plain Line Engraving	12	30 or 32 in.	7¾ to 8	42.00
6K140	No. 2	3-Blade Damascus	Game and Scroll Engraving	12	30 or 32 in.	7¾ to 8	56.00

Weight, packed for shipment, about 14 pounds.

OUR REMINGTON AUTOMATIC SELF LOADING MAGAZINE SHOTGUN, $30.00

$30.00

FOR $30.00 we will furnish you this standard Remington Automatic Loading and Automatic Cocking Single Barrel Magazine Shotgun, manufactured by the celebrated Remington Arms Co., of Ilion, N. Y., one of the oldest manufacturers of fire arms in the United States; a company whose guarantee goes out with every gun and rifle which it makes; a company which is well known to all hunters, trap shooters and sportsmen as well as all governments of the world. They have not only made fire arms for the hunter and trap shooter, but they have made rifles for a great many foreign governments, and have made thousands of rifles and revolvers for the United States Government during the Civil War. This $30.00 Remington Automatic Shotgun is the latest creation in fire arms. The gun was invented by Mr. Browning, of Ogden, Utah, and is now being made exclusively by the Remington Arms Co., under the Browning patents for the United States trade. This $30.00 Remington Automatic Self Loading, Self Cocking Shotgun is exactly as its description implies. It is a five-shot self loading shotgun. You place four loaded shells in the magazine and one in the chamber, then press the little button on the right hand side and the breech block closes. After you fire your first shot, the recoil of the shell opens the breech block, throws out the empty shell, places a new shell in the chamber from the magazine and closes the breech block, and all you have to do is to pull the trigger each time you fire a shot. When the last shell leaves the magazine and is fired, the breech block remains open, which tells you that there are no more shells in the magazine.

OUR $30.00 Remington Automatic Self Loading and Self Cocking Magazine Single Barrel Shotgun is fitted with well seasoned, straight grained, pistol grip, imported walnut stock, and the fore end is made of the same quality walnut. The frame is finished in a military blue of the very best quality workmanship, is bored and machined out of a solid bar of extra quality of steel and is beautifully matted on the top to guide the eye to the front sight. The barrel is of standard length, which is, in this gun, 28 inches long, beautifully tapered from the breech to the muzzle, giving the most metal at the breech; choke bored on the celebrated Remington system, and the gun weighs about 7¾ pounds. It is fitted with a patent safety device in front of the trigger, so that the trigger can be locked or unlocked instantly, as the shooter may desire. We predict a large sale for these guns, and for rapid shooting at the trap or in the field they have no equal, since you can shoot as fast as you can pull the trigger.

No. 6K161 Our No. 1 Grade Remington Automatic Self Loading Shotgun is made in 12-gauge only; 28-inch barrel; weight, about 7¾ pounds, 5-shot. Factory price, $40.00; our price $30.00

Weight, packed for shipment, about 14 pounds.

REMINGTON "K" GRADE DOUBLE BARREL HAMMERLESS SHOTGUNS

Globe Sight FREE with this Gun.

The "K" Grade has patent snap fore end.

Priced at **$23.50**

The "K" Grade Remington Double Barrel Hammerless Shotgun is a plain, well built substantial gun built for service, and like all Remington guns the greatest care is given to every piece and part. It is fitted with blue armory steel barrels, matted nitro extension rib, top snap action; strong forged frame beautifully case hardened, straight grained walnut stock and fore end nicely checkered; a plain finished gun but a good one. **State length of barrels wanted.** Weight, packed for shipment, about 14 pounds.

Cat. No.	Grade	Style of Barrels	Style of Extractor	Gauge	Length Barrels	Weight, Lbs.	Price
6K166	K	Blued Armory Steel	Regular	12	30 or 32 in	7¼ to 7¾	$23.50

No. 3 GRADE REMINGTON DOUBLE BARREL SHOTGUNS PRICED AT $25.00

GLOBE SIGHT free with this Gun.

DESCRIPTION.

All No. 3 Grade Remington Double Barrel Shotguns have two-blade Damascus barrels, matted rib, double bolt locks, extension rib, rebounding hammers, checkered pistol grip stock and fore end, top snap action, choke bored on the latest improved system for nitro or black powder, frame beautifully case hardened. All parts are interchangeable. All hammer guns have Deeley & Edge patent fore end. State length of barrels wanted. Order by catalogue number in full.

Catalogue Number	Grade	Style of Barrels	Gauge	Length, Barrels	Weight	Price
6K167A	No. 3	Damascus	12	30 or 32 inches	7¼ to 8 lbs.	$25.00
6K167D	No. 3	Damascus	10	32 inches	9 to 9¾ lbs.	

Weight, packed for shipment, about 14 pounds.

OUR REMINGTON AUTOMATIC SHELL EJECTING DOUBLE BARREL SHOTGUN, ONLY $31.50

GLOBE SIGHT FREE with this Gun.

REMEMBER, these are the genuine Remington Shotguns, manufactured by the Remington Arms Company, of Ilion, N. Y., one of the oldest and most reliable manufacturers of arms; a company which has made arms a study for many years; a company which has manufactured arms for the hunter as well as for the United States and other governments, and the name Remington on a fire arm is a guarantee of first class workmanship, high grade rifles and shotguns and arms which can be depended upon

$31.50

AT $31.50 we furnish this celebrated Remington Double Barrel Hammerless Shotgun, fitted with top snap break, genuine two-blade Damascus barrels; nicely milled engine turned matted rib, with nitro bite on the extension, making it safe for black, smokeless or nitro powder; strong cocking device which cocks the hammers when opening the gun; patent safety slide, making the gun perfectly safe until you are ready to shoot, bored true and smooth to the Remington gauge and taper choke bored for black or nitro powder; steel forged frame beautifully mottled and case hardened; well seasoned, straight grained walnut stock with the pistol grip nicely checkered; walnut patent snap fore end, also checkered and fitted with the Remington latest patent automatic shell ejector.

Send 10c for our booklet, Useful Information to Shooters

No. 6K172

The above illustration, engraved by our artist direct from a photograph, will give you some idea of this celebrated Remington Automatic Shell Ejecting Hammerless Shotgun.

$31.50 is the lowest price ever named on a standard, hammerless, double barrel, breech loading shotgun, fitted with an automatic shell ejector and genuine two-blade Damascus barrels.

$31.50

ABOUT THE AUTOMATIC SHELL EJECTOR.

The Remington Automatic Shell Ejector is constructed with a "split extractor," so when you open the gun it ejects only the shell which is fired and the unfired shell remains in the gun. If you fire both shells, the gun ejects both upon opening it. In addition to this the ejector is so constructed that should anything happen to the automatic ejector device, the gun will act as a plain extractor, pushing the shells out far enough so that they can be removed by the thumb and first finger. This is an improvement which very few ejector guns have. Don't miss this opportunity to buy a high grade gun at a low price. Mention weight wanted when ordering.

Cat. No.	Grade	Style of Barrels	Style of Extractor	Gauge	Length of Barrels	Weight Lbs.	Price
6K172	KED	2-Blade Damascus	Automatic	12	30 in.	7½ to 8	$31.50

Shipping weight, about 14 pounds when packed.

ITHACA NEW MODEL BREECH LOAD-ING SHOTGUNS.

MANUFACTURED BY THE ITHACA GUN CO., ITHACA, N.Y.

The manufacturer fixes the selling price of these guns and will not allow us or any other house to sell them lower.

ILLUSTRATION shows the heavy breech of Ithaca guns. This illustration is intended to show our customers the double thick breech of Ithaca guns. All guns made for us by the Ithaca Gun Co. have this reinforced breech and are made extra strong for any proper load of black or nitro powder. We charge you nothing for boxing guns for shipment, as some houses do.

Our Patent Globe Sight free with these guns.

ITHACA FIELD GRADE HAMMERLESS SHOTGUN.
$18.00

No. 6K174A

Bored for Black or Nitro Powder.

THE ITHACA FIELD GRADE HAMMERLESS SHOTGUN is the latest creation of the Ithaca Gun Co., Ithaca, N. Y., and is put on the market with a view to giving our customers a lower priced gun, and at the same time a good, honest, substantial gun at a lower price than we have heretofore been able to offer in this make. The lock, working parts and frame are essentially the same as on the high grade guns and the principal difference between the Field grade and the No. 1 grade is the style of barrels. The Field grade is fitted with smokeless steel barrels, while the No. 1 grade is fitted with the twist barrel, and we recommend the Field grade gun as one of the best medium priced hammerless shotguns made. State length of barrels wanted. Weight, packed for shipment, about 14 pounds.

Catalogue Number	Grade	Style of Barrels	Gauge	Length, Barrels	Weight	Price
6K174 A	Field	Smokeless Steel	12	30 or 32 inches	7½ to 8 lbs.	$18.00
6K174 D	Field	Smokeless Steel	10	32 inches	9 to 9¾ lbs.	

RUSTED AND DAMAGED GUNS.
Do not return to us a gun, revolver or rifle which is rusted, pitted or has the finish worn off, for we have no way of selling these guns. If you have a gun, revolver or rifle which needs repairing, first write us, fully describing the article and what is broken, as we may be able to send you the part necessary, thus saving the express charges on the gun both ways.

All Bored for Nitro or Black Powder.

Globe Sight free with this gun.

ITHACA HAMMERLESS SHOTGUNS.
$24.00 AND $29.50

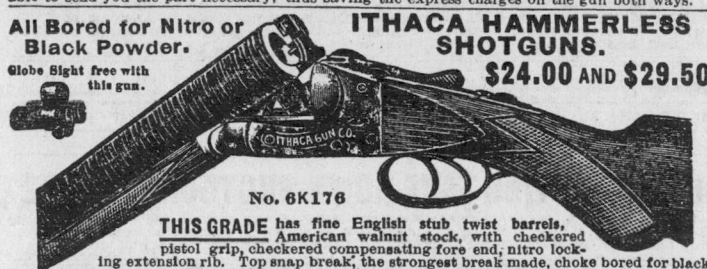

No. 6K176

THIS GRADE has fine English stub twist barrels, American walnut stock, with checkered pistol grip, checkered compensating fore end, nitro locking extension rib. Top snap break, the strongest break made, choke bored for black or nitro powder and long range shooting, fancy tapered and matted rib. A good, strong, honest gun in every way. All barrels are bored and guaranteed for all proper loads of smokeless powder. The No. 1½ grade is the same as the No. 1 grade, but fitted with Damascus barrels. Weight, packed for shipment, about 14 pounds. Mention length of barrels desired.

Catalogue Number	Grade	Style of Barrels	Gauge	Length, Barrels	Weight	Price
6K176	No. 1	Stub Twist	12	30 or 32 inches	7½ to 8 lbs.	$24.00
6K178	No. 1½	Damascus	12	30 or 32 inches	7½ to 8 lbs.	29.50

OUR GLOBE SIGHT free with every Ithaca gun.

ITHACA HAMMER GUNS.

Illustration of No. 6K175A

GENERAL DESCRIPTION. All of our Ithaca guns are fitted with the best grade of selected barrels, nicely case hardened breech, beautiful matted rib, top snatch action, selected walnut stock, extension rib, blued mountings, compensating patent fore end, and choke bored for trap and long range shooting. The shooting qualities of the Ithaca guns cannot be surpassed and for penetration and long range shooting are equal to any guns regardless of price. All are bored for black or nitro powder and all barrels have heavy breech. Shipping weight, when packed, about 14 pounds. State length of barrels desired.

Catalogue Number	Grade	Style of Barrels	Gauge	Length, Barrels	Weight	Price
6K175A	A	Stub Twist	12	30 or 32 inches	7½ to 8 lbs.	$19.00
6K175D	A	Stub Twist	10	32 inches	9 to 9¾ lbs.	
6K177A	AA	Damascus	12	30 or 32 inches	7½ to 8 lbs.	21.00
6K177D	AA	Damascus	10	32 inches	9 to 9¾ lbs.	

$5.95 Our SPECIAL SINGLE BARREL HAMMERLESS SHOTGUN

Compare this price of $5.95 with that asked by other dealers for single barrel hammerless shotguns of equal or inferior grade. You could not purchase a gun of this description from any dealer for less than $10.00.

Made for us under contract by one of the most famous manufacturers of single barrel guns. Fitted with a taper choke bored barrel, patent snap metal joint fore end, case hardened drop forged frame, improved style top snap lever, positive automatic shell ejecting device, improved patented safety locking device which automatically locks the trigger, making this gun absolutely safe. Fitted with selected walnut full pistol grip stock with rubber cap and fancy rubber butt plate, and finely checkered walnut fore end.

Be sure to state length of barrel wanted.
A high grade, first class gun, guaranteed to give satisfaction. Next to the A. J. Aubrey Single Barrel Hammerless Gun, this is the best single barrel hammerless gun on the market today.

No. 6K210 12-gauge, 30 or 32-inch steel barrel. Price..........$5.95
No. 6K211 12-gauge, 30 or 32-inch twist barrel. Price.......... 6.95

BAKER SHOTGUNS.

Manufactured by BAKER GUN & FORGING CO., Batavia, N. Y.

THESE GUNS ARE TOO WELL KNOWN TO REQUIRE ANY LENGTHY INTRODUCTION.
They have been on the market for years and have always given satisfaction. The Baker guns are all bored for nitro powder, and they all have the celebrated Baker Nitro Cross Bite Matted Extension Rib. The workmanship, finish and material are of the best. All our Baker guns are of the improved model and are guaranteed both by us and the Baker Gun & Forging Co. against defective material and construction.

THE BAKER HAMMER SHOTGUN.

Our patent Globe Sight free with this gun.

$22.50

No. 6K183

FITTED WITH THE HIGHEST QUALITY TWIST BARRELS, selected walnut stock, checkered pistol grip, compensating fore end, choke bored, adapted to either nitro or black powder. A high grade, well made, strong shooting gun. State length of barrels desired.

Catalogue Number	Grade	Style of Barrels	Gauge	Length of Barrels	Weight of Gun	Price
6K183	Hammer	Twist	12	30 or 32 in.	7¼ to 8 lbs.	$22.50

BAKER HAMMERLESS SHOTGUNS.

The New Batavia Leader

$22.50

Our Patent Globe Sight furnished free with this and other shotguns. It positively doubles the shooting value of any shotgun.

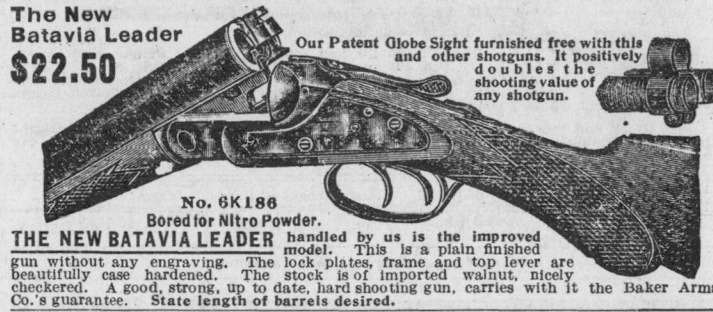

No. 6K186

Bored for Nitro Powder.

THE NEW BATAVIA LEADER handled by us is the improved model. This is a plain finished gun without any engraving. The lock plates, frame and top lever are beautifully case hardened. The stock is of imported walnut, nicely checkered. A good, strong, up to date, hard shooting gun, carries with it the Baker Arms Co.'s guarantee. State length of barrels desired.

Catalogue Number	Grade	Style of Barrels	Gauge	Length of Barrels	Weight of Gun	Finish	Price
6K186	Leader	Twist	12	30 inches	7½ to 8 lbs.		$22.50
6K188	Model B	Twist	12	30 or 32 in.	7½ to 8 lbs.	Engr'd Special	37.35
6K190	Model A	Damascus	12	30 or 32 in.	7½ to 8 lbs.	Engr'd	45.00

THE BAKER AUTOMATIC SHELL EJECTING SHOTGUN.

BORED FOR NITRO POWDER.

$31.50

No. 6K192

THIS IS THE LATEST MODEL GUN made by the celebrated Baker Arms & Forging Co., the improved 1908 model Batavia Leader, fitted with the new style check hook, roller bearing cocking levers and automatic shell ejectors. The ejector device on this gun is entirely new and positive. The ejector will throw either or both shells clear of the breech when the gun is opened. The gun is fitted with the finest decarbonized steel barrels, 12-gauge, 30-inch, selected walnut checkered pistol grip stock, checkered fore end, positive automatic safety trigger locking device, taper choke bored. A high class gun, fully guaranteed by the Baker Gun Co. as well as ourselves.

No. 6K192 Batavia Leader Automatic Ejector, 12 gauge, 30-inch steel barrel. Weight, 7½ to 8 pounds. Price....................$31.50

HOW GUN BARRELS BURST AND CAUTION TO SHOOTERS.

FOLLOW THESE DO NOT'S and you will never have a burst gun or rifle barrel. Do not accidentally put two charges of smokeless powder in the shell; always look through the barrels before loading and see that there is nothing in them. Don't ram the wad edgewise into the powder, nor crimp the shell more than ¼ inch.

DON'T USE A MALLET for ramming the powder; use hand pressure. Don't rest the muzzle on the ground, nor leave the gun in the bottom of a boat or buggy, for something is liable to get into the barrel in this way. When using 12-gauge brass shells use 10-gauge wads, so they will not get loose in the shell and bulge the barrel. If you get a bullet stuck in the barrel don't try to shoot it out or you may bulge the barrel. No manufacturer is held responsible for a burst gun or rifle barrel, because barrels are made to withstand a greater bursting strain than you can possibly get from any factory loaded ammunition. When a gun barrel bursts at the breech or chamber it is caused by an overload of nitro powder, and when it bursts forward of the chamber it is caused by some obstruction, such as a dent, snow, water, moss, mud, etc., and will generally show a distinct ring inside the barrel. Nitro powder should only be used by people familiar with it; and dense nitro powder should be weighed by an apothecary's scale and not measured. Chlorate of potash powder should never be used. We will not guarantee any gun with chlorate powders.

GUN AND RIFLE BARRELS can only burst by having some obstruction in the barrel or by overloading with nitro powder. We would like our customers to read this, for it will prevent accidents.

WINCHESTER REPEATING SHOTGUNS, MODEL 1897

$20.00

No. 6K215

Model 1897.
12-Gauge, 30-inch Barrel.

No. 6K216

$21.60

THE PRICES on these goods are fixed by the manufacturers, and we are compelled to sell them at these prices. Every Winchester Gun is doubly guaranteed, both by the factory and ourselves, and in addition to the rigid examination given them by the factory, they are furthermore carefully inspected by our inspectors, and every Winchester Gun we sell is guaranteed to be perfect in material, workmanship and mechanical construction.

THIS IS THE IMPROVED MODEL WITH DOUBLE EXTRACTORS, constructed so that accidental discharge is impossible. The gun is operated by the sliding forearm, which, when pushed back, unlocks the breech box, ejects the empty shell, places another shell in the carrier, and cocks the hammer. To open gun when full cocked, press button at right side of frame. The stock is 13¾ inches long, 2½-inch drop. The gun is fitted with blued steel barrel, chambered for 2¾-inch and 2⅝-inch shells. The take down gun can be taken apart in a moment's time, and as quickly assembled. There are no screws to lose, as when taken apart the gun is in two parts namely, the barrel and magazine, and stock and frame.

Catalogue No.	GRADE	Length of Barrel	Number of Shots	Weight	Price
6K215	Model 1897, Solid Frame	30 inches	6	7¾ pounds	$20.00
6K216	Model 1897, Take Down	30 inches	6	7¾ pounds	21.60

MARLIN REPEATING SHOTGUNS

THE MARLIN SOLID FRAME REPEATING 12-GAUGE SHOTGUNS, $19.00.

For $19.00 we furnish the latest model Solid Frame Six-Shot Marlin Repeating Shotgun, the latest creation of the well known Marlin Fire Arms Co., of New Haven, Conn., as illustrated and described. The $19.00 shotgun is known as the Model No. 17, which was brought out in 1905 by the Marlin Fire Arms Co. in response to a demand for one of the best solid frame shotguns which mechanical skill, a well equipped factory and the finest gun making machinery can produce.

If you want the best repeating rifle or shotgun made, buy a MARLIN and you will make no mistake. The MODEL No. 17 GUN is fitted with very best special rolled decarbonized blued steel barrel, taper choke bored on the latest taper system, made in 12-gauge, 30-inch barrel. Weight, about 7 pounds.

The stock and fore end are made from the very best quality of well seasoned straight grained black walnut which the Marlin Company is able to obtain. The magazine holds five shells and with one shell in the chamber it makes a six-shot repeating gun.

Catalogue Number	Model	Style of Barrel	Gauge	Length of Barrel	Weight	Price
6K219	No. 17	Special Rolled Decarbonized Steel	12	30 inches	7 pounds	$19.00

Weight, packed for shipment, 14 pounds.

MODEL No. 21, GRADE C, MARLIN FANCY REPEATING SHOTGUN, $35.50.

At $35.50 we offer you the latest Model No. 21, Grade C, Marlin Fancy Repeating Take Down Shotgun as the best fancy finished repeating shotgun ever offered by any house at any price. In the construction of this new model No. 21, grade C, repeating shotgun, every care has been taken and every detail of workmanship, finish, appearance, general construction has been carefully studied and only the very best mechanics in the factory are placed upon this class of work. The barrel is made from the very best grade of special smokeless steel, the finest quality to be had at any price, having a tensile strength of about one hundred thousand pounds to the square inch, special care is given to the boring, polishing and finishing of this grade gun. The stock and forearm are made from the very best selected fancy figured walnut, which is given an extra high finish and extra polish, the fore end and stock are extra finely checkered, as shown in the illustration. The frame is engraved by one of the best engravers in New Haven, and the design is laid out in a very neat, handsome and tasty game pattern, which we illustrate above to the best of our ability; but the gun must be seen and examined to get a good idea of the handsome workmanship, engraving and checkering, etc., which this gun possesses. Our Model No. 21, Grade C, Repeating Take Down Shotgun comes in 12-gauge only, 30-inch barrel, shoots six shots without reloading and weighs about 7 pounds; is an extra fine, well finished gun, one which will please you.

Catalogue Number	Model	Grade	Style of Barrel	Gauge	Length of Barrel	Weight	Finish	Price
6K226	No. 21	C	Smokeless Steel	12	30 inches	7 pounds	Fancy	$35.50

Weight, packed for shipment, about 14 pounds.

MARLIN Model No. 19, 6-SHOT REPEATING TAKE DOWN SHOTGUNS, $21.32

The Marlin Take Down Repeating Shotgun, No. 19, Grade A, can be taken apart and put together very quickly and easily. Made in 12-gauge, 30-inch barrel only. Weight, about 7 pounds. Barrel made of blued smokeless steel, choke bored, guaranteed for nitro powder. Pistol grip stock. This gun has been tried and thoroughly tested by the best shooters in the country and found to be perfect in every detail. Magazine holds five shells, and one in the chamber, making six shots.

We can recommend Marlin goods very highly. None but the best material enters into the construction and only the best skilled workmen are employed in the factory. Guaranteed both by us and the Marlin Fire Arms Co. to give perfect satisfaction.

Catalogue Number	Model	Grade	Style of Barrel	Gauge	Length of Barrel	Weight	Price
6K224	No. 19	A	Smokeless Steel	12	30 inches	7 pounds	$21.32

Weight, packed for shipment, 14 pounds.

OUR NEW LONG RANGE SINGLE BARREL 10-GAUGE GOOSE GUNS, $13.00.

The Best Low Priced Gun for Long Range Shooting Ever Made. For Geese and Large Game.

36-inch Twist Steel Barrels.

10-GAUGE

$13.00

This gun is designed and built for the shooter who desires a single barrel gun for shooting large game and for extreme long range shooting. It is made in 10-gauge with 36-inch genuine twist barrel. The barrel of this gun is reinforced by the breech, is extra heavy, and will stand heavy loads of black or nitro powder. The gun throughout is built for the most severe kind of service. The gun is full choke bored, insuring enormous penetration and excellent target. It is fitted with a fine pistol grip, checkered walnut stock and fine walnut fore end, and the case is nicely case hardened. The bolting action is very strong and positive. This gun at our price of $13.00 is unquestionably excellent value. This price includes one of our patent globe sights.

No. 6K230 Long Range 10-gauge Single Barrel Gun. 36-inch twist barrel; weight, 9 pounds. Price, with our patent globe sight........ **$13.00**

Weight, packed for shipment, 14 pounds.

OUR LADIES' LITTLE BREECH LOADING DOUBLE BARREL SHOTGUN.

REDUCED TO $9.95

A 44-Caliber, or 40-85 Caliber Shotgun.

No. 6K241

We have had this little gun built for ladies or boys who like to hunt and for whom a 12-gauge gun kicks too hard. It is very effective for squirrels, birds or small game, and is made to take the 44 XL shot cartridge No. 6K2717. It can also be furnished to take the 40-85 primed shell, which is about 3 inches long, and can be loaded heavier than the 44 XL shot cartridges are loaded. We cannot furnish the 40-85 shells loaded. The 40-85 shells are large enough to take about 40 grains of black powder and ½-ounce of shot, while the 44 XL will use only about one-half as much powder and shot. This little breech loader is fitted with 25-inch barrels and weighs about 4 pounds. Our patent globe sight is not made small enough for this gun.

This gun is fitted with twist finished barrels, checkered pistol grip stock and checkered fore end, rebounding locks, top snap break, extension rib; a neat, well made and good looking, small, double barrel breech loader, suitable for small game such as quail, squirrels, etc.

Catalogue Number	ARTICLE	Caliber	Quantity	Price
6K241	Our Ladies' Breech Loader........	44 or 40-85	Each	$9.95
6K2717	Shot Cartridges	44 XL	Per 100	1.50
6K3230	Empty Brass Shells (not loaded)........	40-85	Per 100	2.50
6K977	Loading Tools, consisting of Recapper, Decapper, Wad Cutter and Charge Cup........	40-85	Per Set	.55

This gun alone, when packed for shipment, weighs about 8 pounds.

OUR BELGIAN MUZZLE LOADING DOUBLE BARREL SHOTGUN WITH POWDER FLASK

REDUCED TO $7.00

Many of our customers still like the old reliable muzzle loading double barrel shotgun and in order to please them we import a limited quantity each year, as we realize that when a man has his mind made up for a certain article he likes to have just what he wants, and we are offering the best muzzle loader which we can buy abroad, regardless of price.

These guns are imported direct from Belgium, and all have the Belgian government test, same as our breech loaders.

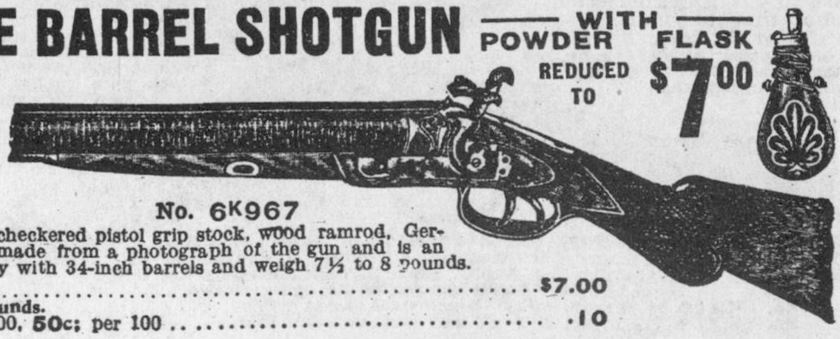

No. 6K967

Our Bar Lock Gun has genuine patent breech, genuine twist barrels, case hardened bar lock plates, checkered pistol grip stock, wood ramrod, German silver escutcheons, iron butt plate, case hardened and blued mountings. This illustration is made from a photograph of the gun and is an exact copy. With each gun we give free one Powder Flask. These guns are made in 12-gauge only with 34-inch barrels and weigh 7½ to 8 pounds.

No. 6K967 The Gun and Powder Flask (two articles.) Price........ $7.00

Weight, packed for shipment, about 13 pounds.

No. 6K3226 Gun Caps for the above muzzle loader (caps cannot go by mail). Price, per 1,000, 50c; per 100........ .10

NEW ENGLAND SINGLE BARREL AUTOMATIC EJECTOR SHOTGUN

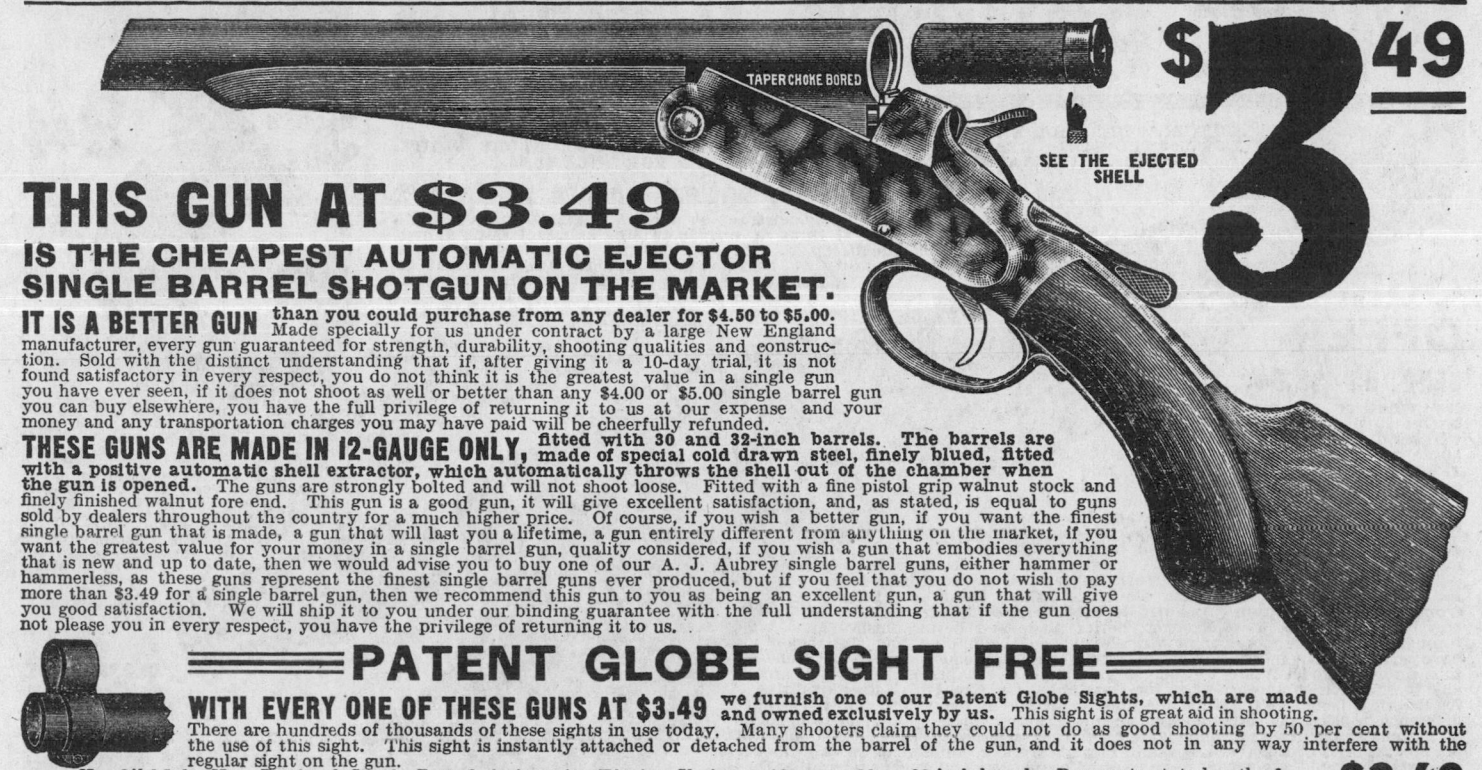

$3.49

TAPER CHOKE BORED

SEE THE EJECTED SHELL

THIS GUN AT $3.49
IS THE CHEAPEST AUTOMATIC EJECTOR SINGLE BARREL SHOTGUN ON THE MARKET.

IT IS A BETTER GUN than you could purchase from any dealer for $4.50 to $5.00. Made specially for us under contract by a large New England manufacturer, every gun guaranteed for strength, durability, shooting qualities and construction. Sold with the distinct understanding that if, after giving it a 10-day trial, it is not found satisfactory in every respect, you do not think it is the greatest value in a single gun you have ever seen, if it does not shoot as well or better than any $4.00 or $5.00 single barrel gun you can buy elsewhere, you have the full privilege of returning it to us at our expense and your money and any transportation charges you may have paid will be cheerfully refunded.

THESE GUNS ARE MADE IN 12-GAUGE ONLY, fitted with 30 and 32-inch barrels. The barrels are made of special cold drawn steel, finely blued, fitted with a positive automatic shell extractor, which automatically throws the shell out of the chamber when the gun is opened. The guns are strongly bolted and will not shoot loose. Fitted with a fine pistol grip walnut stock and finely finished walnut fore end. This gun is a good gun, it will give excellent satisfaction, and, as stated, is equal to guns sold by dealers throughout the country for a much higher price. Of course, if you wish a better gun, if you want the finest single barrel gun that is made, a gun that will last you a lifetime, a gun entirely different from anything on the market, if you want the greatest value for your money in a single barrel gun, quality considered, if you wish a gun that embodies everything that is new and up to date, then we would advise you to buy one of our A. J. Aubrey single barrel guns, either hammer or hammerless, as these guns represent the finest single barrel guns ever produced, but if you feel that you do not wish to pay more than $3.49 for a single barrel gun, then we recommend this gun to you as being an excellent gun, a gun that will give you good satisfaction. We will ship it to you under our binding guarantee with the full understanding that if the gun does not please you in every respect, you have the privilege of returning it to us.

PATENT GLOBE SIGHT FREE

WITH EVERY ONE OF THESE GUNS AT $3.49 we furnish one of our Patent Globe Sights, which are made and owned exclusively by us. This sight is of great aid in shooting. There are hundreds of thousands of these sights in use today. Many shooters claim they could not do as good shooting by 50 per cent without the use of this sight. This sight is instantly attached or detached from the barrel of the gun, and it does not in any way interfere with the regular sight on the gun.

No. 6K404 New England Single Barrel Automatic Ejector Shotgun, 12-gauge, 30 or 32-inch barrel. Be sure to state length of barrel wanted. Weight, about 6¾ pounds. Price...**$3.49**

$4.76 BUYS A COMPLETE SINGLE BARREL SHOTGUN OUTFIT

WORTH $10.00

OUR PATENT GLOBE SIGHT IS FREE WITH THIS GUN

TAPER CHOKE BORED

25 LOADED SHELLS

OUR PRICE OF **$4.76** for this high grade single barrel shotgun and outfit is less by $2.00 to $3.00 than you would have to pay for a shotgun alone were you to purchase it from a dealer. With this shotgun we furnish a high grade set of gun cleaning and shell loading implements, powder and shot measure, loader, rammer, decapper and recapper, crimper, 20-hole shell loading block, wad cutter and extractor, a fine quality web shell belt with shoulder strap, a box of 25 machine loaded shells and a fine take down Victoria style canvas gun cover with leather handle.

TO APPRECIATE THE WONDERFUL VALUE we are offering in this combination shotgun and outfit, we suggest that you take this outfit item by item and price it according to the prices you would have to pay any other house for the single items. For the gun you would have to pay anywhere from $5.00 to $8.00; the loading tools purchased singly from any dealer would cost you approximately $3.00; the canvas gun cover could not be duplicated for less than 50 cents to $1.00; the shell belt would retail for about 50 cents; the 25 loaded shells of a quality equal to those we furnish would cost you not less than 50 cents.

HOW WE ARE ABLE TO MAKE SUCH AN EXTRAORDINARY OFFER Our business in shotguns is the largest gun business in the world today. Our sales on guns exceeds the combined sales on guns of all the mail order houses in the United States. We own and control at Meriden, Conn., the largest gun factory of its kind in the world. We further contract for guns with other factories in quantities five times as great as any other house. Selling such enormous quantities of guns gives us the minimum cost, a cost far lower than that enjoyed by any other concern. This enormous saving in the cost of our guns results in your direct benefit, as we ask but one small margin of profit over the actual cost, thereby furnishing you a gun for less than half of what you would have to pay elsewhere for a gun of equal grade. We also manufacture all of the gun cleaning and shell loading implements we sell. We are the only concern in the country today manufacturing its own gun cleaning and loading implements. Our selling price on these goods is less than your local dealer's cost. We control the output of one of the largest manufacturers of hunting clothing, gun cases and canvas goods in the United States. It is these conditions that make it possible for us to give you $10.00 value for $4.76.

OUR LIBERAL TRIAL OFFER.

SEND US $4.76 and we will send you this complete outfit as described and illustrated herewith, with the full understanding and agreement that you can give the gun ten days' trial, during which time compare it with other guns sold for more than you paid for the complete outfit, test its shooting qualities, note the pattern and penetration, compare the finish, workmanship and construction with that of any other single barrel gun in your neighborhood, examine the outfit carefully, and if you, for any reason, are not satisfied with the gun or the outfit, if you are not pleased with your purchase, if you do not think you have received the greatest possible value, if you do not think that this outfit fulfills our description, or in other words, if you are dissatisfied in any way with your purchase, return this gun and outfit to us at our expense, and we will immediately refund the $4.76, together with any express charges you may have paid.

DESCRIPTION OF THE GUN.

THE GUN is furnished in 12-gauge only. **THE BARREL** is made of the highest quality armory steel, bored specially for nitro powder. This gun is bored on the celebrated taper system, insuring uniform target and enormous penetration. **THIS GUN** is fitted with an improved Automatic Shell Ejector, the strongest ejector ever placed on a single barrel gun, and absolutely positive in its action; will automatically throw the shell clear of the breech when the gun is opened. **THE FRAME** of this gun is a heavy drop forging, beautifully case hardened and finished. **THE MECHANISM** is the simplest, yet strongest, found in any single barrel gun on the market. Improved top snap action. **THE BOLT** is of a special design, particularly adapted for the use of nitro powder. This gun is bolted so that it will not shoot loose. **THE STOCK** is of fine quality walnut, fitted with a neat, shapely pistol grip. **THE FORE END** is of neat design and finely finished. **SHOOTING QUALITIES.**—This gun is guaranteed to outshoot any single barrel gun on the market today ranging in price from $5.00 to $8.00. Special attention has been paid to the shooting qualities of this gun, and we know that after you have had an opportunity to try and test this gun you will be more than pleased with its shooting qualities.

THE OUTFIT which accompanies this gun is first class in every respect; nothing cheap or shoddy in the entire outfit. The gun cleaning and loading implements are all made in our own factory, of the very best material, and are better goods than you could purchase at retail at any price.

UNDERSTAND, if you purchase this outfit at our price of $4.76 and are for any reason dissatisfied, you have the privilege of returning it to us and your money and charges will be refunded. It is sent you under our binding guarantee, which fully protects you in case you are for any reason dissatisfied with your purchase.

No. 6K411 Our high grade Single Barrel Shotgun and Outfit, 12-gauge, with 32-inch barrel. Price, complete..................
Weight, packed for shipment, about 16 pounds. **$4.76**

OUR LATEST 1908 IMPROVED MODEL WHITE POWDER WONDER

$3.94

AN AUTOMATIC SHELL EJECTING SINGLE BARREL BREECH LOADING SHOTGUN, AS ILLUSTRATED AND DESCRIBED HEREON, COMPLETE WITH OUR GLOBE SIGHT, AS ALSO ILLUSTRATED HEREON, IS NOW OFFERED FOR ONLY $3.94.

THE NEW IMPROVED WHITE POWDER WONDER as offered on this page, is now made for us under contract by a New England maker, made on the general lines of our $3.49 single barrel guns shown on another page, but a better gun throughout, a better quality of barrel and a general improvement in gunsmith making from beginning to end, and our $3.94 price barely covers the cost to us, with but our one small percentage of profit added.

$7.00 was the old price of the White Powder Wonder. We afterwards were able to reduce the price to $4.40, but now and under our latest contract we can offer the new model gun, with a number of improvements, as furnished us by the famous New England gun maker for only $3.94. If you want to buy a good single barrel shotgun at a low price, and you want something a little better, stronger, safer, better made and better finished than the ordinary single barrel shotgun that is being sold generally at retail at $5.00 to $7.00 and $8.00, it will certainly pay you to accept the following liberal offer, a liberal offer on this, our New Model White Powder Wonder Gun which we offer at $3.94.

GENUINE ARMORY STEEL

CHOKE BORED

NEW WHITE POWDER WONDER

OUR OFFER

SEND US $3.94, say whether you wish the barrel 30 or 32 inches long, we will send this gun to you and include with it free our removable globe sight, as illustrated hereon, you can examine the gun and use it for ten days, compare it with other guns that you can buy at within several dollars of our price, and if you are not perfectly satisfied with your purchase, you can return the gun to us at our expense, and we will immediately return your money together with any express charges you may have paid.

IN CONTRACTING with the New England Gun Company for this gun, we have asked them to get away from the more common guns and to use a higher grade of steel in the barrel, to give us a stronger, better made and better finished gun throughout than the more common single guns on the market, and this they have certainly done in our New Model White Powder Wonder, and as between this, the New Model White Powder Wonder, and a cheaper gun which we are able to offer you on another page, for durability, for strength, lasting qualities, for shooting, penetration, safety, for general service in every way, for the slight difference in price, the difference between the lowest price we are able to make on an automatic shell ejecting single gun, as shown on another page, $3.49, and this, our special price of $3.94 on the White Powder Wonder, a difference of only 45 cents, we certainly would advise you to pay the 45 cents extra and send us your order for this, our New Model White Powder Wonder at only $3.94.

IN YOUR OWN INTEREST, and before you buy a single gun of any kind from us or any other house, any make at any price, please let us call your attention to the Aubrey Hammerless Flat Water Table Automatic Shell Ejecting Breech Loading Shotgun, shown on another page in this catalogue, and offered by us for $7.95.

THIS $7.95 AUBREY HAMMERLESS EJECTOR SINGLE GUN so far outclasses in every possible respect any and every single barrel breech loading shotgun we have ever seen that we honestly feel it our duty, before presenting any other single gun, to call our customers' attention to this most extraordinary gun value. Really, it's the only single gun made that we know of that is made on exactly the same lines, the same qualities of material, the same workmanship and finish, the same safeguarding, the same strength, the same wonderful shooting qualities as mark the highest grade double barrel hammerless breech loading shotguns; therefore, when about to buy a single gun, even though you do not at first feel like paying more than $3.49, the prices we are able to make on our lowest priced single guns, or if you are considering this, the White Powder Wonder at $3.94, which, by the way, is a much better gun than the more common single barrel guns, we, however, urge you to think seriously of our $7.95 Aubrey, try to add the few additional dollars and see how much more you will get for your money, and if you do this and you are not pleased, if you don't think you have made a wonderful investment in the Aubrey gun, if you don't think it is worth more than twice as much as any other single gun made, return it to us any time within sixty days at our expense and we will immediately return your money, together with any express charges paid by you.

WE KNOW THESE GUNS, know them all, we have examined them, we have had them all apart, we know all the guns made in America and in Europe, our Gun Department has gone over them in every detail, we, therefore, know what the Aubrey guns are, the single and the double. We know if anyone wants a single gun the Aubrey gun is really on its merit the only gun to buy. If anyone is in the market for a double gun, hammer or hammerless, we know the Aubrey Double Hammerless is the only gun to buy. However, if you don't feel like investing as much as $7.95 in a single gun and getting the best single gun ever made, then let us send you this $3.94 gun, our White Powder Wonder, and if it isn't perfectly satisfactory, if you are not convinced you have gotten a much better single gun for $3.94 than you could have gotten elsewhere at two or three dollars more, of course, we want you to return it to us at our expense and we will immediately return your money.

THIS GLOBE SIGHT, which can be instantly attached and removed, and which is a wonderful aid in shooting, especially wing shooting, is furnished free with this, our White Powder Wonder at $3.94.

WHEN DECIDING on a single barrel shotgun as between this the New Model White Powder Wonder, furnished us by a New England maker, and the cheaper grade automatic ejector guns shown on another page, which we furnish for only $3.49, we would advise in your own interest that you pay the slight difference of 45 cents more and order the White Powder Wonder and get something better than the ordinary single barrel shotgun; but still better, and greatly to your interest, don't forget what we have to say here and throughout the book about the Aubrey guns, and if you want a single gun, don't overlook the $7.95 Aubrey single gun shown on another page. Quality considered, the Aubrey is, in fact, really the only high grade single gun standing in a class by itself, and as for use as compared with any of the more common guns worth even twice the $7.95 price we ask.

PLEASE READ ALL ABOUT THE AUBREY GUN AS SHOWN ON A PAGE BY ITSELF ELSEWHERE IN THIS DEPARTMENT.

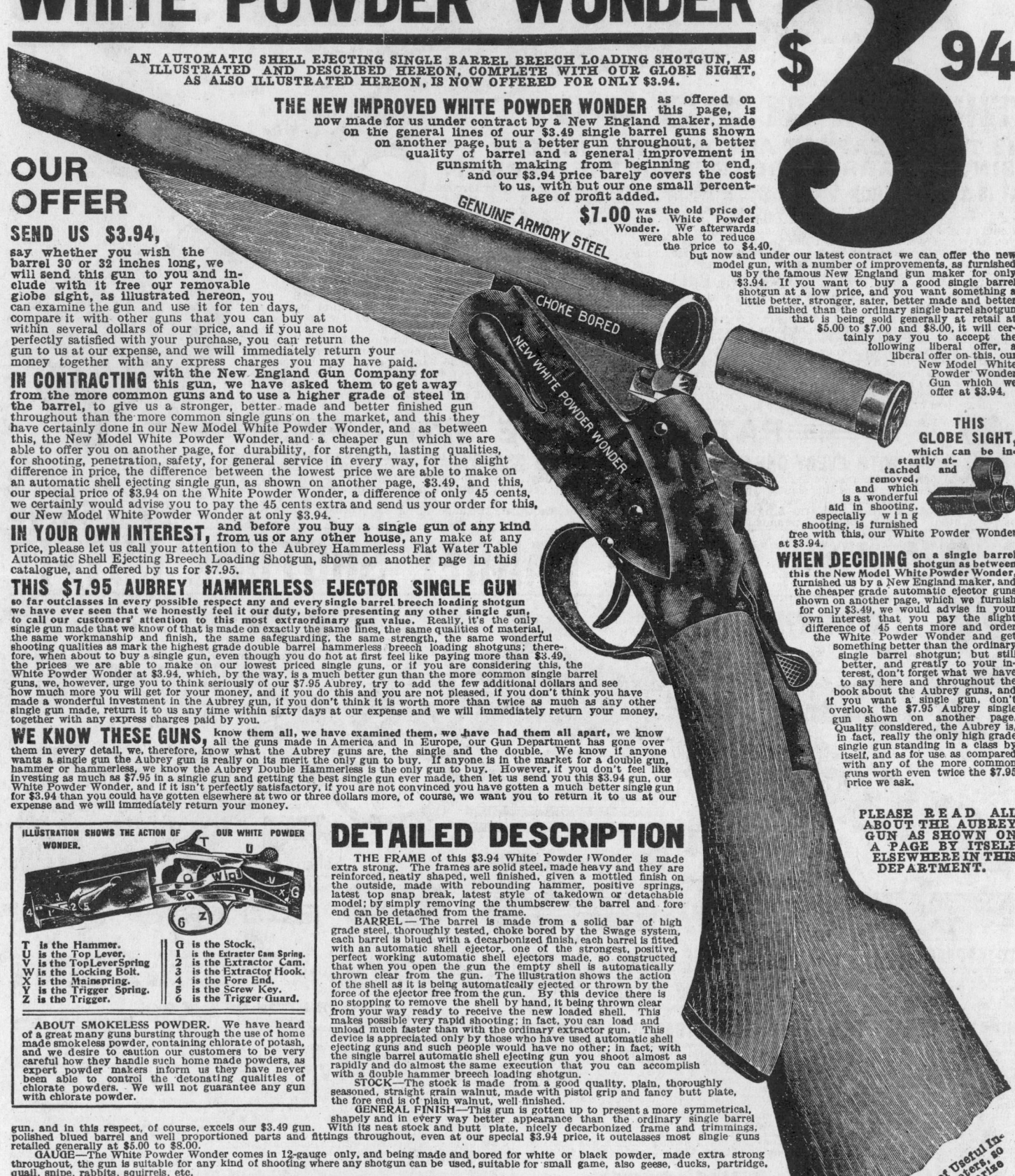

ILLUSTRATION SHOWS THE ACTION OF OUR WHITE POWDER WONDER.

T is the Hammer.	**G** is the Stock.
U is the Top Lever.	**O** is the Extractor Cam Spring.
V is the Top Lever Spring.	**1** is the Extractor Cam.
W is the Locking Bolt.	**2** is the Extractor Hook.
X is the Mainspring.	**4** is the Fore End.
Y is the Trigger Spring.	**5** is the Screw Key.
Z is the Trigger.	**6** is the Trigger Guard.

ABOUT SMOKELESS POWDER. We have heard of a great many guns bursting through the use of home made smokeless powder, containing chlorate of potash, and we desire to caution our customers to be very careful how they handle such home made powders, as expert powder makers inform us they have never been able to control the detonating qualities of chlorate powders. We will not guarantee any gun with chlorate powder.

DETAILED DESCRIPTION

THE FRAME of this $3.94 White Powder Wonder is made extra strong. The frames are solid steel, made heavy and they are reinforced, neatly shaped, well finished, given a mottled finish on the outside, made with rebounding hammer, positive springs, latest top snap break, latest style of takedown or detachable model; by simply removing the thumbscrew the barrel and fore end can be detached from the frame.

BARREL—The barrel is made from a solid bar of high grade steel, thoroughly tested, choke bored by the Swage system, each barrel is blued with a decarbonized finish, each barrel is fitted with an automatic shell ejector, one of the strongest, positive, perfect working automatic shell ejectors made, so constructed that when you open the gun the empty shell is automatically thrown clear from the gun. The illustration shows the action of the shell as it is being automatically ejected or thrown by the force of the ejector free from the gun. By this device there is no stopping to remove the shell by hand, it being thrown clear from your way ready to receive the new loaded shell. This makes possible very rapid shooting; in fact, you can load and unload much faster than with the ordinary extractor gun. This device is appreciated only by those who have used automatic shell ejecting guns and such people would have no other; in fact, with the single barrel automatic shell ejecting gun you shoot almost as rapidly and do almost the same execution that you can accomplish with a double hammer breech loading shotgun.

STOCK—The stock is made from a good quality, plain, thoroughly seasoned, straight grain walnut, made with pistol grip and fancy butt plate, the fore end is of plain walnut, well finished.

GENERAL FINISH—This gun is gotten up to present a more symmetrical, shapely and in every way better appearance than the ordinary single barrel gun, and in this respect, of course, excels our $3.49 gun. With its neat stock and butt plate, nicely decarbonized frame and trimmings, polished blued barrel and well proportioned parts and fittings throughout, even at our special $3.94 price, it outclasses most single guns retailed generally at $5.00 to $8.00.

GAUGE—The White Powder Wonder comes in 12-gauge only, and being made and bored for white or black powder, made extra strong throughout, the gun is suitable for any kind of shooting where any shotgun can be used, suitable for small game, also geese, ducks, partridge, quail, snipe, rabbits, squirrels, etc.

LENGTH OF BARRELS—The barrel comes in 30 or 32-inch length, as desired. When ordering be sure to state length of barrel wanted.

THE GUNS are made with especially selected steel barrels, bored from solid bar steel, choke bored, best automatic ejector, self bolted, self locking, self compensating, interchangeable parts, well case hardened, reinforced frame, barrel is detachable from frame, rebounding hammer, latest top snap break, selected straight grain full pistol grip walnut stock. The gun weighs about 6½ pounds, and at our special $3.94 price we furnish it as follows:

No. 6K414 SPECIAL SELECTED STEEL BARREL, 30 OR 32 INCHES AS DESIRED; WEIGHT, ABOUT 6½ POUNDS. OUR SPECIAL PRICE .... **$3.94** Weight, packed for shipment, about 12 pounds.

Read our booklet of Useful Information to shooters, so you will familiarize yourself with fire arms, and you will have no accidents.

NITRO KING AUTOMATIC EJECTOR ONLY $4.75

THE FIRST TIME A HIGH PRESSURE, NON-EXPLODING, REINFORCED BARREL CONSTRUCTION HAS EVER BEEN OFFERED IN A SINGLE BARREL SHOTGUN AT ANYTHING LIKE OUR $4.75 PRICE.

WHILE WE SELL A VERY GOOD SINGLE BARREL SHOTGUN AS LOW AS $3.49 and another at $3.94, and we offer the highest grade single barrel shotgun made, the A. J. Aubrey Hammerless, as shown on another page, for only $7.95, we have recognized a demand for a single hammer, automatic shell ejecting, breech loading shotgun, built along a higher grade, better, stronger and more shapely lines than anything heretofore offered, and as a result we have had gotten out for us under contract by one of the large American gunmakers this special single gun, a very special single gun, improved construction throughout, which we are able to offer for only $4.75.

OUR CUSTOMERS have from time to time requested a single barrel hammer breech loading shotgun, made from a much higher grade of steel than is commonly used in other single or double barrel guns, a steel that is practically non-destructible, the highest possible pressure test or tensile strain, a gun made with reinforced barrels, with the highest grade, strongest and most positive automatic shell ejecting mechanism, a gun made with a stronger bolt construction, a gun made with a stronger, heavier and better frame and locking mechanism, a single gun that has been given more than ordinary attention in the shooting qualities, in all the essentials that go to make up a thoroughly reliable single gun.

COMPARE OUR $4.75 PRICE WITH THE PRICES CHARGED BY OTHERS.

IN COMPARING OUR SPECIAL NITRO KING GUN which we offer at $4.75 with any gun you can buy from any dealer at home or elsewhere, don't overlook the difference in construction, the quality of material used, the workmanship and finish, for as we can furnish you for only $3.49 a single gun that will compare favorably with any single gun you can buy elsewhere at $4.00 to $5.00, we assure you that the same relative difference, the same difference in value, will be found between our $4.75 Nitro King and any of the cheaper single guns on the market.

SINGLE HAMMER BREECH LOADING SHOTGUNS have not and are not, in fact, generally made along the same grade of workmanship, finish or material as are the high grade double guns; in fact, we know of but one exception and that is our A. J. Aubrey Hammerless, which we sell at $7.95, but in getting out this Nitro King we have called for a quality of material, workmanship, an alignment, especially a barrel steel, a reinforcement, a locking mechanism, a bolt construction, a general hang, finish and all such as is not found on other single guns but found only in the higher grade double guns.

HOW TO SELECT A SINGLE BARREL SHOTGUN.

IF YOU WANT A CHEAP SINGLE BARREL SHOTGUN, one that will compare favorably with guns that retail generally at $4.00 to $6.00, the gun that we show in our catalogue at $3.49 we guarantee will compare favorably in every way. If you want a single gun that will compare favorably in every way with guns that retail generally at $5.00 to $8.00, then order our $3.94 White Powder Wonder or our $4.85 World's Challenge Ejector. If you want a single hammer breech loading shotgun that differs from all others, differs in its construction throughout, much higher grade barrel, better frame, lock and mechanical construction throughout, better alignment, a safer, stronger and more reliable gun for nitro, white or black powder, a gun that will outwear two of the ordinary single guns on the market, then we advise by all means, in selecting a single barrel breech loading shotgun, that you send us your order for this, our new 1908 Model Nitro King at $4.75.

OUR GUARANTEE FREE TRIAL AND MONEY RETURN OFFER

AS A GUARANTEE that this is a better gun than you can buy elsewhere at anything like the price, as an assurance that it will pay you to pick out a stronger, better made and more reliable single gun, to convince you that you can get from us for $4.75 a far better single gun than you would likely be able to buy from your dealer at home at any price, we make you this most extraordinary offer:

IN ORDERING A SINGLE HAMMER GUN, order this, our 1908 Model Nitro King, enclose our special price, $4.75, we will send the gun to you with the understanding and agreement that you can put it to every test, compare it with guns sold by others at about double our price, and if you are not satisfied you have gotten better value than you could get elsewhere, if you are not more than pleased that you paid the little difference between our lowest price, $3.49 and this, our $4.75 price; in short, if you are not more than pleased with your purchase, you can return the gun to us at our expense and we will immediately return your $4.75, together with any express charges you may have paid.

THESE PICTURES, engraved by our artist from a photograph, will give you a general appearance of the gun, although it is a gun that must be seen, tried, tested and compared with other guns, put to the severest kind of test and use to appreciate how much better it is than the ordinary, cheap, single gun commonly sold at $4.00 to $7.00.

GLOBE SIGHT FREE

With every Nitro King Shotgun at $4.75 we include FREE one of our special patented Globe Sights. This sight is endorsed by thousands of shooters. It is an excellent aid for wing shooting, some shooters claiming that it has improved their marksmanship over 50 per cent. This sight is manufactured, owned and controlled exclusively by us. Remember, that with every Nitro King Shotgun you obtain one of these patented Globe Sights free.

on another page at $4.85; look our line over carefully, and if you have about made up your mind to order a gun from us or some other house, consider our proposition on this, the new 1908 Model Nitro King, carefully. This gun comes in 30 or 32-inch barrel, as desired, 12-gauge only, and with every one of these guns at $4.75 we furnish free one of our own special Globe sight, and remember, this is the one single gun in our entire line, a single hammer breech loading shotgun that is built of the highest grade, high pressure, non-explodable steel, and therefore in your own interest, in deciding between the different guns to buy, to get the strongest, safest, and by far the best shooting single gun, we advise you to order this, our $4.75 Nitro King. In ordering state preference in length of barrel.

NOTE OUR PRICE OF $19.00 A THOUSAND for the improved long base Pointer shell, the highest quality shell made, regardless of name, make or price. For best results shoot Pointer shells. We guarantee all fire arms sold by us to give excellent results when used with Pointer ammunition. We are the largest distributors of ammunition in the world dealing direct with the consumer, and we guarantee our ammunition to be equal in every respect to any ammunition on the market, regardless of price. Once shoot Pointer ammunition, and you will never shoot any other.

$4.75

DETAILED DESCRIPTION.

BARRELS. The barrels are made from specially high grade, high pressure steel, and are a grade of barrels found only on the higher grade double guns, but the demand from our customers for something out of the ordinary in a single gun, a grade of barrel steel such as is not used by other manufacturers of single barrel guns, something that can be depended upon for accurate target, a barrel that can be so choke bored by the taper system that you get the same shooting effect, the same accuracy, the same penetration and long range killing effect that you get in the highest grade double guns, a grade of steel that can be worked so that we can give you the heavy breech construction and our special bolt and automatic shell ejecting mechanism, a grade of steel that makes the gun perfectly safe for high explosive powders, such as nitro or white powder as well as black powder, a grade of steel that does not rust easily or pit easily, a grade of steel that enables you to keep the gun clean and in perfect condition; a grade of steel that insures for you a gun, after having five years' usage, that will present a barrel much smoother, better kept and more satisfactory than the ordinary gun barrel as it first comes from the factory.

STOCK. The stocks are made from selected walnut, straight grained, full pistol grip, and the pistol grip is beautifully checkered by hand. The fore ends are carefully made of selected stock, also beautifully checkered by hand. The frames are high grade, reinforced, beautifully finished by fancy mottled case hardening; has a top snap break, a special interchangeable lock mechanism, made with rebounding hammers which automatically come back to half cock, made so the hammer strikes the firing pin squarely in the center, absolutely insuring against misfires.

ALIGNMENT. Much attention has been given to this gun in the way of alignment, the way it will come to the shoulder for quick and accurate wing shooting. In this particular in the cheaper grades of single guns, such as are sold generally at $4.00 to $6.00, little or no attention has been given, and as a result in all other single guns you hear the complaint that it doesn't hang well, it doesn't come to the shoulder as the higher priced double guns do. This has all been overcome in our new 1908 Model Nitro King Gun.

COMPARE OUR PRICES WITH OTHERS. Begin with our $3.49 single gun and compare it with this, with the prices charged by others for single guns and the White Powder Wonder which we offer at $3.94, and compare our World's Challenge Ejector which we offer

THE LARGE ILLUSTRATION shows the gun open, the shell being thrown from the gun by the self acting shell ejector, which, by the way, is the strongest, most positive and best shell ejector used on any single gun. The small illustration shows the breech construction. The breech construction differs from all the single guns, in that it is reinforced, is heavier, made especially for nitro or white powders, so constructed and so locked to the frame that it is practically impossible to shoot loose, perfectly safe for high explosive powders, a stronger lug, a better locking and bolting mechanism than on any of the ordinary single barrel guns. The reinforced breech, the bolt, the locking mechanism and the ejector system alone make the gun worth more than the slight difference we ask in price.

$4.75

No. 6K415 Nitro King Automatic Ejector, 12-gauge, 30 or 32-inch barrel. (State length wanted.) Price......... **$4.75**

A. J. AUBREY ENTIRELY NEW

FINEST GUN EVER MADE IN A SINGLE BARREL BREECH LOADING HAMMER SHOTGUN

$6.95

The first time a strictly high grade, full finished, flat water table, full milled, wide double frame, hammer single barrel breech loading shotgun was ever made or offered for sale, and the only hammer single barrel breech loading shotgun ever built or offered that was manufactured on exactly the same lines, the same frame construction, the same breaking, locking and lever construction, the same bolt, breaking and locking mechanism of the highest grade double barrel hammer breech loading shotguns.

THE AUBREY IS THE ONLY single barrel breech loading shotgun on the market that is made of best material, made on lines and with workmanship and finish that makes it in quality, strength, shooting qualities and all, in every way the equal of a high grade double gun. On another page we show the A. J. Aubrey Hammerless Single Barrel Breech Loading Shotgun which we offer for $7.95.

ON THIS PAGE we show practically the exact same gun, excepting in the hammer gun in place of the hammerless, the same high grade construction throughout, and these two A. J. Aubrey single barrel guns, the $7.95 single barrel hammerless shown on two pages in this book, and this $6.95 A. J. Aubrey Hammer Single Barrel Breech Loading Shotgun, are the two highest grade single barrel guns made. They are worth a dozen of the cheaper grades; in fact, no such a single barrel gun was ever before turned out, there is nothing on the market that will in any way compare with them.

PLEASE TAKE OUR ADVICE IN THIS:

If you want a single barrel breech loading shotgun, and it is true that many prefer a single gun to a double gun, since they are lighter (therefore easier to carry and handle), then by all means buy the best single barrel gun made in America. True, we can sell you a very good single barrel breech loader for $3.49, but in your own interest, to get the most value possible for your money, to get a thoroughly safe arm, a strong shooting gun, a gun with all the advantages of material, workmanship, finish, fit, safety, lasting qualities, strong shooting and target making, by all means pay a little extra and get a genuine A. J. Aubrey single gun, either our A. J. Aubrey Hammerless shown on another page at $7.95, or this A. J. Aubrey Hammer Single Gun, which we offer at $6.95. They are alike in quality, much alike throughout, in fact, many of the parts are identical and interchangeable, the hammer with the hammerless; but this gun at $6.95 is far cheaper than any of the cheaper or lower grade single barrel guns even at half the price we are compelled to get for them. If you are about to buy a single barrel gun, rather than pay $3.49 to $4.00, or rather than pay come one else from $4.00 to $6.00 for an ordinary gun, add the necessary dollar or two to make the price $6.95 and thus in intrinsic value get three times as much for your money as you would otherwise be getting. In the interest of safety alone, to say nothing of shooting qualities, ease in handling, perfect balance, perfect alignment and adjustment, ideal hang, pay the few dollars extra and get the best thing made, this, the genuine A. J. Aubrey at $6.95.

WHY WE CAN GIVE YOU TWICE AS MUCH VALUE FOR YOUR MONEY IN THIS THAN IN ANY OTHER SINGLE GUN WE OFFER

THIS, OUR $6.95, AND THE $7.95 HAMMERLESS shown on another page, are genuine A. J. Aubrey guns. They are made in our own factory, the Meriden Fire Arms Company of Meriden, Conn., they are made under the direct control and supervision of Mr. A. J. Aubrey, President and General Manager of our factory. We are able to control the quality of material, the fit, the finish, everything that goes into the gun. We are able, under our direct control to make the best guns made in America, and these guns, made in our own factory, cost us just the money we pay out for pay roll, that is, labor and material, not one penny of profit to go to any one, and the price we ask you is the actual cost to us, the cost of material and labor, plus only our one small percentage of profit, and as a result, we not only give you vastly more in quality, material, workmanship and finish, in safety, comfort and pleasure, but we make your dollar go really twice as far in an Aubrey gun as it is possible for us to give in any of the lower grade single guns. This is an entirely new departure, but it's something never before attempted in a single barrel hammer breech loading shotgun. We have gotten away from the lines and grades of all other makers.

HOW WE CAME TO MAKE THIS HAMMER SINGLE BARREL BREECH LOADING SHOTGUN, WHICH WE NOW OFFER YOU FOR $6.95.

A few years ago we asked Mr. Aubrey to design, model and arrange to build for us the highest grade single barrel hammerless breech loading shotgun it was possible for him to turn out, making it in every respect the equal of the highest grade double barrel hammerless guns, and as a result, we were soon able to offer our trade our $7.95 single barrel hammerless shown on two pages in this department of the catalogue. This gun was such a departure from anything ever before attempted, it was so much better than any other single gun on the market; it was really to the user worth a dozen of the ordinary cheap single guns, and this being the case the demand for this $7.95 single barrel hammerless Aubrey was many times greater than we expected. Where one gun was sold other orders immediately followed, but since there are many who prefer a hammer gun to a hammerless, we receive a great many calls for a hammer single barrel gun built on the lines of the $7.95 hammerless, equally as well made as to material, workmanship and finish, just as high grade in every particular, and as a result, we have brought out for our customers this beautiful hammer single barrel breech loader which we offer for

$6.95

OUR 60 DAYS' FREE TRIAL OFFER

As a guarantee that this is by far the best single barrel gun ever made, that it is far cheaper at $6.95 than any of the ordinary single barrel guns would be even at $2.00 apiece, as a guarantee that it is in every way the equal of the highest grade hammerless double barrel breech loading shotgun, we make you this offer:

SEND US YOUR ORDER FOR THIS GUN, enclose $6.95, we will send the gun to you with the understanding and agreement that you can give it sixty days' trial, during which time you can put it to every possible test, try it for long range killing, long distance shooting, for target, pattern and penetration, compare it with any double guns for shooting, compare it with any of the ordinary single barrel guns which you can buy for $3.50 to $8.00, and if you don't think it is worth a dozen of the cheaper grades, in short, if you are not perfectly satisfied with your purchase in every way, you can return the gun to us at our expense, and we will immediately return your money.

OUR 20-YEAR BINDING GUARANTEE

Every one of these hammer single barrel breech loading shotguns is covered by our written binding twenty-year guarantee, by the terms and conditions of which, if any piece or part gives out within twenty years, by reason of defect in material or workmanship, we will repair or replace it free of cost to the buyer or owner.

IT IS BUILT ON THE SAME HIGH GRADE LINES as the $7.95 single barrel hammerless, in that we use only the very finest crystal steel barrels and the barrels are heavily reinforced at the breech, they are choke bored by the best known taper system, they are fitted with very heavy, full finished and polished flat water table lugs, they have the strongest ejector used on any gun, and the ejector works on a square bolt instead of a round bolt, so it is impossible for it to ever get out of place; automatic and positive in its action. The heavy water table and the heavy lug construction, with the reinforced breech, makes this an ideal gun for white powder, smokeless powder or other high explosives, as well as for black powder, and in its construction it is so made that there is next to no recoil or kicking. All barrels being made of the finest crystal steel, full polished, they are nothing like as susceptible to rust or pitting with any kind of ammunition as are the more common grades of steel barrels.

DESCRIPTION.

FRAME—The frame of this $6.95 hammer gun, like the frame of the $7.95 hammerless shown on another page, is made from the finest drop steel forgings, full milled and full finished and has a flat water table, the only hammer single barrel breech loading shotgun made with the flat water table construction. It has a double bolt and automatic wedge lock action, highest grade top snap break lever, extra long and finest tang, the frame, lock, tang, etc., is full case hardened, beautiful mottled finish.

STOCK—Stock is made of carefully selected walnut, beautifully finished, has full checkered pistol grip, fancy rubber butt plate to grip and stock.

FORE END—The fore end is made of carefully selected walnut, full finished, neatly checkered, and is equipped with the Aubrey automatic self locking mechanism, which automatically locks the fore end to the barrel and frame. The fore end, of course, has a full blued short long tang, metal tip.

GAUGE—These guns come in 12-gauge only, barrels are either 30 or 32 inches long, as desired. Be sure to state length wanted. The alignment, the shape and the hang, the adjustment, balance and all of this, our $6.95 Aubrey single barrel gun, is exactly the same as on the $7.95 hammerless. Built on the lines of the highest grade double barrel hammerless breech loading shotguns made, there is nothing lacking, nothing left undone to make this the best single barrel shotgun possible to produce.

SEE PAGE 725 which shows the working parts and general construction of the A. J. Aubrey $7.95 Hammerless Single Barrel Breech Loading Shotgun, and except only for the absence of the hammer and the safety mechanism shown on the $7.95 single barrel hammerless, this, our $6.95 single barrel hammer gun, is almost identically the same gun.

We furnish this gun exactly as illustrated and described, under our twenty-year binding guarantee and sixty days' free trial offer, for $6.95 and $7.95, according to grade of barrels, as listed below.

No. 6K426 Gun, complete with special crystal steel, full finished, blued barrel, 12-gauge; length of barrel, 30 or 32 inches (state length wanted); weight, about 6½ pounds. Price......... **$6.95**

No. 6K429 The exact same gun furnished with genuine imported Liege double turned, twist steel barrel, 12-gauge; length of barrel, 30 or 32 inches (state length wanted); weight, 6½ pounds. Price......... **7.95** Weight, packed for shipment, about 14 pounds.

For general illustration of the parts of this special $6.95 gun, see page 725, showing parts of the $7.95 Aubrey Hammerless, for in most respects these parts are interchangeable and identical.

No. 6K426

A. J. AUBREY   HAMMERLESS SINGLE BARREL   SHOTGUN

TO GIVE YOU TWICE AS MUCH VALUE for your money, to give you more gun value for a dollar than you could get in any cheaper single barrel gun for $2.00, to give you for only $7.95 a single barrel breech loading shotgun that is worth ten times as much as any of the common grades of single guns that usually sell at $4.00 to $8.00, we have built in our own factory at Meriden, Conn. (the Meriden Fire Arms Company), under the direction of Mr. A. J. Aubrey, president and general manager of the gun company, this, our special $7.95 flat water table hammerless breech loading shotgun, taking a long step ahead in single gun making, making a gun that will grade only with the highest grade hammerless double barrel breech loading shotguns, a gun with features of workmanship, a gun in which material, labor, workmanship and finish, a gun in which strength, safety, lasting qualities and shooting qualities are fully equal to the highest grade hammerless double barrel breech loading shotguns, a gun that outclasses and outmatches any single gun made by any maker.

TAPER CHOKE BORED

A. J. AUBREY

$7.95

THE ADVANTAGES OF THE SINGLE BARREL SHOTGUN.

WE BELIEVE that many who heretofore would not use a single gun, for the reason that they could not get such a gun of the high quality wanted, would grasp at the opportunity of buying an A. J. Aubrey Single Barrel Gun if gotten out on the same lines and quality of workmanship and finish as the highest grade hammerless double barrel breech loading shotguns, and our belief was supported by the great number of orders we have received, even beyond our expectations. The demand for this gun has been so great that we have at times been unable to keep pace at the factory. Where we sell one we are sure to sell others, and everyone seeing an A. J. Aubrey single gun would not think of buying any of the cheaper guns on the market.

THERE ARE THOUSANDS of shooters who prefer a single barrel gun to a double for numerous reasons, but who, owing to the lack of a high grade single barrel gun, have been compelled to shoot double guns.

WHILE WE CAN SELL YOU A SINGLE BARREL SHOTGUN for as little as $3.59, and even our $3.59 single barrel shotgun is vastly better in quality than most of the ordinary single barrel guns sold at $5.00 to $8.00, still in the A. J. Aubrey single guns, and in this, the $7.95 hammerless, and in our $6.95 hammer single barrel we can really give you twice as much for your money as in any of the lower grade guns shown in this catalogue. If you want to buy a single barrel shotgun of any kind, at any price, just take our advice on this one subject.

THIS AUBREY HAMMERLESS SINGLE BARREL GUN ANSWERS THE REQUIREMENTS OF EVERY SHOOTER DESIRING A HIGH CLASS, RELIABLE, SINGLE BARREL SHOTGUN

IN THIS GUN we offer something that has never been offered before, namely, the same high quality of material and construction, and almost the identical mechanism found in the highest grade double barrel hammerless gun. A single barrel gun possesses the following features which are not found in a double gun, namely, the light weight, which is preferred by many shooters who object to the heavy weight of a double barrel gun, particularly boys and men whose strength handicaps them in the handling of a heavy gun weighing 8 pounds or more. Another feature peculiar to a single barrel gun, particularly the A. J. Aubrey, is the direct sight or line procured on the object when shooting. On a double gun the sight is placed in the center of the rib, between the two barrels. On a single gun the sight is placed directly in the center of the barrel, making it unnecessary to make any allowance, as in sighting a single barrel gun you hold directly on the object. Providing you point your gun squarely at the object, you will hit it.

THE A. J. AUBREY HAMMERLESS SINGLE BARREL SHOTGUN can be operated as fast as an ordinary double barrel hammer gun. By this we mean that after you become accustomed to the A. J. Aubrey Single Barrel Hammerless Shotgun you can fire ten shots with this gun as fast as anyone can with any ordinary double barrel hammer gun. One operation in opening the gun causes the shell to be automatically ejected and the gun cocked. You can shoot, reload and shoot a second time faster than the average shooter can load, cock both hammers and pull both triggers of a double barrel hammer gun.

THIS A. J. AUBREY SINGLE BARREL HAMMERLESS SHOTGUN at our price of $7.95 is unquestionably the greatest value ever offered in a single barrel gun. There is no single barrel gun on the market today that in any way compares with this gun. The illustration shown on this page gives you but a faint idea of the beautiful, symmetrical proportions of this gun. The average single barrel gun is built with no idea of proportion, it has no balance or hang to it. The average single barrel shotgun feels as much like a club in your hands as it does like a shotgun. The Aubrey Hammerless Gun is designed and built by the greatest gun designer in the country, namely, Mr. A. J. Aubrey. The weight of this gun is evenly distributed from butt plate to muzzle. There is no dead weight anywhere. The gun tapers in natural and graceful lines from end to end. When you have this gun in your hand, the way in which it hangs, the way it comes up to your shoulder, gives you a confidence in this gun that enables you to accomplish 50 per cent more than you could with any ordinary single barrel gun.

REFER TO NEXT PAGE and note carefully the illustrations and descriptions of the various parts entering into the construction of this gun. We have endeavored to tell you all about this gun. The more you know about it the more certain we are that you will buy it. At the best, the illustrations we show in this catalogue and what we say of this gun cannot do it more than half justice, for in order to really appreciate what a wonderful gun this is, to realize what wonderful value this price of $7.95 represents, to grasp its superiority over all other single barrel guns, it is necessary that you see the gun, handle it, shoot it, and actually compare it with any other single barrel gun in your neighborhood, and give it a thorough test. You will then realize better than we can possibly tell you in this catalogue what a wonderful gun the A. J. Aubrey Single Barrel Hammerless Shotgun is.

WE FURNISH THIS GUN exactly as illustrated and described, with beautiful long stock, full pistol grip, checkered grip and fore end, beautifully shaped stock and fore end, 12-gauge only; barrels 30 or 32 inches long as desired, our latest model with all improvements, brought right up to date, the highest grade single barrel gun on the market, the only automatic shell ejecting hammerless single barrel breech loading shotgun to buy, in fact, the only single barrel gun of any kind that you can really afford to buy, and we offer it for only $7.95. We offer it in two styles, as listed below.

THE DETAILED DESCRIPTION

of this gun will be found on the following page, together with illustrations of the various parts; in short, we would say that all these guns are 12-gauge, have 30 or 32-inch barrels as desired (be sure to state length wanted); they are the best that can possibly be produced, and are really the only single guns for anyone to buy.

FROM THE DAY we first offered this single hammerless gun to our trade the demand has gone on with leaps and bounds. We have been compelled, as rapidly as we could accumulate tools and machinery, to increase our manufacturing capacity, for such a single gun as this was never seen before, and we have found where we have sold one in a neighborhood more orders have immediately followed from those who have seen this gun.

DON'T THINK OF BUYING a cheap shotgun. If you want a single barrel shotgun by all means buy an A. J. Aubrey, worth five times as much, and yet will cost you very little, if any, more than the cheap, low grade, ordinary single gun, and really there are very few others on the market.

THIS IS OUR ADVICE

IF YOU ARE THINKING of buying a single barrel breech loading shotgun, either send us your order for this, our $7.95 Aubrey Hammerless Single Barrel, or the $6.95 Aubrey Hammer Single Barrel shown on another page, enclose our price, let us send you the gun with the understanding and agreement that you can give it sixty days' trial, during which time you can put it to every reasonable test, and if you are not perfectly satisfied with your purchase, return the gun to us at our expense and get your money back.

IN YOUR OWN INTEREST we advise you not to buy a cheaper gun, since in this genuine Aubrey you get so very much more real value for your money than it would be possible for us to give you in any cheaper grade or lower priced gun. The slight difference in cost between this, the genuine A. J. Aubrey, and the cheaper guns shown in this catalogue will soon be forgotten, but the fact that you have the best single gun made in America, the safest arm, one that you can depend upon under all circumstances, the handsomest single gun and the best shooting gun possible to build, will ever be a satisfaction to you. You will always be very glad that you took our advice and bought the best single gun possible to produce.

When ordering, state length of barrel preferred.

THIS GLOBE SIGHT FREE

With every A. J. Aubrey Shotgun we include one of our famous Globe Sights which is a valuable aid to the shooter. This sight can be instantly attached to the muzzle of the gun and as quickly detached. The use of this sight does not in any way interfere with the regular sight on the gun. We have many letters from shooters advising us that this Globe Sight, which is owned and controlled by us exclusively, has improved their shooting qualities from 25 to 50 per cent. We give one of these Globe Sights free with every A. J. Aubrey Gun.

No. 6K424 Gun, complete with special crystal steel barrel, full blued finish, 12-gauge; length of barrel, 30 or 32 inches (state length preferred); weight, 6½ pounds. Price........................ **$7.95**

No. 6K425 The exact same gun, furnished with the very finest improved genuine Liege double blade, full finished, twist steel barrel, 12-gauge; length of barrel, 30 or 32 inches (state length preferred); weight, 6½ pounds. Price........................ **8.95**

A. J. AUBREY HAMMERLESS SINGLE BARREL SHOTGUN

ON THIS PAGE WE SHOW ILLUSTRATIONS OR PICTURES

of a number of the important parts and the way the A. J. Aubrey Hammerless Single Barrel Breech Loading Shotgun is constructed, and if you will compare these illustrations and descriptions with any other single barrel breech loading shotgun you ever saw or heard of, you will appreciate in some degree the quality and kind of a gun we are furnishing for only $7.95. Observe these illustrations carefully, read the descriptions also, and you will see that we are offering in this $7.95 Hammerless Aubrey Gun, with all the up to date, high grade features, all the workmanship, fit and finish, all the strong and essential parts of the most expensive, the highest grade double hammerless breech loading shotguns made, in fact, the only single barrel gun on the market that is in the high grade double barrel hammerless class.

A FEW POINTS OF SUPERIORITY of this single barrel gun over any other single barrel gun made will be shown more clearly in the following illustrations.

REINFORCED EXTRA BREECH, big square barrel lug, extra strong automatic shell ejector which throws the shell clear from the gun when it is open or broke, square shouldered bolt to automatic shell ejector so that it can never become loose or misplaced, fancy crystal steel barrel, latest choke bore system, finest steel frame, automatic safety, exactly the same as used on the highest priced double barrel breech loading shotguns made, finest top lever break action, double bolt construction, locking mechanism, long tang.

SEE EVERY ILLUSTRATION, every picture, read the full description, and then, when you are about to order a single barrel breech loading shotgun, by all means order this, the A. J. Aubrey Hammerless Single Barrel Breech Loading Shotgun at $7.95, or the Aubrey Hammer Single Gun at $6.95. They are really the only single barrel shotguns for anyone to buy.

$7.95

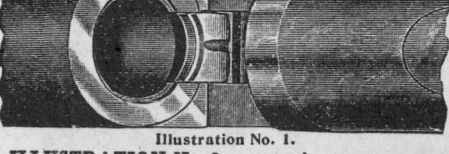
Illustration No. 1.

ILLUSTRATION No. 1 will give you a little idea of the barrel construction. It is made extra heavy, reinforced at the breech, making it an ideal and safe gun for white, smokeless or black powder, reducing the recoil or kick to the very minimum.

ILLUSTRATION No. 2, engraved from a photograph, will give you an idea of the lug and automatic shell ejector and the flat water table construction of this gun. This is the exact same class of work that is found in the most expensive double hammerless guns made. Nothing ever before turned out that will in any way compare with it.

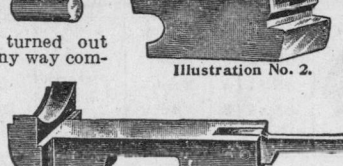
Illustration No. 2.

ILLUSTRATION No. 3 shows the automatic ejector as it goes into the barrel of the gun, and you will note it goes into the square shouldered bolt instead of the common round bolt, locking it firmly in place, making it safe, sure and everlasting.

Illustration No. 3.

ILLUSTRATION No. 4. This frame, as before explained, is made from the very finest steel forging, full milled and full finished. Note the flat water table and the heavy locking bolt. This is the exact same grade of material, the exact same construction as is used in the highest grade double barrel hammerless shotguns made. Nothing like it has ever before been seen in a single barrel gun.

Illustration No. 4.

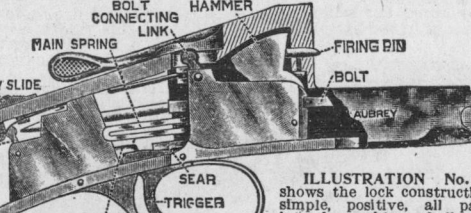
BOLT CONNECTING LINK — HAMMER — MAIN SPRING — SAFETY SLIDE — FIRING PIN — BOLT — AUBREY — SAFETY CATCH LEVER — SAFETY CATCH BLOCKING TRIGGER — SEAR — TRIGGER
Illustration No. 5.

ILLUSTRATION No. 5 shows the lock construction, simple, positive, all parts interchangeable, and all parts that contact being of the finest tool steel, perfectly tempered.

ILLUSTRATION No. 6 shows the automatic safety, the exact same safety construction as is furnished on the highest grade hammerless double barrel shotguns. Nothing better in any gun made, even though sold at $100.00, and with this safety construction, which is the only single gun made with safety construction, you really have a gun worth double that of any hammer gun made. In fact you can operate this gun almost as quickly, shoot almost as many shots in a given time, as with the ordinary double barrel hammer breech loader, and the factor of safety alone makes this gun really the only single barrel gun to buy. The moment the gun is broke or open it is on safe and is so indicated by the safety, and on safe it is impossible to pull the trigger or shoot the gun. This means that even if your gun is loaded, if you should stumble in going over a fence or under a fence, through the weeds or otherwise, there is no possible chance of accidental discharge. Danger of raising and lowering the hammer, especially on a cold day, when the hammer may slip from the thumb and cause accidental discharge, is entirely removed. A touch with the thumb on the safety when you are

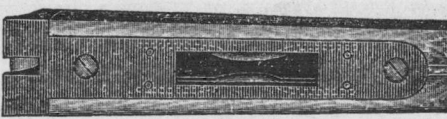
Illustration No. 6.

ready to shoot, the same touch that pushes the safety back and your gun is locked, the trigger cannot be pulled and accidental discharge of the gun is an impossibility.

ILLUSTRATION No. 7, showing top lever, is the exact same grade of top lever as is used on the highest grade double barrel breech loading shotguns made, positive in its action, beautiful in its lines, the best that can be produced.

Illustration No. 7.

ILLUSTRATION No. 8 shows handsomely shaped, full finished, full walnut fore end with fancy checkered ornamentation.

Illustration No. 8.

ILLUSTRATION No. 9 shows the automatic wire locking device which securely and automatically locks the fore end to the barrel. No possible danger of its shooting loose, for the fore end is finished with a full steel metal tip, with long strong tang.

Illustration No. 9.

WALNUT STOCK. These guns are furnished with a specially high grade black walnut stock, beautifully shaped full pistol grip; the butt plate to the grip is a fancy rubber plate; butt plate to the gun is also a fancy rubber butt plate.

SEE OUR $6.95 AUBREY GUN ON ANOTHER PAGE

ON ANOTHER PAGE we show an Aubrey Single Barrel Breech Loading Hammer Gun at $6.95, and in all essential parts, save only for the hammerless feature, it is the exact same gun as the $7.95 Aubrey Hammerless Single Barrel Breech Loader shown on this and the preceding page. Like this gun, it has the same automatic shell ejector, the same style of frame, the same barrels, bolting, locking mechanism, etc., the same alignment, the same stock, the same flat water table construction; so when buying a single barrel breech loading shotgun you have your choice between the two greatest guns ever produced, this, the $7.95 hammerless Aubrey, and the $6.95 hammer Aubrey shown on another page, and when you are ready to order a single barrel breech loading shotgun be sure to order one of these.

ON THE PRECEDING PAGE we show an illustration of this $7.95 gun complete, and on this page we show some of the most important parts. These two pages are devoted to illustrating and describing the $7.95 Aubrey, but remember it's so good, so out of the ordinary, that it must be seen, examined and compared with other guns to appreciate the real value we are giving.

EXCEPT FOR THE FACT THAT THIS $7.95 GUN is a single barrel gun, it looks exactly the same as the highest priced and finest hammerless double barrel breech loading shotguns, perfect in alignment, perfect in hang and drop, balanced exactly right, choke bored by the best known system, practically no recoil or kick, no longer, stronger or better shooting gun made, no gun ever produced that will make a better pattern, better target or greater penetration. It combines the good qualities of every high grade gun made with the defects of none; the finest barrel, finest frame, stock and fore end, the best construction throughout, elaborately finished, beautifully checkered, richly mounted, beautifully case hardened frame, mottled effect, graceful lines from the stock to the fore end of the barrel, the finest and really the only single barrel breech loading shotgun to buy. Comes in 12-gauge only, 30 or 32-inch barrel as desired, full pistol grip, automatic shell ejector by which when the gun is open the shell is thrown clear from the gun, the strongest ejector ever produced, yet sent out on 60 days' free trial, covered by our written binding 20-year guarantee.

WE FURNISH THIS GUN EXACTLY AS ILLUSTRATED on this and the preceding page with beautiful walnut stock, full pistol grip, full checkered grip and fore end, beautifully shaped stock and fore end, 12-gauge only, barrel 30 or 32 inches long (state length preferred), the very latest model with all improvements, brought right up to date, the highest grade possible to produce, at the following special prices:

| No. 6K424 | Gun, complete, with special crystal steel, full choke barrel, 12-gauge; length of barrel, 30 or 32 inches (state length preferred). Weight, 6½ pounds. Price. | $7.95 |
| No. 6K425 | With the very finest imported Liege double blade bar twist steel barrel, full finished, 12-gauge, 30 or 32 inches (state length preferred). Weight, 6½ pounds. Price | 8.95 |

FOR ILLUSTRATION OF THE GUN COMPLETE, SEE OPPOSITE PAGE.

SPECIAL 36-INCH AND 40-INCH LONG BARREL SINGLE GUNS 12 AND 16-GAUGE $5.70

IN ANSWER TO A GENERAL DEMAND for a high grade single barrel gun with an extra long barrel, a barrel from 6 to 8 inches longer than the regular barrel, we have made this special single barrel gun with 36-inch and 40-inch barrel. The demand for these long barrel guns was particularly heavy from sections of the country where a gun of extreme long range is desired, hunting geese, turkeys, ducks, jack rabbits, etc. We are always desirous of meeting our customers' views as far as it is possible, and in the gun line we have facilities for manufacturing and obtaining guns such as are enjoyed by no other concern.

THIS LONG BARREL GUN has been sold by us for several seasons. We have improved it one season over another. The gun we offer you today at $5.70 is the improved model gun, a better gun than you could possibly obtain from any dealer for $7.00 or $8.00; in fact, we doubt if you can obtain a gun of this kind elsewhere, as they are manufactured especially for us under contract by one of the largest manufacturers of single barrel guns in the United States. The enormous business we have on this long barrel gun has enabled us to contract for them in enormous quantities, thereby obtaining the lowest possible cost, of which we, at our price of $5.70, give you the direct benefit.

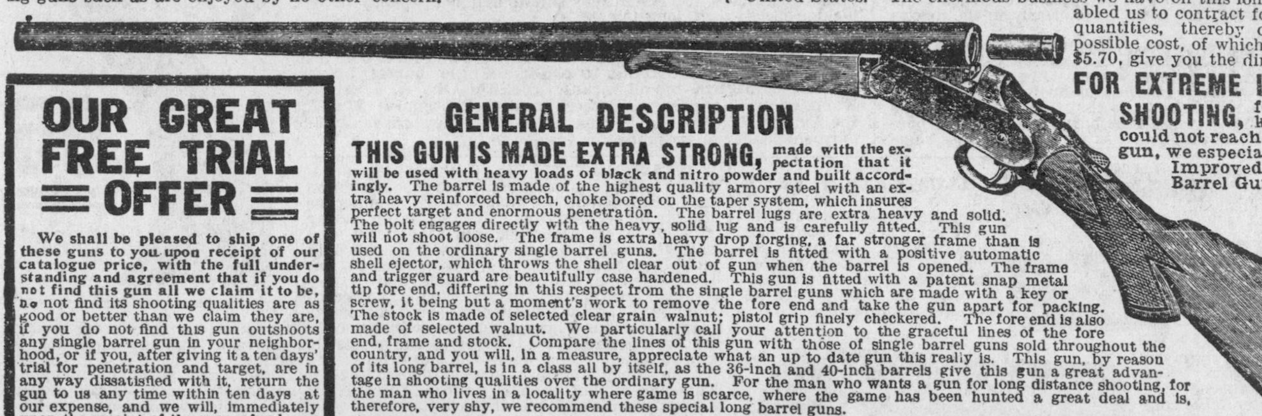

FOR EXTREME LONG DISTANCE SHOOTING, for a gun which will kill game where you could not reach it with an ordinary gun, we especially recommend our Improved 1908 Model Long Barrel Gun.

OUR GREAT FREE TRIAL OFFER

We shall be pleased to ship one of these guns to you upon receipt of our catalogue price, with the full understanding and agreement that if you do not find this gun all we claim it to be, do not find its shooting qualities are as good or better than we claim they are, if you do not find this gun outshoots any single barrel gun in your neighborhood, or if you, after giving it a ten days' trial for penetration and target, are in any way dissatisfied with it, return the gun to us any time within ten days at our expense, and we will, immediately upon the receipt of the gun, refund you your money together with any express charges you may have paid.

GENERAL DESCRIPTION

THIS GUN IS MADE EXTRA STRONG, made with the expectation that it will be used with heavy loads of black and nitro powder and built accordingly. The barrel is made of the highest quality armory steel with an extra heavy reinforced breech, choke bored on the taper system, which insures perfect target and enormous penetration. The barrel lugs are extra heavy and solid. The bolt engages directly with the heavy, solid lug and is carefully fitted. This gun will not shoot loose. The frame is extra heavy drop forging, a far stronger frame than is used on the ordinary single barrel guns. The barrel is fitted with a positive automatic shell ejector, which throws the shell clear out of gun when the barrel is opened. The frame and trigger guard are beautifully case hardened. This gun is fitted with a patent snap metal tip fore end, differing in this respect from the single barrel guns which are made with a key or screw, it being but a moment's work to remove the fore end and take the gun apart for packing. The stock is made of selected clear grain walnut; pistol grip finely checkered. The fore end is also made of selected walnut. We particularly call your attention to the graceful lines of the fore end, frame and stock. Compare the lines of this gun with those of single barrel guns sold throughout the country, and you will, in a measure, appreciate what an up to date gun this really is. This gun, by reason of its long barrel, is in a class all by itself, as the 36-inch and 40-inch barrels give this gun a great advantage in shooting qualities over the ordinary gun. For the man who wants a gun for long distance shooting, for the man who lives in a locality where game is scarce, where the game has been hunted a great deal and is, therefore, very shy, we recommend these special long barrel guns.

REMEMBER that if you order one of these guns it will be shipped to you with the understanding that, if it does not please you, you may return it at our expense and we will immediately return your money.

WE FURNISH FREE, at our price of $5.70 for the 36-inch barrel gun and $6.20 for the 40-inch barrel gun, our Special Globe Sight, which is manufactured and controlled exclusively by us. This sight can be instantly attached or detached from the gun barrel, and does not in any way interfere with the regular sight on the barrel. There are several thousands of these sights now in use, as we have been furnishing shooters with them for a number of seasons; and, the majority of shooters who have once used this sight depend on it entirely, claiming that the use of this sight improves the marksmanship from 33⅓ per cent to 50 per cent. This sight is of particular value on this long barrel gun, as it enables you to center your game directly in the globe of the sight, giving you a direct line that you would not obtain sighting in the ordinary way. This sight, as stated, is furnished free with these single barrel guns.

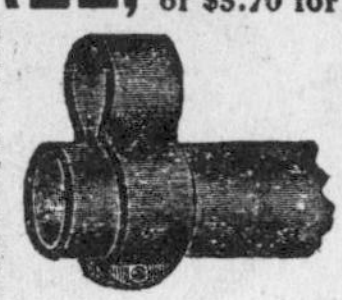

Catalogue Number	Grade	Style of Barrel	Gauge	Length of Barrel	Weight of Guns	Price
6K510A	Ejector	Genuine Armory Steel	12	36 inches, Choke Bored	7 to 7¼ lbs.	$5.70
6K510B	Ejector		16	36 inches, Choke Bored	6¾ to 7 lbs.	5.70
6K511A	Ejector		12	40 inches, Choke Bored	7¼ to 7½ lbs.	6.20
6K511B	Ejector		16	40 inches, Choke Bored	7 to 7¼ lbs.	6.20

Weight, packed for shipment, about 14 pounds.

IMPROVED 1908 MODEL ATLAS RIFLE $1.48

22-CALIBER AND 22-INCH BARREL

REDUCED FROM $1.98 TO $1.48

FOR $1.48, 22-CALIBER WITH 22-INCH BARREL, we furnish the Improved 1908 Model Atlas Rifle, which we have greatly improved over the original model. This improved 1908 model as we offer it today is a better rifle by 25 per cent than the previous models. We have improved the quality and construction of this rifle without increasing the cost to you. The enormous business we have had on this rifle during past seasons has enabled us to demand certain improvements and changes in this rifle which the manufacturer, by reason of the enormous quantity we have ordered, has been able to furnish us with but a slight increase in the cost, and as it is our desire to furnish the greatest value in a 22-caliber rifle and make this the cheapest and best 22-caliber rifle on the market, we have not advanced our selling price. No other house is able to offer such wonderful value. This rifle at this price stands in a class all by itself. The material in the barrel and mechanism of this rifle is as good as that employed in any $4.00 or $5.00 rifle on the market. The rifle is carefully and well made and neatly finished. We guarantee it to give entire satisfaction. 22-caliber, 22-inch barrel, accurately rifled, will shoot 22-short BB or CB caps, black or smokeless powder.

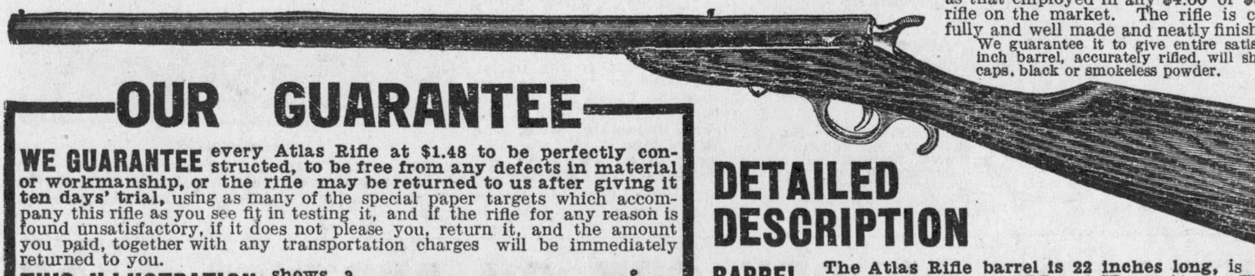

OUR GUARANTEE

WE GUARANTEE every Atlas Rifle at $1.48 to be perfectly constructed, to be free from any defects in material or workmanship, or the rifle may be returned to us after giving it ten days' trial, using as many of the special paper targets which accompany this rifle as you see fit in testing it, and if the rifle for any reason is found unsatisfactory, if it does not please you, return it, and the amount you paid, together with any transportation charges will be immediately returned to you.

THIS ILLUSTRATION shows a cross section of the heavy steel barrel of this rifle and also shows the rifling, which rifling is the same as that found in any of the higher priced rifles, causing this rifle to shoot just as accurately as any rifle you could buy for twice our price of $1.48.

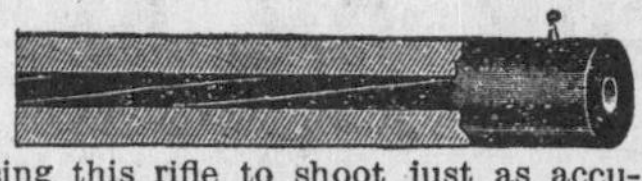

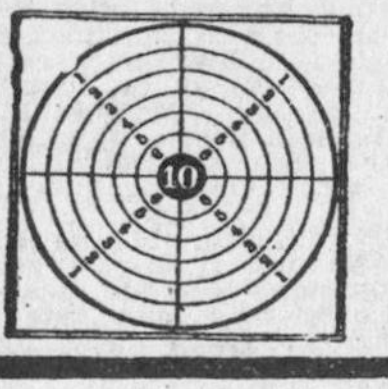

25 SPECIAL TARGETS FREE

We furnish you free with the Atlas Rifle at $1.48 twenty-five of these special white paper rifle targets, of which we herewith show a small illustration. These targets are printed on heavy white paper and are the best paper targets made. With every Atlas Rifle we furnish twenty-five of these targets free.

DETAILED DESCRIPTION

BARREL. The Atlas Rifle barrel is 22 inches long, is chambered for 22-short BB and CB cartridges. The barrel is made of the finest crystal carbon steel, the same grade of steel used in the highest priced rifle barrels. The barrels are rifled by an automatic rifling machine and every barrel is rifled in identically the same manner. The twist in the rifling is not too great nor too light. It is just right, insuring the greatest possible penetration. The barrel is fitted with neat open sights which are especially adapted for quick and accurate shooting, making this rifle suitable for either target practice or for small game, such as squirrels, rabbits, birds, etc.

THE EXTRACTOR is positive. It is worked with a straight pull, made of one solid piece, and while exceedingly simple, is a better extractor and more positive than the many complicated extractors used on high priced rifles.

THE STOCK is made of fine straight grained seasoned walnut, nicely finished and shaped.

THE TAKE DOWN FEATURE is very simple. The one screw in the fore end and in front of the trigger guard is all that it is necessary to remove in order to separate the stock from the barrel.

IN PURCHASING ONE OR MORE ATLAS RIFLES AT $1.48 and a few thousands of the highest quality 22-short cartridges at 21 cents per hundred, together with the paper targets we furnish free, you have a complete outfit to start a shooting gallery. Your outlay would be very small and the profits you would make in a day or two would more than pay for the entire outfit.

Do not forget that twenty-five paper targets are sent free with every Atlas Rifle at $1.48.

No. 6K664 Our special price for the rifle complete, including twenty-five special paper targets $1.48

No. 6K2336 22-Short Black Powder Cartridges. Price, per 1,000, $2.00; per 100 .... 21c

TARGET RIFLES, 22-CALIBER

QUACKENBUSH SAFETY CARTRIDGE RIFLE.

$3.90 WITH 22-INCH BARREL.

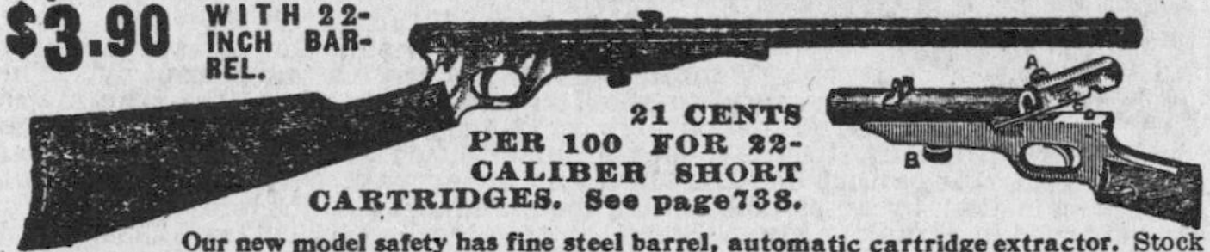

21 CENTS PER 100 FOR 22-CALIBER SHORT CARTRIDGES. See page 738.

Our new model safety has fine steel barrel, automatic cartridge extractor. Stock is black walnut, handsomely finished, and so fastened to the barrel that the two may be easily and quickly separated, making the rifle handy to carry in a trunk, valise or package. The barrel is rifled and durably blued, except the breech block, which is case hardened in color. Whole length, 33 inches, has 22-inch barrel, 22-caliber. Shoots cartridges Nos. 6K2336, 6K2338, 6K2340, or 6K2535; good for 35 to 100 yards. Plain open sights, as shown in illustration. Weight, about 4½ pounds. Guaranteed good shooter. We have discontinued selling this rifle with an 18-inch barrel, as the 22-inch costs only a few cents more and is the best all around rifle.

Catalogue No.	Caliber	Barrel, inches	Shoots Cartridge	Good for	Price
6K676	22 Rim Fire	22	No. 6K2336 No. 6K2338 No. 6K2340 No. 6K2535	35 to 100 yards	$3.90

Weight, packed for shipment, about 8 pounds.
Notice our prices on Rifle Rods. It saves the rifle to keep it clean.
No. 6K4716 Cover fits this rifle. See page 743.

OUR NEW No. 4 REMINGTON TAKE DOWN RIFLE, $5.00.

21 CENTS PER 100 FOR 22-CALIBER SHORT CARTRIDGES. SEE PAGE 738.

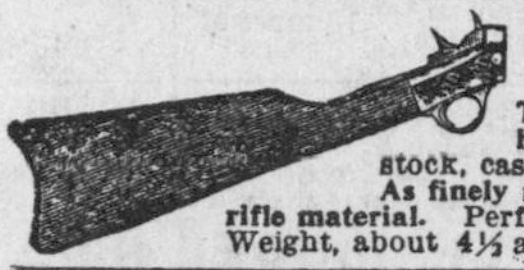

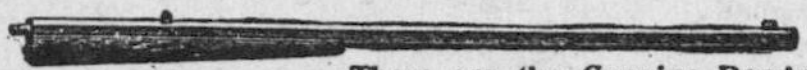

These are the Genuine Remington Take Down Rifles. Don't buy imitations offered by many houses. They are worthless. All Remingtons have walnut stock, case hardened frame and mountings, open front and rear sights. As finely rifled as any rifle in the market, and made of the very best rifle material. Perfectly accurate and every one warranted as represented. Weight, about 4½ and 5½ pounds. 22 and 32-caliber. RIM FIRE.

Cat. No.	Caliber	Barrel	Shoots Cartridge	Good for	Price
6K678	22 Short or Long Rim Fire	22½ in.	No. 6K2336 No. 6K2340	35 to 100 yards	$5.00
6K680	32 Short or Long	24 in.	No. 6K2352 No. 6K2353	100 to 125 yards	5.00

Weight, packed for shipment, about 8 pounds.
Notice our prices on Rifle Rods. It saves the rifle to keep it clean.
No. 6K4716 Cover fits this rifle. See page 743.

OUR NEW No. 6 REMINGTON TAKE DOWN RIFLE, $3.00

The New Remington No. 6 Take Down Rifle is placed upon the market with the view of giving the best possible value at a low price. This new No. 6 Remington Rifle is made from the best material that money can buy, and the shooting quality is of a high order, and each rifle is bored and rifled with the same accuracy and precision that follows the entire line of Remington rifles, which have become famous for their shooting qualities. It is made in 22-caliber only, shoots the 22-caliber cartridges Nos. 6K2336 or 6K2338, and is good for 35 yds.

No. 6K681 Remington Rifle No. 6, 22-caliber, 20-inch round barrel; weight, 3½ pounds; walnut stock and fore end; case hardened frame; take down model. Weight, packed for shipment, about 8 pounds. Price..........**$3.00**

Nos. 6K4698 and 6K4716 Covers fit these rifles. See page 743.

RUSTED AND DAMAGED GUNS.

Do not return to us a gun, revolver or rifle which is rusted, pitted or has the finish worn off, for we have no way of selling these guns. If you have a gun, revolver or rifle which needs repairing, first write us fully describing the article and what is broken, as we may be able to send you the part necessary, thus saving the express charges on the gun both ways.

HOPKINS & ALLEN TAKE DOWN RIFLE, $2.35.

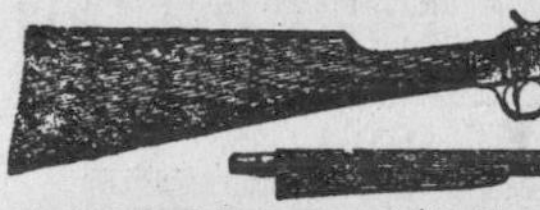

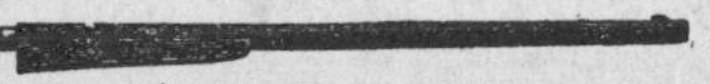

For $2.35 we offer you the latest model Hopkins & Allen Take Down Rifle, factory No. 722. Description—This Hopkins & Allen Take Down Rifle has a finely rifled steel barrel. The frame, breech and trigger guard, as well as all working parts, are case hardened, making them durable. The stock and fore end are of selected straight grain walnut. The rifle is fitted with fancy butt plate and plain open sights. In order to take the barrel from the frame, remove the screw in front of the trigger guard.

No. 6K695 Hopkins & Allen Rifle, 22-caliber, suitable for cartridges Nos. 6K2336 and 6K2338, 19-inch barrel, weight, about 3½ pounds. Weight, packed for shipment, about 8 pounds. The factory price, $3.50 our price..........**$2.35**

Notice our prices on Rifle Rods. It saves the rifle to keep it clean.

THE OLD RELIABLE HOPKINS & ALLEN JUNIOR RIFLE, $4.50.

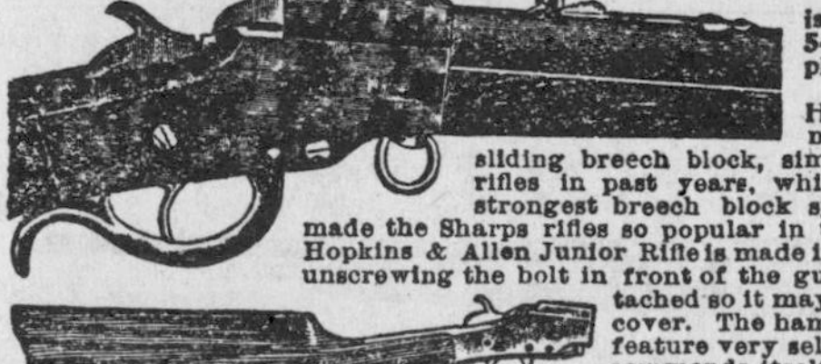

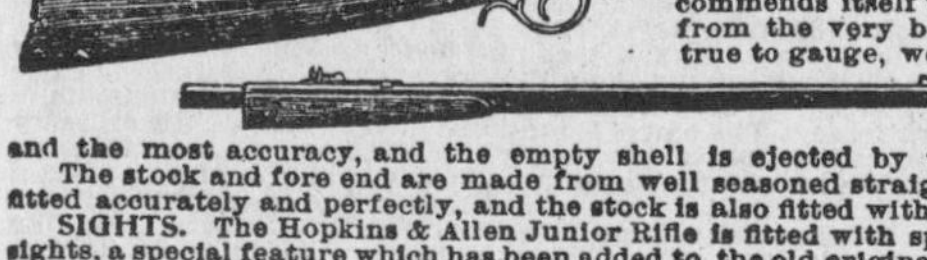

The Hopkins & Allen Junior Rifle is one of the most popular 4½ to 5-pound rifles that has ever been placed on the American market.

GENERAL DESCRIPTION. The Hopkins & Allen Junior Rifle is made with the celebrated vertical sliding breech block, similar to that used on the Sharps rifles in past years, which is conceded to be one of the strongest breech block systems ever invented and which made the Sharps rifles so popular in the large calibers years ago. The Hopkins & Allen Junior Rifle is made in the take down model, so that by unscrewing the bolt in front of the guard lever the barrel may be detached so it may be carried in a Victoria style gun cover. The hammer of this rifle is rebounding, a feature very seldom found on rifles and one which commends itself to the user. The barrel is made from the very best quality crucible steel, bored true to gauge, well rifled with the proper amount of twist and the proper depth of rifle grooves to give the very best possible execution and the most accuracy, and the empty shell is ejected by throwing the lever forward.

The stock and fore end are made from well seasoned straight grained lumber, finished and fitted accurately and perfectly, and the stock is also fitted with rubber butt plate.

SIGHTS. The Hopkins & Allen Junior Rifle is fitted with sporting rear and sporting front sights, a special feature which has been added to the old original rifle, and a feature which makes it far better than any rifle made at this price.

Cat. No.	Grade No.	Caliber	Barrel	Shoots Cartridge	Good for	Price
6K697	922	22 Rim Fire	22 inches	No. 6K2336 No. 6K2340	35 to 100 yds.	$4.50
6K698	932	32 Rim Fire	22 inches	No. 6K2352	100 to 200 yds.	

Weight, packed for shipment, about 8 pounds.
Buy a Rifle Cleaner. It saves your rifle to keep it clean inside.
Nos. 6K4698 and 6K4716 Covers fit this rifle. See page 743.

HOPKINS & ALLEN'S LATEST REPEATING RIFLE, 22-CALIBER.

$7.75

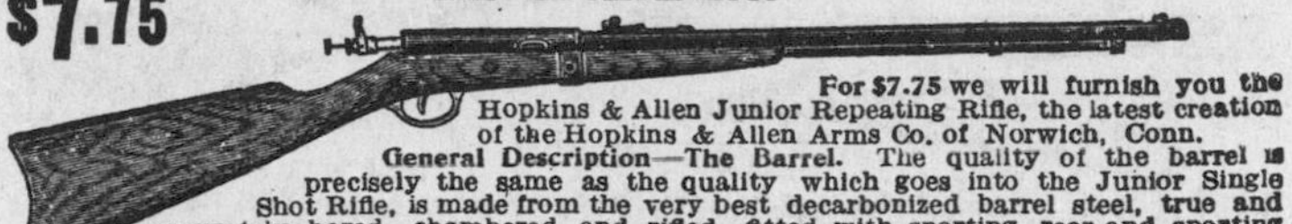

For $7.75 we will furnish you the Hopkins & Allen Junior Repeating Rifle, the latest creation of the Hopkins & Allen Arms Co. of Norwich, Conn.

General Description—The Barrel. The quality of the barrel is precisely the same as the quality which goes into the Junior Single Shot Rifle, is made from the very best decarbonized barrel steel, true and accurately bored, chambered and rifled, fitted with sporting rear and sporting front sight and is handsomely blued and military finish.

The Stock is made from well seasoned, selected, straight grained walnut, handsomely polished and finished, fitted with metal butt plate. The fore end is made from the same quality of lumber and finished in the same manner.

The Action. The action is what is known as the military style bolt action and works very much like the action of the Mauser rifles which were used so successfully in the Spanish-American war. To operate the action, turn the bolt lever up, as shown in the illustration, draw the bolt back toward the butt plate, then push it forward toward the muzzle and turn to the right to lock it, and the rifle is ready to shoot.

The Take Down Feature. The take down feature of our $7.75 repeating rifle is the simplest take down feature yet produced. A small knurled screw at the left hand side of the receiver is all there is to the take down action. By simply turning the screw to the left a few times, you release the barrel from the receiver and it is ready to take down.

Safety. This $7.75 Hopkins & Allen Junior Repeating Rifle has a patent safety device, whereby the trigger cannot be pulled until the breech bolt is home, seated and locked.

The Magazine. The magazine will hold sixteen 22-caliber short cartridges and twelve 22-caliber long rifle cartridges. To load the rifle, pull out the magazine tube about 13 inches, to uncover the cartridge receiver, insert the cartridges, bullet pointing toward the muzzle, then replace the tube in the same way you found it.

Catalogue Number	Caliber all Rim Fire	Round Barrel	Weight	Shoots Cartridge No.	Number of Shots	Price
6K700	22 Short 22 Long 22 Long Rifle	22 inches	5¾ lbs.	6K2336 6K2338 6K2340	12 to 16	$7.75

Weight, packed for shipment, about 15 pounds.
Buy a rifle cleaning rod. It saves the rifle to keep it clean.

STEVENS' FAVORITE RIFLE WITH DETACHABLE BARREL.

All our Stevens' Favorite Rifles are carefully selected for finish, accuracy and workmanship, and we do not send out any rifle which has not passed a rigid inspection at the factory. The manufacturer fixes the price at which we shall sell these rifles, and will positively not allow our house to sell them cheaper. The prices are guaranteed to be as low as offered by any reliable house in the United States, and should you be offered these rifles lower by any dealer, you will confer a great favor by advising us, to give us an opportunity of adjusting the prices.

21 CENTS PER 100 FOR 22-CALIBER SHORT CARTRIDGES. SEE PAGE 738.

$5.40

THE FAVORITE is guaranteed as well finished and rifled a barrel as found in the most costly rifles. Entirely new model. The barrel is held to stock by a set screw, and is easily separated or put together. Rifling and quality of barrel same as the higher cost rifle. All have case hardened frames, walnut stock, finely finished, warranted accurate; all shoot rim fire cartridges and are fitted with sporting rear sight. The Favorite has 22-inch barrel and weighs about 4½ pounds.

Catalogue No.	Caliber	Barrel	Shoots Cartridge	Good for	Price
6K708	22 Rim Fire	22 inches	No. 6K2336 No. 6K2338 No. 6K2340	35 to 100 yards	$5.40
6K709	25 Rim Fire	22 inches	No. 6K2346	75 to 150 yards	
6K710	32 Rim Fire	22 inches	No. 6K2352	100 to 125 yards	

Weight, packed for shipment, about 8 pounds.
For fitting Lyman sights, add 25 cents to cost of sights.
ANY DEVIATION FROM THIS CATALOGUE MAY CAUSE A DELAY IN YOUR ORDER.
Buy a Rifle Cleaner. It saves your rifle to keep it clean inside.

STEVENS' LATEST MODEL IDEAL RIFLE.

The Ideal Rifle is manufactured by the Stevens Arm & Tool Co., Chicopee Falls, Mass. The barrel is made so that it can be instantly detached from the frame and put into a Victoria gun cover. The rifling in the barrel is equal to any rifle made, regardless of price, and the Ideal Rifle, as made for us, will be found extremely accurate. Finish—The barrel is blued and fitted with sporting rear and sporting front sight; the frame is handsomely case hardened, and the lock works are hardened to insure them being good wearing parts; stock and fore end are made from selected straight grain well seasoned walnut, and in fact, the Ideal Rifle is all that its name implies, an Ideal Rifle. The manufacturer fixes the price at which we shall sell these rifles and will not allow us to sell them cheaper. NOTE OUR PRICES ON POINTER SMOKELESS SHELLS. NO HOUSE CAN COMPETE WITH US.

21 CENTS PER 100 FOR 22-CALIBER SHORT CARTRIDGES. SEE PAGE 738.

$8.25

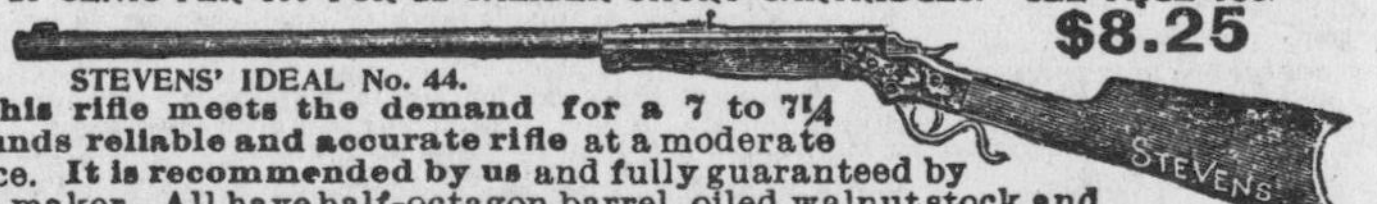

STEVENS' IDEAL No. 44. This rifle meets the demand for a 7 to 7¼ pounds reliable and accurate rifle at a moderate price. It is recommended by us and fully guaranteed by the maker. All have half-octagon barrel, oiled walnut stock and fore end, rifle butt, sporting rear and Rocky Mountain front sights.

Catalog No.	Grade No.	Caliber	Length Barrel	Shoots Cartridge	Good for	Weight about	Price
6K718	44	22 Rim Fire	24 inch.	6K2336 6K2338 6K2340	35 to 100 yds.	7¼ lbs.	$8.25
6K720	44	25-20 O.F.S.S.	26 inch.	6K2373	200 to 300 yds.	7 lbs.	

Weight, packed for shipment, about 12 pounds.
If wanted with Lyman Sights, add 25 cents to cost of sights, for fitting.
We quote 38-40 caliber at $7.25 as long as our stock holds out. They are no longer made.
Buy a Rifle Cleaner. It saves your rifle to keep it clean inside.

MARLIN TAKE DOWN MODEL 1897 RIFLE, $15.10.

FITTED WITH IVORY BEAD FRONT SIGHT AND SPORTING REAR SIGHT. 22-CALIBER.

The New Marlin Model '97 Take Down Rifle is the latest 22-caliber arm of its class on the market. This rifle is practically the model '92 with the addition of the "take down" feature and many other valuable improvements. It has finely tapered barrel, and a neat rubber butt plate; the receiver is made of special steel, same as used in the high power smokeless rifles, and is finely case hardened. This rifle is very easily cleaned: simply removing the side plate (by use of the thumbscrew for the purpose), makes ready access to the inside of this rifle. It comes in 22-caliber only. Magazine holds 25 cartridges 22-caliber short, 20 cartridges 22-caliber long, and 18 cartridges 22-caliber long rifle. Shoots cartridges 6K2336, No. 6K2338 or No. 6K2340.

Catalogue Number	Caliber	Length of Barrel	Shoots Cartridge	Number of Shots	Good for	Weight	Price
6K734	22 rim fire	24-inch Octagon	6K2336 6K2338 6K2340	25	35 to 100 yards	5¾ lbs.	$16.45
6K735	22 rim fire	24-inch Round		20 18	35 to 100 yards	5½ lbs.	15.10

Weight, packed for shipment, 14 pounds.
For fitting Lyman Sights, add 25 cents to the cost of the sights.

MARLIN'S NEW MODEL No. 20 TAKE DOWN REPEATING RIFLE, $11.75.

22-CALIBER.

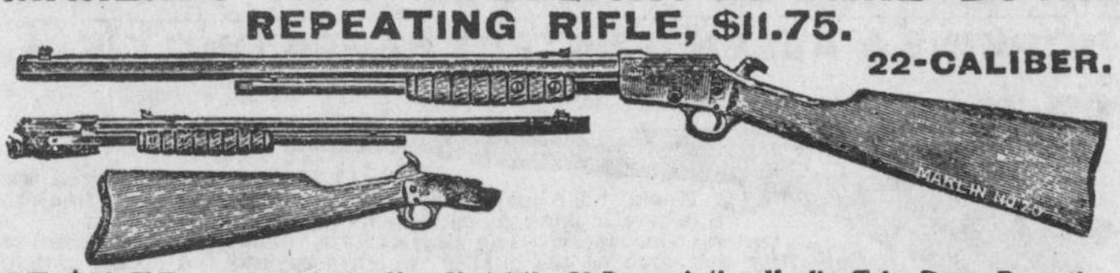

AT $11.75 we furnish the New Model No. 20 Pump Action Marlin Take Down Repeating Rifle, the latest product of the well known Marlin Fire Arms Co., New Haven, Conn. This New Model No. 20 Repeating Rifle is fitted with ivory bead front sight and Marlin's new patent sporting rear sight, the latter being the best rear sight ever placed upon any rifle. It is made to adjust with a small screw and when once set to range, cannot be changed except at the wish of the shooter. The No. 20 rifle is fitted with 22-inch octagon steel barrel, of the best Marlin rifle steel, accurately bored, chambered and rifled for fine shooting up to 200 yards; the frame is made from a special quality of gun frame steel, nicely blued, finely machined and finished in every particular. The take down action is similar to the popular model 1897, and is taken down by pulling hammer to half cock and unscrewing the knurled screw on the right side of the frame. The stock is made from very best straight grained, well seasoned and selected walnut, the fore end is also made from well seasoned, straight grained selected walnut. All the working parts are accurately milled, drilled, fitted and tempered, and should last a lifetime with the proper care. It is the only pump or fore end action repeater on the market which shoots the 22 short, 22 long and 22 long rifle rim fire cartridges in the same rifle. The magazine has a capacity to hold fifteen 22 short cartridges, twelve 22 long cartridges, or eleven 22 long rifle cartridges. The cartridges are extracted from the side of the frame and it is the only pump action rifle which has an ivory bead front sight and the celebrated special Marlin rear sight.

Catalogue Number	Caliber	Barrel	Weight	Shoots Cartridge Number	Number of Shots	Price
6K736	22 Rim Fire	22-inch octagon	4¼ lbs.	6K2236 6K2238 6K2240	15 12 11	$11.75

Weight, packed for shipment, about 10 pounds.
For fitting Lyman Sights, add 25 cents to cost of sights for fitting.
Nos. 6K4698, 6K4701 and 6K4716 Covers fit any the above rifles. See page 743.

MARLIN REPEATING RIFLES, MODEL 1892.

All Model 1892 Rifles have BLUED FRAMES, Sporting rear sights, Rocky Mountain front sights.

$12.15 $13.16

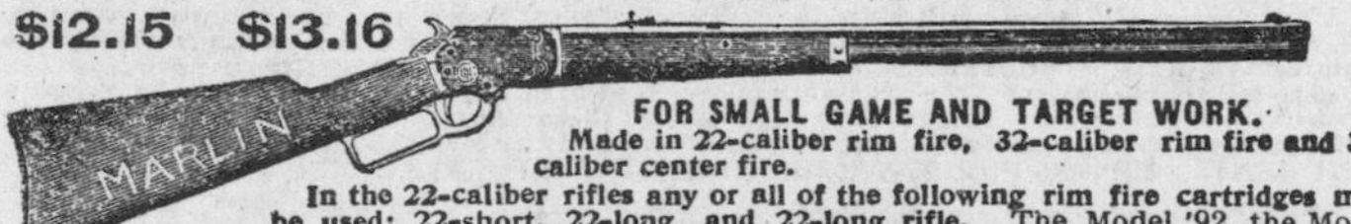

FOR SMALL GAME AND TARGET WORK. Made in 22-caliber rim fire, 32-caliber rim fire and 32-caliber center fire.

In the 22-caliber rifles any or all of the following rim fire cartridges may be used; 22-short, 22-long and 22-long rifle. The Model '92, the Model '97 and Model 20 Marlin are the only repeaters that will do this. Other systems require two or three rifles to do this same work. This model takes entirely to pieces without tools, allowing of perfect cleaning. The magazine holds 25 cartridges 22-short, 20 cartridges 22-long and 18 cartridges 22-long rifle.

All 32-caliber rifles are sent out with two firing pins. This rifle is so made that in the same rifle may be used 32-short rim fire, 32-long rim fire cartridges, and by changing the firing pin, 32-short and 32-long center fire cartridges may be used. The magazine holds 18 cartridges 32-caliber short and 15 cartridges 32-caliber long. This ammunition is cheap, and as compared to repeaters using the 32-20 cartridge will save the entire cost of the rifle on first 2,000 cartridges. Always clean your rifle after shooting. It will last longer. A rifle cleaning rod is a good investment.

Catalogue Number	Caliber	Length of Barrel	Shoots Cartridges	Good for	Weight	Price
6K740	22 rim fire	24-in. Octagon	6K2336 6K2338 6K2340	35 to 100 yds.	5¾ lbs.	$13.16
6K741	22 rim fire	24-in. Round		35 to 100 yds.	5¾ lbs.	12.15
6K742	32-caliber rim or center fire.	24-in. Octagon	6K2352 6K2353	100 to 200 yds.	6 lbs.	$13.16
6K743	32-caliber rim or center fire.	24-in. Round	6K2380 6K2381	100 to 200 yds.	6 lbs.	12.15

Weight, packed for shipment, 14 pounds.
For fitting Lyman Sights, add 25 cents to the cost of the sights for fitting.

MARLIN REPEATING RIFLES, MODEL 1894.

$12.15
13.16

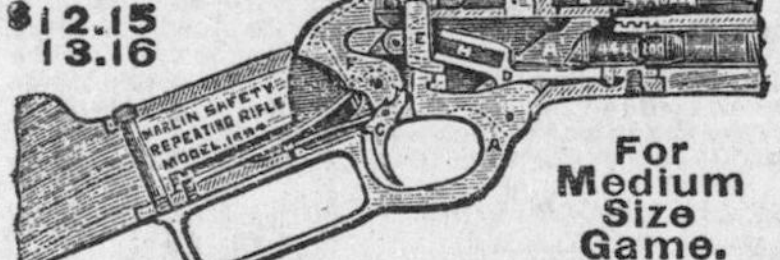

For Medium Size Game.

ALL HAVE CASE HARDENED FRAMES

This illustration shows the action of the Model 1894 Marlin Repeating Rifle. This is the latest and most improved repeating rifle to use the popular 25-20, 32-20, and 38-40 caliber center fire cartridges, and is the natural successor to the well known Model 1889. In the Model 1894 rifle every desirable feature of the 1889 which tended to make that arm the sportsman's favorite wherever used, is retained and the improvements suggested by five more years of experience and experiment are added. This rifle is practically the Model 1893 rifle adapted to the shorter cartridges and good for 100 to 300 yards. Always clean your rifle after shooting. It will last longer. A rifle cleaning rod is a good investment.

Catalogue No.	Caliber	Barrel	Using Cartridge No.	Weight	No. of Shots	Price
6K750	25-20	Octagon, 24-inch	6K2374	6⅞ lbs.	14	$13.16
6K751	25-20	Round, 24-inch	6K2374	7⅛ lbs.	14	12.15
6K752	32-20	Octagon, 24-inch	6K2384	6⅞ lbs.	14	13.16
6K753	32-20	Round, 24-inch	6K2384	7⅛ lbs.	14	12.15
6K754	38-40	Octagon, 24-inch	6K2396	6⅞ lbs.	14	13.16

Weight, packed for shipment, 14 pounds.
For fitting Lyman Sights, add 25 cents to the cost of the sights for fitting.

MARLIN REPEATING RIFLES, MODEL 1893.

$12.15 TO $15.53

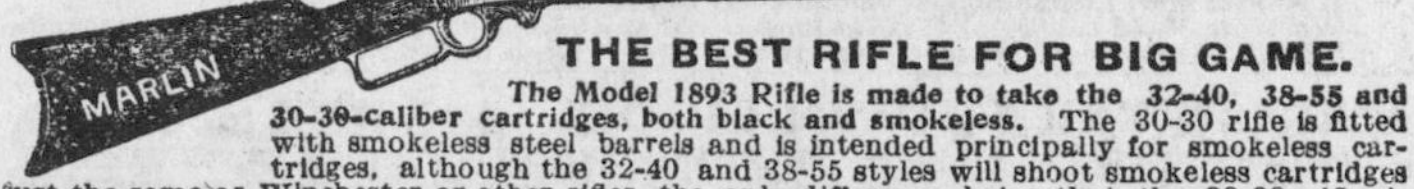

THE BEST RIFLE FOR BIG GAME.

The Model 1893 Rifle is made to take the 32-40, 38-55 and 30-30-caliber cartridges, both black and smokeless. The 30-30 rifle is fitted with smokeless steel barrels and is intended principally for smokeless cartridges, although the 32-40 and 38-55 styles will shoot smokeless cartridges just the same as Winchester or other rifles, the only difference being that the 30-30 rifle is fitted with a smokeless steel barrel, which is somewhat harder than the regular steel barrel, and will shoot more metal patched bullets without injuring the rifling than the regular steel barrel rifle. If you intend to shoot black powder cartridges most of the time and wish to shoot smokeless occasionally, the regular rifle will answer the same purpose as the smokeless steel barrel rifle. From all the information which we can gather the smokeless steel barrel is intended to shoot about 1,000 rounds of metal patched cartridges before the rifling begins to wear, while the regular steel barrel will shoot about 600 or 700 rounds before the rifling begins to wear.

Catalogue Number	Caliber	Style Steel Barrels	Using Cartridge No.	Weight	Good for Yards	No. of Shots	Price
6K758	32-40	Octagon, 26-inch	6K2429	7¾ lbs.	100 to 400	10	$13.16
6K759	32-40	Round, 26-inch	6K2429	7¾ lbs.	100 to 400	10	12.15
6K760	38-55	Octagon, 26-inch	6K2432	7¾ lbs.	100 to 400	10	13.16
6K761	38-55	Round, 26-inch	6K2432	7¾ lbs.	100 to 400	10	12.15
6K766	30-30	Octagon, 26-inch	6K2607	7¾ lbs.	100 to 600	10	15.53

Weight, packed for shipment, 14 pounds.
For fitting Lyman Sights, add 25 cents to the cost of the sights for fitting.
Always clean your rifle after shooting. It will last longer. A rifle cleaning rod is a good investment.

THE NEW WINCHESTER 22-CALIBER RIFLE, MODEL 1902, $3.50.

$3.50

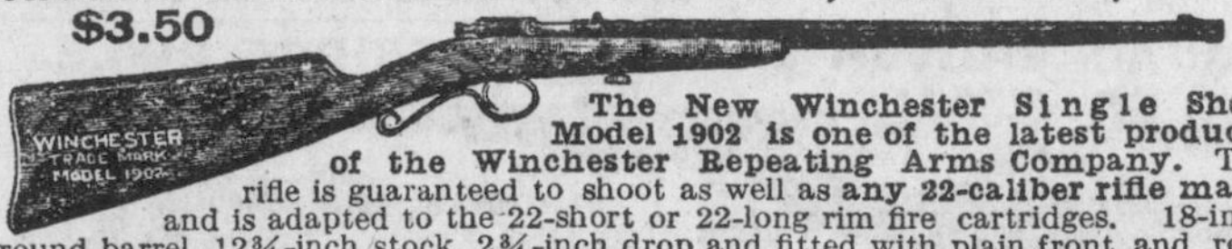

The New Winchester Single Shot, Model 1902 is one of the latest products of the Winchester Repeating Arms Company. The rifle is guaranteed to shoot as well as **any 22-caliber rifle made** and is adapted to the 22-short or 22-long rim fire cartridges. 18-inch round barrel, 12¾-inch stock, 2¾-inch drop and fitted with plain front and rear sights. **This rifle cannot be furnished any other way.** The rifle can be taken apart in an instant by simply unscrewing the thumbscrew on the fore end, so that it can be carried in a trunk or a grip. Shoots cartridges Nos. 6K2336 or 6K2338. Good for 35 to 100 yards. **Weight, packed for shipment, about 6 pounds.**

No. 6K778 Price, 18-inch barrel; weight, 3 pounds........... **$3.50**

WINCHESTER REPEATERS, MODEL 1906, $8.50.

21 CENTS PER 100 FOR 22-CALIBER SHORT CARTRIDGES. SEE PAGE 738.

Made in 22-Caliber Short only.

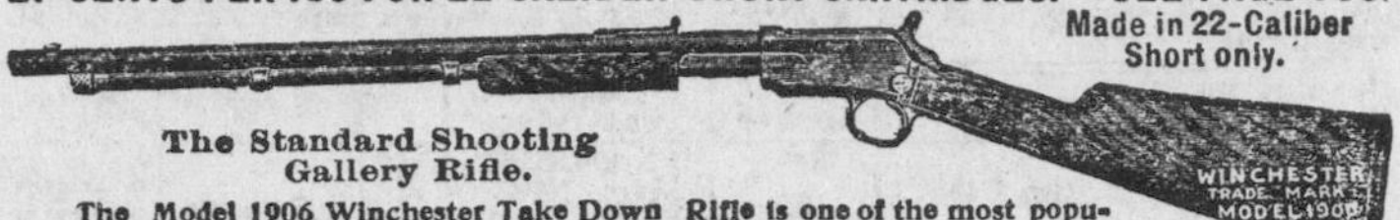

The Standard Shooting Gallery Rifle.

The Model 1906 Winchester Take Down Rifle is one of the most popular 22-caliber repeating rifles on the market. The rifle is cocked and loaded by a sliding action of the forearm and is fitted with 20-inch round barrel, adjustable, Model 1906, rear sight, weighs about 5 pounds, can be easily and quickly taken apart by unscrewing a thumbscrew on the left side of the frame, is made in 22-caliber short rim fire only and is a very popular shooting gallery rifle. The 22-caliber short is good for 35 yards.

THE MODEL 1906 RIFLE is similar to the Model 1890 except it has a plain fore end, round barrel, 20 inches long instead of octagon barrel 24 inches long and shotgun butt instead of rifle butt. Otherwise it is identical with the Model 1890. These rifles cannot be furnished in any other way.

Catalogue Number	Model	Caliber all Rim Fire	Barrel	Weight	Shoots Cartridge Number	Number of Shots	Price
6K781	1906	22-Short	20-in. Round	5 lbs.	6K2336 only	15	$8.50

Weight, packed for shipment, 14 pounds.
For fitting Lyman Sights on any of the above rifles, add 25 cents to the cost of sights for fitting. We box and pack guns free of cost to you. Some houses charge extra for this.

WINCHESTER REPEATING RIFLE, MODEL 1890.

Made in 22-Caliber only.

$10.80

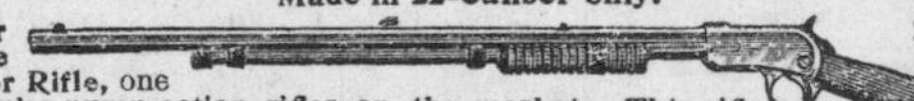

Winchester Model 1890 Take Down 22-Caliber Rifle, one of the most popular pump action rifles on the market. This rifle is cocked and loaded by the action of the forearm; fitted with 24-inch blued octagon barrel; adjustable rear sight, sporting front sight. The rifle is quickly taken apart by unscrewing thumbscrew on the left side of frame. Made in 22-caliber rim fire only, and although made for three different sizes of 22-caliber rim fire cartridges, one rifle will chamber but one size cartridge. A rifle chambered for 22-short cartridges will not take 22-long.

Catalogue No.	Model	Caliber	Barrel, Inches	Weight	Shoots Cartridges Number	No. of Shots	Price
6K784	1890	22-Short	24, Octagon	5¾ pounds	6K2336	15	$10.80
6K786	1890	22-Long	24, Octagon	5¾ pounds	6K2338	12	10.80
6K788	1890	22 Winch. Special	24, Octagon	5¾ pounds	6K2344	10	10.80

Weight, packed for shipment, 14 pounds.
Nos. 6K4698, 6K4701 and 6K4716 Covers fit the above rifle. See page 743.

WINCHESTER MODEL 1892 REPEATING RIFLE.

$12.15 $13.16

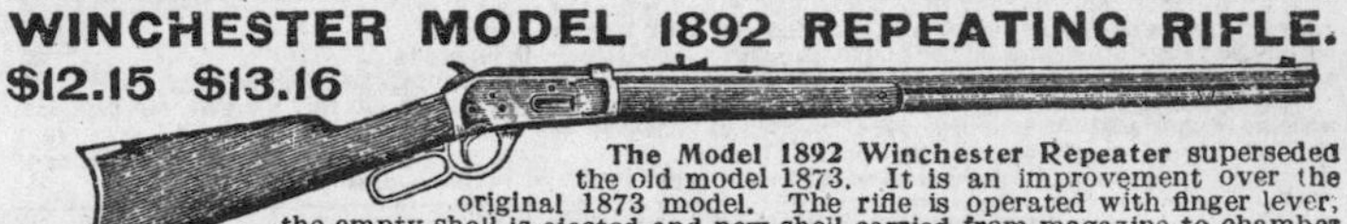

The Model 1892 Winchester Repeater superseded the old model 1873. It is an improvement over the original 1873 model. The rifle is operated with finger lever, the empty shell is ejected and new shell carried from magazine to chamber by the operation of the lever. This gun is light, strong and handsome, and the range varies from 200 to 400 yards, according to caliber.

Catalogue Number	Caliber	Barrel	Weight	Shoots Cartridges Number	No. of Shots	Price
6K790	44-40 W. C. F.	Octagon, 24 in.	6¾ lbs.	6K2409	15	$13.16
6K792	38-40 W. C. F.	Octagon, 24 in.	6¾ lbs.	6K2396	15	13.16
6K794	32-20 W. C. F.	Octagon, 24 in.	6¾ lbs.	6K2384	15	13.16
6K796	25-20 W. C. F.	Octagon, 24 in.	6¾ lbs.	6K2374	15	13.16
6K797	25-20 W. C. F.	Round, 24 in.	6½ lbs.	6K2374	15	12.15

WINCHESTER MODEL 1894.

$13.16 $15.53

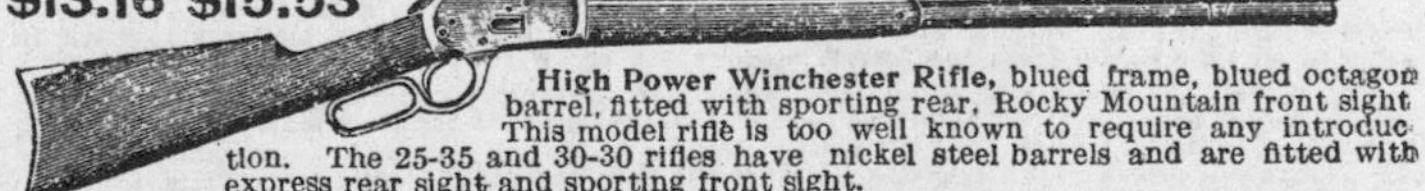

High Power Winchester Rifle, blued frame, blued octagon barrel, fitted with sporting rear, Rocky Mountain front sight. This model rifle is too well known to require any introduction. The 25-35 and 30-30 rifles have nickel steel barrels and are fitted with express rear sight and sporting front sight.

Catalogue Number	Caliber	Barrel	Weight	Shoots Cartridges Number	Number of Shots	Price
6K830	32-40 C. F.	Octagon, 26 in.	7½ lbs.	6K2429	10	$13.16
6K832	38-55 C. F.	Octagon, 26 in.	7½ lbs.	6K2432	10	13.16
6K836	30-30 Winch.	Octagon, 26 in.	7½ lbs.	6K2607	10	15.53
6K838	25-35 Winch.	Octagon, 26 in.	7½ lbs.	6K2601	10	15.53

WINCHESTER MODEL 1907 SELF LOADING RIFLE.

.351-Caliber. High Power.

$18.90

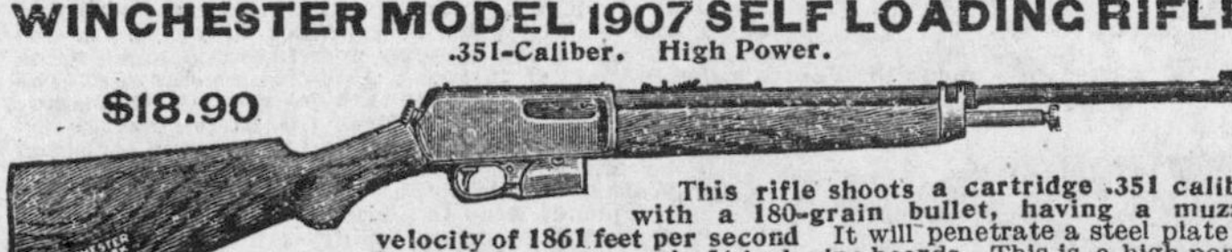

This rifle shoots a cartridge .351 caliber with a 180-grain bullet, having a muzzle velocity of 1861 feet per second. It will penetrate a steel plate ¼ inch thick or twenty-six ⅞-inch pine boards. This is a high power rifle of the latest type, powerful enough for the largest game. The working parts of this rifle are few and strong. There are no moving projections on the outside of the rifle, no pins or screws to work loose. The barrel is stationary like that of an ordinary rifle. The recoil of the exploded cartridge ejects the empty shell, cocks the hammer, and feeds a fresh cartridge from the magazine into the chamber. This rifle is provided with a trigger lock, allowing it to be carried with the hammer at full cock. The take down feature of this rifle is simple. By giving the screw at the rear of the receiver a few turns, the rifle is separated into two parts. This rifle is fitted with a 20-inch round nickeled steel barrel, with sporting front and rear sights.

Catalogue Number	Caliber	Barrel	Weight	Shoots Cartridges Number	Number of Shots	Price
6K841	.351 High Power	20-in. Round	7¾ lbs.	6K2627 6K2628	6	$18.90

Nos. 6K4698 or 6K4701 Covers fit this rifle. See page 743.

A HIGH POWER 6-SHOT SMOKELESS BIG GAME REPEATING RIFLE, NOW ONLY

$7.00

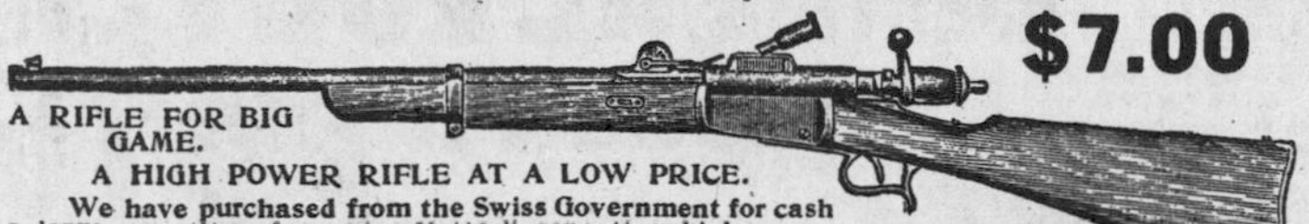

A RIFLE FOR BIG GAME.

A HIGH POWER RIFLE AT A LOW PRICE.

We have purchased from the Swiss Government for cash a large quantity of genuine Vetterli repeating high power rifles, such as were used by the Swiss Government and known as the Model 1881, which we have transformed into sporting rifles, as illustrated above.

The Vetterli Repeating Rifles, as they came to us from the Swiss Government, weighed about 12 pounds, had 33-inch barrels and were only 12 inches from the trigger to the center of the butt plate, which is too short a stock for the average man, and we have transformed these rifles by cutting off the barrel to 26 inches, fitting new stocks, making them 13½ inches from trigger to center of butt, revamped the fore end and transformed it into a 6-shot repeating rifle weighing about 8 pounds, which is very much more desirable and balances much better and looks much better than the original Vetterli rifles when they reached us from Switzerland. **For $7.00 we furnish this Vetterli Repeating Rifle, and 20 rounds of cartridges go free with each rifle,** making an outfit ready to hunt big game at a very low price. Remember, this is not a cheap rifle. It is a rifle which originally cost the Swiss Government at least $16.00 to make, is made from the best high grade material that money can buy, has the Mauser type bolt lever repeating action, one of the strongest bolt actions made, carries five cartridges in the magazine and one in the chamber, making it a 6-shot repeating rifle, and shoots the 41-caliber Swiss smokeless powder cartridges, which may be compared in power to the 30-30 smokeless cartridges, but the bullet is 7-16 inch diameter, weighs 300 grains and strikes a very powerful blow. You will notice the 30-30 bullet is 5-16 inch in diameter and weighs 160 grains. **Remember, $7.00 is our price for the genuine Vetterli smokeless high power rifle, and with each rifle we send 20 cartridges free;** also remember, this is not the heavy, clumsy Vetterli rifle which we purchased from the Swiss Government, but is the transformed Vetterli rifle, which is much more shapely, much better balanced, longer stock, and in every way much more up to date and more desirable. Weight, packed for shipment, about 14 pounds.

No. 6K850 Our Vetterli Smokeless High Power Repeating Rifle, with 20 cartridges. Price.... **$7.00**

No. 6K852 Extra Smokeless Cartridges, 41-caliber Swiss, for the above rifle. Price, per 100.... **$1.95**

OUR 45-70 CALIBER SPRINGFIELD GOVERNMENT BREECH LOADING RIFLE, REDUCED TO $2.75.

$2.75

With Leaf Sight and 20 Rounds of Ammunition Free With Each Rifle.

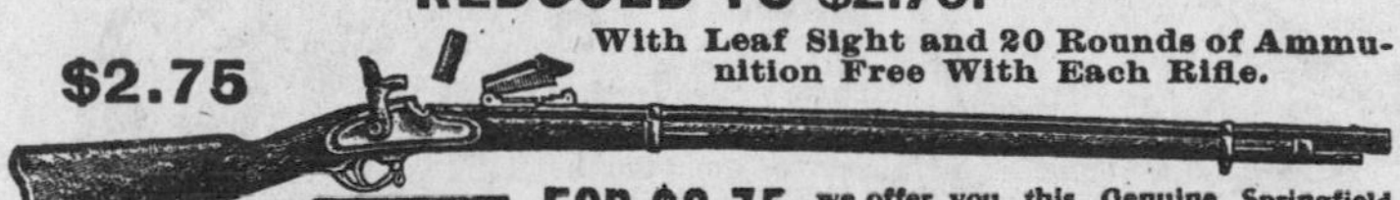

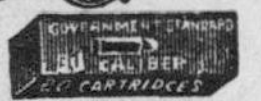

FOR $2.75 we offer you this Genuine Springfield Government Breech Loading Rifle and we give 20 rounds of ammunition free with each rifle. This rifle cost originally from $12.00 to $15.00 to produce. They were made by the United States Government and bear the government stamp. We have just bought a large lot of these guns direct from the U. S. Government Arsenal at Rock Island, Ill., for cash, and while they last we will sell them at $2.75. These are the Genuine Springfield Breech Loading Rifles, taking the 45-70 caliber government cartridge, and any of our customers who have been in the civil war will know that there are no better rifles made at any price, for these are the same rifles that were used in our civil war.

These Genuine Springfield Rifles have 33-inch steel barrels; the empty shell is thrown out when you open the breech block, ready for a new cartridge; they are fitted with sling swivels; the very best quality walnut stock; have the finest quality steel barrels; can be had with or without angular or rod bayonets at the same price in case some of our customers wish to use them for G. A. R. purposes. In case you do not wish the bayonet mention it in your order. These rifles will kill all kinds of game, and our special $2.75 price is within the reach of everybody. You cannot afford to be without a rifle at this price, and we would advise you to send your order early as we anticipate a heavy sale on this new lot of rifles and we may not be able to get any more after these are sold. **Order by number. Weight, packed in box ready for shipment, about 18 pounds.**

No. 6K886 Our Springfield Breech Loading Rifle, with 20 rounds of government ammunition free with each rifle, gives you an outfit ready to go hunting. Price........ **$2.75**

Buy a rifle cleaning rod. It saves the rifle to keep it clean.

OUR SPRINGFIELD SPORTING RIFLE. REDUCED PRICE, $3.75

A RIFLE FOR BIG GAME AT A SMALL PRICE.

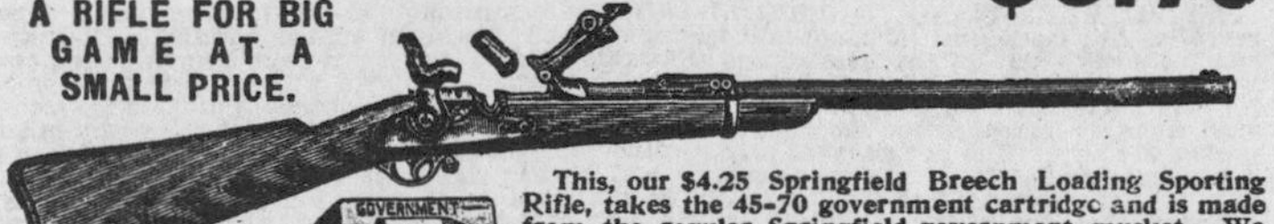

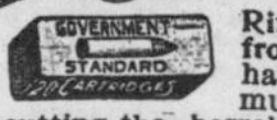

This, our $4.25 Springfield Breech Loading Sporting Rifle, takes the 45-70 government cartridge and is made from the regular Springfield government musket. We have taken the 45-caliber Springfield breech loading musket, which has a 33-inch barrel and weighs 9¼ pounds and transformed it by cutting the barrel down to 26 inches, which is the regular sporting length, cut off the fore stock in such a manner as to make a neat appearing sporting rifle, fitted a sporting front sight instead of the musket sight, and in this manner we have reduced the weight to about 8 pounds, which is a more desirable weight for hunting purposes, especially for big game. The attached illustration will give you a good idea of the appearance of our Springfield breech loading sporting rifle, which we offer for only $3.75. It is without exception the best value ever offered. We bought them direct from the government for cash at a price which permits of our offering this very superior rifle, which could not be duplicated for three times the price we ask, by any factory, and with this rifle we furnish free, twenty rounds of cartridges, making an outfit ready to go hunting for big game at a popular price of only $3.75.

No. 6K888 Our Springfield Breech Loading Sporting Rifle, 26-inch blued steel barrel, weight about 8 pounds and twenty rounds of government cartridges. Price for rifle and cartridges only ....(Weight, packed for shipment, about 14 pounds) **$3.75**

Buy a rifle cleaning rod. It saves the rifle to keep it clean.

OUR AUXILIARY RIFLE BARREL, CALIBER 38-55, FOR 12-GAUGE SHOTGUNS, REDUCED TO $4.75.

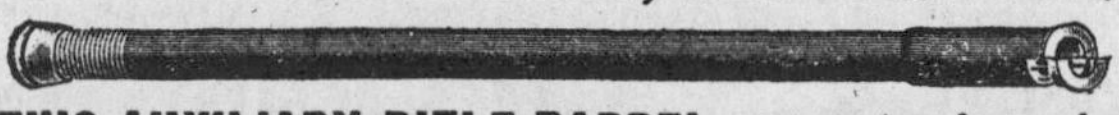

WITH THIS AUXILIARY RIFLE BARREL you can transform a double barrel shotgun into a combination rifle and shotgun by inserting the auxiliary barrel into the shotgun barrel and it will enable you to shoot a 12-gauge shot shell with the one barrel and a rifle cartridge with the other. It may also be used in a single barrel shotgun but it is not intended to be used in magazine repeating shotguns.

UNDERSTAND, that for fine target shooting this barrel is impracticable, but, for large game shooting, a hunter can, with little practice, bring down large game at a distance of 50 to 100 yards by using the shotgun front sight and sighting over the rib of the gun instead of using a rear sight.

No. 6K984 Auxiliary Rifle Barrel, 38-55 caliber, to fit a 30 or 32-inch 12-gauge shotgun. State length and gauge of barrel wanted. Weight, 1¾ to 2 pounds. Price.. **$4.75**

If by registered mail, postage extra, 40 cents.

BURST GUN BARRELS. Gun barrels can only burst either by overloading nitro powder or having an obstruction in the barrel, and we are not responsible for burst gun or rifle barrel. For further information see page 717.

SHIP GUNS BY FREIGHT. We advise ordering fifty pounds or a hundred pounds of ammunition or other goods with a gun and ship by freight instead of express, which will make a big saving to you in the transportation charges.

RUSTY OR SHOPWORN GUNS. We cannot accept guns which are rusty, damaged or have the finish worn off. Do not return such guns, but write us when you have such a gun to return, and we will advise you what to do.

AIR RIFLES

THE NEW QUACKENBUSH AIR RIFLE

$3.00

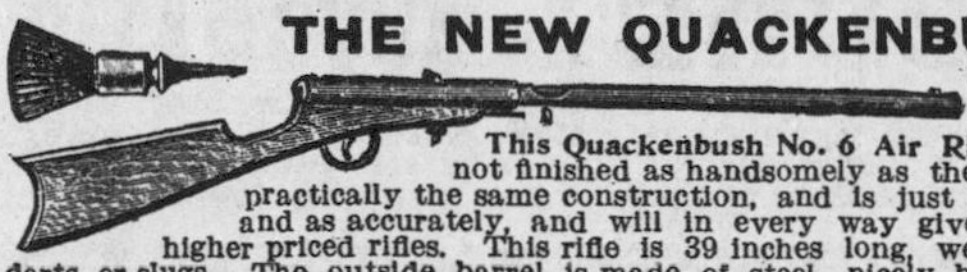

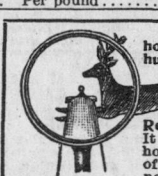

This Quackenbush No. 6 Air Rifle, very latest model, while not finished as handsomely as their higher priced model, is of practically the same construction, and is just as strong, will shoot as hard and as accurately, and will in every way give as good satisfaction as the higher priced rifles. This rifle is 39 inches long, weighs 43 ounces, shoots either darts or slugs. The outside barrel is made of steel, nicely blued; the inside barrel is of brass; the stock is made of black walnut, neatly finished. No cast iron or soft metal used in this rifle. This rifle shoots size 17-100 darts and slugs. Each rifle is packed in a neat paper box, with six steel darts, three paper targets and one cleaning rod.

No. 6K905 No. 6 Air Rifle, blued finish. Price.... **$3.00**

No. 6K912 Caliber 17-100 Darts, for above rifle. Price per dozen.... **23c**

No. 6K914 Slugs, caliber 17-100, for Quackenbush Air Rifle. Price per 100.. **9c**

THE NEW MODEL KING AIR RIFLE, SINGLE SHOT, 65 CENTS.

Our King Rifles we Guarantee the Highest Grade Made.

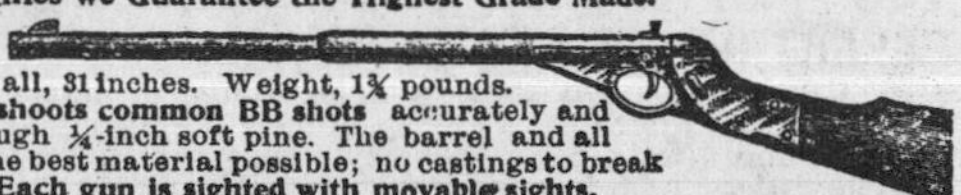

All metal, nickel plated, shoots BB shot. Length of barrel, 19 inches; length over all, 31 inches. Weight, 1¾ pounds. **The New Model King Air Rifle shoots common BB shots** accurately and with sufficient force to go through ¾-inch soft pine. The barrel and all working parts are made from the best material possible; no castings to break in case it falls to the ground. **Each gun is sighted with movable sights.**

No. 6K932 The New Model King Air Rifle. Price.... **64c**

If by mail, postage extra, 35 cents.

No. 6K3615 BB Shot for this Air Rifle. Per pound.... **13c**

THE COLUMBIAN 1,000-SHOT AIR RIFLE, $1.22.

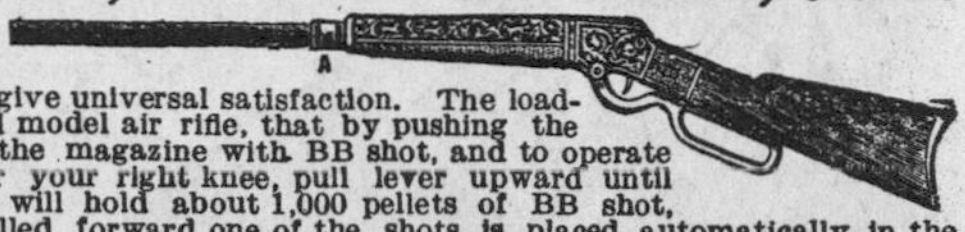

The Columbian 1,000-Shot Air Rifle, as now made, with improved lock parts and magazine, is a rifle which will give universal satisfaction. The loading device is similar to the old model air rifle, that by pushing the sleeve "A" forward you fill the magazine with BB shot, and to operate the rifle place the butt under your right knee, pull lever upward until the trigger catches. This rifle will hold about 1,000 pellets of BB shot, and every time the lever is pulled forward one of the shots is placed automatically in the barrel. Should an imperfect shot get into the barrel, it can easily be removed by cocking the rifle and inserting a wire from the muzzle, which pushes the shot into the chamber, from which it can be easily removed. The entire length of the Columbian 1,000-Shot Air Rifle is 35 inches; the barrel is nickel plated and the frame is japanned; the stock is of good seasoned hardwood. This rifle weighs about 4¼ pounds. It looks like a Winchester, works like a Winchester and pleases the boys. Cannot be sent by mail, as the postoffice will not take anything over 4 pounds.

No. 6K946 The Columbian Air Rifle. Price.... **$1.22**

No. 6K3615 BB Shot for this Air Rifle. Per pound.... **13c**

COMBINATION No. 1 REAR SIGHTS.

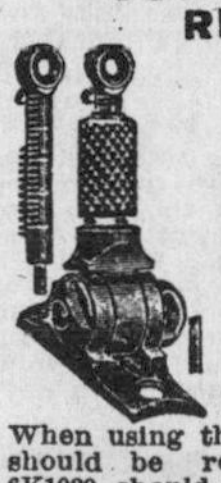

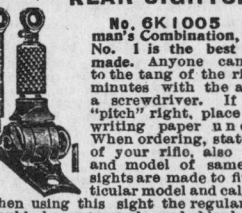

No. 6K1005 Our Rifleman's Combination, Rear Sight No. 1 is the best rear sight made. Anyone can attach it to the tang of the rifle in a few minutes with the assistance of a screwdriver. If they don't "pitch" right, place a piece of writing paper under them. When ordering, state the name of your rifle, also the caliber and model of same, as these sights are made to fit each particular model and caliber of rifle. When using this sight the regular rear sight should be removed and blank piece No. 6K1030 should be used. Price.... **$2.00**

Extra for fitting sight to rifle, allow.... **.25**

If by mail, postage extra, 6 cents.

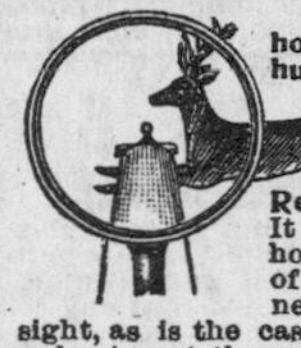

This illustration shows how game appears to the hunter when using the Lyman Patent Combination Rear Sight when sighting. It resembles a ring or hoop and when using one of these sights it is not necessary to get a real fine sight, as is the case with open sights, in order to get the game. When the game is seen in the ring or hoop, like the illustration, pull the trigger and you generally get it.

TO REMOVE SIGHTS drive from left to right, facing the muzzle, and use a brass or copper punch so that it will not deface the sight. To put on a sight, drive from right to left.

NOTICE

WHEN ORDERING, GIVE THE NAME AND CALIBER OF YOUR RIFLE, ALSO, IF POSSIBLE, GIVE THE MODEL OF SAME SO WE CAN SEND YOU THE CORRECT SIGHTS.

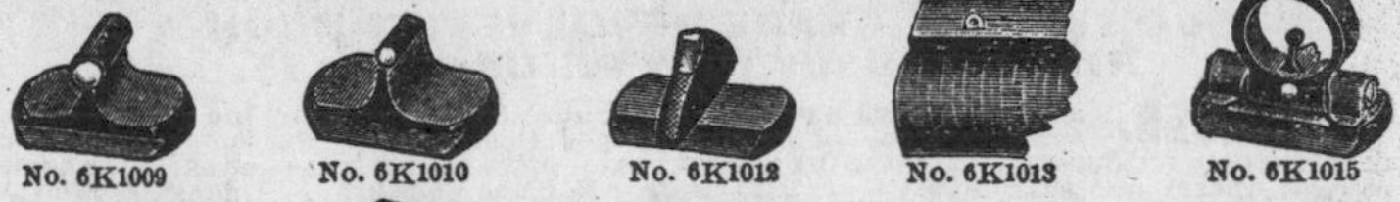

No. 6K1009 No. 6K1010 No. 6K1012 No. 6K1013 No. 6K1015

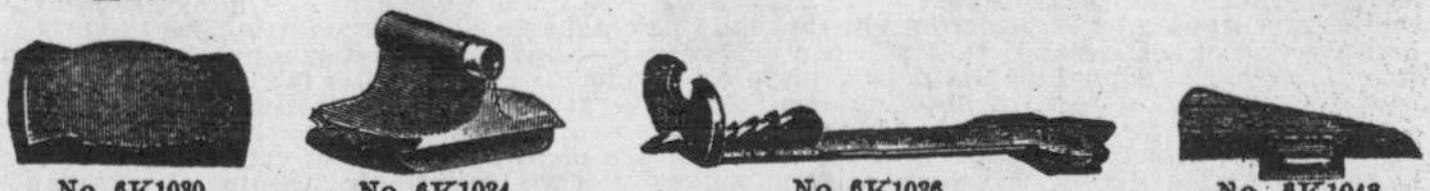

No. 6K1030 No. 6K1034 No. 6K1036 No. 6K1048

NOTICE—Always mention caliber, brand and model of rifle when ordering.

Catalogue Number	Factory Number	Name of Sight	Kind of Sight	Notice	Price of Sight	Postage, extra
6K1009	20	Ivory Jack Sight	Front	Always mention caliber, brand and model of Rifle when ordering Sights.	69c	2 cents
6K1010	3	Ivory Bead Sight	Front		69c	2 cents
6K1012	4	Ivory Hunting Sight	Front		34c	3 cents
6K1013	10	Ivory Shotgun Sight	Front		30c	2 cents
6K1014	11	Ivory Shotgun Sight	Rear		30c	2 cents
6K1015	5	Ivory Folding Globe	Front		69c	3 cents
6K1030	12	Blank Piece, to replace rear sight	Rear		15c	3 cents
6K1034	S. R. S.	Coin Silver Bead	Front		50c	2 cents
6K1035	S. R. G.	Solid Gold Bead	Front		70c	2 cents
6K1036	S. R.	Sporting Rear	Rear		48c	2 cents
6K1048	K. B.	German Silver Rocky Mountain	Front		45c	2 cents

NOTICE—The Coin Silver and Solid Gold Bead Sights are much used by Rocky Mountain hunters. They are very effective in the woods, open country as well as for dark days and twilight shooting. The diameter of bead is about 3-32 of an inch.

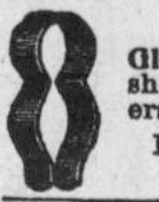

No. 6K1055 Our Own Patent Globe Front Sight for single barrel shotguns, a wonderful help to shooters. Made for 10, 12 and 16-gauge guns. Price.... **38c**

If by mail, postage extra, 2 cents.

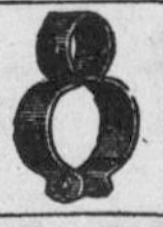

No. 6K1057 Our Own Patent Globe Front Sight for double barrel shotguns, a sight which is greatly appreciated by shooters. For 10, 12 and 16-gauge double barrel breech loaders. Price.... **40c**

If by mail, postage extra, 2 cents.

THE L. H. FOSTER REAR SIGHT FOR SINGLE BARREL SHOTGUNS.

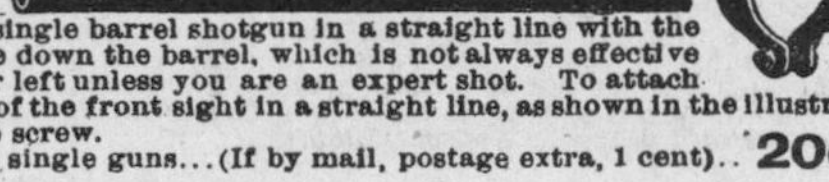

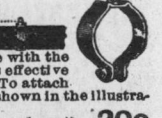

No. 6K1060 Our L. H. Foster Rear Sight for Single Barrel Shotguns is a wonderful assistance to shooters. It helps you to "line up" a single barrel shotgun in a straight line with the object, whereas you now cast your eye down the barrel, which is not always effective and causes you to shoot to the right or left unless you are an expert shot. To attach the sight, place it 12 to 14 inches back of the front sight in a straight line, as shown in the illustration, and fasten it in position with the screw.

Price, each, for all 12 and 16-gauge single guns...(If by mail, postage extra, 1 cent).. **20c**

A. J. AUBREY AUTOMATIC ENGRAVED REVOLVER IMPROVED MODEL, REDUCED TO $4.25

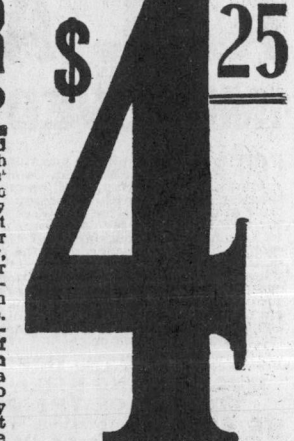

$4.25 IS OUR PRICE for this **A. J. Aubrey Automatic Self-Cocking Automatic Shell Ejecting Revolver,** elaborately hand engraved, beautifully finished, either blued or nickel plated. Compare this handsome automatic engraved revolver at $4.25 with any of the plain finished automatic revolvers offered in competition for far more money, and you will realize what wonderful value we are offering in this revolver at this price, which represents actual factory cost for material and labor with but one small margin of profit added.

DON'T BUY A CHEAP LITTLE 22-CALIBER PISTOL, don't buy any one of these ordinary double action revolvers that are not automatic shell ejecting, just because you can buy them for a few cents less money, and in selecting a revolver don't select one of the more common makes. If you are going to buy a revolver get a safe one, get a good one and one that you will enjoy and keep forever, one that is made on scientific mechanical lines, get one of the very best, get the most for your money, or an A. J. Aubrey Revolver.

IF YOU WILL SEND US $4.25, let us send you this handsome full hand engraved 32 or 38-caliber revolver, we will send it to you with the understanding and agreement that you can give it ninety days' (three months') free trial test, during which time you can put it to every sort of a test, and if for any reason you are not perfectly satisfied with your purchase, you can return the revolver to us at our expense, and we will immediately return your money, together with any express charges you may have paid; and remember, when we send you the revolver we will also send with it our written binding twenty-year guarantee, by the terms and conditions of which if any piece or part gives out by reason of defect in material or workmanship, we will replace or repair it free of charge.

WHILE WE AIM to handle nearly all the so-called standard makes of revolvers, and a number of them we are able to sell at prices very much lower than you can possibly buy elsewhere in any quantity, and on a few we, unfortunately, by reason of contracts we must enter into with the manufacturers in order to get the revolvers, we can only promise on some few makes a price only as low as the very lowest that anyone else can name; but at a price far lower than anyone else can possibly give you, a price that means about double for your money what you can get elsewhere we can sell you an A. J. Aubrey under our binding guarantee, with every possible assurance; so when you are thinking of buying a revolver take time to go into it thoroughly, take time to consider and even if it costs a few cents more on the start you will forever be glad that you paid the few cents more and ordered a high grade genuine A. J. Aubrey as illustrated on this and other pages in this department.

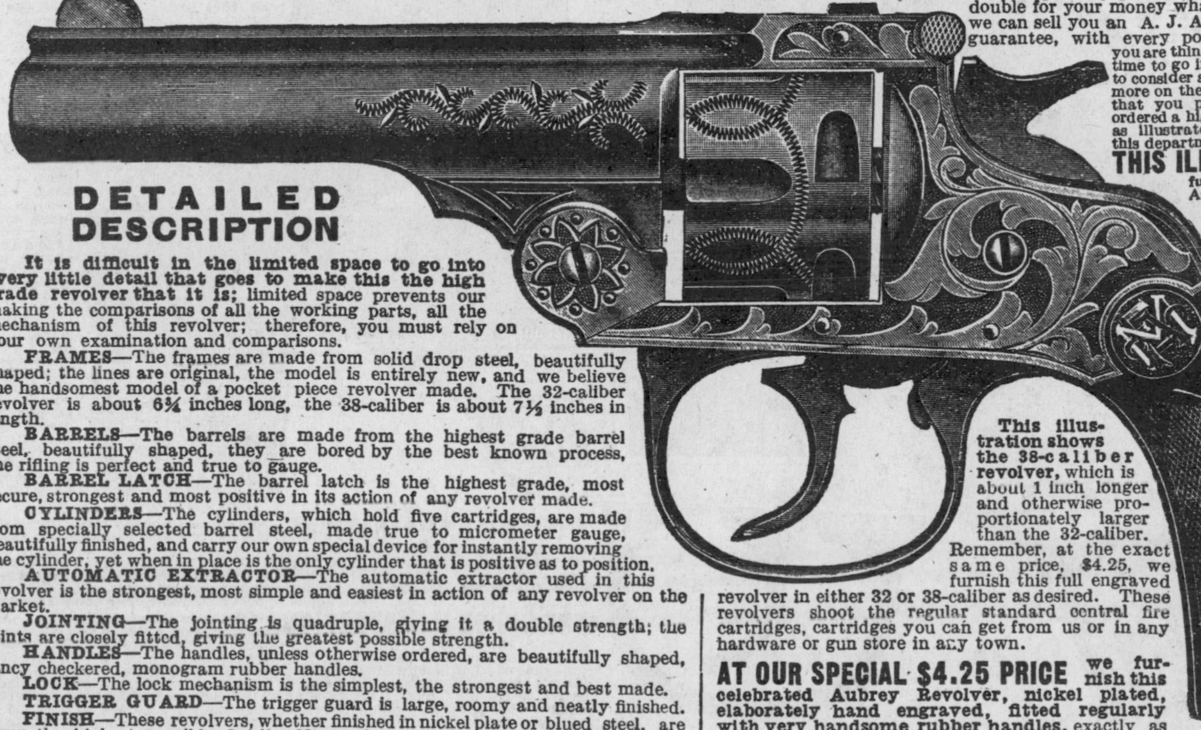

THIS ILLUSTRATION of our 38-caliber, full hand engraved, genuine Aubrey hammer, automatic self cocking revolver will give you but a fair idea of the appearance of the arm; you must see it to appreciate its real worth; to know just how much we are giving for your money; you must see, examine it and compare it with guns that sell at double our price.

This illustration shows the 38-caliber revolver, which is about 1 inch longer and otherwise proportionately larger than the 32-caliber. Remember, at the exact same price, $4.25, we furnish this full engraved revolver in either 32 or 38-caliber as desired. These revolvers shoot the regular standard central fire cartridges, cartridges you can get from us or in any hardware or gun store in any town.

DETAILED DESCRIPTION

It is difficult in the limited space to go into every little detail that goes to make this the high grade revolver that it is; limited space prevents our making the comparisons of all the working parts, all the mechanism of this revolver; therefore, you must rely on your own examination and comparisons.

FRAMES—The frames are made from solid drop steel, beautifully shaped; the lines are original, the model is entirely new, and we believe the handsomest model of a pocket piece revolver made. The 32-caliber revolver is about 6¾ inches long, the 38-caliber is about 7½ inches in length.

BARRELS—The barrels are made from the highest grade barrel steel, beautifully shaped, they are bored by the best known process, the rifling is perfect and true to gauge.

BARREL LATCH—The barrel latch is the highest grade, most secure, strongest and most positive in its action of any revolver made.

CYLINDERS—The cylinders, which hold five cartridges, are made from specially selected barrel steel, made true to micrometer gauge, beautifully finished, and carry our own special device for instantly removing the cylinder, yet when in place is the only cylinder that is positive as to position.

AUTOMATIC EXTRACTOR—The automatic extractor used in this revolver is the strongest, most simple and easiest in action of any revolver on the market.

JOINTING—The jointing is quadruple, giving it a double strength; the joints are closely fitted, giving the greatest possible strength.

HANDLES—The handles, unless otherwise ordered, are beautifully shaped, fancy checkered, monogram rubber handles.

LOCK—The lock mechanism is the simplest, the strongest and best made.

TRIGGER GUARD—The trigger guard is large, roomy and neatly finished.

FINISH—These revolvers, whether finished in nickel plate or blued steel, are given the highest possible finish. No revolver can be made carrying a more elaborate finish than do the Aubrey Revolvers. These revolvers are either 32 or 38-caliber and combine every high grade, up to date feature of every other high grade revolver, with the defects of none. Only the very best of material is used throughout. When every piece and part is in the rough it is first tested to gauge, and in every operation every piece and part is worked through the machines in jigs and, when completed, again tested to gauge, and as a result you have the finest effect in a finished revolver possible to produce.

HAND ENGRAVING—The elaborate hand engraving shown on this revolver, which we furnish at $4.25 in either 32 or 38-caliber, is done in our own factory at Meriden by a special artist. Every line, every ornamentation, every figure shown in this hand engraving is cut with a sharp tool at the hands of an artist engraver. Unfortunately, you can get but a slight idea of the beautiful effect worked out in this hand engraving from the illustration, but the revolver is engraved in all its parts, especially is the frame elaborately engraved on both sides, the barrel, barrel tips, the joints, the hinge and the cylinder. It is completed throughout with a view of giving you such a revolver as you could not buy elsewhere, even at double the price.

AT OUR SPECIAL $4.25 PRICE we furnish this **celebrated Aubrey Revolver, nickel plated, elaborately hand engraved, fitted regularly with very handsome rubber handles,** exactly as illustrated hereon, send it to you with the understanding and agreement that if it is not perfectly satisfactory you can return it to us at any time within ninety days (three months), and we will immediately return your money, together with any express charges you may have paid. With every revolver we send our written binding twenty-year guarantee, by the terms and conditions of which if any piece or part gives out by reason of defect in material or workmanship within twenty years we will replace or repair it free of charge.

We furnish this handsome, full engraved, hammer, automatic self cocking, self ejecting revolver at $4.25 and at the following prices, according to finish.

Catalogue No.	Caliber, Center Fire	Length of Barrel	Finish, All Hand Engraved	No. of Shots	Shoots Cartridge No.	Weight, ounces	Handles	Price
6K1121	32 c. f.	3 in.	Nickel Plated	5	6K2377	12	Rubber	$4.25
6K1122	38 c. f.	3¼ in.	Nickel Plated	5	6K2388	15	Rubber	
6K1123	32 c. f.	3 in.	Blued Steel	5	6K2377	12	Rubber	$4.50
6K1124	38 c. f.	3¼ in.	Blued Steel	5	6K2388	15	Rubber	

Extra for pearl handles on any of the above revolvers..............................**$1.00**

If by mail, postage extra, 32-caliber, 18 cents; 38-caliber, 22 cents.

If by insured mail, add 5 cents to postage rate and say, "ship by insured mail."

FOR $1.00 EXTRA WE WILL FURNISH YOU THIS REVOLVER FITTED WITH A PAIR OF BEAUTIFUL FULL FINISHED, HANDSOMELY MOTTLED PEARL HANDLES, IN PLACE OF THE RUBBER HANDLES, AS ILLUSTRATED.

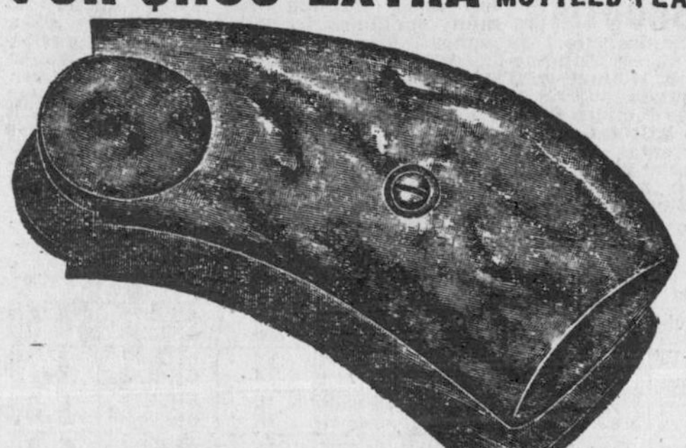

IF YOU WANT A VERY HANDSOME REVOLVER, a revolver that will have a strictly different appearance from any ordinary revolver, we advise you in your own interest, especially when ordering an Aubrey Revolver, that you include $1.00 extra and let us fit to the revolver a pair of these beautiful pearl handles.

UNFORTUNATELY, this illustration, printed on an ordinary printing press, with common paper, will in nowise do these handles justice. It will give you but a faint idea of the appearance that we can bring out in the finished revolver fitted with these pearl handles.

IF YOU SEND US $1.00 EXTRA with your order and ask us to put on a special pair of pearl handles, we know that you will be more than satisfied with your purchase. We know that after you have seen and examined the revolver you will have with these specially finished, beautiful pearl handles, you would not part with the pearl handles and take the rubber handle revolver even if the difference in price was several times $1.00. Our special price of $1.00 for an extra pair of pearl handles, the kind of pearl handles we put on, is a most extraordinary offer. We are very glad, indeed, to fit the Aubrey Revolver with specially fine pearl handles, handles that have been specially selected and of the highest grade, even if in so fitting the $1.00 only covers the actual difference in cost to us, for it adds so much to the general appearance of the revolver. We know the customer buying will be so much better pleased at having had a specially selected pair of pearl handles fitted that it will tend to make the Aubrey Revolver especially conspicuous; it will be sure to delight the buyer and will ever after be to our advantage as an advertisement of this celebrated Aubrey Revolver.

REMEMBER, with every Aubrey Revolver or other fire arm bearing the name of A. J. Aubrey you get our twenty-year written binding guarantee, and you have the privilege of returning the revolver or gun to us at any time within three months and getting your money back.

A. J. AUBREY HAMMERLESS $4.50
IMPROVED MODEL REVOLVERS REDUCED TO $4.50

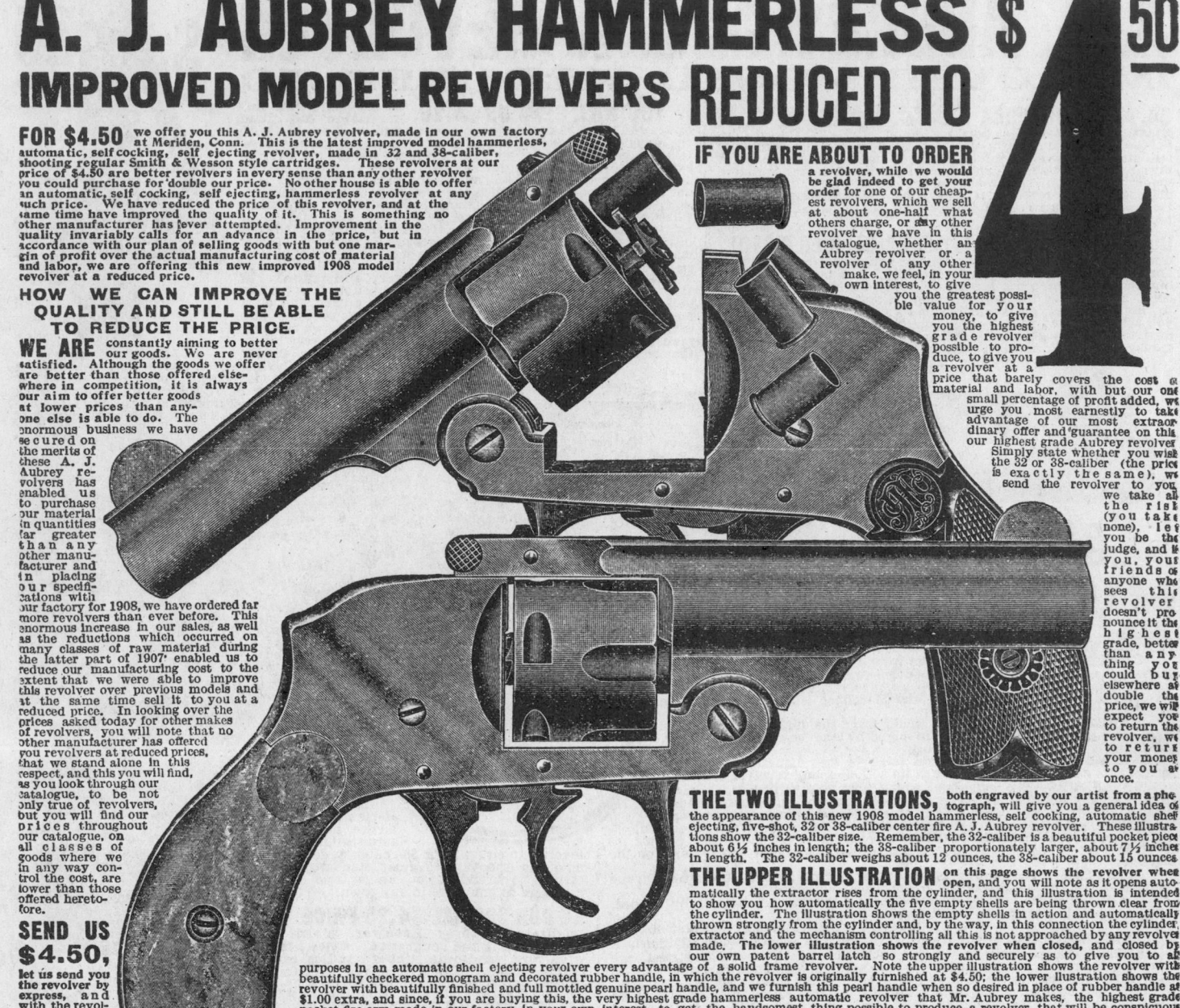

FOR $4.50 we offer you this A. J. Aubrey revolver, made in our own factory at Meriden, Conn. This is the latest improved model hammerless, automatic, self cocking, self ejecting revolver, made in 32 and 38-caliber, shooting regular Smith & Wesson style cartridges. These revolvers at our price of $4.50 are better revolvers in every sense than any other revolver you could purchase for double our price. No other house is able to offer an automatic, self cocking, self ejecting, hammerless revolver at any such price. We have reduced the price of this revolver, and at the same time have improved the quality of it. This is something no other manufacturer has ever attempted. Improvement in the quality invariably calls for an advance in the price, but in accordance with our plan of selling goods with but one margin of profit over the actual manufacturing cost of material and labor, we are offering this new improved 1908 model revolver at a reduced price.

HOW WE CAN IMPROVE THE QUALITY AND STILL BE ABLE TO REDUCE THE PRICE.

WE ARE constantly aiming to better our goods. We are never satisfied. Although the goods we offer are better than those offered elsewhere in competition, it is always our aim to offer better goods at lower prices than anyone else is able to do. The enormous business we have secured on the merits of these A. J. Aubrey revolvers has enabled us to purchase our material in quantities far greater than any other manufacturer and in placing our specifications with our factory for 1908, we have ordered far more revolvers than ever before. This enormous increase in our sales, as well as the reductions which occurred on many classes of raw material during the latter part of 1907 enabled us to reduce our manufacturing cost to the extent that we were able to improve this revolver over previous models and at the same time sell it to you at a reduced price. In looking over the prices asked today for other makes of revolvers, you will note that no other manufacturer has offered you revolvers at reduced prices, that we stand alone in this respect, and this you will find, as you look through our catalogue, to be not only true of revolvers, but you will find our prices throughout our catalogue, on all classes of goods where we in any way control the cost, are lower than those offered heretofore.

SEND US $4.50,

let us send you the revolver by express, and with the revolver, of course, send you our written binding twenty years' guarantee, a guarantee given by no other maker, a guarantee that goes with no other goods, a guarantee that is furnished only with the A. J. Aubrey goods; let us send you the revolver with the understanding and agreement that after you receive it you are to have your own time to examine it, that you are to have the privilege of putting it to every possible test, compare it for shooting, for strength, compare it in every way with revolvers of other makes, even though the price be double the price we ask, and if during the ninety days you have any

IF YOU ARE ABOUT TO ORDER

a revolver, while we would be glad indeed to get your order for one of our cheapest revolvers, which we sell at about one-half what others charge, or any other revolver we have in this catalogue, whether an Aubrey revolver or a revolver of any other make, we feel, in your own interest, to give you the greatest possible value for your money, to give you the highest grade revolver possible to produce, to give you a revolver at a price that barely covers the cost of material and labor, with but our one small percentage of profit added, we urge you most earnestly to take advantage of our most extraordinary offer and guarantee on this our highest grade Aubrey revolver. Simply state whether you wish the 32 or 38-caliber (the price is exactly the same), we send the revolver to you, we take the risk (you take none), let you be the judge, and let you, your friends or anyone who sees this revolver doesn't pronounce it the highest grade, better than anything you could buy elsewhere at double the price, we will expect you to return the revolver, we to return your money to you at once.

THE TWO ILLUSTRATIONS, both engraved by our artist from a photograph, will give you a general idea of the appearance of this new 1908 model hammerless, self cocking, automatic shell ejecting, five-shot, 32 or 38-caliber center fire A. J. Aubrey revolver. These illustrations show the 32-caliber size. Remember, the 32-caliber is a beautiful pocket piece about 6½ inches in length; the 38-caliber proportionately larger, about 7½ inches in length. The 32-caliber weighs about 12 ounces, the 38-caliber about 15 ounces.

THE UPPER ILLUSTRATION on this page shows the revolver when open, and you will note as it opens automatically the extractor rises from the cylinder, and this illustration is intended to show you how automatically the five empty shells are being thrown clear from the cylinder. The illustration shows the empty shells in action and automatically thrown strongly from the cylinder and, by the way, in this connection the cylinder, extractor and the mechanism controlling all this is not approached by any revolver made. The lower illustration shows the revolver when closed, and closed by our own patent barrel latch so strongly and securely as to give you to all purposes in an automatic shell ejecting revolver every advantage of a solid frame revolver. Note the upper illustration shows the revolver with beautifully checkered monogram and decorated rubber handle, in which the revolver is originally furnished at $4.50; the lower illustration shows the revolver with beautifully finished and full mottled genuine pearl handle, and we furnish this pearl handle when so desired in place of rubber handle at $1.00 extra, and since, if you are buying this, the very highest grade hammerless automatic revolver that Mr. Aubrey makes, the highest grade pocket fire arm made in our factory, in your own interest, to get the handsomest thing possible to produce, a revolver that will be conspicuous among other revolvers for its beauty, we urge you, in your own interest, when ordering this revolver to enclose $1.00 extra and ask us to send you the revolver with this specially finished, specially mottled pearl handle.

REMEMBER, the illustration shows the 32-caliber, but the price is exactly the same whether you order a 32 or 38-caliber. The 38-caliber differs from the 32 only in that it is somewhat larger and somewhat heavier, as mentioned above.

reason to be dissatisfied with your purchase, if you don't think this revolver cheaper in price, a better value, a better purchase at $4.50 than any ordinary revolver made by other makers even at $10.00; in short, if there is any reason in the world why you do not wish to keep the revolver, you need not give your reasons to us, simply return the revolver to us at our expense and we will immediately return your money.

OUR WRITTEN BINDING 20 YEARS' CERTIFICATE OF GUARANTEE.

NO OTHER MANUFACTURER of revolvers will guarantee his product for 20 years. We alone have enough confidence and faith in these A. J. Aubrey revolvers to offer them under such liberal conditions. Remember, every A. J. Aubrey revolver is guaranteed for 20 years against defective material or workmanship. We will repair or replace any defective parts free of cost.

WON'T YOU LET US SEND YOU ONE OF THESE REVOLVERS TO TRY?

WE WOULD LIKE SO MUCH to send you a pearl handle hammerless revolver as illustrated and described hereon. Unfortunately the illustration does not do this beautiful pearl handle revolver justice. It must be seen to be appreciated.

IF YOU WILL LET US SEND YOU this pearl handle revolver to try, then won't you please send us $5.50 and tell us to send you the pearl handle revolver, as illustrated? Order by catalogue number, enclose $5.50, and we will send the revolver to you with the understanding and agreement that you can give it three months' trial, during which time you can put it to every possible test, compare it with revolvers that sell generally at double our price, and if for any reason you are not perfectly satisfied with your purchase, if you don't feel that you have gotten such revolver value as you could not have gotten elsewhere, you can return the revolver to us at our expense, and we will immediately return your money.

THIS REDUCED PRICE OF $4.50 for this revolver, 32 or 38-caliber, nickel plated with rubber handles, or $5.50 for the same revolver fitted with selected, highest quality pearl handles, is based on the actual factory cost of material and labor with but one small percentage of profit added. These revolvers, as stated, are all made in our own factory at Meriden, Conn. In figuring the cost of these revolvers, we have no expense of salesmen's salaries or traveling expenses to consider, no fancy advertising, no big office force, and therefore, our cost is naturally far lower than that of any other factory. Selling these goods on our one small profit plan accounts for the big difference in price between the A. J. Aubrey revolvers and any other make offered in competition.

FOR ACCURATE SHOOTING, for rapid shooting, for every factor of safety, for finish, for alignment, beauty, style, construction, for fine mechanical effect throughout, this revolver has positively no superior, and since you can buy it at less than one-half the price at which revolvers that will in no way compare with it sell, we urge you, in your own interest, when selecting a revolver, to order this, the highest grade revolver Mr. Aubrey makes, the highest grade revolver made in our factory, the Meriden Fire Arms Company, of Meriden, Connecticut. Buy it on the lowest price basis calculation possible to operate on, buy it for just what it costs us, plus our one small percentage of profit. We furnish this revolver exactly as illustrated above, one exactly the same as the other, excepting the difference in the handle, one revolver being shown with the highest grade rubber handle, the other with the highest grade genuine pearl handle made. We furnish this revolver in either 32 or 38-caliber, as desired, as listed below. In ordering be sure to order by the number as listed below.

Catalogue Number	Caliber	Length of Barrels	Finish	Handles	No. of Shots	Weight, ounces	Shoots Cartridge	Price
6K1141	32 C.F.	3 inches	Nickel Plated	Rubber	5-shot	12	6K2377	$4.50
6K1142	38 C.F.	3¼ inches	Nickel Plated	Rubber	5-shot	15	6K2388	
6K1143	32 C.F.	3 inches	Blued Steel	Rubber	5-shot	12	6K2377	4.75
6K1144	38 C.F.	3¼ inches	Blued Steel	Rubber	5-shot	15	6K2388	
6K1145	32 C.F.	5 inches	Nickel Plated	Rubber	5-shot	15	6K2377	5.00
6K1146	38 C.F.	5 inches	Nickel Plated	Rubber	5-shot	18	6K2388	
6K1147	32 C.F.	5 inches	Blued Steel	Rubber	5-shot	15	6K2377	5.25
6K1148	38 C.F.	5 inches	Blued Steel	Rubber	5-shot	18	6K2388	

Pearl Handle, extra, $1.00.
If by mail, postage extra, 32-caliber, 18 to 22 cents; 38-caliber, 22 to 26 cents.

REVOLVERS

WE ARE THE LARGEST HANDLERS OF REVOLVERS IN THE WORLD SELLING DIRECT TO THE CONSUMER

YOU WILL FIND on the following pages a very complete line of revolvers of all makes, calibers and descriptions. In selecting the revolvers shown on the following pages, we have been careful to select only such makes, styles and sizes as we know are practical and will give satisfaction. The values we offer in revolvers shown on the following pages are excelled only by the values we offer in the Aubrey revolvers shown on the previous pages.

OUR GUARANTEE. Every revolver we sell is carefully inspected and examined by experienced gunsmiths, and we guarantee every revolver sold by us, regardless of price, against defective material or workmanship. It is sold with the understanding that if not entirely satisfactory in every way, it may be returned to us at our expense, and we will refund your money and any transportation charges you may have paid.

INSURED MAIL. We advise where a revolver only is ordered, that you have the revolver sent by insured mail, which guarantees delivery, and which costs but 5 cents extra over the regular postage for each revolver under $5.00, and 10 cents extra over the regular postage for a revolver costing over $10.00. High priced revolvers, such as Smith & Wesson and the Colt, we recommend being sent by registered mail, which costs 8 cents over the regular rate of postage, or by express.

REMEMBER that the postoffice does not guarantee delivery on revolvers or any other goods lost in the regular mail, but by sending goods either by insured or registered mail, delivery is guaranteed.

DOUBLE ACTION, SELF-COCKING REVOLVERS.

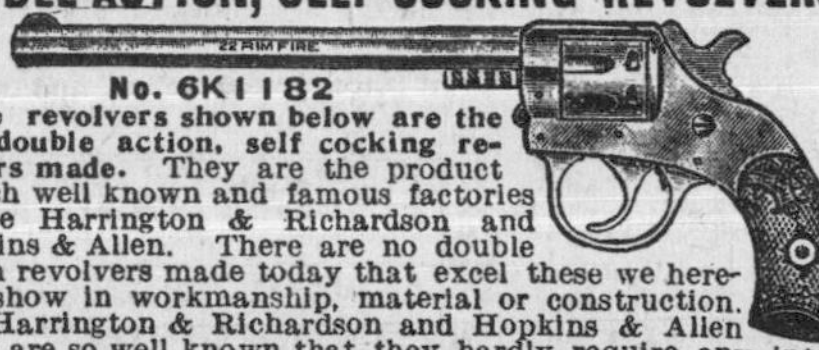

No. 6K1182

The revolvers shown below are the best double action, self cocking revolvers made. They are the product of such well known and famous factories as the Harrington & Richardson and Hopkins & Allen. There are no double action revolvers made today that excel these we herewith show in workmanship, material or construction. The Harrington & Richardson and Hopkins & Allen goods are so well known that they hardly require any introduction. These revolvers all have octagon rifled barrels, are full nickel plated and fitted with neat rubber stocks, and the cylinders are all nicely fluted. By pulling the trigger, the revolver is cocked automatically.

22-CALIBER DOUBLE ACTION REVOLVERS.

See above for full description of these revolvers.

Cat. No.	Caliber	Length of Barrel	Style of Barrel	No. of Shots	Shoots Cartridges No.	Weight	Price
6K1181	22 r. f.	2½ in.	Octagon	7	6K2336 6K2338 6K2535	12 oz.	Rubber Stocks $2.34 Pearl Stocks $3.30
6K1182	22 r. f.	6 in.	Octagon	7	6K2336 6K2338 6K2535	13 oz.	Rubber Stocks $2.95 Pearl Stocks $3.85

If by mail, postage extra, on No. 6K1181, 15 cents.
If by mail, postage extra, on No. 6K1182, 16 cents.
See remarks about insured and registered mail at top of page.

32-CALIBER DOUBLE ACTION REVOLVERS

$2.34

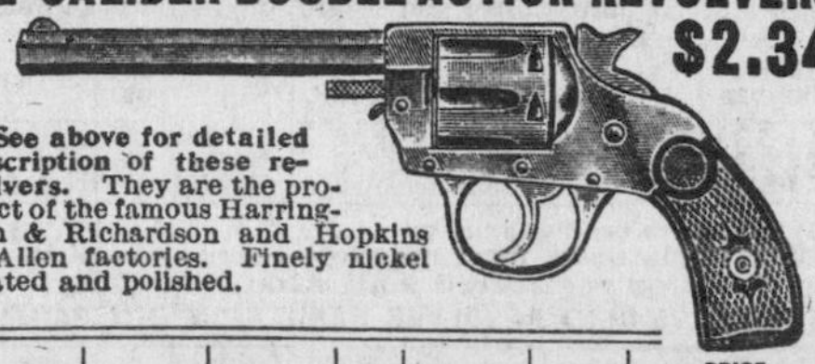

See above for detailed description of these revolvers. They are the product of the famous Harrington & Richardson and Hopkins & Allen factories. Finely nickel plated and polished.

Cat. No.	Caliber	Length of Barrel	No. of Shots	Shoots Cartridges No.	Weight oz.	PRICE Rubber Stocks	PRICE Pearl Stocks
6K1195	32 C. F.	2½ in.	6	6K2377	15	$2.34	$3.30
6K1200	32 C. F.	4½ in.	6	6K2377	19	2.59	3.55
6K1201	32 C. F.	6 in.	6	6K2377	19	2.84	3.85

If by mail, postage extra, No. 6K1195, 18 cents.
If by mail, postage extra, No. 6K1200, 22 cents.
If by mail, postage extra, No. 6K1201, 22 cents.
See remarks about insured and registered mail at top of page.

38-CALIBER DOUBLE ACTION REVOLVERS

$2.34

These revolvers, the same as the 32 and 22-caliber revolvers above described, are made by the well known Hopkins & Allen and Harrington & Richardson Companies, the manufacturers of the best double action revolvers on the market today. See above for further description of these revolvers.

Cat. No.	Caliber	Length of Barrel	No. of Shots	Shoots Cartridges No.	Weight oz.	PRICE Rubber Stocks	PRICE Pearl Stocks
6K1206	38 C. F.	2½ in.	5	6K2388	15	$2.34	$3.30
6K1210	38 C. F.	4½ in.	5	6K2388	19	2.59	3.55
6K1212	38 C. F.	6 in.	5	6K2388	19	2.85	3.85

If by mail, postage extra, No. 6K1206, 18 cents.
If by mail, postage extra, No. 6K1210, 22 cents.
If by mail, postage extra, No. 6K1212, 22 cents.
See remarks about insured and registered mail at top of page.

DOUBLE ACTION REVOLVERS WITH SAFETY HAMMER.

$2.34

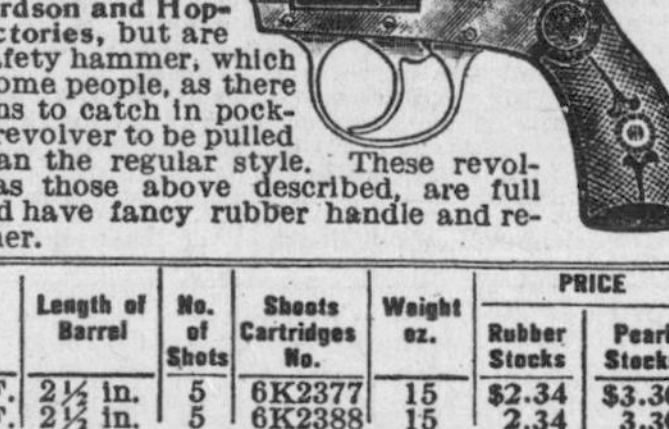

These revolvers, the same as those above described, are the product of the celebrated Harrington & Richardson and Hopkins & Allen factories, but are fitted with the safety hammer, which is preferred by some people, as there are no projections to catch in pocket, enabling this revolver to be pulled more quickly than the regular style. These revolvers, the same as those above described, are full nickel plated and have fancy rubber handle and rebounding hammer.

Cat. No.	Caliber	Length of Barrel	No. of Shots	Shoots Cartridges No.	Weight oz.	PRICE Rubber Stocks	PRICE Pearl Stocks
6K1217	32 C. F.	2½ in.	5	6K2377	15	$2.34	$3.30
6K1218	38 C. F.	2½ in.	5	6K2388	15	2.34	3.30

If by mail, postage extra, each, 18 cents.
See remarks about insured and registered mail at top of page.

IVER JOHNSON REVOLVERS.

32 and 38-Caliber.

$4.80

HAMMER THE HAMMER

70c and 90c per 100 for Cartridges. See page 738.

This revolver is manufactured by the Iver Johnson Arms & Cycle Co., of Fitchburg, Mass., and is widely known and widely advertised as the "hammer the hammer" revolver. It is known as an automatic shell ejecting hinge revolver, so when you open the barrel at the top, the shells are automatically extracted by the shell extractor. It is manufactured from the best material that money can buy, fitted with a rifled steel barrel, fluted cylinder, front and rear sights, full nickel plated throughout, fancy rubber handle, may be fitted with pearl handle at the price quoted below; all working parts are tempered, case hardened and interchangeable, so that if you accidentally break a part, you can order it from the factory at a small cost; shoots cartridges caliber 32 S. & W., our No. 6K2377, or 38 S. & W., our No. 6K2388, and no other cartridges can be used in this revolver. It is safe, reliable and a good shooter.

Catalogue Number	Caliber	Length of Barrel	Finish	No. of Sh'ts	Shoots Cartridge No.	Weight, Ounces	Price
6K1253	32 c.f.	3 in.	Nickel Plated	5	6K2377	13	$4.80
6K1254	38 c.f.	3¼ in.		5	6K2388	18	
6K1255	32 c.f.	3 in.	Blued	5	6K2377	13	5.17
6K1256	38 c.f.	3¼ in.	Blued	5	6K2388	18	

If fitted with Pearl handles, extra $1.00
Postage extra, 17 to 22 cents. See top of page about insured mail.

IVER JOHNSON HAMMERLESS REVOLVERS AT REDUCED PRICES.

32 and 38-Caliber.

$5.43

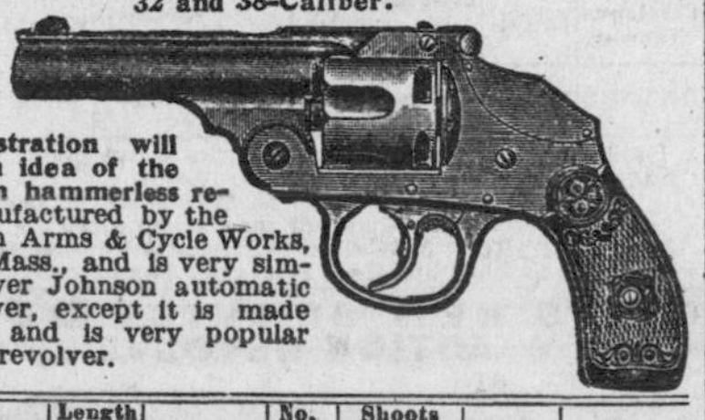

This illustration will give you an idea of the Iver Johnson hammerless revolver, manufactured by the Iver Johnson Arms & Cycle Works, Fitchburg, Mass., and is very similar to the Iver Johnson automatic hinge revolver, except it is made hammerless and is very popular as a pocket revolver.

Catalogue Number	Caliber	Length of Barrel	Finish	No. of Sh'ts	Shoots Cartridge No.	Weight	Price
6K1263	32 c.f.	3 in.	Nickel Plated	5	6K2377	13 oz.	$5.43
6K1264	38 c.f.	3¼ in.		5	6K2388	18 oz.	
6K1265	32 c.f.	3 in.	Blued	5	6K2377	13 oz.	5.80
6K1266	38 c.f.	3¼ in.	Blued	5	6K2388	18 oz.	

If fitted with pearl handles, extra $1.00
Postage extra, 17 to 22c. Read top of page about insured mail.

REMINGTON DERRINGERS.

This is genuine Remington Double Derringer. Don't buy imitations. The Remington Double Derringer, 41-caliber short, rim fire, takes cartridge No. 6K2360; checkered rubber stock; length of barrel, 3 inches; entire length of pistol, 5 inches; nickel plated.

No. 6K1347 Price, nickel plated $5.00
No. 6K1348 Same blued, price $5.00
If fitted with pearl handles, extra $1.00
If by mail, postage extra 17 cents.

THE STEVENS' TIP UP PISTOL, $2.45

22-CALIBER CARTRIDGES, 21c PER 100. SEE PAGE 738.

22-caliber only. 3½-inch barrel.

$2.45

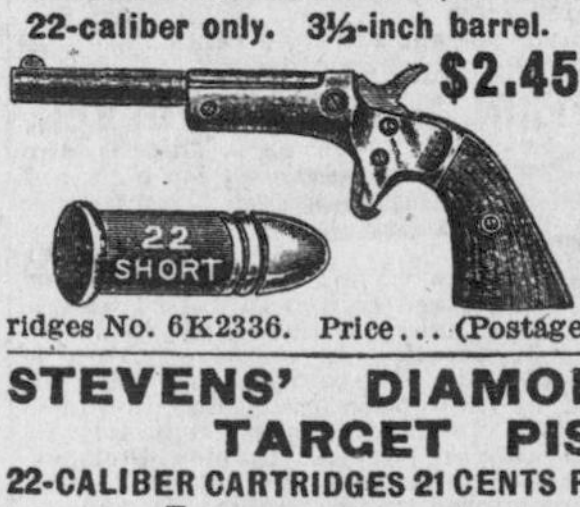

Stevens' Single Shot Pistol. Tip up barrel, nickel plated finish, 3½-inch blued steel barrel, 22-caliber only, rim fire. No better material put in rifles. A fine target pistol. Rifled barrel and well made throughout.

No. 6K1343 For 22-caliber short cartridges No. 6K2336. Price.... (Postage extra, 15c.)....$2.45

STEVENS' DIAMOND MODEL TARGET PISTOL.

22-CALIBER CARTRIDGES 21 CENTS PER 100. SEE PAGE 738

$4.06

The Celebrated Stevens Target Pistol, the best pistol made for fine close shooting. It has fine blued barrel, nickel plated frame, rosewood stock, 6-inch tip up barrel; fitted with fine globe or open target sights, 22-caliber, rim fire. Shoots either 22 long rifle or 22 short cartridges; good for 50 yards, 22-caliber, 6-inch barrel.

No. 6K1344 Diamond model, globe and peep sights. Price.......................$4.04
No. 6K1345 The same pistol, but with open sights. Price,......(If by mail, postage extra, 15c).......$4.06

NEW MODEL HARRINGTON & RICHARDSON 22-CALIBER REVOLVERS.

$4.80

This revolver is made by the Harrington & Richardson Co., Worcester, Mass., and is known as the Premier Small Frame Model, being the very latest production in a 22-caliber revolver. The frame is small, neat and nicely balanced. This revolver is made of the same high quality as all other Harrington & Richardson revolvers, is well finished, the barrel is finely rifled, the cylinder is very neatly fluted, self cocking, automatic shell extractor. We can furnish this revolver with 3-inch or 5-inch barrel, nickel plated or blued, at the prices as given below. This revolver shoots 22 short, 22 long or 22 long rifle cartridges, either black or smokeless powder.

Cat. No.	Caliber	Length of Barrel	Finish	No. of Shots	Shoots Cartridge No.	Price with Rubber Stocks	Price with Pearl Stocks
6K1370	22 r. f.	3 inches	Nick'l	7	6K2336 6K2535	$4.80	$5.80
6K1371	22 r. f.	3 inches	Blued	7	6K2338 6K2340	5.12	6.10

5-INCH BARREL

REDUCED TO $5.32

Same revolver as above, fitted with 5-inch barrel.

Cat. No.	Caliber	Length of Barrel	Finish	No. of Shots	Shoots Cartridge No.	Price with Rubber Stocks	Price with Pearl Stocks
6K1374	22 r. f.	5 inches	Nick'l	7	6K2336 6K2535	$5.32	$6.35
6K1375	22 r. f.	5 inches	Blued	7	6K2338 6K2340	5.68	6.75

If by mail, postage extra, 22 cents.
See top of pages for insured mail.

H. & R. AUTOMATIC REVOLVERS.

70 AND 90 CENTS PER 100 FOR CARTRIDGES. SEE PAGE 738.

32 and 38-Caliber.

Over 3,500,000 Harrington & Richardson's Revolvers now in use.

Hinge Revolvers are not intended for smokeless powder.

OUR $4.80 H. & R. AUTOMATIC REVOLVER.

This revolver is manufactured by the Harrington & Richardson Arms Co., of Worcester, Mass., one of the oldest revolver manufacturers in the United States and is known as the H. & R. Automatic Shell Ejecting Hinge Revolver. It is made from first class material throughout; has a steel rifled barrel, front and rear sights, fluted cylinder; all working parts are tempered, case hardened and interchangeable, so that if you accidentally break one of them it may be replaced at a small cost by writing to the manufacturers. Full nickel plated or blued steel finish throughout, fitted with fancy hard rubber handle. A good, safe, reliable revolver, which takes the 32 S. & W. cartridge, our No. 6K2377 or the 38 S. & W. cartridge, our No. 6K2388. The 32-caliber is 6-shot and the 38-caliber is 5-shot and no other cartridges will fit this revolver, so if you order cartridges with the revolver, be sure to state that the cartridges are for this revolver.

Catalogue Number	Caliber	Length of Barrel	Finish	No. of Sh'ts	Shoots Cartridge	Weight, Ounces	Price
6K1385	32 c.f.	3¼ in.	Nickel Plated	6	6K2377	18½	$4.80
6K1386	38 c.f.	3¼ in.		5	6K2388	18½	
6K1387	32 c.f.	3¼ in.	Blued Steel	6	6K2377	18½	5.12
6K1388	38 c.f.	3¼ in.		5	6K2388	18½	

Pearl handle on above revolvers, extra.................$1.20
If by mail, postage extra, 20 cents.
See top of page for insured mail.

H. & R. HAMMERLESS REVOLVERS.

70 AND 90 CENTS PER 100 FOR CARTRIDGES. SEE PAGE 738.

32 or 38-Caliber. Adapted to S. & W. Cartridges.

$5.43 AND 5.79

The H. & R. Hammerless manufactured by the Harrington & Richardson Arms Co., of Worcester, Mass., one of the oldest revolver manufacturers in the United States and is known as the H. & R. Hammerless Shell Ejecting Hinge Revolver. It is made from first class material throughout; has a steel rifled barrel, front and rear sights, fluted cylinder; all working parts are tempered, case hardened and interchangeable, so that if you accidentally break one of them it may be replaced at a small cost by writing to the manufacturers. Full nickel plated or blued steel finish throughout, fitted with fancy hard rubber handle. A good, safe, reliable revolver, which takes the 32 S. & W. cartridge, our No. 6K2377 or the 38 S. & W. cartridge, our No. 6K2388. The 32-caliber is 5-shot and the 38-caliber is 5-shot and no other cartridges will fit this revolver, so if you order cartridges with the revolver be sure to state that the cartridges are for this revolver. 32-caliber has a small, light frame, making it a fine, good, convenient pocket size.

Notice our 75c Revolver Stock, No. 6K1488.

Catalogue Number	Caliber	Length of Barrel	Finish	No. of Sh'ts	Shoots Cartridge	Weight	Price
6K1411	32 c.f.	3 in.	Nickel Plated	5	6K2377	13 oz.	$5.43
6K1412	38 c.f.	3¼ in.		5	6K2388	18 oz.	
6K1413	32 c.f.	3 in.	Blued Steel	5	6K2377	13 oz.	5.79
6K1414	38 c.f.	3¼ in.		5	6K2388	18 oz.	

Pearl handle on above revolvers, extra........................$1.20
If by mail, postage extra, 18 to 24 cents.
See top of page for insured mail.

44-CALIBER FRONTIER REVOLVER.

Reduced Price **$3.75**

Takes Cartridge 6K2409

This revolver is known as the imported Frontier Revolver shoots the 44-40 caliber cartridge, and is the only low priced revolver taking this cartridge. We cannot recommend this revolver as highly as we can the Colt's revolver for it is a much cheaper revolver, consequently not as good, but it is the only cheap revolver which we can buy that shoots the 44-40 cartridge. It is made with a solid frame, as shown in the illustration, has 5½-inch barrel, is a 6-shooter; fancy rubber handle, full nickel plated or blued steel finish throughout, and for a person who does not do very much shooting, this revolver will probably answer the purpose of a large caliber, low priced revolver, but if you are so situated that you do considerable shooting we recommend by all means that you purchase a Colt's revolver either the Single Action Army or the Bisley Model, which are built for hard use.

Catalogue Number	Caliber	No. of Shots	Finish	Length of Barrel	Price
6K1434	44-40	6	Nickeled	5½ in.	$3.75
6K1436	44-40	6	Blued	5½ in.	3.95

If by mail, postage extra, 40 cents. Insured mail, 45 cents.

OUR IMPROVED REVOLVER RIFLE STOCK.

75c

Our Revolver Rifle Stock converts a revolver into a magazine rifle by attaching this skeleton stock to the butt of any revolver, which can be instantly done by giving the screw on the skeleton stock a few turns to the right. You can shoot at short range as accurately with an ordinary pistol as you can with any rifle. With the aid of this stock and any ordinary revolver, you can have all the enjoyment of shooting a magazine rifle at a cost at least $5.00 lower than you could purchase the cheapest rifle for. The jaws of this stock are covered with leather, so they will not mar the revolver. The stock is nicely nickel plated and finished. Length of stock, 14½ ins.; weight of stock, 16 oz. This stock will not take a Colt's Automatic Pistol on account of the magazine in the handle of this pistol.

No. 6K1488 Revolver Rifle Stock. Price........75c

If by mail, postage extra, 20 cents; insured mail, 25 cents.

THE NEW LIBERTY 22-CALIBER REVOLVER. $1.29

We have a large demand for a revolver at a lower price than the double action revolver costs, and in order to fill the demand we have gotten out the New Liberty Revolver in 22-caliber. The Liberty Revolver is fitted with a 2½-inch smooth bored barrel, 7-shot, fancy rubber handle, nickel plated throughout, and shoots the 22-caliber short rim fire cartridge. Weighs about 7 ounces and is 5¾ inches long. It is as well made as any single action revolver selling generally for $1.50 to $2.00.

Catalogue Number	Caliber	Length of Barrel	Finish	No. of Shots	Weight	Price
6K1489.	22 rim	2½ in.	Nickeled	7	7 ozs.	$1.29

If by mail, postage extra, 10 cents. Insured mail, 15 cents.

COLT'S NEW ARMY MODEL 1892.

38 and 41-Caliber. **$14.00**

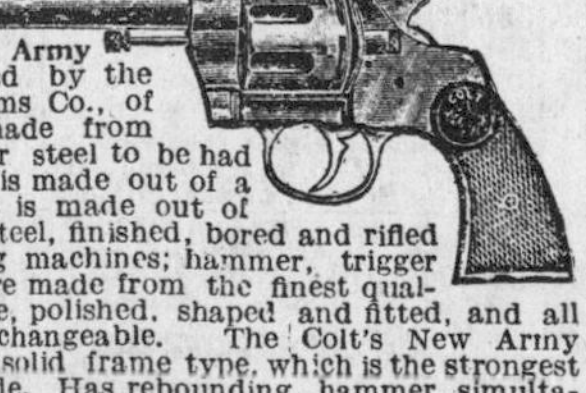

Colt's 6-Shot New Army Revolver, manufactured by the Colt's Patent Fire Arms Co., of Hartford, Conn., is made from the very best revolver steel to be had at any price, the frame is made out of a solid forging, the barrel is made out of the very best revolver steel, finished, bored and rifled on the latest type rifling machines; hammer, trigger and all working parts are made from the finest quality steel, made to gauge, polished, shaped and fitted, and all parts are made interchangeable. The Colt's New Army Revolver is made on the solid frame type, which is the strongest frame for revolvers made. Has rebounding hammer, simultaneous side ejector so that by turning the cylinder out of the frame the cartridges may be instantly extracted. Made in blued steel finish, has a splendid grip, fitted with fancy rubber handle; made to take the 38 short Colt's center fire, 38 long Colt's center fire and 41 long Colt's center fire cartridges, a 6-shooter and a good one. When ordering state which caliber and length of barrel you desire.

COLT'S NEW NAVY REVOLVER

Is precisely the same as the Colt's New Army Revolver, the only difference between the two revolvers is, the Colt's New Navy Revolver has a different monogram in the handle, as you will notice by the above illustration, but the shape of the handles is identical. The handle of one will go on the other.

Catalogue Number	Calibre	Le'th of Barrel	Finish	No. of Shots	Shoots Cartr'ge No.	Wt. oz.	Price
6K1541	38 c. f.	4½ in.	Blued	6	6K2392	32	$14.00
6K1543	38 c. f.	6 in.	Blued	6	6K2392	32	
6K1545	41 c. f.	4½ in.	Blued	6	6K2401	32	14.00
6K1547	41 c. f.	6 in.	Blued	6	6K2401	32	

If fitted with pearl handle, extra $2.75

If by registered mail, postage extra, 50 cents.

Mention registered mail when ordering.

SEE OUR 75-CENT REVOLVER HANDLE ABOVE.

COMPARE THE LOWER PRICES

IN THIS CATALOGUE WITH THE PRICES QUOTED BY US IN PREVIOUS CATALOGUES AND WITH THE PRICES QUOTED BY ANY OTHER HOUSE, AND NOTE HOW MUCH WE SAVE YOU ON ANY NEEDED ARTICLE.

COLT'S AUTOMATIC MAGAZINE PISTOL, 32-CALIBER 9-SHOT, $15.00.

The opposite illustration engraved direct from a photograph, will give you some idea of the Colt's Automatic Pistol, made in caliber 32 to shoot smokeless cartridges for powerful long range shooting. Specifications: The entire pistol is made from the very best grade of crucible steel which can be procured regardless of price, the parts are simple and strong; the barrel is finely rifled for long range shooting; all metal parts are handsomely blued, fancy rubber handle, latest improved safety on the grip; the entire length of the Colt's Automatic Pistol is 7 inches, the weight is 24 ounces, will hold 8 cartridges in the magazine and 1 in the barrel, making it a 9-shot pistol, is accurate up to 300 yards, and will penetrate five 1-inch pine boards at a distance of 15 feet. Each shot throws out the shell and puts in a new cartridge. All you have to do is pull the trigger.

No. 6K1500 Colt's Automatic Pistol, 32-caliber, 4-inch barrel. Weight, 24 ounces, 9-shot. Price................$15.00

If fitted with pearl handle, extra........................ 1.75

Extra magazine for the above pistol. Price......... .90

If by registered mail, postage extra, 38 cents.

Mention registered mail when ordering.

No. 6K2560 32-Caliber Automatic Smokeless, Rimless Cartridges with metal patched bullet. Price, per box of 50..72c

Cartridges cannot be sent by mail.

COLT'S AUTOMATIC MAGAZINE, 38-CALIBER, 8-SHOT PISTOL.

$20.00

One of the strongest pistols ever produced, 8 shots may be fired in eight seconds, has a range of 500 to 1,000 yards, shoots the latest 38-caliber Colt's Automatic high pressure cartridge, and has a velocity of 1,050 feet per second, and will penetrate nine 1-inch pine boards. The magazine is in the handle, and it has no cylinder, whereby it differs from revolvers. To operate this pistol, place seven cartridges in the magazine, and one in the chamber, raise the hammer, and all you have to do after that is to pull the trigger, for the pistol cocks itself by its own recoil after each shot is fired, ejects the cartridge which has been fired, places a new cartridge in the chamber, and is ready to shoot again as soon as you are ready to pull the trigger; the entire eight loads may be fired in eight seconds.

The Colt's Automatic Pocket Pistol has 4½-inch barrel.

Catalogue Number	Caliber	Length of Barrel	Finish	No. of Sh'ts	Shoots Cartridge	Weight	Price
6K1508	38 aut.	4½ in.	Blued	8	6K2580	31 ozs.	$20.00

Extra for pearl handle, fitted to the above pistol.....$2.00

Extra magazines for above pistol. Each............. 1.35

If by registered mail, postage extra, 52 cents.

Mention registered mail when ordering.

No. 6K2580 38-Caliber Automatic Smokeless Cartridges with metal patched bullets. Price, per box of 50.......$1.03

COLT'S NEW SERVICE DOUBLE ACTION REVOLVER.

45 Caliber

The Colt's New Service Revolver, manufactured by the Colt's Patent Fire Arms Co. A heavy, strong, substantial belt revolver, taking the 45-caliber cartridge, which is one of the most powerful black powder cartridges used in any revolver. Has a good grip, which is a leading feature with all Colt's revolvers. The New Service Double Action Revolver is made on the jointless solid frame type, has the simultaneous side ejector, rebounding hammer, fluted and chambered cylinder, barrel made of the best rifle steel, finely rifled, all parts interchangeable so that if you accidentally break or lose a part, you need not send the revolver to be repaired but you can order the part wanted from the factory and can replace it yourself very readily. Fitted with fancy rubber handle, pearl handle may be fitted at price quoted below, blued steel finish throughout, takes the 45-caliber Colt's cartridge, is a 6-shooter, weighs about 36 ounces and is one of the most powerful shooting revolvers made shooting black powder cartridges.

Catalogue Number	Caliber	Length of Barrel	Finish	No. of Sh'ts	Shoots Cartridge No.	Wgt. Oz.	Price
6K1563	45 c.f.	7½in.	Blued Steel	6	6K2413	36	$16.75

If fitted with pearl handle, extra $5.50

If by registered mail, postage extra, 60 cents.

Mention registered mail when ordering.

COLT'S SPECIAL PEARL HANDLE REVOLVER.

Single Action Frontier.

This is our Special Cowboy's Six-Shooter with pearl handle. The right handle has an Ox Head carved in raised design and makes a handsome revolver. This illustration is engraved from a photograph of the revolver and will give you some idea of its appearance. Made in blued steel finish only. We handle these regularly in 32-20 and 44-40-calibers but can furnish them on special order in caliber 41 c. f. or 45 Colt's c. f. with 5½ or 7½-inch barrel at price quoted below. Weight, 41 ounces. When ordering, say which length barrel you prefer.

Catalogue Number	Caliber C. F.	Length of Barrel	Finish	No. of Sh'ts	Shoots Cartridge No.	Wgt. Oz.	Price
6K1587	32-20	5½in.	Blued Steel	6	6K2384	41	$22.50
6K1589	32-20	7½in.		6	6K2384	41	
6K1591	44-40	5½in.	Blued Steel	6	6K2409	41	22.50
6K1593	44-40	7½in.		6	6K2409	41	

If by registered mail, postage extra, 59 to 69 cents

Mention registered mail when ordering.

Weight, packed for shipment, 3 pounds.

COLT'S POLICE POSITIVE REVOLVER.

32 and 38-Caliber.

The Colt's Police Positive Revolver is made on the solid frame, side ejecting, jointless pattern, the same as the Colt's New Army and New Navy. Has the side ejecting device for extracting the shells from the cylinder, patent safety lock device in the frame, made so that the firing pin cannot strike the primer of the cartridge until you pull the trigger. It is a 6-shooter made to take the 32 short Colt's center fire, 32 long Colt's center fire and 38 Smith & Wesson cartridges. The 32-caliber revolver weighs about 18 ounces and the 38-caliber revolver weighs about 20 ounces. Has a splendid grip, smooth working action, blued steel finish, with fancy rubber handle, but may be fitted with pearl handle at price quoted below, and is the revolver which is adopted by the city police departments of New York and other large cities.

Catalogue No.	Caliber	Lgth of Brl.	Finish	No. of Shots	Shoots Cart'ge	Weight	Price
6K1511	32 c. f.	4 in.	Blued	6-shot	6K2380, 6K2381	18 ozs.	$14.00
6K1518	38 c. f.	4 in.	Blued	6-shot	6K2388	20 ozs.	

If fitted with pearl handle, extra $2.00

If by registered mail, postage extra, 33 to 35 cents.

Mention registered mail when ordering.

COLT'S DOUBLE ACTION REVOLVER.

38 and 41 Caliber

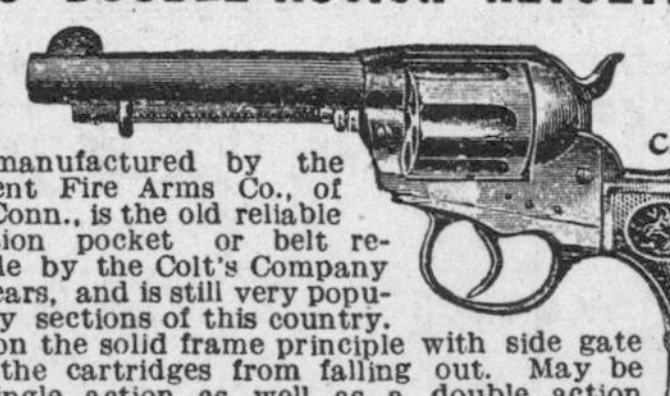

Colt's 6-Shot Double Action Sliding Side Ejecting Revolver, manufactured by the Colt's Patent Fire Arms Co., of Hartford, Conn., is the old reliable double action pocket or belt revolver made by the Colt's Company for many years, and is still very popular in many sections of this country. It is made on the solid frame principle with side gate to prevent the cartridges from falling out. May be used as a single action as well as a double action revolver. Made from the very best quality of revolver steel, fluted and chambered cylinder, barrel made from the very best rifle barrel steel, accurately bored and correctly rifled, fitted with fancy rubber handle, blued steel finish. Is a 6-shooter and takes the 38 short Colt's center fire, 38 long Colt's center fire or 41 long Colt's center fire cartridges. When ordering state caliber and length of barrel you prefer.

Catalogue Number	Caliber	Le'th of Barrel	Finish	No. of Shots	Shoots Cartr'ge No.	Wt. oz.	Price
6K1531	38 c. f.	4½ in.	Blued	6	6K2392	26	$12.00
6K1533	38 c. f.	6 in.	Blued	6	6K2392	28	
6K1537	41 c. f.	6 in.	Blued	6	6K2401	28	13.25

If fitted with pearl handle, extra $2.75

If by registered mail, postage extra, 48 cents.

Mention registered mail when ordering.

SEE OUR 75-CENT REVOLVER HANDLE ON THIS PAGE.

COLT'S SINGLE ACTION COWBOYS' FRONTIER ARMY.

32, 44 and 45-Caliber. **$15.50**

This is the old reliable Cowboys' Gun, and our price is $15.50 for all calibers and lengths of barrels; furnished in blued steel finish only. Colt's single action army revolver is a 6-shooter, rubber handle, solid frame, the best quality of steel and finish; warranted perfect and accurate in every detail. Barrel, 5½ or 7½ inches; 32, 44 or 45-caliber, as desired. We can furnish these in blued finish only.

Catalogue Number	Caliber C. F.	Length of Barrel	Finish	No. of Sh'ts	Shoots Cartridge No.	Wgt. Oz.	Price
6K1571	32-20	5½in.	Blued Steel	6	6K2384	40	$15.50
6K1573	32-20	7½in.		6	6K2384	40	
6K1579	44-40	5½in.	Blued Steel	6	6K2409	40	15.50
6K1581	44-40	7½in.		6	6K2409	40	
6K1583	45 c. f.	5½in.	Blued Steel	6	6K2413	40	15.50
6K1585	45 c. f.	7½in.		6	6K2413	40	

Pearl handle on any of the above revolvers, extra..$4.00

If by registered mail, postage extra, 60 cents.

Mention registered mail when ordering.

COLT'S SINGLE ACTION BISLEY MODEL.

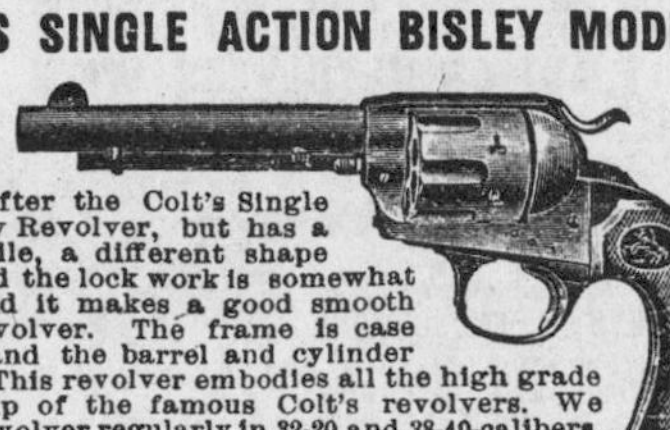

The Colt's Bisley Model Revolver is patterned after the Colt's Single Action Army Revolver, but has a longer handle, a different shape hammer, and the lock work is somewhat different, and it makes a good smooth working revolver. The frame is case hardened, and the barrel and cylinder are blued. This revolver embodies all the high grade workmanship of the famous Colt's revolvers. We carry this revolver regularly in 32-20 and 38-40-calibers, but can furnish it in 45-caliber to special order.

Catalogue Number	Caliber	Length of Barrel	Finish	No. of Sh'ts	Shoots Cartridge No.	Weight Ounces	Price
6K1610	32-20	5½in.	Blued Steel	6	6K2384	40	$15.50
6K1611	32-20	7½in.		6	6K2384	40	
6K1612	38-40	5½in.	Blued Steel	6	6K2396	40	15.50
6K1613	38-40	7½in.		6	6K2396	40	

If by registered mail, postage extra, 60 cents.

Mention registered mail when ordering.

COLT'S OFFICERS' MODEL TARGET REVOLVERS.

38-Caliber.

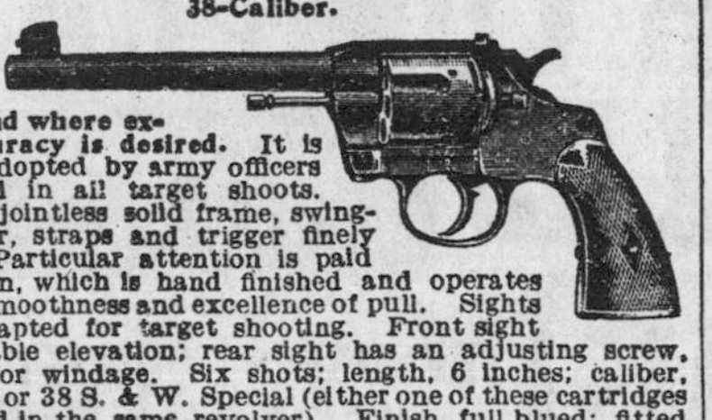

This revolver is designed for target shooting and where extreme accuracy is desired. It is generally adopted by army officers and is used in all target shoots. Made with jointless solid frame, swing-out cylinder, straps and trigger finely checked. Particular attention is paid to the action, which is hand finished and operates with great smoothness and excellence of pull. Sights specially adapted for target shooting. Front sight has adjustable elevation; rear sight has an adjusting screw, adjustable for windage. Six shots; length, 6 inches; caliber, 38 long colt or 38 S. & W. Special (either one of these cartridges may be used in the same revolver). Finish, full blued; fitted with finely checked full walnut stocks. Weight, 32 ounces. Length over all, 11½ inches.

Catalogue No.	Caliber	Length of Barrel	No. of Shots	Shoots Cart'ges No.	Weight, ounces	Price
6K1625	38 Long Colt	6 inches	6	6K2392	32	$18.50

If by registered mail, postage extra, 52 cents. Mention registered mail when ordering. Weight, packed for shipment, 3 pounds.

LUGER AUTOMATIC PISTOL, $24.45

30-CALIBER, 8 SHOTS.

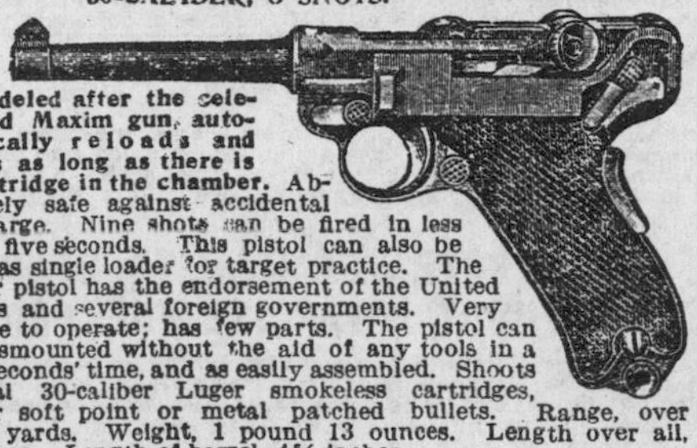

Modeled after the celebrated Maxim gun, automatically reloads and cocks as long as there is a cartridge in the chamber. Absolutely safe against accidental discharge. Nine shots can be fired in less than five seconds. This pistol can also be used as single loader for target practice. The Luger pistol has the endorsement of the United States and several foreign governments. Very simple to operate; has few parts. The pistol can be dismounted without the aid of any tools in a few seconds' time, and as easily assembled. Shoots special 30-caliber Luger smokeless cartridges, either soft point or metal patched bullets. Range, over 1,500 yards. Weight, 1 pound 13 ounces. Length over all, 9 inches. Length of barrel, 4¾ inches.

No. 6K1640 30-Caliber Luger Automatic Pistol. Price $24.45

If by mail, postage extra, 48 cents.

No. 6K2582 30-Caliber Luger Cartridges, soft point. Price, per box of 50 ....$1.03

No. 6K2583 30-Caliber Luger Cartridges, metal patched. Price, per box of 50 ....$1.04

GENUINE SMITH & WESSON REVOLVERS.

OUR 22-CALIBER SMITH & WESSON SIDE EJECTING REVOLVER.

This revolver is double action, has fluted cylinder, rifled steel barrel, rebounding hammer, rubber handle, blued steel or nickel plated finish; made in 22-caliber, taking rim fire cartridges. This is the latest Smith & Wesson revolver, and the highest grade 22-caliber revolver made.

Catalogue Number	Caliber	Length of Barrel	Finish	No. of Sh'ts	Shoots Cartridge No.	Wgt. Oz.	Price
6K1700	22 Rim	3½ in.	Nickel	7	6K2336 or 6K2338	10	$11.85
6K1701	22 Rim	3½ in.	Blued	7	6K2336 or 6K2338	10	$11.85

If fitted with pearl handle, extra 90c

If by registered mail, postage extra, 25 cents. Weight, packed for shipment, about 1 pound.

S. & W. SIDE EJECTING REVOLVERS.

32-38 Caliber.

The Side Ejecting Smith & Wesson Revolver is self cocking, and being the side ejecting type makes a strong, substantial revolver. It is center fire, 6-shot, with solid frame, swing-out cylinder. This revolver is Smith & Wesson's latest creation and is a revolver that is built for business. It will withstand hard usage. They are highly recommended for target shooting, and made in blued steel or nickel plated finish, fitted with rubber handle.

Catalogue No.	Caliber	Length Barrel	Finish	No. of Shots	Shoots Cart'ge	Weight	Price
6K1704	32 c.f.	4¼ in.	Nickel	6-shot	6K2376	19 oz.	$13.80
6K1705	32 c.f.	4¼ in.	Blued	6-shot	6K2376	19 oz.	$13.80
6K1706	32 c.f.	6 in.	Nickel	6-shot	6K2376	20 oz.	13.85
6K1707	32 c.f.	6 in.	Blued	6-shot	6K2376	20 oz.	13.85
6K1714	38 c f	5 in.	Nickel	6-shot	6K2392	30 oz.	14.98
6K1715	38c.f.	5 in.	Blued	6-shot	6K2392	30 oz.	14.98
6K1716	38 c.f.	6½ in.	Nickel	6-shot	6K2392	32 oz.	15.00
6K1717	38 c.f.	6½ in.	Blued	6-shot	6K2392	32 oz.	15.00

FIRST QUALITY PEARL HANDLE ON THE ABOVE, EXTRA, 32-caliber, $1.00; 38-caliber $2.00

If by registered mail, postage extra, 32-caliber, 35c; 38-caliber, 48c.

We cannot furnish Smith & Wesson Revolvers for 38-40 and 32-20 cartridges.

35c RELOADING TOOLS, 38-LONG COLT.

Made by the Bridgeport Gun Implement Co., consist of the following articles: No. 1 is the recapper; No. 2 charge cup; No. 3 decapper; No. 4 bullet mould, and No. 6 is the base block. The bullet mould alone is worth as much as we ask for the complete set. We bought all the factory had, and there will be no more after these are sold.

No. 6K4279 For 38-caliber Colt's long center fire revolver cartridges. Price, per set 35c

If by mail, postage extra, per set, 18 cents.

S. & W. DOUBLE ACTION REVOLVERS.

These revolvers are warranted genuine Smith & Wesson. All are self cocking and double action, with automatic shell extractor, finely rifled steel barrel, fine rubber stocks, nickel plated or blued steel finish. Made of the finest material that money can buy and the workmanship is equal in finish to that of any ordinary watch. If you want the best work for your money buy a Smith & Wesson.

Catalogue No.	Caliber	Length Barrel	Finish	No. of Shots	Shoots Cart'ge	Weight	Price
6K1724	32 c.f.	3½ in.	Nickel	5-shot	6K2377	13 oz.	$12.74
6K1725	32 c.f.	3½ in.	Blued	5-shot	6K2377	13 oz.	$12.74
6K1726	32 c.f.	6 in.	Nickel	5-shot	6K2377	15 oz.	12.75
6K1727	32 c.f.	6 in.	Blued	5-shot	6K2377	15 oz.	12.75
6K1732	38 c.f.	4 in.	Nickel	5-shot	6K2388	18 oz.	13.83
6K1733	38 c.f.	4 in.	Blued	5-shot	6K2388	18 oz.	13.83
6K1734	38 c.f.	5 in.	Nickel	5-shot	6K2388	19 oz.	13.84
6K1735	38 c.f.	5 in.	Blued	5-shot	6K2388	19 oz.	13.84
6K1736	38 c.f.	6 in.	Nickel	5-shot	6K2388	20 oz.	13.85
6K1737	38 c.f.	6 in.	Blued	5-shot	6K2388	20 oz.	13.85

FIRST QUALITY PEARL HANDLE, EXTRA $1.00

If by registered mail, 32-caliber, 30 cents: 38-caliber, 35 cents. Mention registered mail when ordering. Weight, packed for shipment, about 2 pounds.

SMITH & WESSON HAMMERLESS

Made by Smith & Wesson, Springfield, Mass. Latest type new model hammerless, automatic shell ejector, patent safety catch, self cocking rebounding hammer, double action, blued steel or nickel plated finish, fitted with rubber handle. This is positively the best hammerless revolver made.

Improved Safety Trigger Locking Device which automatically releases as trigger is pulled. Accidental discharge impossible.

Catalogue No.	Caliber	Length Barrel	Finish	No. of Shots	Shoots Cart'ge	Weight	Price
6K1756	32 c.f.	3½ in.	Nickel	5-shot	6K2377	15 oz.	$13.80
6K1757	32 c.f.	3½ in.	Blued	5-shot	6K2377	15 oz.	$13.80
6K1762	38 c.f.	4 in.	Nickel	5-shot	6K2388	18 oz.	14.90
6K1763	38 c.f.	4 in.	Blued	5-shot	6K2388	18 oz.	14.90
6K1764	38 c.f.	5 in.	Nickel	5-shot	6K2388	19 oz.	14.91
6K1765	38 c.f.	5 in.	Blued	5-shot	6K2388	19 oz.	14.91
6K1766	38 c.f.	6 in.	Nickel	5-shot	6K2388	19 oz.	14.92
6K1767	38 c.f.	6 in.	Blued	5-shot	6K2388	19 oz.	14.92

FIRST QUALITY PEARL HANDLE, EXTRA $1.00

If by registered mail, postage extra, 32-caliber, 30 cents 38-caliber, 37 cents. ☞ See our prices on cartridges.

BLACK POWDER LOADED SHOTGUN SHELLS, $1.49

AT $1.49 PER HUNDRED we furnish the highest quality black powder loaded shotgun shells. No better black powder shells made at any price. We ask that you compare this price of $1.49 and up with the prices asked by other dealers for various grades of black powder shells, and if you will furthermore avail yourself of the opportunity of comparing the quality of our shells with those sold by others, you will realize that our shells at our prices are the greatest value ever offered in this line. These extraordinary prices, quality considered, are only made possible by the fact that we are the largest handlers of shotgun and rifle ammunition selling direct to the consumer in the world. Our sales in loaded shells, both black and smokeless, are greater than the combined sales of any ten retail houses or catalogue houses. This gigantic business places us in a position to contract for these goods in enormous quantities, insuring us the minimum cost, a cost which, on account of the enormous volume, is lower than that of any other ammunition factory in the country.

YOU ARE BENEFITED DIRECTLY by this low cost, for at our prices, ranging from $1.49 up, we have added but one small profit over the actual cost of material and labor, furnishing you these shells, quality considered, from 50 cents to 75 cents a hundred less than you could purchase shells of like quality elsewhere.

Powder.

IN THESE BLACK POWDER SHELLS we use a special black powder of a hard grain, which burns rapidly and leaves far less residue in the barrel than any other black powder. It has enormous penetration with a minimum breech pressure, and is really the cleanest, strongest and safest black powder ever used in shotgun ammunition. These shells are all loaded by automatic machinery, and one shell is identically like the other. One of the valuable features of these shells is their great uniformity. The good results you get with one shell, you can get with the other 24 in the box, or the other 499 out of the same case.

ANTICIPATE YOUR WANTS IN SHOTGUN SHELLS. Do not wait until the season is here before you order, as our business in shells is enormous, and while we guarantee to take care of your order at any time, still we desire that you place your orders early, for with the opening of the shooting season, our business in shotgun ammunition takes an enormous increase, at times testing the utmost capacity of the factory.

Goods Shipped by Freight.

OWING TO THE WEIGHT OF SHOTGUN SHELLS, we strongly advise sending all shells by freight instead of express, as freight is far cheaper, and it is very easy for you to make up an order of 50 or 100 pounds for a freight shipment, as there are doubtless many other things in our large book that you need, and you will thereby get the minimum freight rate, and the transportation charges on each item will amount to practically nothing.

Our Guarantee.

WE ABSOLUTELY GUARANTEE every loaded shotgun shell we sell against misfire, hang fire, or blow backs. We guarantee the maximum of penetration and the greatest possible uniformity in pattern. We further guarantee that our shells will give better satisfaction and are better value than those you can buy elsewhere, and to give you an opportunity of satisfying yourself that our shells are the best made, we will accept your order for 100 or more shells, and you can shoot one full box of them, and if you have any fault to find with these shells, if you do not find they have greater penetration make a better target and give better results in every way you may return the balance to us at our expense, and your money and any transportation charges you may have paid will be refunded.

NUMBER OF PELLETS TO ONE OUNCE OF SHOT.

We give below the number of pellets to one ounce of shot. The number is approximate. It may vary ten or more pellets.

Size of shot	No. 10	No. 9	No. 8	No. 7½	No. 7	No. 6	No. 5	No. 4	No. 3	No. 2	No. 1	BB
1 ounce contains pellets	850	570	390	335	290	220	170	130	105	85	70	60

OUR LINE OF BLACK POWDER LOADED SHELLS.

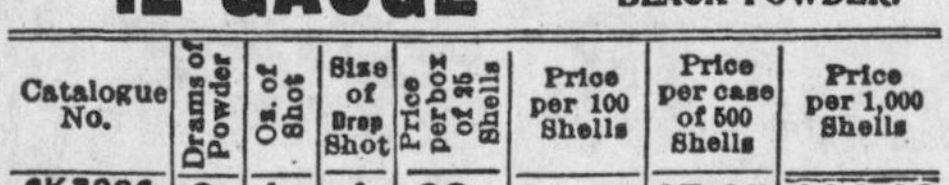

Why not get your friends to join with you and buy shells by the case or 1,000 and ship by freight? It will save you money on freight charges, besides they are cheaper in case lots.

OUR CASE PRICE is for one size and one gauge in a case, just as it comes to us from the factory. We cannot sell less than a case at the case price, nor can we assort the case with different loads.

A case of 500 shells, 12-gauge, weighs about 65 pounds.
A case of 500 shells, 10-gauge, weighs about 75 pounds.
A case of 500 shells, 16-gauge, weighs about 53 pounds.
Our terms on loaded shells are cash with order.

We have taken great pains to select loads which are suitable for most purposes and these loads should meet all requirements. WE DO NOT SEND SHELLS C. O. D.

ALWAYS GIVE CATALOGUE NUMBER WHEN ORDERING.

12-GAUGE

LOADED WITH SPECIAL BLACK POWDER.

Catalogue No.	Drams of Powder	Oz. of Shot	Size of Drop Shot	Price per box of 25 Shells	Price per 100 Shells	Price per case of 500 Shells	Price per 1,000 Shells
6K2006 6K2008	3	1	6 8	38c	$1.49	$7.05	$14.10
6K2014 6K2016 6K2018	3	$1\frac{1}{8}$	4 6 8	40c	1.57	7.45	14.90
6K2022 6K2024 6K2025 6K2026 6K2027	$3\frac{1}{4}$	$1\frac{1}{8}$	2 4 5 6 7	41c	1.61	7.65	15.30
6K2034 6K2036	$3\frac{1}{2}$	$1\frac{1}{8}$	4 6	42c	1.65	7.85	15.70
6K2040B	$3\frac{3}{4}$	$1\frac{1}{8}$	BB	48c	1.89	9.05	18.10

ALWAYS GIVE CATALOGUE NUMBER WHEN ORDERING.

10-GAUGE

LOADED WITH SPECIAL BLACK POWDER.

Catalogue No.	Drams of Powder	Oz. of Shot	Size of Dr'p Shot	Price per box of 25 Shells	Price per 100 Shells	Price per Case of 500 Shells	Price per 1,000 Shells
6K2072 6K2074 6K2076 6K2077	$4\frac{1}{4}$	$1\frac{1}{8}$	2 4 6 7	46c	$1.80	$8.50	$17.00
6K2078 6K2079	5	$1\frac{1}{4}$	8 BB	50c	1.90	9.25	19.50

ALWAYS GIVE CATALOGUE NUMBER WHEN ORDERING

16-GAUGE

LOADED WITH SPECIAL BLACK POWDER.

Catalogue No.	Drams of Powder	Oz. of Shot	Size of Drop Shot	Price per box of 25 Shells	Price per 100 Shells	Price per Case of 500 Shells	Price per 1,000 Shells
6K2086 6K2088	$2\frac{3}{4}$	1	4 6 8	40c	$1.58	$7.60	$15.20

ALWAYS GIVE CATALOGUE NUMBER WHEN ORDERING.

20-GAUGE

LOADED WITH SPECIAL BLACK POWDER.

Catalogue No.	Drams of Powder	Oz. of Shot	Size of Drop Shot	Price per box of 25 Shells	Price per 100 Shells	Price per Case of 500 Shells	Price per 1,000 Shells
6K2096 6K2098	$2\frac{1}{2}$	$\frac{7}{8}$	6 8	47c	$1.85	$8.90	$17.80

ALWAYS GIVE CATALOGUE NUMBER WHEN ORDERING.

THE NEW IMPROVED POINTER LONG BASE SMOKELESS SHELLS

PRIMED WITH
No. 3 NITRO PRIMER
and loaded with
TRIUMPH,
the New Smokeless Powder.

$2.00 PER 100

$9.50 PER CASE OF 500

50C PER BOX OF 25

THE HIGHEST QUALITY SHOTGUN SHELLS MADE.

**GREATER PENETRATION,
BETTER TARGET,
MORE UNIFORM RESULTS**

than in any smokeless powder shotgun shell ever made, regardless of name, make or price.

THE NEW POINTER SHELL is entirely different from the old Pointer Shell. It is similar in name only. We have improved the old Pointer Shell over 100 per cent. The old Short Base Pointer Shell was a good shell, was a better shell than you could have obtained elsewhere for considerably more money, and with this in mind you will appreciate what an excellent shell this New Improved Long Base Pointer Shell is, and what wonderful value we are offering in these shells at $9.50 per case of 500 shells.

THE ADVANTAGES OF THE LONG BRASS CUP

THIS SPECIAL LONG BRASS CUP makes our Pointer Shell the safest shell to use. This cup of heavy brass, extending almost half the length of the entire shell, prevents bursting of shell and obviates all possibilities of the paper pulling away from the head, as occasionally occurs with the short cup shell. The long cup guards against blow-outs and obviates entirely the swelling of the shell after being shot and sticking in chamber, making this the ideal shell for repeating guns as well as all double and single barrel guns. Considering the construction of our Pointer Shells, this shell at 25 per cent more than our price would be the most economical shell to use, as it is so strongly constructed that it can be loaded far oftener than any other shell on the market.

THE PAPER IN OUR POINTER SHELLS is a strong, tough paper, especially made for this purpose, thoroughly waterproof, and is the very best that money can buy.

PRIMER. Special No. 3 Nitro Primer, a very strong, quick primer, insuring instantaneous ignition, and absolutely guaranteeing against hanging or misfire in our Pointer Shells. This primer is set in a special battery cup, as shown in the illustration on this page. The Pointer Battery Cup is a distinctive feature of the Pointer Shell, and adds greatly to the cost and value of same. This cup, as shown in the illustration on this page, reinforces the primer pocket, in fact, serves as the pocket itself, unlike most other smokeless shells, where the primer is placed directly in the head of the shell without any reinforcement such as that afforded by our special battery cup. The value of the battery cup is evident to all shooters, as it not only reinforces the head of the shell, but prevents loss of gas through leakage, a common trouble with almost all other shells, causing a loss of powder and penetration. The Pointer Battery Cup further prevents blow-backs and blowing out firing pins, which accidents invariably injure the shooter. The tapered construction of our battery cup concentrates the fire of the primer and carries it directly to the center of the shell saving the full force of the primer explosion and insuring immediate and uniform combustion of the powder, causing instantaneous discharge and consequent enormous penetration.

THE WADS IN OUR POINTER SHELLS are made of the finest elastic felt, seated squarely over the powder with uniform pressure.

SHOT. Every grain guaranteed a perfect sphere, loaded by special machines with the greatest possible uniformity, and we invite you to cut open one of our Pointer Shells and compare the arrangement of shot with that of any other shell. The manner in which our shot is loaded in the shells largely accounts for the evenness of the pattern made by the Pointer Shell.

HOW WE ARE ABLE TO IMPROVE THE QUALITY OF OUR SHELLS 100 PER CENT WITHOUT ADVANCING THE PRICE.

OUR SALES on the original Low Base Pointer Shells were the largest ever known in the ammunition business. We specified for these shells in quantities of 10,000,000 and over, handling during the season as high as three and four carloads a day. While the old Pointer Shell was an excellent shell, a better shell than you could obtain elsewhere for from 50c to 75c a hundred more, we were not entirely satisfied, and we determined to improve the quality, estimating that if we could improve the quality of our Pointer Shells and make them without question the finest shells ever produced, we would more than treble our already enormous business, and with this in mind, we specified for a quantity of the New Improved Pointer Shells greater than the combined sales of any ten houses handling ammunition, a quantity so enormous as to enable the factory to run the year around, supplying us with shells. This enormous quantity has enabled our factory to purchase raw material such as paper, brass, copper, lead and felt, in quantities three times as great as they were able to purchase them heretofore, with a consequent reduction in the price of the raw material. This enormous quantity has further enabled us to reduce the overhead expense at the factory, so that with these economies and savings in manufacturing in mind, we are able to furnish you the New Improved Long Base Pointer Shell, loaded with Triumph powder, not charging you a cent in advance of what we formerly asked for our Low Base Pointer Shell, a price 25 per cent to 50 per cent below that asked by other dealers for a shell that would in no way stand comparison with our high grade Pointer Shell.

TRIUMPH POWDER.

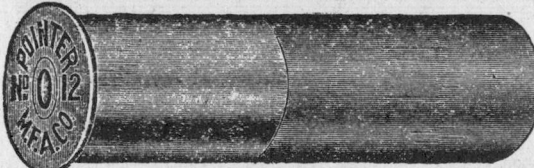

The Ordinary Smokeless Shell.

The Pointer Long Base Shell.

These illustrations show the difference between the Pointer Smokeless Shell and the ordinary shells sold throughout the country at $2.25 a hundred and upward. Note the long brass reinforcements on our Pointer Shell against the short cup on the shells offered in competition. The advantages are many and it will pay you to read what we say about them.

THE NEW IMPROVED POINTER SHELLS are loaded with the famous Triumph powder. This powder is procured from Birmingham, England, where the finest powder in the world is made. We could save at least 20 per cent by loading our shells with any of the American grades of smokeless powder, as the duty on Triumph powder alone is a large item in its cost, but in our aim to give our customers highest quality in a smokeless powder shotgun shell, we have insisted that, above all things, the powder, on which most depends, be absolutely the best that money can buy.

TRIUMPH POWDER IS A BULK POWDER. It is not an acid powder, such as most of the dense powders used so extensively by most manufacturers. There is no acid in Triumph to eat your gun barrel or to create an enormous breech pressure, which is apt to endanger your life. The advantages a bulk powder has over a dense powder are many, and as Triumph is the finest bulk powder made, you can appreciate that in our New Improved Long Base Pointer Shells we are giving the very best that money can buy. Triumph has a very hard grain; does not absorb moisture; there is no disagreeable odor attending the use of this powder, and no unburned particles to blow back in the face of the shooter. We guarantee that Triumph does not contain any gun cotton or nitro glycerine, and we claim that this powder has greater penetration with less breech pressure than any powder made. This being a bulk powder, and owing to the hard, fine grain the combustion is uniform, and there is less recoil to Pointer Shells than to any others.

YOU CANNOT AFFORD TO SHOOT BLACK POWDER SHELLS

when you can get Pointer Smokeless Loaded Shells at $2.00 a hundred, nor can you afford to use any of the common grades of smokeless shells when we offer you the Pointer Shell at these prices, shells which will outshoot any other on the market, regardless of price.

YOU WILL BE SURPRISED AT THE RESULTS

you will obtain from the use of Pointer Shells. You will be able to drop birds that you formerly thought out of range. Your marksmanship will improve from 25 to 50 per cent, depending on your present ability, with the use of Pointer Smokeless Shells.

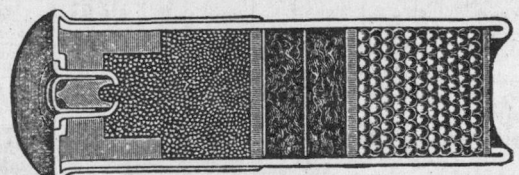

This is an illustration of the Battery Cup used in our Pointer Smokeless Shell. This is a valuable feature and adds greatly to the value of the shell, and is fully described elsewhere on this page. This powder cup prevents the loss of gas, prevents blowing out firing pin, and greatly reinforces the head of the shell. Read what we say about it, as it is a distinctive feature of the Pointer Smokeless Shell.

UNIFORM RESULTS ARE ABSOLUTELY GUARANTEED WITH POINTER SMOKELESS SHELLS

ONE SHELL IS GUARANTEED TO BE LIKE THE OTHER. What you can do with one shell you can do with the other 24 out of the same box, or the other 999 out of the same case. With our special automatic loading machines absolute regularity and uniformity is obtained in the loading of shells, and we guarantee for our Pointer Smokeless Shells greater penetration, better pattern, instantaneous and complete combustion, and longer range than can be obtained through the use of any other shells.

50C PER BOX OF 25
ONE BOX FREE

OUR TERMS: FREE TRIAL, COMPARATIVE TEST AND GUARANTEE OFFER ON ORDER FOR ONE CASE OF 500 OR MORE.

SEND US AN ORDER FOR 500 SHELLS OR MORE, and we will send the shells to you with the understanding and agreement that you can shoot one box of 25 shells for careful test, and if you do not find them by far the best shells you ever used, you can return the balance to us by freight at our expense and we will immediately return your money, including any freight charges you paid, and we will make no charge for the 25 shells you used for test; these 25 shells will be FREE to you.

This illustration shows a box of 25, the way in which our Pointer Shells are put up, 25 in a box, each box sealed with a handsome colored lithographed label. Always look for the Pointer dog on the label to get the genuine. The label is registered in Washington, D. C. Inside, outside, in appearance, finish, safety, regularity, comfort, shooting qualities, in every particular Pointer Smokeless Shells stand ALONE.

THE NEW IMPROVED POINTER LONG BASE SMOKELESS LOADED SHELL

LOADED WITH TRIUMPH

THE NEW BULK SMOKELESS POWDER

PRIMED WITH A No. 3 NITRO PRIMER.

$9.50 PER CASE OF 500 SHELLS

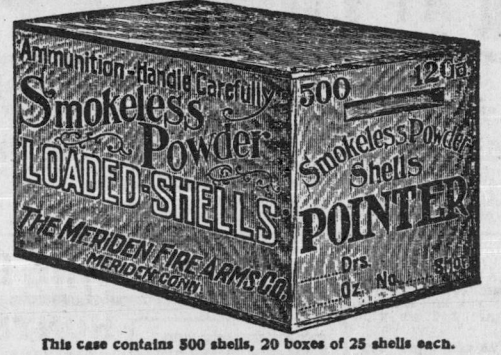

This case contains 500 shells, 20 boxes of 25 shells each.

$19.00 PER 1,000

THESE SPECIAL PRICES ARE OFFERED TO DEALERS, GUN CLUBS, MARKET HUNTERS,

OR ANY SHOOTER WHO WISHES TO TAKE ADVANTAGE OF OUR SPECIAL QUANTITY PRICES

WE ADVISE EVERY SHOOTER to order at least one case of 500 shells, even though he does not use this quantity for some time, as thereby he gets the advantage of our special quantity price, and these shells will keep indefinitely. They are not subject to climatic changes, and you will get as good results from these shells after you have had them a year as you would if you used them the day you receive them. It is, therefore, to your interest to buy them in quantities of 500 or more and obtain the benefit of our special price of $9.50 a case. If you cannot use the entire quantity, get your neighbors to help you make up a quantity of 500 or a 1,000 shells, and divide the saving you effect among yourselves. **THE NEW IMPROVED POINTER SHELL** is loaded with Triumph, the highest quality bulk smokeless powder known, and primed with a No. 3 Nitro Primer, which is the strongest primer ever used in shotgun shells. These shells are absolutely guaranteed against misfire, hangfire or blow backs.

Regardless of what success you have had with other shells, and regardless of the satisfaction the original Pointer shells doubtless gave you, the New Improved Pointer Shell as herewith described, illustrated and quoted, will give you better satisfaction and better results. It is absolutely the best shell on the market regardless of price. **THE NEW IMPROVED POINTER SHELL AT $19.00** per thousand for shells loaded with 3 drams of powder, 1 ounce of shot, is, considering the quality of the shells, certainly the greatest value ever offered in shotgun ammunition. This price of $19.00 per thousand is made only when shells are ordered in full case lots. We will not split cases of shells at these prices. Dealers can handle these shells to their best advantage, as the demand for them is greater than for any other known brand of shells, and they can be sold at a good profit to the dealer. Our name does not appear in any way on the boxes or the labels. The cases and boxes are marked exactly as shown in the illustrations on these pages.

THE NEW IMPROVED POINTER SHELL IS PRIMED WITH A No. 3 NITRO PRIMER AND IS ABSOLUTELY GUARANTEED AGAINST MISFIRES, HANGFIRES OR BLOW BACKS

POINTER SHELLS ADOPTED BY BIG GUN CLUB.

Denver, Colo.
Sears, Roebuck & Co.,
Chicago, Ill.
Gentlemen:
Having used your Pointer Shell quite extensively in the Remington Automatic No. 12-gauge shotgun, find it particularly adapted to that gun. Have shot your Pointers without a single shell breaking or sticking or in any manner interfering with the mechanism. You are probably aware that a great deal of inconvenience is caused by the breaking of certain grades of shells in this gun; in fact, almost every make of shell. Have been using your Pointer, 1-ounce No. 8 drop shot, for trap shooting. My object in writing you is to ascertain if you can furnish me with a load conforming more to the regulation trap load. Quote price and shipping charges. Will thank you for an early reply.
Yours truly,
L. F. NELL,
2558 W. 32d Ave

Mr. Wilt says our Pointer Shells kill at longer range, and are the best shells on the market.

Portage, Penna.
Sears, Roebuck & Co.,
Chicago, Ill.
Gentlemen:
Your smokeless shells are number ONE. I shall use no other make as long as I can get the Pointer shell. Have tried all other makes and find the Pointer shell the best for long range and dead shot; have killed birds from 80 to 100 yards with No. 5 shot. Your shells make better pattern and greater execution, will kill at longer range than any shell I have used before, they are the best shell on the market. Shall order more in next order.
Yours respectfully,
THOMAS WILT.

Twin Lakes, Minn.
Sears, Roebuck & Co.,
Chicago, Ill.
Gentlemen:
I bought from you some time ago the Pointer Smokeless Shotgun Shells. I must say that I was well pleased with what I received from you. I have used the highest priced shells made, the Winchester Leader, U. M. C., Arrow, etc., but cannot find a shell I like better than the Pointer made by the Meriden Fire Arms Company.
Yours, ever a customer,
H. G. DALE.

Sears, Roebuck & Co., Chicago, Ill.
Gentlemen: I purchased a case of Pointer shells from you about a month ago. I have given the shells a thorough test, as we have several others, and we unanimously agree that they are superior to any shells we have ever used. I distributed the shells among my friends, also among all the trap shooters of my acquaintance, and they all agree with me that they are the best shells we ever used, barring none. We were so impressed with the shooting qualities of the shells that we called our newly organized club the Pointer Club. We shot the Winchester Leader shell against the Pointer shell and the Pointer shell won out. We are going to use the Pointer shells exclusively and we want you to give us the rock bottom club prices on the different loads. The captain of our club, Mr. Clarence Thomas, sent you an order for 1,000 Pointer shells last Friday. After trying the Pointer shells myself and finding them superior to all others I used my untiring efforts to show their real value and I am very well pleased with the foothold I have given the Pointer shells in our town. I believe that I am the first man to introduce them in Johnstown. I found that the shooters at first considered the shells too cheap to be good and they did not want to bother trying them. I insisted that they try them, which they did, and were so pleased with the results that they insisted on having Pointer shells. Write a return as soon as you can, giving us your very lowest club prices on all the different loads.
Yours truly, JOHN E. GREEN, 621 Highland Ave.

Johnstown, Pa.

Mr. Fisher says our Pointer Shells at 50 cents are far better than Peters' Shells sold at 60 cents per box.

Sunny Side, N. J.
Sears, Roebuck & Co.,
Chicago, Ill.
Gentlemen:
I received some of your special smokeless powder shotgun shells (the Pointer). I am greatly pleased with them for various reasons. First, they have a good penetration; second, they will kill at longer range; third, they have but little jar; fourth, they are quick and sure fire; fifth, they are much cheaper in price than any shells I have ever seen or bought. Your shells sell at 50 cents per box, while the Peters' Cartridge Company shells sell at 60 cents and are not so good a grade of goods. In fact, the Pointer shells are a better shell in every respect than any other shells I have ever used.
Yours respectfully,
JAMES R. FISHER.

Mr. Tice gets better results from our Pointer Shells than any shells he ever used.

Buford, N. D.
Sears, Roebuck & Co.,
Chicago, Ill.
Gentlemen:
I am well pleased with the Pointer Smokeless Shells I received from you. They will carry a great deal further and give much better penetration than any shell I have ever used. I have been using U. M. C. Nitro Club and Winchester Leader, and have no luck at all with them, as they would not carry far enough, so I gave your Pointer shells a trial, and have been more than pleased with the results I get. I remain,
Ever your customer,
WALTER TICE.

Mr. Gates likes our Pointer Shells better than the Winchester, U. M. C. or Peters'.

Columbia Cross Roads, Pa
Sears, Roebuck & Co.,
Chicago, Ill.
Gentlemen:
The Pointer shells I got from you are the best shells I ever used. I have tried all kinds of shells, the Winchester, U. M. C., Peters' and several other makes, but I like Pointer shells the best for penetration and pattern, especially the three-dram and 1¼-ounce shot load. Will order some more as soon as I need them.
Yours truly,
G. W. GATES.

PRICES ON POINTER SMOKELESS SHELLS
ALWAYS GIVE CATALOGUE NUMBER.

Please notice we furnish only one size and one load in a case, just as they come to us from the factory, at the case price. Order by catalogue number in full.

WEIGHT OF SHELLS IN CASE.
A case of 500 shells, 12-gauge, weight about 65 pounds.
A case of 500 shells, 10-gauge, weight about 75 pounds.
A case of 500 shells, 16-gauge, weight about 53 pounds.
Our terms on loaded shells are cash with order. We do not ship them C. O. D.

POINTER SMOKELESS SHELLS, LOADED WITH DROP SHOT.
Always give Catalogue Number.

12-GAUGE — LOADED WITH SMOKELESS POWDER.

Cat. No.	Grains of Smokeless Powder Equal to	Wt. of shot	Size of Drop Shot	Price per box of 25 Shells	Price per 100 Shells	Price per Case of 500 Shells	Price per 1,000 Shells
6K1920	3 Drams	1 Oz.	No. 6 No. 4 No. 8	50c	$2.00	$9.50	19.00
6K1920	3 Drams	1⅛ Oz.	No. 2 No. 4 No. 5 No. 6 No. 7 No. 8	52c	$2.08	$9.90	19.80
6K1920	3¼ Drams	1⅛	No. 4 No. 6	55c	2.20	10.50	21.00

Always give Catalogue Number.

10-GAUGE — POINTER SMOKELESS SHELLS.

Cat. No.	Grains of Smokeless Powder Equal to	Wt. of shot	Size of Drop Shot	Price per box of 25 Shells	Price per 100 Shells	Price per case of 500 Shells	Price per 1,000 Shells
6K1921	3¼ Drams	1⅛ Oz.	No. 2 No. 4 No. 6 No. 8	57c	$2.28	10.83	21.66

Always give Catalogue Number.

16-GAUGE — LOADED WITH SMOKELESS POWDER.

Cat. No.	Grains of Smokeless Powder equal to	Oz. of shot	Size of Drop Shot	Price per box of 25 Shells	Price per 100 Shells	Price per box of 500 Shells	Price per 1,000 Shells
6K1922	2½ Drams	1	4 6 8	49c	$1.96	$9.24	18.48

POINTER SMOKELESS SHELLS, LOADED WITH CHILLED SHOT.
Shells loaded with smokeless powder and chilled shot give better penetration and more even patterns than drop shot. Loaded in 12-gauge only. The No. 7½ shot is our celebrated trap load. Order by catalogue number.

12-GAUGE, CHILLED SHOT — LOADED WITH SMOKELESS POWDER.

Cat. No.	Grains of Smokeless Powder equal to	Ozs. of shot	Size of Chilled Shot	Price per box of 25 Shells	Price per 100 Shells	Price per case of 500 Shells	Price per 1,000 Shells
6K1923	3 Drams	1⅛	No. 4 No. 6 No. 7½ No. 8	56c	$2.24	10.56	21.12
6K1923	3¼ Drams	1⅛	No. 4 No. 6	58c	$2.32	11.02	22.04

Always give Catalogue Number.

8-GAUGE — HAND LOADED WITH SMOKELESS POWDER.

Cat. No.	Grains of Smokeless Powder equal to	Oz. of shot	Size of Drop Shot	Price per box of 25 Shells	Price per 100 Shells	Price per case of 500 Shells	Price per 1,000 Shells
6K1924	5½ Drams	1⅞	BB	$1.37	$5.48	$25.55	$51.20

Always give Catalogue Number.

WE DO NOT DEEM IT WISE TO ADVERTISE HEAVIER LOADS, SINCE HEAVIER LOADS PRODUCE TOO MUCH HEAT AND ARE LIABLE TO "BALL" THE SHOT OR CAUSE THE SHELL TO BREAK OFF AT THE BRASS WHEN SHOOTING AND GIVE VERY POOR PATTERNS.

NOTICE OUR PRICES ON METALLIC AMMUNITION, GUNS, RIFLES AND REVOLVERS. OUR PRICES ARE BELOW ALL COMPETITION.

HIGHEST QUALITY RIFLE AND PISTOL AMMUNITION AT LOWEST PRICES

21C PER 100; $2.00 PER 1,000 for the highest grade 22-caliber short, black powder, rim fire, loaded metallic cartridges made in the world.

24C PER 100; $2.30 PER 1,000; $22.00 per case of 10,000 for highest grade 22-caliber short smokeless cartridges, the best in the world. (See No. 6K2535)

70C PER 100; $7.00 PER 1,000 for highest grade 32-caliber central fire, S. & W. loaded metallic cartridges, the best made in the world.

90C PER 100; $9.00 PER 1,000 for highest grade 38-caliber central fire, S. & W., loaded metallic cartridges, the best made in the world.

These illustrations show the exact size of the 22, 32 and 38-caliber cartridges that we offer as our leaders in our high grade metallic ammunition at the lowest prices ever known.

THESE ARE THE LOWEST PRICES ever heard of, and we guarantee this ammunition to be equal to the very best on the market, regardless of name, make or price.

WE GUARANTEE the quality of our metallic ammunition in every way. We guarantee it the equal, if not the superior, of any you have ever used, any ammunition you can get from any other dealer or catalogue house. You can send us your order with the understanding that if you do not find our ammunition strictly high grade in every way, the very best ammunition it is possible to make; if you find it inferior in any particular, you are at liberty to return it to us at our expense and we will promptly refund your money.

21 CENTS per 100 for 22-caliber short black powder, 24 cents per 100 for 22 short smokeless, 70 cents per 100 for 32-caliber, and 90 cents per 100 for 38-caliber; these are the lowest prices ever heard of for high grade loaded pistol and rifle cartridges, each and every one shipped under our binding guarantee for quality.

24c PER HUNDRED BUYS THE HIGHEST GRADE SMOKELESS 22-CALIBER SHORT RIM FIRE CARTRIDGES.

For 24 cents per 100, $2.30 per 1,000, or $22.00 per case of 10,000 we will send you our Meriden 22-caliber short rim fire smokeless cartridges with the understanding and agreement that if you do not find them better than any other 22-caliber smokeless cartridges, short or long, more true and accurate, more powerful than any other cartridges you can buy elsewhere, if you do not find them quicker and having more velocity, and shooting stronger, then you are at liberty to return them to us at our expense and we will immediately refund your money. Compare our price on 22-caliber short smokeless rim fire cartridges with prices offered by other houses and you will find that we are 20 to 40 per cent lower in price and superior in quality to any 22-caliber short smokeless cartridges made, regardless of name, make or price. The illustrations will give you an idea of the boxes and the way our 22-caliber short smokeless cartridges are put up. They come fifty in a box and two boxes to the hundred and we recommend by all means that you give these cartridges a trial for we know that you will like them, and we know that if you will try them, it means that you will send us further orders for Meriden smokeless 22-caliber short rim fire cartridges. Only the highest grade smokeless powder is used in these cartridges and we send them out under our binding guarantee; and if you do not find them superior to any other cartridges made, regardless of name, make or price, you are at liberty to return them to us at our expense and we will immediately refund your money. We guarantee our 22 short smokeless to be stronger than 22 long smokeless made by other factories. We are the only house in the United States selling to consumers who buy 22-caliber cartridges in carload lots.

21C PER 100
FOR BLACK POWDER 22-CALIBER SHORT CARTRIDGES

24C PER 100
FOR SMOKELESS POWDER 22-CALIBER CARTRIDGES

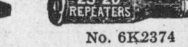

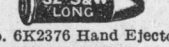

50 SHORT RIM FIRE 22 SMOKELESS METALLIC CARTRIDGES — MERIDEN FIRE ARMS CO. MERIDEN, CONN.

50 22-CAL. SHORT RIFLE & PISTOL CARTRIDGES — HIGHEST GRADE METALLIC AMMUNITION

50 32-CAL. S & W CENTRAL FIRE CARTRIDGES — HIGHEST GRADE METALLIC AMMUNITION

50 38-CAL. S & W CENTRAL FIRE CARTRIDGES — HIGHEST GRADE METALLIC AMMUNITION

These illustrations show the method in which our metallic ammunition is put up, 50 in a box, every box and cartridge guaranteed perfect, the best metallic ammunition that ever went out of any factory. In the larger quantities the 22-caliber comes 500 cartridges in a carton (10 boxes of 50 each) and the 32 and 38-caliber come 250 cartridges in a carton (5 boxes of 50 each).

SHOOTING GALLERIES
please notice these extremely low prices for 22, 32 and 38-caliber CARTRIDGES.

HUNTERS, TARGET SHOOTERS everyone using metallic ammunition, do not fail to take advantage of our wonderfully low prices and send us an order for the quantity of cartridges you use.

OUR FREE TRIAL OFFER
WE ARE SO CONFIDENT that our cartridges will please you, that you will find them better cartridges than you ever shot before, regardless of name, make or price, that we make you this liberal offer: Order 1,000 cartridges and get the benefit of our special quantity price. We will ship the cartridges to you promptly, as we endeavor at all times to carry a complete stock. When ordering these cartridges of us, you will save almost half of what you would have to pay elsewhere. The freight charges amount to but a few cents. We will ship the cartridges to you with the understanding that if you do not find, after testing one box of them, that they are the best cartridges you have ever used, if you do not get better results from them than any you have ever obtained from any other cartridges—in short, if you are not entirely satisfied with the cartridges—return them to us at our expense, and we will promptly return you your money and whatever transportation charges you might have paid, and will make no charge for the box of 50 or 20 you used in testing them.

WHEN WE FIRST INTRODUCED our line of metallic ammunition, particularly 22-caliber, 32 and 38 Smith & Wesson Cartridges, on which sizes there is the largest sale, there was some prejudice among shooters against the new make of ammunition, and for a time a number of these shooters paid 25% to 50% more for cartridges not as good as ours because they could not understand how we were able to sell good ammunition at such low prices. Shooters throughout the country have now been educated to the fact that the name does not make the cartridge, and that there is absolutely no reason for paying a premium of from 5 cents to 20 cents a box for the name that appears thereon. The millions of cartridges we have sold, the thousands of testimonials we have received, and the fact that our ammunition business today is the largest ammunition business in the United States dealing direct with the consumer, bespeak of the quality of our ammunition.

WE GUARANTEE OUR AMMUNITION to be equal, if not superior, to any ammunition made, regardless of name, make or price, and any ammunition you order of us is shipped to you with this distinct understanding. If you do not find it as good or better than any other ammunition you have ever used after testing one box of it, return the balance, and we will refund you the price you paid for the entire lot, as well as any transportation charges you might have paid.

OUR HIGH GRADE RIM FIRE CARTRIDGES.
LOADED WITH BLACK POWDER. Cannot be sent by mail.
If in doubt about the caliber, send a sample shell which has been shot, with your order, or send the cover of the box.

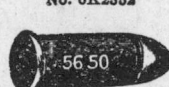

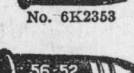

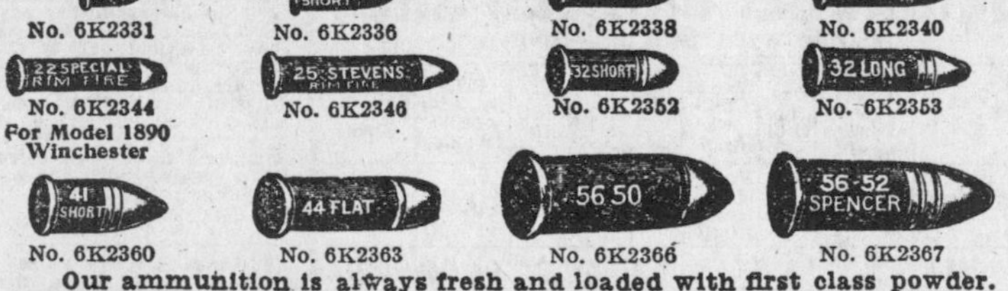

No. 6K2331   No. 6K2336   No. 6K2338   No. 6K2340
No. 6K2344 (22 SPECIAL RIM FIRE, For Model 1890 Winchester)   No. 6K2346 (25 STEVENS RIM FIRE)   No. 6K2352 (32 SHORT)   No. 6K2353 (32 LONG)
No. 6K2360 (41 SHORT)   No. 6K2363 (44 FLAT)   No. 6K2366 (56 50)   No. 6K2367 (56-52 SPENCER)

Our ammunition is always fresh and loaded with first class powder. **OUR TERMS ARE CASH WITH ORDER. WE CANNOT SEND CARTRIDGES C. O. D. nor by MAIL.**

No.	CARTRIDGES Cannot be sent by mail. Caliber	Good for Yards	Grains of Powder	Grains of Lead	Weight Per 100	Price for 50	Price for 100	Price for 1,000
6K2331	B. B. Caps (Round ball) Rim	15	..	21	7 oz.	......	$0.15	$1.44
6K2336	22 Short Rim Fire	35	3	30	9 oz.	.21	.21	2.00
6K2338	22 Long Rim Fire	50	5	29	11 oz.	.31	.31	3.07
6K2340	22 Long Rifle Rim Fire	60	5	40	14 oz.	.31	.31	3.07
6K2344	22 Special for Mod. 1890 Winc.	125	7	45	18 oz.	$0.24	.47	4.61
6K2346	25 Stevens Rim Fire	150	11	65	29 oz.	.36	.72	7.17
6K2352	32 Short Rim Fire	100	9	82	27 oz.	.26	.52	5.13
6K2353	32 Long Rim Fire	100	13	90	30 oz.	.30	.59	5.89
6K2360	41 Short Remington Derringe	125	13	130	40 oz.	.40	.80	8.00
6K2363	44 Flat Rim Fire	300	28	200	64 oz.	.63	1.24	12.30
6K2364	44 Long Ballard Rim Fire	300	28	220	4½ lbs.	.67	1.30	12.80
6K2366	56-50 Spencer Rim Fire	400	45	350	7 lbs.	1.06	2.10	20.52
6K2367	56-52 Spencer Rim Fire	400	45	386	7 lbs.	1.06	2.10	20.52

CENTRAL FIRE PISTOL AND RIFLE CARTRIDGES.
LOADED WITH BLACK POWDER. Explosives cannot be sent by mail.
These illustrations show about the half size of cartridges. If you are in doubt about the caliber send a sample shell which has been shot, with your order, or send the cover of the box.

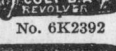

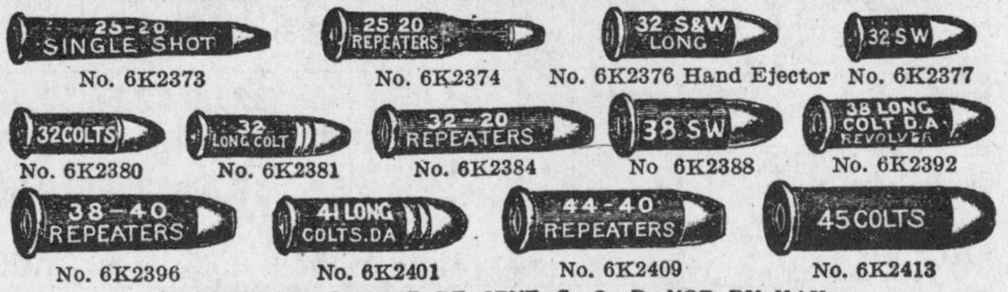

No. 6K2373 (25-20 SINGLE SHOT)   No. 6K2374 (25 20 REPEATERS)   No. 6K2376 Hand Ejector (32 S&W LONG)   No. 6K2377 (32 S W)
No. 6K2380 (32 COLTS)   No. 6K2381 (32 LONG COLT)   No. 6K2384 (32-20 REPEATERS)   No. 6K2388 (38 S W)   No. 6K2392 (38 LONG COLT D.A. REVOLVER)
No. 6K2396 (38-40 REPEATERS)   No. 6K2401 (41 LONG COLTS D.A.)   No. 6K2409 (44-40 REPEATERS)   No. 6K2413 (45 COLTS)

CARTRIDGES CANNOT BE SENT C. O. D. NOR BY MAIL.

No.	CARTRIDGES Cannot be sent by mail. Caliber for following Rifles or Revolvers	Good for Yards	Grains of Powder	Grains of Lead	Weight Per 100	Price for 50	Price for 100
6K2373	25-20 Single Shot Rifles	200	19	86	2½ lbs.	71c	$1.42
6K2374	25-20 Repeating Rifles	200	17	86	2½ lbs.	62c	1.24
6K2376	32 Smith & Wesson Long	125	9	98	2½ lbs.	47c	.94
6K2377	32 Smith & Wesson	75	9	85	1½ lbs.	37c	.70
6K2380	32 Short Colt's Revolver	75	9	82	1½ lbs.	43c	.86
6K2381	32 Long Colt's Revolver	125	13	90	2 lbs.	47c	.94
6K2382	32 Extra Long Ballard	150	18	105	2½ lbs.	70c	1.40
6K2384	32-20 Repeating Rifles	200	20	115	3 lbs.	62c	1.24
6K2388	38 Smith & Wesson	100	14	145	3½ lbs.	47c	.90
6K2392	38 Long Colt's Revolver	175	19	150	3½ lbs.	57c	1.14
6K2396	38-40 Repeating Rifles	300	40	180	4½ lbs.	73c	1.46
6K2401	41 Long Colt's Revolver	175	21	200	4¼ lbs.	68c	1.36
6K2409	44-40 Repeating Rifles	300	40	200	5½ lbs.	73c	1.46
6K2413	45 Colt's Revolver	300	40	260	5½ lbs.	87c	1.74

The above cartridges are reloadable and may be reloaded with Ideal Mfg. Co.'s loading tools.

RIFLE, PISTOL AND REVOLVER AMMUNITION

HIGHEST QUALITY—LOWEST PRICES

WE GUARANTEE the cartridges described on this page to be equal in shooting qualities, penetration, accuracy and uniformity to any cartridges made, regardless of name, make or price. The low prices we name are not occasioned by any difference between the quality of our ammunition and that sold by others for far more money. Our prices are made possible by the fact that we sell more ammunition than any ten houses combined selling direct to the consumer, consequently we enjoy a lower cost. We are not at the mercy of any so called trust, and as we are content with but one small margin of profit we, quality considered, give you better value in ammunition of any kind than you could possibly obtain elsewhere.

CENTER FIRE MILITARY AND SPORTING CARTRIDGES.

LOADED WITH BLACK POWDER.

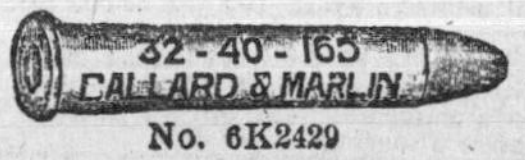

No. 6K2429

No. 6K2432

These illustrations are one-half size of cartridges. If you are in doubt about the correct caliber, send a sample shell, which has been shot, with your order, or send the cover of the box. Cartridges cannot be sent by mail.

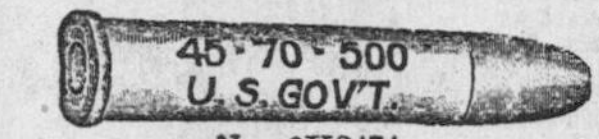

No. 6K2474

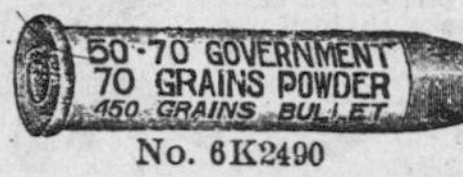

No. 6K2490

ALL THESE CARTRIDGES have lead bullets only, and are good for 200 to 1,000 yards. Explosives cannot be sent by mail. Cartridges cannot be sent C. O. D.

No.	Cartridges cannot be sent C. O. D. or by mail. Caliber Kind	Grains of Powd'r	Grains of Lead	Good for Y'rds	Weight per 100	Price for 20	Price for 100
6K2429	32-40 Ballard and Marlin..	40	165	400	6 lbs	45c	$2.24
6K2432	38-55 Ballard and Marlin..	55	255	500	7 lbs	56c	2.77
6K2466	45-70-405 Government......	70	405	700	11 lbs	50c	2.40
6K2474	45-70-500 Government......	70	500	700	12¼ lbs	57c	2.77
6K2490	50-70 Government..........	70	450	1,000	11½ lbs	59c	2.89

The above cartridges may be reloaded with Ideal tools, No. 6K4293 or No. 6K4294.

SMOKELESS CARTRIDGES.

Metallic Cartridges, loaded with Smokeless Powder, are all the same shape and size as regular Black Powder Cartridges, but have less grains of Powder than Black Powder Cartridges and are much stronger and much more powerful and have a greater velocity.

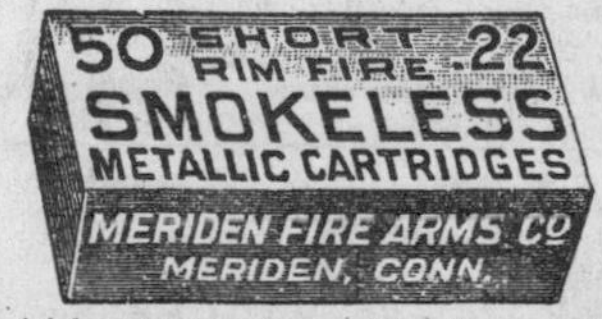

24 CENTS PER 100 FOR 22-CALIBER

RIM FIRE MERIDEN SMOKELESS CARTRIDGES, $2.30 per 1,000 or $22.00 per case of 10,000. These are positively the highest grade 22-caliber short rim fire smokeless cartridges made, regardless of name, make or price, and are as strong as 22-caliber long smokeless cartridges made by other factories.

OUR GUARANTEE. Send us your order for some of these high grade 22-caliber rim fire smokeless cartridges; state whether you wish 100, 1,000 or a case, give them a good, fair trial, compare them with other smokeless cartridges, long or short, sold by other houses at a much higher price, and if you do not find them much better in strength, accuracy and penetration, more especially in penetration, you are at liberty to return them at our expense. No other house will give you such a strong guarantee on 22-caliber short rim fire smokeless cartridges. Our 22 short smokeless penetrates as well as any other make of 22 long smokeless.

OUR ONE BOX FREE PROPOSITION. Send us your order for 1,000 or one case of these Meriden 22-caliber short rim fire smokeless cartridges, inclose our price, and we will ship them to you by freight or express, as you prefer. Try one box of 50 cartridges in any good rifle, and if you do not find them better than any other cartridges made, you may return the balance of your shipment to us by freight, and we will immediately refund your money and the transportation charges paid by you.

No. 6K2535 This is our catalogue number for these celebrated 22-caliber short rim fire smokeless cartridges, and when ordering mention the catalogue number and state whether you wish 100, 1,000, or a case of 10,000, and we will ship them to you by express or freight, as you prefer, but if you order these cartridges in case lots, we recommend that you ship them by freight, since the transportation charges on a case of cartridges is a very small item compared with the large saving you will make in the price which we print on these cartridges.

A thousand Meriden cartridges weigh about 6½ pounds. The weight of a case of 10,000 cartridges is about 65 pounds.

RIM FIRE SMOKELESS. COME WITH LEAD BULLETS ONLY.

This illustration is full size of the cartridge. If you are in doubt about correct caliber, send us a sample shell that has been shot, with your order, or send cover of box.

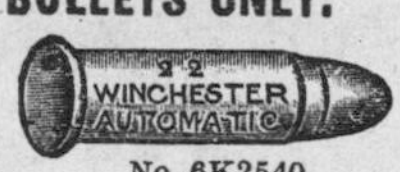

No. 6K2540

No.	Caliber	Grains of Powd'r	Grains of Lead	Weight per 100	Price for 100	Price for case of 1,000	Price for case of 10,000
6K2535	22 Short Rim Fire.........	2	30	10 oz.	$0.24	$ 2.30	$22.00
6K2540	22 Winchester Automatic	......	45 Greaseless	12 oz.	.54	5.30	....
6K2542	41 Swiss for Vetterli Rifle	20	310	7 lbs.	1.95	19.50	....

How to Load Paper Shells to Get the Best Results.

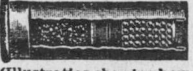

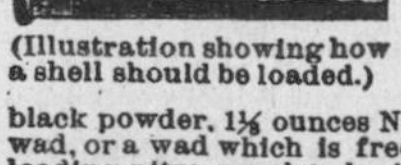
(Illustration showing how a shell should be loaded.)

Our experience is that the loading of shells is largely responsible for good or poor targets. Some guns will make a good pattern with a certain size of shot, and a poor pattern with another size, but nearly all guns will do better when the shell is properly loaded. Try the following rules if you load your own shells: For black powder—first, put in the powder; second, one thick cardboard wad; third, two ¼-inch felt wads; fourth, another card wad; fifth, the shot; sixth, one thin card wad. Test load for 12-gauge, 3 drams black powder, 1⅛ ounces No. 8 shot. For nitro powder use the same rules, except put a thin card wad, or a wad which is free from grease, over the powder instead of a thick card wad. When loading nitro powder don't put in a heavier charge than the directions on the can. Guns are usually tested on a 30-inch circle, at forty yards distance.

CENTER FIRE SMOKELESS CARTRIDGES. RIFLE AND PISTOL SIZES.

CARTRIDGES CANNOT BE SENT BY MAIL OR C. O. D.

All Smokeless Cartridges are the same style and size as Black Powder Cartridges, but they have less grains of powder than Black Powder Cartridges and are much stronger and much more powerful, and have a greater velocity.

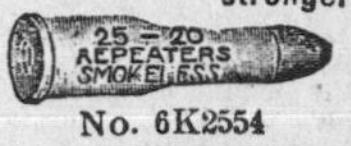

No. 6K2554

No. 6K2560

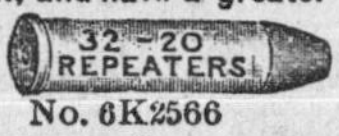

No. 6K2566

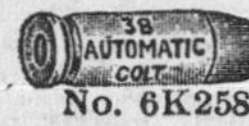

No. 6K2580

NOTICE: M. P. means Metal Patched Bullet. S. P. means Soft Point Bullet. Cartridges cannot be sent by mail.

The powder weight which we quote is Laflin & Rand's of their various brands. It may vary in other brands.

No.	Cartridges cannot be sent C. O. D. or by mail. Caliber Kind	Grains of Powder	Grains of Lead	Weig't per 100	Price for 50	Price for 100
6K2554	25-20 For Repeating Rifles......	4	86 S. P	2¼ lbs.	$0.79	$1.58
6K2560	32 Colt's Automatic Pistol......	2½	71 M.P.	2½ lbs.	.72	1.44
6K2566	32-20 For Repeating Rifles......	5	115 M.P	3 lbs.	.79	1.58
6K2568	32-20 For Repeating Rifles......	5	115 S. P.	3 lbs.	.80	1.60
6K2580	38 Colt's Automatic Pistol......	4½	105 M.P.	3 lbs.	1.03	2.06

SMOKELESS SPORTING RIFLE AND MILITARY CARTRIDGES.

FOR LARGE GAME HUNTING.

All smokeless cartridges are the same style and size as regular black powder cartridges but they have less grains of powder than black powder cartridges and are much more powerful and have a greater velocity. Cartridges cannot be sent C. O. D. or by mail.

These illustrations are half size of cartridges. If you are in doubt about the correct caliber, send us a shell that has been shot, with your order, or send the cover of the box with the label on it.

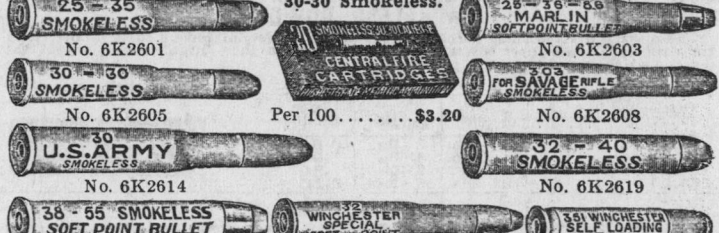

No. 6K2601

30-30 Smokeless.

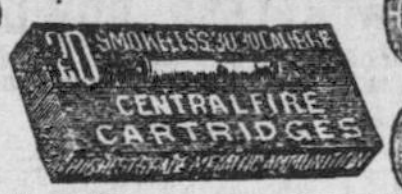

Per 100..........$3.20

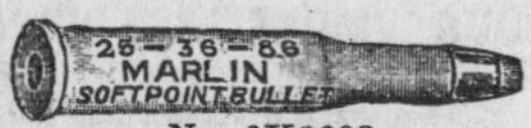

No. 6K2603

No. 6K2605

No. 6K2608

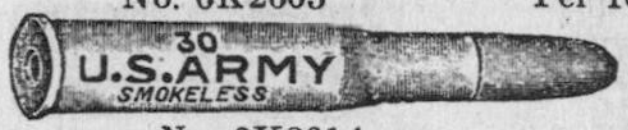

No. 6K2614

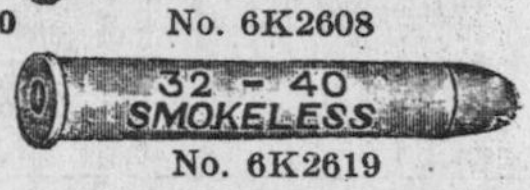

No. 6K2619

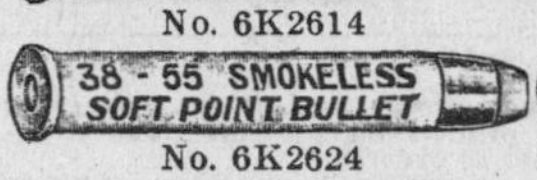

No. 6K2624

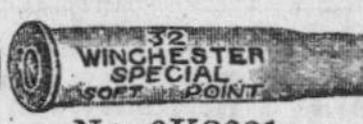

No. 6K2621

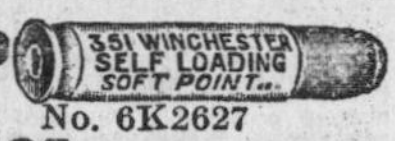

No. 6K2627

SEE OUR PRICES ON **LOADED SHELLS.**

NOTICE.

M. P. MEANS METAL PATCHED BULLET.

S. P. MEANS SOFT POINT BULLET.

The powder weight which we quote is Laflin & Rand's of their various brands. It may vary in other brands.

No.	Cartridges cannot be sent C. O. D. or by mail. Caliber Kind	Grains of Powd'r	Grains of Lead	Weig't per 100	Price for 20	Price for 100
6K2600	25-35 For Winchester Rifles..	19	117 M. P.	4¼ lbs	56c	$2.80
6K2601	25-35 For Winchester Rifles..	19	117 S. P.	4¼ lbs	56c	2.80
6K2602	25-36 For Marlin Rifles......	19	117 M. P.	4¼ lbs	56c	2.80
6K2603	25-36 For Marlin Rifles......	19	117 S. P.	4¼ lbs	56c	2.80
6K2605	30-30 For Repeating Rifles....	23	160 M. P.	6 lbs	64c	3.20
6K2607	30-30 For Repeating Rifles....	23	160 S. P.	6 lbs	64c	3.20
6K2608	303 Savage Repeating Rifle...	27	180 M. P.	6¼ lbs	64c	3.20
6K2609	303 Savage Repeating Rifle...	27	180 S. P.	6¼ lbs	64c	3.20
6K2614	30 U. S. Army..............	35	220 S. P.	7½ lbs	85c	4.22
6K2619	32-40 For Repeating Rifles....	24	165 M. P.	5½ lbs	54c	2.70
6K2620	32-40 For Repeating Rifles....	24	165 S. P.	5½ lbs	54c	2.70
6K2621	32 Winchester Special		170 M. P.	5¾ lbs	64c	3.20
6K2622	32 Winchester Special		170 S. P.	5¾ lbs	64c	3.20
6K2623	38-55 For Repeating Rifles....	26	255 M. P.	7 lbs	67c	3.35
6K2624	38-55 For Repeating Rifles....	26	255 S. P.	7 lbs	67c	3.35
6K2627	351 Self Loading............		180 M. P.	6¼ lbs	64c	3.20
6K2628	351 Self Loading............		180 S. P,	6¼ lbs	64c	3.20

We handle only fresh ammunition, loaded with best grades of powder. Cartridges cannot be sent by mail. They must be sent by express or freight. We cannot send cartridges C. O. D.

SHOT CARTRIDGES.

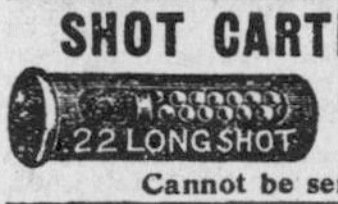

Loaded with shot instead of ball. For use in rifles and revolvers.

Cannot be sent by mail.

Catalogue No.	Caliber	Weight per 100	Price, per 100
6K2719	22 Long, R. F..	¾ lb.	$0.49
6K2717	44 XL C. F.....	5 lbs.	1.43

BLANK CARTRIDGES.

Primed with regular powder charges, but without bullets. For 4th of July and celebrations.

Catalogue No.	Caliber	For	Weight, per 100	Price per 100	Price per 1,000
6K2762	22 Rim	Pistols	4 ounces	15c	$1.50
6K2764	32 S. & W.	Pistols	12 ounces	51c	5.10
6K2765	38 S. & W.	Pistols	15 ounces	65c	6.50

CANNOT GO BY MAIL.

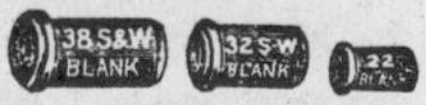

OUR APOTHECARY SCALES WITH WEIGHTS.

FOR WEIGHING SMOKELESS POWDER.

Will weigh from 2 grains to 120 grains. The little weights made of sheet brass are the grain weights, weighing from 2 to 6 grains; the 10-grain weights are made of aluminum and stamped 10 grains. In addition to the above weights we also furnish the regular apothecary scruples and dram weights for druggists, 1 scruple being equal to 20 grains. These scales have a 2-inch pan and scoop, come put up in a box 5½ inches long, 2½ inches wide and 1¼ inches deep.

No 6K3451 Price 44c
If by mail, postage extra, 6 cents.

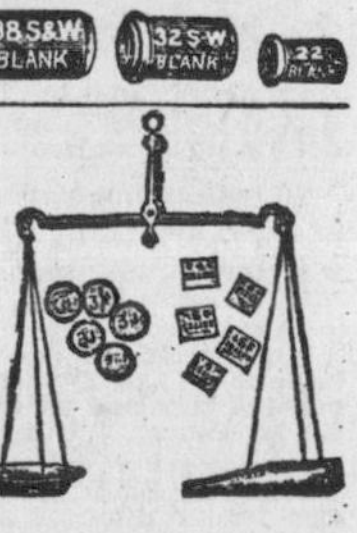

HIGHEST QUALITY EMPTY BRASS SHELLS.

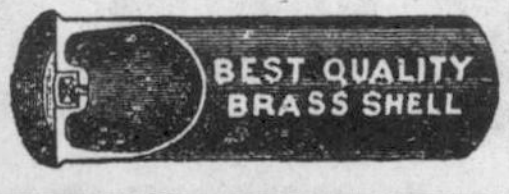

Not loaded. We cannot furnish brass shells loaded These shells come in first quality only, are durable, serviceable shells and may be reloaded many times. These shells come put up 25 shells in a paper box and all use the No. 2 primer and cannot be used in the magazine of repeating shotguns.

Catalogue Number	Gauge of Shell	Length of Shell	Weight Per Box of 25	Price Per Box of 25
6K2103	10	2⅞ in.	1⅞ lbs.	$1.15
6K2104	12	2⅝ in.	1⅞ lbs.	1.08
6K2107	16	2½ in.	1⅛ lbs.	1.09
6K2108	20	2½ in.	1⅛ lbs.	1.10

Brass shells cannot be sent by mail.

OUR BLACK POWDER EMPTY PAPER SHELLS, SUITABLE FOR BLACK POWDER LOADING.

These shells come packed 100 shells in a box and we cannot sell less than 100 shells of one size. All these shells take No. 2 primer. If you wish to shoot smokeless powder in these shells put 2 grains of black powder into the shell before you put in the smokeless powder. Two grains is about half as much as a 22-caliber rim fire cartridge shell will hold. This is called "priming the shell" with black powder. Empty shells cannot be sent by mail.

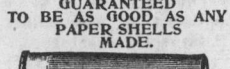

GUARANTEED TO BE AS GOOD AS ANY PAPER SHELLS MADE.

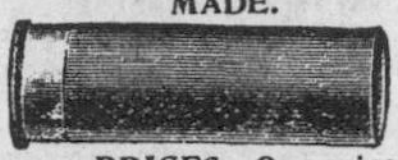

Catalogue No.	Gauge	Length of Shell	Weight per 100	Takes Primer	Price, per 100
6K2128	12	2⅝ in.	3 lbs.	No. 2	63c
6K2129	10	2⅞ in.	3 lbs.	No. 2	70c
6K2131	16	2 9-16 in.	2½ lbs.	No. 2	60c
6K2132	20	2½ in.	2¼ lbs.	No. 2	62c

PRICES—Our prices are ROCK BOTTOM. Positively no reduction made for quantity.

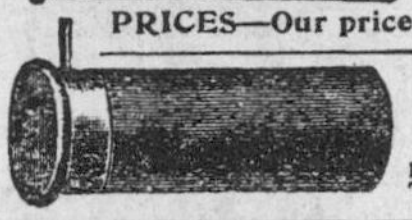

EMPTY PIN FIRE PAPER SHELLS.

We cannot furnish these loaded. Order your ammunition and reloading tools from us and load your own shells to your own liking. These shells come 100 in a box and we cannot sell less than a box.

Catalogue Number	Gauge	Weight, per 100	Price, per 100
6K2150	20 Pin Fire	1⅛ pounds	60c
6K2152	16 Pin Fire	1¾ pounds	60c
6K2153	12 Pin Fire	2 pounds	70c

Shells cannot be sent by mail.

OUR SMOKELESS POWDER EMPTY PAPER SHELLS FOR BULK SMOKELESS POWDER.

These shells are especially adapted to smokeless powder, all have a quick primer. They come put up 100 in a paper box, and we cannot sell less than 100 of a size, except the 8-gauge which come 50 in a box.

These shells cannot be sent by mail.

Catalogue No.	Gauge	Length of Shell	Weight per 100	Price, per 100
6K2133	12	2⅝ in.	3 lbs.	$0.84
6K2134	10	2⅞ in.	3 lbs.	.93
6K2135	16	2 9-16 in.	2½ lbs.	.80
6K2136	8	3¼ in.	5 lbs.	2.20

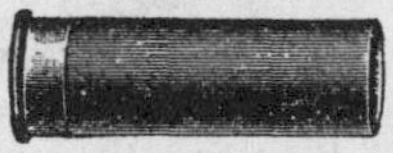

PRIMERS.

AN EXPLANATION ABOUT PRIMERS.

There are at least fifty to sixty styles of primers manufactured, and it becomes confusing to customers as to which style of primer to order.

WHEN ORDERING give the number of primer or name of shells which you wish to load.

Illustrations show the exact size of primers. Primers cannot be sent by mail. Be sure to mention caliber and make of shell for which primers are wanted.

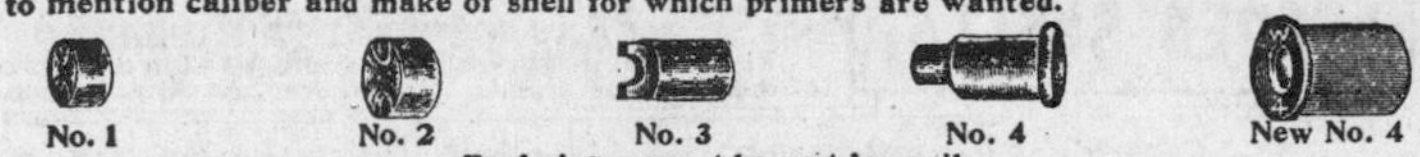

No. 1 No. 2 No. 3 No. 4 New No. 4

Explosives cannot be sent by mail.

NOTICE—All No. 2 primers are alike in size and are used for black powder paper or brass shells.

Catalogue No.	Factory No.	For Powder	Primers, per box	Price, per box	Price, per 1,000
6K2111	1	Black	250	40c	$1.50
6K2111	1W	Smokeless	100	18c	1.50
6K2111	1½	Black	250	40c	1.50
6K2111	3	Smokeless	100	16c	1.50
6K2111	7	Smokeless	250	40c	1.50
6K2111	8½	Smokeless	250	40c	1.50
6K2111	2	Black	100	15c	1.40
6K2111	2½	Black	250	40c	1.50
6K2111	4	Smokeless	100	18c	1.60
6K2111	New 4	Smokeless	100	18c	1.60

SHOT AND BAR LEAD.

Subject to market changes without notice.

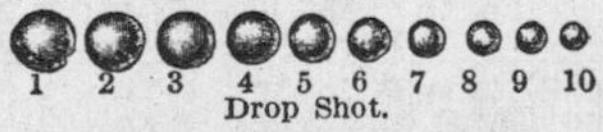

1 2 3 4 5 6 7 8 9 10
Drop Shot.

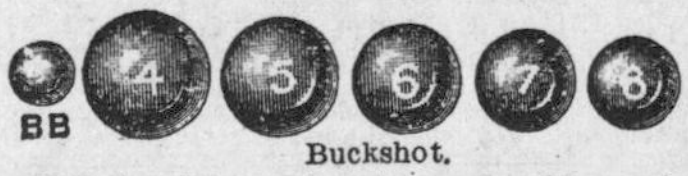

BB
Buckshot.

Chilled and dropped shot in sacks of 5 pounds and 25 pounds at lowest market rates. We do not sell less than a sack. The price of shot fluctuates so much that we cannot quote permanent prices. Prices are subject to change without notice. Always mention size wanted.

WE CANNOT SELL SHOT IN 5-POUND SACKS AT 25-POUND SACK RATE.

Catalogue Number	Kind of Shot	Size of Shot	Wt. of Sack	Per Sack
6K3601	Drop	4, 5, 6, 7, 8, 10	25 lbs.	$2.19
6K3603	Drop	1 to 10	5 lbs.	.54
6K3605	Chilled	4, 5, 6, 7½	25 lbs.	2.40
6K3607	Chilled	1 to 10	5 lbs.	.60
6K3610	Buck Drop	8 to 4	5 lbs.	
6K3612	Buck Drop	BB	5 lbs.	

In case of fluctuation chilled shot is always 25 cents higher in 25-pound sacks and 5 cents higher in 5-pound sacks than drop shot. We will always bill shot at the lowest market rate.

No. 6K3613 F BAR LEAD for running bullets. Take 1 part tin (or solder) to 40 parts of this lead for bullets. If too soft add tin (or solder). Price, per pound 10c

No. 6K3615 BB SHOT in 1-pound packages for air rifles. Price, per pound 13c

GUN WADS.

A FEW WORDS ABOUT GUN WADS

There is considerable difference of opinion among shooters about the best method of loading shells, with reference to the wadding. We have gone into this matter extensively, and our experience is as follows: That if you place one cardboard wad next to the powder, then use one or two ¼-inch black edge wads (according to the length of the shell), after this put another cardboard wad over the black edge wad, then put in your shot and a thin cardboard wad over the shot, leaving about ¼-inch of the shell to be crimped, you will get good results.

The main scientific principle in shooting is to confine the gas generated by the burning powder behind the shot. If loading as above mentioned does not give the proper pattern we advise you to try one size larger felt wads.

CARDBOARD GUN WADS.

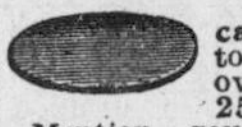

Made from specially prepared cardboard. To be used next to the powder, and may be used over the shot also. They come 250 in a box.

Mention gauge and catalogue number wanted when ordering.

Catalogue Number	Gauge	Weight per box	Price, per box of 250	Price, per 1,000
6K3300	7 or 8	7 oz.	8c	26c
	9 or 10	6 oz.	7c	22c
	11 or 12	5 oz.	6c	18c
	14 or 16	5 oz.	6c	18c
	18 or 20	5 oz.	6c	18c

If by mail, postage extra, per ounce, 1 cent.

BLACK EDGE GUN WADS.

For use over black or smokeless powder. See above instructions about loading. Always put a card wad next to the powder. They come 250 wads in a box. Made in ⅛-inch and ¼-inch thickness. Mention gauge wanted.

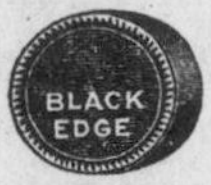

Catalogue No.	Gauge	Thickness	Wt. per box	Price, per box of 250	Price, per 1,000
6K3330	6	⅛ in.	10oz	35c	$1.20
	7 or 8		9oz	25c	.80
	9 or 10		8oz	20c	.70
	11 or 12		7oz	17c	.60
	14 or 16		7oz	17c	.60
	18 or 20		7oz	17c	.60
6K3340	9 or 10	¼ in.	9oz	30c	$1.05
	11 or 12		9oz	25c	.90
	14 or 16			25c	.90

If by mail, postage extra, per ounce, 1 cent.

☞NOTICE—In 12-gauge brass shells use 10-gauge wads. In paper shells use wads the same size of shell. Always put the wad down to place flat and evenly, otherwise the shooting qualities of your gun will be greatly impaired.

NEW IDEAL RELOADING TOOL No. 1, $1.43.

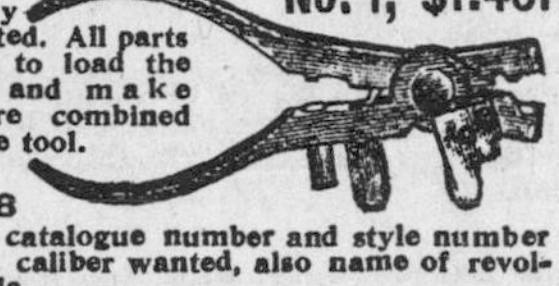

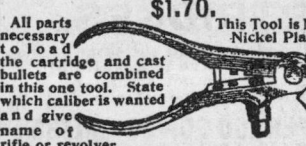

This tool is nicely nickel plated. All parts necessary to load the cartridge and make bullets are combined in this one tool.

No. 6K4288 Order by catalogue number and style number and state caliber wanted, also name of revolver or rifle.

Style	Caliber (All are Center Fire)	For	Price per Set
CC	32 Long	Colt's Revolver	$1.43
EE	32 S. & W.	Revolvers	
LS	38 S. & W.	Revolvers	
GG	38 Long Colts	Colt's Center Fire	1.43
SE	38 Short	Colt's Center Fire	
NN	41 Long	Colt's Revolver	

If by mail, postage extra, per set, 23 to 25 cents.

NOTE—If you want to load S. & W. Cartridges buy tools for S. & W. No other tool will load them. Mention style number.

IDEAL RELOADING TOOL No. 4, $1.70.

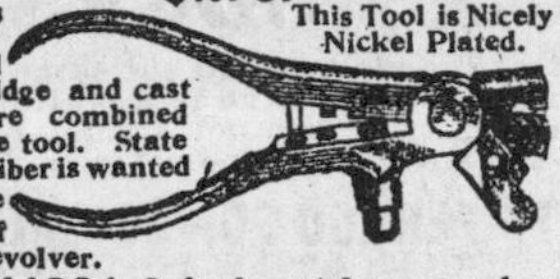

All parts necessary to load the cartridge and cast bullets are combined in this one tool. State which caliber is wanted and give name of rifle or revolver.

This Tool is Nicely Nickel Plated.

No. 6K4291 Order by catalogue number, and style number, and state caliber wanted, also name of rifle or revolver.

Style	Caliber	For Mention style wanted	Price, per Set
A	25-20 Single Shot.	Single Shot Rifles only This tool will not load Repeater Shells.	$1.70
B	25-20 Rep'r.	Repeating Rifles only	$1.70
C	32 S.&W.L.	Smith & Wesson Long, Hand Ejector	
E	32-20	Repeaters and Single Shot	1.70
F	38-40	Repeaters and Single Shot	1.70
H	44-40	Repeaters and Single Shot	1.70
N	45 C. F	Colt's Revolvers	1.70

If by mail, postage extra, per set, 28 to 30 cents.

NEW IDEAL TOOL No. 6, ADJUSTABLE, $2.03.

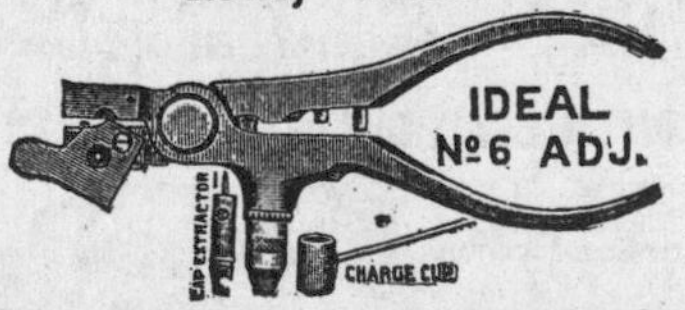

Ideal Reloading Tool No. 6, adjustable, complete, with bullet mould. This tool is substantially the same as No. 6K4294, with an adjustable chamber to accommodate various lengths of shells, and contains all the necessary appliances to make bullets, decap and recap shells, load and seat the bullets, and is without doubt the best tool made. The mould will cast grooved bullets only. Order by catalogue number. State caliber wanted.

Cat. No.	Caliber	For	Per Set
6K4293 B	25-35	Winchester.	$2.03
6K4293 C	30-30	Marlin	
6K4293 D	30-30	Winchester.	
6K4293 E	303	Savage......	2.03
6K4293 F	32-40	Marlin	
6K4293 G	32-40	Winchester.	
6K4293 H	38-55	Marlin	2.03
6K4293 J	38-55	Winchester	

If by mail, postage extra, per set, 32 cents.

IDEAL TOOL No. 6, $2.01.

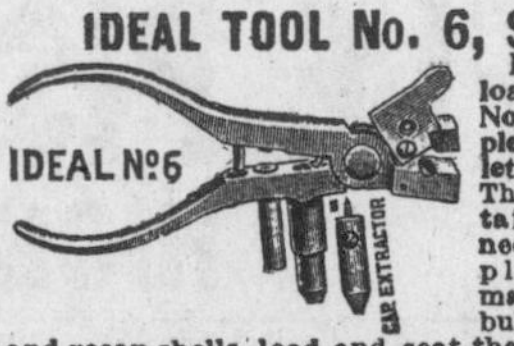

Ideal Reloading Tool No. 6, complete with bullet moulds. This tool contains all the necessary appliances to make grooved bullets, decap and recap shells, load and seat the bullets, and is without doubt the best tool made. Order by catalogue number. State caliber wanted.

Cat. No.	Caliber	For	Per set
6K4294 A	38-56	Winchester	$2.01
6K4294 C	40-82	Winchester	
6K9294 D	40-65	Winchester or Marlin	

If by mail, postage extra, per set, 32 cents.

6K4294 H	45-70-405	Government	$2.01
6K4294 K	45-70-500	Government	
6K4294 L	50-70-450	Government	

If by mail, postage extra, per set, about 39c.

TO PRESERVE SHELLS, always wash them out with hot soapsuds or hot soda water and take out the primers as soon after shooting as possible.

Shell Reducer and Resizer.

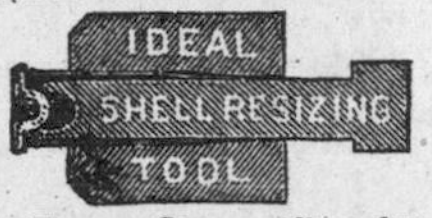

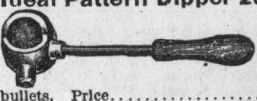

No. 6K4296 Shell Reducer and Resizer for any size from 25 to 45 caliber and larger; will resize shells which have become bulged. Shipped from New Haven, Conn. Allow for postage. State size wanted. Price..$1.34
If by mail, postage extra, 15 cents.

WINCHESTER MAKE LOADING TOOLS, $1.00.

No. 6K4298 Order by catalogue number and state style wanted.

Caliber	Style	Price
38	Colt's Short Center Fire....	$1.00
38- 90	Express	1.00
40- 90	Sharp's Straight.............	1.00
40-110	Express	1.00
50- 95	Express	1.00
303	Savage, without mould....	1.00

If by mail, postage extra, 45 cents.

Ideal Pattern Dipper 25 Cents.

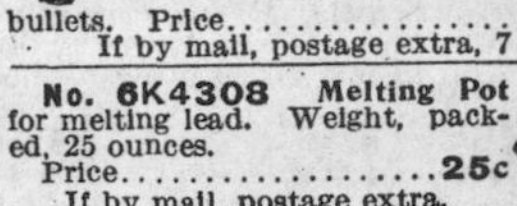

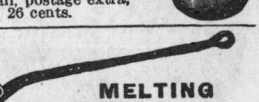

No. 6K4307 Ideal Pattern Dipper for running bullets. Price..........................25c
If by mail, postage extra, 7 cents.

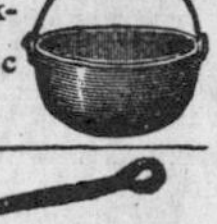

No. 6K4308 Melting Pot for melting lead. Weight, packed, 25 ounces.
Price..........................25c
If by mail, postage extra, 26 cents.

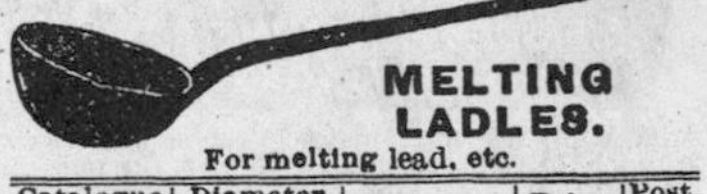

MELTING LADLES.

For melting lead, etc.

Catalogue No.	Diameter of bowl	Weight	Price	Postage
6K4312	4 inches	15 ounces	24c	16c
6K4314	6 inches	26 ounces	32c	27c

CAST STEEL WAD CUTTERS.

When cutting wads always use a hardwood block and cut into the end of the grain to get best results. Be sure to state gauge wanted.

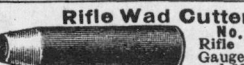

Catalogue Number	Gauge	Price	Postage extra
6K4319	8 or 9	14c	5c
6K4320	10, 11, 12, 14, 15, 16, 19, 20	10c	5c

Hand Forged Steel Wad Cutters.

6K4321½	7, 12, 14, 16, 18, 20	35c	5c

Rifle Wad Cutters.

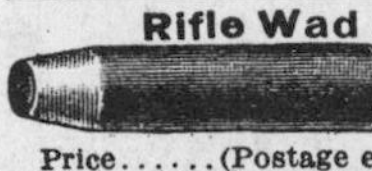

No. 6K4321 Rifle Wad Cutter. Gauge, 32, 38, 44, 45 and 50 caliber.
Price......(Postage extra, 3c.)....28c
Always mention gauge or caliber wanted.

Our Supplemental Chamber.

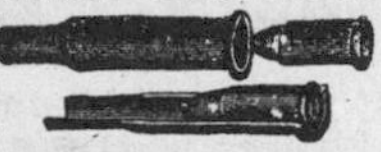

No. 6K4322 Our Supplemental Chamber, to be used in 30-30-caliber rifles. This is an ingenious device which admits of your shooting the 32 S. & W. cartridge in a 30-30-caliber rifle. The supplemental chamber is made exactly like a 30-30-caliber shell, and it is chambered to take a 32-caliber S. & W. cartridge, so that if you own a 30-30-caliber rifle you can insert a 32 S. & W. cartridge in this supplemental chamber, put it in the barrel and use your rifle for short range practice. These supplemental chambers take the regular 32 S. & W. cartridges, No. 6K2377, and are made from brass, nicely nickel plated. Price. 48c
If by mail, postage extra, 2 cents.

INSURED MAIL. We recommend our customers to send articles of value by insured mail, which costs 5 cents extra on articles costing $5.00 or less, and will cost 10 cents extra on articles costing from $5.00 to $10.00. When you do not order goods by insured or registered mail if the article is lost neither the postoffice nor ourselves are responsible; but if it is sent by insured mail you are entitled to another article if lost in the mail.

OUR DEFIANCE PAPER SHELL CRIMPER, 30 CENTS.

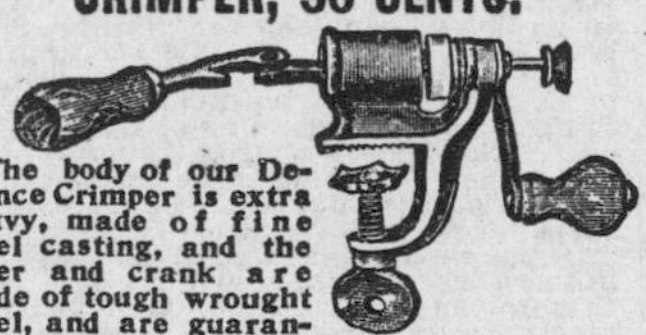

The body of our Defiance Crimper is extra heavy, made of fine steel casting, and the lever and crank are made of tough wrought steel, and are guaranteed never to break. In the crimping cup of our crimper lies the vast superiority of this crimper over all others. This crimping cup is made of solid brass turned from the solid bar, fitted with steel crimping pins, will never wear out and will, therefore, outlast a dozen of the ordinary crimping cups. These crimpers are all fitted with an expelling pin. The shell chamber is extra long, preventing any possibility of the shell bending or buckling, which frequently occurs in crimpers having a short shell chamber. The crimpers are all beautifully finished—the body is finished in heavy enameled japan, and the handles are heavily japanned. Each crimper is put up in a separate paper box. To produce perfect crimp, turn fast and feed slowly. Made 10, 12, 16 and 20-gauge. Be sure to state gauge wanted.

Catalogue Number	For Shells	Price	Postage extra
6K4358A	12-gauge	30c	18c
6K4358B	16-gauge	30c	18c
6K4358C	20-gauge	30c	18c
6K4358D	10-gauge	30c	18c

SHELL LOADING BLOCKS, $1.11.

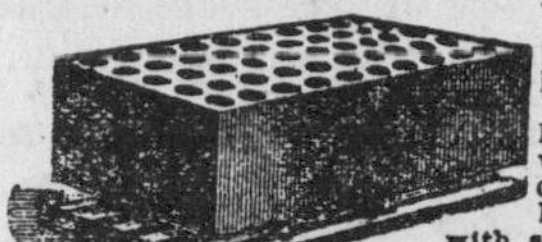

Our 50-Hole Shell Loading Block. Made of well seasoned wood, holesbored with shoulder to fit the entire length of shell. The top of hole is reamed out to act as a wad starter; shell does not come within ½ inch from top of block; shells cannot bulge or break down. With this block you can load 50 shells in half the time you could in the old way, and no danger of upsetting the shells when half loaded. Weight, about 3 pounds. State gauge wanted.

Catalogue No.	Holds	Gauge	Price
6K4362A	50 shells	12	$1.11
6K4362½	50 shells	16	
6K4362D	50 shells	10	

If by mail, postage extra, each, 53 cents.

THE DALY GUN CLEANER AND POLISHER.

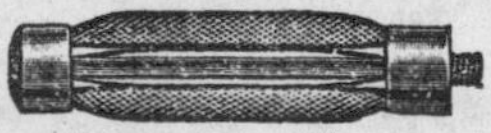

The Daly Gun Cleaner and Polisher is the most practical gun cleaner on the market. All parts are made of brass. Brass being softer than steel, it will not scratch the inside of the barrel. This cleaner not only takes out all burned powder, but polishes the inside surface of the barrels and keeps them in a clean and smooth condition. The sides of this cleaner are made of brass wire gauze, and when worn out may be replaced. This cleaner is made in 16, 12 and 10-gauge, and will fit any jointed rod.

No. 6K4379 10, 12 or 16-gauge. Price, each....41c
If by mail, postage extra, 5 cents.

No. 6K4379½ Extra Wire Gauze Sides. Price, per pair....8c
If by mail, postage extra, each, 2 cents.

THE A B C SHOTGUN CLEANER.

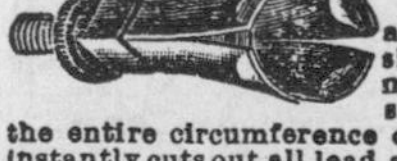

No. 6K4380 This is the latest and one of the best shotgun cleaners made. It has broad, sharp blades covering the entire circumference of gun barrel, which instantly cuts out all lead and burnt powder. Is made of brass, nickeled, will not harm the finest barrel. When used for holding cloth for wiping, and brass strainer cloth for burnishing, it is the finest burnisher made. Constant use only makes it sharper. Turning thumb nut adjusts it to 10 or 12-gauge.

Price, nickel plated....38c
If by mail, postage extra, 4 cents

BRASS WIRE BRUSHES.

10, 12, 16 or 20-GAUGE.

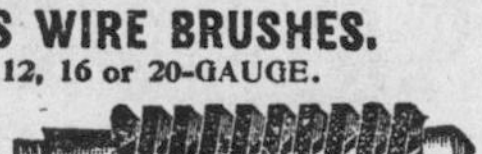

No. 6K4381 Best Quality Brass Wire Brush for removing lead, powder caking and rust spots; can be attached to any jointed rod, 10, 12, 16 or 20-gauge. Order by gauge, as one brush will fit but one gauge. Price, 39c
If by mail, postage extra, 2 cents.

BRASS RIFLE BRUSHES.

22 to 50-CALIBER.

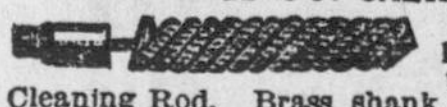

No. 6K4396 Brass Wire Brush to fit No. 6K4398 Cleaning Rod. Brass shank especially made for cleaning rust and burnt powder out of rifles. Made in 22, 25, 30, 32, 38, 40, 44, 45 and 50-calibers. State caliber wanted.

Price.....(Postage extra, 2c)........13c

THE SURPRISINGLY LOW REDUCED PRICES prevailing in this catalogue mean greater savings to our customers than ever before.

OUR 4-PIECE BRASS JOINTED CLEANING ROD, 24 CENTS.

Brass rods will not injure a rifle.

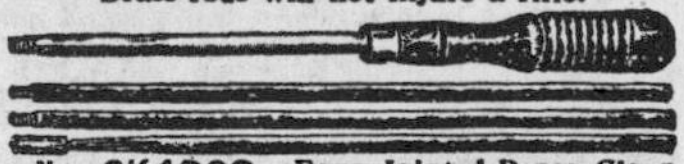

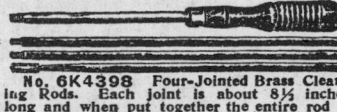

No. 6K4398 Four-Jointed Brass Cleaning Rods. Each joint is about 8½ inches long and when put together the entire rod is about 33 inches long. It may be carried in the pocket and has a revolving handle so the brush or cleaning rag follows the rifled grooves. Made for 22, 25, 30, 32, 38, 44, 45 and 50-caliber. State caliber wanted.

Price.......(Postage extra, 10c).......24c

U. S. GOVERNMENT POCKET CLEANER.

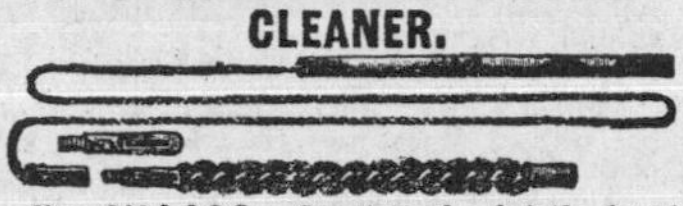

No. 6K4400 Consists of a bristle brush and slotted wiper, with detachable cord and weight for dropping through barrel; a separate slotted wiper for drawing through a dry cloth and for oiling. Made in 22, 25, 30, 32, 38, 45 or 50-caliber. State caliber wanted, as one caliber will fit only one rifle. Price..............25c
If by mail, postage extra, 4 cents.

Gun Cleaning Implements.

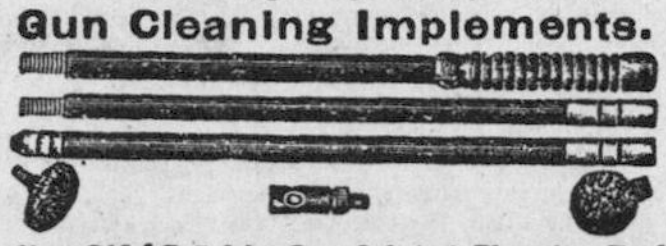

No. 6K4364A Our Jointed Cleaning Rods made of beech or maple wood; patent brass joints and three implements, swab, scratch brush and wiper; 10, 12 or 16-gauge. Weight, packed, 13 ounces. Full length 36 inches.

Price per set. (Postage extra, 10 cents)..25c
No. 6K4365B The same rod 48 inches long. Price....(Postage extra, 13 cents)....30c

OUR 8-PIECE LOADING SET, REDUCED PRICE, $1.09.

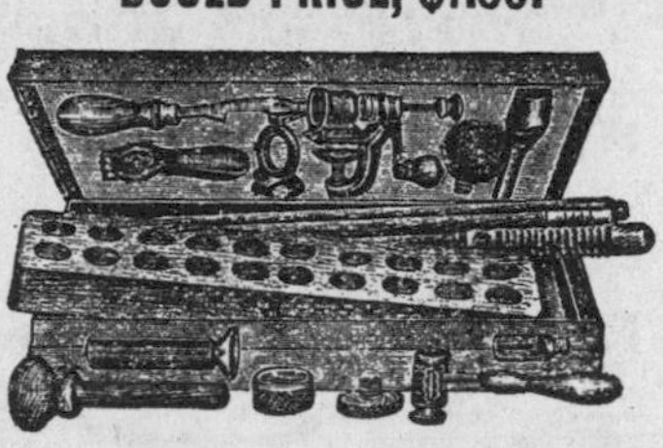

This complete 8-Piece Gun Implement Set for loading paper shells and cleaning a gun, as illustrated and described, comes in a strong box, size, 5x13 inches, each implement is made of good material and recommends itself to every owner of a breech loading shotgun. A retail dealer would charge for—

1 Shell Loading Block, with 20 holes	$0.30
1 Jointed Cleaning Rod, with attachments	.35
1 Paper Shell Crimper Japanned, with Expelling Pin	.45
1 Combined Powder and Shot Measure	.15
1 Rammer, Decapper (take off the knob to find decapper pin) and Nickel Loading Tube	.20
1 Shell Recapper, japanned	.15
1 Ring Shell Extractor, nickeled	.15
1 Steel Wad Cutter	.15
Eight pieces, making a total of	$1.90

While our price for the complete 8-piece 12-gauge set is $1.09, or nearly 35 per cent less than you would have to pay, and the quality of our set is much better than offered by others. Our crimpers are wrought iron and steel, while others are gray iron. Our crimper cups are turned from solid bars of brass, with steel pins while others are common stampings.

Catalogue No.	Gauge	Weight of Set	Price, per Set	Postage extra
6K4401A	12	42 oz.	$1.09	45c
6K4401B	16	37 oz.	1.10	40c
6K4401C	20	41 oz.	1.11	44c
6K4401D	10	42 oz.	1.12	45c

OUR 7-PIECE LOADING SET, 91c.

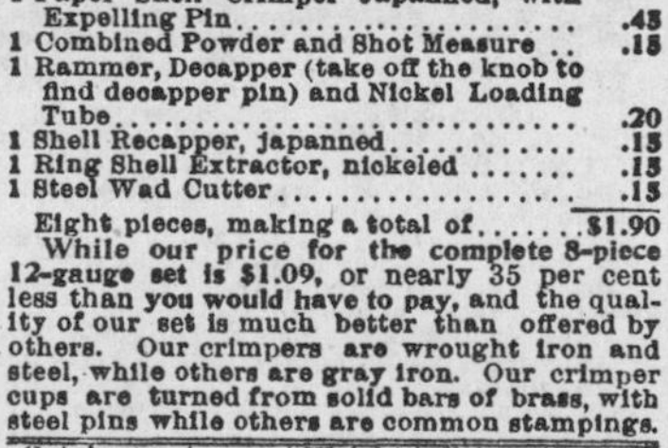

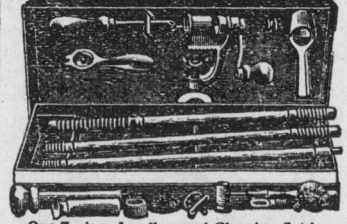

Our 7-piece Loading and Cleaning Set is put up in a nice box 5x13 inches and is practically the same quality in every way as our 8-piece set, with the exception that it has no shell loading block, otherwise it is as high grade and of the same exceptional value.

Catalogue No.	Gauge	Weight, per Set	Price, perSet	Postage Extra
6K4403A	12	33 oz.	91c	35 cents
6K4403B	16	33 oz.	92c	35 cents
6K4403C	20	33 oz.	93c	35 cents
6K4403D	10	33 oz.	94c	35 cents

OUR 6-PIECE LOADING SET. 59c

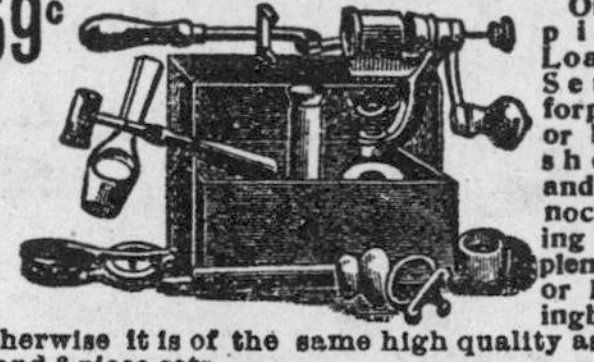

Our 6-piece Loading Set is for paper or brass shells and has no cleaning implements or loading block otherwise it is of the same high quality as our 7 and 8-piece sets.

A retail dealer would charge for—

1 Paper Shell Crimper with Expelling Pin	$0.45
1 Combined Powder and Shot Measure	.15
1 Rammer, Decapper (take off knob to find decapper pin) and Loading Tube	.20
1 Shell Recapper	.15
1 Ring Shell Extractor	.15
1 Steel Wad Cutter	.15
Six pieces, making a total of	$1.25

OUR PRICES on this 6-piece outfit. Order by catalogue number and mention gauge wanted. If by mail, allow for postage.

Catalogue No.	Gauge	Weight, per Set	Price, perSet	Postage Extra
6K4406A	12	21 oz.	59c	22 cents
6K4406B	16	20 oz.	60c	23 cents
6K4406C	20	20 oz.	61c	23 cents
6K4406D	10	24 oz.	62c	26 cents

OUR 4-PIECE LOADING SET.

75-CENT VALUE FOR 30 CENTS.

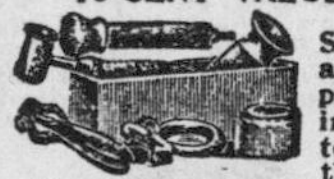

Our 4-piece Loading Set is for brass shells only and has no cleaning implements, crimper or loading block or wad cutter, otherwise it is of the same high quality as our 6, 7 and 8-piece sets.

Catalogue No.	Gauge	Weight, per Set	Price, per Set	Postage Extra
6K4407A	12	8 oz.	30c	10c
6K4407B	16	8 oz.	31c	10c
6K4407C	20	8 oz.	32c	10c
6K4407D	10	8 oz.	33c	10c

OUR BLUE ROCK TARGETS.

NOTE OUR PRICES of $2.34 for 500, $4.59 for 1,000, and you will observe our price is below all others. Our terms are cash with order on these goods.

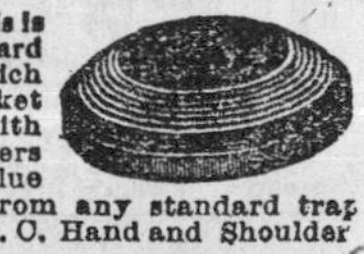

No. 6K4427 This is the old original, standard Blue Rock Target which has been on the market for many years and with which all trap shooters are familiar. The Blue Rock Target will fly from any standard trap such as the Empire, J. C. Hand and Shoulder White Flyer, etc.

Price, per barrel (500). Wgt., 150 lbs $2.34
Price, per 1,000. Weight, 300 pounds, 4.59
Our terms are cash with order on these goods

NEW EMPIRE EXPERT TRAP, $4.25

Made in Our Own Factory. Controlled Exclusively by Us.

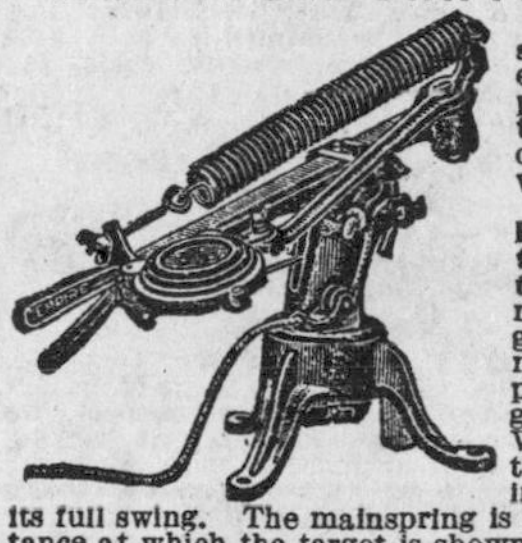

Never before has an Expert Trap been offered at any such price. The lowest price that a trap of this kind has ever been sold for is $6.00. This price of $4.25 is only possible by the fact that we have bought all the patents on this trap, and absolutely control it and manufacture it in our own shop, therefore enjoy the minimum cost, to which we have added but one small percentage of profit.

We have greatly improved this trap, and while the old Empire Trap was considered the best trap on the market, the new Empire Trap, sold by us at $4.25, is a much better trap than the original Empire, and it is therefore a much better trap than any trap on the market today, regardless of price. Among the many improvements we have made on this trap is the trigger pull, which is direct and positive, the rope pulling directly on the trigger. The trigger works easily, making this the easiest pulling trap made. We have improved the hand that holds the clay target, so that it takes a firm hold of the target, and at the same time instantly and positively releases the instant the arm reaches its full swing. The mainspring is adjustable to various tensions, thereby regulating the distance at which the target is shown.

The new Empire Trap has an extra large, heavy base, giving this trap great strength and a solid substantial appearance, contrasting strongly with the many light weight traps which are on the market sold for far more money.

The new Empire Expert Trap will take any of the standard targets, such as the Blue Rock, White Flyer, Tribune, Dickey Bird and others.

No 6K4424 New Empire Expert Trap. Price..........$4.25
Weight, packed for shipment, about 40 pounds.

THE IMPROVED 1908 MODEL J. C. HAND TRAP.

Oxidized Copper Finish.

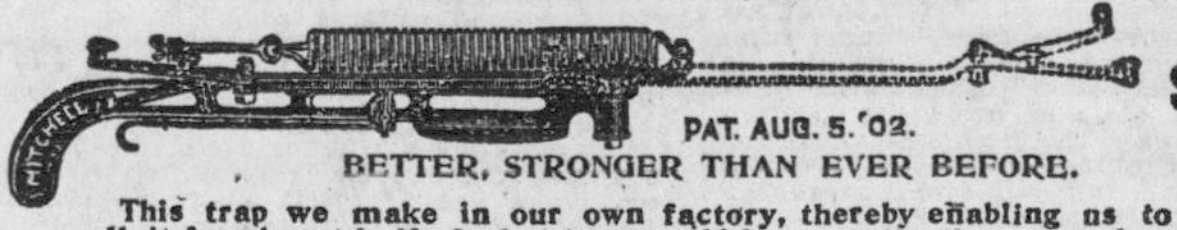

NOW ONLY **$2.40**

BETTER, STRONGER THAN EVER BEFORE.

This trap we make in our own factory, thereby enabling us to sell it for almost half of what it was sold for up to the time we undertook to manufacture it. The value of this trap as against any of the other traps lies in the fact that it is portable and can be carried in an ordinary suit case or wrapped up and carried as any ordinary package.

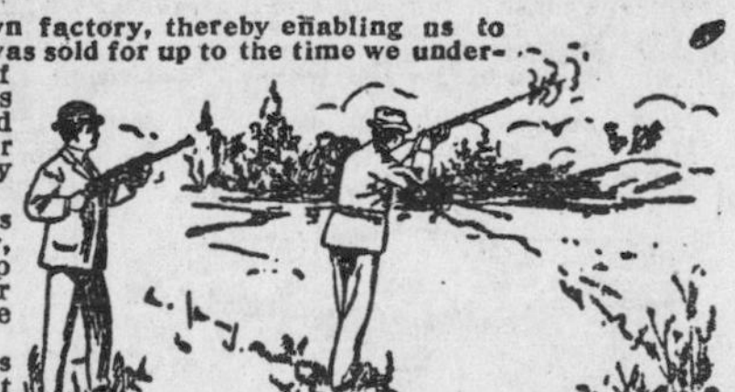

This trap will throw a target just as accurately and as far as the heavy, stationary traps. It is a very easy trap to operate. The large hand grip under the spring, as well as the pistol grip, give the operator a good firm hold.

The construction of this trap is such that when sprung, there is but little vibration or jerk. The operator can throw any quantity of birds without being put to any strain or jar whatsoever. Any 16-year old boy can operate this trap. Operating the trap by hand permits a great range of angles in throwing the target. The frame of this trap is made of the finest steel casting. The mainspring is a finely tempered spring. The tension of the spring is regulated by thumbscrew. The hand is made of steel with rubber covered posts. The trap when sprung is 39 inches long, and when set for shooting 24 inches long. Finished in a beautiful oxidized finish. Weight, packed for shipment, about 9 pounds.

No. 6K4430 Improved 1908 Model J. C. Hand Trap, finished in oxidized copper gun metal finish. Price..........$2.40

GUN GREASE, GUN OIL, ETC.

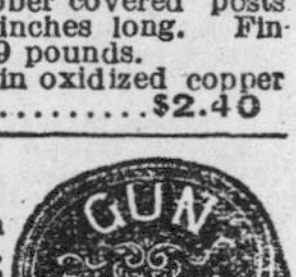

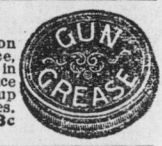

No. 6K4544 The Famous Gun Grease is the best gun grease ever put on the market by any house. It prevents rust on a steel or polished surface, such as the inside and outside of gun or rifle barrels, cutlery, razors; in fact, it is invaluable for all polished surfaces of steel or iron, and our price is lower than you can possibly buy from any other dealer. It is put up in a neat tin box so it may be carried in the pocket. Weight, 2 ounces.

Price, per box..........8c
Postage extra, per box, 3 cents.

Shooting Gallery Targets.

Round Steel Face Plain and Figure Targets.

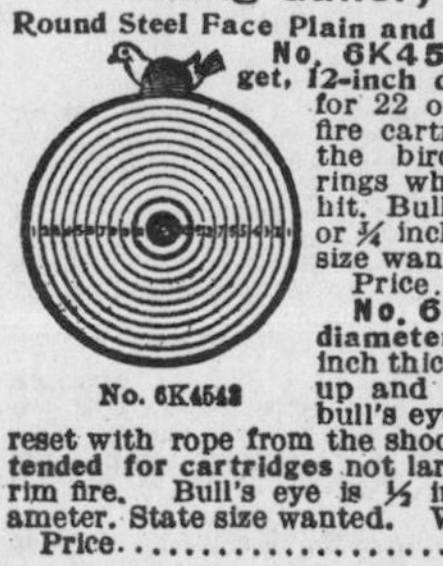

No. 6K4543

No. 6K4541 Steel Target, 12-inch diameter, heavy, for 22 or 32 caliber rim fire cartridges. Without the bird figure, but it rings when bull's eye is hit. Bull's eye is ½ inch or ¾ inch diameter. State size wanted. Wt., 15 lbs. Price..........$1.45

No. 6K4543 12-inch diameter, steel face ¼ inch thick. Bird is thrown up and bell rings when bull's eye is hit. May be reset with rope from the shooting stand. Intended for cartridges not larger than 32 long rim fire. Bull's eye is ½ inch or ¾ inch diameter. State size wanted. Weight, 12½ lbs. Price..........$2.20

Highest Quality of Gun Oil.

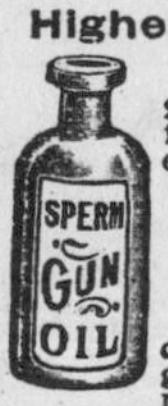

No. 6K4546 Highest Quality Sperm Gun Oil; put up exclusively for guns, gun locks and fine machinery, prevents rust and will not gum. Price, per 2-ounce bottle...8c
Postage extra, 8 cents.

3 In 1 Oil.

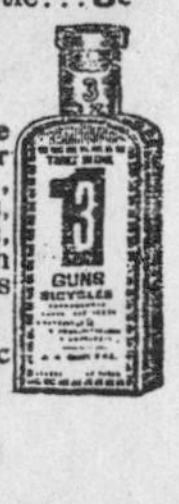

No. 6K4547 The celebrated 3 in 1 Oil for guns, revolvers, reels, razors, razor strops, hones, sewing machines, clocks, bicycles and graphophones, and an excellent polish for gun stocks and furniture.

Price, per 3-oz. bottle......13c
If by mail, postage extra, 9 cents.

GENUINE NEWHOUSE TRAPS.

The Genuine Newhouse Game Traps are branded on the pan "S. Newhouse," and are manufactured by The Oneida Community, (Limited), at Kenwood, N. Y. They are the standard for excellence the world over and are fully guaranteed.

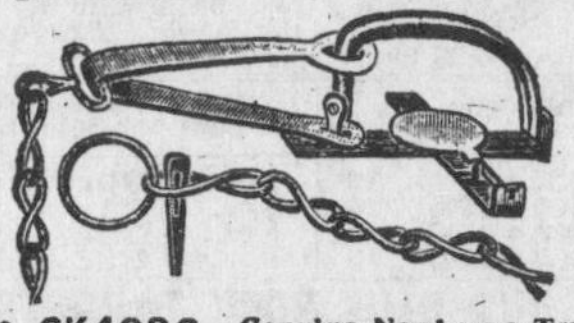

No. 6K4026 Genuine Newhouse Traps. Spread of jaws, 3½ inches; with chain. Size No. 0. Weight, 9 ounces. Price, each..$0.21
Per dozen........................2.42
If by mail, postage extra, each, 16 cents.

No. 6K4027 Genuine Newhouse Traps. Spread of jaws, 4 inches; with chain. Size No. 1. This is the size most used. Weight, 13 ounces.
Price, per dozen, $2.60; each..........22c
If by mail, postage extra, each, 18 cents.

No. 6K4028 Genuine Newhouse Traps. Spread of jaws, 4½ inches; with chain. Size No. 1½. This is called the mink trap. Often used for catching foxes. Weight, 1 pound 3 ounces.
Price, per dozen, $4.28; each..........36c
If by mail, postage extra, each, 26 cents.

Newhouse Double Jaw Trap.

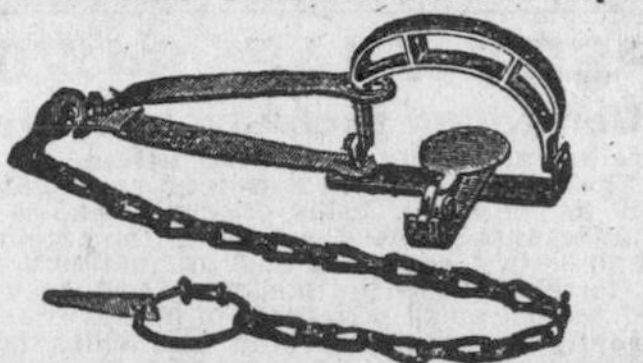

No. 6K4033 The double jaws take an easy and firm grip on a muskrat or skunk so that he cannot twist or gnaw out. Newhouse No. 91, same size as No. 1 Newhouse; jaws spread 4 inches. Complete with chain. Weight, 14 ounces.
Price, per dozen, $3.42; each..........29c
If by mail, postage extra, each, 20 cents.

No. 6K4034 Trap as above, Newhouse No. 91½, corresponds in size with the No. 1½ Newhouse. Weight, 1 pound 4 ounces.
Price, per dozen, $5.13; each..........43c
If by mail, postage extra, each, 26 cents.

Newhouse Webbed-Jaw Trap

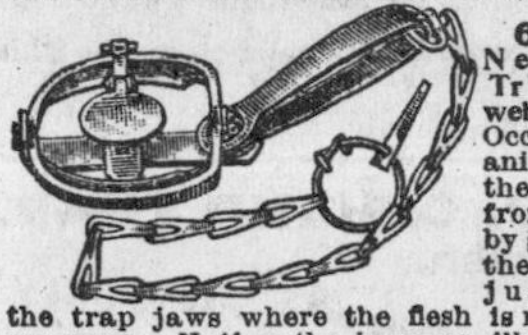

No. 6K4035 Newhouse Trap with webbed jaws. Occasionally animals free themselves from traps by gnawing their legs off just below the trap jaws where the flesh is numb from pressure. Noting the jaws, as illustrated, it is plain the animal can only gnaw off its leg at a point quite a distance below the meeting edges of the jaws. The flesh left above the point of amputation and below the jaws will swell, and make it impossible to draw the leg stump out of the trap. Made in Newhouse quality only and in only one size, Newhouse No. 81. Spread of jaws, 4 inches. Weight, 13 ounces.
Price, per dozen, $3.14; each..........27c
If by mail, postage extra, each, 20 cents.

Newhouse Fox Traps.

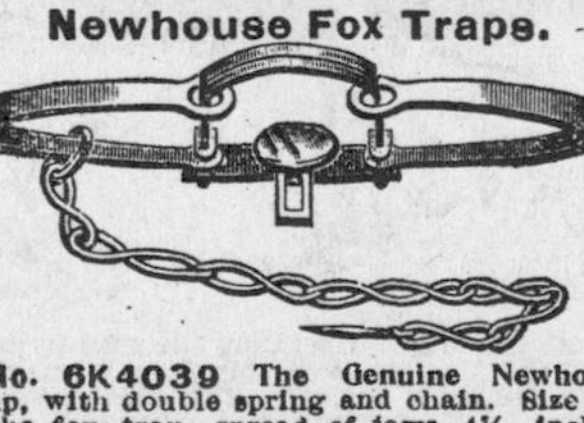

No. 6K4039 The Genuine Newhouse Trap, with double spring and chain. Size No. 2, the fox trap; spread of jaws, 4½ inches. Weight, 1 pound 7 ounces.
Price, per dozen, $5.99; each..........50c
If by mail, postage extra, each, 32 cents.

Newhouse Otter Traps.

No. 6K4040 The Genuine Newhouse Trap, with double spring and chain. Size No. 3, the otter trap; spread of jaws, 5½ inches. Weight, 2 pounds 5 ounces.
Price, per dozen, $7.98; each..........67c
If by mail, postage extra, each, 48 cents.

Newhouse Beaver Traps.

No. 6K4041 The Genuine Newhouse Trap, with double spring and chain. Size No. 4, the beaver trap; spread of jaws, 6½ inches. Weight, 3 pounds 2 ounces.
Price, per dozen, $9.41; each..........79c
If by mail, postage extra, each, 60 cents.

Newhouse Deer Trap.

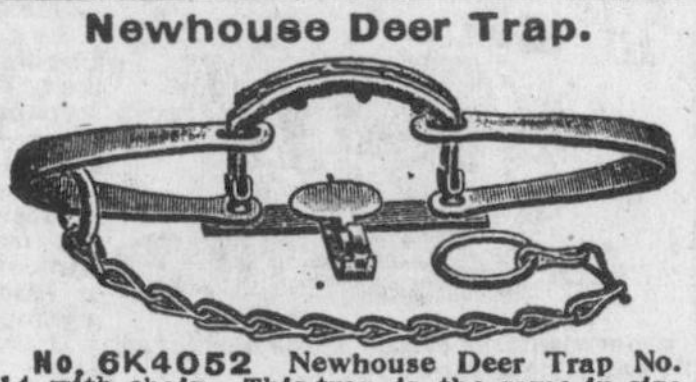

No. 6K4052 Newhouse Deer Trap No. 14, with chain. This trap is the same in size as the No. 6K4041, but has heavier and stiffer springs, and offset jaws, which allow the springs to rise higher when the animal's leg is in the trap, and is furnished with teeth sufficiently close to prevent the animal from drawing its foot out. Spread of jaws, 6½ inches. Weight, 3 pounds 2 ounces.
Price, 6 for $4.99; each..........84c
If by mail, postage extra, each, 64 cents.

Wolf Traps.

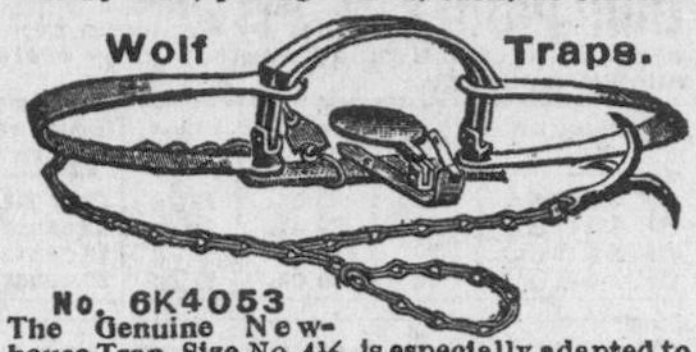

No. 6K4053 The Genuine Newhouse Trap, Size No. 4½, is especially adapted to catching wolves. This trap has 8-inch spread of jaws, with the other parts in proportion, and is provided with a pronged drag, a heavy snap and an extra heavy steel swivel and chain, 5 feet long, warranted to hold 2,000 pounds. The trap, complete with chain and drag will weigh 8 pounds 5 ounces.
Price, 6 for $11.40; each..........$1.90

Bear Traps.

No. 6K4061 Newhouse Bear Trap No. 15, with chain. To meet the views of certain hunters whose judgment we respect, we designed a style of jaw for this trap, making an offset of ¾ of an inch, so as to allow the springs to come up higher when the bear's leg is in the trap. This trap is an improvement over the old No. 5 Newhouse. This gives the spring a better grip. Spread of jaws, 11¾ inches. Weight, 20 pounds.
Price..........$5.70

Hawley & Norton Traps.

The Hawley & Norton Game Traps are manufactured by The Oneida Community (Limited), at Kenwood, N. Y., the makers of the genuine Newhouse traps.

The Hawley & Norton, while almost identical in form, is made somewhat lighter than the Newhouse throughout, and therefore cheaper; but it is a good, reliable trap.

No. 6K4066 The Hawley & Norton Game Trap, size 1, with chain. Spread of jaws, 4 inches. Weight, 10 ounces.
Price, per dozen, $2.00; each..........17c
If by mail, postage extra, each, 18 cents.

No. 6K4067 The Hawley & Norton Game Trap, size 1½, with chain. Spread of jaws, 4½ inches. Weight, 1 pound.
Price, per dozen, $3.00 each..........25c
If by mail, postage extra, each, 24 cents.

No. 6K4068 The Hawley & Norton Game Trap, Size 2, with chain. Double spring. Spread of jaws, 4½ inches. Weight, 1 pound 5 ounces. Price, per dozen, $4.20; each, 35c
If by mail, postage extra, each, 26 cents.

No. 6K4072 The Hawley & Norton Game Trap, size 4, with chain. Double spring. Spread of jaws, 6½ inches. Weight, 2 pounds 5 ounces. Price, per dozen, $6.60; each, 55c
If by mail, postage extra, each, 48 cents.

We Handle Raw Furs.

After receiving thousands of letters from our customers asking us to give them the names of reliable fur dealers, we have decided to open this department for the accommodation of our customers.

We do not buy these furs ourselves,

but immediately upon receipt of them we notify a number of fur dealers who bid against each other, and we dispose of them to the highest bidder.

The amount received is immediately sent to you, less the express charges which we paid upon receipt of the goods. If you prepaid the express charges, the full amount received is sent to you. We deduct no commission, as this department is soley for your accommodation.

Write us for price list and instructions for shipping.

Single Spring Otter Traps.

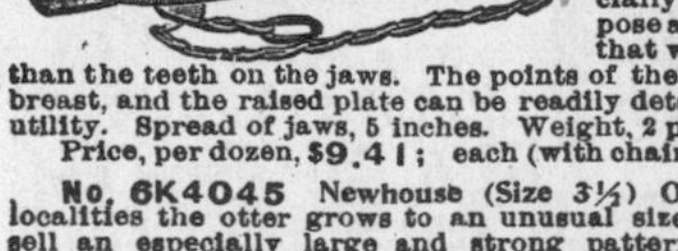

No. 6K4044 Newhouse (Size 2½) Single Spring Otter Trap was designed in response to requests from old and experienced trappers. It is used more especially for catching otter on their "slides." For this purpose a thin, raised plate of steel is adjusted to the pan so that when the trap is set the plate will be a trifle higher than the teeth on the jaws. The points of the teeth are made very sharp, to pierce the animal's breast, and the raised plate can be readily detached if desired, making the trap one of general utility. Spread of jaws, 5 inches. Weight, 2 pounds.
Price, per dozen, $9.41; each (with chain)..(If by mail, postage extra, each, 40 cents.)..79c

No. 6K4045 Newhouse (Size 3½) Otter Trap, single spring, with chain. In some localities the otter grows to an unusual size, with great proportionate strength so that we sell an especially large and strong pattern for those who prefer a single spring trap. The No. 3½ Newhouse was designed to meet these requirements. All the parts are heavier than the No. 2½, the spread of jaws is greater, and the spring stiffer. Spread of jaws, 6½ inches. Weight, 2 pounds 11 ounces, short chain; 3 pounds 1 ounce, long chain.
Price, per dozen, $10.55; each......(If by mail, postage extra, each, 60 cents.)......88c

Victor Brand Traps.

The Victor Brand Traps are made by The Oneida Community and are sold to compete with the various imitations of their Newhouse traps. This is an excellent trap and we guarantee it to give satisfaction.

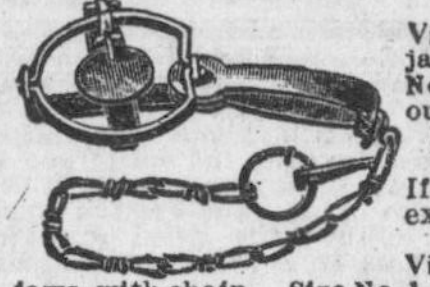

No. 6K4076 Victor Traps, 3½-inch jaws, with chain. Size No. 0. Weight, 7 ounces.
Price, each..$0.10
Per dozen.. 1.10
If by mail, postage extra, each, 12 cents.

No. 6K4077 Victor Traps, 4-inch jaws, with chain. Size No. 1. Weight, 9 ounces.
Price, per dozen, $1.30; each..........11c
If by mail, postage extra, each, 16 cents.

No. 6K4078 Victor Traps. Size No. 1½, mink trap; 4½-inch jaws; single spring, with chain. Weight, 15 ounces.
Price, per dozen, $1.95; each..........17c
If by mail, postage extra, each, 22 cents.

No. 6K4079 Victor Traps. Size No. 2, fox trap; 4½-inch jaws; double spring, with chain. Weight, 17 ounces.
Price, per dozen, $2.73; each..........23c
If by mail, postage extra, each, 24 cents.

No. 6K4080 Victor Traps. Size No. 3, the otter trap; 5½-inch jaws; double spring, with chain. Weight, 2 pounds.
Price, per dozen, $3.64; each..........31c
If by mail, postage extra, each, 40 cents.

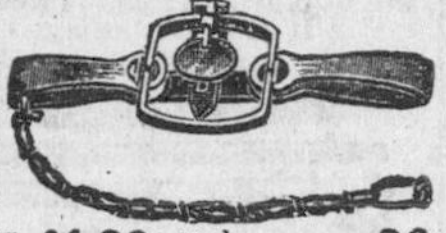

No. 6K4081 Victor Traps. Size No. 4, the beaver trap; 6½-inch jaws; double spring, with chain. Weight, 2 pounds.
Price, per dozen, $4.29; each..........36c
If by mail, postage, extra, each, 40 cents.

Setting Clamps.

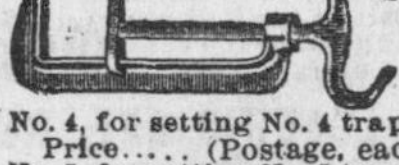

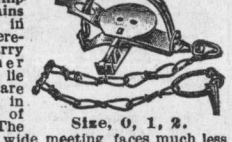

No. 6K4089 For setting game traps. Mention number wanted when ordering.

No. 4, for setting No. 4 trap. Weight, 3 ounces
Price......(Postage, each, 4 cents.)...11c
No. 5, for setting No. 5 trap. Weight, 15 ounces.
Price....(Postage, each, 18 cents.)....26c
No. 6, for setting No. 6 trap. Weight, 26 ounces.
Price....(Postage, each, 30 cents.)....44c

The Oneida Jump Traps, with Chains.

The Oneida Community Jump Traps with chains are lighter in weight and therefore easier to carry than the other styles. They lie very flat and are easily secreted in the runways of animals. The jaws have full, wide meeting faces much less likely to break the animal's leg than are other makes of this pattern. These traps are warranted in every respect.

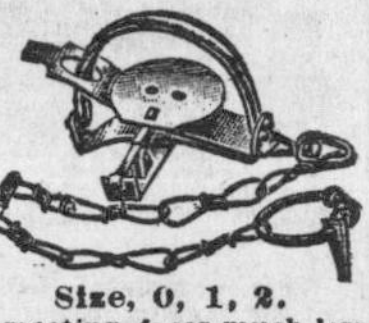

Size, 0, 1, 2.

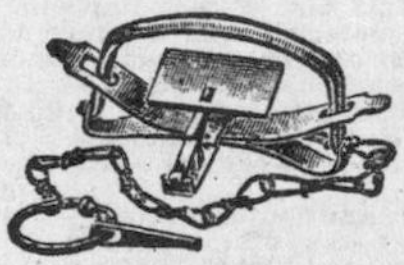

Sizes, 3, 4.

No. 6K4107 Rat or Gopher Trap, size 0, with chain. Weight, 6 ounces.
Price, per dozen, $1.45; each..........13c
If by mail, postage extra, each, 10 cents.

No. 6K4108 Muskrat Trap, size 1, with chain. Weight, 9 ounces.
Price, per dozen, $1.69; each..........15c
If by mail, postage extra, each, 13 cents.

No. 6K4109 Mink Trap, size 2, with chain. Weight, 10 ounces.
Price, per dozen, $3.59; each..........30c
If by mail, postage extra, each, 14 cents.

No. 6K4111 Fox or Otter Trap, size 3, with chain. Weight, 1 pound 5 ounces.
Price, per dozen, $4.79; each..........40c
If by mail, postage extra, each, 30 cents.

No. 6K4112 Beaver or Wildcat Trap, size 4, with chain. Weight, 1 pound 11 ounces. Price, per dozen, $5.64; each, 47c
If by mail, postage extra, each, 36 cents.

Tree Traps.

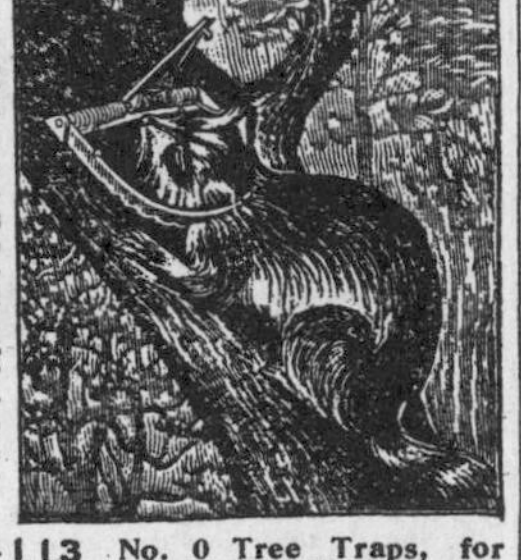

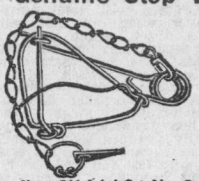

This Tree Trap is made of finely tempered steel, is an excellent trap for mink, marten, raccoon and opossum. This trap can be fastened securely and quickly with 6d nails. It is never snowed under, easy to locate and will kill instantly.

No. 6K4113 No. 0 Tree Traps, for Weasel, Ermine, etc. Weight 17 ounces.
Price, 6 for $1.00; each..........17c
If by mail, postage extra, each, 20 cents.

No. 6K4114 No. 1 Tree Trap, for Mink, Marten, etc. Weight, 20 ounces.
Price, 6 for $1.19; each..........20c
If by mail, postage extra, each, 25 cents.

No. 6K4115 No. 2 Tree Trap, for Coon, Skunk and Opossum. Weight, 23 ounces.
Price, 6 for $1.38; each..........23c
If by mail, postage extra, each, 30 cents.

SPRING WIRE TRAPS.

We carry two styles of Spring Wire Traps, namely, the well known original Stop Thief Trap and the Foster Spring Wire Trap, which is of the same pattern as the Stop Thief, and which we guarantee to be equal, if not superior, to any trap of this construction, regardless of name, make or price. The factory controls the price on the Stop Thief Traps, hence we cannot make any special price, but on the Foster Steel Wire Traps we are able to name exceedingly low prices, as we have contracted for these traps in enormous quantities and are able to sell them to you for less money than you could purchase a trap of like quality elsewhere. All our Spring Wire Traps come fitted with chains.

Genuine Stop Thief Traps.

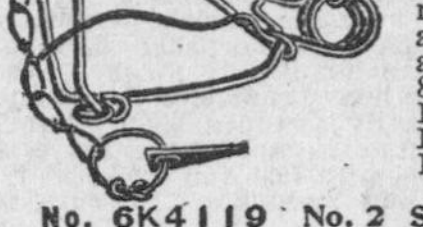

No. 6K4118 No. 1 Genuine Stop Thief Trap with chain, for rats, ground squirrels, gophers, and all small burrowing animals. Weight, 8 ounces.
Price, ea, $0.09
Per dozen, 1.05
If by mail, postage extra, each, 9c.

No. 6K4119 No. 2 Spring Wire Stop Thief Trap, medium size, for rabbits, mink, muskrats, weasels, etc. Weight, 12 ounces.
Price, per dozen, $1.35; each....12c
If by mail, postage extra, each, 17 cents.

No. 6K4120 No. 3 Stop Thief Trap, large size, for skunk, Southern raccoon, etc. Weight, 15 ounces.
Price, per dozen, $1.75; each....15c
If by mail, postage extra, each, 22 cents.

No. 6K4123 No. 3½ Stop Thief Trap, extra large size for Northern raccoon, opossum and can also be used for skunk and mink. Weight, 1 pound 10 ounces.
Price, per dozen, $2.50; each....21c
If by mail, postage extra, each, 35 cents.

The Foster Spring Wire Trap.

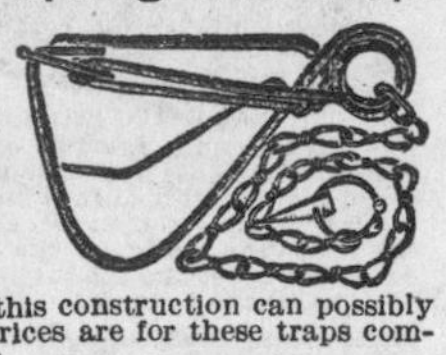

Same construction as the celebrated Stop Thief. These traps are guaranteed to be made of the best tempered steel spring wire, finely finished, and to be as effective as any trap of this construction can possibly be made. The prices are for these traps complete with chains.

No 6K4138 No. 1 Foster Spring Wire Trap, small size, for rats, ground squirrels and small animals.
Price, each, including chain..........7c
Per dozen..........79c
If by mail, postage extra, each, 9 cents.

No. 6K4139 No. 2 Foster Spring Wire Trap, medium size, for rabbits, mink, skunk, etc. Weight, 12 ounces.
Price, each, including chains..........9c
Per dozen..........92c
If by mail, postage extra, each, 17 cents.

No. 6K4140 No. 3 Foster Spring Wire Trap, large size, for skunk, raccoons and similar sized animals. Weight, 15 ounces.
Price, each, including chain......$0.11
Per dozen..........1.18
If by mail, postage extra, each, 22 cents.

Gopher Traps.

Prices Reduced

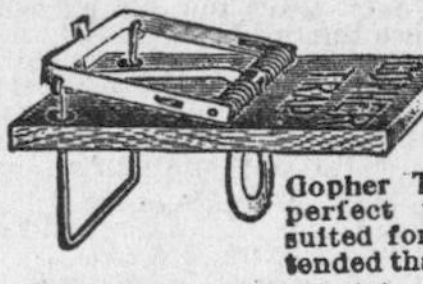

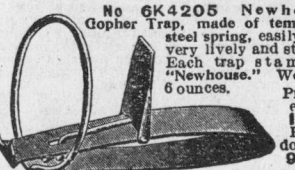

No. 6K4197 Gopher Traps. This is a perfect trap and better suited for the purpose intended than all other makes.
Price, each,......$0.11
Per dozen......1.24
Postage extra, each, 9c.

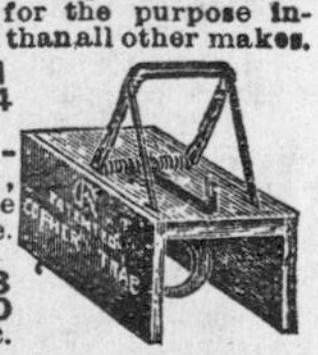

No. 6K4204 Improved Gopher Traps, with wood sides. Can be set easier than above. Weight, 12 ounces.
Price, each......$0.13
Per dozen......1.50
Postage extra, each, 17c.

Newhouse Gopher Trap.

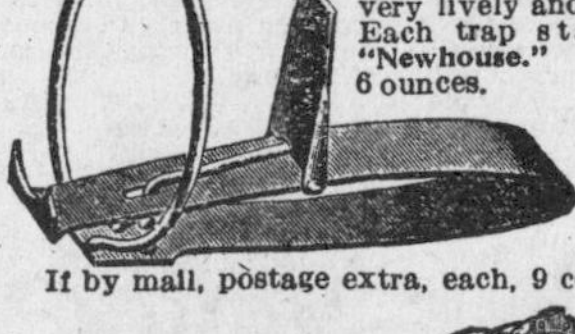

No 6K4205 Newhouse Gopher Trap, made of tempered steel spring, easily set, very lively and strong. Each trap stamped "Newhouse." Weight, 6 ounces.
Price, each, 10c
Per dozen, 99c
If by mail, postage extra, each, 9 cents.

Mole Traps.

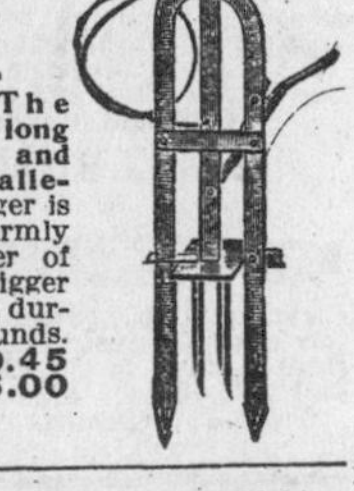

No. 6K4213 The spears are 4½ inches long made of hard steel, and are firmly set in a malleable plate. The plunger is made of hard steel, is firmly fastened in the center of the spear plate. The trigger and trip are simple and durable. Weight, 2¼ pounds.
Price, each......$0.45
Per dozen......5.00

We Buy Your Raw Furs and Skins. Write for Prices and Instructions.

Our Adjustable Steel Fur Stretcher.

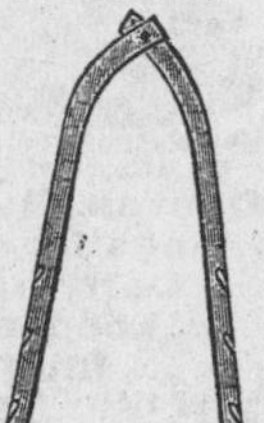

These stretchers are made of carefully selected steel, 3/8x12 gauge; adjustable to fit any size pelt, drying it in its correct shape and in one-third the time of other stretchers. Will fold up to a small space when not in use. By using these stretchers your furs will not only dry in one-third the time but will be in better shape and bring you more money than you could possibly get under any other circumstances.

No. 6K4230 Muskrat Stretchers, weight per ½-doz., 6 lbs. Price, per ½-dozen..**57c**
No. 6K4231 Skunk Stretchers, weight per ½-doz., 7 lbs. Price, per ½-dozen..**95c**
No. 6K4232 Mink Stretchers, weight per ½-doz., 7 lbs. Price, per ½-dozen..**96c**

Lightning Tanner.

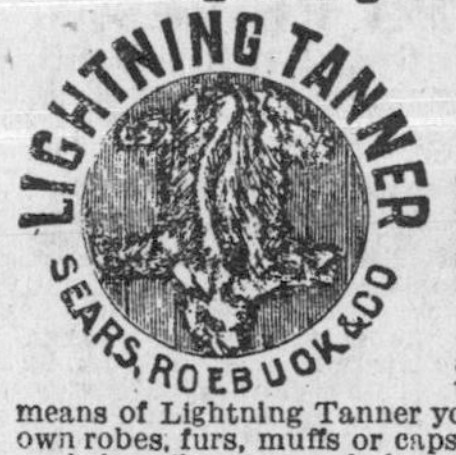

Lightning Tanner is the very latest mixture for quickly and perfectly tanning furs and skins of every description in from 24 to 36 hours. Very simple to use, requires no experience and first class results can always be obtained. By means of Lightning Tanner you can make your own robes, furs, muffs or caps and your leather belts, tie straps, halters, etc. Does not, like many other tanning compounds, rot or weaken the leather, but makes it tough, soft and pliable. Full directions for preparing the hides and tanning are furnished with each package.

No. 8K670 Box with powder sufficient to tan two raccoon skins in 36 hours. Price..........**18c**
If by mail, postage extra, 6 cents.

No. 8K671 Box containing three times the above and sufficient for deer skin. Price..........**37c**
If by mail, postage extra, 10 cents.

No. 8K672 Box holding about twelve times the above and sufficient for horse or cow hide. Price.....(Unmailable)....**85c**

Rat Traps.

(See No. 6K4266.)

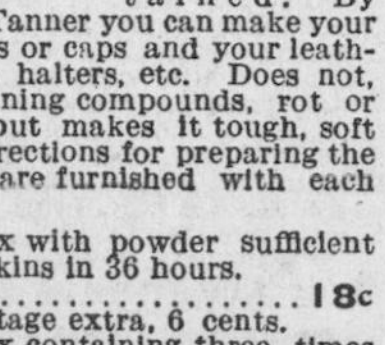

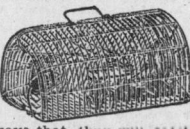

No. 6K4215 The Genuine French Marty Rat Trap is a wonderfully effective rat catcher. Is used in the leading hotels, market houses and public institutions. Many testimonials prove that they will catch rats up to their full capacity night after night, as long as the rats hold out. Family size, 16 inches long; capacity, 20 rats. Weight, 2 pounds.
Price..........**58c**
If by mail, postage extra, 38 cents.

Mouse Traps.

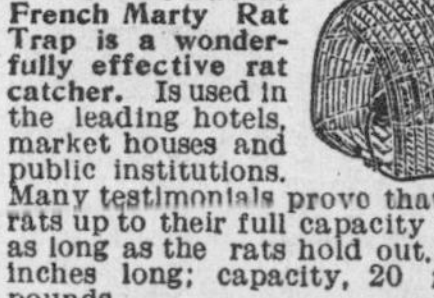

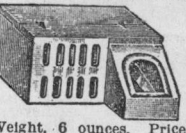

No. 6K4220 Mouse Trap. This is the most successful mouse catcher ever invented. One mouse sets the trap for the next one that comes along; will hold several. Weight, 6 ounces. Price..........**9c**
If by mail, postage extra, 13 cents.

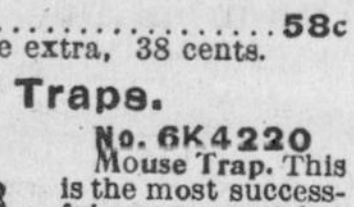

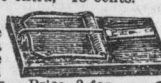

No. 6K4224 Mouse Trap. As a sure mouse catcher it is a certain thing. Mice can't touch the bait and live. Weight, 2 ounces. Price, 3 for.....**8c**
If by mail, postage extra for three, 5 cents.

No. 6K4225 Rat Trap same as No. 6K4224 only larger in size, a sure catch and easy to set. Weight, 5 ounces. Price.....**9c**
If by mail, postage extra, 6 cents.

Animal Scents.

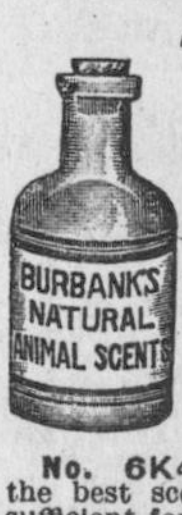

In answer to a large demand for animal scents we have made a contract whereby we are able to offer the famous Burbank Natural Animal Scents at prices lower than those they have ever been sold at before, which prices, considering the superiority of Burbank Scents over all others made, places us in a position where no dealers are able to offer us competition. These scents are not made from drugs, but from parts of the animals they are intended to catch and from their favorite food.

No. 6K4260 Burbank's Trout Oil, the best scent made for mink. One bottle sufficient for 120 sets. Price, per bottle, **70c**

No. 6K4261 Burbank's New Labrador Fox Scent. Made from the formula of a famous Indian trapper. Unquestionably the best fox scent made. Price, per bottle..........**71c**

No. 6K4263 Burbank's Beaver Castor. Triple extract of beaver castor for mink, coon, bear and for making other scents.
Price, per ounce..........**78c**

No. 6K4264 Burbank's Hudson Bay Marten Scent. One bottle sufficient for 120 sets. Price, per bottle..........**72c**

No. 6K4266 Burbank's Rat and Mouse Scent for house rats and mice; four or five drops will intice them into the trap. Bottle contains about 40 sets, with full directions.
Price, per bottle..........**21c**
Postage extra on above, per bottle, 6 cents.

DUCK, TURKEY AND HAWK CALLS.

Kankakee Marsh Duck Call.

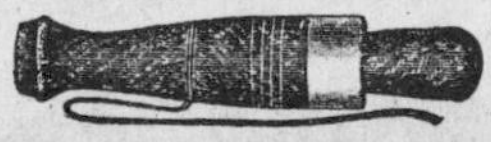

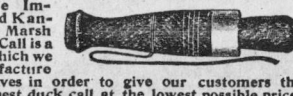

The Improved Kankakee Marsh Duck Call is a call which we manufacture ourselves in order to give our customers the very best duck call at the lowest possible price. We guarantee the call to be equal to any call made regardless of name, make or price. These calls are fitted with best quality German silver reeds and have not the metallic sounds found in many duck calls and sounds which are unnatural to the tones of wild duck, each call is toned by an old experienced duck hunter when it leaves us and should not be altered in any way. With a little practice an amateur will soon learn to call ducks as well as an old experienced hunter. Directions for calling accompany each call.

No. 6K4461 Our Kankakee Marsh Duck Call, made so that it can be carried by a string fastened in the buttonhole when hunting.
Price...(If by mail, postage extra, 2c)...**32c**

Our Crow Caller, 30 Cents.

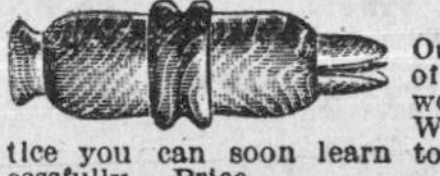

No. 6K4463 Our Crow Call, made of well seasoned wood, fine reed. With a little practice you can soon learn to call crows successfully. Price..........**30c**
If by mail, postage extra, 2 cents.

Our Latest Turkey Caller.

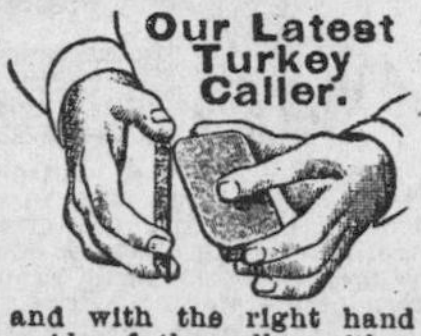

No. 6K4464 Our Turkey Caller is made from well seasoned wood, adapted to make the proper sound for decoying wild or domestic turkeys. Hold the caller in the left hand, as shown in the illustration, and with the right hand rub the slate on the side of the caller, either with the edge or with the flat side, and after a little practice you will be able to decoy turkeys successfully. This caller is 4⅛ inches long, 2⅛ inches wide, and may be carried in the pocket. Price...(Postage extra, 8c)...**48c**

Our Hawk Call, 46 Cents.

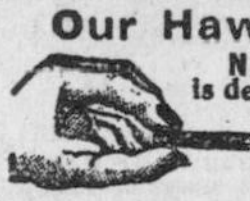

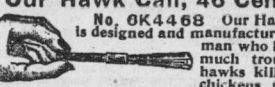

No. 6K4468 Our Hawk Call is designed and manufactured by a man who has had much trouble by hawks killing his chickens, and the hawk caller pays for itself many times over every time a hawk is killed. Hold the caller in the left hand, as shown in the illustration, and by blowing through it you can soon become expert in decoying hawks toward you.
Price....(If by mail, postage extra, 2c)..**46c**

CEDAR WOOD DECOY DUCKS.

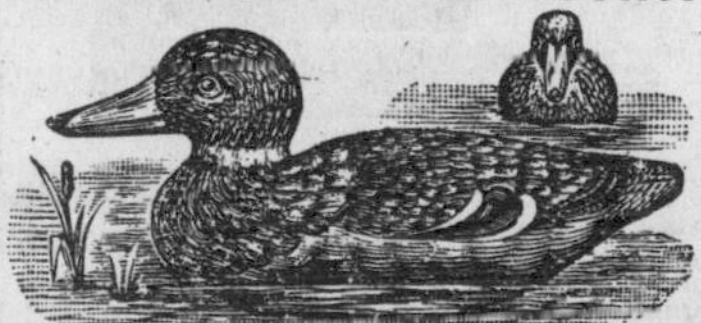

In making these decoys great care has been used to select only sound white cedar for their construction and to secure a perfect balance. They are light, substantial and naturally painted. They will not sink if you shoot them. $2.85 and $4.20 per dozen. Each dozen contains 8 drakes and 4 hens. We cannot furnish them any other way except by special order, which causes delay. Decoys below these prices cannot be properly made and painted to look natural. For highest grade wood decoy ducks, these prices are BELOW ANY COMPETITION.

They come in mallard, canvasback, redhead, bluebill, teal or pintail. Weight, 35 to 40 pounds per dozen. State which style you wish.

REMEMBER—We can only furnish 8 drakes and 4 females in each dozen.

No. 6K4495 No. 10, our best decoy ducks with glass eyes. These decoys are as nicely painted and as well shaped as most decoys which sell at $6.00 to $7.50 per dozen in regular stores. They are really fine decoys and will please you. State which style you wish.
Price, per dozen, **$4.20**; each..........**40c**

No. 6K4496 No. 30, good decoy ducks, nicely painted in natural colors with painted eyes. These decoys are not quite as well painted nor shaped as the No. 1 but are excellent value for the money. State which style you wish.
Price, per dozen, **$2.85**; each..........**30c**

No. 6K4497 Anchors with cord to fasten to breast so they will swim like the natural bird when in the water.
Price, per dozen..........**45c**

OUR CROW DECOYS.

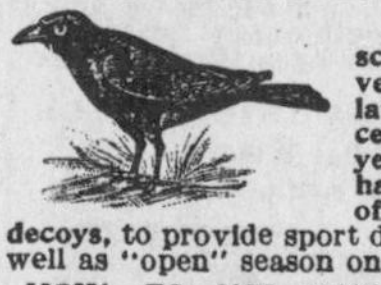

On account of the scarcity of game and the very stringent game laws, now existing at certain seasons of the year in some states, we have conceived the idea of manufacturing crow decoys, to provide sport during the "closed" as well as "open" season on game.

HOW TO USE OUR CROW DECOYS SUCCESSFULLY.

In "setting out" decoys, we suggest you place them on high ground, stumps, logs or fences (by sticking their sharp leg in same), where they may be seen for a long distance. Then find a good hiding place, as the crow has very keen eyes and long range of sight.

No. 6K4610 Crow Decoys.
Price, 3 for **$1.00**; each..........**37c**
Weight, packed for shipment, about 2 pounds each.

GUN AND RIFLE COVERS

The following gun and rifle covers are made according to our specifications and are the best covers and the greatest values on the market. Our styles have been copied and other covers have been offered as being the same as ours, but owing to our enormous business in gun and rifle covers, as well as hunting clothing, we are able to give value in these goods that cannot be equaled by any other dealer. Our canvas covers are made of special woven canvas, full weight and are well made and finished throughout. Our leather covers and cases are made of selected leather. We use no sheepskin or imitation of calf or cowhide, we use only the very best selected cowhide stock and our leather cases are better finished and have more style and are sold for less money, quality considered, than any other cases on the market.

When ordering give us the name of your gun or rifle, also length of barrel, and state whether your gun is single or double barrel, also whether it is a repeater, and we will furnish you a cover that will be an exact fit.

Special lengths not mentioned in this catalogue will have to be made to order and require from a week to ten days to make them.

NOTICE.—8-ounce canvas means a yard weighs 8 ounces; 10-ounce canvas means a yard weighs 10 ounces; 12-ounce canvas means a yard weighs 12 ounces.

The more ounces to the yard, the heavier the canvas.

Mention length of barrel and name of gun or rifle when ordering a gun cover.

Special Value for 67 Cents.

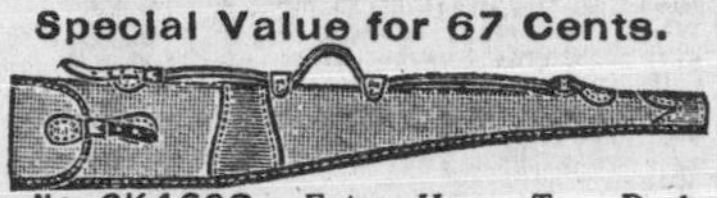

No. 6K4698 Extra Heavy Tan Duck Cover, for rifles and shotguns. Full chase leather bound, with heavy sole leather lock and muzzle protector, with handle and sling. For 24, 26, 28, 30 or 32-inch barrels. State length wanted. Price..(Postage extra, 15c.)....**67c**

Our $1.64 Leather Rifle and Shotgun Cover.

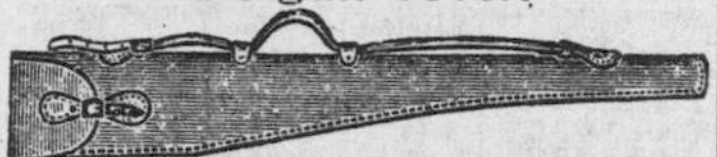

No. 6K4701 Soft Leather Cover, made of heavy, soft russet bag leather, with combined sling and handle. Bright trimmings. For 24, 26, 28, 30 or 32-inch barrels; give length of barrel and name of gun or rifle when ordering. Absolutely waterproof. The finest gun cover made. Price....(Postage extra, 20c.)....**$1.64**
Give name of rifle or shotgun and length of barrel when ordering.

Rifle and Carbine Sheath.

$1.20

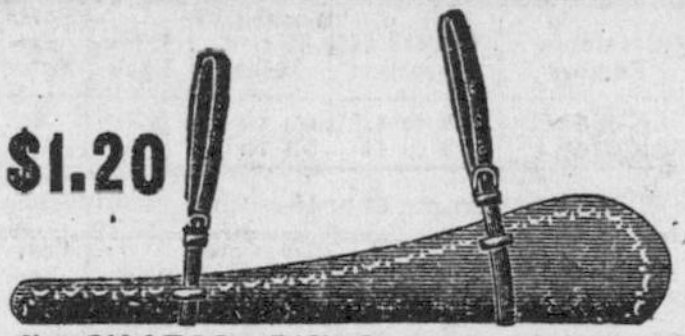

No. 6K4703 Rifle Sheath, made of best russet leather, for sporting rifles. These sheaths are not full length covers, but are intended for carrying rifle on saddle, leaving stock of rifle exposed so it may be easily grasped when needed. Be sure to give name of rifle, model and length of barrel when ordering, as different makes require different sheaths. We furnish these for 24, 26 and 28-inch barrel rifles only. Price..........**$1.20**
If by mail, postage extra, 30 cents.

No. 6K4704 The same identical sheath for carbines. State name of carbine and length of barrel when ordering. We furnish these for 20 and 22-inch barrel carbines only. Price..........**$1.15**
If by mail, postage extra, 25 cents.

Our Victoria Style Canvas Case

85c

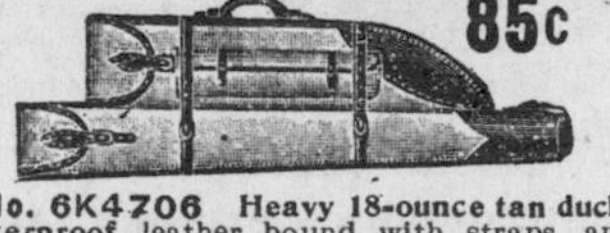

No. 6K4706 Heavy 18-ounce tan duck, waterproof, leather bound with straps and tool pocket, leather lock and muzzle protector, flannel lined, for 28, 30 or 32-inch barrels. State length wanted. Price..........**85c**
If by mail, postage extra, 30 cents.

Victoria Gun Case with Bag.

98c

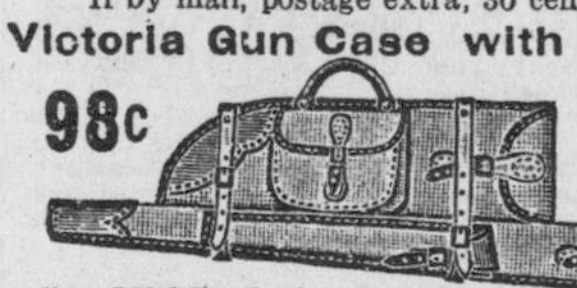

18 OZ. DUCK.

No. 6K4707 Victoria Gun Case, heavy 18-ounce waterproof canvas, reinforced, with leather lock and muzzle protector and pocket for cleaning rod; also shell bag to hold 50 shells. The most complete cover offered to sportsmen and trap shooters. For 30 or 32-inch barrels. State length wanted. Price...**98c**
If by mail, postage extra, 27 cents.

8-Ounce Duck Gun Case, 40c.

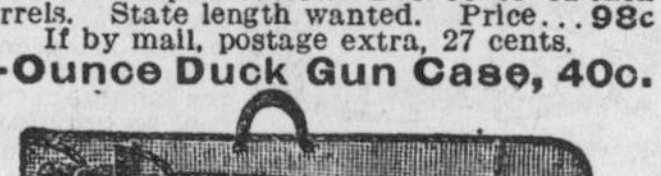

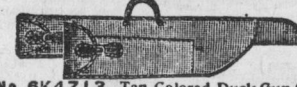

No. 6K4713 Tan Colored Duck Gun Case, for take down shotguns, with rod pocket, made of 8-ounce canvas. Canton flannel lined. For 30 or 32-inch barrels. Give length of barrel.
Price..........**40c**
If by mail, postage extra, 12 cents.
Give length of barrel when ordering.

Folding Gun Case.

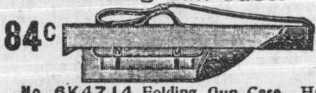

84c

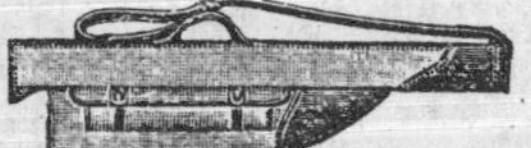

No. 6K4714 Folding Gun Case. Heavy 18-ounce tan colored canvas, reinforced ends, leather muzzle protector, with sling strap and handle. Mention length of barrel when ordering. For 30 and 32-inch barrels.
Price..........**84c**
If by mail, postage extra, 20 cents.

Covers for Take Down Rifles.

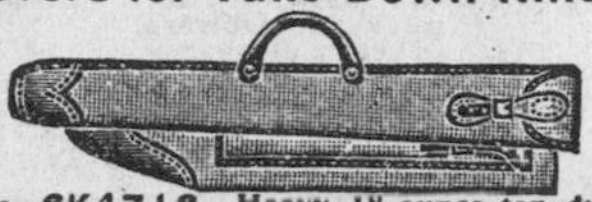

No. 6K4716 Heavy 18-ounce tan duck, with lock and muzzle protector, rod pocket on the side, Victoria style, flannel lined, well made. This case is made for take down rifles only and the Ladies' Little Double Gun. When ordering state for which gun or rifle you wish it, and say if barrel is 24, 26 or 28 inches long. Give length of barrel and model and name of rifle when ordering. Price..........**71c**
If by mail, postage extra, 16 cents.

Our Leather Victoria Gun Case

$2.20

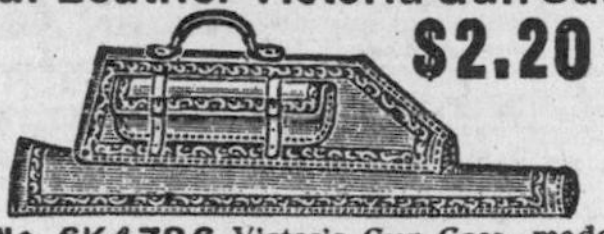

No. 6K4726 Victoria Gun Case, made of heavy russet leather, embossed, strongly stitched, with rod pocket, making it very strong and durable. For 30 and 32-inch barrels. State length wanted. Price..........**$2.20**
If by mail, postage extra, 50 cents.

> IF YOU OWN A FINE GUN it pays to have a sole leather cover, as it protects the gun from bruises, dents, etc., when carrying it in a wagon, etc. For special lengths, not mentioned in this catalogue, allow us a week's time to make.

Our Oak Tanned Russet Leather Gun Case.

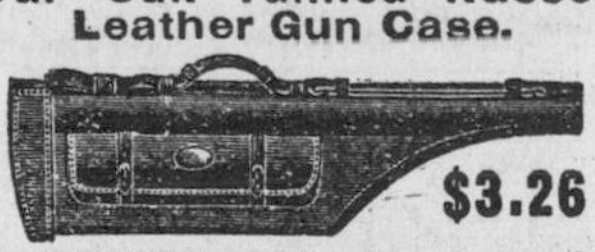

$3.26

No. 6K4733 English Victoria Gun Case, leg of mutton shape, made of oak tanned russet color sole leather, brass trimmings, with lock, buckle and name plate, handle and sling. Flannel lined. Outside rod pocket. For 26, 28, 30 or 32-inch barrels. State length wanted. Price..........**$3.26**
If by mail, postage extra, 64 cents.

No. 6K4733½ Same as above, to fit Remington automatic shotgun. Price...**$3.50**

No. 6K4734 Same as above, for two sets of barrels. Price..........**$4.35**

New Style Leather Case, $3.15

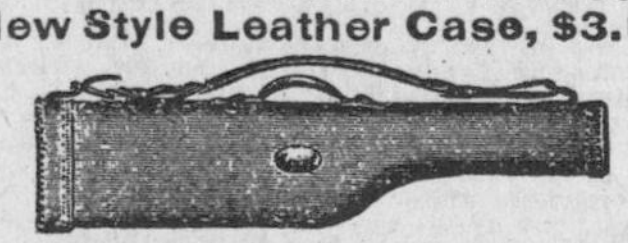

Our New Style Leather Case is different from all other leather cases, as it is fitted with a patented, movable, hinged partition between the stock and the barrel compartments, and will fit all single and double, as well as repeating take down shotguns, and makes a neater, more compact and better balanced case than the old style leg of mutton cases. This case is made of fine quality oak tanned colored leather. Canton flannel lined, fitted with leather suit case handle, adjustable shoulder sling, polished brass trimmings, and lock buckle. Weight, about 4 pounds. The style of this case has been patented and it is one of the best cases on the market—good enough for $50.00 to $100.00 guns, made for 26, 28, 30 or 32-inch barrels. Mention length wanted when ordering.

No. 6K4737 Price for our leather gun case for 30 or 32-inch barrel guns...**$3.15**
If by mail, postage extra, 54 cents.

No. 6K4737½ Same as above, to fit Remington automatic shotgun. Price..**$3.30**

WE HANDLE RAW FURS

TO ACCOMMODATE OUR CUSTOMERS.

Send us your raw furs if you want to secure every cent they are worth. See our reasons for handling raw furs as explained on page 742.

REVOLVER AND PISTOL HOLSTERS.

When ordering holsters, always give the name of your revolver, length of barrel and caliber, to enable us to give you the exact size; for these holsters vary in size, according to caliber and length of barrel.

Our Acme Rubber Pocket Holsters.

Made of black rubber and lined with drilling, soft and pliable, with nickel plated clasp to hook to pocket, and made for pocket size revolvers only up to 4-inch barrel. Order by catalogue number in full.

Catalogue Number	Caliber of Revolver	Length of Barrel, Inches	Price	Postage Extra
6K4755B	32	3 to 4	19c	3c
6K4755E	38	3¼ to 4	21c	4c
6K4755G	44	4 to 5	24c	5c

Our Leather Flap and Open Top Holsters

Made of best quality russet leather, nicely embossed, with loop for belt. When ordering, state make, caliber and length of barrel of your revolver. Order by catalogue number in full.

Flap Holster No. 6K4756
Open Top Holster No. 6K4761
For America double action and Premier revolvers.

Caliber of Revolver	Length of Barrel, Inches	Catalogue No. 6K4756 Flap Holster Price, each	Catalogue No. 6K4761 Open Top Holster Price, each	Postage Extra
32	3 to 4	20c	15c	4c
38		21c	16c	4c

For Smith & Wesson, Harrington & Richardson, Hopkins & Allen, Forehand, Iver Johnson, Colt's New Pocket, Colt's Police, Colt's Automatic Pistols and our own revolvers. Order by catalogue number in full.

Caliber of Revolver	Length of Barrel, Inches	Catalogue No. 6K4756 Flap Holster Price, each	Catalogue No. 6K4761 Open Top Holster Price, each	Postage Extra
32	3 to 4	22c	16c	6c
32	4½ to 5	23c	17c	6c
32	5¼ to 6	24c	18c	6c
38	3¼ to 4	26c	19c	6c
38	4½ to 5	27c	21c	7c
38	5½ to 6	28c	22c	7c
38 Colt	4½ to 6	34c	24c	7c
38 Auto	4½ to 6	35c	35c	7c

For Colt's New Navy, Colt's New Army, Colt's Double Action and Smith & Wesson Military revolvers. Order by catalogue number in full.

Caliber of Revolver	Length of Barrel, Inches	Catalogue No. 6K4756 Flap Holster Price, each	Catalogue No. 6K4761 Open Top Holster Price, each	Postage Extra
38 or 41	4½ to 5	32c	23c	8c
38 or 41	5½ to 6½	32c	24c	8c

For large frame revolvers, such as Colt's Frontier, Army, Single Action and Double Action, 32-20, 38-40, 44 and 45-caliber. Order by catalogue number in full.

Caliber of Revolver	Length of Barrel, Inches	Catalogue No. 6K4756 Flap Holster Price, each	Catalogue No. 6K4761 Open Top Holster Price, each	Postage Extra
32-20 to 45	4½ to 5	34c	24c	8c
32-20 to 45	5½ to 6	35c	25c	8c
32-20 to 45	7½	37c	26c	8c

Our Hand Carved Mexican Style Cowboy Holsters.

Made of heavy russet saddle leather, to match our fancy cowboys' saddle. These holsters are all hand carved, and are not to be compared with the holsters that other houses sell as the fine cowboy holster, which are embossed under a large press; but these are the most handsome and best holsters in the market.

The following holsters are made to fit the Smith & Wesson, Harrington & Richardson, Hopkins & Allen, Colt's New Pocket, and New Police and our own make revolvers in 38-caliber only. They are not made for 32-caliber revolvers. When ordering, give the catalogue number in full.

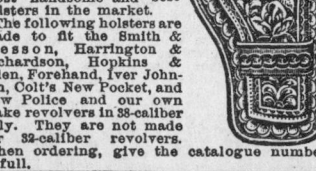

Catalogue Number	Caliber of Revolver	Length of Barrel, Inches	Price, Each	Postage Extra
6K4767E	38	3¼ to 4	$1.00	8c
6K4767F	38	4½ to 5	1.05	8c
6K4767G	38	5½ to 6½	1.15	8c

The following holsters are made to fit the Colt's Double Action, Colt's New Navy and New Army revolvers and Smith & Wesson Military and Police revolvers.

Catalogue Number	Caliber of Revolver	Length of Barrel, Inches	Price, Each	Postage Extra
6K4767H	38 or 41	4½ to 5	$1.28	10c
6K4767J	38 or 41	5½ to 6½	1.33	10c

No. 6K4767K See top of next column.

Cowboy Holsters—Cont'd.

The following holsters are made to fit the large Frontier and Army frame revolvers, 32-20, 38-40, 44-40 and 45-caliber.

Catalogue Number	Caliber of Revolver	Length of Barrel, Inches	Price, Each	Postage Extra
6K4767K	32-20 to 45	4½ to 5	$1.35	10c
6K4767L	32-20 to 45	5½ to 6	1.43	10c
6K4767M	32-20 to 45	7½	1.45	10c

Texas Shoulder Holster.

Keeps revolver always safe and ready. Made of fine soft russet leather, nicely embossed, with leather strap to pass around the chest to hold holster on shoulder, as shown in the illustration. When ordering, always give catalogue number in full and state the make and style of your revolver, give length of barrel, and we will fit your revolver.

No. 6K4768A For 22-Caliber and Young America Revolvers. Mention length of barrel wanted. Price....(Postage extra, 5c.)....43c

For Smith & Wesson, Harrington & Richardson, Hopkins & Allen, Forehand, Iver Johnson, Colt's New Pocket and New Police, Colt's Automatic Pistols, and our own revolvers.

Catalogue Number	Revolver Caliber	Length of Barrel, Inches	Price, Each	Postage Extra
6K4768B	32	3 to 4	45c	5c
6K4768C	32	4½ to 5	46c	5c
6K4768D	38	3½ to 4	47c	5c
6K4768E	38	3½ to 4	48c	5c
6K4768F	38	4½ to 5	49c	5c
6K4768G	32 Colt	5½ to 6	50c	5c
6K4768AU	32 Colt	4½ to 6	54c	8c
6K4768AU	38 Auto	4½ to 6	60c	8c

To fit Colt's Double Action New Navy and New Army, 38 and 41-caliber, and Smith & Wesson Military and Police revolvers.

Catalogue Number	Caliber of Revolver	Length of Barrel, Inches	Price, Each	Postage Extra
6K4768H	38 or 41	4½ to 5	53c	8c
6K4768J	38 or 41	5½ to 6½	54c	8c

To fit large frame 44 or 45-caliber revolvers.

Catalogue Number	Caliber of Revolver	Length of Barrel, Inches	Price, Each	Postage Extra
6K4768K	32-20 to 45	4½ to 5	55c	8c
6K4768L	32-20 to 45	5½ to 6	56c	8c
6K4768M	32-20 to 45	7½	58c	8c

OUR HOLSTER AND CARTRIDGE BELTS.

Our leather goods are the best in the market. Always give waist measure and caliber when ordering.

No. 6K4771 Plain Leather Holster Belt (no loop), 1¼ inches wide, 28 to 44 inches waist measure. Price................18c
If by mail, postage extra, 8 cents.

No. 6K4772 Holster Belt, russet leather, nicely embossed edge, with loops for cartridges; 22, 32, 38, 41 or 44-caliber, 1½ inches wide, plain roller buckle, 30 to 46 inches long. Give length and caliber wanted. Price................27c
If by mail, postage extra, 5 cents.

Combination Cartridge and Money Belt, $1.14.

No. 6K4775 The Cowboy Combined Cartridge and Money Belt. Made of heavy russet tanned leather; strong and durable; nicely embossed; edges double stitched; designed to match our cowboy scabbard and holster; 32, 38, 44 or 45-caliber. Mention caliber wanted and give waist measure. Price................$1.14
If by mail, postage extra, 18 cents.

Shell Belts for Shotgun Shells.

Shell Belts with loops for carrying shotgun shells. Made of web and russet leather and with shoulder straps to go over the shoulder. Order by number and give waist measure.

No. 6K4786A

Catalogue Number	Made of	Size Gauge	Price	Post'g extra
6K4786A	Web	12	30c	8c
6K4786C	Web	16	31c	8c
6K4787A	Rus. Leather	12	43c	10c
6K4787B	Rus. Leather	10	45c	10c
6K4787C	Rus. Leather	16	46c	10c

We cannot furnish any other sizes.

THE IMPROVED MILLS WOVEN SHELL BELTS, $1.17

No. 6K4791 In these Anson Mills Belts the loops are woven into the belts, making them very strong and durable in all kinds of weather; 12-gauge only, with shoulder strap and game hooks. Price................$1.17
If by mail, postage extra, 26 cents.

MILLS HUNTERS' BELTS, 80c.

No. 6K4794 Anson Mills Hunters' Belt. The loops are woven, closed at the bottom, protecting the crimped end of the shell; no sewing whatever on the belt; 10,12 or 16-gauge. This belt has no shoulder straps. Mention gauge wanted. Price................80c
If by mail, postage extra, 12 cents.

Money Belts.

No. 6K4795 Money Belts, made of soft chamois skin; to be worn around the waist, under the clothing; the safest way to keep money. It is soft and comfortable, and made with three compartments. Price................42c
If by mail, postage extra, 3 cents.

No. 6K4796 Money Belts. Made of soft tanned horsehide; same style as above. Extra strong and durable. Price................59c
If by mail, postage extra, 5 cents.

No. 6K4798 Money and Gold Dust Belt. Four inches wide; made of the very finest oil tanned calfskin; very soft and pliable; will never get stiff and is just the thing to carry money or gold dust in; it is double stitched all around; made with three compartments; the center pocket is 8 inches long; the two end pockets are 5 inches long each; the outside cover folds over very closely and is fastened by snap buttons. Nothing to tear or wear out the clothing. This is the finest belt on the market for the purpose. Price................$1.03
If by mail, postage extra, 6 cents.

Rubber Cushion Leather Recoil Pads.

Give length of butt plates.

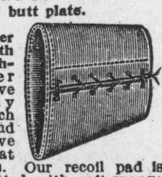

No. 6K5003 The only leather recoil pad with soft rubber cushion. All other leather pads have felt or shoddy cushions which become hard and which do not give the protection that the rubber cushion does. Our recoil pad is made of fine leather fitted with soft sponge rubber cushion, as stated, and is undoubtedly the best finished, most serviceable recoil pad on the market. Give length of butt plate when ordering. Price......(Postage extra, 5c.)......42c

No. 6K5005 The Acme Pure Red Rubber Recoil Pad. The best pad in the market. Lined with elastic cloth so it will not stick to the varnish on the gun stock. They come in three sizes: No. 2 is 5 inches long; No. 3 is 5¼ inches long and No. 4 is 5½ inches long. Mention length of butt plate. Price, (Postage extra, 5c) 59c

Our Combined Leather Cheek and Recoil Pad.

Give length of butt plate.

No. 6K5012 The Combined Leather Cheek and Recoil Pad, made of soft russet leather, oil tanned, will protect the cheek and the stock and at the same time protect the cheek and shoulder of the shooter. It will fit any gun stock. This pad is fitted with a soft sponge rubber cushion, the same as that used on the best recoil pads. The cheek pad is on the comb of stock is left open at one end so that the shooter can remove or add padding as he desires. Price........58c
If by mail, postage extra, 4 cents.

Hunting or Driving Gloves.

No. 6K5014 One Finger Shooting Gloves, made of soft pliable glove leather, fleece lined, close fitting elastic, wool wrist. Price per, pair, 70c
If by mail, postage extra, 8 cents.

Canvas Shell Bags for Carrying Loaded Shells.

Extra Heavy Brown Canvas Bags, leather bound, with pocket and adjustable leather carrying strap.

Catalogue No.	Holds	Price
6K5067	75 Shells	34c
6K5068	100 Shells	36c

If by mail, postage extra, each, 8 to 12 cents.

HUNTING KNIVES.

Perfect Hunting Knife, $1.65.

This style knife is very well known, and while the knife we offer is far lower in price than any knife of similar design on the market, we guarantee our knife to be equal to any knife of its style and pattern on the market, regardless of price. The Perfect Hunting Knife has best quality hand forged, concave blade, with heavy back, fitted with a stag handle, wound with leather. Length of blade, 6 inches, length over all, 10½ inches. Each knife furnished with a fine russet leather sheath with loop to attach to belt.
No. 6K4513 Price, complete with full length sheath................$1.65
If by mail, postage extra, 11 cents.

Our Arkansaw Bowie Knives.

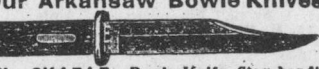

No. 6K4515 Bowie Knife, stag handle, 6-inch steel clip blade, leather sheath, with loop to attach to belt; entire length, 11 inches. Price................64c
No. 6K4516 Bowie Knife, with 7-inch blade. Price, with leather sheath....75c
No. 6K4517 Bowie Knife, with 8-inch blade. Price, with leather sheath....85c

Guides' Hunting Knife.

No. 6K4518 This knife has 6-inch heavy swaged and polished blade of best tempered steel, solid guard and fancy bolster. Finely scored ebony handle. A good serviceable all around knife for camp or trail. Complete with leather sheath. Price................53c
If by mail, postage extra, 10 cents.

Genuine Deerfoot Hunting Knives.

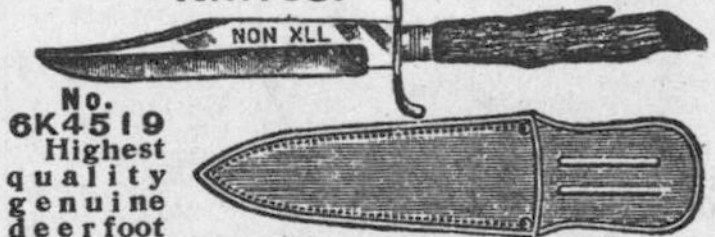

No. 6K4519 Highest quality genuine deerfoot handle (with hair left on (polished hoof, with German silver cap and German silver ferrule, fine polished, fancy, 2¾-inch guard, clip blade ground by hand, keen edge, heavy back, finely swaged, tempered and polished. These knives are imported by us direct from Sheffield, England, and are not to be compared with the cheap German and French knives offered in competition. Price includes fine, heavy leather, sewed sheath with loop for attaching to belt. The highest quality deerfoot hunting knife on the market.
Price, complete with sheath, 6-inch..$1.07
Price, 7-inch................1.15

Hunters' Pocket Knives.

59c

No. 6K16965 Wilbert Hunters' Pride Knife. It has stag handle, long, heavy German silver bolsters, cap and shield, brass lining, highly finished inside and out. The blades open and close freely without wearing. The knife blade is always true in the center, and it is these little points, to which we pay so much attention, that cause our knives to give better satisfaction than those you can procure from any other dealer. Length of handle, 4½ inches; length with large blade open, 8 inches. Price................59c
If by mail, postage extra, 6 cents.

No. 6K16976 Wilbert Hudson Bay Hunting Knife. A very nicely finished hunting knife. Clip point saber blade, flush lock back, curved stag handle, fancy German silver bolsters, caps and linings. Length of handle, 5½ inches. Length with blade open, 9¾ inches. Price...(Postage extra, 7c) $1.12

Sportsmen's Folding Lock Blade Knife.

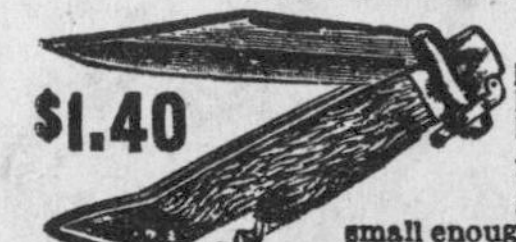

$1.40

No. 6K4521 Deer Foot Folding Lock Blade Knife. A strong, compact, serviceable knife small enough to be carried in the pocket and large enough to be serviceable for the hunter or trapper. This knife has an extra heavy 4¾-inch swaged, finely tempered clip blade, which, when opened, is firmly locked in position and cannot close accidentally. Fitted with a 5-inch genuine deer foot handle, brass lined, German silver bolster and polished corkscrew. Full length of knife when open, 9½ inches. Price............$1.40
If by mail, postage extra, 7 cents.

Pearl and Stag Handle Daggers.

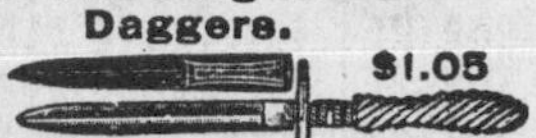

No. 6K4523 Our Finest Quality Ladies' Dagger. $1.05 This is a little beauty, with the very finest quality of steel in blade. Length of blade, 4 inches, both edges sharp, with beautiful pearl handle and German silver guard and fancy bolster, furnished with fine leather sheath. This is the finest quality of a dirk knife, and the metal is warranted.
Price......(Postage extra, 4c)......$1.05

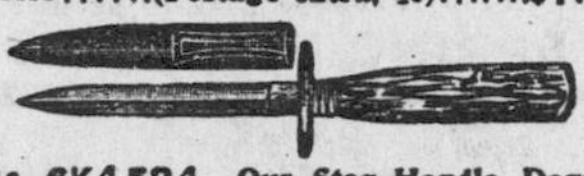

No. 6K4524 Our Stag Handle Dagger, 4-inch blade of good quality steel, with leather sheath. Price......(Postage extra, 5c.).....62c

Hunting Knife Sheath.

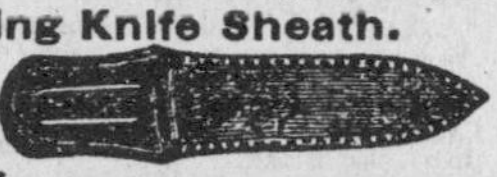

No. 6K4530 Leather Hunting Knife Sheaths.
For 6-inch Bowie, 20c | For 8-inch Bowie, 28c
For 7-inch Bowie, 24c | For 9-inch Bowie, 32c
If by mail, postage extra, 4 cents.
No. 6K4571 Leather Belts for knife sheaths, 1½ inches wide. Price............18c
If by mail, postage extra, 8 cents.

Hunters' Axes.

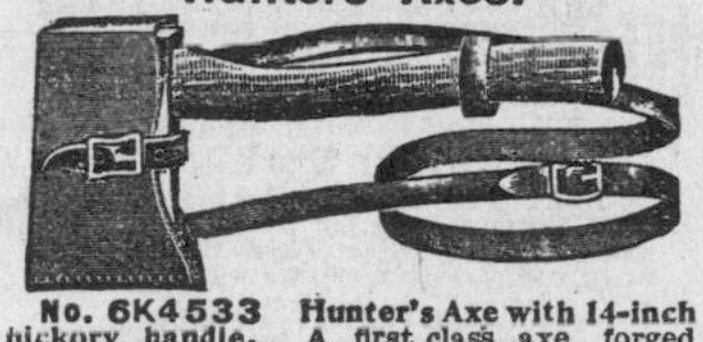

No. 6K4533 Hunter's Axe with 14-inch hickory handle. A first class axe, forged from a solid bar of tool steel. Finely ground and tempered, with solid leather sheath having adjustable shoulder strap for carrying. This is a first class tool and a necessity in every hunter's and camper's outfit. Total length, 16 inches; total weight, 2 pounds.
Price..............................78c
If by mail, postage extra, 45 cents.

Thomas' Nipper No. 4.

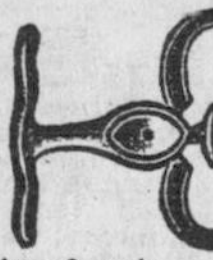

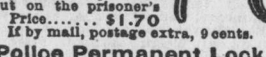

No. 6K4552 Thomas' Nipper, nicely finished and nickel plated. This nipper locks automatically when it is put on the prisoner's wrist. Price......... $1.70
If by mail, postage extra, 9 cents.

Police Permanent Lock Handcuffs.

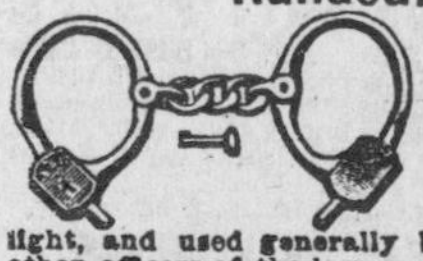

These handcuffs unlock with a key but lock automatically and are adjustable to any size wrist. They are made of good quality steel, are light, and used generally by detectives and other officers of the law.
No. 6K4555 Nicely polished and finished. Price, per pair. $2.75
No. 6K4556 Nicely polished and nickel plated. Price, per pair...............$3.20
If by mail, postage extra, 19 cents.

Police Billies.

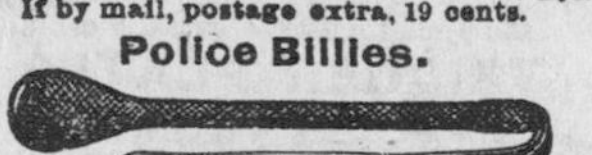

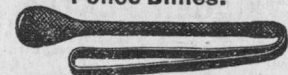

No. 6K4573 Plaited Billy, leather covered head. Weight, about 5 ounces, hand made.
Price..............................17c
If by mail, postage extra, 7 cents.

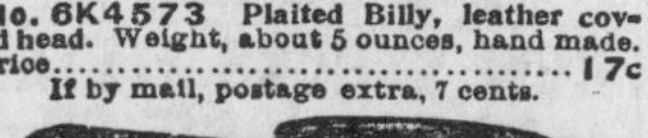

No. 6K4576 Leather Billy, sewed down the side, loaded with shot, made of the best material and cannot be equaled for the price. Length, 9 inches. Weight, about 9 ounces.
Price...(If by mail, postage extra, 12c.)..34c

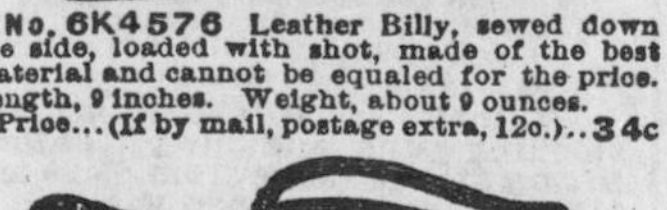

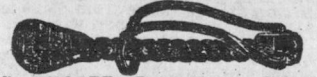

No. 6K4577 Russet Leather Billy, 8½ inches long, with sliding leather handle, filled with shot, sewed down the side and well made. Weight, about 9 ounces. Price............65c
If by mail, postage extra, 12 cents.

HUNTERS' CLOTHING

We are the largest handlers of high grade hunting clothing in the United States; our business exceeds that of any other five mail order houses combined. Our hunting clothing is made of the best selected full weight canvas and leather, the material used is especially selected for this purpose and you will find that our hunting clothing has quality, strength, style and finish not found in any other line. Owing to our enormous business in hunting clothing, we are able to operate the factory the year around. Our purchases of raw material are enormous, consequently we are able to sell our hunting clothing for far less money than you can possibly buy elsewhere. There are many imitations of our goods on the market sold at or even below our prices, but we know you cannot equal the quality of our goods within 25 or 50 per cent of our prices.

When ordering give chest measurement and do not forget that hunting clothing is generally worn over other heavy clothing, consequently should be ordered one size larger than the regular clothing, to allow plenty of freedom. SPECIAL SIZES not mentioned in the following descriptions will have to be made to order and require from ten days' to two weeks' time, and cost 35 per cent more than the prices named below.

Our Gold Medal Hunting Coat, $3.82.

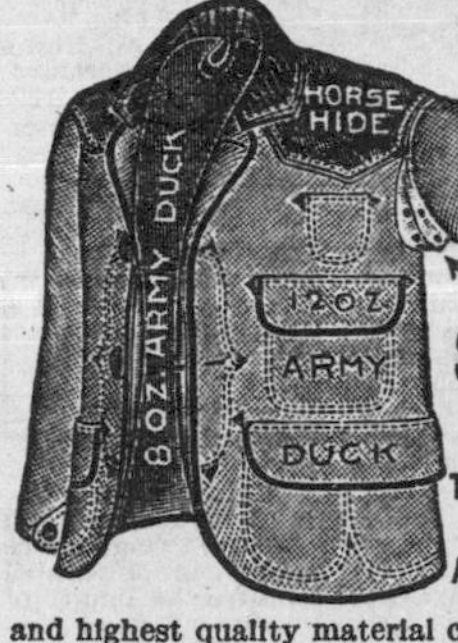

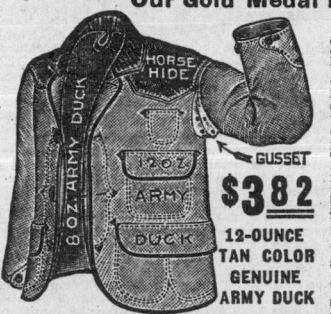

$3.82
12-OUNCE TAN COLOR GENUINE ARMY DUCK

WIND AND WATERPROOF.

No. 6K5130 Gold Medal Canvas Hunting Coat, made of the highest grade genuine United States Government army duck, the finest, strongest, toughest duck made. The construction of this coat is such that it combines practically two coats in one, the outer coat being made of 12-ounce tan color genuine army duck and lined throughout with 8-ounce army duck; sleeves lined with the celebrated Walker sateen. Cut on a very large, full pattern, with an extra large, roomy skirt. The coat does not bind anywhere. All the weight is on the shoulders. The sleeves are cut on a very roomy pattern with special gussets under the arm, giving absolute freedom to the arms. The cuffs are adjustable, with deep inside facing of corduroy. Large oil tanned horsehide pads on the shoulders, well padded, giving the greatest possible protection to the shoulders and adding greatly to the strength and appearance. Full size, narrow corduroy collar, large fancy bone buttons, silk stitched button holes, hand worked silk crow feet pocket stays, full leather bound, double stitched throughout. The finest hunting coat that skilled labor and highest quality material can produce. Sizes, 36 to 48 inches. Give chest measure when ordering. Price..$3.82
This coat is too heavy to go by mail; weight, about 4½ pounds.

DRYBACK COAT, $3.05.

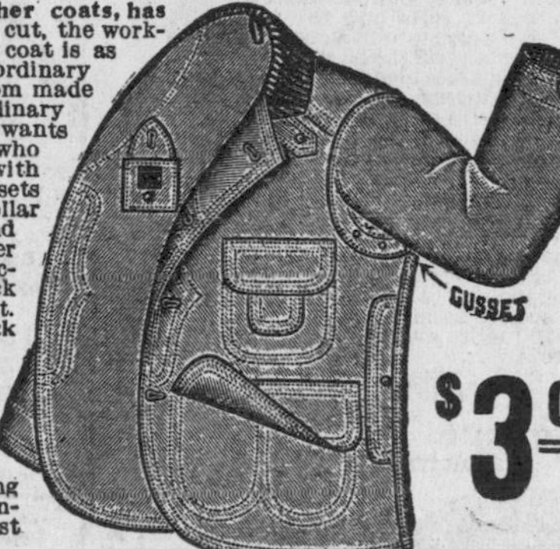

$3.05

This Dryback Coat is unlike all other coats, has a distinctive style all of its own. The cut, the workmanship and the general finish of this coat is as much different from that found in the ordinary hunting coat sold by dealers as the custom made tailored suit is different from the ordinary ready made. Made for the man who wants comfort, who wishes to look neat, who wishes wearing qualities combined with style. The manner in which this coat sets across the shoulder, the fit of the collar around the neck, and the comfort and ease derived from the large gussets under the sleeves are all features which are practical and which make this, our Dryback Coat, the greatest seller on the market.

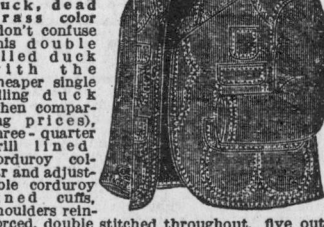

Our price of $3.05 for the Dryback Coat is exceedingly low, considering the quality of material employed and the high class workmanship. For the small difference in price between this and any other canvas coat we strongly advise that, if you can afford to pay $3.05 for a hunting coat, you should buy this Dryback Coat, for its wearing qualities and its excellent reinforced construction will make it by far the cheapest coat in the end.

The material of which this coat is made is genuine army standard 10-ounce khaki, full lined with standard 8-ounce army khaki. Khaki is the material adopted by the United States government for army clothing on account of its enormous strength, its wonderful wearing qualities, its smooth finish, and its peculiar weave, which makes it almost impervious to rain. We have gone even farther than the government in making these coats waterproof, and have had the khaki treated with a patent waterproofing process which renders it as near waterproof as it is possible for any fabric to be.

The color of our Dryback Coat is one of its features, the color being a sage green, the same as that used by the United States army on account of its neutrality, rendering a man at 40 yards invisible against any background. This sage green color harmonizes equally well with the green leaves, rushes or dead grass, making it the ideal coat for either Spring or Fall shooting.

The style or pattern is extra large and full, allowing plenty of comfort. The coat hangs free from the shoulder and does not bind anywhere. It has four buttons in front and a 4-inch collar with tap to button under chin.

The sleeves are cut on a new, special, extra wide pattern, with gussets under the arms, allowing the wearer to freely raise his arms without being compelled to raise the full weight in the pockets, as is the case with the ordinary coats. The sleeves are lined with a fine quality of sateen, have adjustable cuffs with a deep lining of corduroy.

The pockets are extra large and spacious, very strongly sewed, and guaranteed not to rip. There are six outside pockets with broad flaps and one inside match pocket with scratcher. The entrances to the game pockets are from the front edge of the coat and at the side seams under the arms, the side entrances having buttons to keep them closed.

Everything we could possibly do to this coat to make it more comfortable, more durable and a better coat in every way than you could buy elsewhere, has been done. We are satisfied that this coat at $3.05 is second only in strength, finish and style to our No. 6K5130 Coat, above described. The difference between this coat and the No. 6K5130 lies in the extra heavy material employed in the higher priced coat and the special hand work.

No. 6K5136 Dryback Coat, sizes, 36 to 48. Give size when ordering. Price..$3.05
If by mail, postage extra, 45 to 64 cents.

Our Extra Grade Leather Bound 10-Ounce Army Duck Coat, $2.35.

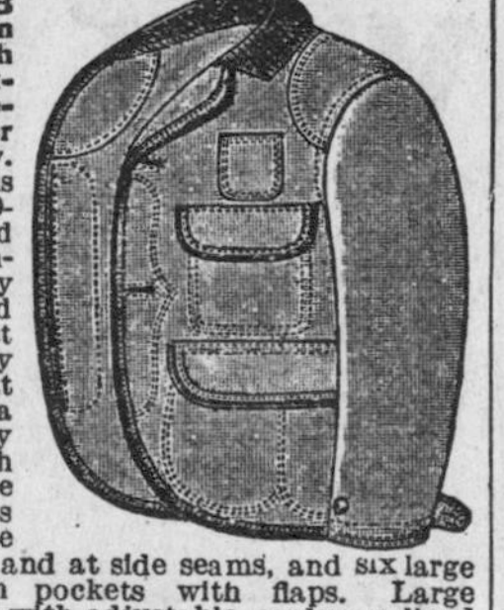

No. 6K5138 We offer in this high grade Hunting Coat special value for the money. This coat is made of 10-ounce dead grass color genuine army duck, full lined with the best 8-ounce army duck. The coat is cut on a large, roomy pattern, with three large game pockets with entrance on front edge and at side seams, and six large outside cut-in pockets with flaps. Large roomy sleeves with adjustable corduroy lined cuffs, reinforced shoulders and corduroy collar. This coat is full leather bound and double stitched throughout. The canvas of which it is made is a genuine army duck, made in accordance with the specifications of the U. S. Government, and we will guarantee that it will stand the government test. Sizes, 36 to 48 inches. Price..........................$2.35
If by mail, postage extra, 45 to 55 cents.

Our 10-Ounce Canvas Special Value Coat for $1.80.

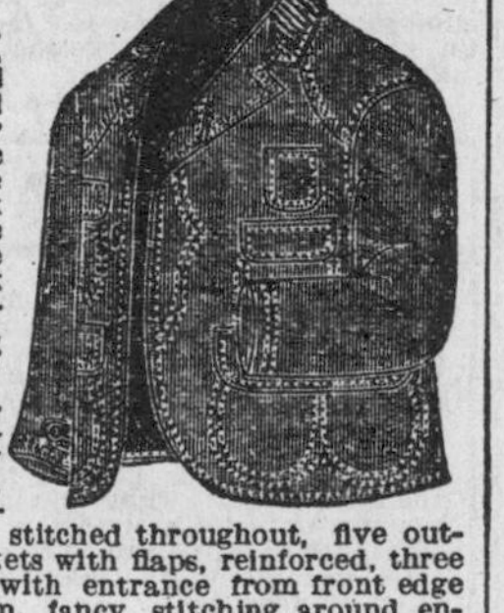

No. 6K5139 Hunting Coat, made of 10-oz. double filled duck, dead grass color (don't confuse this double filled duck with the cheaper single filling duck when comparing prices), three-quarter drill lined corduroy collar and adjustable corduroy lined cuffs, shoulders reinforced, double stitched throughout, five outside shell pockets with flaps, reinforced, three game pockets with entrance from front edge and side seam, fancy stitching around entrance to game pockets. Sizes, chest measure, from 36 to 48 inches. Give chest measure when ordering. Price.......$1.80
If by mail, postage extra, 35 to 45 cents.

Order your Hunting Coat one size larger than your dress coat, to allow plenty of freedom.

Our 10-Ounce Sage Green Hunting Coat for $1.78.

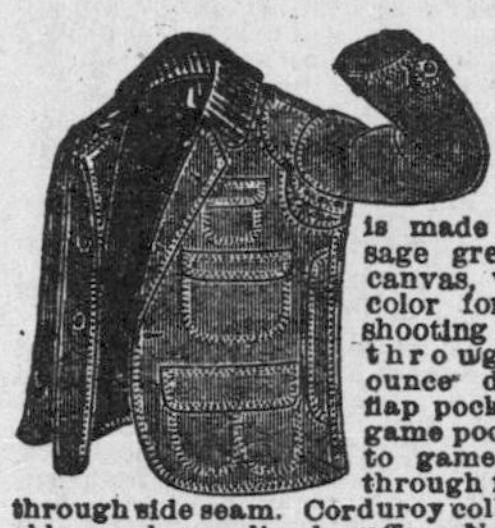

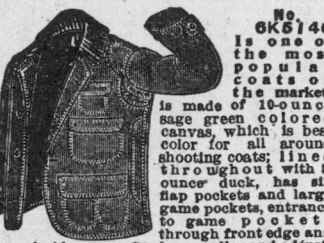

No. 6K5140 Is one of the most popular coats on the market, is made of 10-ounce sage green colored canvas, which is best color for all around shooting coats; lined throughout with 8-ounce duck, has six flap pockets and large game pockets, entrance to game pockets through front edge and through side seam. Corduroy collar and adjustable corduroy lined cuffs. Note the gusset under the sleeves; this is a special feature and enables you to raise your arm without lifting the entire weight of shells and game in the pockets. Sizes, chest measure, 36 to 46 inches. Give chest measure when ordering.
Price...................................$1.78
If by mail, postage extra, 35 to 50 cents.

Our Medium Weight Hunting Coat, $1 38.

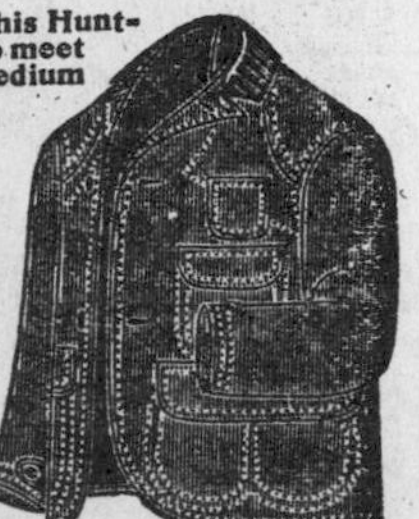

No. 6K5142 This Hunting Coat is made to meet the demand for a medium weight coat. Made of 8-ounce tan color Lindale duck, which is one of the nicest 8-ounce ducks on the market. The skirt is drill lined and the coat has six outside cut-in pockets with flaps, three game pockets with entrance at front and side seams. The shoulders are reinforced, corduroy collar, adjustable corduroy lined cuffs, coat is double stitched throughout. The high grade material used and our price of $1.38 makes this one of the most popular sellers in our line. It comes in sizes, 36 to 46 inches. Give chest measure when ordering. Price....$1.38
If by mail, postage extra, 30 to 40 cents.

Light Weight Coat, 63 Cents.

No. 6K5147 Made of heavy drill, dead grass color, five outside pockets, two inside skirt game pockets. A nice, light hunting and fishing coat for mild weather. Sizes, chest measure, 36 to 46 inches. Give chest measure when ordering. Price.................63c
If by mail, postage extra, 16 to 22 cents.

Our Boys' Hunting Coat, $1.35.

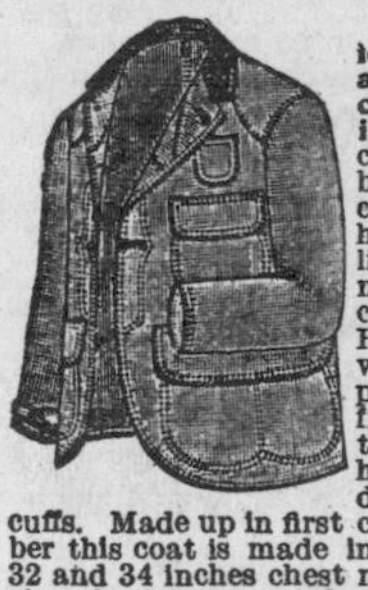

No. 6K5151 Made identically the same as the regular hunting clothing, but is made in boys' sizes only. By confining the line to boys' sizes, we were enabled to furnish a high-grade coat for little money. It is made of 10 ounce tan color canvas, drill lined. Has five outside pockets with flaps, two game pockets with entrance from front and back, the same as our regular hunting clothing. Corduroy lined adjustable cuffs. Made up in first class manner. Remember this coat is made in boys' sizes only—30, 32 and 34 inches chest measure. Be sure to give chest measure when ordering.
Price...........................$1.35

Our $2.78 Corduroy Coat.

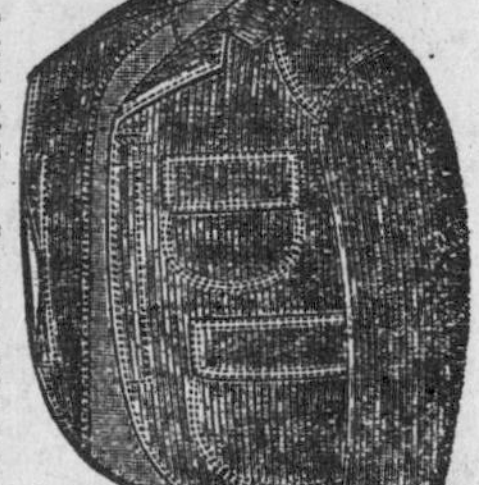

No. 6K5152 Good Quality Corduroy Coat drab color, full lined with drill, four large outside pockets with flaps, game pockets with entrance on front edge, double stitched reinforced shoulders. An excellent coat for little money. May be used by shooters or for all other general purposes. Made in sizes 36 to 48 inches chest measure. Give chest measure when ordering.
Price...........................$2.78
If by mail, postage extra, 38 to 48 cents.

Hunting Vest, 65 Cents.

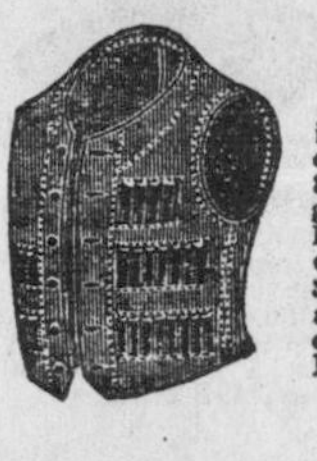

No. 6K5155 Hunting Vest, with loops for cartridges. Made of 8-ounce duck, dead grass color, unlined, holds about 36 shells, 10 or 12-gauge. Sizes, from 32 to 46 inches. Give gauge and chest measure when ordering. Price..65c
If by mail, postage extra, 10 to 20 cents.

Duck Hunting Pants.

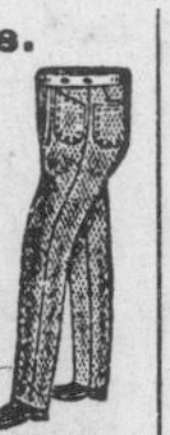

No. 6K5158 Hunting Pants. Made of 8-ounce duck; dead grass color, with four patch pockets. Sizes, from 28 to 44 inches waist measure. Give waist measure and leg measure of inseam when ordering. Price, per pair.......78c
If by mail, postage extra, 22 to 26c.

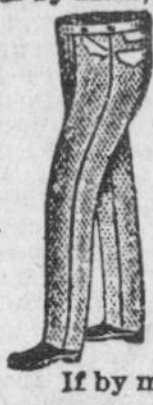

10-oz. Army Duck Pants, $1.29.

No. 6K5159 Duck Hunting Pants. Made of 10-ounce army duck, dead grass color, business style. Two front and two back cut-in pockets. Sizes, from 30 to 44 inches waist measure. Give waist measure and inseam measure of leg when ordering. Price, per pair...$1.29
If by mail, postage extra, 30 to 35 cents.

No. 6K5161 Sage Green Duck Hunting Pants made of finest quality 8-ounce canvas, sage green color to match our No. 6K5141 hunting coats, with cut-in front and hip pockets. Cut business style. Give waist measure and inseam measure of leg when ordering. Price, per pair......................$1.12
If by mail, postage extra, 24 to 35 cents.

Corduroy Hunting Suit, $9.80.

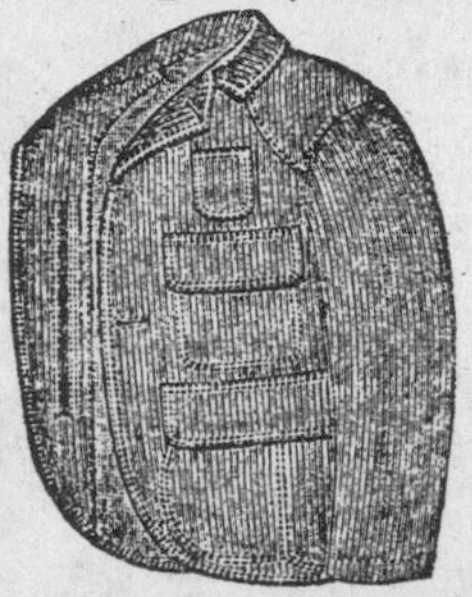

No. 6K5172 Corduroy Coat, made of the best heavy corduroy, drab color, full lined with heavy sateen, reinforced shoulders, adjustable cuffs, made on a large full pattern, six cut-in outside pockets with flaps, spacious game pockets with entrance from front edge and seams under arms. This is as fine a corduroy coat as can be made. The material and workmanship are the best obtainable. This coat is equal to anything on the market, regardless of price. Sizes, 36 to 46 inches chest measure. Give chest measure when ordering.
Price..$4.75
Cannot be sent by mail.

No. 6K5174 Corduroy Vest. Business style, with pockets, to match above coat. Give chest measure when ordering. Price...$2.00
If by mail, postage extra, 23 to 32 cents.

No. 6K5175 Corduroy Pants. Business style. To match above coat. Give waist measure and inseam of leg measure when ordering. Price, per pair...............................$3.20
If by mail, postage extra, 45 to 60 cents.

No. 6K5176 Suit complete, coat, vest and pants. Price..........................$9.80
Cannot be sent by mail.

Japanese Grass Suits, $1.00

Thousands are being worn by sportsmen everywhere.

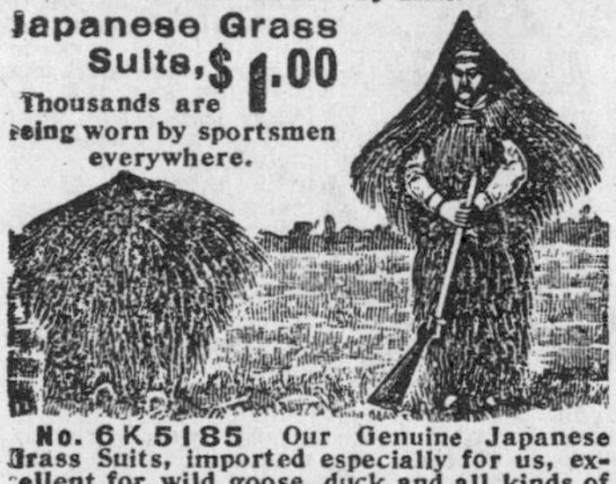

No. 6K5185 Our Genuine Japanese Grass Suits, imported especially for us, excellent for wild goose, duck and all kinds of shore bird shooting, made from long, tough imported marsh grass into a cape coat with hood. They weigh about 4 pounds and are very convenient to wear for hunting. They also make good waterproofs in rainy weather, are easily packed and carried. Hunters appreciate the value of these suits, as no blind or bough house is necessary when shooting on marshes or field.
Price, per suit.............................$1.00
If by mail, postage extra, 64 cents.

HUNTING HATS AND CAPS.

Canvas Cape Cap, 35 Cents.

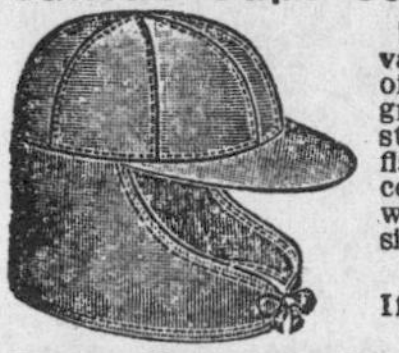

No. 6K5189 Canvas Cape Cap, made of 8-ounce duck, dead grass color, single stiff visor, full cape, flannel lined, an excellent rough or cold weather cap. State size wanted.
Price........35c
If by mail, postage extra, 9 cents.

8-oz. Canvas Duck Hat, 34c.

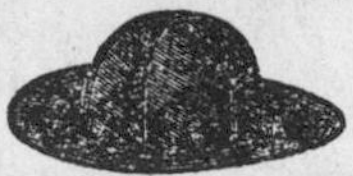

No. 6K5192 Made of 8-ounce duck, dead grass color, round top, taped seams, double stitched, stitched brim. State size wanted.
Price...34c
If by mail, postage extra, 7 cents.

Our Windsor Style Cap, 49c.

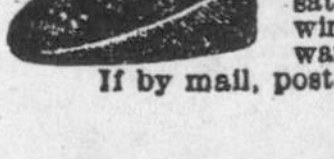

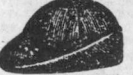

No. 6K5195 Made of heavy imported corduroy. Windsor style, silk finish, sateen lined. An excellent winter cap. State size wanted. Price......49c
If by mail, postage extra, 8 cents.

Our Eureka Hunting and Blizzard Cap.

THREE CAPS IN ONE.

$1.30

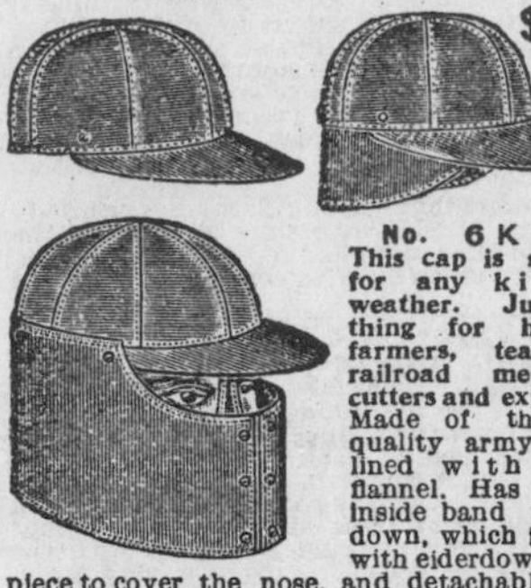

No. 6K5198 This cap is suitable for any kind of weather. Just the thing for hunters, farmers, teamsters, railroad men, ice cutters and explorers. Made of the best quality army duck, lined with domet flannel. Has patent inside band to pull down, which is lined with eiderdown, nosepiece to cover the nose, and detachable cape lined with the finest quality all wool eiderdown. This is the best cap made, and it can be worn as a regular cap in mild weather; the inside band can be pulled down over the ears in fresh, snappy weather, and the detachable cape can be readily put in place for extremely cold and blizzardy weather when you wish to cover up everything but the eyes. There is no unpleasant, musty sheepskin smell about this cap, and the cape is fastened on with patent snap fasteners and is easily detached and can be rolled in a very neat, small package and carried in the pocket. When ordering, be sure to state size wanted. Price..$1.30
If by mail, postage extra, 13 cents.

OUR AMERICAN PEDOMETER.

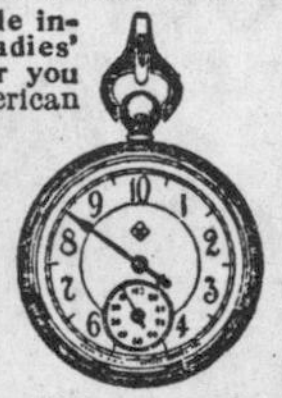

No. 6K5229 This little instrument looks like a ladies' watch, but it tells how far you walk. To operate our American Pedometer take off the back bezel with a knife blade and you will find the figures for your step. Directions for setting the pedometer come with each one. Hang the pedometer in your watch pocket, and every step you take will register. The figures on the face of the pedometer indicate the miles or fraction of a mile which you walk. This pedometer has a dial like illustration and a second hand like on a watch and registers 100 miles and repeats.
Price...80c
If by mail, postage extra, 4 cents. Insured mail, 5 cents extra.

Aluminum Telescope Collapsing Cup, 17c.

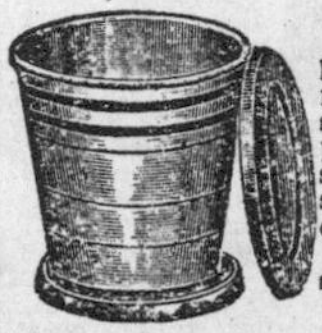

No. 6K5230 Our Aluminum Collapsing Cup. It can be folded into a very small space and carried in vest pocket. Neat and substantial. Handsome satin finish. Size of an ordinary tumbler.
Large size, aluminum; satin finish. Price..17c
Postage extra, 3 cents.

The Lanz Canteen Reduced to 95 Cents.

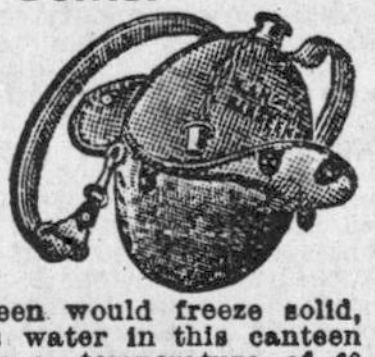

No. 6K5292 The only canteen which will keep water in palatable condition in any climate. With the Lanz Canteen you can always have a cool drink of water in summer, or warm coffee or tea in winter. Where water in an ordinary canteen would freeze solid, under like conditions water in this canteen would not fall below a temperature of 60 degrees. The same theory applies to this canteen used in hot climates. Where water in an ordinary government canteen would reach a temperature of 125 degrees, water in this canteen would not exceed a temperature of 82 degrees. Endorsed by doctors, explorers, soldiers and government officials. The canteen is made of heavy tin covered with a layer of felt, which in turn is covered with a removable canvas cover. Fitted with an adjustable web sling strap. The canteen is 9 inches in diameter, holds 45 fluid ounces, weighs about 1 pound.
Price, now only..............................95c
If by mail, postage extra, 26 cents.

GUN REPAIRS.

We catalogue only the parts for which there is the greatest demand, but we carry a full line of gun repairs, such as mainsprings, trigger springs, hammers, butt plates, trigger guards, etc., consisting of a very large and varied line, and if you are needing any gun repairs we suggest that you write for our circular of gun repairs and at the same time advise us what style of repair you wish, give us the name of the fire arm, state whether it is a gun, rifle, revolver or pistol, say whether it is a muzzle loader or a breech loader and you will assist us materially in taking care of your order intelligently.

There have been many millions of guns, revolvers and rifles made in the past fifty years, and all are different from each other and it will be necessary for us to know exactly what you wish and for what kind of a fire arm it is intended.

Write us and say, "Send me your Circular No. 225H of GUN REPAIRS."

BREECH LOADING GUN LOCKS.

When ordering locks, give us the length of your old lock, make a drawing of it on a piece of paper and attach it to your order, and we will send you, as near as we can, a lock to match it; but you must not expect a lock that will fit exactly in your gun. It may fit exactly or it may require some little work to make it fit your gun. When ordering do not forget to give us the size and a drawing of your gun lock.

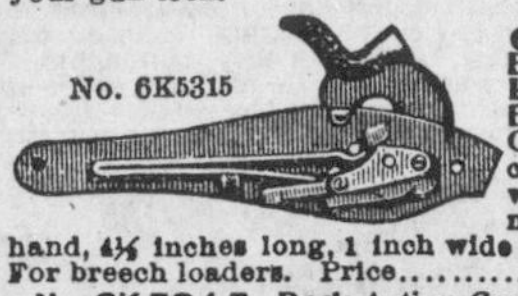

No. 6K5315

No. 6K5314 Breech Loading, Back Action Gun Lock, complete with hammer. Right hand, 4½ inches long, 1 inch wide at hammer. For breech loaders. Price..................98c

No. 6K5315 Back Action Gun Lock, complete with hammer. Left hand, 4½ inches long, 1 inch wide at hammer. For breech loaders. Price..99c
If by mail, postage extra, 7 cents.

NOTICE—Gun repairs are not finished nor ready to put into guns and must be fitted by a gunsmith or mechanic. Send us a sketch of the broken part, so we can better match it.

MUZZLE LOADING GUN LOCKS.

THESE GUN LOCKS are finished, but will have to be fitted to your gun. No two guns are exactly alike and therefore we cannot furnish gun locks to fit exactly. Measure the length of your gun lock and tell us how long it is, or send us a drawing of the lock plate, and we will send you the nearest we have to it. We usually send them a trifle longer, because it is easy to cut out the stocks a little more to make them fit. Gun locks usually measure 4½ to 5 inches from end to end.

BACK ACTION, POLISHED.

FOR MUZZLE LOADERS.

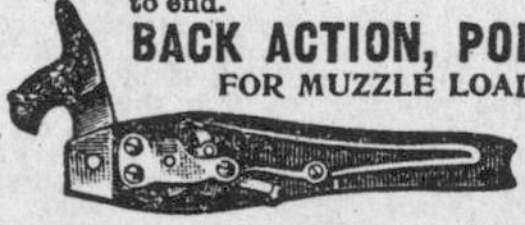

Mention Length Wanted.

Cat. No.	Style	Kind	Length, inches	Price
6K5340	Back	Rt. hand	4½, 4¾, 5	48c
6K5341	Action	Left hand	4½, 4¾, 5	50c

If by mail, postage extra, 6c. Insured mail, 11c.

FOR MUZZLE LOADERS

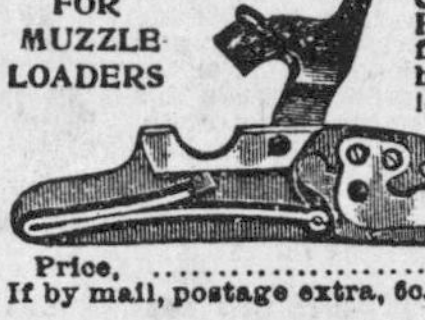

No. 6K5345 C. P. American Forward Action, cut for plug, right hand, for muzzle loading rifles, 4½, 4¾ or 5 inches long; give length wanted.
Price,..65c
If by mail, postage extra, 6c. Insured mail, 11c.

FULL BAR ACTION GUN LOCKS.

FOR MUZZLE LOADERS.

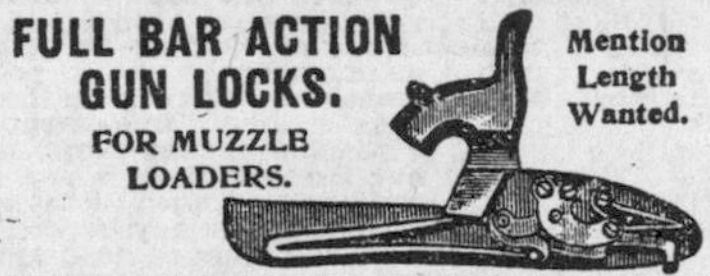

Mention Length Wanted.

Cat. No.	Style	Kind	Length, inches	Price
6K5346	Bar	Rt. hand	4½, 4¾, 5	55c
6K5347	Action	Left hand	4½, 4¾, 5	57c

If by mail, postage extra, 6c. Insured mail, 11c.

TUMBLER PINS.

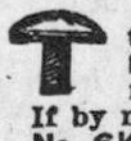

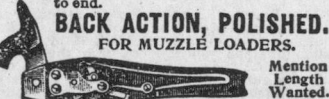

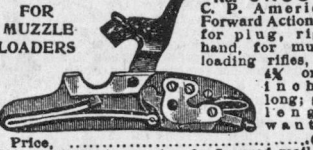

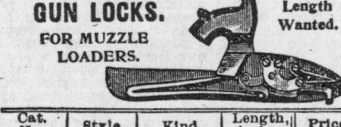

No. 6K5369 Tumbler Pins, threaded, for muzzle loading locks. Send sample, showing size, so we can match it. Price, per pair........10c
If by mail, postage extra, per pair, 1 cent.

No. 6K5370 Tumbler Pins, threaded for American made guns. Mention for which gun it is wanted. Price, per pair...............12c
If by mail, postage extra, per pair, 1 cent.

TOP LEVER SPRINGS.

Order by Catalogue Number.

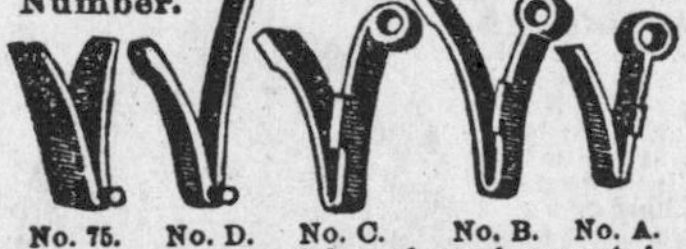

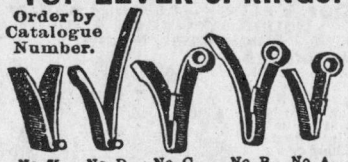

No. 75. No. D. No. C. No. B. No. A.

Be sure to state style and number wanted.

Cat. No.	Style	For	Price
6K5376	No. A	English Guns	24c
6K5377	No. B	Bonehill Guns	25c
6K5378	No. C	English Guns	26c
6K5379	No. D	Tolley Guns	27c
6K5380	No. 75	Belgian Guns	20c

If by mail, postage extra, each, 2 cents.

Fore End Iron. Extractor.

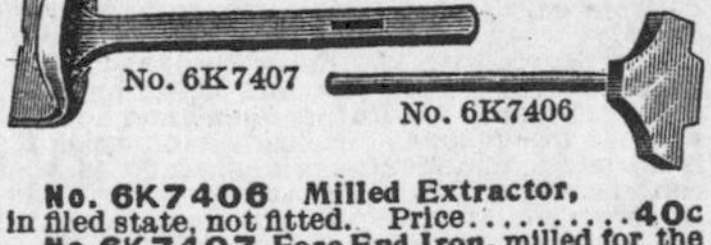

No. 6K7407 No. 6K7406

No. 6K7406 Milled Extractor, in filed state, not fitted. Price..........40c

No. 6K7407 Fore End Iron, milled for the frame of double guns, not fitted. Price...45c
If by mail, postage extra, 4 to 5 cents.

BREECH LOADING GUN HAMMERS

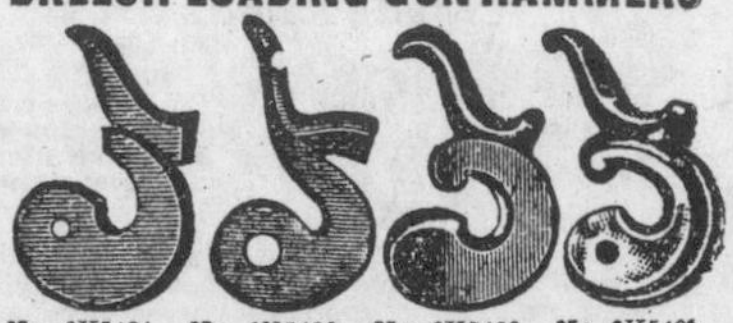

No. 6K5484 Flat Body. No. 6K5486 Round Body. No. 6K5490 Circular Plain. No. 6K5492 Circular Concave.

Hammers are measured from center of hole to middle of nose. State which size and which hand you wish. These hammers are not fitted and must be fitted by a gunsmith or mechanic.

Catalogue No.	Style Body	Size State size wanted	Hand	Price
6K5484	Flat	1 to 1¼ in.	Right	19c
6K5485	Flat	1 to 1¼ in.	Left	20c
6K5486	Round	1 to 1¼ in.	Right	22c
6K5487	Round	1 to 1¼ in.	Left	23c
6K5490	Circular	1 to 1¼ in.	Right	24c
6K5491	Circular	1 to 1¼ in.	Left	25c
6K5492	Concave	1 to 1¼ in.	Right	35c
6K5493	Concave	1 to 1¼ in.	Left	36c

If by mail, postage extra, each, 3 cents.

If you wish one of these hammers fitted, send old sample and allow 75 cents extra for fitting.

For fitting special hammers not listed above allow $1.25 to $1.50 for fitting each hammer.

Allow 3 to 6 days' time for fitting.

SPRING PLUNGERS.

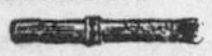

No. 6K5495 For Old Style Spring Plunger Guns, not fitted. Price, per pair, 15c; each........9c

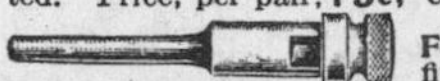

No. 6K5496 For Zulu Guns, not fitted.
Price, per pair, 25c; each..........15c
If by mail, postage extra, each, 1 cent.

NITRO FIRING PINS.

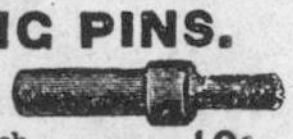

No. 6K5497 For Latest Style Belgian Guns, not fitted.
Price, per pair, 17c; each..........10c
If by mail, postage extra, per pair, 1 cent.

STEEL FIRING PINS.

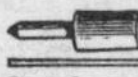

Catalogue No.	Diam. of Head	Length, inches	Price, each	Price, per pair
6K5498	8-32 in.	1¼ in	11c	19c
6K5499	9-32 in.	1¼ in	12c	20c
6K5500	10-32 in.	1¼ in	13c	24c
6K5501	11-32 in.	1⅜ in	14c	26c

If by mail, postage extra, per pair, 1 cent.

Plunger Springs.

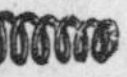

No. 6K5502 Taper, for Old Style Double Guns. Price, per pair, 15c

No. 6K5503 For Zulu Gun.
Price, each. (Postage extra, each, 1c.) 11c

Plunger Seats.

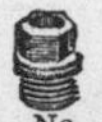

No. 6K5504 For English Guns, 6-cornered shoulder, not fitted.
Price, each..........................10c

No. 6K5506 Seats for Firing Pins No. 6K5495. Price, each..10c

No. 6K5504 If by mail, postage extra, per pair, 1c.

ROUGH TURNED WALNUT GUN STOCKS.

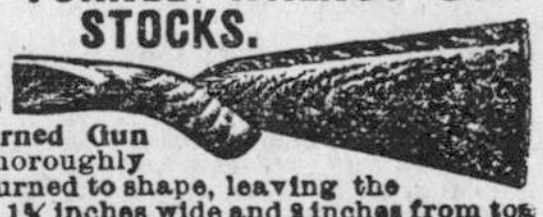

No. 6K5538 Rough Turned Gun Stocks, thoroughly seasoned, turned to shape, leaving the square end 1¾ inches wide and 3 inches from top to bottom, length, 16½ inches, butt measure, 5⅛x1⅜ inches. Made of good American walnut, not fitted, just shaped, for double barrel breech loading guns. Weight, 20 ounces. Price, 58c
If by mail, postage extra, 28 cents.

COMPOSITION BUTT PLATES.

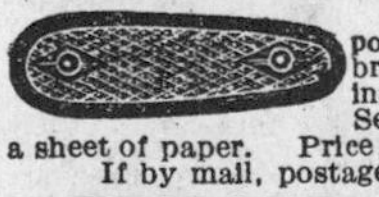

No. 6K5539 Composition Butt Plates for breech or muzzle loading guns; not fitted. Send drawing of size on a sheet of paper. Price..................29c
If by mail, postage extra, 5 cents.

TRIGGER GUARDS.

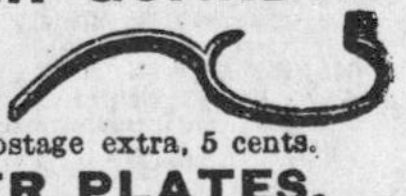

No. 6K5540 Breech Loading Guards, filed and threaded, not fitted.
Price.........38c
If by mail, postage extra, 5 cents.

TRIGGER PLATES.

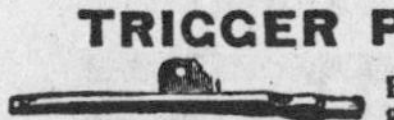

No. 6K5541 Breech Loading Trigger Plates, filed and tapped; not fitted. Price...............45c
If by mail, postage extra, 5 cents.

NEW STOCKS FITTED

$5.00 TO $15.00

We have one of the most complete, best equipped and most up to date gun shops in the country, and are prepared to do all kinds of gun repairing.

We make a specialty of restocking guns, and our prices for fitting stocks range from $5.00 to $15.00, depending upon the quality of wood, finish and labor required, which is in accordance with the quality of the gun. Fore ends fitted from $2.75 to $4.00. Customer to pay transportation charges on gun both ways.

Roller Skates, 38 Cents.

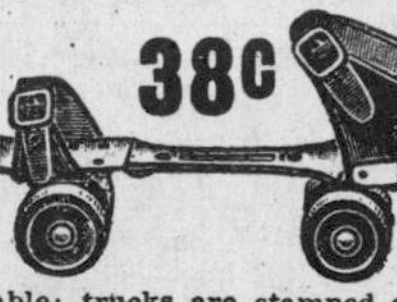

No. 6K5820 Improved Extension Sidewalk Skate, full strapped. Has high grade homogeneous steel tops, is strong and durable; trucks are stamped and corrugated and made from Swedish steel, are very light and strong. Trimmed with black pebbled leather straps, tongue buckles. Maple wheels. This skate is an extension, is easily adjusted to any size shoe and will stay where it is put and gives no trouble.

Price, per pair....................38c

If by mail, postage extra, 33 cents.

Men's Plain Bearing Roller Skates, 97 Cents.

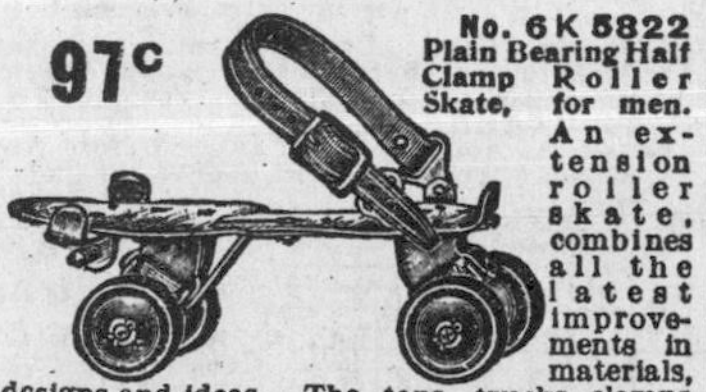

No. 6K5822 Plain Bearing Half Clamp Roller Skate, for men. An extension roller skate, combines all the latest improvements in materials, designs and ideas. The tops, trucks, clamps and stampings being made of the best cold rolled Swedish steel insures fine appearance and strength. Trucks are oscillating, with best rubber cushions, and turn in three-foot circle. Clamps are neat, easily removed for repairs, cleaning or side adjustment and will hold to the shoe like a vise. Skate will extend and fit all sizes from 8½ to 11½ inches. Adjustment is easily made and will hold.

Price, per pair, with steel rolls.......97c

If by mail, postage extra, 64 cents.

THE SURPRISINGLY LOW REDUCED PRICES prevailing in this catalogue mean greater savings to our customers than ever before.

Women's Plain Bearing Roller Skates, 96c.

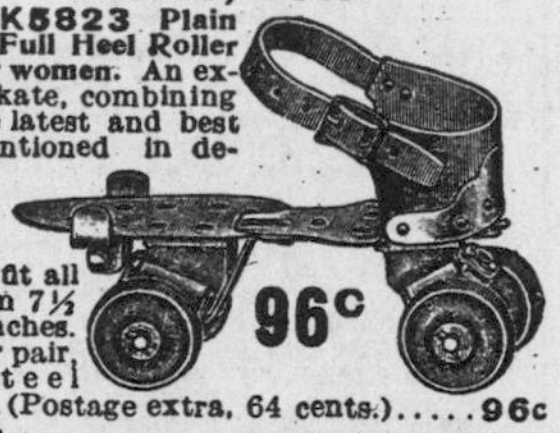

No. 6K5823 Plain Bearing Full Heel Roller Skate, for women. An extension skate, combining all of the latest and best ideas mentioned in description of No. 6K5822. Skate extends to fit all sizes from 7½ to 10½ inches. Price, per pair, with steel rolls.....(Postage extra, 64 cents.).....96c

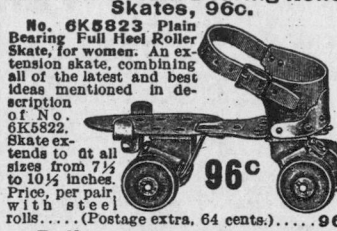

Ball Bearing Extension Skates, $2.40.

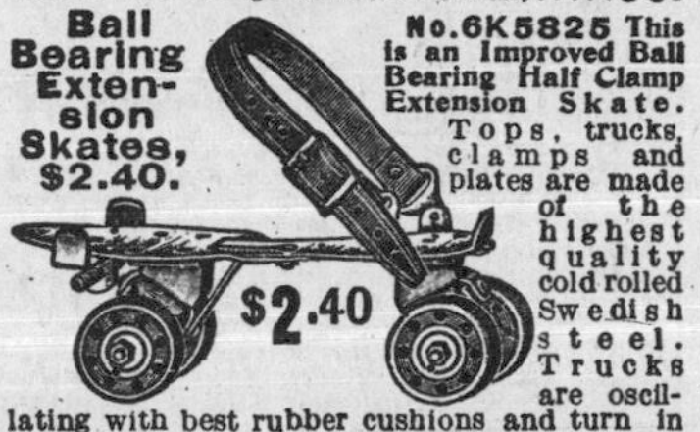

No. 6K5825 This is an Improved Ball Bearing Half Clamp Extension Skate. Tops, trucks, clamps and plates are made of the highest quality cold rolled Swedish steel. Trucks are oscillating with best rubber cushions and turn in three-foot circle. The straps are best russet grade leather, nickel buckles and trimmings. They are strong, handsome and a finely finished skate, and extend to fit any size from 8½ to 11 inches. Price, per pair, with steel rolls......(Weight, 4½ pounds.).....$2.40

Ladies' Ball Bearing Roller Skates, $2.41.

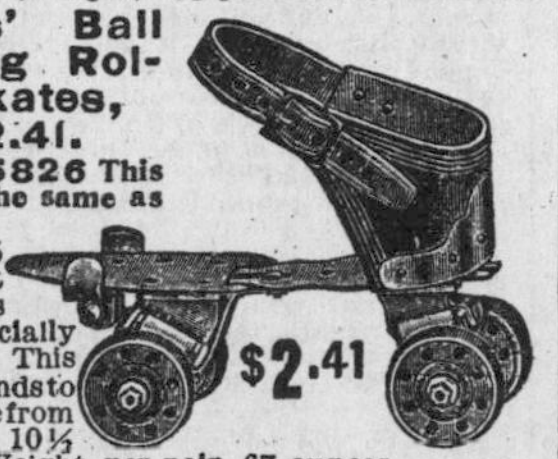

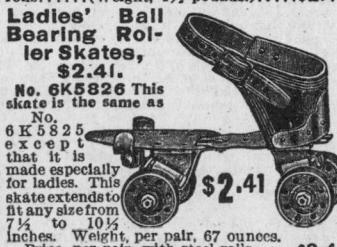

No. 6K5826 This skate is the same as No. 6K5825 except that it is made especially for ladies. This skate extends to fit any size from 7½ to 10½ inches. Weight, per pair, 67 ounces.

Price, per pair, with steel rolls.....$2.41

Ball Bearing Half Clamp Rink Skates.

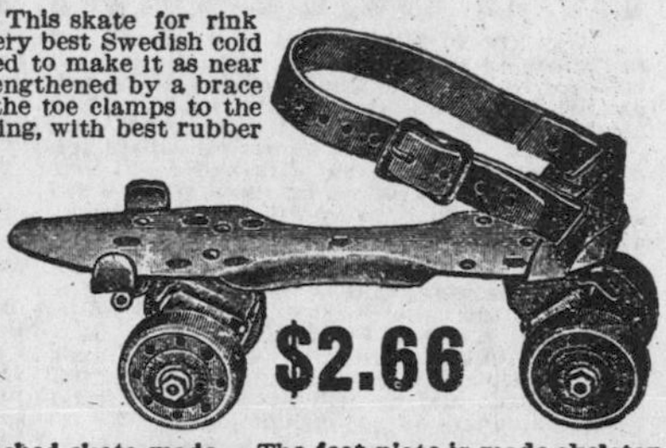

Ball Bearing Men's Rink Skates. This skate for rink work has no equal. It is made of the very best Swedish cold rolled steel, and no expense has been spared to make it as near perfect as possible. The foot plate is strengthened by a brace which is riveted to it, extending from the toe clamps to the back of the heel. The trucks are oscillating, with best rubber cushions, and turn in three-foot circle. Give size of shoe worn, also length of shoe in inches. Weight, 75 ounces.

No. 6K5828 Price, per pair, with steel rolls......................$2.66

No. 6K5831 Same as above, for women. Price, per pair, with steel rolls.......................$2.65

Knight Roller Skate.

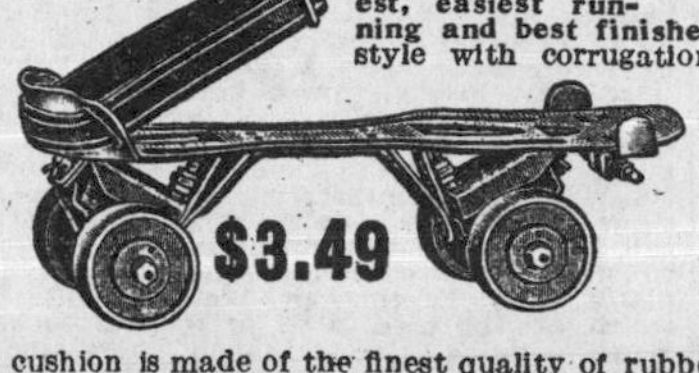

The Knight Roller Skate is the lightest, strongest, easiest running and best finished skate made. The foot plate is made skeleton style with corrugations from cold rolled machine steel, and has a rib truss brace firmly riveted to the bottom and connected with both front and back roller carriers, strengthening the foot plate and bracing the carriers, making this the most rigid skate made. This brace is designed to give the greatest possible strength and rigidity to the skate with the least possible weight. The carriers are made on the box pattern with the solid steel axle passing through and riveted to the lower side. The upper side holds the large solid rubber cushion upon which the skate rests. The cushion is made of the finest quality of rubber. It eliminates all jar and prevents wearing of bearings and bending of axles. The oscillating action on the roller carriers can be made as rigid or as sensitive as possible by simply loosening or tightening the set screw over the plate on the cushion. The adjusting screw is accessible from top of skate.

The rollers have triple thick rims, cut from cold drawn carbon steel seamless tubing, and are shouldered on the inside to receive the side plates, which makes the best wearing rollers. All parts of the Knight Skate are highly polished and nickel plated, and they have an appearance equaled by no other skate on the market. This skate is suitable for both ladies and gentlemen, having a toe clamp and a strap to go over the ankle. When ordering, give length of shoe. Weight, 94 ounces.

No. 6K5836 Knight Roller Skates. Price per pair..................$3.49

Rollers.

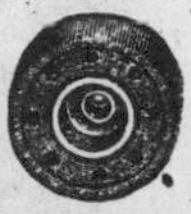

No. 6K5840 Maple Rolls, regular. Price, per set of eight.........12c
If by mail, postage extra, 8 cents per set of eight.

No. 6K5844 Plain Bearing Steel Rolls. Price, per set of eight....43c

No. 6K5845 Steel Ball Bearing Rolls. Price, per set of eight.....75c

Ball bearing rolls will not fit plain bearing skates. Prices are for wheels only.
If by mail, postage extra, 30 cents per set of eight.

No. 6K5848 3-16-inch Steel Balls. Per dozen..................5c

WE HAVE DISCONTINUED THE SALE OF ROLLER SKATES WITH COMPOSITION OR HEMACITE ROLLS OWING TO THEIR POOR WEARING QUALITIES. WE AIM TO HANDLE ONLY SUCH GOODS AS WE KNOW WILL GIVE SATISFACTION.

ICE SKATES

THE SIZE OF ICE SKATES IS SAME AS THE LENGTH OF SHOE SOLE FROM HEEL TO TOE MEASURED IN INCHES.

When Ordering Ice Skates Give Length of Shoe in Inches.

In measuring shoe, place heel of shoe against the wall and measure from wall to end of toe.

We often receive orders like the following: "Send me one pair of skates, No. 9." We do not know if it is for a No. 9 child's shoe, a No. 9 man's shoe, or a 9-inch shoe. We will not attempt to fill orders for skates unless size wanted is given in inches. State length of shoe in inches when ordering.

We guarantee all our skates to be equal to the best goods made. The average weight of a pair of our skates is 40 ounces. They can be sent by mail to any part of the United States. The average express charges are from 25 cents to 45 cents to almost any part of the United States. Postage must be paid in advance.

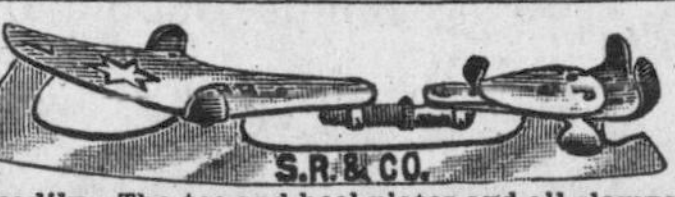

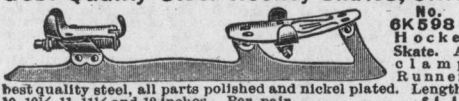

No. 6K5950 The runner of this skate is made of the very best cold rolled cast steel, which does not lose its edge readily. The toe and heel plates and all clamps are made of the best quality of cold rolled homogeneous steel. The clamping mechanism has been proven to be perfect. Sizes from 8 to 12 inches. Price, per pair..........................54c
If by mail, postage extra, 34 to 50 cents.
When ordering skates give length of shoe in inches.

No. 6K5954 Hardened Skate. The steel used in this skate contains a higher percentage of carbon, and the runner is carefully hardened and highly polished. Toe and heel plates and clamps are made of the best quality cold rolled open hearth steel. Sizes, 8 to 12 inches. Price, per pair..................87c
If by mail, postage extra, 35 to 50 cents.
When ordering skates give length of shoe in inches.

Racing Skates, $2.32.

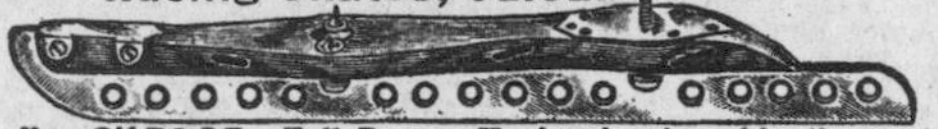

No. 6K5965 Full Racer. Used and endorsed by the most noted fast skaters in the United States and Canada. Tops are made of selected close grain beechwood, varnished, with highly nickel plated toe, heel and center plates. Runners are made of high grade cast steel, ⅛ inch thick and are bored, making the lightest possible skate; made with 14, 16 and 18-inch runners.
Price, per pair...(Postage extra, 40 to 48 cents.)....$2.32
When ordering skates give length of runners desired.

Full Rocker Skates, $1.34.

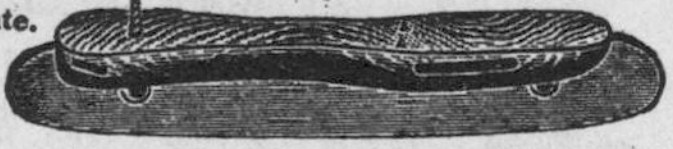

No. 6K5977 Full Rocker Skate. Correct in every detail. Tops are made of selected beechwood and runners from best rolled steel. All runners are fastened to top by a brass thimble, which prevents the wood from splitting. We furnish black straps, ⅝x20 inches for heel and 1⅛-inch broad toe straps with every pair. Sizes, 9½ to 12 inches. Price, per pair....... $1.34
If by mail, postage extra, 36 to 48 cents.
When ordering skates give length of shoe in inches.

Best Quality Steel Hockey Skates, $1.10.

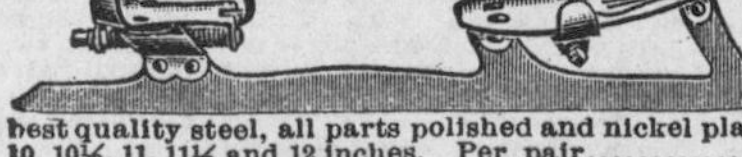

No. 6K5981 Hockey Skate. All clamp. Runners best quality steel, all parts polished and nickel plated. Lengths, 10, 10½, 11, 11½ and 12 inches. Per pair......................$1.10
If by mail, postage extra, 46 to 54 cents
When ordering skates give length of shoe in inches.

High Grade Hockey Skates, $2.60.

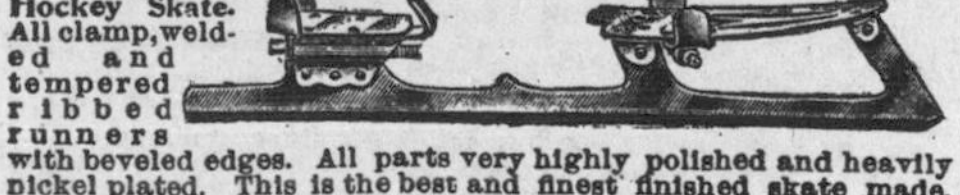

No. 6K5985 Hockey Skate. All clamp, welded and tempered ribbed runners with beveled edges. All parts very highly polished and heavily nickel plated. This is the best and finest finished skate made. Lengths, 10, 10½, 11, 11½ and 12 inches. Price, per pair..$2.60
If by mail, postage extra, 43 to 52 cents.
When ordering skates give length of shoe in inches.

Expert Tubular Hockey and Racing Skates, $4.65.

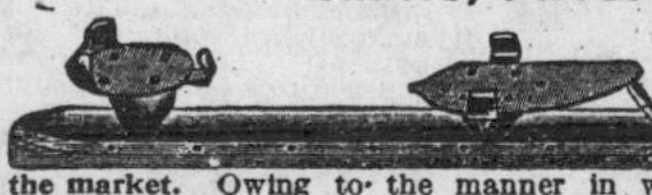

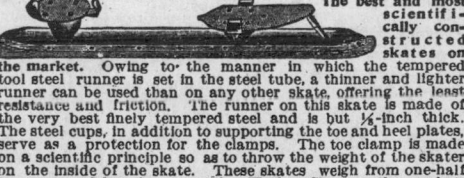

No. 6K5987 The best and most scientifically constructed skates on the market. Owing to the manner in which the tempered tool steel runner is set in the steel tube, a thinner and lighter runner can be used than on any other skate, offering the least resistance and friction. The runner on this skate is made of the very best finely tempered steel and is but ⅛-inch thick. The steel cups, in addition to supporting the toe and heel plates, serve as a protection for the clamps. The toe clamp is made on a scientific principle so as to throw the weight of the skater on the inside of the skate. These skates weigh from one-half to one pound less than any other Hockey Skate on the market. These skates are finely nickel plated and polished. Length, 10, 10½, 11, 11½ and 12 inches. Price, per pair......$4.65
If by mail, postage extra, 45 to 50 cents.
When ordering skates give length of shoe in inches.

Ladies' Skates, 70 Cents.

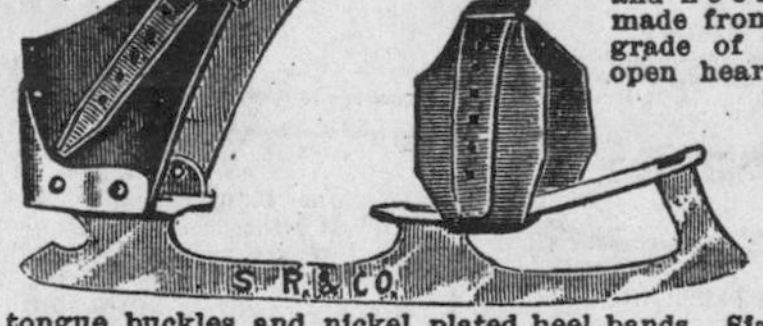

No. 6K5990 Ladies' Strap Skate. Runner is made of cold rolled steel, is highly polished with finely ground cutting edge. The foot and heel plates are made from the best grade of cold rolled open hearth homogeneous steel. The heel and toe straps are of the best oak tanned russet grain leather, tongue buckles and nickel plated heel bands. Sizes, 8 to 11½ inches. Price, per pair.............................70c
If by mail, postage extra, 32 to 40 cents.
When ordering skates give length of shoe in inches.

High Grade Ladies' Club Skates, 94 Cents.

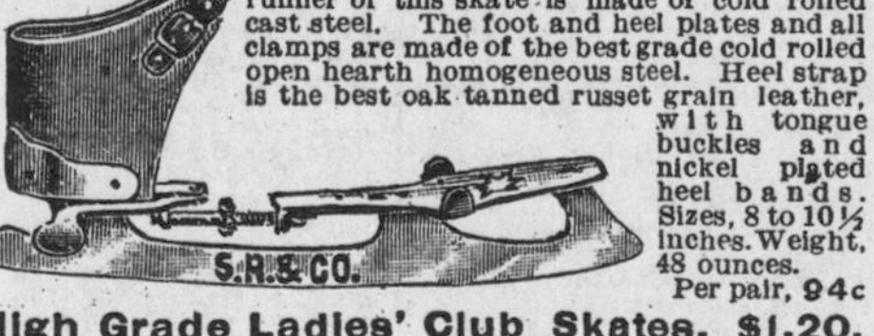

No. 6K5992 Ladies' Club Skate. The runner of this skate is made of cold rolled cast steel. The foot and heel plates and all clamps are made of the best grade cold rolled open hearth homogeneous steel. Heel strap is the best oak tanned russet grain leather, with tongue buckles and nickel plated heel bands. Sizes, 8 to 10½ inches. Weight, 48 ounces.
Per pair, 94c

High Grade Ladies' Club Skates, $1.20.

No. 6K5993 Hardened Runners. Full Nickel Plated. The runner of this skate is made of cold rolled steel. The toe and heel plates and all clamps are made of high grade cold rolled open hearth homogeneous steel. Heel strap best quality oak tanned russet grain leather, with tongue buckles and nickel plated heel bands. Size, 8 to 10½ inches.
Price, per pair...................................$1.20
Postage extra, 36 to 44 cents, according to the size.

Children's Skates, 34 Cents.

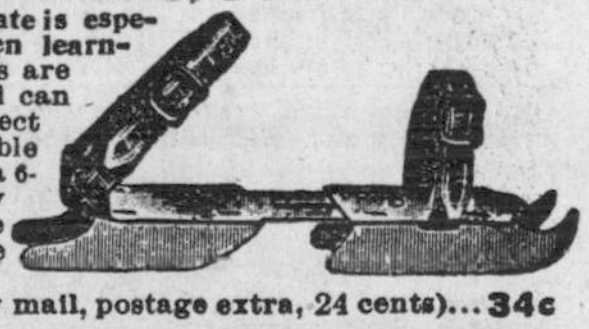

No. 6K6012 This skate is especially adapted for children learning to skate. The runners are so wide apart that a child can stand on them with perfect ease. They are adjustable and can be made from a 6-inch to an 8-inch skate by simply adjusting the thumb screw under the front foot plate.
Price, per pair.. (If by mail, postage extra, 24 cents)...34c

Skaters' Ankle Braces, 49c.

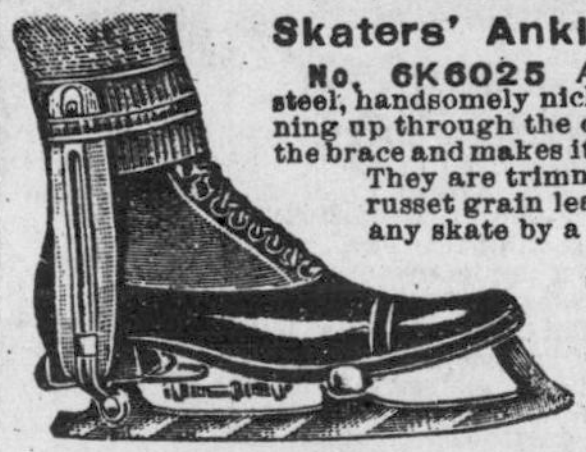

No. 6K6025 Ankle Brace. It is made of steel, handsomely nickel plated with a rib running up through the center, which strengthens the brace and makes it light, strong and durable. They are trimmed with the best quality russet grain leather. Can be attached to any skate by a blacksmith. Price is for braces only without skates.
Price, per pair...49c
If by mail, postage extra, 10 cents.

Skaters' Ankle Support.

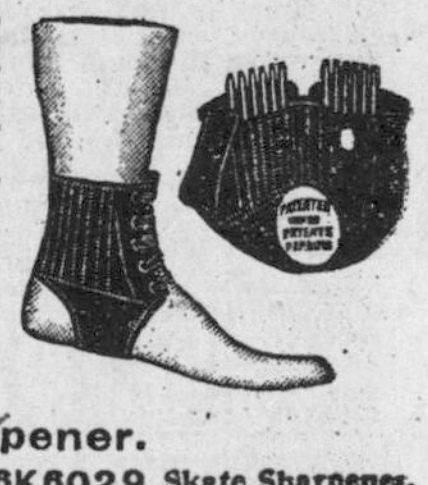

No. 6K6027 This Ankle Support is made of fine soft tanned leather, and has steel stays or stiffeners so arranged in pockets that they are removable, so that one or all may be removed to relieve the pressure on any part that might be sensitive. These supports add great strength to weak ankles, and should be worn by all skaters, either ice or roller.
When ordering, give size of shoe worn.
Price, per pair...........73c
If by mail, postage extra, 3 cents.

Skate Sharpener.

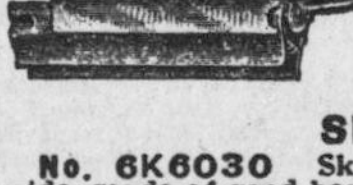

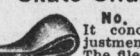

No. 6K6029 Skate Sharpener. It concaves a skate runner. Its adjustment to any skate is automatic. The files are cut on four sides—two flat sides and two convex. It is nickel plated. Price...........12c
If by mail, postage extra, 5 cents.

Skate Straps.

No. 6K6030 Skate Straps, 21 inches long, ¾ inch wide, made of good heavy black leather with buckle.
Price, per pair..................................9c

No. 6K6031 24-inch Skate Straps, same as above.
Price, per pair..................................11c
If by mail, postage extra, per pair, 3 cents.

THE SURPRISINGLY LOW REDUCED PRICES prevailing in this catalogue mean GREATER SAVINGS TO OUR CUSTOMERS than ever before.

Sig. 45—1st Ed.

DOG COLLARS. BIG BARGAINS

Our line of Dog Collars consists of the best grades of collars made, and we offer them at prices 40 per cent lower than those asked by other concerns. All our collars are constructed of the best grades of full stock oak tanned heavy grain leather. The trimmings are the best obtainable for the various styles, and no pains or expense have been spared to make this THE MOST UP TO DATE, HIGH GRADE LINE OF DOG COLLARS ON THE MARKET. We engrave names on collars for 3 cents per letter. Cash with order. If you wish a name engraved on the name plate, write the name PLAINLY, so we will not get it wrong.

IMPORTANT. Always give exact measurement around the dog's neck. Sizes given below are the sizes of a dog's neck the collars will fit when buckled to smallest size. DON'T MEASURE THE OLD COLLAR, but measure the dog's neck with tape measure or string, and give us actual measurement and we will fit him every time. Prices on collars do not include locks.

Our Chain Dog Collars.

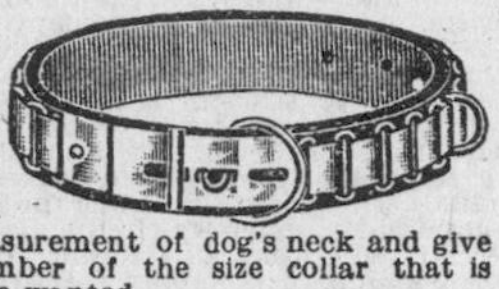

These collars have nickel plated flat links, as shown in illustration, lined with leather. When ordering. give measurement of dog's neck and give catalogue number of the size collar that is nearest to size wanted.

Catalogue Number	Neck Measure	Width of Collar	Price of Collar	Postage Extra
6K6260	11 inches	½ inch	19c	3c
6K6262	13 inches	¾ inch	24c	5c
6K6264	15 inches	1 inch	30c	7c
6K6266	17 inches	1 inch	35c	8c

Our Studded Dog Collars.

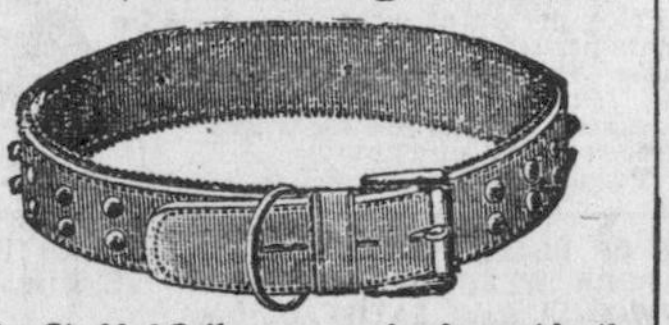

Our Studded Collars are made of russet leather, one row of round studs on the small collars and two rows on the large ones, made to look and all have name plate. When ordering, give measure of dog's neck and give catalogue number of the size collar that is nearest to size wanted.

Catalogue Number	Neck Measure	Width of Collar	Price of Collar	Postage Extra
6K6290	7 inches	½ inch	18c	2c
6K6292	9 inches	½ inch	20c	3c
6K6294	11 inches	¾ inch	24c	4c
6K6296	13 inches	¾ inch	28c	4c
6K6298	15 inches	1 inch	33c	5c
6K6300	17 inches	1 inch	40c	5c
6K6302	19 inches	1 inch	44c	5c

Engraving extra, 3 cents per letter. Write name plainly and send cash with order.

Bull Terrier Spike Collars.

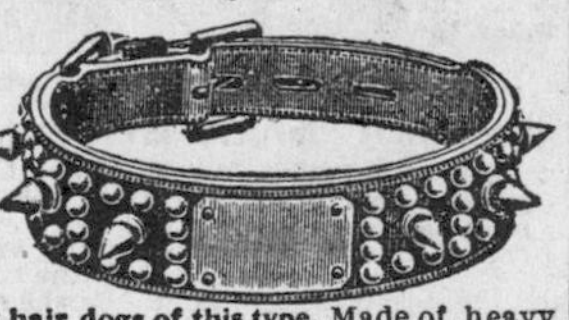

These collars are particularly suited to bullterriers, English bull dogs and short hair dogs of this type. Made of heavy black calf leather, leather lined. The 11, 13 and 15-inch collars have a single row of pointed brass spikes, ⅝-inch long, and a double row of brass ⅜-inch studs. The 17-inch collar has a double row of spikes, treble row of studs. The 19-inch collar has a double row of brass spikes, each spike surrounded with a cluster of brass studs with additional clusters of studs between the spikes. These collars are fitted with burnished brass name plates, brass "D" rings, patent brass lock buckles, which can be used with or without locks as desired. Guaranteed the best line of spike collars on the market. When ordering give catalogue number and size of the collar that is nearest to the measurement around your dog's neck.

Catalogue Number	Neck Measure	Width of Collar, inches	Price of Collar	Postage Extra
6K6320	11 inches	1½	$0.88	7c
6K6321	13 inches	1½	.93	8c
6K6322	15 inches	1½	.94	12c
6K6324	17 inches	2	1.30	17c
6K6326	19 inches	2¼	1.40	19c

Engraving extra, 3 cents per letter. Write name plainly and send cash with order.

Pearl Studded Collars.

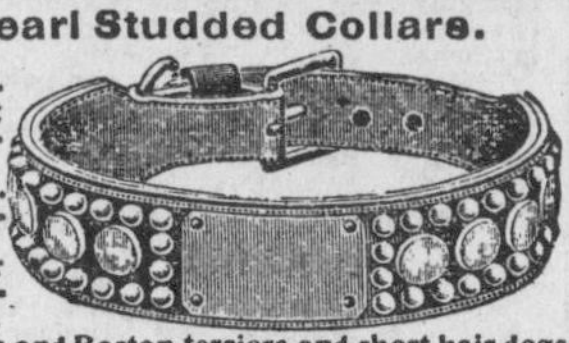

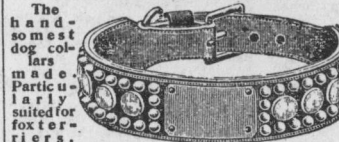

The handsomest dog collars made. Particularly suited for fox terriers, bull dogs and Boston terriers and short hair dogs up to 15 inches in neck measurement. These collars are made of black calf leather, leather lined. Have a single row of best quality pearl studs with a double row of burnished brass studs. The 9, 11 and 13-inch collars have pearl studs, ⅜ inch in diameter. The 15-inch collar has ½-inch pearl studs. The large pearl studs, the polished brass studs and the black calf leather make a beautiful contrast. These collars are fitted with large square brass name plates, brass "D" rings and brass lock buckles which can be used with or without locks. When ordering, give catalogue number and the size collar that is nearest to the measurement around your dog's neck.

Catalogue No.	Neck Measurement	Width of Collar	Price of Collar	Postage Extra
6K6330	9 inches	⅞ inch	$0.88	4c
6K6331	11 inches	⅞ inch	.92	4c
6K6332	13 inches	⅞ inch	.94	5c
6K6335	15 inches	1½ inch	1.02	8c
6K6336	17 inches	1½ inch	1.25	10c

Engraving extra, 3 cents per letter. Write name plainly and send cash with order.

Drilled Key Dog Collar Locks.

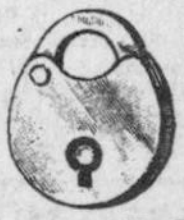

No. 6K6340 Padlock, 1x¾ inch, all nickel plated, with key. Price..................... 15c

If by mail, postage extra, 3 cents.

DOG MUZZLES.

NOTICE—When ordering dog muzzles, please give measurement around the dog's neck and around snout, 1 inch from the tip of the nose, and the length from tip of the nose to the top of head where the strap goes around his neck, and you will assist us in fitting the muzzle, for muzzles vary considerably in size.

Leather Strap Dog Muzzle.

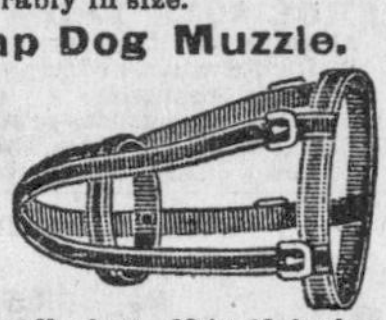

Leather Strap Dog Muzzle, to buckle around neck and buckles to take up length around head if too large. Give measure when ordering.

No. 6K6347 Small sizes, 12 to 16 inches around neck. Price......................20c

No. 6K6348 Large sizes, 17 to 26 inches around neck. Price......................30c

If by mail, postage extra, 5 to 10 cents.

Combination Whistle and Compass.

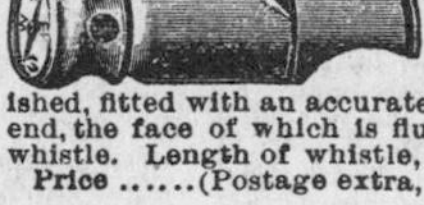

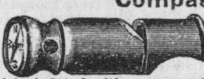

No. 6K6377 This is the ideal whistle, made of horn; loud and shrill, finely finished, fitted with an accurate compass in lower end, the face of which is flush with the top of whistle. Length of whistle, about 2¾ inches.

Price ......(Postage extra, 2 cents).......26c

Dog Leads.

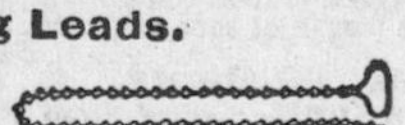

No. 6K6408 Four-foot Nickel Plated Steel Dog Chains with swivel snap and strong handle. An excellent, strong and well finished chain. Price, (Postage extra, 3c), 18c

Kennel Chains.

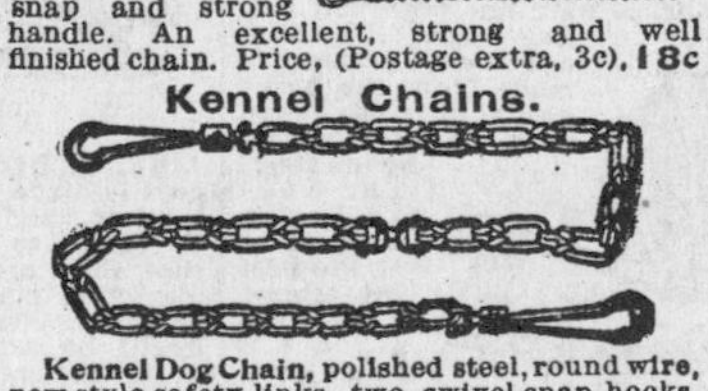

Kennel Dog Chain, polished steel, round wire, new style safety links, two swivel snap hooks, so it will not kink; well made and durable; no dog can break it; comes in two lengths and two sizes. Order by catalogue number.

Catalogue No.	Size Links	Length Chain	Price	Postage Extra
6K6420	Medium	4½ feet	21c	10c
6K6425	Heavy	6 feet	33c	19c

Our Heavy Collars for Mastiffs and Large Dogs.

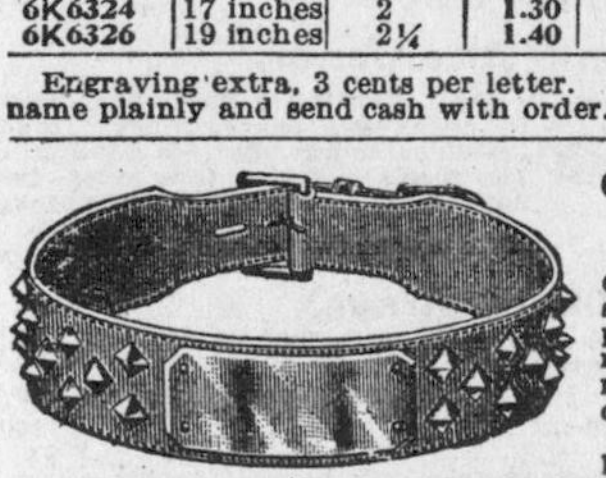

Our Heavy, Russet Color, Double Harness Leather Collar, fine russet finish. Double stitched. Heavily studded, with nickeled studs, solid "D" rings, nickel plated. Nickeled name plate, staple and trimmings, made to lock; for large dogs. When ordering give measurement of dog's neck and give catalogue number of the size collar that is nearest to size wanted.

Engraving extra, 3 cents per letter. Write name plainly to avoid error, and send cash with order.

Catalogue Number	Neck Measure	Width of Collar, inches	Price of Collar	Postage Extra	Catalogue Number	Neck Measure	Width of Collar, inches	Price of Collar	Postage Extra
6K6306	15 inches	1¼	$0.58	5c	6K6312	21 inches	1½	$0.88	8c
6K6308	17 inches	1¼	.60	6c	6K6314	23 inches	1½	.90	9c
6K6310	19 inches	1¼	.65	7c	6K6316	24 inches	2	1.15	10c

LAWN TENNIS GOODS

The Famous Harvard Brand Tennis Rackets.

Known Throughout the Entire Country as the Highest Quality Rackets Made and the Greatest Value for the Money.

We have the exclusive sale of these famous rackets. From the cheapest to the best, all have hand polished, selected second growth, straight grain ash frames, strung with the finest Oriental and American gut. The fitting, finish, swing and balance of these rackets is as near perfection as it is possible for high class labor, most improved automatic machinery and the best quality of material to produce.

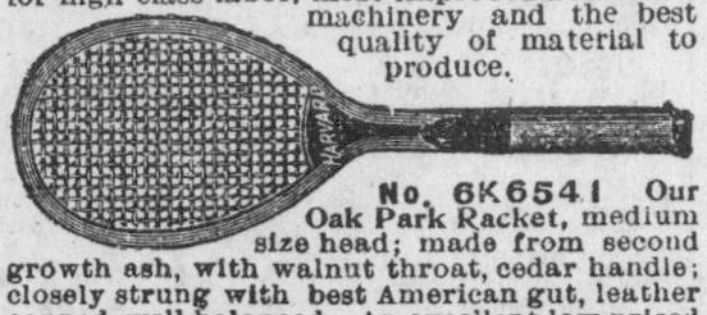

No. 6K6541 Our Oak Park Racket, medium size head; made from second growth ash, with walnut throat, cedar handle; closely strung with best American gut, leather capped, well balanced. An excellent low priced racket for youths and misses. Price..$1.22

If by mail, postage extra, 22 cents.

No. 6K6542 Our Service Racket, full size head; made from selected second growth ash, with walnut throat, cedar handle; strung with good quality selected imported gut, leather capped. Designed for rapid, effective work, well strung and well balanced. Price..$1.74

If by mail, postage extra, 28 cents.

No. 6K6543 Our Volley Racket, full size, highly polished head; is made from selected second growth ash, five-piece walnut and maple throat, polished and scored cedar handle, closely strung with a fine quality imported gut, leather capped and well balanced. A racket suitable for amateur or professional work.

Price ...(Postage extra, 28 cents.)..$2.42

No. 6K6544 Our Improved Champion Racket, latest 1908 model. This is a full sized racket, large popular shaped head and full 5-inch grip. Frame made of second growth white ash, fitted with five-piece throat, scored cedar handle. Strung with the highest grade Oriental gut, trimmed at throat and at top of racket. Guaranteed to be the equal in finish, service, balance and quality to any of the $5.00 or $6.00 rackets on the market.

Price..$3.00

If by mail, postage extra, 28 cents.

The Improved Harvard Expert Racket.

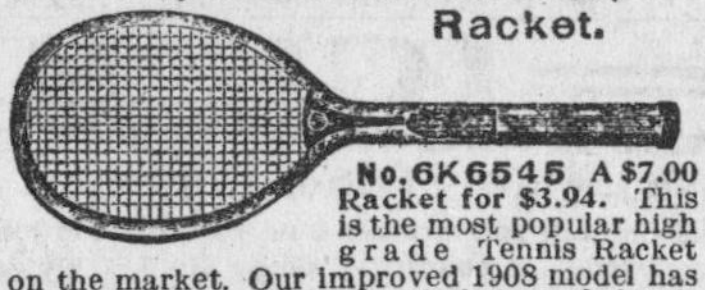

No. 6K6545 A $7.00 Racket for $3.94. This is the most popular high grade Tennis Racket on the market. Our improved 1908 model has a large, extra full size, well balanced head, heavy shoulder. This racket is made of the finest selected second growth, air dried ash. The frames after being bent, are kept in clamps for ten months, guaranteeing this racket, when completed, against warping or twisting. The frame is nicely beveled, hand polished to a beautiful piano finish, fitted with five-piece walnut and maple throat, and finely scored, full size, genuine cedar handle. Specially strung so as to give this racket great driving power. The strings in the center are again as close as the ordinary racket. This racket is designed specially for professional and tournament work, and is guaranteed to be equal to any on the market, regardless of name, make or price. We can furnish 13, 13½, 14 and 14½ oz. weights.

Price..(Postage 20c to 25c extra)..$3.94

No. 6K6546 Our Improved Harvard Special Expert, the same pattern and design as 6K6545, extra finely finished, fitted with a full cane handle and reinforced, cane inlaid throat, the cane inlaying running the full length of the throat, adding greatly to the strength of this racket. Guaranteed to be equal to any $8.00 racket on the market. 13, 13½, 14 and 14½ ounce weights.

Price $4.65

If by mail, postage extra, 20 cents to 25 cents. Rackets restrung with best clear gut, $1.50.

Racket Cover.

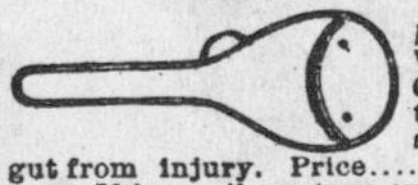

No. 6K6556 Mackintosh Cloth Waterproof Racket Cover. Keeps moisture from racket, saves racket and gut from injury. Price......................52c

If by mail, postage extra, 10 cents.

Lawn Tennis Balls.

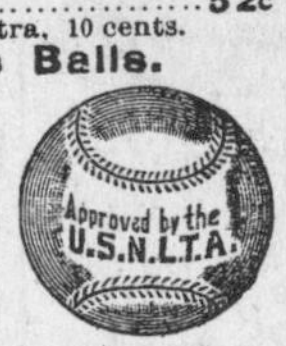

No. 6K6558 Our Country Club. Imported English ball, felt cover, full size, guaranteed to give satisfaction.

Price, each.......$0.20
Per dozen.......2.25

No. 6K6559 Goodrich Championship Tennis Balls. Regular retail price 40 cents.

Price, per dozen, $3.90; each.........34c

No. 6K6560 Wright & Ditson Championship Tennis Balls. Price, each..$0.36
Per dozen..................................$4.15

If by mail, postage extra, each 3 cents.

No. 6K6561 J. C. Higgins Championship Tennis Ball. Specially designed for professional and tournament use. No better tennis ball made at any price. Made specially for us and imported from Manchester, England, where the finest tennis balls are made. Made with the best pure rubber center, covered with finest felt cover, firmly cemented and sewed according to an improved patent stock stitch process. We guarantee this ball to be livelier, to wear better, and to give better satisfaction than any tennis ball on the market, regardless of name, make or price. The J. C. Higgins Tennis Ball is sold only by us. Price, each........$0.32
Price, per dozen.........................3.75

If by mail, postage extra, 3 cents.

Lawn Tennis Nets.

Note our hand made double center net for $2.75.

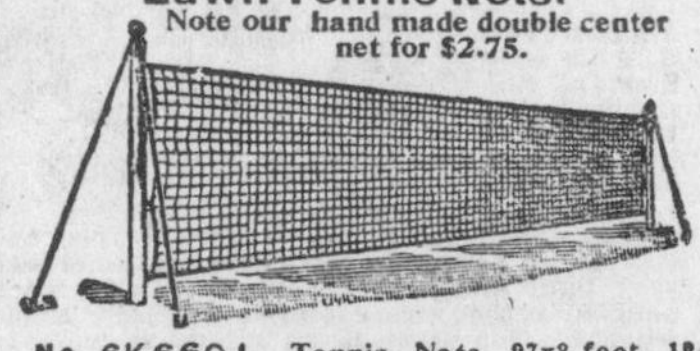

No. 6K6601 Tennis Nets, 27x3 feet, 18-thread. Price..(Postage extra, 31 cents).65c

No. 6K6602 Tennis Nets, 36x3 feet, 15 thread. Price..(Postage extra, 40 cents).92c

No. 6K6603½ Tennis Nets, 36x3 feet, 15-thread, canvas bound. Price....$1.27

If by mail, postage extra, 50 cents.

No. 6K6604 Tennis Nets, 42x3 feet, 15-thread, canvas bound. Price........$1.50

If by mail, postage extra, 48 cents.

No. 6K6605 Double Center Net, 42x3 feet, 21-thread, hand made, canvas bound. Weight, packed, about 6¼ lbs. Price..$2.75

No. 6K6606 Back Stop Net, to prevent balls from rolling out of grounds, 50x8 feet, 18-thread. Weight, packed, about 6¾ pounds.

Price $2.20

Canvas Center Strap

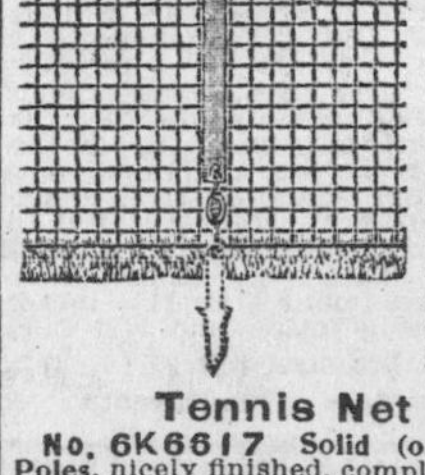

No. 6K6610 Canvas Center Strap for holding center of net at regulation height. Superior to the ordinary center iron, as it does not chafe the net and cause the ball to glance off and strike out of court.

Price, each, 85c

Tennis Net Poles.

No. 6K6617 Solid (one piece) Tennis Poles, nicely finished, complete with guy ropes and pegs. Weight, 4 lbs. Price, per pair.85c

Dry Tennis Court Marker.

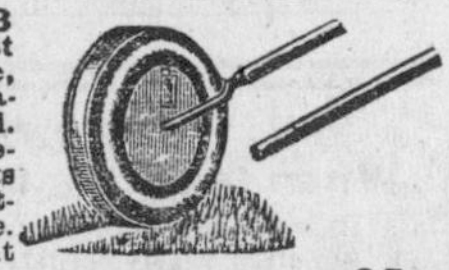

No. 6K6628 Uses marble dust or air slaked lime, no mixing of material required. The wheel revolves on its axle. Comes fitted with handle. Weight, about 6 pounds. Price..............................95c

Tennis Double Court Marking Tapes.

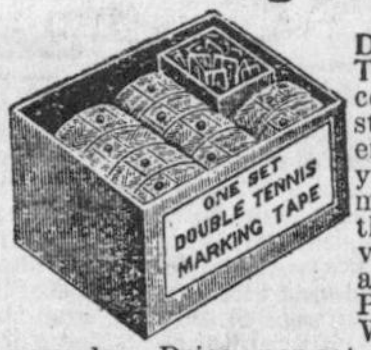

No. 6K6629 Double Court Lawn Tennis Marking Tapes, complete with pins and staples. These tapes enable you to lay out your court in a few minutes' time and show the boundary lines very prominently on all kinds of grounds. Put up in paper box. Weight, about 7½ pounds. Price, per set..........$2.95

Croquet Sets, 54 Cents.

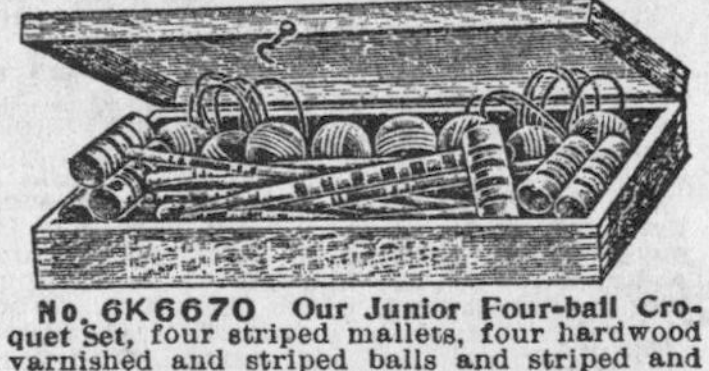

No. 6K6670 Our Junior Four-ball Croquet Set, four striped mallets, four hardwood varnished and striped balls and striped and varnished stakes, ten wire arches; put up in neat, strong wood box with hinged cover. Weight, about 13 pounds. Price, per set 54c

No. 6K6672 Our Amateur Eight-ball Croquet Set, eight striped mallets, eight hardwood varnished and striped balls, two striped and varnished stakes, ten wire arches; put up in a strong wood box with hinged cover. Weight, about 22 pounds. Price, per set..........80c

No. 6K6674 Our Favorite Eight-ball Croquet Set, consists of eight nicely painted and varnished mallets with 5-inch heads, eight striped and varnished balls, two large fancy striped stakes, heavy wire arches; an excellent set at a low price; put up in a strong, durable wood box with hinged cover. Weight, about 24 pounds. Price, per set..............$1.27

No. 6K6676 Our Champion Eight-ball Croquet Set, consisting of eight finely finished striped mallets, with 8-inch heads, eight hard maple striped and varnished balls, two striped fancy stakes, heavy pointed wire arches; well made and finished set in every respect; put up in strong wood box with hinged cover. Weight, about 27 pounds.

Price, per set..................................$1.57

Our Expert Croquet Set.

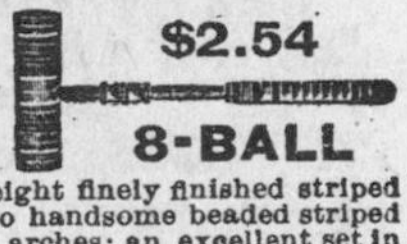

$2.54

8-BALL

No. 6K6678 Our Expert Eight-ball Croquet Set, consisting of eight finely finished varnished and striped mallets, with 8-inch heads, eight finely finished striped hardwood balls, two handsome beaded striped stakes, heavy wire arches; an excellent set in every respect; put up in a strong wood box, hinged cover. Weight, about 31 pounds.

Price, per set $2.54

BOXING GLOVES

We are the largest handlers of boxing gloves in the United States, selling more gloves direct to the consumer than any other house. We have made the requirements of the pugilist a careful study and you will find that our GLOVES fit better, last longer, and quality and construction considered, are cheaper than any other gloves on the market.

We send free a copy of the Marquis of Queensbury Rules with every set. A set consists of four gloves, two pairs, packed in a box.

80c

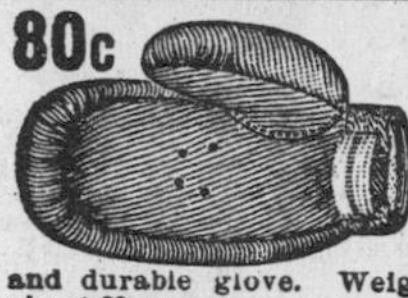

No. 6K6800 Boys' size, made of soft tanned kid leather, ecru color, stuffed with good quality short hair, ventilated palm, elastic wristband, good shape, a well made and durable glove. Weight, per set, boxed, about 28 ounces.

Price, per set of four gloves............80c

If by mail, postage extra, 28 cents.

$1.22

No. 6K6801 Boy's extra quality. About 5 ounces. Made of wine colored kid leather, soft and pliable, stuffed with good quality curled hair; stitched fingers, laced wristband, ventilated palm. Weight, per set boxed, about 29 ounces.

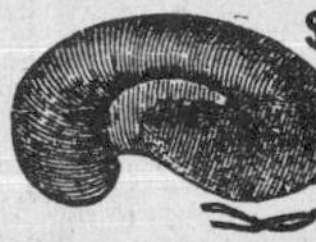

Price, per set of four gloves..........$1.22

If by mail, postage extra, 32 cents.

$1.40

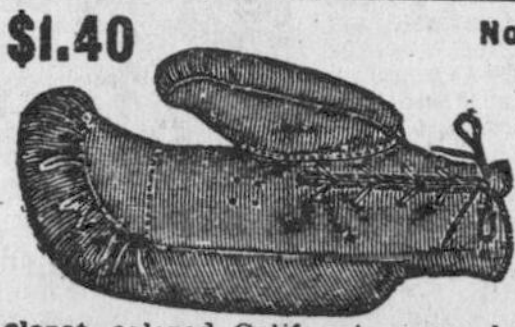

No. 6K6803 Our Frank Snyder Glove. Men's 8-ounce Standard Pattern. Improved. Made of claret colored California napa leather, with padded finger ends, ventilated palm, split and laced wrist, stuffed with good quality curled hair, drill lined. Weight, per set, boxed, about 40 ounces.

Price, per set of four gloves.........$1.40

If by mail, postage extra, 40 cents.

Corbett Pattern. $1.65

No. 6K6804 Our Ben Hoerstal Corbett pattern 8-ounce Glove. Claret back, palm and wrist; ventilated palm, drill lined, laced wristband, stuffed with good quality curled hair. Price, per set of four gloves....$1.65

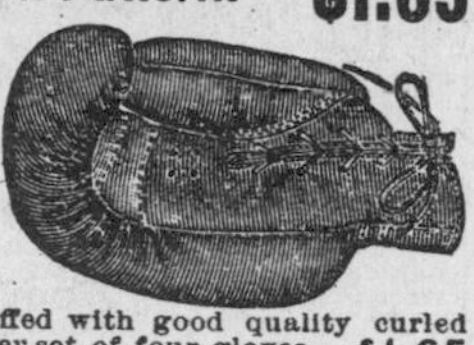

If by mail, postage extra, 48 cents.

Original Corbett Pattern. $1.80

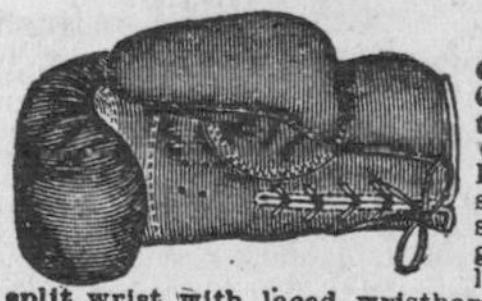

No. 6K6805 Our Original Corbett Pattern. Made of wine colored kid leather, serge lining, stitched fingers, ventilated palm, split wrist with laced wristband and padded cuffs; stuffed with best quality curled hair. Weight, per glove, about 8 ounces.

Price, per set of four gloves..........$1.80

If by mail, postage extra, 45 cents.

Instructor's Pattern. $3.10

No. 6K6808 Instructor's Pattern 8-oz. Glove. Made of selected especially tanned wine color kid, laced wrist, padded cuff, leather bound; best serge lining, ventilated palm, stuffed with extra quality curled hair, double silk stitched, with finger grip. Price, per set of four gloves....$3.10

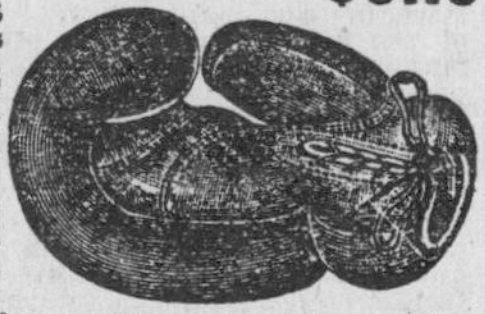

If by mail, postage extra, 52 cents.

Pupil's Glove. $3.20

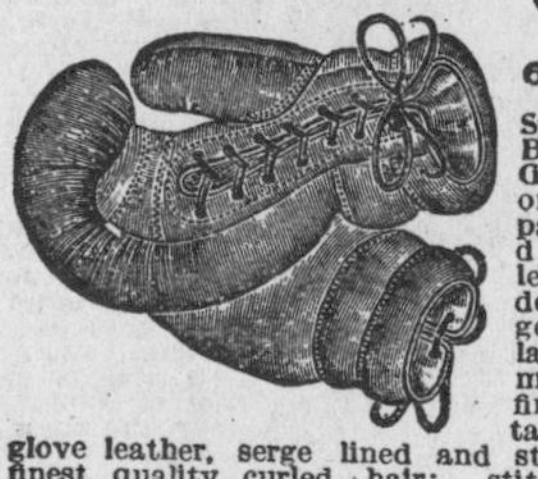

No. 6K6809 Pupil's Special Style Boxing Gloves, cut on Corbett pattern, with double length padded cuff, finger grip and laced wrists; made of the finest quality tan color glove leather, serge lined and stuffed with finest quality curled hair; stitched with best linen thread; made up in the strongest and best possible manner to withstand the severe usage always given boxing gloves by amateurs. These gloves are designed with extra long cuff to give the user all the protection possible. Weight, each, 8 ounces.

Price, per set of four gloves.........$3.20

If by mail, postage extra, 60 cents.

The Dudley Club Special. $4.05

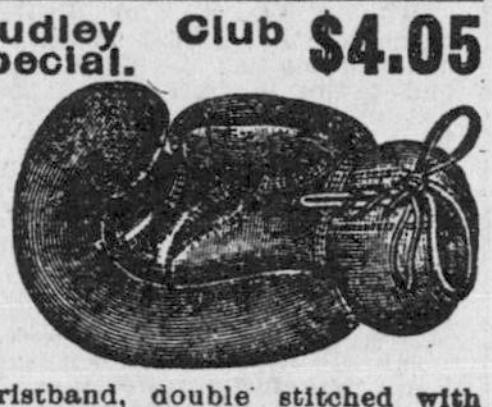

No. 6K6811 The Dudley Club Special 9-oz. Boxing Glove. Corbett pattern, full heel pad below the lacing, center palm grip, full padded cuff, laced wristband, double stitched with silk; made from special selected, tan color, California tanned kid, stuffed with finest quality white curled hair, a new departure in boxing gloves, the latest on the market.

Price, per set of four gloves..........$4.05

If by mail, postage extra 52 cents.

Approved Pattern Gloves. $2.25

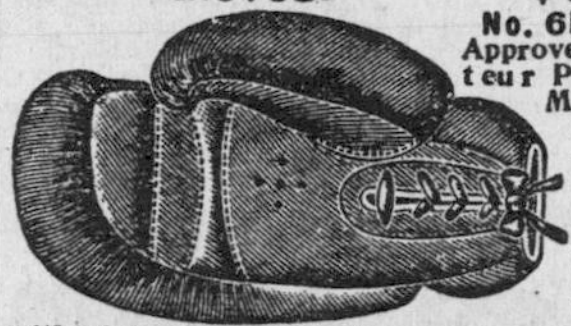

No. 6K6813 Approved Amateur Pattern Men's Size Gloves, made of best wine color California kid leather, with finger grip and toe padded, ventilated palm, padded wrist, best serge lining, leather binding, laced wrist, stuffed with best quality curled hair, double stitched throughout. An 8-ounce glove. A good sparring glove.

Price, per set of four..................$2.25

If by mail, postage extra, 48 cents.

Professional Fighting Gloves. $2.22

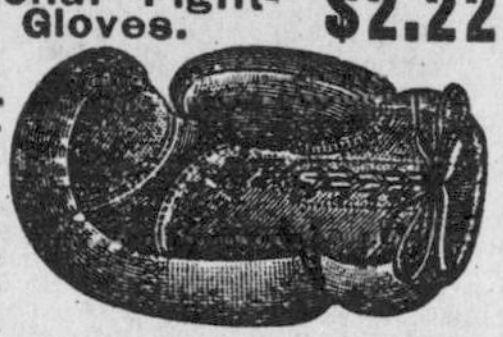

No. 6K6815 Our Official Professional Fighting Glove. Made of selected green California napa leather, with grip in center and toe pad, ventilated palm, lined throughout, laced and leather bound wrist; stuffed with very best quality curled hair, made extra strong for hard usage, double stitched with linen thread, padded cuff. Weight, per set, boxed, about 45 ounces.

Price, per set of four gloves..........$2.22

If by mail, postage extra, 40 cents.

5-Ounce Boxing Gloves. $2.28

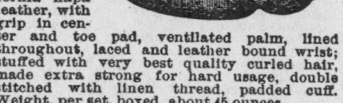

No. 6K6817 Same pattern of glove as above, except 5-ounce weight, for finish fights. Made of selected stock and guaranteed not to rip. Price, per set of four gloves..$2.28

If by mail, postage extra. 40 cents.

Wisconsin Striking Bag Platform. $2.15

Noiseless, No-Jar, Lightweight.

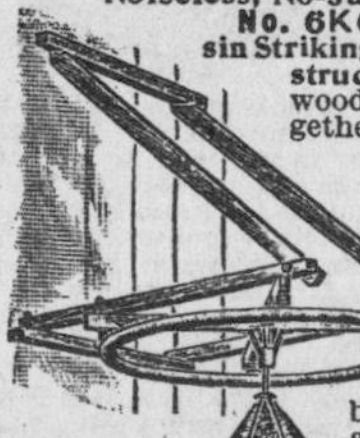

$2.15

No. 6K6848 The Wisconsin Striking Bag Platform is constructed of selected hardwood, securely bolted together; the rim is of maple, one piece, 23 inches in diameter, oil finished; has four rubber pad washers between the rim and frame. The washers act as a cushion and absorb all vibration, besides making the action of the bag extremely lively. The swivel is of new design, made of metal, and is noiseless. The platform is easily adjusted to a wall or ceiling and is very rigid when in position for use. Weight of platform, 7½ pounds.

Price, without bag........................$2.15

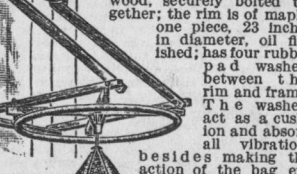

Our Improved Chicago Bag Platform. $3.55

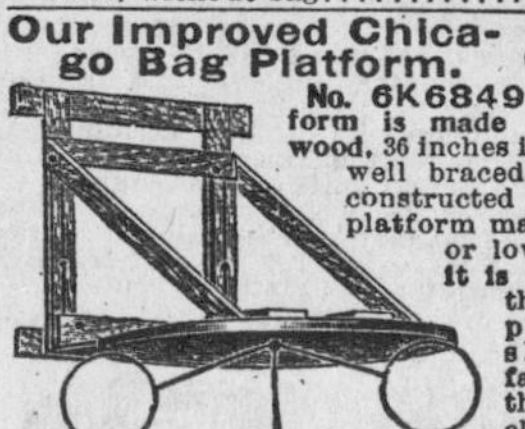

$3.55

No. 6K6849 This platform is made of selected wood, 36 inches in diameter, well braced, and is so constructed that the platform may be raised or lowered after it is fastened to the wall. The platform should be fastened so that the circle will be about 6¼ feet from the floor. Price does not include the punching bag or swivel.

Price..........$3.55

Weight, crated for shipment, about 85 pounds.

Elastic Floor Attachments.

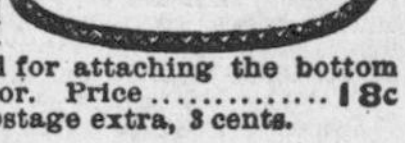

No. 6K6842 Elastic Floor Attachments for Double End Bags, made of elastic and covered with braided cotton and used for attaching the bottom of the bag to the floor. Price..............18c

If by mail, postage extra, 3 cents.

STRIKING OR PUNCHING BAGS, 97c TO $2.81.

Our Combination Single and Double End Bags.

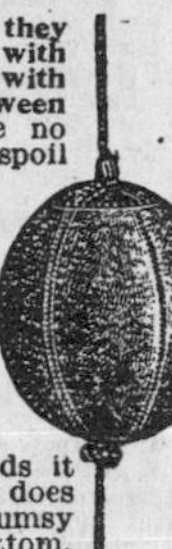

These bags are all made so they can be used either as single end with platform, or as double end bags with rope and elastic, suspended between floor and ceiling. They have no clumsy loop on the bottom to spoil the looks or throw them out of balance when used as single end bags with platform. To make the double end bag, you simply pass the elastic cord through two holes in the round piece usually found on the bottom of all bags. This end piece on all our bags has an extra heavy reinforcement over which the elastic is passed and which holds it securely and does away with the clumsy loop at the bottom. This neat construction makes it possible to change our bags from either double or single end in a moment's time without any inconvenience.

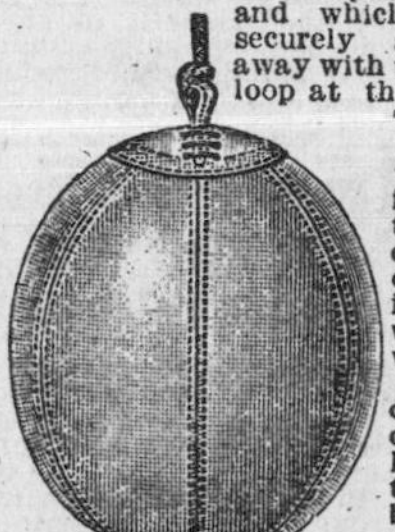

In the construction of our bags we use only the very best leather suitable for the purpose that can be procured, and this, combined with the best quality linings, workmanship and finish, make them the best striking bags on the market today that money can buy. Our bags have been used in many gymnasiums throughout the country for years and are highly endorsed by all amateurs and professionals. The prices quoted below are for the bags complete with bladder, rope, elastic and screw eyes.

No. 6K6824 Made of good strong leather, drill lined, strong loop, all well made. This is a good practice bag for a very little money. Weight, about 10 ounces. Price, complete..97c

No. 6K6825 Made of gold tan napa leather with strong loop. Drill lined, good, desirable and strong. 30 inches circumference when inflated. Weight, complete, about 10 ounces. Price, complete...............$1.20

No. 6K6829 Best quality claret color, soft tanned leather, strong loop, drill lined, triple seams, making an extra strong bag, one of the best sellers, 32 inches circumference when inflated. Weight, complete, about 14 ounces. Price, complete.......................$1.56

No. 6K6835 Soft tan satin calf, drill lined, triple seams welted, strong loop, one-piece top. A good article, retails for $3.50. 32 inches circumference when inflated. Weight, complete, about 14 ounces.

Price, complete.................................$2.35

No. 6K6836 Expert Bag, made of special selected oil tan horsehide, very strong and tough. Drill lined, triple seams, welted, strong loop, one-piece top, made up first class in every respect; very fast and the finest bag made. 32 inches circumference when inflated. Weight, complete, about 14 ounces.

Price, complete...........................$2.60

If by mail, postage extra, 20 to 25 cents.

Prices on Leather Goods.

In spite of the fact that leather such as we use in our striking bags, boxing gloves and base ball goods has been advanced five times during the past year and there has also been advances in the cost of rubber bladders, we have made no advance in price on these goods. Advantageous purchases in leather the early part of the season and economies effected in manufacturing, have enabled us to continue offering striking bags, boxing gloves and base ball goods at prices as low, and in some cases lower than we have sold them heretofore. All other dealers have advanced their prices from 15 per cent to 25 per cent. We alone have made no advance in our selling prices on these goods, but on the contrary, have made a number of reductions. Quality considered, we offer these goods from 25 per cent to 50 per cent less than you could purchase them elsewhere.

Pear Shape Single End Bag.

This is the latest thing in punching bags. The pear shape bag is so made that the strain is on all sections of the bag instead of one place. The top and bottom are stitched by hand and the bag is built to withstand constant use—in fact, the bag is built for work.

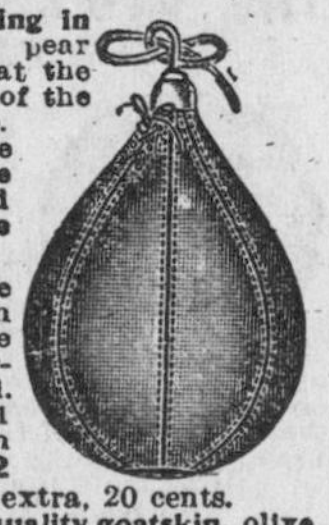

No. 6K6838 Made of napa leather, plain seams, canvas lined, wine color, 30 inches circumference when inflated. Weight, complete, 11 ounces. Price, with bladder..........$1.42

If by mail, postage extra, 20 cents.

No. 6K6839 Fine quality goatskin, olive green color, napa tanned, bound lips, eyeleted lace holes, welted triple seams, canvas lined, 32 inches circumference when inflated. Weight, complete, 11 ounces.

Price, with bladder.....................$1.80

If by mail, postage extra, 20 cents.

No. 6K6840 Fine quality selected horsehide, tan color, patent swivel top, bound lips, eyeleted lace holes, welted seams, canvas lined, 33 inches in circumference when inflated, hand stitched bottom, with very best quality of rubber bladder that can be had; just the bag for professional bag punchers. Weight, complete, 11 ounces. Price, with bladder....$2.81

If by mail, postage extra, 28 cents.

Expert Striking Bag Swivel.

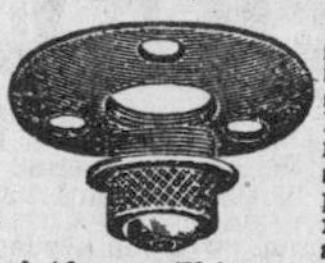

No. 6K6850 The Expert Striking Bag Swivel is undoubtedly the best swivel on the market. Bag can be instantly removed or a new rope inserted by unscrewing the projecting stem from the round disk, which is screwed securely to the platform. This swivel consists of three parts, namely, flat disk 3½ inches in diameter, a projecting threaded stem and a half round metal ball, which revolves inside of the projecting stem. The swivel is nicely oxidized and is as rapid and accurate a swivel as any on the market. Put up in a neat paper box complete with screws. Price...........................37c

If by mail, postage extra, 10 cents.

Rubber Striking Bag and Football Bladders.

No. 6K6852 10-inch Bladders, made of pure Para rubber, for 30-inch striking bags and Association footballs. Price....(Postage extra, 5c.).....53c

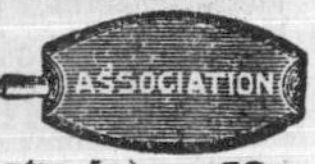

No. 6K6853 12-inch Bladders, made of finest quality pure rubber, for bags 33 inches in circumference. Price.....................59c

If by mail, postage extra, 5 cents.

Striking Bag Mitts.

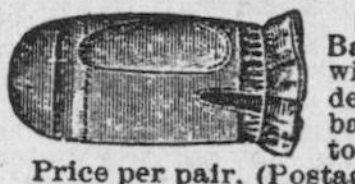

No. 6K6858 Striking Bag Mitts, made of kid, with grip in center, padded back, elastic wristband. This is the best mitt to use for bag punching.

Price per pair, (Postage extra, 6 cents.)52c

Whiteley Chest Pull.

Just the thing to broaden

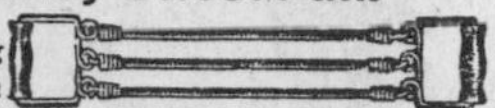

your shoulders and to strengthen the muscles of your back and arms. More beneficial than the heavy chest weights, and far less expensive. Made of three strands of elastic cable, attached to two wood handles with nickel plated trimmings. Comes in three tensions.

No. 6K6866 Light tension, for ladies and children, 27 inches. Price...............45c

No. 6K6867 Medium tension, for youths, 30 inches. Price...............50c

No. 6K6868 Heavy tension for men, 33 inches. Price(Postage extra, each, 16c) 55c

No. 6K6869 Five Strands, extra heavy tension. The couplings on these strands are made so that one or two strands may be removed, if desired, to change the tension.

Price.......................................$1.10

If by mail, postage extra, 20 cents.

The Whiteley Pattern Exercisers.

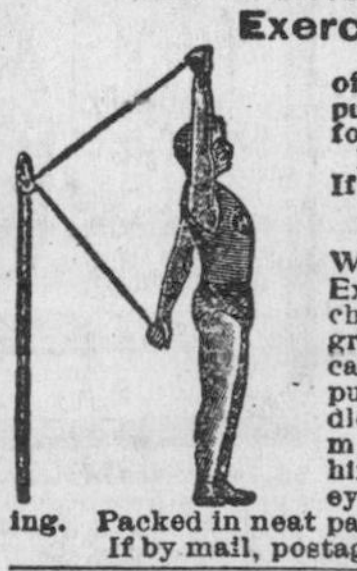

No. 6K6873 Made of elastic cord with wood pulleys, plain handles and foot attachment.

Price.........$1.25

If by mail, postage extra, 22 cents.

No. 6K6877 Whiteley Pattern Special Exercisers, for adults or children, full size, OO grade, made of elastic cable with plain wood pulleys and wood handles, nickel plated trimmings, complete with hinge attachments, screw eyes, also chart of exercising. Packed in neat paper box. Price..85c

If by mail, postage extra, 20 cents.

Exercising or Swinging Rings.

No. 6K6879 Wooden Rings, three pieces, made of walnut and maple glued together, 6 inches in diameter.

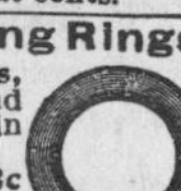

Price, per pair..................48c

If by mail, postage extra, 5 cents.

Old Apple Tree Swing.

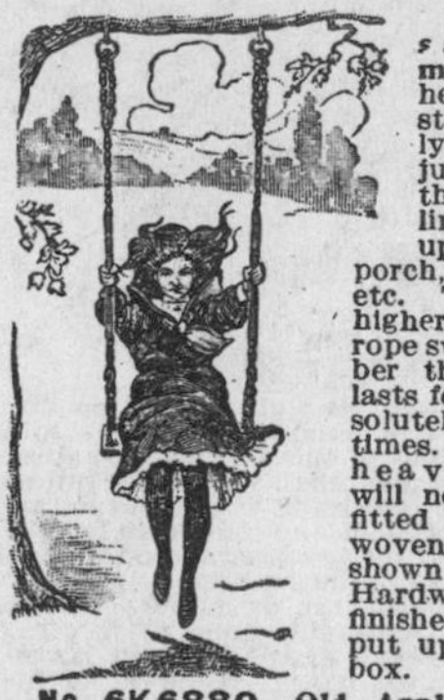

The best and safest swing made. Fitted with heavy galvanized steel chains, quickly put up and adjusted by hooking the S hook into links. Can be put up anywhere—on porch, trees, in the attic, etc. The first cost is higher than that of a rope swing, but remember that this swing lasts forever and is absolutely safe at all times. The chains are heavily galvanized, will not rust, and are fitted with two heavy woven hand grips, as shown in illustration. Hardwood seat, nicely finished. Each swing put up in a neat paper box.

No. 6K6880 Old Apple Tree Swing. Size seat, 16 inches long, 6½ inches wide, with 7½-foot chains. Price..........$1.24

Weight, packed for shipment, 5½ pounds.

No. 6K6881 Old Apple Tree Swing. Same as above, with 10-foot heavy chains. Price.......................................$1.72

Weight, packed for shipment, 6 pounds.

NO SUCH PRICE REDUCTIONS have ever been made by any firm or individual as we have made in the pages of this Big Catalogue on the HIGHEST GRADE MERCHANDISE.

BASEBALL GOODS

THE FAMOUS J. C. HIGGINS LINE of baseball and athletic goods, known and celebrated throughout the country for their sterling qualities, are now owned and controlled exclusively by us. These goods are all made on honor. These goods are made under the direct supervision of practical men, who have made athletic requirements a life study and who work absolutely on the theory of making goods in accordance with the needs of the user, unlike most other manufacturers in this line, who attempt to shape the requirements of the purchaser to their goods. You will find that the J. C. Higgins line of baseball goods have a style, design and finish to them unlike any other goods. The mitts and gloves of this famous brand have a comfortable fit to them, different from any other make. There are no goods on the market today, under any name or brand or sold at any price, that in any way compare with this famous J. C. Higgins line.

OUR GUARANTEE.

WE GUARANTEE every baseball glove or mitt bearing the J. C. Higgins brand against defective material, workmanship or faulty design or construction. Any glove or mitt bearing this brand found unsatisfactory in these particulars or for any reason whatsoever, may be returned to us and money will be immediately refunded. We further guarantee the J. C. Higgins Brand of athletic goods to be the highest grade goods on the market today and the greatest value for the money.

IF YOU PURCHASE ANY ARTICLE FROM US bearing this brand and do not find it exactly as represented, the greatest value for the money, better value than you could possibly obtain elsewhere, do not find the workmanship and material better than that found in other goods of supposedly the same grade, you may return the article to us at once, and your money and any charges you may have paid will be immediately refunded.

BASEBALL UNIFORMS.

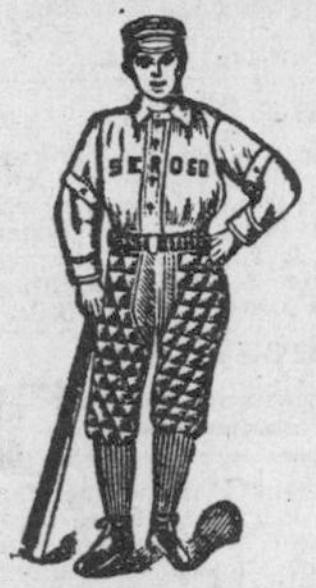

OUR BASEBALL UNIFORM SAMPLE BOOK, OF WHICH WE HEREWITH SHOW A SMALL ILLUSTRATION, IS ABSOLUTELY FREE. SEND US A POSTAL CARD STATING, "SEND ME YOUR BASEBALL SAMPLE BOOK," AND IT WILL BE SENT TO YOU AT ONCE, POSTPAID.

Our Baseball Uniform Business is so enormous that we find it necessary to issue a special illustrated catalogue to do full justice to the large and varied line of uniforms we are handling. We make our own uniforms and buy our own material, and therefore positively guarantee our uniforms to be the superior in quality, workmanship and to be lower in price than any other uniforms on the market. In this special catalogue, which we will send you free upon receipt of your request, we describe, illustrate and furnish samples of different grades of uniforms at **$2.10, $2.55, $3.50, $4.30, $5.40, $6.60 AND $7.95** per uniform complete. These prices include lettering.

WE CAN MAKE YOU 10 SUITS TO ORDER AND SHIP IN SIX DAYS

IF YOU ARE INTERESTED IN BASEBALL UNIFORMS,

Don't Fail to Send for this Free Catalogue.

Send us a postal card for our

SAMPLE BOOK OF BASEBALL UNIFORMS,

and we will send it to you postpaid, together with an order blank and instructions for taking measurements.

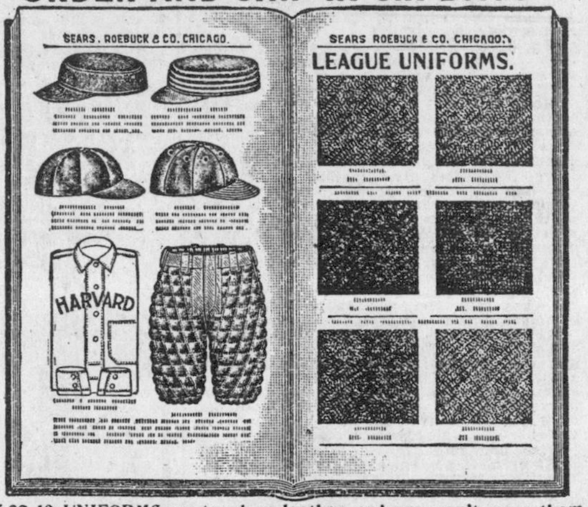

OUR EVER READY $2.10 UNIFORMS are tough as leather and you can't wear them out. Carried in stock in gray, maroon and navy blue colors, in sizes 26, 28, 30, 32, 34 and 36 inches, chest measure, made of a special, heavy baseball cloth. Button front shirt, elbow sleeves, padded pants, college style caps web belt, and black cotton stockings.

No. 6K80 Ever Ready Uniform. Price, per suit....$2.10

NOTE.—We do not letter the shirts of our $2.10 uniforms.

BASEBALLS.

The J. C. Higgins Official League Ball.

85c

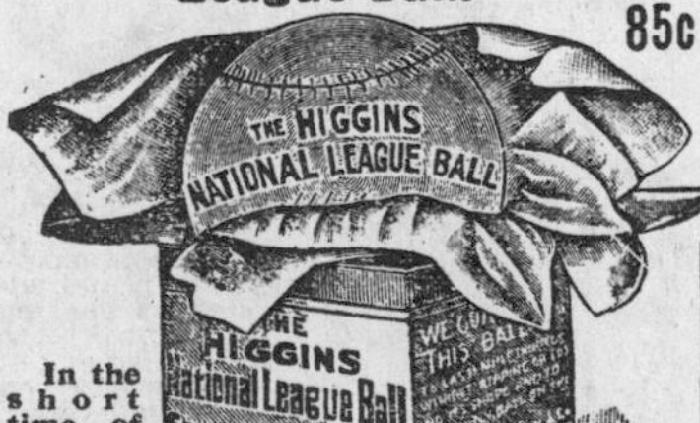

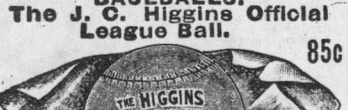

In the short time of two years, this ball has become as popular and as well known as any league ball on the market. We have sold thousands of dozens of this ball. Guaranteed to be equal to any baseball made, regardless of name, make or price, and to be in exact accordance with National and American League specifications, and further guaranteed to last a full game of nine innings without ripping or tearing. Made with the best pure rubber center, wrapped with the finest wool yarn, covered with selected, special tanned horsehide cover, sewed by hand. Made in identically the same way, by the same machinery and by the same class of workmen that make the $1.50 league balls. Our enormous business on this ball and the fact that we have no great selling expense, and the fact that we pay no bonus to any league for adopting this ball, enables us to sell it at 85 cents, where you would have to pay $1.50 for any other ball of equal grade. Each ball is wrapped in tinfoil and tissue paper, and packed in a sealed box. The Higgins League Ball is guaranteed to be the equal of any ball made, regardless of name, make or price.

No 6K6883 The Higgins National League Ball. Price, per dozen, $9.50; each....85c

If by mail, postage extra, each, 8 cents.

Reach Official American League.

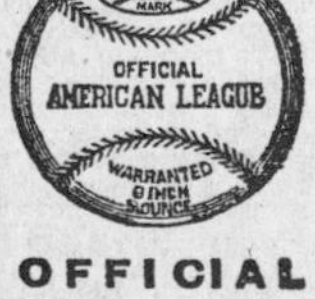

No. 6K6884 The Reach Official American League Ball. Officially adopted by the American League and officially recognized by the National League. Sold everywhere for $1.50. Each...$1.20

If by mail, postage extra, each, 8 cents.

THE VICTOR OFFICIAL LEAGUE BALL.

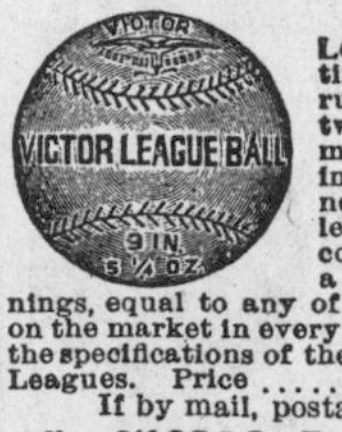

No. 6K6885 Victor League Ball. Made entirely by hand, best Para rubber center, best quality two-piece horsehide cover made of the best material in the best possible manner, adopted by various leagues throughout the country. Guaranteed for a full game of nine innings, equal to any of the higher priced balls on the market in every respect. Conforms with the specifications of the National and American Leagues. Price....95c

If by mail, postage extra, 8 cents.

No. 6K6886 For those who wish the Spalding League Balls we have them at Price, each..(Postage extra, 8 cents)..$1.20

No. 6K6889 Our Boys' League Ball, Rubber Center, yarn wrapped, horsehide cover. A lively, high grade ball, 8½ inches in circumference, weighs 4½ ounces. Price.....44c

If by mail, postage extra, 8 cents.

No. 6K6890 Our Pitchers' Pride. A beauty, has horsehide cover, well made; each in a separate box, sealed. A fine ball for boys. Price....22c

If by mail, postage extra, 8 cents.

No. 6K6892 Our Little Victor, the best ball ever offered for the money. Price....9c

If by mail, postage extra, each, 7 cents.

Baseball Bats.

Our line of Baseball Bats is the best in the country. Our bats are made from Michigan white ash, dried under cover. Every bat is hand finished and is turned in a manner to give it the swing and balance not to be found in any other line of bats.

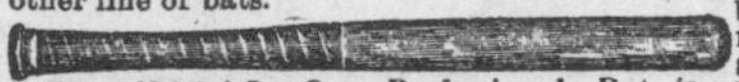

No. 6K6912 Our Professional Bat is made from selected second growth white ash and has just the right taper from end to end, giving it proper swing and balance. This bat is hand made and finely finished, showing the clear, straight grain of the wood. No better bat on the market. Length, 33 and 34 inches. Weight, about 2¼ pounds. Price....60c

No. 6K6913 Same as above, with tape wound handle. Price....62c

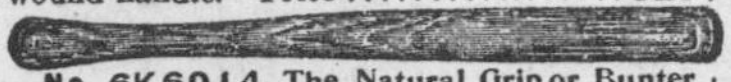

No. 6K6914 The Natural Grip or Bunter Bat, the favorite professional bat. Made from finest Michigan second growth white ash, flame burnt finish, highly polished. No better bat made at any price. Length, 33 and 34 inches. Weight, about 2⅜ pounds. Price....57c

No. 6K6916 Men's Champion Bat. A good, durable, well balanced ash bat, flame burnt finish. Length, 33 and 34 inches. Regularly sells for 50 cents. Weight, about 2½ pounds. Price....35c

No. 6K6917 Antique. This is a full sized white ash bat, dark antique polished finish, well balanced and a finely finished bat. Length, 33 inches. Weight, about 2¼ pounds. Price, 20c

No. 6K6919 Boy's Choice. Made from selected hardwood, fine oil finish. Length, 30 inches. Will give good satisfaction. Weight, 1½ pounds. Price....10c

The New Sullivan Professional Catchers' Mitt.

$4.00

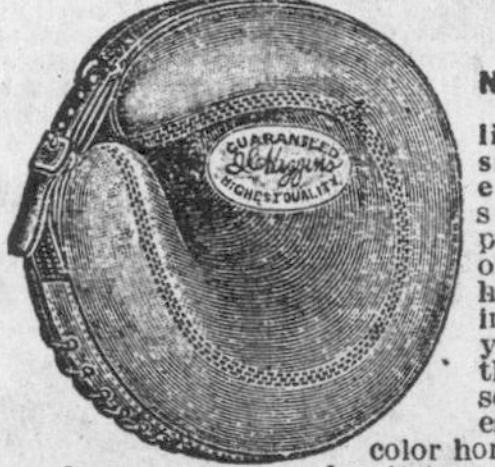

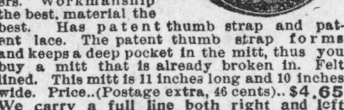

No. 6K6922 The New Sullivan Professional Catchers' Mitt has several improvements over the one we have been selling in past years. Made of the very finest, selected, highest grade drab color horsehide. It is made on an improved pattern with reinforced palm, double piped edge, patent adjustable thumb strap, laced heel, strap and buckle at wrist, leather bound, double band in front, padded with the very best asbestos felt, hand quilted and tailored into shape, with deep round pocket. This mitt is made "ready broke" and is guaranteed to always keep its shape. Double stitched throughout. It carries our J. C. Higgins autograph trade mark, which is our guarantee of highest quality. This mitt is our leader and has no equal at any price. Price....$4.00

If my mail, postage extra, 52 cents

$4.65

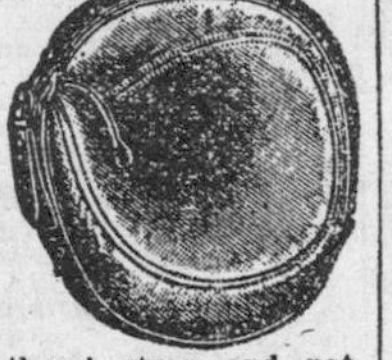

No. 6K6925 The Victor Professional Mitt, made of the highest grade drab horsehide. This mitt is designed especially for professionals and embodies suggestions received from many of the league catchers. Workmanship the best, material the best. Has patent thumb strap and patent lace. The patent thumb strap forms and keeps a deep pocket in the mitt, thus you buy a mitt that is already broken in. Felt lined. This mitt is 11 inches long and 10 inches wide. Price..(Postage extra, 46 cents)..$4.65

We carry a full line both right and left hand mitts.

$3.30

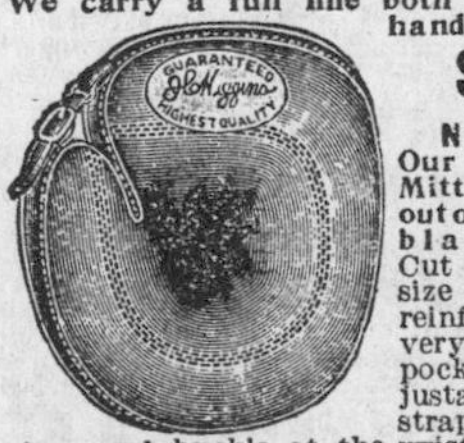

No. 6K6929 Our New Collegiate Mitt, made throughout of the very finest black horsehide. Cut on a regular size pattern, with reinforced palm, very deep, natural pocket, patent adjustable thumb strap, laced heel, strap and buckle at the wrist, the very best asbestos felt padding, tailored and quilted into shape by hand stitching. This mitt is leather bound, double stitched throughout, made up in first class manner, of high grade workmanship. This mitt carries our J. C. Higgins trade mark, which guarantees it to be the highest quality in material and workmanship. Price....$3.30

If by mail, postage extra, 46 cents.

$2.35 American League Mitt.

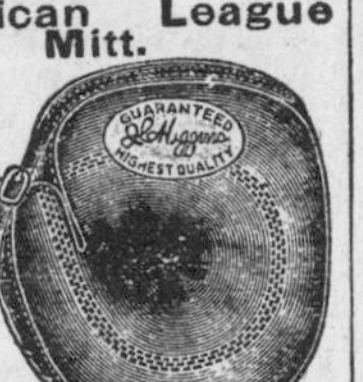

No. 6K6930 Our American League Mitt, regular size pattern, made of the finest oil tanned calf leather throughout. This leather is a beautiful tan color, very soft and exceptionally tough stock. This mitt is double stitched throughout, leather bound, has patent adjustable thumb strap, strap and buckle at the wrist, laced heel and asbestos felt pad. It is so constructed that it has a large, deep, natural pocket that will never come out.

Price...(Postage extra, 44 cents)..$2.35

$1.95

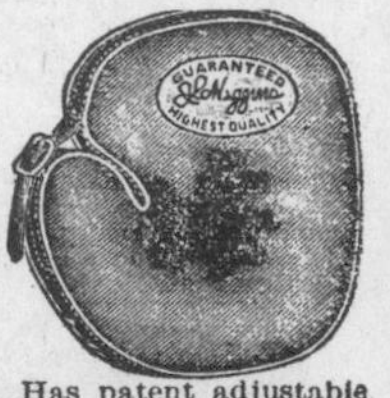

No. 6K6932 Minor League Special, a fine mitt, regular size; palm, band and fingers made of the finest grade heavy buckskin; the back is made of a heavy goatskin; leather bound, double stitched throughout. Has patent adjustable thumb strap with strap and buckle at the wrist; best felt padding. This is made up in first class manner in every respect, and is one of the best medium priced mitts on the market. Price..(Postage extra, 36 cents)..$1.95

$1.68

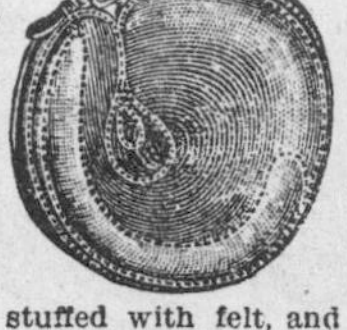

No. 6K6934 Our Chelsea Mitt, raindeer palm and band, back and fingers of selected goatskin, leather bound around the edge, thumb adjustable, crescent heel pad, with deep cup shape palm. An excellent mitt for little money. All are stuffed with felt, and the workmanship is first class. An excellent mitt for school clubs. Price....(Postage extra, 40c)...$1.68

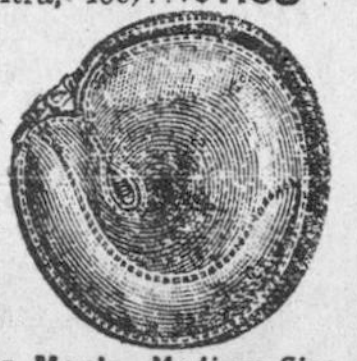

No. 6K6937 Our Medium Size Junior Cub Mitt. Palm is made of selected horsehide, back is made of selected glove leather, leather bound around the edge, crescent heel pad, medium deep pocket in the palm and well stuffed. Price.........$1.22

If by mail, postage extra, 32 cents.

No. 6K6938 Our Men's Medium Size Amateur Mitt. Palm is made of asbestos buckskin, back is made of light tan color glove leather, leather bound around the edges, well stuffed, with medium size pocket in the palm. An excellent glove for young men for amateur games. Price...(Postage extra, 30c)..75c

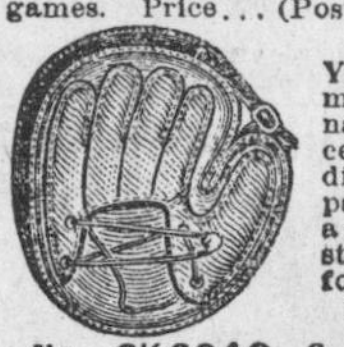

No. 6K6939 Our Youths' Large Size Mitt, made from very strong napa tanned leather, crescent heel pad, with medium deep pocket in the palm, machine stitched around the edges, well stuffed. An excellent mitt for youths. Price, 38c

Postage extra, 20 cents.

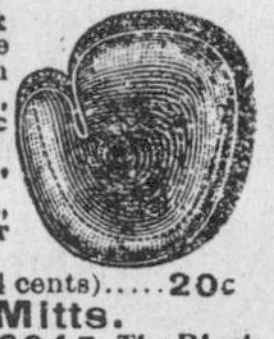

No. 6K6940 S., R & Co.'s Youths' Mitt, made of selected tan leather, with fingers well padded. A good, strong mitt. Price......30c

Postage extra, 16 cents.

No. 6K6941 Boys' Mitt, made with leather palm, canvas back and leather fingers, well padded.

Price.....(Postage extra, 14 cents).....20c

Basemen's Mitts.

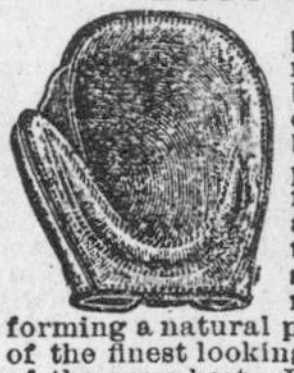

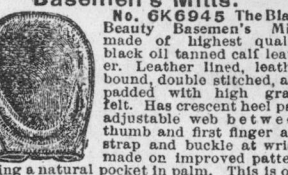

No. 6K6945 The Black Beauty Basemen's Mitt, made of highest quality black oil tanned calf leather. Leather lined, leather bound, double stitched, and padded with high grade felt. Has crescent heel pad, adjustable web between thumb and first finger and strap and buckle at wrist; made on improved pattern forming a natural pocket in palm. This is one of the finest looking mitts made, as well as one of the very best. Price....$1.62

If by mail, postage extra, 21 cents.

Outfielders' Mitt, $1.00

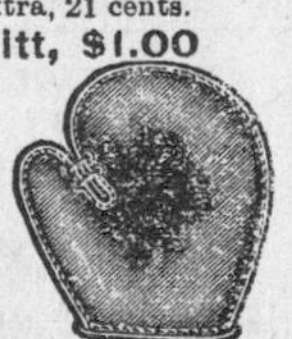

No. 6K6947 Outfielders' or Basemen's Mitt, an exact reproduction of the mitts used by the major league players. The palm is made of the highest grade drab buckskin, with fine glove leather back, leather lined, soft pliable felt padding, piped around the edge, and full leather bound. This is a very soft, pliable, active mitt, one which we guarantee to give satisfaction in every respect. A high grade mitt for a little money. Price each.....$1.00

If by mail, postage extra, 18 cents.

Fielders' Gloves.

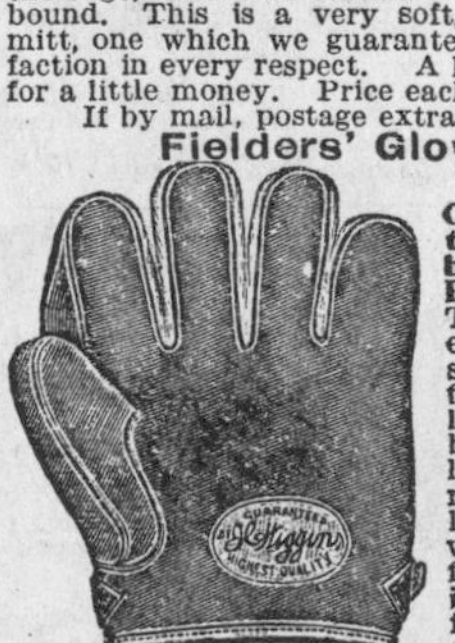

No. 6K6948 Our J.C. Higgins trade mark brand League Fielders' Glove. The best glove ever made. Constructed of very finest high grade light drab color buck, on the latest improved model, extra large size pattern with large little finger and large inside heel pad, forming large, deep pockets in the palm; leather lined, leather bound, welted seams, strap and buckle at the wrist, web between thumb and first finger. This glove contains all of the best features of the most popular gloves on the market and the quality of the stock and workmanship are the best obtainable and comes "ready broke." Made for right or left hand. We send glove for left hand unless otherwise ordered.

Price....(Postage extra, 20c)....$2.50

We carry all gloves and mitts, for both right and left hand.

$2.20 "Black Cub" Professional Glove.

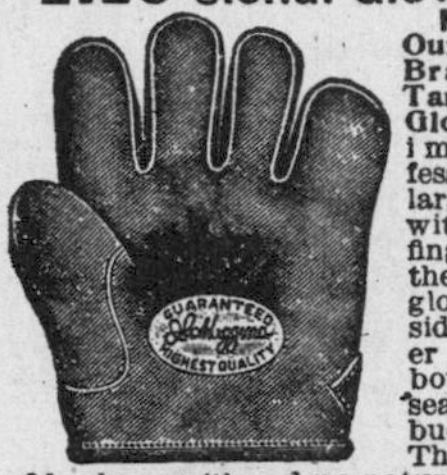

No. 6K6953 Our J. C. Higgins Brand, Black, Oil Tanned, Horsehide Glove, the latest improved professional style, large size pattern with large little finger, padded with the finest quality of glove felt, with inside heel pad, leather lined, leather bound, welted seams, strap and buckle at the wrist. This is a very pliable glove, with a deep natural pocket "ready broke" when you get it. We guarantee this in every respect to be the very best black glove on the market, the equal of any $3.50 glove sold by any retail house. Very popular. Price....(Postage extra, 20c).....$2.20

$1.90

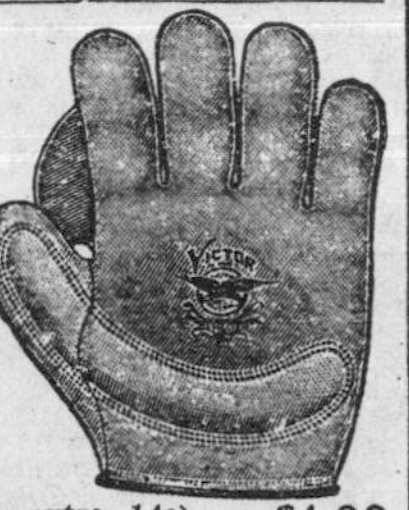

No. 6K6954 The Victor Professional Fielders' Glove. Made of horsehide, correctly padded, crescent pad extending in a semicircle around palm, with adjustable web between the thumb and first finger, as shown in the illustration, making a deep pocket, correctly padded. Price.....(Postage extra, 14c).......$1.90

$1.55

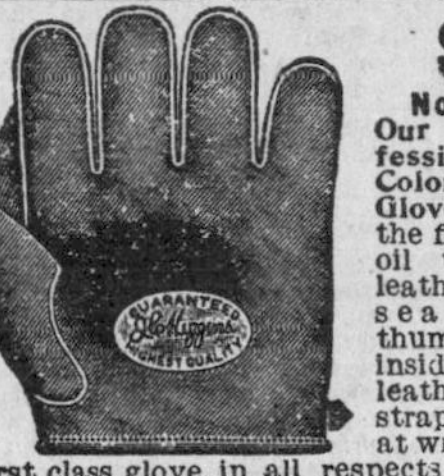

No. 6K6955 Our Young Professional Tan Color Fielders' Glove, made of the finest quality oil tanned calf leather, welted seams, web thumb, felt lined, inside heel pad, leather lined, strap and buckle at wrist. This is a first class glove in all respects and carries our guarantee. Price(Postage extra, 14c)$1.55

$1.25

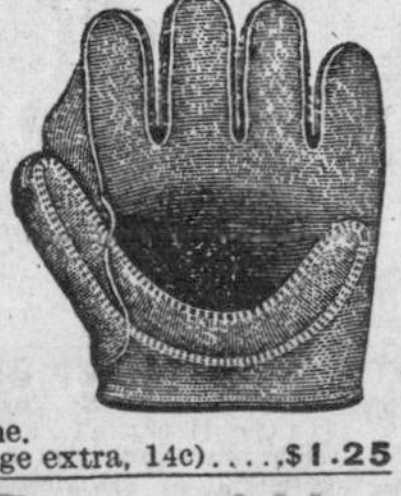

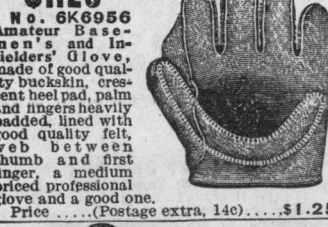

No. 6K6956 Amateur Basemen's and Infielders' Glove, made of good quality buckskin, crescent heel pad, palm and fingers heavily padded, lined with good quality felt, web between thumb and first finger, a medium priced professional glove and a good one. Price .....(Postage extra, 14c).....$1.25

98c

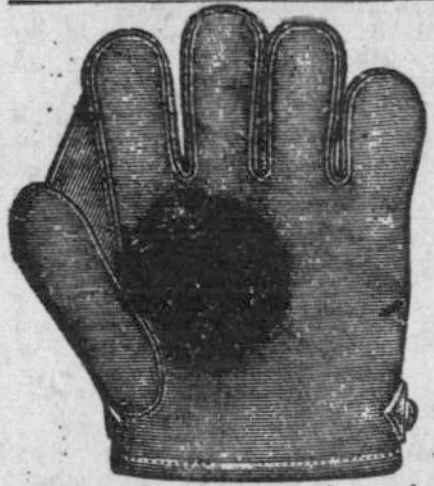

No. 6K6957 Our Black Bargain Infielders' Glove is the best glove ever offered for so little money, made professional style of extra strong, tanned black leather, welted seams, web thumb, felt lined, inside heel pad, leather bound, strap and buckle at the wrist. This is a large size glove and is made up in a first class manner, but we are offering it as one of our leaders. Price...(Postage extra, 14c)...98c

75c

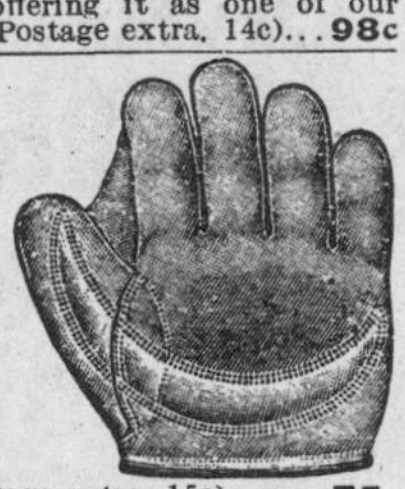

No. 6K6959 Made in men's large size, of buckskin leather, felt lined, crescent heel pad, heavily padded palm, web thumb and first finger, leather bound edges, button wrist. A first class semi-professional glove. Price......(Postage extra, 15c)......75c

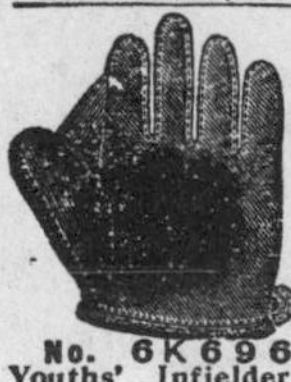

No. 6K6961 Made of napa tanned glove leather; felt padded palm and fingers, padded heel, leather bound edges, button wristband. Price.........40c If by mail, postage extra, 5 cents.

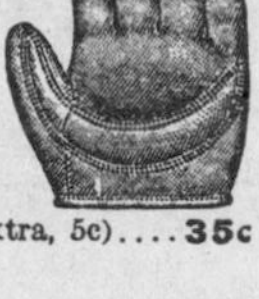

No. 6K6964 Our Youths' Infielders' Glove, made of finest oil tanned leather, heavily padded crescent heel pad, leather bound all around, button fastener. A regular boys' professional glove. Price....(Postage extra, 5c)....35c

Boys' Glove 18c

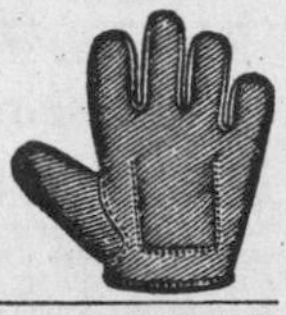

No. 6K6966 Our Boys' Infielders' Glove, made of finest colored sheepskin, palm is felt lined and padded, well stitched seams, button wrist. Price.......18c Postage, extra, 3 cents.

Neck Protecting Rubber Pad Mask. $2.10

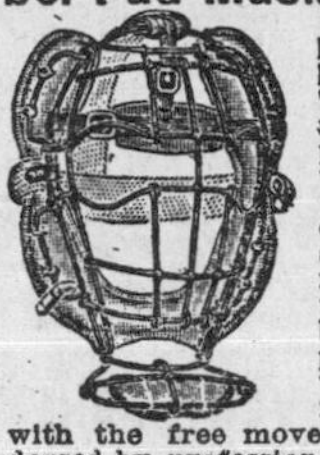

No. 6K6972 Our Patent Neck Protecting Pneumatic Pad Mask. The best mask on the market, fitted with our pneumatic pads made of the best annealed steel wire of extra heavy gauge, covered with black enamel to prevent the reflection of light. Fitted with an extension at the bottom of mask to give protection to the neck, which extension does not in any way interfere with the free movement of the head. Indorsed by professional and amateur players throughout the country. Price......$2.10 If by mail, postage extra, 42 cents.

$1.85 Professional League Mask.

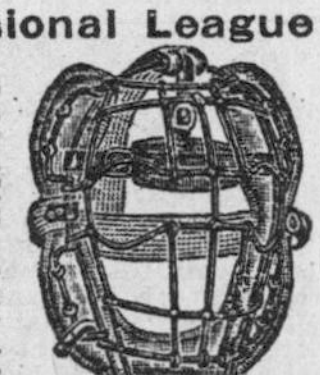

No. 6K6973 Men's Professional League Mask, fitted with our pneumatic pad. This mask is full size, made of black enamel wire, 5-32 and 6-32 inch in diameter. The pneumatic pad extends around the face and across the chin, making this mask more comfortable and better fitting than any other mask. This mask is 10½ inches long, 7½ inches wide and weighs about 24 ounces. Price....$1.85 If by mail, postage extra, 38 cents.

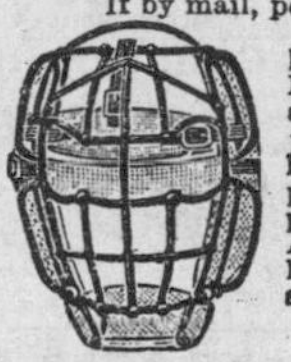

No. 6K6977 Men's Professional League Mask. Black enameled wire of 5-32 and 6-32 inch diameter, which prevents the reflection of the light; temple and cheek pads, with head and chin pieces; weight, 22 ounces; an A1 quality mask; 10½ inches long. 7½ inches wide. A strong mask. Price...$1.25 If by mail, postage extra, 35 cents.

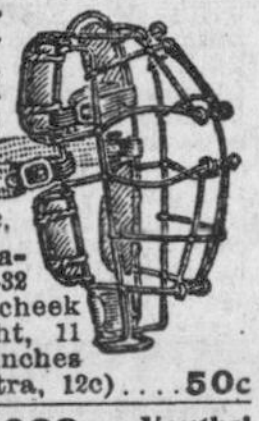

No. 6K6978 Men's Professional Mask. Black enameled wire, 5-32 inch in diameter, temple and cheek pads, head and chin pieces; well made; weight, 18 ounces; 10 inches long, 7 inches wide. Price ....90c If by mail, postage extra, 22c.

No. 6K6980 Men's Amateur Mask. Bright wire, 4-32 inch in diameter; temple and cheek pads; nicely finished; weight, 11 ounces; 10 inches long, 7 inches wide. Price....(Postage extra, 12c)....50c

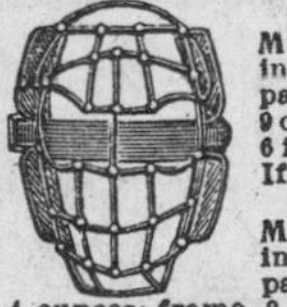

No. 6K6983 Youths' Mask. Bright wire, 3-32 inch in diameter; temple and cheek pads; nicely finished; weight, 9 ounces; frame, 10 inches long, 6 inches wide. Price.....35c If by mail, postage extra, 10c.

No. 6K6984 Boys' Mask. Bright wire, 3-32 inch in diameter; temple and cheek pads; nicely finished; weight, 4 ounces; frame, 9 inches long, 5 inches wide. Price ..(If by mail, postage extra, 6c) ..19c

Baseball Catchers' Body Protectors.

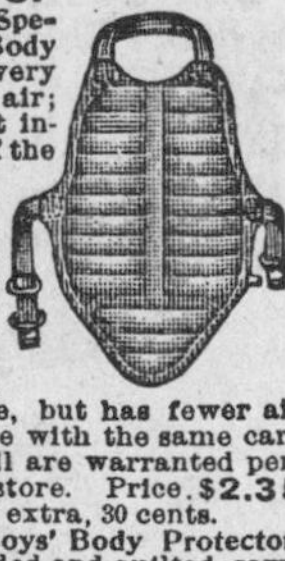

No. 6K6990 Our Special Professional League Body Protector, made of the very best rubber, inflated with air; light, pliable, and does not interfere with movements of the wearer. When not in use air may be let out and the protector rolled into a small package. Price ....$3.40 Postage extra, 42 cents.

No. 6K6991 Our Special Amateur Body Protector, inflated with air, similar to our league, but has fewer air compartments. It is made with the same care as our professional and all are warranted perfect when they leave our store. Price.$2.35 If by mail, postage extra, 30 cents.

No. 6K6992 Our Boys' Body Protector, made of canvas, well padded and quilted, same shape as our league but smaller, for boys. Price .(If by mail, postage extra, 22c) ..58c

No. 6K6993 Our Men's Body Protector, made of canvas, with soft leather front, padded and quilted. Price. (Postage extra, 30c).$1.05

"World's Champion" Baseball Shoes, $1.69.

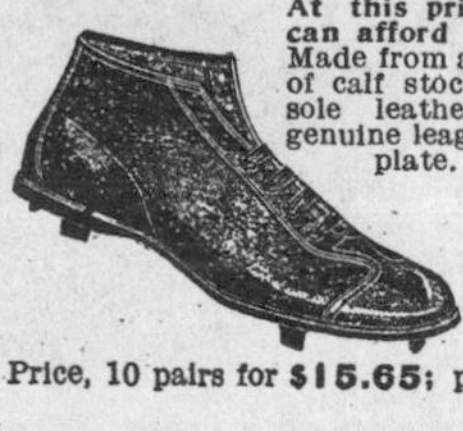

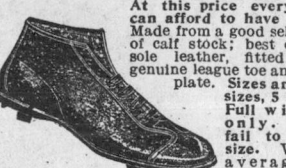

No. 6K0697 At this price every club can afford to have them. Made from a good selection of calf stock; best of oak sole leather, fitted with genuine league toe and heel plate. Sizes and half sizes, 5 to 11. Full widths only. Don't fail to state size. Weight averages 28 ounces.

Price, 10 pairs for $15.65; per pair, $1.69

Professional Shoe Plates.

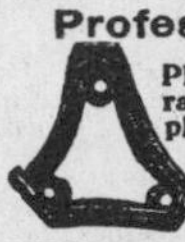

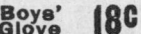

Our Professional League Shoe Plates are made of finest tempered razor steel, guaranteed the best shoe plates on the market. Come put up in an envelope complete with screws.

No. 6K6996 Professional League Razor Steel Toe Plates. Price, per pair. (Postage extra, 3 cents.)..30c

No. 6K6997 Professional League Razor Steel Heel Plates. Price, per pair.... 31c If by mail, postage extra, 3 cents.

Amateur Shoe Plates.

No. 6K7001 Amateur Toe Plates, complete with screws. Price, per pair. ....9c 6 pairs for....................................50c

No. 6K7002 Amateur Heel Plates. Price, 6 pairs for 45c; per pair. ....8c If by mail, postage extra, 3 cents.

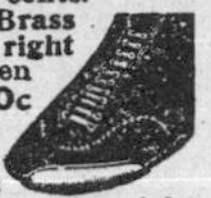

No. 6K7003 Pitchers' Brass Toe Plate. For either left or right foot. State which is wanted when ordering. Price, each.........20c If by mail, postage extra, 3 cents.

No. 6K7004 Pitchers' Aluminum Toe Plate, same as above, except made of aluminum; for right or left foot. Price, each..............20c If by mail, postage extra, 2 cents.

Athletic Guides and Rules.

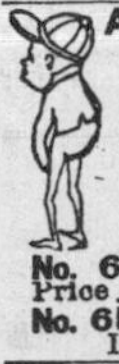

No. 6K7028 Annual Baseball Guide, giving official rules of this game. Not issued before April 1st of each year. Price.................10c If by mail, postage extra, 4 cents

No. 6K7029 Annual Tennis Guide, giving rules and instructions. Price..(Postage extra, 5 cents).10c

No. 6K7039 Annual Basketball Guide. Price..(If by mail, postage extra, 5c)..10c

No. 6K7040 Annual Football Guide, 10c If by mail, postage extra, 6 cents.

Indoor Baseball.

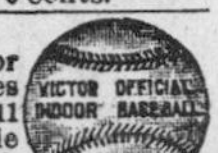

No. 6K7048 The Victor Official Indoor Baseball. 16 inches in circumference; weight, 11 ounces; best quality horsehide cover. The official ball. Price $1.00 If by mail, postage extra, 18 cents.

No. 6K7049 Regulation Indoor Bat, for indoor baseball, made from second growth hickory, with tape wound handle. Price..(If by mail, postage extra. 22c)..35c

Association or Soccer Footballs.

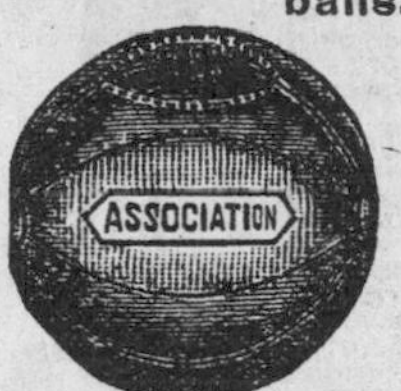

No. 6K7085 The High School Association Football, made of the best American tanned grain leather, hand sewed, canvas lined, rawhide lace, regulation size. Price, with bladder....$2.10 If by mail, postage extra, 24 cents.

No. 6K7086 Association Football, made of good quality pebbled cowhide, canvas lined, rawhide lace and bladder. A very strong, well made ball, that retails at $2.00. Our price ...(Postage extra, 24c.).....$1.59

For Association Football Bladders, see No. 6K6852.

The Victor Rugby Football.

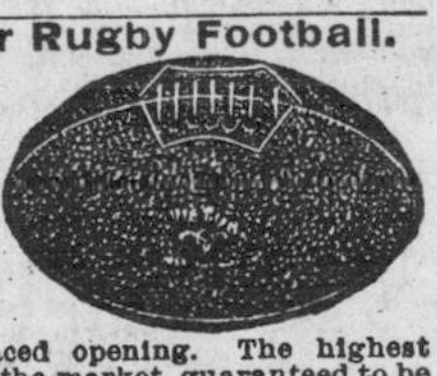

No. 6K7087 The Victor Intercollegiate Official Rugby Football, made of best imported English grain leather with all possible stretch removed, stitched with wax thread and has patent double laced opening. The highest grade football on the market, guaranteed to be equal to any football selling for $5.00 and $6.00. Put up one in a box, with pure gum bladder, lacing needle and pump. Price..........$4.20 If by mail, postage extra, 28 cents.

No. 6K7088 Rugby Football, made of the best quality selected American grain pebbled leather, lined with canvas, stitched on lock stitch machine, with waxed thread, furnished with rawhide lace, lacing needle and pure rubber bladder. An extra strong regulation size ball. Price. (Postage extra, 24 cents.) .$1.50

No. 6K7089 Rugby Football, made of good quality pebbled cowhide, canvas lined, full size and well made. Rawhide lace and bladder. A very good strong ball for a little money, that looks like a $2.50 ball. Price..........$1.20 If by mail, postage extra, 20 cents.

No. 6K7090 Our Leader Rugby Football, made of good quality pebbled leather, well lined and well made, a genuine bargain for the boys. Will give them satisfaction. Price, with bladder (Postage extra, 15c) 82c

Rugby Bladders.

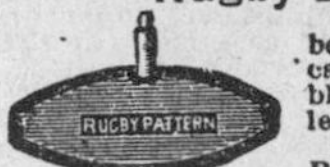

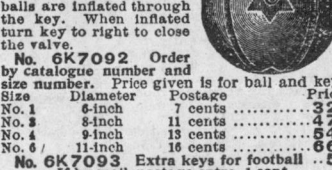

Our Bladders are all the best grade. We do not carry cheap composition bladders. They are worthless.

No. 6K7091 Rugby Bladder. Pure rubber for regulation Rugby footballs. Price..........52c If by mail, postage extra, 5 cents.

For Association Football Bladders see No. 6K6852 and No. 6K6853.

Black Rubber Footballs.

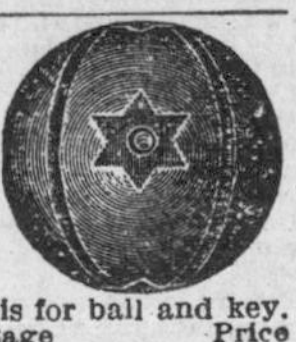

American Round Rubber Footballs. These footballs are inflated through the key. When inflated turn key to right to close the valve.

No. 6K7092 Order by catalogue number and size number. Price given is for ball and key.

Size	Diameter	Postage	Price
No. 1	6-inch	7 cents	32c
No. 3	8-inch	11 cents	47c
No. 4	9-inch	13 cents	54c
No. 6	11-inch	16 cents	66c

No. 6K7093 Extra keys for football ..5c If by mail, postage extra, 1 cent.

Football and Striking Bag Inflaters.

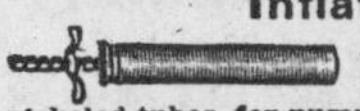

No. 6K7094 Pocket Football and Striking Bag Inflaters, nickeled tubes, for pumping up bladders. Price..(If by mail, postage extra, 4c) .17c

Basket Balls.

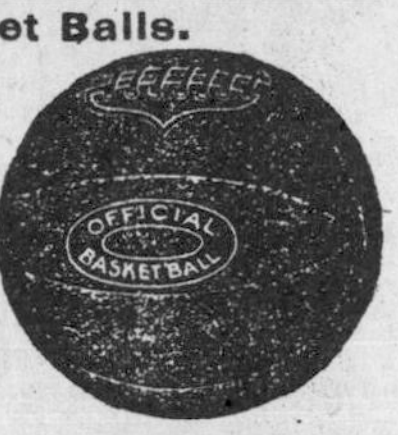

No. 6K7095 Amateur Basket Ball, made of high grade pebbled leather, canvas lined and well made, cheapest basket ball on the market. Will give good service and worth much more than we ask for it. Price, with bladder....$1.45 If by mail, postage extra, 18 cents.

No. 6K7096 Our Regulation Basket Ball, made of best quality American grain pebbled leather, best lining and stitched with waxed linen thread, furnished with rawhide laces and pure rubber bladder. A ball that will stand lots of hard service. Price..................$2.70 If by mail, postage extra, 27 cents.

No. 6K7097 Pure Rubber Bladders for Basket Balls. Price..........58c If by mail, postage extra, 5 cents.

Basket Ball Goals.

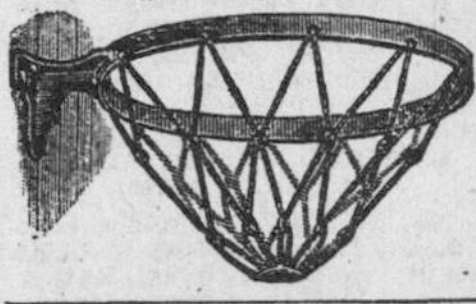

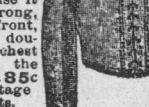

No. 6K7098 Basket Ball Goals, regulation style, made of iron frame with cotton netting. Weight, per pair, 12 lbs. Price, per pair..$2.74

FOOTBALL GOODS.

Football Jackets, Full Sleeves.

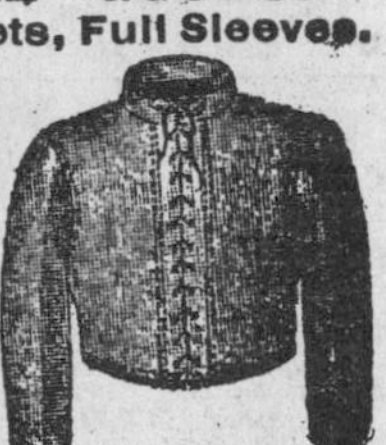

No. 6K7102 Made of very best quality tan colored army khaki cloth, which is growing in favor as football material, because it is light and strong, made in laced front, reinforced with double seams; give chest measure under the arms. Price....85c If by mail, postage extra, 19 cents.

Sleeveless Football Jackets.

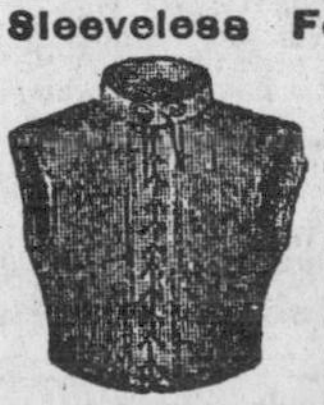

No. 6K7107 Made of finest quality heavy white twilled drilling, laced front, well sewed; a good strong jacket; give chest measurement under the arms. Price...38c If by mail, postage extra, 11 cents.

No. 6K7110 Made of very best quality tan colored army khaki cloth, which is the coming material for football clothing, made with laced front, double seams, reinforced, well made and well finished; give chest measure under the arms. Price.......70c If by mail, postage extra, 12 cents.

Superior Football Pants.

The knees and hips of all our pants are heavily padded and all have elastic bottoms.

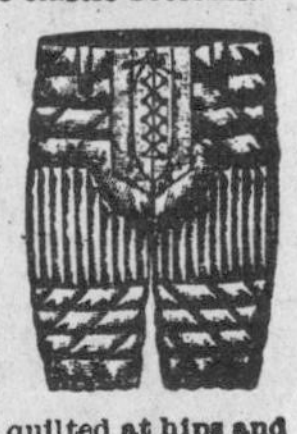

No. 6K7116 Made of finest quality heavy white twilled drilling, laced front, quilted; give waist measure. Price, per pair............60c

No. 6K7118 Made of fine quality sage green 8-ounce duck, laced front, cane reeds at thighs, large loose padding at hips and knees, well made; give waist measure. Price, per pair $1.25

No. 6K7119 Made of very best quality tan colored army khaki cloth, made laced front, full padded and quilted at hips and knees, cane reeds at thighs, the latest thing in football pants; well made and well finished; give waist measure. Price, per pair ......$1.60 If by mail, postage extra, 34 to 48 cents.

For a complete line of Football Shoes, see our Shoe Department.

Boys' Complete Football Uniform, Reduced to $1.20.

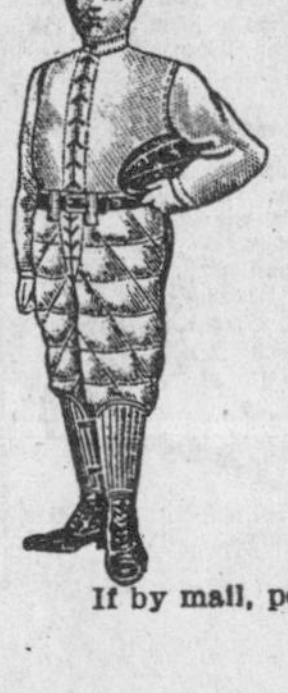

No. 6K7121 Boys' Complete Football Uniform, consisting of full sleeve canvas jacket, full padded canvas pants, strong cotton web belt, heavy cotton ribbed stockings, canvas shin guards. Jacket and pants made of best quality canvas drill, finely finished and reinforced, shin guards have rattan reeds in them and are fitted with adjustable straps. This is a first class outfit in every respect. The items if purchased singly would aggregate double the price of this complete outfit. When ordering give waist measurement. Sizes, 24 to 32. Not made larger than 32 inches waist measure. Price, complete, without ball ....$1.20 If by mail, postage extra, 45 cents.

FOOTBALL SUNDRIES.

Rubber Nose Mask.

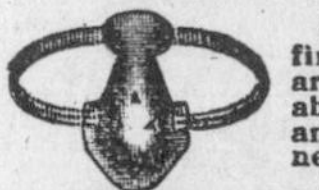

No. 6K7122 Made of finest rubber. Fastens around the head. Gives absolute protection to nose and teeth, and hangs by neck band when not in use. Price..............$1.40
If by mail, postage extra, 14 cents.

The Favorite Head Harness.

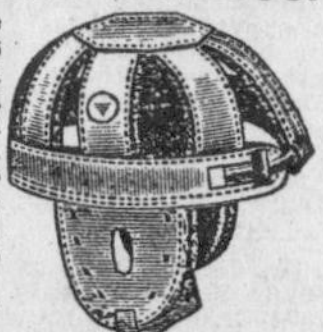

No. 6K7123 The Favorite Head Harness is made of heavy, tanned sewed leather strips, and is lined with all wool soft white felt padding. It is so constructed as to afford full protection to the head and ears, and at the same time permit free circulation of air around the head. The ear pad surrounds the ear, protecting it fully, and does not obstruct the hearing. The head band is made self-adjusting, so that the helmet always fits snugly.
Price..............$1.10
If by mail, postage extra, 13 cents.

Shin Guards.

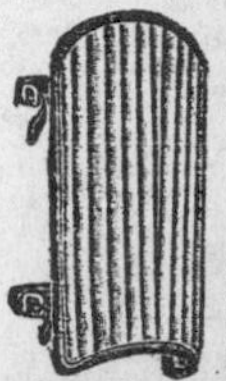

No. 6K7124 Boys' Shin Guards, 9 inches long, made of light weight canvas, padded and stiffened with reeds. A good, well made, durable shin guard. Price, per pair.......35c
If by mail, postage extra, per pair, 8 cents.

No. 6K7125 Men's Shin Guards, 12 inches long, made of heavy weight canvas, leather bound, leather straps, padded and stiffened with reeds. A first class shin guard and very substantial in every respect.
Price, per pair..........................58c
If by mail, postage extra, per pair, 15 cents.

Football Stockings.

No. 6K7134 Medium Weight Ribbed Cotton Stockings, black only. State size wanted. Price, per pair..............23c
No. 6K7135 Heavy Ribbed Cotton Stockings, colors, black, navy or maroon. State size and color wanted. Per pair..30c
No. 6K7136 Medium Weight Wool Ribbed Stockings with cotton feet. Colors, black, navy or maroon. State size and color wanted. Price, per pair.......50c
No. 6K7137 Fine Heavy Wool Ribbed Stockings, black, navy or maroon. State size and color wanted. Price, per pair.......60c
No. 6K7138 Very Fine Worsted Ribbed Stockings, black, navy or maroon. State size and color wanted. Price, per pair.......75c
If by mail, postage extra, per pair, 6 to 8 cents.

Morton's Supporters.

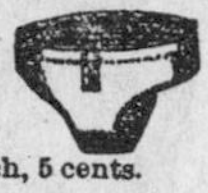

No. 6K7139 Improved Morton Supporter. Made of canton flannel, lace front. Give waist measure when ordering.
Price, each..............18c
3 for..............50c
If by mail, postage extra, each, 5 cents.

Admiral Elastic Supporters.

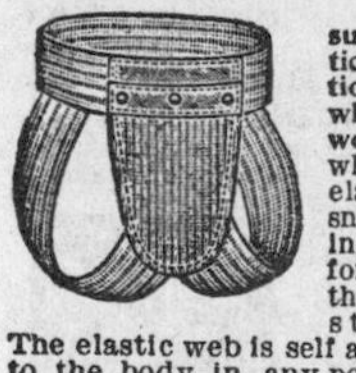

No. 6K7142 This supporter is made of elastic web with the exception of the front piece, which is open mesh, finely woven, washable fabric, which is attached to the elastic belt with three snap glove fasteners, making this the most comfortable, most sanitary, the most practical jockey strap on the market. The elastic web is self adjusting and conforms to the body in any position. This supporter can be washed in lukewarm water. When ordering give waist measure. Price....44c
If by mail, postage extra, 6 cents.

ATHLETIC ELASTIC BANDAGES.

See our Drug Department.

Leather Wrist Supporter.

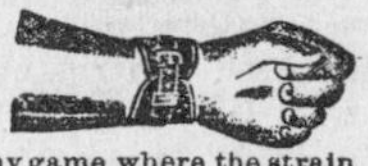

No. 6K7146 A perfect support and protection to the wrist. Invaluable to baseball, tennis and cricket players or in any game where the strain is on the wrist. In domestic grain leather, tan or black. State color wanted. Price, each..16c
If by mail, postage extra, 2 cents.

The Hackey Ankle Supporter.

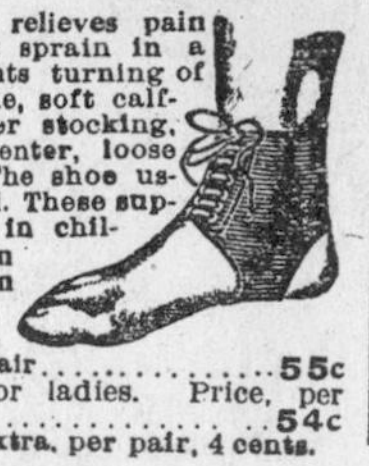

Hackey Supporter relieves pain immediately, cures a sprain in a short time and prevents turning of the ankle. Made of fine, soft calfskin and is worn over stocking, lacing very tight in center, loose at top and bottom. The shoe usually worn can be used. These supporters are not made in children's sizes. Mention size shoe you wear when ordering.
No. 6K7150 For men. Price, per pair..........55c
No. 6K7151 For ladies. Price, per pair..........54c
If by mail, postage extra, per pair, 4 cents.

Quarter Sleeve Shirts.

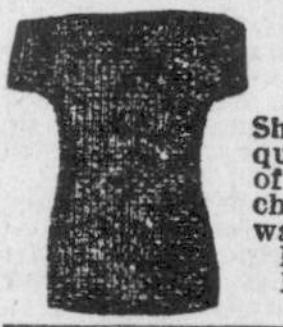

No. 6K7197 Cotton Shirt, quarter sleeves, good quality. Made in solid colors of black or navy blue. Give chest measure and color wanted when ordering.
Price..................35c
If by mail, postage extra, 10 cents.

Athletic Knee Tights.

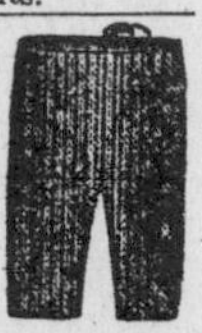

No. 6K7204 Cotton Tights. Good quality cotton tights, made in solid colors of black or navy blue. Sizes, 26 to 36 inches waist measure. Give waist measure and color wanted.
Price, per pair............30c
If by mail, postage extra, 6 cents.

BATHING SUITS.

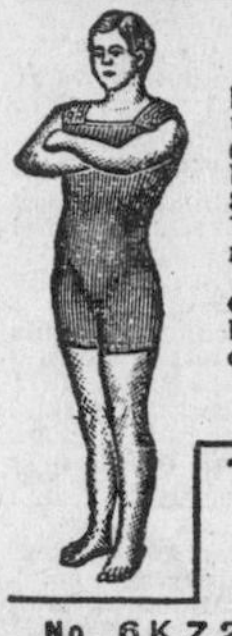

Our One-Piece Best Cotton Bathing Suit is made like a union suit (buttons over shoulder). Made in solid navy blue only; ranging in size from 32 to 44 inches chest measure. When ordering give chest measure.
No. 6K7208 Cotton One-Piece Suit, in solid navy blue color. Be sure to give chest measure.
Price, per suit...........65c
If by mail, postage extra, 10c.

Two-Piece Bathing Suits.

GIVE CHEST AND WAIST MEASURE.

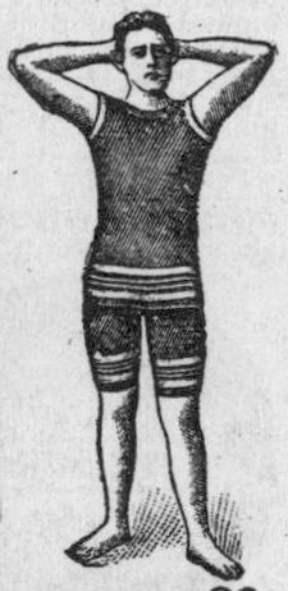

No. 6K7216 Two-Piece Cotton Bathing Suit, consisting of quarter sleeve shirt and knee pants, made in black or navy blue colors. Give chest and waist measure and color wanted.
Price, per suit..........55c
If by mail, postage extra, 10c
No. 6K7217 Consisting of Sleeveless Shirt and Trunks, made of highest quality heavy weight cotton. Colors, black, navy blue with fancy stripes around bottom of garments and around armholes, making the most handsome as well as the best cotton bathing suit on the market. Give color and chest measure when ordering. Price, per suit..........80c
If by mail, postage extra, 12c.
No. 6K7218 High Grade Worsted Two-Piece Bathing Suit, consisting of sleeveless shirt with V shaped neck and trunks. Navy blue or black with fancy trimming around the bottom of the garments and armholes and the neck. Most up to date and best bargain on the market, retailing everywhere for $3.00 to $3.25. If you wear a worsted suit, you will not experience that chill so disagreeable to bathers. Give chest measure and color wanted.
Price, per suit.....................$2.35
If by mail, postage extra, 18 cents.

Our Swimming Trunks.

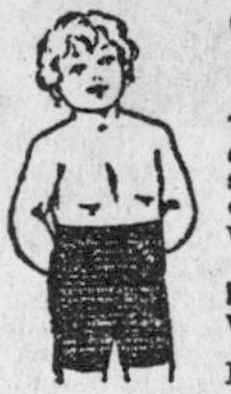

Our Cotton Swimming Trunks, made up in assorted designs of stripes, with draw string; assorted sizes for men or boys. When ordering, give waist measure.
No. 6K7219 Men's and Boys' Swimming Trunks. Give waist measure.
Price, per pair.........20c
Postage, extra, per pair, 4 cents.

LADIES' BATHING SUITS. SEE INDEX.

Ayvad's Water Wings, 20 cts.

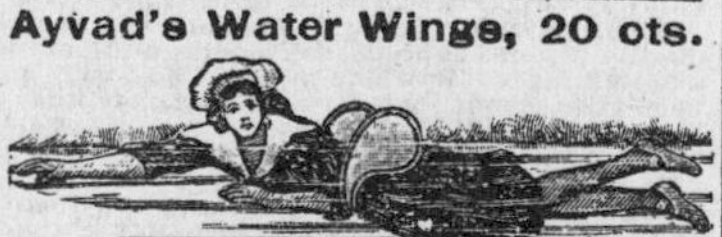

No. 6K7221 Afford great sport for bathers, and are of the greatest assistance to beginners. When inflated, will support a man of 250 lbs. as easily as a child at the proper level for comfortable swimming. When deflated, it can be rolled into a package small enough to carry in a vest pocket.
Price....(Postage extra, 4 cents)....20c

Capoc Swimming Jacket.

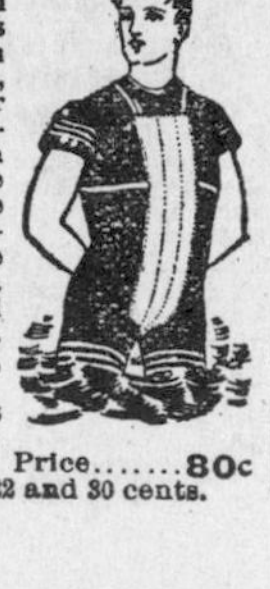

This jacket, as shown in the illustration, is made in two parts, front and back. It is 9½ inches wide, length of each half about 25 inches. Weight, about 2 pounds. It is hung over the shoulders with tapes, fastened round the body in such a manner as not to interfere with the free movement of the limbs. Can be instantly removed. Capoc is a vegetable wool and is very buoyant. These jackets are guaranteed to support any average person. Comes in two styles; for men, and for ladies and children.
No. 6K7225 For ladies and children. Price......75c
No. 6K7226 For men Price.......80c
If by mail, postage extra, 22 and 30 cents.

HAMMOCKS

Made in our own factory according to our own design and patterns.

OUR HAMMOCK BUSINESS has assumed such an enormous size that a year ago we felt that we could no longer depend on the regular market for these goods, the same as other dealers are compelled to do, and give our customers the quality, value and service that we would like to. We accordingly started a factory of our own for the manufacture of hammocks, and by reason of this factory, we today are able to offer you better goods and better value in hammocks than you could possibly obtain elsewhere. By making these goods in our own factory, we enjoy the minimum cost, and owing to the enormous quantity of these goods we use, our cost is lower than that of most other manufacturers, and as we are content with but one small margin of profit over the cost of material and labor, you are directly benefited by this enormous saving in the cost of our hammocks. To appreciate the wonderful values we are offering, it is neccessary that you see the hammocks and examine them carefully, note the workmanship and particularly note the weave, and you will find that our hammocks run from four to five more yarns to the inch than any hammocks offered within 25 to 50 per cent of our prices. In other words, you will find our hammocks contain more material, and consequently have greater strength than those sold by others.

OUR HAMMOCKS are all made according to our special method. We absolutely guarantee them not to pull out at the head or foot, a fault common with all other hammocks. The weight is distributed equally in our hammocks. The strain is equalized, as the ropes supporting the hammocks engage directly with the spreader at the head and foot, unlike other makes, where these ropes are attached to the woven part of the hammock, which does not permit of any adjustment and causes the woven part of the body of the hammock to break.

WE HAVE BEEN VERY CAREFUL in selecting our combinations of colors, and have selected such colors as blend harmoniously and which will contrast with any surrounding. In our hammocks we have studiously avoided violent combinations of green and purple, pink and blue, and all other colors which contrast harshly.

Wire Pillow for Hammocks.

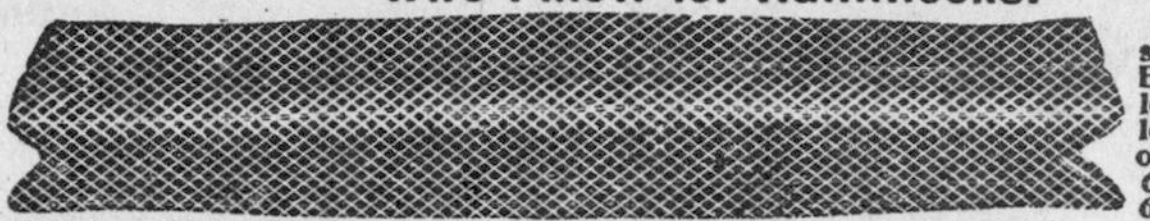

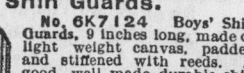

This illustration shows the Torsion Braided Wire Pillow used on the following three styles of hammocks, No. 6K7343, No. 6K7344 and No. 6K7345. This pillow is undoubtedly the greatest improvement on hammocks within the past five years. It is entirely free from the heat and stuffiness of the ordinary pillow, self ventilating, very soft and comfortable and accommodates itself to every movement of the head. It will always retain its shape and elasticity and will not rust. Other manufacturers charge from 50 cents to $1.00 more for a pillow of this kind. We are furnishing the above mentioned three numbers of hammocks fitted with our spring pillow for less money than other dealers charge for the same quality of hammock with the ordinary stuffed pillow.

WE GUARANTEE our hammocks against defective workmanship, and we further guarantee them to be the greatest value ever offered or they can be returned and your money and transportation charges will be cheerfully refunded.

Our Child's Hammock, 49 Cents.

49c

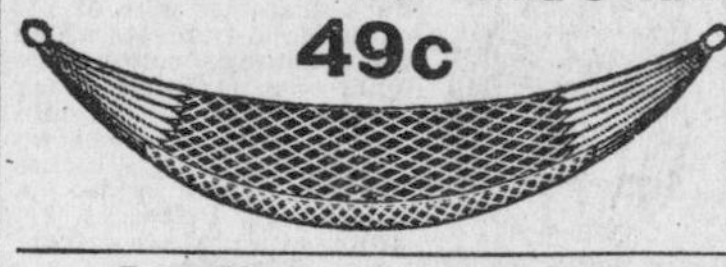

No. 6K7329 This hammock is particularly desirable for babies and small children, as it is a very strong hammock, made of heavy seine twine, knitted by hand and made with sufficient slack so that child cannot roll out. Full length of hammock, 8½ feet; length of bed, 5 feet. This hammock is furnished without spreaders. Price..............49c
If by mail, postage extra, 14 cents.

Our Hand Knitted Seine Twine Hammock, 92 Cents.

92c

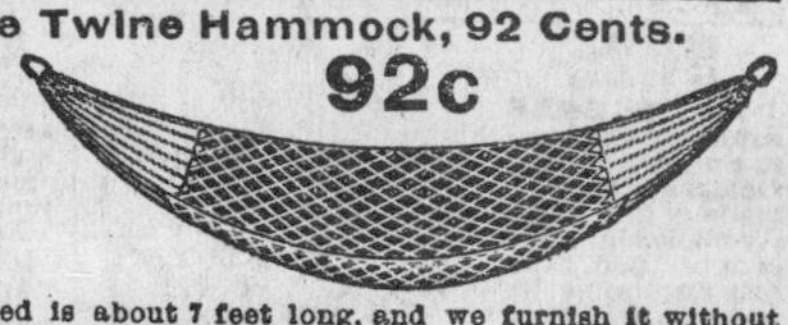

No. 6K7330 Our hand made double seine twine hammock. This hammock is knitted by hand, of double seine twine, forming a 2-inch square mesh, and each hammock is made in white and one other neat attractive color. The edge on each side is chain braided, and interwoven into the meshes, making a strong, substantial and durable hammock, and with ordinary care will last a number of years. The entire hammock is about 13 feet long and the bed is about 7 feet long, and we furnish it without spreaders. Price..92c
If by mail, postage extra, 32 cents.

Shenton's Patent Canvas Hammock, $1.48.

The features of a Morris Chair embodied in a Hammock.

$1.48

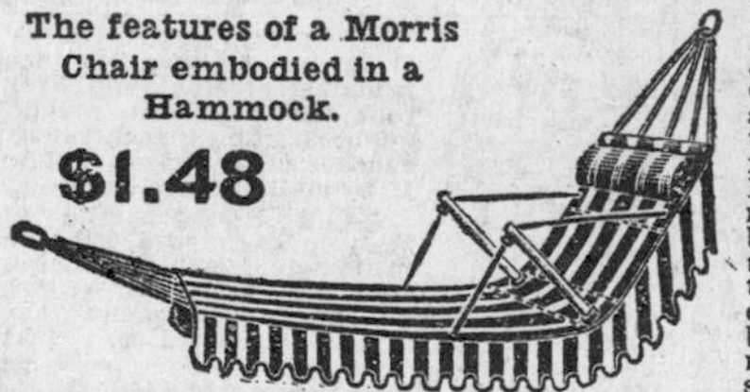

No. 6K7334 The Shenton Patented Hammock is the latest and most comfortable hammock yet produced. It is so constructed that by simply moving the arm-rests from one place to another along the ropes, the hammock may be changed from one position to another instantly. By removing the arm rests the hammock may be used as a regular hammock; and by inserting the arm rests, as shown in the illustration, the hammock has the effect of a reclining chair, and is an excellent thing for invalids, as well as being one of the most comfortable hammocks on the market. All are made of striped canvas. Bed is 30 inches wide and 78 inches long and weighs about 7½ pounds. Made of striped canvas, with spreader, pillow and valance.
Price..............$1.48
When hanging a hammock always hang it so that the head will be higher than the foot.

Canvas Weave Hammock with Pillow and Spreader.

98c

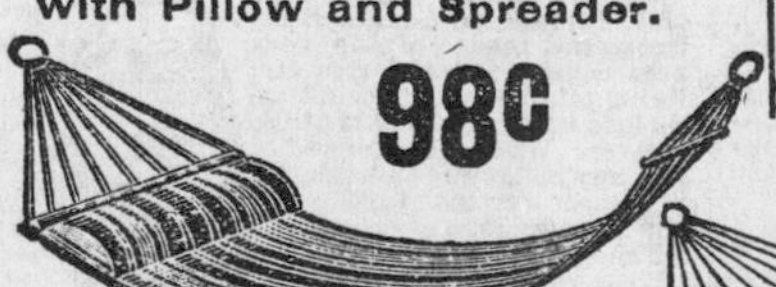

No. 6K7339 Hammock made of closest fancy canvas weave, in full fancy bright colors. Made with three-ply warps with fancy colored pillow and spreader. A very strong hammock. Retails from $1.75 to $2.00. Size of bed, 6½ feet long, 3 feet wide. Weight, 3½ pounds.
Price..........98c
If by mail, postage extra, 61 cents.

Close Woven Hammock with Pillow and Spreader.

85c

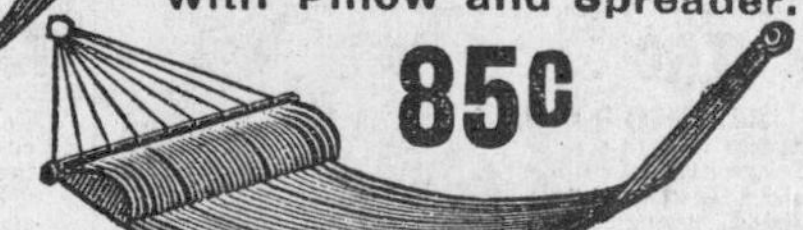

No. 6K7337 Cotton Hammock, with close woven body of the best cotton weave, full fancy colors, with spreader and pillow. Size of bed, 6½ feet long, 3 feet wide. A hammock that sells regularly at $1.25 to $1.50. Weight, 3½ pounds. Price, with fancy pillow and spreader.....85c
If by mail, postage extra, 58 cents.

Our Leader, $2.25 Value for $1.52

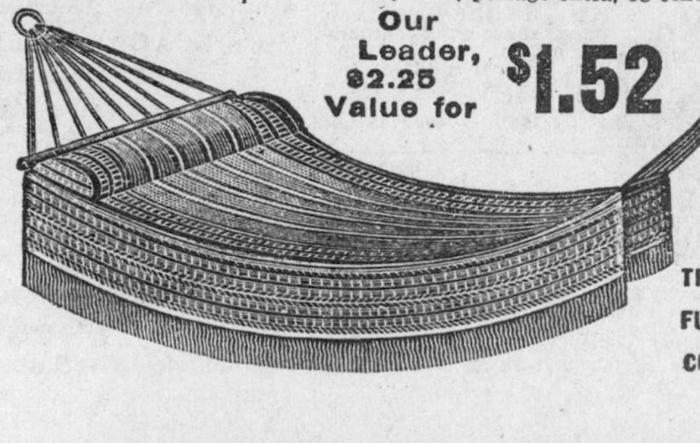

No. 6K7342 Fine Canvas Weave Hammock, has deep woven valance with fringe, full fancy bright colors, with one spreader and one pillow. Size of bed, 6½ feet long, 3 feet wide. A beauty for the money. Weight, about 5 pounds.
Price..$1.52

NOTE THE DEEP, FULL SIZE CURTAIN.

OUR 1908 LEADER WITH TORSION SPRING PILLOW $1.89

No. 6K7343 Our Leader Hammock at $1.89 is the most wonderful value in hammocks for the season of 1908. Beautiful pattern, very closely woven, special weave, four-ply special long fiber firmly twisted yarn. Not to be compared with the open weave hammocks of soft yarn offered in competition. Wide torsion spring pillow, the most comfortable and sanitary pillow ever placed on a hammock. Simple, but beautiful pattern; the stripes are of contrasting colors beautifully blended. Made with extra large, full curtain, with long fringe. The end ropes are connected directly with the spreaders at the head and foot, and are of improved construction, guaranteeing this hammock against pulling out or tearing, all strain being placed on the spreader instead of on the hammock—as in all other makes. Size of bed, 40x86 inches. Weight, 6½ pounds. A $3.00 hammock for $1.89. Price...$1.89

OUR 1908 OFFER OF A $4.00 HAMMOCK FOR $2.54

No. 6K7344 Made in our own factory, extra large size, beautiful new damask weave, handsome design of stripes and checks, beautiful contrasting colors of old gold and black. Constructed of a fine, long fiber, firmly twisted yarn, very closely packed together, giving this hammock enormous strength, and bringing out the full beauty of its pattern and color. Unlike other hammocks sold for $1.00 to $2.00 more money, this hammock has a firm body, no loose threads to catch in the clothing, no large holes or meshes, has the strength of a heavy piece of duck, and all the beauty in color and design of a beautiful Oriental rug. Fitted with our sanitary spring pillow, improved construction; spreader at head and foot; extra full deep curtain, fine heavy fringe. Size of bed, 40x82 inches. Could not be duplicated elsewhere for less than $4.00. Weight, 10 pounds. Our price......$2.54

OUR EXTRA LARGE, DOUBLE SIZE HAMMOCK $3.38

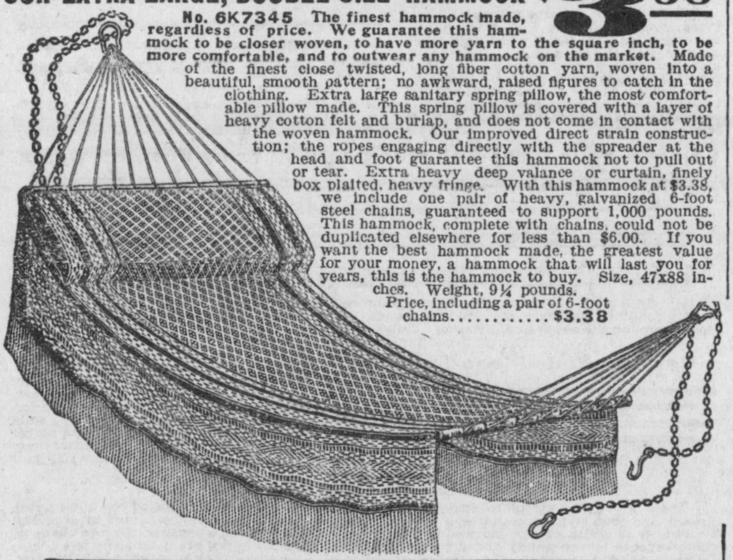

No. 6K7345 The finest hammock made, regardless of price. We guarantee this hammock to be closer woven, to have more yarn to the square inch, to be more comfortable, and to outwear any hammock on the market. Made of the finest close twisted, long fiber cotton yarn, woven into a beautiful, smooth pattern; no awkward, raised figures to catch in the clothing. Extra large sanitary spring pillow, the most comfortable pillow made. This spring pillow is covered with a layer of heavy cotton felt and burlap, and does not come in contact with the woven hammock. Our improved direct strain construction; the ropes engaging directly with the spreader at the head and foot guarantee this hammock not to pull out or tear. Extra heavy deep valance or curtain, finely box plaited, heavy fringe. With this hammock at $3.38, we include one pair of heavy, galvanized 6-foot steel chains, guaranteed to support 1,000 pounds. This hammock, complete with chains, could not be duplicated elsewhere for less than $6.00. If you want the best hammock made, the greatest value for your money, a hammock that will last you for years, this is the hammock to buy. Size, 47x88 inches. Weight, 9¼ pounds. Price, including a pair of 6-foot chains..........$3.38

Hammock Ropes.
No. 6K7349 Hammock Ropes, 6½ feet long, adjustable anchor fastening that remains where you place it; no knots to tie after attached to hammock; no slipping in hammock. Hammock can be raised and lowered in an instant. Price, per pair....15c If by mail, postage extra, per pair, 12 cents.

Hammook Hooks.
No. 6K7346 Screw Hammock Hooks, tinned, 7-16 inch diameter, screw in. Price, per pair..9c Postage extra, per pair, 9 cents.
No. 6K7347 Plate Hammock Hooks, tinned, 7-16 inch in diameter to fasten with screws. Price, per pair...11c
No. 6K7347 If by mail, postage extra, per pair, 11 cents.

Our Acme Folding Lawn or Porch Settee, 83 Cents.
No. 6K7384 For 83 cents we offer you our Acme Lawn Settee, made of selected wood, painted in a bright, attractive color, the seat is in natural wood finish. Unlike other settees, the slats are not nailed but are screwed to the frame. This lawn settee is made so it may be folded up and set away during the winter or it may be left on a porch, as desired. The Acme lawn settee is a very useful and desirable article and will recommend itself to our customers; in fact, it requires no care or attention and saves many times its value in the wear and tear of regular household furniture. Our Acme lawn settee, 3½ feet long, painted. Weight, 20 pounds. Price...................83c

LAWN SWINGS, $3.45 and $4.24.
For Children and Adults.

$3.45

Best lawn swings on the market. Made especially for us according to our own specifications and guaranteed to be superior to any swing sold within $2.00 of our price. These swings are made of selected pine, braced, full bolted, far superior to the cheap nailed swings. Each piece of lumber is selected straight grain stock, no rough edges. These swings have a greater spread than the ordinary swings, allowing plenty of room between the seats. Four-passenger swings will comfortably seat four people, which is not the case with the majority of so called four-passenger swings offered in competition with ours. The swings are finely painted and varnished and present a handsome appearance. There are no swings on the market that will give you better service or as good value as those sold by us. These swings are shipped from our factory in Illinois and cannot be sent with other goods. Cannot be sent C. O. D.

No. 6K7371 Adults' size, about 8½ feet high. The seat is 20 inches wide, which is wider than the ordinary chair, and will hold two grown persons or four children. Weight, about 100 pounds. Shipped from our factory and cannot be sent with other goods. Price..$3.45

No. 6K7372 Large size, 8½ feet high, seat 33 inches wide, large enough to seat four adults or six children. Flat arm rests, hardwood throughout; easiest swinging swing made. Price, $4.24

Wt., about 120 lbs. Shipped from our factory and cannot be sent with other goods.

Our Four-Passenger Porch Swing.
REDUCED TO $6.85

No. 6K7375 The ideal swing for use on a porch or lawn as it occupies just half of the room of the ordinary high swing. Swings with an easy motion and is as comfortable as a rocking chair. Frame is constructed entirely of selected hardwood; has broad comfortable arm rests; the slats, seats and back are of heavy selected stock. Length of frame on ground, 7 feet 6 inches; width of frame, 36 inches; seats are fully 31 inches wide, extra high 33-inch back. This swing folds compactly in shipping, is easily set up and when set up is very strong and rigid. Beautifully painted and varnished in contrasting colors. The best low down swing on the market. Weight, packed for shipment, about 100 pounds. Price..........$6.85

These swings are shipped from our factory in Illinois.

$8.15

Our Steel Lawn Swing, $8.15.

No. 6K7376 Never before has a high class steel lawn swing been offered at any such price. This swing is made specially for us under contract, and we guarantee it to be equal in strength and construction to any steel swing on the market, regardless of price. The swing is 8 feet high, 5 feet, 9 inches wide, and will comfortably hold four passengers. The seats are made of hardwood mission style, 34 inches wide, securely bolted to the steel frame. This swing is not to be compared with the cheap steel swings made of common strap steel. The frame is made of the best wrought angle iron, and the braces are steel. This swing will last a lifetime. The hangers and frame are finely finished with two heavy coats of paint, and the seat and foot board are nicely finished in the natural wood. Weight of swing, about 155 pounds.
Price, without canopy......$8.15
Price, with canopy.......9.00
Shipped from factory in Northern Illinois.

The Chicago Folding Porch Chair, 78 Cents.
No. 6K7378 The Chicago Folding Porch Chair, made of wood frame with denim body. All joints riveted and when not in use folded when not in use. Weighs about 10½ pounds and the back may be adjusted to various angles for comfort. All have arm rests and high back, are easily carried about and save the household furniture.
Price..................78c

Baby Jumpers.
This Jumper combines in one article a swing, reclining chair, crib and jumper; strong and large enough for a child six years old; child cannot fall out.
No. 6K7353 Baby Jumper, complete, with springs and cotton rope and hooks, with veneered seat and back, not upholstered. Shipping weight, 15 pounds. Price.........$1.47
No. 6K7354 Baby Jumper, complete, with springs, rope and hooks, upholstered in cretonne, as illustration. Shipping weight, 16 pounds. Price.........$1.87

Benner's Baby Jumper.
REDUCED TO $1.40
No. 6K7356 A Swing and Walker combined. Develops the baby at the same time gives hours of pleasure and rest to the parents. Being adjustable, it can be used as a swing until the child is five years old. The seat or saddle is constructed on scientific lines, relieving all pressure or strain from the child, the spiral springs protecting it from jar. The child can stand or walk about freely with it and when tired standing, it has a comfortable seat to sit on. Shipping weight, 3 pounds. Price..(Postage extra, 48 cents)...$1.40

Jumper With Stand.
No. 6K7357 The stand is made on the best mechanical principles; will support a tested weight of 150 pounds. The only baby jumper that has a perfect reclining chair and foot rest and is adjustable. You can make a chair cradle or crib by a single movement. All material used in the construction of the stand and chair is the best selected hardwood. Can be folded up when not in use and laid to one side. Height, ready for use, 4 feet 9 inches. You would not take three times the price and be without it after having used same. Shipping weight, 30 pounds. Price..................$3.45

Baby Walker, $1.80.
No. 6K7359 Our Combined Baby Walker, Table and Swing is constructed on a hardwood base, 22x22 inches, resting on casters so that the child can push from place to place about the room. The circular frame and table are supported above the base by three curved springs. The seat is suspended from the frame by adjustable straps, which allows the seat to be lowered and raised to fit the height of the child. The seat is always in position and never in the child's way when walking, so that the child can sit or walk about the room at his own pleasure. The material used in the construction is the best hardwood throughout, finished in natural color. The springs are of the best flat spring steel, ⅛ inch by ¾ inch wide. This walker allows the child the liberty of the entire room and does not confine him to one small area as the other style walkers. Shipping weight, about 8 pounds. Price..................$1.80

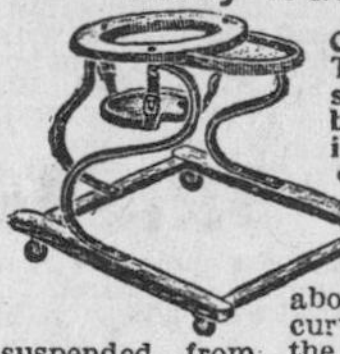

Baby Swings.
No. 6K7351 Baby Swing, has hardwood seat, 11 inches square, upholstered in cretonne; intended to be hung in a doorway; furnished with cotton rope and two hooks to hang it on; has no springs. Shipping weight, 3 pounds. Price..................37c

FISHING TACKLE AT GREATLY REDUCED PRICES

WE HAVE ON A GREAT MANY ARTICLES been able to reduce our prices on fishing tackle, such as rods, reels, lines and bait, and in some instances, where our price remains the same, we have greatly improved the article without making any change in the selling price. The various lines, reels, hooks, baits, etc., described and illustrated on the following pages, are all high class. They are guaranteed to give satisfaction, to be practical, and to possess meritorious features. We have studiously avoided any freak ideas in fishing tackle, being careful to handle only such articles as we, from our own experience, know will be absolutely satisfactory, and give the customer full returns for the money invested. Quality considered, no other house can compete with us in this line. Our business in fishing tackle exceeds that of any five mail order houses combined. It is the largest tackle business in the United States today selling direct to the consumer.

STEEL FISHING RODS AT LOWEST PRICES.

We call attention to the wonderfully low prices we are quoting on our line of guaranteed steel rods. The following steel rods are made specially for us under contract, and we guarantee them to be equal to any steel rods on the market, regardless of name, make or price. We guarantee each and every rod for one year against defective material or workmanship and will replace any joints broken through either of the above causes. These rods are made of special cold drawn steel tubing, finely finished with three coats of baked enamel, fitted with a swelled, solid ringed, cork grasp. The reel seat and butt cap are heavily nickel plated on copper. Special attention is paid to the balance and life of these rods. You will find our rods are livelier and balanced better than the heavy, stiff, club-like steel rods offered in competition at much higher prices.

Our 10-Foot Jointed Steel Fly Rod, $1.75.

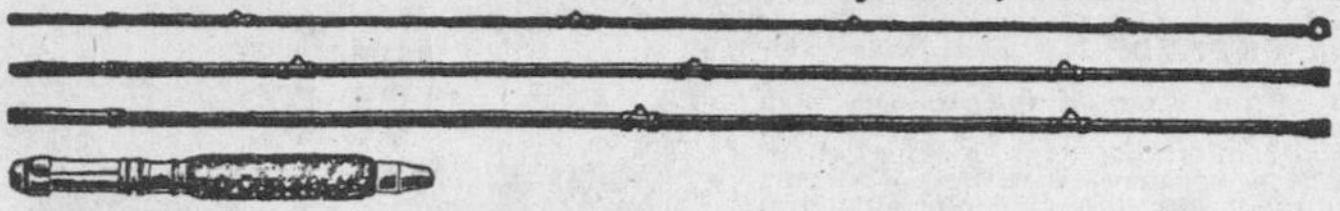

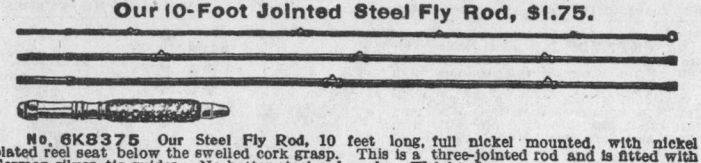

No. 6K8375 Our Steel Fly Rod, 10 feet long, full nickel mounted, with nickel plated reel seat below the swelled cork grasp. This is a three-jointed rod and is fitted with German silver tie guides. No better steel rod made. Weight, 9 ounces. Price.................. (If by mail, postage extra, 15 cents)................ $1.75

Our 8½-Foot Steel Bait Rod, $1.74.

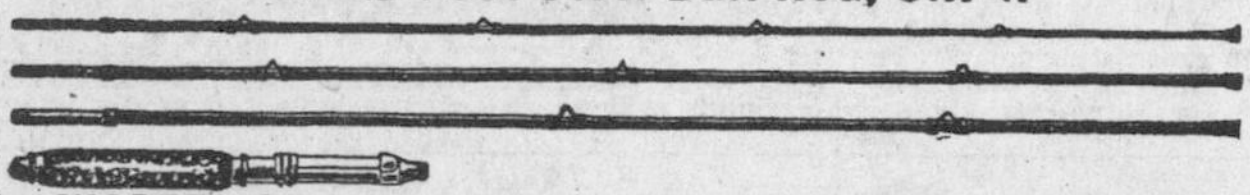

No. 6K8377 Our 8½-foot Steel Bait Casting Rod, three-jointed, cork grasp, with nickel plated reel seat above grasp, German silver standing guides, three-ring frictionless tip, enameled a deep black, put up in a neat cloth partition bag. Price.............. $1.74
If by mail, postage extra, 16 cents.

Our Expert 6½-Foot Steel Bass Casting Rod, $1.69.

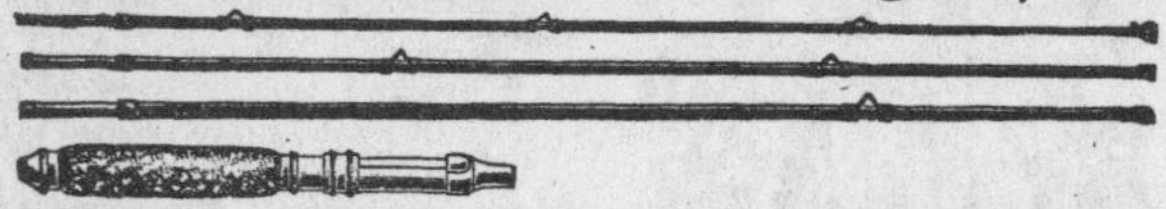

No. 6K8380 For $1.69 we offer this high quality 6½-foot, three-jointed, nickel mounted Bait Casting Rod, with solid nickel plated reel seat above cork grasp, joints fitted with German silver frictionless guides. An excellent lively rod for bait casting. We guarantee this rod to be equal in strength, balance and finish to any steel rod made. Put up in a cloth partition bag. Price............(If by mail, postage extra, 14 cents)............ $1.69

Kalamazoo Steel Bait Casting Rod, $2.58.

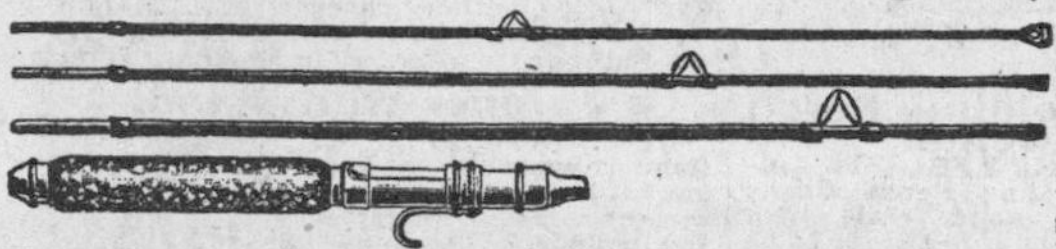

No. 6K8386 Our 5-foot Kalamazoo Bait Casting Rod, three joints, detachable cork grasp, fitted with solid nickel plated reel seat and finger hook, which enables you to obtain a firmer grasp on the rod and reel when playing your fish. This rod is fitted with large two-ring German silver guides, extra large agate tip. Put up in a cloth compartment bag. Weight, 8 ounces. Price.................. $2.58
If by mail, postage extra, 14 cents

Kalamazoo Full Agate Mounted, $3.70.

No. 6K8387 The same rod as above, 5 feet long, fitted with all agate guides. All guides on this rod have extra large agates and extra large agate tip, making this the finest bait casting rod on the market. Price....(If by mail, postage extra, 15 cents)........ $3.70

Our 5½-Foot Steel Bass Rod, Agate Guide and Tip, $2.87.

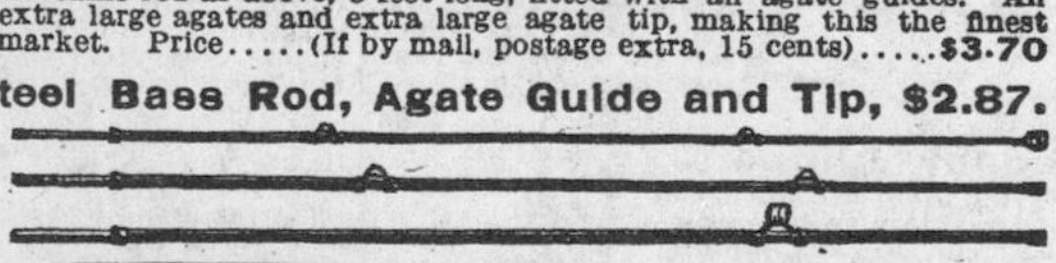

No. 6K8389 This rod is 5½ feet long, three joints, fitted with German silver trumpet guides, agate guide on first joint and agate tip. This Steel Bait Casting Rod cannot be excelled. The German silver trumpet guides and agate guide and tip permit the line to run free without friction, enabling you to get unequaled results in casting with this rod. Solid brass reel seat, finely nickel plated, cork grip. Rod is nicely tapered from butt to tip and workmanship and material are the best that money can buy. Length, 5½ feet. Weight, 8 ounces. Price.............. $2.87
If by mail, postage extra, 13 cents.

GENUINE BRISTOL STEEL RODS

The following three numbers and styles of rods are the genuine Bristol Steel Rods made by the Horton Manufacturing Co., of Bristol, Conn. Each and every rod bears the Bristol trade mark and is guaranteed by the Horton Manufacturing Co., against defective material or workmanship.

Bristol High Grade 10-Foot Jointed Steel Fly Rod, $3.54.

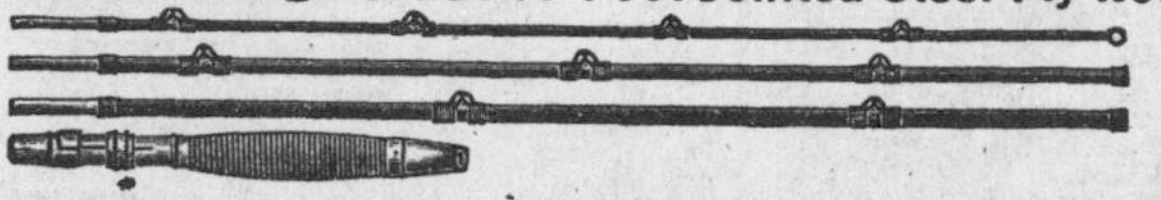

No. 6K8474 Genuine Bristol Steel Fly Rod, 10 feet long, full nickel mounted, with solid reel seat below the hand. This rod is jointed and fitted with two-ring German silver tie guides and one-ring German silver fly tip. Is made with three pieces and handle; each joint being 38 inches long. Does not telescope. Weight, 10½ ounces. With genuine celluloid wound handle. Price..................... $3.54
If by mail, postage extra, 20 cents.

The Genuine Expert 6½-Foot Steel Bass Rod, $3.25.

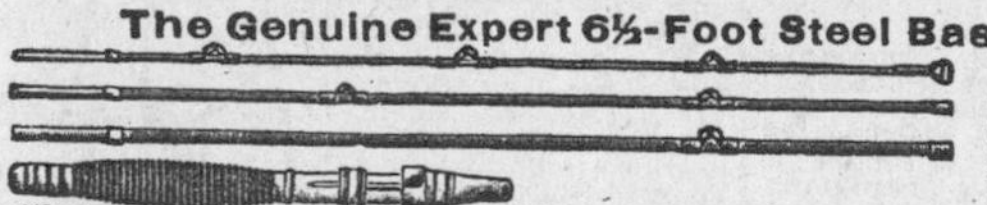

No. 6K8480 The Bristol Expert Steel Bait Casting Rod, 6½ feet long, full nickel mounted, with solid reel seat above the hand. This rod is jointed and fitted with two-ring German silver tie guides and German silver three-ring tip. It is made with three pieces and handle; the joints are 24 inches long. This is a fine rod for long casts and for heavy work. Does not telescope, but is jointed. Weight, 9½ ounces. With genuine celluloid wound handle. Price..........(If by mail, postage extra, 26 cents.)................ $3.25

The Kalamazoo Bristol Steel Casting Rod, $4.95.

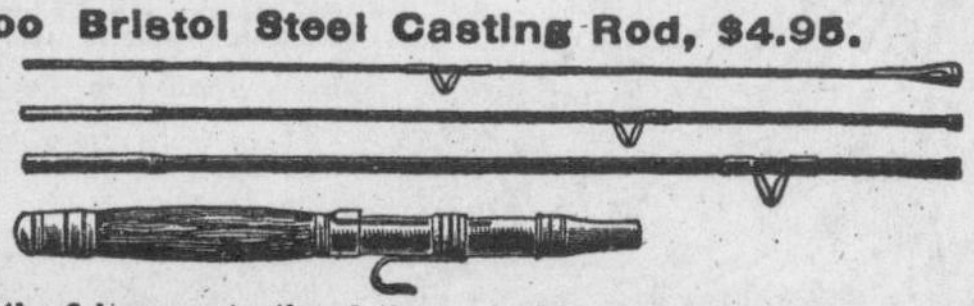

No. 6K8485 Guaranteed Genuine Bristol Steel Rod. This rod has a short cork grip, patent detachable finger hook, large polished German silver two-ring guides, and large solid agate double hole tip. The reel seat is so arranged that the reel is brought close to the grip, which, with the aid of the finger hook, enables the fisherman to thumb the reel without tiring his hand. The free running qualities of the large guides and tip are such that a novice can cast from 75 to 100 feet after a few trials. Length, 5¼ feet. Weight, 8¼ ounces. Price.................. $4.95
If by mail, postage extra, 15 cents.

Emergency Tip.

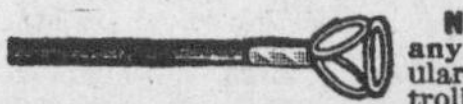

No. 6K8490 Our new German silver adjustable tip will fit any jointed steel fishing rod made, in case of accident to the regular tip joint or in place of the tip joint, to make a very stiff trolling rod. Can be carried in the vest pocket. About 2½ inches long. Every owner of a steel rod should have one. Price........................ 12c
If by mail, postage extra, 2 cents.

Steel Rod Shortener, 15c.

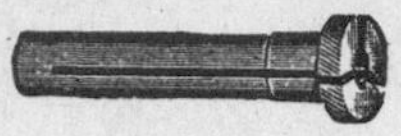

No. 6K8495 Our Gun Metal Finish Steel Rod Shortener. This shortener is made so it will fit in the grip of any jointed steel rod made and in doing so takes only the two smallest joints, leaving out the joint which fits in the grip. With this shortener you can make an 8½-foot rod 6 feet long. Price.............. 15c
If by mail, postage extra, 2 cents.

Japanese Two-Piece Rod with Zylonite Butt, 7 to 8 Feet, 45c.

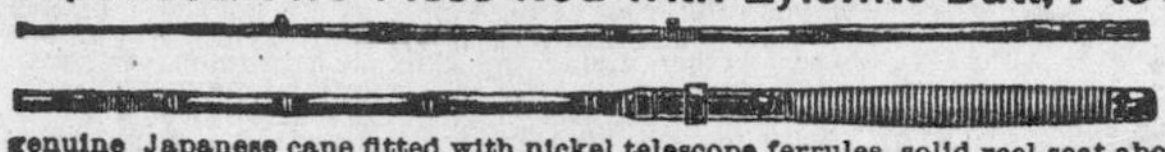

No. 6K8600 Japanese Two-Piece Rod, about 7½ feet long. Made of genuine Japanese cane fitted with nickel telescope ferrules, solid reel seat above the grip, black zylonite butt, line guides for line. The best rod on the market for the money. Weight, about 10 ounces. Price .... (If by mail, postage extra, 15 cents).............. 45c

Japanese Three-Piece Rod with Zylonite Butt, 8½ to 9 Ft., 57c.

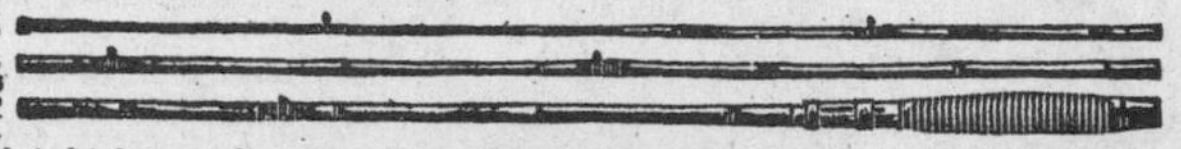

No. 6K8602 Japanese Three-Piece Rod, about 8½ to 9 feet long, made of genuine Japanese cane, nickel plated telescope ferrules, solid reel seat above the grip, black zylonite butt, line guides and tip for the line. The best 3-piece rod on the market for the money. Weight, about 13 ounces. Price.............(If by mail, postage extra, 17 cents).............. 57c

Japanese Four-Piece Rod with Zylonite Butt, 12 to 14 Ft., 84c.

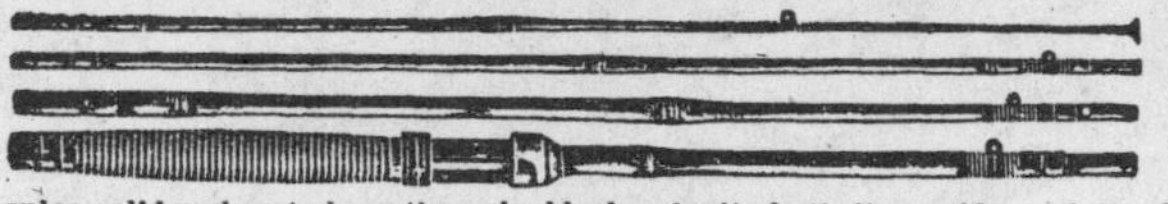

No. 6K8604 Japanese Four-Piece Rod, 12 to 14 feet long, made of genuine Japanese cane, fitted with nickel plated telescope ferrules, solid reel seat above the grip, black zylonite butt, line guides and tip for line. The best long rod on the market for the money. A good rod to fish from the shore. Weight, about 20 oz. Price.................. ...(If by mail, postage extra, 26 cents).................. 84c

Japanese Mottled Three-Piece Casting Rod, 92 Cents.

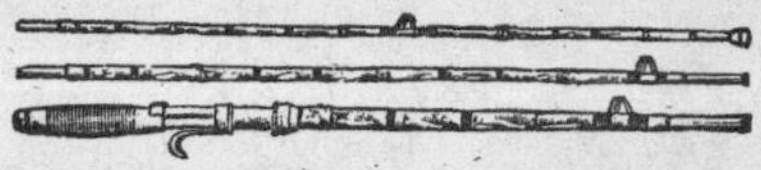

No. 6K8605 Our Japanese Three-Piece Bamboo Casting Rod is a handsome mottled rod, fitted with large Kalamazoo ring guides and tip, full nickel mounted throughout, with solid nickel plated reel seat and finger hook and cord wound grip. This rod is silk wrapped between the guides, which greatly strengthens the rod and adds to its appearance. Three joints, each 24 inches long, total length, 6 feet. Put up in neat partitioned cloth bag. Weight, about 10 ounces. Price..............(If by mail, postage extra, 14 cents).................... 92c

Calcutta Four-Piece Splashing Rod, 12 to 16 Feet, 85 Cents.

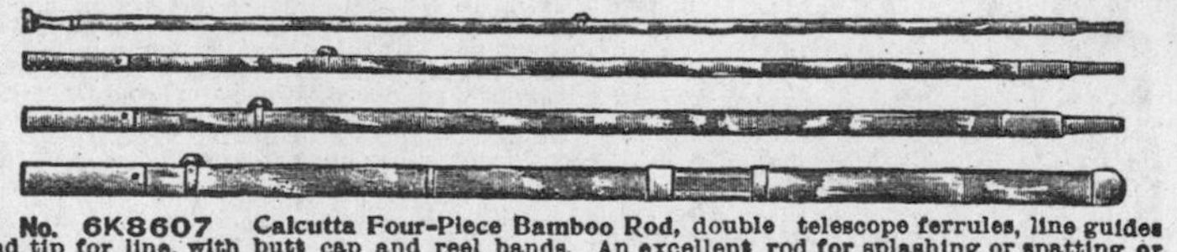

No. 6K8607 Calcutta Four-Piece Bamboo Rod, double telescope ferrules, line guides and tip for line, with butt cap and reel bands. An excellent rod for splashing or spatting or trolling among the weeds and lily pads. Length, 12 to 16 feet. Weight, about 2 pounds. Price .... (If by mail, postage extra, 37 cents).............. 85c

Calcutta Four-Piece Trunk Rod, About 8 Feet, 72 Cents.

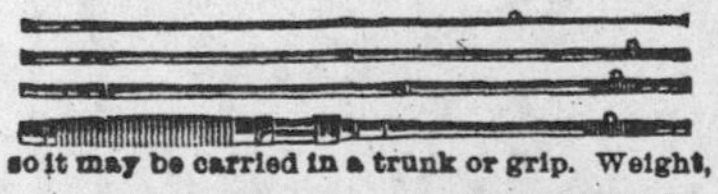

No. 6K8608 Calcutta Four-Piece Trunk Rod. 7½ to 8 feet long. Made of genuine mottled Calcutta cane, nickel plated telescope ferrules, strong line guides and tip, solid reel seat above the grip, zylonite butt, nickel plated trimmings. Each piece is 24 inches long, so it may be carried in a trunk or grip. Weight, 10 oz. Price....(Postage extra, 15 cents).. 72c

LANCEWOOD RODS.

There are about thirty to fifty styles of lancewood rods manufactured by the various makers, and each style necessitates a change in equipment, machinery, etc., and by reducing the number of styles of our lancewood rods, we are able to save the expense of these changes, which expense is necessarily added to the rods when so many styles are handled by one house. We have decided to reduce the number of styles of lancewood rods in order to handle a few.

St. Croix River Lancewood Fly Rod, 10 to 10½ Feet, 80 Cents.

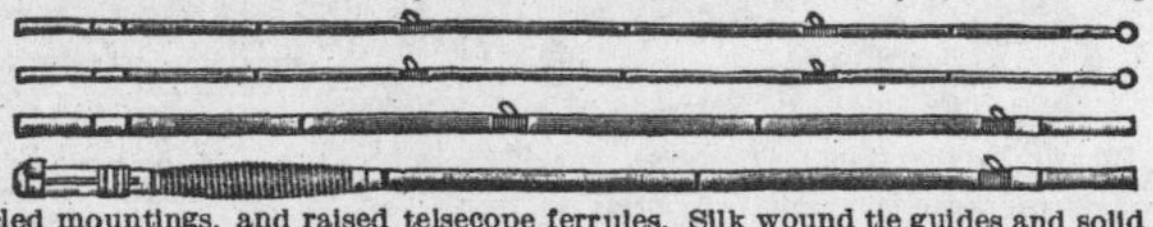

No. 6K8616 Our St. Croix River Lancewood Fly Rod, made in three pieces, with an extra tip, genuine lancewood throughout, nickeled mountings, and raised telescope ferrules. Silk wound tie guides and solid tip and silk wrapping at and between each mounting. Solid reel seat below hand. Zylonite corrugated grip. Length, about 10 to 10½ feet. Put up in neat partioned cloth bag. A fine looking rod. Weight, about 12 ounces. Price.(If by mail, postage extra, 18c). 80c

Genuine Lancewood Bait Casting Rod for 74 Cents.

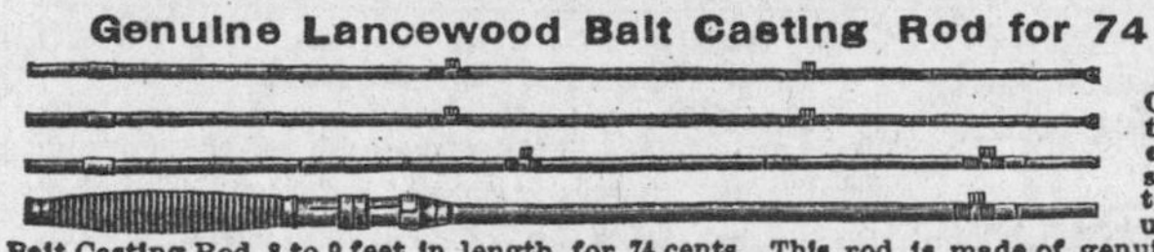

No. 6K8621 Owing to a contract we placed early in the season we are able to furnish a genuine Lancewood Bait Casting Rod, 8 to 9 feet in length, for 74 cents. This rod is made of genuine lancewood, 3 joints, with extra tip, has double shouldered nickel plated telescope ferrules, select silk wound round wire tie guides, which are guaranteed not to cut the lines, is nicely wrapped with silk, solid nickel plated reel seat above handsome corrugated zylonite grip. Weight, about 11 ounces. This rod is put up in a neat, partitioned cloth bag, is a fine looking rod, very strong and pliable, a regular $1.50 to $2.00 rod. Our price..........(If by mail, postage extra, 18 cents)........ 74c

Agate Tip fitted to this rod, 65 cents extra; Agate Guide fitted to this rod, 65 cents extra; Agate Tip and Guide, $1.20 extra over the stated price of the rod.

Our Lancewood Kalamazoo Casting Rod, $1.29.

No. 6K8622 This is a Two-Jointed 5½-Foot Genuine Lancewood Casting Rod. Fitted with double cork grip, nickel plated reel seat and finger hook, large Kalamazoo frictionless guides, extra large 20th century tip. This rod is nicely tapered from butt to tip, closely wrapped with silk of various colors, full nickel mounted with welded shouldered ferrules. An excellent bait casting rod at a low price, put up in a neat cloth bag. Weight, 9 ounces. Price......(If by mail, postage extra, 15 cents).....$1.29

OUR SPLIT BAMBOO RODS.

This illustration will give you, as near as it is possible, an idea of how a split bamboo rod is made. At first the bamboo cane is split in a sort of triangular shape, as shown in illustration, and glued together, forming a hexagonal shape. This is where the rod derives its name—Split Bamboo—the bamboo is split and glued together.

Our New Expert Split Bamboo Bass Rod, 5 Feet, $2.25.

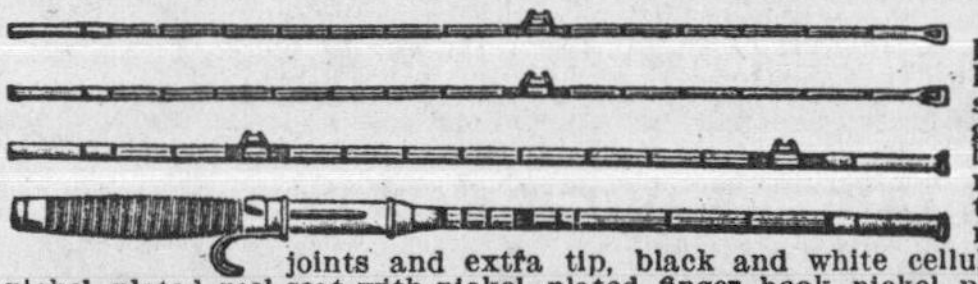

No. 6K8628 Our new Expert Bamboo Bait Casting Rod is made of specially selected, clear, straight grain, hand split bamboo, by one of the largest rod manufacturers in this country, employing the best skilled men. Five feet long three joints and extra tip, black and white celluloid corrugated grip, highly nickel plated reel seat with nickel plated finger hook, nickel plated butt cap, heavy nickel plated shouldered ferrules. The guides are German silver trumpets and double hole tip. The windings are of red and black silk, closely wound at short intervals, highly varnished. Put up in a neat, flannel, partitioned bag. This 5-foot rod is most used nowadays by expert fishermen. The above rod is generally sold for from $4.00 to $5.00; owing to the large quantity we have contracted for, we are able to sell this rod at about one-half the regular price. Price......(If by mail, postage extra, 14 cents).....$2.25

Agate tip fitted to this rod 65 cents extra, agate guide fitted to this rod, 65 cents extra; agate guide and tip fitted to this rod, $1.20 extra over the stated price of rod.

Our Climax Split Bamboo Bass Rod, 8 to 9 Feet, 72 Cents.

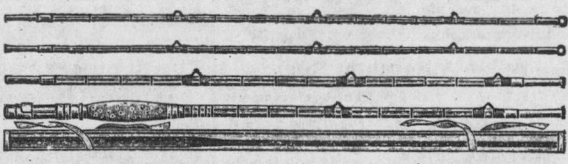

No. 6K8630

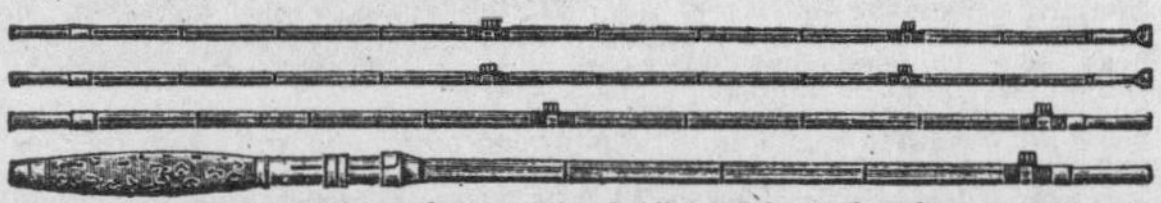

This rod is one that we are making a run on at an exceedingly low price and are positive the rod cannot be duplicated for twice the amount anywhere in the country. Split and glued bamboo bass rods, nickel plated, telescope ferrule, silk wound line guides and tip, with alternate wrappings, solid reel seat above the hand, nickeled mountings, three pieces, with an extra tip. Put up on a wooden form in a cloth bag. About 8 to 9 feet long. Weight, about 11 ounces. Price...(If by mail, postage extra, 22 cents).....72c

Agate tip fitted to this rod, 65 cents extra; agate guide fitted to this rod 65 cents extra; agate tip and guide fitted to this rod, $1.20 extra over stated price of this rod.

Our Acme Split Bamboo Fly Rod, 9½ to 10 Feet, 79 Cents.

No. 6K8634 Solid reel seat below the hand. This rod is the same quality as our Climax, except that the reel seat is below the hand for trout and light fishing. Has silk wound ring guides, with wrappings of fine silk every few inches; solid reel seat and nickel plated telescope ferrules and mountings. Length, about 9½ to 10 feet. Weight, about 11 ounces. Worth $1.75 anywhere. Comes in three pieces, and an extra tip, on a wood form in a cloth bag. Price.....79c
If by mail, postage extra, 22 cents.

The Willownook Split Bamboo Fly Rod, 9½ to 10 Feet, $1.43.

No. 6K8641 Solid reel seat below the hand. This rod is made of special selected bamboo, hexagonal in shape, snake guides with close wrappings of colored silk; full nickel plated telescope ferrules and mountings, cork wood form and in a neat bag. Length, about 9½ to 10 feet. A rod that retails at $3.00 in stores. Weight, 6 ounces. grasp. Put up in three pieces with an extra tip on a fine covered wood form and in a neat bag. Length, about 9½ to 10 feet. A rod that retails at $3.00 in stores. Weight, 6 ounces.
Price..........(If by mail, postage extra, 22 cents).....$1.43

Sunday Pocket Fly Rod, $2.79.

No. 6K8645 This is an ideal rod for the man who wants a rod he can carry in his pocket or in a small grip. The joints of this rod are but 13 inches long, made of select split bamboo, closely wound with two colors of silk, fitted with improved snake guides, welded ferrules, nickel plated reel seat, below the cork grip. With the heavy tip you can make a short six-piece rod, 6 feet long, by placing the heavy tip in the fifth joint. By using the light tip you can make a seven-piece rod, 7 feet long. This is a high grade rod in every respect, and while the joints are short they do not in any way injure the life and spring of the rod. The rod has as much life as any rod with joints twice as long. Put up in neat partitioned cloth bag.
Price...............(If by mail; postage extra, 10 cents)...............$2.79

Walton Hand Split Bamboo Fly Rod, 9½ to 10 Feet Long, $3.49.

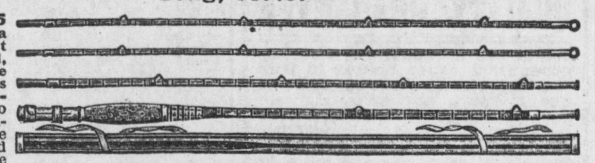

No. 6K8665 This is strictly a high grade Split Bamboo Fly Rod, and could not be bought for less than $7.00 elsewhere. Owing to the large quantity of these we have contracted for we are able to have them made at about half the cost. Our Walton Fly Rod is made from the very best selected split bamboo, split and glued together by hand by experienced rod makers. To give this rod extra strength, we had strips of cedar inlaid between the bamboo at the butt, giving this rod extra strength and beauty which you could not find in any other rod at double the price. The reel seat, butt cap, ferrules and snake guides are all German silver. The wrappings are of colored silk closely wound at short intervals. This rod has three coats of the best varnish to preserve the split bamboo and silk winding. Weight, about 7 ounces. Very lively and strongly built. If you want an up to date fly rod, order one of these. Has cork grasp, three joints, with an extra tip. Put up in a handsome covered wood form and in a flannel bag. Price...............(If by mail, posatge extra, 20 cents)...............$3.49

Eight in One Combination Lancewood Rod, Reduced to $2.45.

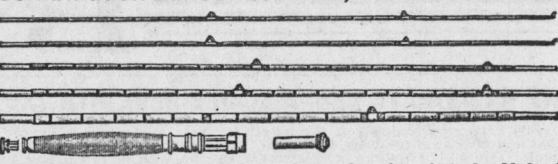

No. 6K8623 The best combination rod on the market. You can make eight different rods of this rod, can place the reel seat above or below the handle, and with the aid of the shortener carried in the butt of rod, can make a short, medium or long bait casting rod or a fly rod, as desired. Made of the best grade lancewood solid nickel reel seat, nickel mounted throughout, fitted with frictionless guides, beautifully wrapped at close intersections with silk. Comes put up four joints and extra fly tip, making five joints in all, with detachable cord wound grip, in a neat partitioned cloth bag. Price...............$2.45

If by mail, postage extra, 20 cents.

TACKLE OUTFITS.

We offer these complete tackle outfits at lower prices than ever before. We have been able, by reason of the enormous increase in our business, to reduce the cost of these outfits, and we are offering them to you at lower prices than we have ever sold them before, prices so low that were you to buy the various articles separately, you could not duplicate any outfit for less than twice the price we ask for the complete outfit. These outfits are practical. They are intended as a convenience to our customers, as every outfit is complete in itself and the various items in the outfit are all high class and guaranteed to give full satisfaction.

Our Tackle Outfit, Reduced to 92 Cents.

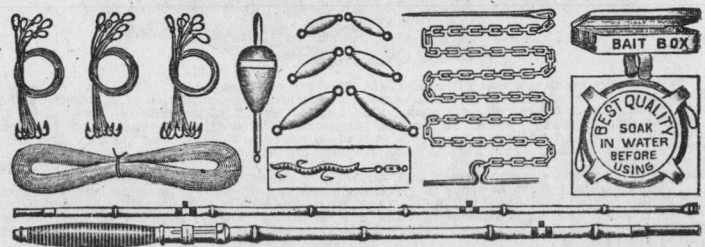

No. 6K8673 An excellent outfit for still fishing for perch, blue gills, rock bass, etc. This outfit is suitable for either shore or boat use, and consists of a high grade two-piece Japanese bamboo rod 7½ feet long, nickel plated ferrules and handsome nickel plated brass reel seat, fine black scored zylonite grasp, with nickel plated butt cap, 84 feet of braided line, 1½ dozen gut hooks, 3 ft. gut leader, soft rubber angle worm, ½ dozen adjustable sinkers, fancy adjustable float, strong nickel plated chain, fish stringer with pointed needle, patent combination bait and hook box to be attached to butt end of rod to carry hook in when not in use without taking hooks from line, all complete.
Price................(If by mail, postage extra, 42 cents)....................92c

A Complete Tackle Outfit.   Reduced Price, $2.24.

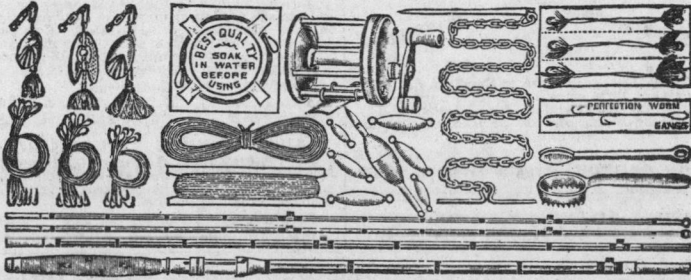

No. 6K8726 This is a first class outfit, one that will please any fisherman, no matter how critical. Same consists of a split bamboo bait casting rod, 8 feet long, three joints and extra tip, cork grip, anti-friction tie guides, mounted wood frame in cloth bag, excellent 60-yard wide spool quadruple reel, fitted with click and drag, full nickel plated fancy bone balance handle; 25 yards of hard silk braided casting line, one linen line suitable for trolling or still fishing, one and a half dozen assorted gut hooks, three popular attractive artificial baits, half a dozen trout flies, half a dozen assorted sinkers, one 3-foot double gut leader, one worm gang, one chain fish stringer, one fancy float, one fish scaler, one disgorger; all put up in a durable pasteboard box. This outfit, if the items were purchased separately, would cost about $3.75. Our price for above outfit as stated.......(If by mail, postage extra, 48 cents).....$2.24

Our Complete Bait Casting Outfit.   Now Only $5.98.

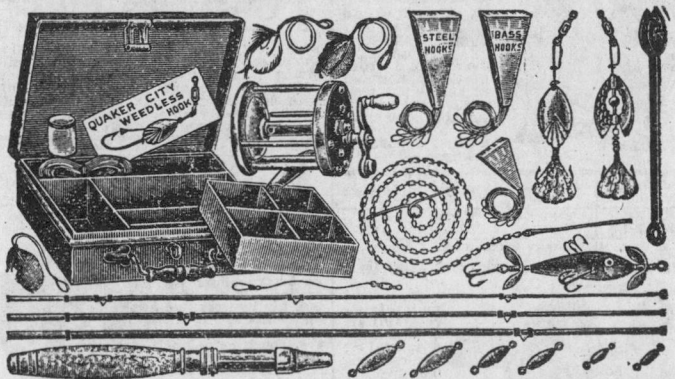

No. 6K8683 This is a complete outfit suitable for bait casting or trolling, and contains everything necessary for catching pickerel, pike, bass and other game fish. Everything in this outfit is best quality, and guaranteed to give satisfaction. This outfit consists of one 6½-foot 3-jointed steel casting rod fitted with cork grasp, nickel plated reel seat, frictionless line guides, one expert rubber plate jeweled quadruple reel, one of the finest reels made, 50 yards Italian silk bass casting line, 25 yards highest quality hard braided linen line, 1½ dozen assorted best quality double gut hooks, three most popular spoon baits, one wooden minnow, one disgorger, one chain fish stringer, ½ dozen assorted sinkers, one 3-foot double gut leader, one worm gang. This tackle is packed in one of our best metal tackle boxes, 9½ inches long, 3½ inches high and 7 inches wide, fitted with four compartments and one large compartment for reel, extra tray with four additional compartments. This is unquestionably the greatest value in a tackle outfit ever offered.
Price, outfit complete .....(Weight, 4½ pounds. Cannot be sent by mail.)...$5.98

BOATS

WE ILLUSTRATE AND DESCRIBE HEREWITH three steel boats which represent the highest types of steel boats made. STEEL BOATS are so well known now that it is hardly necessary to dwell at any length on their superior qualities. We might only say that a steel boat never rusts, leaks, warps, or rots; it outlasts three or four ordinary wood boats; it does not require a boat house; it can be used in rough and rocky water, where it would be impossible to use a wood boat; and what is worthy of greatest consideration is that it will absolutely not sink.

OUR DUCK BOATS, as well as our rowboats, are fitted with patent, steel, air-tight chambers which we positively guarantee to float the boat as well as all occupants in case the boat is capsized, although the construction of the boats is such that they can only be capsized through deliberate carelessness, and they are guaranteed to ride any sea with perfect safety.

OUR WHITE FLYER ROWBOAT is shipped direct from our factory at Detroit, Mich., and the Bustle and "Get There" Duck Boats are shipped from Salem, Ohio. The prices we quote are F. O. B. factory.

OUR 14-FOOT WHITE FLYER SQUARE STERN STEEL CLINKER BOAT, $27.50.

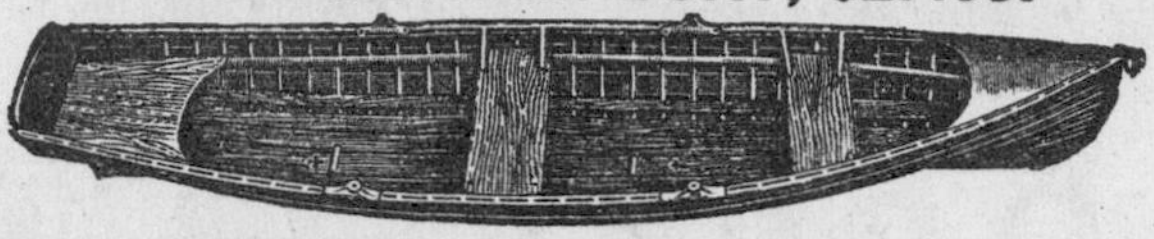

This is the ideal rowboat for high class delivery or family use. This boat embodies the maximum of strength, capacity and safety, and at our price of $27.50 is undoubtedly the greatest value ever offered in a rowboat. The hull of this boat is made of Apollo steel of special construction; the plates, or strakes, run parallel with the keel, and are guaranteed never to buckle; the seams are positively warranted never to open or break loose. This boat never requires calking. It is always dry and ready for use. It will never leak, snag, warp, crack, or wear loose, and will last a lifetime. The bow, stern and seats of this boat are made of cypress, the gunwales are of oak, all finely finished in the natural wood.

The illustration given conveys to you but a faint idea of the symmetrical and beautiful lines of this boat. It glides through the water with one-third less friction than a wood boat, and being fitted with air chambers at either end, it cannot sink. The hull of this boat is painted with white pegamoid, and imported waterproof paint, the same as that used by the United States navy.

SPECIFICATIONS—Length, 14 feet; width amidship, 43½ inches; depth amidship, 14 inches; height of bow, 22 inches; height of stern, 24 inches; weight about 150 pounds; crated for shipment, about 200 pounds.

No. 6K8700 Price, including one pair of oars and oarlocks.......... $27.50
Rudder for this boat, extra.......... 1.75

THE "GET THERE" DUCK BOAT.

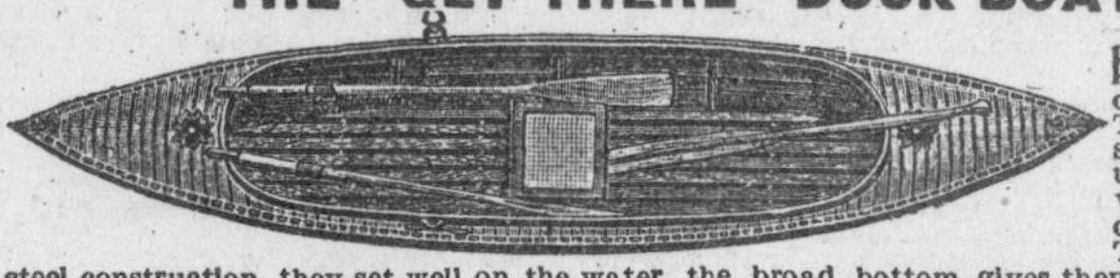

These boats are probably the best known duck boats on the market. There are thousands of them in use, and they invariably give first class satisfaction. These boats are of steel construction, they set well on the water, the broad bottom gives them great stability, and being fitted with air chambers at both ends, they are absolutely safe. Painted a dead grass color. The steel "Get There" Duck Boat will outlast any four or five wood boats, they are safer and easier to handle as they glide through the water with one-third less friction than a wood boat. Our price of $20.00 includes the boat, complete with hardwood bottom board, removable seat, one pair of oars and oarlocks, and one long or short paddle.

SPECIFICATIONS—Length, 14 feet; beam, 36 inches; height to top of coaming, 12½ inches; height amidship, 10 inches; cock pit, 9 feet long and 30 inches wide; weight, about 100 pounds; weight, packed for shipment, 120 pounds. Shipped direct from factory at Salem, Ohio.

No. 6K8703 Price, including one pair of oars and oarlocks, and one short or long paddle.......... $20.00

THE BUSTLE DUCK BOAT.

$27.00

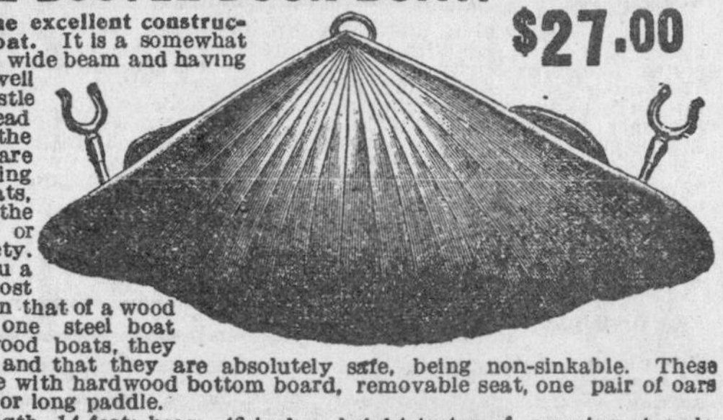

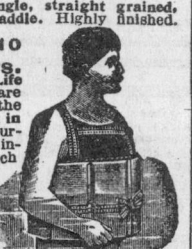

This boat is of the same excellent construction as the "Get There" Boat. It is a somewhat larger boat, having an extra wide beam and having air chambers at the sides as well as at both ends. The Bustle steel Boats are painted a dead grass color. On account of the wide beam, these boats are particularly adapted as fishing boats as well as hunting boats, as the wide beam enables the user to stand up and cast or shoot with perfect safety. One Bustle Boat will last you a lifetime. While the initial cost of a steel boat is higher than that of a wood boat, bear in mind that one steel boat will outlast three or four wood boats, they require no special attention, and that they are absolutely safe, being non-sinkable. These boats are furnished complete with hardwood bottom board, removable seat, one pair of oars and oarlocks, and one short or long paddle.

SPECIFICATIONS—Length, 14 feet; beam, 46 inches; height to top of coaming at ends, 12½ inches; height amidship, 10 inches; cock pit, 9 feet long and 30 inches wide; weight, about 120 pounds; packed for shipment, 140 lbs. Shipped direct from factory at Salem, Ohio.

No. 6K8704 Price.......... $27.00

NORTHERN FIR COPPER TIPPED OARS.

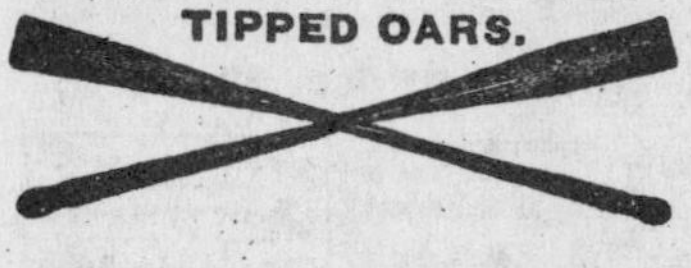

These Oars are made of Northern fir. They weigh but little more than spruce, have greater uniform strength and are far lighter than ash. They are guaranteed to be selected straight grain, well turned and finished.

No. 6K8708 Length given is length of each oar.

Length	6 ft.	6½ ft.	7 ft.	7½ ft.	8 ft.	8½ ft.
Price, pair	92c	98c	$1.07	$1.14	$1.22	$1.30

Ash Oars, Copper Tipped.

Our Ash Oars are made of the best selected straight grain stock. There are no better oars made. We do not handle seconds, or what is known as culls, we handle only selected oars, and owing to our enormous purchases we are able to sell for less money than you can buy inferior oars from other dealers. One pair of 6-foot oars weighs about 6 pounds, and a pair of 8½-foot oars weighs about 13 pounds. The length given is the length of each oar.

No. 6K8711 Copper tipped

Length	6 ft.	7 ft.	8 ft.	8½ ft.
Price, per pair	$1.06	$1.26	$1.42	$1.50

Copper Tipped Spruce Oars.

No. 6K8713 Genuine Adirondack Spruce Oars. Lighter than ash oars and strong; copper tipped. Weight per pair, 6 foot, 5½ pounds; 7 foot, 6 pounds.

Length	6 feet	7 feet	8 feet
Price, per pair	$1.12	$1.32	$1.46

Spruce Paddles.

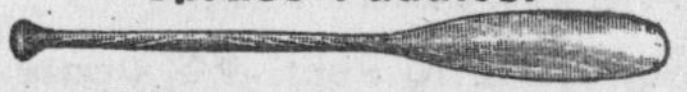

No. 6K8712 Single, straight grained, first quality Spruce Paddle. Highly finished. None better made.
Price, each.... $1.10

Life Preservers.

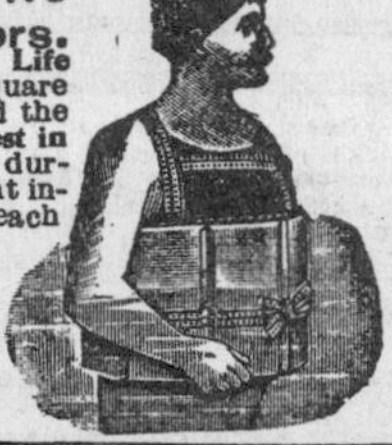

No. 6K8720 Life Belts, made of square blocks of cork around the body. One of the best in the market; safe and durable. The government inspector's stamp on each one. Weight, 7 lbs.
Price.... $1.20

NOTICE—We do not use granulated cork in our life preservers—we use solid block cork only.

Oar Locks.

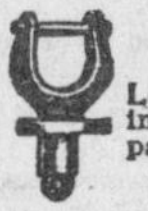

No. 6K8714 North River Oar Lock, galvanized malleable iron, 2 inches between horns. Weight, per pair, about 3 pounds.
Price, per pair.......... 19c

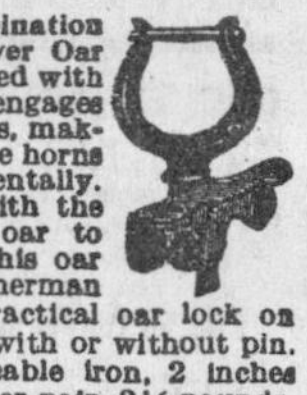

No. 6K8716 Combination Side Plate and North River Oar Lock. This oar lock is fitted with a spring, which spring engages with the shank of the horns, making it impossible to pull the horns out of the socket accidentally. This feature, together with the pin which attaches the oar to the oar lock, commends this oar lock to every boatman, fisherman and hunter as the most practical oar lock on the market; can be used with or without pin. Made of galvanized malleable iron, 2 inches between horns. Weight, per pair, 2½ pounds.
Price, per pair.......... 32c

OUR POSITION AS THE GREATEST MERCHANDISING INSTITUTION IN THE WORLD is emphasized by the wonderful REDUCTION IN PRICES which we have been able to make on thousands of articles quoted in this catalogue.

Double Multiplying Reel, 35 Cents.

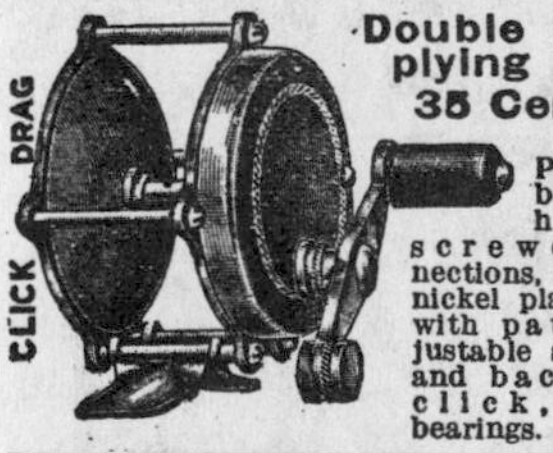

Raised Pillar, balance handle, screwed connections, brass and nickel plated reel, with patent adjustable slide drag and back sliding click, polished bearings.

Catalogue No.	Holds No. 4 Line	Finish	Price
6K8743	40 yards	Nickel	35c
6K8744	60 yards	Nickel	40c

If by mail, postage extra, 8 and 9 cents.

Rubber Cap Reel, 45 Cents.

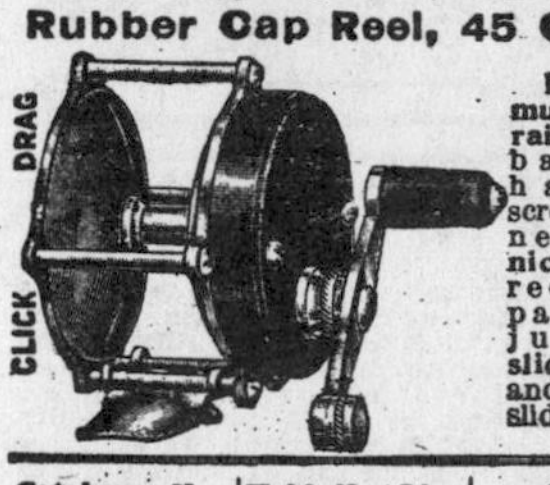

Double multiplying raised pillar, balance handle, screwed connections, nickel plated reels, with patent adjustable slide drag and back sliding click.

Catalogue No.	Holds No. 4 Line	Price
6K8746	40 yards	45c
6K8747	60 yards	50c

If by mail, postage extra, 8 and 10 cents.

Our Ideal Quadruple Reel.

94c

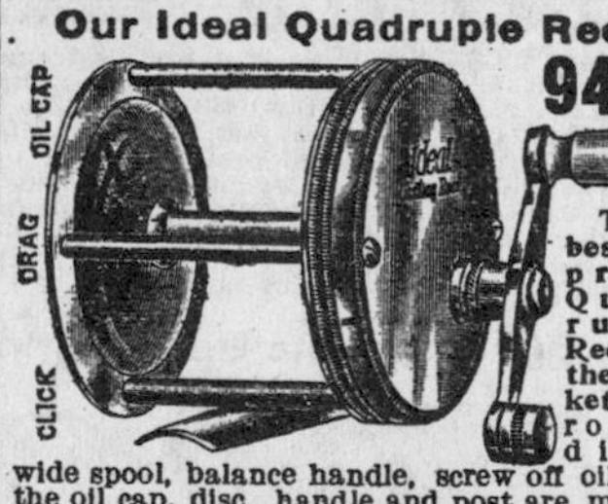

The best low price Quadruple Reel on the market, has round disc, wide spool, balance handle, screw off oil cap, the oil cap, disc, handle and post are milled, giving it a handsome appearance; is fitted with steel axle and steel pinion, also fitted with click and drag, making it a very durable, handsome reel; each reel is carefully examined, guaranteed to run absolutely true.

Catalogue No.	Holds No. 4 Line	Price
6K8750	40 yards	$0.94
6K8751	60 yards	1.10
6K8752	80 yards	1.20

If by mail, postage extra, 11 to 13 cents.

Carlton Ideal Reels.

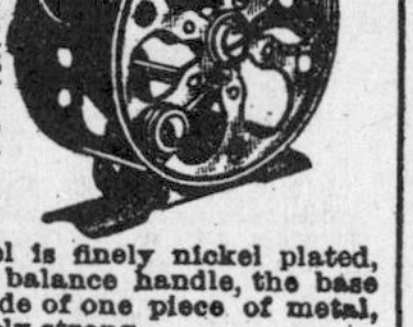

No. 6K8753 The Carlton Ideal Reel is an ideal reel for fly casting. It is doubtless the lightest reel on the market. It is a single action reel, but the construction of the spool enables this reel to reel in the line as fast as a multiplying reel, also thoroughly dries the line, as the air can easily get at same. The reel is finely nickel plated, fitted with click and balance handle, the base and side plate are made of one piece of metal, making the reel doubly strong.
Price, 80 yards.......... $0.84
Price, 120 yards, large size.......... 1.20
If by mail, postage extra, 8 and 12 cents.

THE SURPRISINGLY LOW REDUCED PRICES prevailing in this catalogue mean greater savings to our customers than ever before.

Kelso Automatic Reel.

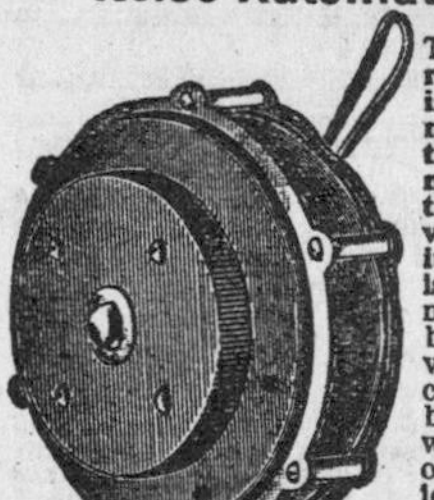

No. 6K8754 The best automatic reel made, possessing all the improvements embodied in the various automatic reels in addition to various valuable features of its own. This reel is made of aluminum and weighs but 7 ounces. Is very simple in construction, has but few parts and will not get out of order. This is an ideal real for fly casting; can also be used for trolling. (Cannot be used for bait casting). A slight pressure on the brake causes reel to rapidly take in the line, keeping the line taut at all times. Will handle 100 feet of line with one winding. Spool will hold 100 yards of No. 6 or H line. The tension of the mainspring is automatically thrown of, which relieves the wear and strain on the spring and allows the line to unwind, even if the spring is wound up tight. This reel is 3½ inches in diameter, 1 inch wide. Price.......... $3.28
If by mail, postage extra, 15 cents.

QUALITY GUARANTEE

WE HAVE A SYSTEM of securing goods from other houses in this city and elsewhere to compare in quality with our own, and we have invariably found where a similar article is offered by any other house at as low or lower a price than ours, it is at a great sacrifice in quality.
REMEMBER, if any other dealers appear to sell any article at as low a price as we, we challenge them on the question of quality, and if you do not find our quality far superior at the same price, we want you to return the goods at our expense.

The Kentucky Pattern Jeweled Reel.

$3.00

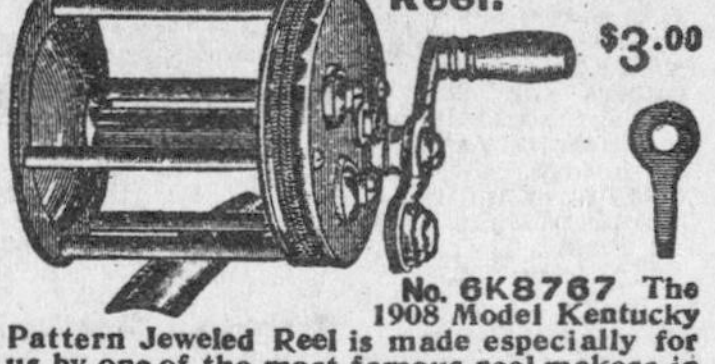

No. 6K8767 The 1908 Model Kentucky Pattern Jeweled Reel is made especially for us by one of the most famous reel makers in the country. Greatly improved. This reel is full quadrupled, 80-yard size, extra wide 1⅛-inch spool, steel pinion and steel axle. The pinion and gear wheel are securely bridged and locked so as to obviate all lost motion and to insure smooth, frictionless running qualities not found in reels that sell for twice its price. The pillars extend clear through the front and rear plates, thus insuring greater strength and rigidity in this reel than found in any other reel of the same pattern. The click and drag are on the handle side and are of an improved positive type. The steel axle bears on jewels at either end, which are fitted by hand with the same degree of accuracy as is employed in fitting jewels in a watch. The mechanism of this reel is quickly accessible by removing two small screws, for which purpose a small flat steel screwdriver (which can be carried on a key ring) is furnished with each reel. Reel is beautifully finished in nickel plate throughout, screw off agate oil caps are nicely knurled, fitted with handsome large size bone balance handle and improved cross blade. Each reel put up in neat box, complete with screwdriver, as shown in the illustration.
Price . . . (Postage extra, 13c.) . . . $3.00

One Drop Never Leak Oiler.

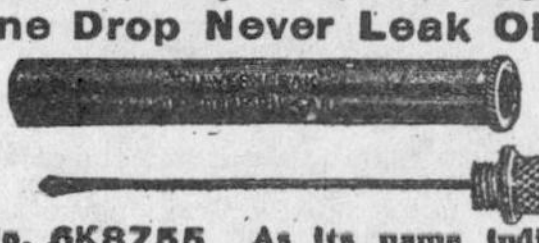

No. 6K8755 As its name indicates, gives one drop only and just where wanted. Will not leak. No waste and no wiping of superfluous oil. Can be carried in pocket or case without soiling other articles. 3½ inches long.
Price, each . . . (Postage extra, 2c.) . . . 9c
Oils suitable for reels quoted on page 741.

The Beaver Quadruple Reel.

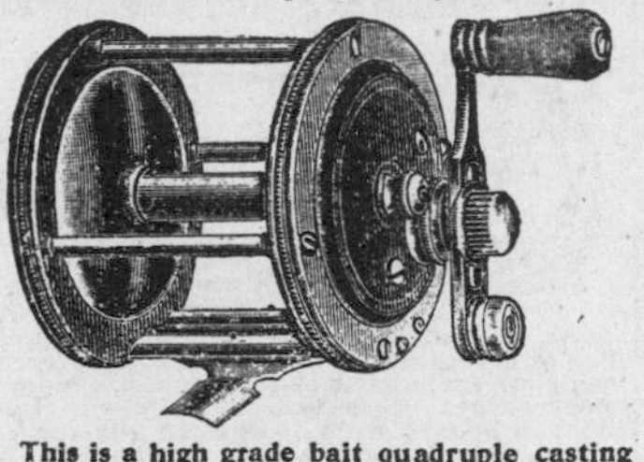

This is a high grade bait quadruple casting reel of an improved type. Made one size only, 80 yards, wide spool pattern, shouldered pillars, pure black rubber cap, heavy nickel plated discs, improved cross plate, extra large bone extension handle. This extension handle gives you greater purchase and enables you to better handle large gamy fish. Fitted with strong, positive, new style click, steel pinion and axle, bridged over gear; wheel, handle, post and screw off oil caps nicely knurled. The reel is fitted and adjusted with the precision of a high grade watch and is one of the handsomest, most up to date, easy running reels on the market.

No. 6K8772 Plain bearing. 80 yards. Price $2.58

No. 6K8773 Jeweled bearing. 80 yards. Price $3.05

If by mail, postage extra, 12 cents.

The Expert Jeweled Bearing Rubber Plate Metal Bound Quadruple Reel.

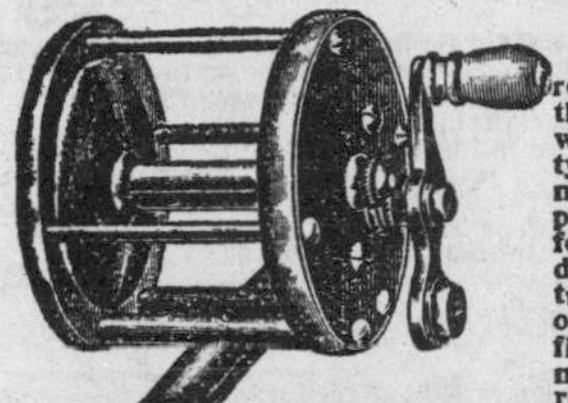

These reels are of the latest widespool type, are made especially for us under contract. It is one of the finest reels made, a reel that would ordinarily sell for twice the price we are asking for same. Rubber plates incased with nickel bands, jeweled bearings, the jewels being accurately adjusted to the axle; has handsome white bone milled balance handle; is bridged to prevent action from becoming loose, insuring smooth running qualities; gears are carefully cut and adjusted by experts; finely finished, being extra heavily nickel plated; new style cross blade, fitted with click and drag. Made in 60 and 80-yard sizes.

No. 6K8775 60-yard size. Price .. $1.88

No. 6K8776 80-yard size. Price .. 2.15

If by mail, postage extra, 11 cents.

The Shakespeare Service Takeapart Reel.

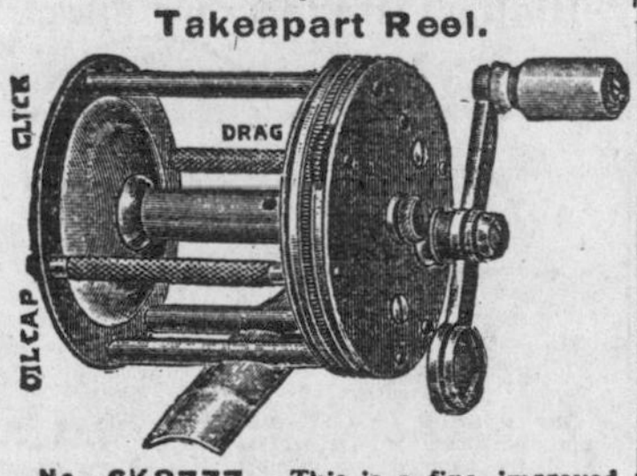

No. 6K8777 This is a fine improved model reel, made with the celebrated Shakespeare take down feature, which is the simplest take down on the market. When taken down there are only three parts; no small pieces or screws to become lost. Can be taken apart in a few seconds and as quickly put together without the aid of any tools by giving the two knurled pillars in front and back a few turns. This reel is handsomely finished in nickel and is a full quadruple. Fancy knurled screw off oil caps, steel pinion and steel axle. The click is on the left side, the adjustable graduated drag is on the top of the right disc, as shown in the illustration. These reels are built for service, are very strong and rigid and possess free running qualities. Extra long spool. Weight, about 7 ounces.

Price, 80-yard size $3.60

If by mail, postage extra, 11 cents.

The Shakespeare Standard Takeapart Reel.

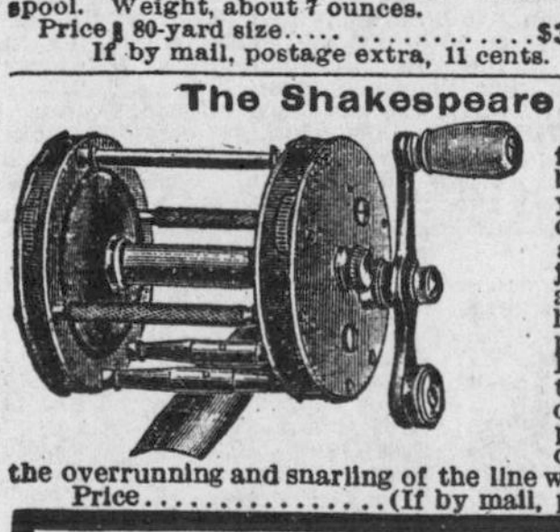

No. 6K8778 This reel held the world's record for long distance bait casting. Made with the celebrated Shakespeare take down feature, which enables you to take the reel apart in a few seconds' time and as quickly put it together again. When taken apart there are but three parts, no screws to get lost or out of adjustment. This is a beautifully finished reel, made as accurately and carefully as a watch; hard rubber heads mounted between turned plates, heavily silver plated and oxidized on hard drawn rolled brass with English silver steel journal and pinions. Is fitted with the harmonic click and adjustable drag, both being operated by knurled wheels placed in a convenient position on the edge of a head and end plates, full quadruple. The adjustable graduated drag prevents the overrunning and snarling of the line when casting. Extra long spool pattern, 80-yard size.

Price ....(If by mail, postage extra, 11 cents.) $5.40

THE SURPRISINGLY LOW REDUCED PRICES PREVAILING IN THIS CATALOGUE MEAN GREATER SAVINGS TO OUR CUSTOMERS THAN EVER BEFORE.

The New Tri-Part Reel.

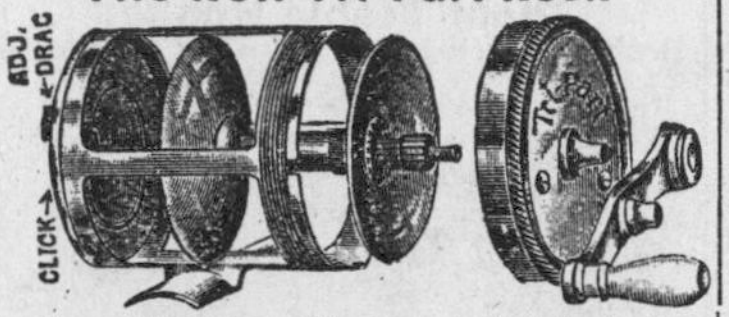

No. 6K8780 The latest, best and simplest takeapart reel on the market, wide spoon, 80 yards, quadruple with German silver spool, very light. No screwdriver required to take this reel apart. This reel is taken apart in a few seconds by simply unscrewing the metal bands on the right hand side and the spool can be lifted out for cleaning or taking a tangle out of your spool. The pivots of this reel are turned on the solid steel shaft which extends the entire length of the spool. The bronzed gear wheel is securely braced and bridged. This reel is fitted with a special friction cap, enabling the fisherman to regulate the speed of the reel and prevent back lashing. This reel is of a wide spool pattern, made by one of the oldest and best known reel makers in the country. Beautifully finished in nickel, fitted with large white bone handle, and with strong and positive click. We guarantee it to be equal in strength, material, workmanship and smooth running qualities to any reel offered at twice the price. One size only, 80 yards.

Price $3.35

If by mail, postage extra, 14 cents.

FISH LINES.

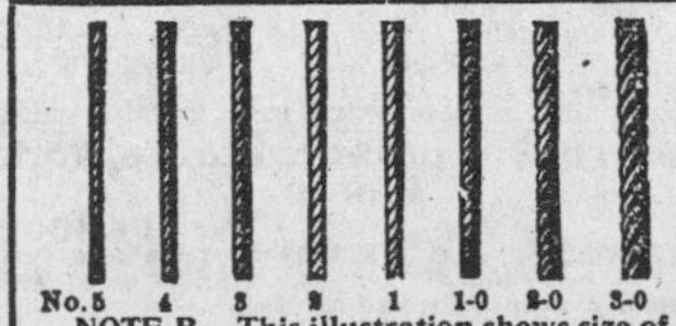

NOTE B. This illustration shows size of braided lines as near as it is possible to print sizes or to illustrate them. Order by catalogue number and state size you wish.

Excellent Braided Line.

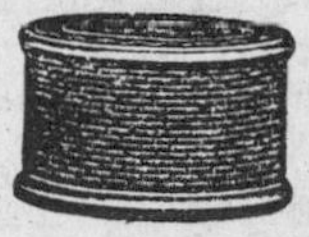

No. 6K8785 Excellent Braided Linen Finished Line. This is a beautifully mottled hard braided line, very strong, put up 50 yards on a nicely finished spool, comes in three sizes. Be sure to state size wanted. Sizes 4 5 6

Per spool 17c 17c 17c

If by mail, postage extra, 4 cents.

Our Rival Waterproof Mixed Silk Line.

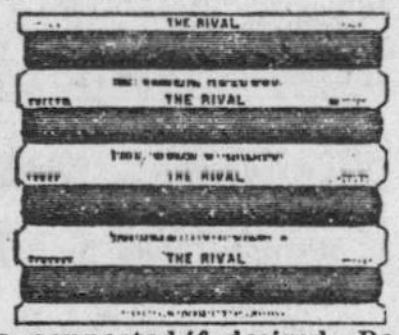

No. 6K8788 This is an excellent mixed silk mottled line, which has been waterproofed. A fine strong line at a very low price, good for fly casting, trolling or still fishing. Comes 25 yards on a card. Can be furnished 100 yards connected if desired. Be sure to state size wanted.

Sizes	3	4	5
Price, per 25 yards	16c	16c	16c
Per 100 yards connected			62c

If by mail, postage extra, 3 cents.

Braided Cotton Lines.

No. 6K8796 Braided Cotton Lines, put up 84 feet in a coil, strong and durable; made of best Sea Island cotton, guaranteed first quality and even strength. Mention size wanted. See note B for sizes.

Size, Nos.	5	4	3	2	1	1-0	2-0	3-0
Price, per coil	6c	6c	6c	7c	8c	10c	11c	12c

If by mail, postage extra, 2 to 4 cents. each. The No. 5 is tested to 10 pounds, the No. 3-0 is tested to 40 pounds pull. All others are tested in proportion.

THE SURPRISINGLY LOW REDUCED PRICES prevailing in this catalogue mean greater savings to our customers than ever before.

THREE QUALITIES.

Every manufacturer of cotton and linen lines makes three qualities — first, second and third. We handle only the first quality in all our fish lines, which are guaranteed to have 33⅓ per cent to 75 per cent more strength and smoother finish than the second and third grades sold by other dealers at apparently competitive prices. Quality considered, our prices are by far the lowest.

Hard Braided Linen Lines.

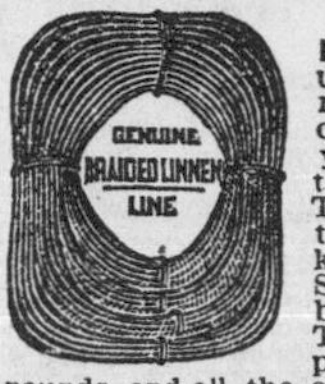

No. 6K8798 Hard Braided Linen Lines put up 25 yards in a coil and may be had four coils connected, making 100 yards. Much stronger than twisted or laid lines. The best bass and pickerel trolling line in the market. Made from best Scotch linen fiber evenly braided and well finished. The No. 5 is tested to 25 pounds; the No. 2-0 to 50 pounds, and all the other sizes are tested in proportion. See illustration Note B for sizes. State size wanted. Order by catalogue number and size number.

Size, Nos.	5	4	3	2	1	1-0	2-0
Per coil	12c	13c	13c	15c	15c	17c	18c

If by mail, postage extra, 2 to 4 cents.

NOTE C. This illustration shows as near as possible the size of our silk lines. It is impossible to show the exact size by illustration.

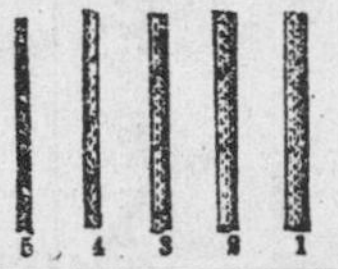

Braided Bronze Wire Fishing Line. Something Entirely New in Fishing Lines.

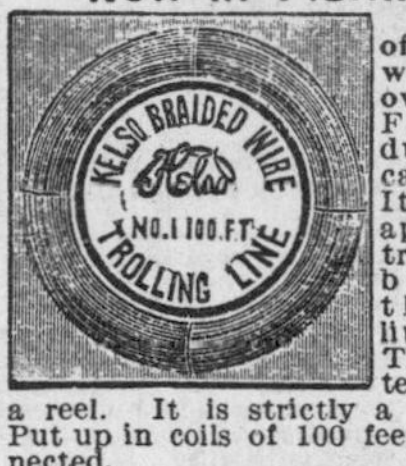

This line is made of very fine bronze wire, closely braided over a silk center. For strength and durability this line cannot be excelled. It is particularly adapted for deep water trolling, no sinker being required, as the weight of this line will sink the bait. This line is not intended to be used on a reel. It is strictly a hand trolling line. Put up in coils of 100 feet, three coils connected.

No. 6K8802

Price per coil of 100 feet 50c

If by mail, postage extra, per coil, 4 cents.

Our Famous Braided Oil Silk Lines in Coils.

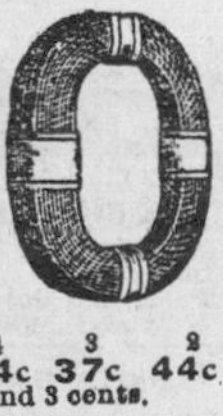

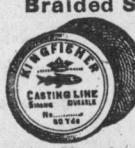

No. 6K8810 Fine Quality Braided Oil Silk Lines, put up 25 yards in a coil and may be had four coils connected, making 100 yards. This is a very strong line, closely braided, of the finest silk, oiled, making it a waterproof line; soft and pliable. A good line for trolling and fly casting. For sizes, see illustration Note C. State size wanted. Order by catalogue number and size number.

Size, Nos.	5	4	3	2
Price, per 25 yards	24c	34c	37c	44c

If by mail, postage extra, 2 and 3 cents.

The Genuine Kingfisher Braided Silk Casting Line.

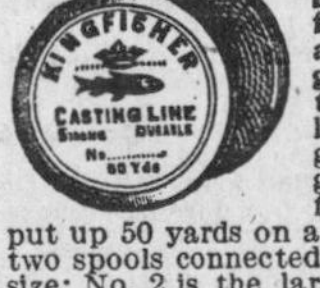

Kingfisher Casting Lines are well and favorably known. They are high class lines and give perfect satisfaction. The Kingfisher lines we handle are guaranteed to be the genuine, original Kingfisher Lines. They come put up 50 yards on a spool, and may be had two spools connected. No. 5 is the smallest size; No. 2 is the largest. No. 2 line is intended for large, heavy fish only, such as muskallonge. Order by catalogue number and size number.

Catalogue Number	Size	Breaking Strength	Price, per Spool
No. 6K8811	No. 5	12 pounds	59c
No. 6K8811	No. 4	16 pounds	67c
No. 6K8811	No. 3	23 pounds	80c
No. 6K8811	No. 2	28 pounds	98c

If by mail, postage extra, 3 cents.

Our Special Enameled Silk Trout and Bass Line.

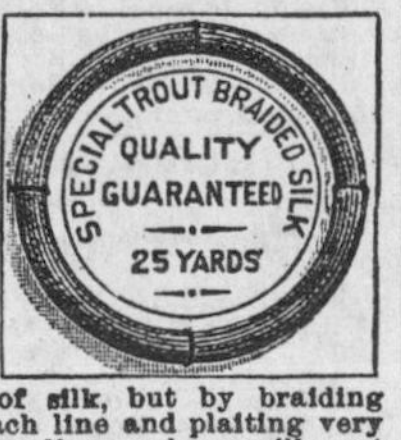

No. 6K8814 Our Extra Quality Enameled Oil Silk Trout Lines are giving excellent satisfaction and the demand for these lines is becoming greater each season, they being of small diameter and possessing great strength. This result is obtained not only by using the highest grade of silk, but by braiding more strands into each line and plaiting very close. Try one of these lines and you will want more. 25 yards on neat card. Mention size.

A—Trout sizes. Price, 25 yards 31c

B—Bass sizes. Price, 25 yards 40c

If by mail, postage extra, 25 yards, 2 cents.

Our Italian Enameled Silk Fly Casting Line.

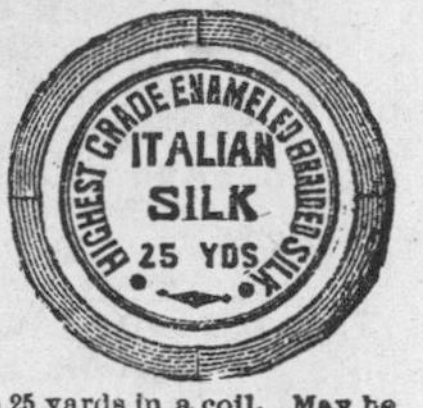

No. 6K8816 Our Italian Enameled Silk Waterproof Flexible Fly Casting Line made from the best Italian silk, braided over a silk core. It is undoubtedly the best fly casting line on the market. The enamel is guaranteed not to crack or become sticky as is the case with many enameled silk lines. Put up 25 yards in a coil. May be had four coils connected if desired. Be sure to state size wanted.

Sizes	6	5	4	3
Price, per 25 yards	47c	55c	60c	69c

If by mail, postage extra, 2 and 3 cents.

The Beaver Highest Quality Braided Silk Casting Line.

Formerly called Badger.

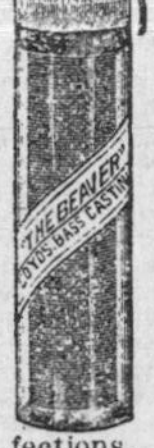

No. 6K8817 We have so greatly improved the quality of this line, which we formerly sold under the Badger brand, that we have decided to call the new improved line the Beaver. This line is the same as the line we formerly sold under the Badger brand, except that it is a better line. No better silk line made at any price. These lines are especially braided for us of a long fiber stock and possess finish, smoothness and hardness not found in any other line. The strength of these lines is enormous. They are braided over a natural color silk core and guaranteed to be free from any imperfections. Each line of 50 yards put up in an airtight glass tube, insuring it reaching the purchaser in excellent condition. If you want the best line that money can buy, buy this Beaver Silk Line and you will not be disappointed.

Bass size. Price, 50 yards $1.02

Trout size. Price, 50 yards ...... .90

If by mail, postage extra, 6 cents.

Genuine Italian Braided Silk Bass and Trout Lines.

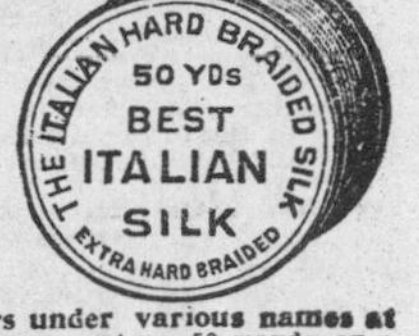

Our Genuine Italian Braided Silk Line is intended for expert fishermen, for the man who wants the best line that money can buy. This line is made from selected stock perfectly braided over a silk core, is a hard line, free from any imperfections. This same line is sold by dealers under various names at $1.50 a spool. It comes put up 50 yards on a spool, two spools connected.

Catalogue Number	For	Yards on Spool	Price, per Spool
6K8818B	Bass	50 Yards	84c
6K8818T	Trout	50 Yards	72c

If by mail, postage extra, 3 cents.

The Beaver Cuttyhunk Linen Lines.

Quality Guaranteed. The Strongest Reel Lines Made.

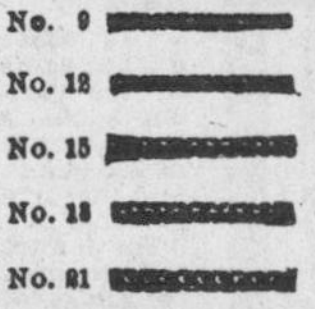

No. 6K8820 Our Cuttyhunk Linen Reel Lines, the old reliable, the strongest for their size and are the best lines made. There are several lines called the Cuttyhunk but they are only cheap linen lines, labeled Cuttyhunk. Our Beaver line is made of the finest quality of Scotch linen, always runs smooth and even and never kinks. The best linen reel line on the market. Put up 150 feet on a spool, or may be had two spools connected, making 300 feet of line.

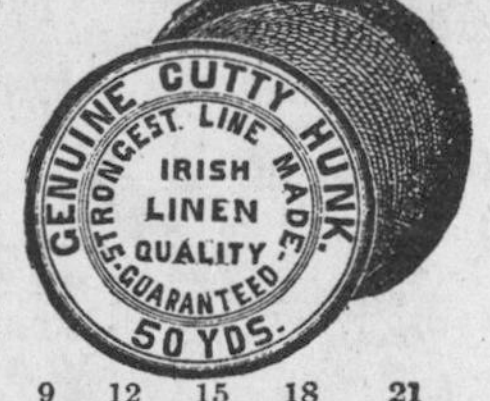

This line is twisted, and when used with swivel on end will not untwist. Can be used same as a braided line. See illustration for sizes. Order by catalogue number and size number.

Size Nos.	9	12	15	18	21
Price, per 150 ft.	24c	27c	32c	36c	39c

If by mail, postage extra, 4 cents.

Crystal Lake Green Linen Lines.

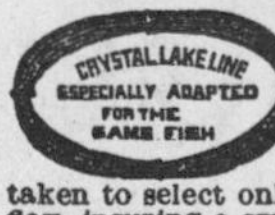

No. 6K8825 This line is made of the finest quality Scotch flax, is green in color, is especially adapted for game fish. In the manufacture of this line great care is taken to select only the best long fiber Scotch flax, insuring a smooth, perfect line that will not kink, free from all knots; will run free on any reel. Comes in three sizes: No. 9, breaking strength, 18 pounds; No. 12, breaking strength, 24 pounds, and No. 15, breaking strength, 30 pounds. Put up 50 feet on the coil, six coils connected if desired. Order by catalogue number and size number.

Size	No. 9	No. 12	No. 15
Price, per coil	15c	17c	18c

If by mail, postage extra, 2 cents.

Our 13-Cent Rigged Silk Line.

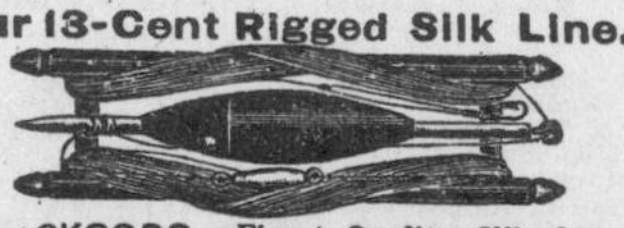

No. 6K8832 Finest Quality Silk Line, rigged complete, with gut hook, fancy barrel shape adjustable cork float and adjustable sinker, for still fishing. Price........13c
Postage extra, 3 cents.

The Maloney Weedless Bass Hook, 8 Cents.

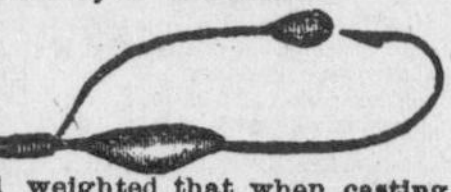

No. 6K8855 This is the latest and most practical weedless hook on the market. It is so made and weighted that when casting for bass, the frog or minnow is always right side up. They are made in sizes 3-0, 4-0 and 5-0. See illustration of ringed hooks for sizes, and state size wanted. Price..............8c
If by mail, postage extra, 2 cents.

Improved Greer's Lever Hooks.

Illustration shows the hook when set and also when sprung.

No. 6K8857 Greer's Patent Lever Fish Hooks. No more fish lost and baits to reset, no coming, home without your largest fish; a dead sure thing on getting your fish if it bites. It is easily adjusted to all kinds of fishing, by sliding the little clamp on the rod. Made of 1-0 and 3-0 Carlisle hooks.

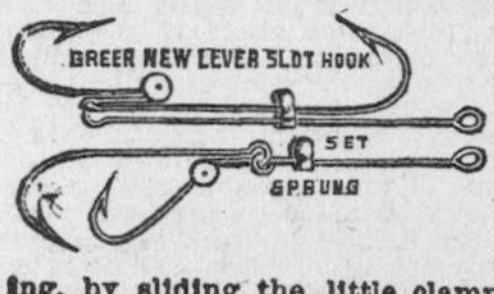
GREER NEW LEVER SLOT HOOK
SET
SPRUNG

Size, 1-0. Price..........................7c
Size, 3-0. Price..........................8c
If by mail, postage extra, 2 cents.

For lowest prices on steel and wood row boats, canvas covered canoes, sail boats, sails, marine engines and accessories, send for our Free Boat Catalogue.

Spring Fish Hooks.

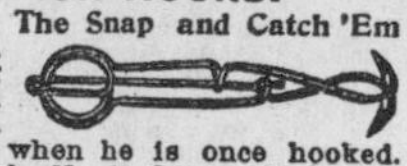

No. 6K8858 The Snap and Catch 'Em Spring Fish Hook. The hook's spring points outward, and it is easily set. Fish cannot get away when he is once hooked. No. 20, for small fish; No. 19, for medium size fish; No. 18, for large fish. Say which you want. Price....(Postage extra, 2 cents.)..........8c

Fish Hooks, Double Refined and Tempered Steel.

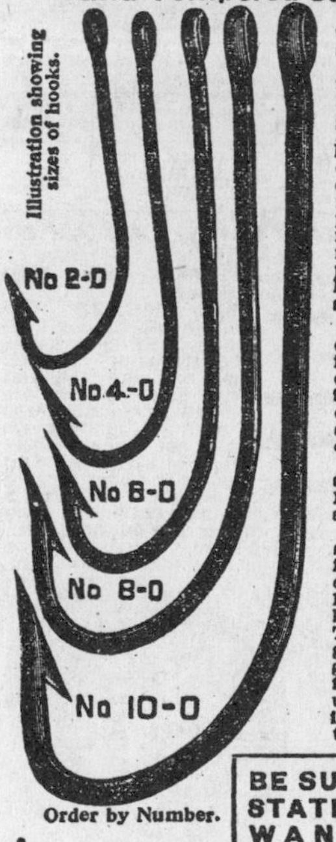
Illustration showing sizes of hooks.
No 2-0
No 4-0
No 6-0
No 8-0
No 10-0

Order by Number.

This illustration shows the exact size of the ringed hooks, such as Limerick, Kirby, Carlisle and all other kinds of hooks, as nearly as possible, measuring from the point of the hook to the shank.

The other difference in the various hooks is in the length of the shank and the style of bend.

We cannot sell less than 100 hooks of a size.

On above sizes, No. 2-0 is the smallest and No. 10-0 is the largest size. The sizes grow larger gradually from No. 2-0 up, as shown in this illustration.

BE SURE TO STATE SIZE WANTED.

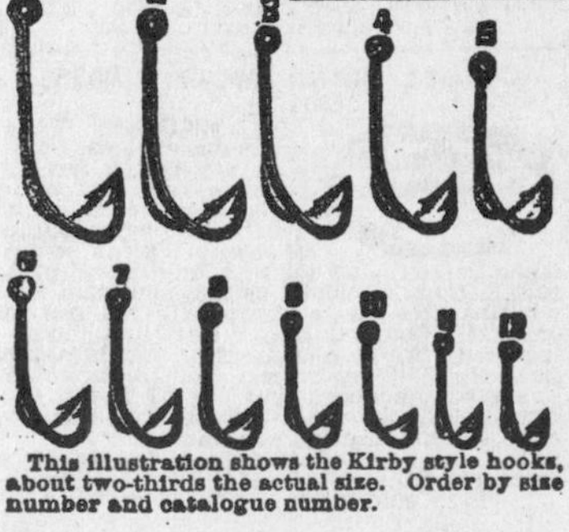

This illustration shows the Kirby style hooks, about two-thirds the actual size. Order by size number and catalogue number.

Ringed Fish Hooks.

Kirby, Limerick and Carlisle, made of superfine steel, ringed. Put up in a box of 100 each. We cannot sell less than 100 of a size, but our price is the same whether you buy 100 or 1,000. We give the lowest price always. See illustration of sizes on this page and state size wanted. Order by catalogue number and size number.

Our Carlisle hooks are the Celebrated Milward English "Iron Arm" brand. No better hooks made.

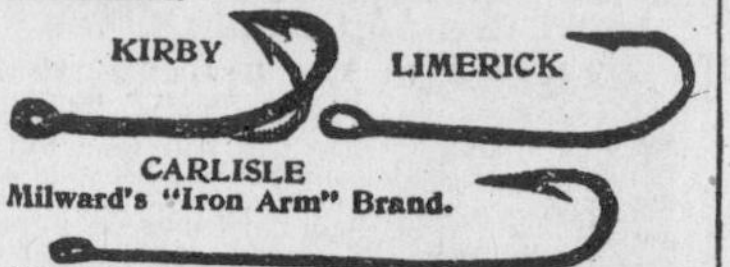
KIRBY
LIMERICK
CARLISLE

Milward's "Iron Arm" Brand.

We do not sell less than 100 hooks of a size.

Size No.	KIRBY Catalogue Number 6K8848 Price for Box of 100	LIMERICK Catalogue Number 6K8850 Price for Box of 100	CARLISLE Catalogue Number 6K8853 Price for Box of 100
12	5c	6c	9c
11	5c	6c	9c
10	5c	6c	9c
9	5c	6c	9c
8	5c	6c	9c
7	5c	6c	9c
6	5c	6c	9c
5	5c	6c	9c
4	5c	6c	9c
3	5c	6c	9c
2	5c	6c	9c
1	5c	6c	9c
1-0	7c	8c	11c
2-0	8c	9c	12c
3-0	10c	10c	15c
4-0	11c	11c	18c
5-0	13c	12c	20c
6-0	14c	13c	25c
8-0	20c	19c	32c
10-0	35c	......	......

POSTAGE ON HOOKS.

Sizes	Per box	Sizes	Per box
1 to 12	3c	8-0	13c
1-0 to 4-0	5c	9-0	17c
5-0 and 6-0	7c	10-0	23c
7-0	9c		

NOTICE—The above prices are not the prices of hooks but are the postage necessary to send hooks by mail.

SNELLED HOOKS.

Our snelled hooks are put up one-half dozen of a size in a package, and we cannot sell less than one-half dozen of a size. All our snelled hooks are specially hand tied and no house can compete with us in quality and prices. All our gut hooks are tied with silk.

Limerick Spear Point Snelled Hooks.

Tied to best quality single and double gut, full length. We cannot sell less than one-half dozen of a size.

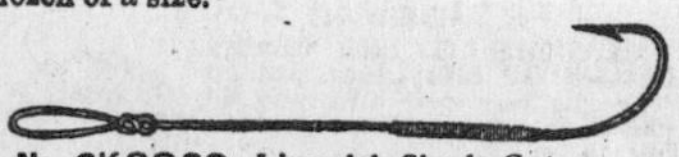

No. 6K8860 Limerick Single Gut.
Size No. 1 to 8. Price, per dozen..........9c
If by mail, postage extra, per dozen, 2 and 3c.

No. 6K8862 Limerick Double Gut.
Size No. 1 to 4. Price, per dozen..........12c

Size No.	1-0	2-0	3-0
Price, per dozen	15c	16c	18c

If by mail, postage extra, per dozen, 2 and 3c.

Carlisle Snelled Hooks.

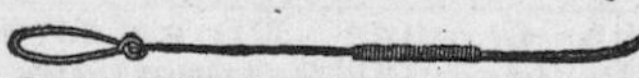

Carlisle Spring Steel Hooks, special quality, silk tied to full length single or double gut. We cannot sell less than one-half dozen of a size.

No. 6K8867 Carlisle Single Gut.
Size No. 1 to 8. Price, per dozen..........15c

No. 6K8369 Carlisle Double Gut.

Size No.	1	2	3	4	1-0
Price, per doz.	19c	19c	19c	19c	21c
Size No.	2-0	3-0	4-0	5-0	6-0
Price, per doz.	23c	26c	30c	34c	40c

If by mail, postage extra, per dozen, 2 and 3c.

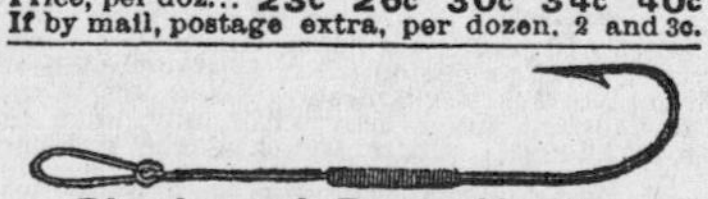

Cincinnati Bass Hooks, Snelled.

No. 6K8875 Cincinnati Bass Hooks. Double Gut, silk tied to best quality double gut, full length, and warranted the best hooks in the market for the money. We cannot sell less than half dozen of a size.

Size No. 24 equal to No. 3, per dozen....19c
Size No. 23 equal to No. 2, per dozen....19c
Size No. 22 equal to No. 1, per dozen....19c
Size No. 21 equal to No. 1-0, per dozen....21c
Size No. 20 equal to No. 2-0, per dozen....22c
Size No. 19 equal to No. 3-0, per dozen....24c
Size No. 18 equal to No. 4-0, per dozen....28c
Size No. 17 equal to No. 5-0, per dozen....30c
Size No. 16 equal to No. 6-0, per dozen....32c
If by mail, postage extra, per dozen, 2 and 3c.

Kelso Worm Gang.

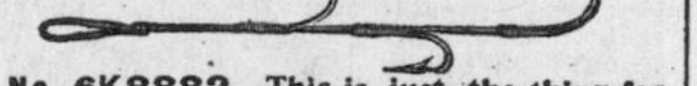

No. 6K8882 This is just the thing for still fishing and will catch the nibbler every time. As shown in the illustration, this bait consists of three No. 8 hooks tied to a piece of gut same as an ordinary snell hook, except you have three hooks around which you twine your angle worm. You will not have your bait nibbled off if you use the Kelso Worm Gang when you go still fishing.
Price, 6 for 36c; each..........7c
If by mail, postage extra, each, 1 cent.

Plain Treble Hooks.

Don't throw away your spoon bait or minnow if you have broken or lost the hook, but buy a hook for it.

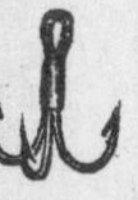

No. 6K8884 Plain Treble Hooks, ringed, made of best quality spring steel and well finished. Sizes compare with regular fish hooks.
Sizes, 1 to 4. Price 3 for.........5c
Sizes, 1-0, 2-0, 3-0. Price 3 for..8c
Sizes, 4-0, 5-0, 6-0, 7-0.
Price, 3 for..............12c
If by mail, postage extra, 1 to 3 cents.

Feathered Treble Hooks.

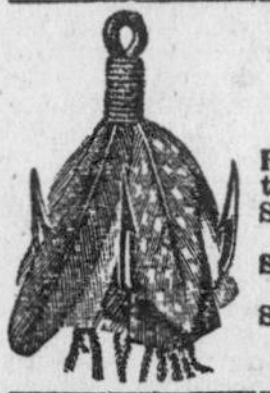

No. 6K8885 Heavily Feathered, well tied, best quality hooks.
Sizes, 1, 2, 3, 4, 5.
Price, 3 for..................8c
Sizes, 1-0, 2-0, 3-0, 4-0.
Price, 3 for..................11c
Sizes, 6-0, 8-0.
Price, 3 for..................15c
Postage extra, each, 2 to 5c.

Bucktail Treble Hooks.

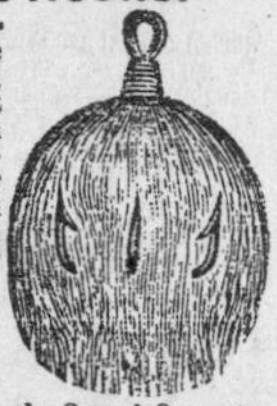

No. 6K8886 Our Bucktail Treble Hooks, made from genuine deertail hair, can be attached to almost any spoon bait, makes an excellent hook to interchange with the regular feathered treble hook, an excellent hook for bass, used the same as a frog, either for trolling or casting.
Sizes, 2, 4 and 6.
Price, each..........9c
Sizes, 1-0 and 2-0.
each..............10c
If by mail, postage extra, each, 2 and 3 cents.

Barrel Shape Adjustable Cork Floats.

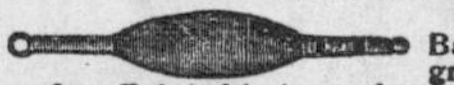

No. 6K8892 Barrel shape, best grade cork, well made. Painted in two colors.

Length, inches	2	3	4
Weight, ounces	1/4	1/3	3/4
Price, each	4c	5c	8c

If by mail, postage extra, each, 1 and 2 cents.

Brass Box Swivels.

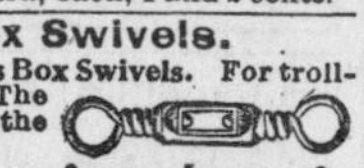

No. 6K8895 Brass Box Swivels. For trolling spoon baits, etc. The length mentioned is the entire length.

No.	8	5	2
Length, inch	1/2	3/4	1
Price, per dozen	14c	14c	14c
No.	1-0	2-0	3-0
Length, inches	1 1/4	1 1/2	1 3/4
Price, per dozen	16c	21c	35c

If by mail, postage extra, per dozen, 2 and 3c.

Patent Spring Swivels.

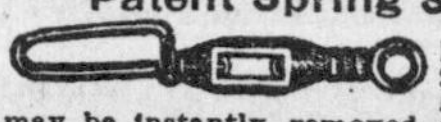

No. 6K8896 Patent Spring Swivel. A broken hook or spoon may be instantly removed without untying the line.

Nos.	6	4	1-0
Length, inches	1	1 3/8	1 3/4
Price, per dozen	26c	28c	34c

If by mail, postage extra, per dozen, 2 and 3c.

Adjustable Sinkers.

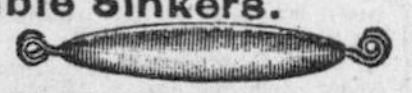

No. 6K8898 Patent Adjusable Sinkers. These can be attached or detached by a single turn of the line. Note the two end wire coils to adjustable line.

Nos.	1	2	4	5	6
Length, inches	3/4	1	1 1/4	1 1/2	1 3/4
Weight, dozen, oz.	2	3	4	5	6
Price, per dozen	5c	6c	9c	11c	13c

If by mail, postage extra, 1 cent per ounce.

Dipsey Sinkers.

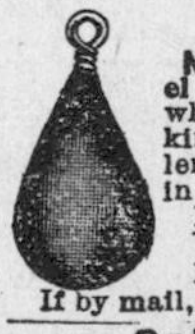

No. 6K8899 The Dipsey Swivel Lead Sinkers, an excellent sinker when casting or trolling. Will not kink the line. No. 6 sinker is excellent for bait casting practice. Sold in any quantity at dozen prices.

Nos.	2	4	6	8	10
Wt., ea., ozs.	2	1	1/2	1/4	1/12
Price, 1/2 doz.	29c	23c	18c	16c	15c

If by mail, postage extra, 1 cent per ounce.

Split Shot Sinkers.

For light sinkers and fly casting when it is windy.

No. 6K8902 Split shot for sinkers, two dozen in wood box.
Price, per box..........3c
If by mail, postage extra, per box, 1 cent.

Mackinac Adjustable Screw Sinkers.

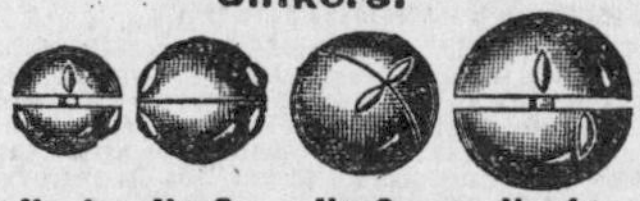

No. 1 No. 2 No. 3 No. 4

No. 6K8903 Is adjustable by screwing the two parts together. Order by catalogue number and mention size wanted.

Nos.	1	2	3	4
Weight, dozen, ounces	1	2	3	5
Price, per dozen	12c	14c	16c	19c

If by mail, postage extra, 1 cent per ounce.

Our Aluminum Leader Box.

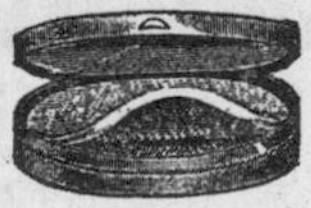

No. 6K8905 Our Aluminum Leader Box, 4 inches in diameter, with two felt pads for keeping the leaders moist, cannot rust, hinge cover, light and convenient to carry in the pocket. No fisherman should be without one, as leaders should always be kept moist when in use. Price, 18c
If by mail, postage extra, 3 cents.

Our Standard Gut Leaders.

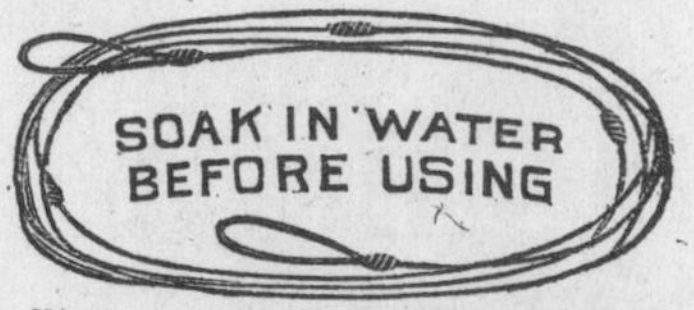
SOAK IN WATER BEFORE USING

We have an entirely new and much superior line of gut leaders for this season. We carry a complete assortment of the highest grades in stock always. These leaders will not peel and weaken, but are made of selected gut and you run no risk of breakage and loss of sport. Imported from Italy and Spain. Leaders should be kept moist when in use. Mist colored. Be sure to mention length of leader wanted.

Catalogue Number	L'g'th of L'der	Kind of Gut	Size for	Per Doz.	Price, Each
6K8906 Mist Color.	3 ft. 6 ft.	Single Single	Trout Trout	$0.50 .72	5c 7c
6K8908 Mist Color.	3 ft. 6 ft.	Double Double	Trout Trout	.68 1.35	6c 12c
6K8916 Mist Color.	3 ft. 6 ft.	Double Double	Salm'n Salm'n	1.35 2.76	12c 24c

If by mail, postage extra, 1 cent.

Wire Leaders.

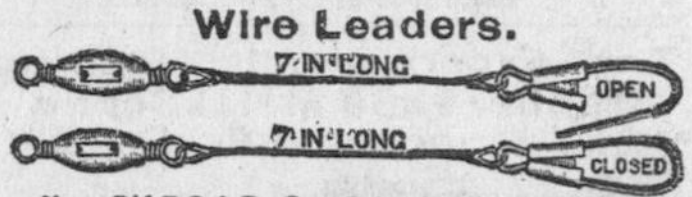
7-IN-LONG
OPEN
7-IN-LONG
CLOSED

No. 6K8918 Our 7-inch wire leader made of finely tempered wire, fitted with brass box swivel at one end and patent snap at the other, permitting quick changing of baits. This leader is just the right thing for bait casting, and will prevent pickerel, pike and other game fish from biting the line and is guaranteed not to kink or break. Price..........9c
If by mail, postage extra, 1 cent.

Silkworm Gut Leaders.

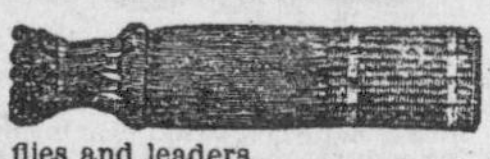

Put up 100 in a bunch, for fishermen who make their own snelled hooks, flies and leaders.

No. 6K8920 Size 12, is 11 inches long, superior quality, medium size.
Price, per bunch..................30c

No. 6K8920½ Size 8, is 12 inches long, select Padron first quality, none better, heavy and very strong.
Price, per bunch..................68c
If by mail, postage extra, per bunch, 2 cents

TROUT FLIES.

Highest Grade Trout Flies.

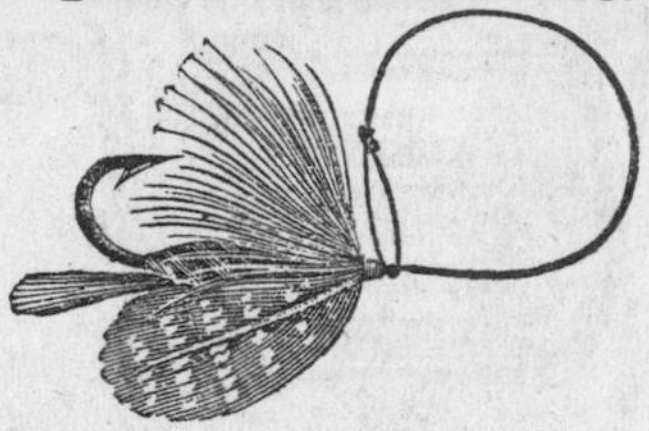

Our line of Trout and Bass Flies has been selected with great care. We have carefully selected only such flies as we know from experience to be killers, and know that our flies cannot be excelled for beauty, quality and workmanship. We do not sell anything cheaper than an all silk body fly, knowing that the cheaper grades do not give satisfaction.

B GRADE is a Silk Body Fly, plain wings, finely finished, tied to full length clear gut and good quality hook.
Price, per dozen..................30c
If by mail, postage extra, per dozen, 2 cents.

D GRADE highest quality, full silk body reversed wing trout flies. By reversed wing we mean the wing is tied twice which makes it impossible to whip off. The ends of the wing are tied and the wing is bent back toward the point of the hook and tied again. These flies are all tied with silk and have high quality hollow pointed imported English hooks, tied to best quality selected full length clear round gut. Regular price, $1.00 per dozen; our price per dozen..........60c
If by mail, postage extra, per dozen, 2 cents.

NOTICE—When ordering, give size of hooks wanted and state whether B or D grade. We cannot sell less than one-half dozen flies nor less than two flies of one kind and size of hook.

	NAME	Size of Hooks
No. 6K8921	Rube Wood	6, 8 or 10
No. 6K8922	Professor	6, 8 or 10
No. 6K8923	Governor	6, 8 or 10
No. 6K8924	Golden Spinner	6, 8 or 10
No. 6K8925	Silver Doctor	6, 8 or 10
No. 6K8926	Seth Green	6, 8 or 10
No. 6K8928	Cow Dung	6, 8 or 10
No. 6K8929	Queen of Waters	6, 8 or 10
No. 6K8930	King of Waters	6, 8 or 10
No. 6K8931	Grizzly King	6, 8 or 10
No. 6K8934	Brown Hackle	6, 8 or 10
No. 6K8935	Gray Hackle	6, 8 or 10
No. 6K8936	Coachman	6, 8 or 10
No. 6K8937	Royal Coachman	6, 8 or 10
No. 6K8939	Parmachenee Belle	6, 8 or 10
No. 6K8940	Montreal	6, 8 or 10
No. 6K8941	Black Gnat	6, 8 or 10
No. 6K8953	White Miller	6, 8 or 10
No. 6K8959	Yellow May	6, 8 or 10

Midget Trout Flies.

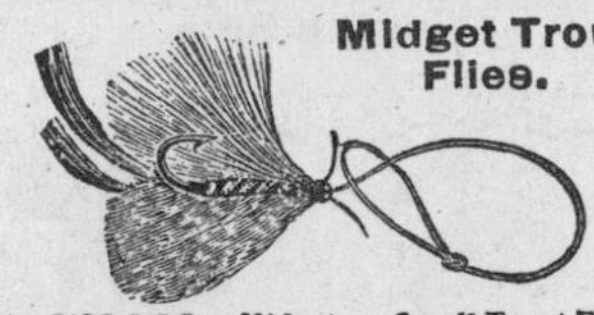

No. 6K8960 Midget, or Small Trout Flies. Superior midget flies, tied on sproat hooks Nos. 12 and 14, of which the following is a list. Silk body—silk tied. State style wanted.

Professor	Gray Hackle
Governor	Coachman
Golden Spinner	Royal Coachman
Cow Dung	Black Gnat
Queen of Waters	White Miller
Grizzly King	Yellow May
Brown Hackle	March Brown

The above selections are "killers."
Price, per dozen.......................35c
If by mail, postage extra, per dozen, 2 cents.

Our Red Beauty Weighted Bass Fly.

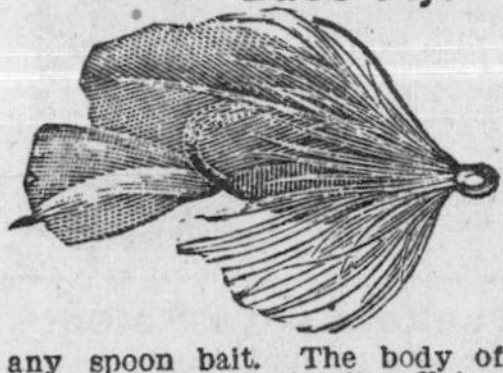

No. 6K8962 Highest Quality Silk Body Fly, monunted on a 4-0 sproat hook with an extra large eye. Can be used alone or on any spoon bait. The body of this fly is weighted so as to give it sufficient weight as a casting bait. The feathers protect the point of the hook, making it practically weedless. Comes in two styles, Ibis and Coachman. State style wanted. One size only.
Price, 6 for 70c; each.......13c
If by mail, postage extra, each, 2 cents.

Our Genuine Bucktail Bass and Trout Flies.

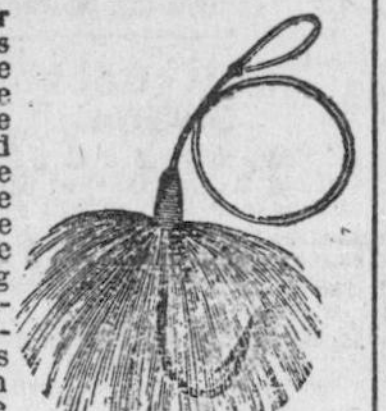

No. 6K8964 Our Bucktail Bass Flies are guaranteed to be made from genuine bucktail hair, all have hollow point hooks and first quality double gut, well tied, and are so constructed that the hair almost covers the entire hook, making one of the best bucktail bass flies ever produced. Made in sizes 1, 1-0 and 2-0. When ordering state size wanted.
Price, each.......................12c
6 for.......................65c
If by mail, postage extra, each, 2 cents.
No. 6K8965 Bucktail Trout Flies. Sizes, 4, 6 and 8. State size wanted. Each.. 9c
6 for.......................50c
If by mail, postage extra, each, 2 cents.

SPOON AND ARTIFICIAL BAITS.

SIZES OF SPOON BAITS.

NOTE K—The spoons of spoon baits come in various lengths, and the following is a list showing the length of the spoons on baits from Nos. 1 to 8. They may vary a trifle either way, for no two manufacturers make them exactly alike. When ordering state size wanted.

Nos.	1	2	3	4	4½
Length, inches	1	1⅛	1¼	1½	1⅝
Nos	4¾	5	6	7	8
Length, inches	1⅞	2⅛	2⅜	2½	2⅝

American Spinner Bait.

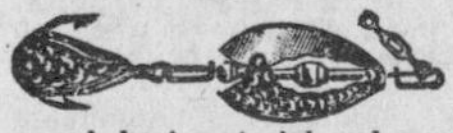

No. 6K8967 Best Plated Spoon, one-half hammered, best material and a rapid spinner, for bass, pickerel, etc. Nos. 2, 3, 4 and 5. See Note K for sizes. These spoons will measure ½-inch larger than Note K measurement.
Price.......................11c
If by mail, postage extra, 3 cents.

Fluted Spoon Bait for Bass.

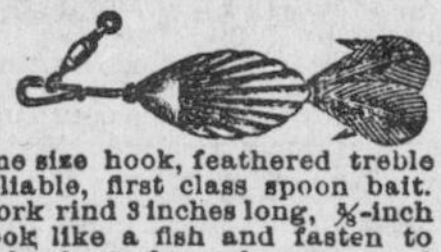

The Old Reliable Fluted Trolling Spoon, full nickel plated, inside painted red, same shape spoon as Skinner's and same size hook, feathered treble hook, an old, reliable, first class spoon bait. Take a piece of pork rind 3 inches long, ⅜-inch wide, cut it to look like a fish and fasten to one of the treble hooks and you have a good bass or pickerel bait. Order by catalogue number and state size wanted.
No. 6K8968 For small size fish, 1 to 3 pounds. Nos. 2, 3 and 4. Price.......8c
No. 6K8968½ For medium size fish, 3 to 6 pounds. Nos. 4½, 4¾ and 5. Price.......9c
No. 6K8968¾ For large size fish, 6 pounds and upward. Nos. 6, 7 and 8. Price.......10c
If by mail, postage extra, 2 to 4 cents.

OUR ALREADY LOWEST PRICES have been still FURTHER REDUCED in this Big Catalogue. Just compare the prices in this book with the prices quoted by us in previous catalogues and note the additional savings we make for you.

Skinner's Spoon Bait for Bass.

14c No. 6K8969 The Genuine Skinner Spoon. All have hollow point hooks. Don't be fooled by imitations. Every spoon bears maker's name. Be sure to state size wanted.
Nos. 1, 2, 3, 4, 4½, 4¾, for black bass, trout, etc. Price, each.......14c
Nos. 5 and 6, for pickerel, pike, lake trout, etc. Price, each.......18c
Nos. 7 and 8, for muskallonge. Price, ea. 25c
If by mail, postage extra, each, 2 to 4 cents.

Weedless Trolling or Casting Spoon.

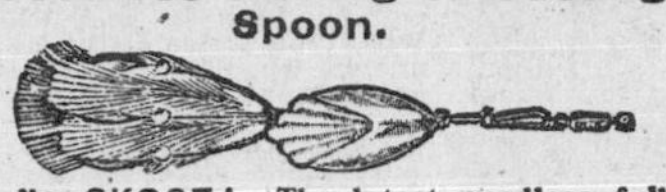

No. 6K8971 The latest weedless, full feathered, treble hook on the market; feathered with duck, peacock and guinea feathers. Nickel plated spoon and brass box swivel. A sure catch and a weedless bait. None better. Be sure to state size wanted.
Sizes, 4 and 4½. Price, each.......30c
Sizes, 5 and 6. Price, each.......35c
If by mail, postage extra, 3 cents.

The Q.C. Weedless Spoon Bait.

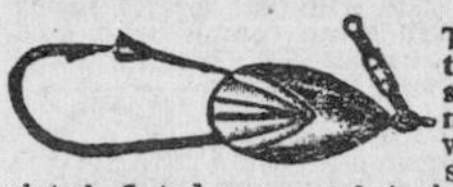

No. 6K8974 This is doubtless the best weedless spoon bait on the market. Fitted with brass box swivel, heavily plated, fluted spoon and single weighted weedless hook. This bait can be used alone or a frog or shiner can be attached to same with excellent results. Sizes, 4-0, 5-0, 6-0. State size wanted. Price, each.......14c
If by mail, postage extra, each, 2 cents.

The Muskallonge or Tarpon Bait.

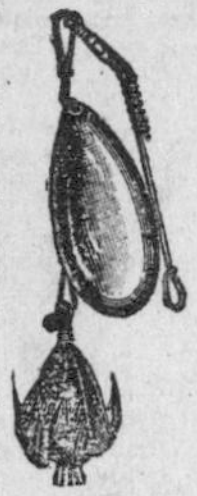

The herculean strength of this bait will tell its own story to the fisherman in pursuit of large gamy fish. For the St. Lawrence, the western lakes and rivers and the coast of Florida, they will fill the bill to perfection. Mention size wanted.
No. 6K8978 Fine Nickel Plated Spoon, treble hook, feathered, very best material.
2¼-inch spoon for 10 to 20-pound fish. Price, each......18c
3¼-inch spoon, for 20 to 100-pound fish. Price, each.......22c
If by mail, postage extra, each, 5 cents.

The Improved Colorado Spinner.

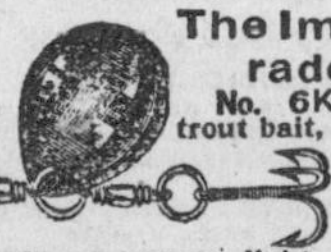

No. 6K8990 An ideal trout bait, in many cases found superior to flies for trout fishing. Hollow point hooks, two small barrel swivels, a very light attractive spoon, nothing but the very best material used in the above spoon. Comes one size only.
Price.......................12c
If by mail, postage extra, 2 cents.

Our Spinning Coachman.

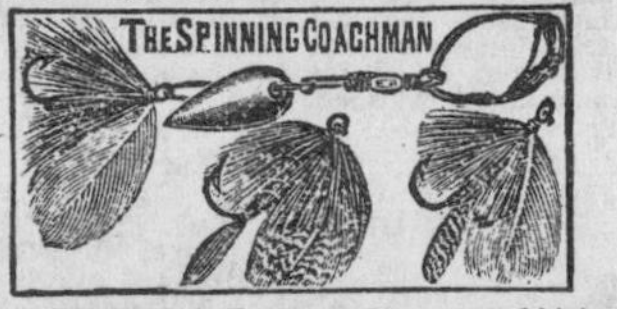

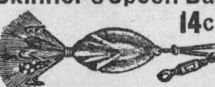

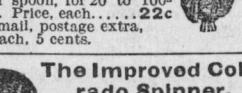

No. 6K8991 First quality, with 1⅛-inch highly nickel plated spoon. No. 1 hook, tied with double gut, nickel plated box swivel. Each bait comes with a coachman and two other popular bass flies mounted on a handsome enameled card. One of the best bass baits on the market. Price, per card...20c
If by mail, postage extra, 3 cents.

The New Joliet Aluminum Spinner Bait, 23 Cents.

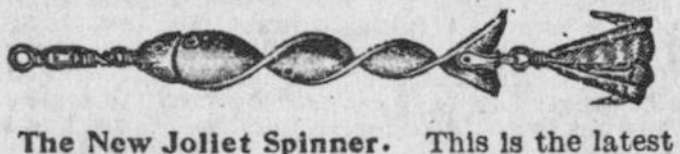

The New Joliet Spinner. This is the latest and best bass and pickerel bait, made of aluminum, on the principle of a wood auger, which causes it to be an excellent spinner in the water, resembling a bright shinner. A very effective bait.
No. 6K8994 For bass and pickerel, 2½ inches long. Price.......................23c
If by mail, postage extra, 2 cents.

Our Bucktail Casting Spoon.

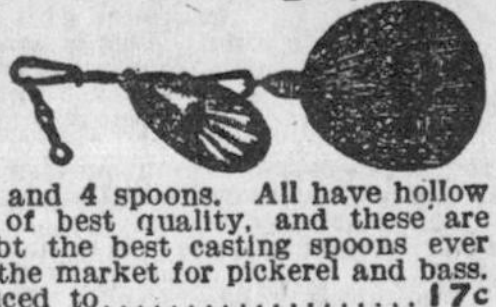

No. 6K8998 Our Genuine Bucktail Casting Spoon is made with Nos. 1, 2, 3 and 4 spoons. All have hollow point hooks of best quality, and these are without doubt the best casting spoons ever placed upon the market for pickerel and bass.
Price, reduced to.......................17c
If by mail, postage extra, 3 cents.

Luminous Tandem Spinner.

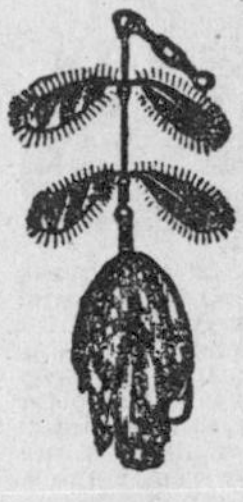

No. 6K9002 This Spinner is considered the most successful spinner used today for bass or pickerel fishing. Blades revolve in opposite directions, giving a perfect imitation of a struggling minnow. This spinner is luminous, making it doubly attractive on dark days or in deep water. The blades are fine German silver polished, and the treble hook is heavily feathered, making a very handsome bait. Made so that the hooks can be easily removed and changed. When unsuccessful with other baits try a tandem spinner. Expose in daylight a few minutes before using.
No. 1. Price.......................30c
No. 2. Price.......................34c
If by mail, postage extra, 3 cents.

Steel Pliers.

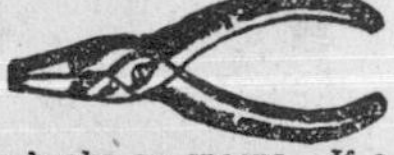

No. 6K9004 Steel Pliers, 4 inches long, weight 2 ounces. Every fisherman should have a pair in his tackle box to replace hooks on spoons. If a hook catches in clothes break it off.
Price.......................9c

The New Winner Wood Minnow, 38c.

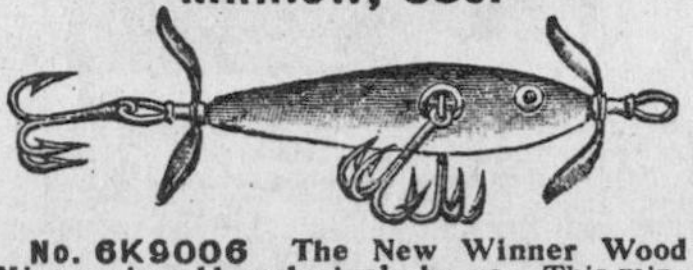

No. 6K9006 The New Winner Wood Minnow is sold exclusively by us. This minnow, as you will note in the illustration above, has the new patented link and detachable hooks. In case you break a hook you can put a new one on in a few seconds by turning the center rod at the head a few turns to the left, which releases the new patent link. This minnow has a 3-inch body and is weighted, so that it will always stay right side up. Nicely enameled; has green back and white belly. Guaranteed to hold its color and not to crack. Has three treble hooks and two nickel plated cut water spinners. Put up in a neat wood box. Could not be duplicated elsewhere for less than 75 cents. Our price.......38c
If by mail, postage extra, 4 cents.

Phantom Minnows.

Water-proof Silk.

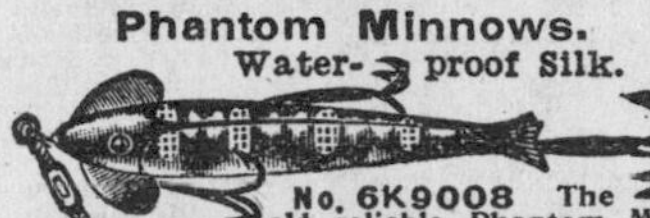

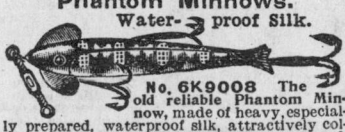

No. 6K9008 The old reliable Phantom Minnow, made of heavy, especially prepared, waterproof silk, attractively colored and striped with indestructible metal head, two projecting metal flanges, as illustrated, which creates a commotion in the water, attracting the attention of all game fish. This minnow is fitted with brass box swivel and three sets of treble hooks attached to the head and tail of minnow, with heavy, twisted gut leaders, allowing sufficient play and preventing the hooks from being twisted off. There are several grades of phantom minnows. We guarantee those handled by us to be absolutely the best. Order by catalogue number and give size of minnow wanted when ordering.

Sizes	1	3	4	5	6	8
Length, inches	2	2¾	3	3½	4	4½
Price, each	22c	24c	26c	27c	30c	34c

If by mail, postage extra, 2 to 4 cents.

Luminous Minnows.

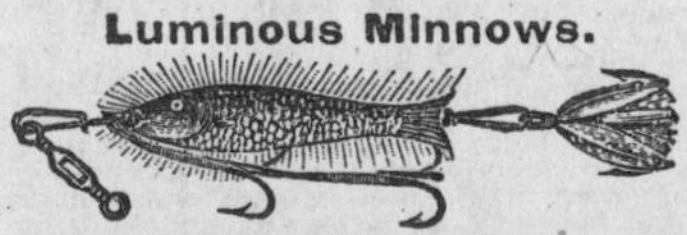

No. 6K9010 Soft Rubber Luminous Minnows, made of one piece solid, soft rubber, with one feathered treble hook at tail and one plain treble at center. The No. 9 has two plain trebles at side, as shown above, with brass wire running clear through center. Fitted with brass box swivel. The luminous body of this minnow is very attractive and will catch fish when other baits fail. Very attractive on dark days. Can be used for casting or trolling. Put up in a neat box. Expose in daylight a few minutes before using.
No. 7 Full length 5 inches. Price...30c
No. 8 Full length 6 inches. Price...34c
No. 9 Full length 7 inches. Price...40c
If by mail, postage extra, 3 cents.

RUBBER BAITS.

Excellent Substitutes Where the Natural Bait Cannot Readily be Found

Helgamites.

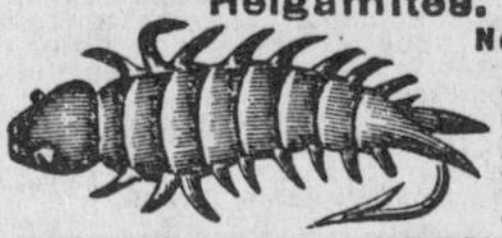

No. 6K9014 Helgamite, or Dobson, soft rubber, with swivel. Price....16c
Postage extra, 3 cents.

Special Fly Minnow.

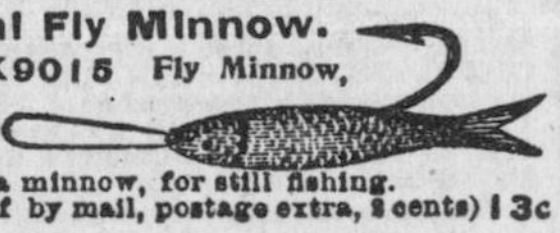

No. 6K9015 Fly Minnow, 1¼ inches long, a good imitation of a minnow, for still fishing.
Price (If by mail, postage extra, 2 cents) 13c

The Kalamazoo Swimming Frog.

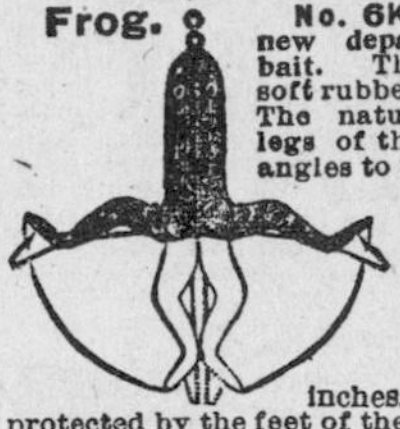

No. 6K9018 This is a new departure in artificial bait. This frog is made of soft rubber with hollow body. The natural position of the legs of this frog are at right angles to the body. In pulling the frog through the water the legs kick backwards with identically the same motion used by a live frog when swimming. Length when extended, 3¾ inches. The hooks being protected by the feet of the frog are practically weedless. Finished in exact imitation of a live frog. Very durable, will catch fish wherever they are to be found. Price.......................70c
(Postage extra, 3c)

Grasshopper Bait.

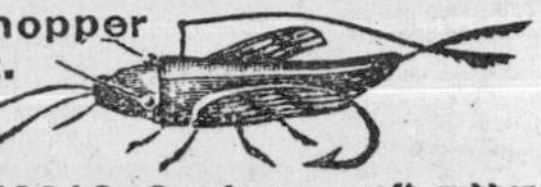

No. 6K9019 Grasshopper, soft rubber, 1¼ inches long, quite natural. Price, ea. 12c
If by mail, postage extra, each, 2 cents.

Floating Meadow Frog.

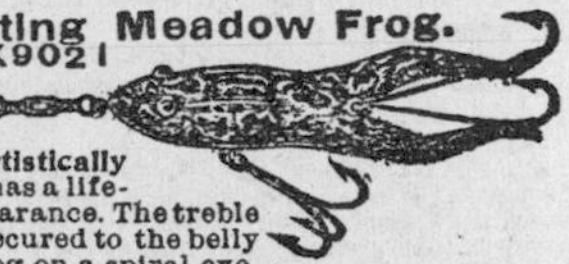

No. 6K9021 Made of satin cork, very artistically painted, has a lifelike appearance. The treble hook is secured to the belly of the frog on a spiral eye, enabling fishermen to change hooks when desired. This treble hook insures hooking your fish when he strikes. Entire length, 3 inches.
Price (If by mail, postage extra, 4c)...23c

Soft Red Rubber Angle Worms.

No. 6K9022 Angle Worms; a perfect imitation of red, live worms; about 3 inches long.
Each. 14c
If by mail, postage extra, each, 2 cents.

Genuine Dowagiac Wood Minnows.

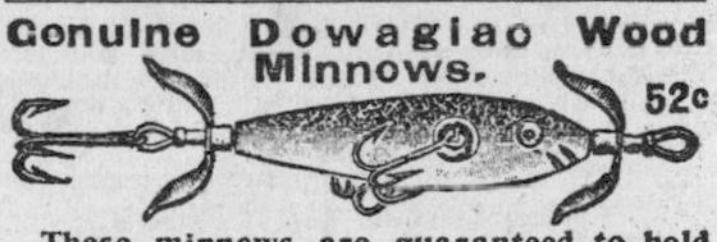

52c

These minnows are guaranteed to hold their color and not to chip or crack. They are beautifully finished with mottled green back and white belly. The patent socket device prevents the hooks from interlocking. Spinners at either end revolve freely. This minnow always comes in right side up and is guaranteed to retain its finish and color.
No. 6K9025 Dowagiac Minnow, 2¾ inches long, fancy back and fitted with three treble hooks and two spinners. Suitable for bass, pike and pickerel. Price. (Postage, 4c.).52c
No. 6K9026 Dowagiac Minnow, large size, 3½ inches long, fancy mottled back fitted with five treble hooks and two spinners, suitable for large fish, including muskallonge.
Price.......(Postage extra, 5c.).......67c

Shakespeare Revolution Bait.

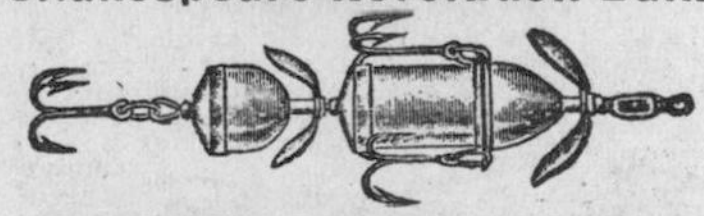

No. 6K9032 This is one of the most popular baits on the market. It is made entirely of aluminum with two paddles and three treble hooks. The body, head and paddles revolve rapidly when the bait is drawn through the water, resembling a fish, making a very attractive lure. This bait has been on the market but a short time, but its killing qualities has made it one of the most popular baits now on the market. 4 inches long. Price.......................39c
If by mail, postage extra, 3 cents.

Our Sure Catch Minnow Trap.

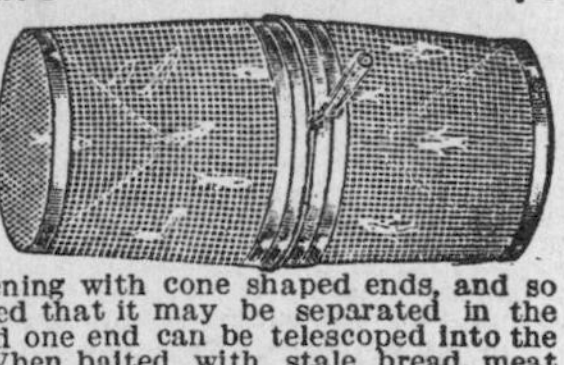

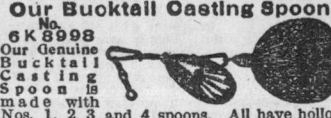

No. 6K9033 Our Sure Catch Minnow Trap is made of galvanized sheet steel and wire screening with cone shaped ends, and so constructed that it may be separated in the center and one end can be telescoped into the other. When baited with stale bread, meat or other bait, the bait is exposed to view through the wire screen and when the minnows, crawfish or other small fish once get into this trap it is difficult for them to find their way out. The Sure Catch Minnow Trap is 18 inches long, 10 inches in diameter and weighs about 2 pounds. Price.......64c
If by mail, postage extra, 44 cents.

Keystone Fish Stringers.

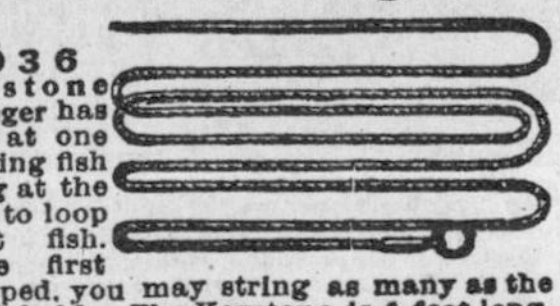

No. 6K9036 The Keystone Fish Stringer has a needle at one end to string fish and a ring at the other end to loop the first fish. After the first fish is looped, you may string as many as the string will hold. The Keystone is 6 feet long.
Price.......................12c
If by mail, postage extra, 4 cents.

Chain Fish Stringers.

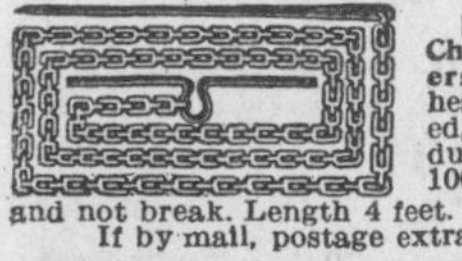

No. 6K9038 Chain Fish Stringers, strong links, heavy nickel plated, strong and durable; will hold 100 pounds of fish and not break. Length 4 feet. Price.....11c
If by mail, postage extra, 3 cents.

Fish or Frog Spears.

At reduced prices.

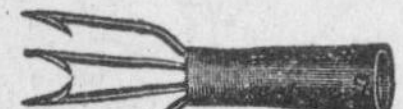

No. 6K9046 Has four tines, 2¾ inches long, with socket for pole. Price.....12c
If by mail, postage extra, 6 cents.

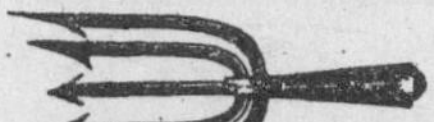

No. 6K9049 Has five prongs, 5 inches long, with socket for pole. Price......41c
If by mail, postage extra, 22 cents.

Our Hand Forged Spear.

The best spear on the market.

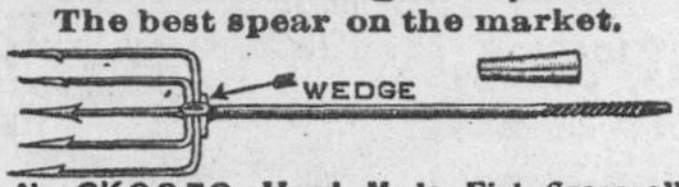

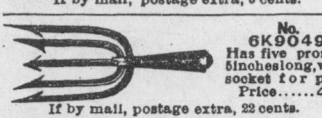

No. 6K9050 Hand Made Fish Spear, all best steel socket and wedge as shown above; beards of each tine made on solid shank, screws into socket and makes its own thread in wood (of handle); the outside tines can be removed if smaller spear is wanted at any time by putting in larger wedge. Width about 4⅛ to 4⅜ inches; entire length of tines, about 6½ inches; entire length, 22 inches. Weight, about 18 ounces. None better.
Price.....$1.30
If by mail, postage extra, 35 cents.

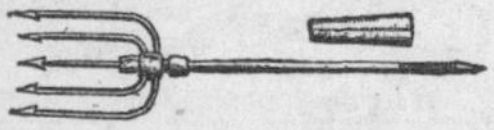

No. 6K9052 Five-Tine Spear. Tines are not removable but are set in heavy head of brass threaded to screw into handle, with socket. Weight, 12 ounces. Total length, 15 inches; length of tines, 4½ inches; width across tines, 3½ inches. An excellent spear.
Price......(Postage extra, 23 cents.)......64c

Take Down Gaff Hook.

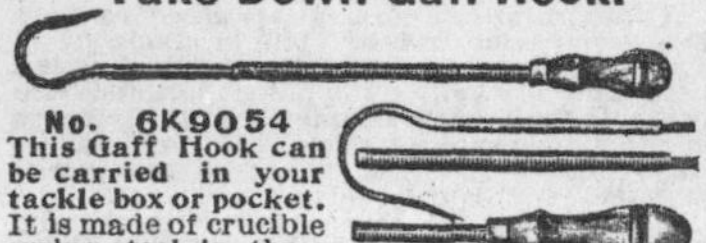

No. 6K9054 This Gaff Hook can be carried in your tackle box or pocket. It is made of crucible spring steel in three sections, screwed firmly together, fitted with black enameled handle, and is very strong. All fishermen who fish for gamey fish should have one. Full length, 20 inches; taken apart, 7 inches. Comes put up in a neat box.
Price.....46c
If by mail, postage extra, 10 cents.

The Lion Gaff.

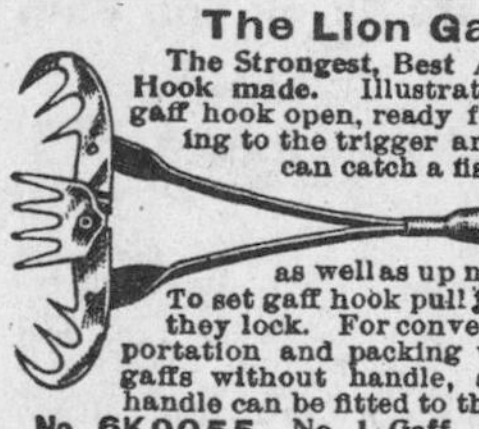

The Strongest, Best Automatic Gaff Hook made. Illustration shows the gaff hook open, ready for action. Owing to the trigger arrangement you can catch a fish lying close to the bottom of the lake as well as up near the surface. To set gaff hook pull jaws apart until they lock. For convenience in transportation and packing we furnish our gaffs without handle, as any broom handle can be fitted to the socket.

No. 6K9055 No. 1 Gaff, blued finish, measuring 8½ inches between the points of jaws when open. Price.....94c
If by mail, postage extra, 28 cents.

Tackle Boxes.

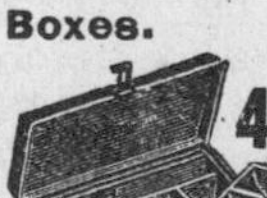

48c

No. 6K9060 An Excellent Tackle Box, 10½ inches long, 4 inches high and 5½ inches wide. Hinged cover with improved locking device. This box is finished on the outside with golden brown Japan and ornamented with neat gold stripes; inside the box is black; has one compartment suitable for snelled hooks, floats, spoons, etc.; one compartment large enough to hold one 100-yard reel; one compartment suitable for lines, leaders, etc.; one tray divided into five spaces. Price.....48c
If by mail, postage extra, 40 cents.

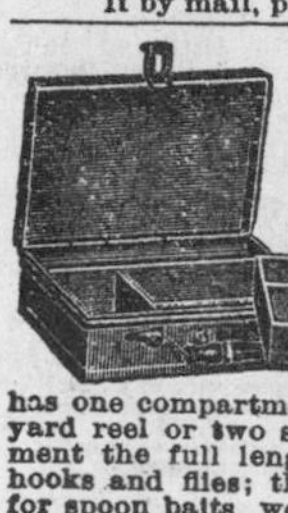

67c

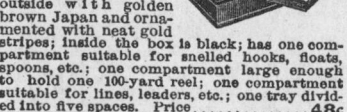

No. 6K9061 This box was designed for a fisherman desiring a flat box that can be packed in a suit case or large grip. This box is 9½ inches long, 3¼ inches high, 7 inches wide, with handle on the side, the same as a suit case, finish same as No. 6K9062; has one compartment large enough for a 100-yard reel or two smaller reels; one compartment the full length of the box for snelled hooks and flies; three smaller compartments for spoon baits, wood minnows, etc., and one tray divided into four compartments. A strong, well made, finely finished box. Price.....67c
If by mail, postage extra, 45 cents.

Tackle Box.

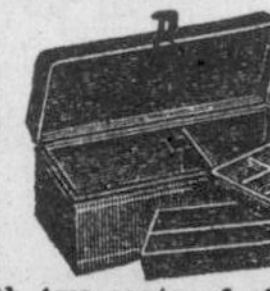

73c

No. 6K9062 Our Full Size Box, 12¼ inches long, 5½ inches wide, 6½ inches high. This is an extra strong box, with hinged cover, with strong hasp, with handle on top of box. Finished on the outside with two coats of rich green enamel, gold striped, and finished inside in jet black. Has one compartment large enough for two or three reels; one compartment suitable for leader box, fly book, lines, etc.; one tray divided into three compartments suitable for snelled hooks, spoon baits, floats, etc.; one small tray, as shown in the illustration, divided into six compartments suitable for swivels, sinkers, etc. This is the best box for fishermen desiring a large, roomy box. Do not compare this box with other cheap light tin boxes. Price.....73c
If by mail, postage extra, 55 cents.

Tackle Box.

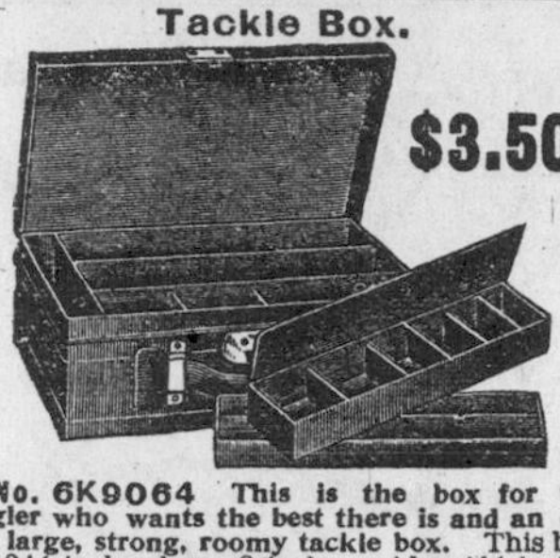

$3.50

No. 6K9064 This is the box for the angler who wants the best there is and an extra large, strong, roomy tackle box. This box is 12½ inches long, 8 inches wide, 4½ inches deep, made of extra heavy tin plate, beautifully enameled and striped. Fitted with nickel plated Yale lock and heavy leather suit case handle. Has compartments for three reels, two compartments for lines and floats, one compartment for tackle book; also has a tray for hooks and one covered tray with six compartments suitable for swivels, sinkers, small baits, etc. No stronger, more serviceable or handsomer box on the market.
Price.....$3.50

Fly and Tackle Book.

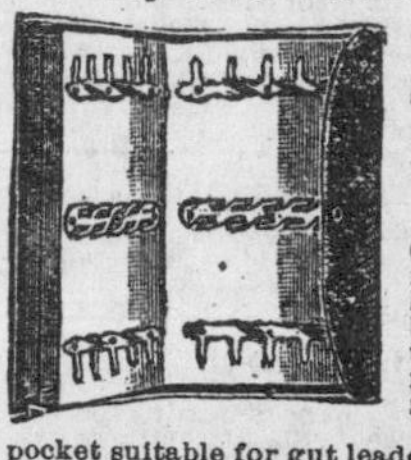

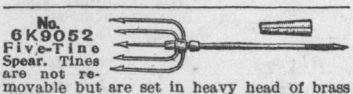

No. 6K9071 Tackle Book. Made to hold snelled hooks or flies. This book has durable pebbled leather cover, made with pocketbook fastening. Size, 6x3½ inches. Has four sheets of yellow parchment with bar and center clips to hold four dozen flies, with two flannel leaves for drying, has also deep pocket suitable for gut leaders. This is a neat, durable book, just the right size for the pocket.
Price.....40c
If by mail, postage extra, 5 cents.

Our Bray Style Fly Book.

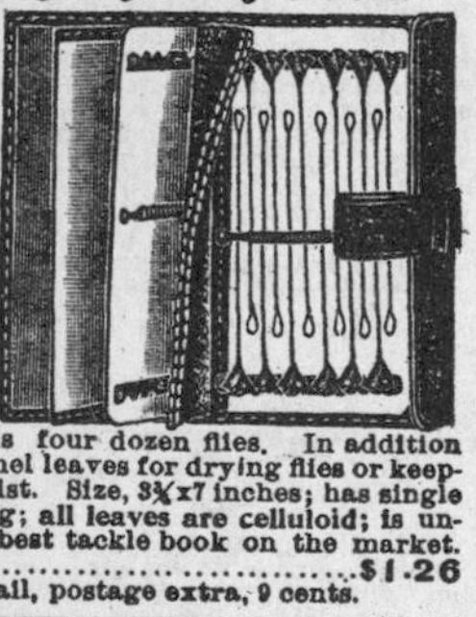

No. 6K9072 The cover of this book is heavy calf leather, lined with soft glove leather, has two leather pockets, also two celluloid envelopes. This book has celluloid leaves. Bray style spring in center, holds four dozen flies. In addition it has two flannel leaves for drying flies or keeping leaders moist. Size, 3¾x7 inches; has single strap fastening; all leaves are celluloid; is undoubtedly the best tackle book on the market.
Price.....$1.26
If by mail, postage extra, 9 cents.

Chicago Tackle Book.

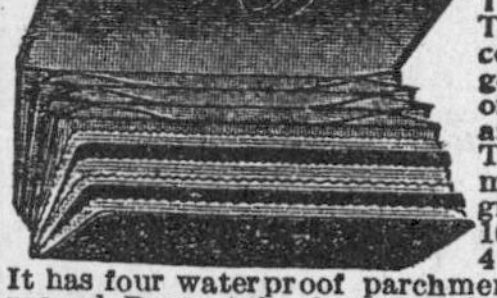

No. 6K9074 The Chicago Tackle Book combines the good qualities of a fly book and tackle box. This book is made of black grain leather, 10 inches long, 4 inches wide. It has four waterproof parchment leaves, improved Bray style fastening, for eight dozen flies; with felt dryers between the leaves; and single strap fastening and five large waterproof canvas pockets 10 inches long, 4 inches wide; three small pockets in which a large number of spoon hooks, sinkers, swivels, etc., can be carried. The book is well and strongly made and is the ideal tackle book for the fly or bait fisherman. Price.....$1.42
If by mail, postage extra, 9 cents.

OUR POSITION AS THE GREATEST MERCHANDISING INSTITUTION IN THE WORLD is emphasized by the wonderful REDUCTION IN PRICES which we have been able to make on thousands of articles quoted in this catalogue.

Bait Box.

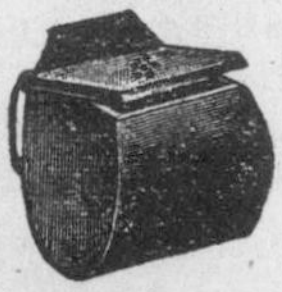

No. 6K9079 The Padlock Bait Box. 3½ inches wide, 3 inches deep, shaped very much like a fish basket, with a top cover and a safety pin on the back so it can be pinned to the coat. No losing of bait or upsetting of bait box.
Price.....10c
If by mail, postage extra, 4 cents.

Never Sink Floating Minnow Bucket.

No. 6K9085 All fishermen who use live minnows, frogs or craw fish should have one of the Never Sink Floating Buckets, as it will pay for itself in one trip. When you arrive at the lake or river where you intend to fish, pull out the inside bucket tie a short piece of string to the handle so it will not float away. The air chamber at the top of this bucket is air tight, with an opening at the top with a self locking hinged, perforated cover to allow you to get at your minnows very easily. The top of the inside bucket floats two inches above the water, made of galvanized wire, permitting plenty of fresh air. The cover of the outside bucket has a strong hinge and locking latch, perforated sunk in cover for putting ice on when in transit on hot days. Made of IX heavy tin plate, with wire bail handle, nicely finished in rich dark green enamel with gold bands and fancy decorations. Weight, 3 and 3½ pounds. Be sure to state size wanted.
8-qt. bucket complete.....69c
10-qt. bucket complete.....84c

Our Keep-Alive Nets, to Keep Fish Alive When Caught.

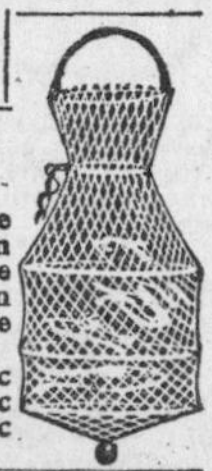

No. 6K9088 These nets are made with wire hoops and green knotted netting, are collapsible and take up very little room. An excellent thing to keep fish alive and fresh when caught.
Price, 10 inches diameter.....26c
Price, 12 inches diameter.....31c
Price, 14 inches diameter.....36c
Postage extra, 14 to 18 cents.

Minnow Dip Nets.

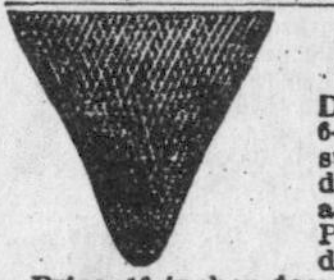

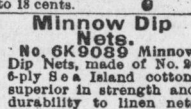

No. 6K9089 Minnow Dip Nets, made of No. 20 6-ply Sea Island cotton, superior in strength and durability to linen nets and far less expensive. Prices are for nets only; do not include frames.
Price, 16 inches deep.....17c
Price, 18 inches deep.....21c
Price, 20 inches deep.....25c
Price, 24 inches deep.....31c
Price, 30 inches deep.....41c
Price, 36 inches deep.....50c
If by mail, postage extra, 2 to 4 cents.

Linen Landing Nets.

No. 6K9090 Price is for netting only, and does not include frame. For landing large fish.
Price, 20 inches deep.....16c
Price, 24 inches deep.....20c
Price, 30 inches deep.....30c
If by mail, postage extra, 2 cents.

Our Chicago Landing and Minnow Net.

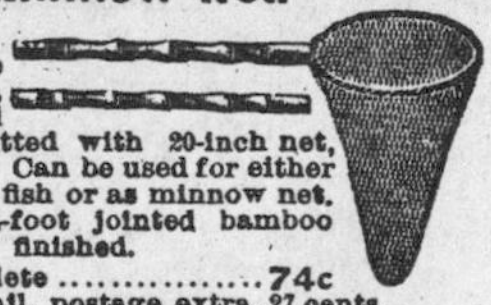

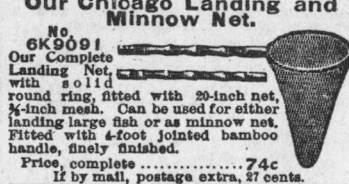

No. 6K9091 Our Complete Landing Net, with solid round ring, fitted with 20-inch net, ⅜-inch mesh. Can be used for either landing large fish or as minnow net. Fitted with 4-foot jointed bamboo handle, finely finished.
Price, complete.....74c
If by mail, postage extra, 27 cents.

The Otter Folding Catch All Minnow Net.

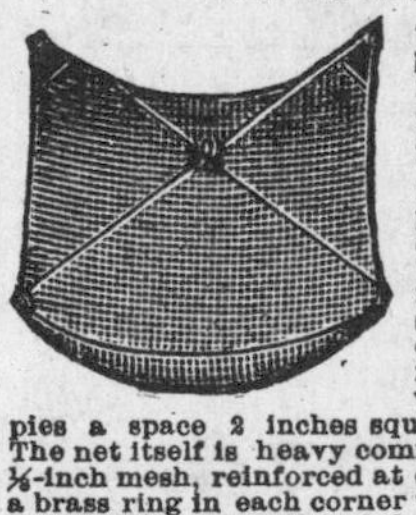

No. 6K9092 This net supplies a long felt want. A minnow net that can be folded into a small space and when spread out is large enough to be practically used as a minnow dip net. This net has a steel frame, 3½ feet square. This frame can be folded in a moment's time; when folded occupies a space 2 inches square, 2½ feet long. The net itself is heavy common sense netting, ⅜-inch mesh, reinforced at corners, fitted with a brass ring in each corner to attach to frame. This net is not fitted with handle; frame has a large ring to which a handle or rope can be attached. Price, complete with bag.....$1.13
If by mail, postage extra, 25 cents.

The Superior Folding Landing Net, Complete, $1.34.

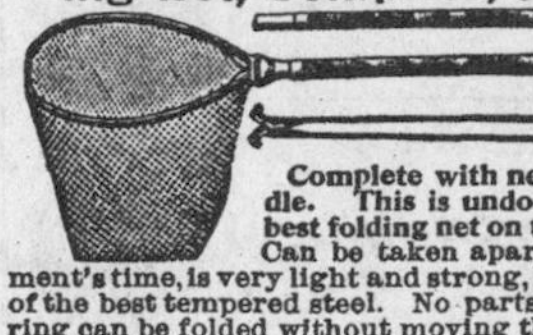

Complete with net and handle. This is undoubtedly the best folding net on the market. Can be taken apart in a moment's time, is very light and strong, being made of the best tempered steel. No parts to get lost, ring can be folded without moving the net. Put up in neat partitioned cloth bag.

No. 6K9095 No. 1 Ring, 14x15 inches, mounted with a square bottom linen waterproof net, ⅜-inch mesh, fitted with 4-foot jointed, nicely finished handle. Price.....$1.34
If by mail, postage extra, 20 cents.

Fishing Hats.

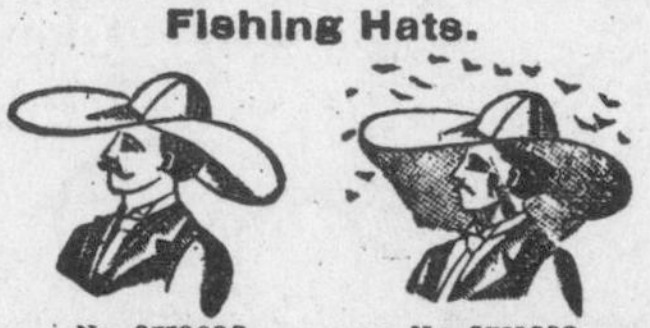

No. 6K9098 No. 6K9099

No. 6K9098 Collapsible Brown Muslin, green lined, rolls up and may be carried flat in the pocket. On a windy day pin it fast to coat collar. The finest thing out, cool and light.
Price.....20c

No. 6K9099 Same as the above, with a mosquito shield; a mosquito proof hat.
Price..(If by mail, postage extra, 4c.)..34c

Mosquito and Bee Head Nets, 35 Cents.

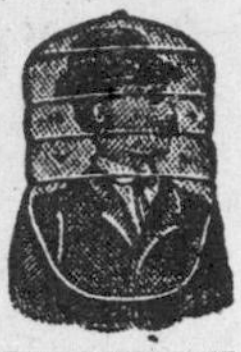

No. 6K9100 To be worn over the hat or cap. Made of good tarletan. Fitted with four light steel springs, bottom weighted with shot so as to set close to shoulders. Can be folded up and put in an ordinary coat pocket.
Price.....35c
If by mail, postage extra, 5c.
Everybody intending to camp or fish should have a Mosquito Head Net.

Trout Baskets with Patent Metal Fastening.

Our baskets are made from select French willow, very strong and light.

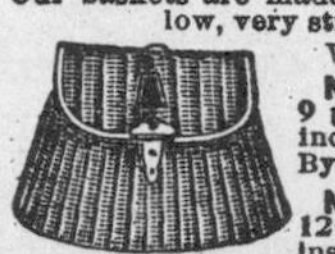

Weight, 1 to 1¾ pounds.
No. 6K9103 Capacity, 9 pounds; measures 7¼x12 inches on back. Price.99c
By mail, postage extra, 15c.
No. 6K9104 Capacity, 12 pounds; measuring 9x13 ins. on back. Price.$1.16
If by mail, postage extra, 20 cents.

Trout Basket Straps.

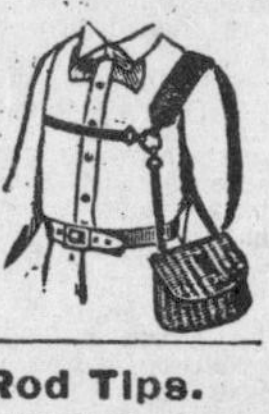

No. 6K9109 Patent Trout Basket Strap, the best trout basket strap made; made of webbing and leather, leaves the arms free. See illustration opposite.
Price.....20c
If by mail, postage extra, 4 cents.

Genuine Agate Rod Tips.

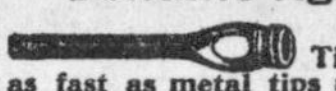

No. 6K9122 Agate Tips do not wear out a line as fast as metal tips and make line run more smoothly. Made for rod tips of the following diameters:

Size No.	4	3	1	1
Diameter, inch	3-32	4-32	5-32	6-32

Give size number when ordering.
Price.....51c
If by mail, postage extra, 2 cents.

Genuine Agate Guides for Rods.

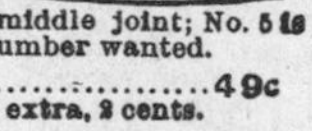

No. 6K9124 Does not wear out the line like metal guides and makes it run smoothly. No. 7 is for tip joint; No. 6 is for middle joint; No. 5 is for grip joint. Mention number wanted.
Price, each.....49c
If by mail, postage extra, 2 cents.

Foard's Disgorger.

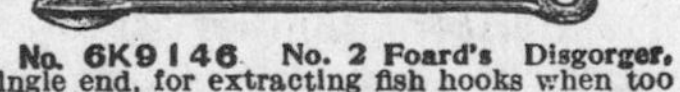

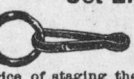

No. 6K9146 No. 2 Foard's Disgorger, single end, for extracting fish hooks when too far in mouth of fish and cannot be taken out by hand. Price.....9c

No. 6K9147 Double End Aluminum Disgorger. Very light, will not rust.
Price.....16c
If by mail, postage extra, 3 cents.

Acme Spring Balances.

WEIGH YOUR FISH.

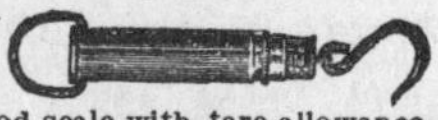

No. 6K9150 Acme Spring Balance, weighs from 1 to 10 lbs. by ¼ lbs. A good scale with tare allowance. Every scale warranted perfect. Price.....24c
If by mail, postage extra, 3 cents.

Set Line Snaps.

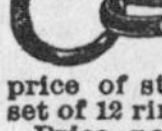

No. 6K9153 These snaps save tying on your hooks, permit hooks to be changed instantly, more than save their cost in the price of staging they save. Price, per dozen, set of 12 rings and 12 snaps.....$0.12
Price, per gross.....1.35
If by mail, postage extra, per dozen, 2 cents.

The Lightning Fish Scaler, 9c.

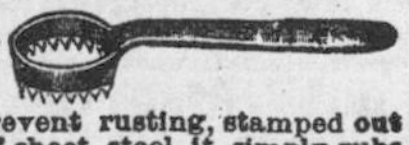

No. 6K9166 The best and most rapid scaler on the market. Neatly made, tinned to prevent rusting, stamped out of one solid piece of sheet steel, it simply rubs the scales off; also excellent for shredding codfish, preparing hamburger steak, etc.
Price.....9c
If by mail, postage extra, 3 cents.

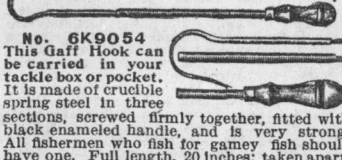

SEINES, TRAMMEL NETS, GILL NETS, HOOP NETS AND NETTING
WE ARE THE LARGEST DISTRIBUTERS OF FISH NETS IN THE UNITED STATES.

YOU WILL FIND OUR FISH NETS in use all over the country. Our business is so enormous that we take practically the entire output of one of the largest fish net factories in the world. Quality considered, our prices are from 25 to 50 per cent lower than those asked by other houses. By using a lower grade cotton in our seines and nets, or by hanging them with less slack than we do, we could easily sell them for one-third less than the prices we quote, but our nets as herewith described are hung with all necessary slack and are made of the very best long fiber cotton and linen twine. The rigging, or hanging, is done by experienced people. All our seines are hung on manila rope, double full reverse twist to prevent rolling. We use the full quantity of floats and leads, so that the seines and nets will stay properly in the water. In short, we aim to give you a net that will satisfy you in every particular, a net that we know is practical and will fully answer the purpose for which it is made, bought and sold, a net which, at our price, would be better value than it would be possible for you to obtain elsewhere.

OWING TO THE LARGE NUMBER OF SIZES and the varying demands one season over another for the different sizes, we do not stock the entire line of nets and seines, but make the big majority of them specially to order. Such nets as are carried in stock we so specify in the descriptions covering these particular nets. Gill nets, trammel nets, cotton and gill netting, and all hoop nets over 3 feet in diameter are not carried in stock, but are made specially to order. Therefore, when ordering, allow from four to eight days for us to make and ship the nets.

WE ADVISE anticipating your requirements in fish nets, inasmuch as the bulk of these goods are made to order, and although we have great capacity at our factory, at the same time this capacity, at the best, is limited, and if you wait until the last moment before ordering netting, seines or nets, your order is apt to come in with hundreds of others, and consequently will be subject to some delay which, if you are in urgent need of the nets, might put you to some inconvenience. Understand that we are able to take care of your order at any time, but when the season is at its full height, we naturally cannot fill orders as promptly as we are able to when the rush of orders is not so heavy.

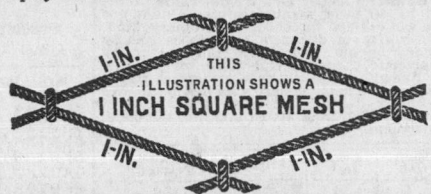

THIS ILLUSTRATION SHOWS A 1 INCH SQUARE MESH

Note—A seine mesh is diamond shaped, and a 1-inch square mesh measures 1 inch on each of the four sides. A 1½-inch square mesh measures 1½ inches on each of the four sides, etc. One-inch square mesh is 2 inches stretched mesh; 1½-inch square mesh is 3 inches stretched mesh.

The following seines are hung with leads and lines ready for use, except hauling lines. Compare our prices and quality with other houses, and you will find that we beat them all.

Weight: A 50-foot seine weighs about 20 pounds; a 100-foot seine weighs about 40 pounds; a 150-foot seine weighs about 80 pounds; a 300-foot seine weighs about 180 pounds.

SUPERIOR TAPERED DRAG SEINES

12-THREAD COTTON SEINE TWINE—SQUARE MESH.

Catalogue No.	Length, feet	Depth, Center, feet	Depth at ends, feet	1-inch Mesh, Price	1¼-inch Mesh, Price	1½-inch Mesh, Price
6K9685	20	4	3	$ 1.03	$ 0.88	$0.79
6K9686	30	4	3	1.44	1.30	1.19
6K9687	40	5	4	2.38	2.00	1.72
6K9688	50	6	4	3.00	2.49	2.20
6K9689	60	6	5	4.04	3.34	2.90
6K9690	72	7	6	5.45	4.40	3.85
6K9691	90	8	7	7.50	6.10	5.10
6K9692	100	8	7	8.34	6.78	5.75
6K9693	120	10	8	11.70	9.15	7.70
6K9694	150	12	10	16.70	13.15	10.99

We cannot ship seines C. O. D. Allow 4 to 8 days for us to make and ship your seine.

16-THREAD COTTON SEINE TWINE—SQUARE MESH.

Catalogue No.	Length feet	Depth, Center, feet	Depth at ends, feet	1-inch Mesh, Price	1¼-inch Mesh, Price	1½-inch Mesh, Price	2-inch Mesh, Price
6K9699	20	4	3	$ 1.12	$ 0.98	$ 0.87	$ 0.77
6K9700	30	4	3	1.74	1.44	1.32	1.15
6K9701	40	5	4	2.70	2.24	1.96	1.65
6K9702	50	5	5	3.38	2.80	2.40	2.13
6K9703	60	6	5	4.65	3.77	3.20	2.79
6K9704	72	7	6	6.25	5.03	4.35	3.63
6K9706	100	8	7	9.70	7.70	6.55	5.39
6K9707	120	10	8	13.39	10.50	8.90	7.25
6K9709	180	12	10	24.32	18.85	15.80	12.31
6K9710	200	14	10	28.00	21.70	18.19	14.51
6K9712	300	14	10	42.24	32.54	27.00	21.76

We cannot ship seines C. O. D. Allow 4 to 8 days for us to make and ship your seine.

Cotton Seine Netting.

This netting is intended for fishermen who wish to repair or make their own nets. Price quoted is for the netting only, and does not include the floats, leads or lines. This netting is made of white seine twine. When ordering, be sure to give the depth, size of mesh and catalogue number of netting desired. We can furnish any depth desired. Cannot be returned if made as ordered. Allow 4 to 8 days to make and ship your netting.

No. 6K9727 Cotton Netting No. 12, soft or medium twine, 1-inch square mesh or larger. Price, per pound....42c
No. 6K9728 Cotton Netting No. 16, soft twine, 1-inch square mesh or larger. Price, per pound................39c
Don't fail to state the depth and the size of mesh of netting wanted.

Straight Seines "Superior Quality."
9-12-16 TWINE.

The depths given are straight from end to end and do not taper. Hung with leads and floats. Made of best soft laid twine. Send cash in full with order. Seines or netting cannot be returned if sent as ordered. Expect a delay of from 4 to 8 days.
NOTE—All our seines are square mesh.

Mesh, inches	No. 6K9716 Price, per running yard. 12-thread—Soft. Sq. Mesh.				No. 6K9717 Price, running yd. 16-thread—Soft Sq. Mesh.			
	1	1¼	1½	2	1	1¼	1½	2
6 ft. deep	22c	19c	16c	18c	25c	21c	18c	14c
8 ft. deep	28c	23c	18c	16c	33c	26c	21c	18c
10 ft. deep	31c	25c	22c	17c	37c	29c	25c	20c
12 ft. deep	36c	29c	24c	21c	44c	33c	28c	23c
14 ft. deep	40c	34c	27c	22c	63c	39c	33c	25c

Lake or River Drag Seines, made of Woodbury's best white cotton, soft laid seine twine. No better seine made at any price. Hung with leads, floats, and line ready for use. Square mesh. These seines are straight from end to end and do not taper. All complete and ready for use.

No. 6K9721 9-thread medium laid twine.

Length	Depth	⅞-inch Mesh Price	1-inch Mesh Price	1¼-inch Mesh Price
20 feet	4 feet	$1.41	$1.01	$0.89
30 feet	5 feet	2.46	1.69	1.50
40 feet	6 feet	3.75	2.53	2.19
50 feet	7 feet	5.24	3.51	2.99
60 feet	8 feet	7.06	4.58	3.90

No. 6K9722 12-thread soft laid twine.

Length	Depth	⅞-inch Mesh Price	1-inch Mesh Price	1¼-inch Mesh Price	1½-inch Mesh Price
20 feet	4 feet	$1.72	$1.09	$0.94	$0.80
30 feet	5 feet	2.99	1.90	1.54	1.32
40 feet	6 feet	4.63	2.85	2.32	2.05
50 feet	7 feet	6.64	3.94	3.19	2.75
60 feet	8 feet	8.95	5.25	4.20	3.55
75 feet	8 feet	10.85	6.55	5.20	4.45

No. 6K9723 16-thread soft laid twine.

Length	Depth	1-inch Mesh Price	1¼-inch Mesh Price	1½-inch Mesh Price
20 feet	4 feet	$1.24	$1.05	$0.90
30 feet	5 feet	2.20	1.77	1.54
40 feet	6 feet	3.30	2.60	2.30
50 feet	7 feet	4.60	3.67	3.15
60 feet	8 feet	6.00	4.80	4.09
75 feet	8 feet	7.54	6.00	5.13

Superior Creek Seines. All fitted with floats and sinkers.

No.	Lengths		4 Ft. Deep	5 Ft. Deep	6 Ft. Deep	7 Ft. Deep
6K9735	10 ft.		$0.54	$0.65	$0.74	$0.85
6K9736	15 ft.	1-2 in. center, 1 in. at ends.	.84	.96	1.10	1.28
6K9737	20 ft.		1.10	1.30	1.46	1.69
6K9738	25 ft.		1.40	1.62	1.85	2.05
6K9739	30 ft.		1.72	2.05	2.28	2.50

Each end of a creek seine is of 1-inch square mesh, No. 9 twine, and one-third the length of the seine in center is ½-inch square mesh, No. 14-6 twine. When ordering seines give size and price as well as catalogue number. Seines and netting cannot be returned if sent as ordered.

WHEN YOU SEND US AN ORDER for merchandise please be very careful to give catalogue number in full, including any letter, and when you have finished writing your order, please check it over carefully to see that it is correct. This will make it easy for us to fill your order correctly.

Superior Minnow Seines.

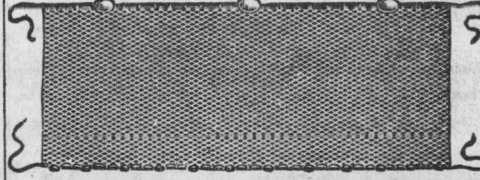

These minnow seines are hung complete with leads and floats, made in ⅜-inch, ¼-inch and ½-inch square mesh. Prices on other lengths or depths quoted upon application. When ordering give catalogue number, length, depth and size of mesh. Minnow seines ⅜ and ¼-inch mesh are made of No. 20-6 twine. Minnow seines with ½-inch square mesh are made of No. 14-6 twine. Allow 4 to 8 days to make.

Number	D'pth Feet	Size Square Mesh	L'gth 10 feet	L'gth 15 feet	L'gth 20 feet	L'gth 25 feet	L'gth 30 feet
6K9740 A	3	⅜-inch	$0.72	$1.08	$1.45	$1.80	$2.39
6K9740 B	4	⅜-inch	.89	1.35	1.80	2.20	3.00
6K9740 C	5	⅜-inch	1.09	1.65	2.15	2.67	3.50
6K9746 D	3	¼-inch	1.20	1.85	2.40	3.00	3.70
6K9746 E	4	¼-inch	1.55	2.33	3.08	3.89	4.95
6K9746 H	5	¼-inch	1.89	2.85	3.75	4.75	5.90
6K9752 I	3	½-inch	.65	.99	1.32	1.69	2.00
6K9752 J	4	½-inch	.82	1.22	1.68	2.04	2.40
6K9752 K	5	½-inch	.96	1.39	1.93	2.42	2.90

Minnow Netting.

Minnow Netting, made of cotton twine. The prices are for the netting only; not rigged with sinkers, floats or lines. Price is by the running yard, hung measure. Cannot be returned if sent as ordered.

Catalogue Number	Size, Square Mesh	Per Yard 4 Feet Deep	Per Yard 5 Feet Deep	Per Yard 6 Feet Deep
6K9755A	¼-inch	40c	52c	64c
6K9755B	⅜-inch	20c	29c	34c
6K9755C	½-inch	19c	23c	28c

The Charles Minnow Trap.

No. 6K9756 This Minnow Trap is made on the order of a fyke net, made of extra heavy woven netting, ⅞-inch square mesh, the hoop at mouth of trap is 12 inches in diameter, the body of trap is 3 feet long, the wings measure 20 feet from end to end. This net can be set in any stream with stakes, and is an excellent trap for capturing minnows and small fish. Price $1.65

$1.65

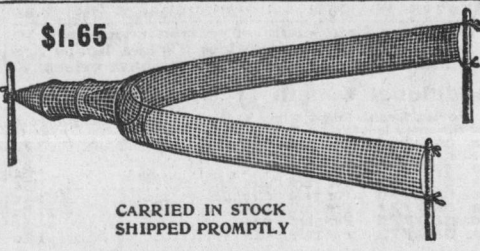

CARRIED IN STOCK SHIPPED PROMPTLY

WE GUARANTEE SATISFACTION to our customers on every transaction they have with us and we will fill your orders with the best merchandise at money saving prices.

Improved Good Sense Minnow Seines, 3-16-Inch Mesh.

The Good Sense Minnow Seines sold by us are entirely unlike those sold elsewhere, as our nets are not made of the flimsy netting used by all other manufacturers. One of our Good Sense Nets will outlast three of the ordinary kind. Considering the superiority of our nets over those sold by other dealers, in comparing our prices with those asked by others, you will appreciate the wonderful values we are offering in these goods. We also claim our nets are better rigged than those sold elsewhere. These nets are all 4 feet deep. We cannot furnish any other depth. We carry a full stock of these nets, all orders are filled from stock, and we, therefore, guarantee prompt shipment.

Catalogue No.	Long, feet	Deep, feet	Price	If by mail, Postage
6K9758A	4	4	$ .23	14c
6K9758B	6	4	.34	19c
6K9758C	10	4	.55	24c
6K9758D	12	4	.68	34c
6K9758E	15	4	.84	42c
6K9758F	20	4	1.10	64c
6K9758G	25	4	1.30	Not
6K9758H	30	4	1.59	Mailable

Good Sense Netting, 10 Cents.

No. 6K9759 Improved Good Sense Netting only, without floats, leads or lines, made only 4 feet deep, 3-16-inch mesh. We cannot furnish this any other depth. Price, per yard.. 10c

Superior Brook and Creek Funnel Nets.

Brook Nets are carried in stock and are shipped promptly.

Our New Brook and Creek Funnel Nets, made expressly for fishing in brooks or small streams. The first or large hoop is made D shape to set flat on the bottom of the stream. These nets are set in the stream and require no wings. Will catch and hold all medium size fish. These nets weigh about 4½ lbs.

Catalogue No.	Style of Throat	Height of Mouth Ft.	Width of Mouth Ft.	Length Ft	Number of Hoops No.	Size of Twine No.	Size Mesh Front In.	Size Mesh Middle In.	Size Mesh Tail In.	Price
6K9760	Double	1¼	3	6	8	9	1¼	¾	¾	$0.65
6K9761	Double	1¾	3½	7	9	9	1¼	¾	¾	.89
6K9762	Double	1½	4½	7	9	16-12	1¼	¾	¾	1.19
6K9763	Double	1¾	5	8	6	16	1½	¾	¾	1.35

The Superior Fyke or Hoop Net.

Lengths which we give on wings are for each wing. Hoops are on outside of netting, thus greatly saving the same. Made of best quality cotton twine. Hung ready for use. Netting can be furnished without hoops to your order if desired. Expect a delay of from 4 to 8 days. Cannot be returned if made as ordered.

Wts.	ft	lbs
Wts. 2	ft.	10 lbs.
Wts. 2½	ft.	12 lbs.
Wts. 3	ft.	20 lbs.
Wts. 4	ft.	25 lbs.
Wts. 5	ft.	35 lbs.
Wts. 6	ft.	46 lbs.

No.	Style Throat	Height, Mouth ft	Length of Net ft	Number of Hoops	L'gth Right Wing ft	Length Left Wing ft	Size of Twine No	Size of Mesh, Inches Square Front	Middle	Tail	White Twine Price
6K9765	Single	2	6	4	6	6	9	¾	¾	¾	$1.69
6K9766	Single	3	10	6	9	9	24	1¼	1¼	1¼	2.66
6K9768	Double	2½	8	6	6	6	16	1¼	1¼	1¼	2.35
6K9769	Double	3	10	6	9	9	24	1¼	1¼	1¼	2.75
6K9770	Double	4	16	7	12	12	24	2	1¾	1½	3.77
6K9771	Double	4½	18	8	15	15	24	2½	2	1½	5.29
6K9772	Double	5	18	8	15	15	28	2½	2	1½	5.65
6K9773	Double	6	18	8	18	18	28	2½	2½	1½	7.65

For Fyke Nets made of tarred twine add 10 per cent to the above prices. When hoops are not wanted deduct one-fifth from above prices.

Additional Length of Wings for Above

We can furnish longer wings at the following prices per yard for the extra length:

No. 6K9765	Per yard extra	5c
No. 6K9766	Per yard extra	5c
No. 6K9768	Per yard extra	6c
No. 6K9769	Per yard extra	5c
No. 6K9770	Per yard extra	4c
No. 6K9771	Per yard extra	5c
No. 6K9772	Per yard extra	5c
No. 6K9773	Per yard extra	7c

SUPERIOR FUNNEL OR HOOP NETS, WITHOUT WINGS.

With hoops complete. Made of the best quality cotton twine. When ordering nets, give size, price and catalogue number, to avoid error. Expect a delay of from 4 to 8 days.

Description No.	Style Throat	Weight, lbs.	Height Mouth ft.	Length of Net ft	Number Hoops No	Size of Twine No	Size of Mesh, Inches Square Front in.	Middle in.	Tail in.	Price
6K9780	Single	7	3	6	4	9	¾	¾	¾	$1.05
6K9783	Double	9	2½	8	6	16	1	¾	1	1.55
6K9784	Double	15	3	10	6	24	1¼	1¼	¾	2.00
6K9785	Double	20	4	16	7	24	2	1¾	1½	2.67
6K9786	Double	25	4½	18	8	24	2	2	1½	3.83
6K9787	Double	30	5	18	8	28	2½	2	1½	4.15
6K9788	Double	35	6	18	8	28	2½	2½	1½	5.45

SUPERIOR LINEN GILL NETTING.

NETTING ONLY WITHOUT FLOATS, LEADS OR LINES.

The best linen netting for all gill nets or for inside of trammel nets, made of best silver gray, 3-cord linen twine. Any depth required. Mention depth when ordering. This netting is for gill or set nets, and not for drag seines, the twine being too small for such use. Cannot be returned when made to order.

No. 6K9810 Size of Twine	1-inch square mesh, per lb.	1¼-inch square mesh, per lb.	1½-inch square mesh, per lb.	1¾-inch square mesh, per lb.	2-inch square mesh, per lb.
18 x 3 cord	$1.75	$1.67	$1.60	$1.51	$1.45
25 x 3 cord	2.05	1.89	1.80	1.72	1.71
30 x 3 cord	2.15	2.10	2.01	1.89	1.90
35 x 3 cord	2.39	2.30	2.20	2.17	2.14
40 x 3 cord	2.61	2.49	2.48	2.41	2.35

Size 25x3-cord, 1-inch mesh, contains about 180 square feet to the pound. Size 40x3-cord, 1-inch mesh, contains about 380 square feet to the pound. Larger mesh contains more square feet to the pound in proportion.

BEST QUALITY TRAMMEL NETS.

Our prices are below any competition, quality considered. The Superior Trammel Net has three nets hung upon a single top and a single bottom line. Of the three nets the two outside have large meshes of cotton seine twine. The inside net is made of best linen gilling twine, which is hung slack, forming a bag in which fish coming from either side are caught and unable to escape. These nets are not "drag seines," but are to be "set" stationary in the water, the same as a gill net.

Price is per running yard in length, hung measure, for the net complete. The mesh sizes are square mesh. Weight per yard, about ⅓-pound. Nets cannot be returned when made as ordered. Expect a delay of from 4 to 8 days.

These nets are sold by the yard, running measure. Multiply the price per yard by the number of yards wanted.

No.	Depth Feet	Outside Mesh Inches	Inside Mesh Inches	Inside Linen Twine No.	Outside Cotton Twine No.	Price per running Yd
6K9820	3½	6	¾	25		26c
6K9821	3½	6	1	25		20c
6K9822	3½	6	1¼	25		18c
6K9823	4	6	1	25		23c
6K9824	4	6	1¼	25		20c
6K9826	4½	7	1¼	25		21c
6K9827	4½	7	1¾	18		17c
6K9829	4½	7	2	18		15c
6K9830	5	8	1	25		26c
6K9831	5	8	1¼	18		19c
6K9832	5	8	2½	18		16c
6K9834	6	8	1	18		31c
6K9835	6	8	1¼	18		23c
6K9836	6	8	1½	18		19c
6K9837	6	8	2½	18		18c
6K9838	7	8	1¼	25		29c
6K9839	7	8	1½	18		28c
6K9840	7	8	2	18		22c
6K9842	8	8	1¼	25		33c
6K9843	8	8	1½	18		30c
6K9844	8	8	1¾	18		27c
6K9846	8	8	2½	18		23c
6K9847	8	8	3	18		20c

All No. 16-Thread Soft Laid Twine.

Other styles made to order. Meshes as given above are diamond square. Hung complete for use except hauling lines. When ordering nets, give size, price and catalogue number. Allow us 4 to 8 days to make.

NOTE—Trammel Nets are made to order only, and if order is filled correctly we cannot take the goods back, as we seldom have any two orders just alike in every particular. Consequently if the net were returned it would be a dead loss to us.

NOTICE—If you intend to use your net in water where there is a very swift current, same must be rigged accordingly. We can rig trammel nets extra heavy with leads and floats at an additional expense of 20 per cent over catalogue prices.

SUPERIOR SQUARE COTTON DIP NETS.

No. 6K9850 Made of cotton seine twine. Roped all around edges, with loops at corners. All are made 1-inch square mesh of No. 12 soft twine. Price is for netting only. No frame comes with these nets. Give size wanted. These nets are carried in stock and can be shipped promptly.

	Price	Postage extra
4x 4 feet, square shape	$0.22	10c
5x 5 feet, square shape	.34	12c
6x 6 feet, square shape	.45	16c
8x 8 feet, square shape	.78	28c
10x10 feet, square shape	1.15	38c
12x12 feet, square shape	1.65	48c

NOTICE—The meshes as given in this catalogue are all square mesh. One-inch square mesh is equal to 2-inch stretched mesh. Two-inch square mesh is equal to 4-inch stretched mesh. Be sure you are not ordering a larger mesh than you really want when you are placing your order.

LINEN GILL OR SET NETS.

A gill net is a single net, hung with floats and leads complete, without hauling lines. Made of best imported linen twine. These nets cannot be used for drag seines, the twine being too fine. They are set in the water and allowed to remain from 5 to 24 hours.

The fish are caught by the gills, hence the name gill or set nets.

Rigged complete ready for use. Made of linen twine. Price per running yard in length, hung measure. Weight, per yard, about ¼ pound.

NOTICE—The twine in these nets is very fine, not much thicker than heavy thread, therefore not suitable for dragging or use among snags and stumps.

Nets cannot be returned if sent as ordered. Allow us four to eight days to make.

No.	Depth feet	Size Linen Twine	Sq. Mesh, 1 inch Price, pr. yd.	Sq. Mesh, 1¼ in. Price, pr. yd.	Sq. Mesh, 1½ in. Price, pr. yd.	Sq. Mesh, 2 in. Price, pr. yd.	Sq. Mesh, 2½ in. Price, pr. yd.
6K9860	3½		14c	13c	10c	8c	
6K9861	4		16c	14c	12c	9c	9c
6K9866	5	All 40-3 Cord	16c	14c	12c	9c	9c
6K9873	6		19c	15c	14c	11c	10c
6K9880	7				15c	12c	
6K9883	8				16c	13c	

Other styles made to order. Our gill nets are made of Knox best Scotch linen twine.

NOTICE—The meshes as given in this catalogue are all square mesh. One-inch square mesh is equal to 2-inch stretched mesh. Two-inch square mesh is equal to 4-inch stretched mesh. Be sure you are not ordering a larger mesh than you really want when you are placing your order.

SUPERIOR COTTON TROT LINES.

Cotton Trot Lines, to use as set lines and top and bottom lines on small nets; in 50-foot coils, six rolls connected or 300 feet. Best quality. Sold in any quantity at dozen rates. Mention number when ordering. Carried in stock and can be shipped promptly.

NOTICE—We guarantee our trot lines to run full 50 feet to the coil. Endeavoring to meet our price, other dealers sometimes sell 35 or 40 feet coils for 50 feet. Measure your line and see that you get what you are paying for.

No. 6K9900

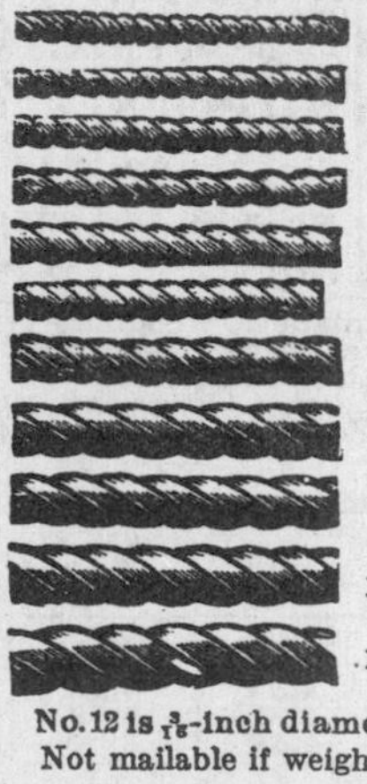

No.	Weight per doz.	Price, per doz. coils or 600 ft.	Postage per doz. coils.
1	15 oz	$0.24	$0.16
2	16 oz	.30	.17
3	19 oz	.39	.21
4	20 oz	.49	.31
5	23 oz	.55	.40
6	24 oz	.75	.44
7	32 oz	.86	.46
8	36 oz	1.00	.48
9	44 oz	1.20	.52
10	52 oz	1.38	.60
11	56 oz	1.60	

No. 12 is ¼-inch diameter..96 oz... 2.00
Not mailable if weighing over 4 lbs.

DEPARTMENT OF TENTS, WAGON, STACK AND MACHINE COVERS AND AWNINGS

WE OWN AND CONTROL ONE OF THE LARGEST EXCLUSIVE TENT, FLAG AND AWNING FACTORIES IN THE UNITED STATES. WE ARE ABLE TO RUN THIS FACTORY THE YEAR AROUND MANUFACTURING THESE GOODS, WHICH WE OFFER YOU, QUALITY CONSIDERED, AT PRICES FROM 25 TO 50 PER CENT LOWER THAN YOU COULD PURCHASE THE SAME GRADE OF GOODS ELSEWHERE. OUR TENT, COVER AND AWNING BUSINESS IS THE LARGEST IN THE UNITED STATES TODAY OF ANY HOUSE DEALING DIRECT WITH THE CONSUMER.

SOME YEARS AGO we were buying tents and covers the same as other dealers are buying them today—in the open market; but we found that we could not, as our business increased, give our customers goods which we could safely guarantee at all times to be up to grade. There is no business today that is so demoralized as the tent and awning business. Nine out of ten dealers today sacrifice quality in these goods in order to offer competitive and attractive prices. It was this condition that practically forced us into the tent manufacturing business. When we found that we could not safely recommend the tents and covers we were buying in the open market, when we thoroughly realized the conditions under which these goods were manufactured and sold throughout the country, we resolved that either we would sell honest tents and honest covers, or we would quit the business, and we found that the only way in which we could sell honest goods in this line, goods that we could absolutely guarantee to be full size and full weight, was to manufacture them ourselves. We accordingly started a factory of our own, and in the short time of three years this factory has grown to be one of the largest factories of its kind in the United States. Our growth in this business is not due to the fact that we have sold certain size tents and covers for less money than other houses, but is due entirely to the fact that the tents, covers, awnings and flags we sell are exactly as we represent them to be in every particular, and that when we state a tent is 9½ feet wide by 12 feet long, the tent will be found exactly in accordance with these measurements, and not 6 inches short in the width and 5 inches in the length, height of wall or height of center.

THE AVERAGE MAN who buys a tent or cover knows little about what he is buying. He is apt to assume that a tent is a tent and a cover is a cover, and in making his selection will, naturally, be guided largely by the price. Lack of space will not permit us to explain in full in how many ways a tent is "skinned" by unscrupulous dealers and manufacturers in order to be sold at or below our price. For your guidance we will state a few methods employed by most of the manufacturers and dealers today: The average 8-ounce tent sold by other dealers is made of 7-ounce duck; 9-ounce duck is invariably substituted for 10-ounce. A tent properly made, such as ours, ought to be made of 29-inch duck; this is the standard width, but in order to effect a saving, many manufacturers, in order to substantiate their claim that their tents are made of 8-ounce duck, use duck 36 inches wide. The wider the duck, naturally the lighter the material. Eight-ounce duck 36 inches wide is not as good a piece of material as 8-ounce duck 29 inches wide, such as we use. A common plan of deception is to make the door of the tent of lighter canvas than the body of the tent. All our tents are made with doors from 15 to 30 inches wide, in proportion to the size of the tent, and you will find the same material in the door of the tent as you will find in the roof or body. Jute rope is also used very extensively in competitive tents. Jute rope is entirely unfit for tents, as it rots very quickly and becomes hard and stiff, and there is always the danger of having your tent blown down at the risk of considerable inconvenience and possibly danger, when jute rope is used. We use the very best pure sisal and manila rope, and in all tents over 12x18 feet, and in all refreshment and photographers' tents we use the best pure manila rope.

WE WANT YOU to know all about our tents, covers and awnings. The more you know about them, the more certain we are of receiving your order. To aid you to buy to your best interest, we will send you upon request a free sample card of canvas, showing the quality of duck we use in our tents and covers, also giving on the reverse side of the card instructions on "How to judge a tent."

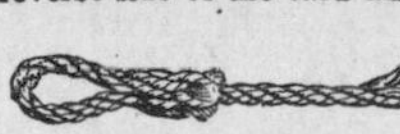

Fulton Brands.

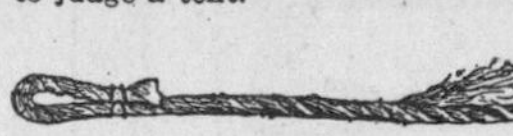

Other Makes.

THIS ILLUSTRATION will give you some idea of the relative qualities of jute rope, used by other manufacturers, and pure manila and sisal, used on all our Fulton Tents and Covers. Note the short, scanty fiber in the jute rope, indicating that the rope has absolutely no body to it, consequently no strength. Also note the common wire splice used by almost all other manufacturers. Compare this with the rope we use, as shown in the illustration, and note the long, full fiber stock, giving this rope enormous strength, and also note the hand worked sailor splice we use as compared with the wire splice used by others.

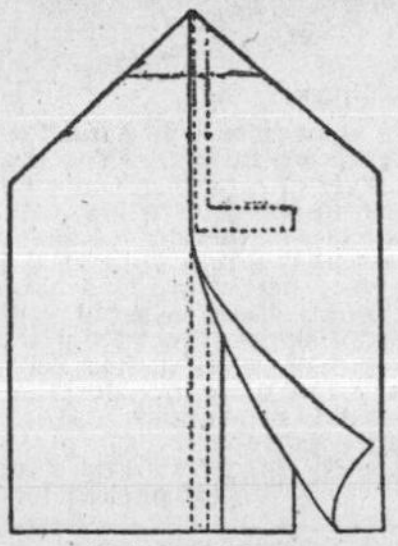

A Fulton Tent.

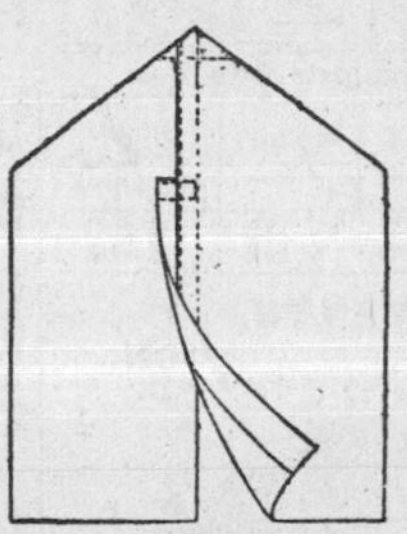

Other Tents.

THIS ILLUSTRATION shows the difference between a Fulton Tent as compared with any other make. Note the large, full door flap used by us, and note that our door laps over almost a full width of canvas, whereas the doors offered on other tents lap over but a few inches. We could reduce the price of our tents materially by making a cheap door, the same as that shown in the competitive tent, but in our Fulton Tents and Covers, we aim to represent only the highest quality that can be made in this line. Our object is not to see how cheap we can furnish these goods, but rather how good we can make them and then make the price consistent with the high class of material, labor and workmanship employed.

TWO DOORS. On all wall tents that are 16x24 feet or larger we will furnish a door at both ends without additional charge. We believe that a tent 16x24 feet or larger ought to have a door at both ends on account of its size, as a matter of convenience and to secure proper ventilation. We, therefore, will furnish all tents 16x24 feet with a door at each end, if desired, at the regular price quoted. Be sure to state whether you want two doors in your tent if you order a tent 16x24 feet or larger. On tents smaller than 16x24 feet we will furnish an extra door for 60 cents.

PRECAUTION. Be sure to slacken your guy ropes on your tent after or immediately before a rain storm, otherwise when your tent dries, the canvas will naturally shrink somewhat during the drying, and your tight guy ropes will pull the tent out of shape. Slacken the guy ropes until the tent is thoroughly dry, then again make them taut.

QUALITY AND PRICE GUARANTEE. We guarantee every tent in this catalogue to be lower in price than the same quality of goods can be bought elsewhere. If any house ever meets or cuts our price on any article, they do it at the expense of quality. If you do not find this so by comparing the goods, or if you ever buy anything from us that is not lower in price than the same high quality of goods can be bought from any other house, you are especially requested to return our goods at our expense and get your money back at once. We guarantee our tents and covers to be exactly as described in our catalogue. We guarantee them to be full weight 29-inch canvas, and to be full size. We guarantee the door of the tent to be of the same weight canvas as the rest of the tent. If you purchase a tent of us and do not find it exactly as we represent it, you have the privilege of returning it to us at our expense and your money and transportation charges will be refunded to you. Weigh one of our tents or covers and one of our competitors' make and note which weighs the most.

DELIVERIES. We carry all sizes of tents from 7x7 to 12x12 feet in stock and make prompt shipment, and on all other sizes allow three to five days' time to make the tent. In June and July allow from four to eight days.

FULTON WALL TENTS.

HIGHEST QUALITY.

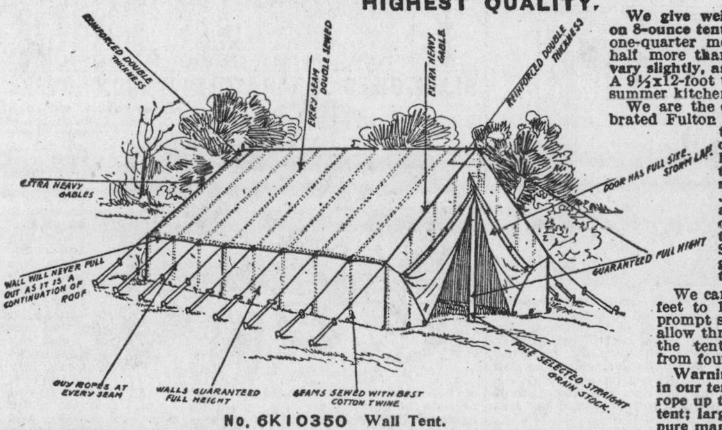

No. 6K10350 Wall Tent.

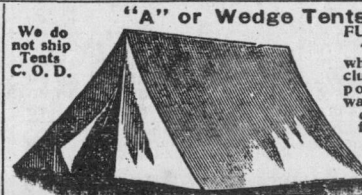

We give weight of tents with poles below on 8-ounce tents. 10-ounce will weigh about one-quarter more and 12-ounce about one-half more than 8-ounce. The weights may vary slightly, as poles do not always run alike. A 9½x12-foot tent makes a good outhouse or summer kitchen.

We are the only manufacturers of the celebrated Fulton Wall Tents. We warrant them to be exactly as represented. In ordering, give catalogue number, length, breadth and price. Allow three to five days' time for making tents, and in June and July allow four to eight days, according to the number of orders we have on hand at the time we receive your order. Send for samples of canvas which goes into our tents and instructions on "How to Judge a Tent."

We carry all sizes of tents from 7x7 feet to 12x12 feet in stock and make prompt shipment, and on all other sizes allow three to five days' time to make the tent. In June and July allow from four to eight days.

Warning—We do not use jute rope in our tents. We use the best pure sisal rope up to and including the 12x18-foot tent; larger than 12x18, we use the best pure manila rope. On all wall tents size 12x12 and larger, we furnish top guy ropes at each end. Order by catalogue number and give size of tent and weight of duck wanted.

No. 6K10350

Length and Breadth	Height of Wall	Height of Pole	Weight, 8-ounce	Our Prices include Poles, Pegs, Guys, Guy Ropes, etc., complete, ready to set up.		
Feet	Feet	Feet	Pounds	8-oz. Duck	10-oz. S. F. Duck	12-oz. S. F. Duck
7 x 7	3	7	30	$ 5.60	$ 6.70	$ 7.90
7 x 9	3	7	35	6.65	7.84	9.40
9 x 9	3	7½	40	8.00	9.54	11.44
9½x12	3	7½	45	9.00	11.00	13.15
9½x14	3	7½	50	10.40	12.50	14.90
12 x12	3½	8	55	11.15	13.20	16.00
12 x14	3½	8	60	12.50	14.95	17.90
12 x16	3½	8	70	13.80	16.50	19.90
12 x18	3½	8	70	15.30	18.34	22.28
14 x14	4	9	70	14.99	18.17	21.69
14 x16	4	9	80	16.35	19.68	23.75
14 x18	4	9	85	17.75	21.09	25.49
14 x20	4	9	100	19.01	22.98	27.56
14 x24	4	9	120	21.80	26.23	31.49
16 x16	5	11	90	20.24	24.30	29.23
16 x18	5	11	110	22.10	26.40	31.59
16 x20	5	11	120	24.70	29.35	35.19
16 x24	5	11	145	27.70	32.68	39.07
16 x30	5	11	170	32.90	38.83	46.90
18 x20	5	11	175	27.20	32.59	38.94
18 x24	5	11	180	29.90	36.25	42.63
18 x30	5	11	240	35.00	41.90	49.18
18 x35	5	11	290	41.10	47.80	57.39

Extras for Tents.

For wall tents made of 10-ounce double filled duck, add 5 per cent to the price of tents made of 12-oz. single filled duck. Where higher wall than regularly quoted is wanted, add 5 per cent of the cost of tent for each additional 6 inches.

Door at each end of tent can be furnished on all tents over 12x12 feet at an additional charge of 60 cents. Poles and pins are included with tents at the price quoted. When poles are not wanted, we will allow 5 per cent of the 8-ounce price. Stove pipe hole cut in tent with metal pipe ring sewed in, 80 cents extra.

A sod cloth on a tent is sewed to the bottom of the ends and sides of the tent, upon which is placed stones or earth to keep out wind, flies, etc. In measuring amount of sod cloth required, measure distance around the tent. A 12x16-foot tent would require 56 lineal feet of sod cloth. 9-Inch Sod Cloth. Price per lineal foot..........2c

Tent Flies.

A fly for a tent is an extra, removable roof, which is spread over the regular roof and staked down, which serves the purpose of making the roof of the tent thoroughly waterproof and also affords protection from the sun and makes the tent warmer in winter time. If you have an old tent with a leaky roof, buy a tent fly. The cost of a fly for a wall tent is one-half (½) the price of the tent of corresponding size and weight of duck. For example, a fly for a $10.00 tent will cost $5.00. Tents cannot be returned if sent as ordered.

"A" or Wedge Tents.

We do not ship Tents C. O. D.

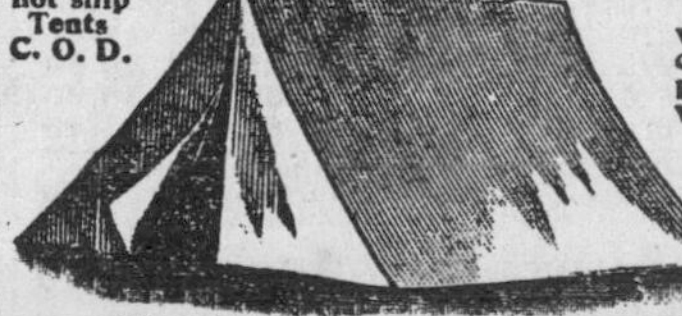

FULTON BRAND

The weight which we give includes poles. When poles are not wanted with tents deduct 5 per cent from the price of 8-ounce tent. Give catalogue number and style wanted.

No. 6K10340 The following prices include poles:

Style No.	Length and Breadth	Weight, 8-oz.	Height	Price, 8-oz. Duck	Price. 10-oz. Duck	12-oz. S. F. Duck
A	7 x 7 ft.	25 lbs.	7 ft.	$4.59	$5.50	$ 6.40
B	7 x 9 ft.	27 lbs.	7 ft.	5.63	6.73	7.96
C	9 x 9 ft.	32 lbs.	7 ft.	6.31	7.57	9.02
D	9½x12 ft.	38 lbs.	7½ ft.	7.61	9.00	10.92

The Fulton Rope Ridge Wedge Tents.

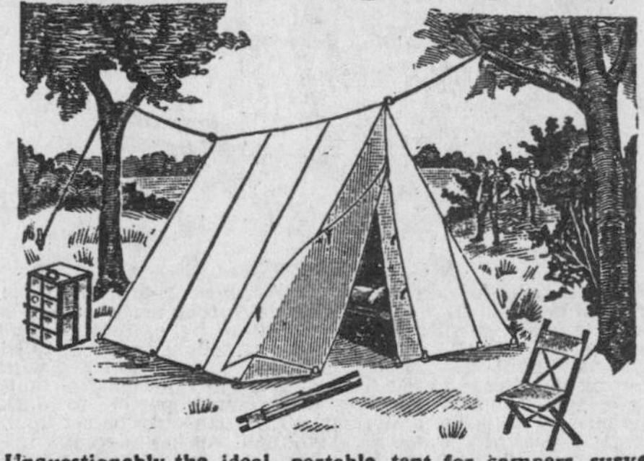

Unquestionably the ideal portable tent for campers, surveyors, prospectors, etc. No poles required with this tent. The rope ridge enables you to stretch this tent up between two trees or two forked sticks or in any manner that you can fasten the two end ropes so as to hold the ridge taut. This tent possesses an advantage over the tent with poles, as it can be easily toted from one place to another; the heavy, bulky poles being unnecessary. The following prices do not include the rope for fastening to trees, etc. The rope furnished with the tent is sewed in the ridge and terminates at each end of the tent in a spliced loop, making it easy for the user to attach additional ropes in accordance with his requirements. The 5x7-foot 8-ounce tent weighs 12 pounds. The 7x7-foot 8-ounce tent weighs 14 pounds. The 7x9-foot 8-ounce tent weighs 17 pounds. Mention size and weight wanted.

No. 6K10341	Size	Height	8-ounce	10-ounce	12-oz. Single Filled
	5x7 feet	6 feet	$3.76	$4.64	$5.50
	7x7 feet	7 feet	4.64	5.57	6.63
	7x9 feet	7 feet	5.79	6.90	8.21

WE ALWAYS UNDERSELL

outdistance and outclass all competition. Following our well established policy of steadily lowering prices we have still further reduced them in this catalogue.

500 SEARS, ROEBUCK & CO., CHICAGO, IL. CATALOGUE No. 117.

Miners' Tents.

FULTON BRAND.

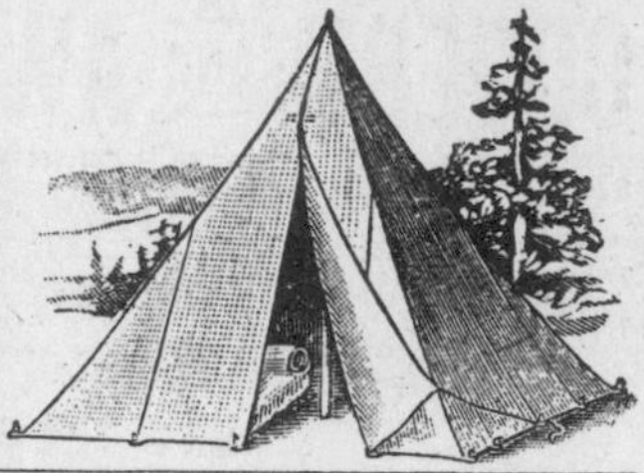

For Miners, Prospectors, or may be used as play tents for children. The weight which we give includes poles. Without pole, deduct 15 cents from price quoted. Tents are not shipped C. O. D. Give style number.

No. 6K10342		Weight, 8-ounce	Price, Complete with Pole			
Style No.	We do not ship Tents C. O. D. Size of Base		Ht.	8-oz. Duck	10-oz. Duck	Single Filled 12-oz. Duck
A	7x7 feet	15 lbs.	7 ft.	$3.30	$4.03	$4.80
C	9x9 feet	22 lbs.	8 ft.	4.80	5.85	6.97

REFRESHMENT TENTS.

FULTON BRAND.

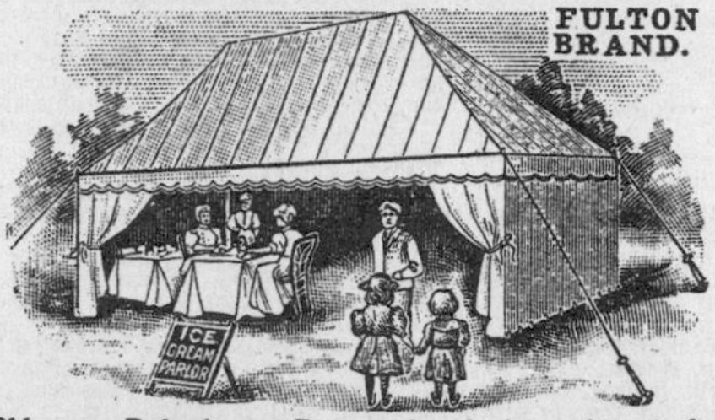

Oblong or Refreshment Tent, made of plain white duck, as shown in illustration. Price includes poles, pins, guy ropes, etc., complete, ready to set up. We furnish all refreshment tents with double corner guy ropes made of best manila and fitted with our patent non-breakable, non-slip metal slides. This illustration shows front open and folded at the sides; the front may be closed or stretched out in front for an awning or taken off altogether, as it is put on with hooks for these changes. Tents are made to order and cannot be returned if made as ordered.

No. 6K10344 Cannot be shipped C. O. D. Order by catalogue number and size. Allow five to eight days to make.

Size	Weight. 8-oz.	Height	Height, Center	8-oz. White Duck	10-oz. White Duck	12-oz. Single or 10-oz. Double Filled Duck
9x14	50 lbs.	6ft.	10 ft.	$15.50	$18.25	$21.95
9x19	80 lbs.	6ft.	10 ft.	19.70	23.30	27.45
12x19	100 lbs.	6ft.	11 ft.	21.80	25.59	30.50
14x21½	125 lbs.	6ft.	11 ft.	27.15	32.15	38.20
14x23½	130 lbs.	6ft.	11 ft.	29.25	34.70	41.15

Tents Without Poles, deduct 5 per cent of the 8-ounce price.

Send for free samples of canvas and instructions on "How to Judge a Tent."

THE FULTON PHOTOGRAPHERS' TENTS

Tents cannot be returned, as they are made to order. It takes three to five days, and in June and July five to ten days to fill tent orders. Send for free samples of canvas used in our tents and covers. We do not ship tents C. O. D.

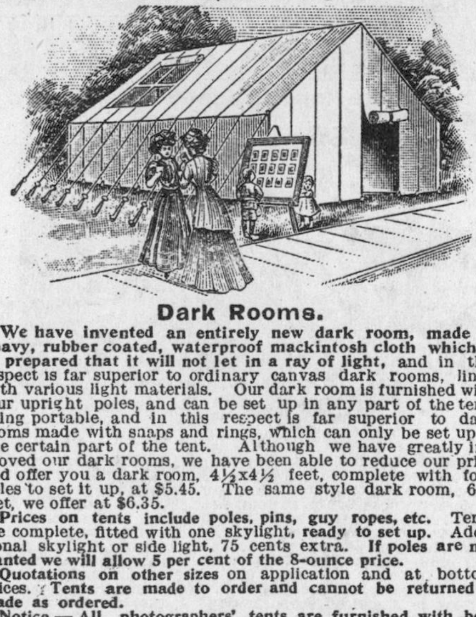

Dark Rooms.

We have invented an entirely new dark room, made of heavy, rubber coated, waterproof mackintosh cloth which is so prepared that it will not let in a ray of light, and in this respect is far superior to ordinary canvas dark rooms, lined with various light materials. Our dark room is furnished with four upright poles, and can be set up in any part of the tent, being portable, and in this respect is far superior to dark rooms made with snaps and rings, which can only be set up in one certain part of the tent. Although we have greatly improved our dark rooms, we have been able to reduce our price and offer you a dark room, 4½x4½ feet, complete with four poles to set it up, at $5.45. The same style dark room, 6x6 feet, we offer at $6.35.

Prices on tents include poles, pins, guy ropes, etc. Tents are complete, fitted with one skylight, ready to set up. Additional skylight or side light, 75 cents extra. If poles are not wanted we will allow 5 per cent of the 8-ounce price.

Quotations on other sizes on application and at bottom prices. Tents are made to order and cannot be returned if made as ordered.

Notice — All photographers' tents are furnished with best manila rope and our patent non-breakable, non-slip metal tent slides.

No. 6K10360 Weight given below includes poles and may vary on account of poles not always being alike.

Order by Catalogue Number and Size — Size	Weight of 8-oz. pounds.	Pole	Wall	Price, Complete, Without Dark Room — 8-oz. Single Filling Duck	10-oz. Single Filling Duck	12-oz. Single or 10-oz. Double Filled Duck
12x16 ft.	135	11 ft.	6 ft.	$18.72	$22.36	$26 96
12x21 ft.	155	11 ft.	6 ft.	23.05	27.35	32.85
12x24 ft.	175	11 ft.	6 ft.	25.00	29.68	35.16
14x24 ft.	230	12 ft.	6 ft.	28.06	33.50	40.35
14x28 ft.	240	12 ft.	6 ft.	32.31	38 49	46.20

Tom Sawyer's Play Tent.

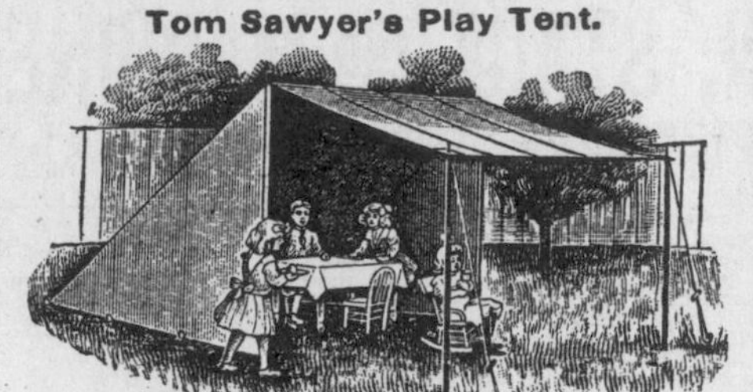

In answer to a demand for a boys' tent, we offer this tent, which is an ideal tent for the purpose. This tent is made on the style of a lumberman's tent. The front of the tent, as shown in the illustration, can be raised as an awning, or can be let down, thereby having the tent closed on all four sides. This tent is 6 feet wide by 6 feet long; height of upright pole, 5½ feet; height of extra poles used to support the awning, 4½ foot. Made without wall, as shown in the illustration the roof slopes direct from the ridge to the ground. Made of heavy drill, well finished throughout, the same as any regular tent. The price includes the tent complete with four poles, necessary ropes and stakes. Carried in stock and can be shipped promptly.

No. 6K10361 Size 6x6 feet. Price............$3.65
Weight packed for shipment, 26 pounds.

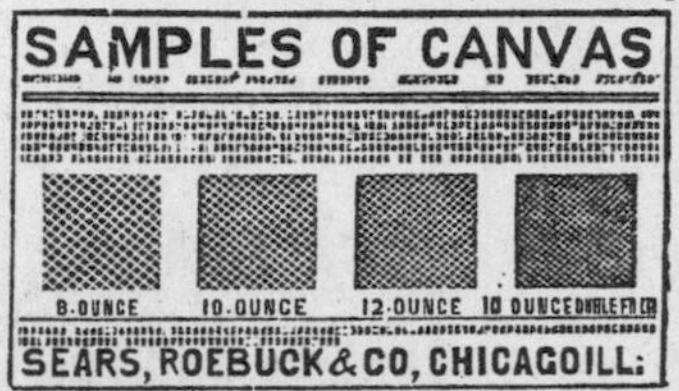

Send for this free sample card showing the grades and qualities of duck used in our tents and covers. It also contains complete information on How to Judge a Tent, placing you in a position to buy intelligently and to your best interests. Send us a postal card asking for our Tent Sample Card, and the same will be sent to you at once by return mail.

Our Patent Tent Slide.

This illustration shows our patent tent slide used on all our tents. This slide is is far superior to the wood slide used by all other manufacturers. It is made of coppered wire, it positively will not slip, it is instantly adjusted, cannot break, will not rust, cannot be lost from the guy rope. These patent slides greatly add to the value of the tent and are furnished on all of our tents without any extra charge whatsoever.

Cowboys' Brown Waterproof, Wool Lined Bed Sheet.

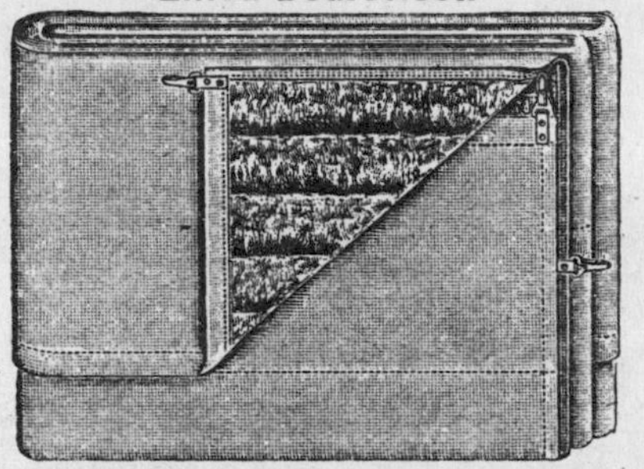

No. 6K10363 The best bed sheet made for herders, prospectors, explorers, who are compelled to sleep in a tent or on the ground. This bed sheet is made of 11-ounce brown waterproof canvas, 34 inches wide, lined with best quality wool blanket. The waterproof canvas will keep the moisture out from above and below, the wool blanket will keep you warm. Fitted with snaps and rings, possessing every advantage of a sleeping bag and none of the disadvantages of weight and bulk, in addition to being waterproof and far less expensive. State size wanted.

Size, 6x12 feet. Price..........................$4.80
Size, 7x16 feet. Price..........................7.36

8-ounce duck means a yard will weigh 8 ounces.
10-ounce duck means a yard will weigh 10 ounces.
12-ounce duck means a yard will weigh 12 ounces, etc.

Gospel Tents.

We will be pleased to quote prices. We have made a great many and if you will give us width, length and weight of duck preferred, or advise us how many people you wish to provide room for, and give us a sketch of the seating arrangement, we will be glad to quote you prices upon receipt of your inquiry.

Merry-Go-Round Tops and Circus Tents.

We can make them and will be pleased to quote prices on receipt of specifications. Our large experience in this line will enable us to quote you better prices and make you a better top than can be procured elsewhere.

Stable Tents.

We are supplying the leading contractors, herders and ranchmen in the country with stable tents, and know that we could satisfy you with a better tent at a lower price, quality considered, than you could get elsewhere. Tell us what you want and we will quote you a price.

Rubber Blankets.

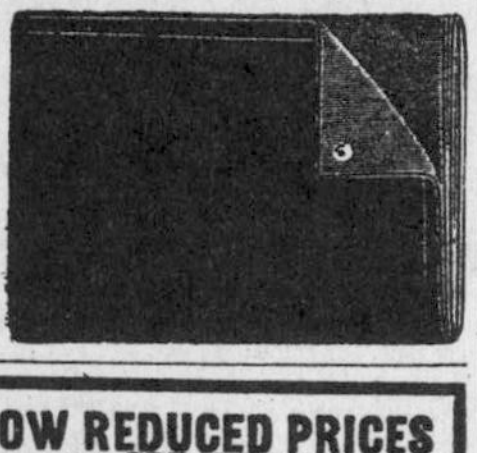

No. 6K10364 Black Rubber Blanket, lined with white sheeting, 3¾ feet wide and 6 feet long. Weight, about 3 pounds. Price..........$1.32

No. 6K10366 Black Rubber Blanket, lined with black cotton fleece cloth, 4½ feet wide and 8 feet long. Weight, about 4½ pounds. Price $3.15

THE SURPRISINGLY LOW REDUCED PRICES prevailing in this catalogue mean GREATER SAVINGS TO OUR CUSTOMERS than ever before.

Rubber Ponchos, $1.45.

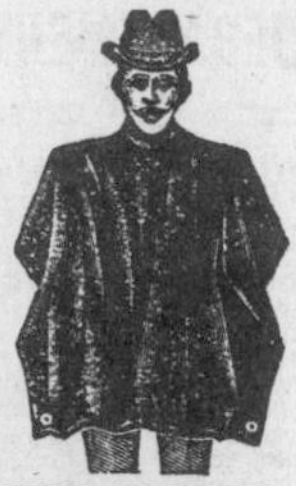

No. 6K10368 Our Luster Ponchos, made of finest quality rubber, lined with fine sheeting and have a hole in center, covered with heavy flap. By using this hole and drawing the poncho over the head, it forms a large rubber cape, protecting the entire body. It is absolutely waterproof and may also be used as a rubber blanket. Size, 45x72 inches. Weight, 3½ pounds.
Price.........................$1.45

PAULINS OR STACK AND MACHINE COVERS.

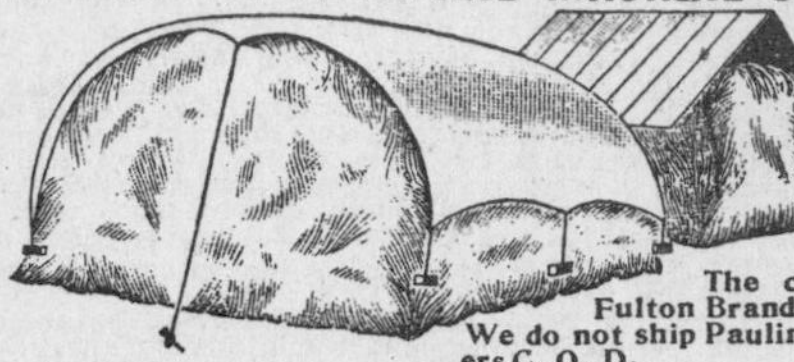

The celebrated Fulton Brand. We do not ship Paulins or Covers C. O. D.

Made of white duck. Always state size wanted when ordering. These goods are not tents, but paulins or stack covers. Stack covers have short ropes, BUT NO POLES; machine and merchandise covers have eyelets around side. Paulins are made to order and cannot be returned if sent as ordered. Write for samples of canvas which goes into our covers.

No. 6K10370 Be sure to state size wanted.

Style No.	Size, Feet	Wgt. of 8-oz.	8-oz. Duck	10-oz. Duck	12-oz. Duck
A	10x16	11 lbs.	$ 3.48	$ 4.10	$5.05
B	10x18	12 lbs.	3.92	4.80	5.80
C	12x14	12 lbs.	3.79	4.45	5.50
D	12x16	13 lbs.	4.35	5.35	6.35
E	12x18	16 lbs.	4.90	6.00	7.35
F	12x20	17 lbs.	5.30	6.65	8.00
G	14x16	16 lbs.	5.00	6.35	7.80
H	14x18	18 lbs.	5.85	7.15	8.85
J	14x20	20 lbs.	6.36	7.84	9.60
K	14x24	25 lbs.	7.60	9.30	11.53
L	16x16	18 lbs.	5.98	7.30	8.98
M	16x18	19 lbs.	6.50	8.00	9.90
N	16x20	23 lbs.	7.00	8.55	10.65
P	16x24	26 lbs.	8.70	10.60	13.00
Q	18x20	25 lbs.	8.12	9.90	12.00
R	18x24	30 lbs.	9.70	11.90	14 60
S	18x28	36 lbs.	11.50	14.20	17.40
T	18x30	39 lbs.	12.20	15.10	18.50
U	20x24	34 lbs.	11.00	13.50	16.60
V	20x36	51 lbs.	16.29	20.00	24.60
W	24x30	51 lbs.	16.01	19.60	24.20
X	24x40	68 lbs.	21.05	25.55	31.70
Y	24x50	84 lbs.	26.90	33.20	40.90

BLACK OILED OR TARPAULIN WAGON COVERS

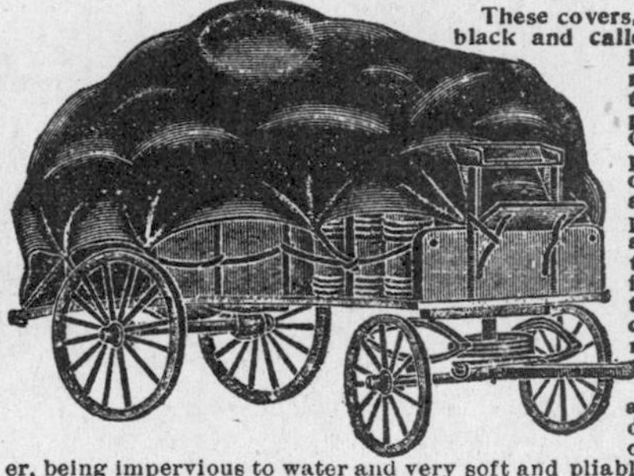

These covers, although black and called tarpaulins, have no tar in their composition. Our waterproof dressing is an oil preparation and is entirely free from anything calculated to rot or burn the canvas, but adds to the durability of the cover, being impervious to water and very soft and pliable. It will neither rot nor mildew from damp, or break from being too hard. They are invaluable to persons who are shipping and receiving goods that are liable to be damaged by wet weather. In ordering, give catalogue number, size and price. Weight, 9 to 28 lbs.; 6x12, 12 lbs.; 6x9, 9 lbs.; 7x12, 16 lbs.; 7x14, 19 lbs.

Allow from two to five days to make.

No.	Size, ft.	Price	Size, ft.	Price	Size, ft.	Price
6K10375	6x 8	$2.27	7x 9	$2.99	8x10	$3.82
	6x 9	2.52	7x10	3.32	8x12	4.62
	6x10	2.89	7x12	3.95	8x14	5.38
	6x12	3.40	7x14	4.73	8x16	6.18
	6x14	4.00	....	......	9x14	6.07

Prices given on other sizes upon application.

WHITE DUCK EMIGRANT WAGON COVERS.

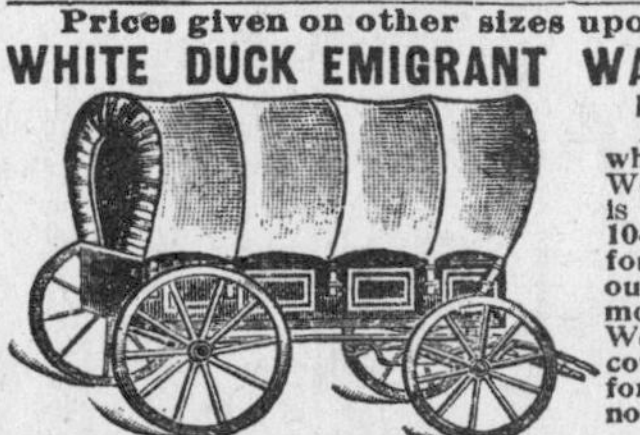

FULTON BRAND.

Always give size when ordering. Weight given below is on 8-ounce covers. 10-ounce weighs one-fourth more and 12-ounce about one-half more than 8-ounce. We do not send wagon covers C. O. D. Write for prices on covers not quoted in this list.

No. 6K10380

Size, Feet	Lbs.	8-oz. Duck	10-oz. Duck	12-oz. Duck
10x10	7	$2.19	$3.02	$3.68
10x12	7½	2.63	3.25	4.20
10x14	7¾	3.09	4.00	4.99
10x16	9	3.86	4.70	5.85
11x13	9	3.41	4.00	5.15
11x15	10	3.70	4.65	5.90
12x15	20	4.40	5.45	6.60
12x16	25	4.65	5.70	7.00
12x20	30	5.75	7.10	8.65

Allow from two to five days to make.

AWNINGS—Fulton Adjustable Window Awning.

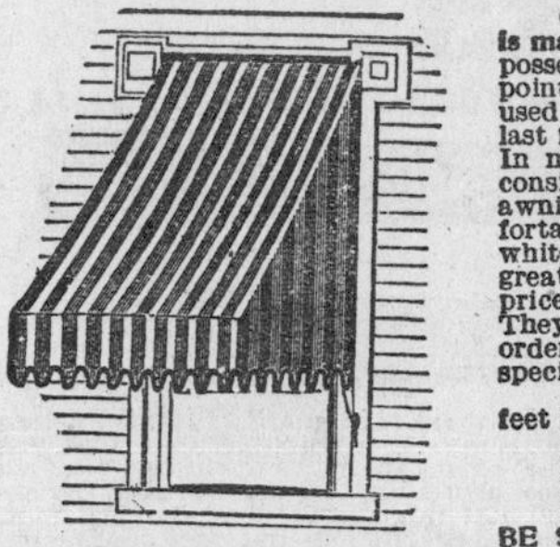

Can be attached in three minutes by anyone, and as quickly removed. This awning is manufactured and sold by us exclusively. No other house has the Fulton awning, which possesses distinct features of its own not found in any other awning. The particular points of merit are the quick adjustment, the rigidity of the frame, the quality of the stripe used and the excellent workmanship. This awning is high grade in every way and will last for several years and is guaranteed to fully answer the purpose for which it was made. In making these awnings at our own factory we enjoy the first cost, consequently, quality considered, are able to offer them to you at lower prices than you could possibly procure awnings of inferior quality. For very small expense you can make your house very comfortable during the hot summer months. These awnings are made of handsome blue and white full weight awning stripe with scalloped curtain, as shown in the illustration, and greatly add to the appearance of the house. They come complete, ready to hang up. The price includes rope, screws and cleat. All you need to attach the awning is a screwdriver. They come in five sizes to fit windows 2 feet 4 inches to 4 feet 6 inches wide. When ordering, give width of your window from center to center of casing on each side and specify number of awning you desire.

No. 6K10399 No. 1 Awning will fit any size window from 2 feet 4 inches to 2 feet 7 inches. Price $1.64
No. 2 Awning will fit any window from 2 feet 8 inches to 3 feet. Price 1.70
No. 3 Awning will fit any window from 3 feet 1 inch to 3 feet 6 inches. Price .. 1.80
No. 4 Awning will fit any window from 3 feet 7 inches to 4 feet. Price 1.88
No. 5 Awning will fit any window from 4 feet 1 inch to 4 feet 6 inches. Price .. 1.95
BE SURE to order awning WIDE ENOUGH.

We can make anything in Canvas Covers, Tents, Walls, Partitions, etc. Send us your specifications and diagram and we will quote prices.

Malleable Iron Tent Pegs.

They last a lifetime. Cannot be broken.

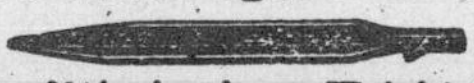

No. 6K10387 Short Peg, 8¾ inches long. Weight, about 4½ ounces each. Price, per dozen.........50c
No. 6K10388 Long Peg, 13½ inches long. Weight, about 7¼ ounces each. Price, per dozen.........69c

Our Palmetto Lawn Tents.

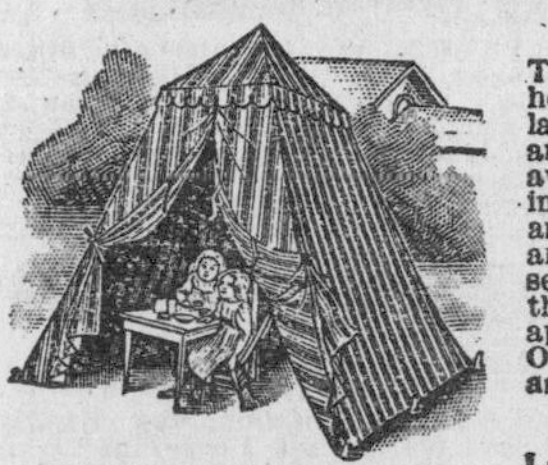

These Palmetto Lawn Tents intended for playhouses for children, for lawn parties, fairs, etc. They are made of about 8-ounce awning material and come in stripes of blue and white, are set up with one pole, and a light iron frame sewed into the tent around the eaves; are handsome in appearance upon the lawn. Order by catalogue number and state size wanted.

WARNING — There are Lawn Tents on the market quoted as being the same size as ours, but which are 6 inches shorter in height of center and size of top.

No. 6K10393

Size of Base	Size of Top	Height at Center	Height at Side	Wgt., lbs.	Price
7x 7 ft.	2 ft. 4 in.	7 ft. 6 in.	6 ft.	17	$4.54
8x 8 ft.	2 ft. 4 in.	8 ft.	6 ft. 6 in.	19	5.60
10x10 ft.	3 ft. 6 in.	9 ft.	7 ft. 6 in.	26	8.20

PORCH CURTAINS.

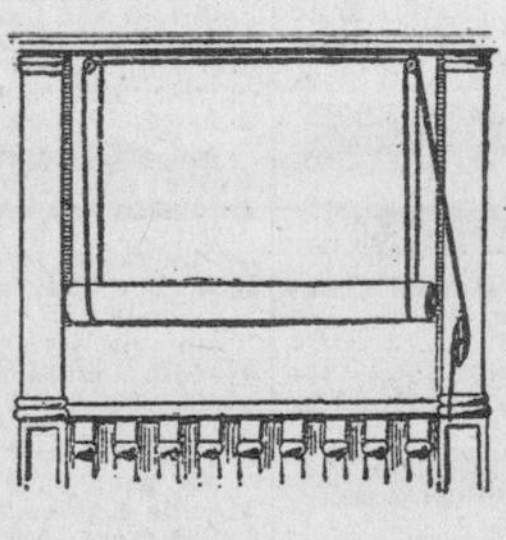

If you have a porch or piazza, a porch curtain will enable you to enjoy the full benefit of same, as it will protect you from the heat of the sun; will also keep out dust and rain, and will help to make your porch very comfortable during the summer months.

Our porch curtains are made of fancy striped or plain white duck, furnished complete with pulleys, ropes and roller, and all necessary screws and adjustments ready to attach to your porch. No experience is required to put up one of these curtains. This curtain is made with double pulleys—the roller is at the bottom. By pulling the rope you revolve the roller, the curtain being raised or lowered, as desired.

When ordering, give actual height and width of the opening for which you desire the curtain. These curtains are made to order. Cannot be returned if made as ordered. We sell these curtains by the square foot, the price per square foot includes all accessories. A curtain 10 feet high and 16 feet wide would contain 160 square feet, and at 6 cents per square foot would cost $9.60. Plain White Striped Duck

No. 6K10397 Price, per sq. ft. 4½c 6c

STORE AND PORCH AWNINGS.

We are headquarters for awnings of all kinds.

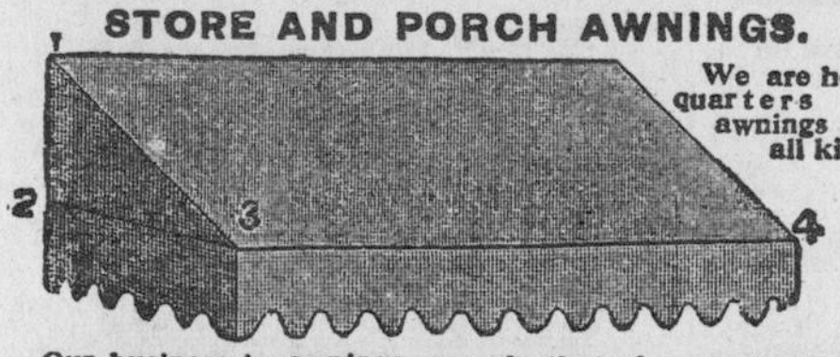

Our business in awnings exceeds that of any other house. Our awnings are made of the best full weight canvas, and all exposed metal parts are either japanned or galvanized. The quality, workmanship and material in our awnings are superior to that in awnings furnished by any other house. We herewith quote prices on a few of the most popular sizes of store awnings. On any awning not quoted in the following list we will be pleased to quote prices on receipt of specifications. The prices quoted herewith are for awnings complete, ready to be set up and include all the necessary fittings.

No. 6K10405 The following prices are for awnings made of plain white duck, blue and white or brown and white. (State which color is desired when ordering.)

Height from 1 to 2	Projection from 2 to 3	Width of Front—from 3 to 4					
		10 Feet	12 Feet	14 Feet	16 Feet	18 Feet	20 Feet
4 ft.	4 ft.	$5.80	$6.47	$7.00	$ 7.60	$ 8.27	$ 8.93
4 ft. 6 in.	4 ft. 6 in.	6.33	7.00	7.60	8.27	8.94	9.67
5 ft.	5 ft.	6.87	7.53	8.20	8.87	9.60	10.60
5 ft. 6 in.	5 ft. 6 in.	7.60	8.27	8.87	9.67	10.60	11.47
6 ft.	6 ft.	8.33	8.93	9.67	10.60	11.53	12.47

If cover only is wanted, deduct 20 per cent or one-fifth from the above price. Lettering roof of awning, 6 cents per letter extra. Lettering on curtain, 4 cents a letter extra.

Camp Chairs and Stools.

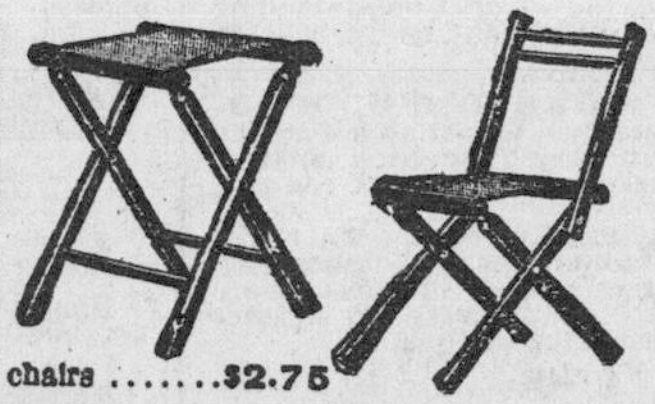

No. 6K10431 Canvas Top Camp Stool, well made. Weight, 2¾ lbs.
Each 20c
Per crate of 12 stools ..$2.00
No. 6K10432 Canvas Top Camp Chair, same as No. 6K10431, with back. Weight, 3¾ pounds.
Price, each 27c
Per crate of 12 chairs $2.75

The Bradley Folding Chair.

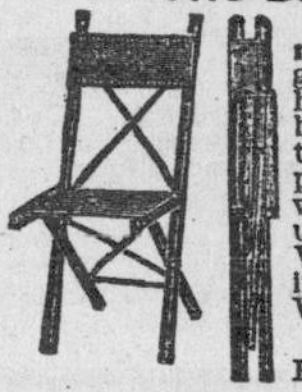

The Most Compact Folding Chair on the market. Frame is made of the best straight grain white maple, seat and back made of heavy brown duck. It has best quality blue steel braces. This chair is guaranteed not to collapse. It will hold 300 pounds without straining the chair in any way. Can be instantly folded without the use of any tools or loosening any screws. When folded it occupies a space of 36 inches long and 12 inches circumference. Weight, 5¼ pounds.

No. 6K10433 The Bradley Chair. Price 58c

Our Portable Folding Cot and Litter.

The Strongest, Most Compact Cot on the Market.

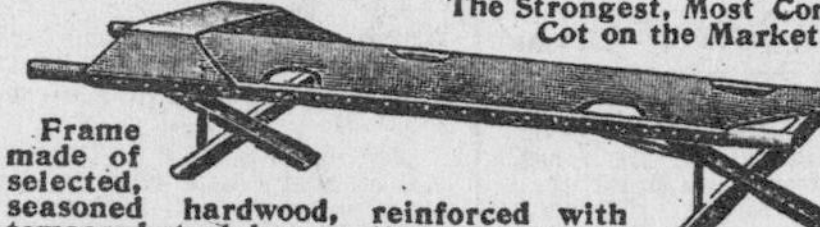

Frame made of selected, seasoned hardwood, reinforced with tempered steel braces, side rails project as shown in the illustration, so that the cot, if necessary, can also be used as a litter or stretcher. The top is made of special weave, full weight, 10-ounce brown duck, with patent pillow casing, so made that it can be stuffed with hay, straw or clothing. Length, 6 feet 3 inches; width, 29 inches; size when folded, 6 feet 3 inches long, 5 inches wide, 2 inches thick. Weight, 15 pounds.

No. 6K10435 Price $1.56

Improved Gold Medal Folding Camp Bed.

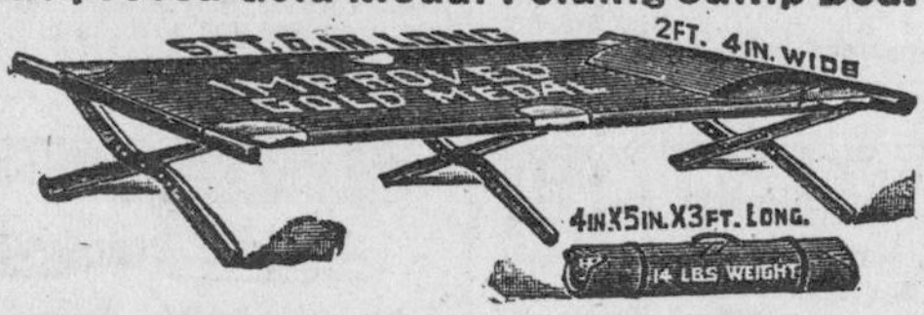

This is positively one of the most substantial, well made and well finished folding cots upon the market. It is so constructed that it may be folded into a parcel 3 feet long and about 5 inches in diameter, and is guaranteed to hold 1,000 pounds. The frame is made strong and substantial, and is covered with heavy brown canvas and has a pillow casing which may be stuffed with straw, hay or clothing to act as a pillow. It is about 6½ feet long and 2½ feet wide and weighs about 14 pounds.

No. 6K10438 Gold Medal Folding Camp Bed. Price, $2.15
No. 6K10439 Gold Medal Bed, same as above, but extra wide; 36 inches wide, 20 inches high, 6 feet 5 inches long; weighs 20 pounds. Price $3.15

CAMPING OUTFIT COMPLETE AT $5.48

No. 6K10455

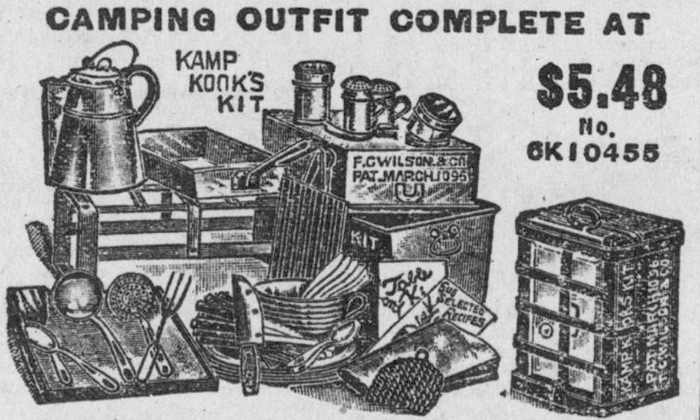

Illustration of kit unpacked. Kit packed for shipment.

No. 6K10455 Wilson's Improved Kamp Kook's Kit. Just the thing for camping out. 53 pieces. Fire jack, two boilers suitable for using as an oven, fry pan, coffee pot and all utensils and tableware for a party of six. Everything first class. Boilers are made of 26-gauge smooth steel. The entire kit nests in small space, and when packed ready for shipment makes a package 14½x10½x8 inches, all nested together and can be firmly locked up by an ordinary padlock. Weight, complete, 20 pounds. Price, complete $5.48

This outfit can be packed inside of either the oven or the fire box of our No. 6K10470 Stove, making the most complete, compact and serviceable combined outfit on the market.

Our Camp Cutlery Outfit Reduced to $1.55.

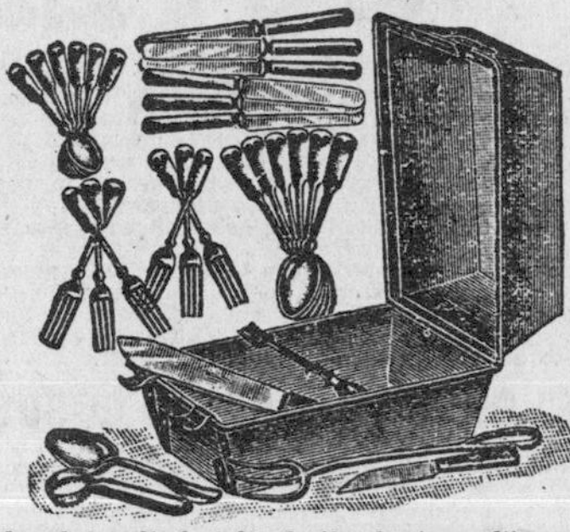

No. 6K10458 Our 31-piece Camp Cutlery Outfit contains everything needed in cutlery for camping purposes for a party of six people. This outfit consists of six each good quality tinned knives and forks, six heavy tinned table spoons, six tea spoons, one 11-inch aluminum mixing or basting spoon, one 12½-inch heavy three-tined tinned fork, one fine 7-inch beech handle butcher knife, best quality paring knife, lightning fish scaler, improved can opener, all packed in one of our Acme roasting pans which is the strongest and best made. The bottom is strengthened by two ribs and has a heavy rack to keep the meat out of the gravy. This pan is suitable for baking or roasting, and makes an excellent case for the above described cutlery. Every item in this outfit is practical, serviceable and will give satisfaction. Weight, 7 pounds.

Price, per outfit, complete as described $1.55

Our Rival Camp Stove, $3.08.

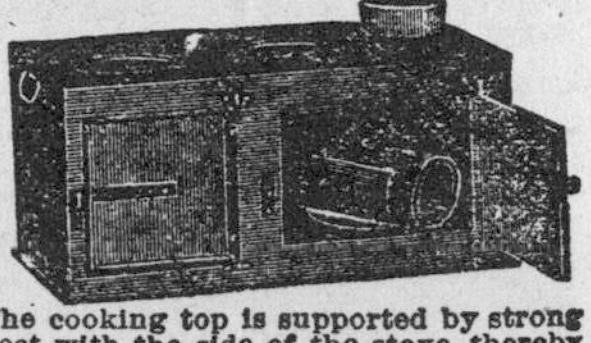

No. 6K10470 Perfect baker, good heater. This stove is made of heavy sheet steel, has heavy ½-inch rolls all around bottom line of body, the corners are well mitered, are well braced inside; also has half-inch rolls around the doors to stiffen them, strong steel latches for each door. The cooking top is supported by strong angle braces which connect with the side of the stove, thereby preventing warpage from the weight of cooking vessels. The pipe collar is in the corner, increasing the space for top cooking. The bake oven is corrugated to prevent warping, and an air space formed by a double wall is made between the fire and the oven; this prevents burning of food in the oven. The stove pipe is nested in six short lengths, so as to pack inside of either the fire box or oven. This stove burns wood; fire is placed on the ground; burns equally well inside or outside of the tent; is an excellent heater; will hold fire all night and keep the tent very comfortable; is undoubtedly the best stove of this kind on the market. The stove is not only for campers, but good for contractors, surveyors, cattlemen, people of all occupations who are compelled to stay in the open air and move from place to place. Length of stove, 29 inches; width, 16 inches; height, 14 inches. Size of oven, height, 9 inches; depth, 16 inches; width, 12 inches. Size of pot holes on top, 7 inches. Weight, crated for shipment, about 40 pounds. Price $3.08

Our No. 6K10455 outfit can be packed inside of either the fire box or oven of this stove, making one compact piece of baggage.

For a complete line of Blue Flame Oil Stoves, hard and soft coal Cooking and Heating Stoves, see our Stove Catalogue.

FLAGS.

REDUCED PRICES.

Made in our own factory, guaranteed full size and weight.

United States Cotton Bunting Flags.

Not Mounted.

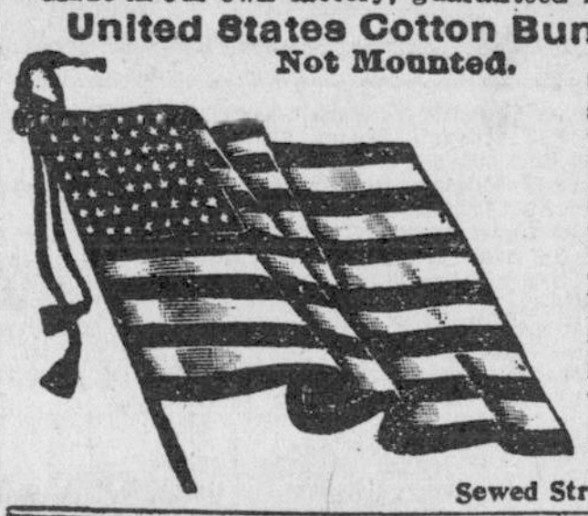

Standard Cotton Bunting, sewed stars and stripes, fast colors full number of stars, sewed on both sides. All have heavy canvas head, with grommets according to size. All flags have extra heavy hems, which prevent ripping and fraying. Do not confuse these flags with the cheap cotton printed flags.

Full number of stars, forty-six; a star for every State.

Sewed Stripes and Sewed Stars.

Catalogue No.	Length, feet	Price	Postage, each
6K10523	5	$0.64	8c
6K10524	6	.79	13c
6K10525	8	1.12	19c
6K10527	10	1.65	26c
6K10528	12	2.50	50c
6K10530	15	3.65	Not mailable

Sewed Wool Bunting U. S. Flags.

Not Mounted. Made of Best Navy Bunting.

FORTY-SIX STARS.

The best finished and strongest wool bunting flag ever offered to the trade. Seams all double stitched. Full complement of stars sewed on both sides of the field, placed Government regulation. The regulation schoolhouse flag is 8 feet. 4-foot flag has only thirteen stars.

Catalogue No.	Length, feet	Price	Postage, each
6K10540	4	$0.94	6c
6K10541	5	1.32	10c
6K10543	6	1.66	12c
6K10545	7	1.95	16c
6K10547	8	2.45	21c
6K10549	10	3.55	30c
6K10551	12	4.75	46c
6K10552	14	6.50	60c
6K10553	16	8.00	Not mailable

National Decorating Bunting.

No. 6K10560 Fast Color Cotton Bunting. 23 inches wide, red, white and blue stripes with or without stars as desired.

Price, per yard 4c
By the piece of about 60 yards. Price, per yard....3⅛c

BURGEES, PENNANTS and YACHT ENSIGNS made to special order in our own factory. Send sketch showing lettering and size desired and we will quote prices.

CUTLERY AND RAZORS

New Goods, Greater Variety, at Greatly Reduced Prices.

WE ARE CONSTANTLY IMPROVING and changing our line of cutlery in order to conform with new ideas and in order to retain the lead we have over all other cutlers in the amount of business we do, the quality of our goods, and in the wonderful values we are offering. You will find our prices are greatly reduced. You will find that we offer values in this line, quality considered, that could not be found elsewhere. It is an easy matter for any house to offer cutlery of similar style and design for less money than we ask for our goods, but bear in mind that every article of cutlery we handle, whether butcher knife, pocket knife, shear, scissor or razor, is guaranteed to be exactly as represented and described, guaranteed to give satisfaction, and guaranteed to be better value than you could get elsewhere, or money will be refunded. We make no attempt to sell cheap cutlery, but we do sell the highest quality of cutlery for less money than any other house on earth. Our Cutlery Department is in charge of experienced cutlers, and our method of inspection is the best in the country—every article we handle is carefully inspected.

WILBERT AND DIAMOND A BRAND GOODS are the highest quality goods made. Every pocket knife, shear, scissor, butcher knife or razor bearing either of these brands is guaranteed to be absolutely the highest quality. The workmanship, material, grinding and temper are absolutely the best that skilled labor, up to date manufacturing methods and finest quality raw material will produce.

OUR CUTLERY BUSINESS is the largest cutlery business in the world today dealing direct with the consumer. Buying cutlery in quantities from five to ten times as great as any other house, we enjoy the minimum of cost, and by selling these goods with but one small margin of profit added to the actual cost we are, quality considered, able to give you better value than it would be possible for you to obtain anywhere else. We solicit your business on cutlery with the distinct understanding that if the goods are not found entirely satisfactory in every way they may be returned to us, and money and transportation charges will be cheerfully refunded.

Prices Reduced on Silver Plated Knives, Forks and Spoons.

We illustrate and quote prices on the Rogers Brand and on our own special made Paragon Brand here. For a more complete line, showing the different brands and the latest patterns in silver plated ware, for a complete line of fruit dishes, cake baskets, berry sets and tea sets, turn to pages 332 to 343.

Knives, forks, spoons, etc., all come in the regulation length. Knives are 9¼ inches long, forks are 7½ inches long, teaspoons are 6 inches long and tablespoons are 8 inches long. The Paragon Brand is the one we recommend above all other makes. The blanks are heavier made, more silver deposited, higher finished, finer trimmed and in every way superior to brands being sold for 30 to 50 per cent more than we ask, considering the quality.

12-Pennyweight Knives and Forks.

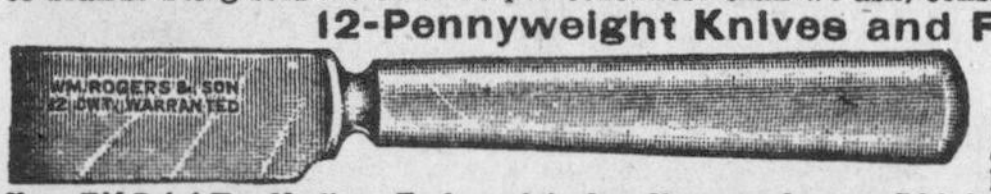

ROGERS BRAND.

No. 5K0115 Medium Knives, plain handle, per dozen, 9¼ inches long....$2.76
No. 5K0117 Medium Forks, plain handle, per dozen, 7½ inches long........2.76

PARAGON BRAND.

No. 5K0104 Medium Knives, plain handle, per dozen, 9¼ inches long..........2.68
No. 5K0106 Medium Forks, plain handle, per dozen, 7½ inches long..........2.68

1847 ROGERS BRAND.

No. 5K0142 Medium Knives, plain handle, per dozen, 9¼ inches long..........3.35
No. 5K0144 Medium Forks, plain handle, per dozen, 7½ inches long..........3.35
Postage extra, per dozen, 48 cents.

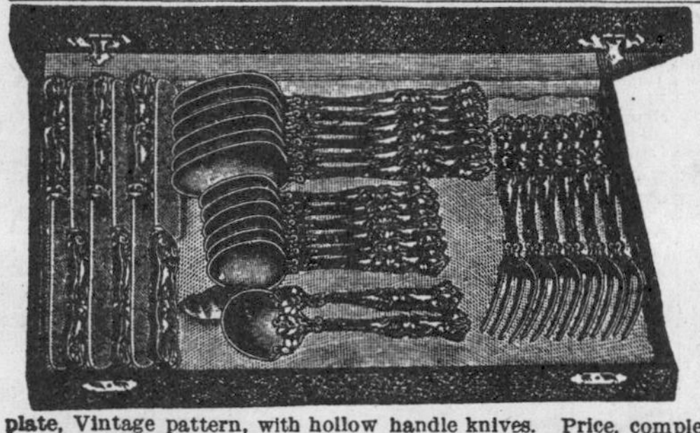

GREAT REDUCTION IN PRICES ON 26-PIECE DINNER SETS.

COMPLETE DINNER OUTFIT FOR SIX PEOPLE, consisting of six teaspoons, six tablespoons, six forks, six knives, one sugar shell and one butter knife, in a fancy lined leatherette case. **Shipping weight, about 7 lbs.**

No. 5K01002 1847 Rogers Bros.' brand, extra plate, Vintage Pattern, with hollow handle knives. Price, complete........$12.50
No. 5K01004 1847 Rogers Bros.' brand, triple plate, Vintage pattern, with hollow handle knives. Price, complete..............$14.90
No. 5K0898 1847 Rogers brand, extra plate, Vintage pattern, with plain handle, 12-pennyweight knives and forks. Price, complete..........$8.68
No. 5K0899 1847 Rogers brand, triple plate, Vintage pattern, with plain handle 12-pennyweight knives and forks. Price, complete..........$10.12
No. 5K0586 Paragon brand, triple plate, Fleur de Lis pattern, guaranteed for fifteen years, with hollow handle knives. Price, complete..........$10.88
No. 5K0585 Paragon brand, extra plate, Fleur de Lis pattern, guaranteed for fifteen years, with plain handle, 16-pennyweight knives. Price, complete..........$8.59
No. 5K0891 Rogers brand, extra plate, Oxford pattern, medium weight, with plain handle, 12-pennyweight knives. Price, complete..........$5.45
No 5K0893 Rogers brand, triple plate, Oxford pattern, medium weight, with plain handle, 12-pennyweight knives. Price, complete..........$7.25

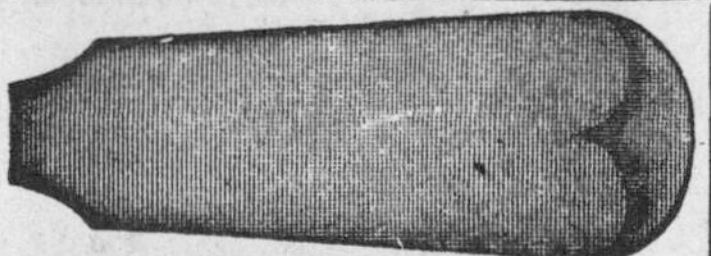

TIPPED PATTERN.

We only show the handle of the spoon, but they come in the regular lengths, 6 inches long. Be sure to state pattern desired.

ROGERS BRAND.		Extra plate, per doz.	Triple plate, per doz.
No. 5K800	Teaspoons...	$0.98	$1.68
No. 5K815	Tablespoons	1.96	3.36
No. 5K819	Medium Forks	1.96	3.36

PARAGON BRAND.		Extra plate, per doz.	Triple plate, per doz.
No. 5K500	Teaspoons...	$1.46	$2.06
No. 5K515	Tablespoons	2.92	4.12
No. 5K519	Medium Forks	2.92	4.12

1847 ROGERS BRAND.		Extra plate, per doz.	Triple plate, per doz.
No. 5K900	Teaspoons...	$2 34	$3.30
No. 5K915	Tablespoons	4.68	6.60
No. 5K919	Medium Forks	4.68	6.60

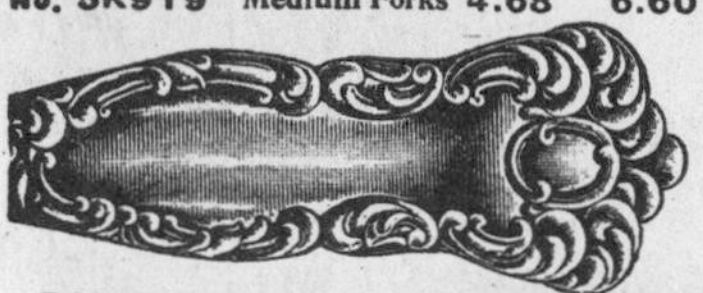

ROGERS BRAND—OXFORD PATTERN.

		Extra plate, per doz.	Triple plate, per doz.
No. 5K800	Teaspoons...	$1.18	$1.90
No. 5K815	Tablespoons..	2.36	3.80
No. 5K819	Medium Forks	2.36	3.80

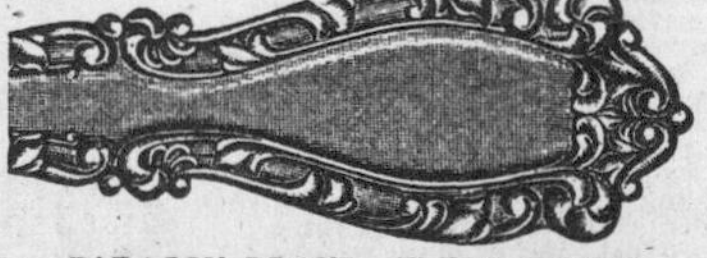

PARAGON BRAND—FLEUR DE LIS PATTERN.

		Extra plate, per doz.	Triple plate, per doz.
No. 5K500	Teaspoons...	$1.78	$2.44
No. 5K515	Tablespoons..	3.56	4.88
No. 5K519	Medium Forks	3.56	4.88

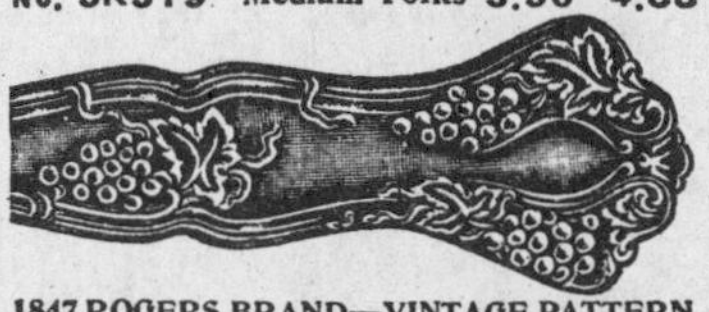

1847 ROGERS BRAND—VINTAGE PATTERN

		Extra plate, per doz.	Triple plate, per doz.
No. 5K900	Teaspoons....	$2.62	$3.58
No. 5K915	Tablespoons..	5.24	7.16
No. 5K919	Medium Forks	5.24	7.16

Postage on silverware sent by mail will be extra per dozen, as follows:

Teaspoons..........17 cents.
Tablespoons........22 cents.
Medium Forks.......22 cents.

FOR A FULL LINE OF SILVERWARE in all makes and grades, including flatware as well as casters, cake dishes and hollow ware, at prices unheard of before, see our Silverware Department, pages 332 to 343.

FRENCH PATTERN TABLE KNIVES WITH FOUR-TINE FORKS, $1.14.

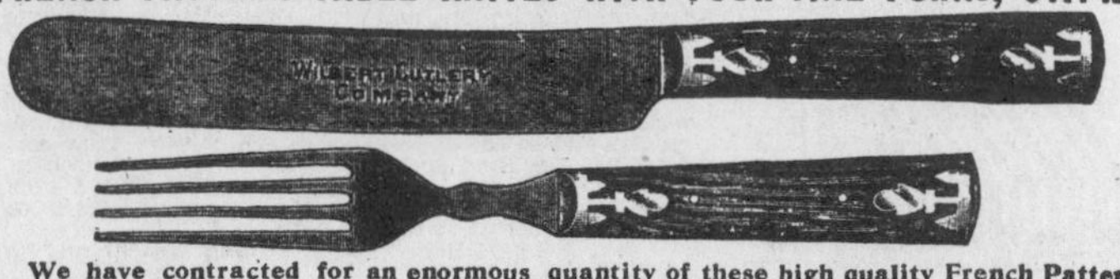

We have contracted for an enormous quantity of these high quality French Pattern Table Knives and Forks, and are able to offer them at prices lower by 50 per cent than you could purchase goods of like quality elsewhere. The knives are made of the finest carved steel, finely swaged and finished. The scimiter shape blades are ground by hand by experienced workmen. Fitted with fancy double French pattern metal bolsters and the finest genuine cocobolo and ebony handles. The forks are the latest style four-tine pattern, finished to match the knives. The steel in these knives and forks is absolutely the best, the tempering is perfect and the workmanship is equal to that found in any goods selling for more than twice the price we ask.

No. 6K16214 Cocobolo Handle Knives, with Four-Tine Forks. Price, per set of 6 knives and 6 forks..........$1.14
No. 6K16215 Knives only. Price, per half dozen..........67
No. 6K16216 Ebony Handle Knives and Forks. Price, per set of 6 knives and 6 forks..........$1.24
No. 6K16217 Knives only. Price, per half dozen..........76

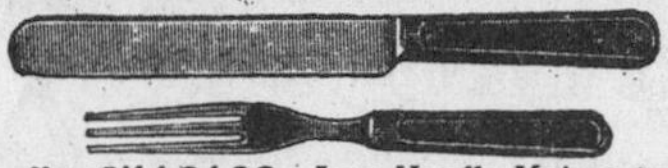

No. 6K16100 Iron Handle Knives and Forks. Price, per set, 6 knives and 6 forks, 40c
No. 6K16101 Knives only. Price, per half dozen..........26c

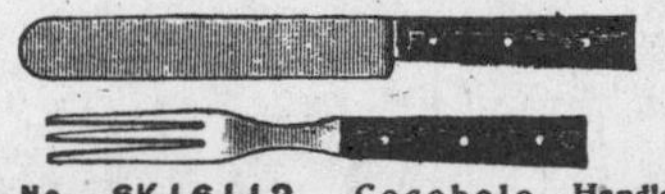

No. 6K16112 Cocobolo Handle Knives and Forks, no bolster. Price, per set, 6 knives and 6 forks..........38c
No. 6K16113 Knives only. Price, per half dozen..........26c
No. 6K16114 White Bone Handle Knives and Forks, no bolster. Price, per set, 6 knives and 6 forks..........67c

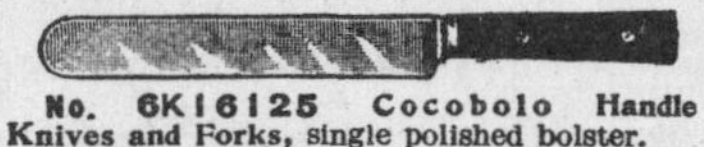

No. 6K16125 Cocobolo Handle Knives and Forks, single polished bolster. Price, per set, 6 knives and 6 forks....56c
No. 6K16126 Knives only. Price, per half dozen..........36c
No. 6K16127 White Bone Handle Knives and Forks, single bolster. Price, per set, 6 knives and 6 forks..........82c
If knives and forks are sent by mail, postage extra, from 35 to 40 cents per set.

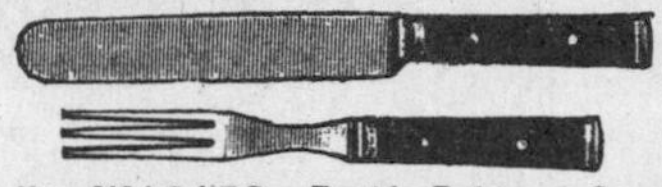

No. 6K16152 Double Bolstered Cocobolo Handle Knives and Forks. Price, per set, 6 knives and 6 forks..........69c
No. 6K16153 Knives only. Price, per half dozen..........43c

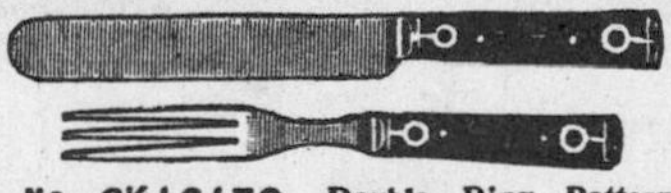

No. 6K16170 Double Ring Pattern Knives and Forks, cocobolo handles. Price, per set, 6 knives and 6 forks....88c
No. 6K16171 Knives only. Price, per half dozen..........50c

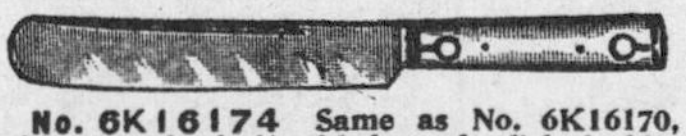

No. 6K16174 Same as No. 6K16170, with swaged scimiter blades and polished white bone handles. Price, per set, 6 knives and 6 forks..$1.26
No. 6K16175 Knives only. Price, per half dozen..........72c

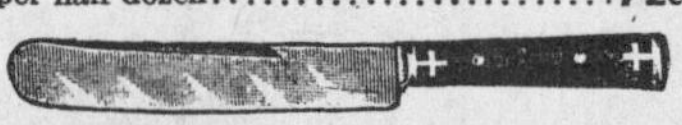

No. 6K16188 Cross Pattern, Double Bolstered Cocobolo Handle Knives and Three-Tine Forks, swaged scimiter blades. Price, per set, 6 knives and 6 forks....99c
No. 6K16191 Knives only. Price, per half dozen..........60c

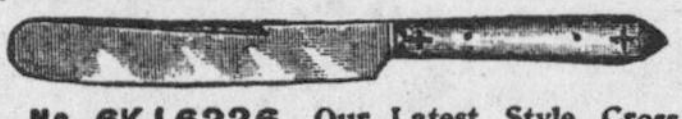

No. 6K16226 Our Latest Style Cross Pattern, white bone handles, swaged scimiter blades. Price, per set, 6 knives and 6 forks..$1.71
If by mail, postage on knives and forks is from 35 cents to 40 cents extra per set.

Knives and Four-Tine Forks

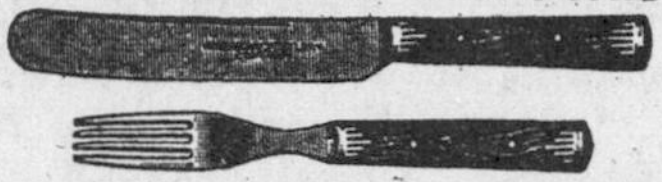

No. 6K16228 Vienna pattern scimiter shape swaged blade knife with four-tine fork. Blade finely tempered and ground, fitted with genuine cocobolo handle with fancy bolsters, as shown in the illustration. Four-tine forks to match the knives. Price, per set, 6 knives and 6 forks.$1.06

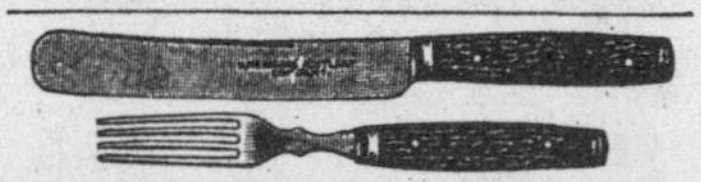

No. 6K16265 Imitation Stag Handle, Double Bolster Knives and Four-Tine Forks, swaged scimiter blades. Price, per set, 6 knives and 6 forks..........$1.32
No. 6K16267 Knives only. Price, per half dozen..........76c

Solid Handle Knives and Forks

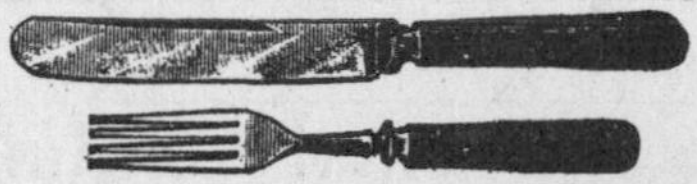

The solid handle goods are furnished in celluloid and hard rubber. The handles are made in one piece; there are no cracks or rivet holes to permit the water to soak in. Most sanitary knives made. Highly polished and finished. No better goods made at any price.

No. 6K16272 Solid Hard Rubber Handle Knives and Four-Tine Forks, swaged blades, ground by hand, with fancy solid steel, polished bolsters. This is a high class knife. The workmanship, material and finish are absolutely the best. Price, per set of 6 knives and 6 forks.$2.89
No. 6K16273 Solid Hard Rubber Handle Knives only, the ideal individual steak knife, used in all fashionable metropolitan restaurants, knives only. Price, per half dozen..........$1.50
No. 6K16274 Solid White Celluloid Handle Knives with Four-Tine forks. Will never crack, warp or change color, and are therefore superior to bone. Highly polished and ground by hand. No better knife made. Price, per set 6 knives and 6 forks$2.90
No. 6K16275 White Celluloid Handle Knives only, same as above described. Price, per half dozen..........$1.55

Tinned Knives and Forks.

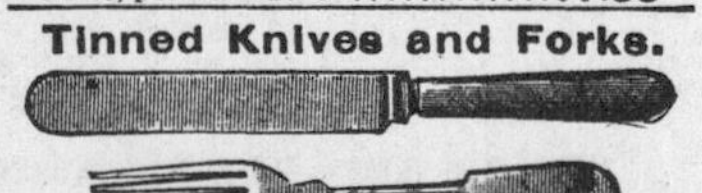

No. 6K16283 Tinned Steel Knives and Forks. Forged from steel, and are heavily coated with pure block tin to prevent rust. We do not break sets. Price, per set, 6 knives and 6 forks..45c

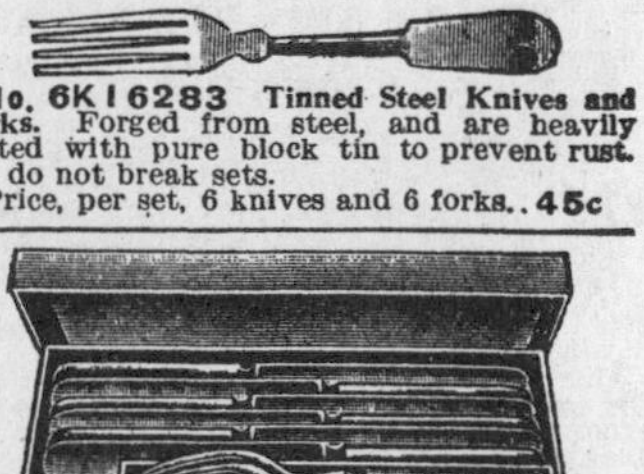

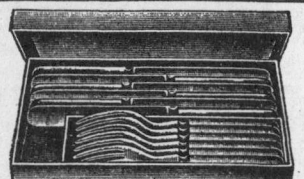

No. 6K16287 Tinned Steel Table Knives and Forks. Put up in cardboard case, as illustrated. Handles of forks are same as knives. We do not break sets. Price, per set, 6 knives and 6 forks..71c
If by mail, postage extra, 35 cents.

Solid Handle French Steak Knife.

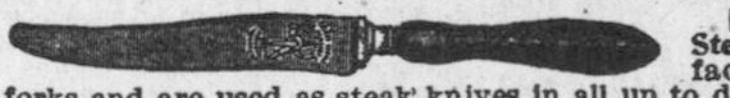

No. 6K16269 Genuine Imported French Steak Knives. Every knife branded with manufacturer's name. These knives come without forks and are used as steak knives in all up to date homes and restaurants. This blade has a peculiar shape, giving the full benefit of the cutting edge from heel to point. The blades are ground by hand. The blade and the heavy steel guard bolster are forged in one piece. The material and tempering are of the best. Fancy polished ferrule, solid round black wood handle. Every knife guaranteed. Price, per half dozen, knives only..........80c

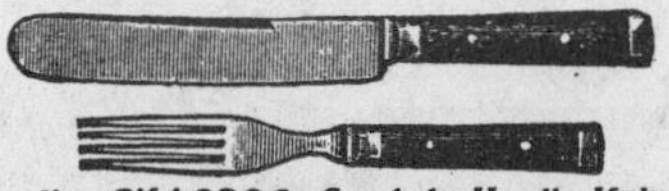

No. 6K16296 Cocobolo Handle Knives and Four-Tined Forks. Double bolster; swaged scimiter blade. A handsome and durable article.
Price, per set, 6 knives and 6 forks..**$1.07**
No. 6K16298 Same as above with fine white bone handle.
Price, per set, 6 knives and 6 forks..**$1.44**

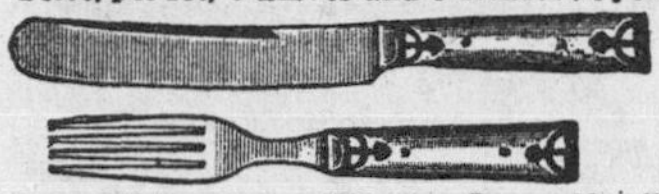

No. 6K16300 White Bone Handle Knives and Four-Tined Forks. Double fancy bolsters; swaged scimiter blades.
Price, per set, 6 knives and 6 forks..**$1.65**
No. 6K16301 Knives only. Price, per half dozen **89c**

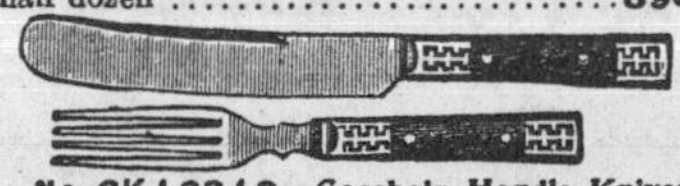

No. 6K16310 Cocobolo Handle Knives and Four-Tined Forks. Double fancy bolsters; swaged scimiter blades. A very neat and attractive pattern.
Price, per set, 6 knives and 6 forks..**$1.42**

IF SENT BY MAIL, Postage on Knives and Forks is from 35 cents to 40 cents extra, per set.

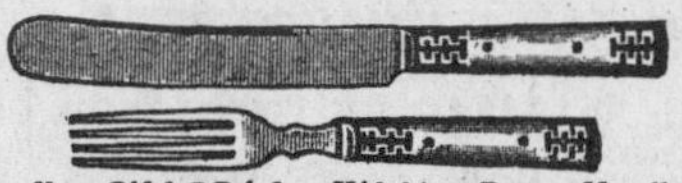

No. 6K16314 White Bone Handle Knives and Four-Tined Forks. Double fancy bolsters; swaged scimiter blades. Price, per set, 6 knives and 6 forks..........**$1.88**
No. 6K16315 Knives only. Price, per half dozen **$1.05**

Dessert Knives.

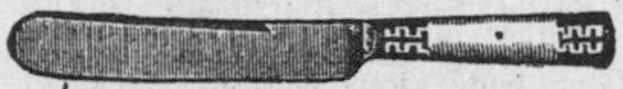

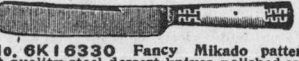

No. 6K16330 Fancy Mikado pattern, best quality steel dessert knives, polished caps and bolsters, 5-inch scimiter blades and three-tined forks. Fine polished cocobolo handles.
Price, per set, 6 knives and 6 forks..**$1.26**
No. 6K16332 Same as above, fitted with fine bone handles. Price, per set, 6 knives and 6 forks...............**$1.76**
If by mail, postage extra, 35 cents.

Children's Knife and Fork Sets. Reduced to 20c.

The blade of knife measures 4½ inches. Entire length, 7½ inches. If by mail, allow 5 cents for postage.

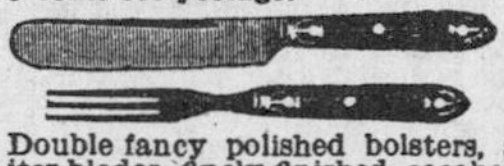

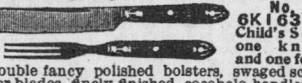

No. 6K16368 Child's Set, one knife and one fork. Double fancy polished bolsters, swaged scimiter blades, finely finished cocobolo handles.
Price, per set **20c**
No. 6K16369 Child's Set, one knife and one fork. Same pattern as above, with genuine white bone handles. Price, per set..**25c**

CARVING KNIVES AND FORKS.
REDUCED PRICES.

We contract with one of the largest and oldest manufacturers of carving knives and forks in the country. This contract calls for a larger quantity of high class carvers than has ever been purchased by any house selling direct to the consumer, and places us in a position to give you better value in carving sets than you could possibly procure elsewhere. We lay particular stress on the fact that all our carvers, from the cheapest to the best, are sharp and absolutely guaranteed in workmanship, finish and material, or they can be returned and money refunded. No sharpening or grinding necessary. They are shipped to you with an edge as keen as a razor's, ready for use. We describe the goods just as they are. They are shipped with the understanding that if you do not find them the best value you have ever received, they can be returned at our expense.

Our 98-Cent Carver.

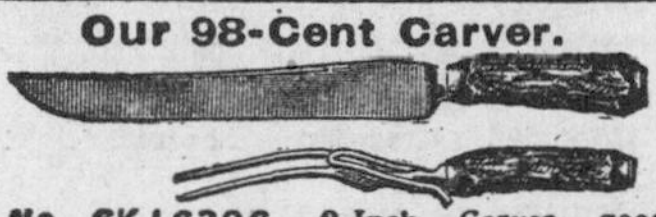

No. 6K16396 9-Inch Carver, good quality stag handle, polished cap and bolster; spring guard fork, blade finely tempered and ground. This carving set could not be duplicated for less than $1.50, and at our price of 98 cents is extraordinary value.
Price, per pair..........................**98c**
If by mail, postage extra, 15 cents.

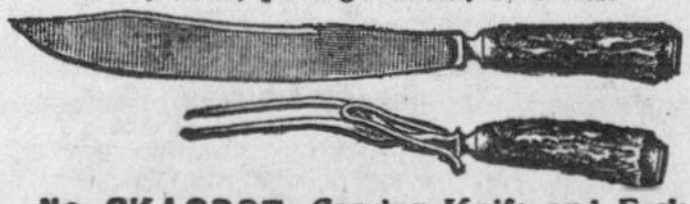

No. 6K16397 Carving Knife and Fork, 9-inch blade, nicely swaged, fancy polished hollow bolster, polished cap; spring guard fork, good medium grade stag handle. An excellent value at $1.75 per pair.
Our price, per pair......................**$1.18**
If by mail, postage extra, 14 cents.

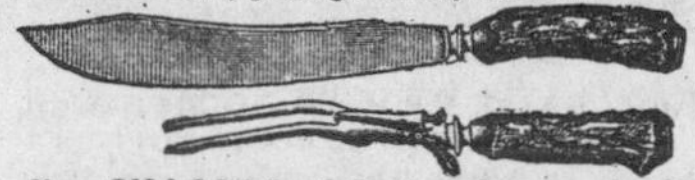

No. 6K16398 9-Inch Carver, blade finely tempered and ground, guaranteed to cut as well as any carver made. Full size, good quality stag handles, fancy double hollow forged bolsters; fork has good, heavy tines, finely finished. Price, per pair........**$1.74**
If by mail, postage extra, 18 cents.

Game and Steak Carver, $1.35.

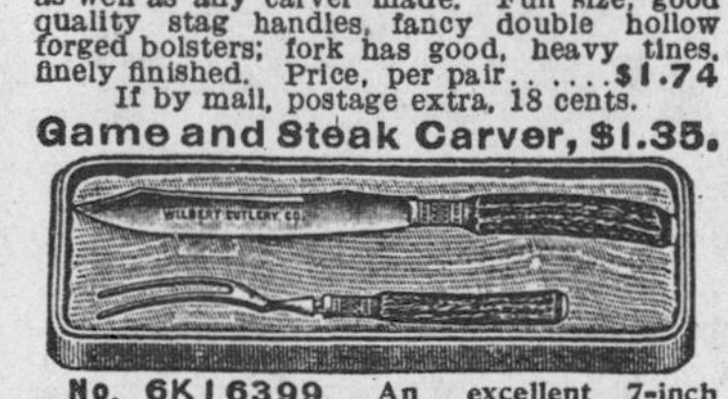

No. 6K16399 An excellent 7-inch Carver, for cutting small roasts, steaks and poultry. Finely forged blade, tempered and ground in a manner equal to the highest priced goods. Fork made without guard. Fancy German silver ferrules, polished caps, good quality stag handles. Bird and game carvers are becoming more popular every season, and at our price of $1.35 this pair of carvers will unquestionably have an enormous sale.
Price, per pair, put up in fancy lined box..(If by mail, postage extra, 19c)..**$1.35**

Game and Steak Carver, 87c.

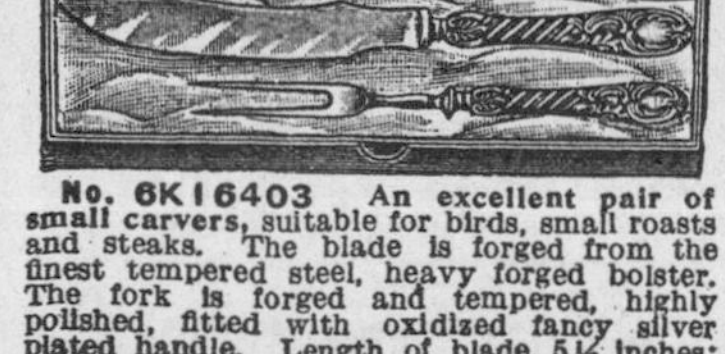

No. 6K16403 An excellent pair of small carvers, suitable for birds, small roasts and steaks. The blade is forged from the finest tempered steel, heavy forged bolster. The fork is forged and tempered, highly polished, fitted with oxidized fancy silver plated handle. Length of blade, 5½ inches; length over all, 10 inches. Put up in neat, cloth lined box. Price, per set..........**87c**
If by mail, postage extra, 11 cents.

Geo. Wostenholm English Carvers at Reduced Prices.

The Genuine IXL Carving Knives and Forks, stamped Geo. Wostenholm & Sons' Celebrated IXL Cutlery, Sheffield, England. Every blade is hand forged from the finest double shear steel, hand tempered to cut and hold an edge. Finely finished and fully warranted. The reputation of this brand makes it unnecessary for us to say very much about the quality, for the goods are known as the standard the world over. They are guaranteed to be genuine IXL goods.

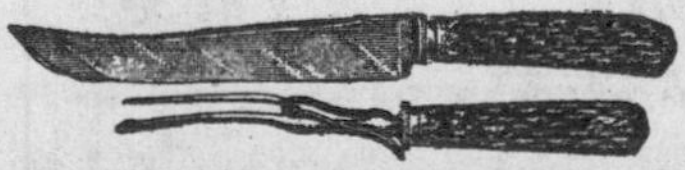

No. 6K16430 Geo. Wostenholm & Sons' Celebrated IXL Carving Knife and Fork. Imitation stag handles. Fancy solid forged steel bolsters with finest electro silver plated ferrules. Length of blade, 8 inches. A very handsome pair of carvers of the very best quality. Price, per pair...............**$1.80**
If by mail, postage extra, 16 cents.

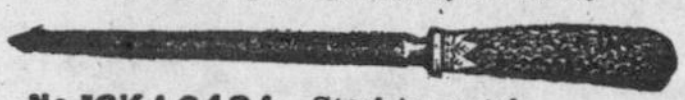

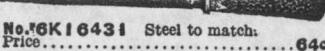

No. 6K16431 Steel to match.
Price **64c**
If by mail, postage extra, 10 cents.

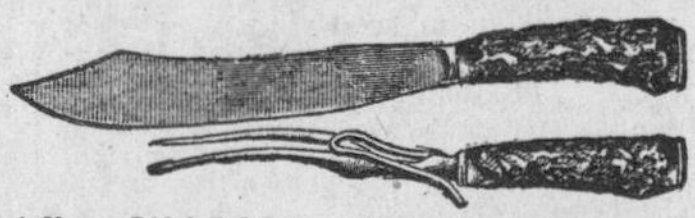

No. 6K16434 Geo. Wostenholm & Sons' Celebrated IXL Carving Knife and Fork. Genuine stag handles, steel bolsters and butts, with 8-inch blade. It is one of the most popular shaped blades made and is fully warranted. Price, per pair...............**$1.42**
If by mail, postage extra, 16 cents.

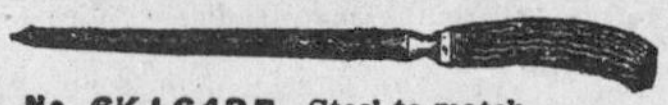

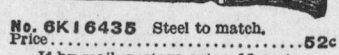

No. 6K16435 Steel to match.
Price **52c**
If by mail, postage extra, 10 cents.

Three-Piece Stag Handle Carving Set, $1.88.

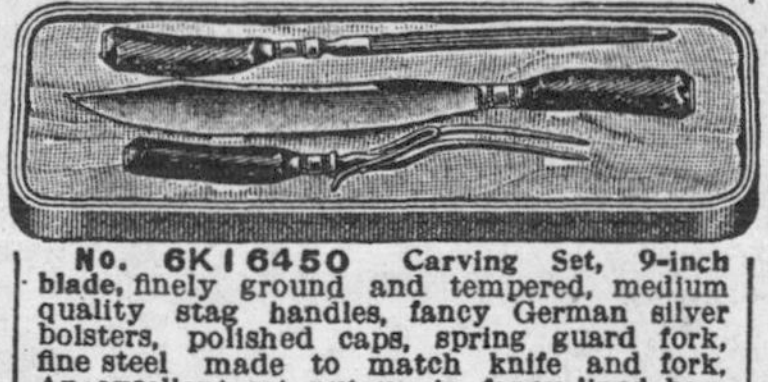

No. 6K16450 Carving Set, 9-inch blade, finely ground and tempered, medium quality stag handles, fancy German silver bolsters, polished caps, spring guard fork, fine steel made to match knife and fork. An excellent set, put up in fancy lined box.
Price, per set **$1.88**
If by mail, postage extra, per set, 38 cents.

THREE-PIECE CARVING SETS IN FANCY LINED BOXES.
Our Optimo Carving Set, $2.37.

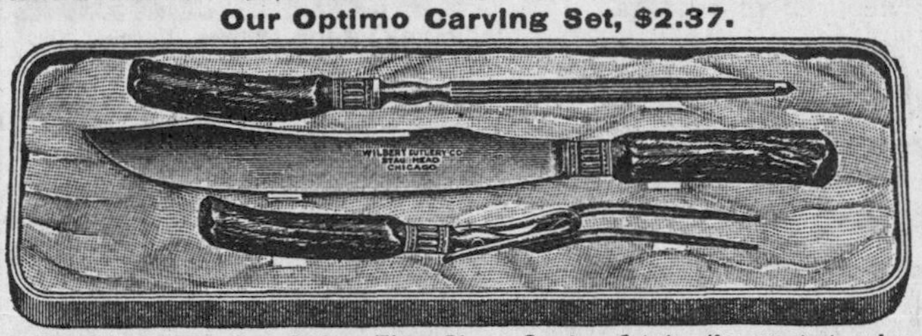

ALL WILBERT CUTLERY IS GUARANTEED.

No. 6K16457 Our Optimo Three-Piece Carving Set is the greatest value ever offered in this line; 9-inch blade, double shear steel, finely tempered and ground and guaranteed to cut. Full size, good quality stag handles, spring guard fork, with steel to match knife and fork. Fancy heavy German silver ferrules, a well made and finely finished set throughout. Put up in fancy lined box. Price, per set....(Postage extra, 40c.)...**$2.37**

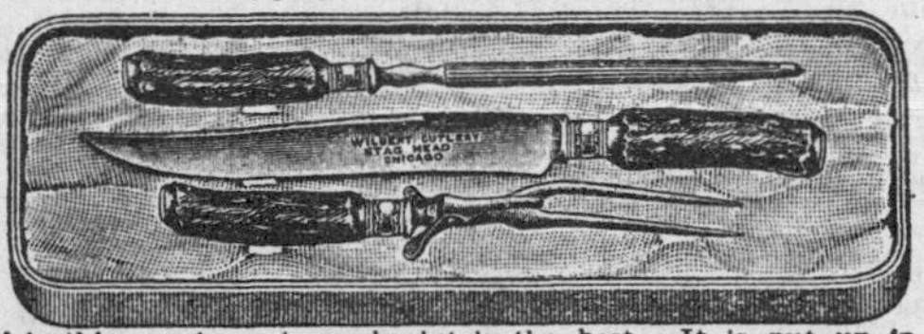

No. 6K16459 Three-Piece Carving Set, 9-inch new style blade. This peculiar style blade gives you the benefit of full cutting edge from heel to point. The blade is made of the finest double shear steel, ground and tempered by most experienced workmen, selected stag handles, patent spring guard fork, heavy sterling silver ferrules and silver caps. The workmanship and material in this carving set are absolutely the best. It is put up in fine cloth lined case. Price, per set........(Postage extra, per set, 42 cents.)..........**$3.00**

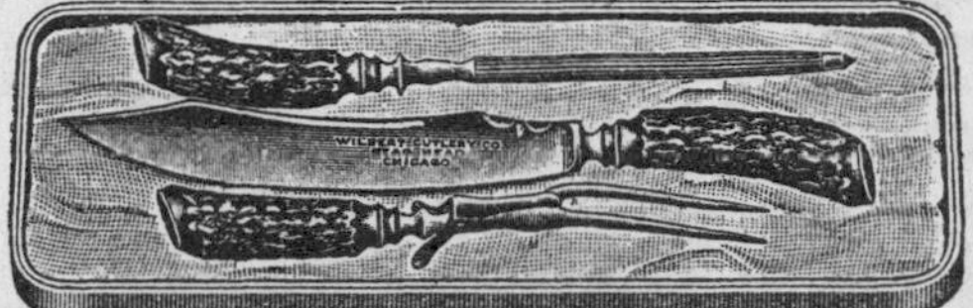

No. 6K16462 Three-Piece, 9-Inch Carving Set, beautiful set, blade forged of the finest steel. The tempering and grinding are absolutely the best. The blade is made particularly attractive by a heavy swage and three fancy indentations near heel, heavy forged fancy bolsters, selected stag handles, nicely turned and finished to match the fancy bolsters, polished caps, fork fitted with forged spring guard, steel made to match knife and fork. An excellent set, guaranteed to give satisfaction. Put up in fine cloth lined box.
Price, per set.........(If by mail, postage extra, per set, 45 cents.).........**$3.90**

Our Highest Quality Three-Piece Carving Set, $4.75.

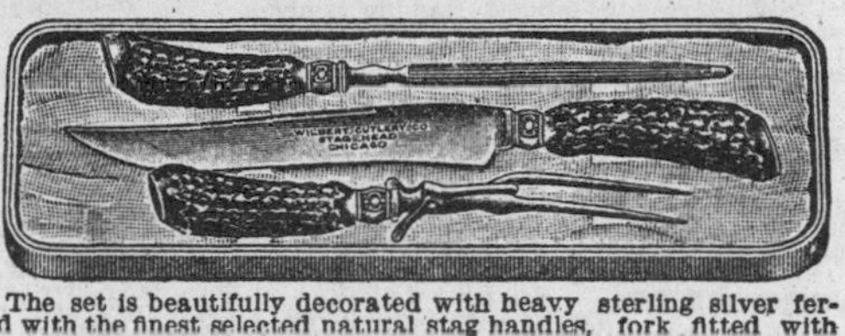

No. 6K16464 Our highest quality carving set is the finest product of our factory. No better goods made at any price. 9-inch blade tapers from heel to point and is shaped so that the entire edge is used. The blade is hand forged of the best double shear steel. Blade and bolster are forged from a solid bar. Blades are not only ground, but they are honed so as to insure perfect cutting edge. The set is beautifully decorated with heavy sterling silver ferrules, polished silver caps, fitted with the finest selected natural stag handles, fork fitted with forged spring guard, tines on fork 3¼ inches long; finely tempered steel, made and finished to match knife and fork. The set is put up in a handsome cloth lined box.
Price, per set of three pieces........(Postage extra, per set, 45 cents.).......**$4.75**

Our 16-Piece Stag Handle Knife Set, Reduced to $4.65.

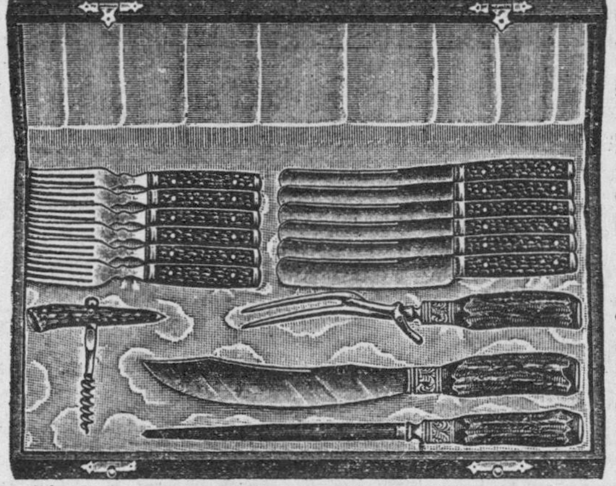

No. 6K16550 We originated this style set two years ago, and it has met with a sale so large that other houses are offering sets similar in design, and in order to offset the wonderful value we give in this set they have sacrificed quality in order to make an attractive price. At $4.65 this sixteen-piece set is the greatest value ever offered in a set of this kind. Buying the knives and forks and a carver separately, you could not duplicate this set for less than $6.00 or $7.00. We could cheapen this set and sell a set of similar design for half of our price, but we will positively not sacrifice quality for price, and we accordingly offer you this set at $4.65 as being better value and containing better goods than you could possibly obtain elsewhere within from $2.00 to $3.00 of the price we ask. This set consists of six stag handled swaged blade knives with forks to match. The forks, you will note, are four-tine forks, and not three-tine, as offered by others. The knives are made of the finest crucible tempered steel, highly polished and swaged, and not to be compared with the cheap, straight blade knives with which the market is flooded. The carver is made of the best double shear steel, finely forged, tempered and ground, fitted with genuine solid stag handles, silver cap and bolster. The carver fork has patent folding guard. The steel is finished and fitted to match the knife and fork. The corkscrew has forged steel shank highly polished, with neat stag handle. This set of sixteen pieces is put up in a handsome, strong, cloth lined box with two fancy metal clasps. Weight, 6 pounds. Price, per set..............**$4.65**

Bread Knives and Slicers.

No. 6K16578 The Hurd Patent Bread Knife. This knife is so shaped and protected at each end that it is impossible to cut the table or table cloth. Blade is finely ground, 10 inches long, made of the best quality steel, finely tempered. Fitted with a hollow malleable handle. This knife will keep sharp longer than any other knife, and it is very easily sharpened when dull. Price **16c**
If by mail, postage extra, 11 cents.

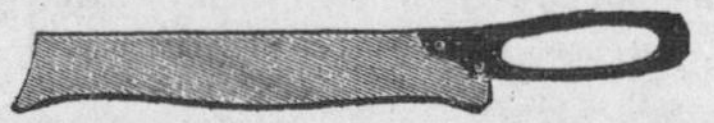

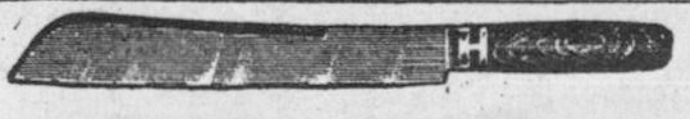

No. 6K16576 Wilbert solid cocoa handle fancy bolster, best crucible steel blade slicer or bread knife. Blade is 9 inches long, made of the best crucible steel, swaged and finely polished. A better blade could not be made. Price.................................**35c**
If by mail, postage extra, 12 cents.

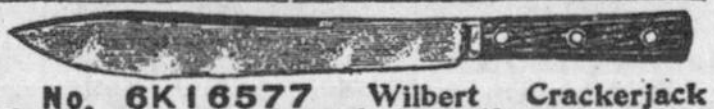

No. 6K16577 Wilbert Crackerjack Slicer, or general household knife, cocoa handle, three large head brass rivets, single bolster, clip point, swaged blade. Length of blade, 9½ inches. The blade of this knife is made of the best crucible steel. A better blade could not be made, and it is fully guaranteed. Price **34c**
If by mail, postage extra, 12 cents.

Complete Kitchen Cutlery.
REDUCED TO 70 CENTS.

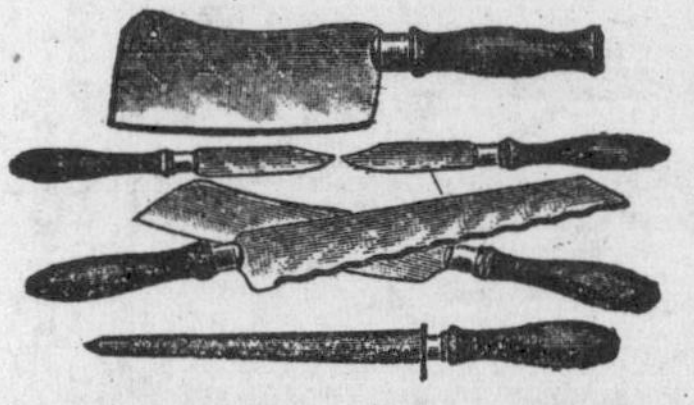

No. 6K16587 Our Six-Piece Complete Kitchen Outfit consists of one 7-inch cleaver with fine steel blade, nickel plated ferrule and round ebonized handle, one 8-inch butcher knife, finely tempered steel blade and nickel plated ferrule, one serrated edge 9-inch bread knife, finely finished, ebonized handle, one 8-inch best quality emery steel with guard and nickel plated ferrule, and two paring knives with nickel plated ferrule, solid ebonized handles, making a total of six pieces. All of the articles mentioned in this list have solid wood handles, ebony finish. They are made in first class manner and the material used is the best, and we know this set will give satisfaction. These items, if bought singly, would aggregate a cost of at least $1.00.
Price, per set, complete, put up in a neat paper box 70c
If by mail, postage extra, 32 cents.

Christy Knife Sets.

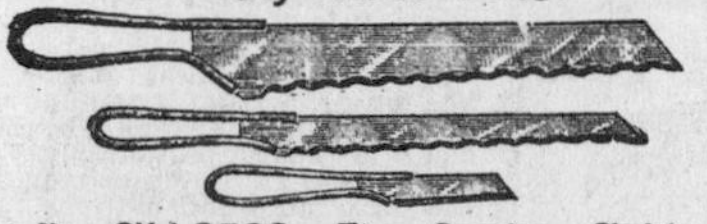

No. 6K16583 The Genuine Christy Knife Sets. Every knife warranted to be made of the best cutlery steel. Bread, cake and paring knife.
Price, per set of three knives 47c
If by mail, postage extra, 12 cents.
No. 6K16586 Serrated Edge Knife Sets, similar in design and pattern to the No. 6K16583. Made of the best cold rolled nickel steel. Will give satisfaction. Handles firmly swaged to the blade and will never come loose. Set consists of bread, cake and paring knife.
Price, per set of three knives 17c
If by mail, postage extra, 12 cents.

Kitchen or Paring Knives.

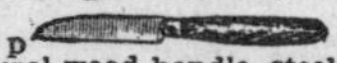

No. 6K16590 Kitchen Knife, sharp point, steel ferrule, natural wood handle, steel blade. Length of blade, 3 inches. Price..4c
If by mail, postage extra, 3 cents.

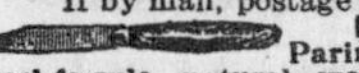

No. 6K16592 Paring Knife, clip point, steel ferrule, natural wood handle. Length of blade, 3 inches. Steel blade. Price....4c
If by mail, postage extra, 3 cents.

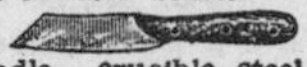

No. 6K16594 Paring Knife, diagonal point, fancy curved handle, crucible steel blade. Length of blade, 3 inches. Price 6c
If by mail, postage extra, 3 cents.

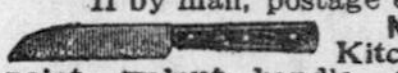

No. 6K16595 Kitchen Knife, sharp point, walnut handle, three brass rivets, swaged blade. This knife is made of the very best crucible steel, and is far better than any knife we have ever seen. Price.......8c
If by mail, postage extra, 3 cents.

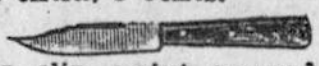

No. 6K16596 Kitchen Knife, walnut handle, three brass rivets, clip point, swaged blade. This knife is made of the best crucible steel, and will cut and hold its edge.
Price...(If by mail, postage extra, 3c)..8c

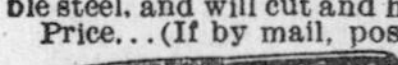

No. 6K16597 Imported French Kitchen Knife. Every knife branded with the French manufacturer's name, sabatier pattern, black handle. The material and workmanship in this knife are first class. Length over all, 7½ inches. Length of blade, 4 inches. Price....(Postage extra, 3c)...9c

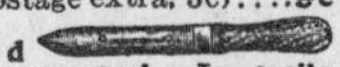

No. 6K16598 Vegetable Parer and Corer. Takes off an even peel. Is easily sharpened and cleaned. Just the thing for Saratoga chips. Price.(Postage extra, 3c)..5c

Butcher Knives.

Wilbert Butcher Knives, guaranteed first quality or money refunded. The following line of butcher knives is very complete; every number represents the highest quality of that particular pattern. The value of butcher knives is in the blade. The blades in the following line of knives are forged of the best steel, finely tempered and ground. Every knife guaranteed to give satisfaction or money refunded.
If butcher knives are sent by mail, postage extra is 7 cents to 14 cents.

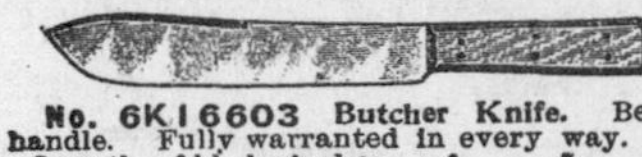

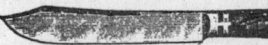

No. 6K16603 Butcher Knife. Beech handle. Fully warranted in every way.

Length of blade, inches	6	7	8
Price	11c	14c	17c
Length of blade, inches	10	12	
Price	26c	39c	

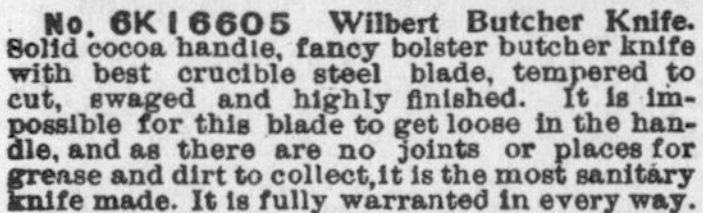

No. 6K16605 Wilbert Butcher Knife. Solid cocoa handle, fancy bolster butcher knife with best crucible steel blade, tempered to cut, swaged and highly finished. It is impossible for this blade to get loose in the handle, and as there are no joints or places for grease and dirt to collect, it is the most sanitary knife made. It is fully warranted in every way.

Length of blade, inches	6	7	8
Price	20c	25c	34c

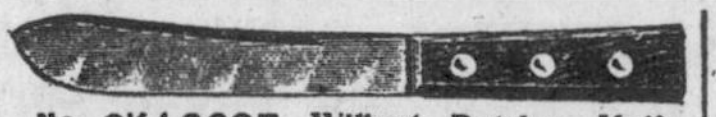

No. 6K16607 Wilbert Butcher Knife. Best quality swaged steel blade, three ridge brass shield rivets, cocobolo handle, high grade serviceable knife, guaranteed.

Length of blade, inches	6	7	8
Price	24c	28c	36c

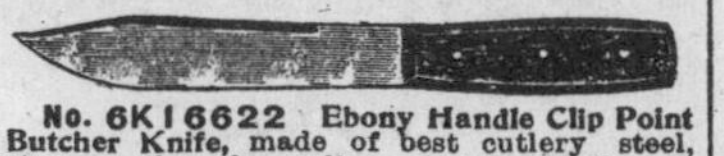

No. 6K16622 Ebony Handle Clip Point Butcher Knife, made of best cutlery steel, stronger than the ordinary butcher knife. It is made the same pattern as a hunting knife for rough, heavy work.

Length of blade, inches	6	7
Price	22c	28c

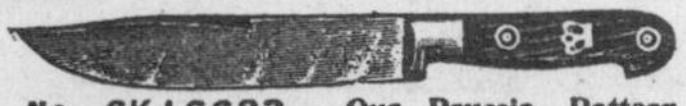

No. 6K16623 Our Prussia Pattern Butcher Knife. Forged from the bar, ground and finished by hand, and fully guaranteed. It has cocobolo handle, large head brass rivets. Warranted.

Length of blade, inches	6	7	8
Price	23c	27c	28c

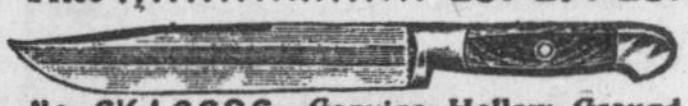

No. 6K16626 Genuine Hollow Ground French Butcher Knife. Every blade stamped with French manufacturer's name. Has cocobolo handle, large head, copper rivet, metal bolsters and butt. Nicely finished. The finest knife we have ever seen.

Length of blade, inches	6	7	8
Price	26c	29c	32c

BUTCHER KNIVES.
The Genuine Diamond A Butcher Knives.

GENUINE A WARRANTED

No brand of Butcher Knives is better known today than the famous, genuine Diamond A Brand, which has been on the market for over fifty years, and in which the quality has been upheld since this brand was first introduced. These knives are made specially for the butcher trade who not only want a knife of the best material, but desire a knife of just the right shape and proper balance to do good work. Every Diamond A Knife is forged from the solid bar by hand and ground by experienced workmen who grind nothing but butcher knives, and honed to an edge as keen as a razor's. Every Diamond A Knife is carefully inspected before leaving the factory, and they are guaranteed to give satisfaction and to be the highest quality it is possible to produce, or they may be returned after being given a thorough trial and money and transportation charges will be refunded. Once buy Diamond A Butcher Knives and you will never be satisfied with any other brand.

Genuine Diamond A Butcher Knives.

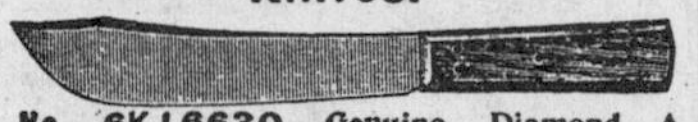

No. 6K16630 Genuine Diamond A Butcher Knives, beechwood handles. Hand forged blades. Fully warranted.

Length of blade, inches	6	7	8	9	10	12
Price	19c	27c	32c	41c	59c	79c

Skinning Knives.

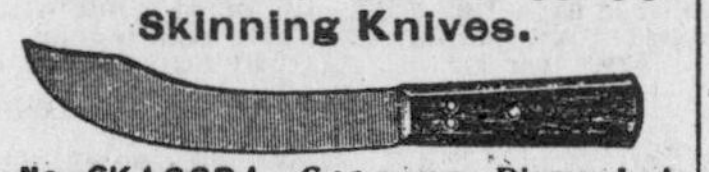

No. 6K16631 Genuine Diamond A Skinning Knives, beechwood handles. Every knife of this brand fully guaranteed.

Length of blade, in.	5½	6	6½	7
Price	22c	26c	27c	33c

Sticking Knives.

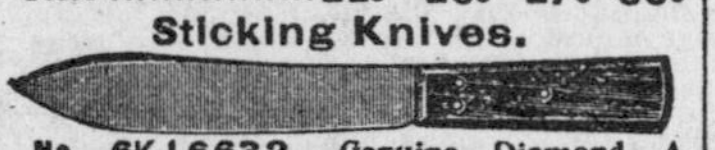

No. 6K16632 Genuine Diamond A Sticking Knives, best beechwood handles. Guaranteed hand forged from best steel.

Length of blade, inches	6	7
Price	20c	25c

Boning Knives.

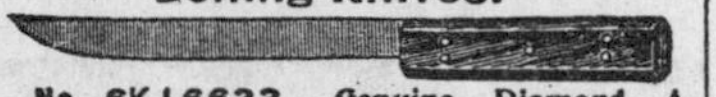

No. 6K16633 Genuine Diamond A Boning Knives, beechwood handles. This shape is a favorite with the butchers everywhere.

Length of blade, inches	6	6½
Price	27c	29c

Scimiter Steak Knives.

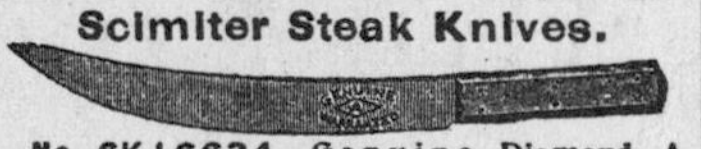

No. 6K16634 Genuine Diamond A Steak Knives, beechwood handles securely riveted through blade, best hand forged steel blades. Right shape and right temper guaranteed.

Length of blade, inches	10	12	14
Price	70c	81c	$1.16

If by mail, postage extra, 10 to 20 cents.

Genuine Wilson Butcher Knives.

Stamped I. Wilson.
Imitations of this knife are frequently sold. If not stamped on blade I. WILSON they are counterfeits.

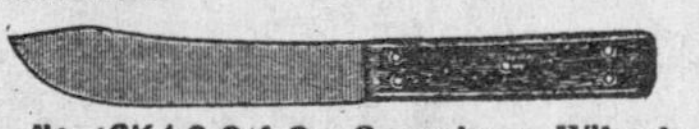

No. 6K16640 Genuine Wilson's Butcher Knives, beechwood handles.

Length of blade, inches	6	7	8	10
Price	24c	36c	48c	70c

Sticking Knives.

No. 6K16641 Genuine Wilson's Sticking Knives, beechwood handles.

Length of blade, inches	6	6½
Price	26c	32c

Skinning Knives.

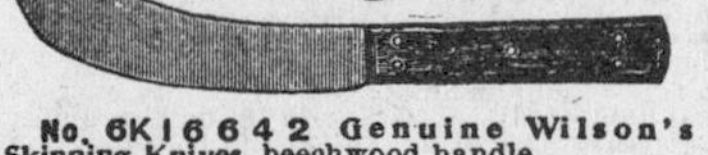

No. 6K16642 Genuine Wilson's Skinning Knives, beechwood handle.

Length of blade, inches	6	7
Price	28c	37c

Steak Knives.

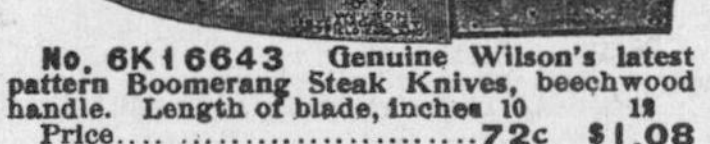

No. 6K16643 Genuine Wilson's latest pattern Boomerang Steak Knives, beechwood handle. Length of blade, inches 10 12
Price........72c $1.08
If by mail, postage extra, 6 to 18 cents.

Genuine Wilson Butchers' Steels.

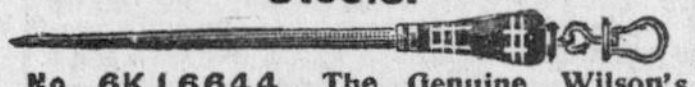

No. 6K16644 The Genuine Wilson's Butchers' Steel, cocoa handle, very best material and finish; the favorite with butchers in all parts of the world.

Length, inches	10	12	14
Price	82c	$1.00	$1.20

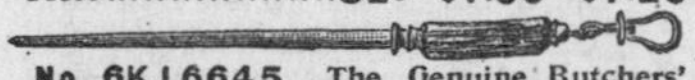

No. 6K16645 The Genuine Butchers' Steel, stag handle, finest quality, best finish.

Length, inches	10	12	14
Price	92c	$1.05	$1.25

Sheffield Butcher Steels.

These steels are guaranteed in both quality and workmanship and will give as good satisfaction as any steel made, regardless of price.
No. 6K16648 Sheffield Butcher Steels, cocoa handle.

Size, inches	10	12	14
Price	65c	80c	94c

No. 6K16649 Sheffield Butcher Steels, with select heavy stag handle.

Size, inches	10	12	14
Price	70c	84c	95c

If by mail, postage extra, 20 to 26 cents.

Butchers' Saws.
REDUCED PRICES.

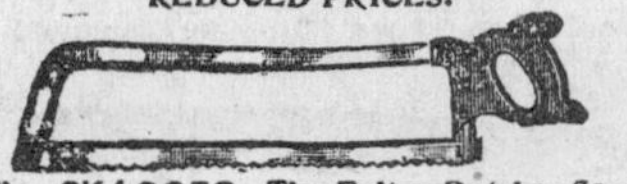

No. 6K16652 The Fulton Butcher Saw, with flat, polished steel frame ¾ inch wide, ¼ inch thick, with beech handle, varnished edges, fastened with three large brass screws, fitted with blued clock spring ¾-inch steel blade, specially tempered for butcher saws. An excellent saw, guaranteed to give satisfaction.

Size, length in.	18	20	22	24
Weight, pounds	1⅝	1¾	1⅞	2
Price	59c	65c	71c	77c

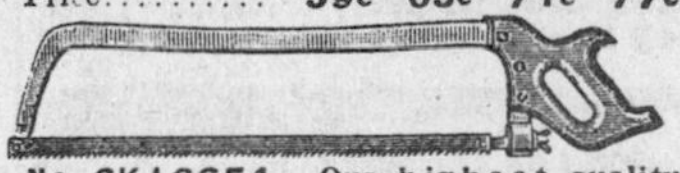

No. 6K16654 Our highest quality Butcher Saw, the best butcher saw made. Frame, 1 inch wide, ¼ inch thick, nicely polished handle made of beechwood and fastened by three large brass screws that go clear through handle. The blades are made of specially tempered steel, expressly made for butcher saws. Will do lots of cutting with one filing. The blades are ¾ inch wide and finely polished. This saw has just the right hang and shape, and will please the professional butcher.
Price List of Frames, with one ¾-inch Blade.

Size, length, inches	18	20	22	24	26
Weight, lbs.	2¼	2¾	2¾	3	3¼
Price	98c	99c	$1.05	$1.12	$1.18

No. 6K16655 Butcher Saw Blades, made of a special quality of spring steel, specially tempered for butcher saws, finely ground and bright polished. These blades are filed and set, ready for immediate use. ¾ inch wide.

Size, length, inches	18	20	22	24	26
Price, each	$0.12	$0.13	$0.14	$0.15	$0.18
Per dozen	1.35	1.36	1.50	1.52	1.80

Star Butcher Saw Blades.

No. 6K16656 Butcher Saw Blades. While wearing out one of these blades it would be necessary to file an old style blade five or six times, hence we claim that though these blades must be thrown away when worn out, they are cheaper in the end. Will fit any frame. Weight, 1 to 3 ounces. Width, ⅝ inch.

Length, ins.	18	20	22	24	26
Price, each	$0.09	$0.09	$0.10	$0.10	$0.12
Per dozen	1.04	1.05	1.11	1.12	1.22

Beef Splitting Saw $2.75.

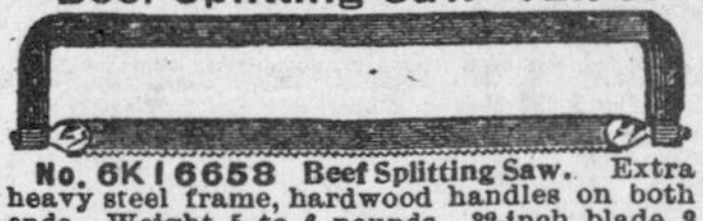

No. 6K16658 Beef Splitting Saw. Extra heavy steel frame, hardwood handles on both ends. Weight, 5 to 6 pounds. 32-inch blade, 2 inches wide. Price $2.75
No. 6K16659 Extra Blades for Beef Splitting Saws, 32x2 inches. Price..........43c

Kitchen Saws, 18 Cents.

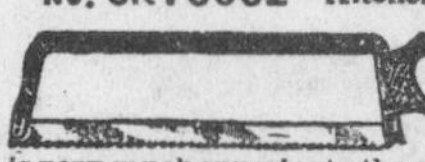

No. 6K16662 Kitchen Saws. Flat steel frame. Good steel blade. Beech handle with two screws. This frame is very much superior to the round or oval frame commonly sold.

Size, inches	14	16
Weight, ounces	11	13
Price	18c	20c

No. 6K16664 Boss Kitchen Saw. Flat steel frame with beech handle. They have what most other kitchen saws do not have—an arrangement for tightening blade, which adds much to their value. Length of blade, 14 inches; width, ½ inch. Weight, 15 ounces. Price, frame with one blade.....29c
No. 6K16665 Extra Blades for Boss Kitchen Saws. Price 8c

Hand Forged Butchers' Cleavers.

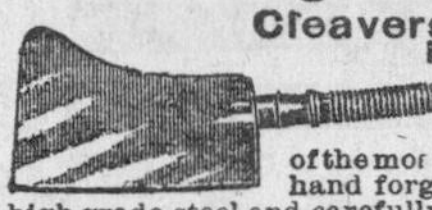

No. 6K16670 Our Butchers' Market Cleavers are of the most desirable pattern, hand forged from a special high grade steel and carefully tempered. Blades are extra strong and heavy and have best varnished hickory handles that never get loose. Every one fully warranted. The best cleaver made regardless of price.

Cut, inches,	7	8	9	10	12
Weight, lbs.	1½	1¾	2¼	3¼	4¾
Price	57c	67c	74c	$1.10	$1.42

The Family Cleaver, 19c.

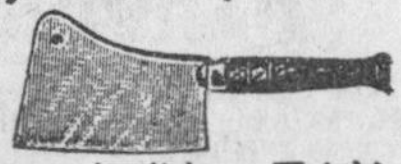

No. 6K16681 Family Cleaver, cast steel blade forged and hardened. Is a very handy household article and should be in everyone's kitchen. Weight, 14 ounces. Price 19c
If by mail, postage extra, 22 cents.

Hog Hook.

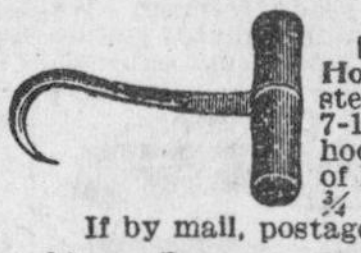

No. 6K16683 Hog Hooks, forged from best steel; diameter of steel, 7-16 inch. Length of hook, 7¼ inches; length of handle, 9 inches. Wt., ¾ pound. Price..25c
If by mail, postage extra, 22 cents.

Hog Scraper.

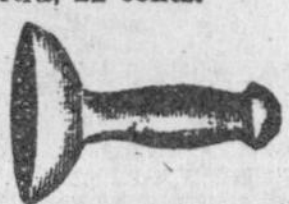

No. 6K16686 Hog Scraper. Will pay for itself the first time used. Wood handle with bolt extending through scraper. Made of No. 18 sheet steel. Weight, 8 ounces. Price..........21c
If by mail, postage extra, 13 cents.

Knife, Scissors and Skate Sharpener.

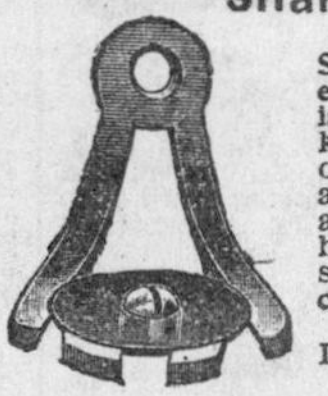

No. 6K16702 Knife, Scissors and Skate Sharpener. A few seconds only is required to sharpen the kitchen knives or a pair of scissors. Screwed to a small block of wood of a suitable size for the hand, it makes a neat skate sharpener that will concave the skate runner.
Price..........5c
If by mail, postage extra, 3 cents.

Silver Steel Knife Sharpener.
REDUCED TO 22 CENTS.

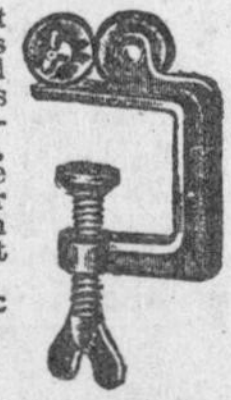

No. 6K16704 The best Sharpener for knives, scissors and tools. Instantly attached to any bench or table. This sharpener has two 1-inch hardened silver steel beveled wheels, which are adjustable to take up wear. Passing the knife or scissors a few times between these wheels will place a first class edge.
Price 22c
If by mail, postage extra, 8 cents.

Cork Screws.

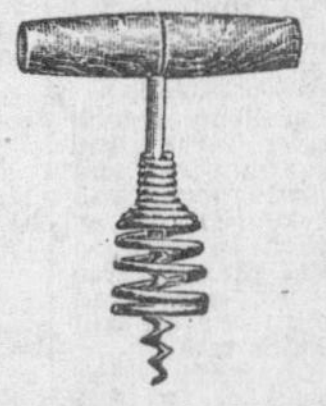

No. 6K16708 Nickel Plated Cork Screw. No pulling necessary, the coil spring guard automatically pulls the cork. A fine polished wood handle. Handle guaranteed not to pull off. Weight, 4 ounces.
Price..........12c
If by mail, postage extra, 5 cents.

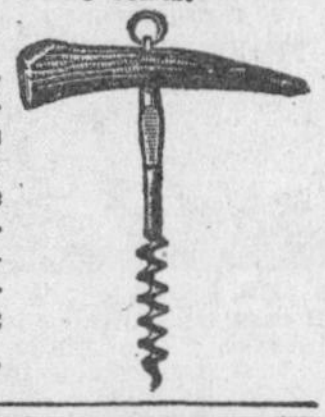

No. 6K16711 Stag Handle Cork Screw. Screw is of finely tempered steel, 4½ inches long, nickel plated and polished, handle is made of tip stag. A handsome cork screw, serviceable as well as ornamental. Price.....30c
If by mail, postage extra, 3 cents.

THE SURPRISINGLY LOW REDUCED PRICES prevailing in this catalogue mean greater savings to our customers than ever before.

Tea and Tablespoons.

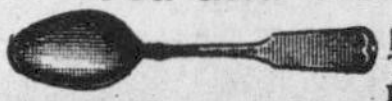

No. 6K16714 Heavy Retinned Steel Teaspoons, tipped pattern. Weight, per ½ dozen, 5 ounces. Price, per ½ dozen.....6c
If by mail, postage extra, per ½ dozen, 6c.

No. 6K16715 Heavy Retinned Steel Tablespoons, tipped pattern. Weight, per ½ dozen, 9 ounces. Price, per ½ dozen.....12c
If by mail, postage extra, per ½ dozen, 11c.

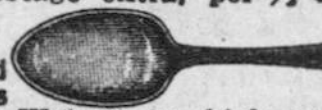

No. 6K16717 Heavy Retinned Steel Teaspoons fancy pattern. Weight, per ½ dozen, 5 ounces. Price, per ½ dozen.....8c
If by mail, postage extra, per ½ dozen, 6c.

No. 6K16718 Heavy Retinned Steel Tablespoons, fancy pattern. Weight, per ½ dozen, 10 ounces. Price, per ½ dozen...15c
If by mail, postage extra, per ½ dozen, 11c.

Aluminum Spoons.

These spoons are highly polished and in appearance are equal to the best solid silver goods, and as they are made of the same material throughout (having no plating to wear off) they will not tarnish nor corrode, but will have the appearance of new goods even after years of use.

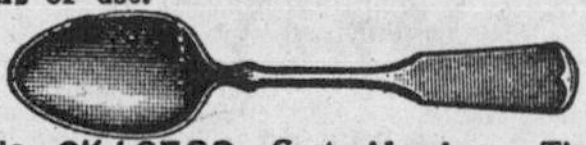

No. 6K16723 Cast Aluminum Tipped Teaspoons. Full size. Very finely finished. Pure as solid silver. Never wear out or tarnish. Price, per set of six.....28c
If by mail, postage extra, 4 cents.

No. 6K16724 Cast Aluminum Tipped Tablespoons. Full size in every way. Length, 8¼ inches. Price, per set of six.....48c
If by mail, postage extra, 7 cents.

Basting Spoons.

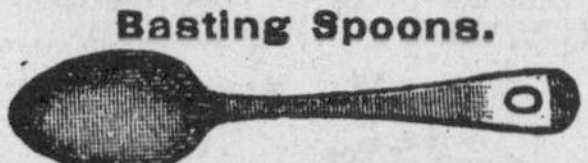

No. 6K16728 Forged Steel Basting Spoons, strong, heavy and durable. Heavily tinned.
10-inch. Weight, 3½ ounces. Price.....5c
If by mail, postage extra, 5 cents.
12-inch. Weight, 4 ounces. Price.....6c
If by mail, postage extra, 11 cents.
14-inch. Weight, 6 ounces. Price.....8c
If by mail, postage extra, 13 cents.
18-inch. Weight, 7½ ounces. Price.....12c
If by mail, postage extra, 16 cents.

Slotted Mixing Spoon, 9c.

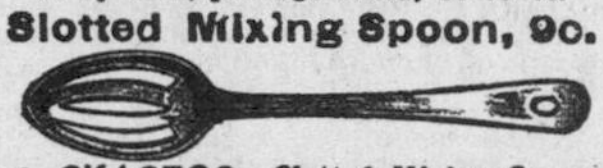

No. 6K16729 Slotted Mixing Spoon or Cake Beater. Forged from one piece of steel and heavily retinned. Smooth and easily cleaned. Length, 11½ inches. Weight, 4 ounces. Price.....9c
If by mail, postage extra, 11 cents.

WILBERT BRAND SHEARS AND SCISSORS.

Wilbert Shears and Scissors are guaranteed to be the highest quality shears and scissors on the market. We guarantee each pair for uniformity of temper, cutting quality, finish, material and workmanship. Our shears are steel laid, which means that they have a plate of crucible tempered steel welded to a malleable frame, making these the toughest, strongest, best cutting shears on the market. They are carefully selected and any shears with the slightest imperfection are not branded "WILBERT." We do not sell the so called second or medium quality shears or scissors. We have but one quality which is the very best that skilled labor and modern machinery and best material can produce. Remember, that every shear and scissor bearing the trade mark "WILBERT," which signifies highest quality, is absolutely guaranteed by our binding guarantee.

GUARANTEE. We guarantee every pair of Wilbert Shears and Scissors to be perfect workmanship and material and will replace any defective Wilbert Shears or Scissors for one year after date of purchase. We guarantee the grinding, tempering, fitting and finishing to be equal, if not superior to the finest goods of this kind on the market, and if found otherwise, they can be returned at our expense and the price paid, together with transportation charges, will be refunded. Wilbert Shears and Scissors are guaranteed to cut clean from heel to point. They remain sharp longer than any other shears or scissors on the market.

Wilbert Shears, Straight Trimmers.

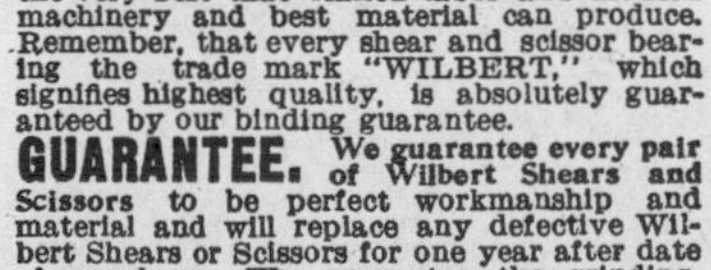

Wilbert Shears (Straight Trimmers). Steel laid blades. Will cut clear to the points and keep sharp longer than any other we know of. Fully warranted, as explained in heading above.

Whole length, inches....	6	7	8	9	10
Length of cut....	2¾	3¼	3¾	4¼	5

No. 6K16751 Japanned handles.

Price....	34c	39c	45c	54c	70c

No. 6K16752 Full nickel plated.

Price....	38c	47c	54c	65c	79c

No. 6K16753 Wilbert Left Hand Straight Trimmers. Full nickel plated; fully warranted.

Whole length, inches....	7½	8½
Length of cut, inches....	3¼	3¾
Price....	57c	68c

If by mail, postage extra, 5 to 14 cents.

Wilbert Bent Trimmers.

THE BEST ON EARTH.

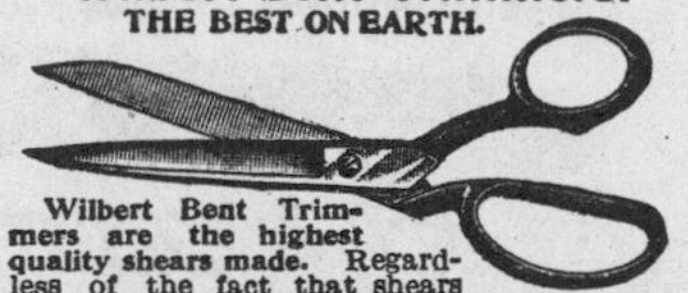

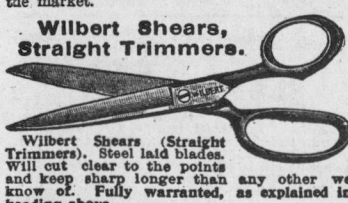

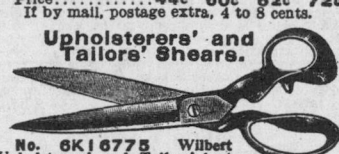

Wilbert Bent Trimmers are the highest quality shears made. Regardless of the fact that shears are offered at prices far in advance of what we are asking for our line of Wilbert Shears, we guarantee the material and workmanship in our line of Wilbert Shears and Trimmers to be the very best on the market or your money and transportation charges refunded. Our business in shears is the largest in the United States and we are therefore in a position to have shears made in accordance with our ideas and are able to undersell any legitimate competition. These bent trimmers are made especially for cutting cloth on a table; the bent handle enables the user to follow a line without the handle coming in contact with the table. Remember, all Wilbert Shears are guaranteed to give satisfaction and to cut from heel to point or money and transportation charges refunded.

No. 6K16763 Bent Trimmers, japanned handles.

Whole length, inches..	8	9	10
Length of cut, inches..	3¾	4¼	5
Price....	49c	65c	74c

No. 6K16764 Bent Trimmers, full nickel plated.

Whole length, inches..	8	9	10
Length of cut, inches..	3¾	4¼	5
Price....	58c	76c	89c

No. 6K16765 Wilbert Left Hand Bent Trimmers, full nickel plated. Full length, 9 inches. Price.....77c
If by mail, postage extra, 8 to 13 cents.

Heinisch Straight Trimmers.

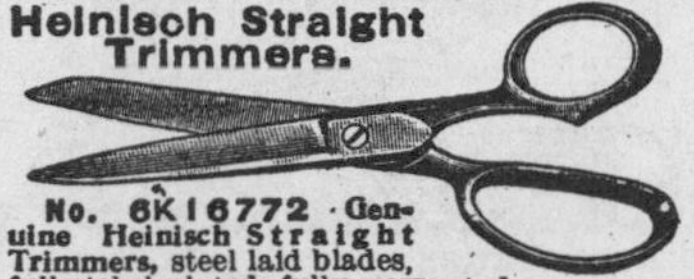

No. 6K16772 Genuine Heinisch Straight Trimmers, steel laid blades, full nickel plated fully warranted.

Size, inches....	6	7	8	9
Price....	44c	60c	62c	72c

If by mail, postage extra, 4 to 8 cents.

Upholsterers' and Tailors' Shears.

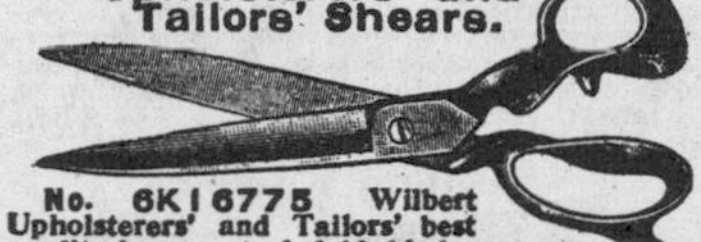

No. 6K16775 Wilbert Upholsterers' and Tailors' best quality heavy steel laid blades with japanned handles. Fitted with strong steel screw and nut. The equal in cutting quality, material and workmanship of shears sold at double our price. Each pair is guaranteed to give satisfaction or your money refunded.

Length, inches	10½	11½	12	12½
Price....	$1.32	$1.48	$1.60	$1.95

If by mail, postage extra, 19 to 34 cents.

Wilbert Barbers' Shears,

QUALITY GUARANTEED.

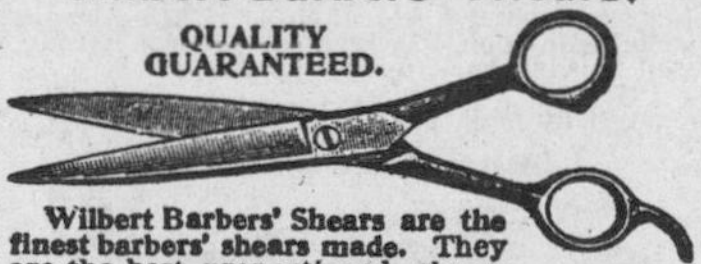

Wilbert Barbers' Shears are the finest barbers' shears made. They are the best proportioned shears on the market, fit the hand perfectly, work easily, smoothly, and are guaranteed to cut from heel to point. Blades are laid with special steel, tempered in a manner that insures a uniform temper. The finish and workmanship are the very best and we guarantee these shears to be the equal in material and workmanship of any shears made, even though offered at double the price. If you do not find these shears to be the best you ever had, return them and your money and transportation charges will be refunded.

No. 6K16778 Full nickel plated.

Whole length, in..	7	7½	8	8½	9
Length of cut, in..	3	3¼	3½	3¾	4½
Price....	48c	50c	55c	56c	61c

No. 6K16779 Japanned handle.

Whole length, inches....	7½	8
Length of cut, inches....	3¼	3½
Price....	40c	45c

If by mail, postage extra, 4 to 6 cents.

No. 6K16781 Wilbert Left Hand Steel Laid Barbers' Shears, full nickel plated. Whole length, 8½ inches; length of cut, 3¾ inches. Price.....70c
If by mail, postage extra, 6 cents.

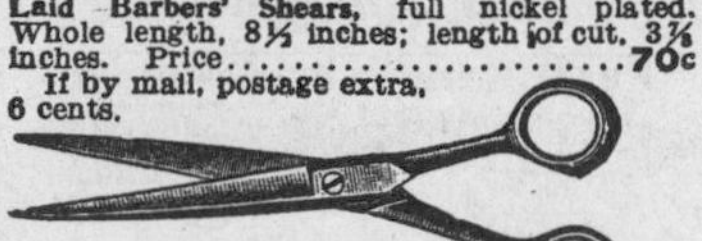

No. 6K16780 Wilbert Highest Quality Solid Steel Barbers' Shears, highly polished. Each pair guaranteed to give absolute satisfaction or money refunded. The material in these shears is the very best, the workmanship, grinding and tempering are absolutely perfect. They are made in a manner that we know will please any barber. Each pair fully guaranteed.

Whole length, inches.	7	7½	8	8½
Length of cut, inches	3¼	3½	3¾	4
Price....	65c	70c	74c	78c

If by mail, postage extra, 4 to 6 cents.

Heinisch Barbers' Shears.

No. 6K16786 Heinisch Barbers' Shears. Finely polished and full nickel plated; steel laid blades. Every pair warranted.

Size, inches....	8	8½	9
Price....	55c	60c	65c

If by mail, postage extra, 5 cents.

Wilbert Pocket Scissors.

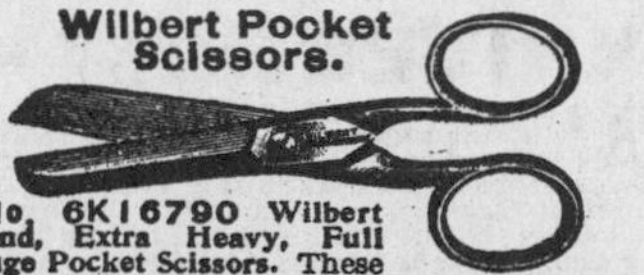

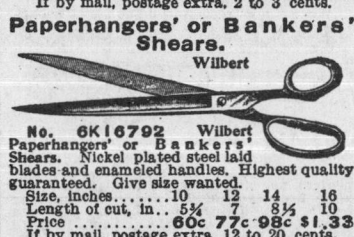

No. 6K16790 Wilbert Brand, Extra Heavy, Full Gauge Pocket Scissors. These scissors have finely swaged blades. They are made of the best material and guaranteed superior to any pocket scissors on the market. Each pair is guaranteed to give satisfaction or money refunded. Give size wanted.

Full length, inches....	4	4½	5
Length of cut....	1¾	2	2¼
Price....	33c	36c	38c

If by mail, postage extra, 2 to 3 cents.

Paperhangers' or Bankers' Shears.

Wilbert

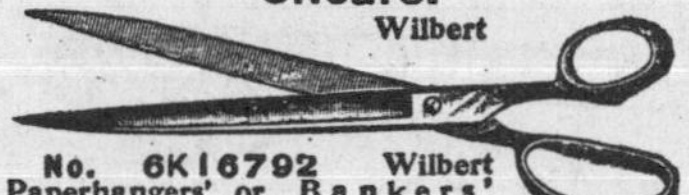

No. 6K16792 Wilbert Paperhangers' or Bankers' Shears. Nickel plated steel laid blades and enameled handles. Highest quality guaranteed. Give size wanted.

Size, inches....	10	12	14	16
Length of cut, in..	5¾	7	8½	10
Price....	60c	77c	98c	$1.33

If by mail, postage extra, 12 to 20 cents.

REMEMBER, all Wilbert Shears are guaranteed to be absolutely perfect or they can be returned and your money and transportation charges will be refunded. We guarantee Wilbert Shears and Scissors to be the superior of any other line of shears and scissors on the market. If you do not find them so, return them and your money will be refunded.

LADIES' SCISSORS.

Wilbert Brand.

The following patterns represent the highest quality of solid steel ladies' imported scissors. There are numerous grades of scissors on the market, both of American and foreign make, and it is an easy matter for any dealer to sell scissors at lower prices than those we quote, but it is impossible for any dealer to sell the grade of scissors we are handling at the prices that will in any way compare with those we quote. The following scissors, all solid steel goods, are made by the best factory in Germany. These scissors are fitted and finished and ground in a manner superior to that found in any other line of either American or foreign manufacture. We guarantee every pair of scissors to be perfect in material, cutting qualities, workmanship and finish or money and transportation charges will be refunded.

The Famous Wilbert Scissors.

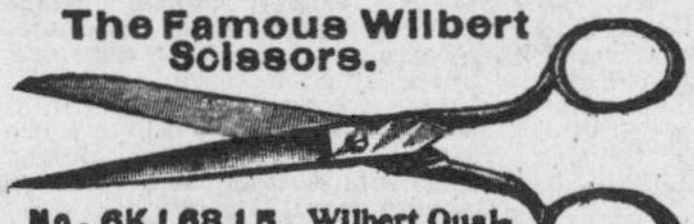

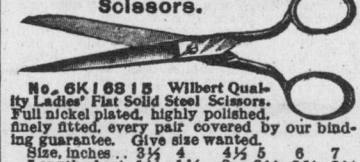

No. 6K16815 Wilbert Quality Ladies' Flat Solid Steel Scissors. Full nickel plated, highly polished, finely fitted, every pair covered by our binding guarantee. Give size wanted.

Size, inches..	3½	4	4½	5	6	7
Length of cut.	1¼	1¾	2	2¼	2¾	3½
Price....	30c	32c	36c	40c	47c	55c

If by mail, postage extra, 2 to 4 cents.

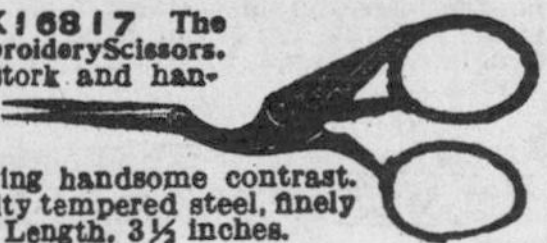

No. 6K16817 The Stork Embroidery Scissors. Body of stork and handles fancy gilt, bill polished steel, making handsome contrast. Best quality tempered steel, finely finished. Length, 3½ inches. Price.....35c
If by mail, postage extra, 2 cents.

Ladies' Fancy Solid Steel Scissors.

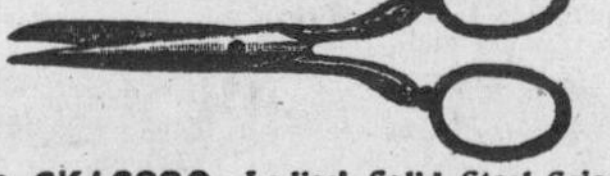

No. 6K16820 Ladies' Solid Steel Scissors, fancy gilt handle. Every pair guaranteed to give satisfaction. Handles are finely engraved and finished in gold, which makes a handsome contrast to the highly polished oval nickel plated blades. Give size wanted.

Size, inches....	3½	4½	5½
Price....	33c	37c	42c

If by mail, postage extra, 2 and 3 cents.

Buttonhole Scissors.

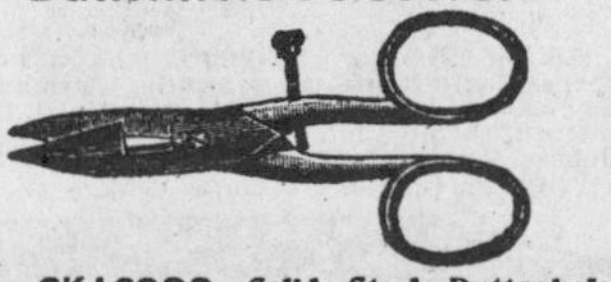

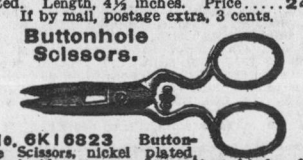

No. 6K16822 Solid Steel Buttonhole Scissors, with adjustable thumbscrew, as illustrated. Length, 4½ inches. Price.....24c
If by mail, postage extra, 3 cents.

Buttonhole Scissors.

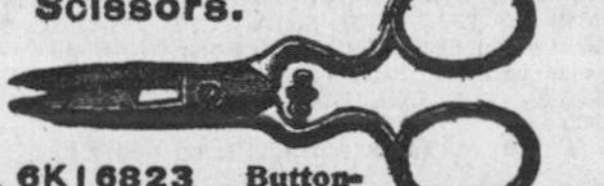

No. 6K16823 Buttonhole Scissors, nickel plated, with inside set screw to adjust blades for cutting. Length, 4½ inches.
Price..(By mail, postage extra, 3c)....34c

Adjustable Buttonhole Scissors.

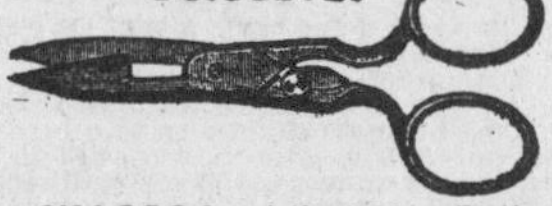

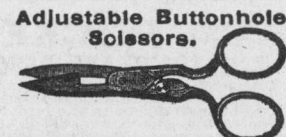

No. 6K16824 Adjustable Buttonhole Scissors, solid steel, nickel plated and polished, finely fitted, adjusted by means of a small notched brass wheel fitted inside of shank. Six different adjustments, each notch numbered, which guarantees uniformity in cutting the various sized buttonholes.
Price.....49c
If by mail, postage extra, 3 cents.

Scissors Sharpener.

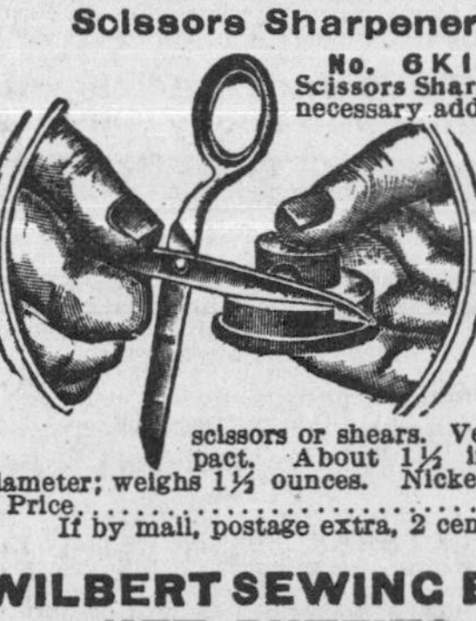

No. 6K16826 Scissors Sharpener, a necessary addition to every work box. Easily operated. A few strokes will put the correct bevel on your scissors or shears. Very compact. About 1½ inches in diameter; weighs 1½ ounces. Nickel plated. Price.....34c
If by mail, postage extra, 2 cents.

WILBERT SEWING BASKET OUTFITS.

The Wilbert Queen Outfit, $3.85

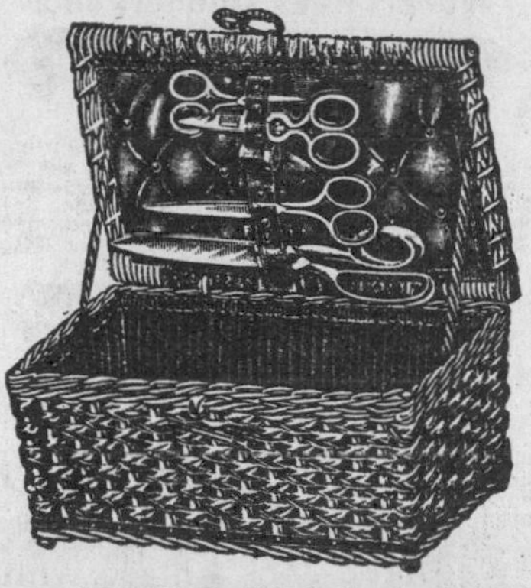

No. 6K16828 This is the handsomest and best sewing basket outfit ever placed on the market. The basket is imported from France, and is artistically woven of French willow and rattan. Size, 11 inches long, 7 inches wide, 5½ inches high. Lined throughout with the finest red satin; the top and bottom of basket are tufted, the sides are laid in folds. The basket alone would almost sell for what we ask for the complete outfit. This basket contains one pair of 8-inch Wilbert quality full nickel plated straight trimmers, one pair of Wilbert quality 6-inch solid steel scissors, one Wilbert solid steel 3½-inch lace or embroidery scissor, one highest quality imported button hole scissor, and one sterling silver thimble. When considering this outfit, bear in mind that Wilbert shears and scissors are the highest quality goods made. They are absolutely guaranteed to be the best or money will be refunded. Weight, 1 pound 12 ounces.
Price, outfit complete, as described, $3.85
If by mail, postage extra, 34 cents.

The Wilbert Princess Sewing Basket Outfit.

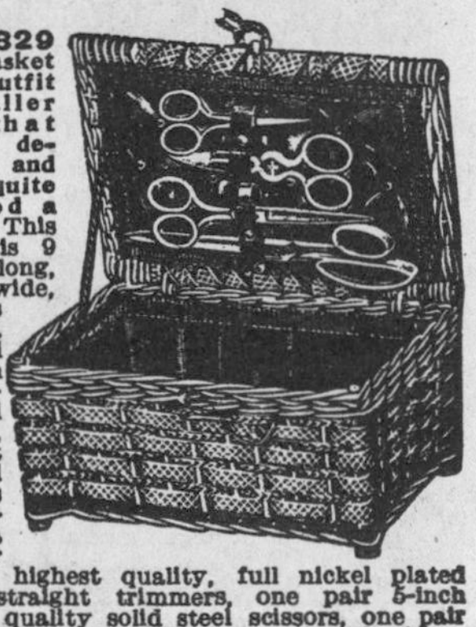

No. 6K16829 The basket of this outfit is smaller than that above described and is not quite as good a basket. This basket is 9 inches long, 6 inches wide, 4 inches high. Lined with beautiful red satin, biscuit tufted lid. This set includes a pair Wilbert highest quality, full nickel plated 7-inch straight trimmers, one pair 5-inch Wilbert quality solid steel scissors, one pair 3½-inch Wilbert quality lace or embroidery scissors, one pair highest quality imported button hole scissors, and one sterling silver thimble. This outfit could not be duplicated, quality considered, for less than $4.00. Weight, 1 pound 4 ounces.
Price, outfit complete, as described, $2.74
If by mail, postage extra, 26 cents.

NEW PATTERNS. **POCKET KNIVES.** LOWER PRICES.

WE ILLUSTRATE AND DESCRIBE a large line of jack and pen knives on the following pages, a line sufficiently large to suit all requirements. The pocket knives we handle are made specially for us under contract according to our own specifications by one of the oldest manufacturers in this country. Our enormous business enables us to control the output of this factory, and as our business on pocket knives is greater than that of any five mail order houses combined and is the largest pocket knife business today selling direct to the consumer, we naturally enjoy the very lowest cost, both in material and in the cost of manufacturing, consequently, quality considered, are able to give you better value than you could possibly procure elsewhere. Every Wilbert knife is guaranteed. If found unsatisfactory, it may be returned and money will be refunded.

THE BLADES in all Wilbert knives are forged from the finest S. C. Wardlow's English steel, tempered by electricity, insuring an even temper from heel to point. The grinding is done by experienced workmen who grind nothing but pocket knives, and are, therefore, able to turn out better work than is usually turned out in a factory whose business is not large enough to confine itself exclusively to pocket cutlery. We guarantee the springs and blades in our knives against breakage through flaws in material or temper. We, of course, do not guarantee them against misuse. We do not recommend the use of pocket knives for such purposes where a chisel, screwdriver or hammer would be better adapted.

Oil your knife once a month at the joints, so that the blades will not wear into the springs.

Two-Blade Jack Knives with Cocobolo and Ebony Handles.

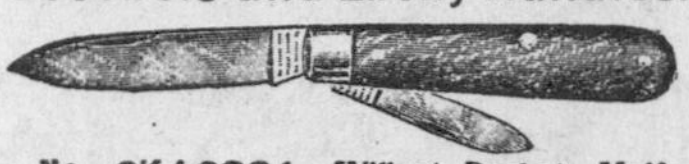

No. 6K16831 Wilbert Pocket Knife. Has rosewood handle, steel lining, iron bolster. Length of handle, 3½ inches. Length, with large blade open, 6 inches. Price........20c
If by mail, postage extra, 4 cents.

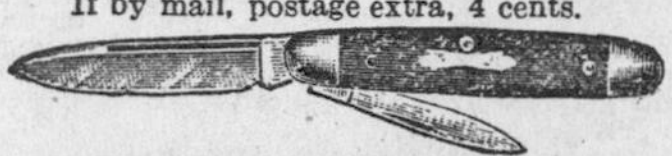

No. 6K16835 Wilbert Equal End Pocket Knife. Has cocoa handle, German silver bolsters, caps and shield, brass lined, finished inside and out. Length of handle, 3⅜ inches. Length, with large blade open, 5⅞ inches. Price........39c
If by mail, postage extra, 5 cents.

Wilbert Easy Opener, 48c.

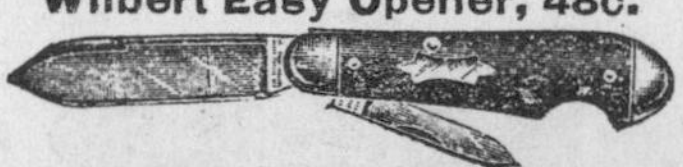

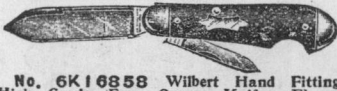

No. 6K16858 Wilbert Hand Fitting High Grade Easy Opener Knife. Ebony handle, German silver bolsters, caps and shield, brass lined. Length of handle, 3¼ inches. Length, with large blade open, 6½ inches. Price........48c
If by mail, postage extra, 5 cents.

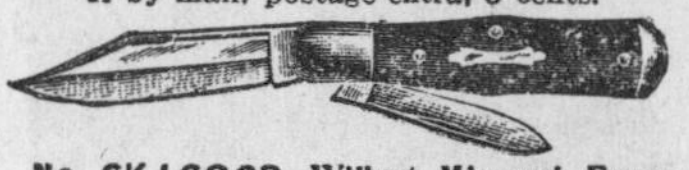

No. 6K16863 Wilbert Missouri Favorite, has clip point saber blade, made of full 12-gauge steel. Has ebony handle, long German silver bolsters, caps and shield, brass lined, finished inside and out. Length of handle, 3¾ inches. Length, with large blade open, 6⅝ inches. Price........49c
If by mail, postage extra, 6 cents.

Two-Blade Jack Knives with Stag Handles.

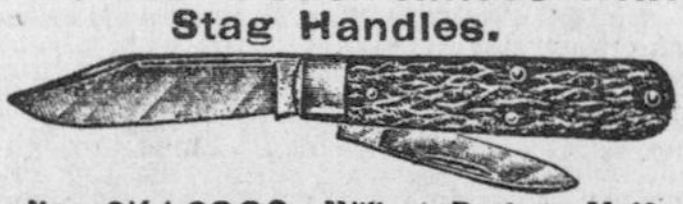

No. 6K16880 Wilbert Pocket Knife, clip point, stag handle, two blades, steel lining, iron bolster. This is a standard size, full weight knife; is durable, and will give splendid satisfaction. Length of handle, 3½ inches. Length, with large blade open, 6⅛ inches. Price........23c
If by mail, postage extra, 5 cents.

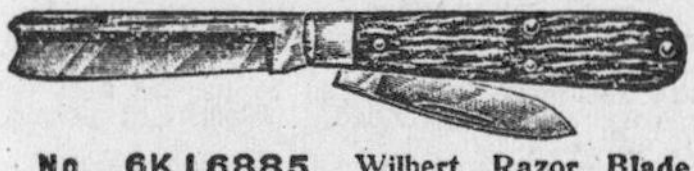

No. 6K16885 Wilbert Razor Blade Jack Knife, stag handle, steel lining, iron bolster. Length of handle, 3½ inches. Length, with large blade open, 6 inches. Price...33c
If by mail, postage extra, 5 cents.

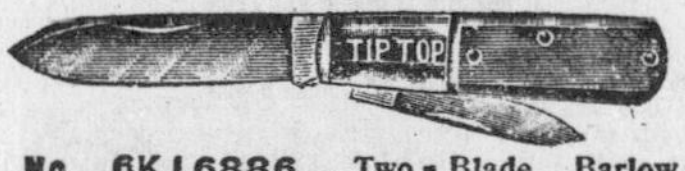

No. 6K16886 Two-Blade Barlow Pattern Jack Knife, steel lined, 1¼-inch iron bolster, bone handle. This is the original Barlow pattern. Length of knife, 3½ inches. Length, with spear blade open, 6 inches. Price........25c
If by mail, postage extra, 5 cents.

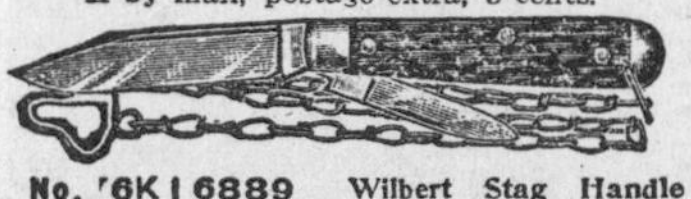

No. 6K16889 Wilbert Stag Handle Chain Knife, clip point, two blades, steel lining, iron bolsters and caps, German silver shield, with chain of suitable length to fasten over button. Length of handle, 3¾ inches. Length, with large blade open, 6⅛ inches. Price........38c
If by mail, postage extra, 6 cents.

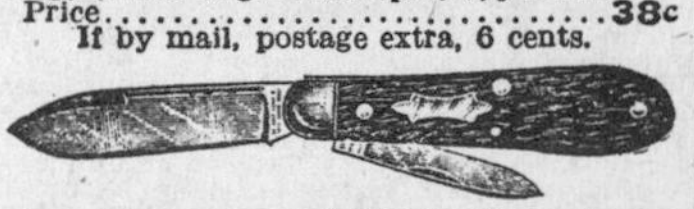

No. 6K16894 Wilbert Jack Knife, stag handle, swell butt, steel lining, iron bolster, German silver shield. Length of handle, 3⅜ inches. Length with large blade open, 6½ inches. Price........37c
If by mail, postage extra, 5 cents.

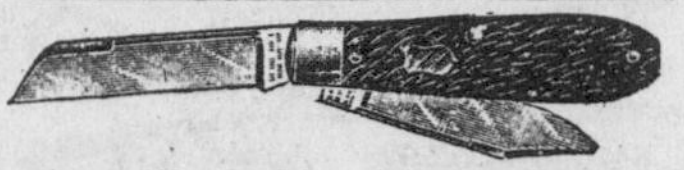

No. 6K16902 Wilbert Carpenters' Sensible Knife, having two large blades, one with clip point and one sheep's foot or carpenter's marking blade. The blades of this knife are made of 11-gauge steel; has stag handle, steel lining, iron bolster, German silver shield, finished inside and out. Length of handle, 3½ inches. Length, with large blade open, 6⅛ inches. Price........43c
If by mail, postage extra, 5 cents.

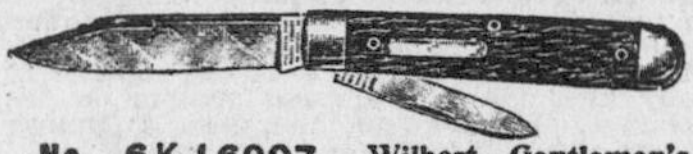

No. 6K16907 Wilbert Gentlemen's Jack Knife, stag handle, German silver bolsters, caps and shield, brass lining, thoroughly finished in every particular, inside and out. Length of handle, 3⅜ inches. Length with large blade open, 5⅞ inches. Price.....(Postage extra, 5 cents.)....42c

Wilbert Cutlery is guaranteed, and if found unsatisfactory money and transportation charges will be refunded. Wilbert Cutlery is sold exclusively by us.

Two-Blade Stag Handle Jack Knives, 45 Cents.

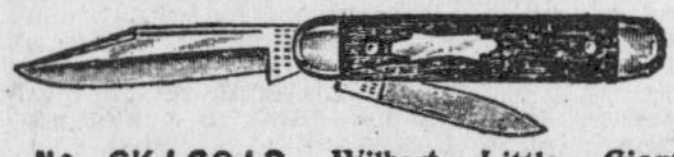

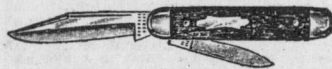

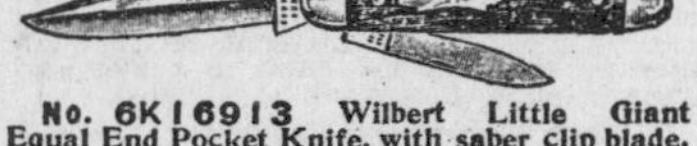

No. 6K16913 Wilbert Little Giant Equal End Pocket Knife, with saber clip blade, stag handle, German silver bolsters, caps and shield, brass lined, finished inside and out. The amount of work which this knife will do is something never before attained in a knife of its size. Length of handle, 3⅜ inches. Length with large blade open, 5¾ inches. Price....(Postage extra, 5 cents)....45c

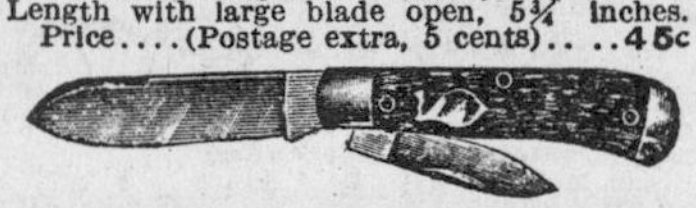

No. 6K16917 Wilbert Easy Opener Pocket Knife, with stag handle, German silver bolsters, caps and shield, brass lining. Finished inside and out. Length of handle, 3⅜ inches. Length with large blade open, 6¼ inches. Price........47c
If by mail, postage extra, 5 cents.

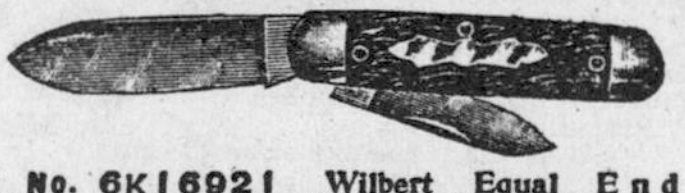

No. 6K16921 Wilbert Equal End Knife, has stag handle, brass lining, German silver bolsters, caps and shield. Length of handle, 3⅜ inches. Length with large blade open, 6¼ inches. Price........46c
If by mail, postage extra, 5 cents.

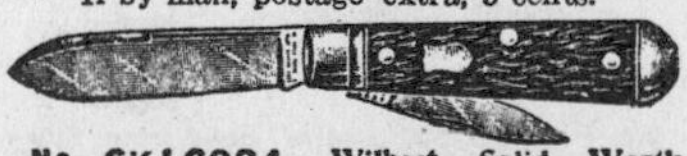

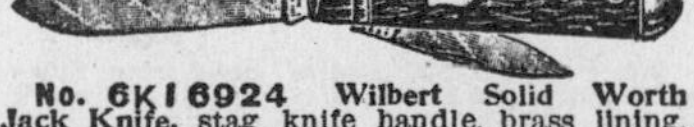

No. 6K16924 Wilbert Solid Worth Jack Knife, stag knife handle, brass lining, finished inside and out, iron bolsters and caps, German silver shield. Length of handle, 3½ inches. Length with large blade open 6¼ inches. Price..(Postage extra, 5 cents)..42c

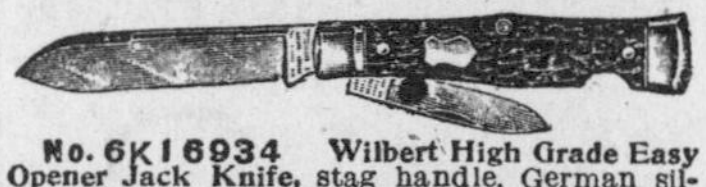

No. 6K16934 Wilbert High Grade Easy Opener Jack Knife, stag handle, German silver bolsters, caps and shield, brass lined, finely finished throughout. Length of handle, 3⅝ inches. Length with blade open, 6⅛ inches. Price....(Postage extra, 5 cents.)....50c

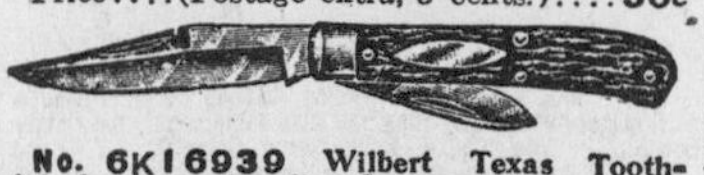

No. 6K16939 Wilbert Texas Toothpick, has stag handle, German silver bolster and shield, brass lining, finely finished inside and out. Clip point saber blade. While the blade is long and slim, the peculiar shape makes it very strong and durable as well as an excellent whittler. Length of handle, 3⅞ inches. Length with large blade open, 7 inches.
Price....(Postage extra, 5 cents.)....51c

THE SURPRISINGLY LOW REDUCED PRICES prevailing in this catalogue mean greater savings to our customers than ever before.

The Wilbert Dakota Cowboys' Knife, 60 Cents.

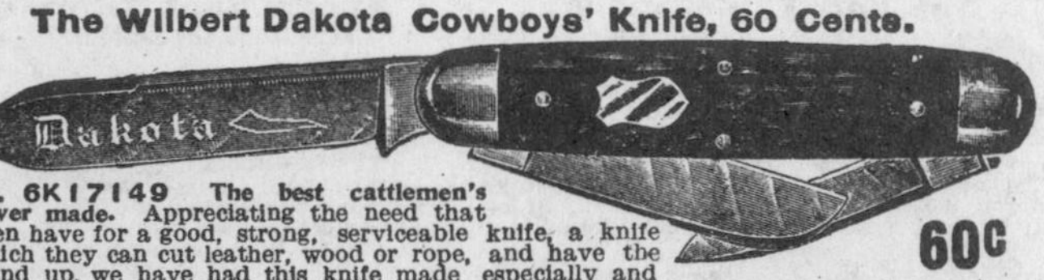

60c

No. 6K17149 The best cattlemen's knife ever made. Appreciating the need that cattlemen have for a good, strong, serviceable knife, a knife with which they can cut leather, wood or rope, and have the edge stand up, we have had this knife made especially and offer it as the best cattlemen's knife ever made. The steel used in these knives is extra heavy gauge and is the very best English steel suitable for this purpose. The blades are tempered by electricity, insuring uniform temper from heel to point. The grinding, finish and cutler's work in this knife cannot be surpassed. It has three blades; spear point blade, sheep's foot, and pen blade; fine stag handle, fitted with German silver shield, heavy German silver polished bolsters, full brass lined and finely finished inside and out. This is an extra strong, heavy knife for the stockman, hunter or trapper, who requires a dependable knife. We guarantee it to give absolute satisfaction or money refunded. It is a knife that would ordinarily sell for $1.25. Length of handle, 3⅝ inches; length, with large blade open, 6½ inches. Our price..............(If by mail, postage extra, 6 cents.)..............60c

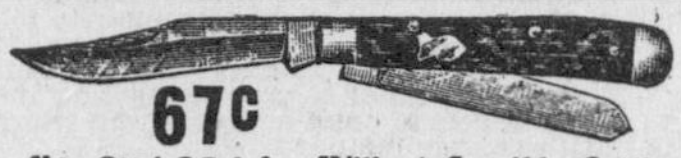

67c

No. 6K16944 Wilbert Sensible Cattlemen's Knife with saber clip point blade and spaying blade 3 inches long from bolster. The practical man will readily see the great advantage in the length of spaying blade in this knife. Has stag handle, German silver bolsters and shield, brass lined, highly finished throughout. Length of handle, 4 inches. Length, with clip point blade open, 7 inches. Price........67c
If by mail, postage extra, 5 cents.

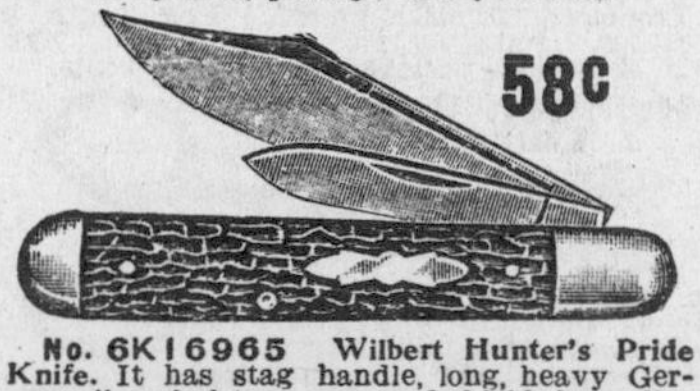

58c

No. 6K16965 Wilbert Hunter's Pride Knife. It has stag handle, long, heavy German silver bolsters, caps and shield, brass lining, highly finished inside and out. The blades open and close freely without wearing. The knife blade is always true in the center, and it is these little points, to which we pay so much attention, that cause our knives to give better satisfaction than those you can procure from any other dealer. Length of handle, 4½ inches. Length with large blade open, 8 inches. Price........58c
If by mail, postage extra, 6 cents.

Hunting Knives.

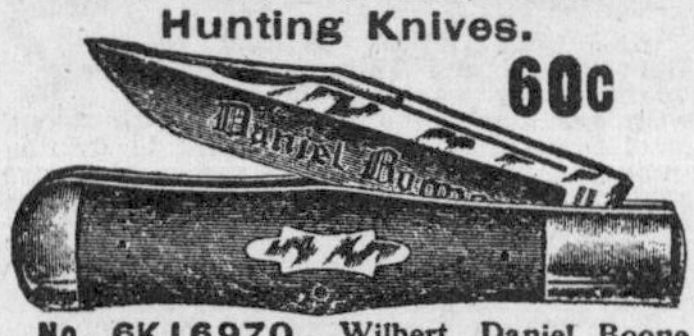

60c

No. 6K16970 Wilbert Daniel Boone Hunting Knife. Cocobolo handle, steel lined, iron bolsters and caps, saber clip point blade. Length of handle, 5¼ inches. Entire length with blade open, 9½ inches. A large, strong, well finished knife, fully warranted. Price........60c
If by mail, postage extra, 7 cents.

Lock Blade Hunter.

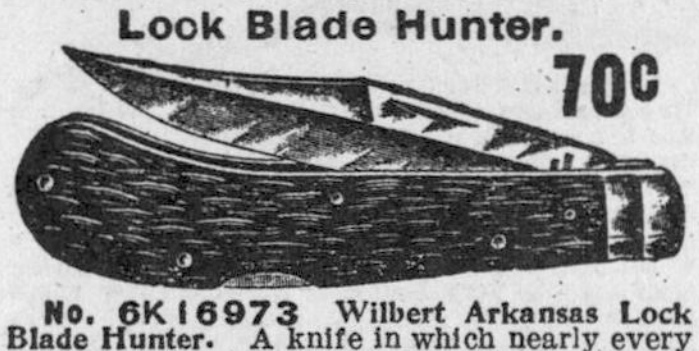

70c

No. 6K16973 Wilbert Arkansas Lock Blade Hunter. A knife in which nearly every cent of the cost is spent in quality and not looks. It has clip point saber blade, flush lock back so blade cannot shut on the fingers, curved stag handle which just fits the hand nicely, fancy iron bolsters, steel lining. Length of handle, 4⅝ inches. Length with blade open, 8⅛ inches. Price........70c
If by mail, postage extra, 7 cents.

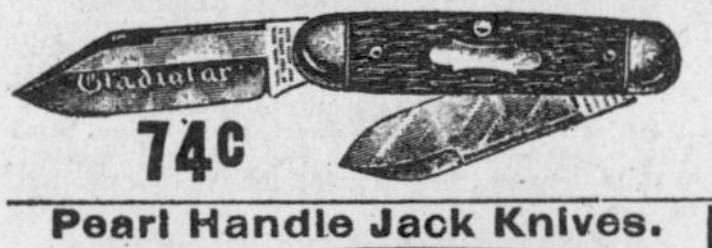

74c

No. 6K16997 Wilbert Gladiator Double Ender, has stag handle, German silver bolsters and shield, brass lined and finely finished throughout. Has saber clip and spear point blades. Length of handle, 4¼ inches. Length with spear blade open, 7½ inches. Price, 74c
If by mail, postage extra, 5 cents.

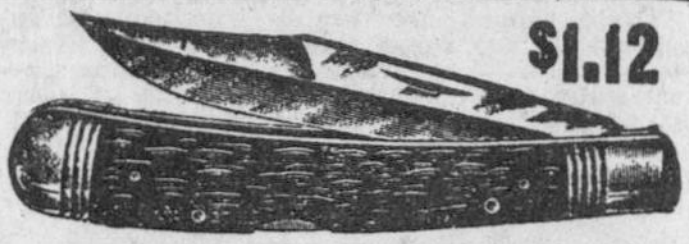

$1.12

No. 6K16976 Wilbert Hudson Bay Hunting Knife. A very nicely finished hunting knife. Clip point saber blade, flush lock back, curved stag handle, fancy German silver bolsters, caps and linings. Length of handle, 5¼ inches. Length with blade open, 9¾ inches. Price........$1.12
If by mail, postage extra, 7 cents.

For other Hunting Knives and a full line of Hunter's Goods see Sporting Goods Department.

Pruning Knives.

35c

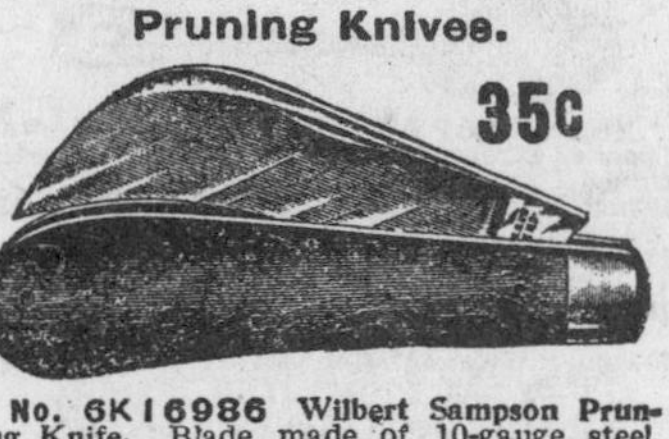

No. 6K16986 Wilbert Sampson Pruning Knife. Blade made of 10-gauge steel. The shape of blade, method of grinding, etc., being according to the ideas of one of the best fruit growers in the country, who had the original made just exactly the way he wanted it regardless of expense. Has cocobolo handle. Length of handle, 4 inches. Length with blade open, 7 inches. Price........35c
If by mail, postage extra, each, 6 cents.

Two-Blade Double End Knives with Stag Handles.

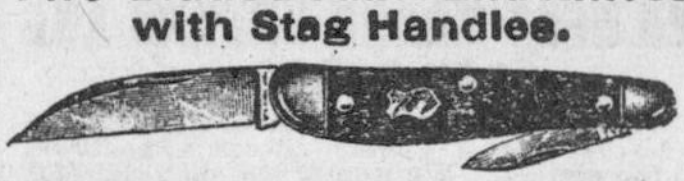

No. 6K16991 Wilbert New England Workmen's Knife. A great favorite with carpenters, cabinet makers and other woodworkers. It has stag handle, German silver bolsters and shield, brass lining, finely finished and polished inside and out. Length of handle, 3¾ inches. Length with large blade open, 6⅛ inches. Price........52c
If by mail, postage extra, 4 cents.

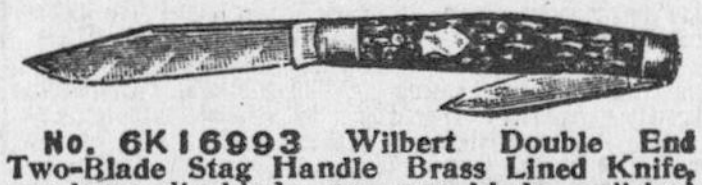

No. 6K16993 Wilbert Double End Two-Blade Stag Handle Brass Lined Knife, one large clip blade, one pen blade, polished brass bolsters and shield. Length of handle, 3½ inches; length with large blade open, 6 inches. This is a well finished and fitted knife, guaranteed to give satisfaction. Price........49c
If by mail, postage extra, 4 cents.

Pearl Handle Jack Knives.

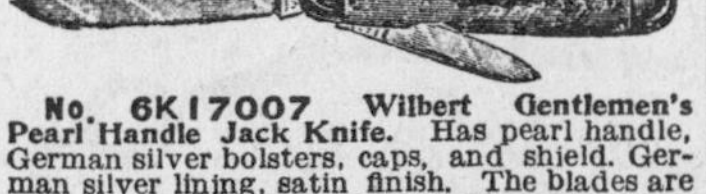

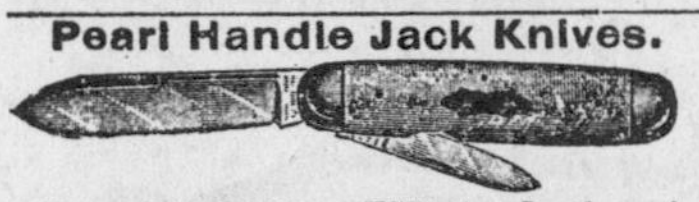

No. 6K17007 Wilbert Gentlemen's Pearl Handle Jack Knife. Has pearl handle, German silver bolsters, caps, and shield. German silver lining, satin finish. The blades are full crocus polished. The knife is in every way finished as finely as the best penknife you ever saw. Length of handle, 3⅜ inches; length with large blade open, 5⅞ inches. Price........90c
If by mail, postage extra, 5 cents.

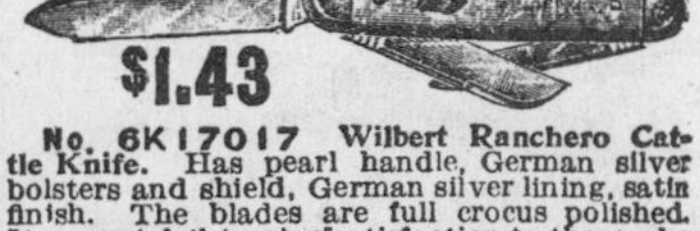

$1.43

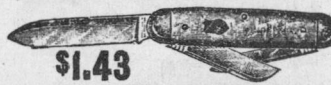

No. 6K17017 Wilbert Ranchero Cattle Knife. Has pearl handle, German silver bolsters and shield, German silver lining, satin finish. The blades are full crocus polished. It cannot fail to give satisfaction to those who want a knife of superior cutting qualities, workmanship and beauty. Length of handle, 3⅝ inches; length with large blade open, 6⅜ inches. Price........$1.43
If by mail, postage extra, 5 cents.

No. 6K17025 Wilbert Montana Beauty Stockmen's Knife.

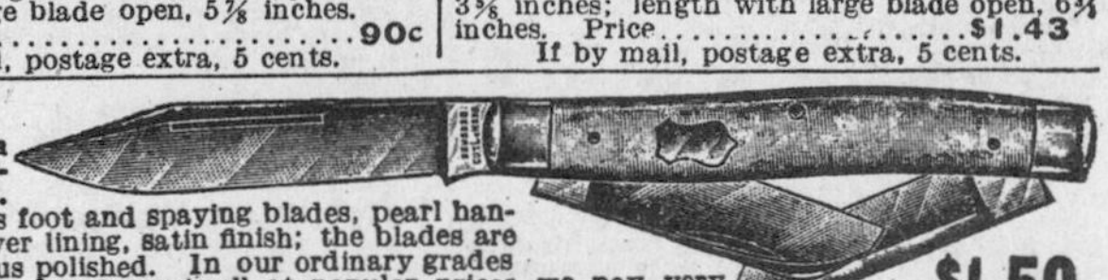

$1.50

Has clip, sheep's foot and spaying blades, pearl handle, German silver lining, satin finish; the blades are beautifully crocus polished. In our ordinary grades of knives, knives which must sell at popular prices, we pay very much more attention to quality and workmanship than we do to beauty and finish, but in this particular knife we excel all others in finish as well as in quality. Length of handle, 3⅞ inches; length with large blade open, 6¾ inches. Price..........(If by mail, postage extra, 5 cents)..........$1.50

The Arc Magnetic Razor.

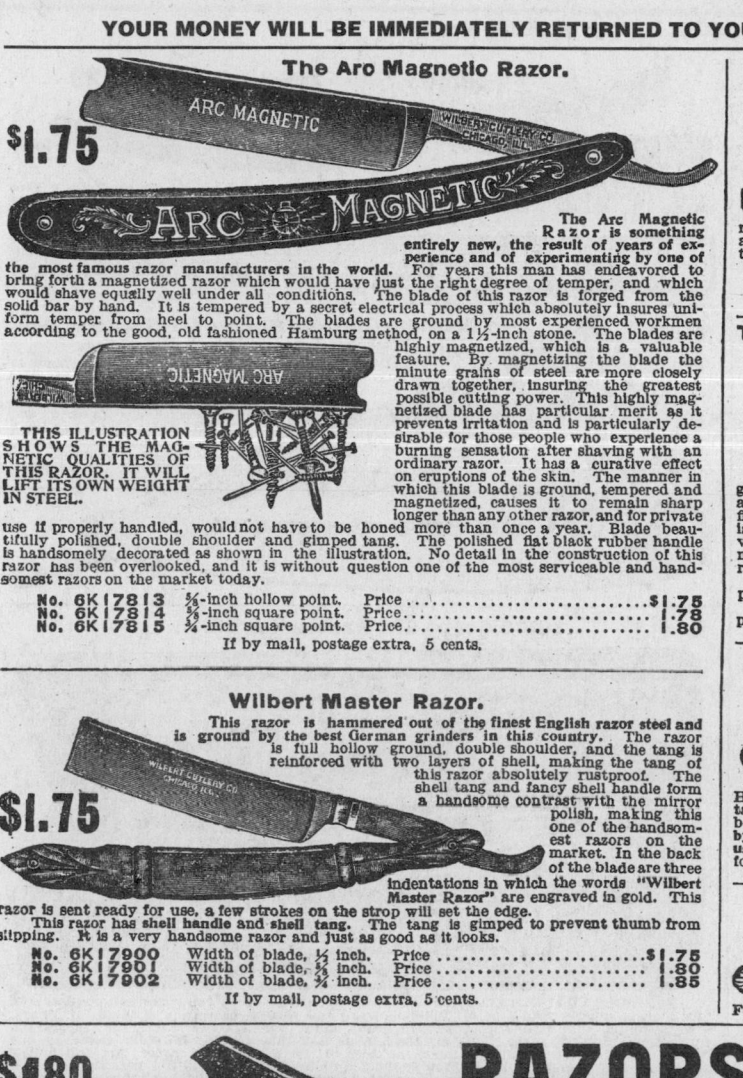

$1.75

The Arc Magnetic Razor is something entirely new, the result of years of experience and of experimenting by one of the most famous razor manufacturers in the world. For years this man has endeavored to bring forth a magnetized razor which would have just the right degree of temper, and which would shave equally well under all conditions. The blade of this razor is forged from the solid bar by hand. It is tempered by a secret electrical process which absolutely insures uniform temper from heel to point. The blades are ground by most experienced workmen according to the good, old fashioned Hamburg method, on a 1½-inch stone. The blades are highly magnetized, which is a valuable feature. By magnetizing the blade the minute grains of steel are more closely drawn together, insuring the greatest possible cutting power. This highly magnetized blade has particular merit as it prevents irritation and is particularly desirable for those people who experience a burning sensation after shaving with an ordinary razor. It has a curative effect on eruptions of the skin. The manner in which this blade is ground, tempered and magnetized, causes it to remain sharp longer than any other razor, and for private

THIS ILLUSTRATION SHOWS THE MAGNETIC QUALITIES OF THIS RAZOR. IT WILL LIFT ITS OWN WEIGHT IN STEEL.

use if properly handled, would not have to be honed more than once a year. Blade beautifully polished, double shoulder and gimped tang. The polished flat black rubber handle is handsomely decorated as shown in the illustration. No detail in the construction of this razor has been overlooked, and it is without question one of the most serviceable and handsomest razors on the market today.

No. 6K17813 ⅝-inch hollow point. Price $1.75
No. 6K17814 ⅝-inch square point. Price 1.78
No. 6K17815 ¾-inch square point. Price 1.80

If by mail, postage extra, 5 cents.

Wilbert Master Razor.

$1.75

This razor is hammered out of the finest English razor steel and is ground by the best German grinders in this country. The razor is full hollow ground, double shoulder, and the tang is reinforced with two layers of shell, making the tang of this razor absolutely rustproof. The shell tang and fancy shell handle form a handsome contrast with the mirror polish, making this one of the handsomest razors on the market. In the back of the blade are three indentations in which the words "Wilbert Master Razor" are engraved in gold. This razor is sent ready for use, a few strokes on the strop will set the edge. This razor has shell handle and shell tang. The tang is gimped to prevent thumb from slipping. It is a very handsome razor and just as good as it looks.

No. 6K17900 Width of blade, ½ inch. Price $1.75
No. 6K17901 Width of blade, ⅝ inch. Price 1.80
No. 6K17902 Width of blade, ¾ inch. Price 1.85

If by mail, postage extra, 5 cents.

Wilbert High Art Razor.

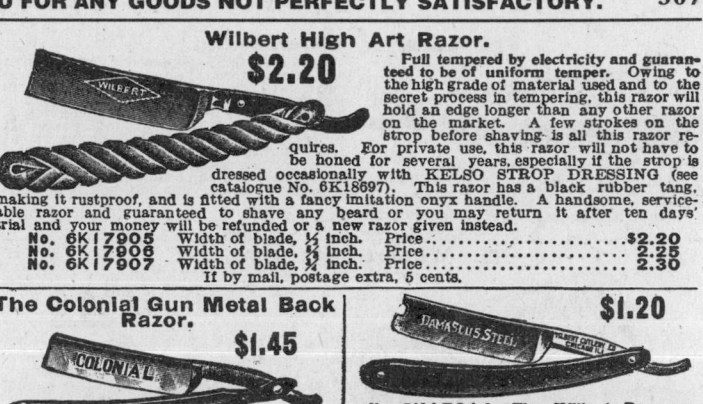

$2.20

Full tempered by electricity and guaranteed to be of uniform temper. Owing to the high grade of material used and to the secret process in tempering, this razor will hold an edge longer than any other razor on the market. A few strokes on the strop before shaving is all this razor requires. For private use, this razor will not have to be honed for several years, especially if the strop is dressed occasionally with KELSO STROP DRESSING (see catalogue No. 6K18697), making it rustproof, and is fitted with a fancy imitation onyx handle. A handsome, serviceable razor and guaranteed to shave any beard or you may return it after ten days' trial and your money will be refunded or a new razor given instead.

No. 6K17905 Width of blade, ½ inch. Price $2.20
No. 6K17906 Width of blade, ⅝ inch. Price 2.25
No. 6K17907 Width of blade, ¾ inch. Price 2.30

If by mail, postage extra, 5 cents.

The Colonial Gun Metal Back Razor.

$1.45

The Wilbert Colonial Razor, full hollow ground, with gun metal, non-rustable tang and back. The tang is shaped to fit the fingers, finely gimped. This razor is full polished; an excellent razor for barbers' or private use. The gun metal tang and back are non-rustable, and with ordinary care this razor will last a lifetime.

No. 6K17908 ½-inch blade, square point. Price $1.45
No. 6K17911 ⅝-inch blade, square point. Price $1.50

If by mail, postage extra, 5 cents.

$1.20

No. 6K17914 The Wilbert Damascus Steel Razor.—Regular English ground, ¾-inch blade, black rubber handle. This razor has a heavy back and a very stiff edge, and is expressly recommended to those having a hard beard or who shave but once a week. It is a razor that gives satisfaction to everyone, but for the coarse, heavy beard, it will give better satisfaction than a lighter razor. It is finely finished and fully guaranteed. Price $1.20

If by mail, postage extra, 5 cents.

Wilbert Acme Razor.

96c

No. 6K17912 The Wilbert Acme Razor. Hollow ground, ⅝-inch blade, heavy gimped tang. This razor will probably "fit" more beards than any razor we sell. It is ground by experts and is suitable for barbers' or private use. A better razor than those usually sold for $1.50. Our price 96c

If by mail, postage extra, 5 cents.

Winner Round Point.

$1.30

No. 6K17919 The Winner, fancy pattern, polished white bone handle, hollow ground ⅝-inch round point, full polished blade, graceful double gimped tang, blade finely tempered and ground by experienced workmen. Guaranteed to give satisfaction. An excellent razor for barbers' and private use. Price ....$1.30 (Postage extra, 5 cents.)

WILBERT CUTLERY IS GUARANTEED TO GIVE SATISFACTION.

$1.75

WILBERT CUTLERY IS SHARP

No. 6K17932 The Wilbert Autocrat Razor, has fancy white ivoroid handle, ⅝-inch blade, full crocus polished, full concaved. Is suitable for barbers' or private use, and is best value ever offered in a high grade razor.

Fully warranted. Price ....(If by mail, postage extra, 5 cents.) $1.75

RAZORS MADE TO ORDER
HAVE A RAZOR MADE TO FIT YOUR BEARD

$1.80

WITH YOUR NAME ENGRAVED ON THE BLADE IN GOLD LETTERS

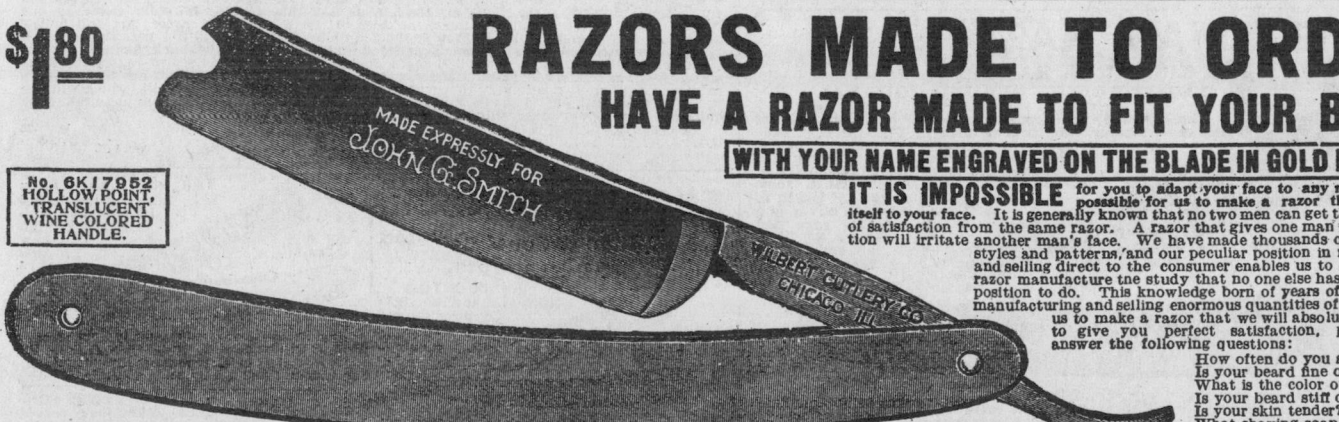

No. 6K17952 HOLLOW POINT, TRANSLUCENT WINE COLORED HANDLE.

No. 6K17950 SQUARE POINT, BLACK RUBBER HANDLE.

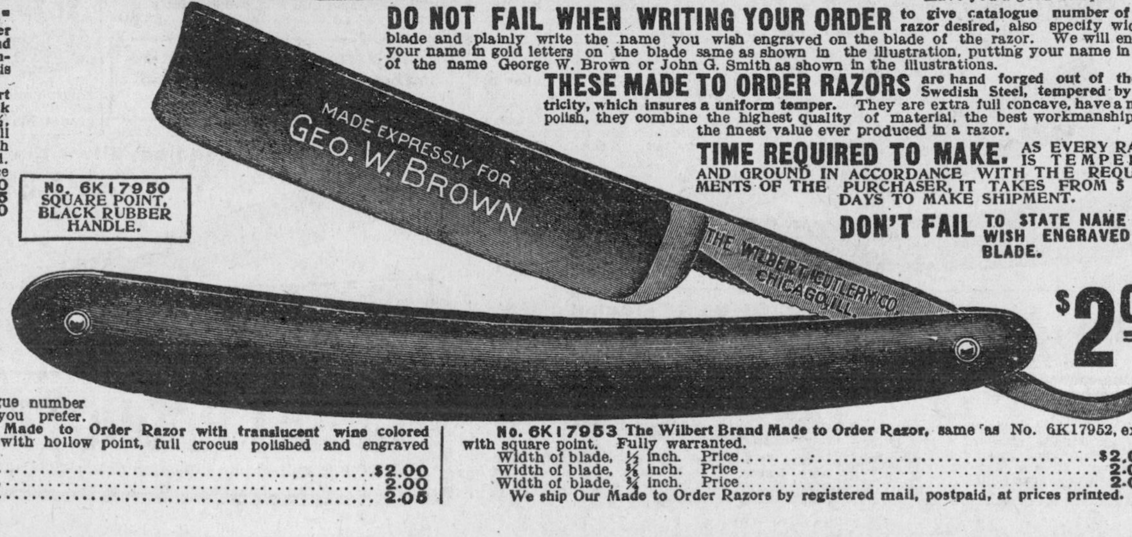

IT IS IMPOSSIBLE for you to adapt your face to any razor, but it is possible for us to make a razor that will adapt itself to your face. It is generally known that no two men can get the same degree of satisfaction from the same razor. A razor that gives one man entire satisfaction will irritate another man's face. We have made thousands of razors, in all styles and patterns, and our peculiar position in manufacturing and selling direct to the consumer enables us to give the art of razor manufacture the study that no one else has ever been in a position to do. This knowledge born of years of experience in manufacturing and selling enormous quantities of razors enables us to make a razor that we will absolutely guarantee to give you perfect satisfaction, provided you answer the following questions:

How often do you shave?
Is your beard fine or coarse?
What is the color of your beard?
Is your beard stiff or soft?
Is your skin tender?
What shaving soap do you use?
Have you a good strop?

THE LOWER ILLUSTRATION shows our Made to Order Razor with square point and black rubber handle with name engraved on blade. We also furnish this razor with hollow point if desired.

No. 6K17950 The Wilbert Brand Made to Order Razor with black rubber handle, and blade either ½, ⅝ or ¾-inch wide, square point, full crocus polished and engraved with your name in gold. Fully warranted.

Price
Width of blade, ½ inch $1.80
Width of blade, ⅝ inch 1.85
Width of blade, ¾ inch 1.90

No. 6K17951 The Wilbert Brand Made to Order Razor, same as No. 6K17950, except with hollow point. Warranted.

Price
Width of blade, ½ inch .. $1.80
Width of blade, ⅝ inch .. 1.85
Width of blade, ¾ inch .. 1.90

THE UPPER ILLUSTRATION shows our Made to Order Razor with hollow point and translucent wine colored handle. We furnish this razor with square point if desired. Be sure and designate by catalogue number which point and which handle you prefer.

No. 6K17952 The Wilbert Made to Order Razor with translucent wine colored handle, and blade ½, ⅝ or ¾-inch, with hollow point, full crocus polished and engraved with name in gold. Warranted.

Width of blade, ½ inch. Price $2.00
Width of blade, ⅝ inch. Price 2.00
Width of blade, ¾ inch. Price 2.05

DO NOT FAIL WHEN WRITING YOUR ORDER to give catalogue number of your razor desired, also specify width of blade and plainly write the name you wish engraved on the blade of the razor. We will engrave your name in gold letters on the blade same as shown in the illustration, putting your name in place of the name George W. Brown or John G. Smith as shown in the illustrations.

THESE MADE TO ORDER RAZORS are hand forged out of the best Swedish Steel, tempered by electricity, which insures a uniform temper. They are extra full concave, have a mirror polish, they combine the highest quality of material, the best workmanship and the finest value ever produced in a razor.

TIME REQUIRED TO MAKE. AS EVERY RAZOR IS TEMPERED AND GROUND IN ACCORDANCE WITH THE REQUIREMENTS OF THE PURCHASER, IT TAKES FROM 5 TO 8 DAYS TO MAKE SHIPMENT.

DON'T FAIL TO STATE NAME YOU WISH ENGRAVED ON BLADE.

$2.00

No. 6K17953 The Wilbert Brand Made to Order Razor, same as No. 6K17952, except with square point. Fully warranted.

Width of blade, ½ inch. Price $2.00
Width of blade, ⅝ inch. Price 2.00
Width of blade, ¾ inch. Price 2.05

We ship Our Made to Order Razors by registered mail, postpaid, at prices printed.

The Surprise Razor, $1.95.

No. 6K17927 Something entirely new; never been offered by any house. The Surprise razor is well named, for no matter how carefully we might describe this razor, you would still be surprised at its beauty upon receiving it. This razor is full hollow ground by most experienced workmen, the blade double shouldered, and is full polished. The tang of this razor is gold plated with 14-ka. at gold. The handle is green celluloid, the green transparent celluloid harmonizing beautifully with the heavily plated gold tang and beautiful mirror polished blade. This razor is as good as it looks. The workmanship is the very best, and it is guaranteed to shave any beard.
Price, ⅝-inch blade, special square point....................................$1.95
If by mail, postage extra, 5 cents.

The Wilbert Regal Razor.

$2.00

No. 6K17933 The Wilbert Regal Razor has ivory tang, fancy imitation ivory handle, has ⅝-inch blade, is full crocus polished, full hollow ground, fancy diamond back. One of the neatest looking razors made and makes an elegant present, while for shaving qualities and workmanship it cannot be excelled. Fully warranted. Price..................$2.00
If by mail, postage extra, 5 cents.

Antiseptic Felt Pad Razor.

$2.44

No. 6K17938 This razor, as indicated by the name, is an antiseptic razor; in fact, the best antiseptic razor made. The flat rubber handles are lined with felt pads which are saturated with an antiseptic oil (Parmoline), which protects the sensitive edge of the blade from rust and keeps it sanitary and sharp. The Antiseptic Razor keeps sharp longer than other razor as the edge is kept free from rust. For private use this razor ought not require honing more than once a year. Every razor is thoroughly tested and inspected before being shipped. Guaranteed to give satisfaction. ⅝-inch full hollow ground blade, square point, double shoulder, broad comfortable tang, flat polished black rubber handle, well finished throughout. Price, each, including nickel plated oiler filled with Parmoline....$2.44
If by mail, postage extra, 5 cents.

50c

No. 6K18019 Wilbert Medium Hollow Ground Razor. Hollow blade, black rubber handle. A good razor, equal to those sold by all dealers for $1.00. Price.................50c
If by mail, postage extra, 5 cents.

75c

No. 6K18020 Our Wilbert Reliable Razor, ⅝-inch blade, hollow ground, hollow point, fancy thumb hold, imitation tortoise shell handle. Guaranteed to give satisfaction. Price.......................75c
If by mail, postage extra, 5 cents.

GERMAN RAZORS.

THE BISMARCK RAZOR.
DOUBLE HOLLOW GROUND. GUARANTEED.

NOTE THE RIDGE OR BACKBONE.

$1.34

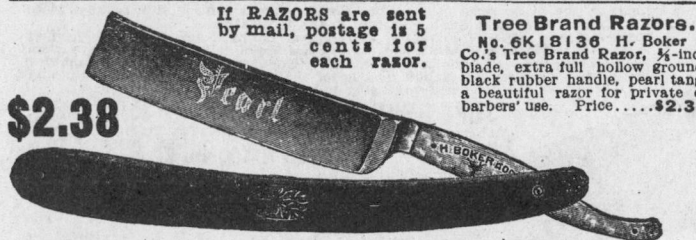

The Bismarck Razor represents the best production of one of the most famous factories in Germany. This razor is made complete in Germany and imported by us. We offer it as the finest razor of its type on the market. It is extra full ground and, as shown in the illustration, has a ridge extending the full length of the blade, which serves as a backbone to the edge and gives the blade strength, life and cutting power not found in any of the other German razors on the market. The material, workmanship and finish of this razor are perfect, and we guarantee it to give absolute satisfaction or your money and transportation charges refunded. Fitted with a polished black rubber handle. Each razor branded BISMARCK, as shown in the illustration.
No. 6K18090 "Bismarck" Razor. Width of blade, ¾ inch. Price.........$1.35
No. 6K18091 "Bismarck" Razor. Width of blade, ⅝ inch. Price.........1.34
If by mail, postage extra on each razor is 5 cents.

If RAZORS are sent by mail, postage is 5 cents for each razor.

Tree Brand Razors.
No. 6K18136 H. Boker & Co.'s Tree Brand Razor, ⅝-inch blade, extra full hollow ground, black rubber handle, pearl tang; a beautiful razor for private or barbers' use. Price.....$2.38

$2.38

30c

No. 61K8165 A Fair Grade German Razor, ⅝-inch blade, medium hollow ground, engraved, "fully warranted," but not warranted by us. It is a razor that is usually sold at from 50 cents to $1.00. Price.................30c

Our 65-Cent Magnetic German Razor.

65c

No. 6K18166 A Good Quality German Razor, ⅝-inch blade. Finely ground, made of best steel, polished and gimped tang, magnetized, warranted. Price.....65c

---

$1.50

No. 6K18135 H. Boker & Co.'s Tree Brand Razor, extra full hollow ground, black rubber handle. Width of blade, ⅝ inch. Price..................$1.50

THE SURPRISINGLY LOW REDUCED PRICES prevailing in this catalogue mean greater savings to our customers than ever before.

$1.29

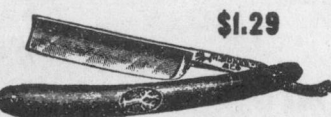

No. 6K18137 H. Boker & Co.'s Tree Brand Razor, extra stiff for the man with the heavy beard who shaves but once or twice a week. ⅝-inch blade, square point, beautifully polished, fully hollow ground, file tang, double shoulder and fitted with oval black rubber handles. This razor is made especially for us, and we guarantee it to be equal to any $2.00 razor on the market. Price..............$1.29

Genuine German Razors for Barbers' Use.
The Figaro Razor. Our Own Importation.

$1.50

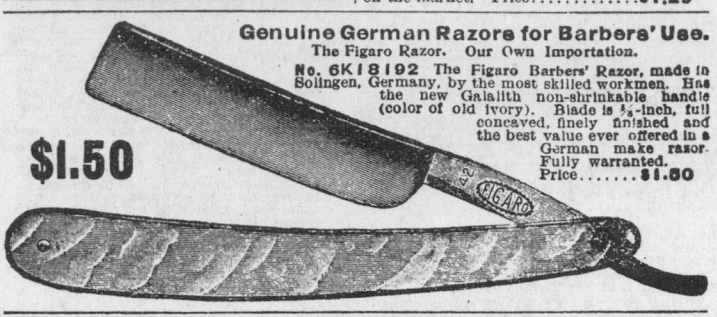

No. 6K18192 The Figaro Barbers' Razor, made in Solingen, Germany, by the most skilled workmen. Has the new Galalith non-shrinkable handle (color of old ivory). Blade is ⅝-inch, full concaved, finely finished and the best value ever offered in a German make razor. Fully warranted. Price........$1.50

$8.00 Set of Ern Razors for $3.94.

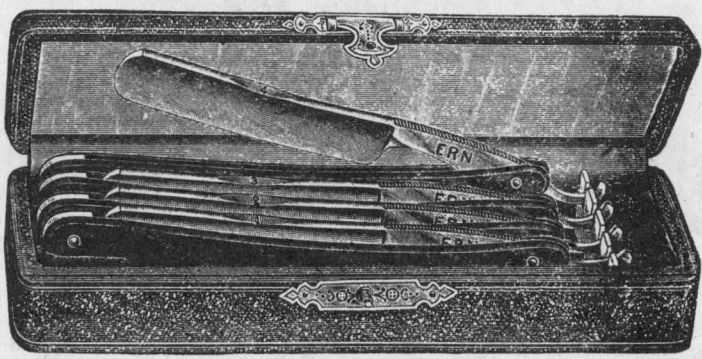

No. 6K18194 For $3.94 we furnish this beautiful four-piece razor set, consisting of four highest quality round point, full hollow ground razors, packed in a beautiful hinged, satin lined, partitioned, leather box, with heavy metal clasp. These razors, sold separately, would retail for $2.00 each. They are the famous Ern razors, made in Wald, Germany, one of the oldest and most famous razor factories in the world. The razors are full hollow ground, ⅝-inch round point, with double gimped finger fitting tang, fitted with flat, polished black rubber handle. These razors have small indentations on the back, as shown in the illustration, and are numbered 1, 2, 3 and 4, respectively. Buy this set of razors for $3.94 and you will have a set that will last for several generations. You will always have a sharp razor and a different razor every time you shave. Compare this set of razors, which will last you a lifetime, with any of the $5.00 safety razors on the market for which you are continually obliged to buy new blades, calling for a continuous additional expenditure.
Price of set of four razors, packed in a beautiful satin lined, partitioned, hinged, leather box.................................$3.94
If by mail, postage extra, 13 cents.

ENGLISH RAZORS.
Jos. Allen & Sons' Celebrated NON-XLL Razors.

60c

No. 6K18199 NON-XLL medium hollow ground ⅝-inch square point razor with oval black rubber handle. Blade is nicely etched and finished. This is a good, stiff, heavy razor and will give satisfaction. Price.................60c

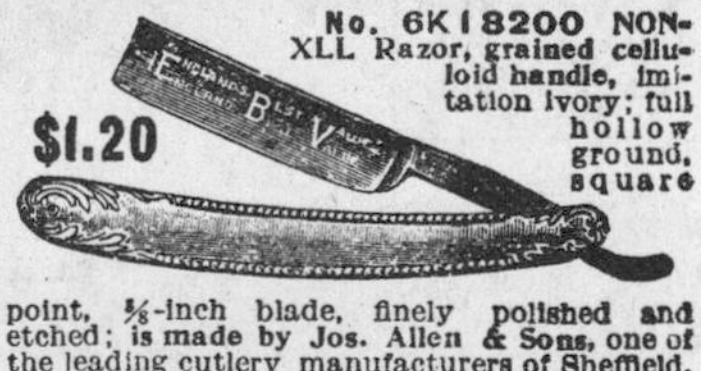

No. 6K18200 NON-XLL Razor, grained celluloid handle, imitation ivory; full hollow ground, square

$1.20

point, ⅝-inch blade, finely polished and etched; is made by Jos. Allen & Sons, one of the leading cutlery manufacturers of Sheffield, England, and is fully warranted. Price.$1.20

No. 6K18202 NON-XLL Razor, fancy carved celluloid handle, ⅝-inch blade with round point, full

$1.25

hollow ground, polished and etched. A razor which is warranted and which cannot fail to give satisfaction. Price...........$1.25

All Razors illustrated and described on this page, if by mail, postage extra, each, 5 cents.

Pearl Handled, Silver Lined Razor.

$2.87

No. 6K18203 Joseph Allen & Sons' NON-XLL Pearl Handled Razor. The handle of this razor is genuine pearl, reinforced with fine German silver lining. The blade is full polished, making this one of the finest appearing razors on the market. ⅝-inch hollow point blade, heavy round back, file tang, ground so as to fit any beard. Guaranteed to give satisfaction. This is one of the finest razors ever turned out by the old firm of Jos. Allen & Sons, whose name alone signifies quality. Price.................$2.87

THE GREAT REDUCTIONS IN THE PRICES SHOWN IN THE PAGES OF THIS CATALOGUE we feel sure will be very pleasing to our millions of customers.

George Wostenholm Imported English Razors.

REDUCED PRICES.

We offer a line of razors made by George Wostenholm & Sons, of Sheffield, England, manufacturers of the genuine IXL cutlery and the Pipe Brand Razors, which are so widely known all over the world.

No. 6K18255 George Wostenholm & Sons' Genuine, Original and True Pipe Razor, medium hollow ground,

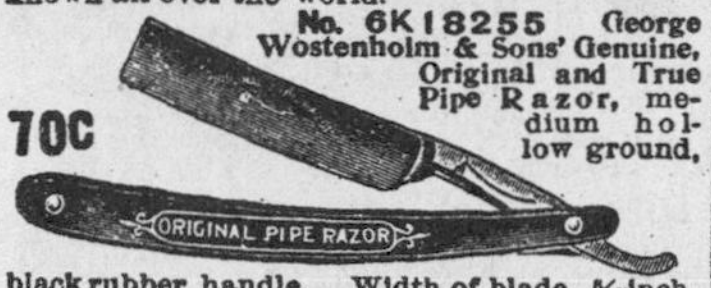

70c

black rubber handle. Width of blade, ⅝-inch. This razor is known all over the world and has established a most enviable reputation. Price.......................70c

No. 6K18257 George Wostenholm & Sons' Original Pipe Razor, hollow ground. Width of blade, ⅝-inch,

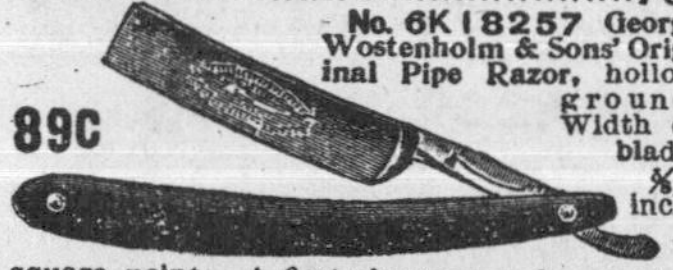

89c

square point. A first-class razor for general use. Price.......................89c

No. 6K18258 George Wostenholm & Sons' Original and True Pipe

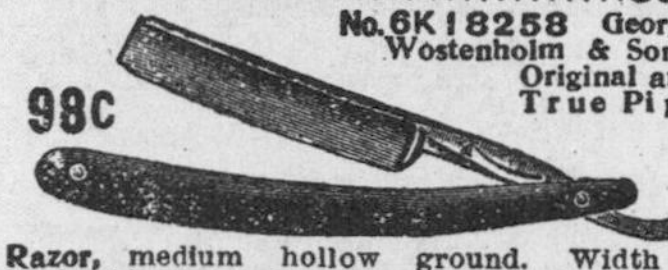

98c

Razor, medium hollow ground. Width of blade, ½ inch. A fine razor for the beginner; also used for shaving a second time over; has black rubber handle, file cut tang. Price.......................98c

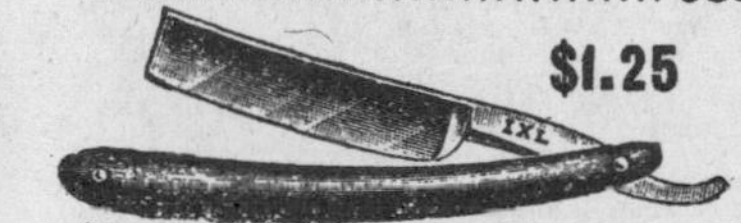

$1.25

No. 6K18261 George Wostenholm & Sons' Celebrated IXL Razor, all hollow ground, black rubber handle. Width of blade, ⅝-inch. Price.......................$1.25

$1.50

No. 6K18265 George Wostenholm & Sons' Celebrated IXL Razor, ⅝-inch blade, hollow ground, round point, imitation ivory handle; an excellent razor for private use. Price.......................$1.50

$2.00

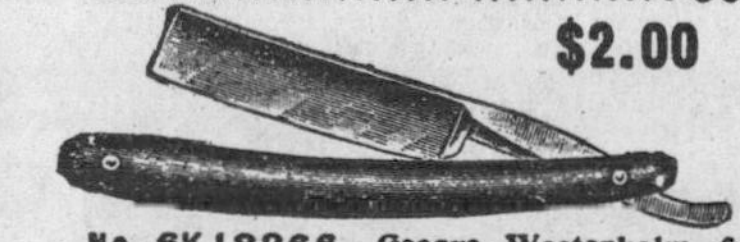

No. 6K18266 George Wostenholm & Sons' Original and True Pipe Razor, ⅝-inch blade, the best razor Wostenholm makes. Black rubber handle, file cut, gimped back tang. A razor that if properly cared for will give the very best satisfaction. Price.......................$2.00

If by mail, postage extra, 5 cents.

Wade & Butcher's Razors.

No. 6K18315 Wade & Butcher's Hollow Point, Medium Hollow Ground Razor, rubber handle.

74c

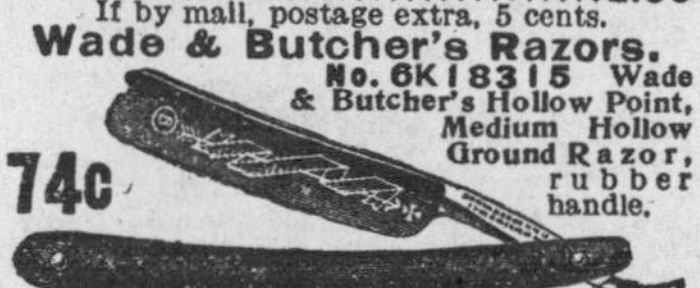

Fully warranted and a superior cutter, ⅝-inch blade. Price.......................74c

No. 6K18321 Wade & Butcher's Special Razor. Full hollow ground. A super-

$1.35

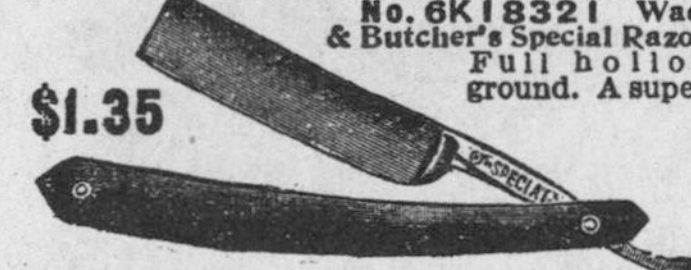

fine barbers' razor. Black rubber handle. Width of blade, ⅝-inch. Price.......$1.35

No. 6K18322 Wade & Butcher's Special Razor. Same as above, except blade is ¾-inch wide. Price.......................$1.40

Swedish Razors.

These razors are genuine Swedish razors imported by us direct from Sweden. They are not to be compared with the many cheap imitations that are offered in competition with these high grade razors.

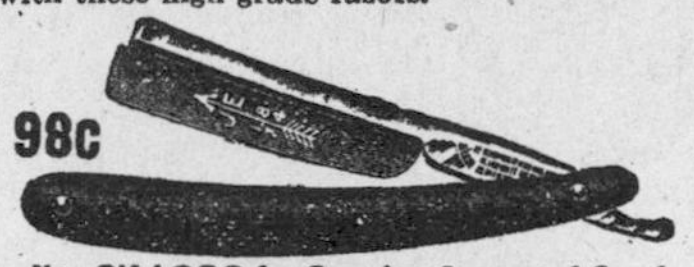

98c

No. 6K18334 Genuine Imported Swedish Razor. The blade of this razor is forged separately from the back. The blade is straight ground, finely tempered steel, firmly set in the round quill back. While this blade is comparatively thin, it is very stiff and will shave any beard. ⅝-inch square point. Fully guaranteed. Price.......................98c

If by mail, postage extra, 6 cents.

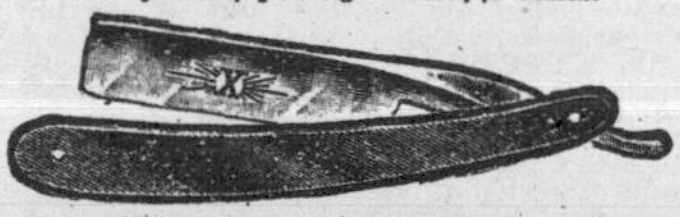

No. 6K18335 Our Special Hand Forged Swedish Razor, manufactured by Klaas Tornblom, Eskilstuna, Sweden. This is one of the finest razors manufactured in this large and famous factory. The blade is straight ground, full round quill back, beautifully polished and etched. This razor is guaranteed to shave any beard. Made of high carbon Swedish steel and ground by the most experienced workmen. With ordinary care this razor will last a lifetime. ⅝-inch square point blade; fitted with flat, polished, black rubber handles. Price, each.......................$1.75

If by mail, postage extra, 6 cents.

Adjustable Razor Guard

No. 6K18339 The "Shavezy" Razor Guard, reversible and adjustable to any razor. Makes a perfect safety razor of your own favorite blade. Full directions accompany each guard. It is finely finished and heavily nickel plated. Price.......................15c

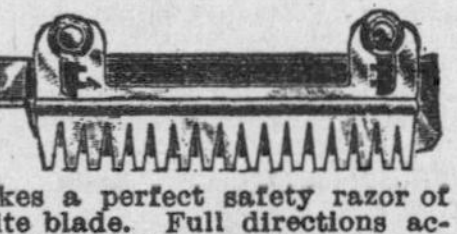

If by mail, postage extra, 2 cents.

Razor Handles.

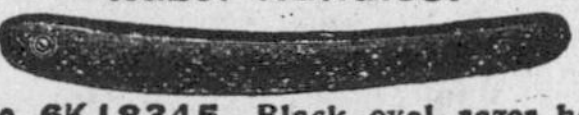

No. 6K18345 Black oval razor handles. Price, complete with rivets......11c

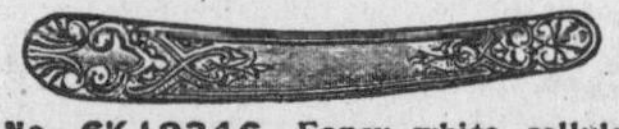

No. 6K18346 Fancy white celluloid razor handles. Price, complete with rivets..........24c

If by mail, postage extra, each, 1 cent.

Combination Shaving Outfit.

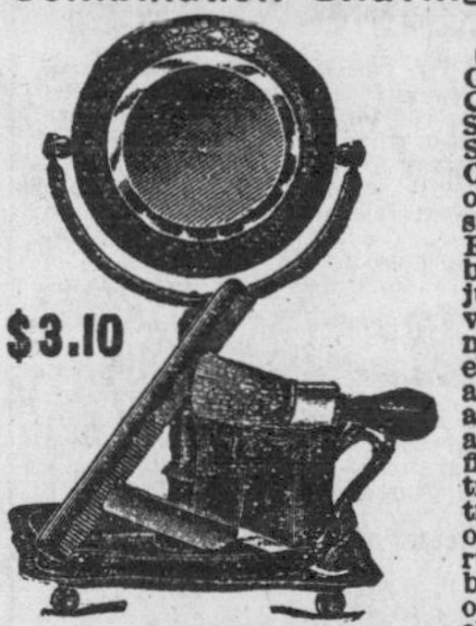

$3.10

No. 6K18397 Our Ebonoid Combination Shaving Stand and Outfit. This outfit consists of a French beveled adjustable, silver mounted mirror, fine ebony frame and stand attached to an ebony finish metal tray. This tray contains one fine hard rubber barber comb, one fancy china finish shaving mug, one first quality shaving brush and one full hollow ground, high grade razor. This is a handsome, well finished set, one that we know will give the purchaser or user satisfaction. Put up in a neat pasteboard box. Price, per set.......................$3.10

If by mail, postage extra, 56 cents.

WE DO NOT EXCHANGE NEW SAFETY RAZOR BLADES FOR OLD ONES.

Ever Ready Safety Razor Outfit.

TWELVE BLADES.

No. 6K18421 Our Improved Ever Ready Safety Razor Outfit with twelve blades at 93 cents. We furnish the safety razor frame with handle and holder for stropping the blades and twelve blades complete in a neat imitation leather case, as illustrated. The blades may be stropped and honed same as any blade, if desired. We sell this outfit on a 30-day trial offer. Shave with the razor for 30 days and, if you are not perfectly satisfied with it and if you do not think it is the best thin blade safety razor you ever saw, return it to us and we will refund the price you paid us and stand the cost of transportation charges both ways. The blades are made from the very best crucible steel, tempered the same as an ordinary razor, not too hard nor too soft, but just right to shave smoothly and hold an edge.

Price, complete outfit as described......93c

If by mail, postage extra, 6 cents.

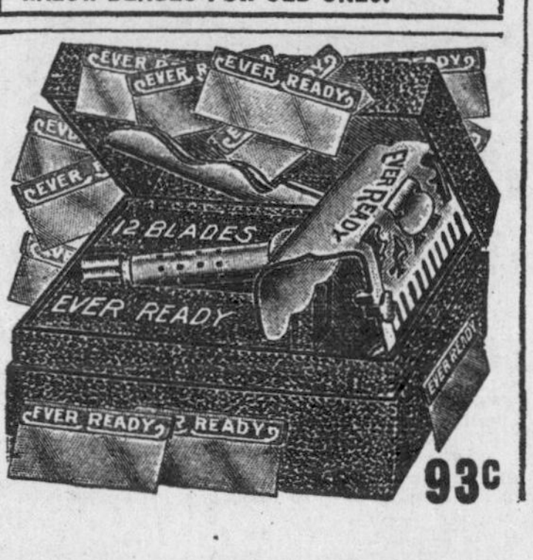

93c

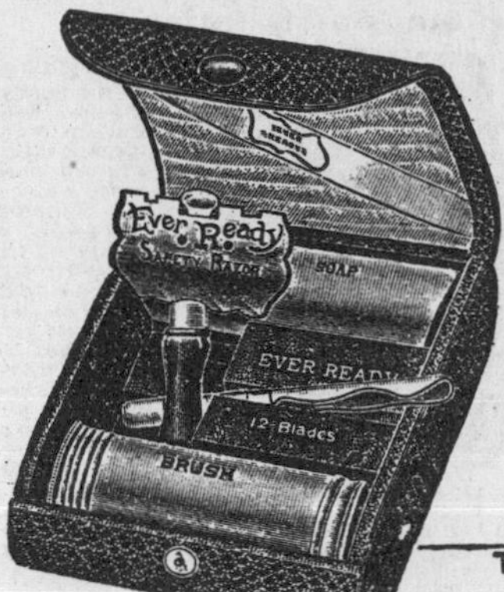

No. 6K18422 Extra blades for the Ever Ready Safety Razor at one-half the price it costs to have blades honed. Those who cannot hone blades themselves will find it cheaper and better to buy new blades when the blades which they buy with the razor become dull. We furnish blades for the Ever Ready Safety Razor put up in a neat case containing one dozen blades. Price, per dozen...(Postage extra, 2c)...58c

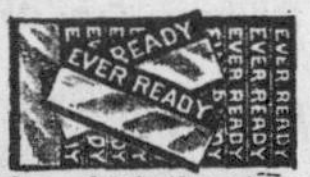

Ever Ready Travelers' Outfit.

REDUCED TO $3.35.

TWELVE BLADES.

No. 6K18424 The Ever Ready Travelers' Outfit. One ebony handle safety razor with twelve blades, one nickel plated soap holder, containing a stick of the best shaving soap, one nickel plated best quality folding travelers' shaving brush, put up in a silk lined, best quality black grain leather case, 5 inches long by 3 inches wide. This is strictly a high grade set, guaranteed to give satisfaction. Price, per set.......................$3.35

If by mail, postage extra, 15 cents

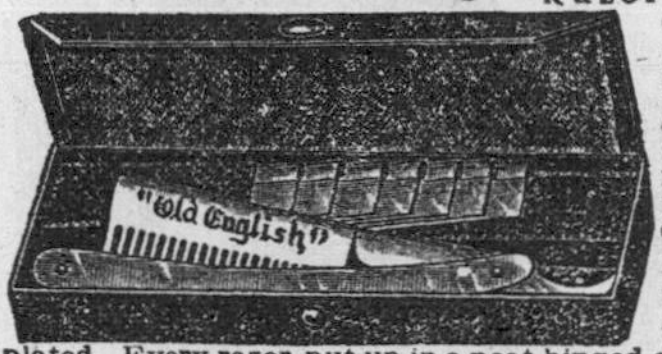

The Old English Safety Razor.

REDUCED TO $1.32.

No. 6K18336 The Old English Safety Razor, with seven blades. A blade for every day in the week. This razor can be used with or without the safety guard as desired. The blades are instantly slipped into the holder and when in position are firmly locked, same as the blade on a regular razor. These blades can be honed and stropped same as the regular old fashioned razor; in fact, this razor has all the advantages of the old safety razor with the additional advantage of having a safety guard and the blades being interchangeable. The blades are made of the best English steel; the blade itself is 2¾ inches long, ⅝ inch wide, square point; frame and handle of the razor are made of brass, heavily nickel plated. Every razor put up in a neat hinged cover box with 7 blades. Price, complete.$1.32

If by mail, postage extra, 6 cents.

SHAVING OUTFITS.

No. 6K18372 Our Acme Shaving Set consists of a high grade hollow ground razor, a good double swing horsehide and prepared web razor strop, a good shaving brush, a seamless hand engraved aluminum shaving mug, and a cake of Williams' Yankee shaving soap. Remember, the razor is fully warranted. Put up in neat paper box.

Price, complete set.......................$1.70

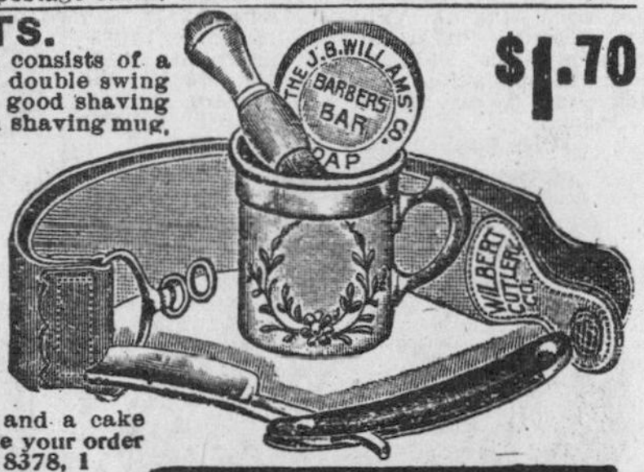

$1.70

We cannot furnish made to order razors with shaving outfits.

No. 6K18378 Our Bon Ton Shaving Set consists of your choice of any razor quoted by us, at $2.00 or less, except the made to order razor, which we do not furnish with outfits, a good leather and prepared web double swing strop, a fancy celluloid handle shaving brush, a seamless hand engraved aluminum shaving mug and a cake of Williams' Yankee shaving soap. Make your order for the above shaving set thus: "No. 6K18378, 1 shaving set with No..........razor," filling in the blank with the catalogue number of the razor you select. Put up in neat black pasteboard box.

Price for complete set.......................$2.69

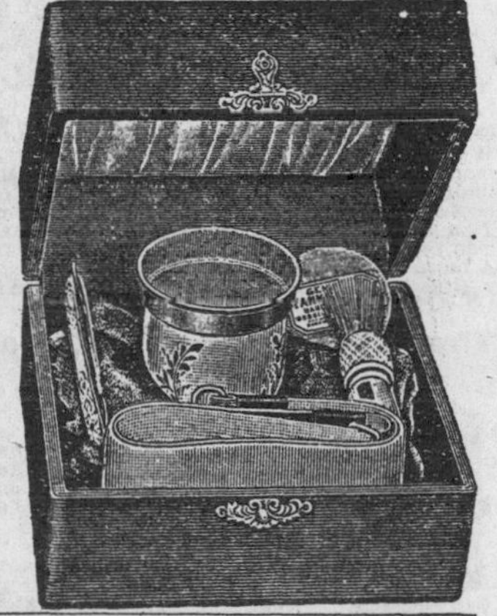

No. 6K18387 Our Autocrat Shaving Set in Case, is made up of No. 6K17938 razor, a seamless aluminum cup, No. 6K18572 shaving brush, a fine double swing strop, and a cake of the genuine Williams' Yankee soap, all packed in an imitation leather covered case, nicely lined.

Price for complete set.......................$3.25

No. 6K18395 Our Figaro Shaving Set consists of one Figaro genuine Solingen razor, a double swing strop, an engraved pure aluminum shaving mug, a Nox-All mounted razor hone, a shavers' pride lather brush and a cake of Williams' Yankee shaving soap. All in neat imitation leather case. The best assortment ever offered in a shaving set. Dimensions of case, 9 x 9 x 5 inches.

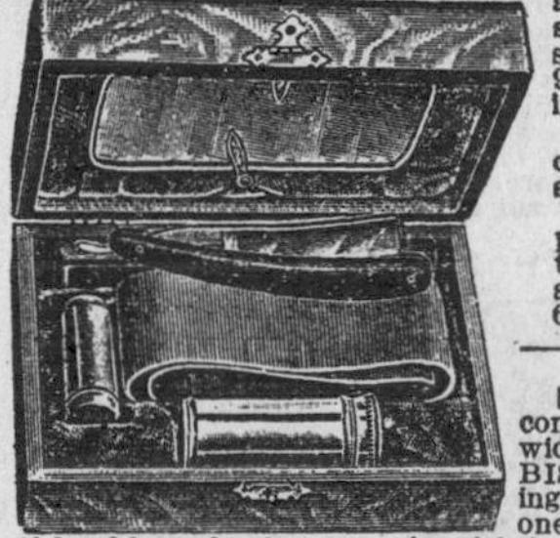

Price for complete set..$4.20

If by mail, postage extra, any of above sets, 60 cents.

Oak Case Travelers' Set, $3.27.

No. 6K18396 Travelers' Shaving Set, put up in a compact, finely finished oak case, 7¼ inches long, 5¼ inches wide and 2½ inches high. The case contains one famous BISMARCK Razor, one genuine badger hair folding shaving brush with brass ferrule and handle finely nickel plated, one highest quality single swing shell horsehide strop, one stick of best shaving soap in nickel plated screw top box, and one 5¼-inch shaving mirror with imitation tortoise shell back, which can be either hung or stood up. This is a high grade shaving set; every article in this set is of highest quality. We guarantee this set to give satisfaction or money refunded. Price, per set....(Postage extra, 40 cents.).....$3.27

The New Wilbert Safety Razor.

IMPROVED MODEL.

No. 6K18437 The New 1908 Model Wilbert Safety Razor is not a freak idea, but it is a substantial, well made razor with a blade that is absolutely guaranteed to shave any beard and which with ordinary care will last a lifetime. We do not limit this blade to five, six or a dozen velvet shaves, but guarantee it, if properly cared for, to last a lifetime. The blade of this razor is the same thickness as a blade of a regular razor, it is hand forged, ground on a small stone, tempered and finished in the same manner as the highest priced razor on the market. This blade can be stropped and honed the same as the regular blade. The solid, one-piece frame of the Wilbert Razor is strong and rigid. Two-jointed nickel plated handle with additional joint to hold blade for stropping. Each razor is put up in a neat metal case with complete instructions. We guarantee every Wilbert Razor to be perfect in material, finish and workmanship, and to give the user a clean, comfortable shave, or the razor can be returned to us and your money and transportation charges will be cheerfully refunded. It is impossible to cut yourself with the Wilbert Razor. Price.......................94c

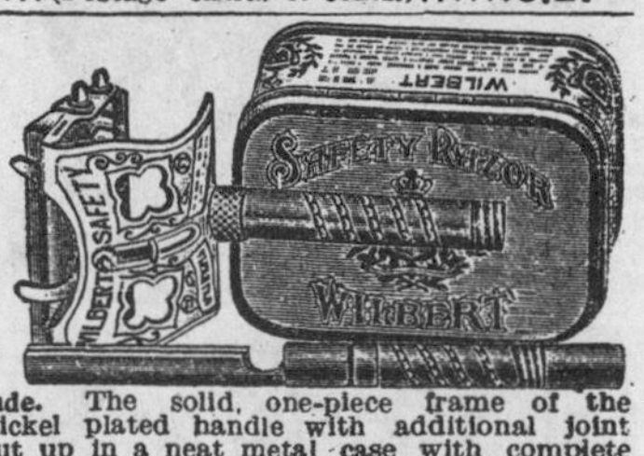

If by mail, postage extra, 6 cents.

No. 6K18438 Extra blades for the Wilbert Razor. Price, each..........50c

If by mail, postage extra, each, 3 cents.

The Wilbert Stropping Machine Reduced to 80c.

No. 6K18439 No better stropping machine made. Will strop blades for the Wilbert, Winner, Yankee and Star; in fact, will strop any razor blades from 1-16 to 3-16 inch thick. The handle can be unscrewed, making this machine very compact. Length, 6 inches. Length, when folded, 3½ inches. Fine nickel plated with solid ebony handle. Guaranteed to give satisfaction.

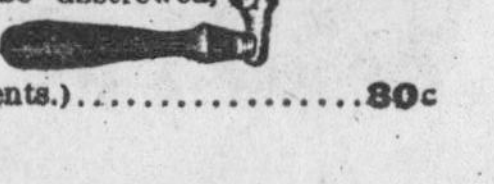

Price.......................(If by mail, postage extra, 7 cents.).......80c

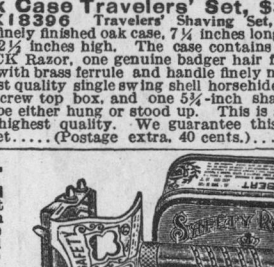

Safety Razor Double Swing Strop, 40 Cents.

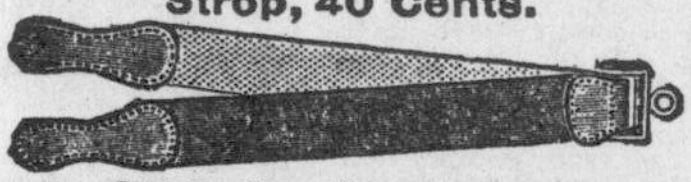

No. 6K18440 This strop is made specially for safety razors, such as the Star, Wilbert, Ever Ready, and any of the forged blade safety razors. It has just the right width and length to properly strop a safety razor blade. Double swing. One side finest quality Irish linen, specially prepared to put a keen edge on a razor; the other side of selected shell horsehide for finishing. Fitted with sewed leather handle, sewed leather end and nickel-plated swivel. Length of stropping surface, 12 inches; length over all, 18 inches.
Price 40c
If by mail, postage extra, 5 cents.

Wilbert Safety Razor Set.

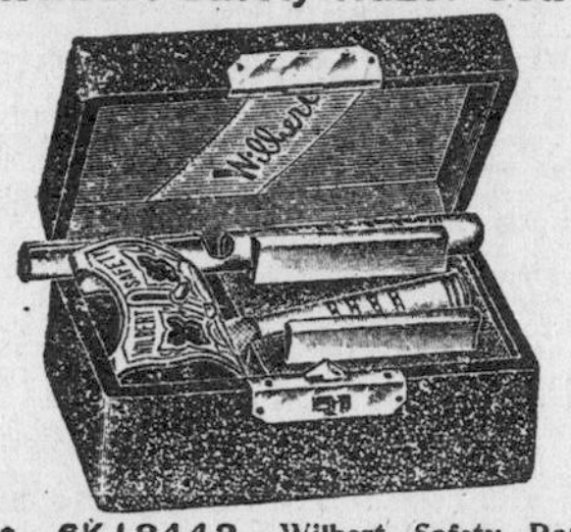

No. 6K18442 Wilbert Safety Razor Set, consisting of Wilbert Safety Razor and two blades. Put up in fine hinge cover imitation morocco leather case, lined with satin and chamois skin. An excellent set for the traveler. It also makes a handsome present.
Price $2.00
If by mail, postage extra, 6 cents.

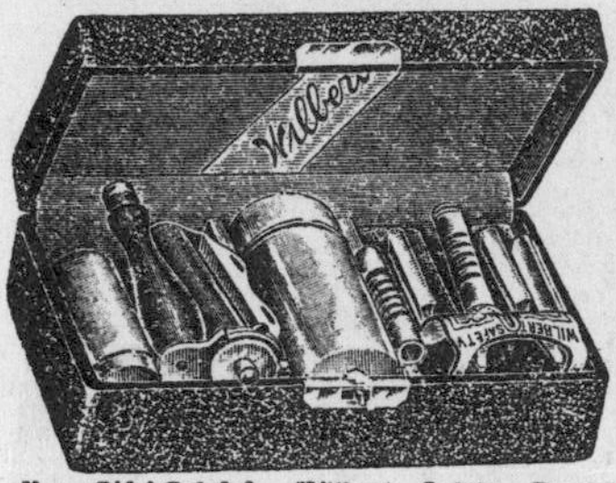

No. 6K18444 Wilbert Safety Razor Combination Set, consisting of high grade Wilbert Safety Razor, two blades, stropping machine, one best quality genuine badger hair folding handle shaving brush, one stick of best shaving soap in fine nickel plated tube. This set is put up in a fine satin lined imitation morocco case, hinge cover, patent clasp. A handsome and serviceable set.
Price $3.65
If by mail, postage extra, 14 cents.

The Genuine Star Safety Razor

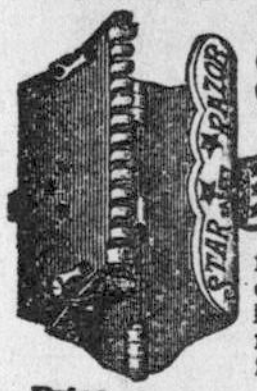

$1.50

No. 6K18449 Star Safety Razor, with the latest improved frame. Blades of best steel and full concave which can be easily removed and placed in handle for stropping. Full nickel plated, packed in latest improved box.
Price $1.50
If by mail, postage extra, 5 cents.
No. 6K18451 Extra Blades for Star Safety Razor. Price, each, postpaid.... 85c

Our $2.00 Star Safety Razor Set.

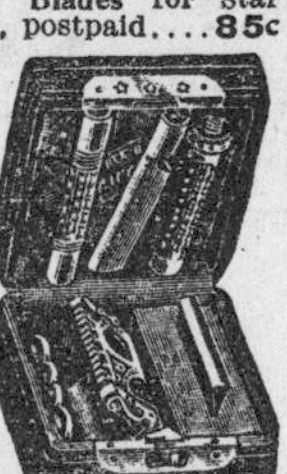

No. 6K18465 Star Safety Razor Set. Put up in elegant satin lined morocco case and contains one safety frame and one blade.
Price, postpaid, $2.00

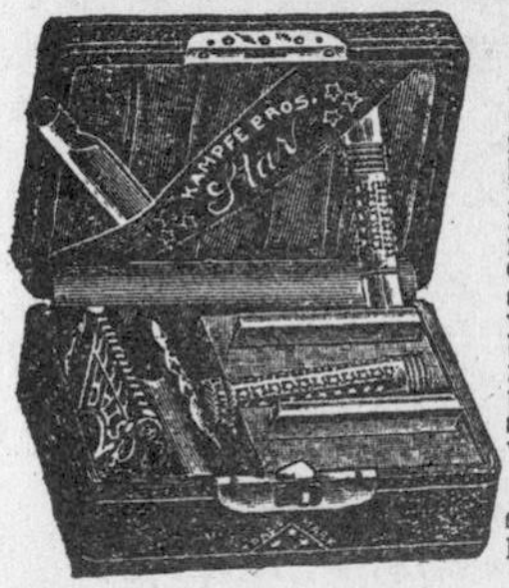

No. 6K18467 Star Safety Razor Set. Elegantly finished in morocco. Contains one safety frame with two blades, and is a gem in the full sense of the word.
Price, per set, postpaid, $3.10

Star Safety Razor Set.

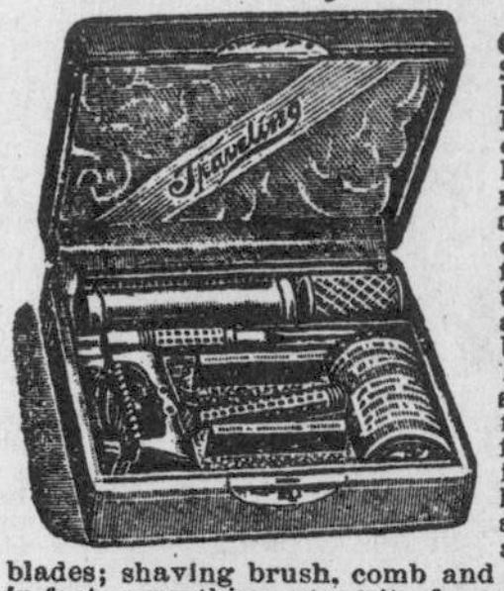

No. 6K18469 Star Safety Razor Set. Put up in an elegant satin lined morocco case, and contains one safety frame with two perfectly adjusted blades of fine silver steel; box of finely perfumed shaving soap; holder for stropping and honing blades; shaving brush, comb and cosmetique; in fact, everything requisite for an easy, quick and luxurious shave.
Price, per set, postage paid $5.00

Star Safety Razor Pocket Set.

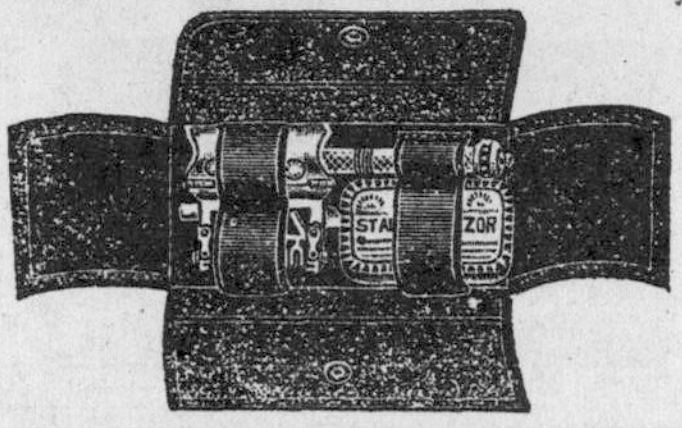

No. 6K18472 Star Safety Razor Pocket Set. A neat and compact flexible leather case, lined with black velvet, containing Star Safety Razor complete, frame and handle; handle can be used with the frame or for stropping the blade. Price, per set, postage paid... $2.00

Gillette Safety Razor Set.

$5.00

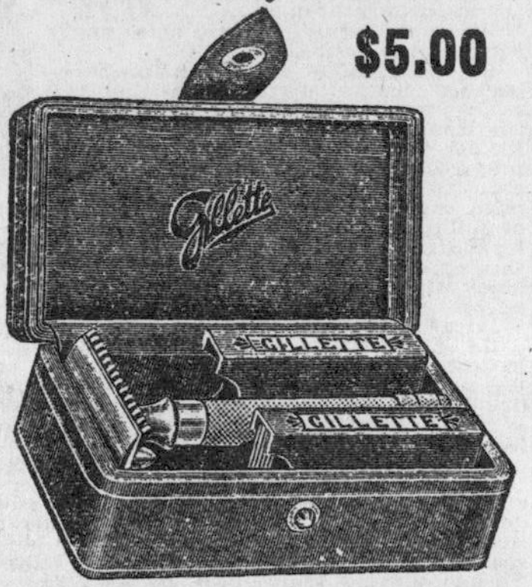

No. 6K18475 The well known Gillette Safety Razor, three-piece silver plated frame with 12 double edge steel blades, all packed in a leather box with snap button fastener. This is the genuine Gillette Razor. Full instructions accompany each razor.
Price, postpaid $5.00
No. 6K18476 Blades for the Gillette Safety Razor, 10 for 50c
We do not exchange old blades.

China Shaving Mugs.

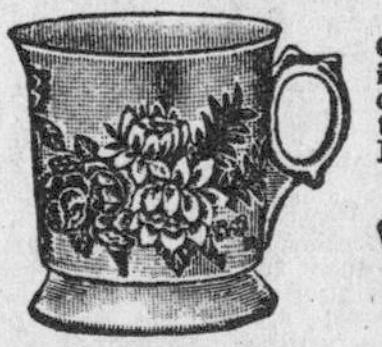

No. 6K18490 Carlsbad China Shaving Mug. Floral decorations. Gold trimmed. Price, 12c
If by mail, postage extra, 15 cents.

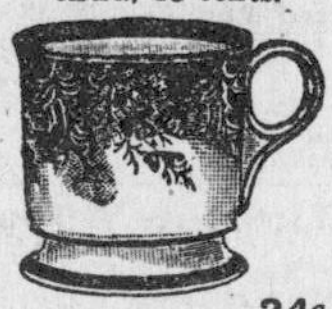

No. 6K18492 Genuine Austrian China Shaving Mug. Beautiful floral decorations. Heavily gold decorated.
Price 24c
If by mail, postage extra, 16 cents.

Aluminum Shaving Mugs.

Engraving initials on aluminum shaving mugs, extra per letter 5 cents.

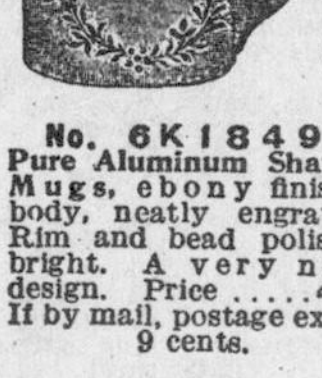

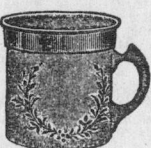

No. 6K18496 Pure Aluminum Shaving Mugs. Size, 3¼ x 3¼ inches. Cast aluminum handles strongly riveted to cup. Satin finish body neatly engraved. Bead and band polished bright. Very strong and serviceable. Price 40c
If by mail, postage extra, 8 cents.

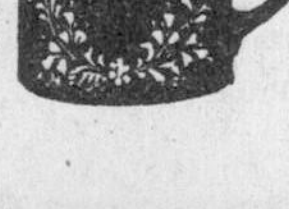

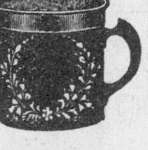

No. 6K18498 Pure Aluminum Shaving Mugs, ebony finished body, neatly engraved. Rim and bead polished bright. A very neat design. Price 44c
If by mail, postage extra, 9 cents.

Aluminum Shaving Soap Box.

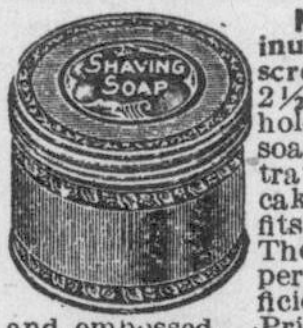

No. 6K18500 Aluminum Shaving Soap Box, with screw top cover, 2 inches high, 2½ inches in diameter, will hold several cakes of shaving soap or can be used as a traveling shaving mug. A cake of Williams' Soap just fits in the bottom of this box. The box is sufficiently deep to permit the working up of sufficient lather. Finely finished and embossed. Price 12c
If by mail, postage extra, 3 cents.

Shaving Brushes.

Aluminum Ferrule Shaving Brushes, Nos. 6K18544 and 6K18548, are put together with waterproof cement under heavy pressure and will wear to the ferrule without shedding bristles. They have no twine to foul, no metal that will corrode, no horn to crack. Made from sterilized, odorless, fine French bristles, with non-corrosive aluminum ferrule, ebonoid handle. They are the best line of shaving brushes we have seen.

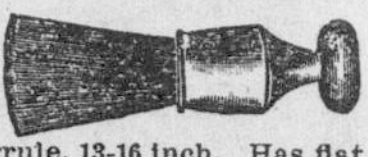

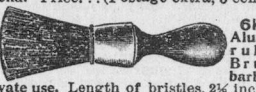

No. 6K18544 Aluminum Ferrule Shaving Brush for private use. Length of bristles, 1⅞ inches. Inside diameter of ferrule, 13-16 inch. Has flat end handle permitting brush to be stood on end. Price...(Postage extra, 3 cents.)... 14c

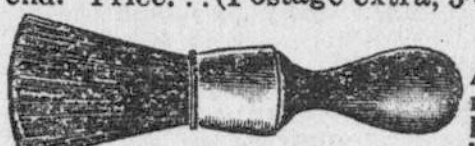

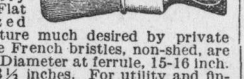

No. 6K18548 Aluminum Ferrule Shaving Brush, for barbers' or private use. Length of bristles, 2⅛ inches. Inside diameter of ferrule, 15-16 inch. Price... 24c
If by mail, postage extra, 5 cents.

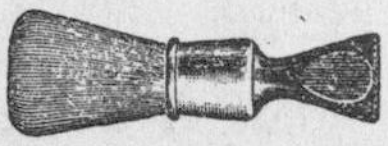

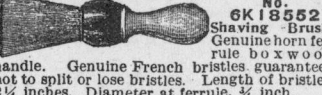

No. 6K18551 Our Kant Kum Out Brush. Solid brass ferrule, heavily nickel plated. Flat end ebonized handle. A feature much desired by private users. Genuine French bristles, non-shed, are 2 inches long. Diameter at ferrule, 15-16 inch. Entire length, 3½ inches. For utility and finish this brush cannot be excelled. Price... 21c
If by mail, postage extra, 5 cents.

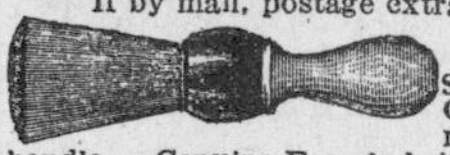

No. 6K18552 Shaving Brush. Genuine horn ferrule boxwood handle. Genuine French bristles guaranteed not to split or lose bristles. Length of bristles, 2¼ inches. Diameter at ferrule, ¾ inch.
Price....(Postage extra, 5 cents.) 20c

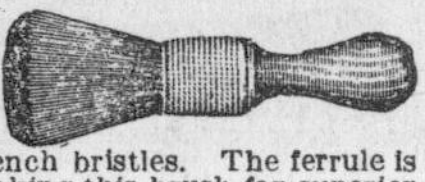

No. 6K18554 Our Wire Ferrule Shaving Brush, with brown enameled handle, selected white French bristles. The ferrule is enameled wire, making this brush far superior to the wood ferrule brushes, which swell and crack. A good, serviceable brush. Length of bristles, 1⅞ inches. Diameter of brush at ferrule, ¾ inch. Price 9c
If by mail, postage extra, 3 cents.

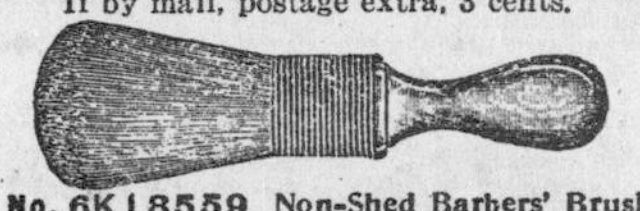

No. 6K18559 Non-Shed Barbers' Brush, twine bound, walnut handle. Fine boiled French bristles, reinforced with patent metal plate under twine, which prevents corrosion or fouling. Will wear to ferrule and not lose a bristle. A favorite with barbers. Length of bristles, 2½ inches. Diameter of ferrule, 1 inch.
Price 34c
If by mail, postage extra, 4 cents.

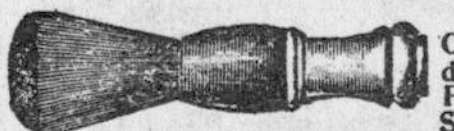

No. 6K18572 Our Fancy Handle Lily White French Bristle Shaving Brush, with fine white bone handle, ferrule of pure, natural black horn. This is a very neat, handsome brush, guaranteed not to spread, swell or crack, and will give satisfaction. Length of bristles, 2⅛ inches. Length of entire brush, 5 inches. Diameter of ferrule, ⅞ inch.
Price 25c
If by mail, postage extra, 3 cents.

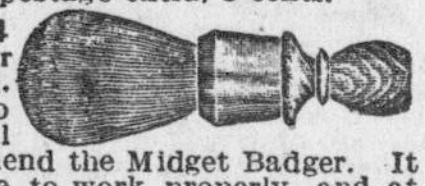

No. 6K18574 Midget Badger Shaving Brush. For the man who prefers a small brush, we recommend the Midget Badger. It is sufficiently large to work properly, and at the same time has not that bulk that most people object to. This is a very neat brush, made of pure badger bristle, fine horn ferrule, cocobolo handle; length over all, 3½ inches; diameter of ferrule, ⅞ inch. Price...... 47c
If by mail, postage extra, 3 cents.

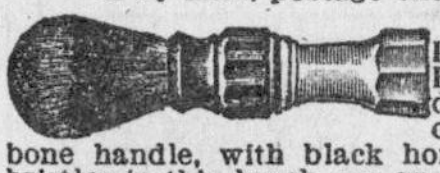

No. 6K18578 Pure Badger Hair Brush. Our latest design. Double octagon white bone handle, with black horn ferrule. The bristles in this brush are guaranteed genuine badger hair and are 2 inches long. Diameter of ferrule, ¾ inch. This brush is guaranteed to give satisfaction. Price.... 75c
If by mail, postage extra, 5 cents.

Williams' Shaving Soap.

The Genuine World Renowned Standard Shaving Soap.

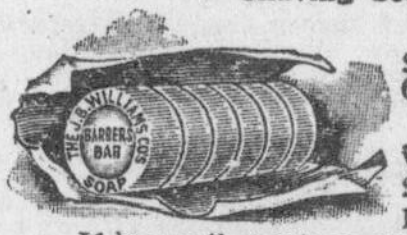

Williams' Shaving Soap, finest made, 6 cakes to pound.
No. 6K18595 Williams' Shaving Soap. Price, per pound 35c
If by mail, postage extra, 20 cents.
No. 6K18596 Williams' Shaving Soap, per 10-pound box $3.25

Williams' Shaving Sticks

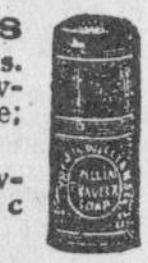

Genuine Williams' Shaving Sticks. In leatherette box; handy when traveling; also for home use. No waste; always clean and ready for use.
No. 6K18597 Williams' Shaving Sticks. Price, per box 21c
If by mail, postage extra, 5 cents.

RAZOR STROPS.

The best razor is no good without a first class strop.

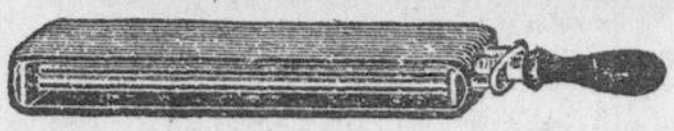

No. 6K18653 Belt Two-Side Extension Razor Strop. A fair grade strop. Full length, 13 inches. Price 23c
If by mail, postage extra, 10 cents.

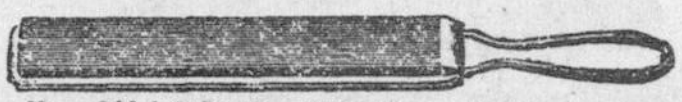

No. 6K18655 The Twentieth Century Cushion Razor Strop, one of the finest cushion strops made. Guaranteed to be equal to any of the cushion strops of similar design sold for twice our price. It has a stropping surface of 8½ inches, length over all 13 inches. One side fine heavy red leather for honing, the other side white buff for finishing. Heavy wire handle, wire bound, giving this strop protection and strength, a feature not found in ordinary cushion strops. Weight, 7¼ ounces. Price 49c
If by mail, postage extra, 10 cents.

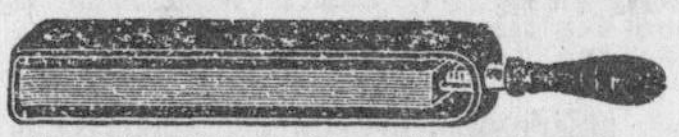

No. 6K18656 Combination Four-Side Extension Razor Strop with cushion buff. A fine strop. Full length, 13 inches. Price, 35c
If by mail, postage extra, 12 cents.

No. 6K18657 Cushion Strop, Four-Side. This is a very superior strop of this old favorite style, solid enameled wood handle. Full length, 14 inches. Price 52c
If by mail, postage extra, 14 cents.

Freeman's Celebrated Metallic Strop, 64 Cents.

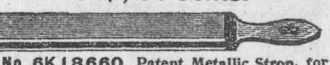

No. 6K18660 Patent Metallic Strop, for razors and surgical instruments, will quickly put a razor in condition to split a hair and shave easy, sharp as the best hone without its harshness. You cannot spoil your razor with this strop. Full length, 13 inches.
Price 64c
If by mail, postage extra, 7 cents.

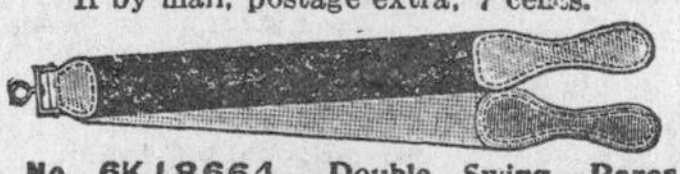

No. 6K18664 Double Swing Razor Strop, black leather on one side, tubular cotton hose on the other; has swivel and stitched fashioned handle. Width, 2 inches; entire length, 22½ inches. Price 25c
If by mail, postage extra, 6 cents.

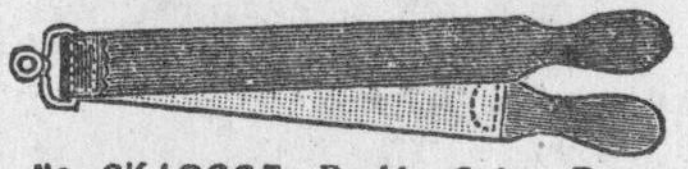

No. 6K18665 Double Swing Razor Strop. Porpoise hide oil finished leather on one side and prepared tubular cotton hose on the other; has a swivel and fashioned handle. Width, 2 inches; entire length, 23 inches.
Price 34c
If by mail, postage extra, 6 cents.

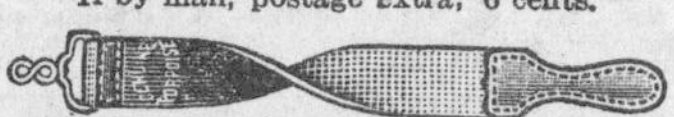

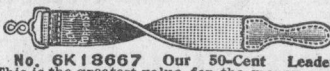

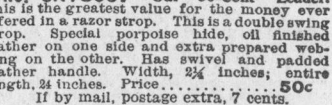

No. 6K18667 Our 50-Cent Leader. This is the greatest value for the money ever offered in a razor strop. This is a double swing strop. Special porpoise hide, oil finished leather on one side and extra prepared webbing on the other. Has swivel and padded leather handle. Width, 2¼ inches; entire length, 24 inches. Price 50c
If by mail, postage extra, 7 cents.

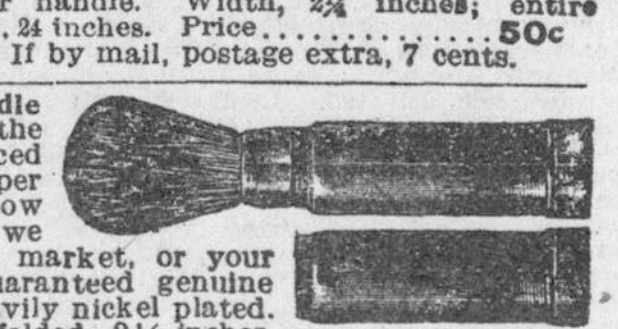

No. 6K18582 Genuine Badger Hair Folding Handle Travelers' or Tourists' Shaving Brush. As shown in the illustration, this brush can be folded and the bristles placed in the hollow nickel plated handle. There are cheaper shaving brushes of this kind on the market, but we know the traveler has great need for a perfect brush, and we offer this brush as being the best folding brush on the market, or your money refunded. The bristles of this brush are guaranteed genuine badger hair, the handle and ferrule made of brass, heavily nickel plated. Length of brush complete, 4½ inches; length when folded, 2½ inches.
Price .... (If by mail, postage extra, 3 cents.) 34c
When you are through using your shaving brush always stand same with the handle down and bristles up. Do not leave your brush stand resting on the bristles, as this spoils the shape of the brush and also ruins the bristles.

The New Black Beauty Self Honing Strop, $1.17

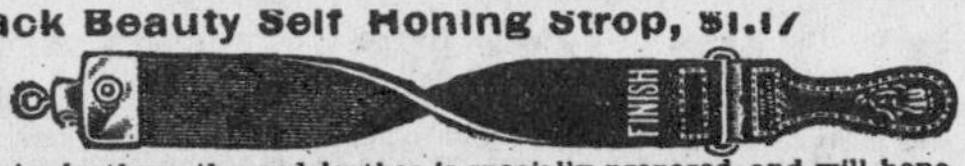

No. 6K18693 Our Black Beauty Combination Double Swing Razor Strop. 25 inches long; 2¼ inches wide. This strop is made of extra heavy red and black fine grain leather; the red leather is specially prepared and will hone and sharpen the dullest razor. The black leather is the very best selected, oiled, fine grain stock for finishing. The leather in this strop is extra heavy imported stock and will last a lifetime. We guarantee this strop to be equal to any strop made. This strop is finished with finest leather trimmings, full padded sewed leather handle and flat nickel plated polished swivel.
Price.... ... .(If by mail, postage extra, 14 cents.)....................$1.17

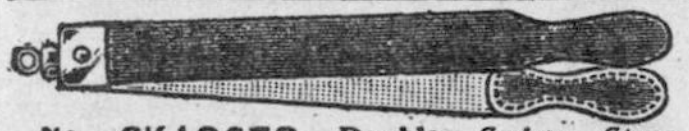

No. 6K18672 Double Swing Strop. Porpoise hide, oil finished leather on one side and pure Irish linen hose, prepared and polished, on the other. Nickel plated removable swivel, fashioned handle. A fine strop for professional barbers. Width, 2¼ inches; entire length, 25 inches. Price 75c
If by mail, postage extra, 9 cents.

DoubleSwing Horsehide, $1.00

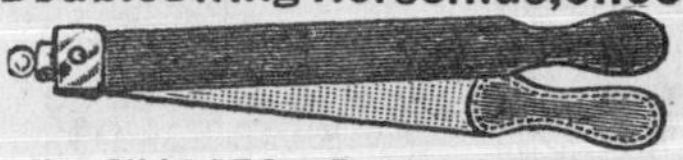

No. 6K18676 Double Swing Strop, very extra quality, satin finished genuine horsehide leather on one side and pure Irish linen hose, prepared and polished, on the other. Removable nickel plated swivel, fashioned handle. A superior strop, good and durable, for any use. Width, 2¼ inches; entire length, 25 inches. Price (If by mail, postage extra, 8c) $1.00

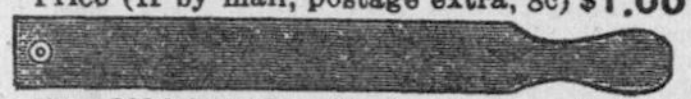

No. 6K18680 Single Swing Barbers' Strop, porpoise hide, oil finished prepared leather. The strop that barbers buy. Fashioned handle and eyelet. Width, 2¼ inches; entire length, 24 inches. Price 26c
If by mail, postage extra, 4 cents.

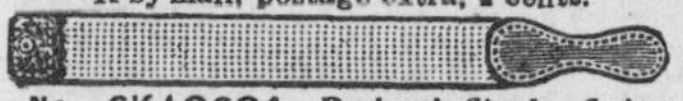

No. 6K18684 Barbers' Single Swing, Irish Linen Web Strop. Pure Irish linen, prepared and polished especially for professional barbers' use. Fashioned leather handle and eyelet. Width, 2¼ inches; entire length, 24 inches. Price..(If by mail, postage extra, 5c.).. 35c

Patent Single Swing Steel Back Horsehide Strop.

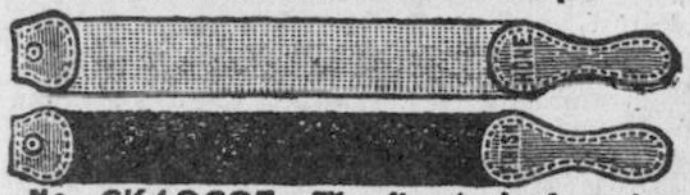

No. 6K18685 The finest single swing horsehide strop made. This strop will keep a razor in perfect condition, and practically dispenses with honing. The reverse side, as shown in the above illustration, is covered with numerous perforations, which extend half way through the strop. These holes or perforations are filled with most minute particles of prepared steel. It requires but a few strokes over the steel side of the strop to put a perfect cutting edge on the razor, then by reversing the strop and using the finishing side, the razor is put in perfect condition. Fitted with heavy sewed leather end and handle. We guarantee it to give satisfaction.
Price..(If by mail, postage extra, 4c.)..90c

Shell Horsehide, 72 Cents.

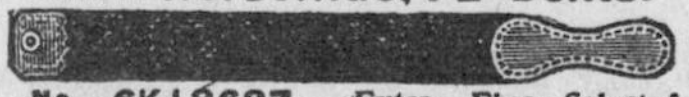

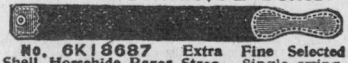

No. 6K18687 Extra Fine Selected Shell Horsehide Razor Strop. Single swing. Width, 2¼ inches; entire length, 24 inches. Used by first class barbers. Price.......72c
If by mail, postage extra, 4 cents.

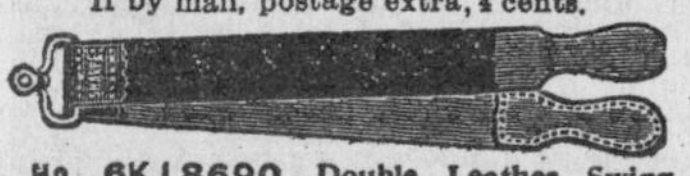

No. 6K18690 Double Leather Swing Razor Strop. Width, 2 inches. Length of stropping surface, 12½ inches; length over all, 19½ inches. Both strops are leather—one for sharpening, the other for finishing. Nickel plated swivel; sewed on handle. Price..........47c
If by mail, postage extra, 7 cents.

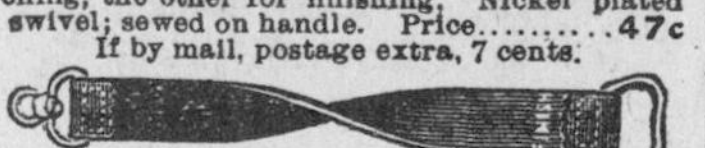

No. 6K18691 Double Leather Swing Razor Strop. Army and Navy style. Width, 2 inches. Length of stropping surface, 14 inches; length over all, 20 inches. Both strops are leather, one for sharpening, the other for finishing. Heavy nickel plated swivel. Heavy nickel plated loop for handle. Price....................67c
If by mail, postage extra, 8 cents.

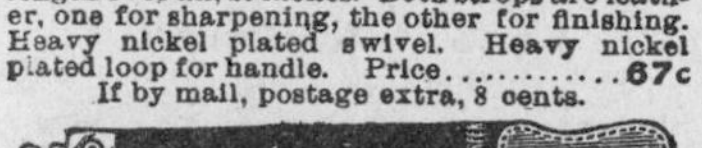

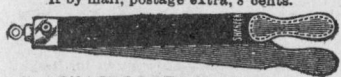

No. 6K18692 Double Leather Swing Razor Strop. Width, 2 inches. Length of stropping surface, 17½ inches; length over all, 23 inches. Both strops are leather—one for sharpening, the other for finishing. Nickel plated bolt swivel; sewed on handle on one strop; fashioned handle on the other.
Price..(If by mail, postage extra, 10c.)..85c

The Perfect Stropping Machine and Strop.

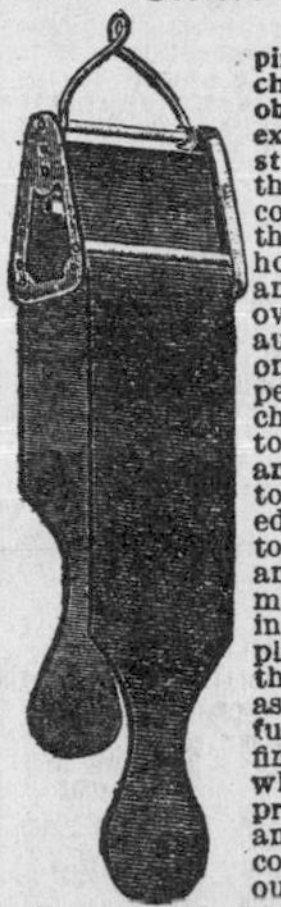

No. 6K18694 A Stropping Machine with which a child can strop a razor and obtain better results than an expert on any other kind of strop. This machine shown in the illustration is furnished complete with strop. Place the razor in the holder, grasp hold of each end of the strop and as the strop is pulled over the rollers, the razor is automatically moved from one side to the other and is perfectly stropped. This machine is absolutely guaranteed to perfectly strop any razor and is further guaranteed not to cut the strop or turn the edge of the razor. No springs to get out of order and guaranteed to last a lifetime. The machine is made of brass, 3½ inches square, highly nickel plated, fitted with handle so that it can be hung up same as a regular strop. Machine furnished complete with a fine specially tanned calf strop which alone is worth the price we ask for the machine and strop combined. Weight, complete with strop, 10 ounces.
Price....(Postage extra, 12 cents)....94c

Kelso's Strop Dressing.

REDUCED TO 10 CENTS.

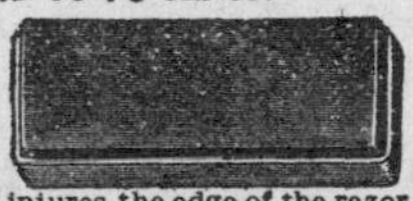

No. 6K18697 The greatest preparation of its kind in the world. All other strop dressings possess a grit that injures the edge of the razor and contain more or less animal and vegetable matter which decays and is subject to climatic changes. Kelso's Strop Dressing is entirely a mineral dressing. Various ingredients are formed together in a compound which possesses just the right amount of hardness and grit to put an edge on the razor. Put up in cakes 2 inches long, ¾-inch wide, and can be applied to the strop without removing from the box. One cake of this dressing will last a year or more and, if used according to directions, will keep your razor in perfect condition and make it unnecessary to hone or grind.
Price, per cake..(Postage extra, 1c)...10c

Razor Hones.

RAZOR HONES ARE LIABLE TO BE BROKEN IF SENT BY MAIL.

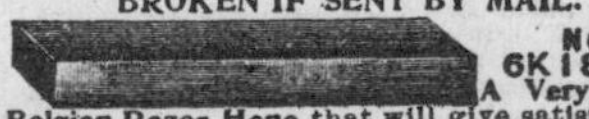

No. 6K18700 A Very Good Belgian Razor Hone that will give satisfaction in private use. We sell them for the same amount of money you must pay to have your razor honed once. Price (Postage extra, 10c).24c

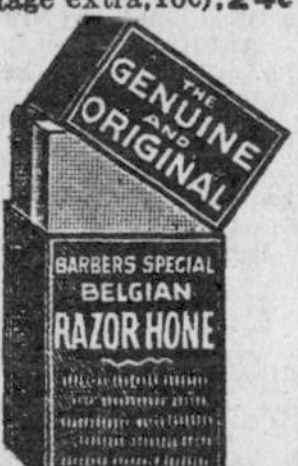

No. 6K18702 A Superfine Belgian Razor Hone. Special selection for our trade. Each hone packed in neat cardboard case; every one perfect; suitable for private or barbers' use. Price..50c
Postage extra, 14 cents.

No. 6K18706 Barbers' Special Belgian Hone. Selected especially for the best barbers' trade. In quality it is the very best and in shape the most convenient for barbers' use. Each hone packed in strong paper box. Size, 5x2½ inches. Price....................$1.65
If by mail, postage extra, 20 cents.

No. 6K18707 Barbers' Special Belgian Hone. Same as above, only smaller. Size, 4x2 inches. Price (Postage extra, 14c). $1.00

Genuine Swaty Hones.

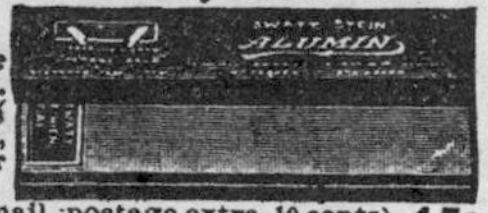

No. 6K18710 The Genuine Swaty Hones. Length, 5¼ inches; width, 2 inches. For private use.
Price..(If by mail, postage extra, 10 cents).45c

No. 6K18712 The Genuine Swaty Hones. For barbers' use. Length, 8 inches; width, 2 inches. Price 72c
If by mail, postage extra, 14 cents.

Emery Razor Hones.

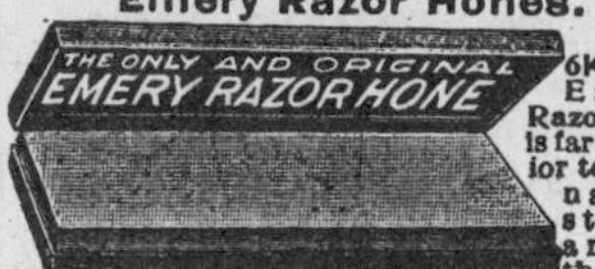

No. 6K18715 Emery Razor Hone is far superior to most natural stones and at the same time much lower in price. Size, 5½x2x1½ inches. Price..(Postage extra, 12c)....39c

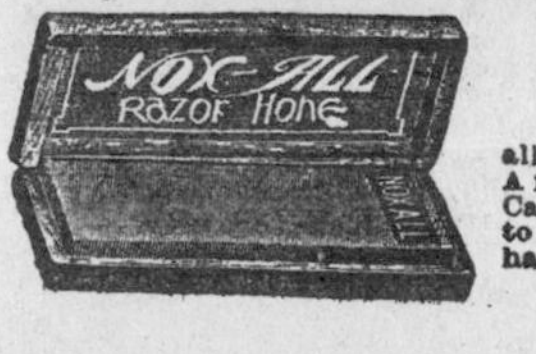

Our Nox-All Mounted Razor Hone.

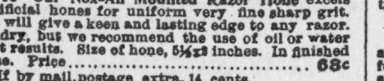

No. 6K18716 Our Nox-All Mounted Razor Hone excels all other artificial hones for uniform very fine sharp grit. A few strokes will give a keen and lasting edge to any razor. Can be used dry, but we recommend the use of oil or water to get the best results. Size of hone, 5¼x3 inches. In finished hardwood case. Price....................68c
If by mail, postage extra, 14 cents.

The Famous Raven Hone, 75 Cents.

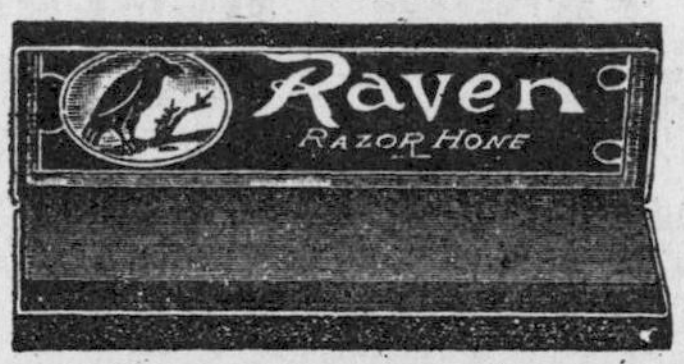

No. 6K18720 The Raven Hone is manufactured for and sold exclusively by us. The marvelous success of the Raven hone has brought many imitations on the market, but there is only one Raven, both in name and in quality. In spite of the fact that there are hundreds of different hones on the market sold under various names, the Raven hone in the short space of two years has attained a success not equaled by hones which have been on the market for years. It is manufactured according to a secret process by one of the most famous hone manufacturers. Our enormous business enables us to contract for this hone in such large quantities as to be able to sell it at the ridiculously low price of 75 cents, although hones of far inferior grade are sold for twice our price. The Raven hone, as the name would indicate, is a jet black hone, contains no veins or emery grit, and has just the right degree of hardness to place an edge on a razor which will insure a velvet shave. Each hone is packed in a neat hinged cover box. Size of hone, 5½x2 inches. Price....................75c
If by mail, postage extra, 10 cents.

German Water Hones, 24c.

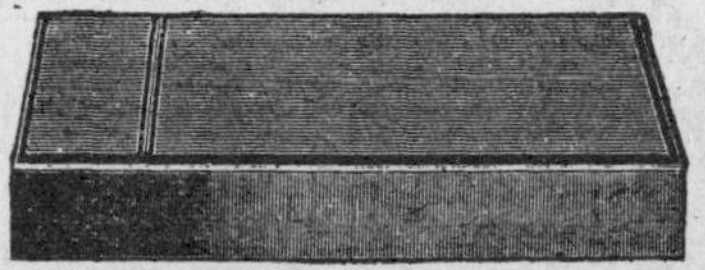

No. 6K18728 Dark Blue German Water Hones, with "rubbers." Length, 7 inches. Price.....(Postage extra, 20 cents).......24c

No. 6K18729 Barbers' Gem German Water Hones, especially selected for barbers' use. Size, 5x2¼ inches. Put up in a strong paper box. Price..(Postage extra, 25c.)..54c

Barbers' Hair Clippers.

For Human Hair Only. For Horse and Dog Clippers, see Harness Department.

SPECIAL NOTICE—When ordering repairs for clippers be sure to give us the NAME of the clipper and all marks that appear on it. We do not furnish springs or repairs for any clipper except those that have been purchased from us.

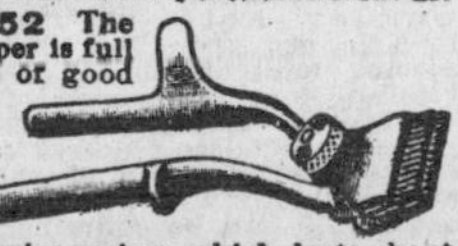

No. 6K18852 The Fulton Hair Clipper is full size, well made of good steel, properly tempered, finely finished and nickel plated. It has concealed three-coil music wire spring, which lasts about five times as long as ordinary springs and can be easily replaced if broken. Cuts hair ⅛-inch long. Price.....(Postage extra, 12c).......52c

No. 6K18853 Springs for the Fulton Hair Clipper. Price 5c
If by mail, postage extra, 2 cents.

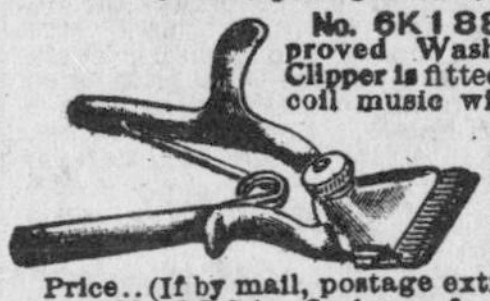

No. 6K18860 The Improved Washington Hair Clipper is fitted with a three coil music wire spring between the handles. Highly nickel plated and polished. Will do fine work.
Price..(If by mail, postage extra, 12c)...64c

No. 6K18861 Springs for the Washington Hair Clipper. Price 9c
If by mail, postage extra, 2 cents.

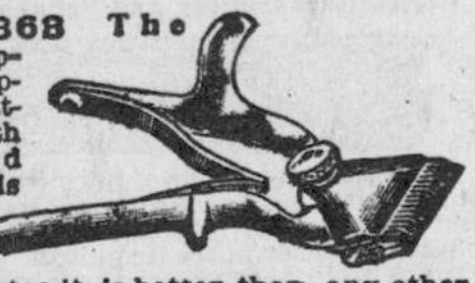

No. 6K18868 The Scott Hair Clipper is the old popular French pattern clipper with flat tempered steel springs. It is very carefully made, tempered to cut, and we guarantee it is better than any other clipper of this pattern in the market. Finely finished and heavily nickel plated. Cuts hair ⅛-inch long. Price....................79c
If by mail, postage extra, 12 cents.

No. 6K18869 Springs for the Scott Hair Clipper, with notch in end. Price....10c

No. 6K18870 Springs for the Scott Hair Clipper, with projection on end. Price....10c
If by mail, postage extra, 2 cents.

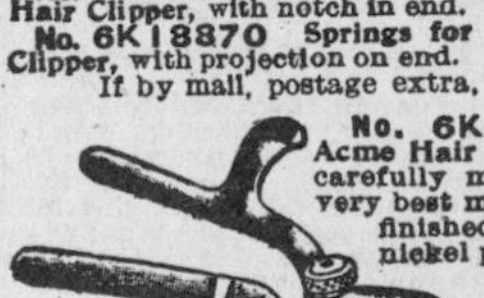

No. 6K18880 The Acme Hair Clipper is very carefully made from the very best material, finely finished and heavily nickel plated. It has a fluted and hollow bottom plate fitting the head, which makes it easy cutting. This clipper is recommended to professional barbers as one which will please. Price..(Postage extra, 12c)...81c

No. 6K18881 Springs for the Acme Hair Clipper.
Price....................7c

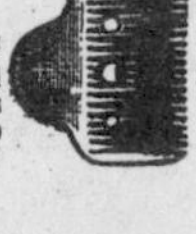

This illustration shows the fluted and curved bottom plate which is furnished on our Keene, Acme and Waldorf Clippers.

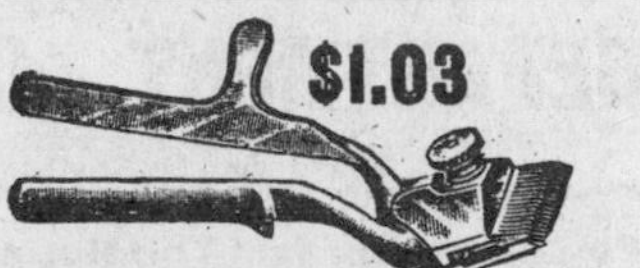

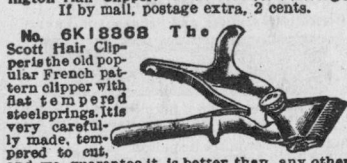

No. 6K18900 The Keene Barbers' Hair Clipper was designed by a barber who knew what a barber required in a clipper. It is made from the very best material. The main tension bolt is set forward almost directly over the teeth, and it is a double tension clipper, insuring ease and perfection of working. The bottom plate is grooved and hollowed, so only the points of teeth touch the scalp. The clipper is finely finished and heavily nickel plated, and is guaranteed to be better than some that are sold at double our price. Cuts hair ⅛-inch long.
Price....................$1.03

No. 6K18901 The Keene Barbers' Hair Clipper, same as above, only to cut very close—almost equal to shaving. Price.......$1.12
If by mail, postage extra, 15 cents.

No. 6K18903 Springs for Keene Hair Clipper. Price ..(Postage extra, 2c)....5c

The Waldorf Ball Bearing Clipper with Adjustable Comb.

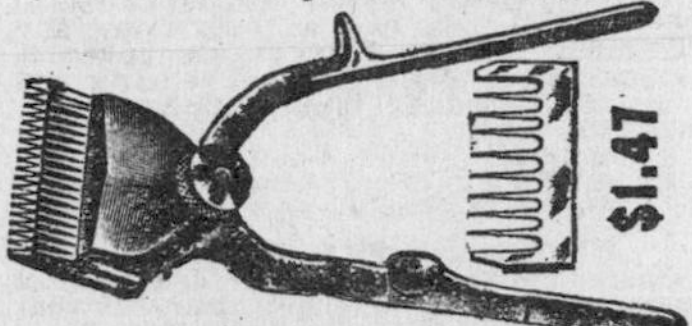

No. 6K18908 Waldorf Ball Bearing Barbers' Clipper, one of the finest clippers on the market, made specially for us under contract by the best clipper manufacturer in the United States. There is no cast iron in this clipper. The entire frame is made of the best malleable steel, which takes this clipper out of comparison with the large number of gray iron clippers sold by dealers throughout the country. The Waldorf Clipper has a fine fluted curved bottom plate finely finished, no rough edges, hand made three coil tempered wire spring, which is guaranteed to last five times as long as the ordinary wire springs. The teeth are finely finished and beveled with just the right taper. The assembling nut is nicely knurled and polished. This clipper is full ball bearing, the easiest operating clipper on the market, heavily nickel plated and polished. Every Waldorf Clipper is furnished with an additional adjustable comb, which can be instantly attached to the clipper and can be adjusted to increase the cut from ⅛-inch to ⅝-inch. If you want the best, most practical and most serviceable clipper made, buy the Waldorf Clipper. It is guaranteed to give satisfaction.
Price, with adjustable comb. $1.47
If by mail, postage extra, 13 cents.

No. 6K18909 Springs for Waldorf Hair Clipper. Price. ..(Postage extra, 2c)....5c

Adjustable Comb, 24 Cents.

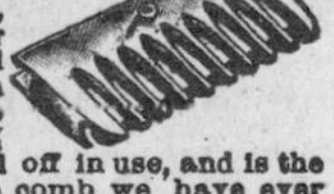

No. 6K18915 Adjustable Comb to fit either the Fulton, Washington, Acme, Keene, Scott or Waldorf Clippers. Will not fit other makes. Can be adjusted instantly to increase the cut from ⅛ to ⅝-inch. It does not fall off in use, and is the only practical adjustable comb we have ever seen. It is finely finished and full nickel plated. Price....................24c
If by mail, postage extra, 4 cents.

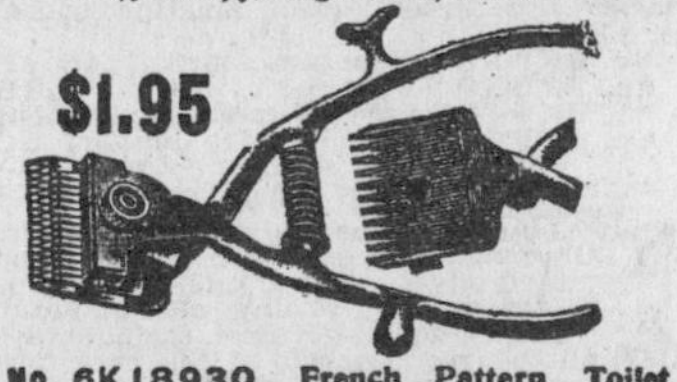

No. 6K18930 French Pattern Toilet Clipper. Modeled on the lines of the original French Toilet Clipper. Has excellent cutting qualities. Workmanship and finish first class. Spring has adjustable tension. Cuts ⅛-inch. Price (If by mail, postage extra, 15c.). $1.95

No. 6K18933 Springs for French Pattern Toilet Clipper. Price....................10c
If by mail, postage extra, 2 cents.

Neck Shave Clipper.

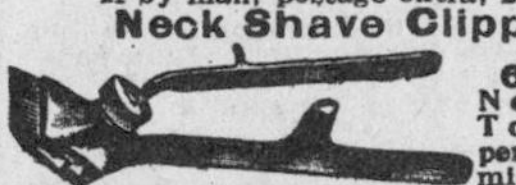

No. 6K18938 Neck Shave Toilet Clipper. For trimming the beard and neck. Has corrugated bottom plate. Very carefully made; light and a favorite with barbers. Cuts very close, almost equal to shaving. Heavily nickel plated. Price........$1.85
If by mail, postage extra, 9 cents.

No. 6K18939 Springs for Neck Shave Clipper. Price....(Postage extra, 2c)...10c

Brown & Sharpe's Barbers' Clippers, Bressant Pattern.

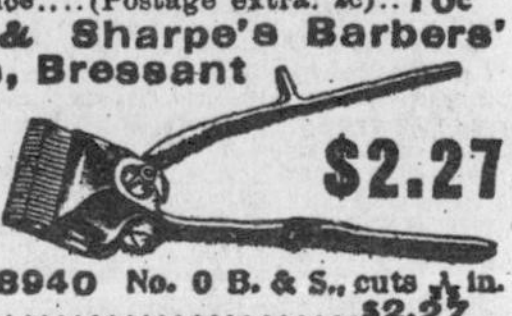

No. 6K18940 No. 0 B. & S., cuts ⅛ in.
Price....................$2.27

No. 6K18941 No. 1 B. & S., cuts ⅛ in.
Price....................$2.30

No. 6K18942 No. 2 B. & S., cuts ⅛ in.
Price....................$2.65
If by mail, postage extra, each, 15 cents.

No. 6K18944 Springs for above clipper.
Price, each....................5c

DEPARTMENT OF FAMILY REMEDIES AND ITEMS FOR THE HOME

MAILING CHARGES—2-ounce bottle, tube and postage, extra, 12 cents; 4-ounce bottle, tube and postage, extra, 16 cents; 8-ounce and 16-ounce bottles unmailable on account of weight. Remember, the pure food law in effect January 1, 1907, is your only safeguard. This applies only to drugs shipped from one state to the other and has no reference to goods sold in your own state. Therefore, buy your drugs from reliable mail order houses whose drugs are guaranteed absolutely pure and pass every pure food law in the United States, either state or national.

Powdered Borax. The Housekeeper's Friend.

No. 8K505 Price, 1-pound carton...9c

Paregoric, U. S. P.

No. 8K508 Full directions with each bottle. Price, 4-ounce bottle.........17c
Mailable sizes, see note above.

Tasteless Castor Oil.

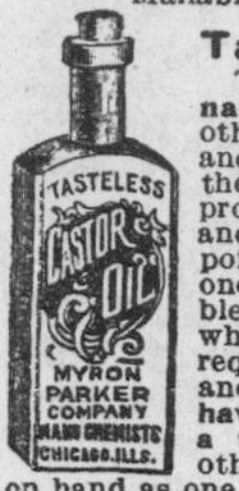

This preparation is a combination of pure castor oil with other substances and aromatics and made in such a manner that the nauseating and objectionable properties are largely eliminated and yet it possesses all the good points that have made castor oil one of the most certain and reliable cathartics that can be used when a remedy of this kind is required. Can be taken by adults and children alike. After you have given our Tasteless Castor Oil a trial you will never use any other, and you will always keep it on hand as one of the standard cathartic and household remedies. (See medicine spoon, page 788.)

No. 8K511 Price, 4-ounce bottle..19c
No. 8K512 Price, 8-ounce bottle..36c
Mailable sizes, see note above.

Sweet Spirits of Nitre.

Guaranteed absolutely pure, fresh and of full strength. Much more reliable than that generally offered for sale in drug stores.

No. 8K516 Price, 4-ounce bottle..20c
No. 8K517 Price, 1-pint bottle....73c
Mailable sizes, see above note.

Essence Peppermint, U. S. P.

Pure, strong and of full strength. Full directions with each bottle.

No. 8K521 Price, 4-ounce bottle...19c
Mailable sizes, see note above.

Essence Jamaica Ginger, U. S. P.

Prepared of great strength from the finest quality of Jamaica ginger. Full directions with each bottle.

No. 8K526 Price, 4-ounce bottle..21c
Mailable sizes, see note above.

Essence of Pepsin.

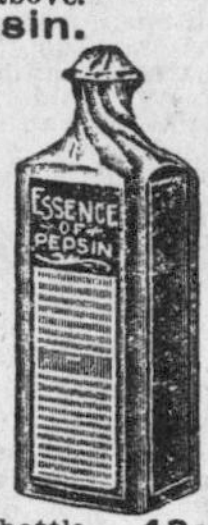

A preparation regularly prescribed by physicians, and usually recommended for the treatment of indigestion, sour stomach, dyspepsia, bad breath and in all conditions arising from a lack of gastric juice to properly digest and assimilate the food. A teaspoonful before or after meals will aid digestion and assimilation of food, and affords prompt relief when suffering from indigestion, as well as the distressing attacks to which chronic sufferers from dyspepsia are subject; also largely used for making junket, whey, etc. for invalids.

No. 8K530 Price, 8-ounce bottle...43c
Mailable sizes, see note above.

Neutralizing Cordial.

A well known household remedy. An ideal children's remedy for many bowel complaints.

No. 8K535 Price, 4-ounce bottle...18c
Mailable sizes, see note above.

Castor Oil.

Cold pressed and almost tasteless. Exceptionally fine grade. (See medicine spoon, page 788.)

No. 8K538 Price, 4-oz. bottle...$0.15
No. 8K539 Price, 1-pint bottle... .35
No. 8K540 Price, ½-gallon jug... .88
No. 8K541 Price, 1-gallon jug.. 1.50
Mailable sizes, see note above.

Imported Olive Oil.

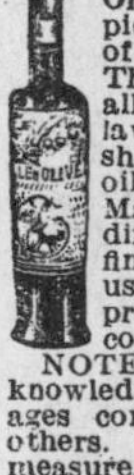

This is genuine Chiris Imported Pure Olive Oil, pressed from choice hand picked olives and guaranteed to be one of the very finest olive oils produced. This oil is absolutely pure, complies with all the requirements of the pure food laws, either state or national. This should not be compared with the olive oils heretofore sold under the name of Malaga Olive Oil, etc., as it is an entirely different product. It is an exceptionally fine flavor and absolutely pure. Largely used for internal use as well as the preparation of salads and general cooking.

NOTE—This is the only brand to our knowledge that is full measure. These packages contain 25 to 40 per cent more than others. When buying be sure to get full measure.

No. 8K546 1 pt., original bottle...$0.72
No. 8K547 1 quart, original can.. 1.25
No. 8K549 1 gallon, original can.. 3.25
All sizes unmailable on account of weight.

Spirits of Camphor, U. S. P.

No. 8K551 Price, 4-ounce bottle...20c
No. 8K552 Price, 1-pint bottle...63c
Mailable sizes, see note above.

Camphorated Oil, U. S. P.

An excellent article for rubbing on children's and grown up persons' chests and throats in cases of croup, difficulty in breathing, sore throat, coughs. A small quantity of pure spirits of turpentine added to it will increase its effectiveness in many cases.

No. 8K561 Price, 4-ounce bottle...17c
No. 8K562 Price, 8-ounce bottle...28c
Mailable sizes, see note above.

Glycerine.

Warranted absolutely pure. Can be used either externally or internally.

No. 8K571 Price, 4 ounces.....$0.15
No. 8K572 Price, ½ pound...... .23
No. 8K573 Price, 1 pound ...... .39
No. 8K574 Price, per gallon jug.. 2.38
Mailable sizes, see note above.

Carbolic Acid.

A 5 per cent solution of Carbolic Acid for disinfecting purposes, destroying contagion, cleansing purposes, etc. Excellent for keeping away disease, destroying bad odors. Put up expressly for household use.

No. 8K576 Price, 1-pound bottle..16c
Unmailable.

Tincture of Arnica, U. S. P.

The value of arnica is well known as an application to bruises, sprains, cuts, swellings, etc., but to secure any benefit it is necessary to have a strong, well prepared tincture such as ours.

No. 8K580 Price, 4-ounce bottle...19c
No. 8K581 Price, ½-pint bottle....36c
No. 8K582 Price, 1-pint bottle....63c
Unmailable.

Household Ammonia.

Standard quality. Extra purity and strength. Put up expressly for home use. It lightens work and brightens the home. Makes the washing cleaner and polishing easier.

In pint bottles, with full directions for use in the laundry, for the toilet, and for cleaning glass, crockery, paint, taking out stains, etc.

No. 8K585 Price, per pint bottle..11c
No. 8K586 Price, per gallon jug....75c
Unmailable on account of weight.

Violet Ammonia.

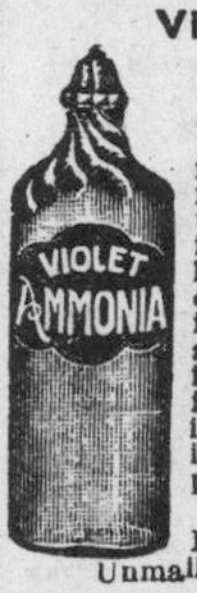

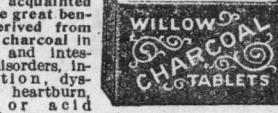

For the toilet and bath. Violet Ammonia is a comparatively new article for toilet and bathing purposes, which has won the favor of every lady and gentleman who has given it a trial. Once used you would never be without it. We furnish Violet Ammonia in liquid form and in the very best condition for toilet and bath. It is inexpensive and a few drops added to the water before washing will be sufficient to perfume it, intensify the cleansing and invigorating effects greatly, leaving a mild but lasting odor always pleasing and refreshing.

No. 8K588 Violet Ammonia. Price, 1-pint bottle.........17c
Unmailable on account of weight.

Willow Charcoal Tablets.

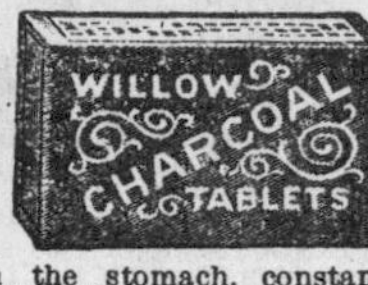

Every person is well acquainted with the great benefit derived from willow charcoal in gastric and intestinal disorders, indigestion, dyspepsia, heartburn, sour or acid stomach, gas upon the stomach, constant belching, fetid breath, all gaseous complications and for the removal of the offensive odor from the breath after smoking.

These tablets are prepared from the purest carefully treated willow charcoal and will not interfere in any way with the action of other medicines. Can be conveniently carried in the pocket. Regular price, per box, 25 cents.

No. 8K380 Our price, two boxes for..25c
If by mail, postage extra, per box, 2 cents.

Genuine Witch Hazel Extract.

A universal all healing remedy. Should be in every household; useful for sore throat, hemorrhage, wounds, sprains, bruises, sore eyes, stiff joints, burns, and in nearly every accident that one can have. Our price is so low that every family can afford to keep a supply in their homes. Look at our prices.

No. 8K590 ½-pint bottle.......$0.16
No. 8K591 1-pint bottle........ .25
No. 8K592 1-quart bottle....... .43
No. 8K593 ½-gallon............ .72
No. 8K594 1-gallon............ 1.20
Unmailable on account of weight.

Baby Soothing Syrup.

Perfectly Harmless and Pleasant to Take.

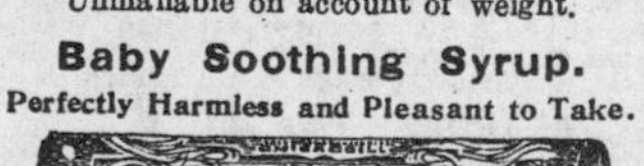

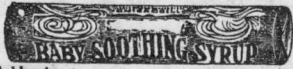

A blessing to parents, harmless and effectual in soothing and quieting children of any age. We guarantee it to contain no opium or morphine, or other narcotic poison. It is prepared from simple herbs and has a wonderful effect in soothing and quieting a child who may be cross, no matter from what reason. A very beneficial remedy for children during teething period.

No. 8K2110 Our price, per bottle..18c
If by mail, postage and tube extra, 12 cents.

M. P. Corn Remover.

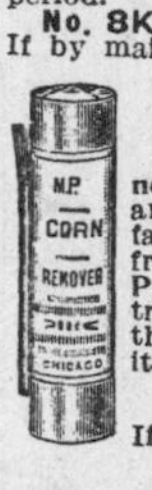

The great M. P. Corn Remover never fails to give immediate relief, and will remove corns if directions are faithfully followed. No one suffering from corns should fail to give this M. P. Corn Remover a trial. We have tried it ourselves and found relief, therefore can testify knowingly as to its great merits.

No. 8K139 Our price.....10c
If by mail, postage extra, 3 cents.

Powdered Alum.

This largely used chemical we guarantee of full strength and efficiency. Will immediately stop bleeding, and largely used around the home for removing canker of the mouth, a small amount placed on canker causing it to disappear. Also used for astringent washes and douches.

No. 8K625 Price, per pound carton.......................11c

Bromo Vichy.

(EFFERVESCENT HEADACHE SALTS.)
The best manufactured.

A morning bracer. A headache reliever. A brain clearer. A nerve steadier.

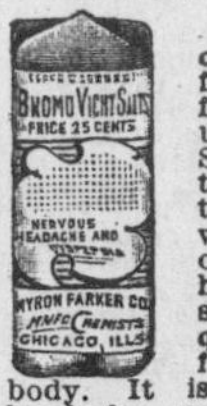

This is a very reliable effervescent headache preparation. It is free from acetanilid and all harmful substances. Its sale is entirely unrestricted by National and State Pure Food Laws. One or two teaspoonfuls of the bromo taken in a half tumbler of cold water will shortly dispel sickness of the stomach, relieve a severe headache, clear up the brain and steady the nerves. It is a thirst quencher, and causes a pleasant feeling to prevail all through the body. It is a quick remedy for nervous headaches, neuralgia, sleeplessness, over brain work, depression following alcoholic excesses, and all nervous troubles. A little should always be on one's bureau or table for use in the morning or at night.

No. 8K137 Price, 25-cent size....18c
No. 8K138 Price, 50-cent size....37c
Unmailable.

Glycerine Suppositories.

Harmless, certain and agreeable, and contain 95 per cent glycerine.

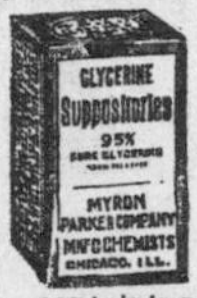

The best treatment for constipation, producing painless, prompt and copious evacuation of the bowels without disturbing the stomach and whole system. The ideal method of emptying the lower bowels. Easy to apply and will keep indefinitely. The best remedy for constipated children. Full directions with each bottle.

No. 8K23 Price, per bottle, containing 12 adult suppositories.................17c
If by mail, postage extra, per bottle, 10 cents.

Boil Remedy.

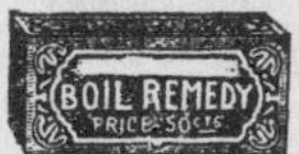

A preparation composed mainly of calcium sulphide, and which has for years been known to quickly check and free the system from boils. Many persons are subject to them periodically, they being caused by a peculiar condition of the system. The remedy is perfectly safe and it seems certain in its effects. No trouble, easy to take, the results are all that can be expected. Don't wait until you are tortured with a boil. Be ready for the trouble. Keep a package on hand. It never spoils. Retail price, 50 cents.

No. 8K64 Our price, per box......24c
If by mail, postage extra, per box, 5 cents.

Santol Perles.

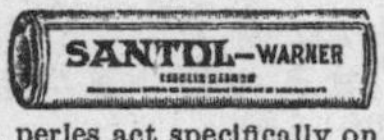

Each perle contains five minims of the purest East India santalwood oil.

These well known perles act specifically on the inflamed mucous surface, rendering the urine less acrid and lessens the quantity passed, hence a reduction of irritation.

Santol Perles should be taken at once upon the appearance of the first symptoms. By being prompt in taking the remedy the disease will be cut off in its earliest stages. The medicine should be continued for some time after the symptoms have entirely disappeared, so as to thoroughly cleanse the system. 40 perles in a bottle. Regular price, $1.00.

No. 8K382 Our special price, each..67c
If by mail, postage extra, 8 cents.

Compound Cathartic Pills.

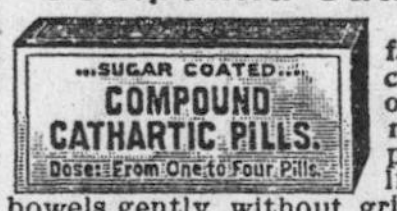

This is the old-fashioned sugar coated Cathartic Pill of the U. S. Pharmacopoeia. They act principally on the liver, and move the bowels gently without griping. Retail price, 25 cents.

No. 8K67 Our price, per box......9c
If by mail, postage extra, per box, 2 cents.

Menthol Cough Drops.

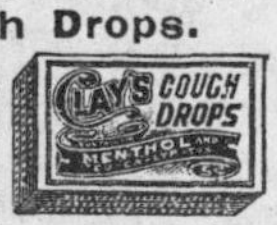

Unexcelled for coughs, colds, sore throat, hoarseness, tickling in the throat, etc. Pleasant to the taste and slowly dissolving in the mouth, the medicaments are so distributed that the beneficial effects continue as long as the tablet dissolves. Much better than the average cough drop.

No. 8K72 Price, 3 boxes for.......12c
If by mail, postage extra, per box, 4 cents.

Carbolic Arnica Salve.

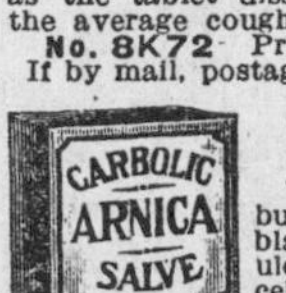

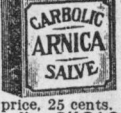

The best in the world for burns, flesh wounds, chilblains, boils, felons, sores, ulcers and fever sores. Excellent for salt rheum, eczema and ringworm. Regular price, 25 cents.

No. 8K610 Our price, per box.....15c
If by mail, postage extra, per box, 4 cents.

Tincture Iodine U.S.P.

For external use only. Universally recommended for reducing swelling and inflammation resulting from sprains and bruises, also highly endorsed by physicians for the treatment of goitre and erysipelas. Always apply by painting the affected parts with a camel's hair brush.

No. 8K645 Price, 2-ounce bottle...17c
No. 8K646 Price, 4-ounce bottle...29c
Not mailable.

Pure Norwegian Cod Liver Oil.

A PURE OIL FOR MEDICINAL PURPOSES.

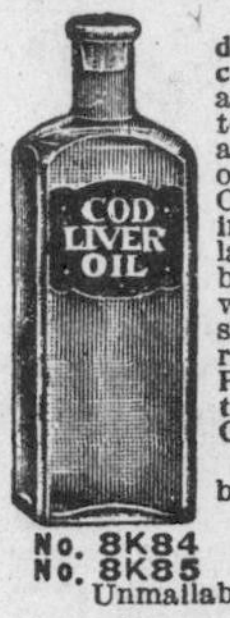

In the treatment of wasting diseases where the body has become emaciated, where patients are losing flesh, where the system is constantly weakening and reaches a state of debility, our Pure Norwegian Cod Liver Oil will not only act as a food, increasing properly the assimilation of all food partaken of, but the medicinal properties which it contains will at the same time produce a quick restoration to general health. For severe colds, lung and throat troubles, Norwegian Cod Liver Oil should be taken regularly.

No. 8K83 Price, per bottle.................$0.53
3 pint bottles for.. 1.50
No. 8K84 Price, per ½ gallon 1.70
No. 8K85 Price, per 1 gallon.. 2.95
Unmailable on account of weight.

Blackberry Cordial.

Formerly known as Blackberry Brandy.

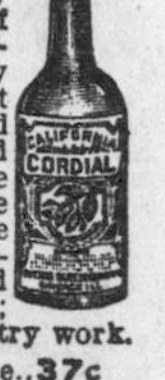

An exceptionally fine and Pure Blackberry Cordial, made from the ripe blackberry; fine dark red color, heavy body and combined with the juice of the blackberry. Held by manufacturers as absolutely pure. Many grades of blackberry cordial are not pure, but our product is guaranteed by the manufacturers. Used and prescribed by many physicians as one of the simplest and most effective remedies for all derangements of the stomach and bowels. Does not constipate. Fine in taste, agreeable and tones up and invigorates the system; also largely used for cooking and pastry work.

No. 8K128 Price, per pint bottle..37c
No. 8K130 Price, per quart bottle.62c
All sizes unmailable on account of weight.

Leininger's Formaldehyde and Menthol Inhaler.

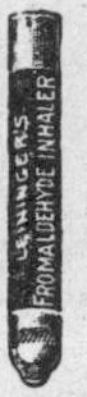

Leininger's Formaldehyde and Menthol Inhaler is a scientific combination for treating hay fever, catarrh, asthma and all germ diseases of the nose, throat and lungs.

Leininger's Formaldehyde and Menthol Inhaler is recognized as the only reliable treatment by inhalation for the purposes for which they are indicated. If you are a sufferer from hay fever and catarrh and so far have been unable to obtain relief, we recommend Leininger's Formaldehyde and Menthol Inhaler, which has proved effective where many other treatments have been found inadequate.

Furnished in a handsome aluminum tube, with a closely fitting cap to prevent evaporation. Contains a two to three months' treatment. Regular price, 25 cents.

No. 8K316 Our price..........19c
If by mail, postage extra, 2 cents.

Effervescent Lithia Tablets.

SCHIEFFELIN & CO. BRAND.

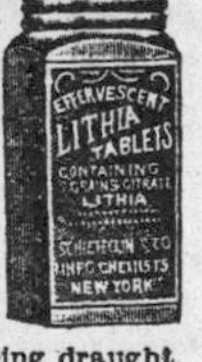

Lithia Salts have for years been recognized as one of the standard remedies for the treatment of subacute and chronic rheumatism, gout, uric acid, irritable bladder and all kidney affections depending upon an excess of uric acid in the system. Schieffelin's Lithia Tablets are absolutely pure, convenient, and accurate in dosage and possess many advantages not embraced by other forms of administration. One tablet dissolved in a glass of water makes a very agreeable, refreshing and beneficial effervescing draught.

No. 8K186 Price, per bottle, 3-grain tablets, 40 in bottle...............18c
No. 8K187 Price, per bottle, 5-grain tablets, 40 in bottle...............23c
If by mail, postage extra, 15 cents.

Refined Camphor.

(GUM CAMPHOR.)

No. 8K614 Price, 1-ounce cake.... 9c
No. 8K615 Price, 1-pound pkg....95c
Subject to market changes.

Boric Acid—Pure

(BORACIC ACID.)

Guaranteed highest purity powder, a popular, valuable and aseptic healing dressing and protective for cuts, wounds, ulcers, sores, bruises and all inflamed and irritated surfaces, a healing and soothing application for chafed and harsh, dry or rough skin.

No. 8K620 Price, 1-pound airtight container.......................20c

Genuine Bathsweet Bath Powder.

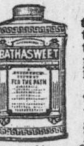

A highly perfumed luxury for the bath. A scientific preparation for softening and perfuming the water. It adds value and pleasure to the bath, by making it more agreeable and refreshing. You will never know or appreciate the real luxury of such a bath with its refreshing, stimulating and exhilarating effect until you have used this delightful toilet necessity. Sold the country over for 25 cents.

No. 8K321 Our price, per package, 17c
If by mail, postage extra, 6 cents.

GRANULAR EFFERVESCENT SALTS.

Headache Salts, see Bromo Vichy, page 787.

Kissingen Salt.

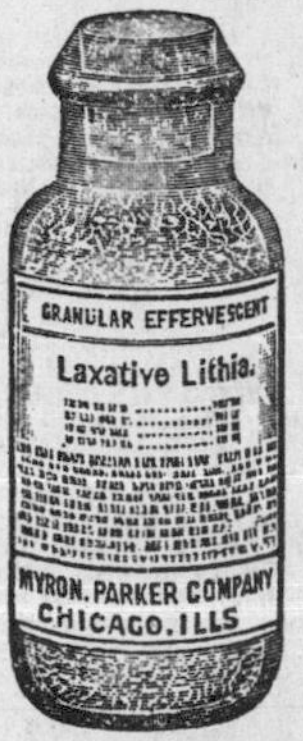

Each heaping teaspoonful dissolved in half a tumblerful of water forms a refreshing and agreeable draught, similar to the natural water. Very beneficial as a table water in all gouty and liver derangements. Highly recommended in daily alternation with Vichy by Dr. Wm. T. Cathell, of Baltimore, for the successful treatment of obesity. The dose of Kissingen Salt is taken in water twenty to thirty minutes after each meal one day, and a similar dose of Vichy after each meal the next day, and this treatment continued week after week, until patient is relieved of the discomforts of overflesh. When near the desired weight, gradually reduce the dose, and at last stop treatment entirely.

No. 8K365 Price, 12-ounce bottle..**36c**
Unmailable on account of weight.

Laxative Lithia.

Each dessertspoonful contains potassium citrate 30 grains, sodium phosphate 30 grains, lithium citrate 5 grains. Laxative, refrigerant, diuretic and antacid. This double salt of lithium is highly recommended for relieving excess of acid existing in the secretions, and hence is indicated in rheumatism, gout neurasthenia, cystitis, gravel and in all similar affections arising from a uric acid diathesis. A very beneficial laxative for use by rheumatic patients.

No. 8K368 Price, 12-ounce bottle ...**36c**
Unmailable on account of weight.

Sodium Phosphate.

Each heaping teaspoonful contains 30 grains sodium phosphate. This well known medicinal agent is one of the very best in the treatment of liver trouble, jaundice, obesity, rickets, constipation, diarrhea in small children, and in all cases requiring a saline laxative. Dose: One or two heaping teaspoonfuls in half glass water before breakfast and teaspoonful before dinner, if necessary.

No. 8K372 Price, 12-oz. bottle......**36c**
Unmailable on account of weight.

Vichy.

Made after the French governmental analysis of the famous Vichy Springs adding to our product all the valuable therapeutic properties contained therein. Each teaspoonful of this salt when added to a glass of water forms a grateful and refreshing draught, similar to the natural water. Highly recommended in daily alternation with Kissingen, by Dr. Wm. T. Cathell, of Baltimore, for the treatment of obesity. The dose of Vichy salt in water is taken twenty to thirty minutes after each meal one day, and a similar dose of Kissingen after each meal the next day, and this treatment continued week after week, until patient is relieved of the discomforts of overflesh. When near the desired weight, gradually reduce the dose, and at last stop treatment altogether.

No. 8K376 Price, 12-oz. bottle......**36c**
Unmailable on account of weight.

Magnesium Sulphate.

Effervescent Epsom Salts.

Each heaping teaspoonful contains 30 grains magnesium sulphate. Laxative, cathartic, refrigerant, antacid. This effervescent form affords a pleasant method of taking Epsom salts. For laxative effect, take one or more tablespoonfuls in small glass of water and drink while effervescing. For cathartic effect, take two or more tablespoonfuls in the same manner.

No. 8K370 Price, 12-oz. bottle......**36c**
Unmailable on account of weight.

Old English Wart Remover.

GUARANTEED TO GIVE SATISFACTION.

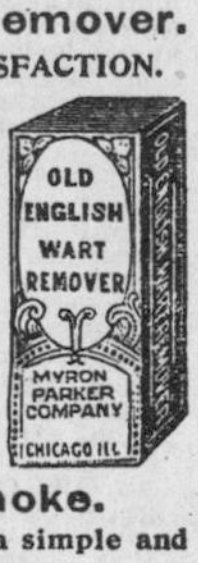

This is a very reliable and harmless remedy for the removal of all kinds of warts. After the first application the wart commences to shrink and after the treatment is continued for a reasonable length of time the wart will drop off without leaving any scar. The treatment is perfectly painless and harmless. Regular price, 25 cents.

No. 8K318 Our price..**17c**
If by mail, postage extra, 4c.

Liquid Hickory Smoke.

For smoking meats and fish in a simple and inexpensive manner.

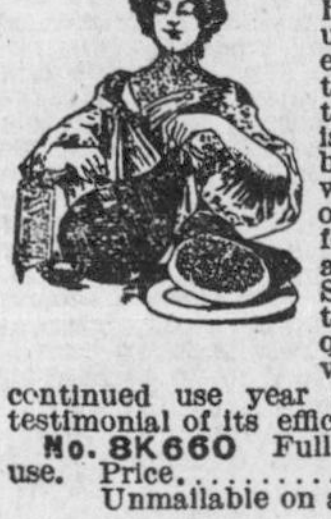

This preparation, sold under the name of Liquid Hickory Smoke, has been upon the market for several years and during that time we have sold thousands of bottles. It is not only a meat smoker but a meat preserver and will accomplish the work of the smoke house in a few hours. A brush and a bottle of Hickory Smoke and you are ready to flavor the hams quickly and we believe very satisfactorily. The continued use year after year is the best testimonial of its efficiency.

No. 8K660 Full quart bottles ready for use. Price..........**41c**
Unmailable on account of weight.

Seroco Egg Preserver.

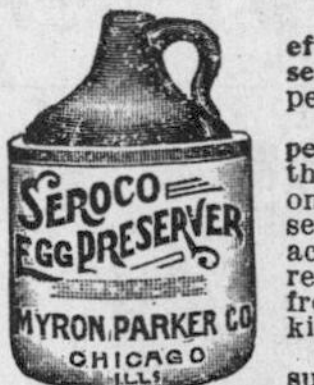

One of the best and most effective means for preserving eggs for a limited period of time.

Carefully conducted experiments have shown that the Seroco Egg Preserver is one of the few egg preservers of today that will accomplish all that can reasonably be expected from a preparation of this kind.

Seroco Egg Preserver is supplied in gallon jugs; this quantity is sufficient for the preserving of forty to fifty dozen of eggs. Complete directions furnished with each gallon of the preservative.

No. 8K665 Price, per gallon.......**64c**
Unmailable on account of weight.

Lightning Tanner.

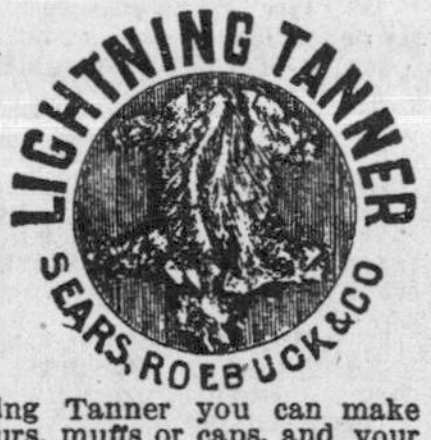

Lightning Tanner is the very latest mixture for quickly and perfectly tanning furs and skins of every description in from 24 to 36 hours. Very simple to use, requires no experience and first class results can always be obtained. By means of Lightning Tanner you can make your own robes, furs, muffs or caps, and your leather belts, tie straps, halters, etc. Does not, like many other tanning compounds, rot or weaken the leather, but makes it tough, soft and pliable. Full directions for preparing the hides and tanning are furnished with each package.

No. 8K670 Box with powder sufficient to tan two raccoon skins in 36 hours. Price............................**17c**
If by mail, postage extra, 2 cents.

No. 8K671 Box containing three times the above and sufficient for deerskin. Price..............................**35c**
If by mail, postage extra, 4 cents.

No. 8K672 Box holding about twelve times the above and sufficient for horse or cow hide.........(Unmailable).........**81c**

Quinine Pills.

Two grains each, sugar or gelatine coated. Full weight and strength and with absolutely pure quinine.

No. 8K675 Price, per bottle of 100 pills...(If by mail, postage extra, 8c.)...**19c**

Quinine.

(QUININE SULPHATE, GUARANTEED ABSOLUTELY PURE.)

No. 8K680 Price, 1-ounce........**39c**
If by mail, postage extra, per ounce, 6 cents.

Furniture Polish.

A handy and valuable household article of the greatest perfection for polishing and restoring all kinds of furniture. Quickly removes scratches, stains and marks of wear, and makes the furniture look like new. Full directions with each bottle.

No. 8K685 Price, per 4-ounce bottle, **13c**
Postage and mailing tube extra, 16 cents.

Seidlitz Powders.

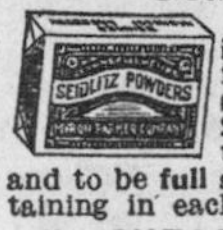

Most of the powders bought in stores are worthless from being kept too long; they lose their strength. We guarantee all Seidlitz Powders we send out to be made from pure materials and to be full strength. Put up in boxes containing in each 10 blue and 10 white papers.

No. 8K700 Price, per box........**18c**
If by mail, postage extra, per box, 5 cents.

Methylene Blue Compound Perles.

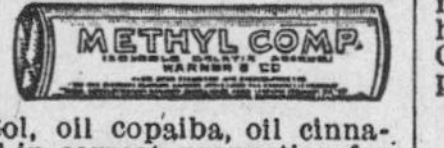

These well known and highly efficient Gelatine Perles, composed of methylene blue, oil East India santol, oil copaiba, oil cinnamon and Harlem oil in correct proportion for speedy relief. In the genito-urinary tract it exerts an active antiseptic action by its peculiar penetrating power, and affects both superficial and deep structure as well. It renders the urine blue and antiseptic and rapidly kills the micro-organisms present. Especially indicated in gonorrhea and its complications. Packed 40 perles in bottle. Regular price, $1.00.

No. 8K385 Our special price......**69c**
If by mail, postage extra, 8 cents.

Jerkin's Medicine Spoon.

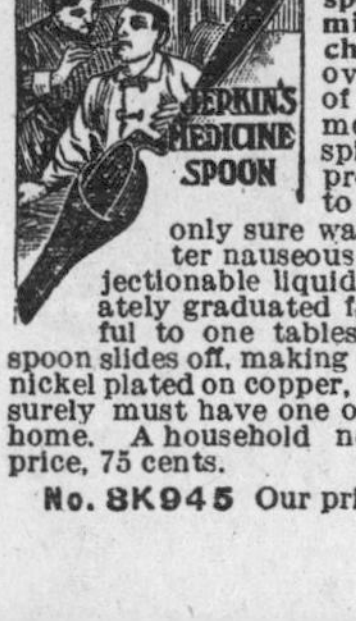

The most convenient spoon ever made for administering medicine to children and adults. It overcomes the bad taste of medicine through the medium of the tongue; no spilling, no spitting out, protects the teeth, sure to be swallowed. The only sure way to give castor oil, bitter nauseous medicines or other objectionable liquids. Each spoon accurately graduated from one-half teaspoonful to one tablespoonful. The top of spoon slides off, making cleansing easy, heavily nickel plated on copper, will not corrode. You surely must have one of these spoons in your home. A household necessity. Regular price, 75 cents.

No. 8K945 Our price (Postage, 6c.), **59c**

Milk Sugar—Pure.

(SUGAR OF MILK.)

Especially recommended for making modified milk as a food for infants. Practically indispensable in all cases where babies are brought up by the bottle. Full directions for infant feeding on each package. Furnished in airtight 1-pound packages.

No. 8K595 Per 1-pound package...**28c**

Seroco Fast and Stainless Dyes.

Dyes Evenly Cotton, Wool, Silk and Mixed Goods, All in the Same Bath.

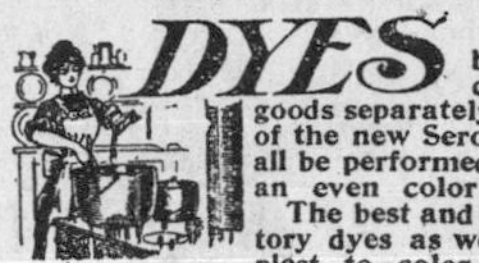

No more trouble with dyeing cotton and wool goods separately, as by means of the new Seroco Dyes it can all be performed together and an even color be obtained. The best and most satisfactory dyes as well as the simplest to color, of any dyes ever offered to a customer. Simple and easy to use, produces bright fadeless colors and will not stain the hands or the container. Will color from one to six pounds of goods according to the shade desired.

The New Seroco Fast and Stainless Dyes can be successfully used for coloring dress goods, coats, carpet rags, ribbons, feathers, yarns, silk fabrics, grass and basket material, moss, and in general for coloring all forms of material. Furnished in the following beautiful shades: Pink, wine, orange, cardinal, heliotrope, myrtle green, pale blue, seal brown, cerise, lemon, brown, old rose, light green, navy blue, royal purple, tan, yellow, drab, olive green, turkey red, black, emerald green, royal blue, salmon. A direction booklet is furnished free with each package of dye. In it is contained a fund of valuable information, including general directions, detection of cotton from wool or mixed goods, cleaning goods before dyeing, using the dye, preparing the goods, preparing the dye bath, boiling, removing goods from bath, various shades of color, ripping the goods, drying, pressing, dyeing light shades, etc., and ending with a complete list of colors produced by dyeing over various shades of cloth. Be sure to state color wanted.

No. 8K730 Regular price, per package, 10 cents; our price, 2 packages for......**14c**
If by mail, postage extra, for 2, 2 cents.

Epsom Salts.

No. 8K740 Price, 1-lb. carton.... **3c**
No. 8K741 Price, 5-lb. package... **12c**
No. 8K742 Price, 10-lb. package... **21c**
No. 8K743 Price, 25-lb. package... **49c**

Rochelle Salts.

No. 8K750 Price, ¼-lb. package... **9c**
No. 8K751 Price, ½-lb. package... **13c**
No. 8K752 Price, 1-lb. package... **23c**
All sizes unmailable.

Sublimed Sulphur.

No. 8K760 Price, 1-lb. carton..**$0.04**
No. 8K761 Price, 5-lb. package. **.19**
No. 8K762 Price, 10-lb. pkg.... **.37**
No. 8K763 Price, 25-lb. pkg.... **.88**
No. 8K765 Price, 100-lb. bag... **2.50**
No. 8K766 Price, 175-lb. bbl... **4.25**
All sizes unmailable on account of weight.

Petroleum Jelly.

VASELINE OR COSMOLINE.

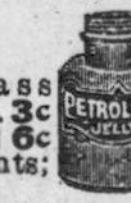

No. 8K780 Price, 2-oz. glass jar..................**3c**
No. 8K781 Price, 1-lb. can, **16c**
Postage extra, each, small, 8 cents; large, 20 cents.

Carbolized Petroleum Jelly.

This is the same as the above, with the addition of 3 per cent pure carbolic acid which increases to a great extent its powers of healing.

No. 8K785 Price, 2-oz. bottle......**4c**
No. 8K786 Price, 1-pound can......**16c**
Postage extra, each, small, 8c; large 20c.

Carron Oil for Burns.

This is one of the household remedies that ought to be ordered by every housewife and kept on hand ready for immediate use.

Our Carron Oil is the safest and most reliable treatment for fresh burns of every description. It stops the pain and smarting at once, prevents inflammation when used without delay, and in case where the inflammation has started, it will reduce it quickly, healing the burns in the shortest possible time. Complete directions are furnished with each package.

No. 8K800 Price, 4-ounce bottle, **14c**
Postage and tube extra, each, 16 cents.

Earache Drops.

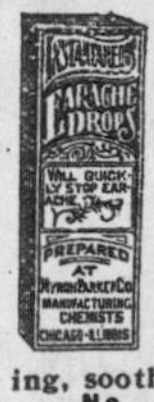

A few drops applied on a piece of medicated cotton and inserted into the ear will relieve earache in a comparatively short time, removing the cause of the pain. INSTANTANEOUS EARACHE DROPS ARE VERY PENETRATING and, when properly applied, will reach all parts of the organism. While earache drops are intended for relieving earache, they will also be found useful for removal of hardened ear wax deposit. Instantaneous earache drops are penetrating, healing, soothing and emollient.

No. 8K71 Instantaneous Earache Drops, 2-dram vials. Price..........**17c**
If by mail, postage extra, per vial, 2 cents.

Hydrogen Peroxide.

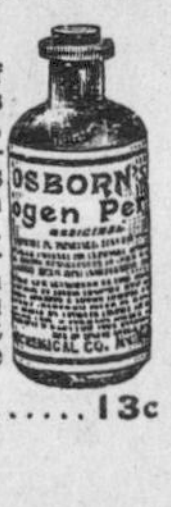

The old time long tried and one of the very best all around antiseptics for the home. Kills disease germs, bubbling as it cleanses, is unsurpassed for washing out fresh cuts and wounds, diluted as a tooth wash or throat gargle, is free from odor, absolutely harmless in unexperienced hands and after once used in the home you will wonder how you have ever before been able to get along without it. Put up in 4-ounce bottles.

No. 8K805 Price..............**13c**

China Cement.

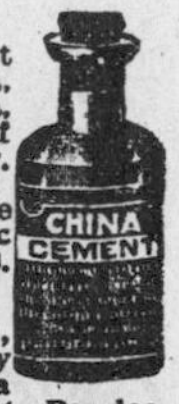

China Cement. One of the best cements for mending glass, china, ivory, shell, marble, fur, terra cotta, meerschaum, porcelain, plaster of paris, wood alabaster and leather. Does the work well and quickly.

No. 8K810 Price, ½-ounce bottle, per bottle..............**8c**
If by mail, postage extra, 4 cents.

Seroco Foot Powder.

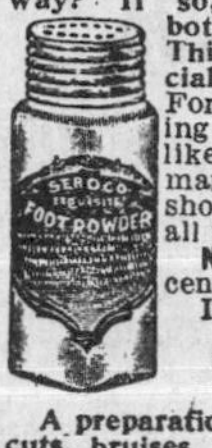

Do your feet get tired, ache, perspire or hurt, annoy you in any way? If so, buy at once a bottle of Seroco Foot Powder. This powder is particularly beneficial to those inclined to perspiration. For destroying bad odors and giving comfort to sore feet nothing like it has hitherto been put on the market. A little shaken in the shoes keeps the feet comfortable at all times.

No. 8K820 Regular price, 25 cents; our price, per box....**13c**
If by mail, postage extra, 3c.

Liquid Skin.

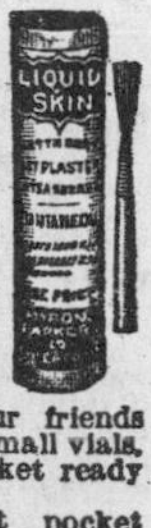

A preparation to be used for all cuts, bruises and abrasions. Acts instantaneously. Better, cheaper and quicker than any other antiseptic bandage, court plaster or other method usually applied for stopping loss of blood in minor wounds. Can be applied in a few seconds, forming at once a new skin over the cut, bruise or abrasion, protecting the wound from all foreign matter and healing it without a moment's delay or danger. No person should be without this valuable yet inexpensive remedy. It may save your life or that of your friends almost any day. Put up neatly in small vials, so it can be carried in the vest pocket ready for immediate use.

No. 8K830 Liquid Skin, vest pocket size. Price.(If by mail, postage extra, 3c.).**8c**

Loofah Flesh Brush.

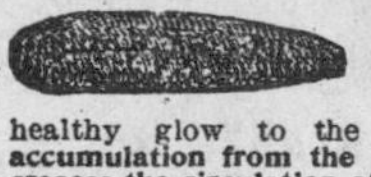

The Loofah is the fibrous part of a gourd that grows in the south of Japan. Their use gives a healthy glow to the body, removes the accumulation from the pores of the skin, increases the circulation of the blood and leaves a pleasant sensation.

No. 8K2632 Large 14-inch size. Price. (If by mail, postage extra, 3c.).**8c**

The Celebrated Dry Powder Fire Fighters.

Do not risk your house by buying a cheap one. Our fighter costs a little more than others, but it pays to buy the best.

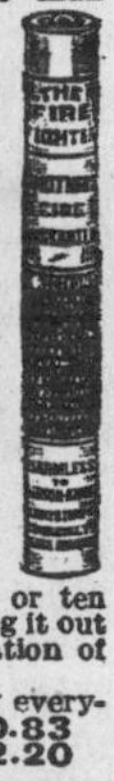

The Fire Fighter is a dry powder fire extinguisher, put up for use in a metallic tube 22 inches long and 2 inches in diameter. One end of the tube is fitted with a cover, held in place by natural tension and fitted with a ring by which the tube is hung from a strong hook, attached for this purpose to a wall, column, door or window frame. By grasping the tube firmly and jerking it, it will immediately be released from the cover, which remains hanging on the hook, leaving the tube open at the upper end and its contents free for immediate use. The dry powder is thrown into the fire by a sweeping motion in accordance with complete instructions furnished with each Fire Fighter. Anyone, even children, can use a Fire Fighter with perfect safety and never failing success. It will extinguish the fire, not in five minutes or ten minutes, but instantaneously by blotting it out in a few seconds after proper application of the dry powder has been made.

No. 8K324 Fire Fighters, retailing everywhere at $3.00 each; our price, each, **$0.83**
3 for......(Not mailable)...... **2.20**

Copper and Nickel Polish.

Put up in paste form. No dust, no dirt, no grit, but a reliable and inexpensive preparation for cleaning and polishing copper, brass and nickel. A necessity to every particular housekeeper. Put up convenient for use in 1 and 2-ounce tin boxes.

No. 8K860 Price, 1-ounce box...**13c**
If by mail, postage extra, 3 cents.
No. 8K861 Price, 2-ounce box...**21c**
If by mail, postage extra, 5 cents.

Seroco Silver Polish.

A preparation for cleansing, renewing, polishing and preserving silver and all silver plated articles. This preparation will not evaporate and change with time, and the last drop in the bottle will be just as efficient as the first part used, giving the same brilliant polish and excellent results.

No. 8K865 Price, per bottle.....**14c**
Postage and tube extra, 13 cents.

Spot and Stain Eradicator.

(NON-INFLAMMABLE.)

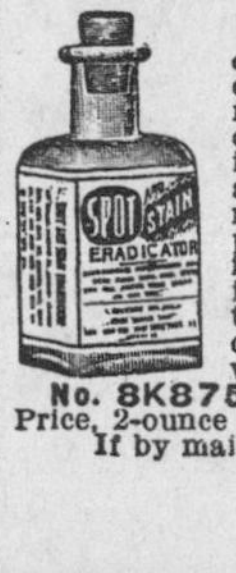

An absolute necessity for the careful housekeeper. The most efficient and safest liquid preparation for the prompt removal of spots and stains from clothing, carpets, linen, woolens and all kinds of fabrics. Will remove stains caused by iodine, paint, iron rust, fruit, etc. It is colorless, odorless and noninflammable. Guaranteed to do the work quickly and thoroughly. Complete directions with each bottle.

No. 8K875 Spot and Stain Eradicator. Price, 2-ounce bottle..............**14c**
If by mail, postage extra, 12 cents.

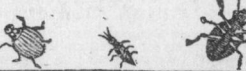

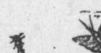

INSECTICIDES

QUICK DEATH BUG KILLER AND FERTILIZER.

Absolute Death to All Insect Life. Cheaper than Any other Insecticide Known. A Good Fertilizer. Any Child can Apply It. Not Dangerous to Handle. Ready for Immediate Use. No Mixing or Preparation Required.

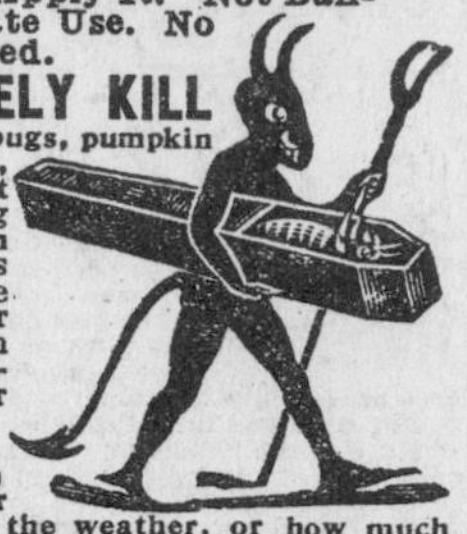

QUICK DEATH WILL POSITIVELY KILL potato bugs, squash bugs, pumpkin bugs, watermelon bugs, rose bugs, currant worms, cabbage worms, etc. It will kill all kinds of creeping things that eat the leaves of vegetables or plants. Quick Death has been on the market for six years, during which time it has met with unprecedented success wherever introduced all over the United States. It has proven to be the most successful destroyer of all insects, bugs or beetles that live on vegetation. We can recommend this preparation to our customers with every confidence; we can assure them it is a better and cheaper insect powder than they have ever used and it operates with certainty.

A GOOD CROP OF POTATOES, CABBAGE, or any other vegetable cannot be obtained, no matter how good your soil and seeds may be, or how favorable the weather, or how much labor or care you expend on them, unless the vines and leaves are kept vigorous and healthy. Such a condition cannot be kept up unless all insects and bugs are destroyed as fast as they appear. Any cause that injures the leaves hurts the plants, and anything that destroys the foliage affects the roots also and poisons the crops. Nothing, therefore, is more necessary than that the growing vines and trees be kept free from the ravages of insects and bugs.

QUICK DEATH KILLS POTATO BUGS IMMEDIATELY. The potato bug is the greatest enemy the potato grower has. This bug eats the leaves off the plants. He is fitted with powerful upper and under jaws and works the greatest ravages in a field of potatoes. Quick Death sprinkled on the leaves kills him with neatness and dispatch. Three crops of eggs are laid each year. Prompt action is therefore necessary. Just as soon as the potato bug makes his appearance, dust the potato vines thoroughly and carefully with Quick Death and your plants are safe from destruction. Kill off the first arrivals and you will have no further trouble, pursuing the same course in the case of other bugs and insects. Dust the leaves of the plants as soon as there is the slightest indication of their presence and save your crop from destruction.

THE WAY TO APPLY QUICK DEATH.

THE BEST WAY is to shake QUICK DEATH on the vine dry (never mix with water), early in the morning when the plants are damp with the dew, or otherwise, but do not apply it when the plants are dry. It can be applied with a sifter, or can be put on with a small burlap bag or sack made of moderately coarse cloth. In this way the powder is not unnecessarily wasted. Be on the lookout for the first appearance of the bugs, as at that time a few pounds will do the work of a much larger quantity later. One application will usually exterminate all the bugs for the entire season, but sometimes two applications are necessary.

AMOUNT NECESSARY. We recommend that you apply 10 to 15 pounds per acre for potatoes, but 20 to 30 pounds can be applied with safety and the expense of it will be many times returned in the greatly increased crop.

EVERY POTATO GROWER, every cabbage grower, every farmer, every market gardener, every grower of roses and flowers and plants of any kind, should give QUICK DEATH a fair trial. If it is once used, it will always be used. DO NOT FAIL TO GIVE IT A TRIAL.

SPECIAL PRICES:

No. 8K2035	Quick Death. Per 5-pound package,	$0.22
No. 8K2036	Quick Death. Per 10-pound package,	.39
No. 8K2037	Quick Death. Per 25-pound package,	.87
No. 8K2038	Quick Death. Per 50-pound package,	1.55
No. 8K2039	Quick Death. Per 100-pound package,	3.10
No. 8K2040	Quick Death. Per 300-pound barrel,	8.25

LIQUID FORMALDEHYDE PREVENTS SMUT

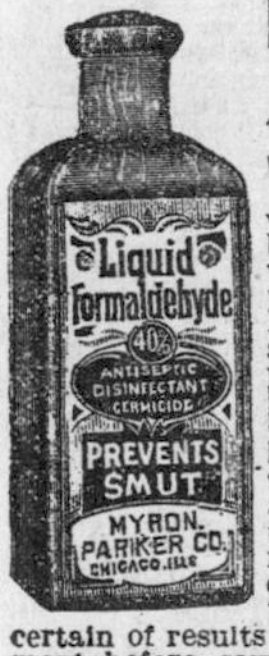

RECOMMENDED BY U. S. GOVERNMENT

AS A PREVENTIVE OF SMUT IN WHEAT, OATS, BARLEY AND OTHER GRAINS, ALSO OF THE POTATO SCAB.

VERY LOW IN COST. A very small expense, for one pint is sufficient to use in fifty gallons (a barrel) of water. Used in a very simple manner. Just spread your seed out on the barn floor and sprinkle with the Formaldehyde after it has been diluted with water, one part of Formaldehyde to ten thousand parts of water (about a pint to a barrel of water), then let the seed dry before sowing or planting. In this way, at the very small expense of a few cents, you can treat your seed and protect your crop of wheat, oats, barley, etc., from smut and your potatoes from scab in the most effective manner.

MILLIONS OF DOLLARS SAVED FOR FARMERS. Bulletin No. 91 of Wisconsin states that the loss from smut in the oat crop in the year 1901 in that state alone was approximately $6,387,500.00, and that all this vast sum of money could have been saved had the farmers treated their seed with Liquid Formaldehyde. Thousands of dollars are lost by the farmers every season in the loss of the crops caused by smut and other germ diseases. Formaldehyde treatment is the only preventive and cure, very much better than the poisonous sprays, has many advantages, always certain of results and is perfectly harmless. Every bushel of seed should receive this treatment before sowing, as it guarantees freedom from diseases and largely increased crops in every case. Wheat, oats, corn, barley, tobacco, cotton, flax and potatoes are all subject to certain destroying diseases, and for these, Formaldehyde is the only certain cure.

FULL 40 PER CENT SOLUTION. We guarantee our Liquid Formaldehyde to contain a full 40 per cent quantity of formaldehyde gas and is so recognized by the pure food and drug laws of every state. This cannot be said of many other formaldehyde solutions, which are diluted with water and which are thereby debarred from entering certain states. We guarantee our Liquid Formaldehyde to be full strength.

REMEMBER, with each package we send you a pamphlet, "Usefulness of Liquid Formaldehyde on the Farm," giving the various uses and dilutions necessary for best results. Don't fail to include a bottle with your next order.

No. 8K1995	Price, per pint	$0.31
No. 8K1996	Price, per gallon jug	1.83
No. 8K1998	Price, per dozen pints....(Unmailable on account of weight)	3.00

Sulphur Candles.

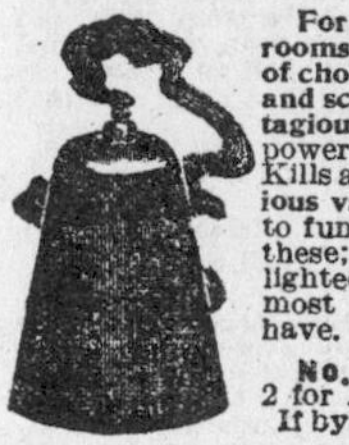

For fumigating infected rooms and clothing in times of cholera, diphtheria, typhoid and scarlet fevers and all contagious diseases. The most powerful disinfectant known. Kills all insects. Destroys noxious vapors. When you wish to fumigate with sulphur, use these; no danger of fire, easily lighted, burns steadily. A most convenient article to have.

No. 8K840 Price, 2 for........16c
If by mail, postage, extra, 5c.

Bed Bug Exterminator

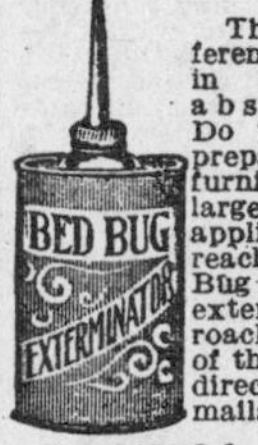

This product is entirely different from most other products, in being more effective and absolutely non-inflammable. Do you want the best? This preparation is in liquid form and furnished in a patent can with large spout, which makes its application easy and sure to reach the smallest opening. Bed Bug Exterminator will not only exterminate every bed bug and roach, but rid a room or building of these little pests entirely. Full directions with each can. Unmailable.

No. 8K894	Price, ½-pint can	$0.17
No. 8K895	Price, one pint	.27
No. 8K896	Price, one gallon	1.85

Flake Tar Moth Destroyer.

ALSO KNOWN AS CHEMICAL CAMPHOR.

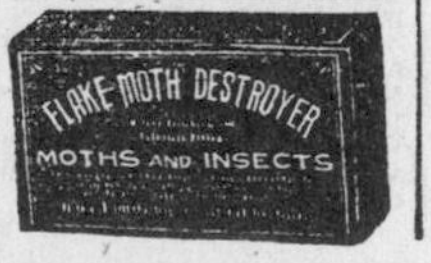

A chemically pure product of coal tar for the preservation of furs, clothing, etc., from moths. It will not injure the most delicate fabrics and is a certain preventive of moth attacks which are so destructive to clothing, woolen goods especially.

No. 8K885 Price, 1-lb. package........9c
If by mail, postage extra, 18 cents.

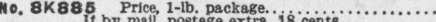

The Daisy Fly Killer.

The Cleanest, Best and Most Effective Fly Killer Known. It is a Beauty.

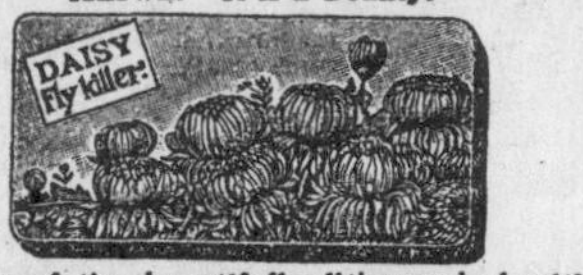

Made of tin, beautifully lithographed with daisies in colors attracting the flies and they drinking the poison through the small sponge in center of each daisy. Will not injure or soil anything. Will effectually kill flies in a room. HARMLESS TO PERSONS.

Will last all the season. It is cheaper than fly paper, clean, neat, ornamental. Try it.

No. 8K910 Price, each........$0.13
Per dozen........1.25
If by mail, postage extra, each, 4 cents.

Sticky Fly Paper.

We guarantee absolutely that STICKY will catch flies all the time.

It will bear exposure and remain in a fly catching condition indefinitely. Having stuck them, it holds them there. They cannot pull away.

IT WILL NOT GRANULATE OR DRY UP.

No. 8K912 Packed 25 double sheets to carton. Regular price, 75 cents.
Our price, per carton........38c

Poison Fly Paper.

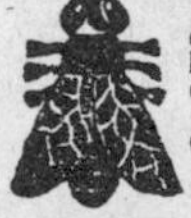

Guaranteed one of the strongest and most effective Poison Fly Papers on the market. Put up eight sheets in each envelope.

No. 8K915 Price, 4 envelopes for........9c
Per dozen envelopes........20c
Unmailable.

Rat Killer.

THE GREAT VERMIN DESTROYER.

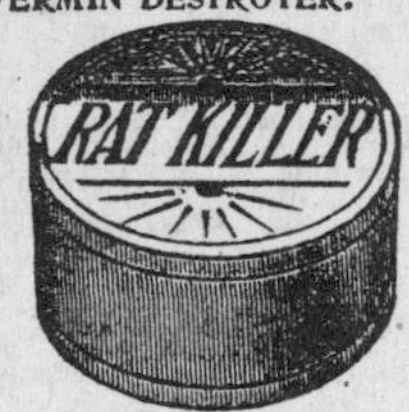

The most efficient poison for rats, mice, cockroaches, ants, flies, squirrels, crows, bed bugs, and all kinds of troublesome vermin. This is a sure destroyer. Rats and mice do not die in the house after eating it, but go outside for air and water.

No. 8K925 Price, per box........8c
This article being poisonous, cannot be sent through the mail.

Acme Roach Powder.

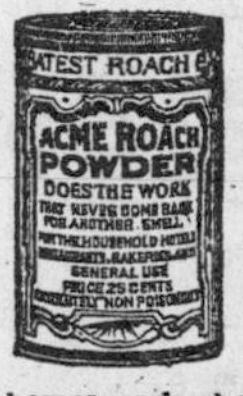

A powder that really kills roaches. Are you troubled with roaches, water bugs, or other troublesome pests? Buy Acme Roach Powder at once. It will quickly kill them and prevent their return. We have tried the powder to demonstrate claims of the manufacturer and give you our word it is the only roach powder to our knowledge that actually does the work. Should be used by all bakeries, restaurants, hotels and homes, and wherever the pest is found. We will guarantee the results. Regular price, per can, 25 cents.

No. 8K927 Our price. (Unmailable). 18c

Insect Powder.

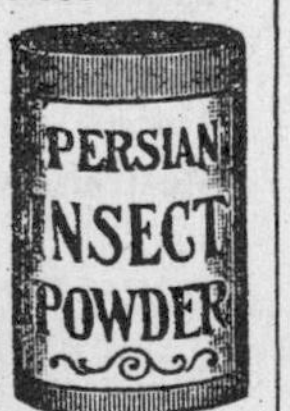

A true Dalmatian Insect Powder, warranted free from all adulterations. Fresh and strong. Sure death to bed bugs, croton bugs, potato bugs, cockroaches, fleas, lice, moths, flies, ants and all insects. This article is very much subject to adulteration. Buy from us and get it pure.

No. 8K929 Price, ¼-lb. carton........12c
No. 8K930 Price, 1-lb. carton........30c
Unmailable.

Insect Powder Gun.

For using Insect Powder No. 8K930.

No. 8K934 Price........3c
If by mail, postage extra, 4 cents.

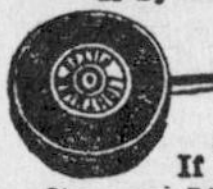

Large or Jumbo Powder Gun, holds ¼ pound of powder, button and spout screw off. Large opening for filling.

No. 8K935 Price......14c
If by mail, postage extra, 6 cents.

Acme Moth-Proof Powder.

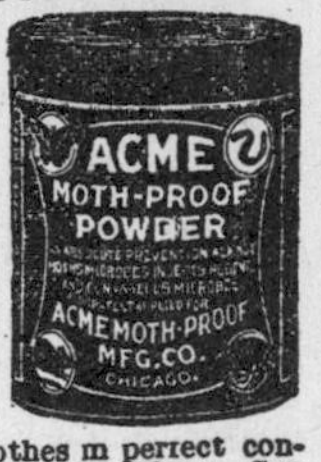

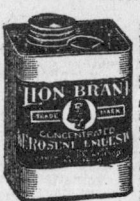

An absolute prevention against moths, microbes, insects, rodents or any other insect affecting cloth. Unsurpassed for the storing and keeping of furs and wearing apparel and guaranteed to keep them free from all insects. It is a mixture of long tried ingredients and not a simple compound like others on the market. This powder not only disinfects and purifies the clothes but also kills foreign odors, cleanses and keeps the clothes in perfect condition. Does not oil or spot like others. Can be brushed clean in a moment.

No. 8K944 Price, 10-cent size....8c
No. 8K945 Price, 25-cent size....18c
Both sizes unmailable.

Paris Green, Powder Form.

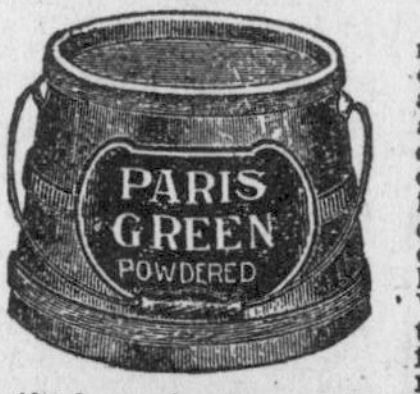

Paris Green is recognized as one of the most important insecticides and is used for destroying insects of all kinds, either in wet or dry conditions, but in all cases it is first largely diluted. When it is used in the dry or powder form, it should be mixed with plaster, sifted wood ashes or flour. The strength of the mixture should depend upon the plants and insects to which it is to be applied but at no time should more than 1 pound of Paris Green be added to 50 pounds of mixture, as that is usually sufficient. Care should be taken when using Paris Green mixed with water that the liquid is constantly stirred up when it is used for spraying, as otherwise the Paris Green will settle and the last quantity in the bottom of the cask will be so strong as to be liable of doing serious damage.

No. 8K2002 Price, per pound..28c
No. 8K2003 Per 2-pound package. Price, per pound........27c
No. 8K2004 Per 5-pound package. Price, per pound........27c
No. 8K2005 Price, per pound in 14, 28 and 56-pound kits........27c
No. 8K2006 Price, per pound in 100-pound kegs........26c
The above prices are subject to market changes.

Seroco Sifter.

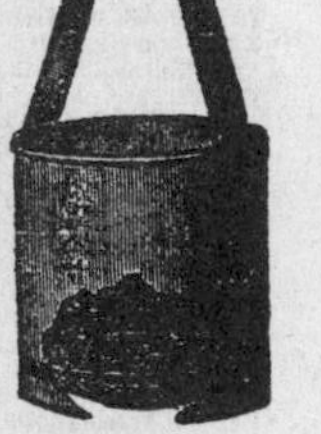

The illustration here shown represents the Seroco Sifter with which to apply the famous Quick Death and other dry powder insecticides. To obtain best results fill the sifter only about half full. This sifter is positively the best on the market. Patent applied for.

No. 8K2045 Seroco Sifter. 2-quart.
Price........29c
Unmailable.

Kerosene Emulsion.

CONCENTRATED.

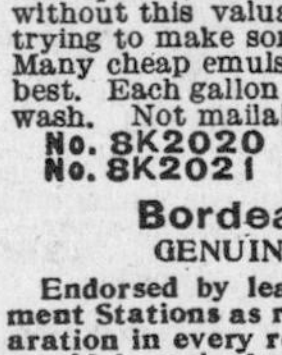

A perfect, reliable and safe concentrated emulsion that does not separate. Can be reduced by adding ten to thirty parts of water, and is at all times ready for use. The trouble with so many so called emulsions, as well as formulas handed out by experimental stations is that they do not make a perfect emulsion and when diluted with water part of the kerosene separates, and in spraying you get clear kerosene in some parts and clear water in others. The clear water has no effect and the clear oil damages the plant or leaves. Buy the only safe, reliable, perfect and effective emulsion. Will kill all suctorial insects, such as plant lice, bark lice, and all true bugs, as tree bugs, squash bugs, red spiders, scabs, mealy bugs. Do not go without this valuable remedy or waste time trying to make something like it. You can't. Many cheap emulsions are offered, but buy the best. Each gallon can sufficient for 50 gallons wash. Not mailable on account of weight.

No. 8K2020 Price, per quart can, 35c
No. 8K2021 Price, per gallon can, 89c

Bordeaux Mixture.

GENUINE LION BRAND.

Endorsed by leading Agricultural Experiment Stations as reliable and a superior preparation in every respect. Compounded from an old formula, but by a new process, making a usable and practical mixture, and by simply adding water and stirring it is ready for use. Destroys all fungus growth on vegetation, prevents blight, rot, mildew and rust. Should be diluted fifty times with water before using. Actual cost of spray less than 1 cent per gallon. Use little or much, remainder is always ready for use. The only Bordeaux mixture that has stood the test of years. Do not waste your time and money on cheap and worthless products. The easiest man convinced is the one who has seen the results of spraying on his neighbor's potatoes, grape or cucumber vines. The results are very profitable. You cannot afford to be without it.

No. 8K2025	Price, per quart can,	$0.35
No. 8K2026	Price, per gallon can,	.89
No. 8K2027	Price, per 5-gal. can,	4.00

California Wash.

LIME, SULPHUR AND SALT.

Used by thousands of fruit growers and recommended by all the leading experimental stations. Millions of fruit trees are being destroyed annually by the San Jose scale and millions of others are infested with it and are the breeding places for others. Use California Wash and stop the spread of the pest. One gallon makes 20 to 40 gallons, depending on trees to be sprayed. Always ready for use by simply adding water. Use what you want out of can; balance good at any time. Trees should be sprayed first time in March or April and a few weeks later go over them a second time to be sure every part is covered. Reasonable in price, effective in results, keeps permanently. You cannot afford to be without it.

No. 8K2015	Price, per quart can,	$0.35
No. 8K2016	Price, per gallon can,	.89
No. 8K2017	Price, per 5-gallon can	4.00

SYRINGES, WATER BOTTLES AND DOUCHES

Gem Fountain Syringe.
GUARANTEED FULL CAPACITY

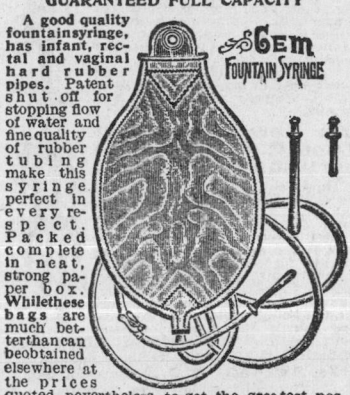

A good quality fountain syringe, has infant, rectal and vaginal hard rubber pipes. Patent shut off for stopping flow of water and fine quality of rubber tubing make this syringe perfect in every respect. Packed complete in neat, strong paper box. While these bags are much better than can be obtained elsewhere at the prices quoted, nevertheless, to get the greatest possible value for your money, we advise you by all means to add 50 cents to $1.00 extra and order one of the Never Leak or "Wearever" syringes. In rubber goods especially it pays to buy the best. All rubber goods being employed for personal use cannot, for sanitary reasons, if once used, be returned for exchange or credit.

No. 8K2300 2 quarts. Our price..70c
No. 8K2301 3 quarts. Our price..81c
No. 8K2302 4 quarts. Our price..88c
If by mail, postage extra, 16 cents.

No. 8K2305 2-quart Gem, in neat, finely polished wooden box.................92c
No. 8K2306 3-quart Gem, in neat, finely polished wooden box (Postage extra, 21c.)$1.03
No. 8K2307 4-quart Gem, in neat, finely polished wooden box.................$1.10

Our Guaranteed Rapid Flow Perfection Fountain Syringe.

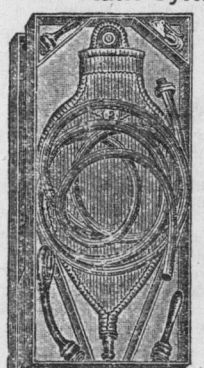

GUARANTEED FULL CAPACITY.
The Rapid Flow Syringe is fitted with ¼-inch tubing for flushing, and for this reason is a special favorite. Four hard rubber screw pipes, infant, rectal, bent vaginal and irrigator. The bag is full capacity, made from heavy white ribbed rubber, heavily reinforced seams and fully guaranteed. Packed in fine box, wrapped and complete, at one-half usual price charged. All rubber goods being employed for personal use cannot for sanitary reasons, if once used, be returned for exchange or credit.

No. 8K2310 2 quarts. Price...$1.08
No. 8K2311 3 quarts. Price... 1.17
No. 8K2312 4 quarts. Price... 1.20
If by mail, postage extra, 27 cents.

Imperial Rapid Flow Fountain Syringe.
GUARANTEED FULL CAPACITY.

A Combination Syringe and Hot Water Bottle. Is fitted with three hard rubber, rapid flow slip pipes, including infant, rectal and bent vaginal pipes. Quarter-inch fine quality tubing, with rolled end or socket for the pipes. Patent shut off and hard rubber combination attachment. The hot water bottle is made of a fine quality white rubber, handsomely embossed with floral design. Each packed complete in handsome flat box with partition for pipes. For sanitary reasons, syringes, being used for personal purposes cannot, if once used, be returned for credit or exchange.

No. 8K2315 2 quarts. Price..$1.50
No. 8K2316 3 quarts. Price... 1.60
If by mail, postage extra, 32 cents.

THE FAULTLESS "WEAREVER" COMBINATION SYRINGE AND HOT WATER BOTTLE

GUARANTEED FULL CAPACITY. AN UP TO DATE DEPARTURE FROM ANTIQUATED IDEAS.

AN ARTICLE combining the best features of the most approved style of fountain syringes, together with the advantages of a durable and serviceable hot water bottle. Made from the finest of maroon rubber, tastefully trimmed and reinforced with specially selected native black rubber, making it the most attractive combination on the market. We add to the bottle a generous length of pure red rubber tubing, harmonizing with the general color scheme and quality; a patent shut off. Four pipes of extra fine quality hard rubber, consisting of one infant pipe, one rectal pipe, one fluted and bent vaginal pipe, and one fluted irrigator pipe, all of which have been made according to designs furnished by the foremost physicians. Our purpose in making this the most durable as well as attractive article of its kind ever offered has been carried even to the accessories. This combination should not be compared to any other on the market. In a class by itself. Its demonstrated positive merits have made it already the most popular and best seller ever offered. The very best in quality and attractiveness and efficiency. Will outwear any three of the cheaper kind and can always be depended upon when needed. It pays to buy the best. All syringes being used for personal purposes cannot, after once used, be returned for credit or exchange, unless defective in some particular.

No. 8K2320 2 quarts. Regular price, $2.65; our price.................$1.95
No. 8K2321 3 quarts. Regular price, $3.25; our price.................. 2.20
If by mail, postage extra, 21 cents.

Acme Bulb Syringe.

No. 8K2335 Acme Bulb Syringe. Put up in a nice pasteboard box. Good quality rubber, two hard rubber pipes. This item being for personal use cannot, if once used, be returned for credit. Drug store price, 50c for same quality. Our price. (Postage extra, 10c.)..37c

Faultless Never Leak Syringe.
THE BEST THAT MONEY CAN BUY.

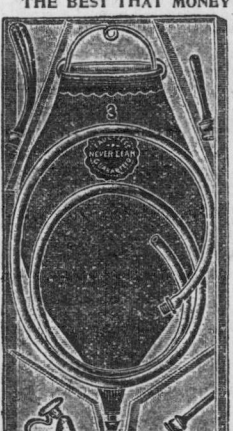

Very latest and up to date syringe made, thoroughly guaranteed. Perfectly sanitary. Wide opening for the water. Non-corrosive metal handle which is a splendid feature. You can hang this syringe anywhere. Very attractive in appearance. Absolutely seamless in construction, consequently cannot leak. Made of the very best quality rubber and practically indestructible. Three screw pipes, infant, rectal and vaginal. Five and one-half feet very best rubber tubing. Patent shut off. By reason of its shape and rapid flow outlet, this bag will empty quicker than any other syringe made. Just as the name indicates, faultless in every particular. This syringe will give satisfaction in every case. It is as good as fine material and workmanship can produce; as perfect as money can buy. Fully guaranteed. Regular price, $2.00 and $2.50.

No. 8K2325 2 quarts. Price..$1.50
No. 8K2326 3 quarts. Price.. 1.70
If by mail, postage extra, 21 cents.

"Wearever" Water Bottle.

This beautiful attractive water bottle is made of the same high grade "Wearever" maroon rubber as used in Wearever combination, tastefully trimmed and reinforced with specially selected native black rubber. Wearever stands for all its name would indicate. Beautiful in appearance and quality, absolutely guaranteed. Positively the best value and highest grade on the market for the prices quoted. Full capacity.

No. 8K2405 2 quarts. Regular price, $1.75. Our price.........$1.20
No. 8K2406 3 quarts. Regular price, $2.00. Our price..........$1.30
If by mail, postage extra, 16c.

Never Leak Water Bottle.
THE BEST THAT MONEY CAN BUY.

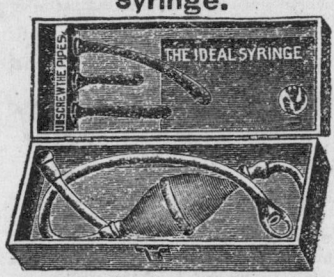

Very latest and up to date bottle made. Handsome in appearance, being made of pure gum red rubber; absolutely seamless in construction, consequently cannot leak. Perfectly sanitary, with wide opening for filling. Covers a larger surface when filled than any other water bottle made, thus giving a more uniform application of heat, which point particularly is a marked advantage. Practically indestructible, just as the name indicates, faultless in every particular. The kind you will be pleased to show and recommend to your friends. No description can do this bottle justice. Should be in every home. Regular price, $2.50.

No. 8K2408 Our price.........$1.55
If by mail, postage extra, 16 cents.

Flannel Covered Water Bottle.

Our Flannel Covered Hot Water Bottles are the most perfect made. Are pure gum rubber with fine flannel cover which keeps an even temperature and will not irritate the most delicate skin. Guaranteed perfect in every respect. If once used cannot be returned for credit unless defective. This is your protection as well as our own.

No. 8K2385 2 quarts. Price....88c
No. 8K2386 3 quarts. Price....99c
If by mail, postage extra, 15 cents.

Excelsior Hot Water Bottle.

All rubber, embossed floral design, exceptional value. Each in a box. Fully guaranteed. While these bags are much better than can be obtained elsewhere at 25 to 50 cents extra, to get the greatest possible value for your money we advise you by all means to add a small advance and obtain one of our higher price bags. If once used cannot be returned for credit unless defective. This is your protection as well as our own.

No. 8K2390 2 quarts. Price....72c
No. 8K2391 3 quarts. Price....77c
If by mail, postage extra, 2 quarts, 11 cents; 3 quarts, 13 cents.

Our 65-Cent Ideal Syringe.

No. 8K2340 The Celebrated Ideal Syringe, with three hard rubber screw pipes, put up in a neat wooden box. This item being for personal use cannot, if once used, be returned for credit. Druggists usually ask $1.00 for this syringe. Our price..........55c
If by mail, postage extra, 12 cents.

THE SPLENDID REDUCTIONS IN PRICE made by us in this catalogue must prove to our customers our ability to undersell all competition.

Eye, Ear and Ulcer Syringe.

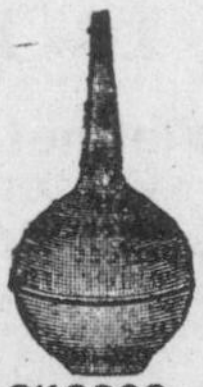

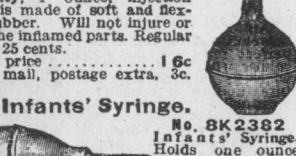

No. 8K2380 Eye, Ear, Ulcer and Abscess Syringe. Capacity, 1 ounce; injection pipe is made of soft and flexible rubber. Will not injure or pain the inflamed parts. Regular price, 25 cents.
Our price **16c**
If by mail, postage extra, 3c.

Infants' Syringe.

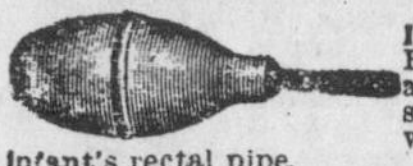

No. 8K2382 Infants' Syringe. Holds one ounce and is made of a soft rubber bulb, with hard rubber infant's rectal pipe.
Price ..(Postage extra, 5 cents) **17c**

Teething Rings.

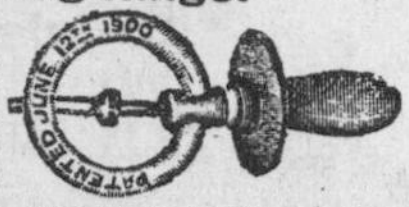

New Style Teething Ring or Pacifier. The new style teething ring or pacifier is a bone ring and bone guard with a soft rubber nipple, having a silk cord for attaching to the baby's arm so the ring cannot be lost. Regular price, each, 15 cents. Should always have two in the house.
No. 8K2122 Our price, 2 for **16c**
If by mail, postage extra, each, 2 cents.

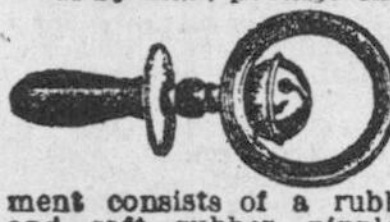

Combination Teething Ring or Pacifier with Bell Attachment. The combination teething ring or pacifier with bell attachment consists of a rubber ring, bone guard and soft rubber nipple. It pacifies and amuses the baby at the same time. Should always have two in the house. Regular price, 10 cents each.
No. 8K2126 Our price, 2 for...... **15c**
If by mail, postage extra, each, 2 cents.

The Whistling Bird Rattle and Pacifier.

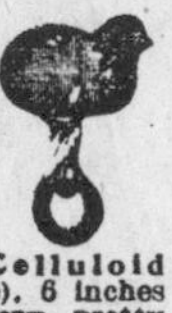

This Rattle is made of pure white rubber, and will amuse and entertain the baby. It has a teething ring at handle end, making it doubly valuable. Regular price, 15 cents.
No. 8K2128 Our price . **11c**
If by mail, postage extra, 2 cents.

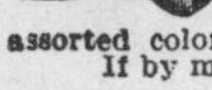

No. 8K2130 Celluloid Rattle (with whistle), 6 inches long, comes in very pretty assorted colors. Price **20c**
If by mail, postage extra, 5 cents.

Glass Nipple Shield.

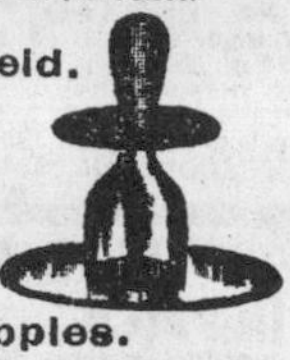

Glass Nipple Shield with white rubber nipple and bone guard.
No. 8K2160
Price **8c**
Unmailable.

Rubber Nipples.

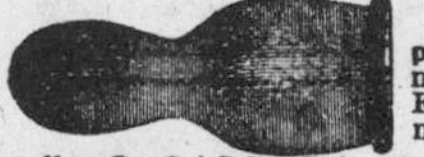

Best Rubber Nipples to fit over nursing bottle. Furnished only in maroon.
No. 8K2135 Price, 6 for......... **18c**
If by mail, postage extra, for six, 4 cents.

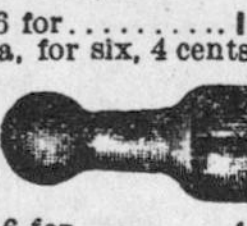

Health Nipples. Made from the finest Para rubber, is constructed so that the infant can obtain a strong hold and renders nursing easy.
No. 8K2136 Price, 6 for......... **18c**
If by mail, postage extra, for six, 4 cents.

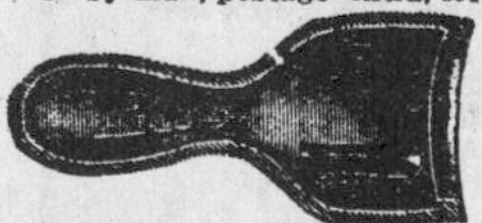

Mizpah Valve Nipple. Making nursing easy. Allows the food to flow easily. Prevents colic. Regular price, 10 cents each.
No. 8K2140 Our price, each **7c**
Per dozen **75c**
If by mail, postage extra, for six, 4 cents.

Kant-Choke Nipple.

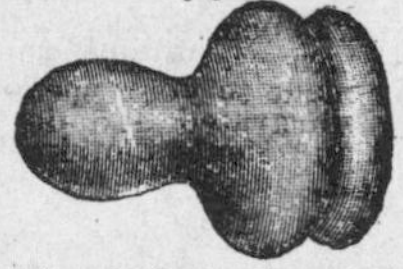

The latest invention in a nipple. Easily fits nursing bottles, but on account of peculiar construction cannot be removed by direct pulling, thus preventing children spilling the milk. The length of the nipple is short thus preventing choking. Once used you would have no other. Regular price, 10 cents each.
No. 8K2141 Our price, 3 for ... **21c**
If by mail, postage extra, for three, 4 cents.

Sterilized Antiseptic Nipple.

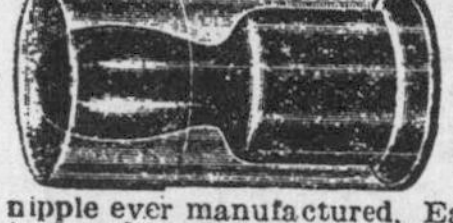

These nipples are the famous Seamless Sterilized Nipples. Made of the very best material, absolutely pure gum, and by far the very best nipple ever manufactured. Each one is sterilized and packed in airproof gelatine capsule so as to keep them perfectly free from all disease germs or other contamination. By using these nipples received in this condition, you need have no fear of giving your baby any diseases.
No. 8K2138 Price, 2 for.......... **17c**
If by mail, postage extra, for two, 2 cents.

Graduated Nursing Flasks.

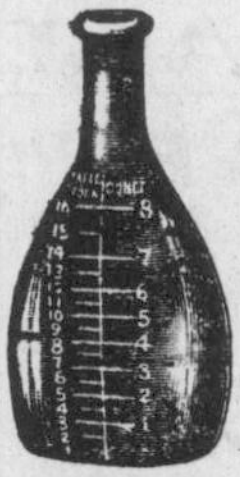

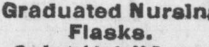

Graduated to hold 8 ounces, oval shape, straight with sloping sides. No corners, therefore easy to clean. As nursing bottles are easily broken it is always best to have two in stock. Weight, 14 ounces.
No. 8K2144 Price, 2 for **8c**
Unmailable.

Nursing Bottle Fittings.

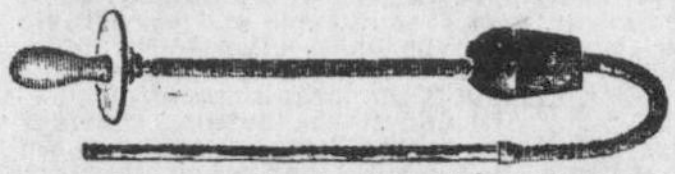

Best quality, all complete, in white, black or maroon.
No. 8K2164 Price, 2 for **8c**
If by mail, postage extra, 4 cents.

Hygeia Nursing Bottle.

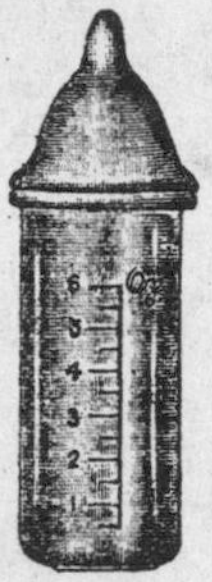

The most up to date, cleanly, antiseptic Nursing Bottle, and the only one with a breast attachment. Easy to clean and fill. Bottle is without a neck or angle, needs no brush to clean or funnel to fill and can be wiped out like a tumbler. Rubber attachment is large, soft and yielding like the mother's breast. Babies do not detect the difference and hence can be weaned from the breast without a struggle. 6 ounces capacity. Retail price, 50 cents.
No. 8K2150 Our price, bottle complete **31c**
No. 8K2151 Extra breasts or bottles can be supplied.
Price **17c**
Unmailable.

S., R. & Co.'s Complete Nurser.

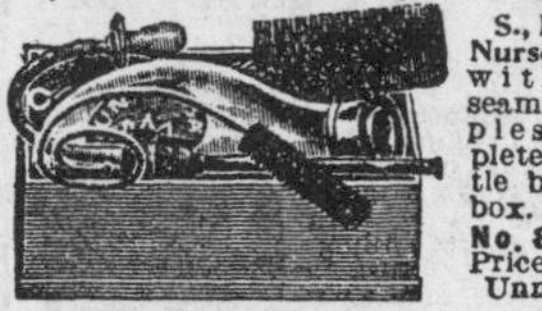

S., R. & Co.'s Nurser. Fitted with good seamless nipples. Complete with bottle brush in box.
No. 8K2153
Price **15c**
Unmailable.

Yankee Bottle Brush.

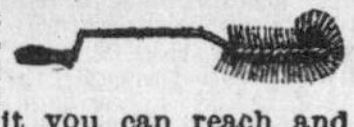

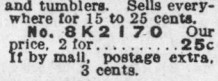

The most ingenious and practically constructed, general all around cleaning brush ever produced. With it you can reach and clean every bend, every corner; in fact, all shapes of inner and outer surfaces of fruit jars, water bottles, milk bottles, chimneys, caster bottles, graduates, sterilizing bottles, molasses pitchers and tumblers. Sells everywhere for 15 to 25 cents.
No. 8K2170 Our price, 2 for **25c**
If by mail, postage extra, 3 cents.

English Breast Pump.

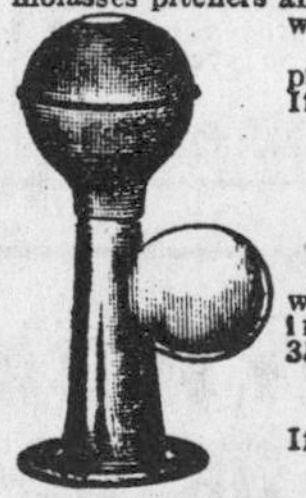

English Breast Pump, with white rubber bulb. One in box. Regular price, 35 cents.
No. 8K2172
Our price **25c**
If by mail, postage extra, 8 cents.

Sterilized Rubber Sheeting.

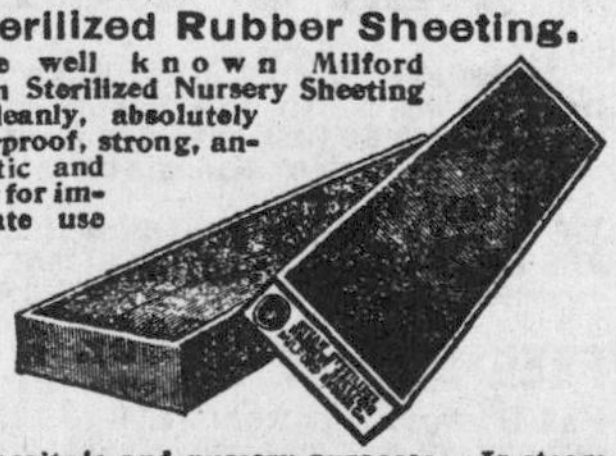

The well known Milford Steam Sterilized Nursery Sheeting is cleanly, absolutely waterproof, strong, antiseptic and ready for immediate use for hospitals and nursery purposes. Is steam sterilized before being packed, carefully wrapped in antiseptic paper and placed in a light telescope box and sealed. The only sheeting offered where same is cleanly and steam sterilized. Cut in squares of assorted sizes and packed one square in a box.

No. 8K2183	Square,	¾x¾ yd.,	**$0.39**
No. 8K2184	Square,	1x1 yd.,	**.57**
No. 8K2184½	Piece,	1x2 yds.,	**.97**
No. 8K2185	Square,	1¼x1¼ yd.,	**.89**
No. 8K2185½	Square,	1½x1½ yd.,	**1.25**

No. 8K2186 Tan cambric coated with pure rubber, soft as silk, finest made, 1 yard square **79c**
No. 8K2186½ Piece Tan, 1x2 yds. Price, (Postage extra, per yard, 18c.) **$1.47**

Rubber Tubing.

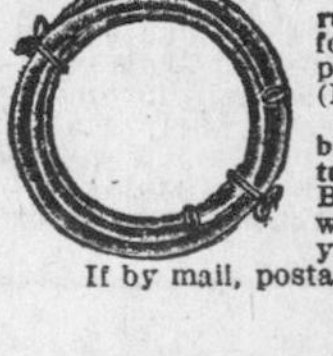

No. 8K2189 Corrugated, for bulb and fountain syringes. Price, per 5½-foot length .**32c**
(Postage extra, 15 cents.)
No. 8K2191 White, black or maroon rubber tubing for nursing bottles. Be sure to state color wanted. Sold only in 1-yard lengths. Price. **14c**
If by mail, postage extra, 10 cents.

Hygienic Sanitary Protector.

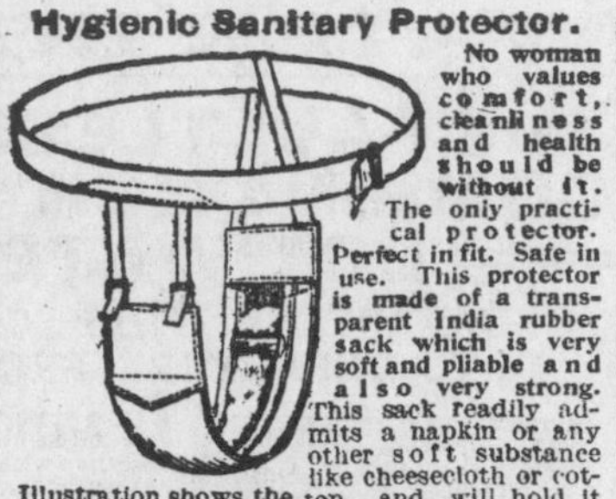

Illustration shows the napkin in place, ready for use.

No woman who values comfort, cleanliness and health should be without it. The only practical protector. Perfect in fit. Safe in use. This protector is made of a transparent India rubber sack which is very soft and pliable and also very strong. This sack readily admits a napkin or any other soft substance like cheesecloth or cotton and will hold it securely in the proper position. The belt is made of the very best lisle, non-elastic. The strap to which the sack is buckled is made of a superior grade of lisle elastic, which gives with the different movements of the body, thus keeping the protector always in the right place. It is perfectly sanitary, comfortable, pliable and non-irritating; easily adjusted and readjusted and indispensable to women walking, riding or traveling. Always clean and ready for use. Feels cool in summer and protects the wearer from cold in inclement weather. This protector will save many times its cost in washing and bleaching. It is absolutely waterproof and thereby positively prevents soiling of the underwear. Each protector comes put up in a neatly finished box with full and explicit directions. With proper use will last a lifetime. After use each month all that is necessary is to clean it with a damp cloth or sponge. In ordering give waist measure. Regular price, $1.00.
No. 8K3505 Our price **34c**
If by mail, postage extra, 3 cents.

Famous H. & H. Bust Forms.

The only bust form made which defies detection.

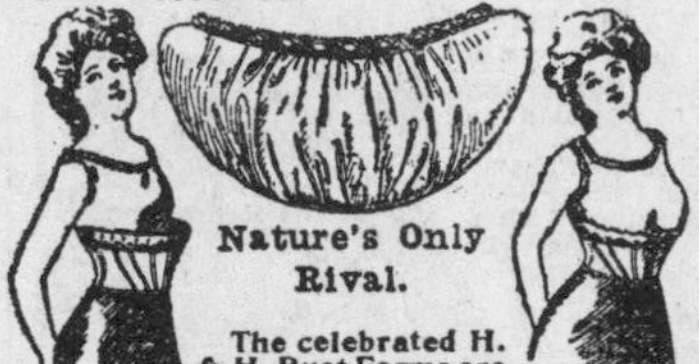

Nature's Only Rival.

The celebrated H. & H. Bust Forms are now so perfect that they cannot be detected from the natural bust, whether by sight or touch. Strikingly stylish, a source of relief, delight and pride to the wearer and of admiration to others. Very durable, economic and hygienic. These forms do away with all unsightly, unhealthy and uncomfortable padding. They produce perfectly the full bust and slender waist decreed by the latest fashion. Positively the only device which perfectly simulates flesh and blood. Applied in an instant; made of white rubber, invisible with any costume; neither sight nor touch reveals their use. They accurately fit the form, are enclosed in fine muslin cover, lace trimmed, cannot get out of place, and can be made any desired size. Be admired. A fine form is admired by all. Why then wear heavy pads, wire forms or be flat chested, all of which are unnatural and plainly detected when so natural a form as this is within your reach? Light as air, takes all the motions of the body and cannot be detected. Do not delay any longer, but buy a bust form, make it the desired size and have a perfect figure.
No. 8K2475 Price, round form .. **$1.37**
No. 8K2476 Price, oblong form, which fills out the hollows under the arm and more like natural bust **$1.83**
If by mail, postage extra, 8 cents.
No. 8K2477 Repair outfit for above. Our price.... (Postage extra, 3 cents.)... **17c**

Invalid Air Cushions.

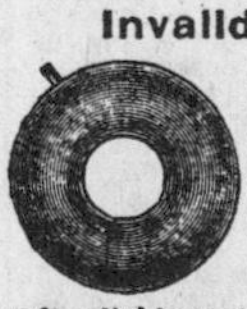

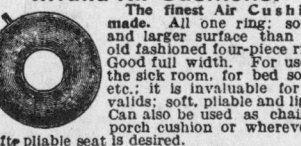

The finest Air Cushion made. All one ring; softer and larger surface than the old fashioned four-piece ring. Good full width. For use in the sick room, for bed sores, etc.; it is invaluable for invalids; soft, pliable and light. Can also be used as chair or porch cushion or wherever a soft pliable seat is desired.

No. 8K2420 12 inches diameter.
Price **$1.58**
No. 8K2421 14 inches diameter.
Price **1.78**
No. 8K2422 16 inches diameter.
Price **2.04**
No. 8K2423 18 inches diameter.
Price **2.20**
If by mail, postage extra, 20 cents.

Home Tooth Forceps.

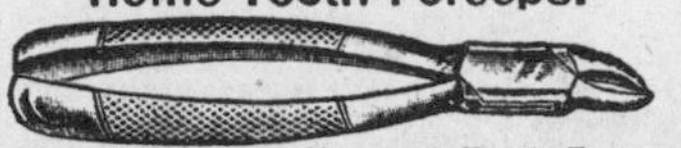

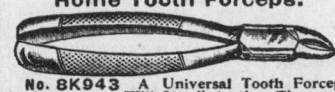

No. 8K943 A Universal Tooth Forceps for home use. Will fit all teeth. The same instrument as used by dentists. Can be used for extracting with ease all children's teeth and save all dentist's fees. Finely nickel plated. Price **$1.13**
If by mail, postage extra, 7 cents.

Soft Rubber Urinal Bags.

FOR MEN, WOMEN, BOYS AND GIRLS.

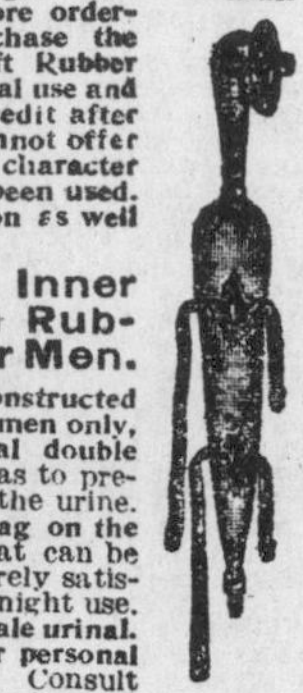

For bed wetting and general incontinence of urine. For male and female children and adults. For day and night use. Consult your family physician before ordering, that you may purchase the proper article, because Soft Rubber Urinal Bags are for personal use and cannot be returned for credit after leaving our store. We cannot offer for sale articles of this character which have or may have been used. This is for your protection as well as ours.

Our New Safety Inner Tube Pure Gum Rubber Urinal Bag For Men.

This Urinal Bag is constructed for day and night use, for men only, and is fitted with special double valve and inner tube, so as to prevent the return flow of the urine. This is the only urinal bag on the market for male use that can be guaranteed to prove entirely satisfactory for both day and night use. The only absolutely safe male urinal. Urinals being employed for personal use cannot be returned. Consult your physician before ordering. This is your protection as well as our own.
No. 8K2450 Price **$2.50**
If by mail, postage extra, 10 cents.

Our New Safety Inner Tube Pure Gum Rubber Urinal Bag.

FOR WOMEN.

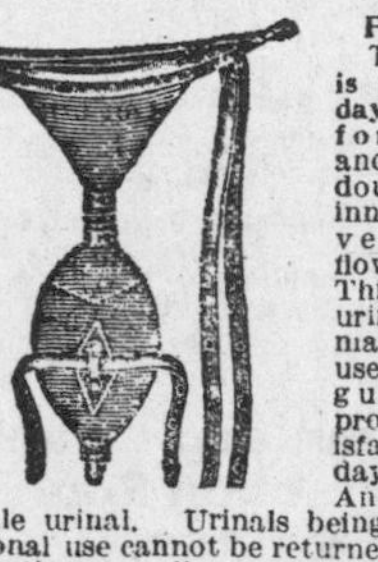

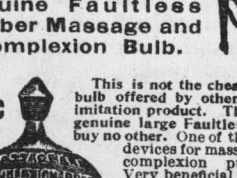

This Urinal Bag is constructed for day and night use, for women only, and is fitted with double valve and inner tube to prevent the return flow of the urine. This is the only urinal bag on the market for female use that can be guaranteed to prove entirely satisfactory for both day and night use. An absolutely safe female urinal. Urinals being employed for personal use cannot be returned. This is your protection as well as our own. Consult your physician before ordering. Regular price, $4.50.
No. 8K2451 Our price **$2.85**
If by mail, postage extra, 10 cents.

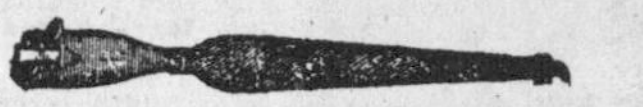

Soft Rubber Urinal Bag, the most comfortable pattern made, of the best material, for male, day or night use. The long tube fits in trouser leg and facilitates easy emptying. Urinals being employed for personal use cannot be returned. This is your protection as well as our own. Consult your physician before ordering. Regular price, $2.00.
No. 8K2453 Our price **$1.55**
No. 8K2454 Short, for boy .. **1.40**
If by mail, postage extra, 8 cents.

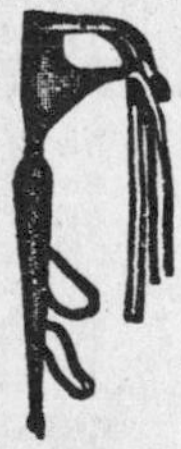

No. 8K2456 Soft Rubber Urinal Bag, day and night use for male; improved French Pattern, with waist belt ready to use without other attachments. Urinals being employed for personal use cannot be returned. This is your protection as well as our own. Consult your physician before ordering. Regular price, $3.50.
Our price **$2.55**
If by mail, postage extra, 20 cents.

Genuine Faultless Rubber Massage and Complexion Bulb.

28c

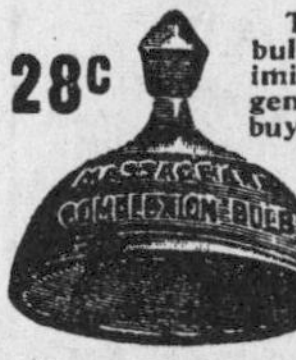

This is not the cheap small bulb offered by others as an imitation product. This is the genuine large Faultless bulb; buy no other. One of the latest devices for massage and complexion purposes. Very beneficial for filling out the hollows of the cheeks and making them plump and rosy. Very popular. Regular price, 50 cents.
No. 8K2458 Our price **28c**
If by mail, postage extra, 2 cents.

THE GREAT REDUCTIONS in the prices shown in the pages of this catalogue we feel sure will be very pleasing to our millions of customers.

OUR PAINT SAMPLE BOOKS ARE FREE, and if you are going to do any painting, don't think of ordering Ready Mixed House Paints of any kind until you have first sent for our free paint books. They describe Seroco Ready Mixed House Paints, the best house paints manufactured, guaranteed by us for ten years; made in our own paint factory and sold at about half the prices asked for Ready Mixed Paints which do not compare with Seroco Ready Mixed House Paints in spreading qualities, in brilliancy of color, luster and durability. Write us a postal card or a letter and say, "Send me your Paint Sample Books" and we will send them to you by return mail free and postpaid.

Genuine Faultless Beauty Brush for the Complexion.

32c

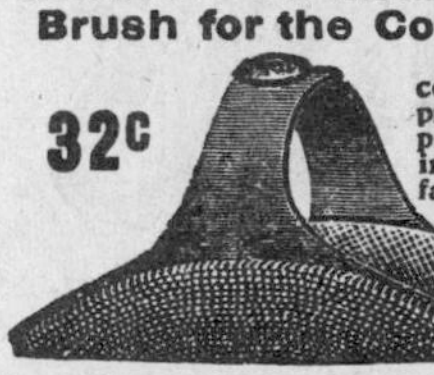

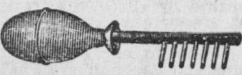

It is especially constructed for improving the complexion and removing all forms of facial blemishes. It removes all roughness and dead cuticle, smoothing out the wrinkles, rendering the skin soft, pliant, and tinted with a healthy glow. Let your skin breathe. If you have pimples, blackheads, blotches, freckles, etc., it is because your skin is choked with dirt and cannot breathe. Your skin, like your lungs, must breathe to be healthy. Cleanse the 12,965,832 pores of your skin and give them a chance to breathe. The most thorough, most sanitary and most efficient way to clean them is by using the famous Faultless Toilet Brush. It is designed especially for this purpose, has just the right texture to soften the dirt and coax it out from its hiding places without irritating the most delicate skin. Use this freely with old fashioned buttermilk soap and water and you will never again be troubled with skin blemishes. This is not the cheap kind often offered at a cheaper price, which is made square of black rubber, and a few days after use loses the teeth and becomes worthless. This is the genuine hand shaped famous Faultless maroon brush, guaranteed for one year. Remember, your complexion is at stake, therefore buy the best. Regular price, 50 cents.

No. 8K2460 Our price............32c
If by mail, postage extra, 3 cents.

Hair Growing Fountain Comb.

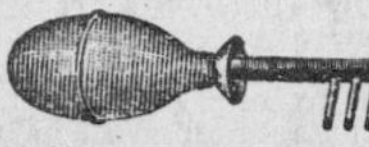

For applying hair tonics, eau de quinine, bleaches, etc. The comb being hollow and with pressure on the bulb the liquid will flow through the teeth to the scalp, applying the remedy to the roots of the hair where it will do the most good. The use of the comb will prevent getting tonic all through the hair unless it is desired to do so. You can apply the tonic rapidly and thoroughly without soiling the hands or badly ruffling up the hair. Every lady will appreciate this advantage. The comb may be used for applying bleaches to the hair by spraying. Packed complete in neat case with full directions for using.

No. 8K2465 Price...............74c
If by mail, postage extra, 8 cents.

OUR POSITION AS THE GREATEST MERCHANDISING INSTITUTION IN THE WORLD is emphasized by the wonderful REDUCTION IN PRICES which we have been able to make on thousands of articles quoted in this catalogue.

Wrinkle Eradicator.

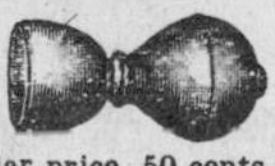

This convenient little article will remove wrinkles from around the eyes and nose and any part of the face. It invigorates the skin and keeps a perfect contour of the face. Regular price, 50 cents.

No. 8K2485 Our price...........28c
If by mail, postage extra, 6 cents.

Magic Flesh Builder and Cupper.

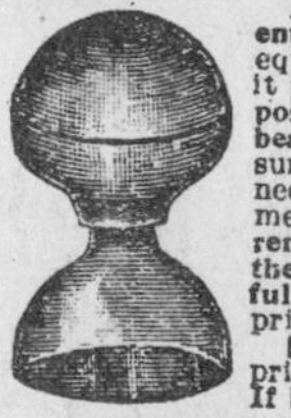

An entirely new and scientific invention. Has no equal as a developer. Makes it possible for every lady to possess a well rounded, plump, beautiful figure. Rebuilds sunken tissues of the bust, neck, arms, and the only method which permanently removes wrinkles and makes the sunken cheeks smooth, full and developed. Regular price, 50 cents.

No. 8K2490 Our price...........30c
If by mail, postage extra, 9c.

Faultless Toilet and Complexion Mask.

The Art of Beautifying the Complexion.

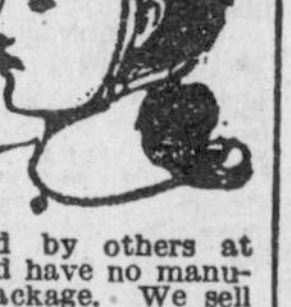

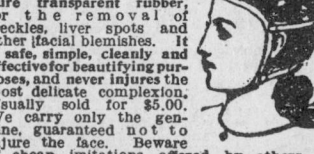

Many ladies praise the value of a mask made of pure transparent rubber, for the removal of freckles, liver spots and other facial blemishes. It is safe, simple, cleanly and effective for beautifying purposes, and never injures the most delicate complexion. Usually sold for $5.00. We carry only the genuine, guaranteed not to injure the face. Beware of cheap imitations offered by others at less prices, and when received have no manufacturer's name upon the package. We sell only the genuine Faultless mask. Made in three sizes, small, medium and large. Always state size desired.

No. 8K2492 Price.............$1.08
If by mail, postage extra, 4 cents.

OUR ALREADY LOWEST PRICES have been still FURTHER REDUCED in this Big Catalogue. Just compare the prices in this book with the prices quoted by us in previous catalogues and note the additional savings we make for you.

Famous Non-Pa-Reil Household Rubber Gloves.

86c

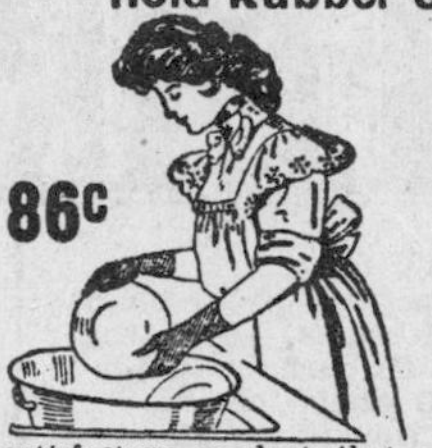

These Gloves are known the world over as the best household glove made. They are not the cheap grade sold at 35 to 75 cents a pair but the best glove manufactured. The name Non-Pa-Reil on rubber gloves stands for the best material and workmanship, the most satisfactory product that master craftsmen by the most modern methods have produced. If you ever wash dishes, scrub floors, develop photographic negatives, wash windows, trim plants, work in the garden, dye any fabrics, blacken stoves, do a hundred and one other household duties, then for your hands sake you need a pair of Non-Pa-Reil gloves. They keep the hands soft and white and are unequaled for ladies' use in doing general housework. They are strong, soft and pliable, and can be worn without the slightest inconvenience in doing work of the most delicate nature. Every pair fully guaranteed. Order one size larger than your kid glove number. These gloves are the best produced, and therefore if once used cannot be returned. Follow closely the directions for keeping them clean found on cover of each box. Especially note effect of oil and grease. Regular price, $1.25 per pair.

No. 8K2496 Our price, per pair...86c
If by mail, postage extra, per pair, 10 cents.

Chamois Skin.

There are many kinds of chamois skins upon the market. We have discontinued handling the cheap oil tanned yellow kind and now furnish nothing except the fine soft oil tanned world renowned skins. They cost about double the cheaper kind but are worth five times as much.

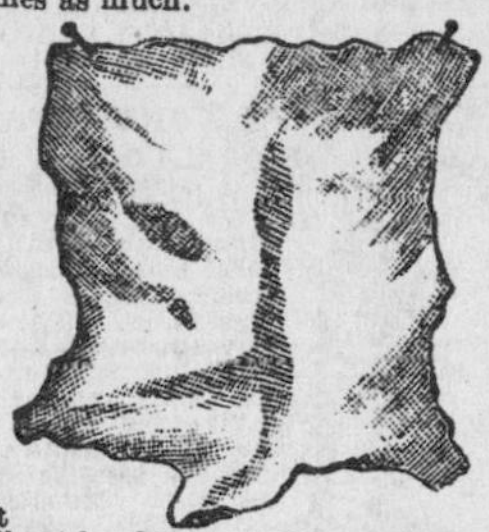

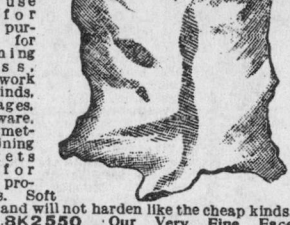

Chamois Skins are used as follows: Ladies use them for toilet purposes, for cleaning glass, wood work of all kinds, carriages, silverware, or any metal, lining pockets and for chest protectors. Soft as silk and will not harden like the cheap kinds.

No. 8K2550 Our Very Fine Face Chamois, for applying powder, etc., to the face. Size, about 5x6 inches. Price.......5c
No. 8K2551 Face Chamois. Size, 6½x 8½ inches.......9c
No. 8K2552 Size, 9x11 inches.......11c
Postage on any of the above, 3 cents.
No. 8K2553 Size, 12x12 inches..$0.18
No. 8K2554 Size, 17x17 inches.. .53
No. 8K2555 Size, 24x24 inches.. .95
No. 8K2556 Size, 29x29 inches.. 1.05
If by mail, postage extra, each, 6 cents.

Medicinal Atomizers.

38c

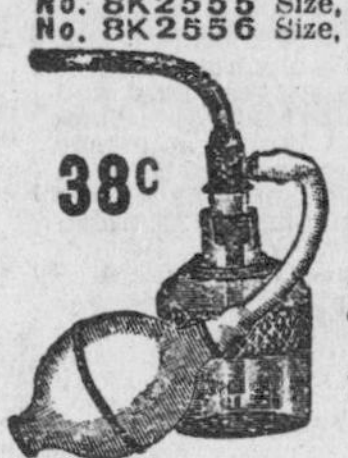

Atomizer for medicinal use. Hard rubber nozzle, rubber bulb of fine quality. Continuous spray.

No. 8K2650 Our price.........38c
If by mail postage extra, 14 cents.

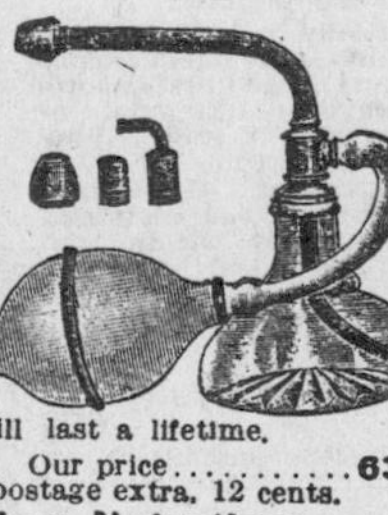

The most reliable and useful Atomizer in the world. Has three hard rubber tips. Can be used for disinfecting a sick room, or applying medicine to the throat or in the nose. It is made of the best materials, and with care will last a lifetime.

No. 8K2652 Our price............63c
If by mail, postage extra, 12 cents.

Atomizing Nebulizer.

$1.13

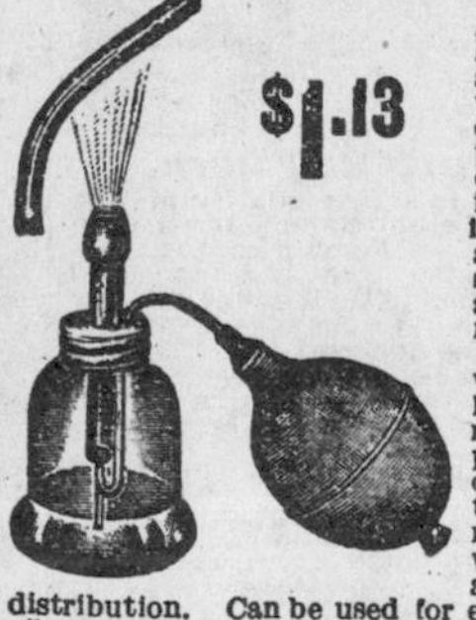

No. 8K174 Atomizing Nebulizer. This atomizer, which is a decided improvement over all other instruments of its kind, throws a very light spray, in fact, almost a nebula, being invaluable where a very light spray is required. Applies oils or other liquids to the entire nasal cavity without force and with equal distribution. Can be used for either water or oil sprays. The throat tube is so made that either end will fit the atomizer.

Price (If by mail, postage extra, 10c) $1.13

Perfume Atomizers.

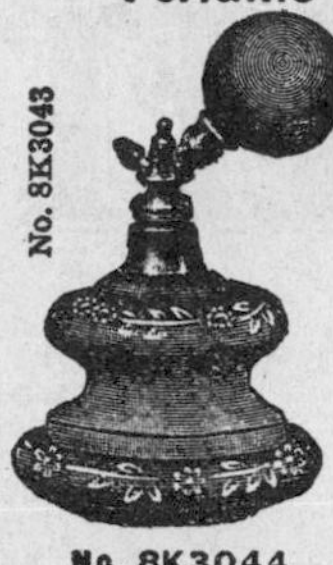

No. 8K3043 Fancy Shape Perfume Atomizer with raised floral design. Fitted with brass top and good red rubber bulb. Excellent value at our special price. Regular price, 50 cents.
Our price..........29c
Unmailable.

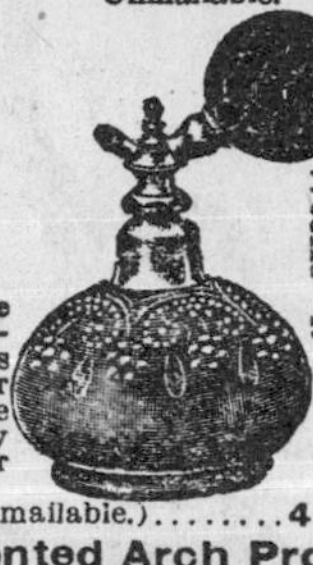

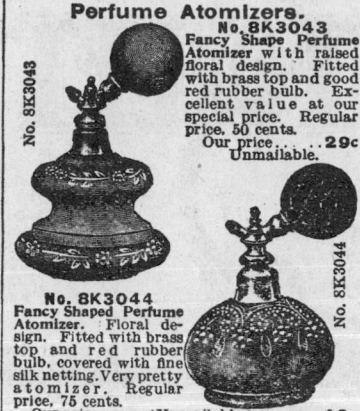

No. 8K3044 Fancy Shaped Perfume Atomizer. Floral design. Fitted with brass top and red rubber bulb, covered with fine silk netting. Very pretty atomizer. Regular price, 75 cents.
Our price......(Unmailable.)........40c

Dunbar's Patented Arch Prop for Flat Feet.

The Great Boon for Persons Troubled with Flat Feet, Broken Arch or Deformed Insteps.

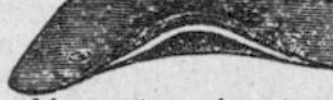

The Dunbar's Arch Prop is the very best made and is manufactured in various sizes to accommodate the various conditions of the feet. By persistent wearing of this new arch prop a normal condition of the foot is guaranteed. They can be worn without pain to the patient and no danger of the arch breaking or giving away. It is made of German silver and is the strongest and best arch on the market. In ordering, state whether for men or women, whether for right or left foot and whether low, medium or high arch is desired.

No. 8K2700 Regular price, per pair $3.00.
Our price, per pair $2.20
Single Arch, each...................1.25
If by mail, postage extra, 7 cents.

Silver Polishing Chamois.

ALWAYS READY, SAVES TIME AND MONEY FOR THE HOUSEWIFE.

Guaranteed for 5 years, if directions are followed. The cloth used by all jewelers.

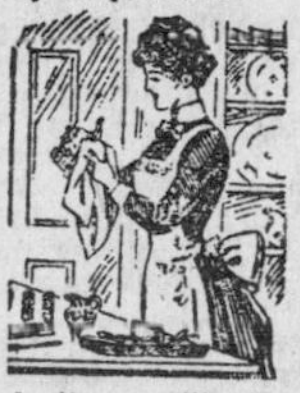

The Stilboma Chamois polisher for silverware and service. No polishing powder, polishing paste or polishing liquid required. With this especially prepared polishing chamois you can keep your tableware, gold, silver, and nickel clean and free from corrosion, tarnish, dirt, etc., by simply rubbing the articles with this cloth. Stilboma, although free from grit, when applied to tarnished silver, will give it a perfectly smooth, bright polished surface and a luster like new. It protects and preserves the metal and never scratches. This is the genuine Stilboma chamois used by jewelers the country over for polishing either silver or gold. Full directions with each package. Regular price, $1.00, each.

No. 8K880 Metal Polishing Chamois, the handy polisher. Price(Postage extra,6c.)..71c

Fischer Bunion Protector.

39c

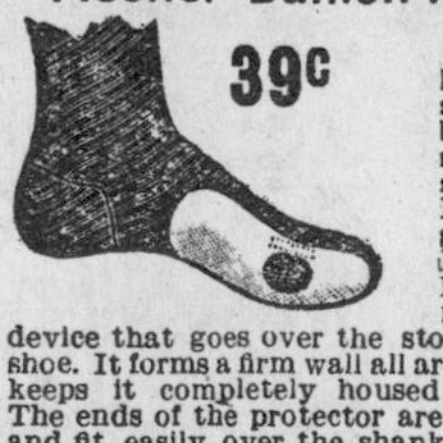

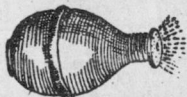

Fits all feet, relieves pain instantly; cures bunions permanently, and keeps shoes in shape. Perfect comfort guaranteed. The Fischer Bunion Protector is a neat, soft leather device that goes over the stocking inside the shoe. It forms a firm wall all around the bunion, keeps it completely housed and protected. The ends of the protector are soft and pliable and fit easily over the shank and toe. Once used you would never be without them. It relieves pain instantly. It effects an absolute and permanent cure. Fits any foot and can be worn with perfect comfort. Ladies' sizes, 2 to 6. Gents' sizes, 6 to 12. In ordering, give size of shoe and whether right or left. Regular price, 50 cents.

No. 8K2525 Ladies' right........39c
No. 8K2526 Ladies' left..........39c
No. 8K2527 Men's right..........39c
No. 8K2528 Men's left 39c
If by mail, postage extra, each, 4 cents.

Seamless Para Rubber Gloves.

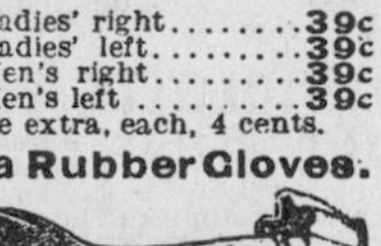

Seamless Para Rubber Gloves. By wearing them at night during sleep you will obtain a hand as fair as an infant's without the least injury. They will remove wrinkles, tan, sallowness, freckles and discoloration of the skin. With care they will last for years. Made of the pure transparent rubber, same as face mask. Order one size larger than your kid glove number.

No. 8K2494 Price, per pair.......95c
If by mail, postage extra, per pair, 6 cents.

Goodyear Plant Sprinkler.

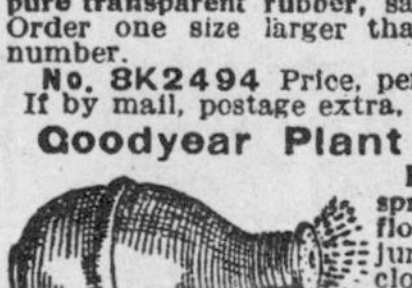

Plant sprinkler for spraying plants and flowers without injury, for sprinkling clothing in the laundry, spraying carpets and clothing to prevent moths, spraying disinfectants in the sick room, etc.

No. 8K2512 Capacity, 6 oz. Price...87c
If by mail, postage extra, 10 cents.

SPONGES.

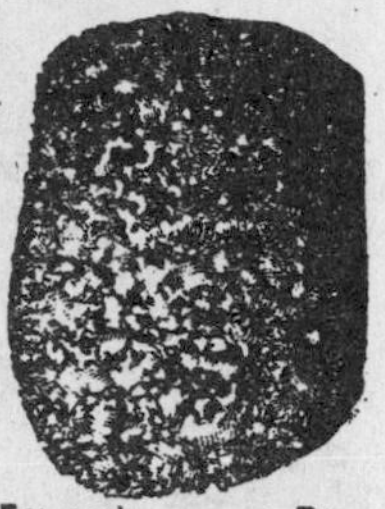

Our Sponges are obtained direct from the Mediterranean Sea, Cuba and Florida, and are the finest quality and size obtainable. Our prices are 25 per cent to 40 per cent lower than the usual prices for the same quality of goods.

No. 8K2575 Small Silk Toilet or Eye Sponge, can be used for surgical purposes, application of face lotions, shaving, etc.
Price, per dozen, 55c; each..........5c

No. 8K2577 Extra fine Elephant's Ear Sponge, a fine article for toilet and bath, specially shaped to fit the hand. Price, 17c

No. 8K2579 Baby Toilet Sponge. A fine soft silk sponge for nursery use and for shaving. Price..................29c

No. 8K2581 Ladies' Silk Sponge. A very fine special form.
Our price..........................27c

No. 8K2583 Ladies' Extra Fine Cup Shaped Sponge. Each in a box. Price, 35c

No. 8K2585 Ladies' Superfine Cup Shaped Sponge, specially selected forms. Each in a box. Price..........................50c

Sheep's Wool Bath Sponge.

No. 8K2589 A Fine Bleached Sheep's Wool Sponge. Soft, cleanly and with great wearing qualities. Medium size for bath use. Price.................................28c

No. 8K2606 Large circumference. Price.................................45c

Unbleached Sheep's Wool Sponges.

For cleaning fine carriages, automobiles or furniture. Largely used by painters and wall paper hangers for wall use. Tough, durable sponges; something you can hardly wear out.

No. 8K2608 Extra large circumference. Regular $1.00 sponge. Our price.....75c

No. 8K2610 Large Cleaning Sponge, 15 to 24 inches in circumference. Suitable for rough work, house cleaning, bailing boats, cleaning walls, woodwork, etc. Price..12c

India Rubber Bath Sponges.

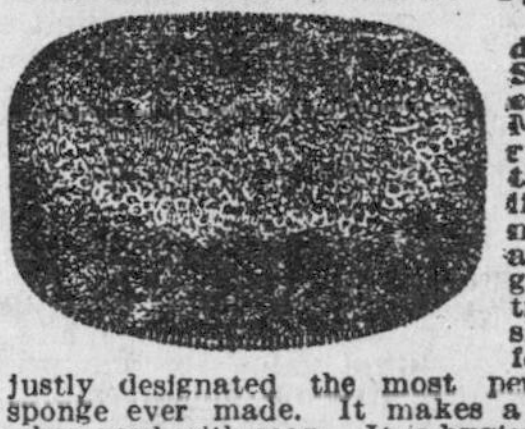

The finest, durable Bath Sponge in existence. Made of pure rubber, will take water like an ordinary sponge and gives a gentle friction to the skin, therefore being justly designated the most perfect toilet sponge ever made. It makes a fine lather when used with soap. It is hygienic, will not harden and is very durable; will last for years. We offer these sponges at nearly one-half the prices at which they are sold elsewhere. These are the genuine imported rubber sponges and not the cheap, putty like imitations offered by others.

No. 8K2615 Small. Price.....35c
No. 8K2618 Medium. Price.....52c
No. 8K2620 Large. Price.....83c
If by mail, postage extra, each, 4 cents.

PLASTERS.

Porous and Medicated.

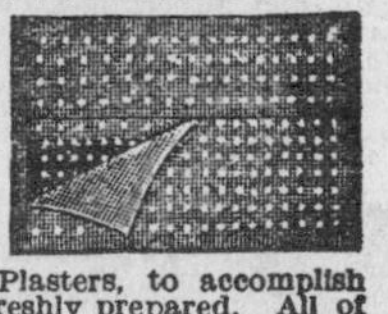

WE GUARANTEE all our Plasters to be full strength and fresh. They are recommended for pains in the back, chest or other parts of the body, arising from colds, rheumatism, sprains, etc. Plasters, to accomplish any good, must be freshly prepared. All of our plasters are made by one of the best plaster and gauze makers in the country and bear their name and guarantee. Regular price, 25c each.

Plasters. Price

No. 8K3825 Arnica.......2 for 33c
No. 8K3826 Belladona.......2 for 33c
No. 8K3827 Strengthening..2 for 33c
No. 8K3828 Poor Man's......2 for 33c
No. 8K3829 Capsicum.......2 for 33c
No. 8K3830 Belladona and Capsicum. Price, 2 for..................33c
No. 8K3831 Dr. King's Kidney Plaster, extra large, to cover both kidneys. Price, 2 for...................39c
No. 8K3832 Rheumatic. Spread on Canton flannel; a great relief for local rheumatic pains. Price, 2 for..............39c
If by mail, postage extra, per dozen, 5 cents.

OUR DRUG DEPARTMENT

Is conducted on a very high plane and the merchandise offered in the drug section of this Big General Catalogue comprises only high class, standard remedies and household necessities offered at a price in keeping with our policy of selling at manufacturing cost with a small profit added. If you will compare our prices on drugs, toilet articles and household necessities, such as are usually sold in a retail drug store, with the prices asked at retail you will make the discovery that we can give you two items for the usual retail price of one.

TOILET PREPARATIONS

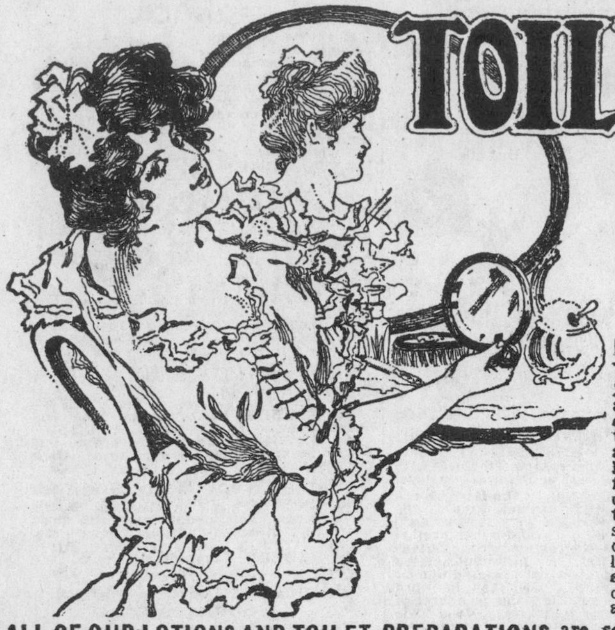

All the latest and best preparations of the beauty doctors by the world's masters, including Eastman, of Cincinnati, Hilbert, of Milwaukee, Mrs. Gervaise Graham, of Chicago, the famous Bourjois, of Paris, and Honore Payan, of Grasse, France. Every package bears their signature and guarantee.

RECOGNIZING THAT UP TO DATE TOILET AND BEAUTIFYING PREPARATIONS are largely adulterated, many containing harmful ingredients that are injurious to the skin, we have taken the initial start in offering our customers an opportunity to obtain from us all the very latest beneficial standard beauty articles free from any harmful substances. Our assortment comprises well known lotions and articles of merit, they being either products of the art and skill of some of the best United States perfumers or imported direct from France. Knowing all about our various lotions and being assured that nothing but the best and purest goods are used therein, our customers can feel a sense of security in using these pure articles.

ALL OF OUR LOTIONS AND TOILET PREPARATIONS are scientifically prepared, strictly up to date, finely perfumed, possess merit and will give satisfaction when used for the purpose for which they are intended. We guarantee every product we sell, as well as giving our customers the positive assurance that in making their selection from the following pages they will obtain not only the latest and best toilet preparations, but they will save considerable in price on every article.

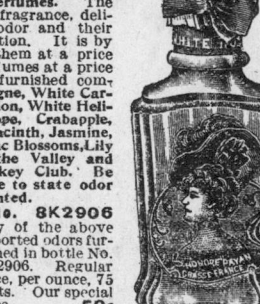

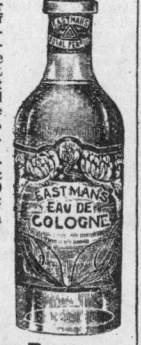

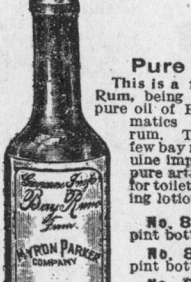

Eastman's Violet Cold Cream.

A PERFECTLY PURE AND SWEETLY PERFUMED COLD CREAM.

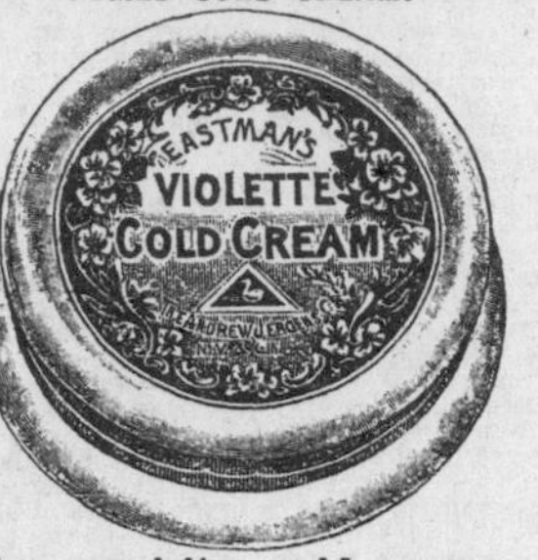

This exquisite cold cream is manufactured by the well known Eastman Perfume Co., of Cincinnati, and is guaranteed by them to be the best that money can buy. By means of its healing action upon the skin it preserves that freshness and whiteness of the skin so much admired by all. This cream is pure and free from all injurious substances. Those using cold cream should be careful to apply only a pure cold cream, and Eastman's Violet Cold Cream is pure, the purest of all cold creams made. Eastman's Violet Cold Cream is different from all other cold creams, it being so absolutely pure and white that it never turns rancid. The last particle out of the jar is just as sweet and delicately perfumed as a fresh jar. **Does not grow hair.** Impure cold creams contain largely, as a base, vaseline or other ingredients that promote the growth of hair. No refined woman desires a growth of hair upon her face, neck or arms, and hence every careful woman will restrict herself to a high grade cold cream the composition of which guarantees absolute protection against this danger. This cream contains no vaseline or other harmful ingredients. **Its uses**—Eastman's Violet Cold Cream affords an excellent application for tan and sunburn, for chapped lips and hands, **for scalds and burns and as a general soothing agent.** When again in need of cold cream, order a jar of Eastman's Violet Cold Cream. After you have convinced yourself of the purity and elegance of this preparation, we know that you will use no other in the future.

No. 8K3049 Regular 4-ounce jar; our price, 2 jars for............**45c**
No. 8K3050 Regular 2-ounce jar; our price, 2 jars for............**28c**
Unmailable on account of weight.

LA DORE PERFUMES.

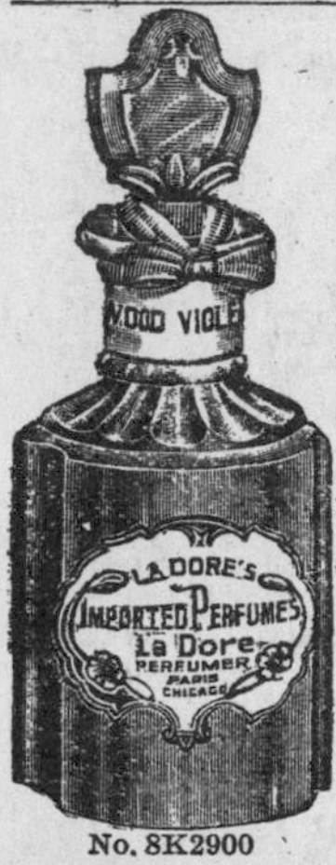

No. 8K2900

The La Dore line of perfumes is manufactured by one of America's best perfumers and is the same grade of perfume retailed at 50 cents and 60 cents per ounce in bulk at retail drug stores.

THE ODORS ARE ALL SWEET, delicate and lasting. They are put up in beautiful 1 and 2-ounce glass stoppered bottles, as shown in illustrations. Each bottle is neatly capped with fine kid and tied with fancy ribbon, and makes a very neat and pretty appearance.

The odors furnished are as follows: **Violet, White Rose, Carnation, Heliotrope, Crabapple, Lily of the Valley, Jockey Club.** While this line of perfume is exceptionally fine value for the price quoted, it can in no way compare with our higher priced perfumes.

No. 8K2900 Any of the above odors. **(Be sure to state odor wanted.)** Price, per 1-ounce bottle.......**35c**
If by mail, postage and mailing tube, extra, 12 cents.
No. 8K2904 Price, per 2-ounce bottle...........**55c**
If by mail, postage and mailing tube, extra, 20 cents.

PAYAN'S IMPORTED PERFUMES.

We have now made arrangements with Honore Payan of Grasse, France, for the selling in America of his well known line of imported triple extract concentrated perfumes. The Payan line of perfumes, on account of their delightful fragrance, delicate blend, lasting qualities, true representation of odor and their high quality, have won for them a world wide reputation. It is by importing these perfumes direct that we can obtain them at a price enabling us to offer our customers these high grade perfumes at a price never before heard of in this country. The fine odors furnished comprise **Trefle, White Rose, La France Violet, Peau de Espagne, White Carnation, White Heliotrope, Crabapple, Hyacinth, Jasmine, Lilac Blossoms, Lily of the Valley and Jockey Club. Be sure to state odor wanted.**

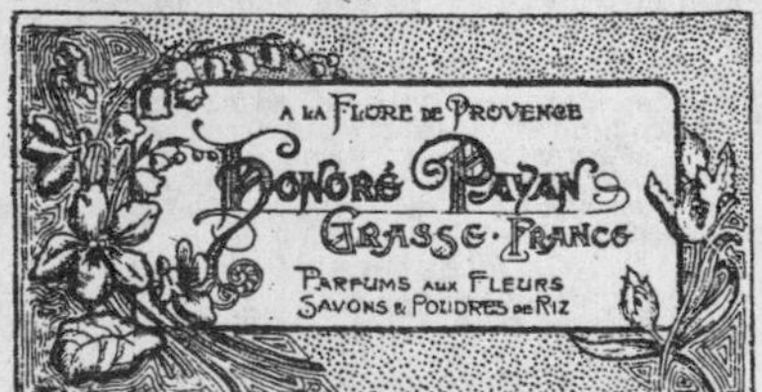

No. 8K2906 Any of the above imported odors furnished in bottle No. 8K2906. Regular price, per ounce, 75 cents. Our special price........**50c**

If by mail, postage and mailing extra, 12 cents.

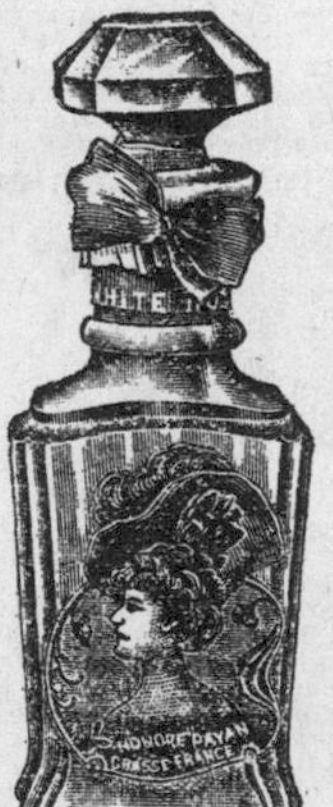

No. 8K2906

BOURJOIS' IMPORTED VIOLETTE DE PARME.

THIS WORLD WIDE FAMOUS PERFUME, manufactured by A. Bourjois & Co., of Paris, France, is put up in graceful and delicate flagons, holding 1½ fluid ounces actual capacity perfume. Beautiful cut faced stopper. The package is trimmed with purple and violet kid and ribbons in harmony with the label, which is in two shades of violet and silver. Each bottle carefully packed in cotton in neat violet colored perfume box. This perfume is very delicate and lasting and a true representation of the flower odor. This is considered the best violet perfume manufactured and is appreciated by everyone. Every drop of this magnificent article is equal to the perfume from several violets and a single drop is sufficient for several hours. Buy the best.

No. 8K2910 Regular price, $1.50; our price.......................**89c**
If by mail, postage and mailing tube, extra, 25 cents.

BOURJOIS' MANON LESCAUT.

This world famous perfume represents the finest article manufactured by any Paris perfumer. The perfume odor is not that of any particular flower but represents the fragrance from the combined flowers of France. This perfume, therefore, has many times been called the Pride of France. The perfume is put up in beautiful colored embossed bottles holding by actual measurement 1½ fluid ounces. The bottles are of irregular design characteristic of imported goods and trimmed with colored kid and rich silk. Each bottle put up in handsome colored lithographed fancy box. This perfume is very rich in odor, sweet and refined in character and wonderfully lasting, a few drops being sufficient to perfume an entire room.

No. 8K2920 Our special price........................**$1.67**
If by mail, postage and mailing tube, extra, 26 cents.

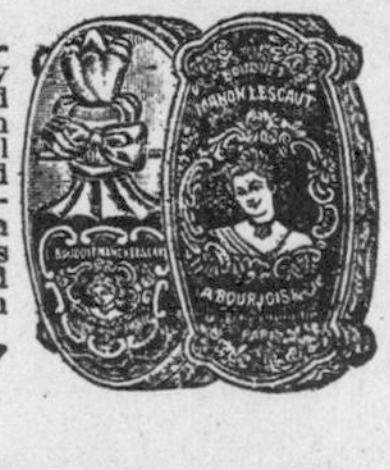

Eastman's Toilet Waters.

BEAUTIFUL FLORAL ODORS OF LONG LASTING QUALITIES.

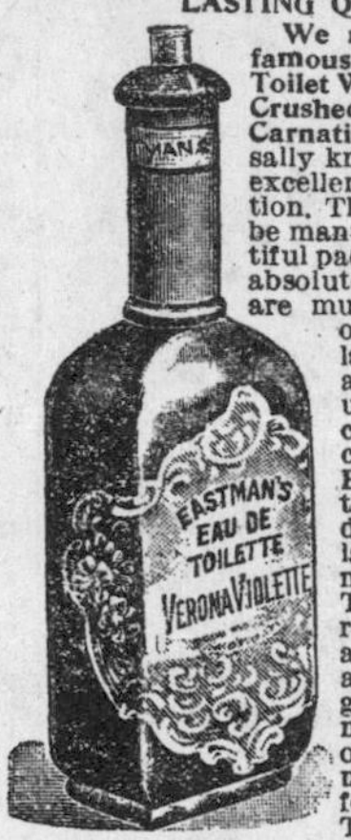

We now carry in stock the famous Eastman Big Three Toilet Waters, Verona Violette, Crushed Roses and Crushed Carnations. Their universally known high standard of excellence needs no introduction. They are as fine as can be manufactured, are in beautiful packages and always give absolute satisfaction. They are much stronger in flower odor, sweetness and lasting quality than the average toilet water upon the market and cannot but be appreciated wherever used. Put a few drops on the hands, and their delicate, sweet and lasting odor causes admiration by all. Violet Toilet Water has now replaced Florida Water and is much more agreeable. Every lady and gentleman of refinement desires an article of exceptionally high merit and it is always found in the Eastman Toilet Water. Be sure to state odor wanted.

No. 8K3055 Regular 75-cent size; our price.........................**42c**
No. 8K3056 Regular $1.00 size; our price........(Unmailable.).........**74c**

Eastman's Eau De Cologne.

Especially prepared for the toilet and handkerchief and equal to the finest imported colognes. It is very refreshing and of great value in the sick room, where it can be used as a disinfectant for destroying bad odors and rendering the air in the room fresh and pleasant, giving it a nice perfume. A very superior article.

No. 8K3060 Price, 50-cent size..................**36c**
No. 8K3061 Price, $1.00 size.....................**69c**
Both sizes unmailable on account of weight.

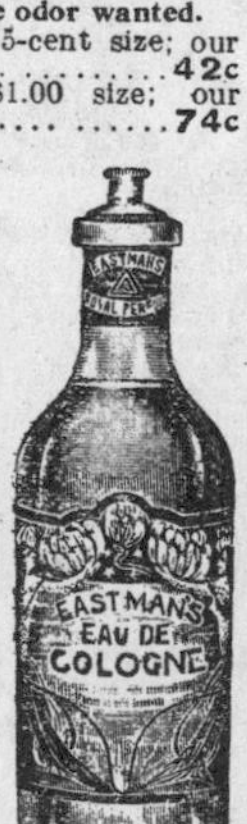

Pure Bay Rum.

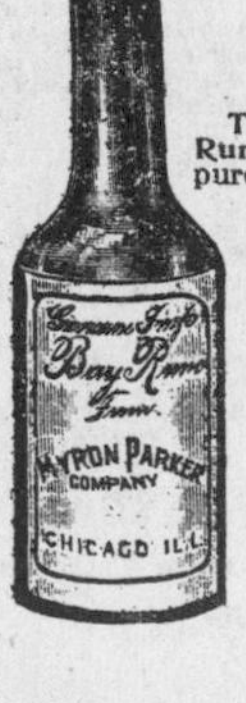

This is a fine quality of Bay Rum, being manufactured from pure oil of Porto Rico bay, aromatics and pure imported rum. This is one of the very few bay rums made from genuine imported rum. Being a pure article it is very useful for toilet purposes. A refreshing lotion for the skin.

No. 8K3066 Price, ½-pint bottle...........**33c**
No. 8K3067 Price, 1-pint bottle..............**60c**
No. 8K3068 Price, 1-quart bottle.........**$1.10**
All sizes unmailable on account of weight.

Witch Hazel with Violet Perfume.

A face and hand application, a delicacy after shaving, and a general perfumed antiseptic. Violet Witch Hazel is a comparatively new product combining the exquisite odor of violets with the antiseptic properties of pure extract of witch hazel. This is not regular witch hazel but a combination especially prepared for the purpose indicated. **No household antiseptic can compare with extract of witch hazel, and when sweetly perfumed with odor of violets, makes an article that has won the favor of every lady and gentleman that has ever given it a trial.** When used for perfuming the hands and face, or as a delicacy after shaving, it removes inflammation, makes the parts antiseptic and leaves that exquisite odor of violets about the person.

No. 8K3072 Our price, 8-ounce bottle...........**28c**
Unmailable on account of weight.

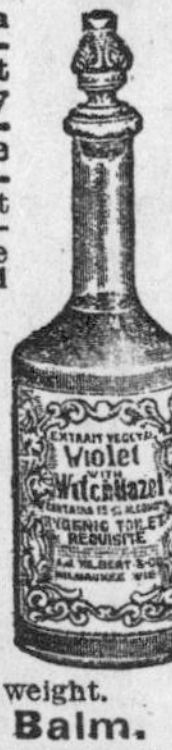

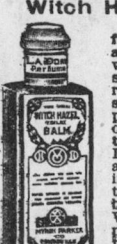

Witch Hazel Toilet Balm.

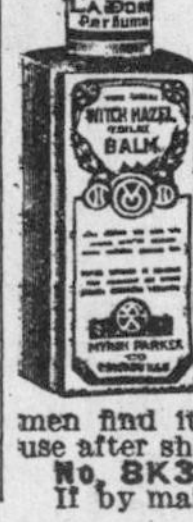

This is an elegant preparation for the skin when it is chapped and rough. A few applications well rubbed in make the skin soft and velvety. It is also recommended for removing sunburn and freckles. It will prevent the skin from chapping or coloring when exposed to the cold if used before going out. It does not leave the skin greasy and sticky. Gloves can be used immediately after each application, the balm being absorbed by the skin very quickly. The Witch Hazel Balm is a very popular, healing and soothing toilet requisite for harsh, dry, cracked or rough skin. Gentlemen find it a lotion highly satisfactory for use after shaving.

No. 8K3078 Price, per bottle...**17c**
If by mail, postage and tube extra, 16c.

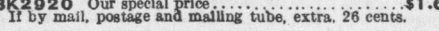

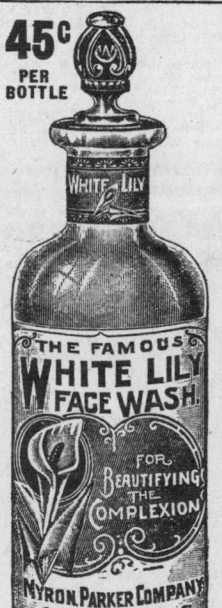

Toilette Liquid Depilatory for Removing Superfluous Hair.

Toilette Liquid Depilatory has long been known to be a very effective and reliable means for quickly removing superfluous hair from the face, neck or arms. It is a liquid preparation which is applied with a pellet of cotton, which is included with each package, which by merely moistening and applying to the part, and leaving on for a period of two to three minutes and then washed off, will remove with it the superfluous hair. The part is then thoroughly washed with lukewarm water, cold cream applied, and if the directions are closely adhered to, it will be absolutely impossible for anyone to detect that you have been using a depilatory for removing the hair. **Hair on the neck, face or arms, so embarrassing to ladies of refinement, can be removed easily and quickly, and for only 76 cents.** This depilatory removes the hair wherever applied and gives in the majority of cases perfect satisfaction. The greatest drawback of perfect loveliness in woman is a superfluous, unnatural growth of hair where nature never intended it. The prettiest face is marred or disfigured by hair on the lips, cheeks or chin. By means of this liquid depilatory every vestige of hair is removed. A perfectly clean, smooth, soft, beautiful skin is assured when directions are followed. No unpleasant effects follow its use. One application is sufficient for the complete removal of the hair. It is considered by many superior to the electric needle, which is a very painful operation. No matter what you have tried before, we believe you ought to give this Toilette Liquid Depilatory a fair trial. This price of 76 cents per bottle is much cheaper than you can obtain an equally good product elsewhere. Why, therefore, pay from $2.00 to $3.00 for a so called hair remover when for 76 cents you can obtain a reliable preparation, and one that with careful attention will give as good results as can be expected from a preparation of this nature? Of course, any depilatory must be used with care, as if left on longer than the time specified is apt to cause irritation of the skin, and this is the reason we specifically specify that directions should be closely followed. **No toilet is complete without a depilatory** and ladies of refinement everywhere should have it upon the dressing table, to be used at any time desired. We will allow you, if you are bothered with superfluous hair, whether on the face, neck or arms, and you want a smooth skin, to buy a bottle of this depilatory, try it, and if after you have used the bottle you are not entirely satisfied with the results obtained, all you have to do is to write us to that effect and we will cheerfully refund your money.

No. 8K3105 Our special price **76c**
If by mail, postage and mailing tube extra, 8 cents.

Orange Flower Skin Food.

CREME MARQUISE.

This celebrated preparation has quickly grown into popular favor, and is today, by ladies of fashion, considered an indispensable toilet article. It acts as a skin nourisher and wrinkle remover, smoothes roughness and fills out hollow cheeks, giving the natural healthy glow and beauty to the skin. Our Orange Flower Skin Food, on account of its fine silky texture and sweet odor of genuine orange flowers, is not to be compared with the many so called orange flower foods made from cheap vaseline, etc. We believe this to be the finest made. Orange Flower Skin Food is today often preferred and used instead of preparations that would cost three and four times the price at which we can furnish same to our lady customers.

No. 8K3160 Price, 2-ounce jar.... **19c**
If by mail, postage extra, regular size, 15 cents.
No. 8K3161 Price, 4-ounce jars... **36c**
Not mailable.

Smooth Up.

A scientific treatment for removing wrinkles. Wrinkles are caused by a lack of nutrition of the tissues underlying the skin, and muscular contraction. Smooth Up is a medicated court plaster and is the result of over 20 years' experience of a prominent facial specialist. It rebuilds the depleted tissues, increases the surface fat, holds the skin smooth and assists nature to permanently remove the wrinkles. It preserves the youthful appearance of the skin indefinitely, and removes wrinkles of all ages. Full directions with each package. Retail price, 25 cents.

No. 8K3163 Our price.......... **18c**
If by mail, postage extra, 2 cents.

Famous Myrka Powder.

We have now made arrangements whereby we can furnish you the world famous Imported Myrka Face Powder. A very fine and highly appreciated powder, and very delicately perfumed. Ingredients are harmless and chemically pure. Stands unquestioned as one of the finest and best powders for constant use. Gives that velvet softness to the skin so much admired by all. Comes in three colors, white, flesh and brunette. Be sure to state shade wanted. Regular price, 50 cents per box.

No. 8K3175 Our price, per box..... **33c**
If by mail, postage extra, per box, 5 cents.

Decorated Glass Puff Box.

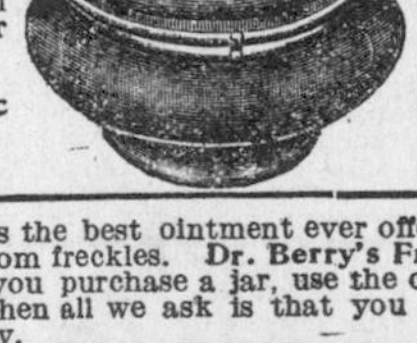

Beautiful Bohemian glass, assorted colors, fancy metallic clasp. Top of box of elaborate design. A very beautiful puff box. Regular price, 75 cents.

No. 8K3189
Our price..... **45c**
Unmailable.

Bourjois' Poudre Manon Lescaut.

IF YOU WANT THE BEST BUY THIS.

This world famous powder has been named after the beautiful heroine of the Abbe Prevost. This is the most famous of all face powders, highly and sweetly perfumed and made of the finest Oriental rice which is bolted many times until it has become perfectly impalpable. This is combined with other ingredients, all of which are absolutely harmless to the most delicate complexion, yet when used upon the face become perfectly invisible. This powder is made by and represents the highest skill of the world's master in face powders.

No. 8K3177 Price, per box...... **$0.93**
2 boxes for....... **1.75**
If by mail, postage extra, per box, 5 cents.

World Famous Java Rice Powder.

We guarantee this to be the genuine imported Java Rice Face Powder. It is made by A. Bourjois & Cie., Paris, France. Used almost exclusively by the theatrical profession. Absolutely pure. Delightful and lasting perfume. Absolutely free from injurious substances. The most adherent powder in the world. Almost double the powder found in any other box. Regular price, 50 cents.

No. 8K3180 Our price, per box..... **27c**
If by mail, postage extra, per box, 5 cents.

C. H. Berry Freckle Ointment.

For the Removal of Freckles, Moth Patches, Muddy Complexion or Discoloration of the Skin.

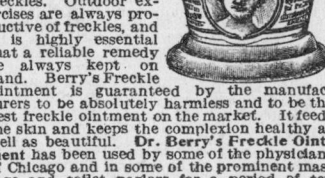

Nothing makes or mars a woman's face more than the quality of her complexion and it is absolutely impossible for any lady to have a really pretty face, a complexion the envy of her friends, if the face is covered with freckles. Outdoor exercises are always productive of freckles, and it is highly essential that a reliable remedy be always kept on hand. Berry's Freckle Ointment is guaranteed by the manufacturers to be absolutely harmless and to be the best freckle ointment on the market. It feeds the skin and keeps the complexion healthy as well as beautiful. **Dr. Berry's Freckle Ointment** has been used by some of the physicians of Chicago and in some of the prominent massage and toilet parlors for a period of ten years, and we have testimonials of persons who have used it repeatedly, who state that without doubt it is the best ointment ever offered. Each $1.00 jar is sufficient to completely clean one's face from freckles. **Dr. Berry's Freckle Ointment** is guaranteed to be exactly as represented. If you purchase a jar, use the contents, and are not entirely satisfied with the results obtained, then all we ask is that you write us to that effect and we will cheerfully refund your money.

No. 8K3073 Regular $1.00 size jar; our special price............ **79c**
If by mail, postage extra, 10 cents.

DO YOU WANT TO BE BEAUTIFUL?

Floral Massage Cream is Now Regarded as Very Essential to Beauty.

A very necessary toilet preparation. A beautifying, antiseptic cleansing and beautifying massage cream. A most excellent product. Used to bring back the color of youth and remove the telltale marks of time. **Floral Massage Cream** is a very high grade toilet preparation equal to, in our opinion, any of the similar preparations upon the market, and much superior in quality and effectiveness to many others offered at much more than our prices. **Floral Massage Cream** is a luxury which no woman, young, middle aged or old, should deny herself. It is composed of the purest ingredients, perfectly harmless to the most delicate skin and free from all irritating effects. It is free from glycerine, almond oil, minerals, mercury, or any injurious ingredients; its emollient effects are great, its cleansing and beautifying results are gratifying. Very beneficial and only appreciated by those who have once given it a trial.

The Floral Massage Cream of today is the result of extended experiments and experience and is successfully used today by many of the leading professional masseurs in the massage parlors of several of our large cities, and is sold by us exclusively to many of our customers for home massage. The preparation is put up in a very unique package, tied with fancy ribbon, carefully sealed to prevent the entrance of air, and when properly corked and protected will keep indefinitely. It is a preparation that should appeal to all ladies of refinement who are particular regarding their appearance, and many prefer it to the oily massage creams so common of today. It is just as necessary an adjunct to the dressing table as a bottle of fine perfume, just as important to the toilet as a tooth brush. **Floral Massage Cream** is used in massage for the removal of the horizontal lines from the brow, for taking out the laughing wrinkles and crowsfeet, for removing the wrinkles under the eyes, for making the cheeks plump and round, for cleaning the skin of all dirt, soot and impurities, for making the complexion what you want it to be, healthy, clear and rosy. It brings fresh bloom to faded faces, and by proper massaging will smooth away many of the age lines and care marks. With every jar of this massage cream is furnished free a booklet giving you a complete course on massage treatment, illustrated throughout with pictures and diagrams showing the regular course of treatment society ladies receive in the city massage parlors. This booklet explains the exact way to massage the face, the various movements, the position of the hands, etc., so that anyone, by following the plain and simple instructions and the method as shown by the pictures, can get the same delightful, wonderful and improving effects from facial massage that makes this treatment so much appreciated by ladies of refinement and fashion everywhere. **Remember this massage cream is offered purely on merit,** and we will allow you to buy a jar, use the contents according to directions, experience its beautifying effects, and if, after the last part of your jar has been used, you do not feel satisfied with the results received, do not believe that the beautifying effects have been noticeable in your own case, then all we ask is that you write us to that effect and we will cheerfully refund your money.

No. 8K3110 Regular 2-ounce jar. Price............ **37c**
If by mail, postage extra, per jar, 14 cents.
No. 8K3111 Large jar, holds more than three times the quantity of the smaller, **71c**
Unmailable.

Satinette Face Powder.

This imported face powder is made by one of the best perfumers in Paris, France. It is manufactured from the very finest sifted rice flour and delightfully perfumed. Absolutely guaranteed free from any harmful ingredients. It is a very popular powder and is the genuine imported article. Furnished in three shades, white, flesh and brunette. Be sure to state shade desired. Regular price, per box, 25c.

No. 8K3170 Our price, 2 boxes for **25c**
If by mail, postage extra, per box, 5 cents.

Trefle Complexion Powder.

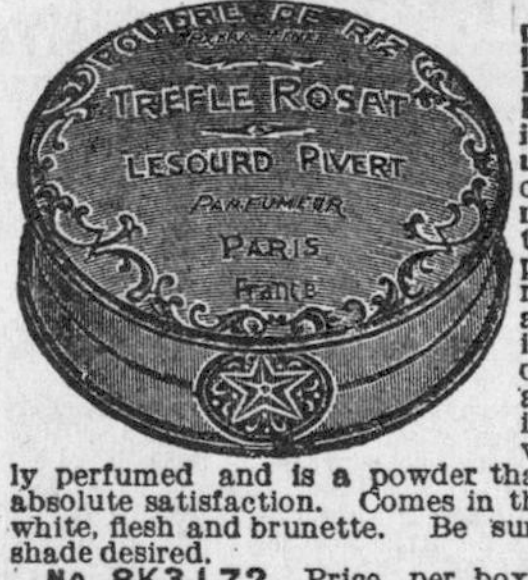

This highly praised and largely used Parisian Powder is imported by us, enabling our customers to obtain the powder so much used abroad. It is composed of the purest and best ingredients, very sweetly perfumed and is a powder that will give absolute satisfaction. Comes in three shades, white, flesh and brunette. Be sure to state shade desired.

No. 8K3172 Price, per box....... **21c**
If by mail, postage extra, per box, 5 cents.

Pocketbook Toilet Case.

Handy Little Toilet Case. Appeals to every woman. Small silver plated box, hinged cover with mirror within; small down puff with handle. Being small enough to carry in pocketbook, is just the article for parties, traveling, etc.

No. 8K3193 Price............ **19c**
If by mail, postage extra, 2 cents.

KOSMEO FACE POWDER

SEE PAGE 794.

Rouge de Theatre.

This is not the cheap American rouge but the genuine Imported Bourjois Rouge put up in round wooden boxes. This is positively the best, giving a natural and lifelike glow, never injures the skin, is today considered by the theatrical profession the only safe and satisfactory rouge, and used by them almost exclusively owing to the fine distributive qualities which it possesses so that it can never be noticed or detected. Be sure to get the genuine.

No. 8K3197 Price, per box....... **19c**
If by mail, postage extra, per box, 6 cents.

GENTLEMEN'S SHAVING AND TOILET OUTFIT

EVERY GENTLEMAN should take pride in his personal appearance. A clean shaven face, properly treated afterward with Violet Witch Hazel, Talcum and toilets is a joy and pleasure to the man himself and admired by all with whom he comes in contact.

THOUSANDS OF MEN SHAVE THEMSELVES, but it is only within the last few years that shaving lotions have been largely employed. How many have experienced that delightful cooling sensation of Violet Witch Hazel after bathing the face in warm water? It removes the irritation caused by shaving, cools and makes antiseptic the thousands of pores on the face, prevents chapping and leaves that exquisite lasting odor of fresh violets about the person. **In like manner every item given in this list has an indispensable use.** No shaving gentleman can afford to miss this opportunity. The list comprises the following: **One pound Williams' Genuine World Renowned Shaving Soap. One Styptic Pencil** for stopping bleeding in case of cuts. **One bottle of Bellezaire Genuine Brilliantine** for perfuming the mustache and hair. A very exquisite article and appreciated only by those who have used it. **One stick Williams' Genuine French Cosmetique** for fixing and giving gloss and softness to the mustache and whiskers. **One jar Crystal Shampoo Jelly,** a superior article for shampooing the hair. **One bottle Eastman's Genuine Eau de Cologne,** fine and refreshing, a superior gentleman's toilet requisite. **A fine Bleach Sponge** for removing the soap and lather after shaving. **One Genuine Faultless Beauty Brush** for coaxing the dirt out of its hiding places and for removing blackheads and all facial blemishes, and producing a fine, clear, clean complexion and healthy glow. **One bottle Genuine Violet Witch Hazel** for application to the face after shaving. **Two bottles of the well known Wood Violet Talcum,** made by the well known Hilbert perfumers, of Milwaukee, Wisconsin.

JUST THINK of receiving ten toilet requisites indispensable to every gentleman at this astonishingly low price. Not only indispensable to a gentleman shaving himself but to every man as a general toilet requisite. Just consider their retail prices and then compare them with the price at which we quote the complete outfit.

Include this outfit in your next freight or express order.

No. 8K3014 Special price.......(Unmailable on account of weight.)...... **$1.79**

YOUR MONEY WILL BE IMMEDIATELY RETURNED TO YOU FOR ANY GOODS NOT PERFECTLY SATISFACTORY.

521

DO YOU WANT TO BUY A GOOD
HAIR TONIC?

PER BOTTLE 63c

THE WORLD FAMED Princess HAIR TONIC

JONES, MARTIN & CO. CHICAGO, ILLS

A GOOD HAIR TONIC IS A HOUSEHOLD NECESSITY

AND PRINCESS HAIR TONIC WILL DO EVERYTHING WHICH AN HONEST HAIR TONIC CAN POSSIBLY DO. WHEN THE HAIR IS DEAD, NOTHING ON EARTH CAN BRING IT TO LIFE. WE, THEREFORE, DO NOT GUARANTEE THAT PRINCESS HAIR TONIC WILL GROW HAIR ON THE BACK FENCE, OR MAKE LONG FLOWING HAIR WITH TWO OR THREE WEEKS' USE, OR COVER A BALD HEAD WITH A TWO-INCH GROWTH OF HAIR WITH A WEEK'S USE OF OUR REMEDY. NO, ALL WE CLAIM IS THAT PRINCESS HAIR TONIC IS THE BEST HAIR TONIC AND HAIR GROWER EVER PRODUCED, AND IF USED AS DIRECTED, WILL DO ALL ANY HAIR TONIC CAN DO.

PRINCESS HAIR TONIC IS A RELIABLE HAIR TONIC

CAUSES OF FALLING HAIR. The main causes of falling hair are dandruff, eczema of the scalp and improper care of the hair. Dandruff is not only the most common of scalp diseases, but it is one causing at all times an untidy appearance and the one causing the greatest number of cases of baldness. If it is not stopped at once, it destroys the hair roots. While it is scarcely noticeable in its earlier stages, nevertheless, like any other disease it rapidly spreads and eats, the white flakes become larger and more prominent, until before long merely running the fingers through the hair causes a snowy white deposit on the clothes and throughout the hair. If allowed to go unchecked, the disease will go on until the under side of these white flakes will have the appearance of tiny scabs and when this condition is reached, nothing but the promptest action will prevent total baldness. Princess Hair Tonic will destroy the disease germ, remove every trace of dandruff itself and soon make the scalp perfectly healthy. The tonic should be applied once a day, rubbed well into the scalp with the finger tips for at least five minutes and until the liquid is all absorbed by the tissues. This should be continued until the dandruff is entirely gone and then the tonic used twice a week as a preventive and to keep the scalp in a healthy condition, enabling it to produce the fine, silky hair designed by nature.

A REAL FOOD FOR THE HAIR. Princess Hair Tonic preserves and strengthens the hair, promotes its growth, arrests falling hair, feeds and nourishes the roots, removes dandruff and scurf and allays all scalp irritations. A very effective, uniformly successful, perfectly harmless preparation that removes scales and dandruff, soothes irritating, itching surfaces, stimulates the hair follicles, supplies the roots with energy and makes the hair grow.

ARE YOU INCLINED TO BALDNESS? Is your hair thin or falling out? Does your hair come out easily and gather on the comb and brush when you brush it? Does your head itch? Do you have dandruff or scurf, and do white dustlike particles settle on your coat collar? Is your hair stiff and coarse and hard to brush? Is your hair fading or has it turned prematurely gray? If your hair suffers in any one or more of these particulars, order three bottles of **Princess Hair Tonic** as a trial, for speedy relief. Use it according to directions and you will be surprised and delighted at the good results. It acts direct on the tiny roots of the hair, giving them required fresh nourishment, starts quick, energetic circulation in every hair cell, tones up the scalp, freshens the pores, stops falling hair, changes thin hair to a fine heavy growth, puts new life in dormant, sluggish hair cells.

PRINCESS HAIR TONIC. It is not a dye. It can be applied to the most delicate hair; it will not stain the daintiest head dress. Princess Hair Tonic is made under a special process, is perfectly pure and clear, without any sulphur sediment, and containing the following named ingredients, recognized as constituents of highest efficiency for hair and scalp treatment: quinine sulphate, soluble sulphur natrium muriate, resorcin cantharides, lead acetate, cayenne, glycerine, alcohol and perfume.

No. 8K3125 Our price, 3 bottles for **$1.55**; per bottle **63c**

NOTE ON ACCOUNT OF WEIGHT THIS ARTICLE CANNOT BE SHIPPED BY MAIL. MUST BE SHIPPED BY EXPRESS OR ORDERED WITH OTHER GOODS

Ruby Salve.

Ruby Salve is a refined and harmless rouge prepared in the form of a cream for tinting the cheeks, lips and fingers, leaves a perfectly natural stain or glow and can never be detected. The majority of ladies prefer rouge in this form, as it is put up in a very convenient manner and easily applied.

RUBY SALVE

No. 8K3202 Price, per box.......**17c**
If by mail, postage extra, per box, 5 cents.

Eyebrow Pencils.

For darkening the eyebrows and lashes. The genuine imported pencils. Unsurpassed for slightly darkening the eyebrows and lashes in a manner so natural that cannot be detected. Absolutely harmless and largely used by theatrical people to bring out the beauty of the eye. Specify whether brown or black is desired. Regular price, 25 cents.

No. 8K3205 Our price, 2 pencils for **31c**
If by mail, postage extra, each, 2 cents.

Eastman's Camphor Ice.

A salve of remarkable healing qualities. Of great value when the skin is chapped from cold; it will heal up the cracks and make the skin soft and smooth again; also it cannot be excelled as a soothing and healing application to burns, and dressing for abrasions of the skin, pimples, boils, etc.

EASTMAN'S CAMPHOR ICE

No. 8K3208 Price, per box.......**14c**
Unmailable.

Styptio Pencils.

STYPTIC PENCILS

Used when shaving. Will instantly stop bleeding. Should be kept on hand by everyone shaving himself.
No. 8K3228 Price, 2 for **8c**
If by mail, postage extra, each, 2 cents.

Perfumed Scalp Food.

PERFUMED SCALP FOOD

A highly beneficial and absolutely harmless hair dressing for invigorating the scalp, preventing the falling of the hair and for keeping it soft and glossy. Perfumed Scalp Food should be applied to the scalp after each treatment with Princess Hair Tonic. It materially aids the hair tonic in performing its work and leaves the scalp and hair in a clean antiseptic condition. Full directions with each jar.
No. 8K3130 Price, per jar....**40c**
If by mail, postage extra, 15 cents.

Barbers' Favorite Shampoo.

This shampoo is the highest grade of shampoo preparations used by the first class barbers in the large cities, and is very popular in every part of the country. As a gentleman's shampoo it is unequaled, makes clean and healthy hair, removes itching of the scalp, and is guaranteed not to contain, like most shampoos, any alkali, which leaves the hair harsh and dry. Our Barbers' Shampoo renders the hair soft, smooth and fluffy.

BARBERS FAVORITE SHAMPOO

No. 8K3216 Price, 8-oz. round shampoo bottle....**21c**
Unmailable on account of weight.

Pomade Philocome.

An exquisite dressing for the hair and mustache, nicely perfumed, and high quality, in 2-ounce large mouthed screw top bottle, very convenient for making application. This pomade is very satisfactory and continually used when once given a trial.

POMADE PHILOCOME

No. 8K3222 Price, per bottle **16c**
If by mail, postage extra, 5 cents.

Hair Curling Fluid.

CURLING FLUID

This preparation will keep the hair in curl during the dampest or warmest weather; quite harmless to the hair; directions on each bottle.
No. 8K3230 Price, per bottle..............**14c**
If by mail, postage extra, including tube, 18 cents.

Crystal Shampoo Jelly.

Removes dandruff, leaves the hair soft and keeps the scalp in a healthy condition; produces the finest foam, is the most economical shampoo and is excellent as a cleanser.

CRYSTAL SHAMPOO JELLY

No. 8K3237 Price, per large size jar................**24c**
If by mail, postage extra, 17 cents.

Bellezaire Brilliantine.

Genuine Bellezaire Brilliantine, a sweetly perfumed hair oil for making the hair soft and glossy. Gentlemen use it with advantage on the mustache to keep the hair in place and make it glossy. Buy this genuine product.

BRILLIANTINE

No. 8K3240 Price, per bottle..............**21c**
If by mail, postage and tube extra, 15 cents.

Perfect Combination Hair Dye.

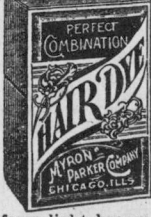

PERFECT COMBINATION HAIR DYE

The Perfect Combination Hair Dye is a really perfect dye for dyeing the hair, mustache or whiskers quickly, easily and satisfactorily, all shades of brown to a deep black. Consists of two different preparations which when used in combination will always insure satisfactory results. Can be used to dye from light brown to jet black. Explicit and complete directions are furnished with each package. State color wanted.
No. 8K3242 Our price....**83c**
If by mail, postage extra, 17 cents.

TOOTH AND NAIL SUNDRIES

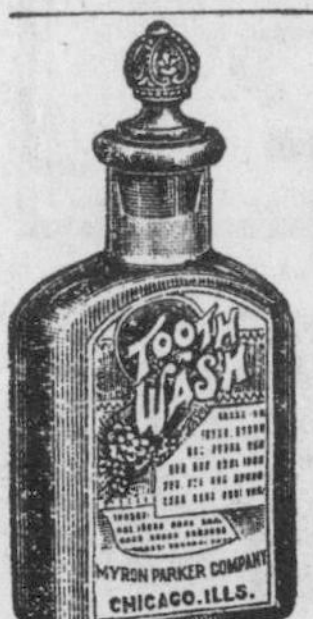

Tooth Wash.

A most perfect preparation for the teeth. Will keep them entirely free from stains and discolorations. It will remove the tartar, harden the gums and keep the teeth as lovely as pearls, leaving a delicious aftertaste in the mouth for hours. Preserves the teeth and kills the germs of decay.

No. 8K3250 Regular 25-cent bottle; our price, 2 bottles for..**25c**
Unprofitable by mail.

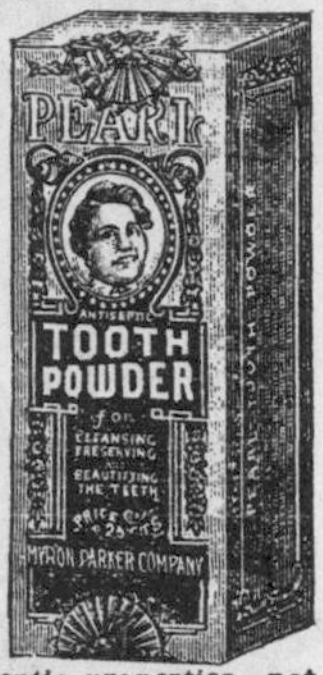

Pearl Tooth Powder.

In patent silverette finish metal can. Dustproof and dampproof and most convenient.

Pearl Tooth Powder is prepared in accordance with a valuable formula for beautifying and preserving the teeth. Approved, recommended and used by dentists and physicians. Cleanses, brightens, whitens the teeth and prevents decay. Contains nothing injurious; is far superior to many other preparations owing to its antiseptic properties, not found in many tooth powders on the market. Regular price, per can, 25 cents.

No. 8K3252 Our price, 2 cans for..**25c**
If by mail, postage extra, per can, 4 cents.

Albi-Denta Tooth Soap.

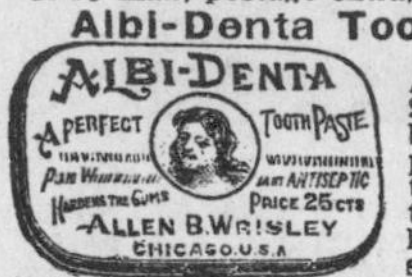

The genuine Albi-Denta Tooth Soap for cleaning, beautifying and preserving the teeth, hardening the gums, and keeping the breath sweet; warranted not injurious; in metallic box. One of the best tooth soaps made. Retail price, per box, 25 cents.

No. 8K3254 Our price, 2 boxes for **25c**
If by mail, postage extra, per box, 3 cents.

Septol Tooth Paste.

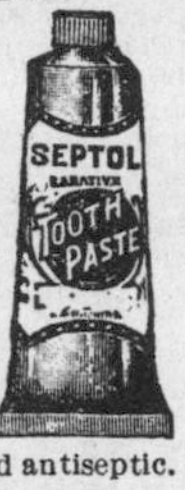

This well known tooth paste is in our opinion one of the finest tooth preparations in paste form. Furnished in metal tubes, and whitens, preserves and beautifies the teeth in the most satisfactory and effective manner. The metal tube style is a very convenient way of using a tooth preparation and is favored by many ladies and gentlemen who prefer it to tooth powders and tooth washes. This splendid preparation is the same high grade as those that always retail at 25 cents and has never before been sold for less than 25 cents. Each tube placed in beautiful sliding box to keep it clean and antiseptic. Regular 25-cent size.

No. 8K3256 Our price..........**17c**
If by mail, postage extra, 5 cents.

Dr. Griffith's Toothache Remedy.

Prepared From the Best and Surest Remedies Known to the Dentist for the Prevention and Cure of Toothache.

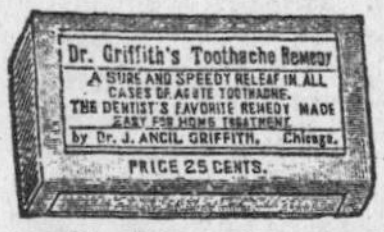

Put up in simple form, convenient for home treatment, and guaranteed if used as directed. The nature of toothache is such that a remedy to meet all requirements must consist of two separate parts. (1) A combined remedy that will stop the ache, cure the inflammation and check decay. (2) A preparation that will seal the remedy in place, close the cavity securely from food and moisture, become hard and remain so indefinitely until you have an opportunity to have the tooth filled. In this remedy we have both these requirements, simple in form and easy to apply, making it a perfect remedy. Superior to all others in so much as the effect of other remedies are soon lost by the cavity being left open to food and moisture. **Seal this remedy in as directed, keep the cavity closed and toothache will not return.** Non-aching cavities treated as above checks the decay and prevents the ache. It is not a cheap gum or wax nor an evaporating liquid, but a sure and lasting remedy. Prepared only by Dr. Griffith and used by thousands of dentists for the prevention and cure of toothache; non-poisonous, reliable, quick to act and safe for young and old. Full directions in each box. Regular price, per box, 25 cents.

No. 8K3261 Our price..........**12c**

Tooth Brushes.

We are now importing directly from Japan and France our Tooth and Nail Brushes, and for this reason are able to supply the finest brushes at the very lowest prices. To appreciate the values we offer, you have only to compare our brushes with those for which you pay two or three times our prices elsewhere.

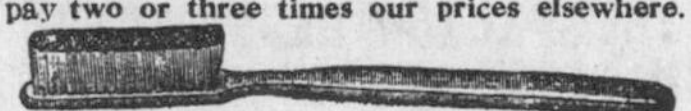

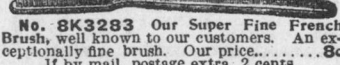

No. 8K3283 Our Super Fine French Brush, well known to our customers. An exceptionally fine brush. Our price........**8c**
If by mail, postage extra, 2 cents.

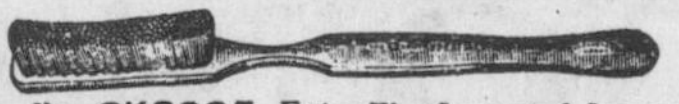

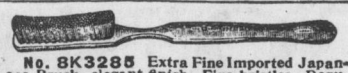

No. 8K3285 Extra Fine Imported Japanese Brush, elegant finish. Fine bristles. Regular 20-cent quality. Our price..........**11c**
If by mail, postage extra, 2 cents.

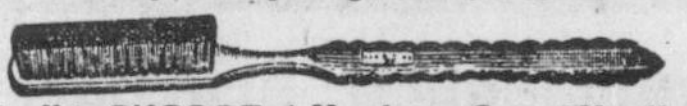

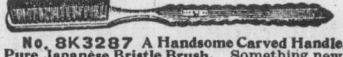

No. 8K3287 A Handsome Carved Handle, Pure Japanese Bristle Brush. Something new. Regular price, 20 and 25 cents.
Our price..(Postage extra, 2 cents)..**15c**

Child's Brush.

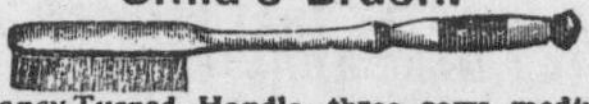

Fancy Turned Handle, three rows medium firm pure bristles. Just the thing to clean the teeth of growing children without hurting the gums. Regular 10 to 15-cent quality.

No. 8K3294 Our price..........**8c**
If by mail, postage extra, 2 cents.

Genuine Aseptic Tooth Brush.

The best brush made. You will make no mistake by buying this brush.

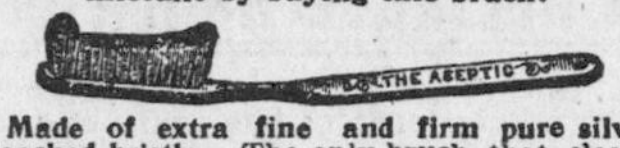

Made of extra fine and firm pure silver bleached bristle. The only brush that cleans the teeth properly, as it is made to clean and remove all food and tartar. Patent bent handle with hole for hanging. Being the finest brush manufactured, we especially recommend it to our customers. Regular price, 35 cents.

No. 8K3296 Our price..........**17c**
If by mail, postage extra, 2 cents.

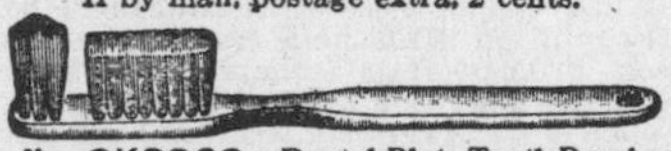

No. 8K3298 Dental Plate Tooth Brushes for cleaning artificial teeth. Price.......**19c**
If by mail, postage extra, 2 cents.

The Genuine Prophylactic Tooth Brush.

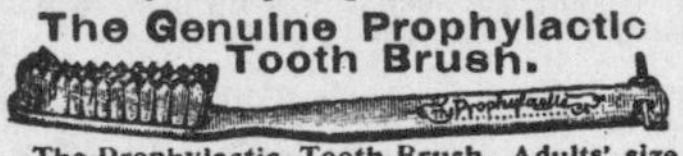

The Prophylactic Tooth Brush, Adults' size, is a perfect tooth brush. Directions for use are given with each brush. It is furnished with new style patent hanger, so that the bristles may dry quickly and keep sweet and clean. Regular price, 35 cents.

No. 8K3300 Our price..........**19c**
If by mail, postage extra, 3 cents.

Nail Brushes.

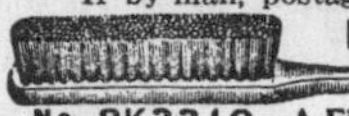

No. 8K3310 A Fine Five-Row Nail and Finger Brush, pure bristles and smooth bone handle. Regular 15-cent quality.
Price....(Postage extra, 2 cents)....**9c**

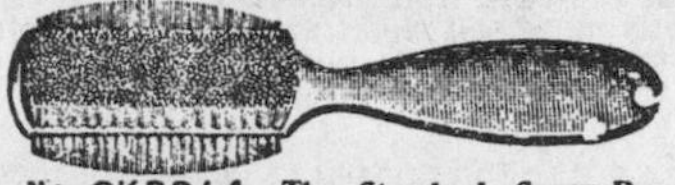

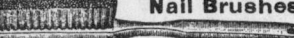

No. 8K3314 The Standard Seven-Row Nail and Hand Brush, with wings on each edge for cleaning finger nails, **superfine bone handle.** Good 25-cent value.
Price. (If by mail, postage extra, 4c.). **18c**

Hand and Finger Brush.

Polished Boxwood Handle, curved top, set with five rows of short firm bristles which clean the nails and finger tips perfectly. Bottom has four rows of extra long and firm silver bleached bristles for cleaning the hands. An exceptionally fine brush.

No. 8K3318 Price..........**21c**
If by mail, postage extra, 3 cents.

Nail and Hand Brush.

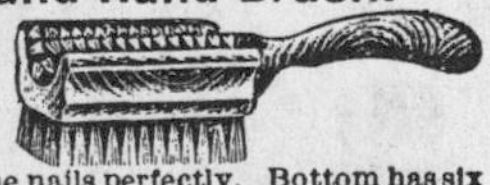

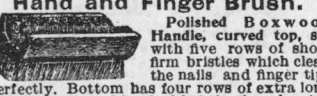

Polished handle with curved top, set with five rows of short, firm bristles, which clean the nails perfectly. Bottom has six rows of extra long white bristles. A very convenient and desirable brush.

No. 8K3321 Price.(Unmailable).**29c**

Polished Hand Brush.

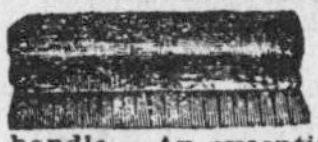

No. 8K3324 Five-Row Stiff, Imported black China Bristle Hand Brush, with fine white imported wood handle. An exceptional 15-cent hand brush.
Price....(Postage extra, 5 cents)....**11c**

Saratoga Hand Scrub.

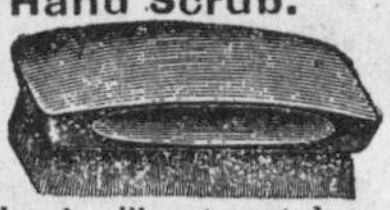

An exceptionally fine 50-cent brush, 7 rows, heavy, pure black, china imported bristles, firmly set in thick white polished holly handle. This brush will not mat down when wet, and will last for years.

No. 8K3325 Regular 50-cent brush. Our price....(Postage extra, 5 cents)....**31c**

Flesh and Bath Brushes.

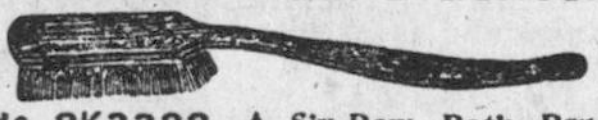

No. 8K3328 A Six-Row Bath Brush, long curved one-piece varnished handle and good black domestic bristles. Cannot break or warp when wet. Shipping weight, 12 ounces. Price..........**24c**

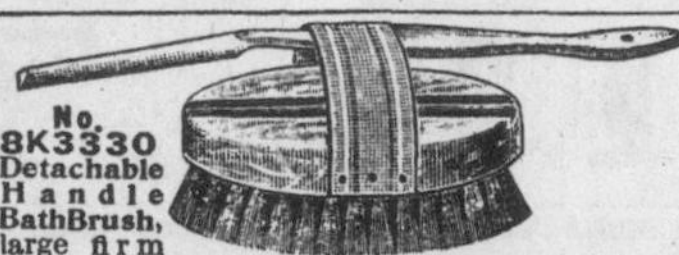

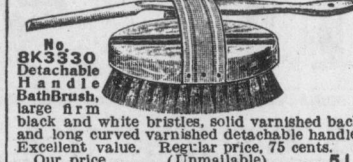

No. 8K3330 Detachable Handle BathBrush, large firm black and white bristles, solid varnished back and long curved varnished detachable handle. Excellent value. Regular price, 75 cents.
Our price.......(Unmailable).......**51c**

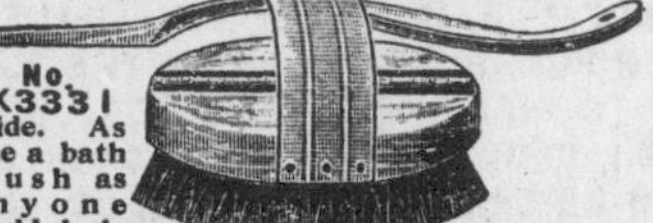

No. 8K3331 Pride. As fine a bath brush as anyone could desire. Long black China imported bristles, firm yet fine, solid back, and long double curved detachable holly handle. Can be used without handle as flesh brush or with handle for bath or back brush. Will not mat down when wet. Will last a lifetime. Cannot be bought elsewhere for double the money. Regular price, $1.00 to $1.25.
Our price.......(Unmailable).......**81c**

No. 8K3333 American Beauty. Same style brush as No. 8K3331, except much larger brush and pure white bristle, handle and back of brush the finest white holly wood. Justly called the American Beauty, as it is the best brush made. With proper care will last a lifetime. Each brush in box. It pays to buy the best. Regular price, $1.50 to $1.75.
Our price......(Unmailable)......**$1.19**

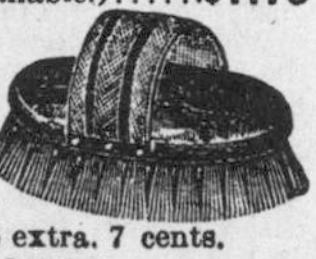

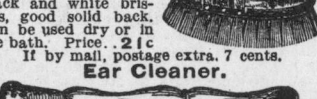

No. 8K3332 An Excellent Flesh Brush, 5½ inches long, with strap. Large, firm black and white bristles, good solid back. Can be used dry or in the bath. Price..**21c**
If by mail, postage extra, 7 cents.

Ear Cleaner.

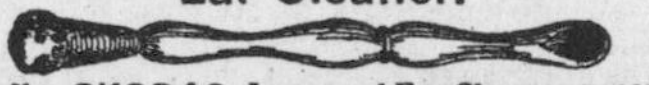

No. 8K3340 Improved Ear Cleaner, spoon and ear sponge combined. A very useful and pretty ivory toilet article. Price........**8c**
If by mail, postage extra, 1 cent.

Manicure Sets.

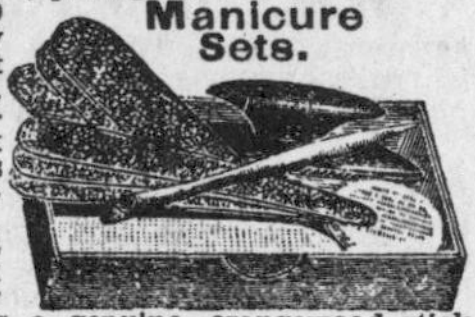

No. 8K3359 A very handy and convenient combination. The set consists of one box of Requa's Rose Nail Polishing Powder, one piece toilet pumice, six cloth center emery nail files, a genuine orangewood stick and a fine ebony chamois buffer. A bargain at double the price. Price, per set.....**19c**
If by mail, postage extra, 4 cents.

Vanity Manicure Set.

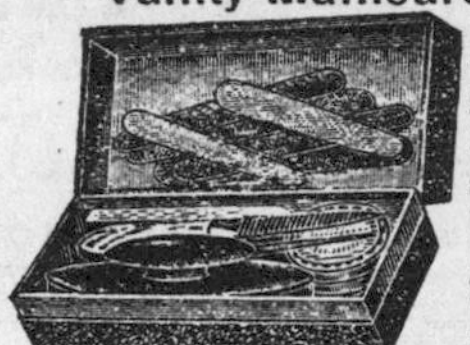

A more complete and much better set than the above. Contains a better chamois ebony buffer, box nail powder, one piece toilet pumice, six cloth center emery nail files, genuine orangewood stick and a fine bone handle nail file and cleaner. A special bargain at price quoted.

No. 8K3361 Price, per set...... **43c**
If by mail, postage extra, 7 cents.

Toilet Pumice Stone.

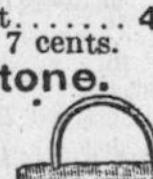

Toilet Pumice Stone, fitted with convenient handle. Very useful for manicuring, removing calloused or rough skin, ink stains, etc., from the hands, making them soft and smooth, and for all toilet purposes. Water should be used with the pumice stone.

No. 8K3360 Price (Postage extra,6c.) **9c**

Ebony Nail Buffer.

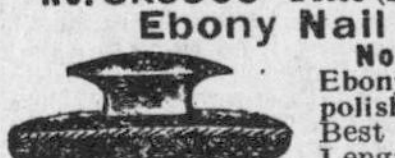

No. 8K3365 A fine Ebony Nail Buffer for polishing the finger nails. Best quality of chamois. Length, about 4 inches.
Price.... (Postage extra, 5 cents.)....**20c**

MANICURE INSTRUMENT DEPARTMENT.

Manicure and Pedicure Instruments.

We list below a high grade line of manicure and pedicure instruments. The general demand is for high grade instruments and we are therefore prompted to offer the highest grade of steel is used in the manufacture of these instruments and they are beautifully polished and finished. Each article is sold under our positive guarantee.

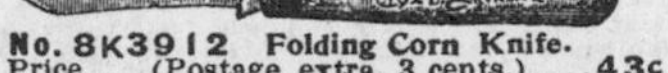

No. 8K3912 Folding Corn Knife.
Price....(Postage extra, 3 cents.)....**43c**

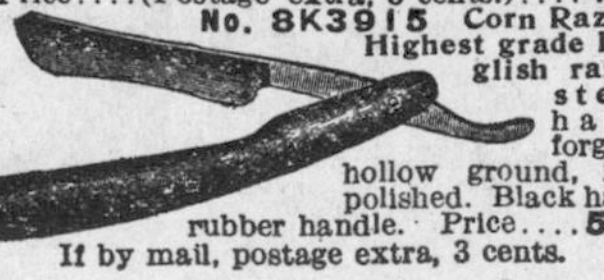

No. 8K3915 Corn Razor. Highest grade English razor steel, hand forged, hollow ground, full polished. Black hard rubber handle. Price....**55c**
If by mail, postage extra, 3 cents.

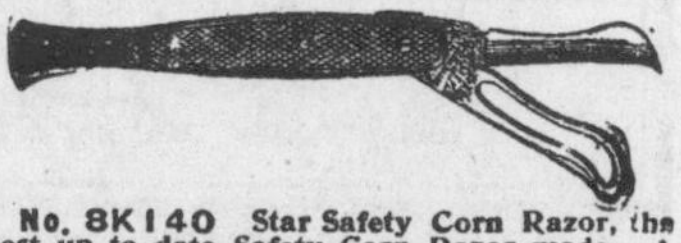

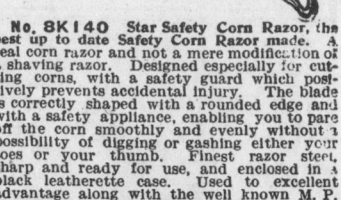

No. 8K140 Star Safety Corn Razor, the best up to date Safety Corn Razor made. A real corn razor and not a mere modification of a shaving razor. Designed especially for cutting corns, with a safety guard which positively prevents accidental injury. The blade is correctly shaped with a rounded edge and with a safety appliance, enabling you to pare off the corn smoothly and evenly without a possibility of digging or gashing either your toes or your thumb. Finest razor steel, sharp and ready for use, and enclosed in a black leatherette case. Used to excellent advantage along with the well known M. P. Corn Remover, catalogue No. 8K139.
Price..........**93c**
If by mail, postage extra, 3 cents.

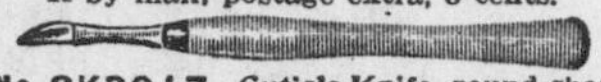

No. 8K3917 Cuticle Knife, round shank, carefully hardened and tempered, full polished long white bone handle. Price......**39c**
If by mail, postage extra, 3 cents.

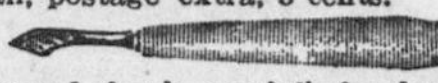

No. 8K3920 Cuticle Knife, round shank, carefully hardened and tempered, full polished short white bone handle. Price..........**27c**
If by mail, postage extra, 3 cents.

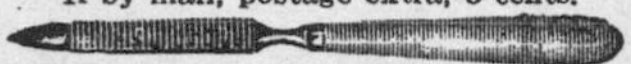

No. 8K3922 Nail File. Stiff nail file in long white bone handle, single cut on one side and double on the other; double grooved. Regular price, 75 cents. Our price.....**36c**
If by mail, postage extra, 3 cents.

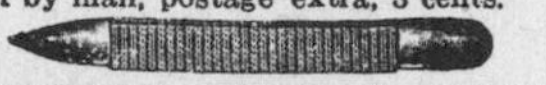

No. 8K3927 Fine Cleaning Point Nail Files. Both sides grooved, full polish, single velvet cut, hard crown. Length, 3 inches. Each in pocket case. Price......**16c**
If by mail, postage extra, 2 cents.

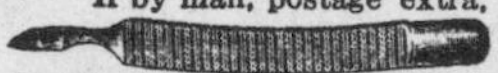

No. 8K3929 Combined Cuticle Knife and Nail File. Stiff curved file double and single cut, one groove in side, hard crown; full polish. Length, 3½ inches. Each in pocket case.
Price..........**25c**
If by mail, postage extra, 2 cents.

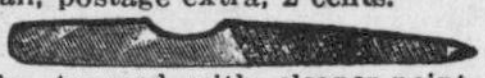

No. 8K3931 Stiff Nail File, tapered with cleaner point, Sheffield steel, a dead smooth double velvet cut, hard crown, full polish. Length, 5 inches.
Price..........**33c**
If by mail, postage extra, 2 cents.

No. 8K3933 Flexible Nail File, with nail cleaning point, same shape as No. 8K3931 Length, 5 inches. Price..........**22c**
If by mail, postage extra, 2 cents.

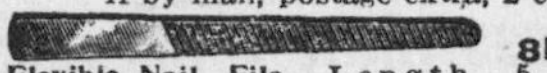

No. 8K3935 Flexible Nail File. Length, 5 inches.
Price..........**19c**
If by mail, postage extra, 2 cents.

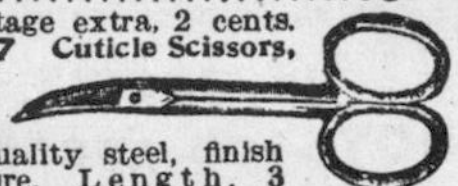

No. 8K3937 Cuticle Scissors, Genuine Wester Bros. scissors of Germany, and are the best quality steel, finish and manufacture. Length, 3 inches; highly nickel plated. Price...**41c**
If by mail, postage extra, 2 cents.

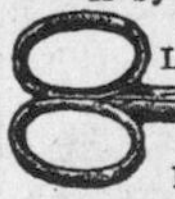

No. 8K3941 Cuticle Scissors. Length, 4 inches; nickel plated.
Price..........**46c**
If by mail, postage extra, 2 cents.

No. 8K3943 Nail Scissors. Genuine Wester Bros. scissors of Germany, and are the best quality steel, finish and manufacture. Length, 3½ inches. Best quality, nickel plated.

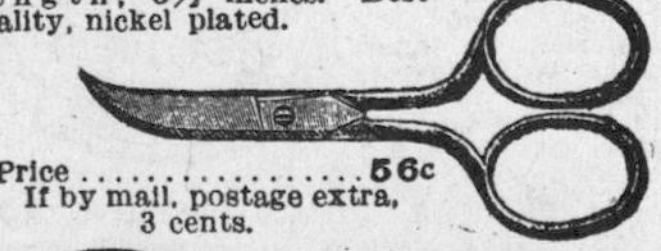

Price..........**56c**
If by mail, postage extra, 3 cents.

No. 8K3945 Nail Nipper, with spring.

High grade steel.
Price.....**51c**
If by mail, postage extra, 5 cents.

No. 8K3947 Nail Nipper, heavy, with patent spiral springs. Best grade steel, nickel plated. Price..........**$1.20**
If by mail, postage extra, 7 cents.

No. 8K3949 Una's Double Comodone or Blackhead Extracting Curette, nickel plated.
Price..........**41c**
If by mail, postage extra, 3 cents.

No. 8K3951 Una's Comodone or Blackhead Extracting Curette and Lance, nickel plated. Price..........**41c**
If by mail, postage extra, 3 cents.

TOILET SOAP DEPARTMENT

Dutch Sandalwood.

One of the best and most popular toilet soaps on the market. The stock used is of the very best and the odor (sandalwood) is particularly pleasing. Packed 3 cakes in box, as illustrated.

No. 8K3403 Our price, 2 boxes (of 3 cakes each) for .....(Unmailable.).....41c

Necessaire Complexion Soap.

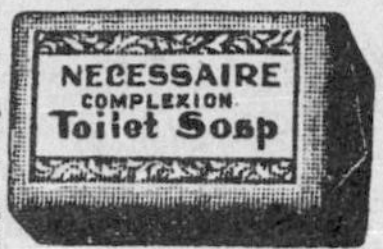

Necessaire (the needful) is the name given to this soap, it being an exceptional combination. It is composed of the purest soap making ingredients, combined in correct proportions. It is the perfection of soap to give the skin a healthy appearance and is free from injurious ingredients which are so irritating, annoying and disfiguring. A very finely perfumed product.

No. 8K3405 Our price, per box of 3 cakes....(Postage extra, 14 cents).....24c

Genuine Witch Hazel Soap.

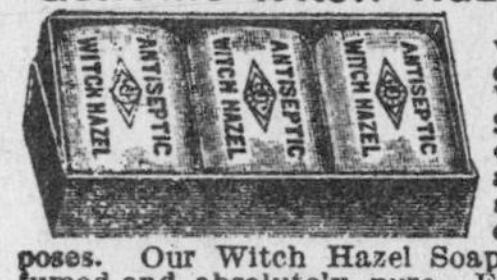

One of our very best sellers. This Witch Hazel Soap is without a peer among the soaps for medicinal purposes. Our Witch Hazel Soap is finely perfumed and absolutely pure. For healing the skin and improving the complexion it is without an equal. Large cakes, nicely milled and perfumed. A great bargain at the price. Not the cheap grade usually sold.

No. 8K3410 Our price, 2 boxes (6 cakes) for........(Unmailable)........19c

English Oatmeal.

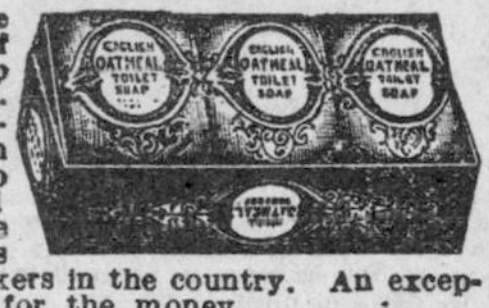

This is the finest piece of Oatmeal Soap on the market. It is the genuine English Oatmeal Soap manufactured by one of the best perfumers and soap makers in the country. An exceptional value for the money.

No. 8K3413 Our price, 2 boxes of 3 cakes each for..........................25c

If by mail, postage extra, per box, 14 cents.

Colgate's Cashmere Bouquet.

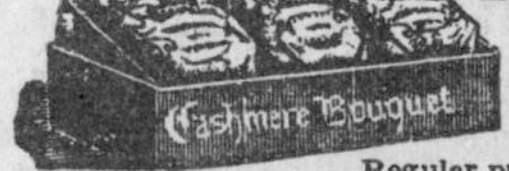

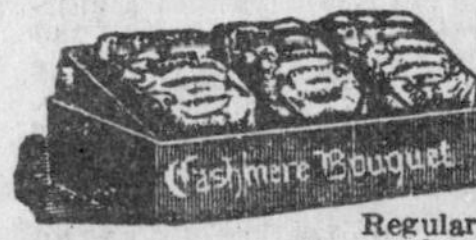

Colgate's Cashmere Bouquet, undoubtedly one of the finest and sweetest perfumed toilet soaps made. Regular price, 75 cents per box.

No. 8K3417 Our price, less than box, per cake...........................19c

No. 8K3418 Per box of 3 cakes....57c

If by mail, postage extra, per box, 14 cents.

Carbolic Soap.

An excellent Carbolic Soap. Why pay 25 cents per cake for certain advertised Green Carbolic Soaps when this can be purchased for 19 cents per box of 3 cakes?

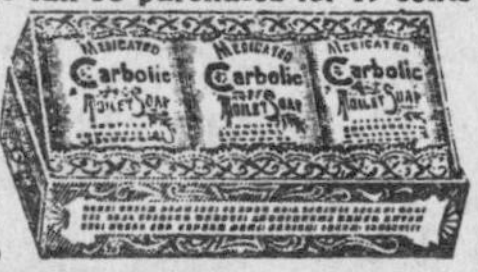

We guarantee this the highest grade carbolic acid soap on the market. Very beneficial where carbolic acid soap is required.

No. 8K3415 Our price, per box of 3 cakes.............................19c

If by mail, postage extra, per box, 14 cents.

Violette De Parme.

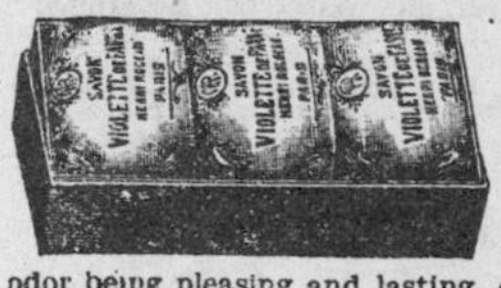

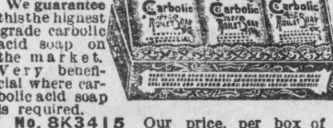

This artistically designed soap is especially prepared for ladies having a preference for green stem violet odor, the odor being pleasing and lasting, characteristic of this high grade article. This soap is of exceptionally fine stock and finely perfumed, and is, in our opinion, one of the finest violet soaps ever sold at reasonable prices.

No. 8K3419 Our price, per box....27c

If by mail, postage extra, per box, 14 cents.

Woodbury's Facial Soap.

The Best Medicated Skin Soap Manufactured.

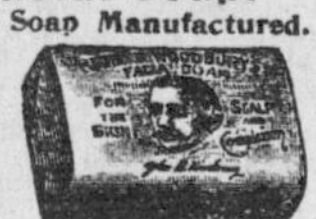

This widely advertised and well known medicated soap is without doubt one of the best curative skin soaps made. Sold everywhere for 25 cents per cake. Preferred by many to any other advertised skin or medicated soap manufactured.

No. 8K3439 Our price, per cake....19c

No. 8K3440 Per box of 3 cakes....57c

If by mail, postage extra, per cake, 3 cents; per box, 10 cents.

Antiseptic Soap Sheets.

Germs readily adhere to wet soap and many skin diseases are contracted from its use.

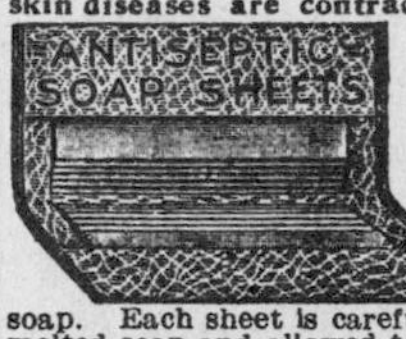

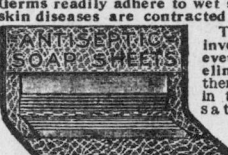

This very handy invention enables every person traveling to carry with them at all times in their pocket, satchel or grip, forty sheets of antiseptic highly perfumed toilet soap. Each sheet is carefully dipped in the melted soap and allowed to harden, and these forty sheets are packed in a pocket, double folding imitation leather case. Each case contains the equivalent of a large cake of 10-cent soap, and at the same time prevents the person from catching diseases in hotels, restaurants or wherever they may use soap. Keeps indefinitely and when placed in the hand, together with a small amount of water, will give a copious cleansing lather. Regular price, per case of 40 sheets, 15 cents.

No. 8K3414 Our price, 3 cases for..21c

If by mail, postage extra, 5 cents.

Garland Glycerine Tar Soap.

THE FARMER'S BAR.

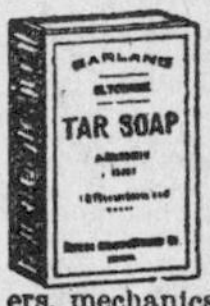

The great healing, cleansing and antiseptic soap. It is a special combination of pure refined glycerine, boric acid, pure refined tar and other antiseptics. It removes dirt and grease easily, heals the wounds on the hands, makes them soft, and is the one soap that combines the best healing and cleansing agents. A great friend to farmers, mechanics and others whose hands require a good cleansing, neutral and healing soap. This soap is without an equal as a general household, medicinal and toilet soap. Cleans the skin easily, is antiseptic, heals all wounds and admired by all who once use it. Considering the extra price offered on this soap, it should be used in every home. Lathers freely in hot, cold, hard or soft water. Large 6-ounce cake, or one-half more soap than others.

No. 8K3431 Price, 6 cakes for.....25c

Armour's Transparent Tar Soap.

The Well Known Shampoo Tar Soap.

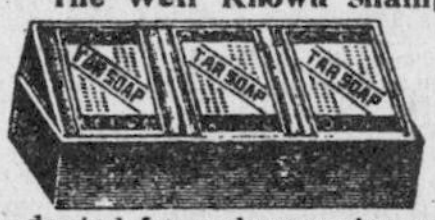

A scientific combination of pure refined pine tar, glycerine and other medicinal ingredients. This soap is particularly adapted for a shampooing soap. If used regularly will keep the scalp free from dandruff and will keep the hair soft and in good condition. Also a first class toilet soap for general use. Packed three cakes in box. Each cake wrapped in tinfoil.

No. 8K3425 Our price, per box.30c

If by mail, postage extra, per box, 10 cents.

Toyland Baby Soap.

FINE FOR BABY'S BATH.

A new and unequaled value. A perfect soap, delightfully perfumed. A most unique and attractive package. Wrapped in colored and gold embossed wrapper and box. Regular price, per box, 25 cents.

No. 8K3476 Our price, per box. 19c

If by mail, postage extra, per box, 12 cents.

Lily Series Soap.

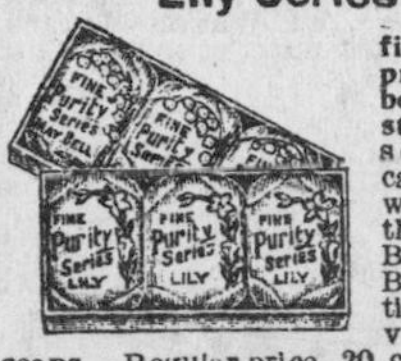

Two boxes of very fine violet soap at the price of an ordinary box in your home store. Fine perfumed soap, 3½-ounce cakes, each cake wrapped and packed three cakes to box. Both Lily and May Bell odors. Exceptional values and very satisfactory soaps. Regular price, 20 cents per box.

No. 8K3451 Our price, 2 boxes for (unmailable on account of weight)....25c

Force Pumiss Soap.

THE ONE STANDARD.

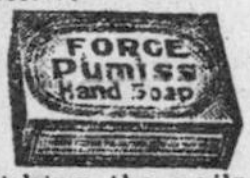

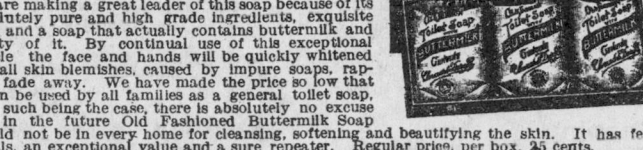

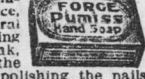

A new scientific combination of pure powdered pumice, salts of tartar and pure neutral cleansing soap. Just the thing for quickly removing ink, paint or grease stains from the hands, hard callous skin, polishing the nails and other general toilet purposes. Does not scratch, is free from acids and should be in every home.

No. 8K3465 Price, 3 cakes for..13c

If by mail, postage extra, 4 cents.

Transparent Glycerine.

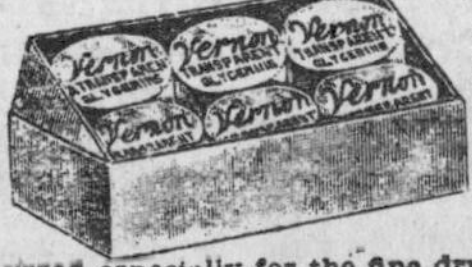

This sweetly perfumed, transparent glycerine soap is a marvelous value and we shall look forward to many repeated orders. Prepared especially for the fine drug trade.

No. 8K3468 Price, per box of 12 cakes.45c

Turkish Bath Soap.

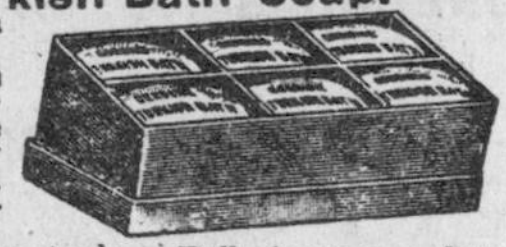

This is a genuine Turkish Bath Soap, made from pure stock, nicely perfumed and especially prepared for fine drug trade. Full 4-ounce cakes. Packed 12 cakes in a neat pasteboard box.

No. 8K3483 Our price, per box of 12 cakes. (Unmailable on account of weight).....46c

Pure Green Oil Soap.

This soap is unequaled for general toilet purposes. Is highly recommended as a soap for shampooing. It is a strictly pure vegetable soap. Contains no animal fats whatever, and is used by many in preference to all other soaps. Also unequaled for a cleansing soap for fine furniture, pianos, etc. Merely wash by making a good lather and you will be very much surprised at the fine results obtained. Then wipe dry and polish with dry soft chamois. Put up in 16-ounce glass screw top jars.

No. 8K3492 Per 16-ounce jar....22c

OUR GREAT LEADERS.

VIOLET GLYCERINE SOAP, 2 BOXES FOR 39 CENTS.

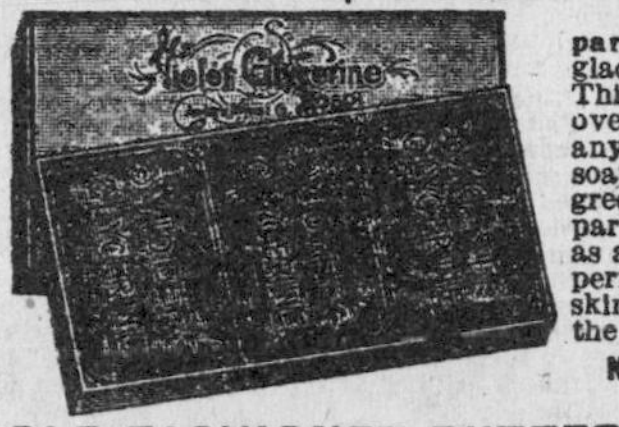

To the thousands of persons preferring a transparent, exceptionally high grade toilet soap, we are glad to offer them the genuine Jergens' Violet Glycerine. This soap has of late spread with wonderful rapidity over the country, and once used you would never have any other. Preferred by many to imported glycerine soaps. Each cake is perfectly clear, transparent pale green color and perfumed with violet odor. The last part of each cake is just as sweet, just as refreshing as a new box. The soap is of absolutely pure materials, perfectly neutral and will not irritate the most tender skin. Large 4-ounce cakes and packed three cakes to the box. Retail price, 25 to 30 cents per box.

No. 8K3437 Two boxes (three cakes each).39c

Unmailable on account of weight.

OLD FASHIONED BUTTERMILK SOAP, The Ladies' Friend. 4 Boxes for 49 Cents.

Ladies particular regarding their complexion must be very careful about the grade of soap they use, as by continually washing the face and hands several times a day with cheap soaps the various pores of the skin absorb the impure products found in such soap and make a perfectly spotless complexion impossible. We are glad to offer the ladies of America Jergens' Genuine Old Fashioned Buttermilk Soap. Every cake of this soap is made out of the very purest white edible tallow. We are making a great leader of this soap because of its absolutely pure and high grade ingredients, exquisite odor and a soap that actually contains buttermilk and plenty of it. By continual use of this exceptional article the face and hands will be quickly whitened and all skin blemishes, caused by impure soaps, rapidly fade away. We have made the price so low that it can be used by all families as a general toilet soap, and such being the case, there is absolutely no excuse why in the future Old Fashioned Buttermilk Soap should not be in every home for cleansing, softening and beautifying the skin. It has few equals, an exceptional value and a sure repeater. Regular price, per box, 25 cents.

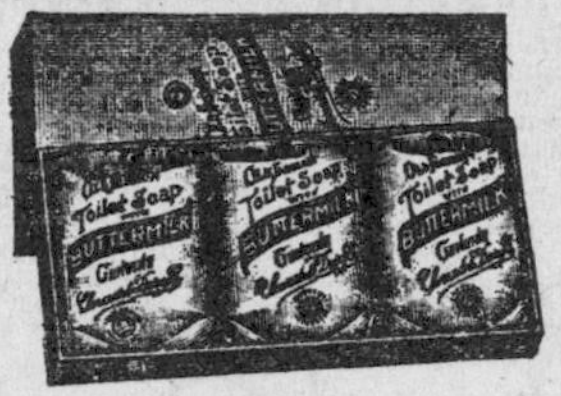

No. 8K3455 On account of the exceptionally low price at which this soap is quoted, and to enable all of our customers to use this exceptionally high class soap, we will sell four boxes, 12 cakes (retail price, $1.00) for...................................49c

Unmailable on account of weight.

GENUINE COLD CREAM SOAP. 12 Cakes for 47 Cents.

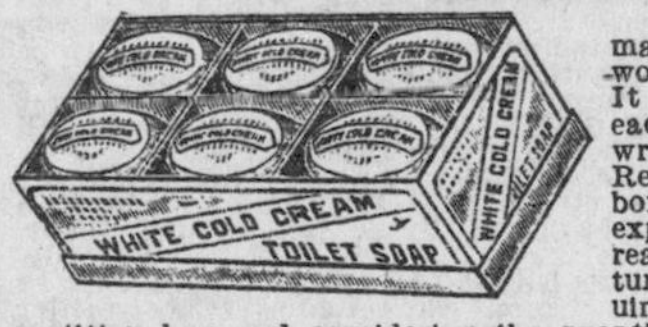

Genuine Cold Cream Soap has been upon the market for several years, and during that time has won for itself thousands and thousands of friends. It has always been packed three cakes in a box, each cake wrapped in a beautiful lithographed wrapper and packed in a box of artistic design. Retail price of this soap is from 25 to 30 cents per box. In order to enable our customers to use this expensive soap, and yet to put the price within the reach of all, we have finally persuaded the manufacturers to put up for us, twelve cakes of this same Genuine Cold Cream Soap, packed twelve cakes in a white partition box, and considering the quantity we would sell, to enable us to reduce the price within the reach of all. We, therefore, are offering for the first time Genuine Cold Cream Soap, full 4-ounce cakes, absolutely pure ingredients, finely milled and pressed, exquisitely perfumed and containing same ingredients as are used in the manufacture of all high grade cold creams. Just think of getting three pounds of absolutely pure, highly perfumed cold cream soap, which would cost you at a retail store from $1.00 to $1.25, at a price never before heard of for this high grade material! We trust our various customers will appreciate this offer and include one or two boxes in their next order.

No. 8K3450 12 cakes in a box. Our price, per box.........................47c

GENUINE IMPORTED OLIVE OIL CASTILE SOAP.

This is the genuine imported olive oil castile soap and the highest grade manufactured. Beautiful hard white imported oil castile. This is not the cheaper grade castile made of olive oil foots and cheap greases offered by others for olive oil castile, but is the very finest imported Olive Oil Castile Soap that we can buy. Unsurpassed for washing sores, scars, skin diseases, tender skin, baby's bath, for washing silks, fine colored ribbons or wherever a strictly pure neutral soap is required. We sell this superior soap at the same price that others ask for the cheap castile, in order to enable our customers to have the very best at the prices asked by others. It pays to buy the best.

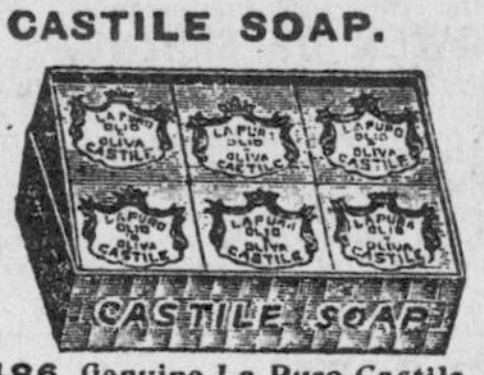

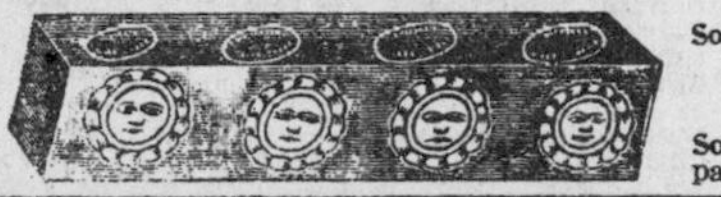

No. 8K3486 Genuine La Puro Castile Soap, packed twelve 4-ounce cakes in a box. Price.......................................57c

No. 8K3487 Genuine La Puro Castile Soap, 2-pound bar. Each one wrapped in oil paper and packed in carton. Price......38c

Hard Water Cocoa Castile Soap

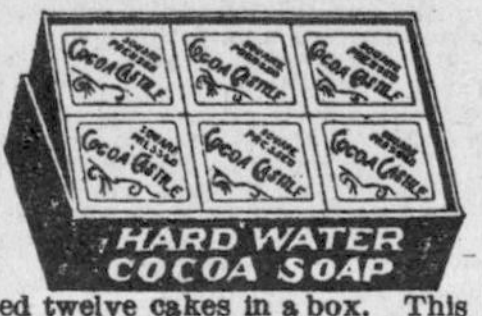

Made of the finest East Indian Cocoa Oil. Lathers freely and is the only soap that produces a good lather in hard water. Large 3½-oz. square pressed cakes and packed twelve cakes in a box. This soap is guaranteed not to turn rancid or yellow which is so common among so called cocoa soaps.

No. 8K3427 Our price, per box...45c

Unmailable.

Forest Queen Soap.

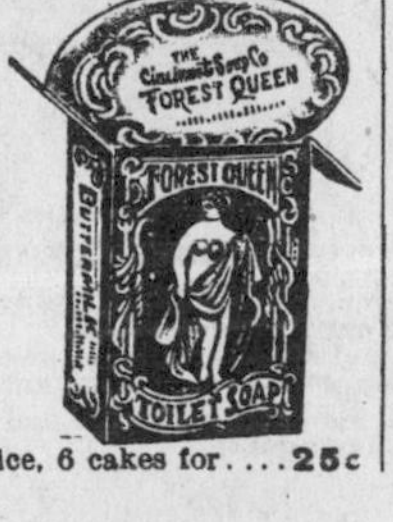

This well known Forest Queen, Buttermilk and Witch Hazel Soap is a pure French milled product made of absolutely pure materials and delightfully perfumed. Each cake wrapped in tissue and packed in handsome individual cartons. Full 4-ounce cakes. A ready seller, quick repeater and always satisfactory.

No. 8K3477 Price, 6 cakes for....25c

Shaving Soaps.

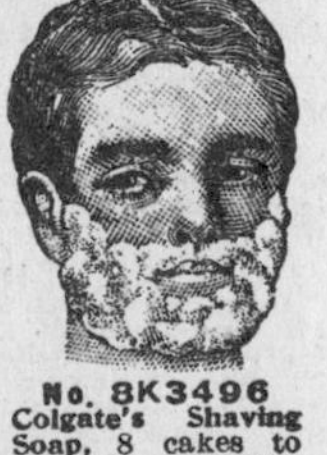

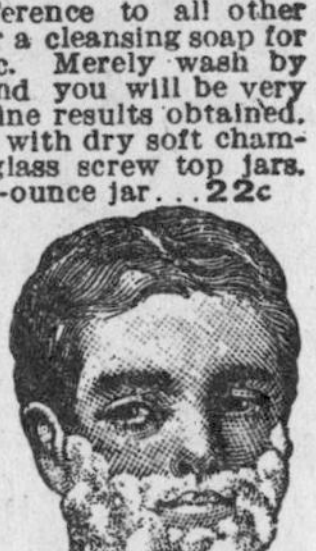

The Genuine World Renowned Standard Shaving Soaps.

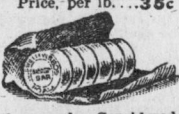

No. 8K3495 Williams' Shaving Soap. 6 cakes to a pound.

Price, per lb....35c

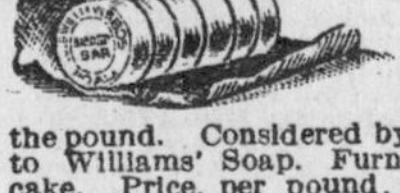

No. 8K3496 Colgate's Shaving Soap, 8 cakes to the pound. Considered by many far superior to Williams' Soap. Furnished in new form cake. Price, per pound..............37c

See also our Gents' Shaving Outfit, page 795

Shaving Sticks.

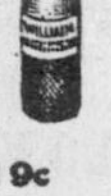

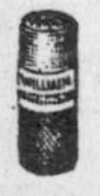

No. 8K3497 Genuine Williams' Shaving Sticks. In leatherette box; handy when traveling; also for home use. No waste; always clean and ready for use. Price, per box...........19c

No. 8K3498 Colgate's Shaving Stick in nickel plated metal case. An excellent piece of shaving soap.

Price, per box....................19c

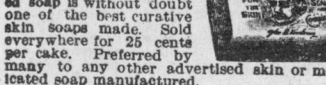

DIVISION OF TRUSSES.

IMPORTANT FACTS REGARDING TRUSSES AND TRUSS PRICES.

THERE IS PROBABLY NO OTHER ARTICLE OF MERCHANDISE, nothing in the medical or surgical line in which there are so many grades or which sell at such exorbitant prices, as trusses, nothing in which the original cost of manufacture has been so utterly disregarded in arriving at a selling price. It seems ever since trusses have been made, it has been the custom for manufacturer, jobber, surgical supply house, physicians and retailer, each to add one or two dollars to the original cost until the truss we now sell you for 50 cents will cost you elsewhere $1.00 to $2.50, and our $2.50 truss from $5.00 to $15.00, depending how much money you have and are able to pay.

WE CHANGE ALL THIS. Knowing the injustice done to thousands and thousands of customers, we made arrangements with the best truss factory in the country for furnishing us the following line of highest grade trusses and considering the quantity we could sell, we obtained their cost price with small profit added. We in turn offer these same high grade trusses to our customers at our cost plus one small profit for handling and that is the reason we offer trusses at the exceptional prices quoted. Remember we furnish you nothing but the very best in every line and guarantee the quality of our trusses to be beyond all competition.

GROSSLY IMITATED. Our truss business has grown until we today sell more trusses than all other mail order houses combined. Remember we buy only the very best trusses, fill your orders accurately and make the various trusses fit your particular requirements. We now have a reputation throughout the United States for furnishing the very best trusses at half or less than half the prices on equal quality trusses over many other concerns in the country. The vast experience of the manufacturers have enabled them to study the various forms of rupture and make the most reliable styles of leather covered, elastic and hard rubber trusses, whose springs and pads are strong, correctly shaped and the entire workmanship of the very best. We do not fear competition in this line, for our high class line has never been duplicated at anywhere near our prices, and we invite comparison of our trusses with those you buy of others for double our prices quoted.

OUR UNQUALIFIED GUARANTEE. We guarantee every truss sent out by our firm to be strictly as represented and of the highest grade of its kind.

WE GUARANTEE that our prices are very much lower than those charged by others and that, taking each style as a class, you cannot get a higher grade, finer or more substantial material or better fitting truss, no matter what price you would be willing to pay. We will send any of our trusses on request for comparison with trusses of other houses, and, if you do not find that our appliances, are better in material, workmanship and fit; if you cannot see at a glance that you can save one half the price on our trusses (the saving depending on the style of the truss you wear), you can return our truss at our expense and the full amount you have paid for it will be returned to you for the asking.

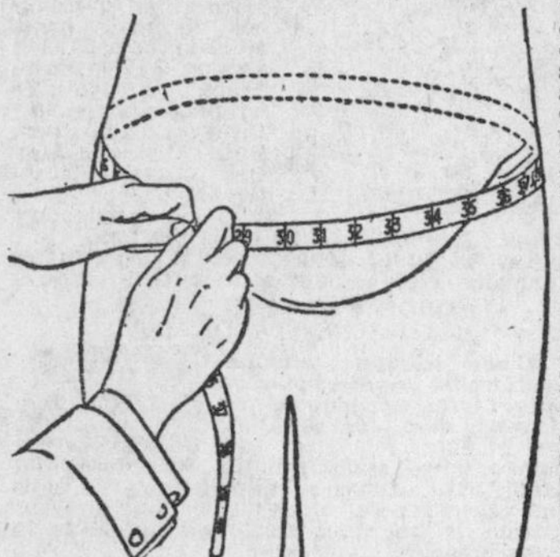

Fig. 1.

HOW TO ORDER.

MEASUREMENTS AND SPECIAL INFORMATION. In ordering trusses state plainly if for adults, youths or children; whether for single or double rupture. If for single rupture, name the side afflicted. Also state how long you have been ruptured, if rupture is round or flat, large or small, and if rupture is on right, left or both sides. Give full circumference of body in line of rupture, or 2 inches below the top of hip bones, avoiding the fullness of the abdomen. (See Fig. 1.) Full information as to sex, age, weight, height and occupation should be given, as it better enables us to successfully meet your requirements and select a truss for your special case. Always put a truss on body from the opposite or well side of body.

Directions for Fitting and Shaping Leather Covered Steel Spring Trusses

IT IS IMPORTANT that the spring should be properly fitted to shape of person at all points by manipulation, using all fingers, the thumb doing the bending, while the fingers hold and brace the spring and spread the strain, thus lessening the chances of breaking in shaping. Never give the spring a sharp bend or force the shape too rapidly, but bend slowly and carefully, as illustrated in Fig. 2, as it is important to hold the strength required in spring as long as possible.

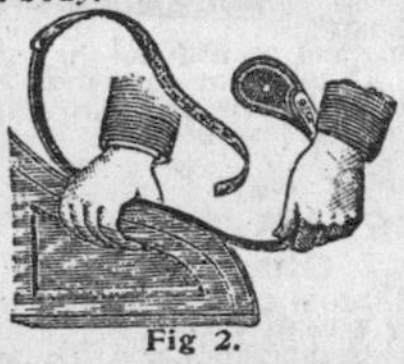

Fig 2.

Directions for Shaping and Fitting Hard Rubber Trusses.

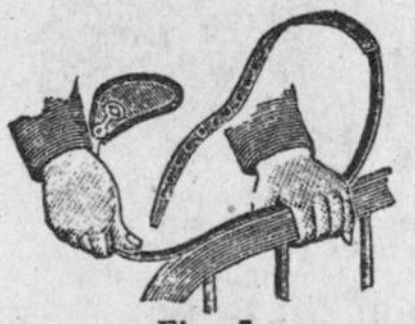

Fig. 5.

TO INCREASE POWER OF SPRING. This may be done in a variety of ways; by placing it over a register for a few moments; holding it near a stove; dipping it in hot water; passing it gradually through flame—gas jet, candle or lamp. (See Fig.3.) It is not necessary to have it near enough to scorch the polish, which will have no other injurious effect than to impair the looks. Before beginning to bend, warm the whole length excepting the pads, regardless of the fact that possibly only a slight bend at some particular point may be necessary. Having the material warmed, gently coil the spring, making the coil smaller, thus making the pressure stronger. (See Fig. 4.)

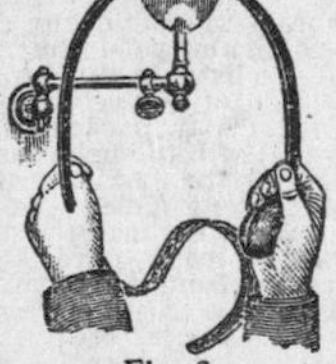

Fig. 3.

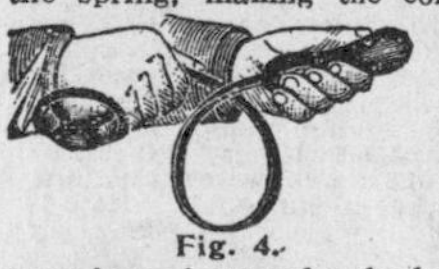

Fig. 4.

TO WEAKEN POWER OF SPRING. Warm the spring as directed, then uncoil gradually with hand, or bending over arm of chair or desk. (See Fig. 5.)

FITTING TO FORM. Warm spring as directed, shaping with hands or over arm of chair or desk (see Fig. 5) until you have secured the shape required. Never give a spring a sharp bend over a sharp corner.

Never attempt to bend or shape a spring until thoroughly warm; it may break. We will not accept in return trusses that have been damaged or broken by manipulation.

ELASTIC TRUSSES.

Trusses with elastic bands are excellent styles for use at night to continue the support given by a Spring Truss during the day; this assists in a radical cure, and a cure is only accomplished by giving a continuing support to the hernia, not allowing its protrusion at any time, which permits nature to make the cure by contracting the opening.

The Genuine New York Elastic Truss.

Is made of an extra good quality web elastic 1¾ inches wide, of great strength and durability. Fitted with nickel fastenings, solid front and fine enamel pad, which is reversible, so it can be arranged for either right or left side. Remember that this truss is fitted with the very best improved safety clutch fastenings, the most reliable fastener made. The price of this style of truss elsewhere is from $1.00 to $2.50. We guarantee it to be superior in quality, workmanship and finish, and it will cost you but 49 cents.

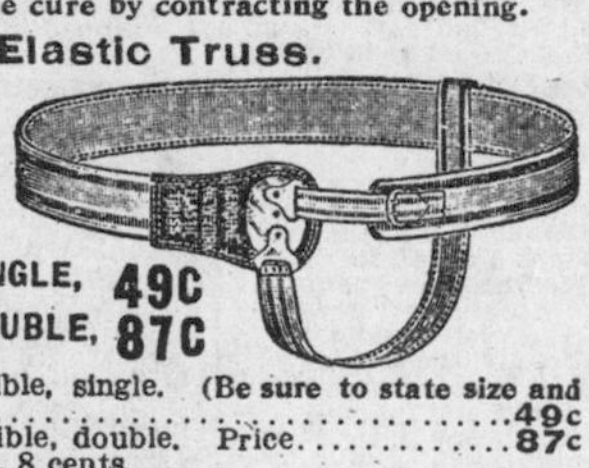

SINGLE, 49c
DOUBLE, 87c

No. 8K3510 New York Elastic Truss, reversible, single. (Be sure to state size and side.) Price....49c

No. 8K3511 New York Elastic Truss, reversible, double. Price....87c

If by mail, postage extra, 8 cents.

The above truss can be furnished in youths' and adult sizes at the prices quoted. Be sure to send with your order measurement around body on a line with rupture.

DO NOT FAIL to state on which side the rupture is located and give measurement around body on a line with the rupture.

Walker's Approved French Pad Single Elastic Truss, $1.95.

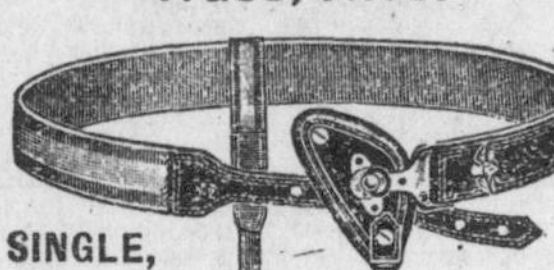

SINGLE, $1.95

An exceptional fine elastic truss. Composed of fine strong, extra wide elastic, to which is attached the improved Walker pad or pads combined with strong elastic understraps. It is by far the best elastic truss ever made. This truss is fitted across the body, the full part of the pad facing the center. The advantages of this style of truss over other elastic trusses are as follows:

First—By fitting across the body and fastening on the center steel posts on the back of pad a center draft over the top of pad is produced, insuring in all cases the right kind of pressure.

Second—By hooking on the tie strap the pad tips produce upward and inward pressure at the same time. Walker's Approved French Pad Elastic Truss is, therefore, especially adapted for rupture which comes out egg shape, usually known as inguinal hernia, or light cases of scrotal rupture, where the intestines go down into the scrotum, called inguinal scrotal rupture. Fitted with rubber tubing understraps. Can be furnished in stuffed pad or water pad. In ordering state which kind is desired. Made of the finest, extra wide and heavy web elastic. Handsomely trimmed and stitched. This truss is reversible and adjustable.

No. 8K3512 Walker's Approved French Pad Single Elastic Truss. (Be sure to state size and side.) Price....$1.95

No. 8K3513 Walker's Approved Truss, with Special Radical Cure Center Spring Pad. (Be sure to state size and side.) Price....$3.10

If by mail, postage extra, 8 cents.

Walker's Approved French Pad Double Elastic Truss, $2.90.

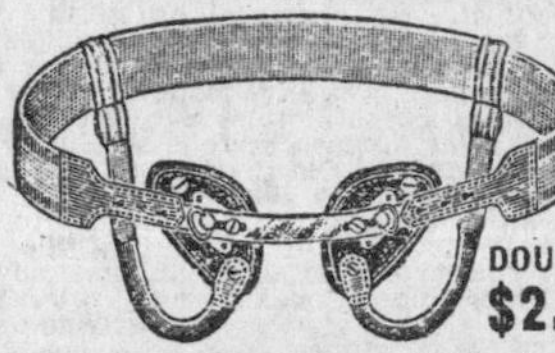

DOUBLE, $2.90

Has all the advantages as explained in the description of the single truss, and is furnished with double rubber tubing understraps. It is adjustable in width, and also enables you to get the proper angle in the groin, thus making this double elastic truss the easiest and most comfortable in existence.

No. 8K3519 Walker's Approved French Pad Double Elastic Truss. Price....$2.90

No. 8K3520 Walker's Approved Double Elastic Truss with Water Pads. Price....$3.65

No. 8K3521 Walker's Double Elastic Truss, with Radical Cure Center Spring Pad, for adults only. Price...$5.25

If by mail, postage extra, 12 cents.

Lea's Special Elastic Truss.

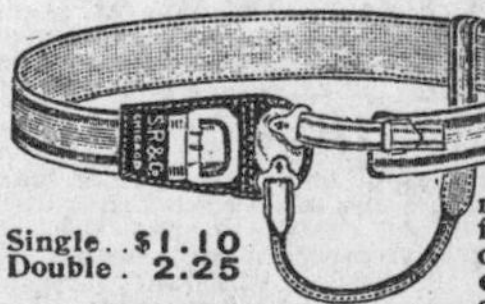

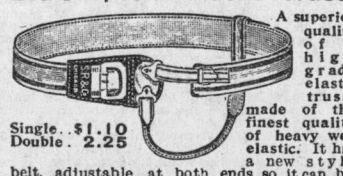

Single..$1.10
Double. 2.25

A superior quality of a high grade elastic truss, made of the finest quality of heavy web elastic. It has a new style belt, adjustable at both ends so it can be lengthened or shortened as may be desired. It is fitted with improved safety clutch fastenings. Complete with the celebrated water pads, which can be supplied either leather or silk covered. These water pads are very popular, comfortable, are reversible, so that they can be arranged for either right or left side. This class of truss is never sold by others for less than $2.50 or $4.00, single, and as high as $4.00 to $6.00 for the double truss. We furnish them with a positive guarantee to our customers that they cannot get a better truss of this style, no matter how much they would be willing to pay, at the following low prices:

No. 8K3514 Lea Special Elastic Truss, youths' or adults' sizes, single. (Be sure to state size and side.) Price....$1.10

No. 8K3515 Lea Special Elastic Single Truss, with Special Radical Cure Center Spring Pad, for adults only. (Be sure to state size and side.) Price....$2.25

No. 8K3516 Lea Special Elastic Truss, youths' or adults' sizes, double. Price....$2.25

No. 8K3517 Lea Special Elastic Double Truss with Special Radical Cure Center Spring Pad, for adults only. Price....$3.25

If by mail, postage extra, 10 cents.

Be sure to send with your order measurement around the waist on a line with rupture, also state whether leather or silk covered pads are desired.

The Genuine Lever Elastic Truss.

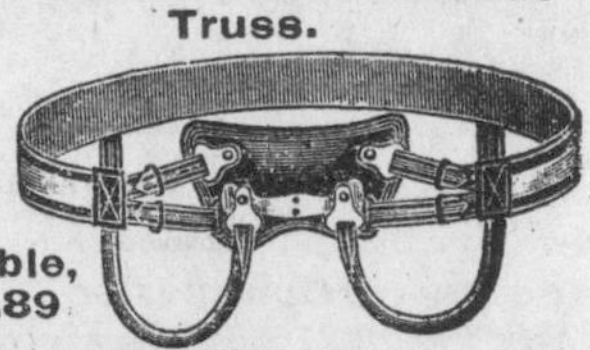

Double, $2.89

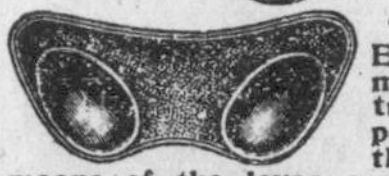

This Genuine Lever Elastic Truss has many valuable features, the most important of which is the fact that by means of the lever appliance extra pressure may be obtained in cases of severe rupture. The Lever Elastic Truss always gives satisfaction. Can be used for both single and double rupture. The belt is 2 inches wide, made of the very best web elastic. Solid leather casing and brass trimmings. Fine enameled finished double pads on one plate, as shown in illustration.

No. 8K3525 The Genuine Lever Elastic Truss. (Be sure to state size and side.) Price, complete....$2.89

No. 8K3526 The Genuine Lever Elastic Truss, with Water Pad. (Be sure to state size and side.) Price....$3.65

No. 8K3527 The Genuine Lever Elastic Truss, with Radical Cure Center Spring Pad, for adults only. (Be sure to state size and side.) Price....$5.40

If by mail postage extra, 12 cents.

NOTICE — The Radical Cure Spring Pad is for use of adults.

SPRING TRUSSES.

Calf Leather Covered French Spring Truss.

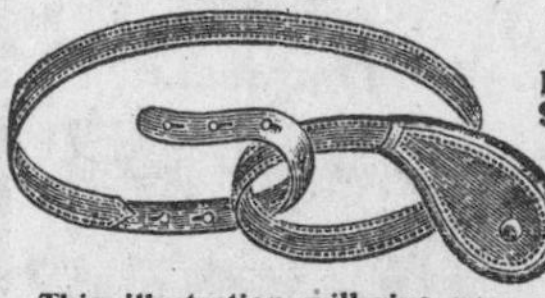

Single, 67c
Double, $1.25

This illustration will give you an idea of the appearance of our single calf leather covered French truss, which we can furnish you at the extremely small price of 67 cents. The double plain leather covered French truss costs only $1.25. These trusses cannot be duplicated at double the price if bought elsewhere, and, although we supply them to our customers at a nominal figure, they are high grade, well made, leather covered spring trusses and give good satisfaction. Even at our low prices we sell this truss with a guarantee that it will fit perfectly, and, if not entirely satisfactory when you receive it, you can return it at our expense and we will cheerfully refund your money.

NOTE — Do not confuse this truss with those in other catalogues. Our truss is covered with genuine calfskin and not with cheap colored leather.

No. 8K3528 Calf Leather Covered Spring French Truss, single. (Be sure to state size and side.) Price....67c

No. 8K3529 Calf Leather Covered Spring French Truss, double. Price....$1.25

If by mail, postage extra, 14 cents.

In ordering the single truss, be sure to state where the rupture is located, whether on the right or left side. Also give in all cases the measurement around body on a line with rupture.

Walker's Approved Fine French Leather Covered Spring Truss.

Single, $1.95

This truss has fine Russia calf covering and is furnished with fine water pad or stuffed pad to make it soft and comfortable for wearer. This truss has a special feature by which it may be adjusted to any angle to suit the position of the rupture, by releasing the thumbscrew that goes through the nickel steel neck into the pad, thereby allowing pad to revolve as on a pivot.

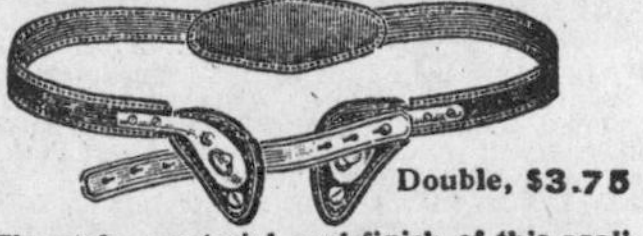

Double, $3.75

The style, material and finish of this appliance is the same as the single Walker's Fine Leather Covered Truss, but with the additional spring back pad, as shown in illustration, which is soft, pliable, and makes this double truss very comfortable.

No. 8K3540 Walker's Approved Fine Leather Covered Spring Truss, single. (State size and side). Price....$1.95

If by mail, postage extra, 12 cents.

No. 8K3550 Walker's Approved Fine French Leather Covered Spring Double Truss. Price....$3.75

If by mail, postage extra, 12 cents.

In ordering, state where rupture is located, whether on right or left side; also give measurement around body on line with rupture.

OUR GREAT LEADER.
A Truss that Meets Nearly all Requirements.
THE BEST THAT MONEY CAN BUY.

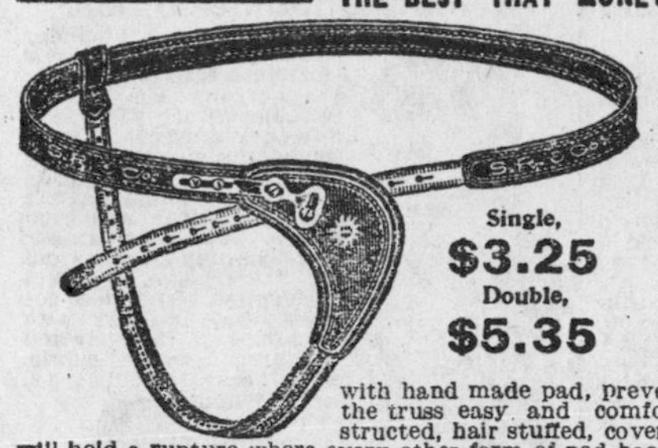

Single, **$3.25**
Double, **$5.35**

WE HAVE SELECTED as a leader the genuine full calf covered scrotal truss, manufactured by J. Ellwood Lee Co. of Conshohocken, Penna. A truss that can be used either for regular or scrotal rupture. This truss is sold by every surgical instrument and physicians' supply dealer in the country at practically double our prices.

EVERY PART OF THE TRUSS is selected with special care. The springs are the very best steel and carefully tempered. The covering over the spring is heavy calfskin, padded inside and fine casing, double silk stitched, with hand made pad, preventing its cutting the body and making the truss easy and comfortable. The pad is especially constructed, hair stuffed, covered with soft leather, large in size and will hold a rupture where every other form of pad has failed. It has a rubber covered elastic understrap which keeps the pad in perfect shape and prevents its slipping or shifting.

THIS TRUSS is the very best truss that can be made and we guarantee will give satisfaction in every case. Rupture is very dangerous unless properly held and we strongly recommend this truss for your particular case. It is a truss that will hold the rupture wherever located; is the best truss made and will outwear all others. We offer you the single truss for $3.25 and the double truss for $5.35. We offer you this excellent truss at these low prices in order to bring the best truss within the reach of all.

IT PAYS TO BUY THE BEST

NOTE—No other mail order house in the country is able to offer you this same high grade truss for less than double our prices. Duplicate pictures are easy to make, but do not confuse pictures that look like this or low prices with this article because no other mail order house has the genuine article. If you want the best and at a price that others charge you for a cheaper imitation, then take no risk, but buy this truss at once. Remember your own life is at stake, therefore buy the best. For cheaper scrotal truss, see German Scrotal No. 8K3552.

No. 8K3541 Lee's Fine Single Scrotal Truss. (Be sure to state size and side.) Price....$3.25
No. 8K3543 Lee's Double Scrotal Truss. Price....5.35
If by mail, postage extra, 24 cents.

IN ORDERING please give side on which rupture is located; also measurement around body on a line with the rupture. Sold under a positive guarantee that no better truss of this style could be obtained anywhere no matter what price you would be willing to pay.

Appendicitis Truss.

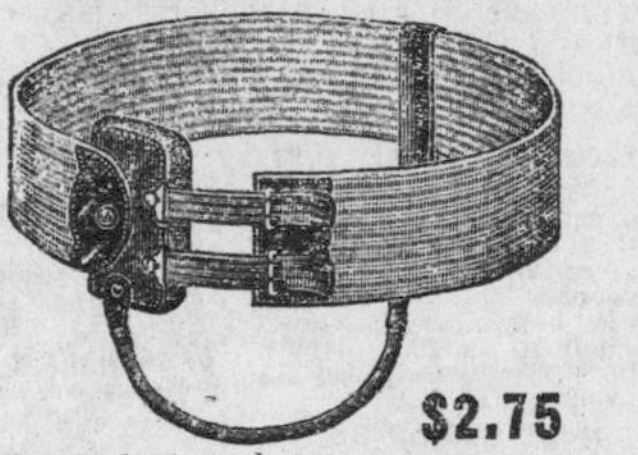

$2.75

This newly invented truss now meets a long felt want. It affords just the right pressure and protection needed for all persons subject to attacks of this dangerous disease. The large soft chamois pad is 4½ inches long by 2½ inches wide, and is attached to body by means of the very best 3½-inch elastic. The understrap is of best material and prevents slipping. The pad is adjustable, is soft, easy and comfortable and a great protection against cold or subsequent attacks. This truss can also be used for holding difficult ruptures and for protection after operation of abdomen or lower parts. If you have ever experienced appendicitis or desire to protect the part from cold or rubbing, we believe this truss will give you satisfaction.

No. 8K3570 Price....$2.75
If by mail, postage extra, 10 cents.

Fine German Truss.

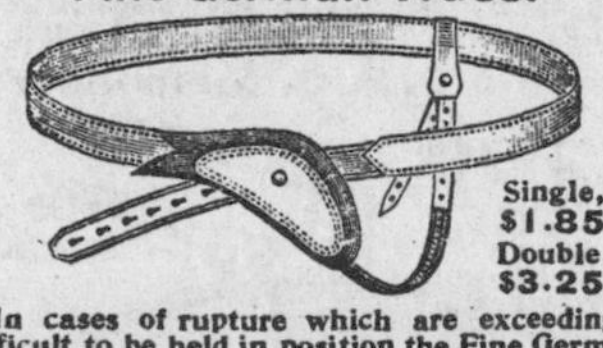

Single, **$1.85**
Double, **$3.25**

In cases of rupture which are exceedingly difficult to be held in position the Fine German Truss is especially recommended. This is a spring truss, leather covered, with scrotal pad. It is fitted with an additional understrap which holds the pad in position and which prevents the moving of the pad. Consequently it will hold the rupture better than most any other style of belt, yet it is comfortable and very effective in the treatment of rupture.

No. 8K3552 Fine German Truss, for rupture that is difficult to hold, single. (Be sure to give size and side.) Price....$1.85
No. 8K3554 Fine German Truss, for double rupture. Price....$3.25
If by mail, postage extra, 14 cents.

In ordering the Single Fine German Truss be sure to state the side on which the rupture is located, whether right or left; also give measurement around body on a line with rupture in all cases. Sold under a positive guarantee that no better truss of this style could be obtained anywhere, no matter what price you would be willing to pay.

Ball and Socket Truss.

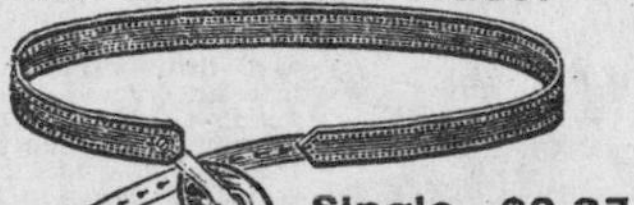

Single, **$2.37**
Double, **3.57**

Ball and Socket Truss or Set Screw Imperial. Made of the finest tested steel springs, covered with Russia leather; highly polished nickel mountings; is reversible; can be arranged for either right or left side, and the pads can be placed in any position desired, and when so placed are held firmly by a perfect fastener. This style of truss has in late years found many admirers, and those who have given same a trial prefer it often to any other style of appliance for the treatment of rupture. The fact that the pad can be placed in almost any position is a very good feature, appreciated by all.

No. 8K3567 Ball and Socket Truss, single. (Be sure to give size and side.) Price....$2.37
No. 8K3568 Ball and Socket Truss, double. Price....$3.57
If by mail, postage extra, 14 cents.

In ordering, always give measurement around body on line with rupture.

HARD RUBBER TRUSSES.

Hard Rubber Trusses have many advantages, and a large number of our customers prefer this style of appliance. They are always clean, are not affected by perspiration nor heat or cold.

They are free from any unpleasant odor and can be easily shaped and adjusted. We carry only the finest grade of hard rubber trusses and supply them at such very low prices that even those in moderate circumstances can now afford to secure for themselves the very best, the very finest hard rubber trusses at the extremely low prices offered below.

Walker's Oval Pad Hard Rubber Truss.

Single, **$1.85**

Especially recommended where the rupture comes out shaped like an egg. This small oval pad will easily fit in the right place, and will retain that class of ruptures better than any other style of pad. When applied constantly for at least a reasonable length of time a complete cure can be established. Adjustable pad; high grade hard rubber spring; finely finished nickel plated attachments; hard rubber oval pad, with one set screw.

No. 8K3580 Walker's Oval Pad Hard Rubber Truss, single. (Be sure to give size and side.) Price....$1.85

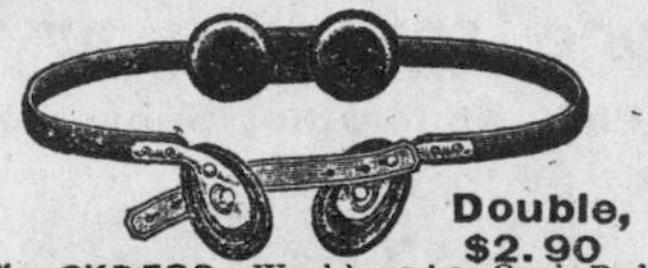

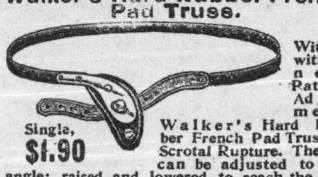

Double, **$2.90**

No. 8K3582 Walker's Oval Pad Hard Rubber Truss, double. Price....$2.90
If by mail, postage extra, 12 cents.

When ordering, state location of rupture, whether on right or left side; also give measurement around body on line with rupture.

Sold under a positive guarantee that no better truss of this style could be obtained anywhere, no matter what price you would be willing to pay.

Walker's Hard Rubber French Pad Truss.

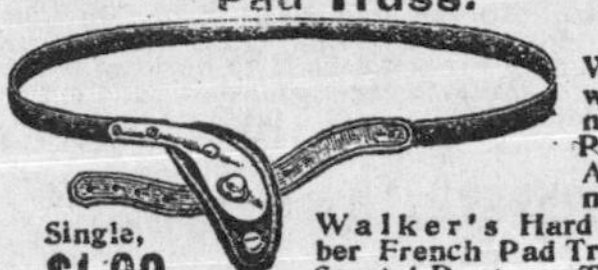

With or without new Patent Adjustment.

Single, **$1.90**

Walker's Hard Rubber French Pad Truss for Scrotal Rupture. The pad can be adjusted to any angle; raised and lowered to reach the conditions of the patient. The shank attachment is so called malleable, and can be bent to suit. Fine hard rubber springs; highly finished nickel plated attachments; hard rubber French pad. Clean and comfortable.

No. 8K3586 Walker's Hard Rubber French Pad Truss, single. (Be sure to give size and side.) Price....$1.90
No. 8K3588 Walker's Hard Rubber French Pad Truss, double. Price....$3.20
If by mail, postage extra, 16 cents.

In ordering, state location of rupture, whether on right or left side, also give number of inches around body on a line with the rupture.

The Solid Comfort (Hood's) Hard Rubber Truss.

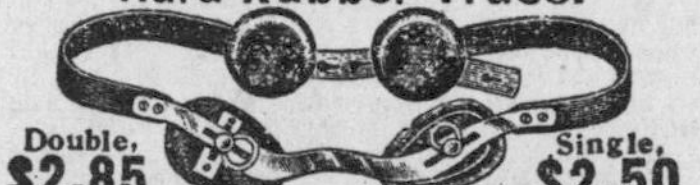

Double, **$2.85**
Single, **$2.50**

This is an elegant hard rubber single truss, especially recommended by all truss experts and scientific truss fitters of the world. Before putting on this truss, the rupture should always be returned into the inguinal ring, placing truss in position, the pad right over the spot where the rupture is located. Then fasten the truss at the back. This truss not only checks rupture quicker than any other appliance, but prevents a breach or rupture on the opposite side. It has a small flat pad on the opposite side from the rupture, known as a "blind" pad, which will save you from a double rupture. Once adjusted it usually proves to be the most comfortable and safest truss for single rupture. Regular price, $9.00 to $15.00.

No. 8K3590 The Solid Comfort Hard Rubber Truss, for single rupture. (Be sure to give size and side.) Our price....$2.50
No. 8K3592 Double Truss. Our price....$2.85
If by mail, postage extra, 16 cents.

This truss can be fitted with Radical Cure pads at 75 cents each, extra.

In ordering, state location of rupture, whether on right or left side, also give number of inches around body on a line with the rupture.

The Genuine Radical Cure Truss.
For adults only.

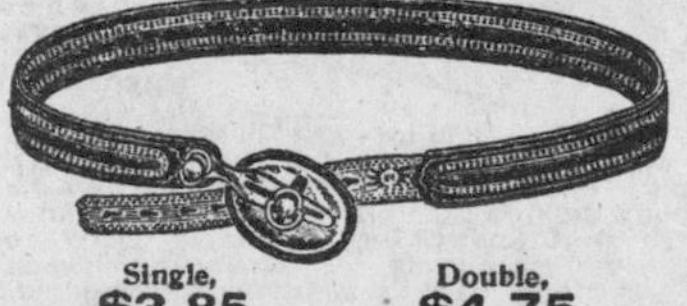

Single, **$3.85**
Double, **$4.75**

There are many so called Radical Cure Trusses on the market but very few possess the merit claimed for them and that can positively be found in our genuine Radical Cure Truss. Owing to the wonderful influence of the pad, which is constructed on the most advanced ideas of truss experts, the Radical Cure Truss will not only serve the purpose of holding up the rupture better than any other similar appliance, but it will, even in cases of old standing, reduce the rupture and gradually effect an absolute cure in many of the most difficult cases, if worn properly for a reasonable length of time.

The Radical Cure Truss is made of best spring steel with a wide orange calfskin leather cover, padded inside, top and bottom edges of the new style roll finish, that will prevent the edges from cutting into the skin. A handsome practical truss made of the best materials, in the most approved manner, for which truss fitters everywhere charge from $10.00 to $15.00. We furnish it to you for $3.85, with full adjustment, so that the pad can be placed in the exact position required; that is, higher up, or lower down, or more toward the right, or more toward the left, making it possible for the patient to shift the pad to any position within reasonable limits, so that you can fit yourself to perfection and save for yourself from $5.00 to $10.00, which truss fitters usually charge for this service.

This Radical Pad has a soft leather covered outer rim with a stationary hard rubber inner pad on metal plate back, adjustable in every direction and can be used for either the right or left side.

No. 8K3598 Radical Cure Truss with stationary hard rubber center pad, single. (Be sure to give size and side.) Price....$3.85
No. 8K3599 Radical Cure Truss with stationary hard rubber center pad, double. Price....$4.75
If by mail, postage extra, 24 cents.

SPECIAL NOTICE. Do not be misled by houses imitating our illustrations of trusses and quoting apparently low prices, furnishing you a different, inferior, cheaply made article, without guarantee of fit or wear.

Infants' Umbilical Truss.

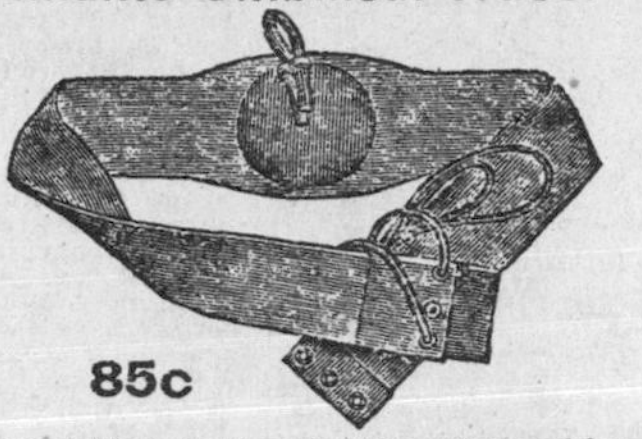

85c

Infants' Soft Rubber Umbilical Truss with an inflatable pad. An excellent truss for very young infants. Sizes, 10 to 17 inches inclusive. It consists of a soft rubber belt which laces in the back. The pad, which covers the navel, is inflated through the rubber tube and when filled, the tube is tied with a soft string to prevent the escape of air from the pad. Be sure to give size around body when ordering.

No. 8K3602 Price....85c
If by mail, postage extra, 3 cents.

Umbilical Trusses.
Regular $5.00 Truss for $2.25.

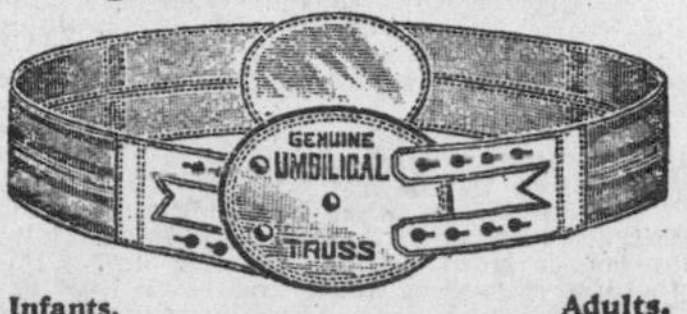

Infants, **$1.95**
Adults, **$2.25**

We show in this illustration the Genuine Elastic Umbilical Truss which is recommended by physicians as the very best truss for umbilical rupture. It is made of the strongest quality of elastic truss webbing, calf and kid pads. A more comfortable truss cannot be found to wear. If in need of such a truss send to us for it and examine it. You will be satisfied and save lots of money.

No. 8K3604 Adults' size. (Be sure to give size around body.) Price....$2.25
No. 8K3605 Infants' size. (Be sure to give size around body.) Price....$1.95
If by mail, postage extra, 12 cents.

Randolph Umbilical Belt.

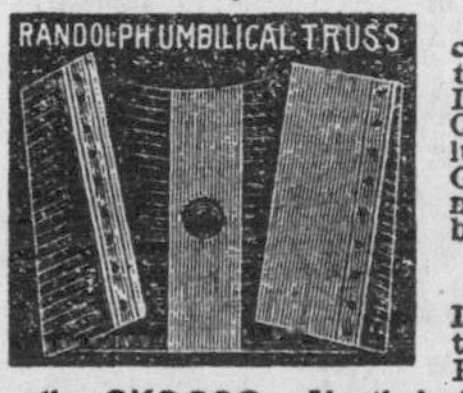

Made of strong covered elastic thread, with pad. Light and airy. Can be washed in lukewarm water. Give measurement around the body.

No. 8K3607 Infants' sizes, up to 19 inches, Price....80c
No. 8K3608 Youths' sizes, up to 29 inches. Price....$1.37
No. 8K3609 Adults' sizes up to 60 inches. Price....$1.87
If by mail, postage extra, 12 cents.

Heavy Elastic Truss Webbing.

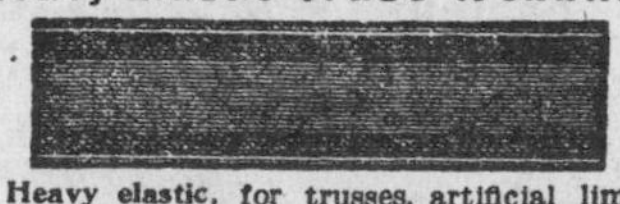

Heavy elastic, for trusses, artificial limbs, etc., furnished only in 1 or 2-yard lengths, 2 yards just double the 1-yard price.

No. 8K3613 Width, ¾ inch. Price, per yard....9c
No. 8K3614 Width, 1 inch. Price, per yard....13c
No. 8K3615 Width, 1¼ inches. Price, per yard....19c
No. 8K3616 Width, 1¾ inches. Price, per yard....22c
No. 8K3617 Width, 2 inches. Price, per yard....31c
If by mail, postage extra, per yard, 2 cents.

Covered Elastic Bandages.

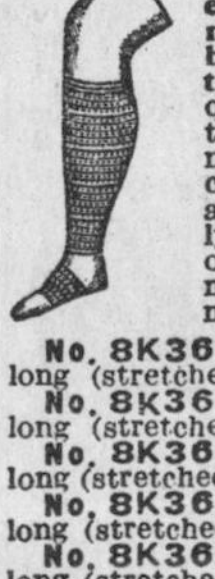

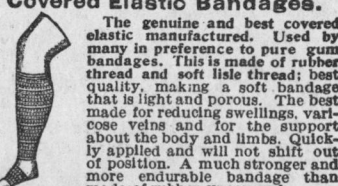

The genuine and best covered elastic manufactured. Used by many in preference to pure gum bandages. This is made of rubber thread and soft lisle thread; best quality, making a soft bandage that is light and porous. The best made for reducing swellings, varicose veins and for the support about the body and limbs. Quickly applied and will not shift out of position. A much stronger and more endurable bandage than made of rubber uncovered.

No. 8K3619 2 inches wide by 9 feet long (stretched). Price....34c
No. 8K3620 2 inches wide by 15 feet long (stretched). Price....48c
No. 8K3621 2 inches wide by 24 feet long (stretched). Price....73c
No. 8K3622 2½ inches wide by 9 feet long (stretched). Price....44c
No. 8K3623 2½ inches wide by 15 feet long (stretched). Price....58c
No. 8K3624 3 inches wide by 9 feet long (stretched). Price....59c
No. 8K3625 3 inches wide by 15 feet long (stretched). Price....92c
If by mail, postage extra, each, 2 cents.

The Peerless Improved French Extension Spring Truss.

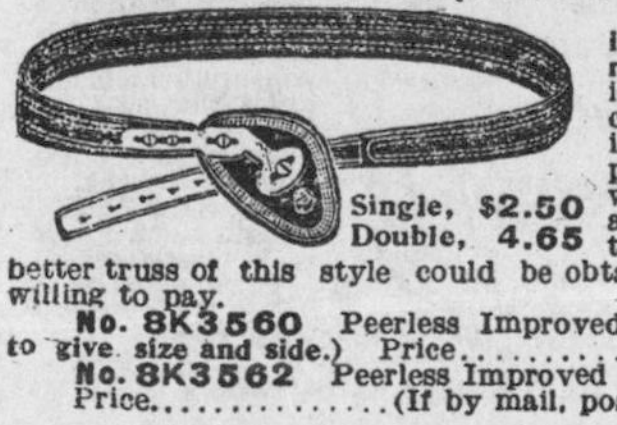

Single, **$2.50**
Double, **4.65**

This truss is manufactured of heavy calfskin, padded inside and tire casing, double silk stitched, with hand made hair pad preventing its cutting the body. The belt is of the finest spring steel, leather covered, easy and comfortable. Pad can be extended and placed exactly in the proper position. Fine nickel trimmings. The pad is not reversible, but adjustable. Always state where rupture is located, whether on right or left side, and give measurement around body on a line with the rupture. Sold under a positive guarantee that no better truss of this style could be obtained anywhere, no matter what price you would be willing to pay.

No. 8K3560 Peerless Improved French Extension Spring Truss, single. (Be sure to give size and side.) Price....$2.50
No. 8K3562 Peerless Improved French Extension Spring Truss, double. Price....(If by mail, postage extra, 16 cents)....4.65

ELASTIC STOCKINGS, ABDOMINAL BELTS, SHOULDER BRACES AND SUSPENSORIES

Elastic Stockings and Special Makes.

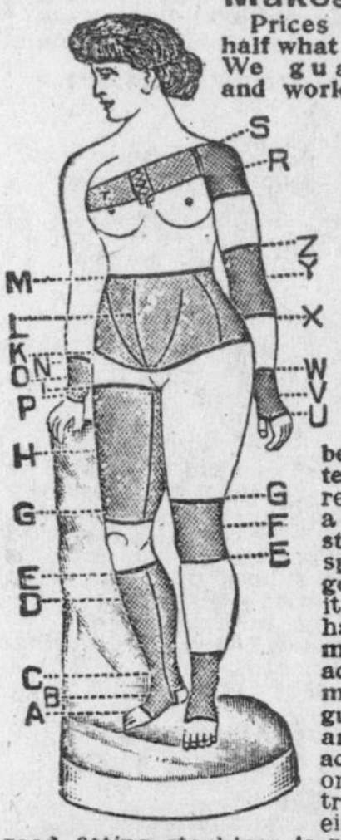

Prices only about one-half what other firms charge. We guarantee quality and workmanship to be the best. You can get nothing better at double the price at which we sell these goods.

For the relief of varicose veins; weak, swollen or ulcerated limbs; corpulency; abdominal weakness and tumors. Asrubber goods spoil with age, these Elastic Stockings and Belts to wear well should be made of fresh material. As soon as we receive an order from a customer for elastic stockings, or other special make elastic goods, we at once send it to the factory and have the article manufactured exactly according to measurements given. We guarantee perfect fit and goods that are actually fresh. Anyone who has had trouble in obtaining either serviceable or good fitting stockings is requested to give us a trial.

Take measurements carefully at each letter as indicated in the illustration; also give the length from the lowest letter to the highest. For example: A garter stocking you would take circumference at A, B, C, D and E; also the length from floor to E inside limb. For stockings extending above and below knee BE SURE TO TAKE SIZE AT F, ALSO LENGTH FROM LOWEST POINT TO F, AND FROM F TO HIGHEST POINT. For thigh knee cap give circumference at E, F, G, H and I; also length from E to F and from F to I. For hand piece give circumference at U, V, W, and length from U to W; also state whether for right or left hand. Give us the exact measurements which should be taken, if possible, in the morning. We allow for expansion.

PRICES FOR SINGLE STOCKINGS OR PIECES.

No. 8K3630 Hand Piece, U, V, W. Fine merc. silk, $1.75; cotton......$1.30
No. 8K3631 Shoulder Piece, S to U. Fine merc. silk, $5.40; cotton......$4.20
No. 8K3632 Thigh Stocking, A to I. Fine merc. silk, $7.55; cotton......$5.35
No. 8K3633 Thigh Legging, C to I. Fine merc. silk, $6.55; cotton......$4.35
No. 8K3634 Thigh Piece, G to I. Fine merc. silk, $2.10; cotton......$1.40
No. 8K3635 Knee Stocking, A to G. Fine merc. silk, $5.40; cotton......$3.85
No. 8K3636 Knee Legging, C to G. Fine silk, $3.10; cotton......$2.60
No. 8K3637 Knee Cap, E to G. Fine merc. silk, $2.10; cotton......$1.55
No. 8K3638 Garter Stocking, A to E. Fine merc. silk, $2.50; cotton......$1.75
No. 8K3639 Garter Legging, C to E. Fine merc. silk, $2.10; cotton......$1.55
No. 8K3640 Anklet, A to C. Fine merc. silk, $2.10; cotton......$1.55
No. 8K3641 Wristlet, N to P. Fine merc. silk, 75c; cotton......55c
No. 8K3642 Abdominal Belt, K to M. Fine merc. silk, $7.10; cotton......$5.45
No. 8K3643 Thigh Knee Cap, E to I. Fine merc. silk, $3.75; cotton......$2.70
If by mail, postage extra, each, 8 cents.

Abdominal Supporters.

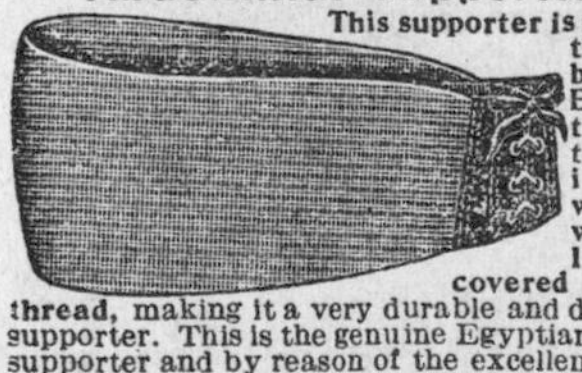

This supporter is made of the very best Egyptian thread, interwoven with soft lisle covered rubber thread, making it a very durable and desirable supporter. This is the genuine Egyptian thread supporter and by reason of the excellent material used in its manufacture, it can be washed in lukewarm water and be kept clean and antiseptic. Made of the best Egyptian thread, fine elastic and firm sateen back, giving excellent support. A very comfortable supporter in cases of corpulency and pregnancy. We allow for pressure. Give measurement around the abdomen

No. 8K3650 Sizes, 30 to and including 38 inches, 8 inches wide. Regular price, $2.50. Our price......98c
No. 8K3651 Sizes, 38 to 44 inches, 10 inches wide. Regular price, $2.75. Our price......$1.23
No. 8K3652 Sizes, 44 to 58 inches, 12 inches wide. Regular price, $3.00. Our price (Postage extra, each, 10 cents)...$1.48

Favorite Obesity Belt.

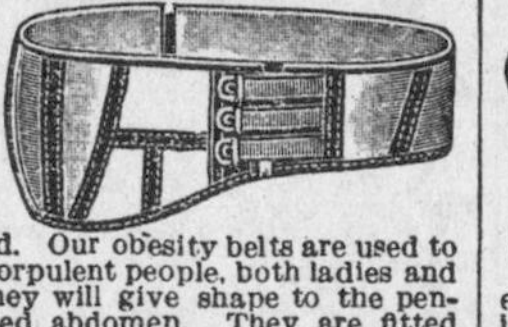

Made of strong mole-skin cloth that yields sufficiently to assist shaping the abdomen, thereby giving comfort and the support required. Our obesity belts are used to advantage by corpulent people, both ladies and gentlemen. They will give shape to the pendulous or relaxed abdomen. They are fitted with strong side straps and stays. In sending your order be sure to give your measure at the largest circumference around the abdomen. Regular price, $3.00 to $5.00.

No. 8K3704 Price............$1.47
If by mail, postage extra, 12 cents.

Pink Abdominal Supporters.

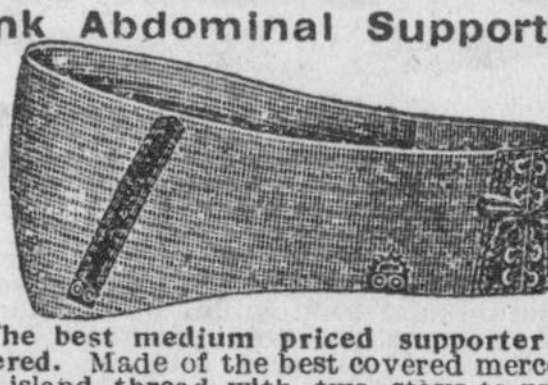

The best medium priced supporter ever offered. Made of the best covered mercerized sea island thread with two stays to prevent wrinkling, and with four attachments for understraps if desired. Stays and back of best pink leather. Quickly applied, conforming readily to the abdomen. Especially knit much wider in front than back, thereby preventing any tucks in back to hurt the body. A supporter giving excellent service and entire satisfaction. We allow for pressure. Sizes, 30 to 56 inches. Give measurement around the body.

No. 8K3695 Sizes, 30 to and including 38 inches, 8 inches wide. Regular price, $3.00. Our price......$1.75
No. 8K3696 Sizes, 40 to 46 inches, 10 inches wide. Regular price, $3.25. Our price......$2.00
No. 8K3697 Sizes, 46 to 56 inches, 12 inches wide. Regular price, $4.00. Our price......$2.50
If by mail, postage extra, each, 10 cents.

Canvas Abdominal Belt.

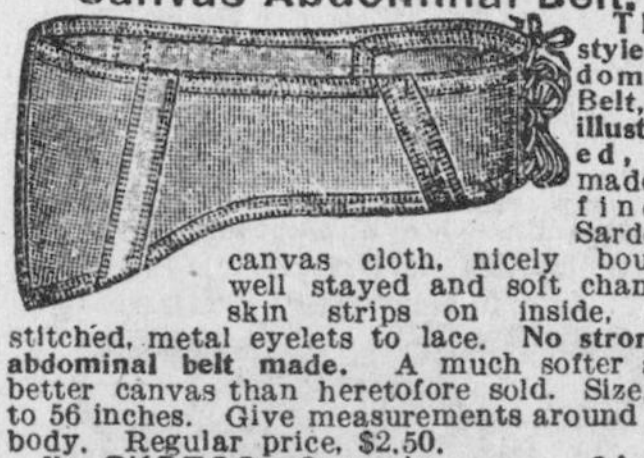

This style Abdominal Belt, as illustrated, is made of finest Sarden's canvas cloth, nicely bound, well stayed and soft chamois skin strips on inside, silk stitched, metal eyelets to lace. No stronger abdominal belt made. A much softer and better canvas than heretofore sold. Size, 32 to 56 inches. Give measurements around the body. Regular price, $2.50.

No. 8K3700 Our price.........$1.35
If by mail, postage extra, 10 cents.

Ideal Abdominal Belt.

Buckling at sides affords easy adjustment.

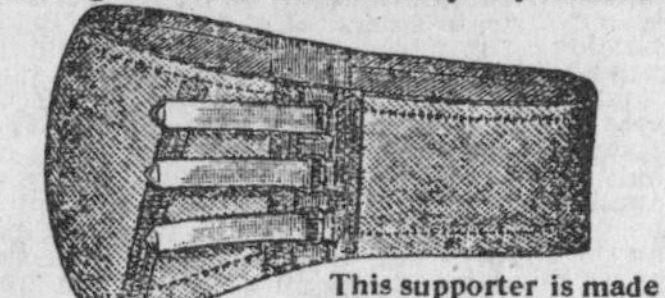

This supporter is made of best pink mercerized sea island thread, full leather trimmings, pads are of soft leather and chamois lined, buckled at sides. Full fashioned front, extra heavy at top and bottom to prevent wrinkling. Give measurements at largest part of abdomen. We allow for pressure. Made in all sizes and in 8, 10 and 11-inch fronts. Be sure to give all measurements. All belts over 54 inches in length or 11 inches front are extra sizes, for which 25 cents extra must be charged to cover material and time in making.

No. 8K3701 Price............$3.67
If by mail, postage extra, 13 cents.

Our Garland Abdominal Belt.

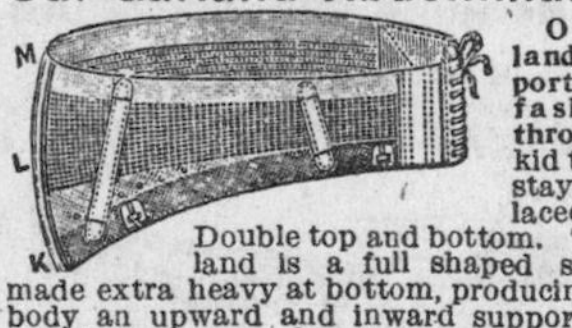

Our Garland Supporter is full fashioned throughout, kid trimmed, stayed and laced in back. Double top and bottom. The Garland is a full shaped supporter made extra heavy at bottom, producing on the body an upward and inward support and is the best known for holding in place excessive corpulency or strained abdomen. Steel stays. Freely ventilated. These pink supporters having a bright lustre are usually called silk, but we tell you the plain truth that the material mentioned has through experience found to wear much longer and give better satisfaction. Sold everywhere from $6.00 to $8.00.

No. 8K3702 Sizes up to and including 42 inches, 8-inch width. Price......$3.00
Sizes, 44 and 46 inches, 10-inch width. Price......$3.50
Sizes, 48 to 58 inches, 12-inch width. Price......$4.00
If by mail, postage extra, each, 13 cents.

Improved Elastic Supporter.

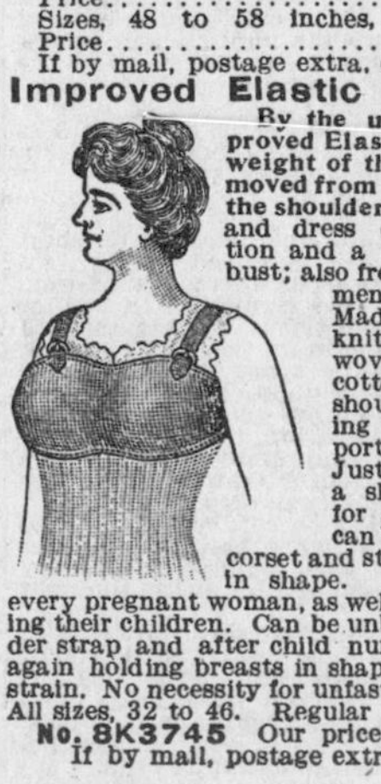

By the use of this Improved Elastic Supporter the weight of the breasts is removed from the dress waist to the shoulders, giving coolness and dress comfort, ventilation and a perfectly shaped bust; also free and easy movement of the body. Made of the very best knitted elastic, interwoven with silk or cotton; the back and shoulder straps making it an ideal supporter for the purpose. Just as important for a slender woman as for a fleshy one, and can be worn without a corset and still keep the figure in shape. A necessity for every pregnant woman, as well as women nursing their children. Can be unbuckled at shoulder strap and after child nurses, be buckled again holding breasts in shape without undue strain. No necessity for unfastening the corset. All sizes, 32 to 46. Regular price, $3.50.

No. 8K3745 Our price.........$1.45
If by mail, postage extra, 10 cents.

Improved Abdominal and Uterine Supporter.

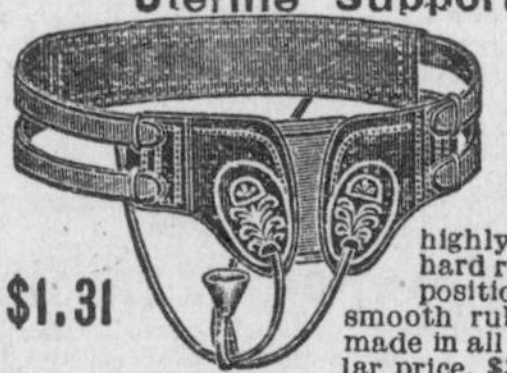

$1.31

Extra fine pebbled morocco or russet leather with elastic side straps. Cup form pessary of highly polished hard rubber held in position by strong smooth rubber tubing; made in all sizes. Regular price, $3.50 to $5.00.

No. 8K3750 Our price.........$1.31
If by mail, postage extra, 20 cents.
When ordering, give circumference of abdomen at largest part.
Extra Tubes. Price, per pair.......25
Extra Hard Rubber Pessaries. Price, each.......40

The London Abdominal Supporter.

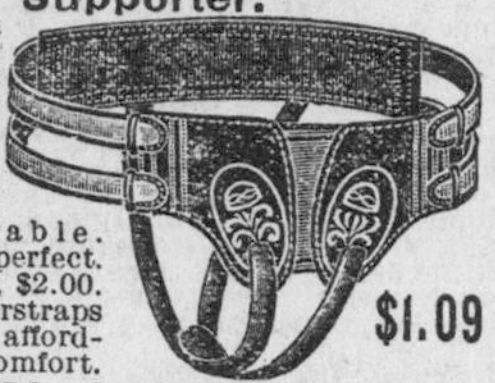

$1.09

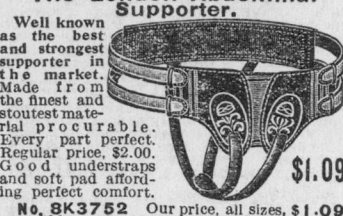

Well known as the best and strongest supporter in the market. Made from the finest and stoutest material procurable. Every part perfect. Regular price, $2.00. Good understraps and soft pad affording perfect comfort.

No. 8K3752 Our price, all sizes, $1.09
If by mail, postage extra, 20 cents.
When ordering, give circumference of abdomen at largest part.

Laced Spinal Shoulder Brace.

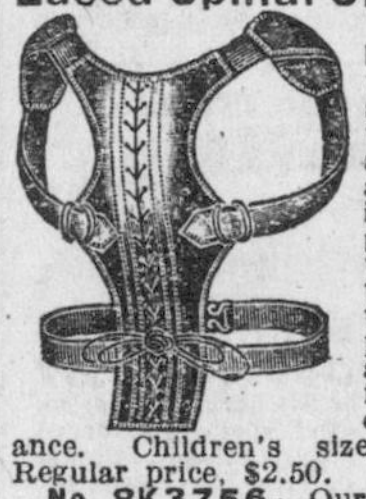

This is a perfect brace for supporting the back, and at the same time drawing the shoulders back so as to expand the chest and throw the body into an erect, graceful position. All tendency to round shoulders is thus avoided, and this to young people in the period when the bones and muscles are growing and hardening, is of the utmost importance. Children's sizes from 5 years up. Regular price, $2.50.

No. 8K3756 Our price.........$1.16
If by mail, postage extra, 19 cents.
Order small, medium or large length if wanted for adults and give age and length of brace if for children.

Washington Shoulder Brace.

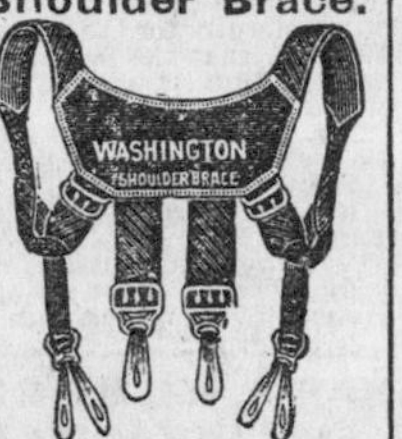

This brace is well arranged to draw the shoulders gently back without cutting or chafing under the arms, thus inclining the body to a graceful, correct position, expanding the chest and correcting all tendency to stooping or round shoulders. Made of strong webbing, calf back; webbing rolled under arms so as not to cut. Suspender attachment is of the strongest material. Regular price, $2.50.

No. 8K3759 Our price.........94c
If by mail, postage extra, 15 cents.
Order small, medium or large length as wanted.

Gamble Shoulder Brace.

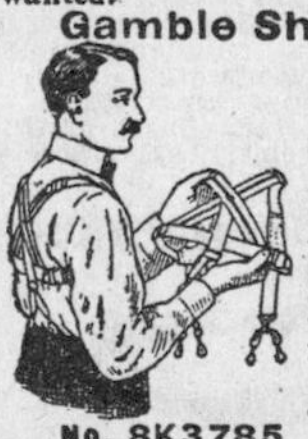

The most comfortable and most effective shoulder brace ever made, steel springs, a leverage that pushes in the protuding shoulder blades. They do the work and do no hurt. Arm pads lined with chamois skin and filled with hair to prevent soreness. Sizes, 26 to 54.

Be sure to state size and style wanted.

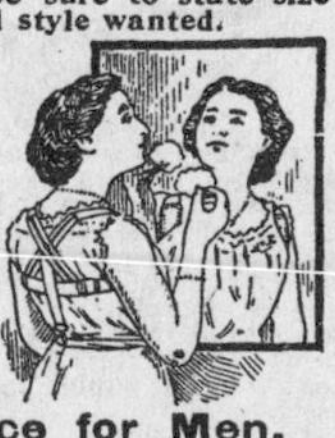

No. 8K3785 Men's sizes, 32 to 54. Price......$1.10
No. 8K3786 Youths' sizes, 26 to 30. Price......89c
No. 8K3787 Ladies' sizes, 30 to 44. Price......$1.10
8K3788 Misses' size, 26 to 30. Price......89c
If by mail, postage extra, each, 8 cents.

Shoulder Brace for Men, Women, Girls and Boys.

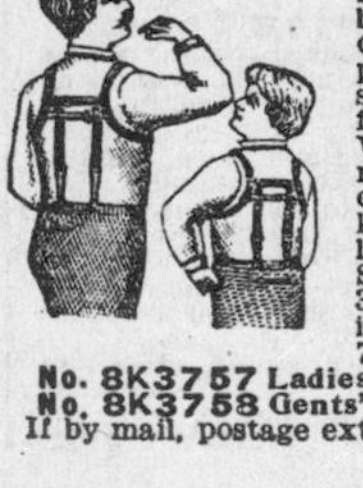

These braces are the best cheap shoulder braces ever made. Gents' serve as a supporter for the trousers and women's brace for skirt support. Women's made of best nonelastic web and can be washed and kept clean. Men's of light colored web. Sizes: 24, 26, 28, 30, 32, 34, 36, 38 and 40 inches. Regular price, 75 cents. Give size.

No. 8K3757 Ladies'. Price, per pair 41c
No. 8K3758 Gents'. Price, per pair, 41c
If by mail, postage extra, per pair, 5 cents.

Radium Shoulder Brace.

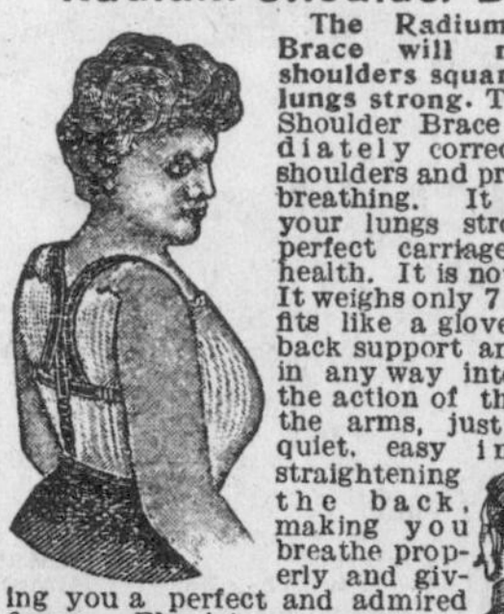

The Radium Shoulder Brace will make your shoulders square and your lungs strong. The Radium Shoulder Brace will immediately correct stooping shoulders and promote deep breathing. It will make your lungs strong, assure perfect carriage and good health. It is not a harness. It weighs only 7 ounces and fits like a glove. A perfect back support and does not in any way interfere with the action of the body and the arms, just a subtle, quiet, easy influence, straightening the back, making you breathe properly and giving you a perfect and admired figure. Physicians recommend them. Now worn by thousands and valuable to men of business, society women, housewives, school children and persons in every walk of life. Once worn you would never be without it. In ordering give chest measure around the body under the arms.

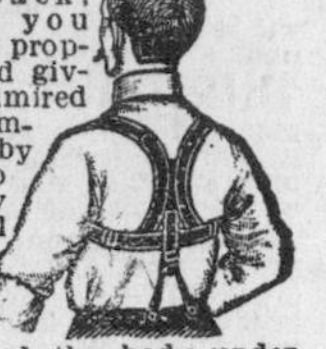

No. 8K3740 Men's or boys' sizes, 28 to 40 inches. Price.............86c
No. 8K3742 Ladies' or misses' sizes, 26 to 38 inches. Price.............86c
If by mail, postage extra, each, 8 cents.

SUSPENSORIES.

We are now carrying for the first time the well known line of the largest and best suspensory manufacturers in the United States. They are all guaranteed first class, easy fit and the best made. The prices are much less than you can obtain them elsewhere.

Continental Army and Navy.

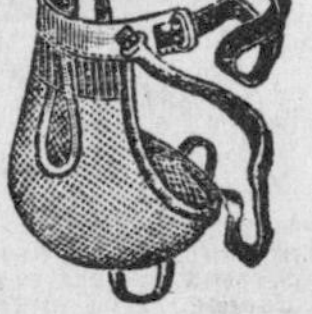

This well known suspensory is so constructed that it fits perfectly and gives the best possible support in any position the body may assume. Each in a flat display box. Regular price, 35 to 50 cents.

No. 8K3762 English web Sack, elastic bands. Our price.........26c
No. 8K3764 Bolting Silk Sack, elastic bands. Our price.........39c
If by mail, postage extra, each, 5 cents.

Genuine J. P. Suspensory, Single Band.

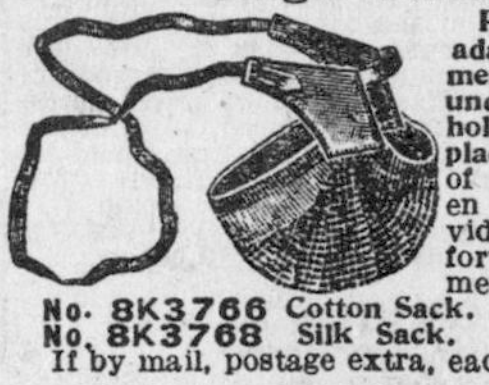

Particularly adapted for slim men, requiring no understraps to hold the pouch in place. The edge of pouch is woven elastic, providing for comfortable adjustment.

No. 8K3766 Cotton Sack. Price, 13c
No. 8K3768 Silk Sack. Price..22c
If by mail, postage extra, each, 4 cents.

Genuine O. P. C. Suspensory.

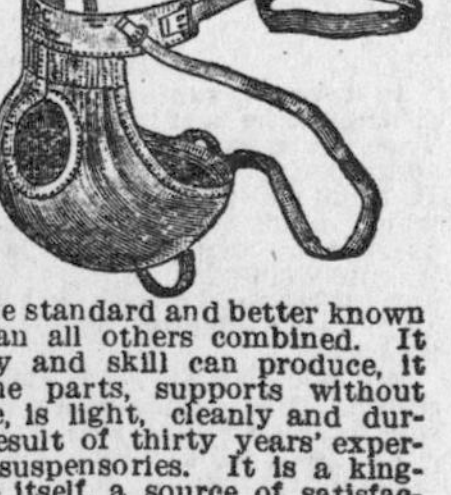

The best suspensory made. This is the one to buy. This Genuine O. P. C. Suspensory should be worn by every healthy normal man. The vital organs need a suspensory to sustain the nervous vitality, energy and force and prevent strain. The O. P. C. is the standard and better known and more sold than all others combined. It is the best money and skill can produce, it accurately fits the parts, supports without strain or pressure, is light, cleanly and durable, and is the result of thirty years' experience in making suspensories. It is a kingdom of comfort in itself, a source of satisfaction at all times. Automatically adjustable and never fails to fit and give entire satisfaction.

No. 8K3770 Lisle. Price....$0.75
No. 8K3772 Silk. Price.... 1.05
No. 8K3774 All Silk. Price, 1.35
If by mail, postage extra, each, 4 cents.

Safety Suspensory.

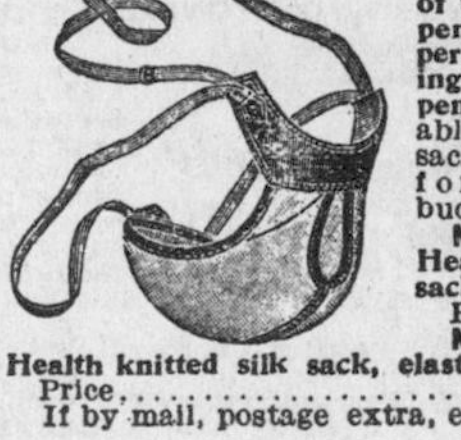

The construction of the Safety Suspensory secures a perfect self adjusting sliding loop suspensory, which enables the seamless sack to be detached for washing; no buckles on sack.

No. 8K3780 Health bolting silk sack, elastic band. Price......55c
No. 8K3782 Health knitted silk sack, elastic band. Price......65c
If by mail, postage extra, each, 2 cents.

THE GENUINE OLD COMFORT BODY BRACE $1.89

SOLD BY OTHERS FOR $5.00 TO $8.00

We have Discontinued Handling the Old Fashioned Brace, and Now Offer the Well Known and Long Tried Old Comfort Body Brace, Sold Under our Personal Guarantee. The Highest Grade, Most Perfect Woman's Brace for Only $1.89. Manufactured and Guaranteed to be Not Only Equal, but Far Superior to Any Other Body Brace, Regardless of the Price at Which They are Sold.

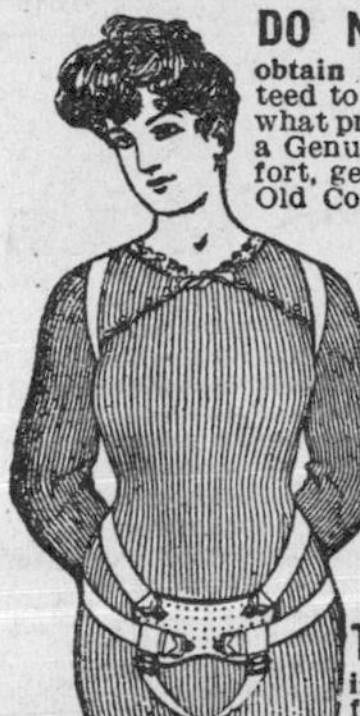

DO NOT PAY $5.00, $6.00 OR $8.00 for an inferior body brace, when you can obtain from us the Genuine Old Comfort Body Brace for only $1.89, guaranteed to render equal and better service than any other body brace, no matter what price you would be willing to pay for the same. You will never know what a Genuine Old Comfort Body Brace means to a woman, as regards her comfort, general health and well feeling, until you possess one of these Genuine Old Comfort Body Braces, the greatest boon to weak, suffering womankind.

A WOMAN'S GENERAL HEALTH, strength, grace, erectness and beauty of form are regained and retained by wearing a properly adjusted Genuine Old Comfort Body Brace. It will meet and remove the cause of weaknesses and organic displacements by applying its strengthening influence and natural support to parts of the body where it is most needed.

THE GENUINE OLD COMFORT BODY BRACE is highly recommended by physicians for all women suffering from general weaknesses, to persons whose shoulders droop and whose posture is neither natural nor correct. It is a proper and comfortable brace for fat people. A large abdomen is often reduced a few inches per month as a result of relief afforded by the brace to the stretched and overloaded muscles.

THE GENUINE OLD COMFORT BODY BRACE is an abdominal supporter and shoulder brace combined, constructed so as to form a natural support to every organ of the body. The supporting, strengthening and healing influence of the Genuine Old Comfort Body Brace has seldom been approached by any other appliance. It assures to the wearer comfort, vigor, health, elasticity, ease; all of the utmost importance to women subject to physical changes, in all conditions and in every walk in life. The Genuine Old Comfort Body Brace is made of good material and is adjustable, thus always insuring a perfect fit. The upper portion of belt and shoulder pads consists of strong elastic webbing. The lower belt is non-elastic, and as a result you will find in this appliance perfect support, yet absolute freedom for every movement of the body.

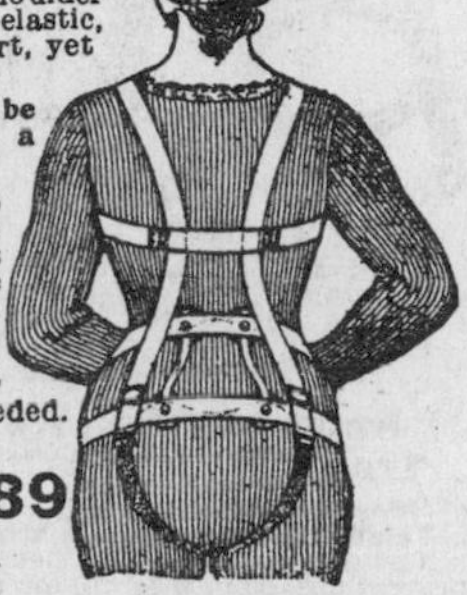

WHITE MATERIAL is used throughout, which can easily be laundered and kept clean and in a sanitary condition.

YOU CAN WEAR the Genuine Old Comfort Body Brace to suit your own convenience and as you may prefer, either under corset, over vest, under closed drawers or over open drawers. The adjustable features of this brace make it possible to wear the same appliance at all times.

An extra set of understraps is furnished with each body brace, free of charge, to be used when the first set is in the laundry, thus enabling the wearer to use the Genuine Old Comfort Body Brace without interruption during the time when it is most needed. Give size around body about 2 inches below top of hip bones.

No. 8K3500 The Genuine Old Comfort Body Brace, complete, only **$1.89**

(State size desired.) If by mail, postage extra, 20 cents.

INVALID CHAIRS

SPECIAL CATALOGUE FREE.

THE FINEST INVALID CHAIRS MANUFACTURED, AND AT A PRICE WITHIN THE REACH OF ALL. SEND FOR OUR SPECIAL FREE CATALOGUE.

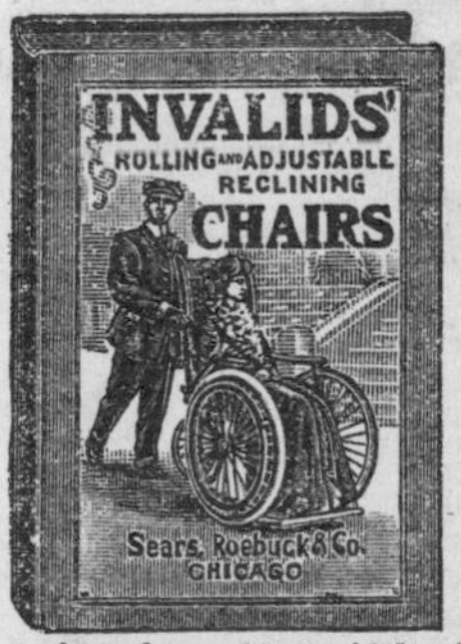

THIS INVALID CHAIR CATALOGUE IS FREE

This illustration shows our big Free Invalid Chair Catalogue, a Special Catalogue containing large illustrations of some 31 reclining, propelling, folding, combination, reed, car, traveling and carrying chairs, the finest line of invalid chairs offered by any firm or dealer; it gives you full and accurate information concerning each one, tells you just the purposes for which they are designed, and if you require an invalid chair for any purpose whatsoever, before you order from any other dealer, be sure to send to us a postal and ask for this big catalogue, which we shall be glad to send you free and postpaid. It tells all about our fine line of invalid chairs, IT QUOTES THE LOWEST PRICES EVER NAMED BY ANY FIRM OR INDIVIDUAL, it gives the freight rates to various parts of every state in the union, it answers every possible question that you might ask concerning invalid chairs; in short this big book is an authority, and it will give you such information as you cannot obtain from any other source. We sell invalid chairs just as we sell other merchandise, that is to say, our prices represent the cost of materials and labor when made in large quantities, plus one small percentage of profit. Dealers generally charge very high prices for invalid chairs, but we have changed all this, as explained in the pages of this BIG FREE CATALOGUE.

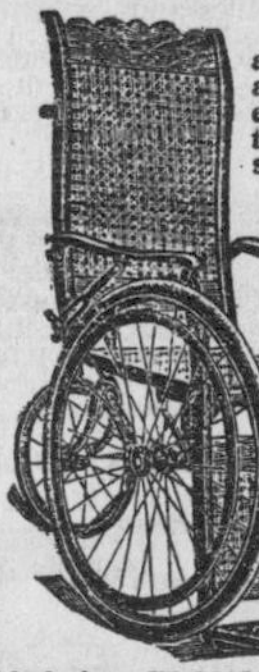

More comfort and pleasure for all invalids than ever before thought possible.

ARE YOU AN INVALID, or have you a relative or friend who needs a reclining or rolling chair, built especially for the comfort of invalids? We carry a complete line of standard styles of invalid chairs which are supplied to our customers at about half the prices at which these chairs have heretofore been sold. You need not pay from $40.00 to $60.00 for an invalid chair. We furnish you the best invalid chairs that can be manufactured. They are made by the same factory and are the same chairs sold to the wholesale dealers throughout the country. Our sales, however, are nearly one-half of all sold in the United States, and for that reason we can furnish you chairs much cheaper than your dealer can buy them from the factory. They are the same chairs he would buy, except that you pay him double what you can buy them for from us direct. We furnish these invalid chairs under a binding guarantee that they are the highest grade of invalid chairs that can be made; that their style, arrangement, adjustment, workmanship and finish are equal to and in many cases better than that of many invalid chairs sold at much more than our special low prices. Send for our special Invalid Chair Catalogue, giving every form of chair.

AT OUR NEVER BEFORE HEARD OF LOW PRICES, every home that needs one can afford an invalid chair. For a comparatively small outlay you can brighten the hours and days of an invalid sufferer, make his or her condition less burdensome, supplying comforts which cannot be had without these specially designed invalid chairs, and thus contribute in the greatest measure possible to the relief, comfort, contentment and happiness of the patient.

SEND FOR OUR INVALID CHAIR CATALOGUE TODAY.

SAVED HALF; WOULDN'T TAKE $100.00 FOR IT.

Sears, Roebuck & Co., Chicago, Ill. Sheridan, Wis.

Gentlemen:—In regard to the Invalid Chair I purchased from you, wish to say that it is a better chair in every respect than we expected, and father is much pleased with it. He goes all over the house in it, and we think we have saved about one-half on it. Father says he would not take $100.00 for his chair if he could not get another one. He is 88 years old and can handle it easily.

Yours truly, MRS. MARY C. MACK.

STEEL FRAME BATH CABINETS.

NOTE. We no longer handle the old fashioned cheap wood frame cabinets. They were used years ago before a steel cabinet could be made, but today are old fashioned and in our opinion nowhere near as good as a steel frame. Most wood frames are clumsy, warp with steam, break easily, occupy much more room, and are much cheaper to make than the up to date steel frame cabinet. Do you want a few wooden slats nailed together or an up to date steel constructed frame? We are proud to say we do not handle old wood frame cabinets.

THE VAPOR BATH is a very reliable means for effectively opening the pores of the skin and causing proper elimination of the poisons and waste matter present. The kidneys and liver get new life and activity, the blood becomes purified, the digestive organs improve, the nerves become strengthened and the health of the person improves from the very first.

WITH A QUAKER CABINET you can take a Turkish bath in the privacy of your own home just before retiring, consequently there is no exposure afterward. You avoid any danger from this source and also save much valuable time and have the bath ready for immediate use when most needed, save the expense of public baths, but most important of all, breathe the fresh air while bathing, air not polluted with poisons exhaled from others.

IF YOU DESIRE a home treatment for opening the pores of the skin, for producing a clear beautiful complexion, a perfect skin, a healthy body, in short if you want perfect health buy a Quaker Cabinet. It is an investment you will never regret. We carry three grades of bath cabinets, depending upon the covering material and appliances desired as follows:

PEERLESS BATH CABINET.

THE PEERLESS CABINET. represents the best low priced cabinet. It is a four-wall, rubber lined room fitted with galvanized steel wire frame. Size cabinet, 28x30½x42 inches. The coating is the best rubber lined muslin. We, however, will sell you this genuine Peerless Bath Cabinet for $2.25, complete with alcohol heater and vaporizing pan. Full directions how to prepare for and take Turkish, Russian, hot air, steam or vapor, perfumed or medicated baths accompany each cabinet. Weight, boxed, 40 pounds. While the Peerless is the best low priced cabinet made, it can in no way compare with the Quaker in efficiency, wear and durability.

No. 8K4000 Peerless Bath Cabinet. Price.. **$2.25**

THE QUAKER BATH CABINET No. 1, $4.25

With a $2.00 book, "THE GUIDE BOOK TO HEALTH AND BEAUTY," furnished free.

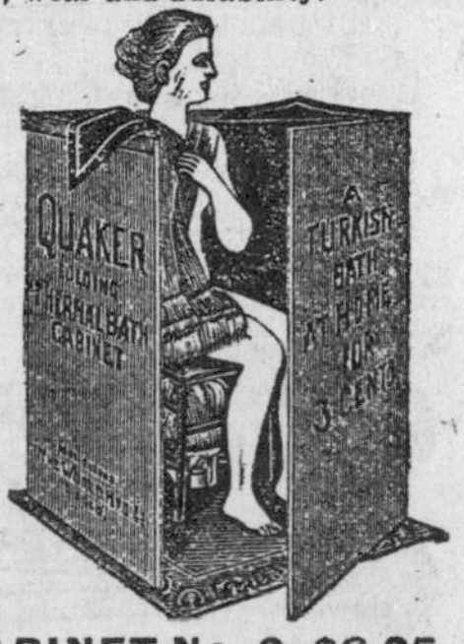

THE SPECIAL QUAKER CABINET No. 1 is made of the very best material and made on the most scientific principles. It is a cabinet large enough to enable you to take a foot bath while you are taking a Turkish bath. The top of the Quaker Cabinet No. 1 is in two pieces. The Quaker top is a very great convenience in entering, as well as in cooling off. The construction of our Quaker Cabinet No. 1 is most substantial. The covering is of special cabinet material (rubber coating inside, checked drill outside) that never stretches, thoroughly vaporproof. The frame is of the best steel construction, and, unlike old fashioned wood frames, does not warp or break. In cooling off, both sides of the top may be unbuttoned and thrown back. The whole cabinet is so jointed and hinged it can be put away in the smallest possible space. When you have finished using the cabinet, simply loosen the braces, tip the frame and it folds up completely. Any child can open and close it in a minute.

No. 8K4005 Our price.......................... **$4.25**

THE HIGHEST GRADE QUAKER BATH CABINET No. 2, $6.25.

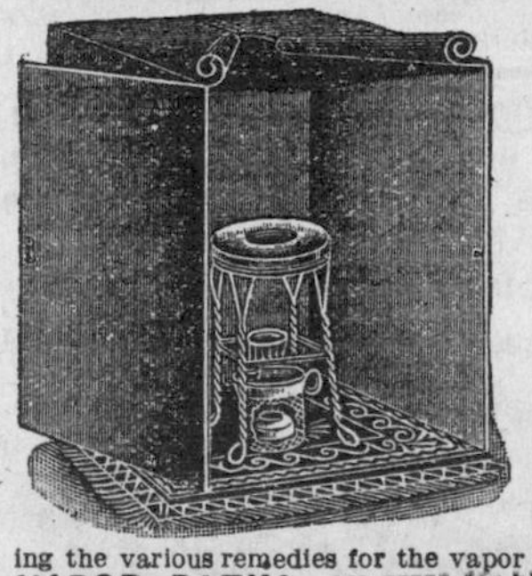

FOR $6.25 we offer the highest grade bath cabinet of the celebrated Quaker make, as the very finest and highest grade bath cabinet made. There is no better bath cabinet construction possible.

OUR $6.25 BATH CABINET is constructed with double walls of the best rubber coated material that can be made, everlasting and always new. The construction of our special $6.25 cabinet is without doubt the best ever shown.

FACE STEAMER FREE. A celebrated Quaker Face Steamer, improved style, as shown in illustration below, will be included with each No. 2 Quaker Bath Cabinet free. For treatment of the complexion the Quaker Face Steamer is one of the most important parts of a vapor bath cabinet. If same is wanted with other cabinets, price is $1.00 extra.

WE FURNISH FREE with this, our best Quaker Bath Cabinet No. 2, one copyrighted $2.00, 100-page book, published and edited by the manufacturer of the cabinet, as described in No. 8K4005, giving formulas and directions for making the various remedies for the vapor treatment of various diseases.

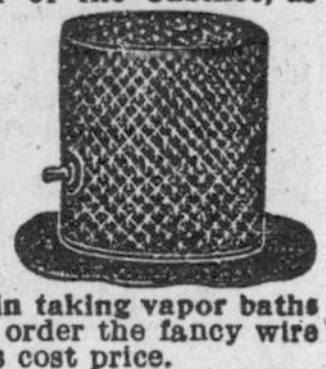

VAPOR BATHS are great for blood and skin diseases. For rheumatism and neuralgia, chronic, acute or inflammatory, our vapor baths have been known to benefit where everything else had failed to give relief. You'll be surprised and delighted at the improvement in your health, feelings and complexion. Weight, boxed, 40 pounds.

No. 8K4010 Retail price, $12.00; our price, (without metal bath stool, as illustrated) **$6.25**

CANE SEAT CHAIRS or ordinary kitchen chairs can be employed in taking vapor baths in these cabinets. Customers wishing to order the fancy wire metal stool illustrated above can get the same from us at manufacturer's cost price.

No. 8K4011 Wire Metal Vapor Bath Stool. Price.......................... **$1.45**

CRUTCHES.

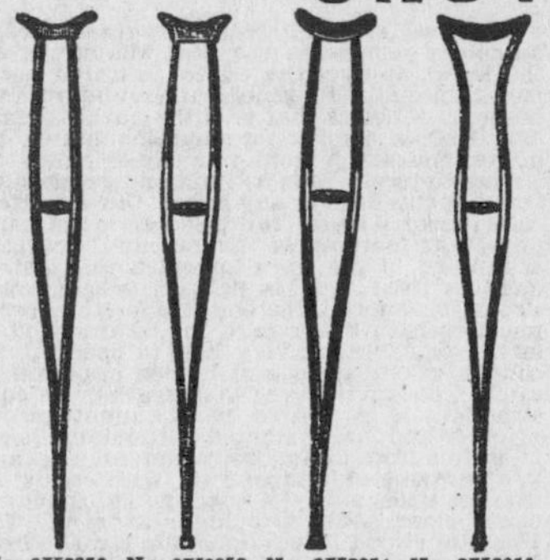

No. 8K3850 No. 8K3852 No. 8K3854 No. 8K3856

Plain; made of maple. The staff is split two-thirds its length from the top, bent to shape and held in shape by a hardwood hand piece, riveted and mortised to the arm piece; no ferrule. Made in sizes from 36 to 60 inches.

No. 8K3850 Price, per pair....... **98c**

Selected maple stock; made of two pieces, glued together at lower third of crutch and reinforced by ferrules. Bent and held in shape by hardwood hand piece, riveted and mortised arm piece. Nickel plated screw ferrule at the bottom and supplied with a screw rubber tip. Made in sizes from 36 to 60 inches.

No. 8K3852 Price, per pair ..**$1.67**

Selected shaped maple stock; made similar to No. 8K3852. The staff is shaped and finely finished. The arm piece is well rounded and most comfortable. Known as the "Cow Horn" crutch. Nickel plated screw ferrule and screw rubber tip. Made in sizes from 36 to 60 inches.

No. 8K3854 Price, per pair...**$3.19**

Extra selected maple stock; made similar to No. 8K3852, except instead of having a hardwood arm piece it is supplied with an elastic leather arm piece, filled with curled hair. The wood is of highly polished natural finish. At the lower end is supplied a clutch socket, into which a special rubber tip is secured. Made in sizes 36 to 60 inches.

No. 8K3856 Price, per pair...**$4.98**

Selected rosewood stock; otherwise the same as No. 8K3856. Made in sizes from 36 to 58 inches

No. 8K3858 Price, per pair...**$6.67**

Crutch Rubbers.

All kinds and all sizes. State whether screw, jaw or slip rubbers are desired and whether large, medium or small.

No. 8K3861 Price, per pair.......................... **35c**

THE SPLENDID REDUCTIONS IN PRICE

MADE BY US IN THIS CATALOGUE MUST PROVE TO OUR CUSTOMERS OUR ABILITY TO UNDERSELL ALL COMPETITION.

VETERINARY INSTRUMENTS. FOR THE SURGEON, THE STOCK RAISER AND THE FARMER.

THE FOLLOWING LIST of high class veterinary instruments represents the best line of these instruments ever offered. They are not the cheap, inferior, imperfect instruments often sold and called veterinary instruments, but represent in every case the very best. The list comprises only such instruments as are required by stock raisers generally and every instrument listed below should be found in every up to date stable ready for emergency cases. What better insurance can you have upon your stock than a few good veterinary instruments ready for an emergency? They will well repay the investment many times a year.

THE PRICES WE QUOTE upon these high grade instruments are very much lower than can be obtained from instrument dealers generally upon the same grade of material and workmanship, and we trust you will appreciate the real value offers given below. All these instruments are sold upon our binding guarantee that for value, workmanship and material, the prices can nowhere be duplicated, and they are all sent to you with the distinct understanding that after they are received, if you do not think them good value for the money or in any other way are not satisfied with them, merely write us to that effect, return the instruments to us, and your money will be cheerfully refunded.

PLEASE DO NOT CONFUSE ILLUSTRATIONS and think that all instruments quoted by others at about our prices are the same grade instrument. You want the very best, they well repay the investment, and take no chances but order them from the following list. We guarantee these goods.

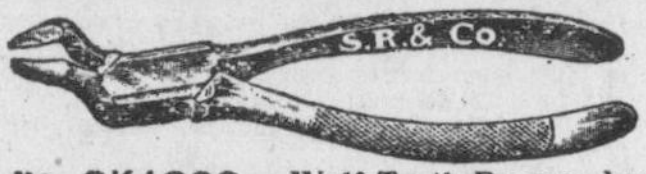

No. 8K1836 Wolf Tooth Forceps, bayonet pattern. Heavily nickel plated steel. Length, 13 inches. Price............$2.89
If by mail, postage extra, 17 cents.

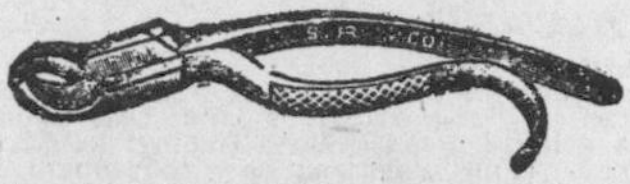

No. 8K1841 Wolf Tooth Forceps, curved. Heavily nickel plated steel. Length, 9 inches. Price..................$2.25
If by mail, postage extra, 17 cents.

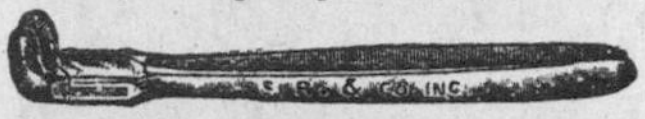

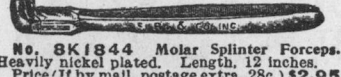

No. 8K1844 Molar Splinter Forceps. Heavily nickel plated. Length, 12 inches.
Price (If by mail, postage extra, 28c.) $2.95
Note that instruments Nos. 8K1850, 8K1853, 8K1854 and 8K1855 require extra handles to complete them. These handles are interchangeable and may be used with either one of the instruments.

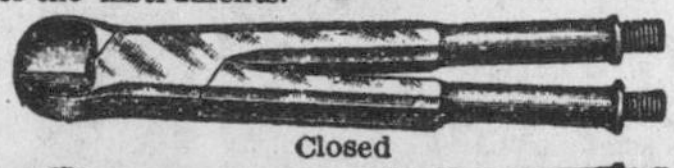
Closed

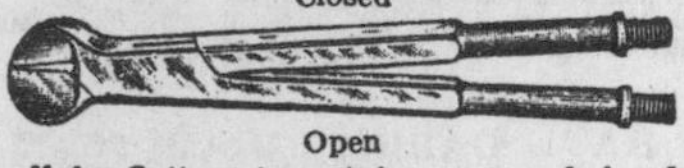
Open

Molar Cutters, two styles, open and closed. Heavily nickel plated steel. Length, with handle 18½ inches. When ordering mention the kind wanted. Handles extra. See No. 8K1856.
No. 8K1853 Closed. Price....$5.69
No. 8K1854 Open. Price.... 5.69
Cannot be sent by mail.

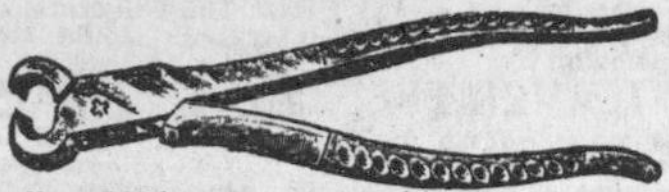

No. 8K1847 Straight Incisor Cutters. Heavily nickel plated. Length, 9 inches.
Price...(Postage extra, 17 cents.)...$2.27

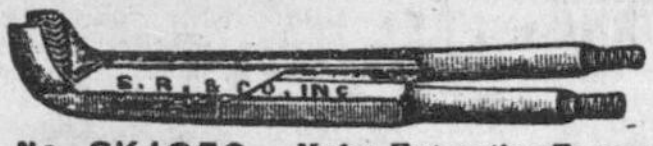

No. 8K1850 Molar Extracting Forceps. Heavily nickel plated. Length, with handles, 18½ inches. Handles extra. Price, ...$5.69
If by mail, postage extra, 20 cents.

Mead's Lever Open Molar Cutter, Without Handles.

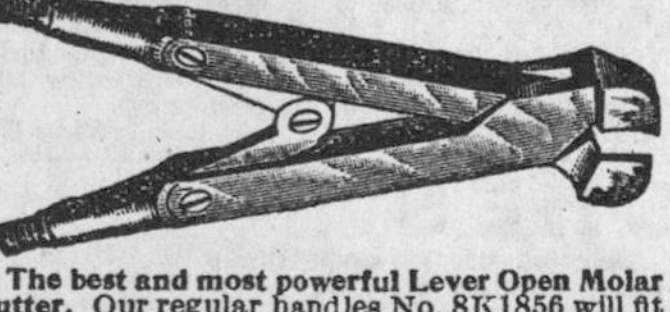

The best and most powerful Lever Open Molar Cutter. Our regular handles No. 8K1856 will fit them. Usual price $13.50 to $15.00. We can furnish you the best steel Mead's Lever Open Molar Cutter that can be made for only $11.50.
No. 8K1855 Mead's Lever Open Molar Cutter. Price.....(Unmailable)....$11.50

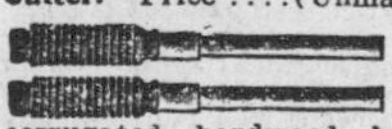

No. 8K1856 Handles for Cutters and Extractors. Length, 9 inches, corrugated hardwood handles and heavily nickeled shanks. Can be used for open and closed molar cutters, also for molar extractors.
Price, per pair...(Unmailable)......$2.79

Our Special Jointed Handle Horse Tooth Rasp.

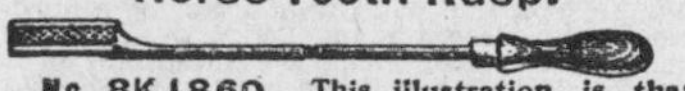

No. 8K1860 This illustration is that of House's Patent Horse Tooth Rasp. As shown in the illustration, it has a jointed handle, a very desirable feature. It is finely polished and nickel plated, complete with reversible file and ready for use. Weight, about 1 pound. Price............................97c
If by mail, postage extra, 16 cents.

Our New Jointed Mouth Horse Tooth Rasp.

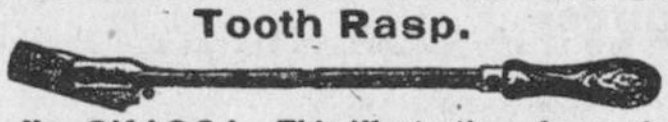

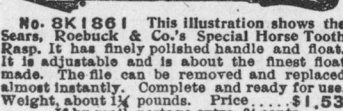

No. 8K1861 This illustration shows the Sears, Roebuck & Co.'s Special Horse Tooth Rasp. It has finely polished handle and float. It is adjustable and is about the finest float made. The file can be removed and replaced almost instantly. Complete and ready for use. Weight, about 1¼ pounds. Price.....$1.53
If by mail, postage extra, 24 cents.

Combination Mouth Float.

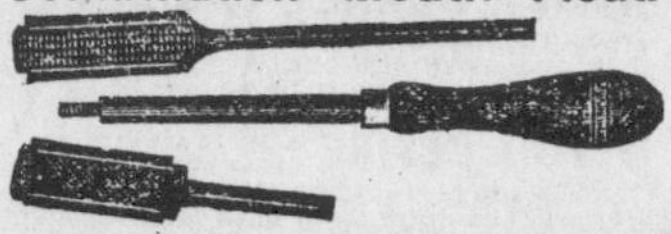

No. 8K1862 Combination Horse Mouth Float. Jointed, copper plated, fine nickel finish and adjustable. Consists of three pieces, straight and angular, with two separate files. Can be used for upper and lower molars, also for first molar teeth. With this float you can reach any part of the mouth.
Price, per set.......................$2.29
Extra blades can be furnished for this float. Cannot be sent by mail.
No. 8K1863 Extra Steel Files, 3½ inches long, for any of the above horse tooth rasps. Weight, about 4 ounces. Price, each......13c
If by mail, postage extra, each, 4 cents.

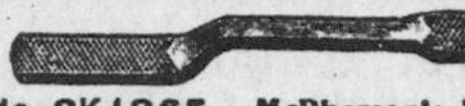

No. 8K1865 McPherson's Double End File. Has 4 different degrees of cutting surfaces. Length, 12 inches. Price........79c
If by mail, postage extra, 14 cents.

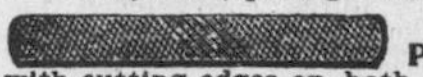

No. 8K1868 Plain Double File, with cutting edges on both sides and ends of different degrees of fineness. Length, 10 inches. Price..............................48c
If by mail, postage extra, 15 cents.

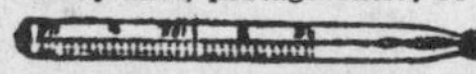

No. 8K1869 Veterinary Thermometer, 5-inch, sensitive, self registering; in hard rubber pocket case. Price..................73c
If by mail, postage extra, 4 cents.
No. 8K1870 Veterinary Thermometer, 6-inch, sensitive, self registering; in hard rubber pocket case. Price..................87c
If by mail, postage extra, 5 cents.

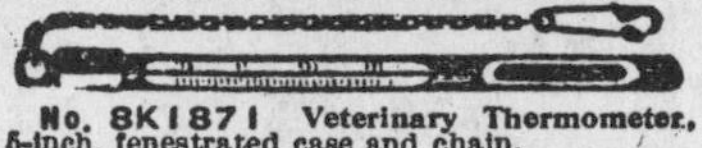

No. 8K1871 Veterinary Thermometer, 5-inch, fenestrated case and chain.
Price...................................$1.10
If by mail, postage extra, 8 cents.

Hercules Horse Mouth Speculum.

THE BEST SPECULUM MADE REGARDLESS OF PRICE.

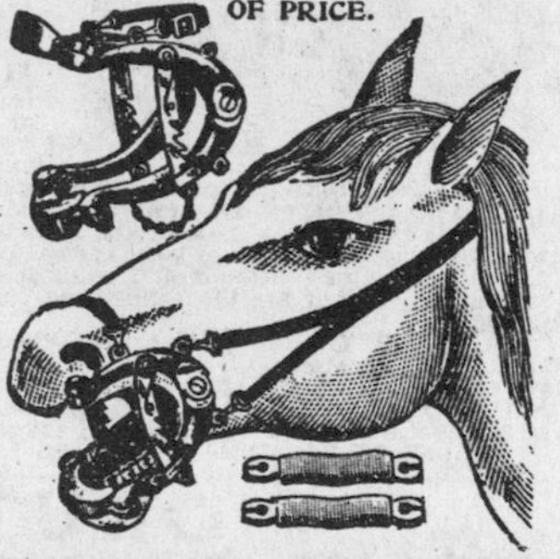

This new Hercules Patented Veterinary Mouth Speculum represents the best, the strongest, the safest and yet the easiest operated horse mouth speculum for general all around work on the teeth of horses that is in the market today. You simply cannot get anything better, no matter how much more you pay or would be willing to pay. In fact, you could get nothing better of this kind at any price. Our new Hercules Patented Horse Mouth Speculum has many important features of distinct and desirable advantage in the work for which this instrument is used. It is light in weight, very strong in material, thereby safe for the operator, aseptic in every part, not complicated, is interchangeable and very easy to operate. It can be taken apart and carried in pocket or satchel, occupying very little space. Its construction is so simple that it cannot get out of order and has patented self locking joint. It is free from every obstruction on sides and it allows operator to operate with ease from front or either side. A single pull of the lower chain closes the speculum instantly. The Hercules Horse Mouth Speculum is made from the best and finest steel hand forged and is handsomely finished, nickel plated and is really the best, strongest and also the cheapest instrument of its kind. If you need a horse mouth speculum we recommend that you send for the Hercules Patented Horse Mouth Speculum, compare it with other speculums that sell at $12.00 to $15.00 and you will prefer the Hercules Patented Speculum every time. The merits and advantages of this instrument are so apparent that everyone can see them. Send us your order for the Hercules Patented Horse Mouth Speculum with remittance to cover; examine it, use it, and if it is not entirely satisfactory you can send it back in ten days and we will refund every cent you have paid for it and transportation besides.
No. 8K1886 Hercules Patented Horse Mouth Speculum. Price..............$7.79
Cannot be sent by mail.

Hart's Improved Drenching Bit

FOR GIVING MEDICINE TO HORSES, COWS, CALVES, SHEEP AND HOGS.

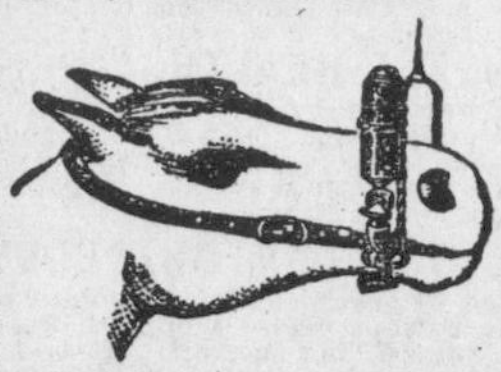

This bit has a container with a screw cap so that the animal cannot spill medicine. A shut-off valve allows the medicine to be turned on and off at will. You may take container from bit, fill it with medicine, and screw into position after the bit has been adjusted to animal's head. The bit keeps the animal's head up and keeps his mouth shut. He has to swallow every drop after you open valve. A perfectly made, compact, strong veterinary appliance. Will last a lifetime.

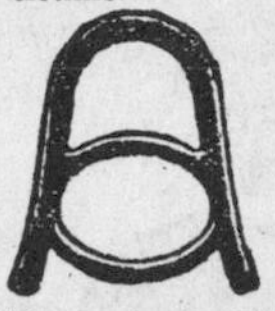

No. 8K1875 Hart's Bit. Price........$2.25
Postage extra, 30 cents.
No. 8K1878 Balling Iron. Weight, 1¼ pounds. Plain. Price..........75c
Postage extra, 18 cents.
No. 8K1879 Nickel plated. Price.....$1.08
Postage extra, 18 cents.

Veterinary Trachea Tube.

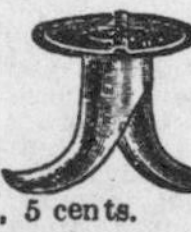

Veterinary Trachea Tube, self retaining. Nickel plated.
No. 8K1880
Price..............$2.00
If by mail, postage extra, 5 cents.

Improved Self Retaining Trachea Tube With Sieve.

SAME AS No. 8K1880, WITH SIEVE.

This tube, as can be readily seen by its shape, is self retaining, and contains sieve attachment to prevent dust from entering the trachea. Tube should be inserted when animal is to be speeded or worked hard. The insertion of this tube in a roarer or broken winded horse will transform him into a useful and profitable animal.
No. 8K1882 Improved Self Retaining Trachea Tube. Nickel plated. Price..$2.55
If by mail, postage extra, 5 cents.

Improved Ecraseur.

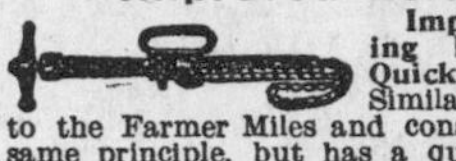

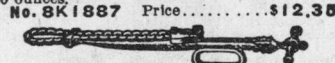

Improved Castrating Ecraseur with Quick Chain Release. Similar in appearance to the Farmer Miles and constructed on the same principle, but has a quick adjustment for the chain, allowing quick and easy manipulation. Very best material, heavily nickel plated and is the best ecraseur made. Weight, 30 ounces.
No. 8K1887 Price..........$12.35

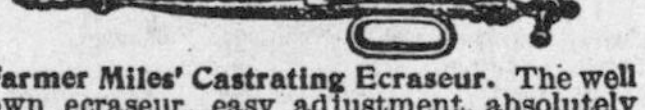

Farmer Miles' Castrating Ecraseur. The well known ecraseur, easy adjustment, absolutely certain, best material and finely nickel plated. Weight, 1 pound.
No. 8K1888 Price............$6.70

Spaying Emasculator.

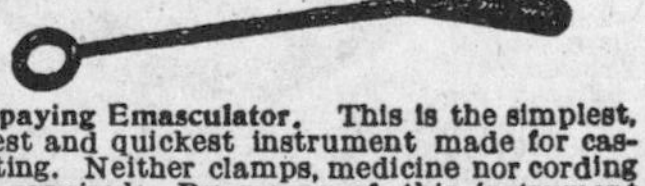

Spaying Emasculator. This is the simplest, safest and quickest instrument made for castrating. Neither clamps, medicine nor cording are required. By means of this instrument the spermatic cord is severed by torsion, completely preventing the loss of blood. Length, 15 inches. Weight, 18 ounces.
No. 8K1889 Price..........$12.00

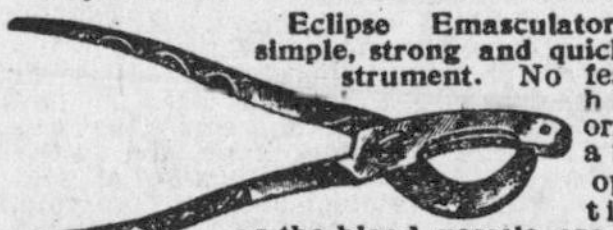

Eclipse Emasculator. A simple, strong and quick instrument. No fear of hemorrhage after operations, as the blood vessels are completely closed. A poor instrument has caused the loss of many a good and expensive horse. It pays to buy the Eclipse. Weight, 18 ounces.
No. 8K1890 Straight. 12 inches long. Price...................................$5.75
No. 8K1891 Curved (for standing operations). 11 inches long. Price..$5.75

Castrating Knives.

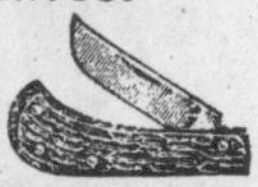

Castrating Knife. Spring back. Metal handle.
No. 8K1892
Price..................75c
If by mail, postage extra, 2 cents.

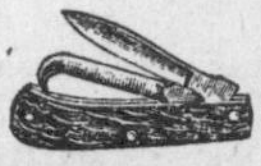

Ziegler's Castrating Knife. Metal handle.
No. 8K1893
Price...............$1.25
If by mail, postage extra, 4 cents.

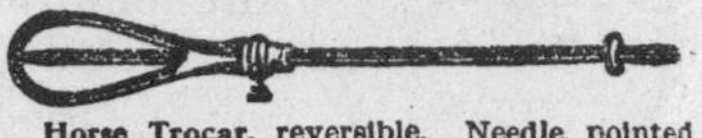

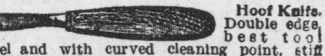

Horse Trocar, reversible. Needle pointed blade, protection handle, nickel plated.
No. 8K1900 Price...........93c
If by mail, postage extra, 8 cents.

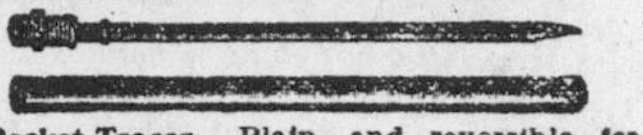

Pocket Trocar. Plain, and reversible, for general veterinary use.
No. 8K1902 Price............88c
If by mail, postage extra, 3 cents.

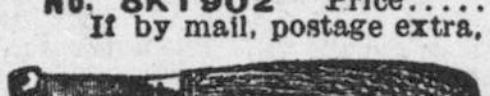

Hoof Knife. Double edge, best tool steel and with curved cleaning point, stiff handle.
No. 8K1904 Price..........$1.19
If by mail, postage extra, 5 cents.

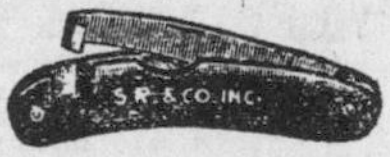

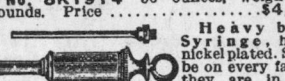

Hoof Knife. Folding, finest tool steel, curved cleaning point, ebony handle.
No. 8K1906 Price...........$1.48
If by mail, postage extra, 5 cents.

Horse Fleams.

Horse Fleams, brass handles.
No. 8K1908
Price, one blade..48c
Price, two blades 54c
Price, three blades 73c
If by mail, postage extra, 5 cents.

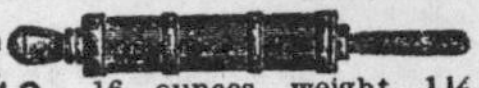

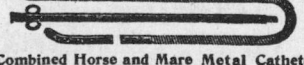

Injection Syringe, metal.
No. 8K1910 16 ounces, weight, 1½ pounds. Price.......................$2.75
No. 8K1912 24 ounces, weight, 2½ pounds. Price.......................$3.65
No. 8K1914 36 ounces, weight, 3½ pounds. Price.......................$4.55

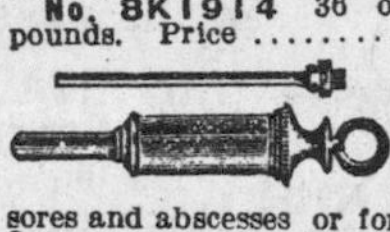

Heavy brass Syringe, heavily nickel plated. Should be on every farm as they are in daily need for washing out sores and abscesses or for quittor in the feet. 2-ounce capacity. Weight, 1 pound.
No. 8K1918 Price...........$1.71
If by mail, postage extra, 15 cents.

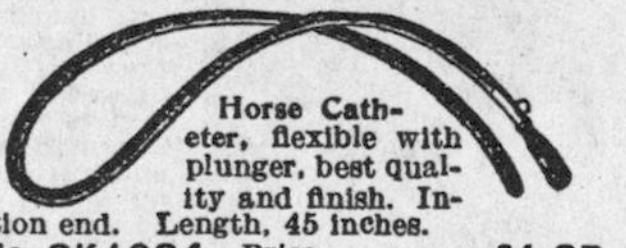

Horse Catheter, flexible with plunger, best quality and finish. Insertion end. Length, 45 inches.
No. 8K1924 Price...........$1.27
If by mail, postage extra, 10 cents.

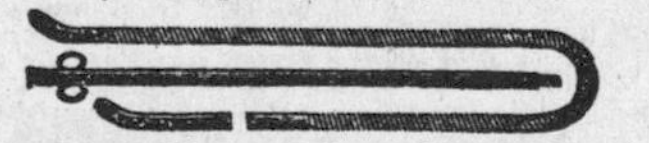

Combined Horse and Mare Metal Catheter, spiral construction, finely finished and nickel plated.
No. 8K1926 Price...........$2.19
If by mail, postage extra, 22 cents.

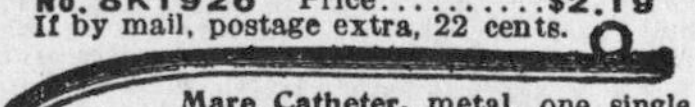

Mare Catheter, metal, one single piece; the regular standard mare catheter, nickel plated.
No. 8K1927 Price..........$1.18
Mare Catheter, metal, jointed.
No. 8K1928 Price........... 1.48
If by mail, postage extra, 8 cents.

OUR ALREADY LOWEST PRICES have been still FURTHER REDUCED in this Big Catalogue. Just compare the prices in this book with the prices quoted by us in previous catalogues and note the additional savings we make for you.

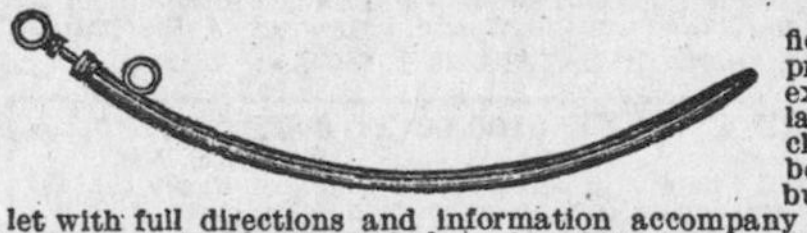

Southerland Impregnation Syringe. Artificial impregnation is now successfully practised by thousands experienced and expensive stallion owners. The Southerland Impregnation Syringe is not the cheapest syringe on the market, but the best, and for the uses required, run no risk but buy the best. A very interesting booklet with full directions and information accompany each syringe. The stallion owner will more than double his profit by using this impregnator. Two or more mares can be impregnated with one service of horse, thereby saving his vitality. Weight, 30 ounces.
No. 8K1930 Price...........(If by mail, postage extra, 15 cents.).........$3.65

Operating Scissors.

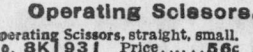

Operating Scissors, straight, small.
No. 8K1931 Price......56c

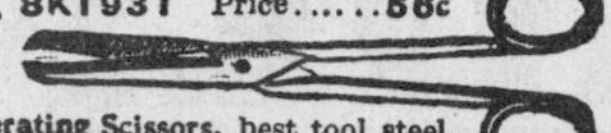

Operating Scissors, best tool steel, blunt nose, straight, large.
No. 8K1932 Price.....66c
Operating Scissors, curved, small.
No. 8K1933 Price.......... $0.82
Operating Scissors, curved, large.
No. 8K1934 Price........... 1.03
If by mail, postage extra, 4 cents.

Breeders' Bag.

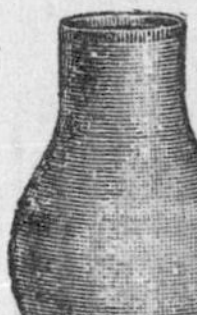

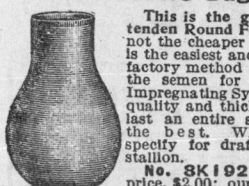

This is the genuine Crittenden Round Form Bag and not the cheaper flat kind. It is the easiest and most satisfactory method of collecting the semen for use with the Impregnating Syringe. Extra quality and thickness. Will last an entire season. Buy the best. When ordering specify for draft or roadster stallion.

No. 8K1929 Regular price, $2.00; our price..89c
If by mail, postage extra, 8c.

Impregnating Dilator.

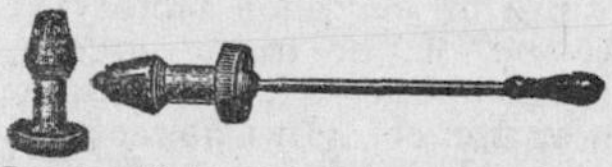

Genuine Crittenden Safety Impregnator and Dilator. This has the corrigations for holding in place and the only one that can be depended upon. Easy to apply and the only sure means for assisting the stallion in getting so called barren and irregular breeding mares in foal. This item is grossly imitated. Buy the dilator with corrigations for holding in place. The increased number of foaled mares and the saving on the horse will repay the cost a hundred times. Each carefully packed in long hinged box. Directions with each outfit. Regular price, $7.50.

No. 8K1920 Our price........$6.75
If by mail, postage extra, 25 cents.

Artery Forceps, plain, 4½-inch.
No. 8K1936 Price..... 59c
Artery Forceps, plain, 6-inch.
No. 8K1938 Price..$1.15
If by mail, postage extra, 4 cents.

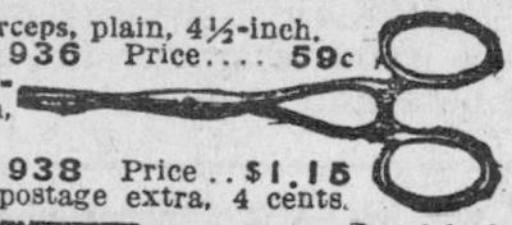

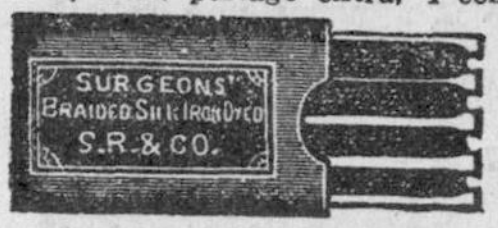

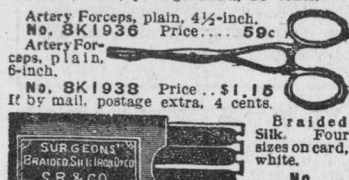

Braided Silk. Four sizes on card, white.
No. 8K1952 Price, per card... 45c
If by mail, postage extra, 2 cents.

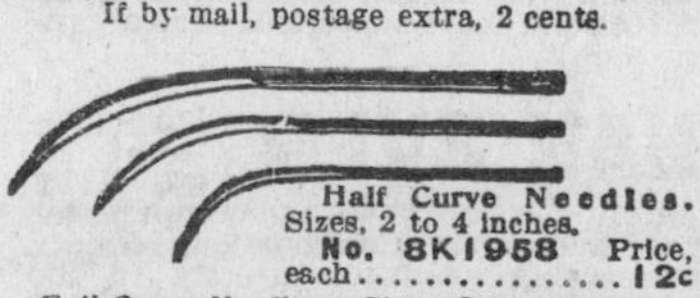

Half Curve Needles. Sizes, 2 to 4 inches.
No. 8K1958 Price, each.......... 12c
Full Curve Needles. Sizes, 2 to 4 inches.
No. 8K1960 Price, each.......... 12c
If by mail, postage extra, 2 cents.

Veterinary Hypodermic Syringe and Aspirator.

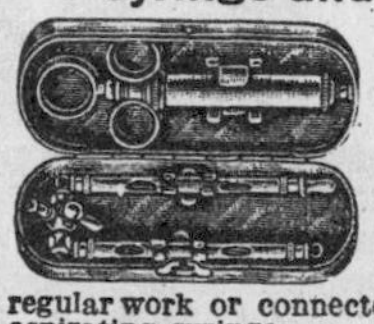

No. 8K1962 Veterinary Hypodermic Syringe and Aspirator, all metal, aseptic, in pocket case, fitted with three finger rings, adjustable cock, three sizes of needles, trocar and canula. Syringe can be used alone for regular work or connected with aspirator for aspirating syringe.
Price, complete....................$2.99
If by mail, postage extra, 16 cents.

Pig Extractor.

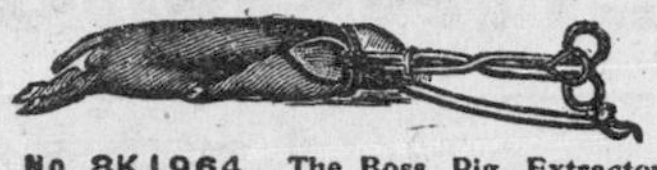

No. 8K1964 The Boss Pig Extractor. This instrument was given first premium at the Iowa State Fair, 1895, and is the most valuable invention of the kind. Suitable for use on large or small sows. Made of heavily polished rods with cord loops. The outfit is put up neatly in a box, and complete, weighs only 18 ounces. Once tried always used, is the general prediction. Price, complete.......98c
If by mail, postage extra, 22 cents.

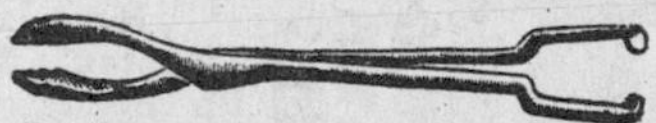

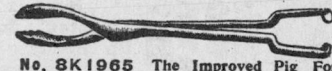

No. 8K1965 The Improved Pig Forceps has points of excellence which make it a most practical instrument, and may be used upon either small or large sows with equal satisfaction. The instrument is made of malleable iron, tinned to prevent rusting; will not tear the sow or otherwise injure the animal in operation. Price.................91c
If by mail, postage extra, 18 cents.

Keystone Dehorning Clippers.

The latest improved and most wonderful instrument manufactured for dehorning cattle.

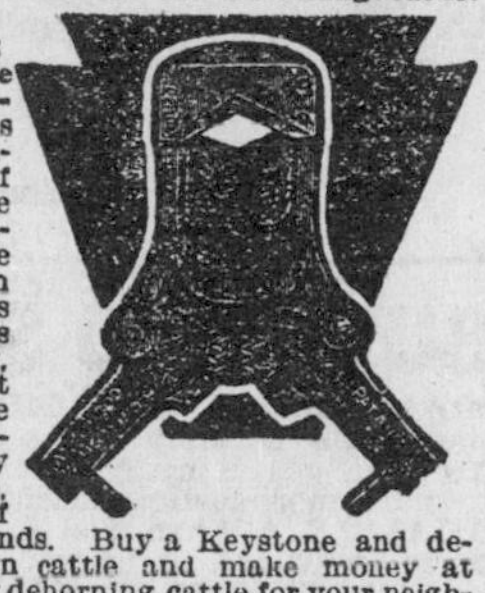

No. 8K1968 The Keystone Dehorner Clipper. This is the best instrument made. If you want one that gives satisfaction, one that you can use two years from date as well as today, an instrument that is made for this purpose, then buy the Keystone, worth three of the cheaper kinds. Buy a Keystone and dehorn your own cattle and make money at spare time by dehorning cattle for your neighbors. Fully guaranteed.
Price for clipper complete, with leader and extra blades and screws..........$10.85
Unmailable.

OUR ALREADY LOWEST PRICES have been still FURTHER REDUCED in this Big Catalogue. Just compare the prices in this book with the prices quoted by us in previous catalogues and note the additional savings we make for you.

Calf Dehorner.

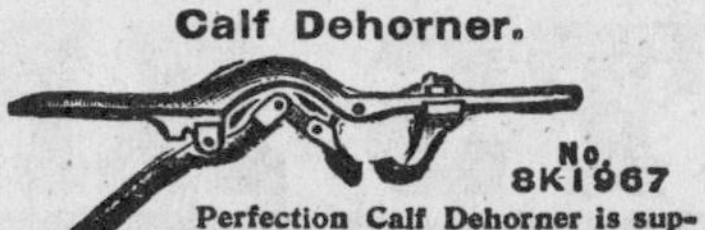

No. 8K1967 Perfection Calf Dehorner is supplied with two curved blades, the stationary one being drawn into the flesh at the base of the horn, thereby holding the instrument in position while the movable blade which does most of the cutting, is hinged so that it cuts with a downward and then an upward cut. Equally as good for dehorning lambs. So simple that it can be operated by anyone. So cheap it is within reach of all.
Price, nickel plated..............$3.85
Unmailable.

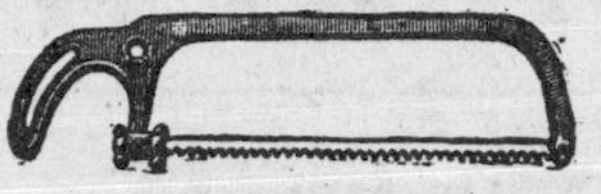

No. 8K1971 Dehorning Saw, nickel plated. Price....................$1.60
If by mail, postage extra, 32 cents.

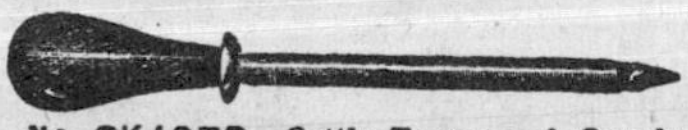

No. 8K1973 Cattle Trocar and Canula (Bull Punch). For opening and draining abscesses, etc. Price.................48c
If by mail, postage extra, 8 cents.

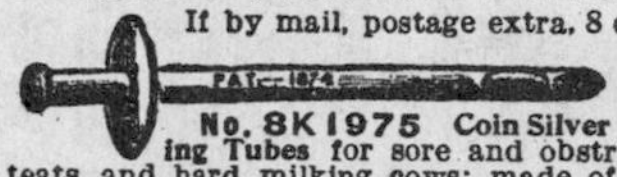

No. 8K1975 Coin Silver Milking Tubes for sore and obstructed teats and hard milking cows; made of pure coin silver, and can be used with absolute safety. Set of four tubes, 2¼ inches long, in a neat box, with full directions for use.
Price, per set, coin silver..........$1.60
Single tubes. Price, each.......... .45
Single tubes, special length, 3¼ inches.
Price, each......................... .45
If by mail, postage extra, 2 cents.

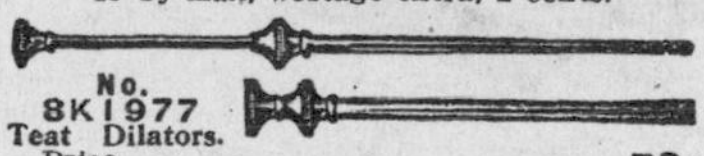

No. 8K1977 Teat Dilators.
Price...............................73c
If by mail, postage extra, 2 cents.

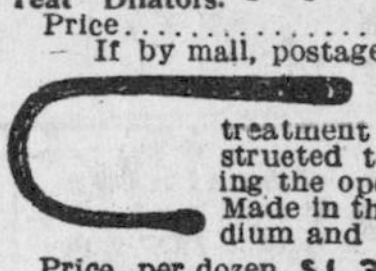

No. 8K1978 Lead Probes, for treatment of stricture and obstructed teats, also for enlarging the opening in cows' teats. Made in three sizes, small, medium and large. State size.
Price, per dozen, $1.35; each.........12c
If by mail, postage extra, each, 3 cents.

No. 8K1980 Cow Teat Slitter, for cutting the stricture or stoppages in cows' teats. This is the best remedy for hard milking cows. Best implement steel; nickeled sheath; length 4 inches. Price.......89c
Postage extra, 3 cents.

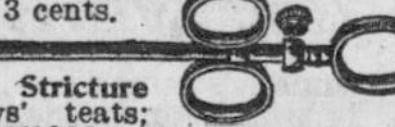

No. 8K1984 Stricture Cutter, for cows' teats; same uses as No. 8K1980, but a much better instrument; length, 7 inches, made of best implement steel; finely nickel plated.
Price.............................$1.45
If by mail, postage extra, 3 cents.

Poultry Instruments.

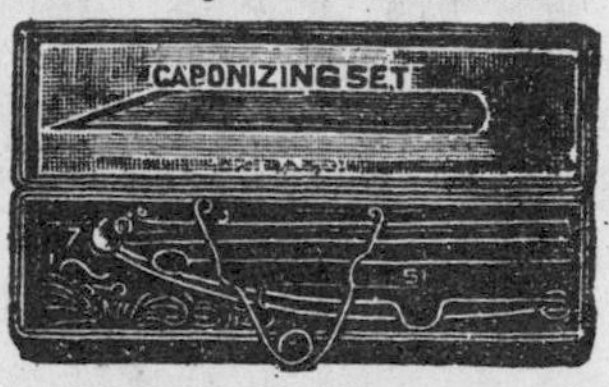

No. 8K1985 Poultrymen can double their profits by caponizing their chicks. The operation is very simple, the instructions being so explicit that anyone, after a careful reading, can do it with these instruments. The complete caponizing set contains the best instruments, and at the at price which they are offered no one who keeps chickens can afford to neglect this opportunity of increasing his profits.
Price, per set, in velvet lined case, with book, "Instructions for Caponizing" $2.45
If by mail, postage extra, 10 cents.

Poultry Killing Knives.

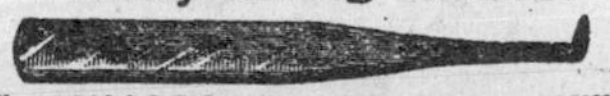

No. 8K1989 Angular Poultry Killing Knife. The shape of this knife permits making incisions which are impossible with any other instrument. Price............48c
If by mail, postage extra, 5 cents.

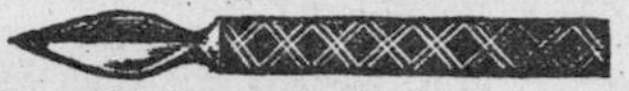

No. 8K1990 French Poultry Killing Knife. Every poultry raiser should have one. They are made of finely tempered instrument steel, with nickeled handle. Price...33c
If by mail, postage extra, 5 cents.

Poultry Marker.

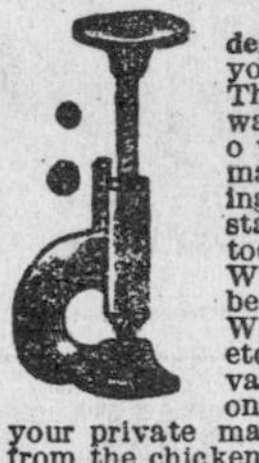

No. 8K1991 The Philadelphia Poultry Marker. Do you keep a record of chickens? There is no better or quicker way than by this marker, as over two hundred different marks can be made by punching between the toes; for instance, between first and second toes of right foot can mean Wyandotte or Plymouth Rock; between second and third toes, White Leghorn or Langshan, etc.; so that hundreds of private marks can be made, not only to keep records, but by your private marks you can secure yourself from the chicken thief. They are well made; with steel spring and cutter, nicely nickel plated. Price...................19c
If by mail, postage extra, 4 cents.

Gape Worm Extractor.

No. 8K1992 Gape Worm Extractor. The disease commonly known as gapes is caused by a small worm in the windpipe of the fowls. When the chick seems to gasp frequently it is a sure sign of gapes and it should receive attention at once. The only certain cure is to remove the worms by mechanical means. You will save time and money by having on hand a Gape Worm Extractor. The extractor quickly removes, without injury to the chick, the worms and the matter from the windpipe and effects an instant cure. One chick saved, pays price of instrument.
Price.................................19c
If by mail, postage extra, 2 cents.

MILK FEVER=AND ITS TREATMENT

$2.50

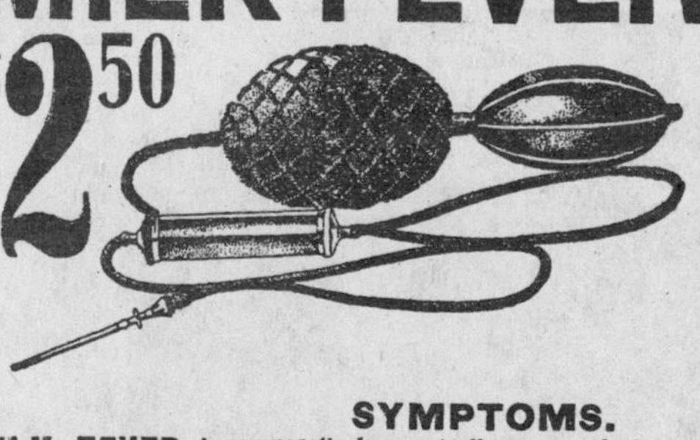

Is your best cow worth $2.50? What would you do if that fancy cow of yours was to become afflicted with milk fever when she drops her calf? Do you know that this disease is fatal in 95 per cent of the cases? Do you know that drugs internally are practically useless? Do you know that the only successful treatment is that prescribed by the Bureau of Animal Industry of the Department of Agriculture of Washington, D. C.?

THE DAVIS MILK FEVER OUTFIT is made according to the specifications of the Bureau of Animal Industry of the Government, and is fully described in Farmers' Bulletin No. 206, issued by the United States Department of Agriculture. The fact that you have never lost a cow from milk fever is no guarantee that you will not. Send us an order for the Davis Milk Fever Outfit today.

MILK FEVER is a very common and heretofore very fatal disease, affecting cows. It has been a particular hardship to the stockman, owing to the fact that it usually attacks the best milking members of the herd at a time when the milk flows most freely, and it has caused extremely severe losses in the dairy industry. It is, therefore, of the utmost importance that the stockman or the dairyman should have at hand at all times an effective and successful method of treatment. Without this treatment, 90 per cent of cases will prove fatal. With the Davis Milk Fever Outfit 90 per cent of the cows can be saved, and, at an expenditure of $2.50, there is absolutely no reason for any stockman to have loss of animals from milk fever. It is the cheapest and best insurance on earth for this disease.

SYMPTOMS.

MILK FEVER is comparatively easy to diagnose, and almost every stockman and dairyman knows it immediately. It usually occurs within two days after the birth of the calf, and is seldom if ever seen after the second week. In isolated cases it has been observed a few days before calving. At the commencement of the attack the cow usually exhibits excitement, is restless, treads with her hind feet, switches the tail, stares anxiously about the stall, bellows occasionally, shows colicky symptoms and makes ineffectual attempts at relieving the bowels. The owner seldom recognizes these symptoms, but they are followed within a few hours by a beginning of paralysis, indicated by a staggering gait and a weakening of the knees and fetlocks in front. The cow becomes quieter, the gait more staggering, and she goes down and is unable to rise. Paralysis by this time is general, the cow lies quiet, her eyes partly closed; she pays no attention to the calf or her surroundings, and flies may light with impunity on all parts of the body. While down, the patient assumes a characteristic position. The head is turned to the side, usually the left, and rests on the chest. Should the head be drawn out straight, it immediately flops around to the side when force is removed. There are symptoms of paralysis of the muscles of the throat, so that swallowing is impossible. Bowels are weak; in some cases there is a rise of temperature. In cases that recover, convalescence is rapid, and on the day following the onset of the disease, or even a few hours after, those that recover will be up and going. A few cases, however, continue to show a slight paralysis for a week or longer. In fatal cases the animal may remain perfectly quiet and die in a comatose condition from complete paralysis. Very frequently, however, there is agitation and excitement prior to death, with tossing about of the head. Death, like recovery, usually occurs in from eighteen to seventy-two hours, after the onset of the malady.

TREATMENT.

THIS TREATMENT is the most successful ever discovered for milk fever. It consists of the injection of sterilized atmospheric air into the udder. It is simple, practical and harmless and will cure 90 per cent of the cases. The Davis Milk Fever Outfit consists of a metal cylinder with milled screw caps on both ends. The cap may be removed in order to place sterilized absorbent cotton within the cylinder. To this cap a pair of rubber bellows is connected by nine inches of rubber tubing. The cap on the end toward the milking tube is to be removed together with the eighteen inches of rubber hose at the free end of which is the self retaining milking tube, for the purpose of disinfection before treating each case. The pulling on or off of the tubing of the nozzles of the milled caps is thus rendered unnecessary. Within the metal cylinder is a wire net, which prevents the obstruction of the outlet of the chamber by holding back the sterilized cotton, and also permits of the unscrewing of the lower cap and the disinfection of this portion of the apparatus, including the milking tube without contaminating the packing. Absorbent cotton, impregnated with carbolic acid (carbolized cotton) or other suitable disinfectants can be purchased from the drug stores in most localities, and is better, though slightly more expensive, than plain cotton.

THIS IS A BRIEF DESCRIPTION of the Davis Milk Fever Outfit. Every farmer, stockman or dairyman owning cows should send for one at once. The fact that you have never had a case of milk fever does not mean that you will not be troubled with it in the future. The extremely low price of the Davis Milk Fever Outfit is such that you cannot afford to be without it in case of emergency. Remember, there is nothing to wear out; that full and complete directions for its use are on every box. Send for it today. Do not wait until that best cow of yours dies; for when she does get milk fever, you will be willing to pay ten times what we are asking for the outfit if you only had it on hand. Full directions and information with each outfit.

No. 8K1250 Complete outfit, as illustrated. Price..$2.50

BOOTS AND SHOES

20,000 PAIRS OF SHOES
OUR DAILY AVERAGE SALES

Our Shoe Factory at Littleton, N. H.

THE REASON IS BRIEFLY TOLD ON THIS PAGE

Here is a picture of our shoe factory at Littleton, N. H., one of the most modern, up to date and complete shoe making establishments in existence. In this factory, equipped with every known device for the improvement of shoe quality and the reduction of shoe cost, we are daily turning out thousands of those **Shoes of Quality** that have made the name of Sears, Roebuck & Co. pre-eminent in shoe selling. Shoes of such quality that in a few short years we have built up the greatest volume of shoe business in the world dealing directly with the real wearers of the shoes, not with jobbers or middlemen, and saving the real wearers every cent of the unnecessary profits usually exacted by jobbers and dealers.

CONTRAST THE METHODS
of this factory, buying the finest raw materials at the lowest cost, manufacturing by the most modern and improved methods, using styles created by the leading designers, and selling directly to you, the actual wearer of the shoes, at prices based on the lowest manufacturing cost with only one small profit added; consider these facts and contrast these methods with the methods of the average dealer, and you will understand at once why we have no real competitors in the shoe business.

QUALITY COUNTS.
We have built up the largest shoe business in the world (over $4,500,000 last year) by our untiring efforts to give our customers **QUALITY**. **QUALITY** is what our leather experts have in mind when they go into the markets to buy their material. **QUALITY** of products is our factory superintendent's aim when he hires his workmen or buys new machinery. **QUALITY** is what our trained corps of inspectors never forget for one moment, as they carefully examine every shoe before shipment, insuring to every purchaser a perfect shoe, free from the slightest imperfection, absolutely satisfactory in every detail.

BUY GOOD SHOES
We make it a point not only to look to the quality in our shoe factory but to talk QUALITY to our customers. **BUY GOOD SHOES.** If two styles suit you equally well, give the **better quality** the preference every time, even if the cost is a little more. You will get so much more wear, so much better style, so much greater comfort, so much more lasting satisfaction, that you will always remember the benefits of **QUALITY**. When you order from us you get the benefit **in QUALITY, in style, in fit and in price** of the world's greatest and most successful shoe organization. **BUY GOOD SHOES.**

PRICES LOWER THAN EVER.
Improvement in quality is not the only benefit of our perfected shoe organization. Compare our prices with those quoted in former catalogues and you will see how our reduced cost, due to improved methods of manufacturing, operates directly to the advantage of our customers. The plain fact is that our prices are so low that competition is impossible.

HOW TO ORDER

Be sure to state size wanted. If shoes go by mail, send cash in full, including enough extra to cover postage, which is 1 cent per ounce. If too much is sent we refund the difference. Weight is given under each article.

OUR SHOE GUARANTEE

Any shoes purchased from us which are not fully up to your expectations, and **BETTER VALUE** than you can possibly obtain elsewhere, may be returned to us, and the purchase price, together with all transportation charges, **will be** promptly refunded to you.

DAILY SCENE IN EXAMINING DIVISION OF OUR SHOE DEPARTMENT

All our footwear is thoroughly examined by our trained shoe experts, assuring the customer a perfect shoe in every detail.

LADIES' STYLISH OXFORDS AT INCOMPARABLE PRICES.

THE LATEST CREATION.

No. 15K177

$1.68

PER PAIR

DON'T FAIL TO STATE SIZE.

The season's latest creation is this Patent Colt Blucher Cut Oxford, with dull mat kid top. Has flexible soles, military heels and silk stitched button holes, making it a thoroughly up to date low shoe. Sizes and half sizes, 2½ to 8. Widths, C, D, E and EE. Weight, 20 ounces.

THE POMPEY PUMP.

No. 15K185

$1.49

PER PAIR

DON'T FAIL TO STATE SIZE.

A dainty pump of patent coltskin, much in favor with fashionable women. Made with the new short vamp effect, with elastic instep, making it a shoe that will fit the foot like a glove. Very dressy. Sizes and half sizes, 2½ to 8. Widths, C, D, E and EE. Weight, 22 ounces.

ALL PATENT COLT.

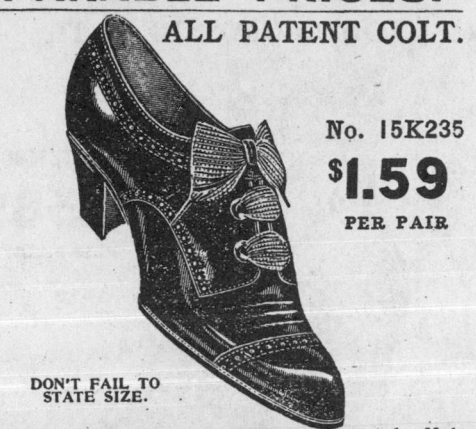

No. 15K235

$1.59

PER PAIR

DON'T FAIL TO STATE SIZE.

A handsome Blucher style artistically perforated. Made over a stylish last with military heel and light flexible soles. Very popular and indeed a shoe that must be seen to be appreciated. Sizes and half sizes, 2½ to 8. Widths, C, D, E and EE. Weight, 20 ounces.

VERY NOBBY.

No. 15K176

$1.58

PER PAIR

DON'T FAIL TO STATE SIZE.

A nobby, serviceable Oxford that has all the characteristics of a $3.00 shoe. Made with the latest short vamp of patent colt, with quarter and top of dull mat kid. Flexible soles and high Cuban heel. Sizes and half sizes, 2½ to 8. Widths, C, D, E and EE. Weight, 20 ounces.

CORONA RIBBON.

No. 15K181

$1.52

PER PAIR

DON'T FAIL TO STATE SIZE.

Another new style destined to be all the rage this season. Made of patent Corona coltskin, with dull mat calf top and medium weight sole cut out of first class leather. A foot-fitting low shoe, hard to beat for the money. Sizes and half sizes, 2½ to 8. Widths, D, E and EE. Weight averages 23 ounces.

THE CASTILIAN.

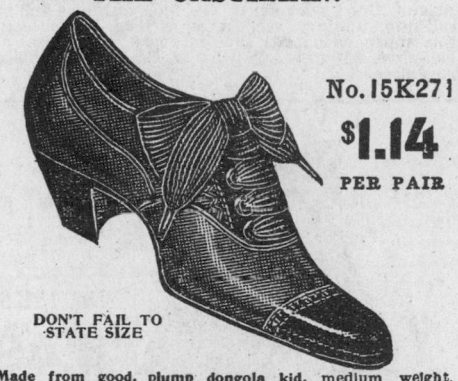

No. 15K271

$1.14

PER PAIR

DON'T FAIL TO STATE SIZE

Made from good, plump dongola kid, medium weight, opera toe, with patent leather tip. In this shoe we give extra good value. Sizes and half sizes, 2½ to 8. Full widths. Weight averages 22 ounces.

GUNMETAL LEADER.

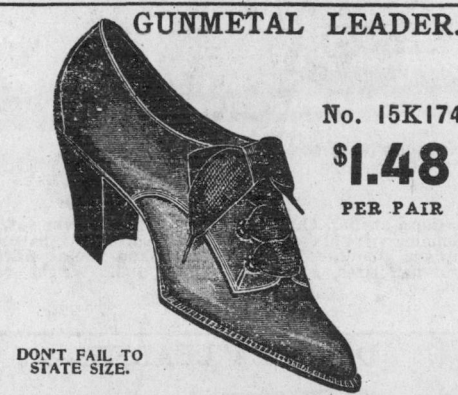

No. 15K174

$1.48

PER PAIR

DON'T FAIL TO STATE SIZE.

This Gunmetal Blucher Oxford has proved to be the popular low shoe of the season. Has light flexible soles, high Cuban heels and large eyelets, making it a delight to the eye and very serviceable. Sizes and half sizes, 2½ to 8. Widths, C, D and E. Weight, 20 ounces.

LATEST OXFORD.

No. 15K241

$1.39

PER PAIR

DON'T FAIL TO STATE SIZE.

We make this Oxford of fine, soft vici kid stock, which is very durable and at the same time very comfortable. Made over the mannish last, neatly perforated, with patent tip and is a good wearing low shoe. Sizes and half sizes, 2½ to 8. Widths, D, E and EE. Weight, 26 ounces.

A BIG SELLER.

No. 15K253

$1.19

PER PAIR

DON'T FAIL TO STATE SIZE.

This number has proven a big seller. No wonder, for where can you find it duplicated at the price? Genuine patent colt, Blucher pattern, flexible sole, Cuban heel, and fitted with large eyelets. Sizes and half sizes, 2½ to 8. Full widths. Weight, 24 ounces.

A NEW SIDE LACE.

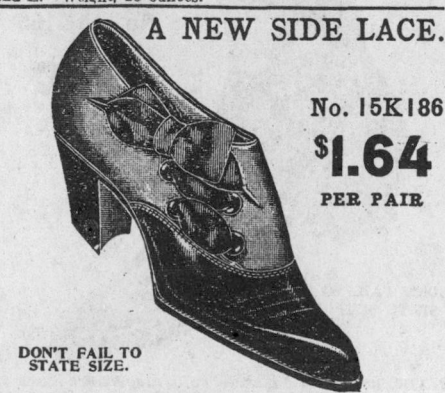

No. 15K186

$1.64

PER PAIR

DON'T FAIL TO STATE SIZE.

One of the season's prize winners is this fine Patent Colt Oxford, with dull mat kid top. It has an artistic side lace of fine Barathea silk and is easy to fit to the foot. A shoe full of value. Sizes and half sizes, 2½ to 8. Widths, C, D and EE. Weight, 20 ounces.

EMPRESS OXFORD.

No. 15K211

$1.49

PER PAIR

DON'T FAIL TO STATE SIZE.

Made of fine mellow vici kid, with dull mat top and patent leather tip. A Blucher cut low shoe, built for style and fitting qualities, while the wear is an essential feature. Sizes and half sizes, 2½ to 8. Widths, D, E and EE. Weight, 22 ounces.

A SURE FITTER.

No. 15K279

92c

PER PAIR

DON'T FAIL TO STATE SIZE.

Made of vici kid with a patent tip and large eyelets over a very nobby glove fitting last. In every way an up to date Oxford that would compare favorably with the shoes you buy elsewhere at $1.50. Sizes, 2½ to 8. Widths, D and E only. Weight averages .20 ounces.

LADIES' STYLISH, SERVICEABLE SHOES AT LOW PRICES.

YOU CANNOT BEAT IT.

No. 15K90
$1.58
PER PAIR

DON'T FAIL TO
STATE SIZE.

An extremely stylish shoe at a most reasonable price. Good selection of vici kid, with nice dull mat calf top, military heel, large eyelets, Union leather sole and a well made shoe in every way. Sizes and half sizes, 2½ to 8. Widths, D, E and EE. Weight, 28 ounces.

ELASTIC INSTEP.

No. 15K66
$1.49
PER PAIR

DON'T FAIL TO
STATE SIZE.

An elastic instep shoe of vici kid stock, with patent tip. The elastic goring at the instep yields to every action of the muscles of the foot, making it a real health shoe. Absolutely all solid and serviceable. Sizes and half sizes, 2½ to 8. Widths, D, E and EE. Weight averages 28 ounces.

GRAND LEADER.

No. 15K132
$1.34
PER PAIR

DON'T FAIL TO
STATE SIZE.

Made over the Rochester last of genuine dongola kid, with patent leather tip and flexible outer sole. We honestly believe it is better value than those you buy elsewhere at $1.75. Sizes and half sizes, 2½ to 8. Widths, D, E and EE. Weight averages 28 ounces.

A WORLD BEATER.

No. 15K95
$1.49
PER PAIR

DON'T FAIL TO
STATE SIZE.

Our enormous shoe output makes it possible for you to secure this world beater at this low price. Patent leather stock, dull kid top and medium heel. Slightly extended soles stitched all around and guaranteed counter and inner sole. Sizes and half sizes, 2½ to 8. Widths, D, E and EE. Weight averages 26 ounces.

FANCY PATENT.

No. 15K119
$1.27
PER PAIR

DON'T FAIL TO
STATE SIZE

A graceful little shoe impossible to equal at this price. Patent leather stock, dongola kid top and fancy inlaid figured velvet lace stay. Carries a Cuban heel, light sole and reliable counter and inner sole. Sizes and half sizes, 2½ to 8. Widths, D, E and EE. Weight averages 28 ounces.

A GOOD WEARER.

No. 15K157
$1.18
PER PAIR

DON'T FAIL TO
STATE SIZE.

More stylish than any $1.50 shoe we ever saw. Genuine vici kid stock, firm, good wearing sole, patent tip and guaranteed leather counter and insole. Sizes and half sizes, 2½ to 8. Widths, full. Weight, 25 ounces.

ESMERALDA.

No. 15K96
$1.48
PER PAIR

DON'T FAIL TO
STATE SIZE.

No manufacturer would furnish it to you cheaper. No retailer can excel it under $2.00. Blucher style made of soft vici kid, with dull mat top. Medium height heel, good wearing soles and a handsome, foot fitting, durable shoe. Sizes and half sizes, 2½ to 8. Widths, D, E and EE. Weight averages 26 ounces.

A RARE VALUE.

No. 15K122
$1.49
PER PAIR

DON'T FAIL TO
STATE SIZE.

A dandy little shoe is this Ladies' Blucher, made from a good selection of dongola leather and fitted with patent tip, outside backstay, good quality soles and fancy lace stay. Sizes and half sizes, 2½ to 8. Widths, D, E and EE. Weight, 28 ounces.

DONGOLA LEADER.

No. 15K169
97c
PER PAIR

DON'T FAIL TO
STATE SIZE

The usual $1.50 shoe sold elsewhere does not excel this genuine dongola shoe we offer you at 97 cents. Two-piece leather counter and inner sole and has also a good, firm outer sole. Sizes and half sizes, 2½ to 8. Widths, E and EE. Weight averages 28 ounces.

YOUR MONEY WILL BE IMMEDIATELY RETURNED TO YOU FOR ANY GOODS NOT PERFECTLY SATISFACTORY.

533

EXTRA VALUES IN MEN'S SERVICEABLE TAN SHOES.

"WORLD'S CHAMPION" BASEBALL SHOES.

No. 15K697

$1.69

PER PAIR

DON'T FAIL TO STATE SIZE.

SEE OUR BASEBALL UNIFORM CATALOGUE.

At this price every club can afford to have them. Made from a good selection of calf stock; best of oak sole leather, fitted with genuine league toe and heel plates. Sizes and half sizes, 5 to 11. Full widths only. Weight averages 28 ounces.

Price, ten pairs for $15.65

BOYS' BLIZZARD PROOF.

No. 15K4983

$2.49

PER PAIR

BE SURE TO STATE SIZE.

A special value. Made of russet tan storm calf, 7½ inches high, rawhide laces. Strong oilized outside sole, large eyelets, making it practically indestructible and just the thing when the wintry breezes blow. Sizes and half sizes, 1 to 5½. Widths, E and EE. Weight, 40 ounces.

THE NEW YORKER.

No. 15K4805

$1.95

PER PAIR

BE SURE TO STATE SIZE.

This Men's Patent Leather Shoe is made for giving special good service, as it is cut from an extra plump grade of prime patent leather and the top is also well selected and very serviceable. The shoe is made over a nobby, new and up to date last, and we are only able to offer it at the price we do by making it in our own factory. Sizes and half sizes, 5 to 11. Widths, D, E and EE. Weight, 38 ounces.

No. 15K5006 Boys' sizes and half sizes, 1 to 5½. Widths, D, E and EE. Weight, 30 ounces.

Price, per pair.........................$1.59

U. S. A. KHAKI HI-CUT.

No. 15K4984

$1.98

PER PAIR

BE SURE TO STATE SIZE.

A 14-inch Khaki Cloth Hi-Cut Shoe, with pigskin trimmings Full bellows tongue, large eyelets, strong laces and genuine oilized sole. The same khaki cloth as used in the United States Army. Good enough for Uncle Sam, good enough for you. The most desirable Hi-Cut shoe for all seasons, especially spring and summer wear. Full sizes, 6 to 11. Full widths. Weight averages 39 ounces.

WE HAVE OUR OWN SHOE FACTORY. THAT IS THE REASON WE ARE ABLE TO OFFER YOU SHOES OF QUALITY. WE GUARANTEE OUR PRICES BELOW ANY AND ALL COMPETITION.

HI-CUT CREEDMORE.

No. 15K827

$2.85

PER PAIR

BE SURE TO STATE SIZE.

This shoe is made on the same pattern and last as our high grade welt shoes, but the sole on this shoe is fastened with the latest improved double clinch fastening, making it impossible to rip. The upper stock is an A1 plump kangaroo side stock, and the sole leather is the best slaughter. It seems almost incredible that so much actual merit can be put into a two-buckle extra high cut Blucher for such a low price as we offer it at. But quantity is what does it, and we cheerfully give our patrons the benefits we derive from these large contracts. Sizes, 5 to 12; no half sizes. Full widths only. Don't fail to state size wanted. Weight, 70 ounces. Height, 12 inches.

REDUCING PRICES IS A HABIT WITH US, and if you will examine the pages of this Shoe Department and compare the prices quoted herein with the prices we have quoted in previous catalogues, you will find that in hundreds of cases we have still further reduced our already lowest prices.

TAN DRY SOX.

No. 15K703½

$2.65

PER PAIR

BE SURE TO STATE SIZE.

This is an extra fine, plump quality of tan calfskin, made hand nailed, with full double sole viscolized and full bellows tongue. An exceptionally good shoe for all the year around wear, and built over a shapely and well fitting last, especially for surveyors, prospectors and others who want the very best of wearing material, but do not like the high cut pattern. Sizes and half sizes, 5 to 11. Full widths only. Weight averages 45 ounces.

The name Dry Sox means it will keep the feet dry.

FOR THE HUNTER.

No. 15K4988

$2.75

PER PAIR

BE SURE TO STATE SIZE.

This is a 12-inch Lace Boot, made from red horn calf, a stock that will stand the hardest kind of wear that hunter or prospector can give it. The soles are cut from the best grade of home grown slaughter hemlock sole leather and are fastened by the double clinch machine, making it absolutely ripproof. Those looking for a first class hunting boot at a moderate price need go no farther. Sizes, 5 to 11; no half sizes Widths, full. Don't fail to state size wanted. Weight averages 55 ounces.

MEN'S RED HORN CALF.

No. 15K4940

$1.68

PER PAIR

BE SURE TO STATE SIZE.

An extra sturdy and well made double sole pegged shoe that will stand the roughest usage, yet is a comfortable fitting, shapely shoe. We would suggest purchasers taking advantage of this rare value, as this is the kind of leather the great advance in price has been made in, and we may be compelled to either raise our price or withdraw this number before the season is over. Sizes, 6 to 11; no half sizes. Full widths only. Weight averages 45 to 50 ounces.

FOOT WANTS FOR THE LITTLE PEOPLE OF THE HOUSEHOLD

JUST LIKE MAMMA'S.

74c AND 64c

DON'T FAIL TO STATE SIZE.

This child's shoe is made of vici kid, with a good wearing turned sole sewed on by the Goodyear machine, and low heel. Is a remarkable bargain at the price we offer it. Weight averages 16 ounces.
No. 15K496 Full widths only. Sizes and half sizes, 4 to 8. Price, per pair...74c
No. 15K497 Infant's sizes (no heel), 2 to 5. Price, per pair.............64c

FELT TOP LACE.

69c AND 55c

DON'T FAIL TO STATE SIZE.

A vici kid, warmly lined shoe for infants and children. Felt top, fleece lined to the toe, hand turned sole and spring heel. Kid tip and very comfortable and durable. Weight averages 12 ounces.
No. 15K550 Sizes and half sizes, 4 to 8, Price, per pair..................69c
No. 15K552 Infants' sizes (no heel), 2 to 5 Price, per pair...............55c

RED AND BLACK.

ONLY 68c PER PAIR

DON'T FAIL TO STATE SIZE.

The latest pattern in a child's scroll vesting lace shoe. Chrome vici kid stock, red or black, with fancy vesting top to match. The soles are strictly hand turned and the shoe is high grade in every particular. Sizes and half sizes, 4 to 8. Widths, C, D, E and EE. Weight averages 12 ounces.
No. 15K543 Bright red. Price, per pair....................68c
No. 15K547 Black. Price, per pair....................68c

WHITE CANVAS OXFORD.

DON'T FAIL TO STATE SIZE.

A most serviceable shoe for children, made of a prime quality duck, light in weight, but strong in texture, with a light sole, making as desirable a summer or outing shoe for a child as can be offered. Weight, 8 to 12 ounces.
No. 15K505 Full widths only. Sizes and half sizes, 5 to 8. Price, per pair...49c
No. 15K506 Infants' sizes (no heel), 2 to 5. Price, per pair..................43c

CHILDREN'S VICI.

No. 15K494
98c PER PAIR

DON'T FAIL TO STATE SIZE.

A fine velvet finish vici kid stock, nature's own foot form last, late style Blucher cut, and fitted with patent leather tip. Soles are slightly extended. A strictly $1.50 value for 98 cents. Sizes and half sizes, 5 to 8. Widths, D, E and EE. Weight, 14 ounces.

PARIS KID.

No. 15K556
69c PER PAIR

DON'T FAIL TO STATE SIZE.

Child's very fine Paris Kid Lace Shoe, pretty coin toe last, patent leather tip and heel foxing. Soles hand turned, fitted with wedge heel, and a very dressy and durable little shoe. Sizes and half sizes, 4 to 8. Widths, full. Weight, 12 ounces.

LITTLE MISS MUFFETT.

No. 15K568
49c PER PAIR

DON'T FAIL TO STATE SIZE.

Child's Kid Button, made from soft, glove like stock, spring heel, flexible soles, patent leather tip, all solid and durable. Widths, full. Sizes and half sizes, 4 to 8. Weight, about 13 ounces.

CHILD'S KID LACE.

No. 15K569
50c PER PAIR

DON'T FAIL TO STATE SIZE.

Made from soft kid stock, patent leather tip, spring heel and turned sole, solid counter and a durable shoe. Sizes and half sizes, 4 to 8. Widths, full. Weight, 12 ounces.

THE NO HEEL.

No. 15K576
48c PER PAIR

DON'T FAIL TO STATE SIZE.

Infant's Vici Kid Lace, no heel, patent tip, lace stay and quarter, very dressy and serviceable. Sizes and half sizes, 2, 2½, 3, 3½, 4, 4½, and 5. Weight, 10 ounces.

CHILD'S MERIT SHOE.

No. 15K502
79c PER PAIR

DON'T FAIL TO STATE SIZE.

A merit made vici kid shoe, half double sole, fair stitched, spring heel. This shoe is made alongside our fine misses' goods and is serviceable. Sizes and half sizes, 5 to 8. Widths, full. Weight, 14 ounces.

INFANTS' THREE STRAP.

No. 15K541
55c PER PAIR

DON'T FAIL TO STATE SIZE.

The price is usually from 75 cents up, but we're always lower. Patent vamp, turned sole, kid quarter and a sandal that will outwear a half dozen pairs of soft soles. Sizes and half sizes, 2 to 5. Weight, 8 ounces.

PRICES LOWER,
QUALITY BETTER.

Never before have we been able to offer such exceptional shoe values as those quoted in this book.

TAN MOCCASINS.

No. 15K592
44c FOR THREE PAIRS

DON'T FAIL TO STATE SIZE.

Just the thing for the baby. Made of soft leather, fleece lined, well made, nicely stitched and a good fitter. Easy to put on. Sizes, 1, 2, 3 and 4. Weight, 6 ounces.

INFANTS' VELVET TOP.

NOTE BIG REDUCTION.

No. 15K551
49c PER PAIR

DON'T FAIL TO STATE SIZE.

Finest vici kid, with patent leather tip, imported velvet top and hand turned oak soles. Sizes and half sizes, 2 to 5. Widths, full. Weight, 10 ounces.

BABIES' DELIGHT.

No. 15K579
98c THREE PAIRS

WHITE   PINK   BLUE

DON'T FAIL TO STATE SIZE.

Just the thing for the sweet little dearies. Patent leather stock, quilted top and white fur trimming. They come in three colors, white, pink and blue. Three pairs in a box. We do not sell single pairs. A wonderful bargain for baby. Full sizes, 1, 2, 3, 4. Weight, per three pairs, 9 ounces.

No. 15K578
59c THREE PAIRS

PINK   WHITE   BLUE

DON'T FAIL TO STATE SIZE.

Patent leather, soft soles, ornament on vamp. Blue, pink and white stitched tops, so baby will have shoes to match dresses. The usual price is much more. Packed three pairs of one size to the box. We cannot change assortment. Sizes, 1, 2, 3, 4. Weight, per three pairs, 9 ounces. We do not sell less than three pairs.

No. 15K580
59c FOR THREE PAIRS

BLUE   TAN   BLACK

DON'T FAIL TO STATE SIZE.

Blue, tan and black stitched tops, patent leather vamp and foxing, ornament on vamp, soft soles. Usually cost from 25 cents to 40 cents per pair. We cannot furnish different colors from the ones named. Sizes, 1, 2, 3, 4. Weight, per three pairs, 9 ounces. We do not sell less than three pairs.

No. 15K597
46c THREE PAIRS

BLACK   TAN   RED

DON'T FAIL TO STATE SIZE.

Infants' Lamb Lace, black, tan and red, made with soft sole; equal to those usually sold at double our price. Sizes, 1, 2, 3 and 4. No half sizes. Weight, 6 ounces. We do not sell less than three pairs. Assorted colors.

No. 15K583
29c PER PAIR

DON'T FAIL TO STATE SIZE.

Patent leather vamp, heel foxing and lace stay, imported figured velvet top, soft sole, making a handsome shoe for baby. Sizes, 1, 2, 3 and 4. Weight, 4 ounces.

SHOES FOR SMALL BOYS, MADE JUST LIKE PAPA'S.

LITTLE PRINCE.

No. 15K485

$1.25

PER PAIR

BE SURE TO STATE SIZE.

Made of patent leather with dull calf top, and the same pattern as our men's $3.50 shoe. Suitable for dress or street wear and will give the little fellows excellent satisfaction. Sizes and half sizes, 9 to 13½. Full widths. Weight averages 25 ounces.

LITTLE SANDOW.

No. 15K472

$1.25

PER PAIR

BE SURE TO STATE SIZE.

A Little Gents' Box Calf Blucher which will certainly please the little fellows. Made with extra heavy sole and will stand the hard knocks that the youngsters give a shoe. Made in our White Mountain factory. You know what that means. Sizes and half sizes, 9 to 13½. Full widths. Weight, 22 ounces.

LITTLE MEN'S CALF.

No. 15K477

$1.14

PER PAIR

BE SURE TO STATE SIZE.

Blucher pattern, good box calf stock, half double sole, custom back stay and lined throughout with leather. Made absolutely all solid and to give the kind of service a shoe should give to satisfy both the youngster and his parents. Sizes and half sizes, 9 to 13½. Widths, full. Weight, 22 ounces.

LITTLE GENTS' DELIGHT.

No. 15K473

99c

PER PAIR

BE SURE TO STATE SIZE.

A nice soft finish vici kid stock is used for this shoe, making a fine shoe for those boys with tender feet. Made over a full round toe last, perforated tip, short outside back stay, low heel, good durable sole, an exceptional value at the price quoted. Sizes and half sizes, 9 to 13½. Widths, full. Weight averages 22 ounces.

FOR YEARS WE HAVE CARRIED THE STRONGEST LINE OF MEN'S HIGH CUT SHOES IT IS POSSIBLE TO MANUFACTURE. SEE PAGE 842.

THE HEEL THAT WON'T COME OFF.

Nailed through and clinched on the inside. Put on all shoes intended for hard wear.

GEO. WASHINGTON JR.

No. 15K482

$1.29

PER PAIR

BE SURE TO STATE SIZE.

Just the proper caper for the little men. Made in the Blucher style of best patent coltskin with dull calf top and perforated tip. Carries a low heel, outside back stay and is a low shoe that is exquisite in style and one the little fellows are bound to appreciate. Sizes and half sizes, 9 to 13½. Full widths. Weight, 22 ounces.

LITTLE GENTS' HIGH CUT.

No. 15K483

$1.25

PER PAIR

BE SURE TO STATE SIZE.

This Little Gents' High Cut Box Calf Shoe is designed for fall and winter wear, so that the little fellows may enjoy the same comforts as their larger brothers. Made of first class stock, sole leather counter and inner sole, plump outsole, and built for service, at the same time not clumsy. Height, 7 inches. Sizes and half sizes, 9 to 13½. Full widths. Weight, 27 ounces.

Notwithstanding the fact that the quality of our shoes is greatly improved, THE PRICES ARE LOWER THAN EVER BEFORE

OUR SERO-KALF.

No. 15K484

87c

PER PAIR

BE SURE TO STATE SIZE.

This Little Gent's Shoe is not intended for grown up people. The stock is good quality Sero-Kalf with fine dongola top. All seams are protected from ripping by an extra row of stitching. The inner soles and counters are of solid leather and to make it doubly serviceable we include a durable outside back stay. Made exactly like our high grade men's shoes. Sizes and half sizes, 7 to 13½. Full widths. Weight averages 24 ounces.

LITTLE GENTS' SEAMLESS.

No. 15K475

$1.00

PER PAIR

BE SURE TO STATE SIZE.

Made from genuine kangaroo grain leather, over coin toe last, with best sole leather counter and inner sole, durable outsole, and the low two-lift heel. This shoe is made seamless pattern, will not rip, the soles being fastened on with the McKay machine, making the shoe practically indestructible. Sizes and half sizes, 9 to 13½. Widths, full. Weight averages 24 ounces.

BLAKELY'S BABY BOY.

No. 15K487

84c

PER PAIR

BE SURE TO STATE SIZE.

A dandy little shoe for little gents, cut from an extra selection of box calfskin with dull kid top. Fitted with a sensible low heel, outside back stay and wear resisting leather outsole. Cut in a Blucher pattern, making it a stylish, durable shoe and one that the little fellow will like. Sizes and half sizes, 6 to 9. Full widths. Weight averages 22 ounces.

BABY BOYS' FAVORITE.

No. 15K489

79c

PER PAIR

BE SURE TO STATE SIZE.

This is made from good quality vici kid, but otherwise is built sturdily for wear as healthy young boys give to their shoes. It is fine enough for a Sunday shoe, yet strong enough for everyday wear. Sizes and half sizes, 6 to 9. Weight averages 22 ounces.

OUR FAMOUS CONVINCER SHOES FOR MEN

THESE SHOES WERE THE GREATEST VALUES EVER OFFERED AT $2.65, NOW REDUCED TO $2.50. EVERY PAIR MADE IN OUR OWN FACTORY AND STAMPED "CONVINCER" ON THE SOLE. GUARANTEED $3.50 VALUE.

BUTTON CONVINCER.

No. 15K717
$2.50
PER PAIR

DON'T FAIL TO STATE SIZE.

Our famous Convincer is much in favor with swell dressers. Made of guaranteed Corona patent coltskin, with dull box kid top, military heel and first grade welted soles. The name Convincer guarantees a $3.50 value in style, fit and wear. Sizes and half sizes, 5 to 11. Widths, C, D, E and EE. Weight, 34 ounces.

THE POTAY.

No. 15K711
$2.50
PER PAIR

DON'T FAIL TO STATE SIZE.

There is no shoe in our whole line that covers so many points looked for as this one. Made from an extra good quality of patent coltskin with dull calf top, and the best of Union leather for outsoles. The Potay last as made over has never been equaled for style and fitting qualities. It would be cheap at $4.00, but we offer it at a bed rock price of $2.50. Sizes and half sizes, 5 to 11. Widths, C, D, E and EE. Weight averages 37 ounces.

THE ROOSEVELT.

No. 15K786
$2.50
PER PAIR

DON'T FAIL TO STATE SIZE.

Another high priced shoe added to our famous CONVINCER line. A vici kid vamp, tip and heel foxing, smooth glove calf top, and a nice medium weight pure oak sole, best custom finished. A handsome shoe that will give the best of satisfaction. Sizes and half sizes, 5 to 11. Widths, C, D, E and EE. Don't fail to state size wanted. Weight, 39 ounces.

CUSHION SOLE.

No. 15K789
$2.50
PER PAIR

DON'T FAIL TO STATE SIZE.

Made in our own shoe factory and guaranteed to be as good a cushion sole shoe as you can get at any price. Best box calfskin and strictly first class grade sole leather. Nothing better than the cushion sole shoe for ease, comfort and wear. Sizes and half sizes, 5 to 12. Widths, D, E and EE. Weight, 45 ounces.

FULL OF QUALITY.

No. 15K821
$2.50
PER PAIR

DON'T FAIL TO STATE SIZE.

The stock from which this shoe is made is a genuine kangaroo, but is finished bright, making one of the handsomest leathers we have ever seen, at the same time containing all of the toughness that the genuine kangaroo has always been noted for. It is made over a medium English last, with tip toe, best of oak sole leather, genuine Goodyear welt, and trimmed in the best manner throughout. The name Convincer means high merit. Sizes and half sizes, 5 to 11. Widths, C, D, E and EE. Weight averages 35 ounces.

GENUINE CORK FILLED.

No. 15K829
$2.50
PER PAIR

DON'T FAIL TO STATE SIZE.

For $2.50 who ever heard of a shoe with a genuine Goodyear welt, cork filled sole, leather lined, solid double oak sole, popular box calf stock as near waterproof as leather can be made? We offer you here a shoe made over a stylish last with modern toe and tip, seams sewed with silk and linen thread that will not rip. Sizes and half sizes, 5 to 12. Widths, C, D, E and EE. Weight averages 39 ounces.

FOR TENDER FEET.

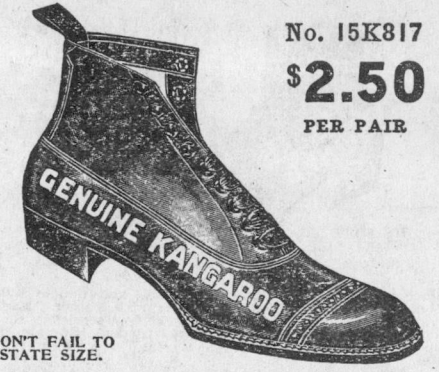

No. 15K817
$2.50
PER PAIR

Made of genuine kangaroo leather, very soft and pliable, yet durable. We make this shoe alongside our best goods, over the fashionable Boston last, with tip toe. It is fitted with custom back stay, best duck lining, trimmed in the best possible manner, has good oak soles sewed on by the Goodyear welt process, making them at once flexible and producing a perfectly smooth inner sole. Sizes and half sizes, 5 to 12. Widths, D, E and EE. Don't fail to state size wanted. Weight averages 35 ounces.

VERY BEST CONGRESS.

No. 15K819
$2.50
PER PAIR

DON'T FAIL TO STATE SIZE.

MADE EXPRESSLY FOR TENDER FEET.

Two of our most famous CONVINCERS are these genuine Australian kangaroo shoes. This leather is very soft and pliable and at the same time as tough as any leather tanned. The soles are cut from the very best of sole leather, and being Goodyear welt sewn assures the wearer a smooth inner sole and a comfortable shoe throughout. Nothing better is manufactured for tender feet than these we offer you herewith. Every pair is stamped "Convincer" on the sole, which means it is better than any $3.00 shoe on the market and the equal of any $3.50 shoe. They are fitted with best duck lining which is the best made and alone will help prolong the life of one's socks. We recommend these shoes highly as being truly foot easers of rare value. Sizes and half sizes, 5 to 12. Widths, D, E and EE. Weight averages 35 ounces.

A WONDER OF VALUE.

No. 15K825
$2.50
PER PAIR

DON'T FAIL TO STATE SIZE.

BUILT FOR WEAR.

NOTE REDUCTION.

No. 15K927

$2.15

PER PAIR

BE SURE TO STATE SIZE.

A hand nailed western made Blucher, made of the best kangaroo calfskin and the finest sole leather procurable. Full bellows tongue, large Klondike eyelets, rawhide laces and a shoe we guarantee to give the best of wear. Full sizes, 6 to 12. Full widths. Weight, 50 to 55 ounces.

SEAL CALF WORKER.

NOTE REDUCTION.

No. 15K1042

$1.68

PER PAIR

BE SURE TO STATE SIZE.

Made from seal calf, with bellows tongue and heavy soles, fastened on by the newest process, known as the double clinch. Two rivets are used where the vamp and quarters meet, making ripping next to impossible. Especially built for hard usage, yet made over a last that is as easy fitting as a high grade shoe. Full sizes, 5 to 12. Full widths. Weight, 50 ounces.

NEVER BEFORE HAVE WE QUOTED PRICES SO LOW (QUALITY CONSIDERED) AS IN THIS BOOK.

KANGAROO PLOW SHOE.

No. 15K944

$1.59

PER PAIR

BE SURE TO STATE SIZE.

The most popular shoe for general wear ever made. Kangaroo side leather, absolutely solid sole, leather inner sole and guaranteed counter. Fitted with full bellows tongue, large eyelets and rawhide laces. Full sizes, 6 to 12. Weight averages 44 ounces.

YOUR NEIGHBOR WILL TELL YOU THAT OUR SHOES ARE THE BEST ON EARTH FOR THE MONEY.

THE DOM PEDRO.

NOTE REDUCTION.

FOR MEN AND BOYS.

DON'T FAIL TO STATE SIZE.

This shoe is made from Milwaukee oil grain stock, has guaranteed counters and insole, is soft and pliable and will not get hard when wet. It has bellows tongue, which makes it dirtproof, and outside tap sole. Full sizes. Widths, full. Weight, about 45 ounces.

No. 15K1032   Men's sizes, 6 to 12.
Price, per pair.........................$1.19
              Sizes 13 and 14, 25 cents extra.
No. 15K1033   Boys' sizes, 1 to 5.
Price, per pair.........................$1.09

IDEAL PLOW SHOE.

NOTE REDUCTION.

No. 15K1029

$1.35

PER PAIR

DON'T FAIL TO STATE SIZE.

Made from Milwaukee oil grain leather, half double sole, absolutely reliable as regards wear and quality. Has large brass eyelets, strong buckskin laces which will last as long as the shoe and to complete this excellent quality we have fitted it with a **crimped tongue.** Sizes, 6 to 12; no half sizes. Full widths. Weight averages 47 ounces.

OIL GRAIN CREOLE.

NOTE REDUCTION.

No. 15K1030

$1.19

PER PAIR

DON'T FAIL TO STATE SIZE.

Made from the best Milwaukee oil grain stock, is very soft and pliable, has guaranteed counter and inner sole and a good, heavy outer sole, cut from the best stock. When you see this shoe you will know that quality counts. Sizes, 6 to 14; no half sizes. Width, full. Weight, about 42 ounces.

THE LABORERS' FRIEND.

No. 15K1035

$1.58

PER PAIR

BE SURE TO STATE SIZE.

This shoe is cut from the very best selection of kangaroo kip and slaughter sole leather, soft as a glove and tough as iron. The shank is also reinforced and the soles are fastened on with second growth hickory pegs. It is well worth $2.50. Sizes, 6 to 12; no half sizes. Full widths. Weight averages 45 ounces.

THE LONG LIFE.

No. 15K920

$1.57

PER PAIR

BE SURE TO STATE SIZE.

The wearing qualities of this shoe are known the country over, but it is always sold at $2.50 elsewhere. Made of the famous kangaroo side leather, soft as a glove, yet tough as cowhide. Heavy soles, standard screw fastened and fitted with large eyelets. A record breaking value. Sizes, 6 to 12; no half sizes. Widths, D, E and EE. Weight averages 53 ounces.

A STARTLING VALUE.

NOTE REDUCTION.

No. 15K1025

$1.15

PER PAIR

BE SURE TO STATE SIZE.

A men's Split Creedmore Shoe for such a ridiculously low figure seems hard to believe, but we have an immense stock ready for you all, and it is only by purchasing in such quantities that we can quote these bed rock prices. Sizes, 6 to 12; no half sizes. Full widths only. Weight, 48 ounces.

RUBBER FOOTWEAR

THE RUBBER FOOTWEAR shown by us in these pages is strictly first grade, produced by manufacturers of standard well known brands sold by us at prices lower than are quoted by others for second quality rubber footwear. For the reason that we sell our rubber footwear at such ridiculously low prices and because of our contract to protect the manufacturer, it is not possible for us to mention the brand we handle. This brand has been on the market many years. It has so well established a reputation that the manufacturer to protect himself must keep it up to the highest standard of quality and in addition to the manufacturer's guarantee, you have our guarantee that there is no better rubber footwear sold at any price.

THERE ARE TWO QUALITIES OF RUBBER FOOTWEAR, first quality and second quality. The rubber footwear sold by us is all first quality, unless otherwise stated in the description. For your information and guidance in the purchase of rubber footwear, we give you herewith a list of manufacturers of first and second quality rubber. We do this so that you may know exactly what you are getting, whether you buy from us or some other firm or individual. Second quality goods should cost ten per cent less than first quality and if you will bear in mind the names of these manufacturers, you will be able to get all that you pay for. If you buy these goods from us, however, you will not only get the exact quality we represent in our catalogue, but you will get new, fresh goods, as our sales are so large that our stock is new all the time, and as all users of rubber footwear know, new goods have greater wearing qualities than those that are shelf worn.

FIRST QUALITY.

WOONSOCKET RUBBER CO.

American Rubber Co.
Candee Rubber Co.
Wales Goodyear Rubber Co.
Boston Rubber Shoe Co.
Lycoming Rubber Co. Meyer Rubber Co.
Goodyear India Rubber Glove Co.
Bannigan Rubber Co.
Beacon Falls Rubber Shoe Co.
Apsley Rubber Co.

SECOND QUALITY.

RHODE ISLAND RUBBER CO.

Para Rubber Co.
Federal Rubber Co.
Keystone Rubber Co.
Connecticut Rubber Co.
Bay State Rubber Co.
New Jersey Rubber Co.
Granite Rubber Co.
Hudson Rubber Co.

SNOW EXCLUDING GAITERS.

MEN'S, WOMEN'S, MISSES', BOYS', YOUTHS' AND CHILDREN'S.

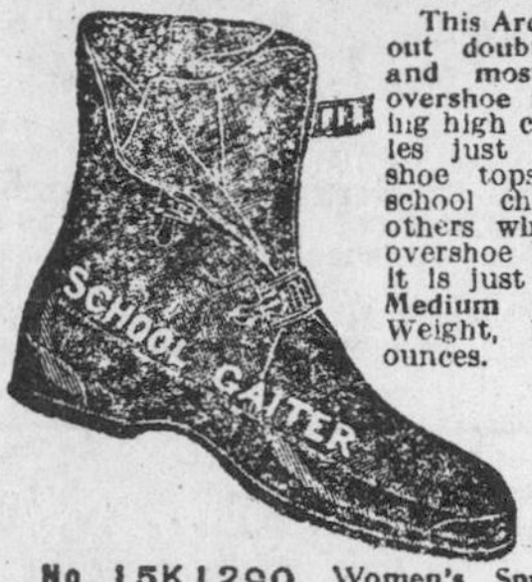

This Arctic is without doubt the best and most practical overshoe made. Being high cut, it buckles just above the shoe tops, and for school children and others who give an overshoe hard wear, it is just the thing. Medium quality. Weight, 16 to 40 ounces. Sizes and half sizes.

STATE SIZE.

No. 15K1290 Women's Spring Heel. Sizes, 2½ to 8. Price, per pair......$1.05
No. 15K1291 Misses' Spring Heel. Sizes, 11 to 2. Price, per pair......92c
No. 15K1292 Children's Spring Heel. Sizes, 6 to 10½. Price, per pair......82c
No. 15K1293 Women's Heel. Sizes, 2½ to 8. Price, per pair......$1.05
No. 15K1294 Boys' full sizes, 1 to 6. Price, per pair......$1.18
No. 15K1295 Youths' full sizes, 11 to 13. Price, per pair......98c
No. 15K1296 Men's full sizes, 6 to 12. Price, per pair......$1.41

MEN'S ALL RUBBER ARCTICS.

FIRST QUALITY.

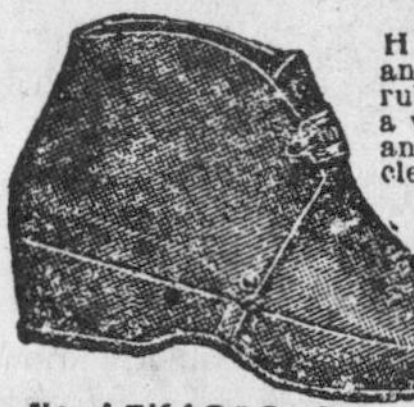

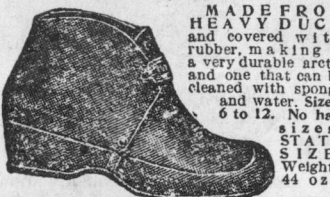

MADE FROM HEAVY DUCK and covered with rubber, making it a very durable arctic and one that can be cleaned with sponge and water. Sizes, 6 to 12. No half sizes. STATE SIZE. Weight, 44 ozs.

No. 15K1298 Price, per pair......$1.53
For postage rate see page 10.

HEAVY BUCKLE ARCTICS.

MEN'S, WOMEN'S, MISSES', BOYS', YOUTHS' AND CHILDREN'S. FIRST QUALITY.

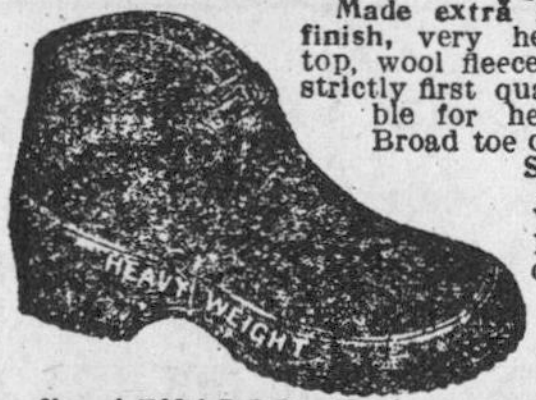

Made extra heavy, dull finish, very heavy cloth top, wool fleece lined and strictly first quality suitable for heavy wear. Broad toe only. STATE SIZE. Weight, 14 to 38 ounces.

No. 15K1300 Men's sizes, 6 to 13. Price, per pair......$1.27
No. 15K1302 Boys' sizes, 1 to 6. Price, per pair......$1.08
No. 15K1304 Youths' sizes, 11 to 13. Price, per pair......86c
No. 15K1306 Women's sizes, 2½ to 8. Price, per pair......91c
No. 15K1308 Misses' sizes, spring heel, 11 to 2. Price, per pair......76c
No. 15K1310 Childs' sizes, spring heel, 5 to 10½. Price, per pair......60c

SNOW EXCLUDING ARCTICS.

MEN'S FOUR BUCKLE, $2.11

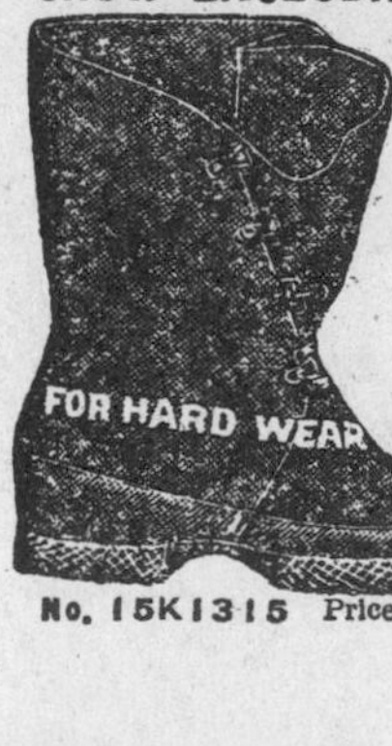

Made with rolled sole and heel. Absolutely coldproof and wearproof. Has fast color cloth tops, lined with wool. This article is made of pure gum rubber, and is of first quality. Full sizes, 6 to 12. STATE SIZE. Weight, 54 ounces.

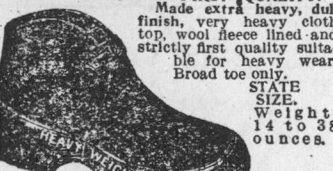

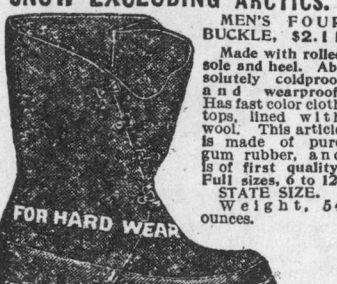

No. 15K1315 Price, per pair...$2.11

LIGHT BUCKLE ARCTICS.

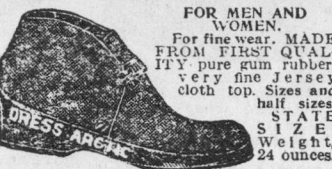

FOR MEN AND WOMEN.

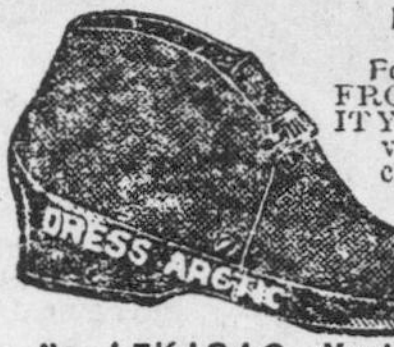

For fine wear. MADE FROM FIRST QUALITY pure gum rubber, very fine Jersey cloth top. Sizes and half sizes. STATE SIZE. Weight, 24 ounces.

No. 15K1316 Men's sizes, 6 to 12. Price, per pair......$1.29
No. 15K1318 Women's sizes, 2½ to 8. Price, per pair......93c

STORM ARCTICS.

FOR MEN AND WOMEN.

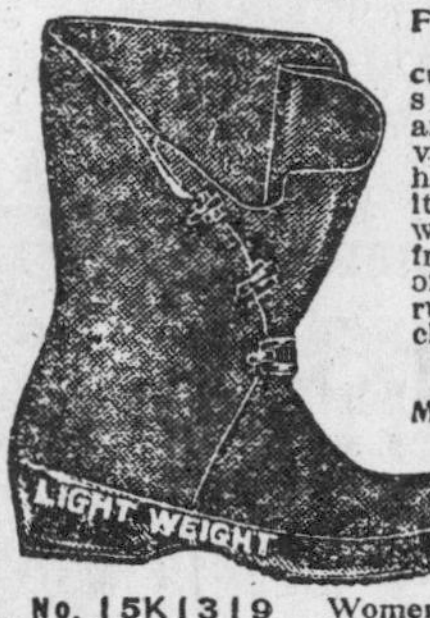

FIRST QUALITY. This shoe is cut extra high, is snow excluding, and being impervious to water over half way up, makes it a very dry and warm shoe. Made from the very best of first quality rubber, with fine cloth top. STATE SIZE.

No. 15K1320 Men's four-buckle. Sizes, 6 to 12. Weight, 40 ounces. Price, per pair..$2.18
No. 15K1319 Women's three-buckle. Sizes, 2½ to 8. Weight, 24 ounces. Price, per pair......$1.72

DUCK PERFECTION, $1.66.

MEN'S, FIRST QUALITY.

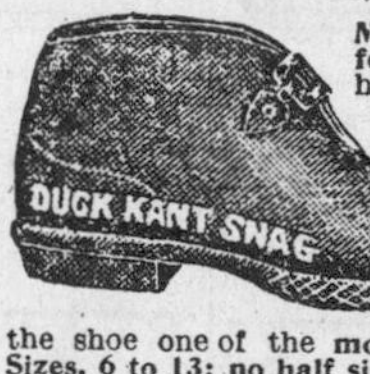

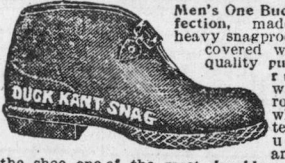

Men's One Buckle Perfection, made from heavy snagproof duck, covered with first quality pure gum rubber with rolledsole, which protects the uppers and makes the shoe one of the most durable ever sold. Sizes, 6 to 13; no half sizes. For wool boots only. STATE SIZE. Weight, 56 ounces.

No. 15K1392 Price, per pair......$1.66

DUCK LUMBER KING, $1.96.

MEN'S, FIRST QUALITY.

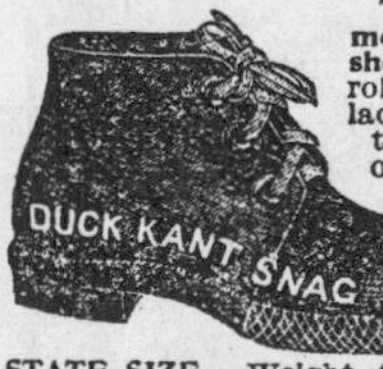

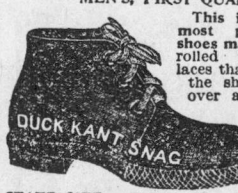

This is one of the most popular rubber shoes made. Built with rolled soles, rawhide laces that will outwear the shoe, and made over a heavy duck cloth, making it a snagproof shoe. Full Sizes, 6 to 12. F width; for socks only. STATE SIZE Weight, 60 ounces.

No. 15K1393 Price, per pair...$1.96

GUM CAPTAIN, $1.77.

MEN'S, FIRST QUALITY.

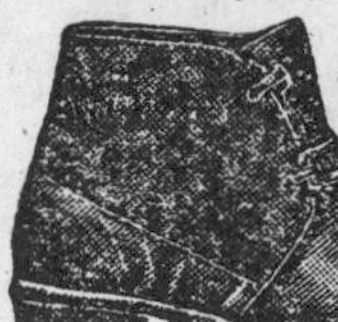

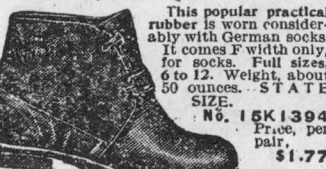

This popular practical rubber is worn considerably with German socks. It comes F width only, for socks. Full sizes, 6 to 12. Weight, about 50 ounces. STATE SIZE.

No. 15K1394 Price, per pair, $1.77

WE ALWAYS UNDERSELL outdistance and outclass all competition. Following our well established policy of steadily lowering prices we have still further reduced them in this catalogue.

EXTRA HEAVY ARCTICS, $1.38.

MEN'S ROLLED SOLE.

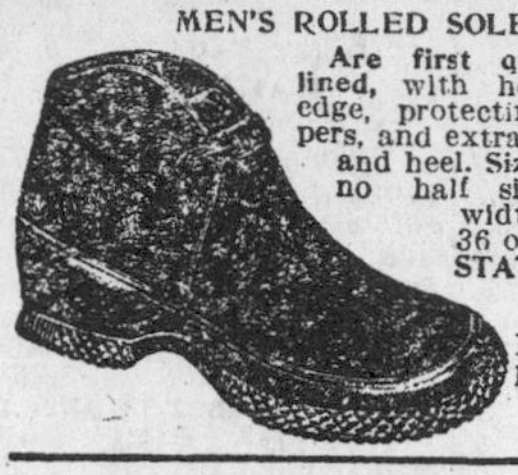

Are first quality wool lined, with heavy rolled edge, protecting the uppers, and extra heavy sole and heel. Sizes, 6 to 13, no half sizes. Full widths. Weight, 36 ounces. STATE SIZE.

No. 15K1396 Price per pair, $1.38

LUMBERMEN'S PERFECTION.

FOR MEN AND BOYS.

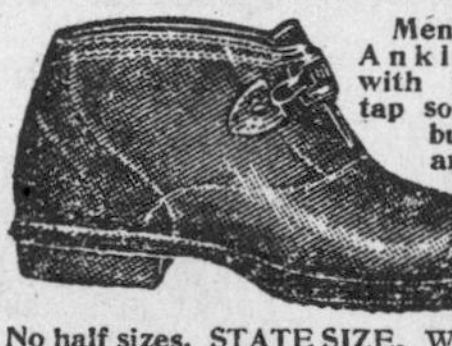

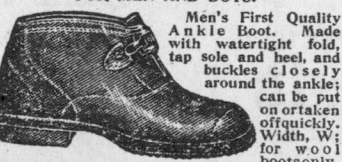

Men's First Quality Ankle Boot. Made with watertight fold, tap sole and heel, and buckles closely around the ankle; can be put on or taken off quickly. Width, W; for wool boots only. No half sizes. STATE SIZE. Weight, 50 ounces.

No. 15K1398 Men's sizes, 6 to 13. Price, per pair......$1.54
No. 15K1399 Boys' sizes, 2 to 6; W width only. Price, per pair......$1.25

DUCK PERFECTION.

FIRST QUALITY.

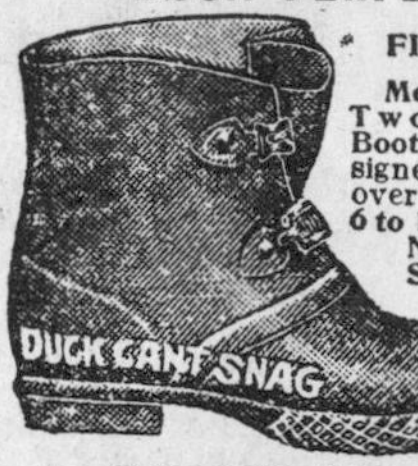

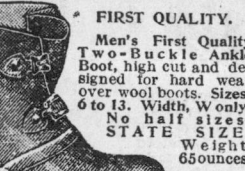

Men's First Quality Two-Buckle Ankle Boot, high cut and designed for hard wear over wool boots. Sizes, 6 to 13. Width, W only. No half sizes. STATE SIZE. Weight, 65 ounces.

No. 15K1400 Price, per pair...$2.13

GUM HURONS.

MEN'S, BOYS' AND YOUTHS'.

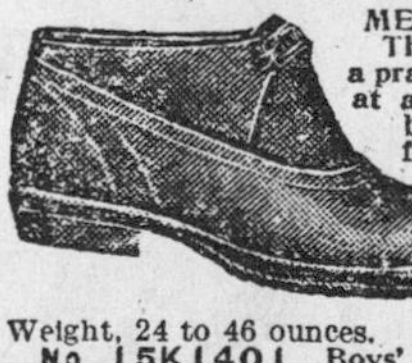

MEDIUM QUALITY. This Huron is at once a practical shoe and one at a low cost. It can be worn over wool felt boots, as well as lumbermen's socks. No half sizes. STATE SIZE.

Weight, 24 to 46 ounces.

No. 15K1401 Boys' F, for socks. Sizes, 1 to 6. Price, per pair......$1.00
No. 15K1402 Boys' W, widths full, for felt boots Sizes, 1 to 6. Price, per pair, $1.00
No. 15K1403 Youths' W, for felt boots. Sizes, 11 to 13. Price, per pair......84c
No. 15K1404 Men's W, for felt boots. Sizes, 6 to 13. Price, per pair......$1.26
No. 15K1405 Men's F, for socks. Sizes, 6 to 12. Price, per pair......$1.26

SHORT BOOTS.

FOR BOYS.

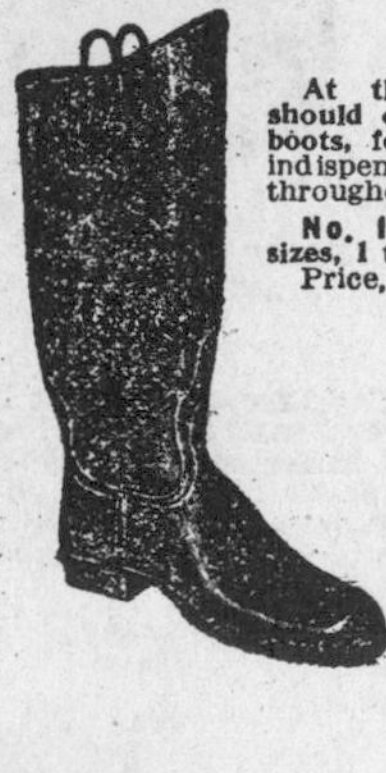

At this price everyone should own a pair of rubber boots, for at times they are indispensable. Friction lined throughout. No half sizes.

No. 15K1406 Boys' sizes, 1 to 6. Price, per pair.... $2.10

The surprisingly low reduced prices prevailing in this catalogue mean greater savings to our customers than ever before.

ROLLED SOLE RUBBER SHOE.

FOR MEN AND BOYS.

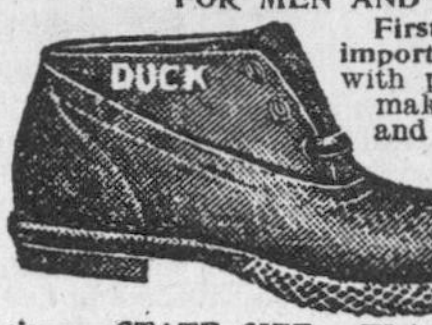

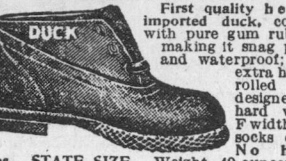

First quality heavy imported duck, coated with pure gum rubber, making it snag proof and waterproof; has extra heavy rolled sole, designed for hard wear. F width; for socks only. No half sizes. STATE SIZE. Weight, 40 ounces.

No. 15K1408 Men's sizes, 6 to 12. Price, per pair......$1.55
No. 15K1409 Boys' sizes, 3 to 6. Price, per pair......$1.29
For postage rate see page 10.

STORM ALASKAS.

MEN'S AND WOMEN'S.

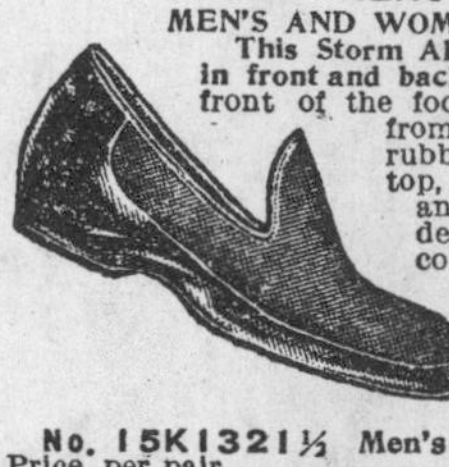

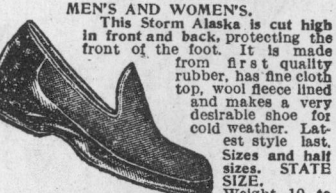

This Storm Alaska is cut high in front and back, protecting the front of the foot. It is made from first quality rubber, has fine cloth top, wool fleece lined and makes a very desirable shoe for cold weather. Latest style last. Sizes and half sizes. STATE SIZE. Weight 10 to 24 ounces.

No. 15K1321½ Men's sizes, 6 to 12. Price, per pair......99c
No. 15K1322 Women's sizes, 2½ to 8. Price, per pair......77c
No. 15K1324 Women's Spring Heel Sizes, 2½ to 8. Price, per pair......77c

GUARANTEED STOCKINGS

Do not fail to turn to page 951, in this catalogue and read about our **"WORTHMORE" STOCKING** for Ladies, which we will positively guarantee to give **wear and satisfaction.** If it does not, we will within six months of the date of purchase, guarantee to replace the stockings. This is one of the biggest offers we have ever made in our Hosiery Department.

STORMY WEATHER RUBBERS.

FOR MEN AND WOMEN, MISSES AND CHILDREN.

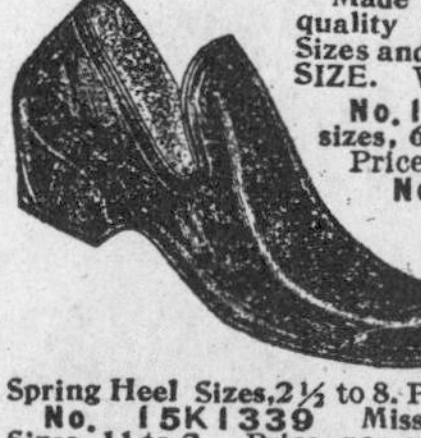

Made from light, first quality rubber, net lined. Sizes and half sizes. STATE SIZE. Weight, 8 to 18 ozs.

No. 15K1336 Men's sizes, 6 to 12. Price, per pair..71c
No. 15K1338 Women's sizes, 2½ to 8. Price, per pair......54c
No. 15K1338½ Women's Spring Heel Sizes, 2½ to 8. Price, per pr..54c
No. 15K1339 Misses' Spring Heel Sizes, 11 to 2. Price, per pair......47c
No. 15K1339½ Child's Spring Heel Sizes, 5 to 10½. Price, per pair......39c
No. 15K1336½ Boy's sizes, 1 to 5½. Price, per pair......59c
For postage rate see page 10.

SELF ACTING SANDALS, 67c.

FOR MEN.

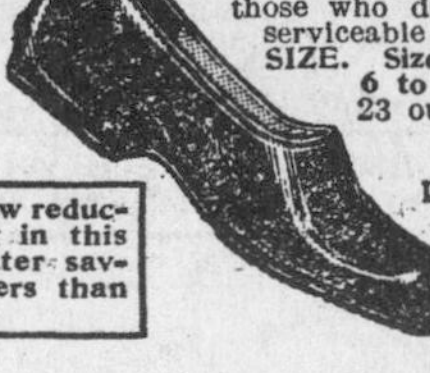

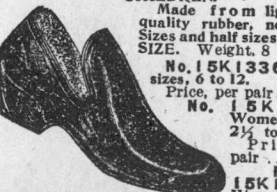

A first quality sandal and a very popular and sensible rubber. Especially adapted for those who desire a light yet serviceable rubber. STATE SIZE. Sizes and half sizes, 6 to 12. Weight, 23 ounces.

No. 15K1340 Price per pair......67c

SANDAL RUBBERS.
FOR MEN AND WOMEN.

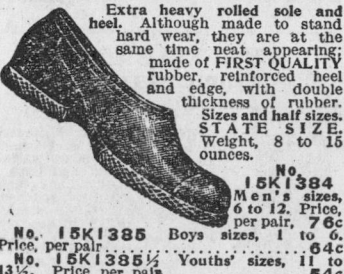

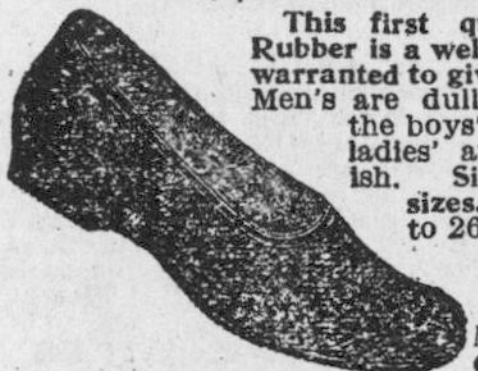

This first quality Sandal Rubber is a well known style, warranted to give satisfaction. Men's are dull finish, while the boys', youths' and ladies' are bright finish. Sizes and half sizes. Weight, 12 to 26 ounces.
STATE SIZE
No. 15K1341
Men's sizes, 6 to 13.
Price, per pair................67c
No. 15K1345 Ladies' sizes, 2½ to 8.
Price, per pair................47c

FIRST QUALITY CROQUET, 49c.

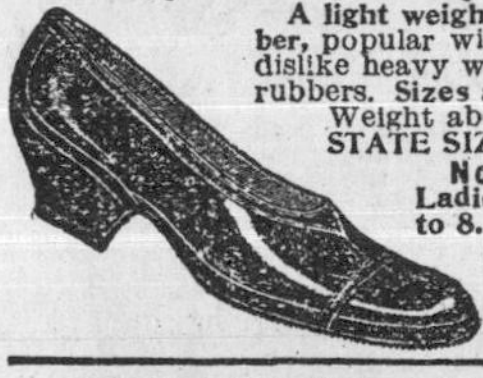

A light weight sensible rubber, popular with ladies who dislike heavy weight or storm rubbers. Sizes and half sizes. Weight about 11 ounces.
STATE SIZE.
No. 15K1343
Ladies' sizes, 2½ to 8. Price, per pair.....49c

ROLLED SOLE RUBBERS.
MEN'S, BOYS', YOUTHS' AND WOMEN'S.

Extra heavy rolled sole and heel. Although made to stand hard wear, they are at the same time neat appearing; made of FIRST QUALITY rubber, reinforced heel and edge, with double thickness of rubber. Sizes and half sizes.
STATE SIZE.
Weight, 8 to 15 ounces.
No. 15K1384
Men's sizes, 6 to 12. Price, per pair, 76c
No. 15K1385 Boys' sizes, 1 to 6.
Price, per pair................64c
No. 15K1385½ Youths' sizes, 11 to 13½. Price, per pair................64c
No. 15K1386 Women's sizes, 2½ to 8.
Price, per pair................57c

THE SURPRISINGLY LOW REDUCED PRICES prevailing in this catalogue mean greater savings to our customers than ever before.

TENNIS SHOES.

Made of canvas cloth with rubber sole. Two colors, white and black. Sizes and half sizes. Don't fail to state size and color wanted. Weight, 12 to 22 ounces.

BLACK.
No. 15K1502 Men's sizes, 6 to 12. Price, per pair................54c
No. 15K1504 Boys' sizes, 1 to 5½.
Price, per pair................49c
No. 15K1506 Women's sizes, 3 to 8.
Price, per pair................49c
WHITE.
No. 15K1502½ Men's sizes, 6 to 12.
Price, per pair................54c
No. 15K1504½ Boys' sizes, 1 to 5½.
Price, per pair................49c
No. 15K1506½ Women's sizes, 3 to 8.
Price, per pair................49c

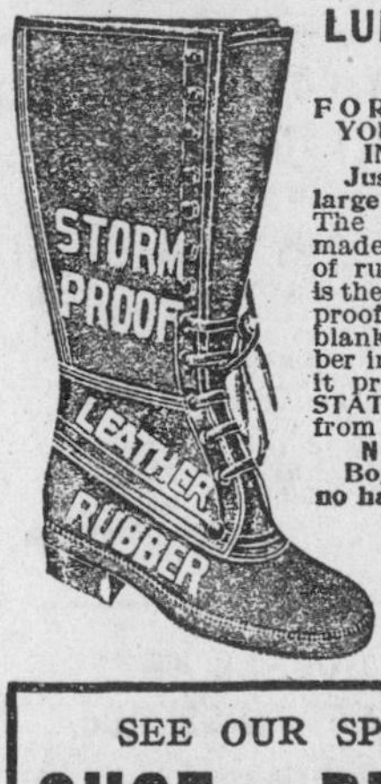

LUMBERMEN'S OVERS.

FOR BOYS AND YOUTHS, 12 and 14 INCHES HIGH.
Just the thing for large and small boys. The rubber shoe is made of good quality of rubber and the top is the celebrated stormproof canvas with blanket lining and rubber interlining, making it proof against cold.
STATE SIZE. Weight, from 50 to 55 ounces.
No. 15K1413
Boys' sizes, 1 to 6; no half sizes.
Per pair, $1.49
No. 15K1414
Youths' sizes, 11 to 13; no half sizes.
Price, per pair.....$1.29

SEE OUR SPECIAL
SHOE AND RUBBER COMBINATIONS
Quoted on Forward Pages.

PEBBLE LEG SHORT BOOTS.
FOR MEN AND YOUTHS, LADIES, MISSES AND CHILDREN.

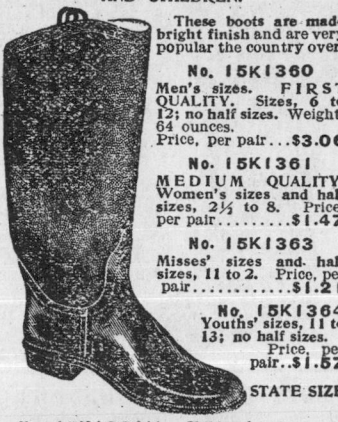

These boots are made bright finish and are very popular the country over.
No. 15K1360
Men's sizes. FIRST QUALITY. Sizes, 6 to 12; no half sizes. Weight, 64 ounces. Price, per pair...$3.06
No. 15K1361
MEDIUM QUALITY. Women's sizes and half sizes, 2½ to 8. Price, per pair........$1.47
No. 15K1363
Misses' sizes and half sizes, 11 to 2. Price, per pair............$1.21
No. 15K1364
Youths' sizes, 11 to 13; no half sizes. Price, per pair..$1.57

STATE SIZE
No. 15K1364½ Children's sizes and half sizes, 5 to 10½. Weight, 24 to 38 ounces. Price, per pair............$1.01

MEN'S GUM HIP BOOTS, $4.37.

Men's Dull Finish Hip Boots. Made from strictly first class quality rubber, very serviceable. Every pair warranted to be as good as any on the market. Friction lined only. Sizes, 6 to 12; no half sizes. STATE SIZE. Weight, about 6½ pounds.
No. 15K1366
Price, per pair...$4.37

STORM KING BOOTS.
MEN'S AND BOYS' MEDIUM QUALITY.

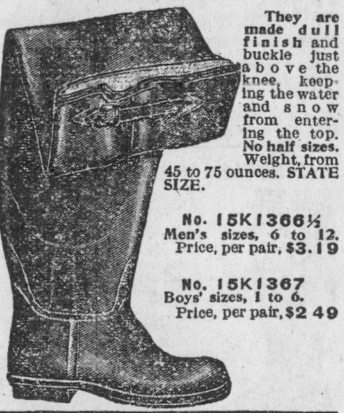

They are made dull finish and buckle just above the knee, keeping the water and snow from entering the top. No half sizes. Weight, from 45 to 75 ounces. STATE SIZE.
No. 15K1366½
Men's sizes, 6 to 12. Price, per pair..$3.19
No. 15K1367
Boys' sizes, 1 to 6. Price, per pair, $2.49

MEN'S GUM SPORTING BOOTS, $4.37.

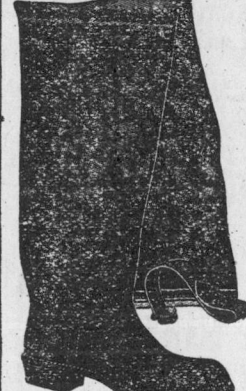

Men's Dull Finish Thigh or Sporting Boots. Made from strictly first quality rubber, just the thing for fishing and hunting and all purposes where a high top boot is wanted. Net lined only. Sizes, 6 to 12; no half sizes. STATE SIZE. Weight, 6½ pounds.
No. 15K1368
Price, per pair, $4.37

MEN'S DUCK FOOT HIP BOOTS.
FIRST QUALITY POLAR SOCKS FREE.

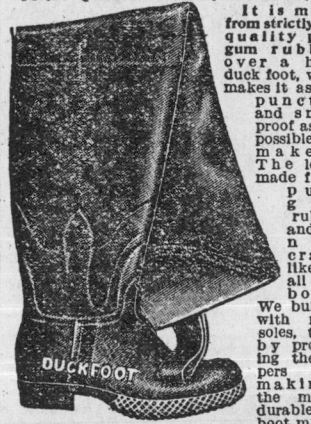

It is made from strictly first quality pure gum rubber, over a heavy duck foot, which makes it as near puncture and snagproof as it is possible to make it. The leg is made from pure gum rubber and will not crack, like the all duck boots. We build it with rolled soles, thereby protecting the uppers and making it the most durable hip boot made, regardless of price. Friction lined only. A PAIR OF POLAR SOCKS FREE WITH EACH PAIR. Sizes, 6 to 13; no half sizes. Widths, full. STATE SIZE. Weight, 104 to 116 ounces.
No. 15K1368½ Price, per pair, $4.57

MEN'S DUCK FOOT SHORT BOOT, $3.19.
ROLLED SOLES, FIRST QUALITY.

Made over a heavy duck cloth, with pure gum rubber, thereby producing a boot which is thoroughly waterproof. We make this boot with heavy rolled soles. The leg is made of pure gum rubber and will not crack. Friction lined only. Pair Polar Socks Free. This sock can be removed at night and thoroughly dried and will give, together with this boot, much better satisfaction than the old fashioned felt lined boot. Sizes, 6 to 13; no half sizes. STATE SIZE. Weight, 80 ounces.
No. 15K1369
Price, per pair, $3.19

DUCK FOOT SHORT BOOTS, $2.69.
MEN'S SECOND QUALITY.

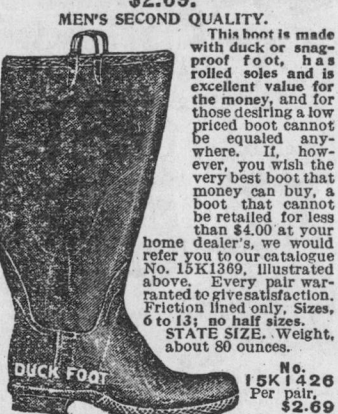

This boot is made with duck or snagproof foot, has rolled soles and is excellent value for the money, and for those desiring a low priced boot cannot be equaled anywhere. If, however, you wish the very best boot that money can buy, a boot that cannot be retailed for less than $4.00 at your home dealer's, we would refer you to our catalogue No. 15K1369, illustrated above. Every pair warranted to give satisfaction. Friction lined only. Sizes, 6 to 13; no half sizes. STATE SIZE. Weight, about 80 ounces.
No. 15K1426
Per pair, $2.69

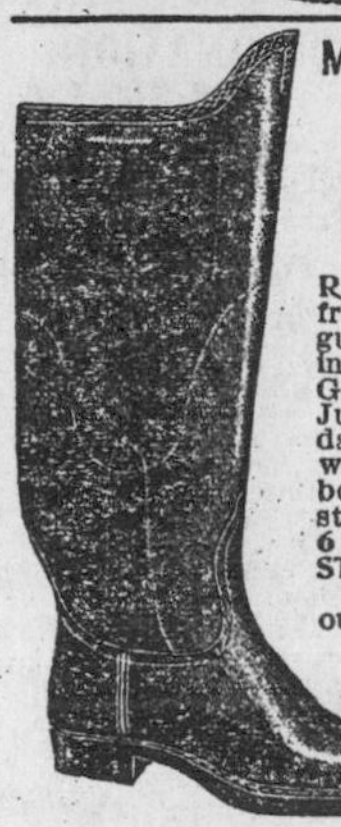

MEN'S RUBBER BOOTS, $4.95.
FIRST QUALITY. LEATHER SOLE.

Men's Leather Sole Rubber Short Boots, made from first quality pure gum rubber with leather insole and heavy leather Goodyear welt outsole. Just the thing for miners, dairymen and railroad work where a waterproof boot is required that will stand the wear. Sizes, 6 to 12; no half sizes. STATE SIZE. Weight, about 90 ounces.
No. 15K1424
Price, per pair.....$4.95

LUMBERMEN'S ERIE, $2.40.
ROLLED SOLE.

Made from first quality pure gum, over a heavy imported duck, making it one of the most durable shoes ever sold. It has extra heavy sole, solid heel, rawhide laces, felt lining, and is snow excluding to the top. To make it doubly strong, we build it with rolled soles. Sizes, 6 to 12; no half sizes. Width, F; for socks only. STATE SIZE. Weight, 65 ounces.
No. 15K1382½ Price, per pair, $2.40

LUMBERMEN'S OVERS, $1.98.
FOR MEN.

Made 10 inches high of first quality rubber, with rolled soles; the leather top is securely stitched to vamp and fitted with full bellows tongue and rawhide laces. Sizes, 6 to 12; no half sizes. STATE SIZE. Weight, from 45 to 55 ounces.
No. 15K1410
Price, per pair, $1.98

GOOD QUALITY SHOES

are the kind we sell. LOW PRICE is next in importance, and we positively guarantee our prices to be lower than anywhere else on earth, and lower in this catalogue than ever before.

BETTER SHOES FOR LESS MONEY IS OUR MOTTO

LUMBERMEN'S OVERS, $2.75.
LEATHER TOP.

This shoe is made of first quality rubber with rolled soles, and is as near snagproof as can be made. The leather top is an excellent grade, and warranted to give satisfaction. Sizes, 6 to 12; no half sizes. STATE SIZE. Weight, 55 ounces. Height, 16 inches.
No. 15K1411
Price, per pair, $2.75

LUMBERMEN'S OVERS, $2.39.
STORMPROOF TOPS.

Something new, which we believe will meet with general approval. The rubber is a snagproof, first quality rubber, and the top is made of stout canvas blanket lined with an interlining of rubber, making it cold-proof. Sizes, 6 to 12; no half sizes. STATE SIZE. Height, 17 inches. Weight, about 55 ounces.
No. 15K1412
Price, per pair, $2.39

SNOW EXCLUDING COMBINATION, $2.25.

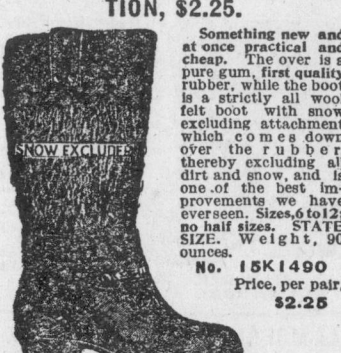

Something new and at once practical and cheap. The over is a pure gum, first quality rubber, while the boot is a strictly all wool felt boot with snow excluding attachment which comes down over the rubber, thereby excluding all dirt and snow, and is one of the best improvements we have ever seen. Sizes, 6 to 12; no half sizes. STATE SIZE. Weight, 90 ounces.

No. 15K1490 Price, per pair, $2.25

KNIT BOOT COMBINATION, $2.49

ALL WOOL, FOR MEN.

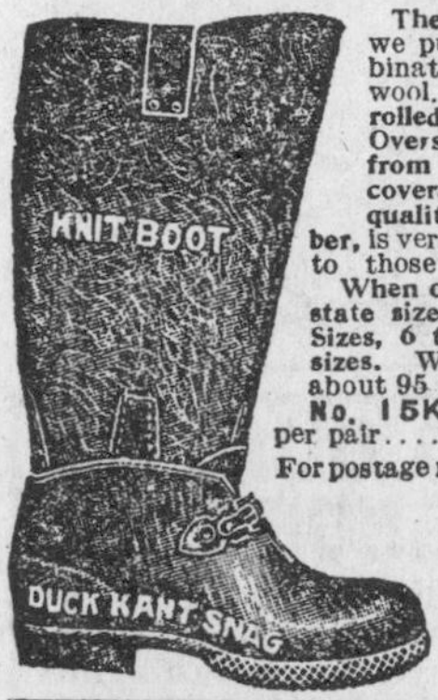

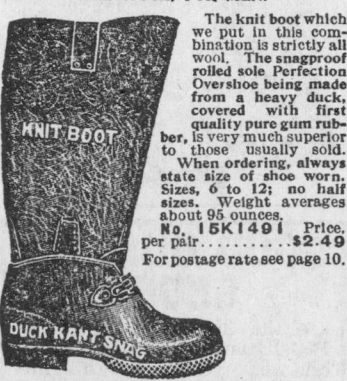

The knit boot which we put in this combination is strictly all wool. The snagproof rolled sole Perfection Overshoe being made from a heavy duck, covered with first quality pure gum rubber, is very much superior to those usually sold. When ordering, always state size of shoe worn. Sizes, 6 to 12; no half sizes. Weight averages about 95 ounces.

No. 15K1491 Price, per pair............$2.49

For postage rate see page 10.

OUR "BB" COMBINATION BEST BLUE BOOT, $2.98.

FIRST QUALITY.

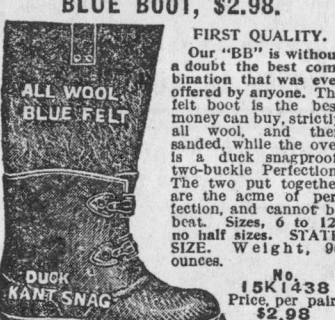

Our "BB" is without a doubt the best combination that was ever offered by anyone. The felt boot is the best money can buy, strictly all wool, and then sanded, while the over is a duck snagproof, two-buckle Perfection. The two put together are the acme of perfection, and cannot be beat. Sizes, 6 to 12; no half sizes. STATE SIZE. Weight, 96 ounces.

No. 15K1438 Price, per pair, $2.98

OUR HERCULES COMBINATION, $2.69.

FIRST QUALITY.

This combination is one that we are justly proud of. Everything that goes into it is strictly first class in every respect. The rubber is a duck snagproof shoe, with rolled soles, and has 10-inch western oil grain leather top, while the sock is all wool, half tufted and has a leather heel piece, giving service where it needs it most. Sizes, 6 to 12; no half sizes. STATE SIZE. Weight, 60 ounces.

No. 15K1440 Price, per pair....$2.69

WOOL SHEEP PACS.

FOR MEN AND BOYS.

Fitted with eyelets and laces; an excellent article for lumbermen's overs. Height, 6 inches. Weight, per pair, averages 9 ounces. STATE SIZE. Full sizes only.

No. 15K1240 Men's sizes, 6 to 11. Price, per pair..........................65c

No. 15K1241 Boys' sizes 1 to 5. Price, per pair..........................49c

LACE-IT COMBINATION.

FOR MEN AND BOYS. FIRST QUALITY.

We have added this Lace-it and Sock Combination because we believe it fills a long felt want. The price we sell it for is the cheapest for a good combination we have ever seen. The over is an all duck, rolled sole, snagproof shoe, and the sock is good value and will give excellent service. STATE SIZE.

No. 15K1446 Men's sizes, 6 to 12; no half sizes. Weight, 65 ounces. Price, per pair..$1.98

No. 15K1447 Boys' sizes, 3 to 6; no half sizes. Price, per pair. $1.69

ALASKA SOCK, $2.59

COMBINATION FOR MEN.

This combination is composed of our Two-Buckle Captain and our all wool Detroit Alaska Sock. A feature of this sock is that it is made with double foot, and two stocking feet knitted into one. The Captain is first quality and together make an excellent combination. Sizes, 6 to 12; no half sizes. Color, black only. STATE SIZE WANTED. Weight, about 60 ounces.

No. 15K1448 Price, per pair........$2.59

16 INCHES HIGH.

MEN'S SHEEPSKIN BOOT COMBINATION. $2.98

The sheepskin boot is made with leather sole and heel and the rubber overshoe is a rolled sole heavy, first quality arctic, warranted. This outfit would cost you elsewhere $4.00. Sizes, 5 to 12; no half sizes. STATE SIZE. Weight, 75 ounces.

No. 15K1450 Price, per pair...$2.98

9 INCHES HIGH.

MEN'S SHEEPSKIN BOOT COMBINATION. $2.19

This combination is composed of fair quality arctic shoe and 9-inch sheepskin boot with leather sole and heel. We guarantee the quality in every way. Sizes, 5 to 12; no half sizes. STATE SIZE. Weight, 60 ounces.

No. 15K1454 Price, per pair...$2.19

STORMPROOF COMBINATION.

FOR MEN. FIRST QUALITY.

A combination that is a great seller for the reason that it is chock full of merit.

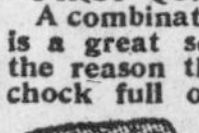

The sheepskin pac is 6 inches high, the stormproof shoe is our No. 15K1412. This combination would cost you at least $3.50 to $3.75 at your dealers. Sizes, 6 to 12; no half sizes. STATE SIZE. Weight, about 80 ounces.

No. 15K1460 Price, per pair...$2.98

STORMPROOF COMBINATIONS.

BOYS' AND YOUTHS'.

These combinations will fill a long felt want for the large and small boys, since they are practical and cheap. It consists of our 6-inch sheepskin pac and our

high quality stormproof shoe. You could not buy these two articles of equal quality from any retail dealer for less than $2.00 to $2.50. STATE SIZE. Weight, from 40 to 50 ounces.

No. 15K1462 Boys' sizes, 1 to 6; no half sizes. Price, per pair......$1.92

BOYS' COMBINATION, $1.69.

FIRST QUALITY.

This combination is composed of a strictly all wool felt boot, made with calf stays and the lumbermen's one-buckle rubber ankle boot. Both the felt boot and the rubber ankle boot are strictly first quality, guaranteed to give perfect satisfaction. When ordering, state size of shoe worn and we will send you the same size wool boot with the Perfection Overshoe to fit. which is one size larger than boot. STATE SIZE. Weight, 64 ounces.

No. 15K1489 Boys' sizes, 1 to 5; no half sizes. Price, per pair...$1.69

LUMBERMEN'S SOCKS, 95c.

LEATHER HEEL.

No. 15K1279 An extra good wearing sock, which is all wool half tufted. The process which makes it one of the best wearing socks is known as the shrinking process. Gigantic size socks are knitted in the usual manner, after which they are shrunk from this very large size to a regular full size sock, making them non-shrinkable and of finely knitted texture. In addition to being a finely knitted sock it has a leather heel stay, making it a sock intended for warmth and hard service. Sizes, 6 to 12. STATE SIZE. Weight, 15 ounces. Price, per pair..............95c

MEN'S ALASKA SOCKS, 90c.

ALL WOOL.

No. 15K1280 This is the genuine Detroit Alaska Lumbermen's Sock. Made from all wool, with double foot, and two stocking feet knitted into one, which makes the most durable sock that money can buy. Color, black foot and gray and black stripe leg. Sizes, 6 to 12. STATE SIZE. Weight, 17 ounces. Price, per pair.....90c

BARGAIN SOCKS.

FOR MEN AND BOYS.

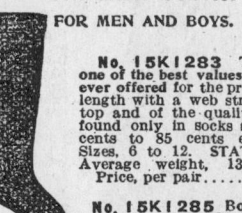

No. 15K1283 This sock, one of the best values we have ever offered for the price, is full length with a web strap at the top and of the quality that is found only in socks sold at 75 cents to 85 cents elsewhere. Sizes, 6 to 12. STATE SIZE. Average weight, 13 ounces. Price, per pair..........60c

No. 15K1285 Boys' socks. Sizes, 1 to 6. Weight, 9 ounces. Price, per pair.........50c

WE HAVE AGAIN BEEN ABLE TO
REDUCE MANY PRICES
IN OUR SHOE DEPARTMENT AS SHOWN BY THESE PAGES.

RIDING LEGGINGS, $1.90.

MEN'S PUTTEE.

No. 15K1236 Made from a very handsome shade of English russet sole leather. This is not a cheap legging as the price would indicate, but the genuine English legging usually sold for about $5.00 per pair. Splendid fitting and easily put on. Sizes, 14 to 18 inches calf measurement. STATE SIZE. Weight, 20 ounces. Price, per pair.....$1.90

THE SNOW EXCLUDER, 45c.

MEN'S CANVAS LACE.

No. 15K1262 A high grade extra heavy Tan Canvas Legging that prevents and keeps out snow and dirt. The excluder is made of the same grade canvas as the legging itself and is 9 inches wide. Some leggings on the market in this style have a much narrower excluder, making it difficult to put on. Full size 17-inch knee legging that will give excellent wear. Sizes, 14, 15, 16, 17 and 18 inches. STATE SIZE Weight averages 14 ounces. Price, per pair.......45c

KNEE LEGGINGS, 65 CENTS.

WATERPROOF.

No. 15K1261 Made lace style, with hook and grummets. Strongly bound at the top and bottom, and have a reinforced heel. The seams are double felled and stitched, heavy leather foot straps. Sizes, 14 to 18 inches calf measure. STATE SIZE. Weight averages 14 ounces. Price, per pair.....65c

LACE LEGGINGS, 35c.

FOR BOYS.

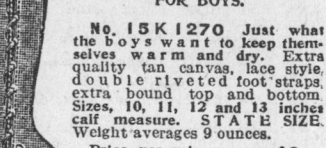

No. 15K1272 Boys' Army Lace Leggings with grummet eyelets and hooks to match. Made from extra heavy tan canvas, with bound top and bottom, double riveted russet leather foot straps, full size knee length. A very serviceable legging for a boy. Sizes, 10, 11, 12 and 13 inches calf measure. STATE SIZE. Weight averages 9 ounces. Price, per pair.........35c

THIGH LEGGINGS, 40c.

FOR BOYS.

No. 15K1270 Just what the boys want to keep themselves warm and dry. Extra quality tan canvas, lace style, double riveted foot straps, extra bound top and bottom. Sizes, 10, 11, 12 and 13 inches calf measure. STATE SIZE. Weight averages 9 ounces. Price, per pair........40c

WATERPROOF LEGGINGS 38 CENTS.

FOR MEN.

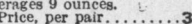

No. 15K1232 These leggings are made similar to the mackintosh cloth, outside facing of covert, blanket fleece lined throughout, with an interlining of rubber. Made to lace on the side with hooks and grummets. Strongly bound top and bottom; double riveted foot straps. Sizes, 14 to 18 inches calf measure. STATE SIZE. Weight averages 19 ounces. Price, per pair.........38c

BUCKLE KNEE LEGGINGS, 49c.

Made extra bound at the top and bottom with five buckle straps and reinforced heel. Double riveted foot straps and in all a dandy legging for the money.

No. 15K1259 Sizes, 14 to 18 inches calf measure. Weight averages 18 ounces. STATE SIZE. Price, per pair....49c

LEATHER, SHOE FINDINGS AND COBBLERS' OUTFITS

WHITTEMORE'S DRESSING, 18c.

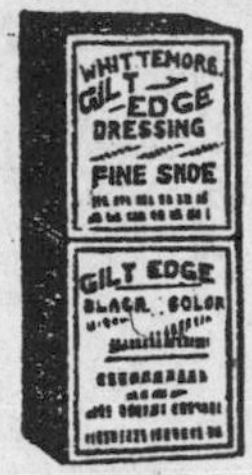

REGULAR 25-CENT SIZE.

No. 15K2010 Ladies' Gilt Edge Shoe Dressing is very useful for a great many things besides shoes. It will make your old rubbers, shopping bags and black kid gloves look equal to new.

Price, per bottle..... 18c

Unmailable.

WATERPROOF POLISH, 15 CENTS.

SOLD ELSEWHERE FOR 25 CENTS.

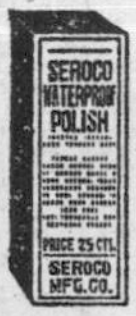

No. 15K2016 Seroco Waterproof Polish is the only polish that is absolutely waterproof, and produces a jet black polish without brushing. Men or boys who dislike rubbers should use this, as it sheds water like a rubber.

Price, per bottle.......... 15c

Unmailable.

FRANK MILLER'S BLACKING, 15 CENTS.

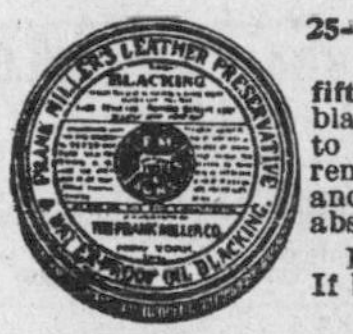

25-CENT SIZE, 15 CENTS.

No. 15K2018 Over fifty years in use. This blacking is not designed to produce a polish, but renders the leather soft and pliable and makes it absolutely waterproof.

Price, per box.... 15c

If by mail, postage extra, 8 cents.

PARROT SHINE, 5 CENTS.

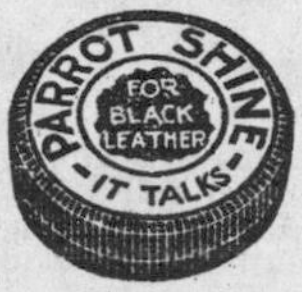

No. 15K2032 Combines the qualities of liquid and paste polish. Never hardens, cracks or forms a crust on the leather, but keeps the shoes soft and pliable.

Price, per box.... 5c
Per dozen....... 50c

If by mail, postage extra, 3 cents.

SHOE LACES

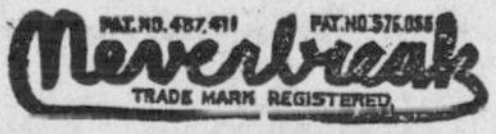

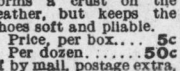

A patented shoe lace adopted by the War Department for the U. S. Army.

No. 15K2044 36 inches. For men's and boys' shoes. Dozen pairs.......$0.25
Per gross laces.............. 1.25

Postage extra, per dozen pairs, 4 cents.

PATON'S HAND SPIRAL TAGGED 40-INCH LACE, 30 CENTS.

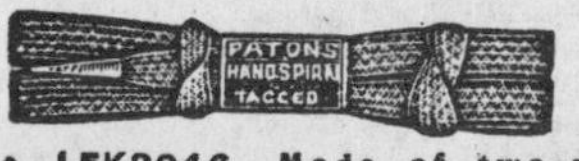

No. 15K2046 Made of two-ply combed sea island cotton, dressy, durable and the best imported lace on the market. Put up 1 dozen pairs in a box. For men's, women's and boys' shoes.

Price, per dozen pairs............... 30c

WATERPROOF ARMY SHOE LACE.

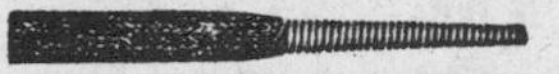

No. 15K2058 This lace is made from the best of linen, woven very close, is about ⅛ inch wide, 1 yard long, with spiral tags. Used by the U. S. Government.

Price, per dozen pairs............. 18c
Per gross laces................. 95c

Postage extra, per dozen pairs, 4 cents.

BEST PORPOISE LACES.

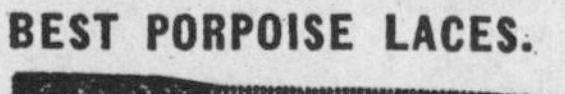

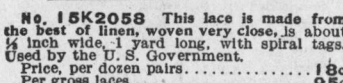

Best English Porpoise Laces, with spiral tags, the strongest and best made at any price.

No. 15K2060 36-inch.
Price, per dozen pairs.............$0.38
Per gross, laces................ 2.00

No. 15K2062 45-inch.
Price, per dozen pairs.............$0.48
Per gross, laces................ 2.60

Postage extra, per dozen pairs, 6 cents.

MEN'S, LADIES', BOYS' AND MISSES' FLAT TUBULAR LACES.

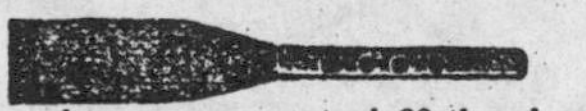

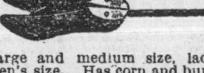

These laces are guaranteed, 88-thread and full lengths. The best domestic tubular lace made, and usually sold at 5 cents per pair.

No. 15K2066 27-inch, for children's shoes and men's and women's Oxfords. Black only. Per gross, 62c; per dozen pairs..12c

No. 15K2072 36-inch, black.
Per gross, 79c; per dozen pairs........ 14c

No. 15K2074 45-inch, black.
Per gross, 90c; per dozen pairs........ 16c

No. 15K2078 54-inch, black.
Per gross $1.00; per dozen pairs........ 18c

Postage extra, per dozen pairs, 4 cents.

SHOE STRETCHERS, 50 CENTS.

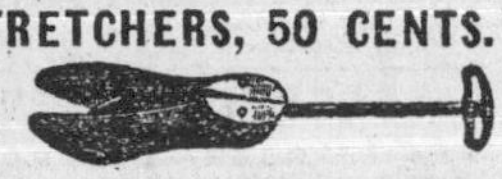

No. 15K2142 Wood Shoe Stretcher, made in four sizes, men's large and medium size, ladies' size and children's size. Has corn and bunion attachments. Price.................. 50c

If by mail, postage extra, 30 cents.

BEST HEEL STIFFENERS, 30c.

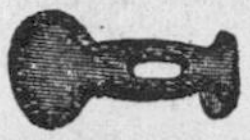

No. 15K2150 Prevents boots and shoes from running over.

Price, per dozen pairs, 30c

Postage extra, per pair, 2c.

PARKER'S ARCTIC SOCKS, 17c.

Fleece lined, unequaled for house, chamber, bathroom, and especially desirable for inside of rubber boots.

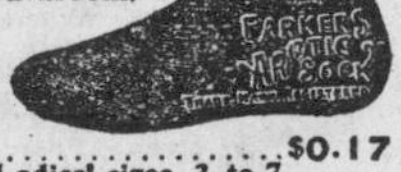

No. 15K2424 Men's sizes, 6 to 11.
Price, per pair......................$0.17

No. 15K2426 Ladies' sizes, 3 to 7.
Price, per pair........................ .17
Per dozen pairs........................ 1.85

If by mail, postage extra, per pair, 2 cents.

RUBBER BOOT OR SHOE ICE CREEPERS, 21 CENTS.

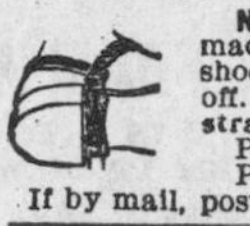

No. 15K2162 Especially made to use with rubber boots or shoes, and easy to put on or take off. Each pair has adjustable straps.

Price, per pair........$0.21
Per dozen pairs.......... 2.25

If by mail, postage extra, per pair, 7 cents.

BEST RUBBER CEMENT.

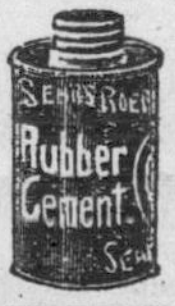

Rubber Cement is used for repairing all kinds of rubber boots and shoes, rubber clothing, mackintoshes, etc. Ours is warranted.

No. 15K2528 4 ounces.
Price, per can............ 8c
Per dozen cans........... 90c

Unmailable on account of postal laws.

STOCKING KNEE PROTECTORS.

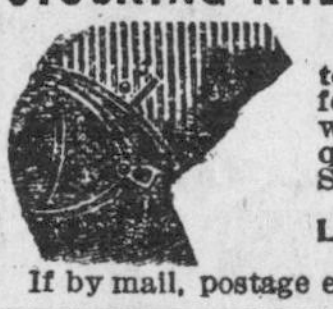

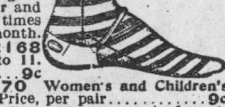

Stocking Knee Protectors are very desirable for boys and girls who wear their stockings out quickly at the knees. State age when ordering.

No. 15K2166 Leather.
Price, per pair.... 16c

If by mail, postage extra, per pair, 2 cents.

STOCKING HEEL PROTECTORS, 9 CENTS.

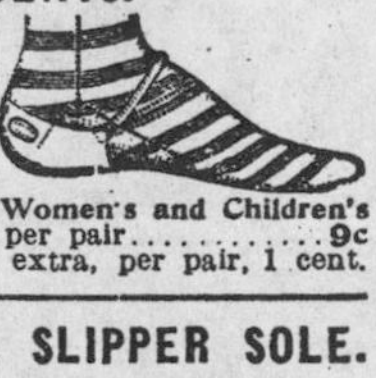

Made from a good grade of leather and will save many times its cost every month.

No. 15K2168 Men's sizes, 6 to 11.
Per pair............. 9c

No. 15K2170 Women's and Children's sizes, 2 to 7. Price, per pair.............. 9c

If by mail, postage extra, per pair, 1 cent.

LAMBS' WOOL SLIPPER SOLE.

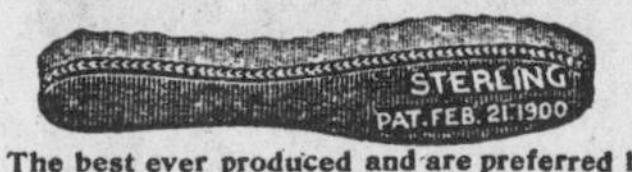

The best ever produced and are preferred by most women for crocheted and knit and toilet slippers. Unlike all others, the stitch or cord of the Sterling is exactly on the upper edge. The needle can thus be thrust directly through the meshes of the stitch and not on an angle, with the risk of breaking the needle as with other soles where the cord is too far over the edge.

No. 15K2176 Men's sizes, 6 to 11.
Price, per pair.................... 30c

No. 15K2178 Women's sizes, 3 to 7.
Price, per pair.................... 20c

No. 15K2180 Misses' sizes, 11 to 2.
Price, per pair.................... 18c

No. 15K2182 Children's sizes, 5 to 10.
Price, per pair.................... 16c

If by mail, postage extra, per pair, 3 cents.

OUR STAR LEATHER OUTFITS, $1.25.

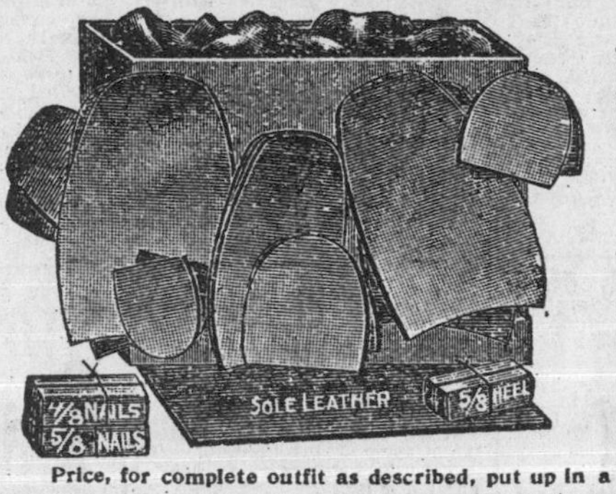

No. 15K2900 For only $1.25 we offer you this Outfit, made from best quality hemlock half soles and heel lifts; also enough patching leather to do the cobbler work of the entire family.

Notice the large sizes of soles and the big variety.

- 1 pair men's boot taps, size 14.
- 1 pair men's best half soles, size 12.
- 1 pair boys' half soles, size 7.
- 1 pair women's best half soles, size 7.
- 1 piece square cut sole, size 6½x8½.
- 1 pair men's best largest size heel lifts.
- 1 pair boys' best largest size heel lifts.
- 1 pair women's best largest size heel lifts.
- 1 package each of 4-8 and 5-8 clinch nails and 1 package 5-8 heel nails, also a small quantity of patching leather. Weight, 3 pounds.

Price, for complete outfit as described, put up in a neat pasteboard carton.....$1.25

A FEW FACTS ABOUT LEATHER HALF SOLES.

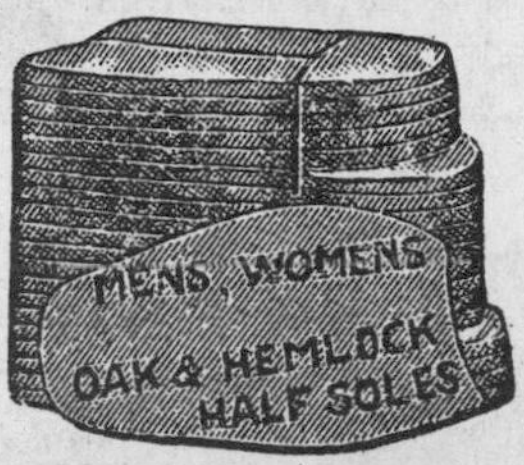

As a safeguard to the consumer when buying leather cut soles, or half soles, we hereby state a few facts about the different selections these half soles are made in. The best quality soles are always stamped on the top of every dozen F, or fine; the second quality (sometimes sold by other firms as the best quality), are stamped M, or medium, and the third selection are all stamped C, or coarse.

We call your attention to the above facts in order that you may know positively what you are getting, no matter where you buy.

HEMLOCK TANNED HALF SOLES.

All our hemlock half soles and heel top pieces are cut from slaughter sole leather made from packer hides. We do not handle dry hide soles, on which it is easy to quote low prices. Each pair carefully selected. Assorted sizes in dozens. Will cover wide shoes.

MEN'S HEMLOCK HALF SOLES.

No. 15K2306 Best quality, 6-inch thickness, per dozen pairs. Per pair..$0.29
Per dozen pairs.......................... 3.25

No. 15K2309 Best quality, 5½-inch thickness, per dozen pairs. Per pair..$0.26
Per dozen pairs.......................... 3.05

No. 15K2312 Good quality, 5-inch thickness, per dozen pairs. Per pair..$0.19
Per dozen pairs.......................... 2.15

No. 15K2313 Medium quality, 4½-inch thickness, per dozen pairs. Per pair..$0.15
Per dozen pairs.......................... 1.60

Weight, 3½ to 4½ pounds to the dozen pairs.

MEN'S BEST OAK TANNED HALF SOLES.

No. 15K2330 Best quality, extra 6-inch thickness. Price, per pair..........$0.30
Per dozen pairs.......................... 3.50

Weight, 4½ pounds to the dozen pairs.

WOMEN'S HEMLOCK HALF SOLES.

No. 15K2324 Best quality, 4½-inch thickness. Price, per pair..........$0.16
Per dozen pairs.......................... 1.66

Weight, 2 pounds to the dozen pairs.

No. 15K2328 Good quality, 3½-inch thickness. Price, per pair..........$0.10
Per dozen pairs.......................... 1.00

WOMEN'S OAK HALF SOLES.

No. 15K2334 Best quality, 4-inch thickness. Price, per pair..........$0.13
Per dozen pairs.......................... 1.47

Weight, 2 pounds to the dozen pairs.

SHOE NAILS.

Remember, our price is per pound. Some concerns quote theirs per package, which means per half pound.

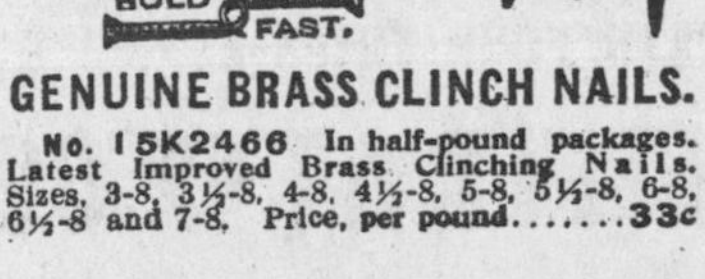

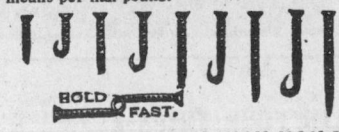

GENUINE BRASS CLINCH NAILS.

No. 15K2466 In half-pound packages. Latest Improved Brass Clinching Nails. Sizes, 3-8, 3½-8, 4-8, 4½-8, 5-8, 5½-8, 6-8, 6½-8 and 7-8. Price, per pound....... 33c

WHITE OAK JUMBO SOLES.

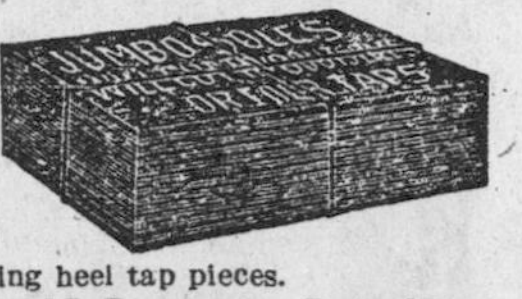

Sizes, 8¼ x12½ inches. Each piece will cut two large pairs of men's half soles or three pairs of women's half soles. Also used for making heel tap pieces.

No. 15K2343 Best grade. Extra heavy substance, weighing 10 pounds to the dozen pieces. Price, each..............$0.55
Per dozen pieces.................. 6.00

No. 15K2344 Best grade. Heavy substance, weighing 9 pounds to the dozen.
Price, each......................$0.48
Per dozen pieces.................. 5.25

No. 15K2345 Best grade. Medium substance, weighing 8 pounds to the dozen.
Price, each......................$0.45
Per dozen pieces.................. 4.80

No. 15K2346 Best grade. Light substance, weighing 7 pounds to the dozen.
Price, each......................$0.40
Per dozen pieces.................. 4.25

HEMLOCK HEELS.

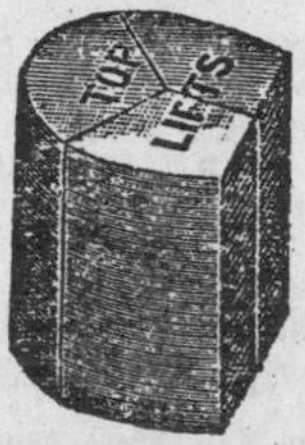

No. 15K2347, Good quality, 5-inch thickness.

Price, per dozen pairs............ 49c

Weight, ⅝ pound to the dozen pairs.

SOLE LEATHER STRIPS.

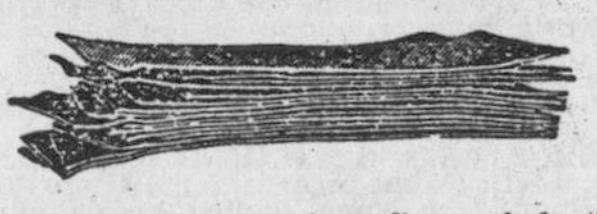

These strips are cut from firm sole leather sides and are in every way the most practical for family shoe repair work. All the various shaped soles and heel tap pieces can be cut from these strips to good advantage. Each strip is about 8 inches wide and varies in length from 1½ to 2½ feet. Prices quoted are for average strips. We will charge you only for exact weight at the lowest market price. Shipping weight averages from 1 to 2 pounds per strip.

HEMLOCK SOLE LEATHER STRIPS.

No. 15K2368 Best quality, heavy thickness. Per piece, about.............. 60c

No. 15K2369 Best quality, medium thickness. Per piece, about............. 50c

OAK SOLE LEATHER STRIPS.

No. 15K2371 Best quality, heavy thickness. Per piece, about.............. 65c

No. 15K2372 Best quality, medium thickness. Per piece, about............. 55c

CORK HAIR CUSHION INSOLES.

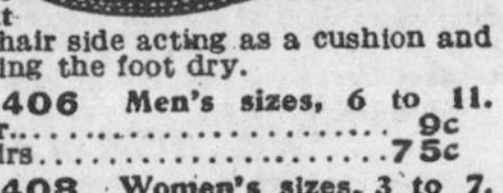

Can be used as a cork cushion insole by having the cork side of the insole next the foot, the hair side acting as a cushion and the cork keeping the foot dry.

No. 15K2406 Men's sizes, 6 to 11.
Price, per pair.......................... 9c
Per dozen pairs.......................... 75c

No. 15K2408 Women's sizes, 3 to 7.
Price, per pair.......................... 7c
Per dozen pairs.......................... 75c

If by mail, postage extra, per pair, 3 cents.

MEN'S MACKINTOSH LEGGINGS, 48 CENTS.

No. 15K1231 Made of gray mackintosh cloth, blanket fleece lined throughout, and fastened with automatic snap buckles. It is one of the strongest leggings manufactured, and absolutely waterproof. Men's sizes only, 14 to 18 inches calf measure. STATE SIZE. Weight, 20 ounces.

Price, per pair................48c
For postage rate see page 10.

HIGH CUT OVERGAITERS, 45c.
FOR MEN.

No. 15K1226 Made from heavy weight kersey, felt lined, very warm and comfortable for winter wear. Sizes, 6 to 11. STATE SIZE. Weight, 8 to 12 ounces, according to size. No half sizes.

Price, per pair....45c

JERSEY LEGGINGS.
LADIES', MISSES' AND CHILDREN'S.

This is an all wool Jersey Legging and buttons above the knee, being easily put on and taken off. Is perfect fitting and a legging that will assure its wearer comfort and warmth. STATE SIZE. Weight, about 9 ounces. No half sizes.

No. 15K1206 Ladies' and Misses' sizes, 3 to 7.
Price, per pair........59c
No. 15K1208 Misses' sizes, 11 to 2.
Price, per pair........48c
No. 15K1210 Children's sizes, 6 to 10.
Price, per pair.....39c

OVERKNEE LEGGINGS, 45c.
FOR LARGE OR SMALL BOYS.

No. 15K1273 This Legging is warm in cold weather, as it is made of a heavy covert, blanket fleece lining, with an interlining of rubber, which makes it absolutely waterproof. The seams are double felled and stitched; heavy foot straps, made of the best leather. Sizes, 10 to 13 inches calf measure. STATE SIZE. Weight averages 15 ounces.
Price, per pair:........45c

LEATHER LEGGINGS, $1.25.
FOR MEN.

No. 15K1227 Made from the best grade of black grain leather. Napoleon style with the latest style spring fastener. This legging is very popular; can be put on much quicker than any other style and is very durable. Sizes, 14 to 18 inches calf measure. STATE SIZE. Weight, per pair, averages 20 ounces.

Price, per pair........$1.25
For postage rate see page 10.

OVERGAITERS.
FOR WOMEN.

No. 15K1211 Ladies' Fine Overgaiters, made heavy for fall and winter wear. Shoe sizes, 3 to 7. STATE SIZE. Weight, 7 ounces. No half sizes.
Price, per pair....19c
No. 15K1215 Ladies' 7-button imported Kersey, the nobbiest and unexcelled overgaiter. Sizes, 3 to 7. Price, per pair....35c

SAMPSON SEAM FASTENER OR HAND STAPLING TOOL.

By means of small staples especially made for this seam fastener, shoes are prevented from ripping in the seam. These staples when clinched are almost invisible and will outwear the shoe. They are the most perfect made and will not tear the threads as other kinds do if put directly over the seams or stitching. No family should be without one of these tools and a box of staples to prevent and repair ripped seams.
No. 15K2516 Seam Fastener.
Price................85c
No. 15K2517 Staples or Fasteners to be used with No. 15K2516. Made in three sizes, short No. 1, medium No. 2 and long No. 3. Medium or No. 2 is the size mostly used. 576 staples in box.
Price, per box............20c

BEST LEATHER CEMENT.

No. 15K2522 1 ounce.
Price, per bottle............5c
Per dozen.............55c
Unmailable on account of postal laws.

RUBBER HEELS.
WE DO NOT PUT ON RUBBER HEELS.
SEROCO CUSHION HEELS, 10 CENTS PER PAIR.
Equal to many heels sold at 25 cents per pair.

Can furnish to fit any shoe and are recommended by physicians for men and women from the fact that it relieves the jar from the base of the spinal column. When ordering send outline of heel.
No. 15K2430 Men's sizes. Price, per pair............10c
No. 15K2432 Women's sizes. Price, per pair............9c
If by mail, postage extra, per pair, 5 cents.

24-INCH MALLEABLE STAND, 80 CENTS.

No. 15K2702 24-inch stand with four lasts. Malleable iron, warranted unbreakable, and the best that is made, regardless of price. Weight, 19 pounds. Price, per set... 80c

POLAR SOCKS, 6 CENTS.
FOR INSIDE OF RUBBER BOOTS.

No. 15K2420 Fleece Lined Polar Socks for house, chamber, bathroom, and various uses. Men's sizes, 6 to 11.
Price, per pair..................6c
Per dozen pairs................70c
If by mail, postage extra, per pair, 2 cents.

STEEL HEEL AND TOE PLATES.

Crescent Heel and Toe Plates, cut out of hardened sheet steel, cannot break. No. 2, for women's shoes. No. 3 for men's shoes. Weight, 7 ounces.
No. 15K2460 Price, per box of 1½ dozen pairs, No. 2....7c
No. 15K2462 Price, per box of 1 dozen pairs, No. 3....7c

BAKER'S CELEBRATED "HOLD FAST" NAILS.
IN HALF-POUND PACKAGES.

No. 15K2468 Baker's Patent Wire Clinch Nails. Sizes, 3-8, 3½-8, 4-8, 4½-8, 5-8, 5½-8, 6-8, 6½-8 and 7-8.
Price, per pound..................10c

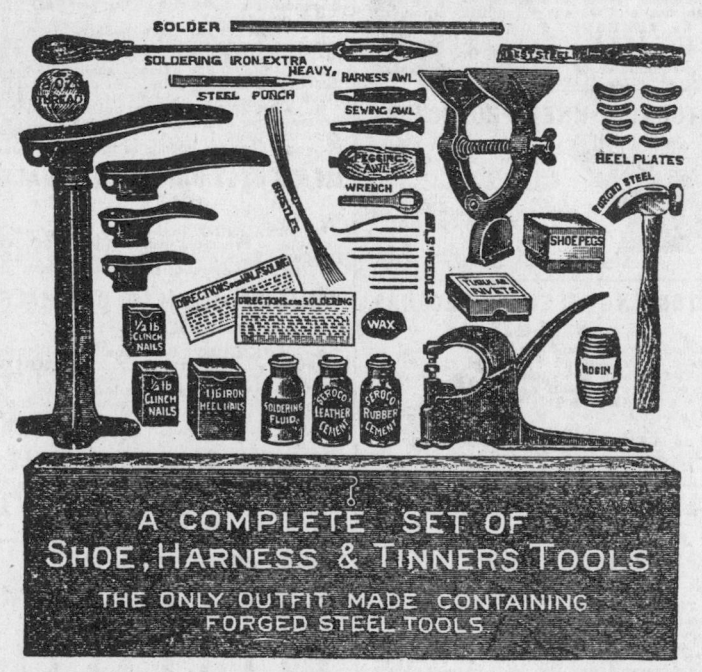

CARPETS, RUGS, AND CURTAINS

WE ASK YOUR TRADE on the strength of our qualities in each and every class of merchandise in this line. Buying in enormous quantities direct from the mills enables us to place our own experts there to supervise the actual manufacturing of our goods and we absolutely protect you against any kind of defective goods whatsoever. We accept no material but what comes strictly up to our contracts. We offer you carpets, rugs and everything in this line of house furnishings, of strictly the best grades produced by any mill. It's easy for dealers to offer, for example, a carpet in which the manufacturer has cheapened the quality enough to make an extra profit of several cents a yard and yet it does not show in the appearance of the carpet. But it will show in the wear after you have had the carpet for some time. Then again it's easy to skimp a little, for example on the width of a carpet or the size of a rug, making a little narrower or a little smaller than is actually supposed to be. We protect you against all such defects and guarantee our qualities and sizes to be just as represented, the best and highest grade materials obtainable, pure goods and full measure throughout, and if you don't find it just as we state, we ask you as a favor to us to return the goods at our expense and we will refund to you both the price and any transportation charges you paid.

WE FURNISH CARPET SAMPLES FREE, to show the quality of any carpet we offer, as explained on page 853, and we also furnish free a Special Catalogue of House Furnishings as explained on page 852, showing the actual colors of all these goods, the largest, most complete and most wonderfully beautiful book of colored illustrations ever produced. Read about it. We guarantee to satisfy you perfectly if you order from the following pages in this catalogue, but if you would like to see the actual colors shown in the latest three-color photography process now perfected, write for our Special Carpet and Rug Catalogue.

OUR PRICES are absolutely the lowest ever quoted on house furnishings simply because we buy direct from the mills at mill prices, buying more goods than the exclusive house furnishing jobbers, getting lower prices from the mills, consequently quoting lower prices to you than your dealers pay the jobbers and thus vastly underselling everybody else in this line. Don't pay retail prices for house furnishings of any kind. Not only are our qualities the finest and our line the most complete, but we save you all retailers' profits and expenses and more besides. Look this line over and see for yourself.

THIS IS BY FAR THE LARGEST AND MOST COMPLETE LINE of house furnishings in the country. Nowhere else will you find anywhere near the assortment to choose from. It represents the results of years of experience of the most expert buyers to be found. We are perfectly sure that, no matter what your tastes are, we can perfectly please you both in quality and coloring while at the same time we will save you a surprising amount of money as compared with what you will pay at retail. It is an education and a treat to householders to look through this great line and especially as shown in our Special Catalogue illustrated on page 852.

REMEMBER OUR LIBERAL OFFER AND GUARANTEE that you can send your order for any of these goods with the distinct understanding that if you find them unsatisfactory in any way at all, you are perfectly at liberty to return them to us at our expense and we will return to you both the price and any transportation charges you paid. You will not lose a single penny.

OUR VERY LOW PRICES FOR CUTTING, MATCHING AND SEWING CARPETS.

2 CENTS PER YARD FOR INGRAIN CARPET. At 2 cents per yard extra we will match and sew any 36-inch Ingrain, Rag or Granite Carpet to fit any room.

3 CENTS PER YARD FOR TAPESTRY, VELVET AND AXMINSTER CARPET. For 3 cents per yard extra we will cut, match and sew any of our 27-inch carpets to fit any room.

10 CENTS PER YARD FOR BORDER CARPETS. At 10 cents per yard we will cut, match and sew any Tapestry, Velvet or Axminster Carpet where there is a border to match. For example, in making a rug from a Tapestry, Velvet or Axminster Carpet in which there is a border on four sides, or in making a border carpet to fit any size room, we make a charge of 10 cents per yard for matching, making and sewing.

OUR SPECIAL PRICES of 2, 3 and 10 cents per yard for matching and sewing, according to the kind of carpet, are very much lower than the same work is being done by any other house, and the demand for made up carpets has grown to where we are now doing this work by automatic machinery on so large a scale that we have been able to reduce the cost of matching, making and sewing, and we feel like giving our customers the benefit of this saving.

WASTAGE IN MATCHING CARPETS. Where you order a carpet cut, matched and sewed you must make a little allowance for wastage in matching the patterns exactly. We require that you allow 1½ yards wastage in matching for each 25 yards. For example, if you wish a carpet made for a room that measures 25 yards, you should pay for 26½ yards; or if you wish a carpet made for a room measuring 12 yards, you should pay for 12¾ yards. We will cut with just as little waste as possible, and if we can make it up wasting less than the amount you allow for—namely, 1½ yards to every 25, we will give you the benefit of the saving and return the difference to you in cash. **There will be less waste and better matching where we make the carpet for you,** even though you were to buy it and match and make it yourself, for the reason that where we are cutting up hundreds of rolls we can always make a saving of waste by cutting and matching from several rolls, giving you the benefit of this saving. Where there is any waste in matching we send you the waste pieces with the carpet so that you can verify the wastage and possibly make use of the small pieces for mats, coverings, etc.

HOW WE CUT, MATCH AND SEW CARPETS. We have a large organization for doing this work, which alone makes possible our special 2, 3 and 10-cent per yard price. Only expert carpet sewers are employed in this department. We have several large special electric carpet sewing machines, where the carpets come edge to edge, insuring a perfect match, and preventing their having ridges, which injures the appearance and wears out at the seam. At our special prices of 2, 3 and 10 cents per yard and with our facilities for making up and matching with the very minimum of wastage, you will find it cheaper to let us make the carpet for you than to buy it in the piece. In ordering carpet cut, matched and made for a square room it is only necessary to give the length and width of the room, but if the room is irregular in shape, such as a bay window, alcove, fireplace or like irregular lines, you should make a drawing on a piece of paper showing the dimensions, being sure to give exact measurements and mark the front of the room so we can cut the carpet to the best advantage.

WE FURNISH SAMPLES OF ANY KIND OF CARPET FREE

WE ALSO FURNISH A LARGE SPECIAL CATALOGUE OF HOUSE FURNISHINGS SHOWING THE ACTUAL COLORS AND DESIGNS FREE. SEE THIS GREAT OFFER ON PAGE 852.

IN ORDERING CARPETS MATCHED AND SEWED BE CAREFUL TO GIVE THE EXACT SIZE OF ROOM OR ROOMS. If an odd size, having a fireplace, bay window or offset, be sure to send a diagram with exact measurements, also be sure to state where entrance and front of room is; also to allow 1½ yards in every 25 yards for wastage in matching.

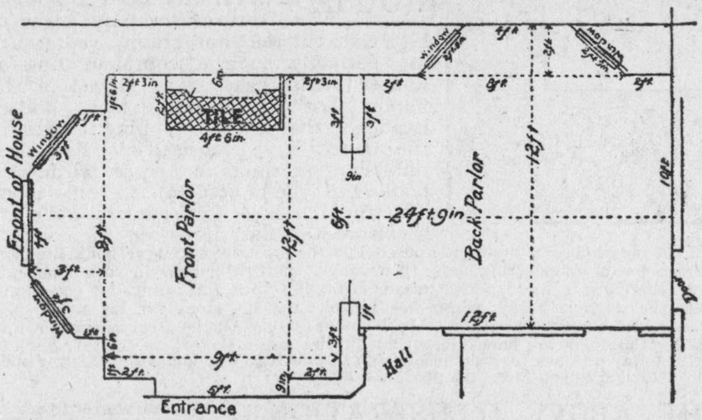

The illustration herewith shows you how a diagram should be made. This diagram came to us with an order for carpet for a front and back parlor. You will notice that every window and door is plainly marked and all measurements are clearly shown for our information. When you send us an order for carpet, if you will make a diagram, with all measurements carefully taken and marked on the diagram in the same careful manner, it will not be possible for us to make a mistake in cutting and fitting your carpet for you.

A FEW SIMPLE INSTRUCTIONS MAKING IT EASY TO TELL HOW MUCH CARPET YOU NEED.

ON PAGE 854 WE GIVE A LIST OF DIFFERENT SIZED ROOMS and have figured the number of yards of 36-inch ingrain carpet, 27-inch Brussels, velvet or Axminster carpets made plain without border, also Brussels, velvet or Axminster carpets made with border, that would be required. If the size of your room is not given in this list and you wish to order carpet at once, we advise you to allow enough money to pay for the next larger size and we will cut the carpet with the least possible waste and only charge you with the exact amount of carpet used in the cutting. In figuring the amount of carpet used in fitting these rooms we have included the ordinary waste, but if we can cut the carpet with less waste when your order is received we will do so and will refund whatever balance you have at the time the shipment is made. Perhaps you will wonder why there should be waste used in matching a carpet. Let us explain that the patterns of different style carpets do not match at exactly the same distance, some patterns being 30 inches apart, some 32, 34 and 36 inches. Take for instance a room size 14x15 feet, and you will readily see that it requires 5 widths of 36-inch ingrain carpet, each width being 14 feet long. This would be the actual amount of carpet used to cover the room. We find when we go to cut this carpet that the patterns will not match at 14 feet exact, but that this pattern cuts at 14 feet 9 inches, and you will readily see that each strip will have to be cut 14 feet 9 inches long to make the patterns match on every strip. On five widths of carpet we would be obliged to use 45 inches more carpet than is actually needed to cover the room and you would be charged with 1¼ yards waste used in matching. This also applies to rooms of different sizes and also applies to Brussels, velvet and Axminster carpets as well as ingrain carpets. Should your room be size 14x14 feet, you will see that we are obliged to use five widths of carpet to cover the room and there will be a strip of one foot on the side that you will either have to turn under, or, in a great many cases, our customers use this extra amount of carpet used in matching to be placed at threshold, or will save these pieces to be used in case a hole is burned in the carpet, as quite often occurs. Remember, Brussels, velvets and Axminster carpets are only 27 inches wide; borders used on carpets are only 22½ inches wide. Ingrain carpets are 36 inches wide. If your room is odd shaped, having a bay window, fireplace or offset, and you do not feel that you can figure the exact amount of carpet in it, we would advise you to send us a diagram of the room, giving all measurements, and we will be pleased to quote you a price on any carpet you may wish. You will note that two rooms of different sizes will require the same amount of carpet. For example, a room 14x14 feet will require 24¼ yards of ingrain carpet. For a room 15x14 feet it will require 24¼ yards of ingrain carpet. On each of these rooms we are obliged to use five widths of carpet, each width 14 feet long, which, of course, does not include the waste used in matching. You will readily see that for the room size 14x14 feet you will have 1 foot of carpet 14 feet long that you will either have to turn under or can cut it off and use at the threshold as above stated.

SEE PAGE 854 FOR FULL INSTRUCTIONS FOR MEASURING A ROOM AND COMPLETE TABLE OF ROOM SIZES, WHICH WILL HELP YOU TELL HOW MUCH CARPET YOU NEED. ALWAYS BE CAREFUL TO STATE EXACT SIZE OF ROOM.

CARPETS AND RUGS IN COLORS FREE
THIS GREAT BOOK SHOWS

THE ACTUAL COLORS AND DESIGNS OF OUR CARPETS, RUGS, LINOLEUMS, OILCLOTHS, MATTINGS, DRAPERIES, ETC. IT IS A REAL WORK OF ART AND A TRIUMPH IN THE SCIENCE OF COLORED PHOTOGRAPHY, THE MOST COMPLETE AND INTERESTING BOOK ON HOUSE FURNISHINGS EVER PUBLISHED.

WRITE FOR IT TODAY

JUST WRITE AND SAY "Send me your Special Carpet and Rug Color Catalogue," and this big book with its numerous pages of beautiful colored photograph plates and complete information on house furnishings, all our great offers, will go to you free and postpaid at once, showing you exactly how any carpet or rug or any floor covering or drapery will look in your room, making it very simple and easy to make a selection.

IN THE PAGES OF THIS BIG CATALOGUE we describe and illustrate all our complete line of carpets, rugs, floor coverings of all kinds, draperies, etc., as accurately and carefully as the limitations of space and printing methods of this book permit, and you can select and order your carpet or rug direct from the catalogue under our guarantee that the goods will please you perfectly or we will immediately refund your money. However, if you have any difficulty whatever in making your selection from these pages, don't buy a dollar's worth of house furnishings of any kind anywhere else at any price, because we know that if you will send for this great book, showing our complete line of house furnishings in their actual colors, that you will be perfectly sure of selecting your goods from our line. Our values are wonderful. This beautiful book makes it very simple and easy to choose, shows you the exact colors, the shades in the background and exactly how the various patterns are worked out in their beautiful color combinations, thus permitting you to judge accurately just what carpet or rug or drapery, etc., would harmonize with the colorings of the walls, furnishings, etc., in your rooms. Just write and ask for our Special Carpet and Rug Color Catalogue and we will at once mail this wonderfully artistic book to you free and postpaid.

POSITIVELY NO OTHER HOUSE has ever attempted to publish a book of so many pages of high class colored photography, representing perfectly such a complete line of house furnishings, to be placed in the hands of the consumer. Only houses handling the largest jobbing trades in the country have ever used such high class publishing methods as represented in this book and their books have only gone into the hands of the dealers. We are therefore the first house in the country and the only house to show the householder the most advanced methods, the most perfect means of selecting house furnishings. With this book in your home you have therefore a more perfect means of buying your furnishings for your home than the average retail dealer has in selecting his stock for his store. No householder should be without this valuable book. All the great offers shown in this Big Catalogue are here brought out in the actual colorings of the designs. Write today and ask for our Special Carpet and Rug Catalogue and this big book will be mailed to you free and postpaid at once.

DON'T YOU WANT TO SEE EXACTLY how any rug, carpet, floor covering of any kind or drapery would look in your room? Don't you wish to see the best qualities of house furnishings ever assembled in one line, shown in their actual colors, exactly how the goods look? Wouldn't you like to see, for example, some of our finest rugs in a colored photograph occupying an entire page of this big book, which has pages as large as the pages of this Big Catalogue, and showing the complete rug, the entire body and entire border? Wouldn't you like to see the real shading of the background in our rugs, carpets, etc., and how the beautiful floral scroll and panel effects are brought out in actual colors? Don't you want to be perfectly informed about the best things produced in house furnishings nowadays? Wouldn't you like to get some fine suggestions about furnishing your home? Wouldn't you like to see absolutely the largest assortment of floor coverings and draperies that it is possible for you to see in this country and all illustrated in the most beautiful, artistic, high class and perfect manner that it is possible to show? Then don't fail to write today and just ask for our FREE Special Catalogue of Carpets, Rugs, Draperies, etc.

THE ABOVE ILLUSTRATION gives you some idea of this complete book of house furnishings in which we show more pages of high class colored photograph plates of house furnishings than ever before placed in the hands of the general public. The cover design is the work of a master artist and suggests what beautiful work is contained in this book, as each and every colored plate in it represents the best professional work in the science of colored photography. Write for it. It's free.

SEE OUR GREAT FREE CARPET SAMPLE OFFER ON THE NEXT PAGE.

CARPET SAMPLES FREE

JUST WRITE AND TELL US WHAT KIND OF CARPET YOU WANT TO BUY, WHETHER INGRAIN CARPET (SEE SET No. 1) OR BRUSSELS CARPET (SEE SET No. 2) OR AXMINSTER, WILTON VELVET OR WILTON CARPET (SEE SET No 3), AND WE WILL MAIL YOU A SET OF SAMPLES, AS ILLUSTRATED, OF THE KIND OF CARPET YOU WANT, SHOWING YOU EXACT QUALITY OF EACH AND EVERY GRADE IN THAT KIND AND AT THE SAME TIME WILL MAIL YOU OUR BEAUTIFUL COLOR BOOK, AS SHOWN ON THE OPPOSITE PAGE, SO THAT YOU MAY SEE THE EXACT COLOR OF EACH DESIGN IN WHICH THE CARPET COMES, ALL FREE AND POSTPAID.

Set No. 1 CONTAINS SAMPLES OF EACH AND EVERY QUALITY WE CARRY IN INGRAIN CARPETS AND IS SENT FREE ON REQUEST.

IF YOU ARE THINKING OF BUYING anything in Ingrain Carpets such as we show on pages 855 to 861 in this catalogue and would like to see the actual quality of the goods before buying, as well as see the actual colors of the designs in which these various qualities come, just write and say, "Send me Set No. 1 of Ingrain Carpet Samples Free," and we will mail you free and postpaid at once this complete set of samples, as illustrated opposite, showing you a fair size sample of each and every quality of Ingrain carpets that we carry from our lowest priced number to our highest priced Ingrain, and at the same time will mail you our great Color Book illustrated and described on the opposite page, thus giving you the most perfect means of selecting your carpets that one could possibly desire, enabling you to see exactly what you are getting in the way of quality and exactly what color combination you can have in each quality.

IF YOU DON'T SELECT YOUR CARPET from this big catalogue don't buy any carpet at any price anywhere else until you get a set of samples and our Color Book, because we are quoting the lowest prices ever named on carpets, quality considered. You can save big money by buying everything in carpets from us.

Set No. 2 CONTAINS SAMPLES OF EACH AND EVERY QUALITY WE CARRY IN BRUSSELS CARPETS AND WILL BE MAILED TO YOU FREE ON REQUEST.

DO YOU WISH TO GET ANY BRUSSELS CARPET? Then don't buy anything of the kind at any furnishing store without testing the remarkable values we are offering in this catalogue. We guarantee to satisfy you or refund your money if you select your carpets from this big catalogue, as our descriptions are accurate and complete; but if you don't feel sure that you can get a good idea from the description in this catalogue, as to exactly how the carpet looks, or if you don't know enough about the quality when you read our descriptions and you want to buy Brussels carpet just write a post card or letter and say, "Please mail me, free and postpaid, Set No. 2 of Brussels Carpet Samples," and we will at once send you this complete set of Brussels Samples, as illustrated opposite, showing you a good sized sample of each and every quality we carry in Brussels carpet from our lowest priced Brussels to the highest grade Brussels in our line so that you may see exactly what quality you are getting and at the same time we will mail you free and postpaid our wonderfully artistic Color Book, described and illustrated on opposite page, in which you will find the exact colors and designs in which each of the qualities of Brussels carpet come. You can therefore make a perfect choice, knowing exactly what you are getting, both in quality and in color.

LOOK THROUGH OUR BIG LINE OF BRUSSELS CARPET in this catalogue. Note the astonishing offers we are making through our methods of controlling the output of big mills and offering our carpet to you on the barest small margin of profit over the actual mill cost of the carpet. If you want the best values ever heard of in Brussels carpet, write for this set of samples and let us show you the actual quality of these goods.

Set No. 3 CONTAINS SAMPLES OF EACH AND EVERY QUALITY WE CARRY IN AXMINSTER, WILTON VELVET AND WILTON CARPET AND WILL BE MAILED TO YOU FREE ON REQUEST.

DON'T BUY AXMINSTER, WILTON VELVET OR WILTON CARPET anywhere else before you see this set of samples. We are offering astonishing values, as compared with retail values in furnishing stores, on this class of goods. These high class carpets are sold on exceptionally big profits at retail; but our wide trade and enormous sales on carpets of all kinds enable us to sell more of these goods than any of the big jobbing houses, so that we get the materials direct from the mills at the lowest mill price ever paid by any house and as we add just one bare small margin of profit our values are truly remarkable. Look through our line of Axminster, Wilton Velvet and Wilton carpets on pages 862 to 866 in this catalogue. Our descriptions are very carefully written and we endeavor to convey the exact idea of each carpet, but if you have the slightest difficulty in forming a perfect idea of the appearance and quality of the goods by all means write to us at once and just say, "Send me Set No. 3 of free samples of Axminster, Wilton Velvet and Wilton carpets," and this complete set of quality samples illustrated opposite will be mailed to you at once free and postpaid and at the same time we will mail you free and postpaid our complete Color Book, as illustrated on opposite page, showing you the actual colors that you can have in each quality of carpet represented by the sample, thus making the most perfect means, the easiest way imaginable of selecting your carpet. The colored photograph plates show exactly how the various floral patterns, panel designs, etc., are worked out in their exact shades, how they are set in the background of various shades.

THESE SAMPLES WILL CONVINCE YOU THAT THE QUALITY of our goods is absolutely the best ever seen at the price. Quality considered, we are quoting the lowest price ever named on carpet. Won't you write and ask for a set of these samples so that we may prove that we save you big money on carpet?

THIS TABLE OF ROOM SIZES WILL HELP YOU TO TELL HOW MUCH CARPET YOU NEED.

WE GIVE A FULL EXPLANATION of this table on the preceding page. If the size of your room is not given in this list, we advise you to allow enough money to pay for the next larger size and we will cut the carpet with the least possible waste and charge only for the exact amount of carpet used in the cutting. In this table we have figured in the waste used in fitting the room, but if in cutting the carpet there happens to be less waste, we will refund whatever balance is due you at the time the shipment is made.

Size of Room, Feet	Yards of Ingrain Carpet (36 inches wide) Needed	Yards of Brussels or Velvet (27 inches wide) Needed	Yards of Brussels or Velvet, Made With Border (including border) Needed	Size of Room, Feet	Yards of Ingrain Carpet (36 inches wide) Needed	Yards of Brussels or Velvet (27 inches wide) Needed	Yards of Brussels or Velvet, Made With Border (including border) Needed	Size of Room, Feet	Yards of Ingrain Carpet (36 inches wide) Needed	Yards of Brussels or Velvet (27 inches wide) Needed	Yards of Brussels or Velvet, Made With Border (including border) Needed	Size of Room, Feet	Yards of Ingrain Carpet (36 inches wide) Needed	Yards of Brussels or Velvet (27 inches wide) Needed	Yards of Brussels or Velvet, Made With Border (including border) Needed
9x9	9½	12¾	17¼	9x17½	18½	24½	31	10x18	21½	28	34½	12x12½	17½	24	29½
9x9½	10	13¼	18	9x18	18½	25	31½	11x11	15½	19½	24½	12x13	18½	25	30½
9x10	10½	14	18½	10x10	12½	16	21	11x11½	15½	20½	25½	12x13½	18¾	26	31½
9x10½	11	14¾	19½	10x10½	13	16¾	21½	11x12	15½	21	26½	12x14	19½	27	32½
9x11	11½	15½	20½	10x11	14½	17¾	22¾	11x12½	17½	21	27½	12x14½	20¼	27¾	33½
9x11½	12	16	21	10x11½	14½	18	23	11x13	18	22¾	28¾	12x15	21¼	28½	34½
9x12	12½	16½	21½	10x12	14½	19	24¼	11x13½	18¾	23½	29¾	12x15½	21¾	29½	35½
9x12½	13	17½	22¾	10x12½	15½	20	25	11x14	19¾	24½	30	12x16	22½	30½	36½
9x13	13½	18	24	10x13	16	20½	25½	11x14½	20½	25½	30¾	12x16½	23	31½	37¾
9x13½	14	18½	25	10x13½	16½	21½	26½	11x15	21	26	32	12x17	23¾	32½	39
9x14	14½	19½	26¼	10x14	17½	22	27½	11x15½	21½	26¾	32½	12x18	25½	34½	40¾
9x14½	15	20½	26¾	10x14½	17½	22½	28½	11x16	22½	27¾	33⅓	13x13	20½	27½	32
9x15	16	21	27	10x15	18½	23½	29½	11x16½	23	28½	34	13x13½	21¼	28½	33
9x15½	16½	21¾	27¾	10x15½	19½	24½	30½	11x17	23¾	29¼	35¼	13x14	22	29½	34
9x16	16½	22¾	28½	10x16	20	25	31	11x17½	24½	30½	36¼	13x14½	22¾	30½	35¼
9x16½	17	23	29¾	10x16½	20½	26	32½	11x18	25	31	37½	13x15	23½	31½	36⅓
9x17	17½	23½	30½	10x17	21	26½	33½	12x12	21½	23¼	28½	13x15½	23¾	32¼	37½

As we have placed several improved carpet sewing machines in our Carpet Department and each machine is in charge of an expert operator we are positive that the carpets will be sewed much better than you can have the work done yourself and we can do it much cheaper for you than you can have the work done. The cost of sewing carpets ordered from us is as follows: Ingrain carpets, per yard...........2c. Brussels, Velvet or Axminster carpets, without border, per yard........3c.   Brussels, Velvet or Axminster carpets, with border, per yard.............10c.

WHEN ORDERING CARPET MADE WITH A BORDER be sure and allow enough money to pay for same, as it will avoid any delay in writing for money to cover cost of goods. Remember, the border is only 22½ inches wide. The body of the carpet is 27 inches wide. The diagram shown on this page is of a room 10 feet 6 inches by 10 feet 6 inches and if you will follow instructions given we do not think you will experience any trouble in allowing enough to pay for carpet and border to fit the room.

Measure the distance around the room in yards, which gives the exact number of yards of border required. In this instance it would be four times 10 feet 6 inches or 42 feet, which is 14 yards of border.

To get the number of strips of carpet, deduct the width of two strips of border or 45 inches from 10 feet 6 inches, which leaves 6 feet 9 inches, or 81 inches. Divide by 27 inches, which is the width of one strip of carpet, which gives the number of strips of carpet needed.

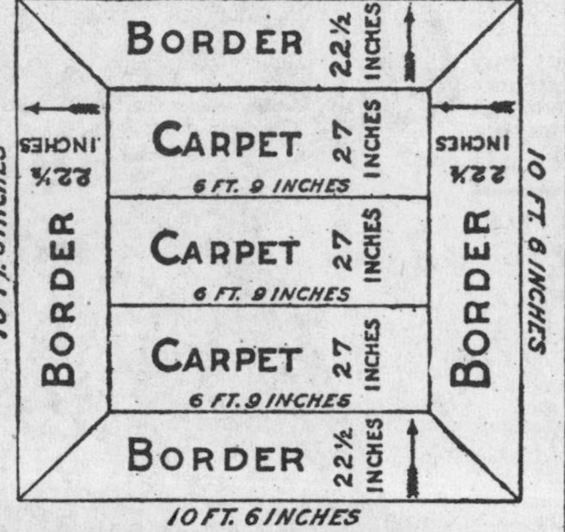

To get the length of the strips, deduct the width of two strips of border or 45 inches from length of room or 10 feet 6 inches, which gives the length of strips, or 6 feet 9 inches. Three strips 6 feet 9 inches would be 20 feet 3 inches or 6¾ yards.

Allow 1½ yards for matching patterns, which would make the total amount of carpet and border to fit a room 10 feet 6 inches by 10 feet 6 inches—22¼ yards. The cost of sewing carpet with border is 10 cents per yard extra.

If your room should require more than an equal number of strips and less than 13 inches in width, you should allow for one-half width of carpet. If more than 13 inches is needed you should allow for one width.

When ordering carpet with border be sure to allow 1½ yards for matching and if we can cut the carpet with less waste we will do so and will only charge for the exact amount of carpet used in cutting. Whatever waste is left will be sent you with balance of goods.

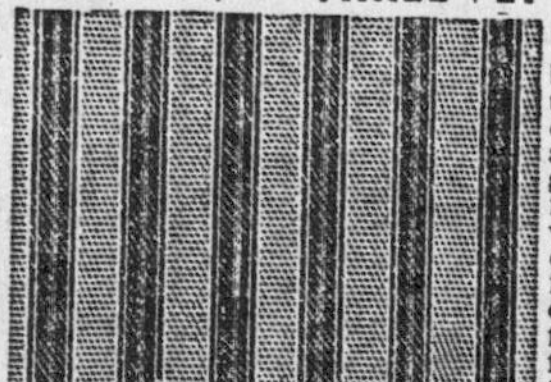

Diagram (center): 10 FT. 6 INCHES — BORDER 22½ INCHES — CARPET 27 INCHES 6 FT. 9 INCHES — CARPET 27 INCHES 6 FT. 9 INCHES — CARPET 27 INCHES 6 FT. 9 INCHES — BORDER 22½ INCHES — 10 FT. 6 INCHES

BELOW WE GIVE AN EXAMPLE of how we figure the amount of carpet and border for a room 10 feet 6 inches by 12 feet 6 inches.

```
10 feet 6 inches
10 feet 6 inches
12 feet 6 inches
12 feet 6 inches
46 feet border, or 15⅓ yards.
10 feet 6 inches, width of room,
 3 feet 9 inches, width of 2 strips of border,
 6 feet 9 inches, width of body of carpet,
12 inches
72 inches
 9 inches
27 | 81 inches, width of body of carpet.
 3, number of strips of carpet required.
```

```
by 12 ft. 6 in., length of room.
by 3 ft. 9 in., width 2 strips border.
 8 ft. 9 in., length of strips.
 3, number of strips.
3 | 26 feet 3 inches
 8¾ yds. carpet.
15⅓ yds. border.
 1½ yds. for matching.
25⁷⁄₁₂ yds. carp't and bor'r.
```

If you wish Brussels, velvet or Axminster carpet made without border, get the width of the room in inches and divide by 27, which gives the number of strips of carpet.

Multiply the number of strips by the length of each strip in feet, which gives the number of feet of carpet. Divide by 3 which leaves the number of yards. For every 25 yards ordered allow 1½ yards for matching.

If the room is odd shaped, having a bay window, fireplace or offset, be sure to send a diagram; also state where entrance and front of room is.

To protect you against any possible dissatisfaction, any chance of loss, to save you time and the slightest disappointment in selecting any carpet from our big line, as shown in this catalogue, we accept any carpet order with this distinct understanding and agreement that if the carpet you receive from us is not even better value than you expected to get, you are at liberty to return it to us at our expense of transportation charges both ways, and we will promptly refund your money.

SPECIAL NOTICE. In ordering carpet matched and sewed, be careful to give the exact size of room or rooms. If an odd size, having a fireplace, bay window or offset, be sure to send a diagram, also indicate on diagram where entrance and front of room is.

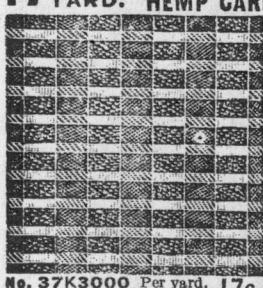

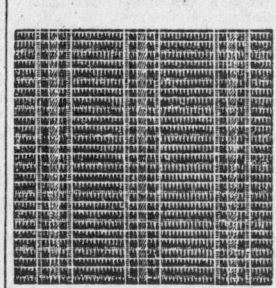
WHEN ORDERING CARPET SEWED OR MADE UP BY US, BE SURE TO GIVE EXACT MEASUREMENTS OF THE ROOM
IF AN ODD SIZE, SEND DIAGRAM, ALSO STATE WHERE ENTRANCE AND FRONT OF ROOM IS.

25 CENTS PER YARD IS OUR LATEST REDUCED PRICE ON THIS SERVICEABLE GRANITE CARPET

THIS No. 37K3032 REPRESENTS the best made Granite Carpet obtainable, and it is guaranteed to you as such. We have determined not to take any chances in failing to satisfy our customers in any carpet quality we furnish. We handle only such grades as will give honest and reliable service. While we could offer you some granite qualities at a lower price than this, and much lower than anyone else would quote on any given quality, yet we figure that when we can offer you a good, standard, perfectly reliable carpet at 25 cents per yard we are doing just the thing that will bring us the carpet trade of the country. By filling an order for one person we are then perfectly sure of the orders from his friends and neighbors, and that is exactly what is happening in this particular case. This is the best grade of granite carpet, a quality we sold at 27 cents last season to over fifteen thousand customers. We are making a reduction of nearly 10 per cent for our new 1908 price, a mill cash price direct to our customers.

WE ADVISE that, in selecting a carpet from us, you look over the line carefully, because you can get some very choice qualities here always at such a low price, as compared with retail prices, that you could readily afford to buy some of our best grades, even though it might cost you just a little more than the quality you thought of buying. It will pay you in the end.

This neat design comes in green and oak; also in red and green.

THIS FLORAL GRANITE CARPET has full 2,000 ends of warp, composed of the very finest prepared cotton and jute. This illustration gives you some idea of the beautiful pattern, an exceedingly rich and stylish floral design, the exact same quality of which we sold over 200,000 yards last season at 27 cents per yard. Reduced to our challenge quality price of 25 cents per yard. **The Colors**—It comes in different color combinations. We have some with neat green and oak colored shades, and some in beautiful effects of red and green. These colors are arranged, in the order of the illustration, in a scroll and floral design showing the leaves plainly, and bringing out a pattern and color effect that harmonizes and is most pleasing. We know that you will consider it, both from the standpoint of quality and pattern, the biggest carpet value ever heard of in granite carpet, and it certainly is. Our price represents just the actual cost of the material and the making of the carpet (the cost in large quantities) with just a bare small margin of profit added. Be sure to tell us in what colors you want this carpet when you order. For an illustration of this pattern in the actual colors, see page 859.

No. 37K3032   Width, 36 inches.
Price, per yard..........................   **25c**

---

30 CENTS PER YARD. TAKE YOUR CHOICE FROM THESE TWO NEW 1908 PATTERNS IN OUR GREAT LEADER CROWN UNION QUALITY INGRAIN CARPET

THIS IS AN EXTRA HEAVY QUALITY that can be depended upon to wear and look well for a very long time. We would be pleased to have you order this quality in either of the patterns described and illustrated below, and compare it with anything to be had elsewhere at much higher prices and you will then see the great saving we can make for you by handling vast quantities of carpet, getting it direct from the weavers and selling it to you on one very small margin of profit. We simply knock off retail profits and expenses and let you get your carpet at as low prices as the dealer pays the jobber.

IF YOU WANT TO SEE THE EXACT QUALITY of this carpet, please be sure to write and ask for free samples of our Ingrain Carpet. See page 853 where we make this offer. While you are perfectly safe in ordering this carpet direct from this description, and we guarantee to please you perfectly or refund your money, yet,

if you prefer to see samples, don't hesitate in the least, but write at once and we will mail you our Set No. 1 of Ingrain Carpets together with our big Special Carpet Catalogue which shows the exact colors and exact designs of the two patterns described and illustrated below.

PLEASE DON'T CONSIDER that this price makes this a poor quality of carpet. Just remember that it is just as fine a carpet as dealers offer at much higher prices, because ours are as low as wholesale prices, and in some cases lower. Remember, if others offer you an ingrain carpet at as low a price as this, it can by no means be of near as good a quality as this is, because they have not the facilities and not the output to enable them to sell a carpet of this quality at as low a price. We are positively the only concern in a position to make this wonderful offer.

DON'T FAIL TO SEND FOR FREE SAMPLES, as shown on page 853. If you would like to see the actual quality of the material.

---

30 CENTS PER YARD. OUR CROWN UNION CARPET IN A NEAT RED AND GREEN, IN A PLEASING LEAF EFFECT.

THIS ILLUSTRATION shows you the general design of one of the pat- terns we offer in our Crown Union Carpet at 30 cents per yard. It is a beautiful red ground with large leaves brought out in pleasing green colors. It is very suitable for any room and is quite stylish and up to date. We are able to offer richer patterns even in our low priced qualities than others use in high priced grades, because we use so much carpet that the mills are willing to put better designing in for us than is commonly put into the average carpet sold at retail. You can order direct from this description, knowing that we guarantee to please you, or you may write and get our Special Carpet Catalogue, shown on page 852, where you will see the actual designs and colors.

No. 37K3036   Width, 36 inches.   Price, per yard..............   **30c**

30 CENTS PER YARD. OUR GREAT CROWN UNION QUALITY IN GREEN AND OAK SCROLL AND LEAF EFFECT.

THIS ILLUSTRATION shows you the layout of the pattern, and if you will examine it carefully and consider that the background is a neat empire green shade with a fine scroll and leaf effect worked out in oak, you can readily understand just about how the color combination looks. For a parlor or bedroom, or the like, this is quite appropriate, and we wish you to remember that, merely because we ask 30 cents per yard for it, it is not the ordinary low priced carpet. It's a much better quality than is being offered at retail for a great deal higher price. We guarantee to please you if you order from this description. For illustration of this pattern in the actual colors, see page 859.

No. 37K3040   Width, 36 inches.   Price, per yard..............   **30c**

65 CENTS PER YARD.

OUR ROYAL EXTRA HEAVY SUPER ALL WOOL REVERSIBLE INGRAIN CARPET

IN TEN RICH DESIGNS TO CHOOSE FROM ON THIS AND THE NEXT PAGE.

THIS SPLENDID QUALITY ALL WOOL REVERSIBLE INGRAIN CARPET at 65 cents per yard is better carpet than is being offered at retail in furnishing stores at 80 to 90 cents per yard. It is woven from all wool, thoroughly cleansed high grade yarn and every yard is perfectly inspected before leaving the mill. It is closely woven and has a fine luster. When you can get such an excellent quality as this at 65 cents per yard and get it in such beautiful color combinations and rich designs as appear on this and on the next page, it will certainly pay you to select this for your job of carpeting. WE WILL MAIL YOU A SET OF SAMPLES FREE on request together with our great color catalogue as explained on page 853, and if desired we will cut, match and sew the carpet to fit any room at only 2 cents per yard. Be sure to give us the size of your room.

---

65 CENTS PER YARD. OUR ROYAL ALL WOOL INGRAIN CARPET IN DARK GREEN AND A FLORAL DESIGN OF SCARLET IN A VERY FINE SHADE.

THIS ILLUSTRATION shows you the floral design very clearly and when you consider that this is worked out in the rich shades of green and scarlet arranged in perfect harmony you can imagine pretty clearly the stylish effect. We guarantee to satisfy you perfectly if you order direct from this description, but will gladly send our free Special Carpet Catalogue on request, as stated on page 852. We consider this number one of the very neat designs in our assortment of ten designs in this 65-cent quality of ingrain. It is perfectly reversible, the other side having a scarlet ground with dark green floral effects. State the size of room if you want the carpet cut and matched.

No. 37K3072
Width, 36 inches.
Price, per yard 65c

65 CENTS PER YARD. OUR ROYAL EXTRA HEAVY SUPER ALL WOOL INGRAIN CARPET IN DELICATE TAN WITH ARTISTIC FLORAL AND SCROLL DESIGN AND FERN LEAVES.

A GREAT FEATURE of our 65-cent ingrain is the fine Moresque yarn used and its very close weave, giving it a luster not usually found in ingrain. Note the illustration. This effect is worked out in a delicate shade of tan. The design consists of an artistic scroll with a floral effect and fern leaves. This is by no means a flashy or gaudy carpet that will offend good taste, but is just the rich, very neat plain and stylish design so much liked by householders of modest taste. While we are perfectly sure we can satisfy you by ordering from this catalogue, yet if you have any doubts as to the appearance of the goods we will gladly mail you our free Special Carpet Catalogue, on request, showing the actual colors. Free samples also if desired.

No. 37K3084
Width, 36 inches.
Price, per yard 65c

---

65 CENTS PER YARD. OUR ROYAL HIGH GRADE ALL WOOL INGRAIN CARPET IN TAN WITH LEAF FLORAL DESIGN IN BROWN AND GREEN.

OUR ILLUSTRATIONS show you how each pattern is arranged. This one has a small leaf floral design in brown and green shading on a background of tan, a very modest, tasteful and restful combination of colors. This design is selected by us as one that will harmonize with almost any surroundings. There is nothing in it to mar the neatness and harmony of colors in any room. If you want a very choice, neat and attractive design for your dining room, library or parlor you certainly have it in this number. We show you the actual colors of this carpet on page 859 of this catalogue.

No. 37K3076
Width, 36 inches.
Price, per yard 65c

65 CENTS PER YARD. OUR ROYAL EXTRA FINE ALL WOOL REVERSIBLE INGRAIN CARPET IN A RED GROUND, WITH GREEN SCROLL AND LEAF EFFECT.

YOU will not find high class patterns of this nature elsewhere, because this is one of our own exclusive designs, a handsome effect brought out by the mill according to our own directions. We consider it one of the most pleasing and up to date effects on the market. We show its actual colors on page 859 of this catalogue. It is arranged like illustration, the ground being a handsome red and the scroll and small leaf effect brought out in green, an entirely new arrangement that we know will be perfectly satisfactory in any room. We design our patterns so that they will harmonize with the general house furnishings to be found anywhere.

No. 37K3088
Width, 36 inches.
Price, per yard 65c

---

65 CENTS PER YARD. ROYAL EXTRA SUPER ALL WOOL INGRAIN CARPET IN TAN WITH LIGHT BROWN AND OLIVE SCROLLS

REMEMBER, our carpet is made under our own supervision and we guarantee the quality throughout and offer only the neatest and choicest designs of the season. This Royal two-ply all wool carpet comes in a fine shade of tan ground with a combination of light brown and olive scrolls and floral effects, which harmonize very beautifully with any class of furnishings in your room. We feel quite sure that if you told us to send you our 65-cent quality and didn't say anything about the color and we sent you this one, you would be satisfied. It is well adapted for the quality, and it pleases practically everybody.

No. 37K3080
Width, 36 inches.
Price, per yard 65c

65 CENTS PER YARD. A MOST PLEASING EFFECT IN OUR ROYAL EXTRA HEAVY REVERSIBLE INGRAIN CARPET.

REMEMBER, our 65-cent ingrain is a guaranteed two-ply firmly woven carpet, perfectly reversible, that is, can be used on both sides. This is a decidedly pleasing combination. The ground is a neat tan shade with scrolls and leaves brought out in fine shades of green and oak, their natural colors. Tan, brown and green effects are exceedingly popular, because they are modest and generally harmonize beautifully with the surroundings of the average room. One of the great features of our carpet department is that you can get choicer designs at lower prices than you will get in much higher priced carpet at retail. Remember, we will send our Special Carpet Catalogue, showing colors and a set of samples free on request.

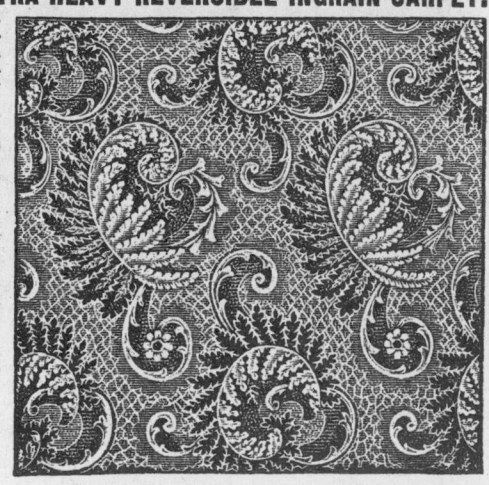

No. 37K3092
Width, 36 inches.
Price, per yard 65c

YOUR MONEY WILL BE IMMEDIATELY RETURNED TO YOU FOR ANY GOODS NOT PERFECTLY SATISFACTORY.

549

OUR HIGHEST GRADE BRUSSELS CARPETS

87c PER YARD. OUR WONDERFUL VALUE IN TEN-WIRE TAPESTRY BRUSSELS AND TWO SPLENDID DESIGNS TO CHOOSE FROM.

This is one of our extra good qualities, a high grade ten-wire Tapestry Brussels Carpet and comes in two handsome designs and color effects, illustrated and described directly below in this column. WE GUARANTEE TO SAVE YOU FROM 20 TO 40 PER CENT ON THIS GRADE. WE WILL MAIL YOU A SAMPLE OF IT FREE ON REQUEST.

87c PER YARD. OUR TEN-WIRE TAPESTRY BRUSSELS PARLOR CARPET IN A RICH BOUQUET AND FOLIAGE DESIGN.

NOTE THIS ILLUSTRATION and you will see that it forms the basis for a very pleasing color combination. The background is a rich dark green. In this a fine scroll and bouquet of roses in red and yellow are worked out, intermingled with foliage shading from a deep, rich dark green to a beautiful shade of nile green. Green grounds and floral effects of this nature are exceedingly popular. They form restful effects and give a fashionable appearance to any room. We guarantee to please you or refund your money if you order direct from

this discription, but if you would like to see the actual colors before ordering, write for our free Special Carpet Catalogue, shown on page 852.

No. 37K3144 Width, 27 inches. Price, per yard..87c
No. 37K3144 Border to match. Width, 22½ inches. Price, per yard............87c

87c PER YARD. BUYS OUR BEAUTIFUL TAN GROUND GENUINE TEN-WIRE TAPESTRY BRUSSELS CARPET.

THIS NUMBER makes a decidedly beautiful floor covering for a parlor. It's the same quality as the above number, an extra heavy, well made long wearing, serviceable material. The illustration shows the pattern. The ground is a beautiful tan shade with a design of large red roses and green leaves intermingled with a scroll of tobacco brown, which harmonizes very nicely. Consider this color effect and the fact that it is a ten-wire guaranteed high grade Brussels at the same time, and you will understand something of the re-

markable values we offer. Do you want a good, substantial carpet? Then we wish to especially recommend this one. Remember, we are always glad to furnish samples free on request, together with our Special Carpet Catalogue, to show the color.

No. 37K3148 Width, 27 inches. Price, per yard............87c
No. 37K3148 Border to match. Width, 22½ inches. Price, per yard............87c

---

WHEN YOU CAN GET GOOD QUALITIES OF BRUSSELS CARPETS like these for such low prices, prices that are much lower than the price you pay at retail for very inferior qualities, surely it needs no argument to prove that it really pays big to buy these in place of the cheaper qualities. While our lower priced carpets are absolutely the best value that money will bring in such qualities and will last a surprisingly long time considering the price you pay, yet for very little more money, as you see, we can offer the very best Tapestry Brussels Carpets, which will last so much longer and always look so much better that you will never regret having paid the difference for them. Our sales for the past two years have been steadily turning to our best carpets until now we have enormous sales on our best qualities throughout the entire line, that being one reason why we can make such wonderfully low prices on the highest grades. We handle more high grade carpets than the big exclusive jobbing houses handle in all grades combined.

> SAMPLES OF THESE CARPETS will be mailed free on request, together with our Special Carpet Catalogue, showing the actual colors. See our great offer on pages 852 and 853.

74c PER YARD. OUR GREAT OFFER IN NINE-WIRE TAPESTRY BRUSSELS HALL AND STAIR CARPET.

COMES IN THE CHOICE DESIGN HERE ILLUSTRATED, BUT IN THREE DIFFERENT COLORS, GREEN, TAN AND RED.

DO YOU WANT THE BEST VALUES OBTAINABLE

in Brussels Hall and Stair Carpet? Here we certainly offer you a carpet that will stand plenty of wear and tear and is expressly woven to stand the extra wear always given to hall and stair carpets, especially made to withstand the constant service given to hall or stair carpet placed where it always gets the most wear and tear of any carpet in the house. It is strictly the finest nine-wire tapestry hall or stair carpet on the market. It is the best, both in quality and in design and coloring. When you know that we handle and contract for enormous quantities with the mills at rock bottom prices and offer it to you on a very small margin of profit, you can see why it is possible to offer it at 74 cents per yard.

Note the colors as quoted below: Green, tan and red; they all come in this same design, of which this illustration is a perfect reproduction. It is a neat, attractive, modest effect that will be liked by everybody.

Order the number below which represents the color you want and the hall or stair carpet you want. The hall carpet has no border at the sides, as shown in the stair carpet above.

All this hall and stair carpet is 27 inches wide and comes in the above illustrated design but in the following variety of colors:

No. 37K3160	Green, Hall Carpet. Price, per yard..74c
No. 37K3164	Green, Stair Carpet. Price, per yard..74c
No. 37K3168	Tan, Hall Carpet. Price, per yard..74c
No. 37K3172	Tan, Stair Carpet. Price, per yard..74c
No. 37K3176	Red, Hall Carpet. Price, per yard..74c
No. 37K3180	Red, Stair Carpet. Price, per yard..74c

No border to match this carpet.

FOR 3 CENTS PER YARD

we cut, match and sew our Brussels Carpet to fit any room. BE SURE TO GIVE THE SIZE OF THE ROOM, which is simply explained on page 854.

96c PER YARD. OUR HIGHEST GRADE BRUSSELS CARPET, MADE FROM FINE WORSTED YARN AND OFFERED IN ORIENTAL AND FLORAL DESIGNS.

When you get this carpet you absolutely know that you have something that will last almost a lifetime and will always look well. THE RICH QUALITY AND THE DISTINCTIVE HIGH CLASS PATTERNS and COLORINGS appeal to everybody at a glance. You will not duplicate this quality under $1.50 at retail. WE WILL GLADLY FURNISH SAMPLES FREE to prove this statement.

96c PER YARD. OUR HIGHEST GRADE BRUSSELS IN THIS FASHIONABLE ORIENTAL DESIGN.

THIS is an entirely new pattern made expressly for us and we were careful in making the selection ourselves to secure an original high class oriental effect. It is a decidedly rich design for the parlor or library. It has the very latest style of colorings in the rich oriental colors of medium cardinal ground and tan with fine green shades and a spray of brown and dark olive in the relief. We are positively sure that you will not equal the effect in quality and pattern under $1.50 per yard at retail. We guarantee to perfectly satisfy you if you order from this description,

but we will also be more than pleased to have you favor us with your request for free samples and free Special Carpet Catalogue.

No. 37K3152 Width, 27 inches. Price, per yard..96c
No. 37K3152 Border to match. Width, 22½ inches. Price, per yard............96c

96c PER YARD. OUR HIGHEST GRADE BRUSSELS CARPET IN OUR OWN EXCLUSIVE FLORAL DESIGN.

NOTICE the pleasing and new effect in the pattern shown in the illustration. It is a design worked out in our own carpet department. The ground is a rich shade of dark tan with a floral design in pink flowers and green leaves, the colors harmonizing beautifully and producing a modest, restful and very stylish effect in any room. At a glance your friends and neighbors will recognize this as a very high grade Brussels. It shows the quality plainly and unless you would actually show them the price you paid they would hardly consider it possible

that you got it for 96 cents per yard if they did not know of Sears, Roebuck & Co.'s carpet values. We furnish a neat border to match, which adds greatly to a finely furnished room, much as a frame does to a picture.

No. 37K3156 Width, 27 inches. Price, per yard............96c
No. 37K3156 Border to match. Width, 22½ inches. Price, per yard............96c

$1.14 PER YARD THE HIGHEST GRADE AXMINSTER CARPET

MADE IN TWO OF THE RICHEST DESIGNS EVER BROUGHT OUT.

THIS IS OUR VERY BEST AXMINSTER CARPET, one that it will pay you to buy, because it will serve you the rest of your life. It is composed of the very finest yarn, has a very high pile, soft, luxuriant and will lie smoothly on the floor, because it is made of very heavy material. Before buying any carpet, figure which is the best to buy in the long run. You don't want to buy carpet often. This carpet will last two and three times as long as other grades and it's only $1.14 per yard. WRITE AND ASK FOR A FREE SAMPLE AND WE WILL BE GLAD TO MAIL IT TO YOU AT ONCE. SEE PAGE 853.

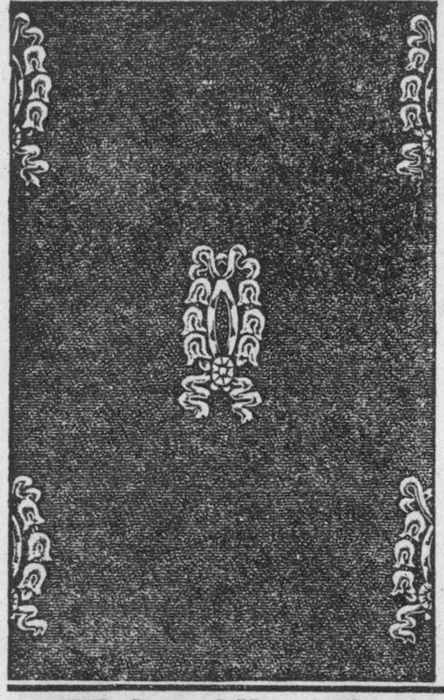

$1.14 PER YARD OUR HIGHEST GRADE AXMINSTER IN LUXURIANT MOTTLED GREEN WITH A UNIQUE DAINTY FIGURE IN BROWN AND ECRU.

IT TAKES RICH CARPET QUALITY in order to produce the most fashionable and high class designs and colorings. Here is one of exceptionally fine taste. It is very modest, with very little figure in it, but that very fact will make it exceedingly popular with those who are looking for simply **plain elegance. The background** is a fine mottled green, perfectly plain and the dainty figure shown in the illustration is in brown and ecru color, these figures being eighteen inches apart. You can very readily grasp the appearance of this even without seeing it in actual colors, but we will be especially glad if you will give us the opportunity to send you our Special Carpet Catalogue, free, as illustrated on page 852, so that you can see something of the richness of this pattern. There is a very neat border also offered to match it and which has a beautiful floral green edge which sets off the carpet magnificently. **Remember, this carpet doesn't cost as much as other carpets, considering its lasting qualities.**

No. 37K3244 Width, 27 inches. Price, per yard........ **$1.14**

No. 37K3244 Border to match. Width, 22½ inches. Price, per yard.................. **$1.14**

$1.14 PER YARD OUR HIGHEST GRADE AXMINSTER IN OUR GRAND PERSIAN DESIGN. THE LOWEST PRICE WE EVER MADE.

THIS IS CERTAINLY the newest style and most fashionable design obtainable in Axminster. Persian effects are considered the very latest and we have selected the best design of this class made this season. Because of using enormous quantities we are always permitted to get the choice of the best designs by the highest class artists. **The background** is a beautiful dark tan with neat set figures in red, ecru, cardinal and green. The illustration here shows you the general plan. Remember, this carpet and the one illustrated on the left are our best Axminsters, the best goods of that kind produced, with a rich, high pile and a quality of the heaviest kind. The carpet will last a lifetime and give your room a most decidedly rich appearance. You need not be particularly anxious about your other furnishings in the room if you have a carpet of this high grade on your floor. Alone it will give your room a finished appearance. **Always state size of room in ordering.**

No. 37K3248 Width, 27 inches. Price, per yard........ **$1.14**

No. 37K3248 Border to match Width, 22½ inches. Price, per yard.............. **$1.14**

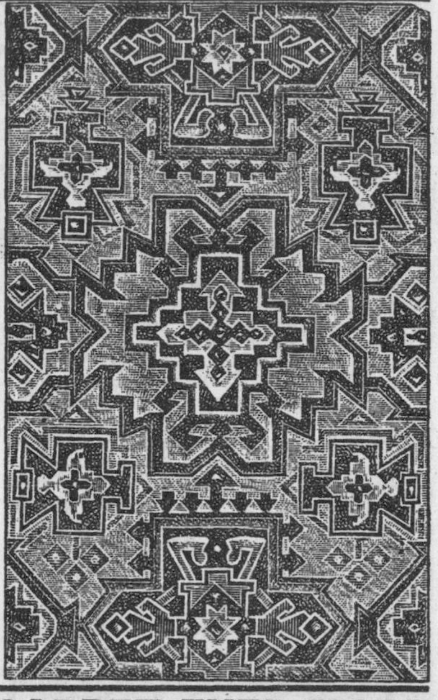

$1.29 PER YARD OUR REDUCED PRICE FOR THE BEST WILTON CARPET EVER MADE

EVERY CENT YOU PAY OVER $1.29 A YARD FOR CARPET IS WASTED MONEY. Wilton Carpet is offered at as high as $2.50 a yard in furnishing stores throughout the country, but no matter what the price, there is no better grade than ours at $1.29 per yard, offered in these two elegant and fashionable designs here illustrated. **$1.29 IS OUR DIRECT FROM THE LOOM PRICE.** Just the same one small profit added to mill cost as we make on our 25-cent Granite Carpet. We sold thousands upon thousands of yards of this same best quality last season at $1.31 per yard. A contract for a greatly increased quantity has enabled us to save on the mill cost, and our rigid policy price rule of only one small profit enables us to bring it down this season to $1.29 per yard. There is nothing better, nothing superior in quality to this our highest grade heavy luxuriant Wilton Carpet, composed of the finest worsted yarn. Quality sample free on request

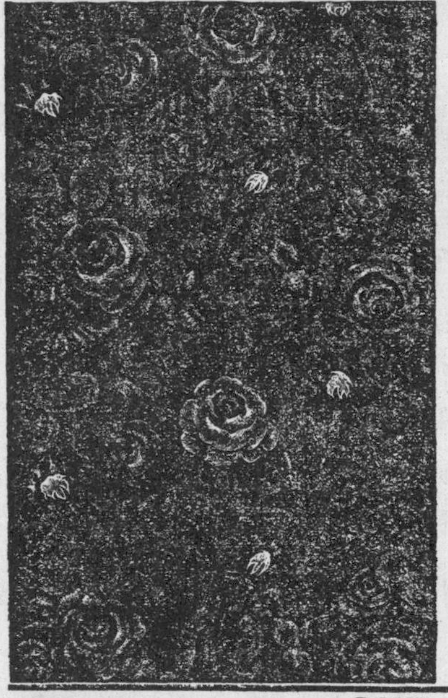

$1.29 PER YARD OUR SPECIAL HIGHEST GRADE WILTON CARPET IN FINE DARK GREEN AND SELECT HARMONIZING COLORS.

REMEMBER, this is the best Wilton Carpet made, composed of the very finest worsted yarn with a rich, soft, glossy finish and is a very much finer class than the Wilton velvets at the highest prices offered at retail. You can, therefore, realize how splendid the following pattern comes out in such a quality. The background is an exceedingly fine dark green, deeper and richer than you can get in ordinary carpet. In this are set the neat, small blossoms shown in the illustration here, which are in pink with neat olive effects and shades of nile green harmonizing most beautifully. Nothing short of seeing the carpet yourself could do it justice, although we guarantee to satisfy you if you order from this description, and we will be more than glad, if you don't feel like ordering it from the description, **if you will write for our free Special Carpet Catalogue,** illustrated on page 852, in which we show this high class carpet in the actual colors. You can't find such beautiful designs in retail stores. With a limited means they can't command such designs as these.

No. 37K3252 Width, 27 inches. Price, per yard........ **$1.29**

No. 37K3252 Border to match. Width, 22½ inches. Price, per yard.............. **$1.29**

$1.29 PER YARD OUR HIGHEST GRADE WILTON IN THE VERY LATEST RICH PERSIAN EFFECT.

PLEASE CONSIDER when buying carpet that it is something that you prefer to buy only once in a long time. You don't wish to be obliged to buy carpet very soon again. This high grade Wilton is something that will last you a lifetime and it really costs you less at $1.29 per yard than the average carpet costs at half the price, because it wears from two to three times as long as ordinary carpet, and remember, this grade would cost you an exceedingly fancy price if you could get it at all in any furnishing store. The design is one of the most select and artistic Persian effects we could find among all the designs of the best artists this season. It comes in the lasting colors of green, brown, cardinal and ecru arranged in the most perfect harmony and in the quaint Persian style so universally admired. Remember, when you put this on the floor of the parlor it will add a dignity and style to the room that nothing else could, not even the finest furniture could express so well the desired effect of elegance as this carpet. We offer, too, a rich border which will set this carpet off with great distinction.

No. 37K3256 Width, 27 inches. Price, per yard........ **$1.29**

No. 37K3256 Border to match. Width, 22½ inches. Price, per yard.............. **$1.29**

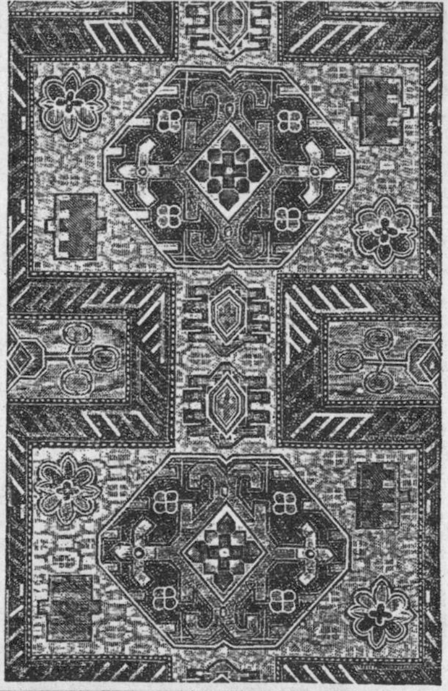

OUR LATEST BIG VALUES IN STAIR CARPETS

11c Per Yard THE GREATEST POSSIBLE VALUE TO BE HAD IN HEMP STAIR CARPET.

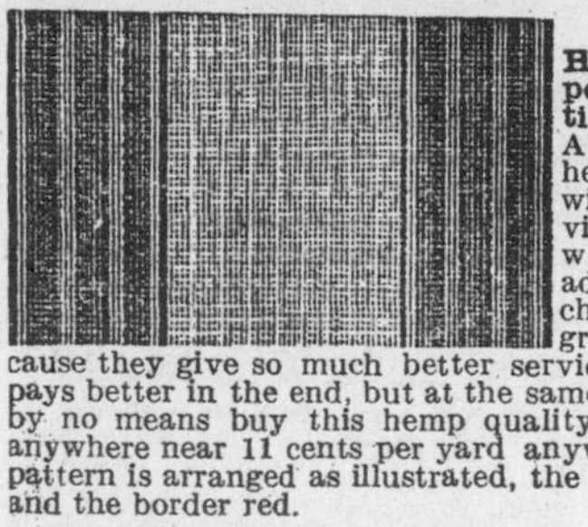

This 18-inch Hemp Stair Carpet is an exceptional bargain. Although only hemp carpet, you will find it very serviceable. Of course, we naturally advise the purchase of better grade carpets, because they give so much better service that it really pays better in the end, but at the same time you could by no means buy this hemp quality stair carpet for anywhere near 11 cents per yard anywhere else. The pattern is arranged as illustrated, the center being tan and the border red.

No. 37K3260 Width, 18 inches. Price, per yard........................ **11c**

20c Per Yard EXTRA HEAVY GRANITE STAIR CARPET.

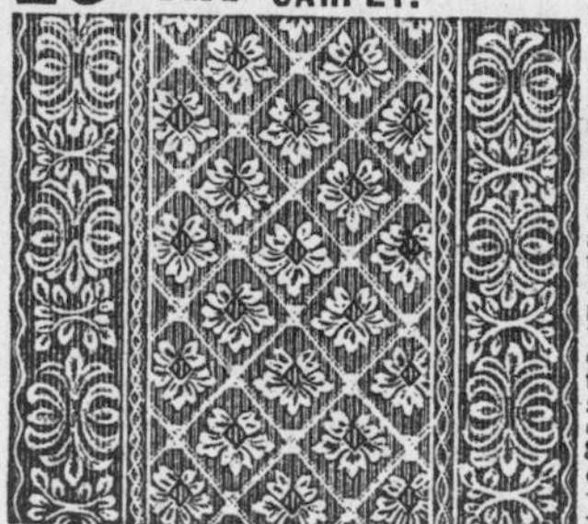

This 22½-inch extra heavy Granite Stair Carpet in a fancy design and good colors is certainly priced extremely low at 20 cents. It is furnished in a rich combination of red and tan or green and tan, as preferred. It is a fine quality of granite carpet and unless you wish to order one of our better stair carpets, such as the one on the right or those on pages 863 and 864, you will certainly get big value out of this. It wears well and has every appearance of a much higher priced material.

No. 37K3264 Width, 22½ inches. Price, per yard........................ **20c**

36c Per Yard OUR BEST QUALITY INGRAIN STAIR CARPET.

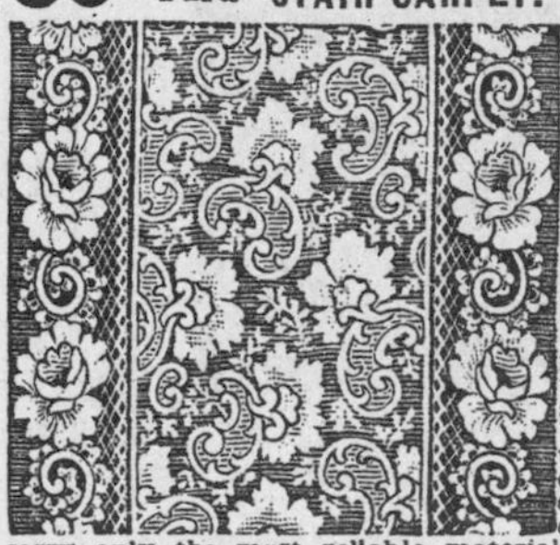

This fine 22½-inch Ingrain Stair Carpet is positively the most remarkable quality offered to you at such a price as 36 cents per yard. Order it and compare with what you get at retail at 50 cents per yard and we guarantee you can get nothing finer than this. It comes in the staple colors of red and green, red and tan, green and tan, scarlet and green and in two-toned red. We guarantee to positively please you in every way with the quality and appearance of these goods. We carry only the most reliable materials on the market and protect you against all defects.

No. 37K3268 Width, 22½ inches. Price, per yard.. **36c**

OUR BIG OFFERS IN IMPORTED MATTINGS

OUR CHINA, JAPANESE AND OTHER MATTINGS are imported direct by us. We don't depend on jobbers at all. We save their profits and expenses and give you the benefit of it, quoting you as low prices as the dealer himself ordinarily pays the jobber at wholesale. Thus we vastly undersell all others in mattings.

WE CARRY ONLY HIGH GRADE STOCK throughout, and here offer you a larger variety than any furnishing store in your neighborhood carries. We guarantee these to be the latest and freshest goods obtainable.

OUR FOUR SELECT QUALITIES IN IMPORTED CHINA MATTINGS

18c PER YARD. FANCY JOINTLESS CHINA MATTING.

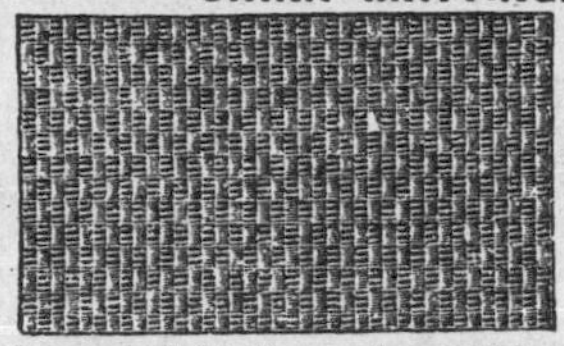

Guaranteed jointless and a good fancy imported quality. Comes in a variety of fancy patterns and colorings of which the illustration is one. The patterns are small, medium and large and colors are green, red, blue, red and tan, or green and tan. State color wanted. By buying a full piece of 40 yards it costs you 1 cent per yard less.

No. 37K3272 Width, 36 inches.
Price, per yard............$0.18
Price, per roll of 40 yards...... 6.80

20c PER YARD. EXTRA QUALITY FANCY MATTING.

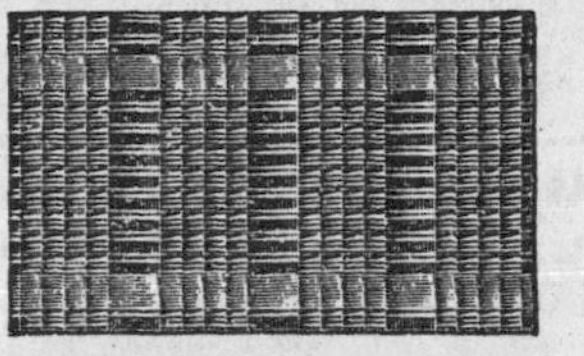

A much better matting than usually offered by dealers at 30 cents per yard. Imported direct by us from Canton, China. Very closely woven and comes in various designs and colors in patterns either small, medium or large. The colors are green, red or blue. State the color you prefer.

No. 37K3276 Width, 36 inches.
Price, per yard..............$0.20
Price, per roll of 40 yards...... 7.60

23c PER YARD BUYS THIS EXTRA FINE IMPORTED CHINA MATTING.

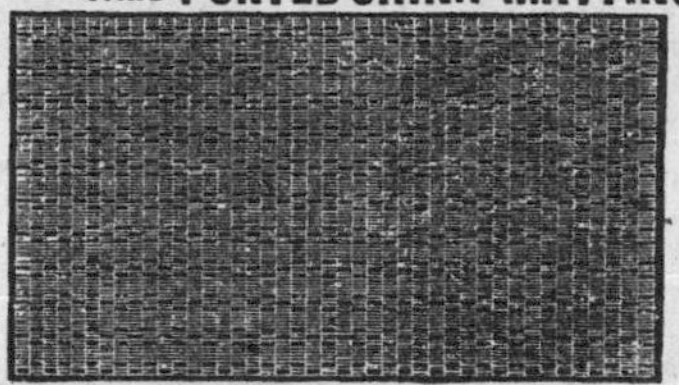

Do you want a China Matting that gives extra good service and always looks neat and clean? This is the kind. It is an extra heavy quality and comes in fancy patterns in such colors as red, green or blue. State color wanted. A full roll costs you $8.80 but of course we sell any quantity you desire. Quantities less than a full roll cost 23 cents per yard.

No. 37K3280 Width, 36 inches.
Price, per yard.........................$0.23
Price, per roll of 40 yards...................... 8.80

27c Per Yard. OUR VERY BEST SPECIAL QUALITY IMPORTED CHINA MATTING.

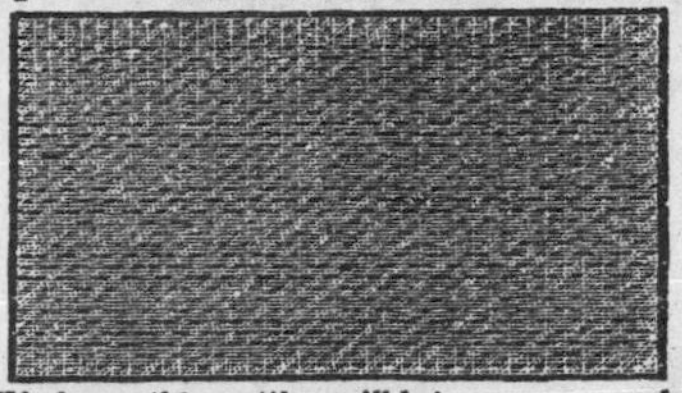

We know this matting will bring us more orders from each locality to which we ship it, because it is an astonishing value for quality, weight, and neatness of pattern. It is far better than mattings sold at retail at from 35 to 40 cents per yard. Our sales on it vastly increase each season and this season we offer a better value than ever. The colors are red, green or blue. State color wanted. The patterns are especially neat and attractive.

No. 37K3284 Width, 36 inches.
Price, per yard...........................$ 0.27
Price, per roll of 40 yards..................... 10.40

98c PER YARD. OUR CORRUGATED HEAVY RUBBER MATTING.

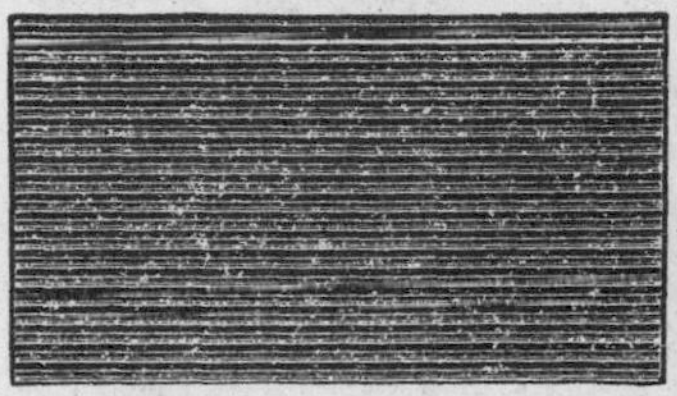

Rubber matting is used principally for the aisles in halls, churches, restaurants, or any public place, as it deadens the noise, and being extra heavy will give good wear.

Weight, about 6½ to 7 pounds per yard. You make a saving of 40 per cent by buying of us.

No. 37K3456 Width, 36 inches.
Price, per yard................98c

HIGH GRADE IMPORTED FANCY WOVEN JAPANESE MATTING.

We import these goods direct from Kobe, Japan. They are the finest goods made and our prices are less than the dealer ordinarily pays at wholesale.

23c Per Yard. OUR SPECIAL POPULAR SELLING JAPANESE MATTING

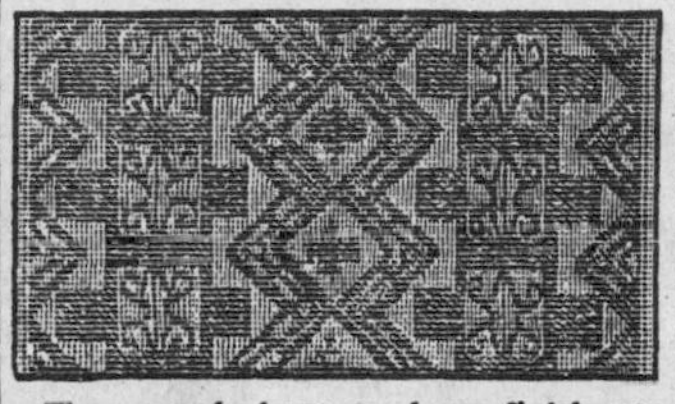

These goods have a glossy finish, are neatly woven and sell at a much higher price at retail. The patterns come in endless varieties, are small, medium and large; and the colors come in red, green or blue. State color wanted. They make a very tasteful, neat and sanitary covering for the floors in the kitchen, bedroom, hall, etc., and wear splendidly. We import all these goods direct and our values are accordingly most remarkable.

No. 37K3288 Width, 36 inches.
Price, per yard...............$0.23
Price, per roll of 40 yards........ 8.80

25c Per Yard. AN EXCEPTIONALLY GOOD QUALITY IMPORTED JAPANESE MATTING.

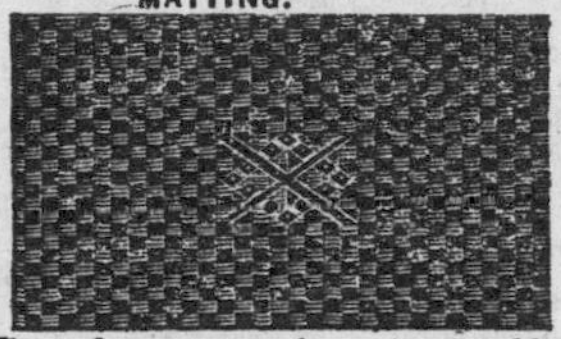

These Japanese goods are imported by us direct from Kobe, Japan, and our price barely covers the actual cost. We handle such vast quantities that we allow ourselves a profit so small that the furnishing houses would not call it a profit at all. We offer them by the yard or roll at lower prices than dealers pay in quantities at wholesale. This special grade has a fine lustrous finish and comes in various designs, on the order of illustration, and the colors are in red, green or blue. State color wanted. It makes a decidedly pleasing and sanitary floor covering.

No. 37K3292 Width, 36 inches.
Price, per yard........................$0.25
Price, per roll of 40 yards.......... 9.60

27c Per Yard. SELECTED QUALITY OF FINE JAPANESE MATTING.

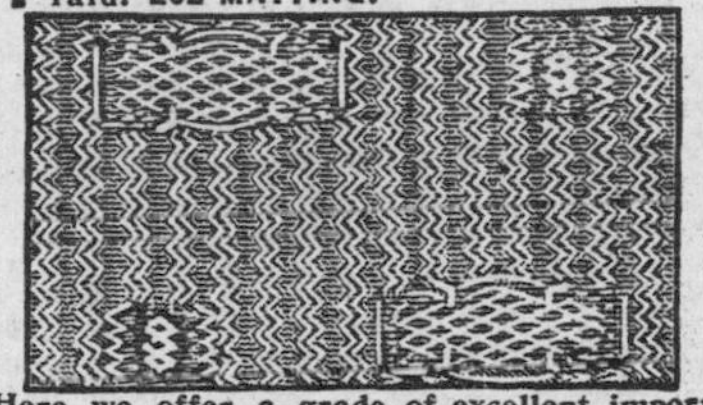

Here we offer a grade of excellent imported goods, very closely woven, of smooth finish and made of the very best selected straw. It comes in a great variety of pretty designs, one of which we illustrate and the colors are in red, green or blue. State color wanted. We are at least saving you 10 to 15 cents per yard on these mattings. We are endeavoring to save our customers as much as possible in every line and we know that we have accomplished great economies for you in Japanese matting. It is a floor covering of world wide reputation as being neat, clean and economical, and we know this quality will give you any amount of service.

No. 37K3296 Width, 36 inches.
Price, per yard............................$ 0.27
Price, per roll of 40 yards.................. 10.40

Zinc Ends.
(Riveted on to Matting)

No. 37K3328 For 18-inch width. Price for each end.......12c
No. 37K3332 For 27-inch width. Price for each end.......19c
No. 37K3336 For 36-inch width. Price for each end.......24c
No. 37K3340 For 45-inch width. Price for each end.......31c
No. 37K3344 For 54-inch width. Price for each end.......36c

Zinc Ends.
(Not Riveted on to Matting).
PRICES INCLUDE RIVETS AND BURRS.

No. 37K3328 For 18-inch width. Price for each end....... 8c
No. 37K3332 For 27-inch width. Price for each end.......12c
No. 37K3336 For 36-inch width. Price for each end.......16c
No. 37K3340 For 45-inch width. Price for each end.......20c
No. 37K3344 For 54-inch width. Price for each end.......24c

27c PER YARD. OUR NEW JAPANESE SUMA MATTING IN SPECIALLY BEAUTIFUL DESIGNS AND COLORINGS.

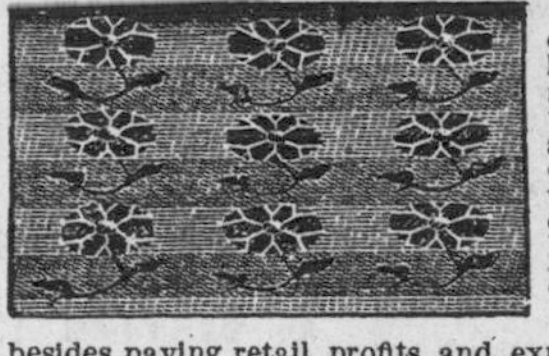

Our direct importations of this special brand in large quantities some months ago have enabled us to quote you a remarkably low price when you consider what the goods would cost under the present conditions of the market and you will certainly pay the long price if you buy this quality in furnishing stores elsewhere, for besides paying retail profits and expenses, you will pay the present rate for imported goods. **The patterns are exceptionally beautiful**, one of which we illustrate. They come in rich shades of red and tan background with red figure and green leaf effect while the reverse side is red and green. We can't guarantee to furnish any one particular pattern but will certainly furnish one equally as beautiful as this.

No. 37K3300 Width, 36 inches. Price, per yd..$ 0.27
Price, per roll of 40 yards.................. 10.40

28c PER YARD. SOMETHING FANCY. A VERY LIGHT TAN INLAID FIGURE JAPANESE MATTING.

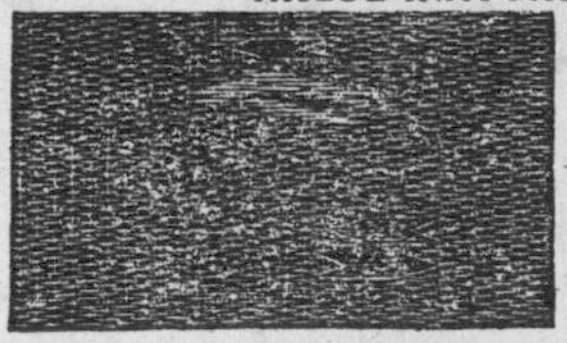

This is our finest high grade imported Japanese goods, an exceedingly stylish floor covering, gotten up for us by our foreign connections, on the most favorable terms, thus enabling us to offer an exclusive, very fashionable material at an extremely low price. It is a better, finer finished cotton warp matting than was ever sold at less than 50 cents per yard. **It comes in a very light or whitish tan color with a fancy inlaid figure** and is very beautiful. A room looks 100 per cent better after you put this matting in as it has a dainty and artistic appearance and yet is strong and very serviceable. If you want something high class and durable, order this.

No. 37K3304 Width, 36 inches.
Price, per yard...............................$ 0.28
Price, per roll of 40 yards...................... 10.80

OUR LINE OF MATTINGS ADAPTED FOR AISLES IN CHURCHES, SCHOOLS AND PUBLIC HALLS

20 TO 60 Cents Per Yard. OUR IMPERIAL NAPIER MATTING IN AN EXTRA HEAVY QUALITY.

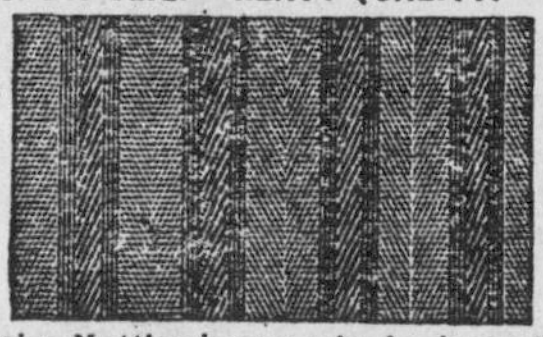

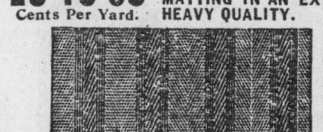

Napier Matting is recognized principally as a floor covering for church aisles, lodge rooms, halls or public places of any kind where there is a great deal of walking done. We are offering an extra heavy grade of Napier matting at from 20 to 60 cents per yard, according to width. From the illustration you will get an idea of the stripe effect it comes in. It is a medium sized stripe, and comes in colors of red and tan only.

No. 37K3308 Width, 18 inches. Price, per yard.........................20c
No. 37K3312 Width, 27 inches. Price, per yard.........................30c
No. 37K3316 Width, 36 inches. Price, per yard.........................40c
No. 37K3320 Width, 45 inches. Price, per yard.........................50c
No. 37K3324 Width, 54 inches. Price, per yard.........................60c

27c TO 81c PER YARD. OUR DOUBLE TWILL MALABAR INDIA MATTING. THE BEST MADE.

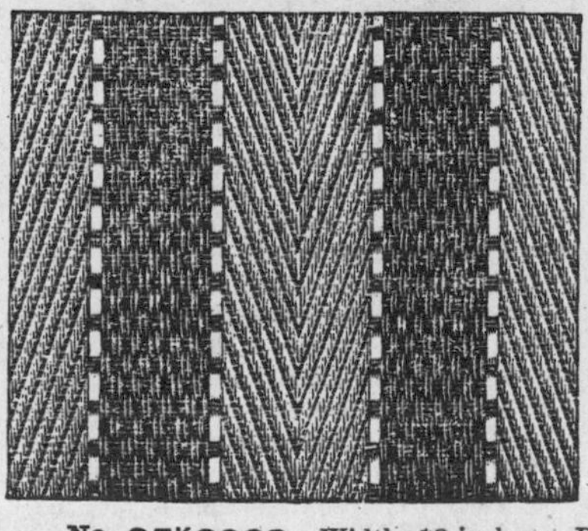

Everyone knows how well cocoa matting wears and you can get some idea of this quality when you understand that we guarantee this double twill Malabar India Matting to be positively the strongest, most durable and neatest cocoa matting made. It is reversible and can be worn on either side, so that it will give extraordinarily long service. The illustration here shows you the way the pattern runs and you can see the neat stripe effect in which it comes and see how closely it is woven. **The color is a neat effect in red and tan.** It is both a handsome and a practical color combination. Don't pay fancy retail prices for these goods when you can buy them from us at prices as low as dealers pay at wholesale. If you or any of your friends are interested in churches, public halls or schools, etc., **this represents a big value for you.**

No. 37K3368	Width, 18 inches.	Price, per yard..........27c
No. 37K3372	Width, 27 inches.	Price, per yard..........41c
No. 37K3376	Width, 36 inches.	Price, per yard..........54c
No. 37K3380	Width, 45 inches.	Price, per yard..........68c
No. 37K3384	Width, 54 inches.	Price, per yard..........81c

19 TO 57 Cents Per Yard. OUR PEERLESS EXTRA HEAVY REVERSIBLE COCOA MATTING.

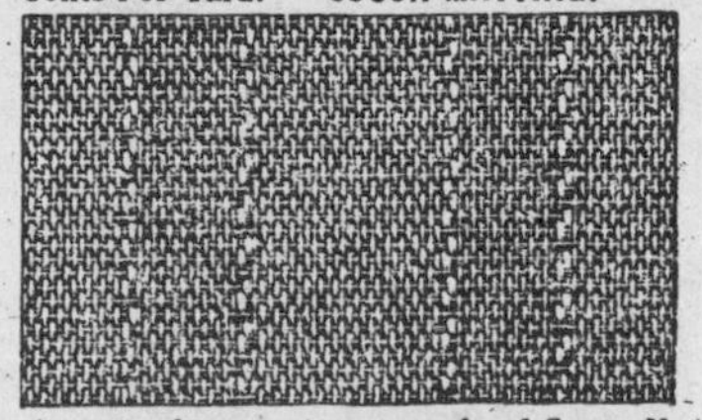

An extra heavy, strong grade of Cocoa Matting especially suitable for places that get hard wear, such as aisles in churches, public halls, lodges, etc. It can be reversed, that is, worn on both sides, thus giving double service. **The color is tan with a red stripe.** When zinc ends are attached it is easily taken up and cleaned, making a very sanitary floor covering. Full roll contains about 53 running yards. Price for full roll will be 3 cents per square yard less.

		Price per Yard.
No. 37K3348	Width, 18 inches.	19c
No. 37K3352	Width, 27 inches.	29c
No. 37K3356	Width, 36 inches.	38c
No. 37K3360	Width, 45 inches.	48c
No. 37K3364	Width, 54 inches.	57c

FLOOR OILCLOTHS AND LINOLEUMS

WE ASK FOR YOUR ORDER BECAUSE OUR QUALITIES ARE THE VERY BEST TO BE HAD ON THE MARKET. OUR PRICES MAKE SUCH QUALITIES MOST WONDERFUL VALUES. WE GUARANTEE TO MORE THAN SATISFY YOU. OUR INLAID LINOLEUMS ARE THE BEST IN THE WORLD. IF YOU PREFER TO SEE THE ACTUAL COLORS BEFORE ORDERING, WRITE FOR OUR FREE SPECIAL CARPET CATALOGUE. SEE PAGE 852.

29 TO 56 CENTS PER YARD — FINE NEW FLOOR OILCLOTH.

Good durable oilcloth, furnished in the pattern illustrated, with tan and olive background and figures in red and green. It can't be bought for less in wholesale lots from jobbers. Remarkable value. No. 37K3388.

Width, yards	1	1½	2
Price, per running yard	29c	42c	56c

32 TO 76 CENTS PER YARD — EXTRA HEAVY BEST QUALITY FLOOR OILCLOTH.

The very best oilcloth and furnished in this decidedly rich design. Made expressly for us. Background is a nice tan shade and figures are in red and olive. We offer great economies on our small profit plan. No. 37K3392.

Width, yards	1	1½	2	2½
Price, per running yard	32c	47c	61c	76c

87c FOR 1½ YARDS SQUARE — EXTRA HEAVY QUALITY OILCLOTH STOVE SQUARES. — $1.54 FOR 2 YARDS SQUARE.

These Oilcloth Stove Squares, or in other words stove rugs, are the best quality obtainable. They come in an assortment of neat patterns. We illustrate a part of one here. It is an extra heavy grade and will wear for a very long time. The colors are usually a tan ground with harmonizing colors in the pattern.

No. 37K3440   1½ yards square.   Price..................$0.87
No. 37K3444   2 yards square.   Price.................... 1.54

METALLIC OILCLOTH BINDING.

No. 37K3448 Brass Oilcloth Binding, to ornament, protect and fasten down the edges of oilcloth stove squares. Sold only in sets, complete with corners and tacks, as follows:

	Weight	Price
Set of 4 yards.	4 ounces...	9c
Set of 5 yards.	5 ounces...	12c
Set of 6 yards.	6 ounces...	14c
Set of 8 yards.	8 ounces...	18c

No. 37K3452 Zinc Oilcloth Binding, put up in sets, same as above.

	Weight	Price
Set of 4 yards.	4 ounces...	5c
Set of 5 yards.	5 ounces...	6c
Set of 6 yards.	6 ounces...	7c
Set of 8 yards.	8 ounces...	10c

87c PER YARD — STRONG DURABLE LINOLEUM IN A NEW FLORAL DESIGN.

While not as good as other linoleums we offer, it is certainly remarkable value at this price. It is made especially for us to meet the needs of those who do not require the very best grades. The pattern is a medium brown with small figures in red and white. It comes in 2-yard widths only. No. 37K3396 Width, 2 yards. Price, per running yard....87c

87c PER YARD — ANOTHER NEAT PATTERN IN OUR SPECIAL GRADE LINOLEUM.

Specially made for the needs of those not requiring our best qualities. An extraordinary value for wear. The pattern is a medium tan ground with a figure of red and green. Dealers pay as much at wholesale as our price to you. No. 37K3400 Width, 2 yards. Price, per running yard....87c

98c TO $2.40 PER YARD — FINE QUALITY LINOLEUM IN A HANDSOME DESIGN.

An exceedingly pretty piece of goods. The pattern has a brown background with tiny specks of black, just enough to relieve it neatly and the figure is in peacock green and tan (really light yellow), most pleasing, harmonizing colors. We show the actual colors in our Special Carpet Catalogue offered free on page 852. Comes in three widths, as quoted below. No. 37K3404

Width, yards	Price, per running yard
2	$0.98
2½	1.22
4	2.40

98c TO $2.40 PER YARD — PRIZE DESIGN IN HEAVY QUALITY LINOLEUM.

Perfect in material and workmanship, the kind of pattern to please particular people. Background, a cream color with figures in olive green, red, white and brown, decidedly artistic and fashionable. You would pay a fancy price at retail for it. Comes in three widths, as quoted below. No. 37K3408

Width, yards	Price, per running yard
2	$0.98
2½	1.22
4	2.40

98c TO $2.40 PER YARD — EXTRA HEAVY LINOLEUM IN A GRAND FLORAL DESIGN.

Very attractive goods and one of our best qualities. Our own special design. Colors in background are light brown and ecru with leaves of green and flowers of deep red and white with a slight tinge of golden yellow. Considering quality, pattern and price, we need hardly mention that this is a great offer. Comes in three widths, as quoted below. No. 37K3412

Width, yards	Price, per running yard
2	$0.98
2½	1.22
4	2.40

98c TO $2.40 PER YARD — EXTRA HEAVY GEOMETRICAL AND FLORAL DESIGN LINOLEUM.

An exceedingly popular pattern in beautifully harmonizing colors. Dark olive and ecru background with green, tan and red floral and geometrical combination design, considered one of the most practical and generally pleasing of all patterns. A quality that will wear an exceedingly long time. Comes in three widths, as quoted below. No. 37K3416

Width, yards	Price, per running yard
2	$0.98
2½	1.22
4	2.40

98c TO $2.40 PER YARD — EXTRA QUALITY LINOLEUM IN DARK BROWN WITH TERRA COTTA AND WHITE FIGURE.

An exceptionally fine grade of linoleum that will give you more wear than you would expect from material costing 40 per cent more. The pattern comes, as illustrated, with a background in dark brown and the figure in terra cotta and white. Order now. We guarantee to satisfy you, but if you wish we will mail you free our Special Carpet Catalogue, showing the colors. Comes in three widths, as quoted below. No. 37K3420

Width, yards	2	2½	4
Price, per running yard	98c	$1.22	$2.40

$2.46 PER YARD — HANDSOME INLAID LINOLEUM, THE SEASON'S LEADER.

Equal to the imported kind that is sold at double the price we ask. Don't pay duty and freight on no better imported goods. The design is, as illustrated, a mottled effect in colors of beautiful ecru shade and peacock green with small white square. Quite luxurious and high class appearance. The best goods manufactured in the world. Our Special Carpet Catalogue shows the actual color effects. No. 37K3424 Width, 2 yards. Price, per running yard..................$2.46

$2.46 PER YARD — FANCY INLAID LINOLEUM IN GREEN AND WHITE OR BLUE AND WHITE.

Absolutely the best linoleum in the world. Will wear right to the back, as colors run right through. Always looks bright and clean. Fine for kitchens, bathrooms, hotels, etc. Pattern as illustrated. Comes in small block design in green and white or blue and white, as preferred.

No. 37K3428 Green and White. Width, 2 yards. Price, per running yard.....$2.46
No. 37K3432 Blue and White. Width, 2 yards. Price, per running yard.....$2.46

$2.46 PER YARD — OUR POPULAR HIGH GRADE MOTTLED INLAID LINOLEUM.

A prize winning design, very beautiful. For the hall, dining room or any place requiring absolutely the best wearing material, these inlaid linoleums are just the thing. The pattern has a groundwork of green with ecru and terra cotta coloring worked out in the order of illustration and harmonizing in a very artistic fashion. Don't look elsewhere for finer linoleums. These inlaid goods are absolutely the best. No. 37K3436 Width, 2 yards. Price, per running yard.........$2.46

OUR HIGH GRADE RUGS ARE WONDERFUL VALUES

WE ARE OFFERING THE FINEST RUG QUALITIES to be found in the largest furnishing stores and are quoting prices on them that we know will surprise everybody who is interested in buying a rug. Our rug sales, it is hardly necessary to say, are really enormous and that enables us to sell them at an exceedingly close margin of profit over their actual cost to us and their cost to us is lower than the average price paid by exclusive rug houses, because we have more direct connections with the manufacturers and buy in larger quantities. That is why we name prices so far below retail prices and at the same time furnish you the very best qualities in rugs and we guarantee to satisfy you in the quality, design, coloring and value or refund your money.

WHILE OUR LOWEST PRICED RUGS are positively remarkable values at the prices quoted, yet our higher grade rugs, such as we show on pages 773 to 778, are so much better and the price on them so very low that you can hardly help seeing that it really pays to buy the better grades. You get far more value out of them for the little extra money they cost than for the money invested in a cheaper rug. Turn to pages 873 to 878 and read about our very fine qualities. We show all of these rugs in their actual colors in our Special Carpet Catalogue, described on page 852 and some of them are shown in colors in this catalogue on page 860.

OUR EXTRAORDINARY OFFERS IN THE SMALLER SIZE RUGS.

97c OUR GREAT JUTE SMYRNA RUG BARGAIN.

This rug is made exactly like a wool Smyrna rug, only with a jute filling. It is perfectly reversible, being the same on both sides. It comes in red, green, blue or tan combinations, and at our price of 97 cents is without an exception the greatest value ever offered by any house. Be sure to state color wanted.

No. 37K3460 Size, 30x60 inches. Price.....97c

49c AND $1.20 OUR FINE KERSEK HEAVY REVERSIBLE RUG OFFER.

In this you will find something very useful. It is one of our many bargains, something entirely new, and at the very low price we ask for it we know it cannot be surpassed. It is a fine combination of wool and cotton woven very closely, making it a firm and durable rug. It comes in the most beautiful color effects, such as reds and greens. They come in sizes very suitable for odd spaces in the house. Be sure to state color wanted.

No. 37K3464 Size, 20x36 inches. Price......$0.49
No. 37K3468 Size, 30x60 inches. Price......1.20

$1.38 OUR NEW VELVET RUG.

This is positively the best velvet rug ever sold for anything like our price in this size. The pattern and color effects brought out in this rug are elegant, and surpass all other rugs on the market that sell for double the price. It comes in red, green and tan combinations. Be sure to order one or more of these rugs, for we know they will please you. Very handy for floor spaces here and there. Be sure to state color wanted.

No. 37K3472 Size, 27x54 inches. Price.$1.38

$1.65 AND $1.95 OUR ANIMAL PATTERN WOOL SMYRNA RUGS.

The above illustration is only one of the handsome animal patterns this wool Smyrna rug comes in. We can also furnish it in a peacock or sheep design. Especially liked by children. They are perfectly reversible, being the same on both sides. The colors are mostly tan in background with effects in shades of red and green. Be sure to state pattern wanted.

No. 37K3476 Size, 26x54 inches. Price......$1.65
No. 37K3480 Size, 30x60 inches. Price......1.95

$2.15 OUR ANIMAL PATTERN AXMINSTER RUG.

This attractive Axminster Animal Pattern Rug comes in two designs, the one above illustrated and another with a Newfoundland dog. The cat and puppy design comes with a green ground with shades of red and tan to harmonize. The Newfoundland dog design comes in a tan ground with red and green shading. It is certainly one of the prettiest animal rugs to be found anywhere and especially delights the children. The value we offer is remarkable. Be sure to state design wanted.

No. 37K3484 Size, 27x60 inches. Price......$2.15

$1.70 AND $2.87 OUR FINE MENDORA PLUSH RUGS.

In offering this very strikingly stylish plush rug we cannot recommend it too highly as it is absolutely one of the greatest values ever put on the market. It is manufactured under our own supervision with the utmost care, and we guarantee it to be the best value obtainable for the very low price we ask for it. It comes in fine Oriental designs; colors are red, green, tan or blue. Be sure to state color wanted.

No. 37K3488 Size, 27x54 inches. Price......$1.70
No. 37K3492 Size, 36x72 inches. Price......2.87

$1.70 AND $2.75 OUR SPLENDID WILTON RUGS. A RARE BARGAIN.

The above illustration is only one of the pretty designs this elegant velvet rug comes in. It is made of fine worsted yarn, is strong and durable, and will wear for years. It comes in a variety of colors, such as red, green or tan, in Persian and medallion patterns. It has been one of our largest selling rugs the past season. We guarantee it to give entire satisfaction or we will cheerfully refund your money. Be sure to state color wanted.

No. 37K3496 Size, 27x54 inches. Price......$1.70
No. 37K3500 Size, 36x63 inches. Price......2.75

$3.50 AND $5.80 ROYAL WILTON RUGS. OUR BEST SMALL RUGS.

This is one of the finest qualities of Wilton rugs manufactured. This illustration shows only one of the many beautiful designs in which it comes. It is made of the very finest worsted yarn; a rug that will wear for years and always look well. We can furnish it in an endless variety of patterns in rich Persian or Oriental designs in pretty color combinations of red, green, blue or tan. Just give us an idea of the colors wanted and we will guarantee to please you.

No. 37K3504 Size, 27x54 inches. Price......$3.50
No. 37K3508 Size, 36x63 inches. Price......5.80

$1.55 WASHABLE COTTON BATH RUG.

This rug is made of a nice fine quality of cotton, made on the same principle as a Smyrna rug; is reversible, both sides being finished alike. Colors are green and white, red and white, blue and white, pink and white and guaranteed fast. Be sure to state colors desired.

No. 37K3512 Size, 30x60 inches. Price......$1.55

$2.75 FUR RUGS AT BARGAIN PRICES.

White Unlined Chinese Goat Rug, made of the best quality skins, have good thick hair and are good value at our price.
No. 37K3536 30x60 inches. Price.......$2.75
Gray Unlined Chinese Goat Rugs, same quality as above.
No. 37K3540 30x60 inches. Price.......$2.75

77c TO $1.45 SPECIAL VALUES IN SMALL RUGS MADE FROM SHORT ENDS OF CARPET FINISHED INTO RUGS AND OFFERED AT EXTREMELY LOW PRICES TO DISPOSE OF THEM QUICKLY.

AS WE CUT ENORMOUS QUANTITIES OF CARPET EACH SEASON, we, of course, have a lot of short ends left from the various rolls, ends of 1½ to 3 yards in length. We have made them into rugs 1½ yards long and fringed them nicely at both ends with wool rug fringe, and to dispose of them quickly we are offering them at prices much below their actual value. They are made from ends of carpet 27 inches wide and borders 22½ inches wide, ranging in quality from our cheapest Tapestry Brussels to our best Wilton and Axminsters. Be sure to include one or more of these great values in your order. They come in mighty handy for odd places about the house and as you see cost merely a trifle.

No. 37K3516 8-wire Tapestry Carpet. Price........................$0.77
No. 37K3520 9-wire Tapestry Carpet or Border. Price...........98
No. 37K3524 10-wire Tapestry Carpet or Border. Price........1.10
No. 37K3528 Wilton Velvet Carpet or Border. Price...........1.45
No. 37K3532 Axminster Carpet or Border. Price...............1.45

$4.38 TWO-TONED "LINED" CHINESE GOAT RUG.

These rugs are made of selected skins, are heavily padded and lined with a good quality of silesia, are exceptional value and come in the following color combinations: Black and white, gray and white, black and gray, brown and white; also in solid colors of white, black, gray or brown. Be sure to give color or combination wanted.

No. 37K3544 Size, 30x60 inches. Price.......$4.38

$11.00 — OUR 7x9 — TAPESTRY BRUSSELS RUG
VERY BEST QUALITY

IF YOU WANT A RUG OF JUST THE PROPER SIZE for a bedroom or library and want a particularly high class material this best grade tapestry Brussels 7 x 9 rug at $11.00 will certainly meet your needs exactly and prove a most remarkable value. If you have heretofore been patronizing retail furnishing stores for your house furnishings you will undoubtedly at first be inclined to think it is impossible that this should be such a wonderfully good rug for only $11.00.

BUT REMEMBER THIS, that we sell the best grades of all the various classes of rugs on the same one very small margin of profit. We never attempt to put a big profit on anything, because we are building our business on uniformly great values throughout our whole line. You also have our positive guarantee that if you are disappointed in the appearance or quality or in any way, with any rug we offer and if you don't think it is absolutely the very best value you ever saw in rugs, you may return it to us at our expense and we will refund both the price and any transportation charges you paid.

WE SHOW TWO OF THE ACTUAL COLOR EFFECTS OF THESE RUGS IN OUR SPECIAL CARPET CATALOGUE FREE ON REQUEST, AS OFFERED ON PAGE 852.

THE ACCOMPANYING ILLUSTRATION shows just one of the designs in which this stylish Tapestry Brussels rug comes. We can furnish it in a small floral design like illustration in green or tan background; also in small allover designs in red, green, tan, delf or peacock blue background, with neat effects in harmonizing colors.

GIVE US JUST AN IDEA of the pattern and color effect that you like best and we will guarantee to positively satisfy you on this matter, because we have variety enough in this assortment to meet your tastes. If you don't quite know what you really would like best and would like to somewhat leave the matter to us, we can make a very fine choice for you. If you will tell us something of the color effects of the walls, etc., in your room, the style of furniture, etc., we will select something to match beautifully.

No. 37K3672   Size, 7x9 feet.
Price..................... **$11.00**

IF YOU PAY A PENNY MORE than the reduced prices we quote in these pages for the best merchandise you are simply throwing money away.

OUR BEST TAPESTRY BRUSSELS QUALITY $17.48
IN 9x12 ROOM SIZE IN TWO STYLISH DESIGNS WITH A GREAT VARIETY OF COLORINGS IN EACH.

This is absolutely the biggest tapestry Brussels value ever quoted by any house. This is not a boast but a proven fact. We sell the best grades on the same one small profit plan as we do the cheaper grades, which certainly makes such qualities as this the most remarkable values of all, as they last twice as long as the average grades.

THIS HIGH CLASS 10-WIRE TAPESTRY BRUSSELS is composed of the finest worsted yarn and will outwear any other tapestry Brussels. While for a few dollars less you can buy from us most extraordinary values, yet this $17.48 rug will give you just about twice the wear and satisfaction of a lower priced rug, and therefore costs you considerably less in the long run. The excellent quality brings out decidedly artistic and beautiful color effects. We have this quality in two distinct designs, both illustrated here, and each of these designs comes in a fine variety of color combinations. Kindly select either the floral pattern on the left or the Oriental pattern on the right, and suggest the color effect you like best. We positively guarantee to furnish you a rug that will please you or it may be returned to us and we will refund both price and transportation charges.

WE OFFER EACH OF THESE RUGS with green, tan or red backgrounds, the pattern being worked out in beautiful harmonizing colors. A suggestion from you about the shadings in your room will help us to decide on a good color combination for you.

No. 37K3688 Medallion design. Size, 9x12 feet. Price, **$17.48**

No. 37K3690 Oriental design. Size, 9x12 feet. Price, **$17.48**

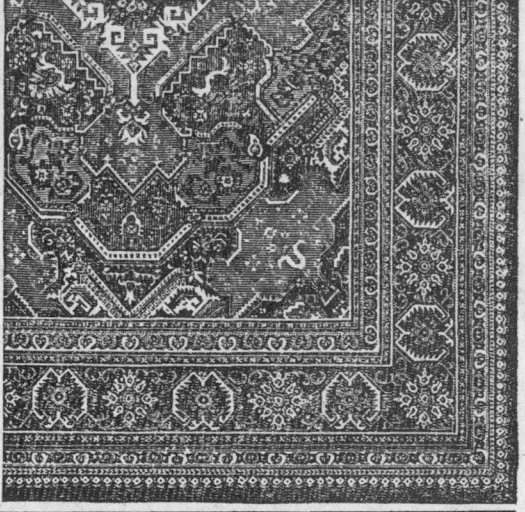

$23.89 — OUR GENUINE BODY BRUSSELS 9x12 PARLOR RUG
PROVING THAT FOR QUALITY NO ONE CAN MEET OUR PRICES.

Body Brussels Rugs are made of the finest selected worsted yarn and are the most carefully made and thoroughly woven rugs of all in point of wearing quality, and their fine material enables the manufacturer to bring out in them the most fashionable and artistic design and colorings that any particular householder could desire.

IF YOU WANT A RUG for long service and stylish effect and prefer the hard finish of the Body Brussels Rug which makes it wear such an extraordinarily long time, this must be your choice, for we guarantee it to you as the best body Brussels rug manufactured. It is composed of the finest of stock, closely woven, and comes in an elegant line of patterns with the richest of colorings. You can suggest what coloring you like the best or if you tell us something of the kind of room you want it for, the shadings of the walls, etc., we will be able to select just the proper thing to suit, if you would like something to harmonize particularly well with the surroundings.

THESE RUGS COME IN TWO DESIGNS, the allover design illustrated on the left and medallion design illustrated on the right, and each design is to be had in numerous fine effects with backgrounds of red, green or tan and the patterns brought out with rich shadings to harmonize. (See page 852 about our great free Special Carpet Catalogue.) Send us your order and we will guarantee to please you perfectly or refund your money.

No. 37K3692 Allover design. Size, 9x12 feet. Price, **$23.89**

No. 37K3694 Medallion design. Size, 9x12 feet. Price, **$23.89**

OUR GREAT WINDOW SHADE VALUES

THIS IS A MORE COMPLETE LINE than we have ever before had and is a more select and complete line to choose from than you will find in any furnishing store elsewhere. We have added this season the celebrated duplex or two color window shades, one color on one side and a different color on the other. Our line comprises plain, fringed, lace trimmed and lace and insertion window shades in all sizes and colors, all quoted at the lowest prices ever heard of.

AN ALLOWANCE OF ABOUT 6 INCHES must be made from lengths quoted. For example, a 3x6 foot shade is cut 6 feet long before mounted. Hemming and mounting take up about 6 inches. A 6-foot mounted shade will therefore measure but 5½ feet; or a 7-foot shade would measure about 6½ feet. Our shades are all mounted and ready to hang. We don't sell them any other way. **Note particularly that lengths quoted are manufacturer's measurements.**

REGULAR STOCK SIZE is 3 feet wide in window shades. Shades wider than 3 feet or narrower than 3 feet must be made to order specially, therefore costing more in proportion.

BRACKETS AND SLATS are included in prices quoted, but shade pulls, etc., are extra and you can select them from our general house furnishing supplies on next page.

LETTERING ON WINDOW SHADES with gold letters is 35 cents per running foot. Shade cloth 48 inches and wider is made of a heavy fabric and will not always match colors in narrower and cheaper cloth.

WE GUARANTEE OUR QUALITIES to satisfy you perfectly or we refund your money, as we get these goods direct from two of the largest manufacturers in the country. The quality of the shade cloth and of workmanship and finish is the best obtainable.

Plain Opaque Window Shades.

No. 37K3792 Plain Water Color Opaque Window Shades. Mounted on patent spring rollers. Made plain without fringe or dado. Colors, light olive, pea green, terra cotta, dark green, light buff, dark olive, slate or white. **Always state color desired.** Size, 3x6 feet (manufacturer's measurement).
Price........................27c

No. 37K3796 Plain Water Color Opaque Window Shades, same as above, but cut down less than 3 feet wide.
Price........................32c

No. 37K3800 Plain Opaque Shades, same quality and colors as above. Size, 3x7 feet (manufacturers' measurement).
Price........................30c

No. 37K3804 Same as No. 37K3800, cut down to less than 3 feet wide.
Price........................35c

No. 37K3808 Plain Water Color Opaque Window Shades. Exactly same quality as above. Size, 3x8 feet.
Price........................35c

Fringed Window Shades.

No. 37K3836 Fringed Water Color Opaque Window Shades with very handsome 3¼-inch fringe at bottom. Mounted on patent spring rollers. Colors, same as No. 37K3792. **Always state color wanted.** Size, 3x6 feet (manufacturer's measurement).
Price........................33c

No. 37K3840 Fringed Water Color Opaque Window Shades. Same quality as above, but cut down to less than 3 feet wide.
Price........................37c

No. 37K3844 Fringed Water Color Opaque Window Shades. Same quality as No. 37K3836, but 7 feet long. Price.....36c

No. 37K3848 Fringed Water Color Opaque Window Shades. Same as No. 37K3844, but cut down to less than 3 feet wide.
Price........................40c

No. 37K3852 Fringed Opaque Window Shades. Same as No. 37K3844, but size 3x8 feet. Price........41c

All shades, from Nos. 37K3792 to 37K3852 inclusive, are not made wider than 3 feet.

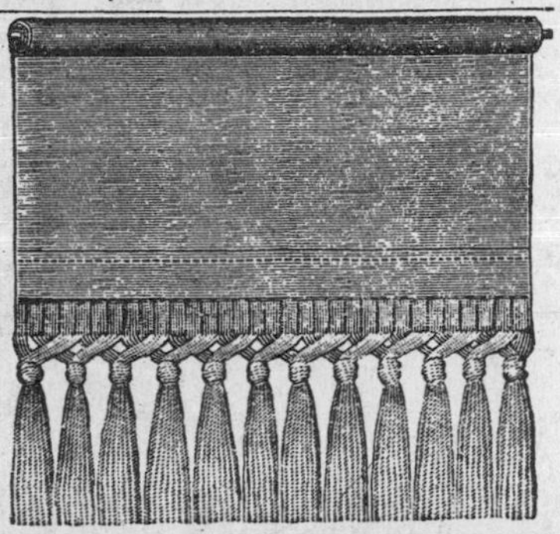

BEST QUALITY PLAIN Oil Opaque Window Shades.

No. 37K3812 Plain Opaque Shades. Made from very best grade oil opaque, and mounted on patent spring rollers. Plain, without fringe or dado. Colors, same as No. 37K3792. **Always state color wanted.** Size, 3x6 feet. Price........39c

No. 37K3816 Plain Opaque Shades. Same as above, cut down to less than 3 feet wide. Price........43c

No. 37K3820 Plain Opaque Shades. Same quality as No. 37K3812, but 3x7 feet.
Price........................43c

No. 37K3824 Same as No. 37K3820, but cut down to less than 3 feet wide.
Price........................47c

No. 37K3828 Plain Opaque Shades. Same quality as No. 37K3812, but 3x8 feet.
Price........................50c

Following are prices on the above shades made to order in the following widths and 7 feet long:

No. 37K3832 Over 36 inches wide up to 42 inches wide. Price........87c
Over 42 inches wide up to 45 inches wide.
Price........................98c
Over 45 inches wide up to 48 inches wide.
Price........................$1.11
Over 48 inches wide up to 54 inches wide.
Price........................$1.33

Above sizes 8 feet long at 10 cents, each, extra.

Lace Trimmed Window Shades.

GENUINE HAND MADE.

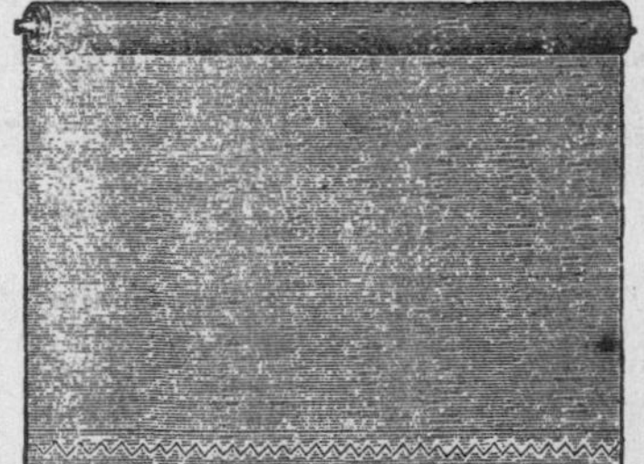

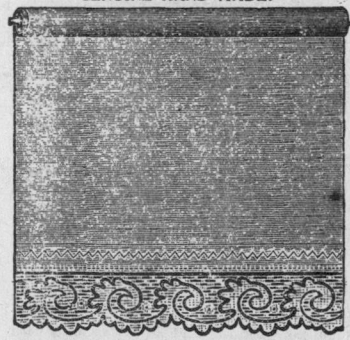

No. 37K3924 Lace Trimmed Window Shades. Made from very best quality oil opaque shade cloth, mounted on patent spring rollers. Beautiful lace edging on bottom, 4¼ inches deep. Colors same as No. 37K3792. **Always state color wanted.** Size, 3x6 feet (manufacturer's measurement). Price....57c

No. 37K3928 Lace Trimmed Window Shades. Same as No. 37K3924, but cut down to less than 3 feet wide. Price........61c

No. 37K3932 Lace Trimmed Window Shades. Same as No. 37K3924, but 7 feet long.
Price........................62c

No. 37K3936 Same exactly as No. 37K3932, but cut down to less than 3 feet wide.
Price........................67c

No. 37K3940 Lace Trimmed Window Shades. Same quality as preceding numbers, but size 3x8 feet. Price........70c

Following are same quality as No. 37K3940, made to order in the following widths and 6 feet long.

No. 37K3944 Over 36 inches wide up to 42 inches wide inclusive. Price....$1.04
Over 42 inches wide up to 45 inches wide.
Price........................$1.12
Over 45 inches wide up to 48 inches wide.
Price........................$1.26
Over 48 inches wide up to 54 inches wide.
Price........................$1.51
Over 54 inches wide up to 63 inches wide.
Price........................$1.85

We can furnish the above sizes in shades 7 and 8 feet long, at 10 cents each extra for the 7-foot and 20 cents extra for the 8-foot.

Do not fail to state color of shades wanted.

BEST QUALITY FRINGED DUPLEX (DOUBLE FACED) OPAQUE SHADES.

Genuine Hand Made.

THIS IS A NEW AND UP TO DATE LINE which we have added this season, owing to the demands of our customers. We have selected a very fine grade of goods, and if you want a window shade that has the style and fashion now so very popular, we heartily recommend our Duplex Shades. Our prices are wonderfully low, as compared with prices for these shades elsewhere.

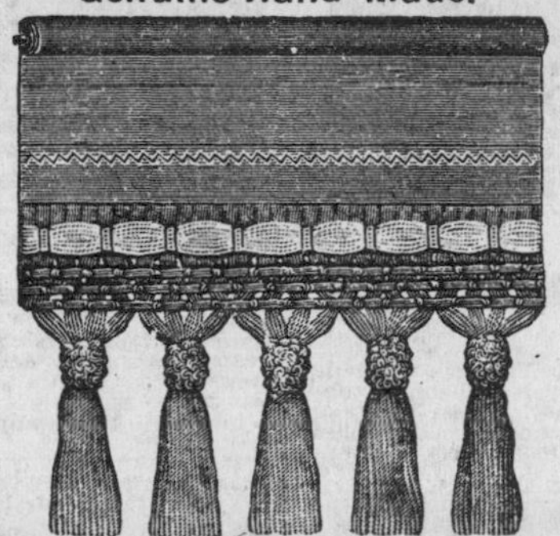

FROM A DECORATIVE STANDPOINT DUPLEX OPAQUE IS PRACTICALLY INDISPENSABLE. By its use, a color to match the outside color of a house and also a neutral color to harmonize with the interior furnishings can be obtained.

No. 37K3880 38 in. by 7 ft. One side dark green, reverse side white. Price..82c
No. 37K3884 38 in. by 7 ft. One side dark green, reverse side cream. Price..82c
No. 37K3888 38 in. by 7 ft. One side olive green, reverse side white. Price..82c
No. 37K3892 38 in. by 7 ft. One side olive green, reverse side cream. Price..82c

No. 37K3896 Fringed Duplex Shades, same quality as above, made to order in the following widths and 7 feet long. **Be sure to state colors wanted.**

Width, inches	42	45	48	54	63
Price	$1.35	$1.55	$1.85	$2.25	$2.85

BEST QUALITY PLAIN DUPLEX (DOUBLE FACED) OPAQUE SHADES.

Genuine Hand Made.

No. 37K3900 38 in. by 7 ft. One side dark green, reverse side white. Price..72c
No. 37K3904 38 in. by 7 ft. One side dark green, reverse side cream. Price..72c
No. 37K3908 38 in. by 7 ft. One side olive green, reverse side white. Price..72c
No. 37K3912 38 in. by 7 ft. One side olive green, reverse side cream. Price..72c

No. 37K3920 Special Size Duplex Shades, made to order. If the exact size you wish is not given in the following schedule, the next larger size will be charged, but the shade will be cut the exact size you order.

Width, inches	38	42	45	48	54	63
Length, 5 feet	$0.87	$1.26	$1.30	$1.48	$1.74	$2.21
Length, 6 feet	.95	1.39	1.46	1.65	1.93	2.48
Length, 7 feet	1.06	1.53	1.62	1.85	2.16	2.73
Length, 8 feet	1.23	1.67	1.76	2.02	2.37	3.01

NOTE—All of the above shades are mounted on the very best quality of spring rollers.

Be sure to state colors wanted.

SPECIAL SIZE MADE TO ORDER SHADES.

FOR STORES, OFFICES AND RESIDENCES. The following shades we make to order from the very best quality hand made oil painted opaque shade cloth. It usually requires about four days to have special size shades made to order. We require the full amount of cash with the order in every instance.

SHADES MADE TO SPECIAL ORDER CANNOT BE RETURNED IF SENT AS ORDERED.

COLORS—Special size shades are made only in the following colors: Dark green, olive, terra cotta, slate, pea green and light buff.

State whether width you desire is width of cloth or roller measure. Roller measure means from end to end of tips. We quote the width of cloth complete.

Lettering.

Price for lettering window shades with Shaded Gilt Lettering is 35 cents per running foot, EXTRA. Shade cloth 48 inches and wider, is made of heavier fabric and will not always exactly match colors of smaller shades.

If the exact size you wish is not given in the following schedule, the next larger size will be charged, but the shade will be cut the exact size you order.

No. 37K3976 **Order by number, size and price, and be sure to state color wanted.**

Lgth. in Feet	WIDTH IN INCHES.										
	38	42	45	48	54	63	72	81	90	104	120
4	$0.49	$0.67	$0.73	$0.81	$0.97	$1.26	$1.82	$2.17	$2.45	$3.01	$ 5.60
5	.56	.76	.84	.92	1.11	1.44	2.03	2.45	2.74	3.39	6.30
6	.63	.84	.95	1.04	1.25	1.62	2.24	2.73	3.04	3.77	7.00
7	.70	.92	1.06	1.15	1.39	1.81	2.45	2.94	3.33	4.14	7.70
8	.77	1.01	1.18	1.26	1.53	1.99	2.66	3.15	3.63	4.52	8.40
9	.91	1.09	1.29	1.37	1.67	2.31	2.87	3.36	3.92	4.90	9.10
10	.98	1.18	1.40	1.48	1.81	2.48	3.08	3.57	4.21	5.28	9.80
11	1.05	1.26	1.51	1.62	2.02	2.67	3.29	3.78	4.51	7.13	10.50
12	1.12	1.34	1.62	1.74	2.23	2.86	3.50	4.06	4.80	7.50	11.20

BEST QUALITY FRINGED Oil Opaque Window Shades.

No. 37K3856 Fringed Oil Opaque Window Shades. Made from best quality oil opaque cloth, same fringe as illustrated in our cheaper shades. Colors same as No. 37K3792. **Always state color wanted.** Size, 3x6 feet.
Price........................44c

No. 37K3860 Same shade as No. 37K3856 but cut down to less than 3 feet wide. Price........48c

No. 37K3864 Fringed Oil Opaque Window Shades. Made from best quality oil opaque cloth, same fringe as No. 37K3836 shades. Colors, same as No. 37K3792. **Always state color wanted.** Size, 3x7 feet. Price..48c

No. 37K3868 Same as No. 37K3864, but cut down to less than 3 feet wide.
Price........................53c

No. 37K3872 Fringed Shades, same quality as above, made to order in the following widths and 7 feet long:
Over 36 inches wide up to 42 inches wide.
Price........................98c
Over 42 inches wide up to 45 inches wide.
Price........................$1.08
Over 45 inches wide up to 48 inches wide.
Price........................$1.25
Over 48 inches wide up to 54 inches wide.
Price........................$1.50

Above sizes 8 feet long, at 10 cents, each, extra.

No. 37K3876 Fringed Oil Opaque Window Shades, Same as No. 37K3864, but 8 feet long. Price........55c

Lace and Insertion Window Shades.

GENUINE HAND MADE.

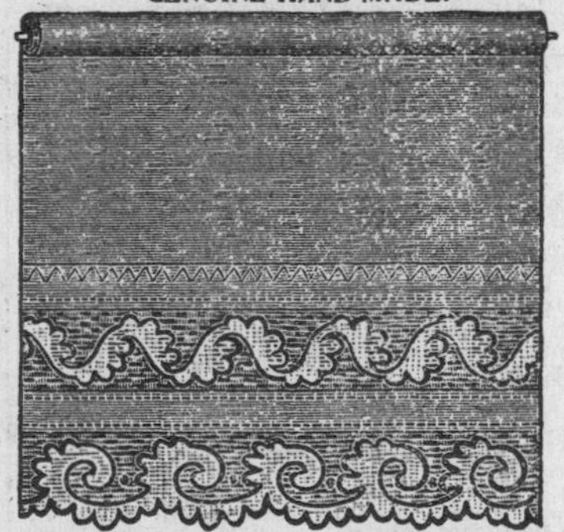

No. 37K3948 Best Quality Oil Opaque Window Shades with lace and insertion, as per illustration. One of the richest things to be had in shades. Colors, same as No. 37K3792. **Always state color wanted.** Size, 3x6 feet.
Price........................68c

No. 37K3952 Same shade as No. 37K3948, but cut down to less than 3 feet wide.
Price........................72c

No. 37K3956 Same shade as above, but size 3x7 feet. Price........74c

No. 37K3960 Same as above, cut down to less than 3 feet wide. Price........78c

No. 37K3964 Lace and Insertion Shade, Same quality as No. 37K3948, but size 3x8 feet. Price........82c

No. 37K3968 Same shade as No. 37K3964, cut down to less than 3 feet wide.
Price........................86c

Following are prices on Best Oil Opaque Window Shades with lace and insertion, same quality as preceding numbers, made to order in the following widths and 6 feet long.

No. 37K3972 Over 36 inches wide up to 42 inches wide. Price........$1.25
Over 42 inches wide up to 45 inches wide.
Price........................$1.34
Over 45 inches wide up to 48 inches wide.
Price........................$1.48
Over 48 inches wide up to 54 inches wide.
Price........................$1.76
Over 54 inches wide up to 63 inches wide.
Price........................$2.16

We can furnish the above sizes in shades 7 and 8 feet long, at 10 cents each extra for the 7-foot and 20 cents each extra for the 8-foot.

THE LATEST WATER COLOR OPAQUE WINDOW SHADES

THE NEWEST AND MOST ARTISTIC EFFECTS IN WINDOW SHADES to be found elsewhere only in the most fashionable furnishing stores in the big cities. The small illustrations will give you only an idea of the pattern; it is impossible to show the beautiful colorings. The shades have all the appearance of hand painted water color panels and are very novel and beautiful. They are made of an extra good quality of shade material and the water color decoration is everlasting, will never fade out, the colors are bright and rich and the work is really artistic. The shades are 3 feet wide and 7 feet long. **The illustrations show only a section of the shade,** the beautiful water color design running the full length. Come complete with spring ready to put up.

59c Fringed Water Color Opaque Shades, come in dark green color only, with a beautiful rose design dado, brought out in their natural color effects.
No. 37K3980 Size, 3x7 only. Price, each, 59c

52c Plain Water Color Opaque Shades Without Fringe, same design and color as one listed above.
No. 37K3984 Size, 3x7 only. Price, each, 52c

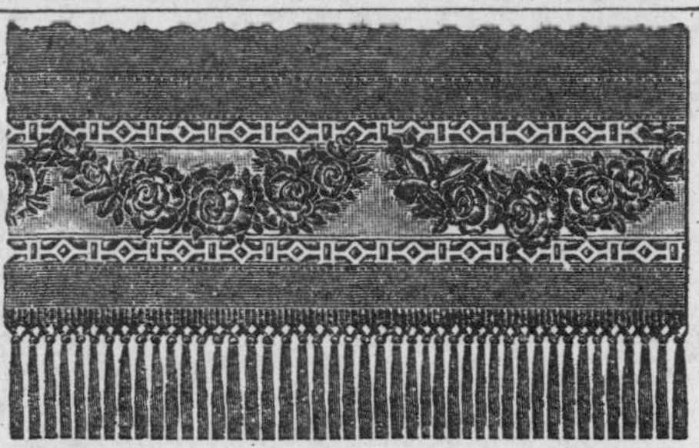

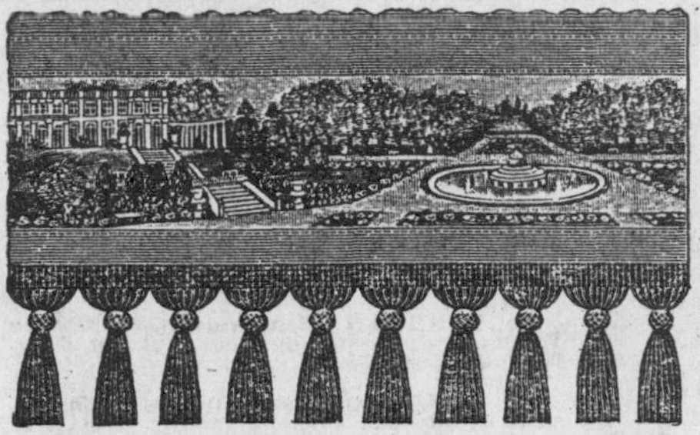

62c Fringed Water Color Opaque Shades, come in dark olive green color only, with a beautiful landscape scenery design dado, reproduced in its natural color effects.
No. 37K3988 Size, 3x7 only. Price, each, 62c

52c Plain Water Color Shades Without Fringe, same design and color as one listed above.
No. 37K3992 Size, 3x7 only. Price, each, 52c

62c Fringed Water Color Opaque Shades, come in white only, with an elegant rose design dado in all its natural color effects.
No. 37K3996 Size, 3x7 only. Price, each, 62c

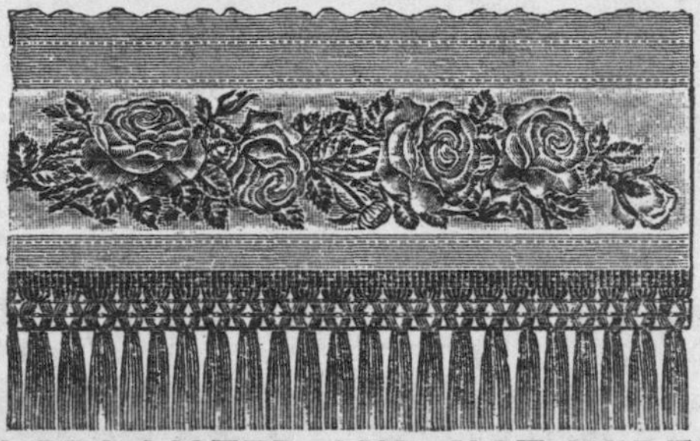

62c Fringed Water Color Opaque Shades, come in buff color only, with a swell "American Beauty" rose design dado, brought out in all its beautiful array of color effects.
No. 37K4000 Size, 3x7 only. Price, each, 62c

WE CAN FURNISH THESE SHADES ONLY IN COLORS LISTED AND NOT WIDER THAN 3 FEET.

GREAT VALUES IN GENERAL HOUSE FURNISHING SUPPLIES

Shade Pulls.

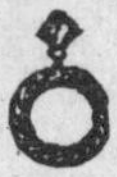

No. 37K4004 Ring Shade Pulls. Handsome silver and copper finish. Shipping weight, 1 ounce. Price 5c

Spiral Bar Shade Pulls.

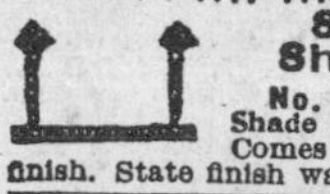

No. 37K4008 Spiral Bar Shade Pulls, with drop chains. Comes in silver, copper or gilt finish. State finish wanted. Price 6c

Vestibule Rods for Sash Curtains.

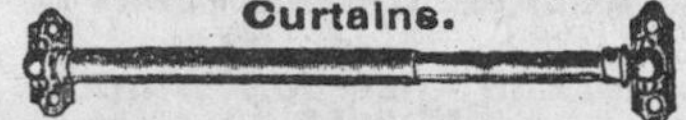

No. 37K4012 Brass Vestibule Rods, made complete with brackets; can be adjusted inside or outside of casing; ⅜ inch in diameter, and will extend from 24 to 44 inches. Price 9c

Our Heavy Brass Telescope or Extension Rod, with Fancy Polished Brass Ends.

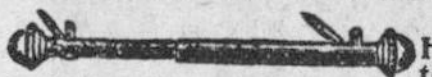

No. 37K4016 Heavy Brass Extension Rods, ½ inch in diameter; will extend from 27 to 54 inches; just the thing for lace curtains. Price 9c

No. 37K4020 Same rod as No. 37K4016. Extends from 54 to 78 inches. Price, complete with brackets 13c

Telescope Vestibule Rods.

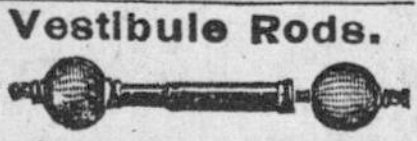

No. 37K4024 Telescope Vestibule Rods, with pretty corrugated ball ends, as per illustration; a very fancy rod, complete with brackets. Will extend 28 to 54 inches. Price 10c

No. 37K4028 Same rod as No. 37K4024 Extends from 54 to 78 inches. Price, complete 12c

Extension Pole Brackets.

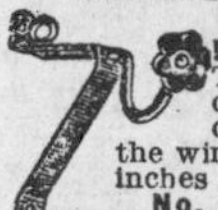

Adjustable Brass Extension Pole Brackets for 1⅜-inch poles. These are used to support the curtain poles so that your lace curtains may hang away from the window. Come in two sizes, 4 to 7 inches and 7 to 12 inches.

No. 37K4032 Extend from 4 to 7 inches. Price, per pair 9c

No. 37K4036 Extend from 7 to 12 inches. Price, per pair 12c

Brass Vestibule Curtain Rod Rings.

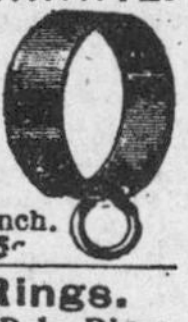

No. 37K4040 This is one of the most serviceable brass rings on the market. State size wanted.

Size	⅜ inch	½ inch	¾ inch	⅞ inch
Per doz.	8c	10c	12c	15c

Curtain Pole Rings.

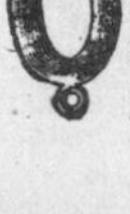

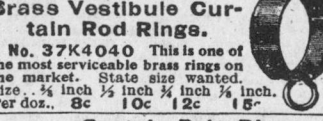

Heavy Brass Curtain Pole Rings, suitable for draperies, etc., made in two sizes.

No. 37K4044 Size, 1¼ inches. Price, per dozen 25c

No. 37K4048 Size, 1¾ inches. Price, per dozen 30c

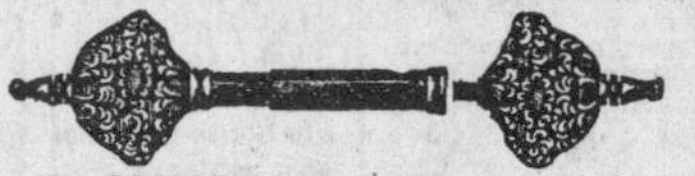

No. 37K4052 Fancy Telescope Vestibule Rods. Are made of heavy ½-inch brass tubing with fancy silver ends with brass band and tip, like illustration; extends from 27 inches to 54 inches; complete with brackets. Price 20c

Stair Pads.

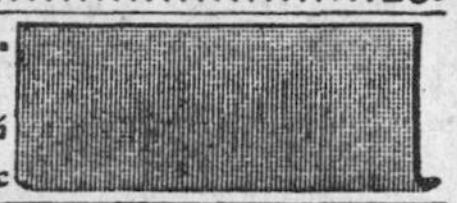

No. 37K4056 Stair Pads, 22½ inches long. Per dozen . . 98c

Curtain Poles and Trimmings.

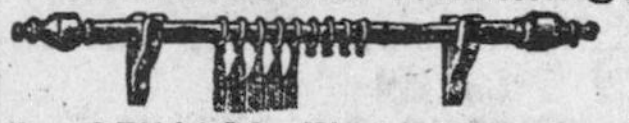

No. 37K4060 Wood Trimmed Curtain Poles, 1⅜-inch, finished in California walnut, mahogany, oak or ebony. Price includes two turned wooden ends, two brackets for ends and sufficient quantity of rings for pole. Don't fail to mention kind of finish wanted.

Length	5 feet	6 feet	7 feet	8 feet	9 feet
Price	25c	29c	32c	36c	40c

No. 37K4064 Wood Pole Trimmings. Same as is used with No. 37K4060 poles. Price, per set 14c

Curtain Poles.

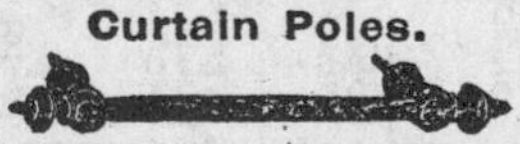

No. 37K4068 Wood Curtain Poles, suitable for bedrooms or sash curtains, ¾ inch, finished antique oak only. Price includes brackets and ends. No rings included.
Length, 4 feet. Price 9c
Length, 5 feet. Price 11c

No. 37K4072 Brass Trimmed Curtain Poles, 1⅜-inch poles, finished in oak, mahogany, walnut or ebony, complete with two brass ends, two brass brackets and sufficient quantity of rings for pole. State finish wanted.

Length	5 feet	6 feet	7 feet	8 feet	9 feet
Price	19c	23c	26c	29c	32c

No. 37K4076 Brass Pole Trimmings. Same as used with No. 37K4072 poles. Price, per set 12c

Curtain Poles and Sockets.

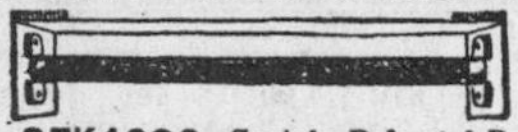

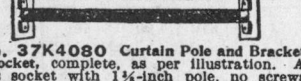

No. 37K4080 Curtain Pole and Bracket or Socket, complete, as per illustration. A brass socket with 1⅜-inch pole, no screws or nails required. It fits on inside of casing and has rubber ends. Cut pole ¾ inch shorter than space between opening and attach brackets. Complete with poles.

Length	5 feet	6 feet	7 feet	8 feet	9 feet
Price	22c	26c	29c	33c	36c

No. 37K4088 Socket without pole. Price, per pair 12c

White Enameled Curtain Poles

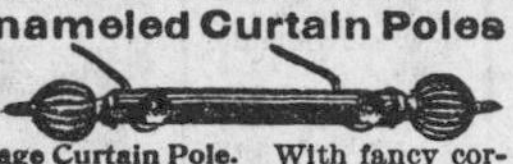

No. 37K4092 White Enameled Corrugated Cottage Curtain Pole. With fancy corrugated ball ends, and also fancy rosette screws, as per illustration. This is the prettiest rod in the market and is sure to please. ¾-inch rod, 4 feet only. Complete with fixtures. Price 10c

Our New ¾-inch Brass Curtain Poles.

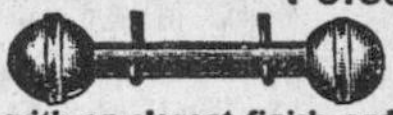

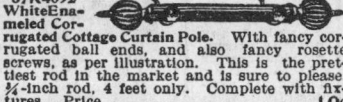

No. 37K4096 This is a very heavy brass pole with an elegant finish, and the heavy brass ends of this pole are 1½ inches in diameter. They come with brackets, as per illustration. This is an entirely new pole and we consider it one of our most showy and serviceable poles. Size, ¾-inch pole, length, 4 feet. Complete with trimmings. Price 25c

Our New ¾-inch Brass Extension Rods.

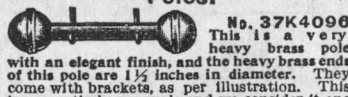

This elegant rod is exactly the same as curtain pole No. 37K4096 listed above, only comes in an extension rod instead of solid pole.

No. 37K4100 Size, 30 to 54 inches. Price 30c

No. 37K4104 Size, 40 to 78 inches. Price 35c

Our New ¾-inch Oxidized Extension Rod.

This rod is exactly the same as one listed above only comes in oxidized finish.

No. 37K4108 Size, 30 to 54 inches. Price 37c

No. 37K4112 Size, 40 to 78 inches. Price 42c

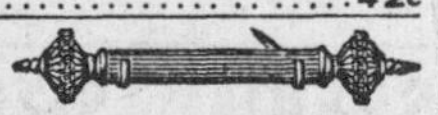

No. 37K4116 Our Fancy White Enameled Pole with silver ends and polished gilt band and tip, like illustration. The pole is ¾ inch in diameter and 4 feet long. Complete with trimmings. Price, 18c

No. 37K4120 Corrugated White Enameled Pole, 1⅜ inches in diameter. Complete with trimmings. State length wanted.

Length	4 feet	5 feet	6 feet	7 feet	8 feet
Price	25c	27c	29c	31c	33c

Curtain Pole Trimmings.

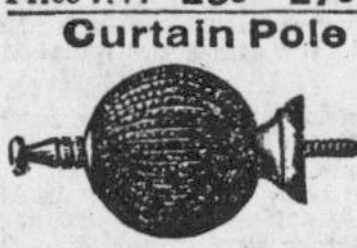

No. 37K4124 Corrugated Silver Ball Trimmings, with gilt tip, same as used with No. 37K4120 poles, complete with brackets and rings. Price, per set, 20c

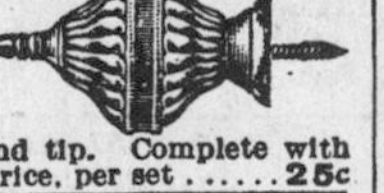

No. 37K4128 Our Fancy Pole Trimmings for 1⅜-inch pole, like illustration, are finished in silver and have polished brass band and tip. Complete with brackets and rings. Price, per set 25c

Stair Buttons.

No. 37K4132 Stair Buttons. Are 1¾ inches in diameter and are finished silver, copper or gilt. State finish wanted. Price, per dozen 10c

Z Cut Brass Stair Corners.

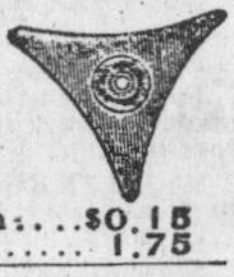

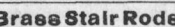

No. 37K4136 These corners prevent dust from accumulating in the corners of stairs where it is hard to sweep. It takes but one nail to fasten these corners. Price, per dozen . . . $0.15
Per gross 1.75

Brass Stair Rods.

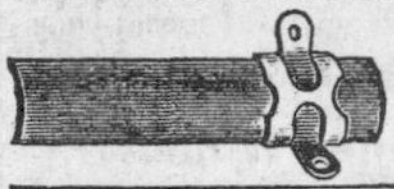

No. 37K4140 Brass Stair Rods, 24-inch. Price, per dozen, 65c
26-inch, Price, per dozen, 70c
30-inch, Price, per dozen, 85c

Polished Steel Stair Rods.

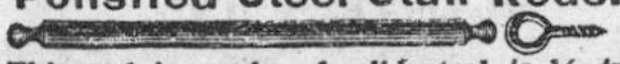

This rod is made of solid steel, is ⅜ inch in diameter, and is nicely polished, and is one of the latest and most durable rods made. They are fastened to the stair with a screw eye. Comes in brass, nickel or oxidized finish.

No. 37K4144 26 inches. Price, per dozen $0.80

No. 37K4148 28 inches. Price, per dozen 90

No. 37K4152 30 inches. Price, per dozen 1.00

Brass Drapery Hooks.

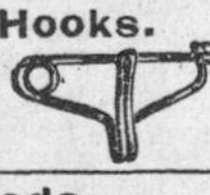

No. 37K4156 Like illustration.
Price, for two dozen . . 5c
Per gross 25c

Wood Stair Rods.

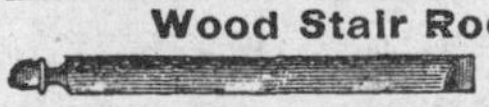

No. 37K4160 Wood Stair Rods, acorn tip, finely finished. Come in antique oak only, 27 and 30 inches long, with screws. State length wanted. Price 4c

Brass Tassel Hooks.

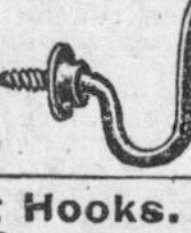

No. 37K4164 Nicely Polished. Price, each . . . 5c

Picture Moulding Hooks.

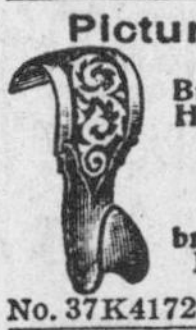

No. 37K4168 Brass Plate Picture Hooks. Price, per doz. . 5c

No. 37K4172 This is the solid brass Moulding Hook. Per dozen 12c

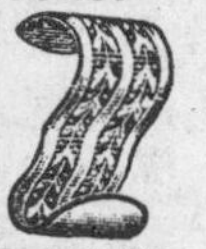

No. 37K4172 No. 37K4168

Rug Fasteners.

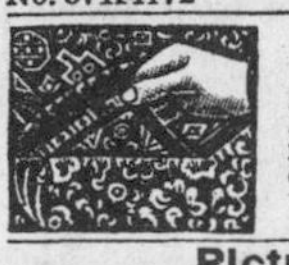

No. 37K4176 The New Patent Rug Fastener. Just the article to keep rugs and art squares fastened to the floor. Price, per dozen . . 25c

Picture Nails.

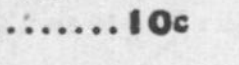

No. 37K4180 Picture Nails, with white porcelain heads, brass trimmed. Price, per dozen 10c

GENERAL HOUSE FURNISHING SUPPLIES—Continued from Preceding Page.

Curtain Loops and Chains.

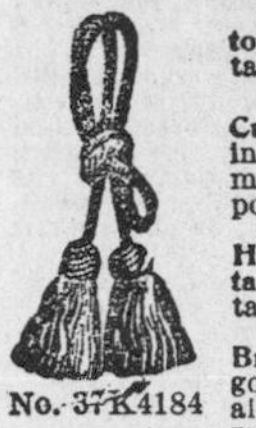

No. 37K4184

No. 37K4184 White Cotton Curtain Loops, cord and tassels. Price, per pair 8c

No. 37K4188 Tapestry Curtain Loops, good quality, in all staple colors to match our tapestry portieres. Per pair. 15c

No. 37K4192 Heavy Chenille Curtain Loops, cord and tassels. Per pair .. 19c

No. 37K4196 Brass Curtain Chain, a good strong chain, usually sold for very much more money. Price, per pair 10c

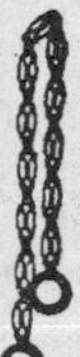

No. 37K4196

No. 37K4200 Spiral Curtain Chains, pretty, strong and durable. Price, per pair 14c

No. 37K4204 Heavy Mercerized Curtain Loops, to match our mercerized portiere. Price, per pair .. 40c

Rug Fringes.

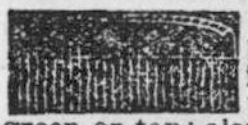

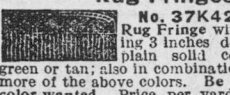

No. 37K4208 Wool Rug Fringe with gimp heading 3 inches deep. Made in plain solid colors of red, green or tan; also in combinations of two- or more of the above colors. Be sure to state color wanted. Price, per yard..........6c

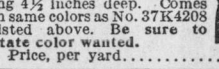

No. 37K4212 Knotted Rug Fringe with gimp heading 4½ inches deep. Comes in same colors as No. 37K4208 listed above. Be sure to state color wanted.

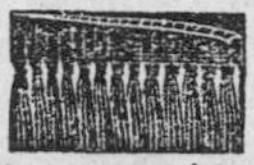

Price, per yard......................10c

Furniture Fringes.

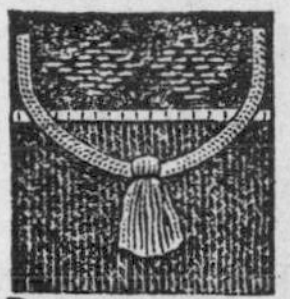

No. 37K4216 Cotton Furniture Fringe made with a good firm heading and 7 inches deep. Comes in the following colors: Bright red, dark red, myrtle, olive or empire green; also dark tan. A very pretty and durable fringe for the money. Be sure to state color wanted. Price, per yard......................10c

Furniture Gimp.

No. 37K4228 Best quality of silk furniture gimp, ½ inch wide, in all staple colors. Price, per yard 4c
Full piece of about 36 yards 80c

Worsted Furniture Fringe.

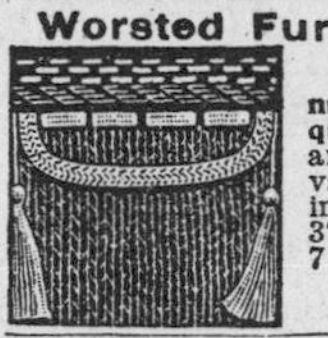

No. 37K4220 This number is made of a nice quality of worsted yarn, and is an exceptional value at our price. Comes in same colors as No. 37K4216. Full width, 7 inches. State color. Price, per yard .. 15c

Our Best Quality Furniture Fringe.

No. 37K4224 This is the very best quality we handle. It is made of a fine quality of worsted yarn, has a good firm heading with heavy strands and tassels; a fringe that is sure to please. Comes in same colors as No. 37K4216. Full width, 7 inches. State color. Price, per yard..........20c

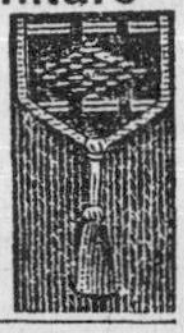

Hassocks and Foot Rests
Children's Hassocks.

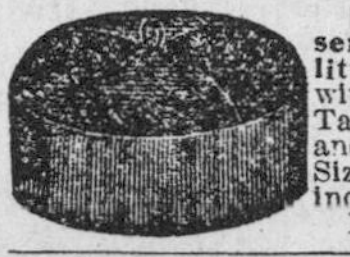

No. 37K4236 This serviceable and pretty little hassock is covered with a good quality of Tapestry Brussels carpet, and is certainly a bargain. Size, 9x9 inches and 4 inches high. Price, each.......19c

A Leader in a Low Priced Hassock at 29 Cents.

No. 37K4240 This is one of our most popular low priced hassocks. It is 12 inches in diameter and 5½ inches high, covered with fine Tapestry Brussels carpet. Be sure to order one or more of these beautiful hassocks. Price, each........29c

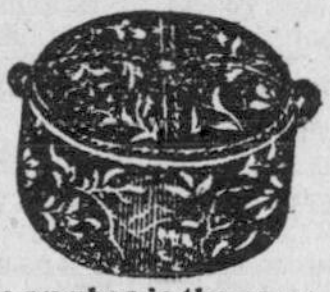

No. 37K4244 This number is the same as one listed above, only covered with velvet or moquette carpet. Price, each..........35c

Furniture Cord.

No. 36K4232 Best quality of silk furniture cord in all staple colors. Price, per yard 4c
Full piece of 18 yards............60c

Our 49-Cent Hassock.

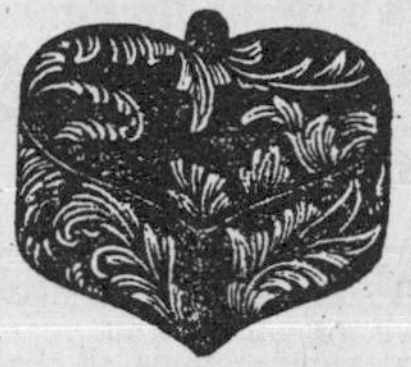

No. 37K4248 The illustration represents the choicest and most stylish original shape hassock in our collection. Size, 12x14 inches, 6 inches high. Covered with a good quality of Brussels carpet. Price, each.. 49c

Special Extraordinary.

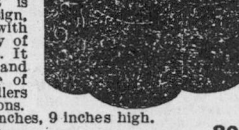

No. 37K4252 This swell hassock is an ornament to any room. It is novel in design, and covered with a fine quality of velvet carpet. It is well made and has been one of our largest sellers in past seasons. Size, 15x15 inches, 9 inches high. Price, each 80c

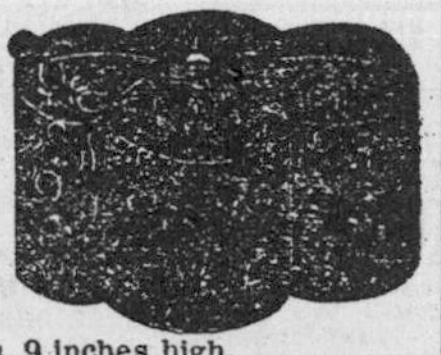

Our Great Bargain in Hassock and Slipper Box Combined.

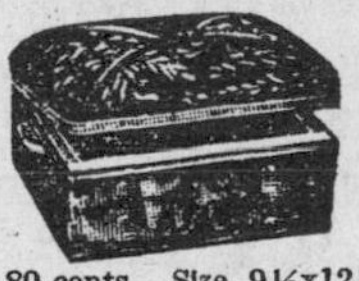

No. 37K4256 This beautiful slipper box is not only useful but ornamental. It is strongly made and covered with the best Brussels carpet, and is certainly a bargain at our special price of 89 cents. Size, 9½x12½ inches and 7 inches high. Price, each..................89c

No. 37K4260 Same as above, only covered with velvet carpet. Price, each, 98c

Our Leader in a Beautiful Parlor Stool at 49 Cents Each.

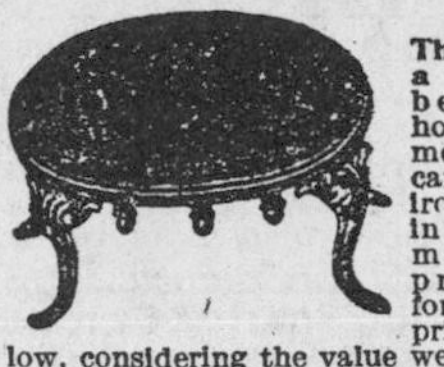

No. 37K4264 These stools have a wooden top, beautifully upholstered with moquette or velvet carpet, malleable iron legs, finished in gold bronze, and makes a useful pretty ornament for any house. Our price is extremely low, considering the value we give you in one of these pretty foot rests. Sizes, 11x11 inches, 7 inches high. Price, each..........49c

Our Commode for Use in Bedrooms.

This is one of the most useful articles that could be in any house. Convenient for children or in case of sickness. These commodes are made of fine imitation oak, with a beautiful Brussels carpet covered top. Size, 15½ inches high, and 14½ inches square. These commodes are something that should certainly be in every well regulated house. The convenience for one week would overcome the expense.

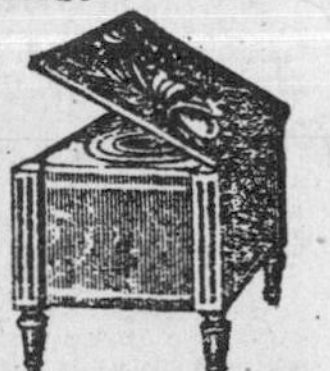

No. 37K4268 Price, each, without pan $1.98
No. 37K4272 Price, with pan, 2.48

THE SPLENDID REDUCTIONS IN PRICE made by us in this catalogue must prove to our customers our ability to undersell all competition.

OUR LATEST BLANKET AND COMFORTER OFFERS

EVERY QUALITY, COLOR AND WEIGHT IS OFFERED IN THIS LINE, FROM THE LOWEST PRICED COTTON BLANKETS, TO THE HIGHEST GRADE WOOL BLANKETS, INCLUDING THE FINEST IMPORTED FANCY GOODS, A BIGGER LINE THAN IS TO BE FOUND IN ANY RETAIL STORE IN THE SMALL TOWNS, AND ALL OFFERED TO YOU AT AS LOW PRICES AS DEALERS PAY AT WHOLESALE.

WE GUARANTEE THE QUALITY of each and every article in this line. Although our prices are the lowest ever heard of, you must understand that our immense sales and direct connections with the biggest sources of supply enable us to offer you the best goods made at these astonishingly low prices. **You will save a very large sum of money** by buying all your house furnishings from us. If these goods are not found perfectly satisfactory, you can return them to us at our expense and we will refund your money.

No. 37K4276 Fancy Colored Cotton Blankets. Colors, red, blue, pink, gray or tan. Stripes on white ground. Size, 54x72 inches. Weight, about 2 pounds. State color wanted. Price, per pair....75c

Gray Cotton Bed Blankets.

No. 37K4280 Gray Cotton Blankets, nice quality. Size, 50 x 72 inches, weight, about 2 pounds. Price, per pair 59c

No. 37K4284 Gray Cotton Blankets. Our most popular priced blanket. Size, 60x76 inches. Weight about 2½ pounds. Price, per pair......75c

No. 37K4288 Gray Cotton Blankets. One of our best values. Size, 64x76 inches. Weight, about 3 pounds. Price, per pair 98c

No. 37K4292 Gray Cotton Blankets. Our leader, the greatest seller in our catalogue. Size, 72x80 inches. Weight, 4 pounds. Price, per pair $1.30

No. 37K4296 Gray Cotton Blankets. Exceptional value. Size, 72x80 inches. Weight, 5 pounds. Price, per pair..................$1.65

White Cotton Bed Blankets.

No. 37K4300 White Cotton Blankets, nice quality. Size, 50x72 inches. Weight, about 2 pounds. Price, per pair..................59c

No. 37K4304 White Cotton Blankets. Our most popular priced blanket. Size, 60x76 inches. Weight, about 2½ pounds. Price, per pair.....75c

No. 37K4308 White Cotton Blankets. One of our best values. Size, 64x76 inches. Weight, about 3 pounds. Price, per pair..................98c

No. 37K4312 White Cotton Blankets. Our leader, the greatest seller in our catalogue. Size, 72x80 inches. Weight 4 pounds. Price, per pair..................$1.30

No. 37K4316 White Cotton Blankets. Exceptional value. Size, 72x80 inches. Weight, 5 pounds. Price, per pair..................$1.65

Our Leader in a 5-Pound, Silver Gray Camping Blanket at $1.10 per Pair.

No. 37K4320 Color, silver gray. Size, 56x76 inches. Price, per pair..................$1.10

No. 37K4324 Special Extraordinary Heavy, 6-Pound Double Blankets. Color, gray. Size, 70x78 inches. Price, per pair..................$1.58

White All Wool Blankets.

No. 37K4328 White All Wool Blankets. Our leader in a low priced blanket. Weight, 4 pounds. Size, 60x76 inches. Price, per pair..........$3.19

No. 37K4332 White All Wool Blankets. Our largest seller in past seasons. Same quality as No. 37K4328. Weight, 5 pounds. Size, 68x78 inches. Price, per pair..................$3.98

No. 37K4336 White All Wool Blankets. Extra fine quality, one of the best values in our catalogue. Weight, 5 pounds. Size, 70x80 inches. Price, per pair..................$4.98

Gray All Wool Blankets.

No. 37K4340 Gray All Wool Blankets. Our leader in a low priced blanket. Weight, 4 pounds. Size, 60x76 inches. Price, per pair..........$3.19

No. 37K4344 Gray All Wool Blankets. Our largest seller in past seasons. Same quality as No. 37K4340. Weight, 5 pounds. Size, 68x78 inches. Price, per pair..................$3.98

No. 37K4348 Gray All Wool Blankets. Extra fine quality, one of the best values in our catalogue. Weight, 5 pounds. Size, 70x80 inches. Price, per pair..................$4.98

Scarlet All Wool Blankets.

No. 37K4352 Scarlet All Wool Blankets. Our leader in a low priced blanket. Weight, 4 pounds. Size, 60x76 inches. Price, per pair..........$3.19

No. 37K4356 Scarlet All Wool Blankets. Our largest seller in past seasons. Same quality as No. 37K4352. Weight, 5 pounds. Size, 68x78 inches. Price, per pair..................$3.98

No. 37K4360 Scarlet All Wool Blankets. Extra fine quality; one of the best values in our catalogue. Weight, 5 pounds. Size, 70x80 inches. Price, per pair..................$4.98

No. 37K4364 Extra Heavy, 5-Pound, Soft Finish, Heavy Nap, Wool Filled Gray Blankets. Color, gray. Size, 72x80 inches. Price, per pair..................$2.45

White California Wool Blankets.

No. 37K4368 Color, white. Size, 60x76 inches. Weight, 4 pounds. Price, per pair..........$4.95

No. 37K4372 Color, white. Size, 70x80 inches. Weight, 5 pounds. Price, per pair..........$5.65

Our Special Extra Value in a Large 11-4 Five-Pound Heavy Wool Blanket.

No. 37K4376 Color, white. Size, 70x80 inches. Weight, 5 pounds. Price, per pair..........$3.29

No. 37K4380 Color, gray. Size, 70x80 inches. Weight, 5 pounds. Price, per pair..........$3.29

Our Celebrated 11-4 5-Pound Blankets, in White or Gray. This Blanket Has a Fine Cotton Warp with a Strictly All Wool Filling.

No. 37K4384 Color, white. Size, 70x80 inches. Price, per pair..................$4.65

No. 37K4388 Color, gray. Size, 70x80 inches. Price, per pair..................$4.65

White Superfine All Wool Blankets.

No. 37K4392 White All Wool Blankets, a very fine quality. Size, 72x84 inches. Weight, 6 pounds. Price, per pair..................$7.25

No. 37K4396 White All Wool Blankets, a finer quality than one listed above, exceptional value. Size, 72x84 inches. Weight, 6 pounds. Price, per pair $8.75

Gray Superfine All Wool Blankets.

No. 37K4400 Gray All Wool Blankets, a very fine quality. Size, 72x84 inches. Weight, 6 pounds. Price, per pair $7.25

No. 37K4404 Gray All Wool Blankets, a finer quality than one listed above, exceptional value. Size, 72x84 inches. Weight, 6 pounds. Price, per pair $8.75

Scarlet Superfine All Wool Blankets.

No. 37K4408 Scarlet All Wool Blankets, a very fine quality. Size, 72x84 inches. Weight, 6 pounds. Price, per pair..................$7.25

No. 37K4412 Scarlet All Wool Blankets, a finer quality than one listed above, exceptional value. Size, 72x84 inches. Weight, 6 pounds. Price, per pair $8.75

Our Finest Grade California Lamb's Wool Bed Blankets

No. 37K4416 White only. Size, 80x90. Weight, 6 pounds. Price, per pair.......$12.50

Our Celebrated Heavy "Jack Frost" Gray Wool Blankets at $2.50 and $2.98 per Pair.

No. 37K4420 Color, gray. Size, 60x72 inches. Weight, 4 pounds. Price, per pair........$2.50

No. 37K4424 Color, gray. Size, 67x80 inches. Weight, 5 pounds. Price, per pair........$2.98

Our Extra Heavy Dark Blue Klondike Wool Camping Blankets at $2.85 and $3.98 Per Pair.

No. 37K4428 Color, dark blue. Size, 58x72 inches. Weight, 5 pounds. Price, per pair..$2.85

No. 37K4432 Color, dark blue. Size, 68x78 inches. Weight, 7 pounds. Price, per pair...$3.98

Our Single 5-Pound Indestructible Camping or Bed Blankets at $2.75 Each.

No. 37K4436 Color, natural gray. Size, 62x82 inches. Price, each..................$2.75

Our Great Big Scarlet Camping Blanket at $5.35 per Pair.

No. 37K4440 Color, red. Size, 80x90 inches. Weight, 6 pounds. Price, per pair.........$5.35

Our 10-Pound Dark Blue Klondike Camping Blanket at $6.00 per Pair.

No. 37K4444 Color, dark blue. Size, 62x82 inches. Price, per pair..................$6.00

Regulation United States Army Blankets at $7.25 per Pair.

No. 37K4448 Color, silver gray. Size, 62x82 inches. Weight, 10 pounds. Price, per pair, ...$7.25

Our Leader In a Fancy Plaid Wool Blanket at $2.50 and $2.85 per Pair.

We consider the above number one of the best values in our catalogue at the prices asked. While this blanket is not all wool, for service and durability it cannot be surpassed. We can furnish it in black and white or red and black only. This blanket has been on the market for over 20 years, which speaks for itself. We look for it to be a big seller and have bought it in very large quantities. If you order this blanket and are not satisfied with your bargain it can be returned at our expense, and your money will be refunded. In ordering be sure to state color combination wanted.

No. 37K4452 Size, 60x78 inches. Weight, 4 pounds. Price, per pair......................$2.50

No. 37K4456 Size, 68x78 inches. Weight, 4½ pounds. Price, per pair......................$2.85

Fancy All Wool Plaid Blankets at $4.75 per Pair.

We have them in a very handsome assortment and combination of colorings, including black and red, black and white, pink and white, blue and white, tan and white or gray and white. These blankets are extra large size, 70x80 inches, and weigh fully 4½ pounds to the pair. These are made of the very finest of selected, perfectly scoured clean wool. We guarantee them not to shrink. They are extra well finished and are equal to a great many plaid blankets in the market that sell as high as $10.00. Be sure to state color combination wanted.

No. 37K4460 Size, 70x80 inches. Weight, 4½ pounds. Price, per pair $4.75

Our Extra Fine California Lamb's Wool Plaid Blankets at $6.98 per pair. Such Blankets Cannot be Equaled in Retail Stores for Less Than $10.00 per Pair.

Nothing handsomer than these beautiful all wool plaid blankets, made of fine selected stock, very soft and fleecy, and come in pretty color combinations of pink and white, blue and white, black and white or black and red. Be sure to state color wanted. We have sold this blanket for several years and can strongly recommend it to any one wanting a high class article.

No. 37K4464 Size, 70x80 inches. Weight, 5 pounds. Price, per pair......................$6.98

IMPORTED ROBE OR FANCY BLANKET.

One of the latest novelties in blankets. These special robes or fancy blankets are a comparatively recent article on the market. They are manufactured in Germany and imported direct by us, so that we are able to offer you these high grade goods at as low as wholesale prices.

The color effects are beautiful. While the goods are cotton, they have the appearance and the feeling of all wool blankets, this being a special feature of their high grade imported quality.

Fancy blankets can be used for many different purposes, but principally are worked into bath robes, smoking jackets, shawls, or chair wraps. Be sure to take advantage of the great values we are giving in this number as it cannot be found elsewhere at anywhere near as low a price. We guarantee to satisfy you or refund your money.

$1.98 Our Leader Imported Fancy Colored Blanket.

One of the handsome designs we brought out last season, and at our price of $1.98 was a big seller. It comes in an unusually large line of color combinations—Red, Green, Blue, Black, Gray, Brown or Tan grounds with other pretty contrasting colors. Be sure to give color desired when ordering. This is an extremely low price for this beautiful robe. Sold singly.

No. 37K4564 Size, 70x86 inches. Price, each..$1.98

BABIES' CRIB BLANKETS.
Our Leader, an Imported Fancy Crib Blanket at 42 Cents Each.

Happy Dreams

This blanket is made in Germany, and we import it direct in very large quantities. It is made of a very fine quality of cotton, and has the appearance and finish of an all wool blanket. It comes in pretty color combinations of baby blue and white, pink and white, also tan and white. In ordering be sure to state color desired.

No. 37K4468 Size, 30x40 inches. Price, each.............................42c

No. 37K4472 White Cotton Crib Blanket. This is made of a nice quality of cotton, is soft and fleecy, comes with pink or blue borders, and is a bargain at our special price of 55 cents. Size, 34x54 inches. Price, per pair......................55c

No. 37K4476 White Wool Mixed Blanket. This number we have sold for a great many seasons and it has always given good service. It is nicely made and comes with fancy colored striped borders. Size, 30x40 inches. Price, per pair.............80c

No. 37K4480 Extra Fine Quality California Wool Filled Crib Blanket. This blanket is nicely made, has an all wool filling with a fine cotton warp. It is very soft and fleecy and has all the wearing qualities of an all wool blanket. It has fancy colored borders, and at our special price of $1.49 is a bargain. Size, 30x40 inches. Price, per pair.......$1.49

No. 37K4484 This number is same quality as No. 37K4480, only comes in an extra large size, being 36x54 inches. Price, per pair...............$1.98

No. 37K4486 Our Very Finest Quality in a California All Wool Crib Blanket. This is one of the finest crib blankets on the market, a blanket that would ordinarily sell from $4.50 to $5.00. It is beautifully made and nicely finished. It is very soft and fleecy and comes with handsome colored borders. If you want something real good do not overlook this number. Size, 36x54 inches. Price per pair..$2.98

OUR GREAT OFFERS IN COMFORTERS.

No. 37K4504 Fancy Print, Reversible Bed Comforters, Size, 54x72 inches. Price, each........................75c

No. 37K4508 Fancy Tufted, Reversible, Silkoline, Medium Weight Comforters. Size, 66x72 inches. Price, each...........................$1.00

No. 37K4512 Handsome Tufted, Silkoline Covered, Reversible Comforters. Size, 68x75 inches. Price, each..$1.25

No. 37K4516 Our New Design Handsome Silkoline, Fancy Stitched Comforters. Size, 66x76 inches. Price, each.............................$1.45

No. 37K4520 Extra Weight, Fancy Stitched, Reversible, Heavy India Cloth Covered Comforters. Size, 68x78 inches. Price, each.......................$1.75

No. 37K4524 Our Specially Pretty Design Extra Fine Quality Silkoline Tufted Comforters. Size, 72x82 inches. Price each.............................$1.98

No. 37K4528 Our Rich, Handsome, Reversible, India Cloth Comforters. Size, 68x78 inches. Price, each....$2.25

No. 37K4532 Our Genuine English Oil Boiled Turkey Red Chintz Comforters. Size, 68x78 inches. Price, each...........................$2.35

No. 37K4536 Extra Size, Reversible, Heavy India Cloth Covered, Fancy Stitched Comforters. Size, 77x87 inches. Price, each............................$2.50

No. 37K4540 Large Size, Handsomely Quilted, Reversible Sateen Comforters. Size, 72x82 inches. Price, each...........................$2.75

No. 37K4544 Our New Persian Design Figured Sateen Comforter. Size, 70x78 inches. Price, each.......$3.35

Our Leader In a Lamb's Wool Comforter at $3.45 Each.

Weight, about 4 pounds. No. 37K4548 Size, 72x78 inches. Price, each....$3.45

Australian Lamb's Wool Filled Comforter, at $4.75 Each.

Weight, about 3½ pounds. No. 37K4552 Size, 70x78 inches. Price, each....$4.75

Our Highest Grade, Mercerized Silk Finished Sateen, Down Filled Comforter at $6.50 Each.

No. 37K4556 Weight, 4 pounds. Size, 70x80 inches. Price, each.............................$6.50

Fancy Jacquard Woven Cotton Bed Comforters or Spreads at $2.35, $2.65, $2.95 Each.

These comforters are manufactured in Germany. We import them direct in large quantities and can save you at least 33 1-3 to 50 per cent on them. They are called "sanitary" for the reason that the colors are fast. They will wash and launder beautifully. They are equally adapted for a wedding present, a sick room, or for any purpose for which a comforter or bed spread is used. Warm, bountiful in size, beautiful in design and colorings, with a range from the strictly useful to the dainty ornament. If you are looking for something real swell, a medium weight covering, order one of these. If you are not delighted with it return it at our expense.

This illustration can give you but a faint idea of the pretty design this comforter is made in. It comes in a beautiful line of colors, including red, green, blue, pink or fawn grounds, with other pretty contrasting colors. It has the appearance and feeling of an all wool article, and is handsome beyond description. Be sure to state color desired. Weight, about 2½ lbs. Size, 70x80 inches. No. 37K4492 Price, each ..$2.35

You can form some idea from the accompanying illustration of the beautiful floral medallion design this comforter comes in. It has a pretty medallion center with a floral border. We consider it one of the swellest shown this season. Comes in a beautiful line of colors, including, red, green, blue or tan grounds, with pretty contrasting colors, and we look for this number to be a very large seller. Be sure to state color desired. Weight, about 3 pounds. Size, 70x80 inches. No. 37K4496 Price, each....$2.65

The accompanying illustration does not do justice to this beautiful comforter, it being the handsomest design brought out this season, both in view of pattern and color effects. It comes in red, green, blue, tan, pink and fawn grounds, with other pretty contrasting colors. No matter what we would try to say about these comforters, we could not do justice in trying to describe them, as they must be seen to be appreciated. Now, we would like you to order one of these, and if it is not away beyond your expectations and more beautiful in every way than you expected to receive, you may return it at our expense. Be sure to state color desired. Weight, about 3 pounds. Size, 70x84 inches. No. 37K4500 Price, each ..$2.95

OUR GREAT LINE OF LACE CURTAINS

NOTTINGHAM LACE	DAINTY IRISH POINT	BRUSSELS NET
BATTENBERG LACE	PLAIN MUSLIN	RUFFLED MUSLIN

OUR PRICES TO YOU ARE AS LOW AS THE PRICES QUOTED BY WHOLESALE HOUSES TO RETAIL DEALERS, BECAUSE WE BUY DIRECT FROM THE MANUFACTURERS THE SAME AS THE WHOLESALE HOUSE. IN MANY CASES, ON ACCOUNT OF BUYING MUCH LARGER QUANTITIES THAN ANY WHOLESALE HOUSE CAN HANDLE, WE ARE ABLE TO GET LOWER PRICES FROM MANUFACTURERS AND HENCE WE EVEN UNDERSELL THE WHOLESALE HOUSE.

OUR IMMENSE VARIETY comprises the finest grades of both domestic and foreign products and no matter for what purpose, whether for bedroom, dining room, library or parlor, or whether you want a very plain curtain or one of the fancy varieties or an ordinary grade or a strictly high class extra fine quality, you will find this line to exactly meet your needs. You can't find as complete an assortment to choose from in any of the big furnishing stores in the largest cities near you. As our trade covers the entire country, you can readily see that to meet such a varied trade we must have the widest possible variety in curtains. You will find in this line varieties that no furnishing store elsewhere can offer at any price, so that aside from the fact that we quote the lowest prices ever heard of, you have the distinct advantage of being able to choose from the most complete line of curtains ever assembled in one assortment. This line completely meets the needs of any household in country, town or city anywhere on the continent.

27 CENTS EACH. NOTTINGHAM LACE LAMBREQUIN.

This Nottingham Lace Lambrequin at 27 cents is wonderful value. It is used at the top of a window, and makes a very effective drape. **Comes in white only.** Size, 40 inches long by 50 inches wide.
No. 37K4576 Price, each............27c

OUR GUARANTEE OF QUALITY

WE POSITIVELY GUARANTEE that the quality of our curtains, in fact all our house furnishings, are the best standard grades on the market. We are offering only the strictly reliable, well known makes of goods. Our Nottinghams, Irish Points, Brussels Nets, Battenberg Laces and Muslins are made by manufacturers of worldwide reputation for the best curtains produced. The curtains you see illustrated and described in these pages are exactly the same high grade qualities that you will find offered by retail furnishing stores at fancy retail prices and you must not think that because our prices are astonishingly low as compared with the prices you ordinarily see quoted elsewhere that it means inferior quality in the curtain. The fact that we quote lower prices means merely that we are taking the place of the wholesale house and letting you have your curtains without having retail prices and expenses added, so that you are buying your curtains from us on the same basis as the dealer buys his store supply, and you can buy one pair or a dozen pairs or any number of pairs as you choose at these same prices.

QUALITY CONSIDERED, there is absolutely no house in the country that can offer curtains to you at such extremely low prices as these. No other house has the facilities or factory connections to enable them to accomplish it.

IF YOU ARE NOT PERFECTLY SATISFIED with any curtain you receive from us, if you don't conclude it is the best curtain value you could possibly get in the world you may return the goods to us at our expense and we will refund both the price and any transportation charges you paid on the shipment.

37 CENTS EACH. OUR BEST NOTTINGHAM LACE LAMBREQUIN.

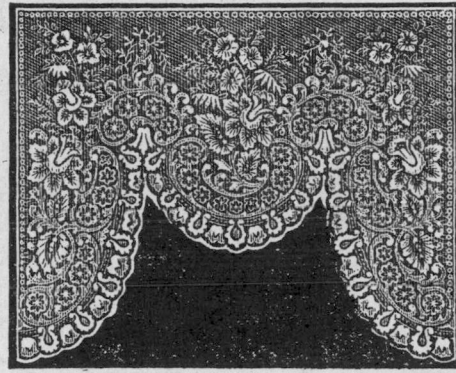

This Lambrequin is made of an extra quality of Nottingham lace, and at our extremely low price of 37 cents is selling very large quantities of it. **Comes in white only.** Size, 48 inches long by 57 inches wide.
No. 37K4580 Price, each.............37c

57 CENTS EACH. OUR LEADER IN A LOW PRICED NOVELTY LACE CURTAIN.

This curtain has the effect of two curtains, while in fact it is only one solid piece of lace. The design is entirely new, and one of the prettiest novelties recently brought out. It is made of a nice quality of Nottingham lace, and we know at our extremely low price it cannot be duplicated by any other house. **Comes in white or cream color. Be sure to give color desired.** Size, 3 yards long by 52 inches wide.
No. 37K4584 Price, each............57c

69 CENTS EACH. OUR BONNE FEMME NOTTINGHAM LACE CURTAIN. A NEAT STYLE.

This pretty Bonne Femme Curtain has been just recently introduced on the market. It is made of a nice quality of net and has the appearance and effect of a curtain that sells for double our price. From the illustration you can form some idea of this pretty curtain. The flounce effect on the bottom is woven so as to give it a heavy ruffle, while in reality it is one solid piece of lace. It comes in white or Arabian. Be sure to state color wanted. Size, 3 yards long by 54 inches wide.
No. 37K4588 Price, each.............69c

79 CENTS EACH. OUR NEW SOLID LACE ROPE PORTIERE EFFECT NOVELTY LACE CURTAINS.

This is a new style of lace curtain, and is positively an exceptional value. The illustration will give you some idea of the style of this curtain. It is made of one solid piece of lace fastened in the center so as to be draped to each side. This curtain has the style and beauty of curtains that sell at more than double the price we ask. It comes in white or cream. Be sure to state color wanted. Size, 3¼ yards long by 56 inches wide.
No. 37K4592 Price, each...................79c

89 CENTS PER PAIR.

OUR BEAUTIFUL POINT D'ESPRIT NOTTINGHAM LACE CURTAIN THAT IS SELLING WITH GREAT RAPIDITY.

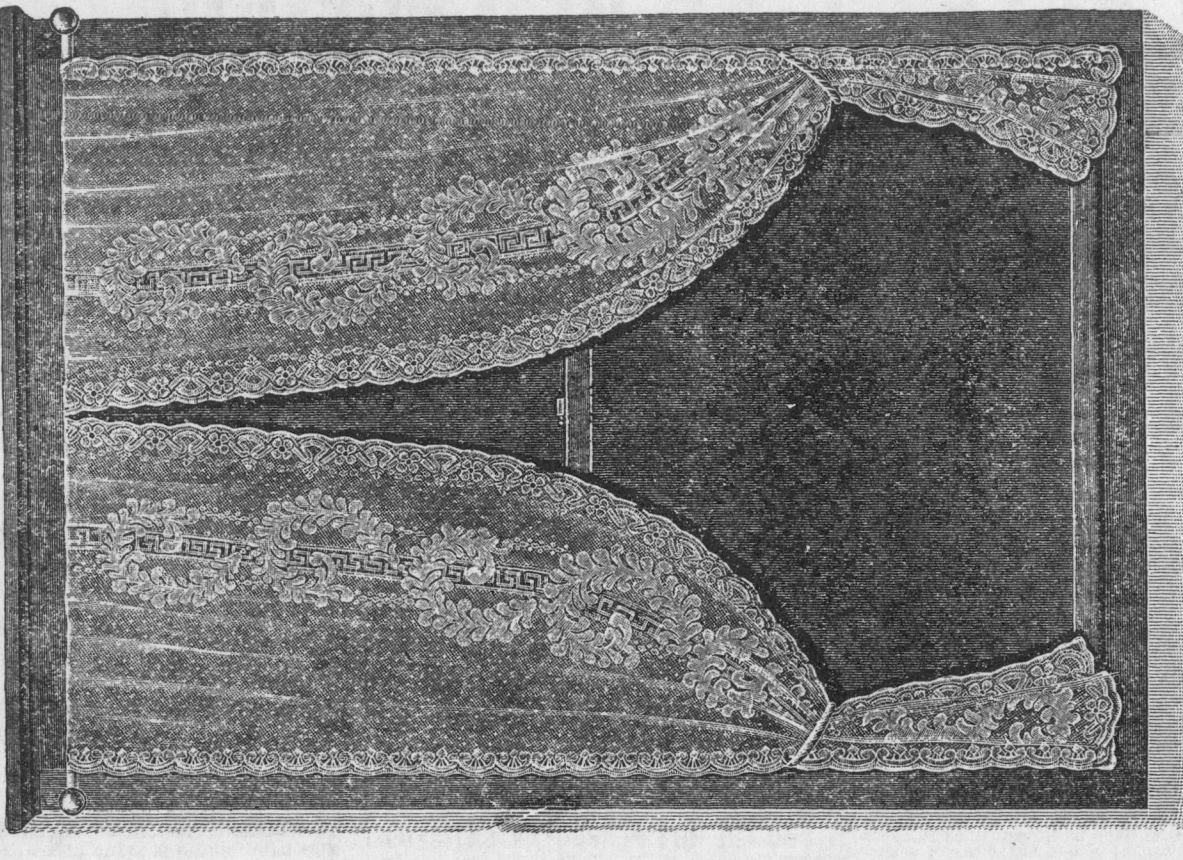

This curtained window illustration shows why our **Point d'Esprit Nottingham at 89 cents is so popular.** If you did not know that we sell vast quantities of all kinds of curtains and particularly large quantities of some special styles and that we place our contracts direct with the manufacturers, you would indeed wonder at this price. **We guarantee** however that our facilities, immense sales and very small profits especially in cases of such exceedingly popular curtains as this, enable us **to offer you the most astonishing values ever heard of.** Note the clever border design and neat point d'esprit weave in the center. It comes **in white or cream. Be sure to state color wanted.** Size, 3 yards long by 48 inches wide.

No. 37K4612   Price, per pair **89c**

78 CENTS PER PAIR.

ONE OF OUR GREATEST OFFERS FOR THE SEASON IN NOTTINGHAM LACE CURTAINS. A WONDER FOR THE PRICE.

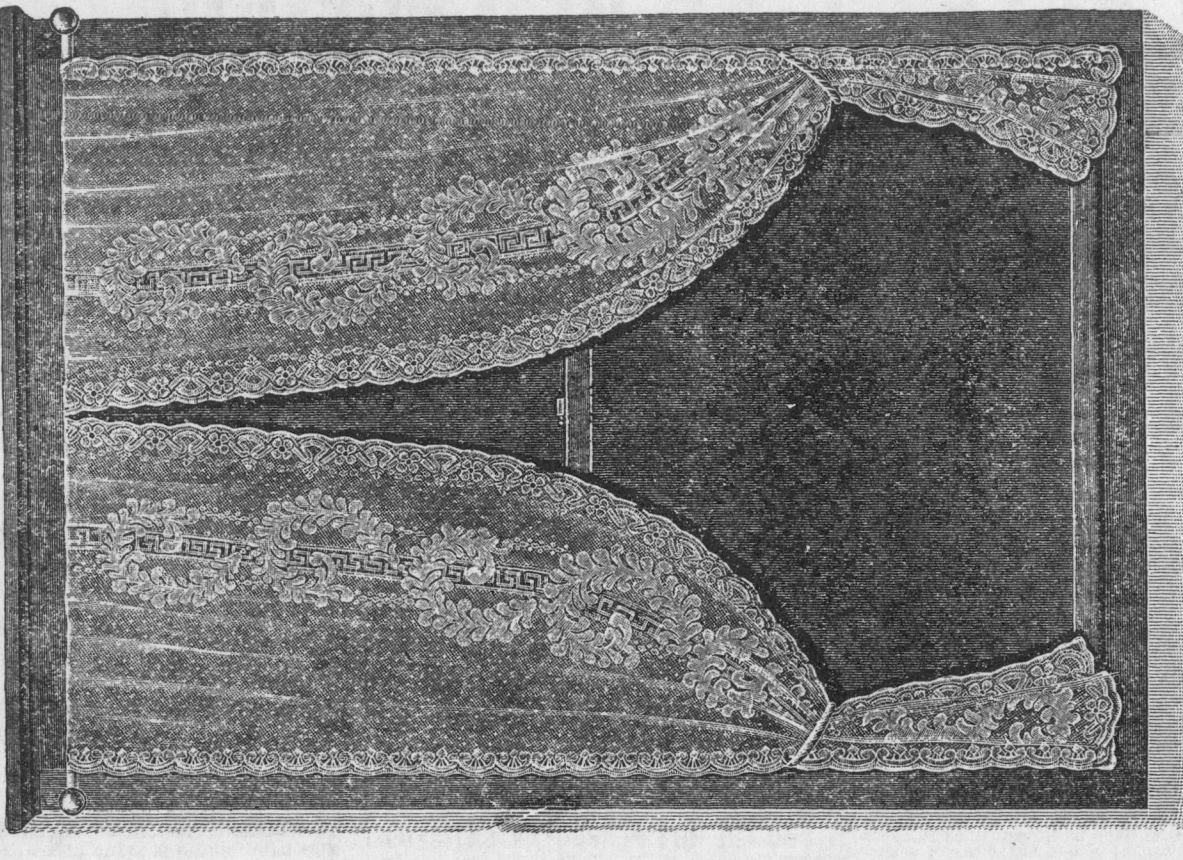

The neatness of the above design, the very effective drape it makes on a window and the splendid quality of Nottingham lace in it at this very low price makes this one of our great wonders in curtain values. Our sales on it are extraordinarily large so that, because of placing contracts direct with the manufacturer for extraordinary large quantities and getting lower prices than even the jobbers pay, we are able even to give you a lower price on this quality than the actual wholesale price. We therefore recommend this to you as one of our unusually great offers. It comes **in white or cream, and in ordering be sure to state the color wanted.** Size, 3 yards long by 38 inches wide.

No. 37K4605   Price, per pair **78c**

$2.14 PER PAIR. IF YOU LIKE A DEEP BORDER DESIGN IN NOTTINGHAM LACE CURTAINS HERE IS A VALUE OF SURPRISING MERIT.

This is a strong, well made Nottingham Lace Curtain, with an 18-inch border in a very fashionable effect with a neat, small figure in the body of the curtain, making it one of the most stylish and attractive drapes one could possibly desire for the parlor window. While, of course, we have dozens of extraordinary values both in qualities not as good and in still better qualities than this and have them in a great variety of designs, as you will find in the various pages, yet taking everything into consideration, this number is entitled to more than ordinary consideration. We are selling unusually large quantities of it and are thus able to give you a shade better value than usual. **You can have it in white or cream as desired.** Size, 3½ yards long by 58 inches wide.
Don't forget to state color preferred.
No. 37K4672 Price per pair............................$2.14

$1.92 PER PAIR. JUDGING THE DESIGN, QUALITY AND FINISH, THIS PRICE IS FULLY 40 PER CENT BELOW RETAIL QUOTATIONS.

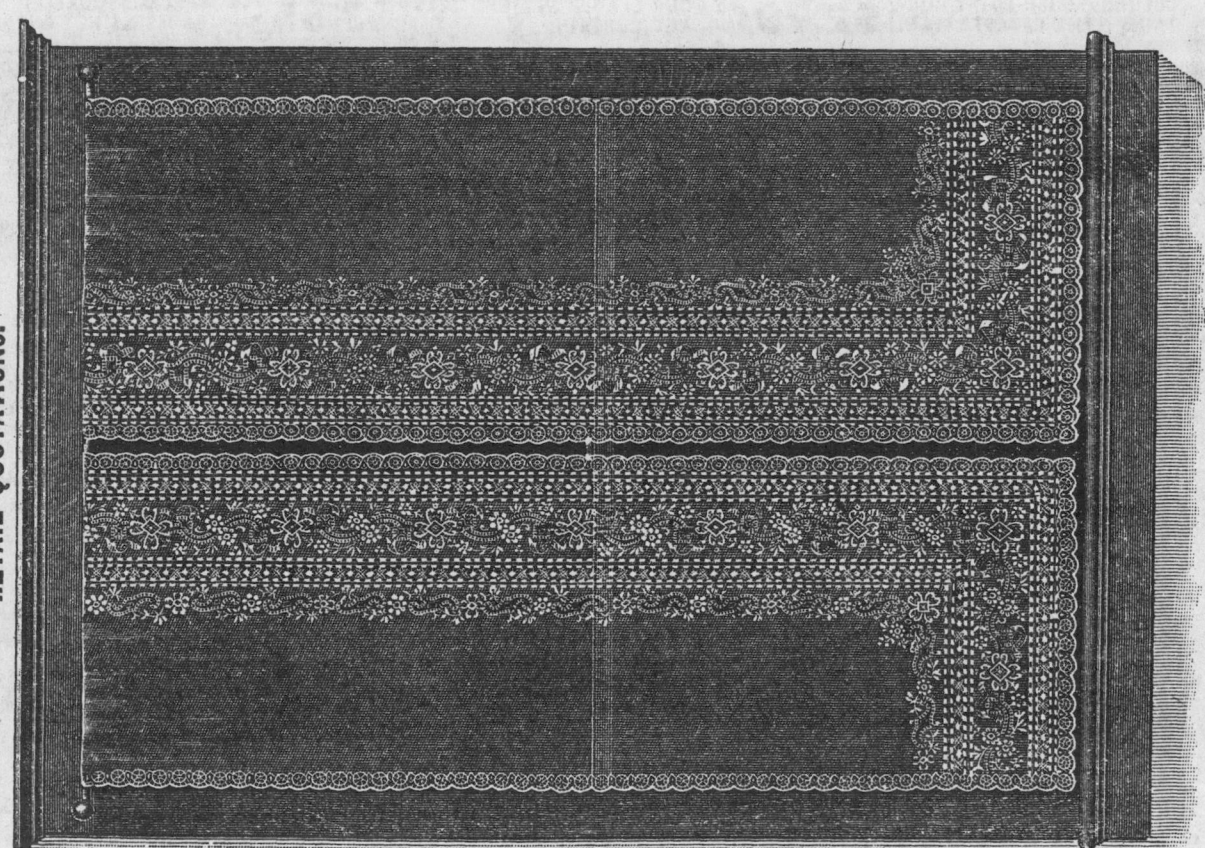

The manufacturer who makes these curtains for us has a world wide reputation for the best standard goods produced and furnishes the curtains that are sold in the foremost retail furnishing stores in the big cities, at fancy prices. This quality is sold right here in Chicago at not less than $2.75. Our enormous quantity order from the manufacturer has enabled us to quote the closest price by our one small profit plan that has ever been quoted by any wholesale jobber. It is an extra fine quality of net, a neat artistic design and this illustration will show you its unusually fine appearance on the window. We guarantee to please you perfectly or refund your money. **We offer it in white or cream color. State which you want.** Size, 3½ yards long by 52 inches wide.
No. 37K4661 Price, per pair............................$1.92

$2.98 PER PAIR. OUR LEADER IN A PRETTY IRISH POINT CURTAIN.

This is a very low price for this dainty Irish Point Curtain. It is made of a good quality of Brussels net. It has a very pretty border with neat figured center, as per illustration. It makes a rich parlor curtain at the price, and we are sure it will interest you. **Comes in white only.** Size, 3 yards long by 48 inches wide.

No. 37K4716   Price, per pair.........$2.98

$3.97 PER PAIR. SPECIAL VALUE IN IRISH POINT CURTAINS.

From the illustration you can form some idea of the fashionable, up to date design this curtain comes in. It is made of a fine quality of net, and the pretty applique work in border and edge gives it a very rich effect. If you want a stylish parlor curtain we know this will please you. **Comes in white only.** Size, 3½ yards long by 46 inches wide.

No. 37K4720   Price, per pair.........$3.97

$5.84 PER PAIR. OUR BEST IRISH POINT LACE CURTAINS.

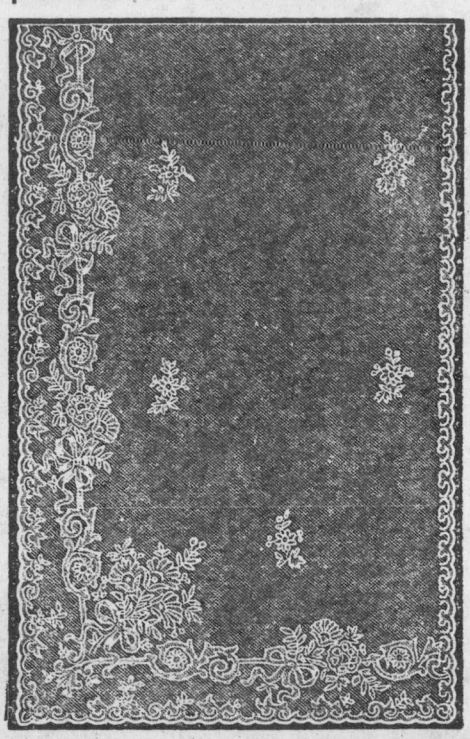

In this beautiful Irish Point Lace Curtain we offer one of the very best values ever presented to our customers at anything like the price. It is made of an extra fine quality of net, and is the richest and most elaborately designed curtain in our store. The border is exceedingly rich, showing an abundance of high art. We can strongly recommend this to anyone wanting a high class parlor curtain. It comes in white only. Size, 3½ yards long by 48 inches wide.

No. 37K4725   Price, per pair...............$5.84

$3.87 PER PAIR. COLORED IRISH POINT CURTAINS. THE LATEST STYLE.

Colored Irish Point Curtains are very much in demand at the present time. The illustration above shows this very handsome pattern made of a fine quality of net. **Comes in ecru color only**, the design being appliqued in red or green on the ecru ground. Be sure to state color of design desired. Size, 3½ yards long by 46 inches wide.

No. 37K4728   Price, per pair.........$3.87

$2.79 PER PAIR. OUR LEADER IN A BRUSSELS NET CURTAIN.

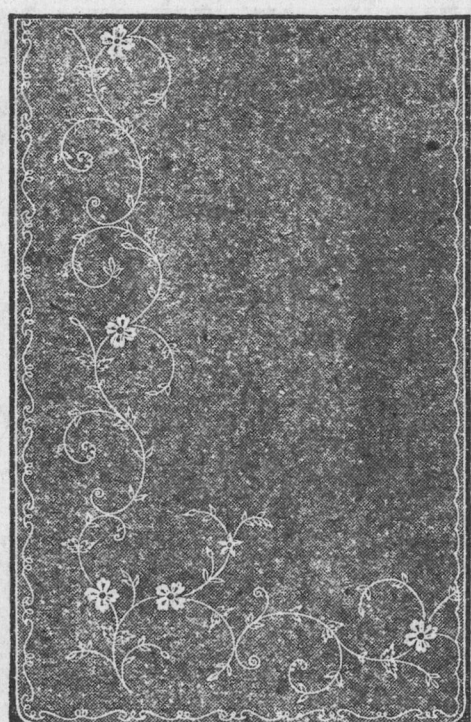

This Brussels Net Curtain is made of a very fine quality net. The scroll design border is very handsome and dainty. We are perfectly sure that by comparison it will be found that this is the best value ever offered in a low priced Brussels net curtain. It makes a very dainty drapery considering the low price. **Comes in white only.** Size, 3 yards long by 43 inches wide.

No. 37K4732   Price, per pair.........$2.79

$3.95 PER PAIR. SPECIAL QUALITY DAINTY BRUSSELS NET CURTAINS.

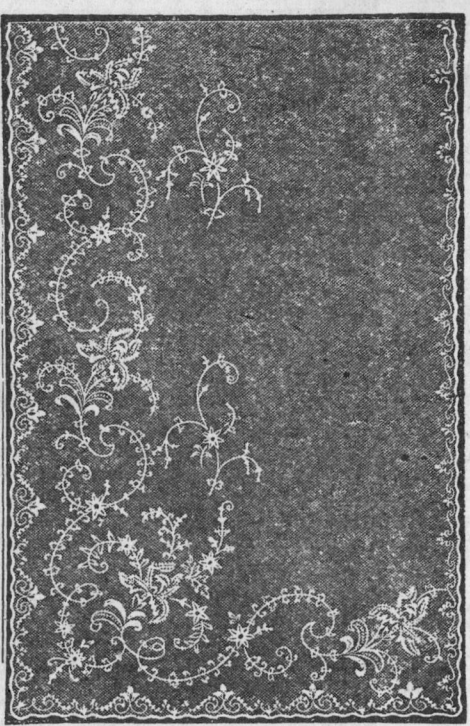

This is one of the prettiest and daintiest Brussels Net Curtains shown this season, and makes a very handsome parlor curtain at a medium price. The quality of net in this curtain will give splendid service. **Comes in white only.** Size, 3 yards long by 48 inches wide.

No. 37K4736   Price, per pair.......$3.95

OUR GREAT ASSORTMENT OF VALUES IN
CHENILLE, TAPESTRY AND MERCERIZED SILK TABLE COVERS, COUCH COVERS, ROPE PORTIERES, ETC.

$1.30 AND $1.80 FASHIONABLE AND RICH MERCERIZED SILK TABLE COVERS.

This is a heavy material that has been made to look like silk through a process patented by a man called Mercer. While not silk, it has the rich appearance of the real silk. It is very heavy. Anyone buying one of these covers will find it one of the richest and handsomest covers that they have ever had the opportunity of seeing. These covers come in beautiful shades and combinations of light and dark reds, empire green and gold, or olive and rose. Be sure to state color combination wanted.

No. 37K5114 Size, 57x58 inches, including fringe. Price...........$1.30
No. 37K5118 Size, 67x67 inches, including fringe. Price...........$1.80

39c TO $1.25 A GREAT VALUE IN TAPESTRY TABLE COVERS.

These covers are made of pretty silky cotton and the patterns are handsome, better than anything we have ever been able to present before in this popular line of covers. They are fringed all around. All of the tapestry table covers come in assorted colors, reds, greens or blues. Be sure to state color wanted.

No. 37K5142 Size, 39x39 inches. Price.........39c
No. 37K5146 Size, 54x54 inches. Price.........79c
No. 37K5150 Size, 54x54 inches. In a very heavy and stylish design. Price.........98c
No. 37K5154 Size, 70x70 inches; in one of the prettiest and richest tapestry table covers procurable. Price...$1.25

$1.19 AND $1.55 OUR NEW WASHABLE TAPESTRY TABLE COVERS.

In offering this cover to the public we are giving them wonderful value for their money, as it is the only cover manufactured today that we can guarantee to wash and hold its color. It is made of a very fine quality of cotton yarn and is nicely finished and perfectly reversible. It comes in green and white, red and white, or blue and white. Be sure to state color combination wanted.

No. 37K5166 Size, 52x52 inches. Price.....$1.19
No. 37K5170 Size, 65x65 inches. Price.....1.55

$1.59 AND $2.75 ORIENTAL TAPESTRY TABLE COVERS

This handsome oriental table cover is made of a heavy quality of tapestry, is reversible, and can be used on either side. It is a very rich pattern, and finished with a heavy tassel fringe. Colors are red, green or blue, with other harmonizing colors. Be sure to state color wanted.

No.37K5122 Size, 54x54 in. Price, $1.59
No.37K5126 Size, 70x70 in. Price, 2.75

95c AN ATTRACTIVE CHENILLE COVER.

From the illustration you can form some idea of this pretty chenille cover and at our special price of 95 cents it is certainly a winner. It is made of a nice quality of chenille and has a knotted fringe all around and comes in pretty combinations of colorings. Size, 54x54 inches, including fringe.

No. 37K5158 Price...........95c

$1.35 OUR VERY BEST CHENILLE TABLE COVER.

This cover is made of the best quality of chenille manufactured and is very heavy and closely woven. There is nothing better to be had at any price and the color combinations brought out in this cover are beautiful. Be sure to order one of these covers. Size, 54x54 inches, including fringe.

No. 37K5162 Price...........$1.35

50c TO $1.70 OUR LINE OF RICH, HEAVY OTTOMAN TABLE COVERS.

These Ottoman Table Covers come in beautiful combinations and styles, of which the accompanying illustration will give you an idea. The colors are reds, greens or blues. State preference of color when ordering.

No. 37K5130 Size, 36x36 inches. Price.........$0.50
No. 37K5134 Size, 54x54 inches. Price.........1.20
No. 37K5138 Size, 70x70 inches. Price.........1.70

BE SURE TO STATE COLOR WANTED

$1.65 OUR NEW OTTOMAN, FANCY STRIPED COUCH COVER.

This is our leader in a low priced couch cover. It is made of an extra good quality of tapestry goods, is extra heavy, and closely woven, and is the greatest value ever put out of any house at anything like our price. It is 50 inches wide by 3 yards long, nicely finished all around with a heavy knotted fringe, is reversible, and can be used on either side. This cover comes in a handsome stripe effect, and colors are red and green, with other pretty harmonizing colors. Give us an idea of color effect desired, and we will send you a cover that will please you. Size, 3 yards long by 50 inches wide.
No. 37K5174 Price.........$1.65

$1.98 STYLISH TAPESTRY COUCH COVER.

This couch cover is 3 yards long by 60 inches wide. It makes an ample, rich covering for couches. This pretty couch cover comes in handsome stripe effects. The colorings are red, green or blue, with other pretty contrasting colors. When ordering, state whether you wish red, green or blue to predominate, and we will select one of our handsome styles that will be sure to please.
No. 37K5178 Price.........$1.98

$2.59 RICH PERSIAN STRIPED COUCH COVER.

This is a couch cover that would be an ornament in any room. It comes in a large assortment of variegated contrasting stripes. It comes in shades of olive, deep Indian red or porcelain with harmonizing, contrasting color effects. The size is 58 inches wide by 3 yards long.
No. 37K5182 Price.........$2.59

$2.75 RICH ORIENTAL COUCH COVER.

Without exception one of the handsomest and most durable couch covers ever put on the American market. We strongly recommend it. The design and colorings are truly those of the Orient, and the fabric is of exceptional weight. No matter in what period a room is decorated, an Oriental rug or couch cover is always in good taste. Size, 3 yards long by 58 inches wide. Colorings are a combination of deep reds, dark greens, tans and blues.
No. 37K5186 Price.........$2.75

$3.50 RICH ORIENTAL COUCH COVER.

This is one of the heaviest and richest Oriental couch covers ever put on the market. The design and colors are truly those of the Orient. Colorings are a combination of red, green, blue, black and gold, beautifully blended. It is 3 yards long by 60 inches wide. This cover is not fringed. It is reversible and can be used on either side. We strongly recommend this couch cover. We consider it the greatest value we have ever been able to give our customers at the price. Size, 3 yards long by 60 inches wide. Give color combination wanted.
No. 37K5190 Price.........$3.50

$5.25 HEAVY, RICH ORIENTAL COUCH COVER.

This handsome, rich oriental couch cover is one of the very best qualities manufactured. It is an elegant design, rich in colorings, and almost indestructible. It is 3 yards long and 60 inches wide, perfectly reversible, and finished with a heavy knotted fringe, and just the thing for library, cozy corner or parlor. Colors are green and red, red and green, with other pretty contrasting colors. Send us your order for one of these beautiful covers, and if not entirely satisfactory you may return it at our expense. Size 3 yards long by 60 inches wide. Give color combination wanted.
No. 37K5194 Price.........$5.25

ROPE PORTIERES AND VALANCES AT EXTREMELY LOW PRICES

This handsome Valance makes a very pretty and inexpensive drape. It is made of a ½-inch chenille cord. Comes in the following color combinations: Red and green, green and red, green and rose, green and gold. Be sure to state colors wanted. These rope valances are adaptable to any size door, and can be adjusted to fit any space up to 6 feet wide.

No. 37K5198 Price, each, $1.29
We can also furnish same design as No. 37K5198 listed above, in ½-inch velour cord. This makes an extremely rich drape for so low a price. Comes in the following colors: Empire green, two-toned green, myrtle green, also in combination of red and green. State color wanted.
No. 37K5202 Price, each...$1.29

This beautiful Valance is made of a ½-inch solid cord, and makes a very heavy, rich drape at the price, and has always been one of our best sellers. Comes in the following color combinations: Light and dark green and red; red, green and pink; red, green, gold, black and blue in oriental combination; or green and gold. Be sure to state colors wanted. Can be adjusted to fit a space up to 6 feet wide.

No. 37K5206 Price, each $2.25
We can also furnish same design as No. 37K5206 listed above, in ½-inch velour cord. This makes a very heavy, rich drape for the price, and one that is sure to please you. Comes in the following colors: Empire green, two-toned green, myrtle green, also in combination of red and green.
No. 37K5210 Price, each, $2.25

This elegant Rope Portiere is made of a ¾-inch solid cord, made expressly for single doorways, and makes a beautiful drape for any room. Comes in the following color combinations: Light and dark green and red; red and green; green and red; light and dark green, pink and olive; red, green, gold, black and blue in oriental combination; or green and gold. Be sure to state colors wanted.
No. 37K5214 Price, each.....$2.10
We can also furnish same design as No. 37K5214 listed above, in ½-inch velour cord. This makes a very rich and effective drape. Comes in the following colors: Empire green, two-toned myrtle green, also in combination of red and green.
No. 37K5218 Price, each.....$2.10

SEE OUR LINE OF ROPE PORTIERES CONTINUED ON NEXT PAGE.

Don't pay retail prices for anything in the line of house furnishings. Buy your carpets, rugs linoleums, mattings, curtains, portieres, etc., from us at as low prices as the dealer pays at wholesale. We cut out all expenses and profits of retailers and therefore offer you immense savings in every line of house furnishing. Look through this great line if you want anything in the way of house furnishings.

ROPE PORTIERES=CONTINUED FROM PRECEDING PAGE.

This handsome portiere is made of a ½-inch solid cord, and is one of the strongest numbers in our line. Comes in the following color combinations: light and dark green and red, dark green; red and pink; red, green, gold, blue and black in oriental combination; or green and gold. Be sure to state color wanted. These ropes are adjustable and will fit any space up to 6 feet wide.

No. 37K5222 Price, each.....................$2.75

We can also furnish same design as No. 37K5222 listed above, in ¾-inch velour cord. This is certainly a beautiful drape for the price, and we know it will please you. Send us your order for one of these drapes, and if you are not delighted with your bargain, return it at our expense. Comes in the following combination of red and green. Be sure to state color wanted. colors: empire green, two-toned green, myrtle green, also in combination of red and green.

No. 37K5226 Price, each.....................$2.75

From the illustration you can form some idea of the beautiful design this portiere comes in. It is made of a ¾-inch solid cord, and is one of the most popular numbers in our catalogue. A rope of this quality would ordinarily sell for about double our price. Comes in the following color combinations: light and dark green and red; red, green and pink; light and dark green; red and pink or green and gold. Be sure to state colors wanted.

No. 37K5230 Price, each.....................$3.98

We can also furnish same design as No. 37K5230 listed above, in ¾-inch velour cord. We strongly recommend this rope if you want something exceedingly rich for the price. It is a beauty, and we know you will not be disappointed if you send us your order for it. Comes in the following colors: empire green, two-toned green, myrtle green, also in combination of red and green. State color.

No. 37K5234 Price, each.....................$3.98

This is a very rich portiere, and one of the finest qualities manufactured. It is made of a ¾-inch solid cord, and makes a very heavy massive looking drape. Comes in the following color combinations: light and dark green and red; red and green; green and red; light and dark green; pink and olive; red, green, gold, black and blue in oriental combination, or green and gold. Be sure to state colors wanted.

No. 37K5238 Price, each.....................$4.35

We can also furnish same design as No. 37K5238, above listed, in ¾-inch velour cord. This makes a very swell drape, and one that is sure to please. Send us your order, and if not entirely satisfactory, return it at our expense. Comes in the following colors: empire green, two-toned green, myrtle green, also in combination of red and green. State color.

No. 37K5242 Price, each.....................$4.35

OUR LATEST OFFERINGS IN PIANO AND MANTEL DRAPES

$1.98 OUR PURE SILK MANTEL OR PIANO DRAPE.

This beautiful drape is made of an extra good quality of China silk, is finished all around with a six-inch knotted tassel fringe, with draw cords and tassels, as per illustration. This is a very handsome silk drape, and an exceptional value at our price of $1.98 each. Comes in beautiful floral and oriental designs. Colors are red, myrtle green, nile green, pink, light blue or cream. Be sure to state color wanted. Size, 30x81 inches.

No. 37K5246 Price, each.....................$1.98

98c OUR BEAUTIFUL FRENCH SATEEN SILK FINISHED MANTEL OR PIANO DRAPE.

This pretty style of drape is 36 inches deep by 99 inches long, including fringe. It comes in very beautiful colors, including green, red, nile, pink, light blue or cream. Be sure to state color wanted. The color effect of each of the shades is very pretty and the pattern represents lovers' knots and bunches of roses in ribbon effect.

No. 37K5258 Price, each.....................98c

$1.85 OUR BEST VELOUR PIANO OR MANTEL DRAPE.

This is one of the newest and handsomest drapes shown this season. It is made of an extra fine quality velour, trimmed all around with a 6-inch knotted silk fringe. It has a beautiful pond lily design in border, and is certainly a stylish drape at our special price of $1.85. Colors are red, green or blue. Be sure to state color wanted. Size, 27x81 inches.

No. 37K5250 Price, each.....................$1.85

48c OUR POPULAR PRICED, HANDSOME FLORAL DESIGN, SATEEN MANTEL OR PIANO DRAPE.

This beautiful drape comes in size 34 inches deep by 90 inches long, including fringe. It comes in a pretty floral design, and is exceptional value. Colors are red, light blue, cream, nile or myrtle green. Be sure to state color wanted.

No. 37K5262 Price, each.....................48c

$1.39 OUR NOBBIEST STYLE OF FRENCH SILK FINISHED SATEEN PIANO OR MANTEL DRAPE.

This beautiful drape has a plain center with a heavy printed border of American beauty roses and foliage, and comes in delicate colors of red, green, nile, pink, pale blue or cream. Be sure to state color wanted. Size, 42 inches wide by 96 inches long, including fringe.

No. 37K5254 Price, each.....................$1.39

25c OUR LEADER IN PRETTY SATEEN MANTEL DRAPE.

This very pretty drape is 19 inches wide by 80 inches long, nicely finished with a 4-inch fringe. It comes in a bright floral design. Colors are red, myrtle green, nile, pink, light blue or cream. Be sure to state color wanted.

No. 37K5266 Price, each.....................25c

YOUR CHOICE OF THESE GREAT VALUES IN CHENILLE PORTIERES

$1.98 PER PAIR. OUR HANDSOME NEW CHENILLE PORTIERES.

This is our leader in low priced Chenille Portieres. It is made of a nice quality of chenille, is closely woven, and makes a very pretty drape considering the extremely low price. It comes in handsome shades of red, green, blue or dark tan, with a pretty dado border at top and bottom, as per illustration, and finished with a nice heavy tassel fringe. Be sure to state color desired when ordering. Size, 3 yards long by 34 inches wide.

No. 37K5270 Price, per pair..$1.98

$2.95 PER PAIR. ONE OF THE LATEST STYLES IN CHENILLE PORTIERES.

At $2.95 per pair we here offer you one of the richest and prettiest Chenille Portieres ever put on the market. It is made of a fine quality chenille, is closely woven, and comes in an elegant line of colors, such as red, green, blue or dark tan; has a rich Oriental dado border at top and bottom, worked out in beautiful harmonizing colors, and finished with a good heavy tassel fringe. Be sure to state color wanted. Size, 3 yards long by 40 inches wide.

No. 37K5274 Price, per pair..$2.95

$3.75 PER PAIR. OUR EXTRA HEAVY QUALITY CHENILLE PORTIERES.

This elegant Chenille Portiere is one of the handsomest shown this season. It is made of the best quality chenille, has a beautiful double dado border at bottom, and is nicely fringed at top, and makes a very heavy rich drape at a medium price. These curtains come in a variety of beautiful colorings, such as red, green, blue or dark tan. Be sure to state color desired. Size, 3 yards long by 46 inches wide.

No. 37K5278 Price, per pair..$3.75

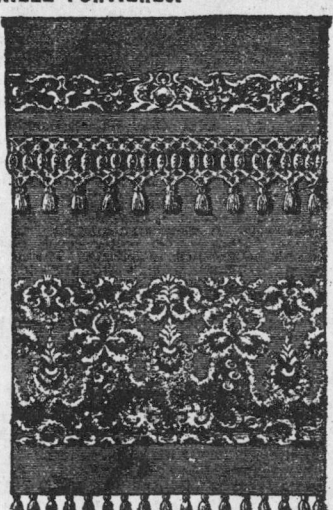

$4.75 PER PAIR. OUR VERY BEST QUALITY CHENILLE PORTIERES.

We guarantee this number to be the very best quality money can buy. Made of the finest quality chenille, is closely woven, and has an extremely rich dado border at bottom, and is finished with a very heavy tassel fringe at top. Comes in colors of red, green, blue or dark tan, with beautiful colors to harmonize in border. This is a very rich curtain and one that will drape beautifully. Be sure to state color wanted. Size, 3 yards long by 48 inches wide.

No. 37K5282 Price, per pair..$4.75

DRESS GOODS

ASTRAKHANS, ALBATROSS, BATISTES, BEDFORD CORDS, BEARSKINS, BRILLIANTINES, BROADCLOTH, CASHMERES, CHALLIES, CHEVIOTS, DRAPE DE PARIS, EOLIENNES, FLANNELS, GRIFFONETTE RAIN CLOTH, HENRIETTAS, KERSEYS, LADIES' CLOTHS, MOHAIRS, MELTONS, NUNS' VEILINGS, PANAMAS, PLAIDS, POPLINS, SAN TOYS, SERGES, SICILIANS, SKIRTINGS, SUITINGS, SUBLIMES, THIBETS, VOILES, WOOL PEAU DE SOIES, WOOL TAFFETAS, WAISTINGS.

Look through this great line of fabrics, note the excellent qualities we carry. Consider the great saving we offer, and remember that we guarantee the quality of every fabric. See our quality guarantee at bottom of this page.

WHY BUY YOUR DRESS GOODS AT RETAIL WHEN WE WILL SELL THEM TO YOU AT WHOLESALE PRICES?

WE ARE THE LARGEST CONSUMERS of Dress Goods and Silks in the world, and we buy more of these goods direct from the manufacturer than most jobbers and wholesalers. That is why we can sell you in many instanees at less than your retailer can buy the goods from his jobber. We therefore save you all the profits of the retail dealers, and even more than that. **Remember that the prices we quote you are not retail prices,** and that when you are ordering any cloth from us, you can feel assured that the same goods at retail will cost you from 25 to 33⅓ per cent more money than we are asking you. You have the same privilege of looking at the goods if you buy from us that you do at home, for we will mail you a free sample of any number listed in our catalogue (see our sample card offer below), and you have the additional advantage of a much larger assortment to select from than is shown in the average retail store. We list only the best high grade and standard fabrics in these pages.

FREE — WE WILL SEND YOU, POSTPAID WITHOUT ANY EXPENSE TO YOU WHATEVER, A CARD LIKE THE ONE SHOWN BELOW, TO WHICH IS ATTACHED SAMPLES OF ALL THE COLORS WE CARRY IN ANY NUMBER SELECTED FROM THIS CATALOGUE. — FREE

WE OFFER FREE A SAMPLE CARD like this illustration from any dress goods fabric we offer in the following pages. Just write and say, "Send me a sample card of your Dress Goods No.________." Give the number of the fabric as it appears in this catalogue on the following pages, and we will send you a card like this, showing you fair size cloth samples of each and every color we carry in that fabric. We would be glad to send you several cards if you need them. **Don't hesitate** to write for any samples you may need. We would, of course, like to have you confine your request to as few sample cards as you can, but we want to have you feel perfectly free to ask for what you need, **as we want to show you what great values these are.**

REMEMBER, we guarantee to satisfy you perfectly if you order your dress goods direct from this catalogue. You take no risk whatever. The descriptions are accurate and carefully written, but if you have the slightest difficulty in making your selection from the descriptions, **remember you can have samples of any number you wish.**

ON A POSTAL CARD OR IN A LETTER JUST SAY, "SEND ME A SAMPLE CARD OF No.________," give the number of the fabric you wish to see, and a card like this, showing all the colors we carry in that number, will go to you FREE AND POSTPAID AT ONCE.

LOWEST PRICE EVER MADE ON THIS CLOTH.

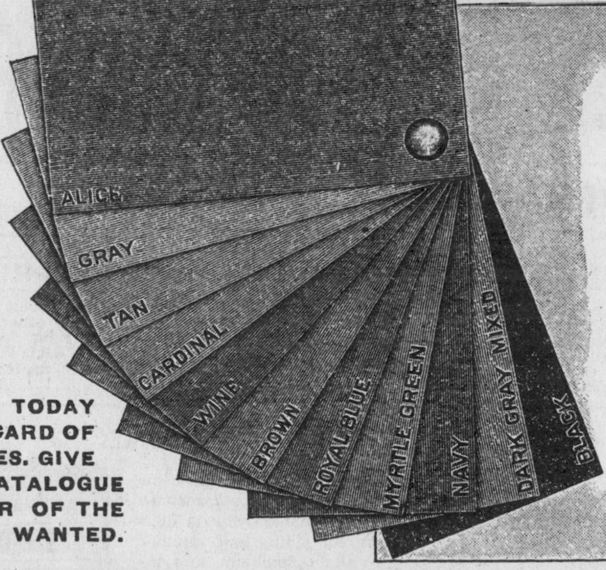

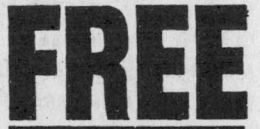

42c PER YARD FOR 54-INCH COTTON WARP BROADCLOTH.

No. 14A5229 Width, 54 inches.

WE ARE OFFERING THIS SPLENDID VALUE, all wool filled cotton warp broadcloth at a lower price than will be asked for it by any wholesaler or jobber. 45 cents per yard is the regular wholesale price for this fabric. We place our large contracts so far in advance that the manufacturer can work on this cloth during his otherwise dull season is the reason we can undersell all others.

WE GUARANTEE the goods we send you to be exactly the same as these samples, which are cut direct from full pieces in stock. Don't fail to state color, catalogue number, and number of yards wanted when you order, also enclose part of the sample selected.

No. 14A5229 Width, 54 inches.
Price, per yard..**42c**

SEARS, ROEBUCK & CO., Chicago, Ill.

WRITE TODAY FOR A CARD OF SAMPLES. GIVE THE CATALOGUE NUMBER OF THE FABRIC WANTED.

PLEASE DON'T COMPARE the values we offer with retail values. There is no comparison. We quote you as low a price per yard as your dealer pays at wholesale. Why should you pay the profits and expenses of unnecessary middlemen?

THE ABOVE ILLUSTRATION shows you a sample card of our great Broadcloth Offer No. 14A5229, which is fully described on page 908 Cloth samples of this Broadcloth, as many samples as there are colors, thus showing all colors, are attached to this card with a full description of the quality and our great offer.

YOU CAN HAVE A SAMPLE CARD LIKE THIS FREE from any number in our dress goods line. Order from this catalogue if you wish, or write for the samples if you prefer. **Always give the catalogue number of the dress goods of which you wish samples.**

WE POSITIVELY GUARANTEE THE QUALITY OF EVERY FABRIC we offer in this line. If you receive any dress goods from us which are unsatisfactory in quality, color or value, or if in any way you are disappointed in the slightest, you are perfectly at liberty to return them to us at our expense, and we will refund both the price and any transportation charges you have paid on the shipment. We take all the risk.

The following table may be found useful in determining quantities of material required for a waist or skirt for the average person:

	Amount required for a Waist	Amount required for a Skirt
If the goods are 18 to 21 inches wide, it requires........	4½ yards	10 yards
If the goods are 26 to 28 inches wide, it requires........	3½ yards	7⅞ yards
If the goods are 34 to 38 inches wide, it requires........	2½ yards	6½ yards
If the goods are 42 to 46 inches wide, it requires........	2 yards	5½ yards
If the goods are 50 to 54 inches wide, it requires........	1¾ yards	4½ yards

COLORED DRESS GOODS

SAMPLES FREE ON REQUEST.

CASHMERES, HENRIETTAS and MOHAIRS.

15c 36-INCH COLORED HENRIETTA.

No. 14K5000 An all cotton cloth, with a fine even twill, giving the appearance of an all wool fabric, and much better wearing than anything in a wool mixture that could be offered at this price. Specially adapted for children's and misses' wear. Comes in a wide range of correct colors.

COLORS—CREAM, PINK, TAN, LIGHT BLUE, NILE GREEN, GRAY, OLIVE GREEN, CARDINAL, WINE, BROWN, ROYAL BLUE, NAVY BLUE OR BLACK. Be sure to state color wanted. Width, 36 inches. Price, per yard......... **15c**

29c 36-INCH WOOL FILLED HENRIETTA.

No. 14K5020 This handsome light weight fabric, suitable for so many purposes, is woven from fine even yarn, carefully selected, and shown in a variety of colors to fill the wants of everybody. The light colors, such as light blue, pink, alice blue, nile green or cream, make beautiful graduating dresses for misses and children, and the dark colors make splendid school suits for children and street dresses for grown folks. It can be washed, and if a little care is exercised, it will neither shrink nor lose any color. It's a standard cloth, and though it costs more than ever, we have maintained our low price, so as to keep it within reach of everybody.

COLORS—LIGHT BLUE, PINK, OLD ROSE, CARDINAL, ALICE BLUE, GRAY, MYRTLE GREEN, TAN, NILE, BROWN, ROYAL BLUE, CREAM, WINE, NAVY BLUE OR BLACK. Send for samples if in doubt and be sure to state color wanted. Width, 36 inches. Price, per yard........ **29c**

51c 36-INCH ALL WOOL HENRIETTA.

No. 14K5030 In the face of an advancing market, we are still able to sell this high grade strictly all wool Henrietta at the old price of 51 cents. It is made from fine even long fiber wool, carefully selected and picked, and consequently as nice a henrietta as can be offered in a retail way at 6⁵ cents. We placed contracts months in advance, and here is the advantage of buying when the market is lowest, and you get the advantage as in this case. If we were to buy these goods now, we could not sell them at the price we now offer them. They come in a big range of colors or black, and are fully guaranteed as to style and wearing qualities, extra high finish, and soft, pliable touch.

COLORS—CREAM, PINK, OLD ROSE, RESEDA, TAN, MYRTLE GREEN, ROYAL BLUE, CARDINAL, NILE, NAVY, LIGHT BLUE, BROWN, WINE, GRAY OR BLACK. Be sure to give color wanted. Width, 36 inches. Price, per yard........ **51c**

69c 42-INCH ALL WOOL HENRIETTA.

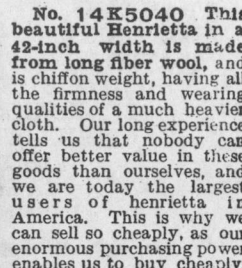

No. 14K5040 This beautiful Henrietta in a 42-inch width is made from long fiber wool, and is chiffon weight, having all the firmness and wearing qualities of a much heavier cloth. Our long experience tells us that nobody can offer better value in these goods than ourselves, and we are today the largest users of henrietta in America. This is why we can sell so cheaply, as our enormous purchasing power enables us to buy cheaply.

COLORS—CREAM, BROWN, ROYAL BLUE, WINE, ALICE BLUE, TAN, GRAY, MYRTLE, CARDINAL, NAVY OR BLACK. Samples free for the asking. Be sure to state color wanted. Width, 42 inches. Price, per yard........ **63c**

87c IMPORTED ALL WOOL SILK FINISHED HENRIETTA

PRICE LOWER THAN EVER BEFORE

PRICE LOWER THAN EVER

THIS HIGH GRADE SILK FINISHED HENRIETTA IS MADE IN GERMANY BY HENRY GLAU & CO., THE BEST MANUFACTURERS IN THE WORLD, AND IN ITS CONSTRUCTION THEY USE ONLY THE FINEST SELECTED YARN, FROM FIRST GRADE OF MERINO WOOL, WHICH ACCOUNTS FOR ITS BEAUTIFUL LUSTER. NOTHING MORE STAPLE IN OUR HOUSE, AND PLEASE NOTE WE ARE OFFERING IT AT A LOWER PRICE THAN EVER BEFORE.

SAMPLES SENT FREE.

PRICE REDUCED

No. 14K5050 We use of this beautiful Henrietta the entire output of one mill, and though we sell an enormous quantity, and though it is the best selling dress material everywhere in this country and Europe, still we have again reduced the price, and are quoting it in this book cheaper than it was ever sold. You cannot buy it in a retail store for less than $1.15 to $1.25 per yard. Think of this saving on this popular fabric, and it is sold as everything else in our line on our just one small margin of profit. It is suitable for spring and summer wear owing to its light weight, and is equally desirable for misses and children's wear, as well as waists, gowns, evening dresses, wraps and blouses for grown folks. The light colors make elegant evening or graduating dresses, and the dark colors make handsome street costumes. You can order from the description with the understanding of getting your money back if the goods don't suit you in every way, or you can write and ask for samples, which we will cheerfully send free.

COLORS—CREAM, LIGHT BLUE, LIGHT GRAY, TAN, ROYAL BLUE, BROWN, ALICE BLUE, PINK, CARDINAL, MYRTLE GREEN, WINE, NAVY OR BLACK. In ordering be sure to state color wanted.

Width, 44 inches. Price, per yard........ **87c**

SAMPLES SENT FREE

87c

COLORED BRILLIANTINES AND SICILIANS

WHOLESALE PRICES **38c YARD WIDE COLORED MOHAIR.** **WHOLESALE PRICES**

No. 14K5065 The best value on the market in a low priced Brilliantine, a fabric that is firmly woven from a good, clear, bright stock of mohair yarns, which produces a lustrous cloth of splendid wearing quality for medium weight dresses for spring and summer wear. It far outclasses any other fabric on the market at anything like the price. We offer our No. 14K5065 colored mohair in comparison with any cloth that is sold over the retail counter for 50 cents per yard. We recommend this for bathing suits as well as street and house dresses for ladies, misses and children. The colors are CREAM, TAN, BROWN, WINE, NAVY, MYRTLE GREEN, GRAY or BLACK. Be sure to state color wanted. Order from this catalogue, or, if you would rather do so, write us for a free sample card of colors. Width, 36 inches. Price, per yard....................... **38c**

44c MOHAIR BRILLIANTINE AT WHOLESALE COST.

No. 14K5070 This Mohair Brilliantine is made in Bradford, England, by the best manufacturer there, and we can guarantee every yard of it to be as nearly perfect as mohair can be made. The stock used in its construction is first quality, clean, pure mohair, which gives a high luster and smooth finish. It is strictly a spring fabric, having that light weight and elegant appearance so desirable for bright weather. To buy an imported mohair at this price is only possible where contracts are placed months in advance, and the goods woven during the dull months. We are showing in this number the best value at the price best value you can buy in America.

It comes in a good range of colors—CREAM, TAN, ROYAL BLUE, BROWN, GRAY, MYRTLE, WINE, NAVY OR BLACK. Be sure to state color wanted. Width, 36 inches. Price, per yard......................... **44c**

69c COLORED MOHAIR BRILLIANTINE.

No. 14K5080 A choice number in a 44-inch Mohair, imported, extra high luster, almost as bright as silk and will wear better. Sheds dust readily and is an ideal fabric for spring and summer wear. We pay special attention to mohairs, and we offer the best value to be found anywhere. The colors are perfect, and the new shades, while similar to the old ones, have a clearer tinge. Many prefer the 44-inch width, as it cuts to better advantage and you cannot match this quality at less than 89 cents per yard. Have no hesitancy in ordering it, as you can have your money back if not suited.

COLORS—CREAM, BROWN, WINE, ROYAL BLUE, GRAY, NAVY OR BLACK. Samples free for the asking. Be sure to state color wanted. Width, 44 inches. Price, per yard......................... **69c**

PRICES REDUCED — PANAMAS AND FANCY DRESS FABRICS — PRICES REDUCED

24c A SPLENDID WEARING PANAMA.

No. 14K5381 This number is half wool and a very popular seller in our line of fashionable dress fabrics, very firm and wiry in weave and about the weight of a French serge. It is really a splendid wearing cloth and one we would recommend for moderate priced dresses, both for ladies' and children's wear. Colors will wash. Comes in CREAM, TAN, CARDINAL, BROWN, WINE, GRAY, MYRTLE GREEN, NAVY or BLACK. Be sure to state color wanted. Width, 36 inches.
Price, per yard.................24c

35c FANCY CHECK PANAMA CLOTH.

No. 14K5385 A very handsome plain colored Panama with a corded over check about 2 inches square. It is a half wool cloth that will present a very pleasing effect when made up, just a little change from the plain cloths that are so much the rage in every style of dress. It is made especially for us from our own designs, and is a better value than you can buy elsewhere for one-third more money. The colors are BROWN, WINE, ROYAL BLUE, RESEDA GREEN, MYRTLE GREEN, NAVY or BLACK. Samples free, postpaid, if you want them. Be sure to state color wanted. Width, 36 inches. Price, per yard.....35c

65c WORSTED PANAMA, 50 INCHES.

No. 14K5400 Panamas still have the lead in fancy weaves for this season's dress fabrics, and they are deservedly popular, for there is no better wearing cloth. This is a medium weight cloth made from all pure wool yarn, woven close and firm, a cloth that will not sag and pull out of shape. It is full 50 inches wide in clear bright colorings in the following shades: LIGHT GRAY, SLATE, TAN, WINE, BROWN, ROYAL BLUE, MYRTLE GREEN, NAVY or BLACK. In ordering, be sure to state color wanted.
Width, 50 inches.   Price, per yard.....65c

77c ALL WOOL CHIFFON PANAMA.

No. 14K5410 This is a fine grade Chiffon Panama, strictly all pure wool. These cloths, while lighter in weight and of finer weave than the regular panama, will wear equally as well. This is a neat even weave that will give excellent service when made into street or house dresses for ladies and misses. We carry it only in the latest up to date shades, as follows: TAN, GRAY, RESEDA GREEN, ROYAL BLUE, MYRTLE GREEN, WINE, NAVY, BROWN or BLACK. Be sure to state color wanted. Ask for samples if you want them; they are free.
Width, 42 inches.   Price, per yard....77c

81c A WONDERFUL VALUE IN IMPORTED WOOL TAFFETA.

No. 14K5411 A very handsome piece of goods in a fine weave, all pure wool Taffeta. We import this beautiful taffeta direct from France and consider it one of the best of its kind on the market and one that we know cannot be matched for less than a dollar per yard at any retail counter. It is a very soft, smooth draping fabric that will give splendid wear on account of its close even weave and being foreign dyed. The colors are the best shades of CREAM, TAN, WINE, ROYAL BLUE, LIGHT BROWN, MEDIUM BROWN, GRAY, WINE, MYRTLE GREEN or BLACK. When sending in your order be sure to state color wanted. Width, 42 inches. Price, per yard.....81c

65c FANCY CHECK CHIFFON PANAMA.

No. 14K5409 One of the neatest patterns offered for sale this season in the fancy weave dress goods line. Fine quality yarns only are used in its construction, the weave and finish are perfect. The ground colors are beautiful shades of CREAM, TAN, CASTOR, GRAY, RESEDA GREEN, ALICE BLUE, WINE, BROWN, MYRTLE GREEN, ROYAL BLUE, NAVY or BLACK. The darker colors are cross lined with plaids in self colorings, while the cream, tan, gray, alice blue, and reseda are cross lined in the dainty plaids with cross lines of cadet blue. When sending in your order be sure to state color wanted. Width, 40 inches. Price, per yard.....65c

84c PLAIN COLORED SHADOW CHECK BATISTE.

No. 14K5417 This is a medium Batiste in plain colors, woven in small shadow check effect, both ways about every 2 inches apart with a twisted cord-like stripe of the same color as shown in the illustration, and which produces a very neat and handsome dress fabric, and a style that is very popular in the larger cities with the high class trade. For light weight dresses for spring and summer you cannot find anything better to wear or neater in appearance. It comes in the following range of colors: TAN, WINE, GRAY, ALICE BLUE, RESEDA GREEN, BROWN, ROYAL BLUE, NAVY or BLACK. Be sure to give color wanted.
Width, 42 inches.
Price, per yard......84c

85c COLORED FRENCH POPLIN.

No. 14K5419 French Poplins are among the prettiest weaves brought out this season for the high class trade. There is no cloth in the novelty dress goods line that smacks more of style and elegance than do these imported fine weave poplins and poplinettes, and their wearing qualities are too well known to need mention. The colors, TAN, GRAY, ALICE BLUE, OLD ROSE, BROWN, CARDINAL, WINE, ROYAL BLUE, NAVY or BLACK. Be sure to give color wanted when you order.   Width, 42 inches.
Price, per yard.................85c

90c 42-INCH FANCY STRIPED PANAMA.

No. 14K5425 Under this number we are offering you one of the best fancy striped Panama suitings ever sold for anything like the price of 90 cents per yard. It is a better value than any retail store in the country will sell for $1.15. It is not a heavy weight cloth, but just the right weight for spring and summer wear. It is a pure wool cloth of solid color, woven in a shadow stripe effect, stripes about ¼ inch apart. Any of the following colors will make a handsome street costume for both ladies and misses: TAN, RESEDA GREEN, ROYAL BLUE, NAVY, GRAY, BROWN, WINE or BLACK. Ask for samples if you want them.
Be sure to state color wanted.
Width, 42 inches.   Price, per yard...90c

84c HANDSOME RIVERA SERGE SUITING.

No. 14K5412 This is one of the prettiest ladies' dress suitings in our Dress Goods Department, made from long fiber pure Australian wool yarns, about the same weight and weave as a serge, but with little chainlike stripes running lengthwise of the goods, about ¼ inch apart. It is just a little change from the plain goods and a cloth that is sure to become very popular with our trade, in fact, it is one of the prettiest novelties shown this season. Colors are GRAY, TAN, BROWN, WINE, MYRTLE GREEN, ROYAL BLUE, NAVY or BLACK. Don't forget to give number of yards and color wanted. Width, 42 inches.   Price, per yard.....84c

88c SHADOW STRIPED POPLIN.

No. 14K5418 Another novelty in plain colored dress goods and a very pretty one at that. The accompanying illustration will give you a good idea of the style of the fabric, though of course it does not do the cloth justice. It is made from all pure wool of the finest grade, poplin weave and has a very neat little shadow stripe running lengthwise of the cloth. It might be considered a plain cloth, but the stripe gives it a character and style. It is very closely woven and will give good serviceable wear. Colors are TAN, ALICE BLUE, ROYAL BLUE, RESEDA GREEN, WINE, GRAY, BROWN, MYRTLE GREEN, NAVY or BLACK. Samples free. Be sure to give color wanted.
Width, 42 inches.   Price, per yard......88c

87c FINE WEAVE MELROSE CLOTH.

No. 14K5420 Melrose weaves are again coming to the front and really there is nothing prettier than a nice gown made from one of our fine melroses. This is an extremely smooth, even and finely woven cloth, nothing but absolutely all pure wool of the finest quality goes into its construction. It will shed the dust and wear like a high grade mohair. These are the colors: TAN, ALICE BLUE, RESEDA GREEN, WINE, NAVY, BROWN or BLACK. Order direct from this description or send for free samples. Be sure to give color wanted when you order.
Width, 41 inches.   Price, per yard...87c

89c EXTRA WIDE CHIFFON PANAMA.

No. 14K5431 Is a quality of 54-inch Chiffon Panama that we offer you at the same price your dealer would ask you for goods that are only 42 inches wide and not one bit better in quality. There is a great saving in using this wide cloth as it cuts to much better advantage. It is all pure wool, very perfect and even in weave; while it is light weight, the construction is firm and it will prove to be an excellent wearing cloth. Comes in TAN, GRAY, BROWN, ROYAL BLUE, WINE, NAVY, MYRTLE GREEN or BLACK.
Be sure to state color wanted.
Width, 54 inches.   Price, per yard .89c

95c HEAVY WEIHT PANAMA.

No. 14K5432 A splendid quality in heavy weight Panama. Not a fine weave cloth like the preceding number, but one that will withstand hard wear and continue to look bright and clear. Made from hard twisted Australian wool yarn of superior strength, one of the best fabrics in our line and we recommend it very highly for ladies' tailored suits or walking skirts. Comes in a range of good serviceable colors as follows: TAN, BROWN, GRAY, WINE, MYRTLE GREEN, NAVY, RESEDA GREEN or BLACK. Be sure to state color.
Width, 50 inches.   Price, per yard...95c

$1.17 54-INCH WORSTED PANAMA.

No. 14K5450 This is the finest grade of pure worsted Panama we carry. It is strictly all wool, even smooth and smooth bright finish, the best that money can buy. For street wear it has no superior and few equals. Comes in the most popular shades of BROWN, WINE, TAN, GRAY, NAVY or BLACK. Be sure to give color wanted. Send for free samples if you don't want to order from this description.
Width, 54 inches.
Price, per yard.................$1.17

$1.29 FANCY HERRINGBONE STRIPE SERGE.

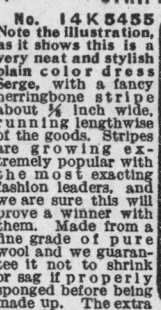

No. 14K5455 Note the illustration, as it shows this is a very neat and stylish plain color dress Serge, with a fancy herringbone stripe about ¼ inch wide, running lengthwise of the goods. Stripes are growing extremely popular with the most exacting fashion leaders, and we are sure this will prove a winner with them. Made from a fine grade of pure wool and we guarantee it not to shrink or sag if properly sponged before being made up. The extra width is a money saver. These are the colors: LIGHT BROWN, MEDIUM BROWN, WINE, OLIVE GREEN, ROYAL BLUE, NAVY or BLACK. Be sure to mention color and number of yards wanted.
Width, 54 inches.
Price, per yard.................$1.29

77c EXTREMELY HANDSOME FANCY MOHAIR.

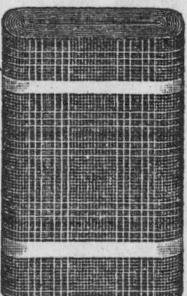

No. 14K5456 These Mohairs are among the prettiest and best wearing fabrics in the medium weight dress goods line. This one is extremely pretty, woven from fine bright mohair yarns into neat hairline plaid and stripe effects in GRAY, TAN or RESEDA GREEN grounds, also in small plaids of DARK GREEN and NAVY BLUE, some of which are cross lined with fine lines of red. All very dressy. Be sure to state color wanted. Samples are free for the asking. Width, 42 inches. Price, per yard.....77c

PRICES REDUCED — BLACK DRESS GOODS DEPARTMENT — PRICES REDUCED

It makes no difference how exacting you may be, in this assortment of black dress goods you will find something that will just suit you. We are spending no end of time and money to make this department replete with every new weave and style as fast as they come into the market. On account of the immense quantities of goods we use, we are in a position to dictate to the manufacturers and weavers, thereby procuring from them the very lowest possible cost price. This is why we can sell you cheaper than most retailers can buy from the wholesaler or jobber. We will send you free samples of anything in the line and you have the same privilege of selecting from the material as if you were buying your goods over the retail counter in any large city store, with the additional advantage of our big saving in price.

15c BLACK COTTON HENRIETTA.

No. 14K5690 This is an all cotton, yard wide Henrietta, with a fine even twill, good firm weight and has all the appearance of being a pure wool fabric. It is much better wearing cloth than the low priced part wool cloth, and will wash well. Much used for linings, underskirts, petticoats, as well as for house dresses. Samples free if you write for them.
Width, 36 inches.
Price, per yard............... **15c**

29c FINE WEAVE WOOL FILLED BLACK HENRIETTA.

No. 14K5710 An excellent wearing light weight Henrietta or Cashmere, made of a fine grade cotton warp, and a pure all wool filling. It is undoubtedly the best low priced wool filled cloth on the market. We have carried this for several seasons past, and have yet to receive a complaint on its wearing qualities. It is full 36 inches wide and comes in a **CLEAR BRIGHT BLACK.**
Price, per yard............. **29c**

BLACK CASHMERES AND HENRIETTAS.

We are showing in this line the most complete assortment of black Cashmeres and Henriettas that we have ever been able to offer our customers. They are the products of the very best domestic and foreign looms and we are offering them to you at a saving of at least 33½ per cent over the prices asked for them in the retail stores.

51c PURE WOOL BLACK HENRIETTA.

No. 14K5720

Though prices on wool goods have advanced materially, we are able to offer our customers this splendid all pure wool henrietta at a lower price than last season, by reason of the fact that we placed our contract on these goods so far in advance. It is made from a fine grade of long fiber wool yarns, smooth and even in finish, warranted to give service and wear. **Color, BLACK.**
Width, 36 inches.
Price, per yard........ **51c**

69c WIDE ALL WOOL BLACK HENRIETTA.

No. 14K5730

This is a handsome fine weave Henrietta of more than ordinary value. It is firm in weave and of good weight, made from a fine quality imported merino wool yarns. The weave is absolutely perfect, and for a medium priced henrietta there is nothing on the market to equal it, taking the 42-inch henrietta into consideration. Samples free for the asking.
Width, 42 inches.
Price per yard........ **69c**

87c IMPORTED ALL WOOL BLACK HENRIETTA.

No. 14K5740 This is a regular $1.15 German Henrietta, and at our price we are saving you 25 per cent. It is the best all pure wool henrietta to be found in any market, being made from the finest selected yarns and woven in a very fine even twill, which is only done to perfection by foreign weavers. It is the best wearing cloth for all kinds of black dresses and especially for mourning purposes. Width, 44 inches. Price, per yard............ **87c**

$1.15 SILK WARP BLACK HENRIETTA.

No. 14K5750 If you want something rich and stylish looking in a plain weave fabric, you can do no better than send for one of our silk warp henriettas. This is a splendid wearing cloth of good medium weight, woven from fine grade of black silk finished all wool yarns and a pure silk warp, which produces a cloth of handsome luster and splendid wearing qualities. It is very much in demand for fine mourning gowns as well as for regular wear.
Width, 44 inches. Price, per yard, **$1.15**

$1.38 FINEST QUALITY SILK WARP HENRIETTA.

No. 14K5760 Of all the numbers in our line there is none that we would be more pleased to have you order than this, for we know the material so well that you could not help being satisfied. It is the very best imported pure silk warp henrietta that is manufactured on foreign looms and a splendid wearing cloth. It is of good weight, suitable for all year around wear. It is a very bright and lustrous cloth in color and there is no finer weave cloth on the market that will give better wear than this one.
Width, 44 inches. Price, per yard. **$1.38**

FINE WEAVE BLACK FABRICS

17c HALF WOOL BLACK CHALLIE OR NUN'S VEILING.

No. 14K5770 This is a fine wearing, low priced black Challie, cotton warp all pure wool filling, and a cloth that will give splendid wear and service. It has the appearance of being all wool, and we recommend it for separate skirts and dresses to those that want inexpensive good wearing cloth.
Width, 27 inches. Price, per yd.. **17c**

44c YARD WIDE BLACK WOOL BATISTE.

No. 14K5780 This is all pure wool plain even weave black Batiste, a splendid light weight material for spring and summer wear. It is closely woven and, while it is a good firm cloth, it is soft to the touch, and will drape beautifully. For those clinging black house gowns, or for evening wear there is nothing prettier. We will be glad to send you free samples if you write for them.
Width, 36 inches. Price, per yard... **44c**

59c OUR SUPERBA BLACK BATISTE.

No. 14K5782 This is the best wearing Batiste on the market, very soft in texture and the weave is perfect. It is 42 inches wide and positively all pure wool. It has proven itself to be a splendid wearing cloth and one that we guarantee not to pull and sag out of shape after being made up. It is much used for heavy mourning veils as well as all around dress purposes. Retailers everywhere will ask you 80 cents per yard for the same cloth. Comes in a clear bright BLACK.
Width, 42 inches. Price, per yard..... **59c**

45c BLACK WOOL ALBATROSS.

No. 14K5800 This is a very pretty soft crepe weave fabric that is among the neatest and most dressy light weight fabrics we are offering this season, a value that cannot be sold for less than 55 cents per yard at retail. It will lend itself nicely to the dressmaker's art and make up beautifully for house dresses or trimmed costumes for evening wear.
Width, 36 inches. Price, per yard... **45c**

$1.23 BLACK SILK WARP TAFFALINE.

No. 14K5816 This elegant material is one of the swellest dress fabrics ever put on the market for dress purposes. It is made from the finest imported wool yarns combined with a bright lustrous silk warp. It is on the order of a sublime or lansdowne, but is a firmer and much better wearing cloth than either of these. Samples free for the asking.
Width, 40 inches. Price, per yard. **$1.23**

$1.29 BLACK SILK STRIPE EOLIENNE.

No. 14K5818 Something new in the line of silk warp fabrics, so rich in luster that it looks like an all silk eolienne, one of the prettiest cloths in our Black Goods Department. Made from the finest grade materials, so woven that it has shadow stripes of pure silk running the up and down way of the cloth. Light in weight, and will be very popular for street and evening gowns this season when stripes are so much in vogue.
Width, 42 inches.
Price, per yard.................. **$1.29**

35c BLACK COTTON VOILE.

No. 14K5803 A good wearing cotton Voile, made from hard twisted cotton yarns, almost as rich looking as a wool voile. It is good firm weight and an all around good wearing cloth that will wash well. These voiles are much used, in fact, they are taking the place of such sheer weave fabrics as organdies, silk mulls, etc. Write for samples.
Width, 36 inches.
Price, per yard...... **35c**

89c FINE FRENCH BLACK VOILE.

No. 14K5810 This is a very handsome all pure wool French Voile, made from a fine grade of bright, lustrous and hard twisted yarn, fine even weave and of good firm weight, a cloth that we guarantee to hold its shape when made up, one that will not turn gray as do many of the cheaper grades. It is extremely popular for separate skirts as well as complete costumes for street and house wear.
Width, 43 inches.
Price, per yard.................. **89c**

58c EXTREMELY HANDSOME BLACK LISLE VOILE.

No. 14K5804 These lisle Voiles are imported direct from France, and there is no light weight fabric that will show off better and give better service than these. The weave is smooth, even and perfect, and they are so bright and lustrous that it is hard to distinguish them from pure silk voiles. There is nothing richer for street or house wear than one of these lisle voiles made over a silk foundation. **Color, BLACK.**
Width, 42 inches.
Price, per yard...... **58c**

$1.23 OUR BEST BLACK VOILE.

No. 14K5815 We import this fine grade all wool Voile direct from France, and it is the finest grade we handle, being made from specially selected hard twisted yarns. It is very strong and smooth in finish, and it is absolutely free from knots and short ends so noticeable in the domestic voiles. Compare this cloth with what your dealer offers you for $1.75 per yard and you will readily send us your order, at the saving of at least 30 per cent. Comes in BLACK only.
Width, 44 inches.
Price, per yard.................. **$1.23**

BLACK MOHAIR BRILLIANTINES AND SICILIANS

Our mohair business has increased to such an extent that we import direct from Bradford, England, more of these justly famous cloths than any house in America. We pay special attention to this end of the Dress Goods Department, and owing to the orders we place, we have many numbers made specially for us, and buying them direct, we save all importer's and jobber's profits, and can sell them to you as cheap as the jobber here can sell to the retailer. Our mohairs are all guaranteed to be strictly first class in weave, luster and quality, each piece is carefully examined before being accepted, and you can feel assured when you buy a mohair from us, you are getting the best value that money can buy, besides getting as perfect a piece of goods as the weaver can turn out. We show them in a big range of prices to suit every purse, and warrant our cheap numbers as well as the better ones. They will be more popular this spring than ever, and we are better equipped to serve you than ever before.

A trial order will convince you of where to buy mohairs, brilliantines and sicilians.

40c CLEAR BLACK MOHAIR BRILLIANTINE.

No. 14K5821 A very bright clear black Brilliantine, made of good stock and will give much better wear than any cloth of domestic manufacture at this price. It will give splendid wear and sheds dust easily, so is as desirable as any fabric for summer skirts or long coats for children and misses. Samples free for the asking.
Width, 37 inches. Price, per yard..... **40c**

48c BLACK MOHAIR BRILLIANTINE.

No. 14K5840 This is a very elegant cloth made from pure mohair, bright smooth finish and will give excellent wear. Like the other numbers it is made especially for us, and we can guarantee every yard of it. Samples free on request.
Width, 38 inches. Price, per yard... **48c**

72c 44-INCH BRILLIANTINE MOHAIR.

No. 14K5855 This close, even weave Brilliantine is extra bright and light weight, but loses nothing in the wearing qualities, as the warp is much better grade of yarn than is usually shown in a mohair at this price. It has a rich, lustrous finish that makes it so desirable for street wear, and will shed dust readily. For a waist, skirt or walking suit it is ideal and is used by many for long outside coats. Samples free on request.
Width, 44 inches. Price, per yard... **72c**

$1.19 FINEST QUALITY BLACK TAMISE MOHAIR.

No. 14K5870 These Tamise Mohairs are the finest quality goods manufactured from mohair yarns, they are the same weave and construction as a brilliantine but slightly lighter in weight, as it is made from a fine yarn and so bright and lustrous, it is hard to distinguish it from a pure silk fabric.
Width, 45 inches. Price, per yard, **$1.19**

71c WIDE BLACK SICILIAN.

No. 14K5890 This is a splendid quality of imported black Mohair Sicilian, full 50 inches wide and a good firm weight cloth, slightly heavier than a brilliantine and preferred by many on this account. There is no cloth manufactured that will shed the dust and wear to better advantage in either complete suits or separate skirts than one of these sicilians.
Width, 50 inches. Price, per yard... **71c**

44c HIGH GRADE LUSTER MOHAIR BRILLIANTINE.

No. 14K5830 This handsome Mohair has a regular silk luster, being made from a fine yarn, so bright that at a short distance it often is taken for silk and will wear better. For suits, skirts, gymnasium and bathing suits it has no superior at half again as much money. Every yard guaranteed. Samples free on request.
Width, 38 inches. Price, per yard... **44c**

59c LUSTROUS BLACK MOHAIR BRILLIANTINE.

No. 14K5850 This is a wider Mohair and preferred by many on that account, and we can assure you of its exceptional quality for this price. It would sell ordinarily at retail for 75 cents per yard, but all this saving is yours, if you want it. For a skirt or dress we can offer you nothing in a medium priced article that will give you the satisfaction in worth and wear that this number will. Order and be convinced.
Width, 44 inches. Price, per yard... **59c**

89c 44-INCH BLACK MOHAIR BRILLIANTINE.

No. 14K5860 This is a handsome quality silk finished Mohair Brilliantine, exceptionally bright in finish and luster. Nothing but the best long fibered silk finished mohair yarn is used in its construction. We offer this cloth in comparison with what retailers everywhere are asking $1.25 per yard. Samples are free if you want them.
Width, 44 inches. Price, per yard... **89c**

$1.05 BLACK SILK LUSTER MOHAIR BRILLIANTINE.

No. 14K5880 This is the best quality we carry in a wide black Mohair Brilliantine, one that cuts to good advantage when making up. For smooth, even weave and rich silk luster this cloth has no equal on the market. It will keep its rich appearance almost indefinitely, and we guarantee its wearing qualities. Samples are free for the asking.
Width, 50 inches. Price, per yard, **$1.05**

97c OUR BEST QUALITY BLACK SICILIAN.

No. 14K5910 This is the best grade of Mohair Sicilian we carry and that we guarantee in every respect. Good in weight, perfect in weave, firm in texture, and of a rich lustrous finish. You cannot match it anywhere for less than $1.25 per yard.
Width, 50 inches. Price, per yard... **97c**

PLAIN COLORED TAFFETA SILKS. PRICES REDUCED ON EVERY NUMBER ON THIS PAGE.

34c PER YARD — COLORED SILK TAFFETALINE.

No. 14K6201 The best value ever sold in an all pure silk Taffetaline for less than 40 cents per yard. A very good wearing silk fabric, same weight and weave as a regular taffeta but not quite so lustrous, very desirable for waists, dresses and underskirts, also much used for fine lining. It will not break or crack and has all the rustle and swish of the taffeta.

We show it in a beautiful range of up to date shades and colorings, all of which we guarantee. WHITE, CREAM, LIGHT BLUE, PINK, NILE, TAN, OLD ROSE, GRAY, RESEDA GREEN, CARDINAL, WINE, TURQUOISE, LAVENDER, GOLDEN BROWN, DARK BROWN, ROYAL BLUE, CADET, MYRTLE GREEN, NAVY OR BLACK.

Be sure to state color wanted.
Width, 18½ inches. Price, per yard **34c**

FOR LINING SILKS SEE PAGE 920.

57c — ALL SILK COLORED TAFFETA.

PURE SILK TAFFETA

No. 14K6210 The best Taffeta Silk in America for the price. Our experience has taught us to be very careful in buying taffetas; we handle only reliable ones and despite the fact of the enormous advance in raw silk, we placed our orders months ago and we are able to offer you this fabric now at what the small merchant has to pay for it. This same taffeta is sold today by the best houses in the country at 75 cents; is absolutely all silk, very high luster, suitable for waists, gowns, drop skirts, linings, etc., and comes in a beautiful range of colorings. If you want a good taffeta at little money, order this. COLORS—WHITE, CREAM, LIGHT BLUE, PINK, NILE, OLD ROSE, GRAY, TAN, BROWN, RESEDA GREEN, LAVENDER, ALICE BLUE, MYRTLE GREEN, CARDINAL, WINE, ROYAL BLUE, NAVY OR BLACK. Also comes in changeables—BLACK AND BLUE, BLACK AND BROWN, BLACK AND RED OR BLACK AND GREEN.

Be sure to state color wanted.
Width, 19 inches. Price, per yard **57c**

74c PER YARD — COLORED GUARANTEED TAFFETA AT A BIG REDUCTION IN PRICE.

No. 14K6220 All pure silk guaranteed Taffeta in colors and black. This cloth is made by the best silk manufacturer in this country and sold by all leading dry goods stores at 90 cents. Is a heavy weight, smooth finish and very high luster. Every piece is tested, so you need have no doubt as to its wearing qualities. It makes a handsome gown, waist or skirt and will give satisfaction for whatever purpose you use it.

Comes in the following COLORS—WHITE, CREAM, LIGHT BLUE, PINK, NILE, OLD ROSE, TAN, PEARL GRAY, MYRTLE GREEN, LAVENDER, RESEDA GREEN, CARDINAL, WINE, BROWN, ALICE BLUE, ROYAL BLUE, NAVY BLUE OR BLACK.

Be sure to state color wanted.
Width, 19 inches. Price, per yard **74c**

WE ARE ASKING LESS MONEY FOR SILKS THAN EVER BEFORE.

(Sample card colors shown): CREAM, OLD ROSE, WHITE, BROWN, PINK, WINE, CARDINAL, LIGHT BLUE, MYRTLE GREEN, NILE, RESEDA GREEN, LAVENDER, ROYAL BLUE, TAN, NAVY, ALICE BLUE, GRAY, BLACK & GREEN, RED & BLACK, BLACK & BROWN

WE CARRY ONLY THE BEST QUALITIES IN EVERY KIND OF SILK.

A CARD OF SAMPLES OF ANY OF OUR SILKS FREE

WRITE AND ASK FOR A SAMPLE of any silk you wish to see. Never before have we been able to quote these handsome all pure silk taffetas for so little money. Owing to the enormous sales in our silk department for the past season, we have placed the largest contracts ever given by any silk handlers in the history of the country. This is the reason we can sell you these silks for less money than ever before, this is why we can sell you these handsome silks for less money than your home dealer pays for them from his wholesaler. We want to prove that we are saving you all the profits and expenses of retail dealers and are offering these fabrics at wholesale prices. You can order these goods from this catalogue if you wish. You are just as safe in doing so as in ordering from samples because we guarantee to satisfy you perfectly or refund your money, but if you have any difficulty in making a selection, or any doubt at all about the matter, please write and let us send you samples of the number in which you are interested. Write today. We will mail you a card like the one illustrated, showing every color in the actual material (a sample for each color). PRICE REDUCED.

57c PER YARD BUYS THE BEST VALUE IN ALL SILK COLORED TAFFETA OFFERED THIS SEASON.

No. 14A6210 Width, 19 Inches.

THIS GENUINE ALL SILK TAFFETA is offered to you here at the price the small merchant has to pay for it wholesale. It can't be equaled in quality at retail for less than 75 cents per yard. It is a wonderful offer in the face of the great advance in the price of raw silk, but we were able to place our orders for vast quantities before the advance in price and have made you an exceptionally great saving.

IT IS ABSOLUTELY ALL SILK and you can see for yourself its high luster and understand what a beautiful fabric it is for waists, gowns, drop skirts, linings, etc. Note the wide range of colors and the rich effects in which it comes.

ATTACH A PIECE OF THE SAMPLE to your order, thus showing the color you wish, state how many yards you want, enclose the price required at 57 cents per yard and we will send you this remarkable value. If it isn't all that we claim and perfectly satisfactory in every way, you may return the goods to us at our expense and we will refund your money.

WE TAKE ALL THE RISK.

No. 14A6210 Width, 19 inches. Price, per yard...... **57c**
SEARS, ROEBUCK & CO., Chicago, Illinois.

THIS ILLUSTRATION SHOWS YOU A CARD OF SAMPLES OF OUR No. 14K6210

OUR GREAT OFFER IN ALL SILK COLORED TAFFETAS AT 57 CENTS PER YARD. COLORS—White, Cream, Light Blue, Pink, Nile, Old Rose, Gray, Tan, Brown, Reseda Green, Lavender, Alice Blue, Myrtle Green, Cardinal, Wine, Royal Blue, Navy or Black; also Black and Blue, Black and Brown, Black and Red and Black and Green, Changeables. Order these goods direct from our description here, or if you wish, write and ask for this card and we will be more than pleased to send it to you free and postpaid, so that you may be convinced that we are offering positively THE GREATEST VALUES EVER HEARD OF IN DRESS GOODS AND SILKS.

74c CHANGEABLE COLOR TAFFETA SILK AT A BIG REDUCTION IN PRICE.

No. 14K6230 Changeable Taffetas are still in vogue for many purposes, and justly so, as their iridescent effects impart a richness not to be found in a plain fabric. We offer you the best changeable taffeta to be had, in the best color combinations made, at a price unequaled in the country and expect your patronage only on our merits. This season will see many of these used for coats and jackets as well as rich linings, waists and underskirts.

COMBINATIONS ARE—BROWN AND GREEN, BLUE AND CARDINAL, GREEN AND CARDINAL, GREEN AND BLACK, RED AND BLACK, ROYAL AND BLACK, WHITE AND BLACK OR BROWN AND BLACK.

Order without hesitancy; money back if desired. Samples free for the asking.
Be sure to state color wanted.
Width, 19 inches. Price, per yard..................... **74c**

77c SILK BROADCLOTH OR TAFFETA IMPERIAL.

No. 14K6235 The prettiest fabric for a waist or gown in a medium priced silk to be had. Smooth finish, soft touch, all silk. Wear guaranteed. Can be used for the same purposes as an ordinary taffeta but will wear much better. Money back if not in every way satisfactory. Samples free for the asking.

COLORS—WHITE, CREAM, LIGHT BLUE, PINK, NILE, LILAC, GRAY, OLD ROSE, RESEDA, ALICE, TAN, CARDINAL, WINE, LIGHT BROWN, DARK BROWN, MYRTLE, ROYAL, NAVY OR BLACK.

Be sure to state color wanted.
Width, 19 inches. Price, per yard .. **77c**

$1.22 36-INCH PLAIN COLORED TAFFETA.

No. 14K6240 This is an especially fine, firm all silk Taffeta, as bright as an imported one and will wear better; many like it as it cuts to better advantage for some garments than the narrow width. We can highly recommend it as far as wearing qualities are concerned. Samples free for the asking.

Comes in the following COLORS—IVORY, OLD ROSE, SLATE, TAN, CARDINAL, WINE, GOLDEN BROWN, DARK BROWN, HUNTER GREEN, NAVY OR BLACK.

Be sure to state color wanted.
Width, 36 inches. Price, per yard. **$1.22**

SATINS, JAPANESE SILKS, PONGEES AND FOULARDS

COLORED JAPANESE SILKS AT REDUCED PRICES.

35c 20-INCH COLORED JAPANESE SILK.

No. 14K6250 This silk is made in Japan, perfect in weave and gives splendid satisfaction in wear, as the purest kind of silk is used in its natural state, no adulteration of any kind. We import these goods direct and are in a position to offer you values not obtainable anywhere else in America. Send for samples and compare. The following COLORS—WHITE, CREAM, TURQUOISE, LIGHT BLUE, PINK, OLD ROSE, NILE, LILAC, PURPLE, YELLOW, BRIGHT CARDINAL, MEDIUM CARDINAL, ALICE BLUE, WINE, MEDIUM BLUE, ROYAL BLUE, NAVY BLUE, EMERALD GREEN, GRAY, ECRU, BROWN OR BLACK. State color wanted.
Width, 20 inches.
Price, per yard.... **35c**

45c 27-INCH COLORED JAPANESE SILK.

No. 14K6260 This is the same silk in every way as the previous number, only in the wider cloth. It comes in the same range of colors and black, and is suitable for children's dresses, waists or sashes, as well as for gowns for ladies and misses. Order and be convinced. Samples free for the asking.
The colors are clear and perfect shades of WHITE, CREAM, LIGHT BLUE, TURQUOISE, PINK, OLD ROSE, NILE, LILAC, PURPLE, YELLOW, BRIGHT CARDINAL, MEDIUM CARDINAL, WINE, MEDIUM BLUE, ROYAL BLUE, NAVY BLUE, EMERALD GREEN, GRAY, ECRU, ALICE BLUE, BROWN OR BLACK. **Be sure to give color wanted.**
Width, 27 inches. Price, per yard.. **45c**

WHITE JAPANESE SILKS

A BEAUTIFUL QUALITY RANGE OF THESE DESIRABLE SILKS, SO ADAPTABLE TO THE MANY REQUIREMENTS OF THE WARDROBE. We show them to you just as they are made, no dyeing or finishing, but that beautiful sheen of the natural silk. They wash like cotton goods and wear better than any other silk made. They come in a shade of ivory that combines with any color to advantage.

37c PER YARD THIS HANDSOME CREAM COLORED JAPANESE SILK

It is 23 inches wide and the best quality offered anywhere in the country for less than 50 cents per yard.

MADE IN JAPAN FROM PURE RAW SILK. WE IMPORT THEM FROM THE WEAVERS DIRECT.

No. 14K6275 We import and sell more Japanese Silk than any other house in America, and are, therefore, in a position to sell you these silks for less money by far than you can buy them for elsewhere. Every yard of these silks must pass through the United States Government inspection for quality, and you need no better proof than this, that they are the best that money can buy. This number is absolutely pure silk, just as it comes from the weavers' looms, guaranteed not to crack. It drapes beautifully and for waists, summer or evening dresses there is no silk that we can recommend to give better satisfaction. It will launder as well as a piece of linen. We will be glad to send you a free sample of this handsome silk. **Comes in CREAM WHITE only.**
Width, 23 inches. Price, per yard.... **37c**

33c 20-INCH CREAM JAPANESE SILK.

No. 14K6270 This natural **Habutai or Japanese Silk is not the flimsy light weight cloth that retailers sell for 35 and 40 cents per yard;** it is a good firm cloth, closely woven and one that will wash well and not slip on the warp. Very handsome and will give good serviceable wear, splendid for children's dresses, as well as separate waists for ladies. Write for free samples.
Width, 20 inches. Price, per yd., **33c**

42c 27-INCH NATURAL CREAM JAPANESE SILK.

No. 14K6280 We cannot say too much in commendation of our imported natural Habutai or Japanese Silks, for they are without a doubt the best line of these natural colored silks in the market, a soft, serviceable silk and will wear and wash, just the right weight for waists and dresses. A grade that sells everywhere for 59 cents and worth every cent of it. On account of the immense quantities we use, we are able to offer it to you for 42 cents per yard. We will send you free samples if you will write for them.
Width, 27 inches. Price, per yard.. **42c**

53c YARD WIDE CREAM JAPANESE SILK.

No. 14K6290 This natural **Habutai or Japanese Silk is full 36 inches wide,** made on hand looms from the very finest of high grade luster silk. It will stand the test of the tub and wear splendidly on account of the extra width. It cuts to good advantage when used for graduating dresses or waists. We guarantee that you will be satisfied; your money back if you are not. **Samples are free.**
Width, 36 inches. Price, per yd., **53c**

59c HEAVY 27-INCH JAPANESE SILK

No. 14K6300 We take special pride in being able to offer this heavy weight 27-inch Japanese Silk at this price. We import them ourselves, that is how we are able to do it. Retailers that have to buy their goods from wholesalers and jobbers never ask less than 75 cents for the same identical quality. It is a heavy quality that will stand the hard usage required of it in shirts and underwear. Remember, there is no dye in these natural finished silks, so there is no danger of them splitting or cracking.
Width, 27 inches. Price, per yard.... **59c**

79c EXTRA HEAVY CREAM WHITE JAPANESE SILK

No. 14K6310 This silk is made on hand looms by the most expert silk weavers in Japan. It is very closely woven and has a good firm leathery touch and very bright lustrous finish. It is a very heavy quality, especially adapted for men's and boys' shirts and blouses, as well as for ladies' wear. Every yard of it is guaranteed to wear. Write for free samples.
Width, 27 inches. Price, per yard.... **79c**

PONGEE SILKS.

39c 27-INCH PLAIN PONGEE SILK.

No. 14K6330 A beautiful fabric though not all silk, made of fine Egyptian yarn and dry spun silk, as lustrous as any silk and will wear well. Can be laundered like cotton goods and retains its finish. For waists, dresses and evening gowns it has no equal in a low priced silk. Samples free for the asking.
Comes in the following COLORS—CREAM, PINK, LIGHT BLUE, TAN, ALICE, GRAY, LIGHT BROWN, DARK BROWN, GARNET, CARDINAL, RESEDA, NAVY OR BLACK. State color wanted.
Width, 27 inches. Price, per yard... **39c**

59c 27-INCH COLORED PUNJAB SILK.

No. 14K6340 A heavy, rough part silk fabric, giving that rich effect so desirable for dresses and long coats. It is strictly high grade and will wear like worsted, having all the desirable qualities of heavy material without its weight. It is popular for street and house wear; sold for 85 cents everywhere. Samples free on request.
Full range of COLORS—CREAM, PINK, CADET BLUE, MEDIUM BROWN, RESEDA, TAN, LILAC, OLD ROSE, LIGHT BLUE, LIGHT GRAY, CARDINAL, NAVY BLUE OR BLACK. Be sure to state color wanted.
Width, 27 inches. Price, per yard.. **59c**

63c SATIN CROSS BARRED PONGEE SILK.

No. 14K6345 These fancy Pongees are the latest up to date fancy silks brought out for this season's swell trade. Made from natural color raw silk, warranted not to split or crack, and it will wash well. Ground color is tan cross lined with narrow satin stripes about 1¼ inches apart, in either WHITE, RESEDA, ALICE, ROYAL BLUE, CARDINAL, BROWN OR BLACK. It will make the swellest kind of fancy waists or dresses. Be sure to give color wanted.
Width, 19 inches. Price, per yard.. **63c**

48c SILK PEAU DU CYGNE.

No. 14K6320 All pure silk twilled back Peau du Cygne in plain solid colors, a silk of beautiful, soft, clinging texture that will make up with unusually rich and stylish effect.
COLORS—WHITE, CREAM, LIGHT BLUE, PINK, TURQUOISE, RESEDA, GREEN, ALICE BLUE, TAN, BROWN, GRAY, ROYAL BLUE, MYRTLE, WINE, NAVY OR CARDINAL. Be sure to give color wanted.
Width, 20 inches. Price, per yard.. **48c**

44c CHIFFON POPLIN.

No. 14K6400 A very pretty silk and cotton cloth with fine pin cord, same on both sides, soft, lustrous fabric that drapes beautifully and wears well, makes a handsome gown, waist or skirt and can be used to advantage for linings. Samples free for the asking.
COLORS—WHITE, CREAM, LIGHT BLUE, PINK, TAN, GRAY, CARDINAL, BROWN, MYRTLE GREEN, NAVY BLUE OR BLACK. Be sure to state color wanted.
Width, 18 inches. Price, per yard.. **44c**

CREAM WHITE and COLORED SATINS.

37c PLAIN SILK FACED SATIN.

No. 14K6350 A good grade of plain Satin for lining, fancy work and inexpensive party dresses, half silk, wears well and comes in the following colors:
WHITE, CREAM, PINK, LIGHT BLUE, TURQUOISE, PURPLE, PEARL GRAY, OLD ROSE, CARDINAL, WINE, NAVY, MYRTLE, TAN, BROWN OR BLACK.
Samples free for the asking. Be sure to give color in your order.
Width, 18 inches. Price, per yard.. **37c**

95c YARD WIDE COLORED SATIN.

No. 14K6370 **This is a high grade Satin that we guarantee for two seasons' wear,** and one that is equally desirable for both dresses and waists as well as for lining purposes where our customers want something above the ordinary. It has a very close, perfectly woven silk face with a twilled back. Send for a free sample of this beautiful satin.
COLORS—CREAM, TAN, BROWN, NAVY BLUE, WINE, GRAY OR BLACK. Be sure to give color wanted.
Width, 36 inches. Price, per yard.. **95c**

58c ALL SILK LIBERTY SATIN.

No. 14K6361 A pure silk twilled back Liberty Satin in plain solid colors. A satin of beautiful, soft, clinging texture that will make up into very rich and stylish waists and dresses. It is particularly adapted for evening wear as it comes in a beautiful range of evening colors as well as the darker shades as follows:
WHITE, PINK, NILE, LAVENDER, TAN, CARDINAL, NAVY BLUE, BLACK, CREAM, LIGHT BLUE, GRAY, OLD ROSE, GOBELIN BLUE, WINE OR BROWN.
Samples free for the asking. Don't forget to give color wanted.
Width, 19 inches. Price, per yard... **58c**

$1.00 BEAUTIFUL CREAM DUCHESS SATIN.

No. 14K6371 This is a very handsome all pure silk Satin Duchess, very lustrous and bright; the weave is perfect. No fabric is so much used for wedding dresses as the beautiful cream white satin. Also very desirable for fancy waists or evening gowns.
Width, 21 inches. Price, per yard.... **$1.00**

FOULARD SILKS.

49c ALL SILK FOULARDS.

No. 14K6375 These pretty small figured silk Foulards are very desirable for waists and dresses for ladies and misses; they are light, cool and extremely dainty. The patterns are small black and white checks, dots or stripes on LIGHT GRAY, LIGHT BLUE, LIGHT GREEN, BROWN, LAVENDER, CARDINAL OR NAVY BLUE GROUNDS. Send for free samples. Be sure to give color wanted.
Width, 23 inches. Price, per yard... **49c**

59c 22-INCH SILK FOULARDS.

No. 14K6377 This Foulard is a little heavier in weight and construction than No. 14K6375, made from bright thrown silk yarn, in a line of swell neat patterns. Splendid for children's wear as well as grown folks. The ground colors are TAN, BROWN, RESEDA GREEN, ALICE BLUE, NAVY, GRAY, WINE OR BLACK. Be sure to give color wanted.
Width, 22 inches. Price, per yard... **59c**

73c CHOICE FOULARDS.

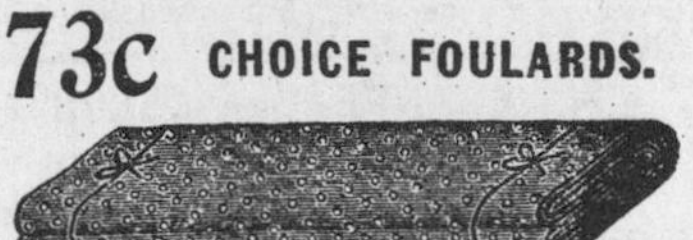

No. 14K6380 Handsome polka dot Foulard, strictly all silk. Satin finish, suitable for either street or evening wear and makes the most desirable gown a lady can wear, besides being much used for waists. In the wanted shades of NAVY BLUE, WINE, BROWN, MYRTLE OR BLACK with white dots. Be sure to state color wanted.
Width, 23 inches. Price, per yard... **73c**

YOUR MONEY WILL BE IMMEDIATELY RETURNED TO YOU FOR ANY GOODS NOT PERFECTLY SATISFACTORY.

571

REALLY WONDERFUL VALUES IN HIGH CLASS FANCY SILKS

WE ARE BETTER ABLE TO SAVE YOU MONEY on these luxuries than any house in the country. Realizing they are luxuries, the retailers make big profits on these beautiful dress fabrics, but owing to the enormous quantities we buy, we are in a position to sell them to you on the same basis which we sell you wool and cotton dress goods, at a saving of from 25 to 30 per cent. **We buy direct from the mill.** **WE GUARANTEE OUR SILKS.** We guarantee all our silks to be exactly as represented. We carry only the best qualities and the latest styles. Remember, these are regular wholesale prices.

39c CREPE DE SUMA.

No. 14K6410 A handsome Crepe, part cotton, but as bright as an all silk, and owing to its price is extra popular for party dresses and children's wear, though specially made for street dresses. It has all the soft clinging qualities of an all silk crepe and is identical in appearance. Order it and it will satisfy you. Samples free for the asking.

Comes in these colors, WHITE, IVORY, LIGHT BLUE, PINK, MAIZE, LILAC, ALICE, PEARL GRAY, DARK GRAY, CARDINAL, GARNET, TURQUOISE, LIGHT BROWN, OLD ROSE, RESEDA, NAVY or BLACK. State color wanted. Width, 24 inches.
Price, per yard...........39c

69c BEAUTIFUL CREPE DE CHINE.

No. 14K6420 One of the richest creations of the weaver's art in the silk industry. It is soft and lustrous, made on box looms from the finest grade of yarn and is dyed so that it can be laundered, thus making it almost indispensable for scarfs and trimmings where constant use makes washing a necessity. For evening wear, wedding gowns and fancy waists it has no equal, and the dark colors are exceedingly popular for street costumes.

It comes in the following wide range of colors: WHITE, CREAM, PINK, LIGHT BLUE, NILE, LAVENDER, PEARL GRAY, TAN, CARDINAL, BROWN, ROYAL BLUE or BLACK. Be sure to give the color you want.
Width, 24 inches. Price, per yard.. 69c

48c COLORED SHEPHERD CHECKS.

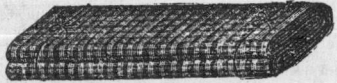

No. 14K6428 This is a good quality of pure silk Louisine weave, a silk that will give good service, as these Louisine silks do not crack or split. Comes in small, modest shepherd checks about ⅛ of an inch in size, in either BROWN and WHITE, BLUE and WHITE or BLACK and WHITE. Be sure to state colors wanted.
Width. 18 inches. Price, per yard, 48c

59c FANCY LOUISINE SILK.

No. 14K6429 A very fine quality in a good weight of pure silk. It is a bright and lustrous cloth in the Louisine weave. Will make durable silk shirtwaist suits. We guarantee the silk to give satisfaction. The patterns are all neat, small broken checks on either WHITE, LIGHT GREEN, LIGHT BLUE, TAN, ALICE, CARDINAL, ROYAL BLUE, RESEDA, MYRTLE or NAVY grounds. Be sure to state color wanted.
Width, 18 inches. Price per yard...........59c

61c BLACK AND WHITE, BLUE AND WHITE, BROWN AND WHITE LOUISINE CHECKS.

GIVE SECOND CHOICE

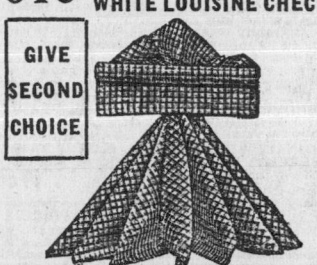

No. 14K6430 An exceptionally fine fabric for this money; something that will cost you a fancy price at retail. It is 19 inches wide, strictly all silk, rich, soft and pliable; a distinctly beautiful fabric, that wears well. It comes in a choice variety of checks.

Colors, BLACK and WHITE, BLUE and WHITE or BROWN and WHITE. Be sure to state colors wanted.

The shepherd checks come in two sizes, medium and large. If you would like to see the samples of this pretty silk, we will gladly furnish you a card of it free on request. Of course, if you order from this catalogue we guarantee to please you just the same. You take no risk at all. In ordering, kindly be sure to state the colors wanted, as well as the size of the check you prefer.
Width of goods, 19 inches.
Price, per yard................61c

63c HANDSOME SATIN STRIPED SILK.

No. 14K6431 This is a very handsome as well as stylish fancy silk, will make the swellest kind of fancy waists or summer and evening dresses. The body of the silk is either light or dark gray, with little narrow satin stripes running lengthwise of the silk, about ½ inch apart.

The stripes are LIGHT BLUE, ALICE, LIGHT GREEN, WINE, LIGHT GRAY or ROYAL BLUE. Be sure to state color wanted. Very swell. Send for free samples.
Width, 19 inches. Price, per yard...........63c

69c FANCY PLAID SILK.

No. 14K6440 An exceptional value in choice handsome satin barred Louisine or taffeta plaid silk, a regular 85-cent plaid silk for 69 cents.

Predominating colors are WHITE and BLACK; BLUE and BROWN; GREEN, RED and BROWN; BLUE, RED and BROWN; WHITE, BLACK and RED, or ALICE, WHITE and BLACK. Be sure to state colors wanted.
Width, 18 inches. Price, per yard...........69c

39c PER YARD FOR THIS HANDSOME CORDED HABUTAI OR JAPANESE SILK

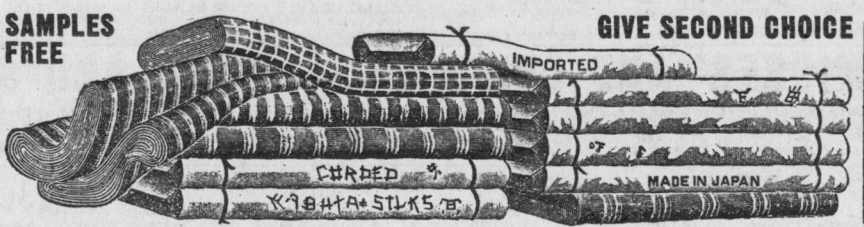

THEY ARE THE BEST VALUES OFFERED THIS SEASON IN WASH SILKS

SAMPLES FREE

GIVE SECOND CHOICE

WE IMPORT THESE SILKS DIRECT FROM JAPAN OURSELVES AND GIVE YOU THE BENEFIT OF OUR SAVING IN PRICE

AT THIS PRICE, 39 CENTS PER YARD, we are selling them to you at less money than they can be imported for today from Japan. Over a year ago we placed our contract direct with the foreign manufacturers of these corded wash silks. That was before the rise came on raw silk, or else we could not now be selling these silks for less than 50 or 55 cents per yard. The silk is closely woven and of firm weight, that will wash and iron as well as linen.

The colorings are beautiful shades of CREAM, PINK, LIGHT BLUE, TAN, NILE, LAVENDER, CARDINAL, GRAY, WHITE and BLACK combinations or PLAIN BLACK. Be sure to state color wanted.

The best silk made for hard wear, much used for children's as well as ladies' waists or dresses. Every yard is guaranteed to give satisfaction or money refunded. Width, 20 inches.
No. 14K6390 Price, per yard..........**39c**

61c CROSSLINED FANCY SILKS.

No. 14K6449 One of the prettiest pattern designs shown this season in a medium priced fancy silk. It is a silk that we guarantee to wear well, very bright, lustrous and closely woven, Louisine weave that will not slip on the warp.

It is a splendid value for the money, and one that you cannot duplicate for less than 75 cents per yard elsewhere. We especially recommend this for fancy waists and evening dresses. The ground color is WHITE, crosslined with LIGHT BLUE, NAVY, BROWN, GREEN or BLACK. State color wanted. Write for samples; they are free.
Price, per yard.............61c

93c STYLISH PLAID SILKS.

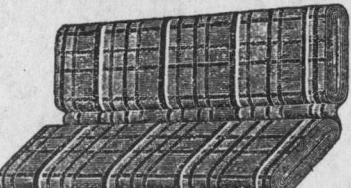

No. 14K6450 A very beautiful piece of silk, good, firm weight in rich, handsome coloring. The designs are the latest color combinations. They make the richest kind of fancy waists.

To be had in GREEN, BROWN and WHITE, CARDINAL, BLUE and BROWN, or CARDINAL, GREEN, BLACK and WHITE. Be sure to state colors wanted.
Width, 20 inches. Price, per yard...........93c

98c HANDSOME CORD STRIPE TAFFETA.

No. 14K6453 This is a very neat, solid color pure Taffeta silk with a little raised color stripe running crosswise of the goods, very similar to a faille or poplin. Will make handsome waists and dresses for those who are in search of something exclusive as well as rich and stylish. We recommend this beautiful silk.

TAN, BROWN, WINE, MYRTLE or NAVY are the colors. Be sure to state color wanted. Let us send you a free sample; we know you will be pleased with it.
Width, 19 inches. Price, per yard...........98c

$1.05 WIDE CROSSBAR CHECK LOUISINE.

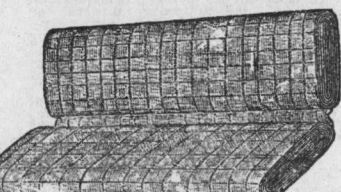

No. 14K6454 This is one of the handsomest fancy colored silks we have been able to offer our customers for many seasons past. It is 27 inches wide, and at our price we are saving you 25 cents on every yard. It is a soft, rich, handsome silk, woven in small check designs. Will not crack.

The ground colors are RESEDA, ALICE, BROWN, NAVY or BLACK cross lined with WHITE. Be sure to state color wanted. Satisfaction guaranteed or money back. Width, 27 inches. Price, per yard....$1.05

DEPARTMENT OF LININGS

CAMBRICS — MERCERIZED SATEENS — HEATHERBLOOM — MOREENS — SHADOW SILKS — PERCALINE — SATINS — SHIMMER SILK — SILESIAS

WE DO MORE BUSINESS IN OUR DRESS LINING DEPARTMENT than any store in the country, and we are in a position to sell you these materials for less money by far, than you can buy them for elsewhere. We use larger quantities than the average wholesale house, and in selling them direct to you at prices that allow us only a bare small margin of profit over the actual cost, we can save you about 30 per cent on every number listed below, as against the prices quoted at retail. Prices reduced.

WE GUARANTEE EVERY LINING WE OFFER and if you receive from us any fabric that is unsatisfactory in any way, or if you do not believe that you have received the greatest possible values obtainable in linings, you are at liberty to return the material to us at our expense and we will refund your money. We take the risk. While we do not sample linings, since these are a class of fabrics well understood and commonly known to everybody, and because the prices are so exceedingly small as compared with dress fabrics in general, **you understand our guarantee protects you perfectly.**

5c BEST QUALITY KID FINISHED CAMBRIC.

No. 14K6980 Kid finished Lining Cambric. Ours is the best 64x64 cloth. COLORS—White, Cream, Yellow, Nile Green, Lavender, Pink, Light Blue, Purple, Light Gray, Slate, Tan, Brown, Myrtle Green, Cardinal, Wine, Navy or Black. Be sure to give color wanted.
Width, 25 inches. Price, per yard....5c

10c TWILLED SATEEN WAIST LINING.

No. 14K6990 A good heavy weight Waist Lining that is too well known to require much of any description; a lining that is unequaled in its wear resisting qualities. COLORS—White, Gray or Black. Be sure to give color wanted.
Width, 27 inches. Price, per yard...10c

13c FINE QUALITY WAIST PERCALINE.

No. 14K7010 This is a finely woven Percaline, good weight with a highly lustrous beetled surface that will not wear off. Guaranteed not to stretch. COLORS—White, Old Rose, Royal Tan, Light Blue, Reseda Green, Navy, Myrtle, Brown, Pearl, Gray, Slate, Cardinal, Wine or Black. Be sure to give color wanted. Width, 36 inches.
Price, per yard....................13c

13c SHADOW SILK.

No. 14K7020 An excellent quality of Shadow Silk at 13 cents per yard. These rich, silky, rustling linings are very much in demand and we can recommend them for style and durability. COLORS—White, Cream, Pink, Light Blue, Old Rose, Light Gray, Slate, Nile Green, Yellow, Cardinal, Myrtle Green, Navy, Tan, Brown, Wine or Black. Be sure to give color wanted.
Width, 36 inches. Price, per yard....13c

60c COLORED AND BLACK PURE SILK TAFFETA LINING.

No. 14K8210 This lining is intended for those who are in search of a really high class lining, and is positively guaranteed to be all pure silk and very lustrous in finish. Made purposely for lining fine coats and jackets, also very much in demand for underskirts and petticoats. Colors are Cream, Pink, Light Blue, Rose, Gray, Tan, Brown, Navy, Reseda, Myrtle, Cardinal, Wine, Royal Blue or Black. Width, 19 inches wide.
Price, per yard....................60c

17c SHIMMER SILK.

No. 14K7030 This Shimmer Silk Dress Lining is a medium weight, finely woven lining that closely resembles silk, although it has no silk in its make up, being woven from the very finest of sea island cotton. Suitable for lining the very best of dresses. We have this in a beautiful line of colors as follows: WHITE, CREAM, LIGHT BLUE, PINK, LAVENDER, YELLOW, TURQUOISE, PEARL GRAY, OLD ROSE, NILE GREEN, RESEDA GREEN, MYRTLE GREEN, TAN, BROWN, CARDINAL, WINE, PURPLE, SLATE, NAVY OR BLACK. Be sure to give color wanted.
Width, 36 inches.
Price, per yard....................17c

THE SURPRISINGLY LOW REDUCED PRICES prevailing in this catalogue mean greater savings to our customers than ever before.

75c GOOD QUALITY BLACK SATIN LINING.

No. 14K7100 For a moderate priced black Satin Lining we offer this heavy all silk faced especially constructed satin, 36 inches wide. It is heavier and more durable than an all silk satin and will not rough up.
Width, 36 inches.
Price, per yard....................75c

$1.10 BLACK SILK TAFFETA LINING.

No. 14K8520 We do not hesitate to say that this handsome black taffeta is the best pure silk lining made. It is specially constructed and made with the idea in view, of producing pure silk lining that will give good serviceable wear. Width, 35 inches. Price, per yard..........$1.10

32c HEATHERBLOOM. REDUCED IN PRICE.

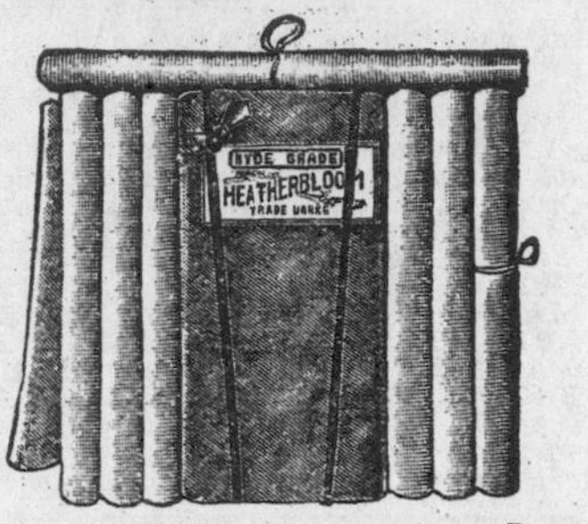

No. 14K7080 Heatherbloom Dress Lining, the neatest and best substitute for silk to be found on the market. Light in weight, highly lustrous and with that crisp rustle that is found in no other lining outside of silk. The weave resembles the genuine taffeta silk, just the foundation wanted for light, open weave fabrics. Comes in WHITE, CREAM, NAVY BLUE, BROWN, TAN, WINE, MYRTLE GREEN, LIGHT GRAY, SLATE, ALICE OR BLACK. Be sure to give color wanted.
Width, 36 inches. Price, per yard...32c

26c 27-INCH BLACK MOREEN SKIRTING.

No. 14K7090 A splendid heavy Watered Moreen for skirting. Exceptionally pretty and effective. Will wear well and looks like silk.
Width, 27 inches. Price, per yard..26c

95c HIGH GRADE COLORED SATIN LINING.

No. 14K7110 This is a fine quality of high grade Lining Satin and one that we guarantee for two seasons' wear. It is heavy weight, twilled back with a pure silk closely woven face. It is in every way equal to the satins that are sold in the retail store for $1.25 per yard. COLORS—CREAM, BROWN, NAVY BLUE, WINE, BLACK, TAN OR GRAY. Be sure to give color wanted.
Width, 36 inches. Price, per yard...95c

MERCERIZED SATEENS.

17c HEAVY MERCERIZED SATEEN SKIRTING.

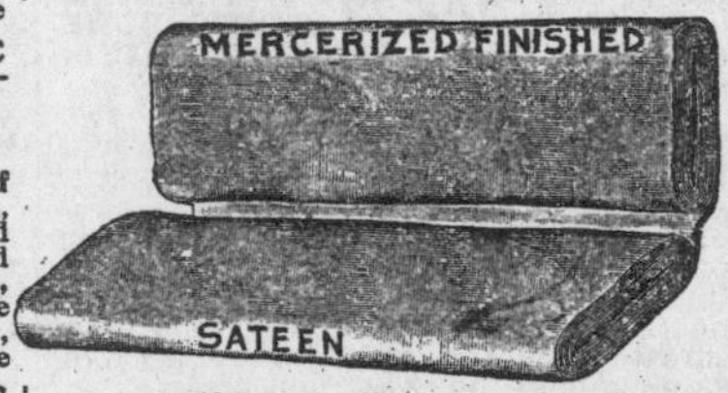

No. 14K7050 These beautiful Mercerized Sateens are guaranteed permanent finish and good firm weight. They have a rich, silky luster that is not equaled in any other lining fabric made. They are well adapted and extensively used for dresses and underskirts also, for they will wear almost for ever. COLORS—White, Tan, Yellow, Medium Brown, Light Blue, Pearl Gray, Pink, Slate, Old Rose, Cardinal, Heliotrope, Purple, Nile Green, Olive Green, Wine, Royal Blue, Navy Blue or Black. Be sure to give color wanted.
Width, 36 inches.
Price, per yard....................17c

12c MERCERIZED SATEEN.

No. 14K7040 A good weight Mercerized Sateen Lining; also very desirable for underskirts and petticoats. A firm, durable cloth that will give good, serviceable wear. COLORS—WHITE, BROWN, LIGHT GRAY, ROYAL BLUE, OLIVE GREEN, SLATE, TAN, WINE, LIGHT BLUE, BLACK, CREAM, CARDINAL, PINK OR NAVY BLUE. Be sure to give color wanted.
Width, 26 inches. Price, per yard....12c

21c MERCERIZED SATEEN.

No. 14K7060 Better than the preceding number. A very handsome satin finished fabric of heavy weight and perfect, even weave. Comes in WHITE, CREAM, TAN, BROWN, WINE, GRAY, NAVY, MYRTLE OR BLACK. Be sure to give color wanted
Width, 36 inches. Price, per yard...21c

32c LUCINTA SATEEN. REDUCED IN PRICE.

No. 14K7070 This is the finest grade of Mercerized Sateen to be found anywhere, nothing better manufactured. Steaming or ironing cannot affect it in any way. Comes in WHITE, CREAM, TAN, BROWN, NAVY, MYRTLE, GRAY, WINE OR BLACK. Be sure to give color wanted.
Width, 36 inches. Price, per yard..32c

—SPECIAL— FABRICS FOR MISSES' AND CHILDREN'S SPRING AND SUMMER WEAR

ON THIS HALF PAGE we have grouped together what in our judgment is the best value (in their particular and individual lines) to be found in any dress goods market. Every number is positively guaranteed to be strictly as represented, as well as to give satisfaction. You can order these goods direct from this description with the assurance that if you do not feel satisfied in every way with your purchase, you are at liberty to return them and get your money back. There is not one number on which we cannot save you more than 25 per cent on each and every yard. You can have the samples of any of these numbers free, postpaid, if you write for them.

32c FANCY CHALLIE.

No. 14K8675 27-inch printed Challies in new designs, half wool, specially adapted for misses' and children's wear. Color guaranteed fast, and all choice styles. They are sold everywhere at 50 cents per yard, and at our price are the best value we show.
The ground colors are PINK, LIGHT GREEN, LIGHT GRAY, LIGHT BLUE, CREAM OR WHITE with Persian designs, polka dots, rings and moss rose buds. Samples free on request. Be sure to state color wanted.
Width, 27 inches. Price, per yard, 32c

17c PLAIN HALF WOOL CHALLIE.

No. 14K8460 This pretty fabric in half wool, makes pretty dresses for misses and children, and is inexpensive, and at the same time a good wearing cloth. It has the appearance of an all wool Challie, and will wash splendidly. For party dresses, graduating gowns and school wear it has no superior.
Comes in this range of colors: CREAM, LIGHT BLUE, PINK, NAVY, CARDINAL, GRAY OR BLACK. Be sure to give color wanted.
Width, 27 inches. Price, per yard, 17c

39c FRENCH WOOL WAISTING.

No. 14K8151 A French twilled waisting, strictly all wool in a big range of choice colorings, suitable for misses' and children's blouses, waists and gymnasium suits, for boys' waists or school suits. It will stand the hardest kind of wear, and we highly recommend it for girls' skirts. Samples free on request.
These colors to choose from: NAVY BLUE, BROWN, CADET, MYRTLE GREEN, BLACK, CREAM, CASTOR, NILE GREEN, WINE, GRAY, CARDINAL, OLD ROSE OR PALE BLUE. Be sure to state color wanted.
Width, 28 inches.
Price, per yard....................39c

44c ALL WOOL BATISTE.

No. 14K8480 This handsome Batiste is strictly all wool, smooth even cloth, and of medium weight. Especially adapted for misses' blouses, skirts, waists or whole suits, and comes in a wide range of colors. It is made for us and we can warrant it in every respect. Samples free on request, or order from our catalogue and save time and expense.
These colors: CREAM, PINK, LIGHT BLUE, TAN, OLD ROSE, RESEDA GREEN, WINE, BROWN, ROYAL BLUE, CADET, NAVY, ALICE BLUE, MYRTLE GREEN, NILE, CARDINAL, LIGHT GRAY OR BLACK. State color wanted.
Width, 36 inches. Price, per yard 44c

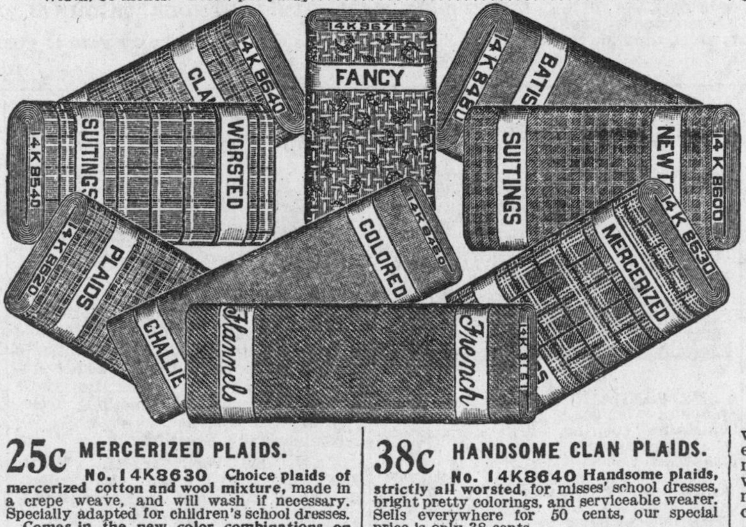

25c MERCERIZED PLAIDS.

No. 14K8630 Choice plaids of mercerized cotton and wool mixture, made in a crepe weave, and will wash if necessary. Specially adapted for children's school dresses.
Comes in the new color combinations on grounds of CARDINAL, GREEN, WINE, BROWN OR BLACK. Be sure to state color wanted.
Width, 32 inches. Price, per yard...25c

38c HANDSOME CLAN PLAIDS.

No. 14K8640 Handsome plaids, strictly all worsted, for misses' school dresses, bright pretty colorings, and serviceable wearer. Sells everywhere for 50 cents, our special price is only 38 cents.
Pretty combinations of ground colors: CARDINAL, GREEN, BROWN, BLUE OR GRAY. Be sure to state color wanted.
Width, 36 inches. Price, per yard....38c

13c NEWTON SUITING.

No. 14K8600 Choice checked patterns in an inexpensive suiting for children's or misses' wear. Made in a granite weave, and a splendid wearer. It is made to resemble an all wool suiting.
Comes in very good color combination checks, viz: RED AND BLACK, BLUE AND BROWN, GREEN AND BLUE, CADET AND BLACK, OR BROWN AND TAN. Be sure to give color wanted.
Width, 28 inches.
Price, per yard....................13c

41c FANCY GRAY SUITINGS.

No. 14K8540 These handsome checked and striped suitings in all the new shadings, strictly all worsted, and a material that will give splendid satisfaction in the wear. It comes in a good range of styles and colorings, all neat and dressy. Good for street wear for misses and children. Goods you will pay 50 cents for everywhere. Samples free for the asking.
Full 38 inches wide.
Price, per yard....................41c

13c SCOTCH PLAIDS.

No. 14K8621 Pretty broken plaids, mostly bright colors, woven on crepe ground that will give excellent wear. Made from selected mercerized yarn, and looks exactly like wool goods, will wash splendidly and make very useful dresses for misses and children.
They come in these ground colors with contrasting combination of colors: GREEN, WINE, BROWN, BLUE OR CARDINAL. Be sure to state color wanted.
Width, 28 inches. Price, per yard....13c

Take Advantage of Wholesale Prices

DOMESTIC DEPARTMENT

Get Away from Retail Prices

NEVER HAVE SUCH GENUINE PRICE REDUCTIONS BEEN MADE ON STRICTLY HIGH GRADE MERCHANDISE.

COTTON BATTING, BED TICKING, BUNTING, CAMBRIC, CARPET WARP, CHEESE AND BUTTER CLOTH

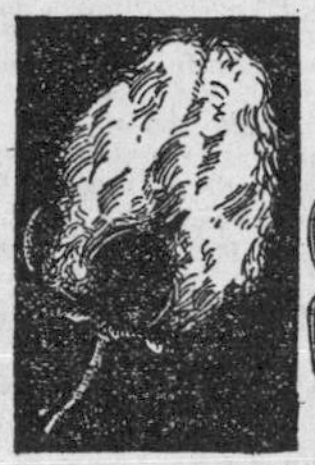

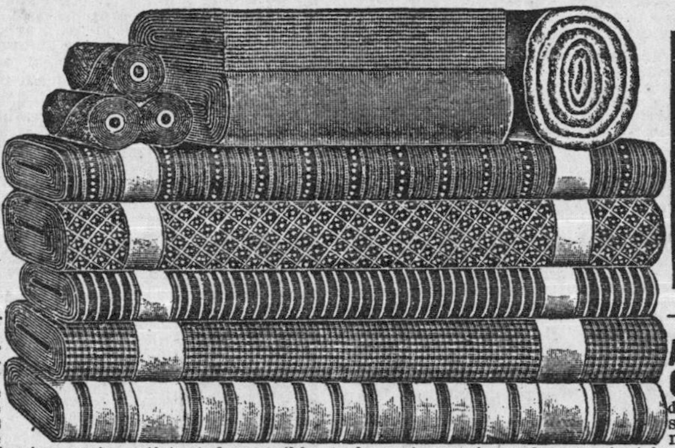

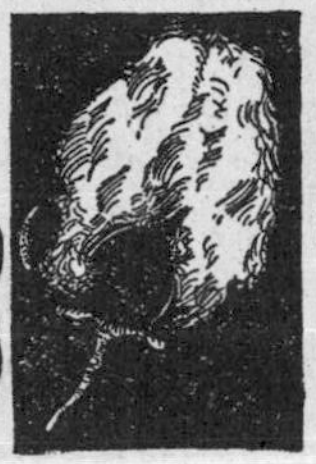

DENIMS, MUSLINS, SHEETINGS, SHEETS AND PILLOW CASES, TABLE, WALL AND SHELF OILCLOTHS, WADDINGS

WE HAVE JUST CONCLUDED the most satisfactory domestic season we have ever experienced, and by satisfactory we mean that we have had a larger and more complete stock of domestics in spite of a known scarcity, and have been able to furnish high standard goods to our customers at a greater saving than ever before. Our plans for the coming season have been laid on even broader lines, and, having again anticipated a possible barrenness of the market on certain popular cottons we will be better able than ever to protect our customers from the lack of needed domestics. Do not delay your order in the hope of securing lower prices later. There is no relief in sight for some months from the scarcity of these goods and no probability of any material change in the market. **You are protected by our guarantee that in the event of any decline in price on the goods we list or similar domestics, we will give you the benefit of any such reduction.**

WE APPRECIATE THE TREMENDOUSLY INCREASED DOMESTIC BUSINESS given us by our friends, and we are determined to show our appreciation by still lower prices for the same high quality, better goods for the same or less money and continued endeavors toward a larger and more complete stock, as well as improved service in filling and shipping it. No user of cotton goods is more exacting as to every detail of manufacture than we are. Every shipment is thoroughly inspected by competent merchandise examiners and extra care is taken at every point to see that none but perfect goods are received, and if, as might rarely happen, such a piece not up to our standard should pass in, we make doubly sure that it is caught before re-shipment. Isn't that a fact worth considering?

IN THESE REDUCED PRICES we believe we have more than anticipated any decline in domestic values to take place for many months. Should there be any further reduction, however, in the price of these or similar goods when your order is received we will voluntarily reduce our price and refund you the difference.

EVERY NUMBER ON THIS PAGE HAS BEEN REDUCED IN PRICE.

AN ARGUMENT THAT CANNOT BUT CONVINCE the woman who wants to save money is to be found in our method of quoting domestics. We can assist you as we have assisted thousands of customers in the selection of universally needed muslins, sheetings, cambrics, etc., by having them put up for us in popular and convenient lengths. This method enables us to save you on an average one-half cent per yard and in some cases as much as one cent per yard additional. The yardage quoted is in each case a very well selected one and is not a hardship on even the smallest user. Saving money on your purchases is easy. Let us demonstrate it to you by filling your domestic wants.

WHY WE DO NOT SAMPLE DOMESTICS! We stand first, last and always for high grade goods and are at all times desirous of having our goods judged solely on their merit and not by price alone. The expense of sampling domestics, as you well know, must become a part of the selling price, and were we to engage in a large distribution of domestic samples, while we would still undersell competition, we could not name the wonderfully low prices we now do, and we have made such a marvelous success of selling domestics direct from the pages of our catalogue, where the goods are fully and clearly described, that we have found it unnecessary to send samples, and by increasing our output we are able each season to still further reduce our prices. Our customers who favor us with their orders season after season, saving a large percentage of their ordinary outlay for these goods, know where we stand on first class merchandise and rely on our guarantee to give them better domestics than can be obtained anywhere else at the same price or the same goods (if high quality) at less money or we will, upon return of the goods, refund the purchase price together with the transportation charges paid by our customer.

WE MAKE NO "LEADERS." Each and every number listed stands on its own merit; make up a trial order from these pages and we are positive we will then be able to enroll you among our thousands of constant customers on domestics.

BROWN OR UNBLEACHED SHEETINGS

In order that we may show you the greatest possible saving in price and at the same time enable you to select your sheetings most conveniently, we have these goods put up in special size pieces, and while, to further assist you in your selection, we state the cost per yard, we cannot sell any smaller cuts than those listed. Please bear in mind that every economy we can make in the handling of our business shows a corresponding reduction in our catalogue price and we assure you that by putting up these sheetings in this way we are enabled to save you from ½ to 1 cent per yard. At the same time the lengths we quote do not impose a hardship on anyone, as these size pieces are the ones in most universal demand.

No. 36K1 Brown or Unbleached Sheeting. Full yard wide. A good quality at a low price. Full piece of 15 yards for........... **79c**
Equal to 5¼ cents per yard.

No. 36K3 Brown or Unbleached Sheeting. Full yard wide. An improved value. Full piece of 30 yards for... **$1.54**
Equal to 5⅛ cents per yard.

No. 36K5 Brown or Unbleached Sheeting. Full yard wide. A quality that seeks comparison with the average 8-cent goods. Full piece of 60 yards for... **$3.00**
Equal to 5 cents per yard.

No. 36K7 Brown or Unbleached Sheeting. A quality far superior to goods usually shown at 25 per cent advance in cost. Full 36 inches in width. 15-yard piece for........ **94c**
Equal to 6¼ cents per yard.

No. 36K9 Brown or Unbleached Sheeting. A surprisingly good quality at such a low figure. Width, 36 inches. 30-yard piece for........... **$1.84**
Equal to 6⅛ cents per yard.

No. 36K11 Brown or Unbleached Sheeting. A value that will bring you back for more. Full yard wide. 60-yard piece for............ **$3.60**
Equal to 6 cents per yard.

No. 36K25 Brown or Unbleached Sheeting. Much heavier and finer than the preceding numbers. Width, 36 inches. 10-yard piece for........... **85c**
Equal to 8½ cents per yard.

No. 36K27 Brown or Unbleached Sheeting. A dependable grade and a tempting value at our special price. Width, 36 inches. 25-yard piece for.......... **$2.07**
Equal to 8¼ cents per yard.

No. 36K29 Brown or Unbleached Sheeting. Sterling value and knows no competition at or near its price. 36 inches wide. 50-yard piece for.............. **$4.00**
Equal to 8 cents per yard.

No. 36K31 Extra Width Brown or Unbleached Sheeting. Superior quality. Fine yarn and a heavy cloth. Very serviceable. Width, 39 inches. 10 yard piece for............... **95c**
Equal to 9½ cents per yard.

No. 36K33 Extra Width Brown or Unbleached Sheeting. A grade we especially recommend as a great investment. Its extra service is an assurance of economy. Fine and strong. Washes nice and white. Width, 39 inches. 25-yard piece for **$2.32**
Equal to 9¼ cents per yard.

No. 36K35 Extra Wide Brown or Unbleached Sheeting. High quality. Only long fiber cotton of established grade and of sufficient strength and smoothness is used in this sheeting. No better goods needed for any purpose. A splendid purchase. Width, 39 inches. 50-yard piece for......... **$4.50**
Equal to 9 cents per yard.

HALF BLEACHED MUSLINS.

By reason of their natural softness these goods are especially well liked by many people, being frequently preferred to the full bleached muslins.

No. 36K69 Yard Wide Muslin. Half bleached finish. Soft, fine and of good weight. Width, 36 inches. 15-yard piece for............. **$1.48**
Equal to 9⅞ cents per yard.

No. 36K71 Half Bleached Muslin. Yard wide, fine and firm yet of a pleasing softness that simplifies your needlework. You'll be delighted with this number which is endorsed by a host of satisfied customers. Bleaches splendidly in washing and gives unusual service. Width, 36 inches. 30-yard piece for............. **$2.93**
Equal to 9¾ cents per yard.

No. 36K73 Another strong argument that demonstrates our ability to save you money on muslins. Extra quality. Fine yarn goods. That nice soft finish so highly desirable. Bleaches well in laundering. You'll like this cloth on sight and it will grow in favor with you every day. We put you in the way of saving $1.80 on this piece of goods. 60-yard piece for **$5.70**
Equal to 9½ cents per yard.

GREAT ECONOMIES IN BLEACHED MUSLINS

Our unequaled mill connections enable us to reduce our old prices. Our stock was never more complete in all grades

No. 36K75 Yard Wide Bleached Muslin. A quality not to be judged by the price. Nicely bleached. Width, 36 inches. 15-yard piece for........ **$1.20**
Equal to 8 cents per yard.

No. 36K77 Yard Wide Bleached Muslin. Represents a saving that ought to interest you. Well made and bleached. 30-yard piece for....... **$2.32**
Equal to 7¾ cents per yard.

No. 36K79 Bleached Muslin, yard wide and pure white. Same quality and width for less money. We use nothing but standard eastern bleached muslins of a pleasing uniformity of color. 60-yard piece for.............. **$4.50**
Equal to 7½ cents per yard.

No. 36K81 Bleached Muslin, full yard wide. Thoroughly dependable in texture and finish. Always makes a hit. Width, 36 inches. 15-yard piece for....... **$1.37**
Equal to 9⅛ cents per yard.

No. 36K83 Bleached Muslin, full yard wide. Good weight and well bleached. Discerning buyers will not be slow in appreciating this value. Width, 36 inches. 30-yard piece for............ **$2.70**
Equal to 9 cents per yard.

No. 36K85 Pure Bleached Muslin. That nice, soft finished cloth that recommends itself to the needle. Our muslins are all cotton and not loaded with adulterants. 60-yard piece for............... **$5.33**
Equal to 8⅞ cents per yard.

No. 36K87 Soft Finished Bleached Muslin. An excellent quality for general purposes, having enough weight to make it very desirable. One of our deservedly popular numbers last season. Our new price should promote an even larger sale. Width, 36 inches. 10-yard piece for... **99c**
Equal to 9⅞ cents per yard.

No. 36K89 Extra Quality Soft Bleached Muslin, one of those values that have done much to establish this department as a recognized economy center. You will call for this number regularly if once used. Width, 36 inches. 30-yard piece for. **$2.93**
Equal to 9¾ cents per yard.

No. 36K91 A Surprising Value in Pure White, Soft, Bleached Muslin. Has a pleasing weight and is altogether a cloth without a disappointment. A muslin that is the same all the way through. Nothing but fine, long cotton. Our reduced price adds attractiveness to the offering and makes this a purchase well worth while. Width, 36 inches. 60-yard piece for........... **$5.70**
Equal to 9½ cents per yard.

No. 36K93 Our Best All Pure Soft Bleached Muslin. A quality without a peer and a cloth that can be selected without hesitancy for the finest use. Excellent weight. Nice, smooth, soft finish. Very durable. Width, 36 inches. 10-yard piece for............ **$1.09**
Equal to 10⅞ cents per yard.

No. 36K95 If you want the Best, Pure White, Soft Finished Muslin, a cloth that lends itself readily to any purpose and is good enough to meet the most exacting requirements we especially recommend this number which is a "seek no further" grade. Beautifully fine and of substantial weight, assuring purchaser of splendid service. Width, 36 inches. 30-yard piece for **$3.19**
Equal to 10⅝ cents per yard.

No. 36K97 Those who buy this number don't come back for it often—they don't need to. It has a world of service and satisfaction. Hard to wear it out. Try a piece and be convinced. This is really, when considering the extra service to be had, our greatest value in the entire line. This cloth is brimful of welcome features which make new friends for it everywhere. Width, 36 inches. 60-yard piece for.............. **$6.23**
Equal to 10⅜ cents per yard.

BIG VALUES IN FINE WHITE CAMBRIC MUSLINS.

Our Cambrics are all bleached and finished by the very best bleachery in New England and have no superiors in any respect.

No. 36K99 Yard Wide Fine White Cambric. A splendid value. Width, 36 inches. 10-yard piece for........... **90c**
Equal to 9 cents per yard.

No. 36K101 Fine White Cambric. A cloth that really has no superior at 15 cents per yard in the ordinary retail way. Made from good stock and well finished. Width, 36 inches. 30-yard piece for.. **$2.67**
Equal to 8⅞ cents per yard.

No. 36K103 Pure White Cambric of a quality that would draw attention to it at much higher prices anywhere. Splendid for ladies' and children's underwear, etc. Fine and soft. Width, 36 inches. 60-yard piece for.............. **$5.10**
Equal to 8½ cents per yard.

No. 36K105 Superior White Cambric. Fine finish and an honest piece of goods all the way through. Free from adulteration. Width, 36 inches. 10-yard piece for................ **$1.20**
Equal to 12 cents per yard.

No. 36K107 One of our most popular Cambrics. That soft, fine and yet durable quality that makes up so tastefully in undergarments. A money saving purchase of great interest to every consumer. Width, 36 inches. 25-yard piece for....... **$2.94**
Equal to 11¾ cents per yard.

No. 36K109 Very Fine White Cambric. All pure cotton. Not filled with starch or clay. A quality we readily endorse for general use. Good enough for the best undergarments, yet low enough in price to fit a popular need. Width, 36 inches. 60-yard piece for............ **$6.90**
Equal to 11½ cents per yard.

No. 36K111 Wamsutta Cambric. The best goods made. A quality that is too good in the estimation of many underwear makers to put into even their best garments. You know what you're getting when you make them up yourself from our goods. Pure Sea Island Cotton. Width, 36 inches. 10-yard piece for............ **$1.40**
Equal to 14 cents per yard.

No. 36K113 Sea Island White Cambric. Wamsutta goods. That's really all we need say to anyone who has used it. Made from high class Sea Island Cotton. None better—nor as good. Beautifully fine and soft and every fiber is intended to give lasting satisfaction to the purchaser. Width, 36 inches. 30-yard piece for............ **$4.13**
Equal to 13¾ cents per yard.

No. 36K116 Unequaled Wamsutta Cambric. Elegant in its softness and purity, and why not? Couldn't put any better stock in it than the selected Sea Island Cotton that it is built of and, contrary to market conditions, we have reduced our already low price. Width, 36 inches. 60-yard piece for.............. **$8.10**
Equal to 13½ cents per yard.

TABLE LINENS, NAPKINS, TOWELS, TOWELINGS, ETC.

WE WANT YOUR HOUSEKEEPING LINEN ORDERS THIS SEASON. Never before in the history of this department, the growth of which has been constant and marvelously rapid, have we been able to make you such important offerings in dependable linens of all kinds. Our contracts with Irish, Scotch, German and Austrian manufacturers have been larger than ever and our line as shown in these pages is more extensive than any we have heretofore brought to your notice. No effort has been spared to keep our assortment new and strictly up to date by replacing old patterns with newer and more attractive designs and increasing the desirability of staple items by improving their quality, color or width.

IF WE CAN SAVE YOU MONEY on a trial order, we know you will appreciate it by continuing to favor us with your housekeeping linen orders. None but goods we are willing to personally guarantee for service find their way into the pages of our catalogue. You can readily see why this is so. We warrant our goods to give satisfaction and we could not afford to risk our reputation by handling questionable merchandise. No one else can sell you as good quality for as little money. No one else can offer you the assortment of linens that we do. Every number has been as carefully considered in the making, designing and finishing and placing in its position in our line as though it were the only number in our catalogue. This ought to be an important feature for you to consider when purchasing linens whether you are ordering a pair of towels, a fine matched table set or any one of the many useful linen items described.

WE KNOW WE CAN MAKE GOOD EVERY statement made in our description of the various damasks, padding, pattern cloths, center covers, napkins, etc., listed here. No exaggeration has been used to influence you in your selection, but each article quoted will be found on arrival to be not only as good as we describe it but in nearly every instance better, for the reason that black ink on white paper cannot do justice to the merchandise and we are glad that it is so, for we would by far prefer that you order the goods from our catalogue description, satisfied that you are getting a square deal and reaping the benefit of our immense buying powers by reason of which the very cream of each class of goods is laid before you, thus adding convenience of selection to economy in purchase and then be gladly surprised when the carefully packed goods are opened up and found to be even better than you had imagined. The risk is all ours. While we have made our descriptions as clear and complete as possible so that you may feel just as safe in ordering from this catalogue as though you saw the goods themselves, and while we have underestimated rather than exaggerated the quality of the goods quoted, you take no chance whatever because, if for any reason the merchandise is not up to description, if you are not certain that we have given you better goods and more goods for the same money or less than you have to pay anyone else, we ask you to return your purchase to us and we will exchange it for any other goods or refund the purchase price and any transportation charges you may have paid.

TURKEY RED TABLE DAMASKS.

21c TURKEY RED FLORAL TABLE DAMASK.

No. 36K667 Turkey Red Table Damask in new and attractive patterns, all florals with appropriate borders. Not the cheap goods that have neither stability or character to recommend them but a quality that contrasts strongly with a low price. Warranted fast color and to be far superior to the regular quarter cloth. We have added a few new patterns. Width, 58 inches.
Price, per yard.. **21c**

22c TURKEY RED DICE TABLE DAMASK.

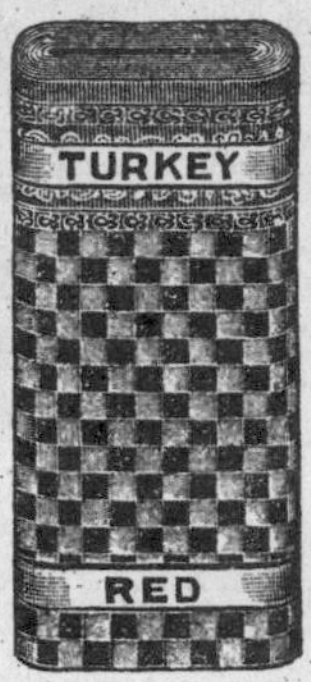

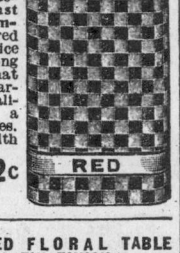

No. 36K677 Those who are in the habit of selecting by price alone will meet with a pleasant surprise in this fast color Turkey Red Damask. It comes in red and white 1-inch dice pattern and is a strong value, having merit that will entitle it to comparison with 30-cent qualities elsewhere. Has a good width 58 inches. Dice pattern only, with floral borders like illustration.
Price, per yard.. **22c**

32c TURKEY RED FLORAL TABLE DAMASK. SATIN FINISH.

No. 36K697 Our guaranteed oil boiled Turkey Red Damask will give you that service that finds expression in a hearty recommendation to your friends. Many so called turkey red damasks are turkey red in name only. We guarantee ours to be oil boiled, and have never had a complaint from a customer, although we handle many thousands of yards each season. The range of patterns covers a wide field of floral work, each pattern has neat borders to match. Fine satin finish. Width, 58 inches.
Price, per yard.. **32c**

32c TURKEY RED DICE TABLE DAMASK.

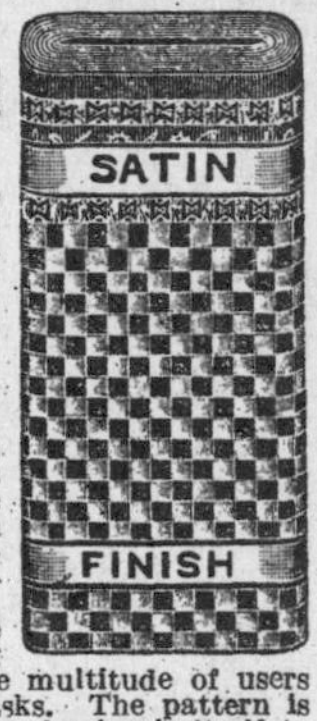

No. 36K707 Dice Pattern Turkey Red Damask. Special satin finish not usually found in goods anywhere near our price. Every yard of these turkey red damasks is thoroughly oil boiled and guaranteed by us. Good weight and a damask that always meets with favor. Comes only in a red and white dice pattern 1 inch square, similar to illustration. Borders are attractive floral ideas. Width, 58 inches. These dice designs are growing steadily in favor with the multitude of users of turkey red table damasks. The pattern is neat and while sufficiently pleasing in itself to merit consideration its desirability is increased by the addition of the floral border designs giving you a combination of the best work in each class of designing. You will be surprised to see so much style in a cloth of this kind and at such a low price.
Price, per yard **32c**

42c EXTRA QUALITY TURKEY RED TABLE DAMASK. CHOICE STYLES.

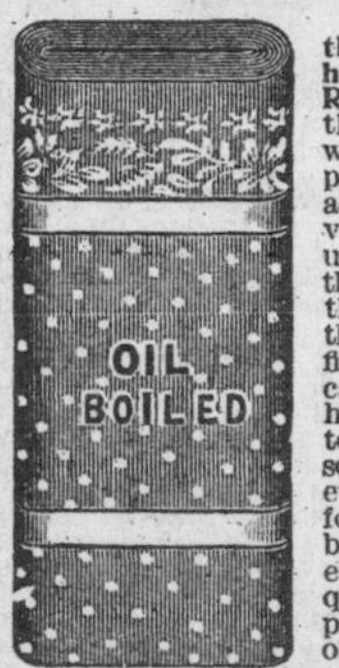

No. 36K737 To those who want the very highest grade Turkey Red Damask made in this wide land and are willing to pay a few cents per yard more for the added beauty and service thereby gained we unhesitatingly endorse this number. Everything that comes into use in the manufacture and finish of these goods is carefully selected and high class. We have yet to see a half dollar article so good. Our customers evidently agree with us for the demand keeps us busy caring for it. However, we never cut the quality nor hurry the process. Guaranteed full oil boiled damask. High satin finish. Lustrous and heavy. Elegant floral or spot patterns with either floral or open borders. Width, 58 inches. Price, per yard........... **42c**

42c EXTRA QUALITY TURKEY RED DICE DAMASK. GUARANTEED OIL BOILED. HIGH LUSTER.

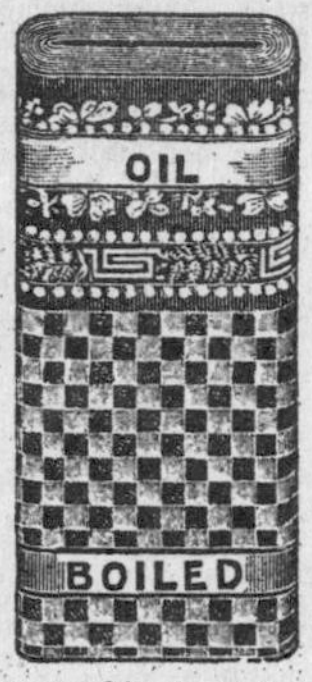

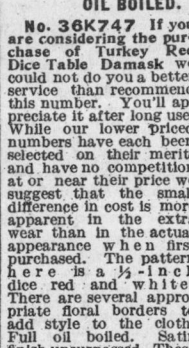

No. 36K747 If you are considering the purchase of Turkey Red Dice Table Damask we could not do you a better service than recommend this number. You'll appreciate it after long use. While our lower priced numbers have each been selected on their merits and have no competition at or near their price we suggest that the small difference in cost is more apparent in the extra wear than in the actual appearance when first purchased. The pattern here is a ½-inch dice red and white. There are several appropriate floral borders to add style to the cloth. Full oil boiled. Satin finish unsurpassed. These dice designs are growing steadily in favor with the multitude of users of turkey red table damasks. The pattern is neat and while sufficiently pleasing in itself to merit consideration its desirability is increased by the addition of the floral border designs, giving you a combination of the best work in each class of designing. You will be surprised to see so much style in a cloth of this kind and at such a low price. Width, 58 inches. Price, per yard............. **42c**

43c HIGH GRADE RED AND GREEN TABLE DAMASK BOTH FLORAL AND DICE PATTERNS.

No. 36K749 Turkey Red and Green Table Damask. We only list one quality and that the best, still the price is low enough for ordinary purposes. The cloth has a good weight, satin finish and will wear well. Will not wash out, because it is oil boiled, every yard. Nice patterns, either dice or floral. Be sure to state which is wanted. Width, 58 inches.
Price, per yard **43c**

Be sure to see what we are doing on Wash Voiles. We have a carefully selected range of these delightful fabrics listed on page 936.

SAMPLES MAILED FREE ON REQUEST.

CREAM OR HALF BLEACHED TABLE DAMASKS.

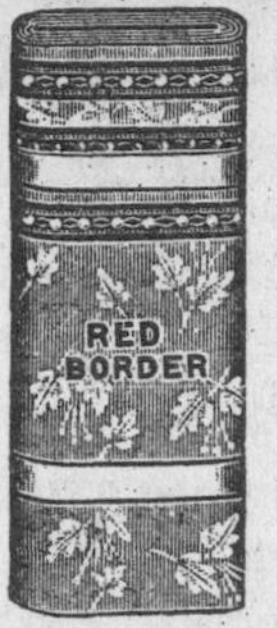

31c RED BORDER HALF BLEACHED TABLE DAMASK.

No. 36K757 Cream or Half Bleached Table Damask in a good selection of patterns like and similar to illustration. All floral effects. Each pattern has a fast turkey red border which may be seen in the illustration. Our importation of these damasks enables us to create prices that are difficult for any competition to solve. 54-inch red bordered cream damask.
Price, per yard.... **31c**

25c HALF BLEACHED TABLE DAMASK.

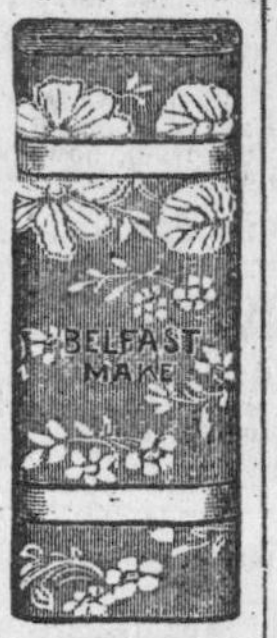

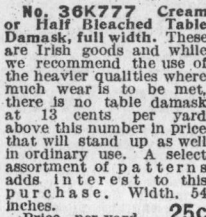

No. 36K777 Cream or Half Bleached Table Damask, full width. These are Irish goods and while we recommend the use of the heavier qualities where much wear is to be met, there is no table damask at 13 cents per yard above this number in price that will stand up as well in ordinary use. A select assortment of patterns adds interest to this purchase. Width, 54 inches.
Price, per yard... **25c**

53c 58-INCH HALF BLEACHED ALL LINEN TABLE DAMASK.

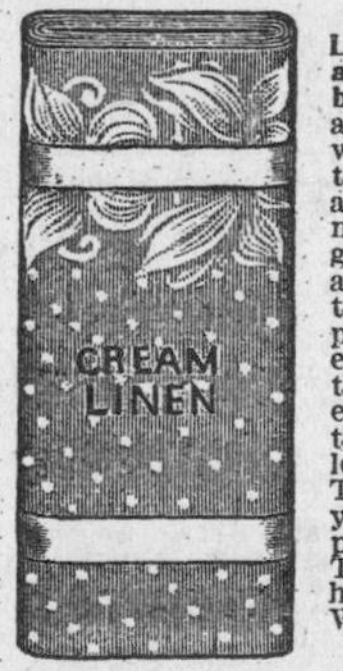

No. 36K787 All Linen Table Damask in a clear cream or half bleach finish. These appeal to many people who really prefer them to the bleached goods and to those who have never used the cream goods we might say that a few launderings bring them out white. This price really underestimates the value of the cloth so we ask you especially not to judge them that way but buy a length and try it out. The expense is ours if you are dissatisfied. The patterns will please you. They are all good. A heavy cloth, all linen. Width, 58 inches.
Price, per yard........ **53c**

58c 64-INCH ALL LINEN HALF BLEACHED DAMASK.

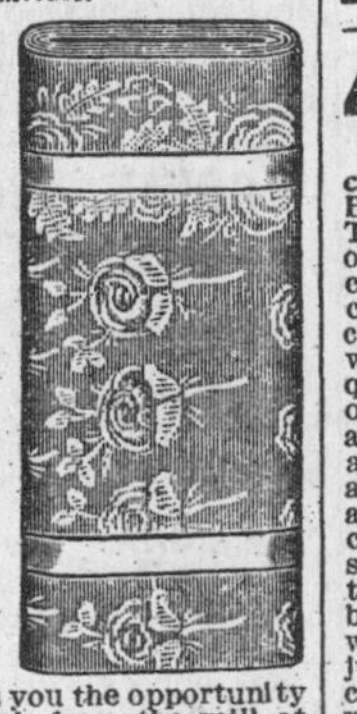

No. 36K797 Wide Table Damask. All linen and a nice half bleached or cream finish. These are Irish linens and are not filled up to mislead you as to weight. A stocky cloth coming in a well selected range of patterns, spot, floral, etc. A serviceable grade whose true value will be most apparent in service. It requires but a few washings to render the damask a good white color. These cream bleached damasks are manufactured in Belfast, Ireland, and imported directly by ourselves in sufficiently large quantities to enable us to secure the very lowest cost of manufacture and transportation; this plus our one small percentage of profit gives you the opportunity of securing the goods fresh from the mill at all times and at a price which is frequently less than that at which the retail dealer buys the same quality from his jobber. Width, 64 inches. Price, per yard.... **58c**

63c 70-INCH ALL LINEN HALF BLEACHED TABLE DAMASK.

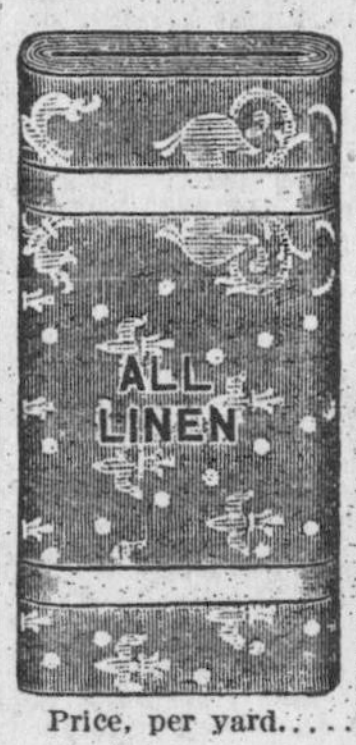

No. 36K807 Extra Wide and Heavy All Linen Half Bleached Damask. Invaluable for the larger tables and where exposed to hard service, frequent laundering, etc. Never fails to give the purchaser satisfaction. A new selection of patterns in dots, florals, etc. These cream bleached goods have a steady sale among a wide field of customers who appreciate the fact that after laundering once or twice the cloth bleaches nicely. We have everything desirable in spots, florals, etc. An investment that assures a steady return in service and satisfaction. Width, 70 inches.
Price, per yard.................... **63c**

BLEACHED TABLE DAMASKS.

21c BLEACHED TABLE DAMASK, 58 INCHES WIDE.

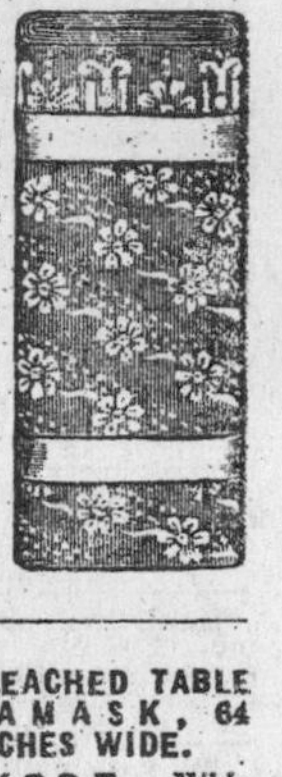

No. 36K827 Bleached Table Damask. The grade that many dealers make a noise on at a quarter. Pure white. Good patterns, a lot of goods for a small price. Width, 58 inches.
Price, per yard **21c**

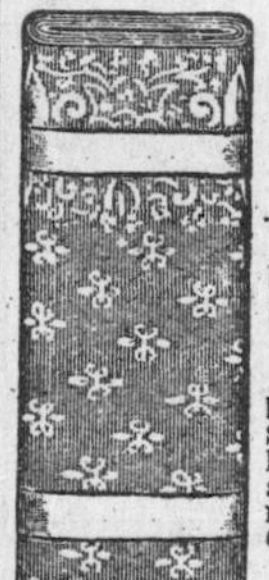

25c BLEACHED TABLE DAMASK, 64 INCHES WIDE.

No. 36K837 Wide Bleached Table Damask. Snow white bleach. Same low price regardless of market advances. Comes in a choice range of patterns. Width, 64 inches.
Price, per yard....... **25c**

WE ALWAYS UNDERSELL outdistance and outclass all competition. Following our well established policy of steadily lowering prices we have still further reduced them in this catalogue.

45c MERCERIZED PURE WHITE SATIN TABLE DAMASK, 64 INCHES WIDE.

No. 36K841 Mercerized Table Damask. Bleached Pure White. The fact that we list but one number in these goods causes us to be unusually careful in selecting the cloth for width and weight as well as for quality. It is the opinion of many large users that a good mercerized damask is to be preferred to a low priced linen cloth and as a result the mercerized goods find strong support among proprietors of hotels, clubs, boarding houses, etc. The weight of our damask is just right, a good, stocky cloth made from selected yarns well bleached and patterned in a way that would do justice to a fine imported all linen damask. Width, 64 inches. Price, per yard.... **45c**

HIGH GRADE TABLE NAPKINS AT MONEY SAVING PRICES

45c BLEACHED TABLE NAPKINS.

No. 36K1237 Bleached Table Napkins made in Ireland and imported by us. This is not an all linen napkin but at such a low price is a value intended to impress you favorably as to what we can do for you on the better goods. Size, 14½x15 inches. Good patterns.
Price, per dozen........ **45c**

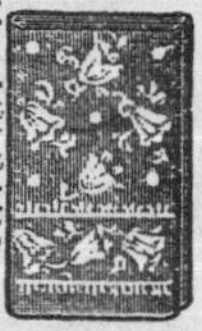

78c BLEACHED TABLE NAPKINS.

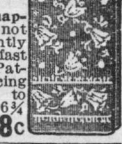

No. 36K1257 A big napkin at a small price. It is not all linen though it frequently passes as such. Made in Belfast and bleached pure white. Patterns are very good, embracing several floral ideas similar to illustration. Size, 16¾ x 16¾ inches.
Price, per dozen........ **78c**

$1.14 ALL LINEN TABLE NAPKINS, BLEACHED. GOOD STYLES.

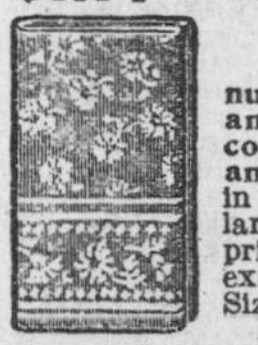

No. 36K1267 Our first number in All Linen Napkins and an article that would really command much more money anywhere than we ask. Made in Scotland for us and is our largest seller among the low priced qualities. Patterns are excellent. Pure white bleach. Size, 16½x16½ inches.
Price, per dozen........ **$1.14**

$1.21 ALL LINEN BLEACHED TABLE NAPKINS. SPECIAL WEIGHT.

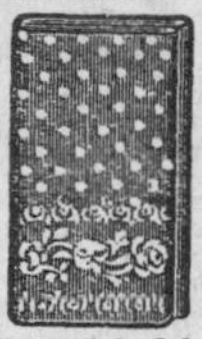

No. 36K1277 We are prepared to save you at least 21 cents per dozen on these napkins. This should interest you into sending for a dozen and testing the truth of our statement. The napkin is all linen, warranted, bleached pure white. A much heavier napkin than the usual $1.50 grade, so much so that you'll be agreeably surprised. Patterns are very good florals, scrolls, spots, etc. Size, 16¾x16¾ inches. State pattern. Price, per dozen........ **$1.21**

$1.53 BLEACHED ALL LINEN TABLE NAPKINS. PLEASING WEIGHT.

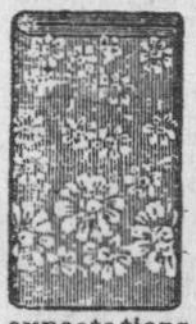

No. 36K1287 On our line of imported napkins we hesitate to make our statements as strong as we really should for fear of exciting doubt in the minds of some prospective purchaser who may not fully appreciate our advantage in importing the goods ourselves direct from the mill in Scotland. You will, therefore, be delighted when the napkins open up and exceed both our claims and your expectations. This is a good weight, pure white napkin, in marguerite, spot, fleur de lis, etc., patterns and will match our 66-inch bleached damask No. 36K869. Size of napkin, 19x19 inches. State pattern.
Price, per dozen................ **$1.53**

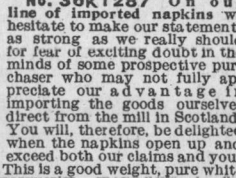

$1.61 FINE ALL LINEN SCOTCH DAMASK TABLE NAPKINS.

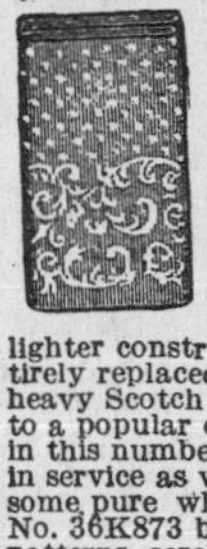

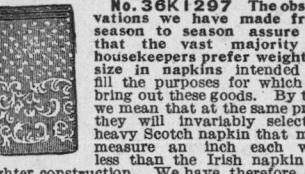

No. 36K1297 The observations we have made from season to season assure us that the vast majority of housekeepers prefer weight to size in napkins intended to fill the purposes for which we bring out these goods. By this we mean that at the same price they will invariably select a heavy Scotch napkin that may measure an inch each way less than the Irish napkin of lighter construction. We have, therefore, entirely replaced the lighter napkins with our heavy Scotch goods and still kept the size up to a popular one. We are proud of the value in this number and we know we can please you in service as well as save you in cost. A handsome pure white napkin which matches our No. 36K873 bleached damask, coming in spot patterns, scrolls, etc. Size of napkin, 19x19 inches. State pattern.
Price, per dozen................ **$1.61**

$2.47 ALL LINEN BLEACHED TABLE NAPKINS. CHOICE GOODS.

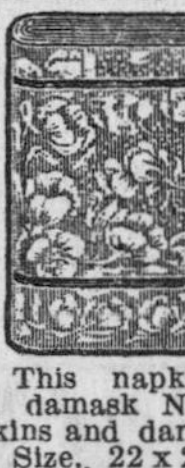

No. 36K1307 A larger napkin than anything we have quoted in the preceding numbers and really an increasing value. Full of fine flax and Scotch sincerity. You are invited to compare this napkin with the ordinary $3.00 grade. If you do this you'll appreciate the value more than ever. The variety of patterns leaves nothing to be desired. We have rose, carnation, pansy, hydrangea, crocus and fleur de lis, tastefully designed. This napkin matches our 71-inch bleached damask No. 36K877. You may order napkins and damask together or separately. Size, 22 x 22 inches. State pattern.
Price, per dozen................ **$2.47**

$2.55 BLEACHED ALL LINEN TABLE NAPKINS. EXCELLENT STOCK.

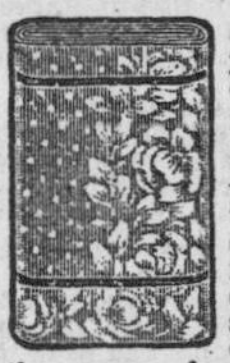

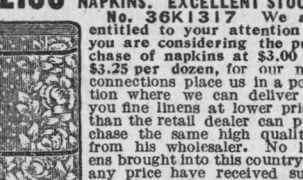

No. 36K1317 We are entitled to your attention if you are considering the purchase of napkins at $3.00 to $3.25 per dozen, for our mill connections place us in a position where we can deliver to you fine linens at lower prices than the retail dealer can purchase the same high qualities from his wholesaler. No linens brought into this country at any price have received such critical attention all through the course of manufacture as our goods, and as a result not alone do we excel in quality and price, but in the many details that in themselves are small but go toward imparting to the napkin in its design and general character that snappy touch of true merit and class that appeals to the eye of the careful and exacting user. A remarkably well balanced napkin having just the right weight and size to class it as a wonderfully convenient and serviceable article. This napkin is all pure linen, snow white and has a charming selection of patterns, chief among which are several popular spots, fleur de lis, florals, etc., matching our 71-inch bleached damask No. 36K887. Size, 22x22 inches. State pattern.
Price, per dozen................ **$2.55**

$1.57 ALL LINEN TABLE NAPKINS. GRASS BLEACHED SCOTCH GOODS

To match our Pattern Cloths Nos. 36K1047, 36K1052 and 36K1057.

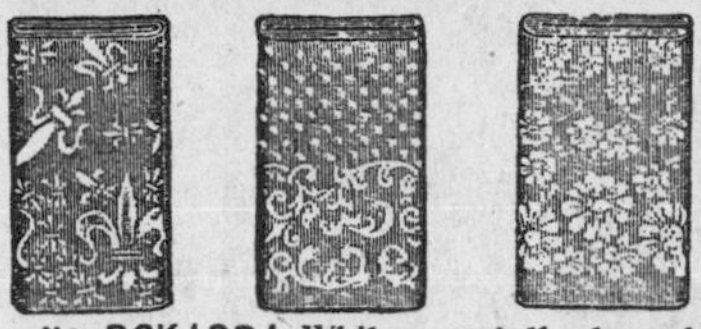

No. 36K1331 While especially planned to match our pattern cloths Nos. 36K1047, 36K1052 and 36K1057, this napkin will be found equally desirable to those who may need napkins only, as they are built on merit and intended to give greater service and more satisfaction than can be found in much higher priced napkins in the usual way. It is all pure linen of fine texture, good weight and pretty patterns, such as marguerite, spot, fleur de lis, etc. Size, 19x19 inches. State pattern. Price, per dozen........ **$1.57**

$2.49 EXTRA FINE ALL LINEN BLEACHED TABLE NAPKINS.

To match our Pattern Cloths Nos. 36K1062, 36K1067 and 36K1072.

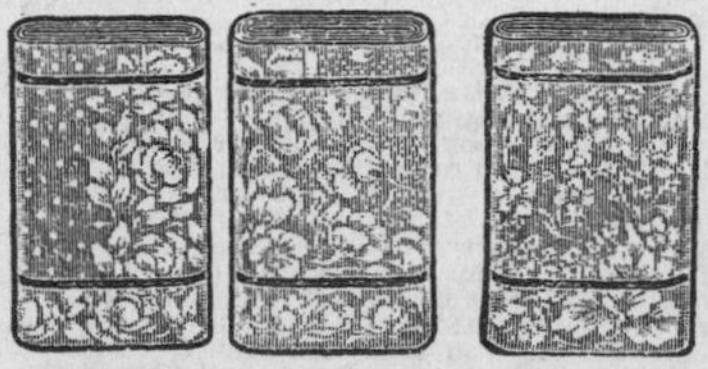

No. 36K1334 Do you ever realize what an important item quality is? Many people don't. The time you fully appreciate it is when you allow yourself to be a little careless, or too hurried in making a purchase. We have taken every precaution to safeguard quality. You could run through our catalogue with your eyes shut without ever putting your finger on a number that isn't built on quality. If you are particular about your table napkins and wish something of superior weight, quality and beauty of style and are in the habit of paying $3.50 per dozen, let us save you $1.01 and you will have made a good purchase. This napkin is designed to match our pattern cloths Nos. 36K1062, 36K1067 and 36K1072, and will match them in every way, making a reasonable priced set of extra merit and affording you an opportunity of choosing from three sizes of cloth. Among the patterns are crocus, rose, hydrangea, pansy, fleur de lis, spot, etc. Size, 22x22 inches. State pattern.
Price, per dozen................ **$2.49**

THE LOWER PRICES QUOTED IN THIS CATALOGUE will be more interesting to you than the prices quoted by any other firm or individual.

$3.40 FINEST QUALITY BLEACHED DAMASK TABLE NAPKINS.

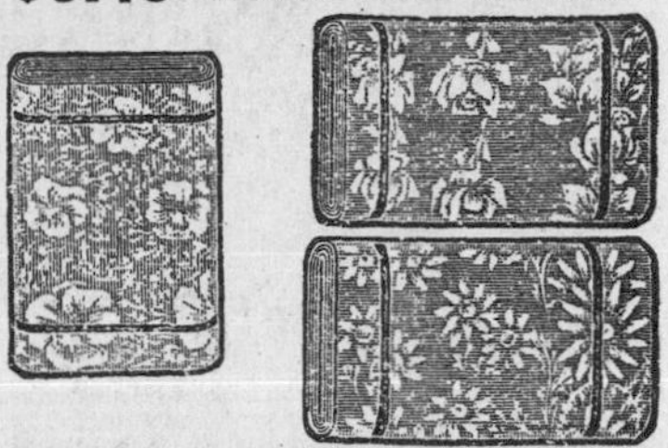

No. 36K1337 Extra size and super quality fine Scotch Satin Damask Table Napkins. Our very best quality heavy damask and a value that knows no competition. Pure snow white and comes in the most elegant designs imaginable. Some patterns are rose, pansy, marguerite, etc., but so far superior in the way they are worked out as to be totally different from any other patterns of the same name. You can match our No. 36K907 damask with these goods. A napkin that will wear for years after you've forgotten the price you paid for it. If you were to go to Europe and at a great expense of time and money should visit every one of several leading flax manufacturers and having before you the cream of each mill's production, should then go over the different lines critically and make a selection based on quality, style, size and price, you would probably have had an interesting experience, but you really would have gained nothing so far as securing values in fine table linen is concerned over our catalogue offerings, for we give you the exact same benefits you would derive from a visit to the mills by bringing to you the best of each class of linens and not only save you money on your purchase but likewise make your selecting a matter of great convenience. This division is really an exposition of linen goods and rarely is such an opportunity for great values offered. Size, 24x24 inches. State pattern. Price, per dozen........ **$3.40**

$1.05 GOOD SIZE BLEACHED NAPKINS. FINE MERCERIZED DAMASK.

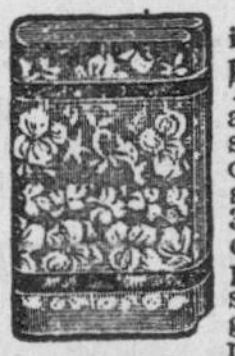

No. 36K1347 Mercerized Damask Table Napkins, pure white and of good weight. These are splendidly patterned and finished napkins of generous size and will be appreciated by our customers. They are the same quality cloth as our Nos. 36K1077 to 36K1097 pattern cloths and come in the same patterns, fleur de lis, pansy and spot, making the lowest cost good set we know of. You really could not get any better patterns in higher priced napkins for we have had these designs copied from the highest types of fine imported damasks at four times the price of this number. These patterns are unquestionably the most popular in damask cloths and napkins, so that those who purchase these fine mercerized napkins may rest assured of getting the greatest satisfaction from their investment. Size, 20x20 inches. State pattern.
Price, per dozen........ **$1.05**

TOWELS AND TOWELINGS

BARBER TOWELS, BATH TOWELS, FRINGED; BATH TOWELS, HEMMED; DAMASK TOWELS, HONEYCOMB TOWELS, HUCK TOWELS, WASH CLOTHES.

WE HAVE AIMED TO MAKE THIS DIVISION of our Linen Department a department in itself, and to that end, have devoted especial attention to the selection of the various items which go to make up what we have every reason to believe is the most complete assortment of towels and towelings ever gathered together by ourselves or any dealer.

HAD WE BEEN SATISFIED to show so many numbers of Bath Towels, so many Huck Towels, so many Damask Towels, etc., and so make up a line, we might have filled up much more space, but we have worked from a different starting point. There is hardly an article of household use that is so subject to either criticism or praise as a towel. We use them every day and if after one washing we find the towel or toweling comes out little more than half its original weight, leaving behind it in the tub a quantity of starch or china clay, or if after short use the towel becomes tender and will not bear the ordinary usage which a towel must meet, we justly find fault with it.

WITH A FULL KNOWLEDGE, THEREFORE, OF WHAT IS EXPECTED of a towel, either ready made or in the yard goods, we have built our line, number by number, each and every item being subjected to a rigid test, and the result is that we have every confidence in the goods we offer you, and we are willing that you should select any number or numbers and thoroughly satisfy yourself by every practical test, that we give you the best possible towels and towelings at the lowest possible prices, and if we can't save you money we don't want your orders.

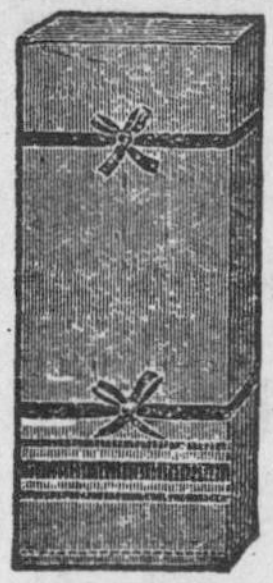

46c HEMMED DUCK WEAVE TOWELS, EXCELLENT ARTICLE FOR BARBERS' USE.

No. 36K1600 Bleached Duck Weave Towels. Soft finish and very absorbent. Enormous quantities sold every year for use as a barbers' towel. Fast turkey red borders. Hemmed ends. Size, 12½x24 inches.
Price, per dozen .. **46c**

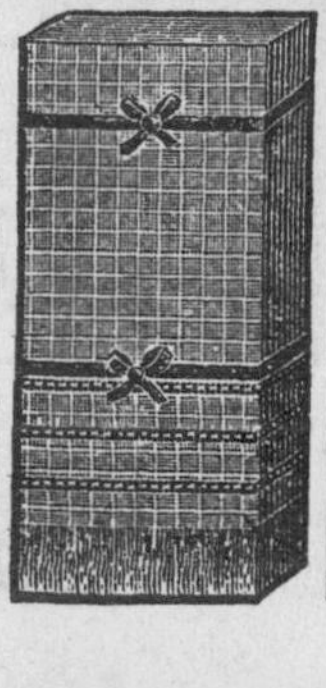

47c COTTON TOWELS, HONEYCOMB WEAVE, FRINGED ENDS.

No. 36K1615 Cream Honeycomb Towels. Used mainly as a dish towel for which purpose it is very well suited. Fast colored borders and fringed ends. Size, 16x36 inches.
Price, per dozen. **47c**

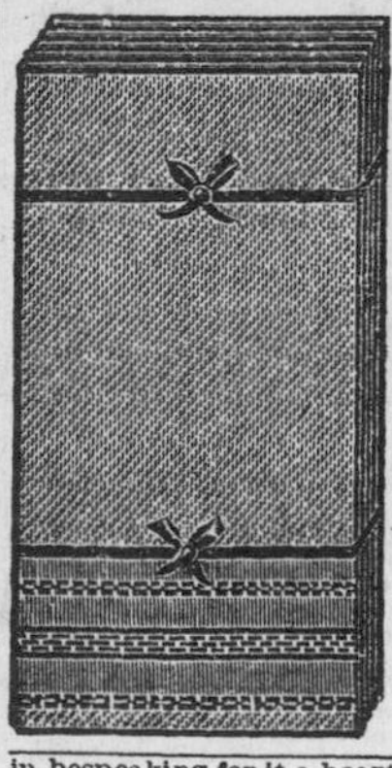

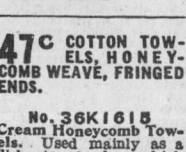

9c COTTON HUCK TOWELS, FAST RED BORDERS AND HEMMED ENDS.

No. 36K1687 Bleached Cotton Huck Towels with hemmed ends and fast color turkey red border. An improved towel this season. This is a fast edge towel that will give great service. Size, 18x36 inches.

Price, each, $0.09
Per dozen.. 1.00

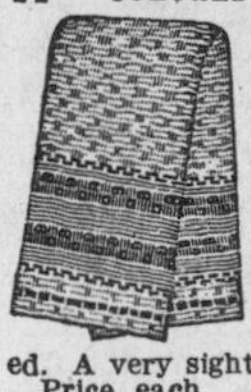

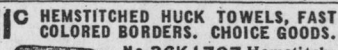

11c HEMSTITCHED HUCK TOWELS, FAST COLORED BORDERS. CHOICE GOODS.

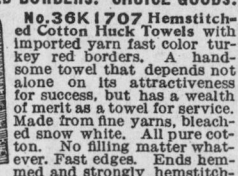

No. 36K1707 Hemstitched Cotton Huck Towels with imported yarn fast color turkey red borders. A handsome towel that depends not alone on its attractiveness for success, but has a wealth of merit as a towel for service. Made from fine yarns, bleached snow white. All pure cotton. No filling matter whatever. Fast edges. Ends hemmed and strongly hemstitched. A very sightly towel. Size, 18x36 inches.
Price, each........ $0.11
Per dozen........ 1.25

13c LINEN FINISH HUCK TOWELS, HEMMED ENDS, TURKEY RED BORDERS.

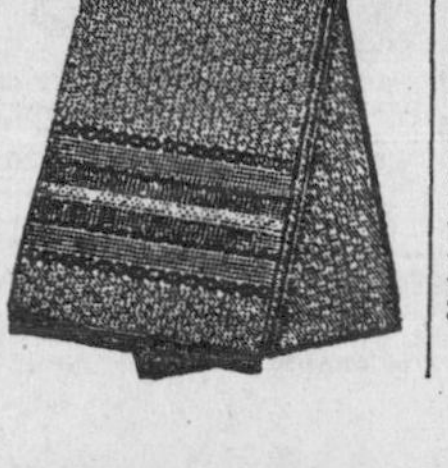

No. 36K1697 We are listing a larger and heavier Cotton Huck Towel this season than ever before and feel warranted in bespeaking for it a hearty reception. It is a towel that we have tested thoroughly and know it will answer its purpose splendidly. Being made of long fiber cotton it will resist wear and give tip top service. Fast selvage; will not tear at the edges. Pure white with hemmed ends and red borders like illustration. Mangle finish; will not wear or wash off and looks like an all linen towel. We use imported turkey red yarns in border. Guaranteed fast color. Size, 20x42 inches. Price, each........ $0.13
Per dozen........ 1.47

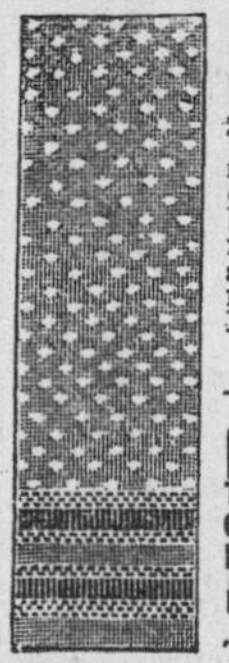

11c LINEN HUCK TOWELS, FAST TURKEY RED BORDERS, NEATLY HEMMED ENDS.

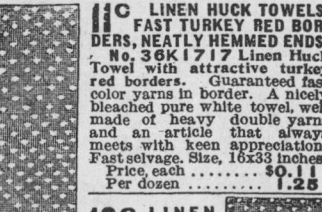

No. 36K1717 Linen Huck Towel with attractive turkey red borders. Guaranteed fast color yarns in border. A nicely bleached pure white towel, well made of heavy double yarns and an article that always meets with keen appreciation. Fast selvage. Size, 16x33 inches.
Price, each........ $0.11
Per dozen........ 1.25

13c LINEN HUCK TOWELS, FAST COLORED BORDERS.

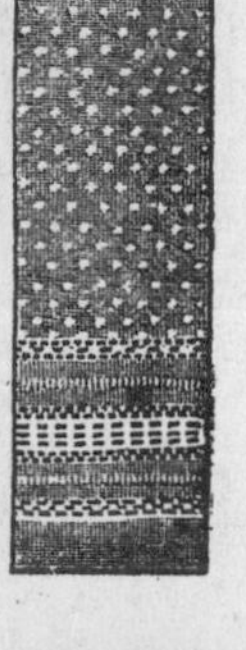

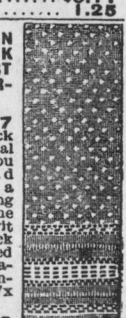

No. 36K1727 Hemmed Huck Towel. Actual comparisons will convince you that this is the best hand towel ever offered at such a price. That's a mighty strong statement to make but the towel is good enough to merit it. Bleached pure white huck with fast color turkey red borders, as shown in illustration. Fast selvage and unusually serviceable. Size, 17x34 inches.
Price, each........ $0.13
Per dozen........ 1.50

WHITE CUT CORNER BEDSPREADS.

WHITE CUT CORNER BEDSPREADS.

$1.73 WHITE CROCHET BEDSPREAD, PERFECTLY CUT OUT CORNERS.

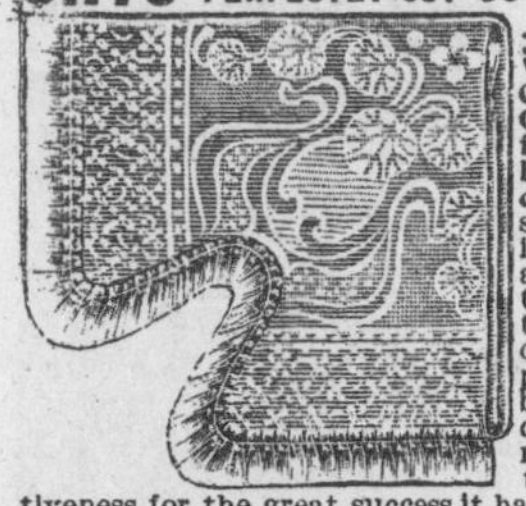

No. 36K2279 White Crochet Quilts, fringed and hand cut corners. A spread having sufficient artistic style to attract the attention of the prospective buyer but depending not alone on this attractiveness for the great success it has won, being possessed of a sterling quality so pronounced as to even exceed the favorable impression created for it by its stylish designs. A stocky spread of full size and being free from adulterants of any kind, will wash and wear splendidly. The corners being cut out by hand will fit around the bed posts perfectly. A luxury at a commonplace price. Size, 88x93 inches. Price, each.............. $ 1.73
Per dozen.............. 19.70

$1.98 WHITE CROCHET BEDSPREAD, HAND CUT CORNERS, SNUG FIT.

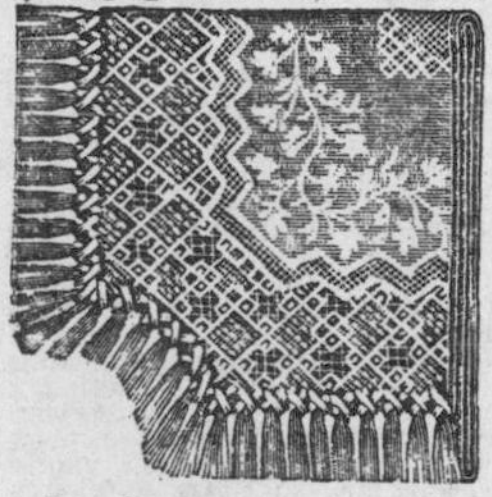

No. 36K2283 The acme of combined elegance and usefulness in a pure white heavy weight fringed crochet quilt with hand cut corners. Three-ply hard twisted yarns of the very choicest stock obtainable are worked into this spread and used in liberal quantities, so that even when judged from a standpoint of weight alone our quilt will be conceded by everyone to have no competition. The patterns are expressions of the highest artistic skill used in work of this kind, and must be seen in their full beauty to be thoroughly appreciated. The corners of the quilt are cut out by hand and are guaranteed to fit perfectly around the posts of the bed, relieving you of the annoyance of tucking in lumps or having gaping spaces around posts as is the case where corners are not accurately cut. Size, 88x91 inches.
Price, each.............. $ 1.98
Per dozen.............. 22.50

WHITE SATIN BEDSPREAD, CUT OUT CORNERS.

$2.05 OUR HIGHEST QUALITY AND MOST HANDSOME WHITE SATIN BEDSPREAD WITH CORNERS CUT OUT SCIENTIFICALLY ACCURATE BY HAND.

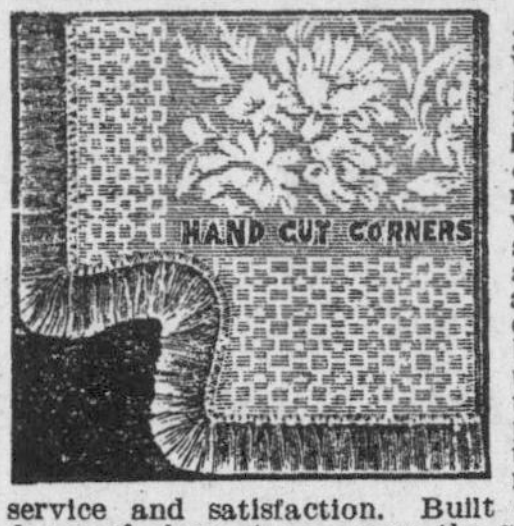

No. 36K2274 White Satin Bedspreads, fringed and hand cut corners, making a very handsome quilt in appearance as well as one that can be relied upon to give the greatest possible return for your money in service and satisfaction. Built of an abundance of clean strong yarns the quilt is naturally heavy, and being free from starch or other filling matter you can see what you are buying without having to wait until the quilt is washed. The corners of this spread are cut out by hand and will fit snugly around bedposts. As for style we need only say that the progressive methods used in this division reflect themselves in the constant addition of new and original patterns which will be found to excel in their tastefulness the designs to be had in any competitive quilt even at a much higher price. Full size, 89x95 inches.
Price, each.............. $ 2.05
Per dozen.............. 23.30

COLORED BEDSPREADS.

Colored Crochet Quilts, Fringed.

$1.19 COLORED CROCHET QUILTS, FRINGED DEEPLY ON FOUR SIDES

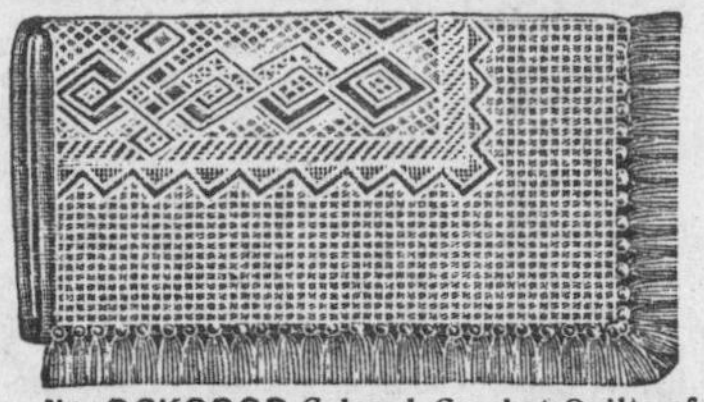

No. 36K2293 Colored Crochet Quilts of liberal weight and size. It is just as true in quilts as anywhere that a low price alone may attract attention and even go so far as to influence the first purchase, but it always takes quality to bring the customer back. We couldn't increase our output of these goods the way we have if that quality that makes for economy were not in evidence in every quilt. If you have never used these colored spreads you may doubt their serviceability or attractiveness. Those who have used this number will agree with us in saying that it is a highly desirable article in every way. Made from choice cotton yarns of uniformity in strength and grade. The patterns are all good, showing up clearly. The colors are bright and full of life. Pretty but not vivid. Navy, red, brown, pink or light blue. Fringed all around four sides with knotted mixed fringe, the navy quilt having alternate strands of navy and white in the tuft, the red having red and white tufts. **Be sure to mention color wanted.** Size, 86x90 inches.
Price, each.............. $ 1.19
Per dozen.............. 13.50

Colored Mitcheline Quilts, Hemmed.

$1.28 COLORED MITCHELINE QUILTS HEMMED, FAST COLORS.

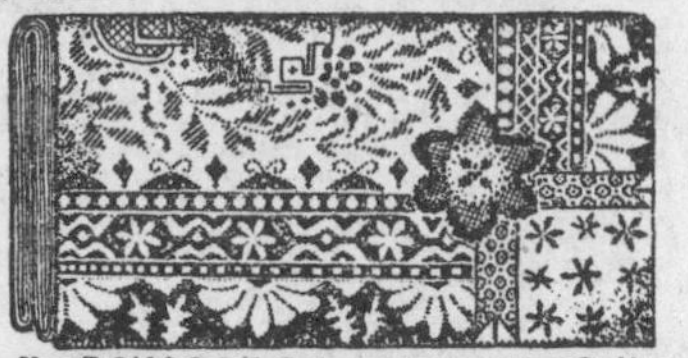

No. 36K2297 Colored Mitcheline Quilts, hemmed. Unquestionably for hard usage the greatest bedspread made, being constructed from heavy round cotton yarns of great durability. While emphasis is deservedly laid on this quilt for wear it is nevertheless a sightly quilt in appearance, the bright fast colors in which the patterns are worked out being tasteful in character. Really the cotton that goes into one of these Mitcheline quilts is worth the price we ask for the spread. We handle the only Mitcheline quilt that can absolutely be guaranteed fast color in all shades, many manufacturers warranting the life of the navy and red, but not of the light colors. You take no risk ordering any color we list, for we guarantee each color fast to soap and light. This is an important point to bear in mind when purchasing Mitcheline quilts. Our quilt is a generous size, weighty spread that cannot fail to make friends for itself on sight. This has been amply demonstrated by the enormous growth of our business on these goods. Colors are pink, light blue, red or navy. **Be sure to mention color wanted.** Size, 72x88 inches.
Price, each.............. $ 1.28
Per dozen.............. 14.60

WHITE INDIA LINONS.

8c WHITE INDIA LINON, FINE, EVEN TEXTURE.

No. 36K2332 White India Linon of fine texture, pure white and very evenly woven. A value that really conflicts with the low price quoted. Width, 30 inches.
Price, per yard.......$0.08
24-yard piece for....... 1.85
Equal to 7 7-10 cents per yard.

11c WHITE INDIA LINON, CHOICE SHEER FINISH.

No. 36K2337 An improved grade of choice White India Linon this season. All our Indias are woven from combed yarns. You would appreciate this fully when our goods are laid side by side with similar linons not so constructed. Width, 30 inches.
Price, per yard.......$0.11
24-piece yard for....... 2.55
Equal to 10⅝ cents per yard.

IN THE MATTER OF QUALITY and price our offerings on this and other pages of our catalogue surpass anything to be found in any other catalogue issued by any other mail order house. Our purchases for this season have been unusually large and we have succeeded in securing price concessions which enable us to quote lower prices on almost every line of merchandise represented in these pages.

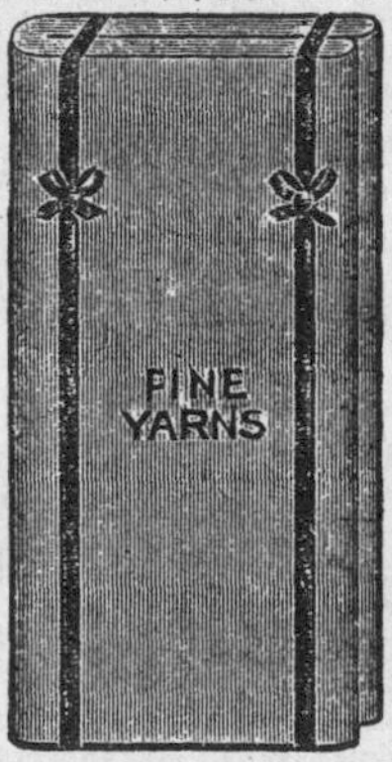

16c WHITE INDIA LINON, VERY FINE GRADE.

No. 36K2342 White India Linon of a superior quality. Fine combed yarn, texture very smooth and even. Pure white, fine and sheer. Will give excellent service. This is a grade that usually sells at a quarter per yard and considered a strong value at that price. Width, 30 inches.
Price, per yard.......$0.16
24-yard piece for....... 3.75
Equal to 15⅝ cents per yard.

22c WHITE INDIA LINON, VERY FINEST GRADE.

No. 36K2352 Our very finest and best pure White India Linon, woven from specially selected Sea Island cotton spun and combed into a fine yarn. Perhaps you have been using imported India linons at fancy prices; if so, we don't want to disturb your ideas as to quality, finish or color, but we do desire to impress you with the money saving features of this number, which is equal to foreign cloths in every way. Beautifully fine and sheer, and makes up charmingly. Width, 30 inches.
Price, per yard.......$0.22
24-yard piece for....... 5.15
Equal to 21½ cents per yard.

WHITE GOODS

NEVER BEFORE HAS SUCH AN ASSORTMENT of white wash dress goods been within the reach of our customers. It is a matter of great pride with us that the constant efforts we have put forth in presenting our line of staple and semi-novelty plain and fancy white fabrics at the lowest prices at which it is possible for us, with our enormous organization working for economy in purchasing and handling expense, to offer such high quality merchandise, have met with such keen appreciation by a host of discerning purchasers. Their valued patronage places us away in the lead in the distribution of popular priced white goods of recognized merit and by thus increasing our purchasing power with the manufacturers enable us to consistently lower the cost of production, the benefit of which returns to you in the shape of reduced catalogue prices, giving you the opportunity to get 25 to 30 per cent more goods for your dollar than would be possible any other way.

QUALITY. You know where we stand on the question of quality. We could not afford with our satisfaction to you or money back policy to adopt any middle ground. We are first, last and always for a high standard of quality, a quality that we could unhesitatingly stand back of, not once, but constantly, and our strong fight against adulterations and depreciation in quality has won us thousands of customers who know that they can depend on getting none but high grade goods at all times, regardless of price movements of raw material or manufactured goods.

ECONOMY. This is a big word and is one that is not always spelled LOW PRICE; in fact, cheapness has a meaning entirely foreign to that of genuine economy. We believe that quality is the keystone of economy and we have made it possible for you to know the real wealth of economy as illustrated by our purpose to sell you reliable goods at as near the actual cost at the mill door as is consistent with high quality. Let us speak a word of advice right here. We honestly believe that it is an evidence of thrift on the part of purchasers today to plan the use of a little better grade of cotton goods than they have previously used. The advance in raw cotton has made itself felt more on the lower grade of manufactured goods where raw material forms the chief value than on the better grades where it is not as much a question of raw material as it is skill in manufacturing. While we, even with our one small percentage above actual mill cost, are consequently compelled to ask a trifle more on the lower grade of cottons today than a year or two ago, we can, and do, furnish the higher qualities at practically old prices. Careful buyers will therefore appreciate that the way to reap the greatest possible benefit from their purchases is to buy a better grade of goods than they have heretofore used.

VARIETY. Our assortment of white goods for this season is a matter of sincere satisfaction to us and will minimize your difficulty of selection.

WE HAVE LISTED a much wider range of popular priced goods than ever before and have covered every sought for weave, finish and style to the best possible advantage, after spending months in looking over the various lines of hundreds of home and foreign manufacturers, and we must say that there never was a season when so many choice fabrics and styles have been produced, especially by our home mills. Therefore, when we say that we have picked out the cream of each maker's goods, you may rest assured that your opportunity for buying new and nobby white goods, both plain and fancy, is by far the greatest you have ever had.

LINEN COLORED INDIA LINONS.

9c LINEN COLORED INDIA LINON, FINE AND SHEER.

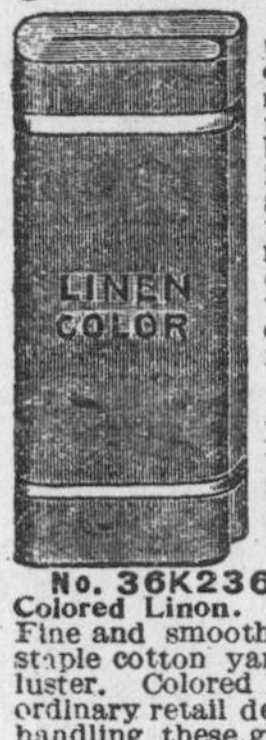

No. 36K2357 Indications are that the Linen Colored India Linons are to be more sought after this season than for some time past. We believe that the special finish imparted to our goods, together with their fine, sheer texture, which is a natural result of using combed yarns only, will create for them a warm welcome. Nice ecru or linen color. Width, 31 inches.
Price, per yard....$0.09
24-yard piece for... 2.10
Equal to 8¾ cents per yard.

13c LINEN COLORED INDIA LINON, SPECIAL QUALITY.

No. 36K2367 Extra High Grade Linen Colored Linon. A good ecru or linen shade. Fine and smooth. Woven from choice long staple cotton yarns of unusual strength and luster. Colored Indias are made to bring the ordinary retail dealer a large profit, but by our handling these goods like everything else, on our one small percentage of profit policy, we are safe in promising you a saving here of 11 cents per yard. Width, 31 inches.
Price, per yard..............$0.13
24-yard piece for.............. 3.03
Equal to 12⅝ cents per yard.

BLACK INDIA LINONS.

9c BLACK INDIA LINON, WARRANTED FAST COLOR. CHOICE STOCK.

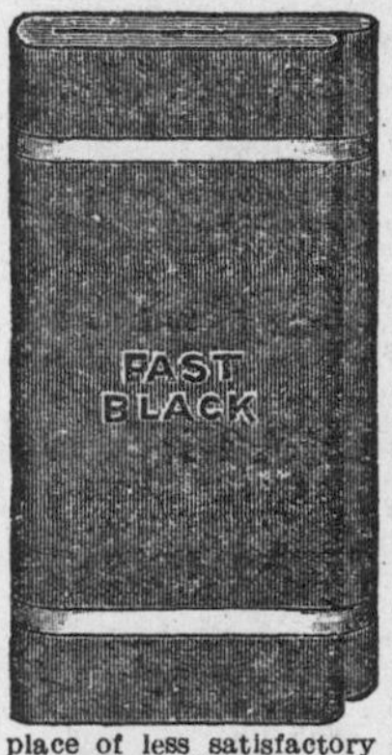

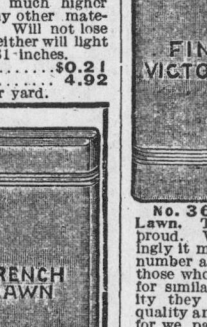

No. 36K2372 Black India Linon of a good quality, well woven and guaranteed fast black. Compares favorably with the 15-cent grades in the ordinary way. Our special finish. Width, 28 inches.
Price, per yd... 9c
24-yard piece for........$2.10
Equal to 8¾ cents per yard.

14c BLACK INDIA LINON, FINE, FAST COLOR

No. 36K2377 Fine Black India Linon. Wider and better quality than the foregoing number. Its inexpensiveness recommends it for use in place of less satisfactory materials, while it has sufficient merit to suggest its use for the best uses. Pure aniline black. Warranted against discoloring through sun or moisture. Width, 31 inches. Price, per yard...$0.14
24-yard piece for.............. 3.27
Equal to 13⅝ cents per yard.

21c BLACK INDIA LINON, BEAUTIFULLY FINE SEA ISLAND COTTON.

No. 36K2387 Our Highest Grade Black India Linon, constructed of choice Sea Island cotton, combed into the finest and most lustrous yarns. The extra select stock used in the manufacture of these goods produces a fabric capable of retaining a much higher finish than is possible with any other materials. Guaranteed fast black. Will not lose its color through laundering; neither will light or moisture affect it. Width, 31 inches.
Price, per yard..............$0.21
24-yard piece for.............. 4.92
Equal to 20½ cents per yard.

22c WHITE FRENCH LAWN, 48 INCHES WIDE, A GREAT ECONOMY.

No. 36K2510 EXTRA WIDE FINE FRENCH LAWNS. Nice sheer finish and a pearly whiteness that attracts the eye by its purity. These fabrics will be found invaluable for separate skirts, bonnets and children's wear. The extra width lends emphasis to the purchase from an economical viewpoint. The texture is very similar to that of a Victoria lawn. Width, 48 inches.

Price, per yard..22c

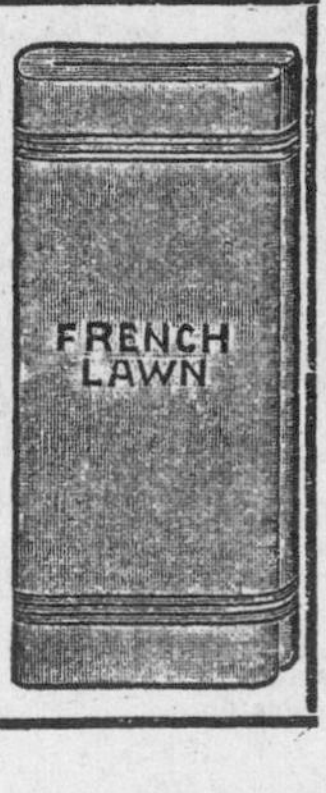

WHITE VICTORIA LAWNS.

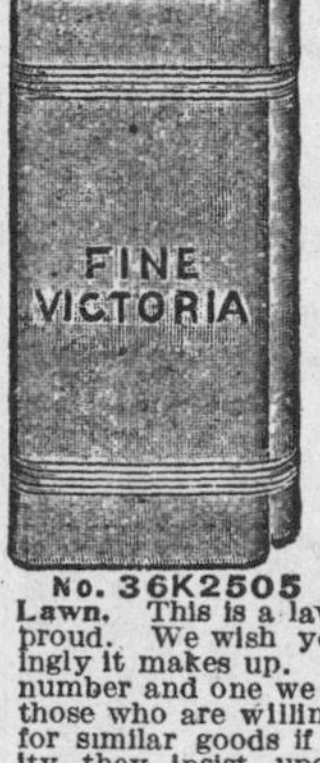

13c WHITE VICTORIA LAWN, WIDE AND FINE, GOOD VALUE.

No. 36K2496 White Victoria Lawn, full apron or skirt width, and a quality that will be readily appreciated by users of these popular fabrics. Medium weight, even texture and sheer. Makes up readily and launders well. Altogether a thoroughly satisfactory fabric. Width, 40 inches. Price, per yd. 13c

17c WHITE VICTORIA LAWN, WIDE, EXTRA FINE, SPLENDID QUALITY

No. 36K2505 Our best White Victoria Lawn. This is a lawn of which we are justly proud. We wish you could see how charmingly it makes up. Finer than the preceding number and one we suggest unhesitatingly to those who are willing to pay 30 cents per yard for similar goods if necessary to get the quality they insist upon. We guarantee the quality and you run no risk of disappointment, for we pay the transportation charges both ways if goods do not please you. This Victoria lawn is 40 inches wide.
Price, per yard.............. 17c

NO SUCH PRICE REDUCTIONS have ever been made by any firm or individual as we have made in the pages of this Big Catalogue on the HIGHEST GRADE MERCHANDISE.

CHECK OVER YOUR ORDER CAREFULLY after you have completed it to see that you have given catalogue numbers in full, including any initial, and that correct quantities are stated in each case. We must have catalogue numbers to enable us to fill your order correctly.

FREE WHITE WASH DRESS GOODS SAMPLES

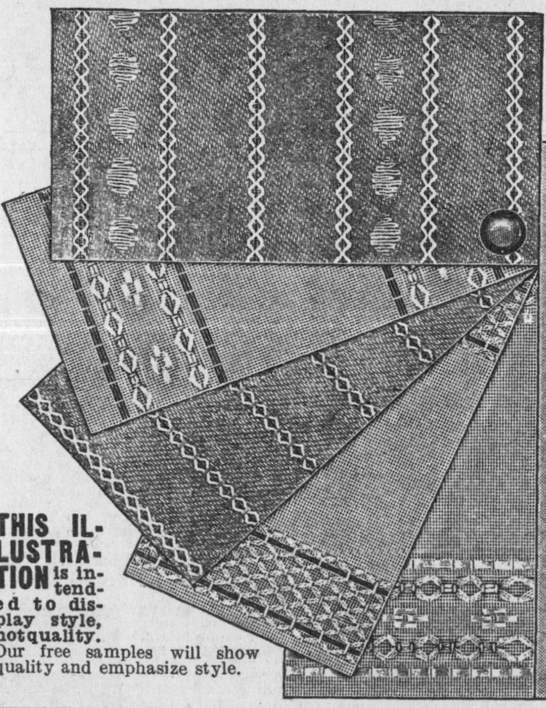

THIS ILLUSTRATION is intended to display style, not quality. Our free samples will show quality and emphasize style.

YOU ARE GOING TO BUY SOME WHITE GOODS THIS YEAR. You can't get along without them. Are you thoroughly decided as to what you want? You may be reasonably well satisfied as to about the price you intend to pay but we have such a wide range of attractions this season you may possibly find it difficult to make your choice. Perhaps you have never ordered any dress fabrics from us and therefore naturally you question our ability to serve you better than anyone else and save you money too. In either case send us a postal asking for free samples of the numbers that attract your notice and they will be mailed postpaid at once and free of all expense to you. To give you an idea just how these samples are put up we ask you to note our No. 36K2837 a wonderful display of fine novelty waistings. Such a value as has never before come your way.

BEAR IN MIND that samples of any number of fancy white goods you may select will be mailed to you on a card just like these waistings and will show in a generous clipping all the patterns, designs and styles we have in our immense stock, which is at all times complete, enabling us to fill all orders no matter how large without a moment's delay. Isn't this worth while considering? Read through these pages and make your selections today. Don't delay in getting your samples. You run no risk in mailing us your order without waiting for samples as the descriptions have been made as complete as possible and we pay the express charges both ways if goods are not in every way satisfactory to you.

FIVE SPLENDID WHITE WAISTING NOVELTIES 22c PER YD.

No. 36W2837 WIDTH, 28 INCHES.

We want every woman who is partial to white waisting stripes (and few there are who are not) to inspect the free samples of this select group of novelties.

NOTHING ORDINARY ABOUT THE GOODS IN ANY WAY although they have a commonplace price. If you allow the low price at which we offer these waistings to unfavorably influence your decision you will have lost an excellent opportunity of seeing some of the very choicest of this year's white waistings and you will also have overlooked a chance to test the truth of our price arguments, as applied to our line of white and colored wash fabrics. These fabrics are of varying weights, some of them closely woven, but medium light weight; others are a little heavier. All of them are peculiarly adapted to waisting use and we only need ask you to look around you in the better shops anywhere and be convinced that stripes will be stronger than ever this year. These novelties are woven of mercerized yarns both ways, fine and soft, draping tastefully. We have plain stripes, a combination of stripes, with pure silk dots and others with bright medium two cord stripes outlined with black or cream. Very beautiful and as lustrous as all pure silk. The greatest value we, or anyone else, ever offered in up to date high class waistings, not a lot of goods we just happened on, but one of the best purchases we ever made for you as you will admit when you see the goods.

No. 36W2837 Width, 28 inches. Price, per yard..................22c

SEARS, ROEBUCK & CO., CHICAGO, ILL.

15c WHITE COTTON CASHMERE, FINE HENRIETTA TWILL.

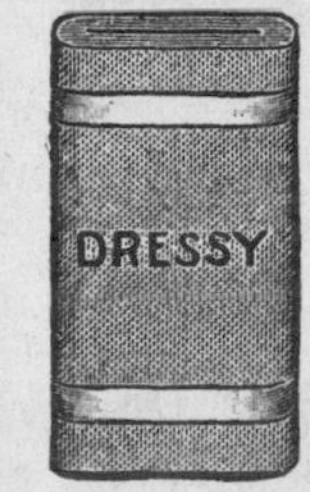

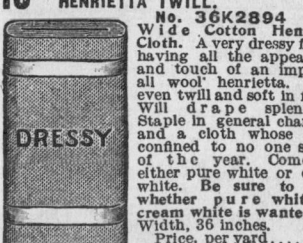

No. 36K2894 Yard Wide Cotton Henrietta Cloth. A very dressy fabric, having all the appearance and touch of an imported all wool henrietta. Fine, even twill and soft in finish. Will drape splendidly. Staple in general character and a cloth whose use is confined to no one season of the year. Comes in either pure white or cream white. Be sure to state whether pure white or cream white is wanted. Width, 36 inches.
Price, per yard..... 15c
Full piece of about 30 yards, per yard..... 14¼c

22c OUR GREAT TWO TO ONE YARN MERCERIZED PONGEE.

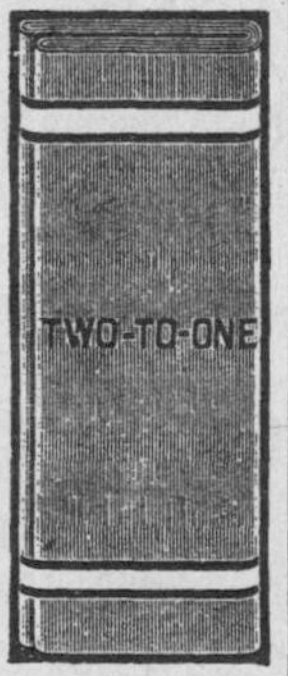

No. 36K2900 We call this our two to one cloth because it is so skillfully made, and from such high class materials that we find by comparison with similar fabrics that ours will wear twice as long and give you double the satisfaction, and we are prepared to save you money as well. This cloth is woven like a pongee in texture and is the result of a liberal use of extra fine Egyptian combed cotton yarns, all of which have been thoroughly mercerized before weaving. This process not only adds a silky luster to the fabric but increases the strength of the cloth, thereby lengthening the life of the garment into which it enters. The beauty and purity can only be appreciated when seen in the piece. The width is a feature not to be overlooked, and lastly, the ordinary price of this cloth anywhere else is 27 to 30 cents per yard. Width, 32 inches. Price, per yard..... 22c
Full piece of about 30 yards, per yard 21½c

23c WHITE MOHAIR BRILLIANTINE, NATURAL FINISHED FABRIC.

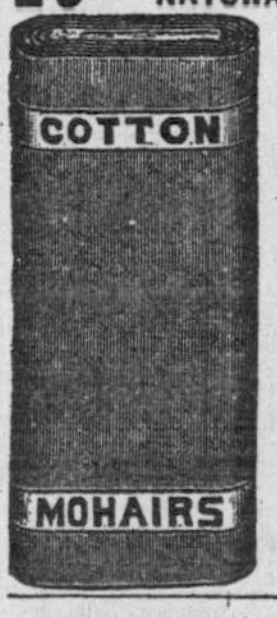

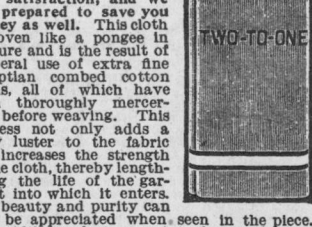

No. 36K2898 In this fabric we believe we have the nearest approach you have ever seen to a real mohair brilliantine, all the desirable features of these exceedingly serviceable fabrics being incorporated in our cloth. To see the two fabrics side by side one could hardly detect the difference. The natural finish imparted to this fabric may be depended on as being permanent, as the manufacturer has made up several thousand pieces of these goods before putting them on the market. Comes in pure white only. Width, 30 inches.
Price, per yard... 23c

17c GIBSON CLOTH, PURE SNOW WHITE.

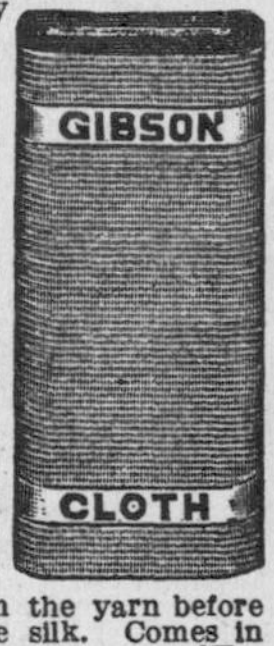

No. 36K2903 A charming waisting or costume cloth of unusual brilliancy and merit. The weave is very similar to that of a wool tricot or Jersey cloth. We appreciate that this is going a long way from home to make a comparison, but the texture is so unique in cotton fabrics that nothing that you have seen before will compare with it. While it may carry some likeness to a rep it is so much finer and softer, so much more of a draping, clinging fabric that it would be unfair to class our Gibson cloth with the reps. The moment you feel the soft silkiness of this fabric you will realize that nothing but the choicest cotton could produce such goods. While fine and dainty, it will nevertheless give good service, outwearing many heavier fabrics. Fully mercerized in the yarn before weaving. Bright as all pure silk. Comes in white only. Width, 28 inches.
Price, per yard........................ 17c

16c COTTON CREPE DE CHINE, MADE FROM POLISHED YARNS.

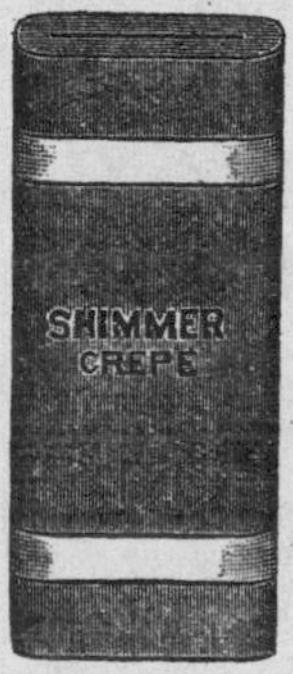

No. 36K2907 Our Cotton Crepe de Chine is a very happy combination of specially twisted and finished yarns which appear to be mercerized but is the result of a new process which hardens the yarn, thus increasing the length of life of the fabric and adding luster. The luster is permanent and is guaranteed to wash and wear as well as a mercerized fabric. Special attention has been given to the construction of this cloth so that it will not pull on the warp. Comes in pure white only. 27 inches wide.
Price, per yard..... 16c

20c MEDIUM WEIGHT POPLIN SUITINGS, HIGHLY LUSTROUS, MERCERIZED FABRIC.

No. 36K2911 Good Poplin is at once a sightly and serviceable suiting. The cloth is just right in weight so that it drapes nicely; being constructed of hard twisted, wiry yarns, it does not soil easily and is at the same time one of the best wearing suitings we know of. Poplins of this character are frequently met with in the ordinary dry goods store at 30 cents per yard and our saving of 9 cents per yard should, therefore, be an item of great interest to you. We assure you such interest will only be intensified by the service the fabric will give you. Comes in pure white only. 28 inches
Price, per yard..... 20c

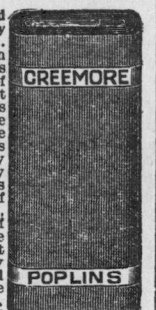

10c WHITE REP SUITINGS, SMALL NEAT FIGURES, CHECKS AND PLAIDS.

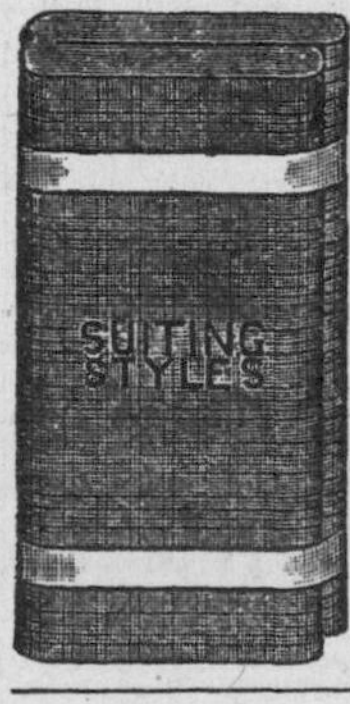

No. 36K2913 A medium weight White Rep Suiting in a good selection of patterns, such as plaids, small figures, etc. Very neat and serviceable. Your interest attracted by a low price will nowise be lessened by its quality, which is really not to be judged by our wholesale price. Width, 26 inches.
Price, per yard.. 10c
Full piece of about 40 yards, per yard.. 9½c

12½c WHITE BRILLIANTINES, NEAT SUITING STYLES.

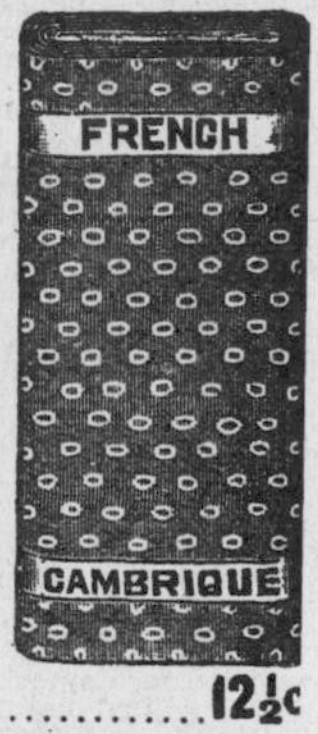

No. 36K2917 It is so difficult to imagine a suiting cloth of any real merit at such a low price that we know we have prepared a great surprise for many of our customers. If you are the least in doubt about it, send at once for our assortment of free samples. This is a closely woven cloth of a soft, clinging nature, well bleached and comes in a line of patterns that while not large covers the needs of every purchaser. There are dots as well as small medium figures. All these patterns are worked out in mercerized yarns, adding considerable beauty to the fabric. Width, 27 inches.
Price, per yard.................. 12½c

16c WHITE MERCERIZED WAISTING, GUARANTEED PERMANENT LUSTER.

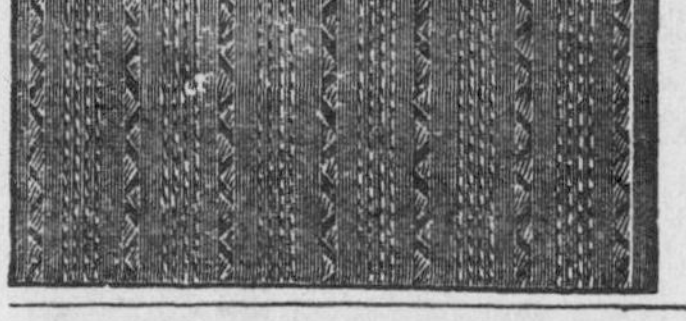

No. 36K2923 White Mercerized Waistings in new tasty striped patterns similar to the one illustrated. We have a great variety of styles and among the samples we mail you free you will be sure to find just the pattern you prefer. This cloth has a plain woven ground of a little better than medium weight. The stripes are all woven of mercerized yarns of a guaranteed brilliancy and life. A close resemblance to silk. A wonderful combination of service and beauty.
Width, 28 inches. Price, per yard..... 16c

NO SUCH PRICE REDUCTIONS HAVE EVER BEEN MADE BY ANY FIRM OR INDIVIDUAL AS WE HAVE MADE IN THE PAGES OF THIS BIG CATALOGUE ON THE HIGHEST GRADE MERCHANDISE.

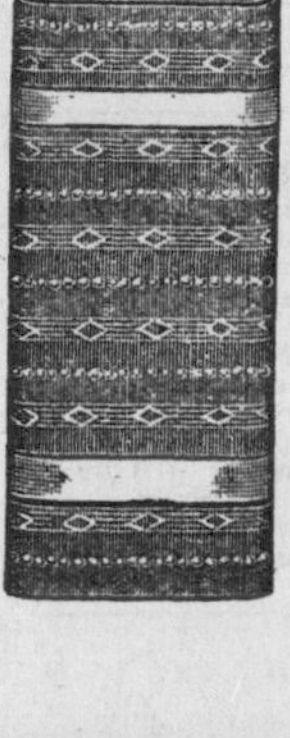

17c WHITE WAISTING, MERCERIZED STRIPES.

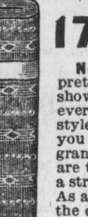

No. 36K2927 New Mercerized Stripe Waisting. One of the prettiest fabrics of the season, and that means a great deal, for we are showing by far the finest and swellest line of these cloths now that we ever have displayed. All pure white made from choice cotton and has a style that takes it out of the class of waistings ordinarily shown. To give you some idea of the manner in which it is woven—it is somewhat of a granite weave ground closely woven and of great durability. The stripes are three-quarters of an inch apart, the first being a row of spots, the next a stripe composed of several hairlines with a set design similar to cut. As all the stripes are woven of silky mercerized yarns of great permanency, the effect can better be imagined than described. The marvelous life of the cloth, together with its style, make a combination that really should bring the regular retailing price of 30 cents per yard. If you have any doubt as to the claims we have made for this cloth, send for our free samples. You run no risk by ordering from this description, however if goods are not entirely satisfactory to you we pay the charges and refund your money. Width, 28 inches.
Price, per yard.................. 17c

PLAIN AND FANCY WASH SUITINGS.

7¾c CHAMBRAY SUITING, CHOICE KNICKERBOCKER EFFECTS.

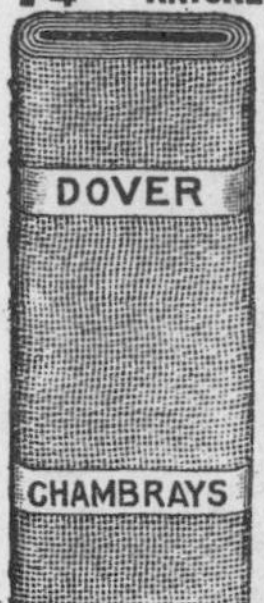

No. 36K3573 It isn't our fault that we run these Chambray Suitings season in and season out. We wouldn't do it if our trade did not insist upon it by their re-orders or if we could find a fabric that would really take their place. They are well made in spite of such a price and are fast colors. With home washing they do splendid service. Printed in knickerbocker splash effect. Colors are tan, brown, nile green, steel gray, pink, red, light blue or navy. **Be sure to mention color wanted.** Width, 25 inches.
Price, per yard 7¾c
Full piece of about 50 yards, per yard 7½c

7¾c CHAMBRAY SUITINGS, FANCY STYLES, ALL NEW IDEAS.

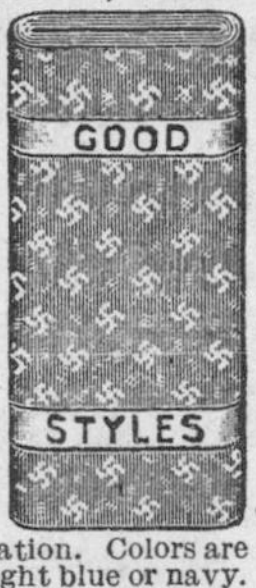

No. 36K3574 It is really surprising what a splendid effort has been put forth by the manufacturers of these Fancy Chambray Suitings this season. We think the styles are just a little better and the character of printing a shade more perfect than ever before. Therefore, we have every reason to believe that their popularity will be again limited only by the capacity of the mill to turn out the goods. The cloth is well put together and the printing is clear and clean. There are several styles similar to illustration. Colors are red, reseda green, steel gray, light blue or navy. **Do not overlook mentioning color in your order.** Width, 25 inches. Price, per yard, 7¾c
Full piece of about 50 yards, per yard. . 7½c

16c FRENCH BLUE SUITINGS. EVERYBODY ASKING FOR THEM.

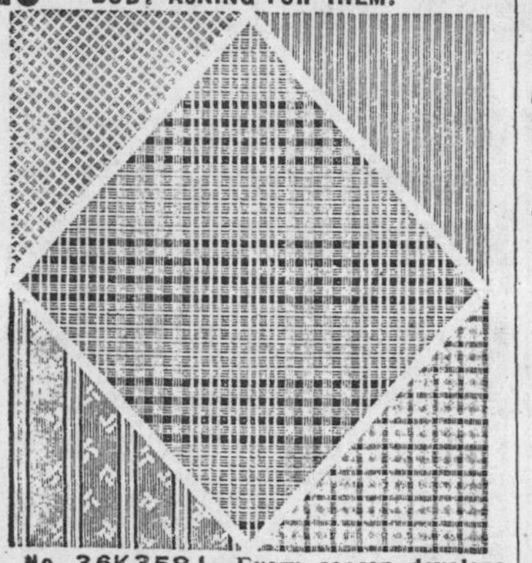

No. 36K3581 Every season develops one color or shade in particular that above everything else gets the call from all quarters. This season it is the French blue. Rarely does fashion set her mark upon a shade that at once combines the essence of durability, economy, comfort and sightliness as is the case with these snappy French blues. The suiting which we are bringing out in this happy tint is a good medium weight, evenly woven fabric, made from the most adaptable yarns it is possible to get, yarns that not only show up smoothly in the finished cloth, but take a color brightly and will wash and wear almost endlessly. Measured by every standard of quality, weight, color and finish, critical buyers will be immediately convinced of the merit of our new French blue suitings. Comfort and economy go hand in hand to endorse this fabric. Each pattern in the line has been as carefully selected as though we depended entirely on that one design for our season's success. All the most favored style touches of the day are here awaiting your selection. We have a most liberal assortment of patterns. Everybody will want French blue suitings. Some will want hairline checks, small, medium or large, others prefer hairline stripes. The fancy stripes with small figures between will be eagerly looked for by their admirers, and plaids in small and medium sizes will attract the attention of a great many women. Note the special width, 34 inches. Price, per yard . . 16c
Full piece of about 30 yards, per yard, 15½c

10½c MANCHESTER CHAMBRAY, FAST COLORING.

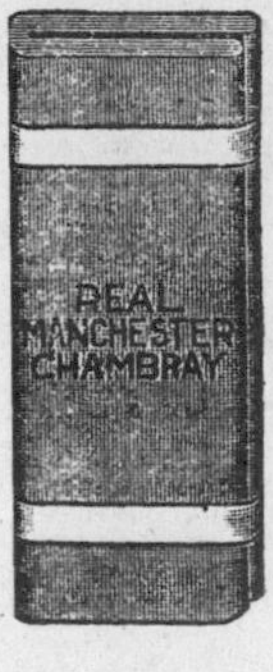

No. 36K3583 The real old fashioned Manchester Chambray. It never loses its interest with a great mass of housekeepers. We have aimed to encourage its use by sticking to our high standard of quality. The cotton used in this chambray is of an excellent grade and takes on a nice full color tone. We carry in stock at all times pink, light blue, dark red, navy, cadet, nile green, tan, dark brown, or steel gray. **Be sure to mention color wanted.** Width, 26 inches.
Price, per yard 10½c
Full piece of about 26 yards, per yard 10c

14c SOFT FINISH CHAMBRAY, WIDE AND FINE. VERY DRESSY.

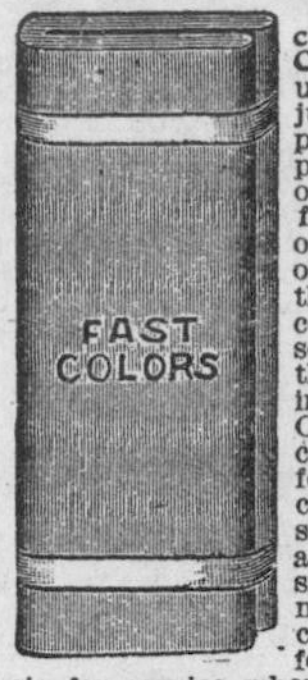

No. 36K3593 In considering this Fine Chambray please do not underrate the quality by judging from a price standpoint alone. Such an impression as you might thus obtain would be misleading for this cloth is really one of the very largest sellers in our line of plain goods and the enormous quantities we contract for enable us to secure a price concession that at once finds its way into our catalogue price. Only very fine, long fiber cotton is spun into yarns for these goods and the cloth when finished being soft and even in its texture and entirely free from any sizing or dressing that might tend to weight the cloth or stiffen it. Will be found a most desirable fabric for service wherever a solid colored cloth of this nature is adaptable. We fully warrant the colors. They are beautifully soft, full tints. Something decidedly distinctive about this cloth. A bully thing for men's and boys' shirts as well as children's wear. Colors are pink, light blue, cadet blue, navy, soft red, nile green, steel gray, tan, champagne, dark brown or black. **Be careful to state color.** Width, 32 inches.
Price, per yard 14c
Full piece of about 40 yards, per yard, 13½c

17c OUR NEW FIGURED HENRIETTA CLOTH OR COTTON CASHMERE.

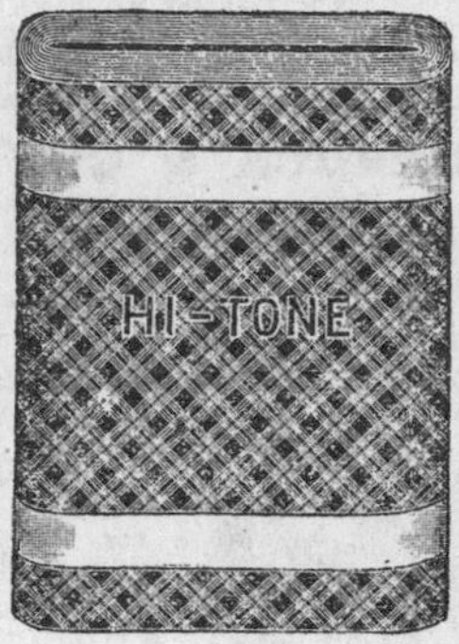

No. 36K3696 Fancy Henrietta Suitings, one of the most noteworthy offerings of our extensive line of wash goods this season, not only on account of the extra saving we are able to make for you due to the excessive profit dealers are expected to have from the sale of these goods, but also from the standpoint of all around satisfaction with quality and character. The weave of this henrietta cloth is so fine that none but the very best materials can be employed in its manufacture and equally true is it that none but the finest yarns could produce such a fine, smooth, soft texture. The fabric really is such a striking likeness of our all wool henrietta that we find it necessary to lay more than usual stress on the fact that it is all cotton of the highest type. The dyeing is done in the very best way the most expert finishers in this country know and the styles leave nothing untouched that one could possibly wish for. Black and white shepherd checks (three sizes), black and white plaids in six or more designs including small, medium and large hairline, two and three-line and block effects. Yes! we have a complete assortment of polka dots also, comprising light blue, red or black dots on cream ground, as well as white dots on dark green, medium brown, dark cardinal, navy or black grounds. **Be sure to state style and color wanted.** Width, 36 inches. Price, per yard 17c

DRESS SATEENS, BLACK AND COLORS.

12c FAST BLACK SATEEN, FINE HENRIETTA FINISH, EVEN TWILL.

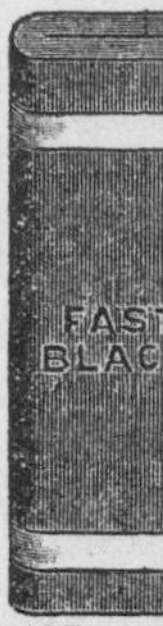

No. 36K3663 Fast Black Dress Sateens Henrietta Finished. Even twill and free from sizing or weighting of any kind. Width, 30 inches.
Price, per yard 12c
Full piece of about 40 yards, per yard 11½c

15c FAST BLACK SATEEN, EXTRA HENRIETTA FINISH.

No. 36K3665 For the small difference in price this cloth represents an economy of appreciable sincerity. Dyed in aniline and warranted fast black. Fine twill and a silky henrietta finish that suggests the cloth as a good purchase for men's and boys' shirts as well as ladies' underskirts, etc. Width, 31 inches.
Price, per yard 15c
Full piece of about 40 yards, per yd., 14½c

THE SURPRISINGLY LOW REDUCED PRICES prevailing in this catalogue mean greater savings to our customers than ever before.

20c BLACK BROCADED SATEENS, NEAT, DRESSY PATTERNS.

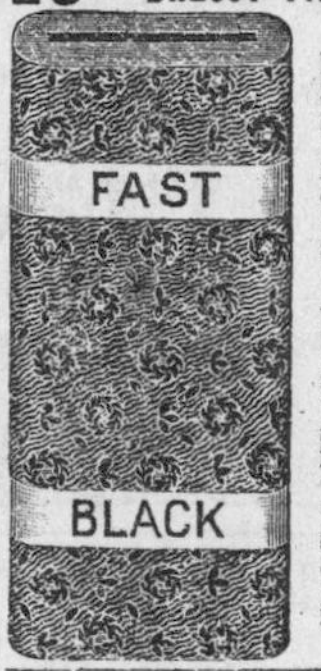

No. 36K3686 Fast Black Brocaded Sateens, a near approach to the silk goods in appearance. A very fine sateen cloth, thoroughly mercerized and having neat brocaded styles similar to illustration. All solid black. Attractive and has a great deal of simple style that is unobtrusive, but still apparent. Wears well as it is just as you see it. Nothing to lose in wear or laundering. Our price is a revelation to many users of these goods as 25 cents is considered low enough elsewhere. Width, 30 inches.
Price, per yard . . 20c

15c COTTON HENRIETTA CLOTH, FINE, EVEN TWILL. WOOL EFFECT.

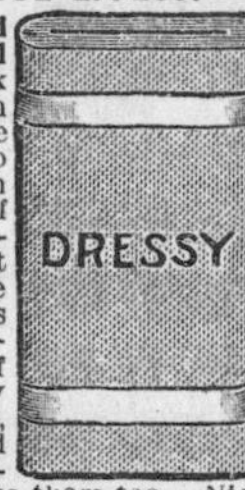

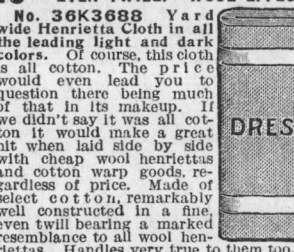

No. 36K3688 Yard wide Henrietta Cloth in all the leading light and dark colors. Of course, this cloth is all cotton. The price would even lead you to question there being much of that in its makeup. If we didn't say it was all cotton it would make a great hit when laid side by side with cheap wool henriettas and cotton warp goods, regardless of price. Made of select cotton, remarkably well constructed in a fine, even twill bearing a marked resemblance to all wool henriettas. Handles very true to them too. Nice medium weight, soft and will drape charmingly. Colors very deep and absolutely fast. We at all times can supply you promptly with any of these shades: Pink, light blue, nile green, purple, old rose, tan, medium brown, pearl gray, slate, myrtle green, light navy, dark navy, dark cardinal, wine, cream white, pure white or black. **Do not overlook color in your order.** Width, 36 inches.
Price, per yard 15c
Full piece of about 35 yards, per yard, 14½c

20c FINE BLACK SATEEN, SUPERIOR SILK FINISH.

No. 36K3667 Extra Quality Black Silk Finished Sateens. Suitable for the better shirts and especially desirable in making fine underskirts. A very fine twill. Soft finished and very pure. Color guaranteed fast, neither light, moisture or laundering will affect color. Aniline dye insures its depth and life. In every way a high class sateen. Width, 31 inches.
Price, per yard 20c

24c EXTRA FINE BLACK SATEEN, SUPERIOR SILK FINISH.

No. 36K3668 Our very finest and highest quality pure aniline dyed Fast Black Silk Finished Henrietta Sateen. A quality that requires close scrutiny in order to tell it from silk. Has a special finish that stamps the fabric with sensational character. It really is too good to be used for underskirts as it has sufficient merit to suggest the advantage of its use for waists. Fine, almost invisible twill and being a closely woven fabric and entirely pure long fiber cotton with no filling matter of any kind it will wear and wash to a degree of perfection unknown to inferior sateens. Width, 31 inches. Price, per yard 24c

14½c COLORED DRESS SATEEN, FINE SILK FINISH, HIGH LUSTER.

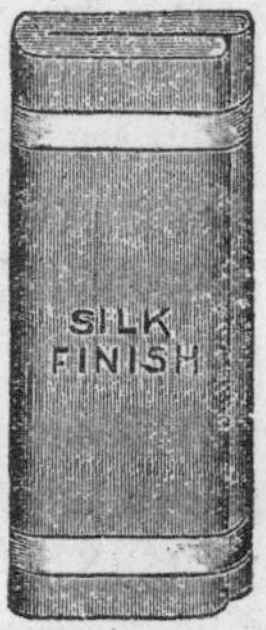

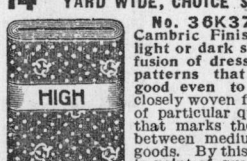

No. 36K3678 Dress Sateens in all colors. Hardly anything new to say about these goods. Everybody knows their qualifications. Some people prefer to confine their use to waists, underskirts, ruffles, etc. Sateens fill the bill satisfactorily, others have found that they add to the life of a garment when used for linings. Good economy. This cloth has a fine twill and a lustrous, silky finish that is very tempting. Being soft, they drape pleasantly. Colors, guaranteed fast, are pink, light blue, nile green, myrtle green, primrose yellow, tan, champagne, medium brown, royal blue, navy, turkey red, dark cardinal, slate, cream white, pure white or black. **State color wanted.** Width, 31 inches.
Price, per yard 14½c
Full piece of about 40 yards, per yard 14c

20c EXTRA SILK FINISH, FINE DRESS SATEENS.

No. 36K3681 In this superior silk finished dress sateen we believe the nearest approach to absolute perfection in weaving and dyeing has been attained. In order to reach the high point of merit shown in every yard yes, every strand, it was necessary to seek out a special grade of long, soft fibered cotton to luster and strength and after spinning into an unusually fine yarn to send it to silk dyers so that the last step in its attempt to equal silk in luster might be the more surely successful. The twill is very nearly invisible and the general effect is that of a fine piece of all silk goods. Nothing in it to wash out. Colors fast and beautifully full rounded out tones that would do credit to any silk fabric. They are pink, light blue, primrose yellow, nile green, myrtle green, tan, champagne, medium brown, royal blue, navy, turkey red, dark cardinal, slate, pearl gray, cream white, pure white or black. **Be sure to state color wanted.** Width, 31 inches. Price, per yard 20c

DOUBLE THE VALUE OF YOUR DOLLAR by purchasing needed articles from us at our greatly reduced prices.

YARD WIDE FINE DRESS PERCALES.

10½c FAST COLOR PERCALES, DARK GROUNDS ONLY.

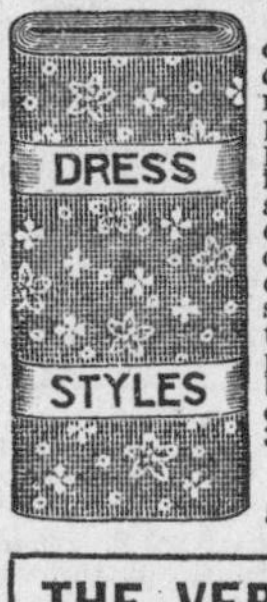

No. 36K3698 Shirting or Dress Percales, all dark colors, full yard wide. A much better fabric than seems possible to bring out at the price when the extra width is considered. The colors are all fast and patterns very enjoyable. There are polka dots, figures, small and medium and a few choice fancy stripes. We at all times aim to carry a full stock of these patterns in navy, wine or black. **Don't forget style and color in your order.** Width, 36 inches—note this.
Price, per yard 10½c
Full piece of about 50 yards, per yard 10c

THE VERY LOW PRICES

we quote on all lines of wash goods shown in this catalogue offer you savings on these necessary materials which you cannot secure from any other dealer at home or elsewhere. Our purchases of wash goods were very fortunate. We secured goods very much below the market and these advantages we give to you in the form of these very low prices. Our splendid qualities will appeal to the discriminating housewife and we will be glad to send samples upon receipt of postal card request asking for them.

11c SHEPHERD CHECK PERCALES, POPULAR SIZED CHECKS.

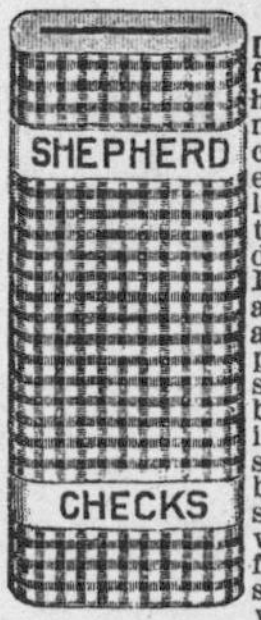

No. 36K3703 Yard Wide Dress Percales in plain and fancy black and white shepherd checks. People really never tire of these neat checked styles. They are so easy to make up and always look right. Requiring practically no trimmings they are decidedly economical, too. For those who are looking for a little variety we have secured a tasteful set of small ring patterns, dots, etc., properly spaced on the checks, all in black and white. We have in addition, of course, all the sizes of even checks. It would be absurd to put so much style into a cheap cloth, and we haven't done so. The fabric is surprisingly well constructed at such a price which will be frequently paid this year for narrow calicos. There is a freshness and charm about these shepherd check percales that will instantly meet your fancy. This is noticeable even in the illustration. An illustration is very helpful in displaying the pattern but there are a few things that illustrations cannot tell. One of these is quality. Quality is a big word and should mean the same today and tomorrow as it did yesterday. Styles change frequently and we reshape our assortments to fit the current demands but we stand pat on quality. This is a feature of our merchandising that means much to you. Fast colors. **Don't forget style and color in your order.** Width, 36 inches. Price, per yard . . 11c
Full piece of about 50 yards, per yard 10½c

14c FINE CAMBRIC FINISHED PERCALE, YARD WIDE, CHOICE STYLES.

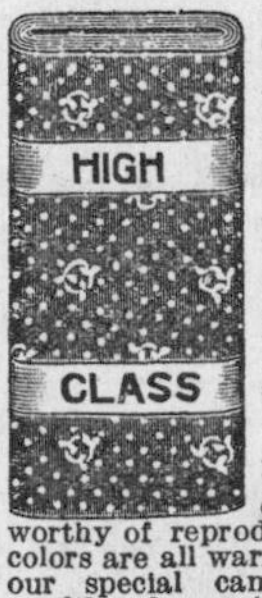

No. 36K3705 Special Cambric Finished Percales, light or dark styles, in a profusion of dress and shirting patterns that will do you good even to look at. A closely woven fine yarn fabric of particular quality and one that marks the dividing line between medium and better goods. By this we mean that in point of quality and style it unquestionably belongs to the high class goods, while we have, by our early contracts, been enabled to keep the price where you would otherwise get an ordinary fabric. Handsome patterns of an excellence in design that makes them worthy of reproduction on such a cloth. The colors are all warranted fast and a purchase of our special cambric finished percale has a wealth of genuine pleasure in store for you. In dark colors we can furnish navy, cadet blue, black or wine with white figures, dots or stripes in small and medium patterns, some suitable for wrappers, others for waists, boys' blouses and girls' dresses. The light colors comprise red, blue or black figures on white grounds, principally shirting styles. Such a large line of patterns we nearly overlooked mentioning black and white shepherd checks. We've got them in several sizes. **Don't forget color and style in your order.** Width, 36 inches.
Price, per yard 14c
Full piece of about 30 yards, per yd., 13½c

NOTE OUR REDUCED PRICES

PLAIN AND PRINTED CALICOS OF ALL DESCRIPTIONS.

6½c DRESS AND SHIRTING PRINTS, FULL STANDARD GOODS.

EVERYTHING KNOWN IN PRINTED CALICO. We have included under this one number our entire line of staple and fancy shirting and dress prints. This enable you to make your selections with greater convenience. Simply state catalogue number and style of print you want and we will please you in the goods you receive, as well as save you money on the purchase.

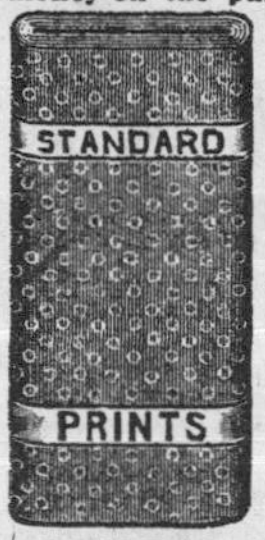
STANDARD
PRINTS

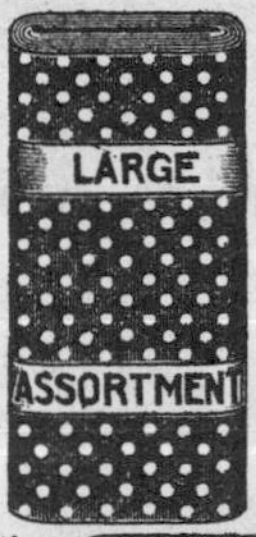
LARGE
ASSORTMENT

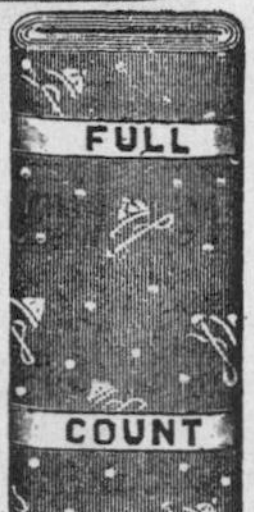
FULL
COUNT

No. 36K3711 Shirting or Dress Prints. All full standard goods in weight, count, and finish. You may frequently be able to buy printed calicos at as low a price as our full standard goods at this special price of 6¾ cents. Don't do it. Save your money by purchasing high grade goods originally. These calicos will last so much longer and always look so much better—in short you'll get so much more real satisfaction out of the use of our goods that the economy of your investment will be at once apparent. We are constantly adding new styles so that the interest our calicos have created wherever they go may not be lessened. New, choice styles, embracing everything that is good in dots, figures, checks and stripes. White grounds with red, blue or black figures, pinks, light blues, Garibaldi red and blacks, black and reds, red and whites, wines, cadets, grays, black and whites, indigo blues, browns, shepherd checks in black and white, pink, blue, green and brown, chambrays, chocolates, madders, beige effects, tans and a full line of plaids, etc. Be sure to state color wanted. Width, 25 inches.

Price, per yard 6½c
Full piece of about 50 yards, per yard. 6⅜c

11c HEAVY GERMAN CALICO, INDIGO BLUE DRESS PATTERNS.

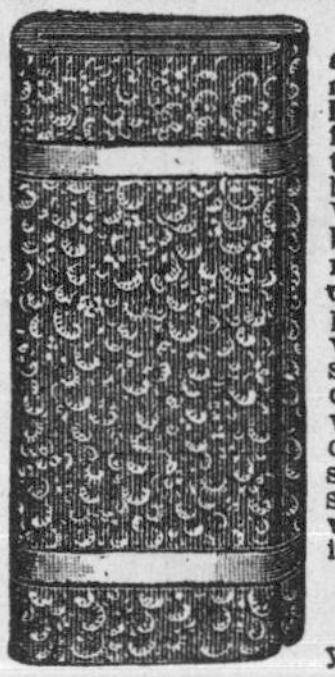

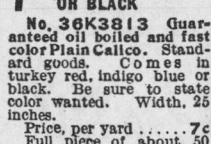

No. 36K3783 Wide and Heavy Pure German Indigo Dress Print. The real old fashioned heavy calico that has been the standby for so many years. Very few manufacturers beside our own have maintained the original quality, and although print cloths have advanced sharply we are still away below all competition on prints as well as all other lines of merchandise. Neat styles, figures, dots and stripes. Mention style wanted. Width, 31 inches.

Price, per yard ... 11c
Full piece of about 45 yards, per yard .. 10½c

7c OIL BOILED CALICO, RED, BLUE OR BLACK

No. 36K3813 Guaranteed oil boiled and fast color Plain Calico. Standard goods. Comes in turkey red, indigo blue or black. Be sure to state color wanted. Width, 25 inches.

Price, per yard 7c
Full piece of about 50 yards, per yard 6¾c

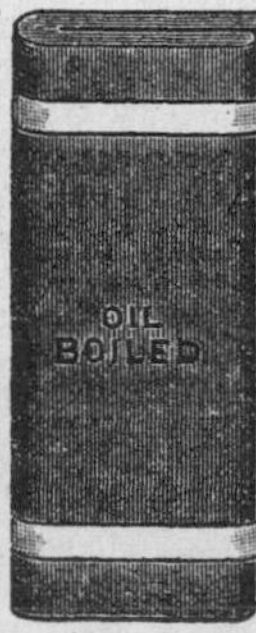
OIL
BOILED

9½c WIDE RED CALICO, OILBOILED COLOR.

No. 36K3817 A nice soft Turkey Red Calico, oil boiled and guaranteed color. A wide cloth at a price usually asked for the narrow goods. Width, 31 inches.

Price, per yard 9½c
Full piece of about 40 yards, per yard 9c

OUR ALREADY LOWEST PRICES have been still FURTHER REDUCED in this Big Catalogue. Just compare the prices in this book with the prices quoted by us in previous catalogues and note the additional savings we make for you.

FIGURED SILKOLINES AND SATEENS FOR COMFORTERS

Comforter Prints.

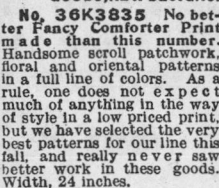

RIVER VIEW
ROBES

6½c FANCY COMFORTER PRINTS, HIGH GRADE GOODS, NEW DESIGNS.

No. 36K3835 No better Fancy Comforter Print made than this number. Handsome scroll patchwork, floral and oriental patterns in a full line of colors. As a rule, one does not expect much of anything in the way of style in a low priced print, but we have selected the very best patterns for our line this fall, and really never saw better work in these goods. Width, 24 inches.

Price, per yard 6½c
Full piece of about 50 yards, per yard 6⅜c

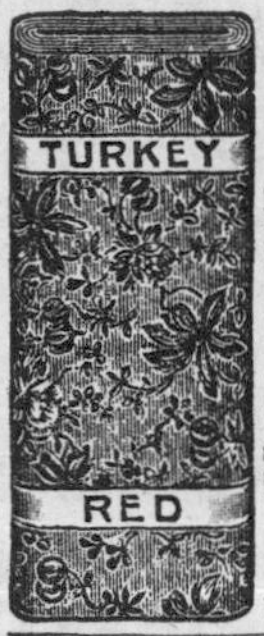
TURKEY
RED

6½c RED AND BLACK FINE COMFORTER PRINTS GUARANTEED OIL RED.

No. 36K3843 Genuine Oil Boiled Comforter Prints. Red grounds with black scroll and other tasty designs. Those who have once used these red and blacks may be counted on for repeated orders. They make friends everywhere. We are showing a variety of new designs this fall, including patchwork patterns. Full standard goods in every respect. Color warranted. Width, 24 inches.

Price, per yard 6½c
Full piece of about 50 yards, per yard...... 6⅜c

11c NEW COMFORTER SILKOLINES, BEAUTIFUL PATTERNS.

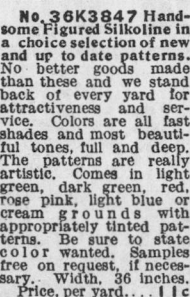

No. 36K3847 Handsome Figured Silkoline in a choice selection of new and up to date patterns. No better goods made than these and we stand back of every yard for attractiveness and service. Colors are all fast shades and most beautiful tones, full and deep. The patterns are really artistic. Comes in light green, dark green, red, rose pink, light blue or cream grounds with appropriately tinted patterns. Be sure to state color wanted. Samples free on request, if necessary. Width, 36 inches.

Price, per yard.... 11c
By the piece of about 42 yards, per yd... 10½c

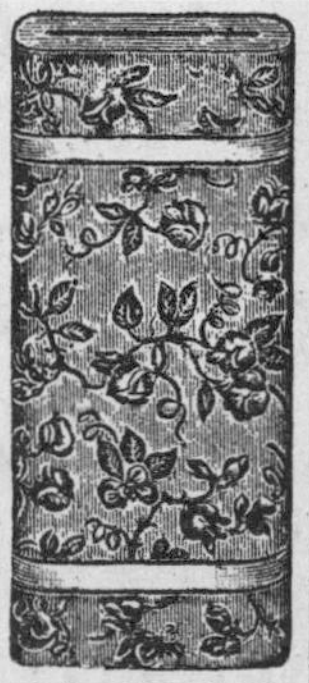

THE leading paper pattern distributors are now bringing out garment patterns especially designed for 24-inch goods. Printed calicos will, therefore, have an increased demand. See our Standard Calico No. 36K3711 on this page.

16c Fancy Comforter Sateens, Handsome Patterns.

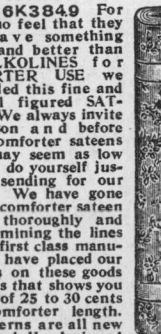

No. 36K3849 For those who feel that they must have something heavier and better than the SILKOLINES for COMFORTER USE we have added this fine and beautiful figured SATEEN. We always invite comparison and before buying comforter sateens which may seem as low as ours, do yourself justice by sending for our samples. We have gone over the comforter sateen market thoroughly and after examining the lines of every first class manufacturer, have placed our contracts on these goods on a basis that shows you a saving of 25 to 30 cents on a comforter length. The patterns are all new and especially designed for comforter work. They will appeal to you the moment you see them. Illustration in black and white cannot do them justice. The colors are dark green, light green, rose pink, light blue, cream, red or white ground with appropriately tinted floral patterns like illustration. Be sure to state color wanted. Samples free on request if necessary. Width, 36 inches.

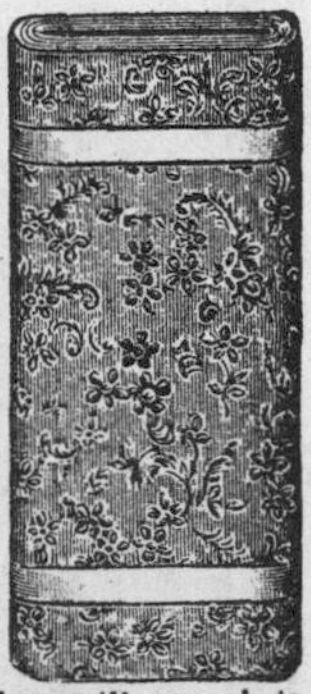

Price, per yard 16c
By the piece of about 40 yards, per yd. 15c

FLANNELS AND FLANNELETTES

Buffalo Shirting Flannels. California Shirting Flannels. Canton Flannels. Domet or Shaker Flannels. Eiderdowns. Embroidered Flannels. Fleeced Back Flannelettes. Guinea Hen Mottled Flannels. Mackinaw Flannels. Outing Flannels, Plain and Fancy. Shirt Patterns, Flannel and Flannelette. White Wool Flannels.

WE WILL BE DISAPPOINTED IF WE CANNOT SAVE YOU AT LEAST ONE FOURTH THE MONEY you intended to spend on those flannels and flannelettes. Stop and consider this for a minute. It may mean a great deal to you. Our various lines have been carefully selected and priced as low as it is possible for us, with our mill to consumer with one small percentage of profit policy, to make them.

FURTHERMORE, WE KNOW OUR GOODS. We sell many thousands of cases of cotton and wool flannels every season, and each yard of goods must pass a rigid examination, and if any are found to be below our specification we turn them back. We have no more loyal customers today on these goods than those who, following up their satisfaction with their first order, have favored us, season after season, with their own orders and their recommendation to friends and neighbors.

IT WOULD BE IMPOSSIBLE FOR US TO DOUBLE OUR FLANNEL BUSINESS AS WE HAVE DONE without the support of our customers of seasons back in continuing to send in their orders, and it would be out of the question for us to expect their stanch loyalty unless we stood pat on the quality and satisfaction question and gave them better goods for the same money or less, or the same high quality at lower prices than it is possible for them to obtain anywhere else.

TO THOSE WHO HAVE NEVER TRIED THESE GOODS we say that only reliable fabrics of known value will be sent out by us, and we stand ready at all times to cheerfully refund the purchase price plus the transportation charges you may have paid on any merchandise with which you are not thoroughly satisfied. If this is fair let us fill your order and start you on Economy Road.

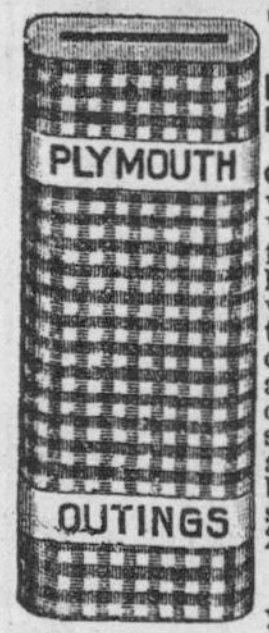
PLYMOUTH
OUTINGS

7½c FANCY OUTING FLANNELS, CHECKS, PLAIDS, STRIPES. GOOD NAP.

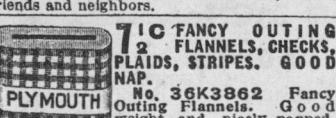

No. 36K3862 Fancy Outing Flannels. Good weight and nicely napped. We could not buy this cloth from the mill today in one hundred case lots at the price we quote you. This only serves to show how you benefit by our anticipation of the market advances. A new assortment of pretty checks, plaids and stripes, both light and dark, as well as plain pink, light blue and cream. Be sure to state color wanted. Width, 27 inches.

Price, per yard 7½c
By the piece of about 50 yards, per yard 7¼c

9c FANCY OUTING FLANNELS, PRETTY CHECKS, PLAIDS AND STRIPES.

No. 36K3868 Extra Weight Fancy Outing Flannel, well napped. Will give excellent service. The cloth is close and nicely finished. The styles are very pleasing, coming in both light and dark in a good variety of checks, plaids and stripes. There are also several fancy bourette styles which are worthy of production in much higher priced qualities. We recommend the purchase of a full piece of these goods which shows you an additional saving of 20 cents on your purchase. Width, 28 inches.

Price, per yard 9c
By the piece of about 40 yards, per yard 8¾c

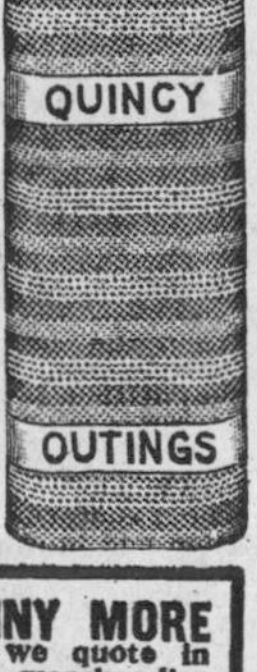
QUINCY
OUTINGS

IF YOU PAY A PENNY MORE than the reduced prices we quote in these pages for the best merchandise you are simply throwing money away.

10½c FANCY OUTING FLANNELS, OUR HEAVIEST AND BEST QUALITY.

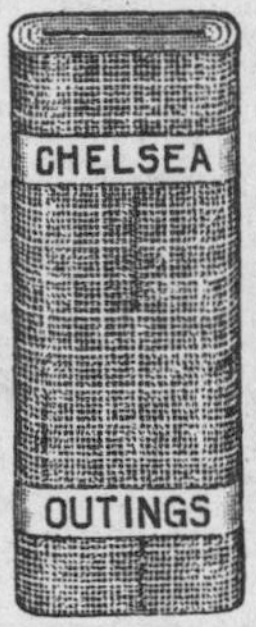
CHELSEA
OUTINGS

No. 36K3872 Our Heaviest and Best Fancy Outing Flannel. This is a cloth that retails ordinarily for 15 cents per yard, and considered good value at that price. The very newest styles in both staple and fancy checks, plaids and stripes are to be found in the assortment, which covers a handsome variety of colorings, light and dark. Many of the styles shown are copied from dress goods patterns. A very warm and durable outing flannel. No better made. Be sure to mention whether light or dark color is wanted. Width, 27 inches.

Price, per yard 10½c
By the piece of about 40 yards, per yard 10c

9½c PLAIN OUTING FLANNELS, DARK, SOLID COLORS. SERVICEABLE.

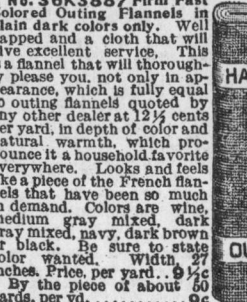

No. 36K3887 Firm Fast Colored Outing Flannels in plain dark colors only. Well napped and a cloth that will give excellent service. This is a flannel that will thoroughly please you, not only in appearance, which is fully equal to outing flannels quoted by any other dealer at 12½ cents per yard, in depth of color and natural warmth, which pronounce it a household favorite everywhere. Looks and feels like a piece of the French flannels that have been so much in demand. Colors are wine, medium gray mixed, dark gray mixed, navy, dark brown or black. Be sure to state color wanted. Width, 27 inches. Price, per yard .. 9½c
By the piece of about 50 yards, per yd. 9c

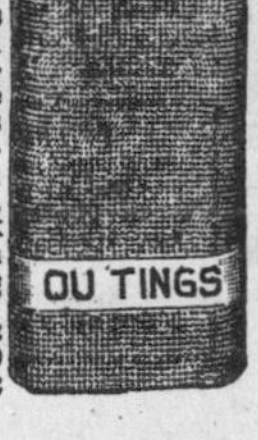
HARMONY
OUTINGS

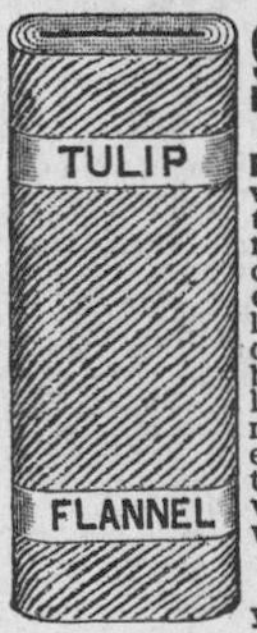
TULIP
FLANNEL

9½c DAISY CLOTH OR BABY FLANNEL. PINK, BLUE, CREAM OR WHITE.

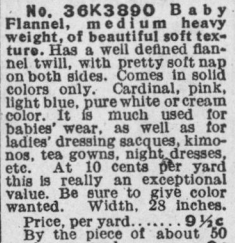

No. 36K3890 Baby Flannel, medium heavy weight, of beautiful soft texture. Has a well defined flannel twill, with pretty soft nap on both sides. Comes in solid colors only. Cardinal, pink, light blue, pure white or cream color. It is much used for babies' wear, as well as for ladies' dressing sacques, kimonos, tea gowns, night dresses, etc. At 10 cents per yard this is really an exceptional value. Be sure to give color wanted. Width, 28 inches.

Price, per yard 9½c
By the piece of about 50 yards, per yard 9c

Fancy Figured Flannelettes.

Samples free on request if necessary.

10c HANDSOME DRESS FLANNELETTES, ALL THE POPULAR NEW STYLES.

No. 36K3930 An elegant assortment of stylish Dress Flannelettes at a very low price. The cloth is firm, well woven and will give extra wear. Has a nice dressy appearance. Back of fabric is lightly napped. Among the many new styles shown will be found several appropriate kimono ideas as well as others adapted for wrappers, waists and children's wear. Colors are navy, wine, cardinal, reseda green, tan, pink, light blue, brown, gray or black. Figures, stripes or dots, as desired. We also have tasty plaids in red, blue, green or brown. Be sure to state color wanted. Width, 28 inches.

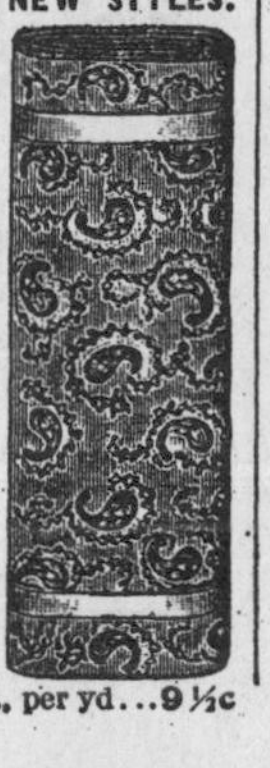

Price, per yard 10c
By the piece of about 40 yds., per yd... 9½c

7c GUINEA HEN FLANNEL, NICE MOTTLED EFFECTS. GOOD WEIGHT.

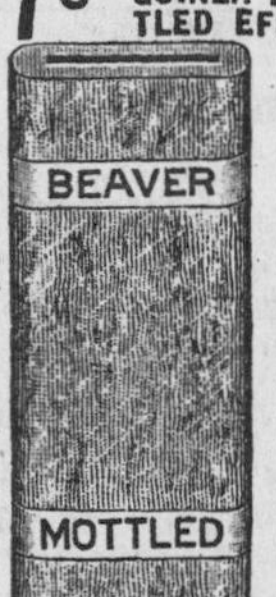
BEAVER
MOTTLED

No. 36K3900 Choice Guinea Hen Flannel. Good stock cloth. Well napped, soft and warm. Wears splendidly. Our Guinea Hen Mottled Flannels are finished on both sides, making a much more desirable cloth than the general run of these goods. Colors are mottled pink, blue, gray or brown. Be sure to state color wanted. Width, 27 inches.

Price, per yard..... 7c
By the piece of about 60 yards, per yard 6¾c

10c GUINEA HEN FLANNEL, EXTRA WARM CLOTH. FOUR COLORS.

No. 36K3925 Our Best and Heaviest Mottled Flannel, or Guinea Hen, as it is commonly called. This is a stout cotton flannel, having a delightfully soft fleece and is wonderfully warm. Gives the greatest service imaginable. Comes in mottled pink, blue, gray or brown. Be sure to state color wanted. Width, 28 inches.

Price, per yard 10c
By the piece of about 55 yards, per yd. 9½c

13c FANCY DRESS FLANNELETTES, EXTRA FINE AND WIDE.

No. 36K3960 Our Best and Widest Fine Dress Flannelette. We have pink, light blue, tan, cardinal, navy, brown or black in figures like illustration, also new and handsome plaids in red, green, blue and brown combinations, black and white shepherd checks, as well as staple dots and a few choice fancy stripes. Be sure to state color wanted. Width, 34½ inches.

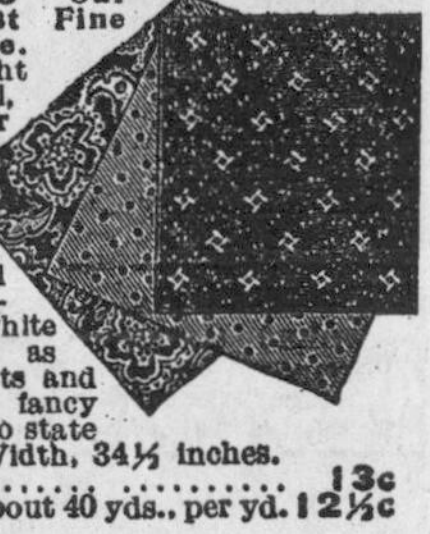

Price, per yard 13c
By the piece of about 40 yds., per yd. 12½c

HOSIERY AND UNDERWEAR
LOWER PRICES AND BETTER VALUES THAN EVER BEFORE

Size of Shoe,	6 and 6½	7 and 7½	8 and 8½	9 and 9½	10 and 10½	11	DO NOT FAIL TO GIVE
Size of Sock,	9½	10	10½	11	11½	12	CORRECT SIZE YOU WEAR

YOUR -SOX- INSURED
WE GUARANTEE THESE TO WEAR 6 MONTHS

WHAT KIND OF SOCKS DO YOU WEAR?

$1.36 FOR BOX OF 6 PAIRS

OUR *Positive-wear* SOX

OUR GUARANTEE

WE WILL GUARANTEE that six pairs of our "Positive-Wear" Sox, if worn alternately and changed two or more times each week will give positive wear and satisfaction. If they do not wear, if they do not give satisfaction, if they are not all that we claim and you have worn them as we advise you, we will, within six months of the date of purchase, give you six new pairs of socks upon receipt of the socks and your letter of complaint.

WE WANT YOU TO BUY SIX PAIRS because we believe the socks will be changed more frequently; this will make your socks wear longer and give far better satisfaction. Our guarantee will be found on the fly leaf of each box.

WE HAVE GIVEN THIS SOCK EVERY TEST, we have worn it ourselves and we are positive that this is one of the biggest values that we have ever offered in our Hosiery Department. We could not make this offer unless we were perfectly satisfied that this sock would wear longer and give far better satisfaction than any sock you have ever purchased. It is far superior to the advertised brands sold six pairs for $2.00.

OUR "POSITIVE-WEAR" SOX are especially made for us from the very finest selected Egyptian cotton yarns; they contain all of our ideas as to how a sock should be made TO GIVE POSITIVE WEAR AND SATISFACTION. It would be IMPOSSIBLE to make a sock that would be WEARPROOF but WE ARE POSITIVE THAT THIS SOCK is one of the best that can be made, THAT IT WILL WEAR LONGER and give FAR BETTER SERVICE than the average sock.

WE MUST CAUTION YOU ABOUT GIVING US THE CORRECT SIZE when you order. If you do not know the size you wear, give us the size of your shoe and we will make every endeavor to fit you satisfactorily. Sizes, 9½, 10, 10½, 11, 11½ and 12.

SIX PAIRS OF ONE SIZE IS POSITIVELY THE SMALLEST QUANTITY WE WILL SELL.

MADE IN COLORS OF BLACK, BLUE, SLATE OR TAN. Guaranteed to be stainless and not to color the feet. If wanted we will assort colors in boxes.

DON'T FORGET TO GIVE US THE CORRECT SIZE YOU WEAR.

I WEAR "POSITIVE-WEAR" SOX.

No. 16K4200—BLACK.   No. 16K4202—TAN.   No. 16K4204—BLUE.   No. 16K4206—SLATE.

PRICE, $1.36 FOR BOX OF SIX PAIRS
If by mail, postage extra for six pairs, 14 cents.

GUARANTEED FAST BLACK COTTON SOCKS FOR MEN

29c FOR 3 PAIRS
GOOD VALUE BLACK COTTON SOCKS.

No. 16K2042
Medium heavy in weight. This is a sock that could not be duplicated for less than 15 cents per pair in the average retail store. Made from selected cotton; full seamless feet; guaranteed fast black. We consider it an unequaled value at this price. Sizes, 9½, 10, 10½, 11 and 11½.

Do not fail to give correct size. Price for 3 pairs........29c
If by mail, postage extra, per pair, 4 cents.

42c FOR 3 PAIRS
FINE BLACK COTTON SOCKS.

No. 16K2044
Extra fine quality Men's Black Cotton Socks. Medium light in weight, which makes it a very trim fitting and neat looking sock for men to wear with low shoes or for summer wear. Highly finished, guaranteed fast black. Sizes, 9½, 10, 10½, 11 and 11½.
Be sure to give size wanted. Price for 3 pairs........42c
If by mail, postage extra, per pair, 4 cents.

42c FOR 2 PAIRS
IMPORTED BLACK COTTON SOCKS.

No. 16K2045
Socks for men, specially imported by us from a German manufacturer, made on full fashioned machinery from the very best selected Egyptian combed yarns. Medium in weight, this sock is made for wear and will give remarkable satisfaction. Guaranteed fast black color. Sizes, 9½, 10, 10½, 11 and 11½.
Do not forget to give size wanted. Price for 2 pairs, 42c
If by mail, postage extra, per pair, 4c.

66c FOR 3 PAIRS
SILK FINISHED SOCKS.

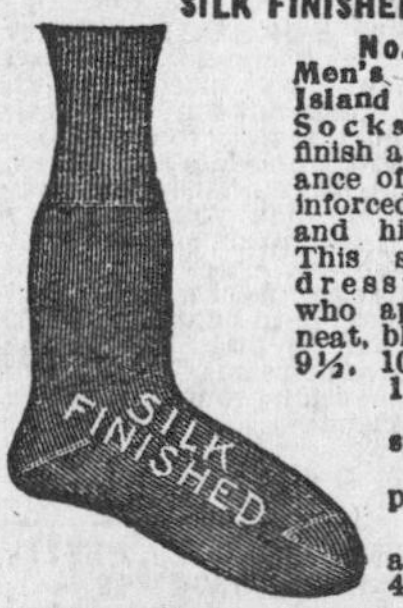

No. 16K2075
Men's Mercerized Sea Island Black Cotton Socks, a sock with the finish and all the appearance of pure silk. Reinforced double sole and high spliced heel. This sock is a very dressy sock for men who appreciate a fine, neat, black sock. Sizes, 9½, 10, 10½, 11 and 11½.
Do not forget to state size.
Price for 3 pairs........66c
If by mail, postage extra, per pair, 4 cents.

34c FOR 3 PAIRS
BLACK COTTON SOCKS MADE FOR WEAR.

No. 16K2043
Socks for men made from double thread of the best Egyptian cotton, reinforced heels and toes, full seamless feet. This sock is built for wear and we will warrant it to give satisfaction. Absolutely fast black color. Sizes, 9½, 10, 10½, 11 and 11½.
Remember to give size.
Price for 3 pairs........34c
If by mail, postage extra, per pair, 4c.

66c FOR 6 PAIRS

Special value in Men's Black or Tan Color Cotton Socks. The price on this sock is as low as your retail dealer can purchase it from his wholesaler or manufacturer. Our immense business, which has rapidly developed on this popular price sock, has placed us in a position to dictate how it should be made and the price we should pay for it. Made from the very best selected yarns, thoroughly reinforced. We will guarantee it to give exceptional wear. We advise the purchase of all hosiery in quantities; by so doing, you can change your socks more

BLACK AND TAN
SPECIAL

often and this will make them wear twice as long. Made in sizes, 9½, 10, 10½, 11 and 11½. Do not forget to give us size.
No. 16K2066 Fast black color.
No. 16K2026 Fast tan color.
Price for 6 pairs.....66c
If by mail, postage extra, for 6 pairs, 15 cents.

Note reduction in price over previous catalogue.

50c FOR 2 PAIRS
FINE BLACK LISLE SOCKS.

No. 16K2037
Socks imported specially for us, made from the very finest lisle yarn, which gives them that sheer, neat and gauzy effect so popular with men who appreciate fine socks for summer wear. The sole, heel and toes are reinforced. The highest finished socks the market affords and the very best in our stock. Sizes, 9½, 10, 10½, 11 and 11½.
Do not forget to give size wanted.
Price for 2 pairs........50c
If by mail, postage extra, per pair, 4c.

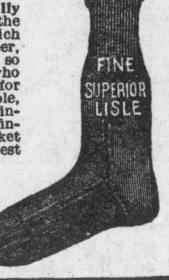

HAVE YOU SEEN OUR "HOT WEATHER" UNDERWEAR FOR MEN ON PAGE 955?

YOUR MONEY WILL BE IMMEDIATELY RETURNED TO YOU FOR ANY GOODS NOT PERFECTLY SATISFACTORY.

581

GREAT VALUES IN LADIES' BLACK COTTON HOSIERY

DO NOT FAIL TO STATE THE CORRECT SIZE YOU WEAR. CONSIDER OUR SPLENDID VALUES IN SUMMER UNDERWEAR WHEN ORDERING YOUR HOSIERY.

SCALE OF SIZES:					
Size of Shoe..	1-2	3-4	5-6	7	7½
Size of Hose..	8½	9	9½	10	10½

PRICES LOWER AND VALUES BETTER THAN IN ANY PREVIOUS CATALOGUE

29c FOR 3 PAIRS
SEAMLESS BLACK COTTON STOCKINGS.

No. 16K2300 One of the largest selling numbers in our catalogue, this is an exceptional value at this low price for women desiring a black cotton seamless stocking. We will guarantee this stocking to be fast color of black. Sizes, 8½, 9, 9½ and 10.

Do not fail to give us correct size.

Price for 3 pairs..................29c
If by mail, postage extra, per pair, 4 cents.

63c FOR 3 PAIRS
EXTRA QUALITY STOCKINGS.

No. 16K2310 Burson Seamless Stocking, made from two threads of the best combed cotton, which gives it just enough weight and body so that it is a remarkable stocking for wear. Sizes, 8½, 9, 9½ and 10.

Do not forget to give correct size.

Price for 3 pairs..................63c
If by mail, postage extra, per pair, 4 cents.

60c FOR 3 PAIRS
ELASTIC RIBBED STOCKINGS.

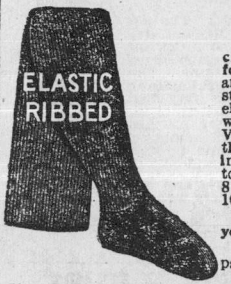

No. 16K2316 Stocking specially adapted for women who are in need of a stocking that is elastic and that will fit properly. Very elastic at the ankle, making it very easy to get on. Sizes, 8½, 9, 9½ and 10.

What size do you wear?

Price for 3 pairs......60c

72c FOR 3 PAIRS
OUR FAMOUS FINE COTTON STOCKINGS.

No. 16K2312 A stocking specially made for us. We have called it our Famous Stocking for some seasons, as we have spared nothing to secure a stocking that is fine in quality and weight that will give thorough wear and satisfaction. Sizes, 8½, 9, 9½ and 10.
Do not forget to give us correct size.

Price for 3 pairs..................72c
If by mail, postage extra, per pair, 4 cents.

39c FOR 3 PAIRS
DOUBLE SOLE STOCKINGS.

No. 16K2301 This is a special value, made expressly for our trade. We purchase this stocking in great quantities and are able to make this very low price. It has a thoroughly reinforced double sole, toe and high spliced heels. This reinforcement will make this stocking wear twice as long. Made from the very best selected cotton, fully seamless, and finished ankle. We will guarantee it to be fast color and are positive it will give good wear. Sizes, 8½, 9, 9½ and 10.

We must have correct size.

Price for 3 pairs ...39c

If by mail, postage extra, per pair, 4 cents.

51c FOR 3 PAIRS
BURSON SEAMLESS STOCKINGS, COLORS, BLACK OR TAN.

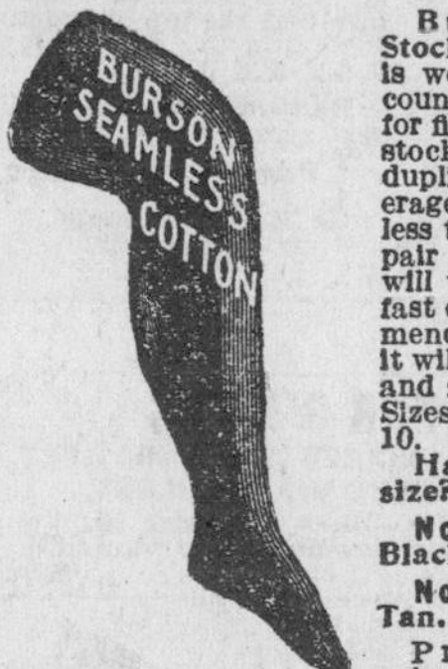

Burson Finished Stocking. This hose is well known on account of its qualities for fit and wear. This stocking could not be duplicated in the average retail store for less than 20 cents per pair or more. We will warrant it to be fast color and recommend it as we know it will give good wear and satisfaction. Sizes, 8½, 9, 9½ and 10.

Have you given us your size?

No. 16K2306 Black.
No. 16K2307 Tan.

Price for 3 pairs.......51c

If by mail, postage extra, per pair, 4 cents.

6 PAIRS GUARANTEED 6 MONTHS

$1 26 FOR BOX OF SIX PAIRS.

OUR WORTHMORE STOCKING for ladies is made especially for us by one of the largest hosiery mills in the country. It is celebrated on account of its wearing qualities and because it is the only stocking that is knit in shape to fit the leg, ankle, heel, foot and toe without seams or uneven thread. Made from the very best selected combed Egyptian yarns. This gives it that finish and elasticity at the tops and ankles so much desired by women.

OUR GUARANTEE

WE WILL GUARANTEE that six pairs of our "Worthmore" Stockings, if worn alternately and changed two or more times each week, will wear longer and give you far better satisfaction than any stocking you have ever purchased. If they do not give you entire satisfaction, if they are not all that we claim, and you have worn them as we have advised you, we will within six months of the date of purchase guarantee to give you six new pairs of stockings in return, upon receipt of the hosiery and your letter of complaint.

WE WANT YOU TO BUY six pairs because we believe the stockings will be changed more frequently. This will make your hosiery wear longer and give far better satisfaction. Our guarantee will be found on the fly leaf of each box.

IS NOT THIS A GREAT OFFER?

WE MUST HAVE THE CORRECT SIZE WHEN YOU ORDER. This stocking comes in sizes 8½, 9, 9½, 10 and 10½. If you do not know the size hose you wear give us the size of your shoe and we will make every endeavor to fit you satisfactorily. In ordering hosiery we would advise you to order them one-half size larger than you usually wear and you will be surprised how much more comfortable they are. We will absolutely warrant the color of these stockings to be fast black and not to color the feet.

CATALOGUE No. 16K4243
Do not forget to give correct size.

$1.26 for Box of Six Pairs.
If by mail, postage extra, 24 cents.

THEY FIT PERFECTLY

"Worthmore"

24c PER PAIR
FINE BLACK LISLE STOCKINGS.

No. 16K2314 This is a beautiful stocking for women who desire a thin gauzy lisle stocking for summer wear. It is specially made for us by the Burson Mills. This alone will guarantee it to fit perfectly, which is so essential in a fine stocking, as it is usually worn with a low shoe. This stocking could not possibly be duplicated for less than 35 cents per pair in the average retail store. Sizes, 8½, 9, 9½ and 10.

Do not forget to give us correct size.

Price, per pair...24c

If by mail, postage extra, per pair, 4 cents.

33c PER PAIR
SILK FINISHED STOCKINGS.

No. 16K2315 Mercerized stocking for ladies. This is a process through which the stocking is put which gives it all the finish, luster and appearance of a fine pure silk stocking. This stocking would retail at 50 cents per pair or more. We consider it a beautiful stocking for women who desire a highly finished hose, and will guarantee it to be a fast black color and to retain its luster. Sizes, 8½, 9, 9½ and 10.

Do not forget to give us correct size.

Price, per pair..................33c

If by mail, postage extra, per pair, 4 cents.

LADIES' UNBLEACHED SOLES AND FEET HOSIERY.

38c FOR 3 PAIRS
UNBLEACHED FEET HOSIERY.

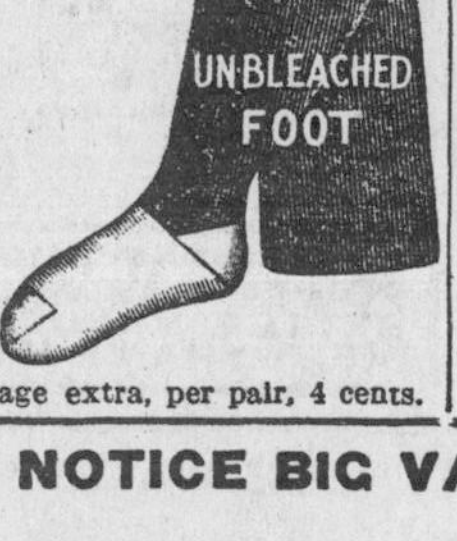

No. 16K2340 This stocking is dyed a stainless fast black to the ankle; the entire foot is made from an unbleached cotton that has not been dyed.

Sizes, 8½, 9, 9½ and 10.

We cannot fill your order unless you give us correct size.

Price for 3 pairs 38c

If by mail, postage extra, per pair, 4 cents.

60c FOR 3 PAIRS
UNBLEACHED SOLES, SEAMLESS.

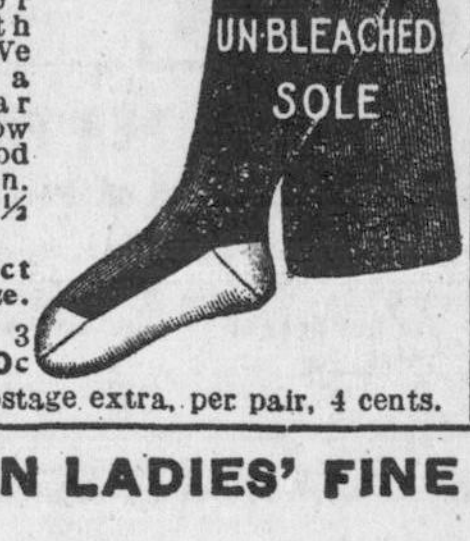

No. 16K2341 A new stocking with us which we have put into our line on account of the growing demand for hosiery with split soles. We consider this a very popular price and know it will give good satisfaction. Sizes, 8½, 9, 9½ and 10.

Do not neglect to give us size.

Price for 3 pairs......60c

If by mail, postage extra, per pair, 4 cents.

72c FOR 3 PAIRS
OUR UNBLEACHED SOLE LEADER.

No. 16K2342 Stocking made expressly for us. We consider it one of the very best values the market affords in a black cotton stocking with unbleached sole, heel and toe. The yarn in the sole being undyed, seems to rest the feet. Sizes, 8½, 9, 9½ and 10.

Do not fail to give us size wanted.

Price, for 3 pairs .72c

If by mail, postage extra, per pair, 4 cents.

EXTRA LARGE SIZE.

35c FOR 3 PAIRS
EXTRA LARGE STOCKINGS.

No. 16K2460 Ladies' Extra Wide Leg Black Cotton Stockings. Sizes, 8½, 9, 9½ and 10. Price for 3 pairs 35c

63c FOR 3 PAIRS

No. 16K2466 Specially adapted for stout women; very elastic, perfectly seamless. Sizes, 8½, 9, 9½ and 10. Do not neglect to give us correct size.

Price for 3 pairs 63c
If by mail, postage extra, per pair, 4 cents.

NOTICE BIG VALUES IN LADIES' FINE VESTS FOR SUMMER. SEE PAGE 960.

LADIES' HOSIERY FOR SUMMER WEAR

BIG REDUCTION IN PRICES | **BETTER VALUES THAN EVER BEFORE**

EMBROIDERED HOSIERY.

35c FOR 3 PAIRS
FANCY STRIPE AND FIGURED DESIGN BLACK COTTON STOCKINGS.

No. 16K2410 Stocking, made from fine cotton with a very pretty design. We carry it in three patterns, a variegated stripe, a polka dot and a fancy boot pattern. Sizes, 8½, 9, 9½ and 10.
Do not forget to give size and style of pattern you want. Price for 3 pairs....35c
If by mail, postage extra, per pair, 5 cents.

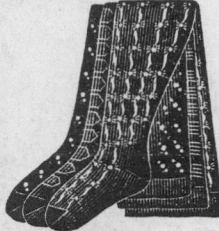

37c PER PAIR
EXTRA FINE SILK EMBROIDERED HOSIERY FOR WOMEN.

No. 16K2422 The best stocking in our line and very popular with women desiring a very finely embroidered black cotton stocking. This stocking is very neat and can be worn by the very best dressers. The pattern of the embroidery is very new and up to date and comes in colors of red, white or pink. Sizes, 8½, 9, 9½ and 10.
Be sure to state size and color of embroidery wanted.
Price, per pair.......37c
If by mail, postage extra, per pair, 5 cents.

63c FOR 3 PAIRS
LADIES' FINE BLACK COTTON EMBROIDERED HOSIERY.

No. 16K2416 Very fine Egyptian cotton stocking with a very neat embroidered pattern of flower design in colors of lavender, red or blue. This stocking is highly finished and will make a very dressy and pretty stocking for summer wear. Sizes, 8½, 9, 9½ and 10.
Be sure to state size and color of embroidery you want.
Price for 3 pairs, 63c
If by mail, postage extra, per pair, 5 cents.

36c FOR 3 PAIRS
LADIES' BLACK COTTON EMBROIDERED HOSIERY. SPECIAL VALUE.

No. 16K2414 Our first season on this stocking. We consider it a splendid value for women desiring a black cotton stocking embroidered with a neat pattern. We have this hose embroidered with either stripe or a dot design in colors of red, white or blue. Sizes, 8½, 9, 9½ and 10.
Be sure to state size, design and color of embroidery wanted. Price for 3 pairs.....36c
If by mail, postage extra, per pair, 5 cents.

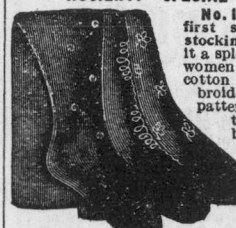

ROCKFORD MIXED.

59c FOR 6 PAIRS
BLUE OR BROWN COTTON MIXED STOCKINGS.

No. 16K2362 This stocking is specially adapted for the use of farm women or women in need of a coarse, heavy cotton stocking. It is made from selected cotton, very soft, comfortable to the wearer, fully seamless with reinforced heels and toes and will give great wear and satisfaction.
Be sure to state color wanted.
Price for 6 pairs....................59c
If by mail, postage extra, per pair, 6 cents.

STOCKING FEET.

39c FOR 6 PAIRS
EXTRA FEET FOR STOCKINGS.

These stocking feet fill a growing demand by women who have worn out the feet of their stockings and desire to replace them at a small cost. How to sew on the feet: Cut off the leg of the stocking at the ankle; turn the stocking and the foot inside out, match the edges together and sew them with a firm fine overcast seam; then turn the stocking back again. Colors, black or cream color. Sizes, 8½, 9, 9½ and 10.
Do not fail to state size wanted.
No. 16K2370 Fast black.
No. 16K2372 Cream color.
Price for 6 pairs...................39c
If by mail, postage extra, for 6 pairs, 10 cents.

LADIES' BLACK LACE HOSIERY.

35c FOR 3 PAIRS
BLACK LACE STOCKING "SPECIAL."

No. 16K2424 Allover lace from toe to top of a very pretty pattern, making it a stocking which is very cool, pretty and attractive for summer. This stocking is bought by us in very large quantities and could not be duplicated in the average retail store for less than 50 cents. Sizes, 8½, 9, 9½ and 10.
Do not fail to give correct size.
Price for 3 pairs...........35c
If by mail, postage extra, per pair, 5 cents.

39c PER PAIR
IMPORTED BLACK LACE HOSIERY.

No. 16K2440 Fine quality black lisle stocking in either an allover or a boot lace pattern, specially imported by us. It is a stocking that positively could not be duplicated in your retail store for less than 50 cents. This is a beautiful stocking for summer wear and the very best hose in our stock. Sizes, 8½, 9, 9½ and 10.
Be sure to state size and pattern of lace you want.
Price, per pair..39c
If by mail, postage extra, per pair, 5 cents.

BOOT LACE

63c FOR 3 PAIRS
ALLOVER LACE LISLE STOCKINGS, EXTRA VALUE.

No. 16K2432 This stocking is an allover lace stocking, made from the very finest lisle. The sole, heel and toe are extra reinforced. The stocking is lace to within about 5 inches of the top, so that you do not have to fasten the garter into the lace of the stocking but have a good firm top to fasten it to. Sizes, 8½, 9, 9½ and 10.
Do not forget to state size wanted.
Price, 3 pairs for 63c
If by mail, postage extra, per pair, 5 cents.

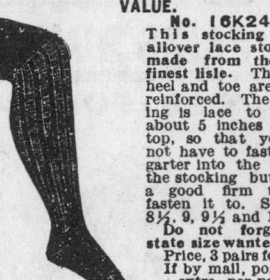

63c FOR 3 PAIRS
BLACK LACE STOCKINGS WITH FANCY EMBROIDERED INSTEP.

No. 16K2426 This is a very neat stocking for summer wear. It is a lace pattern of a very pretty design which reaches to the toe. The instep and ankle are embroidered in a stripe pattern in colors of blue, lavender or red, making it an exceptional value at this low price. Sizes, 8½, 9, 9½ and 10.
Have you given us correct size and color of embroidery you want?
Price for 3 pairs, 63c
If by mail, postage extra, per pair, 5 cents.

FINE WHITE COTTON HOSIERY.

12c PER PAIR
LADIES' WHITE OR BALBRIGGAN COLOR COTTON HOSIERY.

PLAIN WHITE

No. 16K2385 Sizes, 8½, 9, 9½ and 10. Be very careful to state size and color wanted.
Price, per pair.........12c

21c PER PAIR
FINE COMBED WHITE COTTON STOCKINGS.

No. 16K2386 Burson fashioned; this is a perfect fitting and a very fine stocking for women desiring a white hose. Sizes, 8½, 9, 9½ and 10.
Do not forget to give us size.
Price, per pair...21c
If by mail, postage extra, per pair, on either of the above numbers, 5 cents.

21c PER PAIR
FINE WHITE ALLOVER LACE STOCKINGS OF THE VERY LATEST DESIGN.

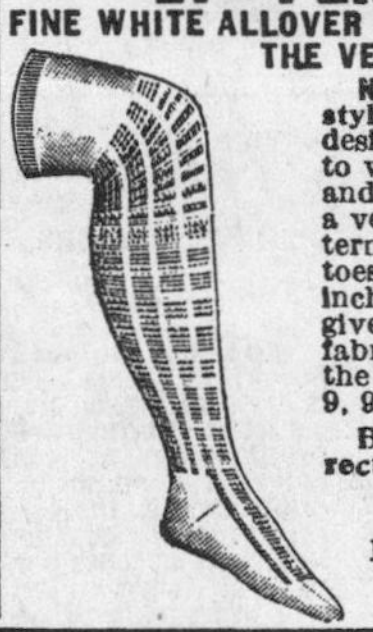

No. 16K2387 Very stylish hose for women desiring a white stocking to wear with white shoes and dress. This hose has a very beautiful lace pattern which extends to the toes, it is lace to within 6 inches of the top. This gives the stocking a firm fabric at the top to fasten the garter to. Sizes, 8½, 9, 9½ and 10.
Be sure to give us correct size.
Price, per pair..21c
If by mail, postage extra, per pair, 5 cents.

LADIES' FINE CASHMERE, WOOL AND FLEECE LINED HOSIERY.

35c FOR 3 PAIRS
LADIES' BLACK COTTON FLEECE LINED STOCKINGS.

No. 16K2472 Sizes, 8½, 9, 9½ and 10. Do not forget to give us size.
Price for 3 pairs....................35c

54c FOR 3 PAIRS
No. 16K2474 Ladies' Heavy Black Cotton Fleece Lined Stockings. Sizes, 8½, 9, 9½ and 10. Have you given us size?
Price for 3 pairs....54c

FLEECE LINED

63c FOR 3 PAIRS
No. 16K2486 Ladies' Fleece Lined Ribbed Top Black Cotton Stockings. Sizes, 8½, 9, 9½ and 10. What size is wanted?
Price for 3 pairs....63c

31c PER PAIR
No. 16K2490 Ladies' Full Fashioned Fleece Lined Black Cotton Stockings. Sizes, 8½, 9, 9½ and 10. Do not forget to give us size.
Price, per pair....31c

57c FOR 3 PAIRS
ELASTIC RIBBED COTTON FLEECE LINED STOCKINGS.

No. 16K2499 Very popular stocking because it is elastic and will fit properly. Sizes, 8½, 9, 9½ and 10. Remember to give size.
Price for 3 pairs....................57c
If by mail, postage extra, per pair, 6 cents.

66c FOR 3 PAIRS
BLACK MERINO WOOL STOCKINGS.

No. 16K2506 Stocking made from a mixture of good wool and cotton. Sizes, 8½, 9, 9½ and 10. Do not fail to give size wanted.
Price for 3 pairs 66c
If by mail, postage extra, per pair, 6 cents.

BLACK COTTON FLEECE LINED STOCKINGS OF EXTRA QUALITY.

No. 16K2476 Made specially for us. It will fit properly, fully seamless and reinforced at the heels and toes. The inside of the stocking has a very soft full fleecing. Sizes, 8½, 9, 9½, and 10. Don't forget to give size wanted.
Price for 2 pairs....48c
If by mail, postage extra, per pair, 6c.

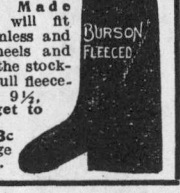
BURSON FLEECED

25c PER PAIR
SPECIAL VALUE IN LADIES' BLACK WOOL STOCKINGS.

No. 16K2509 This is nearly an all wool stocking with the exception of the merino heel and toe. Sizes, 8½, 9, 9½ and 10.
Be sure to give us correct size.
Price, per pair....................25c
If by mail, postage extra, per pair, 6 cents.

41c PER PAIR
HEAVY BLACK WOOL STOCKINGS.

No. 16K2512 Our finest wool stocking; heavy weight. Sizes, 8½, 9, 9½ and 10.
Do not neglect to give size wanted.
Price, per pair.................41c
If by mail, postage extra, per pair, 7 cents.

68c FOR 2 PAIRS
FINE BLACK CASHMERE STOCKINGS.

No. 16K2516 This is a very good stocking for women desiring a fine black cashmere hose. Sizes, 8½, 9, 9½ and 10. Specify size wanted.
Price for 2 pairs....68c
If by mail, postage extra, per pair, 6 cents.

49c PER PAIR
LADIES' FINE BLACK CASHMERE STOCKINGS

No. 16K2517 This is a very fine stocking and is specially made for us from selected fine cashmere. Sizes, 8½, 9, 9½ and 10.
Do not forget to give size wanted.
Price, per pair....................49c
If by mail, postage extra, per pair, 6 cents.

66c FOR 3 PAIRS
LADIES' HEAVY RIBBED WOOL HOSIERY, BLACK OR BLUE MIXED COLORS.

No. 16K2542 Sizes, 9½ and 10. Be sure to state size and color wanted.
Price for 3 pairs....................66c

50c FOR 2 PAIRS
No. 16K2534 Special value in Ladies' Heavy Black Ribbed Wool Hosiery. Sizes, 8½, 9, 9½ and 10.
Remember to give size.
Price for 2 pairs....50c

51c PER PAIR
No. 16K2538 Our extra heavy Women's Dark Blue Color Ribbed Wool Stockings. Sizes, 9½ and 10. Do not fail to give size wanted.
Price, per pair.....51c

RIBBED WOOL

EXTRA SIZE, 22c
No. 16K2521 Ladies' Heavy Black Elastic Ribbed Fleece Lined Cotton Stockings. Sizes, 8½, 9, 9½ and 10. Do not forget to give us size.
Price, per pair....................22c

OUR KNIT UNION SUITS FOR LADIES ARE GUARANTEED TO FIT. SEE PAGE 958.

| Be very careful to give us correct size you want. | **CHILDREN'S, MISSES' AND BOYS' STOCKINGS** | Consider our complete underwear line when you are ordering your hosiery. |

SCALE OF SIZES:

Size of Shoe	4-5	6-7	8-9	10-11	12-13	1-2	2-3	4	5-6	6-7
Size of Hose	5½	6	6½	7	7½	8	8½	9	9½	10

NEVER HAVE WE BEEN ABLE TO QUOTE SUCH LOW PRICES ON OUR CHILDREN'S HOSIERY

28c FOR 3 PAIRS

DOUBLE KNEE, BLACK, RIBBED COTTON STOCKINGS FOR BOYS AND GIRLS.

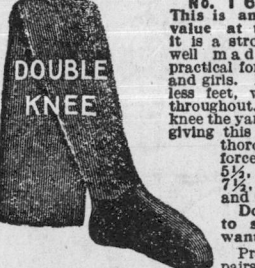

No. 16K2600 This is an excellent value at this price; it is a strong, durable well made stocking, practical for both boys and girls. Fully seamless feet, well made throughout. At the knee the yarn is double, giving this vital part thorough reinforcement. Sizes, 5½, 6, 6½, 7, 7½, 8, 8½, 9 and 9½. Do not fail to state size wanted. Price for 3 pairs......28c

If by mail, postage extra, per pair, 5 cents.

Tear-proof 95c FOR 6 PAIRS

SPECIAL VALUE, HEAVY FINE RIBBED BLACK COTTON STOCKINGS FOR BOTH BOYS AND GIRLS.

No. 16K2608 Stocking of special value for both boys and girls. This stocking is fairly heavy in weight but not too heavy; it has just enough body to it so that we know it will wear and will give great satisfaction. A great many mothers believe that to secure a stocking that will wear, they have to buy an extra heavy hose; this is not so in this stocking, because we know that we have a stocking in this number that will give great wear and satisfaction without the uncomfortable weight of a heavy stocking. Made from the very best carded yarns, fully seamless, shaped ankle, perfectly made throughout. Guaranteed fast black in color. Sizes, 6, 6½, 7, 7½, 8, 8½, 9, 9½ and 10. Be very sure to give us correct size.

Price for 6 pairs...............95c

If by mail, postage extra, for 6 pairs, 35 cents.

57c FOR 3 PAIRS

EXTRA STRONG AND HEAVY STOCKINGS FOR BOYS.

No. 16K2612 One of the biggest selling stockings in our stock. This hose is especially made and adapted for boys because it is made just as strong as it is possible to make a stocking. It has heavy corded ribbed legs, narrow ankles, and fully seamless feet. We will absolutely guarantee it to wear and to give great satisfaction. Sizes, 6, 6½, 7, 7½, 8, 8½, 9, 9½ and 10. Do not fail to state size wanted.

Price for 3 pairs............57c

If by mail, postage extra, per pair, 8 cents.

38c FOR 3 PAIRS

OUR GREAT STOCKING FOR CHILDREN.

No. 16K2604 Fine gauge and fine ribbed stocking. This stocking is especially valuable for girls and the smaller boys. It has just enough weight to make it strong and durable and to give excellent wear. Sizes, 5½, 6, 6½, 7, 7½, 8, 8½, 9 and 9½. Do not fail to state size wanted.

Price for 3 pairs.........38c

If by mail, postage extra, per pair, 6 cents.

63c FOR 3 PAIRS

FINE RIBBED LISLE HOSIERY FOR MISSES.

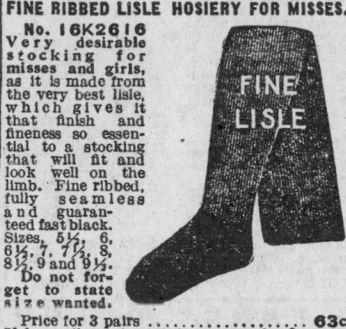

No. 16K2616 Very desirable stocking for misses and girls, as it is made from the very best lisle, which gives it that finish and fineness so essential to a stocking that will fit and look well on the limb. Fine ribbed, fully seamless and guaranteed fast black. Sizes, 5½, 6, 6½, 7, 7½, 8, 8½, 9 and 9½. Do not forget to state size wanted.

Price for 3 pairs..........63c

If by mail, postage extra, per pair, 6 cents.

21c PER PAIR

SILK FINISHED STOCKINGS.

Colors, black, tan or white. Silk finished stockings. This is a stocking that has been put through a mercerizing process which gives it all the finish, luster and feeling of a pure silk stocking, making it very desirable for mothers who want a highly finished stocking for their children. Guaranteed fast colors. Sizes, 5½, 6, 6½, 7, 7½, 8, 8½, 9 and 9½.

What size do you wear?
No. 16K2624 Fast Black.
No. 16K2625 Tan Color.
No. 16K2626 Pure White.

Price, per pair.............21c

If by mail, postage extra, per pair, 6 cents.

21c PER PAIR

ALLOVER LACE BLACK LISLE STOCKINGS.

No. 16K2628 A beautiful stocking for summer wear for the girls and misses. This stocking is openwork lace down to the toe, which is very stylish for the latest styles in low shoes. Fully seamless and absolutely fast black in color. Sizes, 5½, 6, 6½, 7, 7½, 8, 8½, 9 and 9½. Do not forget to state size wanted.

Price, per pair..........21c

If by mail, postage extra, per pair, 6 cents.

CHILDREN'S WOOL AND FLEECED HOSIERY

33c FOR 3 PAIRS

DOUBLE KNEE, FLEECE LINED, RIBBED COTTON STOCKINGS FOR CHILDREN.

No. 16K2661 Sizes, 5½ to 9½. Be sure to state size. Price, for 3 pairs, 33c

39c FOR 3 PAIRS

CHILDREN'S BLACK COTTON FLEECED STOCKINGS OF GOOD WEIGHT. No. 16K2663 Sizes, 5½ to 9½. Tell us what size you wear. Price for 3 pairs 39c

If by mail, postage extra, per pair, 6 cents.

51c FOR 3 PAIRS

HEAVY RIBBED, FLEECE LINED, BLACK COTTON STOCKINGS FOR CHILDREN. No. 16K2664 Sizes, 6 to 10. Do not forget to give us size wanted. Price, for 3 pairs, 51c

60c FOR 3 PAIRS

OUR VERY HEAVIEST FLEECE LINED, BLACK COTTON RIBBED STOCKINGS FOR BOYS, GUARANTEED TO WEAR. No. 16K2668 Sizes, 6 to 10. Be sure to state size wanted. Price for 3 pairs, 60c If by mail, postage extra, per pair, 8 cents.

63c FOR 3 PAIRS

CHILDREN'S HEAVY RIBBED BLACK WOOL STOCKINGS. No. 16K2680 Sizes, 5½ to 9½. Price for 3 pairs......63c

52c FOR 2 PAIRS

No. 16K2682 The very heaviest and best children's Wool Stocking that can be bought. Sizes, 6 to 10. Price for 2 pairs .52c

52c FOR 2 PAIRS

No. 16K2684 Worsted Wool Ribbed Stockings. Sizes, 5½ to 10. Price for 2 pairs, 52c

Be very sure to give us correct size wanted. If by mail, postage extra, per pair, 7 cents.

62c FOR 2 PAIRS

CHILDREN'S WORSTED WOOL RIBBED STOCKINGS.

No. 16K2687 Sizes, 5 to 8½. What size do you wear? Price for 2 pairs, 62c

39c PER PAIR

CHILDREN'S HEAVY BLACK CASHMERE WOOL STOCKINGS. No. 16K2692 Sizes, 6 to 10. Do not forget to give correct size.

Price, per pair, 39c

If by mail, postage extra, per pair, 7 cents.

INFANTS' HOSIERY

REDUCED PRICES — BETTER VALUES

32c FOR 3 PAIRS

BLACK OR WHITE INFANTS' FINE LISLE STOCKINGS.

Very pretty fitting and very satisfactory stockings for infants' wear. Made from fine lisle, which makes the leg of the stocking very elastic. Fully seamless feet.
No. 16K2714 Fast Black.
No. 16K2718 Pure White.
Sizes, 4½, 5, 5½ and 6.
Do not forget to give us correct size.
Price for 3 pairs.............32c
If by mail, postage extra, per pair, 3c.

26c FOR 3 PAIRS

FINE RIBBED BLACK COTTON STOCKINGS FOR INFANTS.
No. 16K2712 Very fine soft cotton, fine ribbed stockings for infants. Fully seamless feet, elastic ribbed legs and very comfortable. Absolutely fast black. Sizes, 4½, 5, 5½ and 6.
Do not forget to give us correct size.
Price for 3 pairs.....(If by mail, postage extra, per pair, 3c.).....26c

16c PER PAIR

SILK FINISHED HOSIERY IN ALL COLORS FOR INFANTS.

Beautiful stocking for infants' wear, finely ribbed, fully seamless.
No. 16K2760 Fast Black.
No. 16K2761 Light Blue.
No. 16K2762 Pink.
No. 16K2763 Pure White.
No. 16K2764 Red.
No. 16K2765 Tan.
Sizes, 4½, 5, 5½ and 6.
Be very sure to state size wanted.
Price, per pair...........16c
If by mail, postage extra, per pair, 3c.

45c FOR 3 PAIRS

WORSTED WOOL RIBBED STOCKINGS FOR INFANTS.
This stocking is made from the very finest worsted wool yarns, with a very small mixture of cotton. Fully seamless and very elastic.
No. 16K2739 Fast Black.
No. 16K2740 Blue.
No. 16K2741 Pink.
No. 16K2742 Pure White.
No. 16K2743 Red.
Do not fail to give us correct size.
Price for 3 pairs..........45c
If by mail, postage extra, per pair, 3c.

35c FOR 3 PAIRS

BLACK OR WHITE COLOR MERINO WOOL STOCKINGS FOR INFANTS.
Very popular with mothers who desire a stocking for infants' wear which is made from a mixture of wool and cotton. Very soft and pliable, fully seamless.
No. 16K2752 Fast Black.
No. 16K2754 Pure White.
Sizes, 4½, 5, 5½ and 6.
Be very sure to state correct size wanted.
Price for 3 pairs.....(If by mail, postage extra, per pair, 3c.)......35c

21c PER PAIR

CASHMERE STOCKINGS OF THE FINEST QUALITY FOR INFANTS.

Made from the very finest cashmere wool. Heels and toes are finished with silk in assorted colors.
No. 16K2774 Fast Black.
No. 16K2775 Light Blue.
No. 16K2776 Pink.
No. 16K2777 Pure White.
No. 16K2778 Red.
Sizes, 4½, 5, 5½ and 6.
Do not forget to give us correct size.
Price, per pair...............21c
If by mail, postage extra, per pair, 3c.

COMPLETE LINE OF INFANTS' VESTS ON PAGE 960.

BALBRIGGAN UNDERWEAR
SUMMER UNDERWEAR FOR MEN.

WE CANNOT FILL YOUR ORDERS UNLESS YOU GIVE CORRECT SIZE.

HOW TO ORDER UNDERWEAR. Undershirt: A close, firm (but not too tight) measure should be taken over vest with coat off, observing that you do not expand the chest. See that tape is close up under arms. Drawers: Measure under vest just above hips.

SINGLE GARMENTS FURNISHED IF DESIRED.

42c BIGGEST VALUE 42c
WE EVER QUOTED IN MEN'S BALBRIGGANUNDERWEAR

IMPROVED QUALITY

SPECIAL VALUE

Balbriggan Underwear for men that we can absolutely guarantee to give positive wear and satisfaction. We make use of several hundred cases of this number in a year; the purchase of this great quantity places us in a position to say how it should be made and what it should be made of and we can assure our customers that we have secured a garment that is made from the very best cotton yarns, perfectly and thoroughly sewed together. The drawers are adjustable in the back with buttoned straps and have a large double seat which gives it thorough reinforcement. The buttons are sewed on to stay. Every piece of underwear in our stock is examined before it is sent out, and we can guarantee this garment to give positive satisfaction. Color, ecru (cream color).

No. 16K5032 Undershirts. Sizes, 34, 36, 38, 40, 42, 44, 46, 48, 50 and 52 inches breast measure.
Price, each 42c
No. 16K5033 Drawers to match above shirts. Sizes, 30, 32, 34, 36, 38, 40, 42, 44, 46, 48, 50 and 52 inches waist measure.
Price, each 42c
We must have size or we cannot fill your order.
If by mail, postage extra, each, 10 cents.

22c PER GARMENT
BALBRIGGAN UNDERWEAR.

BALBRIGGAN

Underwear for men which is in great demand on account of its low price. It is a satisfactory number for wear during the summer for workingmen who are out in the heat and are in need of a light weight, low price garment. It is well made throughout; drawers are double reinforced in the seat. Cream color.

No. 16K5026 Undershirts. Sizes, 34, 36, 38, 40, 42 and 44 inches breast measure.
Price, each...22c
No. 16K5027 Drawers to match above shirts. Sizes, 30, 32, 34, 36, 38, 40 and 42 inches waist measure.
Price, each 22c
Be very positive to give us correct size.
If by mail, postage extra, each, 9 cents.

41c PER GARMENT
MESH STRIPE UNDERWEAR FOR MEN.

MESH WEAVE

There is a growing demand for this style of underwear, and there should be, because it is the most comfortable grade of underwear that was ever originated for summer wear. It is knit so that the shirt and drawers are covered with small holes, this ventilates the body and allows the air to circulate freely under the underwear. Color, an ecru shade (cream color.)

No. 16K5030 Undershirts. Sizes, 34, 36, 38, 40, 42 and 44 inches breast measure.
Price, each 41c
No. 16K5031 Drawers to match above shirts. Sizes, 30, 32, 34, 36, 38, 40 and 42 inches waist measure. Price, each 41c
Be very careful not to forget size wanted.
If by mail, postage extra, each, 10 cents.

34c PER GARMENT
ONE OF OUR LARGEST SELLERS IN MEN'S BALBRIGGAN UNDERWEAR.

BIG VALUE

This is one of our biggest sellers on account of its popular price. We have been able to secure a garment in this number that we believe will give great wear. It is strongly made from good yarn, well sewed throughout. Drawers are double reinforced in the seat. Color, an ecru shade (cream color.)

No. 16K5028 Undershirts. Sizes, 34, 36, 38, 40, 42 and 44 inches breast measure.
Price, each...34c
No. 16K5029 Drawers to match above shirts. Sizes, 30, 32, 34, 36, 38, 40 and 42 inches waist measure.
Price, each 34c
Do not fail to give us correct size.
If by mail, postage extra, each, 11 cents.

39c PER GARMENT
ELASTIC RIBBED ECRU COLOR UNDERWEAR.

ELASTIC RIBBED

Underwear for men that is very satisfactory for spring and summer wear. It is made from very fine cotton on spring needle machines which makes it very elastic and perfect fitting. It is very strongly made, the drawers are reinforced with a large double seat. Cream color.

No. 16K5102 Undershirts. Sizes, 34, 36, 38, 40, 42 and 44 inches breast measure.
Price, each...39c
No. 16K5103 Drawers to match above shirts. Sizes, 30, 32, 34, 36, 38, 40 and 42 inches waist measure. Price, each...39c
Do not fail to give us correct size.
If by mail, postage extra, each, 10 cents.

69c FRENCH BALBRIGGAN UNDERWEAR 69c
FOR MEN. OUR BEST VALUE.

BETTER VALUES

EXTRA QUALITY

Celebrated "Bon Bon" Underwear, made in France. We believe this to be the best grade of underwear that money will buy. Made from the very finest selected Egyptian yarns, fine gauge and medium in weight. It has enough weight so that it will wear and give great satisfaction. It would be impossible to describe this garment because it is so perfect. Trimmed and finished throughout with the very best materials that can be made. Strapped back drawers and the best pearl buttons are used throughout the garment. Color, ecru (cream color.)

No. 16K5086 Undershirts, long sleeve or wing sleeve. Sizes, 34, 36, 38, 40, 42 and 44 inches breast measure. Be sure to state style of sleeve wanted.
Price, each 69c
No. 16K5087 Drawers to match above shirts. Sizes, 30, 32, 34, 36, 38, 40 and 42 inches waist measure.
Price, each 69c
Be very careful to give us correct size when ordering.
If by mail, postage extra, each, 11 cents.

FANCY STRIPED AND FANCY COLORED.

41c PURE WHITE COLOR 41c
FINE COTTON UNDERWEAR.

REDUCED PRICES

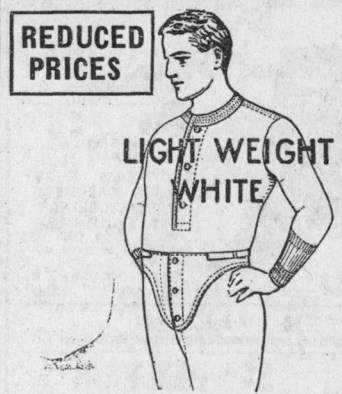

LIGHT WEIGHT WHITE

Pure white underwear has increased in sale until it has reached very large proportions, and in these numbers we believe we have secured a very clean cut and satisfactory grade of underwear. It is made of the very finest combed Egyptian yarns; these yarns give it almost a silk finish appearance. It is very fine, sheer and the most comfortable underwear a man can buy for summer wear. Beautifully made and finished, silk stitched throughout. Pearl buttons well sewed on. Very practical underwear for the hot days during the summer and for men who desire a neat, trim and dressy looking suit for dress-up wear.

No. 16K5036 Undershirts. Sizes, 34, 36, 38, 40, 42 and 44 inches breast measure.
Price, each 41c
No. 16K5037 Drawers to match above shirts. Sizes, 30, 32, 34, 36, 38, 40 and 42 inches waist measure.
Price, each 41c
Do not fail to give us correct size.
If by mail, postage extra, each, 9 cents.

42c PER GARMENT
PURE WHITE UNDERWEAR WITH A FANCY MERCERIZED HORIZONTAL STRIPE.

FANCY STRIPE

Very pretty underwear for summer wear for men who like fancy stripe undergarments. Perfectly made and handsomely finished and trimmed throughout. We will warrant this underwear to be most satisfactory.

No. 16K5078 Undershirts. Sizes, 34, 36, 38, 40, 42 and 44 inches breast measure.
Price, each. 42c
No. 16K5079 Drawers to match above shirts. Sizes, 30, 32, 34, 36, 38, 40 and 42 inches waist measure.
Price, each 42c
Do not fail to give us correct size.
If by mail, postage extra, each, 10 cents.

41c PER GARMENT
BLACK COLOR BALBRIGGAN UNDERWEAR.

BLACK BALBRIGGAN

Underwear for men that is in great demand by miners, farmers and workingmen who want underwear that will not show the soil and who during the hot weather work in this underwear. This underwear is well made and thoroughly reinforced; we will absolutely guarantee it to be fast black in color.

No. 16K5042 Undershirts. Sizes, 34, 36, 38, 40, 42 and 44 inches breast measure.
Price, each 41c
No. 16K5043 Drawers to match above shirts. Sizes, 30, 32, 34, 36, 38, 40 and 42 inches waist measure. Price, each 41c
Do not forget to give size wanted.
If by mail, postage extra, each, 9 cents.

42c PER GARMENT
BLUE COLOR BALBRIGGAN UNDERWEAR FOR MEN.

BLUE BALBRIGGAN

Very stylish underwear for men who like fancy color highly trimmed and highly finished underwear. This number is splendidly trimmed and made throughout. We will guarantee it to be a fast shade of blue.

No. 16K5034 Undershirts. Sizes, 34, 36, 38, 40, 42 and 44 inches breast measure.
Price, each 42c
No. 16K5035 Drawers to match above shirts. Sizes, 30, 32, 34, 36, 38, 40 and 42 inches waist measure.
Price, each 42c
Do not forget to give size.
If by mail, postage extra, each, 10 cents.

41c PER GARMENT
FANCY STRIPE BLACK AND WHITE UNDERWEAR.

FANCY PATTERN

We have had this number in our line for a good many seasons and it has been a very popular selling number. Thoroughly made throughout from fine yarns. It has a very pretty and nobby stripe of black on white, which gives it almost an oxford gray effect.

No. 16K5084 Undershirts. Sizes, 34, 36, 38, 40, 42 and 44 inches breast measure.
Price, each.. 41c
No. 16K5085 Drawers to match above shirts. Sizes, 30, 32, 34, 36, 38, 40 and 42 inches waist measure.
Price, each 41c
Do not neglect to give us correct size.
If by mail, postage extra, each, 10 cents.

81c SILK FINISHED UNDERWEAR 81c
WHITE OR BLUE COLORS.

WE INVITE COMPARISON

SILK FINISHED BLUE OR WHITE

Very best grade of summer underwear in our line. Underwear for men that has been put through the celebrated mercerizing process, which gives it the appearance, feel and all the luster of pure silk underwear. If you bought this underwear in your furnishing goods store you would have to pay $1.00 to $1.25 per garment. This price is a wholesaler's price and there is no question about it being a splendid appearing and splendid made grade of underwear. Worn by the very best dressers and in demand by men who want underwear to wear for dress occasions. Colors are a pure white or light blue. We want to caution our trade that this underwear is not made for rough wear.

No. 16K5040 Undershirts. Sizes, 34, 36, 38, 40, 42 and 44 inches breast measure.
Price, each.......................81c
No. 16K5041 Drawers to match above shirts. Sizes, 30, 32, 34, 36, 38, 40 and 42 inches waist measure.
Price, each 81c
Do not forget to give size and color wanted.
If by mail, postage extra, each, 10 cents.

HAVE YOU HEARD OF "OUR POSITIVE WEAR SOCKS?" SEE PAGE 948.

MEN'S WOOL AND FLEECE LINED UNDERWEAR

WOOL AND COTTON FLEECED UNDERWEAR

41ᶜ PER GARMENT
HEAVY JAEGER COLOR COTTON UNDERWEAR WITH A FLEECE LINING.
No. 16K6064 Undershirts. Sizes, 34 to 46 inches breast measure. Price, each........41c
No. 16K6065 Drawers to match above shirts. Sizes, 30 to 44 inches waist measure.
Price, each........41c
DO NOT FAIL TO GIVE US CORRECT SIZE.

47ᶜ PER GARMENT
SPECIAL VALUE IN EXTRA HEAVY LIGHT BLUE COLOR COTTON UNDERWEAR, WITH A WOOL FLEECING ON THE INSIDE.
No. 16K6080 Undershirts. Sizes, 34 to 46 inches breast measure. Price, each........47c
No. 16K6081 Drawers to match above shirts. Sizes, 30 to 44 inches waist measure.
Price, each........47c
REMEMBER, YOU MUST GIVE SIZE.

84ᶜ PER GARMENT
DR. WRIGHT'S CELEBRATED SANITARY FLEECE LINED GRAY COLOR UNDERWEAR.
No. 16K6092 Undershirts. Sizes, 34 to 44 inches breast measure. Price, each........84c
No. 16K6093 Drawers to match above shirts. Sizes, 30 to 42 inches waist measure.
Price, each........84c
DO NOT FAIL TO STATE CORRECT SIZE.

$1.29 PER GARMENT
DR. WRIGHT'S SANITARY WOOL FLEECED UNDERWEAR.
No. 16K6098 Undershirts. Sizes, 34 to 44 inches breast measure. Price, each........$1.29
No. 16K6099 Drawers to match above shirts. Sizes, 30 to 42 inches waist measure.
Price, each........$1.29
REMEMBER TO GIVE SIZE WANTED.

WOOL UNDERWEAR IN PLAIN COLORS

83ᶜ PER GARMENT
CAMEL'S HAIR COLOR WOOL MIXED UNDERWEAR.
No. 16K6224 Undershirts. Sizes, 34 to 46 inches breast measure. Price, each........83c
No. 16K6225 Drawers to match above shirts. Sizes, 30 to 44 inches waist measure.
Price, each........83c
WHAT SIZE DO YOU TAKE?

$1.00 PER GARMENT
OUR BIGGEST VALUE IN MEN'S CAMEL'S HAIR COLOR WOOL UNDERWEAR.
No. 16K6228 Undershirts. Sizes, 34 to 46 inches breast measure. Price, each........$1.00
No. 16K6229 Drawers to match above shirts. Sizes, 30 to 44 inches waist measure.
Price, each........$1.00
DON'T FAIL TO STATE SIZE WANTED.

$1.74 PER GARMENT
"ROOT'S TIVOLI" CAMEL'S HAIR COLOR UNDERWEAR, FINEST OF WOOL.
No. 16K6234 Undershirts. Sizes, 34 to 44 inches breast measure. Price, each........$1.74
No. 16K6235 Drawers to match above shirts. Sizes, 32 to 42 inches waist measure.
Price, each........$1.74
BE VERY POSITIVE TO GIVE US SIZE.

$1.00 PER GARMENT
FAWN COLOR MERINO WOOL UNDERWEAR.
No. 16K6244 Undershirts. Sizes, 34 to 46 inches breast measure. Price, each........$1.00
No. 16K6245 Drawers to match above shirts. Sizes, 32 to 44 inches waist measure.
Price, each........$1.00
DO NOT FAIL TO STATE SIZE WANTED.

$1.24 PER GARMENT
BUFF COLOR GRADE OF UNDERWEAR. MADE FROM THE FINEST WOOL.
No. 16K6256 Undershirts. Sizes, 34 to 46 inches breast measure. Price, each........$1.24
No. 16K6257 Drawers to match above shirts. Sizes, 32 to 44 inches waist measure.
Price, each........$1.24
DO NOT FAIL TO STATE SIZE WANTED.

84ᶜ PER GARMENT
SCARLET COLOR WOOL MIXED UNDERWEAR.
No. 16K6268 Undershirts. Sizes, 34 to 46 inches breast measure. Price, each........84c
No. 16K6269 Drawers to match above shirts. Sizes, 32 to 42 inches waist measure.
Price, each........84c
DO NOT FAIL TO STATE CORRECT SIZE WANTED.

MEN'S HEAVY WOOL UNDERWEAR

79ᶜ PER GARMENT
HEAVY PLUSH KNIT AND PLUSH LINED NATURAL GRAY WOOL UNDERWEAR.
No. 16K6348 Undershirts. Sizes, 34 to 44 breast measure.
Price, each........79c
No. 16K6349 Drawers to match above shirts. Sizes, 32 to 42 inches waist measure. Price, each........79c

99ᶜ PER GARMENT
HEAVY PLUSH BACK FAWN COLOR WOOL UNDERWEAR.
No. 16K6354 Undershirts. Sizes, 36 to 46 inches breast measure.
Price, each........99c
No. 16K6355 Drawers to match above shirts. Sizes, 32 to 44 inches waist measure. Price, each........99c

$1.15 PER GARMENT
HEAVY DOUBLE FRONT AND DOUBLE BACK FAWN COLOR WOOL UNDERWEAR.
No. 16K6362 Undershirts. Sizes, 36 to 46 inches breast measure.
Price, each........$1.15
No. 16K6363 Drawers to match above shirts. Sizes, 32 to 44 inches waist measure. Price, each........99c

$1.98 OUR "ESQUIMO"
POSITIVELY THE HEAVIEST WOOL PLUSH LINED UNDERWEAR MADE.
No. 16K6414 Undershirts. Sizes, 36 to 46 inches breast measure. Price, each........$1.98
No. 16K6415 Drawers to match above shirts. Sizes, 32 to 44 in. waist measure. Price, ea...$1.98
DO NOT FAIL TO STATE CORRECT SIZE.
If by mail, postage extra, each, 33 cents.

LADIES' WOOL AND FLEECED UNION SUITS

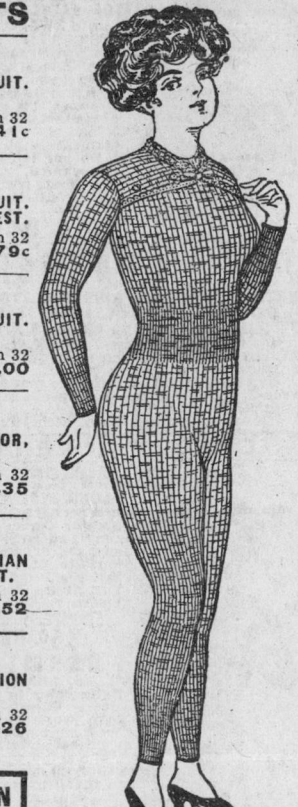

41ᶜ PER SUIT
LADIES' SILVER GRAY COLOR RIBBED COTTON FLEECE LINED UNION SUIT. BUTTONS DOWN THE FRONT.
No. 16K6434 Sizes, 4, 5 and 6, to fit bust from 32 to 40 inches. Price, per suit........41c
DO NOT FAIL TO STATE SIZE WANTED.

72ᶜ PER SUIT
DROP SEAT COTTON RIBBED FLEECE LINED UNION SUIT. BUTTONS DOWN THE FRONT. COLOR, CREAM WHITE.
No. 16K6443 Sizes, 4, 5 and 6, to fit bust from 32 to 40 inches. Price, per suit........72c
WHAT SIZE DO YOU WEAR?

79ᶜ PER SUIT
FINE QUALITY CREAM WHITE COLOR COTTON RIBBED FLEECE LINED UNION SUIT, BUTTONS DOWN THE FRONT.
No. 16K6447 Sizes, 4, 5 and 6, to fit bust from 32 to 40 inches. Price, per suit........79c
YOU MUST BE SURE TO GIVE SIZE.

81ᶜ PER SUIT
WOOL MIXED FLEECE LINED MOTTLED GRAY COLOR UNION SUIT. BUTTONS DOWN THE FRONT.
No. 16K6457 Sizes, 4, 5 and 6, to fit bust from 32 to 40 inches. Price, per suit........81c
DO NOT FAIL TO STATE SIZE WANTED.

$1.00 PER SUIT
WORSTED WOOL NATURAL GRAY COLOR UNION SUIT. BUTTONS DOWN THE FRONT.
No. 16K6459 Sizes, 4, 5 and 6, to fit bust from 32 to 40 inches. Price, per suit........$1.00
YOUR SIZE MUST NOT BE FORGOTTEN.

$1.52 PER SUIT
FINE AUSTRALIAN WOOL UNION SUIT. NATURAL GRAY COLOR. BUTTONS DOWN THE FRONT.
No. 16K6481 Sizes, 4, 5 and 6, to fit bust from 32 to 40 inches. Price, per suit........$1.52
DO NOT FAIL TO STATE SIZE WANTED.
If by mail, postage extra, each, 23 cents.

41ᶜ PER SUIT
ECRU COLOR RIBBED COTTON FLEECED UNION SUIT. BUTTONS ACROSS THE CHEST.
No. 16K6435 Sizes, 4, 5 and 6, to fit bust from 32 to 40 inches. Price, per suit........41c
REMEMBER TO GIVE YOUR SIZE.

79ᶜ PER SUIT
MEDIUM WEIGHT, RIBBED COTTON UNION SUIT. COLOR CREAM WHITE. BUTTONS ACROSS THE CHEST.
No. 16K6437 Sizes, 4, 5 and 6, to fit bust from 32 to 40 inches. Price, per suit........79c
DO NOT FAIL TO STATE SIZE WANTED.

$1.00 PER SUIT
NATURAL GRAY COLOR WOOL MIXED UNION SUIT. BUTTONS ACROSS THE CHEST.
No. 16K6455 Sizes, 4, 5 and 6, to fit bust from 32 to 40 inches. Price, per suit........$1.00
DO NOT FAIL TO STATE SIZE WANTED.

$1.35 PER SUIT
HIGH GRADE WORSTED WOOL UNION SUIT. COLOR, CREAM WHITE. BUTTONS ACROSS THE CHEST.
No. 16K6477 Sizes, 4, 5 and 6, to fit bust from 32 to 40 inches. Price, per suit........$1.35
DO NOT FAIL TO STATE SIZE WANTED.

$1.52 PER SUIT
OUR "LEADER" WHITE COLOR FINE AUSTRALIAN WOOL UNION SUIT. BUTTONS DOWN THE FRONT.
No. 16K6482 Sizes, 4, 5 and 6, to fit bust from 32 to 40 inches. Price, per suit........$1.52
BE SURE TO GIVE CORRECT SIZE.

$2.26 PER SUIT
OUR BEST AUSTRALIAN WORSTED WOOL UNION SUIT. BUTTONS DOWN THE FRONT.
No. 16K6485 Sizes, 4, 5 and 6, to fit bust from 32 to 40 inches. Price, per suit........$2.26
DO NOT FAIL TO STATE SIZE WANTED.
If by mail, postage extra, each, 23 cents.

OUR PRICES IN THIS CATALOGUE ARE LOWER, OUR VALUES ARE BETTER THAN AT ANY TIME IN THE HISTORY OF OUR INSTITUTION.

LADIES' RIBBED AND FLAT KNIT WINTER UNDERWEAR

RIBBED COTTON AND WOOL.

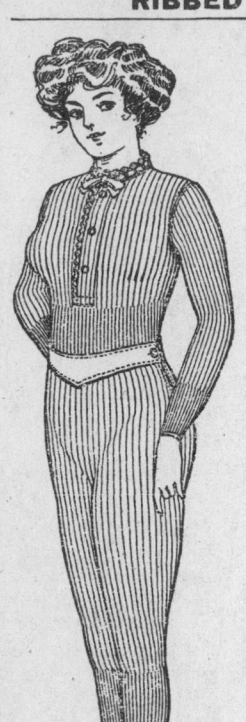

24c PER GARMENT
ECRU COLOR RIBBED COTTON FLEECE LINED UNDERWEAR.
No. 16K6634 Vests. Sizes, 4, 5 and 6, to fit bust from 32 to 40 inches. Price, per garment.........24c
No. 16K6635 Drawers to match above vests. Sizes, 4, 5 and 6. Price, per garment...............24c

42c PER GARMENT
EXCEPTIONAL VALUE IN RIBBED COTTON FLEECE LINED UNDERWEAR. COLOR, CREAM WHITE.
No. 16K6636 Vests. Sizes, 4, 5 and 6, to fit bust from 32 to 40 inches. Price, per garment.........42c
No. 16K6637 Drawers to match above vests. Sizes, 4, 5 and 6. Price, per garment...............42c

42c PER GARMENT
EXTRA HEAVY RIBBED COTTON VELVET FLEECE LINED UNDERWEAR. COLOR, NATURAL GRAY.
No. 16K6638 Vests. Sizes, 4, 5 and 6, to fit bust from 32 to 40 inches. Price, per garment.........42c
No. 16K6639 Drawers to match above vests. Sizes, 4, 5 and 6. Price, per garment...............42c

44c PER GARMENT
WORSTED WOOL MIXED RIBBED UNDERWEAR. COLOR, MIXED GRAY.
No. 16K6642 Vests. Sizes, 4, 5 and 6, to fit bust from 32 to 40 inches. Price, per garment.........44c
No. 16K6643 Drawers to match above vests. Sizes, 4, 5 and 6. Price, per garment...............44c

79c PER GARMENT
FINE WORSTED WOOL FLEECED RIBBED UNDERWEAR. COLOR, SILVER GRAY.
No. 16K6644 Vests. Sizes, 4, 5 and 6, to fit bust from 32 to 40 inches. Price, per garment.........79c
No. 16K6645 Drawers to match above vests. Sizes, 4, 5 and 6. Price, per garment...............79c

$1.00 PER GARMENT
OUR WOOL WORSTED SPECIAL. THIS IS A SPECIAL VALUE IN WOOL WORSTED RIBBED UNDERWEAR. IN COLORS OF CREAM WHITE OR SILVER GRAY.
No. 16K6646 Vest, Cream White.
No. 16K6648 Vest, Silver Gray. Sizes, 4, 5 and 6, to fit bust from 32 to 40 inches. Price, per garment..$1.00
No. 16K6647 Drawers, Cream White.
No. 16K6649 Drawers, Silver Gray. Sizes, 4, 5 and 6. Price, per garment...............$1.00
Do not fail to give proper size or we cannot fill your order. Postage extra, for each of above garments, 16 cents.

FLAT KNIT WOOL AND FLEECED COTTON.

63c PER GARMENT
FLAT KNIT NATURAL GRAY COLOR MERINO WOOL UNDERWEAR.
No. 16K6732 Vests. Sizes to fit from 32 to 44 inches bust measure. Price, per garment..........63c
No. 16K6733 Drawers to match above vests. Sizes, 32 to 44. Price, per garment...............63c

79c PER GARMENT
FLAT KNIT NATURAL GRAY WOOL UNDERWEAR.
No. 16K6734 Vests. Sizes to fit bust from 32 to 44 inches. Price, per garment...........79c
No. 16K6735 Drawers to match above vests. Sizes, 32 to 44. Price, per garment...............79c

$1.12 PER GARMENT
AUSTRALIAN WOOL LEADER, FLAT KNIT NATURAL GRAY WOOL UNDERWEAR.
No. 16K6736 Vests. Sizes to fit bust from 32 to 44 inches. Price, per garment........$1.12
No. 16K6737 Drawers to match above vests. Sizes, 32 to 44. Price, per garment...............$1.12

86c PER GARMENT
CAMEL'S HAIR COLOR FLAT KNIT WOOL UNDERWEAR.
No. 16K6744 Vests. Sizes to fit bust from 32 to 44 inches. Price, per garment...............86c
No. 16K6745 Drawers to match above vests. Sizes, 32 to 44. Price, per garment...............86c

$1.29 PER GARMENT
FLAT KNIT CAMEL'S HAIR COLOR WOOL UNDERWEAR.
No. 16K6746 Vests. Sizes to fit bust from 32 to 44 inches. Price, per garment........$1.29
No. 16K6747 Drawers to match above vests. Sizes, 32 to 44. Price, per garment...............$1.29

42c PER GARMENT
HEAVY COTTON FLAT KNIT, FLEECE LINED UNDERWEAR. JAEGER COLOR.
No. 16K6784 Vests. Sizes to fit bust from 32 to 44 inches. Price, per garment...............42c
No. 16K6785 Drawers to match above vests. Sizes, 32 to 44. Price, per garment...............42c
Please be sure to give size.
Postage extra, for each of above garments, 17 cents.

COMPARE OUR PRICES IN THIS CATALOGUE WITH PREVIOUS CATALOGUES AND YOU WILL NOTE MANY REDUCTIONS IN PRICE ON EVERY PAGE

LADIES' "EXTRA SIZE" FLEECE LINED AND WOOL UNDERWEAR.

26c PER GARMENT
EXTRA LARGE SIZE, ECRU COLOR RIBBED COTTON FLEECE LINED UNDERWEAR.
No. 16K6818 Vests. Sizes, 7, 8 and 9, to fit bust from 42 to 48 inches. Price, per garment.....26c
No. 16K6819 Drawers to match above vests. Sizes, 7, 8 and 9. Price, per garment.....26c
Do not fail to state size wanted. If by mail, postage extra, each, 15 cents.

42c PER GARMENT
EXTRA LARGE SIZE RIBBED COTTON UNDERWEAR WITH A HEAVY FLEECE LINING. COLOR, A CREAM WHITE.
No. 16K6822 Vests. Sizes, 7, 8 and 9, to fit bust from 42 to 48 inches. Price, per garment...............42c
No. 16K6823 Drawers to match above vests. Sizes, 7, 8 and 9. Always give size. Price, per garment...............42c
If by mail, postage extra, each, 16 cents.

49c PER SUIT
EXTRA LARGE SIZE JERSEY RIBBED COTTON FLEECE LINED UNION SUIT. BUTTONS DOWN THE FRONT, COLOR SILVER GRAY.
No. 16K6812 Sizes, 7, 8 and 9, to fit bust from 42 to 48 inches. Do not forget to state size wanted. Price, per suit...............49c
If by mail, postage extra, each, 20 cents.

91c PER SUIT
EXTRA LARGE SIZE JERSEY RIBBED WOOL MIXED FLEECE LINED UNION SUIT. BUTTONS DOWN THE FRONT. COLOR, SILVER GRAY.
No. 16K6814 Sizes, 7, 8 and 9, to fit bust from 42 to 48 inches. Be very careful not to forget size. Price, per suit...............91c
If by mail, postage extra, each, 20 cents.

$1.63 PER SUIT
EXTRA LARGE SIZE JERSEY RIBBED WOOL UNION SUIT.
No. 16K6816 Union Suit which has been especially made for us, from high grade selected Australian wool with a very slight mixture of cotton which is placed on the inside of the garment; this will keep the garment from shrinking, if properly washed, and makes a more comfortable suit, as it will not irritate the skin. This suit is especially adapted for large and stout women, who will find it a most comfortable garment. Very neatly trimmed and well made throughout. Color, natural gray. Sizes, 7, 8 and 9, to fit bust from 42 to 48 inches.
Do not fail to state size wanted.
Price, per suit........$1.63
If by mail, postage extra, each, 24 cents.

51c PER GARMENT
EXTRA LARGE SIZE JERSEY RIBBED WOOL MIXED FLEECED UNDERWEAR. COLOR, NATURAL GRAY.
No. 16K6824 Vests. Sizes, 7, 8 and 9, to fit bust from 42 to 48 inches. Price per garment.....51c
No. 16K6825 Drawers to match above vests. Sizes, 7, 8 and 9. Price, per garment.....51c
Do not forget to give size. If by mail, postage extra, each, 16 cents.

99c PER GARMENT
EXTRA LARGE SIZE JERSEY RIBBED AUSTRALIAN WOOL UNDERWEAR. COLOR, NATURAL GRAY.
No. 16K6826 Vests. Sizes, 7, 8 and 9, to fit bust from 42 to 48 inches. Price, per garment...............99c
No. 16K6827 Drawers to match above vests. Sizes, 7, 8 and 9. Do not fail to state size wanted. Price, per garment...............99c
If by mail, postage extra, each, 15 cents.

CORSET COVERS.

21c PER GARMENT
LONG SLEEVE.
No. 16K6842 Pure white color Corset Cover, medium in weight, neatly trimmed and finished, fashioned to fit the waist. Sizes, 4, 5 and 6, to fit bust from 32 to 40 inches.
Price, each......21c

34c PER GARMENT
No. 16K6843 Extra value in a long sleeve Corset Cover, pure white in color, medium in weight, perfectly finished and trimmed. Sizes, 4, 5 and 6, to fit bust from 32 to 40 inches.
Do not fail to state size.
Price, each...............34c
If by mail, postage extra, each, on either of the above numbers, 7 cents.

LADIES' TIGHTS.

$1.00 EACH
BLACK WORSTED WOOL TIGHTS.
No. 16K6854 Jersey Ribbed Black Tights, made from the finest worsted wool. This garment is practical at all seasons of the year, and no woman should be without a pair of them. They are very elastic and can be worn next to the body or over the underclothing and stockings. Self fitting waist, closed seat. Sizes, 4, 5 and 6. Price, each..$1.00
Be sure to state size. If by mail, postage extra, each, 14 cents.

ORDER YOUR HOSIERY WITH YOUR UNDERWEAR

24c PER PAIR
THE TWO STOCKINGS REPRESENTED IN THIS DESCRIPTION ARE POSITIVELY THE VERY BEST WEARING STOCKINGS THAT WE ARE ABLE TO BUY.
They are expressly made for our trade from the very best selected Egyptian yarns by the "Burson Knitting Mills." Fully seamless and absolutely guaranteed by us to give positive comfort, wear and satisfaction. Sizes, 8½, 9, 9½ and 10.
Do not forget to give us correct size.
No. 16K2312 Plain Black.
No. 16K2342 Plain Black with an unbleached color heel, sole and toe. Price, per pair..24c
If by mail, postage extra, per pair, 4 cents.
SEE PAGES 948 TO 953 FOR OUR COMPLETE LINE OF HOSIERY.

FAMOUS FOR WEAR

LEADER UN-BLEACHED SOLE

DO YOUR CHILDREN WEAR "TEAR PROOF" HOSIERY? SEE PAGE 953.

LADIES' SUMMER UNION SUITS

REDUCTIONS IN PRICE

85c PER SUIT

SILK FINISHED, LOW NECK AND LACE TRIMMED UMBRELLA DRAWERS UNION SUIT.

No. 16K6886 The finest Union Suit for ladies in our line; this suit has been put through the celebrated mercerizing process, which gives it all the luster and the appearance of an all silk garment. Beautifully trimmed, low cut neck and armholes, which are hand finished with silk tape. This suit flares out at the knees (see illustration) and is trimmed with a 2-inch torchon lace of fine pattern. The sale on union suits is growing daily, as women realize the comfort that is found in wearing them. Pure white in color. Sizes, 4, 5 and 6, to fit bust measure from 32 to 40 inches.

Price, per suit..................85c
Do not fail to give correct size.
If by mail, postage extra, each, 10 cents.

42c PER SUIT

OUR POPULAR PRICE LOW NECK AND UMBRELLA LACE TRIMMED DRAWERS UNION SUIT.

No. 16K6878 This suit is our biggest seller and is accounted for by the fact that we have been able to secure an exceptional garment to sell at this very low price. This garment could not be duplicated by the average retail store for less than 50 to 60 cents each. It is made from very fine cotton yarn, which is given a lisle finish, the low cut neck and armholes are finished with mercerized silk tape, beautifully made throughout. Large umbrella bottoms finished with wide lace of a very pretty design. This is a big value in a union suit. Color a pure white. Sizes, 4, 5 and 6, to fit bust measure from 32 to 40 inches.

Price, per suit..................42c
Have you given correct size?
If by mail, postage extra, each, 10 cents.

49c PER SUIT

EXTRA WIDE UNION SUIT FOR STOUT WOMEN.

No. 16K6882 Sleeveless, low cut neck and umbrella lace trimmed drawers Union Suit, made for large or stout women. This is a good big full elastic union suit, and it will give great comfort and satisfaction to large women. Made from fine lisle yarns handsomely finished and trimmed at the neck and armholes with mercerized tape. The umbrella drawers are extra large and finished with wide lace of a new pattern, shaped at the waist. Color, pure white. Sizes, 7, 8 and 9, to fit bust from 42 to 48 inches.

Price, per suit..................49c
We must have your size.
If by mail, postage extra, each, 10 cents.

No. 16K6886   No. 16K6872   No. 16K6875

No. 16K6882

No. 16K6878

No. 16K6879

BIGGER VALUES

58c PER SUIT

LISLE FINISH, LOW CUT NECK, LACE TRIMMED UMBRELLA DRAWERS UNION SUIT.

No. 16K6879 This is a very practical suit for summer wear as it is very sheer and fine. Made from the finest lisle yarns and exquisitely hand finished throughout; the low cut neck is trimmed with a silk ribbon; the umbrella bottom drawers are finished with an imported lace of a new design. (See illustration.) This is positively a big value for ladies who desire a high grade union suit at this remarkably low price. Color, a pure white. Sizes, 4, 5 and 6, to fit bust measure from 32 to 40 inches.

Price, per suit..................58c
Do not forget size wanted.
If by mail, postage extra, each, 10 cents.

42c PER SUIT

TIGHT KNEE, KNEE LENGTH, LOW NECK UNION SUIT.

No. 16K6872 A most practical suit for women desiring a Union Suit that fits the limbs closely. This suit comes a trifle below the knee and is finished so that you can pull the stockings up over the suit. It is sleeveless, with a low cut neck finished with mercerized tape, and is made from the finest yarn which is lisle finished. Well trimmed and perfectly made and finished throughout. All of our union suits are fashioned at the waist, and we will guarantee them to fit perfectly if you give us the correct size. This suit is pure white in color. Sizes, 4, 5 and 6, to fit bust from 32 to 40 inches.

Price, per suit..................42c
Do not forget size wanted.
If by mail, postage extra, each, 9 cents.

42c PER SUIT

ANKLE LENGTH, HIGH NECK AND LONG SLEEVE UNION SUIT.

No. 16K6875 Union Suit, worn by a great many women all the year around. It is very sheer and fine, and is a splendid value at this price. Long sleeves and ankle length, fashioned at the wrist and ankle to fit; high neck, trimmed with a mercerized tape. Buttons down the front to the waist line with seven buttons, fashioned at the waist. We know that this suit will give satisfaction and that it will fit correctly providing you give us the proper size. Color, pure white. Sizes, 4, 5 and 6, to fit bust from 32 to 40 inches.

Price, per suit..................42c
Have you given us the right size?
If by mail, postage extra, each, 12 cents.

LADIES' "SHAPED TO FIT" COTTON VESTS.

21c LONG SLEEVE AND HIGH NECK FINE COTTON VEST. 21c

No. 16K6944 Especially made for us, this is an excellent value at this very low price. The sleeve of this garment is fashioned at the wrist and the body is fashioned at the waist. It is very well made and plenty long enough so that it will come well over the hips and make the skirt fit snugly. Pure white in color. Sizes, 4, 5 and 6, to fit bust from 32 to 40 inches.

Price, per garment..21c

Do not forget to give size.

If by mail, postage extra, each, 6 cents.

42c PER GARMENT

HIGH NECK, LONG SLEEVE HAND FINISHED LISLE VEST.

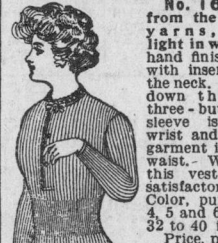

No. 16K6947 Made from the very finest lisle yarns, very sheer and light in weight, beautifully hand finished and trimmed with inserted silk tape at the neck. Buttons part way down the front with a three-button effect. The sleeve is finished at the wrist and the body of the garment is fashioned at the waist. We will guarantee this vest to be a most satisfactory fitting garment. Color, pure white. Sizes, 4, 5 and 6, to fit bust from 32 to 40 inches.

Price, per garment..42c
Do not neglect to give size wanted.
If by mail, postage extra, each, 6 cents.

21c PER GARMENT

WING SLEEVE, HIGH NECK VEST OF FINE COTTON.

No. 16K6949 Very popular and big selling vest with women who desire a high cut neck with a wing sleeve effect for summer wear. This is a most practical garment; it is made from good cotton, thoroughly made and finished throughout. Fashioned at the waist so that it will fit right. Extra long in length so that it will come well over the hips. Pure white in color. Sizes, 4, 5, 6, 7, 8 and 9, to fit bust from 32 to 48 inches.

Price, per garment 21c
Do not fail to give size.
If by mail, postage extra, each, 6 cents.

23c EXTRA LARGE SIZE FOR STOUT WOMEN, LONG SLEEVE, HIGH NECK VEST 23c

No. 16K6952 This vest is made from good cotton, fine and light in weight. It is worn by a great many women at all seasons of the year. Very elastic and fashioned at the waist so that it will fit snugly, long sleeves which are shaped at the wrist to fit properly. Buttons part way down the front with a three-button effect, finished at the neck with mercerized tape. Color, pure white. Sizes, 7, 8 and 9, to fit bust from 42 to 48 inches.

Price, per garment, 23c
Have you given us size?

If by mail, postage extra, each, 6 cents.

DRAWERS—TIGHT KNEE AND LACE TRIMMED FOR SUMMER.

22c LADIES' TIGHT KNEE LENGTH OR ANKLE LENGTH DRAWERS. 22c

The knee length drawers are tight fitting at the knee so that you can pull your stockings over the drawers and they will fit properly. The ankle length drawers are perfect fitting so that the stocking will fit over them neatly. Color, pure white. Sizes, 4, 5, 6, 7, 8 and 9.

If you do not know your size, give us your bust measure and we will fit you correctly.

No. 16K6956 Knee Length.
No. 16K6957 Ankle Length.
Price, per garment...............22c
Do not forget to state size wanted.
If by mail, postage extra, each, 6 cents.

22c PER GARMENT

LADIES' UMBRELLA SHAPED LACE TRIMMED DRAWERS.

No. 16K6960 Pure white in color, Jersey ribbed and very elastic, French band finished waist, umbrella shaped, lace trimmed drawers. Strongly and thoroughly made and finished throughout. We sell large quantities of this style as it is worn by women who wear with it light weight vests; which will be found quoted on other side. Sizes, 4, 5, 6, 7, 8 and 9.

If you do not know your size, send us your bust measure, and we will fit you correctly.
Price, per garment................22c
Do not forget size.
If by mail, postage extra, each, 6 cents.

35c PER GARMENT

UMBRELLA SHAPE LACE TRIMMED DRAWERS.

No. 16K6962 This is a new garment this season. Knit drawers are growing in demand every year as their advantages are discovered. They are a most practical garment to wear with light weight vests, which we quote on other side. This number is perfectly made from the very finest cotton yarns. Umbrella bottoms which are trimmed with a wide lace of new design. Pure white in color. Sizes, 4, 5, 6, 7, 8 and 9.

If you do not know your size, give us your bust measure and we will fit you correctly.
Price, per garment................35c
Do not forget size.
If by mail, postage extra, each, 6 cents.

42c OUR BEST VALUE, UMBRELLA SHAPED, LACE TRIMMED DRAWERS. 42c

No. 16K6990 Hand finished drawers, they are beautifully made and finished throughout, puckering strings at the waist which will make the garment fit snugly. The umbrella bottoms are finished with an extra wide imported torchon lace slightly flaring. These drawers are made from the finest lisle yarns, pure white in color. Sizes, 4, 5, 6, 7, 8 and 9. If you do not know your size, give us your bust measure, and we will fit you correctly.

Price, per garment................42c
Do not forget your size.
If by mail, postage extra, each, 6 cents.

NOTICE—DON'T FAIL TO READ ABOUT OUR "WORTHMORE" HOSE. SEE PAGE 951.

LADIES' LISLE MERCERIZED AND FINE COTTON VESTS

OUR PRICES ARE LOWER THAN EVER BEFORE

10¢ PER GARMENT
OUR BIGGEST SELLER, HIGHLY TRIMMED LADIES' SUMMER VESTS.

No. 16K6918 During the summer months we sell cases of this number a day. This vest is thoroughly made and neatly trimmed. It is a most satisfactory garment for women to wear during the summer months. It is sheer and very fine. Low cut neck and sleeveless. Color, pure white. Sizes, 4, 5 and 6, to fit from 32 to 40 inches.
Do not neglect to give us correct size.
Price, each 10c
If by mail, postage extra, each, 3 cents.

12¢ PER GARMENT
BEAUTIFULLY TRIMMED MERCERIZED TAPED VESTS.

No. 16K6919 Pure white in color. This vest is an exceptional bargain at this very low price. Sleeveless, with a low cut neck and a very neat and pretty lace over the shoulder inserted with a mercerized tape. Sizes, 4, 5 and 6, to fit bust from 32 to 40 inches.
Do not fail to give us size wanted.
Price, each 12c
If by mail, postage extra, each, 3 cents.

15¢ PER GARMENT
HANDSOME LACE TRIMMED, MERCERIZED TAPED VESTS FOR SUMMER WEAR.

No. 16K6921 We use this number in great quantities, because at this price we have been able to secure a vest made from the very finest cotton yarns, sheer and thin. It is sleeveless, with a low cut neck trimmed with a very neat pattern of lace which is inserted with a mercerized tape. Color, pure white. Sizes, 4, 5 and 6, to fit bust from 32 to 40 inches.
Be sure to give us correct size.
Price, each 15c
If by mail, postage extra, each, 3 cents.

12¢ PER GARMENT
WING SLEEVE, LOW CUT NECK VESTS FOR SUMMER WEAR.

No. 16K6935 This vest fulfills a growing demand in a low cut neck vest, with short tight fitting wing sleeves for summer. It is made from the finest cotton yarns, thoroughly finished and trimmed throughout. Pure white in color. Sizes, 4, 5 and 6, to fit bust from 32 to 40 inches.
We must have your size when ordering.
Price, each 12c
If by mail, postage extra, each, 4 cents.

21¢ PER GARMENT
OUR FINEST LISLE, MERCERIZED TAPE INSERTED SUMMER VESTS.

No. 16K6923 Vest for women that is made from the very finest lisle yarns, which makes it a most comfortable garment for summer and hot weather wear. Sleeveless and low cut neck, highly trimmed with an imported lace of new design inserted with mercerized tape. Color, pure white. Sizes, 4, 5 and 6, to fit bust from 32 to 40 inches.
We must have size when ordering.
Price, each 21c
If by mail, postage extra, each, 3 cents.

23¢ PER GARMENT
SILK PLAITED VESTS OF GREAT VALUE

No. 16K6927 This vest is made from the finest mercerized yarns. These yarns give it the finish and all the appearance and luster of a pure silk garment. It is the most satisfactory and comfortable vest a woman can wear during the hot weather. Sleeveless, and low cut neck neatly trimmed. Color, a clean pure white. Sizes, 4, 5 and 6, to fit bust from 32 to 40 inches.
Do not forget to give us size wanted.
Price, each 23c
If by mail, postage extra, each, 3 cents.

39¢ PER GARMENT
MERCERIZED SILK VESTS, THE BEST VALUE IN OUR STOCK.

No. 16K6928 Sleeveless, low cut neck vest which has been made from the very finest mercerized yarns the market affords. This garment positively has all the appearance and luster of pure silk. Beautifully made and trimmed; the shoulders and armholes are inserted with a pure silk tape. Color, pure white. Sizes, 4, 5 and 6, to fit bust from 32 to 40 inches.
We must have your size when you order.
Price, each 39c
If by mail, postage extra, each, 3 cents.

12¢ PER GARMENT
EXTRA SIZE VESTS FOR LARGE WOMEN.

No. 16K6939 Sleeveless, with low cut neck. This vest is extra wide and specially made and suited for large and stout women. Made from the very finest yarns, splendidly made and finished throughout. Color, pure white. Sizes, 7, 8 and 9, to fit bust from 42 to 48 inches.
Do not forget to give size wanted.
Price, each 12c
If by mail, postage extra, each, 4 cents.

19¢ PER GARMENT
WING SLEEVE, LOW CUT NECK, LISLE FINISH VESTS.

No. 16K6936 This vest is made from the finest hard finished lisle yarn, making it a most comfortable and practical garment for the summer and hot weather months. Short tight fitting wing sleeves, low cut neck which is neatly trimmed with a mercerized tape. Color, pure white. Sizes, 4, 5 and 6, to fit bust from 32 to 40 inches. Price, each 19c
Do not fail to give us the right size.
If by mail, postage extra, each, 3 cents.

23¢ PER GARMENT
EXTRA SIZE LISLE FINISHED VESTS, ESPECIALLY MADE FOR LARGE WOMEN.

No. 16K6941 Vest made from the finest lisle finished yarns, a most comfortable garment for large women to wear during the summer months, as it is sheer and very thin, especially adapted for women who suffer with the heat. Sleeveless, with low cut neck, beautifully trimmed and inserted with silk tape. Pure white in color. Sizes, 7, 8 and 9, to fit bust from 42 to 48 inches. Price, each 23c
Do not fail to give us the right size wanted.
If by mail, postage extra, each, 4 cents.

19¢ PER GARMENT
EXTRA SIZE, SLEEVELESS, LOW CUT NECK VESTS FOR LARGE WOMEN.

No. 16K6940 Vest made of finest cotton yarns, sleeveless, with a low cut neck which is neatly trimmed and inserted with a mercerized tape. This vest is very elastic, sheer and fine and the most comfortable garment a large woman could buy for the summer months. Pure white in color. Sizes, 7, 8 and 9, to fit bust from 42 to 48 inches. Price, each 19c
Do not neglect to give us size wanted.
If by mail, postage extra, each, 4 cents.

LOWER PRICES   INFANTS' VESTS   BETTER VALUES

12¢ PER GARMENT
INFANTS' COTTON VESTS FOR SUMMER.

No. 16K7015 This vest is made from fine cotton, with long sleeves and high neck, which is neatly trimmed and inserted with mercerized tape. Buttons down the entire front with five buttons; edges are neatly crocheted. Color, pure white. Sizes, 1, 2, 3, 4, 5 and 6. See table of sizes when ordering.
Do not neglect to give us size wanted.
Price, each 12c

16¢ PER GARMENT
FINE EGYPTIAN COTTON VESTS FOR INFANTS' SUMMER WEAR.

No. 16K7016 Made from the finest combed cotton yarn, long sleeves, high neck, hand finished and inserted with silk tape. Buttons down the entire front with five buttons; the edges are neatly crocheted. Color, pure white. Sizes, 1, 2, 3, 4, 5 and 6. See table of sizes when ordering.
Be very careful to give us correct size.
Price, each 16c

INFANTS' UNDERVESTS. ORDER BY SIZE.

Table of Sizes for Infants' Shirts.

Size	Length, inches	Suitable for
Size 1	9	1 to 3 months
Size 2	10	3 to 6 months
Size 3	12	6 to 9 months
Size 4	14	9 to 12 months
Size 5	15	1 to 2 years
Size 6	16	2 to 3 years
Size 7	18	3 to 4 years

Postage on infants' vests, extra, each, 3 cents.

12¢ PER GARMENT
FLEECE LINED RIBBED COTTON VESTS.

No. 16K7020 Made from good weight cotton with a heavy nap fleecing on the inside. Perfectly made and trimmed throughout; long sleeves and high cut neck; buttons all the way down the front. Sizes, 1, 2, 3, 4, 5 and 6. Cream color.
See table of sizes when ordering.
Price, each 12c

RUBENS INFANTS' SHIRTS.

NO BUTTONS   NO TROUBLE

PAT. Nov. 1894 Nov 15.03

No. 16K7000 Rubens Shirt, made from one-third wool and two-thirds cotton, fine Jersey ribbed; very soft and elastic; the edges and seams are all finished with silk stitching. Color, cream white.

Sizes	1	2
Price, each	24c	27c
Sizes	3	4
Price, each	31c	34c
Sizes	5	6
Price, ea.	37c	39c 41c

See table of sizes when ordering.

No. 16K7005 Rubens Shirt, made from the finest selected white Saxony wool with a very slight mixture of cotton. Color, cream white.

Sizes	1	2	3	4
Price, each	38c	41c	44c	46c
Sizes	5	6	7	
Price, each	49c	52c	55c	

See table of sizes when ordering.

25¢ PER GARMENT
OUR SPECIAL VALUE, INFANTS' CASHMERE VESTS.

No. 16K7032 Wonderful value, this vest is specially made for us from the very finest cashmere wool yarns, mixed with fine cotton. Long sleeves, high cut neck which is neatly trimmed and inserted with a mercerized tape, buttons all the way down the front, crochet edges. Color, cream white. Sizes, 1, 2, 3, 4, 5 and 6.
See table of sizes when ordering.
We must have size when you order.
Price, each 25c

No. 16K7010 Rubens Shirt. Made from the finest and softest Saxony wool. This is the biggest seller in our stock of infants' vests. Color, cream white.

Sizes	1	2
Price, each	47c	49c
Sizes	3	4
Price, each	52c	55c
Sizes	5	6	7
Price, ea.	58c	62c 64c

See table of sizes when ordering.

No. 16K7011 Rubens Shirt, made from a mixture of silk and Saxony wool. Color, cream white.

Sizes	1	2	3
Price, each	88c	97c	$1.06 $1.15
Sizes	5	6	7
Price, each	$1.24	$1.33	$1.42

See table of sizes when ordering.

INFANTS' FINE MERINO WOOL VESTS.

No. 16K7035 Cream white in color, made from the finest merino wool, with a slight mixture of cotton. Elastic ribbed, well made and finished throughout. Long sleeves, high neck and buttons down the front.

Sizes	1	2
Price, each	25c	28c
Sizes	3	4
Price, each	32c	35c
Sizes	5	6
Price, each	38c	40c

See table of sizes when ordering.

FINE SAXONY WOOL VESTS FOR INFANTS.

No. 16K7040 Positively made from the very highest grade Saxony wool, beautifully trimmed and finished. Long sleeves, high neck inserted with silk tape. Buttons all the way down the front. Color, cream white.

Sizes	1	2	3	4	5	6
Price, each	42c	45c	48c	51c	53c	56c

See table of sizes when ordering.

INFANTS' SAXONY WOOL BANDS.

No. 16K7055 Fine ribbed wool bands, made from the best Saxony wool, with a very slight mixture of cotton. Sleeveless, with low cut neck. This garment will stay on without the use of safety pins.

Length, inches	8	9	10	11	12
Price, each	21c	23c	25c	27c	29c

See table of sizes when ordering.

OUR BIGGEST VALUE, OUR "WORTHMORE" HOSE. SEE PAGE 951.

CHILDREN'S UNDERWEAR FOR SUMMER

NEVER BEFORE HAVE WE BEEN ABLE TO SHOW SUCH REMARKABLE VALUES, AND QUOTE SUCH LOW PRICES AS WE HAVE IN THIS CATALOGUE

TABLE OF SIZES FOR CHILDREN'S AND MISSES' UNDERWEAR.

VESTS		PANTALETS	
Sizes inches	For Age	Sizes inches	For Age
16,	1 year and under	16,	1 to 1½ years
18,	1 to 1½ years	18,	1½ to 2 years
20,	1½ to 2 years	20,	2 to 4 years
22,	2 to 4 years	22,	4 to 6 years
24,	4 to 6 years	24,	6 to 8 years
26,	6 to 8 years	26,	8 to 10 years
28,	8 to 10 years	28,	10 to 12 years
30,	10 to 12 years	30,	12 years
32,	12 to 13 years	32,	13 years
34,	13 to 14 years	34,	14 years

8ᶜ PER GARMENT
SLEEVELESS, LOW CUT NECK SUMMER VESTS FOR CHILDREN AND MISSES.

No. 16K7083 Pure white in color, this is a very neat and practical garment for girls' and misses' wear during the summer months. Prettily trimmed with tape insertion around armholes and shoulders. Jersey ribbed, which makes it perfect fitting. Good length, will come well down over the hips. Sizes, 20, 22, 24, 26 and 28 inches breast measure. See table for sizes.

Be very careful to give us the correct size when you order.

Price, each.....................8c
If by mail, postage extra, each, 3 cents.

14ᶜ PER GARMENT
OUR FINEST MISSES' OR GIRLS' VESTS, SLEEVELESS WITH LOW CUT NECK.

No. 16K7091 This is the finest misses' vest in our stock. It is made from very selected combed cotton, very sheer and pretty. Hand finished at the armholes and around the breast with a very neat crochet pattern inserted with a silk tape. This is the most practical garment a mother could buy for her child for summer wear. It is very neat and attractive, pure white in color. Sizes, 18, 20, 22, 24, 26, 28, 30, 32 and 34 inches breast measure. See table for sizes.

Be very careful to give us the correct size.
Price, each 14c
If by mail, postage extra, each, 3 cents.

20ᶜ PER GARMENT
WING SLEEVE, HIGH NECK, FINE JERSEY RIBBED WHITE COTTON VESTS FOR GIRLS AND MISSES.

No. 16K7092 This is a beautifully trimmed vest for girls' and misses' wear, made from the finest Egyptian cotton yarns, Jersey ribbed, elastic fitting. Short wing sleeve, high neck, very prettily crocheted with inserted silk tape. Buttons part way down the front. This is a most satisfactory and comfortable garment for summer wear, as it is very sheer and fine. Color, pure white. Sizes, 18, 20, 22, 24, 26, 28, 30, 32 and 34 inches breast measure. See table for sizes.

Be very careful to give us the correct size you want.
Price, each.....................20c
If by mail, postage extra, each, 4 cents.

12ᶜ PER GARMENT
LONG SLEEVE, HIGH CUT NECK VESTS FOR GIRLS AND MISSES.

No. 16K7084 Jersey Ribbed Vest, made from good cotton yarn. Color, pure white. Buttons part way down the front; edges and neck are neatly crocheted, long sleeves. This is a very popular garment for children to wear during the summer months.

Sizes, 20, 22, 24, 26, 28, 30 and 32 inches breast measure. See table for sizes.

Be very careful to give us the right size when you order.

Price, each.................12c
If by mail, postage extra, each, 4 cents.

12ᶜ PER GARMENT
LACE TRIMMED JERSEY RIBBED COTTON PANTS FOR GIRLS AND MISSES.

No. 16K7085 Very prettily made pants for girls' and misses' wear, strongly and thoroughly made throughout from the very best cotton yarns. Buttons at the side. The waistband of good grade muslin is strongly attached and the bottoms of these pants are finished with a neat lace of a new design. Color, pure white. Sizes 20, 22, 24, 26, 28, 30 and 32 inches waist measure. See table for sizes.

Do not forget to give us size wanted.

Price, each.................12c
If by mail, postage extra, each, 4 cents.

21ᶜ PER GARMENT
LONG SLEEVE, HIGH NECK FINE WHITE RIBBED COTTON VESTS FOR GIRLS AND MISSES.

No. 16K7093 Long sleeve, high neck, perfectly trimmed garment for girls' and misses' wear during the summer months. Jersey ribbed and very elastic, this garment is made from fine cotton, which makes it very sheer. Perfectly trimmed around the neck with crochet effect inserted with a silk ribbon. Buttons part way down the front. Pure white in color. Sizes, 18, 20, 22, 24, 26, 28, 30, 32 and 34 inches breast measure. See table for sizes.

Do not neglect to give the correct size.
Price, each.................21c
If by mail, postage extra, each, 4 cents.

21ᶜ PER GARMENT
KNEE LENGTH PANTS, JERSEY RIBBED, WHITE IN COLOR.

No. 16K7098 Made from the finest combed cotton yarns, perfectly made and finished throughout, strongly sewed on good muslin waistband, buttons at the sides with hand finished buttonholes. This pant comes to the knee and is tight fitting, so that the stockings will fit over it perfectly. This is a most satisfactory and popular garment for summer wear. Pure white in color. Sizes, 18, 20, 22, 24, 26, 28, 30, 32 and 34.

See table for sizes.

Be very careful to give us the right size wanted.

Price, each.........21c
If by mail, postage extra, each, 4 cents.

UNION SUITS FOR GIRLS

41ᶜ PER SUIT
GIRLS' AND MISSES' TIGHT KNEE OR LACE TRIMMED PANT UNION SUITS.

This is our first season in quoting these numbers. We have put them in our catalogue on account of the growing demand that we have had for a moderate priced misses' and girls' union suit. These suits are perfectly made from the very best cotton yarns, all seams are overcast and strongly reinforced. Sleeveless, with low cut neck, the armholes and shoulders are prettily trimmed with tape inserted. Two styles, either lace trimmed pants, or tight fitting knee. Color, pure white.

Sizes	3	4	5
To fit ages	4-5	6-7	8-9
Sizes	6	7	8
To fit ages	10-11	12-13	14-15

No. 16K7096 Suit with lace trimmed pants.
No. 16K7097 Suit with tight fitting knee, knee length.

Price, each.......................41c
Do not forget to give us size when ordering.
If by mail, postage extra, each, 12 cents.

KNIT WAISTS FOR BOYS AND GIRLS

19ᶜ CHILD'S WAISTS 19ᶜ
THE E. Z. WAIST FOR BOYS AND GIRLS.

This waist is thoroughly reinforced over the shoulders and down the back with tubular bands. These bands take all the strain of holding up the clothing; buttons are strongly sewed on at all points of the garment where a button is necessary. We will positively guarantee this waist to give satisfaction and service.
No. 16K7072 Boys' Waist, cream color, sleeveless with high cut neck.
No. 16K7074 Girls' Waist, color white, sleeveless and low cut neck.
Sizes to fit children from 2 to 13 years of age.
Price, each.....................19c

10ᶜ BIG VALUE 10ᶜ
FOR BOYS AND GIRLS.

The biggest seller in our line. This is a big value. No. 16K7070 Especially made for us. We are able to contract for this waist in very large quantities; in this way we secure a splendid garment and are able to make this very low price. Sleeveless with low cut neck, plenty of buttons to hold up the children's clothing. Color, cream. Sizes, to fit children from 2 to 12 years of age.
Price, each.........................10c
Do not forget to give us age of child.
If by mail, postage extra, each, 5 cents.

BOYS' SUMMER UNDERWEAR

23ᶜ
BOYS' SUMMER WEIGHT STRONGLY MADE BALBRIGGAN UNDERWEAR, KNEE LENGTH AND ANKLE LENGTH DRAWERS.

This is beautiful underwear for boys and young men for summer wear, light weight, ecru color, strongly and carefully made throughout from the very best selected cotton yarns. The drawers have large double seats and suspender tapes, in two styles, ankle length and knee length, with tight fitting cuffs at the ankle and knee so that the stockings will fit neatly. We will warrant this underwear to give great satisfaction and service.
No. 16K7410 Undershirts. Sizes, 24 to 34 inches breast measure. Price, each.........23c
No. 16K7411 Drawers, knee length. Sizes, 24 to 34 inches waist measure. Price, each.........23c
No. 16K7413 Drawers, ankle length. Sizes, 24 to 34 inches waist measure. Price, each.........23c
Be very careful to state size wanted.
If by mail, postage extra, each, 6 cents.

52ᶜ
YOUNG MEN'S AND BOYS' UNION SUITS, SHORT SLEEVE, KNEE LENGTH OR LONG SLEEVE AND ANKLE LENGTH.

These suits have been especially made for us and our trade, they are thoroughly and strongly made throughout, and will stand the rough wear a boy usually gives his underwear. Made from fine cotton yarns, cream color; these suits button down the entire front, the buttons are on to stay. In two styles, either short sleeve and knee length, a most practical garment for summer wear, or long sleeve and ankle length. Sizes, 24 to 34 inches breast measure.
Be very careful to give the correct size you want in ordering.
No. 16K7509 Short sleeve and knee length.
No. 16K7510 Long sleeve and ankle length.
Price, per suit 52c
If by mail, postage extra, each, 12 cents.

DO YOUR CHILDREN WEAR OUR "TEARPROOF" HOSIERY? SEE PAGE 953.

Sig. 57—1st Ed.

WOOL AND FLEECE LINED UNDERWEAR FOR CHILDREN

CHILDREN'S TWO-PIECE UNDERWEAR.

CHILDREN'S JERSEY RIBBED COTTON FLEECE LINED UNDERWEAR, ECRU SHADE.

No. 16K7206 Undervests.

Sizes	18	20	22
Each	12c	14c	16c
Sizes	24	26	28
Each	19c	21c	23c
Sizes	30	32	34
Each	25c	28c	30c

No. 16K7207 Pantalets to match above vests, open sides.

Sizes	18	20	22
Each	12c	14c	16c
Sizes	24	26	28
Each	19c	21c	23c
Sizes	30	32	34
Each	25c	28c	30c

Be sure to state size wanted.

If by mail, postage extra, each, 12 cents.

OUR JERSEY RIBBED WOOL SPECIAL FOR CHILDREN.

Positively our best and biggest value in ribbed wool underwear. This garment contains over 70 per cent of the very best domestic wool; the inside of the garment is slightly fleeced.

No. 16K7212 Vests.

Sizes	18	20	22	24	26
Price, each	30c	34c	38c	42c	46c
Sizes		28	30	32	34
Price, each		50c	54c	58c	62c

No. 16K7213 Pantalets to match above vests, open at the sides.

Sizes	18	20	22	24	26
Price, each	30c	34c	38c	42c	46c
Sizes		28	30	32	34
Price, each		50c	54c	58c	62c

Do not fail to state correct size wanted.
If by mail, postage extra, each, 12 cents.

CHILDREN'S HEAVY FLAT KNIT FLEECE LINED SILVER GRAY COLOR COTTON UNDERWEAR.

Extra fleecing on the inside, this garment is very strongly made and finely finished.

No. 16K7214

Sizes	18	20	22
Each	12c	15c	18c
Sizes	24	26	28
Each	20c	22c	24c
Sizes	30	32	34
Each	26c	29c	31c

No. 16K7215 Pantalets to match above vests, open at sides.

Sizes	18	20	22
Each	12c	15c	18c
Sizes	24	26	28
Each	20c	22c	24c
Sizes	30	32	34
Each	26c	29c	31c

Be very careful that you give size.

If by mail, postage extra, each, 12 cents.

CHILDREN'S FLAT KNIT NATURAL GRAY COLOR MERINO WOOL UNDERWEAR.

Thoroughly made and finished.

No. 16K7234 Vests.

Sizes	18	20
Each	24c	27c
Size		22
Each		31c
Sizes	24	26
Each	36c	41c
Sizes	28	30
Each	46c	51c
Sizes	32	34
Each	55c	60c

No. 16K7235 Pantalets to match above vests, open at sides.

Sizes	18	20
Each	24c	27c
Size		22
Each		31c
Sizes	24	26
Each	36c	41c
Sizes	28	30
Each	46c	51c
Sizes	32	34
Price, each	55c	60c

Be very careful to give us correct size.
If by mail, postage extra, each, 12 cents.

FAWN COLOR, FLAT KNIT AUSTRALIAN WOOL UNDERWEAR.

Extra value for children's and misses' wear.

No. 16K7240 Vests.

Sizes	16	18	20	22	24
Price, each	23c	28c	33c	37c	42c
Sizes	26	28	30	32	34
Price, each	47c	52c	56c	61c	66c

No. 16K7241 Pantalets to match above vests, open at the sides.

Sizes	16	18	20	22	24
Price, each	23c	28c	33c	37c	42c
Sizes	26	28	30	32	34
Price, each	47c	52c	56c	61c	66c

We must have size.
If by mail, postage extra, each, 12 cents.

OUR FINEST NATURAL GRAY FLAT KNIT AUSTRALIAN WOOL UNDERWEAR FOR CHILDREN AND MISSES.

No. 16K7260 Vests.

Sizes	16		18
Price, each	33c		38c
Sizes	20		22
Price, each	43c		48c
Sizes	24	26	28
Each	53c	57c	62c
Sizes	30	32	34
Each	67c	71c	76c

No. 16K7261 Pantalets to match above vests, open at sides.

Sizes	16		18
Price, each	33c		38c
Sizes	20		22
Price, each	43c		48c
Sizes	24	26	28
Each	53c	57c	62c
Sizes	30	32	34
Each	67c	71c	76c

Be very positive to give us correct size wanted.
If by mail, postage extra, each, 12 cents.

UNION SUITS, TIGHTS AND SLEEPING GARMENTS.

UNION SUITS, HEAVY RIBBED COTTON, FLEECE LINED, SILVER GRAY COLOR FOR CHILDREN AND MISSES.

Buttons down the front.

No. 16K7305

Length	28	32
Ages	2-3	3-4
Price, each	24c	27c
Length	36	40
Ages	5-6	7-8
Price, each	30c	33c
Length	43	46
Ages	9-10	11-12
Price, each	36c	38c
Length	49	52
Ages	12-13	14-15
Price, each	41c	44c

Do not fail to state size wanted.
If by mail, postage extra, each, 14 cents.

UNION SUITS FOR CHILDREN AND MISSES.

Jersey ribbed, fine cotton, fleece lined, cream color, buttons down the front.

No. 16K7312

Ages	3-4	5-6	7-8	9-10
Length	32	36	40	43
Price, each	37c	40c	43c	46c
Ages		11-12	12-13	14-15
Length		46	49	52
Price, each		49c	51c	54c

What size do you want?
If by mail, postage extra, each, 18 cents.

ADDITIONAL DOUBLE BACK, JERSEY RIBBED COTTON, WOOL FLEECE LINED UNION SUITS FOR CHILDREN.

No. 16K7316 Buttons down the front.

Ages	2-3	4-5	6-7	8-9
Length	28	32	36	40
Price, each	41c	44c	47c	50c
Ages		10-11	12-13	14-15
Length		44	48	52
Price, each		52c	55c	57c

Do not fail to state size wanted.
If by mail, postage extra, each, 16 cents.

JERSEY RIBBED WORSTED WOOL UNION SUITS FOR CHILDREN AND MISSES.

No. 16K7318 Natural gray color. Buttons down the front.

Ages	3	4-5	6-7	8-9	10-11	12-13	14-15
Len.	30	33	36	40	44	48	51
Ea.	83c	83c	83c	83c	99c	99c	99c

We must have the correct size when you order.
If by mail, postage extra, each, 16 cents.

CHILDREN'S AND MISSES' BLACK WORSTED WOOL TIGHTS.

Very practical garment for children at all seasons of the year.

No. 16K7328

Sizes	2	3	4	5
Ages	4	5-6	7-8	9-10
Price, each	47c	51c	55c	59c
Sizes		6	7	8
Ages		11-12	13-14	15-16
Price, each		64c	68c	72c

Be very careful to give correct size.
By mail, postage extra, each, 12c.

BUTTONS ACROSS THE CHEST, JERSEY RIBBED COTTON, FLEECE LINED UNION SUITS FOR CHILDREN AND MISSES. SILVER GRAY COLOR.

No. 16K7322

Sizes	2	3	4	5
Ages	3	4-5	6-7	8-9
Sizes		6	7	8
Ages		10-11	12-13	14-15

Price, each 41c

Do not fail to state size wanted.
If by mail, postage extra, each, 14 cents.

BUTTONS ACROSS THE CHEST, WORSTED WOOL UNION SUITS FOR CHILDREN AND MISSES. SILVER GRAY COLOR.

No. 16K7326

Sizes				2	3
Ages				2-3	4-5
Sizes	4	5	6	7	8
Ages	6-7	8-9	10-11	12-13	14-15

Price, each 79c

Do not fail to state size wanted.
If by mail, postage extra, each, 16 cents.

FLAT KNIT COTTON SLEEPING GARMENTS, FLEECE LINED INSIDE, FOR CHILDREN, SILVER GRAY COLOR.

No. 16K7078 Sizes to fit ages, 1, 2, 4, 6 and 8.

Price, each 41c

Do not fail to state age of child when ordering.

If by mail, postage extra, each, 15 cents.

DR. DENTON'S FAMOUS MERINO WOOL SLEEPING GARMENTS FOR CHILDREN.

No. 16K7079

Ages	2	3	4
Length, ins.	28	30	32
Price, each	55c	55c	70c
Ages	5	6	7
Length, ins.	34	36	38
Price, each	70c	70c	70c
Ages	8	9	10
Length, ins.	40	42	44
Price, each	80c	80c	80c

Do not fail to state age of child when ordering.

If by mail, postage extra, each, 15 cents.

REDUCED PRICES.

BOYS' TWO-PIECE UNDERWEAR.

23c PER GARMENT

BOYS' HEAVY FLAT KNIT COTTON SILVER GRAY COLOR UNDERWEAR.

Fleece lined inside, this is a splendid value for boys. It is very strongly made and will give great service.

No. 16K7442 Undershirts. Sizes, 24 to 34 inches breast measure.
Price, each 23c

No. 16K7443 Drawers to match above shirts. Sizes, 24 to 34 inches waist measure.
Price, each 23c

Be careful to give size wanted.

If by mail, postage extra, each, 15 cents.

44c PER GARMENT

BOYS' NATURAL GRAY WOOL MIXED UNDERWEAR.

This is a big seller and very practical for boys' wear. It is made from a mixture of selected domestic wool and cotton.

No. 16K7452 Undershirts. Sizes, 24 to 34 inches breast measure.
Price, each 44c

No. 16K7453 Drawers to match above shirts. Sizes, 24 to 34 inches waist measure.
Price, each 44c

Do not fail to give size wanted.
If by mail, postage extra, each, 14 cents.

42c PER GARMENT

DR. WRIGHT'S HEAVY FLAT KNIT COTTON UNDERWEAR WITH A WOOL FLEECING INSIDE, MOTTLED GRAY COLOR.

No. 16K7446 Undershirts. Sizes, 24 to 34 inches breast measure.
Price, each 42c

No. 16K7447

Drawers to match above shirts. Sizes, 24 to 34 inches waist measure.

Price, each 42c

Have you given us the correct size you want?

If by mail, postage extra, each, 17 cents.

61c PER GARMENT

AUSTRALIAN WOOL UNDERWEAR FOR BOYS, NATURAL GRAY COLOR.

This garment is made from the highest grade selected Australian wool and is our best value in boys' wool underwear.

No. 16K7456 Undershirts. Sizes, 24 to 34 inches breast measure.
Price, each 61c

No. 16K7457 Drawers to match above shirt. Sizes, 24 to 34 inches waist measure.
Price, each 61c
Give size wanted.
If by mail, postage extra, each, 14 cents.

UNION SUITS FOR BOYS.

42c PER SUIT

BOY'S FLAT KNIT COTTON UNION SUIT, FLEECE LINED INSIDE.

No. 16K7536 This is an extra value, very strongly made, buttons down the entire front, open seat. Jaeger color. Sizes to fit breast measure from 24 to 34 inches.

Do not fail to give size wanted.

Price, per suit 42c
If by mail, postage extra, each, 18 cents.

46c PER SUIT

HEAVY JERSEY RIBBED COTTON UNION SUIT, SLIGHTLY FLEECED INSIDE.

No. 16K7537 This is a very strongly made suit for boys, all seams are double stitched and overcast, buttons down the front, elastic and perfect fitting. Color, silver gray. Sizes to fit breast measure from 24 to 34 inches.

Do not fail to state size wanted.

Price, per suit 46c
If by mail, postage extra, each, 18 cents.

69c PER SUIT

HEAVY JERSEY RIBBED FINE EGYPTIAN COTTON UNION SUIT FOR BOYS.

No. 16K7539 Union Suit made from the finest cotton, good weight, well made and perfectly trimmed, buttons down the entire front. Color, ecru. Sizes to fit breast measure from 24 to 34 inches.

Be very careful to give size wanted.

Price, per suit 69c
If by mail, postage extra, each, 18 cents.

78c PER SUIT

JERSEY RIBBED WORSTED WOOL UNION SUIT FOR BOYS.

No. 16K7540 This suit is very popular with the boys, and it is one of our largest sellers. Made from good quality worsted wool with a very slight mixture of cotton which is placed on the inside of the garment to prevent irritation. Color, mottled gray. Sizes to fit breast measure from 24 to 34 inches.

Be very sure to state size wanted.

Price, per suit 78c
If by mail, postage extra, each, 18 cents.

"TEAR PROOF" HOSIERY FOR CHILDREN WILL WEAR. SEE PAGE 953.

YOUR MONEY WILL BE IMMEDIATELY RETURNED TO YOU FOR ANY GOODS NOT PERFECTLY SATISFACTORY.

591

MEN'S AND BOYS' CLOTHING

SHIRTS, SWEATERS AND CARDIGAN JACKETS, COLLARS AND NECKTIES, BELTS AND SUSPENDERS, HANDKERCHIEFS, MUFFLERS, HATS AND CAPS, LADIES' AND MEN'S GLOVES, TRUNKS AND TRAVELING BAGS

NOTICE OUR PRICES HAVE BEEN MATERIALLY REDUCED. OUR QUALITIES HAVE BEEN RAISED TO THE HIGHEST POSSIBLE STANDARD. THE FINEST POSSIBLE WORKMANSHIP AND FINISH HAS BEEN PUT INTO EVERY GARMENT

THE EXORBITANT PRICES charged and the inferior quality and coarseness of nearly every class of merchandise which most manufacturers have offered during the past twelve months makes this our greatest opportunity and yours to conclusively prove, beyond the question of a doubt, our oft repeated assertion that conditions for which the trusts and combinations are wholly responsible cannot in any way affect our low prices or the standard high quality of our goods; for, with our immense and far reaching organization, we are at all times entirely independent of so called "market conditions" and we are always able to quote the lowest prices on earth for the highest standard qualities.

83c MEN'S LAUNDERED WHITE SHIRTS, PRICED LOWER, BUT BETTER SHIRTS.

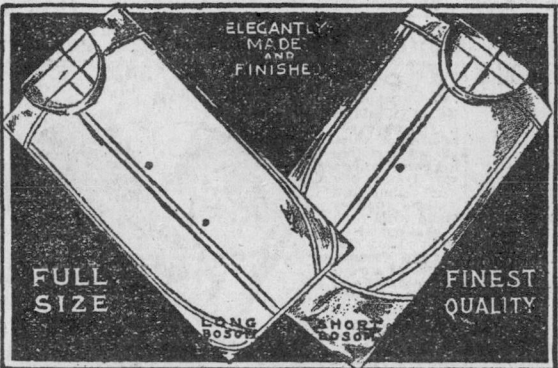

ELEGANTLY MADE AND FINISHED

FULL SIZE — FINEST QUALITY — LONG BOSOM — SHORT BOSOM

HIGHER QUALITIES AND LOWER PRICES than ever before. Notwithstanding so called prevailing "market conditions," the furnishing goods which we here illustrate and describe will be found to be the greatest values ever offered. Our perfect organization, our sources of supply and our wonderful buying power are the explanation.

UNLIMITED GUARANTEE

We guarantee absolutely every article we sell and will refund the full price paid, plus transportation charges, on anything not entirely satisfactory. You take absolutely no risk.

89c PLAIN WHITE OR BLUE PLAITED BOSOM SHIRTS. PRICE REDUCED.

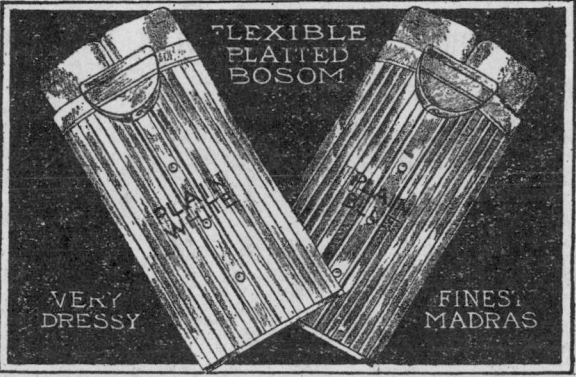

FLEXIBLE PLAITED BOSOM — PLAIN — VERY DRESSY — FINEST MADRAS

Finest quality muslin body, reinforced throughout, three-ply bosom, neckband and wristbands; large full cut body, gathered yoke back, cushion neckband, faced sleeves, flat felled seams. Sizes, 14, 14½, 15, 15½, 16, 16½ and 17. Please state size. Choice of four following styles. Our reduced price, each, now only ... **83c**
If by mail, postage extra, each, 23 cents.

No. 33K7086 Short closed bosom, open back style. Material and make as above described. Sizes 14 to 17. Please state size. Reduced price, each, now only ... **83c**
No. 33K7088 Exactly the same as above style, but with open bosom. Sizes, 14 to 17. Please state size. Reduced price, each, now only ... **83c**
No. 33K7104 Long closed bosom, open back style. Material and make as above described. Sizes 14 to 17. Please state size. Reduced price, each, now only ... **83c**
No. 33K7102 Exactly the same as above style, but with open bosom. Sizes, 14 to 17. Please state size. Reduced price, each, now only ... **83c**

48c UNLAUNDERED WHITE SHIRTS. 67c BETTER QUALITIES AND PRICES REDUCED.

No. 33K7056 Good quality muslin body, cambric bosom Unlaundered Shirts. Reinforced throughout, yoke back, faced sleeves, cushion neckband, medium length closed bosom, open back. Full sizes, 14, 14½, 15, 15½, 16, 16½ and 17. State size wanted. Retail value, 75 cents. Our reduced price, each, now only ... **48c**
(If by mail, postage extra, each, 12 cents.)
No. 33K7062 Finest quality muslin body, medium length cambric bosom, open back, closed front Unlaundered Shirts. Reinforced front and back, yoke back, cushion neckband, faced sleeves, felled seams. Sizes, 14, 14½, 15, 15½, 16, 16½ and 17. State size. $1.00 retail value. Our reduced price, each, now only ... **67c**
If by mail, postage extra, each, 12 cents.

No. 33K7230 Elegant plain blue madras or plain white muslin Plaited Bosom Shirts. The white is made of pure white muslin, soft and fine and of excellent quality, while the blue is of fast color madras of the best grade procurable. These shirts have carefully plaited starched flexible bosoms, extra long and wide, so that edges do not show when worn without a vest. Yoke back, cushion neckband, faced sleeves, attached laundered cuffs. Front closed with three white ocean pearl buttons. Full size and custom fit and workmanship guaranteed. If you are looking for something serviceable as well as dressy, order these shirts. Sizes, 14, 14½, 15, 15½, 16, 16½ and 17. Please give size and state if white or blue is wanted. Retail value, $1.50. Our reduced price, each, now only ... **89c**

89c PLAIN FRONT WHITE OR BLUE MADRAS NEGLIGEE SHIRT. PRICE MATERIALLY REDUCED.
No. 33K7194 Plain Front Negligee Shirt made of fine quality white or blue madras. A fine custom made shirt with attached laundered cuffs and made throughout in the most elegant manner. We particularly recommend this shirt in the white as it is one of the dressiest numbers in our whole line. Sizes, 14, 14½, 15, 15½, 16, 16½, 17 and 17½. State size and color wanted. Our reduced price, each, only ... **89c**

65c FANCY STIFF BOSOM SHIRTS, DETACHED LAUNDERED LINK CUFFS. PRICE REDUCED.
No. 33K7143 A fortunate purchase for spot cash enables us to offer, while they last, 500 dozen men's finest Madras and Percale Fancy Stiff Bosom Shirts, at a price which it is doubtful if we can ever again quote. Neat and handsome shades and patterns, either figured or striped designs. Shirts of the finest finish and most careful detail in make. Made to sell at $1.00 to $1.50. One pair detached laundered link cuffs to match each shirt. Sizes, 14, 14½, 15, 15½, 16, 16½ and 17. Please state size, color and patterns wanted. Our reduced price, each, now only ... (If by mail, postage extra, each, 25 cents.) ... **65c**

48c PLAIN BLUE MADRAS SHIRT. PRICE REDUCED
Two detachable turndown collars to match.

No. 33K7155 Excellent quality fast color plain blue Madras Negligee Shirt with two neat style detachable turndown collars to match. Shirt is cut full size, has gathered yoke back, cushion neckband, and is finished neatly and strongly, double stitched throughout. Popular with railroad men, engineers and stockmen. The collars to our shirts fit the neckbands. Most other makes do not. Sizes, 14, 14½, 15, 15½, 16, 16½ and 17. Please state size. A staple shirt at an exceptional price.
Reduced price, each, now only ... **48c**
If by mail, postage extra, each, 18 cents.

48c PLAIN OR PLAITED BOSOM.
Our Wonderful Leader Equal to Usual $1.00 Quality!
Fine Madras or Percale. — Warranted fast colors.

No. 33K7162 Plain style — FINEST MADRAS — No. 33K7163 Plaited style

State which.

48c FANCY PERCALE SHIRT. PRICE REDUCED.
Two detachable turndown collars to match.

No. 33K7156 A popular style Negligee Shirt with two neat style turndown collars to match. (White linen collar can be worn when desired.) Neat figured and striped effects in medium shades of good quality percales. Shirt is cut full size; made with yoke back, double stitched throughout, cushion neckband, and front closed with pearl buttons. Collars fit the neckband perfectly. Retails at about twice our price. Sizes, 14, 14½, 15, 15½, 16, 16½ and 17. Please state size, colors and patterns preferred.
Reduced price, each, now only ... **48c**
If by mail, postage extra, each, 18 cents.

No. 33K7162 Plain Style Negligee Shirts, made from choicest patterns of finest fast color percales and madras cloths. Handsome figured, checked and striped effects, in light, dark and medium shades. Cut full in size and made with gathered yoke back, faced sleeves, cushion neckband and finished with faced pocket and box plait facing, closed with pearl buttons down the front. Flat felled, double stitched seams throughout. One pair three-ply detached laundered link cuffs to match. In every way these shirts are equal to $1.00 retail values. Sizes are 14, 14½, 15, 15½, 16, 16½ and 17. Please state size and mention shade and pattern wanted when ordering one of the greatest values in our line. This is the plain style, as illustrated by the two shirts at the left in the above illustration.
Our special price, each, only ... (If by mail, postage extra, each, 18 cents.) ... **48c**

No. 33K7163 Stylish plaited bosom, attached cuff Negligee Shirt, as illustrated by the two shirts at the right in above illustration, made from beautiful patterns of fast color percales and fine madras cloths. The shades and patterns and the finish of these shirts are such as were never before shown at less than $1.00 each at retail. This handsome plaited bosom style is made up with the same care in detail and finish and the same full regular size as the plain front style, No. 33K7162, illustrated and described at the left, but this plaited bosom style has no pocket and has attached laundered link cuffs instead of detached cuffs. Sizes, 14, 14½, 15, 15½, 16, 16½ and 17. Please state size, shade and pattern wanted when ordering this exceptional value. Order No. 33K7163, Plaited Bosom.
Our special price, each, only ... (If by mail, postage extra, each, 18 cents.) ... **48c**

REDUCED PRICES FOR THE BEST WORK SHIRTS MADE
INCLUDING GENUINE SATEEN.

WORTH NOTING. Our absolute independence (on account of manufacturing our own shirts) from so called market conditions, enables us to offer these wonderful values. In our recent catalogue we warned our customers against the inferior qualities and mercerized twills and sheetings which are being commonly sold for genuine sateen on account of the scarcity of the latter. As a consequence our sales of these shirts have grown to immense proportions and we are thus enabled to quote more wonderful values than heretofore.

WE GUARANTEE THESE SHIRTS TO BE GENUINE SATEEN. Mercerized sheeting does not compare with genuine sateen in quality, as it washes out and becomes a dingy, sleazy brown, while genuine sateen always retains a high luster and gives the perfect service which has made the reputation for sateen shirts. The four styles shown here are the greatest values ever offered. Many retailers appreciating the fact that our prices are lower than wholesale, purchase these shirts from us.

41c GENUINE BLACK SATEEN SHIRTS. UNDER MANUFACTURER'S COST.

No. 33K7393 A Genuine Black Sateen Shirt that cannot be bought today at wholesale at our low price. You cannot afford to accept cheap mercerized sheeting substitutes for genuine sateens. There is absolutely no comparison in the values. This shirt has the high luster and perfect finish which proves genuine sateen. Full size, strongly made and neatly finished, with pearl buttons and pocket. Sizes, 14½, 15, 15½, 16, 16½ and 17. Please state your size.
Reduced price, each, only........41c
If by mail, postage extra, each, 14 cents.

79c EXTRA WEIGHT GENUINE BLACK SATEEN SHIRTS, PRICE REDUCED.

No. 33K7398 This Genuine Black Sateen Shirt is of extra heavy weight and high luster, finely made, with soft attached collar, gathered yoke back, shaped shoulders, double stitched flat felled seams throughout, faced and extension front and sleeves faced and closed with pearl buttons and shirt is finished with pocket. Big liberal body. Sizes, 14½, 15, 15½, 16, 16½ and 17. Please state size. No retailer can match this value at $1.00. Price, greatly reduced, each, only........79c
If by mail postage extra, each, 17 cents.

96c EXTRA HEAVY GENUINE TAN SATEEN ARMY SHIRT. A "CORKER". PRICE REDUCED.

No. 33K7396 Quality, durability, appearance, weight and workmanship are combined in this Khaki Tan Color Heavy Sateen Shirt, making a most extraordinary value. Note this construction: Large full size, gathered yoke back, shaped shoulders, faced sleeves, faced and extension neckband, soft attached collar and cuffs. Two pockets, closed with pearl buttons, front and cuffs closed with pearl buttons. Double stitched flat felled seams throughout. Sizes, 14½, 15, 15½, 16, 16½ and 17. Please state size.
Our reduced price each, now only........96c
If by mail, postage extra, each, 18 cents.

$1.17 FINEST BLACK SATEEN SHIRT; TIE TO MATCH. PRICE REDUCED.

No. 33K7399 Elegantly made, highest quality Black Sateen Shirt with tie to match. The closest woven, finest finish genuine sateen to be had. Made with yoke back, faced sleeves, attached soft cuffs and collar, finished with string tie, two pockets and double stitched throughout with white, which with the pearl buttons contrasts beautifully with the glossy black fabric. For sportsmen, horsemen, engineers or chauffeurs, the handsomest and most serviceable shirt made. Full sizes, 14½, 15, 15½, 16, 16½ and 17. Please state size.
Reduced price, each, now only........$1.17
If by mail, postage extra, each, 14 cents.

THE MOST DURABLE SHIRTS MADE, IN CASSIMERES, TWILLS, CORDUROYS, ETC. FULL SIZE. SEWED TO STAY.

45c SOFT FINISH COTTON TWILL SHIRTS. PRICE REDUCED BUT NOT QUALITY.

No. 33K7405 We sell annually thousands of dozens of this excellent shirt. Has no equal for service required by lumbermen, miners and all men whose "Falls Twills," known for years as a soft finish cotton material of most wonderful wearing qualities. Neat and pleasing striped and checked patterns. Full size and carefully made with yoke back, double stitched flat felled seams, finished with pocket. Big value if 75 cents each. Sizes, 14½, 15, 15½, 16, 16½ and 17. State size and pattern wanted. Price reduced but not quality of finish.
Our reduced price, each, now only........45c
If by mail, postage extra, each, 18 cents.

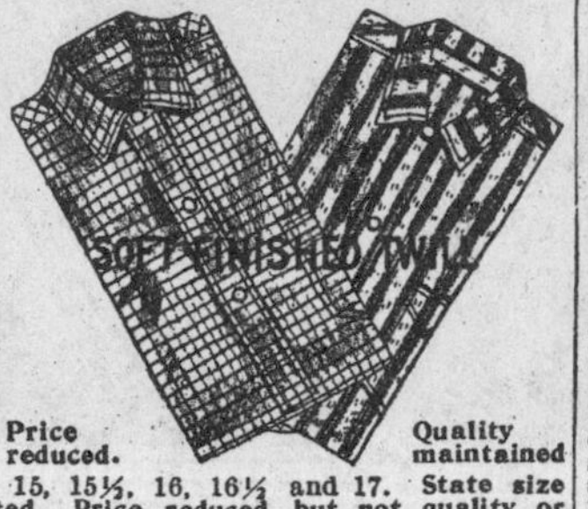

96c FIREMEN'S OR TEAMSTERS' DOUBLE BREASTED BLUE TWILL SHIRT.

No. 33K7391 Warranted fast color Steiffel "A" Blue Cotton Twill Firemen's Regulation Double Breasted Style Shirt, with deep, wide, long pointed collar, buttoned down with large pearl buttons, shirt heavily double stitched throughout, finished with three large white pearl buttons down each side of bosom, deeply stitched, wide, shaped cuffs finished with pearl buttons. Very popular because of its serviceability and construction. Adaptable to many uniformed occupations. Sizes, 14½, 15, 15½, 16, 16½ and 17. State size. 
Reduced price, each, only.. (Postage extra, each, 21c)..96c

73c CELEBRATED "FLANNEL FINISH" COTTON OVERSHIRT.

No. 33K7408 If you have not tried this shirt yet we certainly urge that you do so. Looks like wool flannel and wears better. Made with yoke back, double stitched flat felled seams, pocket, faced sleeves, faced and extension neckband, cut large and full throughout and will not shrink or fade. Sizes, 14½, 15, 15½, 16, 16½ and 17. Gray only, in three shades, light, dark or medium. State size and shade wanted.
Our price, each, only........73c
If by mail, postage extra, each, 17 cents.

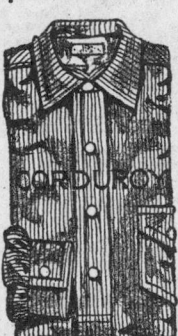

$2.09 WONDERFUL CORDUROY COAT STYLE SHIRT. PRICE REDUCED.

No. 33K7601 Imported drab corduroy, extra heavy and of very fine quality. Has no equal for service required by lumbermen, miners and all men whose work is a severe strain on clothing. Regular coat style, not necessary to pull on or off over the head, but is put on and taken off in the same manner as your coat. Yoke, back double stitched flat felled seams, faced sleeves, front closed with pearl buttons and finished with two pockets with button flaps. Extra large sizes, 14½, 15, 15½, 16, 16½, 17 and 17½. Please state size wanted. Positively a $3.00 retail value. Reduced price, each, only........$2.09
Postage extra, 34c.

42c MADRAS SHIRT, WOVEN COLORS. PRICE REDUCED.

No. 33K7264 Excellent quality woven color madras cloth, medium colored stripes and checks. Made with gathered yoke back, faced and extension neckband, front closed with pearl buttons and finished with a pocket, shaped shoulders, double stitched felled seams and full and regular sizes. Sizes, 14½, 15, 15½, 16, 16½ and 17. State shade and size wanted.
Our reduced price, each, now only........42c
If by mail, postage extra, each, 15 cents.

46c LIGHT WEIGHT FINE FINISH CHAMBRAY. PRICE REDUCED.

No. 33K7265 Fine finish, light weight chambray, color blue or tan. A light weight cotton shirt in a material of extra strength. Gathered yoke back, faced and extension neckband. Finished with pocket and carefully made throughout. Full sizes, 14½, 15, 15½, 16, 16½ and 17. Please state size and color wanted.
Our reduced price, each, now only........46c
If by mail, postage extra, each, 15c.

$1.22 CORDUROY SHIRT. SERVICE WITHOUT LIMIT.

No. 33K7603 Made from medium weight drab, gray or brown corduroy, unequaled for wear. Double stitched, gathered yoke back, pearl buttons, faced and extension neckband and finished with one pocket. Extra full cut. Probably the cheapest shirt on the market because of the practically unlimited service which it will give. Sizes, 14½, 15, 15½, 16, 16½ and 17. State size and color wanted. Retail value, $1.75.
Reduced price, each, now only........$1.22
If by mail, postage extra, each, 22 cents.

MEN'S FANCY CASSIMERE AND FLANNEL OVERSHIRTS.

45c EXCELLENT WEARING CASSIMERE OVERSHIRT. PRICE REDUCED.

No. 33K7401 Outing Flannel Twills for wear and service, never equaled at the price. Soft finish but strong and durable. Yoke back double sewed, full sizes and finished with a pocket. Neat stripes or checks. Sizes 14½, 15, 15½, 16, 16½, 17. State size and patterns wanted.
Reduced price, each, only........45c
If by mail, postage extra, each, 18c.

96c CASSIMERE OVERSHIRT WITH NECKTIE. PRICE REDUCED.

No. 33K7580 Ensley's cotton cassimere, celebrated for wear. Neat stripes and checks in medium shades. Double stitched, yoke back, faced sleeves, finished with a pocket and has necktie to match. Sizes, 14½, 15, 15½, 16, 16½ and 17. State size. Reduced price each, only..96c
Postage extra, 17c.

$1.48 FANCY TRIMMED REPELLANT FLANNEL SHIRT. PRICE GREATLY REDUCED.

No. 33K7575 Medium Weight Extra Fine Australian Wool Flannel Shirt, plain blue, red or green, with contrasting fancy silk embroidered facing, finished with pearl buttons at points of collar and down the front. Made with gathered yoke back, double stitched felled seams, faced and extension neckband, faced sleeves and full size. Sizes, 14½, 15, 15½, 16, 16½ and 17. State size and color wanted.
Reduced price only, $1.48
If by mail, postage extra, each, 13c.

$1.59 FANCY FLANNEL SHIRT. PRICE REDUCED.

No. 33K7582 Highest Grade Imported Fancy Union Flannel Shirt, warm and serviceable. Neat shades in stripes, light, dark and medium. Custom workmanship and fit. Full sizes, 14½, 15, 15½, 16, 16½ and 17. State size and shade wanted. Our reduced price, each only, $1.59
Postage extra, 20 cents.

$1.58 FANCY FLANNEL SHIRT WITHOUT COLLAR.

No. 33K7584 Fancy Lorraine Flannel Shirt, without collar but with non-shrinkable neckband. Blue or tan stripes and figures of the newest and neatest designs. Custom made. Full sizes, 14½, 15, 15½, 16, 16½ and 17. State size, shade and pattern wanted. Reduced price only, $1.58
If by mail, postage extra, each, 15c.

SEE OUR WONDERFUL COTTON WORK SHIRT OFFER ON PAGES 966 AND 967.

FLANNEL AND JERSEY OVERSHIRTS ═══ REDUCED PRICES ═══ MEN'S AND BOYS' NIGHTSHIRTS

Inferior grades of flannel are commonly used because of the cheapness in price, and as they have the same appearance before being worn and washed as standard qualities, you cannot be too careful in buying Flannel Shirts.

$1.08 CHALLENGE OFFER BLUE FLANNEL SHIRTS. $1.23
Single Breasted   REDUCED PRICES.   Double Breasted

STANDARD FLANNEL ONLY.

We do not use one yard of flannel that is not of a standard and reliable quality, and we guarantee every shirt to hold its color and give satisfaction, and if properly washed will not shrink.

$2.69 FINEST FLANNEL SHIRT. No. 33K7574 Highest Standard, imported flannel. Gathered yoke back, felled seams, double stitched, faced sleeves, pearl buttons, faced pocket, shaped shoulders. Regular custom make. Colors, gray, tan or brown. Sizes, 14½, 15, 15½, 16, 16½ and 17. Please state size and color. Price, each.... **$2.69** Postage extra, each, 22 cents.

No. 33K7538 Single Breasted Style Blue Flannel Shirt. We cannot recommend it too highly. Extra large, strongly made and carefully finished, will not shrink or fade, and after being washed has the same smooth and handsome finish as when first worn. Sizes, 14½, 15, 15½, 16, 16½ and 17. State size. Reduced price, each, only **$1.08** If by mail, postage extra, each, 25 cents.

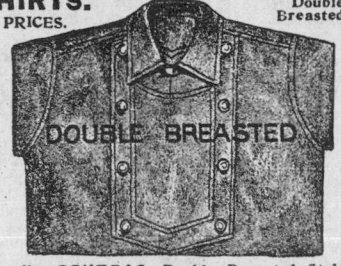

No. 33K7546 Double Breasted Style Leader Blue Flannel Shirt. Has the same careful workmanship, full and regular size and the same in every way as our No. 33K7538, except that this is the double breasted style. Sizes, 14½, 15, 15½, 16, 16½ and 17. Please state size. Reduced price, each, now only **$1.23** If by mail, postage extra, each, 28 cents.

$2.37 FIREMEN'S SPECIAL FLANNEL. Price Reduced. No. 33K7556 Firemen's or Teamsters' Double Breasted Blue Flannel Shirt. Santa Rosa Flannel. Long pointed collar, points buttoned down with large pearl buttons. Faced sleeves and extra wide cuffs, heavily double stitched and closed with three large pearl buttons. Highest quality 6-ounce blue California flannel. Sizes, 14½, 15, 15½, 16, 16½ and 17. Please state your size. Reduced price, each, only...... **$2.37** If by mail, postage extra, each, 26 cents.

$1.68 5 oz. BLUE CALIFORNIA FLANNEL SHIRTS. **$1.96** 6 oz.

No. 33K7539 Five-ounce pure wool California blue flannel Shirts. Best make. Sizes, 14½, 15, 15½, 16, 16½ and 17. State size. Price, each, only...... **$1.68** If by mail, postage extra, each, 21 cents.

No. 33K7541 Six-ounce California Blue Flannel, pure wool. Best make. Sizes, 14½, 15, 15½, 16, 16½ and 17. State size wanted. Reduced price, each, only.... **$1.96** If by mail, postage extra, each, 23 cents.

Qualities Improved   Prices Reduced

$1.68 5 oz. COLORED CALIFORNIA FLANNEL SHIRTS. **$1.96** 6 oz.

No. 33K7568 Five-ounce mixed brown or gray California flannel. Sizes, 14½, 15, 15½, 16, 16½ and 17. State size and color. Price, each.... **$1.68** If by mail, postage extra, each, 20 cents.

No. 33K7569 Six-ounce Standard California Flannel. Brown only. Full sizes, 14½, 15, 15½, 16, 16½ and 17. Be sure to state size. Reduced price, each.... **$1.96**

FINEST PURE WOOL FLANNELS   PRICES REDUCED

If by mail, postage extra, each, 24 cents.

$1.78 5 oz. DOUBLE BREASTED FLANNEL SHIRTS. **$2.11** 6 oz.

No. 33K7550 Five-ounce Double Breasted Blue California Flannel Shirts. Sizes, 14½, 15, 15½, 16, 16½ and 17. State size. Price, each, only.... **$1.78** If by mail, postage extra, each, 22 cents.

No. 33K7552 Six-ounce double breasted blue California flannel. Sizes, 14½, 15, 15½, 16, 16½ and 17. State size. Price, each, only **$2.11**

FINEST PURE WOOL FLANNELS   PRICES REDUCED

If by mail, postage extra, each, 25 cents.

78c LEADER FLANNEL SHIRTS, REGULAR AND EXTRA SIZES. **88c**

No. 33K7535 Wool mixed heavy blue, brown or gray flannel. Full sizes, 14½, 15, 15½, 16, 16½ and 17. State size and color. Reduced price, ea. **78c** If by mail, postage extra, each, 23 cents.

EXTRA SIZES No. 33K7537 Same as above, blue only. Sizes, 17½, 18, 18½ and 19. State size. Reduced price, ea. **88c** If by mail, postage extra, each, 27c.

$1.38 BUFFALO CALIFORNIA FLANNEL OVERSHIRTS. **$1.92**

No. 33K7586 Heavy California Flannel Overshirt. Checked patterns, blue and black, white and black or red and black. Sizes, 14½, 15, 15½, 16, 16½ and 17. State size and color. Price, each. **$1.38** Postage, 23c.

No. 33K7587 Same as above, but heaviest made. Sizes, 14½, 15, 15½, 16, 16½ and 17. State size and color. Price, each **$1.92** If by mail, postage extra, each, 25c.

87c PLAITED FRONT COLORED FLANNEL SHIRT.

No. 33K7573 Golden Star Flannel, one of the best flannels known. Cleanly and carefully made with fancy tape trimmed plaited bosom. Colors, blue, brown or gray. Sizes, 14½, 15, 15½, 16, 16½ and 17. Please state size and color wanted. $1.25 retail value. Reduced price, each, only.... **87c** If by mail, postage extra, each, 25c

$2.37 HIGH GRADE COLORED FLANNEL SHIRT.

No. 33K7571 Extra Fine Heaviest Weight High Grade California Flannel Shirt of finest combed Australian wool. Best workmanship and finish throughout. Colors, gray or brown. Sizes, 14½, 15, 15½, 16, 16½ and 17. Please state size and color. Reduced price, each.... **$2.37** If by mail, postage extra, each, 21 cents.

91c LEADER DOUBLE BREASTED BLUE FLANNEL SHIRT.

No. 33K7544 Double Breasted Blue Flannel Shirt. Contains just enough cotton to insure wearing qualities and prevent shrinkage. Full size and carefully made. Sizes, 14½, 15, 15½, 16, 16½ and 17. State your size. Reduced price, each, only.... **91c** If by mail, postage extra, each, 25 cents.

41c 58c 78c JERSEY SHIRTS.

No. 33K7590 Plain Blue Jersey Shirts. Full size and well made. Sizes, 14½ to 17. Please state size. Our price, each, only.... **41c**

No. 33K7589 Fine Gauge Blue Jersey Shirt. Full size, strongly made. Sizes, 14½ to 17. State size. Reduced price, each, only.... **58c**

No. 33K7591 Wool Fleeced Blue or Gray Jersey Shirt. Full sizes, 14½ to 17. State color and size. Reduced price, each, only **78c** Jersey shirts, by mail, postage extra, each, 25 cents.

HEAVY BLUE JERSEY

Do not fail to state size when ordering shirts.

MEN'S AND BOYS' NIGHTSHIRTS AND PAJAMAS.
Cut large and loose and full length. Nightshirts are not made in half sizes.

43c MEN'S WHITE MUSLIN NIGHTSHIRTS. PRICES REDUCED. **67c**

No. 33K7606 Men's Excellent Nightshirt, with collar and pocket and fancy faced front. Large, full sizes, 14, 15, 16, 17 and 18. Reduced price, each, only.... **43c** If by mail, postage extra, each, 12 cents.

45c MEN'S DOMET FLANNEL NIGHTSHIRTS. **83c**

No. 33K7622 Good Quality Flannelette or Domet Nightshirt, with collar. Well made and full length. Fancy stripes. Sizes, 14, 15, 16, 17 and 18. State size. Our price, each, only.... **45c** If by mail, postage extra, each, 14 cents.

46c DOUBLE BREASTED JERSEY SHIRTS. **96c**

No. 33K7592 Leader Double Breasted Blue Jersey Shirts. Good quality and well made. Sizes, 14½ to 17. State size. Price, each.... **46c**

No. 33K7599 Wool Fleeced Blue or Gray Double Breasted Jersey Shirts. Best quality and make and full sizes, 14½ to 17. State size and color. Reduced price, each, only. Either number, if by mail, postage extra, each, 30c. **96c**

DOUBLE BREASTED BLUE JERSEY

96c MEN'S PAJAMAS.

No. 33K7646 Military Cut Flannel Pajamas, neat patterns. Sizes, 14, 15, 16, 17 and 18. State size. Coat and trousers. Per suit, only.... **96c**

No. 33K7649 French Flannelette Military Pajamas. Coat and trousers. Neat patterns. Sizes, 14, 15, 16, 17 and 18. State size. Per suit, only **$1.45** If by mail, postage extra, per suit, 20c.

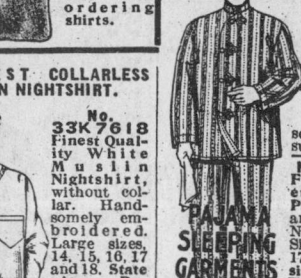

Prices Reduced   PAJAMA SLEEPING GARMENTS

$1.45 MEN'S PAJAMAS.

No. 33K7612 Extra Quality White Muslin Nightshirt. Full size and length. Collar and pocket and fancy front. Sizes, 14, 15, 16, 17 and 18. State size. Reduced price, each, only.... **67c** If by mail, postage extra, each, 13 cents.

No. 33K7628 Extra Heavy Domet Flannel Nightshirt. Large and extra long. Collar and pocket. Striped patterns. Sizes, 14, 15, 16, 17 and 18. State size. Reduced price, each, only.... **83c** If by mail, postage extra, each, 19 cents.

BOYS' NIGHTSHIRTS.

39c BOYS' FLANNEL NIGHTSHIRTS. **53c**

No. 33K7791 Good Quality Domet Flannel Nightshirt with collar, full size. Neat stripes. Sizes, 12, 13 and 14. State size. Price, each.... **39c** Postage, extra, each, 11 cents.

No. 33K7792 Heavy Extra Fine Quality French Flannelette Nightshirt, stripes or checks. Sizes, 12, 13 and 14. State size and pattern. Reduced price, each, only.... **53c** If by mail, postage extra, each, 13c.

39c BOYS' MUSLIN NIGHTSHIRT. No. 33K7781 Good Quality Muslin Nightshirts, full size and full length. Collar and pocket and fancy front. Sizes, 12, 13 and 14. State size. Price, each, only.... **39c** If by mail, postage extra, each, 10c.

97c FINEST COLLARLESS MUSLIN NIGHTSHIRT.

Prices Reduced. No. 33K7618 Finest Quality White Muslin Nightshirt, without collar. Handsomely embroidered. Large sizes, 14, 15, 16, 17 and 18. State size. Reduced price, each, only.... **97c** If by mail, postage extra, each, 14c.

IMPROVED QUALITIES = BOYS' SHIRTS AND SWEATERS = REDUCED PRICES

THE BEST MADE AND BEST WEARING BOYS' SHIRTS THAT CAN BE PRODUCED AT THE LOWEST PRICES EVER QUOTED. BIGGER VALUES THAN EVER BEFORE.

42c BOYS' FANCY MERCERIZED BOSOM NEGLIGEE SHIRT. IMPROVED QUALITY. PRICE GREATLY REDUCED.

No. 33K7680 Body of Finest Percales with handsome black, blue or pink stripes, checks and figures on white backgrounds, while the bosom is of Garner's mercerized Ionia cloth of patterns and shades which match body. Warranted fast colors. Gathered yoke back, front closed with pearl buttons. Perfect fitting and full liberal sizes, 12, 12½, 13, 13½ and 14. Be sure to state size and color or wanted. Good value at 75 cents retail. Our reduced price, each, now only............42c
If by mail, postage extra, each, 10 cents.

39c BOYS' NEGLIGEE SHIRT WITH TWO DETACHED COLLARS. PRICE REDUCED.

No. 33K7678 Mothers appreciate the advantages of this shirt with two neat style detachable turndown collars to match. Materials used are of the best percales, and the shirt is made up in the strongest and most serviceable manner possible, and is finished with a pocket. Comes in medium shades and attractive striped designs. Sizes, 12, 12½, 13, 13½ and 14. Be sure to state the size. A regular 75-cent shirt. Our reduced price, each, now only....39c
If by mail, postage extra, each, 10 cents.

36c BOYS' LEADER FANCY NEGLIGEE SHIRT.

PRICE REDUCED.

No. 33K7675 Boys' Negligee Shirt of excellent quality non-shrinkable fast color madras and percales. Pretty patterns in figures, stripes and checks, light, dark or medium shades. Made with gathered yoke back, double stitched throughout, front closed with pearl buttons and finished with pocket. A well made shirt which cannot be retailed at less than 50 cents. Extraordinary value at our low price. Sizes, 12, 12½, 13, 13½ and 14. State size and colors wanted. 
Our reduced price, each, only.............36c
If by mail, postage extra, each, 9 cents.

72c BOYS' PLAIN WHITE OR NEAT FIGURED SHIRTS, ATTACHED CUFFS.

No. 33K7683 A Strictly Dress Negligee Shirt for Boys. Plain white corded madras of beautiful quality or if preferred white madras neatly figured in blue, black or pink. Excellent wear and neat appearance. Made with yoke back, faced sleeves, attached laundered cuffs and closed with pearl buttons. Sizes, 12½, 13, 13½ and 14. State size and color wanted. Reduced price, each 72c
If by mail, postage extra, each, 10 cents.

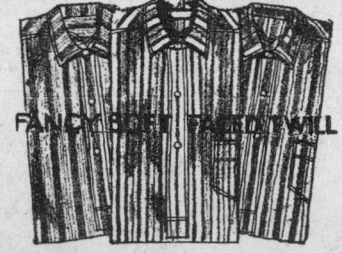

42c BOYS' SOFT FACED TWILL SHIRT. SAME QUALITY, REDUCED PRICE.

No. 33K7702 Boys' Soft Finish Cotton Twill Shirts, in neat stripes and checks. A fortunate purchase of this excellent material which has stood the severest test of hard wear explains wholly the reduced price. Strongest and best make. Sizes, 12½, 13, 13½ and 14. State size and patterns wanted. Our reduced price, each, only. (If by mail, postage extra, each, 12c.) 42c

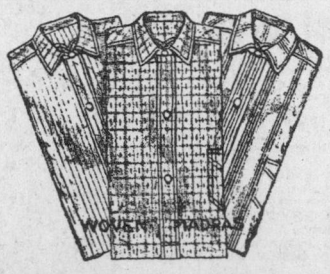

39c BOYS' WOVEN COLOR MADRAS SOFT SHIRT.

No. 33K7685 Extra value in Boys' soft woven color Madras Shirts. Will not fade or shrink. Gathered yoke back, double stitched throughout, and finished with pocket. Stripes and checks in neat colors. Sizes, 12½, 13, 13½ and 14. State size and color. Our price, each, only. 39c
If by mail, postage extra, each, 10 cents.

72c BOYS' PLAIN COLOR PONGEE SHIRT WITH SOFT COLLAR.

No. 33K7692 Beautiful Cream White or Tan Shirt of Pongee, soft as silk and excellent for wear. Yoke back, soft attached collar and cuffs, faced sleeves, pearl buttons and finished with a pocket. The neatest negligee for boys. Sizes, 12½, 13, 13½ and 14. State size and color wanted. Our price, each, only... 72c
If by mail, postage extra, each, 10 cents.

38c BOYS' BLACK SATEEN. PRICE REDUCED.

No. 33K7706 Boys' Guaranteed Best Sateen Shirt. Well made, finished with pocket, yoke back and double stitched. Sizes, 12½, 13, 13½ and 14. State size. Our reduced price each now only...........38c
If by mail, postage extra, each, 6 cents.

37c BOYS' MILITARY CHAMBRAY. PRICE REDUCED.

No. 33K7709 Boys' Standard Defiance Chambray Work Shirts (same as men's, page 966). Military style. Stripes and checks. Sizes, 12½, 13, 13½ and 14. State the size. Our reduced price, each, only.....37c
If by mail, postage extra, each, 10c.

37c BOYS' BLACK AND WHITE DRILL. PRICE REDUCED.

No. 33K7710 Boys' Black and White 2.85 Weight Drill Work Shirts (same as men's, page 967). Exceptional service. Sizes, 12½, 13, 13½ and 14. Retail price, 50 cents. State size. Our reduced price, each, now only.....37c
If by mail, postage extra, each, 10c

37c BOYS' FANCY CHAMBRAY. PRICE REDUCED.

No. 33K7711 Boys' Neat Fancy Pattern Chambray Work Shirts (same as men's, page 966). Best for wear and service. Sizes, 12½, 13, 13½ and 14. State size wanted. Retail price, 50 cents. Our reduced price, each, now 37c only.....
If by mail, postage extra, each, 10c

37c BOYS' BLUE OR TAN CHAMBRAY. PRICE REDUCED.

No. 33K7712 Boys' Defiance Blue or Tan Chambray Work Shirts (same as men's, page 966). Sizes, 12½, 13, 13½ and 14. State size. Our reduced price, each, now 37c
If by mail, postage extra, each, 10c.

BOY'S FLANNEL AND JERSEY SHIRTS.

35c BOYS' BLUE JERSEY SHIRT. Price Reduced.

No. 33K7732 Boys' Heavy Blue Jersey Overshirts, fleece lined and strongly made. Sizes, 12½, 13, 13½ and 14. State size wanted. Better than shirts that retail at 50 cents. Reduced price, each...35c
If by mail, postage extra, each, 16 cents.

71c BOYS' COLORED FLANNEL SHIRT. PRICE REDUCED.

No. 33K7722 Fine Wool Mixed Flannel. Colors, plain blue, brown, gray or tan. If properly washed will not shrink. Strongly and well made. Sizes, 12½, 13, 13½ and 14. State size and color wanted. Reduced price, each...71c
If by mail, postage extra, 17 cents.

BOYS' AND CHILDREN'S SWEATERS.

$1.10 BOYS' COAT SWEATER. PRICE REDUCED.

No. 33K7883 Boys' Pride Coat Style Sweater. Fine wool and worsted. Colors, oxford, cardinal or navy blue. Sizes, 24, 26, 28, 30, 32 and 34 inches breast measure. State size and color wanted. Price, each $1.10
If by mail, postage extra, each, 14 cents.

45c LIGHT WEIGHT JERSEY.

No. 33K7895 Boys' Fine Gauge Jersey Sweater. Very elastic and close fitting. Blue or gray. Fast colors and non-shrinkable. An unequaled garment for boys' hard wear. Sizes 24, 26, 28, 30, 32 and 34 inches breast measure. State size and color wanted. Reduced price, each..45c
If by mail, postage extra, each, 10 cents.

82c State size and color.

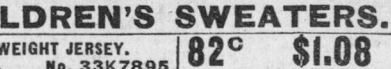

$1.08 $1.58 ROLL NECK SWEATERS.

No. 33K7860 Boys' Wool Mixed Sweaters. Colors, blue, black or cardinal. Sizes, 24, 26, 28, 30, 32 and 34. Price, each, only 82c
No. 33K7862 Boys' Worsted Sweater. Colors, blue, black or cardinal. Sizes, 24 to 34 breast measure. Reduced price, each $1.08
No. 33K7866 Wool Sweater. Colors, cardinal, navy blue or black. Sizes 24 to 34. Price, each, If by mail, postage extra, 18c. $1.58

78c BOYS' FANCY PLAITED FRONT FLANNEL SHIRT.

No. 33K7721 Boys' Wool Mixed Flannel, blue, brown or gray, fancy trimmed plaited bosom. Sizes, 12½, 13, 13½ and 14. State size and color wanted. Reduced price, each. 78c
If by mail, postage extra, 18c.

78c BOYS' DOUBLE BACK AND FRONT BLUE FLANNEL SHIRT.

No. 33K7726 Boys' Flannel Shirt, double back and front style, double warmth and double wear. Sizes, 12½, 13, 13½ and 14. State size. Price, each...78c
If by mail, postage extra, each, 21 cents.

53c CHILD'S WOOL SWEATER. PRICE REDUCED.

No. 33K7885 Child's Ribbed Sweater, buttoned at neck and shoulders. Colors, navy, royal blue, white or scarlet. Ages, 3 to 6 years only. State age and color wanted. Reduced price, each, only... 53c 
If by mail, postage extra, each, 8c.

81c BUSTER BROWN GOLF COAT.

PRICE REDUCED.

No. 33K7891 All Wool Fancy Knitted Golf Coat, trimmed with fancy buttons and attached belt. Contrasting colored vertical stripes, scarlet with white or royal blue with red stripes. Ages, 3 to 6 years only. Be sure to state age and color wanted. Reduced price, each, only......81c
If by mail, postage extra, each, 12c.

68c CHILD'S SWEATER. PRICE REDUCED.

No. 33K7890 Child's Pure Wool Worsted Sweater, plain navy blue, royal blue, white or scarlet. Buttons at neck and shoulders, for 3 to 6 years only. State age and color wanted. Reduced price, each, 68c
Postage extra, each, 10c.

MEN'S SWEATERS, JERSEYS, CARDIGAN JACKETS
AND SMOKING JACKETS—MEN'S AND BOYS' BELTS
REDUCED PRICES

Our Sweaters are made of the best shrunken yarns, closely knitted to keep their shape.

Comparing quality for quality you will find that our prices are much lower than usually quoted for similar grades.

48c LIGHT WEIGHT JERSEY SWEATER

No. 33K7850 Fine Closely Knitted Jersey Sweater. Neatly and cleanly made with over-stitched inner seams. Full size but close fitting and elastic. For warm weather wear when engaged in athletic sports or other active pursuits these garments are practically indispensible. Fast colors, GRAY or BLUE. Sizes, 34, 36, 38, 40, 42 and 44 inches breast measure. Please state size and color wanted. Retails at 75 cents to $1.00. Reduced price, each, now only.....48c

If by mail, postage extra, each, 10 cents.

$1.87 FINE AUSTRALIAN WOOL SWEATER.

State and Size Wanted

No. 33K7812 Fine Heavy Australian Combed Wool Yarn Sweater with heavily ribbed neck, tail and cuffs. Colors, BLACK, RED, GRAY, BLUE, WHITE or TAN. Sizes, 34, 36, 38, 40, 42 and 44 inches breast measure. State size and color wanted. Actually worth $3.00 at retail. Reduced price, each, only..$1.87 If by mail, postage extra, each, 29 cents.

Price Reduced

$3.48 HEAVIEST SHAKER RIBBED SWEATER.

State Size and Color Wanted

No. 33K7818 Finest and Heaviest Athletic Sweater, made of Australian wool yarn, in NAVY, BLUE, GRAY or BUCKSKIN TAN. Sizes, 36, 38, 40, 42 and 44 inches breast measure. Be sure to state size and color. This is the regular $5.00 athletic sweater. Reduced price, each, only..$3.48 If by mail, postage extra, each, 32c.

$1.48 FINEST COAT STYLE JERSEY. RETAILS AT $2.50.

State size wanted

No. 33K7855 Medium Weight Coat Style Jersey Sweater of fine worsted yarn in Gray only. A handsome and very popular garment, the convenience of which you will have occasion to appreciate every time you wear it. Elegantly made and closed with large pearl buttons. Sizes, 34, 36, 38, 40 and 42 inches breast measure. Reduced price, each, only $1.48 Postage extra, each, 10 cents.

83c MEN'S SERVICEABLE SWEATER.

No. 33K7804 Heavy Ribbed Non-shrinkable Three-fourths Wool Sweater. Will give excellent service. Please state size and color wanted

PRICE REDUCED

Colors, BLACK, GRAY, MAROON Sizes, 34, 36, 38, 40, 42 and 44 inches breast measure. Reduced price, each, only..83c. If by mail, postage extra, each, 22c.

87c DOUBLE KNITTED COAT SWEATER.

No. 33K7849 A popular Coat Style Sweater at a price never before quoted on this style of garment. Colors, BLACK or OXFORD GRAY. Sizes, 36, 38, 40, 42 and 44 inches breast measure. State size and color wanted. Reduced price, each, only....87c If by mail, postage extra, each, 24 cents.

PRICE REDUCED

$1.58 FANCY WORSTED SWEATER.

No. 33K7844 Men's Fancy Honeycomb Knitted Sweater. Alternate stripes, NAVY and CARDINAL, BLACK and CARDINAL, GREEN and CARDINAL. Sizes, 34, 36, 38, 40, 42 and 44 inches breast measure. State size and color combinations wanted when ordering. Reduced price each, only, $1.58 If by mail, postage extra, each, 23c.

$2.19 FINEST PURE WORSTED COAT SWEATER.

State size and color wanted. Price Reduced

No. 33K7847 Highest Grade Pure Worsted Sweater. Heavy shaker ribbed. Will highly please because of its many advantages, as well as its excellent quality. Colors, BROWN, BLACK or GRAY. Sizes, 36, 38, 40, 42 and 44 inches breast measure. Reduced price, each, only..$2.19 If by mail, postage extra, each, 30c.

$2.77 HEAVY WEIGHT WOOL SWEATER.

No. 33K7816 Knitted very heavy, extra fine Australian yarn, Pure Worsted Sweater.

State size and color wanted

Colors, NAVY BLUE, BLACK, CARDINAL or WHITE. Sizes, 34, 36, 38, 40, 42 and 44 inches breast measure. One of the best made. Reduced price, each, only $2.77 If by mail, postage extra, each, 28c.

PRICE REDUCED

CARDIGAN JACKETS AND SMOKING JACKETS

$4.39 MEN'S SMOKING JACKET.

No. 33K7899 Neat Double Texture Smoking Jacket, with faced collar and cuffs and pockets, showing the plaid back of the goods. Edges are neatly finished with fancy silk cord to harmonize with the color of the jacket and front is closed with fancy silk cord straps or frogs. Colors, OXFORD GRAY, BROWN, BLUE or GREEN. Sizes, 34, 36, 38, 40, 42 and 44 inches breast measure. A convenient smoking jacket that every man will appreciate. State size and color wanted.

Price Reduced

Reduced price, each only....$4.39 If by mail, postage extra, each, 24 cents.

$1.98 JERSEY KNITTED COAT No. 33K7918

PRICE REDUCED

Made from Black Stockinet Jersey Knitted Cloth. Heavy weight and perfect fitting. Single breasted with double stitched pockets. Made without lining and seams all taped. Sizes, 34, 36, 38, 40, 42 and 44 inches breast measure. State size when ordering. Our reduced price, each, $1.98

If by mail, postage extra, each, 35c.

$1.62 WOOL CARDIGAN JACKET.

No. 33K7905 BLACK or BROWN Wool Cardigan Jacket. Sizes, 34, 36, 38, 40 and 42 inches breast measure. State size and color wanted. Worth $2.00 or more at retail. Price, each, only $1.62 If by mail, postage extra, each, 21 cents.

$1.92 AND $2.89 DOUBLE BREASTED CARDIGAN JACKETS.

No. 33K7910 Double Breasted BLACK or BROWN Worsted Cardigan Jacket in sizes 34 to 42 inches breast measure. State size and color wanted. Reduced price, each, only..$1.92 If by mail, postage extra, each, 28c.

No. 33K7912 Exceptionally Fine Quality All Worsted Double Breasted Jacket. Color, black only. Sizes, 34 to 42 inches breast measure. Be sure to state size. Reduced price, each, only..$2.89 If by mail, postage extra, each, 30c.

PRICE REDUCED

$2.36 GERMAN KNITTED WOOL JACKET.

PRICE REDUCED

No. 33K7908 Single Breasted All Wool Jacket, fancy raised cord effect. Color, solid black. Sizes, 34 to 42 inches breast measure. Please state size wanted. Reduced price, each, only.....$2.36 If by mail, postage extra, each, 25 cents.

MEN'S BELTS.

Sizes, Waist Measure, 30, 32, 34, 36, 38, 40, 42.

If by mail, postage extra, each, 7 cents.

No. 33K8890 Men's Fancy Embossed English Calf Belt, 1¼ inches wide. Colors, GRAY or OLIVE. Sizes, 30 to 42 inches waist measure. A beauty. State size and color wanted. Reduced price, each, now only 43c

No. 33K8877 Fancy Orange Grain Leather Belt, 1¼ inches wide. Sizes, 30, 32, 34, 36, 38, 40, 42 inches waist measure. State size. Reduced price, each, only 21c

No. 33K8886 Imitation Seal Embossed Belt, black only, 1 inch wide. Suede lined. Neat new buckle. Sizes, 30 to 42 inches waist measure. State size wanted. Reduced price, each, only...........46c

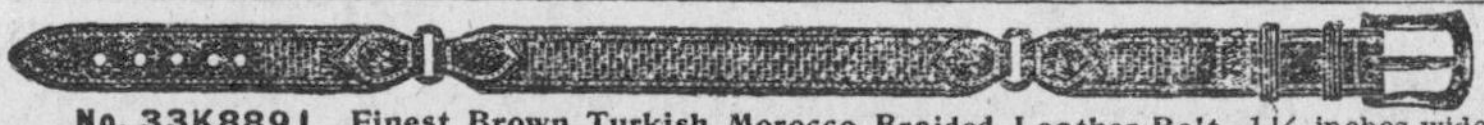

No. 33K8891 Finest Brown Turkish Morocco Braided Leather Belt, 1¼ inches wide. Sizes, 30, 32, 34, 36, 38, 40, 42 inches waist measure. Give size. Reduced price, each, now only 69c

No. 33K8882 Handsome Alligator Embossed Belt, 1¼ inches wide. Suede lined. Colors, BLACK, TAN or GRAY. Sizes, 30, 32, 34, 36, 38, 40, 42 inches waist measure. Be sure to state size and color wanted. One of our handsomest styles. Reduced price, each, now only 48c

No. 33K8876 Men's Fancy Incised Surface Leather Belt, 1 inch wide. Colors, BLACK or BROWN. Sizes, 30 to 42 inches waist measure. State size and color wanted. Reduced price, each, only.........23c

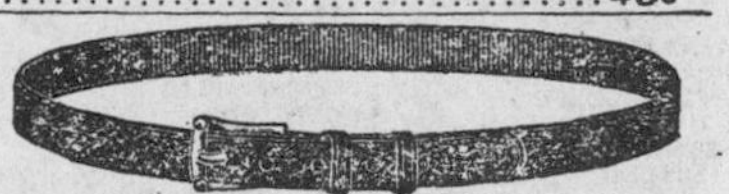

No. 33K8893 Genuine Morocco Leather Belt, calf lined, 1 inch wide with handsome new buckle. Colors, BLACK or BROWN. Sizes, 30, 32, 34, 36, 38, 40, 42 inches waist measure. Exceptional value. State size and color wanted. Reduced price, each, only..........69c

No. 33K8885 Braided Grain Leather Belt, 1¼ inches wide. Colors, BLACK or TAN. Sizes, 30, 32, 34, 36, 38, 40, 42 inches waist measure. State size and color wanted. Reduced price, each, only............39c

BOYS' BELTS.

Sizes, 24 to 30 inches. Don't fail to give waist measure.

If by mail, postage extra, each, 7 cents.

No. 33K8894 Boys' Leather Belt, 1 inch wide. Color, brown only. Sizes, 24 to 30 inches waist measure. Please state size wanted. Special price, each, only............15c

No. 33K8897 Boys' BLACK or BROWN Incised Surface Leather Belt, 1 inch wide. Handsome buckle. Sizes, 24 to 30 inches waist measure. State size and color wanted. Reduced price, each, only............19c

MEN'S AND BOYS' SUSPENDERS AT REDUCED PRICES

Men's Suspenders 36 ins. long | **WE RECOMMEND** No. 33K8663 (or No. 33K8666 Extra Length) and No. 33K8604 as the Best Suspenders EVER SOLD AT 25 CENTS PER PAIR; and No. 33K8698 (or No. 33K8699 Extra Length) and No. 33K8622 as the Best Suspenders EVER SOLD AT ANY PRICE. | Boys' Suspenders 28 ins. long

If by mail, postage on suspenders and braces, men's 8c and boys' 5c per pair. Be sure to allow extra for postage when goods are to be sent by mail.

43c GENUINE PRESIDENT SUSPENDERS.
No. 33K8670 Advertised everywhere. WEB—Full width closely woven, white back, fancy faced, cushion style, very elastic but with strong rebound. MAKE—Separate piece back web with patent continuous adjustable cord connection running from back buttons through swivel loops at back and shoulder webbing as illustrated, thus practically overcoming all direct tension. TRIM—Double take up, non-rusting brass sliding buckles and cast off.
Our cut price, per pair only.....43c

43c RECOMMENDED.
No. 33K8622 Heaviest, Strongest Suspender ever made. WEB—Heaviest 2-inch width, tightly woven special cushion style, exceptionally elastic with strongest rebound of any web ever woven. Unequaled for strength and service. MAKE—Strongly double sewed with heavy leather reinforced cross back and strongest horsehide ends. TRIM—Stout, non-rusting sliding nickel buckles with patent cast off. The best on earth. Furnished in regular and extra lengths. Which do you want?
Our cut price, per pair, only.........43c

Strongest Suspender Made.

32c ELASTIC BACK SILK AND LISLE SUSPENDERS.
No. 33K8704 A Fine Dress Suspender. WEB—Fancy woven non-elastic silk. Elastic back ends. MAKE—Double stitched leather reinforced cross back. TRIM—Fancy satin finish, non-rusting brass buckles. Kid ends and glove button castoff.
Reduced price, per pair 32c

25c RECOMMENDED.
No. 33K8604 Strongest Suspender ever sold for 25c. WEB—Very elastic, 2-inch cushion style, specially woven for us. MAKE—Double stitched, heavy leather reinforcements equal to the usual 50-cent suspender at retail. TRIM—Strong double take up non-rusting sliding nickel buckle and strong pliable grain leather ends.
Our special price, per pair, only.....25c

With a "come back" like a "steel spring"

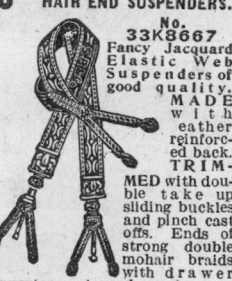

36c ADJUSTABLE SHOULDER BRACES.
No. 33K8770 Best Shoulder Brace Made. WEB—Strongest full width cushion style, very elastic with strong rebound. MAKE—Double stitched leather reinforced police back, adjustable shoulder loops. TRIM—Strongest nickel buckles. Strong, round horsehide ends.
Reduced price, per pair 36c

21c POLICE SUSPENDERS.
No. 33K8607 One of the Best. WEB—1½ inches wide, white back, striped faced, cushion style, strong and elastic. MAKE—Double stitched heavy leather reinforced, police style. TRIM—Strong double take up sliding nickel buckles, glove button leather castoff, and round leather ends.
Special price, per pair, only...21c

35c GUYOT STYLE NON-ELASTIC SUSPENDERS.
No. 33K8671 Celebrated Imported Suspenders. WEB—1 inch wide, white back, striped face, non-elastic. Elastic back ends. MAKE—Linen sewed throughout. TRIM—Patent double take up sliding buckles without teeth, with continuous double sliding loop ends of patterns to match the web.
Our cut price, per pair, only................35c

21c SELF-ADJUSTING SUSPENDERS.
No. 33K8646 A Deservedly Popular Suspender. WEB is full width, white back, fancy faced, cushion style, closely woven, very elastic with strong "kick" or rebound. MAKE—Strongly double stitched. Separate piece back web with continuous self-adjusting cord running through swivel loops as illustrated, thus minimizing the tension. TRIM—Double take up non-rusting brass sliding buckles and metal castoff.
Our special price, per pair, only.....21c

32c BEST POLICE SUSPENDERS.
No. 33K8624 Heaviest and Best Police and Firemen's Suspenders. WEB—2 inches wide, extra strong and elastic with quick rebound, white back, striped face, cushion quality. MAKE—Police style with double stitched heavy leather reinforcements and TRIMMED with flat double take up nickel buckles warranted not to rust. Round grain leather ends running through glove button fastener, leather castoffs.
Reduced price, per pair.....32c

PRICE REDUCED

25c EXTRA LENGTH. RECOMMENDED.
No. 33K8666 Forty inches long, and the same superior WEB used in No. 33K8663 is also used in this extra length suspender. MAKE is identical except that this suspender is 4 inches longer. TRIMMED with brass double take up buckles and best calfskin ends. Second only to 33K8699, elsewhere described.
Special price, per pair, only.........25c

18c JACQUARD WEB MOHAIR END SUSPENDERS.
No. 33K8667 Fancy Jacquard Elastic Web Suspenders of good quality. MADE with leather reinforced back. TRIMMED with double take up sliding buckles and pinch cast offs. Ends of strong double mohair braids with drawer supporters. A good wearing suspender at small cost.
Special price, per pair, only 18c

25c RECOMMENDED.
No. 33K8663 The Best Suspender ever sold for a quarter. WEB is another one of the exceptional values which we can offer because of being satisfied with a small profit. This is the best medium weight suspender that we can produce at the price and is equal to the usual 50c quality at retail. Non-rusting brass buckles and horsehide ends that correspond in value and appearance. We recommend this suspender as second only to 33K8698, elsewhere described. Special price, per pair, only..25c

37c BEAUTIFUL SILK GIFT SUSPENDERS BOXED.
No. 33K8712 Non-elastic Silk Web Suspenders. Elastic in back ends only. Double take up, fancy embossed brass buckles. Round kid ends and loops with glove button castoffs. White only, with black, blue, green or red stripes. Packed one pair in box. State color.
Reduced price, per pair...37c

21c LIGHT WEIGHT LISLE SUSPENDERS.
No. 33K8662 All Elastic Lisle Web Suspenders. WEB of excellent quality and handsome patterns, exceptionally elastic and excellent for service. MADE cross back style, strongly double stitched and TRIMMED with fancy gilt buckles. Genuine hogskin leather ends and glove button castoff.
Special price, per pair, only....21c

83c HAND EMBROIDERED SATIN SUSPENDERS.
No. 33K8716 Elegant Satin Gift Suspenders. Elastic in back ends only. Handsomely embroidered in contrasting colors on black, cream, pink, lavender, garnet, navy or royal blue. One pair in a handsome box. Be sure to state color.
Reduced price per pair..83c

33c FINE LISLE SUSPENDERS.
No. 33K8710 Finest All Elastic Lisle Suspenders. WEB is the lightest weight and neatest for dress suspenders. Remarkable for service and comfort. MADE cross back style, double stitched and TRIMMED with double take up non-rusting brass buckles and round kid ends running through kid loops with glove button castoff.
Special price, per pair, only 33c

42c RECOMMENDED.
No. 33K8698 Our Handsomest and Most Serviceable Suspender. WEB is specially woven for us and is superior to any other on the market. Has a rebound that excels all others and is the "longest lived" suspender made. MADE cross back style, double stitched and finished with artistic gilt buckles, warranted not to rust. Reinforced glove button castoff and ends of soft selected English calfskin. A suspender without an equal. Special price, per pair, only.....42c

Buy These

46c 42 INCHES LONG. RECOMMENDED.
No. 33K8699 Forty-two inches long, (the longest made) and of the same superior WEB as No. 33K8698. The suspender of "longest life" and strongest "kick" or rebound. Made and trimmed same as No. 33K8698 but is 6 inches longer. Unquestionably the best extra length suspender made. Our special price, per pair, only..46c

---

BOYS' SUSPENDERS

9c BOYS' FANCY SUSPENDERS.
No. 33K8755 Leader Boys' Suspender. MADE of good quality fancy web, leather reinforced and TRIMMED with serviceable buckles, good pinch cast-offs and mohair ends. Length, 28 ins.
Special price, per pair, only.....9c

14c BOYS' FANCY MOHAIR END SUSPENDERS.
No. 33K8756 A Remarkable Value. WEB cushion style, strong and serviceable, elastic but firm. MAKE—Double stitched leather reinforced. TRIM—Double take up buckles, patent cast off and strong mohair ends. Length, 28 inches.
Special price, per pair, only 14c

15c BOYS' POLICE SUSPENDERS.
No. 33K8762 Boys' Strongest Suspenders. WEB—Regular Police style in boys' suspender width. MAKE—Strong and durable workmanship and regular police construction same as men's. TRIM—Double take up buckles, round leather ends and leather loops. Length, 28 inches.
Special price, per pair, only...15c

18c BOYS' CROSS BACK SUSPENDERS. PRICE REDUCED.
No. 33K8764 Old Reliable Cross Back Suspenders. WEB—Good width cushion web, very elastic and with strong rebound. MAKE—Double stitched leather reinforced. TRIM—Double take up buckles, round leather ends and glove button castoff.
Our reduced price, per pair, only......18c

18c BOYS' SELF ADJUSTING SUSPENDERS. PRICE REDUCED.
No. 33K8768 The kind that don't pull buttons. WEB—Fancy figured elastic cushion. MAKE—Self adjusting cord connection running through metal loops, connecting back piece and shoulder webbing, thus minimizing the tension. TRIM—Double take up buckles and metal sliding cord ends.
Reduced price, per pair, only..18c

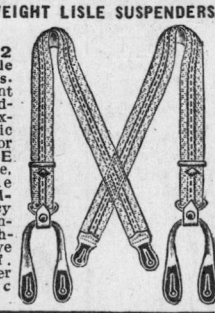
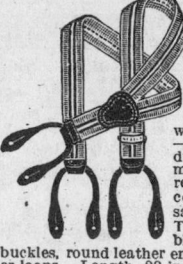

7c EACH

FINE LINEN COLLARS

7c EACH

ONLY THE BEST "TWO FOR A QUARTER" BRANDS, WHICH YOU WILL RECOGNIZE, AND CUFFS THAT NEVER BEFORE SOLD AT LESS THAN 25 CENTS PER PAIR. DON'T BUY INFERIOR 10-CENT COLLARS WHEN WE SELL THE STANDARD 15-CENT BRANDS AT 7 CENTS EACH.
DON'T FORGET TO STATE SIZE WHEN ORDERING COLLARS.
If by mail, postage extra, each, 2 cents; per one-half dozen, 9 cents. Postage on Cuffs, extra, per pair, 3 cents.

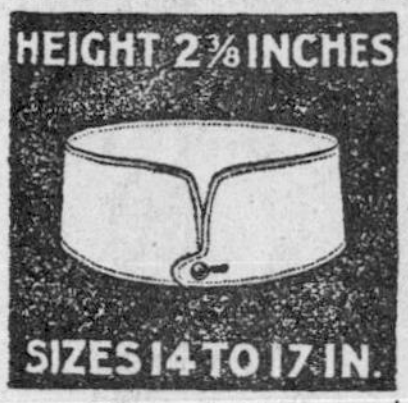
HEIGHT 2⅜ INCHES
SIZES 14 TO 17 IN.

No. 33K8054 The Dressy Polk Style. Sizes, 14, 14½, 15, 15½, 16, 16½ and 17. State size.
Price, each 7c

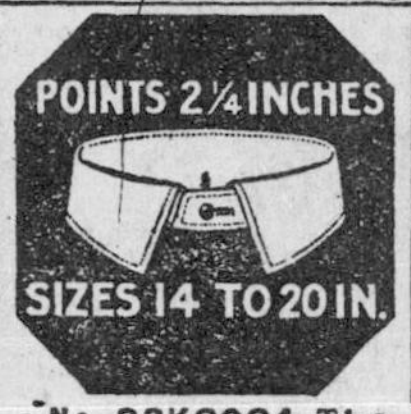
POINTS 2¼ INCHES
SIZES 14 TO 20 IN.

No. 33K8084 The Regular Turn Down Collar. Sizes, 14, 14½, 15, 15½, 16, 16½, 17, 17½, 18, 18½, 19, 19½ and 20. State size.
Price, each 7c

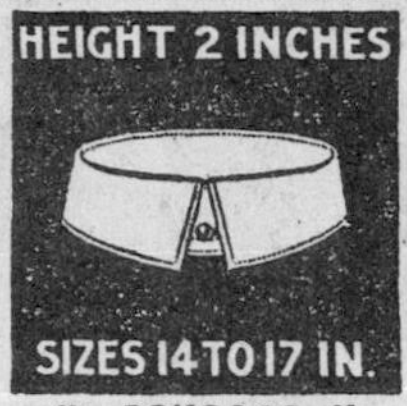
HEIGHT 2 INCHES
SIZES 14 TO 17 IN.

No. 33K8069 Medium Height, Medium Opening, Turn Down Collar. Sizes, 14, 14½, 15, 15½, 16, 16½ and 17. State size.
Price, each 7c

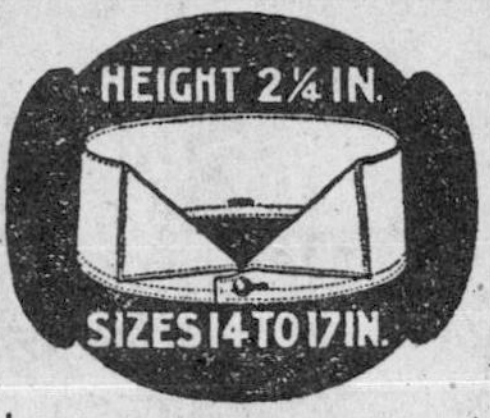
HEIGHT 2¼ IN.
SIZES 14 TO 17 IN.

No. 33K8004 Stylish Wing Collar, dressy height and up to date. Sizes, 14, 14½, 15, 15½, 16, 16½ and 17.
Price, each 7c

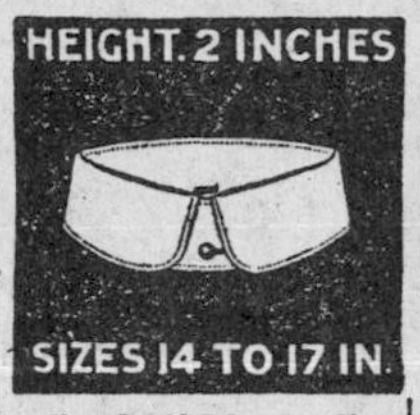
HEIGHT. 2 INCHES
SIZES 14 TO 17 IN.

No. 33K8068 Medium Height, Turn Down Collar. Medium wide opening. Sizes, 14 to 17.
Price, each 7c

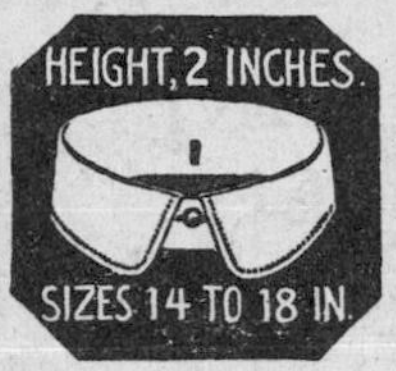
HEIGHT, 2 INCHES.
SIZES 14 TO 18 IN.

No. 33K8076 A Popular Collar for any occasion. Medium height and comfortable. Sizes, 14 to 18.
Price, each 7c

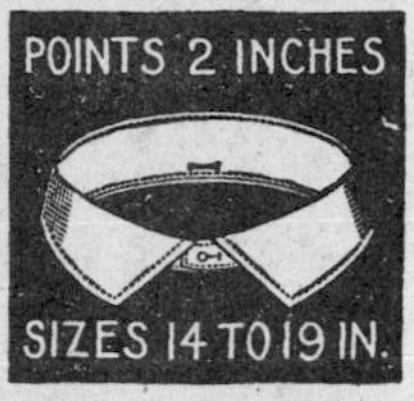
POINTS 2 INCHES
SIZES 14 TO 19 IN.

No. 33K8088 A Neat and Comfortable Turn Down Collar. Medium width. Sizes, 14 to 19.
Price, each 7c

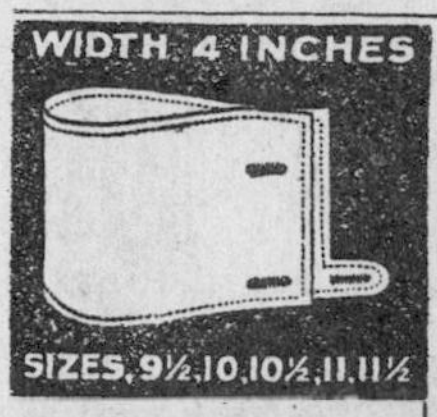
WIDTH 4 INCHES
SIZES, 9½,10,10½,11,11½

No. 33K8110 Square Corner, Linen Link Cuffs. Be sure to state size wanted. Sizes, 9½, 10, 10½, 11 and 11½.
Price, per pair 14c

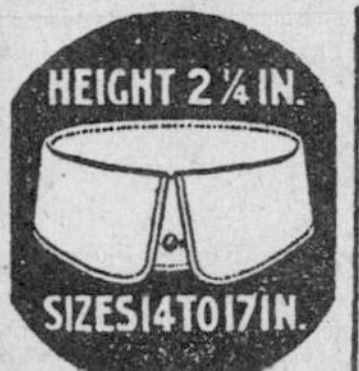
HEIGHT 2¼ IN.
SIZES 14 TO 17 IN.

No. 33K8072 The Higher Style of Turn Down Collar. Sizes, 14 to 17.
Price, each 7c

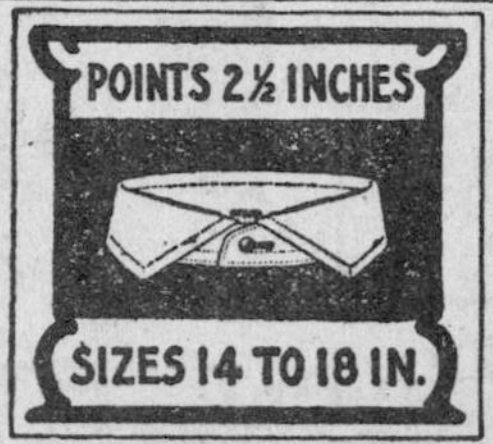
POINTS 2½ INCHES
SIZES 14 TO 18 IN.

No. 33K8000 A Very Popular Style Collar. Sizes, 14 to 18.
Price, each 7c

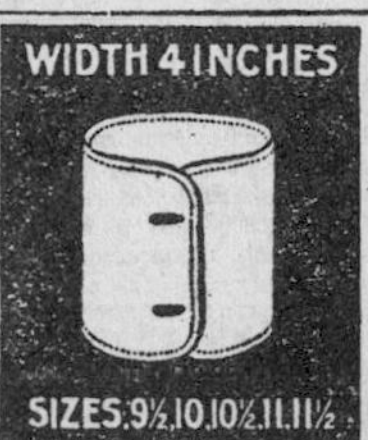
WIDTH 4 INCHES
SIZES 9½,10,10½,11,11½

No. 33K8104 The Regular Round Style Cuffs. Sizes, 9½, 10, 10½, 11 and 11½.
Price, per pair ... 14c

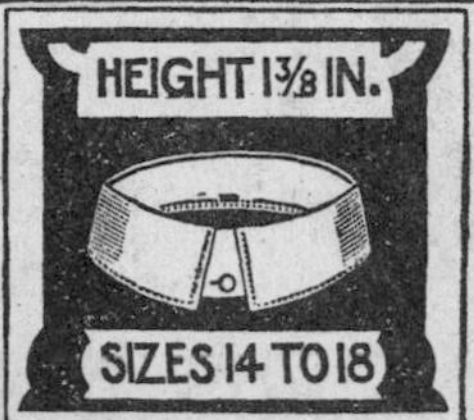
HEIGHT 1⅜ IN.
SIZES 14 TO 18

No. 33K8062 Rather Low Turn Down Collar, but has an appearance of height. Sizes, 14 to 18.
Price, each 7c

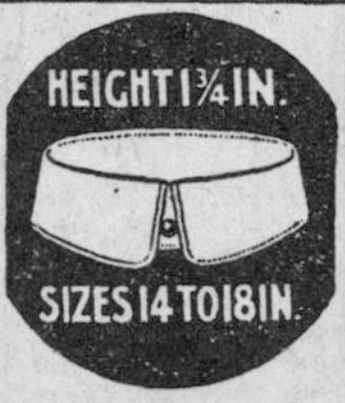
HEIGHT 1¾ IN.
SIZES 14 TO 18 IN.

No. 33K8067 A Neat Collar in the Turn Down Style, medium opening. Sizes, 14 to 18.
Price, each 7c

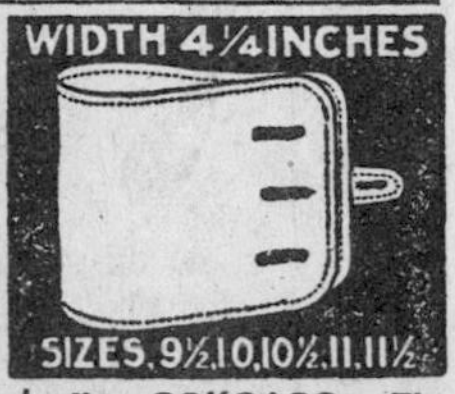
WIDTH 4¼ INCHES
SIZES. 9½,10,10½,11,11½

No. 33K8122 The Reversible, Round Cornered Link Style Cuffs. Double service in this style cuffs. Sizes, 9½, 10, 10½, 11 and 11½.
Price, per pair 14c

Ours is a well known "Two for a quarter" Brand Linen Collar, never before offered at less than 15 cents each or two for a quarter. Beware of collars without a "Brand."

BOYS' LINEN COLLARS, 7c EACH.

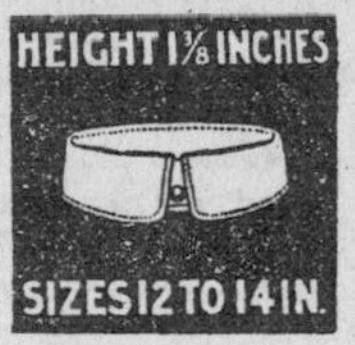
HEIGHT 1⅛ INCHES
SIZES 12 TO 14 IN.

No. 33K8151 Boys' Turn Down Linen Collar. Boys' sizes, 12, 12½, 13, 13½ and 14.
Price, each 7c

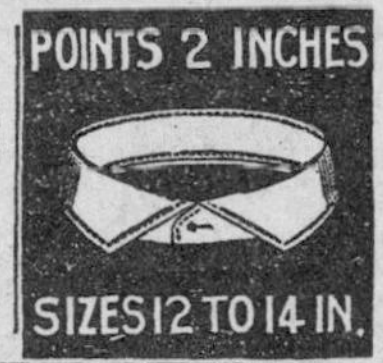
POINTS 2 INCHES
SIZES 12 TO 14 IN.

No. 33K8156 This Comfortable Style Turn Down Linen Collar in boys' sizes, 12 to 14.
Price, each ... 7c

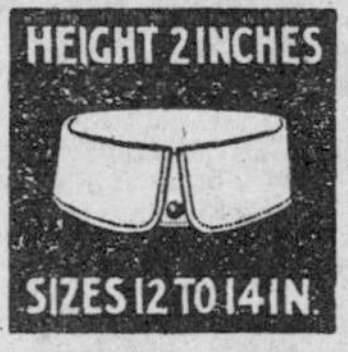
HEIGHT 2 INCHES
SIZES 12 TO 14 IN.

No. 33K8154 Boys' Fair Height, Turn Down Linen Collar. Boys' sizes, 12, 12½, 13, 13½ and 14.
Price, each 7c

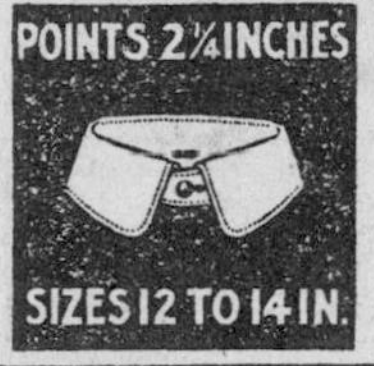
POINTS 2¼ INCHES
SIZES 12 TO 14 IN.

No. 33K8150 Boys' Neat Turn Down Linen Collar, comfortable and sensible. Boys' sizes, 12 to 14.
Price, each ... 7c

BE SURE TO STATE SIZE WHEN ORDERING COLLARS OR CUFFS.

POLISHED OR DULL FINISH.

RUBBER COLLARS AND CUFFS

WILL NOT BREAK OR TURN YELLOW.

POLISHED OR DULL.

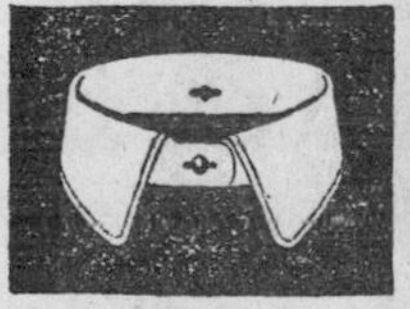

No. 33K8234 Turn Down Style. Polished or dull finish. Sizes, 12 to 20. Price, each 14c
If by mail, postage extra, each, 4 cents.

POLISHED OR DULL.

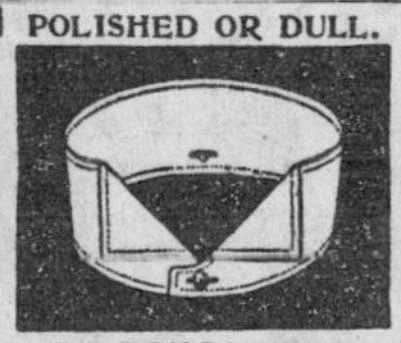

No. 33K8252 Wing Style. Height, 2¼ inches. Polished or dull finish. Sizes, 13½ to 17½.
Price, each 14c
If by mail, postage extra, each, 4 cents.

POLISHED OR DULL.

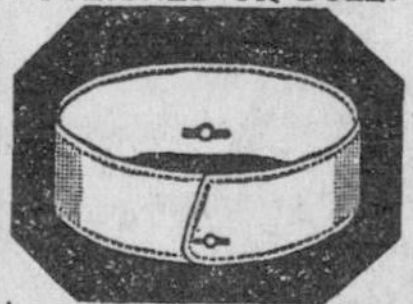

No. 33K8264 Clerical Style Collar. Height, 1¾ inches. Polished or dull finish. Sizes, 12 to 18. Price, each 14c
If by mail, postage extra, each, 2 cents.

PLEASE STATE YOUR SIZE, AND CATALOGUE NUMBER OF STYLE WANTED.

RUBBER SHIRT FRONTS.

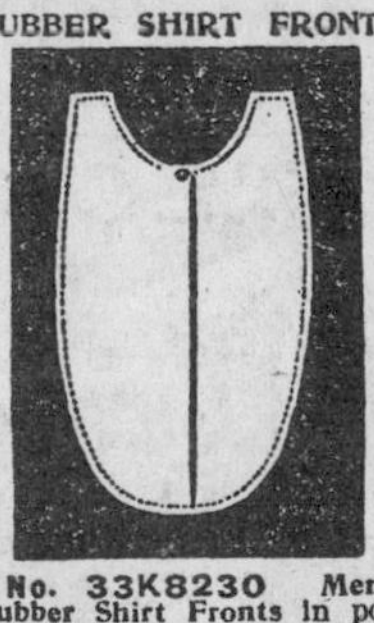

No. 33K8230 Men's Rubber Shirt Fronts in polished or dull finish, medium length. Price, each 35c
Postage extra, each, 8 cents.

POLISHED OR DULL.

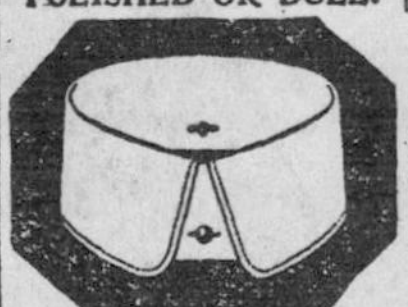

No. 33K8242 Turn Down Style. Height, 2¼ inches. Polished or dull finish. Sizes, 13½ to 17½. Price, each .. 14c
If by mail, postage extra, each, 4 cents.

POLISHED OR DULL.

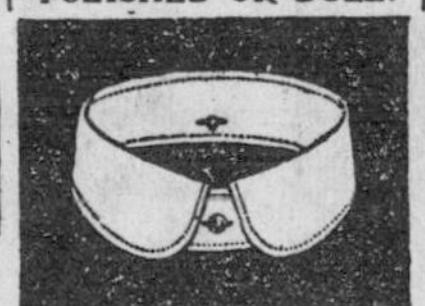

No. 33K8238 Turn Down Collar. Height, 2 inches. Polished or dull finish. Sizes, 12½ to 18½.
Price, each 14c
Postage extra, each, 2c.

POLISHED OR DULL.

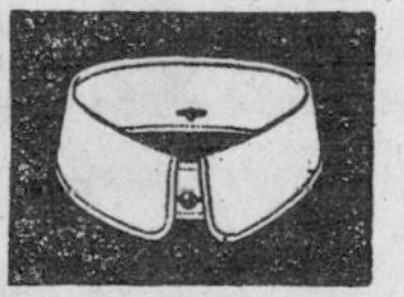

No. 33K8240 Turn Down Style. Height, 1¾ inches. Polished or dull finish. Sizes, 12 to 18. Price, each .. 14c
If by mail, postage extra, each, 4 cents.

POLISHED OR DULL.

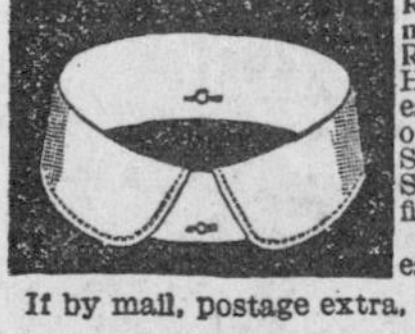

No. 33K8244 Rounded Corner Turn Down Rubber Collar. Height, 2 inches. Polished or dull finish. Sizes, 12 to 18. State size and finish wanted.
Price, each 14c
If by mail, postage extra, each, 4 cents.

POLISHED OR DULL.

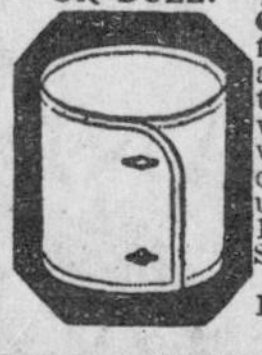

No. 33K8269 Round Style Rubber Cuffs. Polished or dull finish. Rubber collars and cuffs cannot be told from linen, but when soiled can be wiped clean with a damp cloth and are unharmed. Sizes, 9½, 10, 10½, 11 and 11½. State size wanted.
Price, per pair 29c
If by mail, postage extra, pair, 5c.

POLISHED OR DULL.

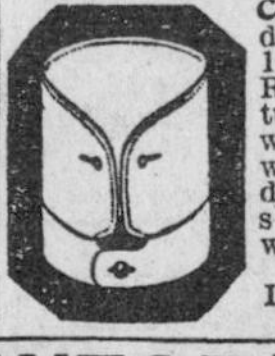

No. 33K8270 Link Style Rubber Cuffs. Polished or dull finish. Sizes, 9½, 10, 10½, 11 and 11½. Rubber cuffs do not turn yellow nor warp and can be wiped clean with a damp cloth. State size and finish wanted.
Price, per pair, 29c
If by mail, postage extra, pair, 5c.

POLISHED OR DULL.

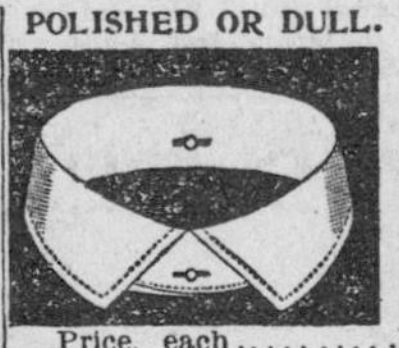

No. 33K8248 Turn Down Rubber Collar, with cut back corners. Height, 2 inches. Polished or dull finish. Sizes, 12 to 18. State size and finish wanted.
Price, each 14c
If by mail, postage extra, each, 4 cents.

BOYS' AND CHILDREN'S SILK NECKWEAR

IF BY MAIL, POSTAGE EXTRA, 2 CENTS.

CHILD'S SILK WINDSOR BOW TIE.

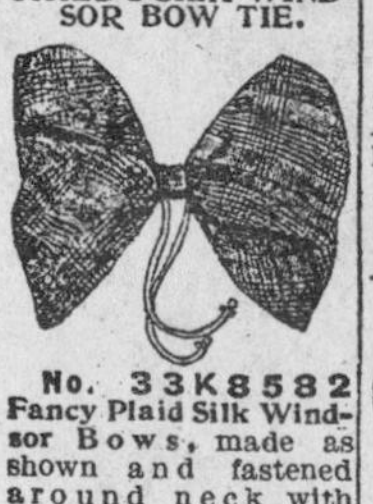

No. 33K8582 Fancy Plaid Silk Windsor Bows, made as shown and fastened around neck with elastic band. Comes in many different colors. State color wanted. Price, each .. 23c

UNEQUALED BARGAINS IN BOYS' SHIRTS SHOWN ON PAGE 970.

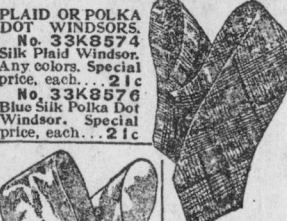

PLAID OR POLKA DOT WINDSORS.
No. 33K8574 Silk Plaid Windsor. Any colors. Special price, each 21c
No. 33K8576 Blue Silk Polka Dot Windsor. Special price, each 21c

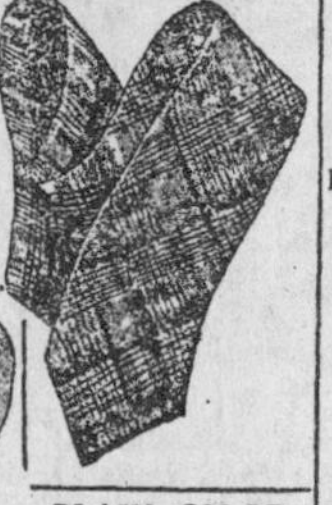

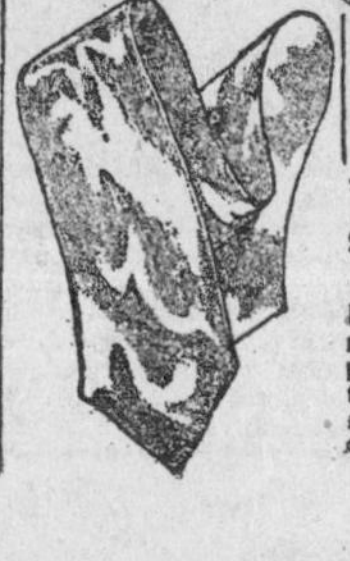

PLAIN COLOR SILK WINDSORS.
No. 33K8578 Plain black, white, navy, orange, pink, blue or red, twilled silk windsor. Be sure to state color wanted.
Price, each, 21c

BOYS' SILK BAND TECKS.

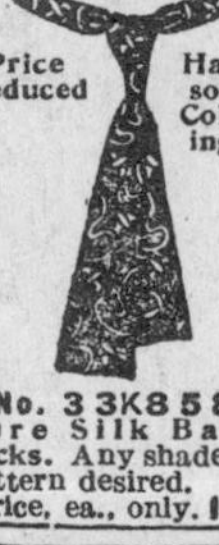
Price Reduced
Handsome Colorings.

No. 33K8586 Pure Silk Band Tecks. Any shade or pattern desired.
Price, ea., only. 17c

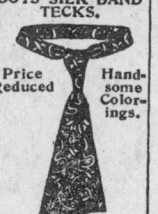

BOYS' SILK FOUR-IN-HANDS.

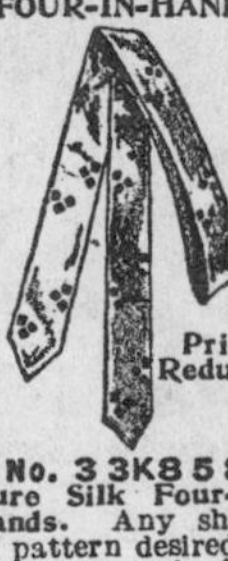
Price Reduced

No. 33K8588 Pure Silk Four-in-hands. Any shade or pattern desired.
Price, ea., only. 17c

BOYS' SILK SHIELD TECKS.

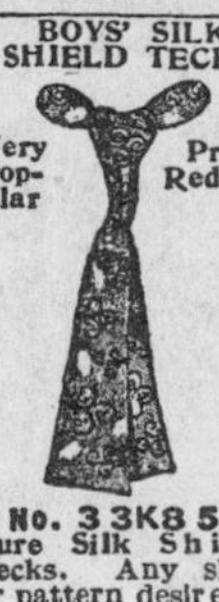
Very Popular
Price Reduced

No. 33K8590 Pure Silk Shield Tecks. Any shade or pattern desired.
Price, ea., only 17c

No. 33K8592 Pure Silk String Ties. Any shade or pattern desired.
Special price, each, only .. 8c

No. 33K8598 Pure Silk Shield Bows.
Any shade or pattern desired.
Special price, each, only .. 8c

MEN'S WASHABLE TIES

MEN'S WHITE LAWN STRING TIES.

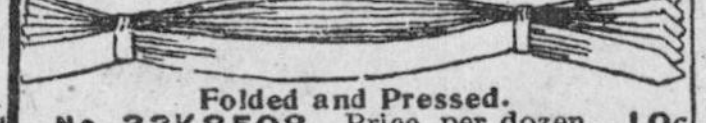

Folded and Pressed.
No. 33K8508 Price, per dozen .. 10c
No. 33K8510 Price, per dozen .. 16c
No. 33K8512 Price, per dozen .. 23c
If by mail, postage extra, per doz., 5 cents.

MEN'S COLORED PERCALE STRING TIES.

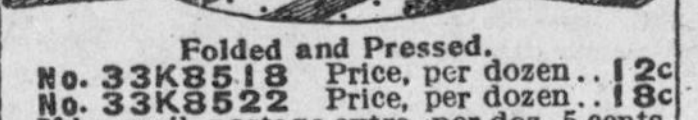

Folded and Pressed.
No. 33K8518 Price, per dozen .. 12c
No. 33K8522 Price, per dozen .. 18c
If by mail, postage extra, per doz., 5 cents.

COLORED MADRAS SHIELD BOWS.
No. 33K8474 Madras Shield Bows.
Price, 6 for ... 25c
If by mail, postage extra for six, 6c.

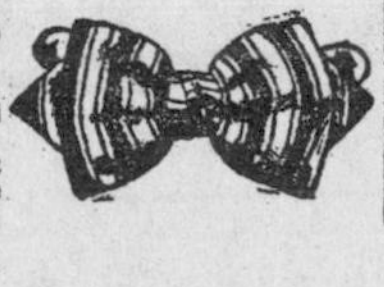

MERCERIZED MADRAS FOUR-IN-HAND TIES

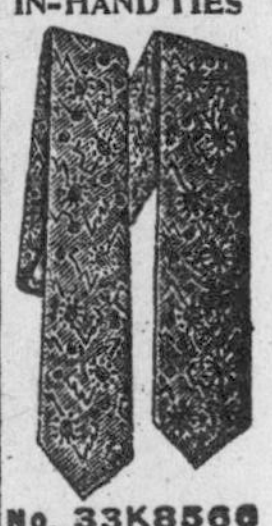

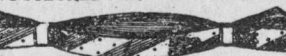

No. 33K8566 Solid Colors, White, black, navy, wine, royal blue, lavender or tan, self figured. Be sure to state color. Each, 19c
If by mail, postage extra, ea., 3c

FINEST SILK NECKWEAR

ELEGANT SILKS   **AT ASTONISHINGLY LOW PRICES**   **HANDSOME STYLES**

Our No-Limit Quantity Contract with the largest neckwear manufacturers in the country whose styles and qualities have for years been recognized as the best, makes possible these low prices.

Ties, if by mail, postage extra, each, 2 cents.
If in a box, 7 cents each.

The finest qualities and most beautiful neckwear produced is here offered. Tell us the colors and designs you like and we will send you ties that retail at more than double our prices.

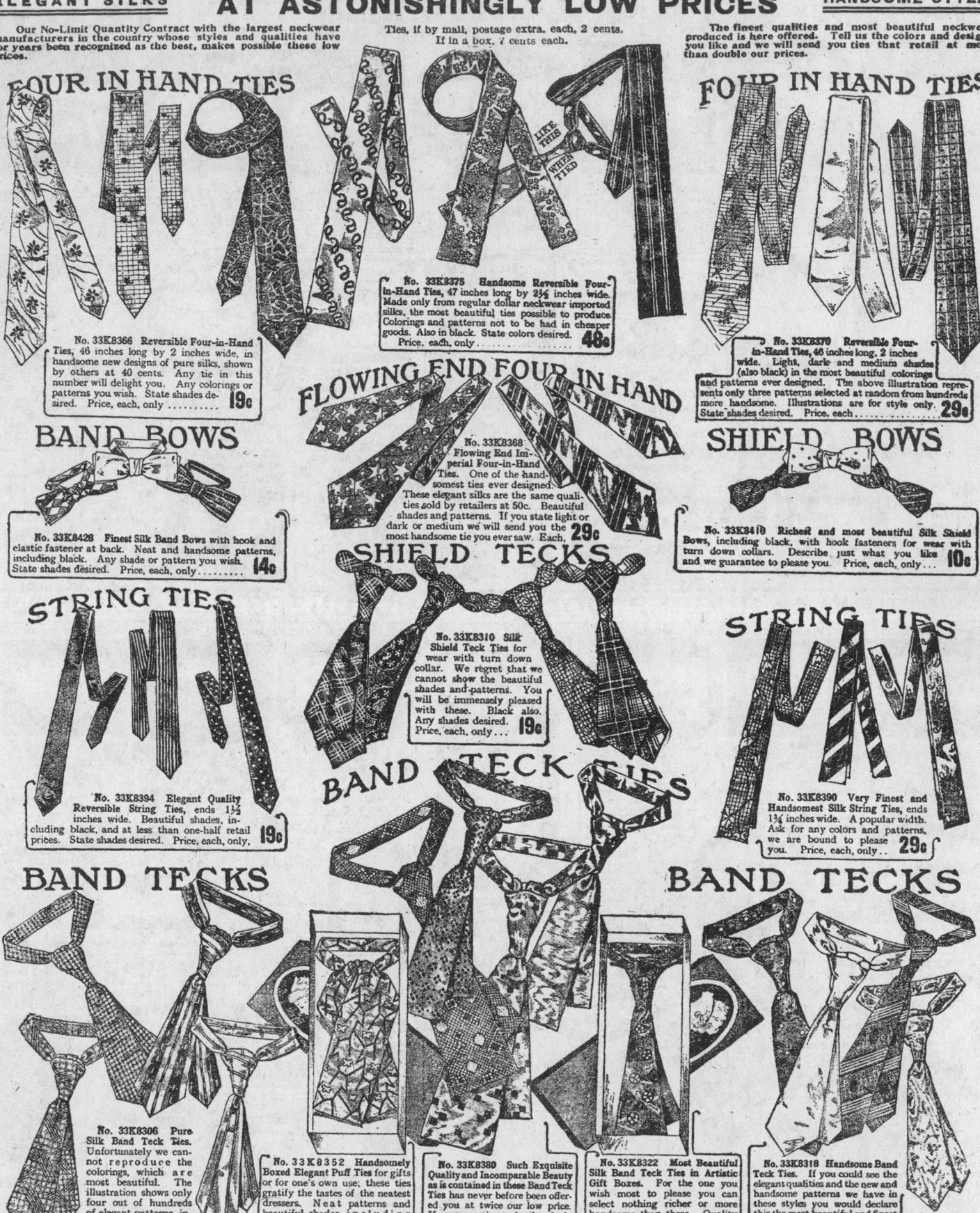

FOUR IN HAND TIES

FOUR IN HAND TIES

No. 33K8366 Reversible Four-in-Hand Ties, 46 inches long by 2 inches wide, in handsome new designs of pure silks, shown by others at 40 cents. Any tie in this number will delight you. Any colorings or patterns you wish. State shades desired. Price, each, only.......... **19c**

No. 33K8375 Handsome Reversible Four-in-Hand Ties, 47 inches long by 2½ inches wide. Made only from regular dollar neckwear imported silks, the most beautiful ties possible to produce. Colorings and patterns not to be had in cheaper goods. Also in black. State colors desired. Price, each, only................... **48c**

No. 33K8370 Reversible Four-in-Hand Ties, 46 inches long, 2 inches wide. Light, dark and medium shades (also black) in the most beautiful colorings and patterns ever designed. The above illustration represents only three patterns selected at random from hundreds more handsome. Illustrations are for style only. State shades desired. Price, each.............. **29c**

BAND BOWS

FLOWING END FOUR IN HAND

SHIELD BOWS

No. 33K8428 Finest Silk Band Bows with hook and elastic fastener at back. Neat and handsome patterns, including black. Any shade or pattern you wish. State shades desired. Price, each, only......... **14c**

No. 33K8368 Flowing End Imperial Four-in-Hand Ties. One of the handsomest ties ever designed. These elegant silks are the same qualities sold by retailers at 50c. Beautiful shades and patterns. If you state light or dark or medium we will send you the most handsome tie you ever saw. Each, **29c**

No. 33K8418 Richest and most beautiful Silk Shield Bows, including black, with hook fasteners for wear with turn down collars. Describe just what you like and we guarantee to please you. Price, each, only... **10c**

SHIELD TECKS

No. 33K8310 Silk Shield Teck Ties for wear with turn down collar. We regret that we cannot show the beautiful shades and patterns. You will be immensely pleased with these. Black also. Any shades desired. Price, each, only... **19c**

STRING TIES

STRING TIES

No. 33K8394 Elegant Quality Reversible String Ties, ends 1½ inches wide. Beautiful shades, including black, and at less than one-half retail prices. State shades desired. Price, each, only, **19c**

No. 33K8390 Very Finest and Handsomest Silk String Ties, ends 1¾ inches wide. A popular width. Ask for any colors and patterns, we are bound to please you. Price, each, only.. **29c**

BAND TECK TIES

BAND TECKS

BAND TECKS

No. 33K8306 Pure Silk Band Teck Ties. Unfortunately we cannot reproduce the colorings, which are most beautiful. The illustration shows only four out of hundreds of elegant patterns, including black. State shades desired. Price, each, only. **19c**

No. 33K8352 Handsomely Boxed Elegant Puff Ties for gifts or for one's own use; these ties gratify the tastes of the neatest dressers. Neat patterns and beautiful shades, including black, or, if desired, more striking patterns and brighter shades. State shades desired. Price, each, only...... **48c**

No. 33K8380 Such Exquisite Quality and Incomparable Beauty as is contained in these Band Teck Ties has never before been offered you at twice our low price. If you mention only the shade desired we will select a tie so handsome that you will never be able to equal it. Black if desired. Price, **48c**

No. 33K8322 Most Beautiful Silk Band Teck Ties in Artistic Gift Boxes. For the one you wish most to please you can select nothing richer or more handsome than these. Quality and design that impresses their exceptional value and beauty. Mention the favorite shade. Price, each, only, **48c**

No. 33K8318 Handsome Band Teck Ties. If you could see the elegant qualities and the new and handsome patterns we have in these styles you would declare this the most beautiful and finest quality neckwear ever shown at double the prices. State what shades you like. Price, each, only............. **29c**

YOUR MONEY WILL BE IMMEDIATELY RETURNED TO YOU FOR ANY GOODS NOT PERFECTLY SATISFACTORY. 599

LADIES' IMPORTED KID AND FABRIC GLOVES = IN ALL THE = STYLISH LENGTHS

PURE SILK, SILK AND LISLE, PLAIN LISLE, AND MERCERIZED COTTON.

OUR GLOVES are guaranteed the best made. As we import direct all our Foreign Kid and Fabric Gloves and Mitts from the best French and German manufacturers we are able to demand and secure absolutely the finest qualities produced.

OUR PRICES are the lowest in this country, as we save all importing jobbers' and middlemen's profits and offer direct to you these finest and handsomest foreign made gloves with only our one small profit added to the cost to produce.

YOU BUY FROM US at lower prices than your dealer pays at wholesale, and we guarantee our qualities to be better than can possibly be secured at retail at any price. We cannot fill dealers' quantity orders at these prices.

LADIES' ELBOW LENGTH GLOVES more popular than ever. While last season we bought immense quantities of kid and fabric gloves we were unable to supply the big demand produced for the longer lengths by our wonderfully low prices. This season we have contracted for hundreds of dozens to be shipped every two weeks by fast steamer and we will be able to fill all orders received.

IMPORTANT TO NOTE: When first trying on kid or fabric gloves, insert first the fingers without the thumb and carefully "rub" on after which insert the thumb and as carefully "rub" on. Do not "pull" your gloves on, as fine gloves are easily torn if not properly tried on. If care is used in fitting the first time our gloves are guaranteed not to rip or tear nor stretch out of shape and will always fit smoothly and give unequaled service. To determine your size measure hand as shown below.

LADIES' LISLE AND COTTON GLOVES.

89c LADIES' MERCERIZED LISLE SIXTEEN-BUTTON LENGTH GLOVES.

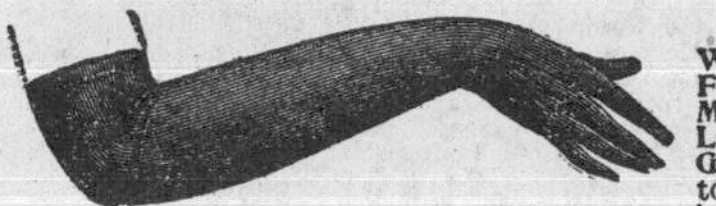

No. 33K5129 Women's Very Fine Quality Mercerized Lisle Imported Gloves, 16-button length (23 inches). The fabric is of highest luster and fineness; appearance equal to pure silk, wears better and stands washing more frequently. Double stitched thumb, three-row silk embroidered backs. Opening at wrist with two clasps. Colors, BLACK, WHITE, GRAY or TAN. Sizes, 6 to 8½. State size and color wanted.
Special price, per pair, only 89c
If by mail, postage extra, per pair, 2 cents.

48c LADIES' LONG LISLE GLOVES. INCLUDES SIZE 5½ FOR LARGE GIRLS.

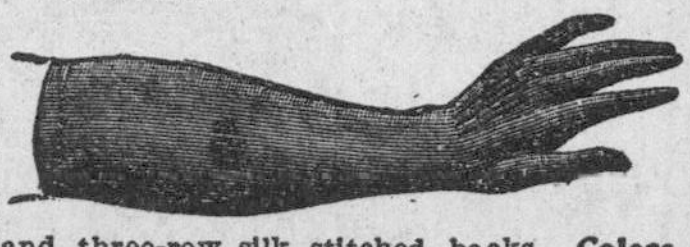

No. 33K5128 Women's Long Lisle Gloves, 12-button length (19 inches), of very good quality. Two clasps at wrist, double stitched thumb and three-row silk stitched backs. Colors, BLACK, WHITE, GRAY or TAN. Sizes, 5½ to 8½. Sizes, 5½ and 6 can be ordered for larger girls. State size and color wanted. Our special price, per pair 48c
If by mail, postage extra, per pair, 2 cents.

29c LADIES' FULL ELBOW LENGTH COTTON GLOVE.

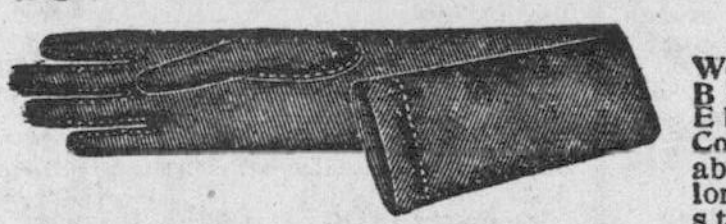

No. 33K5126 Women's Plain Black Full Elbow Length Cotton Gloves, about 21 inches long, three rows stitching on backs, carefully made and of good quality. This is the lowest price ever quoted for a dependable full length fabric glove. Color, BLACK only. Sizes, 6 to 9. Please state size wanted. Retails everywhere at 50 cents.
Our unbeatable price, per pair, only 29c
If by mail, postage extra, per pair, 3 cents.

22c LADIES' FULL ELBOW LENGTH MERCERIZED MITTS. PRICE REDUCED.

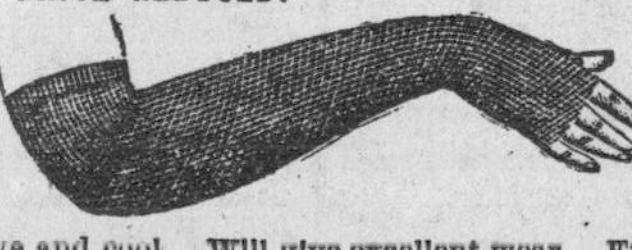

No. 33K5120 Ladies' Beautiful Mesh Weave Mercerized Mitts. The greatest value ever offered in full elbow length mitts. Open weave and cool. Will give excellent wear. Exactly the same as last year and actually lower in price. Colors, BLACK or WHITE. Be sure to state color wanted.
Reduced price, per pair, only 22c
If by mail, postage extra, per pair, 2 cents.

43c LADIES' MILANESE LISLE GLOVES. PRICE REDUCED.

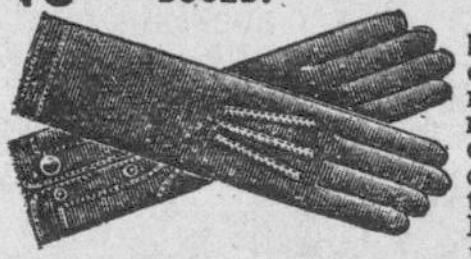

No. 33K5104 Ladies' Extra Fine Quality Milanese Lisle Gloves, of best manufacture. Made with three rows embroidery on back, two clasps at wrist to match color of glove, double stitched thumbs. Length, 11 inches. Lisle gloves are durable and will stand frequent washing. Colors, BLACK, WHITE, GRAY or TAN. Sizes, 6 to 8½. Be sure to state size and color wanted.
Our reduced price, per pair 43c
If by mail, postage extra, per pair, 1 cent.

21c LADIES' LISLE THREAD GLOVES.

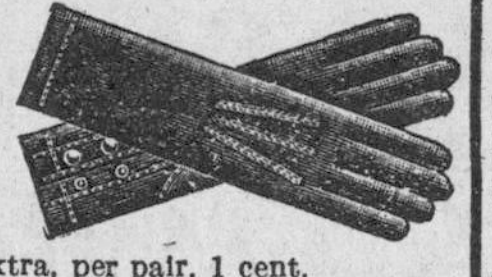

No. 33K5105 Ladies' Lisle Thread Gloves, with three rows embroidered stitching on backs, two clasps to match color of glove, double stitched inserted thumbs. Colors, BLACK or WHITE. Sizes, 6 to 8½. Be sure to state size and color wanted.
Special price, per pair .. 21c
If by mail, postage extra, per pair, 1 cent.

14c MISSES' PLAIN LISLE GLOVES. JERSEY WRISTS.

No. 33K5119 Misses' Plain White or Tan Lisle Gloves, three rows stitching on backs. For ages 6 to 14 years. State age and color wanted. Special price, per pair, only 14c
If by mail, postage extra, per pair, 1 cent.

87c LADIES' KID GAUNTLET DRIVING GLOVES. PRICE REDUCED.

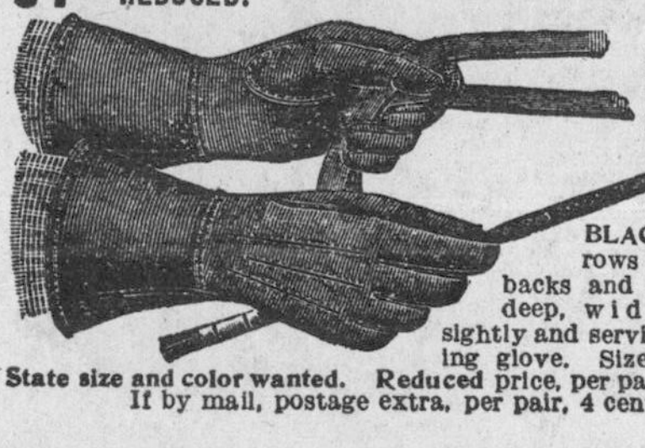

No. 33K5062 Ladies' Fine Kid Gauntlet Driving Gloves in REDDISH BROWN or BLACK. Three rows stitching on backs and silk lined, deep, wide cuffs. A sightly and serviceable driving glove. Sizes, 6 to 8½. State size and color wanted. Reduced price, per pair 87c
If by mail, postage extra, per pair, 4 cents.

HOW TO MEASURE HAND FOR SIZE OF GLOVE.

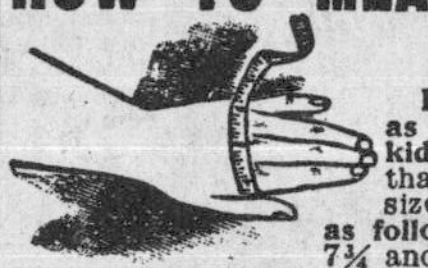

Draw a tape around the knuckles, as shown in the illustration. Ladies' kid gloves are not made in sizes larger than size 8. Ladies' driving gloves to size 8½. Ladies' kid glove sizes are as follows: 6, 6¼, 6½, 6¾, 7, 7¼, 7½, 7¾ and 8. Always state color and size.

LADIES' STYLISH SILK GLOVES.

$1.45 LADIES' PURE SILK SIXTEEN-BUTTON GLOVES.

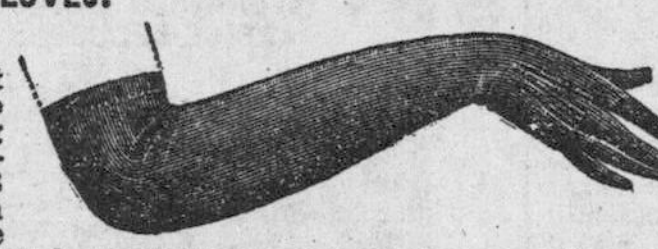

No. 33K5132 Women's Best Quality Fine Pure Silk Long Gloves, 16-button length (23 inches), which comes above the elbow. This is our best quality, equal to those usually sold for $2.00 or more per pair, and we recommend them to the most critical as the glove of gloves at our low price. Double tipped fingers and thumb, three-row silk embroidered backs. Opening at the wrist, with two clasps. Colors, BLACK or WHITE. Sizes, 6 to 8½. Be sure to state size and color wanted.
Special price, per pair $1.45
If by mail, postage extra, per pair, 2 cents.

89c LADIES' PURE SILK LONG GLOVES.

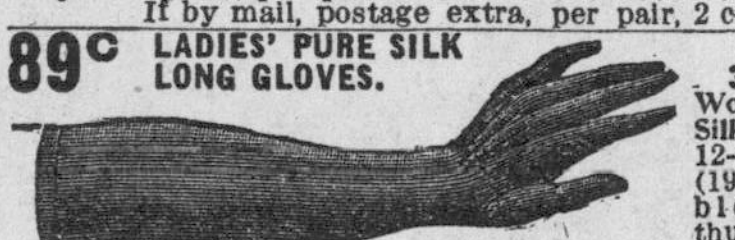

No. 33K5130 Women's Pure Silk Long Gloves, 12-button length (19 inches), double stitched thumb and three rows silk embroidery on backs. Colors, BLACK, WHITE or TAN. Sizes, 6 to 8½. Be sure to state size and color wanted.
Special price, per pair 89c
If by mail, postage extra, per pair, 2 cents.

98c FINEST PURE SILK GLOVES. PRICE REDUCED.

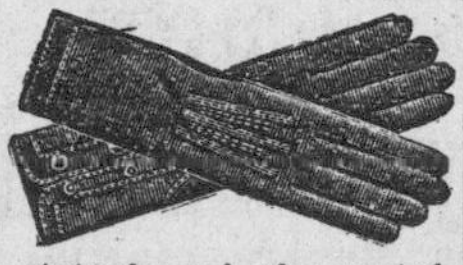

No. 33K5096 Women's Best Quality Finest Pure Silk Gloves, extra double tipped fingers and thumb. Three rows silk embroidery backs, two clasps at wrists, double stitched thumb. Made by the most skilled operators; every pair perfect fitting. Colors, BLACK or WHITE. Sizes 6 to 8½. Please state size and color wanted.
Special price, per pair 98c
If by mail, postage extra, per pair, 1 cent.

75c LADIES' PURE SILK GLOVES.

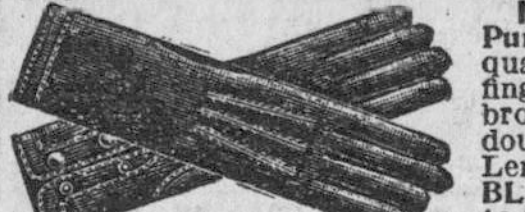

No. 33K5098 Ladies' Pure Silk Gloves. Very fine quality, genuine double tipped fingers, three rows of silk embroidery on backs, and thumbs double stitched. Two clasps. Length, 11 inches. Colors, BLACK or WHITE. Sizes, 6 to 8½. Be sure to state size and color wanted.
Price, per pair .... (Postage extra, per pair, 1 cent) 75c

49c FOR LADIES' PURE SILK GLOVES.

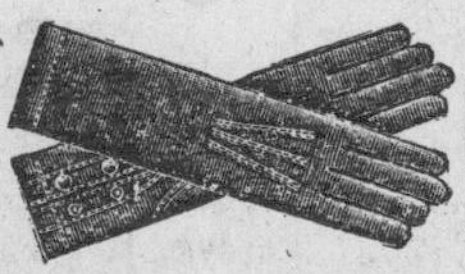

No. 33K5103 Ladies' Pure Silk Gloves, with two patent clasps at wrist. Double tipped fingers and double stitched thumbs. Three rows of embroidery on back. This glove is unequaled at the price. Colors, BLACK or WHITE. Sizes, 6 to 8½. Be sure to state size and color wanted.
Price, per pair ... (Postage extra, per pair, 1 cent) 49c

42c LADIES' PURE SILK MITTS. PRICE REDUCED.

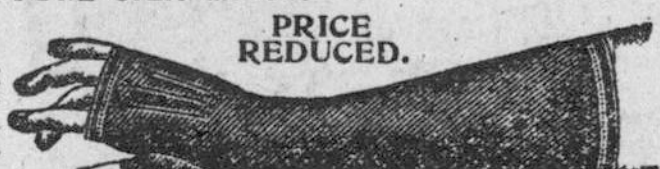

No. 33K5127 Ladies' Pure Silk Black Mitts, 11 inches long. Three rows glove embroidery on backs.
Reduced price, per pair, only 42c
If by mail, postage extra, per pair, 1 cent.

LADIES' GAUNTLET DRIVING GLOVES.

78c FOR LADIES' KID GAUNTLET DRIVING GLOVES. PRICE REDUCED.

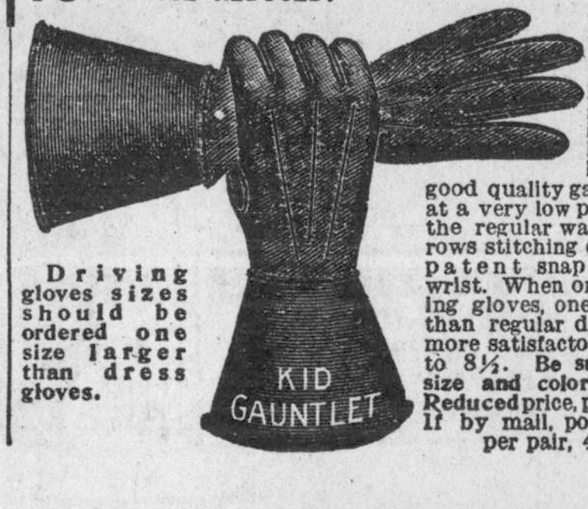

Driving gloves sizes should be ordered one size larger than dress gloves.

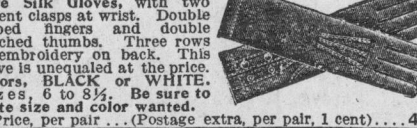

No. 33K5060 Ladies' Kid Gauntlet Driving Gloves in TAN, BROWN or BLACK. A good quality gauntlet glove at a very low price, made in the regular way with three rows stitching on back and patent snap buttons at wrist. When ordering driving gloves, one size larger than regular dress glove is more satisfactory. Sizes, 6 to 8½. Be sure to state size and color wanted.
Reduced price, per pair, 78c
If by mail, postage extra, per pair, 4 cents.

LADIES' KID AND MOCHA GLOVES.

$2.89 SIXTEEN-BUTTON LENGTH REAL FRENCH KID GLOVES. PRICE REDUCED.

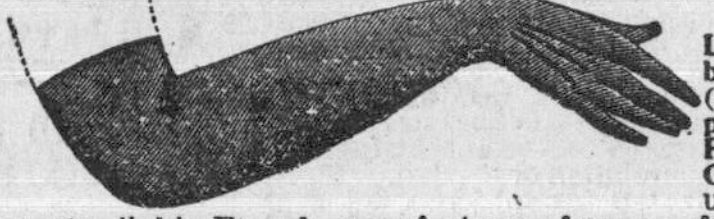

No. 33K5042 Ladies' Full 16-button length (23 inches) Imported Real French Kid Gloves. Made for us by one of the most reliable French manufacturers from carefully selected fine real French kid skins, soft, pliable and perfect fitting and regular full weight stock throughout. Has three buttons at wrist and three rows of silk embroidery on backs. We are able to quote a lower price than ever and we guarantee these gloves to be even better than heretofore. Colors, WHITE or BLACK only. Sizes, 6 to 8. Please state color and size wanted. Retails at $3.50 to $4.00. Reduced price, per pair, only $2.89
If by mail, postage extra, per pair, 3 cents.

$2.19 USUAL ELBOW LENGTH LADIES' KID GLOVES. PRICE REDUCED.

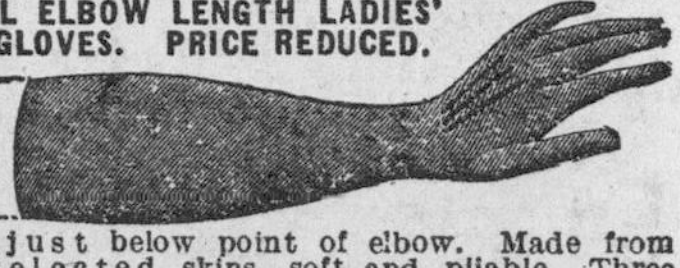

No. 33K5040 Ladies' Fine Imported Kid Gloves, the usual elbow length (20 inches), comes just below point of elbow. Made from fine quality selected skins, soft and pliable. Three buttons at wrist with three rows narrow silk embroidery on back. A high grade glove, made from finest selected stock. Colors, BLACK or WHITE only. Sizes, 6 to 8. State size and color wanted. Again we quote a lower price while guaranteeing the glove to be even better than before. Retails at $3.00. Reduced price, per pair, only $2.19
If by mail, postage extra, per pair, 3 cents.

96c LADIES' IMPORTED KID GLOVES.

BLACK, WHITE, BROWN OR GRAY.

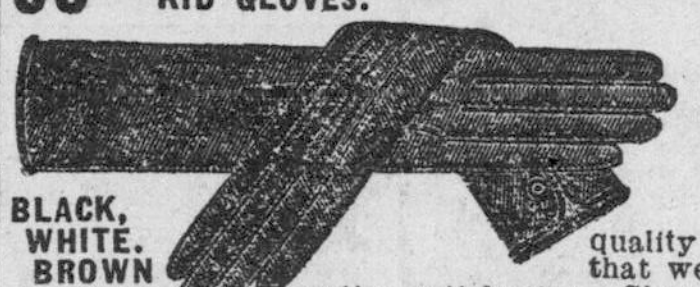

No. 33K5027 Ladies' Fine Imported Kid Gloves, two clasps at wrist, three rows of narrow silk embroidery on backs. An extra quality well made glove that we warrant to give entire satisfaction. Sizes, 6 to 8. State size and color wanted.
Reduced price, per pair, only 96c
If by mail, postage extra, per pair, 2 cents.

$1.39 FINEST FRENCH KID GLOVES. Price Reduced.

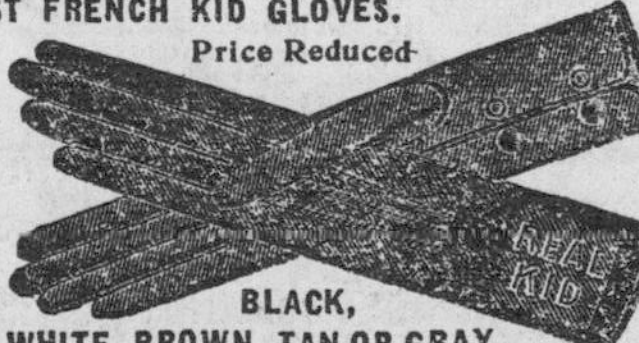

BLACK, WHITE, BROWN, TAN OR GRAY.

No. 33K5030 Ladies' Very Finest Quality Real French Kid Gloves, two clasps at wrist and three rows of embroidery on backs. Every pair made from specially selected elastic pliable real French kid skins. This glove will please the most fastidious woman. Sizes, 6 to 8. State size and color.
Reduced price, per pair, only $1.39
If by mail, postage extra, per pair, 2 cents.

RETAILS AT $1.25.

83c LADIES' UNDRESSED KID GLOVES.

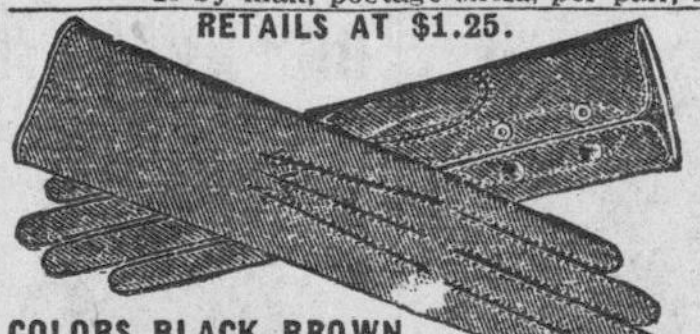

COLORS, BLACK, BROWN OR GRAY.

No. 33K5045 Ladies' Suede Gloves of good quality, made with embroidered backs and two clasps at wrist. Sizes, 6 to 8. State size and color wanted.
Reduced price, per pair, only 83c
If by mail, postage extra, per pair, 2 cents.

$1.12 LADIES' REAL MOCHA GLOVES.

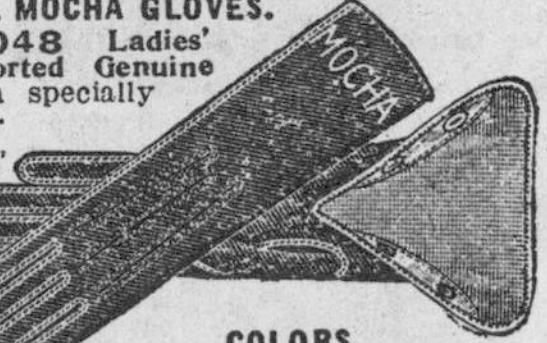

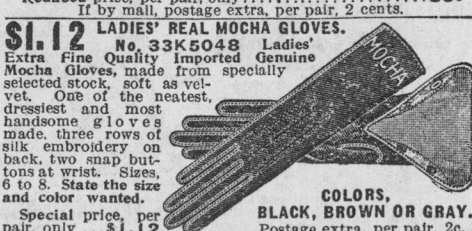

No. 33K5048 Ladies' Extra Fine Quality Imported Genuine Mocha Gloves, made from specially selected stock, soft as velvet. One of the neatest, dressiest and most handsome gloves made, three rows of silk embroidery on back, two snap buttons at wrist. Sizes, 6 to 8. State the size and color wanted.
Special price, per pair, only $1.12

COLORS, BLACK, BROWN OR GRAY.
Postage extra, per pair, 2c.

$1.46 LADIES' BUCKSKIN GAUNTLET GLOVES.

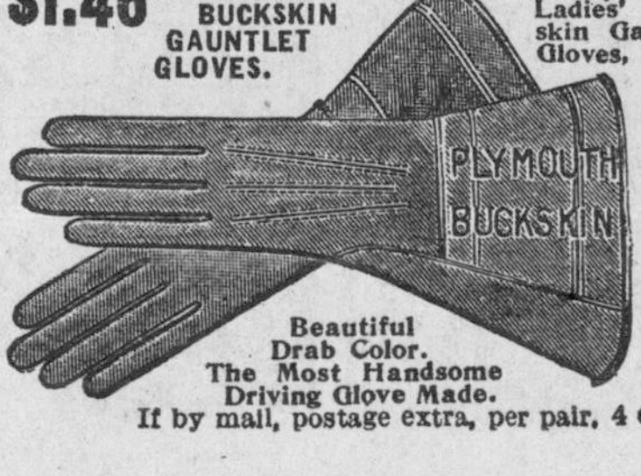

Beautiful Drab Color. The Most Handsome Driving Glove Made.

No. 33K5064 Ladies' Finest Buckskin Gauntlet Driving Gloves, selected light weight genuine Plymouth buckskin, three rows stitching on backs and wide deep fancy stitched leather lined cuffs. Sizes, 6, 6½, 7, 7½, 8, 8½. Please state size wanted. Reduced price, per pair ... $1.46
If by mail, postage extra, per pair, 4 cents.

MEN'S GAUNTLET, DRIVING AND WORKING GLOVES

ALSO HEAVY LINED WORKING GLOVES
PRICES REDUCED—QUALITIES IMPROVED.

$1.98 DRIVING OR AUTOMOBILE GAUNTLET GLOVES.

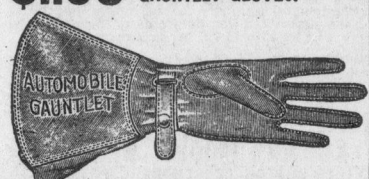

Important to Note: We do not recommend for heavy labor gloves quoted as driving gloves, as the stock in a driving glove is too fine to give the best of satisfaction when put to the severest test of heavy labor, but gloves described as working gloves we guarantee to give the best service for the roughest and hardest kind of labor.

$1.49 BUCKSKIN GAUNTLET DRIVING GLOVES.

PRICE REDUCED BUT BETTER QUALITY.

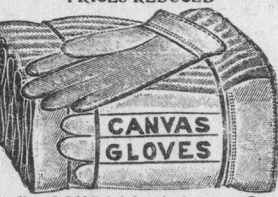

No. 33K5475 Selected English Calf Unlined Automobile Gauntlet Gloves, soft and pliable and finely made and finished. Colors, black or tan. Outseam sewed; spear point stitched backs, bellows cuffs 10 inches wide and snap button strap wrist tightener, as illustrated. Elegant fitting and unequaled for automobiling or driving. Sizes, 8 to 10½. State size. Retails at $3.00. Special price, per pair, only..... **$1.98** If by mail, postage extra, per pair, 9 cents.

92c HORSEHIDE GAUNTLET DRIVING OR WORKING GLOVES.

HORSEHIDE

FIRE AND WATER RESISTING

PRICE REDUCED No. 33K5474 Specially Tanned Horsehide Glove of best selected stock, and will give the best of service for either driving or working purposes. These gloves will remain soft and pliable in any climate and will resist steam and water. Sizes, 8 to 10½. Please state size. Our reduced price, now only **92c** per pair. If by mail, postage extra, per pair, 8 cents.

No. 33K5494 Table Cut Indian Tanned Buff Color Unlined Buckskin Gauntlet Driving Glove. Reinforced forefingers. Embroidered backs, elastic in wrists. Sizes, 8 to 10½. Our reduced price, per pair, now only.... **$1.49** If by mail, postage extra, per pair, 7 cents.

79c HORSEHIDE GAUNTLET WORKING GLOVES.

FIRE AND WATER RESISTING

Price Greatly Reduced

STAYS SOFT AND PLIABLE

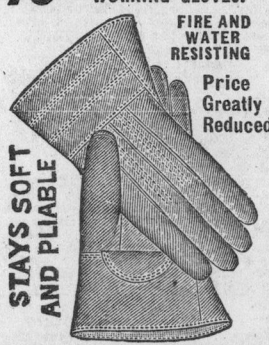

No. 33K5482 Specially Tanned Horsehide Gauntlet Gloves, recommended for teamsters, farmers, brakemen, engineers and laborers; in fact, everybody who requires the best of service in an unlined glove. This leather is specially selected and subjected to a tannage which makes it practically fire and waterproof, and will remain pliable in any climate. This heavy fire and water resisting genuine horsehide glove, made with welted seams, will wear "like iron." Sizes, 8, 8½, 9, 9½, 10 and 10½. Be sure to state size wanted. We warrant this glove to give the best of satisfaction. Retails at $1.25. Reduced price, per pair, only **79c** If by mail, postage extra, per pair, 8 cents.

WONDERFUL WORK SHIRT OFFER ON PAGES 966 AND 967 SAVES YOU MONEY.

49c CALFSKIN FACED GLOVES. PRICE REDUCED.

ELECTRIC TANNED

No. 33K5480 Special Electric Tanned Unlined Gauntlet Glove, extra heavy calfskin palms with sheepskin backs, a low priced glove which will give unequaled service. Sizes, 8 to 10½. Please state size. Retails at 75 cents. Reduced price, per pair, only **49c** If by mail, postage extra, per pair, 8 cents.

$1.38 HORSEHIDE GAUNTLET DRIVING GLOVES.

No. 33K5486

FIRE AND WATER RESISTING

PRICE REDUCED

Unlined Horsehide Gauntlet Driving Gloves, medium weight, heavily embroidered cuffs and backs. Buff color. Fire and water resisting tannage. Sizes, 8 to 10½. Please state size. Reduced price, per pair **$1.38** If by mail, postage extra, per pair, 11 cents.

98c SARANAC BUCKSKIN WORKING GLOVES. PRICE REDUCED.

SARANAC BUCKSKIN

No. 33K5472 Excellent Quality, Heavy Saranac Unlined Drab Buckskin Gauntlet Glove, welted seams. Best wearing leather ever produced for driving or heavy labor. Sizes, 8 to 10½. Please state size. Reduced price, per pair, only **98c** If by mail, postage extra, per pair, 11c.

$1.27 BUCKSKIN GAUNTLET DRIVING GLOVES.

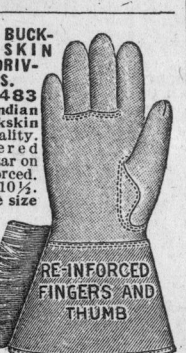

RE-INFORCED FINGERS AND THUMB

No. 33K5483 Buff Color Indian Tanned Buckskin of fine quality. Embroidered backs and star on cuffs. Reinforced. Sizes, 8½ to 10½. Please state size wanted. Our special price, per pair, **$1.27** Postage extra, per pair, 8 cents.

$1.08 HORSEHIDE DRIVING GLOVES. PRICE REDUCED.

No. 33K5484

Extra wide cuff.

Medium Weight Selected Horsehide Driving Gloves. Extra large gauntlet cuffs. Buff color, guaranteed to remain soft and pliable and give wonderful service. Sizes, 8 to 10½. Please state size. Reduced price, per pair, only **$1.08** Postage extra, per pair, 8 cents.

$1.69 PLYMOUTH BUCKSKIN DRIVING GLOVES.

No. 33K5498

Heaviest Unlined Drab Plymouth Buckskin Gauntlet Gloves. Wide fancy stitched cuffs. Handsomest driving gloves made. Sizes, 8 to 10½. Please state size. Special price, per pair, only **$1.69** If by mail, postage extra, per pair, 8c.

CANVAS OR CANTON FLANNEL GLOVES. Owing to our low prices on canvas gloves, we can furnish only in quantities as quoted. PRICES REDUCED

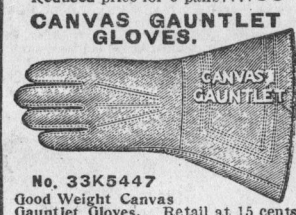

CANVAS GLOVES

No. 33K5444 A 6-ounce Canvas Glove. 10 cents per pair at retail. Reduced price, per dozen pairs, only.... **72c**
No. 33K5445 8-ounce Canvas Gloves, retailed at 15 cents per pair. Reduced price, per dozen pairs, only.... **87c**
No. 33K5446 Heaviest 10-ounce Canvas Gloves, leather tipped fingers and thumb. Reduced price for 6 pairs.... **53c**

CANVAS GAUNTLET GLOVES.

CANVAS GAUNTLET

No. 33K5447 Good Weight Canvas Gauntlet Gloves. Retail at 15 cents. Reduced price, per dozen pairs, **95c**
No. 33K5448 Heaviest Canvas Gauntlet Gloves. Reduced price for 6 pairs **55c**
All canvas gloves if by mail, postage extra, per dozen pairs, 35 cents; for ½ dozen pairs, 20 cents.

MEN'S HEAVY FLEECE AND FUR LINED WORKING GLOVES

87c HORSEHIDE WORKING GLOVES.

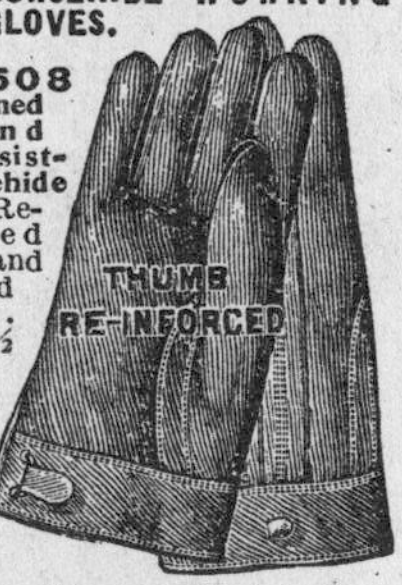

No. 33K5508

THUMB RE-INFORCED

Fleece Lined Fire and Water Resisting Horsehide Gloves. Reinforced thumbs and welted seams. Sizes, 9½ to 10½. Please state size. Reduced price, per pair **87c** Postage extra, per pair, 8 cents.

87c CORDOVAN AND BUCKSKIN GLOVES.

KNIT WRIST

No. 33K5516 Genuine Cordovan Fleece Lined Gloves. Knitted wrists. Sizes, 8½ to 10½. State size. Reduced price, per pair, only... **87c**
No. 33K5520 Heavy Genuine Buckskin Gloves. Fleece lined. Sizes, 8½ to 10½. State size. Reduced price, per pair, only.. **87c** Postage extra, per pair, 10 cents.

89c LINED FIRE AND WATER RESISTING HORSEHIDE GAUNTLET GLOVES.

No. 33K5527

HORSE HIDE

Specially Tanned Fire and Water Resisting Horsehide Gauntlet Gloves. Fleece lined. Recommended for hardest wear. Sizes 8½ to 10½. State size. Special price, per pair **89c** If by mail, postage extra, per pair, 9c.

$1.10 LAMB LINED HORSEHIDE GLOVES.

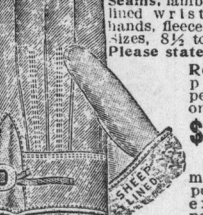

SHEEP LINED

No. 33K5509 Specially Tanned Horsehide, Welted seams, lamb's wool lined wrists and hands, fleece lined. Sizes, 8½ to 10½. Please state size. Reduced price, per pair, only **$1.10** If by mail, postage extra, per pair, 11 cents.

49c MEN'S HEAVY CALFSKIN FACED GLOVES.

THIS GLOVE GIVES WONDERFUL SERVICE

No. 33K5506 Men's Fleece Lined Working Gloves, made with extra heavy genuine calfskin palms and heavy sheepskin backs, with draw string fastener at wrist, as illustrated. For wear and service, in a moderate priced glove, this glove has no equal. Satisfaction guaranteed. Sizes, 8½ to 10½. Please state size. Special price, per pair, only **49c** If by mail, postage extra, per pair, 7 cents.

BEFORE YOU ORDER MEASURE YOUR HAND AND ON YOUR ORDER TELL US WHAT THE MEASUREMENT IS.

$1.21 LINED GENUINE SARANAC BUCKSKIN GAUNTLET GLOVES.

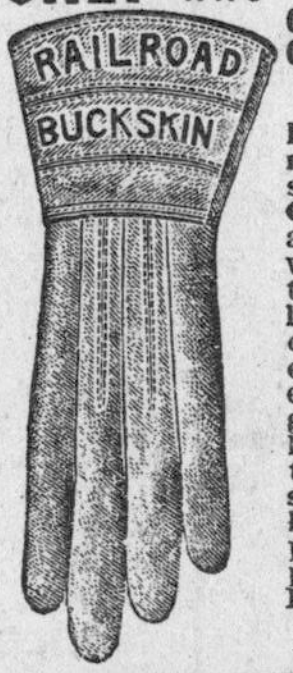

No. 33K5529

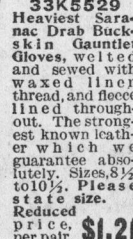

RAILROAD BUCKSKIN

Heaviest Saranac Drab Buckskin Gauntlet Gloves, welted and sewed with waxed linen thread, and fleece lined throughout. The strongest known leather which we guarantee absolutely. Sizes, 8½ to 10½. Please state size. Reduced price, per pair, **$1.21** If by mail, postage extra, per pair, 11 cents.

42c LINED HOGSKIN GLOVES.

No. 33K5522

HOG SKIN FACED

KNIT WRIST

PRICE REDUCED

Heavy Hogskin Fleece Lined Gloves, snug fitting wool wrists. Sizes, 8½ to 10½. Please state size. Reduced price, per pair, only.. **42c** If by mail, postage extra, per pair, 8 cents.

96c SARANAC BUCKSKIN, LINED GLOVES. No. 33K5512

WOOL FLEECE LINED

Heavy Saranac Buckskin Gloves. Waxed thread sewed, welted seams and fleece lined. Very serviceable. Sizes, 8½ to 10½. Color, drab. Please state size. $1.50 gloves at retail. Our price, per pair, only.. **96c** If by mail, postage extra, per pair, 9 cents.

$1.45 SARANAC BUCKSKIN GLOVES. PRICE REDUCED. No. 33K5517

WISH BAND

Heavy Fleece Lined; outseam sewed with waxed thread, double draw string fastener on extra wide band wrist. Sizes, 8½ to 10½. Please state size. Reduced price, per pair only **$1.45** Postage extra, per pair, 11 cents.

MEN'S DRESS AND DRIVING MITTENS
HEAVY WORKING MITTENS—KNITTED WOOL MITTENS

57c FLEECE LINED KID MITTENS. PRICE REDUCED.
No. 33K5691 Dark Brown Kid Mittens, elastic wrists, stitched backs, fleece lined. Sizes, 8 to 10½. Give size. Reduced price, per pair, only . .57c
If by mail, postage extra, per pair, 6 cents.

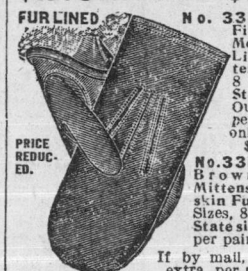

$1.79 FUR LINED MOCHA MITTENS $3.35
FUR LINED. PRICE REDUCED.
No. 33K5699 Fine Brown Mocha Fur Lined Mittens. Sizes, 8 to 10½. State size. Our price, per pair, only . . . $1.79
No. 33K5701 Brown Mocha Mittens. Moleskin Fur Lined. Sizes, 8 to 10½. State size. Price, per pair, $3.35
If by mail, postage extra, per pair, 8c.

91c FUR TOP KID MITTENS. PRICE REDUCED.
CONEY FUR WRIST
No. 33K5694 Finest Brown Kid Mittens. Fleece lined embroidered backs, elastic wrists and fine black fur tops. Sizes, 8 to 10½. State size. Reduced price, per pair, only . . 91c
If by mail, postage extra, per pair, 8 cents.

$1.29 BUCKSKIN MITTENS. $2.39
FUR LINED BUCK
No. 33K5705 Plymouth Buckskin Driving Mittens, fleece lined. Sizes, 8½ to 10½. Price, per pair $1.29
No. 33K5707 Finest Buckskin Driving Mittens. Sizes, 8 to 10½. Price, per pair, only . . . $2.39

58c FUR TOP KID MITTENS.
FUR WRIST
No. 33K5697 Fur Top Elastic Wrist Brown Kid Mittens, fleece lined. Sizes, 8 to 10½. State size. Our price, per pair, only . . 58c
If by mail, postage extra, per pair, 6 cents.

CHALLENGE OFFER.

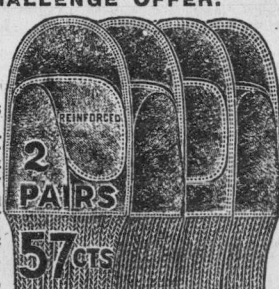

57c FOR TWO PAIRS.
No. 33K5726 Heavy Fleece Lined Leather Working Mittens. Reinforced. Special price, for two pairs, only . .57c
If by mail, postage extra, for two pairs, 15c.
REINFORCED 2 PAIRS 57 CTS

49c ROLL WRIST CALFSKIN PALM MITTENS.
No. 33K5742 Sheepskin backs, welted seams, fleece lined. Knitted wrist rolls over coat sleeve. Special price, per pair, only . . 49c
If by mail, postage extra, per pair, 12 cents.

79c BEST QUALITY HORSEHIDE LEATHER MITTENS.
No. 33K5748 Heavy Fleece Lined. Roll Up Wrist. Special price, per pair, only. . . 79c
If by mail, postage extra, per pair, 13 cents.

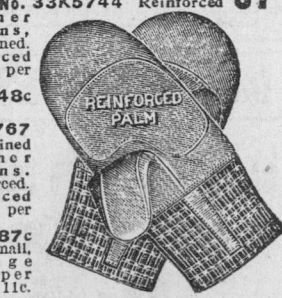

48c PATCH PALM MITTENS. 87c
No. 33K5744 Reinforced Leather Mittens, fleece lined. Reduced price, per pair, only. . . 48c
No. 33K5767 Fleece Lined Leather Mittens. Reinforced. Reduced price, per pair, only. . . 87c
If by mail, postage extra, per pair, 11c.
REINFORCED PALM

46c FLEECE LINED CALFSKIN MITTENS.
No. 33K5730 Extra Large Heavy Calfskin Palm Mittens, sheepskin backs, welted seams, fleece lined. Special value at our price. Reduced price, per pair, only . . . 46c
If by mail postage extra, per pair, 11 cents.

46c 82c 85c 97c KNITTED WOOL WRIST MITTENS.
No. 33K5731 Welted Seam, Calfskin Palm Mittens, fleece lined. Special price, per pair, only . . . 46c
If by mail, postage extra, per pair, 9 cents.
No. 33K5766 Welted Seam, Leather Mittens, fleece lined. Our special price, per pair, only. . . 82c
If by mail, postage extra, per pair, 11 cents.
No. 33K5754 Heavy Fire and Water Resisting Horsehide Mittens, fleece lined. Extra large size. Special price, per pair, only . . . 85c
If by mail, postage extra, per pair, 12 cents.
No. 33K5747 Heavy Horsehide Mittens. Half lamb's wool lined. Special price, per pair, only . . 97c
If by mail, postage extra, per pair, 11 cents.

49c LINED MITTENS, BAND WRISTS. $1.23 $1.69
STEAM AND WATER RESISTING
No. 33K5770 Heavy Calfskin Palm, Sheepskin Back Mittens, fleece lined. Special price, per pair, only. . . 49c
If by mail, postage extra, per pair, 8 cents.
No. 33K5786 Heaviest Buckskin Mittens, lamb's wool lined. Special price, per pair, only . $1.23
If by mail, postage extra, per pair, 12 cents.
No. 33K5787 Best Saranac Buckskin Mittens. Fur lined. Special price, per pair, only . $1.69
Postage extra, per pair, 12 cents.
No. 33K5778 Heavy Lamb Lined Horsehide Mittens. Fire and water resisting. Welted seams and extra wide band wrist. Price, per pair only . . . $1.23
Postage extra, per pair, 12 cents.

49c STORM WRIST MITTENS. $1.23
STORM WRIST STRING FASTENER
No. 33K5746 Wool Wrist Hogskin Palm Mittens, fleece lined. Large sizes. Special price, per pair, only. . . 49c
No. 33K5753 Heaviest and Biggest Mittens made. Buckskin, lamb's wool lined. Price, per pair, only. . . $1.23
If by mail, postage extra, per pair, 14 cents.

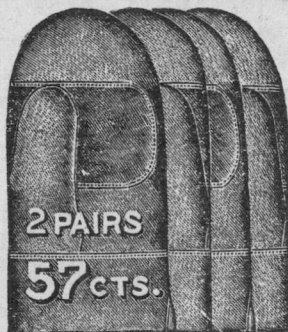

57c FOR TWO PAIRS.
No. 33K5872 Reinforced Palm Unlined Muleskin Mittens. Wonderful wearing qualities. Special price, for 2 pairs, only . . . 57c
If by mail, postage extra, per 2 pairs, 17 cents.
2 PAIRS 57 CTS.

49c COMBINATION MITTEN OFFERS. 96c
Fleeced Inner Mitten
TWO IN ONE
No. 33K5870 Unlined, Calfskin Palm, Sheepskin Back Mittens, sewed with waxed thread, also one pair cotton fleeced inner mittens. Our price, for combination of 2 pairs, only. (Without fleeced inner mitten, 41 cents per pair). .49c
If by mail, postage extra, 10 cents.
No. 33K5874 Unlined Fire and Water Resisting Horsehide Mittens, reinforced riveted thumb, includes Special Fleeced Cotton Mitten. Our price, for combination of 2 pairs, only. (Without fleeced inner mitten, 88 cents per pair)..96c
If by mail, postage extra, 14 cents.

81c GAUNTLET MITTENS. $1.26 PRICE REDUCED.
No. 33K5810 Horsehide Gauntlet Mittens, fleece lined. Our reduced price, per pair, only . . . 81c
If by mail, postage extra, 14 cents.
No. 33K5814 Horsehide Gauntlet Mittens, lamb's wool lined welted seams. Our reduced price, per pair. . . $1.26
If by mail, postage extra, per pair, 17 cents.
LAMBS WOOL LINED HORSEHIDE REINFORCED SEAMS

24c SHOOTING MITTENS.

HUNTERS SPECIAL
No. 33K5833 One-Finger Seamless Gray Wool Shooting Mittens. Special price, per pair, only . . . 24c
Postage extra, per pair, 6 cents.

21c HEAVY YARN MITTENS.
HEAVY WOOL YARN MITTEN
No. 33K5824 Black, Gray or White Heavy Knitted Mittens. Price, per pair, only. . 21c
Postage extra, per pair, 5 cents.

42c WATERPROOF WOOL MITTENS.
WIND AND WATER PROOF
No. 33K5855 Heavy Wool Mittens, fleece lined and waterproof interlining. Price, per pair, only. 42c
Postage extra, per pair 11 cents.

42c PULL OVER SLEEVE MITTENS. 49c BEST PULL OVER SLEEVE MITTENS.
No. 33K5852 Double Knitted Wool Mittens, with double extension wool wrists. Price, per pair, only . . . 42c
If by mail, postage extra, per pair, 15 cents.
No. 33K5858 Best Value Wool Mittens, with double pull over sleeve wrists. Special price, per pair, only. . . . 49c
If by mail, postage extra, per pair, 15 cents.

CANVAS MITTENS. PRICES REDUCED.
No. 33K5880 Eight-Ounce Canvas Mittens. Reduced price, per dozen pairs . . . 73c
No. 33K5882 Ten-Ounce Canvas Mittens. Reduced price, per dozen pairs . . . 97c
Postage extra, for 1 dozen pairs, 35 cents.

7c WRIST STRAPS.
No. 33K5910 Calfskin Wrist Straps, 2½ inches wide. Price, each. . . .7c
Postage extra, each, 2c.

87c UNLINED BUCKSKIN MITTENS. $1.18
No. 33K5876 Saranac Heaviest Unlined Buckskin Mittens. Our reduced price, per pair. . . . 87c
If by mail, postage extra, per pair, 10 cents.
No. 33K5878 Genuine Jack Buckskin Reversible Mittens. Unlined. Reinforced riveted thumbs, double wear. Our reduced price, per pair. . . $1.18
If by mail, postage extra, per pair, 14 cents.

37c WATERPROOF KNITTED MITTENS.

HEAVY WATER AND STORM PROOF
No. 33K5862 Double Wool Mittens, heavy tufted lining, with waterproof interlining. Dark colors. Special price, per pair, only. . . 37c
If by mail, postage extra, per pair, 12 cents.

LESS THAN WHOLESALE PRICES

MEN'S AND BOYS' HATS

BEST HATS MADE AT THE PRICE

HATS IN ALL THE POPULAR AND STAPLE STYLES AT THE LOWEST PRICES EVER QUOTED.

UNDER OUR OWN SUPERVISION every hat we sell is made and we add only our one small margin of profit to the actual cost to make. This is the reason why we can quote these astonishingly low prices for finer hats than were ever sold even at 33⅓ per cent more than our prices. **OUR HATS ARE ALL MADE OF THE FINEST** selected Belgian fur stock, dyed by the best process known, assuring absolutely fast colors that will not change under the rays of the hot sun. They are all made and trimmed in the best possible manner, with finest quality silk bands and best leather sweats, and will not shrink or get out of shape when wet. **WE OFFER THE LATEST AND MOST GENTEEL STYLES.** We do not make or sell freak styles. Note closely our illustrations, which are made from actual photographs of each hat. Read our descriptions carefully, and if you care to refer to the illustrations of hats of different dimensions as shown on different types and ages of men and make your selection accordingly, you can be assured of getting a hat to suit you better than if bought in a store, because, you see, you have our big assortment to choose from, each well illustrated and correctly and fully described, which is far better than buying a hat at retail, because you are likely to decide hastily from the recommendation of the retailer who may not have your interest in view but is trying to sell you a style he is anxious to get rid of.

WE GUARANTEE EVERY HAT WE SELL. Buy our hat, examine it, wear it, try it thoroughly, and if it does not prove exactly what we claim for it in quality and style and as good or better than hats for which you have paid 33⅓ per cent more at retail, return it to us at our expense and we will refund both the price and any transportation charges paid.

BOYS' SIZES, 6½ to 7⅛.
MEN'S SIZES, 6¾ to 7¾.

Hat	Inches around head
Size, 6½; measures	20¾
Size, 6⅝; measures	21
Size, 6¾; measures	21½
Size, 6⅞; measures	21⅝
Size, 7; measures	22¼
Size, 7⅛; measures	22½
Size, 7¼; measures	23
Size, 7⅜; measures	23⅜
Size, 7½; measures	23¾
Size, 7⅝; measures	24
Size, 7¾; measures	24½

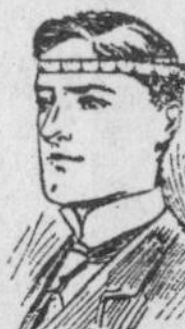

HOW TO MEASURE

Take your measure as above illustrated and either send us this measurement in inches when you order or compare the number of inches your head measures with this scale, which will tell you the size hat you wear.

MEN'S NEWEST AND NEATEST STYLES IN BLACK AND BROWN STIFF HATS

$1.33 FULL SHAPE

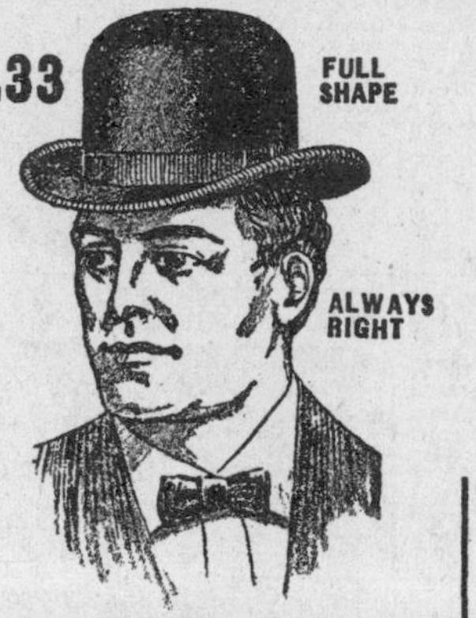

ALWAYS RIGHT

$1.33 FULL SHAPE STAPLE BLACK STIFF HAT.

No. 33K6010 Large Man's Style Black Stiff Hat. Full oval crown 5¾ inches deep, with staple roll brim, 2¼ inches wide front and back. Not an extreme hat but is a well proportioned style of slightly larger dimensions throughout than the hat illustrated and described at the right. Intended for rather large men or men with full features, and for this type of man is one of the most becoming and most appropriate styles ever shown. Sizes, 6¾ to 7¾. **Do not fail to state the size or give measurement of head when ordering hats.** Black only. A $2.00 hat at retail.
Our price, each, only..........**$1.33**
If by mail, postage extra, each, 26 cents.

$1.33 STYLE AND SERVICE

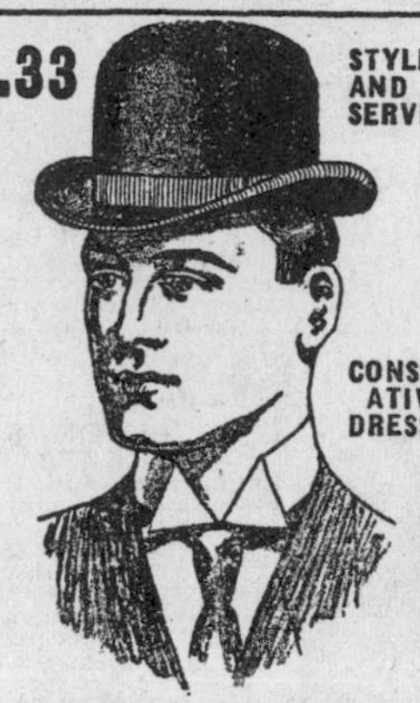

CONSERVATIVE DRESSER

$1.33 FASHIONABLE BLACK STIFF HAT.

No. 33K6005 Conservative Dresser's Black Stiff Hat. Oval crown 5½ inches deep, moderately rolled brim, 2 inches wide front and back. A most becoming style for any man and is a strictly up to date hat in a staple shape which will always remain one of the best style stiff hats that can be made. Sizes, 6¾ to 7½. **Do not fail to give your size.** Black only. A $2.00 hat if bought at retail.
Our price, each, only..........**$1.33**
If by mail, postage extra, each, 26 cents.

$1.69 FITS RIGHT AND LOOKS RIGHT

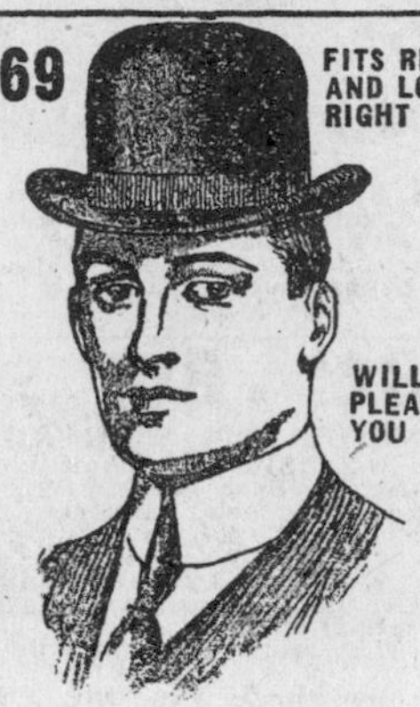

WILL PLEASE YOU

$1.69 FINE AND SERVICEABLE BLACK STIFF HAT.

No. 33K6020 Black Stiff Hat for critical men. Crown 5½ inches deep and neatly but stylishly turned brim 2 inches wide front and back. This is one of the neatest and dressiest hats shown this season and is guaranteed to please the most critical. Sizes, 6¾ to 7½. **Please state size.** Black only. It's an absolute fact that this quality retails at $2.50.
Our price, each, only..........**$1.69**
If by mail, postage extra, for any stiff hat, each, 26 cents.

$1.69 MODERATELY FULL SHAPE

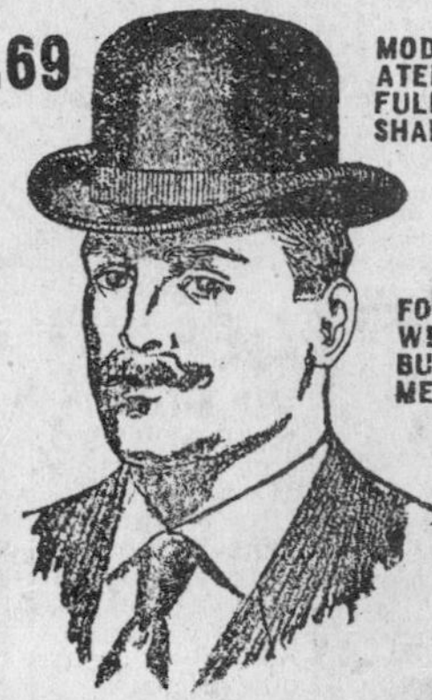

FOR WELL BUILT MEN

$1.69 EXCELLENT QUALITY STYLISH BLACK STIFF HAT.

No. 33K6025 The Larger Shape Black Stiff Hat in the same conservative but stylish block as described at the left but with crown 5½ inches deep, brim 2⅛ inches wide front and back. Sizes, 6¾ to 7¾. This hat is only slightly larger than No. 33K6020. Will suit the average well built man of 180 to 200 pounds. **State the size hat you wear.** Black only. A $2.50 hat.
Our price, each, only.....**$1.69**
If by mail, postage extra, for any stiff hat, each, 26 cents.

$2.19 A HANDSOME HAT

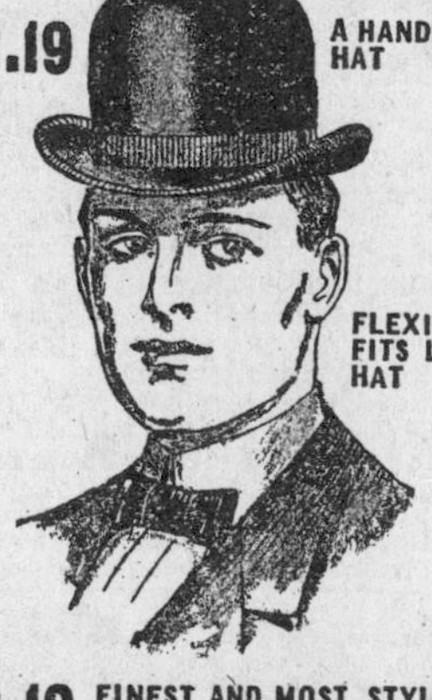

FLEXIBLE BAND, FITS LIKE A SOFT HAT

$2.19 FINEST AND MOST STYLISH PURE BEAVER STIFF HAT.

No. 33K6035 Gentlemen's Dressiest Black Stiff Hat. One of the most conservative styles and handsomest hats ever shown, crown 5½ inches deep, with beautifully curled brim 1⅞ inches wide back and front. Elegant quality with flexible band, **so that hat fits any head as comfortably as a soft hat.** Sizes, 6¾ to 7½. **State size wanted.** Color, Black only. The handsomest hat ever produced. Never less than $3.00.
Our price, each, only..........**$2.19**
If by mail, postage extra on above style, each, 26 cents

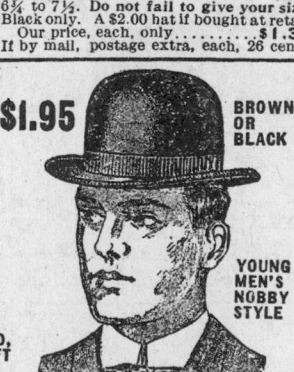

$1.95 BROWN OR BLACK

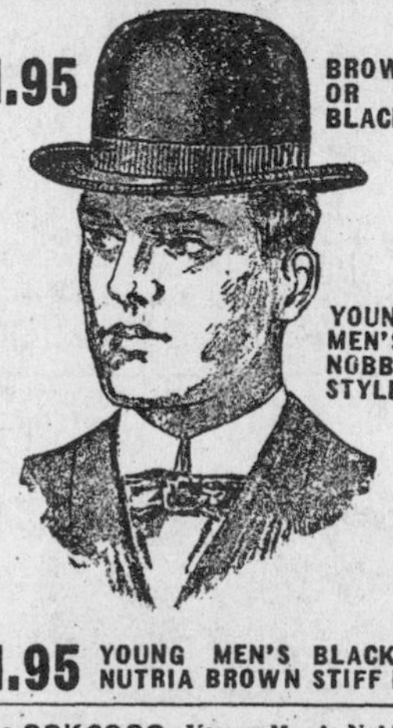

YOUNG MEN'S NOBBY STYLE

$1.95 YOUNG MEN'S BLACK OR NUTRIA BROWN STIFF HAT.

No. 33K6028 Young Man's Nobbiest and Neatest Black or Nutria Brown Stiff Hat. Crown 5¼ inches deep and "snappy" only slightly curled brim 1⅞ inches wide. This is absolutely the newest and most dressy stiff hat for young men who wish to be "up to date" but not extreme. Either black or the latest shade of light tan (nutria brown). Sizes, 6¾ to 7⅜. **Please state size and color wanted.**
Our price, each, only..........**$1.95**
If by mail, postage extra, each, 26 cents.

$1.95 BROWN OR BLACK

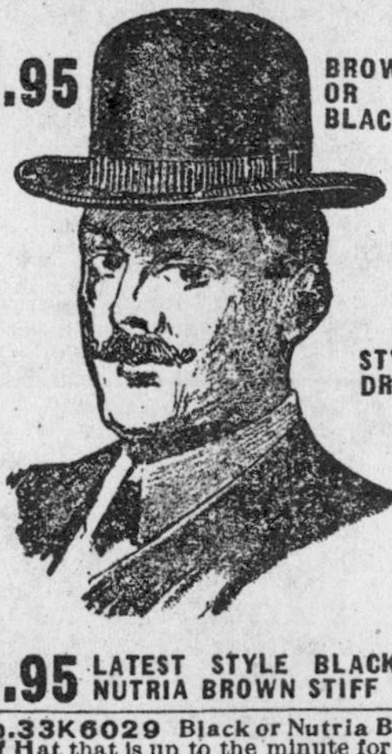

STYLISH DRESSER

$1.95 LATEST STYLE BLACK OR NUTRIA BROWN STIFF HAT.

No. 33K6029 Black or Nutria Brown Stiff Hat that is up to the minute for style and character. The illustration shows this handsome new style just as it is, and the average built man weighing between 140 and 190 pounds cannot select a more handsome hat. Crown is 5½ inches deep, and the brim which is only slightly curled measures 2 inches wide at front and back. Colors, black or nutria brown (light tan). Sizes, 6¾ to 7½. **State size and color wanted.**
Our price, each, only..........**$1.95**
If by mail, postage extra, each, 26 cents.

$2.19 NONE BETTER MADE

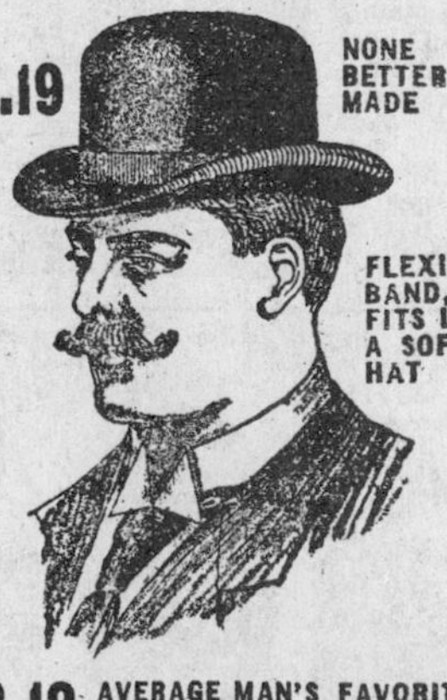

FLEXIBLE BAND, FITS LIKE A SOFT HAT

$2.19 AVERAGE MAN'S FAVORITE STYLE BLACK STIFF HAT.

No. 33K6040 Conservative Style in Black Stiff Hat for Larger Men. Crown 5¾ inches deep, brim 2⅛ inches wide front and back, just enough and not too much fulness to crown and brim to make the most becoming hat ever offered for this type of man. Flexible band which makes this hat fit any head and is as comfortable as a soft hat. Sizes, 6¾ to 7¾. **State size.** Black only. A $3.00 hat.
Our price, each, only..........**$2.19**
If by mail, postage extra on above style, each, 26 cents.

WHY WE SHOULD SELL YOU YOUR HATS: Because we quote only the best styles and quality. We could not afford to do otherwise for our hats must please or they will come back to us. And we guarantee a positive saving to you of 33⅓ per cent. Surely enough said.

MEN'S HOT WEATHER HATS=BOYS' DRESS HATS=MEN'S AND BOYS' CAPS

49c HAIRCLOTH HAT CRUSHER STYLE.

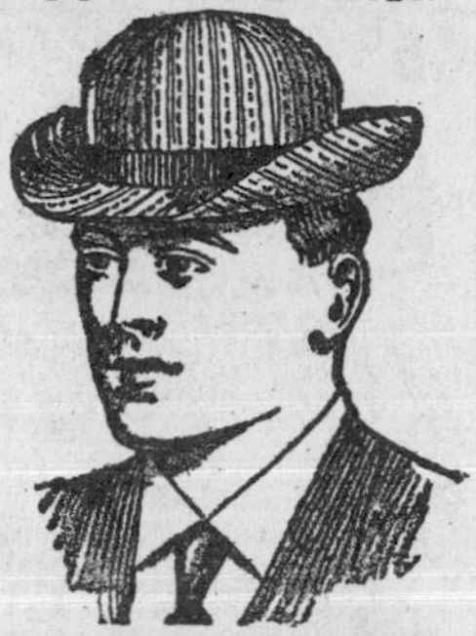

No. 33K6885 Men's Round Crown, Crusher Style Haircloth Hat, fancy light gray color. Made without starch or stiffening and when crushed or wet is not harmed but quickly returns to its original shape. Beats straw. Taped seams, leather sweat. Men's sizes, 6¾ to 7½. State size. Special price, each, only **49c**
If by mail, postage extra, each, 16c.

43c HAIRCLOTH HAT.

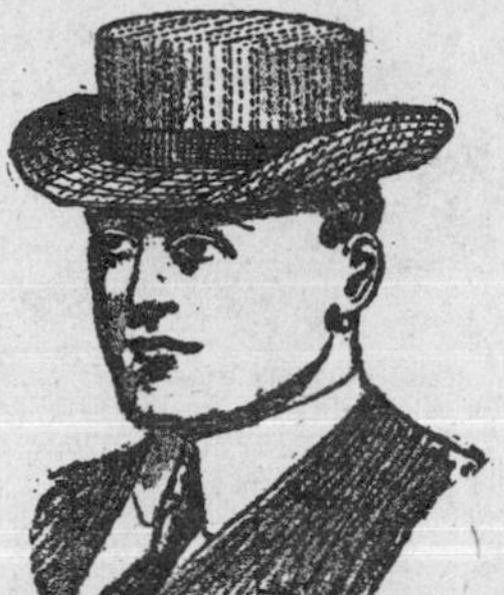

No. 33K6882 Men's Neat and Serviceable Haircloth Summer Hat with absolutely no starch or stiffening. Leather sweat. Light drab color with "invisible" stripes. Men's sizes, 6¾ to 7½. State size. More durable than straw. **43c**
Special price, each, only...
If by mail, postage extra, each, 14c.

75c HAIRCLOTH HAT TELESCOPE STYLE.

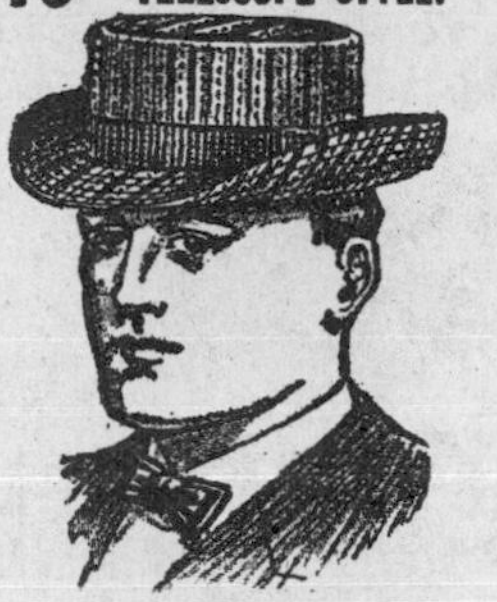

No. 33K6880 Men's Neat Telescope Style Haircloth Hat, "invisible" stripe, straw color. Fine silk ribbon band, closely stitched brim and leather sweat. The most practical hot weather hat ever made. Will keep its shape after being crushed or wet. We strongly recommend this hat. Men's sizes, 6¾ to 7½. State size. Retails at $1.00.
Special price, each, only.... **75c**
If by mail, postage extra, each, 15 cents.

40c MERCERIZED POPLIN HAT.

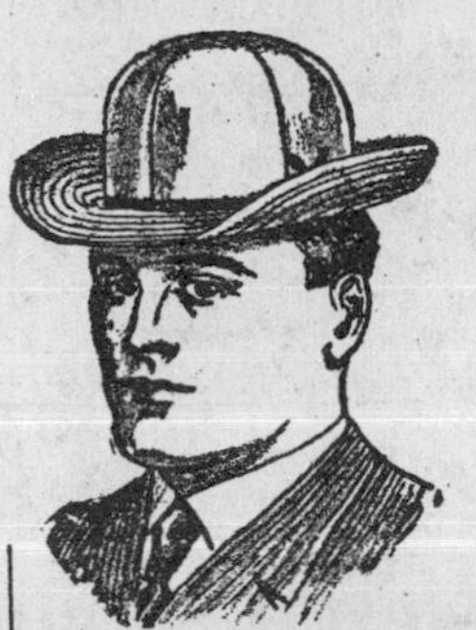

No. 33K6872 Fine White Mercerized Poplin Cloth Hat, with closely stitched brim, four-piece taped seam crown. Exactly as illustrated. Men's sizes, 6¾ to 7½. Be sure to state size wanted. A neat hat for outing wear.
Special price, each, only... **40c**
If by mail, postage extra, each, 24c.

40c REGULATION ARMY BROWN DUCK HAT.

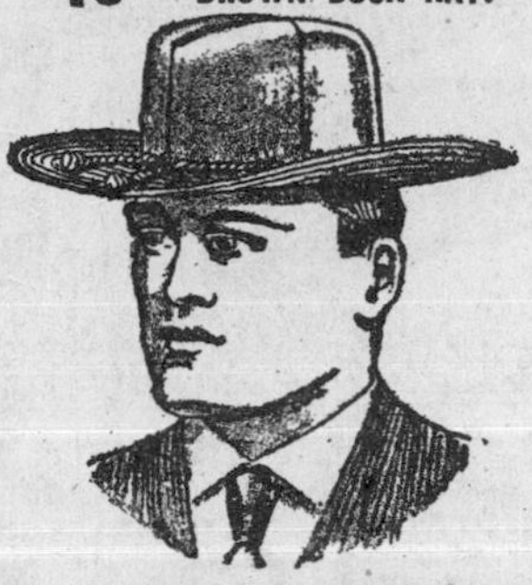

No. 33K6874 Regulation Army Style Brown Twill Duck Hat, for hot weather wear, closely stitched and stiffened brim. A favorite with fishermen. A hat that will stand rough service and protect you from the hot sun. Men's sizes, 6¾ to 7½. Be sure to state size wanted.
Special price, each, only.... **40c**
If by mail, postage extra, each, 25 cents.

41c BOYS' WOOL TELESCOPE.

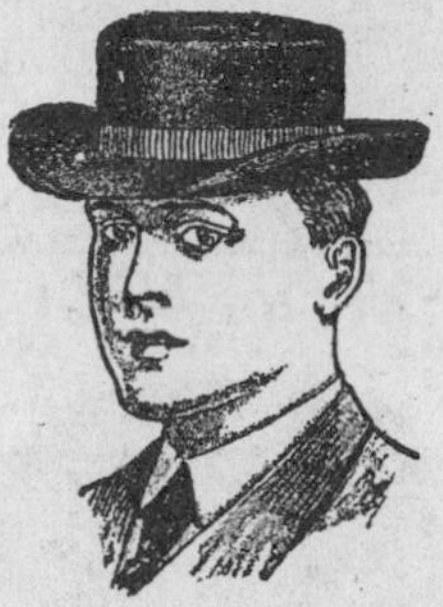

No. 33K6200 Boys' Black Telescope Wool Hat, raw edge brim. Crown, 3 inches deep; brim, 2½ inches wide. Boys' sizes, 6½ to 7. State size.
Price, each, only **41c**
No. 33K6201 Boys' Steel Color Telescope Wool Hat, above style. Boys' sizes, 6½ to 7. State size.
Price, each, only **41c**
If by mail, postage extra, each, 14c.

89c BOYS' PAN BRIM STYLE.

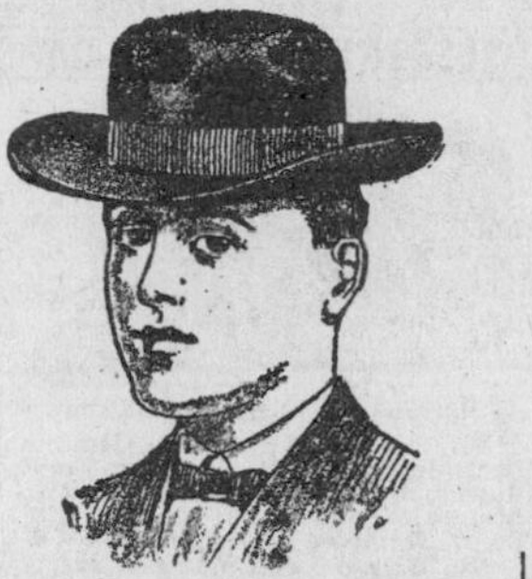

No. 33K6228 Boys' Pan Brim Style Black Soft Hat, raw edge, can be worn telescoped, creased or indented. Crown, 4 inches deep; brim, 2¾ inches wide. A staple style. Boys' sizes, 6½ to 7⅛. Be sure to give size. Color, black only. A $1.25 hat.
Our price, each, only...... **89c**
If by mail, postage extra, each, 25c.

89c BOYS' COLLEGE CRUSHER.

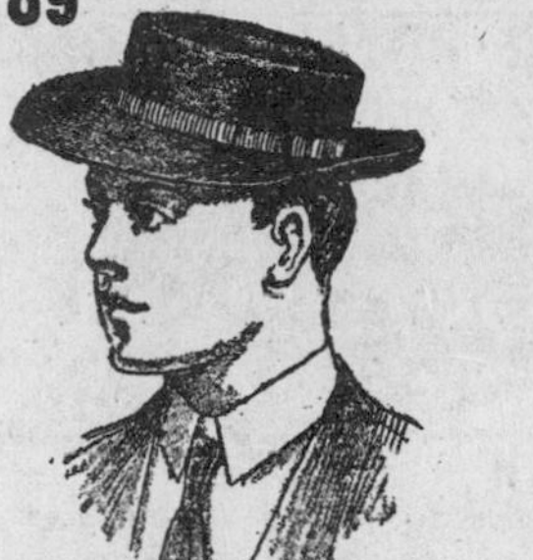

No. 33K6215 Boys' Black Telescope College Crusher, raw edge brim. Crown, 2¾ inches deep; brim, 2½ inches wide. Boys' sizes, 6½ to 7⅛. A typical "Young America" style hat, because no matter how carelessly worn is still becoming to any boy. What size, please? **89c**
Price, each, only ....
No. 33K6216 Boys' Silver Telescope Crusher, above style. State size. Price, each, only... **89c**
If by mail, postage extra, each, 14c.

89c BOYS' BLACK TOURIST.

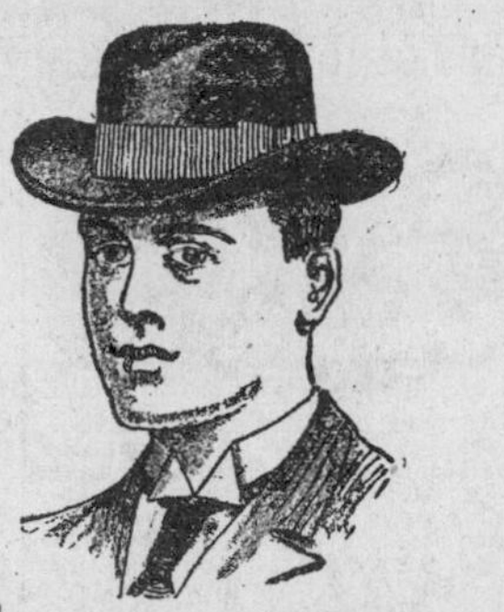

No. 33K6230 Boys' Black Tourist Style Hat, raw edge brim. Crown, 4¾ inches deep; brim, 2½ inches wide. Staple style. Boys' sizes, 6½ to 7⅛. State size wanted. Black only. A $1.25 hat. Our price, each, only... **89c**
If by mail, postage extra, each, 25 cents.

89c BOYS' "SNAP" STYLE.

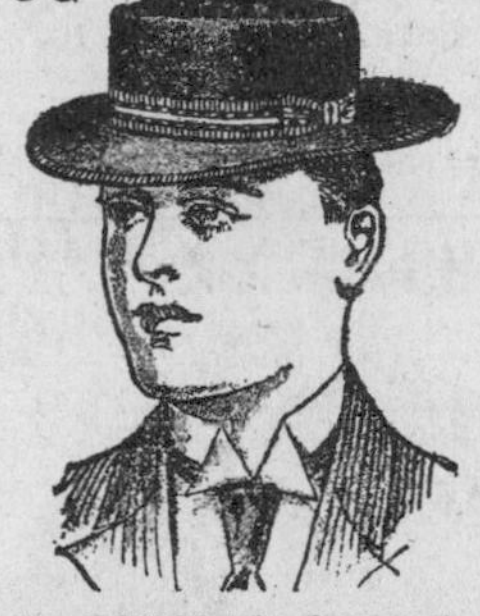

No. 33K6218 Boys' Fancy Band "Snap" Style Black Telescope Hat with flexible brim, bound edge. Crown, 3 inches deep; brim, 2½ inches wide. Boys' sizes, 6½ to 7⅛. State size wanted. $1.25 at retail. Our price, each, only... **89c**
No. 33K6219 Boys' Fancy Band "Snap" Style Silver Color Telescope. Above style. State size wanted.
Our price, each, only........ **89c**
If by mail, postage extra, each, 15c.

45c MEN'S — NEWEST STYLE CAPS. REDUCED PRICES. — 42c BOYS'

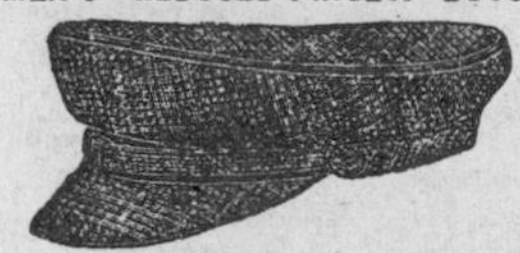

No. 33K6835 Men's Cap in Plain Gray Worsted or Tan Covert Cloth. Leather piped seams and strap, serge lining. Men's sizes, 6¾ to 7¾. State size and color.
Reduced price, each, only... **45c**
No. 33K6755 Boys' Light or Dark Gray Mixed Cassimere Cap, same style as above. Boys' sizes, 6½ to 7⅛. State size and shade.
Reduced price, each, only... **42c**
If by mail, postage extra, each, 14c.

23c BOYS' FANCY GOLF CAP. PRICE REDUCED.

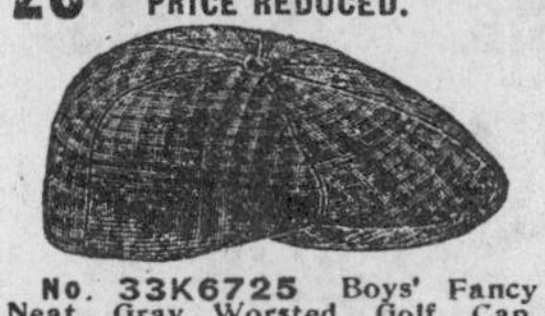

No. 33K6725 Boys' Fancy Neat Gray Worsted Golf Cap, good twill lining. Boys' sizes, 6½ to 7⅛. State size.
Reduced price, each, only... **23c**
If by mail, postage extra, each, 8 cents.

43c MEN'S LEATHER OR SILK ENGINEERS' CAPS.

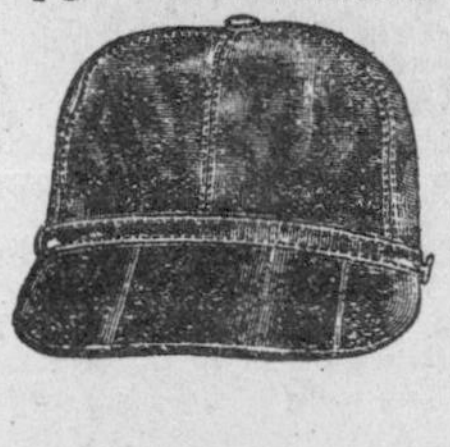

No. 33K6805 Engineers' Fine Quality Black Leather Cap. Sizes, 6¾ to 7¾. State size. Price, each, only... **43c**
No. 33K6810 Engineers' Fine Black Silk Cap, style as illustrated. Sizes, 6¾ to 7¾. State size.
Price, each, only... **43c**
If by mail, postage extra each, 8 cents.

MEN'S AND BOYS' NEWEST STYLE CAPS.

See top of page 984 for how to measure for correct size.

46c MEN'S — BLUE BROADCLOTH GOLF CAPS. — 43c BOYS'

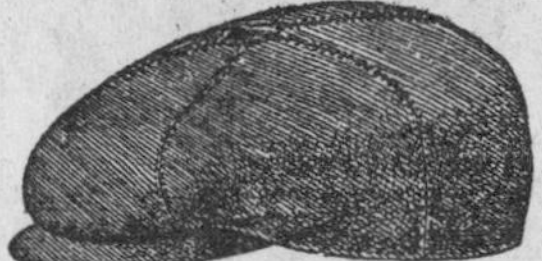

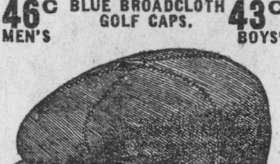

No. 33K6822 Men's Fine Pure Wool Navy Blue Golf Cap, serge lining. Carefully made throughout. Men's sizes, 6¾ to 7¾. State size. Special price, each, only... **46c**
No. 33K6752 Boys' Navy Blue Golf Cap, same as above. Boys' sizes, 6½ to 7⅛. State size.
Special price, each, only... **43c**
If by mail, postage extra, each, 9c.

38c MEN'S FANCY CASSIMERE GOLF CAP. PRICE REDUCED.

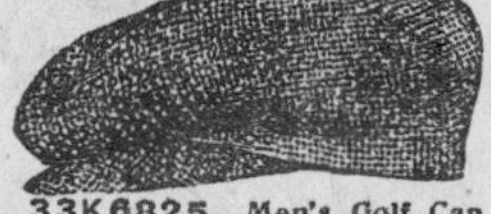

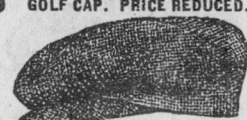

No. 33K6825 Men's Golf Cap of Fine Cassimere Suiting, in handsome plaids and checks, light or dark shades, mercerized serge lining. Men's sizes, 6¾ to 7¾. State size and shade wanted.
Reduced price, each, only... **38c**
If by mail, postage extra, each, 8c.

42c BOYS' LEATHER TRIMMED CAP, PRICE REDUCED.

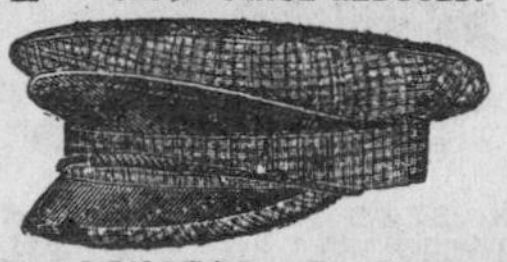

No. 33K6732 Boys' Newest Style Cap, blue or gray, fancy mixed cassimere suitings. Leatherette trimmed. Fancy striped lining, leather sweat. Boys' sizes, 6½ to 7⅛. State size and shade wanted.
Reduced price, each, only... **42c**
If by mail, postage extra, each, 10c.

57c MEN'S LEATHER AUTOMOBILE CAPS. 89c

No. 33K6860 Men's Leather Automobile Cap, good quality black leather; silk braid band, patent leather visor and strap, leather sweat. Men's sizes, 6¾ to 7¾. Please state size.

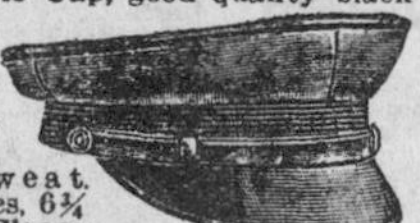

Reduced price, each, only... **57c**
No. 33K6865 Extra Fine Leather Automobile Cap, welted seams, Russian leather sweat, mercerized serge lining, patent leather visor and strap. Men's sizes, 6¾ to 7¾. Please state size. Price reduced.
Reduced price, each, only... **89c**
If by mail, postage extra, each, 15c.

46c MEN'S — BLUE BROADCLOTH YACHT CAPS. — 43c BOYS'

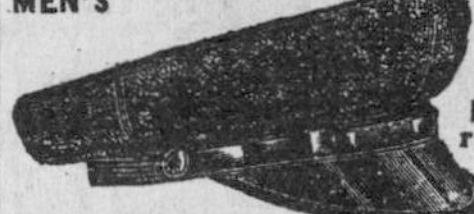

Prices reduced

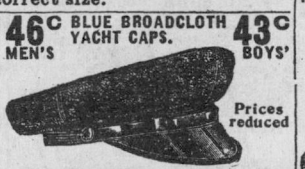

No. 33K6855 Men's Fine Blue Broadcloth Yacht Cap. Patent leather visor and strap, silk braid band and leather sweat, serge lined. Men's sizes, 6¾ to 7¾. State size.
Reduced price, each, only... **46c**
No. 33K6735 Boys' Blue Cap, same as above. Boys' sizes, 6½ to 7⅛. Reduced price, each, only... **43c**
If by mail, postage extra, each, 15c.

48c MEN'S OCTAGON CROWN TOURIST CAP.

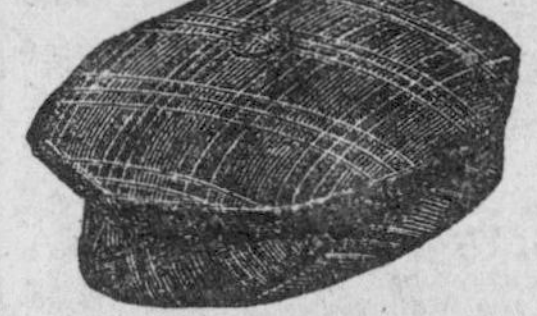

No. 33K6838 Men's Handsome Octagon Shaped Crown Tourist Cap. Fancy light or dark cassimere suiting, patent leather strap. Men's sizes, 6¾ to 7¾. State size and shade. Price, each, only...... **48c**
If by mail, postage extra, each, 14c.

41c MEN'S — COMBINATION CAPS. PRICES REDUCED. — 38c BOYS'

No. 33K6840 Men's White Duck Top Cap, with extra detachable black poplin silk top. Patent leather visor and strap, silk braid band and leather sweat. A dandy. Men's sizes, 6¾ to 7¾. State size.

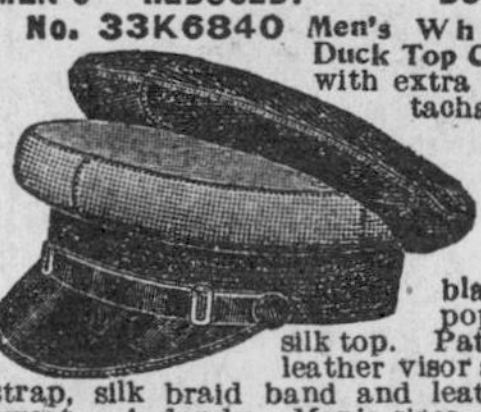

Reduced price, each, only... **41c**
No. 33K6740 Boys' Combination Cap, same as above. Boys' sizes, 6½ to 7⅛. State size.
Reduced price, each, only... **38c**
If by mail, postage extra, each 13c.

36c BOYS' FANCY CASSIMERE GOLF CAP. PRICE REDUCED.

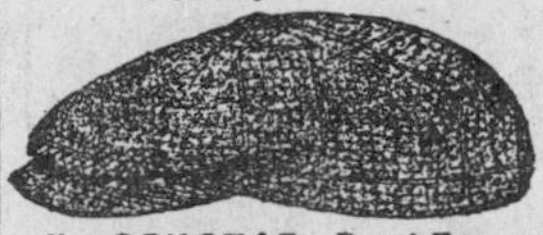

No. 33K6745 Boys' Fancy Gray Cassimere Golf Cap. Mercerized serge lining. Boys' sizes, 6½ to 7⅛. State size. A 50-cent cap. Reduced price, each, only **36c**
If by mail, postage extra, each, 8c.

$1.19 FINE BLACK GROSGRAIN SILK UNIFORM CAP.

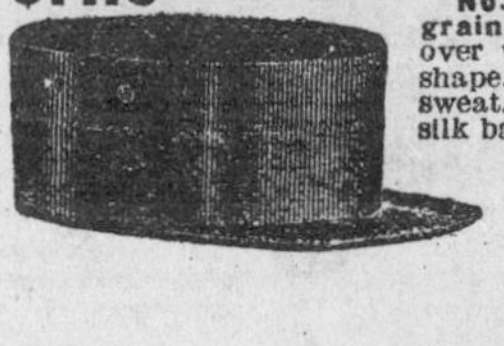

No. 33K6625 Black Grosgrain Silk Uniform Cap. Made over wire frame and will keep its shape. Patent leather visor, leather sweat. Gold wire block letters on silk band, per letter, 7 cents. Sizes, 6¾ to 7¾. State size. Where lettering is desired we require cash in full with order.
Price, each, only... **$1.19**
If by mail, postage extra, 16c.

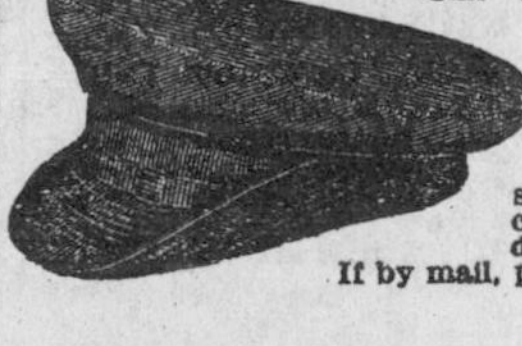

69c POPLIN SILK TOURIST CAP. PRICE REDUCED.

No. 33K6845 Men's Poplin Silk Tourist Cap, heavy black grosgrain weave with closely stitched band and visor and silk strap across front, mercerized serge lining. Men's sizes, 6¾ to 7¾. Please state size. The handsomest traveling or driving cap ever made. Reduced price, each, only **69c**
If by mail, postage extra, each, 14 cents.

MEN'S AND BOYS' FUR, PLUSH AND WOOL CLOTH WINTER CAPS

WHEN ORDERING CAPS STATE SIZE WANTED.

ALSO FUR STORM COLLARS

CAPS, IF BY MAIL, POSTAGE EXTRA, EACH, 12 CENTS.

81c MEN'S SILK PLUSH CAP.

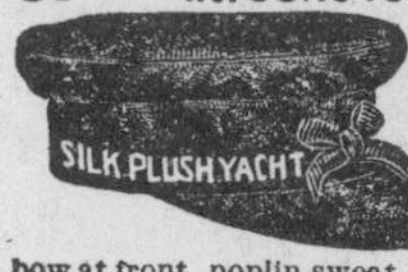

No. 33K6435 Men's Black Silk Plush Yacht Cap, double pull down band, grosgrain silk bow at front, poplin sweat and satin lined. Men's sizes, 6¾ to 7¾. Please state size wanted. Reduced price, each, only.. **81c**

96c FINEST SILK PLUSH CAP.

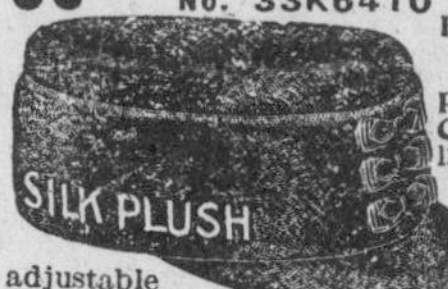

No. 33K6410 Men's Black French Seal Plush Cap, poplin sweat, satin lined, adjustable forehead protector. Men's sizes, 6¾ to 7¾. State size. Reduced price, each, **96c**

87c MEN'S INSIDE FUR BAND SILK PLUSH CAP.

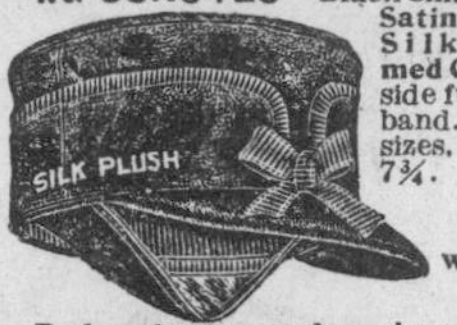

No. 33K6420 Black Silk Plush, Satin Lined, Silk Trimmed Cap; inside fur lined band. Men's sizes, 6¾ to 7¾. State size wanted. Reduced price, each, only.. **87c**

46c BOYS' INSIDE BAND PLUSH CAP.

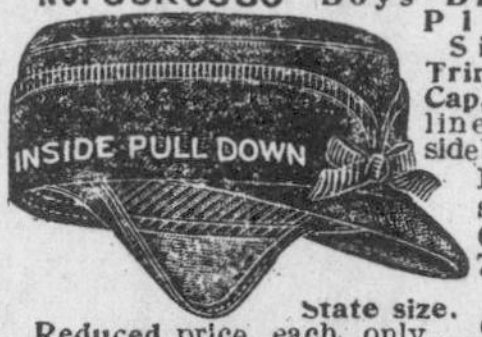

No. 33K6380 Boys' Black Plush Silk Trimmed Cap, felt lined, inside band. Boys' sizes, 6½ to 7⅛. State size. Reduced price, each, only... **46c**

46c BOYS' PLUSH GOLF CAP.

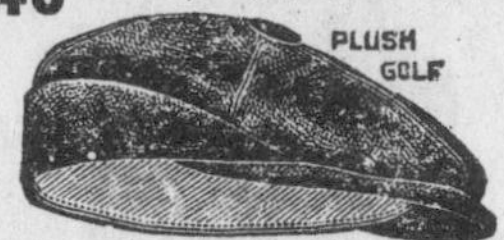

No. 33K6390 Boys' Fine Black Plush Golf Cap, wide double pull down band, serge lining. Boys' sizes, 6½ to 7⅛. State size. Reduced price, each, only **46c**

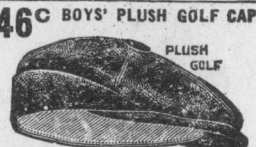

$3.89 MEN'S FUR STORM COLLARS. $4.58

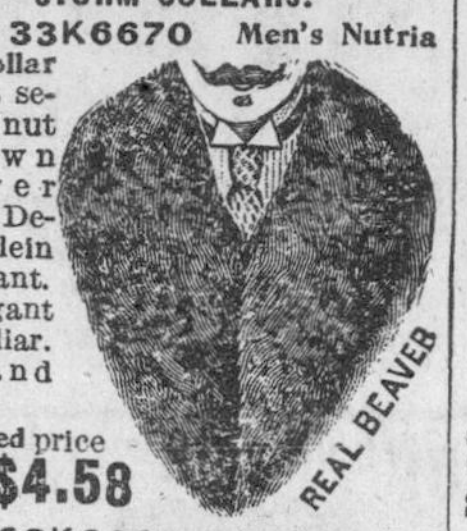

No. 33K6670 Men's Nutria Fur Collar of best selected nut brown beaver fur. Detachable in an instant. An elegant fur collar. Rich and dressy. Reduced price each, only.. **$4.58**

No. 33K6665 Identically same style as above but of genuine selected blended brown muskrat fur. Reduced price, each, only **$3.89**

Collars, by mail, extra, each, 15c.

43c BOYS' PLUSH CAPS. 48c MEN'S

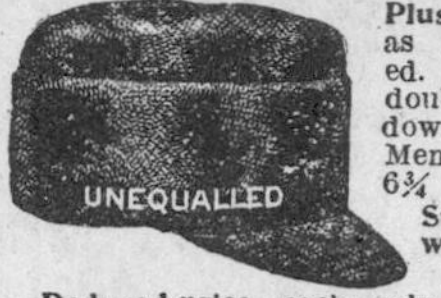

No. 33K6405 Men's Black Plush Cap, as illustrated. Wide double pull down band. Men's sizes, 6¾ to 7¾. State size wanted. Reduced price, each, only... **48c**

No. 33K6378 Boy's Plush Cap, same style as above. Boys' sizes, 6½ to 7⅛. State size. Each, only **43c**

53c MEN'S PLUSH CAPS 69c

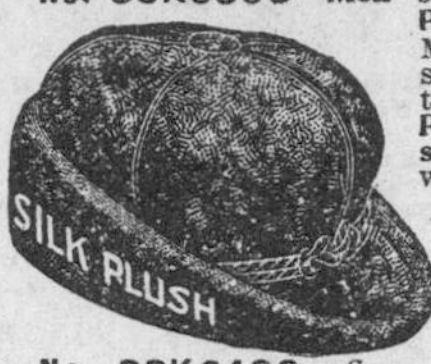

No. 33K6395 Men's Black Plush Cap. Men's sizes, 6¾ to 7¾. Please state size wanted when ordering. Price, ea. **53c**

No. 33K6400 Same style as above, but finer plush, satin lined. Men's sizes, 6¾ to 7¾. State size. Reduced price, each only **69c**

96c MEN'S INSIDE FUR BAND WATERPROOF PLUSH CAP.

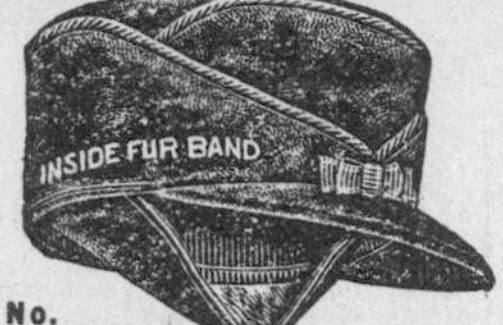

No. 33K6425 Men's French Seal Waterproof Plush Cap, inside fur lined band, silk trimmed and satin lined. Men's sizes, 6¾ to 7¾. State size. Our reduced price, each, only, **96c**

$2.87 MEN'S FUR STORM COLLARS.

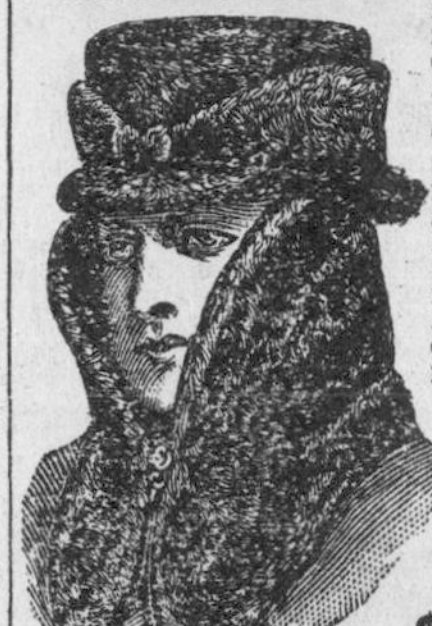

No. 33K6660 Black Baltic Seal Fur Storm Collar, as illustrated. Top of collar fur lined. Satin lined underneath, and fastens in front with nickel plated chain. Reduced price, each, only **$2.87**

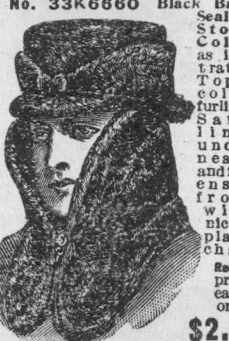

If by mail, postage extra, each, 15c.

$2.83 MEN'S MUSKRAT FUR CAP.

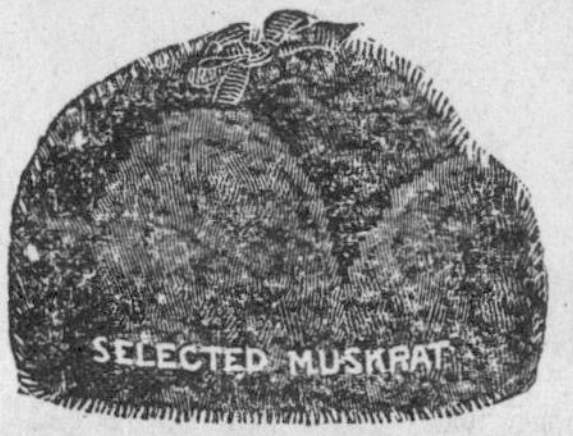

No. 33K6675 Men's Genuine Muskrat Fur Cap, adjustable visor. Men's sizes, 6¾ to 7¾. State size. Price, each... **$2.83**

STATE SIZE WANTED.

MEN'S AND BOYS' FUR CAPS

If by mail, postage extra, each, 12 cents.

MEN'S GENUINE SEALSKIN CAPS AND MEN'S AND BOYS' ELECTRIC SEAL FUR CAPS.

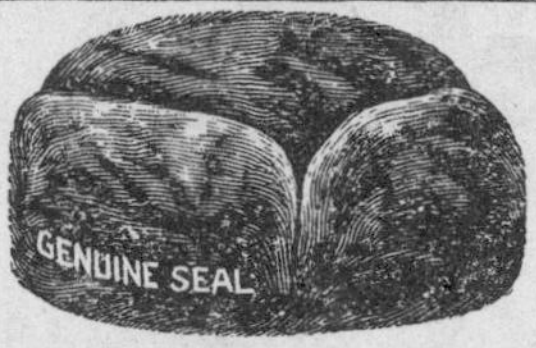

Following numbers all this shape:

No. 33K6640 Men's Genuine Sealskin Cap, satin lined, adjustable visor and wide turndown band. Men's sizes, 6¾ to 7¾. State size. Price, each. **$3.69**

No. 33K6685 Men's Electric Seal Fur Cap, satin lined. Above style. Men's sizes, 6¾ to 7¾. State size. Price, each, **$1.38**

No. 33K6695 Boys' Electric Seal Fur Cap, satin lined. Above style. Boys' sizes, 6½ to 7⅛. State size. Price, each... **$1.27**

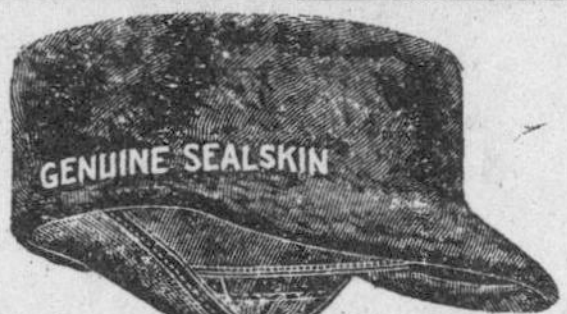

Following numbers all this shape:

No. 33K6650 Men's Genuine Sealskin Cap, satin lined. Inside fur band. One of the most popular styles. Men's sizes, 6¾ to 7¾. State size. Retails at $5.00. Reduced price, each **$3.69**

No. 33K6680 Men's Electric Seal Fur Cap, satin lined. Inside fur band. Above style. Men's sizes, 6¾ to 7¾. Please state size. Reduced price, each...... **$1.38**

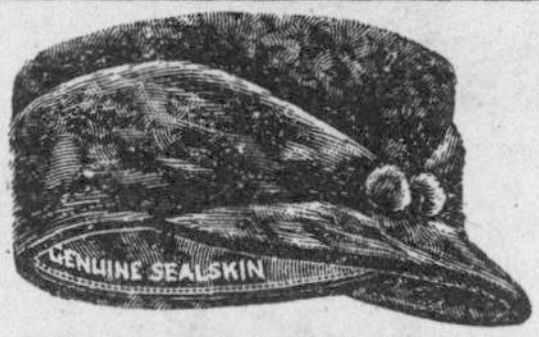

Following numbers all this shape:

No. 33K6645 Men's Genuine Sealskin Cap, satin lined, wide pull down band. Men's sizes, 6¾ to 7¾. State size. Retails at $5.00. Reduced price, each **$3.69**

No. 33K6690 Men's Electric Seal Fur Cap, satin lined. Above style. Men's sizes, 6¾ to 7¾. State size. Price, each. **$1.38**

No. 33K6697 Boys' Electric Seal Fur Cap, satin lined. Above style. Boys' sizes, 6½ to 7⅛. State size. Price, each. **$1.27**

$1.27 BOYS' ELECTRIC SEAL FUR CAPS. $1.32 MEN'S

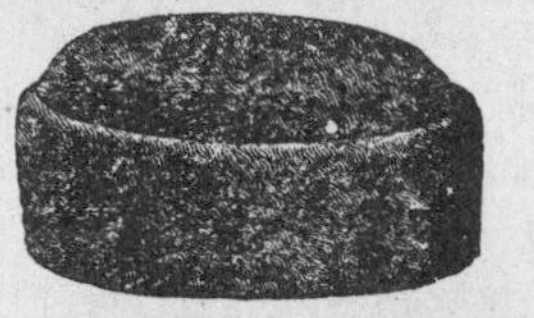

No. 33K6692 Men's Electric Seal Turban Cap, satin lined. Men's sizes, 6¾ to 7¾. State size. Reduced price, each....... **$1.32**

No. 33K6696 Boys', above style. Boys' sizes, 6½ to 7⅛. State size. Reduced price, each...... **$1.27**

MEN'S AND BOYS' CORDUROY AND HEAVY WINTER CAPS

41c 82c MEN'S — 39c BOYS' CAPS WITH FUR LINED BANDS.

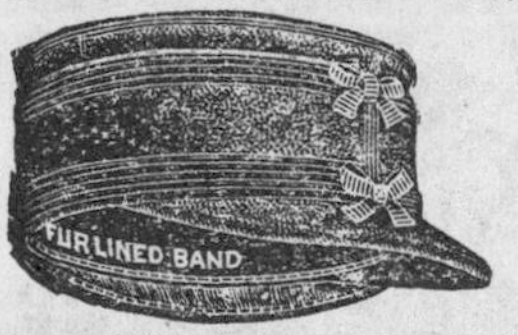

No. 33K6465 Men's Blue Melton Cap. Men's sizes, 6¾ to 7¾. State size. Price, each.. **41c**

No. 33K6518 Men's Black Kersey Cap, satin lined, adjustable forehead protector. Men's sizes, 6¾ to 7¾. State size. Price, each, **82c**

No. 33K6312 Boys' Black Melton Cap. Boy's sizes, 6½ to 7⅛. State size. Price, each.. **39c**

77c MEN'S CAPS, WITH INSIDE LAMB LINED BANDS. 42c BOYS'

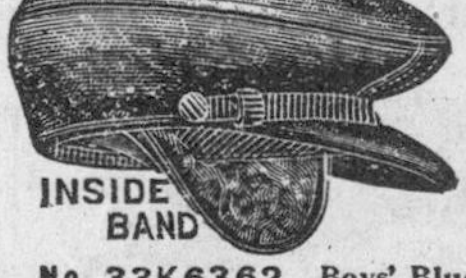

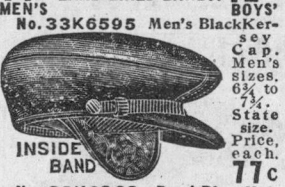

No. 33K6595 Men's Black Kersey Cap. Men's sizes, 6¾ to 7¾. State size. Price, each. **77c**

No. 33K6362 Boys' Blue Melton Cap. Boys' sizes, 6½ to 7⅛. State size. Price, each. **42c**

46c MEN'S 82c — 48c BOYS' CAPS WITH INSIDE FUR BANDS.

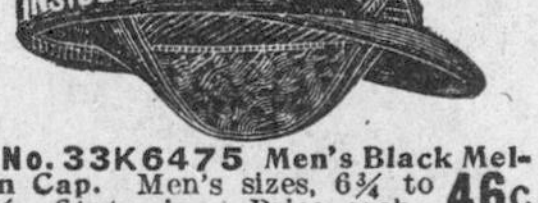

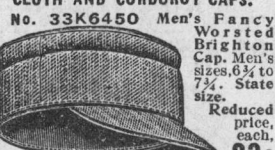

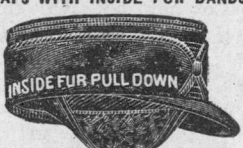

No. 33K6475 Men's Black Melton Cap. Men's sizes, 6¾ to 7¾. State size. Price, each.. **46c**

No. 33K6498 Men's Blue Kersey Cap. Satin lined. Men's sizes, 6¾ to 7¾. State size. Price, each, **82c**

No. 33K6508 Men's Black Kersey Cap. Satin lined. Men's sizes, 6¾ to 7¾. State size. Price, each... **82c**

No. 33K6318 Boys' Black Melton Cap. Boys' sizes, 6½ to 7⅛. State size. Price, each. **48c**

77c MEN'S CAPS WITH INSIDE FUR BANDS. 65c BOYS'

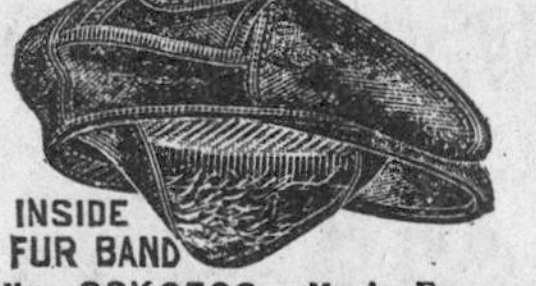

No. 33K6590 Men's Fancy Cassimere Button Top Cap. Men's sizes, 6¾ to 7¾. State size. Reduced price, each........ **77c**

No. 33K6368 Boys' Black Melton Button Top Cap. Boys' sizes, 6½ to 7⅛. Please state size. Special price, each........ **65c**

46c 78c MEN'S — 48c 72c BOYS' CAPS WITH INSIDE FUR BANDS.

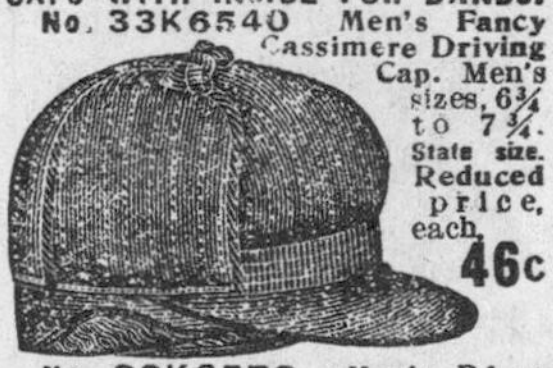

No. 33K6540 Men's Fancy Cassimere Driving Cap. Men's sizes, 6¾ to 7¾. State size. Reduced price, each. **46c**

No. 33K6572 Men's Blue Kersey Cap, satin lined. Men's sizes, 6¾ to 7¾. State size. Reduced price, each **78c**

No. 33K6322 Boys' Fancy Cassimere Cap. Boys' sizes, 6½ to 7⅛. State size. Price, each **48c**

No. 33K6328 Boys' Blue Kersey Cap, satin lined. Boys' sizes, 6½ to 7⅛. State size. Special price, each........ **72c**

23c 39c MEN'S — 25c 35c BOYS' CLOTH AND CORDUROY CAPS.

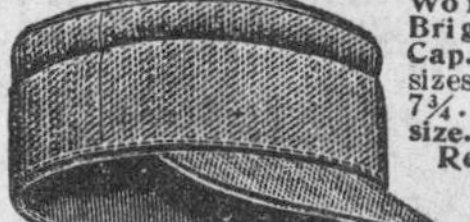

No. 33K6450 Men's Fancy Worsted Brighton Cap. Men's sizes, 6¾ to 7¾. State size. Reduced price, each, **23c**

No. 33K6462 Men's Black Melton Cap. Men's sizes, 6¾ to 7¾. State size. Special price, each.. **39c**

No. 33K6458 Men's Drab Corduroy Cap. Men's sizes, 6¾ to 7¾. State size. Price, each **39c**

No. 33K6302 Boys' Fancy Cassimere Cap. Boys' sizes, 6½ to 7⅛. State size. Price, each. **25c**

No. 33K6308 Boys' Blue Melton Cap. Boys' sizes, 6½ to 7⅛. State size. Price, each **35c**

53c MEN'S HAVELOCK CAPS.

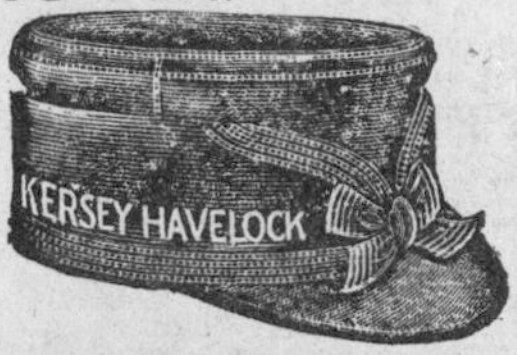

No. 33K6485 Men's Black Kersey Pull Down Band Cap. Men's sizes, 6¾ to 7¾. State size. Reduced price, each........ **53c**

53c MEN'S YACHT CAPS 41c BOYS' WITH PULL DOWN BANDS.

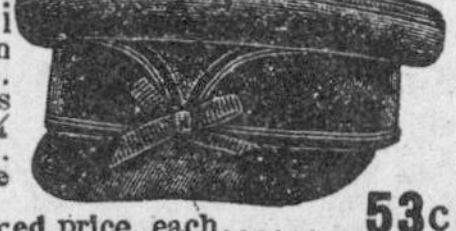

No. 33K6520 Men's Black Melton Cap. Pull down band. Men's sizes, 6¾ to 7¾. State size. Reduced price, each........ **53c**

No. 33K6338 Boys' Black Melton Cap. Pull down band. Boys' sizes, 6½ to 7⅛. State size. Special price, each.............. **41c**

38c MEN'S 49c — 39c BOYS' BUTTON TOP WINTER CAPS.

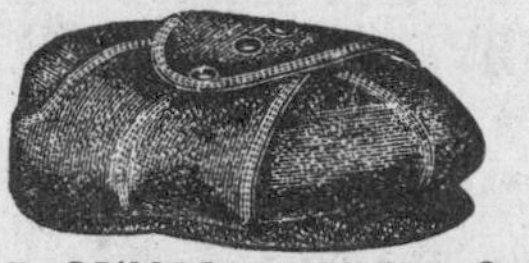

No. 33K6580 Men's Fancy Cassimere Cap. Men's sizes, 6¾ to 7¾. State size. Price, each. **38c**

No. 33K6588 Men's Black Melton Cap. Men's sizes, 6¾ to 7¾. State size. Price, each.. **49c**

No. 33K6358 Boys' Fancy Cassimere Cap. Boys' sizes, 6½ to 7⅛. State size. Price, each.. **39c**

41c MEN'S — 25c BOYS' 38c GOLF CAPS.

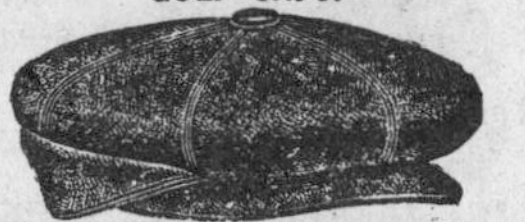

No. 33K6575 Men's Black Melton Cap. Men's sizes, 6¾ to 7¾. State size. Price, each.. **41c**

No. 33K6342 Boys' Fancy Cassimere Cap. Boys' sizes, 6½ to 7⅛. State size. Price, each... **25c**

No. 33K6348 Boys' Blue Kersey Cap. Boys' sizes, 6½ to 7⅛. State size. Price, each.. **38c**

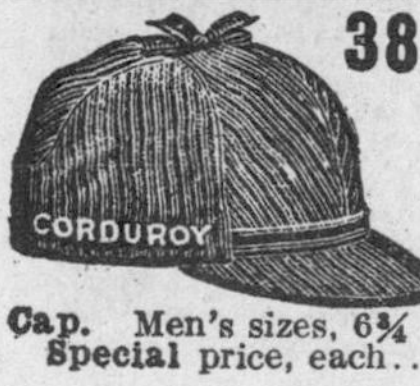

38c MEN'S CLOTH AND CORDUROY CAPS. 42c

No. 33K6535 Men's Drab Corduroy Driving Cap. Men's sizes, 6¾ to 7¾. State size. Reduced price, each, **38c**

No. 33K6548 Men's Fancy Cheviot Driving Cap. Men's sizes, 6¾ to 7¾. State size. Special price, each............ **42c**

77c MEN'S BLUE KERSEY INSIDE FUR BAND CAP.

No. 33K6530 Men's Blue Kersey Yacht Cap. Silk inserted front, fur lined inside band, satin lining. Men's sizes, 6¾ to 7¾. Please state size. Reduced price, each..... **77c**

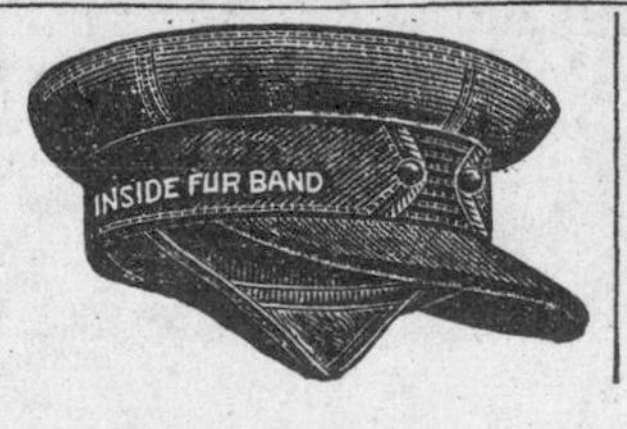

78c MEN'S BLUE MELTON FUR LINED BAND COMBINATION CAP.

No. 33K6490 Men's Blue Melton Combination Cap, six-piece telescope crown, closely stitched tourist band. Inside fur lined band. Men's sizes, 6¾ to 7¾. Please state size. Reduced price, each, **78c**

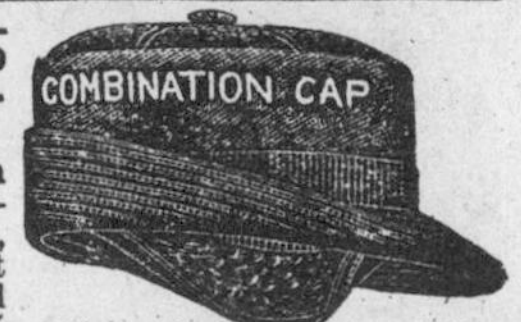

SUIT CASES AND TRAVELING BAGS

Only the finest grades and the toughest and best wearing qualities of selected grain leather. Made over strong steel frames and reinforced underneath with heavy binders' board.

$5.85 BLACK WALRUS GRAIN COWHIDE OXFORD BAG.

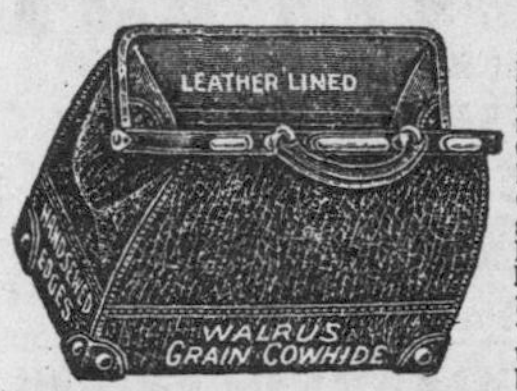

No. 33K1238 Hand Sewed Black Walrus Grain Oxford Bag, leather lined. Only the best selected cowhide bag leather of full 6-ounce weight is used in this bag, but the embossed grain on the leather is such a perfect imitation of genuine walrus that an expert can hardly distinguish the difference. Lined with serviceable buff color leather with pocket inside, and has sewed and riveted corners. English round padded leather handle and strong handsome brassed lock and catches. Large and roomy. State size wanted.

Length, 16 inches. Cut price......$5.85
Length, 18 inches. Cut price...... 6.45

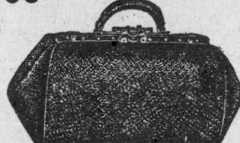

59c BROWN SPLIT LEATHER BAG.

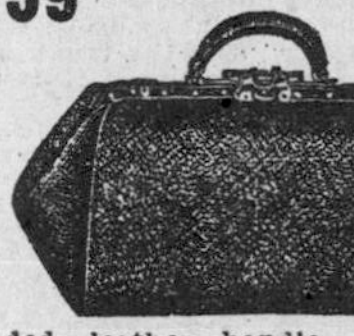

No. 33K1210 Heavy Split Cowhide Leather Club Style Bag. Looks like genuine brown grain leather. Has cloth lining, round padded leather handle, brassed lock and catches and large bell rivets in bottom. Big value at our low price. Be sure to state length wanted.

Length, 10 inches. Special cut price,$0.59
Length, 12 inches. Special cut price, .79
Length, 14 inches. Special cut price, .95
Length, 16 inches. Special cut price, 1.12

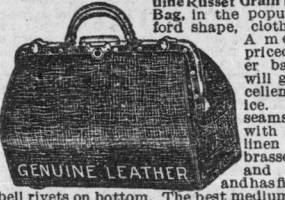

$2.15 GENUINE GRAIN LEATHER BAG.

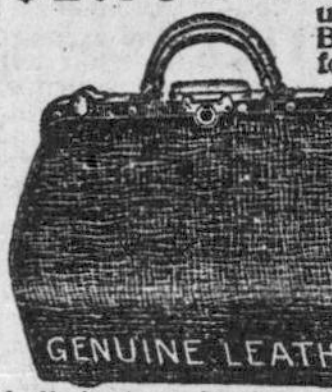

No. 33K1230 Genuine Russet Grain Leather Bag, in the popular Oxford shape, cloth lined. A medium priced leather bag that will give excellent service. Welted seams sewed with waxed linen thread, brassed lock and catches and has five large bell rivets on bottom. The best medium priced genuine leather bag ever shown. State size.

Length, 14 inches. Special price....$2.15
Length, 16 inches. Special price.... 2.55
Length, 18 inches. Special price.... 2.95

$3.45 GRAIN LEATHER OXFORD BAG. PRICES REDUCED.

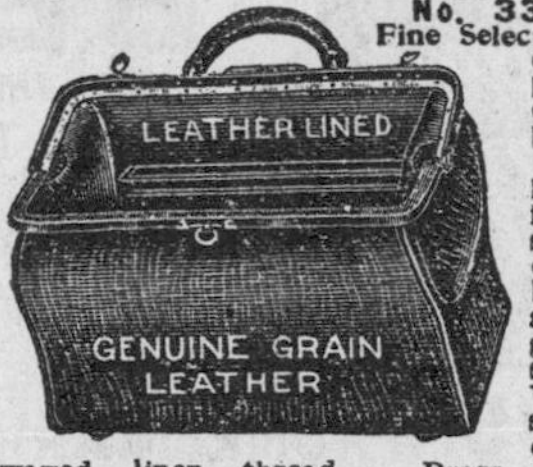

No. 33K1232 Fine Selected Heavy Grain Leather Oxford Bag, with good leather lining and inside pocket. A sightly bag and will give best of service. Welted seams sewed with waxed linen thread. Brass lock and catches, keratol covered steel frame, English round padded leather handle and heavy bell rivets on bottom. State size wanted.

PRICES REDUCED AS FOLLOWS:
Length, 14 inches. Reduced price, now only..................$3.45
Length, 16 inches. Reduced price, now only..................$3.90
Length, 18 inches. Reduced price, now only..................$4.35

$9.95 BEST GENUINE BLACK WALRUS TRAVELING BAG.

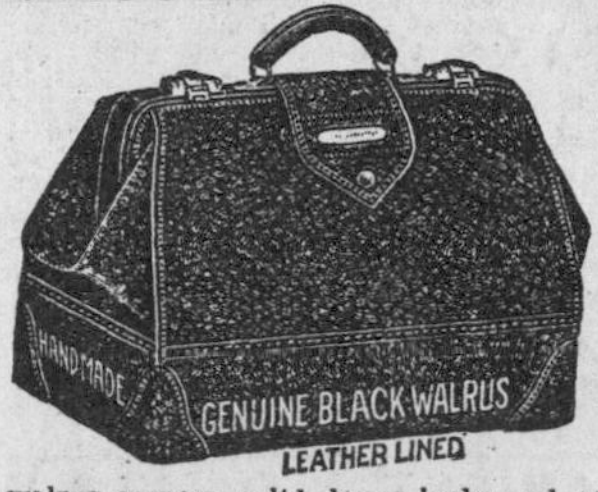

No. 33K1244 Extra Large Shape, First Quality Genuine Walrus Oxford Bag. Genuine black walrus leather distinguished by its deep heavy grain, is absolutely waterproof and the best and handsomest bag leather known. Will wear a lifetime. Sewed with strongest waxed linen thread. Hand made over imported English frame. Lined with best buff color leather and has capacious inside pocket. Hand sewed walrus corners, solid brass locks and catches of the strongest and latest improved pattern. Lock protected by large walrus flap with slot for card or name plate. This handsome black walrus traveling bag is unequaled for service and appearance by any bag retailed at $18.00 to $20.00. State size wanted.

Length, 16 inches. Our special price, only......$ 9.95
Length, 18 inches. Our special price, only...... 10.95
Length, 20 inches. Our special price, only...... 11.95

$6.85 LADIES' LIGHT WEIGHT HAND MADE CASE.

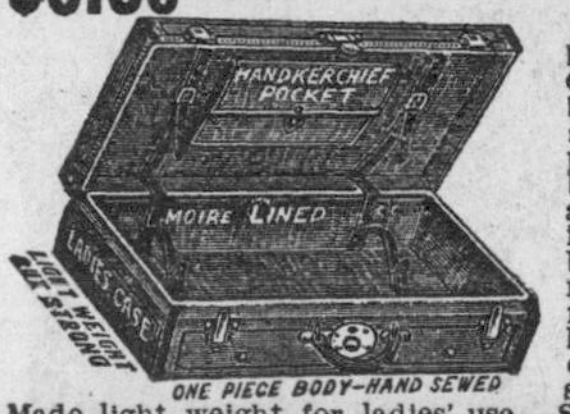

No. 33K1315 Ladies' Light Weight Case of finest selected bridle leather in handsome russet shade. One-piece body, hand made, beautifully hand creased and edges French finished. Satin finished solid brass lock and catches made especially for ladies' finest cases. Moire linen lined and has handkerchief pocket in cover and straps in bottom of case. Made light weight for ladies' use. State size wanted.

Length, 22 inches. Our special price, only........$6.85
Length, 24 inches. Our special price, only........ 7.15

$6.60 FOR FINE LEATHER LINED SUIT CASE. PRICES REDUCED.

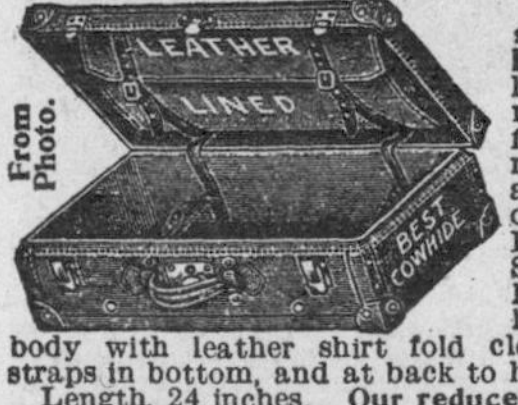

No. 33K1320 Handsome Brown Cowhide Leather Suit Case of heaviest, highly polished bridle leather, made over strong steel frame, finished with heavy brass bell rivets in sole leather corners and on ends, sewed throughout with waxed linen thread. Handsomely creased surface. Solid brass lock, catches and hinges. Padded leather handle. Full leather lined body with leather shirt fold closed with two straps, also straps in bottom, and at back to hold cover. State size.

Length, 24 inches. Our reduced price, now only...$6.60
Length, 26 inches. Our reduced price, now only... 6.85

98c IMITATION LEATHER WATERPROOF SUIT CASE.

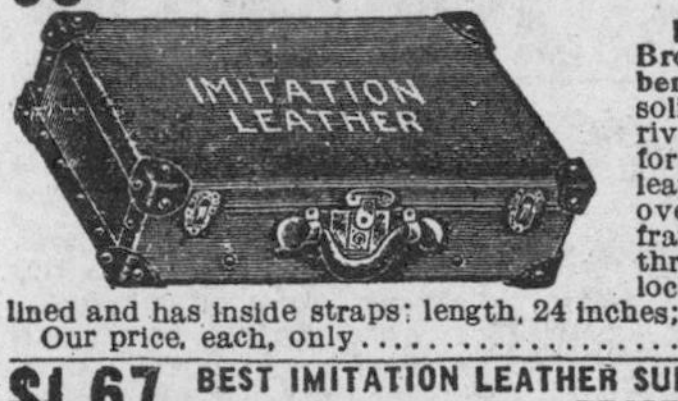

No. 33K1302 Brown Enamel Rubber Cloth Suit Case, solid cowhide leather riveted corners, reinforced round padded leather handle. Made over strong steel frame and riveted throughout, brassed lock and bolts, cloth lined and has inside straps; length, 24 inches; weight 6 pounds.

Our price, each, only..............................98c

$1.67 BEST IMITATION LEATHER SUIT CASE. PRICE REDUCED.

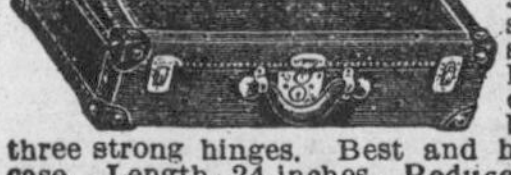

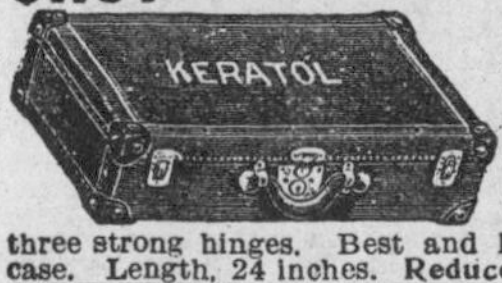

No. 33K1304 Best Waterproof Imitation Brown Grain Leather, Cloth Lined Suit Case, strongly riveted and sewed throughout, made on strong steel frame and has heavy riveted sole leather corners, round padded handle brassed lock and catches, and three strong hinges. Best and handsomest imitation leather case. Length, 24 inches. Reduced price, each, only...$1.67

22c LEATHER RIVETED CANVAS COVERED TELESCOPE.

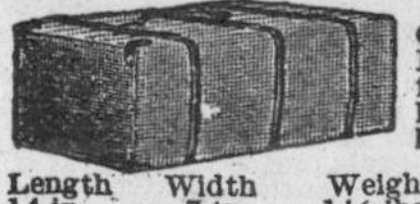

No. 33K1344 Excellent Quality Canvas Covered Telescope. Full size. Corners leather reinforced. Padded and riveted leather handle and three cowhide straps on large sizes. State length wanted.

Length	Width	Weight	Height	Extd.	Price
14 in.	7 in.	1½ lbs.	6 in.	12 in.	22c
18 in.	9 in.	2½ lbs.	7 in.	14 in.	42c
20 in.	10 in.	3 lbs.	7½ in.	15 in.	52c
24 in.	12 in.	4 lbs.	8½ in.	17 in.	72c

$4.85 COWHIDE SUIT CASE WITH SHIRT FOLD. PRICES GREATLY REDUCED.

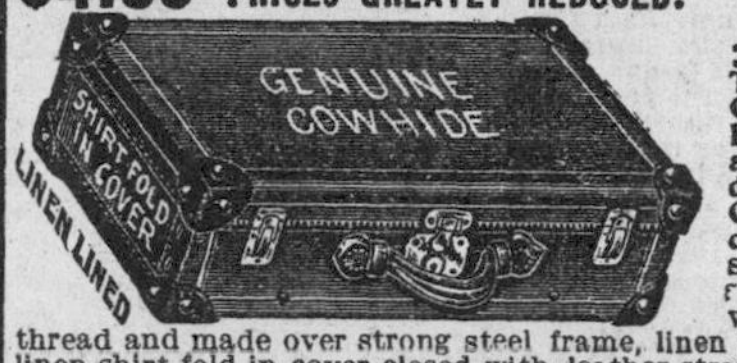

No. 33K1316 This is the Greatest Value Ever Offered in a Genuine Bridle Leather Cowhide Suitcase. Selected stock, strongly sewed with waxed linen thread and made over strong steel frame, linen lined and has linen shirt fold in cover closed with leather straps, also straps in bottom of case and stay straps at back to hold cover when open. Brass lock and catches, bell rivets, padded leather handle and sole leather corners. Artistically creased surface. Color a beautiful olive brown shade. We have materially reduced the price of this case this season, and we are able to supply an even better and handsomer case than before. Please state size wanted.

Length, 24 inches. Reduced price, now only.......$4.85
Length, 26 inches. Reduced price, now only....... 5.10

$5.85 SOLE LEATHER SUIT CASE WITH STRAPS. PRICES REDUCED.

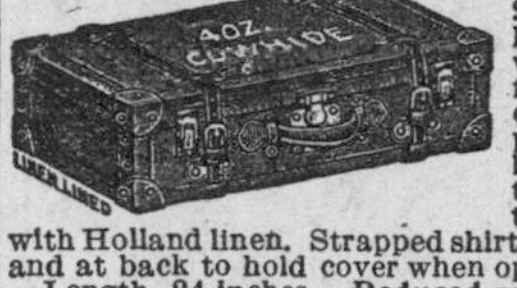

No. 33K1313 Heavy Selected Cowhide Suit Case, hand creased surface, sewed with waxed linen thread, finished with heavy bell riveted sole leather corners, round padded leather handle, brass lock and catches, brass rivets throughout, reinforced with two heavy straps and lined with Holland linen. Strapped shirt fold in top. Straps in bottom and at back to hold cover when open. Color, rich olive brown.

Length, 24 inches. Reduced price, each, now only, $5.85
Length, 26 inches. Reduced price, each, now only, 6.15

$7.95 STRONGEST, MOST ELEGANT BRIDLE LEATHER CASE. EXTRA DEEP. PRICES REDUCED.

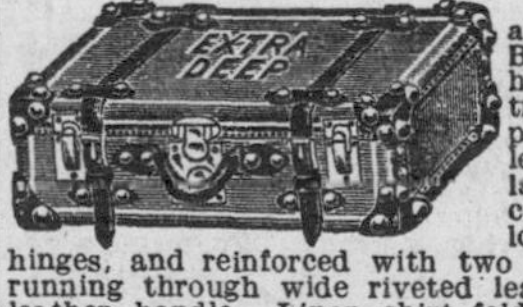

No. 33K1323 Strongest and handsomest Cowhide Bridle Leather Suit Case, highly finished and beautifully trimmed and hand creased, plaid linen lined. Heavy sole leather corners with six extra large brass bell rivets at each corner. Heaviest solid brass lock and catches, three brass hinges, and reinforced with two continuous cowhide straps, running through wide riveted leather loops. Padded solid leather handle. Linen shirt fold in cover, closed with two straps, two straps in bottom and stay strap at back, which holds cover of case when open. Color, the popular olive brown. The deepest and undoubtedly the strongest and one of the handsomest suit cases made. State size.

Length, 24 inches. Depth, 7½ inches. Reduced price, $7.95
Length, 26 inches. Depth, 7½ inches. Reduced price, 8.30

$10.65 ONE-PIECE BODY, HAND MADE CASE.

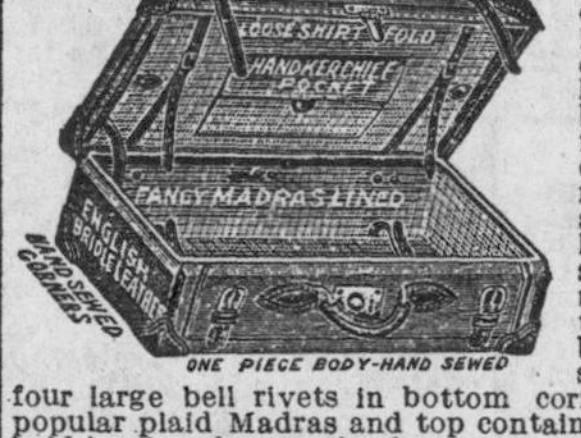

No. 33K1324 The finest Suit Case made. Highest grade 5-ounce English bridle leather, popular russet color, one-piece body, hand sewed throughout, beautifully hand creased, finished with French edges, hand sewed corners, straps and handle and with solid brass lock of latest design. Instead of the usual catches near the ends of case, this case has hand sewed buckled straps; three strong brass hinges and four large bell rivets in bottom corners. Case is lined with popular plaid Madras and top contains removable shirt board held in place by two leather straps and finished with bellows pocket for handkerchiefs, etc. Straps in bottom and strap at end to hold cover when open. This is the most elegant and the highest grade cowhide suit case ever made and retails at $15.00 to $18.00. State length wanted.

Length, 24 inches. Our remarkable price, only....$10.65
Length, 26 inches. Our remarkable price, only.... 11.00

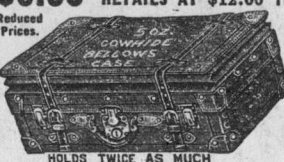

$9.35 FOR ENGLISH BELLOWS COWHIDE CASE. RETAILS AT $12.00 TO $14.00.

Reduced Prices.

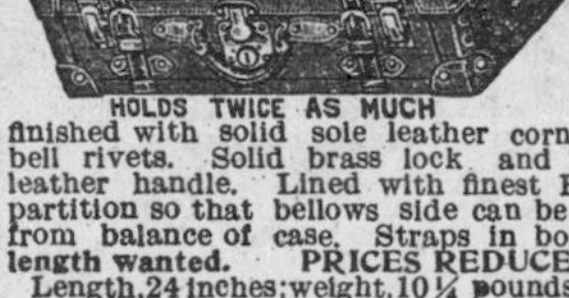

No. 33K1322 English Bellows Case. Made of rich olive brown cowhide leather, selected stock, hand creased and sewed with waxed linen thread. Double bellows side, reinforced with two heavy cowhide straps running through broad riveted leather loops, finished with solid sole leather corners, secured with heavy bell rivets. Solid brass lock and catches, padded round leather handle. Lined with finest Holland linen. Strapped partition so that bellows side can be packed entirely separate from balance of case. Straps in bottom. Be sure to state length wanted. PRICES REDUCED AS FOLLOWS:

Length, 24 inches; weight, 10¼ pounds. Reduced price $ 9.35
Length, 26 inches; weight, 11¼ pounds. Reduced price 9.85
Length, 28 inches; weight, 12¼ pounds. Reduced price 10.35

$8.95 FOR GENUINE BRIDLE LEATHER TRAVELING BAG. PRICES REDUCED.

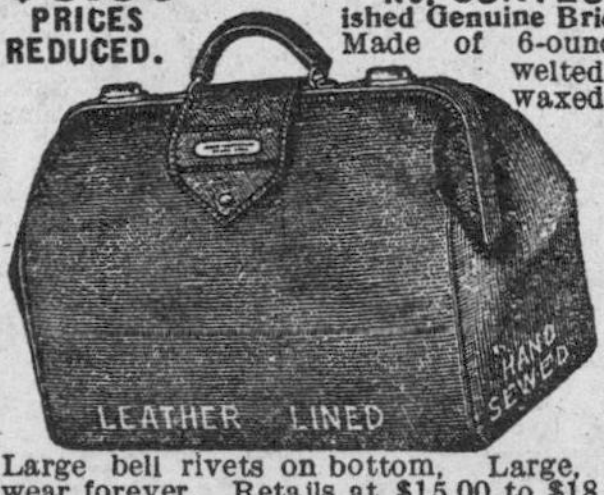

No. 33K1251 Heavy Highly Finished Genuine Bridle Leather Oxford Bag. Made of 6-ounce selected cowhide, welted seams sewed with waxed linen thread. English frame which opens up full width. Lined with fine buff color selected leather and finished with large inside pocket. Round padded English leather handle. Satin finished, solid brass catches, and lock covered with leather flap with slot for name plate or card. Large bell rivets on bottom. Large, roomy shape and will wear forever. Retails at $15.00 to $18.00. Please state size.

Length, 16 inches. Our reduced price, now only..$ 8.95
Length, 18 inches. Our reduced price, now only.. 9.95
Length, 20 inches. Our reduced price, now only.. 10.95

$3.15 CHALLENGE OFFER GENUINE LEATHER DRESS SUIT CASE.

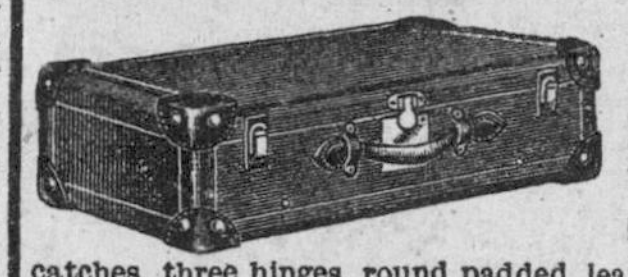

No. 33K1311 Genuine Leather Dress Suit Case of full weight stock, made over strong steel frame, brass riveted and sewed with waxed linen thread. Highly polished and handsomely creased surface. Has brass lock and catches, three hinges, round padded leather handle, solid cowhide riveted corners and is linen lined with full set of leather straps inside. A genuine leather case, which retails at $4.50 to $5.00. Sole leather color only. We have improved the quality of the stock in this case and now challenge anyone to equal it at $1.00 more than our low price. Length, 24 inches.

Our price, now only.................................$3.15

$6.75 CONVENIENTLY FITTED COWHIDE LEATHER SUIT CASE. PRICE REDUCED.

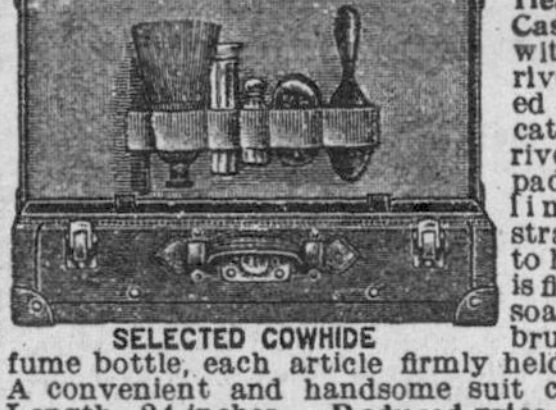

No. 33K1317 Extra Heavy Selected Cowhide Suit Case, hand creased and sewed with waxed linen thread, riveted throughout and finished with best brass lock, catches and hinges, heavy bell riveted cowhide corners and padded leather handle, best linen lining. Has inside straps, including stay straps to hold cover when open and is fitted with hair brush, comb, soap box, tooth and nail brush in glass case and perfume bottle, each article firmly held in place by strong loops. A convenient and handsome suit case. Color, olive brown. Length, 24 inches. Reduced price, now only $6.75

$1.37 FOR BEST IMITATION ALLIGATOR SUIT CASE.

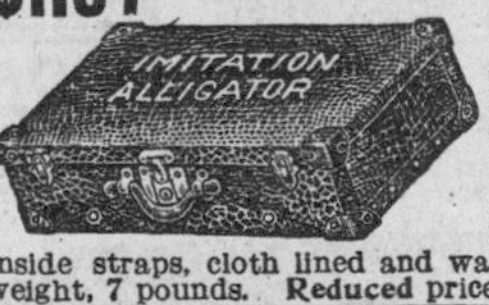

No. 33K1307 Finest Imitation Alligator Suit Case, highly finished surface, and can hardly be distinguished from genuine alligator. Reinforced round padded sole leather handle, riveted ends and brass plated lock and catches, strong steel frame, inside straps, cloth lined and waterproof. Length, 24 inches; weight, 7 pounds. Reduced price, only...........$1.37

$2.15 MATTING SUIT CASE, STRAPS ALL AROUND. LIGHT WEIGHT BUT SERVICEABLE.

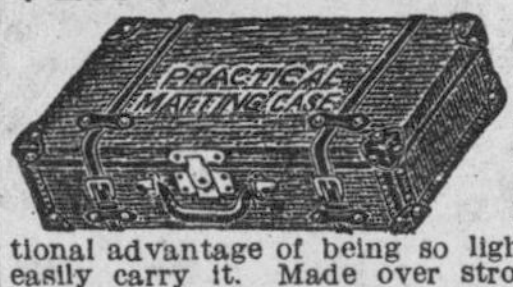

No. 33K1305 Popular Olive Matting Suit Case, leather and leatherette trimmed and with straps all around. Very closely woven and strong Japanese matting braided or woven in such a manner that it is practically waterproof and has the additional advantage of being so light in weight that a child can easily carry it. Made over strong steel frame and finished with riveted cowhide corners, edges and ends neatly bound with leatherette. Strong brassed lock, round padded leather handle and two strong leather straps running all around. One of the most practical cases ever made. Length, 24 inches. This case retails at $3.00. Our price, each, only..........$2.15

49c FULL LEATHER BOUND CANVAS TELESCOPE. PRICES REDUCED.

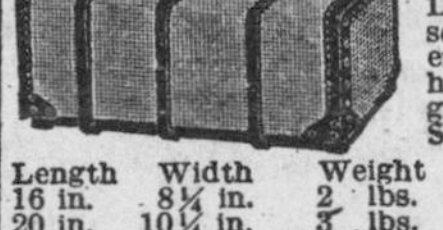

No. 33K1346 Strongest Waterproof Canvas Telescope. Leather bound ends. Strongly sewed and riveted corners and ends, and broad sewed and riveted handle. Finished with three solid grain leather straps on large sizes. State length wanted.

Length	Width	Weight	Height	Extd.	Reduced Prices
16 in.	8¼ in.	2 lbs.	6½ in.	12 in.	$0.49
20 in.	10¼ in.	3 lbs.	8 in.	14 in.	.69
24 in.	12¼ in.	4 lbs.	9½ in.	17 in.	.89
26 in.	13½ in.	4½ lbs.	10½ in.	18½ in.	1.09

Can't Smash Them

BEST TRUNKS ON EARTH

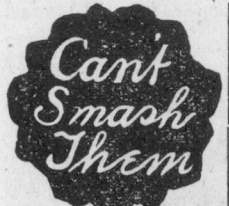

CONVENIENCE AND CAPACITY — REINFORCED AT EVERY DANGER POINT — REPLACED IF UNSATISFACTORY

ONLY THOROUGHLY SEASONED BASSWOOD WHICH WILL NOT SPLIT OR CHECK

OUR TRUNKS are built like battleships, strongly protected and reinforced at every danger point, practically unbreakable. Our first and last consideration in their construction has been to make them as roomy, as strong and as nearly unbreakable as possible. **ABSOLUTELY THE BEST STYLES** and strongest trunks made. If you don't find the trunk or traveling bag you get from us far superior to what will cost you 50 per cent more if purchased elsewhere, we will willingly refund both the price and any transportation charges you paid on the goods on return of the same to us. Read carefully the descriptions, compare every statement with illustrations shown. Every illustration is made from an actual photograph of the trunk described. Note carefully one by one the reinforcements, note size and weight of the trunk and the compartments and fittings, and last but not least, remember the iron clad guarantee on these iron clad trunks.

$1.85 CRYSTALLIZED METAL COVERED TRUNK, BARREL TOP. Reduced Prices.

Strong and Serviceable. Full Size.

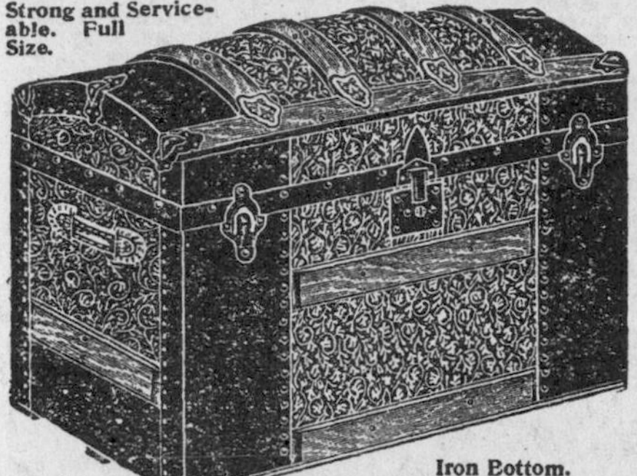

Iron Bottom.

No. 33K1002 Substantially made Barrel Top Trunk, with four hardwood slats over top and two slats on sides and one on each end. Sheet iron bound, japanned steel end clamps, iron bottom, special bar bolts, hinges, rollers and catches and strong hasp lock and leather handles. Contains set up tray with side compartment and covered bonnet box. A full size trunk at a very low price. Cannot be duplicated at $2.00 more than what we ask. But we honestly advise the purchase of a better trunk, as a good trunk lasts many years and always insures safe transportation to its contents, and we recommend to you our No. 33K1014 or No. 33K1050, illustrated and described at bottom of this page. Remember though, for the price, this is the best trunk ever made. State size wanted and give correct catalogue number.

All prices reduced.

Length, 26 in.	Width, 14½ in.	Height, 17½ in.	Weight, 28 lbs.	Reduced price, $1.85
Length, 30 in.	Width, 16½ in.	Height, 19½ in.	Weight, 35 lbs.	Reduced price, 2.45
Length, 34 in.	Width, 18½ in.	Height, 21½ in.	Weight, 42 lbs.	Reduced price, 3.05
Length, 36 in.	Width, 19½ in.	Height, 22½ in.	Weight, 47 lbs.	Reduced price, 3.35

$2.95 LEADER CANVAS COVERED TRUNK

Taken from Photograph.

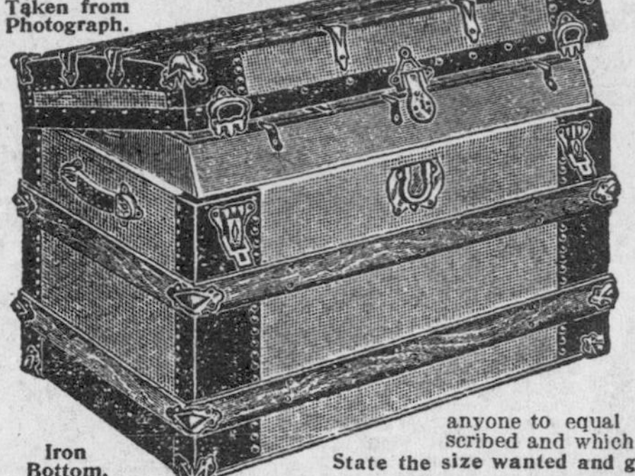

Iron Bottom.

No. 33K1055 Painted Canvas Covered Trunk, with iron bottom, sheet iron bound edges, four hardwood slats on top, two slats on sides and ends, steel clamps, knees and corner bumpers top and bottom. Monitor lock, patent bolts, hinges, catches, rollers, etc., leather handles, deep tray and hat box covered. Large size box, paper lined. A low priced trunk which for service is unequaled. While this trunk for the money is guaranteed to be better than can be bought anywhere else, we strongly recommend the purchase of better trunks, as a good trunk will last indefinitely. If interested in a better trunk, we recommend to you our Nos 33K1058 or 33K1070, both illustrated and described on the following page. Remember, though, that at the price we defy anyone to equal the trunk here illustrated and described and which is guaranteed to give satisfaction. State the size wanted and give catalogue number.

Length, 28 in.	Width, 16¾ in.	Height, 17¾ in.	Weight, 38 lbs.	Special price. $2.95
Length, 32 in.	Width, 18¾ in.	Height, 19¾ in.	Weight, 50 lbs.	Special price. 3.65
Length, 36 in.	Width, 20¾ in.	Height, 21¾ in.	Weight, 57 lbs.	Special price. 4.35
Length, 38 in.	Width, 21¾ in.	Height, 22¾ in.	Weight, 62 lbs.	Special price. 4.70

$3.65 MONITOR TOP STEEL COVERED TRUNK. Prices Reduced

Skirt Tray.

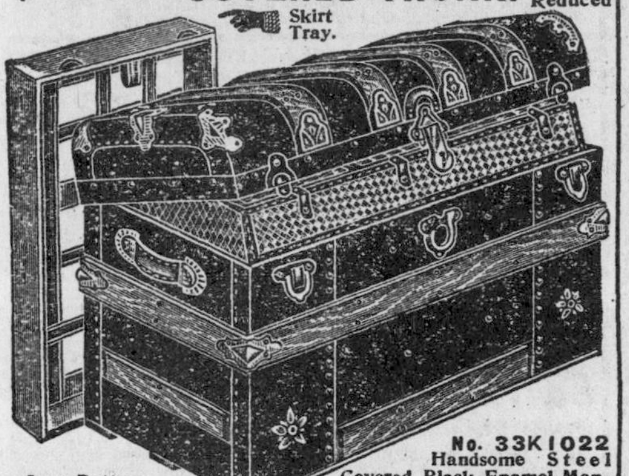

Iron Bottom.

No. 33K1022 Handsome Steel Covered Black Enamel Monitor Top Trunk. Large box made of thick basswood, paper lined, has flat top with rounded edges and is finished with four heavy hardwood bar slats over top and two on sides and around ends. Heavy sheet iron bottom and is thoroughly reinforced and trimmed with metal trimmings, steel end clamps, patent bar bolts, heavy steel hinges and rollers, brass monitor lock and catches, leather handles, and contains tray with separately covered bonnet box and side compartment, also skirt tray which fits underneath first tray and when desired can be inverted and takes up comparatively no room. A trunk that is easily worth $2.00 to $3.00 more than our low price. We gladly offer this trunk as proof of our assertion of absolutely the best trunks ever made at prices which cannot be met. Guaranteed to give absolute satisfaction in every respect or your money back. Be sure to state size wanted. All prices REDUCED as follows:

Length, 28 in.	Width, 16 in.	Height, 18½ in.	Weight, 37 lbs.	Reduced price.. $3.65
Length, 32 in.	Width, 18 in.	Height, 20½ in.	Weight, 47 lbs.	Reduced price.. 4.25
Length, 36 in.	Width, 20 in.	Height, 22½ in.	Weight, 58 lbs.	Reduced price.. 4.85

$6.05 WAGON OR STEAMER TRUNK. CANVAS COVERED. Prices Reduced.

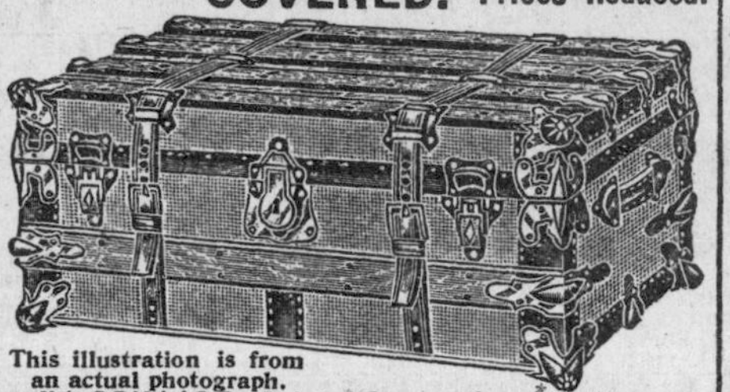

This illustration is from an actual photograph.

No. 33K1136 Painted Canvas Covered Wagon or Steamer Trunk. Four heavy hardwood slats running lengthwise across top, one heavy hardwood slat across front and back, all protected with heavy brass clamps and fancy corner bumpers, brass lock and side bolts. Heavy brass valance clamps at corners where cover meets body. Tray with two compartments separately covered muslin lined throughout. Reinforced as illustrated and strengthened with heavy sole leather straps. Our guarantee: We will replace any trunk of this number which does not prove satisfactory. State size and catalogue number when ordering a trunk. Following are REDUCED PRICES:

Length	Width	Height	Weight	Reduced Prices
32 inches	19 inches	13½ inches	36 pounds	...$6.05
36 inches	20 inches	13½ inches	40 pounds	... 6.70
38 inches	21 inches	13½ inches	43 pounds	... 7.25

$4.95 HEAVIEST MONITOR TOP BLACK ENAMEL STEEL COVERED TRUNK.

ONE OF THE HANDSOMEST and STRONGEST TRUNKS MADE

Intersecting Slat Lengthwise on Top.

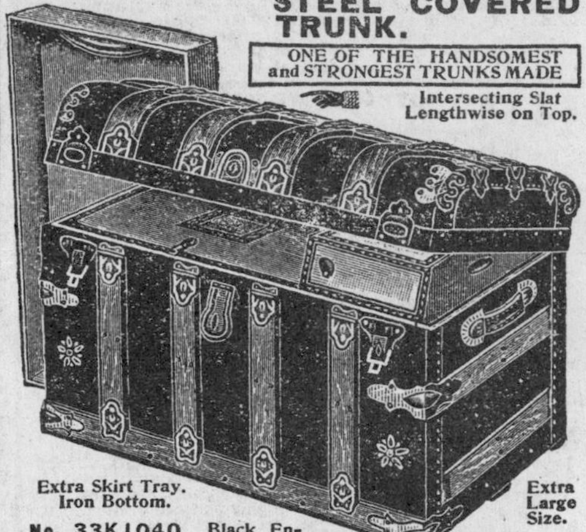

Extra Skirt Tray. Iron Bottom.

Extra Large Size.

No. 33K1040 Black Enamel Steel Covered Monitor Top Trunk. Four heavy hardwood slats over top and down side, two across each end and one lengthwise across top, intersecting cross slats. Extra heavy brass malleable clamps and reinforcements, brass Excelsior lock, heavy patent bolts, rollers, hinges, catches, stitched leather handles, etc. Contains tray with bonnet box and side compartment, fall-in-top compartment in cover, all separately covered. Has extra skirt tray which can be inverted and takes up comparatively no room. Note the heavy malleable trimmings, the number of and width and thickness of the hardwood slats, the strong reinforcements, and remember that this trunk has an iron bottom and is made on extra large size thick basswood box, one of the handsomest and most serviceable trunks made. We are so confident of the strength and the superiority of this trunk that we will, at any time, replace any one that does not give absolute satisfaction. Where is the dealer that offers this guarantee on any trunk he sells? Be sure to state size and catalogue number.

Length, 28 in.	Width, 17 in.	Height, 20 in.	Weight, 45 lbs.	Special price....$4.95
Length, 32 in.	Width, 19 in.	Height, 22 in.	Weight, 55 lbs.	Special price.... 5.65
Length, 36 in.	Width, 21 in.	Height, 24 in.	Weight, 64 lbs.	Special price.... 6.35
Length, 38 in.	Width, 22 in.	Height, 25 in.	Weight, 70 lbs.	Special price.... 6.70

$4.55 BEST BARREL TOP TRUNK, STEEL COVERED. PRICES REDUCED

No. 33K1050 Heaviest, Fancy Metal Covered Trunk, with large barrel top, five heavy hardwood barrel stave slats over top and down side, two hardwood slats across each end. Heavy, malleable trimmings and reinforcements throughout. Brass Monitor lock, strongest malleable iron, patent bolts, rollers, hinges, catches, etc. Leather handles, full finished hinged tray with separately covered compartment and bonnet box, also fall-in cover top compartment and extra skirt tray which fits in underneath first tray. Iron bottom, and made and trimmed and reinforced at every danger point exactly as illustrated. Extra large size, thick basswood box. One of the greatest trunks in this style ever offered. We will, at any time, replace any trunk of this number which fails to give satisfaction. Where else can you get a guarantee like this on trunks? Remember to state the size and catalogue number.

Five Slats on Cover

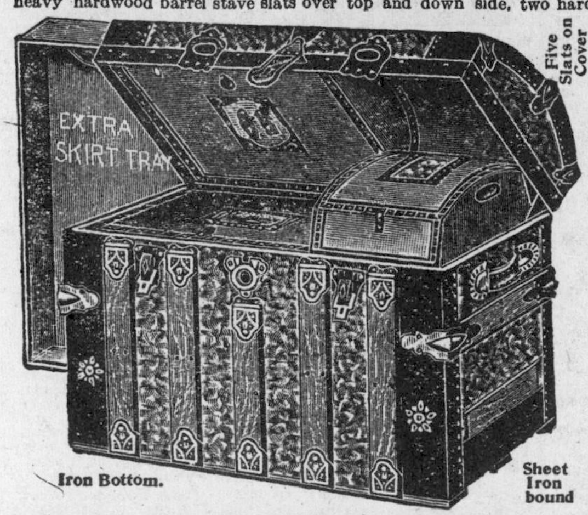

Iron Bottom.

Sheet Iron bound

Length, 28 in.	Width, 16½ in.	Height, 22 in.	Weight, 48 lbs.	Reduced price, now $4.55
Length, 32 in.	Width, 18½ in.	Height, 24 in.	Weight, 51 lbs.	Reduced price, now 5.25
Length, 36 in.	Width, 20½ in.	Height, 26 in.	Weight, 62 lbs.	Reduced price, now 5.95

$3.65 FANCY METAL COVERED BARREL TOP TRUNK

See No. 33K1050 for better barrel top trunk.

Extra Suit or Skirt Tray.

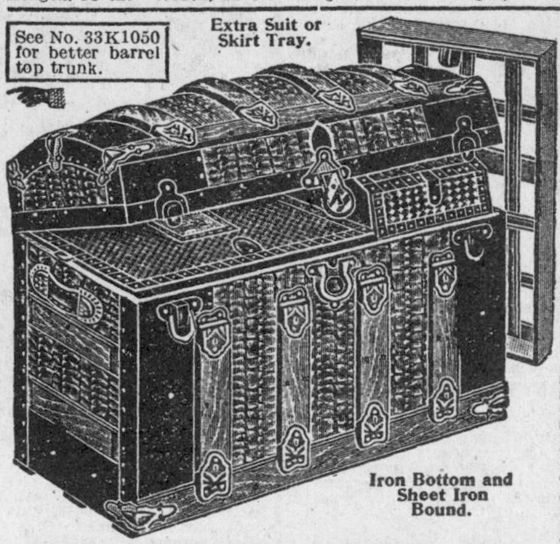

Iron Bottom and Sheet Iron Bound.

No. 33K1014 Fancy Metal Covered Trunk, large thick basswood box, paper lined, large barrel top with four heavy hardwood bar slats over top and on side, and two across each end. Sheet iron bound, and heavy fancy malleable trimmings and reinforcements, Iron bottom, patent bar bolts and rollers, heavy steel hinges and strong end clamps. Strong brass Monitor lock, fancy catches and leather handles, and contains tray with bonnet box and side compartment separately covered, also fall-in covered top compartment. Has skirt tray, which fits in underneath the upper tray and when not in use can be inverted and takes up comparatively no room. This is the greatest value ever offered in a low priced barrel top trunk, and we guarantee it to give satisfaction. Be sure to state the size wanted.

Length, 28 in.	Width, 16½ in.	Height, 20 in.	Weight, 41 lbs.	Price..........$3.65
Length, 32 in.	Width, 18½ in.	Height, 22 in.	Weight, 49 lbs.	Price.......... 4.25
Length, 36 in.	Width, 20½ in.	Height, 24 in.	Weight, 60 lbs.	Price.......... 4.85

$11.85 THE STRONGEST TRUNK MADE

Buy this trunk on our recommendation.

TWO TRAYS.

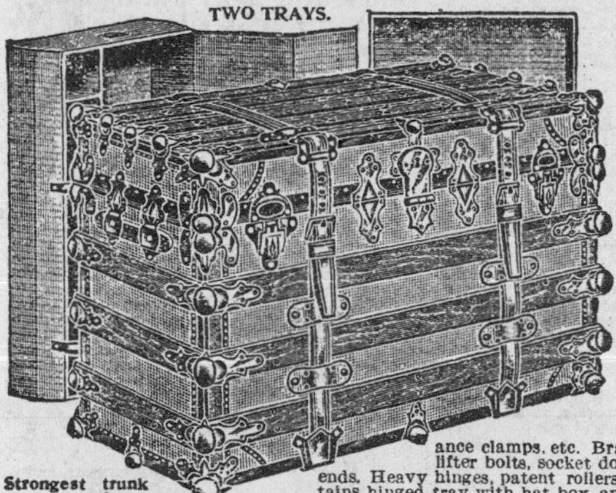

Strongest trunk ever made.

No. 33K1096 Wonderful Leather and Iron Bound Trunk. Built like a battleship because reinforced at every danger point. Extra large and thick basswood box covered with heaviest painted canvas. Flat top, five painted hardwood slats running lengthwise on top, and three heavy hardwood slats running around body of trunk. Front and back angle steel binding, edges heavy cowhide leather bound with fancy leather quarter rounds in corners, heavy leather handles and two heavy cowhide leather straps running through fancy metal and leather loops and tips. Heavy dome set brass plated clamps, knees, corner bumpers, valance clamps, etc. Brass Excelsior lock, patent lifter bolts, socket dowel clamps on front and ends. Heavy hinges, patent rollers, iron bottom, and contains hinged tray with hat box and other compartments, each with folding lid. Additional dress tray, full cloth lined, which fits underneath main tray. You cannot fail to note the thorough manner in which this trunk is made and reinforced. We say, "built like a battleship," and the trunk is sufficient proof of the statement. A great big trunk, which can never be broken in ordinary service. We will replace any trunk so broken. **Do not fail to state the size wanted and catalogue number.**

Length, 32 in.	Width, 18½ in.	Height, 21 in.	Weight, 65 lbs.	Reduced price..$11.85
Length, 34 in.	Width, 19½ in.	Height, 22 in.	Weight, 69 lbs.	Reduced price.. 12.60
Length, 38 in.	Width, 21½ in.	Height, 24 in.	Weight, 82 lbs.	Reduced price.. 14.10
Length, 40 in.	Width, 22½ in.	Height, 25 in.	Weight, 92 lbs.	Reduced price.. 14.85

$5.65 CANVAS COVERED STEEL BOUND TRUNK

TWO TRAYS.

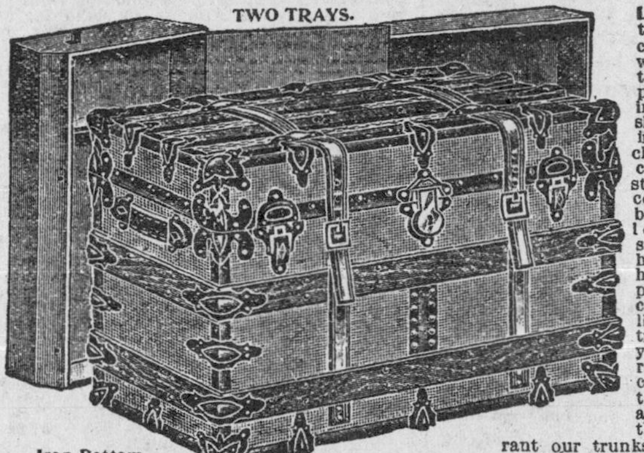

Iron Bottom.

No. 33K1058 Large, Full Size Trunk, thick basswood box, covered with heavy waterproof canvas, entirely bound with japanned angle steel binding, heavy hardwood slats, heavy malleable iron japanned valance clamps, buckle bar bolts, corner bumpers, steel strip clamps, knees, center band and iron bottom, brass Monitor lock, sole leather straps. Contains roomy hinged upper tray with hat box and side compartments separately covered with folding lids and extra skirt tray below. What can you get in the ordinary retail way that will compare in construction, reinforcements and appearance with this trunk? We warrant our trunks absolutely, and this trunk, if it in any way at any time should prove unsatisfactory, we will replace without charge. Please bear in mind the fact that these trunks are built on honor and that we are not afraid to warrant them absolutely. **Remember to give the size wanted and catalogue number when ordering.**

Length, 30 in.	Width, 17½ in.	Height, 19½ in.	Weight, 51 lbs.	Price....$5.65
Length, 32 in.	Width, 18½ in.	Height, 20½ in.	Weight, 56 lbs.	Price.... 6.00
Length, 36 in.	Width, 20½ in.	Height, 22½ in.	Weight, 65 lbs.	Price.... 6.70
Length, 38 in.	Width, 21½ in.	Height, 23½ in.	Weight, 69 lbs.	Price.... 6.95

$5.45 CANVAS COVERED WALL TRUNK

For better Wall Trunks see Nos. 33K1110 and 33K1116

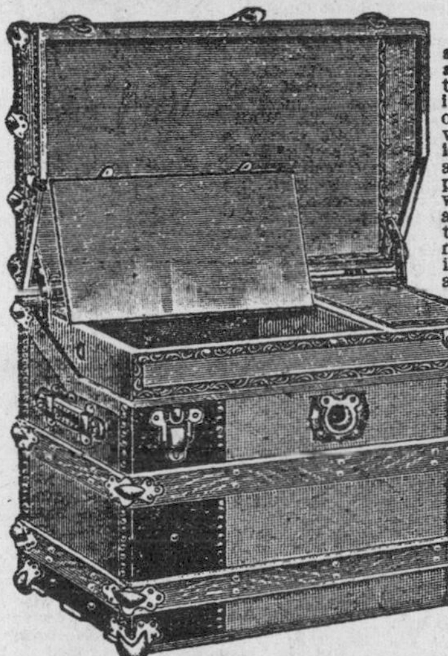

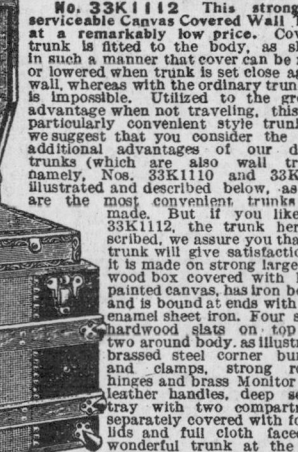

No. 33K1112 This strong and serviceable Canvas Covered Wall Trunk at a remarkably low price. Cover of trunk is fitted to the body, as shown, in such a manner that cover can be raised or lowered when trunk is set close against wall, whereas with the ordinary trunk this is impossible. Utilized to the greatest advantage when not traveling, this is a particularly convenient style trunk, but we suggest that you consider the many additional advantages of our dresser trunks (which are also wall trunks) namely, Nos. 33K1110 and 33K1116, illustrated and described below, as they are the most convenient trunks ever made. But if you like No. 33K1112, the trunk here described, we assure you that this trunk will give satisfaction, as it is made on strong large basswood box covered with heavy painted canvas, has iron bottom and is bound at ends with black enamel sheet iron. Four strong hardwood slats on top and two around body, as illustrated, brassed steel corner bumpers and clamps, strong rollers, hinges and brass Monitor lock, leather handles, deep set up tray with two compartments separately covered with folding lids and full cloth faced. A wonderful trunk at the price and is guaranteed to give satisfaction. **State size wanted.**

REDUCED PRICES:

Length, 32 in.	Width, 18½ in.	Height, 19½ in.	Weight, 50 lbs.	Price..$5.45
Length, 36 in.	Width, 23¾ in.	Height, 21½ in.	Weight, 57 lbs.	Price.. 5.95

$6.85 WONDERFUL CANVAS COVERED TRUNK

Our best medium priced trunk.

From photograph.

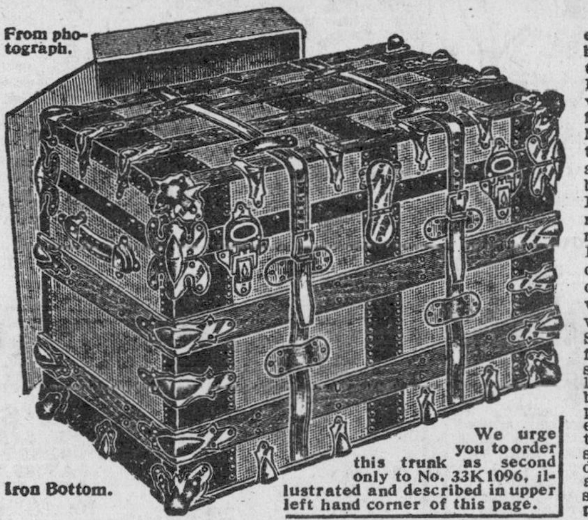

Iron Bottom.

No. 33K1070 The equal of this trunk cannot be bought at retail at twice our remarkable price. Extra large size painted canvas covered trunk. Made with four extra wide and heavy hardwood slats on top, and two body slats running clear around. Heavy sheet iron bottom and binding on ends. Has heaviest and strongest malleable brass clamps and reinforcements at every point. Buckle bar bolts. Brass Excelsior lock. Heavy brass corner bumpers and malleable valance clamps at corners where lid and body meet. Strong rollers, and is reinforced with two extra heavy sole leather straps. Contains large, roomy tray with hat box and large side compartment separately covered. A trunk that has been thoroughly tried by us for several years and has never disappointed. We will replace any trunk which does not give satisfaction. **When ordering please state size.**

We urge you to order this trunk as second only to No. 33K1096, illustrated and described in upper left hand corner of this page.

Length, 32 in.	Width, 21 in.	Height, 23½ in.	Weight, 50 lbs.	Special price..$6.85
Length, 36 in.	Width, 22½ in.	Height, 25 in.	Weight, 60 lbs.	Special price.. 7.55
Length, 38 in.	Width, 23 in.	Height, 25½ in.	Weight, 65 lbs.	Special price.. 7.90
Length, 40 in.	Width, 24 in.	Height, 26 in.	Weight, 72 lbs.	Special price.. 8.25

$10.95 WALL DRESSER TRUNK

We could offer a cheaper dresser trunk, but you would not want it.

PRICES REDUCED.

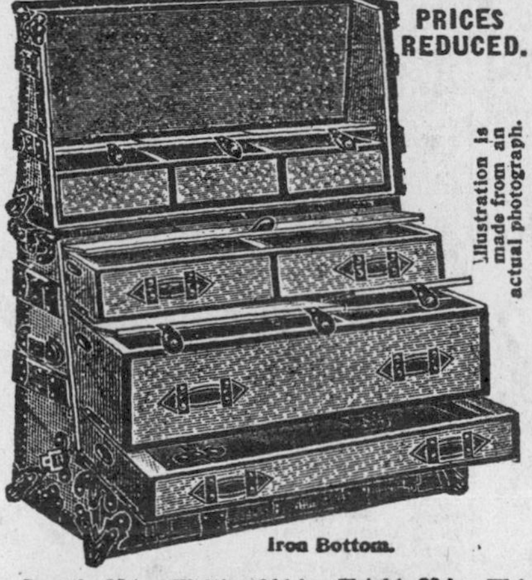

Illustration is made from an actual photograph.

Iron Bottom.

No. 33K1116 Special Wall Dresser Trunk, painted canvas covered large thick basswood box, thoroughly reinforced and protected by heaviest malleable japanned trimmings, with No. 4 buckle bar bolts in front and on ends, has brass Excelsior lock, strong patent catches, hinges and rollers. Valance clamps at corners where cover strikes body. The most convenient style trunk ever made. Any part accessible at all times. Upper part has three compartments and body contains three capacious cloth faced drawers, metal bound, resting on steel supports. Exactly as illustrated. One of the most serviceable and convenient of trunks. Retails at $18.00 to $20.00 and at our price is an exceptional value. A favorite with ladies. We cannot afford to misrepresent. Your money's worth here or your money back. **Please state size wanted.**

Following are Reduced Prices:

Length, 32 in.	Width, 18½ in.	Height, 22 in.	Weight, 62 lbs.	Reduced price...$10.95
Length, 36 in.	Width, 20½ in.	Height, 24 in.	Weight, 74 lbs.	Reduced price... 12.45
Length, 38 in.	Width, 21½ in.	Height, 25 in.	Weight, 80 lbs.	Reduced price... 13.20

$17.95 STRONGEST, MOST CONVENIENT BUREAU TRUNK MADE

Recommended as our best.

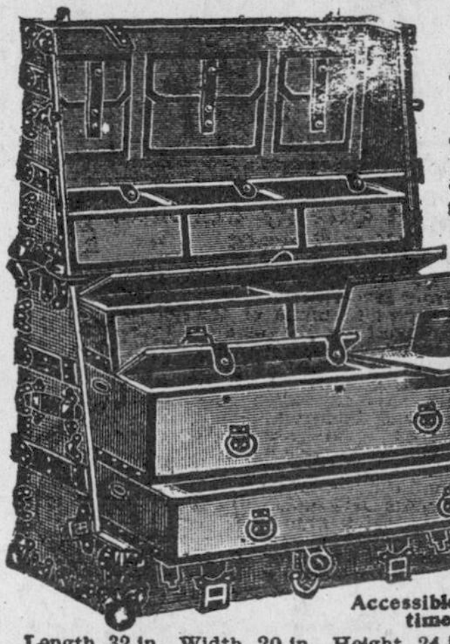

Taken from photograph.

Accessible at all times.

No. 33K1110 The strongest, heaviest and most convenient Wall Dresser Trunk ever made. Extra large thick basswood box covered with heavy waterproof painted canvas and reinforced and protected with olive enameled steel binding. Brass plated heels, corner bumpers and clamps, No. 4 buckle bar bolts, brass Excelsior lock, strongest and heaviest malleable catches, valance clamps at corners of lid and strong socket dowels joining cover and body, four heavy hinges and rollers, and has heavy stitched leather handles, and is reinforced with two heavy sole leather straps, protected with metal and leather strap loops. The illustration is an exact photographic reproduction of this trunk. Linen lined with genuine Holland linen facing, three strapped pockets and three roomy compartments in lid of trunk and has three large, roomy drawers arranged with movable hat form, and extra compartment in bottom of trunk. For strength and durability, coupled with its many convenient features, this trunk stands without a peer. The strongest guarantee ever put upon a trunk; we will replace any trunk if at any time it is proven unsatisfactory. **Please state size wanted.** Sizes as follows:

FOLLOWING ARE REDUCED PRICES:

Length, 32 in.	Width, 20 in.	Height, 24 in.	Weight, 78 lbs.	Reduced price..$17.95
Length, 36 in.	Width, 22 in.	Height, 26 in.	Weight, 88 lbs.	Reduced price.. 20.95
Length, 38 in.	Width, 24 in.	Height, 28 in.	Weight, 98 lbs.	Reduced price.. 22.45
Length, 40 in.	Width, 26 in.	Height, 30 in.	Weight, 108 lbs.	Reduced price.. 23.95

WOMEN'S ACCESSORIES

Be sure to give your size, and do not forget postage if by mail. If you do not know your exact size observe the following rules in taking your measure: If you measure over your corset, deduct 2 inches, thus allowing for spread of lacing in the back. For example, if your waist measure is 23 inches over your corset, you should order corset size 21. DO NOT FAIL TO GIVE THE SIZE.

Our Leading Value in a Popular Priced Corset - 47c

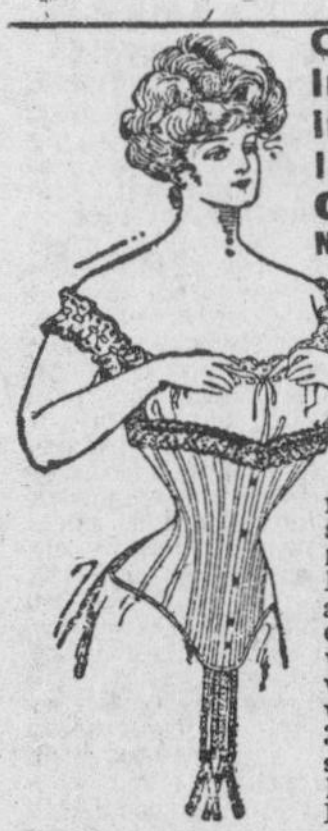

No. 18K101 Designed to improve the slender figure. Medium high bust, rather short over hips. Made of good quality coutil; well boned throughout with non-rusting tipped steels, encased in satin finished sterling cloth. Has five-hook front clasp and front hose supporters. Top is trimmed with dainty lace drawn with baby ribbon. Colors, white or drab. Sizes, 18 to 30. **Be sure to give us your size and color wanted.** Price........ **47c**
Postage extra, 16c.

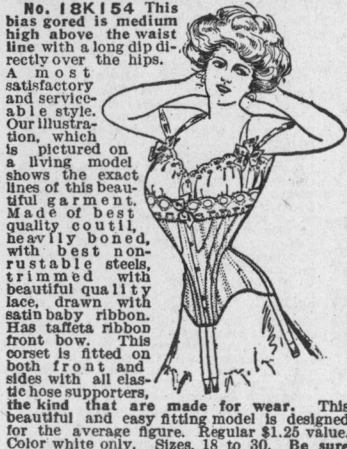

Mercerized Tape Girdle, Easy Fitting and Pretty, 44c

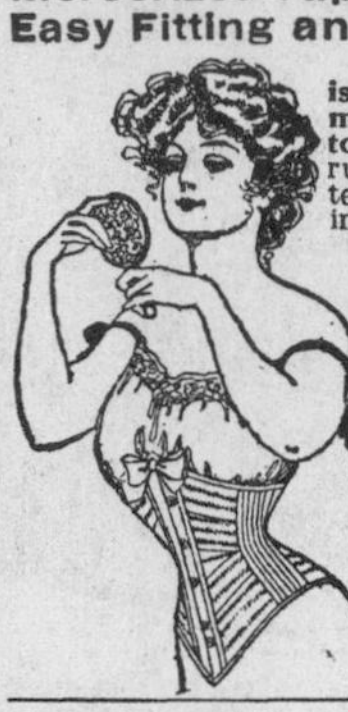

No. 18K130 This is a very dainty girdle, made of mercerized cotton tape, having stripes running through the center resembling silk. Boning set in sections covered with batiste. Boned with non-rusting steels and has aluminum eyelets. Ribbon bow on top. This high grade girdle is equal in style, looks and fit to the $1.00 girdle sold elsewhere. Made in all white only. Sizes, 18 to 26. **Be sure to give size wanted.**
Our price... **44c**
Postage extra, 9c.

Our Batiste Girdle Corset, 47c

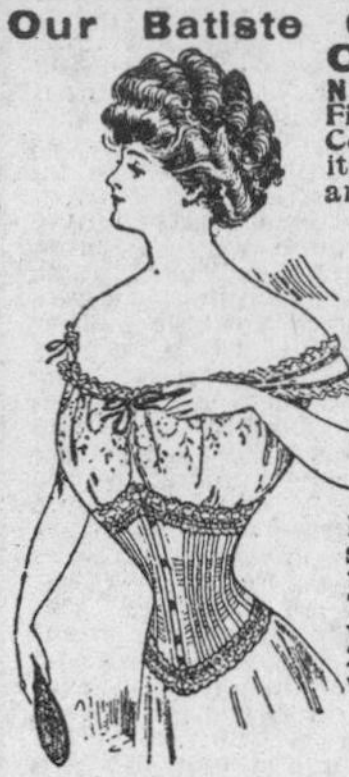

No. 18K135 Five-Hook Short Girdle Corset, made of fine quality batiste. These girdles are extremely popular and extensively worn, allowing the body greatest freedom of movement. Front steel, 10¼ inches long and of great pliability, boned with non-rusting tipped steel, encased in batiste. Trimmed top and bottom with dainty lace. An ideal corset for slender figures. We offer this corset as a regular 75-cent value. Color, white only. Sizes, 18 to 26. **Be sure to give size wanted.**
Price.......... **47c**
If by mail, postage extra, 10 cents.

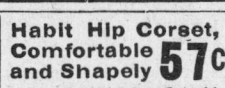

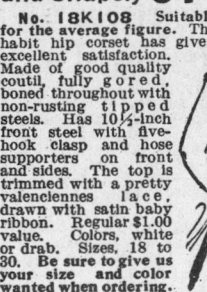

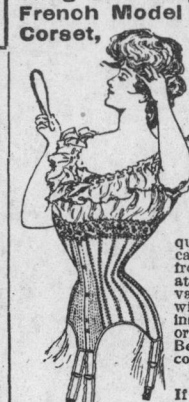

Snug and Easy Fitting French Model Dip Hip Corset, 88c

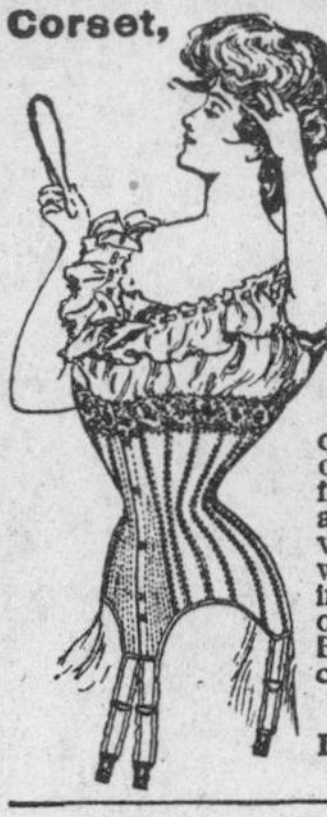

No. 18K160 This corset is a copy of a fine fitting French model sold at $5.00. Made of fine quality French sateen boned with non-rusting tipped steels, straight seamed, medium height bust and tapering waist, long sloping dip hip and back. This gives a graceful, slender figure which is so much desired. Fitted with good quality lisle elastic, patent catch hose supporters on front and sides. Trimmed at the top with a delicate valenciennes lace drawn with satin baby ribbon insertion. Colors, white or drab. Sizes, 18 to 30. **Be sure to give size and color wanted.**
Price.......... **88c**
If by mail, postage extra, 20 cents.

Extra Quality Girdle Top, Straight Front Corset - 93c

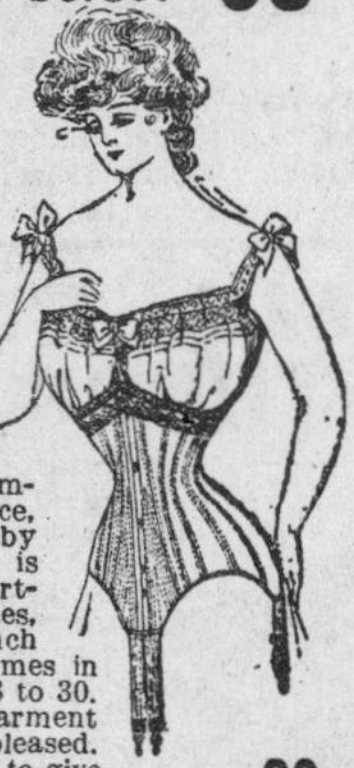

No. 18K151 This Low Bust, Long Hip Corset has proven to be one of our most popular and best selling numbers. The lines upon which it is built insure great comfort and freedom of arm and shoulder movement and it is suitable for the average figure. Made of best quality imported coutil, straight stripped, with non-rusting stays. Trimmed with pretty lace, drawn with satin baby ribbon. This corset is fitted with hose supporters on front and at sides, all made of best 1-inch wide lisle elastic. Comes in white only. Sizes, 18 to 30. If you will try this garment you are bound to be pleased. $1.35 value. **Be sure to give size when ordering.** Price. (Postage, 17c) **93c**

Extra Quality Short Hip Corset, 88c

No. 18K136 This short hip model is designed to improve the average slender figure, in as much as it has a tendency to force the hips out rather than confine them as is the case with the dip hip styles. The bust is medium high, allowing the proper freedom of the arms and shoulders, average length in the back. Made of fine quality white coutil, boned throughout with guaranteed non-rustable steels and has no heavy side steels. The top of the corset is trimmed with dainty lace, drawn with white satin baby ribbon, and set with taffeta ribbon bow. Has lisle elastic two-prong hose supporters in front only. Comes in white only. Sizes, 18 to 26. **Be sure to mention size.** All eyelets are aluminum. Regular $1.25 value.
Our price.. (Postage extra, 16 cents.).. **88c**

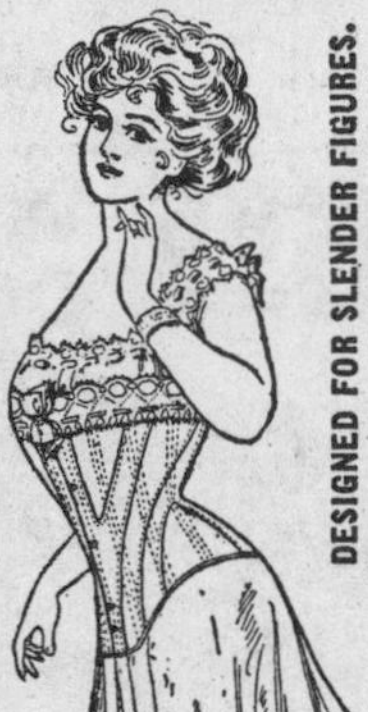

DESIGNED FOR SLENDER FIGURES.

The Armorside Corsets 85c
(Do Not Break Down at Sides.)

No. 18K145 The well known Armorside is one of the most popular corsets made. Constructed of a fine quality coutil, trimmed with rich valenciennes lace with ribbon drawn through. This model will fit a wide range of figures, and is especially adapted for women who have trouble with the corsets breaking down at the sides. Has the Armorside water proof clasp and boned with non-rusting fine steels. Colors, white or drab. Sizes, 18 to 30. Price...... **85c**
If by mail, postage extra, 17c to 22c.

No. 18K150 Extra Size Armorside Corset. Same style as above. Sizes, 31 to 36. Colors, white or drab.
Price...... **$1.00**
If by mail, postage extra, 18c to 22c.

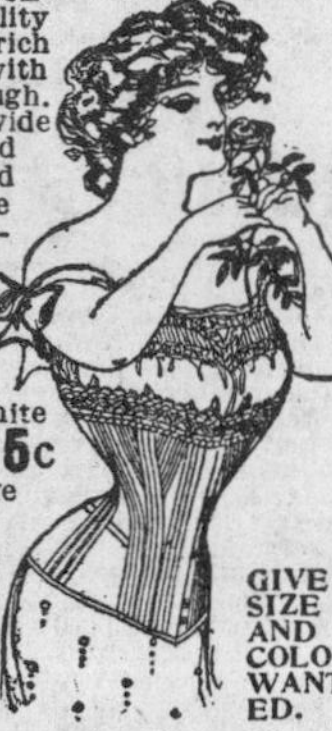

GIVE SIZE AND COLOR WANTED.

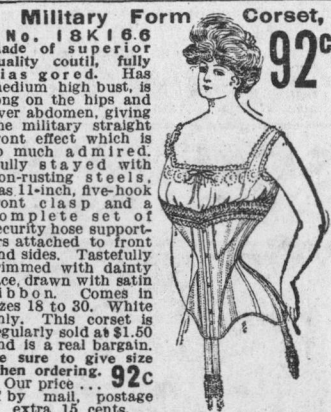

Military Form Corset, 92c

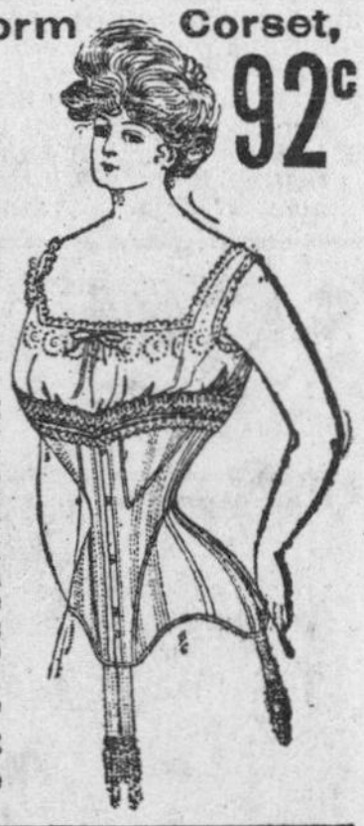

No. 18K166 Made of superior quality coutil, fully bias gored. Has medium high bust, is long on the hips and over abdomen, giving the military straight front effect which is so much admired. Fully stayed with non-rusting steels, has 11-inch, five-hook front clasp and a complete set of security hose supporters attached to front and sides. Tastefully trimmed with dainty lace, drawn with satin ribbon. Comes in sizes 18 to 30. White only. This corset is regularly sold at $1.50 and is a real bargain. **Be sure to give size when ordering.**
Our price ... **92c**
If by mail, postage extra, 15 cents.

Popular Priced Girdle Top Extension Hip Model 50c

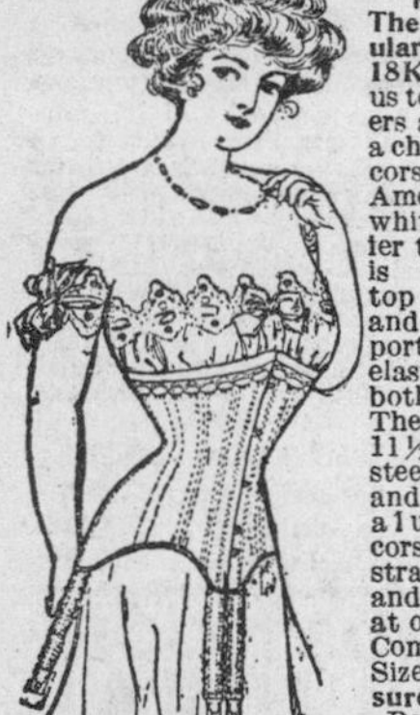

No. 18K112 The tremendous popularity of our No. 18K151, has induced us to offer our customers a similar style in a cheaper corset. This corset is made of good American twill (strong white material heavier than batiste). It is trimmed around top with dainty lace and has hose supporters of frilled elastic attached to both front and sides. The front clasp is 11½ inches long. All steels are non-rusting and all eyelets are aluminum. This corset is strictly straight front effect and great value at our price... **50c**
Comes in white only. Sizes 18 to 26. **Be sure to mention size.**
Postage extra, 16c.

EXTRA SPECIAL OFFER
Regular $1.50 Corset for - - 95c

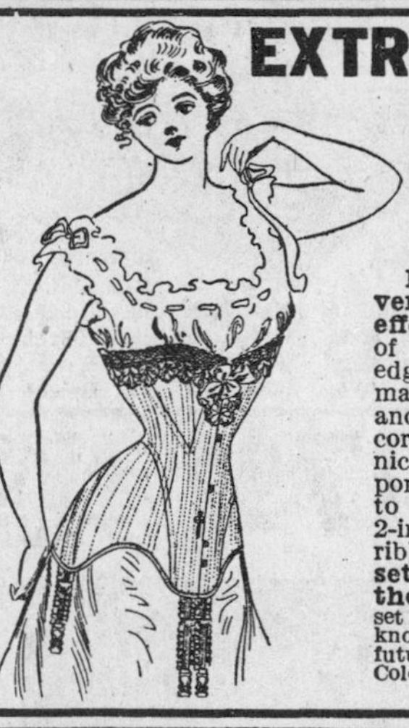

WE SPECIALLY RECOMMEND THIS CORSET AS ONE TO GIVE ABSOLUTE SATISFACTION, BOTH IN FIT AND QUALITY.

No. 18K143 This corset is made in the very popular long hip medium high bust effect and will fit the average figure. Made of the best quality of French coutil, acknowledged by all to be the best wearing corset material. It is fitted with non-rustable stays and aluminum eyelets. The front clasp of the corset is 11 inches long with five hooks and nickel plated skirt fastener. Four hose supporters of the best lisle elastic are attached to the front and sides. Corset is finished with 2-inch wide valenciennes lace drawn with satin ribbon. **We absolutely guarantee this corset to be equal to any $1.50 garment on the market.** The wearing quality of this corset is a particular feature, and if it is once used, we know that we will receive many re-orders in the future. Sizes, 18 to 30. **Be sure to give size.** Color, white only. Price.................. **95c**
If by mail, postage extra, 17 to 21 cents.

Beautiful Girdle Top, Dip Hip Model, $2.00 Value, $1.25

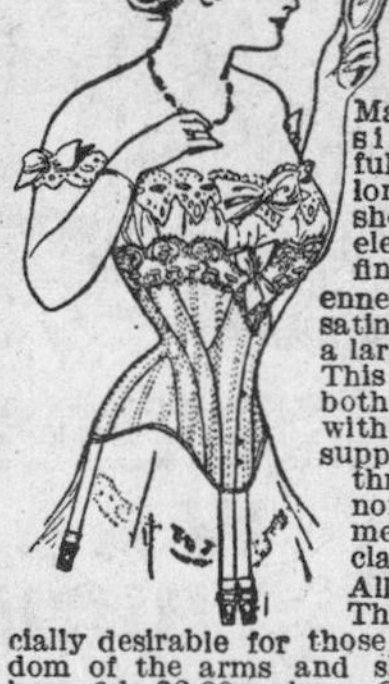

No. 18K182 We offer this beautiful corset as an improvement on our very popular number 18K181, and believe our trade will fully appreciate the great value given. Made of fine quality silk finished batiste, full bias gored, rather long over the hips and short in the back. Is elegantly trimmed with fine quality valenciennes lace, drawn with satin baby ribbon, set with a large satin taffeta bow. This garment is fitted on both sides and in front with good elastic hose supporters and is boned throughout with pliable non-rusting steels in medium weight. Front clasp is 10 inches long. All eyelets aluminum. This garment is especially desirable for those who appreciate freedom of the arms and shoulders, and is a bona fide $2.00 value. Comes in white only. Sizes, 18 to 26. State size. Price.... **$1.25**
If by mail, postage extra, 15 cents.

Strictly Straight Front Dip Hip Model. Special Value - - 85c

No. 18K154 This bias gored is medium high above the waist line with a long dip directly over the hips. A most satisfactory and serviceable style. Our illustration, which is pictured on a living model shows the exact lines of this beautiful garment. Made of best quality coutil, heavily boned, with best non-rustable steels, trimmed with beautiful quality lace, drawn with satin baby ribbon. Has taffeta ribbon front bow. This corset is fitted on both front and sides with all elastic hose supporters, **the kind that are made for wear.** This beautiful and easy fitting model is designed for the average figure. Regular $1.25 value. Color white only. Sizes, 18 to 30. **Be sure to give size.** Our price.................. **85c**
If by mail, postage extra, 16 cents.

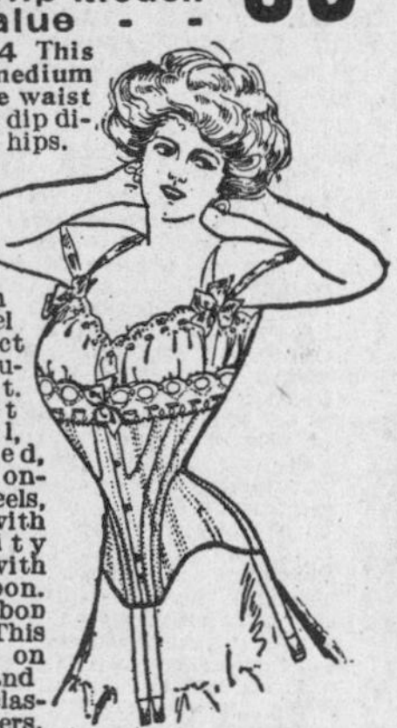

Best Quality Summer Netting Corset - 44c

No. 18K125 Straight Front Five-Hook Summer Corset, made of the strongest quality summer netting, trimmed with lace and baby ribbon insertion. The steels are covered with sateen and it is reinforced with six strips of sateen running across corset. The front clasp is 10½ inches long. Has aluminum eyelets. An excellent corset for those who desire a cool netting corset. Sizes, 18 to 30. White only. **Be sure to give your size.**
Price..... **44c**
If by mail postage extra, 14 cents.

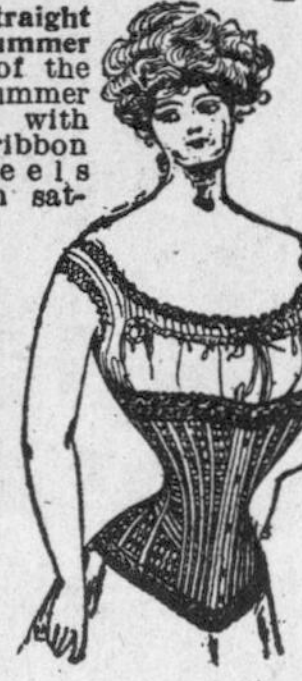

Habit Hip Corset, Comfortable and Shapely 57c

No. 18K108 Suitable for the average figure. The habit hip corset has given excellent satisfaction. Made of good quality coutil, fully gored, boned throughout with non-rusting tipped steels. Has 10½-inch front steel with five-hook clasp and hose supporters on front and sides. The top is trimmed with a pretty valenciennes lace, drawn with satin baby ribbon. Regular $1.00 value. Colors, white or drab. Sizes, 18 to 30. **Be sure to give us your size and color wanted when ordering.**

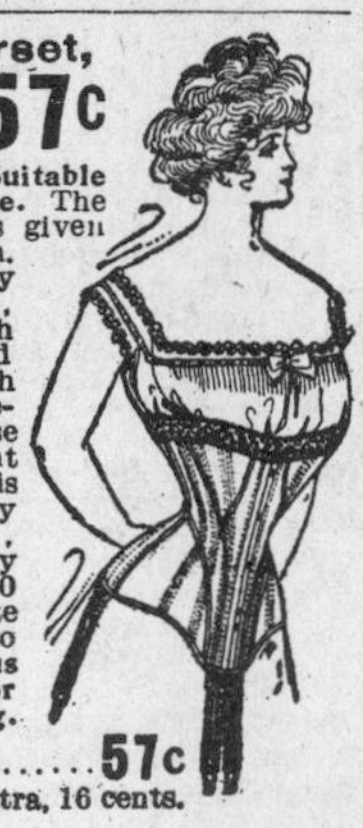

Price.......................... **57c**
If by mail, postage extra, 16 cents.

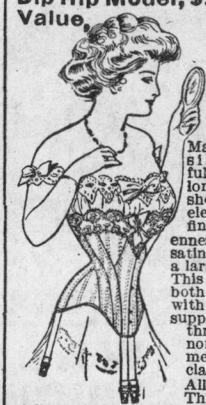

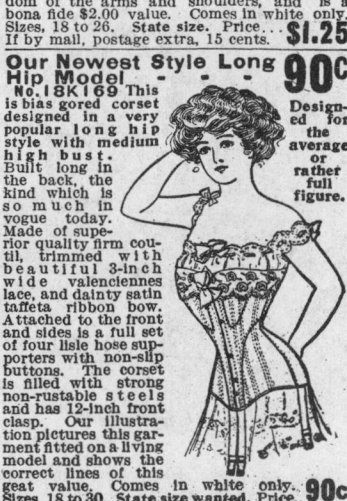

Our Newest Style Long Hip Model - - - 90c

No. 18K169 This is bias gored corset designed in a very popular long hip style with medium high bust. Built long in the back, the kind which is so much in vogue today. Made of superior quality firm coutil, trimmed with beautiful 3-inch wide valenciennes lace, and dainty satin taffeta ribbon bow. Attached to the front and sides is a full set of four lisle hose supporters with non-slip buttons. The corset is filled with strong non-rustable steels and has 12-inch front clasp. Our illustration pictures this garment fitted on a living model and shows the correct lines of this great value. Comes in white only. Sizes, 18 to 30. State size wanted. Price, **90c**
If by mail, postage extra, from 15c to 19c.

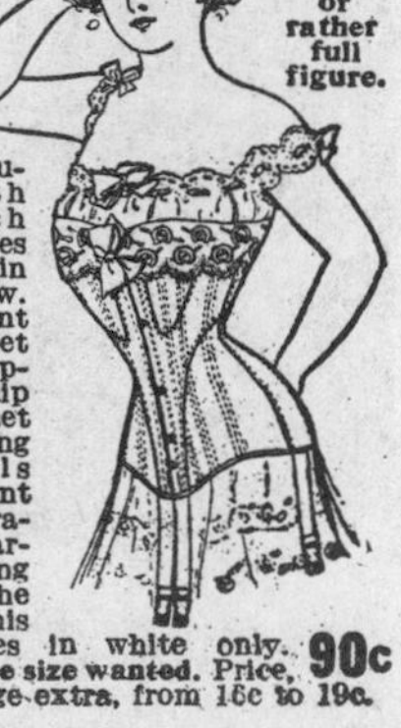

Designed for the average or rather full figure.

PRICED TO SAVE ⅓ FOR YOU

Comfortable Nursing Corset - - - 77c

No. 18K230 "Mothers' Friend" Nursing Corset, four-hook, reinforced clasp. Made of good quality coutil. Entirely new principle, as it is easily adjusted, with patent snap button, and will permit use of nipple without the slightest inconvenience. Very pliable over sensitive parts; a boon to mothers. Boned bust, strong jean girdle, two side steels. Colors, drab or white. Sizes, 18 to 30 inches. Always give size and color wanted. Price....77c

If by mail, postage extra, 16 cents.

Imported Coutil Straight Front Corset - - - $1.38

No. 18K200 An Ideal Corset for use with latest fashion in skirts; designed for the average figure. Straight front dip hip, just the correct height from the waist line, medium bust and taped hips, has 11½-inch five-hook clasp, boned with best non-rusting tipped steels. Made of very fine imported coutil, handsomely trimmed with superfine quality lace with a row of ribbon insertion and large silk ribbon bow. Has nickel plated skirt hook, equipped at front and sides with high grade frilled elastic hose supporters. This corset we can recommend as equal to the regular $3.00 corsets. Colors, white or drab. Sizes, 18 to 30 inches. Always be sure to give size and color wanted. Price....$1.38

If by mail, postage extra, 20 cents.

A Beautiful and Comfortable Fitting High Grade Silk Italian Cloth Corset - - - $2.39

No. 18K205 This is an imported French Model Corset, for medium figures, made of silk Italian cloth with silk flossing, has extra long straight front and dip hips, which gives the long tapering waist with sloping hips. The bottom edge is bound with silk tape and the boning throughout is covered and tipped, absolutely non-rusting. Trimmed at the top with a superior quality wide valenciennes lace with ribbon insertion and large silk ribbon bow. Fitted with superior quality hose supporters with "security clasps" at front and sides. Also fitted with nickel plated skirt hook at front; has best five-hook front clasp. This is the highest art of corset making. Usually retailed for $4.50. Color, white only. Sizes, 18 to 30. Always be sure to give your size. Our price....$2.39

If by mail, postage extra, 22 cents.

Ferris Good Sense Waist - - - 19c

No. 18K255 Comfortable and convenient for children from 4 to 6 years. Buttons for everything and everything easily buttoned; supports the body, healthful, comfortable and natural; easily adjusted and easily washed; made of good quality strong corset jean, nicely corded. Sizes, 21 to 28 inches waist measure. Colors, white or drab. Be sure to give size and color wanted. Price .19c

If by mail, postage extra, ½ cents.

French Model, Front Lacing Corset - - $1.85

No. 18K236 Eventually you will come to this style. Why not buy one now? Front lacing corsets are becoming more popular every day, and if once worn they are sure to prove so satisfactory that you will wear no other. Our corset is copied from a French model which sells for $10.00 and it will give as good satisfaction as the highest price goods. Made of superior quality firm white coutil, boned with best non-rusting wires. Daintily trimmed at the top with beautiful lace, drawn with white satin baby ribbon, set with taffeta ribbon bow. A particular feature of this corset is the hose supporter arrangement. The front hose supporters being doubled in V shape, single supporters on the sides. Sizes, 18 to 26 inches. Be sure to state size. As a foundation for a perfect fitting gown our front lacing corset has no equal. Good dressmakers everywhere advise patrons to use them. Price......$1.85

If by mail, postage extra, 17 cents.

$2.25 ARE YOU TOO STOUT?

THIS GARMENT GUARANTEED TO MAKE YOU SLENDER, TO REDUCE AND CORRECT PROTRUDING ABDOMENS.

No. 18K237 The Sahlin Form Reducer will do for you what an abdominal corset or belt cannot do. The upper part is designed in the same way as the best fitting corsets, while the lower or reducing part is fitted with twelve separate adjustments, which can be tightened or loosened to suit every figure. Unlike any other corset of its kind, it accomplishes the work of reducing and bracing the figure by construction over the hips and abdomen and has no "dragging down" effect. Made of fine quality French coutil, boned with non-rustable steels and well reinforced throughout. The top is elegantly trimmed with best quality wide lace drawn with satin ribbon, has frilled elastic hose supporters on front and sides. We strongly recommend this form reducer and guarantee it to do all that we claim for it. When ordering give size of corset you usually wear. Comes in white only at the following prices:

Sizes, 20-30. Price $2.25
Sizes, 31-36. Price 2.50
Sizes, 37-40. Price 2.75
If by mail, postage extra, each, 22 cents to 33 cents.

Sahlin Perfect Form and Corset Combined.

ONE THOUSAND TWO HUNDRED DOZEN SOLD BY US IN THE LAST YEAR.

No. 18K220 Sahlin Perfect Form and Corset Combined. Retains all the good and avoids the evil of ordinary corsets. Nothing lost in the style or shape. The bust will not cave in, and therefore padding and interlining are avoided. The effect as here shown is an exact reproduction of a perfect form, obtained only by wearing the Sahlin. No corset is necessary, as it is a corset and form combined. Approved and endorsed by physicians and health reformers. Made of good quality corset jean, white or drab. Give bust and waist measure and color wanted. For sizes and how to measure, see below. Price....90c

No. 18K225 Sahlin Perfect Form and Corset Combined. Same as above, made of fancy summer netting, white only. Give bust and waist measure. For sizes and how to measure, see below. Price.....90c

If by mail, postage extra, 15 cents.

No Hooks
No Clasps
No Eyelets
No Strings
No Heavy Steels

90c

How to Give us Your Correct Measure for Sahlin Form.

FOLLOW THESE THREE INSTRUCTIONS CAREFULLY.

1. Give waist measure.   2. Give bust measure.   3. Give underarm measurement from arm pit to waist line.

The Sahlin Perfect Form and Corset Combined is made in the following sizes:

Bust	Waist	Under Arm	Bust	Waist	Under Arm
30 in.	18, 20, 22 in.	7, 8, 9 in.	36 in.	22, 24, 26, 28 in.	7, 8, 9 in.
32 in.	20, 22, 24 in.	7, 8, 9 in.	38 in.	24, 26, 28, 30 in.	7, 8, 9 in.
34 in.	20, 22, 24, 26 in.	7½, 8½, 9¾ in.	40 in.	28, 30, 32 in.	6½, 7½, 8½ in.

WE CAN ONLY FURNISH MEASUREMENTS AS ABOVE. DON'T ASK FOR OTHERS.

Martha Washington Misses' Corset Waist For Girls - - - 48c

Combining all the good qualities of a waist. No. 18K265 The Martha Washington Misses' Corset Waist for misses. Made of fine sateen, button front with adjustable shoulder straps and laces in the back; tab for hose supporter, trimmed at the top with pretty edging; a waist that is helpful and will help the girl grow as she should grow. Colors, white or drab. Sizes, 20 to 28 inches waist measure. Do not fail to give size and color wanted. Price....48c

If by mail, postage extra, 7 cents.

Armorside Nursing Corset - - - 85c

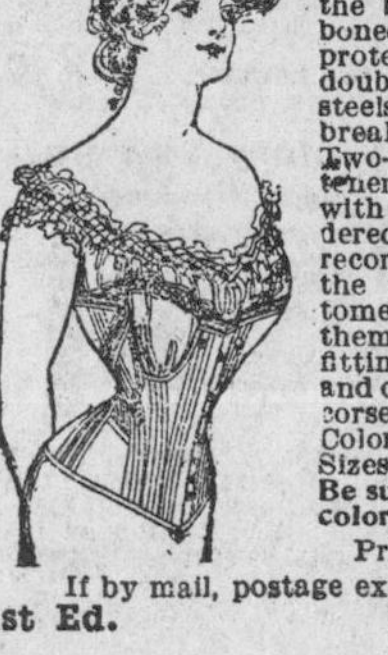

No. 18K235 Armorside Nursing Corset (will not break down on the sides). Made of the best quality coutil, boned with non-rusting protected steels, has the double clasps and side steels, which prevent breaking at the sides. Two-button clasp fasteners, neatly trimmed with a pretty embroidered top. We highly recommend this, as do the thousands of customers who have used them, as being the best fitting, most durable and comfortable nursing corset on the market. Colors, white or drab. Sizes, 18 to 30 inches. Be sure to give size and color wanted. Price........85c

If by mail, postage extra, 20 cents.

Sig. 59—1st Ed.

Misses' Common Sense Waist - - - 55c

A POPULAR STYLE.

No. 18K275 Suitable for girls 12 to 17 years of age. Has plaited bust so arranged as to lay flat or distend. Especially adapted to growing girls of slender form. Made of good quality corset jean, bound top and bottom with tape. Colors, white or drab. Sizes, 19 to 28 inches waist measure. Don't fail to give size and color wanted. Price....55c

If by mail, postage extra, 8 cents.

LOOK AT THIS OFFER $1.98

A good corset is the foundation of a well fitting gown. We positively guarantee to you that you cannot buy this corset in equal quality and style from your dealer for less than $4.00.

No. 18K238 This corset is designed in one of the leading and most popular styles of the day, and will fit any average figure perfectly. It is made of the finest quality brocaded silk twill, in handsome patterns, trimmed around the top with elegant quality valenciennes lace, drawn with double row of satin baby ribbon. It is fitted with best 1¼-inch wide lisle elastic hose supporters on both front and sides. These wide, strong supporters are adjustable in length. The style, as you will see by the illustration, is bias gored, with medium high bust and rather long hips. Strictly straight front effect with a five-hook front clasp. Comes in white only. Sizes, 18 to 30. Be sure to give size. Price....$1.98

If by mail, postage extra, 17 cents.

The Armorside Abdominal Reducing Corset - - - $1.25

No. 18K245 Armorside Abdominal Reducing Corset, straight front. The reducing feature recommends it very strongly for stout figures. The inserting of fine English sateen gores on the side prevents clumsy bunching on the hips, no side laces, no elastic to rot. The Armorside corsets are made to fit and wear. Made of a very fine quality coutil, boned with best non-rusting steels, with the Armorside waterproof clasp in front. The bones and steels are made with a protective covering for the ends which prevents their cutting through. Colors, white or drab. Sizes, 22 to 30 inches. Be sure to give size or color wanted. Price....$1.25

No. 18K250 Extra size Armorside Abdominal Reducing Corset, straight in front. Sizes, 31 to 36. Price....$1.40

If by mail, postage extra, 24 cents.

The Jackson Favorite Waist Is the Best Corset Waist - - - 82c

No. 18K240 The Jackson Waist combines in the highest degree the embodiment of an elegant waist and corset combination. It stays are ample, outlining a most graceful poise of figure, at the same time easy and comfortable; it is also adaptable as a negligee by the removing of all the side steels, which can be replaced at will. Made of good sateen in white or drab. Sizes, 18 to 30 inches. Be sure to give size and color wanted. Price....82c

If by mail, postage extra, 18 cents.

No. 18K241 Jackson Waist. Extra style and quality as No. 18K240. Extra sizes, 31 to 36. Price....$1.11

If by mail, postage extra, 14 cents to 19 cents.

HOSE SUPPORTERS IN SPECIAL STYLES AND VALUES

Easy Catch Hose Supporters.

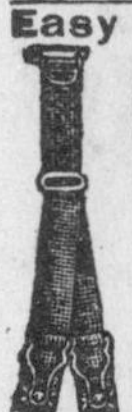

Made of good quality Lisle Elastic Webbing with safety pin top and slide center. Colors, black or white; in four sizes. State color wanted.

No. 18K300 Child's size. Length, 7 inches. Price, per pair..(Postage 2c)...6c

No. 18K302 Misses' size. Length, 9¾ inches. Price, per pair..(Postage 2c)...7c

No. 18K304 Young Ladies' size. Length, 12 inches. Price, per pair..(Postage 2c)...8c

No. 18K306 Ladies' size. Length, 15 inches. Price, per pair 9c

If by mail, postage extra, per pair, 2 cents.

The Indestructible Flexo Grasp Hose Supporter.

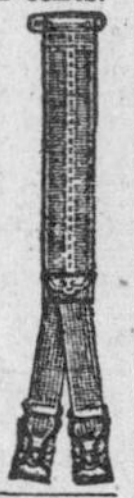

Made of a superior quality one-inch Elastic Lisle Webbing. Trimmed with nickel adjustable slide buckle and fiber button clasp with safety pin top. Colors, black, white, pink or light blue. State color wanted. Comes in three sizes.

No. 18K308 Child's size. Length, 7½ inches. Per pair 9c Postage extra, per pair, 2 cents.

No. 18K311 Misses' size. Length, 9½ inches. Price, per pair..(Postage 2c)...11c

No. 18K313 Young Ladies' size. Length, 11½ inches. Price, per pair..(Postage 2c)...13c

Braces and Hose Supporters.

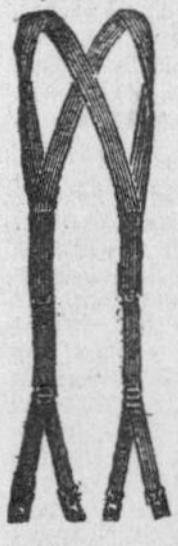

Made of good Lisle Elastic Webbing.

No. 18K316 Ladies' Shoulder Braces, with hose supporters; fitted with adjustable slides; black or white. State color wanted. Price, per pair.........19c Postage, extra, 3 cents.

No. 18K318 Misses' Shoulder Braces, with hose supporters; fitted with adjustable slides; black or white. State color wanted. Price, per pair...........17c Postage, extra, 3 cents.

No. 18K320 Children's Shoulder Braces, with hose supporters; fitted with adjustable slides; black or white. State color wanted. Price, per pair 14c

Postage extra, per pair, 3c.

Children's Combination Waist and Hose Supporter.

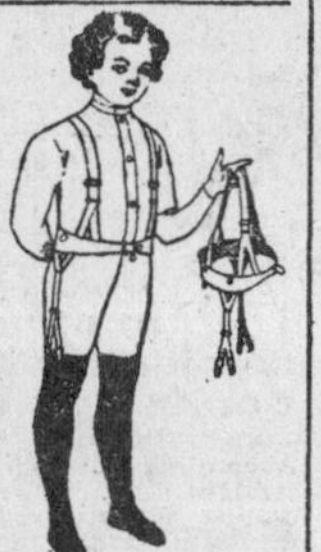

No. 18K322 Combination Belt and Supporters for Boys and Girls. The handiest, safest and most convenient waist and hose supporter on the market. Made of good sateen and lisle elastic sides. Sizes are from 2 to 12 years. Be sure to give age. Comes in white only. Price.......19c

If by mail, postage extra 4 cents.

Ladies' Pin On Supporters.

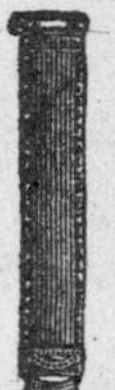

No. 18K324 Ladies' Pin On Supporters. Made of heavy quality lisle webbing with small frill on side. Trimmed with good quality adjustable nickel slide buckle and fiber button clasps. Colors, black, white, pink or light blue. State color. Price, per pair....16c

If by mail, postage extra, per pair, 2 cents.

Great Values in Hose Supporters.

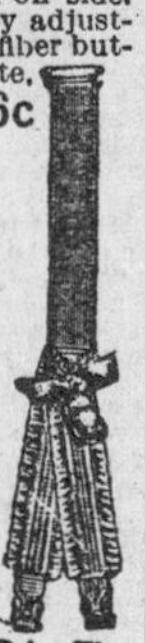

No. 18K326 This is a very beautiful Side Supporter. The top part is 1⅛-inch satin band, stitched on both sides, and the lower part is a beautiful fancy frilled mercerized elastic with pretty bows of silk ribbon, adjustable nickel buckle and fiber button clasp. Colors, black, white, pink or light blue. State color wanted. Regular 35-cent value. Our price, per pair.......21c

Postage extra, per pair, 2 cents.

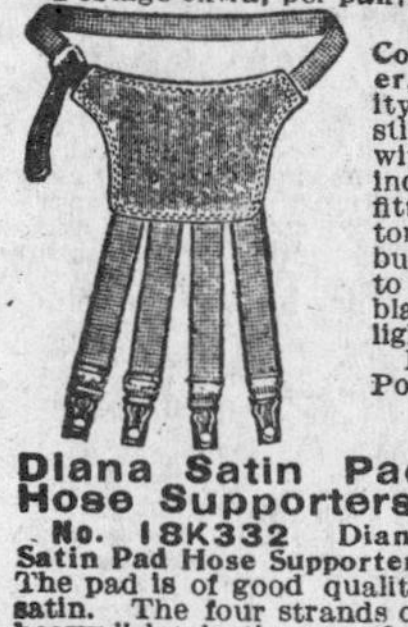

No. 18K331 The Comfort Pad Supporter, made of good quality material, all double stitched. Trimmed with four straps of 1-inch wide lisle elastic fitted with fiber button clasps and nickeled buckles. Adjustable to any size. Colors, black, white, pink or light blue. Price, ...21c

Postage extra, 4 cents.

Diana Satin Pad Hose Supporters.

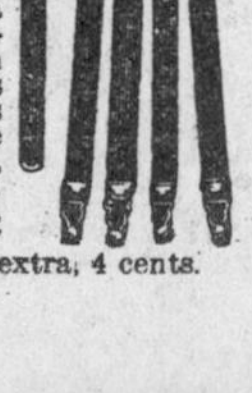

No. 18K332 Diana Satin Pad Hose Supporter. The pad is of good quality satin. The four strands of heavy lisle elastic are of a superior grade. Has fine adjustable nickel buckles, with fiber button clasp. This style of hose supporter is the best made and this value is unexcelled. Colors, black, white, pink or light blue. State color wanted. Price...........25c

If by mail, postage extra, 4 cents.

Exceptional Value at 44 Cents.

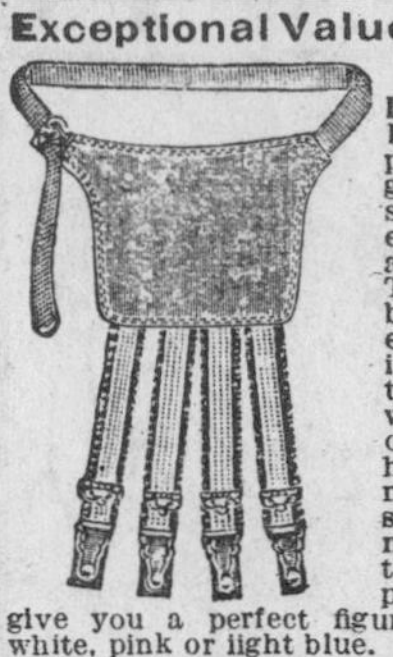

No. 18K334 Diana Satin Pad Hose Supporter. The pad is of a better grade satin, double stitched, with non-elastic belt, adjustable to any size waist. The four strands of beautiful heavy silk elastic are fine quality, has neat, adjustable gilt buckles with fiber button clasp. The Diana hose supporter is the most comfortable pad supporter made, making you assume the correct standing position, and it helps give you a perfect figure. Colors, black, white, pink or light blue. State color wanted. Price........................44c

If by mail, postage extra, 4 cents.

The Model Princess Hose Supporter.

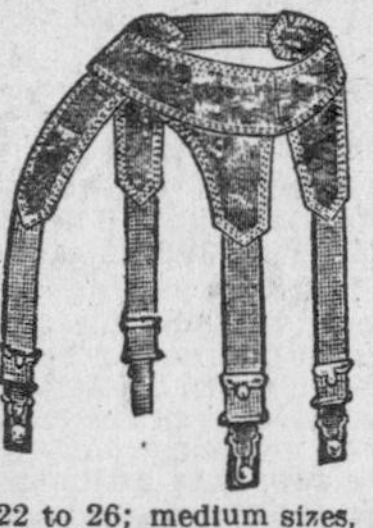

No. 18K338 The Model Princess Hose Supporter, made of good quality twill sateen, in moire effect. The Model Princess is the most satisfactory supporter made for comfort and style. The belt and four tabs are all double stitched and trimmed with best quality lisle elastic 1¼ inches wide fitted with adjustable nickel buckles and fiber buttons. Colors, black, white, pink or light blue. Comes in small sizes, 22 to 26; medium sizes, 27 to 30; large sizes, 31 to 36. Be sure to give size and color. Price.........................44c

If by mail, postage extra, 5 cents.

Ladies' Safety Belts.

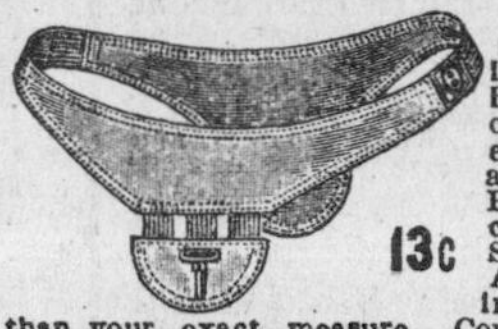

No. 18K340 Ladies' Safety Belts. Made of sateen, with elastic band across hips. Easy and convenient. Sizes, 22 to 36. Ask for one inch larger than your exact measure. Comes in even sizes only. Give waist measure. Color, white only. Price.......13c

If by mail, postage extra, 2 cents.

Washable Cloth Belt.

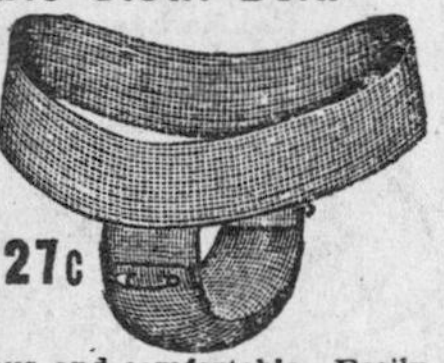

No. 18K342 All Elastic Washable Doily Cloth Belt. Made of high grade elastic, cream color. Has no straps to roll or cut, no buckles to rust or stick, and it can be readily washed and cleaned. It is antiseptic, porous and comfortable. Easily slipped on over the limbs. A regular 50-cent article. Made in four sizes, as follows: Small, 19 to 24 inches. Medium, 25 to 28 inches. Large, 29 to 32 inches. Extra large, 33 to 36 inches. Be sure to state size wanted. Price, for belt with two napkins....27c

Postage extra, per set, 4 cents.

The E Z Sanitary Belt.

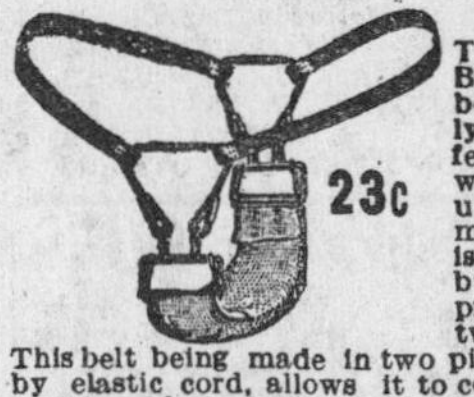

No. 18K344 The E Z Sanitary Belt. It fits the body so smoothly that it is not felt when either worn over or under garments, for there is no button or buckle or other projection between the web. This belt being made in two pieces, connected by elastic cord, allows it to conform to any position of the body. The fastener is made in such a way that the napkin can be inserted or detached very easily. Sizes from 22 to 36. Always give size. Price, for belt and two napkins.....23c

If by mail, postage extra, per set, 5 cents.

Antiseptic Sanitary Towels.

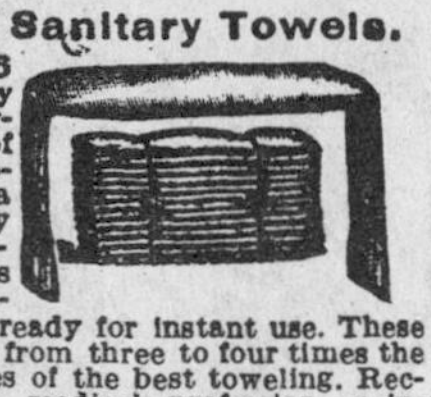

No. 18K346 Serviette Sanitary Cloth. These serviettes are made of the finest absorbent cotton, with a layer of absolutely impervious material, which insures cleanliness. Absolutely antiseptic, ready for instant use. These serviettes possess from three to four times the absorbent qualities of the best toweling. Recommended by the medical profession as indispensable in every lady's wardrobe. Price, PER DOZEN.............30c

If by mail, postage extra, per dozen, 14 cents.

Special Sanitary Supports.

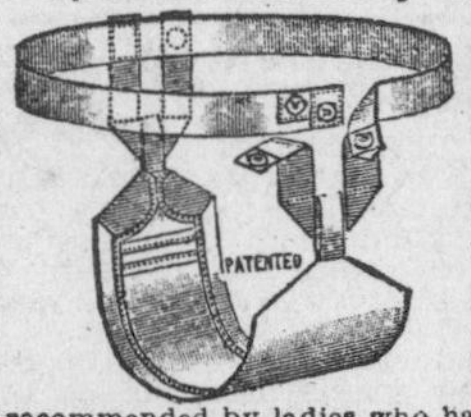

No. 18K348 Special Sanitary Support and Belt for holding serviette or napkin to prevent soiling the clothes. Made of fine waterproof stockinet, which is easily washed; fills a long desired want; highly recommended by ladies who have used them. The belt is made in sizes from 22 to 36. Try one and you will never be without. Give size when ordering. Price, for support and belt combined 59c

If by mail, postage extra, 4 cents.

Elastic Arm Bands.

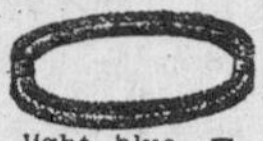

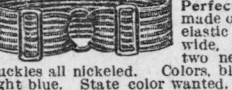

No. 18K350 Mercerized Elastic Arm Band. This is a double row, round, knit elastic band. Very durable and comfortable. Colors, black, white, pink or light blue. State color wanted. Price, per pair.........7c

If by mail, postage extra, per pair, 2 cents.

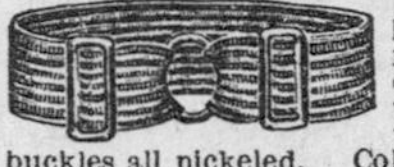

No. 18K351 The Perfect Arm Bands made of silk finished elastic ¾ inches wide, fitted with two neat adjusting buckles all nickeled. Colors, black, white or light blue. State color wanted. Price, per pair......................10c

If by mail, postage extra, per pair, 2 cents.

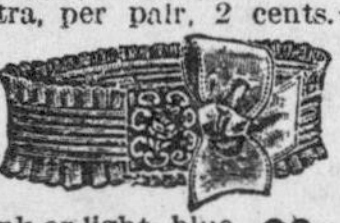

No. 18K353 Ladies' Round Garters made of fancy frilled elastic, trimmed with large satin bows and gilt buckles. Neatly packed in fancy box. Colors, black, pink or light blue. State color wanted. Price, per pair.....22c

If by mail, postage extra, 10 cents.

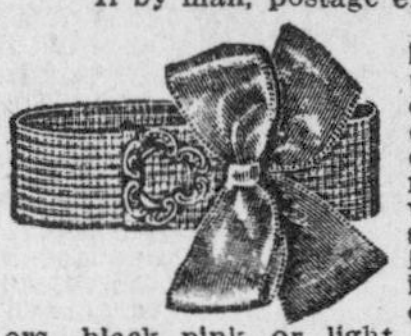

No. 18K355 Ladies' Fancy Garters made of best quality all silk cable web elastic, one inch wide, neatly trimmed with large bows of silk ribbon and fancy gilt buckles in handsome glass covered box. Colors, black, pink or light blue. State color wanted. Price, per pair.........42c

If by mail, postage extra, per pair, 10 cents.

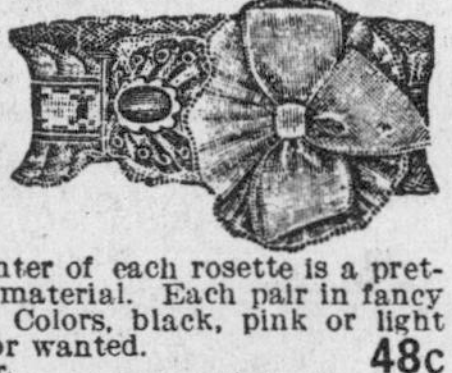

No. 18K352 Ladies' Finest Silk Garters. Made of imported frill elastic. Has pretty gilt buckle and handsome rosettes made of satin taffeta ribbon. In the center of each rosette is a pretty bow of same material. Each pair in fancy glass top box. Colors, black, pink or light blue. State color wanted. Price, per pair...................48c

If by mail, postage extra, per pair, 11 cents.

Ladies' Fancy Elastic Arm Bands.

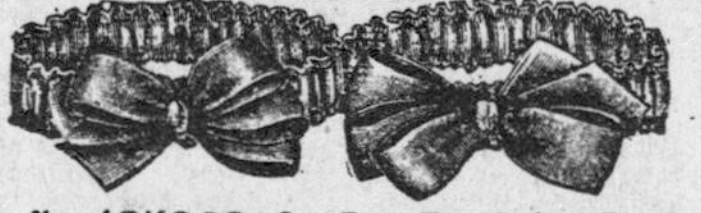

No. 18K368 Our Best Elastic Arm Bands for long gloves and short sleeves. Made of closely shirred satin ribbon over good elastic. Trimmed with bows of fine quality satin taffeta ribbon. Colors, black, white, or blue. State color wanted. Price, per pair 46c

If by mail, postage extra, per pair, 1 cent.

No. 18K370 Elastic Arm Bands. Made of nice quality shirred satin over good elastic with bows of satin taffeta ribbon. Colors, black, white, pink or blue. State color wanted. Price, per pair.........23c

If by mail, postage extra, per pair, 1 cent.

Plain Lisle Elastic.

No. 18K354 Black or White Lisle Loom Garter Elastic, good quality. Width, inches ⅝ ¾ 1

Price, per yard 4c 5c 6c

If by mail, postage extra, per yard, 1 cent.

Non-Elastic Webbing.

No. 18K356 Black or White Non-Elastic Webbing, good quality, used for hose supporters, bandings and belts.

Width, inches ½ ⅝ ¾ 1

Price, PER YARD 2c 2½ 3c 4c

If by mail, postage extra, per yard, 1 cent.

Garter Elastic.

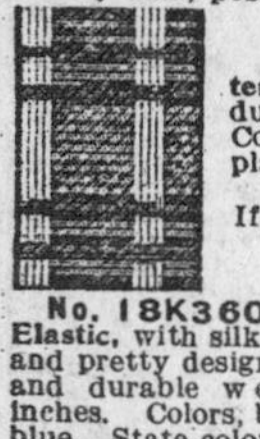

No. 18K358 Plaid Garter Elastic. This is a good, durable web. Width, ¾ inch. Colors, blue, pink, red or black plaid. State color wanted. Price, per yard.........4c

If by mail, postage extra, per yard, 1 cent.

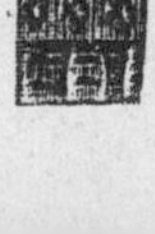

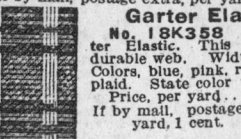

No. 18K360 Fancy Frilled Elastic, with silk overshot. A new and pretty design. This is a strong and durable web. Width, 1¼ inches. Colors, black, pink or light blue. State color wanted. Price, per yard...........5c

If by mail, postage extra, per yard, 1 cent.

Silk Elastic.

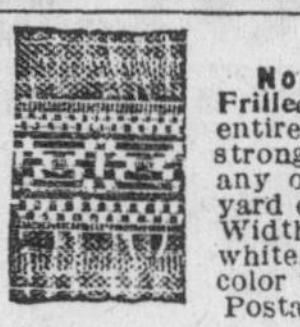

No. 18K362 Our best Frilled Silk Elastic. This is an entirely new pattern. Very strong and durable. Equal to any of the 15 and 20 cents a yard elastics, as sold elsewhere. Width, 1½ inches. Colors, black, white, pink or light blue. State color wanted. Per yard..10c Postage, per yd., 1 cent.

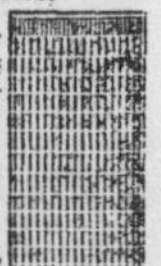

No. 18K364 Best quality Silk Schappe Elastic Web. This is preferred by many to the very expensive silk. Looks just the same and wears splendidly. Width, ⅞ inch. Colors, black, white, pink or light blue. State color wanted. Price, per yard......9c

If by mail, postage extra, per yard, 1 cent.

Ribbed Silk Elastic.

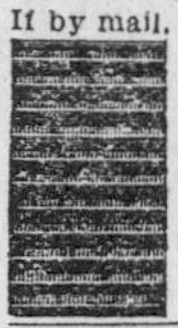

No. 18K366 Heavy Ribbed All Silk Elastic. The highest grade quality; one inch wide. Colors, black, white, pink or light blue. State color wanted. Price, per yard.........23c

If by mail, postage extra, per yard, 1 cent.

Improved Breast Support for Low or High Busts.

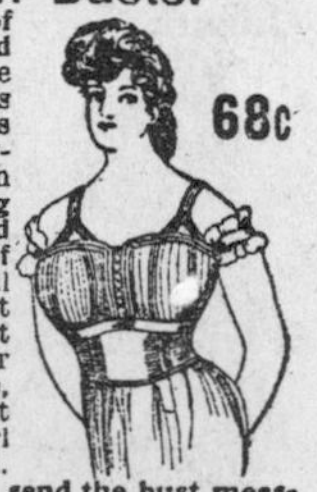

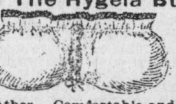

No. 18K372 Made of strong, light material called tampico fiber. By its use the weight of the breast is removed from the dress waist to the shoulders, giving coolness and comfort in warm weather, producing a perfect shaped bust and free and easy movement of the body. By its use all deficiency of development is supplied. They are just as essential for a slender person as for a stout one, and meet a long felt want for every woman and girl from the age of sixteen. When ordering be sure to send the bust measure, and state whether low or high bust is wanted. Sizes, 32 to 46 inches. Price.....(Postage, extra, 5c.).....68c

The Hygeia Bust Forms.

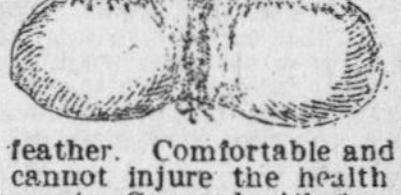

No. 18K374 The Hygeia Bust Forms, made of the finest tempered braided wire. Oval in shape. Adjustable. Light as a feather. Comfortable and nonheating. They cannot injure the health nor retard development. Covered with fine lawn, and in such a way that the forms can be removed and the covering washed. A great improvement over any other form on the market. Covered in white or black. State color wanted. Price.....(Postage extra, 6c.)....44c

The Featherbone Dress Form.

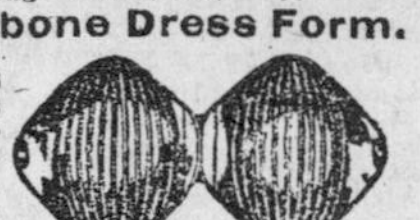

No. 18K376 Featherbone Dress Form. The ribs are made of featherbone with two reinforcing strips, and are adjustable. The most sensible and best dress form on the market. Light and cool. White only. Price..................30c

If by mail, postage extra, 3 cents.

The Parisienne Wire Bustle.

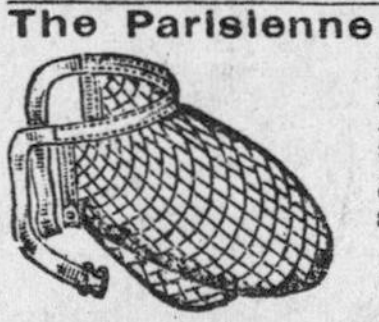

No. 18K378 Parisienne Woven Wire Bustle, made of highly tempered, black enameled woven wire. The best shape. Price, ...20c

If by mail, postage extra, 8 cents.

The New Model Pad.

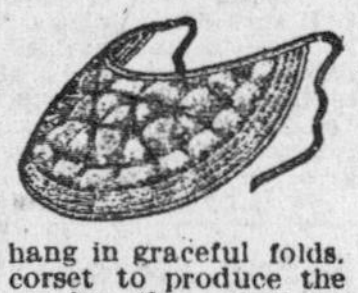

No. 18K381 New Model Pad. This pad is form fitting, invisible, light in weight. Made of sterilized materials in white, drab or black. This new model pad adds grace and symmetry to the figure, allowing the skirt to hang in graceful folds. May be worn over the corset to produce the short waist effect and under the corset for long waist effect. When ordering give color. Price..................23c

If by mail, postage extra, 4 cents.

Hip Pad and Bustle.

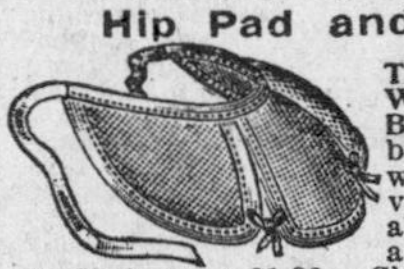

No. 18K383 The Duchess Woven Wire Hip Pad and Bustle, made of the best woven white wire, correct shape, very light and durable, and equal to any sold elsewhere for 75 cents or $1.00. Shipping weight, 15 ounces. Our price.......42c

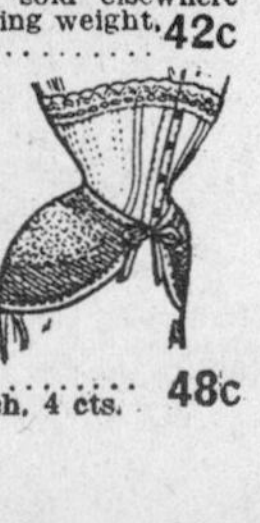

No. 18K385 The Popular Habit Hip Pad and Bustle, made of light tampico, thoroughly hygienic. The only style of hip pad to wear with the new, modish, form fitting skirts which are the prevailing fashion at the present time. Recommended by all the leading dressmakers. Comes in white or gray. State color desired. Price, each...................48c

If by mail, postage extra, each, 4 cts.

STYLISH BELTS DIRECT FROM OUR FACTORY TO YOU

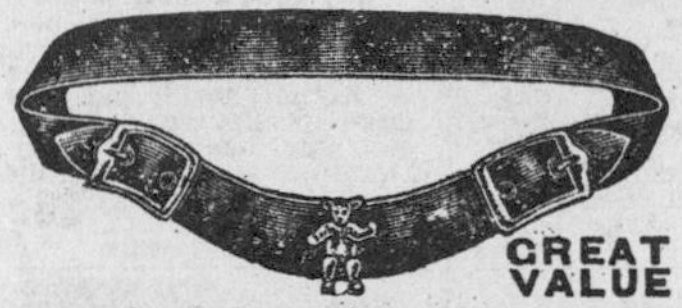

GREAT VALUE

No. 18K602 Teddy Bear Buster Brown Belt, made of soft, pliable double faced patent leather, 1 inch wide, with extreme dip shape front, with two buckles and large size Teddy bear ornament. Especially made for the outside of children's coats. Colors, black, brown or red. Sizes, 26 to 36. Be sure to give size and color wanted. Price........ **23c**
If by mail, postage extra, 5 cents.

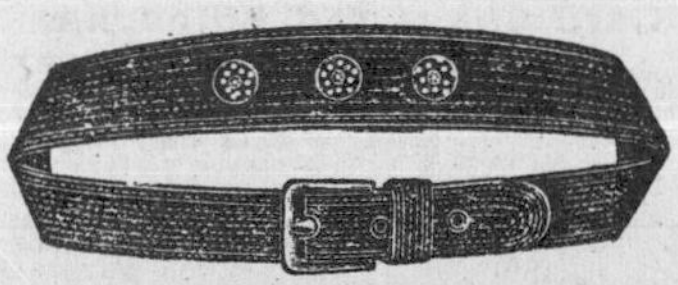

No. 18K607 Ladies' Form Fitting Leather Belt, tailored and stitched throughout. Has three cut steel ornaments in the back and nickel plated harness buckle to match in the front; 1¾ inches wide in the back, tapering to 1-inch width in the front. Black only. Sizes 22 to 30. Be sure to state size wanted. Regular 50-cent value. Our price........ **33c**
If by mail, postage extra, 5 cents.

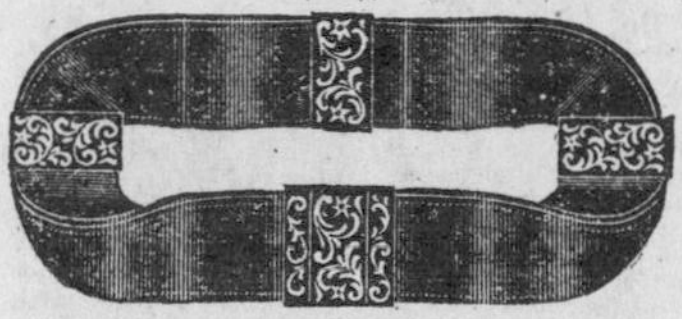

No. 18K610 The New Fluffy Style Belt, 1⅜ inches wide. Made of the best quality soft pliable kid leather, mounted with the new fluffy metal set, ¾-inch wide, handsomely decorated metal slides. Closes in the front with the new fluffy buckle to match. Colors, black, brown or tan. Sizes, 22 to 30 inches. Be sure to state size and color wanted. Price........ **48c**
If by mail, postage extra, 5 cents.

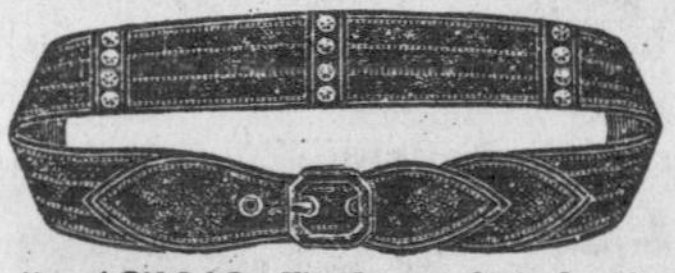

No. 18K613 The Latest Style Leather Belt, made out of the finest quality French calfskin. Is 1½ inches wide in back, and 1¼ inches in front. Stitched throughout with four rows of stitching, and ornamented in the back and sides with creased leather ornaments, set with cut steel studs. Closes in front with patent underclasp and finished with extending pointed ear. Colors, black, brown, green or tan. Sizes, 22 to 34 inches. Be sure to state size and color wanted. Price...... **49c**
If by mail, postage extra, 5 cents.

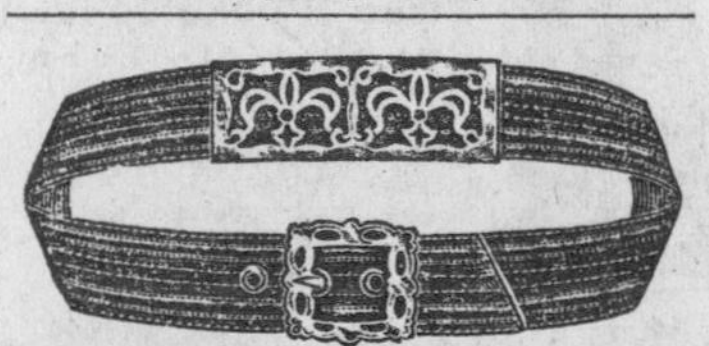

No. 18K615 Fine Quality Leather Belt, 1½ inches wide, made of best quality soft pliable kid leather, has four rows of stitching and two rows of raised cording. The back is ornamented with handsome gilt fleur de lis back piece, 4½ inches long and 1½ inches wide. Closes in the front with handsome openwork buckle to match back piece. Colors, black, brown or tan. Sizes, 22 to 30 inches. Be sure to state size and color wanted. 75-cent value. Our price........ **50c**
If by mail, postage extra, 5 cents.

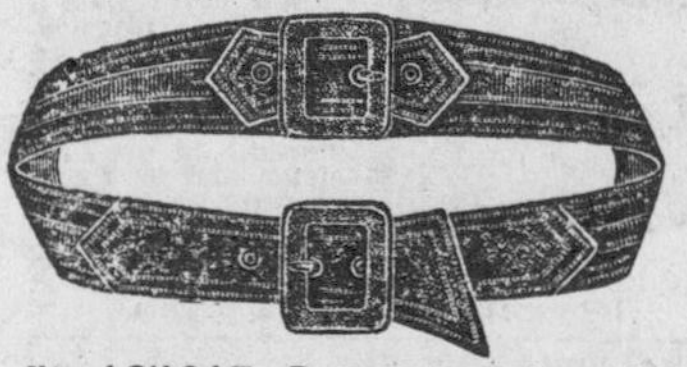

No. 18K617 Beautifully Tailored Kid Leather Belt with overlaid strip running throughout. Ornamented in back with long leather billet set with leather covered harness buckle. Belt is 2 inches wide in back, tapering to 1½ inches in front. Closes with leather covered harness buckle set on pointed ear. One of our finest styles and biggest values. Comes in black, brown or tan. Sizes, 22 to 32 inches. Be sure to state size and color wanted. Price........ **55c**
If by mail, postage extra, 5 cents.

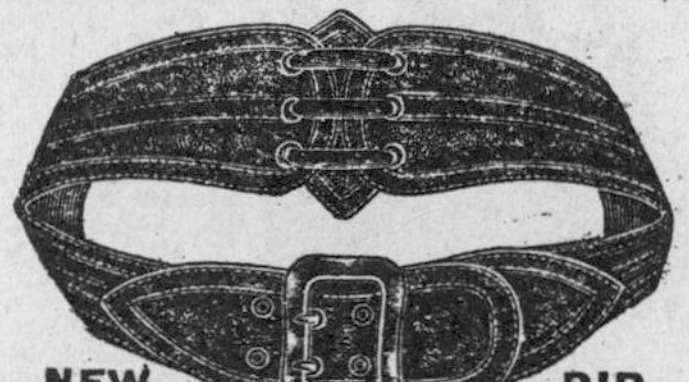

NEW STYLE — DIP FRONT

No. 18K621 The New "Iole" Belt, made out of good quality suede leather trimmed with three ¼-inch smooth leather, tailored strips; has a fancy pointed effect in the back, with three lacings, giving it a V shaped effect. The back is 3¾ inches wide; the sides 1⅜ inches wide. Closes in the front with double prong harness buckle 2 inches wide. Colors, black, brown or green. Sizes, 22 to 32 inches. Be sure to state size and color wanted. Price........ **78c**
If by mail, postage extra, 5 cents.

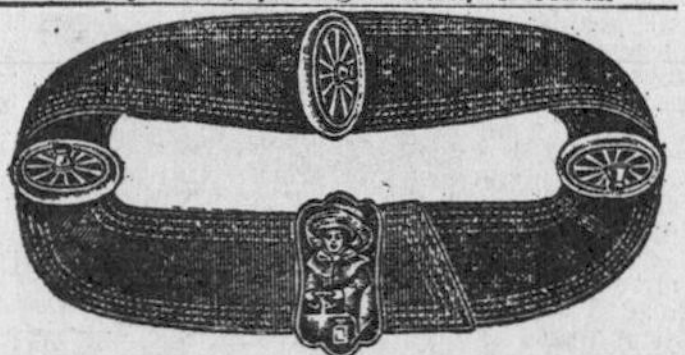

No. 18K623 The New "Fluffy" Automobile Style, made out of 2-inch wide, finest soft leather, turned edges and six rows of stitching. The back and sides are ornamented with heavy metal slides in green gold finish, handsomely engraved into automobile design. Closes in front with the new automobile buckle, showing a handsomely gowned woman in an automobile. Colors, black, brown or tan. Sizes, 22 to 32 inches. Be sure to state size and color wanted. Price........ **98c**
If by mail, postage extra, 5 cents.

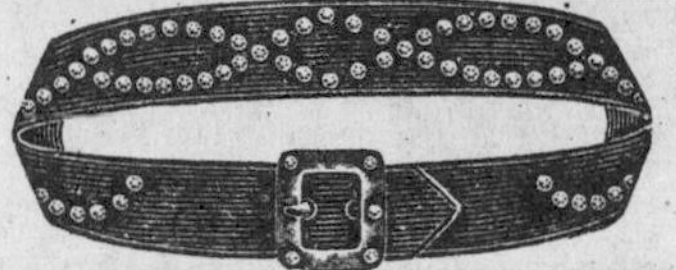

No. 18K625 Our Leading Value Steel Studded Elastic Belt. 1⅜ inches wide, ribbed elastic, studded on back and sides with fifty-seven cut steel studs. The black harness buckle is ornamented with five cut riveted steel studs. Black only. Sizes, 22 to 36 inches. Be sure to state size. Price........ **25c**
If by mail, postage extra, 5 cents.

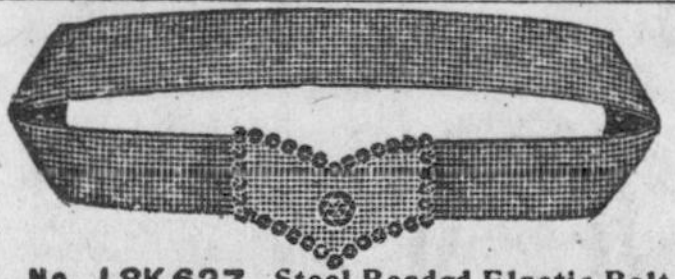

No. 18K627 Steel Beaded Elastic Belt, closely covered entirely with steel beads, 1¼ inches wide, closing in the front with steel beaded dip buckle, ornamented with thirty-four large steel beads and a large steel bead in the center. Hook and eye fastening. Sizes, 22 to 30 inches. Price........ **48c**
If by mail, postage extra, 5 cents.

No. 18K629 Cut Jet Beaded Belt, exact same style as above, only in all black. Sizes, 22 to 30 inches. State size. Price.. **42c**
If by mail, postage extra, 5 cents.

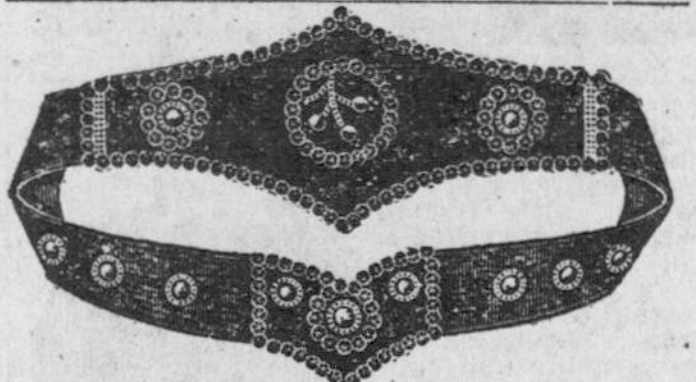

No. 18K631 Beautiful Imported Studded Elastic Belt, 1½ inches wide, with fancy studded back piece, 8½ inches long, smaller ornaments on side and front, buckle to match, a large round fancy piece with jet, steel and coral beads in center of back. Can be had with large turquoise, coral or steel beads set in the ornaments. Black only. Sizes, 22 to 30 inches. Price........ **49c**
If by mail, postage extra, 5 cents.
For our best grade elastic belt see No. 18K635.

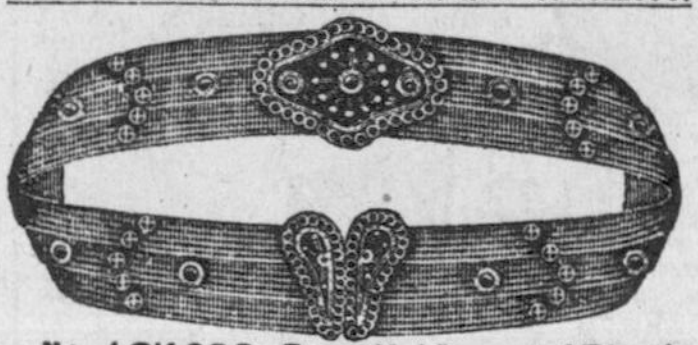

No. 18K633 Beautiful Imported Elastic Belt, made of three strands of ½-inch black ribbed elastic. This belt is beautifully ornamented with a combination of cut jet and steel beads worked around large colored beads, with turquoise or coral settings. Sizes, 22 to 30 inches. Regular $1.00 value. Price. **69c**
If by mail, postage extra, 5 cents.

FINEST QUALTIY

No. 18K635 Steel Studded Silk Elastic Belt, 1½ inches wide with a silk back piece handsomely studded with fancy steel beads in three sizes. The elastic is also studded with six large oval shaped steel beads, each surrounded with eight smaller steel beads. The dip shaped buckle is 3¼ inches long and closes with hook and eye fastening. Black only. Sizes, 22 to 30 inches. Price.... **96c**
If by mail, postage extra, 5 cents.

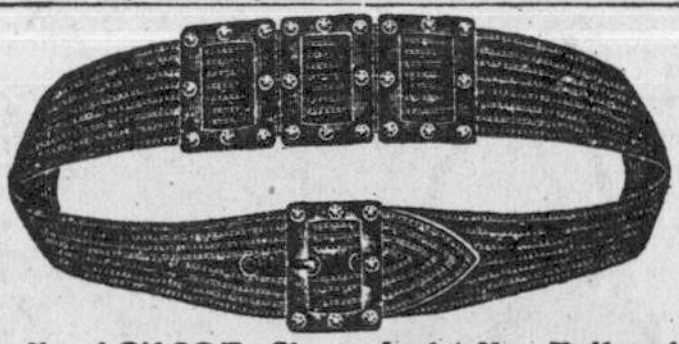

No. 18K637 Chorus Lady, Man Tailored Belt, made out of pure taffeta silk, well lined and interlined throughout. Has eight rows of silk stitching. The back is ornamented with three handsome black metal buckles, each with eight riveted steel studs. Closes in the front with black buckle to match the back pieces. Is 2 inches wide in the back, 1 inch on the sides, and 2 inches in the front. Black only. Sizes, 22 to 32 inches. Be sure to state size wanted. Price........ **48c**
If by mail, postage extra, 5 cents.

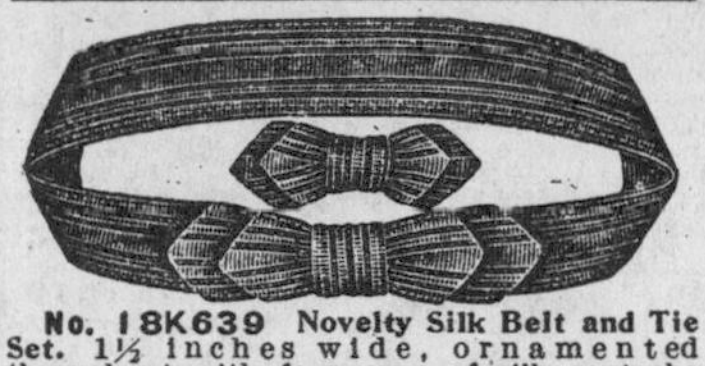

No. 18K639 Novelty Silk Belt and Tie Set. 1½ inches wide, ornamented throughout with four rows of silk soutache braid, lined and interlined with best materials, stitched and turned edges. The front is a fancy double bow effect, ornamented the same as the belt. The double neck bow is made to exactly match the belt. Colors, black, brown or navy blue. Sizes, 22 to 34 inches. Be sure to state size and color wanted. Price, per set........ **48c**
If by mail, postage extra, per set, 5 cents.

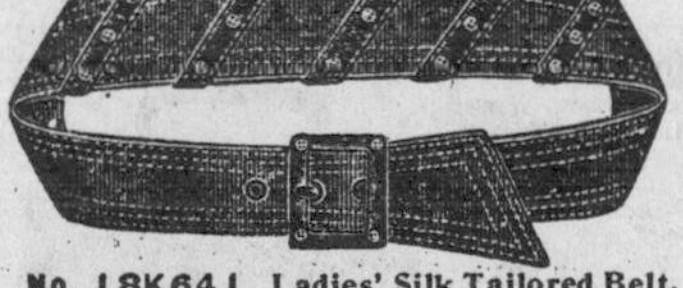

No. 18K641 Ladies' Silk Tailored Belt, made of finest quality pure silk taffeta, silk stitched, lined and interlined throughout. The back and sides are ornamented with five tailored cross pieces, each cross piece having three riveted cut steel studs. 2 inches wide in the back, tapering to 1¼ inches in the front, finished with extending pointed ear, and closing with black harness buckle; studded with five cut steel studs. Black only Sizes, 22 to 34 inches. Be sure to state size wanted. Price........ **49c**
If by mail, postage extra, 5 cents.

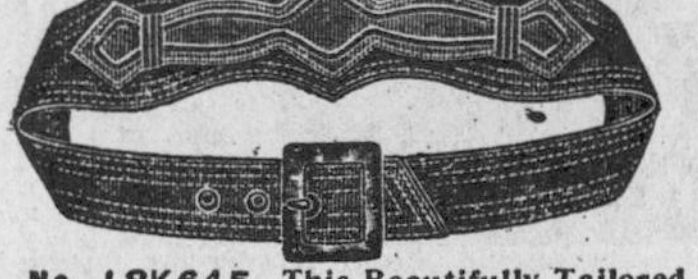

No. 18K645 This Beautifully Tailored Belt is made of best quality pure silk taffeta, stitched, tailored and turned edges throughout. Back has an entirely separate piece set on belt, worked in fancy design and ornamented with black silk soutache braid. Lined and interlined with best materials. The width of the belt in the back is 2¼ inches, and 1¼ inches wide in the front. Closes with new black harness buckle, with patent underclasp. Black only. Sizes, 22 to 34 inches. Be sure to state size wanted. Others ask 75 cents for this belt. Our price........ **58c**
If by mail, postage extra, 5 cents.

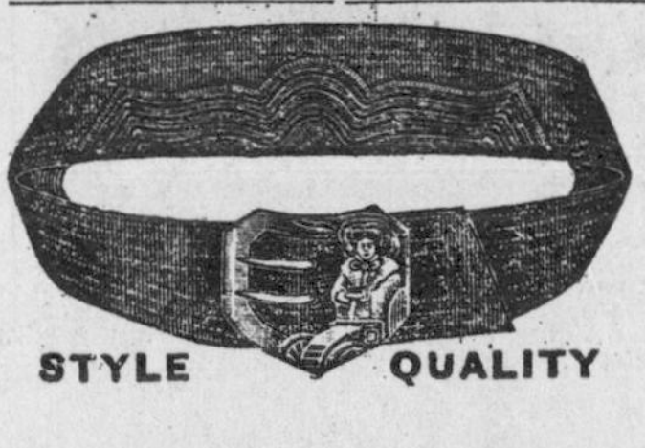

STYLE — QUALITY

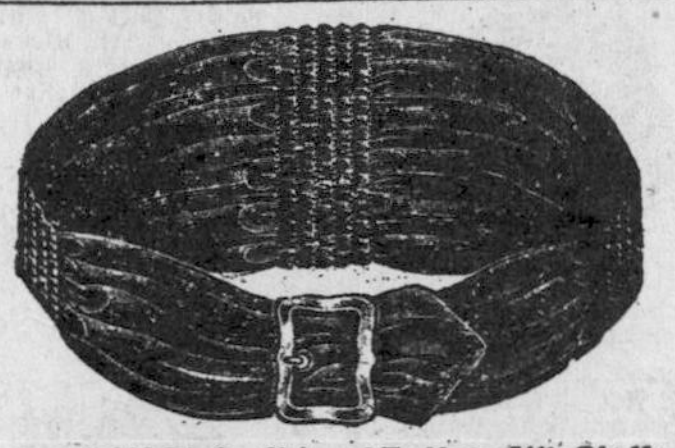

No. 18K653 Shirred Taffeta Silk Girdle, lined throughout. This girdle is 3¾ inches wide in the back, tapering to 1⅝ inches wide in the front and closes with a fancy gold harness buckle and patent underclasp. The back is boned, has six rows of shirring, and the sides are plaited and ornamented on each side with six rows of shirring. This belt is made of good quality taffeta, well lined. Black only. Sizes, 24 to 32 in. Be sure to state size wanted.
Price. (If by mail, postage extra, 5c.). **29c**

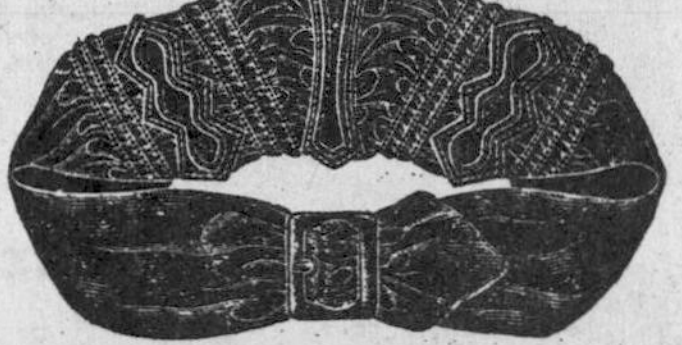

No. 18K658 Our Best Pure Silk Taffeta Princess Girdle, with tailored back pieces. The back has twelve rows of shirring and three fancy silk tailored back pieces, ornamented with silk soutache braid. 3¼ inches wide in the back, tapering to 1½ inches in width in the front, closing with a black harness buckle, with patent underclasp and extending pointed ear Black only. Sizes, 24 to 30 inches. Be sure to state size wanted. 75-cent value. Our price.... **58c**
If by mail, postage extra, 5 cents.

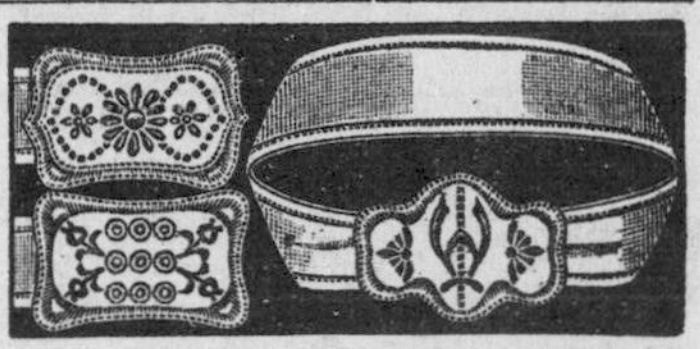

No. 18K660 A Very Special Offer in Ladies' Wash Belts. Made of good quality ribbed poplin. Bound on both edges and lined throughout. The belt is finished in front with a large, handsomely embroidered medallion, with buckle underclasp. Width, 2½ inches. Sold three assorted designs of one size only in set. Color, white only. Sizes, 24 to 32 inches. Be sure to state size wanted. Price. **3 FOR**.. (If by mail, postage extra, 10c.) **25c**

No. 18K680 Lingerie Wash Belt, made of finest quality washable India linon. This belt is handsomely embroidered in openwork design, and has a patent clasp buckle which can be removed before laundering. 2¾ inches wide, fastening in front with extending ear; white only. Sizes, 22 to 34 inches. Be sure to state size wanted. Price........ **25c**
If by mail, postage extra, 5 cents.

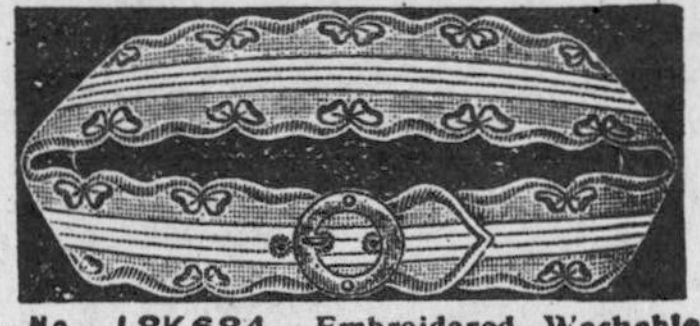

No. 18K684 Embroidered Washable Belt, made of finest imported twill washable fabric, 2 inches wide, embroidered on both sides with large scallops, ornamented with embroidered lovers' knots. Throughout the center of the belt is a ¾-inch wide box plait with two rows of silk stitching. Closes in front with a large pure white ocean pearl buckle, 1¼ inches wide, with patent underclasp. The buckle and underclasp can be removed for laundering purposes. Color, white only. Sizes, 22 to 34 inches. Be sure to state size wanted. Price........ **48c**
If by mail, postage extra, 5 cents.

No. 18K650 Our Very Finest Tailor Made Pure Silk Taffeta Belt, in the new automobile style, lined and interlined throughout with best quality materials. The back is neatly trimmed with overlying design ornamented with four rows of silk soutache braid. Neatly stitched throughout. 2½ inches wide in the back, tapering to 1½ inches in front and closes with a most beautiful buckle in automobile design, in handsome Roman gold finish. The buckle alone on this belt is sold by others for $1.00, and it will wear for years. Colors, black, brown, cardinal or navy. Sizes, 22 to 36 inches. Be sure to state size and color wanted. Our price........ **99c**
If by mail, postage extra, 5 cents.

PURSES.

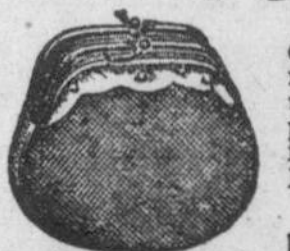

No. 18K1004 Fine Calfskin Purse with nickel riveted frame, and partition; chamois lined; two pockets. Size, 3½x3 inches. Price........ 8c
If by mail, postage extra, 3c.

No. 18K1008 Fine Buck Purse, with gusseted bottom and welts, nickel riveted frame with partition; three-ball catch; chamois lined; two pockets. Size, 3¾x3¾ inches. Price........ 19c
No. 18K1008
If by mail, postage extra, 3 cents.

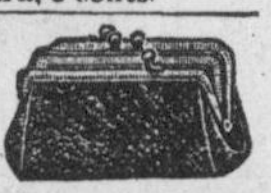

No. 18K1012 Bag Shape, Seal Grain Leather Purse. Fine square frame, nickeled, riveted, with embossed gilt center partition, ball catch, two pockets, chamois lined, stitched edges. Size, 2¾x4 inches. Price........ 23c
If by mail, postage extra, 3 cents.

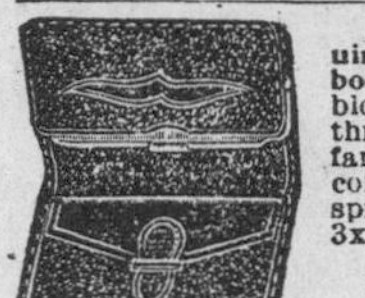

No. 18K1016 Genuine Seal Leather Pocketbook with calf facings; blocked bottom, gusseted, three regular and one fancy card, one tuck and coin pocket with nickel spring catch frame. Size, 3x4½ inches. Price........ 47c
If by mail, postage extra. 3 cents.

Vanity Purses.

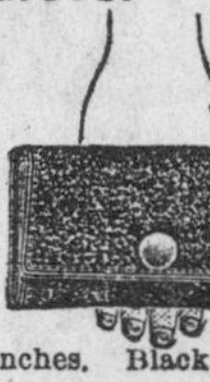

No. 18K1017 57c
Ladies' Strap Handle Vanity Purse. Made of good quality seal grain leather, lined in moire, has two outer pockets and one large coin pocket lined with chamois. The inner pocket is mounted with a fine brass frame and patent catch. The purse closes with a large oriental pearl button snap fastener. Size, 3½x5½ inches. Black only. Price........ 57c
If by mail, postage extra, 5 cents.

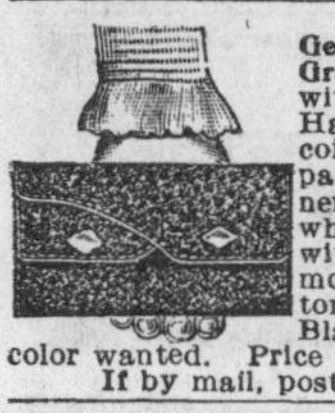

No. 18K1018 Ladies' Genuine Morocco High Grade Leather Vanity Purse with strap handle in back. Has large inner pocket for coin, with nickel frame and patent clasps, has three inner pockets and two flaps which fasten on outside with snap fastener and diamond shaped pearl buttons. Size, 5½x3 inches. Black or tan. State color wanted. Price........ 95c
If by mail, postage extra, 4 cents.

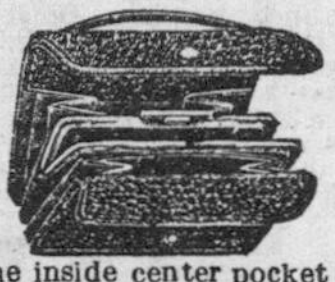

No. 18K1022 Ladies' Seal Grain Leather Vanity Bag, in the new flat shape. Leather gusseted sides and bottom and flat flexible leather handle. Has three spacious inside and one outside pocket, closing with pearl snap fastener. The inside center pocket is made on a gilt frame with patent catch. All pockets are moire lined, while both flaps are entirely lined with leather. Size, 6½x4 inches. Color, black only. Price........ 98c
If by mail, postage extra, 7 cents.

Misses' Novelty Hand Bags.

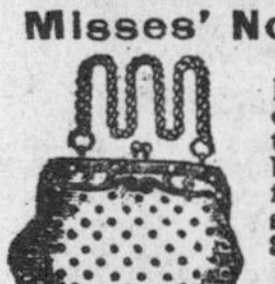

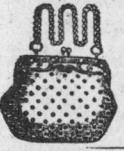

No. 18K1042 Novelty Hand Bag for Misses. Made of imported colored velvetta, trimmed with small colored beads. Has riveted nickel frame and chain handle, faille silk lining. Size of purse, 3¾x3¼ inches. Price........ 22c
If by mail, postage extra, 3 cents.

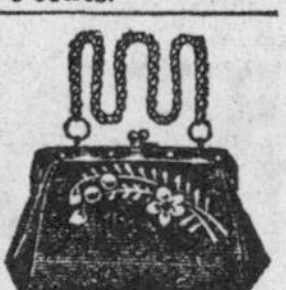

No. 18K1046 Imported Novelty Hand Bag for Misses. Made of real calf leather and calf lined throughout. Has pretty hand painted decorations. Mounted on riveted nickel frame with ball catch fasteners and nickel chain. Size, 4½x3¼ inches. Price........ 25c
If by mail, postage extra, 3 cents.

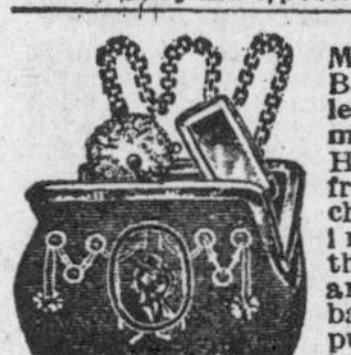

No. 18K1049 Misses' Imported Hand Bag of finest quality leather, beautifully ornamented in gilt colors. Has substantial gilt frame with ball clasp and chain handle. Has two inner pockets lined throughout with moire and fitted with celluloid back mirror and powder puff. Size, 4½x3½ inches. Price........ 42c
If by mail, postage extra, 4 cents.

Newest Styles in Hand Bags.

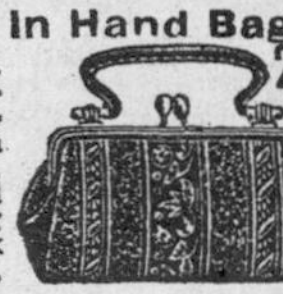

Ladies' Hand Bag, made of fancy embossed leatherette of durable quality; has 7-inch nickel pinch frame, with large pear shaped catch and swinging handle. Color, black only. Size, 8½x4½ in. 23c
No. 18K1054
Price........ 23c
If by mail, postage extra, 11 cents.

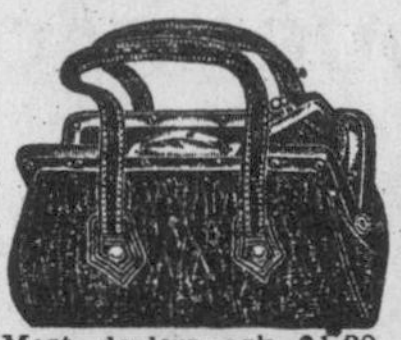

No. 18K1056 Ladies' Hand Bag. Made of genuine leather in seal grain pressing, on 8-inch frame. Has double strap handles. Moire lined throughout and fitted with small coin purse. Size, 10x5½ inches.
Most dealers ask $1.00.
Our price....(Postage extra, 14c)........ 49c

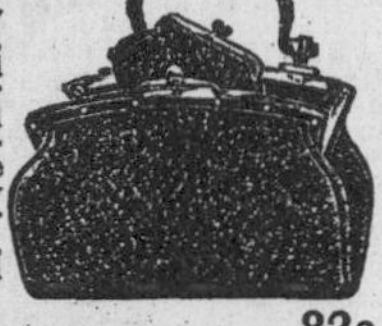

No. 18K1062 82c
Seal Grain Leather Hand Bag. A very attractive shape, moire lined and fitted with leather coin purse. Solid leather military handle on Vienna handle caps, has fancy curved frame, leather covered and riveted, and wide gusseted sides. Size, 8¼x5½ inches. Color, black only. $1.25 value. Our price........ 82c
If by mail, postage extra, 13 cents.

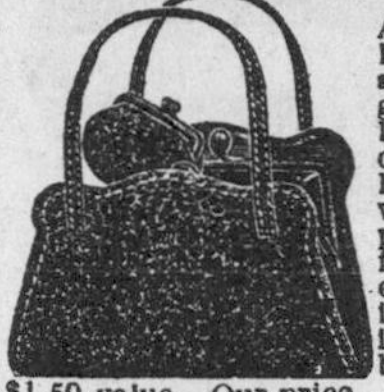

No. 18K1064 A Neat Serviceable Bag in a popular style, made of seal grain leather, moire lined. Has flat, double stitched handles, and is fitted with leather coin purse. Best quality frame with ball fastening. Size, 8½ inches long by 5 inches deep. Color, black only.
$1.50 value. Our price........ 95c
If by mail, postage extra, 13 cents.

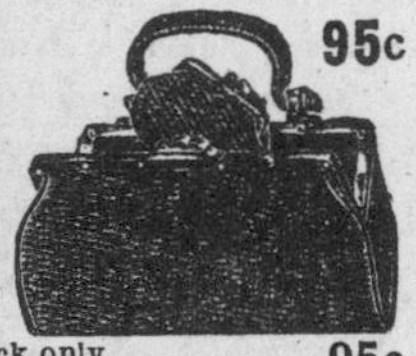

No. 18K1066 95c
Ladies' Hand Bag in diamond pressed leather, full leather lined and gusseted. The bag is fitted with leather coin purse, leather covered riveted frame and flexible swinging handle on Viennahandle caps. Size, 9¾x5½ inches. Color, black only.
Price....(Postage extra, 16c.)........ 95c

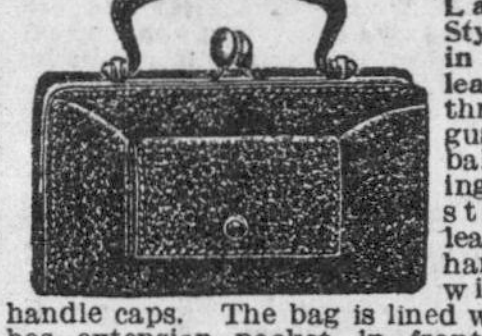

No. 18K1070 Ladies' Flat Style Hand Bag in seal grain leather, stitched throughout, with gusseted sides, ball catch fastening and double stitched soft leather swinging handle fastened with Vienna handle caps. The bag is lined with moire and has extension pocket in front with patent snap fastener. A genteel and serviceable article. Size, 8½x5 inches. Color, black only. Price....(Postage extra, 14c.).... $1.05

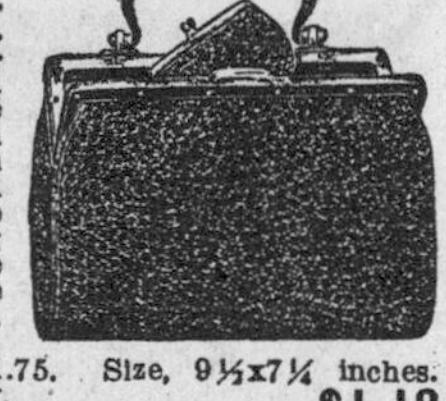

No. 18K1072 The New, Deep Shape Bag, in walrus grain leather. Has leather covered riveted frame, moire lined and fitted with leather coin purse, stitched military handle on swinging Vienna handle caps and wide gusseted sides. Exceptional value, worth $1.75. Size, 9½x7¼ inches. Color, black only.
Our price..(Postage extra, 18c.).. $1.18

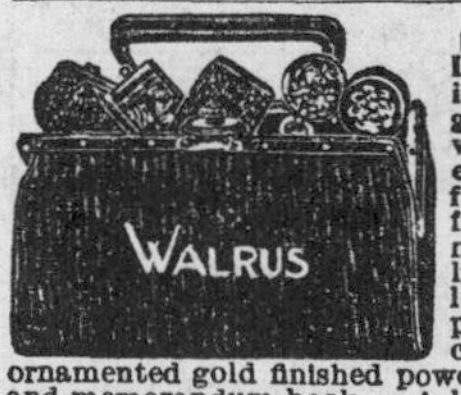

No. 18K1075 Ladies' Hand Bag in fine walrus grain leather with leather covered riveted frame. Contains five compartments, moire lined, fitted with leather coin purse, leather card case, fancy ornamented gold finished powder box, mirror, and memorandum book. A large roomy bag of superior quality, never before sold for less than $2.75. Size, 10¾x6½ inches. Color, black only.
Our price..(Postage extra, 23c.).. $1.89

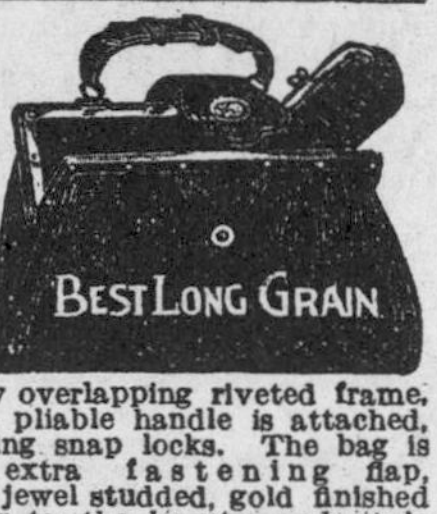

No. 18K1077 An Exclusive Style in Ladies' Bag. Made of finest quality long grain leather, lined throughout with calf. Has large inner pocket fitted with fine leather lined coin purse. Has finest quality overlapping riveted frame, to which the soft, pliable handle is attached, also double sliding snap locks. The bag is made with an extra fastening flap, ornamented with jewel studded, gold finished ornament, adding to the beauty and style of the bag. Size, 9½x6 inches. Color, black only. Value, $3.50.
Price.....(Postage extra, 18c)..... $2.19

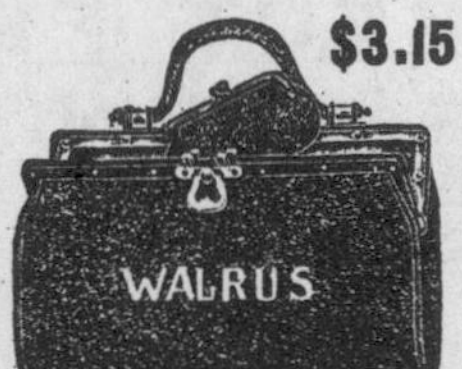

No. 18K1079 $3.15
This Beautiful Ladies' Hand Bag must be seen to be appreciated. We cannot show the quality in the illustration, and the quality of this article is its leading feature. Made of the finest grade walrus grain leather, lined throughout with calfskin. Large stitched inner pocket containing handsomely finished coin purse. Has flexible leather handle fastened to a 10-inch leather covered frame. This is an excellent $4.50 value and should wear for years. Size, 10¾x6 inches. Color, black only.
Our price........ $3.15
If by mail, postage extra, 21 cents.

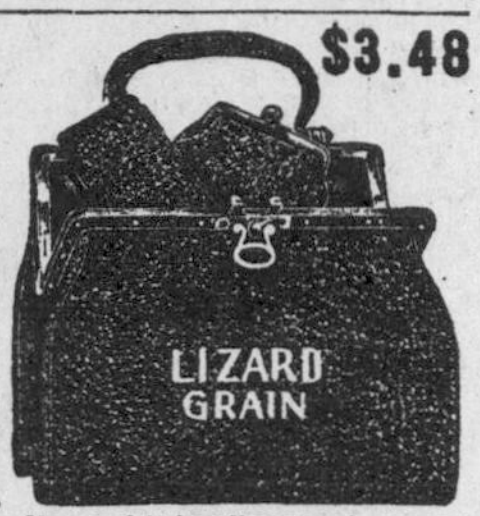

No. 18K1081 $3.48
Our Handsomest Ladies' Hand Bag in a new Kyle shape. Made entirely of one piece finest lizard grain leather. Is full leather lined with two stitched inner pockets, containing leather lined coin purse and card case. Has flexible military handle, and is in all respects a very exclusive style, the finish and workmanship being of the highest standard. This bag is well worth $5.00. Size, 10x7 inches. Color, black only. Our price........ $3.48
If by mail, postage extra, 21 cents.

Ladies' Shopping Bags.

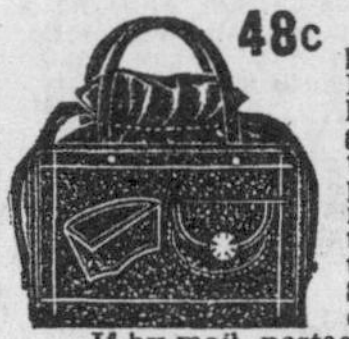

No. 18K1082 48c
Ladies' Shopping Bag. Made of seal grain leatherette, bound with gimp cord all around; two small outside pockets, one with nickeled catch; sateen top with draw strings, two leather handles. Size, 6¾x10 inches. Price........ 48c
If by mail, postage extra, 19 cents.

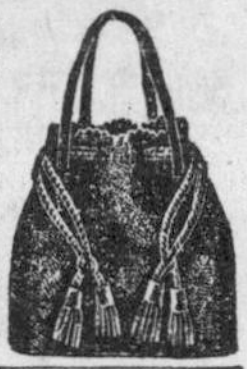

No. 18K1088 Ladies' Leather Squaw Bag with flat sewed bottom, sateen lined and fitted with double strap handles. The bag closes with double silk cable cord, trimmed with four leather tassels. Size, 6½x7½ inches. Colors, black or tan. State color wanted. $1.00 value. Our price........ 59c
If by mail, postage extra, 9 cents.

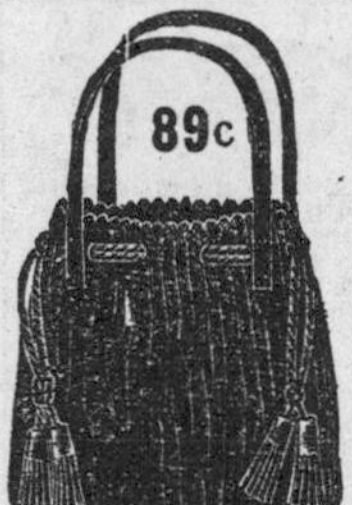

No. 18K1091 89c
The Vassar Frameless Shopping Bag. All the rage. Made of fine smooth natural calf leather, soft and pliable. Sateen lined. Is fitted with soft leather handles and silk drawing cord, with leather tassels. Depth of bag, 9 inches; width, 8¾ inches. Very pretty in brown; also comes in black. State color wanted. Regular $1.50 value. Our price........ 89c
If by mail, postage extra, 9 cents.

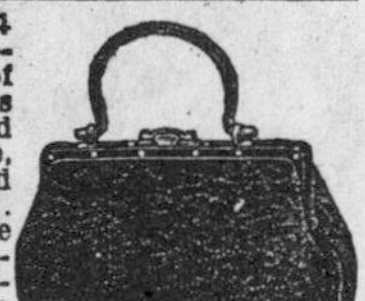

No. 18K1094 Ladies' Boston Shopping Bag. Made of fine quality walrus leather, with riveted leather covered frame, and having improved nickel snap catch. Leather covered handle strap. The inside lining is moire and contains little inside pockets for handkerchief and small articles. A very convenient and handy style of bag. Size, 9½ by 6 inches. Price........ $1.15
If by mail, postage extra, 19 cents.

Quaker Purse.

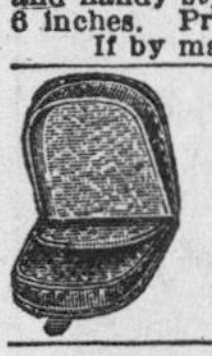

No. 18K1098 Genuine pigskin. Two pockets. Size, 2½x2½ inches. Its peculiar shape and formation admit the handling of coin without danger of losing its contents. Price........ 39c
If by mail, postage extra, 2c.

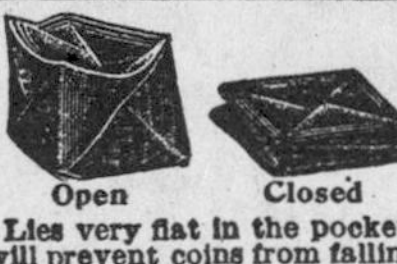

Open Closed

No. 18K1102 Paragon Patent Folding Coin Purse. Made of morocco finished leather. This purse will hold $10.00 in silver. Lies very flat in the pocket, at the same time will prevent coins from falling out. It is one of the best known and handiest coin purses on the market. Size, when folded, 2½x2½ inches, and about ¼ of an inch thick. Price........ 24c
If by mail, postage extra, 2 cents.

WALLETS.

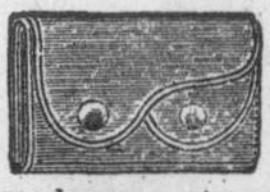

No. 18K1106 Wallet, fine English calf leather, closes with glove button catches on the side; interior is leather lined; has one large pocket for change, etc., and has a specially made compartment for notes and bills. Neatly finished. Size, ¾x2¾x3½ inches. Price........ 23c
If by mail, postage extra, 2 cents.

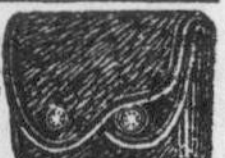

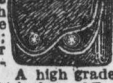

No. 18K1110 Wallet, fine seal grain leather, closes with glove button catches on the side; interior is leather lined; has one large pocket for change, etc., and has a compartment for notes and bills. A high grade book. Size, closed, ¾x2¾x3½ inches. Price........ 45c
If by mail, postage extra, 2 cents.

Card Cases and Billbooks.

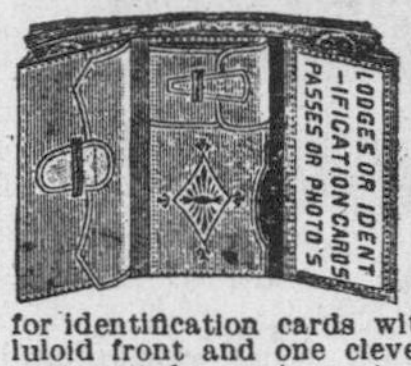

No. 18K1117 Gentlemen's Billbook and Card Case, made of very best quality of heavy English calfskin, soft and pliable. Has one long partition pocket for bills, one coin pocket, two card pockets, a pocket for identification cards with transparent celluloid front and one cleverly arranged compartment for postage stamps. A very neat and compact book. Well worth $1.25. Color, brown only. Size when opened, 8¼x4¾ inches. Size closed, 3x4¾ inches.
Our price........ 85c
If by mail, postage extra, 3 cents.

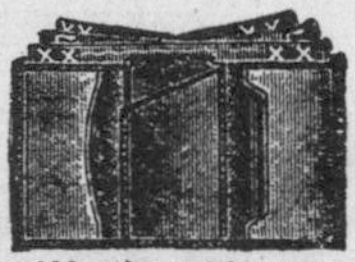

No. 18K1118 Combination Card Case and Billbook. This book has a partition pocket the entire length of book for carrying paper money. Has two side card pockets and extra ticket pocket. In center is a partition of calf leather with memorandum book. Made of fine seal leather with calf facing, extra well stitched and lined. Size, closed, 4½x3¾ inches. Black only. Price........ 98c
If by mail, postage extra, 3 cents.

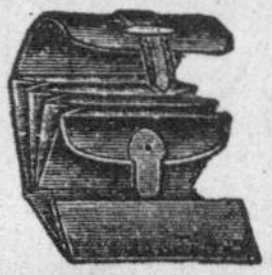

No. 18K1130 Fine calf leather, three pockets and bill fold, with flap and tuck strap. Stitched all around. Size, 2¾x4¾ inches. Price........ 21c
If by mail, postage extra, 3 cents.

English Calfskin Pocketbook.

No. 18K1138 English Calf Pocketbook. A very high grade and finely finished book. Soft leather, very durable, four regular and three small pockets. Bill fold, with flap and tuck strap. Size, 2¾x4¾ inches. Price........ 55c
If by mail, postage extra, 3 cents.

Seal Grain Leather Strap Pocketbook.

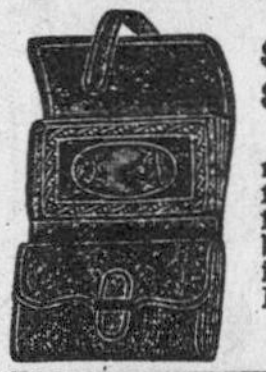

No. 18K1142 Four regular pockets, bill fold, with flap and tuck strap, leather faced. Regular $1.00 pocketbook. Size, 2¾x4¾ inches. Price........ 79c
If by mail, postage extra, 6 cents.

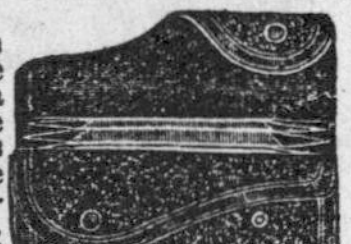

No. 18K1154 Gents' Fine Seal Grain Billbook, with three large pockets, extra bill fold with glove snap fastener. This is the new envelope shape billbook. Convenient in every way, well lined and the best workmanship. Size, 8x3 inches. Price........ 42c
If by mail, postage extra, 3 cents.

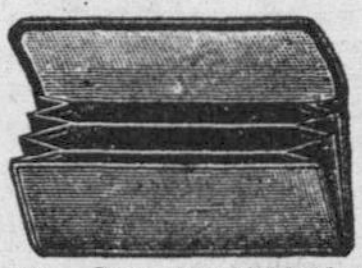

No. 18K1158 Fine Calf Billbook. This is a smooth red calf leather with four large full size pockets. This book is well finished in every detail and very convenient for carrying large papers, bills, etc. Size, 10x4½ inches. Price........ 45c
If by mail, postage extra, 6 cents.

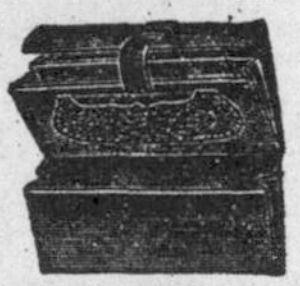

No. 18K1162 The Secret Pocket Billbook. Kid faced and canvas lined; fine morocco grain leather, three large, two small and one secret burglar proof pocket; finely made and finished throughout. Size, 3½x8 inches. Price........ 62c
If by mail, postage extra, 5 cents.

Bankers' and Collectors' Billbook.

No. 18K1164 Extra Fine Morocco Grain Leather Billbook. Eight large pockets alphabetically indexed, also seven smaller pockets for bills and currency; leather faced and canvas lined. Specially adapted for collectors and as a deposit for notes and bills. Large size, 4½x10 inches. Price............ **95c**
If by mail, postage extra, 7 cents.

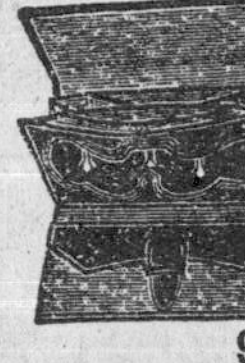

No. 18K1166 Our Highest Grade Genuine Morocco Billbook. Made of finest quality morocco leather, with kid lining, has three large and two smaller pockets for stamps, tickets, etc., also outside card case, has one regular bill fold secured by flap. Highest quality finish and workmanship throughout. Size, 3¾x8 inches. Price............ **98c**
If by mail, postage extra, 6 cents.

Bead Necklaces.

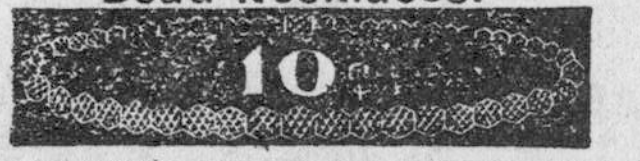

No. 18K1300 Good Quality Graduated Bead Necklace. Large beads in the center, graduating to small in the back. Closes with a large size bead clasp, 16 inches long and comes in the following colors: White, amethyst, amber, medium blue, emerald green, alice blue or cut jet. Be sure to state color wanted. Price............ **10c**
If by mail, postage extra, 3 cents.

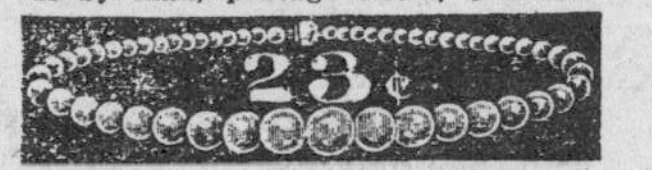

No. 18K1305 Fine Quality Round Graduated Bead Necklace. The front bead is ½ inch in diameter, graduating to ¼-inch bead in diameter in the back. The necklace is 18 inches long of the very finest quality beads, and closes with a bead clasp to match. Can be ordered in light turquoise or dull jet black. Be sure to state color wanted. Price **23c**
If by mail, postage extra, 4 cents.

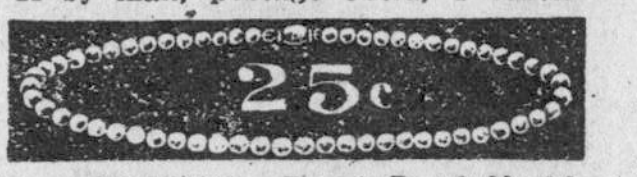

No. 18K1310 Pearl Bead Necklace. Finest quality lustrous pearl. Closes with a pearl bead clasp to match. This necklace is 13½ inches long. White only. Price... **25c**
If by mail, postage extra, 4 cents.

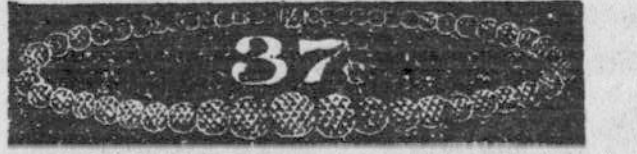

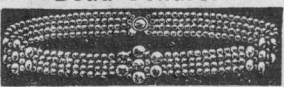

No. 18K1315 Finest Quality Graduated Cut Bead Necklace. The front bead of this necklace is ½ inch in diameter, graduating to ¼-inch bead in the back. Closes with large size bead clasp, ornamented with gilt trimmings. This necklace is full 18 inches long, and comes in the following colors: White, amethyst, amber, medium blue, emerald green, light sapphire or cut jet. Be sure to state color wanted. Price............ **37c**
If by mail, postage extra, 4 cents.

Bead Collars.

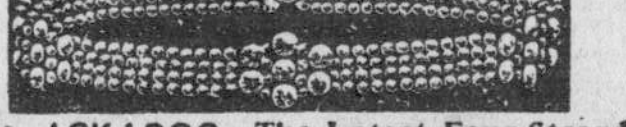

No. 18K1320 The Latest Four-Strand White Bead Collar, having three clusters of seven large pearl beads each on the sides and front. Fastens at the back with a gilt clasp, ornamented with a white bead. Length, about 13½ inches. White only. Price.. **23c**
If by mail, postage extra, 4 cents.

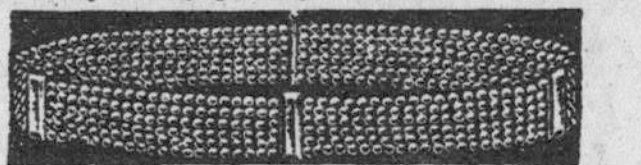

No. 18K1325 New Six-Strand Bead Collar, in beautiful light turquoise or cut jet, with three turquoise or cut jet bars to match, at regular intervals. Beads are all one size. This collar closes in the back with gilt slide and is about 14 inches long. Colors: Turquoise blue or cut jet. Be sure to state color wanted. Price............ **48c**
If by mail, postage extra, 6 cents.

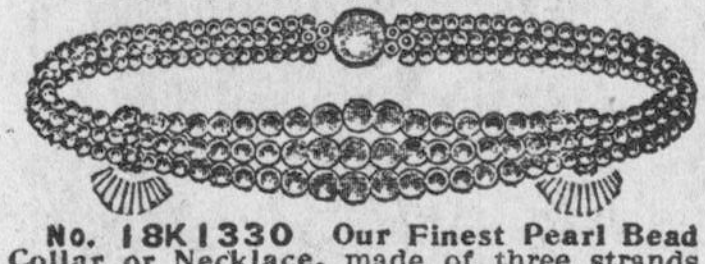

No. 18K1330 Our Finest Pearl Bead Collar or Necklace, made of three strands best quality beads, graduated large in front and small at back, ornamented with a pearl bead clasp in the back and a cross bar or slide with three brilliant rhinestones on each side. This collar is graduated in size, beads being very large in the front and small in the back. Length, about 13½ inches. White only. Price............ **48c**
If by mail, postage extra, 5 cents.

FANS
AT LOWER PRICES THAN EVER BEFORE.

WE IMPORT OUR FANS direct from Europe and Japan and guarantee a saving to you of one-third to one-half on any purchase.

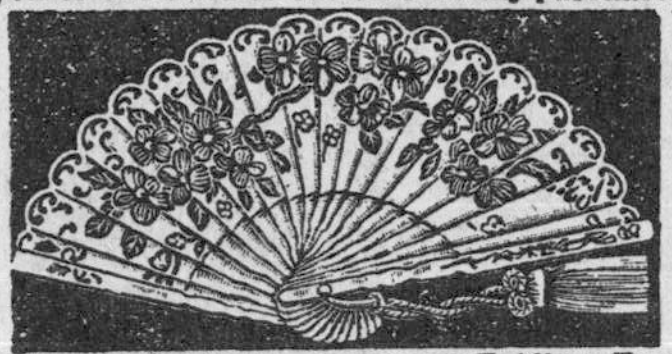

No. 18K1403 Japanese Folding Fan, made of heavy parchment on 8¾-inch decorated sticks. Hand painted decorations in natural color floral designs, finished in center with silk braid and ornamented with silver tinsel. Price............ **10c**
If by mail, postage extra, 2 cents.

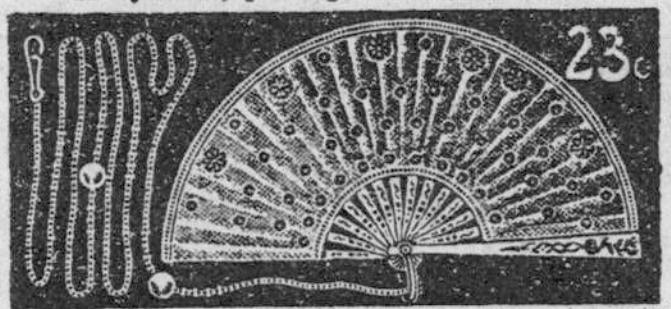

No. 18K1406 Misses' Fan, made of fine quality taffetine, decorated with four rows of small silver spangles, in fancy design, has white enameled sticks, with pressed silver decorations. Attached to the fan is a long beaded neck chain. Length of sticks, 6 inches. White only. Price............ **23c**
If by mail, postage extra, 2 cents.

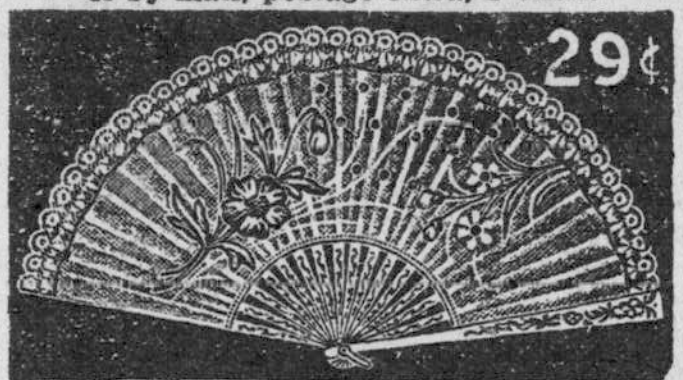

No. 18K1410 White Silk Fan, beautifully decorated with hand painted designs and small silver spangles, edged on top with delicate lace, base of fan is trimmed with purling braid. This fan is mounted on 16 decorated white enameled sticks, 8 inches long. Splendid value. Price............ **29c**
If by mail, postage extra, 2 cents.

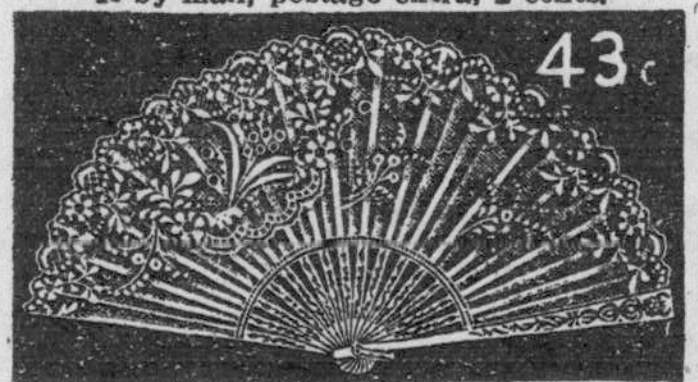

No. 18K1414 White Marcelaine Silk Fan with full lace top, with hand painted decorations, pretty designs and lace applique in a cutout effect. Bottom is edged with lace purling braid, mounted on 16 white enameled sticks with beautiful silver decorations. Length of fan, 8 inches. Price............ **43c**
If by mail, postage extra, 3 cents.

Two Special Values at 48c.

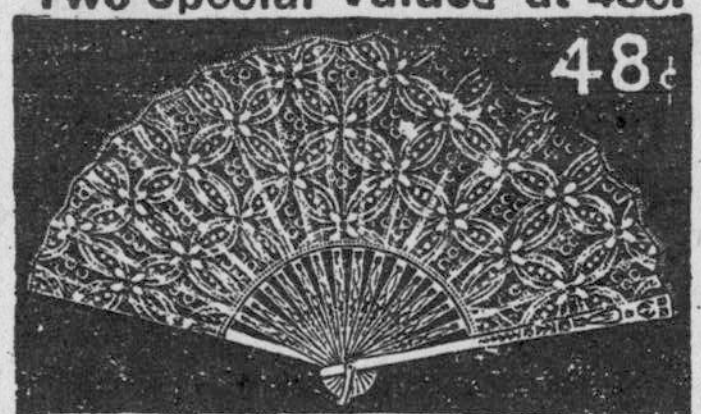

No. 18K1418 This Elegant Fan is made of fine allover lace, in white, richly appliqued with small silver spangles, edged top and bottom with purling braid, has finely decorated sticks. Length of fan, 7½ inches. Price............ **48c**
If by mail, postage extra, 3 cents.

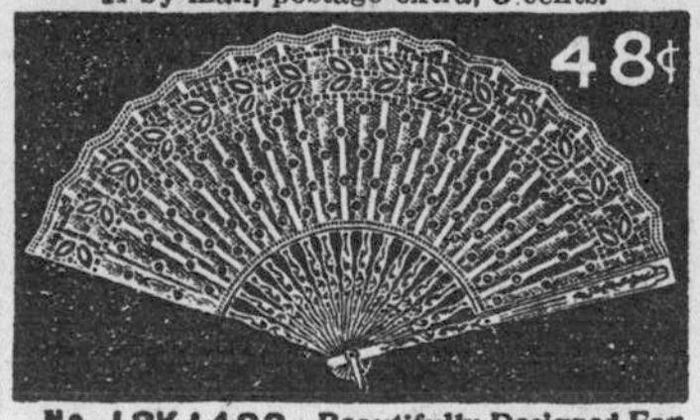

No. 18K1422 Beautifully Designed Fan. Made of fine silk gauze, in white, elaborately trimmed with a large number of small fancy silver spangles worked in various designs. This fan is finished top and bottom with white purling braid and has pressed sticks fully decorated with silver. Length of sticks, 8 inches. Price............ **48c**
If by mail, postage extra, 5 cents.

High Grade Gauze and Silk Fans at Lowest Prices.

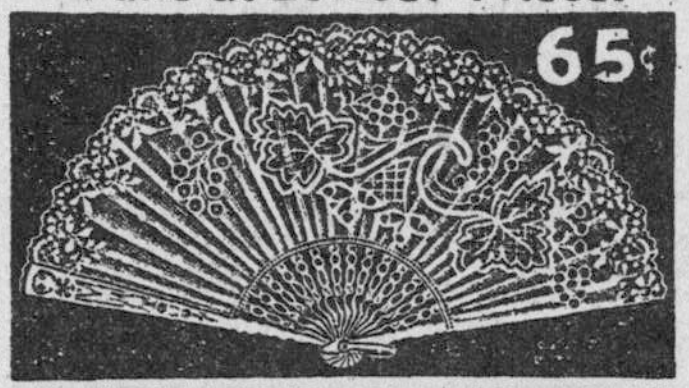

No. 18K1426 This Elegant Fan of white silk gauze is beautifully trimmed with lace edge top and large lace appliqued cutout work. Beautiful hand painted design set with small silver spangles. Has very pretty white sticks decorated in silver. Length of sticks, 8 inches. Price............ **65c**
If by mail, postage extra, 3 cents.

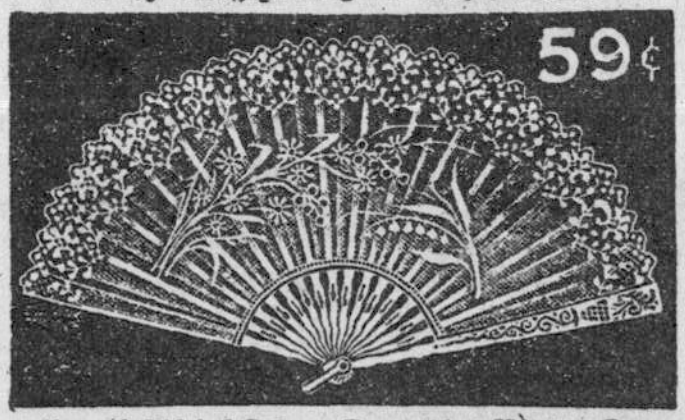

No. 18K1430 Beautiful White Gauze Fan. Very rich looking, being decorated with dainty, hand painted design and tiny silver spangles. Top is trimmed with silk Chantilly lace, bottom is edged with lace purling braid. This fan is mounted on beautifully carved bone sticks, 8 inches long and is an exceptional value. Price............ **59c**
If by mail, postage extra, 3 cents.

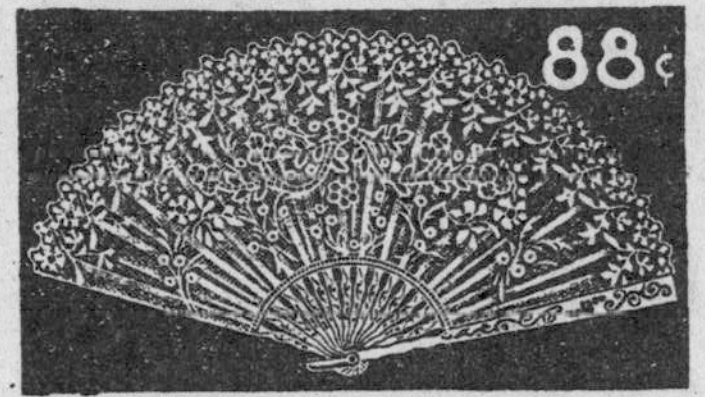

No. 18K1435 White Silk Gauze Fan edged on top with fine silk lace. Handsomely decorated with tiny silver spangles and hand painted design, spangles being worked into a flower pattern. Mounted on carved imitation ivory sticks 8 inches long. A very special offering. Price............ **88c**
If by mail, postage extra, 3 cents.

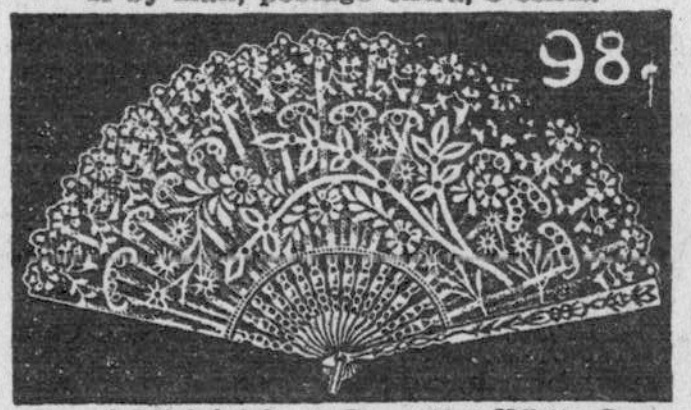

No. 18K1440 A Beautiful White Gauze Fan with white silk Chantilly lace top, all hand painted, and appliqued in designs with tiny honiton braid, set with small silver spangles. Has fancy designed white enameled 8-inch sticks ornamented with pressed silver decorations. This is $2.00 value. Our price............ **98c**
If by mail, postage extra, 3 cents.

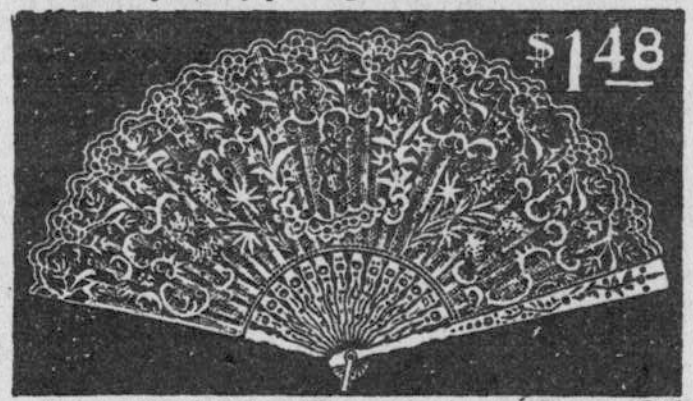

No. 18K1444 This Elaborate White Silk Double Gauze Fan, has wide Chantilly lace insertion top. Hand painted miniature in center, surrounded by lace applique in cutout effect and flower designs in white and silver, beautifully inserted with small silver spangles. Hand carved imitation ivory sticks 8 inches long, inlaid with steel discs. We consider this fan exceptional value at the price. Price............ **$1.48**
If by mail, postage extra, 3 cents.

Black Silk Fan.

25c

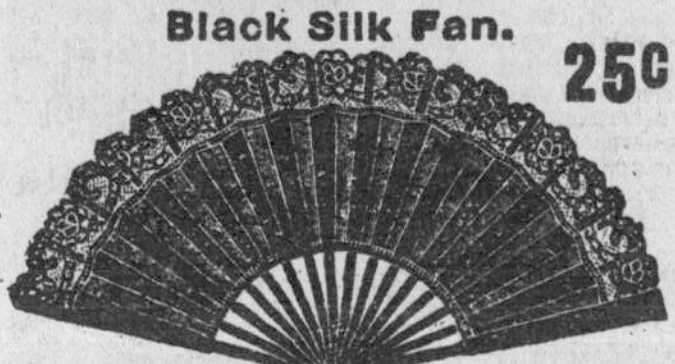

No. 18K1450 Black China Silk Fan with Chantilly lace top. Bottom is trimmed with black purling braid. This is an exceedingly popular and serviceable article, 8 inches long. Regular 50-cent fan. Our price... **25c**
If by mail, postage extra, 3 cents.

Don't Overlook Our 25-Cent Feather Fan.

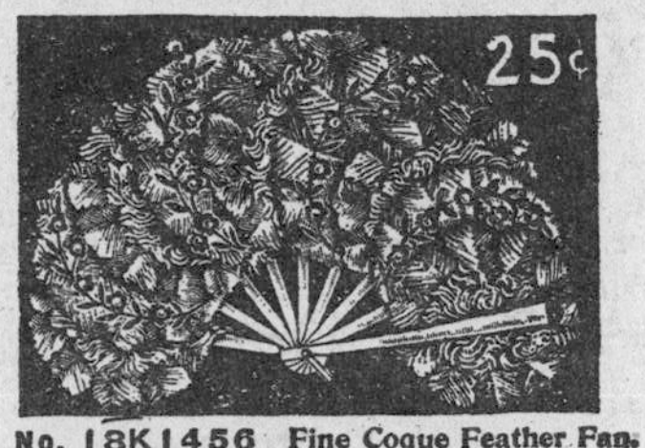

No. 18K1456 Fine Coque Feather Fan. Decorated with hand painted design. Colors, white, pink or light blue. Be sure to state color wanted. Length of fan, 9 inches. Price............ **25c**
If by mail, postage extra, 6 cents.

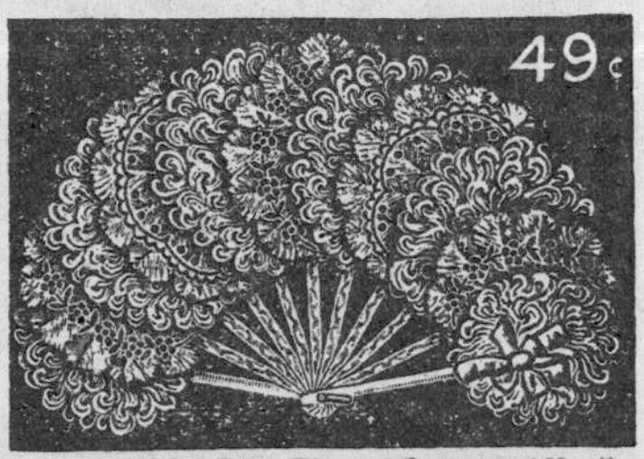

No. 18K1460 Elegant Coque and Marabo Feather Fan, handsomely ornamented with hand painted design and gilt decorations, comes in white, pink or light blue. Be sure to state color wanted. Has pressed enameled sticks, decorated in silver. Entire length, 10 inches. A splendid value. Price............ **49c**
If by mail, postage extra, 6 cents.

Genuine Ostrich Feather Fan, 58 Cents.

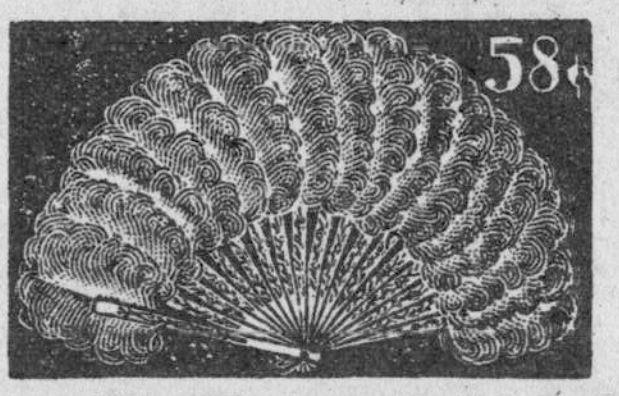

No. 18K1466 Genuine Ostrich Feather Fan, 8½ inches long. Mounted on white enameled sticks nicely decorated with pressed silver design. Will make a very acceptable gift. White only. $1.00 value. Our price............ **58c**
If by mail, postage extra, 4 cents.

Special Value at 82 Cents.

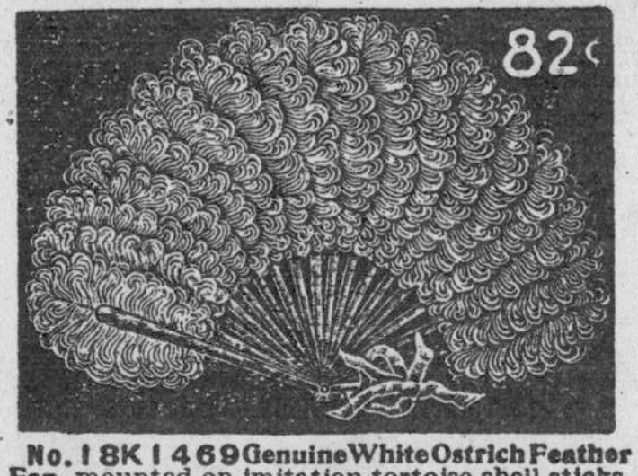

No. 18K1469 Genuine White Ostrich Feather Fan, mounted on imitation tortoise shell sticks. This is an exact reproduction of the very high grade article. A most effective and striking fan. An exceptional bargain. The greatest value in fans ever offered for the money. White only. Length of sticks, 9 inches. Price............ **82c**
If by mail, postage extra, 4 cents.

Our Best at 99 Cents.

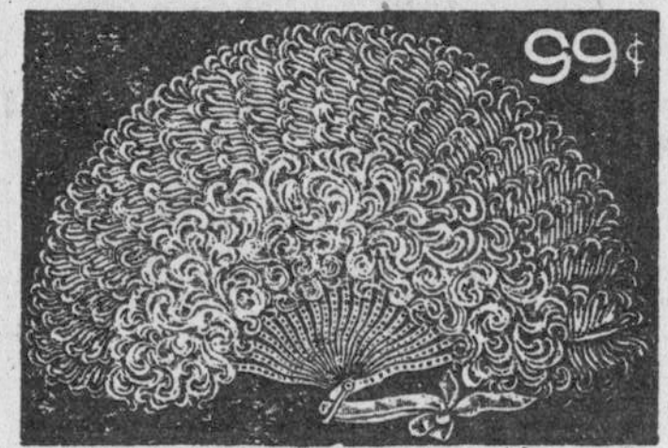

No. 18K1470 Our Finest Quality, Genuine Ostrich Feather Fan, 10 inches long. Fully curled feathers, with the base of fan heavily filled with long ostrich fiber. Mounted on fancy white enameled sticks, with pressed silver decorations. This fan cannot be matched at your dealers for less than $1.75. Colors, white, white and pink or white and light blue. State color wanted. Our price... **99c**
If by mail, postage extra, 5 cents.

Great Bargain in Pin Cabinets.

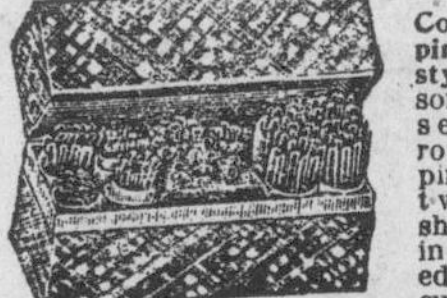

No. 18K1802 Contains 200 hair pins in all sizes and styles. Has an assortment of thirty-seven colored round headed toilet pins, including twelve 2-inch shawl or belt pins in black, all mounted in a velvet pin cushion. Also contains two rolls of adamantine pins, forty black and forty white. The box is finished in plaid paper and gilt edged.
Price 12c
If by mail, postage extra, 7 cents.

Hair Crimpers.

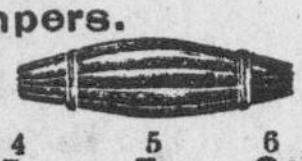

No. 18K1807 Real Kid Hair Crimpers, 12 in a package. State length.

Length, inches	4	5	6
Price, 2 PKGS FOR	5c	7c	8c

Postage extra, for 2 packages, 2 cents.

Aluminum Hair Pins.

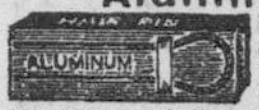

No. 18K1816 The best quality Aluminum Hair Pins; extra heavy fancy twist. Length, 3½ inches. Worth double. Price, 2 DOZEN FOR . . 17c
If by mail, postage extra, per 2 dozen, 2 cents.

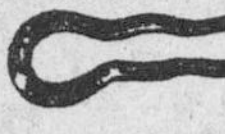

No. 18K1844 Fine Polished Hair Pins. Imitation tortoise shell, an excellent style and shape. Length, 4½ inches.
Price 4c
If by mail, postage extra, 1 cent.

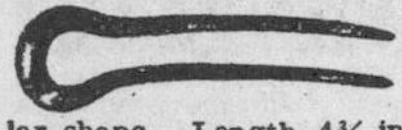

No. 18K1848 Hair Pins. Imitation tortoise shell, new improved pattern, a very popular shape. Length, 4¾ inches.
Price 4c
If by mail, postage extra, 1 cent.

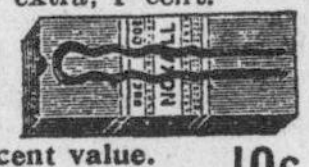

No. 18K1850 Imitation Tortoise Shell Horn Hair Pins, put up one dozen in a box, in either straight or crimped. Length, 3¼ inches. 20-cent value.
Our price, PER DOZEN 10c
If by mail, postage extra, per dozen, 2 cents.

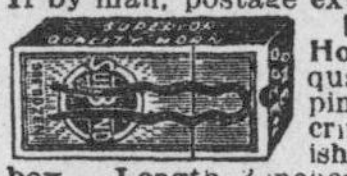

No 18K1852 Prima Horn Hair Pins. Elegant quality imitation shell hair pins, loop tops, straight or crimped, very highly polished. Twelve pins in a box. Length, 3 inches. Also in amber color. State choice. Price, PER DOZEN 21c
If by mail, postage extra, per dozen, 2 cents.

No. 18K1854 Parisienne Celluloid Hair Pins, made in imitation of tortoise shell. This is a 3-inch crimped hair pin, very highly polished. Price, PER DOZEN . . . . (Postage, per dozen, 2c.) 19c

Hair Rolls.

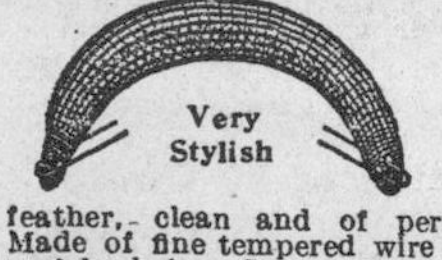

No. 18K1855 Braided Wire Pompadour Hair Rolls. These rolls are very popular at the present time. Light as a feather, clean and of perfect ventilation. Made of fine tempered wire with lace net to match hair. Colors, light brown, medium brown, blonde and black. State size and color wanted. Two sizes, 10-inch and 18-inch.

Size	10-inch	18-inch
Price, each	12c	21c

If by mail, postage extra, 10-inch, 3 cents; 18-inch, 4 cents.

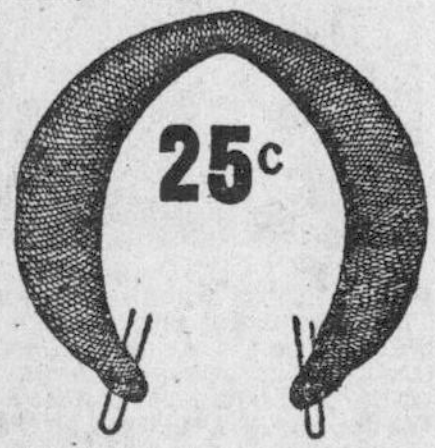

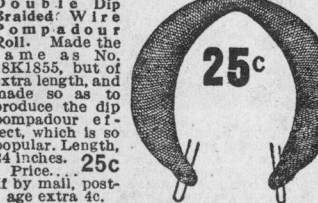

No. 18K1856 Double Dip Braided Wire Pompadour Roll. Made the same as No. 18K1855, but of extra length, and made so as to produce the dip pompadour effect, which is so popular. Length, 24 inches.
Price 25c
If by mail, postage extra 4c.

The "Fluffy Puff" Comb.

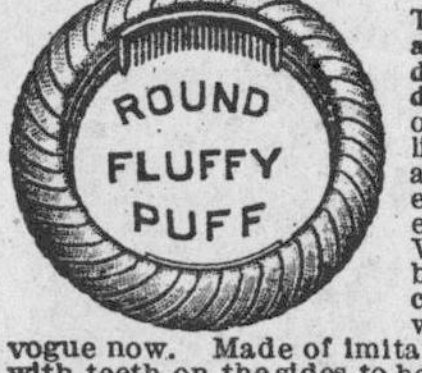

No. 18K1870 To create the new all around pompadour style of hair dressing. Thoroughly hygienic, light in weight, cool and comfortable, entirely new and easily applied. Will give you the beautiful new crown pompadour which is so much in vogue now. Made of imitation tortoise shell with teeth on the sides to hold the pompadour firmly in place.
Price, each . . . (Postage extra, 8c.) 45c

New Pompadour Human Hair Roll.

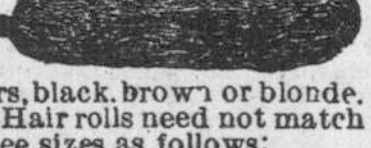

Ladies' New Pompadour Roll to be worn under the hair. Made of clean hair, under sanitary conditions. Colors, black, brown or blonde. State color wanted. Hair rolls need not match exact. Comes in three sizes as follows:

Cat. No.	18K1857	18K1858	18K1859
Length, inches	8	10	12
Price, each	7c	9c	11c

Invisible Hair Nets.

A SERVICEABLE ARTICLE IN HIGH FAVOR WITH NEAT DRESSERS.

Include an order for a package of these nets with your order for a switch or wave, and after using see the neat effect. They confine all the stray hairs, giving a nicely finished appearance to any hair dressing. SPECIFY COLOR WANTED. Comes in two sizes and three colors as follows:.

No. 18K1860 Large size to completely cover the hair. Colors, blonde, medium brown or black. Price, 3 FOR 44c

No. 18K1862 Medium size for partial covering. Colors, blonde, medium brown or black. Price, 3 FOR 35c
If by mail, postage extra, 3 for 3 cents.

Adjustable Puff Comb.

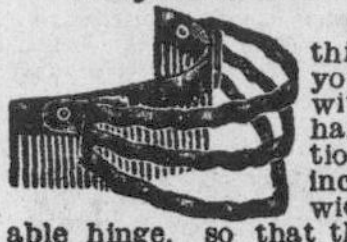

No. 18K1869 With this comb you can dress your hair pompadour style without the use of the hair rats. Made in imitation tortoise shell. 8½ inches long and 1¼ inches wide. Has the adjustable hinge, so that the puff can be worn on top or forward. Price, each 17c
If by mail, postage extra, each, 4 cents.

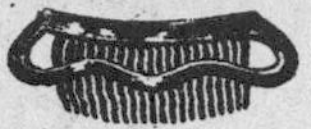

No. 18K1872 New Shaped Hair Barrette. When inserted in the hair it just shows the design with opening, imitation tortoise shell. Size, 4½ inches; very stylish. Price, each 13c
If by mail, postage extra, each, 2 cents.

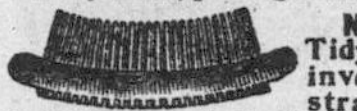

No. 18K1873 Ever Tidy Barrette, a clever invention for holding stray back hairs. Imitation tortoise shell, 4½ inches long. When in the hair the teeth are hidden and only a narrow bar shows. Price, each . . 15c
If by mail, postage extra, each 3 cents.

Side Combs.

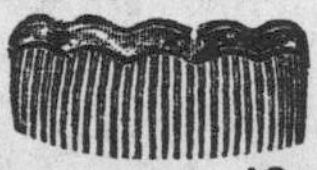

No. 18K1874 Side Combs, made of imitation tortoise shell, highly polished. Length, 4 inches. Has a very pretty scalloped top, as shown.
Price, PER PAIR 10c
If by mail, postage extra, per pair, 2 cents.

No. 18K1875 Ladies' Side Combs. Very highly polished. Heavy top. Imitation of tortoise shell. A good heavy comb. Length, 4¼ inches. 25-cent value.
Our price, PER PAIR 16c
If by mail, postage extra, per pair, 2 cents.

No. 18K1877 Ladies' Side Combs. Imitation tortoise shell, very highly polished, heavy and finely finished teeth. Extra heavy top. The new curved shape. Looks as well as the real shell. Can also be ordered in amber. State choice. 35-cent value. Length, 4¾ inches. Our price, PER PAIR 23c
If by mail, postage extra, per pair, 4 cents.

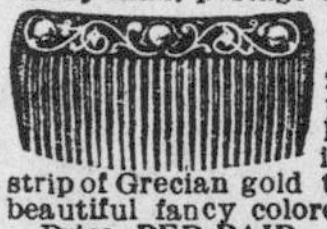

No. 18K1890 Imitation Tortoise Shell Side Combs. Highly polished and finished; length, 4 inches. The top is ornamented with a strip of Grecian gold trimming, set with three beautiful fancy colored jewel stones.
Price, PER PAIR 23c
If by mail, postage extra, per pair, 2 cents.

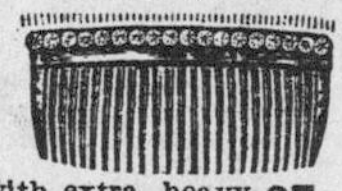

No. 18K1893 Imitation Tortoise Shell Side Combs. Size, 3¾ inches. The top is ornamented with a strip of silver trimming set with rhinestones, well finished with extra heavy top. Price, PER PAIR 27c
If by mail, postage extra, per pair, 2 cents.
For back combs to match, see No. 18K1897.

Ladies' Back Combs.

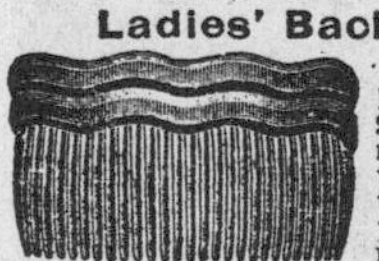

No. 18K1895 Imitation Tortoise Shell Comb. Has nicely rounded teeth and grooved top, which gives it a very handsome appearance. Extra heavy and nicely finished. 4¾ inches long; teeth, 1⅝ inches. Regular 25-cent value.
Our price, each 17c
If by mail, postage extra, each 4 cents.

The Popular Spanish Back Comb.

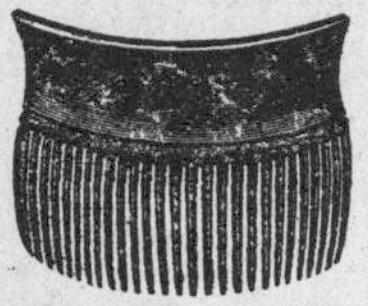

No. 18K1896 Imitation Tortoise Shell Back Comb. 4½ inches long; 1¼-inch top and 2-inch teeth. This is the new style Spanish back comb, very popular at the present time. Extra well finished and good heavy material. 35-cent value.
Our price, each 19c
If by mail, postage extra, each, 4 cents.

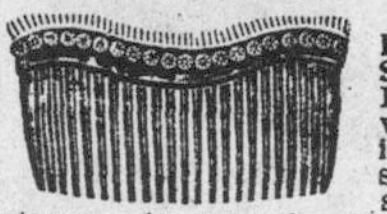

No. 18K1897 Imitation Tortoise Shell Back Comb. Extra heavy and well finished. Top is ornamented with silver strip of twenty-six brilliant rhinestones. An exceptionally attractive number. Length of comb, 4½ inches.
Price, each 21c
If by mail, postage extra, each, 4 cents.

No. 18K1905 Imitation Tortoise Shell Back Comb, 4¾ inches long. Nicely polished and finished. Top is ornamented with beautiful flower design gold finished mounting set with three colored brilliants.
Price, each 23c
If by mail, postage extra, each, 4 cents.

Fluffy Ruffle High Back Comb.

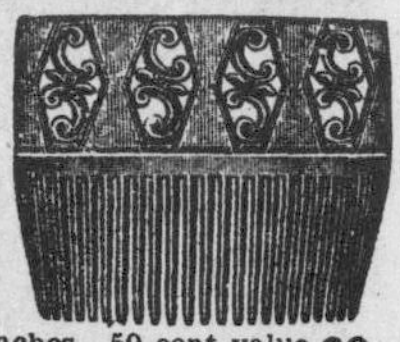

No. 18K1907 Heavy imitation tortoise shell, embossed and fancy carved. A most stylish comb. Length of teeth 2 inches; top 1⅞ inches; width, 4½ inches. 50-cent value.
Our price, each 29c
If by mail, postage extra, each, 4 cents.

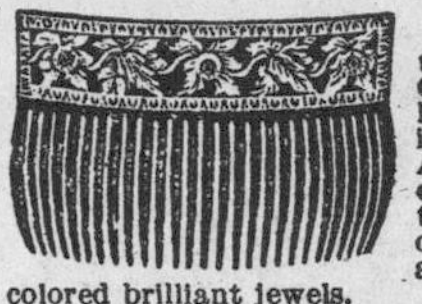

No. 18K1908 Imitation Tortoise Shell Back Comb, 4¾ inches long. Highly polished and finished. A very attractive comb, top being trimmed with gilt oak leaf pattern and set with three colored brilliant jewels.
Price, each 35c
If by mail, postage extra, each, 4 cents.

Mercury Wings All the Rage.

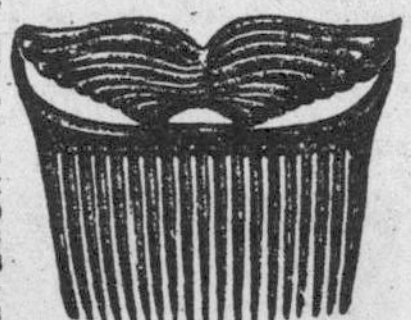

No. 18K1911 The New Mercury Wings Back Comb. One of the prettiest designs being shown this season in hair ornaments. 5 inches long, made of the very finest quality imitation tortoise shell. Highly polished and finished. An exceptionally beautiful comb. One of our newest importations.
Price, each 48c
If by mail, postage extra, each, 4 cents.

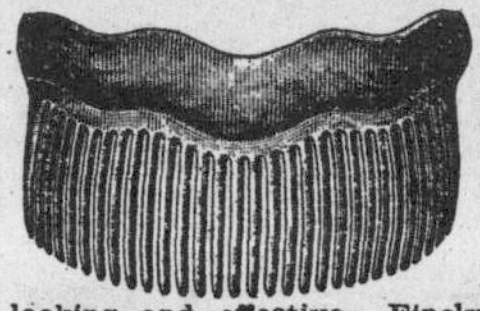

No. 18K1912 Extra Large Fancy Shaped Back Comb, 6 inches wide, made of finest imitation tortoise shell. An easy comb on the head. Rich looking and effective. Finely finished and highly polished. One of the latest combs.
Price, each 48c
If by mail, postage extra, each, 6 cents.
For Side Combs to match see No. 18K1877.

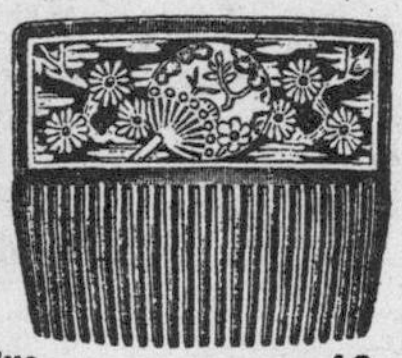

No. 18K1913 Spanish High Back Comb. Heavy imitation tortoise shell with 1¾-inch inlaid gold finished floral design, studded with seven colored and twelve white stones. Highly polished and extra finely finished. Width, 5 inches. Regular 75-cent value.
Our price, each 49c
If by mail, postage extra, each, 3 cents.

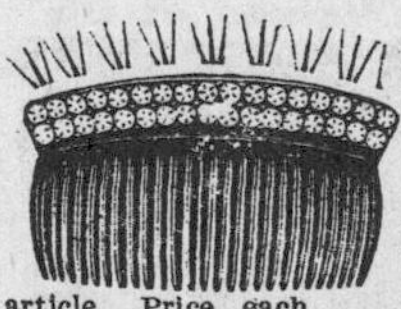

No. 18K1914 Fine Quality Imitation Tortoise Shell Back Comb, beautifully finished teeth. Mounted with a double row of fifty-two brilliant rhinestones. Length of comb, 5 inches. A rich looking article. Price, each 55c
If by mail, postage extra, each, 5 cents.
For Side Combs to match see No. 18K1893.

No. 18K1920 Ladies' Back Comb, imitation tortoise shell, highly polished teeth 2 inches in length, ornamented with a beautiful floral design in gold, set with brilliant rhinestones. Length of comb, 4¾ inches. Price, each 65c
If by mail, postage extra, each, 3 cents.

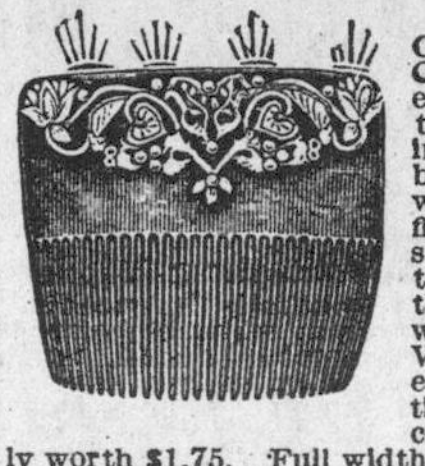

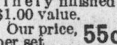

No. 18K1924 Our Best Back Comb. Made of extra heavy imitation tortoise shell, in the Spanish high back style, mounted with a beautiful finished ornament studded with thirteen of the finest quality white rhinestones. Very highly polished. A most beautiful and popular comb, which is easily worth $1.75. Full width, 5 inches.
Our price, each 98c
If by mail, postage extra, each, 10 cents.

Bargains in Comb Sets.

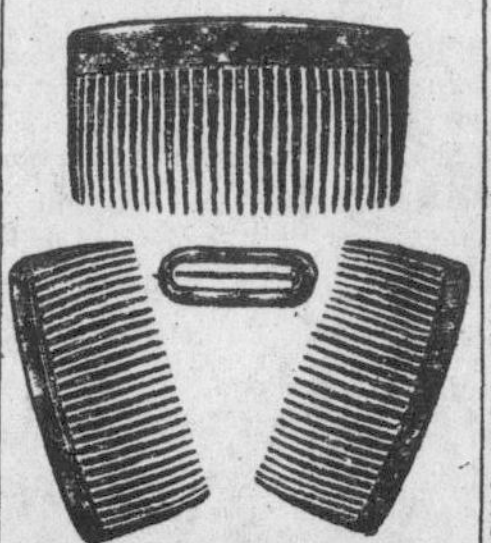

No. 18K1926 Imitation Tortoise Shell Comb Set. Consists of back comb 4½ inches long, pair of side combs 3¼ inches long and barrette 2 inches wide. All made of the good quality imitation tortoise shell and nicely finished. An exceptionally big offer, each set being put on a card and in a box. Would be cheap at 50 cents.
Our price, PER SET 33c
If by mail, postage extra, per set, 6 cents.

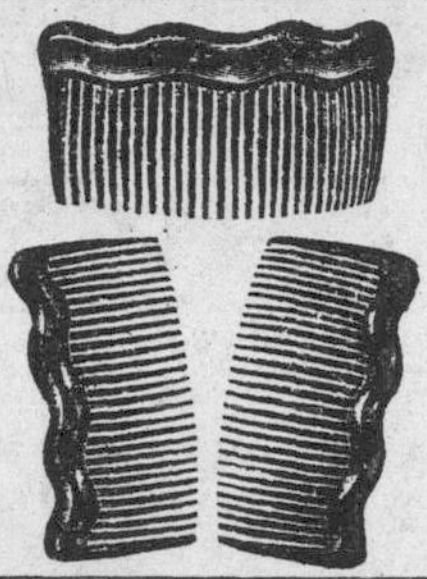

No. 18K1928 Ladies' Back and Side Comb Set. Made of extra heavy imitation tortoise shell, highly polished and finished. Back comb, 5 inches long; side combs, 4¼ inches long. The top of the combs being cut in the new wave design makes an exceptionally attractive and ornamental set.
Price, per set 46c
If by mail, postage extra, per set, 6 cents.

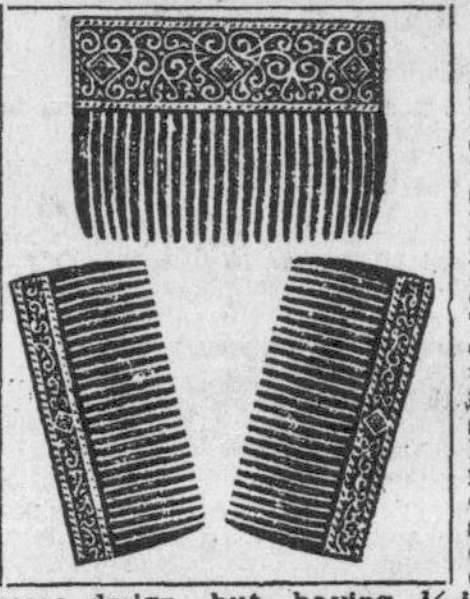

No. 18K1930 Back and Side Comb Set. Made of good quality imitation tortoise shell, highly polished and finished. Length of each comb, 4 inches. Top of comb is ornamented with 1-inch fancy scroll design in gilt, is highly ornamental and set off with three square cut jewel settings. Side combs of the same design, but having ⅝-inch mounting to match. An exceptionally fine set, and one that would be retailed at 75 cents.
Our price, per set 48c
If by mail, postage extra, per set, 6 cents.

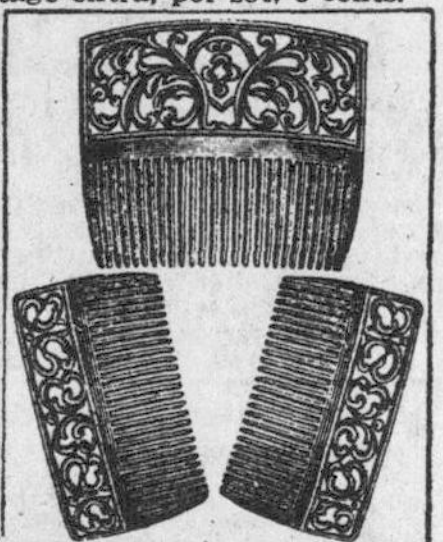

No. 18K1933 Carved Comb Set. Set of the best quality heavy imitation tortoise shell. Back comb 4½ inches in width and pair of 4-inch side combs to match. Both are beautifully carved and decorated in scroll design, a great bargain. Extra highly polished and finely finished. $1.00 value.
Our price, per set 55c
If by mail, postage extra, per set, 8 cents.

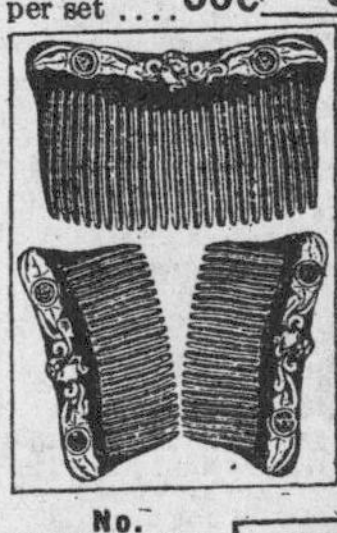

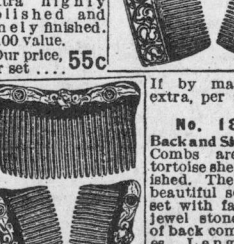

No. 18K1934 Back and Side Comb Set. Combs are imitation tortoise shell highly polished. The mounting is beautiful scroll design, set with fancy colored jewel stones. Length of back comb, 4½ inches. Length of side combs, 4 inches. Price, per set. 67c
If by mail, postage extra, per set, 6 cents.

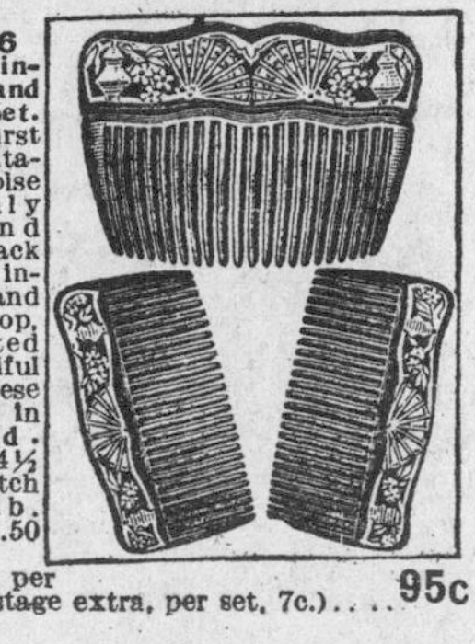

No. 18K1936 Our very finest Back and Side Comb Set. Made of first quality imitation tortoise shell, highly polished and finished. Back comb is 5 inches wide, and has 1-inch top, ornamented with beautiful inlaid Japanese fan design in solid gold. Side combs 4½ inches to match back comb. Regular $1.50 value.
Our price, per set . . . . (Postage extra, per set, 7c.) 95c

Marcelle Hair Waver.

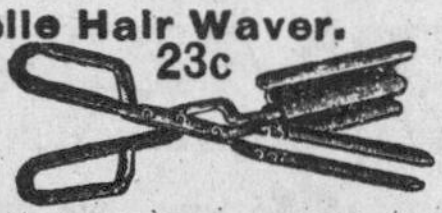

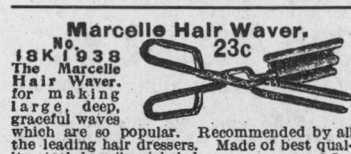

No. 18K1938 23c The Marcelle Hair Waver, for making large, deep, graceful waves which are so popular. Recommended by all the leading hair dressers. Made of best quality steel, heavily nickeled. Our price........ 23c
If by mail, postage extra, 10 cents.

Waving Iron.

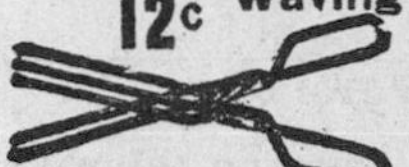

12c No. 18K1974 Five-Prong Waving Iron, for waving the hair, made of good quality metal. Price........ 12c
If by mail, postage extra, 9 cents.

DRESSING COMBS.

6c No. 18K1980 Horn Dressing Comb, 7 inches long. Nickel plated back, coarse and fine teeth. Price........ 6c
If by mail, postage extra, 3 cents.

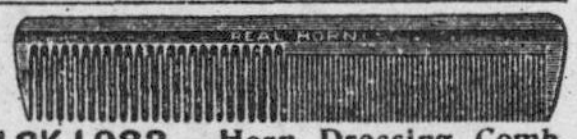

19c No. 18K1982 Horn Dressing Comb. Made of finest quality horn, highly polished. Our own importation. Regular 35-cent value. Length, 7½ inches. Price.... 19c
If by mail, postage extra, 4 cents.

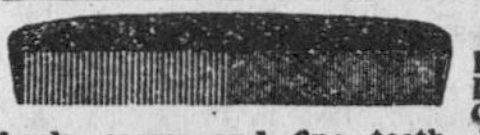

No. 18K1983 Hard Rubber Dressing Comb. Curved back, coarse and fine teeth. Length, 7 inches. Price........ 6c
If by mail, postage extra, 4 cents.

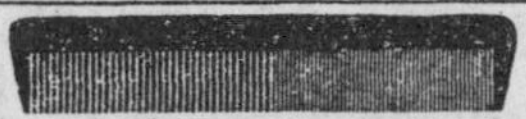

12c No. 18K1986 Strong Hard Rubber Dressing Comb. Heavy square back, rounded teeth, coarse and fine. Length, 8 inches. Price........ 12c
If by mail, postage extra, 3 cents.

14c No. 18K1989 Hard Rubber Dressing Comb. Fancy carved back; coarse and fine teeth. Length, 8 inches. Usually retailed at 25 cents. Our price........ 14c
If by mail, postage extra, 3 cents.

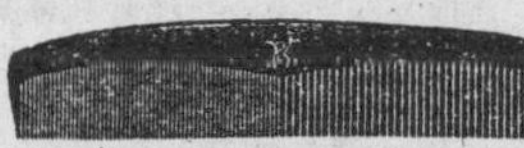

24c No. 18K1998 Hard Rubber Dressing Comb. With best grailed teeth, in coarse and fine, a very high grade comb. Length, 8 inches. Price........ 24c
If by mail, postage extra, 3 cents.

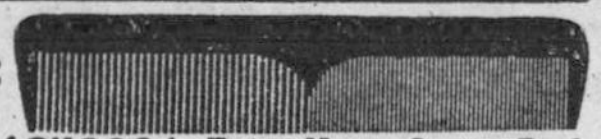

38c No. 18K2001 Extra Heavy Square Back Hard Rubber Dressing Comb. Hand sawed, round finished, coarse and fine teeth. A regular 50-cent comb. Length, 9 inches. Our price........ 38c
If by mail, postage extra, 3 cents.

No. 18K2002 Extra Heavy Square Back Hard Rubber Dressing Comb. Same style and design as No. 18K2001, but all coarse teeth, especially adapted for long, heavy hair; makes hair dressing a pleasure. Length, 9 inches. Price........ 38c
If by mail, postage extra, 3 cents.

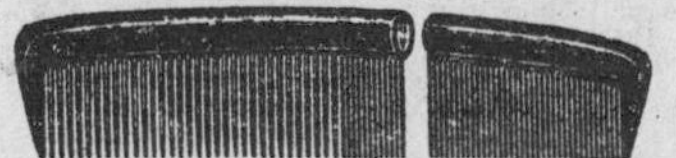

No. 18K2004 Revelation Comb. Light, strong and warranted unbreakable. Made with a hollow back; stronger than solid combs but much lighter, so that it can be handled with ease and comfort. Every comb guaranteed. Fine and coarse teeth. Length, 8¼ inches. Price........ 44c
No. 18K2006 The Revelation Comb, all coarse teeth, same quality and size as No. 18K2004. Price........ 44c
If by mail, postage extra, 4 cents.

No. 18K2007 The Innovation Comb. Different from anything now on the market. The hair is first disentangled with the coarse teeth, after which the semi-coarse part is used; with the Innovation Comb this is done with one operation. Made of the best quality hard rubber. Every comb guaranteed. Length, 8 inches. Price........ 48c
If by mail, postage extra, 3 cents.

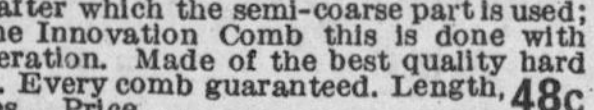

39c No. 18K2013 Hard Rubber Dressing Comb. With handle, giving extra purchase on comb; all coarse teeth; just the thing for heavy and thick hair. Length, 9 inches. Price........ 39c
If by mail, postage extra, 3 cents.

10c No. 18K2016 Extra Super Quality Hard Rubber Barbers' Comb. With graduated coarse and fine teeth. Length, 7 inches. Price........ 10c
If by mail, postage extra, 2 cents.

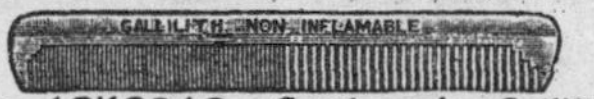

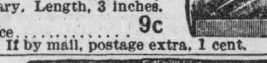

No. 18K2018 Gentlemen's Gallilith Dressing Comb. Made of a newly discovered substance stronger than rubber, and absolutely non-inflammable. The hardest substance now used in making combs. Length, 7 inches. Price........ 19c
If by mail, postage extra, 4 cents.

Imported Horn Comb.

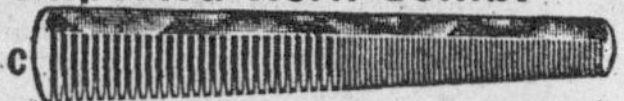

35c No. 18K2019 Highest Grade Imported French Horn Comb. Used particularly by barbers and as a gent's hair dressing comb. Length, 7½ inches. Price........ 35c
If by mail, postage extra, 2 cents.

Rubber Fine Combs.

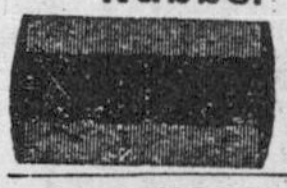

No. 18K2022 Hard Rubber Fine Tooth Comb. Size, 3x1⅜ inches. 10-cent value. Price........ 6c
If by mail, postage extra, 3 cents.

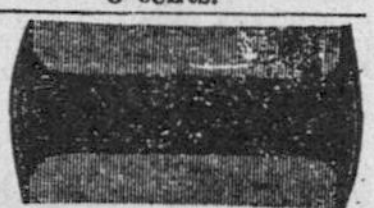

No. 18K2025 Hard Rubber Fine Comb. The 20c kind. Size, 4x2 inches. Our price.... 10c
If by mail, postage extra, 3 cents.

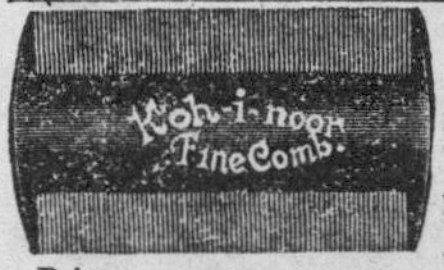

No. 18K2031 Imported Extra Heavy Hard Rubber Fine Tooth Comb. 3-16 inch thick. Highly polished. 35-cent value. Size, 4½x2½ inches. Price........ 22c
If by mail, postage extra, 2 cents.

No. 18K2034 Aluminum Fine Comb. Will not tarnish or break; strictly sanitary. Length, 3 inches. Price........ 9c
If by mail, postage extra, 1 cent.

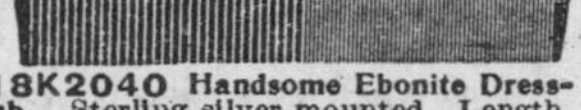

29c No. 18K2040 Handsome Ebonite Dressing Comb. Sterling silver mounted. Length, 7½ inches. Easily worth 40 cents. Our price........ 29c
If by mail, postage extra, 2 cents.

Fiberloid Combs.

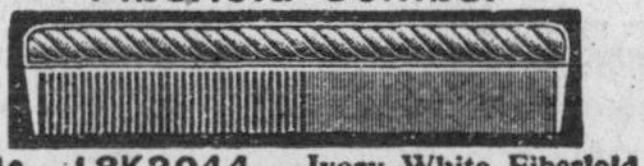

No. 18K2044 Ivory White Fiberloid Dressing Comb, 7 inches long. Heavy squared back, nicely embossed with rope design. Coarse and fine teeth. Exceptional value. Price........ 14c
If by mail, postage extra, 3 cents.

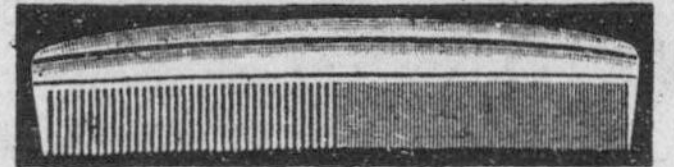

No. 18K2047 A Fine Quality Ivory White Fiberloid Dressing Comb. Has coarse and fine teeth and rounded back. An extra strong comb, 8⅜ inches long. Price........ 23c
If by mail, postage extra, 4 cents.

No. 18K2050 Best Fiberloid Comb in ivory white finish. Fancy curved back, beautifully embossed. Very strong, coarse and fine teeth; length, 7½ inches. Regular 50-cent value. Our price........ 33c
If by mail, postage extra, 2 cents.

Aluminum Combs.

No. 18K2058 Aluminum Dressing Comb. Coarse and fine teeth. Length, 7½ inches; width, 1½ inches. Price........ 10c
If by mail, postage extra, 2 cents.

No. 18K2067 Aluminum Dressing Comb. Extra heavy, with fancy engraving. Highly polished teeth. Length, 7½ inches. Price........ 19c
If by mail, postage extra, 3 cents.

No. 18K2070 Extra Heavy, Square Back, Hard Rubber Pocket Comb. Coarse and fine teeth in leatheroid case. Length, 4½ inches. Price........ 10c
If by mail, postage extra, 2 cents.

Infants' Comb and Brushes.

FINE COMB.

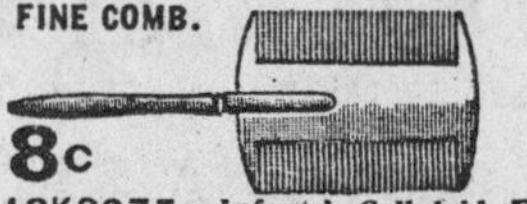

8c No. 18K2075 Infants' Celluloid Fine Comb, with handle. Full length, 4½ inches. Color, white. Price........ 8c
If by mail, postage extra, 1 cent.

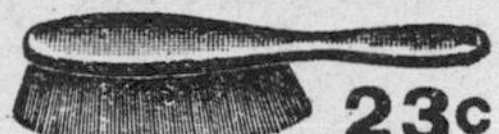

No. 18K2203 Infants' Imported White Bone Brush, with soft, white goat bristles. A splendid infants' hair brush; also suitable for ladies' powder brush. Regular 30-cent value. Our price........ 23c
If by mail, postage extra, 2 cents.
No. 18K2207 Infants' Imported Fine White Bone Goat Hair Brush; also suitable for ladies' toilet powder. Smaller size than above. Price........ 15c
If by mail, postage extra, 3 cents.

HAIR BRUSHES

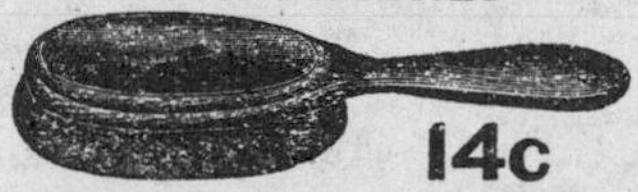

14c No. 18K2211 Medium Size Oval Shape Brush, with eleven rows of good black bristles, concave back, mahogany finish. Regular 25-cent value. Our price........ 14c
If by mail, postage extra, 9 cents.

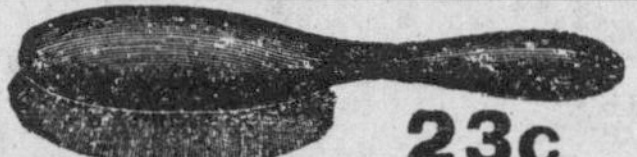

23c No. 18K2215 Eleven Rows Fine, Long Black Russian Bristles, solid oval back in mahogany finish, finely polished. A splendid brush at our price........ 23c
If by mail, postage extra, 7 cents.

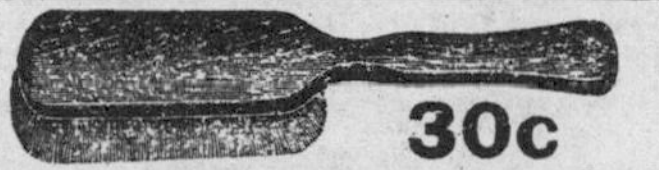

30c No. 18K2219 This Handsome Brush has nine rows of fine white China bristles. Oblong shape, solid back in walnut finish, highly polished with new fancy shape handle. Regular 50-cent value. Our price........ 30c
If by mail, postage extra, 9 cents.

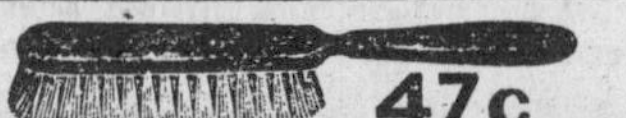

47c No. 18K2224 Our Own Special Design Ladies' Hair Dressing Brush. In using this brush no comb is necessary, as the bristles are stiff enough to penetrate a heavy head of hair; especially adapted for professional hair dressers. Solid wood back of highly polished rosewood, having seven rows of the very best Russian bristles. We especially recommend this brush. Price........ 47c
If by mail, postage extra, 5 cents.

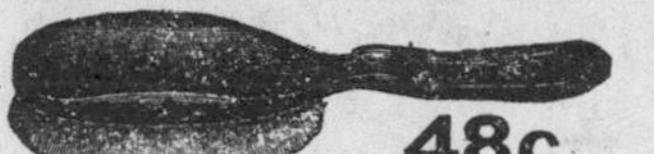

48c No. 18K2229 New Concave Back Hair Brush, made of genuine solid mahogany, highly polished. Has eleven rows of heavy white Russian bristles; the kind that penetrate. Others ask 75 cents. Our price........ 48c
If by mail, postage extra, 7 cents.

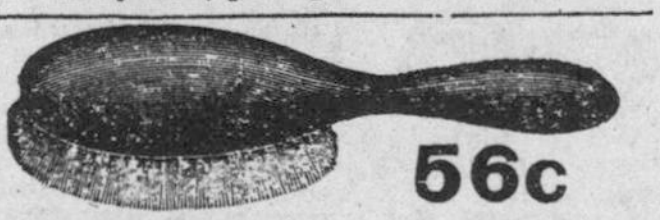

56c No. 18K2233 A Very High Grade Brush. Has thirteen rows of extra quality white China bristles. Oval shaped rounded back in walnut finish, highly polished. One of our leaders. Price........ 56c
If by mail, postage extra, 7 cents.

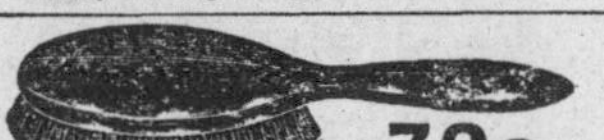

72c No. 18K2236 Our very finest Thirteen-Row Best Black China Bristle Brush, very penetrating and especially adapted as a barbers' brush, such as is sold at $1.25. Highly polished, solid wood, walnut finish back. A very serviceable and high grade brush. Our price........ 72c
If by mail, postage extra, 9 cents.

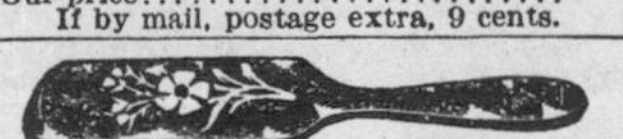

15c No. 18K2244 Ten-Row Metallic Wire Hair Brush. Oval handle, nicely polished and decorated back. Price........ 15c
If by mail, postage extra, 7 cents.

Extra Fine Wire Brush.

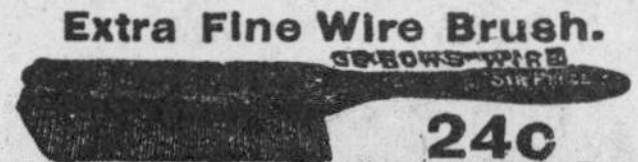

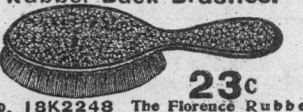

24c No. 18K2246 "Fine Wire" Brush. Imitation ebony, solid back. Made of 36 rows of fine wires set in rubber so that they will not fall out. One of the best brushes made for the treatment of dandruff and for penetrating the hair. Price........ 24c
If by mail, postage extra, 5 cents.

Rubber Back Brushes.

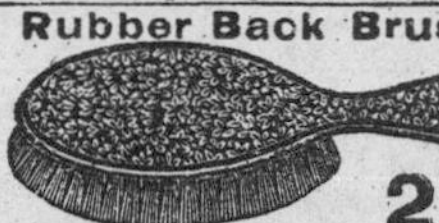

23c No. 18K2248 The Florence Rubber Back, Black Bristle Hair Brush. Nine rows black Russian bristles. Easy to clean; nice to use. Value, 40 cents. Our price........ 23c
If by mail, postage extra, 7 cents.

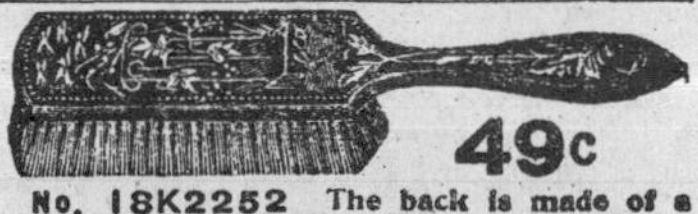

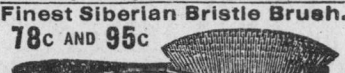

49c No. 18K2252 The back is made of a black composition with fancy embossed designs. Has eleven rows of long, fine white, best penetrating Russian bristles. A very substantial and durable brush; very easily kept clean. Size, 8¾x2⅜ inches. Price........ 49c
If by mail, postage extra, 9 cents.

Finest Siberian Bristle Brush.

78c AND 95c

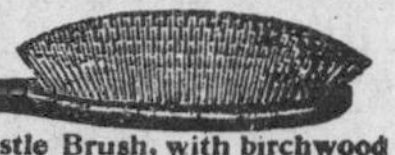

Finest Siberian Bristle Brush, with birchwood back. This is a genuine Siberian bristle brush, with a single bristle substituted for the ordinary tuft, the bristles being set in an elastic air cushioned base. This construction enables it to penetrate the most luxuriant growth of hair without effort. It also prevents the possibility of injuring the hair or scalp. Used effectually in removing dandruff without irritating the scalp. It is clean, light and durable.
No. 18K2256 Medium Size. Price........ 78c
No. 18K2258 Large Size. Price........ 95c
If by mail, postage extra, 8 cents.

The Celebrated "Keep Clean" Brush.

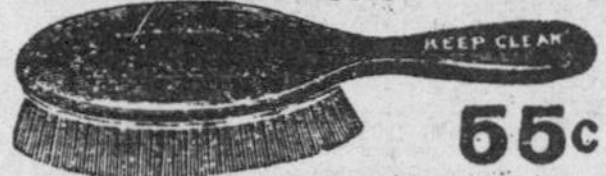

55c No. 18K2260 Keep Clean, large size, oval shaped, Black Ebony Finished Hair Brush, with fifteen rows of medium size black pure bristles, the bristles being set in pure aluminum, which is waterproof and very easy to keep clean. This is the best brush made and cannot become foul by absorbing the water, oil and dirt like an ordinary brush. Size, 9¾x3¼ inches. Price........ 55c
If by mail, postage extra, 12 cents.

"Keep Clean" Military Hair Brushes.

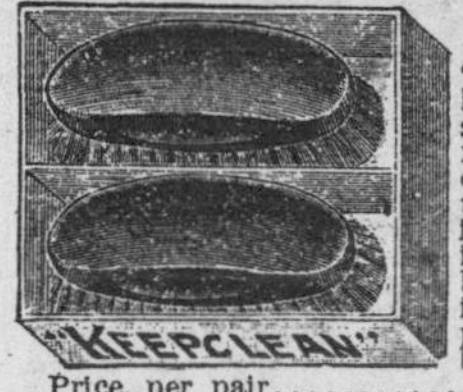

No. 18K2262 The well known "Keep Clean" Brush in a new style. Eleven rows of best quality long bristles set in aluminum block; solid imitation ebony back, neatly finished. Comes put up two in a box. Price, per pair........ 89c
If by mail, postage extra, per pair, 10 cents.

Dr. Scott's Electric Hair Brushes Are Recommended by Leading Physicians.

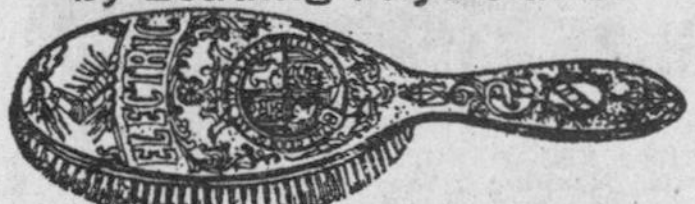

No. 18K2264 Dr. Scott's Electric Hair Brushes are recommended by leading physicians and are extensively known. A wonderful help for headache and neuralgia; splendid to prevent falling hair, dandruff, etc. The curative powers of these brushes have been known and tested for a number of years. We can furnish them in three sizes. Prices range according to size, as follows:
Size No. 1, regular price $1.00. Our price........ $0.79
Size No. 2, regular price $2.00. Our price........ 1.18
Size No. 4, regular price $3.00. Our price........ 1.68
Shipping weight, each, 10 to 15 ounces.

Clothes Brushes.

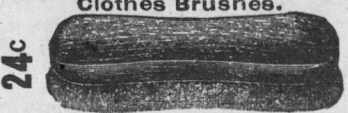

24c

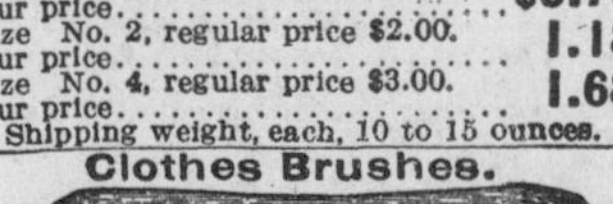

No. 18K2265 Clothes Brush, 6½ inches long, made on heavy satinwood back, highly polished. Bristles are of good quality in black, edged with one row of white. A very showy article. Price........ 24c
If by mail, postage extra, 9 cents.

Clothes Brushes.

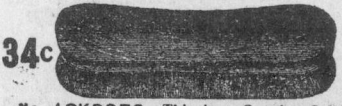

34c

No. 18K2270 This is a Genuine Solid Mahogany Back Clothes Brush, 7¼ inches long with nine rows of fine quality black Russian bristles of extra length. Regular 50-cent value. Our price......... 34c
If by mail, postage extra, 9 cents.

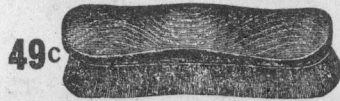

49c

No. 18K2275 For good service, we recommend this brush. Has ten rows of long, black Russian bristles mounted on solid mahogany back; 7¼ inches long, new curved shape; highly polished. A splendid value. Price.................. 49c
If by mail, postage extra, 10 cents.

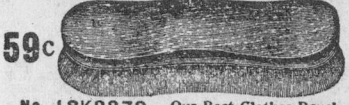

59c

No. 18K2279 Our Best Clothes Brush. Has eleven rows of fine, white China bristles set in solid satinwood back; the new curved shape. Length of brush, 7½ inches. $1.00 value; our price......... 59c
If by mail, postage extra, 11 cents.

Genuine Ebony Back Brushes.

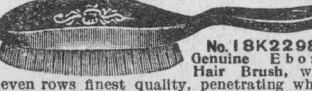

No. 18K2298 Genuine Ebony Hair Brush, with eleven rows finest quality, penetrating white Russian bristles; handsome sterling silver mounting on back. Suitable for ladies or gentlemen. Length, 9½ inches. Guaranteed $2.00 value. Our price.. $1.05
If by mail, postage extra, 8 cents.

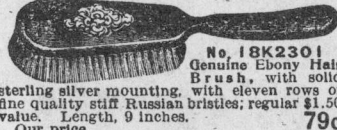

No. 18K2301 Genuine Ebony Hair Brush, with solid sterling silver mounting, with eleven rows of fine quality stiff Russian bristles; regular $1.50 value. Length, 9 inches. Our price.................. 79c
If by mail, postage extra, 8 cents.

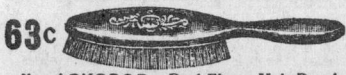

63c

No. 18K2305 Real Ebony Hair Brush, with solid sterling silver mountings, nine rows finest quality imported bristles. Length, 8½ inches. A brush retailed at your jeweler's for $1.00. Our price.. 63c
If by mail, postage extra, 8 cents.

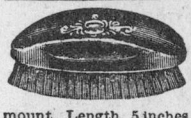

No. 18K2307 Genuine Ebony Military Brush with eleven rows of fine white bristles, extra heavy and highly finished back, with sterling silver mount. Length, 5 inches. Regular $1.50 value
Our price, each.................$0.99
Price, per pair.................1.93
If by mail, postage extra, each, 7 cents.

No. 18K2315 Genuine Ebony Military Brush, with nine rows of fine white bristles; has handsome sterling silver mount. Same style as above. A very sightly brush at a low price. Length, 5 inches.
Price, each.....................$0.67
Price, per pair.................1.29
If by mail, postage extra, each, 7 cents.

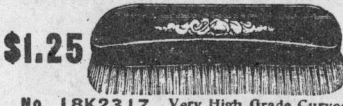

$1.25

No. 18K2317 Very High Grade Curved Back Genuine Ebony Cloth Brush, with 8 rows of extra quality white, long Russian bristles. A superior quality brush in every way. Mounted with heavy silver plate on back. Size, 7 inches.
Price.............................$1.25
If by mail, postage extra, 8 cents.

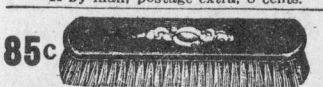

85c

No. 18K2319 Solid Black Genuine Ebony Cloth Brush, having seven rows of pure white Russian bristles; back mounted with sterling silver plate. Length, 6¾ inches. Extra value. Price.................. 85c
If by mail, postage extra, 7 cents.

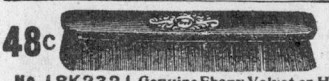

48c

No. 18K2321 Genuine Ebony Velvet or Hat Brush, with long, white imported bristles, very desirable for ladies' or gents' hats, or for fine cloth and velvet. Very acceptable gift for ladies or gents; solid sterling silver mounted. Length, 6 inches. Price.... 48c
If by mail, postage extra, 3 cents.

BUTTON DEPARTMENT.

ALL BUTTONS DESCRIBED IN THE FOLLOWING COLUMNS ARE GUARANTEED TO BE STRICTLY FIRST QUALITIES.

Owing to the very small margin of profit asked on our high grade line of buttons, we cannot accept orders for smaller quantities than those catalogued. The following button scale shows, as near as possible, the size in inches of all buttons which may be quoted by the line:

Lines..............	12	14	16	18	20	22	24
Size, inches......	¼	5/16	⅜	7/16	½	9/16	⅝

Pearl Buttons.

18-line. 16-line.

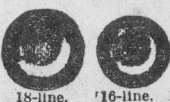

No. 18K3061 Superfine Clear White Pearl Buttons, best quality, cup shape, two-hole. State size wanted.
Size, lines.......... 16 18 20 22 24
Price for 2 DOZEN 8c 9c 11c 12c 13c
If by mail, postage extra, per package, 2 cents.

Small Pearl Trimming Buttons, Ball Shape.

14-line 16-line

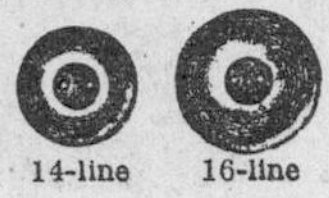

No. 18K3068 Small Ball Pearl Trimming Buttons are very much in demand. Superior quality domestic pearl, half ball shape, two holes. State size wanted.
Size, lines.................. 14 16
Price, per card, 2 DOZEN 13c 15c
If by mail, postage extra, per card, 2 cents.

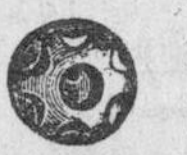

No. 18K3070 Fancy Engraved Two-Hole Pearl Dress and Trimming Buttons. Very dainty and stylish for trimming purposes. State size wanted.
Size, lines..... 12 14 16
Price per card, 2 DOZEN... 15c 17c 19c
If by mail, postage extra, per card, 2 cents.

No. 18K3072 Imported Oriental Pearl Cat's Eye Ball Button, finest quality obtainable, with self shank. A very handsome and dressy button. State size wanted.
Size, lines.................. 12 14 16
Price, per DOZEN.......... 12c 14c 16c
If by mail, postage extra, per dozen, 2 cents.

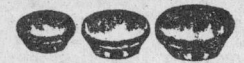

12-line. 14-line. 16-line.

No. 18K3075 Fine Grade Full One-Half Ball Plain White Pearl Trimming Buttons, with self shank. State size wanted.
Size, lines.................. 12 14 16
Price, per card, 2 DOZEN. 18c 21c 23c
If by mail, postage extra, per card, 2 cents.

Fresh Water Fish Eye Pearl Buttons.

14 16

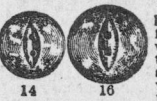

No. 18K3078 Pearl Dress Buttons, in sizes from 12 to 20 lines. Fresh water pearl, fish eye pattern with two holes; suitable for shirts, shirtwaists, etc. State size wanted.
Size, lines......12 14 16 18 20
Price, per card,
2 DOZEN... 9c 12c 14c 16c 18c
If by mail, postage extra, per card, 2 cents.

12c PER DOZEN

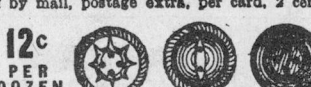

No. 2 No. 3 No. 4

No. 18K3086 Pearl Shirt Waist Buttons. The finest quality imported mother of pearl. Choice of three styles. Size, 16-line. State style wanted.
Price, per DOZEN.................. 12c
If by mail, postage extra, per dozen 1 cent.

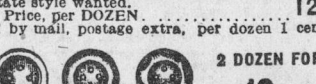

Style 1 Style 2 Style 3

2 DOZEN FOR 19c

No. 18K3090 Finest Real Mother of Pearl. Size, 12-line, small size shirt button. Size of illustrations. Choice of the three styles. State style wanted.
Price, per card of 2 DOZEN........ 19c
If by mail, postage extra, per card, 2 cents.

Stylish Plain Flat Pearl Buttons.

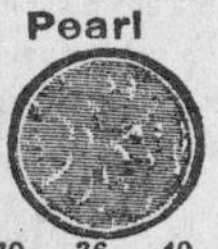

No. 18K3094 Flat Top Pearl Buttons, with metal shank. These buttons are very stylish and popular for shirt waists. State size wanted. Come in the following sizes:
Size, lines......... 22 30 36 40
Inches, diameter..... ½ ¾ ⅞ 1
Price, per DOZEN...... 14c 20c 25c 30c
If by mail, postage extra, per dozen, 2 to 4c.

Pearl Buttons for Cloaks, Jackets and Dresses.

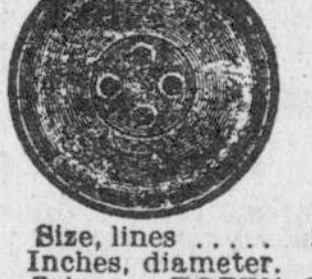

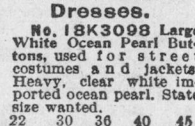

No. 18K3098 Large White Ocean Pearl Buttons, used for street costumes and jackets. Heavy, clear white imported ocean pearl. State size wanted.
Size, lines..... 22 30 36 40 45
Inches, diameter. ½ 11-16 ¾ 1 1⅛
Price, per DOZEN, 23c 39c 50c 65c 80c
If by mail, postage extra, per dozen, 3c to 5c.

Gilt Trimming Buttons.

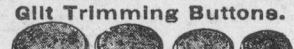

16-line. 14-line. 12-line. 10-line.

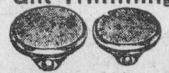

No. 18K3106 Flat Dull Finish Gilt Trimming Buttons with shanks. A very desirable trimming button for various uses. Come in four sizes as per above illustrations, which are actual sizes. State size wanted.
Size, lines........ 16 14 12 10
Price, 2 DOZEN FOR 13c 11c 10c 9c
If by mail, postage extra, per dozen, 2 cents.

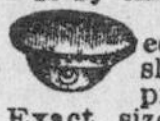

No. 18K3126 Imitation Imported Colored Pearl Buttons, with self shank. Colors, white, light blue, pink, red, brown or navy blue. Exact size as per illustration. Mounted two dozen on a card. State color wanted.
Price, per card, 2 DOZEN......... 11c
If by mail, postage extra, per card, 1 cent.

Silk Covered Buttons.

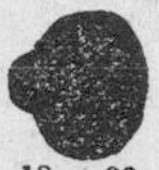

No. 18K3146 Fine Silk Diagonal Covered Buttons for dress trimmings, etc., with self shank. Black only. Put up two dozen in a package. State size wanted.
Size, lines.......... 12 14 16 18 20
Price, 2 DOZEN FOR 8c 9c 10c 11c 12c
If by mail, postage extra, per package, 2 cents.

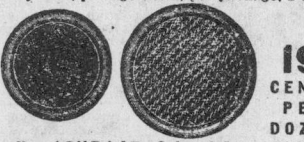

19 CENTS PER DOZEN

No. 18K3147 Colored Ivory Rim Silk Buttons for trimming waists, coats and skirts, Come in two sizes, in the following colors: Black, navy, green, red, brown, tan and gray. State size and color wanted.
Size, lines.............24 30
Price, per DOZEN...... 19c 28c
If by mail, postage extra, per dozen, 24-line, 3 cents; 30-line, 4 cents

Washable Lace Buttons.

10 12 14

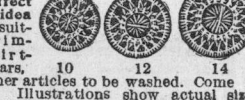

No. 18K3149 Teneriffe effect the latest idea in Buttons suitable for trimming shirt-waists, collars, ties and other articles to be washed. Come in three sizes. Illustrations show actual size. State size wanted.
Size, lines............10 12 14
Price, 2 DOZEN FOR 9c 11c 13c
If by mail, postage extra, per card, 3 cents.

Highest Grade Washable Lace Buttons.

10 12 14

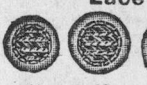

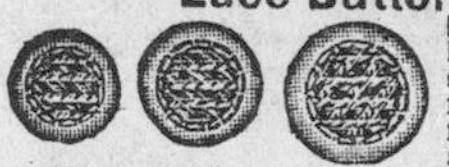

No. 18K3151 Honeycomb design. Suitable for use on the finest grade of articles to be washed. Come in three sizes. Illustrations show actual size. State size wanted.
Size, lines.........10 12 14
Price, per DOZEN.. 9c 10c 12c
If by mail, postage extra, per dozen, 2 cents.

Coat and Vest Buttons.

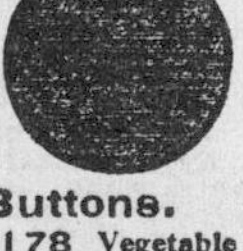

No. 18K3162 Fine Silk Covered Diagonal Buttons. Black only. State size wanted.
Size.....Vest Coat Overcoat
Price, per
DOZEN 6c 10c 13c
Postage extra, per dozen, 2c.

Vegetable Ivory Buttons.

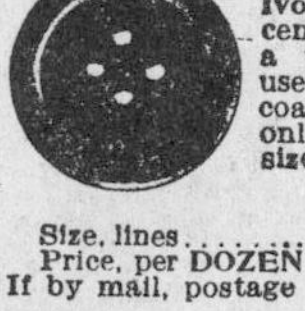

No. 18K3178 Vegetable Ivory Buttons, with dull finish centers and polished rims; a very high grade button, used by the best tailors. Vest, coat and overcoat. Black only. Sizes as follows: State size wanted.
Vest Coat Overcoat
Size, lines.........24 30 36
Price, per DOZEN.......7c 9c 12c
If by mail, postage extra, per dozen, 3 cents.

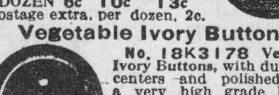

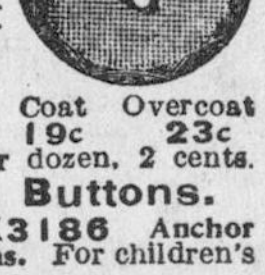

No. 18K3182 Real Vegetable Ivory Buttons, fancy design, dull finish; suitable for the highest grade tailor made clothing. Black only. Come in sizes as follows: State size wanted.
Sizes..................Vest Coat Overcoat
Price, per DOZEN 14c 19c 23c
If by mail, postage extra, per dozen, 2 cents.

Brass Buttons.

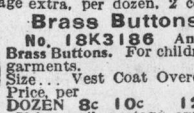

No. 18K3186 Anchor Brass Buttons. For children's garments.
Size... Vest Coat Overcoat
Price, per
DOZEN 8c 10c 12c
If by mail, postage extra, per dozen, 2 cents.

Agate Buttons

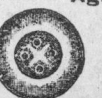

No. 18K3190 Plain White Agate Buttons. See button scale for sizes. State size wanted.
Size, lines...... 16 20 24 28 30
Price, per GROSS. 4c 7c 9c 10c 11c
If by mail, postage extra, per gross, 4c to 12c.

No. 18K3194 Fancy White Pearl Agate Buttons.
Size, lines 16 20 24 28
Price, per
GROSS, 8c 13c 15c 19c
If by mail, postage extra, per gross, 4 to 12 cents.

Thumb and Finger Automatic Button.

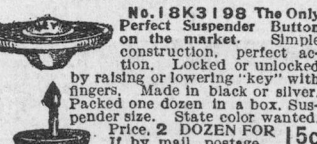

No. 18K3198 The Only Perfect Suspender Button on the market. Simple construction, perfect action. Locked or unlocked by raising or lowering "key" with fingers. Made in black or silver. Packed one dozen in a box. Suspender size. State color wanted.
Price, 2 DOZEN FOR 15c
If by mail, postage extra, two boxes, 3 cents.

Washburne Bachelor Buttons.

No. 18K3202 Washburne Bachelor Buttons. Can be adjusted instantly and removed just as quickly. Comes in blue steel or nickel. State color wanted. Price, PER SET OF 6........... 17c
If by mail, postage extra, per set, 2 cents.

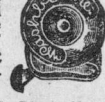

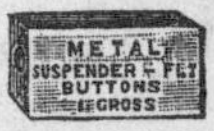

No. 18K3210 Black Metal Buttons, small or fly size.
Price, per GROSS........ 7c
If by mail, postage extra, 4 cents.

No. 18K3214 Black Metal Buttons, suspender size. Per GROSS........ 9c
If by mail, postage extra, 4 cents.

No. 18K3218 Brass Fly Buttons, best quality. Price, per GROSS....... 10c
If by mail, postage extra, 5 cents.

No. 18K3222 Brass Suspender Buttons, best quality. Per GROSS..... 12c
If by mail, postage extra, 5 cents.

Bone Pants Buttons.

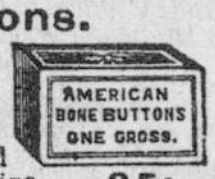

No. 18K3226 Universal Bone Pants Buttons. Black or white; used extensively for underwear, etc. Put up one gross in box, state size and color wanted
Price, per GROSS, suspender size.... 25c
Price, per GROSS, fly size.......... 20c
If by mail, postage extra, per gross, 5 cents.
Pants buttons are put up in one gross boxes. We do not sell less than one box.

Patent Collar and Cuff Button.

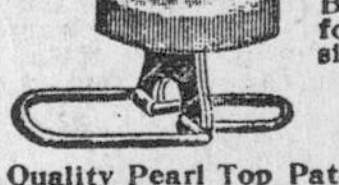

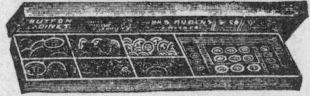

No. 18K3230 Heavy Bone Top Patent Button for Collars and Cuffs. The simplest to adjust.
Price, per DOZEN, 9c

No. 18K3234 Extra Quality Pearl Top Patent Collar and Cuff Buttons. Same style as No. 18K3230.
Price, 6 FOR........................ 17c
If by mail, postage extra, per dozen, 2 cents.

Button Cabinet.

No. 18K3238 Handy Button Cabinet. A button for every emergency. This cabinet is made up for family use, with complete assortment of different style buttons; such as are necessary every day. The cabinet contains assorted sizes of each style of button and consists of: 2 dozen pearl buttons, 2 dozen agate buttons, 1½ dozen ivoreen buttons, 1 dozen trousers buttons, 1 dozen bone buttons, 1 dozen covered buttons, making 8½ dozen in all. We offer THIS ENTIRE CABINET FOR.................. 25c
If by mail, postage extra, 7 cents.

THE SPLENDID REDUCTIONS IN PRICE made by us in this catalogue must prove to our customers our ability to undersell all competition.

WE OFFER ON PAGE 999 BEAUTIFUL STYLES IN LADIES' BELTS AT MANUFACTURERS' COST PLUS ONLY ONE SMALL PERCENTAGE OF PROFIT.

OUR DEPARTMENT OF HUMAN HAIR GOODS

OF SPECIAL INTEREST TO EVERY WOMAN

A BEAUTIFUL HEAD OF HAIR IS A WOMAN'S CROWNING BEAUTY. OUR REMARKABLE HAIR GOODS OFFER ENABLES EVERY WOMAN TO OWN AN ELEGANT SWITCH, POMPADOUR OR WIG AT THE ABSOLUTE COST OF PRODUCTION, PLUS ONLY OUR ONE SMALL PERCENTAGE OF PROFIT. AT PRICES SO LOW THAT THEY ARE WITHIN REACH OF ALL.

DON'T PAY THE FANCY PRICES asked by hair goods establishments elsewhere; let us furnish you a switch, wig or pompadour of genuine human hair of the best guaranteed quality obtainable, at just merely the cost of production, with but our one bare small margin of profit added, just on the same basis as that upon which we sell all the merchandise in this catalogue. If you buy hair goods elsewhere you cannot obtain any finer qualities at any price than we offer right here, and you have to pay big profits, for other hair dealers never offer an article of this character without making an enormous profit. By the very nature of this line of merchandise it is possible for dealers to make bigger profits than on other lines. But we ask only a fraction of the profit on each article that others take, and by selling enormous quantities on the smallest margin of profit ever asked, we can save you big money on hair goods of all kinds.

DON'T BE TEMPTED TO BUY INFERIOR HAIR GOODS at any price, as they are manufactured and dyed to the desired shade. This manufactured hair does not wear well or give satisfaction. Many unscrupulous firms advertise manufactured hair goods at seemingly low prices. Remember that the best is the cheapest in the long run. We guarantee our hair switches, wigs, puffs and pompadours to be made under perfect sanitary conditions and of the best quality human hair. Hair blended by experts to match your sample.

TIME REQUIRED TO FILL ORDERS FOR HAIR GOODS. It takes from five to eight days to make a hair switch, and from ten to twenty days to make a wig. Whenever it is possible to ship the goods in a shorter time, we will, of course, always do so.

HOW TO ORDER HAIR GOODS. Give the catalogue number of the switch, wig or pompadour you wish, mention the size or length you want, send us a large sized sample of your hair, cut as close to the roots as possible, so we can give you a perfect match all the way through, enclose our price, and the required postage extra, 5 cents, 10 cents, or whatever amount is mentioned as the postage on the article, and we will send you the switch, wig or pompadour ordered, by mail, postpaid. We positively guarantee it to match your hair perfectly and to be in every way satisfactory, or you may return it to us at our expense and we will refund your money.

SPECIAL CAUTION. No greases or oil should be used on a hair switch. If your hair switch begins to fade. we advise you to wash it in a solution of cold tea which is very beneficial in restoring it to its original color. By following this suggestion carefully you will surely get complete satisfaction from any hair goods you may buy from us.

WE DO NOT GUARANTEE HAIR SWITCHES AGAINST FADING.

Experience teaches that the hair on the head fades and changes color, which is equally true of the hair switches. No person can guarantee even the best switches against fading. The length of time they will wear and keep from fading depends entirely upon the care they receive.

WE DO NOT MAKE HAIR SWITCHES TO ORDER FROM COMBINGS UNDER ANY CIRCUMSTANCES, AND DO NOT BUY COMBINGS.

Ordinary Shade Hair Switches.

No. 18K4370 This is a short stemmed switch with the exception of the 2-ounce, 20-inch length, which is a long stemmed switch. The prices quoted are for ordinary shades of hair only.

Weight	Length	Price	Weight	Length	Price
2 ounces	20 inches	$0.49	3 ounces	24 inches	$1.65
2 ounces	20 inches	.78	3 ounces	26 inches	2.43
2 ounces	22 inches	.99	4 ounces	28 inches	3.48
8 ounces	22 inches	1.23			

Be Sure to Send Sample of Hair.

Our Extra Quality Hair Switches.

No. 18K4371 No better switches can be sold at any price than this, our XX quality. Don't imagine that because our prices are extremely low our qualities are inferior. We positively guarantee our XX quality to give absolute satisfaction. You can wear this switch 30 days and if you are not perfectly satisfied with it you can return it to us at our expense and we will refund your money or exchange for other merchandise, all transportation charges paid by us. These are all short stemmed switches, in three braids. We strongly recommend these switches as a much better value at a slightly higher price than our No. 18K4370.

Weight	Length	Price	Weight	Length	Price
2 ounces	20 inches	$0.98	3 ounces	24 inches	$2.10
2 ounces	22 inches	1.25	3 ounces	26 inches	3.25
8 ounces	22 inches	1.55	4 ounces	28 inches	4.10

The above prices are for ordinary shades of hair. If your hair is blonde, red, drab or gray shade order them from Nos. 18K4373 or 18K4374.

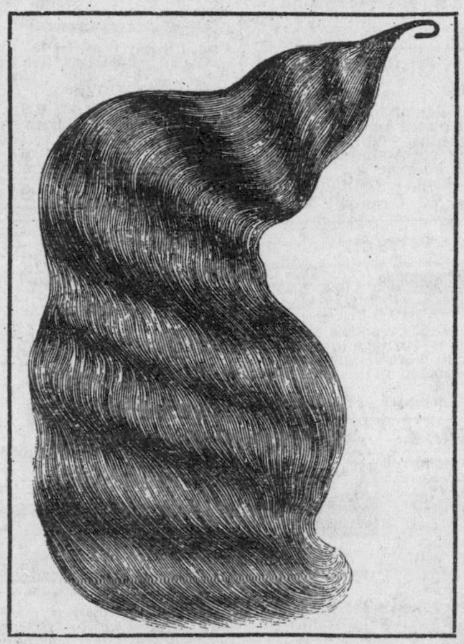

No. 18K4373

Red, blonde for drab shades. Finest quality genuine human hair. Short stems.

Weight	Length	Price	Weight	Length	Price
1½ ounces	18 inches	$1.58	3 ounces	23 inches	$3.48
2 ounces	20 inches	2.29	3 ounces	25 inches	4.47
2½ ounces	22 inches	2.83	3 ounces	27 inches	5.98

No. 18K4374

Gray or gray mixed Switches containing up to three quarters gray hair.

Weight	Length	Price	Weight	Length	Price
1½ ounces	18 inches	$2.19	3 ounces	23 inches	$4.39
2 ounces	20 inches	2.95	3 ounces	25 inches	6.67
2½ ounces	22 inches	3.68	3½ ounces	27 inches	8.89

No. 18K4375

From three-quarters gray up to all white hair switches.

Weight	Length	Price	Weight	Length	Price
1½ ounces	18 inches	$2.88	3 ounces	23 inches	$5.49
2 ounces	20 inches	3.49	3 ounces	25 inches	6.98
2¼ ounces	22 inches	4.18	3½ ounces	27 inches	9.86

No. 18K4377

Natural wavy best quality French hair, short stem switches.

Weight	Length	Price	Weight	Length	Price
1 ounce	18 inches	$1.88	2 ounces	22 inches	$4.95
1 ounce	20 inches	2.29	2½ ounces	24 inches	6.79
1½ ounces	20 inches	3.15	2¾ ounces	26 inches	8.25

Don't forget to send sample of hair.

Pompadours.

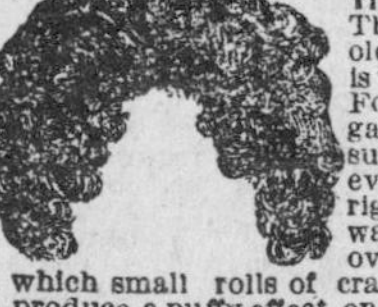

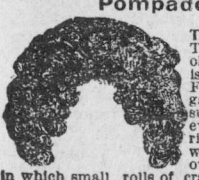

No. 18K4390 The Pompadour. This style, unlike the old style pompadour, is very light in weight. For simplicity, elegance and style is far superior to anything ever shown. It slips right on. The soft wavy hair is combed over one's own hair in which small rolls of crape hair are placed to produce a puffy effect on sides and top.

Price $3.50
Gray or blonde hair 5.75
If by mail, postage extra, each, 8 cents.

No. 18K4394 The Patent Pompadour. It produces the fluffy fullness now so much in vogue. It is made on twisted wire, of the best long hair and weighs only half an ounce. Can be worn with just the ends concealed under the lady's own hair, or may be used in place of the rolls and the wavy ends coiled in with the natural hair. Send Sample of Hair.

Price $1.98
Blonde or gray hair 3.48
If by mail, postage extra, each, 6 cents.

No. 18K4401 Puff Curls, the latest styles of hair dressing. Can be used as puffs or curls as desired. Made of French curly hair to be interlaced with the coiffure or worn in the back.

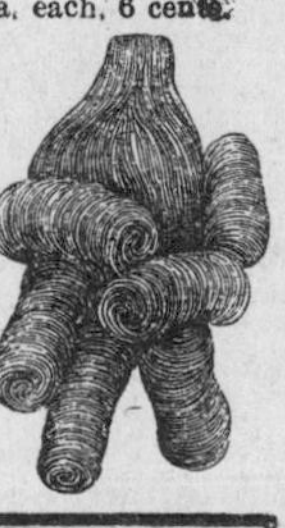

Price, for ordinary shades $2.98
Gray, blonde or drab $4.38
If by mail, postage extra, 6 cents.

THE SURPRISINGLY LOW REDUCED PRICES prevailing in this catalogue mean greater savings to our customers than ever before.

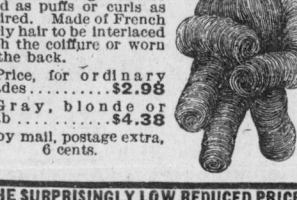

Puffs.

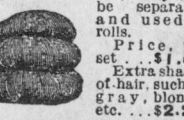

No. 18K4402 Puffs, three in a set. Can be curled over the finger and arranged through the hair, to make a stylish headdress; may also be separated and used as rolls.

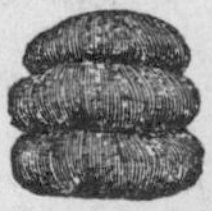

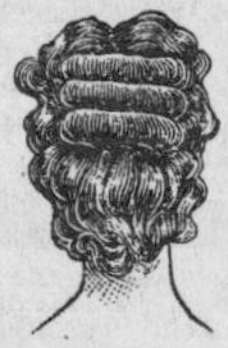

Price, per set ... $1.50
Extra shades of hair, such as gray, blonde, etc. ... $2.25
If by mail, postage extra, 7 cents.

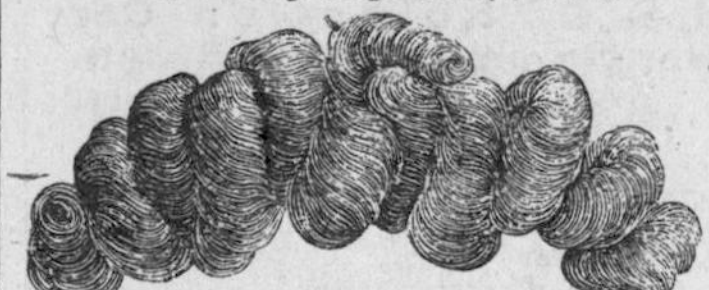

No. 18K4403 Coronet Puffs. Made of natural wavy French hair. Very stylish and beautiful hair dressing to be worn in front or back, as desired.

Price, for ordinary shades $2.98
Gray, blonde or drab 4.48
If by mail, postage extra, 10 cents.

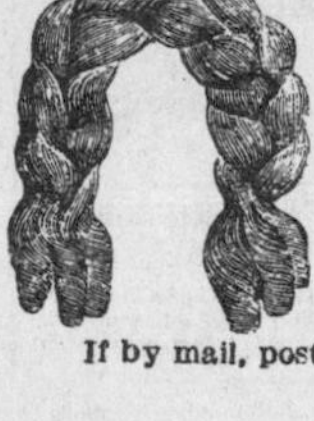

No. 18K4405

Full Coronet Braid. Very stylish and popular. Made of natural wavy French hair with curly ends. Ordinary shades usually sold at $10.00.

Our price, ordinary shades $5.99
Extra shades, 8.67
If by mail, postage extra, 10 cents.

WIGS.

ALL WIGS, TOUPEES, WAVES, ETC., BEING MADE TO ORDER, WE ASK FIVE TO TEN DAYS' TIME IN FILLING YOUR ORDER.

How to Measure All Wigs.

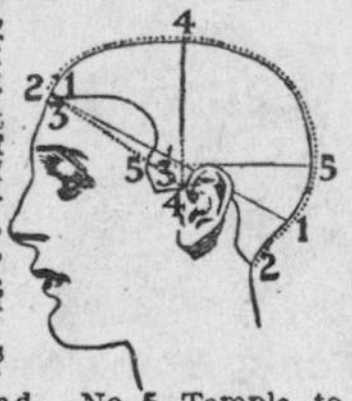

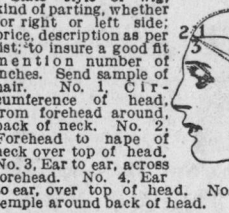

State style of wig, kind of parting, whether for right or left side; price, description as per list; to insure a good fit mention number of inches. Send sample of hair. No. 1, Circumference of head, from forehead around, back of neck. No. 2, Forehead to nape of neck over top of head. No. 3, Ear to ear, across forehead. No. 4, Ear to ear, over top of head. No. 5, Temple to temple around back of head.

Ladies' Wigs—Long Hair.

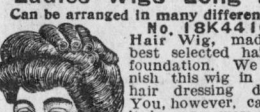

Can be arranged in many different ways.

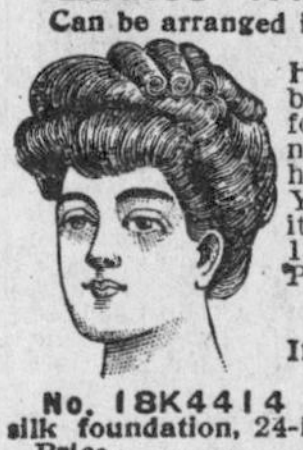

No. 18K4410 Long Hair Wig, made of the best selected hair on silk foundation. We will furnish this wig in any style hair dressing desired. You, however, can arrange it in any way you wish. 18-inch hair.

Price $16.25
Red, gray or blonde $24.75
If by mail, postage extra, 10 cents.

No. 18K4414 Made same as above on silk foundation, 24-inch hair.

Price $19.95
Red, gray or blonde 29.50
If by mail, postage extra, 10 cents.

Gentlemen's Wigs.

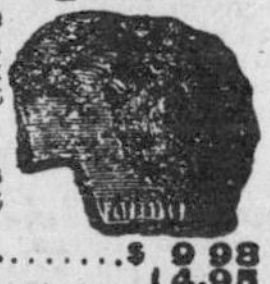

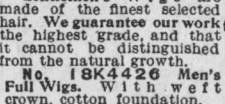

Gentlemen's Wigs are made of the finest selected hair. We guarantee our work the highest grade, and that it cannot be distinguished from the natural growth.

No. 18K4426 Men's Full Wigs. With weft crown, cotton foundation.

Price $9.98
Gray, red or blonde 14.95

No. 18K4430 Men's Full Wigs. Gauze or silk parting. Price $13.50
Gray, red or blonde 19.98

No. 18K4434 Men's Wigs. Ventilated, with hair net parting. The finest wig that money can buy. Price $23.48
Gray, red or blonde 31.50
If by mail, postage extra, each, 8 cents.

Toupees.

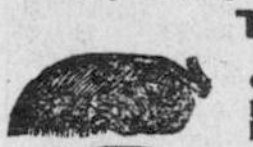

To measure for a Toupee or top piece, cut a piece of paper the exact size of the bald spot, mark the crown and parting, enclose a lock of hair, and state if hair is to be straight or curly.

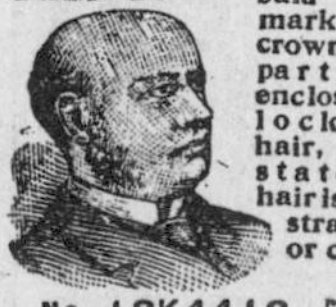

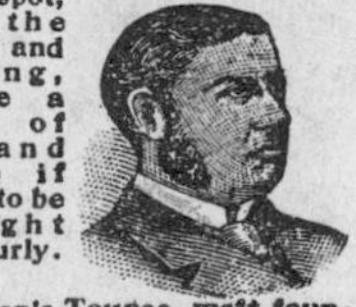

No. 18K4418 Men's Toupee, weft foundation on a cotton net and weft parting suitable for ordinary wear. Price $6.49
Red, gray or blonde 8.97
If by mail, postage extra, 8 cents.

No. 18K4422 Men's Toupee made of finest selected hair, ventilated foundation with natural parting, showing scalp through.

Price $12.75
Red, gray or blonde 17.50
If by mail, postage extra, 8 cents.

Toupee Paste.

No. 18K4423 Toupee Paste, which is used to keep toupee in place; heat and apply. Price, per stick 42c
If by mail, postage extra, 5 cents.

Remember, we guarantee a perfect fit and match if you follow instructions, or your money back.

HIGHEST GRADE STAPLE NOTIONS AT LOWER PRICES THAN EVER BEFORE.

SMALL WARES.

In notions we can save you lots of money. All items on these pages are the most reliable and dependable kind.

Thimbles.

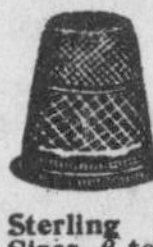

No. 18K3401 Aluminum Thimbles, come one dozen in a box, style like illustration. Assorted sizes, 7 to 10.
Price, PER DOZEN 7c
If by mail, postage extra, per dozen, 1 cent.

No. 18K3408 Genuine Sterling Silver Thimbles. 25-cent value. Sizes, 6 to 11. State size wanted.
Price, each 15c
If by mail, postage extra, 1 cent.

Milliners' Needles.

No. 18K3416 Milliners' Needles. The highest grade, each paper worth 10 cents. Nos. 4, 5, 6 and 7. State size wanted.
Price, for 2 PAPERS 9c
If by mail, postage extra, 3 cents.

Superior Helix Needles.

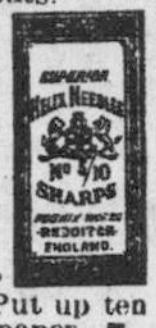

No. 18K3420 The best Helix Needles, made in Redditch, England. Sold elsewhere at 5 cents a paper. All sizes, sharps and betweens. Be sure to give size wanted.
Price for 2 PAPERS 5c
If by mail, postage extra, 1 cent.

Darning Needles.

No. 18K3424 Cloth Stuck. Put up ten to the paper; assorted sizes in each paper.
Price, for 2 PAPERS 5c
If by mail, postage extra, 3 cents.

Knitting Needles.

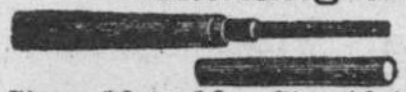

No. 18K3428 Put up five to the set, in wood case. Sizes, 10 to 16. Size 10 is coarsest, size 16 is finest. State size wanted. Price, per set, ... 3c
If by mail, postage extra, per set, 3c.

Crochet Hook Set.

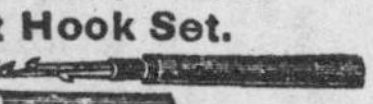

No. 18K3432 Consists of two steel and one bone crochet hooks, put up in round cabinet case.
Price, per set 4c
If by mail, postage extra, per set, 2c.

Wooden Crochet Hooks.

No. 18K3436 Wooden Crochet Hooks. Used to crochet Shetland shawls. Come in three sizes, fine, medium, and large.
Price, per set of 3 NEEDLES 14c
If by mail, postage extra, per set, 4 cents.

Complete Needle Case, 8c.

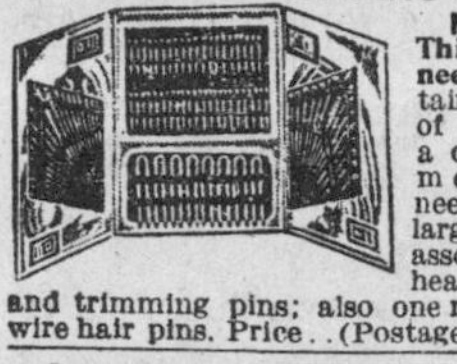

No. 18K3448 This most complete needle case contains four papers of sewing needles, a complete assortment of other needles. It has a large and complete assortment of jet head, toilet, veiling and trimming pins; also one row of black wire hair pins. Price..(Postage extra, 4c) 8c

Ladies' Work Basket, 55c.

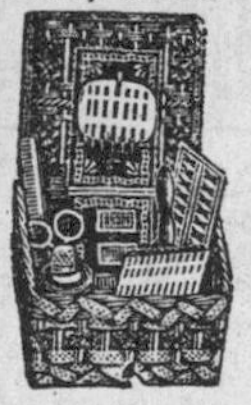

No. 18K3452 The basket is a square shape of fancy imported satin straws, woven in rustic design, with attached lid. Size, 6½x6½x3¾ inches. Contains the following articles: One pair of scissors, four papers of needles with an assortment of needles for darning and fancy work, one dozen shawl pins, one piece mending tissue, one egg darner for gloves and hosiery, one tape measure, one aluminum thimble, one card hooks and eyes, one spool machine thread, one spool linen finished thread, and one spool darning cotton. The basket and contents, at regular retail prices, are worth over $1.00. Weight, packed for shipment, 1½ pounds. Price, 55c

Handy Work Basket, $1.00.

No. 18K3456 Mothers' Handy Work Basket should be in every home. Beautiful fancy basket. Size, 9x9x4½ inches, drawn with ribbons, bottom tufted with satin. Contains the following immense assortment: Pair scissors, egg darner, tape measure, aluminum thimble, two papers of needles, assortment of crewel needles for fancy work, an assortment of pins, hair pins and toilet pins, three crochet hooks, one card hooks and eyes, one dozen black headed shawl pins, one piece mending tissue, one 50-yard spool of silk, two spools machine thread, one spool heavy linen finished thread, two spools darning cotton, one spool red embroidery cotton. Shipping weight, 2½ pounds. Price $1.00

O. K. Skirt Marker and Gauge.

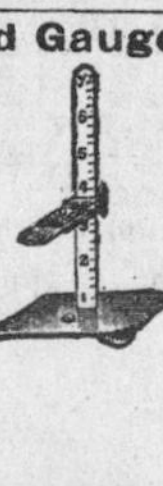

No. 18K3458 Made of solid metal, nickel plated, therefore indestructible. The O. K. Marker measures correctly the distance from the floor to hem of skirt by means of an adjustable gauge, measurements as desired, marking a thin chalk line which insures a perfect fitting skirt. Shipping weight, 1 pound. Price 39c

Tape Measure.

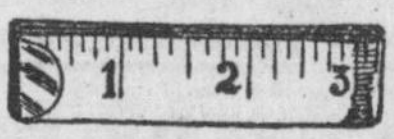

4c

No. 18K3466 Non-Stretchable Tape Measure, made of imported cloth. Will always retain actual measurements, very durable. Length, 60 inches.
Price, each 4c
If by mail, postage extra, 1 cent.

The Mercedes Plaiter.

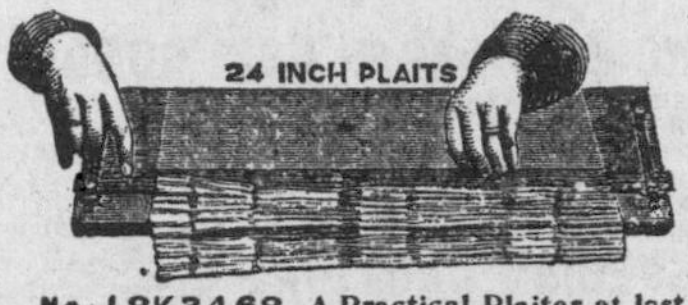

No. 18K3468 A Practical Plaiter at last, and at a price within the reach of all. This is the only machine selling for less than $150.00 that is capable of making perfect plaits up to 24 inches. The Mercedes Plaiter is recommended by all the leading dressmakers, and is indispensable to those wishing a high grade plaiting machine at a price which is less than you would have to pay for having a single garment plaited. Put up in neat box and contains 48 heavily nickeled steel wires 24 inches long, and also directions showing the simplicity in operating this really wonderful machine. Shipping weight, 2¼ pounds. Regular retail price, $3.00.
Our price $1.89

Stocking and Glove Darner.

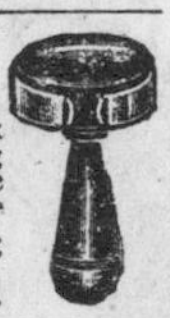

No. 18K3474 Made of black ebonized wood, nickel plated spring to hold stocking or other fabric firmly in place. Does not require to be adjusted until work is completed. Price 8c
If by mail, postage extra, 4 cents.

Tracing Wheel.

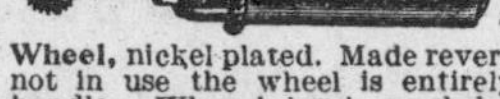

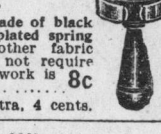

No. 18K3478 Metal Handle Tracing Wheel, nickel plated. Made reversible, so when not in use the wheel is entirely inclosed in handle. When lying in work basket will not injure or become entangled with other articles. Price 8c
If by mail, postage extra, 2 cents.

Adamantine Pins.

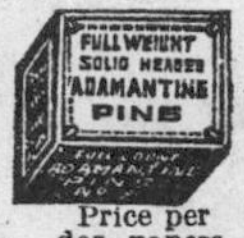

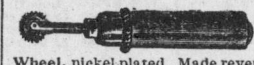

No. 18K3486 Adamantine Pins are put up one dozen papers to the package. State size wanted. Shipping weight, 16 ounces.

Size.	Postage if by mail.	Price per doz. papers.
No. 3, Medium,	14c	15c
No. 2, Large,	15c	17c

No. 18K3494 Ne Plus Ultra Brass Pins. This is the best high grade English pin, with finest needle points. 360 pins on each paper.

Size	M. C. Large	S. C. Medium	F3½ Small
Price, for 3 PAPERS	12c	10c	9c

If by mail, postage extra, 5 cents.

No. 18K3498 The Washington Needle Point Adamantine Pin, polished solid heads. Contains 400 pins to the paper. Put up in gilt edged papers. Shipping weight, 21 ounces. Price, per DOZEN PAPERS 23c

Pin Books.

No. 18K3506 Pin Books, contain 240 pins assorted three sizes, eight rows of 30 pins each, one row is black; all Ne Plus Ultra high grade brass pins.
Price, for 3 BOOKS 11c
If by mail, postage extra, 6 cents.

Fancy Black and Colored Head Pins.

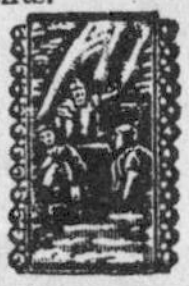

No. 18K3518 Fancy Chromo Pins. Card contains 42 jet head assorted size black pins.
Price, for 3 CARDS (126 pins) 10c
If by mail, postage extra, 3 cents.

18 Gold Pins, 11 Cents.

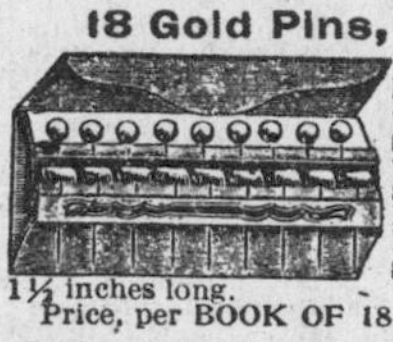

No. 18K3520 French Pin Book. Contains eighteen gold pins, nine of which have a T shaped head and nine have a round shaped head. They are solid gold plated and are 1½ inches long.
Price, per BOOK OF 18 PINS 11c
Postage extra, 2 cents.

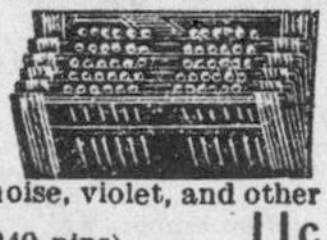

No. 18K3522 Toilet Pins. This is an entirely new pin put up in neat book form, containing about 80 assorted colored head toilet pins. In white, turquoise, violet, and other shades.
Price, for 3 BOOKS (240 pins) 11c
If by mail, postage extra, 4 cents.

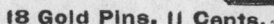

Pearl Lace Pins.

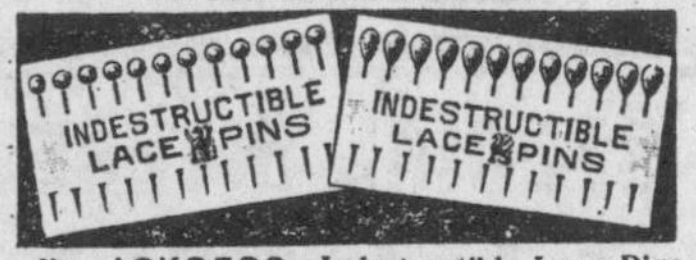

No. 18K3530 Indestructible Lace Pins, round or pear shaped heads, convenient and handy. Regular size, length, 1½ inches. Colors, pearl, pink, lavender or turquoise. State color wanted. Price, for 3 DOZEN 11c
If by mail, postage extra, 3 cents.

No. 18K3534 Cube Pins. Assorted colors. Cube containing 100 pins; black, white and fancy colored heads.
Price, for 2 CUBES (200 pins) 9c
If by mail, postage extra, 2 cents.

No. 18K3538 White Head Toilet Pins. Cube like above containing 100 solid white head toilet pins. Price, 2 CUBES for 11c
If by mail, postage extra, 2 cents.

No. 18K3546 Safety Pin Book, contains two dozen small, medium and large assorted sensible nickeled safety pins. Price, per book, 5c
If by mail, postage extra, 2 cents.

A Sensible Safety Pin.

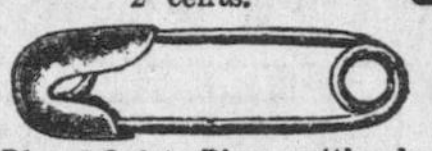

No. 18K3550 Polished Nickel Plated Safety Pins, with double sided shield. We do not sell less than 3 dozen of a number.

	No. 1	No. 2	No. 3
Price, 3 DOZEN	5c	7c	8c

No. 18K3554 Black Japanned Safety Pins. Shields open both sides, as above. Superior quality.

	No. 1	No. 2	No. 3
Price, for 3 DOZEN	5c	7c	8c

If by mail, postage extra, per 3 doz., 3 cents.

Corset Steels.

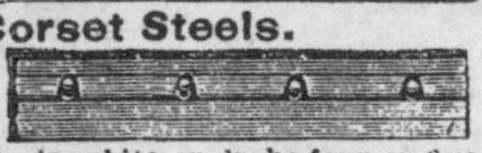

No. 18K3566 Fine French Sateen Covered Corset Steels, in white or drab; four or five hooks. State color wanted. Price, per pair, 8c
If by mail, postage extra, per pair, 6c.

No. 18K3570 The Neverbreak Corset Lace. White or black. State color wanted. 2½ yards long. Price, for 6 LACES 13c
If by mail, postage extra, 2 cents.

Nail Clipper

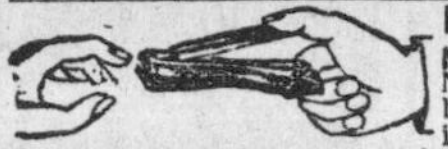

No. 18K3580 Nail Clipper. The best thing ever invented for the purpose. Made of fine steel, nickel plated.
Price 20c
If by mail, postage extra, 2 cents.

Trousers or Skirt Hanger.

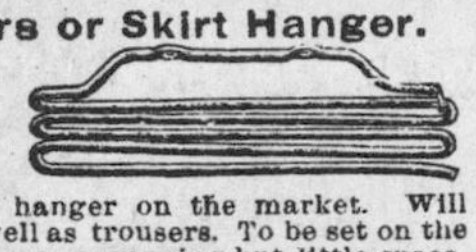

No. 18K3586 The Setwell Trousers or Skirt Hanger. This is the most desirable hanger on the market. Will hold skirts as well as trousers. To be set on the inside of the door, occupying but little space. Holds four garments. Made of 5-16-inch copper Bessemer steel wire, heavily nickel plated, highly finished. Screws attached to each set. Shipping weight, 1½ pounds. Price 22c

Trousers Stretchers and Hangers.

33c FOR 2

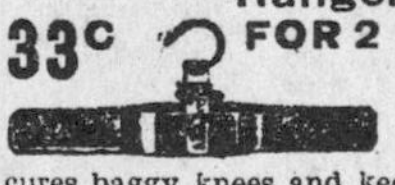

No. 18K3590 The "Setwell" Trousers Stretcher and Pants Hanger. Makes wrinkled clothes smooth, cures baggy knees and keeps your trousers in shape. Made of best steel, heavily nickel plated. The best hanger on the market today. Price, per set (2 HANGERS) 33c
If by mail, postage extra, per set, 12 cents.

Ideal Combination Coat Hanger and Clothes Brush.

25c

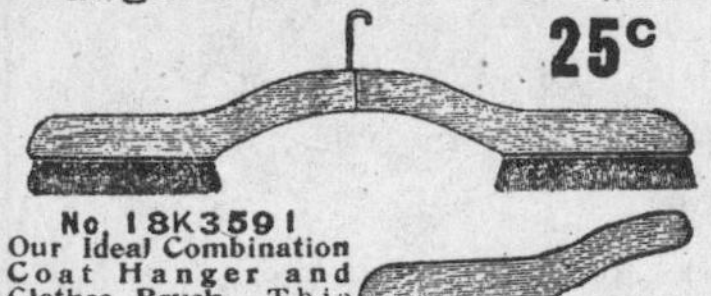

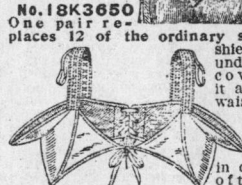

No. 18K3591 Our Ideal Combination Coat Hanger and Clothes Brush. This coat hanger can be folded in the center into a complete hat and clothes brush. The cleverest invention of the year. The Ideal is made of solid maple, and is fitted on each side with a good quality genuine bristle brush. Regular 50-cent article. Our price, 25c
If by mail, postage extra, 8 cents.

Skirt Hanger.

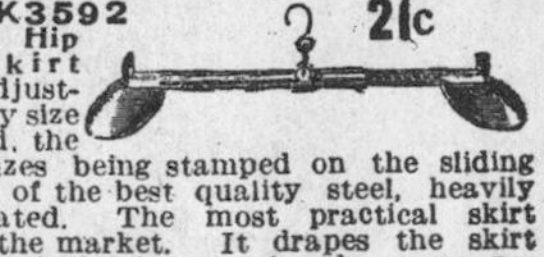

No. 18K3592 The Model Hip to Hip Skirt Hanger, adjustable to any size skirt band, the different sizes being stamped on the sliding bar; made of the best quality steel, heavily nickel plated. The most practical skirt holder on the market. It drapes the skirt over the steel hips in exactly the same position it is in when worn. It is the only skirt hanger having this feature. Price 21c
If by mail, postage extra, 13 cents.

"Cosy Corner" Wardrobe Rack.

$1.33

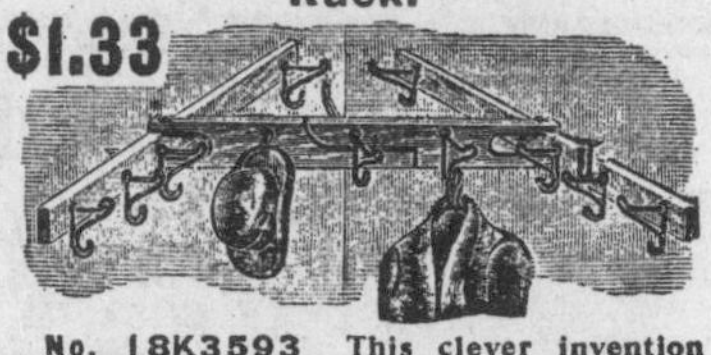

No. 18K3593 This clever invention does away with the old fashioned wardrobe, destroying of walls, etc. No wooden backing required. Can be put on a plastered and papered wall without marring the surface at all. It is put up without the use of nails, hooks or screws; and when sprung into position holds a weight of 200 pounds. It takes but a minute to put it up and a few seconds to take it down. A feature of the rack is its beauty when used with drapery as an ornament to the room. Is made of the finest quality oak, golden finish, hooks and drape rod made of cold rolled steel, beautifully nickeled. Full instructions for use with each rack. Shipping weight, 12 pounds.
Price, complete $1.33

Special "Setwell" Set, 95c.

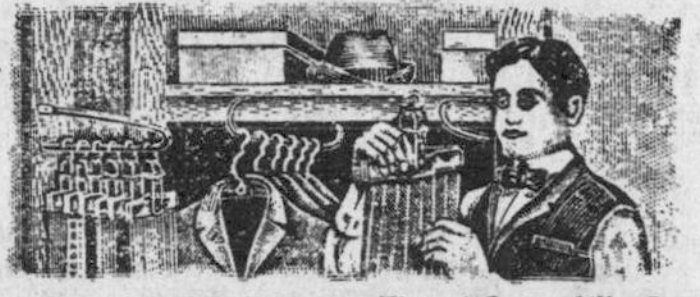

No. 18K3594 The "Setwell" Set Trousers Stretcher and Hanger. Set complete consists of three trousers hangers, same as No. 18K3590, three shaped coat hangers, one shelf bar which will hold four garments, one door loop, with screws and directions how to use. Made of best steel, heavily nickel plated. Shipping weight, 2¾ pounds.
Price, per set, complete 95c

Brush Braid.

No. 18K3626 S., R. & Co.'s Brush Braid and Skirt Protector. We guarantee this braid all wool, heavier than other makes and the best at any price. Colors, black and staple colors. State color wanted.
Price, per piece, 5 YARDS 19c
If by mail, postage extra, per piece, 3 cents.

Skirt Binding.

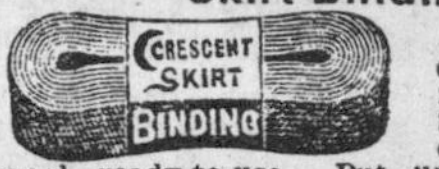

No. 18K3634 Crescent Mohair Skirt Binding. Steam shrunk, dyed in the wool, ready to use. Put up in full 5-yard pieces, enough for a skirt. Colors, black, white, brown, navy, tan, gray, red or green. State color wanted.
Price, per piece 10c
If by mail, postage extra, per piece, 2 cents.

The Kleinert's Simplex Shield and Corset Protector, 46c.

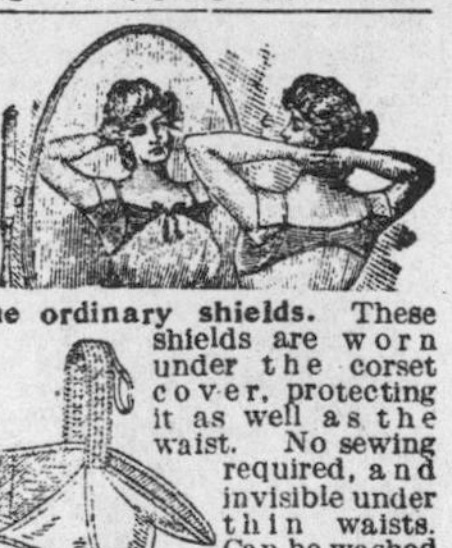

No. 18K3650 One pair replaces 12 of the ordinary shields. These shields are worn under the corset cover, protecting it as well as the waist. No sewing required, and invisible under thin waists. Can be washed in cold water as often as desired. State size wanted.

Bust measure,	28-30	32-34	36-38	40-42-44
Size, No.	2	3	4	5

Price, per pair 46c
If by mail, postage extra, per pair, 3c.

Tade Dress and Corset Protector, 75c.

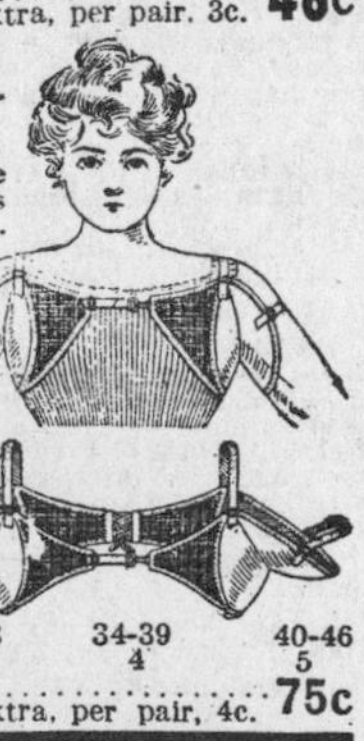

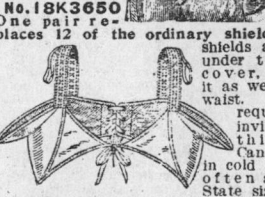

No. 18K3654 The Tade Ventilated Dress and Corset Protector. A complete garment to be worn under the corset, protecting it as well as the waist. Easily removed and washed, being adjustable. One pair will replace 12 pairs of regular dress shields. State size wanted.

Bust measure,	23-33	34-39	40-46
Size, No.	3	4	5

Price, per pair 75c
If by mail, postage extra, per pair, 4c.

NO SUCH PRICE REDUCTIONS have ever been made by any firm or individual as we have made in the pages of this Big Catalogue on the HIGHEST GRADE MERCHANDISE.

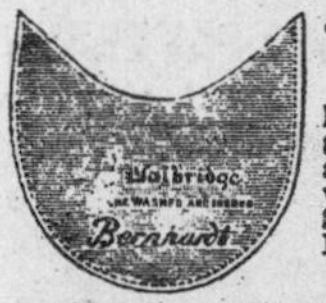

The Bernhardt.

No. 18K3656 Fine Nainsook Dress Shield, guaranteed waterproof and odorless. State size wanted.

Size.... 2 3 4
Per pair 8c 10c 12c
Postage extra, 3 cents.

Kleinert's Dress Shields.

EXQUISITE

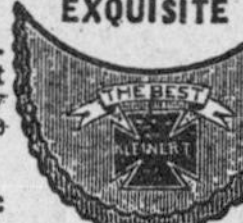

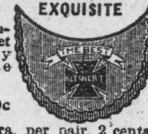

No. 18K3662 Kleinert's Exquisite Stockinet Dress Shields. Every pair warranted. State size wanted.

Size, No. 2 3 4
Per pair 15c 17c 19c

If by mail, postage extra, per pair, 2 cents.

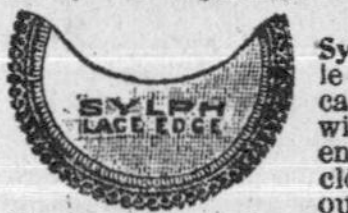

No. 18K3671 The Sylph Shield. For lingerie waists; made of fine cambric and trimmed with a good quality Valenciennes lace, rubber cloth lining and thoroughly cemented seams. Guaranteed waterproof. Can be washed and ironed.

Size, No......... 2 3 4
Price, per pair.... 20c 22c 24c
If by mail, postage extra, per pair, 2 cents.

The S. H. & M. Dress Shields.

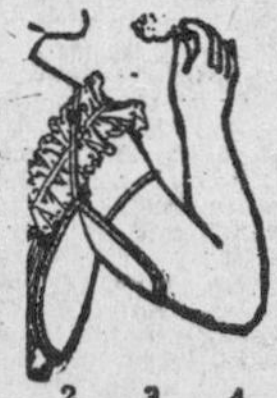

No. 18K3676 The S. H. & M. Light Weight Dress Shield. Especially adapted for shirt waists. Made of the light, strong, waterproof nainsook, adjustable, washable, requires no sewing, most perfect fitting dress shield made, clings to the arm and does not wrinkle. Comes in three sizes. State size wanted.

Size, No. 2 3 4
Price, per pair........20c 23c 25c
If by mail, postage extra, per pair, 2 cents.

Invisible Ball and Socket Fastener.

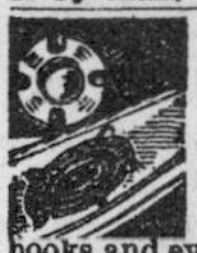

No. 18K3682 This Invisible Sew-on Ball and Socket Fastener. Easy to open. Easy to close. The best made. Skirt size. Never rusts. Used instead of hooks and eyes. Silvered or japanned.
Price, 2 DOZEN FOR............ 11c

No. 18K3686 Invisible Ball and Socket Fastener, small size, used for collars, waists, etc. Same style as above.
Price, 2 DOZEN FOR................ 11c
If by mail, postage extra, 2 cents.

Hold-Fast Skirt Supporter.

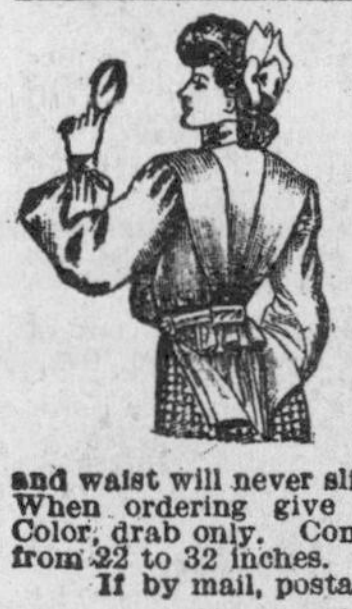

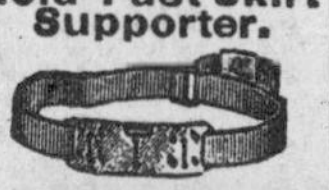

No. 18K3694 Hold-Fast Skirt Supporter and Waist Holder. It is absolutely self adjusting, does not require any hooks, buttons or anything else to be sewed on the skirt or waist. Your skirt and waist will never slip with Hold-Fast Belt. When ordering give your waist measure. Color, drab only. Comes in even sizes from 22 to 32 inches. Price.......... 17c
If by mail, postage extra, 2 cents.

The Disc Belt.

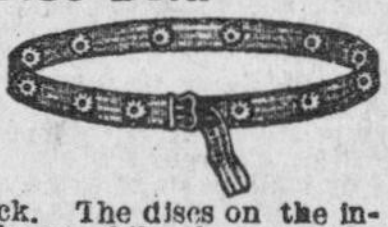

No. 18K3702 The Disc Belt. The only supporter that holds your shirtwaist and skirt in place all the way around, the others do so only in the back. The discs on the inside hold the waist down while those on the outside hold the skirt up. The discs will not rust. Colors, black or white, all sizes. State size and color wanted. Price.... 15c
If by mail, postage extra, 2 cents.

Invisible Eyes and Hooks.

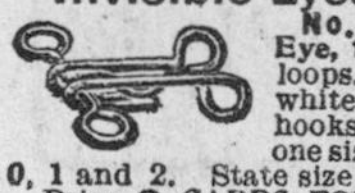

No. 18K3703 Invisible Eye, takes the place of silk loops. Colors, black or white. Put up two dozen hooks and two dozen eyes of one size to the card. Sizes, 0, 1 and 2. State size and color wanted.
Price, 2 CARDS FOR............ 9c
If by mail, postage extra, 2 cents.

Six Dozen Hooks and Eyes, 10c.

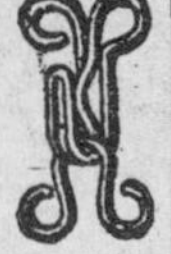

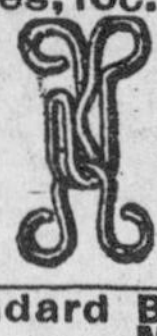

No. 18K3718 The Special Hook and Eye (with a perfect hump). Made of best brass wire, nonrustable, highly finished, silvered or japanned. Two dozen on card. Sizes, 2, 3 and 4. State size and color wanted.
Price, 3 CARDS FOR.... 10c
If by mail, postage extra, 3 cards, 3 cents.

EUREKA SEWING SILK.

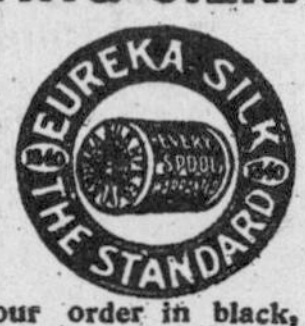

Eureka Silk is warranted full size and full length. We consider it the best silk made. Black spool silks are marked 00, 0, A, B, C and D. No. 00 is the finest; No. 0 is the next coarser, etc. Colored spool silks come in letter A only. If you need only a few colors in threads, fill out the balance of your order in black, thus taking advantage of our unequaled price by the dozen.

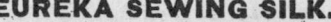

No. 18K3739 Eureka Sewing Silk, 50-yard spools, black, white and all colors. State color wanted. Price, PER DOZEN 45c
If by mail, postage extra, per dozen, 5 cents.

No. 18K3740 Eureka Sewing Silk, 100-yard spools, black, white and all colors. State color wanted. Price, PER DOZEN 85c
If by mail, postage extra, per dozen, 5 cents.

No. 18K3741 Eureka Buttonhole Twist, 10-yard spools, black, white and all colors. State color wanted. Price, 6 SPOOLS... 10c
If by mail, postage extra, per ½ dozen, 2 cents.

Mercerized Machine Thread.

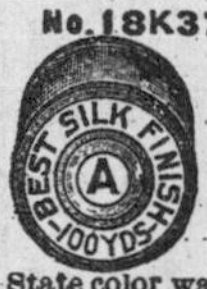

No. 18K3754 Finest quality. This is 100-yard machine thread. Mercerized thread is as good as the best sewing silk and no more expensive than ordinary cotton. Recommended to the trade for its high luster, even of spin, twist and uniform strength, is pure dye, fast color. Made in black, white and all silk shades. State color wanted. In size letter A only.
Price............6 SPOOLS FOR.. 15c
If by mail, postage extra, 6 spools 3 cents.

Sampson Thread.

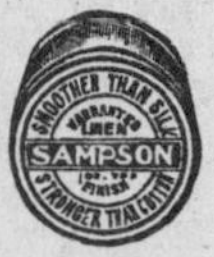

No. 18K3774 Sampson Thread. This thread has a linen finish and is especially adapted for sewing carpets, buttons, etc. Equally as strong as linen, but sews smoother and looks better; 100-yard spools. Comes in black or white. State color wanted.
Price, 6 SPOOLS FOR.. 17c
If by mail, postage extra, for 6 spools, 4 cents.

Barbour's Linen Thread.

No. 18K3776 Barbour's (200-yard spools) Best Linen Thread. Numbers run from No. 25 (coarse) to No. 100 (fine). Colors, black or white. State color wanted.
Price............2 SPOOLS FOR.. 15c
If by mail, postage extra, for 2 spools, 4 cents.

Our "Lustoria" Crochet Cotton.

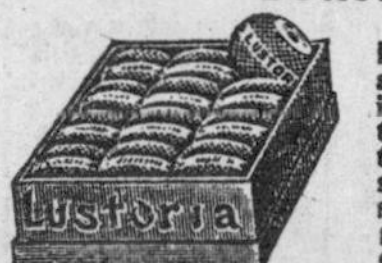

No. 18K3779 Lustoria, a soft, heavy and lustrous Mercerized Crochet Cotton, cannot be distinguished from real silk. Lustoria is absolutely the highest grade of mercerized crochet cotton manufactured. Will outwear any other brand and will retain its luster forever. Put up in full 100-yard spools in colors that are rich and uniform in shade. While we catalogue a cheaper grade of mercerized cotton, our experience has proven that the best is the cheapest. We especially recommend this article and know that if once tried you will use no other. Comes in the following colors: white, light pink, medium pink, violet, purple, cream, light blue, medium blue, brown, light yellow, medium yellow, orange, nile green, moss green, olive green, dark green, scarlet, cardinal, dark garnet, black, also in mixed colors, as follows: White and pink, white and moss green, white and light blue, white and yellow, white and lilac, white, blue and pink and white, green and pink. State color wanted. Price, 6 SPOOLS FOR.... 22c
If by mail, postage extra, 8 cents.

Mercerized Crochet Cotton.

No. 18K3782 Mercerized Crochet Cotton. 83⅓ yards to the spool; for crocheting and embroidering. This is a cotton thread with a silk finish. A cheaper grade than our well known and popular Lustoria Cotton No. 18K3779. Comes in plain and shaded colors as follows: Plain colors, nile green, moss green, olive green, light yellow, medium yellow, orange, scarlet, crimson, light blue, medium blue, light pink, medium pink, lilac, purple, tan, white, cream or black. Shaded colors, white, blue and pink; white and yellow; white, green and pink; white and moss green; white and blue; white and lilac; white and nile green. State color wanted.
Price, 3 SPOOLS FOR.................. 7c
If by mail, postage extra, for 3 spools 4 cents.

H. M. C. Embroidery Cotton.

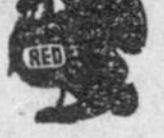

No. 18K3786 H. M. C. Embroidery Cotton on Spools. Color, turkey red only. Nos. 8, 10, 12, 14, 16, 18, 20, 22, and 24. Sold only by the dozen. Will not crock or wash out if washed with ivory soap and lukewarm water. Price, PER DOZEN 16c
If by mail, postage extra, per dozen, 5 cents.

Standard Brands Six-Cord 200-Yard Machine Thread.

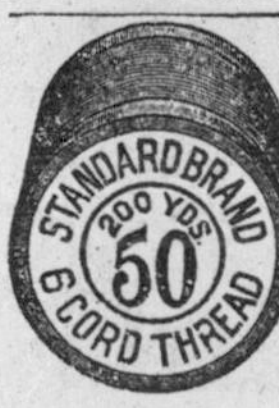

No. 18K3762 We mention no brand on our best six-cord thread, but guarantee that in filling your order we will give you one of the three best known and most standard makes in the United States at a price which you will readily appreciate. We are satisfied with our one small percentage of profit on thread as well as on all other items but the trust objects to our cutting under their price of 6c a spool, and for this reason we quote no brand. Comes in black or white. Sizes 8 to 100. Our price for guaranteed 200 yards, finest quality six-cord machine thread, PER DOZEN SPOOLS.......................... 49c

No. 18K3768 High Grade Basting Spool Cotton (200-yard spools); a very high class basting cotton. Nos. 30 to 60 only. Color, white only. Price, PER DOZEN SPOOLS (Postage extra, 8 to 20c) 23c

HIGHEST GRADE KNITTING YARNS.

German Yarns.

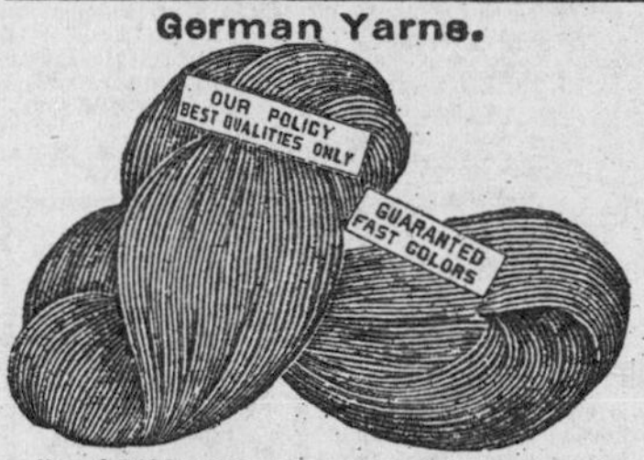

No. 18K3900 German Knitting Worsted Yarn, standard quality, four skeins to the pound, manufacturer's weight. Comes in the following colors: Cardinal, scarlet, medium and navy blue, purple, medium and seal brown, sheep's gray, black mixed, black or white. State color wanted.
Price, per pound 79c
If by mail, postage extra, per pound, 18 cents.

Fleisher's First Quality German Yarn.

No. 18K3902 German Knitting Worsted Yarn. Fleisher's first quality, always runs smooth and always the same, four skeins to the pound, manufacturer's weight. Colors same as No. 18K3900. State color wanted.
Price, all colors, per skein........$0.28
Per lb..(Postage extra, per lb., 19c) 1.07

No. 18K3904 German Knitting Yarn, our best quality high grade yarn, four skeins to the pound, manufacturer's weight. Colors same as No. 18K3900. For a good satisfactory yarn buy this first quality yarn. We recommend it as our best, which contains a long wool filling; and we guarantee every hank sold. State color wanted.
Price, all colors, per skein............ 25c
Per lb...(Postage extra, per lb., 18c).. 96c

Saxony Wool Yarn.

No. 18K3906 Saxony Wool Yarn, Imported. Made of the finest Australian wool; twenty skeins to the pound, manufacturer's weight. Colors, scarlet, cardinal, wine, pink, light, medium or navy blue, medium or seal brown, black or cream white. State color wanted.
Price, per skein 6½c
Per lb..(Postage extra, per lb., 18c).$1.25

No. 18K3908 Spanish Knitting Worsted Yarn, imported, eight skeins to the pound, manufacturer's weight. Colors, cardinal, navy blue, seal brown, black or cream white. State color wanted. Price, per skein..........$0.14
Per lb..(Postage extra, per lb., 17c). 1.10

Crinkled Shetland Floss.

The Highest Grade, Best Quality Yarn.

No. 18K3910 Shetland Floss, fine grade imported wool, twelve skeins to the pound, manufacturer's weight. Colors, light blue, medium blue, light pink, dark pink, lemon, lilac, cardinal, dove, nile green, black, snow white or cream white. State color wanted.
Price, per skein, all colors.................. 7c
Per lb...(Postage extra, per lb., 15c).. 82c

No. 18K3912 Coral Yarn, imported, twelve skeins to the pound, manufacturer's weight. Colors, cardinal, light blue, pink, yellow, garnet, peacock blue, black or cream white. State color wanted.
Price, per pound, $1.40; per skein.. 13c
If by mail, postage extra, per pound, 16 cents.

No. 18K3914 Fairy Floss or Crinkled Yarn. Used for fancy knitting, twelve skeins to the pound, manufacturer's weight. Colors, black or white only. State color wanted. 10c
Price, per pound, $1.10; per skein.
If by mail, postage extra, per pound, 16 cents.

Germantown Yarn.

No. 18K3916 Germantown Wool Yarn, Imported. Sixteen skeins to the pound, manufacturer's weight. Colors, scarlet, cardinal, wine, light, medium or navy blue, pink, seal brown, yellow, green, purple, gray, black, white or cream. State color wanted. 8½c
Price, per pound, $1.30; per skein.
If by mail, postage extra, per pound, 20 cents.

Imported Angora Wool.

No. 18K3918 Angora Wool, best quality imported yarn. Colors, black, white or gray. State color wanted. 16 balls to the box. 8c
Price, per box, $1.25; per ball.........
If by mail, postage extra, per box, 7 cents.

Imported Angora Yarn ½-ounce Balls.

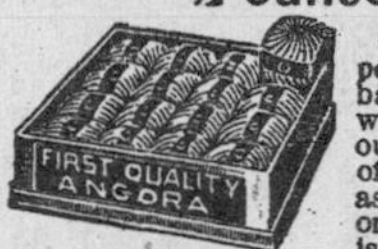

No. 18K3920 Angora Yarn. A superior quality put up 8 balls to the box and will weigh full one-half ounce to the ball. One of these balls will knit as far as 4 balls of the ordinary Angora. This is an advantageous way of buying Angora yarn, as it does away with tying and knotting. Comes in white, gray, black, cardinal or brown. State color wanted.
Price, per ball...............................$0.29
Price, per box of 8 balls................. 2.20
If by mail, postage extra, per box, 9 cents.

Imported Ice Wool.

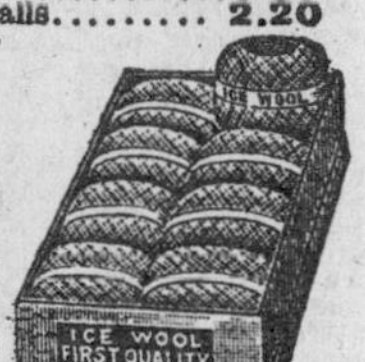

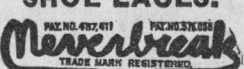

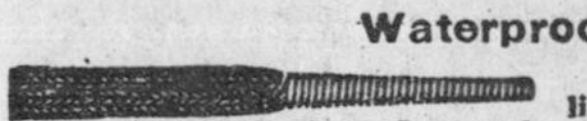

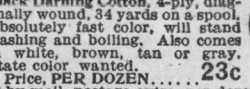

No. 18K3922 Ice Wool, Imported. 1-ounce balls, put up eight balls to the box. Colors, black, white, pink or light blue. Give color wanted.
Price, per ball.... 9c
Price, per box.. 70c
If by mail, postage extra, per box, 8 cents.

Zephyr Worsteds.

No. 18K3924 Zephyr Worsted, imported. Berlin zephyr, 4-ply, called single. For working rug patterns, etc. Colors, scarlet, cardinal, garnet, wine, light pink, dark pink, light, medium and navy blue, nile, medium and dark green, olive, brown, tan, canary, orange, gray, purple, black or cream white. Forty laps to the pound, manufacturer's weight. Give color wanted. Price, per lap............ 3½c
12 laps for...(Postage, per lap, 1c).. 40c

No. 18K3926 Zephyr Worsted, imported Berlin zephyr, 2-ply, called split zephyr. Colors, same as No. 18K3924. Give color wanted. Forty laps to the pound, manufacturer's weight. Price, per lap............ 3½c
12 laps for...(Postage, per lap, 1c)..40c

Crown Knitting Cotton.

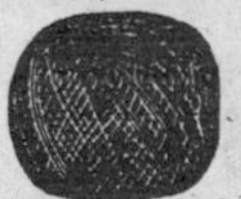

No. 18K3790 Crown White Knitting Cotton. Best quality, 4-thread, put up 10 balls to the pound, manufacturer's weight, and 2 pounds to the box. Nos. 6 to 24.
Price, PER ½ POUND (5 BALLS).... 23c
If by mail, postage extra, 5 balls, 10 cents.

No. 18K3794 Crown Navy Blue Knitting Cotton, same quality as above. Nos. 8 to 16. Price, PER ½ POUND (5 BALLS)........................ 23c
If by mail, postage extra, 5 balls, 10 cents.

No. 18K3798 Crown Blue and White Mixed Knitting Cotton, same quality as above. Nos. 8 to 16. Price, PER ½ POUND (5 BALLS)........................ 23c
If by mail, postage extra, 5 balls, 10 cents.

Darning Cotton.

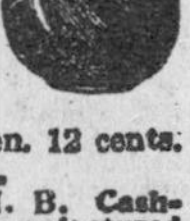

No. 18K3802 Best Fast Black Darning Cotton, 4-ply, diagonally wound, 34 yards on a spool. Absolutely fast color, will stand washing and boiling. Also comes in white, brown, tan or gray. State color wanted.
Price, PER DOZEN........ 23c
If by mail, postage extra, per dozen. 12 cents.

Mending Yarn.

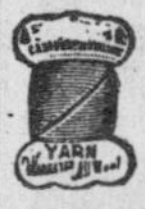

No. 18K3806 H. B. Cashmere Mending Yarn. Manufactured from the very highest grade of scoured wool, 30 yards warranted. Once tried, you will use no other. Colors, brown navy, tan, gray, black or white. State color wanted.
Price, PER DOZEN.................. 24c
If by mail, postage extra, per dozen, 4 cents.

SHOE LACES.

PAT. NO. 487,411 PAT. NO. 37,056
Neverbreak
TRADE MARK REGISTERED

A patented shoe lace adopted by the War Department for the U. S. Army.

No. 18K3808 36 inches. For men's and boys' shoes.
Price, PER DOZEN PAIRS........... 25c
If by mail, postage extra, per doz. pairs, 4 cents.

Paton's Hand Spiral Tagged 40-inch Lace.

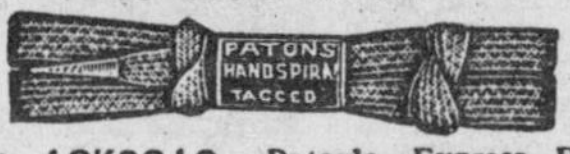

No. 18K3810 Paton's Express Rifle Tubular Laces have spiral tags, made of two-ply combed Sea Island cotton, dressy, durable and the best imported lace on the market. Put up in 1 dozen pairs in a box. For men's, women's and boys' shoes.
Price, PER DOZEN PAIRS........ 30c
If by mail, postage extra, per dozen pairs, 4c.

Best Porpoise Laces.

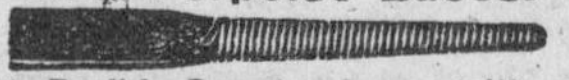

Best English Porpoise Laces, with spiral tags, the strongest and best made at any price.
No. 18K3814 36-inch.
Price, PER DOZEN PAIRS.............. 38c
No. 18K3816 45-inch.
Price, PER DOZEN PAIRS.............. 48c
If by mail, postage extra, per dozen pairs, 6c.

Men's, Ladies', Boys' and Misses' Flat Tubular Laces.

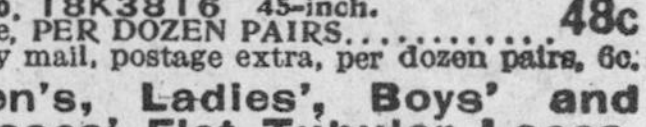

These laces are guaranteed 38-thread and full lengths. The best domestic tubular lace made, and usually sold at 5 cents per pair. Black or tan.

No. 18K3818 27-inch for children's shoes and men's and women's Oxfords. Black only.
Price, PER DOZEN PAIRS.............. 12c
No. 18K3820 36-inch, black.
Price, PER DOZEN PAIRS.............. 14c
No. 18K3822 45-inch, black.
Price, PER DOZEN PAIRS.............. 16c
No. 18K3824 54-inch, black.
Price, PER DOZEN PAIRS.............. 18c
If by mail, postage extra, per dozen pairs, 4c.

Waterproof Army Shoe Lace.

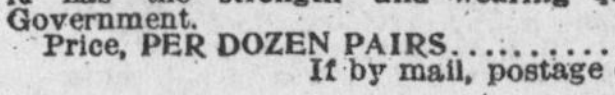

No. 18K3812 This lace is made from the best of linen, woven very close, is about ⅛-inch wide, 1 yard long, with spiral tags. It is without a doubt the best lace ever made for men's shoes, as it has the strength and wearing qualities of the porpoise lace. Used by the U. S. Government.
Price, PER DOZEN PAIRS.................. 18c
If by mail, postage extra, per dozen pairs, 4 cents.

Stamped Pillow Tops.

No. 18K5507 "In the Shade of the Old Apple Tree," motto and landscape design on good quality tan colored ticking front, with drill back. Size, 21 inches.
Price, for front and back without ruffle **23c**
For ruffling to trim above, see catalogue, No. 18K5568.
If by mail, postage extra, each, 6 cents.

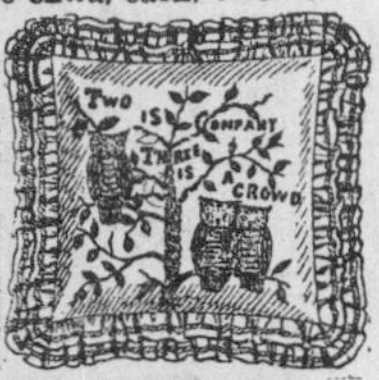

No. 18K5509 "Two is Company, Three is a Crowd." Very attractive motto design on hand painted pillow top. Made of good quality tan colored ticking with drill back. Size, 21 inches.
Price, for front and back without ruffle........ **23c**
For ruffling to trim above, see catalogue No. 18K5568.
If by mail, postage extra, each, 6 cents.

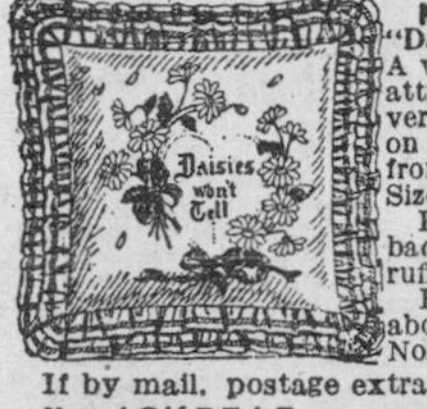

No. 18K5511 "Daisies Won't Tell." A very popular and attractive design in very pretty colorings on light green ticking front with drill back. Size, 21 inches.
Price, for front and back without ruffle **23c**
For ruffling to trim above, see catalogue No. 18K5568.
If by mail, postage extra, each, 6 cents.

No. 18K5515 "Only a Breath of Violets" Pillow. Top and back made of excellent grade ticking. Hand painted basket of violets tinted in natural colors, making this a very attractive pattern. Size, 22x22 inches.
Price, for front and back without ruffle **23c**
For ruffling, see catalogue, No. 18K5568.
If by mail, postage extra, each, 6 cents.

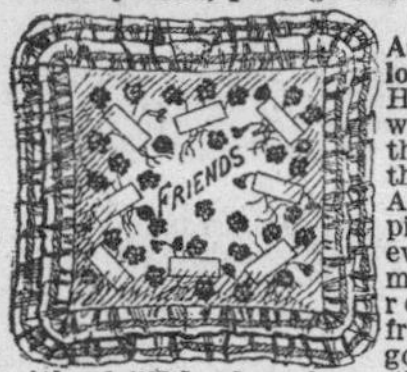

No. 18K5518 Autograph Sofa Pillow, all the rage. Have your friends write their names in the blank spaces, then embroider same. A finished autograph pillow is prized by everybody. Nothing more appropriate to remember your friends by. Made on good quality ticking with drill back and neatly tinted in natural color violets. Size, 22x22 inches.
Price, for front and back, without ruffle........ **23c**
For ruffling to trim above, see catalogue No. 18K5568.
If by mail, postage extra, each, 6 cents.

Birthday Pillow Tops.

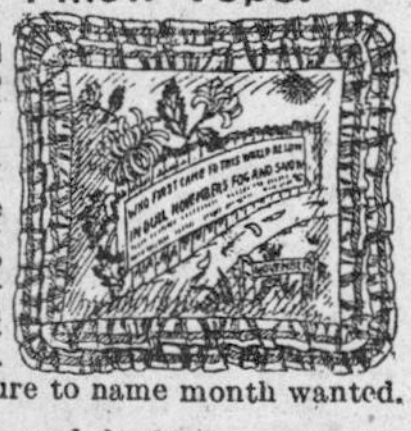

No. 18K5520 Hand Painted Birthday Pillow, top and back on highest grade ticking, beautifully tinted in flower designs, with appropriate birthday motto for each month; also a planet to represent every month in the year. A very appropriate birthday present. Be sure to name month wanted. Size, 22x22 inches.
Price, for front and back in any design, without ruffle........ **23c**
For ruffling to trim above, see catalogue No. 18K5568.
If by mail, postage extra, each, 6 cents.

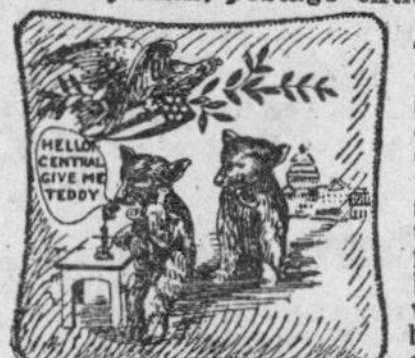

No. 18K5527 Teddy Bears, the latest idea in sofa pillows, made of good quality crash and nicely tinted in design as shown in illustration. The entire front and back are bound and stitched with mercerized bonaz, making this a finished article and ready for use. Size, 22x22 inches.
Price, for front and back........ **23c**
If by mail, postage extra, each, 4 cents.

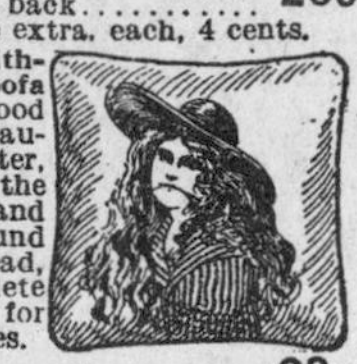

No. 18K5533 Lithograph Pillow Top or Sofa Cushion. Made of good quality ticking with beautiful tinted character, "The Girl From the West." The front and back are neatly bound with mercerized thread, making this a complete sofa pillow and ready for use. Size, 21x21 inches.
Price, for front and back........ **23c**
If by mail, postage extra, each, 4 cents.

THE SURPRISINGLY LOW REDUCED PRICES prevailing in this catalogue mean greater savings to our customers than ever before.

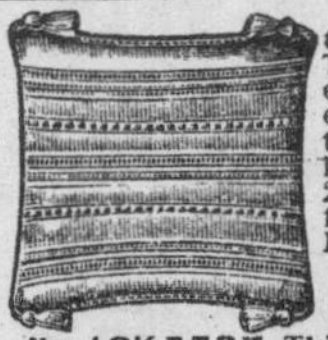

No. 18K5535 Tapestry Pillow Top, in bright Turkish colors, ornamented with four tassels on either end, backed with the same material. Regular 50-cent value. Size, 20x20 in. Price, for front and back.... **22c**
If by mail, postage extra, each, 5 cents.

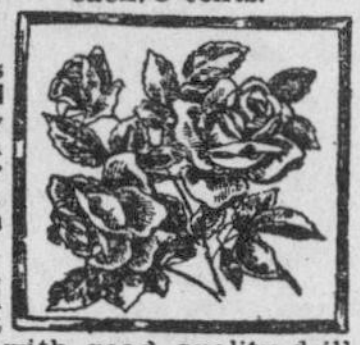

No. 18K5537 This is a Beautiful Hand Painted Cushion Pillow Top. Hand painted on good quality linen color crash, with beautiful, bright, natural colors with large rosebuds, leaves and stems, bound with mercerized tape edge to contrast with top, and backed with good quality drill cloth. Finished complete. Ready to use. Size, 21x21 inches. Price, for front and back **27c**
If by mail, postage extra, each, 6 cents.

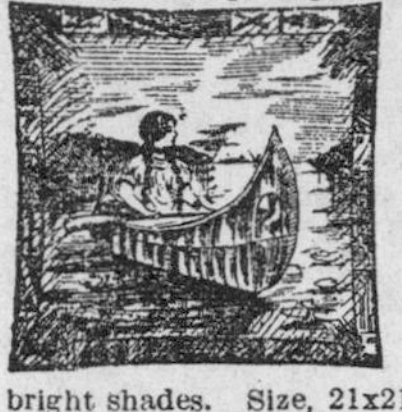

No. 18K5542 Sofa Pillow, made of good quality crash with bound and hemstitched edge ready for use, hand painted sunset scene, showing an Indian maiden paddling a canoe. The entire border is ornamented with various Indian emblems painted in contrasting bright shades. Size, 21x21 inches.
Price, for front and back........ **26c**
If by mail, postage extra, 6 cents.

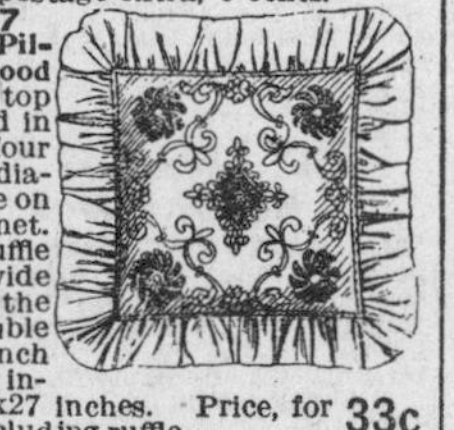

No. 18K5547 White Lawn Sofa Pillow, made of good quality lawn; the top is entirely stitched in bonaz and has four wheels and one diamond design made on good quality lace net. The white lawn ruffle is four inches wide and is fastened to the pillow with a double stitched, half-inch lawn tape. Size, including ruffle, 27x27 inches. Price, for front and back, including ruffle........ **33c**
If by mail, postage extra, 6 cents.

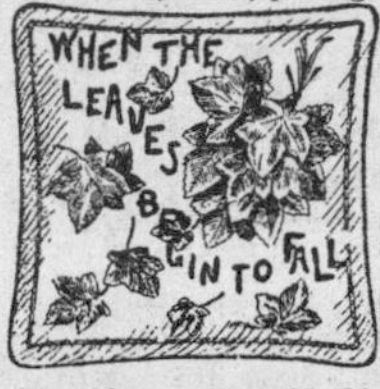

No. 18K5551 Sofa Pillow, on good quality ticking with hand painted oak leaf design and motto, "When the Leaves Begin to Fall." The leaves are tinted in shades as they appear in the fall, which give them a most beautiful effect. The top is bound and stitched and is bordered with silk ribbon. Size, 21x21 inches.
Price, for front and back........ **35c**
If by mail, postage extra, each, 6 cents.

Embroidered Pillow Top.

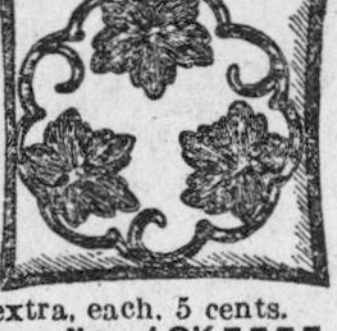

No. 18K5553 Embroidered Bonazed Pillow Top, made of linen colored crash, handsomely embroidered in oak leaf design, with fancy scroll border, all embroidered in bonaz stitching. This pillow top and back is bound and ready for use. Size, 22 inches. Price, for front and back **33c**
If by mail, postage extra, each, 5 cents.

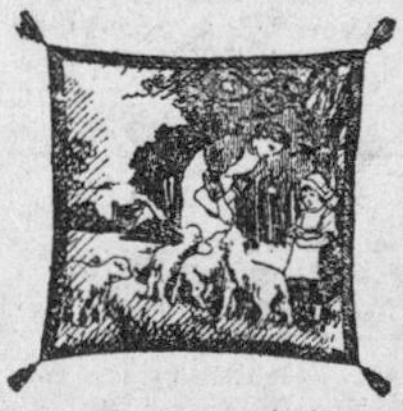

No. 18K5555 Tapestry Sofa Pillow, bound and ready for use, trimmed with four full tassels nicely colored; a good wearing sofa pillow, one that will not soil. The design as illustrated is woven into the cloth. A regular 50-cent value. Size, 20x20 inches. Price, for front and back.... **39c**
Postage, extra, each, 8c.

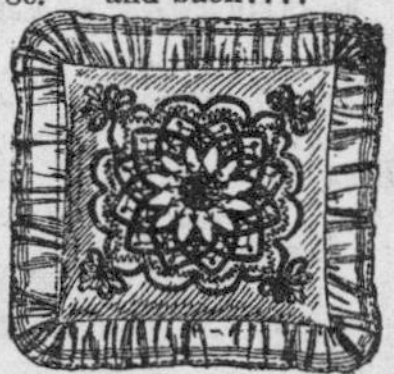

No. 18K5558 Complete Pillow Top, made of cream colored drill, with back to match, trimmed with a green sateen 3½-inch ruffle, with three rows of hemstitching on same. The design is embroidered with a fine silk finished floss. Size of entire pillow, 27 inches.
Price, for front and back........ **49c**
If by mail, postage extra, each, 8 cents.

Hand Painted Satin Pillow Top

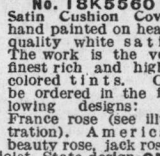

No. 18K5560 Satin Cushion Cover, hand painted on heavy quality white satin. The work is the very finest rich and highly colored tints. Can be ordered in the following designs: La France rose (see illustration). American beauty rose, jack roses, carnation, poppy or violet. State design wanted. Size, 22x22 inches. Price, each, **67c**
If by mail, postage extra, each, 8 cents.

The Very Latest, Real Teddy Bear Pillow Cushion.

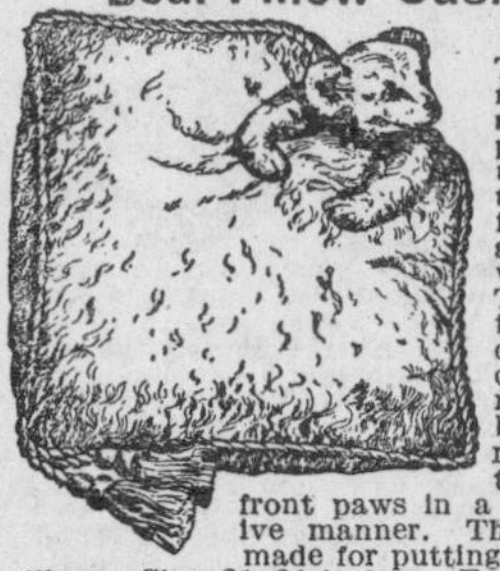

No. 18K5559 This is the newest and most popular pillow top on the market today. The front and back are made of the well known Teddy bear fur with one corner folded over and a real Teddy bear head resting between its two front paws in a very attractive manner. This is already made for putting in the inside pillow. Size, 21x21 inches. Front and back are made of the same material, and it is bound with a mercerized pillow girdle with tassels in color to match pillow. The pillow can be ordered in white only. This pillow top is sold everywhere for $4.50 each.
Our price complete, ready to insert pillow, only........ **$2.75**
If by mail, postage extra, 24 cents.

Make Your Own Teddy Bear.

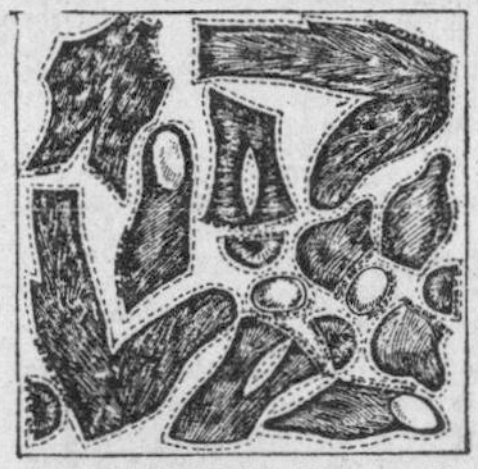

25c

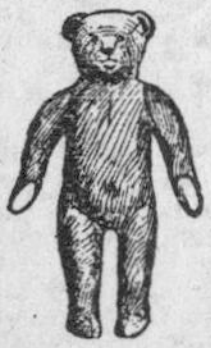

No. 18K5561 The new Teddy Bear Pattern made on good substantial material. The different parts are plainly lithographed and named, making it a very simple process in joining same. Size, when completed, about 12 inches. Price........ **25c**
If by mail, postage extra, 6 cents.

Pillow Shams, Stamped.

No. 18K5562 Made of good quality muslin, one sham stamped "I Slept and Dreamed That Life Was Beauty," and the other sham stamped "I Woke and Found That Life Was Duty." Size, 30x30 inches.
Price, per pair........ **20c**
If by mail, postage extra, per pair, 6 cents.

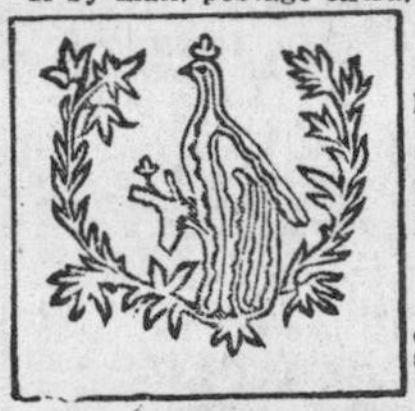

No. 18K5563 White Muslin Pillow Shams. Embroidered in fast color red embroidery cotton. Size, 30x30 inches. Peacock pattern.
Price, per pair **25c**
If by mail, postage extra, per pair, 6 cents.

Pillow Girdles.

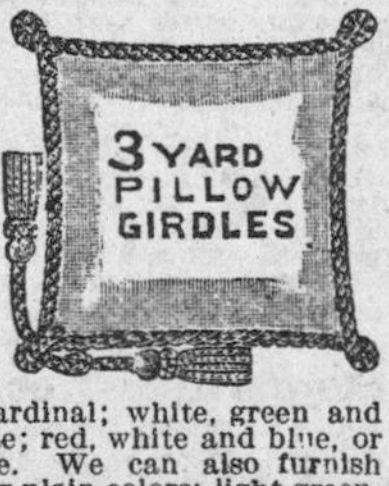

No. 18K5564 A heavy mercerized twisted Cushion Cord with tassels complete. Can be ordered in the following combination of colors: Black and yellow; green, tan and pink; royal blue, tan and yellow; green, tan and cardinal; light blue and yellow; navy blue and orange; black and cardinal; white, green and red; orange and white; red, white and blue, or light blue and white. We can also furnish them in the following plain colors: light green, yellow, or cardinal. Give color wanted. Length, 3 yards. Price, each........ **21c**
If by mail, postage extra, each, 6 cents.

No. 18K5566 Silk Pillow Girdle. A heavy twisted cord with tassels, same as illustration above. Length, 3 yards. In colors, same as No. 18K5564. Price, each.. **31c**
If by mail, postage extra, each, 6 cents.

Pillow Cushion Ribbon.

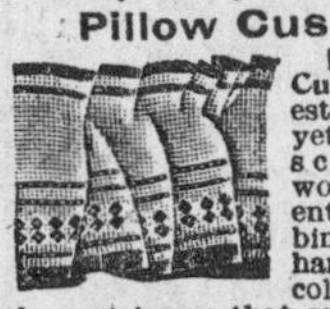

No. 18K5568 Pillow Cushion Ribbon. The newest and most effective ribbon yet designed. Made of linen scrim, beautifully worked with silk in rich oriental designs, and fancy combination colorings that will harmonize with most any color of pillow top. Has draw string so that same can be ruffled on top. When ordering, mention color of your pillow top. Width, 4 inches. Comes only in 4½-yard pieces. Regular price, 50 cents. **33c**
Price, PER PIECE OF 4½ YARDS..
If by mail, postage extra, per piece, 4 cents.

White Lawn Hemmed Pillow Ruffling.

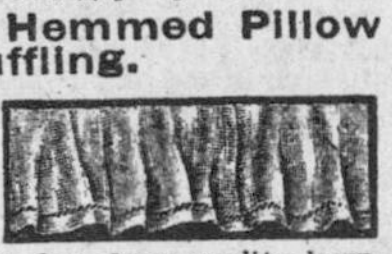

No. 18K5570 White Hemmed Pillow Ruffling is used extensively for shadow embroidery pillow tops. It is made of a fine sheer quality lawn, neatly hemmed. Width, 4 inches. Comes only in 4-yard pieces.
Price, PER PIECE OF 4 YARDS.... **20c**
If by mail, postage extra, per piece, 3 cents.

OTTOMAN BURLAP PATTERNS

For materials for working Burlap Patterns, see Zephyr yarns. Ask for our free circular giving estimates of yarn required for working patterns.

No. 18K5600 Pattern 40. Pretty flower design, burlap rug pattern. Size, 23x41 inches. Price, each........ **24c**
If by mail, postage extra, each, 7 cents.

No. 18K5602 Pattern 9. Ottoman. Large rose leaves and buds with nice border. Size, 18x20 inches. Price, each **12c**
If by mail, postage extra, each, 4 cents.

No. 18K5604 Pattern 53. ⅔x1⅛ yards Arabian Horse and Landscape center, enclosed with an oval line, and oak leaves at each end, new design. Price, each. **31c**
If by mail, postage extra, each, 8 cents.

No. 18K5606 Pattern 19. ½x1 yard. A spaniel dog lying on a box. Very clearly printed in moss and brown colors in center. A branch, with roses, leaves and buds, at each end and a plain border.
Price, each........ **24c**
If by mail, postage extra, each, 8 cents.

No. 18K5610 Pattern 93. ⅔x1⅛ yards. Nice floral center, consisting of red and moss roses, leaves, buds, lilies, etc., beautifully arranged, with a plain scroll surrounding the center, three autumn leaves in each corner and a plain border.
Price, each........ **31c**
If by mail, postage extra, each, 9 cents.

No. 18K5612 Pattern 39. ¾x1½ yards. A cat and two kittens playing on the carpet in the center, enclosed in a plain scroll. Plain border with nice scroll in corners. A very interesting design for those who are fond of pets. All new. Price, each........ **44c**
If by mail, postage extra, each, 13 cents.

No. 18K5614 Pattern 22. ¾x1½ yards. A very pretty scroll border, with a stag standing near a lake of water, very pretty landscape scenery, etc., in the center. A very nice sofa rug. Price, each........ **47c**
If by mail, postage extra, each, 13 cents.

No. 18K5616 Pattern 7. ⅞x1¾ yards. A large lion lying down, and a small lion in the background, with a fine scene of flowers and palm trees. Is very easy to work and makes a nice hearth rug. Price, each........ **55c**
If by mail, postage extra, each, 14 cents.

No. 18K5619 Pattern 12. ½x1 yard Door Mat. Oval chain through center, with word Welcome. Letters transposed, so that when worked with the machine will read properly. Plain border with scroll in corner. Price, each........ **19c**
If by mail, postage extra, each, 6 cents.

Rug Machine.

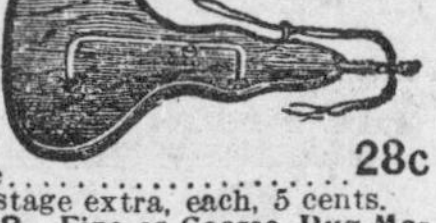

No. 18K5621 The Novelty Rug Machine. For working rugs, ottomans, chair covers, cushions and burlap patterns with full directions. Price........ **28c**
If by mail, postage extra, each, 5 cents.

No. 18K5622 Fine or Coarse Rug Machine Needles. For working on plush, satin, etc. Price, 3 FOR........ **8c**
If by mail, postage extra, 2 cents.

Stamping Pattern Outfits.

Stamp your own linen.

No. 18K5623 The Quintette Stamping Outfit. Consists of five sheets on which are 26 full sized, new and pretty designs in doilies, collars, cuffs, flowers, etc., one complete alphabet, one box of black and one box of white stamping powder; also directions with each set. Price, per outfit... **25c**
If by mail, postage extra, per outfit, 7 cents.

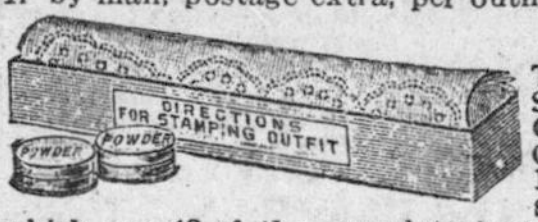

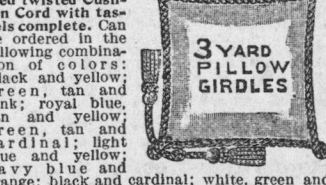

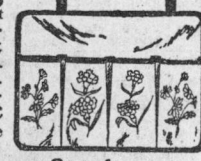

No. 18K5627 The Seroco Stamping Outfit. Consists of 12 large sheets on which are 48 of the very latest patterns for stamping all kinds of linens, shirt waist patterns, sofa pillows, laundry bags, collars, cuffs and all kinds of fancy work; one complete alphabet, and one box each of black and white stamping powder with each set. **48c**
Price, per outfit........
If by mail, postage extra, per outfit, 13 cents.

Shoe Pockets.

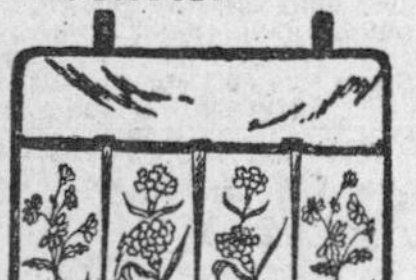

No. 18K5630 Ecru Colored Print Drill Shoe Pocket. Tape bound edges. Stamped in pretty floral designs. Contains four pockets. Size, 14x18 inches.
Price........ **18c**
If by mail, postage extra, 4 cents.

Dresser Scarf.

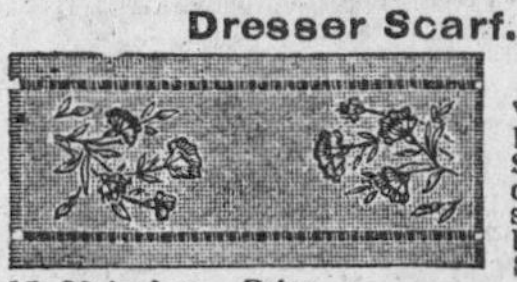

No. 18K5635 White Cotton Duck Dresser Scarf, with drawn insertion on both sides. Size, 16x35 inches. Price........ **14c**
If by mail, postage extra, 4 cents.

Laundry Bag.

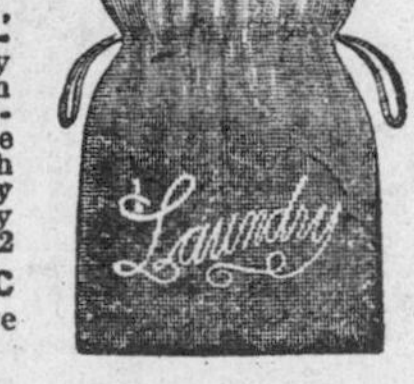

No. 18K5640 Laundry Bag, made of linen colored crash, heavily embroidered with mercerized, periluster thread. Wide hem at top with drawstrings. A very durable and pretty bag. Size, 30x22 inches.
Price........ **33c**
If by mail, postage extra, 7 cents.

DRAWN WORK, RENAISSANCE AND FANCY SPACHTEL GOODS

IF YOU WANT SCARFS, DOILIES, SHAMS, ETC., SENT BY MAIL BE SURE TO ALLOW FROM 2 TO 6 CENTS EXTRA FOR POSTAGE.

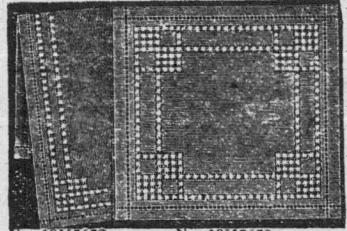

No. 18K5652   **No. 18K5650**
No. 18K5650 Real Japanese Hand Drawn Linen Center Piece, hemstitched on good quality linen, a very neat and showy pattern, an exceptional value. Comes in the following sizes:
Size, ins. 12 18 24 30
Price, each. . . . 27c 59c 95c $1.25
If by mail, postage extra, each, 2 to 4 cents.
No. 18K5652 Real Japanese Hand Drawn Scarf, same material and to match No.18K5650 center piece. Size, 18x54 inches.
Price, each . . . (Postage, 5 cents) . . . **$1.55**

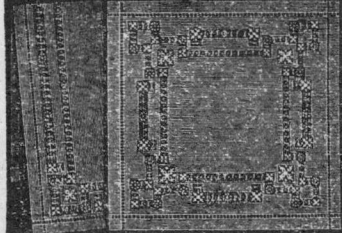

No. 18K5656   **No. 18K5654**
No. 18K5654 Real Japanese Drawn Work Linen Squares, hemstitched on extra quality pure linen. Every thread in the design of this real Japanese drawn center piece is hand drawn. Comes in the following sizes:
Size, inches . . 20 24 30
Price, each . . $1.33 $1.73 $2.25
If by mail, postage extra, each, 4 to 6 cents.
No. 18K5656 Real Japanese Drawn Work Hemstitched Dresser Scarf, made of the same material to match No.18K5654 center piece. Size, 18x54 inches.
Price, each . . (Postage, 6 cents) . . . **$2.79**

No. 18K5660   **No. 18K5658**
No. 18K5658 Hand Made All Battenberg Lace Renaissance Squares, in handsomely designed star center, with border and corners to harmonize. Materials and workmanship are of the best. Comes in the following sizes:
Size, ins. 9 12 18 24 30
Price, each 19c 28c 63c $1.12 $1.69
If by mail, postage extra, 2 to 5 cents.
No. 18K5660 Hand Made All Battenberg Lace Renaissance Scarf, to match No. 18K5658 squares. Size, 18x54 inches. Price, each . (Postage, 6 cents) **$1.69**

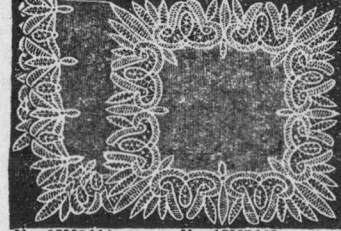

No. 18K5664   **No. 18K5662**
No. 18K5662 Hand Made Battenberg Renaissance Square, a handsomely arranged design in a neat, close worked effect on a fine union linen center. Comes in the following sizes:
Size, ins. 9 12 18 24 30
Price, each 15c 23c 59c $1.09 $1.49
If by mail, postage extra, 2 to 5 cents.
No. 18K5664 Hand Made Battenberg Dresser Scarf, on union linen center, to match square No. 18K5662. Size, 18x54 inches. Price, each . . . (Postage, 6c.) **$1.63**

No. 18K5668   **No. 18K5666**
No. 18K5666 Our Very Latest Idea in Scarfs and Squares. A combination of renaissance and Japanese drawn work. The linen center is worked in a beautiful all hand drawn design and is edged with a battenberg braid, making this a very new and desirable pattern. Comes in the following sizes:
Size, inches . . . 18 24 30
Price, each . . . 67c $1.12 $1.65
No. 18K5668 Combination Japanese Drawn Work and Renaissance Scarf, with three drawn work centers, on fine union linen, to match No. 18K5666 squares. Size, 18x54 inches. Price, each **$1.73**

No. 18K5672   **No. 18K5670**
No. 18K5670 Our Best Grade, All Hand Made Imported Lace, Renaissance Battenberg Pattern, with pure linen center. The braid and stitches are all closely and carefully worked by hand exactly as shown in illustration. Comes in the following sizes:
Size, inches . 12 18 24 30
Price, each . 33c 75c $1.29 $1.89
No. 18K5672 Our Best Grade All Hand Made Dresser Scarf, to match above square. Size, 18x54 inches. Price, each **$2.38**

No. 18K5674 Hand Made Battenberg Lace Renaissance Round Center Piece, on a pure linen center, with a wide border of battenberg lace braid and clusters of battenberg rings arranged in a very artistic design. Comes in the following sizes:
Size, inches 9 12 18 24 30
Price, each 17c 29c 59c 98c $1.69

Pillow Shams and Dresser Scarfs.

No. 18K5678   **No. 18K5676**
No. 18K5676 White Lawn Hemstitched Sham or Table Cover, on good quality material, prettily designed in net and battenberg braid. Size, 32x32 inches. Price, each **26c**
If by mail, postage extra, 3 cents.
No. 18K5678 White Lawn Dresser Scarf, to match No. 18K5676 sham. Size, 18x50 inches. Price, each **26c**

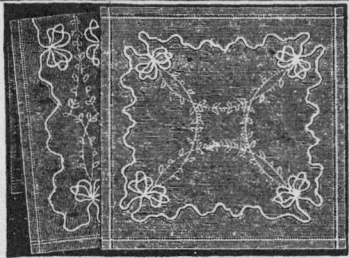

No. 18K5686   **No. 18K5684**
No. 18K5684 Extra Quality White Lawn Hemstitched Sham or Table Cover, handsomely embroidered in bowknot design. Size, 31x31 inches. Price, each **33c**
No. 18K5686 Fine White Lawn Hemstitched Dresser Scarf, to match No. 18K5684 sham. Size, 18x50 inches. Price, each . . . . (Postage, 4 cents) . . . **33c**

No. 18K5690   **No. 18K5688**
No. 18K5688 White Lawn Spachtel Sham or Table Cover, bonaz stitched and ornamented with handsome cutout eyelets and flower design, hemstitched edge. Size, 29x29 inches. Price, each **39c**
If by mail, postage extra, 4 cents.
No. 18K5690 White Lawn Dresser Scarf, to match No. 18K5688 sham. Size, 18x50 inches. Price, each **39c**

No. 18K5698   **No. 18K5696**
No. 18K5696 White Lawn Scalloped Edge Sham or Table Cover, embroidered in the new wide chain stitch in design as shown in illustration. Size, 30x30 inches. Price, each . . . (Postage, 4 cents) . . . **48c**
No. 18K5698 White Lawn Scalloped Edge Dresser Scarf, to match sham No. 18K5696. Size, 18x52 inches. Price, each . . . . (Postage, 4 cents) . . . **48c**

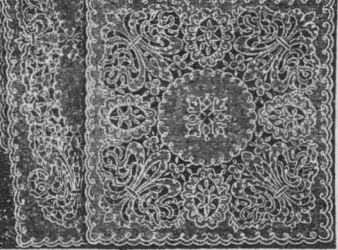

No. 18K5702   **No. 18K5700**
No. 18K5700 White Lawn Irish Point Spachtel Sham or Table Cover, trimmed in a cutout conventional design, embroidered with fancy bonaz stitching. Size, 32x32 inches. Price, each . . . (Postage, 4c.) . . **57c**
No. 18K5702 White Lawn Irish Point Spachtel Scarf, to match No. 18K5700 sham. Size, 18x52 inches. Price, each . . . **57c**

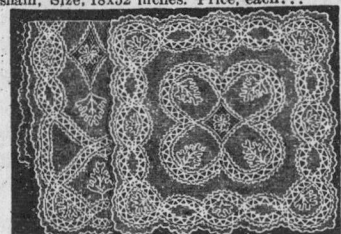

No. 18K5706   **No. 18K5704**
No. 18K5704 White Lawn Irish Point Sham or Table Cover, with neatly worked border and center with battenberg braid and bonaz embroidering. Size, 30x30 inches. Price, each . . . (Postage, 5 cents) . . . **63c**
No. 18K5706 White Lawn Dresser Scarf, to match No. 18K5704 sham. Size, 18x50 inches. Price, each **63c**

No. 18K5710   **No. 18K5708**
No. 18K5708 High Grade Imported Spachtel Sham or Table Cover, made on fine quality lawn, handsomely designed and embroidered as shown in illustration. A handsome cover for table or pillow at a very low price. Size, 31x31 inches. Price, each **69c**
If by mail, postage extra, 4 cents.
No. 18K5710 Dresser Scarf, to match No. 18K5708 sham. Size, 18x52 inches. Price, each . . . (Postage, 4 cents) . . . **69c**

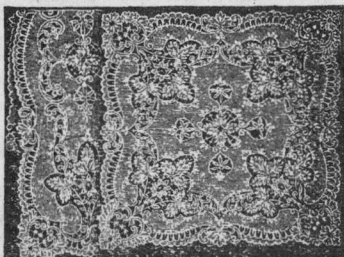

No. 18K5714   **No. 18K5712**
No. 18K5712 Fine White Imported Spachtel Irish Point Sham in White, made on a fine quality lawn. The four corners, as well as the center and center border, are artistically worked in floral and leaf designs, all embroidered with fancy bonaz stitching; can be used for pillow or table cover. Size, 32x32 inches. Price, each **89c**
If by mail, postage extra, 4 cents.
No. 18K5714 Dresser Scarf, to match No. 18K5712 sham. Size, 18x52 inches. Price, each . . . (Postage, 4 cents) . . . **89c**

No. 18K5718   **No. 18K5716**
No. 18K5716 Our Highest Grade Imported Irish Point White Spachtel Sham, made on fine quality lawn, with beautiful flower and leaf design in allover effect. Every leaf and flower is neatly embroidered with bonaz stitching, making this a unique, handsome and serviceable article. Size, 31x31 inches. Price, each . . . (Postage, 5 cents) . . **$1.23**
No. 18K5718 Scarf, to match sham No. 18K5716. Size, 18x52 inches. Price, each . . . (Postage, 5 cents) . . **$1.23**

No. 18K5720 Brussels Net Doily, with beautiful scroll design border and center of fine quality lawn. Comes in three sizes.

Size, inches	Price, each
8x 8	9c
12x12	10c
18x18	15c
Postage, 2 cents.

No. 18K5722 White Lawn Spachtel Doily, as illustrated, with fancy bonaz stitching and pretty lace center. Comes in three sizes.

Size, inches	Price, each
8x8	7c
12x12	15c
18x18	19c
Postage, 2 cents.

No. 18K5724 White Lawn Scalloped Edge Spachtel Doily, with lace corners and heavy raised bowknot design in center. Comes in three sizes.

Size, inches	Price, each
8x 8	10c
12x12	15c
18x18	23c
Postage, 2 cents.

THE BEST EMBROIDERY VALUES EVER SHOWN

Our 1908 importation of embroideries combines style and quality with our well known feature of especially low prices. This season we had our embroideries made on better cloths with daintier and closer work; in fact, made better throughout. The tremendous success of our last seasons sale of improved qualities has led us to make further improvements which we feel confident our customers will appreciate. We offer you highest qualities at prices lower than ever before.

Every price we name is hammered down to the lowest notch. Every pattern shown is selected with the utmost care, so that it will give entire satisfaction. You make no mistake in ordering your embroideries from us. We sell you embroideries with the distinct understanding that if the goods are not satisfactory when you receive them you can return them at our expense and we will cheerfully exchange for other goods or refund your money. The weight of embroideries varies so, according to the pattern and width, that it is impossible for us to state accurately the postage per yard on each pattern. However, if you desire embroideries sent by mail, be sure to allow from 1 to 3 cents per yard for postage. If you send more money than is required, we will refund the difference. We do not sample embroideries

CAMBRIC EMBROIDERY EDGES.

Cambric embroideries are used where a good wearing substantial cloth is desired that will stand the greatest amount of washing and laundering. Especially desirable for children's clothing. The wider widths are used extensively for skirtings and corset covers.

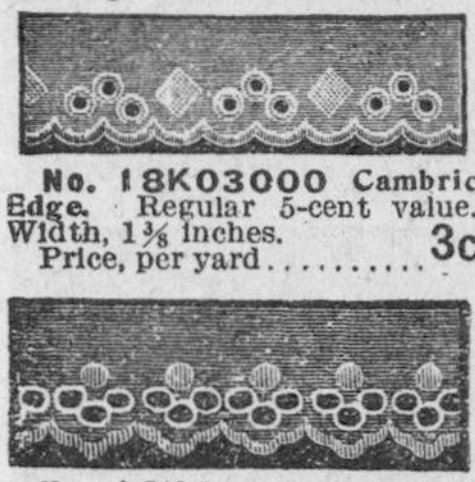

No. 18K03000 Cambric Edge. Regular 5-cent value. Width, 1⅜ inches. Price, per yard 3c

No. 18K03002 Cambric Edge. Neatly worked design. Width, 2⅛ inches. Price, per yard 6c

No. 18K03004 Cambric Edge. Fancy fillet edge design. Would retail at 10 cents per yard. Width, 2¼ inches. Price, per yard 8c

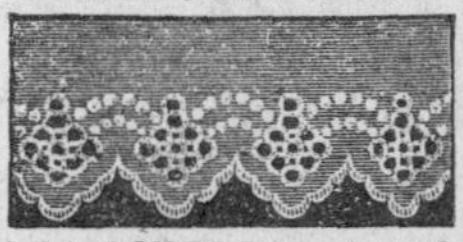

No. 18K03006 Cambric Edge. Nice openwork design. Width, 3 inches. Price, per yard 9c

No. 18K03007 Cambric Edge with beading edge for drawing No. 1 ribbon through. Always sells for 15 cents a yard. Used for edging corset covers. Width, 1⅜ inches. Price, per yard 10c

No. 18K03008 Cambric Edge in fillet mesh crescent design. Width, 3⅜ inches. Price, per yard 10c

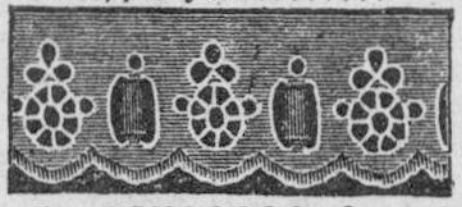

No. 18K03009 Cambric Edge with ribbon edge design for drawing No. 2 ribbon through. This style is used extensively for corset covers as an edging on plain cloth. Width, 3 inches. Price, per yard 12c

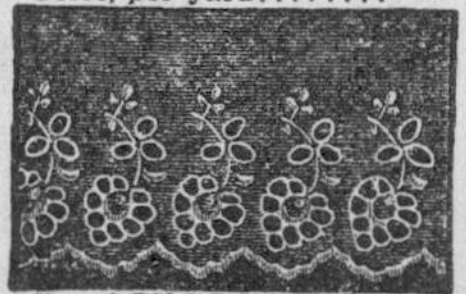

No. 18K03010 Cambric Edge in openwork leaf design. Width, 5 inches. Worth 19 cents. Our price, per yard 13c

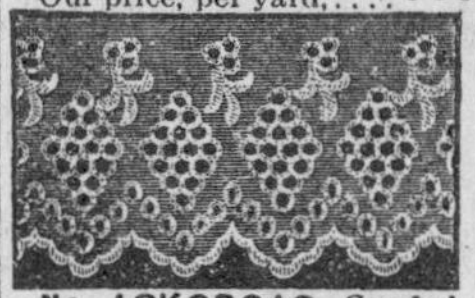

No. 18K03012 Cambric Edge. Very handsome effect. Good wearing edge. Width, 5¼ inches. Price, per yard 15c

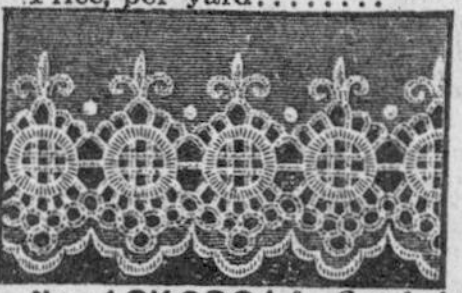

No. 18K03014 Cambric Edge in neat openwork button effect. Width, 5⅝ inches. Price, per yard 17c

No. 18K03016 Cambric Edge in combination fillet half moon and half leaf design. Extra value at the price. Width, 6½ inches. Price, per yard 18c

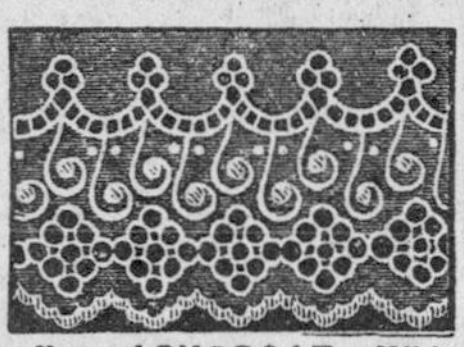

No. 18K03017 White Cambric Embroidery. A neat openwork and festoon design. Width, 7¼ inches. Price, per yard 19c

No. 18K03018 Cambric Edge in a neat heavily worked design. Width, 8½ inches. Price, per yard 19c

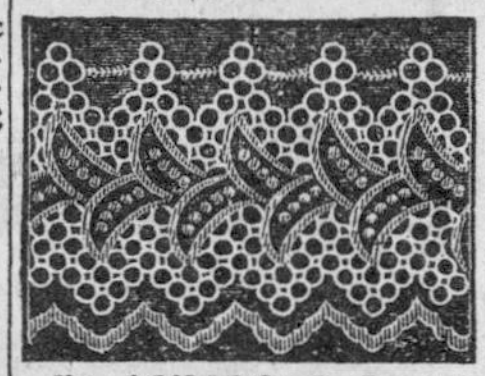

No. 18K03020 Cambric Edge in an extremely handsome openwork design. Would be cheap at 30 cents per yard. Width, 8¼ inches. Price, per yard 21c

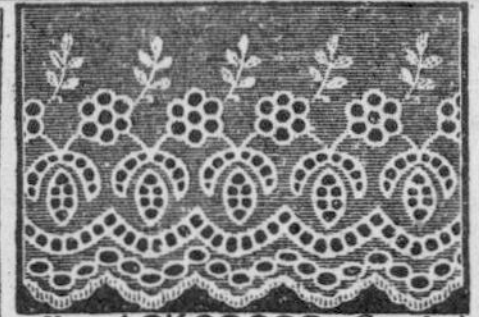

No. 18K03022 Cambric Edge. Openwork design. Closely stitched, very neat, clean pattern. Width, 8¼ inches. Price, per yard 23c

No. 18K03024 Cambric Edge in a neat openwork design. A splendid skirting pattern. Width, 12¼ inches. Price, per yard 25c

No. 18K03026 Cambric Edge. Combination openwork leaf and button design. Suitable for corset covers, skirting, etc. Width, 12⅝ inches. Price, per yard 27c

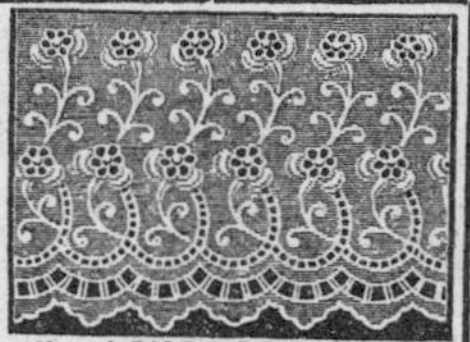

No. 18K03028 Cambric Edge in an exceptionally handsome, well worked leaf design. This is a very fine quality. Width, 10 inches. Price, per yard 31c

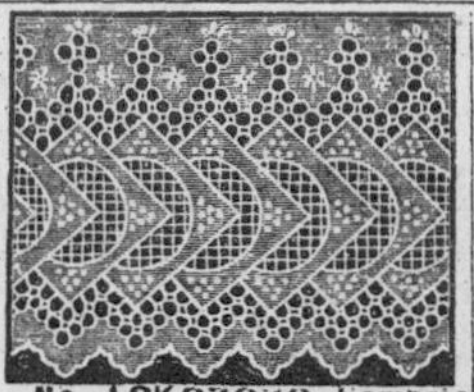

No. 18K03030 Cambric Edge in an entirely new fillet mesh block design. This is our best quality. Width, 13½ inches. Price, per yard 37c

17-Inch Cambric Embroidery.

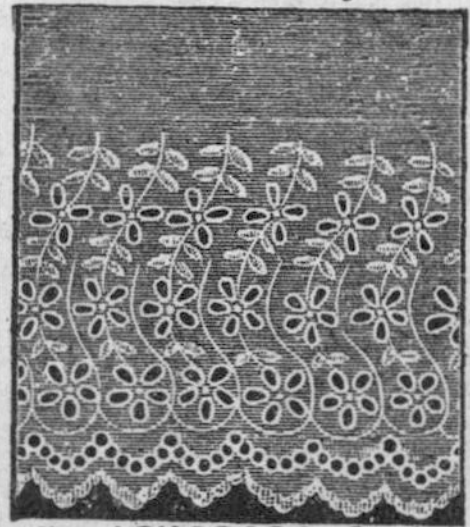

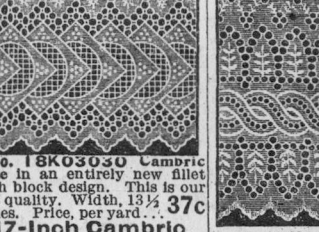

No. 18K03032 Cambric Edge in sweeping floral design. Openwork edge. Width, 17 inches. Price, per yard 32c

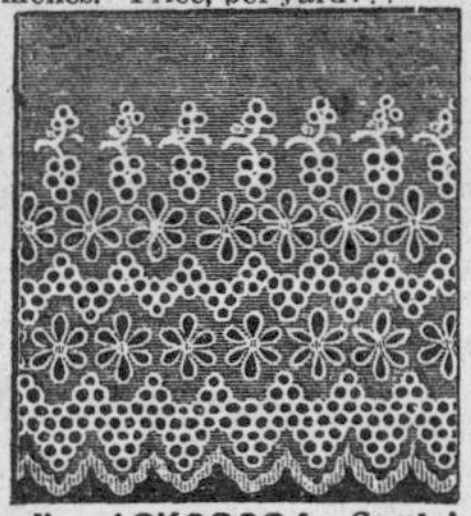

No. 18K03034 Cambric Edge. Exceptionally handsome pattern with a durable edge. Width, 17 inches. Price, per yard 38c

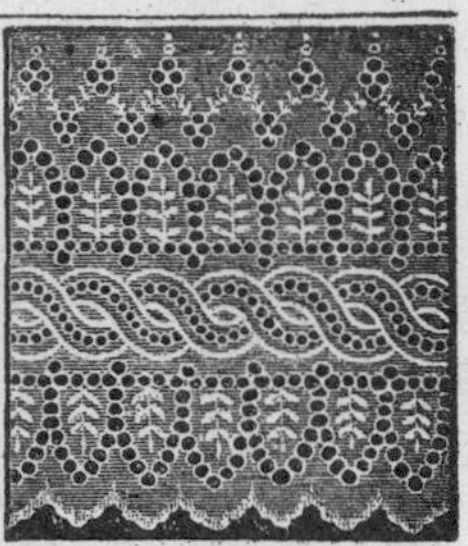

No. 18K03036 Cambric Edge. Fancy escurial openwork pattern. Width of work, 7¼ inches. Entire width of embroidery, 17 inches. Price, per yard 43c

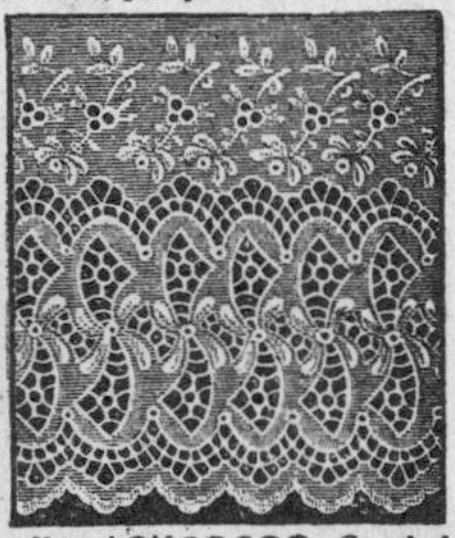

No. 18K03038 Cambric Edge. Openwork design. Width of work, 7½ inches. Entire width of embroidery, 17 inches. This is our best quality and is a regular 60-cent value. Price, per yard 49c

Colored Cambric Embroideries.

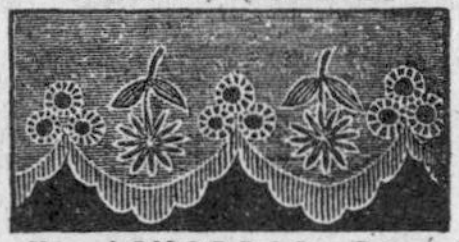

No. 18K03040 Colored Cambric Embroidery. Very neat openwork and floral design worked in colored threads on white cambric. Colors, white, with red, navy, pink and light blue embroidery. Width, 2½ inches. State color wanted. Price, per yard 9c

CAMBRIC INSERTIONS.

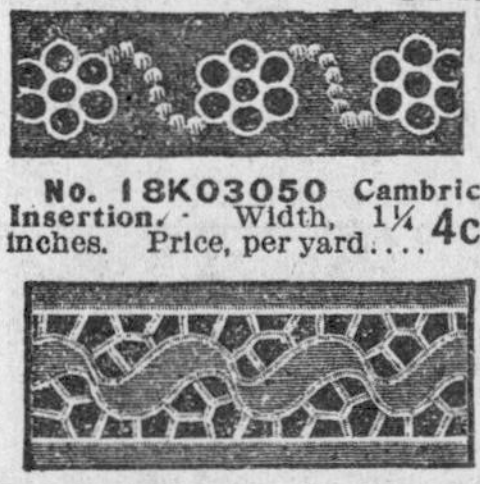

No. 18K03050 Cambric Insertion. Width, 1¼ inches. Price, per yard 4c

No. 18K03052 Cambric Insertion. A 10-cent value. Width, 1¾ inches. Price, per yard 7c

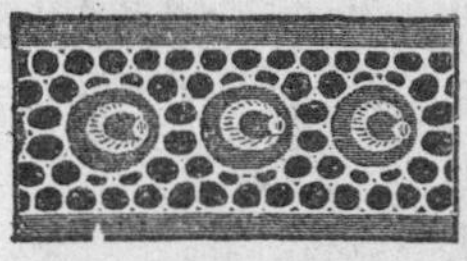

No. 18K03054 Cambric Insertion, suitable for any purpose. Width, 2⅜ inches. Price, per yard 9c

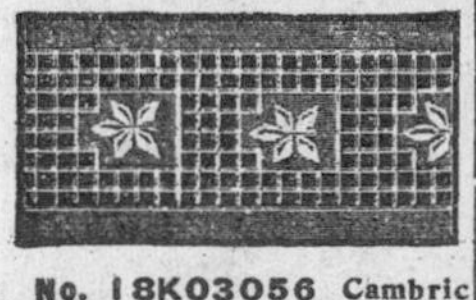

No. 18K03056 Cambric Insertion in a handsome fillet or square mesh design. Width, 2½ inches. Price, per yard 12c

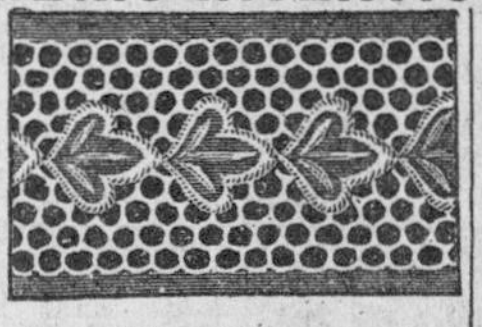

No. 18K03058 Cambric Insertion, good wide openwork effect. Width, 3¾ inches. Price, per yard 14c

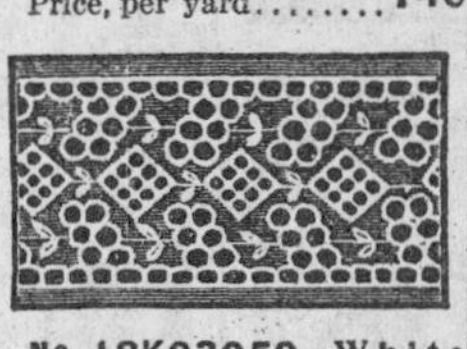

No. 18K03059 White Cambric Insertion. A dainty openwork design, finely worked on good quality cambric. Width 4 inches. Price, per yard 15c

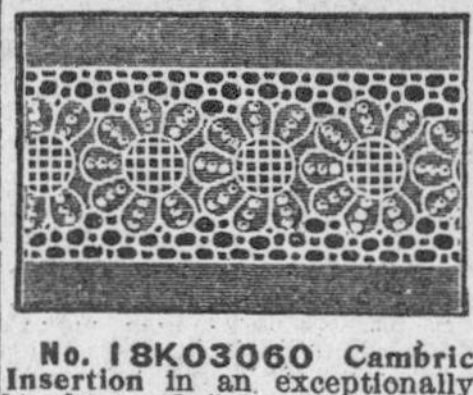

No. 18K03060 Cambric Insertion in an exceptionally handsome design. Very finely worked. Width, 3⅜ inches. Price, per yard 17c

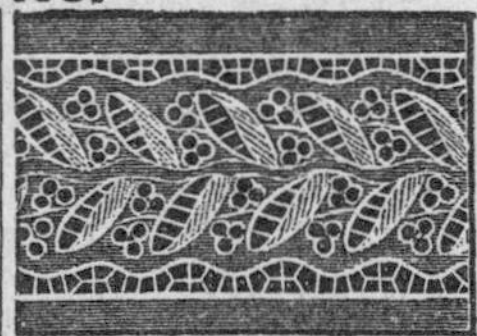

No. 18K03062 Cambric Insertion. Heavily shaded leaf effect center with openwork edge. Width, 4 inches. Price, per yard 20c

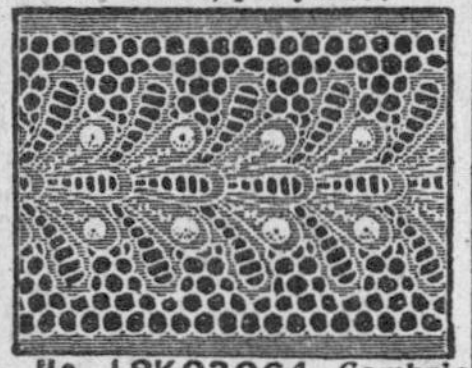

No. 18K03064 Cambric Insertion. Handsome openwork effect. Suitable for skirting or waists. Width, 5⅝ inches. Price, per yard 30c

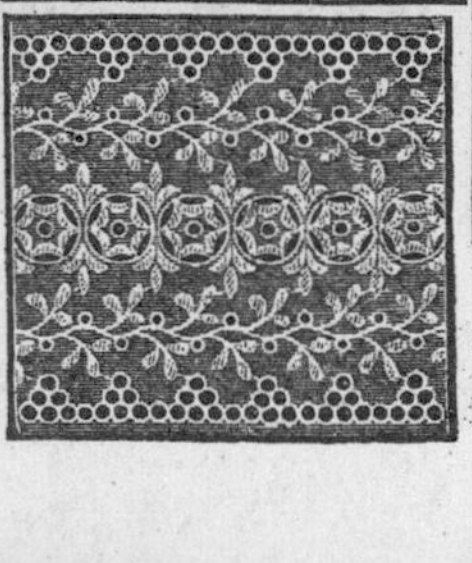

No. 18K03066 Cambric Insertion. One of the new idea waisting or skirting effects with a very wide lace design. Well worth 50 cents per yard. Width, 10 inches. Our price, per yard 38c

SWISS EMBROIDERY EDGES.

Swiss Edges are used extensively for trimming fine lingerie waists and Swiss dresses and the wider widths for corset covers. Swiss is a very light sheer cloth of finest weave and is extremely popular at the present time on account of its adaptability for trimming the white sheer materials that are so fashionable.

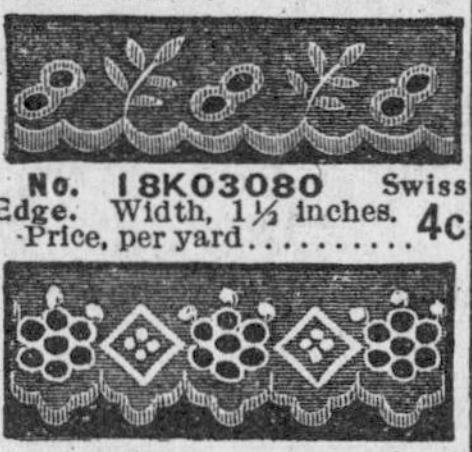

No. 18K03080 Swiss Edge. Width, 1½ inches. Price, per yard 4c

No. 18K03082 Swiss Edge in openwork design. Regular 10-cent value. Width, 2 inches. Price, per yard 8c

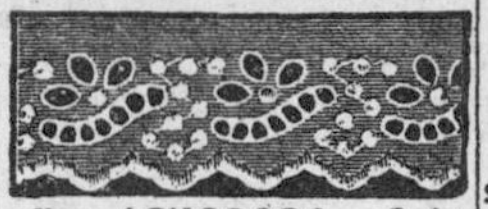

No. 18K03084 Swiss Edge. Very pretty design. Width, 2⅜ inches. Price, per yard 10c

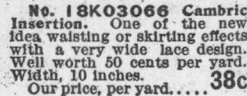

No. 18K03086 Swiss Edge in combination fillet mesh and openwork design. Width, 4 inches. Price, per yard 11c

No. 18K03088 Swiss Edge in fancy floral openwork design with extra well worked edge. Width, 4 inches. Price, per yard 12c

No. 18K03090 White Swiss Embroidery Edging. Very nicely worked with teneriffe wheel design. Width, 3½ inches. Price, per yard 13c

WE DO NOT SAMPLE EMBROIDERIES.

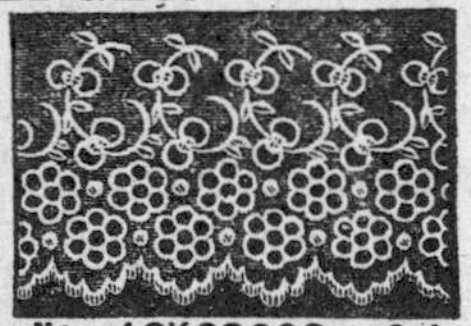

No. 18K03092 Swiss Edge. Handsome openwork design, deeply worked. Very special value at our price. Width, 7¼ inches. Price, per yard 17c

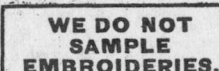

No. 18K03094 Swiss Edge. Wide openwork design in crescent effect. Width, 8½ ins. Price, per yard 20c

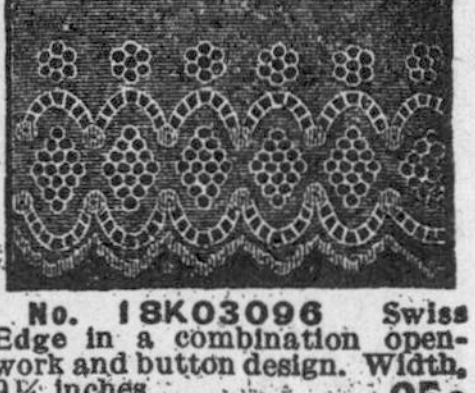

No. 18K03096 Swiss Edge in a combination openwork and button design. Width, 9¼ inches. Price, per yard 25c

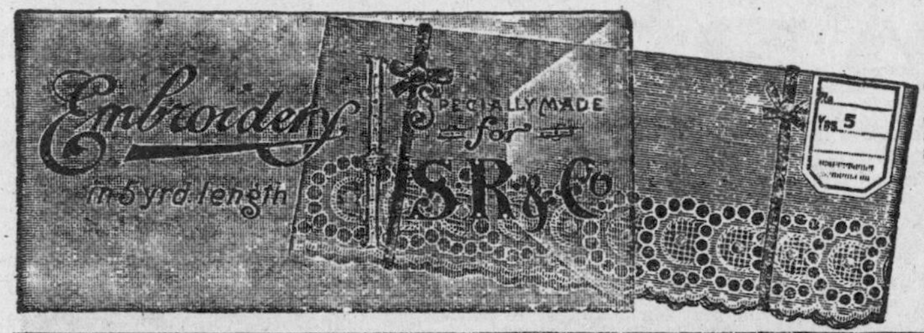

EMBROIDERIES IN 5-YARD LENGTHS

We herewith present an entirely new feature, embroideries put up in 5-yard lengths, neatly carded, folded and enclosed in a special envelope. Every woman knows that embroideries are made in short lengths and pieced together. Sometimes it is not convenient to use pieced embroidery on a garment, and for this reason we have gotten up this special 5-yard package. **The embroideries are made in one continuous length, no jointed seams or pieces, and the embroideries cannot be soiled by handling, as the special envelope fully protects them.** Our special 5-yard package should be appreciated by every woman; aside from the advantage which we have gained by placing exceptionally large orders on the numbers we show in this manner, which consequently permits us to name lower prices to you, the mere fact that **the goods will reach you in the best possible condition, always clean, neat and attractive, should make it a great inducement to every one to purchase their embroideries this way. The illustration which we show gives you an idea of how the package is made up.** The envelope is made of a special transparent paper so that the pattern of the embroidery shows through. Each 5-yard length is carded and tied with ribbon. Undoubtedly it is the neatest embroidery package that has ever been offered to the trade. Where embroideries are shown in 5-yard lengths we will not sell a less quantity. The prices quoted are for the 5-yard pieces.

Cambric Embroidery Edges Put Up in 5-Yard Pieces.

No. 18K03500 Cambric Edge Embroidery in neat openwork design. Width, 1¾ inches. Put up in special 5-yard package. Price, per package **25c**
If by mail, postage extra, per package, 3c.

No. 18K03502 Cambric Edge in dainty openwork design. Put up in 5-yard packages. Width, two inches.
Price, per package **35c**
If by mail, postage extra, per package, 3c.

No. 18K03504 Cambric Edge in fancy openwork design. Put up in 5-yard packages. Width, 2¾ inches.
Price, per package **40c**
If by mail, postage extra, per package, 3c.

No. 18K03506 Cambric Edge in fancy floral and scroll design in 5-yard packages. Width, 3½ inches.
Price, per package **49c**
If by mail, postage extra, per package, 3c.

No. 18K03508 Cambric Edge, openwork design. Sold only in 5-yard packages. Width, 4¼ inches. Price, per package.......... **55c**
If by mail, postage extra, per package, 4c.

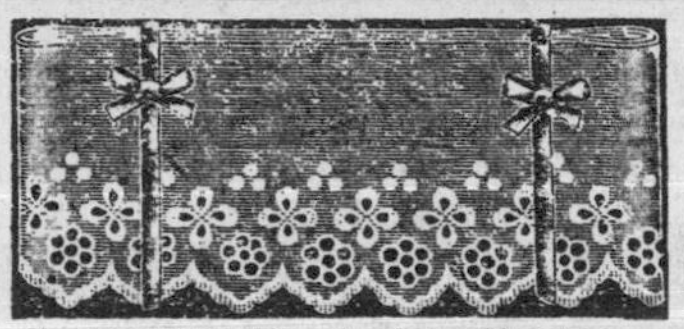

No. 18K03510 Cambric Edge in a very neat design. Sold only in 5-yard packages. Width, 4¾ inches. Price, per package.. **60c**
If by mail, postage extra, per package, 4c.

No. 18K03512 Cambric Edge in dainty fillet mesh wheel design. Very fine quality. Put up in 5-yard packages. Width, 3¾ inches. Price, per package **68c**
If by mail, postage extra, per package, 4c.

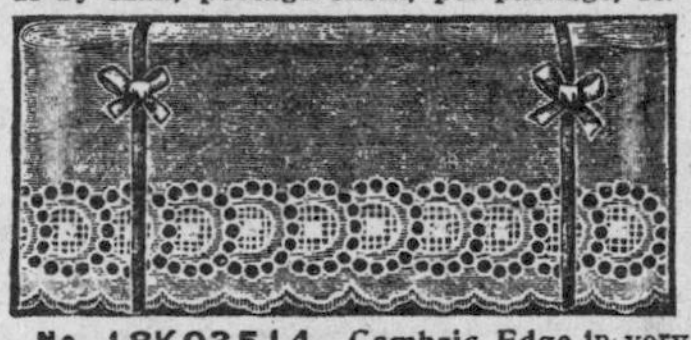

No. 18K03514 Cambric Edge in very dainty fillet mesh crescent design. Put up in 5-yard packages. Width, 4½ inches.
Price, per package.................. **79c**
If by mail, postage extra, per package, 4c.

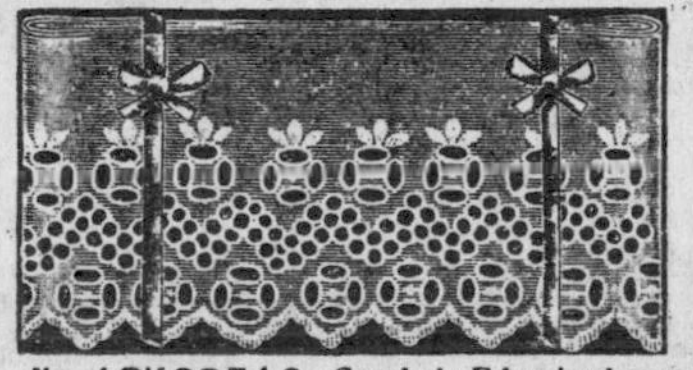

No. 18K03516 Cambric Edge in showy openwork design. Splendid skirting pattern. Width, 7 inches. Sold only in packages of 5 yards. This pattern would sell retail for 25 cents per yard.
Our price, per package.................. **85c**
If by mail, postage extra, per package, 4c.

Swiss Embroidery in 5-Yard Pieces.

No. 18K03520 Swiss Edge in openwork design. Width, 2 inches. Sold only in 5-yard packages. Price, per package... **30c**
If by mail, postage extra, per package, 3c.

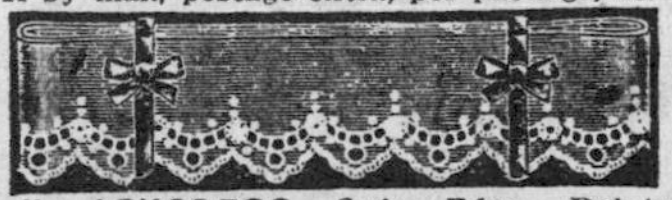

No. 18K03522 Swiss Edge. Dainty button and openwork design. Very finely worked. Width, 2½ inches. Sold only in 5-yard packages. Price, per package.... **40c**
If by mail, postage extra, per package, 3c.

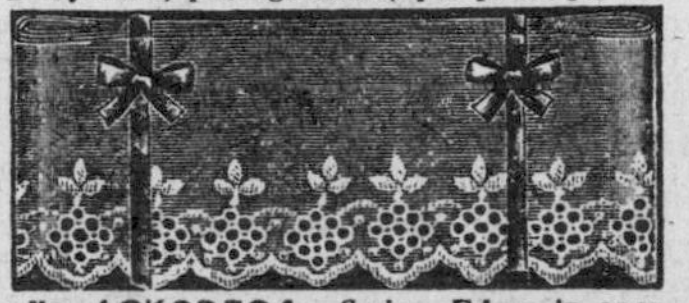

No. 18K03524 Swiss Edge in openwork design in diamond effect. Width, 4½ inches. Sold only in 5-yard packages. Price, per package................ **55c**
If by mail, postage extra, per package, 4c.

No. 18K03526 Swiss Edge in openwork wheel design. Width, 4½ inches. Sold only in 5-yard packages. Price, per package.. **05c**
If by mail, postage extra, per package, 4c.

Nainsook Embroidery in 5-Yard Pieces.

No. 18K03530 Nainsook Edge in circular design with block centers. Width, 2 inches. Sold only in 5-yard packages.
Price, per package **40c**
If by mail, postage extra, per package, 3c.

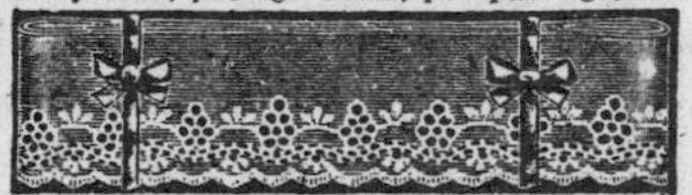

No. 18K03532 Nainsook Edge in very dainty design. Width, 2½ inches. Sold only in 5-yard packages.
Price, per package.............. **45c**
If by mail, postage extra, per package, 3c.

No. 18K03534 Nainsook Edge in very effective openwork design. Width, 4 inches. Sold only in 5-yard packages.
Price, per package.............. **60c**
If by mail, postage extra, per package, 3c.

No. 18K03536 Nainsook Edge. Very attractive Anglaise eyelet design. Splendid trimming for fine dresses. Width, 4½ inches. Price, per package.............. **65c**
If by mail, postage extra, per package, 4c.

Ever Ready Buttonholes.

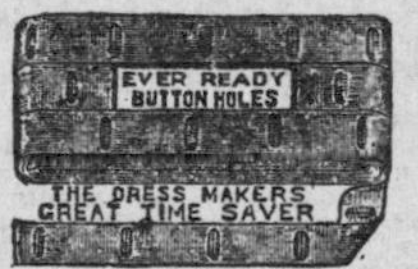

No. 18K03554 Ever Ready Buttonholes are an entirely new idea and a great time saver, relieving dressmakers, in fact, everyone who does sewing, of the tedious and tiresome work of making buttonholes. Ever Ready buttonhoes are made on the finest quality sheer lawn and can be used on the finest waists. The stitches on the button holes are made evener and stronger than could possibly be done by hand at home. Buttonholes are two inches apart and of the correct size for waists, underwear, or any place where buttonholes are used. It requires 18 inches to the waist. Comes in white only. Width, ¾ inch.
Price, per piece of 54 inches, enough for three waists.................. **23c**

COMPLETE CORSET COVER PATTERNS

THE MANY ADVANTAGES GAINED by buying our Complete Corset Cover Patterns will be readily seen by every woman. The shoulder straps always match the embroidery, and we give you three yards of ribbon in the correct width to use as a draw string. We have these complete corset cover patterns made up especially for us according to our own original ideas. We pack each pattern in a neat pasteboard box, which insures the goods reaching you in the best possible condition.

OUR SEMI-MADE CORSET COVER PATTERNS are the most perfect ready to make garment ever offered for sale. They are made on the same style as the regular embroidery corset cover, but have the armholes cut out and closely embroidered around the edges, so that they require no binding and fit perfectly under the arm.

Each complete corset cover pattern consists of 1¼ yards of 17-inch embroidery with 28 inches of galoon insertions for shoulder straps, and three yards of good quality ribbon, which can be ordered in either pink or light blue.

DON'T OVERLOOK THE EXTRAORDINARY LOW PRICES that we name.
Remember, the prices we quote are for the Complete Corset Cover pattern all ready to be made up. The patterns are not made or shaped, but there is sufficient material to make any style of corset cover that may be desired. Order one of these styles from us, you will be more than pleased with the value you receive.

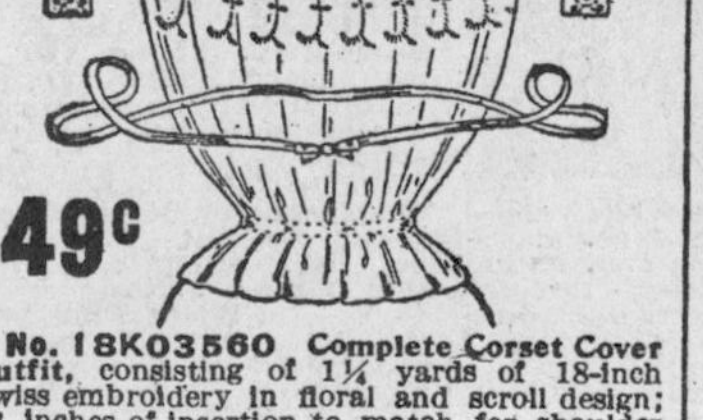

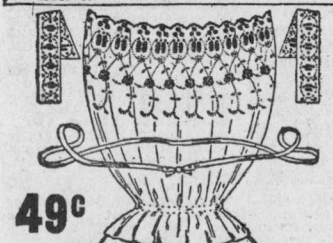

49c

No. 18K03560 Complete Corset Cover Outfit, consisting of 1¼ yards of 18-inch Swiss embroidery in floral and scroll design; 28 inches of insertion to match for shoulder straps, which gives 14 inches for each strap; also 3 yards of extra quality No. 1½ satin ribbon, which can be ordered in either pink or light blue. State color wanted.
Price, complete.................. **49c**
If by mail, postage extra, 5 cents.

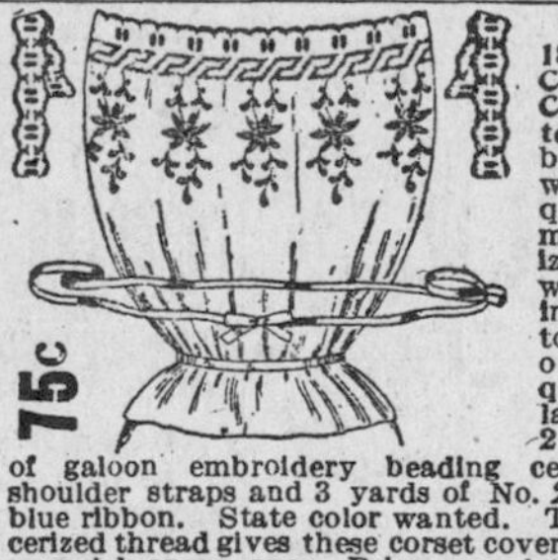

75c

No. 18K03562 Corset Cover Pattern embroidered with fine quality mercerized thread with beading edge top, made of extra quality lawn with 28 inches of galoon embroidery beading center for shoulder straps and 3 yards of No. 2 pink or blue ribbon. State color wanted. The mercerized thread gives these corset covers a very rich appearance. Price, complete... **75c**
If by mail, postage extra, 5 cents.

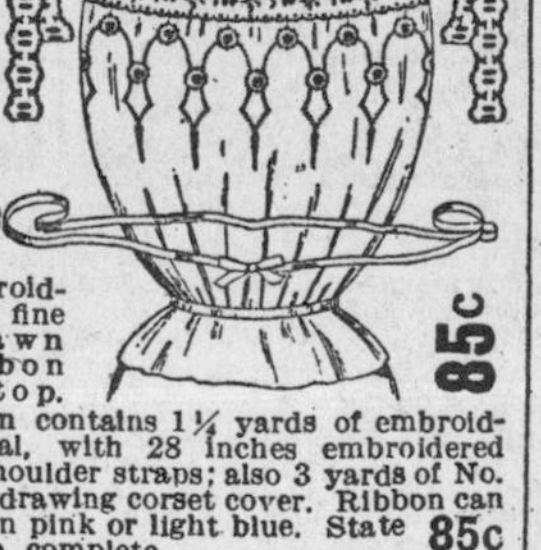

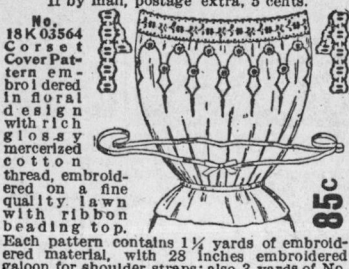

85c

No. 18K03564 Corset Cover Pattern embroidered in floral design with rich glossy mercerized cotton thread, embroidered on a fine quality lawn with ribbon beading top. Each pattern contains 1½ yards of embroidered material, with 28 inches embroidered galoon for shoulder straps; also 3 yards of No. 2 ribbon for drawing corset cover. Ribbon can be ordered in pink or light blue. State color. Price, complete.................. **85c**
If by mail, postage extra, 5 cents.

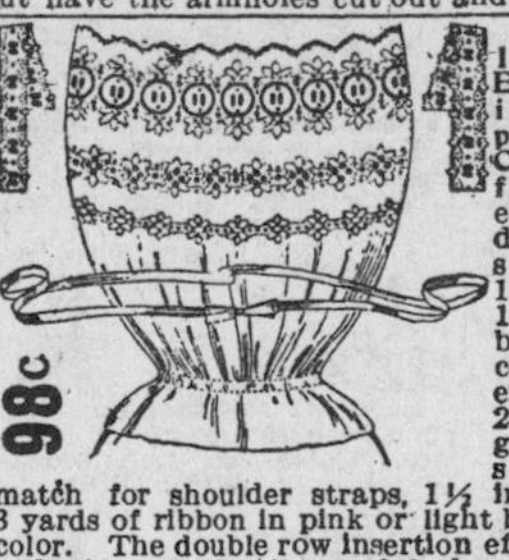

98c

No. 18K03566 Extra quality Complete Corset Cover Outfit in a very elaborate design, consisting of 1¼ yards of 17-inch beading edge corset cover embroidery; 28 inches galoon insertion to match for shoulder straps, 1½ inches wide, 3 yards of ribbon in pink or light blue. State color. The double row insertion effect on this embroidery makes it one of the handsomest designs ever shown. Each complete pattern packed in neat box. Price, complete... **98c**
If by mail, postage extra, 5 cents.

Semi-Made Corset Cover Patterns.

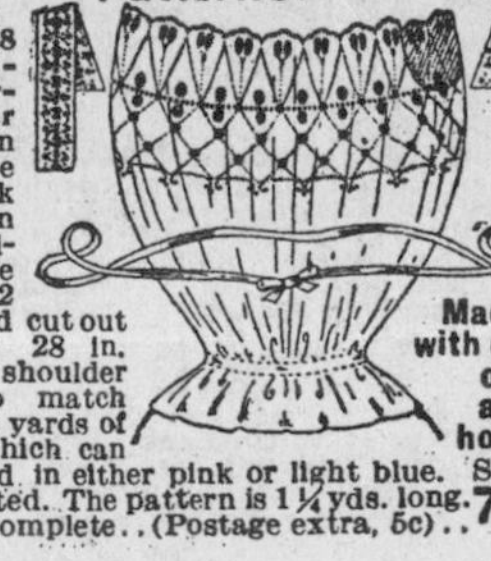

Made with cut-out arm holes.

No. 18K03568 Semi-Made Corset Cover Pattern in handsome openwork design with beading edge for No. 2 ribbon and cut out armholes; 28 in. of galoon shoulder straps to match and three yards of ribbon, which can be ordered in either pink or light blue. State color wanted. The pattern is 1¼ yds. long. **70c**
Price, complete..(Postage extra, 5c)..

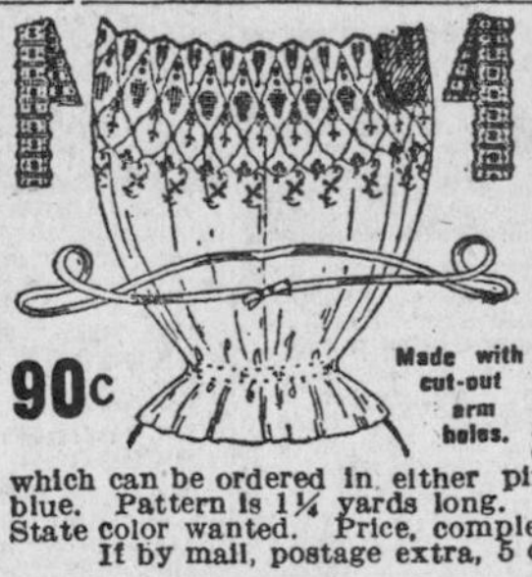

90c

Made with cut-out arm holes.

No. 18K03570 Semi-made Corset Cover Pattern in rich openwork design with beading edge and cut out armholes; also 28 inches of galoon shoulder straps to match, and 3 yards of ribbon, which can be ordered in either pink or light blue. Pattern is 1¼ yards long. State color wanted. Price, complete, **90c**
If by mail, postage extra, 5 cents.

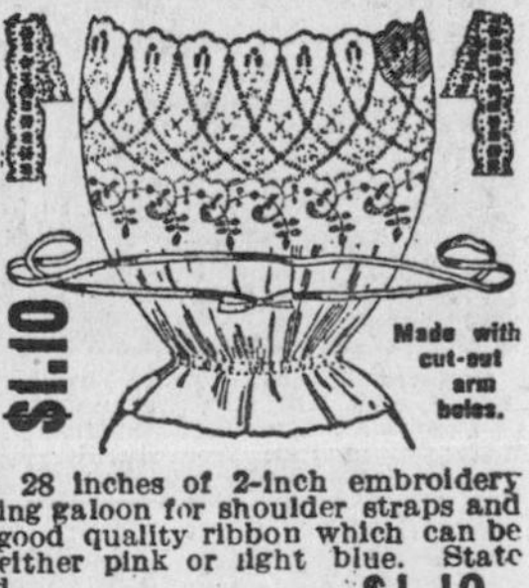

$1.10

Made with cut-out arm holes.

No. 18K03572 Semi-made Corset Cover Pattern in an entirely new fillet mesh design with elaborate embroidery work in very dainty effect. The entire pattern contains 1¼ yards of embroidery; 28 inches of 2-inch embroidery ribbon beading galoon for shoulder straps and 3 yards of good quality ribbon which can be ordered in either pink or light blue. State color wanted.
Price, complete.................. **$1.10**
If by mail, postage extra, 5 cents.

LACE DEPARTMENT

LOWEST PRICES, HIGHEST QUALITIES, NEWEST DESIGNS.

EVERY DAY IS BARGAIN DAY IN OUR LACE DEPARTMENT.

We sell better qualities at lower prices than retail dealers can buy them for. Our styles are the newest and the collections which we now offer represent our new line for this season.

We show a complete line of all staple and fancy laces, including English Nottingham Laces, French Valenciennes Laces, Silk Chantilly Laces, Plauen and Oriental Laces; also an unequaled line of lace allovers. In fact, every style of lace that is in demand or is being used for trimming underwear, waists, dresses, hats, etc. Only high grade qualities are represented in our line this season. In fact, never before have we shown as fine quality laces, and we recognize that the demand of our trade is for better grade goods, and in selecting our lace line we have borne this in mind. You can order the finest qualities of our laces with all confidence as they are suitable for trimming the finest and sheerest materials.

When you send us an order for laces, you are fully protected, as we guarantee all our qualities to be perfectly satisfactory and to be just exactly as represented. If you do not find them so you are at liberty to return them to us at our expense and we will cheerfully exchange for other merchandise or refund your money.

Our prices are so low and our values so extraordinary that we are obliged to sell certain styles of our laces in 12-yard pieces. Wherever we sell lace put up in 12-yard pieces under no consideration can we sell a less quantity. In every instance where we sell lace by the dozen yards it is always such styles as can be used in that quantity, and you will find it economy to buy such laces from us because you will pay the same elsewhere for a few yards that we charge you for twelve.

When you require lace do not overlook the great money saving prices which we name throughout our entire lace department and do not be misled into the belief that our very low prices mean inferior qualities. We assure you that our qualities are satisfactory and considerably better than is usually handled by any retail dealer.

Postage on laces varies according to width and quality, but be sure to allow from 4 to 10 cents per dozen yards extra if you desire lace sent by mail. If you send too much money we will refund it to you. We do not sample laces.

Pillow or American Laces.

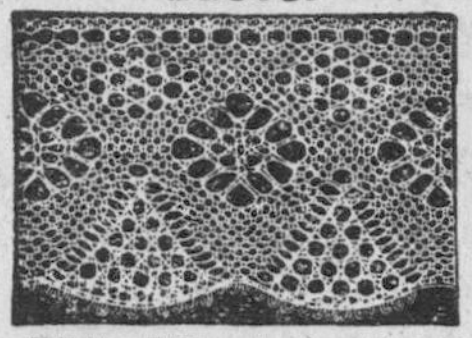

White Pillow Lace. A new double thread pattern, very serviceable quality. Comes in four widths.

Cat. No.	Width, inches	Price, per doz. yards
18K06000	1¼	18c
18K06001	2½	27c
18K06004	3½	35c
18K06005	5⅛	50c

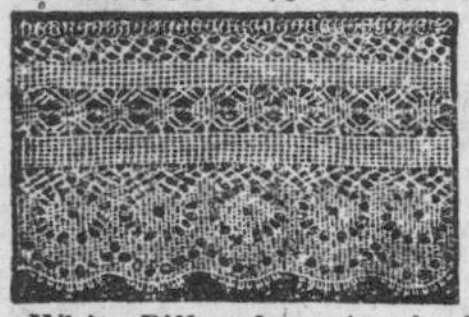

White Pillow Lace in wheel design with heavy insertion effect. A very attractive pattern. Comes in four widths.

Cat. No.	Width, inches	Price, per doz. yards
18K06010	1¼	25c
18K06011	2	33c
18K06013	2¾	42c
18K06014	3¾	53c

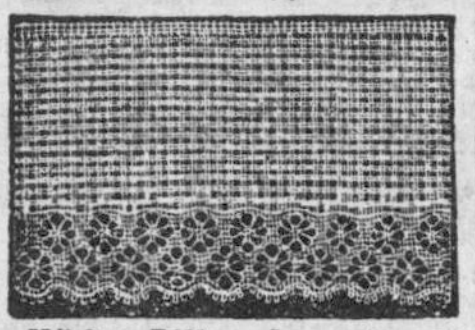

White Pillow Lace in new filet mesh design with wheel pattern edge. This is an exceptionally durable and attractive pattern, and one we highly recommend. Comes in four widths.

Cat. No.	Width, inches	Price, per doz. yards
18K06020	1¼	42c
18K06021	2	59c
18K06023	2¾	70c
18K06024	3½	89c

Everlasting Lace Trimming.

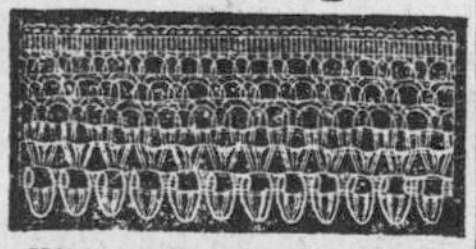

White Everlasting Lace Trimming, made of an extra strong, double cotton thread. This lace is unexcelled for wearing qualities and is used extensively for underwear and children's dresses or where a good wearing lace trimming is desired.

Cat. No.	Width inches	Price, per doz. yards
18K06029	⅝	16c
18K06030	⅞	20c
18K06031	1	26c

German Torchon Laces.

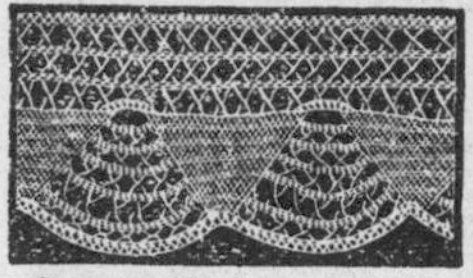

German Machine made Torchon Laces are very popular, as they wash and wear splendidly. Comes in five widths. White only.

Cat. No.	Width, inches	Price, per doz. yards
18K06035	⅜	6c
18K06036	⅝	11c
18K06037	⅞	15c
18K06038	1⅛	18c
18K06039	1⅜	22c

Sevilla Torchon Laces.

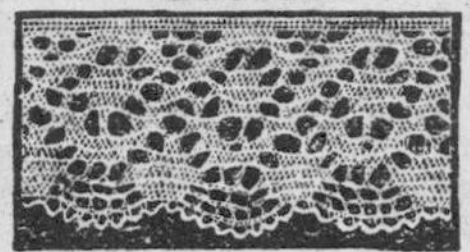

White Sevilla Torchon Lace, made of a very strong but fine thread in neat crochet design. Comes in five width laces with insertion to match.

Cat. No.	Width, inches	Price, per doz. yards
18K06044	½	18c
18K06046	1	24c
18K06047	1¼	36c
18K06048	1¾	48c
18K06049	2¼	56c

No. 18K06050 White Insertion to match above lace, 1⅛ inches. Price, per DOZEN YARDS........ 36c

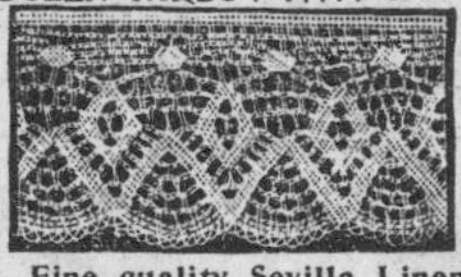

Fine quality Sevilla Linen Torchon Lace in neat craquelle effect. This is a splendid quality for fine underwear and children's dresses. Comes in five widths with insertion to match. White only.

Cat. No.	Width, inches	Price, per doz. yards
18K06054	½	30c
18K06055	¾	42c
18K06057	1¼	58c
18K06058	1¾	69c
18K06059	2¼	90c

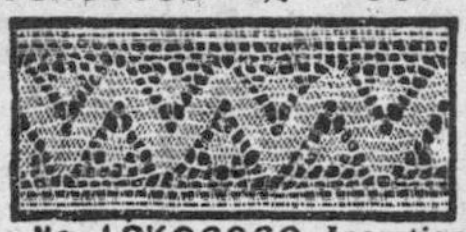

No. 18K06060 Insertion to match above lace. Width, 1¼ inches. White only. Price, per DOZEN YARDS.............. 58c

Real Linen Torchon Laces.

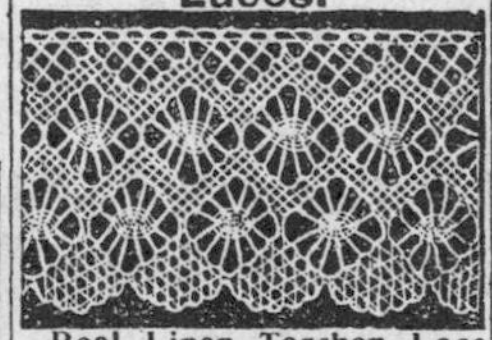

Real Linen Torchon Lace in double thread effect. The most durable lace made. Comes in five widths. White only.

Cat. No.	Width, inches	Price, per yard
18K06065	¾	4c
18K06066	1	7c
18K06067	1¼	10c
18K06068	1¾	12c
18K06069	2	14c

No. 18K06070 Real Linen Torchon Lace Insertion to match above lace. Width, 1¼ inches. White only. Price, per yard........ 8c

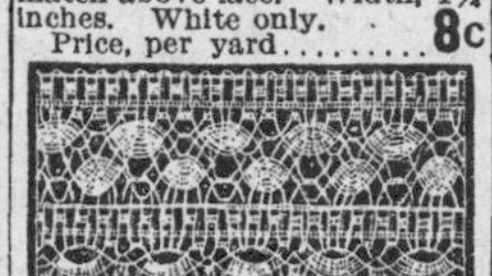

Real Linen Torchon Lace, made of a fine quality double thread. A very attractive pattern. Comes in three widths. White only.

Cat. No.	Width, inches	Price, per yard
18K06075	1	8c
18K06076	1¼	10c
18K06077	1½	13c

No. 18K06078 Real Linen Torchon Insertion to match above lace. Width, 1 inch. White only. Price, per yard........ 8c

Linen Torchon Lace.

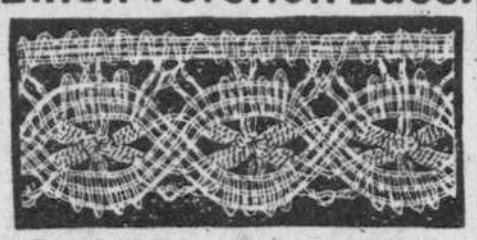

Real Linen Torchon Lace. An entirely new cluny design. This is a very fine quality and a pattern we strongly recommend. Comes in three widths. White only.

Cat. No.	Width, inches	Price, per yard
18K06085	¾	8c
18K06086	1¼	12c
18K06087	1½	15c

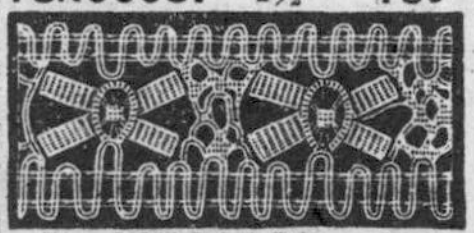

No. 18K06089 Real Linen Torchon Insertion to match above lace. Width, ¾-inch. White only. Price, per yard........ 8c

English Nottingham Torchon Laces.

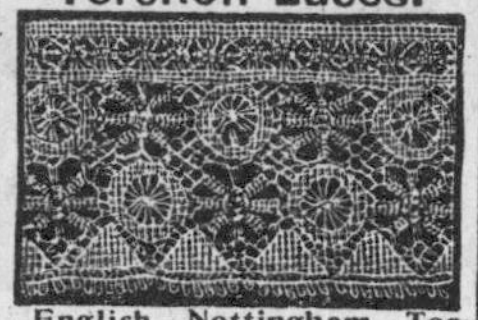

English Nottingham Torchon Lace in new cluny and wheel design. Made of a double thread. Very attractive pattern. Comes in four widths.

Cat. No.	Width, inches	Price, per doz. yards
18K06091	1	25c
18K06096	1¾	36c
18K06097	2½	45c
18K06098	3¼	59c

English Nottingham Torchon Insertion to match above lace. Comes in two widths. White only.

Cat. No.	Width, inches	Price, per doz. yards
18K06099	1¼	29c
18K06101	1¾	39c

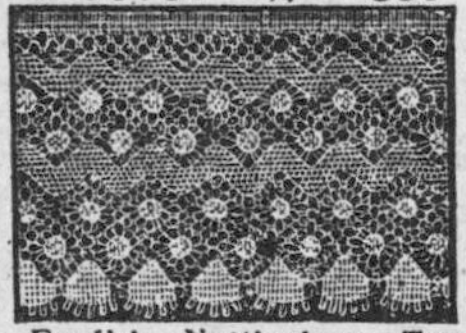

English Nottingham Torchon Lace in handsome baby Irish effect. Comes in four widths. White only.

Cat. No.	Width, inches	Price, per doz. yards
18K06108	1¼	32c
18K06110	1⅞	40c
18K06112	2½	49c
18K06114	3½	70c

English Nottingham Torchon Insertion to match above lace. Comes in two widths. White only.

Cat. No.	Width, inches	Price, per doz. yards
18K06116	1	29c
18K06117	1½	36c

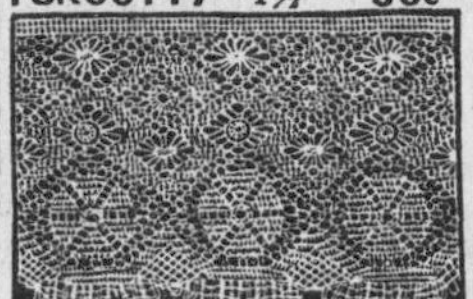

English Nottingham White Torchon Lace in new antique pattern with teneriffe top design. Comes in three widths.

Cat. No.	Width, inches	Price, per doz. yards
18K06126	1½	42c
18K06128	2⅛	49c
18K06129	2¾	69c

No. 18K06131 English Nottingham White Torchon Insertion to match above lace. Width, 1½ inches. Price, per DOZEN YARDS.... 45c

English Torchon Laces.

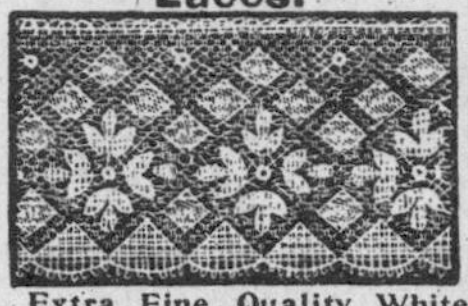

Extra Fine Quality White English Nottingham Torchon Lace. Suitable for the finest underwear. In a very neat combination fleur de lis design. Comes in three widths.

Cat. No.	Width, inches	Price, per doz. yards
18K06135	¾	33c
18K06136	1½	50c
18K06138	2	70c

White English Nottingham Insertion to match above lace. Comes in two widths.

Cat. No.	Width, inches	Price, per doz. yards
18K06139	¾	35c
18K06140	1½	52c

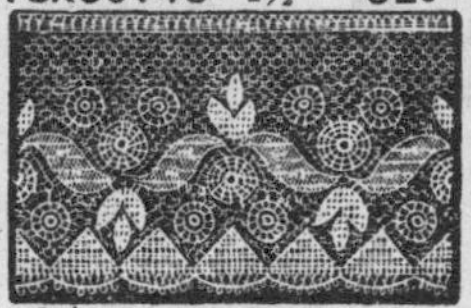

Our Finest Quality White English Nottingham Torchon Lace, in neat ribbon design with round mesh ground. This is a very pretty trimming for the finest underwear or waists. Comes in three widths.

Cat. No.	Width, inches	Price, per doz. yards
18K06145	¾	39c
18K06146	1½	69c
18K06147	2¼	85c

No. 18K06148 English Nottingham White Torchon Insertion, to match above lace. Width, 1 inch. Price, per DOZEN YARDS.............. 47c

Fancy Cluny Laces.

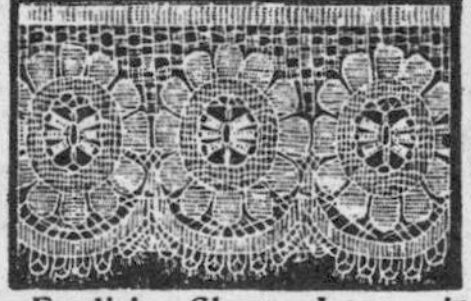

English Cluny Lace, in handsome, bold design, used extensively for fancy work. Comes in three widths. Colors, white or ecru.

Cat. No.	Width, inches	Price, per doz. yards
18K06153	1¾	$0.47
18K06154	2½	.69
18K06155	4½	1.10

English Cluny Insertion, to match above lace. Comes in two widths. Colors, white or ecru.

Cat. No.	Width, inches	Price, per doz. yards
18K06156	1½	47c
18K06157	2½	69c

English Antique Laces.

White English Antique Lace, in a pretty conventional design. This makes a very attractive and inexpensive trimming. Comes in three widths.

Cat. No.	Width, inches	Price, per yard
18K06162	1¾	7c
18K06163	3	11c
18K06164	3½	15c

No. 18K06165 White English Antique Insertion, to match above lace. Width, 2 inches. Price, per yard........ 8c

Fancy Valenciennes Laces.

Fancy Round Mesh White Valenciennes Lace, in tulip design. Comes in four widths.

Cat. No.	Width, inches	Price, per doz. yards
18K06170	1½	$0.45
18K06171	2	.59
18K06172	3	.85
18K06173	4	1.10

Fancy White Valenciennes Insertion, to match above lace. Comes in two widths.

Cat. No.	Width, inches	Price, per doz. yards
18K06174	1	39c
18K06175	1½	46c

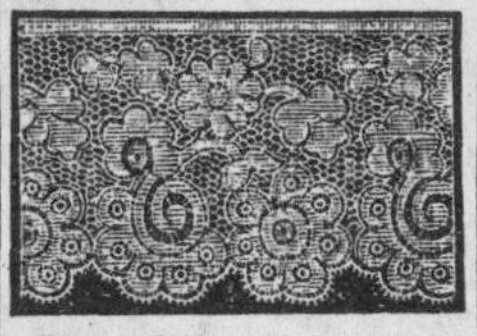

Fancy White Valenciennes Lace. Round mesh ground with fancy floral and scroll design. Comes in three widths.

Cat. No.	Width, inches	Price, per doz. yards
18K06180	1½	$0.69
18K06181	2½	.98
18K06182	3½	1.23

No. 18K06183 Fancy White Valenciennes Insertion, to match the above lace, Width, 1½ inches. Price, per DOZEN YARDS.............. 70c

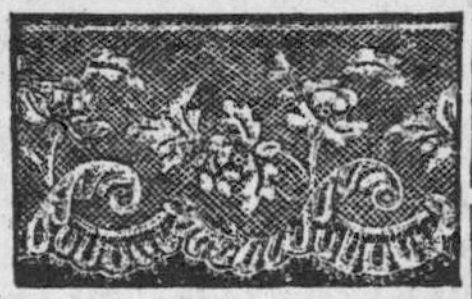

Fancy White Platte Valenciennes Lace, in very handsome floral and leaf design with good strong edge. This is our finest quality. Comes in three widths.

Cat. No.	Width, inches	Price, per doz. yards
18K06188	1¾	$0.75
18K06189	2	1.05
18K06190	3½	1.42

No. 18K06191 Fancy White Platte Insertion, to match the above lace. Width, 1¾ inches. Price, per DOZEN YARDS.............. 75c

Fancy Raised Valenciennes Laces.

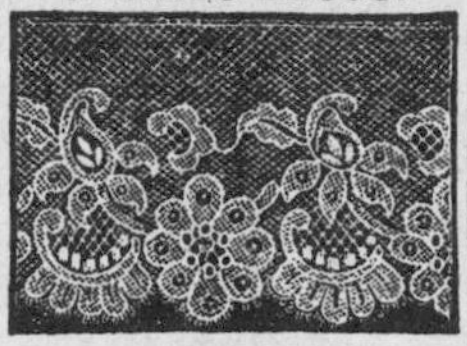

Fancy Raised White Valenciennes Lace, in a new daisy pattern. Comes in four widths.

Cat. No.	Width, inches	Price, per doz. yards
18K06195	1½	42c
18K06197	2½	69c
18K06198	3½	79c
18K06199	4½	98c

No. 18K06201 Fancy Raised White Valenciennes Insertion to match above lace. Width, 1¼ inches. Price, per DOZEN YARDS.............. 45c

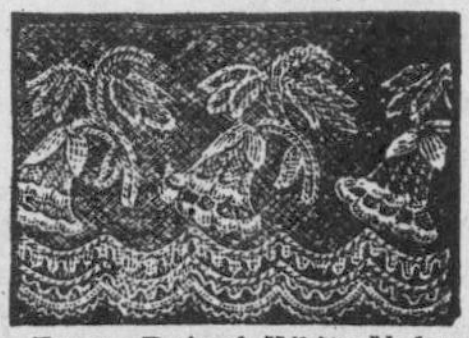

Fancy Raised White Valenciennes Lace, in blue bell design. Comes in four widths.

Cat. No.	Width, inches	Price, per doz. yards
18K06208	1¼	$0.49
18K06210	2	.65
18K06212	3	.98
18K06214	4	1.1?

No. 18K06215 Fancy Raised White Valenciennes Insertion, to match above lace. Width, 1½ inches. Price, per DOZEN YARDS..... 52c

Fancy Raised White Valenciennes Lace, in combination craquelle and diamond mesh ground with floral and leaf design. Comes in three widths.

Cat. No.	Width, inches	Price, per 6-yd. piece
18K06220	1½	29c
18K06221	2½	46c
18K06222	4	69c

No. 18K06223 Fancy Raised White Valenciennes Insertion, to match above lace. Width, 1½ inches. Price, per 6-YARD PIECE.............. 34c

Nottingham Baby Irish Laces.

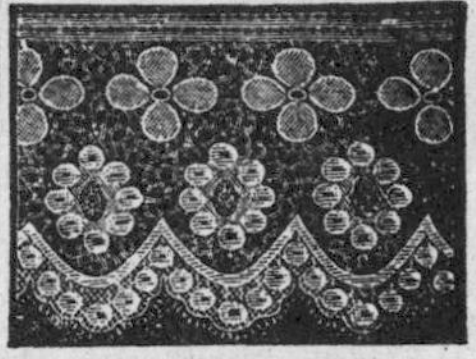

White Nottingham Baby Irish Lace, an entirely new effect. Comes in three widths.

Cat. No.	Width, inches	Price, per 6-yd. piece
18K06230	2½	45c
18K06231	3¼	59c
18K06232	4½	76c

No. 18K06233 White Nottingham Baby Irish Insertion, to match above lace. Width, 1½ inches. Price, per 6-YARD PIECE.............. 38c

Oriental Laces.

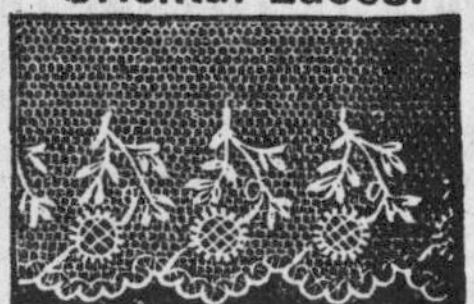

White Oriental or Net Top Lace. Fine quality net with neat floral and spray design. Comes in three widths.

Cat. No.	Width, inches	Price, per yard
18K06238	3½	9c
18K06239	4	12c
18K06240	5¾	15c

No. 18K06242 White Oriental or Net Top Insertion, to match above lace. Width, 1½ inches. Price, per yard........ 9c

Champagne or Butter Color Oriental or Net Top Lace edge. Same pattern as above. Comes in three widths.

Cat. No.	Width, inches	Price, per yard
18K06245	3½	9c
18K06246	4	12c
18K06247	5¾	15c

No. 18K06249 Champagne or Butter Color Oriental or Net Top Insertion, to match above lace. Width, 1½ inches. Price, per yard........ 9c

OUR BIG VALUE LACE ASSORTMENTS

OUR BIG VALUE LACE ASSORTMENTS have been expressly made up at the urgent request of many of our customers, who buy lace from us to use as a profitable line for house to house canvassing. Our sole object in making up these assortments has been to give our customers the greatest lace values they possibly could secure in the most popular styles and best patterns of quick selling laces. You can more than double your money on our big value lace assortments and still sell the goods at a lower price than is usually charged by retail dealers. If you do any canvassing or have a desire to try this pleasing and profitable way of earning money, we know of no better buying opportunity or quicker selling line that will pay as handsome profits as we now offer you in our lace assortments.
SEND US YOUR ORDER for one of our Big Value Lace Assortments. We know you will be more than pleased with the remarkable values you can get in laces from us for so little money. Our lace assortments are packed in special hinged covered strong pasteboard boxes suitable for carrying.

$6.50 LACE ASSORTMENT FOR $3.00

No. 18K010 You can easily get $6.50 or more for this lace assortment and still sell the goods cheaper than your home dealer would. This assortment consists of twelve dozen yards of lace, or in other words 144 yards of lace, at a cost of about 2 cents per yard, for which you can get an average price of 4½ cents per yard, more than double your money. The lace is assorted in the following styles: pillow lace, English torchon lace, everlasting lace, fancy laces; ranging in width from the narrow valenciennes lace to the wide 3½-inch fancy laces. The assortment is made up of nine pieces of one dozen yards each of lace edgings, two pieces of one dozen yards each of lace insertion and one piece of one dozen yards beading.

Complete assortment of 144 yards, only **$3.00**

OUR CHALLENGE $13.00 LACE ASSORTMENT FOR $5.00

No. 18K012 You will have no trouble in getting $13.00 or more for this assortment and still sell the goods under the regular retail price. This assortment consists of twenty-four pieces of one dozen yards each, or a total of 288 yards, at a cost of less than 2 cents per yard, on which you can get an average price of over 4½ cents per yard, or more than double your money. In the assortment we give you seventeen dozen yards lace edging, six dozen yards lace insertion and one dozen yards valenciennes beading in the following style laces: pillow lace, English torchon lace, everlasting lace, German torchon lace, linen torchon lace, fancy raised valenciennes laces, and French valenciennes laces, ranging in width from the narrow valenciennes lace to the wide 3½-inch fancy laces.

CHALLENGE LACE ASSORTMENT EACH $5.00

We show two illustrations of our challenge lace assortments; the one showing the lace in the box, the other showing the lace loose, so as to give you the best possible idea of the widths and styles which we send you.
Our special price for the entire twenty-four pieces, or 288 yards of lace, is only **$5.00**

WAIST AND DRESS NETS.

27-Inch Brussels Net.

No. 18K06800 Black Silk Brussels Net, good quality, in close mesh 27 inches wide. Price, per yard. **29c**

No. 18K06802 Exceptionally Fine Quality Black Silk Brussels Net, 27 inches wide, of good heavy thread and very close mesh. Price, per yard. **39c**

27-Inch White Cotton Wash Blonde Net.

No. 18K06804 White Cotton Wash Blonde Net, close mesh, 27 inches wide, used extensively for waists, etc. Price, per yard. **23c**

No. 18K06806 White Cotton Wash Blonde Net, 27 inches wide. A closer mesh than above number. Price, per yard... **35c**

72-Inch Wash Blonde Net for Waists and Dresses.

No. 18K06808 Soft Finished Cotton Wash Blonde Net of heavy thread, close mesh. The correct style for dresses and waists, etc. Width 72 inches. Regular 75-cent value. White only. Our price, per yard... **50c**

No. 18K06810 An Extra Quality Wash Blonde, very soft finish, can be shirred and tucked in any way desired; the quality we recommend for waists, dresses and all styles of neckwear. Width, 72 inches. Colors, white and Arab. Be sure to state color wanted. Price, per yard... **72c**

45-Inch New Style Fillet Mesh Drapery or Dress Net.

No. 18K06812 White Fillet or Square Mesh Dress Net, good wearing quality, pure white bleached thread, rich in appearance. Width, 45 inches. Price, per yard.. **$1.23**

No. 18K06814 High Grade Quality Ecru Fillet or Square Mesh Net, made of strong substantial thread. Fillet mesh nets are all the rage now. Width, 45 inches. Price, per yard... **$1.35**
Allow from 2 cents to 5 cents per yard for postage on Dress Nets.

Russian Dress Waist or Drapery Nets.

No. 18K06816 All Silk Black La Tosca Net, of medium thread in the new dull finish. This is a very serviceable quality, and where a medium grade is desired, it will be found very satisfactory. Width, 45 inches. Price, per yard. **85c**

No. 18K06818 Our Highest Grade All Silk 45-Inch Black Russian La Tosca Net, of very fine quality, used for trimming the finest waists and dresses. We strongly recommend this quality, as it will undoubtedly give entire satisfaction. Comes in black only. **$1.45**

No. 18K06820 White All Silk La Tosca Net, same quality as above. Width, 45 inches. Price, per yard. **$1.45**

No. 18K06822 Black Russian LaTosca Net, heavy thread, somewhat similar to a fancy allover. Used extensively for skirts and yokes. Width, 42 inches. Guaranteed absolutely fast black. Price, per yard. **27c**

Point D'Esprit Heavy Thread Drapery and Dress Nets.

No. 18K06824 Point D'Esprit Drapery or Dress Net of heavy thread and very closely dotted. At the price we name this quality is unequaled and sells regularly for 80 to 90 cents per yard. Comes in black only. Width, 45 inches. Our price, per yard. **65c**

No. 18K06826 All Silk Point D'Esprit Drapery or Dress Net of good strong thread, closely dotted. This is our most popular number and sells regularly for $2.00 per yard. Black only. Width, 45 inches. Our price, per yard. **$1.45**

No. 18K06828 White Point D'Esprit Drapery or Dress Net, made of good strong heavy thread, closely dotted. Width, 45 inches. Our price, per yard. **70c**

No. 18K06830 All Silk White D'Esprit Dress Net, fine quality thread, closely covered dots. This quality is unexcelled for waists, etc. Width, 45 inches. Worth $1.75. Our price, per yard **$1.15**

EMBLEM SETS.

No. 18K06894 Silk Embroidered Set, consisting of eagle, star and bar, one piece; height, 3 inches. Anchor, 1⅛ inches, and two stars, size, 1½ inches. Colors, red, white and navy or light blue. State color desired. Price, per set..... **15c**
If by mail, postage extra, per set, 3c.

No. 18K06896 The latest craze Teddy Bear Ornaments for jackets, coats, etc. Made of all silk floss. The set consists of a teddy bear, 2½ inches high, holding the American flag in national colors, and two silk stars 1⅜ inches. Colors, red, white, navy or light blue. State color wanted. Price, per set..... **15c**
If by mail, postage extra, 3c.

DRESS BRAIDS, TRIMMINGS AND ORNAMENTS.

No. 18K06858 Fancy Coxcomb All Wool Silk Trimming Braid. Width, ¾ inch. Colors, black, white, brown or navy blue. State color wanted. Price, per yard.... **10c**

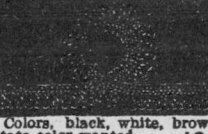
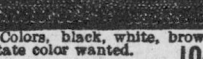

No. 18K06860 Fancy Wood Silk Pull Braid with feather-stitch edge. This braid comes with drawstring. Width, ¾ inch. Colors, black, white, brown or navy blue. Price, per yard. **10c**

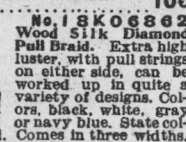

No. 18K06862 Wood Silk Diamond Pull Braid. Extra high luster, with pull strings on either side, can be worked up in quite a variety of designs. Colors, black, white, gray or navy blue. State color and width wanted. Comes in three widths.

Width, inch....	½	¾	1½
Price, per yard..	6c	9c	16c

No. 18K06864 Fancy Brilliant Wood Silk Pull Braid, with fancy basket weave pattern in center. One of the neatest trimmings shown this season. Colors, black or white in three widths. Be sure to state color and width wanted.

Width, inch......	½	¾	1
Price, per yard..	12c	16c	20c

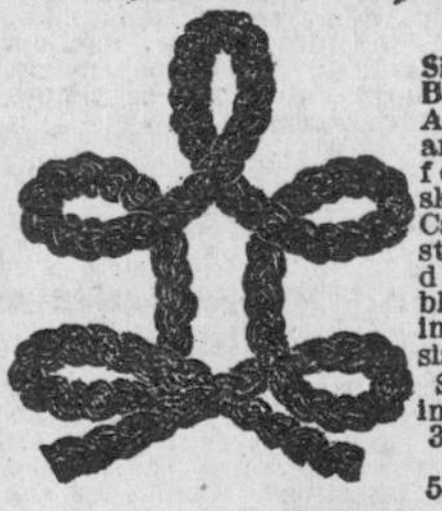

No. 18K06866 Silk Soutache Braided Trimming. A very desirable and stylish braid for trimming skirts, jackets, etc. Can be used for any style of fancy loop design. Color, black only. Comes in three sizes. State size wanted.

Size, inches	Price, per yard
3-16	5c
¾	6c
5-16	8c

No. 18K06868 Silk Drop Effect Dress Trimming, made of best quality all silk soutache braid, with fancy feathered braid drops. This is a specially popular and effective trimming. Size, ¾ inches. Color, black only. Price, per yard **15c**

No. 18K06870 Fancy Wood Silk Braid or Dress Trimming, in new lattice work effect, with satin braid waved center in a beading design, through which ribbon can be drawn if desired. Width, ⅞ inch. Colors, black and white. State color wanted. Price, per yard ... **22c**

Allow about 2 cents per yard for postage on Braids and other Dress Trimmings.

No. 18K06872 Fancy Silk Trimming Braid. This braid is used very effectively for dresses, waists, etc., where a narrow braid is required. Width, ⅛ inch. Colors, black, white, pink, light blue, brown, cardinal or gray. State color wanted. Price, per 12-yard piece **33c**

Silk Hercules Braid.

No. 18K06874 Fine Quality Silk Hercules Braid. Very fine ribbed. To be used for dress and cloak trimming, also desirable for coat binding. Comes in black only in the following widths. State width wanted.

Lines	4	8	12	16
Width, inch.......	3-16	½	¾	1
Price, per yard.....	3c	7c	10c	12c

Soutache Braid

No. 18K06876 White Cotton Soutache Braid (washable). Comes in three widths. This is the better grade soutache. State width wanted.

Width, inch.......	1-16	⅛	3-16
Price, per dozen yards...	6c	9c	12c

If by mail, postage extra, per doz. yds. 2c.

No. 18K06878 Silk Soutache Braid, extra quality. In black and colors. State color wanted. ⅛ inch wide. Price, per dozen yards **18c**
If by mail, postage extra, per doz. yds. 2c.

No. 18K06880 Gold Soutache Braid, good quality for trimming. ⅛ inch wide. Price, per dozen yards **23c**
If by mail, postage extra, per doz. yds., 3c.

No. 18K06882 Silver Soutache Trimming Braid. ⅛ inch wide. Price, per dozen yards........... **28c**
If by mail, postage extra, per doz. yds., 3c.

Dress Ornaments.

No. 18K06884 Fancy Silk Fourglers or Dress Ornaments. A very appropriate trimming for cloaks, coats, etc. Made of silk soutache braid in design as shown, in two sizes. Sold only by the dozen. Color, black only. State size wanted.

Size, inches	¾	1½
Price, per dozen ...	22c	39c

No. 18K06886 Silk Cord Pendant in medallion design, with three silk cord drops. Color, black only. Size, 4½ inches. Price, per pair **18c**

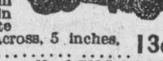

No. 18K06888 Fancy Drop Pendant made of silk braid in clover leaf design, with seven silk cord pendants, three of which are ornamented with silk covered pear shaped drops. Color, black only. Size, 4¾ inches. Price, per pair **35c**

Fancy Frog Loops.

No. 18K06890 Fancy Silk Braid Frog Loop of neat design, as shown in illustration. Comes in black or white. State color desired. Width across, 5 inches. Price.. **13c**

No. 18K06892 Silk Braid Fourgiers or Loop Ornaments. This is a very high grade article, made of fine quality silk braid; fancy pendants; an elegant trimming for jackets, waists, etc. Black or white. State color desired. Length, 6 inches. Price **30c**

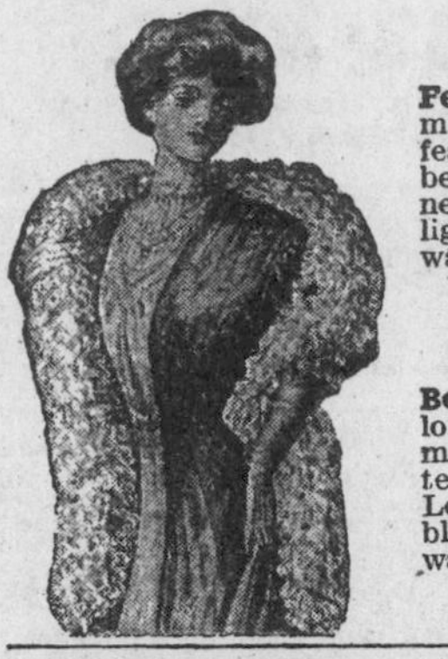

Feather Boas.

No. 18K07084 Ladies' Coque Feather Boa, made of excellent grade long maribo feathers. The demand for maribo feather boas is exceptionally large, many being used for hat trimmings as well as neck boas. Length, 56 inches. Colors, white, light blue, gray, pink or black. State color wanted.
Price **$1.98**
If by mail, postage extra, 15 cents.

No. 18K07086 Ladies' Feather Boa, made of exceptionally good quality long and fluffy maribo feathers, intermingled with Spanish coque feathers, extensively worn by all fashionable dressers. Length, 72 inches. Colors, white, light blue, gray and pink or black. State color wanted.
Price **$2.98**
If by mail, postage extra, 18 cents.

Newest Design in Neck Ruching.

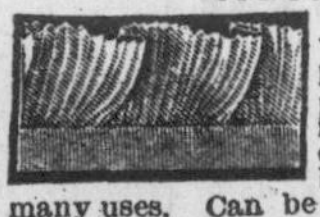

No. 18K07088 Washable Tourist Ruching in 6-yard pieces. This ruching is very popular on account of its being adapted to so many uses. Can be washed and ironed. White only.
Price, per 6-yard piece **22c**
If by mail, postage extra, 4 cents.

Silk Ruchings.

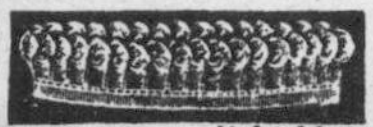

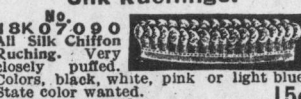

No. 18K07090 All Silk Chiffon Ruching. Very closely puffed. Colors, black, white, pink or light blue. State color wanted.
Price, per yard **15c**
If by mail, postage extra, per yard, 2 cents.

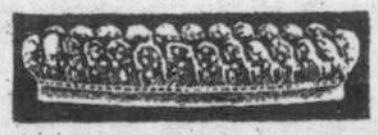

No. 18K07092 Extra Quality Silk Chiffon Ruching, closely puffed. The chiffon is studded with small chenille dots. Can be ordered in white with white dots, white with black dots, black with white dots, pink with white dots and light blue with white dots. State color wanted.
Price, per yard **17c**
If by mail, postage extra, per yard, 2 cents.

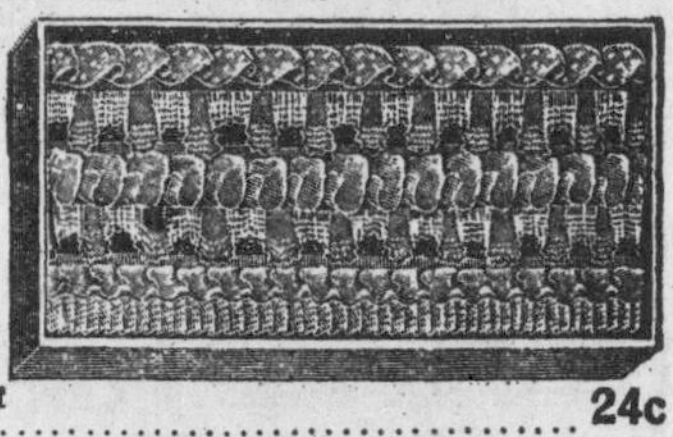

No. 18K07094 Six Pieces Assorted Neck Ruching, each 14 inches in length, put up in fancy lithographed box. The latest patterns. An exceptional bargain for the price. White only.
Price, per box of 6 pieces **24c**
If by mail, postage extra, 4 cents.

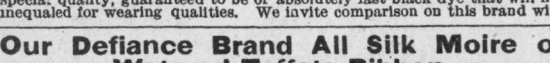

IMPROVED QUALITIES — RIBBONS — LOWER PRICES

WE PRIDE OURSELVES IN THE FACT that we are in position to make the statement to our customers that we are now selling ribbon of better quality at lower prices than could be bought formerly. We have accomplished this by establishing our own special brands and having the goods manufactured exclusively for us from selected silk. **Buying direct from the looms in this manner saves our customers** all middlemen's profit, as you buy ribbons from us at the actual cost of manufacture with only our small percentage of profit added, and it is no exaggeration on our part to say that we can save you from one-fourth to one-third on all ribbons. Send us your ribbon orders and prove for yourself the truth of our statements. We particularly desire to call your attention to our **"Serano Brand"** plain taffeta ribbon and to our **"Lustoria Brand"** satin taffeta ribbon. We absolutely guarantee them to run uniform, to be of even shade and to give entire satisfaction, as they have enough body and weight to them to retain their shape.

A VERY SPECIAL FEATURE of our ribbon department this year is our unequaled **"Midnight Brand"** of fast black taffeta ribbon. This is a special quality, guaranteed to be of absolutely fast black dye that will not crock or fade and unequaled for wearing qualities. We invite comparison on this brand with any ribbon sold elsewhere. We import all our fancy ribbons direct from Europe, and offer you the largest and most varied selection of latest styles at record breaking low prices, and in every instance you will find quality supreme.

REMEMBER, you buy all our ribbons under our binding guarantee of perfect satisfaction, or goods can be returned to us at our expense and we will cheerfully exchange for other merchandise or refund your money.

OUR SPECIAL FREE OFFER. In addition to naming lower prices and giving higher qualities than can be secured elsewhere, we make this most liberal free offer of a special publication entitled, "Simple Methods of Bow Making," written especially for us by an expert. This valuable book is an education on how to make bows for the hair or millinery purposes, and also instructions on how to make a great many fancy articles, such as ribbon girdles, glove boxes, opera bags and floral effects. The publisher's price on this book is 50 cents. We send this to you absolutely free, providing you send us an order for ribbons amounting to One Dollar ($1.00) or more. You can buy as many different styles of ribbon as you desire in any quantity you may wish; the only condition placed upon this offer is that the order must amount to a total of $1.00 or more, then we will send the book free.

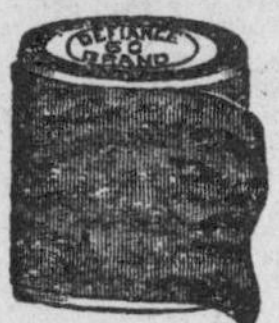

Our Defiance Brand All Silk Moire or Watered Taffeta Ribbon.

No. 18K08000 This is an All Silk Moire Taffeta Ribbon of splendid quality and exceptionally high luster. We have this ribbon moired especially for us, so that we obtain the high luster shade effects so desirable in moire ribbons. Can be ordered in the following colors: black, white, cream, pink, light blue, scarlet, cardinal or navy. When ordering, be sure to state color and width wanted.

Width, Nos.	12	16	22	40	60
Width, inches	2	2⅜	2⅝	3⅛	3½
Price, per yard	12c	15c	18c	21c	24c

Our Serano Brand Highest Grade All Silk Taffeta Ribbon.

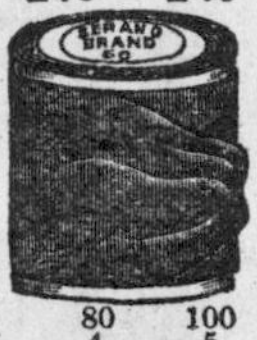

No. 18K08005 This is our best quality All Silk Taffeta Ribbon. Made of a selected silk which has an exceptionally high luster. We strongly recommend this quality as being the best taffeta ribbon for all purposes you could possibly buy. Bows made of this ribbon hold their shape and wear better than of any other quality on the market. Comes in the following colors, black, white, cream, pink, light blue, scarlet, cardinal, navy or brown. Don't forget to state color and width wanted.

Width, Nos.	5	7	9	12	16	22	40	60	80	100
Width, inches	1	1¼	1⅝	2	2⅜	2⅝	3⅛	3½	4	5
Price, per yard	5c	7c	9c	12c	15c	17c	19c	22c	25c	30c

Midnight Brand All Silk Fast Black Taffeta Ribbon.

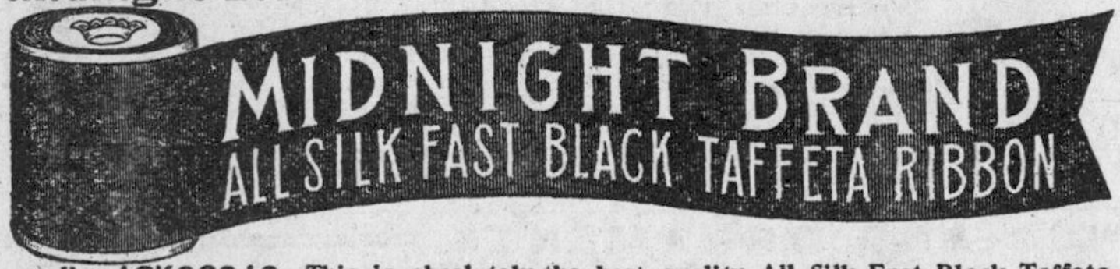

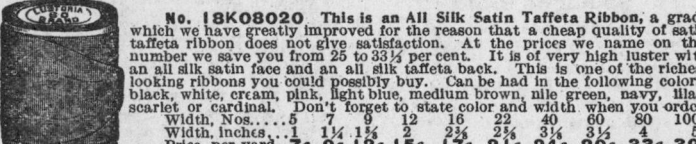

No. 18K08010 This is absolutely the best quality All Silk Fast Black Taffeta Ribbon you could buy. It will not crock or fade and has more weight and body to it than any other ribbon sold at anywhere near our price. If you are looking for a ribbon of quality that can be used for every requirement and retain its beautiful high luster until worn out, we urge you to buy our "Midnight Brand." Comes in black only in the following widths. State width wanted.

Width, Nos.	5	7	9	12	16	22	40	60	80	100
Width, inches	1	1¼	1⅝	2	2⅜	2⅝	3⅛	3½	4	5
Price, per yard	6c	8c	11c	14c	17c	20c	23c	25c	29c	35c

Sunshine Brand Medium Quality All Silk Taffeta Ribbon.

No. 18K08015 Medium quality All Silk Taffeta Ribbon. Can be used for any trimming where a medium quality ribbon will do. The quality which we offer you in this ribbon is a great deal better than the low price which we ask would indicate. Many houses offer this number as their best quality. While we recommend your using our better grade taffeta, we guarantee our "Sunshine Brand" as the best value ever offered at the price named. Comes in the following colors, black, white, cream, pink, light blue, navy or cardinal. Be sure to state color and width wanted when ordering.

Width, Nos.	16	22	40	60	80	100
Width, inches	2⅜	2⅝	3⅛	3½	4	5
Price, per yard	10c	12c	14c	17c	21c	25c

Our Lustoria Brand All Silk Satin Taffeta Ribbon.

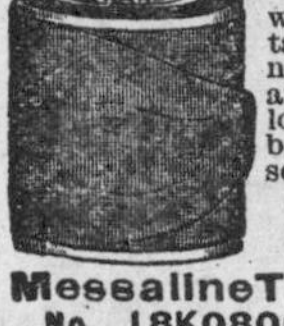

No. 18K08020 This is an All Silk Satin Taffeta Ribbon, a grade which we have greatly improved for the reason that a cheap quality of satin taffeta ribbon does not give satisfaction. At the prices we name on this number we save you from 25 to 33⅓ per cent. It is of very high luster with an all silk satin face and an all silk taffeta back. This is one of the richest looking ribbons you could possibly buy. Can be had in the following colors: black, white, cream, pink, light blue, medium brown, nile green, navy, lilac, scarlet or cardinal. Don't forget to state color and width when you order.

Width, Nos.	5	7	9	12	16	22	40	60	80	100
Width, inches	1	1¼	1⅝	2	2⅜	2⅝	3⅛	3½	4	5
Price, per yard	7c	9c	12c	15c	17c	21c	24c	29c	33c	39c

Messaline Taffeta Silk Ribbon.

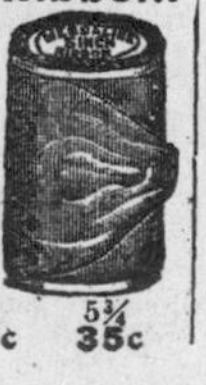

No. 18K08065 All Silk Messaline Taffeta Ribbon of fine soft weave; very lustrous and makes up in neat, graceful folds. Splendid material for ladies' neckwear, bows, millinery trimmings and fancy work. Comes in two widths. Colors, black, white, pink, light blue, scarlet, nile green, medium brown, navy or cardinal. State color and width wanted.

Width, inches	5	5¾
Price, per yard	25c	35c

Mousseline Taffeta Ribbon.

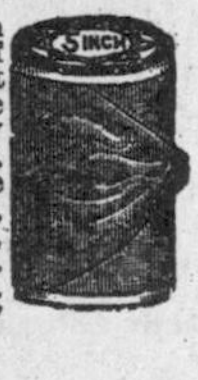

No. 18K08070 This is a very splendid quality ribbon, of a stiffer finish than a messaline, at a very low price and is one of the most popular weaves for millinery trimmings, fancy work and sashes. Width, 5 inches. Comes in the following colors: black, white, cream, pink, light blue, nile green, turquoise, medium brown or navy. Always state color wanted.
Price, per yard **23c**

Narrow Baby Ribbons.

Our Sterling Brand Baby Ribbons are the product of the foremost manufacturer of narrow baby ribbons in the world. The qualities we positively guarantee to give absolute satisfaction. The colors are rich and of even shade. As we name extraordinary low prices on narrow ribbons, we only sell them in 10-yard pieces.

Sterling Brand Satin and Grosgrain Baby Ribbon.

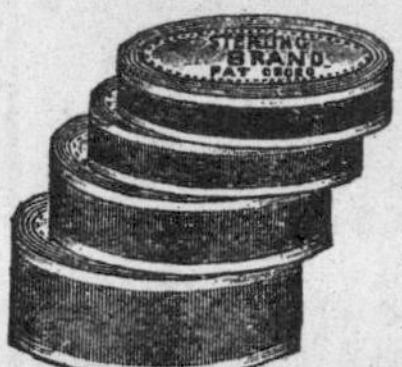

No. 18K08025 Satin and Grosgrain Narrow Baby Ribbons are used extensively for running through embroideries, insertions, corset covers, laces and fancy work. Comes in the following colors, black, white, cream, pink, light blue, nile green, medium brown, medium green, scarlet, cardinal, heliotrope, maize, turquoise, navy, purple, royal blue or yellow. Sold only in 10-yard pieces. State color and width wanted.

Width Nos.	1	1½	2	3
Width, inches	¼	5-16	⅜	⅝
Price, 10-yard piece	10c	16c	22c	30c

Sterling Brand Narrow Taffeta Baby Ribbon.

No. 18K08030 All Silk Narrow Taffeta Baby Ribbon; our own special quality. Sold only in 10-yard pieces. Comes in the following colors: black, white, cream, pink, light blue, nile green, medium brown, medium green, scarlet, cardinal, heliotrope, maize, turquoise, navy, purple, royal blue or yellow. State color and width wanted.

Width Nos.	1	1½	2	3
Width, inches	¼	5-16	⅜	⅝
Price, 10-yard piece	18c	23c	30c	40c

Sterling Brand Narrow Satin Taffeta Baby Ribbons.

No. 18K08035 Sterling Brand Narrow Satin Taffeta Baby Ribbons of superior quality. This class of ribbon is very popular for all kinds of fancy work, corset covers and drawing through insertions. Comes in the same colors as our No. 18K08025. Be sure to state what color and width you want. Sold only in 10-yard pieces.

Width, Nos.	1	1½	2	3
Width, inches	¼	5-16	⅜	⅝
Price, 10-yard piece	16c	21c	30c	37c

Never Fade Brand All Silk Wash Ribbons.

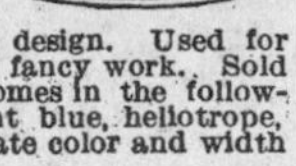

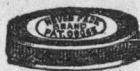

No. 18K08040 Our Never Fade Brand All Silk Wash Ribbons are absolutely fast dye, will not fade or run in washing. A pretty new jacquard or basket weave design. Used for all kinds of underwear and fancy work. Sold only in 10-yard pieces. Comes in the following colors, white, pink, light blue, heliotrope, nile green or maize. State color and width wanted.

Width Nos.	1	1½	2	3
Width, inches	¼	5-16	⅜	⅝
Price, 10-yard piece	23c	32c	45c	55c

No. 18K08047 Taffeta Seam Binding in black and colors. Sold in 6-yard pieces only. State color wanted.
Price, PER 6-YARD PIECE **8c**

Satin Back Velvet Baby Ribbon.

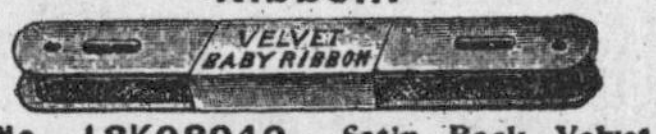

No. 18K08049 Satin Back Velvet Baby Ribbon, fast woven edge. Comes in the following colors, in width Nos. 1 and 1½: Black, white, pink, light blue, scarlet, cardinal, heliotrope, navy or brown. Always give color and width when you order.

No. 1, width about ¼-inch. Price, PER 10-YARD PIECE **29c**

No. 1½, width about ⅜-inch. Price, PER 10-YARD PIECE **39c**

All Silk Satin Back Velvet Ribbons.

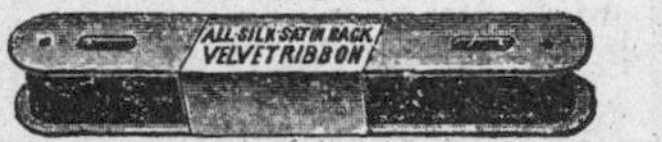

No. 18K08050 This is an All Silk Black Velvet Face Ribbon, with an all silk satin back of extra good quality and absolutely fast black dye. We have this ribbon manufactured especially for us. It is a superior quality to what is usually sold by retail stores, has a fast woven edge which will not unravel, and runs smooth and even. You can save considerable money by ordering this number from us. When ordering be sure to state width wanted. Black only. Widths Nos. 1, 1½ and 2 are sold only in 10-yard pieces.

Price, for 10-YARD PIECE. Width, No. 1, width, inches, 3-16 .... **35c**

Price, for 10-YARD PIECE. Width, No. 1½, width, inches, ¼ **48c**

Price, for 10-YARD PIECE. Width, No. 2, width, inches, ⅜ **65c**

Width, Nos.	3	4	5	7
Width, inches	½	⅝	1	1¼
Price, per yard	8c	10c	12c	15c

Width, Nos.	9	12	16	22	40
Width, inches	1½	2¼	2¾	3	3⅛
Price, per yd.	19c	23c	30c	35c	42c

Linen Back Silk Face Velvet Ribbon.

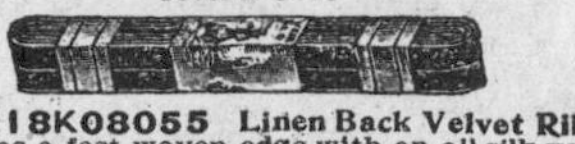

No. 18K08055 Linen Back Velvet Ribbon has a fast woven edge with an all silk velvet face and a pure linen back. Where a serviceable and good wearing grade of velvet ribbon is desired we strongly recommend this number, especially for binding skirts or trimming dresses where the velvet will be exposed to wear. Comes in black only. Be sure to state width wanted when ordering.

Width, Nos.	1¾	2	3
Width, inches	⅜	7-16	⅝
Price, 10-YARD PIECE	30c	40c	50c

Width, Nos.	4	5	7	9	12
Width, inches	¾	1	1¼	1½	2
Price, per yard	7c	8c	13c	17c	20c

Postage on ribbon varies according to width. If you desire ribbons sent by mail allow from 1 to 2 cents per yard extra.

FANCY RIBBONS, PRICED VERY LOW

Fancy Ribbons.

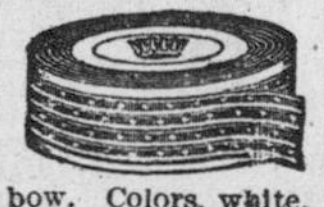

No. 18K08072 Fancy Stripe All Silk Taffeta Ribbon, with small diamond shaped figure running between the stripes. This is a very handsome weave pattern. Makes a very pretty hair bow. Colors, white, light blue, pink, cardinal or black. State color wanted. Width, 1 inch. Sold by the piece only.
Price, per piece of 4½ yards........ **18c**

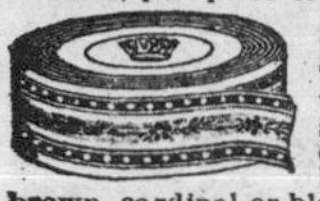

No. 18K08074 Fancy Brocaded Silk Ribbon. The brocaded flowers are woven in natural colors; silk polka dots on outer edge. Colors, white, light blue, pink, lilac, navy, brown, cardinal or black. State color wanted. Width, 1 inch. Sold by the piece only.
Price, per piece of 4½ yards......... **23c**

No. 18K08076 Narrow Fancy Silk Taffeta Ribbon with a zig zag satin stripe intermingled with a fancy brocaded flower. Width, 1 inch. Colors, white, pink, light blue, cardinal, navy or lilac. State color wanted. Sold only in 10-yard pieces.
Price, per piece of 10 yards......... **42c**

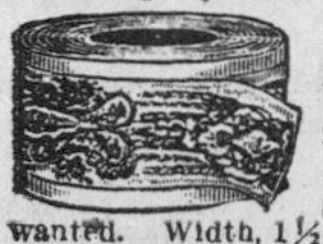

No. 18K08078 Fancy narrow Persian Pattern Taffeta Ribbon. Very rich coloring. Colors, white, pink, light blue, red, green or lavender, all with white background. State color wanted. Width, 1½ inches.
Price, per yard.......... **9c**

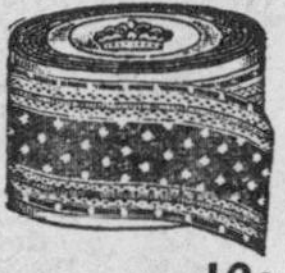

No. 18K08080 Fancy Imported Silk Taffeta Ribbon with small diamond design in center. Fancy corded stripes on edge with open lace work between the stripes. Colors, white, pink, light blue, lilac or black. Be sure to say what color is wanted. Width, 2⅞ inches.
Price, per yard.................. **12c**

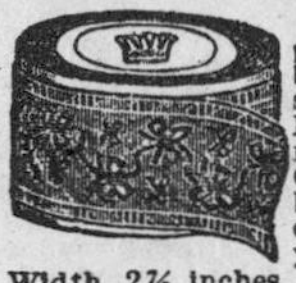

No. 18K08082 Imported Silk Taffeta Ribbon in fancy bowknot design with corded stripes. Edges have lacy effect running between the stripes. Colors, white, pink, light blue, lilac, cardinal or turquoise. Say what color you want when you order. Width, 2⅞ inches.
Price, per yard.......... **14c**

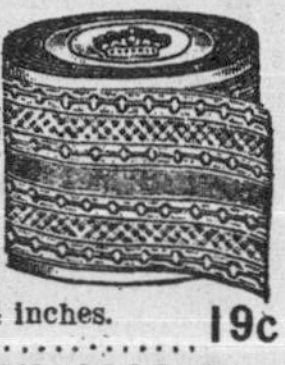

No. 18K08084 Silk Taffeta Ribbon with woven lace effects on either side in combination colors alternating with white. Can be ordered with the following colors predominating, all white, light blue, nile, lilac, maize, turquoise, brown, navy or cardinal. Be sure to give a color selection when you order. Width, 4 inches.
Price, per yard.......... **19c**

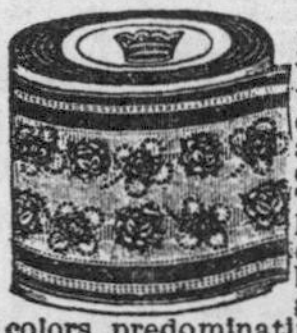

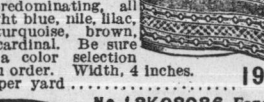

No. 18K08086 Fancy Imported Taffeta Ribbon, with jacquard weave center design in contrasting colors with a stripe border alternating with a lacy effect and white center. This is an exceptionally handsome design. The colorings are beautiful. Can be ordered with white ground with the following colors predominating, all white, light blue, pink, lilac, cardinal or nile green. State color wanted. Width, 3¾ inches. Regular retail price, 35 cents. Our price, per yd. **22c**

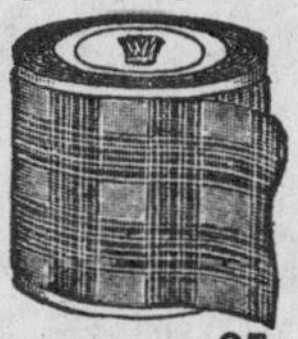

No. 18K08088 Fancy Silk Taffeta Ribbon, in the new broken check design which is so popular at the present time. The ground is white with the following colors predominating, light blue, pink, cardinal, navy, myrtle green, brown or black. Don't forget to say what color you want. Width, 4½ inches.
Our price, per yard.......... **25c**

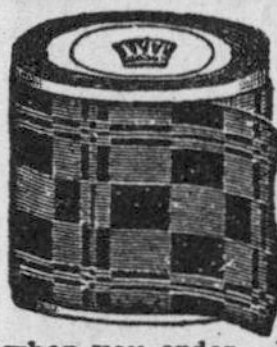

No. 18K08090 Fancy Imported Silk Taffeta Ribbon, in new fancy block check design. The large blocks are brought out in a satin effect which gives this ribbon a very rich appearance. Comes in the following colors: pink, light blue, medium blue, navy, cardinal, medium green or black. Be sure to give the color you want when you order. Width, 4¾ inches. Regular price, 39 cents.
Our price, per yard.............. **29c**

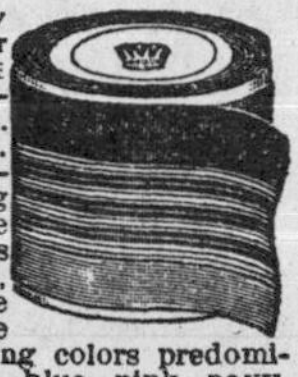

No. 18K08092 Fancy Imported Corded Center Taffeta Ribbon. The corded center comes in contrasting colors in stripes, such as blue and white. The edges also are contrasting colors; one edge being white and the other edge being colored the same as the corded center. Width, 4½ inches. All colors have one white edge and white in the center. The following colors predominate: light blue, medium blue, pink, navy, cardinal, medium green, dark green, brown or black. Always indicate what color you want. Well worth 50 cents per yard.
Our special price, per yard............. **32c**

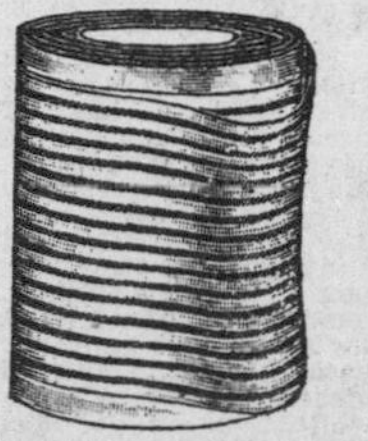

No. 18K08094 All Silk Fancy Taffeta Ribbon, in the new solid bar stripe design. This is one of the handsomest weaves brought out this season. Can be ordered in black and white or navy blue and white. Be sure to give color when you order. Width, 4¾ inches.
Price, per yard.......... **25c**

ALLOW FROM 1 TO 2 CENTS PER YARD FOR POSTAGE ON RIBBON.

Fancy Plaid Ribbons.

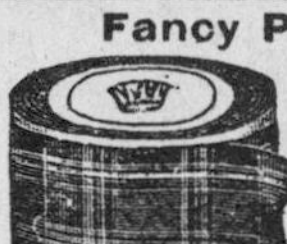

No. 18K08100 An entirely new fancy weave in an All Silk Taffeta Plaid Ribbon of splendid quality. Plaid ribbons are more popular than ever. Comes in the following colors: cardinal, brown, dark blue, green or white. Width, 1½ inches. State color wanted.
Price, per yard............ **9c**

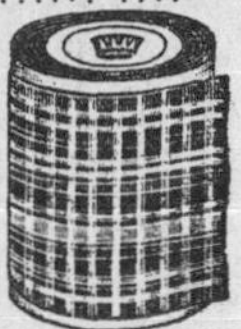

No. 18K08102 All Silk Taffeta Plaid Ribbon in the newest colorings. This is an exceptionally good quality. Woven in a raised effect. Comes in the following colors: cardinal, medium green, light blue, navy, black, scarlet or myrtle green. Be sure to say what color you want. Width, 3½ inches.
Price, per yard........ **19c**

No. 18K08104 Our highest grade quality of All Silk Taffeta Plaid Ribbon, in beautiful narrow stripes in splendid color combinations. This is one of the newest effects shown and is exceptionally cheap at the price we name. Comes in white, black, cardinal, green, brown, navy, light blue or pink. Width, 4 inches. State color wanted. Price, per yard.............. **25c**

Beautiful Warp Print or Floral Persian Ribbons.

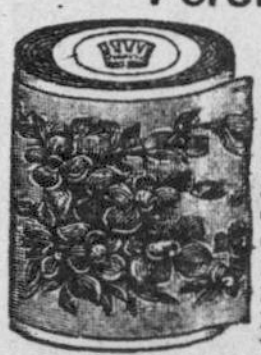

This is a beautiful All Silk Persian Warp Print Taffeta Ribbon in floral designs. These floral effects are not printed, but are woven in the fabric. A print ribbon is considerably cheaper than a woven ribbon. Comes in three different widths in the following colors: pink, light blue, nile green, lilac, cardinal or maize. State color wanted when ordering.

No. 18K08106 Width, 3 inches. Price, per yard.......... **23c**
No. 18K08107 Width, 3¾ inches. Price, per yard.......... **29c**
No. 18K08108 Width, 4⅜ inches. Price, per yard.......... **35c**

LATEST STYLES READY MADE VEILS

ALL OUR READY MADE VEILS CAN BE WORN IN ANY OF THE NEW STYLE DRAPES. WHEN YOU ORDER VEILS BE SURE TO STATE COLOR WANTED IF THE STYLE YOU WANT COMES IN MORE THAN ONE COLOR. IF VEILS ARE TO BE SENT BY MAIL, SEND 4 CENTS EXTRA EACH, FOR POSTAGE.

Ready Made Chiffon Veil, 29 Cents.

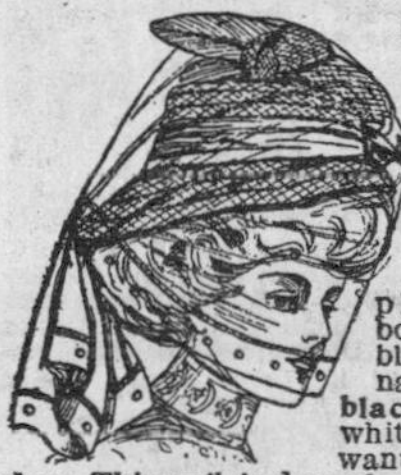

No. 18K08400 A very popular number in a ready made Chiffon Veil with neat chenille dots. Has a plain hemstitched border. Can be had in black, white, brown, navy, white with black dots or black with white dots. State color wanted. Size, 54x17 inches. This veil is draped over our hat No. 18K16016. Price, each.......... **29c**

Beautiful Quality All Silk Chiffon Veil, 59 Cents.

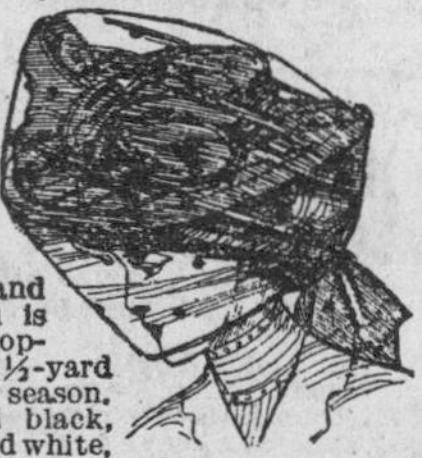

No. 18K08405 This is a very fine quality soft finished All Silk Chiffon Veil. It has a wide hemstitched border, same dotted with large silk chenille dots. It is 1½ yards long and ½ yard wide, and is one of the most popular veils in a 1½-yard length shown this season. Can be had in all black, all white, brown and white, green and white or white with black dots. Be sure to state color wanted. A veil of equal quality chiffon would easily retail for $1.00. These can be used for either face veils or for trimming and draping purposes. This veil is draped over our hat No. 18K16018.
Price.......... **59c**

Tuxedo Veiling With Lace Edge, 55 Cents.

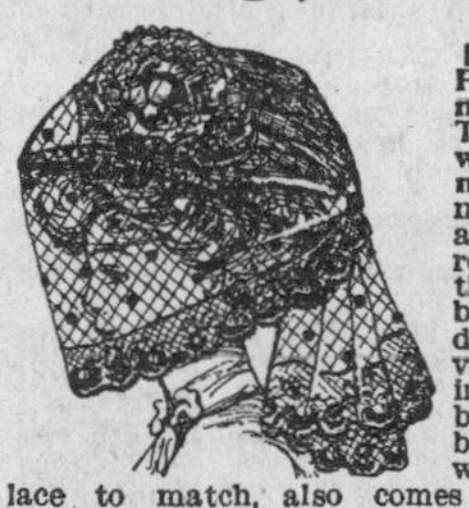

No. 18K08415 Fancy ready made All Silk Tuxedo Veiling with dainty chenille spots, trimmed at bottom and sides with a row of silk chantilly lace. Can be used as a drape or face veil. Size, 18x54 inches. Colors, black, white, brown or navy with dots and lace to match, also comes in white with white dots and black laces. State color wanted. This veil is draped over our hat No. 18K16022.
Price.......... **55c**

Nobby Lace Veil, 62 Cents.

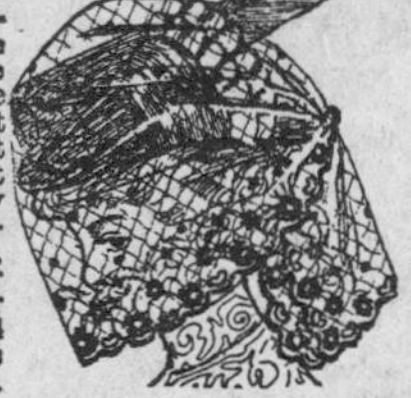

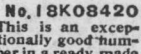

No. 18K08420 This is an exceptionally good number in a ready made Silk Chantilly Lace Veil, made of fine quality silk net with point d'esprit spots, finished at bottom in pretty figured design. Colors, black, white, brown, light blue or navy. State color wanted. Size, 16x54 inches. This veil is draped over hat No. 18K16024.
Price.......... **62c**

Fancy Tuxedo Veil, 85 Cents.

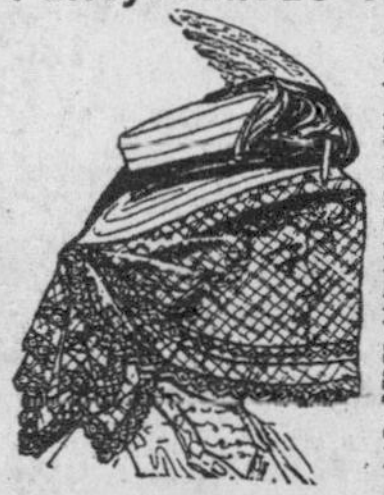

No. 18K08425 Fine Quality Silk Tuxedo Ready Made Veil, with border of insertion and edge of valenciennes lace. A very attractive and rich looking veil. Colors, black, white, navy, brown, or white with black lace trimming, or black with white lace trimming. State color wanted. Size, 18x54 inches. This veil is draped over hat No. 18K16000.
Price....... **85c**

Mourning Veils.

No. 18K08430 Black Silk Grenadine Mourning Veil, with hemstitched and hemmed border. Size, 14x52 inches.
Price.......... **41c**

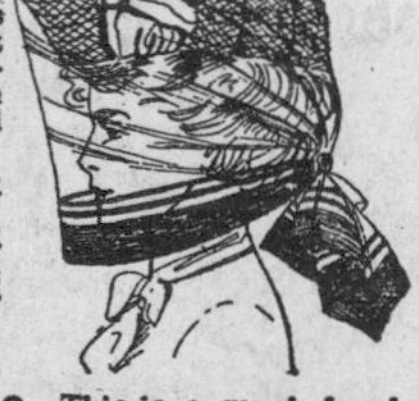

No. 18K08435 This is a good quality Grenadine or Mourning Veil, made exactly as illustrated here. It is finished at bottom and sides with double hemstitched border about 1¼ inches wide. Size, 16 inches wide by 54 inches long. This is a regular $1.25 veil. This veil is draped over hat No. 18K16008.
Price.......... **65c**

No. 18K08440 This is a much handsomer quality Mourning Veil than the above number. It is 18 inches wide by 54 inches long. Is finished with a neat hemstitched border about 2 inches wide. Price.... **95c**

$1.19 Three-Yard, High Grade Silk Chiffon Automobile Veil.

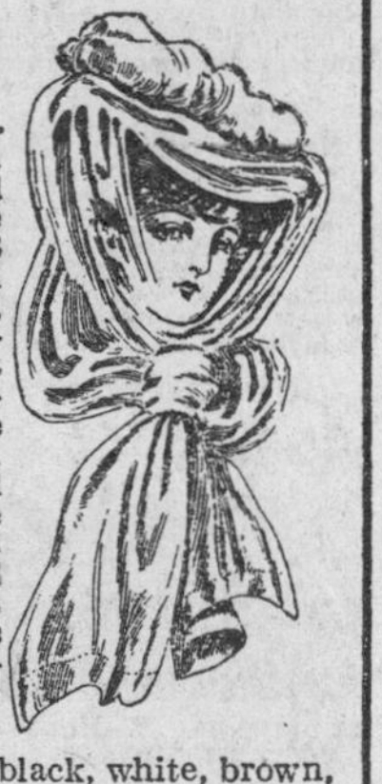

No. 18K08410 The illustration shows a Beautiful Automobile Veil. It is 3 yards in length by ½ yard wide, made of the finest imported soft finished silk chiffon. These are extensively used. You will find this veil will give you excellent service and will drape most beautifully. This veil retails regularly at $2.00

Can be had in black, white, brown, navy, light blue, gray or green. Be sure to state color wanted.
Price, each........... **$1.19**

VEILINGS BY THE YARD

If by mail, postage extra per yard, 1 to 2 cents.

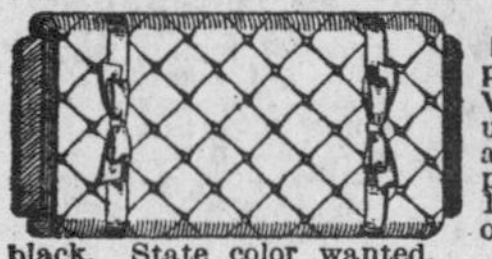

No. 18K08500 Plain Tuxedo Veiling, medium size mesh, all silk. A neat pattern. Size, 18 inches. Colors, white or black. State color wanted.
Price, per yard.......... **10c**

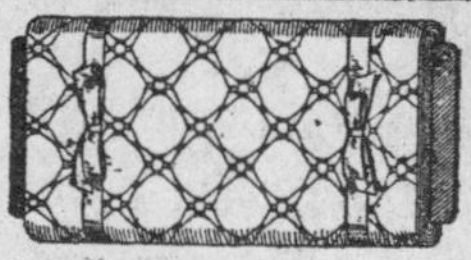

No. 18K08504 Fancy Mesh Tuxedo Veiling, all silk. A very attractive pattern, and a splendid wearing quality. Width, 18 inches. Colors, black, white, brown or navy. State color wanted.
Price, per yard.......... **19c**

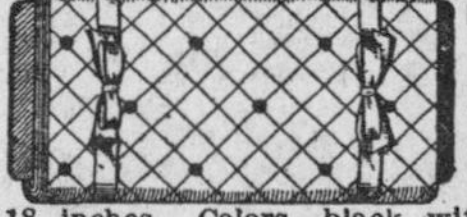

No. 18K08510 Good quality plain mesh Chenille Dot Veiling. All silk. Closely dotted in chenille. Width, 18 inches. Colors, black with black dots, white with black dots. All brown or all navy. State color wanted.
Price, per yard.......... **15c**

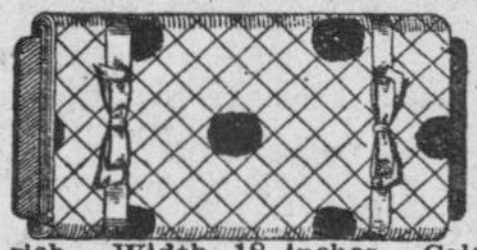

No. 18K08514 Plain mesh all silk Chenille Dot Veiling. Neatly dotted with large silk chenille dots. Something rich. Width, 18 inches. Colors, black with black dots, white with black dots, all brown or all navy. State color wanted.
Price, per yard.......... **20c**

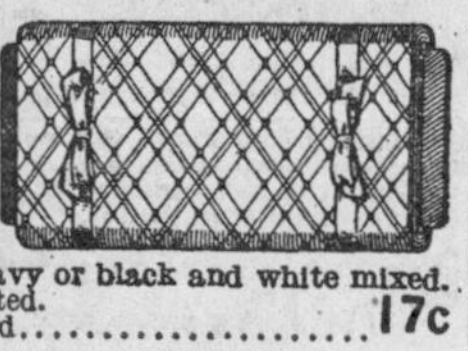

No. 18K08502 Tuxedo Veiling in diamond pattern. Made of all silk in medium size mesh. Width, 18 inches. Colors, black, white, brown, navy or black and white mixed. State color wanted.
Price, per yard.......... **17c**

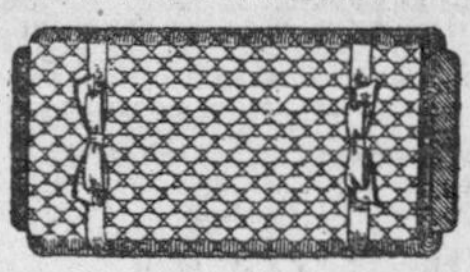

No. 18K08506 All silk Brussels Net Veiling. Excellent quality close mesh. Good value. Width, 18 inches. Colors, black or white only. State color wanted.
Price, per yard.......... **20c**

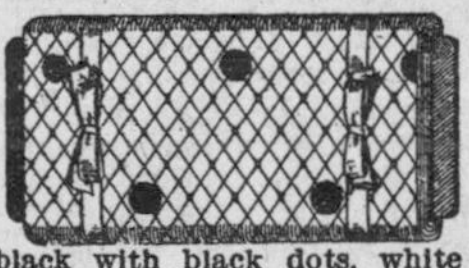

No. 18K08512 Medium mesh all silk Chenille Dot Veiling with neatly arranged chenille dots. Width, 18 inches. Colors, black with black dots, white with black dots, all brown or all navy. State color wanted. Price, per yard... **17c**

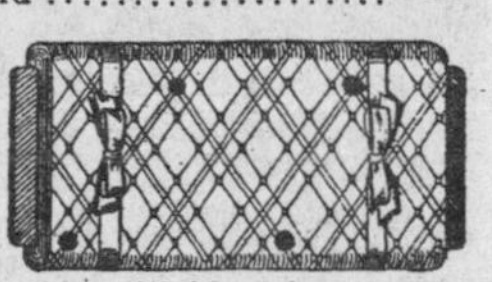

No. 18K08516 Chenille dotted all Silk Tuxedo Veiling, double threaded. A very tasty pattern. Width, 18 inches. Colors, all black or white with black dots. State color wanted. Price, per yard.. **19c**

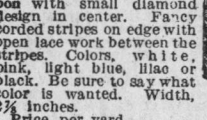

Chenille Dot Veiling.

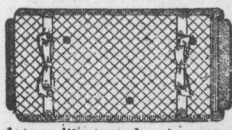

No. 18K08520 Our highest grade all Silk Chenille Dot Veiling. Closely meshed and trimmed with medium and small chenille dots as illustrated. A very satisfactory item. Width, 18 inches. Colors, all black or white with black dots. State color wanted. Price, per yard.................**26c**

Plain Silk Chiffon Veiling.

No. 18K08522 This is a Plain Silk Chiffon Veiling, especially desirable for a plain chiffon veiling or can be used for neck trimming, also for millinery and dress trimming purposes. Has a fast finished border and is of excellent quality. Colors, black, white, brown or navy. Be sure to state color wanted. Width, 18 inches. Price, per yard..................**22c**

No. 18K08524 Fine Quality Chiffon Veiling, lingerie finish suitable for face veils and millinery purposes. Comes in black, white, navy or brown. State color wanted. Width, 18 inches. Price, per yard.....**32c**

Postage on yard goods, 2c per yard extra.

Dotted Chiffon Veiling.

No. 18K08526 Fine Silk Chiffon Veiling with chenille dots. We are offering here a good quality at an unusually low price. Colors are all black, all white, black with white dots, white with black dots, brown with white dots and navy with white dots. Be sure to state color wanted. Width, 18 inches. Price, per yard.................**25c**

Silk Crepe de Chine Veiling.

No. 18K08528 All Silk Crepe de Chine Veiling. This veiling makes up beautifully. Those who desire a soft, draping automobile effect should order this number; also used for face veils. Colors are black, white, brown, navy, light blue or gray. Width, 16 inches. When ordering, be sure to state color wanted. Retail value, 39 cents per yard. Our price, per yard.............**30c**
Postage on yard goods, 2 cents per yard extra.

Sewing Silk Veilings.

No. 18K08530 A 16-inch Plain Sewing Silk Veiling, made with silk border, as shown in illustration. This is a very popular veiling, at an exceptionally low price. Width, 16 inches. We offer a regular 25-cent quality. Colors, black, white, brown or navy. State color wanted. Price, per yard....**18c**

No. 18K08532 This is our best quality Sewing Silk Veiling, finished with silk striped border. This veiling is used extensively. Is a popular number with our customers and always gives entire satisfaction. This quality usually retails at 40 cents per yard. Colors, black, white, navy or brown. State color wanted. 18 inches wide. Our price, per yard.....**25c**

Silk Grenadine Veiling.

No. 18K08534 This is an All Silk Black Grenadine Veiling, finished at bottom with dainty stripes and wide border. Is a popular veiling for either face or draping purposes. Width, 16 inches. Price, per yard.....**25c**

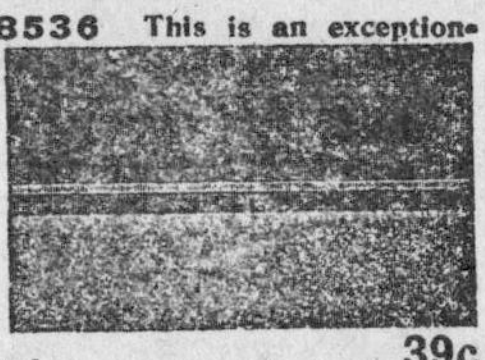

No. 18K08536 This is an exceptionally fine quality All Silk Black Veiling, finished with wide border at bottom. Would retail easily at 60 cents per yard. Width, 18 inches. Price, per yard.....**39c**
Postage on yard goods, 2 cents per yard extra.

Imported Barege Veiling.

No. 18K08540 Fine Imported All Wool Barege Veiling, 23 inches wide. A very excellent quality. Comes in black, navy, myrtle green, brown or gray. When ordering be sure to state color wanted, also catalogue number. Price, per yard.....**38c**

No. 18K08542 All Wool Barege Veiling, 23 inches wide. A good quality. Much better than is sold elsewhere at this price. Colors, black, brown, navy, myrtle green or gray. Be sure to state color wanted. Price, per yard.....**28c**

42-Inch Silk Chiffon.

No. 18K08546 This is our best quality All Silk Chiffon. It is superior to the grade usually sold at 75 cents per yard. It has a soft, lustrous finish, such as is desirable in chiffon. Only high grade qualities possess this feature. This material is very desirable for trimming waists and neckwear. Is especially adapted for all millinery purposes. Colors, black, white, pink or cream. When ordering state color wanted. Width, 42 inches. Price, per yard.....**54c**

No. 18K08548 This is an excellent quality All Silk Chiffon A very unusual grade to be sold at this low price. It has a medium finish and is suitable for all dress and millinery trimming purposes. Can be had in black, white, cream, light blue, pink, yellow, cardinal, heliotrope, nile green, navy, brown and emerald green. When ordering, please state catalogue number and color wanted. Width, 42 inches. Price, per yard.....**42c**

No. 18K08550 All Silk Chiffon at 28 cents. This is a special grade of silk chiffon, our own importation. Is usually sold at 40 cents per yard. Colors, black, white, cream, pink, light blue, corn color, brown, heliotrope, dark green, navy and lilac. Be sure to state color wanted. Width, 40 inches. Our price, per yard.....**28c**
Allow 2 cents per yard extra, if to go by mail.

All Silk Maline Net.

No. 18K08552 Silk Maline Net is very extensively used. It has only been recently that malines have become so popular. Maline net is especially desirable for neck bows, also millinery trimming and numerous other purposes. This is a splendid quality and should retail for at least 25 cents per yard. Width, about 24 inches. Colors, black, white, pink, light blue, navy, maize or garnet. Be sure to state color wanted. Our price, per yard.....**19c**
Postage on yard goods, 2 cents per yard extra.

Silk Finished Mull.

No. 18K08554 This is a good quality Silk Finished Mull. Used especially for hat trimming, also in dress trimming. Width, about 38 inches. Colors, black, white, pink, light blue. State color wanted. This is not the ordinary cheap cotton mull; this quality has a silk finish. Price, per yard.....**12c**

Silk Bridal Illusion.

No. 18K08556 This is an All Silk Illusion or Bridal Veiling, made of very fine quality. Close mesh. Veiling of equal grade would easily sell for $1.50 per yard. We quote an exceedingly low price. Comes in white only. Width, 72 inches. Our price, per yard.....**92c**
Postage extra, per yard, 2 cents.

No. 18K08558 All Silk Illusion or Bridal Veiling of coarser quality than the above number, however, excellent value for the price. Width, 72 inches. Price, per yard.....**55c**
Postage on yard goods, 2 cents per yard extra.

BUCKLES, ORNAMENTS AND HAT PINS.

No. 18K12980 Fancy Steel Cabachon. Neatly cut design. Size, 1⅝ inches in diameter. Price.................**8c**
Postage extra, 2 cents.

No. 18K12982 Fancy Jet Cabachon, with wired back. Size, 1½x2 inches. Price.................**10c**
Postage extra, 2 cents.

No. 18K12986 Oval Shape Rhinestone Buckle, with gilt metal prong. Size, 2⅜x1⅝ inches. Price.................**15c**
Postage extra, 2 cents.

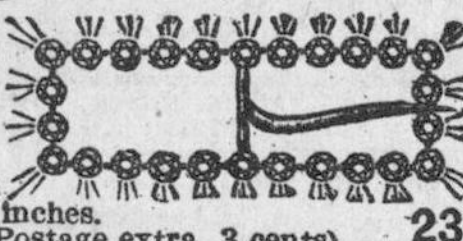

No. 18K12988 Oblong or long shaped Rhinestone Buckle, with metal prong. Size, 3¾x1⅛ inches. (Postage extra, 3 cents)....**23c**

No. 18K12990 Fancy Iridescent Mother of Pearl Buckle, with gilt metal prong. Size, 1½ and 2½ inches. Price.................**25c**
Postage extra, 3c.

Buckles.

No. 18K12992 Fancy Steel Buckle. Riveted corners with polished prong. Size, 2x3 inches. Price.....**15c**
Postage extra, 3c.

No. 18K12994 Diamond Shape Steel Ornament. Extra heavy quality with reinforced bar in center. This is an exceptionally handsome buckle trimming. Length 5¼ inches; width in center, 1½ inches. Price.... (Postage extra, 3 cents)....**25c**

No. 18K12996 Fancy Steel Buckle in lattice pattern with polished prong. Size, 1¼x4⅝ inches. Price.... (Postage extra, 3 cents)....**19c**

No. 18K12998 Jet Ornament in oval design. Length, 4 inches; width in center, 1½ inches. Price.... (Postage extra, 3 cents)....**10c**

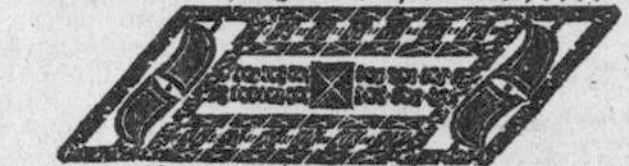

No. 18K13000 Jet Bar Ornament. Very handsome design in an entirely new shape. Size, 5¼x1 inch. Price.... Postage extra, 3 cents.**25c**

No. 18K13002 Square Jet Buckle, with black enameled metal prong. Size, 2 x 3½ inches. Price.....**19c**
Postage extra, 3c.

Hat Pins.

No. 18K13006 This Set of Hat Pins is put up three on a card. In the assortment is a highly polished gilt signet pin, also one set with brilliant colored stone, another set with a large pearl. Length of pins, 8 inches. Our price, PER CARD OF 3.....**27c**
Postage extra, 3 cents.

No. 18K13010 Finely Cut Jewel Pear Shape Hat Pin. Strongly mounted on an 8-inch pin. A regular 10-cent article. Colors, crystal, amethyst or jet. State color wanted. Our price, 2 FOR.....**12c**
Postage extra, each, 3 cents.

No. 18K13012 The New Swastska or Lucky Charm Hat Pin. It is finished in either old gold or silver, set with brilliant colored stones and rhinestone mounted on 8-inch pin. State finish wanted. Regular price, 25 cents. Our price.....**12c**
Postage extra, each, 3 cents.

No. 18K13018 Large Ball Top Cut Jet Hat Pin. The top is 1¼ inches in diameter, and is handsomely cut and mounted on a gilt stem, with gilt cup to hold the pin. Length, 9 in. Price, 2 FOR.....**25c**
Postage extra, each, 3c.

No. 18K13020 Large Ball Top Pearl Hat Pin, 1¼ inches in diameter. Made of smooth lustrous pearl, practically indestructible; mounted in gilt cup setting with long gilt stem. Length 9 inches. Price.....**19c**
Postage extra, each, 3 cents.

No. 18K13022 The latest hand cut Jewel Hat Pin. Oval shape, 1¼ inches long by 1 inch wide. Mounted in large gilt cup setting with gilt stem. Comes in the following colors: amethyst, crystal, ruby or emerald. State color wanted. Length, 9 inches. Price. (Postage extra, 3c).....**25c**

Mirrors.

Square Shape Mirror, in hardwood frame, with polished nickel stand, which can be used as a fastening to hang on the wall or a base to stand on. French beveled plate mirror in highly polished selected hardwood frame, either mahogany or oak. At prices never before quoted for a mirror of this kind. Comes in three sizes. State preference in wood and size of glass wanted.

No.	Size of Glass, inches	Shipping, Wt. lbs.	Price
18K25321	4x 6	1	$0.29
18K25323	6x 8	1½	.59
18K25325	8x10	2	1.00

Oval Mirrors.

Oval Shaped Mirror, with polished nickeled stand for dresser or to hang up; fitted with best French beveled plate mirror in high piano polish finish, selected hardwoods—walnut, santander or ebony finish—state preference in wood and size of glass wanted. Glass comes in following sizes:

No.	Size of Glass, inches	Weight, ounces	Price
18K25327	4x6	16	$0.61
18K25329	5x7	20	.92
18K25331	7x9	30	1.48

Special Value Oval Hand Mirrors.

Hand Mirror with long handle, best quality French beveled mirror, fitted in highly piano polished hardwood frame, in walnut, mahogany or ebony finish. Can be ordered in either wood in different size glass as follows:

No.	Size of Glass, inches	Weight, ounces	Price
18K25333	4x6	30	$0.55
18K25335	5x7	33	.88
18K25337	7x9	38	1.49

Nickel Plated Shaving Mirror.

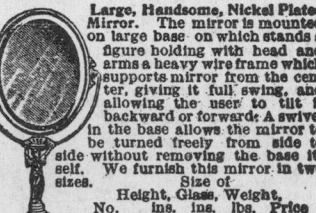

Large, Handsome, Nickel Plated Mirror. The mirror is mounted on large base on which stands a figure holding with head and arms a heavy wire frame which supports mirror from the center, giving it full swing, and allowing the user to tilt it backward or forward. A swivel in the base allows the mirror to be turned freely from side to side without removing the base itself. We furnish this mirror in two sizes.

No.	Height, ins.	Size of Glass, ins.	Weight, lbs.	Price
18K25339	17	6x 8	3	$1.38
18K25341	20	8x10	4	1.89

Triplicate Mirrors.

Beautiful Triplicate Mirror, handsome, heavy hardwood frames, highly polished, with very best quality French plate beveled mirrors, and nickel plated hinges. Can be used either to stand on table, having the little ball stands, or hung on the wall with chains which are furnished with each mirror. Can be ordered in either dark mahogany, English oak frames or dull finished ebony. Comes in three sizes. State preference in finish and size wanted.

No.	Size of Glass, inches	Shipping Weight, lbs.	Price
18K25343	5x 7	5½	$1.65
18K25345	7x 9	7½	2.39
18K25347	8x10	10	2.98

Pocket Toilet Cases.

No. 18K25360 Pocket Toilet Case, vest pocket size. Illustration shows it open. Contains beveled mirror, celluloid comb and nail pick; case handsomely covered with Russia leather, valuable companion. Size, 3½x2½ inches. Price.....**15c**
If by mail, postage extra, 3 cents.

No. 18K25362 Pocket Toilet Case. Seal grain leather covered; contains a heavy beveled mirror, comb, nail and ear pick with celluloid leaf between mirror and small pencil for keeping memorandums. This is a very high grade article at an exceptionally low price. Size, 3½x2¾ inches. Price.....**23c**
If by mail, postage extra, 3 cents.

No. 18K25364 Pocket Toilet Case, made of marble leather with gilt embossed design. Has bevel edge mirror 2x4 inches. Lined with silk, contains good quality horn comb and nail cleaner in leather pockets. Entire size, 2¼x4¼ inches when closed. Price.....**35c**
If by mail, postage extra, 4 cents.

No. 18K25366 Pocket Toilet Case. Genuine calf back, with elegant, embossed design, contains heavy beveled French plate mirror, comb, ear and nail pick, with silk leaflet between. Case is also lined with silk throughout. A very valuable and handy companion. Size, 2½x4¼ inches. Price.....**46c**
If by mail, postage extra, 5 cents.

FLOWERS

WE ARE IN A BETTER POSITION THAN EVER BEFORE TO GIVE YOU THE FINEST FLOWERS ON THE MARKET AT THE LOWEST PRICES.

OUR FLOWER LINE is more complete than it has ever been. This is due to the fact that we have gone into both the American and European markets thoroughly and consequently have the best that they offer at the very lowest prices. We look for the biggest season in the history of flowers as a trimming. Every Parisian model shown is loaded with them, and because of the large hats which are so popular this season, the effect is beautiful and easily executed.

IN SELECTING OUR LINE OF FLOWERS for Spring we have worked to one end and that is to secure an assortment which would be complete in style and that could be easily and artistically applied by an inexperienced trimmer as well as by the most tasty of milliners and we have accomplished that end. No matter what pattern you decide upon you will find no difficulty in getting the desired effect. We want to call your attention to the fact that while our flowers are the best, our prices are lower than ever before. We show a line of flowers at from 9 cents to 88 cents per bunch which we know cannot be duplicated, and we can save you from one-third to one-half on every bunch of flowers you buy from us.

Violets in Pretty Styles.

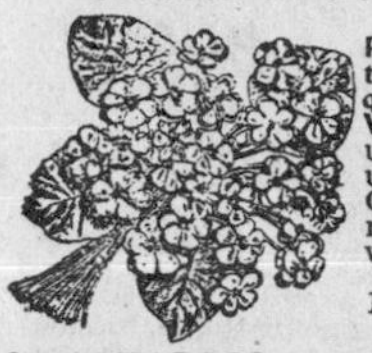

No. 18K13300 Pretty cluster of twenty-four good quality silk centered Violets, with four natural green leaves. Regular 25-cent value. Colors, black, white or natural. State color wanted.
Our price..... 14c
If by mail, postage extra, 5 cents.

No. 18K13302 Beautiful cluster of eighteen double silk and velvet Violets with silk velvet foliage in green. Comes in natural violet shade only.
Price, per bunch..... 23c
If by mail, postage extra, 5 cents.

SILK AND VELVET
35c

No. 18K13305 Our very finest Violet in silk and velvet combination. Is branched in three clusters with natural leaves. Natural violet shade only. Others ask 75 cents for equal value. Our price, per bunch 35c
If by mail, postage extra, 7 cents.

No. 18K13307 This beautiful all silk double Violet is branched in three sprays, containing forty-eight blossoms in all. Is very easily trimmed and gives a beautiful effect. Colors, black, white, light blue, pink, gray, brown or natural violet shades. State color wanted. Price, per bunch... 38c
If by mail, postage extra, 7 cents.

Imported Forget-Me-Nots.

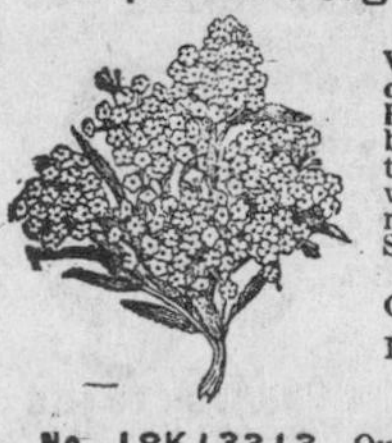

No. 18K13310 Very pretty bunch of imported velvet Forget-Me-Nots, branched in six clusters. Comes in pink, white, light blue or red. 25-cent value. State color wanted.
Our price..... 16c
If by mail, postage extra, 5 cents.

No. 18K13313 Our finest quality imported velvet Forget-Me-Nots, branched in full spray effect. Forget-me-nots are always popular as they make the daintiest of trimmings. Colors, white, pink or light blue. State color wanted.
Price, per bunch... 23c
If by mail, postage extra, 5 cents.

Two Special Values in Lilies.

No. 18K13315 Pretty bunch of Lilies of the Valley with natural green foliage. Suitable for children's hats. Colors, white, pink, or light blue. State color wanted.
Price, per bunch..... 10c
If by mail, postage extra, 5 cents.

No. 18K13317 Finest quality Lilies of the Valley, with green foliage and buds. A dainty, rich trimming. Come in white only.
Price, per bunch..... 21c
If by mail, postage extra, 5 cents.

Artificial Lilacs.

No. 18K13319 Good quality Lilacs at an exceptionally low price. Branched in six sprays. Comes in white, pink, light blue or natural lilac color. State color wanted. Price, per bunch..... 12c
If by mail, postage extra, 5 cents.

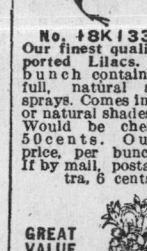

No. 18K13321 Our finest quality imported Lilacs. This bunch contains four full, natural shaped sprays. Comes in white or natural shades only. Would be cheap at 50 cents. Our price, per bunch 29c
If by mail, postage extra, 6 cents.

GREAT VALUE
33
CENTS

No. 18K3323 This beautiful bunch of Imported Hyacinths is branched in drooping effect and makes a very handsome trimming. Comes in light blue, pink or brown, all shaded from light to dark, also solid white. State color wanted.
Price, per bunch..... 33c
If by mail, postage extra, 7 cents.

No. 18K13325 Our leading value in natural centered Daisies. Fine quality double mercerized petals with natural foliage. Comes in white, with brown or yellow centers. Regular retail price, 25 cents. Our price..... 14c
If by mail, postage extra, 6 cents.

Handsome Daisy Wreath.

25c

No. 18K13327 Beautiful long wreath effect of natural centered Daisies with double mercerized petals. Comes in white with yellow centers, or yellow with brown centers. State color wanted.
Price, per wreath..... 25c
If by mail, postage extra, 7 cents.

No. 18K13329 Morning Glories are very stylish. This large, showy bunch is branched in wreathed effect, blossoms being blended in assorted natural shades. Comes in one blended color only as described. Price, per bunch..... 29c
If by mail, postage extra, 8 cents.

No. 18K13332 A dainty spray of Crabapple Blossoms. Makes a beautiful trimming on children's or misses' hats. Colors, white, pink or natural, all delicately shaded. State color wanted.
Price, per bunch..... 19c
If by mail, postage extra, 5 cents.

No. 18K13334 This beautiful imported cluster of Wild Flowers has all silk centers and natural foliage. A very large handsome trimming on children's hats. Comes in white, pink or light blue. State color wanted.
Price, per bunch..... 32c
If by mail, postage extra, 7 cents.

No. 18K13336 Beautiful cluster of three-spray Imported June Roses with all silk centers, branched with foliage, buds and natural moss. A large showy trimming of quality. Colors, pink, white or light blue. State color wanted.
Price..... 38c
If by mail, postage extra, 8 cents.

All Velvet Geraniums.

No. 18K13338 This pretty bunch of Geraniums has all velvet petals and natural green foliage, branched in three-spray cluster effect. Colors, pink, light blue, or natural red. State color wanted.
Price, per bunch..... 19c
If by mail, postage extra, 7 cents.

A STYLISH TRIMMING EASY TO USE

ALL COLORS AT 33c

No. 18K13340 Handsome wreath effect made up of all velvet Geraniums sprayed with beautiful imported foliage and geranium buds. A very showy number. Comes in white, pink, light blue or natural red. State color wanted.
Price, per bunch..... 33c
If by mail, postage extra, 8 cents.

No. 18K13342 Our finest quality all silk and velvet Geraniums, containing eighteen large flowers branched in three clusters with finest imported foliage. A decidedly showy trimming. Regular 75-cent value. Colors, pink, white, light blue or red. State color wanted. Price, per bunch..... 45c
If by mail, postage extra, 7 cents.

All Silk Centered Poppies.

No. 18K13344 Very handsome bunch of double Poppies with full silk centers, sprayed with natural green poppy foliage. Comes in white, pink or red. State color wanted. 33c
Price, per bunch.....
If by mail, postage extra, 6 cents.

Imported Poppy Wreath. Finest Quality, 38 Cents.

38c

No. 18K13347 Beautiful long wreath effect of medium sized silk centered double Poppies. Makes a full trimming. Colors, white, pink or natural red. State color wanted.
Price, per bunch..... 38c
If by mail, postage extra, 7 cents.

Three Extra Special Values in Silk Covered Rose Buds.

No. 18K13349 Exceptional offer in Silk covered half blown Rose Buds, sprayed with natural foliage and moss. Comes in white, pink, tea or American beauty red. State color wanted.
Price, per bunch.. 19c
If by mail, postage extra, 5 cents.

Regular 75c Value, 38 Cents.

No. 18K13351 Our greatest value in silk covered Moss Rose Buds. A great favorite with our customers and one of the best styles in our entire line. Twenty-four beautiful buds branched with natural rose foliage and sea moss. Colors, white, pink, tea or American beauty red. State color wanted. Price, per bunch.. 38c
If by mail, postage extra, 7 cents.

68c

No. 18K13353 Our finest quality Rose Bud Wreath. All silk covered buds, branched with natural moss and sprays of small foliage. A very handsome trimming, easily applied on any hat. Colors, white, pink, tea or American beauty red. State color wanted. Price per bunch..... 68c
If by mail, postage extra, 8 cents.

Imported Foliage.

9c

No. 18K13355 Good quality natural tinted Rose Foliage, contains eighteen muslin leaves in natural green only. Trims prettily with any kind of flower.
MILLINERS ASK 20 CENTS.
Price, per bunch..... 9c
If by mail, postage extra, 4c.

19c

No. 18K13357 Extra fine quality imported muslin Rose Foliage, containing twenty-seven leaves handsomely sprayed. Natural green shade only. Regular 35c value.
Price, per bunch..... 19c
If by mail, postage extra, 7 cents.

Silk Velvet Foliage.

No. 18K13359 Finest quality pure silk Velvet Rose Foliage. This spray contains eighteen beautiful leaves. Just the trimming for use with silk and velvet crush roses. Natural green only.
Price, per bunch... 33c
If by mail, postage extra, 7 cents.

13c CENTS

No. 18K13361 Very pretty bunch of small June Rose Foliage with buds. A very dainty trimming. Natural green color only.
Price, per bunch..... 13c
If by mail, postage extra, 5 cents.

No. 18K3363 Our finest spray of June Rose Foliage branched in three clusters with natural moss and buds. Comes in natural foliage shade only with assorted buds. Very large and showy.
Price, per bunch..... 24c
If by mail, postage extra, 7 cents.

No. 18K13365 A very handsome pattern in Imported Rose Foliage, containing thirty best quality muslin leaves. Autumn tints only. Well worth 50 cents.
Price, per bunch..... 27c
If by mail, postage extra, 8 cents.

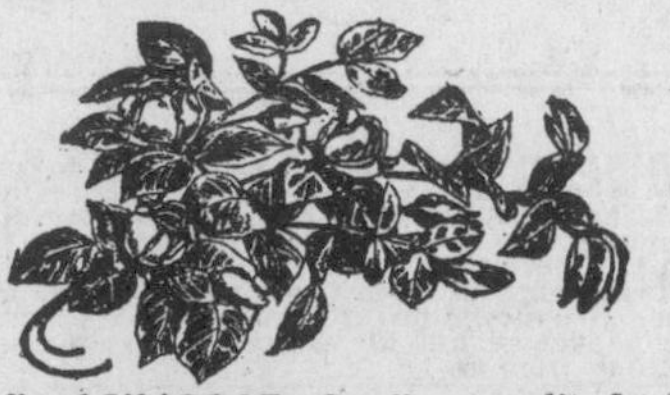

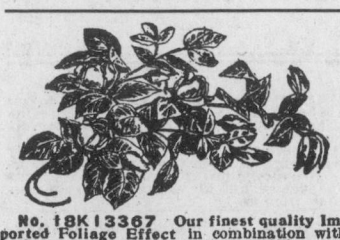

No. 18K13367 Our finest quality Imported Foliage Effect in combination with half blown buds. Good buyers will appreciate this offer. Comes in natural foliage shades with pink, tea or American beauty red buds. State color wanted.
Price, per bunch 48c
If by mail, postage extra, 7 cents.

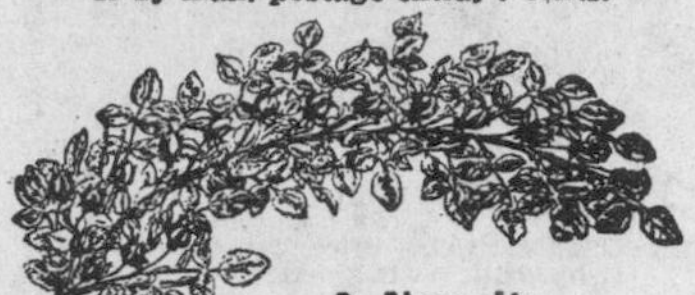

A Novelty Wreath.

No. 18K13369 Foliage Wreath. Full trimming for one hat. Made up of handsome June rose foliage, liberally mixed with tiny buds. Natural shaded foliage with pink, tea, or American beauty red buds as wanted. State color wanted. Price, per wreath. 42c
If by mail, postage extra, 7 cents.

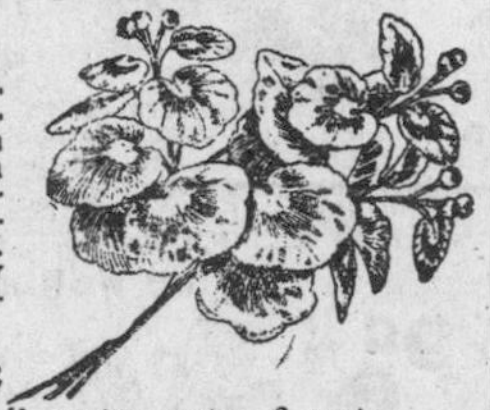

No. 18K13371 Natural shaded, finest quality Geranium Foliage with tiny buds, containing twenty-one leaves. We show only one quality—the best.
Price per bunch 18c
If by mail, postage extra, 6 cents.

Pretty Styles in Fruits with Foliage.

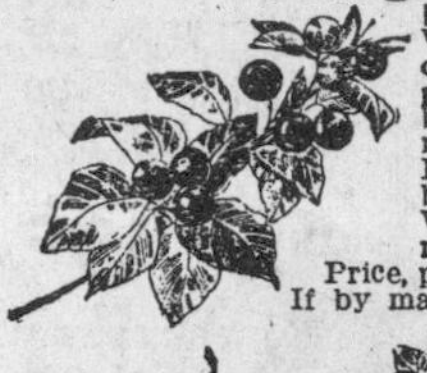

No. 18K13373 Very showy spray of fine quality Imported Cherries, branched with natural foliage. Finest quality unbreakable cherries. Very showy trimming.
Price, per bunch... 21c
If by mail, postage extra, 6 cents.

38c

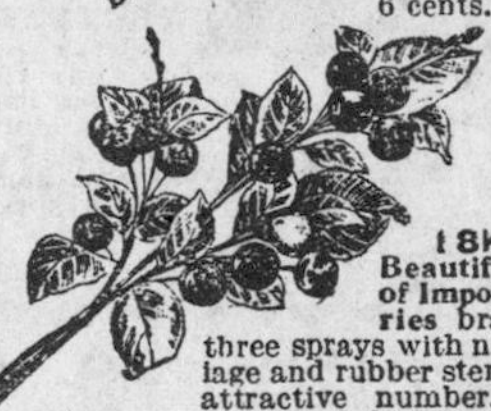

No. 18K13376 Beautiful bunch of Imported Cherries branched in three sprays with natural foliage and rubber stems. Very attractive number. Comes in natural shades only.
Price, per bunch.. (Postage extra 8c). 38c

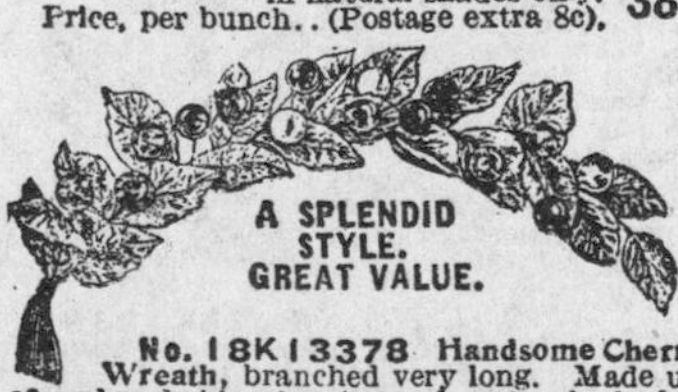

A SPLENDID STYLE. GREAT VALUE.

No. 18K13378 Handsome Cherry Wreath, branched very long. Made up of unbreakable cherries and natural shaded foliage. Exceptional value at our price. Price, per wreath............ 38c
If by mail, postage extra, 8 cents.

48c

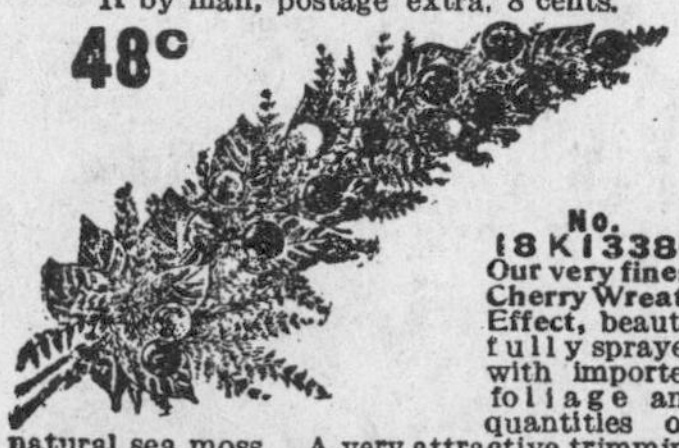

No. 18K13380 Our very finest Cherry Wreath Effect, beautifully sprayed with imported foliage and quantities of natural sea moss. A very attractive trimming in a pretty soft effect. Price, per wreath. (If by mail, postage extra, 8c).. 48c

44c

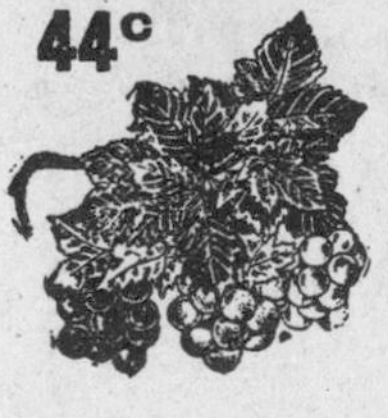

Grapes Are Very Popular.

No. 18K13382 A very pretty cluster of natural shaded Grapes, sprayed with natural grape foliage in rosette effect. Regular 75-cent value.
Price, per bunch......... 44c
If by mail, postage extra, 5 cents.

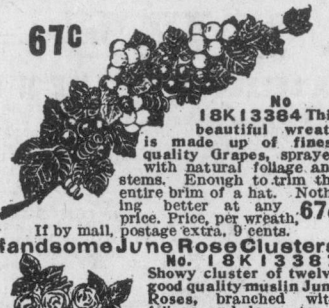

67c

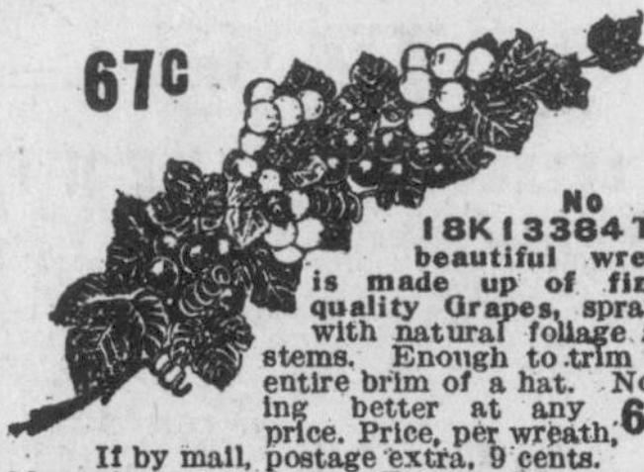

No. 18K13384 This beautiful wreath is made up of finest quality Grapes, sprayed with natural foliage and stems. Enough to trim the entire brim of a hat. Nothing better at any price. Price, per wreath, 67c
If by mail, postage extra, 9 cents.

Handsome June Rose Clusters

No. 18K13387 Showy cluster of twelve good quality muslin June Roses, branched with foliage and long stems. Colors, pink, white, light blue or American beauty red. 25-cent value. State color wanted.
Price, per bunch. 15c
If by mail, postage extra, 5 cents.

38c

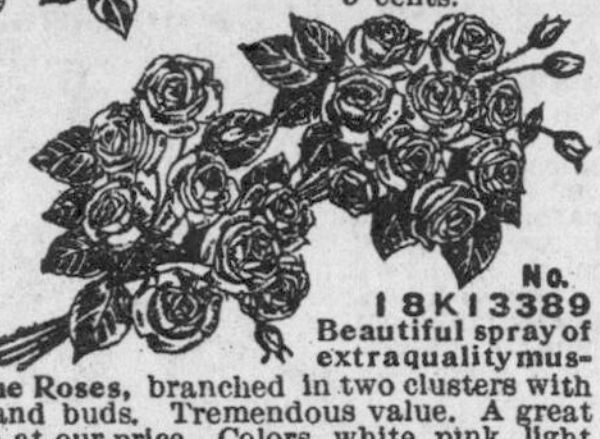

No. 18K13389 Beautiful spray of extra quality muslin June Roses, branched in two clusters with leaves and buds. Tremendous value. A great bargain at our price. Colors, white, pink, light blue or American beauty red. State color wanted. Price, per bunch 38c
If by mail, postage extra, 6 cents.

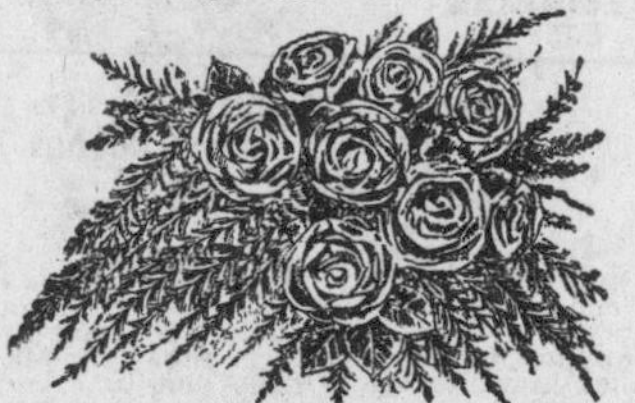

No. 18K13392 Our finest June Rose Effect of best quality silk and muslin flowers in combination with buds and beautiful sea moss. Very handsome front trimming with the present style hats, soft and fluffy. Colors, pink, tea or American beauty red. State color wanted. Price, per bunch, 59c
If by mail, postage extra, 8 cents.

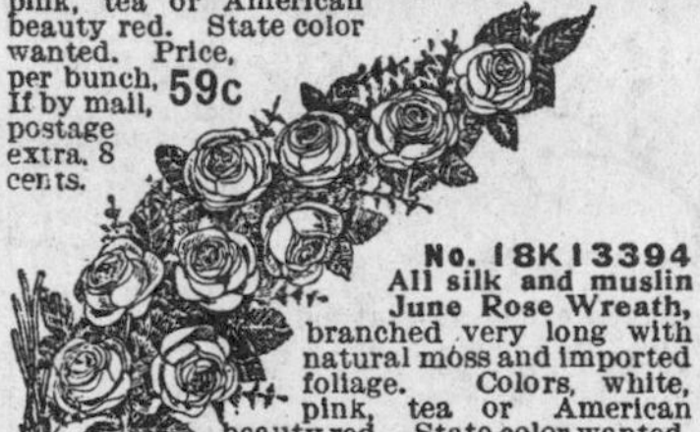

No. 18K13394 All silk and muslin June Rose Wreath, branched very long with natural moss and imported foliage. Colors, white, pink, tea or American beauty red. State color wanted.
Price, per wreath...... 45c
If by mail, postage extra, 8c.

Best Muslin Roses.

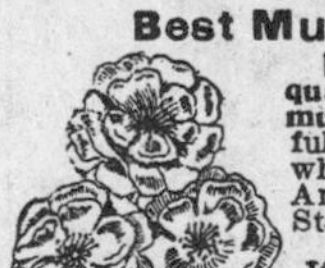

No. 18K13396 Good quality three in a bunch muslin Crush Roses, with full centers. Colors, pink, white, tea, light blue or American beauty red. State color wanted.
Price, per bunch.. 14c
If by mail, postage extra, 5 cents.

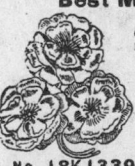

No. 18K13398 Our best quality all muslin, six in a bunch Cup Roses, with rubber stems. Colors, white, pink, light blue or American beauty red. State color wanted.
Price, per bunch... 23c
If by mail, postage extra, 5 cents.

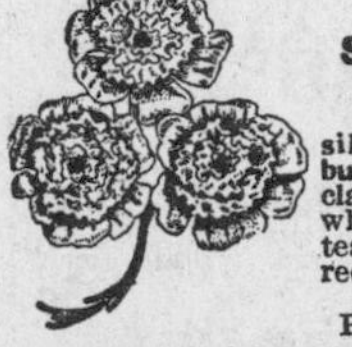

Silk and Velvet Crush Roses.

No. 18K13403 All silk and velvet, three in a bunch Crush Roses. First class materials. Colors, white, pink, light blue, tea or American beauty red. State color wanted.
Price, per bunch.. 13c
Postage extra, 5c.

No. 18K13413 These beautiful three in a bunch Crush Roses are made of a combination of finest quality silk, velvet and muslin. Our illustration does not show its real beauty. Colors, pink, white, or American beauty red, brown shaded with light blue, green shaded with brown. 50-cent value. State color.
Price, per bunch.
Postage extra, 5c. 29c

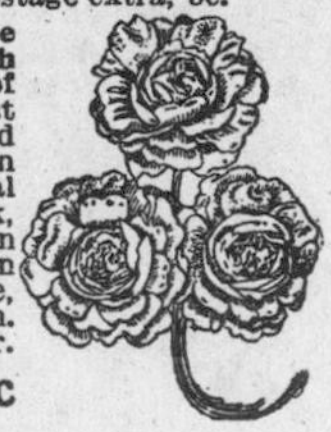

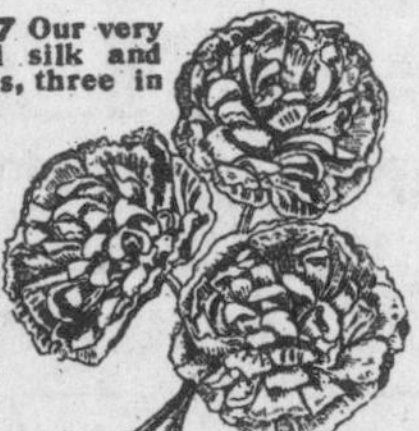

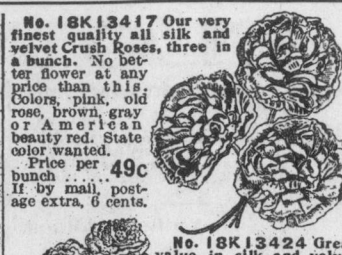

No. 18K13417 Our very finest quality all silk and velvet Crush Roses, three in a bunch. No better flower at any price than this. Colors, pink, old rose, brown, gray or American beauty red. State color wanted.
Price per bunch 49c
If by mail, postage extra, 6 cents.

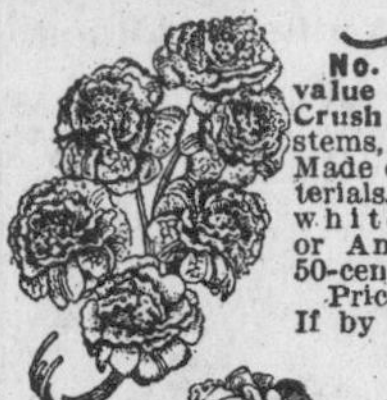

No. 18K13424 Great value in silk and velvet Crush Roses with rubber stems, six in a bunch. Made of good quality materials. Colors, pink, white, light blue, tea, or American beauty red. 50-cent value.
Price, per bunch... 29c
If by mail, postage extra, 7 cents.

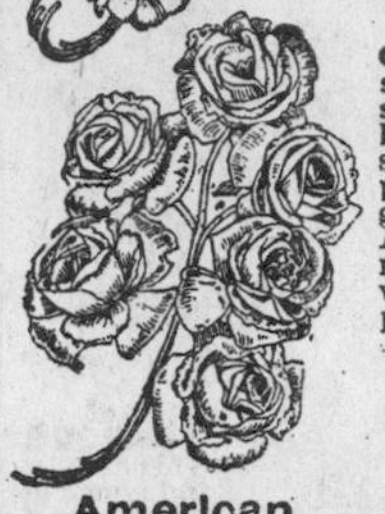

No. 18K13430 Our finest quality six in a bunch all silk and velvet Cup Roses, with rubber stems. Colors, white, pink, light blue, tea, gray, brown or American beauty red. State color wanted. Price, per bunch..... 46c
If by mail, postage extra, 7 cents.

American Beauty Roses.

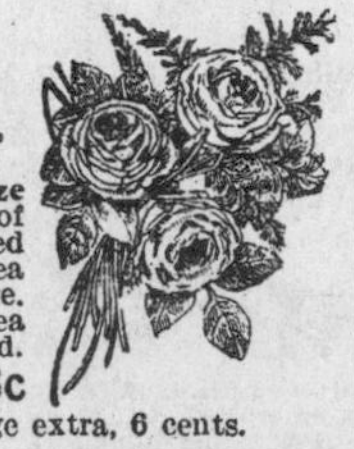

No. 18K13432 Three medium size American Beauty Roses of good quality lawn, sprayed with soft natural sea moss and rose foliage. Colors, white, pink, tea or American beauty red. State color wanted. 18c
Price, per bunch.
If by mail, postage extra, 6 cents.

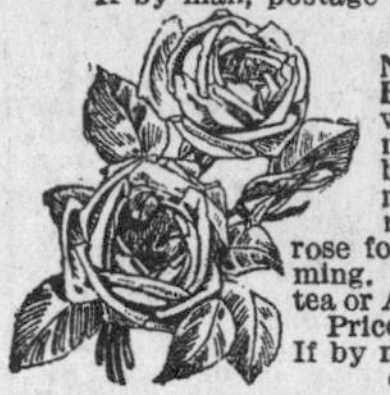

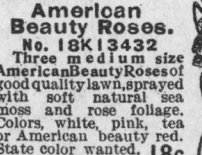

No. 18K13434 Natural American Beauty Roses are always popular. This number contains two beautiful, full blown roses with a bud and natural imported rose foliage. A rich trimming. Colors, white, pink, tea or American beauty red.
Price, per bunch 27c
If by mail, postage extra, 6 cents.

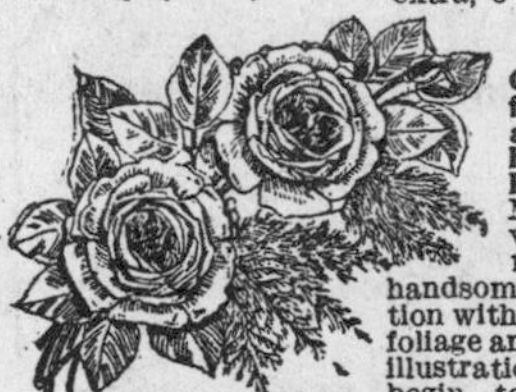

No. 18K13436 Our very finest two in a bunch, Half Blown Rose Effect. Made of silk, velvet and muslin in handsome combination with natural rose foliage and moss. Our illustration does not begin to show the real beauty of these flowers. Comes in white, pink, tea or American beauty red.
Price, per bunch.. (Postage extra, 7c). 46c

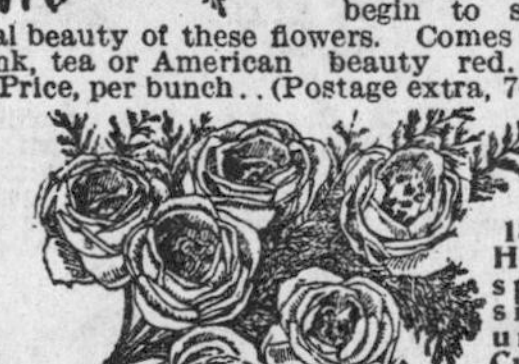

No. 18K13438 Handsome spray of six medium size Cup Roses of fine quality lawn, sprayed with soft sea moss, giving it a very dainty effect. Colors, white, pink, tea or American beauty red. State color wanted. Price, per bunch. (Postage extra, 7c). 33c

Rose Wreaths Trim Easily.

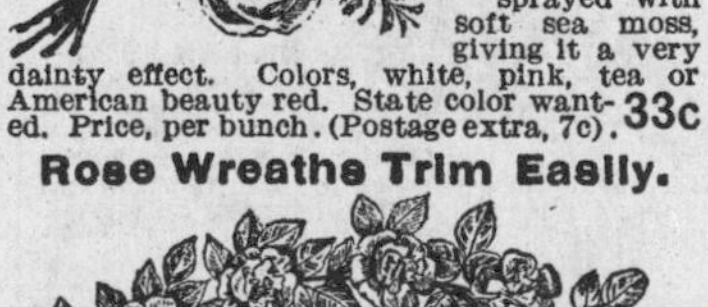

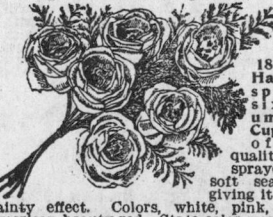

No. 18K13440 Our leading value in velvet and muslin Rose Wreath, six velvet and six muslin roses, wreath effect, sprayed with foliage on chenille stems. One of the biggest bargains ever offered. Colors, white, pink, light blue, tea or American beauty red.
Price, per wreath... (Postage 6c.).... 27c

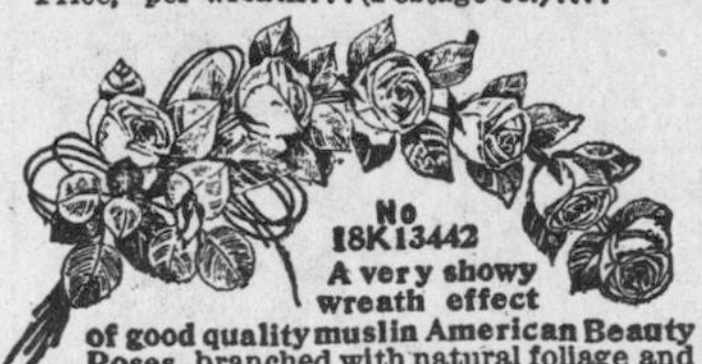

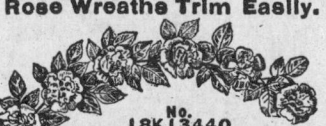

No. 18K13442 A very showy wreath effect of good quality muslin American Beauty Roses, branched with natural foliage and long stems. Colors, white, tea, pink or American beauty red. State color wanted.
Price, per wreath. (Postage extra, 7c). 35c

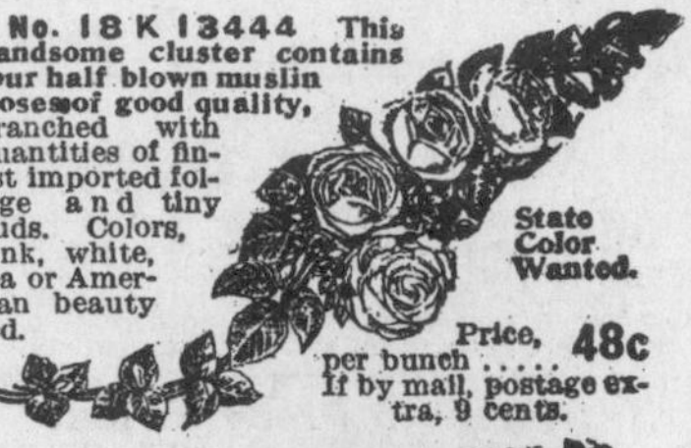

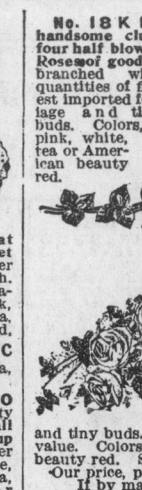

No. 18K13444 This handsome cluster contains four half blown muslin Roses of good quality, branched with quantities of finest imported foliage and tiny buds. Colors, pink, white, tea or American beauty red. State Color Wanted.
Price, per bunch 48c
If by mail, postage extra, 9 cents.

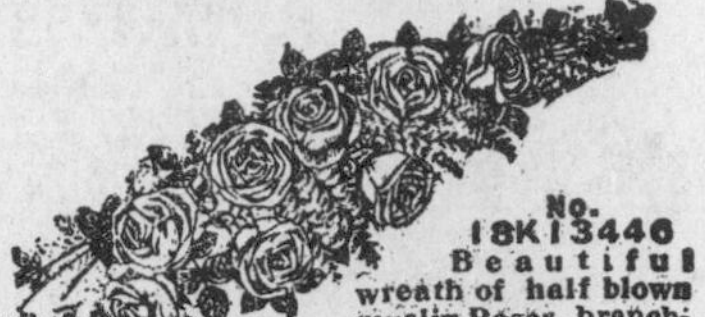

No. 18K13446 Beautiful wreath of half blown muslin Roses, branched with June rose foliage, natural soft moss and tiny buds. Others ask $1.25 for no better value. Colors, pink, white, tea or American beauty red. State color wanted.
Our price, per wreath............ 67c
If by mail, postage extra, 8 cents.

88c

No. 18K13448 Our most beautiful Crush Rose Wreath. The daintiest effect in our complete line. Something entirely new and very attractive. Our illustration does not show the exquisite beauty of these roses. Come in white, pink, tea or American beauty red. State color wanted. Price, per wreath. 88c
If by mail, postage extra, 8 cents.

Black Foliage.

No. 18K13450 Good quality black Mercerized Satin Foliage for use with black crush roses. Regular 35-cent value.
Price, per bunch 19c
If by mail, postage extra, 7 cents.

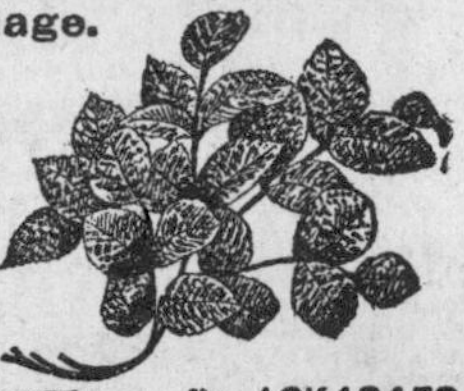

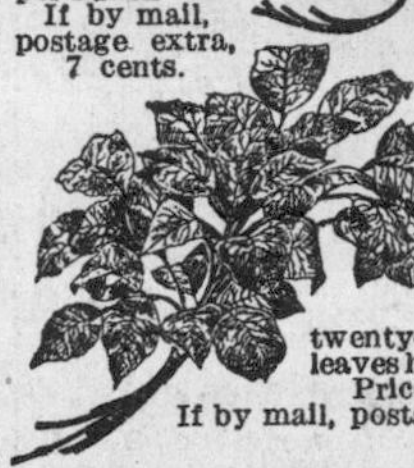

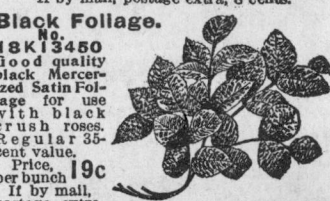

No. 18K13452 Our very finest All Satin Foliage in black only. No better black foliage than this can be bought at any price. Contains twenty-four beautiful leaves handsomely sprayed.
Price, per bunch.. 33c
If by mail, postage extra. 8c.

Best Black Flowers.

No. 18K13454 Good quality black Crush Roses with all silk centers, three in a bunch. Great value at our price.
Price, per bunch .. 14c
If by mail, postage extra, 5 cents.

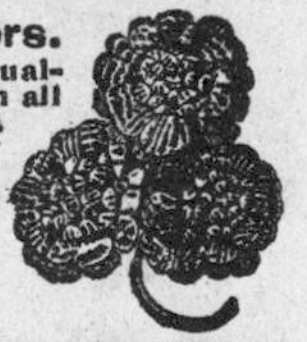

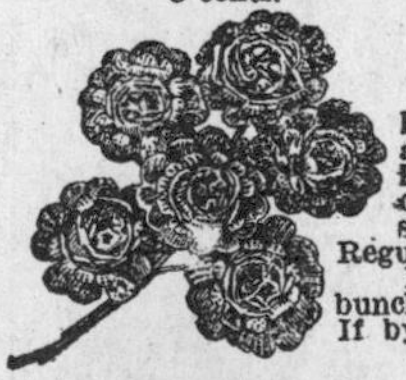

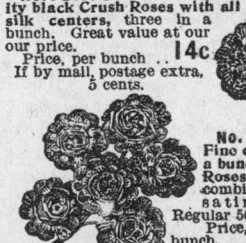

No. 18K13456 Fine quality, six in a bunch, black Cup Roses, made of a combination of silk, satin and muslin. Regular 50-cent value.
Price, per bunch............ 33c
If by mail, postage extra, 5 cents.

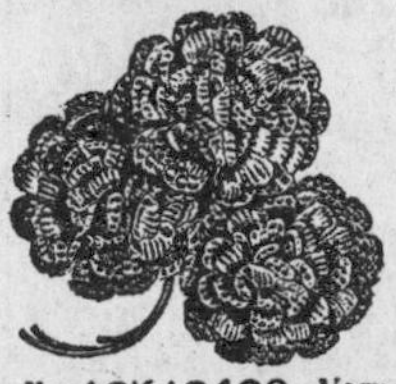

No. 18K13487 Extra fine quality all silk and satin black Crush Roses with very full centers. Three in a bunch.
Price, bunch. 46c
If by mail, postage extra, 5 cents.

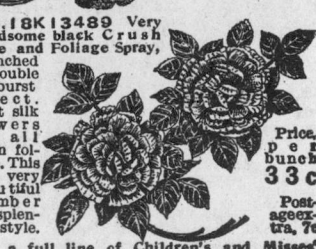

No. 18K13489 Very handsome black Crush Rose and Foliage Spray, branched in double sunburst effect. Best silk flowers and all satin foliage. This is a very beautiful number in splendid style.
Price, per bunch 33c
Postage extra, 7c

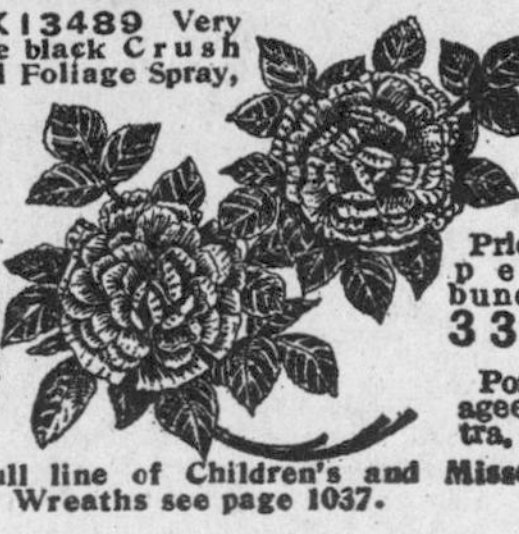

For a full line of Children's and Misses' Wreaths see page 1037.

THE WORLD'S BEST OSTRICH FEATHERS

NEVER BEFORE were ostrich feathers so popular as they are at the present time. Never were good ostrich feathers so easily within the reach of the buying public until we began our great price reducing campaign. In spite of the fact that unfinished feathers have advanced fully 50 per cent in price, owing to the tremendous demand which is much greater than the supply, in spite of this fact we are still able, on account of contracts placed a year ago, to maintain almost without exception our wonderfully low prices, representing an actual saving to you of from one-third to one-half.

THOUSANDS OF SATISFIED PURCHASERS will attest to the wonderful beauty and rich quality of our ostrich plumes, and all who have bought from us need no further introduction. If you have never purchased ostrich goods from us we urge you to give our plumes a trial, and can assure you that you will be more than satisfied. In a few short years we have built up the largest plume business in the country.

HIGHEST QUALITY AT LOWEST PRICE is the secret of our wonderful success. We use only the highest grade hard fiber feathers, which take a more beautiful finish and a higher luster in the dyeing than any other. They hold their curl and will wear season after season if given proper care and attention. With each feather we send directions telling you how to care for your plume. If you will carefully follow these directions you will get excellent results.

OUR WELL KNOWN LIBERAL POLICY of satisfaction or your money back covers every style in our line of plumes, half plumes and tips. You take no chances in ordering from us, for if you do not find our goods all that we claim for them, both as to quality and saving on prices asked by others, we earnestly ask you to return them to us, and we will gladly refund your money or exchange them for other goods. For quick and safe shipments of ostrich plumes we advise express, but if you find it more convenient and wish them sent by mail always allow from 6 cents to 20 cents extra for postage.

THAT OUR VALUES ARE REAL IS PROVEN BY THE FACT THAT OUR SALES OF OSTRICH FEATHERS FOR THE LAST FIVE MONTHS OF 1907 EXCEEDED $100,000.00

REAL FRENCH CURL PLUMES.

FRENCH CURL PLUMES, which we illustrate in the center of this page, are by far the most popular style in use today. They combine all the good features that a plume should have, namely, beauty of form, width in proportion to length, and long hard fibers which take a graceful curl and retain it longer than the cheap soft qualities which are so often forced upon the buyers of ostrich plumes.

WHEN WE SPEAK OF BEAUTY OF FORM, we might say that until the French curl style in plumes was brought out, plumes as a trimming had not begun to reach their present height of popularity, because with the styles then in vogue, it took an expert milliner to procure a graceful effect. The French curl style has removed this obstacle, and the home milliner can procure the finest effects, as this popular plume lends itself easily to any style of trimming.

IN OUR ILLUSTRATION TO THE RIGHT we show three different sizes of our French curl plumes in both black and white colors, and we call your particular attention that length is the most important item in the cost of a plume, for the longer the plume is, the wider it must be to maintain its proportion and beauty.

IN THE COLUMN DIRECTLY OPPOSITE we give a complete price list of our beautiful French Curl Plumes, all of which are made of the finest hard flue stock with the best London dye and finish. In selecting your plumes, take particular notice of the various lengths given and always remember that the best are the cheapest in the long run.

OUR PRICES ON FRENCH CURL PLUMES.

Be sure to state color wanted.
No. 18K13621 A good feather at the price. Length, 15 inches. Colors, black, white or cream. Price, each........$1.99
No. 18K13623 Regular $4.00 value. Length, 16 inches. Colors, black, white or cream. Price, each........$2.98
No. 18K13624 At your dealer's would cost $5.00. Length, 17 inches. Colors, black, white or cream. Price, each........$3.75
No. 18K13625 A most desirable size. Length, 18 inches. Colors, black, white or cream. Price, each........$4.88
No. 18K13627 An Exceptionally Fine Plume. Length, 19 inches. Colors, black, white or cream. Price, each........$5.89
No. 18K13629 Equal qualities sell elsewhere at no less than $12.00. Length, 22 inches. Colors, black, white or cream. Price, each........$7.98
No. 18K13631 Our Very Finest Plume. Length, 24 inches. Colors, black, white or cream. Price, each........$9.49

COLORED FRENCH CURL PLUMES.

Made of the same fine quality stock which is used in our large line of blacks, whites or creams. No finer qualities at any price than those quoted below. Be sure to state color wanted.
No. 18K13633 Never before sold for less than $2.25. Length, 13 inches. Colors, light blue, pink, cardinal, navy, brown or myrtle green. Price, each........$1.48
No. 18K13635 A beautiful feather nicely curled, with fine full head. Length, 15 inches. Comes in light blue, pink, cardinal, navy, brown, corn color or myrtle green. Price, each........$2.29
No. 18K13637 Our Best Colored Ostrich Plume. Regular $5.00 value. Length, 17 inches. Comes in light blue, pink, cardinal, leghorn, brown, navy or myrtle green. Price, each........$3.25

DO NOT FAIL TO STATE COLOR WANTED.

Demi or Half Plumes with Large Full Heads.

These are worn very much this season. Are extensively used in clusters of two or more. They make a showy trimming at a very low cost. If to be sent by mail, include from 6 cents to 12 cents extra for postage.
No. 18K13602 Special Value. 9-Inch Demi Plume, made of good ostrich stock, is nicely curled and will give entire satisfaction for a low priced plume. Comes in black only. Price, each...33c
No. 18K13604 A 10-Inch Demi Plume, made of good quality hard flue ostrich stock, finely curled. Will trim very beautifully. Comes in black, white or cream. When ordering, please state color wanted. Price, each...49c
No. 18K13606 This is one of our popular numbers. 11-Inch Demi Plume with a nicely curled head made of best grade hard flue ostrich stock. Is rich and glossy. A better plume than you can get at retail for $1.25. Comes in white, black or cream. State color wanted. Price, each...79c
No. 18K13608 12-Inch Demi or Half Plume, is rich in appearance. Made of best quality hard flue ostrich stock. Is finely curled. These are extensively used in clusters. Hats are usually trimmed with two or three of these. Colors, black, white or cream. Price, each...99c
No. 18K13610 This is an Exceptionally Fine Quality 13-Inch Plume, made of good glossy stock in rich curl. Plume of equal quality cannot be obtained elsewhere for less than $2.00. Colors, black, white or cream. Be sure to state color wanted. Price, each...$1.29
No. 18K13612 Extra Quality 14-Inch Genuine Ostrich Plume, made in demi style. This is an exceptionally fine plume made of selected stock; is rich in finish. Has a very beautiful curl and a large full head. Colors, black, white, cream, light blue, brown or pink. Please state color wanted. Price, each...$1.59
No. 18K13614 Our Best Quality 15-Inch Demi Plume, made of very best selected stock, genuine ostrich. This has a hard richly curled glossy flue, and is one of our best sellers. This would retail easily for $3.00. Colors, black, white or cream. State color wanted. Price, each...$1.87

Fine Quality Ostrich Tips.

These goods, as shown in illustration, are put up three in a bunch, which gives them a full appearance. Like all our other ostrich goods these tips contain only the finest grade of hard male stock, and the colors are perfect. Tips are in great demand for trimming turbans as well as all kinds of small shapes which will not carry a full plume. In this class of ostrich goods the length is of little consequence as the head of the tip is all that would show after the hat is trimmed. For this reason our tips are especially desirable, as we have worked to this end and are prepared to give you not alone the best stock for your money, but also the most desirable shape plume for every style of trimming. These tips are three separate plumes wired together and can be taken apart and used in any way you desire. We recommend the better grade of goods; for the larger and fuller the plume or tip is, the longer it will keep its curl and rich appearance.

No. 18K13653 An exceptional value at the price. Comes in black only. Price, per bunch of three........30c
No. 18K13655 A larger and fuller bunch than the above. Colors, black, white or cream. State color wanted. Price, per bunch of three........55c
No. 18K13657 An Exceptionally Pretty Bunch of Tips, in the following good colors: Black, white, cream, light blue, brown, pink or red. State color wanted. Price, per bunch of three........99c
No. 18K13659 A Beautiful Bunch of Large Full Tips. Colors, black, white or cream. State color wanted. Price, per bunch of three........$1.50
No. 18K13661 Extra Fine Quality Tips, very full. Colors, black or white. State color wanted. Price, per bunch of three........$1.95
No. 18K13662 These are our Finest Quality Tips. Colors, black or white. State color wanted. Price, per bunch of three........$2.60

Ostrich Quill Stem Holders Free.

With each ostrich plume, half plume or bunch tip, we give our customers absolutely without cost a white or black celluloid quill stem holder to match feather as ordered. It will not be necessary for you to ask for this quill holder as we will include one with each feather ordered when packing the goods.

About Our Method of Packing Plumes, Half Plumes and Tips for Safe Shipment.

A special feature of our Ostrich Department is our method of packing all plumes, half plumes and tips so that they will be sure to reach our customers in absolutely first class condition.

We aim to pack every one of our fine feathers so that it goes into the hands of the transportation company in the best possible shape and should reach you in perfect form.

In our illustration we show one of our No. 18K13625 black plumes as it appears in our specially prepared box ready to be wrapped and packed. We have this box made for this particular purpose at a considerable expense to ourselves and know that you will appreciate our earnest endeavor to have our goods reach

you in perfect shape. We put each plume, half plume or tip in an individual box whether it be an article selling for our lowest or highest price.

If for any reason you find it necessary to return any ostrich plume to us you would do us no greater favor than by repacking it in the same box in which it is received, or at least in a good strong package, so that we will receive the goods in the same condition as they were sent out.

If you can include your order for ostrich feathers with an order for other goods which are to be shipped by freight you will save practically all transportation charges. We can make very quick and safe shipments by express, however, or by mail if it is more convenient for you.

LABOR COSTS JUST AS MUCH ON CHEAP MATERIALS AS ON GOOD

Quality Considered, this Hat Cannot be Duplicated by Your Milliner for Less than $2.25. Our Price, only $1.49.

No. 18K15200 Our leading value in a genteel turban. Hand made on a wire frame of novelty white allover straw braid. This pretty little hat is trimmed with a drape of crimped white lace which falls prettily over the entire brim. On the left side a bunch of pink June roses is set in the midst of loops of good quality Jap silk, which are brought down to the bandeau and there caught in place with a round cut steel cabochon. This hat is very good as described in white with pink roses; can also be ordered in brown with pink roses and white lace; navy blue with jack roses and white lace; light blue with white lace and light blue roses; black with pink roses; black with red roses, or all black. Be sure to state the color you want.

Price $1.49

$1.49

Made on a Fine Quality Straw Shape all Faced With Lace. Great Value at $1.69

$1.69

No. 18K15205 A very attractive and popular style, which is known as the Cheyenne or roll front effect. A pretty hat which is worn off the face by young ladies or misses. The shape is made of a handsome straw braid in white, sewed row and row, being entirely faced with good quality plaited white lace. The brim is rolled high on the left side at the front. Starting at the bandeau and extending almost entirely around the crown appears a wreath effect of pretty blossoms in white. A drape of pink taffeta ribbon twisted among the flowers and around the crown completes the trimming of this stylish popular priced model. Can be ordered in white with white flowers and pink ribbon as described; white with light blue, pink or red flowers; brown with light blue or pink flowers; or navy blue with white flowers; all with ribbon to match. Always state the color you want. Price $1.69

Combination of Imported Braid and Dainty Lace, $1.99

$1.99

No. 18K15210 A drooping brim, large modified mushroom style with high bell crown. A remarkably pretty hat and one suitable for all ages. The wire frame is entirely hand covered with rows of alternating dark green braid and narrow black lace. The facing is made of the same material and the effect obtained is striking and attractive. A pretty trimming is obtained by the use of a large wreath of four half blown pink American beauty roses, sprayed with natural moss and foliage. Entirely overlaying the brim and sides of the crown is a drape of plaited mull, edged with a wide band of finest Jap silk. This drape is artistically folded between the foliage and roses and completely encircles the crown. The hat as described in black and dark green, with contrasting roses in pink is very handsome. May also be ordered in all black with pink or light blue roses; light blue and white with tea roses; white and black with jack roses; or pink and white with pink roses. Be sure to state colors wanted. Price $1.99

This Beautiful All Lace Top Mushroom Style, only $2.15

No. 18K15215 A very handsome short front, dip back, mushroom style, made in the height of fashion. The wire frame is faced in black shirred mull with two rows of tucking. The entire upper brim and large bell crown are covered with good quality plaited black allover lace, shirred and ruffled on the edge. The very handsome style of making helps to trim the hat. The simple but effective trimming consists of a row of black daisies, extending entirely around the bell crown and massed high on the left side. These are intertwined with a knot of black taffeta ribbon. This is a very stylish and attractive hat as described in all black, but may also be ordered in white with white daisies having brown or yellow centers, or all white with yellow daisies. Don't forget to say what colors you want. Price $2.15

$2.15

The Style and Value of this Pattern at $1.98 Will be Readily Appreciated by You.

No. 18K15220 Beautiful shepherdess shape, which we guarantee to be becoming to any face. This hat is

$1.98

hand made on a wire frame of good quality materials. Overlying the upper brim and edge of crown are rows of imported hair braid in brown. A full drape of brown milliners' mull is laid around the crown and extends nearly to the edge of the brim. This mull is gathered in large rosette effect directly on the left side front of the crown and a large crushed rose in pink with buds and natural foliage give beauty and height to the trimming. Peeping from beneath the rosette is a bow of brown satin taffeta ribbon, the ribbon extending in folds around the outer edge of the crown, being brought over the left side of the brim to the bandeau where it ends in a large loop effect. The under facing is of hand laid mull finished around the edge with a row of ruffled brown braid. A splendid hat in brown as described. May also be ordered in navy, champagne or black with trimmings to match. Don't forget to state colors wanted. Price $1.98

We Save One-Third for You in Pricing this Pretty Hat at $1.98.

No. 18K15225 Large mushroom style with French crown in bell effect. This handsome hat is made entirely of a novelty allover straw in brown, brim being edged with fancy brown braid. The dainty trimming is obtained by the use of four crush roses sprayed with foliage massed in front and on left side, in combination with a beautiful drape of imported white plaited lace, which extends entirely around the crown. This hat is very pretty as described in brown with pink roses and white lace; but can also be ordered in light blue with white lace and light blue roses; black with jack roses and black lace; pink with white roses and white lace; or navy blue with white lace and tea roses. Don't forget to say what colors you want. Price $1.98

$1.98

The Best Hat We Have Ever Offered at the Low Price of $1.48.

No. 18K15230 One of the greatest values ever offered to millinery buyers at a low price. This handsome model is strictly hand made on a wire frame, the entire brim and crown being overlaid with fancy allover straw netting in black. Extending around the crown and completely overlaying the upper brim are three deep folds of black milliners' mull. A rosette trimming of the same material centered with two muslin crush roses in American beauty red finish the trimming of this great value. The side bandeau is finished with loops of black ribbon. May be ordered in black with red roses as described or in white, navy or champagne with trimming to match. Always state colors wanted. Price $1.48

$1.48

A Beautiful Spring and Summer Style, $3.00 at Any Milliner's. Our Price, $2.10.

No. 18K15235 Dainty little pattern hat especially designed for misses' and young ladies' wear. This is a handsome combination of lace and milliners' mull. The large balloon crown is made of leghorn colored mull edged with a wide row of plaited white lace which is gathered to the center and falls gracefully over the sides of the crown. The upper brim is entirely covered with plaited white lace and the facing is of plaited leghorn colored mull. The flower trimming consists of a beautiful wreath of tiny June roses and velvet forget me nots in pink, laid around the entire crown. Very pretty in leghorn and white combination with pink flowers as described. May also be ordered in light blue with white lace and light blue flowers; all white with white flowers, or cardinal with white lace and flowers to match. Tell us what colors you want. Price $2.10

$2.10

You Will Appreciate This Quiet and Refined Style, Only $2.15.

No. 18K15240 Large turban effect, close fitting in the back with slightly pointed front. Hand made on a wire frame, the brim being covered with good quality black shirred chiffon. Large crown is overlaid with rows of fancy black silk finished Maline hair braid. The trimming of the hat consists of a beautiful wreath of half blown tiny June roses, all silk and velvet, placed across the front and over the left side where it is held in place with loops of black taffeta ribbon. This ribbon extends to the bandeau in a bow and is caught with a cut steel ornament. Very pretty as described in all black; can also be ordered in navy blue with tea colored roses; brown with pink roses; light blue with jack roses; leather color with tea roses and pink ribbon; pink with cream roses; or all white with pink roses. Be sure to tell us what colors you want. Price $2.15

$2.15

WE SAVE MONEY FOR YOU BY USING HIGH CLASS GOODS

Trimmed Leghorn for Misses and Young Ladies, only $2.38.

$2.38

No. 18K15245 The new Cheyenne or roll front effect is particularly attractive when applied to good leghorns. Our hat as illustrated is made of a good quality imported leghorn with a facing of shirred and tucked leghorn colored mull. The very effective trimming is obtained by the use of brown taffeta ribbon gathered in the center and laid in long loops on the entire front and entirely across the front of the hat. This ribbon extends in folds around the base of the crown. Starting at the left side of the roll, extending back around the crown and down the back of the hat is a wreath of six tea colored crush roses sprayed with natural foliage. Comes in natural leghorn with brown and tea combination trimming as described; leghorn with pink roses and white ribbon; red roses and white ribbon; tea roses and light blue ribbon; light blue roses and light blue ribbon, or pink roses and pink ribbon. Price.......$2.38

One of Our Leading Values at the Special Low Price of $2.19.

$2.19

No. 18K15260 Beautiful pattern hat made in extremely serviceable style, drooping a little in the front and back, and has slightly tilted sides. Wire frame is covered by hand with a layer of black milliners' mull over which are laid rows of imported German braid in black. On the upper and under brims a braid is applied in ruffle effect, giving a soft and pleasing appearance on the face. Entirely around the large full crown is laid a ruche of plaited black mull which is brought into a rosette effect on the left side front of the crown in combination with a wreath of pretty silk centered morning glories in natural purple shade. This hat is especially good as described in black with natural morning glories, but may also be ordered in brown, navy or champagne with trimmings to match. Be sure to say what color you prefer. Price.............................$2.19

A Pretty, Serviceable Style, Trimmed with Cherries, Regular $3.00 Value, only $1.99.

$1.99

No. 18K15275 Very pretty hat for misses or young ladies. This hat is made of a good quality Picot chip braid flat in white, caught up high on the side. Has a dainty little bandeau trimming of narrow red taffeta ribbon applied in loops and caught with a cut steel ornament. In front the upper brim and crown are covered with a trimming comprising an imported wreath of natural cherries, and cardinal ribbon trimming done in rosette effect with long loops. This ribbon trimming is twisted around the crown, giving the hat an effective appearance. May be ordered in white with cardinal trimming as described; white with light blue, pink or navy trimming, or all white; black with red, pink, or light blue trimming; or all black. Cherries and foliage in natural colors on all hats. Price..............$1.99

Great Style is Reflected in this Pattern Hat, Priced Within Reach of all, $2.48.

$2.48

No. 18K15250 Large, slightly drooping brim, bell crown pattern with rather long back. This exquisite model we consider one of our very best values at the price and can highly recommend it to our customers. Strictly hand made over a wire frame. The entire hat is faced with a combination of light blue milliners' mull run with rows of satin Juby ribbon to match. Both the upper and under brim and crown are completely covered with this material laid in very heavy folds running toward the center. The very effective trimming consists of a large cluster of deep cream colored roses massed on the left front of the crown together with quantities of imported green foliage. Handsome combination as described in light blue with cream color roses; may also be ordered in white, champagne or cardinal with roses to match. Price.........................$2.48

Trimmed French Sailor Styles are Very Popular and Fit Well on the Head.

$3.05

No. 18K15255 Large crown French sailor, strictly hand made on a wire frame. The brim and crown of this beautiful sailor effect are entirely covered with combination light blue silk and hair braid run with tiny tuscan cords. The edge of the brim is finished with folds of fine quality tucked chiffon in light blue. The hat is trimmed around the crown in large wreath effect American beauty roses, sprayed with imported foliage and beautiful natural moss. A three-quarter bandeau trimming completes the making of this handsome pattern. Very pretty as described in light blue with deep red flowers. Can also be ordered in champagne with navy edge and tea roses; champagne with edge to match and pink flowers; light gray with white cord and dark red roses; or pretty myrtle green with tuscan cord and pink flowers. Price.......$3.05

One of Our Best Hats at a Popular Price, $2.85.

$2.85

No. 18K15265 The fluffy style of trimming which is so popular. The biggest success of the year. This dainty hat for young ladies is hand made on a wire frame, with a novelty cardinal red braid of silk and hair which is used to cover the crown and upper brim and also to face the hat. The lovely trimming effect is obtained by the use of great quantities of plaited Jap silk in cardinal which completely surrounds the crown. A row of the same material is laid in a ruffle on the edge of brim. On the left side front in the midst of the plaited trimming is set a rosette effect of five half blown American beauty roses in red to match the trimming. This hat is very striking as described in cardinal. It may also be ordered in leather with champagne trimming and deep red roses; white with light blue silk and light blue roses; brown with champagne silk and pink roses; navy with light blue silk and light blue roses, or all black. Price.........................$2.85

This Large Turban Shape is Very Becoming and Fits Well on the Head, $2.65.

No. 18K15270 This beautiful turban effect as illustrated is made on a large wire frame, the brim of which is completely covered with fine quality pink shirred chiffon, made with rows of tuckings. The crown is covered with plaited chantilly lace in white. A large bunch of beautiful June roses and foliage applied on the front of crown is intertwined with narrow taffeta ribbon brought entirely around the crown and over the back where it ends in a bandeau trimming of tiny loops. May be ordered in pink and white with pink flowers as described, or light blue with white crown and jack roses; brown with white crown and tea roses; navy with white crown and light blue roses, or all black with pink or red roses. Price.......$2.65

$2.65

You Will be Pleased with this Hat. Milliners ask $4.50 for Equal Values, $2.89.

$2.89

No. 18K15280 In our illustration we picture a hat of the finest quality, very narrow imported German hair braid sewed in a bell crown, flat shape rolled high in the front. This model has a half facing of the best black gathered chiffon, and is profusely trimmed with black satin taffeta ribbon laid on in large milliners' bows. Extending from the rolled front and over the crown and around the left brim to the back is a wreath of six imported muslin roses in delicate shades of pink. Liberal quantities of natural sea moss and imported leaves are sprayed with the flowers. This hat can be ordered in black with pink flowers as described, or black with white ribbon and white roses, or black with light blue ribbon and tea roses, or black with pink ribbon and shaded pink roses. Always give colors wanted. Price..................$2.89

A Striking and Harmonious Combination of Colors on a Splendid Hat, only $2.38.

$2.38

No. 18K15285 A large flaring mushroom style with long drooping back, the shape being made of fine quality Picot chip braid. A rich and effective trimming is brought about by the use of two rosettes in cardinal and dark green of best quality Jap silk, which appear directly in the front of the crown. Beginning in the center of one of these rosettes and applied gracefully over the left side brim and down the extreme back appears a wreath of fine imported jack roses with natural foliage and large buds. A wide band of dark green velvet encircles the crown and completes the trimming of this stylish model. The colorings as described in white, cardinal and dark green we consider one of the best effects, but the hat may also be ordered in white with tan and light blue silk and trimming of pink roses; all black with pink or jack roses; all brown silk with light blue or pink roses or all navy with light blue or tea roses. Price.......$2.38

YOU MAKE A POSITIVE SAVING OF FROM ONE-THIRD TO

Exceptionally Good Style, Trimmed with Cherries and Ribbon, $3.25.

$3.25

No. 18K15380 A handsome short front mushroom style, beautifully executed on a wire frame. The entire frame is covered by hand with the new Maline silk finished hair braid in white, which is applied in folds around the upper edge of the brim. The trimming of the hat consists of an imported wreath of cherries, laid on from the left side and over the front and down to the right side of the hat. Beautiful folds of finest white taffeta ribbon are placed on the left side front, and the under brim is finished with folds of the same ribbon. This hat is very handsome as described in white with natural cherry wreath, but can also be ordered in black, light blue, brown or navy, all with natural cherry wreaths and ribbon to match. Price.....................$3.25

Simplicity and Quiet Style in Every Line of this Pattern Hat, $3.98.

$3.98

No. 18K15385 A most beautiful creation of all silk finished narrow pyroxylin braid sewed row and row, reflecting a very quiet and rich style which we feel sure will readily appeal to our customers. The hat is strictly hand made over the wire frame and has a full tucked chiffon facing in champagne color. The upper brim and balloon crown are made of narrow pyroxylin braid. The trimming consists of three handsome crush roses sprayed with natural foliage set on left side in a large fluffy rosette of champagne chiffon, which extends in folds around the entire crown of the hat. This hat is very handsome as described in all champagne with tea roses. May also be ordered in white with cream roses; pink with jack roses, or light blue with pink roses. Price..........$3.98

The Popular "Off the Face" Style. Others Ask $6.00, our Price, $3.88.

$3.88

No. 18K15390 This hat is strictly hand made on a buckram frame of fine quality dark brown Japanese silk. The edge of the brim is finished with a double row of wide satin pull braid in dark leather color, producing a very handsome contrasting effect. The simple trimming consists of one beautiful wreath of three shaded roses in jack, pink and tea branched very long with nine buds and natural sea moss and foliage. This wreath extends from the center of the front brim around the entire back brim of the hat. Folds of dark brown velvet are applied around the base of the crown, adding a finishing touch to this exquisite model. A half round bandeau in front is finished with folds of brown taffeta ribbon. The brown and leather combination as described is exceptionally handsome. May also be ordered in navy with Copenhagen blue; champagne with leather edging, or light blue with champagne edging, flowers to match. Always give colors wanted when you order. Price...................$3.88

A Dainty Model, Made of Fine Plaited Chiffon, only $3.48.

No. 18K15395 Short front mushroom style with large bell crown and flaring side. The exquisite lines of this hat are exactly pictured in our illustration. Hand made on a wire frame with a facing of finest quality tucked chiffon in light blue. The upper brim and sides of crown are covered with the same material, while the edge of brim is finished with a wide band of heavy corded light blue silk. Large bunches of tea colored June roses sprayed with foliage are massed on the left side of the crown together with a four-looped bow of fine quality taffeta ribbon, which extends around the crown in folds and is used to finish a very handsome bandeau trimming. This hat is tremendously popular on account of the dainty and graceful lines which it gives on the head. It is conceived in the very latest style. The hat is very pretty as described in all light blue with tea roses. May also be ordered in leather color with pink roses and champagne ribbon; all white with light blue roses, or all black with black violets. Say what colors you want. Price..........$3.48

$3.48

One of Our Handsomest Designs. Made of Elegant Material, $4.25.

No. 18K15400 Beautiful large mushroom sailor effect. Strictly hand made on a wire frame. This beautiful hat is almost entirely made of finest quality heavy Venisse lace, the edge of the brim being covered with folds of finest white chiffon. The trimming of imported pink American beauty roses and green foliage is intertwined with folds of soft finished white chiffon gracefully draped between the flowers and leaves. The simple beauty of this hat and the high quality of materials used recommend it to those who admire quiet elegance. Can be ordered in white with pink roses as described; white with jack roses, or white with tea roses. State colors wanted. Price............$4.25

$4.25

Becoming to Any Face, Rich Looking Dress Hat, only $4.15.

$4.15

No. 18K15405 Something entirely new in the very effective short front, dip back mushroom style. The hat is becoming in the extreme to every face. Has a facing of light blue shirred chiffon with rows of tucking throughout. The upper brim and crown are overlaid with rows of finest silk pyroxylin braid. The balloon crown is completely surrounded with light blue chiffon rosettes, in the center of which are placed beautiful crush roses of finest quality, in shades of Copenhagen blue, one of the leading colors shown for spring and summer wear. On the left side front appear three very long loops of the finest quality satin taffeta ribbon, which most artistically sets off the exquisite beauty of this hat. This is a copy of a genuine imported pattern and represents the highest art of millinery workmanship. Can be ordered in light blue with the new Copenhagen blue roses as described; in champagne with pink shaded roses; white with pink shaded roses; black with pink or jack roses, or all red. Don't forget to say what colors you want. Price............$4.15

A Real Picture Hat Heavily Trimmed, $4.19.

$4.19

No. 18K15410 For those who admire beautiful materials artistically assembled we especially recommend this pattern. The wire frame is entirely covered with finest quality silk and hair combination braid in a dainty pattern. The crown is the large, low French style and the brim rolls slightly on the left side. Massed across the front of the hat and extending to the extreme right edge are great clusters of fine quality silk and muslin cup roses in white. Gracefully intertwined with the flowers are quantities of best quality silk taffeta ribbon in pink, laid in dainty loops and bows. This ribbon extends from the right side of the crown over the back brim and around to the bandeau where it ends in a large lovers' knot. This hat can be ordered in white with white flowers and pink ribbon as described; light blue with tea colored flowers and light blue ribbon; black with light blue flowers and black ribbon, or all black. Price.............$4.19

Beautiful Turban Style, $5.00 Value, only $2.99.

No. 18K15415 Short black turban exquisitely millinered of the finest materials. This pattern is strictly hand made. The brim of the wire frame being overlaid with rows of imported German braid, edged with tiny spangled jet. Between the rows of braid are folds of fine quality black chiffon. The crown is made of black jetted braid and a full drape of chiffon falls in between the brim and the crown. The left side trimming consists of handsome jet centered satin roses sprayed with black satin foliage which are applied in rosette effect in combination with wide satin taffeta ribbon. The ribbon extends over the left side brim and is caught with a jet ornament. Comes in black only. Price..............................$2.99

$2.99

Very Neat Style. A Rich, Dressy Hat Made of Very Good Material, $3.48.

$3.48

No. 18K15420 Very stylish model in slightly drooping brim sailor effect. The wire frame is faced with best quality gathered chiffon with two wide rows of narrow tucks. The upper brim is covered with the same material with one very wide row of tucking. The large bell crown is overlaid with fine imported spangled jet. The trimming consists of a novelty bow made of taffeta ribbon in black, prettily shirred. Intermingled with the ribbon are clusters of silk roses with leaves in black. The ribbon, turning, extending folds around the crown and the side bandeau is set off with loops of the same material. Can be ordered in all black as described or black with violets in natural shade. Price.............$3.48

ONE-HALF ON ANY TRIMMED HATS BOUGHT FROM THESE PAGES.

Well Worth $8.50. A Special Bargain at $5.48.

$5.48

No. 18K15425 One of our finest styles in the new and popular mushroom effect. Hand made on a wire frame, completely overlaid with beautiful white silk and hair braid in dainty pattern. The trimming consists of large milliners' bows of wide pink satin taffeta ribbon laid in deep folds over the entire left side of the hat and brought over the brim to the bandeau where it ends in bow effect. The flower trimming consists of a combination of crushed roses in pink on top of crown, set deep in masses of dainty hyacinths in combination of white, pink and lavender shades. Neither our illustration or description can do justice to the exquisite beauty of this creation. Very handsome, as described, in white with pink ribbon and mixed flowers. May also be ordered in white with light blue ribbon and roses, or white with white ribbon and tea roses. Give color wanted. Price..........$5.48

Most Artistic Combination of Colors in This Pattern at $4.38.

$4.38

No 18K15440 One of the very latest New York styles. This beautiful hat is entirely hand made on a wire frame. The frame is completely covered with crimped navy braid in combination silk and hair effect. Extending around the French crown are beautiful clusters of silk centered geraniums in Copenhagen blue with natural foliage. Milliners' loops of finest wide satin taffeta ribbon in light blue are intertwined from the front and through left side. The satin taffeta ribbon trimming is brought over the brim to the bandeau, where it ends in a dainty bow, completing trimming of hat. Can be ordered in navy with Copenhagen blue, as described; white with tea colored geraniums and white ribbon; cardinal with natural red geraniums and ribbon to match; champagne with natural red geraniums and cardinal ribbon or all black. Always give colors. Price.......................$4.38

This Elegant Picture Hat Could Not Be Equaled at Your Milliner's for Less Than $12.00.

We call your particular attention to the quality of plumes we use.

$7.95

No. 18K15455 Our finest ostrichplumed hat in the ever popular Gainsborough style, being a modification of the prevailing mushroom effect. This beautiful creation is entirely hand made on a wire frame, overlaid with finest black braid in silk and hair combination. The edge of the brim is finished with a wide fold of fine quality silk. The simple trimming consists of two lovely ostrich feathers, reaching from the front center of the crown over the left side brim. They are caught in front with a great rosette bow of wide black taffeta ribbon centered with a large jet ornament. An all around bandeau finished with folds of taffeta ribbon completes the trimming of this stylish model. Comes in all black as described, black with white plumes, or white with white plumes. Say what colors you want. Price........$7.95

Copied from a French Pattern. Great Value at $4.75.

No. 18K15430 This beautiful hat is made of finest champagne novelty braid in combination of silk and hair, the under brim and crown being entirely covered with this material.

$4.75

Beautiful half blown pink roses are applied in cluster effect entirely around the crown. Intertwined with these roses are folds of beautiful soft finished brown chiffon and on the left side of the hat a very handsome trimming of heavy brown corded silk is applied in bow effect, all ends being fringed. This same silk is made into loops and applied against the back of the bandeau with a touch of green foliage. This hat is exquisite as described in champagne with brown silk and pink roses, but may also be ordered in white with pink silk and tea roses; white with light blue silk and jack roses, or navy with navy silk and light blue roses. Price....................$4.75

This Beautiful Pattern, Made of Yards of Finest Chiffon, only $5.98.

No. 18K15445 In offering this pattern hat to our trade we do so knowing that those who appreciate finest quality and style will see an attractive bargain in this value. Strictly hand made on a wire frame. The frame is entirely covered with fine quality light blue chiffon, which is very closely shirred with rows of light blue silk Juby ribbon, the facing being made to match. On the left center of the crown appears a huge bunch of six beautiful white roses sprayed with natural imported foliage and large buds. Ribbon sash of wide light blue taffeta ribbon encircles the crown and ends in a bow directly behind the roses. This hat is exquisite as described in light blue; may also be ordered in white, pink or champagne with trimming to match. A $10.00 value anywhere. Our price....................$5.98

A Beautiful Dress Hat, Stylish and Becoming, only $4.69.

No. 18K15460 The entire hat is hand made, of a combination light blue silk and tuscan braid. The crown is entirely surrounded with six large, full blown, soft crush roses, over which is draped Plauen Venisse lace in beautiful effect. The top of the crown is entirely covered with milliners' loops of finest 4-inch satin taffeta ribbon in light blue, which extends over the brim to the left side to the bandeau, and there ends in beautiful bow effect. The entire side as well as the bandeau is draped with good quality light blue chiffon, which completes the trimming of this hat. Is very beautiful as described in pale blue with Copenhagen blue roses. Can be ordered also in pink and tuscan combination braid with pink roses and ribbon; champagne and tuscan combination braid with American beauty red roses and champagne ribbon, or brown braid with brown ribbon and tea roses. Price..$4.69

Only the Best Materials Used in This Style, $4.98.

$4.98

No. 18K15435 An exquisite creation of lace and silk, hand made on a wire frame. The entire hat is made of rows of beautiful white Plauen Venisse lace, in applique effect. The brim is edged with beautiful corded white silk, as is the edge of the crown. Cluster of pure silk half blown tea roses sprayed with imported foliage is massed on the left front, extending to the left brim. Intertwined with the flowers is a drape of best quality wide white satin taffeta ribbon, which is brought around the crown in folds. The all around bandeau is trimmed with folds of the same ribbon knotted on the side. This dainty creation is very handsome as described in white with tea roses, but may also be ordered in all white with light blue roses and ribbon; all white with pink roses and ribbon, or white with white ribbon and pink roses. Price.$4.98

A Hat You Will Be Proud Of. Well Worth $7.50. Special at $4.88.

$4.88

No 18K15450 This handsome mushroom effect is hand made of the finest quality materials, none betterat any price. The wire frame is completely covered with a white silk and hair combination braid in dainty pattern. Masses of American beauty rosebuds in various sizes shaded from pink to dark red are set on each side, the center effect being brought out by large bunches of June flowers in white with pink tint. Heavy loops of white taffeta ribbon are intertwined among the flowers in pretty bow effects and are brought around the crown of the hat in folds. The ribbon extends over the left side brim to the round bandeau, where it is neatly folded, completing the trimming of this exceedingly rich looking hat. Can be ordered in white, light blue, champagne, brown or navy, with trimming to match. Be sure to say what colors. Price.....$4.88

This Handsome Pattern Hat Reflects a Decidedly Refined Style, $4.15.

$4.15

No. 18K15465 All hand made hat built on a wire frame in a striking and attractive style. The entire frame is overlaid with navy crimped braid of combination silk and hair. The side front trimming consists of two beautiful light blue full blown roses of the best lawn and muslin, between which is set a navy plaited rosette of wide satin taffeta ribbon with a cut steel ornament in the center. The plaited ribbon extends entirely around the crown. The trimming of this hat is completed by a bow of the same ribbon on the bandeau. This pattern can be ordered in navy with blue flowers as described, brown with pink roses, black with jack roses, champagne with pink roses, or light blue with pink roses. Say what colors you want. Price..................$4.15

WE USE FINE SILK LININGS IN ALL OF OUR TRIMMED HATS

This Bonnet Certainly Reflects Good Style. Milliners Ask $3.00.

Our Price, $1.69.

No. 18K15470 Very dainty bonnet at an exceedingly low price. Strictly hand made on a wire frame. The high rolling brim is covered with a row of imported German braid in combination with plaited and shirred milliners' mull. The ball crown and upper brim are finished with this same fine braid sewed row and row. A very stylish trimming effect of feather aigrettes tipped with very tiny spangled petals arise from the center of a ribbon rosette made of the best quality narrow black taffeta ribbon. On the right of the brim appears a cut jet barette.

Ties of No. 12 black taffeta ribbon are applied at the back and complete the trimming of this exceptional model. Can be ordered in all black as described, or black with a touch of lavender or a touch of white. Please mention color. Price......$1.69

Only the Best Materials are Used in this Elegant and Refined Bonnet, $2.68.

No. 18K15485 Our very best bonnet style, particularly designed for middle aged and elderly ladies. The high rolling brim of this beautiful bonnet is made of a combination silk and hair braid, laid in folds around the brim with plaited lace. The round crown is covered with black silk and hair braid. The upper brim is filled with daintily tucked chiffon of the best quality. Three good quality ostrich tips fall gracefully over the left side front of the bonnet and immediately behind the tips is a large three-loop bow of fine quality No. 22 black ribbon. Two long, beautiful taffeta ribbon ties 2½ inches wide complete the trimming of this elegant bonnet. Comes in black only. Price........$2.68

A Clever Style in a Misses' Hat, Beautifully Executed in Good Materials, $1.88.

No. 18K15500 Beautiful large crown mushroom effect particularly designed for misses or young ladies. This dainty style is hand made on a wire frame with gathered mull facing in white.

The crown is made of all silk pyroxylin braid in balloon effect, while on the upper brim appear rows of pretty white mull edged with silk Juby ribbon in pink. The trimming consists of a beautiful large rosette effect which is obtained by the use of white mull edged with pink Juby ribbon, liberally mingled with pink morning glories. The making of this hat brings out a very rich trimming effect and we especially recommend this number as one of our best values. Can be ordered in white and pink combination as described; light blue and white, cardinal and white, all white, or all cardinal with trimming to match. Price......$1.88

All Hand Made Poke Bonnet Style, Beautifully Trimmed, $2.38.

No. 18K15475 Our very finest poke bonnet style for girls up to twelve years of age. This child's hat is strictly hand made on a wire frame with the entire upper and under brim very closely covered with shirred pink milliners' mull with numerous rows of tucking. This gives a soft, fluffy effect and is exceptionally pretty. The large bell crown is entirely covered with silk pyroxylin braid in pink. A large wreath of silk and velvet geraniums in pink with green foliage is artistically applied across the entire upper brim, being bunched heavily in front. A pretty bow of white taffeta ribbon appears in the midst of this wreath. The hat is finished with long ribbon ties in white. This hat can be ordered in pink as described; light blue or cardinal with flowers to match; white with pink or light blue flowers. Do not forget to state colors. Price......$2.38

Pretty "Off the Face" Hat for Children, Trimmed with Cherries, only $1.69.

No. 18K15490 The Cheyenne style as applied to children's hats has proven the biggest success of the season. We offer a very handsome imported leghorn with wide fancy edge, trimmed in a most attractive manner. A pretty facing of gathered light blue mull with two rows of tucks finishes the entire under brim of the hat perfectly. In front and at the edge of the brim a natural cherry wreath with foliage is applied which extends over and around the entire crown. This is daintily set off with a rosette bow effect of narrow taffeta ribbon in light blue. We especially recommend this hat as one of the best values we have ever offered for children's wear. Can be ordered in natural leghorn, trimmed with light blue as described; or with white, pink, cardinal, brown or navy trimming. Always give color wanted. Price......$1.69

The Best Value Ever Offered in Children's Trimmed Leghorns at $1.25.

No. 18K15505 A tremendous value in good quality leghorn hat, attractively trimmed for children. Never before have we offered such an exceptional value as this hat, which we illustrate. We use a very good quality imported leghorn with a fancy edge, the entire under brim being faced with white milliners' mull shirred in with two rows of tiny tucks. Loops of narrow white taffeta ribbon complete a pretty bandeau trimming. A wreath of white daisies with yellow centers extends from the front entirely around the brim to the drooping back of the hat. On the side front of the crown appears a rosette bow of narrow white taffeta ribbon braced with wire. This ribbon is drawn entirely around the crown and gives a decidedly pretty finish to the hat. Comes in natural leghorn with pink, white, light blue or red trimming. Price......$1.25

Poke Bonnet Styles are Dainty and Stylish. This $2.50 Value Only $1.48.

No. 18K15480 For little children and girls up to twelve years of age there is nothing prettier than a poke bonnet style. We illustrate an imported leghorn shaped into this popular effect, having a facing of light blue milliners' mull very closely gathered with eight rows of close tucks. The edge of the hat is bound with light blue silk velvetta. The crown trimming consists of a pretty wreath of tiny white daisies twisted through a very large rosette trimming of light blue mull and light blue taffeta ribbon. Ties of light blue taffeta ribbon extend from the back of the hat, giving a dainty finish to this handsome little style. Can be ordered as described in natural leghorn with light blue trimming; or with white, pink or red trimming. Please state color. Price......$1.48

This Elegant Trimmed Leghorn is an Extra Special Offer at $1.95.

No. 18K15495 One of our very best styles in fancy edged fine imported leghorns for misses and children. The imported leghorn used in this hat is of extra fine quality and will prove highly satisfactory to you. The most effective trimming is obtained by the use of a wreath of imported velvet forget me nots in light blue sprayed with tiny full blown June roses. Fine quality white taffeta ribbon is gathered in rosette effect in the front and entirely around the brim of the hat close to the crown. This dainty little child's hat is exceedingly pretty as described in natural leghorn with light blue trimming; may also be ordered with white, pink or red trimming. Please give color. Price......$1.95

Pretty Imported Body Hat, $1.95.

No. 18K15510 This stylish child's hat is made of an imported body hat in cream color natural straw, and is woven in fancy design.

Body hats allow of most original ideas in shapes and our style as illustrated shows one of the best. The trimmings consist of a large wreath effect of silk centered apple blossoms in pink. Intermingled with the flowers appears a novelty effect of plaited ribbon, edged on mull which is laid around the upper brim of the hat. The bandeau trimming of twisted light blue taffeta ribbon, ending in loops, completes the trimming of this very stylish hat. Can be ordered in natural and light blue as described, or with pink, white or red trimming. Remember to state color. Price......$1.95

Wreaths for Trimming Children's and Misses' Hats.

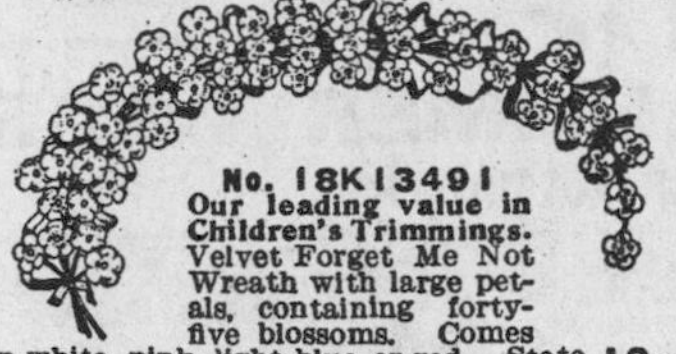

No. 18K13491 Our leading value in Children's Trimmings. Velvet Forget Me Not Wreath with large petals, containing forty-five blossoms. Comes in white, pink, light blue or red. State color wanted. Price, per wreath....... 13c
If by mail, postage extra, 6 cents.

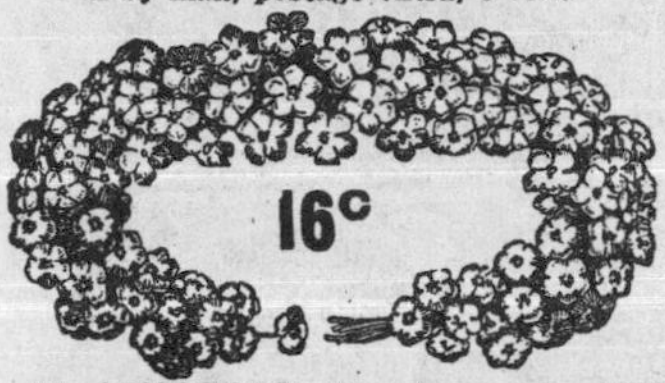

16c

No. 18K13493 Very handsome child's Wreath Effect of Blossoms, very closely sprayed. A dainty trimming. Comes in white, pink, light blue or red. State color wanted. Price, per wreath.......... 16c
If by mail, postage extra, 6 cents.

No. 18K13495 Large full Wreath of Good Muslin Daisies, branched very full at center and tapering at the ends. Makes a showy trimming for a child's hat. Colors, white, pink, light blue, all with yellow centers. State color wanted. Price, per wreath.. 27c
If by mail, postage extra, 7 cents.

29c

No. 18K13497 A big value in muslin June Rose Wreath for trimming misses' and children's hats. More than sixty blossoms in this wreath. Comes in white, pink, light blue or American beauty red. State color wanted. 50-cent value.
Our price, per wreath.................. 29c
If by mail, postage extra, 8 cents.

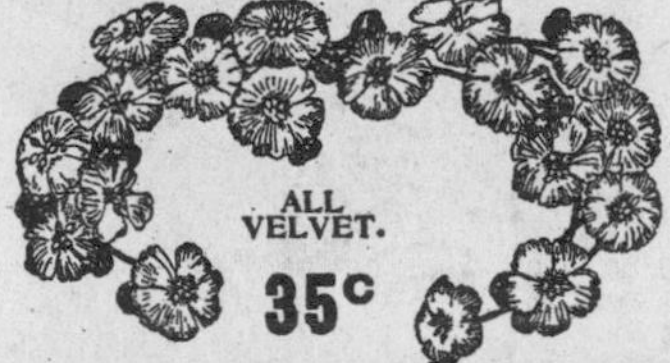

ALL VELVET. 35c

No. 18K13499 Velvet Carnation Wreath, made with all velvet petals, branched on chenille stems with foliage in green. Colors, white, pink, light blue, or white with pink tint. State color wanted.
Price, per wreath.................. 35c
If by mail, postage extra, 9 cents.

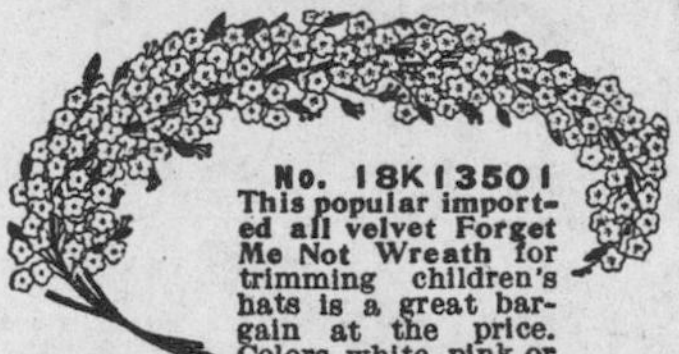

No. 18K13501 This popular imported all velvet Forget Me Not Wreath for trimming children's hats is a great bargain at the price. Colors, white, pink or light blue. State color wanted.
Price, per wreath.................. 17c
If by mail, postage extra, 5 cents.

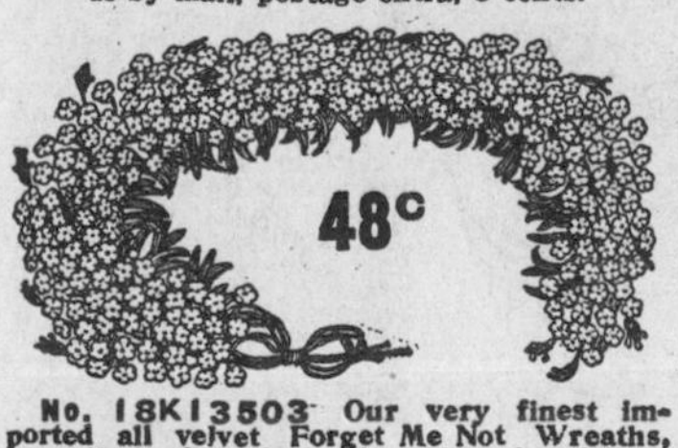

48c

No. 18K13503 Our very finest imported all velvet Forget Me Not Wreaths, beautifully branched with carnation foliage and long stems. Colors, white, pink or light blue. State color wanted.
Price, per wreath.................. 48c
If by mail, postage extra 7 cents.

Bridal Wreaths and Bouquets.

12c

No. 18K13505 This is an exceptional value at the price. Confirmation or Procession Wreath, made of good quality muslin flowers with green leaves. This wreath cannot be duplicated anywhere at the price.
Price, per wreath.................. 12c
If by mail, postage extra, 9 cents.

No. 18K13507 Confirmation Wreath. Larger and fuller than No. 18K13505. Is made of good quality muslin flowers. Very desirable for confirmations or processions of any kind. Price, per wreath... 18c
If by mail, postage extra, 9 cents.

No. 18K13509 Finest quality Confirmation Wreath. Made of wax and muslin flowers with green leaves, very prettily branched. This is larger and fuller than either of the above two numbers. Easily retails at 50 cents. Our price, each.......... 29c
If by mail, postage extra, 9 cents.

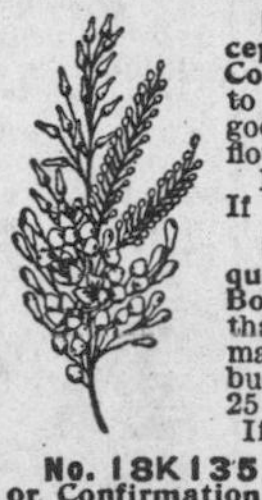

No. 18K13511 An exceptional value. Medium size Confirmation Bouquet. Similar to illustration. Is made of good quality wax and muslin flowers, artistically branched.
Price, each.......... 8c
If by mail, postage extra 4c.

No. 18K13513 Fine quality Bridal or Confirmation Bouquet. Larger and fuller than the above number. Is made of good wax flowers and buds. Regular retail price, 25 cents. Our price, each. 12c
If by mail, postage extra, 4c.

No. 18K13515 Our best quality Bridal or Confirmation Bouquet. Made entirely of wax and muslin flowers and wax buds. Is similar to illustration. Much larger than either of the above two numbers.
Price, each.................. 18c
If by mail, postage extra, 4 cents.

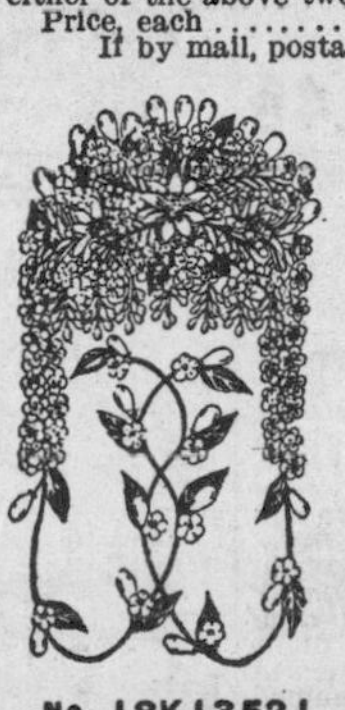

No. 18K13517 Our leader in Bridal Wreaths. A very full showy wreath of fine quality wax flowers and bouquet. Regular retail price of this wreath is $1.00.
Our price, each 78c
If by mail, postage extra, 12 cents.

No. 18K13519 A very beautiful Bridal Wreath with Bouquet. Made of all wax flowers artistically branched. Is larger and fuller than the above number.
Price, per wreath. 98c
If by mail, postage extra, 12 cents.

No. 18K13521 Our very finest quality Bridal Wreath with Bouquet. It is much larger and fuller than either of the above two numbers and is beautifully branched. No finer wreath can be bought at any price.
Price, per wreath.................. $1.65
If by mail, postage extra, 12 cents.

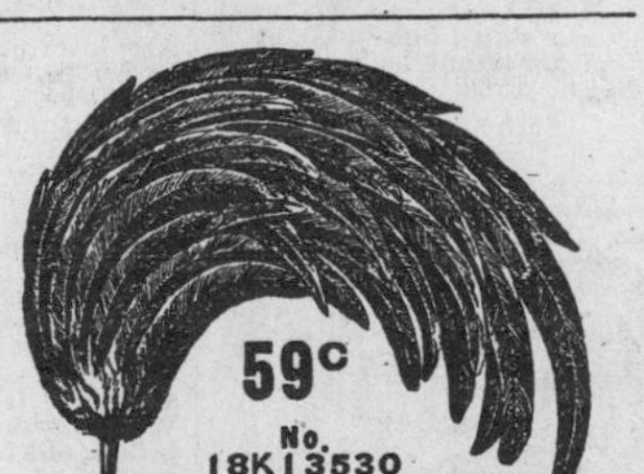

59c

No. 18K13530 A Beautiful Bronze Black Coque Feather, in graceful plume effect. This makes an elegant trimming for any style hat. Can be had in bronze black only. Price, each.......... 59c
If by mail, postage extra, 7 cents.

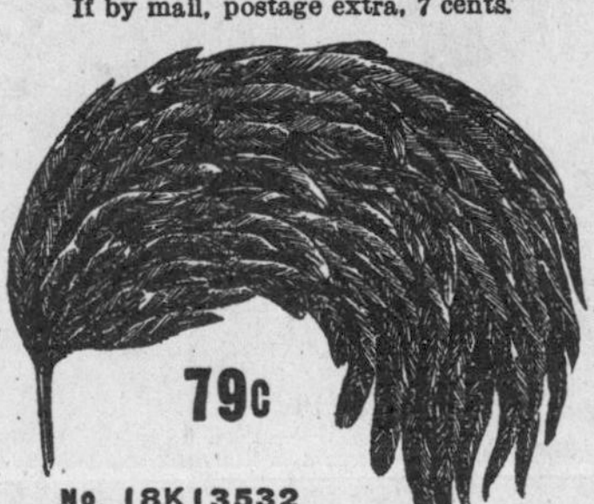

79c

No. 18K13532 Our very finest quality Coque Feather, made in the popular plume shape. The feathers are wired, thus assuring you of a substantial trimming. Comes in the natural bronze black only. 79c
Price, each..........
If by mail, postage extra, 7 cents.

Wings.

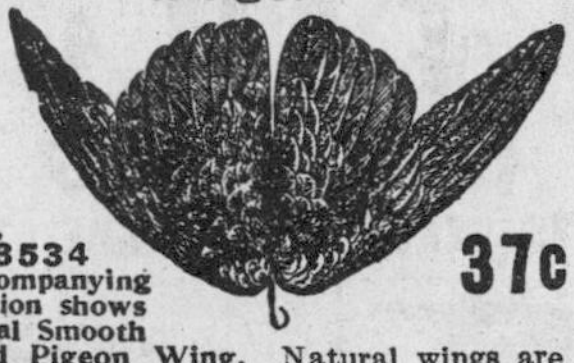

No. 18K13534 The accompanying illustration shows a Natural Smooth Finished Pigeon Wing. Natural wings are very durable. They are quite popular for trimming all styles of hats, and are sure to give entire satisfaction. Colors, black, white, light blue, brown or navy. State color wanted. Price per pair.......... 37c
If by mail, postage extra, 5 cents.

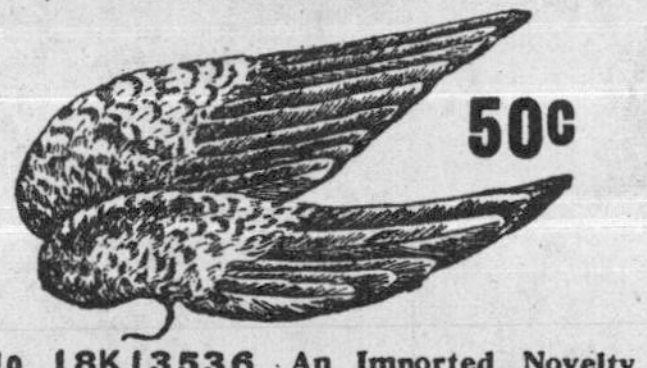

50c

No. 18K13536 An Imported Novelty Wing Effect. Is a durable and stylish trimming. Numerous effects can be produced with this wing. It is particularly well adapted for a side trimming. Can be had in white, black, brown or navy. State color wanted.
Price, per pair.................. 50c
If by mail, postage extra, 6 cents.

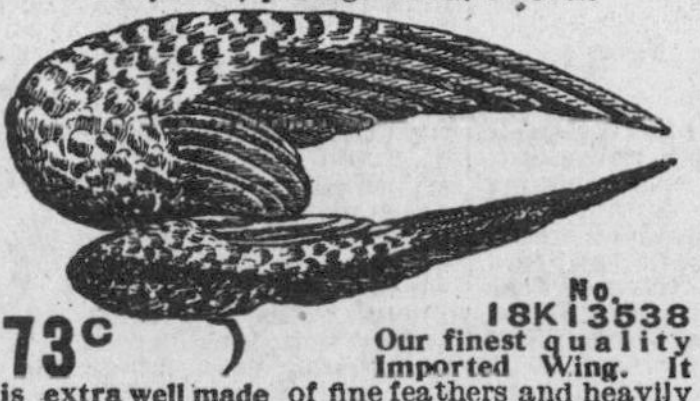

73c

No. 18K13538 Our finest quality Imported Wing. It is extra well made of fine feathers and heavily padded. We are certain it will give absolute satisfaction. Value, $1.50 per pair. Colors, black, white, cardinal, brown or navy. State color wanted. Price, per pair.... 73c
If by mail, postage extra, 13 cents.

Colored Coque Plume.

58c

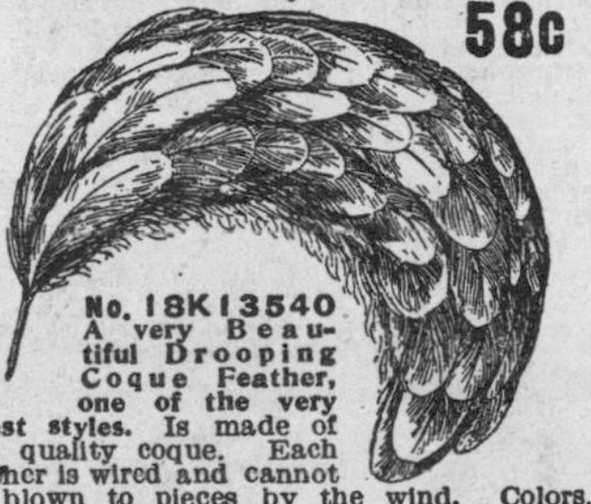

No. 18K13540 A very Beautiful Drooping Coque Feather, one of the very latest styles. Is made of fine quality coque. Each feather is wired and cannot be blown to pieces by the wind. Colors, white, champagne, brown, garnet, navy or light blue. State color wanted. Price, 58c
If by mail, postage extra, 7 cents.

Fancy Edge Imported Leghorns. Suitable for Misses and Children.

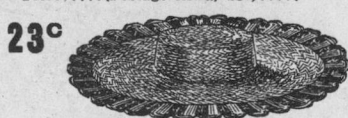

19c

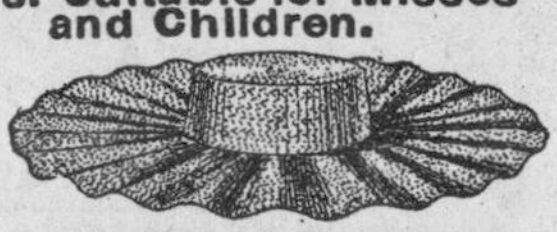

No. 18K16610 Misses' Leghorn Hat, fluted brim. An exceptional value for the price. Comes in white only. Price..... 19c

No. 18K16612 Misses' Plain Brim Leghorn Hat with medium crown. Same quality as No. 18K16610 with straight brim.
Price.....(Postage extra, 18c)..... 19c

23c

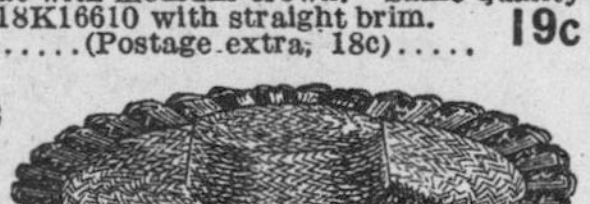

No. 18K16614 Misses' or Child's Fancy Edge Leghorn Hat. Very good quality. Comes in white only. Regular 50-cent value. Price...(Postage extra 20c)... 23c

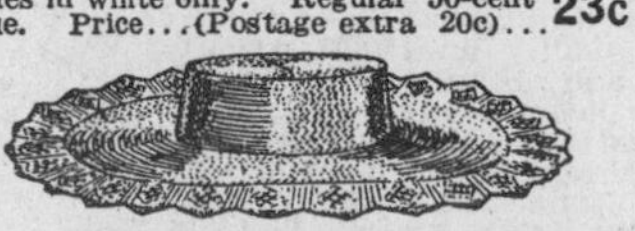

No. 18K16616 This is a Medium High Crown Fancy Edge Leghorn, with a wider edge than our No. 18K16614. Comes in white only. Price....(Postage extra, 20c).... 33c

48c

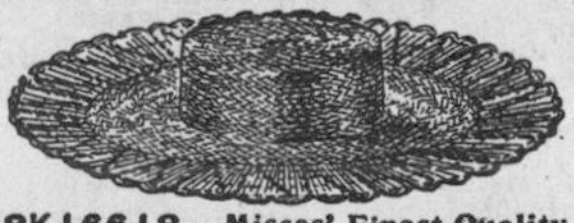

No. 18K16618 Misses' Finest Quality Fancy Edge Imported Leghorn Hat. Our very best fancy edge style. Comes in white only. Large size. Price.......... 48c
If by mail, postage extra, 20 cents.

Medium High Crown Leghorns for Misses and Children.

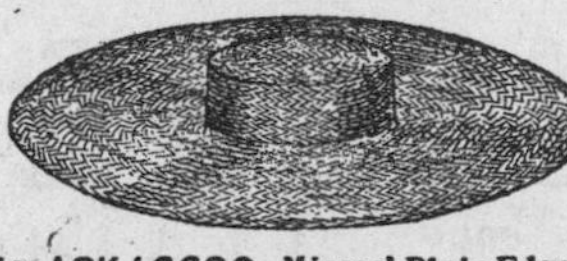

No. 18K16620 Misses' Plain Edge Leghorn Hat, wide brim, medium crown. Comes in white only. Others ask 75 cents for this hat. Our price.......... 46c
If by mail, postage extra, 17 cents.

No. 18K16622 Misses' Good Quality Leghorn Hat, with wide brim. Medium crown. Is closely woven and a very pretty hat. Comes in white only. Price, each.... 67c
If by mail, postage extra, each, 17 cents.

No. 18K16624 Our Finest Quality Misses' Leghorn Hat. Wide brim and medium crown. Made of very finely woven imported leghorn. A very beautiful hat.
Price.................. 98c
If by mail, postage extra, 17 cents.

Imported Leghorn Hats in Shapes Suitable for Ladies and Misses.

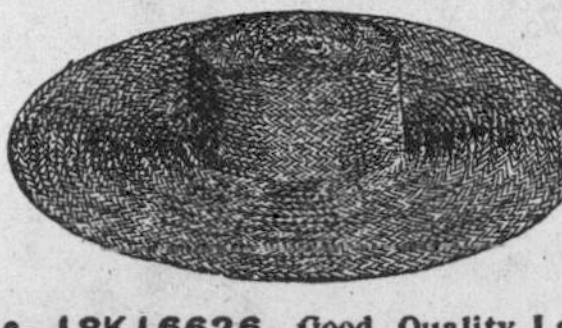

No. 18K16626 Good Quality Ladies' Leghorn, medium brim and high crown. A very popular size and a splendid value for the price we ask. Comes in white only.
Price.................. 46c
If by mail, postage extra, 18 cents.

No. 18K16628 Ladies' or Misses' High Crown, Imported Leghorn Hat. Made of good quality closely woven straw. Comes in white only. Regular $1.00 value. Price. 67c
If by mail, postage extra, 18 cents.

No. 18K16630 Our Finest Quality Ladies' or Misses' High Crown Imported Leghorn. Is made of the finest quality imported straw. This is a beautiful hat. Comes in white only. Price.......... 98c
If by mail, postage extra, 18 cents.

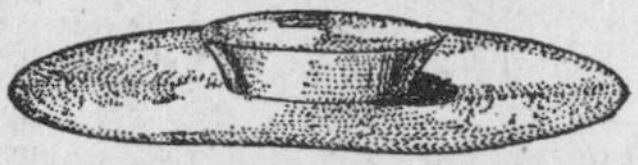

No. 18K16632 Our Finest Quality Misses' or Ladies' Medium High Bell Crown Leghorn, woven of highest grade material. Comes in white only. No better hat at any price than this. Price.......... 98c
If by mail, postage extra, 20 cents.

Latest Styles in Body Hats.

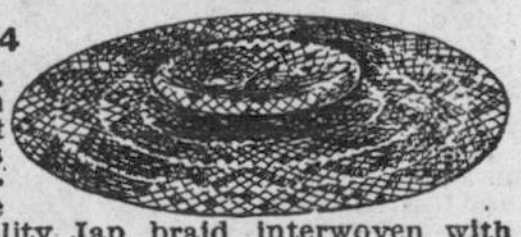

No. 18K16634 BIG VALUE. Bell Crown Body Hat for Misses and Children, made of good quality Jap braid interwoven with fancy stripe. Comes in natural white only. Price.......... 14c
If by mail, postage extra, 16 cents.

33c

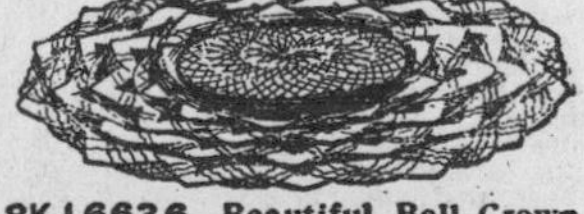

No. 18K16636 Beautiful Bell Crown Body Hat for misses or ladies. The brim is made of four ruffles of silk finished Jap braid interwoven with a twisted straw cord in a very pretty design. A beauty at the price.
Price.................. 33c
If by mail, postage extra, 18 cents.

67c

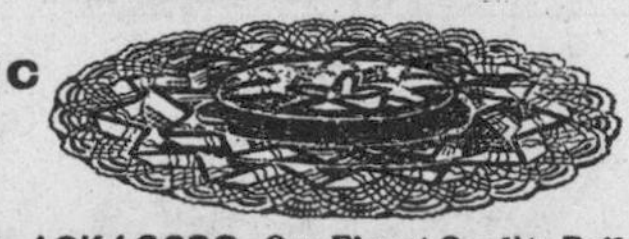

No. 18K16638 Our Finest Quality Bell Crown Body Hat. Is made of a beautiful silk finished braid interwoven with a colored silk stripe and straw cord. Edge is finished in scalloped design of colored silk braid. This is an exceptionally pretty pattern. Colors, white with pink, light blue or maize stripe, or all white. Be sure to state color wanted. Price.................. 67c
If by mail, postage extra, 20 cents.

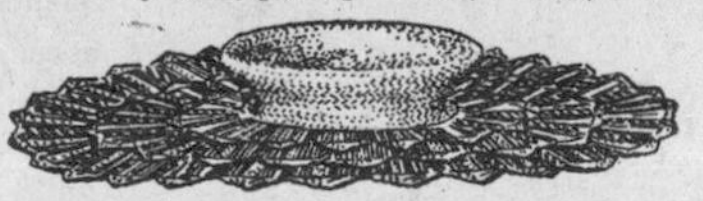

No. 18K16640 New Leather Color Bell Crown Leghorn Hat. A combination natural leghorn crown and Tuscan straw braid brim. The brim has three rows of fancy scalloped Tuscan braid. Comes in natural leghorn color only. Price, each.......... 59c
If by mail, postage extra, each, 20 cents.

Sig. 61—1st Ed.

◼ HAND TAILORED SUIT HATS ◼
PARTICULARLY DESIGNED FOR SPRING OR SUMMER WEAR
VERY LATE STYLES BEAUTIFULLY MADE AT PRICES WHICH WILL INTEREST ALL CAREFUL BUYERS.

No. 18K16000 Ladies' or misses' stylish Street or Suit Hat. Is made of fine quality satin finished Jap braid in short front mushroom shape. Hat is trimmed in front with a large natural wing in large twist of fine quality Jap silk, this silk extending in folds around the base of crown. Hat is finished with a half round bandeau of silk velvet and is silk lined. Colors, white, brown, navy or champagne, all with trimming to match. Be sure to state color wanted.
Price......(If by mail, postage extra, 24 cents.) **$1.19**

No. 18K16002 This stunning Suit Hat at a popular price is made of combination very fine split Jap braid with crown of fine natural Milan braid in white. The edge of braid is draped into a very pleasing mushroom style and caught up very high on the left side with a large crush rosette of silk velvet. Three long quills finish the side trimming. Hat is bound with velvet to match trimming, as is the round bandeau. Comes in natural and brown, natural and navy, natural and dark green, or natural and black. Be sure to state color.
Price...... **$1.49**
If by mail, postage extra, 20 cents.

No. 18K16006 A beautiful mushroom turban effect in a very clever style. Made of a combination of very fine quality split Jap and imported tuscan straw braid, sewed row and row. The brim is caught up all around in a graceful manner, and the trimming consists of a large rosette of silk velvet centered with a fancy effect of very narrow tuscan braid, the rosette being edged with same material. Two handsome quills are brought through the hat to the left side front. A silk velvet drape extends around the crown to the back and ends in a pretty loop effect. Colors, natural tuscan with brown, navy, black, cardinal or green trimmings. $3.00 value. Be sure to state color wanted.
Our price...... **$1.88**
If by mail, postage extra, 20 cents.

No. 18K16008 A close fitting pointed front Turban. A stylish suit hat for ladies or misses. Is made of best quality imported hair braid, the upper crown and under brim being in a pattern effect while the sides are done in perfectly plain narrow braid. A drape of good quality taffeta silk fills the space between the upper edge of crown and brim. This silk is brought over the left side and twisted into a pretty knot effect. Three loops of braid complete the trimming of this very stylish hat. Comes in black, brown or navy.
Price...... **$1.99**
If by mail, postage extra, 16 cents.

No. 18K16010 Ladies' or misses' handsome tailored Suit Hat. Is hand made, on a wire frame, with short front and long, drooping back. Hat is made entirely of all silk pyroxylin braid with large Tam o' Shanter crown. Trimming of this hat is decidedly simple but very swell. It is composed of folds of fine quality chiffon drawn around the crown and finished on left side with four full rosettes of the same material. This is one of the neatest styles shown in our line. Colors, black, brown, navy or champagne, with trimmings to match. Be sure to state color wanted.
Price...... **$2.45**
If by mail, postage extra, 19 cents.

No. 18K16012 Ladies' small modified mushroom style in a beautiful tailored Suit Hat. Is hand made on a wire frame of best quality imported pull braid. The edge of the brim and crown are prettily trimmed with rows of fluted braid. Very stylish combination in the trimming effect is obtained by the use of three quills artistically pierced through front of hat. These quills are intertwined with long loops of fine quality satin taffeta ribbon held in place with two large trimming pins. The ribbon extends in a fold around the entire crown, adding a pretty finishing touch. Colors, black, brown, or navy. Be sure to state color wanted. Regular $3.50 value.
Our price..... **$2.48**
If by mail, postage extra, 20 cents.

No. 18K16014 One of the most stylish tailor made Suit Turbans shown this year; hand made on a wire frame. Crown and sides are made of finest quality all silk pyroxylin braid draped artistically in folds. Under brim is made of the finest quality velvet closely tucked chiffon. Hat is trimmed on left side with two large quills, held in place with three cut ostrich pompons. A band of velvet ribbon brought around right side of the hat and finished with jet buckle completes the trimming of this swell walking hat. Comes in black only.
Price...... **$2.95**
If by mail, postage extra, 20 cents.

No. 18K16016 Elegantly tailored Suit Hat for misses or ladies. This handsome style is hand made on a wire frame with under brim facing of all silk pyroxylin braid, upper brim and crown being made of closely sewed rows of narrow imported hair braid. The simple but effective trimming consists of a wide drape of fine quality black taffeta ribbon laid in folds around the crown and gathered into a twisted drape effect in combination with the braid. On the left side three beautiful quills pierce this rosette. Plain but very stylish model, particularly easy to wear. Comes in black, brown, navy or garnet. Be sure to state color wanted.
Price..... **$2.98**
If by mail, postage extra, 22 cents.

No. 18K16018 The New French Sailor. Wide brim slightly shortened in front. Is entirely made of fine quality taffeta silk with tucks running two ways. This hat is trimmed in front with a large butterfly bow of best taffeta silk to match the hat. A band of folded silk around the crown completes the trimming. The large silk bow is very well wired and will hold its shape. Comes in black, brown, navy or champagne. Be sure to state color wanted.
Price..... **$2.98**
If by mail, postage extra, 20 cents.

Fine Style.

No. 18K16020 Striking new style in rolling front mushroom shape. Made on a buckram frame of fine quality shaded taffeta silk. The simple trimming consists of one very large French bow, all wired, which extends entirely across the front and over the sides of crown. A splendid value at an exceedingly low price. Colors, brown, navy, champagne or black. Be sure to state color wanted.
Price...... **$3.19**
If by mail, postage extra, 25 cents.

All Silk Taffeta.

No. 18K16022 Ladies' or misses' hand made Suit Hat in very stylish toque effect. Our illustration does not begin to show the beauty of this hat. Frame is entirely covered with silk and hair combination braid in pretty pattern, edge of brim and crown being finished with a wide fluted ruffle of braid. Trimming consists of a very large rosette effect made of rows of best taffeta silk and fluted braid laid in alternating folds. Double wing effect protruding from the rosette gives a finishing touch. The rosette is centered with a large ball pin. Wide folds of taffeta silk extend around the entire crown. Comes in black, brown or navy. Be sure to state color wanted. Real $5.00 value.
Our price...(If by mail, postage extra, 21 cents.).. **$3.48**

No. 18K16024 Our very finest and most stylish hand made Suit Hat. Short front, rolling slightly on the left side with slightly drooping brim. Made of fine quality narrow silk and hair braid, sewed row and row. Left side is caught up with a wide band of fancy crimped hair braid with double ruffle of folded and plaited silk. Long quill is drawn through this side trimming. Wide drape crown trimming of crimped hair braid gives a finishing touch to this very handsome hat. Colors, black, brown, navy or leather. Be sure to state color wanted.
Price...... **$3.69**
If by mail, postage extra, 16 cents.

The values offered in our lace and embroidery sections on pages 1014 to 1026 deserve your particular attention.

A COMPLETE LINE OF CAPS FOR CHILDREN AND MISSES.

Children's Trimmed Silk and Mull Hats.

No. 18K16094 Our Leader in Boys' and Girls' Caps. Made of good quality mixed crash with vizor to match, finished off on top with button of the same material. This is a very serviceable cap as it will not show the dirt. Would retail at 50 cents. Colors, navy and white mixture or gray and white mixture. Price. State color wanted. **23c**
If by mail, postage extra, 13 cents.

No. 18K16096 A splendid quality White Pique Tam O'Shanter for Boys or Girls. Is made entirely of good quality white pique, embroidered in front with American eagle in silk and trimmed with good quality satin taffeta ribbon around band. Both wire in the crown and in the band can be removed, making hat washable. This is an exceptional value at the price. Comes in white only. Price. **33c**
If by mail, postage extra, 12 cents.

38c

No. 18K16098 A great value in a Plaid Cloth Cap for boys or girls. Is made of an exceptionally pretty mixed suiting material with a very small stripe running through it. This is a very serviceable cap. Comes in dark gray mixtures only. Price. **38c**
If by mail, postage extra, 13 cents.

No. 18K16100 Our finest quality Silk Poplin Cap with vizor. Finished off on top with button and in front with silk cord. Poplin caps are extremely popular because of the good service they give. Colors, brown, black, navy, cardinal or gray. State color wanted. Price. **44c**
If by mail, postage extra, 13 cents.
No. 18K16102 Same style as above in fine quality white pique. Price. **39c**
If by mail, postage extra, 13 cents.

No. 18K16104 Beautiful all silk crash Tam O'Shanter for boys or girls. Is finished on top with two wide box plaits. Band of material to match is drawn across the top of the cap and finished with two gilt buttons. This cap retails for 75 cents. Comes in brown, tan or gray. State color wanted. Price. **48c**
If by mail, postage extra, 13 cents.

No. 18K16106 A Nobby Flannel Outing Cap. Is made of fine quality black and white checked flannel with vizor to match. Two strips of all silk poplin are drawn over the cap from either side and caught at the top with three gilt buttons. Caps trimmed in front with a gilt buckle. Comes in white and black check, with navy, brown or cardinal trimming. Don't **48c** forget color. Price.
If by mail, postage extra, 14 cents.

No. 18K16108 Something new in a two-tone Silk Poplin Cap with visor. Top is made in scalloped design; finished in center with large poplin button. Is trimmed across front with all silk cord. Comes in the following combination of colors, navy and white, brown and white, champagne, cardinal and white, or all white. Always give color. Price. **48c**
If by mail, postage extra, 14 cents.

No. 18K16110 The new style Navy Cap for boys or girls. Made of extra good quality blue serge, embroidered in front with emblem of U. S. Navy, and has patent leather visor. Is trimmed across front with double silk cord caught at either end with patent leather button. Comes in navy only. Price **48c**
If by mail, postage extra, 13 cents.

No. 18K16114 The most popular Toque for little boys or girls shown this season. Is made entirely of good quality silk poplin. The crown is prettily draped to a point and caught at one side with a military pompon. The trimming consists of three silk cords drawn across the front of the cap, caught at either end with loops of the same material. Colors, brown, navy or cardinal. Be sure to state color. Price, **48c**
If by mail, postage extra, 8 cents.

No. 18K16116 A very stylish Toque for little ones. Made in Napoleon shape of fine quality silk poplin. Edge of crown is finished off with all silk cord. Hat is trimmed in front with horse hair pompon held in place with rosette of silk poplin and gilt button. Colors, brown, navy or cardinal. Always say what color is wanted. Price. **44c**
If by mail, postage extra, 11 cents.

No. 18K16118 A most becoming Misses' Duck Hat. Is made on the mushroom shape, which is so popular and becoming to all. Brim is closely stitched and the large tam crown is wired and will not lose its shape. Is trimmed in front with a double bow of material to match the hat. Comes in white only. Price... (Postage extra 20c) ... **48c**

No. 18K16120 The latest novelty in girls' or misses' headwear. Is made of all silk poplin on the popular close fitting mushroom shape with extreme short front and long back. Hat has a large, full crown and closely stitched brim. Is trimmed in front with numerous loops of fine quality changeable silk. This hat is very stylish. Colors, brown, navy or cardinal. Give color wanted. Price. **98c**
If by mail, postage extra, 17 cents.

No. 18K16130 A Very Pretty Child's Mull Hat. Is made with fluted brim and full bell crown with lace edging and insertion. Regular 25 cent value. Comes in white, pink or light blue. Don't fail to mention color wanted. Price. **19c**
If by mail, postage extra, 9 cents.

No. 18K16132 Child's Mull Hat with fluted brim and full bell crown, trimmed with lace edging and insertion, and finished in center of the crown with bow of mull. Brim is wired and will not lose its shape. Colors, white, pink or light blue. State color desired. Price. **32c**
If by mail, postage extra, 13 cents.

45c

No. 18K16134 An Exceptionally Good Value in a Misses' Mull Hat. Brim is made of two full fluted ruffles, both edged with lace and full bell crown is also trimmed with one ruffle edged with lace to match brim. Brim is wired and will not lose its shape. Comes in white, pink or light blue. Give color wanted. Price. **45c**
If by mail, postage extra, 17 cents.

No. 18K16136 Beautiful Pattern in Child's Silk Embroidered Lingerie Hat. Brim is finished with a wide ruffle of embroidery with scalloped edge in handsome design. Crown is finished on top with panel embroidered in design to match brim. Comes in white only. Price. **48c**
If by mail, postage extra, 17 cents.

No. 18K16138 Our Ever Popular Mull and Silk Hat. Brim is made of two double ruffles of crinkled mull and crown is made of Japanese silk, finished on top with silk cord. Hat is trimmed in front with rosette of mull. This is a very stylish pattern. Colors, white, pink, light blue or red. Mention color. Price. **62c**
If by mail, postage extra, 18 cents.

No. 18K16140 Something Entirely New in Misses' Style Washable Hat. This hat is made of closely woven material and can be washed and ironed without losing its shape. Is trimmed in front with full double bow of white lawn. An exceptionally stylish pattern. Comes in white only. Price..... (Postage extra, 18c)...... **62c**

No. 18K16142 This Beautiful Child's Hat is made of good quality mull and valenciennes lace. Brim is of double fluted ruffles with lace edge. Tam crown is made of six fluted ruffles of mull, each edged with lace. This pretty hat comes in the following colors: white, pink or light blue. Be sure to select color wanted. Price. **75c**
If by mail, postage extra, 17 cents.

No. 18K16144 Misses' Washable Hat. Brim is made of silk embroidered lingerie with scalloped edges. Underbrim and crown are made of dotted Swiss, the latter being trimmed in the center with lace medallion. This hat is made in such a manner that by untying two strings at the back of the hat, same can be taken entirely apart and washed, and is easily put together again, making a very serviceable hat. Comes in white only. Price. **88c**
If by mail, postage extra, 16 cents.

Washable

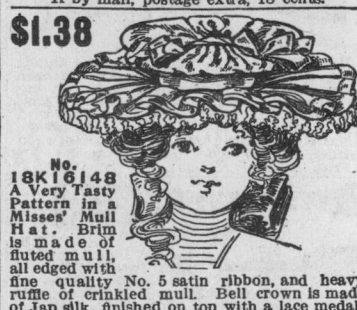

No. 18K16146 Beautiful Poke Bonnet for Misses and Children. Brim is made of tucked mull, and edged with good quality raised valenciennes lace, finished on top with ruffle of fluted mull. Crown is also made of mull trimmed on top with lace and edged with double ruffle of mull. Hat is trimmed at the front with large rosette of mull and satin taffeta ribbon, and at the back with mull bow, and is finished off with two mull streamers. Colors, pink, light blue or white. Name color wanted. Price **99c**
If by mail, postage extra, 18 cents.

$1.38

No. 18K16148 A Very Tasty Pattern in a Misses' Mull Hat. Brim is made of fluted mull, all edged with fine quality No. 5 satin ribbon, and heavy ruffle of crinkled mull. Bell crown is made of Jap silk, finished on top with a lace medallion, and trimmed with two loops of ribbon. This is a very beautiful style. Colors, all white, white with pink, or white with light blue ribbon. Give color wanted. Regular $2.00 value. Price. **$1.38**
If by mail, postage extra, 17 cents.

$1.69 FINE QUALITY

No. 18K16150 One of the nobbiest hats for misses shown this year. Made of a good quality butchers' linen worked in bonaz openwork design with under brim of embroidery. The bell crown is worked in design to match. The brim is drawn up in front and finished off with two loops of satin taffeta ribbon, giving a very stylish effect. Colors, white with pink ribbon, white with light blue ribbon or all white. Remember to state color wanted. Price. **$1.69**
If by mail, postage extra, 19 cents.

GREAT VALUES IN UMBRELLAS AND PARASOLS

Neat, stylish handles, dependable cloths and best workmanship are guaranteed in every umbrella we sell. Our umbrellas look better, wear longer, and cost less for equal quality than any umbrella you can buy from any other dealer.

Umbrellas cannot be sent by mail.

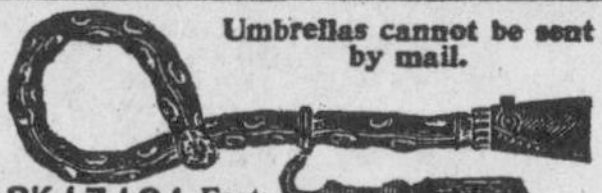

No. 18K17101 Fast Black English Twilled Mercerized Carolo Umbrella. Natural Congo loop or hook handle, 75c value. Size, 26 inches. Price 59c

No. 18K17105 Fast Black English Twilled Mercerized Carolo Umbrella. Paragon frame, steel rod, with natural Congo loop or tied handle, silverine swedge. Size, 26 inches. Price 79c

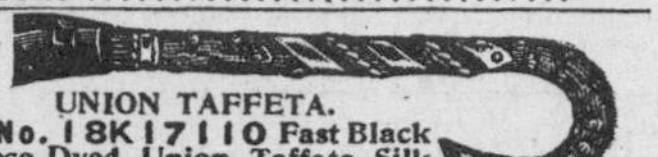

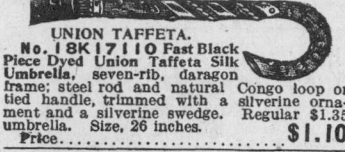

UNION TAFFETA.

No. 18K17110 Fast Black Piece Dyed Union Taffeta Silk Umbrella, seven-rib, daragon frame; steel rod and natural Congo loop or tied handle, trimmed with a silverine ornament and a silverine swedge. Regular $1.35 umbrella. Size, 26 inches. Price $1.10

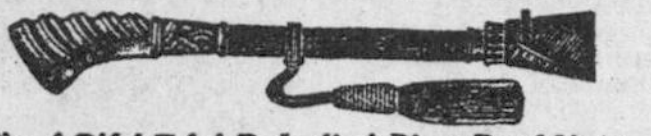

No. 18K17115 Ladies' Piece Dyed Union Taffeta Silk Umbrella. Has best paragon frame, steel rod beautiful fancy pearl chunk handle with gold chased swedge on partridge wood mount, gilt swedge at bottom of handle to match. Size, 26 inches. Black only. Price $1.27

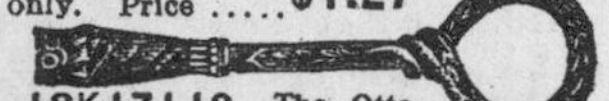

No. 18K17119 The Otto Mueller Piece Dyed Gloria Taffeta Silk Umbrella. Paragon frame, steel rod and black carved rubber handle. Same quality umbrella usually retailed at $1.75. Size, 26 inches. Black only. Price $1.29

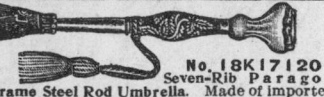

No. 18K17120 Seven-Rib Paragon Frame Steel Rod Umbrella. Made of imported union taffeta silk with chased silverine top and carved gunmetal finish, oval shape post with a large silverine swedge. Case and tassel. Size, 26 inches. Black only. Price $1.49

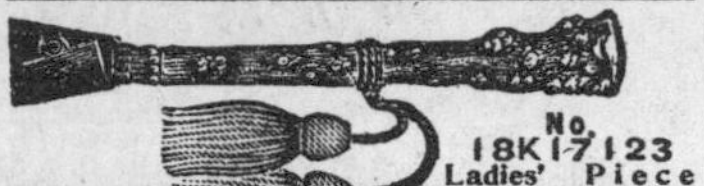

No. 18K17123 Ladies' Piece Dyed Union Taffeta Silk Umbrella, with tape edge, on best paragon frame with steel rod. Beautiful natural boxwood handle in fancy design. Length of handle, 8 inches. Silk case and tassel to match. Very neat and serviceable style. Black only. Size, 26 inches. $2.25 value. Price $1.69

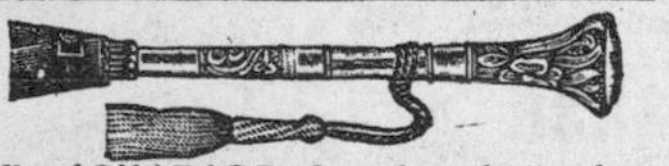

No. 18K17125 One of our best values for quality and style. Seven-Rib Paragon Frame, Steel Rod Umbrella. Made of imported union taffeta silk with tape edge. Case and tassel. Has large art silvered top with mother of pearl post and art silvered swedge in center and long art silvered swedge on bottom. Size, 26 inches. Black only. Price $1.77

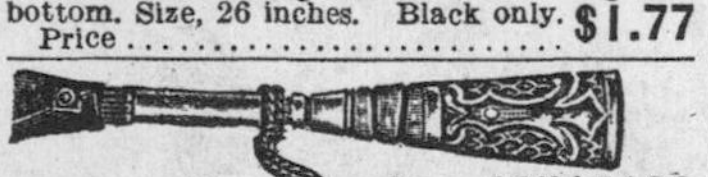

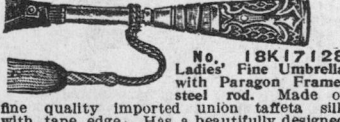

No. 18K17128 Ladies' Fine Umbrella with Paragon Frame, steel rod. Made of fine quality imported union taffeta silk with tape edge. Has a beautifully designed German silver handle; mounted on 1¼-inch oriental pearl post with 3-inch German silver swedge. Has silk case and tassel. Regular $3.00 value. Black only. Price $2.19

Protector Tape Edge Taffeta Silk.

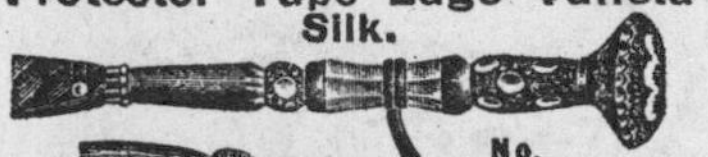

No. 18K17136 This is a Seven-Rib Paragon Frame Umbrella, very best steel rod. Made of the celebrated "Protector" tape edge union taffeta silk, guaranteed for one year. With all silk case and tassel. Has 2-inch chased gold top, mounted on mother of pearl post, with 2-inch chased gold swedge on bottom. We cannot illustrate the real beauty of this umbrella. Black only. Size, 26 inches. Price $2.69

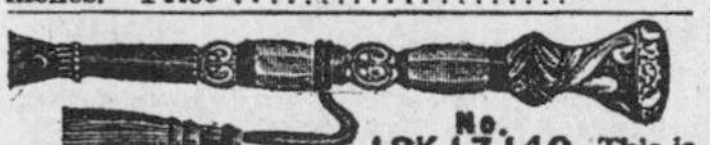

No. 18K17140 This is a Seven-Rib Paragon Frame Umbrella, very best steel rod. Made of imported tape edge taffeta silk, very fine quality and guaranteed for one year. Has tight roll case and tassel. Two-inch finely chased gold top mounted on double barrel pearl post, with chased gold swedge at the center and a 2-inch gold chased swedge at the bottom. Black only. Size, 26 inches. Price $3.25

Famous Herald Square Taffeta Silk.

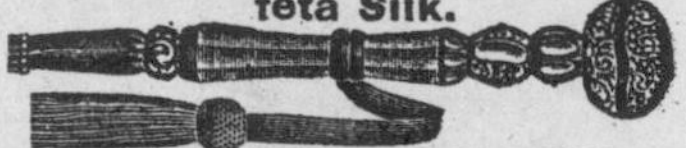

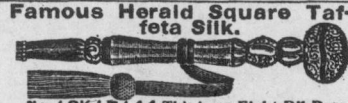

No. 18K17144 This is an Eight-Rib Paragon Frame Umbrella, best steel rod. Made of the celebrated Herald Square tape edge taffeta silk. Guaranteed for one year. Has case and tassel and 3-inch large chased gold ball top mounted on 3½-inch fine mother of pearl post, with 2½-inch gold swedge on bottom. Black only. Size, 26 inches. Price .. $4.48

Colored Umbrella.

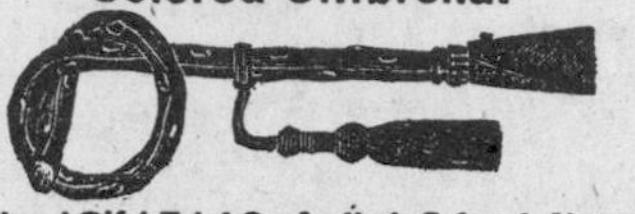

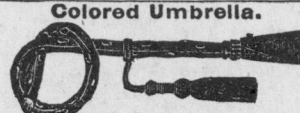

No. 18K17146 Ladies' Colored Union Taffeta Silk Umbrella, with case and tassel to match. Has paragon frame, steel rod, with imported Congo handle. Colors, navy, dark red or dark green. Size, 26 inches. State color wanted. Price $1.15

Self Opening Umbrella.

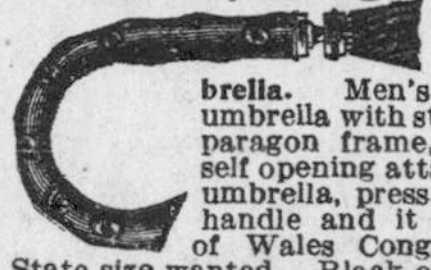

No. 18K17152 New Patent Self Opening Umbrella. Men's mercerized cloth umbrella with steel rod, double rib paragon frame, and new patent self opening attachment. To open umbrella, press spring at base of handle and it flies open. Prince of Wales Congo wood handles. State size wanted. Black only.

Size, inches	26	28
Price	95c	$1.05

Men's Umbrellas.

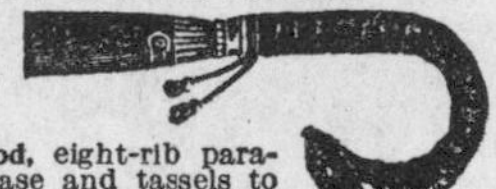

No. 18K17148 Men's Mercerized Cloth Umbrella, with steel rod, eight-rib paragon frame, case and tassels to match. Prince of Wales Congo wood hook handle. Silverine trimmed. We highly recommend this umbrella for looks and durability. Black only. State size wanted.

Size, inches	26	28	30
Price	$1.10	$1.20	$1.30

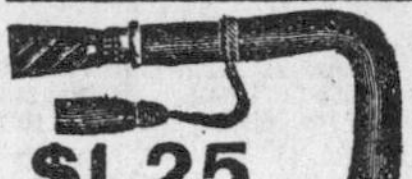

$1.25

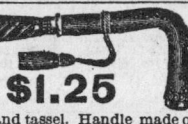

No. 18K17155 Eight-Rib Paragon Frame Steel Rod Umbrella, with imported union taffeta, tape edge, guaranteed fast black. Has case and tassel. Handle made of imported boxwood hooks, with silverine swedge and nose. Black only. State size wanted.

Size, inches	26	28
Price	$1.25	$1.35

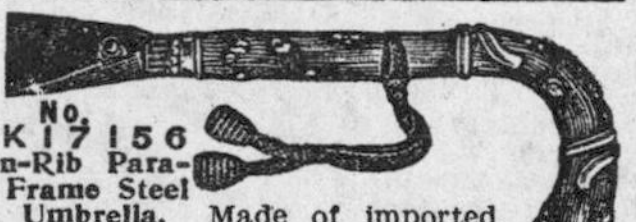

No. 18K17156 Seven-Rib Paragon Frame Steel Rod Umbrella. Made of imported union taffeta silk, with case and tassel to match. The handle is imported boxwood trimmed with fancy German silver wire and German silver swedge. Black only. State size wanted.

Size, inches	26	28
Price	$1.55	$1.65

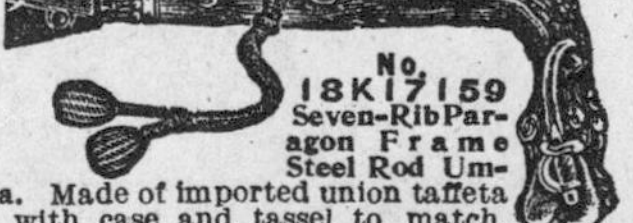

No. 18K17159 Seven-Rib Paragon Frame Steel Rod Umbrella. Made of imported union taffeta silk, with case and tassel to match. The handle is fine quality, made of imported boxwood, trimmed with genuine silver and silver swedge. Black only. State size wanted.

Size, inches	26	28
Price	$1.89	$1.99

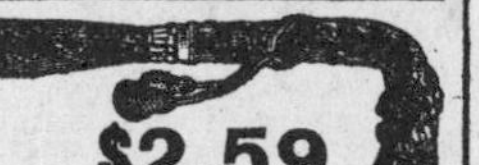

$2.59

No. 18K17166 This is the Famous Herald Square Taffeta Silk Umbrella, guaranteed for wear and appearance. Fine quality taped edge silk, paragon frame, steel rod, mounted with fine imported boxwood handle. A gentleman's very stylish, plain umbrella. Black only. State size wanted.

Size, inches	26	28
Price	$2.59	$2.83

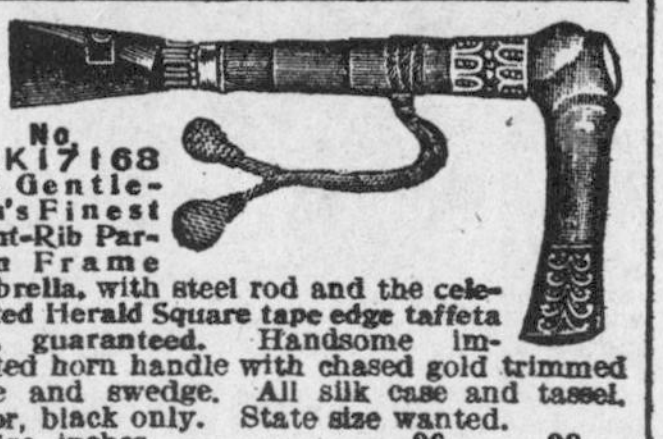

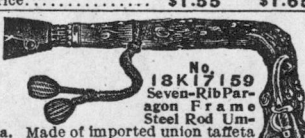

No. 18K17168 Our Gentlemen's Finest Eight-Rib Paragon Frame Umbrella, with steel rod and the celebrated Herald Square tape edge taffeta silk, guaranteed. Handsome imported horn handle with chased gold trimmed nose and swedge. All silk case and tassel. Color, black only. State size wanted.

Size, inches	26	28
Price	$3.75	$4.00

24-inch School Umbrellas for Children.

No. 18K17170 Fast Black English Gloria Silk Umbrella, steel frame, steel rod, with small imported Congo handle, Prince of Wales hooks, etc., for boys, or loops and tie shapes, for girls. Price 47c

No. 18K17174 School Umbrellas for Boys and Girls. This is a fine quality imported, mercerized carola, guaranteed fast black, has paragon frame and steel rod, with pearl hooks, handle mounted on partridgene; also imported Congos with silverine tips. All have silverine swedges. Black only. Price 75c

PARASOLS.

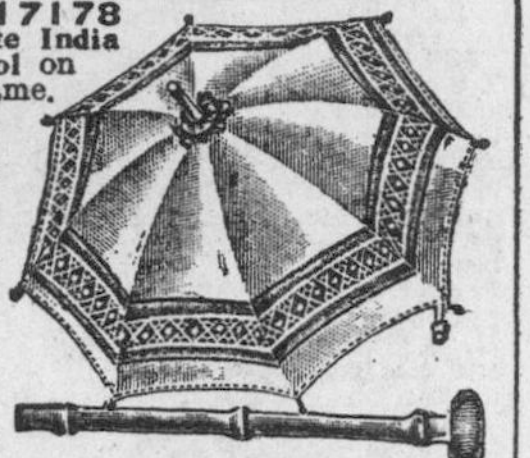

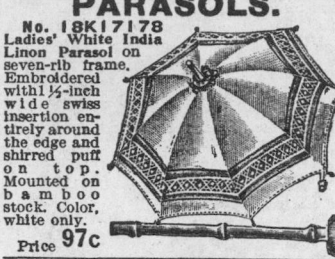

No. 18K17178 Ladies' White India Linon Parasol on seven-rib frame. Embroidered with 1½-inch wide swiss insertion entirely around the edge and shirred puff on top. Mounted on bamboo stock. Color, white only. Price 97c

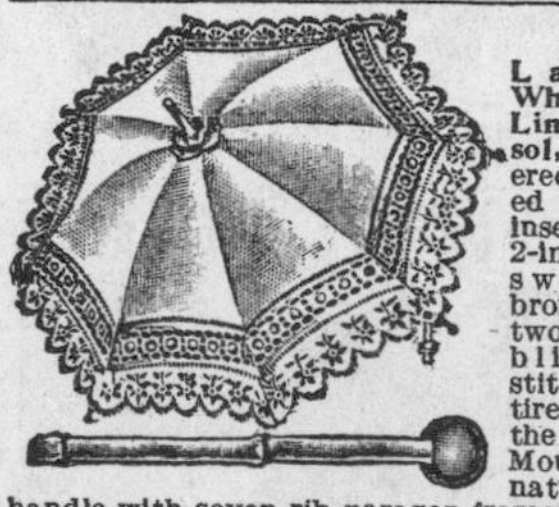

No. 18K17180 Ladies' White India Linon Parasol, embroidered scalloped edge and inserted with 2-inch wide swiss embroidery and two rows of blind hemstitching entirely around the edge. Mounted on natural wood handle with seven-rib paragon frame. $1.75 value. Color, white only. Price $1.29

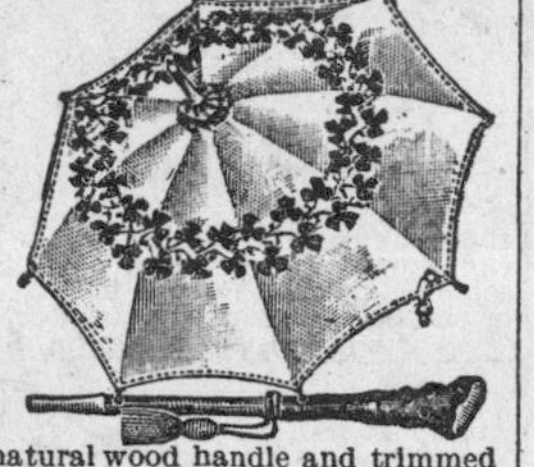

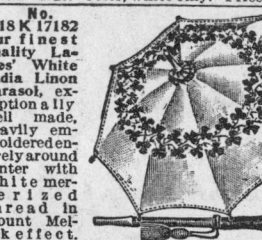

No. 18K17182 Our finest quality Ladies' White India Linon Parasol, exceptionally well made, heavily embroidered entirely around center with white mercerized thread in Mount Mellick effect. Mounted on natural wood handle and trimmed with white silk tassel. Color, white only. Price $1.89

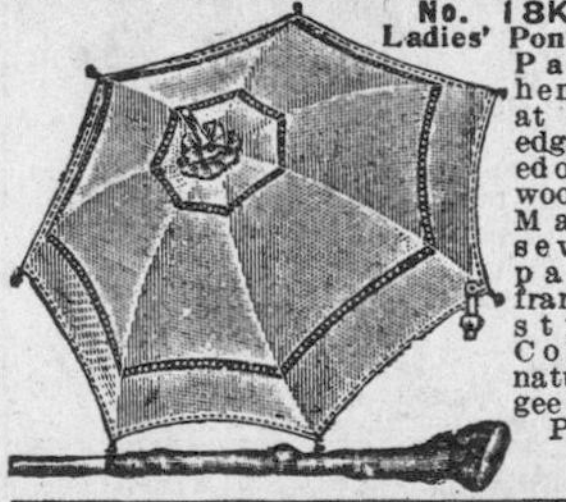

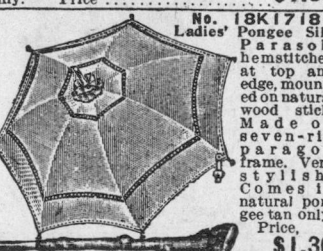

No. 18K17184 Ladies' Pongee Silk Parasol, hemstitched at top and edge, mounted on natural wood stick. Made on seven-rib paragon frame. Very stylish. Comes in natural pongee tan only. Price, $1.30

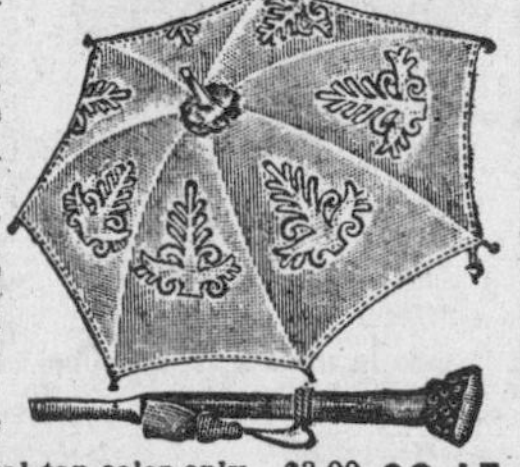

No. 18K17186 Ladies' Pongee Silk Parasol. Our very best quality, made on a seven-rib paragon frame. Handsomely embroidered and ornamented with puff at top and silk pongee tassel on natural wood handle. Pongee parasols are very popular. Natural tan color only. $3.00 value. Our price $2.15

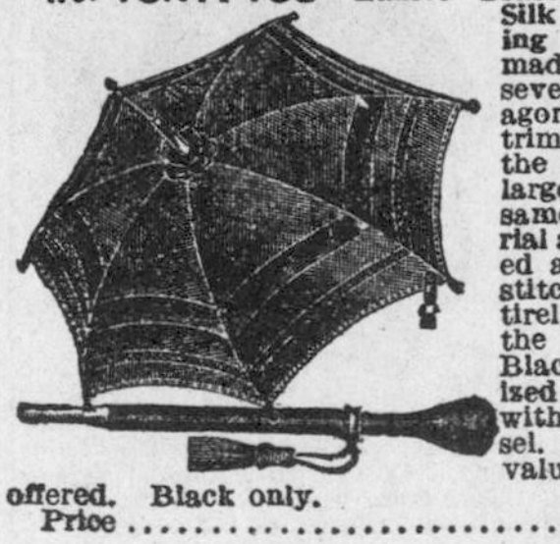

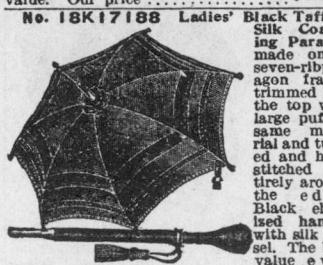

No. 18K17188 Ladies' Black Taffeta Silk Coaching Parasol, made on a seven-rib paragon frame, trimmed at the top with large puff of same material and tucked and hemstitched entirely around the edge. Black ebonized handle, with silk tassel. The best value ever offered. Black only. Price $1.69

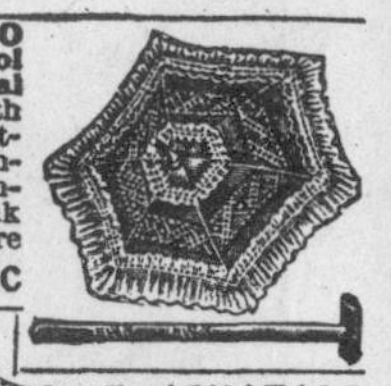

No. 18K17190 Child's Sateen Parasol on good substantial frame, trimmed with ruffles at top and bottom and a row of lace insertion around the center. Colors, white, pink or light blue. Be sure to state color wanted. Price .. 49c

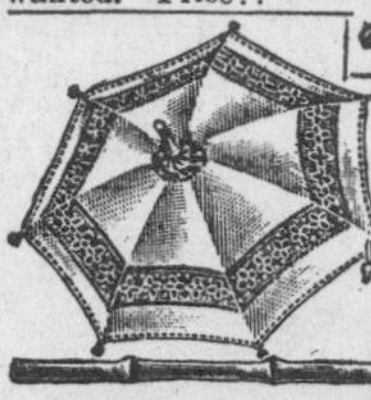

No. 18K17192 Child's White India Linon Parasol. A splendid value. Trimmed with one band of Swiss embroidered insertion and two rows of blind hemstitching and puff at the top. Color, white only. Price .. 78c

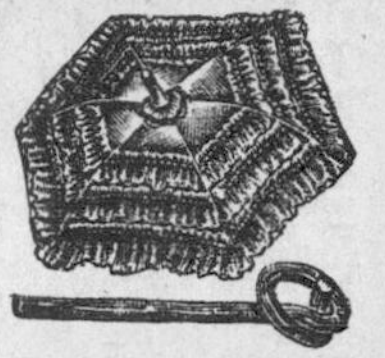

No. 18K17194 Child's China Silk Parasol with three full ruffles and puff of same material, mounted on substantial steel frame and natural handle. A very rich and showy pattern. Colors, white, pink or light blue. Be sure to state color wanted. Price 98c

PIPES.

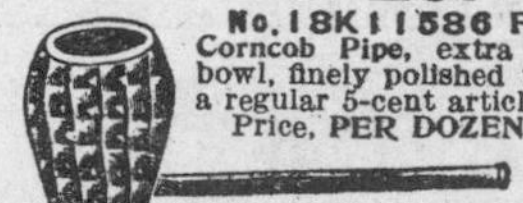

No. 18K11586 Fine Selected Corncob Pipe, extra large size bowl, finely polished reed stems, a regular 5-cent article. Price, PER DOZEN 18c

If by mail, postage extra, per dozen, 12 cents.

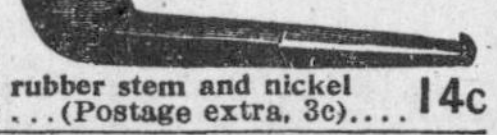

14c

No. 18K11590 Very Elegant Brier Pipe, medium size, 5½ inches long, with polished hard rubber stem and nickel band. Price ... (Postage extra, 3c) 14c

Cartridge Pipe.

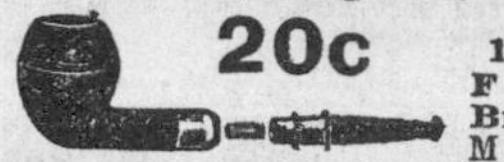

20c

No. 18K11656 French Brier Pipe, Morgan shape, with best vulcanized rubber shove bit. A fine nickel band on stem, holding inside an absorbent paper cartridge, which effectually absorbs the nicotine. Length of pipe, 5 inches. Price .... (Postage extra, 6c) 20c

No. 18K11658 Extra Cartridges to replace used cartridges in above pipe. 10 in a box. Price, 3 BOXES FOR ... 10c

If by mail, postage extra, 3 boxes, 5 cents.

22 Cents for a Self Cleaner.

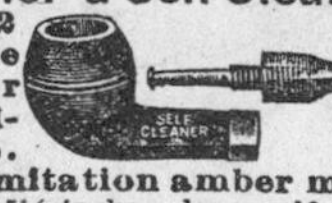

No. 18K11662 A Genuine French Brier English Bulldog Pipe. Handsome imitation amber mouthpiece. Length, 5½ inches, long self cleaner, handsome nickel band, finely made and finished. Price 22c

If by mail, postage extra, 3 cents.

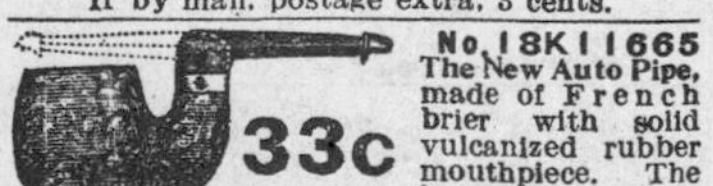

33c

No. 18K11665 The New Auto Pipe, made of French brier with solid vulcanized rubber mouthpiece. The bowl is oval in shape and fitted with a mouthpiece which can be adjusted over the bowl when not in use, making a handy and compact pipe that can be carried in the vest pocket. Length of pipe, 5 inches. Price 33c

If by mail, postage extra, 5 cents.

Chip Meerschaum Bowl.

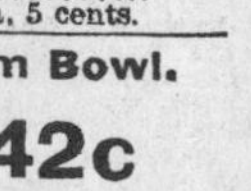

42c

No. 18K11667 Genuine French Brier Pipe, bulldog shape with celluloid mouthpiece. The pipe is fitted with a deep chip meerschaum bowl set in the brier bowl in such a manner as to prevent saliva from mingling with the tobacco, therefore insuring a clean, cool smoke, which is so much desired. Length of pipe, 5 inches. Price 42c

If by mail, postage extra, 5 cents.

The New Ring Pipe.

For a cool smoke and to prevent the nicotine from passing into the mouth.

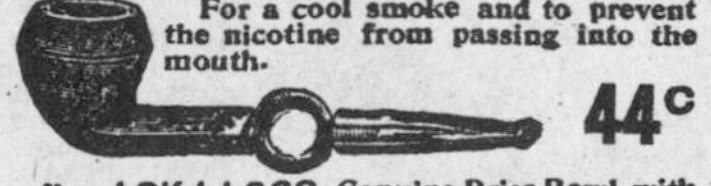

44c

No. 18K11668 Genuine Brier Bowl, with imitation amber mouthpiece, and having the latest invented ring attachment. Tobacco in pipe is always kept dry, insuring a sweet, cool smoke. Easily cleaned. A boon for smokers. Price 44c

If by mail, postage extra, 5 cents.

Chip Meerschaum. 88c

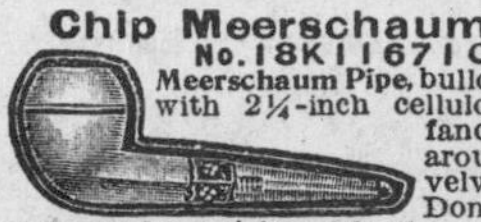

No. 18K11671 Chip Meerschaum Pipe, bulldog shape bowl with 2¼-inch celluloid stem, has fancy nickel band around stem, in velvet lined case. Don't confuse this high grade article with the ordinary cheap pipes. Length of pipe, 5½ inches. Price........ 88c
If by mail, postage extra, 5 cents.

No. 18K11672 French Brier Pipe with bent celluloid mouthpiece and new fancy shaped bowl, studded with small gilt nail heads. Just the thing for those desiring a light and comfortable pipe. Regular 35-cent pipe. Length, 4½ inches. Price........ 23c

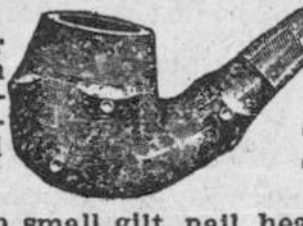

If by mail, postage extra, 5 cents.

Pipes with Curved Bits.

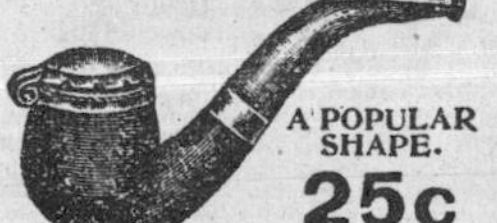

A POPULAR SHAPE. 25c

No. 18K11673 Curved Egg Shape Genuine French Brier, with 2¾-inch horn bit, heavy nickel cover and band. A specially good pipe for farmers and mechanics. Whole length, 5 inches. Price........ 25c
If by mail, postage extra, 5 cents.

The New Reservoir Well Pipe.

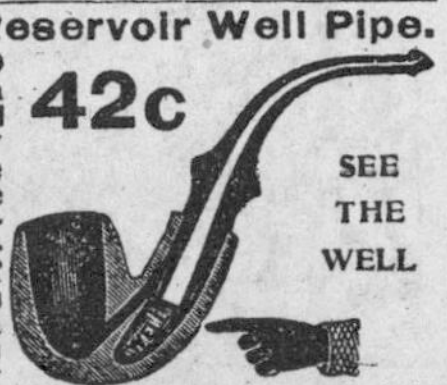

42c SEE THE WELL

No. 18K11679 The Pipe with a Well, for a cool smoke. Easily cleaned. The reservoir pipe offers two important advantages. The well of the bowl collects the saliva and thereby leaves the tobacco dry to the last. The peculiar shaped mouthpiece permits the tongue to rest easily underneath the curve and the upper boring of the draft hole compels the smoke to pass over the tongue and does not irritate the mouth. Made by skilled workmen. Patterned after the famous Peterson, made of the best selected French brier, and the mouthpiece of finest quality hard rubber, has heavy nickel band around stem. Large size. Length, 6¼ inches. Price....(Postage extra, 5c).... 42c

No. 18K11681 The New Reservoir Well Pipe. Made of fine quality genuine French brier with hard rubber bit and heavy nickel band. Smaller size than 18K11679. Length of pipe 5 inches. Price........ 25c
If by mail, postage extra, 5 cents.

An Old Favorite. 29c

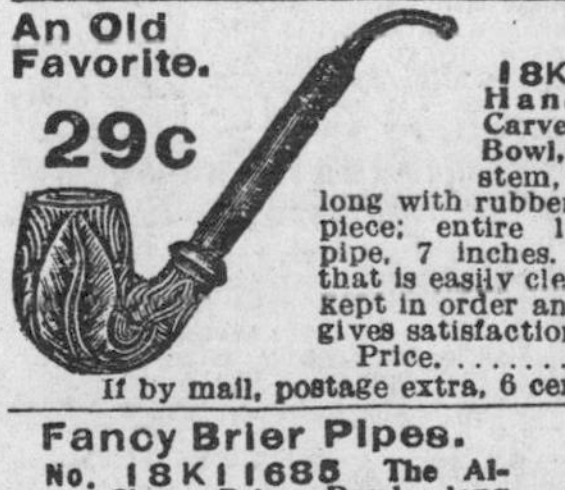

No. 18K11683 Handsomely Carved Brier Bowl, cherry stem, 6 inches long with rubber mouthpiece; entire length of pipe, 7 inches. A pipe that is easily cleaned and kept in order and always gives satisfaction. Price........ 29c
If by mail, postage extra, 6 cents.

Fancy Brier Pipes.

No. 18K11685 The Always Clean Brier Bowl, long rubber stem, with rubber under bowl and nicotine absorber, handsomely decorated cover; a pipe that can be taken apart in four pieces and usually retails for 75 cents. Our price........ 33c
If by mail, postage extra, 7 cents.

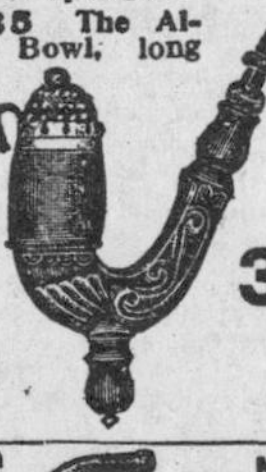

33c

38c

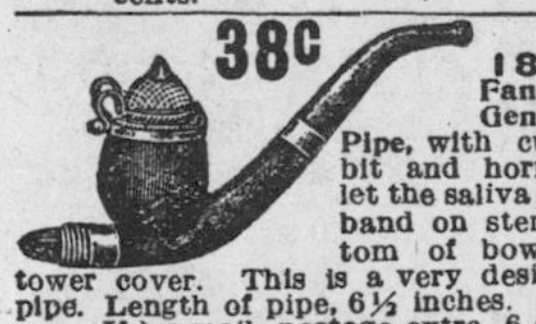

No. 18K11686 Fancy Shaped Genuine Brier Pipe, with curved horn bit and horn screw to let the saliva out. Nickel band on stem and bottom of bowl, fancy tower cover. This is a very desirable pipe. Length of pipe, 6½ inches. Price 38c
If by mail, postage extra, 6 cents.

No. 18K11687 Fine Eagle Claw French Brier Pipe, with fancy curved horn mouthpiece. A large size egg shape bowl. Length of pipe, 6 inches. Price 45c
If by mail, postage extra, 6 cents.

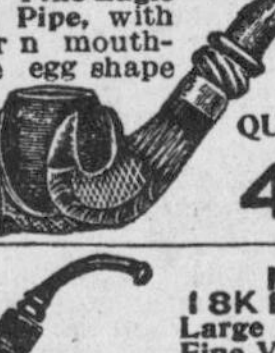

EXTRA FINE QUALITY. 45c

38c REGULAR 75c VALUE.

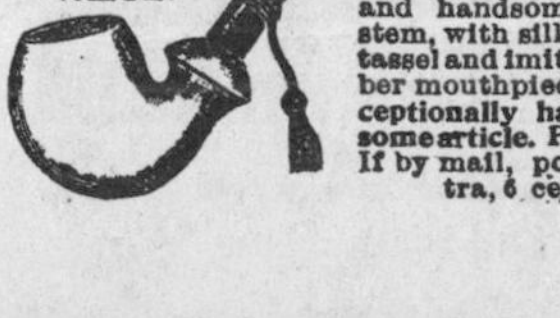

No. 18K11689 Large Sized Fine Vienna Chip Meerschaum Pipe, large egg shaped bowl and handsome cherry stem, with silk cord and tassel and imitation amber mouthpiece. An exceptionally handsome article. Price 38c
If by mail, postage extra, 6 cents.

No. 18K11691 Fancy Shape Vienna Chip Meerschaum Pipe, artistically carved design lady's head. Pipe is boiled in wax and will color like genuine meerschaum if properly handled, has 4-inch cherry stem, with curved celluloid bit. Length of pipe, 8½ inches. Price 65c
If by mail, postage extra, 6 cents.

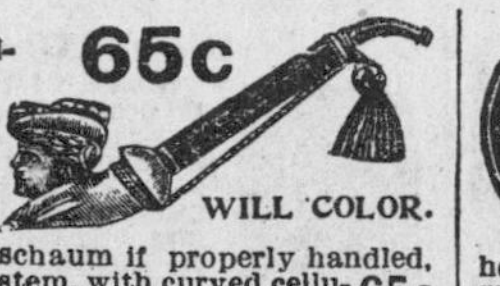

65c WILL COLOR.

Pipe Stems.

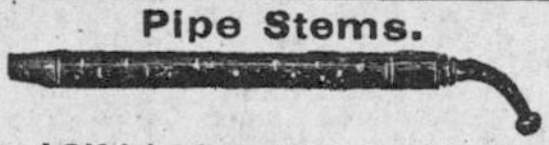

No. 18K11688 6½-inch Weichsel Pipe Stem, with curved rubber mouthpiece. Price........ 13c

No. 18K11690 7-inch Cherry Pipe Stem with curved rubber mouthpiece. Price........ 9c
If by mail, postage extra, each, 3 cents.

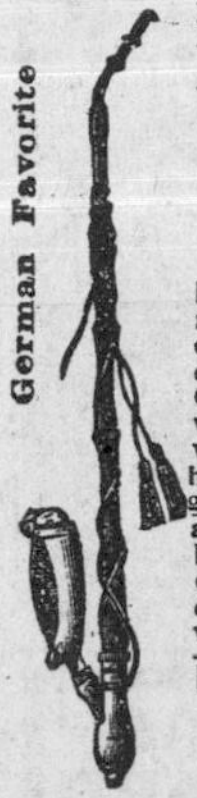

German Favorite

79c German Porcelain Pipes.

No. 18K11695 German Porcelain Pipe, handsomely decorated; just the thing for a good old fashioned smoke. This is an exceptionally fine and handsome German porcelain pipe. Made with very fine long stem, fitted with flexible top and extra fine hard rubber mouthpiece. Long genuine porcelain bowl, artistically and handsomely decorated. The bowl can readily be taken apart for cleaning, thus assuring a clean, cool smoke. Shipping weight, 1¾ pounds. Price........ 79c

Regular $2.00 German Porcelain Pipe, $1.33.

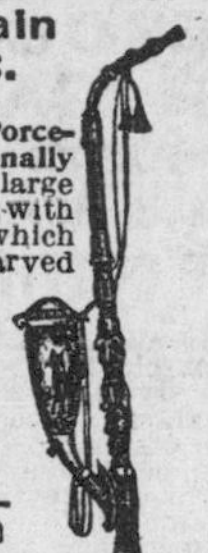

No. 18K11697 German Porcelain Pipe. This is an exceptionally high grade German pipe with a large elaborately decorated bowl, with nicotine receiver on bottom which can be unscrewed, long fancy carved horn stem, fitted with flexible top and fine hard rubber mouthpiece. Trimmed with long silk cord and tassels. All the different parts can be separated, so that you can easily clean. Shipping weight, 1¾ pounds. Price........ $1.33

Genuine French Brier Pipes, 55c.

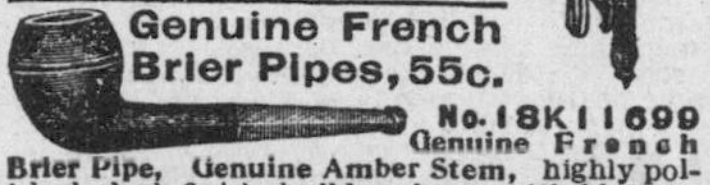

No. 18K11699 Genuine French Brier Pipe, Genuine Amber Stem, highly polished, dark finish, bulldog shape, with 1¾-inch genuine amber straight stem. Length of pipe, 5 inches. 75-cent value. Our price........ 55c
If by mail, postage extra, 7 cents.

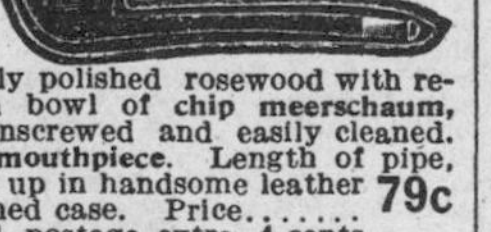

79c

No. 18K11700 This is certainly one of the very handsomest pipes made. It is made from highly polished rosewood with removable set in bowl of chip meerschaum, which can be unscrewed and easily cleaned. Genuine amber mouthpiece. Length of pipe, 5½ inches. Put up in handsome leather covered satin lined case. Price........ 79c
If by mail, postage extra, 4 cents.

Genuine French Brier.

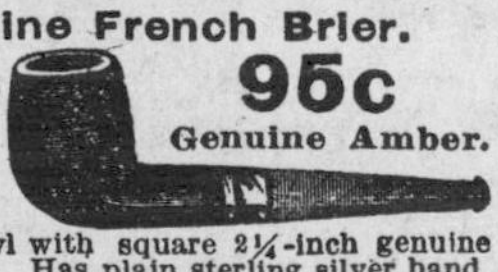

95c Genuine Amber.

No. 18K11703 Excellent Quality Highly Finished Genuine French Brier; egg shape bowl with square 2¼-inch genuine amber stem. Has plain sterling silver band, giving pipe a very pretty appearance. Whole length of pipe, 5 inches. Price........ 95c
If by mail, postage extra, 6 cents.

Extra Value. Genuine Amber. $1.15

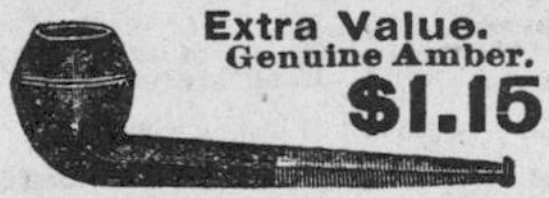

No. 18K11706 Genuine French Brier Pipe, Genuine Amber, highly polished, dark finish, with 3-inch genuine amber straight stem. Bulldog shape. Length of pipe, 6¼ inches. Worth $1.75. Our price........ $1.15
If by mail, postage extra, 7 cents.

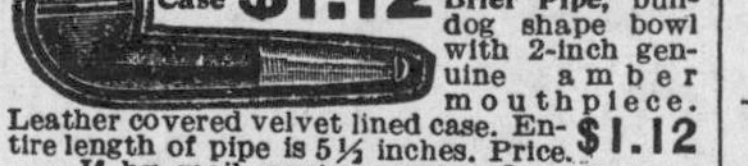

With Case $1.12

No. 18K11711 Selected French Brier Pipe, bulldog shape bowl with 2-inch genuine amber mouthpiece. Leather covered velvet lined case. Entire length of pipe is 5½ inches. Price........ $1.12
If by mail, postage extra, 2 cents.

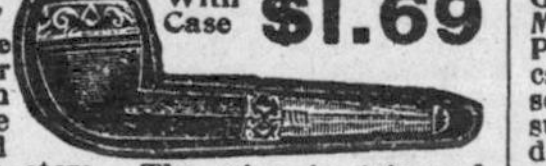

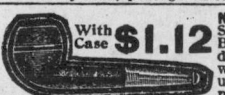

With Case $1.69

No. 18K11717 High Grade French Brier Pipe, with bulldog shape bowl and 2-inch amber stem. The pipe is trimmed with a heavy chased gold band on bowl and stem. Length of pipe, 5¾ inches. In leather covered velvet lined case. Price........ $1.69
If by mail, postage extra, 6 cents.

French Brier Pipes.

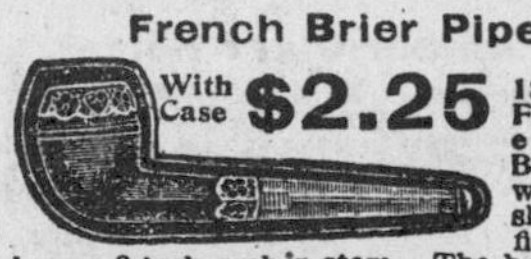

With Case $2.25

No. 18K11721 Fine Imported French Brier Pipe, with bulldog shape bowl fitted with heavy 3-inch amber stem. The bowl is trimmed with beautifully engraved heavy gold top band and the stem with band to match. Entire length of pipe, 6¾ inches. In leather covered silk plush lined case. Price........ $2.25
If by mail, postage extra, 5 cents.

No. 18K11723 High Grade French Brier Pipe with highly polished large bulldog shape bowl. Has extra heavy 3½-inch amber stem. The bowl is mounted with 14-K. gold plated top, with band to match. Entire length of pipe, 7 inches. In chamois covered silk plush lined case. Price........ $2.98
If by mail, postage extra, 5 cents.

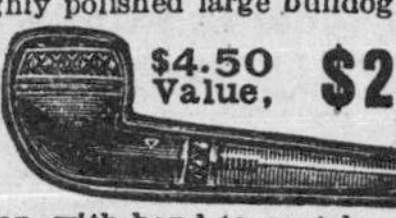

$4.50 Value, $2.98

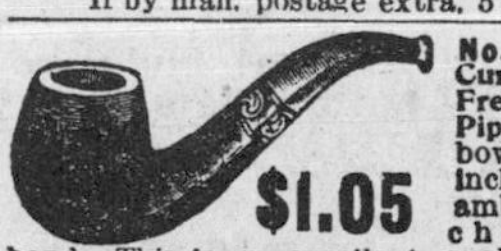

$1.05

No. 18K11724 Curved Genuine French Brier Pipe. Egg shape bowl, with 1⅞-inch genuine amber bit and chased gold band. This is an excellent quality pipe. Whole length, 4½ inches. Price........ $1.05
If by mail, postage extra, 6 cents.

No. 18K11725 Genuine French Brier Pipe, bulldog shape bowl with 1¾-inch genuine amber bit, has engraved gold band around stem. Length of pipe, 4½ inches. In leather covered silk plush lined case. Price........ $1.35
If by mail, postage extra, 5 cents.

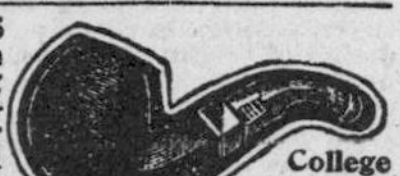

College Style

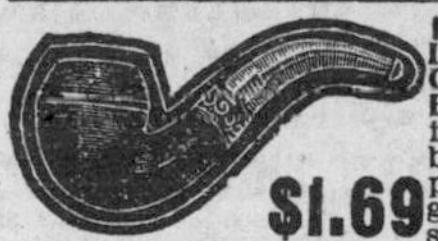

$1.69

No. 18K11727 Large Bulldog Genuine French Brier Pipe with 2-inch genuine amber bent mouthpiece. Has chased gold band around stem. Length of pipe, 4¾ inches. In leather covered silk plush lined case. Price........ $1.69
If by mail, postage extra, 5 cents.

No. 18K11729 Very Fine Quality French Brier Pipe, bulldog shape bowl, has a 2½-inch genuine amber curved mouthpiece. The bowl and stem are mounted with beautifully engraved gold bands, same design. Length of pipe, 5½ inches. In leather covered silk plush lined case. Price........ $2.69
If by mail, postage extra, 5 cents.

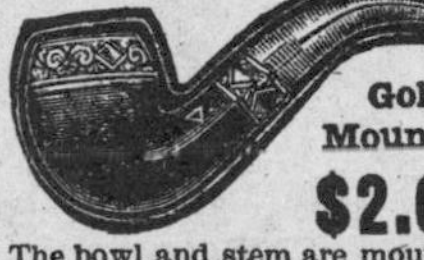

Gold Mounted $2.69

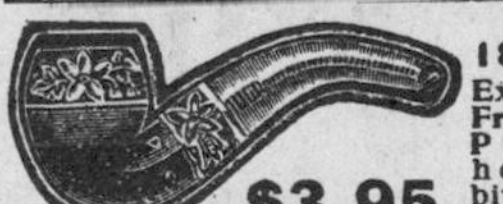

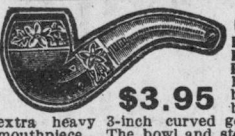

$3.95

No. 18K11731 Extra Quality French Brier Pipe, with heavy bull-bitch shape bowl. Has an extra heavy 3-inch curved genuine amber mouthpiece. The bowl and stem are ornamented with very heavy gold plated band with raised sterling silver ornaments, a new and attractive design. Length of pipe, 6 inches. In fine chamois covered silk plush lined case. $5.00 value. Our price........ $3.95
If by mail, postage extra, 5 cents.

Genuine Meerschaum Pipes.

We guarantee all of our genuine meerschaum pipes to be absolutely first quality.

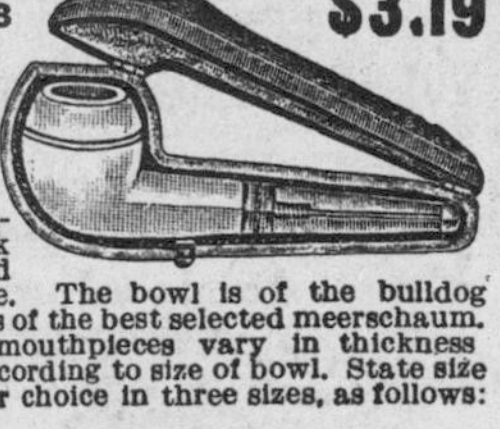

$3.19

No. 18K11733 Genuine Meerschaum Pipes. Guaranteed highest grade meerschaum, with best amber mouthpiece. In silk plush lined chamois case. The bowl is of the bulldog pattern and is of the best selected meerschaum. The amber mouthpieces vary in thickness and length according to size of bowl. State size wanted. Your choice in three sizes, as follows:

Size of bowl, No.	Length of pipe	Price
5	4½ inches	$3.19
7	5½ inches	4.29
8	6 inches	4.88

If by mail, postage extra, each, 8 cents.

Select, Fancy Carved Pipes.

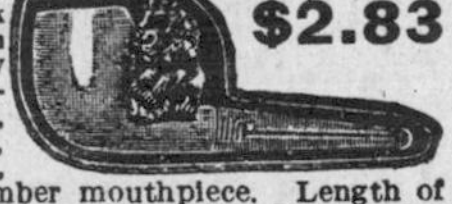

$2.83

No. 18K11735 Genuine Block Meerschaum Pipe, handsomely carved bowl, assorted designs, such as lions, dogs, deer, etc., with genuine amber mouthpiece. Length of pipe, about 5 inches, with a No. 5 bowl in a satin lined case. State design wanted. Price........ $2.83
If by mail, postage extra, 6 cents.

Meerschaum Pipes.

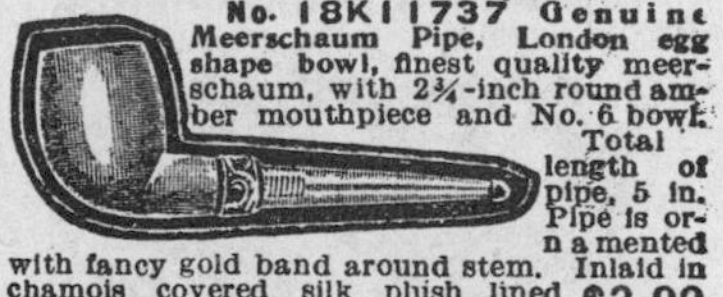

No. 18K11737 Genuine Meerschaum Pipe, London egg shape bowl, finest quality meerschaum, with 2¾-inch round amber mouthpiece and No. 6 bowl. Total length of pipe, 5 in. Pipe is ornamented with fancy gold band around stem. Inlaid in chamois covered silk plush lined case; very high grade. Price........ $3.99
If by mail, postage extra, 5 cents.

Our $5.29 Meerschaum Pipe.

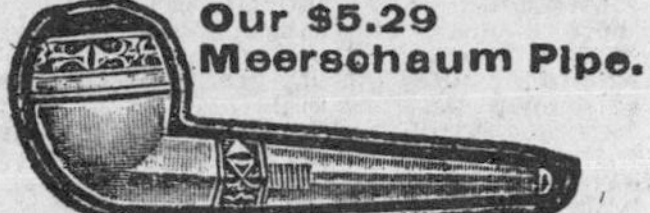

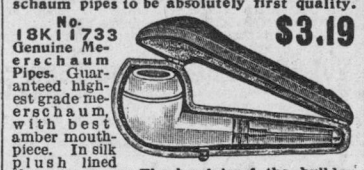

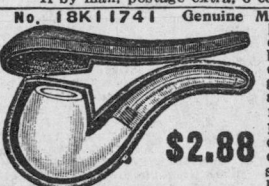

No. 18K11739 Genuine Meerschaum Pipe, straight bulldog shape, with 3-inch genuine amber mouthpiece and No. 7 bowl, heavy chased gold band on stem and bowl; inlaid in finest plush lined chamois covered case. No better pipe at any price. $8.00 value. Our price........ $5.29
If by mail, postage extra, 6 cents.

No. 18K11741 Genuine Meerschaum Pipe with egg shape bowl and curved genuine amber mouthpiece, in chamois covered silk plush lined case. Length of pipe, 5 inches. Price........ $2.88
If by mail, postage extra, 8 cents.

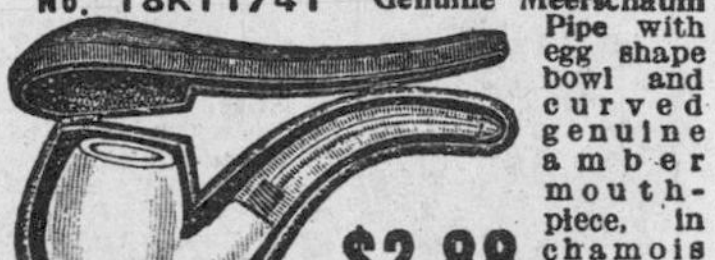

$2.88

No. 18K11742 Fine Imported Meerschaum Pipe, in silk plush lined chamois case. The pipe is made of the highest grade meerschaum and first quality genuine amber mouthpiece. The model is the new Vienna pattern, egg shaped bowl with neat scroll design on the stem. Length of pipe, 5 inches. This pipe is an exceptional value, easily worth $5.50. Our price........ $3.89
If by mail, postage extra, 7 cents.

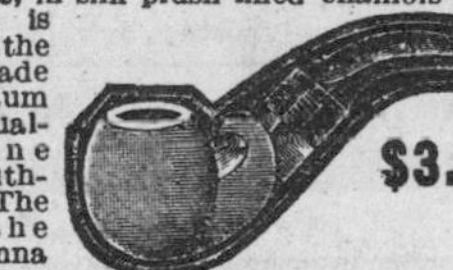

$3.89

Special Value Fancy Shape.

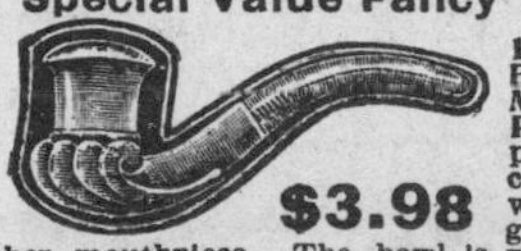

$3.98

No. 18K11745 Best Quality Meerschaum Pipe, in silk plush lined chamois case with a curved genuine amber mouthpiece. The bowl is new and exclusive in shape and ornamented with a pretty Grecian design. For those wishing a high grade pipe, one that will color and insure a cool, pleasant smoke, we recommend this pipe. Length of pipe, 5½ inches. Our price........ $3.98
If by mail, postage extra, 7 cents.

High Grade Meerschaum.

No. 18K11746 High Grade Genuine Meerschaum Pipe with large egg shape, size 6 bowl. Finest Quality. Has a curved, genuine amber mouthpiece 2¾ inches in length. The pipe is trimmed with plain gold band on top of bowl and stem, making a very rich and neat looking pipe. Fitted in morocco leather covered, plush lined case. None better made. Price........ $4.48
If by mail, postage extra, 8 cents.

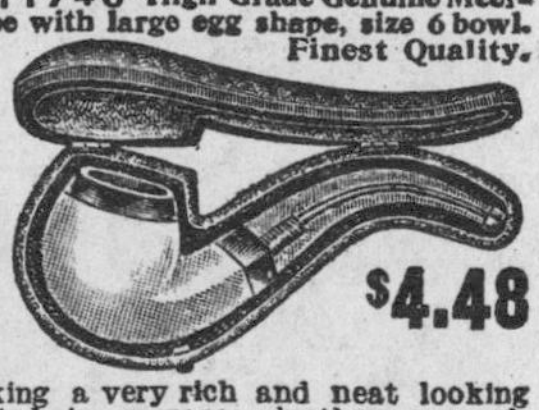

$4.48

Eagle Claw, Exceptional Value.

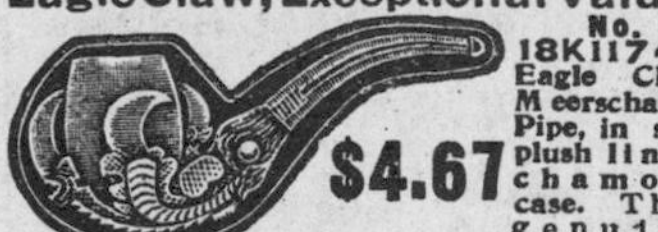

$4.67

No. 18K11747 Eagle Claw Meerschaum Pipe, in silk plush lined chamois case. This genuine meerschaum pipe is very high grade, having curved genuine amber mouthpiece and number 6 bowl. Total length of pipe is 5½ inches. The workmanship is of the very finest, being carved carefully and artistically by the most skilled Austrian workmen. The same pipes are retailed at exclusive pipe stores for $7.50. Our price........ $4.67
If by mail, postage extra, 8 cents.

Gold Mounted Meerschaum Pipe, $5.99.

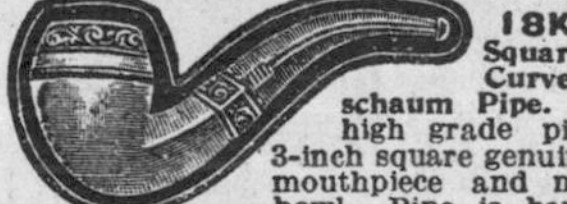

No. 18K11749 Square Stem, Curved Meerschaum Pipe. A very high grade pipe, with 3-inch square genuine amber mouthpiece and number 7 bowl. Pipe is handsomely mounted with gold bands on top of bowl and around stem of pipe. Inlaid in fine chamois, plush lined case. Price........ $5.99
If by mail, postage extra, 6 cents.

642 SEARS, ROEBUCK & CO., CHICAGO, IL. CATALOGUE No. 117.

Our Finest Meerschaum.

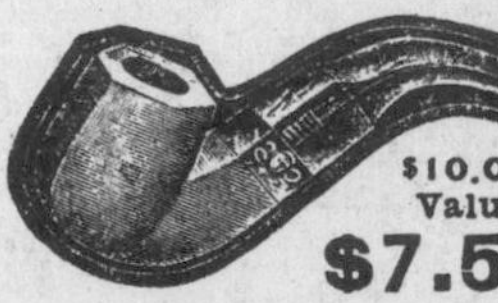

$10.00 Value **$7.50**

No. 18K11751 Highest Grade Genuine Meerschaum Pipe, made of very heavy solid piece of block meerschaum in a fancy shape square design bowl. The mouthpiece is cut square of finest quality genuine amber and is so shaped that the pipe may be held by the stem instead of bowl. The stem is trimmed with a heavy solid gold band with French gray silver ornaments. Length of amber stem, 2¾ inches. In a beautiful Russian leather covered, silk plush lined case.
Our price.......... **$7.50**
If by mail, postage extra, 8 cents.

First Quality Genuine Meerschaum Bowls in Chamois Lined Cases.

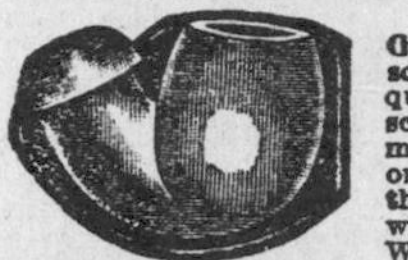

No. 18K11753 Genuine Meerschaum Bowl, finest quality block meerschaum. This style of meerschaum bowl colors quickest, and is the best style for use with the popular Weichsel stem; the finest grade of meerschaums on the market; comes in fine plush lined chamois leather case. Compare our prices. Come in four sizes, as follows:

	Price
No. 5 bowl	$3.48
No. 6 bowl	3.99
No. 7 bowl	4.89
No. 8 bowl	5.69

If by mail, postage extra, 4 cents.

Genuine Weichsel Stem, 52c.

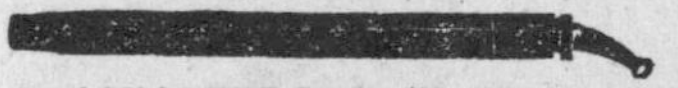

No. 18K11755 Genuine Weichsel Stem with real amber mouthpiece. Length, 6 inches. This stem is used in connection with the meerschaum bowl under preceding No. 18K11753.
Price.......... **52c**
If by mail, postage extra, 2 cents.

Our $4.29 Smoker's Set.

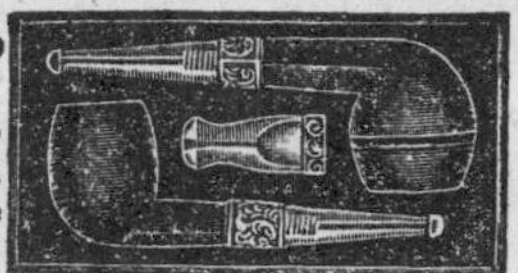

No. 18K11759 Smoker's Set, consisting of two high grade French brier pipes, one bulldog shape and one egg shape, the pipes being 5 inches in length with a 2-inch genuine amber mouthpiece. Has also a 1¾-inch genuine amber cigar holder. All three pieces are trimmed with heavy engraved gold bands, in beautiful chamois covered, silk plush lined case. Price, per set.......... **$4.29**
If by mail, postage extra, per set, 12 cents.

Smoker's Companion.

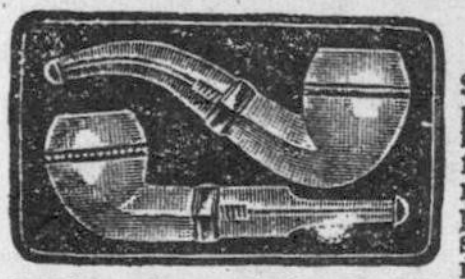

No. 18K11761 Smoker's Companion, containing two genuine first quality meerschaum pipes. One is straight, medium size, bulldog shape, 4½ inches long with a genuine 2¼-inch amber bit, and the other is a bent bulldog shape, 4 inches long with 2¾-inch curved amber bit. Both have plain gold bands. This case is of unique shape, made of chamois leather, silk plush lined.
Price, per set.......... **$5.68**
If by mail, postage extra, per set, 15 cents.

Meerschaum Cigar Holders.

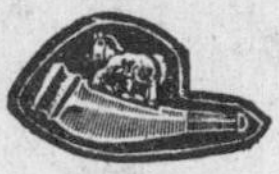

No. 18K11771 Genuine Meerschaum Cigar Holder, fancy carved with real amber bit, each in leather plush lined case. Order by number.
Price.......... **59c**
If by mail, postage extra, 3 cents.

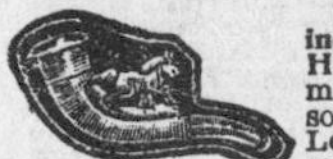

No. 18K11773 Genuine Meerschaum Cigar Holder with real amber mouthpiece in pretty assorted carved designs. Length, 4 inches, in leather covered, silk plush lined case. Price.......... **$1.15**
If by mail, postage extra, 4 cents.

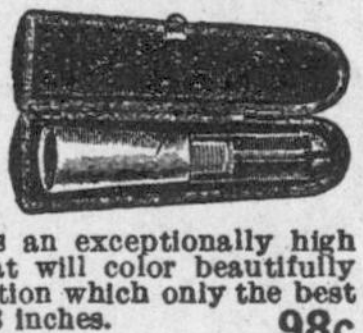

No. 18K11774 Genuine Meerschaum Cigar Holder, made of first quality heavy block meerschaum with genuine amber mouthpiece of select grade, set in a neat silk plush lined chamois case. This is an exceptionally high grade article, one that will color beautifully and give that satisfaction which only the best goods can. Length, 3 inches.
Price.......... **98c**
If by mail, postage extra, 4 cents.

Solid Amber Cigar Holder.

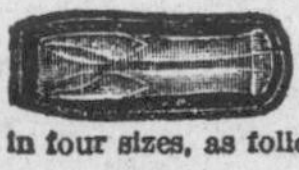

No. 18K11775 Finest Quality Real Amber Cigar Holder, chamois covered and plush lined case, a very fine article. Comes in four sizes, as follows:

	Price
1½-inch length	$0.90
2 -inch length	1.10
2½-inch length	1.25
3 -inch length	1.50

If by mail, postage extra, 2 cents.

Self Closing Rubber Pouch.

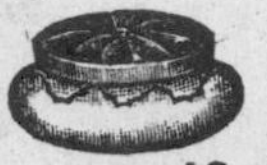

No. 18K11779 Raleigh Velvet Rubber Tobacco Pouch. Self closing, tan color. Diameter, 3⅜ inches. Keeps tobacco moist, clean and sweet. 25-cent value.
Price.......... **18c**
If by mail, postage extra, 3 cents.

Plain Nickel Finished Match Safe.

No. 18K11783 Combination Match Safe and Cigar Cutter. Nickel finish leather covering.
Price.......... **19c**
If by mail, postage extra, 2 cents.

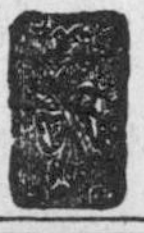

No. 18K11785 This pretty Match Safe is made of German silver, with handsome embossed design of bright silver finish. Very neat and tasty design. 75-cent value. Our price.......... **48c**
If by mail, postage extra, 2 cents.

Cigar Cases.

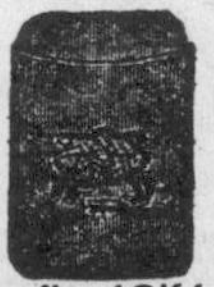

No. 18K11787 Cigar Case, telescope style and moulded into shape, fine polished tan sole leather case, stitched French edges, front embossed in English heraldic design, large size. Size, 1x3¼x5¼ inches. 50-cent value. Our price.. **29c**
If by mail, postage extra, 5c.

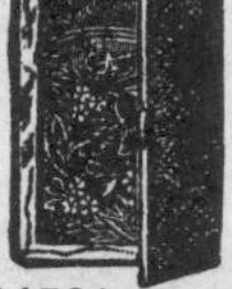

No. 18K11789 Cigar Case, made of morocco grained leather, in black with riveted nickel frame. Silk embroidered inner pocket. Size, 5¼x3¼ inches.
Price.......... **49c**
If by mail, postage extra, 5 cents.

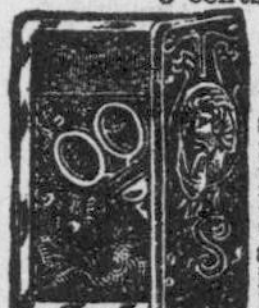

No. 18K11791 Fancy Marbleized Leather Cigar Case with embossed medallion design, fitted with good nickel riveted frame. The inner pockets are made of good material, has small scissors, cigar cutter and match scratcher. Size, 5⅛x3½ inches. Price.......... **89c**
If by mail, postage extra, 5c.

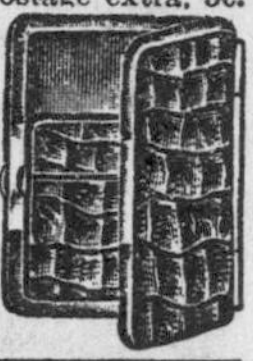

No. 18K11793 Alligator Leather Cigar Case, has fine imported alligator leather covered frame with best nickel spring catch, leather lined throughout. Our best and most serviceable cigar case; makes a most acceptable gift. Regular $2.00 value. Size, 5¼x3½ inches.
Our price.......... **$1.20**
If by mail, postage extra, 5c.

THE IMPROVED SEROCO REVERSIBLE COMBINATION GAME BOARD

WITH A NEW GAME OF BASEBALL ADDED.

Thousands of Satisfied Purchasers of This Board All Through the Country.

No. 18K22072 THIS COMPLETE OUTFIT NOW $1.79. For this year we have improved this game board so that now the best baseball game can be played on it. We furnish in our rule book plain rules for playing this game, so that anyone can easily play, whether they understand the national game of baseball or not. We have in addition increased the number of games to be played on this board from seventy-five to eighty-three, and in addition any game that can be played on any of the other game boards can be played on the Seroco board. We offer the combination game board with revolving stand and complete book of rules for playing all the games for $1.79. Our Seroco combination board is the most popular board on the market and more than equal to the boards that are being sold at from $2.75 to $4.00. It has many features which you will not find on the other higher priced boards; eighty-three distinct games can be played on this elegant combination game board. Board is made of the best three-ply white basswood which we have found by experimenting to be the only wood in game boards that will not warp. All the circles, decorations and checker board are stenciled on in very high colors, thoroughly rubbed and varnished, giving the board a very high and artistic finish. The board is 28 inches square with good net pockets. We furnish a complete set of rings, shooters, dice, ten pins, movable back and baseball men. Some of the games that can be played on this board are Seroco Baseball, Crokinole, various styles of Pool, Ten Pins, Checkers and many others. All the games can be played by from two to eight players. We have spared no expense to make this board absolutely the best on the market.

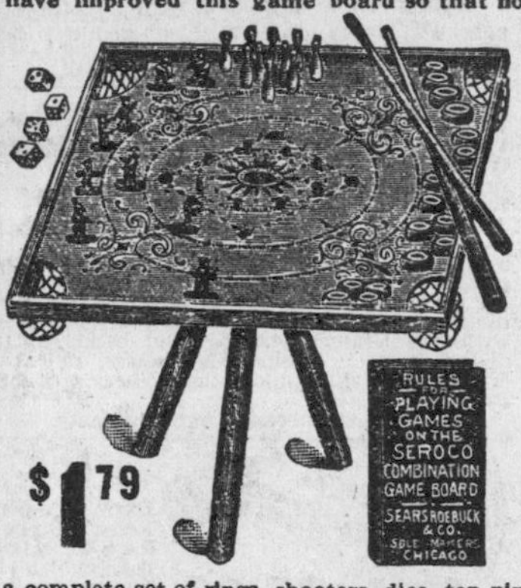

$1.79
RULES FOR PLAYING GAMES ON THE SEROCO COMBINATION GAME BOARD
SEARS, ROEBUCK & CO. SOLE MAKERS CHICAGO

THE GAME BOARD STAND for the Seroco Board is a firm support at the proper height for the players to sit on chairs. Its being revolving, makes it convenient. Folds up in very compact space. The regular selling price for this board only would be $2.75, and for the stand 50 cents. By taking the output of a very large factory and adding our very small percentage of profit, we are enabled to place these boards in the hands of our customers at the extremely low price for both board and stand of $1.79; this is much less than the price charged by other manufacturers to regular dealers for boards which are not nearly so good.

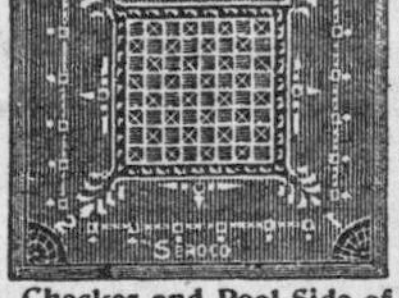

SEROCO

Checker and Pool Side of Board.

EVERY BOARD GUARANTEED as represented and fully equal to the $2.75 and $4.00 boards sold by other concerns. Shipping weight, 14 pounds. Remember, you get a full book of instructions with each game board.
Price for set complete, board, cues, rings, stand and full book of instructions.. **$1.79**

Billie's Parlor Return Pool.

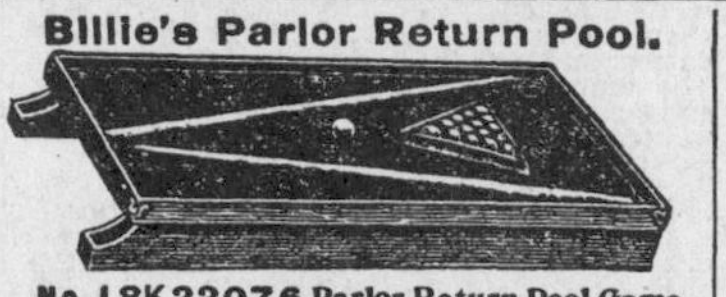

No. 18K22076 Parlor Return Pool Game. A complete miniature pool table; size, 13x23 inches, including triangle, 2 hardwood cues, set of 15 numbered balls, also white cueball. The table has brass finished corners to strengthen and beautify the table. The cushions and bed are covered with genuine green pool table cloth. The brass pockets are removable, so that when playing, the balls after being shot into the open pocket, find their way into an inclined slide from which they return to the player at the front of table. Tables are finished in natural colored cherry and oak. The balls are of a composition. Table can be set on any ordinary table and for real amusement, recreation and excitement has no equal. Shipping weight, 4½ pounds.
Price.......... **$1.10**

Parchesi.

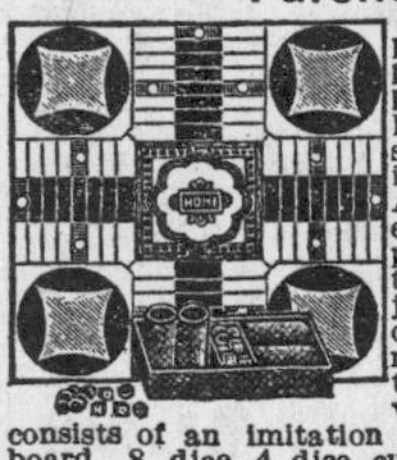

HOME

No. 18K22090 Parchesi, the popular home game and Backgammon game of India. This game as shown in illustration is very interesting. Anyone can very easily learn how to play it; at the same time considerable judgment and skill can be used so as to make each move to the best possible advantage. This game consists of an imitation leatherette covered board, 8 dice, 4 dice cups, various colored counters and all necessary directions. Regular $1.00 game. Shipping weight, 28 ounces. Our price.......... **65c**

WE SELL Highest Grade **DOLLS** only. See our wonderful low prices on pages 1148-1149.

Large Size Ouija, or Egyptian Luck Board.

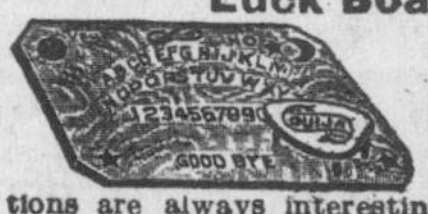

No. 18K22094 Without a doubt the most remarkable, interesting and mystifying production of the age. Its operations are always interesting and sometimes invaluable, answering, as it does, questions concerning the past, present and future. Full directions for operating the Ouija Board accompany each board. Packed, one each in a pasteboard box. Unmailable. Regular $1.00 size. Shipping weight, 3 pounds.
Price.......... **75c**

The Universal Spelling Board.

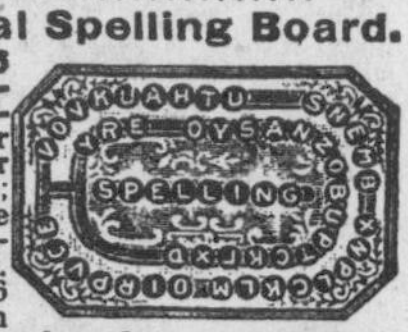

No. 18K22096 One of the most entertaining and educating articles for children ever put on the market; should have a place in every family having small children. The board has 56 lettered blocks which are made of hardwood and very strong and serviceable. They rotate freely in the grooves but cannot be taken out and lost or scattered around the floor. Size of board, 13½ inches long by 9½ inches wide. Shipping weight, 32 ounces. Price.......... **70c**

The Newest Game. Four-Handed Checkers.

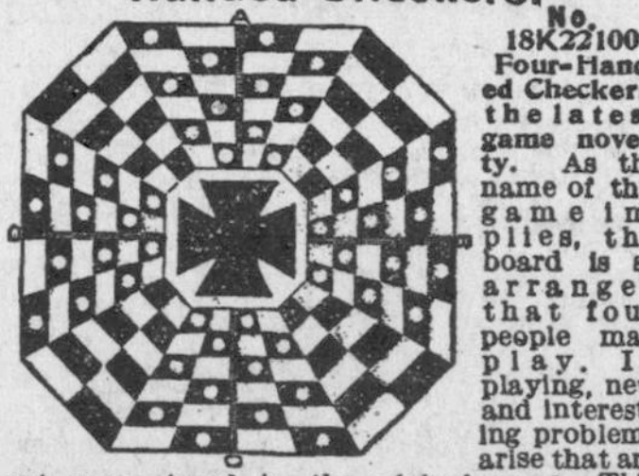

No. 18K22100 Four-Handed Checkers, the latest game novelty. As the name of this game implies, the board is so arranged that four people may play. In playing, new and interesting problems arise that are not encountered in the original game. This game will appeal to anyone, whether he has ever played checkers or not. The rules are very simple and anyone can easily understand them. For two people this game can be played with dummy partners. The board is 17 inches square. Shipping weight, 23 ounces. Regular selling price for this game, 50 cents. Our price.......... **38c**

Chess and Checker Boards.

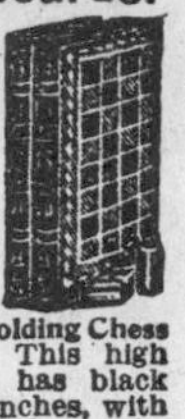

No. 18K22108 Folding Backgammon Board in book form. Squares, 1½ inches. Finished in durable embossed imitation leather. Fitted with dice cups (no dice) and complete set of checkers in separate box. Size of board, 15x15 inches. A high grade board, very durable. Shipping weight, 1½ lbs.
Price, per set.. **45c**

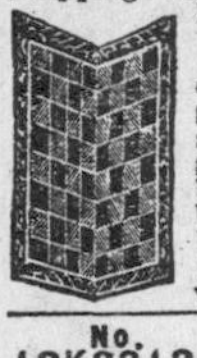

No. 18K22112 Folding Chess or Checker Board. This high grade checker board has black and red squares 1½ inches, with gold lines ⅛ inch wide. The border is 2 inches wide in red, black and gold; covered with fine black embossed paper. Size, 18x18 inches. Shipping weight, 1½ pounds. Price.. **20c**

Chessmen.

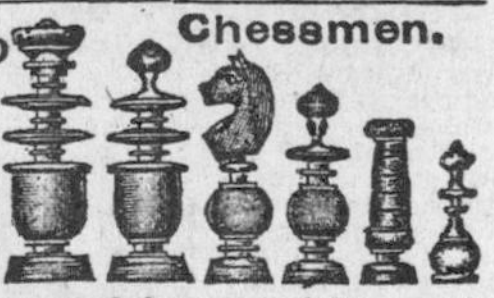

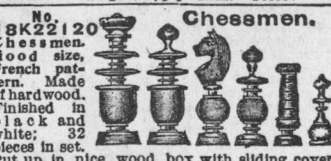

No. 18K22120 Chessmen. Good size, French pattern. Made of hardwood. Finished in black and white; 32 pieces in set. Put up in nice wood box with sliding cover. Shipping weight, 17 ounces.
Price, per set.......... **55c**

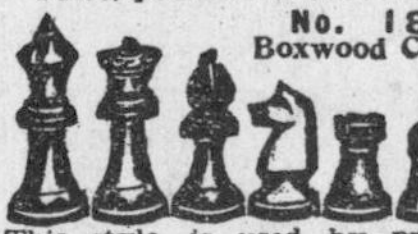

No. 18K22124 Fine Boxwood Chessmen, Staunton pattern. Black and white polished; in dovetailed white wood box with sliding cover. This style is used by professionals. Shipping weight, 14 ozs. Price, per set.. **88c**

Checkers.

No. 18K22136 The Yorkite Embossed Checkers. 1⅛ inches in diameter. A strong composition checker of a new and durable material; 30 to the set. Red and black.
Price, per set.......... **20c**
If by mail, postage extra, per set, 8 cents.

Dominoes.

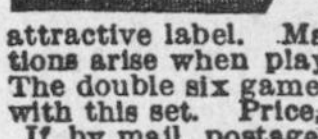

No. 18K22144 Express Dominoes. Double nines. Black adamant dominoes, 55 pieces to the set, with new pattern and attractive label. Many interesting complications arise when playing with a double nine. The double six game can also be played with this set. Price, per set.......... **25c**
If by mail, postage extra, per set, 13 cents.

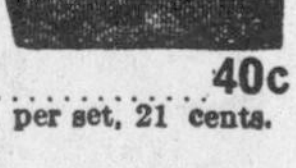

No. 18K22148 Nubian Dominoes. Double nines. 55 pieces. Beautiful arabesque black dominoes. Packed in wood frame box. A high grade set of dominoes.
Price, per set.......... **40c**
If by mail, postage extra, per set, 21 cents.

PLAYING CARDS.

No. 18K22200 Special Linen Finish Playing Cards. With round corners, double index, in large, plain figures, in a pretty back design. This same quality card is frequently sold at 25 cents per pack.
Price, 3 PACKS FOR 29c
If by mail, postage extra, for 3 packs, 12c.

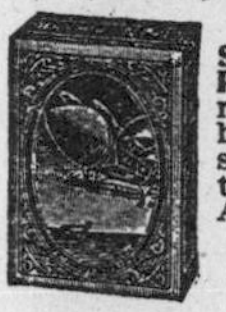

No. 18K22204 Airship Superior Enameled Waterproof Playing Cards. With high radium luster finish. This card has a perfect slip and will not swell. We guarantee it equal to any card on the market. Assorted backs.
Price, 2 PACKS FOR 25c
If by mail, postage extra, for 2 packs, 8 cents.

Special Value, "Strollers," 15c.

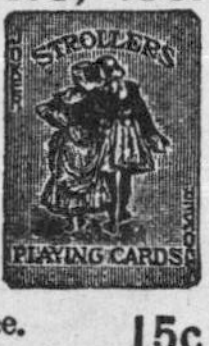
STROLLERS
PLAYING CARDS

No. 18K22209 Strollers' Playing Cards. This is an extra fine quality playing card, made of linen stock, very flexible and superior enameled finish; a card that will give as good a service as any 25-cent card now on the market. The card is put up in a substantial heavy cardboard telescope case; comes in a very good assortment of neat backs. Never before offered at this price.
Price, per pack 15c
If by mail, postage extra, per pack, 6 cents.

Bicycle Playing Cards.

No. 18K22205 Ivory, Enameled Finish Bicycle Playing Cards, all the popular designs. A card that is used by all professionals and universally sold for 25 cents.
Our price, per pack 19c
If by mail, postage extra, per pack, 5 cents.

Art Series Gold Edge Cards.

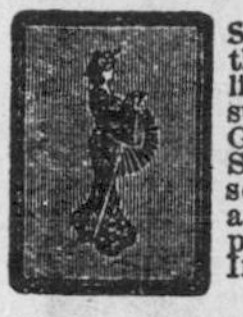

No. 18K22222 The Art Series Gold Edge Cards. Made of the highest grade waterproof linen stock with gold edges. The subjects, "Japanese," "Holland Girls," are very pretty designs. State design wanted. Made to sell at 50 cents. We offer them at the exceptionally low price, per pack 29c
If by mail, postage extra, per pack, 5 cents.

Congress Gold Edge Cards.

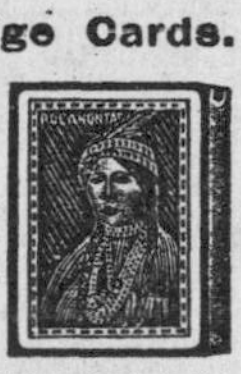
POCAHONTAS

No. 18K22224 Congress Gold Edge Playing Cards. A new and artistic series of backs in high, rich colors, designed especially for card parties, social and home play. Can furnish them in the following backs: Pocahontas, like illustration, Rookwood, Indian, Priscilla, The Old Mill, Rube, Rose, Autumn, etc. The highest grade quality linen. Put up in handsome telescope case. State design wanted. Price, per pack .. 39c
If by mail, postage extra, per pack, 5 cents.

Nile Gold Edge Fortune Telling Cards.

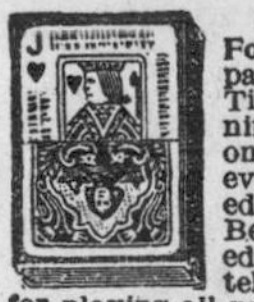

No. 18K22228 The Nile Fortune Telling Cards. A new pack of fortune telling cards. Tinted panel faces with the signification of each card printed on each face. Can be used by everyone. Sphinx backs, printed in high colors. Gold edges. Best linen stock, double enameled. Instructions for fortune telling in each pack. Complete for playing all regular card games.
Price, per pack 35c
If by mail, postage extra, per pack, 5 cents.

Choice of Two Popular 50-cent Card Games, each 19c.

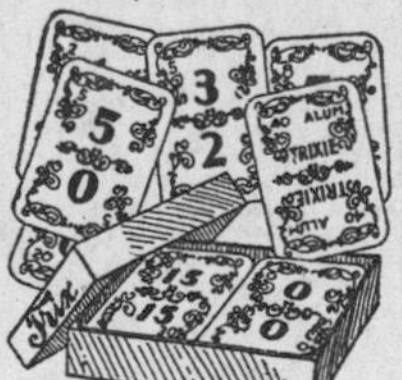

No. 18K22230 Trix. With this game ten entirely new games can be played in addition to any of the popular 50-cent games. Pack contains seventy-two enameled cards. Full book of instructions with each set for playing the various games. Regular price, 50 cents.
Our price.. 19c
If by mail, postage extra, 6 cents.

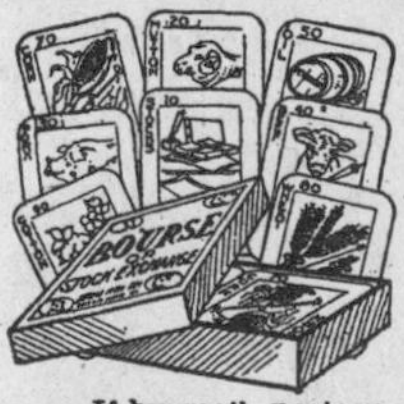
BOURSE

No. 18K22234 Bourse. So called from the French stock exchange. Pack consists of eighty high grade cards, depicting the various commodities, as cotton, beef, pork and mutton; a game that affords endless amusement to any number of players. Can be learned in a few seconds. Regular 50-cent game.
Our price... 19c
If by mail, postage extra, 7 cents.

THE SPLENDID REDUCTIONS IN PRICE made by us in this catalogue must prove to our customers our ability to undersell all competition.

Fan Craze, The Great Baseball Game.

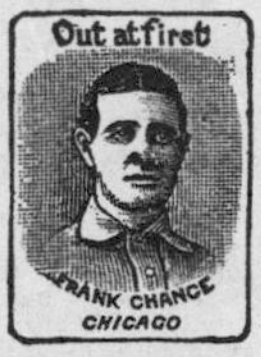
Out at first
FRANK CHANCE
CHICAGO

No. 18K22278 Fan Craze. The latest game of baseball. This game consists of 54 ivory enameled cards, a board for scoring and showing positions, a set of brass pegs, full directions and score cards. With this game, baseball is not only a summer but also a winter sport. The game is being played very extensively throughout the country. Anyone with a fair knowledge of the rules of baseball can learn to play the game in a few minutes. On each card is a halftone picture of a well known baseball player, in either the National or American League. When ordering this game, if you have any preference between the American and National Leagues, mention the one you desire. Our price on this game, per pack 39c
If by mail, postage extra, 9 cents.

Flinch, the Popular Card Game.

No. 18K22284 Flinch. More simple than authors, more scientific than whist. Something entirely new in card games. Each pack consists of 150 cards, finest quality of stock. The combinations resulting, while simple, are so intricate that the game has been pronounced by many to be more scientific than whist. Enjoyed by old and young alike. Regular price, 50 cents.
Our price, per pack 35c
If by mail, postage extra, per pack, 10 cents.

Leather Cases with Gilt Edge Cards.

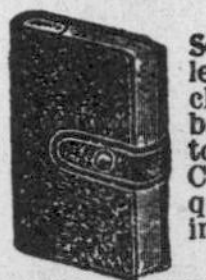

No. 18K22304 Playing Card Set. Book form. Fine seal grain leather, closes with fine gilt metal clasp. Interior is provided at the back with a gilt metal receptacle to securely hold a deck of cards. Contains pack of gilt edge best quality cards. Size, 2⅝x3⅞ inches. Price.......... 49c
If by mail, postage extra, 6c.

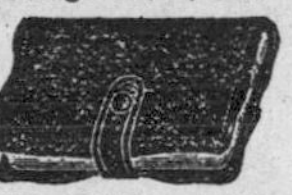

No. 18K22306 Card Case. Neat novelty in book form; in exact imitation of oxford style of binding. Made of fine black seal grain leather, leather lined. Closes with leather clasp and glove button catch. Beautiful genuine sterling silver ornament mounted on the side. Contains a high grade deck of gilt edge playing cards. Size, 3x4 inches.
Price 75c
If by mail, postage extra, 6 cents.

Poker Chips, Best Quality.

No. 18K22320 New Design Poker Chip. Known as the Eclipse. Made of composition with ivory finish. 1½ inches in diameter. A unique pattern. Come put up in boxes of 100, assorted, 50 white, 25 red and 25 blue. Shipping weight, per box, 31 ounces.
Price, PER BOX OF 100 .... 55c

Special Design Poker Chips.

STEER HEAD

No. 18K22332 Special design engraved poker chips. This is a very neat and elegant design. Made of the best quality composition; stack even and will not break easily. Size, 1½ inches in diameter. Assorted 100 in box as follows: 50 white, 25 blue and 25 red. Shipping weight, 30 ounces.
Price, PER BOX OF 100.......... 74c

Inlaid Unbreakable Poker Chips, best quality made.

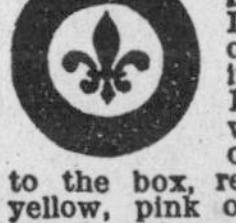

No. 18K22336 Fleur de Lis or Maltese Cross Design. Inlaid celluloid on highest grade of composition ivory. 1 9-16 inches in diameter and put up 100 to the box; assorted, 50 white, 25 red, 25 blue; or can be ordered in the solid colors, 100 to the box, red, white, blue, yellow, pink or brown. State assortment wanted. Absolutely perfect in every respect. Warranted to stack perfectly and used a great deal by professionals. Shipping weight, 30 ounces. State design you wish.

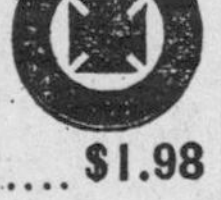

Price, PER BOX OF 100 .... $1.98

Dice.

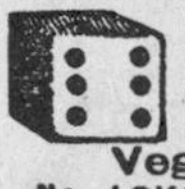

No. 18K22348 Bone Dice. Square corners. Large size.
Price, PER DOZEN 12c
If by mail, postage extra, per dozen, 4 cents.

Vegetable Ivory Dice.

No. 18K22364 This is the latest style in dice. Is made of the pure ivory nut; is absolutely perfect. Size, 11-16 inch.
Price, per set (five dice to set) 25c
If by mail, postage extra, per set, 2 cents.

Transparent Celluloid Dice.

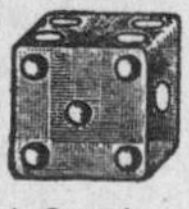

No. 18K22372 Made of pure transparent celluloid. Are as clear as glass. Colors, green, magenta or saffron. Absolutely perfect. State color wanted. Put up five in a box.
Price, per set (five dice to a set) 47c
If by mail, postage extra, per set, 2 cents.

Celluloid Poker Dice.

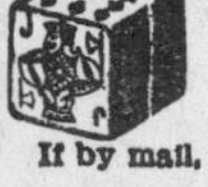

No. 18K22376 Representing Ace, King, Queen, Jack, Ten and Nine Spots. Fine ivory finished celluloid. Perfect goods. Size, ⅝ inch. Set of five dice.
Price, per set of five. 43c
If by mail, postage extra, per set, 2 cents.

Dice Cup and Dice.

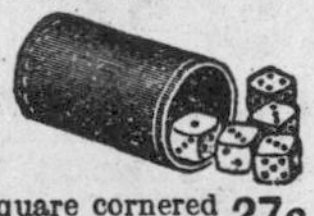

No. 18K22381 Double Sole Leather Dice Cup and Five Dice. Dice cup is two inches in diameter and 3¼ inches deep, made extra strong of double leather. We furnish with this cup five square cornered bone dice without extra charge. Price 27c
If by mail, postage extra, per set, 4 cents.

Complete Cribbage Set.

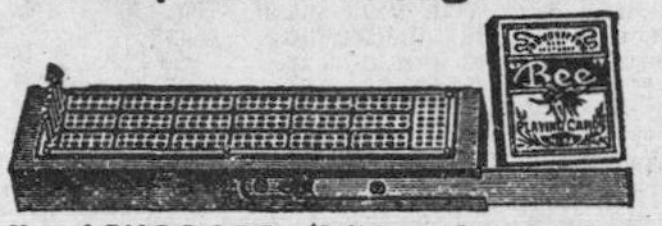
Bee
PLAYING CARDS

No. 18K22403 Cribbage Set, consisting of the well known Le Comte polished metal, nickel plated cribbage board; also a pack of best quality 25-cent playing cards. The board is made to score all card games, including cribbage, pinocle, etc. The bottom of the board is made of polished mahogany with two compartments, one for pack of cards and another containing six steel pegs; top is of best quality nickel plated steel. Size of board, 2¾ by 10½ inches. Shipping weight, 28 ounces.
Price for BOARD AND CARDS complete $1.15

Alphabet Blocks.

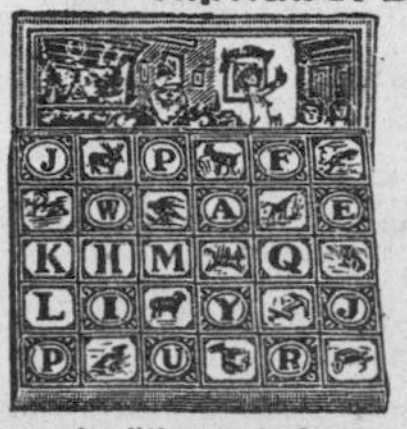

No. 18K22405 Extra Quality Embossed Alphabet Blocks. On two sides of each block are fancy embossed letters from the alphabet, the other sides are decorated with pictures of animals in high colors. Each block is 1¾ inches in diameter; thirty blocks in all, put up in very handsomely lithographed pasteboard box. Shipping weight, 3¼ pounds. Price.. 47c

No. 18K22407 Embossed Alphabet Building Blocks. This set consists of sixteen blocks, each 1¾ inches in diameter. Decorated and embossed similiar to above. This set comes in a very attractively lithographed cardboard box. Shipping weight, 1¾ pounds.
Price 23c

Seroco Savings Bank.

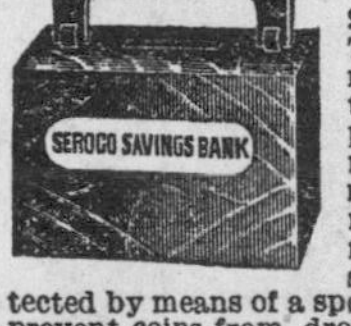
SEROCO SAVINGS BANK

No. 18K22412 Seroco Savings Bank. This bank is the most popular design that has ever been placed on the market; made of the best cold rolled steel with the most perfect oxidized finish, durably constructed and is protected by means of a special patented device to prevent coins from dropping out. Key with each bank. This bank is one which usually sells at $1.00. Size, 4⅜x3¼x2⅜. Shipping weight, 1¼ pounds. Our price.... 65c

Canary Bird Whistle.

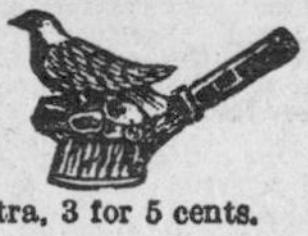

No. 18K22416 The Canary Bird Whistle. Made of metal. All the pretty notes of the canary can be imitated. Lots of fun for boys and girls. Price, 3 FOR 10c
If by mail, postage extra, 3 for 5 cents.

Funny Folks.

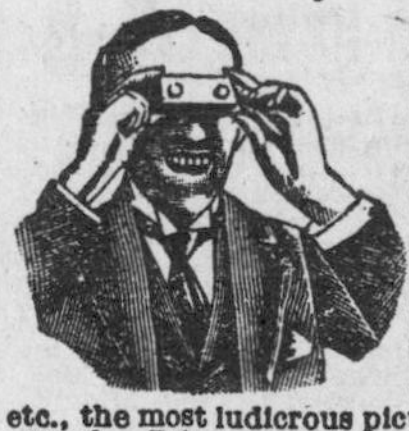

No. 18K22420 A whole passing show. Furnishes more amusement than you would get in a circus. Your friends grotesquely photographed. Stout people look thin and thin people look stout. By getting a focus on passing pedestrians, horses, cars, etc., the most ludicrous pictures are witnessed. Price 10c
If by mail, postage extra, 3 cents.

The Kinematograph.

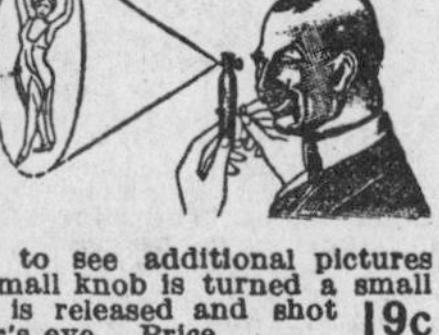

No. 18K22418 The smallest Kinematograph in the world. A positive sensation. By looking through the small eye piece a perfect picture may be seen. Ask your friends to keep turning to see additional pictures and as soon as small knob is turned a small spray of water is released and shot into the operator's eye. Price.......... 19c
If by mail, postage extra, 2 cents.

OUR POSITION AS THE GREATEST MERCHANDISING INSTITUTION IN THE WORLD is emphasized by the wonderful REDUCTION IN PRICES which we have been able to make on thousands of articles quoted in this catalogue.

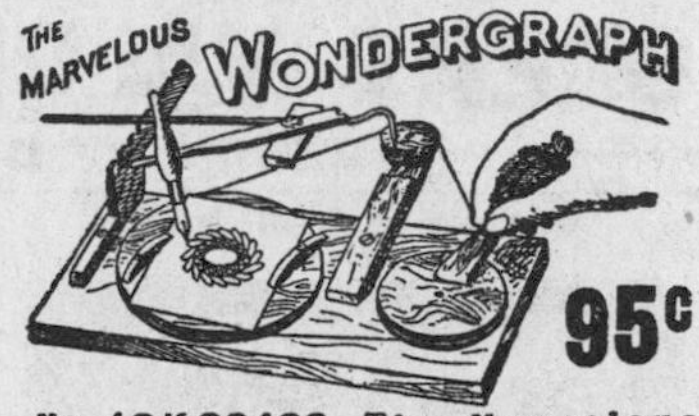
THE MARVELOUS WONDERGRAPH

95c

No. 18K22422 The Marvelous "Wondergraph," a startling invention. A fascinating toy. The Wondergraph makes, as if by magic, beautiful designs, such as no artist could draw. A child can operate it. All that is necessary is to turn the handle and the Wondergraph does the rest. This not only will teach the youngest child how to design very beautiful patterns, but will suggest to a draftsman patterns which he had never thought of before. No two designs will be alike unless desired so by the operator. The illustration will give you an idea of how this Wondergraph machine operates. Shipping weight, 1½ pounds. Price...... 95c

Young Folks' Scroll Saw Outfit.

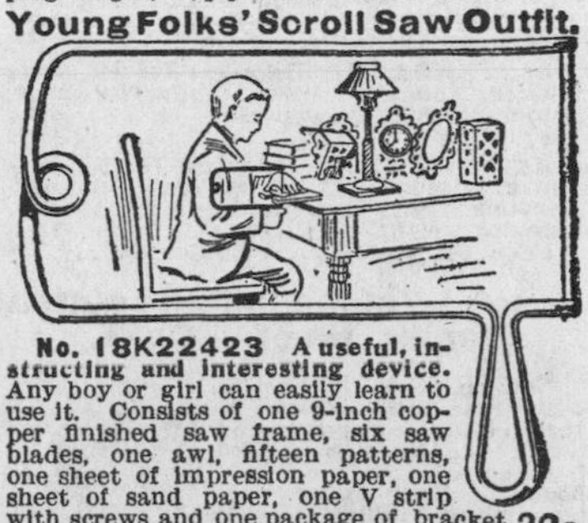

No. 18K22423 A useful, instructing and interesting device. Any boy or girl can easily learn to use it. Consists of one 9-inch copper finished saw frame, six saw blades, one awl, fifteen patterns, one sheet of impression paper, one sheet of sand paper, one V strip with screws and one package of bracket tacks. A regular 50-cent outfit. Our price 32c
If by mail, postage extra, 8 cents.
We furnish saw blades at 10 cents per dozen.

China Tea Sets.

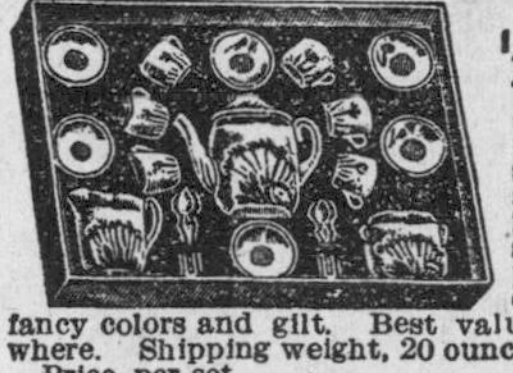

No. 18K22424 Toy China Tea Set, consisting of 22 pieces; cups, saucers, sugar and creamer, including six spoons. All prettily hand decorated in fancy colors and gilt. Best value sold anywhere. Shipping weight, 20 ounces.
Price, per set 23c

No. 18K22428 China Tea Set. Beautifully decorated in hand painting and gilt. Consists of 18 pieces, including cups, saucers, cake dish, tea, sugar and creamer. A nice set, similar to above, but much larger. No such value sold elsewhere. Shipping weight, 41 ounces. Price, per set 47c

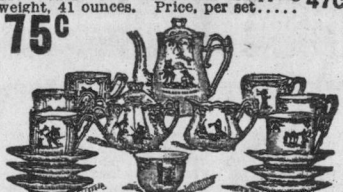

75c

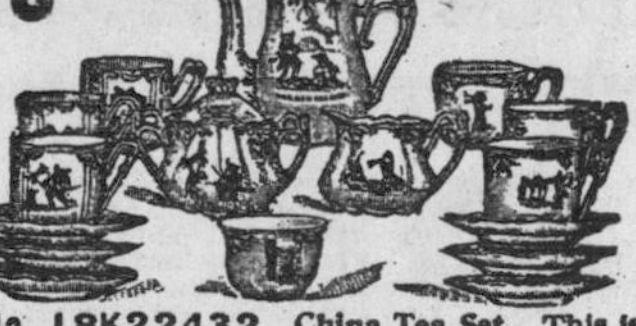

No. 18K22432 China Tea Set. This is a particularly desirable set, made of fine, thin white china with embossed design. Extra large pieces, that can be used practically for an after dinner set. Consists of six cups and saucers, one tea, one sugar, one creamer and bowl. Put up in a nice individual box. No decorations. Extra $1.00 value. Shipping weight, 6 pounds. Our price, per set 75c

No. 18K22436 China Tea Set. This is an elegant, large set, consisting of six cups and saucers, one tea, one sugar, one creamer and bowl. Made of very fine, thin white china, beautifully decorated in enameled picture designs taken from fairy tales. With gold traced edges and handles relieved with floral decorations on the larger pieces. This is a very large size, for practical use, and will be very highly appreciated by the children. Regular $1.50 value. Shipping weight, 6 pounds. Our price, per set $1.00

Decorated Tin Tea Sets.

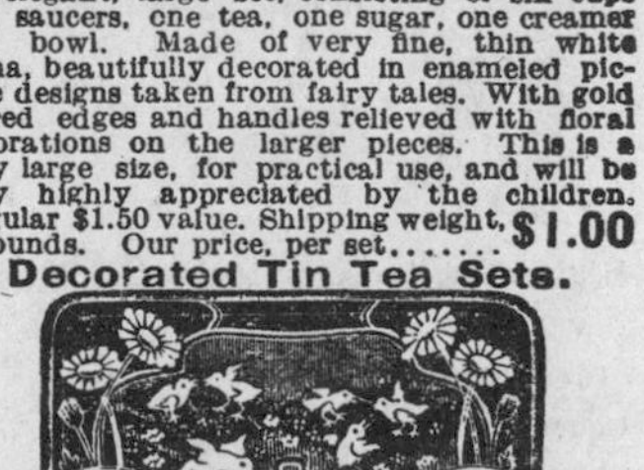

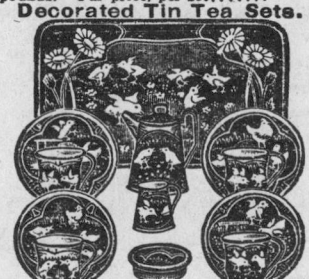

No. 18K22438 Decorated Unbreakable Tea Set, consisting of 13 pieces, four cups and saucers, cream pitcher, teapot with cover and sauce pan. All highly decorated on heavy metal; pictures being of landscapes, country scenes, etc. This is something new and attractive and pleasing to the children, put up in heavy cardboard box. Shipping weight, 2 pounds. Price, per set...... 47c

GREAT VALUES IN DOLLS, ALL STYLES AND SIZES

WE IMPORT DIRECT FROM GERMANY AND SELL YOU AT WHOLESALE PRICES

Britannia Tea Sets.

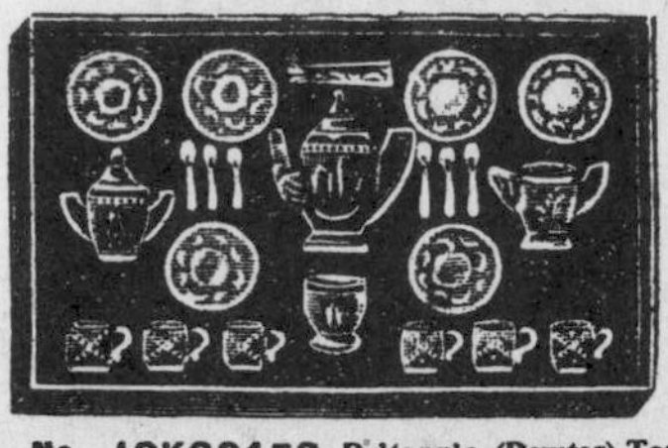

No. 18K22452 Britannia (Pewter) Tea Set. Highly silver finished, with very handsome filigree design. Large cups, saucers and other pieces. Set consists of about 23 pieces. Regular $1.25 size. Shipping weight, 40 ounces. Our price, per set........ **86c**

No. 18K22448 Britannia Tea Set, silver finished, about 24 pieces, similar to above. Shipping weight, 28 ounces. Price, per set.................. **47c**

No. 18K22444 Britannia Tea Set, consisting of about 23 pieces, silver finished, assortment same as above, but a smaller size. Shipping weight, 17 ounces. Price, per set.................. **20c**

Special Values in Full Jointed Papier Mache Dolls.

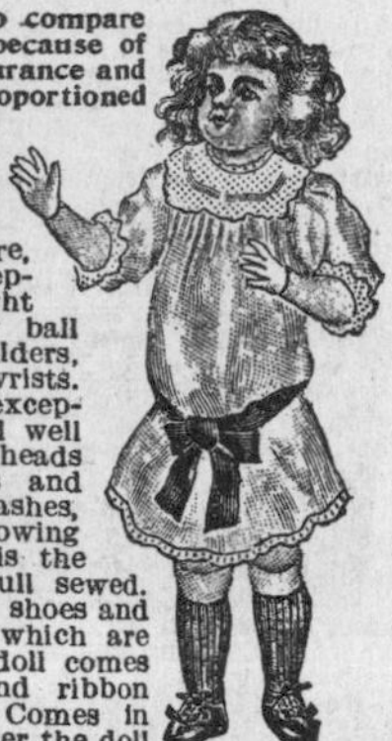

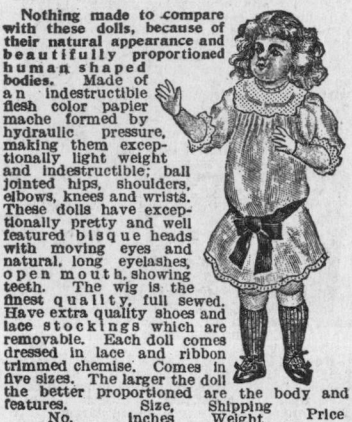

Nothing made to compare with these dolls, because of their natural appearance and beautifully proportioned human shaped bodies. Made of an indestructible flesh color papier mache formed by hydraulic pressure, making them exceptionally light weight and indestructible; ball jointed hips, shoulders, elbows, knees and wrists. These dolls have exceptionally pretty and well featured bisque heads with moving eyes and natural, long eyelashes, open mouth, showing teeth. The wig is the finest quality, full sewed. Have extra quality shoes and lace stockings which are removable. Each doll comes dressed in lace and ribbon trimmed chemise. Comes in five sizes. The larger the doll the better proportioned are the body and features.

No.	Size, inches	Shipping Weight	Price
18K23000	19	3 pounds	$1.19
18K23004	22	4 pounds	1.67
18K23012	24	7 pounds	2.88
18K23016	28	9 pounds	3.99
18K23020	30	18 pounds	4.89

Extra Large Size Kid Body Dolls.

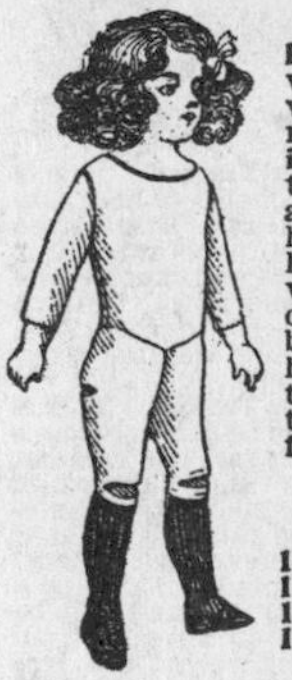

Large Sized Dolls at very low prices. The dolls are very well made and have very pretty faces. They are made of good quality genuine kid and not a poor imitation, of which most dolls at these prices are made, have fine quality bisque heads with moving eyes and very fine mohair wigs, those on the three larger sizes being full sewed and long haired. The larger the doll the better proportioned is the body and the head. We furnish this doll in four sizes.

No.	Size, in	Shipping Weight	Price
18K23024	13	1 lb.	$0.25
18K23028	16	1½ lbs.	.50
18K23032	18½	2½ lbs.	.75
18K23036	21½	3½ lbs.	1.00

High Grade Jointed Kid Body Dolls.

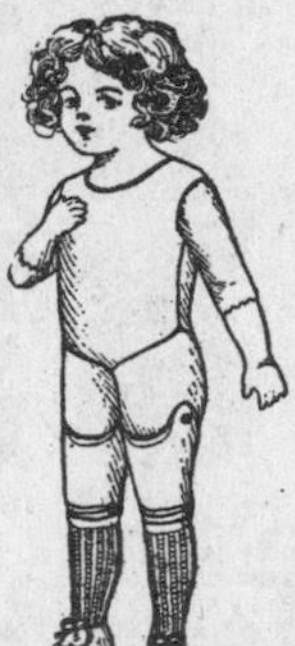

These Dolls are made with riveted joints, fine bisque heads with moving eyes, very pretty faces, full sewed wigs with new style parting tied with ribbon. The dolls have very large, fat bodies made of the best quality kid; beautifully proportioned heads; riveted joints at hips and knees that enable this doll to assume any position. The larger the size of the doll the better featured is the face and the better proportioned is the body. We furnish this doll in four different sizes.

No.	Size, in.	Shipping W't, lbs.	Price
18K23040	15	2	$0.59
18K23044	17	2½	.87
18K23048	21½	3	1.29
18K23056	25	5	1.78

Our Special Value, Half Cork Stuffed Kid Body Dolls, Full Jointed.

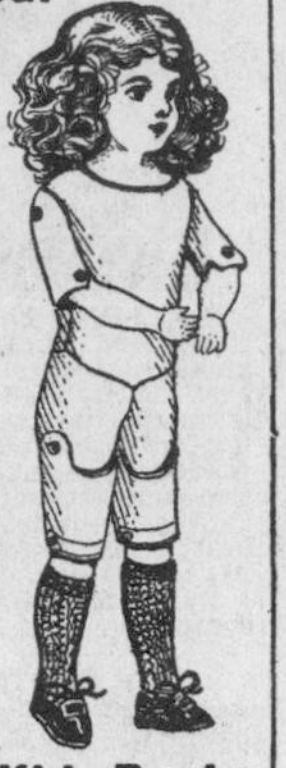

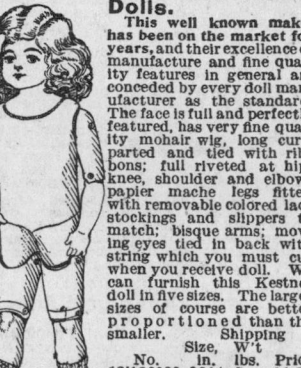

These dolls have very fine extra large bisque heads with moving eyes and full sewed wig with long curls and new style hair dressing, parted on the side and tied with bows of ribbon. The body is of the finest quality white kid, half cork stuffed, making it light weight and very shapely; full riveted hips, arms, elbows and knee joints, allowing the doll to assume any position, removable shoes and lace stockings. The larger the doll the better proportioned are the body and the features of the face. We can furnish this doll in four different sizes, all exceptional values at our very low prices.

No.	Size, in.	Shipping W't, lbs.	Price
18K23064	17½	2½	$1.29
18K23068	21	3½	1.88
18K23072	23	5	2.37
18K23076	27	7	2.99

Genuine Kestner Kid Body Dolls.

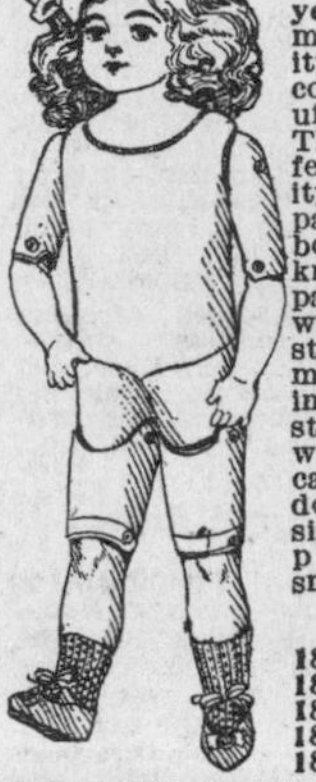

This well known make has been on the market for years, and their excellence of manufacture and fine quality features in general are conceded by every doll manufacturer as the standard. The face is full and perfectly featured, has very fine quality mohair wig, long curls parted and tied with ribbons; full riveted at hip, knee, shoulder and elbow; papier mache legs fitted with removable colored lace stockings and slippers to match; bisque arms; moving eyes tied in back with string which you must cut when you receive doll. We can furnish this Kestner doll in five sizes. The larger sizes of course are better proportioned than the smaller.

No.	Size, in.	W't lbs.	Price
18K23080	18½	3	$1.75
18K23084	20½	5	2.37
18K23088	23½	7	3.45
18K23092	25½	8	4.15
18K23096	28	11	4.98

Metal Head Unbreakable Dolls Are Best For Wear.

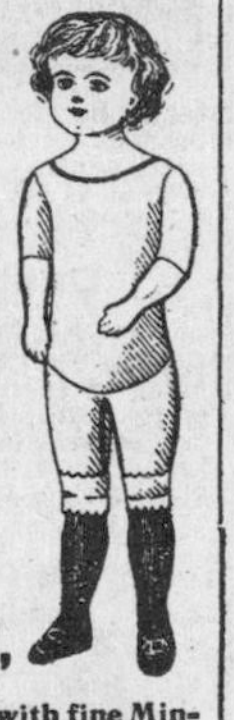

New Unbreakable Dolls, silesia bodies with the fine genuine Minerva metal heads, painted eyes and hair. Body is of the best quality silesia, hair stuffed, with movable knee joints. This doll is absolutely unbreakable and harmless, the most serviceable doll ever produced. We furnish this doll in four different sizes. The larger the doll the better are the proportions.

No.	Size, in.	Shipping Weight	Price
18K23100	11½	¾ lb.	25c
18K23104	14½	1 lb.	44c
18K23108	16	1½ lbs.	59c
18K23112	18	1½ lbs.	67c

Unbreakable Dolls, Metal Heads, With Wigs.

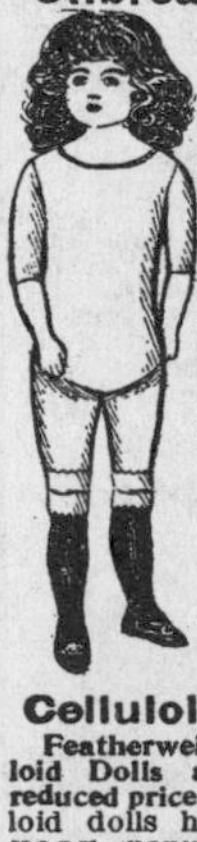

Silesia Body Dolls with fine Minerva metal head with curly hair and glass eyes. These dolls have been recently placed on the market and have at once been a decided success. Every mother is probably familiar with the Minerva metal head and combining this feature with a fine hair stuffed silesia body makes an unbreakable doll and at the same time a very pretty doll. These dolls, with the Minerva heads, flowing curls and glass eyes, with silesia body, we furnish in the following sizes:

No.	Size, in.	Shipping Weight	Price
18K23120	14¾	1 lb	$0.50
18K23124	17	2 lbs.	.75
18K23128	20	3 lbs.	1.00

NOTE—We claim for this doll special value which cannot be equaled elsewhere.

Celluloid Dolls.

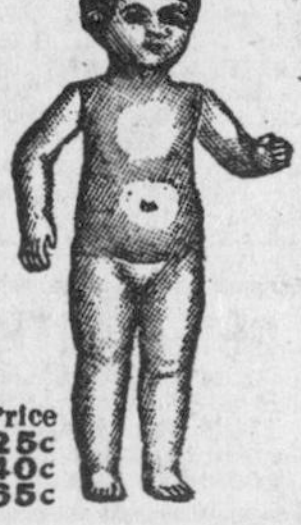

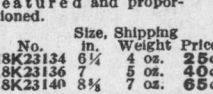

Featherweight Celluloid Dolls at greatly reduced prices. The celluloid dolls have become very popular and are very prettily proportioned and handsome. These celluloid dolls have arm joints so that they can be placed in different positions. We furnish them in three sizes, the larger the size the better featured and proportioned.

No.	Size, in.	Shipping Weight	Price
18K23134	6¼	4 oz.	25c
18K23136	7	5 oz.	40c
18K23140	8¾	7 oz.	65c

Indestructible Rag Dolls, Exceptional Values.

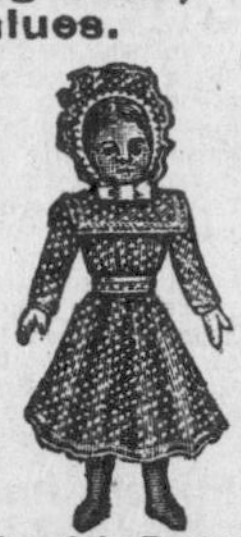

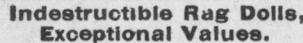

No. 18K23148 Indestructible Rag Doll, well shaped and proportioned. Has nicely made gingham dress in bright, attractive colors and bonnet to match. The face is photographed from life onto cloth, a tremendous improvement over the old style painted faces. Size, 15 inches high. Shipping weight, 13 oz. Price, **25c**

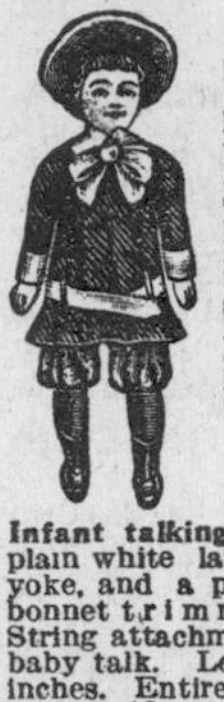

No. 18K23160 Buster Brown Indestructible Rag Doll. A very fine imitation of the Buster Brown you read about. The doll is dressed in a red suit with white collar, cuffs and belt, has Buster Brown cap of red and white, and a large black Windsor tie. This doll will be a delight to the children on account of the popularity of Buster Brown. Length, 15 inches. Price.......... **25c**

If by mail, postage extra 12c.

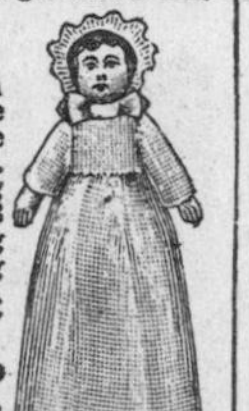

No. 18K23164 Infant talking Doll, dressed in plain white lawn slip with lace yoke, and a pretty little poke bonnet trimmed in ruching. String attachment for producing baby talk. Length of body, 13 inches. Entire length, including dress, 18 inches. Shipping weight, 10 ounces. Price.................... **25c**

Unbreakable Leather Doll, 47 Cents.

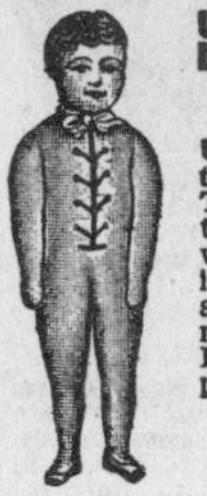

No. 18K23212 Unbreakable Leather Doll of finest workmanship. This is a baby's friend. The leather is very fine and soft. Stuffed with cotton and will always retain its shape. This doll will last baby and also baby's brother. Coloring matter warranted not to come off. Length, 12½ inches. Shipping weight, 15 ounces. Price, **47c**

Wonderful Values in Dressed Dolls.

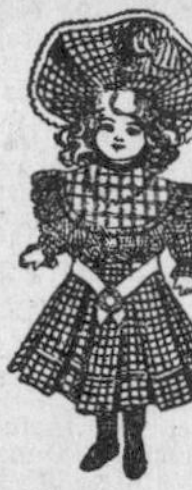

No. 18K23218 Dressed Doll with Jointed Arms and Hips. Has very pretty gingham dress trimmed with lace, also hat to match; removable shoes and stockings. Height of doll, 11½ inches; with hat, 14 inches. Shipping weight, 1 pound. Price.. **25c**

Sailor Doll.

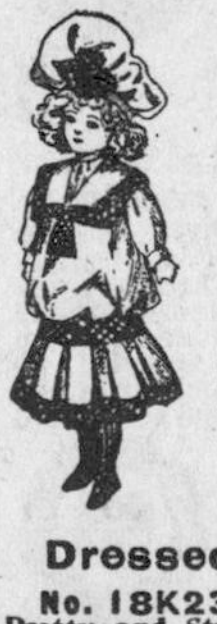

No. 18K23222 Very Pretty Sailor Doll, dressed in pretty cashmere dress with revers collar. Skirt and sailor collar very prettily trimmed with plaid. Has sailor cap to match dress; removable shoes and stockings, bisque head with natural wig; moving eyes and open mouth, showing teeth. This doll at 45c is a regular 75c value. Height of doll, 14½ inches; entire height with cap, 17 inches. Shipping weight, 1½ lbs. Our price **45c**

Dressed Dolls.

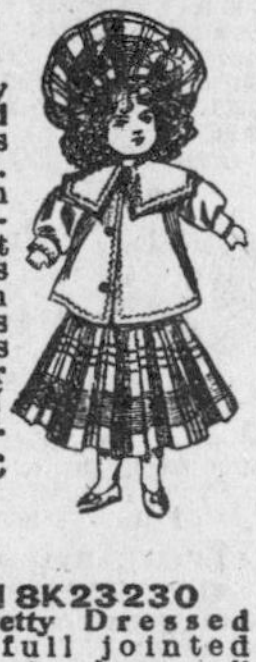

No. 18K23226 A Very Pretty and Stylishly Dressed Doll with moving eyes, has jointed arms and hips. Dressed in gingham with lace trimmed skirt and revers collar, has pretty hat to match dress. The head is of best quality bisque with pretty features, sleeping eyes and natural wig. This doll is an exceptional value at our price. Height of doll, 14½ inches; with hat, 17½ inches. Shipping weight, 2 lbs. Price **57c**

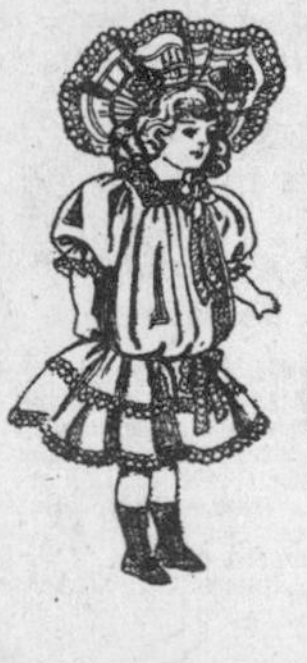

No. 18K23230 Very Pretty Dressed Doll, full jointed throughout, has well featured bisque head with moving eyes and open mouth, showing teeth, and natural wig. Dress is made of white net over colored crepe. Dress as well as underclothes are lace trimmed. Height of doll, including hat, 18½ inches. Shipping weight, 3 pounds. Price. **75c**

Dressed Dolls.

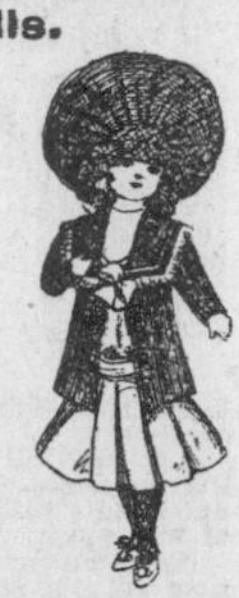

No. 18K23234 Stylishly Dressed Doll, has dress of good quality in blouse design, lined throughout, over which is stylish removable jacket with revers collar and medallion and lace trimmed; hat of material to match dress, with drop veil. Doll is full jointed throughout; has removable shoes and stockings. Good quality bisque head with parted wig; moving eyes and open mouth, showing teeth. Entire height of doll, including hat, 20 inches. Shipping weight, 3 pounds. Price.............. **$1.00**

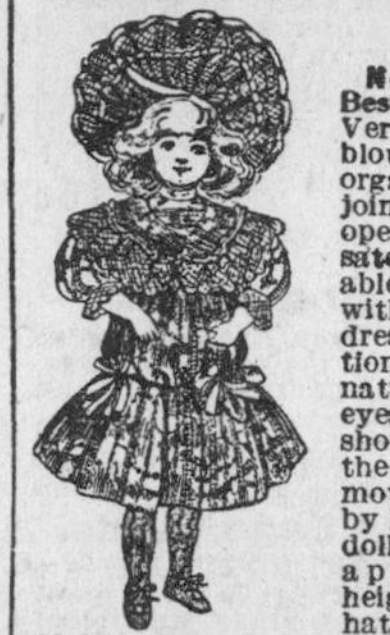

No. 18K23238 Our Best Quality Dressed Doll. Very stylishly dressed in blouse design, flowered organdy dress. Full jointed throughout, has openwork stockings and sateen shoes, both removable. Lace hat trimmed with ribbon to match dress. Very well proportioned head with long natural hair, moving eyes and open mouth, showing teeth. All of the clothes can be removed, being fastened by hooks and eyes. This doll must be seen to be appreciated. Entire height of doll, including hat, 23 inches. Regular $3.00 value. Shipping weight, 5 lbs. Our price.......... **$1.50**

Knockabout Dolls Absolutely Unbreakable.

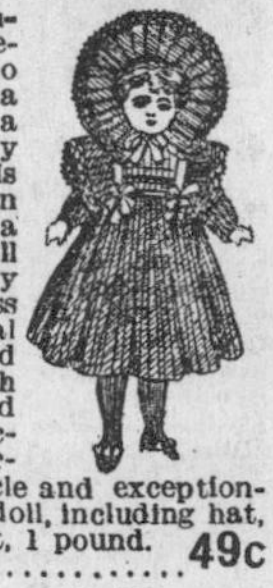

No. 18K23242 Unbreakable Dressed Doll. Something for the young child who appreciates the beauty of a pretty doll and will break a doll that is not absolutely indestructible. This doll is made with a silesia, cotton stuffed body, fitted with a genuine Minerva metal doll head, making it an absolutely indestructible doll. The dress is of good quality material with lace trimmed yoke and collar; also has hat to match and removable shoes and stockings. This doll, on account of its being indestructible is a very desirable article and exceptionally low priced. Height of doll, including hat, 15 inches. Shipping weight, 1 pound. Price.......................... **49c**

Papa and Mama Dolls.

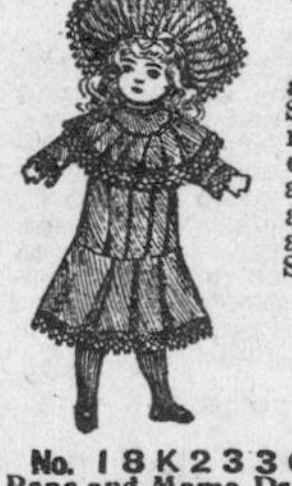

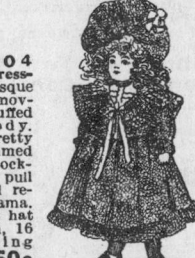

No. 18K23300 Papa and Mama Dressed Doll. Stuffed body, bisque head, moving eyes. Neatly dressed in a pretty gown, shoes and stockings. By pulling a cord, doll repeats papa and mama. Size, 14 inches. Shipping weight, 1 lb. Price.............. **30c**

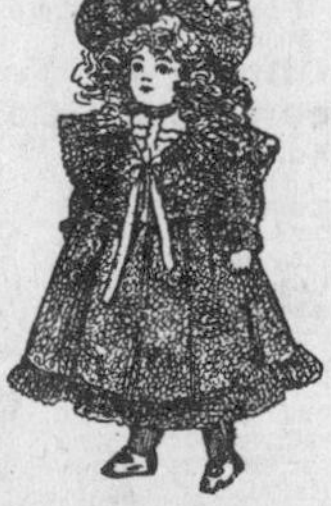

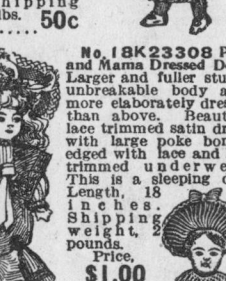

No. 18K23304 Papa and Mama Dressed Dolls. With bisque head, curly hair, moving eyes, and stuffed unbreakable body. Dressed in very pretty fancy sateen trimmed gown, shoes and stockings. When you pull the cord, the doll repeats papa and mama. Fancy sateen dress hat to match. Length, 16 inches. Shipping weight, 1¾ lbs. Price.......... **50c**

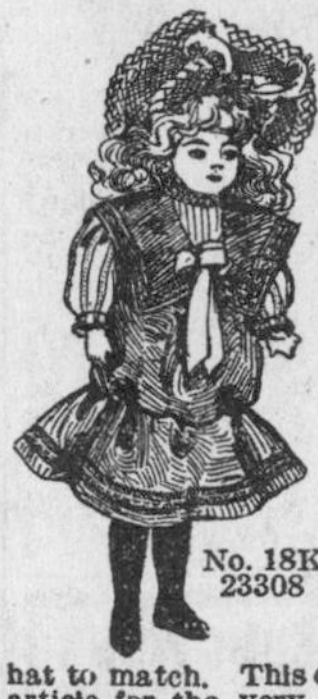

No. 18K 23308

No. 18K23308 Papa and Mama Dressed Dolls. Larger and fuller stuffed unbreakable body and more elaborately dressed than above. Beautiful lace trimmed satin dress, with large poke bonnet edged with lace and lace trimmed underwear. This is a sleeping doll. Length, 18 inches. Shipping weight, 2 pounds. Price, **$1.00**

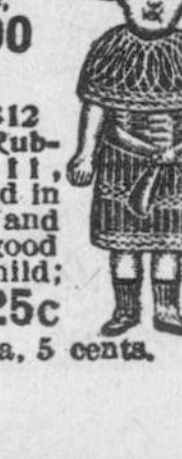

No. 18K23312 White Rubber Doll, dressed in knit suit and hat to match. This doll is a good article for the very young child; 8 inches in height. Price.................. **25c**

If by mail, postage extra, 5 cents.

French Stag Brush and Comb Set, $1.50.

No. 18K25040 Toilet Set, grosgrain lined, containing genuine French unbreakable stag hair brush of eleven rows best quality white bristles, and 7-inch comb to match, both with heavy sterling silver trimmings, in leatherette case. Shipping weight, 18 ounces. Price, per set **$1.50**

New Design Genuine French Stag Comb, Brush and Toilet Set, $2.85.

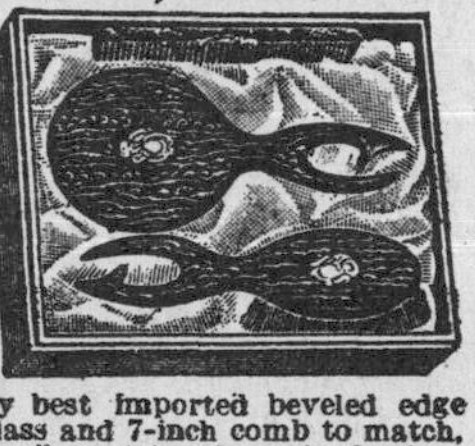

No. 18K25044 Toilet Set, containing genuine French unbreakable stag hair brush of eleven rows best quality white bristles, genuine French stag mirror, with 4½-inch selected quality best imported beveled edge French plate glass and 7-inch comb to match, all with sterling silver trimmings, in leatherette case all grosgrain lined. Shipping weight, 42 ounces. Price, per set **$2.85**

Complete French Stag 7-Piece Toilet and Manicure Set, $4.48.

No. 18K25048 Combination Toilet Set, grosgrain lined, containing genuine French unbreakable stag hair brush of eleven rows best quality white bristles; genuine French stag mirror, with 4½-inch selected quality best imported French plate glass, 7-inch comb, nail polisher, nail file, salve box, cuticle knife; all steel of finest quality hard tempered and carefully ground, with French stag handles, sterling silver mounted in leatherette case. Shipping weight, 3¾ pounds. Price, per set **$4.48**

Genuine French Stag Manicure Sets.

No. 18K25052 Manicure Set. Containing nail polisher, salve box, nail file and manicure scissors, with genuine French stag handles, in leatherette case, neatly lined. weight, 1½ pounds. Price, for four-piece set **$1.18**

No. 18K25054 Manicure Set. Containing nail polisher, two salve boxes, manicure scissors, nail file, and shoe horn, with genuine French stag handles, in leatherette case, handsomely lined. Weight, 29 ounces. Price, per set **$1.65**

French Stag Military Brush Sets. Special Values.

No. 18K25056 Military Set. Containing pair of French stag military brushes of eleven rows best quality white bristles, with heavy sterling silver trimmings, in a lined leatherette case. Weight, 1½ pounds. Price, per set **$2.50**

No. 18K25058 Military Set. Containing pair of genuine French stag military eleven-row brushes, both with best quality white bristles, and stag brush with seven rows best quality white bristles, with heavy sterling silver trimmings, in good quality lined leatherette case. Weight, 2 pounds. Price, per set **$3.50**

Art Silvered Comb and Brush Set, $1.39.

No. 18K25062 Art Silvered Comb and Brush Set, consisting of good thirteen-row hair brush with art silvered back, in fancy rose raised design and a tortoise shell dressing comb with silver plated metal back to match brush. This set is exceptional value at our price, nothing of this kind having ever been sold at this figure. The set is put up in heavy lined fancy box. Price, per set. If by mail, postage extra, 11 cents. **$1.39**

Sterline 5-Piece Manicure Outfit, $2.10.

No. 18K25075 Excellent quality Sterline Manicure Set, consisting of a chamois buffer with sterline silver back, excellent quality manicure scissors with fancy handle, good quality cuticle knife, nail file and glass salve jar with sterline top. This set is put up in lined case with hinged telescope cover, leatherette covering. Shipping weight, 1½ pounds. Price, per set **$2.10**

Celluloid Toilet Cases. Exceptional Values.

No. 18K25130 Toilet Case of very pretty design; desk shape, extension base, lined throughout, with a large mirror in cover. Contains composition back brush and a 6-inch white celluloid comb to match; has brass catch and hinges. Size, 8¼x4½x2½ inches. Shipping weight, 1½ pounds. Price, per set **69c**

Fancy Shape, Exceptional Value at $1.35.

No. 18K25136 Fancy Shape Toilet Case. Extension base with full celluloid top under which is very pretty highly colored floral design, has floral design sides, lined throughout with good quality sateen, contains fancy shape composition back hair brush embossed with chrysanthemum design, bevel edge mirror to match and a 6-inch white celluloid comb. Size, 10¼x6x3¼ inches. Shipping weight, 2 pounds. Price, per set **$1.35**

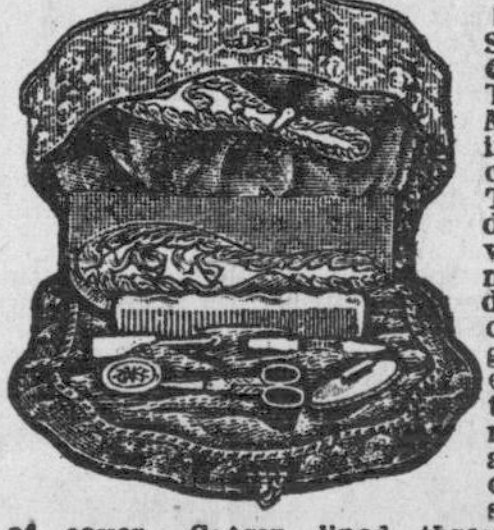

No. 18K25143 Special Value Combination Toilet and Manicure Set in plush and celluloid case. Top of case is decorated with very pretty miniature under transparent celluloid, with gilt embossed edges; has extension base of mottled plush and floral decorations on side and inside of cover. Sateen lined throughout; brass catch and hinges, composition back brush highly decorated in colors with bevel edge mirror to match, salve jar, bone nail file, bone handled buttonhook and chamois buffer, also a 5¾-inch celluloid comb. Size, 11x9x3 inches. Shipping weight, 2½ pounds. This case is a regular $3.50 value. Price, per set **$2.19**

An Exceptionally Attractive Case, $3.79.

$3.79

No. 18K25156 This Case is exceptionally attractive. It is a number that not only contains good, useful articles but is very pretty and an exceptional value at our very low price of $3.79. This combination upright toilet case and manicure outfit has a very artistic shape, covered with fancy combination celluloid and figured plush; two pretty pictures on swinging doors in gilt frame; has a very beautifully decorated top; extension base covered with celluloid. This case is fitted with good quality highly decorated brush with bevel edge mirror to match, also a good quality white celluloid comb, with bone handled file, buttonhook, manicure scissors and chamois buffer. On inside of doors are two bevel edge mirrors in gilt frames. Satin lined throughout. Size, 10½x9½x6½ inches. Shipping weight, 5 pounds. Price, per set **$3.79**

Military Brush Set, $1.50.

No. 18K25167 Military Brush and Case Set. The case is an oval shape, made of fine, black, seal grained leather. Neatly creased and finished. Front flap closes with glove button catch, leather lined throughout. The case is fitted with a pair of genuine ebony nine-row bristle military brushes, with sterling silver mounts on each brush. Size of case, closed, 3½x3¾x5¾ inches. Shipping weight, 13 ounces. Price, per set **$1.50**

Roll Up Traveling and Dresser Sets, $2.19.

No. 18K25169 Exceptional Value Roll Up Case, containing the best quality nine-row ebonoid military brush with soap box, nail brush and tooth brush, also 7-inch barber comb, all sterling silver mounted; put up in good quality seal grain leather case with moire lining, which, when open, measures 15x8 inches and which, rolled up, measures but 8x5x2 inches. A very useful article for tourists or for the dresser. Shipping weight, 1 pound. Price, per set **$2.19**

Shaving Sets, Exceptional Values.

No. 18K25198 Shaving Set, consisting of china mug decorated with hand painted dog head in high colors, with good quality rabbit hair shaving brush to match. This set is put up in leatherette covered case which is sateen lined and has hinged cover. The set is an exceptional value at our price. Size, 4½x6½x6½ inches. Shipping weight, 1¾ lbs. Price, per set **63c**

Seal Grain Shaving Set, 98c.

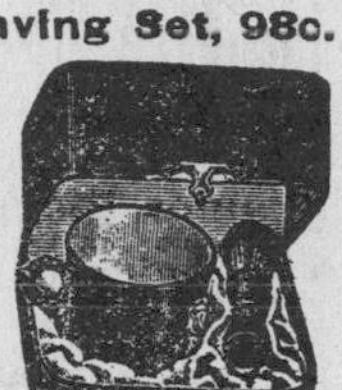

No. 18K25200 Shaving Case, made of seal grain leather, moire lined, containing shaving mug and brush. The mug is black, with white porcelain lining, and has an oxidized silver mounting. The brush has ebonoid handle and rabbit hair tip. Size, 6x6x3¾ inches. Shipping weight, 25 ounces. Price, per set **98c**

$4.00 Value Shaving Set, $2.50.

No. 18K25208 Shaving Case, black seal grain leather, with round edges, white lining fitted with quadruple plate silver shaving mug and good, unexcelled hollow ground razor with black handle, which alone would be worth $1.50, and fine lather brush. Size, 7x5½x4½ inches. Shipping weight, 26 ounces. Price, per set **$2.50**

No. 18K25223 Exceptional Value Fancy Sewing Box. Gilt finish with full celluloid top over very pretty pictures; brass corners; lined with very good quality material and diamond shape mirror on inside of cover; fitted with lock and key and contains six useful sewing articles. A very large and showy box, with plenty of room for such articles as thread, needles, silks and other sewing materials. Size, 9½x7x3½ inches. Shipping weight, 2 pounds. Price, per set **88c**

Fancy Shape Sewing Box.

No. 18K25231 Plush and Celluloid Combination Work Box. Top of box is decorated with very pretty picture under transparent celluloid; full mottled plush sides, floral design front and extension base; lined with sateen, inside of cover has a large mirror; contains six useful sewing articles, with plenty of room for other articles used by one who sews; brass catch and hinges. Size, 10x6½x4 inches. Shipping weight, 2½ pounds. Price, per set **$1.42**

Collar and Cuff Box.

No. 18K25251 Embossed Leatherette Collar and Cuff Box. Very fine rose design, embossed sides, with handsomely decorated top, trimmed with lilies in natural colors. Has separate compartment for collars and cuffs. It is only by importing direct from Europe, a large quantity of this number, that we are enabled to quote it at this very low price. Size, 5x6x6 inches. Shipping weight, 1¼ pounds. Price **45c**

This Very Popular Shape, Best Quality, $1.95.

No. 18K25271 Combination Collar and Cuff Box, large size, hexagon shape. Black walrus grain, padded top, nicely finished, extra quality, satin lined throughout, including inside of drawer for holding small articles. On top of case is suitable ornament, and on inside of cover is a bevel edge mirror. Oxidized metal catches fasten cover. Size 9¾x7x6 inches. Shipping weight, 40 ounces. Price **$1.95**

Special Value, 62 Cents.

No. 18K25287 Our Extra Value Glove or Necktie Box, suitable for either ladies or gentlemen; has full celluloid top handsomely embossed in gilt and bronze with rural scene in center. Fancy bronze and black decorated sides; brass catch and hinges; tufted sateen lining throughout. Exceptional value at our price. Size, 12x3¾x2½ inches. Shipping weight, 1 pound. Price **62c**

Two Boxes, Good Quality, 55 Cents.

No. 18K25293 Glove and Handkerchief Set. Consists of two boxes, one for gloves or neckties and the other for handkerchiefs, suitable for either ladies or gentlemen. Each box is fitted with lock and key and is bronze finished with pretty medallion picture on top. Size of glove box, 11½x3½x2½ inches. Size of handkerchief box, 6x2½x7½ inches. Shipping weight, 24 ounces. Price, per set of two boxes **55c**

Wonderful Value, Three Best Quality Embossed Boxes for 98 Cents

No. 18K25307 Extraordinary Value Dresser Set, consisting of three boxes, one for gloves or neckties, the other for handkerchiefs and the third for small articles or photographs. These boxes are made of taxiderme, the sides being embossed with raised floral designs and the tops being very handsomely decorated with embossed patterns of lilies in natural colors. It is only by a very large purchase that we are enabled to sell this set at the wonderfully low price of 98c. Suitable for either ladies' or gentlemen's use. The size of the handkerchief box is 6x7¼x2¼ inches; the glove box is 12¾x4x2¼ inches; the photo box is 10½x5½x2¼ inches. Shipping weight of set, 2¾ pounds. Price for this set of three boxes, only **98c**

NOTE—For collar and cuff box to match this set see No. 18K25251.

Work Basket, 88 Cents.

No. 18K25309 Ladies' Fancy Work Basket, also suitable for handkerchief box. Made of a very pretty combination of fancy straws, braided in fancy design. The bottom and sides of the basket, which is square shaped, are lined with fancy tufted, heavily padded top, bound with a fancy braid. Size of basket, 8x8 inches and 4½ inches high. Price **88c**

If by mail, postage extra, 24 cents.

Imported Palm Plants.

Fine Imported Palm Plants, extensively used for ornamenting parlors and halls. These plants are naturally prepared and very lasting. They come packed flat, without the pots. Are easily set up. Sizes and prices are as follows:

	No. 18K25311	No. 18K25313
Height, inches	36	40
Branches	4	5
Shipping w't., lbs.	6	8
Price, each	59c	73c

	No. 18K25315	No. 18K25317
Height, inches	45	60
Branches	7	10
Shipping w't., lbs.	8½	10
Price, each	89c	$2.19

The 10-branch palm comes in shape of a tree with removable branches to set in tin tubes, and branches much larger size than the 4, 5 and 7-inch plants.

Red India Rubber Toys. Guaranteed Fast Color.

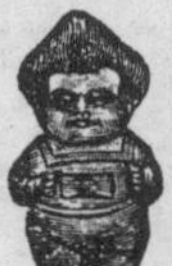

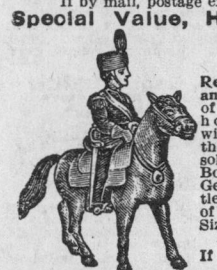

No. 18K23328 Red India Rubber Fat Boy. Made of finest quality red rubber; red will not wear off. Has German silver whistle. Size, 5 inches. Price... 25c
If by mail, postage extra, 3 cents.

No. 18K23328

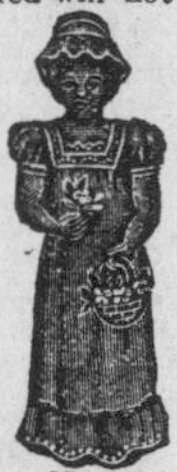

No. 18K23342 Red India Rubber Peasant Girl Doll, made of the best quality red India rubber, the coloring of which will not wear off. This doll, as shown in accompanying illustration, has basket of flowers in one hand and a single flower in the other hand. Has German silver whistle, which is harmless to the child. Size, 5¾ inches. Price... 28c
If by mail, postage extra, 3 cents.

No. 18K23342

Special Value, Horse and Soldier for 50 Cents.

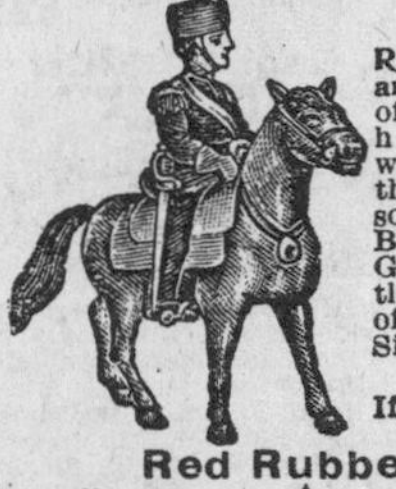

No. 18K23348 Red Rubber Horse and Rider. Consists of two pieces, the horse being fitted with saddle in which the rider, made up in soldier costume, sits. Both pieces have German silver whistles, and are made of the best red rubber. Size, 8 inches.
Price, per set, 50c
If by mail, postage extra, 6 cents.

Red Rubber Dog.

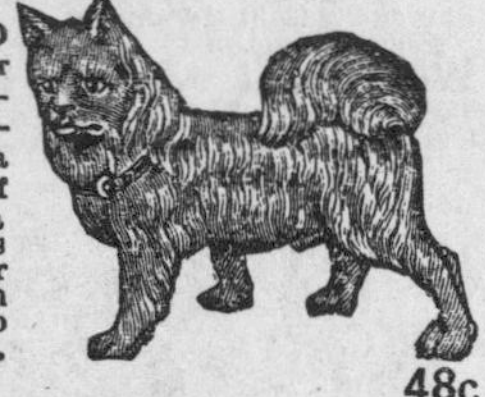

No. 18K23350 Red Rubber Dog. Handsome representation of a dog; made of pure red India rubber; has German silver whistle, which is harmless to the child. Size, 6½ inches.
Price... 48c
If by mail, postage extra, 5 cents.

Red Rubber Cat.

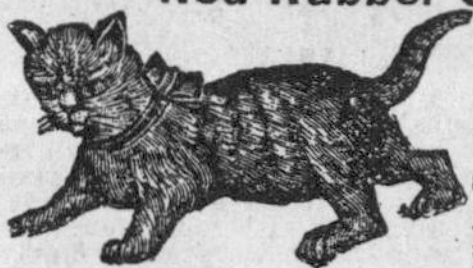

No. 18K23354 Red Rubber Cat. A good and excellent, lifelike representation of a cat, made of pure red India rubber; has German silver whistle. Length, 5¾ inches. Price... 37c
If by mail, postage extra, 5c.

Kid Doll Bodies.

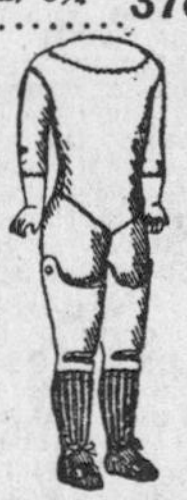

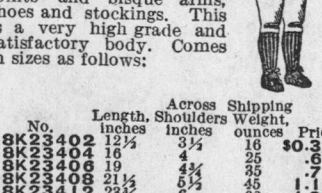

Kid Doll Bodies. Very full size, extra quality cork stuffed, high grade kid bodies, with riveted hip joints and bisque arms, shoes and stockings. This is a very high grade and satisfactory body. Comes in sizes as follows:

No.	Length, inches	Across Shoulders inches	Shipping Weight, ounces	Price
18K23402	12½	3½	16	$0.39
18K23404	16	4	25	.62
18K23406	19	4¾	35	.79
18K23408	21½	5½	45	1.10
18K23412	23¾	6	60	1.39
18K23414	24½	6¼	65	1.58
18K23416	25½	7	75	1.85

Silesia Doll Bodies.

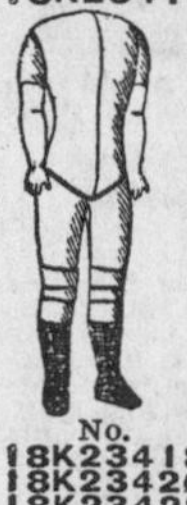

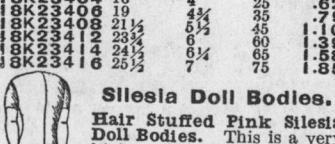

Hair Stuffed Pink Silesia Doll Bodies. This is a very high grade and satisfactory silesia body that will give best of wear and satisfaction; has bisque arms and removable shoes and stockings. Comes in the following sizes:

No.	Length, inches	Inches Across Shoulders	Shipping Weight, oz.	Price
18K23418	12	3¼	10	$0.25
18K23420	15½	4	13	.35
18K23422	16½	4½	11	.44
18K23426	23½	6	30	.69

Sewed Wig and Moving Glass Eyes.

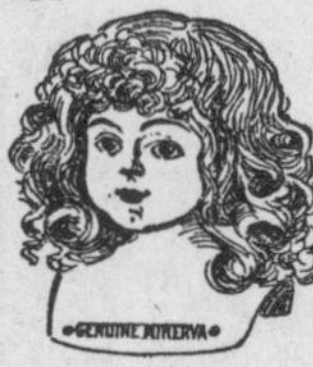

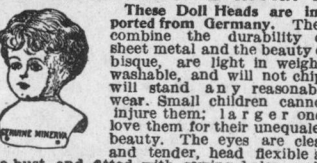

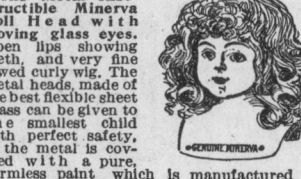

The Metal Indestructible Minerva Doll Head with moving glass eyes. Open lips showing teeth, and very fine sewed curly wig. The metal heads, made of the best flexible sheet brass can be given to the smallest child with perfect safety, as the metal is covered with a pure, harmless paint which is manufactured especially for the purpose. Comes in sizes as follows:

No.	Height, inches	Inches Across Sh'lders	Shipping Weight, oz.	Price
18K23446	4	3	9	$0.38
18K23448	4½	3½	11	.53
18K23450	5½	4½	14	.76
18K23452	6⅝	4⅞	21	1.00

Bisque Doll Heads.

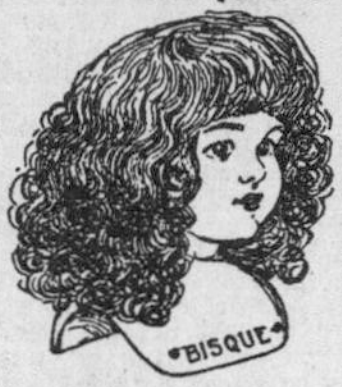

IMMENSE VALUES. COMPARE SIZE AND PRICE.

Bisque Doll Heads. First quality, high grade bisque, with very beautiful moulded faces, showing teeth, with two rows, sewed wig and movable eyes. Either blondes or brunettes. Please mention choice. Comes in sizes as follows:

No.	Height, Inches	Inches Across Sh'lders	Shipping Weight, oz.	Price
18K23454	3⅞	3	9	$0.21
18K23456	4½	3½	13	.35
18K23458	5¼	4¼	15	.45
18K23460	6	5	17	.65
18K23462	7	5½	24	.90
18K23464	8¼	6½	39	1.35
18K23466	9	6¾	42	1.65

Kestner Bisque Doll Heads.

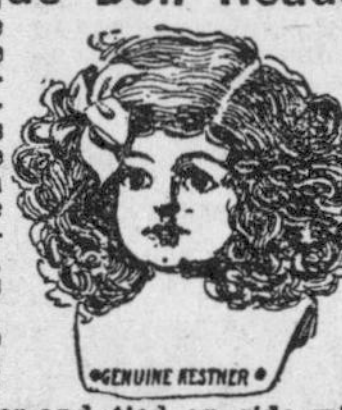

These are the highest grade bisque heads that are manufactured. The Kestner make of dolls is well known, being the best make of dolls in the world. All these heads are very lifelike in appearance, having moving eyes and open mouth, showing teeth. The highest grade full sewed wig with long curls braided in center and tied on side with large silk ribbon bow. We furnish these doll heads in the following sizes:

No.	Height, inches	Inches Across Shoulders	Shipping Weight, oz.	Price
18K23482	4¾	3¼	16	$0.62
18K23484	5½	[illegible]	17	.89
18K23486	6½	4¼	22	1.19
18K23488	7½	4¾	32	1.43
18K23490	8¾	6¼	36	1.96

Celluloid Doll Heads.

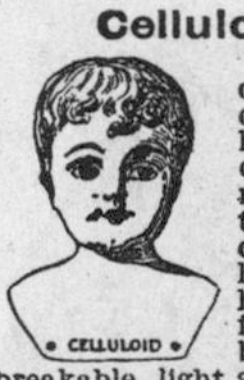

Celluloid Doll Heads. The celluloid doll heads, until recently, have been extremely high priced. We have succeeded in making arrangements so that they are exceptionally cheap, considering the distinct advantages this head has over the ordinary doll head. The faces are beautifully moulded. Made of the best celluloid, absolutely unbreakable, light as a feather and, at the prices we quote, will surely make them exceedingly popular. This style of celluloid doll head has painted hair, glass eyes, with open mouth showing teeth. Come in the following sizes:

No.	Height, inches	Inches Across Shoulders	Shipping Weight, oz.	Price
18K23500	3½	2¾	4	10c
18K23502	3¾	3	6	15c
18K23504	4½	3½	6	29c
18K23506	5	4	8	37c
18K23508	6¼	5¼	11	50c

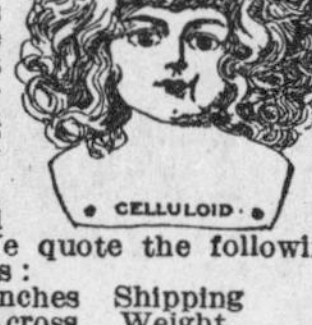

Celluloid Doll Heads, with glass eyes and fine curly sewed wig. The features of this doll are very beautiful. This head combines all the features of the finest bisque head, but is exceptionally light in weight, being made of the finest celluloid. They are unbreakable, making a pretty and durable doll head. We quote the following exceptionally low prices:

No.	Height, Inches	Inches Across Shoulders	Shipping Weight, oz.	Price
18K23510	3½	2¾	4	25c
18K23512	3¾	3	7	37c
18K23514	4¼	3	8	55c
18K23516	5	4	13	68c
18K23518	6¼	5¼	15	82c

Genuine Minerva Metal Doll Heads at Reduced Prices.

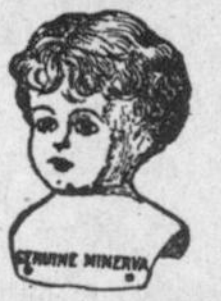

These Doll Heads are imported from Germany. They combine the durability of sheet metal and the beauty of bisque, are light in weight, washable, and will not chip; will stand any reasonable wear. Small children cannot injure them; larger ones love them for their unequaled beauty. The eyes are clear and tender, head flexible at the bust, and fitted with sewing holes, making it easy to adjust and fasten them to body. Comes in sizes as follows:

No.	Height, inches	Inches Across Sh'lders	Shipping Weight, oz.	Price
18K23432	3⅝	2¾	3	14c
18K23434	3¾	3	3	21c
18K23436	4⅛	3⅜	8	28c
18K23438	4½	3⅝	8	35c
18K23440	5	4	9	40c
18K23442	6¼	4¾	14	58c
18K23444	6¾	5½	17	76c

Nos. 18K23442 and 18K23444 have glass eyes and open mouth, showing teeth.

"TEDDY BEARS" ARE ALL THE RAGE

The Best Plaything Ever Invented.

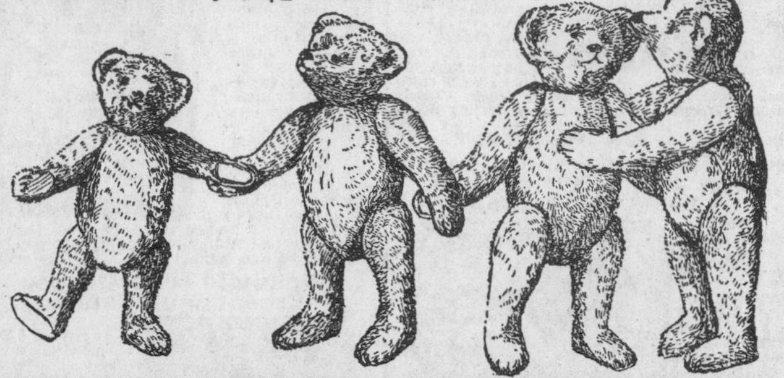

THESE BEARS ARE THE MOST SENSIBLE AND SERVICEABLE toys ever put before the public. Not a fad or campaign article, but something which has come to stay on merit alone. An article which will afford your children and even yourself great amusement and lasting pleasure. Made of the finest quality imported bear plush, they closely resemble the little cubs. They are full jointed and will assume countless different positions (four of which we illustrate). Each bear has a natural voice, produced by slight pressure on the front of body, and they are practically unbreakable. We offer these bears in four sizes. Natural cinnamon color only. The larger the size the better proportioned are the bears. Order one of these bears at once for your boy or girl, and you will find that no toy which you could select would give them more actual pleasure and entertainment.

No.	Size	Shipping Wt.	Price
18K23358	10 inches high	10 ounces	$0.75
18K23360	12 inches high	16 ounces	1.19
18K23362	14 inches high	18 ounces	1.75
18K23364	16 inches high	24 ounces	2.38

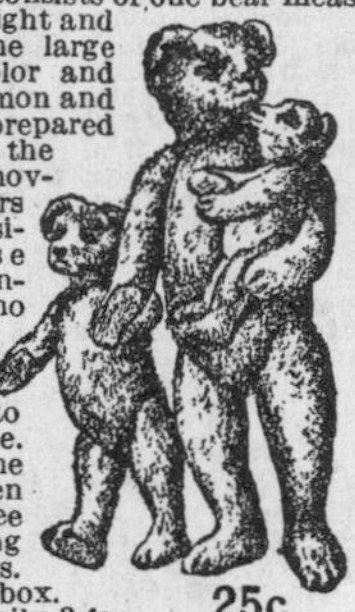

No. 18K23366 The latest idea in bears. This family consists of one bear measuring 7¾ inches in height and two 4½ inches. The large bear is cinnamon color and the smaller are cinnamon and white. Are made of prepared cotton on strong wire, the arms and legs being movable so that the bears will assume any position desired. These bears are practically indestructible, and no matter how roughly used by the children they can always be put back into their original shape. This is the first time that any one has been enabled to sell three bears at the astonishing low price of 25 cents. Come put up in neat box.
Price the entire family 3 for..... 25c
If by mail, postage extra, 6 cents
If you desire the larger stuffed bears with imported bear-skin plush, refer to Nos. 18K23358 to 18K23364.

Brass Wire Doll Bed, 98c

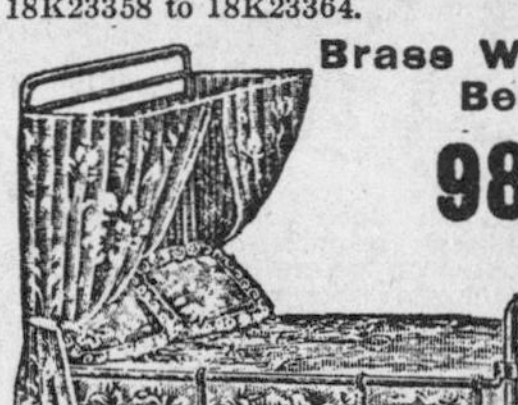

No. 18K23520 Brass Wire Doll Bed. The frame of this doll bed is made entirely of brass finished wire, strongly put together and complete in every detail. Has mattress and two pillows, covered with excellent quality floral pattern silkoline, the back and canopy being trimmed to match. Pillows are trimmed with good quality lace. Entire length of bed is 24 inches. Shipping weight, 4 pounds. This article is unmailable.
Price, for entire bed, complete with mattress, pillows and draperies........ 98c

Comb and Brush Set.

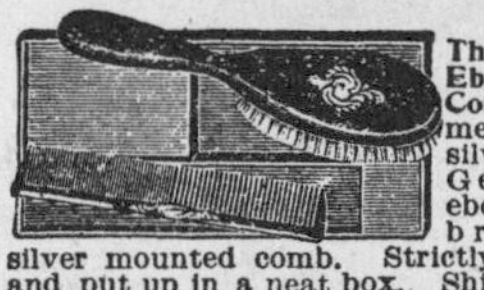

No. 13K25000 This Genuine Ebony Brush and Comb Set is trimmed with sterling silver mountings. Genuine solid ebony back, long bristle, with silver mounted comb. Strictly high grade, and put up in a neat box. Shipping weight, 8 ounces. Worth double our price.
Price, per set, complete............ 69c

$2.00 Value, Genuine Ebony Comb, Brush and Mirror Set, $1.19.

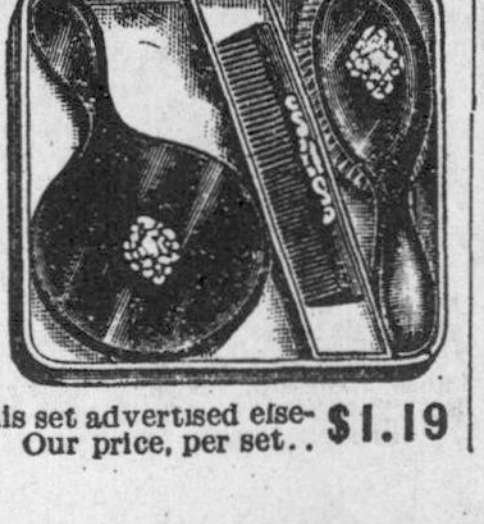

No. 18K25016 Fine Toilet Set, consisting of solid back genuine ebony hair brush, ebonite mirror and comb. All finest sterling silver mounted. Put up in special box, covered with enameled paper. Shipping weight, 1¼ pounds. This set advertised elsewhere for $2.00. Our price, per set.. $1.19

Special Values, Ladies' or Gentlemen's 6-Piece Toilet Sets, only $1.75.

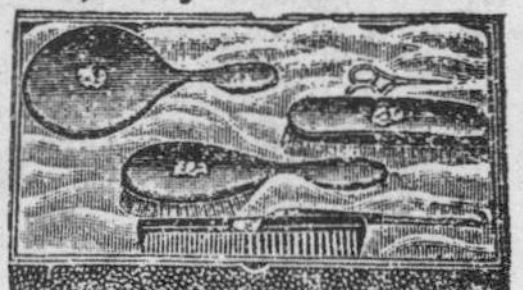

No. 18K25021 High Grade Ladies' Ebonoid Toilet Set in telescope box, lined with good quality grosgrain material, containing nine-row ebonoid hair brush, eight-row cloth brush and bevel edge mirror to match, ebonoid handled buttonhook, manicure scissors and a 7-inch ebonoid comb; all sterling silver mounted. A very attractive set at an exceptionally low price. Size of case, 9½x15½ inches. Shipping weight, 2½ pounds. Price, per set. $1.75

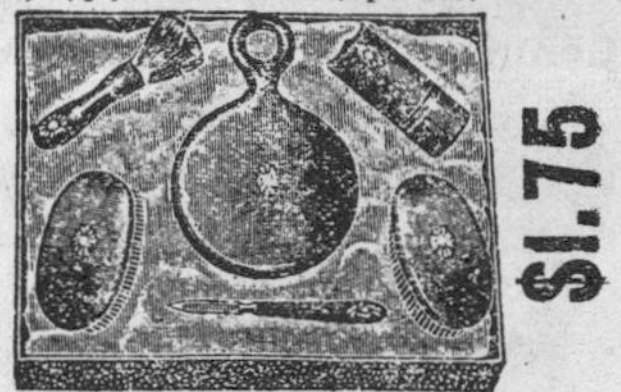

$1.75

No. 18K25023 Finest Quality Gentlemen's Toilet Set, consists of two excellent quality bristle, nine-row military brushes, a ring handled bevel edge plate mirror, ebonoid soap box, rabbit tail ebonoid handled shaving brush and good quality nail file; put up in flat telescope box with excellent quality lining; all pieces sterling silver mounted. A very attractive dresser set which any gentleman will appreciate; at an exceptionally low price. Shipping weight, 3 pounds.
Price, per set........ $1.75

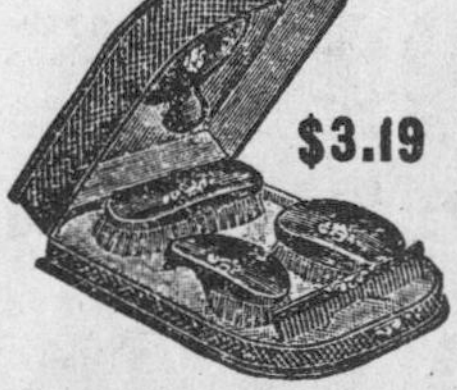

No. 18K25032 Ebonoid Toilet Set, in fancy leatherette case. White satin lined throughout. Contains a pair eleven-row ebonoid military brushes, cloth brush, bevel edge, ring handle mirror and good ebonoid comb, all sterling silver mounted. All brushes are fitted with best quality of bristles. Size of case, 3x9x11 inches. Shipping weight, 4 pounds. Price, per set......... $3.19

Genuine Ebony Toilet Case, $6.00 Value, $3.98.

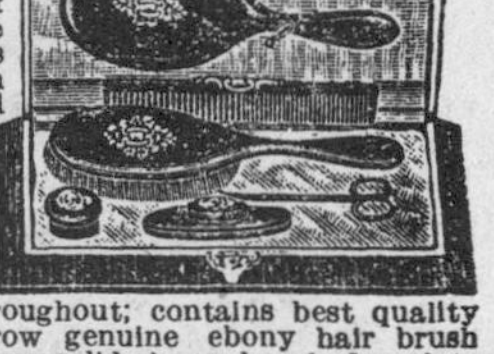

No. 18K25037 Genuine Ebony Toilet and Manicure Case. Case is covered with walrus grained leather with fine large oxidized mounting on top, extension base, best quality satin lined throughout; contains best quality bristle, nine-row genuine ebony hair brush with extra heavy solid ebony bevel edge plate mirror to match; good quality black celluloid comb also chamois buffer and powder jar, all mounted with sterling silver, also good quality manicure scissors; a case that will be liked by anyone who appreciates quality. Size, 11x7x3½ inches. Shipping weight, 3½ pounds. Price, per set............ $3.98

DON'T PAY RETAIL PRICES FOR CLOTHING

WE MANUFACTURE MEN'S AND BOYS' CLOTHING OF ALL KINDS OURSELVES (BOTH MADE-TO-ORDER AND READY MADE) AND SELL IT DIRECT TO ANYBODY AT PRICES THAT JUST INCLUDE THE ACTUAL COST OF THE MATERIAL AND MAKING IN OUR OWN FINELY EQUIPPED PLANT WITH BUT OUR ONE BARE SMALL MARGIN OF PROFIT ADDED, SO THAT WE CUT OUT ALL WHOLESALE AND RETAIL PROFITS ALTOGETHER AND GUARANTEE TO FURNISH YOU THE BEST GRADES OF MEN'S AND BOYS' CLOTHING, MADE FROM ALL THE LATEST HIGH CLASS MATERIALS, AT THE LOWEST PRICES EVER HEARD OF.

WE GUARANTEE our clothing to be better made, of better quality throughout, to be better fitting and of finer appearance, more stylish and up to date than the average clothing retailed at any price elsewhere. You will not be able to equal the quality of our garments under about double the price at retail, and if we fail to please you in any way, if we don't fit you perfectly, or if for any reason the garments are unsatisfactory, you are at perfect liberty to return them to us at our expense and we will refund both the price and any transportation charges you paid. We take all the risk. You can't lose a penny. Why pay the profits and expenses of dealers, agents and wholesale clothiers?

WE SAVE YOU ABOUT HALF THE MONEY YOU WOULD SPEND FOR CLOTHING ANYWHERE ELSE.

LOOK THROUGH OUR GREAT LINE OF CLOTHING IN THIS CATALOGUE
QUALITY CONSIDERED, OUR PRICES ARE LOWER THAN EVER THIS SEASON

ANY SAMPLE BOOK FREE

Write at any time a postal card or letter and just say, "Send me Free Sample Book No. —— (give the number of the book you want, or just tell us what kind of clothing you want), and the big book, including Cloth Samples, Fashion Illustrations, Order Blanks and Tape Measure all complete will go to you free and postpaid at once.

YOU CAN ORDER THIS CLOTHING DIRECT FROM THIS CATALOGUE IF YOU WISH
(See the Following Pages)

But if you wish to see samples before ordering, write and ask for the sample book you want, or tell us the kind of clothing you wish and we will send you the book or books you need, free and postpaid.

No. 81K FREE SAMPLE BOOK OF MEN'S MADE TO ORDER SUITS, PANTS AND SPRING OVERCOATS AT FROM $7.90 TO $25.34.

A high class and beautiful assortment of medium weight and light weight fabrics suitable for spring and summer wear and many of them especially adapted for year around purposes; suitings, trouserings and light overcoatings, including all the fashionable weaves in both domestic and imported fabrics adapted for business men, professional men or anybody wanting a strictly high class made to order suit or overcoat. Includes beautiful correct fashion plates of all the business and dress styles, showing everything that the latest designers of fashions have created. If you want a strictly high class suit, pair of trousers or light overcoat made to your own order in a style of your own selection, with the understanding that we guarantee to perfectly fit you or refund your money, write and ask for free Sample Book No. 81K. See illustration and full description of this handsome book on page 1053. Don't place an order for any tailoring with an agent or home tailor until you have seen this valuable book. Get it and have in your home just as complete information on the fashions of the day as any tailor can obtain from his headquarters. Don't depend upon the recommendation of any salesman, but see these things for yourself and save about half your tailoring expenses.

No. 84K FREE SAMPLE BOOK OF MEN'S READY TO WEAR CIELETTE RAINPROOF SPRING AND FALL OVERCOATS AT FROM $6.48 TO $15.24.

See pages 1076 and 1077 in this catalogue for descriptions and illustrations of these goods; but if you want to see cloth samples of our Cielette raincoats before ordering, write for free Sample Book No. 84K.

No. 86K FREE SAMPLE BOOK OF MEN'S READY TO WEAR LIGHT WEIGHT SUMMER OUTING SUITS FOR WARM WEATHER WEAR.

$2.48 to $13.98 for fine light weight suits of khaki, crash, flannel and fine summer worsted weaves, blue serges, checks, plaids, etc., representing just the kind of materials used by fashionable tailors for making the summer clothes of fine dressers. Unlined coats with pants made in golf bottom style with belt loops, etc. See this fashionable line described and illustrated on pages 1069 to 1072 in this Big Catalogue.

MEN'S FUR COATS, BLANKET AND SHEEP LINED DUCK, CORDUROY AND LEATHER CLOTHING, WORKING GARMENTS, OVERALLS, RUBBER AND OIL SLICKER RAINCOATS, ETC.

We do not sample this class of garments but describe and illustrate them perfectly on pages 1093 to 1102 in this catalogue, making it perfectly satisfactory to order them and guaranteeing to please you or refund your money. We, however, have a special catalogue of this line showing larger illustrations of the winter garments and if you desire to see it we should be glad to furnish it to you free if you will just write and ask for our special **Fur Coat and Duck Clothing Catalogue.**

No. 88K FREE SAMPLE BOOK OF YOUNG MEN'S, BOYS' AND CHILDREN'S CLOTHING

Young Men's Suits, $3.48 to $13.48.   Boys' Long Pants Suits, $3.25 to $6.75. Knee Pants Suits, $1.50 to $6.35.   Little Fellows' Fancy Styles, $1.48 to $3.75.

We show cloth samples of fair size of all goods we offer for young men and boys and colored photographs of our little fellows' fancy styles, showing the actual colors of the goods and trimmings. We have the latest styles for all ages from 21 years down to 2½ years of age, comprising 100 cloth samples and 100 illustrations of fashions. The greatest line of Boys' Clothing ever assembled in one assortment and all quoted at manufacturer's prices. See this great line on pages 1079 to 1092 in this Big Catalogue.

No. 89K OUR GREAT FREE SAMPLE BOOK OF MEN'S READY TO WEAR CLOTHING

SUITS, $3.98 TO $17.93
PANTS, 1.19 TO 5.24

We quote manufacturer's prices, cutting retail prices in two. This is a choice and very large assortment of fabrics in which we furnish a great variety of styles. We offer a greater number of materials and a larger variety of styles to choose from than you can find in any store in your neighborhood. You couldn't equal the selection except by visiting the biggest clothing stores in our greatest cities. See illustration of this great book on page 1056. Don't fail to look through the clothing section of this Big Catalogue. See pages 1055 to 1068. Order direct from this catalogue or write for this Free Sample Book No. 89K, just as you please. We send it free and postpaid with order blanks, tape measure, samples and fashion plates, all complete. It represents the choicest high grade ready to wear clothing to be obtained. Double the prices at retail will not buy any better.

No. 191K FREE SAMPLE CARD OF MAIL CARRIERS' UNIFORMS AT $8.90 TO $10.90 AND GRAND ARMY AND RAILROAD MEN'S UNIFORMS AT $10.47.

We show samples of regulation all wool gray fabrics for mail carriers and navy blue all wool goods for railroad men, which we furnish in well made, up to date regulation style uniforms. Don't pay retail prices for uniforms. Send for this card of remarkable values. Ask for No. 191K.

No. 291K FREE SAMPLE CARD OF MEN'S READY TO WEAR DRESS SUITS, PRINCE ALBERTS, TUXEDOS AND FULL DRESS STYLES AT $20.00 AND $22.00.

While we show an extra fine line of suitings in Sample Book No. 81K for Made to Order Dress Suits, we also have an excellent line of ready made dress garments. If you need such clothing at once and can't wait for a made to order garment, write for free Sample Card No. 291K. Prices are about one-half what clothiers ask.

$14.89

BRINGS YOU A SUIT OF THIS EXCELLENT
MEN'S AND BOYS' SUITS
IN ANY STYLE MADE TO YOUR ORDER

This is the same high grade navy blue serge quality we offered last year at a higher price. We have been able to reduce the price as against a year ago while still maintaining the high standard of quality throughout the whole suit.

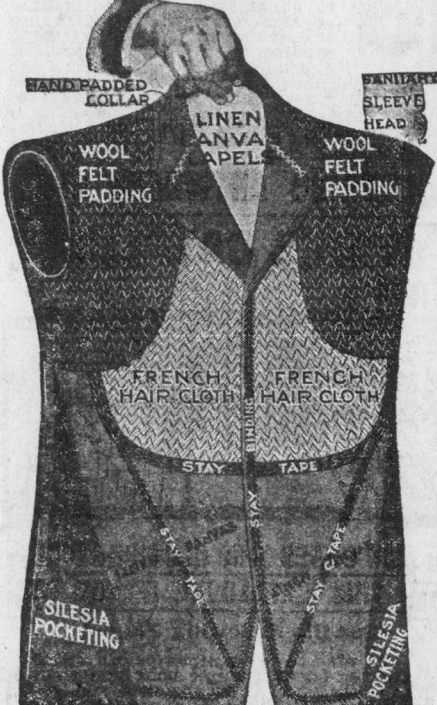

$25.00 PAID TO AN AGENT OF A WHOLESALE TAILORING HOUSE OR PAID TO A HOME TAILOR WON'T BRING YOU A SUIT OF AS FINE A SERGE QUALITY OR REPRESENT AS FINE TAILORING. WE GUARANTEE TO PROVE THIS STATEMENT TO YOUR PERSONAL SATISFACTION ABSOLUTELY OR YOU MAY RETURN THE CLOTHES TO US AT OUR EXPENSE AND WE WILL REFUND BOTH THE PRICE AND ANY TRANSPORTATION CHARGES YOU PAID ON THE SHIPMENT. WE PROVE IT OR YOU PAY NO MONEY.

YOU GENTLEMEN WHO PAY $20.00 TO $30.00 TO AGENTS or home tailors for suits made to your order, won't you accept this liberal quality test offer? (Note the illustration showing the tailoring in our garments.) Just give us your measurements according to the simple plan shown at the bottom of this page, ask for cloth No. 13K6620, tell us what style you wish made (see the following two pages for illustrations of some of the popular styles or write for our Sample Book No. 81K and see all our fashion plates), enclose our price, $14.89, and let us make a suit to your own order and measurements and we guarantee to please you in every way and if you don't feel perfectly satisfied with the quality of the serge, its rich appearance, the way the suit is made, the style of it, and if it doesn't fit you perfectly, or if you don't find it worth at least $25.00 as compared with what you know to be the standard of $25.00 tailoring in suits offered by tailors and agents in your neighborhood, then you can return the suit to us at our expense and we will refund to you both the price, $14.89, and any transportation charges you paid on the shipment. You will not lose a single cent. This is our offer to you, to your neighbor or anybody; no restrictions.

THIS GREAT OFFER IS POSSIBLE BECAUSE the basis upon which we handle the tailoring business is totally different than the basis on which it is handled in any other institution. There is no other institution within one-hundredth the capacity of our made to order clothing department that is doing business direct with the wearer of the clothes. No wholesale tailoring house that does business through agents handles anywhere near the quantity of cloth or tailoring as we handle, so that our tailoring department stands in a class by itself. We control the output of many woolen mills and while the direct effect of this is noticeable in the low prices we quote all through our made to order suits yet it is particularly noticeable on a blue serge of this fine all wool quality, because as a blue serge is a staple material we are able to use astonishingly large quantities of it and get it direct (as we do all our fabrics) from the weavers (not from woolen jobbers), paying only a very slight profit over the actual cost of the wool and weaving. We save you a big item in the cost of the cloth along in any one suit and particularly in a blue serge because vast quantities count in price lowering. Then consider the equipment of our tailoring shops with everything of the latest model manned by the most experienced expert workmen to be found in the trade. The finest workmanship can thus be done without waste of time at any stage and with greatly lessened possibilities for waste of material than in small shops. The cost of the finished garment even though the work is the best that the highest skill can produce is less to us than the same garment with the same class of work would be to a smaller house or to a home tailor. To this cost we add merely our one bare small margin of profit and no one else handles the suit before you. No agents' profits or commissions come in and that fact knocks out $5.00 to $15.00 or even $25.00 according to the grade of garments you buy. We save you on every suit no matter what the material, and save you big money, but we particularly save you big money on a blue serge, a staple, standard, useful material for dress or business wear, every season and all seasons. We have this all wool serge suiting both in navy blue and black. If you want navy blue ask for cloth No. 13K6620, but if you want the black ask for No. 13K6622. Price is same in each case.

YOU CAN COUNT ON GETTING BETTER MADE CLOTHES (see the illustration here), from us than from any other tailoring house or home tailor. We have only to point you to the illustration at the left showing to you the interior workmanship in one of our coats. This blue serge suit will be made exactly as here shown with an interlining just as pictured and marked out in this illustration. In the lapels will be pure linen canvas to keep them in perfect shape, the collar will be hand padded, the shoulders interlined with wool felt padding, rounding them out and giving them the graceful shape and curve, the fronts will contain French haircloth, linen canvas and stay tape. The pockets will be supported from the shoulder, all of which enables the coat to keep its smooth, even stylish shape splendidly. Take just a little care of your clothing and a garment made as we make it will give you perfect satisfaction a most surprisingly long time. You won't feel the need of getting a new suit half as quick when wearing one of ours made this way as you will by investing in tailoring of doubtful make elsewhere. Won't you try a suit from this blue serge, or from some of the goods shown on page 1054, or write for our free Sample Book No. 81K and make your choice from 100 cloth samples of stylish goods?

HIGH GRADE ALL WOOL NAVY BLUE SERGE

This fabric is finely woven from pure all wool worsted yarn, weighs 14 ounces per yard and is therefore suitable for wear at any season of the year and possesses a rich dark navy blue shade. A good blue serge will give you more service than any other suiting you can get and this is a quality that you won't wear out before your wife or mother asks you to let her cut it down for the little boy, and it stands a good show against the hard wear the youngster will give it.

Cloth No. 13K6620

PRICES

Suit	$14.89
Coat and vest	10.07
Coat and pants	12.71
Pants	5.06

We have the same quality of all wool serge in black at same price, $14.89. If you want the black, ask for cloth No. 13K6622.

THIS ILLUSTRATION shows you the interior of one of our made to order coats, THE INTERLINING which goes between the outside cloth and the lining on the inside of the coat and shows you how perfectly you can be of the wearing qualities and the keep-in-shape qualities of our garments. These materials don't make a heavy, bulky suit or a suit that is too warm. They are light, and merely serve to hold shape.

See following two pages for illustrations of some of the up to date styles for the season.

HOW TO MEASURE FOR A SUIT OR OVERCOAT TO BE MADE TO YOUR ORDER.

Use one of our regular custom tailoring order blanks if you have one, or if not, use a plain sheet of paper and mark down the measurements in order as they are called for in the instructions we give here. These instructions are taken from our regular order blank. We guarantee to fit you or refund your money.

COAT OR OVERCOAT MEASUREMENTS

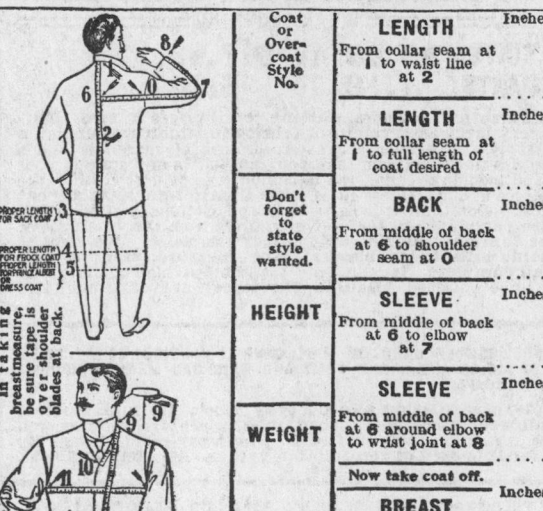

Measuring is as easy as A, B, C. There is no trick or difficulty in it at all. It does not require a tailor's experience. Anybody can do it perfectly by following the simple rules on our tailoring order blanks or the instructions given here. Never fear make a mistake. Even if you do make a mistake, we take the risk just the same. Don't pay tailor's fancy prices elsewhere. Let us furnish you your made to order clothes at half the ordinary price.

Coat or Overcoat Style No.		
	LENGTH From collar seam at 1 to waist line at 2	Inches
	LENGTH From collar seam at 1 to full length of coat desired	Inches
Don't forget to state style wanted.	**BACK** From middle of back at 6 to shoulder seam at 0	Inches
HEIGHT	**SLEEVE** From middle of back at 6 to elbow at 7	Inches
	SLEEVE From middle of back at 6 around elbow to wrist joint at 8	Inches
WEIGHT	Now take coat off.	
	BREAST All around body at 11 over vest only	Inches
AGE	**WAIST** All around body at 12 over vest only	Inches

Give Cloth No.   State whether you want a suit, coat and vest, pants or overcoat   State price of garments you are ordering

EXTRA CHARGES FOR LARGE SIZES.

For sizes larger than 42 inches breast, but not over 45 inches, we charge $1.50 extra, and for sizes over 45 inches, but not over 50 inches breast, we charge $2.00 extra.

EXTRA CHARGES FOR SPECIAL TRIMMING.

For silk or satin lining we charge $5.00 extra, or for silk or satin facing on coat $1.50 extra.

VEST MEASUREMENTS

State style of vest wanted.

OPENING From collar seam at back of neck, 9 to first button at 10	Inches
LENGTH From collar seam at back of neck, 9 to length of vest at 13	Inches

PANTS MEASUREMENTS

Prevailing width for pants legs now in fashion 19 inches knee and 17 inches bottom.

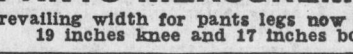

OUTSIDE SEAM From top of waistband at 14 to heel seam of shoe at 15	Inches	**KNEE** Around knee at 20 give size desired	Inches
INSEAM From close up in crotch at 16 to heel seam of shoe at 17	Inches	**BOTTOM** Around bottom at 21 give size desired	Inches
WAIST All around body at 18 over pants only	Inches	**PANTS POCKETS** State kind wanted Side or top	
SEAT All around body at hips, 19 over pants only	Inches	Are your shoulders regular, square or sloping?	
THIGH All around thigh at 22	Inches	When standing naturally, are you erect, regular or stooping? Do you require easy armholes, because of large muscles?	

In taking breastmeasure, be sure tape is over shoulder blades at back.

FREE THIS GREAT CLOTH SAMPLE BOOK
No. 81K OF MEN'S MADE
TO ORDER CLOTHING
AND POSTPAID

WRITE FOR IT NOW, TODAY. JUST SAY ON A POSTAL CARD OR IN A LETTER, "SEND ME FREE SAMPLE BOOK No. 81K," OR JUST ASK FOR OUR SAMPLE BOOK OF MEN'S MADE TO ORDER CLOTHING, AND THIS WONDERFUL BOOK WITH 100 FAIR SIZED SAMPLES OF CLOTH AND ABOUT THIRTY ILLUSTRATIONS OF MEN'S FASHIONS, WITH TAPE MEASURE, ORDER BLANKS, EVERYTHING COMPLETE WITH ALL OUR GREAT OFFERS WILL GO TO YOU FREE AND POSTPAID AT ONCE.

Fashionable Styles for Sunday and Ordinary Dress Wear or for Professional Men

STYLE 5 Four-Button Frock Suit, usually worn with only the top button closed and often called a one-button frock.

STYLE 9 Clerical or Minister's Suit, with clerical vest style 98 as shown on page 8.

STYLE 17 Long Roll Frock Suit, the lapels having a long roll and not intended to button.

STYLE 4 Three-Button Frock, usually worn buttoned as illustrated, no outside pockets, but inside breast and tail pockets. A fashionable dress suit.

$12.48 BRINGS YOU A SUIT TO ORDER FROM THIS MEDIUM GRAY FINE WEARING WORSTED FINISH CASSIMERE

This Cloth No. 13K06514, exactly like sample, is one of the very latest fashionable weaves for this season, being a fair weight for spring, summer and early fall wear, and having a medium plain gray background just dark enough to make it practical for general wear and not show soil readily. The diagonal weave shows a fairly wide twill just about as wide again as the twill in a serge but not prominent, and over this runs a rich mild silver silk effect overplaid which is ¾ of an inch wide and 1¼ inches long, making it a strictly up to date style of goods while at the same time it is, as we have said, practical for general wear. When you consider that we will make a suit of this in any style that you may select to your order for $12.48, you can certainly understand that we are giving you an actual $20.00 value and we guarantee to fit and please you perfectly or refund your money. Won't you order this suit on this liberal offer and guarantee?

Cloth No. 13K06514

SUIT	$12.48
COAT AND VEST	8.47
COAT AND PANTS	10.70
PANTS	4.26

$9.95 $10.85 $14.98 $16.56 $18.63

and that's why we can do it,

the reason why we save you.

this class is not found

such fashionable goods as these.

quantities direct from the mills.

$17.65 $16.94 $19.20 $23.16 $24.20

purpose suit and dress wear.

sure you'll not wear it out.

than an all wool serge.

not do as well any where else.

quantity of high class goods.

THE ABOVE IS A SMALL ILLUSTRATION OF OUR SAMPLE BOOK No. 81K OF MEN'S MADE TO ORDER CLOTHING showing the book open and illustrating the way in which we show the samples and prices and giving an exact description of each cloth and style. This book contains page after page of actual cloth samples showing you the exact quality of the fabric and giving you a perfect idea of the pattern so that you can order with perfect ease and satisfaction, knowing exactly what you are going to get, also containing many pages of fashion plates showing the latest styles for the season and telling you exactly what is suitable for wear, whether for business, Sunday or high class dress purposes.

WE ARE QUOTING LOWER PRICES THAN EVER BEFORE ON THE SAME HIGH GRADE QUALITIES.

$7.90 TO $25.34 IS THE RANGE OF PRICES QUOTED BY US FOR HIGH CLASS MADE TO ORDER CLOTHING and this great book, No. 81K, which is free and postpaid upon request, contains samples of everything in fine grade suitings, trouserings and spring and fall overcoatings, fabrics suitable for spring and summer wear and many suitable for year around wear, all wool goods and all wool and silk mixtures, in shades of the latest gray, gray mixtures, checks, shadow checks, overplaids, brown shades and brown mixtures, navy blue serges, black Thibets, unfinished worsteds, imported dress worsteds, broadcloths, cassimeres, cheviots, tweeds and fancy worsted. Our line represents the entire range of qualities suitable for all purposes, business, everyday, Sunday and dress wear, and we offer to you the best cloth weavers produce, goods such as fashionable merchant tailors offer in their so called high class tailoring at fancy prices.

DON'T PAY AGENTS OR TAILORS FANCY PRICES.

Just take a look at our all wool blue serge suit offer on the preceding page, consider even the offer which you can read on the right page of the sample book here photographed, or see the great offers on the following page in this catalogue. We give you a small selection here, chosen at random from among our great variety of fabrics and describe them accurately and the illustrations give you a good idea of the pattern. If you order your suit direct from our descriptions here we positively guarantee to satisfy you or refund your money, but if you don't order from this catalogue don't place an order with a tailor or agent in your locality until you write and get this great free Sample Book No. 81K. It will open your eyes to the big profit made by home tailors and agents and show you the expenses they tax you with, and enable you to make a saving of about half in the price of tailoring.

ANY OF THESE 100 FABRICS WILL BE MADE TO YOUR ORDER IN ANY STYLE YOU WANT.

WRITE AT ONCE AND ASK FOR FREE SAMPLE BOOK No. 81K

AND WE WILL MAIL YOU FREE AND POSTPAID THIS WONDERFUL BOOK WITH ITS 100 CLOTH SAMPLES, ITS BEAUTIFUL CORRECT AND INSTRUCTIVE FASHION PLATES DRAWN FROM LIFE, ITS FUND OF INFORMATION UPON ALL SUBJECTS THAT A MAN WANTS TO KNOW IN BUYING A SUIT AND INCLUDING A GOOD CLOTH TAPE MEASURE AND SIMPLE ORDER BLANKS, MAKING EVERYTHING SO PLAIN AND EASY TO ORDER THAT YOU SIMPLY CAN'T MAKE A MISTAKE. REMEMBER, WE GUARANTEE TO FIT AND PLEASE YOU PERFECTLY OR REFUND BOTH THE PRICE AND ANY TRANSPORTATION CHARGES YOU PAID. YOU ASSUME NO RISK WHATEVER.

SEE OUR GREAT TAILORING OFFERS BOTH ON THE FOREGOING PAGE AND ON THE FOLLOWING PAGE.

A FEW OF OUR MADE TO ORDER SUIT OFFERINGS

FROM THE VALUES OFFERED ON THIS PAGE and on the two preceding pages you can get a fairly good idea of the remarkably fine quality we give you for every dollar you invest for our tailoring. When you consider that we will make these garments to your individual measurements in any style that suits you and interline them as illustrated on page 1052, and guarantee to satisfy you or refund your money, it proves that you cannot afford to have your tailoring done anywhere else. If you don't see anything in this assortment to suit your taste be sure to write and ask for our free Sample Book No. 81K, illustrated on page 1053.

$10.65 A SPLENDID OFFER IN THE FASHIONABLE GRAY CLUB CHECK SUITING IN ANY STYLE TO YOUR ORDER.

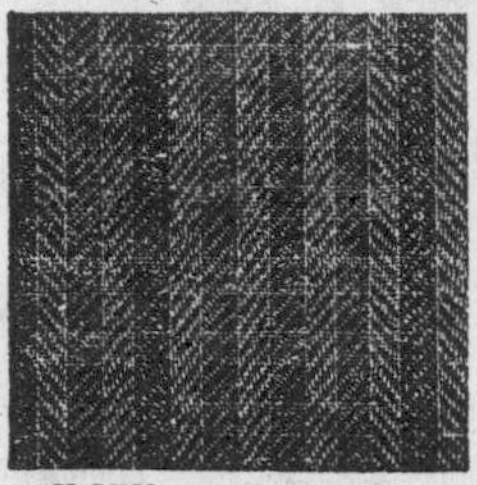

CLOTH No. 13K6504

PRICES

Suit	$10.65
Coat and vest	7.25
Coat and pants	9.18
Pants	3.65

From this picture you can get a good idea of the kind of pattern in this fabric. The background is a medium gray diagonal weave over which are dark gray checks ½ inch square in the nature of shadows. The vertical stripes which form part of the checks have alternately a few brown threads and a few purple and green threads in them, not noticeable unless the cloth is examined closely, yet serving to cast a slight color on the goods other than gray, and making it of a decidedly pleasing effect. The cloth is a good strong worsted weave suitable for spring, summer and fall wear and is really something that a home tailor or agent would ask $15.00 to $18.00 for at least. **Tell us what style you want and give us your measurements according to our simple plan on page 1052**, and we guarantee to fit and please you perfectly or refund your money.

$14.48 VERY STYLISH BLACK AND GRAY FANCY SUITING MADE TO YOUR ORDER IN ANY STYLE OF YOUR CHOICE.

CLOTH No. 13K6526

PRICES

Suit	$14.48
Coat and vest	9.81
Coat and pants	12.37
Pants	4.93

This picture is taken from a photograph of a sample and the pattern is just a little smaller in the picture than in the actual goods, the dark bands are just half as far apart in the picture as they are in the actual cloth. The surface is half diagonal and half small basket weave. The diagonal weave part and the basket weave part are each in the form of bars or stripes, ¼ inch wide and alternating with each other, and both weaves are in rich black. Then over this is a silver silk decoration. The diagonal weave is sifted with very fine pinpoint silver colored silk threads and there are cross bars of silver threads also, bringing out a hardly noticeable silver gray check effect, but as the background is so jet black, the whole pattern is very dark and exceedingly neat. **Mention the style you wish made and send your order for this splendid value.** We will save you $10.00 easily and guarantee perfect satisfaction.

$15.76 VERY DARK CLUB CHECK AND BLACK OVERPLAID FANCY WORSTED SUITING IN ANY STYLE TO ORDER.

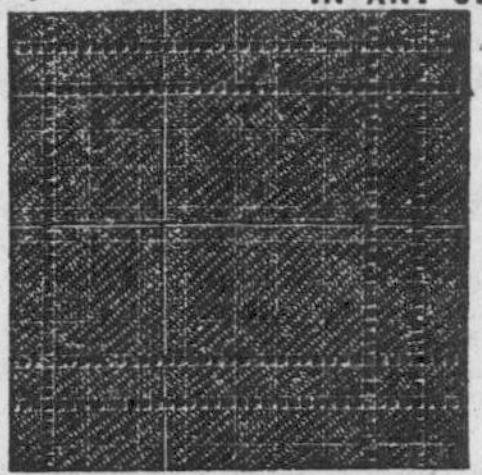

CLOTH No. 13K6528

PRICES

Suit	$15.76
Coat and vest	10.85
Coat and pants	13.63
Pants	5.40

You can get a good idea from this picture as to how the pattern is arranged. This is not a conspicuous or what is termed a loud check, but is a subdued, very neat dark gray suiting with the gray effect brought out in the form of a faint shadowy check on a black background. The checks are about ½ inch square and the vertical and cross stripes forming them are nearly ¼ inch wide and of a very faint gray while the centers are black. There is also a raised black cord effect overplaid about 1⅜ inches square consisting of two parallel small raised black cords ¼ inch apart, thus making the fabric still darker and relieving the plain diagonal weave. There is also a single purple thread overplaid on the surface, but scarcely noticeable, yet lending a slight tint to the gray if you examine the suiting at close range. The fabric is fashionable and dressy, but not too striking for the modest person. **Tell us what style you want** and see page 1052 about our simple rules of measuring.

OUR LATEST LOW PRICE OFFERS ON TAILORING ARE SURPRISING. SEND FOR OUR SAMPLE BOOK No. 81K. SEE PRECEDING PAGE.

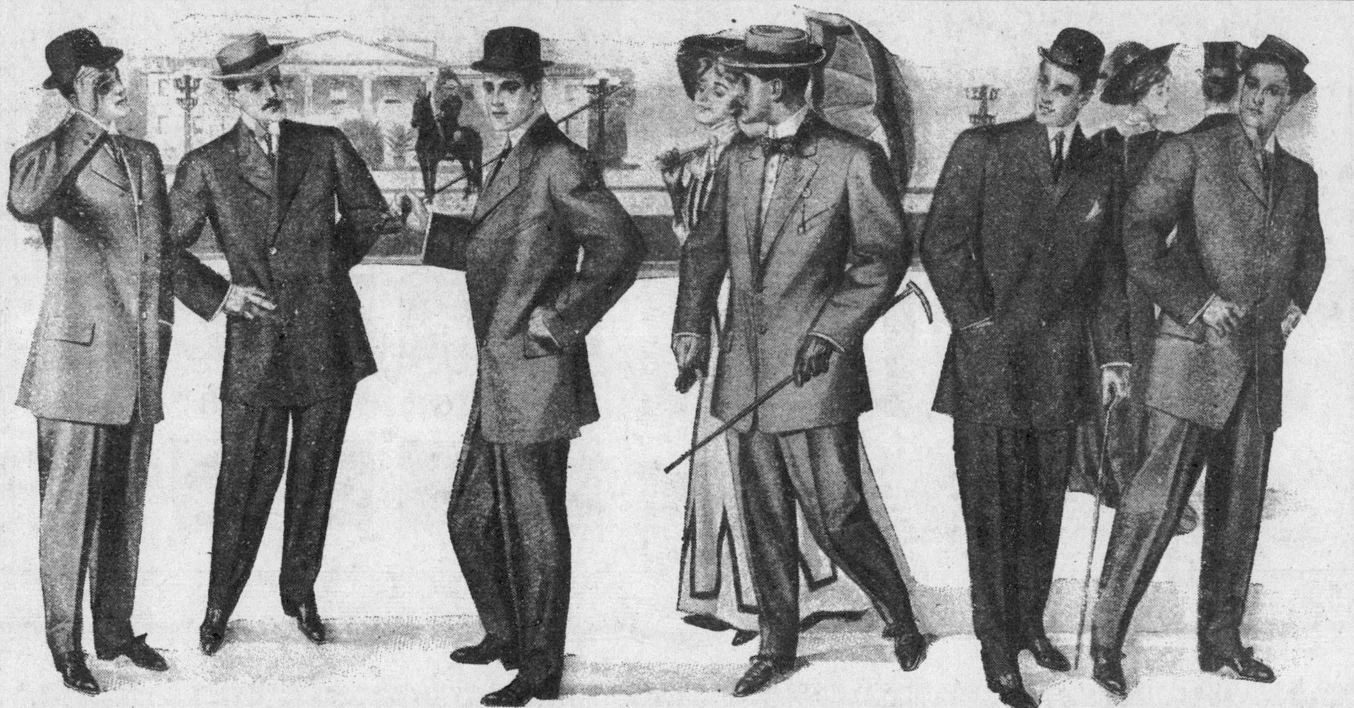

QUALITY CONSIDERED, WE ARE NOW OFFERING THE BIGGEST TAILORING VALUES WE EVER OFFERED.

STYLE 29—Stylish Three-Button Single Breasted Sack Suit with just a slight opening at coat corners at bottom.

STYLE 10—Double Breasted Three-Button Sack Suit, a favorite style.

STYLE 69—Newest Fashionable Three-Button Single Breasted Sack Suit with long lapels and cuff sleeves.

STYLE 24—Fashionable Two-Button Single Breasted Sack Suit with long broad lapels, one of the very latest things out.

STYLE 2—Single Breasted Four-Button Straight Front Sack Suit, always popular.

STYLE 18—Practical Four-Button Cutaway Sack Suit, very popular business style.

THESE ARE A FEW OF THE STYLES that are fashionable for business and dress wear this season, and you can see others in the illustration of our Sample Book on page 1053, but if you don't find the style you want, **write and ask for our FREE SAMPLE BOOK No. 81K**, where our complete fashion plates show everything in men's fashions. For simple instructions on measuring and about extra large sizes, see page 1052.

$17.50 VERY FINE ALL WOOL RICH DARK AND BROWN EFFECT WORSTED SUITING TO YOUR ORDER IN ANY STYLE.

CLOTH No. 13K6554

PRICES

Suit	$17.50
Coat and vest	12.00
Coat and pants	15.08
Pants	5.98

This is an exceedingly fashionable pattern and an excellent wearing cloth, being a finely woven, pure all wool worsted of suitable weight particularly for spring, summer and fall but also usable for winter wear if one does not care for a particularly heavy fabric. As the picture shows, this is a very fine small check effect, but not striking enough to be at all objectionable to the modest taste as the pattern is very subdued and exceedingly neat. The background is a very rich dark brown fine diagonal twill over which run ¼ inch black shadow checks. At intervals of 1 inch run three parallel stripes in faint cord effect, ¼ inch apart, the middle one with one red silk thread and the two outside ones with one green silk thread in each. Half way between these sets of three small stripes runs a small basket weave stripe ⅛ inch wide. These stripes are all very faint and just serve to relieve the weave. Browns are the very latest and this is a very stylish effect in brown. **State the style you want.**

$18.72 EXTRA QUALITY PURE ALL WOOL WORSTED RICH DARK AND GRAY SUITING MADE TO YOUR ORDER IN ANY STYLE.

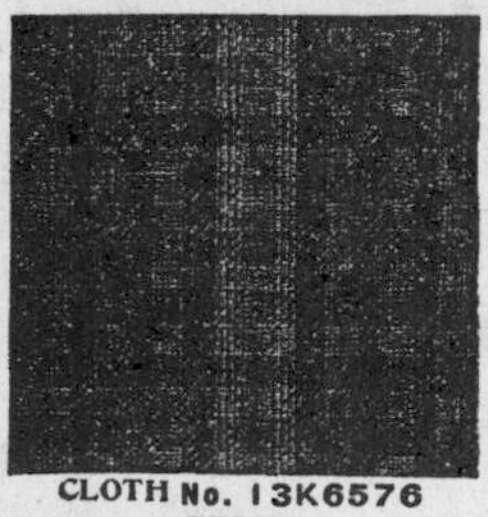

CLOTH No. 13K6576

PRICES

Suit	$18.72
Coat and vest	12.83
Coat and pants	16.10
Pants	6.39

Gray effects and brown effects are the real stylish goods for the season. Both at the left and the right we offer you extra fine brown effects, but here is **one of the real high class gray patterns** of the season. The background is a very fine diagonal twill worsted finish in a dark gray, over which run darker gray checks about ⅜ inch square with a larger check ⅝ inch square nearly black. At intervals of 1½ inches run two parallel sets of fine lines, ¼ inch apart, just serving to relieve the diagonal weave slightly. There is a faint purple thread overplaid which cannot be seen except by close examination, but which slightly relieves the dark gray. It is a pattern that will meet the requirements of those wishing to be strictly up to date and fashionable, as well as not prove any too striking for those of more modest taste. **It is a pure all wool worsted of very fine texture suitable for spring, summer and early fall wear. State what style you want.**

$21.96 ONE OF OUR HIGH CLASS BROWN EFFECTS IN PURE ALL WOOL WORSTED SUCH AS MERCHANT TAILORS USE IN SUITS AT $40.00, TO YOUR ORDER IN ANY STYLE.

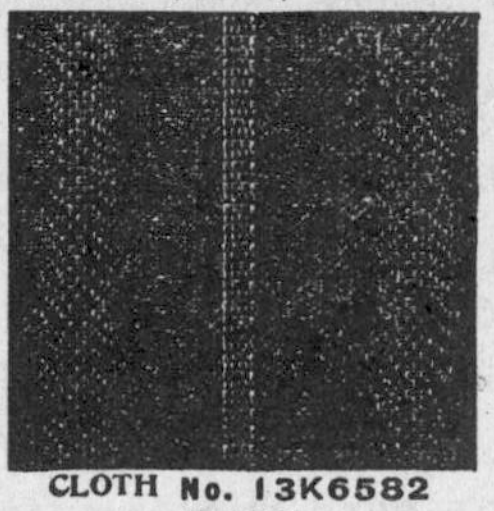

CLOTH No. 13K6582

PRICES

Suit	$21.96
Coat and vest	15.14
Coat and pants	19.05
Pants	7.57

This beautiful cloth is a pure all wool very fine worsted of a weight suitable for spring, summer and early fall wear, or for year around purposes in the milder climates. It is a medium finish, not as hard as the usual finished worsted and not as soft as the unfinished. The background is a rich dark brown with exceedingly faint darker brown shadows in the form of checks about ¼ inch square which are scarcely noticeable but making a very rich and stylish effect. There are birdseye weave stripes of the same dark brown shade ⅛ inch wide and ¾ inch apart. Each alternate stripe has a sprinkling of fine pinpoint gray threads 1-16 of an inch at each side of it and the other stripe has a dark red or maroon thread in each edge, serving to relieve the dark brown shade beautifully. We know you wouldn't get a finer pattern or quality in a $40.00 suit from an agent or home tailor. **State what style you want** and see our simple rules of measuring on page 1052.

MEN'S READY TO WEAR CLOTHING

$3 98 $17 93 to

WE FURNISH THE BEST CLOTHING EVER OFFERED IN READY TO WEAR GARMENTS, saving you about half the price you would pay anywhere else, because we manufacture all of it ourselves in our enormous clothing plant, the biggest and best equipped in the world, and sell the garments at the mere cost of the material and workmanship, with but our one bare small margin of profit added, cutting out woolen jobbers', and wholesale and retail profits and expenses altogether.

Many better qualities than ever before and lower prices than ever on the same qualities.

DON'T PAY RETAIL PRICES FOR CLOTHING

You need pay us the mere cost of labor and material and one small profit only, and not a single cent's worth of expense or profit for anything or anybody is added to the price, as you are the next to own the clothes after us, who are the manufacturers.

WE CONTROL EVERY STAGE OF THE MANUFACTURING from the very weaving of the cloth right through to the sponging and shrinking of it, the drafting, cutting and tailoring, and positively assure your getting the best materials and the best workmanship ever put into clothing. Don't listen to the fine quality talk of the high priced clothing manufacturer elsewhere who sells through dealers, who thus tries to give a reason for asking big prices. With all the advertising they do, they don't furnish any better clothing than is offered to you direct from these pages and from our big Sample Book No. 89K, and they ask about twice our price for it. Our trade is by far greater than that of several of the so called big clothing manufacturers combined, and the immense saving we make for you from our enormous output and small profits is certainly shown in every price and description and illustration in the following pages. Don't buy a dollar's worth of clothing anywhere else at any price until you have either ordered from this catalogue or have seen our big Sample Book No. 89K of Men's Ready to Wear Clothing, which is free and postpaid on request.

STYLES. The clothing offered on the following pages, from page 1056 to page 1078, is all men's ready to wear clothing and can therefore only be furnished in the exact styles as illustrated and described for each fabric. We cannot furnish any fabric in any other style than the style or styles in which the descriptions say it is furnished. If we cannot possibly meet your wishes in this matter from our line of ready to wear clothing please refer to pages 1052 to 1054, from which we offer to make clothing to order in any style desired.

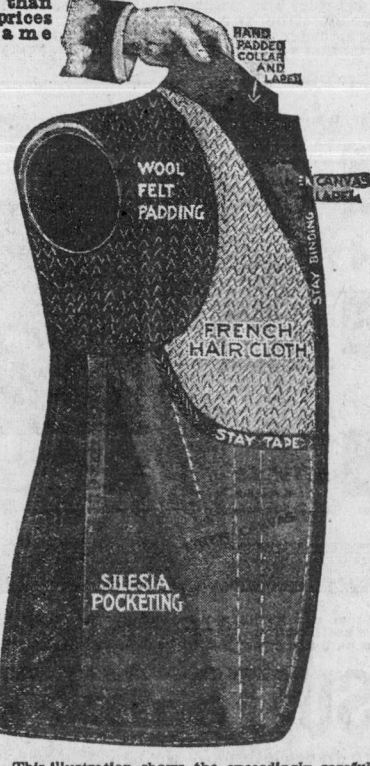

HAND PADDED COLLAR AND LAPEL

WOOL FELT PADDING

CANVAS LABEL

STAY BINDING

FRENCH HAIR CLOTH

STAY TAPE

SILESIA POCKETING

This illustration shows the exceedingly careful workmanship and the excellent foundation we put into the garments we make and shows why our clothing is much better than the average clothing offered on the market.

OUR GREAT GUARANTEE AND MONEY REFUND OFFER ON CLOTHING

WE ABSOLUTELY GUARANTEE TO FIT AND PLEASE YOU perfectly in every way. If you receive from us any clothing that fails to please you in any way at all, we ask you to return it to us at our expense and we will either exchange them for garments that will be satisfactory (and in such cases we will pay the transportation charges both ways), or if you prefer we will send you back your money, including any transportation charges you paid on the shipment. We take all the risk and you can't lose a single penny.

SEND US YOUR ORDER, follow our simple rules below, for measuring, shown enclose our price and we will send the garments to you and guarantee to please you in every way, fit you perfectly and surprise you with the wonderful value, otherwise we stand ready and willing to return your money. You take no risk at all. Don't pay retail prices and thus pay double the actual value of clothes, for we offer you the best clothing made direct from our big clothing manufacturing plant at manufacturer's prices and guarantee you against loss of any kind.

THE ILLUSTRATION HEREWITH shows you the interlinings we put into our suits. These are the materials that go between the outside cloth and the linings on the inside of the coat and are the materials that form the foundation on which the garments are built, and which enable them to keep their shape perfectly and give them the style and fashionable appearance which every person admires in clothing. You can't get better made clothes than these and in most clothing offered at retail such interior work on coats as we here show is not found. We guarantee all our clothing to be made in this careful, thorough and painstaking manner. These clothes will last longer than any clothing bought elsewhere and prove of surprising value for your money.

SIZES. The clothing offered on the following pages, from page 1056 to page 1078, is all men's ready to wear clothing and can therefore be furnished only in the sizes and styles mentioned in each description. Almost all of it comes only in sizes for men of BREAST measurements from 34 inches up to and including 42 inches, and WAIST measurements from 30 inches up to and including 40 inches, INSEAM measurements from 30 to 36 inches. LARGER SIZES in suits are offered only from the fabrics shown on page 1060.

THIS SHOWS YOU HOW EASY IT IS TO MEASURE

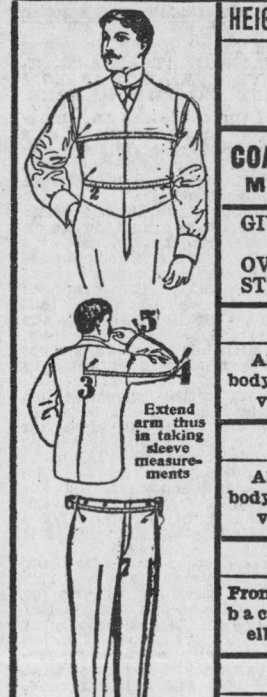

Extend arm thus in taking sleeve measurements

HEIGHT	WEIGHT		AGE

COAT OR OVERCOAT MEASUREMENTS		
GIVE COAT OR OVERCOAT STYLE No.	STYLE No.	
BREAST		
All around body at 1 over vest only	Inches	
WAIST		
All around body at 2 over vest only	Inches	
SLEEVE		
From middle of back at 3 to elbow at 4	Inches	
SLEEVE		
From middle of back at 3 to wrist joint at 5	Inches	

State whether you are ordering a suit, coat and vest, pants or overcoat

Goods No.	
PRICE OF GARMENT	
$	

VEST MEASUREMENTS		
BREAST		
All around body at 1 over vest only	Inches	
WAIST		
All around body at 2 over vest only	Inches	

PANTS MEASUREMENTS		
WAIST		
All around body at 6 over pants only	Inches	
INSEAM		
From close up in crotch at 7 to heel seam of shoe at 8	Inches	

DON'T BE THE LEAST AFRAID on the question of measuring as it is as simple and easy as A, B, C. Very likely you have a measuring tape in the house or can get one readily from a friend, or if you want one you can ask for our free Sample Book No. 89K, as we furnish a tape measure free with the book. Just use one of our order blanks if you happen to have one, or if you have not an order blank just use a plain sheet of paper and write down the measurements just in the way we call for them on this page. You can hardly make a mistake as it is so very easy, and, even if you do make a mistake, we take all the risk. We never ask our customers to accept any garments that are unsatisfactory for any reason whatever. Even if you do make a mistake, and the clothes should not be satisfactory, they may be returned to us at our expense and we will refund your money, both the price and the transportation charges, so you can't lose a cent.

THREE SIMPLE MEASUREMENTS and your height and weight will enable us to fill your order perfectly, and we guarantee to fit and please you with that information. These are your breast measure, taken around body at breast close up under the arms over the vest; waist measure, taken around body at waist over your pants—waist line is right above hip bones; inseam measure for pants, showing length of leg, taken from close up in crotch to heel seam of shoe. See illustrations on this page, which show you where measurements are taken. Give us these simple measurements and your height and weight, and we will fit you perfectly and guarantee to do so or refund your money. We mention other measurements here as well as the above because they will help in some cases where men are of special build, out of the ordinary. They enable us, in connection with the other measurements, to judge the proper proportions still better. If you can readily give the other measurements, we shall be glad to have them.

ABOUT THE TRANSPORTATION CHARGES (Freight, mail or express charges). If you order your suit of clothing or other garments, together with other goods from this catalogue, and the entire shipment is large enough (50 pounds or more) to go by freight, then the cost of freight charges on the clothing alone amounts to practically nothing, and will add nothing to the freight charges on the other goods. If you order only clothing from this catalogue, to be sent by express, the express charges will be very little. Below we give the weight of the different garments, and express charges on a package of clothing to towns within 100 to 500 miles from Chicago will only amount to 25 cents to 75 cents. A package of clothing can be shipped by express to almost any town within 500 miles of Chicago for 50 cents, greater or less distances in proportion.

THE AVERAGE WEIGHT OF CLOTHING. The following table shows you the average weight (packed and ready to ship) of different garments in this season's line:

Complete Suits	6½ pounds each
Pants, per pair	2 pounds each
Spring Overcoats and Cielette Raincoats	2½ pounds each
Winter Overcoats, average length	4½ pounds each
Ulsters	7½ pounds each
	8½ pounds each

ABOUT SENDING GOODS BY MAIL. A suit can be mailed by dividing it into more than one package. The heaviest package that will be carried by mail is 4 pounds, and the rate is 1 cent per ounce or 16 cents per pound. If you wish garments sent by mail, you must always include the postage with your order in addition to the price of the garments. Overcoats and corduroy suits cannot be sent by mail.

FREE

AND POSTPAID

THIS GREAT SAMPLE BOOK
(No. 89K) OF MEN'S READY TO WEAR CLOTHING

Write today and ask for it. Just say on a postal card or in a letter, "Send me free Sample Book No. 89K," or write and ask for our big Sample Book of Men's Ready to Wear Clothing and we will mail you this wonderful book with its 100 cloth samples and numerous illustrations of men's fashions representing our entire line of men's clothing which we describe and illustrate on the following pages in this Big Catalogue, together with free cloth tape measure, order blanks and simple rules for measuring, making everything plain and simple, ALL FREE AND POSTPAID ON REQUEST.

100 ACTUAL CLOTH SAMPLES, with scores of illustrations of men's fashions comprising the most complete line of Men's Ready to Wear Clothing to be seen anywhere this season, and all at a saving of one-third to one-half the money that clothing of such quality costs at retail.

$9.87 AN EXTRAORDINARY SUIT OFFER

THIS HANDSOME DARK MILD STRIPED SILK MIXED FANCY WORSTED EXACTLY LIKE SAMPLE

Goods No. 45K09046

Price for suit $9.87

Order this suit with the understanding that if you don't find it worth almost double what we ask for it, you can return it to us at our expense and we will refund your money. We guarantee to fit you perfectly.

YOU CAN SELECT YOUR GARMENTS from the pages of this Big Catalogue, as our descriptions and illustrations are very accurate and complete, but if you have any difficulty in making your selection don't fail to write at once for Sample Book No. 89K, which shows the actual samples of the cloth.

This small illustration shows our Sample Book No. 89K thrown open and letting you see the way we show page after page of samples and illustrations of styles which enable you to make your selection of cloth for your suit with perfect ease and satisfaction. If you will refer to page 1066 you can see another illustration of this same book thrown open to show other pages. This great book will convince you that we save you half the prices you will pay elsewhere for clothing.

$3.98 TO $17.93 FOR SUITS, $1.19 TO $5.24 FOR PANTS

This represents the range of prices we ask for just such high grade clothing as you see advertised at about double the prices at retail. We describe and illustrate this great line of clothing in the following pages, but if you have the slightest difficulty in making your selection from this catalogue, don't invest a dollar anywhere else for clothing until you write and get our great Sample Book No. 89K, from which we know you can make a selection to your utmost satisfaction and at the same time save half the money you would pay at retail, because we manufacture all this clothing and sell it at the mere cost of material and labor with but our one bare small margin of profit added. Write today and ask for free Sample Book No. 89K.

$5.83 BUYS YOU A SUIT FROM THIS DARK GRAY EFFECT WORSTED
MADE EXACTLY AS HERE ILLUSTRATED

WHILE WE OFFER A SUIT ON THE FOLLOWING PAGE AT EVEN A LOWER PRICE THAN THIS, YET, AS THIS IS A PARTICULARLY FASHIONABLE PATTERN FOR THE SEASON, WE ESPECIALLY RECOMMEND IT AS A GARMENT THAT WILL SHOW YOU CONVINCINGLY WHAT SPLENDID QUALITIES WE CAN GIVE EVEN AT AS LOW A PRICE AS THIS WHEN MAKING GARMENTS OURSELVES AND SELLING THEM DIRECT TO THE WEARER.

If you would like to try this dark gray effect fancy worsted suit in the style as illustrated, send us your measurements according to the simple plan shown on page 1055 and ask for

Goods No. 45K9012

Price for suit	$5.83
Price for coat and vest	4.26
Price for pants	2.13

SIZES. Breast measurements from 34 inches up to and including 42 inches; waist measurements from 30 inches to 40 inches. Inseam, 30 inches to 36 inches. **No larger sizes.**

THESE ILLUSTRATIONS of the coat, vest and pants were drawn from a suit made up from the exact material that you will get if you order this No. 45K9012 and the illustrations give you a very good idea of the pattern. You can't be disappointed if you order directly from this description.

THE STYLE is what we call our style 16, the same style as illustrated on a man's figure on the following page and there described also, coat is a three-button single breasted garment with three outside pockets and a small cash pocket located inside of the right hand outside pocket and one inside pocket. The corners of the coat show just a slight opening, the vest has five buttons and no collar. Pants are made in the latest medium peg top shape, not extreme, but just what the best dressers prefer. You don't get a suit from this number that lacks style in any way. You can expect a neat and thoroughly up to date garment.

THE CLOTH is a fair weight for spring, summer and early fall wear and is a good wearing worsted finish fabric that we are sure will give you splendid satisfaction and is just such goods as will be used in suits offered at retail at as high as $10.00. The background is a medium gray mixture and over this runs an indistinct dark check effect, not pronounced enough to make it conspicuous, but visible enough to bring it within the class of fabrics that are considered stylish and up to date. It is a shade that will give you perfect satisfaction for wear, as it will not show the dust readily.

WON'T YOU ORDER THIS SUIT so as to let us show you that we can actually give the dealers' $10.00 garment to you for $5.83? Of course we would rather sell you one of our better grade suits at $10.00 to $17.93, such as the dealers offer at $20.00 to $30.00, knowing these finer grades will give you better satisfaction, but if you want a suit at a low price, certainly we give you the biggest value for your money that you can possibly get when we offer you this garment.

REMEMBER THAT WE GUARANTEE to perfectly satisfy you in every way with any clothing you buy, guarantee to fit you in every case and we take the entire responsibility. While measuring is very easy, as shown on page 1055, yet even if you do make a mistake we don't ask you to accept any garments that are unsatisfactory in any way. In every case you are invited to return unsatisfactory goods and we will refund both the price and any transportation charges you paid. This is our offer whether you order this suit at $5.83 or our best suit in this line at $17.93.

A PAGE OF SPECIAL VALUES IN SINGLE BREASTED SUITS

THE FOLLOWING EIGHT NUMBERS ARE FURNISHED ONLY IN THIS STYLE 16, SINGLE BREASTED GARMENT, AS ILLUSTRATED, AND CANNOT BE FURNISHED IN ANY OTHER STYLE.

These pictures illustrate accurately the different patterns, and as each is described carefully in order to give you a correct idea of the color, we are sure we can satisfy you right from this catalogue, but if you do not wish to order from our descriptions, send for our big free Sample Book No. 89K, as per our offer on page 1056.

$3.98 OUR GREAT LEADER VALUE IN DARK STRIPED CASSIMERE SUITING. THE LOWEST EVER NAMED FOR A GUARANTEED SUIT.

GOODS No. 45K9010
Price for suit.....$3.98
Price for coat and vest..........2.91
Price for pants..$1.46

Style—This quality comes in our fashionable three-button single breasted garment, style 16, illustrated and described on this page. **Cloth** is a special value at this price, being a firmly woven cassimere, excellent spring and summer weight, and a strong wearing cloth, particularly adapted to business wear. Background is a plain black weave with a mild and pleasing pattern of alternating blue and white broken threads. The effect is a medium gray. **Trimmings** in this suit are of good quality, and garment is substantially interlined and reinforced. While this would be easily a $7.00 retail value, yet we advise you to buy such garments as we sell for about $8.00 and up to obtain the greatest values, but if you are looking for a first class value at the lowest price possible, this number will certainly please you.

SIZES. Breast, from 34 inches up to and including 42 inches. Waist, from 30 to 40 inches. DON'T FORGET TO GIVE YOUR SIZES.

$6.87 A MEDIUM GRAY WORSTED IN THE POPULAR CLUB CHECK PATTERN.

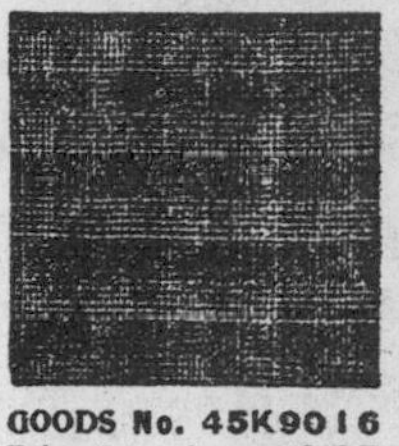

GOODS No. 45K9016
Price for suit....$6.87
Price for coat and vest..........5.04
Price for pants...2.52

Style—We furnish this pattern in our handsome style 16, three-button garment, illustrated and described on this page, with the added feature of belt loops on pants. **Cloth** is a beautiful fancy worsted with a medium gray background, over which are woven at regular intervals, vertical and horizontal shadow stripes ¼ inch wide, forming a nobby club check pattern, not conspicuous, but prominent enough to give this pattern a distinctive style quality. For a sample of the goods, send for our big free Sample Book No. 89K. **Trimmings**—Coat body lining is of good domestic Italian and pants curtain and vest back are of domestic twill. Our garments are all interlined as per the illustration on page 1055 and their lasting shape and style is insured by this careful method of reinforcement.

SIZES. Breast, from 34 up to and including 42 inches. Waist, from 30 to 40 inches. PLEASE STATE YOUR MEASUREMENTS.

$7.26 HANDSOME MEDIUM GRAY WORSTED SUITING IN OUR STYLE 16.

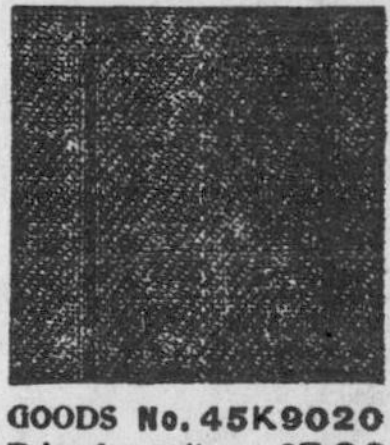

GOODS No. 45K9020
Price for suit....$7.26
Price for coat and vest..........5.32
Price for pants...2.66

Style—We have this suit in our fashionable style 16, as illustrated on this page, with the addition of belt loops on pants. This garment is a common sense business and dress fashion, thoroughly stylish, and in demand everywhere among the tastiest dressers. **Cloth** is one of the handsomest medium priced worsteds in our line, substantially woven from good yarns, and made to withstand long wear. If you are interested in a suit at this medium price, don't fail to consider this one carefully, as this is a style that will surely please you. Background is a plain, medium gray shade, into which are interwoven at intervals of 1 inch, narrow dark stripes half way between which run single silver threads. This is one of the mildest possible patterns in the season's most popular new shade. **Trimmings**—Coat is lined with domestic Italian and the entire trimmings are of an honest, good wearing standard of goods. See page 1055 for an illustration and description of our interlinings which enable the coat to keep permanent shape.

SIZES. Breast, from 34 up to and including 42 inches. Waist, from 30 to 40 inches. DON'T FORGET TO GIVE YOUR MEASUREMENTS.

SEE OUR FREE SAMPLE BOOK OFFERS ON PAGES 1056 AND 1066.

WE GUARANTEE TO FIT YOU. SEE EASY MEASURING PLAN ON PAGE 1055.

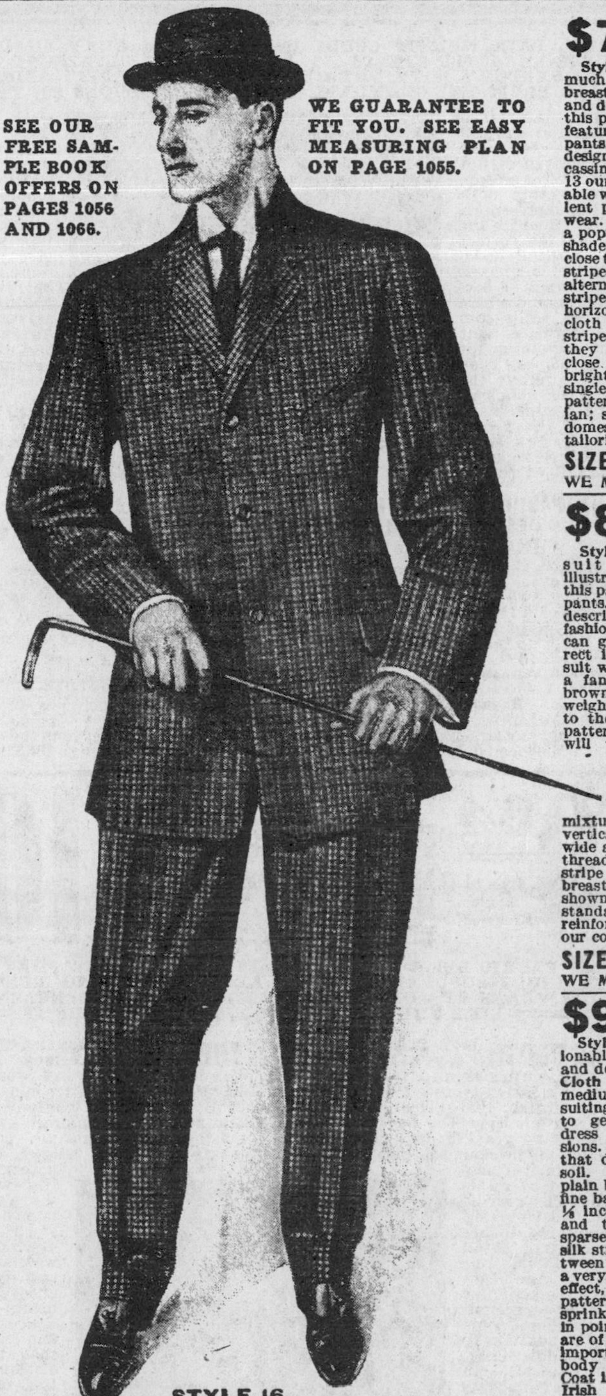

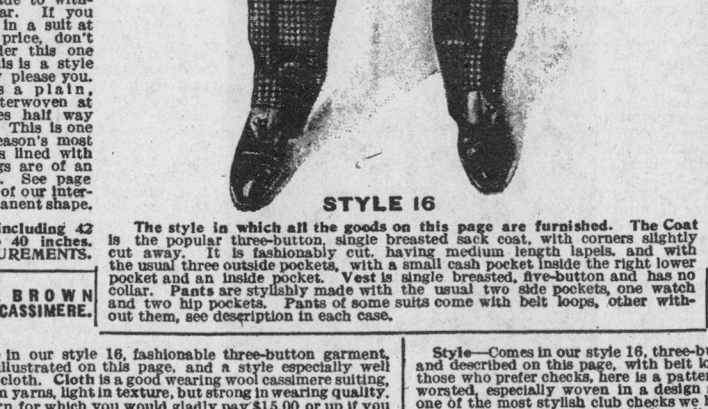

STYLE 16

The style in which all the goods on this page are furnished. The Coat is the popular three-button, single breasted sack coat, with corners slightly cut away. It is fashionably cut, having medium length lapels, and with the usual three outside pockets, with a small cash pocket inside the right lower pocket and an inside pocket. **Vest** is single breasted, five-button and has no collar. **Pants** are stylishly made with the usual two side pockets, one watch and two hip pockets. Pants of some suits come with belt loops, other without them, see description in each case.

$7.68 YOU CAN'T AFFORD TO MISS THIS NOBBY GRAY MIXED WOOL CASSIMERE.

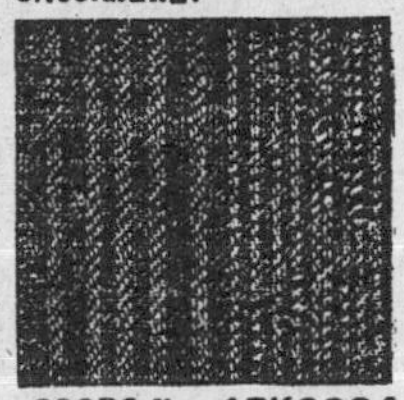

GOODS No. 45K9024
Price for suit....$7.68
Price for coat and vest..........5.62
Price for pants...2.81

Style—Comes in our much favored single breasted style 16, shown and described in detail on this page, with the added feature of belt loops on pants. **Cloth** is a neat design, light weight wool cassimere, weighing about 13 ounces per yard, a suitable weight and an excellent pattern for general wear. Background is of a popular new dark gray shade, over which run close together lighter gray stripes, making a neat alternate light and dark stripe effect. Woven horizontally through the cloth are dark gray stripes, so very faint that they cannot be noticed at a slight distance, but on close observation lending a mild check effect. To brighten up the plain gray, there is an occasional single brown thread running vertically through the pattern. **Trimmings**—Coat is lined with domestic Italian; sleeve lining, vest back and pants curtain are of domestic twill. Interlinings are of good grade and tailoring is first class.

SIZES. Breast, from 34 up to and including 42 inches. Waist, from 30 to 40 inches. WE MUST HAVE YOUR MEASUREMENTS.

$8.73 FOR A HIGH GRADE MIXED WORSTED SUIT IN THE GRAY BROWN SHADE.

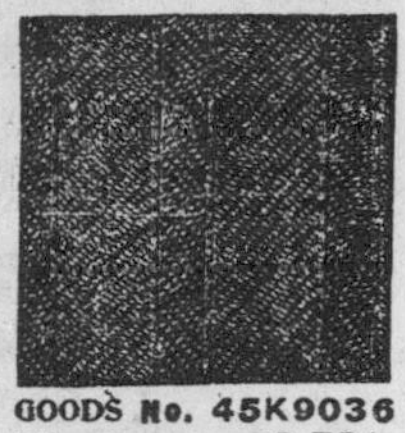

GOODS No. 45K9036
Price for suit...$8.73
Price for coat and vest.....6.40
Price for pants....3.20

Style—We have this suit in our style 16, illustrated and described on this page, with belt loops on pants. Read the detailed description and see the fashion figure and you can get an absolutely correct idea of just what your suit will be like. **Cloth** is a fancy mixed gray and brown mixed worsted, weighing about 13 ounces to the yard, and a splendid pattern and texture that will wear long after you have had them made into pants for the little fellow. The background is a rich dark brown and gray mixture over which run vertical stripes of a darker gray shade, about ⅜ inch wide and ⅝ inch apart, with an almost invisible green thread in each. The general effect is a handsome stripe pattern that looks especially well in this single breasted style 16. Nothing more striking is being shown anywhere. **Trimmings**—Suit lined with fine standard Italian, with our superior interlinings and reinforcements. See page 1055 for a description of our coat making.

SIZES. Breast, from 34 up to and including 42 inches. Waist, from 30 to 40 inches. WE MUST KNOW YOUR SIZE.

$9.87 THIS DARK WORSTED SUITING IN OUR STYLE 16 IS A GREAT VALUE.

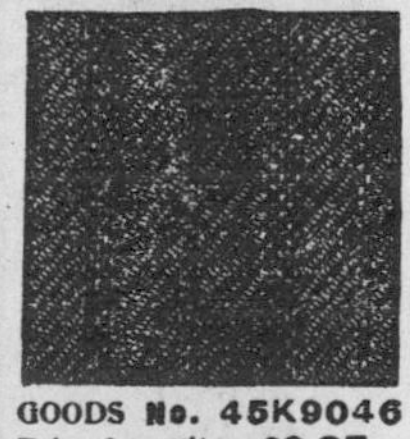

GOODS No. 45K9046
Price for suit...$9.87
Price for coat and vest.....7.24
Price for pants, 3.62

Style—Made in our fashionable style 16, illustrated and described on this page. **Cloth** is a good grade medium weight worsted suiting, especially adapted to general wear for both dress and business occasions. It is the kind of cloth that does not readily show soil. The background is plain black over which run fine basket weave stripes ⅛ inch wide, 1 inch apart, and through which are sparsely interwoven orange silk strands. Half way between these stripes there is a very narrow stripe in cord effect, and over the entire pattern there is a slight sprinkling of silver threads in point effect, and scarcely noticeable. **Trimmings** are of good grade; the coat being lined with fine imported English Italian, with sleeve lining, vest body and pants curtain of best domestic sateen. Coat is well interlined and reinforced with wool felt, Irish canvas and herringbone haircloth. Seams stitched with silk, pockets stayed, and tailoring throughout only the best.

SIZES. Breast, from 34 up to and including 42 inches. Waist, from 30 to 40 inches. PLEASE REMEMBER TO GIVE YOUR SIZE.

$7.43 FOR THIS CHOICE BROWN PLAID IN WOOL CASSIMERE.

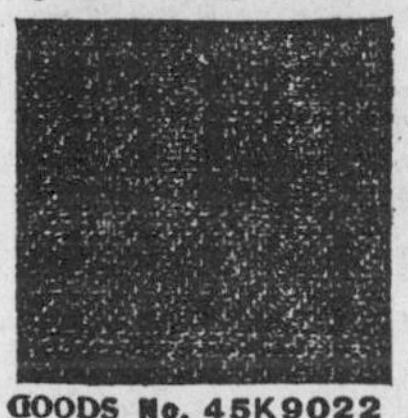

GOODS No. 45K9022
Price for suit....$7.43
Price for coat and vest..........5.44
Price for pants.......2.72

Style—Made in our style 16, fashionable three-button garment, described and illustrated on this page, and a style especially well adapted to this cloth. **Cloth** is a good wearing wool cassimere suiting, woven from firm yarns, light in texture, but strong in wearing quality. This is a pattern for which you would gladly pay $15.00 or up if you didn't know of our splendid values. **Cloth** has a rich, dark brown background, into which are woven at intervals of ½ inch, navy blue stripes, and the plaid is finished by horizontal stripes, made up of three indistinct silver threads. While not conspicuous, the plaid in this pattern is just plain enough to relieve the conventional stripe effect. **Trimmings**—This garment is lined with durable Italian and finished in our usual way, illustrated and fully explained on page 1055. After reading of the way in which we so carefully reinforce and interline our garments, you will be convinced of their matchless wearing qualities.

SIZES. Breast, from 34 up to and including 42 inches. Waist, from 30 to 40 inches. DON'T NEGLECT TO GIVE YOUR SIZES.

$9.76 FOR THIS FINE MEDIUM GRAY CLUB CHECK SUITING.

Style—Comes in our style 16, three-button garment, as illustrated and described on this page, with belt loops on pants. **Cloth**—For those who prefer checks, here is a pattern in a firm, medium weight worsted, especially woven in a design and quality that makes this one of the most stylish club checks we have ever shown. The background is of dark gray, over which run lighter gray stripes ⅛ inch wide and ⅛ inch apart, making an alternate light and dark stripe pattern. This same stripe effect runs horizontally over the pattern, introducing a mild club check, but to relieve the check design, every fifth vertical stripe is in herringbone weave. Send for a copy of our big free Sample Book No. 89K if you wish to see a sample of this number. **Trimmings** are of the best quality, and our garments are interlined as per the drawing and description on page 1055. Remember, if any of our suits fail to satisfy you in any respect, you are at liberty to return them at our expense for a refund or exchange.

SIZES. Breast, from 34 inches up to and including 42 inches. Waist, 30 to 40 inches. BE SURE TO STATE YOUR SIZE.

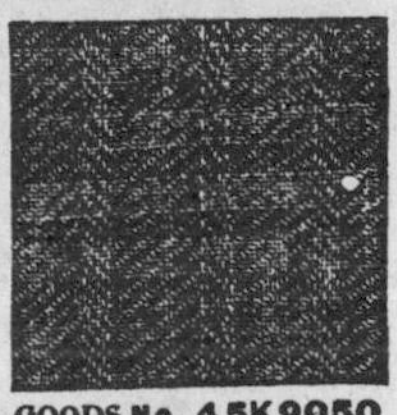

GOODS No. 45K9050
Price for suit...$9.76
Price for coat and vest.....7.18
Price for pants 3.58

$8.97 WOULDN'T YOU LIKE A FASHIONABLE $9.97 GRAY SUIT THIS SEASON?

$8.97 Style 16 Single Breasted

$9.97 Style 30 Double Breasted

HERE WE OFFER A WORSTED FINISH, FAIR WEIGHT GOODS IN A MEDIUM GRAY SHADE WITH A FAINT HERRINGBONE STRIPE EFFECT IN BOTH SINGLE AND DOUBLE BREASTED STYLES AT PRICES THAT REPRESENT JUST THE MERE COST OF THE MATERIAL AND LABOR IN OUR OWN CLOTHING FACTORY WITH BUT OUR ONE SMALL PROFIT ADDED AND REPRESENTING VALUES OF ABOUT $15.00, JUDGING FROM THE STANDARD RETAIL QUOTATIONS ON THE MARKET TODAY.

THIS CLOTH is a firmly woven worsted material of fair weight for spring, summer and fall wear. The shade is a medium gray, not so light as to make it easily soiled and not too dark for attractiveness, but a good standard gray for a fashionable garment this season. **The pattern** is represented fairly by the picture of a sample of the goods shown here. This picture represents a sample 2 inches square of the exact cloth of which the suits are made and shows the actual weave and the correct distances between the faint stripes. The up and down diagonal weave is what is popularly known as a herringbone effect, and where these diagonal twills join you see it forms a faint stripe effect, or what might rather be called lines. They serve merely to relieve the plainness of the goods as they are of the same shade as the rest of the goods. No finer fabrics than these are offered in suits at $15.00 at retail.

See about our Great Free Sample Book No. 89K on pages 1056 and 1066.

THE SUITS FROM THIS FABRIC are lined in body with a fine mercerized Italian cloth of excellent wearing quality and the sleeves are lined with mercerized twill. Turn to page 1055 and you will see how the interlinings are put into the coat. In this case they consist of wool felt padding, Belgian canvas and French elastic in fronts to hold their shape. Pockets are stayed with linen tape and in every way the garment is so made that it will give you the best possible wear, keep its shape nicely and represent the latest fashionable style of the season. By making the clothes ourselves we can positively guarantee to furnish better garments than can ordinarily be obtained at retail, even though you have to pay about twice as much for the clothes that you buy elsewhere. We would like you to try our suits from this fabric as a test of our values.

We Positively Guarantee to Fit and Please you or Refund your Money.

THIS FABRIC IS FURNISHED IN THE TWO STYLES ILLUSTRATED AND DESCRIBED ON THIS PAGE. ORDER BY THE NUMBER THAT REPRESENTS THE STYLE YOU PREFER.

If you want this fashionable gray cloth in our three-button single breasted style 16, as illustrated on the left, ask for

Goods No. 45K9030
PRICES

Suit, style 16	$8.97
Coat and vest, style 16	6.58
Pants	3.29

If you want a suit of this fine gray goods in our three-button double breasted style 30, as illustrated on the right, ask for

Goods No. 45K9031
PRICES

Suit, style 30	$9.97
Coat and vest, style 30	7.58
Pants	3.29

SIZES. **Breast** measurements from 34 inches up to and including 42 inches. **Waist** measurements from 30 to 40 inches. We do not carry any larger sizes in these goods. We furnish larger sizes from the goods shown on page 1060 only. **Measuring is very easy. See page 1055.**

$9.64 PLEASE CONSIDER THIS $10.64 CHOICE VERY MILD SHADOW CHECK AND PLAID EFFECT FANCY WORSTED FOR YOUR SUIT

$9.64 Style 16 Single Breasted

$10.64 Style 30 Double Breasted

THIS FABRIC BELONGS TO A CLASS OF PATTERNS THAT ARE EXCEEDINGLY POPULAR, PARTICULARLY FOR YOUNG MEN FROM 20 TO 35 YEARS OF AGE, IN FACT, MANY OLDER GENTLEMEN WHO LIKE THE LIVELIER GOODS ALSO ADMIRE IT.

THE CLOTH is a fair weight for any climate for spring, summer and fall purposes, and is a fancy worsted with a fairly hard finish that gives it a splendid wearing quality. The background is a fairly dark gray shadow check effect, not at all pronounced, but just enough to make it pleasing, and over this runs a black birdseye weave plaid about 1¼ inches square, not at all too noticeable, but serving to relieve the plainness of the background and giving it some life in addition to the shadow check. There is also an almost invisible overplaid of fine small blue and green threads which you can hardly notice, except by observing the fabric closely, and still they relieve the dark gray neatly. You will like this for a business suit.

THE LININGS consist of fine mercerized Italian in the body and strong wearing twill in sleeves. The interlinings are made of Belgian canvas reinforced with wool felt and again reinforced with French elastic. Shoulders are padded and pockets well stayed, thus guaranteeing a coat that will hold its shape and give the utmost satisfaction from the standpoint of wearing quality and from appearance. Our garments will hold their shape better and wear longer than the average clothing offered on the market and thus prove a splendid investment aside from the fact that we offer them at about half retail prices. See page 1055 for an illustration of the way we make our garments.

STYLE 16

One of the most practical of all styles. Coat is single breasted with three buttons, three outside pockets and a small cash pocket inside the right hand pocket and one inside pocket, and the corners of the coat show just a slight opening. Vest has five buttons and no collar. Pants made in the fashionable medium peg top shape. Each of the two fabrics shown on this page comes in this style. The above illustration shows a man wearing the single breated suit made from the goods shown at the top of this page.

STYLE 30

The very fashionable double breasted sack suit. Coat has two rows of three buttons each and has the stylish broad deep lapels and three outside pockets with small change pocket in right hand pocket, and one inside pocket. Vest has five buttons and no collar. Both the fabrics shown on this page come in this style as well as in the style shown on the opposite side of the page. Pants are made in the fashionable medium peg top shape. The above illustration shows a man wearing the double breasted suit made from the goods shown at the bottom of this page.

THIS CLOTH AS ILLUSTRATED IS FURNISHED IN BOTH SINGLE AND DOUBLE BREASTED STYLES EXACTLY LIKE THE FASHION FIGURES ON THIS PAGE. ORDER BY THE NUMBER THAT REPRESENTS THE STYLE YOU PREFER.

If you want this fabric as illustrated and described, in single breasted style 16 as shown at the left of the page, ask for

Goods No. 45K9044
PRICES

Suit, style 16	$9.64
Coat and vest, style 16	7.06
Pants	3.53

If you want these goods exactly as illustrated and described, in the three-button double breasted style 30 as shown on the right of this page, ask for

Goods No. 45K9045
PRICES

Suit, style 30	$10.64
Coat and vest, style 30	8.06
Pants	3.53

SIZES. **Breast** measurements from 34 inches up to and including 42 inches. **Waist** measurements from 30 to 40 inches. We do not furnish any other sizes from this fabric. If you must have larger sizes we can furnish them only from the goods shown on page 1060.

YOUR MONEY WILL BE IMMEDIATELY RETURNED TO YOU FOR ANY GOODS NOT PERFECTLY SATISFACTORY. 655

ALL SUITS ON THIS PAGE ARE FURNISHED IN STYLE 16

WE HAVE MADE OUR ILLUSTRATIONS AND DESCRIPTIONS OF THE FABRICS ACCURATE AND CLEAR so that they give you a correct idea of the designs and colors of the patterns and that you may very easily make your selection. However, if you have any difficulty in making your selection, be sure to send for our big Sample Book No. 89K, described on pages 1056, and 1066, which we will send you **free and postpaid.**

$12.49 A WONDERFUL VALUE IN AN ALL WOOL AND SILK WORSTED SUITING IN THE LATEST DARK OLIVE BROWN SHADE.

Goods No. 45K9074

PRICES

Suit	$12.49
Coat and vest	9.16
Pants	4.58

STYLE 16 as shown in illustration with belt loops on pants. **THE CLOTH** is a pure wool and silk worsted of a medium weight, suitable for all year around wear. The surface is one-half fine small basket weave and one-half very fine diagonal weave arranged in alternate bars, each ¼ inch wide. A very faint gold pinpoint thread runs through each basket weave bar, but is hardly noticeable. This whole pattern makes an exceedingly neat dark olive brown shade suiting. If you are looking for a handsome suit and one that will give good wear, this one we are positive will please you. **THE TRIMMINGS**—The coat body is lined with fine serge and the vest with a very fine grade of sateen. Shoulders are carefully padded with wool felt. See illustration on page 1055, which shows how our clothing is made. Agents and other dealers sell a suit of this kind regularly at $18.00 and $20.00.

SIZES. Breast, 34 inches up to and including 42 inches. Waist, 30 inches up to and including 40 inches. No larger sizes. **Be sure to give size when ordering.**

$13.38 A VERY NOBBY GRAY MIXED ALL WOOL SUIT MADE IN SINGLE BREASTED SACK STYLE.

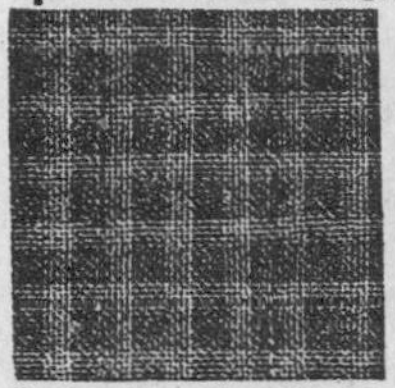

Goods No. 45K9082

PRICES

Suit	$13.38
Coat and vest	9.80
Pants	4.90

THE STYLE—Very fashionable style 16, as shown in the illustration. Look at the illustration and see exactly how the suit is made. We also furnish pants of this number with belt loops and tabs on hip pockets. **THE CLOTH** has an exceedingly beautiful gray mixed background, which is relieved by a very subdued and indistinct shadow check composed of faint vertical and horizontal alternate bars of dark gray, brown and green threads. The texture of the cloth is very firm and a better cloth, combining both style and service cannot be had. It is an all wool worsted adapted for spring, summer and early fall wear. **THE TRIMMINGS** used throughout this garment are of the finest. An imported English serge is used for lining the body of the coat and an imported English sateen for the sleeves. Every coat front is interlined with French canvas and French haircloth. The collars and shoulders are all carefully padded and all seams are sewed with silk.

SIZES. Breast measure, 34 inches up to and including 42 inches. Waist, from 30 inches up to and including 40 inches. No larger sizes. **Remember to give sizes. It is easy. See page 1055.**

$13.63 FOR AN EXCEEDINGLY BEAUTIFUL DARK NAVY BLUE ALL WOOL WORSTED HERRINGBONE WEAVE SUITING.

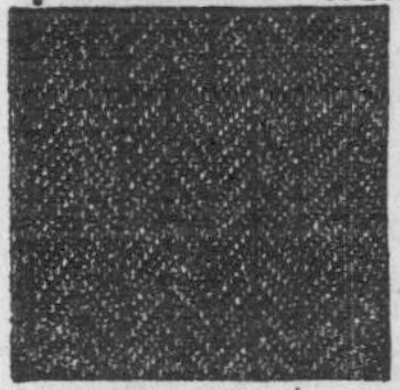

Goods No. 45K9086

PRICES

Suit	$13.63
Coat and vest	10.00
Pants	5.00

THE STYLE—Our style 16, with belt loops on pants and tabs on hip pockets. **THE CLOTH** is a particularly fine grade of all wool dark navy blue worsted woven in ⅛-inch herringbone stripes. While this is a very modest appearing piece of goods, yet when made up in a suit, the effect is very rich and stylish. The texture of the cloth is very firm, and as it is of fairly good weight, the suit is suitable for all year around wear. **THE TRIMMINGS**—Every coat front is interlined with an exceptionally fine grade of French canvas and French haircloth, and the linings are of the very highest grade English sateen and serge. In fact, all the trimmings are those usually only found in high priced tailor made garments. Those who are partial to blue serge suits will find this suit a very pleasing substitute, as it possesses their style and wearing qualities. If you had a blue serge suit last season you will especially like this change this season. Why not order one today?

SIZES. Breast measure, 34 inches up to and including 42 inches. Waist, from 30 inches up to and including 40 inches. No larger sizes. On page 1055 we tell you how to take measurements. It is easy.

$13.79 HERE WE HAVE A RICH DARK FANCY WORSTED SUITING THAT WILL APPEAL TO MEN OF ALL AGES.

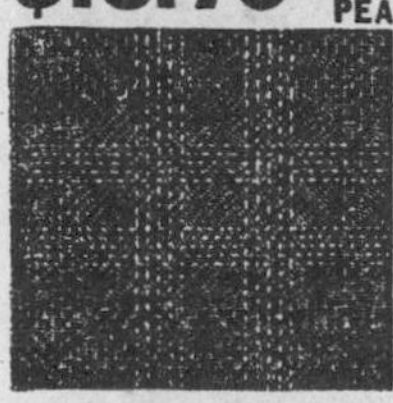

Goods No. 45K9088

PRICES

Suit	$13.79
Coat and vest	10.10
Pants	5.05

THE STYLE—Made in the favorite three-button single breasted sack style 16, as shown in illustration. With belt loops on pants and tabs on hip pockets. **THE CLOTH** is an unusually finely woven dark all worsted, of medium weight. The background is a very fine jet black diagonal weave. Over this run horizontal and vertical birdseye weave bars ⅛ inch wide, forming an overplaid 1¼ inches square. Within every plaid are nine shadow checks formed by very faint gray horizontal and vertical bars each ¼ inch wide, which, however, are not conspicuous, but tend to lighten up the pattern, which otherwise would be a plain black one. **THE TRIMMINGS**—Every seam in this suit is sewed with the very best silk thread. Every pocket is tacked with silk thread and reinforced with linen tape. The coat fronts are interlined with extra quality canvas and haircloth and are guaranteed by us to keep their shape. Lined with fine serge and sateen qualities.

SIZES. Breast measure, 34 inches up to and including 42 inches. Waist, 30 inches up to and including 40 inches. No larger sizes. **Do not fail to give sizes when ordering.**

YOU RUN NO RISK

IF THE GARMENT DOES NOT SATISFY YOU IN EVERY PARTICULAR—WORKMANSHIP, MATERIAL AND VALUE—YOU MAY SEND IT BACK TO US AND WE WILL REFUND YOUR MONEY.

Quality Considered, our Prices are now Lower Than Ever.

We Guarantee to Fit You or Refund Your Money.

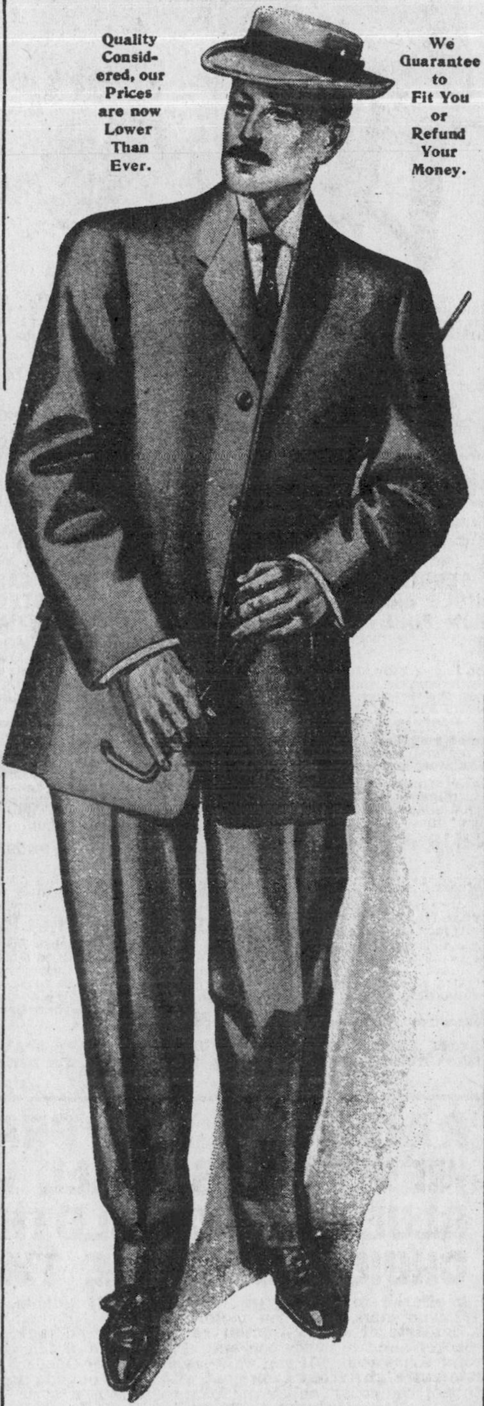

STYLE 16

A VERY STYLISH THREE-BUTTON SINGLE BREASTED SACK STYLE with the corners slightly cut away. **THE COAT** has three outside pockets, with cash pocket inside the lower right hand pocket, also one inside pocket. **THE VEST** is five-button single breasted style, without collar, with the usual pockets. **THE PANTS** are cut in the medium peg top style so much in demand by good dressers. All suits described on this page are furnished in this style only. If you prefer other styles, see other pages of this catalogue.

The pants of some numbers have belt loops and tabs on hip pockets, others have not. See descriptions of each number.

$10.43 A VERY HANDSOME SILK DECORATED BROWN WORSTED, SUITABLE FOR SPRING, SUMMER AND FALL WEAR.

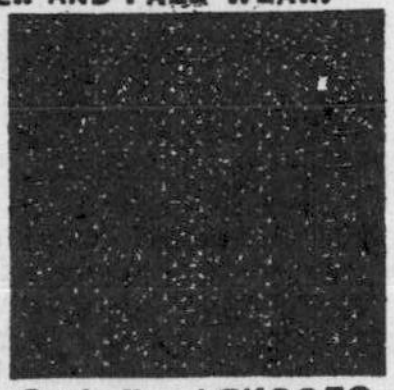

Goods No. 45K9052

PRICES

Suit	$10.43
Coat and vest	7.64
Pants	3.82

THE STYLE is our style 16, the three-button single breasted sack (see illustration). **THE CLOTH** is a worsted finish goods of an excellent wearing quality, suitable for spring, summer and early fall wear. The background is a very dark shade of brown, relieved by a sprinkling of very fine pinpoint silk threads of red, gray and green, which are barely discernable. Over this, running alternately ½ inch apart, are corded stripes 1-16 and ⅛ inch wide, of same shade as background, which, however, are not conspicuous. The cloth is of a very fine texture, is firmly woven and will give good wear. **THE TRIMMINGS**—The coat body is lined with an imported English Italian. Every pocket is carefully tacked with silk and reinforced with linen tape. Read page 1055, which shows and explains how these suits are built up. A suit made in this style and of this material would cost you $15.00 or $18.00 if purchased from dealers.

SIZES. Breast measure, 34 inches up to and including 42 inches. Waist, from 30 inches up to and including 40 inches. No larger sizes. **Be sure to give your measurements.**

$11.98 HERE IS A VERY STYLISH DARK GRAY ALL WOOL WORSTED AND SILK SUITING.

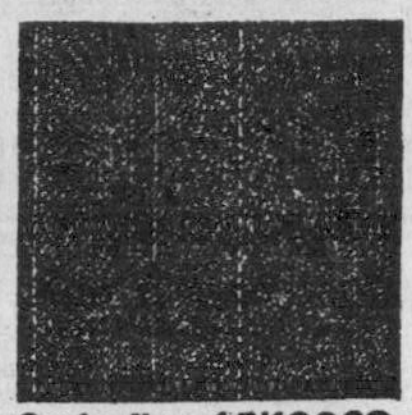

Goods No. 45K9068

PRICES

Suit	$11.98
Coat and vest	8.78
Pants	4.39

THE STYLE—We have this suit in the practical style 16, as per illustration on this page, which is so much in favor with good dressers. **THE CLOTH** is a medium weight dark gray diagonal weave, all wool worsted and silk. The background, which is dark gray, is relieved by very faint stripes composed of three broken lines of silver silk threads running 1 inch apart. Exactly in the middle between these stripes are three hardly noticeable parallel lines of black threads. The stripes and lines are not conspicuous, but serve to relieve the pattern which otherwise would be a very dark gray. **THE TRIMMINGS**—Very high grade domestic serge lining is used for the coat body and an excellent striped mercerized sateen for the sleeves. All of the trimmings are of the kind used by tailors and other dealers in suits that sell at twice the price of this one. Order one today. We guarantee that you will be pleased with it.

SIZES. Breast, 34 inches up to and including 42 inches. Waist, 30 inches up to and including 40 inches. No larger size. **Don't forget to state size.**

$14.26 FASHIONABLE BLACK ALL WOOL WORSTED DIAMOND WEAVE SUITING.

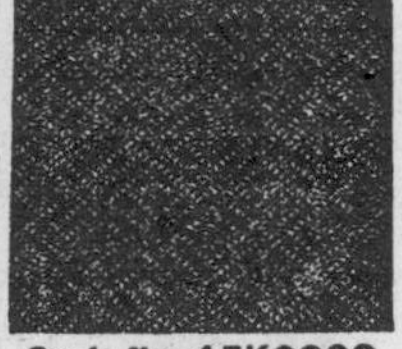

Goods No. 45K9092

PRICES

Suit	$14.26
Coat and vest	10.46
Pants	5.23

THE STYLE—Very popular three-button single breasted sack, style 16, as illustrated, with the addition of belt loops on pants and tabs on hip pockets. **THE CLOTH** is an exceptionally fine grade of black all wool worsted, medium weight, woven in the beautiful diamond design so extensively worn by fashionable dressers. The illustration will give you a very good idea of the pattern. It is specially adapted for spring, summer and early fall wear, but may also be used for a year around suit. **THE TRIMMINGS** used throughout this suit are high class. The body of the coat is lined with the very best imported English serge and the sleeves with an extra quality English sateen. The shoulders are carefully padded with all wool felt and French haircloth. Read page 1055, which tells you how carefully our garments are made in every detail. We do not hesitate to say that you cannot get a suit equal to it from any local dealer, agent or others for less than $25.00.

SIZES. Breast measure, 34 inches up to and including 42 inches. Waist, 30 inches to 40 inches. No larger sizes. **Do not forget to give size when ordering. It is easy.**

$14.94 VERY LATEST DARK GRAY SHADOW CHECK ALL WOOL WORSTED SUITING.

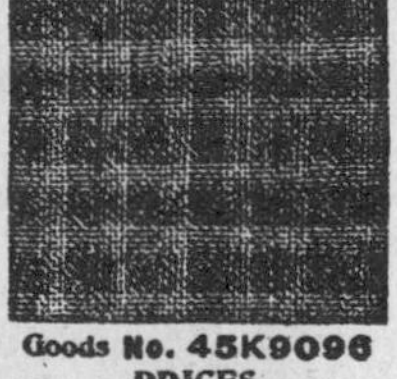

Goods No. 45K9096

PRICES

Suit	$14.94
Coat and vest	10.94
Pants	5.47

THE STYLE as illustrated on this page is the widely popular three-button single breasted sack style 16, with the additional features of belt loops on pants and tabs on hip pockets. **CLOTH** is a medium weight dark gray pure wool worsted. The background is a very fine jet black diagonal weave over which run very indistinct stripes composed of two sets of three parallel lines ¼ inch apart. These stripes run at intervals of 1½ inches. Between these, ¾ inch apart, appear hardly noticeable single vertical lines of green threads. Over the whole appear very dark gray horizontal and vertical bars forming checks ¾ inch square. It is an exceptionally neat suiting, and when made up in our style 16 makes a stylish garment for spring, summer and fall wear. **THE TRIMMINGS** are in keeping with the high quality of the suit, the coat body and sleeve linings being the very finest imported English serge and English sateen. Read page 1055, which tells you how well made our garments are in every detail.

SIZES. Breast, from 34 inches up to and including 42 inches. Waist, 30 inches to 40 inches. **Be sure to mention size when ordering.**

$20.00 FOR TUXEDO OR PRINCE ALBERT SUITS

THESE PRICES BUY YOU THE HIGHEST CLASS READY-TO-WEAR DRESS GARMENTS, MADE FROM IMPORTED ALL WOOL UNFINISHED BLACK DRESS WORSTED AND FACED WITH PURE SILK.

DON'T GO TO THE HIGH PRICED CLOTHIER in your neighborhood, who handles the line of a high priced manufacturer, if you want to get a thoroughly up to date, high grade, finely tailored ready to wear Prince Albert, Tuxedo or full dress suit. We are offering garments in these styles, made from the finest all wool imported dress suiting with high class linings and trimmings and tailored in the most perfect manner, for just about half the price that you will pay at retail, because we offer them to you at just a small profit over the actual cost of material and workmanship.

WE GUARANTEE TO FIT AND PLEASE YOU PERFECTLY

and prove these suits worth $40.00, judging by standard retail values, or you may return them to us at our expense and we will refund both the price and any transportation charges you paid.

If you want the double breasted Prince Albert suit, as above illustrated, faced with silk, ask for

Goods No. 45K9110
PRICES
Suit..........$20.00
Coat and vest 15.00
Pants........ 7.00

If you want this Tuxedo style suit, faced with silk, as illustrated, ask for

Goods No. 45K9112
PRICES
Suit..........$20.00
Coat and vest 15.00
Pants........ 7.00

If you want this full dress style suit, faced with silk, as illustrated, ask for

Goods No. 45K9114
PRICES
Suit..........$22.00
Coat and vest 17.20
Pants........ 7.00

$22.00 FOR FULL DRESS SUITS

THE CLOTH from which these dress suits are made is a genuine imported English unfinished black dress worsted, weighs 17 ounces per yard, thus being suitable for year around purposes. It is a fabric of rich finish and will maintain its high class appearance as long as you wear the suit. It is just such a cloth as would be used in the very finest custom tailored garment made by the most fashionable merchant tailor in big towns and cities. If you wish to see a sample before ordering write and ask for our Sample Card No. 291K.

THE LININGS AND TRIMMINGS ARE AS FOLLOWS: The coat bodies and backs of vests are lined with imported satin finish Venetian, which wears much better than satin or silk and is the most stylish lining obtainable other than silk, and gives much better satisfaction. The sleeves are lined with fine English striped sateen and inside of vests with high grade dove color sateen. The coat lapels and fronts are faced with pure silk. The coats are interlined with all wool felt in shoulders, high grade French haircloth in fronts and sewed with silk throughout. The interlinings shown on page 1055 are carried out to perfection and represent the finest of materials all the way through in the case of these dress garments.

SIZES. We furnish only sizes from 34 inches up to and including 42 inches breast, and from 30 to 40 inches waist, and from 30 to 36 inches inside seam. Just give the same measurements as for an ordinary suit, as shown on page 1055. Remember, we positively guarantee to fit and please you perfectly or refund your money.

SPECIAL VALUES IN MAIL CARRIERS' UNIFORMS

In mail carriers' uniform suits our values are absolutely supreme. We have built up a tremendous patronage among the mail carriers of the country because of the quality of our uniforms, because of the thorough satisfaction they give to the wearer, and because we have always sold them at wonderfully low prices. The steady and enormous increase in the volume of our business in this line has resulted in reducing our cost to the lowest possible figure, and our selling prices represent actual cost with only the very smallest and most necessary margin of profit added. If you wish to see samples of the cloth from which these mail carriers' uniforms are made we will be pleased to mail to you our sample card No. 191K free on request.

$8.90 MAIL CARRIERS' REGULATION SPRING AND SUMMER SINGLE BREASTED UNIFORM, MADE FROM PURE ALL WOOL GRAY SUITING.

THE STYLE consists of the regulation four-button straight front sack coat with three outside pockets and one inside pocket, regulation buttons and corded edges, the style for usual spring and summer wear. Vest is single breasted with six buttons and notched collar and has regulation buttons. Pants in usual style.

THE CLOTH is the regulation all wool pure dye gray uniform goods, especially woven for mail carriers, and is a fair weight especially adapted for spring, summer and early fall wear.

THE TRIMMINGS consist of specially strong, honest wearing fabrics, and the interlinings are as indicated on page 1055, giving lasting qualities, good shape and style to the suit. If you want a suit or other garment of these goods, ask for

Goods No. 45K9118
PRICES
Suit, sizes from 34 to 42 inches breast.................$8.90
Coat and vest, sizes from 34 to 42 inches breast........ 6.52
Pants, sizes from 30 to 40 inches waist................ 3.26

PRICES FOR LARGER SIZES cut to fit heavy set regularly built men only, are as follows:
Suit, sizes, 43 to 50 inches breast....................$11.00
Coat and vest, sizes, 43 to 50 inches breast.......... 8.00
Pants, sizes, 42 to 50 inches waist................... 3.75
This extra cost just covers the actual extra cost to us for making, as we have to make these large sizes to special order. We do not carry them in stock.
Don't fail to give measurements. See our simple plan on page 1055.

$10.90 MAIL CARRIERS' REGULATION DOUBLE BREASTED UNIFORM FROM HEAVY WEIGHT ALL WOOL GRAY CLOTH.

THE STYLE consists of the regulation coat in double breasted style with two rows of five buttons each, corded edges and regulation buttons, and with three outside pockets and one inside pocket. The vest is single breasted and is high cut, especially adapted for fall and winter suit. Pants are made in the usual fashion with usual pockets at each side, one watch and two hip pockets.

THE CLOTH is a good heavy weight pure all wool absolutely fast dye regulation gray material, which will give any amount of wear, and is especially adapted for fall and winter purposes and for any person wanting a heavy weight garment the year around.

THE TRIMMINGS consist of an extra strong lining, and the interlinings are as illustrated on page 1055, making the coat substantial and durable in every respect. If you want this special value uniform, ask for

Goods No. 45K9120
PRICES
Suit, sizes, 34 to 42 inches breast...................$10.90
Coat and vest, sizes, 34 to 42 inches breast.......... 8.00
Pants, sizes, 30 to 40 inches waist................... 4.00

PRICES FOR LARGER SIZES cut to fit heavy set, regularly built men only, are as follows:
Suit, sizes, 43 to 50 inches breast...................$13.00
Coat and vest, sizes, 43 to 50 inches breast.......... 9.50
Pants, sizes, 42 to 50 inches waist................... 4.50
The extra cost just covers the extra cost to us, as we make these large sizes to order. We do not carry them in stock.
Be sure to state your sizes. See our simple plan of measuring on page 1055.

We do not carry in stock larger sizes than 42 inches breast or larger than 40 inches waist in mail carriers' uniforms. The larger sizes must be made to order, after your order arrives, for which we require six to eight days' time.

$10.47 RAILROAD AND GRAND ARMY MEN'S SUITS IN ALL WOOL NAVY BLUE UNIFORM CLOTH AND YOUR CHOICE OF THESE TWO STYLES.

THE STYLES: This fine fabric is offered in two styles, one particularly adapted for Grand Army men and the other suitable for conductors, brakemen, motormen, etc.

STYLE 1, illustrated to the left, consists of a four-button round cornered sack coat with two lower outside pockets, one small cash pocket and two inside pockets. Five-button notch collar vest, with usual pants. This is a style commonly worn by Grand Army men. If you want style 1 ask for Goods No. 45K9116.

STYLE 32 consists of a four-button straight front sack coat with three outside pockets and one inside pocket, and six-button vest with notched collar and usual pants. This is a style commonly worn by railroad men, although Grand Army men also use it. If you want style 32 ask for Goods No. 45K9117.

BOTH STYLES are made with detachable black buttons, so that street car, railroad men or G. A. R. men can detach the black buttons and put regulation buttons on in place of them. We furnish an extra set of G. A. R. buttons along with suit when requested.

CLOTH is the finest medium weight pure all wool navy blue flannel suiting for year around wear, and is guaranteed fast indigo dyed. If you want to see a sample, write for our Sample Card No. 191K.

THE SUITS ARE LINED with good durable Italian body lining and sateen sleeve lining, interlined with wool felt and haircloth as shown on page 1055, and are guaranteed to give the best possible service.

PRICES
Suit in either style, 1 or 32...$10.47
Coat and vest.. 7.68
Pants... 3.84

SIZES. We furnish these suits only in sizes from 34 inches up to and including 42 inches breast and from 30 to 40 inches waist.

STYLE 1
If you want this all wool navy blue uniform goods in round corner sack style 1, as illustrated above, ask for
Goods No. 45K9116

STYLE 32
If you want this all wool navy blue uniform goods in straight front sack style 32, as illustrated above, ask for
Goods No. 45K9117

MEN'S LIGHT WEIGHT SUMMER OUTING SUITS

Stylish Warm Weather Suits, consisting of Coat and Pants only, no vest. Coat, skeleton or half lined only, suit otherwise unlined; Pants made with belt loops, suspender buttons sewed inside the waistband and with turned up or golf bottoms; made from light weight crash flannel worsted and blue serge summer fabrics

DON'T PAY A TAILOR OR CLOTHIER a fancy price for your light weight summer clothes this year. We are furnishing the most fashionable and finely made garments **direct to you at manufacturer's prices** from our great clothing manufacturing plant and we are saving you about half the money you would be obliged to spend elsewhere. **Look through this great line** and select your garments. The styles are carefully illustrated and the fabrics fully described and pictured from actual samples of the cloth.

IF YOU WISH TO SEE ACTUAL CLOTH SAMPLES of our summer outing clothes, write for **free Sample Book No. 86K.** This is a separate line by itself and is represented only by Sample Book No. 86K.

OUTING SUITS (Coat and pants only) **weigh** on an average 59 ounces each, that is, 3 pounds 11 ounces. See front pages about figuring transportation charges. They are very small, and especially so when you have clothing shipped with other goods.

WE FURNISH THESE CLOTHES ONLY IN THE STYLES ILLUSTRATED and described in each case. Certain goods come in certain styles only. No fabric can be had in any other style than the one illustrated and described. While the different styles vary, each summer suit in this line consists only of a coat and pair of pants. We don't furnish a vest and we sell **the coat and pants together only and never separate.**

WE GUARANTEE to fit and please you in every way, and if you receive from us any garment that is unsatisfactory at all you are perfectly at liberty to return it to us at our expense and we will refund both the price and any transportation charges you paid.

SIZES. We furnish these summer garments only in sizes from 34 inches up to and including 42 inches breast measure, from 30 to 40 inches waist and from 30 to 36 inches inseam. We don't furnish any larger sizes in these goods. See page 1055 for our simple system of measuring. Don't forget to give your measurements.

$4.49 VERY LIGHT WEIGHT MEDIUM GRAY ALL WOOL CRASH SUMMER OUTING COAT AND PANTS.

Style—As illustrated on this page, our style 16. Note description and illustration and you will see exactly how it is made. **The Cloth** is an all wool open weave crash of very light weight and of cool and summery **appearance.** It has a medium gray background, over which are distributed irregular bars of a darker gray, showing just a slight pattern, but very indistinct. It makes a stylish and very neat garment, especially when you consider the extremely low price. **Trimmings**—Coat is lined in the sleeves only with domestic twill, but there is no other lining, either in coat or pants. It is neatly finished, all seams being carefully worked, giving the garment a well tailored appearance. If you would like to see a sample of this suiting, as well as the others in this line, write for free Sample Book No. 86K.

GOODS No. 41K1400
Price for coat and pants $4.49

SIZES. Breast measurements from 34 inches up to and including 42 inches. Waist measures from 30 to 40 inches. No larger sizes. Be sure to give measurements.

$5.29 FANCY MEDIUM GRAY AND DARK CHECKED WORSTED SUMMER COAT AND PANTS.

Style—Comes exactly as illustrated in the fashion figure on this page, our style 16. A neat three-button single breasted garment with pants having belt loops and golf or turned up bottoms. This is the only style in which this number comes. **The Cloth** is a light weight fancy worsted weave of good wearing quality and the background is a medium gray shade, while over it run indistinct dark checks about 1/3 inch square. The check effect is not pronounced, but relieves the plainness of the goods and gives it a decidedly nobby and up to date appearance. **Trimmings**—The coat has a sleeve lining of domestic twill, but has no other lining, the garments being made for summer comfort.

GOODS No. 41K1404
Price for coat and pants $5.29

SIZES. Breast measurements from 34 inches up to and including 42 inches. Waist measurements from 30 to 40 inches. No larger sizes. Don't forget measurements.

$8.29 FAIRLY DARK GRAY AND MILD STRIPED WORSTED OUTING COAT AND PANTS.

Style—This neat fabric comes in style 16, exactly as illustrated and described on this page. It is a practical, neat, up to date fashion very much adapted to this class of goods. You can see exactly the kind of garment you will get by examining the illustration and description. **The Cloth** is a fairly dark or what might be called a medium gray worsted finish material of light weight and of fine herringbone weave. There are two parallel stripes about 1/8 inch wide and 1/8 inch apart that run at intervals of 1 1/2 inches, consisting of threads of lighter gray, and the surface between them is divided into three equal parts by one single thread stripe of faint green, another of faint red or maroon, the whole effect being a medium gray relieved slightly by the faint stripes. **Trimmings**—The coat is half lined in body with domestic serge and a neat striped sleeve lining. There is no lining in coat back.

GOODS No. 41K1428
Price for coat and pants $8.29

SIZES. Breast measures from 34 to 42 inches. Waist measures from 30 to 40 inches. We do not furnish any larger sizes. Be sure to give measurements.

$5.98 EXTRA VALUES IN SUMMER OUTING SUITS OF VARIOUS SHADES AND PATTERNS.

The Style—This number represents goods furnished in single breasted sack styles, mostly like style 16 on this page, although some of them have four buttons on the coat instead of three; otherwise the style is made precisely like illustration here. **The Cloth**—We offer a variety of goods here, some gray, some gray and brown and some medium shades and overplaid effects in cassimeres and some fancy worsteds, representing odds and ends of cloth we have left over in our summer tailoring. We offer them to you at real low prices to close them out. While we cannot promise you any exact pattern like we can from the other numbers, yet if you are not over particular in this matter and will leave us to select for you we can give you an exceptional value and undoubtedly please you well. **Trimmings**—The suits are made exactly like our other outing suits. Coats are half lined in body with Italian fabrics and with twill sleeve lining.

GOODS No. 41K1430
Price for coat and pants $5.98

SIZES. We furnish only breast sizes from 34 to 42 inches and waist sizes from 30 to 40 inches. Give sizes.

ALL PANTS in these summer suits have belt loops, buttons sewed inside the waistband, and turned up or golf bottoms.

ALL FABRICS ON THIS PAGE COME IN THIS STYLE

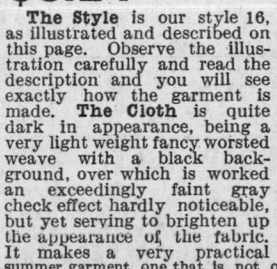

SEE OUR SIMPLE PLAN FOR GIVING MEASUREMENTS ON PAGE 1055.

STYLE 16

Our Three-Button Single Breasted Summer Outing Suit (the style in which all the suits on this page come), consisting of three-button single breasted coat with three outside pockets and pants with belt loops, suspender buttons sewed inside the waistband, and golf or turned up bottoms. Coats are unlined in body and lined in sleeves, according to the quality and class of material. See description of each number for special details. **The above illustration** represents the general fashion of the suit. We sell the coat and pants together only and never separately and don't furnish a vest.

$8.24 VERY DARK MILD GRAY CHECK FANCY WORSTED SUMMER OUTING SUIT.

The Style is our style 16, as illustrated and described on this page. Observe the illustration carefully and read the description and you will see exactly how the garment is made. **The Cloth** is quite dark in appearance, being a very light weight fancy worsted weave with a black background, over which is worked an exceedingly faint gray check effect hardly noticeable, but yet serving to brighten up the appearance of the fabric. It makes a very practical summer garment, one that is not only comfortable but will maintain its good appearance longer than a lighter colored garment. It won't show the dirt so quickly. After the summer is over you could wear the coat in the house or for office purposes all winter. **Trimmings**—Coats are half lined in body with domestic serge. No lining in back. Sleeves lined with striped sateen. Suits are very neatly finished and of excellent fitting qualities for summer garments.

GOODS No. 41K1436
Price for coat and pants $8.24

SIZES. We furnish only breast measurements from 34 inches up to and including 42 inches and waist measurements from 30 to 40 inches. Remember to give sizes.

$6.97 A SPECIAL LOT OF EXTRA VALUES IN SUMMER OUTING SUITS.

Styles—The suits come in styles like style 16 on this page, and others have four buttons, but are essentially like style 16 and made in the summer fashion with golf bottoms on pants, belt loops and suspender buttons sewed inside the waistband, etc. **The Cloth**—In this lot we have dark gray pinchecks patterns, overplaids and medium and dark gray mixed goods in fancy worsteds, cassimeres, flannels, etc. If you leave the matter of choice to us we will pick you as near to what you prefer as possible from the lot, as these suits are made from small ends of cloth left over in our manufacturing department in our summer tailoring, and are offered at low prices to close out the goods, and the suits are made just as neatly and carefully as all others, only, of course, we can't promise you any exact pattern. **Trimmings**—Coats half lined with good Venetian in body; no lining in back, but lined in sleeves with English sateen.

GOODS No. 41K1438
Price for coat and pants $6.97

SIZES. Only breast measures from 34 inches up to and including 42 inches and waist measures from 30 to 40 inches. Be sure to give measurements.

$11.35 OUR VERY FINEST HIGH GRADE ALL WOOL WORSTED NAVY BLUE SERGE.

Style—Comes in style 16, like fashion illustrated and described on this page. In the case of this garment, we have put **side buckles and tabs on the pants** pockets thus adding a strictly up to date and very stylish feature to the suit. **The Cloth** is an exceedingly fine small twill rich dark navy blue serge, **strictly all wool** and a fine light weight, making a decidedly classy and fashionable garment, a suit with the **college air** about it, up to date enough for the young or middle aged man who wishes to wear the very latest. **Trimmings**—Coat is half lined with satin finished Venetian and sleeves are lined with imported French sateen, leaving the back unlined. The tailoring in this garment is decidedly neat and of a highly finished order, all seams being carefully worked and neatly finished. We especially recommend this high grade blue serge suit.

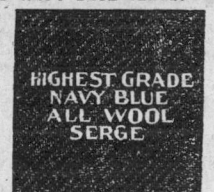

HIGHEST GRADE NAVY BLUE ALL WOOL SERGE

GOODS No. 41K1464
Price for coat and pants $11.35

SIZES. Breast measures from 34 inches up to and including 42 inches. Waist measures from 30 to 40 inches. We furnish only the sizes stated. Remember to give sizes.

$13.98 OUR VERY BEST FINE WEAVE ALL WOOL GRAY WORSTED AND SILK SUMMER OUTING COAT AND PANTS.

Style—Made in style 16, exactly as illustrated and described on this page, only that we have added the up to date feature of side buckles and tabs on pockets of pants. This is the latest thing, and considering the quality of these goods it certainly constitutes a most beautiful and fashionable garment. **The Cloth** is a strictly all pure wool worsted with a very slight mixture of pure silk and of a fine small diagonal weave, with a background of medium gray, over which run vertical and horizontal bars of small very dark gray threads forming a modest overplaid 1 inch square. Very rich and high class in appearance. $25.00 invested at retail would not bring you any finer quality or more fashionable clothes than these. **Trimmings**—Coat half lined in body with PURE SILK, remainder of coat body unlined. Sleeves lined with imported sateen with silk finish. As this is our best summer outing suit and costs only $13.98 it is a most remarkable offer.

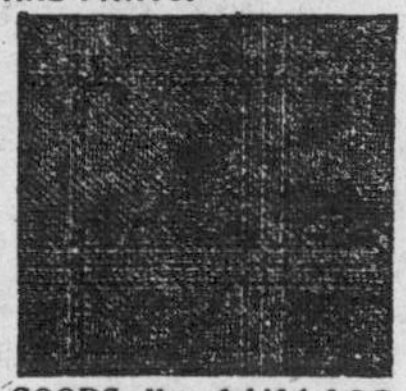

GOODS No. 41K1468
Price for coat and pants $13.98

SIZES. We furnish breast sizes from 34 inches up to and including 42 inches and waist sizes from 30 to 40 inches. We don't furnish any larger sizes. Be sure to give measurements.

$2.48 OUR KHAKI SUMMER SUIT OFFER.

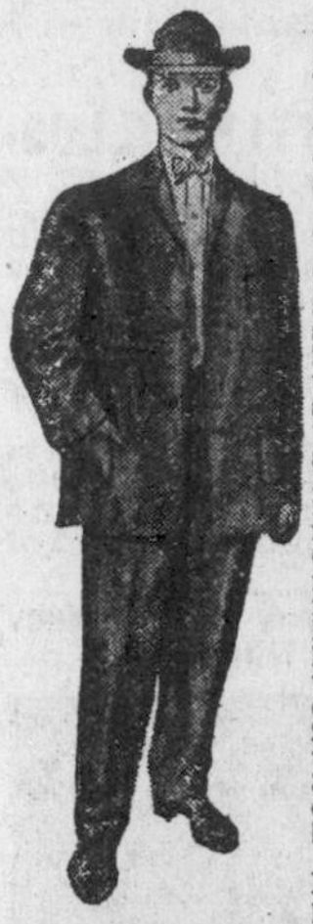

THE STYLE comprises two garments only, the coat and pants, no vest. THE COAT is single breasted with three buttons and straight front, one inside and three outside pockets. NO LINING. Made light and comfortable for summer purposes. THE PANTS have belt loops and seams are taped and extra well sewed. THE MATERIAL is the regulation light weight tan colored khaki similar to that used by the U. S. army for the soldiers' summer uniform. It's a tested, strong wearing, durable fabric and makes garments that are especially suitable for fishing, excursions, ordinary hunting trips or the like, where something of light and comfortable weight and of strong construction is desirable. SIZES—From 34 inches to 42 inches breast and 30 to 40 inches waist. Average weight, 49 ounces. Be sure to give sizes.

Goods No. 41K595 Price for coat and pants.......... $2.48

MEN'S FANCY VEST VALUES.

GIVE SIZE AROUND BODY AT BREAST OVER VEST. SEE PAGE 1055.

$1.19 A CHOICE NEAT WHITE AND DARK STRIPED WASH VEST.

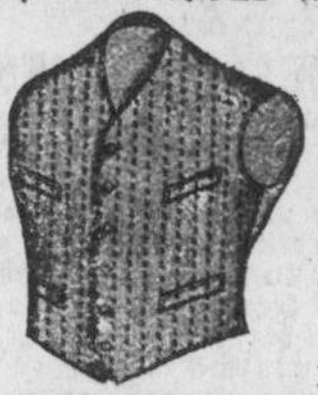

This is a neat, sensible pattern which always is in good taste. The ground work is a plain white weave over which run mild dark stripes. Made with usual pockets, neatly tailored and finished with pearl buttons. Good fitting form. SIZES—From 34 inches to 42 inches breast. State size.

Goods No. 41K46 Price for vest.... $1.19

$1.49 A WHITE DRESS VEST WITH THE LATEST STYLISH EFFECT.

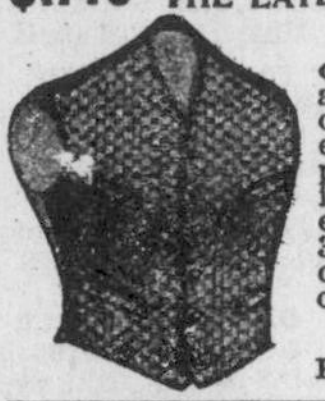

A plain white wash vest of excellent style, suitable for wear on dress occasions. Nicely tailored, neatly trimmed with pearl buttons. The fabric is a plain, neat fine birdseye weave. SIZES—From 34 inches up to and including 42 inches breast only. State size.

Goods No. 41K48 Price for vest.... $1.49

$1.89 OUR ASSORTMENT OF FASHIONABLE COLORED FANCY VESTS.

The lot comprises patterns with dark shades over which run dots or dashes in green or red and various colors. Some have tan or tan shaded backgrounds with combination of figures and dots. They are all dressy designs and the vests are finely made. SIZES—From 34 inches to 42 inches breast measure only.

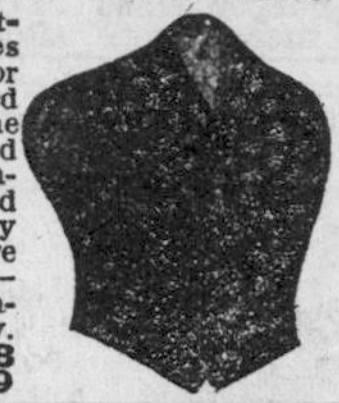

Goods No. 41K58 Price for vest.... $1.89

$2.39 OUR FINEST AND VERY FASHIONABLE PEARL SHADE AND SILK MIXED VEST.

This vest has the rich, grayish white shade or pearl color with silk finish designs worked over the background, bringing out a handsome and stylish appearance. It makes a pleasing contrast with coat and pants in dark shades. SIZES—From 34 inches to 42 inches breast only.

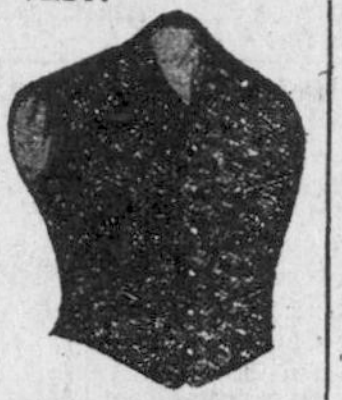

Goods No. 41K66 Price for fancy vest.......... $2.39

98c TAN COLORED OUTING PANTS WITH BELT TO MATCH FROM EITHER COTTON COVERT OR KHAKI CLOTH.

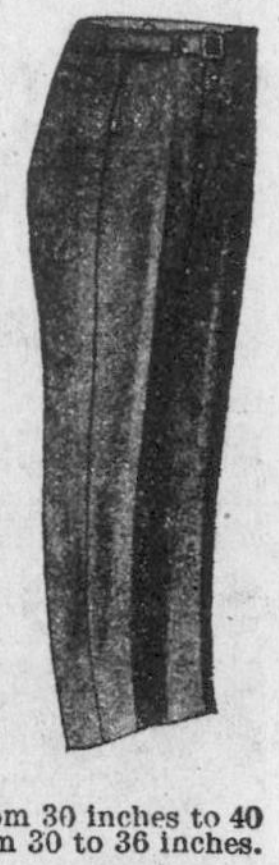

We offer here two different materials in the same style of pants adapted for outing purposes, for summer games like tennis, etc. The pants are firmly sewed and reinforced. Have watch, side and hip pockets and belt loops, with suspender buttons sewed inside the waistband. We furnish belt of the same goods with steel buckle with pants. Take your choice of materials as below.

Light Weight Tan Cotton Covert outing pants, made as described above.

Goods No. 41K598 Price.............. 98c

Light Weight Tan Khaki outing pants, made as described above.

Goods No. 41K599 Price.............. 98c

SIZES—Waist measure from 30 inches to 40 inches; inseam measure from 30 to 36 inches. Be sure to give sizes.

ALPACA, DRAP D'ETE AND BLUE SERGE SUMMER COATS AND COATS AND VESTS.

SIZES—This clothing comes only in sizes from 34 inches up to and including 42 inches breast. We don't furnish any larger or smaller sizes. Give size around body at breast over vest. See our simple measuring plan on page 1055.

WEIGHT AND TRANSPORTATION CHARGES: We give average weight of each class of garments below. See front pages of catalogue about transportation cost. If you wish any garment sent by mail, include postage extra at the rate of 1 cent per ounce.

MEN'S ROUND CUT SACK ALPACA AND SICILIAN COATS.

These eight numbers come in style 49, three-button round cornered sack style with three outside pockets as illustrated. Average length of coat, 32 inches. Average weight, 22 ounces.

$1.00 MEN'S BLACK ALPACA COAT.

A good grade of black alpaca, well made, and for this price represents splendid value. Don't compare it with cheaply made coats retailed at about $1.35. This is better made. Style 49. SIZES—34 to 42 inches chest. State size.

Goods No. 41K6 Price for coat.................. $1.00

$1.50 MEN'S FINE GRADE BLACK ALPACA COAT.

Same style as the above, No. 41K6, only a much finer quality. These coats have two lower pockets and one breast pocket. Length about the same as ordinary dress sack coat. SIZES—34 to 42 inches chest. Be sure to state size.

Goods No. 41K10 Price for coat.................. $1.50

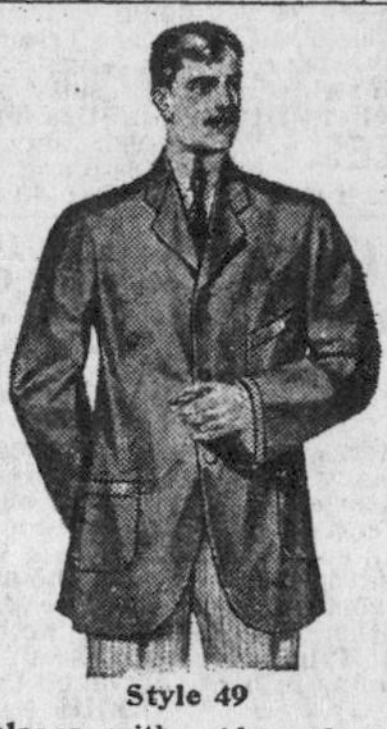

Style 49

$2.00 MEN'S BLACK ALPACA COAT, OF FINE LUSTER.

An excellent quality of black alpaca, with fine luster finish, double stitched seams, usual pockets; $3.00 retail value. Style 49. SIZES—34 to 42 inches chest. State size.

Goods No. 41K14 Price for coat, $2.00

$2.25 EXTRA QUALITY SILVER GRAY ALPACA COAT.

Made from an extra fine grade of silver gray alpaca. Very fine goods and good wearer. Has breast pocket and two lower pockets. Style 49. SIZES—34 to 42 inches chest. Be sure to state size.

Goods No. 41K15 Price for coat, $2.25

$2.50 MEN'S EXTRA FINE QUALITY BLACK ALPACA COAT.

Something extra fine, with a jet black glossy finish; extra well tailored, double stitched throughout, three pockets. Style 49. SIZES—34 to 42 inches chest. Be sure to state size.

Goods No. 41K16 Price for coat, $2.50

$3.00 BUYS OUR VERY FINEST BLACK SACK STYLE ALPACA COAT.

The very best grade of alpaca, good weight, strong, serviceable fabric, with a fine jet black glossy finish of high luster. No wholesale house quotes a finer coat to the dealer for as low as $3.00. Three outside pockets. Style 49. Finely tailored. SIZES—34 to 42 inches chest. Be sure to state size.

Goods No. 41K18 Price for coat.......................... $3.00

$3.45 HIGH CLASS SILK FINISH BLACK SICILIAN COAT.

An extra fine class of goods called black Sicilian cloth, having a finish or gloss resembling silk. Finely sewed and neatly tailored, wide facings. Style 49, three-button sack with three outside pockets and one inside pocket. One of the very finest summer coats imaginable. SIZES—34 to 42 inches chest. Be sure to state size.

Goods No. 41K19 Price for coat, $3.45

$4.25 OUR VERY FINEST SILK FINISH BLACK SICILIAN COAT.

Made the same as the above, No. 41K19, only of the very best grade of silk finish black Sicilian cloth and double ply over shoulders and facings in front, thus making an extra stylish summer garment. Extra well tailored, neatly sewed, something you seldom find at retail at any price. Style 49. SIZES—34 to 42 inches chest. Don't forget to state sizes.

Goods No. 41K21 Price for coat, $4.25

LONG BLACK ALPACA AND DRAP D'ETE COATS FOR PROFESSIONAL MEN, MINISTERS, ETC.

Two of these numbers come in style 51. Average length, 37 inches. Straight front, three outside pockets. Average weight, 22 ounces. For professional men or anybody wanting a fairly long coat.

Three numbers come in style 52, average length, 37½ inches. Same general style as style 51, only longer. The favorite style for ministers. Average weight, 22 ounces.

INCLUDE A
SUMMER COAT OR FANCY VEST
WITH
YOUR ORDER FOR OTHER CLOTHING.

It will add hardly anything to the weight of a package and nothing or next to nothing to the transportation charges and these values are most remarkable. BE SURE TO STATE SIZE WANTED.

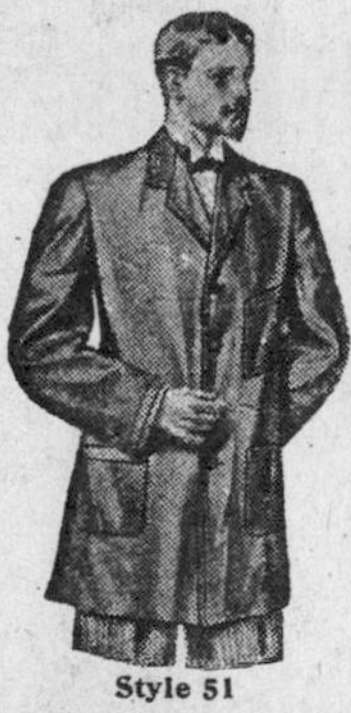

Style 51

$2.00 GOOD GRADE LONG ALPACA COAT.

Made from durable quality of black alpaca cloth, wide facings, neatly trimmed throughout. Style 51. SIZES—34 to 42 inches chest. Be sure to state size.

Goods No. 41K20 Price for coat. $2.00

$3.00 OUR VERY BEST GRADE EXTRA LONG BLACK ALPACA COAT.

Made from a very fine quality of jet black alpaca, seams double stitched, wide facings. Style 51. SIZES—34 to 42 inches chest. State size.

Goods No. 41K24 Price for coat.. $3.00

$2.65 MEN'S MINISTERIAL LONG BLACK ALPACA COAT.

An excellent value; very neatly made from good grade of black alpaca, nicely trimmed and finished; wide facings, neat fitting qualities. Style 52. SIZES—34 to 42 inches chest. Give size.

Goods No. 41K26 Price for coat. $2.65

$3.56 OUR VERY BEST QUALITY MINISTERIAL STYLE BLACK ALPACA COAT.

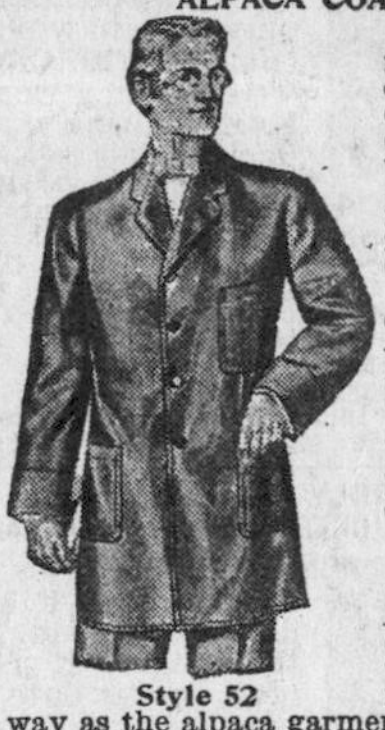

Style 52

Made from extra fine jet black glossy or high luster alpaca of excellent texture, double stitched throughout. Style 52. SIZES—34 to 42 inches chest only. State size.

Goods No. 41K28 Price for coat...... $3.56

$3.98 DRAP D'ETE MINISTERIAL STYLE, EXTRA LONG, FINE BLACK COAT.

Made of a very fine summer drap d'ete material, so well known for its fine quality. It is neatly tailored and made in the same careful way as the alpaca garments; with wide facings and neat trimmings. Style 52. Length averages 38 inches. SIZES—34 to 42 inches chest. State your size.

Goods No. 41K29 Price for coat, $3.98

MEN'S BLACK ALPACA AND SERGE COATS AND VESTS.

Two numbers come in style 50, round cornered sack coat with single breasted vest, as illustrated. Average length of coat, 32 inches. Average weight, 26 ounces. A good style for the general public. Two numbers come in style 51, straight front sack coat with three outside pockets and single breasted vest. Average length of coat, 37 inches. Average weight, 27 ounces. The style of coat and vest used by ministers, professional men, etc., or anyone wanting a longer coat than usual.

$3.00 MEN'S BLACK ALPACA SACK STYLE COAT AND VEST.

Made from fine grade black alpaca, double stitched throughout; wide facings, neatly shaped. Style 50, sack coat with corners cut away and single breasted vest, neatly trimmed. SIZES—34 to 42 inches chest. Be sure to state size.

Goods No. 41K30 Price for coat and vest.. $3.00

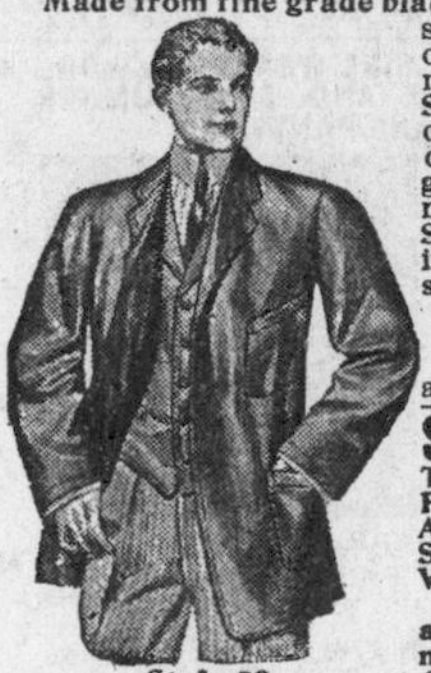

Style 50

$3.95 OUR EXTRA QUALITY FINE BLACK ALPACA SACK STYLE COAT AND VEST.

Made the same as the above number, only of finer grade. Seams double stitched; very fine workmanship throughout. Style 50, sack coat with corners cut away, as illustrated. SIZES—34 to 42 inches chest. Be sure to state your size.

Goods No. 41K32 Price for coat and vest.......................... $3.95

$4.45 MEN'S EXTRA LONG BLACK ALPACA COAT AND VEST.

Made from a splendid grade of black alpaca, double stitched seams, neatly trimmed and finished throughout. Style 51, in extra length coat with single breasted vest. SIZES—34 to 42 inches chest only. Be sure to state size.

Goods No. 41K34 Price for coat and vest........ $4.45

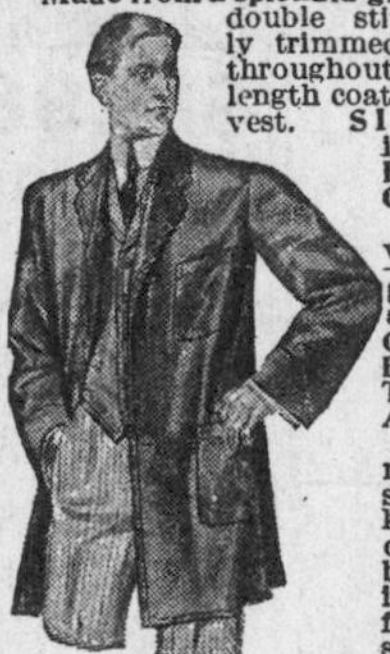

Style 51

$6.96 OUR HIGH GRADE FINE BLACK SERGE EXTRA LONG COAT AND VEST.

This fine fabric needs no special description, as it is well known. It is a high class, beautiful finish black summer quality, made with wide facings, neatly shaped, finely trimmed and finished throughout. Style 51, made extra long, suitable for ministers or anyone wanting a long coat. Vest is made single breasted style. SIZES—34 to 42 inches chest only. Be sure to state size.

Goods No. 41K40 Price for coat and vest.......................... $6.96

MEN'S BLUE SERGE COATS AND COATS AND VESTS.

We furnish two numbers of single coats and two numbers of coats and vests. These garments are unlined and made from very fine light weight blue serge goods in style 18. Cutaway sack coat with three outside pockets and the vest in single breasted style. Average weight of coat alone, 38 ounces. Average weight of coat and vest, 49 ounces.

$4.45 MEN'S NAVY BLUE SERGE SINGLE COAT.

Made from pure worsted fast colored serge of very light weight, durable quality, wide facings and without lining, well sewed. Style 18, as illustrated. SIZES—34 to 42 inches chest only. State size.

Goods No. 41K101 Price for coat alone........ $4.45

$6.45 OUR EXTRA QUALITY BLUE SERGE SINGLE COAT.

Made from extra fine grade all wool worsted navy blue serge, guaranteed fast dye. Sleeves lined, with English sateen. Body half lined with good quality Italian. Nicely tailored, wide facings and a very fine summer coat. Splendid value. Style 18, as illustrated. SIZES—34 to 42 inches chest. Be sure to state size.

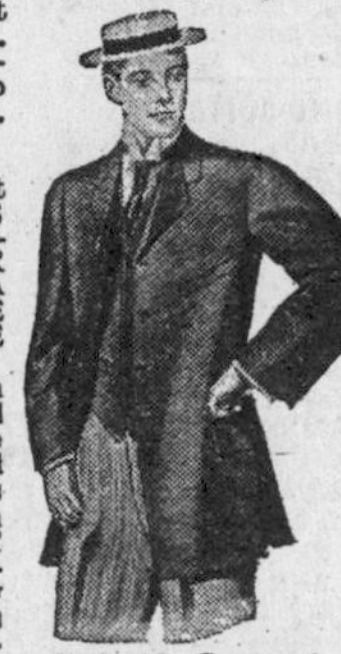

Style 18, Coat only

Goods No. 41K103 Price for coat, $6.45

$6.19 VERY FINE QUALITY BLUE SERGE COAT AND VEST.

Made from fine grade navy blue serge of light weight. Coat has wide facings, but no lining. Made light for hot weather wear and neatly tailored. Style 18, sack coat and five-button single breasted vest. Vest and coat sold together and not separately. SIZES—34 to 42 inches chest. State size.

Goods No. 41K105 Price for coat and vest... $6.19

$8.45 OUR VERY FINEST HIGH GRADE COAT AND VEST.

Made from the finest quality Australian wool worsted serge, standard navy blue shade, fast color, much finer than usually offered at retail in unlined coats and vests. Made with wide facings, lined in sleeves and body half lined with Italian lining. Style 18, cutaway sack, as illustrated. Vest single breasted with five buttons. Coat and vest are sold together, not separately. SIZES—34 to 42 inches chest. Be sure to state size.

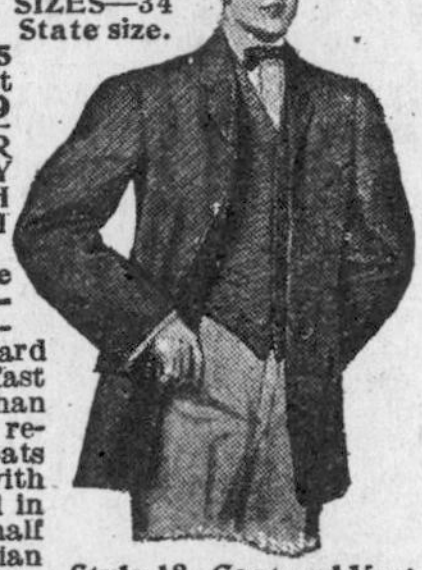

Style 18, Coat and Vest

Goods No. 41K107 Price for coat and vest.......................... $8.45

CORDUROY CLOTHING AND SPECIAL SUIT AND VEST VALUES

Average weight of corduroy clothing packed ready to ship is as follows: Suits, 7 pounds each; pants, 3 pounds per pair; vests, 1½ pounds each.

MEN'S HEAVY CORDUROY SUITS

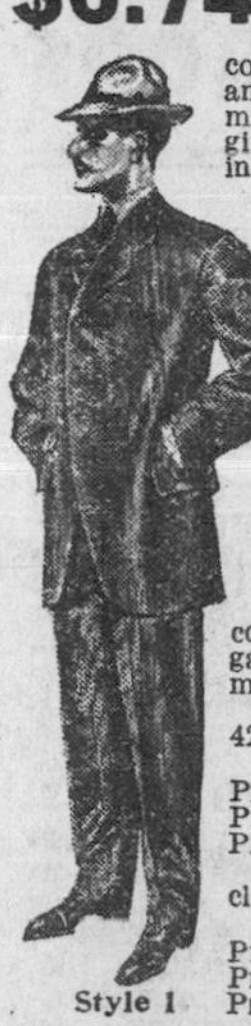

Style 1

$6.74 SPLENDID WEARING HEAVY WEIGHT DRAB CORDUROY SUIT. STYLE — Comes in style 1, round corner four-button sack coat with five-button notch collar vest. The garments are thoroughly made. THE CLOTH is a guaranteed grade of strong wearing corduroy in the popular and serviceable drab shade. TRIMMINGS—Coat body and vest back lined with strong wearing Italian and sleeves with durable material. Suit is carefully interlined, well shaped, firmly sewed, and will give honest and lasting service. SIZES—34 inches up to and including 42 inches breast and 30 to 40 inches waist.

Goods No. 45K9214

Price for suit $6.74
Price for coat and vest 4.94
Price for pants 2.47

$7.67 Regular Sizes — THE BEST VALUE EVER OFFERED IN BROWN CORDUROY SUITS. — **$8.67** Extra Sizes

STYLE—This fabric is furnished only in style 1, as illustrated here. Coat is four-button round cornered sack garment and vest has five buttons and notch collar. THE CLOTH is an excellently made, durable and lasting corduroy in dark brown. We carry a much better line of corduroys than the average retail clothier. We are in a position to obtain better qualities through our immense facilities as manufacturers. TRIMMINGS—Linings consist of excellent quality of Italian body lining and domestic sleeve linings. The garments are well put together, neatly shaped, thoroughly sewed and altogether more finely finished corduroy garments than you ordinarily find on the market.

If you want this brown corduroy in any size from 34 inches up to and including 42 inches chest, and from 30 to 40 inches waist ask for

Goods No. 45K9216

Price for suit $7.67
Price for coat and vest 5.63
Price for pants 2.81

If you want this brown corduroy in any size from 43 inches up to and including 50 inches chest, or from 42 to 50 inches waist ask for

Goods No. 45K9217

Price for suit $8.67
Price for coat and vest 6.36
Price for pants 3.18

$7.93 SINGLE BREASTED — HANDSOME DARK BROWN AND GRAY FLAKED FANCY CORDUROY SUITS. — **$8.93** DOUBLE BREASTED

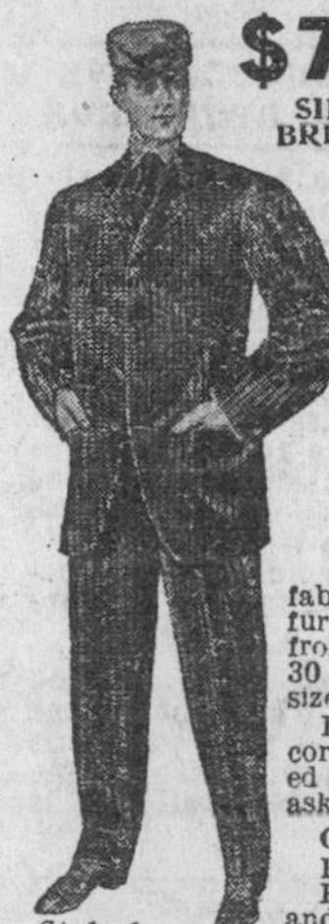

Style 1

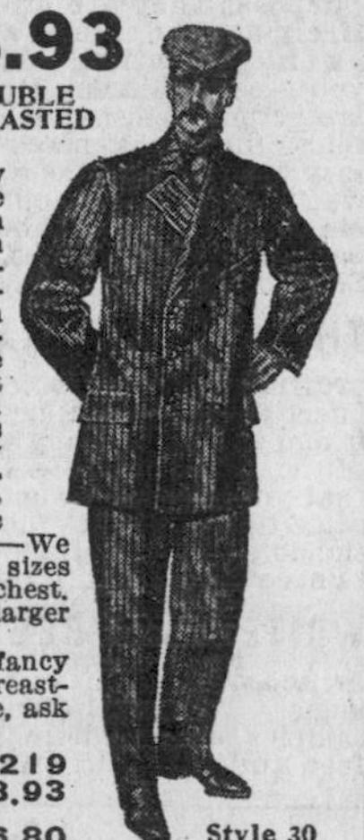

Style 30

STYLES—We furnish this choice quality of fancy corduroy in two styles, our single breasted round cornered sack style 1 and in our double breasted style 30, both illustrated here. THE CLOTH is good, reliable, well made corduroy with a background of rich dark brown, over which run small gray flecks in an irregular order, alternating with spaces where the brown shade alone appears, thus forming a somewhat broken check effect not pronounced and yet just plain enough to bring out what is acknowledged to be one of the neatest fancy corduroys that one could wish. TRIMMINGS—Lined very thoroughly with splendid wearing qualities of Italian and domestic fabrics, carefully interlined and shaped. SIZES—We furnish this fabric in both styles only in regular sizes from 34 inches up to and including 42 inches chest, 30 to 40 inches waist. We cannot furnish any larger sizes.

If you wish this fancy corduroy in single breasted sack style 1 as above, ask for

Goods No. 45K9218
Price for suit.. $7.93
Price for coat and vest 5.80
Price for pants....... 2.90

If you want this fancy corduroy in double breasted style 30 as above, ask for

Goods No. 45K9219
Price for suit.. $8.93
Price for coat and vest 6.80
Price for pants.. 2.90

MEN'S CORDUROY PANTS

$1.64 FOR A PAIR OF CORDUROY PANTS IN A QUALITY WHICH COULD NOT BE BOUGHT FROM ANY OTHER WHOLESALE MANUFACTURER IN DOZEN LOTS FOR A CENT LESS.

THE CLOTH is a strong wearing quality of heavy weight drab color corduroy. The garments are exceptionally well made, thoroughly sewed, of good shape and are not by any means the cheap and common kind ordinarily offered at low prices at retail. They are made with the usual pocket at each side, two hip and one watch pocket. SIZES—From 30 inches up to and including 40 inches waist; no larger sizes.

Goods No. 45K9220 Price for pants....... $1.64

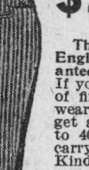

$2.23 Regular Sizes — **$2.73** Extra Sizes

MEN'S EXTRA QUALITY, HEAVY WEIGHT DRAB CORDUROY PANTS.

Here we offer a still finer grade of the popular drab corduroy in an extra well made garment. This is as fine quality as you could possibly obtain in this class of corduroy. The garments are made with the usual pockets and in prevailing style. You will find them much better tailored and shaped than the corduroy clothes offered by the average clothier.

If you want any size from 30 to 40 inches waist ask for Goods No. 45K9222 Price for pants ...$2.23

If you want any size from 42 to 50 inches waist ask for Goods No. 45K9223 Price for pants ...$2.73

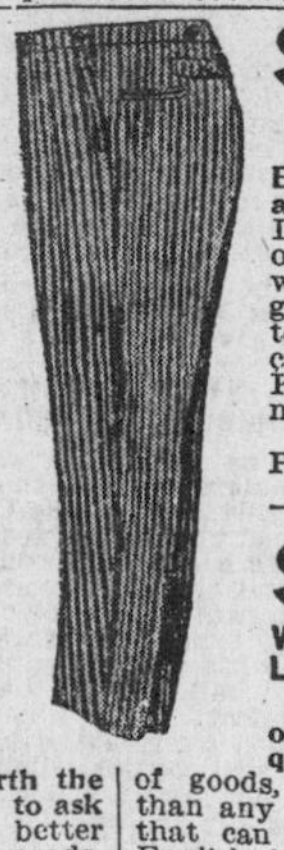

$2.96 HIGH GRADE HEAVY WEIGHT BLACK CORDUROY PANTS.

This is an extra fine quality of English corduroy, which we can guarantee against ripping and breaking. If you want something real good and of fine finish and well tailored, strong wearing corduroy pants, you ought to get a pair of these. SIZES, from 30 to 40 inches waist only. We do not carry larger sizes in this number. Kindly state your waist and inseam measurements.

Goods No. 45K9226
Price for pants $2.96

$2.64 GOOD HEAVY WEIGHT, STRONG WEARING DARK BROWN CORDUROY PANTS.

Our imported qualities are well worth the difference in price that we are obliged to ask for them. They will give you still better satisfaction than any other class of goods. THE CLOTH is a rich dark brown shade, firm and strong. The pants are made extra well, and we can recommend them to you as the best workmanship obtainable. SIZES—We furnish only regular sizes, 30 inches up to and including 40 inches waist measure. Be sure to give your waist and inseam measurements.

Goods No. 45K9224 Price for pants....... $2.64

$3.23 OUR HIGHEST GRADE SPECIAL QUALITY HEAVY WEIGHT LIGHT TAN CRINKLE ENGLISH CORDUROY PANTS.

Here is something that you really ought to see in order to understand its quality. It is an exceedingly fine piece of goods, a better finish, of richer shade than any other corduroy that we can offer or that can be found elsewhere. It is an English fabric of fine rich light tan shade called Tan Crinkle Corduroy. They are well made and guaranteed not to rip or break. They have two hip pockets, the usual pocket on each side and one watch pocket. SIZES, from 30 inches up to and including 40 inches waist and from 30 to 36 inches inside seam. State your measurements.

Goods No. 45K9228 Price for pants....... $3.23

MEN'S CORDUROY VESTS

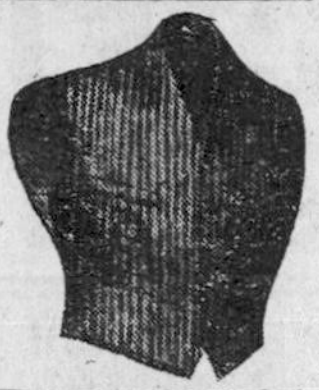

$1.18 A GOOD QUALITY DRAB CORDUROY SINGLE BREASTED VEST. An excellent wearing grade of plain drab corduroy, made in single breasted, five-button style, without collar. We actually offer these vests at prices which are less than the price of a vest in wholesale lots would be to a clothier who buys from other manufacturers. SIZES—34 to 42 inches chest. Be sure to state what size you wear.

Goods No. 45K9232 Price for vest....... $1.18

$1.48 FANCY BLACK AND WHITE DOT CORDUROY SINGLE BREASTED VEST.

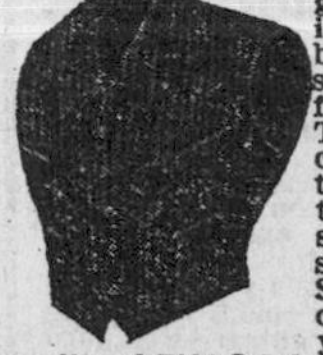

Background is black very thickly dotted with gray at intervals of ½ inch. The dots are white, bringing out an indistinct stripe effect which is very fashionable and pleasing. The corduroy quality is excellent, and you will certainly find this an exceptional value. It comes in single breasted five-button style without collar. SIZES — 34 to 42 inches chest only. State what you measure.

No. 45K9234 Price for vest...$1.48

$1.74 EXTRA QUALITY DOUBLE BREASTED GRAY AND BROWN CHECK FANCY CORDUROY VEST.

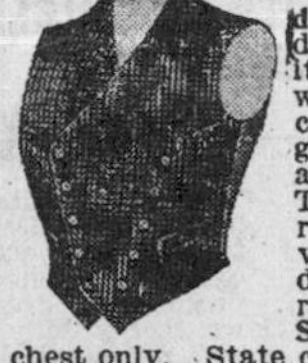

Background is a rich dark brown shade with dark gray dots worked over it in four small groups within ¾-inch square checks of single lines of gray dots. Quite a fashionable and nobby pattern. The quality of the corduroy is very fine and the vest comes in the latest double breasted fashion, two rows of five buttons each. SIZES—34 to 42 inches chest only. State chest measure.

No. 45K9236 Price for vest. $1.74

SPECIAL VALUES IN SUITS AND VESTS FROM ODDS AND ENDS.

AS WE ARE MANUFACTURERS OF CLOTHING we have at times odds and ends of cloth left over and these quantities are too small to catalogue or sample, and to dispose of them we make them up into garments according to the size of the piece of cloth. We make sometimes a vest, sometimes a pair of pants and sometimes a coat and vest and we are here offering them to you at much lower prices than we would be obliged to ask in our regular line, simply because the main point is to dispose of them to make room for other goods. If you are not over particular as to the exact pattern or exact class of goods so long as you get a very fine value, we know that we can please you if you send your order from this assortment and leave the matter of selection of the goods to us according to our stock. We have arranged this lot of bargains in groups or lots according to the quality of the garments. Send us the price of the garment according to the lot from which you select, give us your measurements and we will guarantee to fit and please you or refund your money.

VESTS.

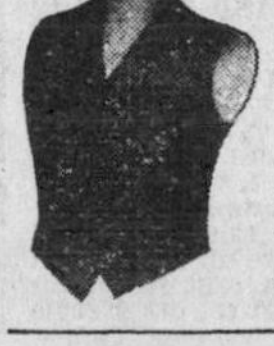

SIZES—From 34 to 42 inches breast.

Goods No. 45K9238 Men's Single Breasted Vests in various shades and mixed patterns, cassimere, cheviots and other weaves, good qualities.
Price for single breasted vest $1.23

Goods No. 45K9240 Men's Single Breasted Vests of a finer grade of remnants, consisting of better qualities of cassimeres, cheviots, worsteds and some suit mixed fabrics.
Price for single breasted vest....... $1.46

Goods No. 45K9242 Men's Single Breasted Vests, our finest grade of remnants in cheviots, tweeds, worsted and silk mixed quality.
Price for single breasted vest $1.63

GREAT VALUES IN SUITS

Consisting of Coats and Vests of one kind of Goods and Pants of Another.

SOME OF THESE GARMENTS are made from odds and ends of cloth and some of them come from our regular stock of suits because as we are more liberal than other clothiers in the matter of breaking a suit to sell a coat and vest or a pair of pants separate from a suit, it leaves us with some coats and vests for which there are no pants to match, or leaves us with pants for which there are no coats and vests to match. These suits, therefore, consist of coats and vests of one kind and pants of another kind of goods. Of course, we have made a special effort to match a pair of pants with a coat and vest of something similar, or something that at least harmonizes to some extent. We have assorted them according to quality so that if you will just send your measurements in the usual way as shown on page 1055 and enclose the price according to the lot from which you select, we will pick out a suit for you that will prove an astonishing value.

SIZES AND STYLES. We furnish these suits only in regular sizes from 34 inches to 42 inches breast and from 30 to 40 inches waist and in sack styles only. While the styles vary a little, we cannot promise a definite style, although they are all sack suits.

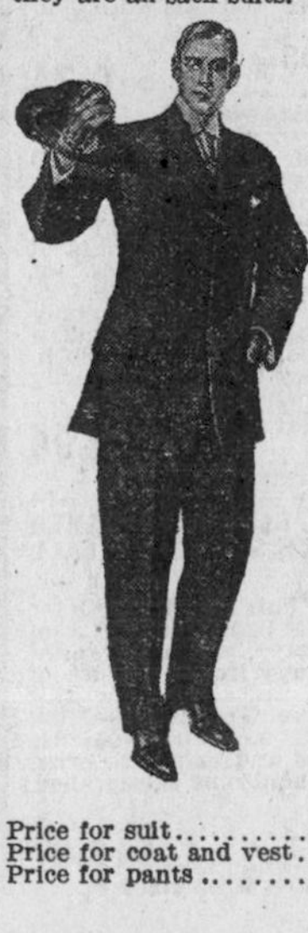

Goods No. 45K9250 Consists of suits with coats and vests of one kind of goods and pants of another, all fancy patterns, that is, no solid shades of black or blue, but a variety of goods from dark to fairly light patterns in cassimeres, etc., that we have been offering in suits at from $5.00 to $7.00, and even more in some cases. They all come in sack styles, although we cannot definitely state the exact features of each style. SIZES—From 34 inches to 42 inches breast only.

PRICES.

Price for suit $4.39
Price for coat and vest 2.93
Price for pants 1.46

Goods No. 45K9252 This lot comprises suits with coats and vests of one kind and pants of another, consisting of somewhat better quality of material than in the foregoing lot, such goods as we have been offering in our line at from $8.00 to $10.00, cassimeres, tweeds and some fancy worsteds, but no solid shades such as black or blue. The patterns vary from dark to light, and there are many very neat designs among them. All the suits are in sack styles. SIZES—From 34 inches to 42 inches breast measure only. Don't forget to give your size.

PRICES.

Price for suit....... $5.82
Price for coat and vest....... 3.88
Price for pants 1.94

Goods No. 45K9254 In this lot the suits, consisting of coats and vests of one kind and pants of another, are made of very good quality such as we have been offering in previous lines at from $11.00 up, and while there are no solid blacks or blues, there are many choice dark shades varying up to light shades in cassimeres, cheviots and fancy worsteds, etc. All suits coming in sack styles, although some of the styles are slightly different from others. SIZES—From 34 to 42 inches breast measure only.

PRICES.

Price for suit....... $7.64
Price for coat and vest....... 5.10
Price for pants 2.55

SPRING AND FALL TOP COATS AND CIELETTE RAINPROOF OVERCOATS

SPRING AND FALL OVERCOATS

NOT RAINPROOF

WE FURNISH TWO STYLES of Spring and Fall Overcoats which are not rainproof. These are the garments that are generally worn for chilly weather at all times of the year when it is not cold enough for a winter overcoat; in fact, in the medium climates of the country these styles are worn to a larger extent and men have more use for them than for winter overcoats.

SIZES. We furnish Spring and Fall Overcoats only in regular sizes for men measuring from 34 to 42 inches breast. Give same breast measure as you would in measuring for a suit. SEE OUR SIMPLE MEASURING PLAN ON PAGE 1055.

THE THREE GARMENTS DESCRIBED IMMEDIATELY BELOW ARE ALL FURNISHED IN STYLE 31, THE UP TO DATE SHORT TOP COAT STYLE.

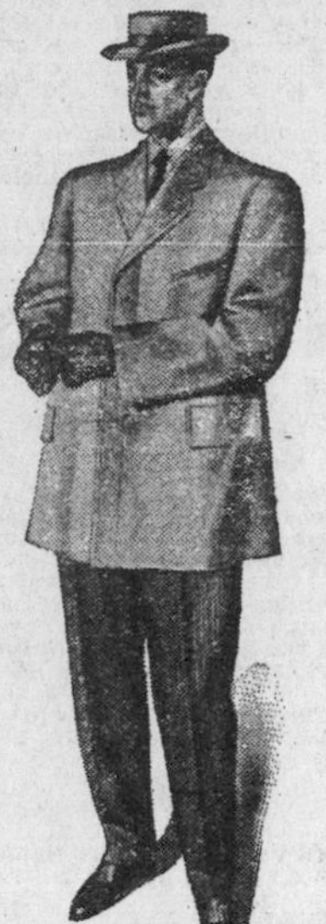

STYLE 31

Spring and Fall Top Coat, plain collar, fly front, one inside and three outside pockets. Average length, 36 to 38 inches. A stylish and comfortable coat to wear at any time of the year when the weather is not cold enough for a winter overcoat.

$8.63 EXCEEDINGLY PRACTICAL DARK OXFORD GRAY COVERT SPRING AND FALL TOP COAT.

Style 31, illustrated here. Average length, 36 to 38 inches. See description below the illustration. The Cloth is fairly light weight, finely woven covert in exceedingly dark oxford gray shade, making a decidedly useful coat either for business or dress wear at any season of the year when the weather is chilly but not what you would call cold. This shade will not show dust or spots readily. Trimmings—Standard Italian lining, interlined with felt and patent canvas, giving perfect shape and good fitting qualities to the garment.

Goods No. 45K9202

Price for top coat, style 31 .... $8.63

SIZES 34 inches to 42 inches breast measure only. State size wanted.

$9.46 EXTRA FINE GRADE ALL WOOL TAN COVERT SPRING AND FALL TOP COAT.

Style 31, as illustrated on the left. Average length, 36 to 38 inches. The cloth is a suitable weight for spring and fall overcoat wear, and is a finely made all wool covert in the popular medium tan shade, a better quality than you would be offered in coats at $15.00 to $18.00 retail. Trimmings—Imported Italian in body and sleeves, interlined with wool felt shoulder padding and patent canvas stiffening in fronts. A garment that will hold its shape and fit splendidly.

Goods No. 45K9204

Price for top coat, style 31 .... $9.46

SIZES From 34 inches up to and including 42 inches breast measure. Tell us the size you wear.

$10.29 MEDIUM WEIGHT GENUINE ALL WOOL BLACK THIBET SPRING AND FALL TOP COAT.

Style 31, as illustrated here. See description below the illustration. Specially designed for service in chilly weather or all times of the year when a winter coat is too heavy. The Cloth is a medium weight, specially suited for year around purposes and is an all wool, genuine good quality black Thibet, very practical for general wear on workdays or Sundays. Trimmings—Excellent wearing gloria cloth in sleeves and body. Coat interlined with felt and patent canvas. These garments are nicely tailored and you'll not get their equal elsewhere for a cent less than $16.00. Our very finest black Thibet is shown in the other style on the bottom of the page.

Goods No. 45K9206

Price for top coat, style 31 .... $10.29

SIZES—34 inches to 42 inches breast measure only. State size.

THIS STYLE 44, AS SHOWN BELOW, IS FURNISHED FROM EACH OF THE THREE FABRICS HERE DESCRIBED.

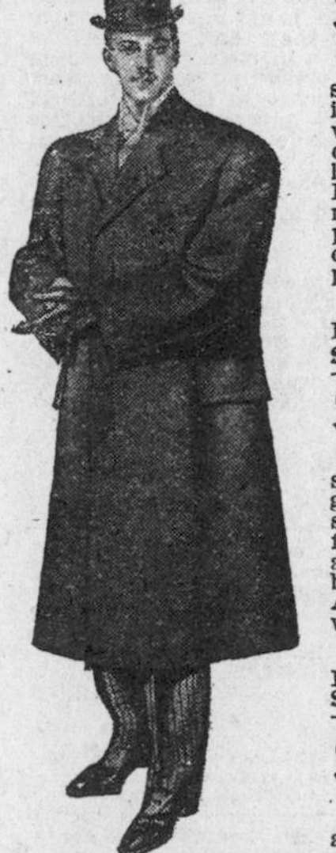

STYLE 44

The very latest Spring and Fall Overcoat. Considered the dressiest style now being worn. Average length, 45 inches, one inside and three outside pockets, plain collar and long vent or opening at back of coat. A very stylish overgarment.

$10.74 LATEST STYLE MEDIUM LENGTH DARK GRAY DIAGONAL WORSTED SPRING AND FALL OVERCOAT.

Style 44, as here illustrated. The latest fashion and a very serviceable overgarment for spring and fall weather. The Cloth is a fairly light weight, very dark gray, a fairly wide diagonal weave or ribbed effect, such cloth as is used in $18.00 to $20.00 coats at retail. Trimmings—Standard splendid wearing Italian linings, plain collar, interlined with wool felt and patent canvas. By making these garments ourselves we know we can give you very much finer work than you ordinarily obtain, because we have compared our tailoring with what you get through ordinary retail channels. We have proved it for ourselves and are willing to prove it to you at our own risk.

Goods No. 45K9208

Price for medium length overcoat $10.74

SIZES—34 to 42 inches breast only. State size wanted.

$11.98 MEDIUM GRAY DIAGONAL WEAVE WORSTED SPRING AND FALL OVERCOAT.

Style 44, as here shown, longer than the usual top coat and shorter than a raincoat. This is a stylish length for this class of garment. The Cloth is a medium gray, the kind that does not show dust readily and is a fairly wide diagonal weave or ribbed effect, something on the order of the number described above, only a lighter gray and of finer material. Trimming—Extra fine Italian body and sleeve lining and interlined with wool felt and haircloth. A well tailored, handsomely made coat in every particular. Easily worth $20.00 retail.

Goods No. 45K9210

Price for medium length overcoat $11.98

SIZES—34 to 42 inches breast only. State size.

$12.87 HIGH CLASS ALL WOOL BLACK UNFINISHED THIBET, MEDIUM LENGTH SPRING AND FALL OVERCOAT.

Style 44, as here illustrated, an exceedingly fashionable length for a spring and fall overcoat. The Cloth is a fairly light weight all wool genuine unfinished black Thibet of very fine weave, making a capital dress overcoat; in fact, suitable for wear at any time. No use of your paying $25.00 for a fine overcoat, because we know this is as fine as you will get for $25.00 elsewhere. Trimmings—High class Venetian body and sleeve lining, interlined with wool felt in shoulders and haircloth in fronts. Tailored and shaped to bring out the most perfect fitting qualities and handsome appearance. Try this excellent garment.

Goods No. 45K9212

Price for overcoat, style 44 .... $12.87

SIZES—34 to 42 inches breast only. Be sure to state size.

MEN'S CIELETTE RAINPROOF OVERCOATS

THESE OVERCOATS DO DOUBLE SERVICE, BEING ADAPTED FOR ALL KINDS OF CHILLY WEATHER, RAIN OR SHINE.

TWO COATS IN ONE is what a Cielette Rainproof Overcoat amounts to. They serve exactly the same purpose as the regular spring and fall overcoat which is adapted for wear in all kinds of weather when it is chilly but not cold enough for a winter overcoat, **and in addition they protect you against the rain,** so that you do not need a rubber coat or mackintosh except only for the severe storming rains or long continued rain. **Our immense sales on these garments prove** that they are a most valuable addition to men's wardrobes, in fact, they are being considered practically indispensable nowadays.

WE DON'T RECOMMEND CIELETTE RAINCOATS FOR HEAVY RAINS, but for all general purposes they are entirely dependable as a rain protection. If you need a garment for protection against severe rains, finding it necessary to be out in them, we refer you to our Mackintoshes and Rubber Coats on other pages. See index.

RAIN-PROOF INTERNATIONAL-WATER-PROOFING-CO. TRADE MARK "CIELETTE" REGISTERED CHICAGO NEW YORK GUARANTEED POROUS TO AIR

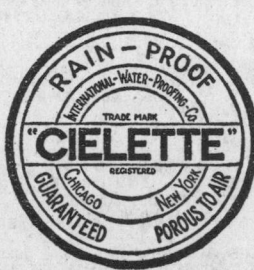

The Trade Mark of the Patent Waterproof Process which we have bought the right to use.

SIZES AND STYLES. These rainproof overcoats come only in sizes from 34 inches to 42 inches breast, and only in style 135, as described and illustrated below and on the next page.

BE SURE TO GIVE SIZE REQUIRED.

Give same breast measure as for a suit.

See our simple plan on page 1055.

THE CIELETTE RAINPROOFING PROCESS consists of applying a patent chemical to any ordinary fabric, which gives it the property of shedding water, but does not affect the quality, appearance or flexibility of the goods. There is no rubber in it and no smell or any other objectionable feature whatever attached to it. One of the great advantages is that the cloth remains flexible and porous to air, so that you have the wonderful feature of a garment that sheds water, while at the same time it admits the air and makes the coat comfortable, avoiding the objectionable quality of the airtight mackintosh or rubber coat. Thus the Cielette raincoat can be worn on a mild rainy day with perfect comfort.

WRITE FOR FREE SAMPLE BOOK No. 84K if you wish to see samples of these raincoats. We have a special sample book in which we sample these garments alone. The descriptions here are accurate and complete, but if you wish to see samples before ordering, don't hesitate to write for Sample Book No. 84K. **It is free and postpaid on request.**

$6.48 OUR LEADER VALUE IN JET BLACK WOOL THIBET RAINPROOF OVERCOAT.

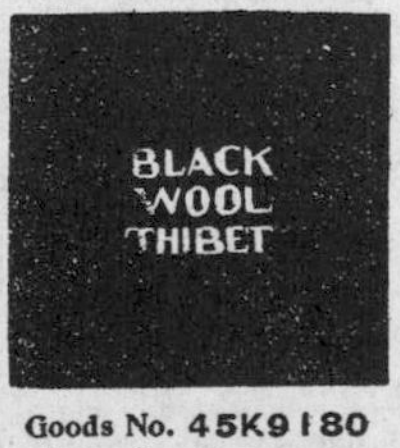

Goods No. 45K9180

Price for rainproof overcoat $6.48

Style—Comes in style 135, as illustrated and described on this page just to the right, specially made for general purposes as an overgarment for any time of the year, rain or shine, when the weather is not cold enough for a winter coat. The Cloth is a very good durable quality of medium weight jet black Thibet, proving an economical coat to invest in because of its color and weight, as it is something that can be worn at any time for dress or business, and its weight particularly adapted for any time of the year. Trimmings—The yoke lining, the facing and the sleeve lining are domestic Italian fabric. The shoulders are padded and fronts reinforced with French elastic and canvas, giving shape and good fitting qualities to the garment. There is no other body lining in the coat. Tailoring is all neat and for $6.48 (the manufacturer's price) it is a wonder.

SIZES. We furnish these coats in sizes for men with breast measurements from 34 inches up to and including 42 inches only. Be sure to give size.

$7.63 FANCY BLACK AND WHITE PINCHECK WORSTED CIELETTE RAINPROOF OVERCOAT.

Style—Is our style 135, exactly as illustrated and described at the right, a garment particularly adapted in length and otherwise for overgarments of this class. The Cloth is medium weight fancy worsted finish weave with a background composed of black and white threads very thickly interwoven, the black predominating, forming a dark gray effect, or what some people call pepper and salt gray, or others a pincheck effect. Over this runs a neat subdued overplaid, consisting of two parallel vertical single gold threads ¼ inch apart, which run at intervals of 1½ inches, and across the fabric horizontally run two faint blue threads ⅜ inch apart, thus forming the overplaid and relieving the gray background neatly. Trimmings—The yoke lining, the facing and the sleeve lining are a domestic Italian fabric. Shoulders are padded and fronts interlined to give excellent fitting effects.

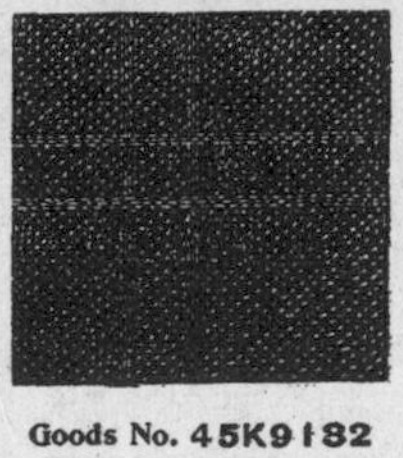

Goods No. 45K9182

Price for rainproof overcoat $7.63

SIZES. We furnish coats with breast sizes from 34 inches up to and including 42 inches only. State size wanted.

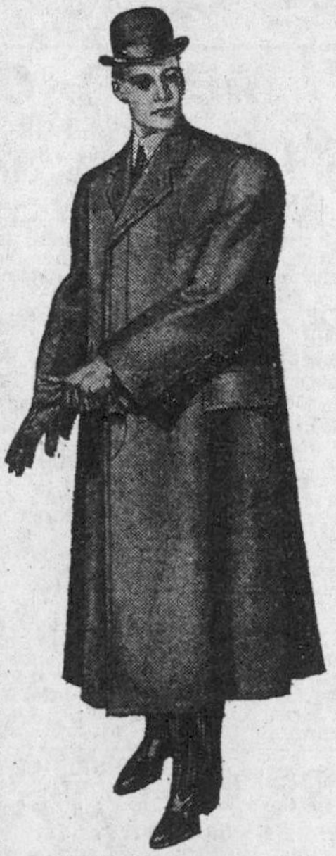

STYLE 135

Long Single Breasted Fly Front Overcoat, averaging 51 inches long, plain collar, three outside pockets and one inside pocket, long vent or opening at back shown on next page. Lined only in sleeves and yoke. No body lining. All our Cielette raincoats come in this style.

MEN'S CIELETTE RAINPROOF OVERCOATS

SEE FULL DESCRIPTION OF OUR CIELETTE RAINPROOF PROCESS ON THE PRECEDING PAGE

ALL THE GARMENTS ON THIS PAGE ARE FURNISHED IN STYLE 135, as here illustrated. If you want to see cloth samples of these goods, write and ask for FREE SAMPLE BOOK No. 84K. Give size around body at breast over vest. Don't measure over a coat.

$8.76 FANCY DARK GRAY AND DARK FAINT STRIPE EFFECT CIELETTE RAINPROOF OVERCOAT.

Style—We furnish these goods only in style 135, exactly as illustrated and described on this page. A very fashionable and practical coat for the purpose. The Cloth is a medium weight fancy worsted finish fabric with plain diagonal weave and a background of dark gray over which run darker gray stripes about ⅜ inch wide and ¼ inch apart, but quite subdued, and alternately they have faint red and blue silk threads in them for slight relief, just making a very neat, dressy and pleasing garment either for one who wishes style or one who wishes a modest garment. Trimmings—Yoke and sleeve lining are of a fine mercerized Italian, shoulders and fronts are neatly shaped with the proper material. A perfect fit is guaranteed.

GOODS No. 45K9184 PRICE FOR RAINPROOF OVERCOAT... $8.76

SIZES These overcoats come in sizes for men with breast measurements from 34 inches up to and including 42 inches. No larger sizes. Don't fail to give size.

$8.96 OUR EXCELLENT VALUE IN ALL WOOL JET BLACK THIBET CIELETTE RAINPROOF OVERCOATS.

Style—This Thibet is made in style 135, like the garment illustrated and described on this page. Note the length and general outlines from the illustration, and read the description below it and you will see exactly the kind of coat you will get, only of course this is plain black. The Cloth is a good quality, pure all wool jet black Thibet of weight suitable for general wear the year around, in place of a winter coat when winter coats would be too heavy. You will have more use for a coat of this kind than for any other overcoat you ever bought. Trimmings—Lined in sleeves and yoke only with mercerized Italian of great wearing quality, interlined in shoulders and fronts, giving perfect fitting qualities.

ALL WOOL BLACK THIBET

GOODS No. 45K9188 PRICE FOR RAINPROOF OVERCOAT... $8.96

SIZES Breast measurements from 34 inches up to and including 42 inches. Don't forget to give your measurements. See simple plan on page 1055.

$10.43 VERY DARK GRAY FANCY WORSTED CIELETTE RAINPROOF OVERCOAT.

Style—Goods comes in style 135, as you will find perfectly illustrated and carefully described on this page, a style particularly adapted for this class of garments. The Cloth is a worsted finish in a faint herringbone weave of a dark gray, which might be termed a stone gray, and over this runs just a slight relief in the form of silk finished silver threads, forming a slight overplaid, which, though not at all pronounced, yet serves to relieve and brighten the dark gray somewhat. It is a practical gray that will not show soil readily, or of which the wearer will not tire quickly. Trimmings—The yoke and sleeve lining is a mercerized Venetian, remainder of body not lined. Shoulders padded and fronts interlined with canvas. A well shaped, carefully tailored, good fitting garment throughout.

GOODS No. 45K9192 PRICE FOR RAINPROOF OVERCOAT... $10.43

SIZES We furnish breast measurements from 34 inches up to and including 42 inches only. Be sure to give size.

$12.37 STYLISH MEDIUM GRAY PATTERN WORSTED CIELETTE RAINPROOF OVERCOAT.

Style—This cloth is made up in our style 135, just as illustrated and described on this page. The Cloth is a medium weight worsted finish, fine herringbone weave. Over this runs an overplaid effect, consisting of vertical and horizontal bars ¼ inch wide of fine small basket weave, forming a plaid 1⅝ inches square. All this background as described, is in a medium gray shade, but in the middle of the plaid run two vertical lines about a ½ inch apart, each with an almost invisible green silk thread in them. These you can hardly notice but they form lines on the goods and thus make a neat relief. The pattern is decidedly stylish and yet not loud at all. There is considerable tone and class to it. Trimmings—Yoke and sleeves lined with silk serge, very dressy goods. No other body lining. Shoulders padded with all wool felt, fronts interlined with haircloth and canvas. A very finely tailored and good fitting garment throughout.

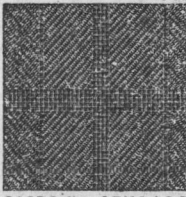

GOODS No. 45K9196 PRICE FOR RAINPROOF OVERCOAT... $12.37

SIZES Breast measurements from 34 inches up to and including 42 inches only. Don't fail to give size.

$13.83 EXTRA GRADE ALL WOOL WORSTED AND SILK DARK CIELETTE RAINPROOF OVERCOAT.

Style—Please note the illustration and description for style 135 on this page. This garment is made like illustration. The Cloth is a medium weight very finely woven all wool worsted, strong wearing material with a slight pure silk mixture for decoration. The background is a plain black small herringbone weave with very faint stripes of small cord effect running ¾ inch apart, hardly noticeable because of the same shade as the background. Alternately midway between these faint dark stripes the surface has lines of blue silk and red silk threads which are very faint, but just serve to relieve and tone up the pattern. It is what one would call rich and dressy. Trimmings—Lined in yoke and sleeves with a very fine silk serge. No body lining. Interlined with all wool felt padding, haircloth and canvas. A handsomely tailored garment in every respect.

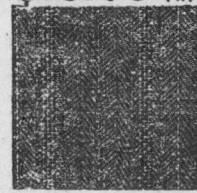

GOODS No. 45K9199 PRICE FOR RAINPROOF OVERCOAT... $13.83

SIZES We furnish breast measurements from 34 inches up to and including 42 inches. Don't forget to give your measurements.

SEE OUR SIMPLE PLAN FOR GIVING MEASUREMENTS ON PAGE 1055.

STYLE 135

Long Single Breasted Fly Front Overcoat. Average length, 51 inches, plain collar, one inside and three outside pockets, and long vent or opening at back of coat, as illustrated above, making it easy for walking purposes. The coat has no body lining, but is lined in sleeves and yoke only. It is not a tight fitting garment, but one that hangs fairly loose from the shoulders down. Thoroughly up to date in make and finish throughout. This illustration is a good representation of this stylish and very practical garment. All our Cielette rainproof overcoats are furnished in this style and only in sizes from 34 inches up to and including 42 inches breast measure.

$9.24 VERY DARK OXFORD GRAY WOOL COVERT CIELETTE RAINPROOF OVERCOAT.

Style—Is our style 135, just as illustrated and described on this page. Remember these garments serve the double purpose of an ordinary medium weight overcoat and a raincoat and can be worn any season of the year when the weather is not chilly enough for a winter overcoat. The Cloth is a medium weight covert weave, just such goods as are commonly used in the light weight short top coat, and the shade is very practical for general purposes, being what is known as a very dark oxford gray. If you don't like a plain black, but want something dark without a pattern in it, this will surely meet your needs. Trimmings consist of a good mercerized Italian lining in yoke and sleeves only. Shoulders and fronts interlined with padding and canvas. Neat tailoring.

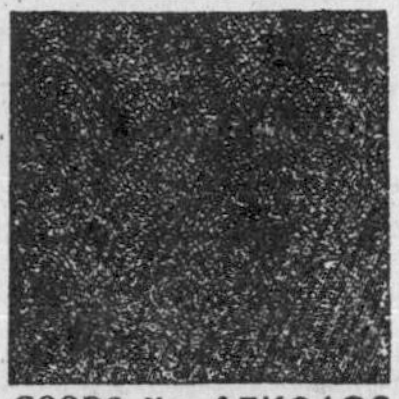

GOODS No. 45K9186 PRICE FOR RAINPROOF OVERCOAT... $9.24

SIZES Comes only in breast sizes from 34 inches up to and including 42 inches. Don't fail to state size.

$9.98 BLACK AND WHITE PINCHECK FANCY WORSTED CIELETTE RAINPROOF OVERCOAT.

Style—This goods is made in style 135, just as illustrated and described on this page. The Cloth is a weight suitable for over garments for ordinary chilly weather the year around. It is a worsted finish weave with a background of black and white. The white consisting of fine pinpoint silk finish threads distributed very close together (1-16 inch apart) all over the black, forming what is usually called a pincheck pattern. The general effect is dark gray. These white threads are more numerous at intervals, forming stripes and cross bars about ½ inch wide and 1 inch apart, thus bringing out a faint but most pleasing overplaid effect. This is a pattern that is very apt to please more people than any other, because it is modest and yet has something of the style that makes it attractive. Trimmings—Sleeves and yoke are lined with good Venetian, shoulders interlined with wool felt and fronts with canvas. No other body lining.

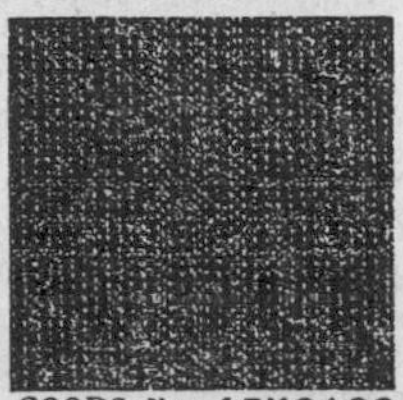

GOODS No. 45K9190 PRICE FOR RAINPROOF OVERCOAT... $9.98

SIZES We furnish only breast measurements from 34 inches up to and including 42 inches. Don't fail to give size.

$11.98 OUR FINEST HIGH GRADE ALL WOOL JET BLACK UNFINISHED WORSTED RAINPROOF CIELETTE OVERCOAT.

Style—The coat comes in style 135 of which we show a good illustration on this page. We also describe it carefully right below the illustration so you can see for yourself the dressy and practical garment you will get. The Cloth is our finest quality medium weight all wool unfinished black worsted, which you can wear either for business or dress purposes, or which you can keep for your fine dress overcoat. $20.00 at retail wouldn't buy you a better one. Trimmings—Yoke and sleeves are lined with imported satin finished Venetian, very fine, dressy material. Remainder of body not lined. Shoulders padded with wool felt and fronts interlined with haircloth. A very finely made and tailored black dress coat. We know the value will be a great surprise to you.

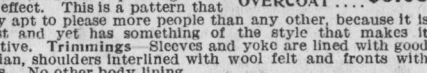

HIGH GRADE ALL WOOL UNFINISHED BLACK WORSTED

GOODS No. 45K9194 PRICE FOR RAINPROOF OVERCOAT... $11.98

SIZES Comes in breast sizes only from 34 inches up to and including 42 inches. Be sure to give measurements.

$12.68 DARK STEEL GRAY WORSTED CIELETTE RAINPROOF OVERCOAT.

Style—This cloth is made up in style 135, just as illustrated and described on this page. The Cloth is a medium weight worsted finish fabric of a close very fine weave in a plain dark steel gray, a fabric specially woven for Cielette rainproof overcoats and of a class that is used for this purpose to a larger extent than any other. It is an exceptionally strong wearing fabric and the shade makes it very practical for general wear and we can promise you a most economical coat in this number. Trimmings—It is beautifully tailored, being lined in yoke and sleeves with silk serge, no other body lining. Shoulders are padded with all wool felt and fronts interlined with haircloth and canvas. When you can get such a garment, so well made and which will serve you rain or shine at any time of the year when the weather is chilly but not cold enough for a winter overcoat for such a price, you can't afford to overlook the opportunity.

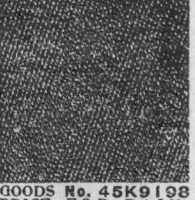

GOODS No. 45K9198 PRICE FOR RAINPROOF OVERCOAT... $12.68

SIZES We furnish breast measurements from 34 inches up to and including 42 inches only. Be sure to give your size.

$15.24 OUR $30.00 GRADE EXTRA FINE ALL WOOL WORSTED DARK BROWN CIELETTE RAINPROOF OVERCOAT.

Style—Our style 135, as illustrated and described on this page. This rich fabric certainly makes a most stylish garment in this style. The Cloth is a medium weight very fine serge weave in a rich very dark brown shade. There are running over this, vertical dark shadow lines running in sets of three, ¼ inch apart at intervals of 1 inch, but so very faint as to be hardly noticeable at all, although serving to lend tone and distinction to the fabric. It is truly a very high class material, being pure all wool worsted and finely woven in every particular. Trimmings—Lined in yoke and sleeves with imported pure silk. Interlined with all wool felt shoulder padding and haircloth and canvas in fronts. A most elegantly tailored and guaranteed perfectly fitting and high class coat throughout.

GOODS No. 45K9200 PRICE FOR RAINPROOF OVERCOAT... $15.24

SIZES We furnish only breast measurements from 34 inches up to and including 42 inches. Be sure to give your measurements. See our simple plan on page 1055.

$4.96 TO $13.46 FOR MEN'S WINTER OVERCOATS

Measure over vest only and not over a coat. See page 1055.

WE OFFER HERE an excellent variety of styles in Men's Winter Overcoats and give you a choice of some excellent fabrics in each style. Remember, we offer all these goods at manufacturer's prices and that they are therefore worth just about twice the price we quote as compared with the standard retail clothing values. SIZES AND STYLES. We furnish overcoats on this page with one exception, only in sizes from 34 inches to 42 inches breast, and only in the style mentioned in each description. Be sure to give your size. See our simple plan for measuring on page 1055. WINTER OVERCOATS WEIGH AS FOLLOWS: Style 34, about 7 pounds; styles 36 and 37, about 7½ pounds each; styles 46 and 56, about 8½ pounds each. See front pages about transportation charges.

THESE FIVE FABRICS ARE FURNISHED IN STYLE 34 AS HERE ILLUSTRATED.

$4.96 GOOD RELIABLE DARK OXFORD GRAY WOOL MELTON OVERCOAT.

Style—This comes in our style 34, which is described and illustrated here. **The Cloth** is a full 28-ounce dark oxford gray wool melton of exceedingly good wearing qualities, considering this extremely low price. No better coat can be had at retail under $8.00. Of course, we can offer you a very much better coat for a little more money. **Trimmings**—Lined with domestic twill, thoroughly interlined, and made in an honest and thorough manner.

Goods No. 45K0602

Price for overcoat...$4.96

SIZES 34 to 42 inches chest measure. Be sure to give your size around body at chest.

$6.53 A $10.00 RETAIL VALUE EASILY; A $12.00 VALUE MOST LIKELY, IN BLACK WOOL FRIEZE.

Style—As here illustrated, this fabric comes in a popular length, average about 42 inches. It is good for both dress and business wear, an exceedingly practical garment. **The Cloth** is a good 28-ounce heavy black wool frieze, which will prove a splendid wearer. We have never gotten better fabrics for overcoating than we have this season. With our immense organization and experience we are able to improve in our qualities from time to time. **Trimmings**—Body and sleeves lined with excellent qualities of Italian fabrics. Shoulders padded, fronts shaped with good grades of interlining. **Our clothes will fit well and hold their shape.**

Goods No. 45K0606

Price for overcoat........$6.53

SIZES Any size from 34 inches up to and including 42 inches chest measure. What's your size?

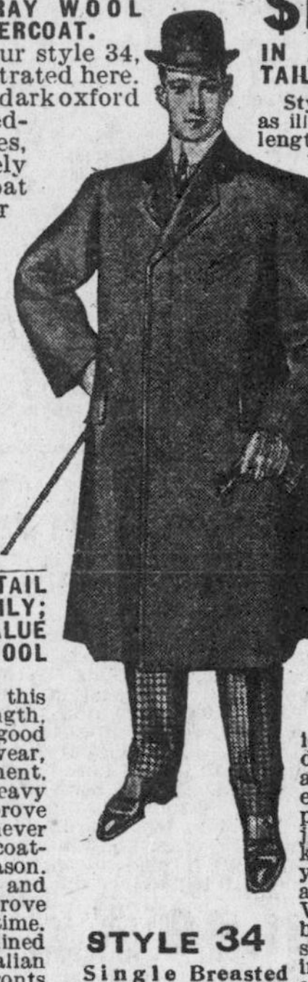

STYLE 34

Single Breasted Overcoat, average length, 42 inches, box back effect, velvet collar, three outside pockets and cash pocket inside the right hand lower pocket and one inside pocket. A fine style for general all around wear.

$10.43 THE HIGHLY FAVORED DARK NAVY BLUE SHADE IN AN ALL WOOL KERSEY WELL TAILORED OVERCOAT.

Style—Comes in the style 34, exactly as illustrated here, a box back medium length coat, very practical for both business and dress wear. A very nice coat for walking purposes. **The Cloth** is an all wool extra good wearing fabric, weighing 28 ounces per yard, something that will endure a great deal of wear and always look well. **Trimmings**—Strong domestic serge body lining, splendid wearing Venetian sleeve lining. Padded shoulders, haircloth stiffened fronts, velveteen pockets, stayed with linen Holland, velvet collar.

Goods No. 45K0614

Price for overcoat..$10.43

SIZES Men's regular sizes from 34 to 42 inches chest. See page 1055 about how easy taking measures is. Be sure to state size.

$12.23 EXTRA FINE ALL WOOL JET BLACK KERSEY OVERCOAT.

Style—Comes in the very fashionable style as here illustrated and described, a coat that is made for all general purposes and one of the easiest garments for walking purposes you can buy. **Cloth** is a rich jet black, firmly woven all wool kersey, weighing 28 ounces per yard, a fabric that will last for years as your winter coat. **Trimmings**—Velvet collar, strong domestic serge body lining, good wearing Venetian sleeve lining, haircloth and wool felt interlinings, velveteen pocketing, and pockets stayed with linen Holland. We'll promise you a better made overcoat in any number in our line than you will ordinarily find in the market at any time.

Goods No. 45K0618

Price for overcoat......$12.23

SIZES 34 to 42 chest only. Be sure to state size.

$7.83 Regular Sizes — A FINE JET BLACK WOOL KERSEY OVERCOAT — $9.83 Extra Sizes

The style is our No. 34, illustrated above. Read the description below the illustration. **The Cloth** is a jet black 28-ounce wool kersey of firm texture and splendid wearing quality. Coats are lined with excellent Italian twill and thoroughly interlined and padded. **SIZES**—We furnish this overcoat in all sizes from 34 inches up to 50 inches chest, but please note the prices below according to the size you take and give the goods number that represents your size.

If you want any size from 34 inches to 42 inches chest, ask for Goods No. 45K0608. Price for overcoat.......$7.83

If you want any size from 42 to 50 inches chest, ask for Goods No. 45K0609. Price for overcoat.......$9.83

THESE THREE OVERCOATINGS COME IN STYLE 36, AS HERE ILLUSTRATED.

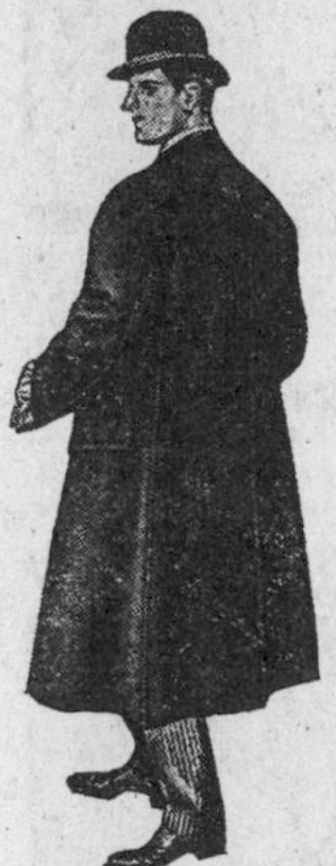

STYLE 36

Single Breasted Overcoat, average length about 45 inches, velvet collar, long vent or opening at back, three outside pockets, cash pocket inside the right hand lower pocket and one inside pocket. A coat of stylish shape and strictly up to date.

$6.87 A VERY STYLISH DARK OXFORD GRAY WOOL FRIEZE OVERCOAT.

Style—Made as illustrated, in style 36; average length, 45 inches; velvet collar and vent at back. An excellent single breasted style that is exceedingly popular. A very good length for an overcoat. **The Cloth** is a good 28-ounce frieze winter overcoating. The shade is dark oxford gray, one of the most favored shades in overcoating. It does not show the dust or dirt readily. This is a fabric that will wear a long time. **Trimmings**—Good Italian body lining and strong wearing sleeve lining and interlined thoroughly.

Goods No. 45K0624

Price for overcoat..........$6.87

SIZES Any size from 34 up to and including 42 inches chest. Tell us your chest measurement.

$8.36 A COMFORTABLE BLACK WOOL KERSEY OVERCOAT, WORTH $15.00 RETAIL.

Style—Comes in style 36, as here illustrated; length is a medium between our styles 34 and 37. A great number of people like it. **The Cloth** is a 28-ounce wool kersey, in a nice rich jet black shade, fine for business or dress wear. A cloth that will give any amount of service. **Trimmings**—Imported wide wale Italian in body and fine mercerized fabric in sleeves. Coat fronts, patent stiffened, shoulders nicely padded, more style and shape to the garment than ordinarily obtained in overcoats. Our workmanship is strictly first class.

Goods No. 45K0628

Price for overcoat..........$8.36

SIZES Any size from 34 to 42 inches chest. Don't forget to state size wanted.

$10.34 FIRMLY WOVEN ALL WOOL DARK OXFORD GRAY MELTON OVERCOAT.

Style—This garment comes in style 36, as illustrated on the left. Read the description below the illustration. **The Cloth** is a 28-ounce all wool dark oxford gray melton that will wear splendidly and the coat is lined with serge in body and Venetian in sleeves, and interlined with wool felt shoulder padding and with haircloth along the lines shown on page 1055. This is an $18.00 retail value.

Goods No. 45K0632

Price for overcoat..........$10.34

SIZES From 34 to 42 inches chest. See page 1055 for our simple system of measuring. We guarantee to fit you. Don't forget to state size wanted.

WE FURNISH THESE THREE MATERIALS IN STYLE 37, WHICH IS HERE SHOWN.

$7.73 A VALUE IN BLACK WOOL MELTON THAT CAN'T BE DUPLICATED UNDER $12.00, GUARANTEED.

Style—37; average length, 50 inches; single breasted. An excellent garment for winter wear if one desires a long overcoat. Long vent in back, making easy walking. **The Cloth** is a firm 28-ounce black wool melton, thoroughly reliable. **Trimmings**—Body lined with fine twill Italian; sleeves with an excellent wearing fabric. Interlining of a good canvas and felt padding. Well tailored and cut over excellent fitting patterns. We know we can fit and please you perfectly. There isn't even a doubt about it. Our experience is wide and varied enough to give us that confidence.

Goods No. 45K0626

Price for overcoat..........$7.73

SIZES From 34 to 42 inches chest only. Don't forget to say what size you wear.

$11.23 HIGH GRADE VERY DARK OXFORD GRAY ALL WOOL LONG OVERCOAT.

Style—Comes in style 37, as here illustrated, with velvet collar, and vent or opening at back of coat, giving a neat appearance and for comfort in walking. **The Cloth** is a good weight, all wool dark oxford gray melton, a weave that will wear as long as you want it. **Trimmings**—Lined in body with strong serge and in sleeves with Venetian, interlinings of wool felt and haircloth, velveteen pocketing. Everything in this coat is good, honest material.

Goods No. 45K0634

Price for overcoat..........$11.23

SIZES 34 to 42 inches chest measure only. Tell us the size you wear.

$13.46 THE BEST ALL WOOL KERSEY OVERCOAT WE OFFER IN THIS FASHIONABLE STYLE.

Style—Comes in single breasted style 37, average length 50 inches. A coat that gives good protection, at the same time is comfortable for walking, not being as heavy as an ulster. 18-inch vent or opening at back. **The Cloth** is a very finely woven smooth jet black finish all wool kersey, weighing 28 ounces per yard. **Trimmings**—Body lining is of fine domestic wide wale serge and sleeves are lined with satin. Shoulders have wool felt padding and fronts are interlined with haircloth, pockets stayed strongly with Irish linen.

Goods No. 45K0638

Price for overcoat..........$13.46

SIZES 34 inches to 42 inches chest measure only. What size do you wear?

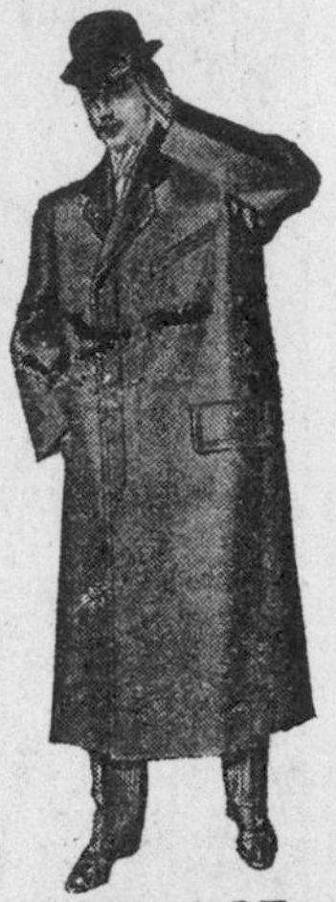

STYLE 37

Single Breasted Overcoat, average length, 50 inches, three outside pockets, cash pocket inside the right hand lower pocket, one inside pocket, velvet collar and long vent or opening at back. A good winter protection.

THIS ULSTER STYLE 46 CAN BE HAD FROM EACH OF THESE TWO FABRICS.

$5.96 REALLY A WONDER IN VALUE, A HEAVY WEIGHT DARK GRAY WOOL FRIEZE ULSTER.

Style—It comes just as illustrated here in style 46. **The Cloth** is a 28-ounce wool frieze in the practical dark oxford shade, something that does not show dust readily. Don't be afraid of this coat because our price is only $5.96. If you wanted to pay $10.00 for an ulster and saw this in a retail store and did not know of these values, you would pay your $10.00 for this one quick. **Trimmings**—Both body and sleeves are exceptionally well lined and interlined, warmer than the average overcoat, and the garment is thoroughly well made.

Goods No. 45K0650

Price for ulster......$5.96

SIZES From 34 to 42 inches chest only. State your chest measurement.

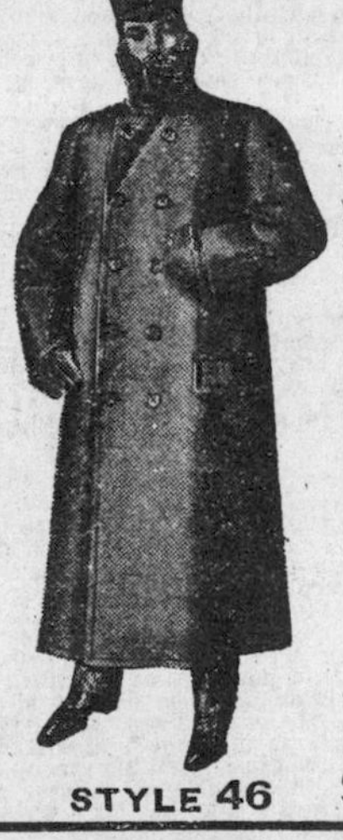

STYLE 46

$8.78 HEAVY DARK OXFORD GRAY WOOL FRIEZE STORM ULSTER

Style—Comes in style 46, as illustrated here. You can see for yourself from the illustration how well the garment is adapted for protection against cold. **The Cloth** is a 28-ounce heavy wool frieze in a dark oxford gray shade, which is well adapted for general wear, being a shade that does not show soil readily. The cloth will give a surprising amount of wear. **Trimmings**—Imported wide wale Italian body lining and strong lusterine sleeve lining. Interlined with wool felt and patent canvas, pockets well stayed and reinforced with linen Holland.

Goods No. 45K0658

Price for ulster.........$8.78

SIZES From 34 inches up to and including 42 inches chest measure only. State size wanted.

THESE TWO FABRICS ARE FURNISHED IN THIS DRESS ULSTER STYLE 56.

$7.89 DARK BROWN MIXED WOOL MELTON DRESS ULSTER.

Style—Comes in double breasted ulster style 56, as illustrated on this page. This style is nearly the same as style 46, as shown above, only that it has no muff pockets, but has a breast pocket instead. Many prefer this for dress purposes. **The Cloth** is a 28-ounce melton, in a very dark brown mixed shade, with a slight bronze tinge, a shade that is considered very neat and up to date. **Trimmings**—Body is lined with diagonal ribbed twill and sleeves with striped lusterine cloth. The shoulders are padded with wool felt, fronts are interlined thoroughly, the garments are cut over excellent fitting patterns.

Goods No. 45K0654

Price for ulster.........$7.89

SIZES Any size from 34 inches up to and including 42 inches chest measure. Don't forget to say what size you wear.

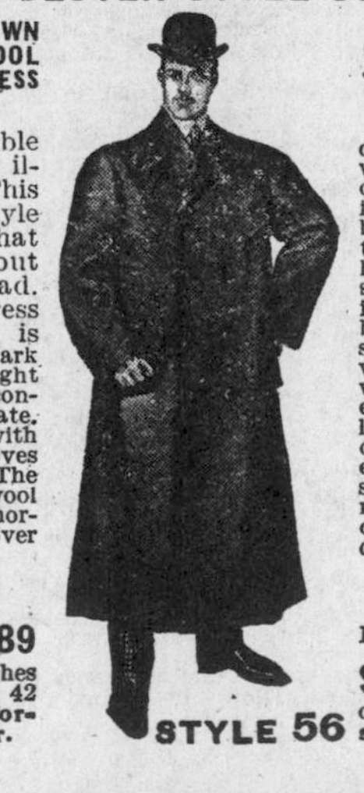

STYLE 56

$9.83 EXTRA HEAVY BLACK WOOL FRIEZE DRESS ULSTER.

Style—Comes in the handsome dress ulster style 56 shown here, with storm collar; average length of coat, 50 inches. This garment is specially designed to combine both the idea of dress and protection. **The Cloth** is an extra heavy weight, exceptionally strong wearing wool frieze, weighing 30 ounces per yard. It is jet black, and therefore specially suitable for dress or business wear. **Trimmings**—Imported wide wale Italian body lining and excellent wearing lusterine sleeve lining. The interlinings consist of wool felt and good French elastic canvas, materials that give shape and durability to any garment, and our tailoring brings out the best possible effects you could have.

Goods No. 45K0660

Price for ulster.........$9.83

SIZES From 34 up to and including 42 inches chest only. Be sure to say what your size is.

YOUNG MEN'S, BOYS' AND CHILDREN'S CLOTHING

SAMPLE BOOK FREE. SEE NEXT PAGE.

GREATER VALUES THAN EVER.

OUR NEW GREAT OFFERS IN YOUNG MEN'S CLOTHING, BOYS' LONG PANTS SUITS, TWO-PIECE AND THREE-PIECE KNEE PANTS SUITS, NORFOLK STYLES, LITTLE FELLOWS' FANCY STYLES, BOYS' WASH SUITS, WAISTS AND PLAY SUITS, ETC. ALL FURNISHED AT AS LOW AND IN SOME CASES LOWER PRICES THAN DEALERS PAY AT WHOLESALE.

WE GUARANTEE TO FURNISH YOU BETTER MADE CLOTHING than you can ordinarily get in retail stores or elsewhere at any price. We manufacture our clothing ourselves, and for that reason are able to govern the quality of cloth we use, the quality of the trimmings and the workmanship. The only way to build up and maintain a lasting, successful boys' clothing business is to absolutely insure that each garment turned out is the best that can be produced for the price,

AND THAT IS EXACTLY WHAT WE ARE DOING.

WE CONTROL WEAVING MILLS in different parts of the country, and these mills make cloth to our order and exactly according to our specifications. We don't pay any commission to commission houses and woolen agents. We get the cloth at mill prices and thus we are perfectly sure not only **of getting it at the lowest prices, but are also sure that the quality is the best obtainable.** We use only the strongest wearing, most substantial and lasting goods.

WHILE WE KNOW you will be better satisfied with our higher grade clothing, yet if you want clothing at the lowest prices possible, even our lowest priced numbers are better in fabrics and style than usually found on the market at vastly higher prices.

WE DON'T SACRIFICE QUALITY TO MAKE A LOW PRICE

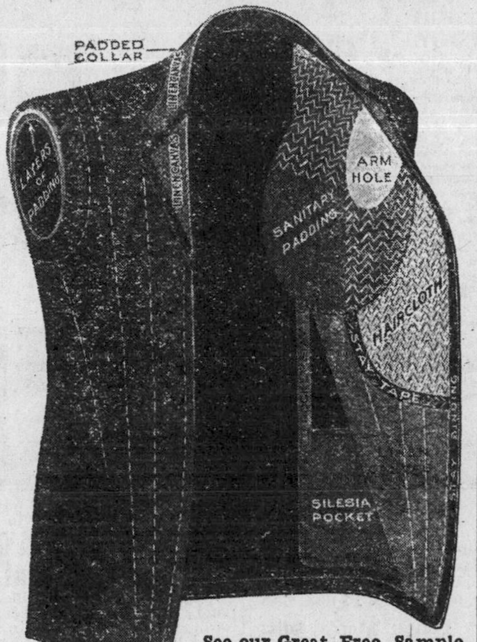
PADDED COLLAR
LAYERS OF PADDING
ARM HOLE
SANITARY PADDING
HAIRCLOTH
STAY TAPE
SILESIA POCKET

See our Great Free Sample Book Offer on next page.

Our Ucanttear Process of making Young Men's and Boys' Clothing.

THIS ILLUSTRATION SHOWS YOU the interior interlinings and trimmings that we put into our garments, and represents what we have called our Ucanttear Process of making boys' clothing.

THE UCANTTEAR PROCESS OF MAKING BOYS' CLOTHING is exclusively our own, and we are perfectly sure that you can't get boys' clothing under double the price at retail that is made anywhere near as well as ours is, represented here by this illustration.

OUR BOYS' CLOTHING is of better shape and will keep its shape longer and look better and wear longer than other clothing you get through retail stores even though we offer at about half what is paid for boys' clothing at retail.

DON'T MISJUDGE OUR CLOTHING from its low price. Don't think it is not good because the price is low. **We have simply shorn off the retailers' profits and expenses,** and are furnishing clothing to you at just actual cost with one bare margin of profit.

THE UCANTTEAR PROCESS insures your getting properly padded shoulders, perfectly shrunk collars, thoroughly interlined coat fronts to prevent their sagging or getting out of shape, all seams double sewed and taped so they won't tear out, pockets well supported and stayed and every vital point reinforced.

THE BEST MADE BOYS' CLOTHING YOU CAN BUY

HOW TO MEASURE AND SEND AN ORDER.

IT IS AS EASY AS A, B, C to make up an order for young men's, boys' or children's clothing. We show you below exactly how measurements should be taken for young men's or boys' long pants suits or overcoats.

THE AGE IS A VERY IMPORTANT THING, which must never be forgotten in any case. Always give this in addition to the measurements for long pants suits and young men's overcoats.

USE ONE OF OUR REGULAR ORDER BLANKS for young men's and boys' clothing if you have one, but if you have not an order blank, just use a plain sheet of paper and give the information according to the copy of our order blank as shown below. It's very easy.

FOR BOYS' KNEE PANTS SUITS AND OVERCOATS and for little fellows, suits, overcoats and other garments, we require to know the age only, and to know whether the boy is large or small for his age. That's all the information we require on these garments.

THE TABLES BELOW tell you the measurements according to which our clothing is cut. By referring to these tables you can tell what size your boy wears, and will greatly assist you to select the proper size required.

A GOOD WAY TO GET CORRECT SIZES on boys' clothing is to keep the size tickets that come attached to the garment, and when another garment is needed you can send for the same size as the ticket shows, or a size larger if it has been some time since the last garment was received.

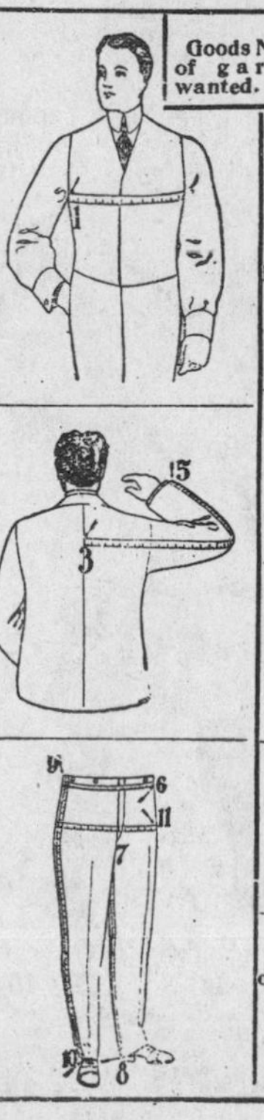

Goods No. of garments wanted.	STYLE	State price of garments you are ordering. $

MEASUREMENTS FOR LONG PANTS SUITS AND YOUNG MEN'S OVERCOATS.

	COAT MEASUREMENTS	
BE SURE to give Age, Height and Weight	**BREAST** All around body close up under arms at 1 over vest only	Inches
AGE	**SLEEVE** From middle of back at 3 around elbow to wrist joint at 5	Inches
HEIGHT	**PANTS MEASUREMENTS**	
	WAIST All around body right above hip bones at 6 over pants only	Inches
WEIGHT	**OUTSIDE SEAM** From top of waistband at 9 to heel seam of shoe at 10	Inches
	HIP All around body at hips at 11	Inches
STYLE NUMBER of Suit or Overcoat	**INSIDE SEAM** From close up in crotch at 7 to heel seam of shoe at 8	Inches

OUR LIBERAL TERMS AND GUARANTEE. Send us your order, give us the goods number found in the description, tell us the sizes in accordance with our simple plan explained here, enclose our price and **we guarantee** to ship you garments that will fit perfectly, please you in every way and prove a surprising value, or you may return them to us at our expense and we will exchange the garments for satisfactory garments, and in such cases we pay the transportation both ways on the goods you return, or if preferred, we will refund both the price and any transportation charges you paid. You can't lose a penny.

ABOUT WEIGHT AND TRANSPORTATION CHARGES. We give the average weight of garments in the heading of each different line of goods. Pages 13 to 17 in this catalogue tell you how to figure cost of express or freight. Any package of clothing not weighing over 4 pounds can be mailed.

POSTAGE RATE is 1 cent per ounce or 16 cents per pound. Transportation costs very little, and where you have clothing shipped with other goods it costs next to nothing.

TABLE OF MEASUREMENTS showing how our Young Men's Suits are cut. Sizes, 32 to 37 inches breast measure.

AGE	COAT		Length of Coat, Inches	PANTS		Weight Pounds
	Chest, Inches	Sleeve, Inches		Waist, Inches	Inseam, Inches	
16	32	29	28½	30	30	110
17	33	30	29	31	31	120
18	34	30½	30	31	32	130
19	35	31	30½	32	32	135
20	36	31½	31	32	33	140
21	37	32	31½	33	33-34	150

The weight and chest measure are for average size young men of this age.

TABLE OF MEASUREMENTS showing how our Long Pants School Suits are made. Sizes, 28 to 31 inches breast measure.

AGE	COAT		Length of Coat, Inches	PANTS		Weight, Pounds
	Chest, Inches	Sleeve, Inches		Waist, Inches	Inseam, Inches	
12	28	26½	24½	26	26	80
13	29	27	25¼	27	27	85
14	30	27½	26	28	28	90
15	31	28½	27	29	29	100

The weight and chest measure are for average size boys of this age.

TABLE OF MEASUREMENTS according to which our Two and Three-Piece Knee Pants Suits are made. A good guide to help you select the proper size suit needed.

AGE	COAT		Length of Coat, Inches	PANTS	
	Chest, Inches	Sleeve, Inches		Inseam, Inches	Outseam, Inches
8	24	22½	20¾	9¼	18
9	25	22¾	21¼	10	18½
10	26	23	21¾	11	19
11	27	23½	22¼	11½	20
12	28	24½	23¼	12	21
13	29	25½	24¼	12¾	21½
14	30	26¼	25¼	13½	22½
15	31	28	26¼	14	24
16	32	28½	26¾	14½	25

Largest breast measure in three-piece suits is 32 inches, and in two-piece suits, 31 inches.

MEASUREMENTS FOR YOUNG MEN'S OVERCOATS should be taken the same as for undercoats, as allowance is made in cutting overcoats so that they will fit over undercoats of the same size.

THE ONLY INFORMATION REQUIRED FOR Boys' Knee Pants Suits, Little Fellows' Suits, Boys' Overcoats and Waists is the correct age and whether boy is large or small or of average size for his age. Give this information below.

AGE OF BOY

Is the boy LARGE OR SMALL or of average size for his age?

FREE
AND POSTPAID

THIS BIG BOOK OF CLOTH SAMPLES (No. 88K) OF YOUNG MEN'S, BOYS' AND CHILDREN'S CLOTHING
INCLUDING ALL OUR GREAT OFFERS

WRITE A POSTAL CARD OR LETTER TO US AND JUST SAY, "Send me free Sample Book No. 88K" or "Send me samples of Young Men's, Boys and Children's Clothing," and this great book with fully one hundred actual cloth samples of young men's and boys suits and a large number of colored photographs of our little fellows' fancy suits, showing the actual colors of the goods and trimmings, including free cloth tape measure, order blanks and everything. making it simple and easy to order, WILL BE MAILED TO YOU AT ONCE FREE AND POSTPAID. WRITE TODAY.

NEARLY A HUNDRED CLOTH SAMPLES AND OVER 100 ILLUSTRATIONS OF FASHIONS, INCLUDING A LARGE NUMBER OF COLORED PHOTOGRAPHS ALL FREE AND POSTPAID IN THIS BOOK.

$3.48 THIS FINE LIGHT WEIGHT ALL WORSTED SERGE

COMES IN THE HANDSOME STYLE HERE ILLUSTRATED, FOR BOYS FROM 3 TO 8 YEARS OF AGE, AND IN BROWN, NAVY BLUE, OR LIGHT BLUE COLORS AS DESIRED.

This great value in little fellows' suits is made from material exactly like sample which is a pure all worsted light weight serge, and you can have your choice of three colors, brown, dark navy blue or a handsome light blue usually called electric blue. Style, made double breasted, trimmed with six white pearl buttons, a beautiful silk embroidered emblem in corners of collar, center of shield and on left arm and a black silk tie and white silk cord and tassel are also furnished. Pants are in bloomer style and lined throughout.

This is one of the most reliable offers in our big line of little fellows' clothing.

ALL WORSTED SERGE

Order the number that represents the color you want.

Goods No.
40K6347 Electric Blue.
40K6348 Rich Brown Shade.
40K6349 Dark Navy Blue.

Price on any of the above colors for sailor blouse suit, as illustrated, for boys from 3 to 8 years of age $3.48

Be sure to state boy's age and the color of serge wanted.

We guarantee to please you in every way and prove this worth $6.00 on the retail basis or refund your money.

This is the Sailor Blouse style in which this worsted serge is furnished for boys from 3 to 8 years of age.

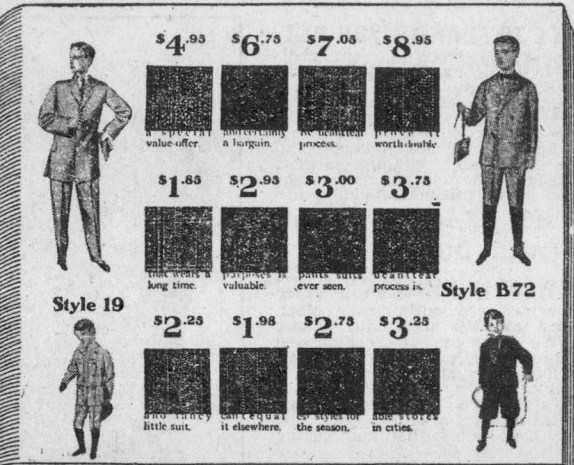

$4.93 $6.75 $7.05 $8.95

$1.85 $2.95 $3.00 $3.75

Style 19   Style B72

$2.25 $1.98 $2.75 $3.25

WE GUARANTEE TO PLEASE YOU PERFECTLY IF YOU ORDER FROM THIS CATALOGUE BUT IF YOU PREFER TO SEE SAMPLES BEFORE BUYING WE WILL MAIL YOU FREE THIS GREAT BOOK SHOWING THE ACTUAL SAMPLES.

THIS SMALL ILLUSTRATION shows you our Sample Book No. 88K thrown open and showing two pages, and while the picture is small, it gives you some idea of the way we show samples and illustrations page after page in this large cloth sample book. In fact, you can read one of our special offers on one of these pages, and can order from it if you wish, as the photograph has not made it too small to read. This book shows you the actual samples, illustrates the styles, and makes everything very plain and simple.

IN THIS BOOK No. 88K we show samples of Young Men's Suits from $3.48 to $13.48, Boys Long Pants Suits from $3.25 to $6.75, Boys' Knee Pants Suits from $1.48 to $6.35, and show Little Fellows' Fancy Styles in the actual colors of the goods and trimmings by the color photography process. You can get a perfect idea as to just how the goods will look.

YOU CAN ORDER ALL THE CLOTHING direct from this Big Catalogue from the following pages, but if you have the slightest difficulty in making your selection, and would like to see a cloth sample or a colored illustration before ordering, don't fail to write and ask for this free Sample Book No. 88K, and it will be mailed at once free and postpaid, all complete.

$3.25 OUR GREAT UCANTTEAR SPECIAL TWO-PIECE KNEE PANTS SUIT FOR BOYS FROM 8 TO 16 YEARS OF AGE

THE ENORMOUS SALES WE MADE LAST SEASON OF A SUIT MADE IN THIS SAME WAY ENABLE US TO OFFER A MORE STYLISH GARMENT YET AT EVEN A LOWER PRICE.

THIS IS THE STRONGEST WEARING SUIT ever made at any price and if you have any boys from 8 to 16 years of age, DON'T FAIL TO TAKE ADVANTAGE OF THIS REMARKABLE OFFER. $3.25 represents the mere cost of material and workmanship with but one bare small margin of profit. Enormous purchases of cloth direct from the mills and enormous sales make this price possible. No use to look elsewhere for anything like it. Read the description below.

WE USE RELIABLE CLOTH and have it in either gray or brown effects with patterns of subdued check, very rich and stylish looking goods that wears like iron. The cloth is rainproofed by a process like described on page 1076, thus having the property of shedding water and keeping out dampness. It is not entirely waterproof like a mackintosh or rubber coat, but is a fine protection to the lad in damp weather.

THE COAT is in the latest double breasted style, with long roll broad lapels, slightly corset fit at waist, with slight flare at the bottom, just like the latest effects in men's suits. Trimmed very strongly. Extra durable linings, seams triple sewed and taped. Won't tear out. Fronts interlined with canvas and haircloth. Shoulders padded. Collars fit neat to the neck.

PANTS made as illustrated below. Every seam taped and double sewed. Fronts lined and knees and seat reinforced with double thicknesses of cloth. Will stand the roughest kind of wear. The pants with suit are straight style, but we furnish knickerbockers at a low price to match if desired, as quoted below.

A CAP in golf style to match suit is also offered at a low price.

Be sure to state age and if large or small for age.

PLEASE STATE COLOR DESIRED AS WE HAVE THEM EITHER IN BROWN OR GRAY EFFECTS.

Goods No. 40K4235
Price for two-piece double breasted suits for boys from 8 to 16 years of age, but not larger than 32 inches breast measure with straight pants...... $3.25

Goods No. 40K4236
Price for extra knickerbocker pants, sizes, 8 to 16 years of age 80c

Goods No. 40K4237
Price for handsome golf caps to match suits, sizes, 6½ to 7 ...... 35c

INSIDE FRONT VIEW   INSIDE BACK VIEW

FRONT CANVAS LINED
DOUBLE KNEE
DOUBLE SEAT
ALL SEAMS DOUBLE SEWED & TAPED

98c OUR TWO GREAT LEADER OFFERS IN BOYS' WASH SUITS $1.25

AN OUTFIT CONSISTING OF SUIT WITH BLOOMER PANTS, AN EXTRA PAIR OF STRAIGHT PANTS AND A JOCKEY CAP TO MATCH, FOR BOYS FROM 3 TO 10 YEARS OLD.

AN OUTFIT CONSISTING OF A DOUBLE BREASTED BELT SUIT WITH KNICKERBOCKER PANTS AND A HANDSOME GOLF CAP TO MATCH, FOR BOYS FROM 8 TO 15 YEARS OLD.

THE MOST WONDERFUL VALUES EVER KNOWN IN WASH GOODS, BECAUSE WE HANDLE GREATER QUANTITIES BY FAR THAN SEVERAL OF THE SO CALLED BIG JOBBING HOUSES COMBINED AND WE SELL DIRECT TO THE CONSUMER ON SMALL MARGIN OF PROFIT AND SAVE YOU ALL RETAIL PROFITS AND EXPENSES.

BOTH THESE OUTFITS are made from the same materials, a natural linen color good weight wash crash, one of the best known washable fabrics and the different outfits are made exactly as described below.

FOR AGES 3 TO 10.

THE OUTFIT FOR BOYS FROM 3 TO 10 YEARS OLD AT 98 CENTS consists of a blouse cut full in double breasted effect, trimmed with six pearl buttons, large plain sailor collar, long white duck detachable shield, with silk emblem in center, outside breast pocket and cord and whistle attached. There are two pairs of pants, one bloomer style and the other straight cut. The seams of all garments are double stitched and strong. A neat jockey cap to match suit is added. The blouse, two pairs of pants and cap all go for 98 cents.

FOR AGES 8 TO 15.

THE OUTFIT FOR BOYS FROM 8 TO 15 AT $1.25 consists of a double breasted belt coat of the latest model, one pair of knickerbocker pants and a handsome golf cap to match the suit. Coat is the latest double style with long roll broad lapels, two outside patch pockets and belt of same goods. Pants are made large and roomy with hip and side pockets, loops for belt and a strap and buckle at the knee. The coat, one pair of pants and cap all go for $1.25. Be sure to state age and if large or small for age.

IF YOU HAVE ANY BOYS FROM 3 TO 15 YEARS OF AGE, YOU CAN TAKE ADVANTAGE EITHER OF ONE OR OF THE OTHER OF THESE GREAT OUTFIT OFFERS. SEE OUR OTHER WASH GOODS OFFERS ON PAGES 1090 TO 1092.

STATE AGE.

Goods No. 40K4452
Price for sailor blouse suit with bloomer pants and extra straight pants and cap to match, for boys from 3 to 10 years of age only 98c

If by mail, postage extra, 22 cents for each outfit.

STATE AGE.

Goods No. 40K4454
Price for two-piece double breasted suit with knickerbocker pants and cap to match, sizes, 8 to 15 years only $1.25

YOUNG MEN'S FASHIONABLE SUITS IN THE LATEST SINGLE BREASTED SACK STYLE AS ILLUSTRATED ON THIS PAGE

SIZES TO FIT YOUNG MEN OF AVERAGE SIZE FROM 16 TO 21 YEARS OF AGE, OR MEASURING FROM 32 TO 37 INCHES BREAST. BREAST SIZES SMALLER THAN 32 INCHES ARE FURNISHED FROM OUR BOYS' SCHOOL SUITS AT A LOWER PRICE ON PAGE 1085.
Give sizes according to our simple plan on page 1079. Average weight of a young man's suit is 4½ pounds.

MEDIUM WEIGHT UNION CASSIMERE SUITS FOR YOUNG MEN FROM 16 TO 21 YEARS OF AGE.

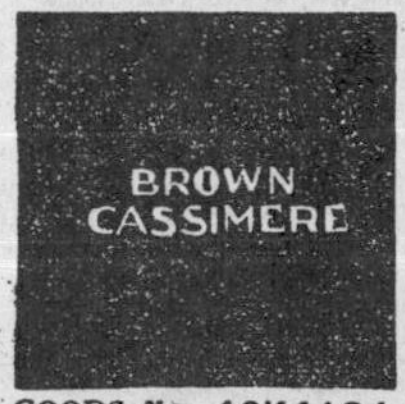

Material—Medium weight, wool and cotton mixed cassimere, a soft finish material suitable for all year around wear. **Color**—Dark brown background with an overplaid in dark maroon. **Style**—Single breasted, three-button sack. **Vest**—Five-button without collar. Pants cut in medium pegtop effect. **Trimmings**—Body of coat and vest back lined with substantial black Italian cloth. Front interlined with canvas, shoulders padded. Substantially tailored garments. **The best possible value for the price in an honest made everyday suit. Be sure to give measurements.**

SEE OUR YOUNG MEN'S FANCY VESTS ON PAGE 1092.

GOODS No. 40K4121
Price for young men's suits, in style 19 only, 32 to 37 inches breast measure, **$3.48**

FANCY GRAY MIXED CHEVIOT YOUNG MEN'S SUITS, SIZES 32 TO 37 INCHES BREAST MEASURE.

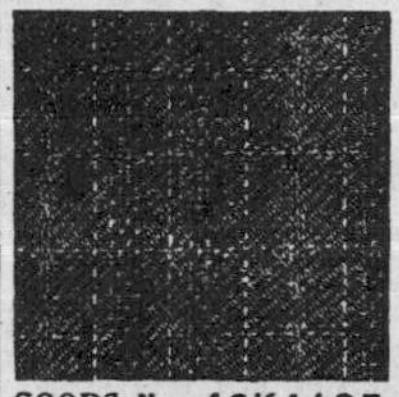

Goods—Double and twist wool and cotton mixed cheviot. **Color**—A mixture of light and dark gray with a stripe effect formed by alternating blue and light brown lines. A very desirable spring and summer suit. **Style**—Three-button sack coat, as illustrated for style 19. Trimmed with a good quality of black Italian cloth to match material, front interlined with canvas, well padded shoulders, bone buttons, three outside and one inside pocket in coat. **Vest**—Five-button without collar. Neatly shaped, roomy half peg top pants, with side pockets, hip pockets and a watch pocket. **Be sure to give measure as described on page 1079.**

GOODS No. 40K4125
Price for young men's suits, in style 19 only, 32 to 37 inches breast measure, **$4.52**

SOFT FINISH UNION CASSIMERE SUITS IN THE POPULAR TAN AND BROWN EFFECT.

Material — Mackintosh's well known union cassimere, one of the most reliable fabrics which can be put in suits offered at the price. **Color**—The latest brown and tan mixed effect relieved by dark blue stripes. **Style**—Latest three-button sack with long broad lapels and cut in correct length. **Workmanship** is the best possible for suits at the price and will be found much better than usually offered. **Trimmings**—Substantial twill lining to match material in body of coat and back of vest, ivory buttons, neatly striped twill sleeve lining. **Coats** have three outside pockets, one inside pocket. **Vests**—Four outside pockets, one inside pocket and are made without collar. **Pants** have side pockets, hip pockets, watch pocket, strap and buckle in the back. **Give size.**

GOODS No. 40K4127
Price for young men's suits, in style 19 only, 32 to 37 inches breast measure, **$5.35**

DARK FANCY MIXED WORSTED SUITS FOR YOUNG MEN FROM 16 TO 21 YEARS OF AGE.

Material is medium weight, worsted front with a cotton chain in the back, which helps to give it a good body. **Color**—Black background relieved by a mixture of blue and white threads and an indistinct stripe effect in black and dark maroon. Well tailored garments, lined with a good quality of black Italian in body and strong neatly striped twill in sleeves. Stylish cut coats with long broad lapels; semi-form fitting, a slight flare at the bottom and in the proper length for the season. **Vest**—Five-button without collar. **Pants**—The popular semi-peg top effect. Nice roomy garments but not too extreme. Side pockets, hip pockets, watch pocket and strap and buckle in the back. An exceptionally neat appearing suit at a popular price. **State size.**

GOODS No. 40K4131
Price for young men's suits, style 19 only, 32 to 37 inches breast measure....... **$6.45**

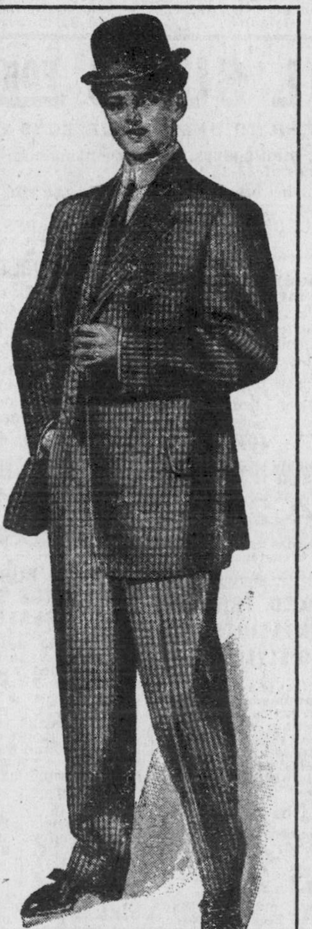

STYLE 19

Three-Button Single Breasted Sack with handsome broad long roll lapels, semi-form fitting effect, a little flare at bottom. Imitation cuffs on sleeves. SIZES, 32 TO 37 INCHES ONLY, OR THE SIZES REQUIRED FOR THE AVERAGE SIZE YOUNG MEN FROM 16 TO 21 YEARS OF AGE.

ABSOLUTELY FAST BLACK THIBET CLOTH SUITS IN SIZES 32 TO 37 INCHES BREAST MEASURE ONLY.

If an honest wearing, substantially tailored black suit is needed, suitable for all year around wear, we are confident that you will be well pleased with this number. **Material** — Soft finish strictly fast black Thibet cloth. **Style 19**, latest effect in three-button sack with nearly square corners. Slightly cut in at waist line and a little flare at bottom. Long roll broad lapels. **Vest**—Without collar, five buttons, four outside pockets and one inside pocket. **Pants**—The latest and extremely popular half peg top style. A full cut, roomy garment, but not too extreme. Side pockets, two hip pockets and a watch pocket. **See description of our Ucanttear make on page 1080, which will give you a good idea as to how the garments are made.** Lined with black Italian cloth, interlined with canvas and haircloth, well stayed, neatly shaped and padded shoulders. **Please take measure carefully as described on page 1079.**

GOODS No. 40K4135
Price for young men's suits, style 19 only, 32 to 37 inches breast measure....... **$5.98**

BEAUTIFUL GRAY STRIPED HERRINGBONE EFFECT ALL WOOL CHEVIOT SUITS.

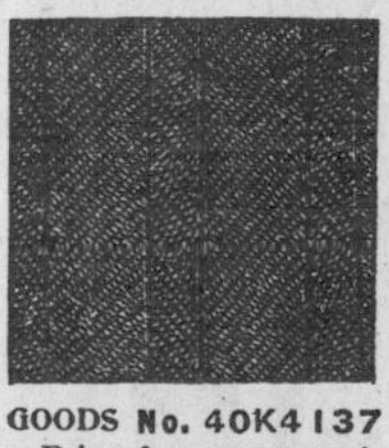

One of the handsomest styles in a medium priced suit, suitable for all year around wear, which we have ever been able to offer. **Material** is nice soft finish cheviot cloth in a herringbone effect weave. **Color**—A mixture of dark and medium gray forming an indistinct stripe effect. Splendidly tailored, fashionable and snappy appearing garments. **Style 19 only**, as illustrated on this page. **Vest** is the latest style, no collar, five buttons. Lower pockets have fancy shaped flaps. **Pants**—Latest effect peg top, nice roomy garments, but not too extreme, with side pockets, two hip pockets, watch pocket and the latest style buckles on sides. **Trimmings**—Fine black Italian cloth, twill sleeve lining, ivory buttons, interlinings and padding, as shown in illustration of our Ucanttear make on page 1079. The enormous increase in our sales of young men's clothing shows that the thoroughness of our make is being appreciated. **Do not fail to give size.**

GOODS No. 40K4137
Price for young men's suits, style 19 only, 32 to 37 inches breast measure **$6.75**

STYLISH MEDIUM GRAY STRIPED WORSTED SUITS FOR YOUNG MEN FROM 16 TO 21 YEARS OF AGE.

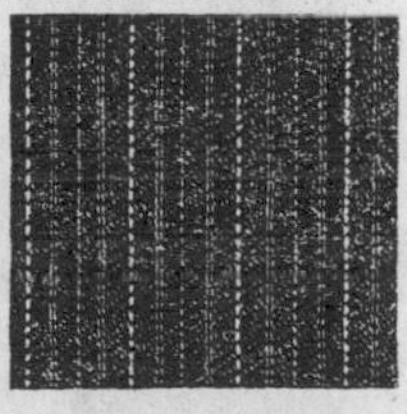

A particularly dressy, especially desirable pattern for stylish young men's suits. **Material**—Is a strong worsted fabric, medium weight. **Color**—A mixture of dark and light gray with a stripe effect formed by black lines about ⅜ inch apart. **Trimmings**—An excellent quality of Italian cloth, near match to material, canvas and haircloth front, which greatly helps to keep the garments in shape; handsomely padded shoulders, ivory buttons. **Style**—The latest effect in single breasted three-button sack style with handsome long roll broad lapels, slight flare at bottom of coat and cut in at waist line sufficient to make garment hang gracefully. **Vest**—Five-button without collar, fancy flaps on lower pockets. **Pants**—Latest peg top effect with side buckles, loops for belt, side pockets, two hip pockets and a watch pocket. **State size.**
See our big offers in young men's fancy vests on page 1092.

GOODS No. 40K4141
Price for young men's suits, style 19 only, 32 to 37 inches breast measure....... **$7.75**

BEAUTIFUL SMALL CHECK WORSTED SUITS, SIZES 32 TO 37 INCHES BREAST MEASURE.

Material—Through and through worsted, medium weight. **Color**—A mixture of gray and brown in a neat small check effect, one of the most popular styles this season. **Lined** with excellent quality imported Italian cloth in body of coat and back of vest. Interlined with canvas and haircloth, padded and neatly shaped shoulders. Ivory buttons. **Style**—Strictly up to date three-button sack semi-form fitting, long broad lapels, imitation cuffs on sleeves. **Vest**—Five-button without collar and with neatly shaped flaps on two lower pockets. **Pants**—The popular roomy, comfortable style called peg top, dressy effect, but not in the extreme width. Side pockets, hip pockets, watch pocket, buckles on the sides and loops for belt. **Be sure to give size.**
Include a fancy vest with your order. See the values on page 1092.

GOODS No. 40K4143
Price for young men's suits, style 19 only, 32 to 37 inches breast measure **$7.85**

LATEST EFFECT IN TAN AND BROWN MIXED STRIPED WORSTED SUITS FOR YOUNG MEN FROM 16 TO 21 YEARS OF AGE.

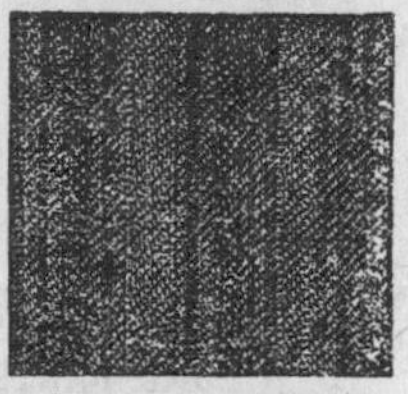

This suit will especially appeal to the young gentlemen who like to dress in the latest fashion, and the price at which we offer it is surely within reach of all. **Material**—Through and through worsted. **Pattern**—A narrow stripe effect. **Color**—A mixture of tan and brown, decorated by occasional silk lines in blue and orange. Lined with the best imported Italian cloth to match material; padded, interlined and stayed, as illustrated for our Ucanttear make on page 1079. The many favorable comments we have had on this make from our customers and the remarkable increase in our young men's clothing business shows plainly that our customers find that there is no better make of medium priced clothing in the market. **Style 19 only. Vest**—Five buttons with neatly shaped flaps on two lower pockets. **Pants**—In the popular peg top effect with side buckles and loops for belt. Imitation cuffs on coats. **Give size.**

GOODS No. 40K4147
Price for young men's suits, style 19 only, 32 to 37 inches breast measure **$8.48**

DARK MIXED THROUGH AND THROUGH WORSTED SUITS FOR YOUNG MEN FROM 16 TO 21 YEARS OF AGE.

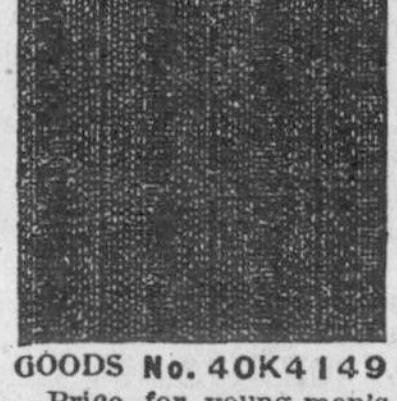

A very dressy style in a medium weight worsted which can be worn at almost all seasons of the year. **Color**—Dark gray mixture in a stripe effect. Made with all the special features which we advertise for our Ucanttear make. **Style** — Three-button sack coats with long broad lapels, nearly square corners, slight flare at bottom and cut in sufficient at waist to conform comfortably to the body. **Lined** with fine black Italian cloth in body and neatly striped twill in sleeves. Imitation cuffs. **Vest**—No collar, four outside pockets with flaps on two lower pockets and five buttons. **Semi-peg top Pants**, the most popular style for young men. Side pockets, hip pockets, watch pocket, loops for belt and the latest style buckles on the sides. **Give size.**

GOODS No. 40K4149
Price for young men's suits, in style 19 only, 32 to 37 inches breast measure **$8.75**

OUR POPULAR DARK DRAB CORDUROY SUITS FOR YOUNG MEN FROM 16 TO 21 YEARS OF AGE.

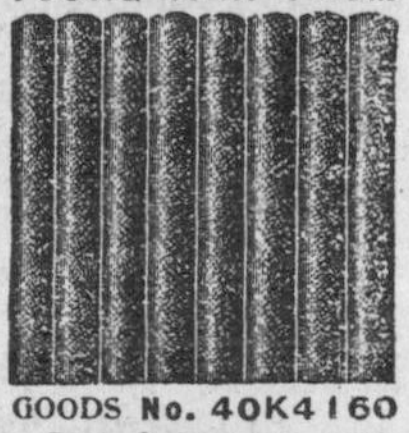

Material—Good weight dark drab corduroy, well filled and odorless. **Style**—Three-button sack coat with three outside pockets, one inside pocket. **Vest**—Five-button. **Pants**—With side pockets, hip pockets and a watch pocket. **Lined** with strong twill lining to match the color of suit. We take special care to tailor our corduroy suits as strong as possible, as we realize that these suits are intended more for hard wear than for dress. **The large quantities which we sell of this number every season is the best recommendation we can give it. Sizes**—32 to 37 inches breast measure, or the sizes usually worn by average size young men from 16 to 21 years of age. **Give measurement.**

GOODS No. 40K4160
Price for young men's suits, in style 19 only, 32 to 37 inches breast measure **$5.25**

OUR PRICES REDUCED OUR SALES WHICH HAVE CONSTANTLY INCREASED ENABLE US TO QUOTE LOWER PRICES THAN EVER BEFORE, QUALITY CONSIDERED. :: :: :: :: :: ::

YOUNG MEN'S CIELETTE RAINPROOF SPRING AND FALL OVERCOATS

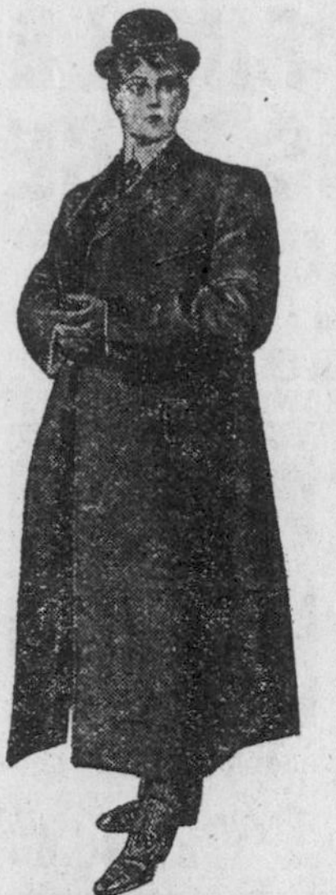

STYLE B63
For ages from 16 to 21.

SIZES—For young men of average size from 16 to 21 years of age, or measuring from 32 to 37 inches breast measure. Give size around body at breast over vest same as for an undercoat. See page 1079.

For a full description of the Cielette Rainproofing Process see page 1076 in our men's line, where we tell you the great value of these garments.

THE GREAT THING IS THAT YOU CAN USE THESE COATS EITHER AS SPRING AND FALL OVERCOATS OR AS RAINCOATS. While they are not strictly waterproof in the same sense as a mackintosh or rubber coat, yet they will protect you perfectly in any ordinary rain and for damp weather are unexcelled. They are the most comfortable, stylish, up to date and useful garments anyone could buy. You will find more use for them than for a winter overcoat because they are just the thing to use in chilly weather at all times of the year when a winter coat would be too heavy.

$5.95 FOR A HANDSOME DOUBLE TWIST CHEVIOT RAINCOAT.

A neat gray mixed pattern with a faint overplaid formed by dark maroon lines. Full cut, well made garments with three outside pockets, one inside pocket and a long slit in the back. They are unlined with the exception of a yoke around neck and shoulders. A very desirable coat, suitable either as a raincoat or spring and fall overcoat. **Sizes,** 32 to 37 inches. **Be sure to give breast measurement.**

Goods No. 40K4524

Price for rainproof overcoats for young men from 16 to 21 years of age, but not larger than 37 inches breast measure, style B63 . . **$5.95**

$6.95 FOR AN ABSOLUTELY FAST BLACK THIBET SPRING AND FALL OVERCOAT.

MATERIAL—A good weight absolutely fast black Thibet, just the right weight for spring and fall wear. Made with a large yoke of black Venetian cloth and lined with the same material in sleeves. Balance of the coat is unlined. Cut in the latest spring style with a long slit in the back, three outside pockets and one inside pocket, throat latch and a collar of same material. Excellent coats for chilly spring and fall days when a heavy overcoat would be uncomfortable. **Sizes,** 32 to 37 inches breast measure only. **Do not fail to give size.**

Goods No. 40K4525

Price for rainproof overcoats for young men from 16 to 21 years of age, but not larger than 37 inches breast measure, in style B63 . . . . **$6.95**

$7.50 FOR A HANDSOME SMALL CHECK EFFECT WORSTED RAINPROOF COAT.

A very stylish, up to date garment in a handsome small check effect. COLOR—A mixture of dark gray and black with a faint overplaid in dark red. Thoroughly tailored coats with large yoke of fine twill serge and sleeves lined with the same material. Three outside pockets, one inside pocket and a long slit in the back. Should you send us an order for one of these coats you would do us a great favor to compare it with coats offered elsewhere for this price and we feel sure that you will recommend our coats to your friends. Size, 32 to 37 inches breast measure. **Be sure to state size wanted.**

Goods No. 40K4526

Price for rainproof overcoats for young men from 16 to 21 years of age, but not larger than 37 inches breast measure, in style B63 . . . . **$7.50**

$8.98 IS THE PRICE OF OUR FINEST WORSTED CIELETTE RAINPROOF OVERCOATS.

MATERIAL—A very fine steel gray cravenette worsted in an indistinct striped effect. A perfectly tailored unlined coat with a yoke and with sleeves lined with black Venetian cloth. All seams felled and double stitched, three outside pockets, one inside pocket, a long slit in the back. If you never have used one of these practical spring and fall rainproof overcoats you have missed some real comfort in damp weather or in weather which is not cold enough for real heavy overcoats. **Be sure to take measure carefully the same as you would for an under coat.**

Goods No. 40K4527

Price for rainproof overcoats for young men from 16 to 21 years of age, but not larger than 37 inches breast measure, in style B63 . . . . **$8.98**

LONG PANTS SCHOOL SUITS FOR BOYS FROM 12 TO 15 YEARS OF AGE

HERE ARE WONDERFUL VALUES FOR THOSE WHO WISH TO DRESS THEIR BOYS FROM 12 TO 15 YEARS OF AGE IN LONG PANTS SUITS.

At retail you pay as much for these sizes as for young men's sizes, but by cutting a large number of garments in these special sizes, adapted for boys of this age, we are able to offer the suits at the surprisingly low prices of $3.25 to $6.75.

SIZES—For boys from 12 to 15 years old, not larger than 31 inches breast measure. **Give age and breast measure.** Average weight of one of these suits, 3¼ pounds.

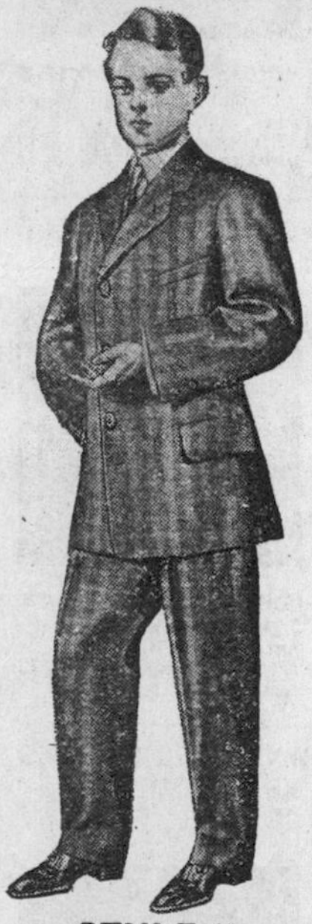

STYLE 11
Single breasted, three-button sack coat, with three outside pockets and one inside pocket. Five-button vest. Pants, side pockets and hip pockets.

DOUBLE OR SINGLE BREASTED SCHOOL SUITS WITH LONG PANTS.

Made of a beautiful dark brown cassimere suiting in a broken check effect with a very faint overplaid in gray and dark blue. A very desirable, dressy suit in medium weight material. Stylish cut garments with long roll broad lapels, lined with strong Italian cloth and sewed in the most substantial manner. Coats have three outside pockets, one inside pocket, bottom facings and are cut in correct length. Pants, roomy garments with side pockets, hip pockets and a watch pocket. **Either double or single breasted style.**

Goods No. 40K4105	Goods No. 40K4106
Price for single breasted suit, Style 11,	Price for double breasted suit, Style 12,
$4.00	**$4.25**

SIZES. For boys from 12 to 15 years of age, not larger than 31 inches breast measure. **Give age and breast measure.**

BEAUTIFUL GRAY AND BLACK MIXED THROUGH AND THROUGH WORSTED LONG PANTS SUITS IN SINGLE OR DOUBLE BREASTED STYLE.

MATERIAL—A very pretty broken check effect in a mixture of dark gray and black relieved by colorings in dark maroon. Stylish cut, well made garments in the latest semi-form fitting effect with broad lapels, padded shoulders, fronts interlined with canvas. Three outside pockets. Imitation cuffs on sleeves. Vest, five-button, no collar. Pants neatly shaped full cut garments with side pockets, hip pockets and a watch pocket. Can be furnished in either double or single breasted styles. **Be sure to state style wanted and note price of each style.**

Goods No. 40K4111	Goods No. 40K4112
Price for single breasted suit, Style 11,	Price for double breasted suit, Style 12,
$4.95	**$5.25**

SIZES For boys from 12 to 15 years of age, not larger than 31 inches breast measure. **Give age and breast measure.**

DRESSY APPEARING WOOL AND COTTON MIXED WORSTED SUITS WITH LONG PANTS, IN DOUBLE OR SINGLE BREASTED STYLE.

COLOR—Dark blue background with a small subdued check effect formed by green dotted lines. STYLE—Double or single breasted sack coats with three outside pockets, padded, interlined and thoroughly tailored garments. Substantially lined with black Italian cloth and made with bottom facings. Five-button vest, no collar. Pants cut medium width with side pockets, hip pockets and a watch pocket. A suit which in same material would sell in men's sizes for about double this price.

Goods No. 40K4107	Goods No. 40K4108
Price for single breasted suit, Style 11,	Price for double breasted suit, Style 12,
$4.48	**$4.65**

SIZES. For boys from 12 to 15 years of age, not over 31 inches breast measure. **Give age and breast measure.**

STRICTLY PURE WORSTED NAVY BLUE OR BLACK SERGE SUITS IN SINGLE OR DOUBLE BREASTED STYLES. For boys from 12 to 15 years of age.

All worsted serge is a very favorite material for boys' clothing. We have these suits in navy blue or black and in double or single breasted styles. Please note which number is described in navy blue and which in black. Splendid tailored, stylishly cut garments, lined with black Italian cloth, interlined with canvas and haircloth, all seams double stitched and taped. Coats have stylish broad lapels and imitation cuffs on sleeves. Vests, five-button, no collar. Pants are cut in the latest roomy effect with side pockets, hip pockets and watch pocket. The navy blue suits are very popular for dressy summer suits and the black suits are especially well suited for confirmation and Sunday suits.

Goods No. 40K4115	Goods No. 40K4116	Goods No. 40K4117	Goods No. 40K4118
Price for single breasted navy blue suit, Style 11,	Price for double breasted navy blue suit, Style 12,	Price for single breasted black serge suit, Style 11,	Price for double breasted black serge suit, Style 12,
$6.45	**$6.75**	**$6.45**	**$6.75**

SIZES. For boys from 12 to 15 years of age, not larger than 31 inches breast measure. **Give age and breast measure.**

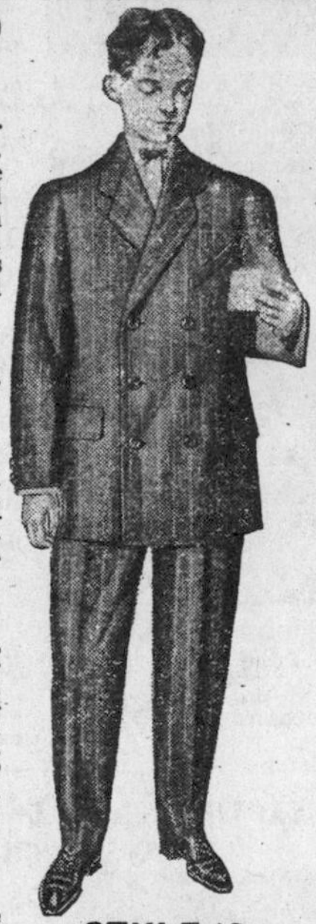

STYLE 12
Double breasted sack coat, three outside pockets, one inside pocket. Five-button vest. Pants, side pockets and hip pockets.

SINGLE BREASTED SCHOOL SUITS WITH LONG PANTS, IN FANCY DARK MIXED COTTON WORSTED.

MATERIAL—A strong cotton worsted fabric. COLOR—A mixture of dark and light gray in a pincheck effect and with an overplaid in green. The most substantial garments which it is possible to produce for the price. Strongly sewed and substantially trimmed suits. Coats made as illustrated for style 11, with three outside pockets, imitation cuffs on sleeves, long broad lapels and cut in correct length. Vest, five-button, no collar. Pants, a good width and neatly shaped and with the usual number of pockets. **Sizes,** for boys 12 to 15 years of age, not larger than 31 inches breast measure. **Be sure to give age and breast measure.**

Goods No. 40K4101

Price for single breasted school suits for boys from 12 to 15 years of age only, style 11 . . . . **$3.25**

SOFT FINISH DARK BLUE CASSIMERE SCHOOL SUITS WITH LONG PANTS.

A medium weight soft finish material. COLOR—Dark navy blue with a striped effect, formed by green and red lines. Heavy enough to be worn all the year around. Coats made in single breasted three-button sack style with three outside pockets, one inside pocket, latest style lapels and imitation cuffs on sleeves. Vests, five-button, without a collar. Pants with side pockets, hip pockets and a watch pocket. Cut in most prevailing style. **Trimmings—**Lined with strong black Italian cloth fronts of coats interlined with canvas, shoulders padded. A nice dark suit for everyday wear. **Sizes,** to fit average size boys from 12 to 15 years of age only, none larger than 31 inches breast measure. **Do not fail to give age and breast measure.**

Goods No. 40K4103

Price for single breasted school suits for boys from 12 to 15 years of age only, style 11 . . . . **$3.75**

STYLISH MEDIUM WEIGHT CHEVIOT SCHOOL SUITS WITH LONG PANTS.

COLOR—A stylish mixture of brown and gray with decorations in light blue and green. A subdued check effect. Splendid made suits which have all the special features of our well known Ucanttear make. Coats cut in single breasted three-button sack style with long roll lapels, semi-form fitting effect and imitation cuffs on sleeves. Vest, five-button, no collar. Pants in the full cut roomy style, with side pockets, hip pockets and a watch pocket. We can especially recommend this number for a dressy spring and summer suit in a reliable, good wearing fabric. **Sizes,** for boys 12 to 15 years of age, not larger than 31 inches breast measure. **Be sure to give age and breast measure.**

Goods No. 40K4109

Price for single breasted school suits for boys from 12 to 15 years of age only, style 11 . . . . **$4.60**

THROUGH AND THROUGH WORSTED SINGLE BREASTED SCHOOL SUITS.

MATERIAL—Medium weight through and through worsted in a diagonal weave and with a handsome striped effect. COLOR—Very dark almost black background with a very little decoration in gray and light blue. A very dressy worsted suit suitable for all year around wear. Stylish cut, handsomely trimmed garments. Coats, three-button single breasted sacks cut in the latest spring effect with imitation cuffs at sleeves. Vest, five-button, no collar. Pants, semi-peg top effect with side pockets, hip pockets and a watch pocket. **Sizes,** 12 to 15 years only, 31 inches breast measure the largest size. **Do not fail to give age and breast measure.**

Goods No. 40K4113

Price for single breasted school suits for boys from 12 to 15 years of age only, style 11 . . . . **$5.50**

WONDERFUL VALUES IN YOUNG MEN'S LONG PANTS

OUR LINE, consisting of pants in Cheviots, Khakis, Cotton Worsteds, Union Cassimeres, Serges and all Worsteds, some cut in regular style and some in the very latest peg top style, is the most complete line we have ever offered and we believe the most complete line ever offered by any clothier or retail dealer in the country. Our prices, ranging from 60 cents to $3.15, are absolutely the lowest, being just about one-half the prices you would have to pay dealers for these pants. Don't miss this chance to include a pair of these pants with your suit order at our wonderful low prices.

60c FOR WASHABLE OTIS CHEVIOT PANTS. Well known strong material, just the thing for an everyday summer pants which will wash perfectly. Cut in regular style with side pockets, one hip pocket, watch pocket, patent suspender buttons, strap and buckle in the back. Color, a mixture of white and light blue in a pincheck effect. **Give measurements.**

GOODS No. 40K4261

Price, per pair, sizes, 28 to 33 inches waist measure only........... 60c

75c UNDOUBTEDLY THE GREATEST VALUE POSSIBLE IN WELL MADE KHAKI CLOTH WASHABLE SUMMER PANTS. Material, strong, washable khaki cloth, which is used so extensively by the United States government. Color, light tan; full cut, comfortable summer pants, made with side pockets, hip pocket, watch pocket, loops for belt and latest suspender buttons. Substantial trimmings and taped through seat.

GOODS No. 40K4263

Price, per pair, sizes, 28 to 33 inches waist measure only........... 75c

98c OUR LINE OF MEDIUM WEIGHT EXTRA STRONG EVERYDAY PANTS. Material, strong wool and cotton mixed cheviot. Color, dark gray mixed in neat striped effects. The most substantial everyday pants we have ever been able to produce. Made extra strong, cut in regular style, side pockets, hip pocket, watch pocket, patent suspender buttons, strap and buckle in the back. **Good weight, suitable for all year around wear. Be sure to state size.**

GOODS No. 40K4265

Price, per pair, sizes, 28 to 33 inches waist measure only 98c

$1.25 FOR DARK NAVY BLUE UNION CASSIMERE PANTS. Material, a medium weight union cassimere, not too heavy but such that it can be worn at almost all seasons. Color, dark navy blue. Full cut, roomy pants in regular style with side pockets, hip pockets, watch pocket, strap and buckle in the back. **Be sure to state size.**

GOODS No. 40K4267

Price, per pair, sizes, 28 to 33 inches waist measure only........ $1.25

$1.25 FOR FAST BLACK UNION CASSIMERE PANTS. Another pants which is suitable for all year around wear. Material, a wool and cotton mixed fabric. Color, fast black. Neatly trimmed and substantially made pants, cut in regular style with side pockets, hip pocket, watch pocket, strap and buckle in the back and patent suspender buttons.

GOODS No. 40K4269

Price, per pair, sizes, 28 to 33 inches waist measure only........... $1.25

$1.50 FOR OUR BEST QUALITY DARK DRAB CORDUROY PANTS. Material, well filled, pure dye dark drab corduroy. Absolutely reliable material. We could sell cheaper corduroy pants but the material would be such that we could not recommend it. **The immense quantities we sell of this number every season is the best recommendation we can give it.** Made in the most substantial manner possible, with side pockets, hip pockets and a watch pocket. **Be sure to state size.**

GOODS No. 40K4271

Price, per pair, sizes, 28 to 33 inches waist measure only........... $1.50

$2.65 OUR NAVY BLUE SERGE PANTS IN PEG TOP STYLE. One of the greatest values we have to offer this season. Material, all worsted navy blue serge. The very thing for comfortable summer pants. Cut in peg top style, full and roomy but not too baggy; made with side pockets, hip pockets with flaps, belt loops and straps and buckles on the side. **Be sure to state size.**

GOODS No. 40K4273

Price, per pair, sizes, 28 to 33 inches waist measure only........... $2.65

$1.00 FOR EXTRA STRONG DARK STRIPED WORSTED PANTS. Color, black background in a striped effect, formed by alternating green and gray lines. A very neat appearing everyday pants, cut in regular style. Side pockets, hip pocket, watch pocket and patent suspender buttons. **Be sure to state size.**

GOODS No. 40K4275

Price, per pair, sizes, 28 to 33 inches waist measure only........... $1.00

$1.25 FOR A FANCY DARK STRIPED WORSTED PANTS. Material, is an extra strong wool and cotton mixed fabric, worsted finish through and through goods. Color, gray and black with decorations in green and orange, a fancy striped pattern. Side pockets, hip pocket, watch pocket, strap and buckle in the back and cut in regular style. **Be sure to state size.**

GOODS No. 40K4277

Price, per pair, sizes, 28 to 33 inches waist measure only $1.25

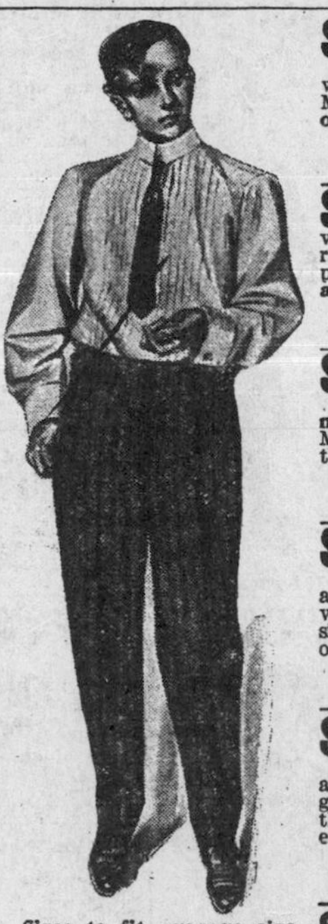

Sizes to fit average size young men, from 14 to 21 years of age, or measuring from 28 to 33 inches in the waist and from 28 to 34 inches inseam. Take measure carefully as described on page 1079.

$1.25 GREATEST POSSIBLE VALUE IN STYLISH PEG TOP SUMMER PANTS. Color, medium gray in a very fancy striped effect. Roomy peg top pants with side pockets, hip pocket, loops for belt and buckles on the side. Material, nice soft finish union cassimere. **One of the most stylish pants ever offered for so little money. Be sure to give size.**

GOODS No. 40K4279

Price, per pair, sizes, 28 to 33 inches waist measure only........ $1.25

$1.85 FANCY DARK BROWN MIXED WORSTED PANTS. Exceptionally dressy appearing worsted finish pants. Color, a very dark brown background with decorations in gray and yellow and with a raised striped effect in black. Nicely shaped pants cut in regular style with side pockets, hip pocket, strap and buckle in the back. **Be sure to take measure as described on page 1079.**

GOODS No. 40K4281

Price, per pair, sizes, 28 to 33 inches waist measure only $1.85

$1.75 FOR A VERY NICE DARK GRAY NARROW STRIPED WORSTED PANTS. Material, splendid quality cotton worsted, exceptionally good wearing material. Color, black background with a narrow striped effect in gray. Made with side pockets, hip pockets, watch pocket and strap and buckle in the back. **A very neat and dressy appearing pants, cut in regular style.**

GOODS No. 40K4283

Price, per pair, sizes, 28 to 33 inches waist measure only $1.75

$1.85 A VERY STYLISH SUMMER PANTS IN THE LATEST PEG TOP EFFECT. Color, medium gray in a fancy striped effect, formed by alternating gray and dark maroon and black dotted lines. Material, tropical worsted. The very thing for dressy, cool and comfortable summer pants. Peg top effect, side pockets, hip pockets, watch pocket, loops for belt and straps and buckles on the sides. **State size.**

GOODS No. 40K4285

Price, per pair, sizes, 28 to 33 inches waist measure only........ $1.85

$2.00 FOR A MEDIUM WEIGHT WORSTED PANTS IN PEG TOP STYLE. Material, all worsted front with a cotton chain in the back. Color, almost black, with a raised stripe effect and very faint decorations in light gray. Stylish cut, neatly trimmed pants in the popular peg top effect, but not the extreme baggy kind. Side buckles, loops for belts, side pockets, hip pockets with flaps. **Exceptionally dressy pants for the price. State size.**

GOODS No. 40K4287

Price, per pair, sizes, 28 to 33 inches waist measure only........ $2.00

$2.58 A VERY NEAT MEDIUM GRAY STRIPED WORSTED PANTS IN PEG TOP STYLE. Worsted finish material. Color, a medium gray mixture with a pretty striped effect. Very nice pants to wear with any dark coat and vest. Stylish peg top garments so popular with young men. Side pockets, hip pockets, straps and buckles on the sides. **Give measurements.**

GOODS No. 40K4289

Price, per pair, sizes, 28 to 33 inches waist measure only........ $2.58

$2.85 FOR STYLISH PEG TOP PANTS IN THE LATEST BROWN EFFECT. Material, all through and through worsted. Color, dark brown with silk decorations in gray and with a striped effect in black. **One of the best values in our line which is sure to please young men who like to dress in the very latest style.** Roomy, full cut peg top effect garments with hip pockets, side pockets, and a watch pocket. **Give measurements.**

GOODS No. 40K4291

Price, per pair, sizes, 28 to 33 inches waist measure only $2.85

$3.15 FOR OUR FINEST WORSTED DRESS PANTS IN STYLISH PEG TOP CUT. Material, all worsted front. Color, a very handsome black and gray mixture in a pretty striped effect. Exceptionally well trimmed and thoroughly tailored garments, cut in the very latest and most stylish peg top effect. **Pants which would sell in men's sizes for at least $5.00.** Side pockets, hip pockets with flaps and a watch pocket. Loops for belt.

GOODS No. 40K4293

Price, per pair, sizes, 28 to 33 inches waist measure only $3.15

OUR UCANTTEAR BOYS' TWO AND THREE-PIECE KNEE PANTS SUITS

OUR BOYS' TWO AND THREE-PIECE KNEE PANTS SUITS on this and on next page are made in the very latest styles in all the popular fabrics and colors. Our great Ucanttear make is acknowledged to be the best make of medium priced clothing in the country. The illustration and explanation of this make on page 1079 will give you a good idea of the careful and substantial construction of these garments. **Be sure to read it.**

SIZES. Two-piece suits are made in sizes to fit young boys 8 to 14 years of age. Three-piece suits for boys 8 to 16 years of age. Order by age only, and be sure to state if boy is large or small for his age.

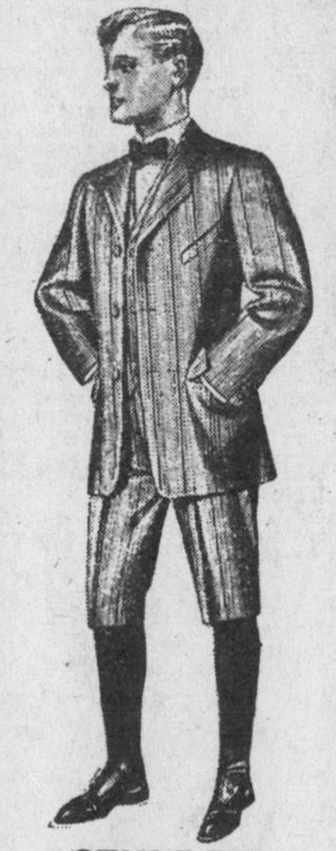

STYLE B71
Single Breasted Three-Piece Knee Pants Suits. Sizes, 8 to 16 years. Three-button single breasted sack coat, stylish broad lapels, corners nearly square, three outside pockets, five-button vest, no collar. Pants cut in regular style.

NEAT DARK GRAY COTTON WORSTED SUITS IN A NARROW STRIPED EFFECT.

Medium weight substantial worsted finish materials. Color, dark gray in a neat striped effect in black. Substantially made, three outside pockets, one inside pocket, trimmed with black Italian cloth. Pants, side pockets, one hip pocket and taped through seat. **An honest made suit at the very lowest possible price. Be sure to state age.**

GOODS No 40K4199

Price for single breasted three-piece knee pants suits, style B71 sizes, 8 to 16 years.............. $1.98

GOODS No 40K4200

Price for double breasted two-piece knee pants suits, style B72 sizes 8 to 14 years.............. $1.48

NICE MEDIUM GRAY PINCHECK EFFECT SUITS IN STRONG, HARD FINISH MATERIAL.

Substantially made and well trimmed garments. Lined with strong Italian lining, cut in the latest effect with padded shoulders and long broad lapels. Coats have three outside pockets, one inside pocket. Pants, side pockets, hip pocket and three buttons at the knee. Extra buttons and a patch piece of the material furnished with each suit. **Compare our prices and make with others and we are confident that you will never buy your boys' clothing anywhere else. Give age.**

GOODS No 40K4201

Price for single breasted three-piece knee pants suits, style B71, sizes, 8 to 16 years.............. $2.25

GOODS No 40K4202

Price for double breasted two-piece knee pants suits, style B72, sizes, 8 to 14 years.............. $1.75

FANCY BROWN MIXED COTTON WORSTED SUITS.

A neat appearing, splendid wearing material in a worsted finish. Color, brown. Pattern, a broken check effect in gray and relieved by colorings in green and dark maroon. Substantially made garments with all seams double stitched and taped, interlined with canvas and lined with strong black Italian cloth. Pants, side pockets, hip pockets and double stitched and taped seams. Extra buttons and a patch piece of material furnished with each suit. **State age of boy.**

GOODS No. 40K4203

Price for single breasted three-piece knee pants suits, style B71, sizes, 8 to 16 years only.............. $2.85

GOODS No. 40K4204

Price for double breasted two-piece knee pants suits, style B72, sizes, 8 to 14 years.............. $2.25

FANCY GRAY MIXED UNION CASSIMERE KNEE PANTS SUITS.

Material, a strong quality of wool and cotton mixed cassimere. Color, a mixture of light and dark gray in a pincheck effect and relieved by colorings in orange and light blue. **A very desirable pattern for a spring and summer suit.** Coats made with three outside pockets, lined with strong Italian cloth, interlined with canvas and made with double stitched and taped seams. Pants cut in regular style, with three buttons at knee and all seams double stitched and taped, side pockets, hip pockets and patent suspender buttons. **State age.**

GOODS No. 40K4205

Price for single breasted three-piece knee pants suits, style B71, sizes, 8 to 16 years.............. $3.00

GOODS No. 40K4206

Price for double breasted two-piece knee pants suits, style B72, sizes, 8 to 14 years.............. $2.35

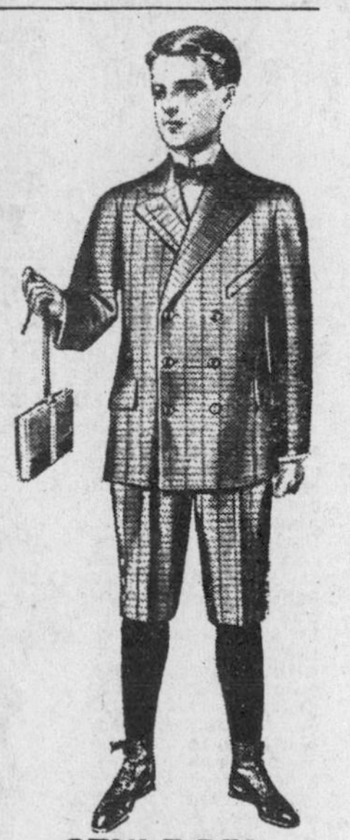

STYLE B72
Two-Piece Double Breasted Knee Pants Suits. Sizes, 8 to 14 years only. Three-button double breasted sack coats with stylish long roll lapels, three outside pockets. Pants cut regular style with side pockets, hip pockets and buttons at the knee.

OUR GREAT ASSORTMENT OF LITTLE FELLOWS' WASHABLE SUITS

By buying our fabrics in large quantities direct from the mills and manufacturing the suits in large numbers, we are able to offer suits made of the best washable fabrics, finest patterns and styles, all made full and roomy, at prices ranging from 38 cents to $1.98, absolutely the lowest prices quoted on this class of goods. Retail clothiers and other dealers cannot as a rule buy this class of goods at wholesale for less than the prices at which we offer them to you.

Do not miss this chance to dress your little fellows in a healtay, cool and comfortable manner at a nominal cost.

SIZES—When ordering, state age of boy and whether he is large or small for his age. Note carefully the sizes mentioned in the descriptions. We do not furnish these suits in sizes other than those mentioned. When suits are to be sent by mail, postage must be allowed, amount of which is stated under each number.

38c FOR A MEDIUM WEIGHT CRASH SUIT IN NATURAL LINEN COLOR.

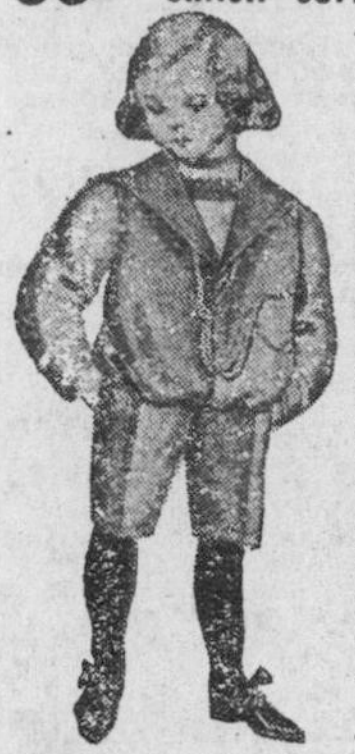

Well made little garment which buttons with a fly, has outside breast pocket, a wide duck sailor collar trimmed with a piece of crash, same material as suit. A detachable neatly trimmed shield and a cord and whistle are furnished with each suit. Pants cut in regular style. Color, natural linen in medium weight washable crash. State age.

No. 40K4402 Price for sailor blouse suits for boys from 3 to 10 years of age only........ 38c
If by mail, postage extra, 14 cents.

45c PRETTY BLUE AND WHITE STRIPED CHAMBRAY SUIT WITH BLOOMER PANTS.

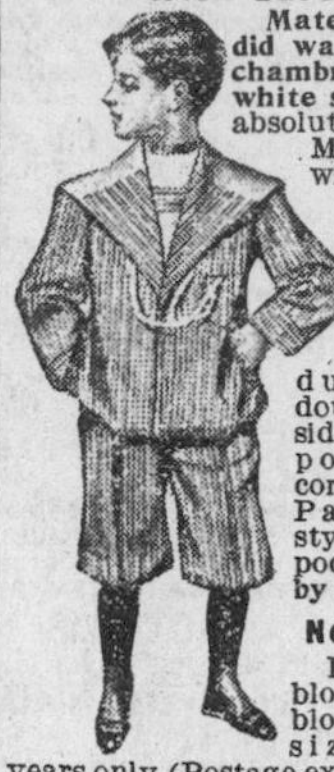

Material, a splendid washable woven chambray in blue and white striped effect, absolutely fast color. Made fly front with white duck sailor collar, front of which is trimmed with same material as suit. White duck shield, double cuffs, outside breast pocket and cord and whistle. Pants bloomer style with side pockets. Order by age.

No. 40K4404 Price for sailor blouse suits with bloomer pants, sizes, 3 to 10 years only. (Postage extra, 15c). 45c

49c GOOD WEIGHT MILITARY BLOUSE SUITS.

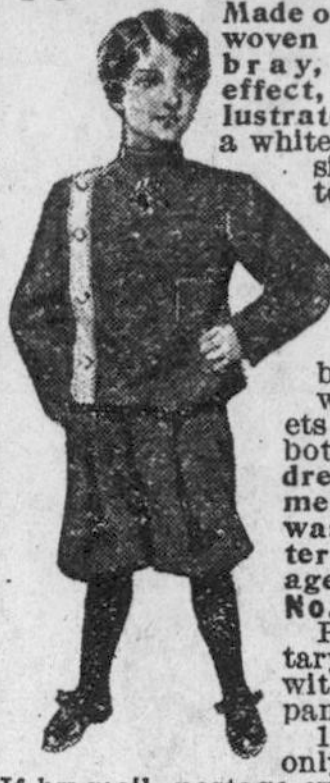

Made of good weight woven blue chambray, in military effect, style as illustrated, buttons on a white band on the side, pearl buttons, one outside breast pocket, cuffs double thickness, the little pants cut in the popular bloomer style with side pockets and elastic at bottom. A very dressy little garment in splendid washable material. State age.

No. 40K4406 Price for military blouse suits with bloomer pants, sizes, 3 to 10 years only........ 49c
If by mail, postage extra, 16 cents.

52c PLAIN WHITE DUCK SAILOR BLOUSE SUIT WITH BLOOMER PANTS.

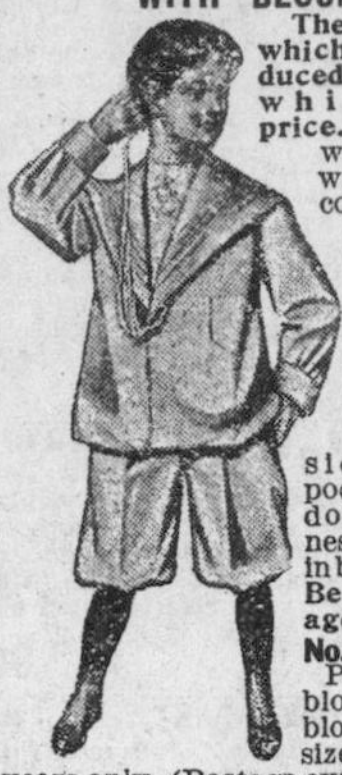

The best suit which can be produced in plain white for the price. Medium weight duck, with sailor collar trimmed with four rows of white soutache, silk embroidered white duck shield and cord and whistle. Fly front, outside breast pocket, cuffs double thickness and pants in bloomer style. Be sure to state age of boy.

No. 40K4408 Price for sailor blouse suit with bloomer pants, sizes, 3 to 10 years only. (Postage extra, 16c). 52c

58c GOOD WEIGHT SAILOR BLOUSE SUIT WITH BLOOMER PANTS IN GALATEA CLOTH.

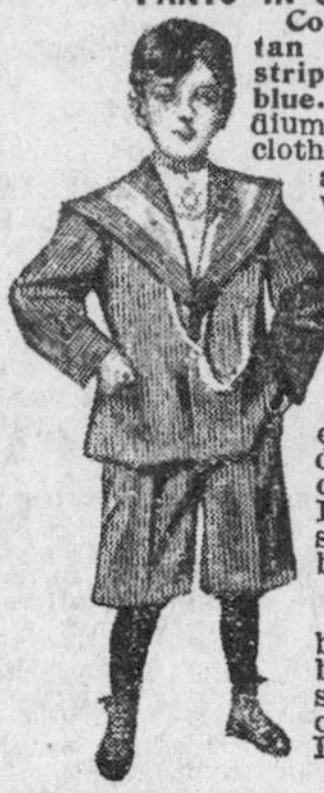

Color, a mixture of tan and white with a striped effect in dark blue. Material, medium weight Galatea cloth, a splendid washable fabric. Made with a sailor collar trimmed with white duck and piped with white soutache. Fly front, one outside pocket, cuffs double thickness. Silk embroidered white duck shield and cord and whistle. Pants bloomer style with elastic at bottom. State age.

No. 40K4410 Price for sailor blouse suits with bloomer pants, sizes, 3 to 10 years only...... 58c
If by mail, postage extra, 16 cents.

70c A BEAUTIFUL BLACK AND WHITE CHECK DOUBLE BREASTED SAILOR SUIT WITH BLOOMER PANTS.

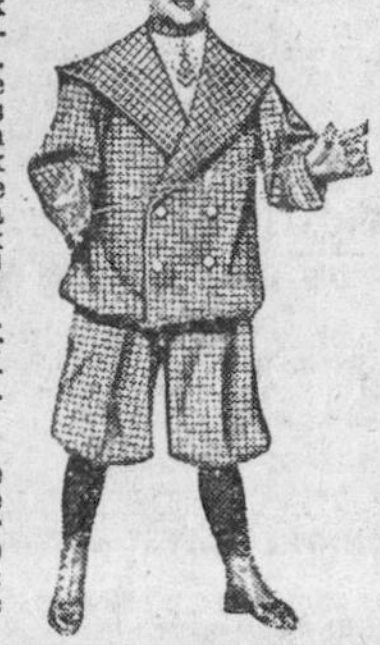

Material, good weight washable cheviot. Color, black and white in a handsome check effect. Full cut double breasted garments with a perfectly plain large sailor collar, six pearl buttons, outside breast pocket, a dickey of white duck which is embroidered with a blue silk emblem in the center. Pants cut bloomer style with side pockets and elastic at bottom. Give age.

No. 40K4412 Price for double breasted sailor blouse suit with bloomer pants, sizes, 3 to 10 years only...... 70c
If by mail, postage extra, 18 cents.

75c A VERY STYLISH BLACK AND WHITE STRIPED SAILOR SUIT WITH BLOOMER PANTS IN GALATEA CLOTH.

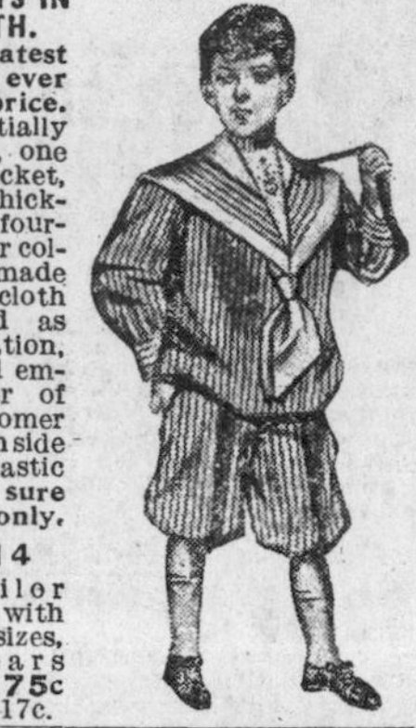

One of the neatest little garments ever shown for the price. Very substantially made, fly front, one outside breast pocket, cuffs double thickness, white linen four-in-hand tie, sailor collar and dickey made of white madras cloth and trimmed as shown in illustration, silk embroidered emblem in center of shield. Pants bloomer style, cut full with side pockets and elastic at bottom. Be sure to order by age only.

No. 40K4414 Price for sailor blouse suits with bloomer pants, sizes, 3 to 10 years only.......... 75c
Postage extra, 17c.

85c A DOUBLE BREASTED WHITE LINEN SUIT.

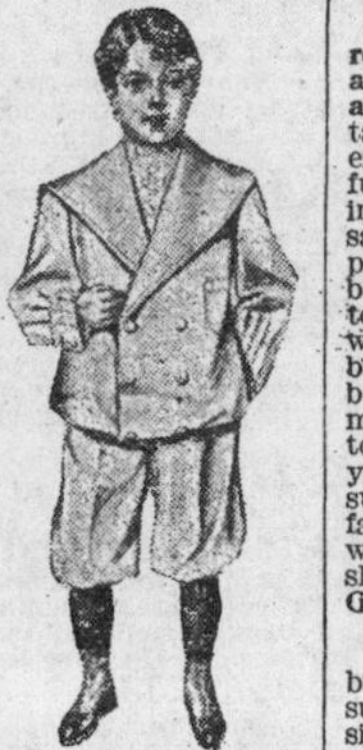

A price heretofore unheard of for well made suits in this material. A splendid quality of linen duck; color, plain white. Extra full cut double breasted garments, trimmed with pearl buttons, sleeves and cuffs plaited and made to button. Outside breast pocket, silk embroidered shield, same material as suit. The large sailor collar is perfectly plain. Well made little pants in bloomer style, side pockets and elastic at bottom. One of the best values ever shown in wash goods. State age.

No. 40K4416 Price for double breasted sailor suits with bloomer pants, sizes, 3 to 10 years only........ 85c
If by mail, postage extra, 20 cents.

95c A HANDSOME DOUBLE BREASTED GALATEA CLOTH SAILOR SUIT IN A STYLISH CHECK EFFECT.

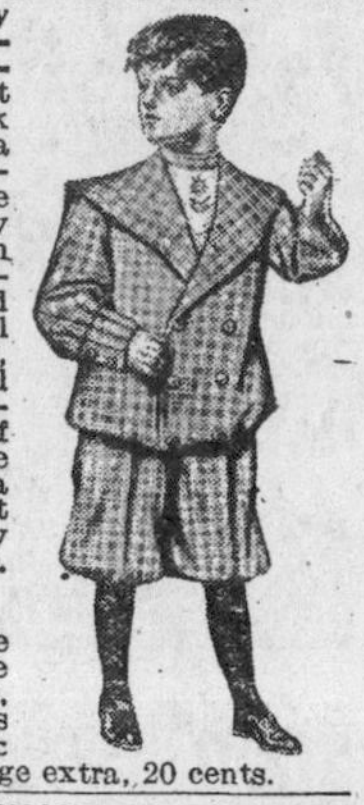

Material, absolutely reliable, splendid washable good weight Galatea cloth. Color, light tan with a pretty check effect in white. Extra full cut, stylish appearing garments, large sailor collar, neatly plaited cuffs which button with two buttons, silk embroidered white linen shield, pearl buttons. Pants roomy, bloomer style, well made, elastic at bottom; side pockets. If you get one of these suits you will do us a favor to compare it with any suit generally shown for about $1.50. Give age.

No. 40K4418 Price for double breasted sailor blouse suit, bloomer pants, sizes, 3 to 10 years only.......... 95c
If by mail, postage extra, 20 cents.

$1.00 THE GREATEST VALUE IN A WHITE LINEN UNITED STATES NAVY SAILOR SUIT.

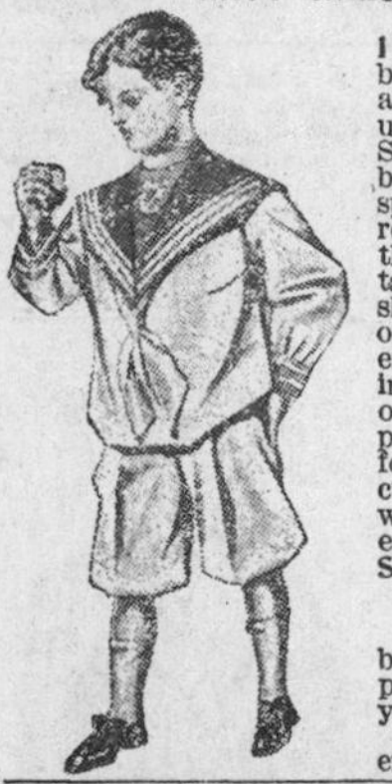

Material, fine white linen. The little blouse is made exactly like the summer uniform of the United States navy. Light blue sailor collar of splendid washable rep, trimmed with three rows of white tape. Cuffs and shield are also made of blue rep. Silk embroidered anchor in front. Fly front, outside breast pocket, white linen four-in-hand tie. Full cut bloomer pants, with side pockets and elastic at bottom. State age.

No. 40K4420 Price for sailor blouse with bloomer pants, sizes, 3 to 10 years only... $1.00
If by mail, postage extra, 19 cents.

98c ONE OF OUR GREAT LEADERS IN WASHABLE SUITS FOR LITTLE FELLOWS FROM 3 TO 10 YEARS OLD.

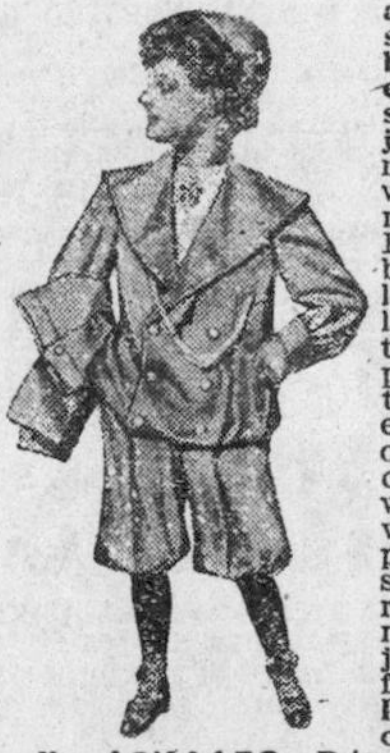

Outfit consists of a double breasted sailor blouse with bloomer pants, an extra pair of straight pants and a jockey cap. Material, good weight washable crash in natural linen color. Blouse cut in double breasted style with a large plain sailor collar, six pearl buttons, outside breas pocket, cuffs double thickness. Neatly embroidered shield of white madras cloth and a cord and whistle furnished with each suit. One pants cut in bloomer style, the other in regular style. A well made, lined little jockey cap is given free with each outfit. Please order by age only.

No. 40K4452 Price for suit with bloomer pants and an extra straight pants and jockey cap to match, for boys from 3 to 10 years of age only...... (Postage extra, 22c)..... 98c

$1.25 STYLISH CUT DOUBLE BREASTED BELT SUIT WITH KNICKERBOCKER PANTS AND GOLF CAP TO MATCH.

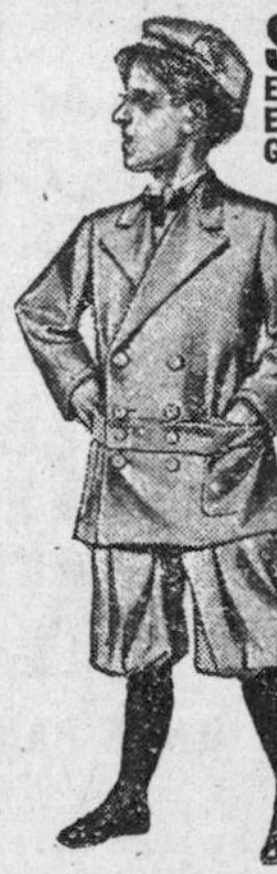

Double breasted belt suits with knickerbocker pants, full cut, roomy, comfortable summer garments for bigger boys. Material, good weight, splendid washable crash in natural linen color. Coat has stylish broad lapels, two outside patch pockets, six buttons and a belt of same material attached. Pants have side pockets, one hip pocket, loops for belts and a strap and buckle at the knee. A latest style golf cap is furnished free with each suit. Order by age.

No. 40K4454 Prico for double breasted belt suits with knickerbocker pants and cap to match, sizes, 8 to 15 years only.................. $1.25
If by mail, postage extra, 22 cents.

$1.25 SPECIAL VALUE IN THE SUMMER SAILOR BLOUSE SUIT WITH BLOOMER PANTS AND A CAP TO MATCH FREE.

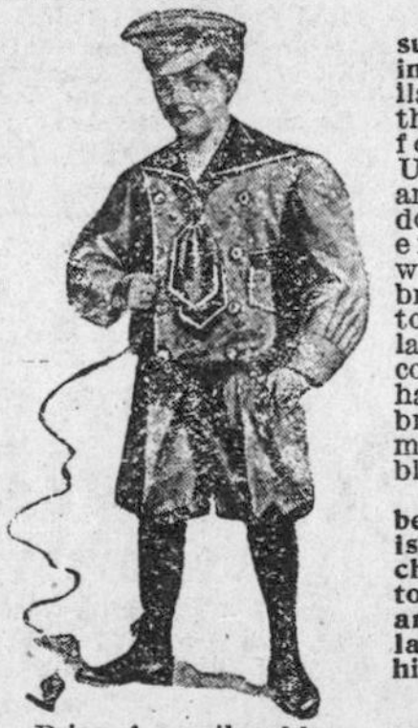

A stylish little suit, sateen finish in a tan color, similar to the color of the summer uniforms of the United States army. Made in double breasted effect, trimmed with eight brass anchor buttons, red sailor collar, made of fast color rep four-in-hand tie, outside breast pocket trimmed in red. Pants bloomer style.

With this number we give a stylish golf cap free of charge. Be sure to state age of boy and whether he is large or small for his age.

No. 40K4421 Price for sailor blouse suit with bloomer pants and cap to match, sizes, 3 to 10 years only.... (Postage extra, 18 cents)... $1.25

$1.35 BEAUTIFUL TAN COLOR IMPORTED ENGLISH REP DOUBLE BREASTED SAILOR SUITS.

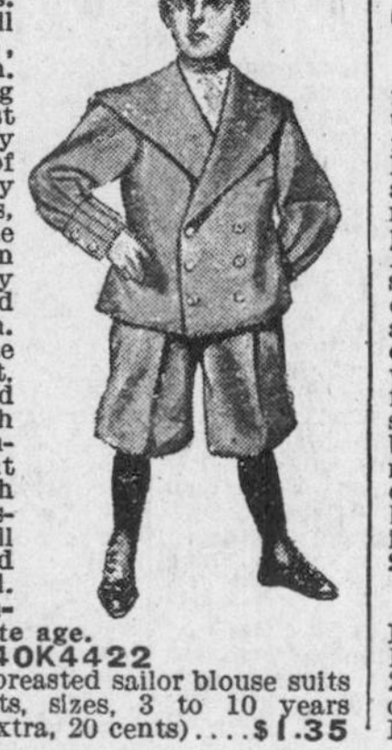

One of the most stylish garments made in wash goods. Material is the well known 696 rep, made in Great Britain. Particularly strong and absolutely fast color. Color, a very handsome shade of tan. Exceptionally full cut garments, thoroughly well made with a large plain sailor collar, nicely plaited sleeves and cuffs made to button. Pearl buttons, one outside breast pocket, a long white shield embroidered with white silk in the center. Pants full cut bloomer style with side pockets and elastic at bottom, all seams double stitched and neatly finished. A high class washable garment. State age.

No. 40K4422 Price for double breasted sailor blouse suits with bloomer pants, sizes, 3 to 10 years only.... (Postage extra, 20 cents).... $1.35

48c LITTLE FELLOWS' RUSSIAN SUITS IN SPLENDID WASHABLE BLUISH GRAY CHAMBRAY.

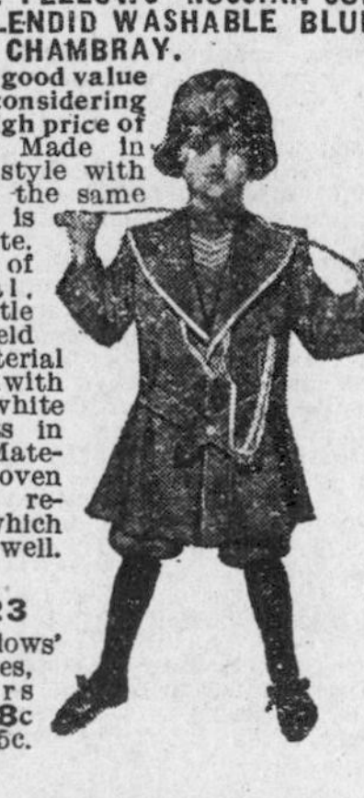

Exceptionally good value for the price, considering the extremely high price of raw material. Made in Russian blouse style with a sailor collar of the same material which is piped in white. Fly front, belt of same material, cord and whistle and with a shield of same material which is trimmed with four rows of white soutache. Pants in bloomer style. Material bluish gray woven chambray. A reliable material which is sure to wash well. State age.

No. 40K4423 Price for little fellows' Russian suits, sizes, 2½ to 6 years only........ 48c
Postage extra, 15c.

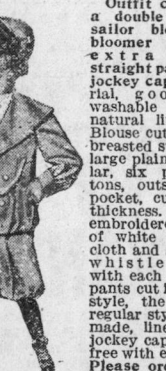

50c OUR BLUE AND WHITE STRIPED CHAMBRAY RUSSIAN SUITS.

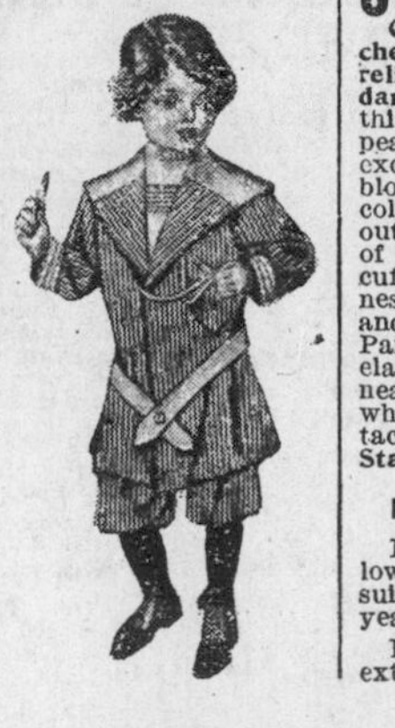

A nice little suit which will wash well and give satisfactory wear. Made fly front with a large white duck sailor collar. A white duck shield with a stripe of same material as suit in the center, one outside pocket, a belt of white duck and made to button with a fly. Little pants are cut in bloomer style. A cord and whistle are given free with each suit. How old is he?

No. 40K4424 Price for little fellows' Russian suits, sizes, 2½ to 6 years only.......... 50c
If by mail, postage extra, 14 cents.

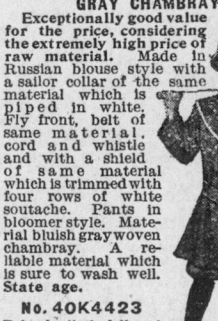

56c A GOOD WEIGHT FANCY CRASH RUSSIAN BLOUSE SUIT.

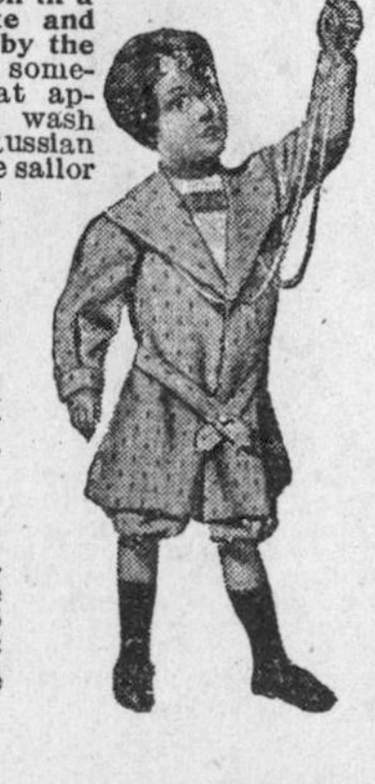

Color, natural linen in a check effect in white and relieved from plain by the dark brown figures, something especially neat appearing which will wash exceptionally well. Russian blouse style with large sailor collar, fly front, one outside pocket, belt of same material, cuffs double thickness and with a cord and whistle attached. Pants bloomer style, elastic at bottom. A neatly trimmed white shield is attached to the collar. State age.

No. 40K4425 Price for little fellows' Russian blouse suits, sizes, 2½ to 6 years only...... 56c
If by mail, postage extra, 16 cents.

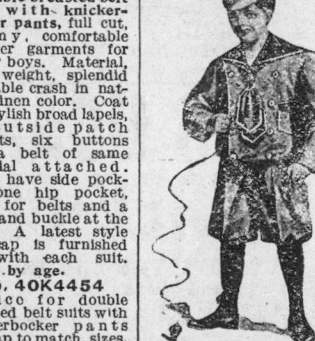

FACTORY PRICES ON MEN'S FUR COATS, BLANKET AND SHEEP LINED CLOTHING AND WORKING GARMENTS OF ALL KINDS

DON'T PAY RETAIL PRICES for any such clothing as we offer on the following pages. We operate the largest fur coat, duck and leather coat and working clothing factory in the United States, and quote you prices that just include the actual cost of material and labor with but our one very small profit added. Dealers cannot buy qualities as good as we offer here from other manufacturers in wholesale lots for a cent less than the prices at which we offer them to you.

OUR LIBERAL TERMS AND MONEY REFUND GUARANTEE offer on fur coats. Send us your order, give us your measurements according to our simple plan mentioned on page 1055, enclose our price, and we will send you the garment you order and guarantee it to fit and please you perfectly, or refund to you the price and any transportation charges you paid on the shipment upon return of the goods to us, or will exchange the unsatisfactory goods and furnish goods that will be satisfactory, and in that case we will pay the transportation charges both ways on the goods returned.

ALL THESE COATS ARE GUARANTEED to leave our establishment in perfect condition and free from all defects, and if not entirely satisfied with the coat when you receive it, you are at liberty to return it to us at our expense and we will refund the price of it, together with any transportation charges you have paid; or, if desired, we will exchange it for a satisfactory coat and pay the transportation charges both ways on the coat you return. **If you have worn the coat and if for any reason you are not entirely satisfied with it and you then return it to us, we reserve the right at our discretion to repair the coat, furnish a new one in its place or refund your money, according to the circumstances.**

FOR MEASUREMENTS give the size around the body at chest, over your vest, close up under your arms, just the same as if you were measuring for a suit. Don't measure over other clothing, as our garments are cut and made with proper allowance for fitting over other clothing. See page 1055 for instructions on measuring clothing.

SIZES. We furnish men's fur coats in any size from 36 inches up to and including 46 inches breast measure. No larger sizes than these are kept in stock. For the average size, our coats run 52 inches in length, and are cut full size, being more roomy than the average fur coat offered elsewhere. We do not skimp in the manufacturing of our garments. Any size over 46 inches chest measure or longer than 52 inches, we call an extra size, for which we make an extra charge, as quoted below.

EXTRA CHARGES FOR EXTRA SIZES. On all fur coats measuring over 46 inches breast measure, up to and including 52 inches breast measure, we charge 10 per cent more than the price quoted for our regular sizes in this catalogue. For fur coats over 52 inches breast measure, up to and including 56 inches breast measure, we charge 20 per cent extra. For fur coats over 52 inches in length, up to and including 56 inches in length, we charge 10 per cent more than the price quoted for regular length in this catalogue. For fur coats over 56 inches in length, up to and including 60 inches in length, we charge 20 per cent extra. For example, if you wish a fur coat of a number, which in regular sizes costs $15.75, and your breast measure is 48 inches, we would charge you 10 per cent more than catalogue price, which is $1.58 extra, making the coat cost you $17.33. Also note that if you want a fur coat which is an extra size as well as an extra length, you must add the two percentages together, as we charge you the combined extra charges for both size and length. Extra sizes have to be made to special order, which requires two weeks' time.

$9.93 A BETTER BUFFALO FUR CLOTH OVERCOAT THAN EVER BEFORE OFFERED.

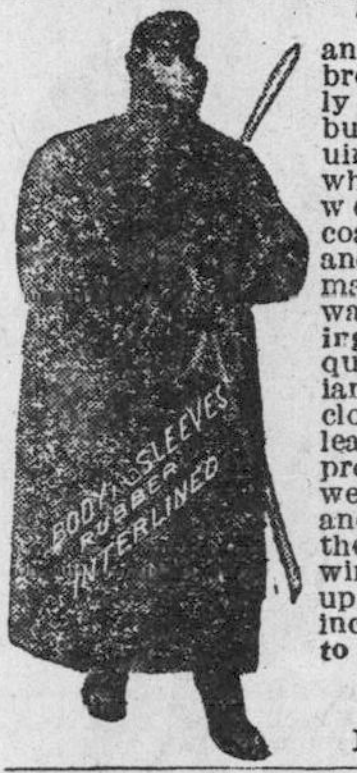

The outside material is an extra heavy rich dark brown buffalo cloth, closely resembling the genuine buffalo fur, and is a genuine stockinette back, which guarantees its wearing quality. The coat is **interlined** in body and sleeves with rubber, making it both wind and waterproof, and the lining next the body is quilted mercerized Italian, and in sleeves, ironcloth. It is made with leather arm shields to protect the lining from wearing at the armholes, and has wristlets inside the cuffs to keep out the wind. Sizes—36 inches up to and including 46 inches breast. **Be sure to give your size.**

No. 41K296
Price........**$9.93**

$14.93 OUR CELEBRATED BROWN CABARETTA FUR OVERCOAT FOR ROUGH WEAR.

Fur—Genuine brown cabaretta, closely resembling the color and fur of the genuine buffalo. A very warm, durable fur. **Trimmings**—Heavy quilted lining throughout body and sleeves. Finished at bottom with a strip of leather, protecting bottom edge from wearing against the shoe, leather arm shields. Coat is double sewed throughout, and fitted in the sleeves with our patent wind excluding wristlets and closes with loops and buttons. Our next coat is a still finer grade. **Sizes**—36 to 46 inches breast, full 52 inches long. **Don't forget sizes.**

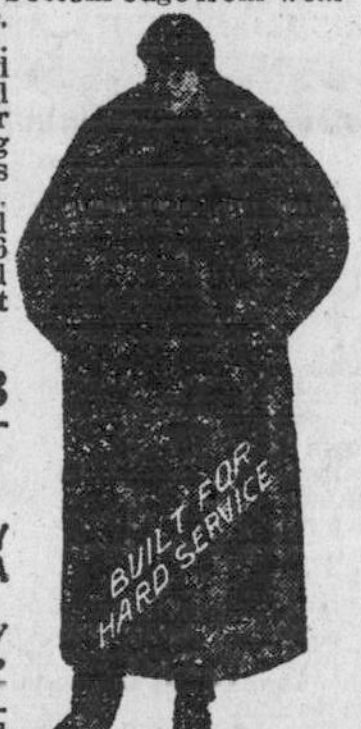

No. 41K297
Price.......**$14.93**

$16.82 EXTRA QUALITY BROWN CABARETTA COAT.

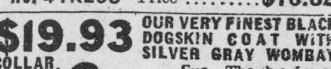

This is our very finest cabaretta coat, much superior to anything of the kind elsewhere. Made and trimmed in exactly the same way as the above coat, only made from the very best selected cabaretta skins. you can't get a better grade of cabaretta skins at any price. **Be sure to state size wanted.**

No. 41K293 Price.........**$16.82**

$19.93 OUR VERY FINEST BLACK DOGSKIN COAT WITH SILVER GRAY WOMBAY COLLAR.

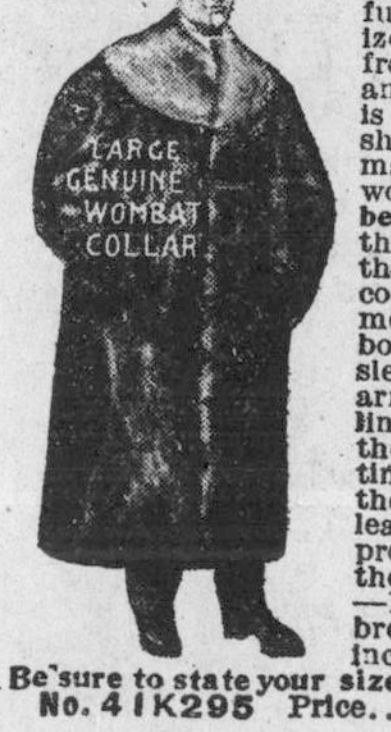

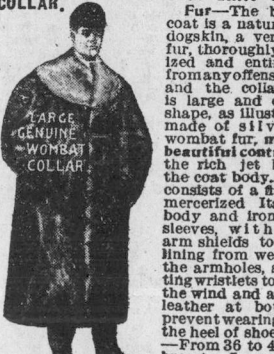

Fur—The body of coat is a natural black dogskin, a very heavy fur, thoroughly deodorized and entirely free from any offensive odor, and the collar, which is large and of shawl shape, as illustrated, is made of silver gray wombat fur, **making a beautiful contrast** with the rich jet black of the coat body. **Lining** consists of a fine grade mercerized Italian in body and ironcloth in sleeves, with leather arm shields to protect lining from wearing at the armholes, snug fitting wristlets to exclude the wind and a strip of leather at bottom to prevent wearing against the heel of shoe. **Sizes**—From 36 to 46 inches breast. Length, 52 inches.

Be sure to state your size.
No. 41K295 Price...........**$19.93**

$16.94 A FINER BLACK CHINA DOGSKIN COAT THAN WE HAVE EVER BEFORE OFFERED.

Fur—Black China dogskins that are perfectly matched, giving the coat the appearance of being made from one hide. Skins all natural color and will wear exceptionally well. **The Make**—Double sewed throughout, quilted lining, leather arm shield, wind excluding wristlets, fitting tight at the wrists. While this is a very fine coat, better than the average dealer handles, if you wish to get our best China dogskin coat, made from the very finest skins obtainable, select the next number below. **Sizes**—36 to 46 inches breast measure. Length, 52 ins. **Don't forget to state your size.**

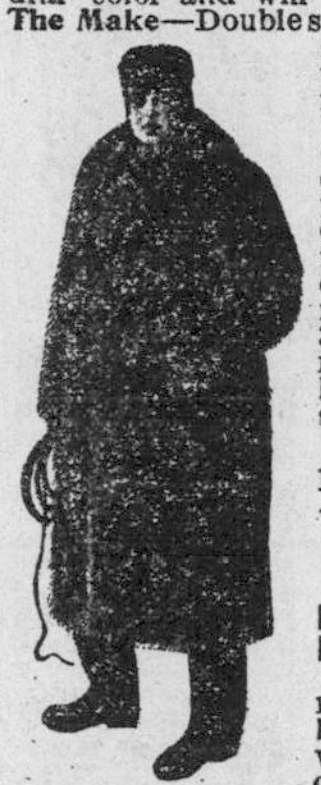

No. 41K299
Price.........**$16.94**

$18.24 BEST QUALITY PLAIN BLACK DOGSKIN COAT.

Fur—The very best and most carefully selected black China dogskins, well worth paying the difference in price for, considering the quality throughout. **The Make**—Exactly the same as the above coat No. 41K299, large and roomy, 52 inches long, made only from extra heavy furred and better skins. **Sizes**—36 to 46 inches chest. **What is your chest measure?**

No. 41K294 Price..........**$18.24**

$14.94 CERTAINLY A WONDERFUL COAT FOR THE MONEY IS THIS GRAY NORWAY DOGSKIN COAT.

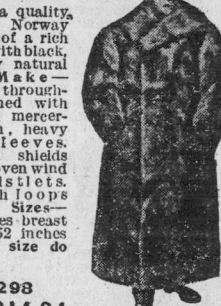

Fur — Extra quality, selected gray Norway wolf dogskin of a rich shade tipped with black, absolutely natural color. **The Make**—Double sewed throughout, body lined with heavy quilted mercerized Italian, heavy ironcloth in sleeves. Leather arm shields and woolen woven wind excluding wristlets. Closes with loops and buttons. **Sizes**—36 to 46 inches breast measure, 52 inches long. **What size do you take?**

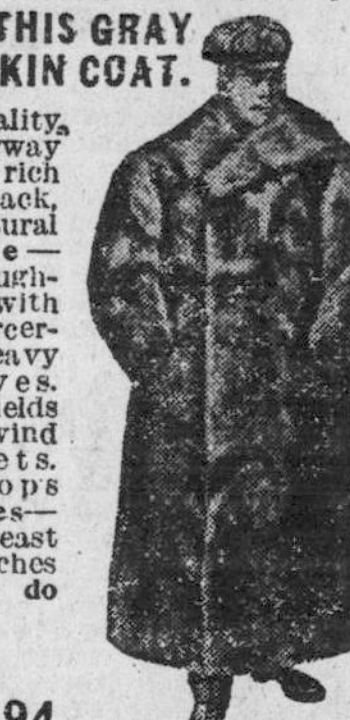

No. 41K298
Price.......**$14.94**

$15.67 THE DEALER PAYS AS MUCH OR MORE FOR A BLACK LAMBSKIN COAT OF THIS QUALITY AS WE ASK FOR IT FROM YOU.

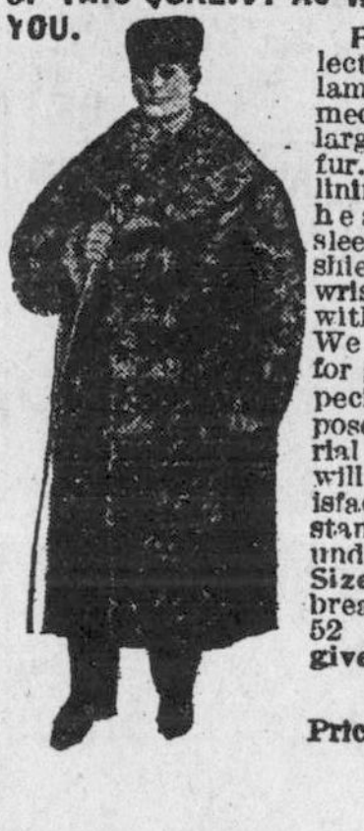

Fur—A carefully selected jet black curly lambskin. A very warm, medium weight fur coat, large shawl collar of same fur. **The Make**—Quilted lining throughout body, heavy ironcloth in sleeves, leather arm shields, wind excluding wristlets, and coat closes with loops and olives. We recommend this coat for general wear and especially for street purposes or driving. Material and workmanship will give you perfect satisfaction, as you understand the coats are made under our own control. **Sizes**—36 to 46 inches breast measure. Length, 52 inches. **Be sure to give your chest measure.**

No. 41K300
Price........**$15.67**

$21.89 BETTER VALUES THAN EVER IN JET BLACK GALLOWAY CALF COATS.

Fur—Jet black galloway calfskins, well selected and matched. A splendid wearing fur, immensely popular with fur coat users, making a comfortable medium weight and warm garment. **The Make**—Cut very full size, double sewed throughout, leather arm shields, woolen woven wind excluding wristlets, heavy quilted Italian lining, large shawl collar and loops and buttons. Bottom of coat faced with leather, protecting it from wear against the shoe. Before buying, look at the next description of a still better coat. **Sizes**—36 to 46 ins. chest. Length, 52 inches. **Remember your size.**

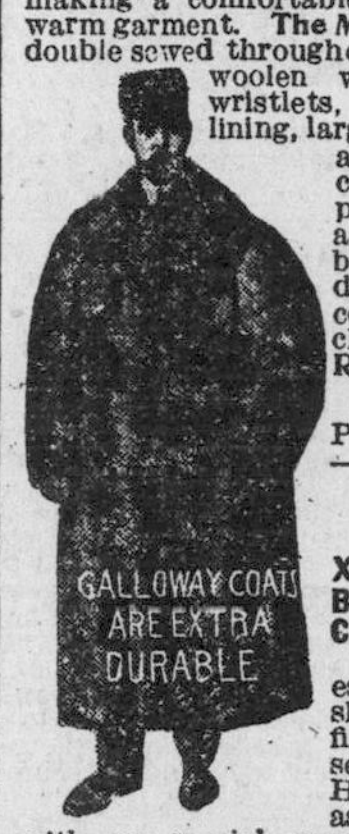

No. 41K304
Price........**$21.89**

$24.35 XXXX QUALITY JET BLACK GALLOWAY CALFSKIN COAT.

Fur—This is the highest priced galloway calfskin coat we sell, the very finest and most carefully selected skins being used. Has a very large, genuine astrakhan collar. Sold with our special guarantee to give absolute satisfaction or money refunded. **The Make**—Otherwise than the better skins and astrakhan collar, it is exactly the same style and make as the above number. **Sizes**—36 to 46 inches chest, cut large and roomy, which avoids the tight feeling across the chest and under arms, which coats of other makes have. Length, 52 ins. **What size coat do you wear?**

No. 41K305 Price.........**$24.35**

$23.11 READ ABOUT OUR JET BLACK CURLY DOGSKIN COAT.

Fur—A jet black domestic skin of extra fine appearance, so fine that unscrupulous manufacturers often sell coats of this class for genuine astrakhan. Skins are carefully matched and thoroughly deodorized by a patent process of our own, guaranteeing it against offensive odor. Fur has a rich, glossy appearance, and at the same time is one of the finest wearing garments in our line. **The Make**—Double sewed throughout, leather arm shields and patent wind excluding wristlets; heavy Italian lining. **Sizes**—36 to 46 inches chest. Length, 52 inches.

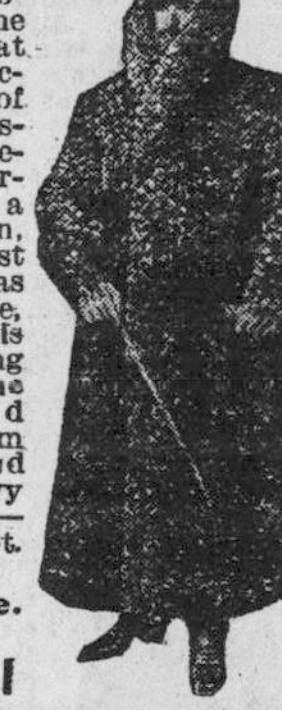

Be sure to state size.
No. 41K306
Price.........**$23.11**

$23.14 THE BEST VALUE JET BLACK SIBERIAN KIP COAT WE EVER QUOTED.

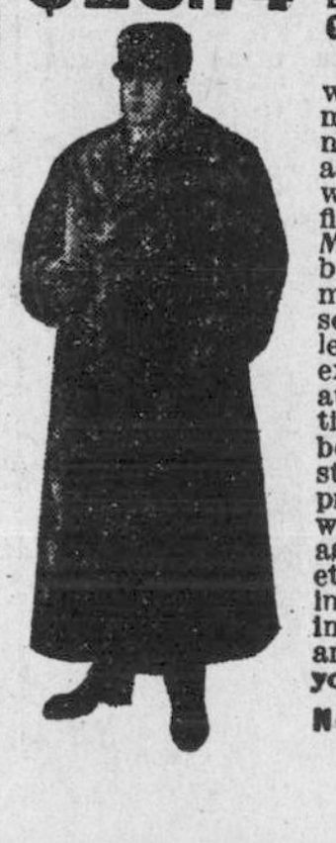

Fur—Siberian kip, which is a hide with a medium length fur and noted for its toughness and wearing qualities, as well as an elegant luster, a fine jet black. **Style and Make**—Lined throughout body with heavy quilted mercerized lining, double sewed all the way through, leather arm shields, wind excluding wristlets, loops and buttons, as illustration shows, and fitted at bottom with our anti-wear strip of leather, which protects the lining from wearing by rubbing against the heel of shoe, etc. **Sizes**—36 to 46 inches breast measure; 52 inches long and cut large and roomy. **Tell us your chest measure.**

No. 41K309
Price.......**$23.14**

$24.96 VERY FINE JET BLACK RUSSIAN CALF COAT.

Fur—A jet black Russian calfskin, with collar and pockets trimmed with southern beaver or what is commonly called nutria, a fine soft fur. **Style and Make**—Lined throughout body with heavy quilted Italian and in sleeves with heavy drill, which has hardly any wear out to it, fitted at cuffs with wind excluding wristers and bottom faced with our anti-wear strip of leather. Coat closes with loops and buttons, as illustrated. A coat that is of great value either for dress or ordinary wear; but if you want a still better coat of this class, our next number below will certainly interest you. **Sizes**—36 to 46 inches breast measure; 52 inches long, cut large and roomy. **Give size.**

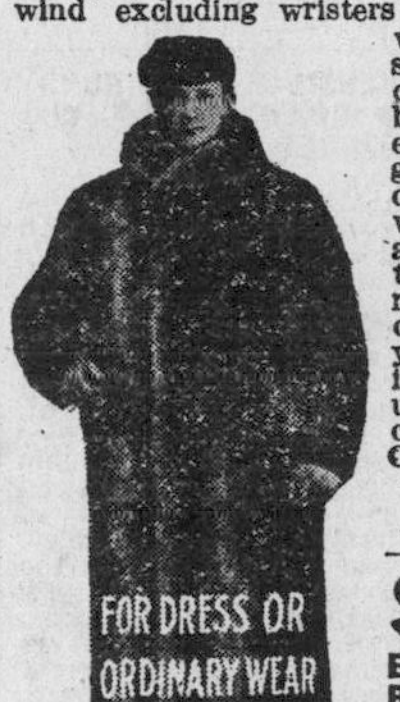

No. 41K310
Price..**$24.96**

$28.29 EXTRA QUALITY JET BLACK RUSSIAN CALF COAT.

Fur — The very finest and most carefully selected jet black Russian calfskins, being the best selected backs from the thousands of Russian calfskins that are bought for our own fur coat factory. Our most careful experts are engaged in the matching of the skins used in this coat, and we are absolutely sure that this is the finest of its kind offered anywhere. We quote an astonishingly low price, considering this extra fine quality. **The Make and Trimmings** are the same as in the above number, the difference being in the special grade of fur. **State size.**

No. 41K311 Price.........**$28.29**

$24.75 OUR POPULAR JET BLACK HAIR SEAL FUR COAT.

Fur—Jet black, glossy hair seal, making a medium weight coat, combining durability and comfort, and the collar, which is a large shawl shape, and the pocket pieces are composed of heavy southern beaver, a rich, soft dark brown fur, harmonizing neatly with the jet black body. **Lined** with an excellent quilted fabric. Closes with worsted ornaments and olives as illustrated, and is fitted at wrist with our wind excluding wristlets and at the bottom with a strip of leather to prevent wearing against the shoe, and with arm shields to prevent wear of the lining at the armholes. We refer you to the next number below for our finest hair seal coat, if you want the best we carry. **Sizes**—From 36 to 46 inches breast. Length, 52 inches. **State your size.**

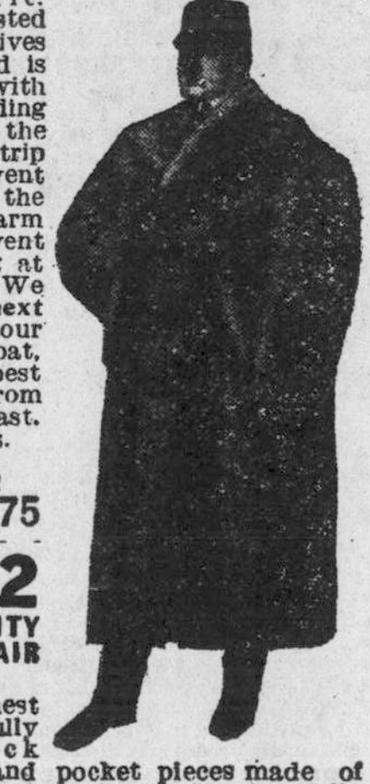

No. 41K312
Price...**$24.75**

$27.42 OUR BEST QUALITY JET BLACK HAIR SEAL COAT.

Fur — The finest and most carefully selected jet black hair seal, collar and pocket pieces made of southern beaver, these furs being specially selected from the best hides of their class. Otherwise the coat is made exactly the same as the above number and as illustrated, the only difference being that you get the pick of the best qualities in the fur in this number. **State size.**

No. 41K317 Price..............**$27.42**

GREAT VALUES IN MEN'S HEAVY LINED WORKING CLOTHING

CONTINUED FROM PRECEDING PAGE.

$2.89 THE TEAMSTER'S FAVORITE WATERPROOF COAT.

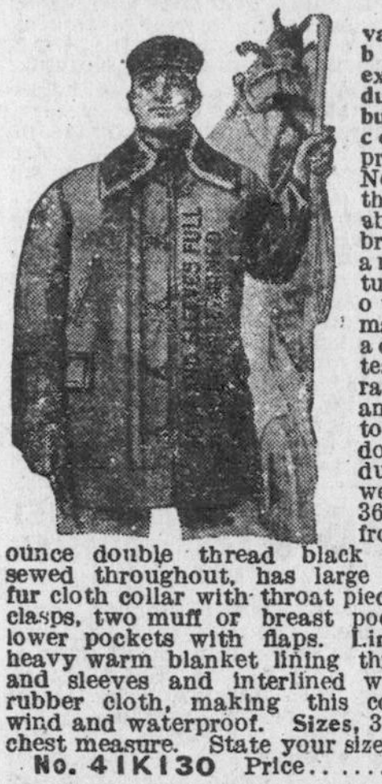

Our great value, full rubber interlined extra length duck coat with buffalo fur cloth collar. This practical coat, No. 41K130, is the most remarkable value ever brought out by any manufacturer. One of our exclusive makes, especially adapted for teamsters, or for railroad men or anybody obliged to be out of doors in his work during severe weather. Made 36 inches long, from full 10-ounce double thread black duck, double sewed throughout, has large 6-inch buffalo fur cloth collar with throat piece, patent auto clasps, two muff or breast pockets and two lower pockets with flaps. Lined with very heavy warm blanket lining throughout body and sleeves and interlined with a genuine rubber cloth, making this coat absolutely wind and waterproof. Sizes, 34 to 46 inches chest measure. State your size.

No. 41K130 Price........ $2.89

$2.88 REVERSIBLE CORDUROY AND GRAY COVERT WATERPROOF COAT.

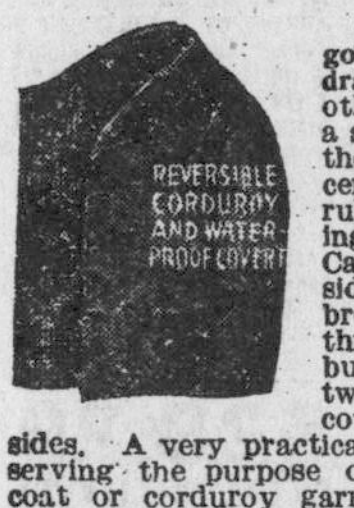

One side is made of a good quality brownish drab color corduroy, the other side of gray covert, a strong wearing fabric, these two fabrics being cemented together by our rubberizing process, making the coat waterproof. Can be worn with either side out. Style, double breasted, double sewed throughout, two rows of buttons and buttonholes, two pockets on both the covert and corduroy sides. A very practical and economical coat, serving the purpose of an ordinary covert coat or corduroy garment, to suit yourself. Sizes, 34 to 46 inches chest. Your size, please?

No. 41K150 Price........... $2.88

$1.25 GRAY PINCHECK WORSTED EFFECT WATERPROOF COAT.

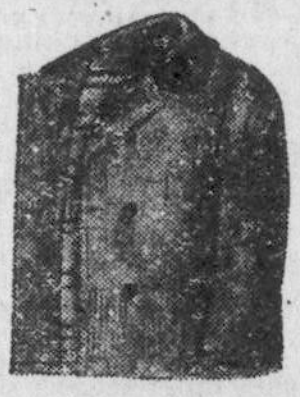

Outside goods is a good quality gray pincheck worsted effect, heavy cottonade, double breasted style, two rows of patent never-come-off buttons and worked buttonholes, two outside pockets with flaps, double stitched throughout, 5-inch corduroy collar. Lined throughout with good blanket lining, which is cemented to the outside material making the coat wind and waterproof. Sizes, 34 to 46 inches breast. What is your size?

No. 41K138 Price $1.25

$2.15 SPECIAL DOUBLE LINED DARK COVERT WATERPROOF COAT.

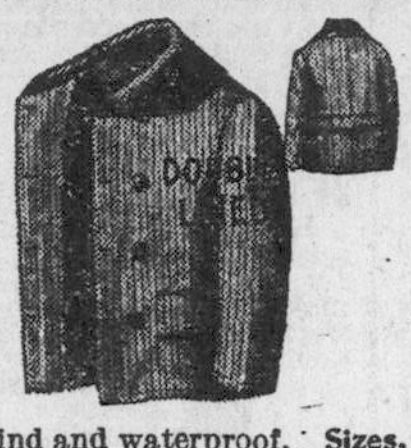

Cloth is a dark gray waterproof covert. Style—Double breasted, all seams double stitched, two rows of patent never-come-off buttons, large rolling corduroy collar, two outside pockets, belt in back. Double lined; one lining is cemented to the outside fabric and the second lining next to body, which is blanketing, is put in in the usual way, which makes the coat both wind and waterproof. Sizes, 34 to 46 inches breast. State your size.

No. 41K148 Price.......... $2.15

$2.29 TEAMSTERS' EXTRA LONG COAT, SHEEPSKIN COLLAR.

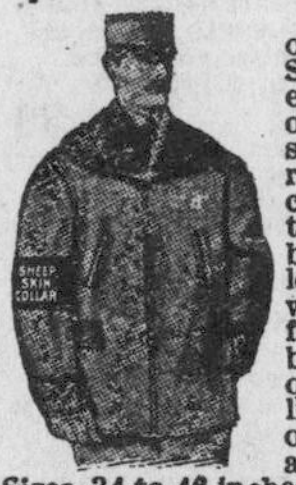

Outside is a cotton worsted of a dark striped pattern. Style—Extra long, 36 inches, especially adapted for teamsters or anyone desiring an extra long sack waterproof coat. Large rolling 6-inch sheepskin shawl collar; cuffs and pocket flaps also trimmed with corduroy; two breast or muff pockets and two lower outside pockets; fastens with Thompson's automatic fasteners. Lined throughout body and sleeves with an extra quality gray striped blanket lining, which is cemented to the outside fabric making the coat absolutely wind and waterproof. Sizes, 34 to 46 inches breast measure. Don't forget to give your breast measure.

No. 41K152 Price.......... $2.29

$1.42 SPECIAL HAIRLINE PATTERN STRIPED WATERPROOF COAT.

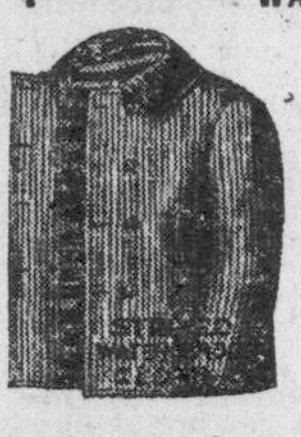

Outside made of black and white striped heavy waterproof cloth, double breasted style, all seams double stitched, two rows of buttons, two outside pockets with flaps, $5\frac{1}{2}$-inch corduroy collar. Lined throughout body with heavy blanket lining, which is cemented to the outside goods by our new rubberizing process, insuring the wearer a warm, comfortable, wind and waterproof coat. Pocket flaps and cuffs faced with good quality black corduroy, as illustrated. A very neat looking, durable coat. Sizes, 34 to 46 inches breast measure. Give your size.

No. 41K140 Price....... $1.42

63c MEN'S DUCK VEST. SURPRISING VALUE.

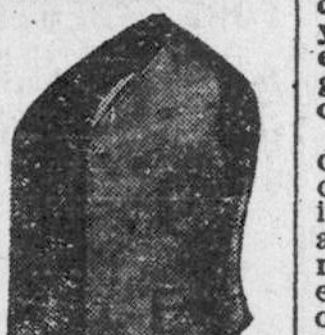

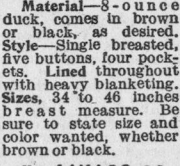

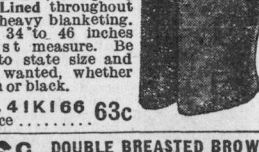

Material—8-ounce duck, comes in brown or black, as desired. Style—Single breasted, five buttons, four pockets. Lined throughout with heavy blanketing. Sizes, 34 to 46 inches breast measure. Be sure to state size and color wanted, whether brown or black.

No. 41K166 Price........ 63c

76c DOUBLE BREASTED BROWN DUCK VEST.

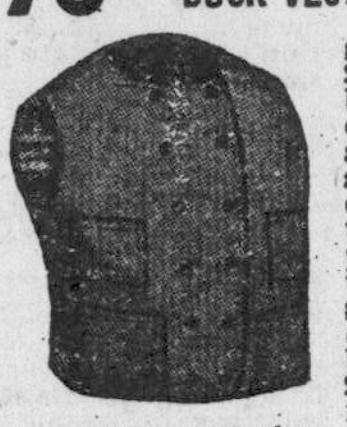

Material—Good grade brown duck. Style—Double breasted, buttons close up to neck, assuring warmth and protection, double sewed throughout, four pockets. Lined throughout with good quality dark colored heavy blanket lining. Sizes, 34 to 46 inches chest measure. State your size.

No. 41K170 Price.......... 76c

$1.69 DARK OXFORD GRAY WATERPROOF COAT, WONDERFULLY POPULAR.

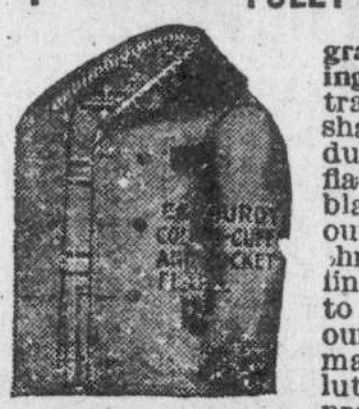

Cloth is a dark oxford gray goods of great wearing quality, style as illustrated, with large rolling shawl collar of black corduroy, cuffs and pocket flaps also trimmed with black corduroy, three outside pockets. Lined throughout with blanket lining which is fastened to the outside fabric by our rubberizing process, making the coat absolutely wind and waterproof. Sizes, 34 to 46 inches chest measure; length, $32\frac{1}{2}$ inches. What is your size?

No. 41K144 Price........ $1.69

$2.79 NEAT, STYLISH, PINCHECK WATERPROOF DRIVING COAT.

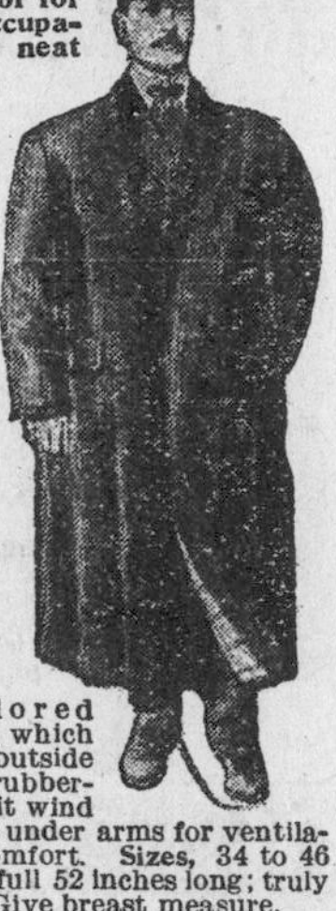

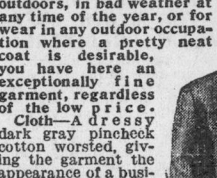

For ordinary dress wear, outdoors, in bad weather at any time of the year, or for wear in any outdoor occupation where a pretty neat coat is desirable, you have here an exceptionally fine garment, regardless of the low price. Cloth—A dressy dark gray pincheck cotton worsted, giving the garment the appearance of a business coat to some extent. Style—Like ordinary long dress overcoat, which it closely resembles, and is excellent for driving purposes; made large and roomy, loose, popular effect, black velvet collar, same as overcoat, two outside pockets with flaps, fly front. Lined throughout body and sleeves with an extra quality medium colored striped blanket lining, which is cemented to the outside fabric by our patent rubberizing process, making it wind and waterproof, eyelets under arms for ventilation, thus insuring comfort. Sizes, 34 to 46 inches breast measure, full 52 inches long; truly a remarkable value. Give breast measure.

No. 41K158 Price.............. $2.79

BOYS' DUCK, CORDUROY, WATERPROOF AND SHEEP LINED COATS.

DO YOU WANT BOYS' PRACTICAL SCHOOL COATS, coats for knocking about, cold weather coats of any kind for boys, little or big? Then look through the specially prepared line on this page of many of our exclusive makes, designed in our own duck and working clothing factory, to meet the requirements of boys for outdoor wear in chilly or cold weather, for school, chores or playing. Please note the ages in which we furnish each coat. VALUES STILL BETTER THAN LAST SEASON.

76c LITTLE BOYS' GRAY WATERPROOF COAT.

Ages 6 to 14 Years.

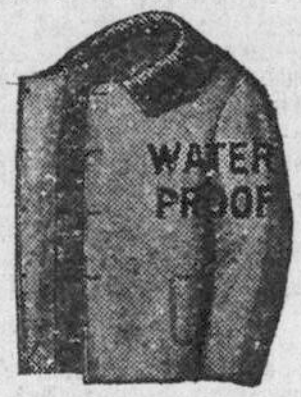

Fabric—Good wearing gray goods, and these coats are waterproofed by the same process as our men's coats. Style—Double breasted, double sewed throughout, two rows of patent never-come-off buttons and worked buttonholes, and two outside pockets with flaps, black corduroy collar. Lined with warm blanketing, which is cemented to the outside fabric by our patent rubberizing process, making it wind and waterproof, makes a serviceable school coat and at this season's price of 78 cents is certainly a big value. Sizes, for boys from 6 to 14 years only. State age.

No. 41K172 Price.............. 76c

86c BOYS' DOUBLE BREASTED GRAY WATERPROOF COAT.

Ages 12 to 18 Years.

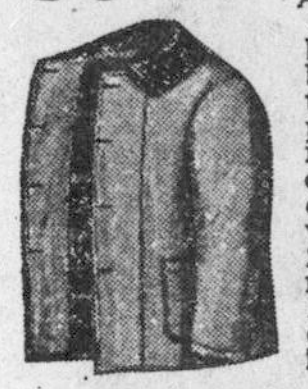

Fabric—Dark gray durable covert. Style—Double breasted, double stitched throughout, two outside pockets with flaps, two rows of patent never-come-off buttons, black corduroy collar. Lined with very warm blanket lining. Sizes, 26 to 34 inches breast measure, or for boys from 12 to 18 years. A great coat for knocking about in. How old is he?

No. 41K176 Price.............. 86c

71c LITTLE BOYS' DUCK REEFER COAT; BLANKET LINED.

Ages 4 to 8 Years.

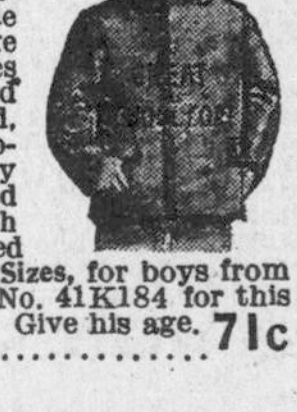

Fabric—7-ounce black duck, wear resisting quality. Style—Double breasted, 5-inch black plush ulster collar, just like regular reefer overcoat. Two outside pockets, two rows of large brass buttons, buttonholes and seams are all stitched with gold colored thread, making an attractive appearance. Lined with heavy blanketing in body and sleeves, pockets lined with flannel. Cannot be equaled for school or rough wear. Sizes, for boys from 4 to 8 years only. See No. 41K184 for this style coat for larger boys. Give his age.

No. 41K180 Price.............. 71c

$1.25 BLANKET LINED CORDUROY COAT.

For Boys from 4 to 8 Years.

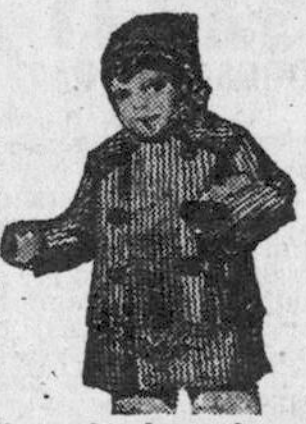

Outside—Made of good quality strong wearing drab colored corduroy. Lined with good grade blanket lining, making a warm garment. Style—Double breasted, two outside set in pockets with flaps, two rows of buttons and loops, large collar to protect ears; coat takes the place of an ordinary reefer, and will stand any amount of hard wear; a neat appearance, too. Great for school purposes or playing. Sizes, for boys from 4 to 8 years old. State age.

No. 41K182 Price.......... $1.25

86c DUCK BLANKET LINED COAT.

For Boys from 10 to 14 Years.

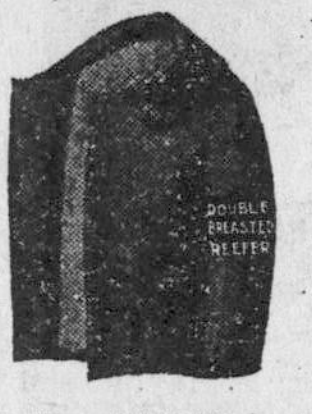

Outside—7-ounce black duck, great for wear. Lined with heavy warm blanketing in body and sleeves. Fine, warm coat that gives any amount of wear. Style—Double breasted, 5-inch black plush ulster collar, two rows of patent never-come-off buttons, in fact, same coat as No. 41K180, only this is made for larger boys. Sizes, for boys from 10 to 14 years only. How old is he?

No. 41K184 Price.......... 86c

93c BOYS' BROWN DUCK BLANKET LINED COAT.

For Boys from 12 to 18 Years.

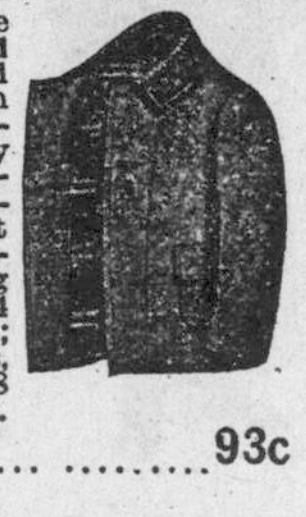

Outside—An 8-ounce brown duck. Lined throughout body and sleeves with heavy warm blanketing. Style—As illustrated, 3-inch corduroy collar, patent never-come-off buttons, worked buttonholes; certainly a great coat for all sorts of outdoor wear and knocking about. Sizes, 28 to 34 inches breast measure; average length, 28 inches, or for boys from 12 to 18 years old. State his age.

No. 41K188 Price.............. 93c

$1.50 BOYS' DOUBLE BREASTED CORDUROY COAT.

For Boys from 10 to 14 Years.

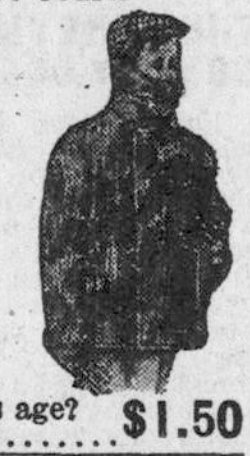

Fabric—Good wearing quality drab colored corduroy. Lined throughout body and sleeves with a good quality heavy blanket lining. Made very strong and guaranteed not to rip. Style—Double breasted, two rows of buttons and worsted loops as illustrated, two outside pockets with flaps, large 5-inch corduroy collar, just the kind of coat for outside work of any kind or school wear. Sizes, for boys from 10 to 14 years old only. What's his age?

No. 41K186 Price.......... $1.50

95c JUVENILE STRIPED WATERPROOF COAT.

For Boys from 6 to 14 Years.

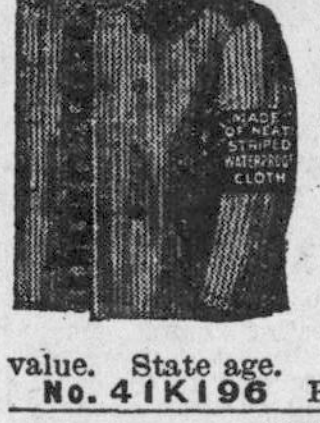

Outside fabric is an extra quality black and white narrow striped waterproof cloth. Lined throughout body and sleeves with a dark red, green and brown domet flannel, which is cemented to the outside fabric by our new rubberizing process, making the coat wind and waterproof. Sizes, for boys from 6 to 14 years old only. You will certainly like this coat. Think of the value. State age.

No. 41K196 Price.............. 95c

$1.20 BOYS' BLACK 9-OUNCE DUCK COAT.

Ages 12 to 18 Years.

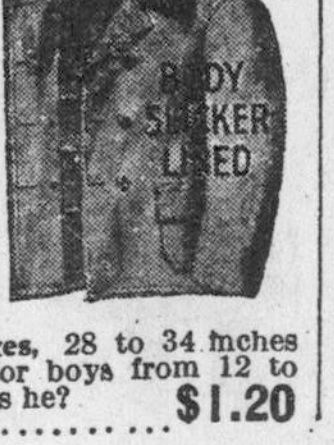

Outside—Good quality black duck, wears like iron. Lined throughout body and sleeves with a heavy, warm blanket lining and interlined with Tower oil slicker cloth, making the coat absolutely wind and waterproof, and very serviceable. Style—Double breasted, double stitched throughout, warranted not to rip; two outside pockets with flaps, never-come-off buttons, $3\frac{1}{2}$-inch corduroy collar. Sizes, 28 to 34 inches breast measure only, or for boys from 12 to 18 years old. How old is he?

No. 41K190 Price.......... $1.20

$1.75 BOYS' DOUBLE BREASTED CORDUROY COAT.

For Boys from 12 to 18 Years.

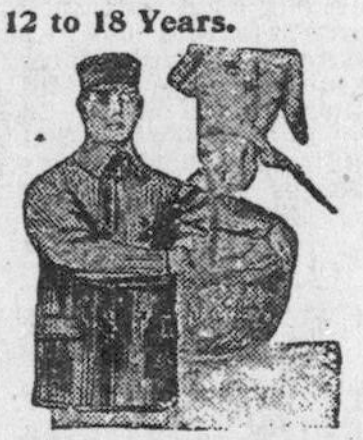

Outside—A good quality of drab corduroy. Lined throughout body and sleeves with a good heavy blanket lining, sleeves faced at bottom with sheepskin wristers. Style—Double breasted, two rows of buttons and worsted loops, two outside pockets, large 5-inch corduroy collar, constructed to stand wear and tear and makes a fine appearance, suitable for working or school purposes. Sizes, for boys from 12 to 18 years, or from 28 to 34 inches chest measure; average length, $27\frac{1}{2}$ inches. State age.

No. 41K192 Price.............. $1.75

$2.46 BOYS' SHEEPSKIN LINED DUCK COAT WITH SHEEPSKIN COLLAR.

For Boys from 12 to 18 Years.

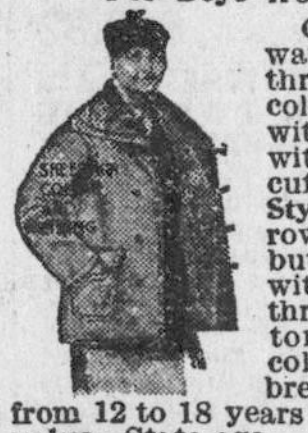

Outside fabric is a heavy waterproof brown duck. Lined throughout with a prime buff colored sheep pelt and sleeves with a heavy husking cloth with sheepskin wristers at cuffs, coat open at bottom. Style—Double breasted, two rows of worsted loops and buttons, two outside pockets with flaps, double sewed throughout. Guaranteed not to rip. Brown sheepskin shawl collar. Sizes, 28 to 34 inches breast measure, or for boys from 12 to 18 years old. Don't overlook this value. State age.

No. 41K200 Price.......... $2.46

$1.92 BOYS' COMBINATION RAINCOAT AND ULSTER BLANKET LINED.

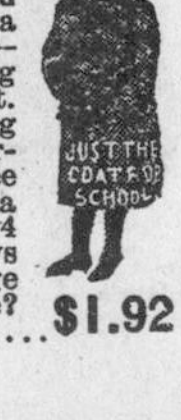

Outside fabric is a neat, dressy, gray pincheck goods. Lined throughout body and sleeves with a fancy striped blanket lining. Style—The prevailing long, loose hanging effect, quite a dressy looking coat. Adapted for school wear, answering all purposes of an ordinary overcoat that would cost you three times our price. Certainly this is a remarkable value. Sizes, 28 to 34 inches breast measure, or for boys from 12 to 18 years old. Average length, 42 inches. How old is he?

No. 41K204 Price.............. $1.92

MEN'S SHEEP LINED DUCK AND CORDUROY WORKING CLOTHING

BETTER QUALITIES AT THE SAME PRICES AS LAST SEASON OR LOWER PRICES ON SAME QUALITIES.

SIZES. Sheep lined clothing comes in sizes from 36 to 46 inches breast measure. We don't furnish from stock any larger sizes than 46 inches chest. Average length, 32 inches. **LARGER SIZES THAN 46 INCHES** will have to be made to order and we charge 50 cents extra per garment for it, which is the exact cost to us, and it will, of course, take extra time to furnish such coats.

MEASUREMENTS. Give your exact breast measure around body at breast, over vest, the same as for an ordinary coat, also give your height and weight. Don't forget to state your sizes.

$4.44 OUR LUMBERMEN'S KING SHEEP LINED DUCK COAT WITH LARGE GENUINE WOMBAT FUR COLLAR.

A BETTER QUALITY THAN WE HAVE EVER BEEN ABLE TO OFFER BEFORE

YOU CAN TAKE THIS COAT HOME AND WEAR IT TEN DAYS, you can show it to your neighbors, give it a good hard test, examine it inside and outside, compare it with anything in this line shown by any other house or any dealer, and if it isn't honestly a wonder to you in value at this price, and if in ten days, as we say, it isn't all we have claimed, return it to us and we will give you back your $4.44 and the transportation charges. That's our offer and we mean it. **THIS COAT IS MADE** of a very heavy 10-ounce waterproof brown duck, in double breasted style, outside pockets with flaps, double sewed throughout and has a large genuine silver gray wombat fur collar, adding to the appearance and value of the garments, lined throughout body with fine grade buff color sheepskin and in sleeves with heavy blue felt, skirt open at bottom and faced with a 2½-inch strip of rubber. Sizes, 36 to 46 inches chest. State size. Average length, 32 inches. **YOUR WORKING CLOTHING** costs you just about half bought at manufacturer's prices from us, coming as it does from our big duck coat factory in the west, where we have every facility for getting the skins and other material and for making these coats, and from the fact that we make them in enormous quantities and always have a heavy stock on hand here. Look through this line. No. 41K423, below, is another astonishing value in a corduroy sheepskin lined coat. Look through our line of mackinaws and overalls. Everything sold on the basis of actual cost and one small profit.

No. 41K421 Price........ $4.44

$2.82 OUR LEADER VALUE SHEEP LINED DUCK COAT—BETTER THAN EVER.

Outside is a heavy waterproof brown duck. Style—Double breasted, double sewed throughout, two rows of patent buttons and loops as illustrated, outside pockets with flaps, corduroy collar. As usual, we lead with a better coat than is sold by other makers. Lined in body with buff sheepskin, fur wristers in cuffs, a better coat than other manufacturers sell at $36.00 per dozen. Sizes, 36 to 46 inches breast. State size.

No. 41K409 Price........ $2.82

$3.33 WONDERFUL VALUE FULL SHEEP LINED DUCK COAT.

Outside is a heavy 9-ounce brown duck. Style — Double breasted, three outside pockets with flaps, double sewed throughout, guaranteed not to rip, patent never-come-off buttons and loops, 5½-inch extra quality corduroy collar. Lined throughout body with extra prime buff sheepskin, sleeves lined with heavy navy blue felt, sheep fleece wristers at cuffs, coat open at bottom of skirt and faced with 2½-inch strip of rubber. Sizes, 36 to 46 inches breast measure; average length, 32 inches. Be sure to state breast measure.

No. 41K411 Price........ $3.33

$5.93 OUR EXTRA QUALITY ROYAL CORDUROY SHEEP PELT LINED COAT WITH WOMBAT FUR COLLAR.

THIS IS OUR VERY BEST SHEEP LINED COAT AND ONE THAT IS WELL KNOWN TO OUR CUSTOMERS.

The outside fabric is an extra quality of strong, durable drab color corduroy, one of the very best wearing grades possible to obtain. The style is double breasted, with three outside pockets with flaps, each pocket leather bound, and has a large rolling collar of genuine wombat fur, giving the coat an excellent appearance as well as making it a decidedly comfortable storm coat. Lined throughout body with best grade of sheep pelt fleece, and in sleeves with a heavy, strong quality, closely woven, warm material. For appearance, comfort and durability and all kinds of heavy wear, we guarantee our Royal Corduroy Coat to give the fullest measure of satisfaction. Sizes, 36 to 46 inches breast measure; average length, 33 inches. State size.

No. 41K424 Price........ $5.93

$3.83 CHALLENGE FULL SHEEP LINED COAT WITH LARGE BROWN SHEEP PELT COLLAR.

Outside is made of full 10-ounce brown duck, double sewed throughout. Style—Double breasted, three outside inserted pockets with flaps, large 6-inch brown sheepskin collar, two rows of patent never-come-off buttons, worsted loops, skirt open at bottom and faced with a 2½-inch strip of rubber. Lined throughout body with first quality buffed sheepskin, sleeves lined with a heavy blue felt. Sizes, 36 to 46 inches breast; average length, 32 inches. Don't forget to give your size.

No. 41K413 Price........ $3.83

$4.95 EXTRA HEAVY WONDERFUL VALUE SHEEP LINED CORDUROY COAT.

Outside fabric is an extra quality of drab color corduroy. Style—Double breasted, with a large sheep pelt collar, three outside pockets with flaps, each pocket leather bound and worsted loops and buttons. Lined throughout the body with sheep pelt of good quality and in sleeves with heavy blue felt, fitted at cuffs with sheep pelt wristers, skirt open at bottom and faced with a 3-inch strip of rubber cloth, which prevents wear. A very warm, guaranteed strong wearing coat. Sizes, 36 to 46 inches breast; average length, 33 inches. See full information about sizes above.

No. 41K423 Price........ $4.95

$1.80 DUCK SHEEP LINED VEST.

Outside is an 8-ounce waterproof brown duck, double stitched throughout; single breasted style, buttons close up to neck; four outside pockets. Lined with buff sheepskin. A very warm garment, and both wind and waterproof; something you ought to have for outdoor work in cold weather. Sizes, 36 to 46 inches breast. Give your size.

No. 41K453 Price........ $1.80

$2.22 SHEEP PELT VEST FOR DOCTORS, LIVERYMEN, CONDUCTORS, MOTORMEN, ETC.

Made of fine sheep pelt with wool or fleecy side to be worn next to body, tanned side exposed; single breasted style; six patent socket fasteners, one upper and two lower pockets; double sewed throughout; very strong and practical for doctors, liverymen, conductors, motormen, etc.; in fact, any man with outdoor work. Our own design, really a wonder in value. Sizes, 36 to 46 inches chest. Give your size.

No. 41K454 Price........ $2.22

THE FINEST LEATHER CLOTHING MADE AND ALL AT FACTORY PRICES

SIZES. Leather goods run in sizes from 36 to 46 inches breast measure for coats and vests. Pants, 30 to 42 inches waist, 30 to 36 inches inside seam. No larger sizes whatever are kept in stock. If you must have a larger size than 46 chest we will only make to order at 75 cents extra per garment and you must allow ten days for making.

WE GUARANTEE all goods to be exactly as represented, and to be the best values you can get or they may be returned to us at our expense and we will refund you your money and transportation charges.

$3.95 OUR LEADER BLACK LEATHER FLANNEL LINED COAT.

Outside is a soft and pliable good quality leather made from genuine Australian skins. Style—As illustrated with corduroy collar, three outside pockets with flaps, patent snap buttons, double stitched throughout. Lined throughout body with all wool flannel and an exceptionally well made coat, nothing to equal it elsewhere at anywhere near the price. Our vest No. 41K472 matches this coat. Sizes, 36 to 46 inches breast measure. Give breast measure.

No. 41K462 Price........ $3.95

$5.80 OUR CELEBRATED FULL SHEEP PELT LINED BLACK LEATHER COAT.

We will send this to you and leave it to your judgment as to whether it is the greatest thing for the money you ever saw, or you can return it to us at our expense, and we will pay you back your $5.80 and whatever it cost for transportation from Chicago.

This coat is made of very fine quality black leather, and is exactly as illustrated, three outside pockets, patent latch fasteners and hooks, large, sheep pelt storm collar. The leather is the best quality of bark tanned Australian skins, guaranteed to keep soft and pliable and stand any amount of wear. Coat is lined throughout body with prime sheep pelt fleece, and in sleeves with woolen goods. We recommend this coat as being especially desirable for motormen, teamsters and similar occupations. Our No. 41K470 is still a better grade, being made of the finest selected hides. If you want the best coat you can get, absolutely the very finest, No. 41K470 is well worth the difference in price, although this coat, No. 41K468, is as good as you will find on the market elsewhere at almost any price. Sizes, 36 to 46 inches breast only. Be sure to give breast measure.

No. 41K468 Price........ $5.80

$4.83 OUR REVERSIBLE CORDUROY AND LEATHER COAT IS A PERFECT MARVEL IN QUALITY AND VALUE.

THIS No. 41K466 AT $4.83 represents our very widely known reversible black leather and corduroy coat, composed on one side of fine grade bark tanned Australian leather and on the other side of fine grade durable drab color corduroy, made exactly as illustrated with two rows of patent snap buttons, three pockets on the leather side and same on the corduroy side and with a reversible corduroy and leather collar. This is a coat that you can wear with either the corduroy or leather side exposed to suit yourself. It is the kind that costs you a great deal more elsewhere and this one is made extra strong and durable. Think of it at $4.83. Sizes, 34 to 46 inches chest. State size.

WE HAVE A VEST TO MATCH THIS, see the bottom of this page, No. 41K474. These two together will make you a fine combination or they can be worn separate just as you choose.

WHETHER YOU WANT A DUCK COAT, a leather coat, a sheepskin lined coat, or overalls or Mackinaw clothing or working garments of any kind, always remember that our whole line is based on just the actual cost of goods and work with but one small profit added. You can't afford to buy such goods anywhere else in the face of such astonishing values as here laid before you, all guaranteed just what we say they are or money refunded.

No. 41K466 Price........ $4.83

PLEASE DON'T FORGET TO STATE YOUR SIZE WHEN YOU SEND AN ORDER FOR ANY KIND OF CLOTHING. GIVE BREAST MEASURE FOR COATS AND VESTS AND WAIST AND INSEAM FOR PANTS. IT IS BEST TO ALSO GIVE HEIGHT AND WEIGHT. WE GUARANTEE TO SEND A GARMENT OF THE RIGHT SIZE FOR YOU.

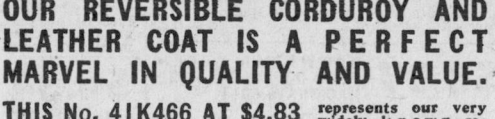

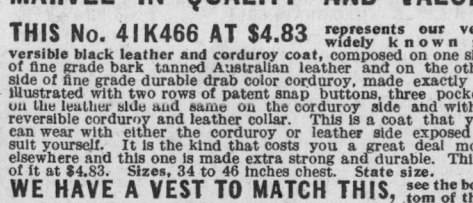

$6.65 EXTRA SPECIAL QUALITY SHEEPSKIN LINED LEATHER COAT WITH SHEEPSKIN COLLAR.

THERE IS ABSOLUTELY NO FINER COAT THAN THIS IN EXISTENCE.

Outside—Very fine black leather; the best bark tanned Australian specially selected skins, guaranteed for wear and to keep soft and pliable. Style—Exactly as illustrated; large brown sheepskin storm collar, three set in heavy drill pockets, patent auto clasp button fasteners; double sewed throughout. Lined throughout body with an extra quality sheep pelt; sleeves lined with heavy blue felt. Our highest grade leather sheepskin lined coat, all material in it being the very finest quality. A better coat than you ordinarily find at any price elsewhere. Just the thing for motormen, teamsters or anybody wanting a very warm coat of the best quality. We guarantee this one to give you the finest service of any coat ever made. Sizes, 36 to 46 inches breast. Give your size.

No. 41K470 Price........ $6.65

$2.35 BLACK AUSTRALIAN LEATHER VEST.

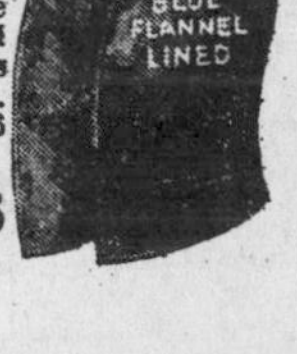

Made from first quality black Australian leather, four outside pockets, patent snap buttons, double stitched throughout. Lined with all wool flannel. This vest matches coat No. 41K462. Sizes, 36 to 46 inches chest. Give size.

No. 41K472 Price $2.35

$2.80 REVERSIBLE CORDUROY AND LEATHER VEST.

One side made of black Australian leather, first quality. Other side is extra quality drab corduroy. Can be worn with either side exposed; three pockets on corduroy side and same on leather side, patent snap fasteners. Sizes, 36 to 46 inches chest. State size. This vest matches coat No. 41K466 shown above.

No. 41K474 Price $2.80

$3.91 EXTRA QUALITY BLACK LEATHER PANTS.

Made of first quality Australian leather, same style as regular pants, patent buttons, two front pockets, pants double stitched throughout but not lined. The best leather pants value ever offered. Sizes, 30 to 42 inches waist and from 30 to 36 inches inside seam, no larger sizes in stock. State sizes. Larger sizes will only be made to order at the extra charge of 75 cents and require ten days to make.

No. 41K770 Price........ $3.91

MEN'S MACKINAW CLOTHING AT FACTORY PRICES

WE GUARANTEE to please you perfectly with any purchase you make from this line, or you may return the goods to us at our expense, and we will refund the price you paid, together with transportation charges. Sizes of Mackinaw clothing run as follows: 34, 36, 38, 40, 42, 44 and 46 inches breast measure. We do not carry any larger sizes than 46 inches breast in our stock. Measure over your vest the same as for an ordinary coat. IF YOU MUST HAVE A LARGER COAT THAN 46 INCHES BREAST we can only make it to order at an extra charge of 50 cents per garment and we require about six days' extra time to make it.

LOOK AT THESE GREAT VALUES IN Mackinaw FROCKS

No. 41K600 Our Leader, 18-ounce Blue Mackinaw Frock, made from 18-ounce blue Mackinaw. Two outside pockets with flaps, large turndown collar faced with Kentucky jeans, throat piece of same material, 2½-inch detachable belt which can be worn back or front or removed entirely from garment. State size wanted.
Price $2.21

No. 41K602 Our 22-ounce Blue Mackinaw Frock, made from 22-ounce all wool Mackinaw. Large turndown collar, two outside pockets, 2½-inch detachable belt; pockets and inside facing of Kentucky jeans; four rows of stitching, reinforced over the shoulders with extra stay. When ordering state size wanted.
Price $2.66

No. 41K604 Our 26-ounce or 2½-point Blue Mackinaw Frock, made from a full 26-ounce or 2½-point all wool Mackinaw flannel. This is a guaranteed all wool Mackinaw, made up with large collar, throat piece of same goods; pockets and flaps as well as inside facings of Kentucky jeans. Cut single breasted style, detachable belt, double sewed throughout; 2-inch Mackinaw strap sewed on shoulder. A thoroughly first class coat. Don't forget to state size.
Price $3.21

No. 41K608 Our Full 30-ounce or 3½-point Blue Mackinaw Frock. This coat is made from full 30-ounce or 3½-point all wool Mackinaw. This frock is made of the very highest grade of all wool Mackinaw flannel and one of our best sellers. This frock is double sewed throughout, large turndown collar, two outside pockets with flaps, all facings of genuine Kentucky jeans, 2½-inch detachable belt, shoulders reinforced with strap of Mackinaw. Always state size wanted.
Price... $3.90

No. 41K610 Our 36-ounce or 4-point Double Breasted Mackinaw Coat, melton lined. This coat is made from a 4-point or 36-ounce all wool blue Mackinaw flannel. Lined throughout body and sleeves with extra quality dark melton, made in double breasted style, double sewed throughout. Has large turndown collar, two outside pockets, 2½-inch detachable belt, all facings of melton, has throat piece of Mackinaw, double row patent buttons and double row of buttonholes. Guaranteed to stand wear. Makes a very warm and sightly Mackinaw coat. When ordering state size wanted.
Price $4.42

No. 41K611 Our Extra Heavy Weight All Wool 40-ounce Blue Mackinaw Frock. This is our highest priced blue Mackinaw frock, made from extra heavy all wool 40-ounce Mackinaw flannel. Better garment than this cannot be obtained, no matter what the cost. Double sewed throughout, large turndown collar, two outside pockets with flaps, all facings of Kentucky jeans. This is guaranteed to be a frock of exceptional value and a frock that will stand hard usage, combining warmth and durability, two very essential points in Mackinaw clothing. State size wanted. Price $4.59

MEN'S BLUE MACKINAW SHIRTS

SIZES, 34 to 46 inches Breast Measure.

No. 41K612 Men's All Wool Blue Mackinaw Flannel Shirts. Made from 16-ounce Mackinaw flannel. Has collar, cuffs and breast pockets. All facings made of Kentucky jeans or melton cloth. State size wanted. Price......... $1.97

No. 41K614 Men's All Wool Blue Mackinaw Flannel Shirts. Made from 22-ounce all wool blue Mackinaw flannel. Double sewed throughout, cut full size, has collar, cuffs and breast pocket. A very good and warm garment. Be sure to give size. Price............ $2.40

No. 41K616 Made from 26-ounce or 2½-point Blue All Wool Mackinaw. This shirt is extra well made, double sewed throughout, has cuffs, collar and breast pockets. All facings of melton and is a splendid garment throughout. In ordering give size wanted. Price........ $2.86

MEN'S BLUE MACKINAW DRAWERS

SIZES, 30 to 42 inches Waist Measure. Regular Lengths to Correspond.

No. 41K634 Blue 18-ounce Mackinaw Drawers. Fly front, patent riveted buttons for suspenders, extra well made, double sewed throughout. State size wanted.
Price, per pair.................. $1.87

No. 41K636 Men's All Wool Blue Mackinaw Drawers. Made from a 22-ounce goods, made same as above, only better material. Be sure to give size wanted.
Price, per pair.......... $2.15

No. 41K638 Men's All Wool Blue Mackinaw Drawers. Made from a 26-ounce or 2½-point all wool blue Mackinaw. These are the best Mackinaw drawers we have quoted. For warmth and durability will recommend this number. All weak points reinforced and double sewed throughout. Be sure to give size wanted.
Price, per pair.................. $2.64

MEN'S MACKINAW PANTS

SIZES, 30 to 42 inches waist measure, 30 to 36 inches inside seam. These are the largest sizes we carry in stock. If a larger size is required we will have to make it to order at an extra charge of 50 cents per garment, and we will require from one week to ten days to make it. Be sure to give your measurements.

No. 41K624 Made from 18-ounce Blue Mackinaw. Made up with patent riveted buttons, extra well made and sewed.
Price of pants, per pair $2.16

No. 41K626 Men's 22-ounce Blue Wool Mackinaw Pants. Have two front pockets, one hip pocket and one watch pocket. Extra well made.
Price of pants, per pair $2.37

No. 41K628 Made from All Wool 26-ounce or 2½-point All Wool Mackinaw. Double sewed throughout, patent riveted buttons, made with continuous fly piece, back seam to be taped and double stitched.
Price of pants, per pair $2.96

No. 41K632 Made from an Extra Quality 30-ounce or 3½-point All Wool Blue Mackinaw. Double sewed throughout, all weak points reinforced; have two outside, one watch and one hip pocket.
Price of pants, per pair $3.40

No. 41K633 Made from our 40-ounce, Extra Heavy Blue Mackinaw. We consider this the best blue Mackinaw that can be bought, no matter what price you may pay. Made the same as all our Mackinaw pants, special attention being paid to reinforcing the weak points. Price of pants, per pair $3.94

GIVE SIZE — MEN'S FANCY HEAVY WEIGHT MACKINAW FROCKS — SIZE, PLEASE?

$2.17 OUR LEADER FANCY MACKINAW FROCK.

No. 41K664 Made of a heavy weight fancy Mackinaw blanket, dark blue check, with smaller checks of white, maroon, drab and medium light blue, making a very pleasing combination of colors. Double stitched throughout, 2½-inch detachable belt, 5-inch turndown collar, two outside pockets with flaps, cut in single breasted style, as illustrated, 2-inch reinforcement over shoulders, pocket facings and collar are faced with genuine Kentucky jeans. Sizes, 34 to 46 inches breast measure. Be sure to state size.
Price $2.17

$2.62 DARK COLOR FANCY MACKINAW FROCK.

No. 41K668 Made of a dark color Mackinaw flannel. The background is a dark green with small broken stripes of brown, red and black, alternated with a very rich shade of oxford gray. We consider this a very neat and desirable pattern and one of the most popular numbers in our line, cut in single breasted style, two outside pockets with flaps, detachable belt which can be worn either back or front or not worn at all, just as desired; 5-inch turndown collar and reinforced over shoulders with 2-inch strips of same material; guaranteed to give excellent service. Sizes, 34 to 46 inches breast measure. Be sure to state your size. Price.......... $2.62

$2.86 FANCY TAN COLOR MACKINAW FROCK.

No. 41K675 A very popular design for a fancy Mackinaw, as it is neither light nor dark but a medium shade; principal color or background is of a very popular shade of tan with marks or stripes of green, red, white and brown. While the illustration is an excellent representation of the pattern, the combination of colors must be seen to be appreciated; cut in single breasted style, double sewed throughout, 5-inch turndown collar and has all the other good features of all our Mackinaws, such as double sewed throughout, reinforced shoulders, facings of Kentucky jeans. Our Mackinaw clothing is sent out with the same guarantee as all our merchandise, to give absolute satisfaction or your money refunded at any time. Sizes, 34 to 46 inches breast measure. What is your breast measure? Price........ $2.86

$3.16 FOR A MACKINAW COAT.

No. 41K676 The pattern consists of a gray and black mottled effect gray background, with a broken black stripe running lengthwise, forming a very pleasing appearance without being too gaudy. Comes in the popular double breasted style, as illustrated, has outside pockets with flaps, large turndown collar, all facings made of extra quality Kentucky jeans, double row of never-come-off buttons and buttonholes, made full and roomy in every respect. A very warm and serviceable coat. Color is also practical; it does not show dirt easily. Sizes, from 34 to 46 inches breast measure. State size. Price.......... $3.16

$3.38 FANCY PLAID DOUBLE BREASTED MACKINAW COAT.

No. 41K678 Made of a very fine quality in a large check of a rich shade of olive brown, the cross check or plaid of a darker brown, smaller checks of green and white, making a combination of colors which are seldom found in Mackinaws. Made in double breasted style as per illustration, two outside pockets with flaps, double row of patent buttons, large turndown collar and a garment that we can recommend in every respect, both for appearance and durability. Made in sizes from 34 to 46 inches breast measure. Be sure to state size.
Price $3.38

$3.97 BROWN AND GREEN PLAID DOUBLE BREASTED MACKINAW COAT.

THE SAME FINE QUALITY AS LAST YEAR AT A STILL LOWER PRICE.

No. 41K680 Made of an extra quality fancy Mackinaw flannel, an extra heavy weight, very warm and durable. Combination of colors being brown, red, yellow and green plaid, 5-inch turndown collar, two outside pockets, cut in double breasted style, all facings are Kentucky jeans, reinforced shoulders, double sewed throughout. Sizes, 34 to 46 inches breast measure. Be sure to state size.
Price $3.97

$4.34 OUR MEN'S BEST FANCY DOUBLE BREASTED MACKINAW COAT.

No. 41K687 Here we offer you absolutely the best heavy weight fancy Mackinaw Coat obtainable. We know that it is of better grade and the workmanship of better quality than has ever been shown by any other manufacturer of Mackinaws. Cut in double breasted style, the background is of a dark sage green and a fancy plaid of tan, red, yellow and green, all facings of a dark gray, all wool dickey kersey cassimere; two lower outside pockets with flaps, all seams are double stitched, reinforced shoulders and large turndown collar with throat piece. Sizes, 34 to 46 inches breast measure. State size. Price.......... $4.34

$4.31 FULL JEAN LINED DOUBLE BREASTED BLIZZARD COAT.

No. 41K690 It will protect the wearer in the most severe weather. Made of a full 36-ounce dark brown or dark olive green Mackinaw flannel, is lined throughout the entire body and sleeves with a very heavy Kentucky jean, which makes it almost impossible for the wind and cold to penetrate. Double breasted style, has two lower and one upper outside pockets and inside breast pocket, double lined throughout, large turndown collar with throat piece, full 33 inches long and made in sizes from 34 to 46 inches breast measure. Do not fail to give color and size desired.
Price $4.31

MEN'S SPECIAL PROCESS ALL WOOL HEAVY KNIT SHIRTS AND COATS

Here we offer an unusually durable and warm line of garments. These shirts and coats are knit throughout on a regular knitting machine, at first being made about double the size of the finished garment and they are then fulled or reduced to the proper size by our patent process. We guarantee these garments against ripping or unraveling. The manner of their construction makes them splendid articles for wear in cold weather, in and around cold buildings and out of doors. Made in sizes from 36 to 46 inches breast. We recommend these garments especially and quote them at prices which represent exceptional values.

$1.82 MEN'S HEAVY KNIT SHIRT.

No. 41K695 This shirt is made from all wool yarn and is knit as above described and then reduced to its present size by a patent process in a fulling machine. It is practically a seamless shirt, there being only one seam over the shoulder and armhole. We guarantee it against ripping or unraveling. Color is a medium light gray and there is one outside pocket, as illustrated. We recommend the shirt for such occupations as lumbermen, teamsters, etc. Tight fitting at wrist. Sizes, from 36 to 46 inches breast. Don't fail to state size wanted.
Price $1.82

$1.97 MEN'S HEAVY KNIT COAT.

No. 41K696 This is made of a heavy all wool yarn, being knit as before described, and fulled or reduced to the correct size, and as the sleeves are tight fitting at the wrist the coat is practically windproof. The color is a dark oxford gray; made in single breasted style with three outside pockets, as illustrated. It is adapted especially for people who are doing work in or around buildings in cold weather, such as storekeepers, lumbermen, etc. It is entirely different from an ordinary knit garment and is guaranteed against unraveling, a coat that we know will give splendid satisfaction. Sizes, from 36 to 46 inches breast measure. Be sure to state size wanted.
Price $1.97

$2.31 MEN'S HEAVY KNIT NORFOLK STYLE COAT.

No. 41K697 Made from all wool yarn, being knit throughout as above described and then fulled to its proper size. Of a medium gray color and cut in Norfolk style, as illustrated, with strap and belt, with patent buckle. The coat is large and roomy, is double sewed throughout and full 31 inches long. It can be worn as an ordinary coat or under an overcoat and is especially adapted for driving. The sleeves fit snug at the wrists and it has two outside pockets. If you want a fine warm coat for outdoor occupations in cold weather, you will do well to order this number. Ours is a lower price and at the same time this is a better coat than you will be able to get elsewhere. Sizes, 36 to 46 inches breast measure. Be sure to state size wanted. Price $2.31

41c AND UP FOR OVERALLS, WORKING PANTS, JUMPERS AND JACKETS OF ALL KINDS

ALL OUR OVERALLS are sewed on lock stitch machines, making it impossible to rip them even with the roughest kind of wear.

BUY YOUR WORKING OVERGARMENTS, OVERALLS, JACKETS, ETC., from us on the basis of factory cost and our one very small margin of profit, and thus put yourself in a better place for values than by ordering anywhere else and take the place of the merchant himself, getting lower prices in many cases than he has to pay another manufacturer for garments that really don't possess all the many good features in our makes.

WE GUARANTEE OUR QUALITIES BETTER AND OUR VALUES GREATER than obtainable from any other source, and if it is not just as we say in your judgment, you are perfectly at liberty to return any garment to us at our expense and we will refund you your money.

THIS IS A BACK VIEW OF THE SUSPENDERS that go with each and all of our Men's Apron Overalls with the exception of Nos. 41K714 and 41K739. It is by far better than you will receive with apron overalls ordinarily sold at retail, because it has a metal crosspiece with 5-inch cord ends, and elastic in back which adjusts itself to the movements of the body just like regular suspenders.

SIZES OF OVERALLS AND JACKETS. Jackets run from 34 to 46 inches chest; overalls from 30 to 44 inches waist and from 30 to 36 inches inseam. No larger sizes are kept in stock. If your chest is larger than 46 inches or waist larger than 44 or your inseam longer than 36 inches, we will only make to measure at an extra charge of 15 cents on all garments under 50 cents in price, and an extra charge of 25 cents on all garments at 50 cents or over. If you want overalls where your waist is larger than 44 and your inseam is longer than 36, then we must charge you just double the above extra charges, that is, we would charge you extra for the larger waist and extra for the inseam.

MEASUREMENTS. Give sizes like this: "Waist 34 and inseam 32." Don't just give the figures, as in some cases we could not tell which was waist and which was inseam. Measure in the same way as you do for a pair of pants. See page 1055.

REDUCED PRICES

ON SAME QUALITIES AND BETTER QUALITIES FOR THE SAME PRICES AS LAST SEASON, BECAUSE OF INCREASING SALES AND OUR ABILITY THEREBY TO REDUCE THE COST OF PRODUCTION.

41c PLAIN OR PANT OVERALLS.

No. 41K698 Made from a 6½-ounce very fine washable blue denim. This overall is especially gotten up for those who desire a light overall and one that has all the good features of a heavier weight overall. Has two front and one hip pocket, all the seams are double stitched, patent never-come-off buttons. Average weight, 21 ounces. State size.
Price, per pair........................41c

48c GRAY STRIPED PANT OVERALLS.

No. 41K702 Made from a gray striped duck of a very neat pattern, and often worn to take the place of a cottonade pant, has every appearance of such. Double sewed throughout, continuous fly piece, reinforced at crotch, patent never-come-off buttons and extra well stayed at all the weak points. Two front, one watch and one hip pocket. This is a very popular number with us and one that we know gives every satisfaction. Average weight, 23 ounces. Give your measurements.
Price, per pair........................48c

50c OUR POPULAR BLUE DENIM PANT OVERALLS.

No. 41K706X Made of extra quality double and twist blue denim, guaranteed absolutely fast color, double lock stitched throughout, inside crotch piece, has continuous fly piece as illustrated, two swinging outside pockets, one watch and one hip pocket, like regular pants; all seams double stitched and felled, thus impossible to rip. Reinforced button pieces which are attached to pocket corners, making pocket stays doubly strong. Average weight, 26 ounces. Jacket No. 41K746 on next page matches this overall. State size.
Price, per pair........................50c

64c OUR HEAVY 9-OUNCE RED BACK DENIM OVERALLS.

No. 41K707 Made of full 9-ounce red back blue denim, and **extra well made.** Has a two-seamed leg, extension fly which will not tear out at the crotch. Two swinging top pockets, one watch, one hip pocket, all stayed with copper rivets at corners, and patent riveted buttons. All seams double stitched. Average weight, 29 ounces. State size.
Price, per pair........................64c

73c DOUBLE FRONT RIVETED OVERALLS.

No. 41K708 Made from a full 9-ounce red back blue denim. The front is doubled from the waistband to below the knee; when the reinforced front is worn out, it can be cut off at stitching at lower end of pocket, as shown in illustration, and the under part is finished so that you will have an ordinary pair of overalls. This is practically two pairs of overalls at the price of one, as the front of the overalls from the pockets to below the knee is always the first part to wear. Continuous fly piece, reinforced crotch stay, two front, one hip, one watch pocket and double sewed throughout. Copper rivets at corner of pockets. See jacket to match this, No. 41K748, on next page. Average weight, 33 ounces. State size. Price, per pair..73c

79c FAMOUS BLACK TEXAS RANGER OVERALLS.

No. 41K710 For those who need an overall of extra heavy material this number is especially recommended; made from an extra quality fast black heavy 10-ounce duck, are made with double front from waistband to below the knee, double seat, continuous fly, extra crotch stay; has two front and two hip pockets with flaps, buttons and buttonholes as per illustration, double stitched and felled seams, are shaped around over hips and waistband the same as an ordinary pair of pants. Average weight, 30 ounces. Give your measurements.
Price, per pair........................79c

95c CAVALRY RIDING PANTS.

No. 41K712 Made of very heavy 10-ounce soft finish mode duck closely resembling government khaki and especially made and reinforced for horseback riding. The entire back half is double, extending between crotch, double stitched throughout, continuous never rip fly, reinforced crotch piece, two back and front pockets, fastened with flaps and buttonholes. Has double seat, and when worn out can be detached from the pants. Average weight, 35 ounces. Be sure to give size when ordering.
Price, per pair........................95c

48c OUR DOUBLE BIB BLUE APRON OVERALLS.

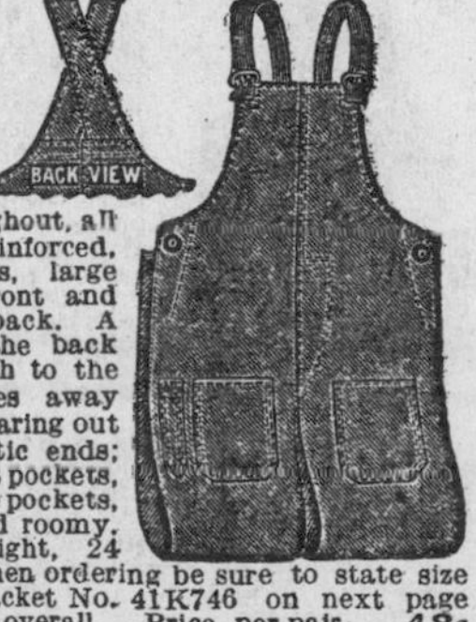

No. 41K714 Made from 7-ounce washable blue denim. Double sewed throughout, all vital parts reinforced, felled seams, large apron in front and wide bib in back. A support for the back adds strength to the overalls, does away with the wearing out of the elastic ends; has two front pockets, back and rule pockets, cut large and roomy. Average weight, 24 ounces. When ordering be sure to state size wanted. Jacket No. 41K746 on next page matches this overall. Price, per pair....48c

50c CARPENTERS' BLACK DUCK OVERALLS.

No. 41K718 Specially adapted for those desiring a working overall heavier than denim. Made from a jet black color 8-ounce black duck, double sewed throughout, all vital parts reinforced, patent buttons, large apron, regular cord and elastic end suspenders, one front, one lower and one back pocket, cut large and roomy and not skimped in size as those offered by other manufacturers. Average weight, 24 ounces. Be sure to give size wanted.
Price, per pair 50c

55c CARPENTERS' SPECIAL BLUE DENIM APRON OVERALLS.

No. 41K719 Good quality 2-40 weight washable blue denim. Large apron front, elastic suspenders in back like illustrated in heading of this page, combination watch and pencil pocket, rule pocket, two front swinging pockets like in pants, one hip pocket. Two buttons at each side, double sewed throughout, an extraordinary value. Matches Jacket No. 41K746 on next page. Average weight, 24 ounces. Sizes, 30 to 44 inches waist. Give size. Price, per pair..........55c

50c GRAY STRIPED DUCK APRON OVERALLS.

No. 41K720 Very neat pattern gray striped duck, has all the appearance of a gray cottonade and material will stand wear; are of the regular carpenter pattern, large apron, one front, one back and one lower pocket, cut full size, all vital points reinforced, patent buttons, all seams are double sewed and felled, impossible to rip; suspenders of same material with 6-inch elastic end, metal cross piece and cord ends. Average weight, 25 ounces. State size when ordering.
Price, per pair........................50c

75c DOUBLE FRONT APRON OVERALLS.

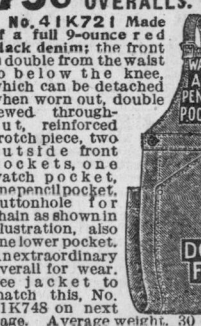

No. 41K721 Made of a full 9-ounce red back denim; the front is double from the waist to below the knee, which can be detached when worn out, double sewed throughout, reinforced crotch piece, two outside front pockets, one watch pocket, one pencil pocket, buttonhole for chain as shown in illustration, also one lower pocket. An extraordinary overall for wear. See jacket to match this, No. 41K748 on next page. Average weight, 30 ounces. Be sure to give size wanted. Price, per pair..75c

79c MEN'S RAILROAD JACKET.

No. 41K734 This coat is especially gotten up for the use of baggagemen, firemen, brakemen or anyone employed in a similar class of work; it is a regular coat jacket made from an extra quality black twilled sateen, buttons close up to the neck as shown in illustration; has combination watch and pencil pockets, watch is inserted in such a way that it cannot fall out in stooping over; has three outside pockets, cuffs button at wrist, buttons are put on with eyelets and can be removed when coat is washed. Sizes, 34 to 46 inches breast measure. Be sure to state size. Average weight, 24 ounces. Price.....79c

85c MECHANICS' AND RAILROAD MEN'S BLUE DENIM APRON OVERALLS.

No. 41K739 Made of extra strong washable 8-ounce blue denim. Double sewed seams throughout, legs with two seams like pants, made full and roomy and thoroughly reinforced at all vital points. Has combination watch and pencil pocket, two front and two hip pockets, front pockets swinging inside same as pants pockets, double brass buckles and double buttons. Suspenders same goods as overalls, back of overalls made same as No. 41K714. Our own design to exactly meet the needs of mechanics and railroad men. Extra heavy and very strongly made. Sizes, 30 to 44 inches waist. Average weight, 26 ounces. Price, per pair, 85c

$1.46 MEN'S STAR PATTERN RAILROAD OVERALL SUIT.

No. 41K737 Made of heavy guaranteed indigo star pattern drill, one of the best fabrics ever made for overall purposes and the color of which we guarantee to be absolutely fast and one we know will not fade. Overalls are made in apron style with extra waistband, swinging top pockets and watch, rule, and hip pockets, suspenders have elastic and cord ends. Are cut large and roomy and button at hips with two detachable gilt buttons. The jacket is made coat shape, has two lower outside pockets, one breast and one combination watch and pencil pocket, extra buttonhole for chain, has five detachable gilt buttons and rings in front of coat, and two detachable buttons on each sleeve. Made in sizes from 34 to 46 inches chest measure for coat, overalls from 30 to 44 inches waist and 30 to 36 inches inseam. Average weight, jacket, 22 ounces, overalls, 22 ounces. Be sure to state size wanted.

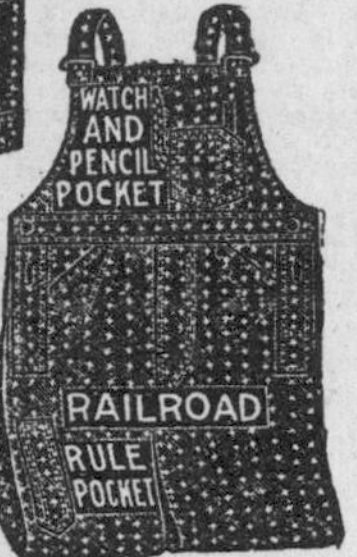

Price for suit........ $1.46
Price for single garment.... .73

50c MEN'S BLUE DENIM JACKETS.

No. 41K746 This jacket is made from full 8-ounce blue denim. Cut full 28 inches long. Buttons close up to collar, patent buttons on sleeves, two lower and one upper outside pocket, shaped shoulders, extra well stayed and sewed. Average weight, 22 ounces. State size wanted. Price........50c

65c No. 41K748 Men's 9-ounce Red Back Blue Denim Jacket. This jacket is made from a full 9-ounce red back blue denim; cut regular coat style with shaped shoulders. Coat is fully 28 inches long, double sewed throughout, has our patent never-come-off buttons, three outside pockets, the top being a combination for watch and lead pencil, as per illustration. This jacket is a match for the Nos. 41K708 and 41K721 overalls. Average weight, 26 ounces. Be sure to state size wanted. Price..........65c

We have made many reductions in prices for this season and in other cases have been able to give better qualities for the same prices.

BLUE AND WHITE CHECK JACKETS.

Sizes from 34 to 46 inches breast measure. For sizes larger than 46 inches we make an extra charge of 15 cents on all jackets that we quote less than 50 cents, and 25 cents for those over 50 cents.

29c No. 41K738 Men's Amoskeag Blue and White Check Jackets. Well made and shaped; two outside pockets. Average weight, 14 ounces. Be sure to state size. Price..........29c

40c No. 41K740 Same color, except made from better material; good, washable blue and white check, well worth the difference in price. A most desirable jacket. Average weight, 16 ounces. State size wanted. Price..........40c

49c No. 41K742 Made from blue and white hairline check denim. A very desirable coat for elevator men, grocers, lumbermen, carpenters, or in fact anybody desiring a jacket of this description; buttons up close to the neck, with neat turndown collar; two lower and one upper outside pocket; cut large and roomy; patent buttons on front of coat and at cuffs. A very desirable coat for indoor or light outside work. Average weight, 17 ounces. Do not fail to state size when ordering. Price..........49c

BE SURE TO STATE SIZE IN ORDERING

WONDERFUL VALUES IN CHILDREN'S BROWNIE OVERALLS.

No Parents Should be Without These Most Durable Overalls.

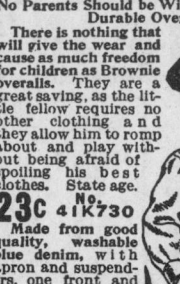

There is nothing that will give the wear and cause as much freedom for children as Brownie overalls. They are a great saving, as the little fellow requires no other clothing and they allow him to romp about and play without being afraid of spoiling his best clothes. State age.

23c No. 41K730 Made from good quality, washable blue denim, with apron and suspenders, one front and one hip pocket; made to fit boys from 3 to 14 years of age. Average weight, 12 ounces. State age of boy. Price, per pair..23c

33c OUR BEST BROWNIE OVERALLS. No. 41K732 Made from fine, smooth finished washable blue denim, double sewed in all vital parts, extra crotch piece, suspenders have elastic ends and made detachable so they can be removed when washing, two front and one hip pocket. This is undoubtedly the best Brownie overall on the market today and we guarantee it to give satisfaction in every respect. Ages, 3 to 14 years. Average weight, 14 ounces. State age. Price, per pair..........33c

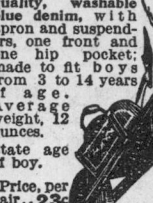

37c OUR NEW "FREE AND EASY" OVERALLS FOR LITTLE GIRLS OR BOYS.

No. 41K733 A fine full, well made washable and comfortable overall for little brother or sister. Great for playing in, and saves their good clothes. Allows them lots of freedom for action. Free and easy in every way. Made of strong blue chambray set off with red or blue trimming, as desired, on front edges of apron, tops of pockets, waist in back, and bottoms of legs. Red or blue supenders. A handsome as well as strong and practical overall. Sizes, for little girls or boys from 1 to 8 years of age. State age of child and color of trimming wanted. Price....37c

MEN'S HEAVY WORKING PANTS.

Our line of working pants are cut large and roomy, and warranted not to rip or break. Sizes in pants run from 30 to 42 inches waist measure, and 30 to 36 inches inseam measure. For extra sizes larger than 42 inches waist measure or longer than 36 inches inseam, there will be an additional charge of 25 cents on all pants up to $1.25 and 50 cents on all pants we quote $1.25 and over.

75c No. 41K750 Men's Gray Jean Cloth Pants, well made, double sewed, printed curtain lining, two front and one back pocket. Average weight, 28 ounces. Be sure to state size wanted. Price, per pair...75c

$1.15 No. 41K760 Extra Fine Quality Heavy Weight Jet Black Jeans. Well made, trimmed and finished, two top, two hip and one watch pocket, double sewed throughout. Average weight, 31 ounces. Be sure to state size wanted. Price, per pair, $1.15

81c VERY NEAT COTTON WORSTED STRIPED PANTS. No. 41K754 Dark colored pattern. Black, white and drab color, white drill curtain lining, swinging pockets, double sewed throughout, taped back seam, patent never-come-off buttons, two front and one hip pocket. Average weight, 31 ounces. Be sure to state size wanted. Price, per pair..........81c

$1.25 No. 41K756 Men's Heavy Gray Cassimere Pants. Made of a very heavy gray striped cassimere, well made, trimmed and finished throughout, double sewed; with two front, two hip and one watch pocket. As they are double sewed throughout, we guarantee them against ripping. Made in sizes from 30 to 42 inches waist measure, and 30 to 36 inches inseam. Average weight, 42 ounces. Be sure to state size wanted. Price, per pair.......... $1.25

$1.25 No. 41K758 Men's Black or Brown Blanket Lined Duck Pants. Made from good quality 8-ounce black or brown duck, double stitched seams throughout, patent never-come-off buttons on waistband and fly, two swinging front and one watch pocket, lined throughout with a good quality heavy blanket lining. Sizes, 32 to 42 inches waist measure, 30 to 36 inches inside seam measure. Average weight, 48 ounces. Be sure to state size and color wanted. Price, per pair.....$1.25

$1.79 No. 41K764 Heavy Weight All Wool Dickey Cassimere Pants. Dark gray stripe pattern; no better or more satisfactory wearing pants can be had at any price; two top, two hip and one watch pocket, good strong lining, double sewed seams, warranted not to rip. Average weight, 38 ounces. Be sure to state size wanted. Price, per pair.......$1.79

$2.49 ICEMEN'S EXTRA HEAVY ALL WOOL PANTS. No. 41K768 Made of an extra heavy all wool dark oxford gray cassimere and guaranteed to weigh full 30 ounces to the yard, are specially adapted for those whose employment compels them to be out in very cold weather; they are double stitched throughout, all seams are double stitched and taped, excellent quality curtain lining, pockets of heavy drill, patent never-come-off buttons, two front swinging, two back and one watch pocket. These are undoubtedly the best pants ever placed on the market, which we absolutely guarantee to be free from any cotton mixtures whatever. Average weight, 44 ounces. Be sure to state size wanted. Price, for these extra quality pants, $2.49

YOUTHS' OVERALLS. MADE EXTRA STRONG TO MEET ALL REQUIREMENTS.

40c BOYS' BLUE APRON OVERALLS. No. 41K727 For boys aged from 12 to 16 years, or 26 to 31 inches waist measure, 26 to 31 inches inseam. Made of 7-ounce blue denim, all seams double sewed, have front and back pockets. In ordering, give measure the same as for men's overalls. Average weight, 17 oz. Price, per pair..40c

50c YOUTHS' RED BACK APRON OVERALLS. No. 41K729 Made of full 9-ounce red back blue denim, double stitched throughout, apron front as per illustration, has two front, one back and one lower pocket. For boys aged from 12 to 16 years, or 26 to 31 inches waist measure, 26 to 31 inches inseam. Average weight, 24 ounces. Give size. Price, per pair..........50c

38c BOYS' BLUE PANT OVERALLS. No. 41K728 Boys' Blue Overalls for boys aged 12 to 17 years, or 26 to 31 inches waist measure, inseam 26 to 31 inches. When ordering give size the same as for men's overalls. Made from 7-ounce blue denim, extra well made, double sewed in all vital parts. The kind that is usually sold for 50 cents. Average weight, 16 ounces. Give size. Price, per pair....38c

50c YOUTHS' RED BACK PANTALOON OVERALLS. No. 41K731 These overalls are made from a 9-ounce red back blue denim, made extra strong, double sewed throughout, patent riveted buttons, has two front swinging and one watch pocket, also hip pocket. As boys usually give overalls hard usage we recommend this number for wear. Sizes same as in above number. Average weight, 22 ounces. Be sure to give size. Price, per pair..........50c

BUTCHERS', BARTENDERS', BARBERS', GROCERS', WAITERS' AND COOKS' JACKETS, APRONS AND COATS

82c WAITERS' HEAVY WHITE DRILL COAT. No. 41K76 Made of a good quality heavy white drill and in double breasted style, has high standing or military collar, three outside pockets, cuffs at sleeves. This coat is not only used by waiters, but is a desirable coat for anybody using a white coat. Average weight, 19 ounces. Sizes, 34 to 44 inches chest. Be sure to state size wanted. Price..........82c

$1.00 HEAVY WHITE DUCK DOUBLE BREASTED COAT. No. 41K78 Coat is cut in double breasted style, the same as an ordinary double breasted coat, three outside pockets, eight detachable buttons, sleeves are fitted at bottom with cuffs. This coat is used exclusively by butchers, bartenders and waiters. Sizes, 34 to 44 inches chest. Average weight, 22 ounces. Be sure to state size wanted. Price.......... $1.00

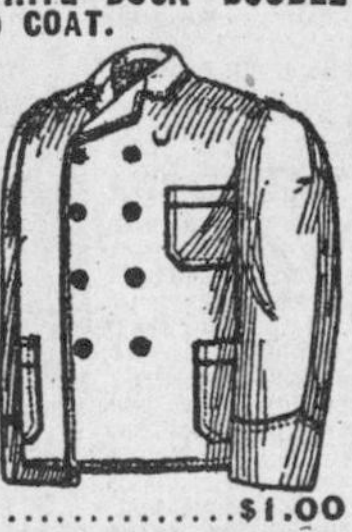

THESE ARE ALL MANUFACTURERS' PRICES. DON'T PAY RETAIL PRICES FOR CLOTHING OF ANY KIND.

73c BARTENDERS' COMBINATION COAT AND VEST. No. 41K83 Made of an extra quality white drill. Made exactly as a vest, with the exception of having sleeves with cuffs. Four outside pockets, six detachable buttons, buckle and strap in back. Sizes, 34 to 44 inches chest. Average weight, 15 ounces. Be sure to state size wanted. Price..........73c

98c No. 41K84 Made exactly as combination vest described above, with the exception of being made of an extra quality heavy white duck. This number in particular we especially recommend, as being laundered frequently, we would suggest that you send for this number in preference to the lighter weight. Made in sizes from 34 to 44 inches breast measure. Average weight, 19 ounces. Be sure to state size wanted. Price..........98c

28c BUTCHERS' BIB APRONS. No. 41K86 Made of heavy white duck to fit over the head. Length, 44, 46, 48 and 50 inches, the measure to be taken from the neck down. Average weight, 14 ounces. Be sure to state length wanted. Price..........28c

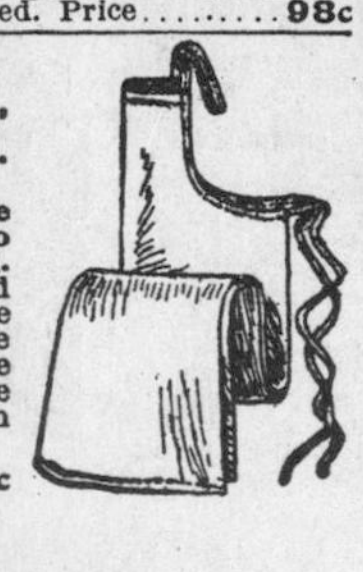

68c BARBERS' HEAVY WHITE DRILL COAT. No. 41K91 Coat is made single breasted style. Three outside pockets; is made of a heavy white drill material and a first class coat for the price, cannot be equaled elsewhere, made exactly as illustrated. Sizes, 34 to 44 inches breast measure only. Average weight, 19 ounces. Be sure to state size wanted. Price..........68c

75c BARBERS' HEAVY WHITE DRILL COAT. WITH BLACK AND WHITE TRIMMING.

No. 41K93 This number is one of our most popular barbers' coats. Made of an excellent quality white drill, cut in single breasted style, two lower and one upper outside pocket; collar, lapel and cuffs are trimmed with black and white striped material, making a coat very pleasing to the eye; has four detachable black buttons. Sizes, 34 to 44 inches, breast measure only. Average weight, 18 ounces. Be sure to state size wanted. Price..........75c

BE SURE YOU DON'T FORGET TO GIVE YOUR SIZE ON YOUR ORDER.

WOMEN'S AND GIRLS' GOWNS AND DRESSES

Our muslin underwear is only made in the most sanitary and labor saving workshops, which are fitted up with the latest appliances known to modern invention, hence WE CAN PRODUCE AN ENORMOUS SUPPLY AT A VERY SMALL COST to manufacture. Every piece is carefully inspected as to workmanship, only the best class being allowed to pass muster. Embroideries, laces and all other trimmings are of the latest importation, of only the newest patterns. Gowns, corset covers and chemises, 32 to 42 inches bust measure. Underskirts, 38 to 42 inches length. Drawers, 23 to 29 inches length. When we quote open and closed styles, always give style desired.

ANOTHER OUTFIT VALUE! SIX PIECES OF MUSLIN UNDERWEAR FOR ONLY $2.98

This outfit is especially designed for those who do not care to buy a more complete one. If your supply of muslin underwear is getting low, here is your golden opportunity to replenish it at a slight cost.

(A) One Muslin Empire Gown made with square neck and lapels which are trimmed with ruffle and insertion of lace, sleeves trimmed with ruffle to match.

(B) One Cambric Gown with square neck; yoke with tucks and, embroidery insertion. Neck and sleeves finished with lawn ruffle.

(C) One Cambric Corset Cover trimmed around neck with ribbon beading and lace; armholes with lace to match; band of embroidery across front, with lace and ribbon insertion.

(E) One Muslin Corset Cover neatly trimmed with two lace insertions, neck with lace and ribbon insertions; neck with lace and ribbon insertion.

(F) One Pair of Drawers made of lawn trimmed with ruffle edged with embroidery.

Sizes, 32 to 42 inches bust measure. Skirt lengths, 38, 40 and 42 inches. Be sure to give bust measure and skirt length when ordering.
No. 38K5556 Price for six-piece outfit.............. **$2.98**
For Matched Trousseau Outfits, see page 1110.

THIS WELL SELECTED OUTFIT OF EIGHT PIECES OF MUSLIN UNDERWEAR, AND THE PRICE IS JUST $3.95

Don't you see what a convenience it is to buy your underwear in outfits and save the time and trouble of selecting each piece separately? You save a great deal on the piece, too, for what we save on the cost of handling these goods we allow you on their price which makes a neat sum on the whole outfit.

(A) One Muslin Gown with square yoke of embroidery insertion and tucks, square neck and sleeves being finished with cambric ruffle.

(B) One Gainsook Gown made with V neck trimmed with hemstitched lawn ruffle; sleeves trimmed to match. Yoke with insertion and cluster of tucks on either side. Plainness in back.

(C) One Corset Cover made of cambric trimmed at neck and armholes with hemstitched lawn, three rows of lace insertion across front.

(D) One Corset Cover made of cambric trimmed around neck and armholes with lace and across front with two rows of insertion and beading with ribbon.

(E) One Underskirt made of muslin with deep lawn ruffle trimmed with wide tucks separated by cluster of pin tucks and finished with hem. Draw string at waist.

(F) One Cambric Underskirt, with lawn ruffle trimmed with cluster of small tucks, row of insertion and lace to match.

(G) One Pair of Muslin Drawers trimmed with lawn ruffle having one cluster of small tucks and hemstitched hem.

(H) One Pair of Drawers made of nice quality muslin trimmed with cluster of tucks and neat ruffle of alternating vertical rows of lace insertion and lawn, edged with lace to match.

Sizes, 32 to 42 inches bust measure. Skirt lengths, 38, 40 and 42 inches. Be sure to give bust measure and skirt length when ordering.
No. 38K5554 Price for outfit of eight pieces........... **$3.95**
WE SHOW A BEAUTIFUL ASSORTMENT OF SEPARATE PIECES ON FOLLOWING PAGES.
See pages 1110 for Matched Trousseau Outfits.

THIS TWELVE-PIECE OUTFIT OF MUSLIN UNDERWEAR AT THE LOW PRICE OF $5.19

Sit right down and figure out the cost of this twelve-piece outfit. What is the result? Could you buy it in separate pieces for $5.19? If we were to sell you these twelve pieces separately we could not do it for this price, but by making up these sets the cost of handling is so much less (one handling for twelve pieces) that we can afford to put a low figure.

(A) Two Gowns made of good quality muslin with yoke of tucks and insertion; neck and sleeves trimmed with lawn ruffle.

(B) One Gown made of cambric with V neck, finished with wide embroidery beading and ribbon; round yoke of tucks and lace insertions finished with herring-bone braid and hemstitched lawn ruffle trimmed with lace to match insertion.

(C) Two Corset Covers trimmed in same manner of muslin with lawn flounce having two rows of torchon lace insertions and lace edge to match.

(D) One Underskirt made of good quality cambric with deep lawn ruffle trimmed with hemstitched tucks and lace.

(E) Two Corset Covers made of cambric and trimmed at neck and armholes with torchon lace.

(F) Two Corset Covers made of cambric trimmed with torchon lace insertion in front and edged with lace to match at neck and armholes.

(G) Two Pairs of Drawers made of cambric with cambric flounce, finished with cluster of tucks and lace.

(H) One Pair of Cambric Drawers trimmed with cluster of tucks and lawn ruffle having one row of insertion and lace edge.

Sizes, 32 to 42 inches bust measure. Skirt lengths, 38, 40 and 42 inches. Be sure to give bust measure and skirt length when ordering.
No. 38K5550 Price for entire set of twelve pieces.......... **$5.19**
FOR SEPARATE PIECES SEE FOLLOWING PAGES.
For Trousseau Outfits with matched trimmings, see page 1110.

MUSLIN, CAMBRIC AND NAINSOOK GOWNS

NOTE THE STYLE AND VARIETY OF THESE GOWNS. WE HAVE AIMED TO COVER THE WHOLE FIELD, FROM THE PLAIN, INEXPENSIVE ONES TO DAINTILY TRIMMED ONES, AND ALL AT VERY LOW PRICES.

MATERIALS AND PRICES TO FIT ALL TASTES AND ALL POCKETBOOKS.

SIZES, 32 TO 42 INCHES BUST MEASURE.

THE WORKMANSHIP AND TRIMMINGS ON THESE GOWNS ARE THE VERY BEST, WITH FULL WIDTHS AND LENGTHS.

ALWAYS GIVE BUST MEASURE WHEN ORDERING.

BE SURE TO GIVE BUST MEASURE.

49c PLAIN MUSLIN GOWN WITH YOKE FORMED BY HEMSTITCHED TUCKS.

The square yoke on this plain Muslin Gown is formed by hemstitched tucks. Neck and sleeves are finished with embroidery. Gown opens at square back, has plain yoke in back. A value at our price. If you want something more fancy see number 38K5574. Sizes, 32 to 42 inches bust measure. Give size.
No. 38K5570 Price.............49c
If by mail, postage extra, 18 cents.

75c DON'T OVERLOOK THIS VALUE. TRIMMED WITH HEMSTITCHED TUCKS AND EMBROIDERY INSERTIONS.

Nice, serviceable gown, made of cambric and neatly trimmed with pointed yoke formed by alternating rows of hemstitched tucks and embroidery insertion. Front trimmed with embroidery beading and ribbon insertion, neck and sleeves trimmed with lawn ruffle. Sizes, 32 to 42 inches bust measure. Size?
No. 38K5574 Price.............75c
If by mail, postage extra, 18 cents.

69c VERY SERVICEABLE MUSLIN GOWN, TRIMMED WITH TUCKS AND EMBROIDERY, AT A VERY LOW PRICE.

This good quality Muslin Gown has yoke of tucks relieved by single row of embroidery insertion, V neck and sleeves finished with ruffle. Opens at center front. For a serviceable gown at a moderate price this has no equal. Sizes, 32 to 42 inches bust measure. Mention size when ordering.
No. 38K5578 Price.............69c
If by mail, postage extra, 18c.

87c VERY DAINTY AND LACY.

If you like a showy lace trimmed Muslin Gown this one will please you. The yoke is trimmed with hemstitched tucks, lace insertion on either side and cambric ruffle edged with lace. Sleeves, neck and front also edged with lace. Well made. Sizes, 32 to 42 inches bust measure. Size, please?
No. 38K5586 Price.............87c
If by mail, postage extra, 17 cents.

98c LACE TRIMMED EMPIRE GOWN.

Collar or rever effect on this Cambric Gown is produced by lace insertion and edge to match. Front trimmed with ruffle. Neck and sleeves finished with ruffle. Full skirt, well finished. Sizes, 32 to 42 inches bust measure. Don't forget measurements.
No. 38K5594 Price.............98c
If by mail, postage extra, 19 cents.

79c LACE AND EMBROIDERY TRIMMED GOWN.

The combination of lace and embroidery on this Cambric Gown is very pretty. Revers and band across front are of embroidery. Lace edged lawn ruffle finishes neck and front, revers and sleeves. Full skirt, well finished. Sizes, 32 to 42 inches bust measure.
No. 38K5598 Price.............79c
If by mail, postage extra, 16 cents.

49c PLAIN MUSLIN GOWN WITH YOKE FORMED A RICH LOOKING GOWN AND AN EXCELLENT VALUE.

There is nothing prettier than an embroidery trimmed Gown, and there is no more popular trimming this season. The square yoke, separated by narrow tucks and is trimmed with ruffle to match. Neck and down front, also sleeves, trimmed with ruffle. Sizes, 32 to 42 inches bust measure. Size?
No. 38K5602 Price.............49c
If by mail, postage extra, 18 cents.

$1.39 VERY DAINTY EMBROIDERY AND LACE TRIMMED SLIP OVER GOWN.

The entire yoke of this pretty slip over Gown is made of double bands of neatly embroidery openwork design with embroidery beading ribbon insertion. Neck is trimmed with lace. The three-quarter length sleeves are trimmed with lace ruffle and edged with lace. Sizes, 32 to 42 inches bust measure. Size, please?
No. 38K5610 Price.............$1.39
If by mail, postage extra, 18 cents.

$1.19 BEST VALUE EVER OFFERED FOR THE PRICE.

For style, comfort and durability there's nothing better than this fine quality Cambric Gown. The yoke is neatly trimmed with clusters of pin tucks, alternating with single wide hemstitched tucks. V neck and sleeves are trimmed with narrow embroidery edge. A neat, serviceable gown. Sizes, 32 to 42 inches bust measure. Always give size.
No. 38K5606 Price.............$1.19
If by mail, postage extra, 22 cents.

$1.48 EMBROIDERY TRIMMED NAINSOOK GOWN.

You can't get a better value for the money anywhere than this dainty Nainsook Gown. The square yoke of embroidery insertion is finished with frill of embroidery to match. Sleeves finished in same manner. A well made gown. It will please you in every detail. Sizes, 32 to 42 inches bust measure. State size.
No. 38K5614 Price.............$1.48
If by mail, postage extra, 18 cents.

75c NAINSOOK GOWN WITH UNUSUALLY PRETTY YOKE.

Two bands of lace insertion separated by ribbon beading set in between clusters of hemstitched tucks form the charming effect of this yoke. V neck and sleeves are finished with lawn ruffle. The material is a good quality. Nicely made. Sizes, 32 to 42 inches bust measure. Your size?
No. 38K5618 Price.............75c
If by mail, postage extra, 18c.

98c CAMBRIC GOWN, EMPIRE STYLE.

The front and revers of this Gown are trimmed with embroidery insertion, while a ruffle to match finishes the neck, revers and sleeves. Gown opens at left of front. You'll like it. Sizes, 32 to 42 inches bust measure. Always give size.
No. 38K5622 Price.............98c
If by mail, postage extra, 18 cents.

83c GOOD VALUE IN A NAINSOOK GOWN.

This pretty gown is made with a fancy yoke of alternating rows of clusters hemstitched tucks and lace insertions. Square neck trimmed with lawn ruffle; sleeves trimmed with ruffle to match; opens at left side to front. Plain yoke in back. Well finished, neat and serviceable. Sizes, 32 to 42 inches bust measure. Always state size wanted.
No. 38K5626 Price.............83c
If by mail, postage extra, 17 cents.

87c AN UNEQUALED VALUE IN A NAINSOOK GOWN.

The unique yoke of lace insertion and hemstitched tucking gives a very charming effect to this good soft finished Nainsook Gown. Neck and sleeve are finished with lawn ruffle; ribbon bow at neck; V cut. This gown is well made and one that, we know will please you. Sizes, 32 to 42 inches bust measure. Give size, please.
No. 38K5582 Price.............87c
If by mail, postage extra, 17 cents.

98c BEAUTIFUL EMBROIDERY TRIMMED EMPIRE GOWN.

Nice Cambric Gown having revers of embroidery, with embroidery ruffle. Front is finished with embroidery beading and ribbon, also embroidery edge. Gown opens at left side of front. Sleeves finished with ruffle. Sizes, 32 to 42 inches bust measure. Please?
No. 38K5590 Price.............98c
If by mail, postage extra, 18c.

EVERY UNDERSKIRT ON THIS PAGE IS A REVELATION IN STYLE, BEAUTY, QUALITY AND PRICE

THEY ARE TRIMMED WITH EMBROIDERY AND COVER A WIDE RANGE OF THE NEWEST AND DAINTIEST IMPORTED PATTERNS AND THERE NEVER WAS A TIME WHEN EMBROIDERY WAS SO POPULAR AS THIS SEASON. LENGTHS, 38, 40 AND 42 INCHES. BE SURE TO STATE LENGTH.

$1.75 **EXTRA VALUE IN AN EMBROIDERY TRIMMED SKIRT.**

The body of this Skirt is of good quality cambric. The lawn flounce is finished with rows of hemstitched tucks and extra deep embroidery flounce in an unusually pretty pattern. Finished at top with adjustable draw string; has dust ruffle. When ordering, give length. Lengths, 38, 40 and 42 inches.
No. 38K5724 Price...$1.75
If by mail, postage extra, 22 cents.

$1.98 **A COMBINATION OF SIMPLICITY AND ELEGANCE.**

This beautiful embroidery trimmed Skirt is sure to please you. It is made of nice quality cambric; the flounce being of wide, heavy embroidery, an exquisite pattern, headed by wide band of embroidery insertion with silk ribbon inserting; has dust ruffle. Lengths, 38, 40 and 42 inches. Give length, please.
No. 38K5728 Price...$1.98
If by mail, postage extra, 20 cents.

$2.19 **ELEGANT EMBROIDERY TRIMMED SKIRT.**

Best quality cambric forms the foundation of this beautiful Skirt. The flounce is a nice quality cambric and is trimmed with three clusters of hemstitched tucks. The wide English embroidery ruffle is an exquisite pattern. We feel sure that you will like it. Lengths, 38, 40 and 42 inches. Don't forget to give length.
No. 38K5732 Price...$2.19
If by mail, postage extra, 21 cents.

$1.98 **CAMBRIC SKIRT WITH DEEP EMBROIDERY TRIMMED FLOUNCE.**

This Skirt is of nice quality cambric. The deep lawn flounce is trimmed with clusters of tucks alternating with rows of embroidery insertions, as shown, and is finished with an excellent embroidery ruffle. This is an unusually durable Skirt. Has dust ruffle. Closes with draw string. Lengths, 38, 40 and 42 inches. Always give length.
No. 38K5736 Price...$1.98
If by mail, postage extra, 21 cents.

$2.48 **THE DAINTIEST OF LINGERIE SKIRTS.**

This exquisite garment is made of good quality cambric with deep flounce of fine quality lawn trimmed with two clusters of pin tucks separated by rows of hemstitching and embroidery insertion, finished at bottom with extra wide ruffle of embroidery in very newest pattern. An unusually attractive skirt. Lengths, 38, 40 and 42 inches. Length, please?
No. 38K5740 Price...$2.48
If by mail, postage extra, 22 cents.

BEAUTIFUL LACE TRIMMED
CORSET COVER
32 TO 42 INCHES BUST MEASURE.

EMBROIDERY TRIMMED SKIRT AND LACE TRIMMED CORSET COVER. EITHER GARMENT AN EXCELLENT VALUE.

No. 38K5972
CORSET COVER
43c

A very pretty Corset Cover, made of soft finished nainsook, trimmed in front with insertions of neat torchon lace, alternating with ribbon inserting. Neck trimmed all around with lace edging to match. Sleeves also trimmed with matched lace edging. Sizes, 32 to 42 inches bust measure. Mention size when ordering.
No. 38K5972 Price..............43c
If by mail, postage extra, 6 cents.

No. 38K5704 SKIRT $1.48

$1.48 **NOTE THE PRICE OF THIS ATTRACTIVE EMBROIDERY SKIRT.**

Here's a Skirt value that should not be permitted to escape you. The body is made of good quality cambric, the flounce is of fine quality lawn trimmed with two clusters of pin tucking, headed by one wide hemstitched tuck and finished with deep embroidery flounce. Draw string at waist, so that skirt can be adjusted to fit. Has dust ruffle. Lengths, 38, 40 and 42 inches. Always order by length.
No. 38K5704 Price..............$1.48
If by mail, postage extra, 21 cents.

89c **YOU COULDN'T BEAT IT AT OUR PRICE.**

The price on this Cambric Skirt is no true index to its value. It is nice and full at bottom, has dust ruffle and deep lawn flounce finished with tucks and ruffle of embroidery. Adjusted at waist by draw string. Lengths, 38, 40 and 42 inches. Always give length.
No. 38K5700 Price...89c
If by mail, postage extra, 19 cents.

$1.19 **AN UNUSUALLY ATTRACTIVE SKIRT.**

Made of good quality cambric. The deep flounce is of good quality lawn, with numerous rows of tucks, and is finished at bottom with wide ruffle of embroidery in attractive design; draw string; has dust ruffle. Lengths, 38, 40 and 42 inches. Give length desired.
No. 38K5708 Price...$1.19
If by mail, postage extra, 21 cents.

$1.69 **A BARGAIN AT OUR PRICE.**

The foundation of this Skirt is made of cambric. The flounce is made of good quality lawn with wide hemstitched tucks and embroidery insertion finished with deep ruffle of neat embroidery. The skirt must be seen to be appreciated. Has dust ruffle. Lengths, 38, 40 and 42 inches. What length, please?
No. 38K5712 Price...$1.69
If by mail, postage extra, 21 cents.

$1.85 **ANOTHER DAINTY EMBROIDERY TRIMMED SKIRT.**

A very pretty effect is produced on this Skirt by the diagonal flounce of alternating clusters of hemstitched tucks and rows of embroidery insertions. Flounce is finished at bottom with ruffle of embroidery in a very dainty pattern. Body is made of cambric, has dust ruffle, is nice and full and finished at waist with draw string. Lengths, 38, 40 and 42 inches. Give length, please.
No. 38K5716 Price...$1.85
If by mail, postage extra, 22 cents.

$1.98 **CAMBRIC SKIRT WITH DOUBLE FLOUNCE.**

A new feature is brought out on this Cambric Skirt by the double flounce which is made of lawn and trimmed with embroidery ruffles and a cluster of tucks. Dust ruffle on body of skirt; draw string at waist. Lengths, 38, 40 and 42 inches. Order by length.
No. 38K5720 Price...$1.98
If by mail, postage extra, 21 cents.

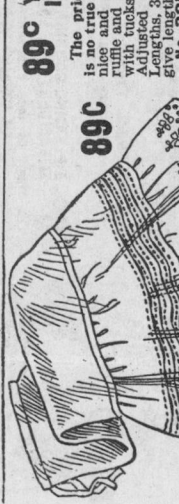

CORSET COVERS

CORSET COVERS

Note the pretty effects in this splendid array of Corset Covers. Laces and embroideries of the very newest patterns. The styles are copies of the very latest French models. Make selections of one or more of these pretty Corset Covers with your supply of Muslin Underwear. You'll like them. Sizes, 32 to 42 inches bust measure.

Isn't this a pretty selection of Corset Covers? We show them to suit all tastes. Order your supply from these beautiful styles, as we know you will surely be pleased. Trimmed Corset Covers will be worn very much this season, as waists of sheer materials and trimmings are very popular and stylish. Sizes, 32 to 42 inches bust measure.

THESE CORSET COVERS REPRESENT THE VERY LATEST STYLES, NEWEST TRIMMINGS, —AT ASTONISHINGLY LOW PRICES.—

48c NEW FLUFFY RUFFLE CORSET COVER.
Made of fine cambric and trimmed with lawn ruffles which are edged with lace to match, with neck and armholes. Beading and ribbon at neck. The ruffles will make perfect shirt waist distender and will give the right contour to the figure. Sizes, 32 to 42 inches bust measure. Always give bust measure.
No. 38K5956 Lace trimmed with three ruffles...48c
Price.
If by mail, postage extra, 5 cents...........26c

95c LACY CORSET COVER WITH FRONT RUFFLE.
Charming effect is produced on this fine nainsook Corset Cover by the combination of valenciennes lace and embroidery insertions together with ribbon beading, lawn ruffle with lace insertion and edged with lace to match. Neck and armholes also finished with lace. Sizes, 32 to 42 inches bust measure. Mention size.
No. 38K5958 Price...........95c
If by mail, postage extra, 5 cents.

18c SERVICEABLE FITTED CORSET COVER AT A REASONABLE PRICE.
Plain fitted Corset Cover. Made of cambric; has V cut neck trimmed with insertions; clusters of hemstitched tucks and lace edge to match. Sizes, 32 to 42 inches bust measure. Give size.
No. 38K5932 Price.............18c
If by mail, postage extra, 4 cents.

21c A BARGAIN AT OUR PRICE.
Made of cambric. Is trimmed across front with three rows of neat torchon lace insertions, trimmed at neck and armholes with hemstitched lawn. Will give you good service. For more elaborately trimmed covers see opposite group. Sizes, 32 to 42 inches bust measure.
No. 38K5936 Price.............21c
If by mail, postage extra, 5 cents.

25c A VERY PRETTY LITTLE CORSET COVER.
Made of cambric, trimmed with two lace insertions, ribbon beading and lace edge to match. Sizes, 32 to 42 inches bust measure. State size.
No. 38K5940 Price............25c
If by mail, postage extra, 5 cents.

23c NEAT CORSET COVER AND A GOOD VALUE.
Cambric Corset Cover, neatly trimmed across front with band of embroidery and around neck with ribbon beading and lace; lace edge in armholes to match. Sizes, 32 to 42 inches bust measure. Don't forget size.
No. 38K5952 Price.............23c
If by mail, postage extra, 5 cents.

27c TRIMMED WITH TORCHON LACE AND INSERTION.
A good quality Cambric Corset Cover trimmed across front with two rows torchon lace insertions, as shown; neck, trimmed with lace to match. A very good value for the price. Sizes, 32 to 42 inches bust measure. State size.
No. 38K5944 Price.............27c
If by mail, postage extra, 5 cents.

39c NEATLY TRIMMED WITH EMBROIDERY AND LACE.
A serviceable Corset Cover made of nainsook, trimmed with set in pieces of embroidery finished with lace insertion to match; neck trimmed with beading and ribbon inserting followed with lace edge. Sizes, 32 to 42 inches bust measure. State bust measure.
No. 38K5954 Price.............39c
If by mail, postage extra, 5 cents.

48c A PLEASING COMBINATION OF EMBROIDERY AND LACE.
The front of this handsome Corset Cover is of wide embroidery while the back is made of fine nainsook and trimmed all around with ribbon inserting, lace. A serviceable corset cover. Shoulder straps of ribbon beading with lace. Sizes, 32 to 42 inches bust measure. State bust measure.
No. 38K5954 Price.............48c
If by mail, postage extra, 5 cents.
ALWAYS GIVE BUST MEASURE WHEN ORDERING.

43c SLIP OVER COR-SET COVER.
If you like a Slip Over Corset Cover we know this will please you. Made of fine nainsook trimmed across front, with embroidered band finished on either side with beading and ribbon with one row extending around neck; armholes edged to match. Sizes, 32 to 42 inches bust measure. Always state size.
No. 38K5960 Price.............43c
If by mail, postage extra, 5c.

48c TRIMMED WITH LACE AND EMBROIDERY.
Band of embroidery between rows of valenciennes lace insertion serves as trimmings on either side of front; trimmed across back with row of lace insertion and around neck with beading and lace edge lace in armholes to match. Sizes, 32 to 42 inches bust measure.
No. 38K5962 Price.............48c
If by mail, postage extra, 5 cents.

$1.19 FLUFFY RUFFLE CORSET COVER, ALL THE RAGE.
Made of fine nainsook; ruffles being of sheer lawn trimmed with tucks, neat valenciennes insertion and edge. Three rows of insertion; upper row extending around back; lower row of lace edge at neck. The full ruffles make a perfect shirt waist distender. Sizes, 32 to 42 inches bust measure. Size?
No. 38K5964 Price..........$1.19
If by mail, postage extra, 5 cents.

98c THE LACIEST OF CORSET COVERS.
This dainty creation is made of sheer lawn alternating with rows of neat valenciennes lace insertions, front and back trimmed alike. Ribbon beading at neck and armholes finished with lace edging. Sizes, 32 to 42 inches bust measure. Size?
No. 38K5966 Price.............98c
If by mail, postage extra, 5 cents.

44c BONED STAY AND CORSET COVER COMBINED.
A Perfect Bust Supporter and Corset Cover, combined. Made of most durable fine batiste lace insertions. Made of good durable lightly boned. It pulls down snugly over the liquid assets to conceal over the straight with boned so one can cheaply straight front, too cheap the bust with no pressure to its proper place. Covers well above the top of corset in back, holding the flesh and shoulder blades in place. Easily laundered. Worn with charming effect under the sheerest lingerie waists. Sizes, 32 to 42 inches bust measure. Never omit bust measure when you order.
No. 38K5968 Price.............44c
If by mail, postage extra, 5 cents.

THESE THREE CORSET COVERS AND SHORT UNDERSKIRTS ARE EXCELLENT VALUES, VERY PRETTILY TRIMMED. SIZES, 32 TO 42 INCHES BUST MEASURE.

34c TRIMMED WITH INSERTION, LACE AND BEADING.
An unusual value in a nainsook Corset Cover. Trimmed as illustrated with insertions of torchon lace. Neck with insertion and edge with beading and ribbon; armholes trimmed with lace to match. Well made. Sizes, 32 to 42 inches bust measure. Give bust measure.
No. 38K5970 Price.............34c
If by mail, postage extra, 5 cents.

43c DAINTILY TRIMMED CORSET COVER.
The Corset Cover shown on figure represents one of our best values. Made of nainsook prettily trimmed with alternating rows of lace insertion and beading, being exactly alike; invisible closing in front. Armholes trimmed with valenciennes lace to match. Sizes, 32 to 42 inches bust measure. Give size.
No. 38K5973 Price.............43c
If by mail, postage extra, 5 cents.

98c HANDSOME EMBROIDERY CORSET COVER.
This Corset Cover is made of beautiful wide pattern of embroidery made on bias, giving V shape neck, front and back being exactly alike; invisible closing in front. Armholes trimmed with valenciennes lace. Sizes, 32 to 42 inches bust measure. Give size.
No. 38K5974 Price.............98c
If by mail, postage extra, 5 cents.

LADIES' SHORT UNDERSKIRTS

Short Underskirts (knee lengths) are very popular. We show in these three styles, the plain, lace and embroidery trimmed. These short skirts can also be worn by girls or misses in the lengths given.

30c IT'S A SMALL PRICE BUT A BIG VALUE.
Serviceable Underskirt made of muslin with cambric flounce ruffle, trimmed with hemstitched tuck and hem. If bought elsewhere it would cost more. Lengths, 26, 28 and 30 inches. Length?
No. 38K5976 Price.............30c
If by mail, postage extra, 10 cents.

69c NICE LACE TRIMMED SKIRT.
Cambric Short Underskirt with French flounce of lawn trimmed with rows of insertions and lace edge. Lengths, 26, 28 and 30 inches. Give length when ordering.
No. 38K5978
Price.............69c
If by mail, postage extra, 12 cents.

75c PRETTY EMBROIDERY TRIMMED SHORT UNDERSKIRT.
Made of good quality cambric with French flounce of lawn, trimmed with cluster of pin tucks and finished with wide ruffle of embroidery. Lengths, 26, 28 and 30 inches. Which length shall we send you?
No. 38K5980 Price.............75c
If by mail, postage extra, 12 cents.

HANDSOME AND SERVICEABLE MUSLIN UNDERWEAR. MUSLIN, NAINSOOK AND CAMBRIC DRAWERS AND COMBINATION GARMENTS.

These Drawers range in quality from those for everyday wear to garments fit for a trousseau. Lengths, 23, 25, 27 and 29 inches. Closed styles furnished only when so stated in description. Don't forget to give length desired.

43c NEATLY TRIMMED CAMBRIC DRAWERS.

These Muslin Drawers are trimmed with cluster of tucks and lawn ruffle, finished with lace edge and insertion. They are excellently made. Open style only. Lengths, 23, 25, 27 and 29 inches. Always order by length.
No. 38K6128 Price....43c
If by mail, postage extra, 9 cents.

75c ELABORATELY TRIMMED WITH LACE INSERTION.

Very pretty Drawers made of fine quality cambric, with deep ruffle of alternating rows of lawn and insertion finished with lace edge to match. The lace in these drawers is a good wearing quality and a dainty pattern. Open style only. Lengths, 23, 25, 27 and 29 inches. Length, please?
No. 38K6136 Price....75c
If by mail, postage extra, 13c.

85c BEAUTIFULLY TRIMMED NAINSOOK DRAWERS.

Just the thing for best or your trousseau are these drawers, made of fine quality nainsook drawers, with lawn ruffle trimmed with tucks, insertion and lace, and headed by insertion to match, under which ribbon is run. Open style only. Lengths, 23, 25, 27 and 29 inches. Don't forget to state length.
No. 38K6140 Price....85c
If by mail, postage extra, 12 cents.

79c DAINTILY TRIMMED WITH EMBROIDERY RUFFLE AND INSERTION.

You could not get a better value than these, fine quality Cambric Drawers, elaborately trimmed with cluster of narrow tucks, embroidery insertion and wide ruffle. Send for them. Open style only. Lengths, 23, 25, 27 and 29 inches. Mention length desired.
No. 38K6144 Price....79c
If by mail, postage extra, 13 cents.

98c A FRENCH STYLE RUFFLE.

If you like dainty underwear these fine Nainsook Drawers with French ruffle will please you. Ruffle is made of sheer lawn trimmed with two rows of hemstitching and wide lace in an exquisite design, and is headed by embroidery beading and ribbon insertion. Open style only. Lengths, 23, 25, 27 and 29 inches. Length, please?
No. 38K6148 Price....98c
If by mail, postage extra, 12 cents.

$1.10 POINT LACE TRIMMED, OPEN OR CLOSED STYLE.

Made of fine soft finish nainsook and trimmed with cluster of tucks, lawn flounce being trimmed with two clusters of neat tucks; trimmed with lace and edge to match, with insertion to match. Lengths, 23, 25, 27 and 29 inches.
No. 38K6152 Open. Price $1.10
No. 38K6153 Closed. Price $1.10
If by mail, postage extra, each, 11c.

98c WILL PLEASE THE MOST FASTIDIOUS.

Soft finished nainsook is used for the body of these Drawers, which are trimmed with cluster of tucks, and extra wide ruffle of beautiful pattern of embroidery. Very handsome and nice enough for the woman of expensive tastes. You'll like them. Open style only. Lengths, 23, 25, 27 and 29 inches. What length, please?
No. 38K6156 Price....98c
If by mail, postage extra, 13 cents.

COMBINATION CORSET COVER AND DRAWERS OR CORSET COVER AND SKIRT

AND THE NEW COMBINATION BRASSIERE.

SIZES: Bust measure, 32 to 42 inches on Combination Garments. Order by bust measure.

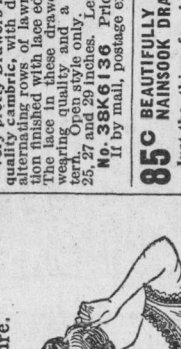

$1.98

98c

98c COMBINATION CORSET COVER AND DRAWERS OR COMBINATION CORSET COVER AND SKIRT.

Combination Garments are more popular than ever and deservedly so, for they simply show you just what the garment really is. They come in fine soft finish nainsook and comes in corset cover and drawers combination like illustration, or in corset cover and skirt (short or knee length) combination, both drawers and skirt being made in the circular French style. Corset cover is trimmed with valenciennes lace insertion, and lace edge to match, also beading and ribbon insertion. Drawers have fine lawn ruffle trimmed with cluster of tucks and edged with lace to match. Skirt is trimmed with lace insertion and edge to match. See number below when ordering. Sizes, 32 to 44 inches bust measure. What size?
No. 38K6160 Corset cover and drawers combination. Price....98c
No. 38K6164 Corset cover and skirt combination. Price....98c
If by mail, postage extra, each, 14c.

$1.98 COMBINATION BRASSIERE AND DRAWERS.

This is truly the garment to accentuate and bring out the graceful lines of the figure. It is made of finest grade cambric; is boned in front to fit snugly and smoothly over the bust, holding it in perfect position without the least discomfort. Eyeletted tab is attached to front at waist line so that it may be hooked down to corset. Surplice effect in back which buttons across shoulders to hold flesh over shoulder blades in perfect style. The drawers are the circular French style with circular ruffle trimmed with lace insertion and edge to match. Brassiere is trimmed at neck and around armholes with beading and lace. Sizes, 32 to 44 inches bust measure. Give size desired.
No. 38K6168 Price....$1.98
If by mail, postage extra, 16 cents.

23c PLAIN DRAWERS, OPEN OR CLOSED STYLE.

These Drawers are made of good muslin, with ruffle trimmed with a cluster of neat tucks and hemstitched hem. They come both open and closed styles. State style preferred. Lengths, 23, 25, 27, and 29 inches. What length please?
No. 38K6100 Open. Price....23c
No. 38K6104 Closed. Price....23c
If by mail, postage extra, each, 7c.

29c OPEN OR CLOSED MUSLIN DRAWERS.

Good quality muslin is used for the body of these Drawers, while the ruffle is of cambric and trimmed with neat hemstitched hem and a row of torchon lace insertion. They come both in open and closed styles. Lengths, 23, 25, 27 and 29 inches. Give length when ordering.
No. 38K6104 Open. Price....29c
No. 38K6108 Closed. Price....29c
If by mail, postage extra, each, 7c.

37c WELL MADE RUFFLE TRIMMED DRAWERS.

These Drawers are made of good quality muslin and trimmed with cambric ruffle which is finished with cluster of tucks and torchon lace. We guarantee these to give best satisfaction. Open style only. Lengths, 23, 25, 27 and 29 inches. Mention length when ordering.
No. 38K6108 Price....37c
If by mail, postage extra, 8 cents.

39c EMBROIDERY TRIMMED RUFFLE DRAWERS.

We recommend these Drawers for their excellent wearing qualities. They are made of good grade muslin with cambric ruffle edged with embroidery. They are well made and are a good value. Open style only. Lengths, 23, 25, 27 and 29 inches. State length, please.
No. 38K6112 Price....39c
If by mail, postage extra, 8 cents.

45c LACE TRIMMED CAMBRIC DRAWERS.

One of our best values is represented in these Cambric Drawers, trimmed with tucks and tucked lawn ruffle edged with wide lace of a good wearing quality. They come in open and closed styles. Lengths, 23, 25, 27 and 29 inches. Give length desired.
No. 38K6116 Open. Price....45c
No. 38K6117 Closed. 45c
If by mail, postage extra, each, 7 cents.

49c NICELY TRIMMED, LOW PRICE.

Fine cambric forms the foundation of these Drawers, which have wide lawn ruffle trimmed with cluster of tucks, two rows of torchon lace insertion and lace edge to match. Open style only. Lengths, 23, 25, 27 and 29 inches. Don't forget to mention length when ordering.
No. 38K6124 Open. Price....49c
No. 38K6125 Closed. 49c
If by mail, postage extra, each, 10c.

47c A REMARKABLE VALUE.

Wide embroidery ruffle and a cluster of tucks are used as a trimming on these Cambric Drawers, which come in either open or closed style. They are well made and will give you the best of service. Lengths, 23, 25, 27 and 29 inches. Mention length desired.
No. 38K6120 Price....47c
If by mail, postage extra, each, 8 cents.

$2.98 VERY NOBBY SICILIAN BATHING SUIT.

The wide sailor collar, four-in-hand tie, belt and facing on bottom of skirt are of white duck, trimmed with braid and rows of soutache braid, the tie being trimmed with embroidered emblem. The bloomers are attached to waist. The Bloomers are attached to waist. This bathing suit will give you the best of satisfaction and could not be bought elsewhere at our price. Sizes, 32 to 42 inches bust measure. Colors, navy blue or black. Be sure to state size and color wanted.

No. 38K6558......$2.98
If by mail, postage extra, 19 cents.

$3.19 NICE MOHAIR BATHING SUIT.

This Bathing Suit is not only a very pretty style, but an excellent bargain. It is made of fine quality mohair and is trimmed around Dutch neck, down opening at left side of front, on short puffed sleeves and skirt with fancy braid. Bloomers are attached to waist. This material sheds water well and does not cling to the figure. Will keep its color. Sizes, 32 to 42 inches bust measure. Colors, black or navy blue. Give color and bust measure when ordering.

No. 38K6562 Price.............$3.19

BATHING OR DUST CAPS.

Bathing or Dust Caps. Has elastic inserting in order to make cap fit perfectly around head. Keeps the hair dry. These caps are also very useful as dust caps when housecleaning, etc.

No. 38K6564 Rubber Bathing Cap, lined with cambric. Colors, black or steel gray. Give color. Price, each...45c
Price, 4 for.................45c

No. 38K6566 Fancy Sateen, lined with rubber. Colors, black or blue polka dots. Give color wanted.
Price, each......................23c
3 for.............................62c

No. 38K6568. This is an excellent Cap, made of oiled silk, making this a strictly waterproof cap, transparent and very light weight. Color is light tan. Price, each......$0.43
3 for by mail, postage extra, each, 4 cents. 1.20

48c BATHING SUIT BAG.

Bathing Suit Bag, made of rubber coated henrietta cloth, with brass ring attachments, and draw string of wide tape. A very handy article to carry the wet bathing suit to and from the bathing beach. Colors, black or royal blue. Give color wanted.

No. 38K6572........$0.48
3 for.......................1.35
Postage extra, each, 3c.

25c DAINTY AFTERNOON OR TEA APRON.

There is nothing nicer than one of these dainty White Lawn Aprons with ruffle trimmed with valenciennes lace and rows of hemstitching. Small pocket trimmed to match. Lawn tie strings. Just the thing to wear when sewing or to protect the dress at any time. White only.

No. 38K6528
Price.............................25c
If by mail, postage extra, 5 cents.

24c WHITE LAWN BIB APRONS.

Bib Apron made of white lawn. Shoulder straps and bib trimmed with neat tucks. Has wide tie strings and deep hem at bottom. Wonderful value.

No. 38K6529
Price, each.............$0.24
Price, 4 for..............1.10
If by mail, postage extra, each, 5 cents.

LADIES' OR MISSES' BATHING SUITS.

These Bathing Suits can also be used as gymnasium suits. We would advise that you purchase your supply of bathing suits, slippers, caps, etc., as early in the season as possible, thus taking advantage of being prepared for the bathing season as soon as it starts. Order by bust measure for ladies' suits, and age for children's suits.

$1.75 A GOOD SUIT FOR A REASONABLE PRICE.

This neat Bathing Suit is made of good quality grade cloth and is trimmed on fancy collar, belt and bottom of skirt with rows of braid and soutache. Bloomers are attached to waist. This is a very popular material for bathing suits and it sheds water nicely and does not cling to the figure. If you want a higher priced one we would refer you to No. 38K6558 or No. 38K6562. Colors, black and navy blue. State size and color wanted.

No. 38K6550
For ladies, size, 32 to 42 inches bust measure.
Price..............................$1.75

No. 38K6552
For girls, aged 8 to 14 years. State age.
Price............................$1.48
If by mail, postage extra, each, 17 cents.

24c BATHING SLIPPERS.

Bathing Slippers, made of heavy quality canvas, bound with tape, fiber lined sole, tape ankle straps. Colors, white or black. Sizes, 3 to 7. Be sure to state size and color wanted.

No. 38K6570.............$0.24
Price, per pair..............24c
6 pairs for.....................1.35
Postage extra, per pair, 4 cents.

43c THE ALLOVER GINGHAM APRON.

This Apron is the ideal dress protector, as it completely coverall, both in back and front. Every woman should wear it for kitchen use and it is especially liked for wear when one is dressed up and wishes to protect the gown while doing some light work. It is 48 inches long. Comes in blue or brown checked gingham. State color preferred when ordering.

No. 38K6508
Price.............................43c
If by mail, postage extra, 8 cents.

20c DESIRABLE BLACK SATEEN APRON.

This nice Work Apron is made of good quality fast black mercerized sateen. It does not require frequent washing, always looks neat. We know that you will like it. It is made with pocket, it is full and long, nicely hemmed. The regular 35-cent apron.

No. 38K6512 Price..20c
If by mail, postage extra, 6 cents.

21c TRIMMED WITH NICE RUFFLE.

Nice Black Mercerized Sateen Apron, made with convenient pocket. Just the thing as a work apron. We guarantee it to give satisfaction and assure you that you could not buy it elsewhere at our price. Length, 25 inches. Color, black only.

No. 38K6516
Price...........................21c
If by mail, postage extra, 5 cents.

12c FOR A WHITE LAWN APRON.

Ladies' Apron, made of good quality white lawn. Nice tie strings. Deep hem at bottom. Length, 32 inches.

No. 38K6518
Price, each..............12c
If by mail, postage extra, each, 5 cents.

39c EMBROIDERY TRIMMED WHITE LAWN APRON.

Very nice White Lawn Apron, made with extra deep hem and finished at top with band of embroidery. Extra long and wide with nice tie strings. Color, white only.

No. 38K6520
Price...........................39c
If by mail, postage extra, 5 cents.

17c NICE SHEER WHITE LAWN APRON.

You can't have too many of these serviceable White Aprons. They are an absolute necessity for wearing in the home, are trimmed at bottom with hem and tucks and deep hem and have extra long and wide tie strings. Length, 29 inches.

No. 38K6524
Price...........................17c
If by mail, postage extra, 5 cents.

69c MADE WITH LACE TRIMMED POINTED FLOUNCE.

A very pretty Tennis Flannel Short Underskirt with wide Van Dyke flounce (pointed) which is edged with ruffle of torchon lace in pretty pattern. These skirts are both serviceable and extremely comfortable. Lengths, 26, 28 and 30 inches. Colors, red, blue or pink stripes. Be sure to state length and color desired when ordering.

No. 38K6464 Price......69c
If by mail, postage extra, 11 cents.

LADIES' GINGHAM, SATEEN AND WHITE LAWN APRONS. KITCHEN APRONS AT NEARLY THE COST OF MATERIAL.

15c SERVICEABLE GINGHAM APRON.

You couldn't buy the material and make this kitchen apron for our price. It is made of good quality checked gingham. It is 34 inches long. Colors, blue or brown checked gingham. State color wanted.

No. 38K6500
Price...........................15c
If by mail, postage extra, 5 cents.

24c BIB APRON MADE OF GOOD GINGHAM.

These Bib Aprons are so convenient for kitchen wear as they give excellent protection to the dress, being made nice and large. They are very neat looking. It really doesn't pay to make them when you can buy them already made as you yourself could do them. Length from waist band, 36 inches. Colors, blue or brown checks. Be sure to give color wanted.

No. 38K6504
Price...........................24c
If by mail, postage extra, 5 cents.

LADIES' FLANNELETTE GOWNS.

We call especial attention to this class of goods. Combined with our low prices you will find in our flannel wear first class workmanship, material and trimming, full length and width, every number is a splendid value. Sizes, 32, 34, 36, 38, 40 and 42 inches bust measure.

75c PRETTY, COMFORTABLE, OUTING FLANNEL GOWN.

It is made in the V neck, as shown, with long sleeves, both neck and sleeves being trimmed with scalloped ruffle headed by fancy braid. Front of yoke is also finished with braid to match. The braid harmonizes in color with the stripe in the goods. Colors, pink, blue or gray. Sizes, 32 to 42 inches bust measure. Don't fail to state size and color wanted.

No. 38K6404
Price...........................75c
If by mail, postage extra, 20c.

OUR 39c AND 48c FLANNEL UNDERSKIRTS.

39c SHORT SKIRT MADE OF OUTING FLANNEL.

These skirts are made of fine quality outing flannel; have wide flounce which is scalloped and stitched with mercerized twist. French waist band with draw strings. First class workmanship. Average lengths, 26, 28, and 30 inches. Fancy blue, gray or pink stripes. Be sure to give length and color.

No. 38K6460 Price..........39c
If by mail, postage extra, 15c.
No. 38K6462 Daisy cloth, solid colors, white, blue or pink. Do not fail to give length and color. Price............48c
If by mail, postage extra, each, 12 cents.

98c FLANNELETTE GOWN.

Ladies' Gown, made of good quality flannelette. Has very neat yoke, trimmed with scalloped ruffle made of daisy cloth and followed with fancy braid. Neck and sleeves trimmed to match. Made extra full. Colors, blue or pink stripes. Don't forget to mention size and color wanted.

No. 38K6408
Price...........................98c
If by mail, postage extra, 19 cents.

$1.10 MADE OF STRIPED TENNIS FLANNEL.

This Tennis Flannel Gown is an excellent value. It is made with plain collar and cuffs to match and is neatly trimmed with rows of fancy braid. Yoke is also finished with braid. Gown is made nice and full with hem at bottom and is good length. We guarantee it to give you excellent service. Sizes, 32 to 42 inches bust measure. Colors, pink or blue stripe. Mention size and color desired when ordering.

No. 38K6412
Price...........................$1.10
Postage extra, 20c.

THE QUEEN OF PETTICOAT FABRICS

Rusleen

NONE GENUINE WITHOUT THIS LABEL.

THESE PETTICOATS ARE JUST AS PRETTY AS THEY LOOK.

TEST THE STATEMENT BY ORDERING ONE OR — MORE OF THEM.

IT IS LIGHT IN WEIGHT, has that silky rustle which marks the wearer as a good dresser, and its wearing qualities are un-equaled.

A dependable cloth especially adapted for petticoats.

LENGTHS, 38, 40 and 42 INCHES.

ADJUSTABLE WAISTS WITH DRAW STRINGS.

DON'T FORGET TO GIVE LENGTH.

$1.19 $1.48 $1.75 $1.98 $1.63 $2.19

No. 38K6600   No. 38K6604   No. 38K6608   No. 38K6612   No. 38K6616   No. 38K6620

$1.19

Rusleen PETTICOAT.

Just think of paying only $1.19 for a Rusleen Petticoat! It is made with a deep flounce in double effect, produced by two puffs headed by two rows of machine cross stitching. The adjustable waist finished with draw strings. We call particular attention to our higher priced Rusleen petticoats, which are the greatest values ever offered. Lengths, 38, 40 and 42 inches. State length when ordering.

No. 38K6600   Color, black.............$1.19
Price.

No. 38K6601   Color, new shade blue.
Price...........................$1.19

No. 38K6602   Color, brown.
Price...........................$1.19

If by mail, postage extra, each, 21 cents.

$1.48

Rusleen LOOKS LIKE TAFFETA.

This Rusleen Petticoat is made with a very pretty flounce trimmed with several rows of narrow straight bands which give the body. The straight rustle of four ruffles set together fullness being graduated to bottom. Dust ruffle. The workmanship on this skirt is perfect and the waist is finished with adjustable draw string. Lengths, 38, 40 and 42 inches. Always give length desired when ordering.

No. 38K6604   Color, black..........$1.48
Price.

No. 38K6605   Color, golden brown.
Price...........................$1.48

No. 38K6606   Color, royal blue.
Price...........................$1.48

If by mail, postage extra, each, 23 cents.

$1.75

Rusleen A VERY NICE PETTICOAT.

There is no nicer material for petticoats than Rusleen cloth, which has the appearance of taffeta and that slight rustle so much liked. It is the best wearing material and will give the wearer real comfort. The deep flounce is trimmed with four tucks, the two lower ones being put on straight and fin-ished with two tucks. Foundation of flounce extends to bottom of lower ruffle. Skirt flares prettily. Is well made and has draw string at waist. Good enough for anyone to wear. It comes in lengths 38, 40 and 42 inches. Don't forget to give length. Price.

No. 38K6608   Color, black....$1.75
Price.

No. 38K6609   Color, new blue.
Price...........................$1.75

No. 38K6610   Color, brown.
Price. (By mail, postage ex., ea., 26c.)$1.75

$1.98

Rusleen WITH PRETTY FLOUNCE.

Pleasing feature of this nice quality Rusleen Petticoat is the deep flounce which is trimmed with three wide shirred ruffles; foundation of flounce extends to bottom of skirt, giving the French flounce is shirred in two clusters, lower part being made of two wavefull feet. The skirt flares at giving good heavy body. The waist is extra well finished and fastens at waist with adjustable draw string. If you want a nice skirt for best at a low price or one that will give you the best of wear for everyday, we strongly advise you to buy this one. Lengths, 38, 40 and 42 inches. What length, please?

No. 38K6612   Color, black..$1.98
No. 38K6613   Color, blue.
Price.

No. 38K6614   Color, popular shade brown. Price..........$1.98
Price.

If by mail, postage extra, each, 24 cents.

$1.63

Rusleen WITH FRENCH FLOUNCE.

This Petticoat is made of good grade Rusleen, that smooth finished, silky looking material which is so much in demand. The upper part of French flounce is shirred in two clusters, lower part being made of two wavefull feet. The skirt flares giving good heavy body. Deep dust ruffle. This is a nice shaped petticoat and gives the skirt that graceful flare so much desired. Waist is finished with adjustable draw string. Lengths, 38, 40 and 42 inches. Give length when ordering.

No. 38K6616   Color, black.
Price...........................$1.63

No. 38K6617   Color, golden brown. Price.............$1.63

No. 38K6618   Color, royal blue.
Price...........................$1.63

If by mail, postage extra, each, 25c.

$2.19

EMBROIDERED TRIMMED Rusleen

Best quality Rusleen is the material used in this pretty petticoat. The upper part of deep French flounce is trimmed with stitched bands, lower tucks and an elaborately embroidered perceeled twist, in pretty design and finished with buttonhole scallops. Nice dust ruffle. An ideal skirt for best. Excellently made and adjustable waist. Is finished with draw string. Lengths, 38, 40 and 42 inches. Always give length when ordering.

No. 38K6620   Color, black.
Price...........................$2.19

No. 38K6621   Color, royal blue.
Price...........................$2.19

No. 38K6622   Color, popular shade brown, red. Price...........$2.19

If by mail, postage extra, each, 25 cents.

HEATHERBLOOM TAFFETA PETTICOATS. A Rustling Fabric with pecially adapted for petticoats. Lengths, 38, 40 and 42 inches, with draw strings adjustable to waist. Always give length desired.

$1.48 PETTICOAT, WITH NEAT TRIMMED FLOUNCE.
The flounce of this Heatherbloom Petticoat is trimmed with four tiny pin tucks separated by fancy machine stitching, finished with ruffle trimmed to match, adjustable draw string at waist. Color, black. Lengths, 38, 40 and 42 inches. Please state length desired.
No. 38K6650   Price.............$1.48
If by mail, postage extra, 23 cents.

HEATHERBLOOM TAFFETA PETTICOATS.

$1.85 MADE OF HEATHER-BLOOM with two clusters of shirring and two pin tucks and ruffle at bottom finished with hemstitching, side plaits give wide, full, graceful rustle. Made and has draw string at waist. Has dust ruffle.
Lengths, 38, 40 and 42 inches. Be sure to give length when ordering.
No. 38K6654   Color, black.   Price.....$1.85
No. 38K6655   Color, royal blue.   Price.....$1.85
Price...(Postage extra, each, 24c) $1.85

MEDIUM WEIGHT SILK PETTICOAT.
This Petticoat is made of medium weight silk, being especially adapted for splendid wearing qualities. Has a wide flounce of spun glass material, with three silk ruffles, each with two rows of cording. Splendid value. Lengths, 38, 40 and 42 inches, each with draw string. Give length desired.
No. 38K6680   Color, black.   Price.....$3.69
No. 38K6681   Color, blue.   Price.....$3.69
No. 38K6682   Color, red.   Price.....$3.69
No. 38K6683   Color, green.   Price.....$3.69
Price...(Postage extra, each, 25c) $3.69

HIP FORM PETTICOATS

That day is past when the slender woman, because of her slenderness must limit her choice to certain styles of outer garments, but with the Hip Form Petticoat her range for choice is boundless. The graceful, perfect figure it gives, permits her to wear almost any gown in vogue.

HIP FORM PETTICOAT. KNEE LENGTH.
This Petticoat, made in the most sensible form to come to the aid of the slender woman in the shape of this ideal Hip Form Skirt. There is no more excuse for an angular, ungraceful form, when by the purchase of this soft finished Lucinta cloth skirt, at our low price, you can secure the graceful contour of a perfect figure. Look at the illustration, see how perfect fitting it is, and how smooth about the hips. The pad is stitched securely so that it cannot slip or lose its place. Opens at left of front. Made of black Lucinta cloth, smooth and close fitting around the hips, and hooks at the side of front. It should be worn not only by slender women, but by all women whose flesh is not properly distributed, and who require a slight pad in back to make a dress skirt hang properly. It is smooth finished black Lucinta cloth which is good wearing and has a slight rustle, with a deep flounce trimmed with tucks. Sizes, 21 to 26 inches waist measure. Give length and waist measure desired.
No. 38K6670   Price............$1.98
If by mail, postage extra, 29 cents.

THE PERFECT FITTING FORM GIVING HIP FORM HEALTH PETTICOAT.
The Ideal Skirt for slender women. It does away with the use of unsanitary easily detected hip pads and produces a well rounded, graceful figure, such as nature herself intended. The padding is in the skirt and is so distributed as to be absolutely impossible of detection and stitched down in such a manner that it cannot get out of place. Skirt is smooth and close fitting around the hips, and hooks at the side of front. It not only be worn by slender women whose flesh is tributed, not properly...

HEATHERBLOOM TAFFETA PETTICOATS, specially adapted for petticoats. Lengths, 38, 40 and 42 inches. Always give length desired.

$2.89 PETTICOAT WITH FANCY TRIMMED FLOUNCE.
Made of Heatherbloom cloth, with deep French flounce; upper part trimmed with ruching as illustrated; lower part being a triple ruffle effect. It is well made and has draw string at waist. Has dust ruffle. Lengths, 38, 40 and 42 inches. Don't forget to give length when ordering.
No. 38K6658   Color, black.
Price..........................$2.48
No. 38K6659   Color, brown. (Postage extra, each, 26c) 2.48
Price. (Postage extra, each, 26c)..2.48

$2.89 PETTICOAT MADE OF HEATHERBLOOM CLOTH
Made with an extra deep flounce; top part having two clusters of shirring, and bottom part with three wide ruffles finished with hemstitching. Always give waist measure. Has dust ruffle. Lengths, 38, 40 and 42 inches. Color, black. Draw string at...
What length, please?
No. 38K6662   Color, black.   Price.....$2.89
No. 38K6663   Color, royal blue.   Price.....2.89

$1.48 HIP FORM PETTICOAT.

EXCELLENT VALUES IN THESE UP TO DATE PETTICOATS.
Made with an extra deep ruffle effect, comes in knee length, an average length of 29 inches. 21 to 26 inches waist measure.
No. 38K6674.
Price............$1.48
If by mail, postage extra, 18 cents.

HEATHERBLOOM TAFFETA PETTICOATS.

$5.98 ONLY THE BEST WEARING GRADES OF RUSTLING TAFFETA SILK IN THESE PETTICOATS.

$5.19 BEAUTIFUL EMBROIDERED FLOUNCE.
Very Pretty Petticoat made of fine rustling taffeta silk, with deep French flounce. Beautifully embroidered in a very neat design. Under flounce and dust ruffle of fine cambric. Exceptionally pretty Petticoat. Lengths, 38, 40 and 42 inches. Always give length desired.
No. 38K6692   Color, black.
Price............................$5.19
No. 38K6693   Color, royal blue.
Price............................5.19
Postage extra, each, 27 cents.

$5.98 EXCELLENT QUALITY OF TAFFETA SILK.
Here is a good quality, rustling Taffeta Silk Petticoat, made with a deep flaring flounce with heading and shirring, trimmed with tucks and double ruffle. We have them in solid, or changeable colors. Lengths, 38, 40 and 42 inches. Be sure to give length, and when ordering.
No. 38K6696   Color, black.   Price.....$5.98
No. 38K6697   Color, blue, newest shade.   Price.....5.98
No. 38K6698   Color, red and green, changeable.   Price.....5.98
If by mail, postage extra, each, 27c.

SILK PETTICOATS

We show a splendid variety of Silk Petticoats at astonishingly low prices, quality, style and workmanship all combined in these petticoats. They are made with draw strings at waist, in lengths 38, 40 and 42 inches.

$6.25 ISN'T THIS A HANDSOME PETTICOAT WITH PRETTY TRIMMED FLOUNCE?
Made of fine quality rustling taffeta silk, with deep plaited flounce, headed with silk ruching. Triple ruffle effect around bottom. Has sixteen dust ruffle. Exceptionally pretty petticoat. Lengths, 38, 40 and 42 inches. State length desired.
No. 38K6688   Color, black.   Price.....$6.25
No. 38K6689   Color, blue.   Price.....6.25
No. 38K6690   Color, brown, stylish shade.   Price.....6.25
Price.......

EMBROIDERED FLOUNCE IS A WORK OF ART.

NOTE THE VARIETY OF STYLES IN THESE PETTICOATS.

$4.98 TAFFETA SILK PETTICOAT.
Good quality rustling Taffeta Silk Petticoat, with deep flounce fluted and trimmed with rows of cording and narrow ruffles around bottom. Lengths, 38, 40 and 42 inches. Always mention length wanted.
No. 38K6684   Color, black.   Price.....$4.98
No. 38K6685   Color, blue.   Price.....4.98
No. 38K6686   Color, red and green.   Price.....4.98

STYLISH SILK PETTICOATS.

changeable.   Price............

YOUR MONEY WILL BE IMMEDIATELY RETURNED TO YOU FOR ANY GOODS NOT PERFECTLY SATISFACTORY.

683

LONG KIMONOS OR NEGLIGEES AND BATH OR LOUNGING ROBES.

YOUR WARDROBE IS NOT COMPLETE WITHOUT ONE OR MORE OF THESE COMFORTABLE GARMENTS. SIZES, 32 TO 44 INCHES BUST MEASURE.

$2.35 A FANCY EIDERDOWN BATH OR LOUNGING ROBE.

The wide sailor collar, kimono sleeves and pockets are bound with satin in blue or crimson shade with colors in robe; fastens at neck with bow of ribbon and loop on front with frogs and loop. Heavy all wool cord with tassel. This is an excellent garment that every woman needs. Colors, light or dark ground with fancy fancy stripe, tan color predominating. Made wide and full. A garment that every woman needs. Give bust measure when ordering. Sizes, 32 to 44 inches bust measure.
No. 38K7100. Price...$2.35
If by mail, postage extra, 46 cents.

$3.19 NICE RIPPLE EIDERDOWN BATH ROBE.

There is no more necessary garment than a warm, comfortable bath or lounging robe. They are just the thing for lounging in one's room. This robe is made with wide sailor collar which is bound with satin ribbon, pointed kimono sleeves and patch pockets are also bound with satin. Heavy wool cord and tassels; fastens at neck with satin and across front with frogs and loop. Extra long and full sweep. Color, cardinal only. Give bust measure when ordering. Sizes, 32 to 44 inches bust measure.
No. 38K7104.
Price...........$3.19
If by mail, postage extra, 54 cents.

$1.85 FANCY DOWN FLANNEL.

This is one of our best values, in long kimonos. Made of fine flannelette, down with alternating light and dark patterns in Japanese effects and figured designs especially adapted for kimonos. It is faced around neck, down front and on sleeves with wide band to match colorings in kimono. Extra long skirt, and nice and wide. Sizes, 32 to 44 inches bust measure. Give bust measure when ordering.
No. 38K7114.
Price..........$1.85
Postage extra, 33c.

Short Kimono. Same style as No. 38K7114. Colors, fancy medium or dark patterns.
Price..38K7150.....79c
If by mail, postage extra, 11 cents.

$1.29 LONG AND SHORT KIMONOS.

$1.29 LONG KIMONO FANCY PATTERNS.

This long Kimono is an extra good value. Is finished around neck, down front and on sleeves with wide band to match colorings in kimono. Made of flannelette. Just what you need for house wear or lounging. Colors are medium or dark patterns in very pretty effects. Sizes, 32 to 44 inches bust measure. When ordering, be sure to state bust measure.
No. 38K7110....$1.29
If by mail, postage extra, 26 cents.

48c SHORT KIMONO. Same style as No. 38K7110. Colors, fancy blue or red patterns.
No. 38K7148........48c
If by mail, postage extra, 11 cents.

$1.25 AN EXCELLENT VALUE AT OUR PRICE.

THE IDEAL HOUSE GARMENT FOR GENERAL WEAR.

It is made of good quality percale, with wide fancy collar trimmed with ruffle; sleeves trimmed to match; gathered at waist line in back; held in place by belt. Nothing so comfortable to work in as this style house garment. Sizes, 32 to 44 inches bust measure. Be sure to give measure when ordering.
No. 38K7132. Color, black ground. Price..$1.25
No. 38K7133. Blue ground. Price....$1.25
If by mail, postage extra, 27 cents.

$1.45 FIGURED LAWN IN ATTRACTIVE PATTERNS

This pretty Kimono made of fancy figured lawn, has wide sailor collar trimmed with ruffle; three-quarter sleeves with plain lawn cuffs; neck is also finished with fancy pointed elbow sleeves are finished with ruffle. White ground with neat floral effects. Sizes, 32 to 44 inches bust measure. Always give bust measure when ordering.
No. 38K7128. Price, $1.45
If by mail, postage extra, 21 cents.

$1.18 FIGURED LAWN IN ATTRACTIVE PATTERNS

Fancy Kimono is made with Dutch neck finished with plain band of lawn to harmonize; three-quarter sleeves with plain band of lawn to harmonize; neck is also finished with lace edge. Flounce on bottom of skirt. This is an ideal garment. White grounds with fancy figured floral effects. Sizes, 32 to 44 inches bust measure. Give bust measure when ordering.
No. 38K7124. Price....$1.18
If by mail, postage extra, 19c.

72c LAWN KIMONO.

Long Kimono made of fancy figured lawn in neat floral effects. Trimmed with collar; has wide kimono sleeves. Made nice and full. Excellent value. Sizes, 32 to 44 inches bust measure. Always give bust measure when ordering.
No. 38K7120 Price....72c
If by mail, postage extra, 19c.

$4.95

No. 38K7114.

$1.89

$1.68 NEW STYLE KIMONO WITH YOKE.

Made of daisy fancy figured lawn. The fancy fancy yoke is trimmed with wide tucks; finished with satin. Neck is trimmed with fancy lace beading and ribbon inserted. New shaped sleeves trimmed to match. White ground with fancy figured effects. Sizes, 32 to 44 inches bust measure. Give bust measure when ordering.
No. 38K7136 Price, $1.68
If by mail, postage extra, 24c

$4.95 LONG OR SHORT JAPS SILK KIMONOS. $2.48

These are the prettiest Kimonos we are showing. The Oriental design is in challie of a neat figured Japanese challie. Shirred front, finished down fronts. Kimono sleeves usually attractive. We quote this style in the short or full length. Give bust measure when ordering. Sizes, 32 to 44 inches bust measure. Color, blue or black ground with fancy Japanese effects.
No. 38K7146 Long Kimono, $4.95
No. 38K7147 Short Kimono, $2.48
If by mail, postage extra, 24c.

$1.89 MADE OF JAPANESE CHALLIE.

This long Kimono is made of a neat figured Japanese challie. The Oriental design is in perfect keeping with the style and is unusually attractive. We quote this style in the short or full length. Give bust measure when ordering. Sizes, 32 to 44 inches bust measure. Color, blue or black ground with fancy Japanese effects. Give inches bust measure when ordering.
No. 38K7140 Price, $1.89
If by mail, postage extra, 24c.

HOUSE DRESSES, TEA GOWNS AND WRAPPERS

SIZES, 32 TO 44 INCHES BUST MEASURE.

THESE NEW ONE-PIECE HOUSE DRESSES ARE THE MOST COMFORTABLE GARMENTS MADE. THEY HAVE THAT DRESSY GENTEEL APPEARANCE, TOGETHER WITH THE NECESSARY COMFORT FOR A GENERAL WEARING GARMENT.

$1.69

$1.69 BLACK MERCERIZED SATEEN WRAPPER.

This neat wrapper is made with pointed yoke in back and square yoke in front. Finished with two rows of narrow ribbon and ruffle, waist being plain in back and, over collar and cuffs, are finished with row of ribbon. Front is plaited at neck; skirt is made with flounce. Sizes, 32 to 44 inches bust measure. Always give bust measure.

No. 38K7204 Color, black only.
Price.................$1.69
If by mail, postage extra, 32c.

$1.85

$1.85 MADE OF FINE STRIPED PERCALE.

A very neat effect is produced on this percale in light ground with neat stripes, the bias front in the new Marie Antoinette style; turnover collar. Sizes, 32 to 44 inches bust measure. Be sure to state size.
No. 38K7231 Color, black stripes. Price....$1.85
No. 38K7232 Color, blue stripes. Price....$1.85
No. 38K7233 Color, red stripes. Price....$1.85
If by mail, postage extra, 26 cents.

$1.69

$1.69 PERCALE HOUSE DRESS WITH DUTCH NECK.

This neat and serviceable one-piece House Dress is a very good value for the money. Made with four tucks in front. Dutch neck is finished with band of self material. Three-quarter sleeve with plain cuff. Nice full skirt is gathered on to attached belt. Sizes, 32 to 44 inches bust measure. When ordering, state bust measure.
No. 38K7228 Color, black with polka dots. Price, $1.69
No. 38K7229 Color, blue with polka dots. Price, $1.69
No. 38K7230 Color, red with polka dots. Price, $1.69
If by mail, postage extra, 21 cents.

$1.15 MADE OF GOOD GRADE PERCALE.

This is one of our unparalleled values in House Dresses. Made of good grade percale in plain style, waist being plain in back and gathered in front. Turnover collar, full length sleeves with button cuff. Nice full skirt is attached to waist by belt. There is nothing better for general wear than one of these dresses. Sizes, 32 to 44 inches bust measure. Always give bust measure when ordering.
No. 38K7224 Color, black ground. Price.........$1.15
No. 38K7225 Color, blue ground. Price.........$1.15
No. 38K7226 Color, red ground. Price.........$1.15
If by mail, postage extra, 23 cents.

ALWAYS GIVE BUST MEASUREMENTS WHEN ORDERING.

HERE IS A NEAT SERVICEABLE HOUSE DRESS IN THE NEW BLACK AND WHITE SHEPHERD CHECKED PERCALE AND VERY NEATLY TRIMMED. **$1.48** THE PRICE IS ONLY

$1.15

No. 38K7220

$1.48 SHEPHERD CHECK PERCALE HOUSE DRESS. $1.48

Very neat House Dress, made of black and white shepherd check percale and trimmed on front in yoke effect with bias band of material piped with red. Plain turnover collar is also piped with red. Three-quarter length sleeves. Full skirt is attached to waist at belt. Lined with good grade cambric. Sizes, 32 to 44 inches bust measure. Always give bust measure.
No. 38K7220 Price.........$1.48
If by mail, postage extra, 25 cents.

$1.75 ONE-PIECE DRESS OF FINE PERCALE.

This pretty House Dress is made of figured percale in very neat style; waist has two box plaits down center of back; front being trimmed with deep folds of the goods and band of fancy percale trimming; full-ness being laid in gathers. Turnover collar trimmed with fancy percale. Plain shirt sleeves with neat button cuff. Full gored skirt is attached to waist by belt. Waist is lined with good grade cambric. As pretty a house dress as you could wish for. Sizes, 32 to 44 inches bust measure. Be sure to state bust measure when ordering.
No. 38K7216 Colors, white ground with blue figures. Price.........$1.75
No. 38K7217 Colors, white ground with black figures. Price.........$1.75
If by mail, postage extra, 24 cents.

$1.75

$3.50 NICE CASHMERE TEA GOWN.

There is no more graceful dress for home wear than one of these pretty tea gowns. Made of cashmere and is neatly trimmed around wide fancy collar and wide lace cuffs, lace to match. Fullness laid in three side plaits on each side. Ribbon tie at neck. Waist is lined with good quality cambric. Sizes, 32 to 44 inches bust measure. Always give bust measure.
No. 38K7200 color, black.
Price.........................$3.50
No. 38K7201 Color, blue.
Price.........................$3.50
No. 38K7202 Color, red.
Price.........................$3.50
If by mail, postage extra, 23c.

$1.48 SERVICEABLE PERCALE HOUSE DRESS.

It is made with plain bias back with a pointed yoke in front made with two side plaits on either side. Cuffs and turnover collar are made on the bias of the goods. Nice full skirt is attached to waist by belt; plain shirt sleeves. Waist is lined with good cambric. Sizes, 32 to 44 inches bust measure. Give bust measure.
No. 38K7212 Color, black ground with fancy figures. Price.........$1.48
No. 38K7213 Color, blue ground, with fancy figures. Price.........$1.48
If by mail, postage extra, 24 cents.

$3.50

$1.48

$1.10 NEAT HOUSE DRESS.

Made of striped gingham. Bias fold across front. Belt is attached at center of back, with deep turnover collar and an ordinary house dress as a nurse's uniform. Sizes, 32 to 44 inches bust measure. Give size.
No. 38K7208 Price.$1.10
If by mail, postage extra, 24 cents.

$1.10

FASHIONS FOR YOUNG FOLKS

GIRLS' TWO-PIECE GUIMPE DRESSES, TWO-PIECE SAILOR SUITS AND GUIMPES, OF WASHABLE MATERIALS. HANDSOME UP TO DATE STYLES. TRIMMINGS AND MATERIALS ARE OF THE VERY NEWEST EFFECTS. WOULD IT PAY YOU TO MAKE THEM AT THESE PRICES? REMEMBER THE GUIMPE DRESSES WE SHOW INCLUDE SEPARATE GUIMPES, AND ADDITIONAL GUIMPES ARE SHOWN ON THIS PAGE. FOR GIRLS, AGES 6 TO 14 YEARS.

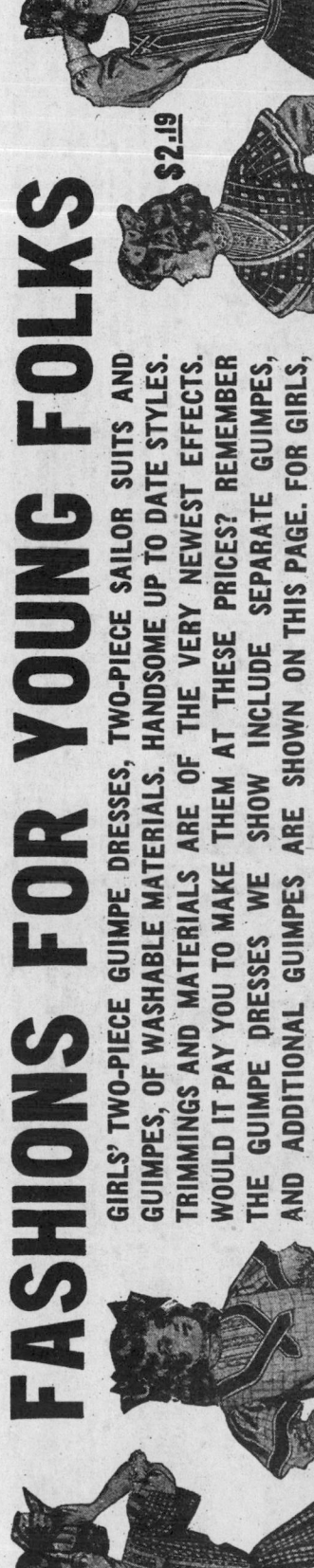

$1.23

$2.19

$1.59

$1.59 GOOD STYLE GUIMPE DRESS

Made of good quality washable gingham, Dutch neck trimmed with pique which extends down front on left side and is finished with fancy braid. Bell sleeves with straps of pique. Box plaits on front. Deep hem on skirt. Guimpe of white lawn, yoke of tucks and embroidery. Sizes, 6 and 14 years. Order by age and color, please.
No. 38K7600 Colors, blue or pink check.
Price $1.59
If by mail, postage extra, 16 cents.

$1.75 NOBBY CHILD'S DRESS MADE OF WASH SUITING.

Made of pretty wash suiting, trimmed as shown, around front, bell sleeves and belt with band of color to harmonize. Skirt with box plaits. White lawn guimpe trimmed with insertion, lace and wide tucks. Sizes, 6 to 14 years. Size and color, please.
No. 38K7604 Colors, white with black or blue check effects.
Price $1.75
If by mail, postage extra, 22 cents.

$1.48 THIS SAILOR SUIT IS A VALUE.

It is made of good quality German linen and is trimmed on sailor collar, cuffs and standing collar with four rows of soutache braid, four-in-hand tie of white linen. Embroidered emblem on dickey. Skirt is plaited in front with box plaits and finished with deep hem. These sailor dresses are just the thing for school wear, and we guarantee them to give you the best of service. Sizes, 6 to 14 years. Don't forget to give age.
No. 38K7634
Colors, blue or tan. Price, $1.48
If by mail, postage extra, 19 cents.

$1.98 ONLY FOR THIS PRETTY GERMAN LINEN DRESS.

There's style, attractiveness and durability in this German linen dress, with separate guimpe, which is made with V cut neck and circular sleeves, both being trimmed with two rows of fancy braid; tucked front skirt; is made with very deep hem with a wide fold. Patent leather belt with buckle. Back has two tucks extending to waist line. Separate white lawn guimpe with yoke of tucks and embroidery. Hemstitched in neck and sleeves. Ages, 6 to 14 years. Give age and color, please.
No. 38K7608 Colors, white or blue
Price $1.98
If by mail, postage extra, 21 cents.

$2.25 STRICTLY UP TO DATE GUIMPE DRESS.

Very pretty Child's Dress, made of white butcher linen and trimmed as shown with bands of plain blue piped on either side with checked gingham. Belt to match. Three box plaits in front of skirt, the side plaits extending around to back. The separate guimpe with this dress is of plain white lawn with pointed yoke of clusters of tucks and band of embroidery. For children from 6 to 14 years old. Always give age when ordering.
No. 38K7612
Price $2.25
If by mail, postage extra, 23 cents.

HERE IS A COMPLETE COAT DRESS OF THREE PIECES

Consisting of a separate skirt, guimpe and coat. Very nobby and stylish, and only $2.98 for the three pieces. For girls, ages, 10, 12 and 14 years. The latest in girls three-piece suits.

$2.98

This Coat Suit of nice quality washably Chambray Gingham is one of the nicest styles that has been put on the market. It is made with a plain full skirt having box plaits with two side plaits on either side in front, belt of self material; and extra deep hem. The coat is made in the plain box style with regulation coat collar and lapels and plain coat sleeves with turn back cuffs. It is double breasted and two sided with six large pearl buttons, has two side pockets with flaps, one breast pocket, etc. The separate skirt waist which comes with the suit is trimmed on neck and sleeves and down front in single band of embroidery insertion front having plait, lawn ruffle. Sizes, 6 to 14 years. Order by age. No. 38K7642
No. 38K7640 Price........$2.98
If by mail, postage extra, 26 cents.

VERY NEAT CHAMBRAY GINGHAM SAILOR SUIT.

A very pretty, sensible Sailor Suit, trimmed around collar with rows of bias Scotch plaid gingham bands; four-in-hand tie to match; one plaid band around collar and cuff bands. Fullness is laid in sleeves in narrow tucks, white pique dickey with silk embroidered emblem. Skirt has box plaits in front. An excellent value and one that we know will please you.
Color blue or ox-blood red. Ages, 6 to 14 years. Always give age and color.
No. 38K7630
Price............98c
If by mail, postage extra, 18 cents.

98c

$1.98

PRETTY GUIMPE SUIT OF ZEPHYR GINGHAM.

If you want an extra pretty dress for your little girl, and one that is really nice enough for almost any occasion, buy this zephyr gingham in Scotch plaid effects. Trimmed around neck, front and bell sleeves with bands of white sheer pique. Full plaited skirt front and side plaits to yoke depth on either side. Plain collar to separate guimpes. Sizes, 6 to 14 years. What size and color, please.
Price $1.23
Postage extra, 19 cents.

$1.23 EXCELLENTLY MADE CHAMBRAY GINGHAM SUSPENDER DRESS.

This is one of the neatest garments you ever saw. The suspender straps are piped with white pique and trimmed with narrow stitched bands to match. The front of skirt, self full skirt, with belt of zephyr stitched around, large peep buttons in front, with waist. The guimpe is made of fine white lawn, trimmed in front with tucks and insertion of embroidery. Collar and cuffs trimmed with embroidery. Ages, 6 to 14 years. Give age, please.
No. 38K7616 ....$1.23
If by mail, postage extra, $2.19

GIRLS' WHITE LAWN GUIMPES OR WAISTS

TO BE WORN WITH EITHER THE SUSPENDER OR GUIMPE DRESSES, AS SHOWN ON THIS PAGE. FOR GIRLS, AGES 6 TO 14 YEARS.

89c

IT IS ALWAYS WELL TO HAVE SEVERAL OF THESE DAINTY WAISTS TO WEAR WITH COLORED GUIMPE DRESSES.

NEAT WHITE LAWN GUIMPE.

Yoke on this White Lawn Guimpe is made of cluster tucks alternating with bands of embroidery. The neck and sleeves are trimmed with hemstitched single band. Sizes, 6 to 14 years. Give age when ordering.
No. 38K7646 Price....48c
If by mail, postage extra, 8 cents.

48c

75c

LACE TRIMMED GUIMPE.

White Lawn Guimpes, very dainty when worn with a guimpe dress. Made with four clusters of tiny tucks with three rows of valenciennes lace insertion. Collar and cuffs edged with lace. Ages, 6 to 14 years. Don't fail to state age.
No. 38K7650
Price............75c
If by mail, postage extra, 10 cents.

This serviceable Guimpe Waist is made of white sheer lawn trimmed with band of embroidery and three clusters of hemstitched tucks. Turnover collar; hemstitched lawn ruffle on sleeves. Ages, 6 to 14 years. Always give age when ordering.
No. 38K7650
Price............89c
If by mail, postage extra, 10 cents.

INFANTS' LONG CLOAKS IN CASHMERE, BEDFORD CORD AND SILK

WE SHOW A COMPLETE LINE IN BOTH PLAIN AND TRIMMED SKIRTS. THEY ARE ALL MADE FULL LENGTH AND SWEEP. WHEN CHANGING BABY'S CLOTHES FROM LONG TO SHORT THESE CLOAKS CAN EASILY BE ALTERED TO THE DESIRED LENGTH. THOSE WITH TRIMMED SKIRTS CAN BE SHORTENED AT THE YOKE, OR THOSE WITH PLAIN SKIRTS CAN BE SHORTENED AT THE BOTTOM.

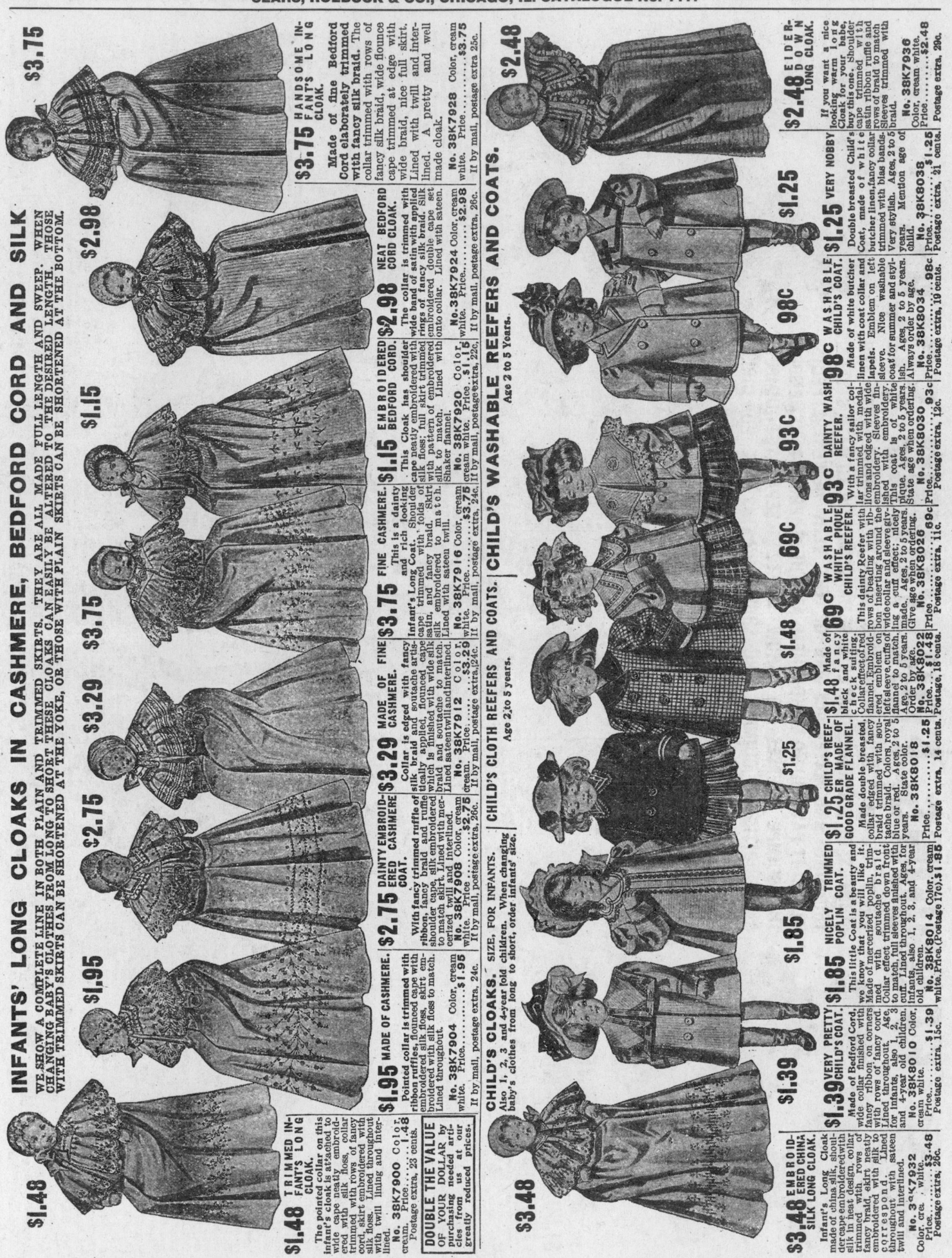

$3.75 HANDSOME INFANT'S LONG CLOAK.

Made of fine Bedford Cord elaborately trimmed with fancy silk braid. The collar trimmed with rows of fancy silk braid, wide flounce cape trimmed at edge with wide braid, nice full skirt. Lined with twill and well lined. A pretty and well made cloak.
No. 38K7928 Color, cream white. Price.........$3.75
If by mail, postage extra 25c.

$2.98 NEAT BEDFORD CORD CLOAK.

The collar is trimmed with cape neatly embroidered with wide band of satin with applied trimmed rings of fancy silk braid. Silk floss; full skirt trimmed with pattern of embroidered double cape set silk to match. Lined with sateen.
No. 38K7924 Color, cream white. Price.........$2.98
If by mail, postage extra, 26c.

$1.15 EMBROIDERED BEDFORD CORD.

This Cloak has shoulder cape neatly embroidered with wide band of satin with applied trimmed rings of fancy silk braid. Silk floss; full skirt finished with wide silk silk to match. Lined with Shaker flannel.
No. 38K7920 Color, cream white. Price..$1.15
If by mail, postage extra, 22c.

$3.75 FINE CASHMERE.

This is a dainty and rich looking Infant's Long Coat. Shoulder cape trimmed with folds of satin, and fancy braid. Skirt embroidered to match. Lined sateen twill and interlined.
No. 38K7916 Color, cream white. Price....$3.75
If by mail, postage extra, 24c.

$3.29 MADE OF FINE CASHMERE.

Collar is edged with fancy silk braid and soutache artistically applied, flounced cape trimmed with wide silk braid and soutache to match. Lined twill and interlined.
No. 38K7912 Color, cream. Price....$3.29
If by mail, postage extra, 26c.

$2.75 DAINTY EMBROIDERED CASHMERE COAT.

With fancy trimmed ruffle of ribbon, fancy braid and ruffle shoulder cape, silk embroidered to match skirt. Lined with mercerized twill and interlined.
No. 38K7908 Color, cream white. Price.........$2.75
If by mail, postage extra, 24c.

$1.95 MADE OF CASHMERE.

Pointed collar is trimmed with ribbon ruffles, flounced cape with embroidered silk floss, skirt embroidered with silk floss to match. Lined throughout.
No. 38K7904 Color, cream white. Price.........$1.95
If by mail, postage extra, 24c.

DOUBLE THE VALUE OF YOUR DOLLAR by purchasing needed articles from us at our greatly reduced prices.

$1.48 TRIMMED INFANT'S LONG CLOAK.

The pointed collar on this infant's cloak is attached to wide cape neatly embroidered with silk floss, collar trimmed with rows of fancy silk cord, skirt embroidered with silk floss. Lined throughout with twill lining and interlined.
No. 38K7900 Color, cream white. Price....1.48
Postage extra, 23 cents.

$3.48 EMBROIDERED CHINA SILK LONG CLOAK.

Infant's Long Cloak made of china silk, shoulder cape embroidered with fancy ribbon and rows of fancy silk cord. Lined throughout. Age, also 1, 2, 3 and 4-year old children.
No. 38K7932 Color, cream white. Price.........$3.48
Postage extra, 26c.

CHILD'S CLOAKS, SIZE, FOR INFANTS.

Also 1, 2, 3 and 4-year old children. When changing baby's clothes from long to short, order infants' size.

CHILD'S CLOTH REEFERS AND COATS. | CHILD'S WASHABLE REEFERS AND COATS.

Age 2 to 5 years.

$1.39 VERY PRETTY CHILD'S COAT.

Made of Bedford Cord, wide collar finished with fancy ribbon and rows of fancy silk cord. Lined throughout. Age, also 1, 2, 3 and 4-year old children.
No. 38K8010 Color, cream white. Price....$1.39
Postage extra, 15c.

$1.85 NICELY TRIMMED POPLIN COAT.

This little Coat is beauty and we know that you will like it. Made with intercolor applique trimmed with soutache braid. Collar effect trimmed down front, to match, full sleeves finished with cuff. Lined throughout. Ages, for Infants, also 1, 2, 3, and 4-year old children.
No. 38K8014 Color, cream white. Price.........$1.85

$1.25 CHILD'S REEFER MADE OF GOOD GRADE FLANNEL.

Made double breasted, collar edged with fancy braid trimmed with soutache braid. Ages, 2 to 5 years. Order by age.
No. 38K8018

$1.48 Made of fancy check suiting.

Collar effect of red black and white check suiting.
No. 38K8022 Price.....$1.48
Postage extra, 18 cents.

69c WASHABLE WHITE PIQUE REEFER.

This dainty Reefer with rows of beading with wide collar and aloud the embroidery.
No. 38K8026 Price.....69c
Postage extra, 11c.

93c DAINTY WASH REEFER.

With a fancy sailor collar trimmed with medallions and edged with wide lapels. Sleeves finished with embroidery. Nice washable coat for summer and stylish. Ages, 2 to 5 years. Give age when ordering.
No. 38K8030 Price.....93c
Postage extra, 12c.

98c WASHABLE CHILD'S COAT.

Made of white butcher linen with coat collar and lapels. Emblem on left sleeve. This coat is of white pique. Ages, 2 to 5 years. Always order by age.
No. 38K8034 Price.....98c
Postage extra, 13c.

$1.25 VERY NOBBY CHILD'S COAT.

Double breasted Child's Coat, made of white butcher linen, fancy collar trimmed with satin ribbon ruffle and rows of braid to match. Sleeves trimmed with braid.
No. 38K8038 Color, cream white. Price.....$1.25
Postage extra, 21 cents.

$2.48 EIDER DOWN LONG CLOAK.

If you want a nice looking, warm long Cloak for your babe, buy this one. Shoulder cape trimmed with satin ribbon ruffle and butcher linen. Very stylish. Mention age of child.
No. 38K7936 Color, cream white. Price.........$2.48
Postage extra, 29c.

Prices: $3.75 $2.98 $1.15 $3.75 $3.29 $2.75 $1.95 $1.48 $2.48 $1.25 $98c $93c $69c $1.48 $1.25 $1.85 $1.39 $3.48

YOUR MONEY WILL BE IMMEDIATELY RETURNED TO YOU FOR ANY GOODS NOT PERFECTLY SATISFACTORY.

687

DEPARTMENT OF INFANTS' WEAR

Two complete outfits for the baby's wardrobe. Almost everything necessary for an infant's wardrobe is comprised in either of these two sets. They not only save the time, trouble and worry of making them or of buying the separate pieces, but they also save you money, for if you bought the pieces of either set separately the outfit would cost you almost double our price. Don't fail to look through these pages of infants' wear for additional pieces. Our line is not only complete but the best and most reasonable in price to be found anywhere.

FREE

ASK FOR OUR INSTRUCTIVE BOOK, "HOW TO TAKE CARE OF THE BABY." A BOOK OF INFORMATION FOR EVERY MOTHER.

This book we include, free of charge, with either of these sets or with every order amounting to $3.00 or more from our Infants' Wear Department. This book is an illustrated treatise on the care and feeding of infants and it is a book no mother can afford to be without. It was especially prepared for us by an eminent woman specialist and its advice may be followed without the least hesitancy. If you want one of these helpful guides, be sure to mention it in your order for infants' wear amounting to $3.00 or more and it will be sent you with the goods.

A COMPLETE OUTFIT OF INFANTS' WEAR, 24 PIECES $5.79 FOR ONLY

In making up this Infants' Set we have been careful to select the most essential pieces of baby's wardrobe and to give the mother just the lowest possible price. It comprises nearly everything needed in this set will be sure to please you. Every piece is well made and very dainty and it comprises baby's robe, and by buying the garments in the manner you get them for almost half what separately as are needed in the following at pleasing prices.

1 Beautiful Cambric Robe, handsomely trimmed with embroidered front panel and insertion with ribbon. Embroidered ruffle around yoke and on bottom of skirt. 1 Fine Quality Nainsook Day Slip, with yoke of point de Paris lace and insertion finished with lace to match, neck and sleeves being trimmed with lace edge; trimmed around bottom with tucks, insertion and lace, as shown. 1 Muslin and embroidery insertion and ruffle, as shown. 1 Muslin Night Slip, with tucked yoke and wide hem. 1 Fine Nainsook Skirt (to match day slip), finished around collar, down front and on sleeves with embroidered twist. 1 Long Flannel Skirt, finished at bottom with fine tucks, lace insertion and wide edge to match. 2 Long Cambric Skirts, finished at bottom with three tucks and good hem. 1 Flannel Shawl, cream color, with handsome flower design in one corner. 2 Bibs, honeycomb pattern trimmed with lace. 1 Silk Bib (quilted) with lace edge. 2 Diapers, made of good quality birdseye absorbent cotton. 1 Rubber Diaper (white), to be used over cloth diaper. 2 Stockinette Diaper. 1 Pair of Bootees, made of all wool zephyr; very dainty and closely knitted. A very fine bootee. 1 Pair of Bootees, made of mercerized twist (looks like silk), closely knitted in artistic pattern. 1 All Wool Knitted Zephyr Sacque; crocheted edge around collar; front and sleeves very closely knitted. Sacque made of fine cashmere, embroidered with silk very pretty and stylish. 1 Sacque made of fleeced flannel or daisy cloth and finished with mercerized twist. 2 Bands, made of flannel. 1 Pinning Blanket or Barrier Coat, made of wool flannel, cambric waist band.

No. 38K8200 Price for complete outfit (24 pieces) including our baby book. Weight, packed for shipment, 6 pounds....................$5.79

INFANTS' HIGH GRADE OUTFIT, 26 PIECES, EVERY PIECE A REAL VALUE $9.65

Our illustration of this beautiful set cannot begin to do it justice. It is an outfit of quality in every detail and if you are particular about your baby's wardrobe the pieces in this set will be sure to please you. Every piece is well made and very dainty and it comprises baby's everything needed for the baby. Such extra pieces as are needed will be found listed in the following and at pleasing prices.

1 Beautiful Cambric Robe, handsomely trimmed with embroidery and insertion, as shown in illustration. 1 Muslin Day Slip, with embroidery trimmed yoke; wide hem as bottom. 1 Fine Quality Slip, with fancy tucked Night Slip, with fancy tucked yoke. 2 Domet Flannel Wrappers, stitched around collar, down front and on yoke and sleeves with mercerized twist. 1 Long Cambric Skirt, finished around bottom with neat tucks. 1 Long Cambric Skirt, trimmed around bottom with cluster of tucks embroidered around bottom with mercerized twist. 1 Domet Flannel Wrapper, finished around collar, down front and on sleeves with fine tucks, lace insertion and beading at bottom with fine tucks, lace insertion and good hem. 1 Long Flannel Skirt, trimmed with three rows of lace insertion, beading with ribbon and lace ruffle; back of yoke is trimmed with cluster of pin tucks. Neck and sleeves are trimmed with beading with ribbon and lace. The skirt is nice and full and is trimmed with insertion, beading with ribbon and wide lace to match. The underskirt is made of Jap silk and is trimmed to match slip; waist of lawn.

No. 38K8204 Complete set (26 pieces), including our baby book, only........(Shipping weight, 6 lbs.) $9.65

SEE FOLLOWING PAGES FOR OUR SPLENDID ARRAY OF SEPARATE PIECES OF BABY'S WEARING APPAREL.

INFANTS' MATCHED SETS, CONSISTING OF LONG SLIP AND SKIRT

A BARGAIN IN INFANTS' SETS. 75c

A very pretty set made with square yoke of hemstitched tucks and embroidered insertion, and back being made with wide cluster of tucks on either side. Hemstitched ruffle around yoke trimmed with lace to match that in neck and sleeves. Skirt is nice and full and is trimmed with lawn ruffle edged with lace. The Skirt to this set is trimmed to match slip and has plain waist of same material. There is nothing nicer for a baby than one or more of these sets.

No. 38K8212
Price of slip...$1.15
No. 38K8213
Price of skirt.....75c
No. 38K8214
Price of set, consisting of both pieces...$1.75
If by mail, postage extra, each, 6 cents.

$1.15

LACE TRIMMED NAINSOOK SET. $1.25 $1.89

This beautiful set is made of fine quality Nainsook with fancy yoke in front and back of lace insertion ribbon beading and with wide ruffle of lace; ribbon and beading around neck at head of ruffle. Neck trimmed with narrow lace edge. Sleeves trimmed with beading and lace. Skirt is made with three clusters of tucks separated by rows of insertion and finished at bottom with wide lace to match. Dainty and pretty enough for any occasion. You'll like it.

No. 38K8216
Price of slip........$1.89
No. 38K8217
Price of skirt.....$1.25
No. 38K8218
Price of set, consisting of both pieces.....$2.98
If by mail, postage extra, each, 6 cents.

BEAUTIFUL JAP SILK SET. $1.75 $2.69

There is nothing nicer than these dainty trimmed Japanese infants' sets. The yoke is trimmed with three rows of lace insertion, beading with ribbon and lace ruffle; back of yoke is trimmed with cluster of pin tucks. Neck and sleeves are trimmed with beading with ribbon and lace. The skirt is nice and full and is trimmed with insertion, beading with ribbon and wide lace to match. The underskirt is made of Jap silk and is trimmed to match slip; waist of lawn.

No. 38K8222
Price of silk slip....$2.69
No. 38K8223
Price of silk skirt.$1.75
No. 38K8224
Price of set, consisting of both pieces.......$4.25
If by mail, postage extra, each, 6 cents.

48c Infants' Long Robe made of daisy cloth or baby flannel. Has pointed collar trimmed with fancy braid. Cuffs to match. Made nice and full. A serviceable wrap for baby. Colors are pink, cream or baby blue. State color wanted.

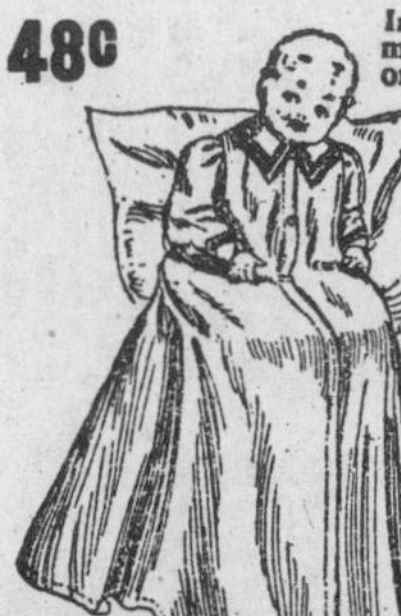

No. 38K8676 Price. .48c
If by mail, postage extra, 9 cents.

Infants' Flannel Wrapper.

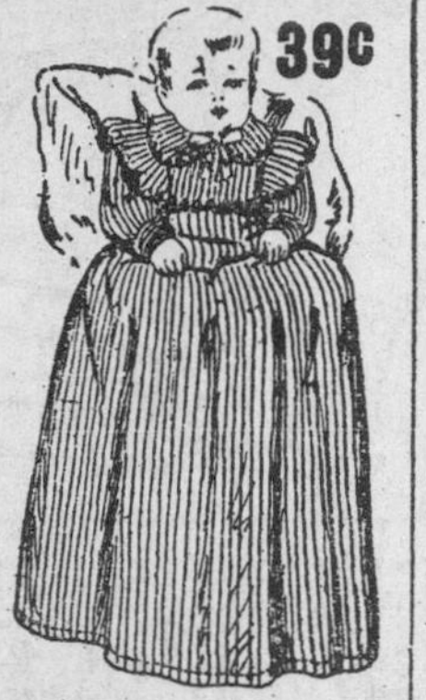

39c

Infants' Wrapper, made of domet flannel, stitched with mercerized twist around the collar and a yoke in front and back; epaulets over shoulders. Colors, pink or blue stripes. State color wanted.

No. 38K8678
Price . . 39c
If by mail, postage extra, 8 cents.

Infants' Flannel Sacque.

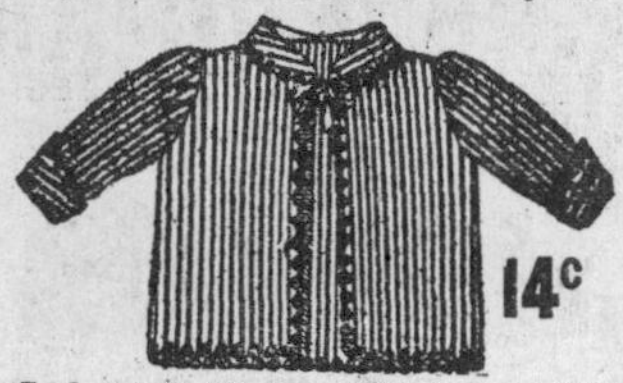

14c

Infants' Flannel Sacque, stitched down front and all around bottom, collar and cuffs with mercerized twist. Wonderful value. Colors, blue or pink stripes. State color wanted.

No. 38K8680 Price........14c
If by mail, postage extra, 4 cents.

39c Infants' Sacques.

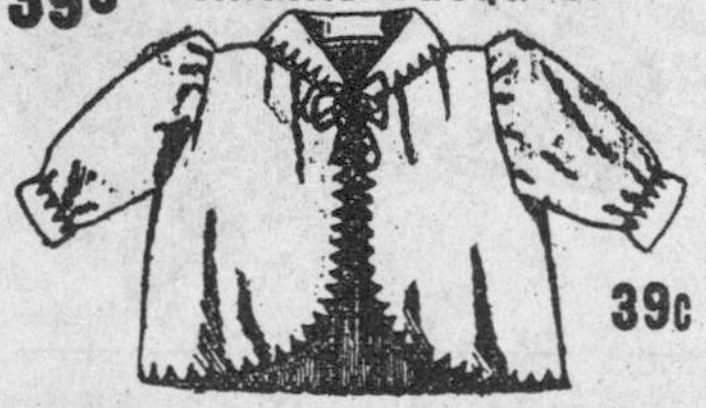

39c

Infants' Sacque, made in either flannel or cashmere; has a wide collar and turnover cuffs, stitched down front, bottom, collar and cuffs with mercerized twist. Silk ribbon tie strings at neck.

No. 38K8684 Made of flannel. Color, cream. Price..............39c
No. 38K8688 Made of fine cashmere. Colors, cream, with blue, pink or cream stitching. State color desired. Price..............................48c
If by mail, postage extra, 5 cents.

39c The Marguerite Sacque.

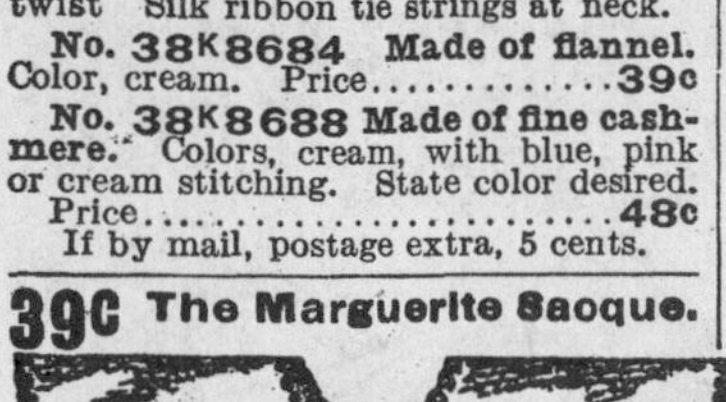

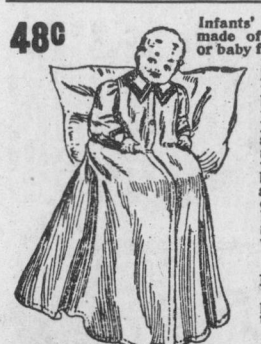

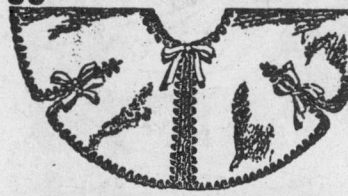

The Marguerite Infants' Sacque, made of one piece good quality baby flannel (daisy cloth) stitched all around with mercerized twist. Can be worn as a cape by tying silk ribbons accordingly, which are also used to tie in order to form the sleeves. Ribbon strings at neck. Color, cream.

No. 38K8690 Price... ...39c
If by mail, postage extra, 4 cents.

A SHAWL FOR BABY IS ONE OF THE MOST NECESSARY ITEMS FOR BABY'S WARDROBE.

INCLUDE ONE OR MORE OF THESE SHAWLS WHEN MAKING UP YOUR ORDER FOR BABY'S CLOTHES.

Made of Fine Quality Flannel and Only 43 Cents.

43c

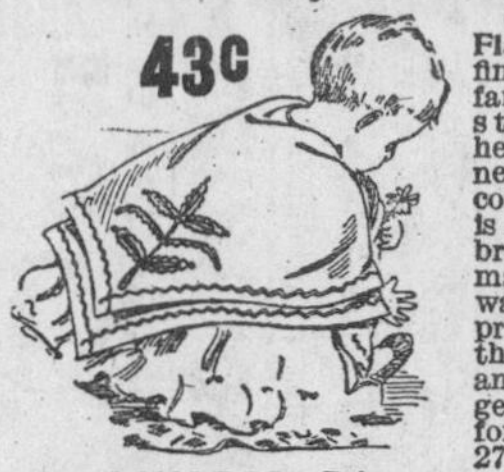

Cream Color Flannel Shawl, finished with fancy machine stitching on hem and with neat design in corner which is machine embroidered. It makes a nice warm shoulder protection for the little one and will give genuine comfort. Size, 27x27 inches.

No. 38K8700 Price..............43c
If by mail, postage extra, 5 cents.

87c Infants' Silk Embroidered Flannel Shawl.

This Infants' Shawl has a beautiful silk hand embroidered design in corner. They are very pretty and serviceable. A baby's wardrobe is not complete without one. Size, 28x28 inches

87c

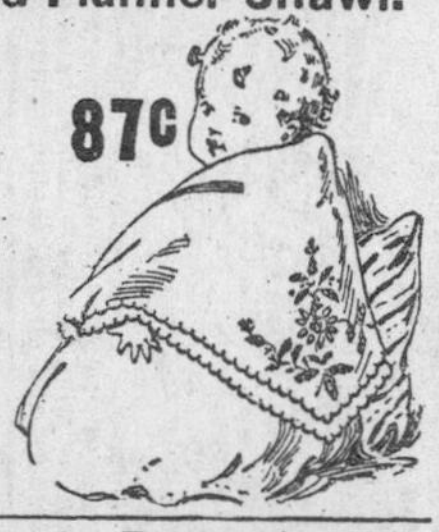

No. 38K8702
Price....87c
If by mail, postage extra, 6c.

$1.39 Hand Embroidered Flannel Shawl.

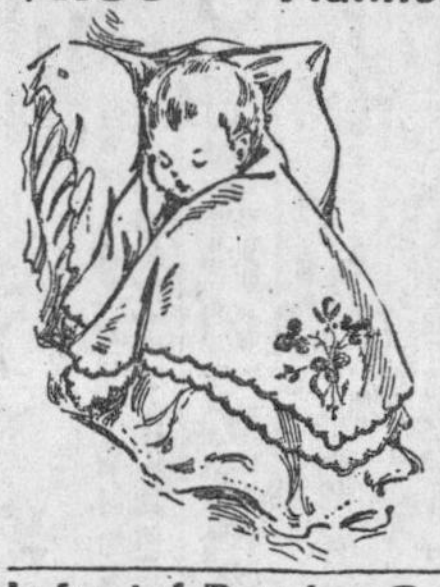

Extra Large Flannel Shawl for Infants with handsome silk hand embroidered floral design in corners. Scalloped edge with silk. Every baby needs one and every baby should have one at our price. Size, 32x32 inches

No. 38K8704
Color, cream.
Price..$1.39
If by mail, postage extra, 6c.

Infants' Barrior Coats or Pinning Blankets.

No. 38K8705 Infants' Barrior Coats or Pinning Blankets, made of Shaker flannel. Well made. Cream color. Price, each..17c
If by mail, postage extra, each, 6 cents.
No. 38K8706 Infants' Barrior Coats or Pinning Blankets, made of wool cream color flannel. Price, each...................39c
If by mail, postage extra, each, 6 cents.
No. 38K8707 Infants' Bands, made of good Shaker flannel. Price, each.........7c
If by mail, postage extra, each, 3 cents.
No. 38K8708 Infants' Bands, made of of wool flannel, scalloped edge. Price, each, 10c
If by mail, postage extra, each, 3 cents.

INFANTS' WOOL AND SILK VEILS.

An Excellent Protection for the Baby's Face.

Fine all Wool Infants' Veil Price, 17c.

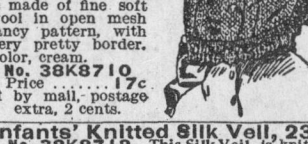

This Infants' Veil, is made of fine soft wool in open mesh fancy pattern, with very pretty border. Color, cream.

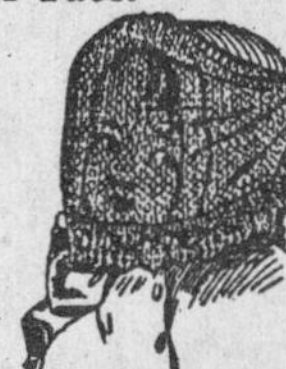

No. 38K8710
Price..........17c
If by mail, postage extra, 2 cents.

Infants' Knitted Silk Veil, 23c.
No. 38K8712 This Silk Veil, is knitted in open pattern, and has wide fancy border. An excellent protection to the face. Color, white. Price.........................23c
If by mail, postage extra, 2 cents.

Infants' Sacques.

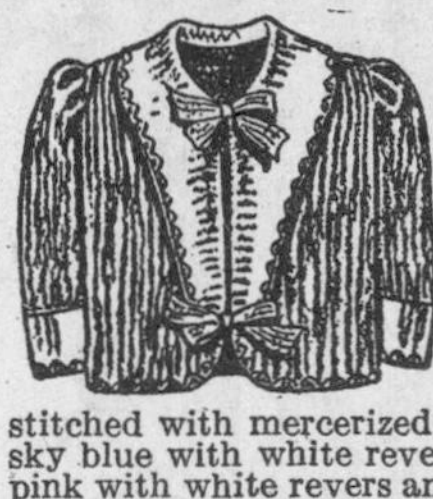

No. 38K8694 **Infants' Sacque, made of ripple eiderdown.** Has very neat revers, with two fancy silk ribbon tie strings. Revers, cuffs and around bottom shell stitched with mercerized twist. Colors, sky blue with white revers and cuffs, or pink with white revers and cuffs. State color wanted. Price...................43c
If by mail, postage extra, 6 cents.

CHILDREN'S BIBS.

Plain White Bibs, 4 for 10c.

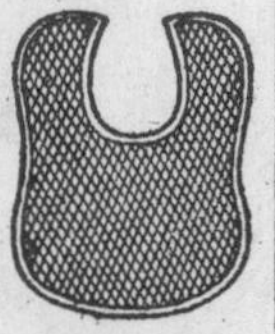

This Serviceable Plain White Bib, is bound with tape. They are heavy enough to protect the dress and their cost is almost nothing.

No. 38K8716
Price, 4 for.......10c
If by mail, postage extra, 4 for 5 cents.

Heavy Jap Silk Bib, 17 Cents.

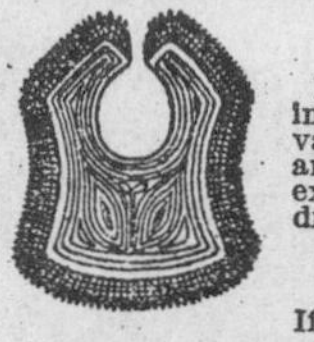

It is artistically stitched, in silk and is edged with valenciennes lace. Is lined and interlined making it an excellent protection to the dress.

No. 38K8726
Price, each.........17c
Three for.............45c
If by mail, postage extra 2c.

The Perfect Diaper.

This Diaper is made of good quality birdseye cloth, interlined with absorbent, medicated cotton, which is cut in one piece and quilted. The medicated cotton used is so treated making it antiseptic, that it renders the diaper odorless. Will not chafe or irritate the tenderest skin. After washing, they are always soft and pliable. Made in two sizes, small or large. State size desired.

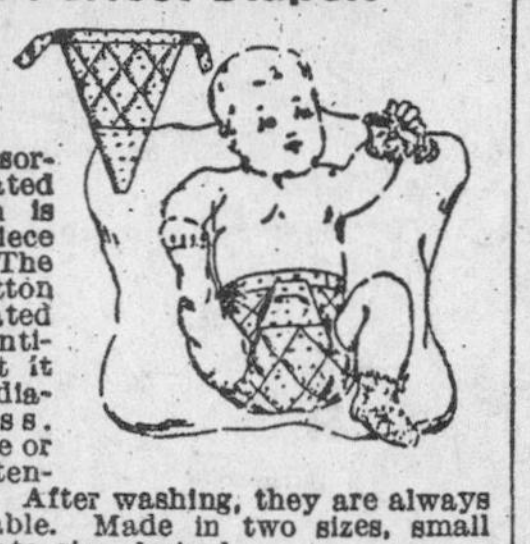

No. 38K8730 Price, 2 for.......23c
If by mail, postage extra, 2 for 7 cents.

Hemmed Purity Diapers, $1.00 and $1.35 Per Dozen.

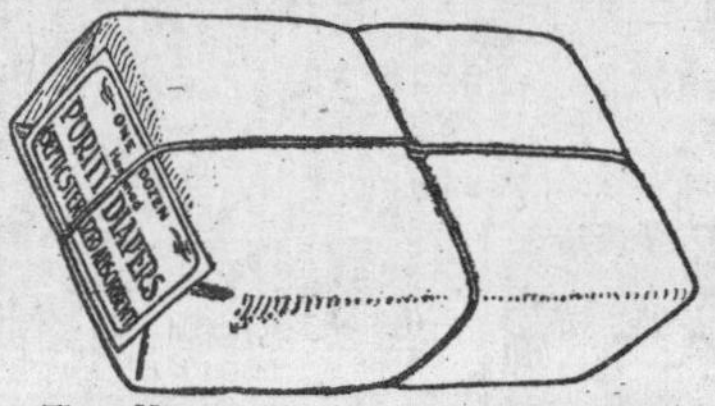

These Hemmed Diapers are a great convenience, being made and ready for use. They are made of antiseptic, absorbent birdseye diaper cloth and are put up and sold only in packages of one dozen in each. They come in two sizes and prices as follows:

No. 38K8731 Size, 18 x 36 inches. Price, per dozen.......................$1.00
No. 38K8732 Size, 22 x 44 inches. Price, per dozen........................$1.35
If by mail, postage extra, per dozen, 34 cents.

The Ideal Diaper Drawers. 2 for 35 Cents.

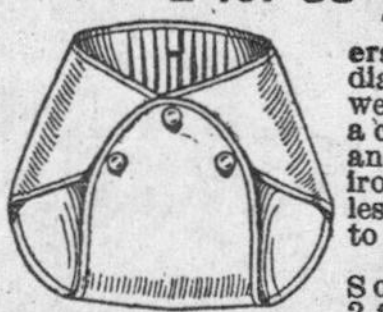

These Diaper Drawers to be worn over the diaper are very light weight, are absolutely acid and waterproof and can be washed and ironed. They are odorless. Have loop in back to hang them up by.

No. 38K8733
Sold only in pairs, 2 for.............35c
If by mail, postage extra, 2 for 6 cents.

39c Waterproof Stockinet Diaper Drawers.

These Stockinet Diaper Drawers are waterproof and the material is very soft and pliable. They give perfect comfort to the child and are washable. Made with wide waistband and draw string. Easily adjusted to any waist. Three sizes, small, medium and large. State which size wanted.

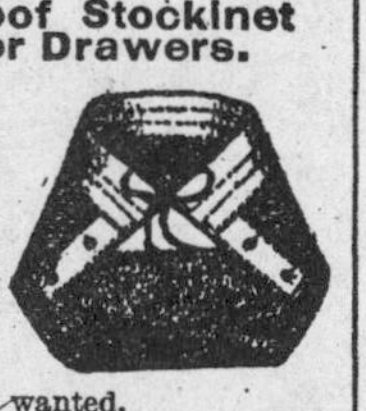

No. 38K8734 Price..............39c
If by mail, postage extra, 5 cents.

48c Rubber Coated Silk Diaper Drawers.

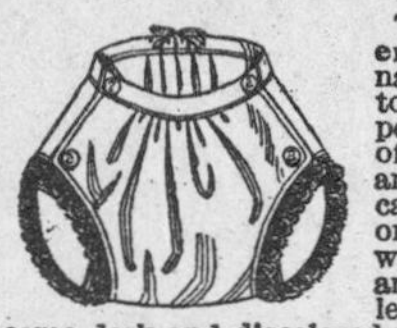

These Diaper Drawers are just what the name specifies. Made to wear over the diaper. They are made of waterproof silk and are so soft that they can be crushed in one's hand. They will wash perfectly, are absolutely odorless and do not become dark and discolored by use. They are neatly trimmed with lace. Fasten with pearl buttons on each side. Made with muslin band and draw string. Three sizes, small, medium and large. State which size.

No. 38K8735 Price..............48c
If by mail, postage extra, 4 cents.

21c Infants' Silk Bonnets, 21c.

Sizes are small, medium or large. Be sure to give size desired.

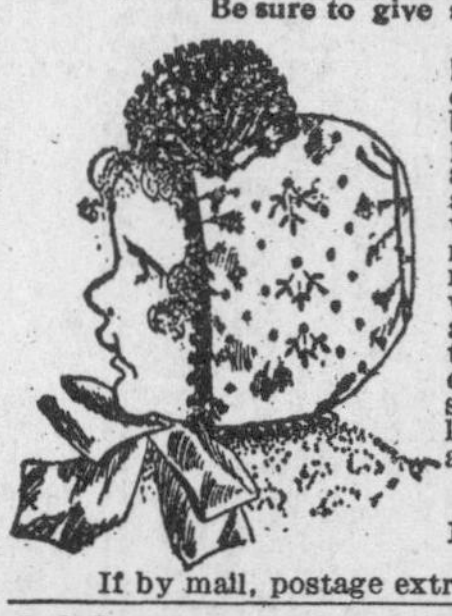

This Infant's Bonnet in Japanese silk is embroidered in pretty design and is finished all around edge with high top ruching to match. It is lined with cambric and has cambric ties. Color, cream. Sizes, small, medium or large. State size and color wanted.

No. 38K8740
Price....21c
If by mail, postage extra, 5 cents.

39c Nice Embroidered Infants' Bonnet.

It is made of Japanese silk and is embroidered in very nice design. Has plaited valenciennes frill all around and full ruching on top with ribbon bows on either side. Lined with fine soft cambric. Wide tie strings. Color, cream only. A very pretty bonnet. Sizes, small, medium or large. State size wanted.

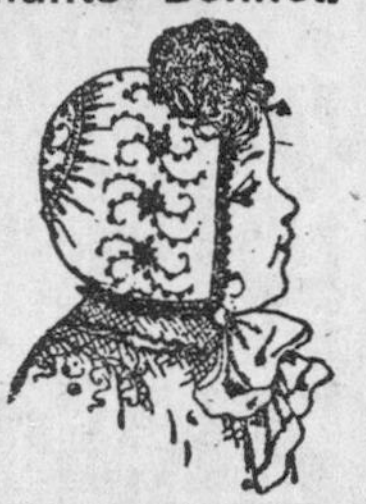

No. 38K8742
Price.........39c
If by mail, postage extra, 6 cents.

69c Made of Jap Silk and Silk Lined.

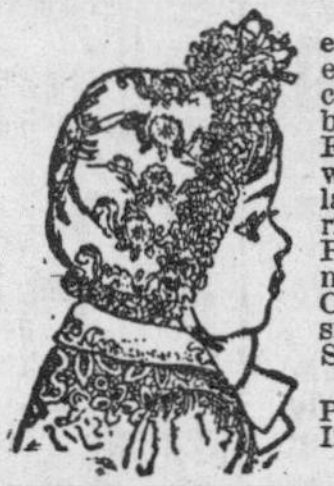

This beautiful Japanese Silk Bonnet is heavily embroidered with silk; crown in back is embroidered to match. Finished around front with ruching and narrow lace edge. Tiny silk ribbon bows on ruching. Ruching around back of neck. Silk string ties. Color, cream only. Sizes, small, medium or large. State size wanted.

No. 38K8744
Price..........69c
If by mail, postage extra, 6 cents.

98c The Daintiest of Jap Silk Baby Bonnets.

Beautifully embroidered with silk, with embroidered crown to match. Finished all around edge with plaited ruffle of fine silk mull. Two rosettes on top of silk mull with centers of baby ribbon. Lined with sateen. Sizes, small, medium or large. Mention size when ordering.

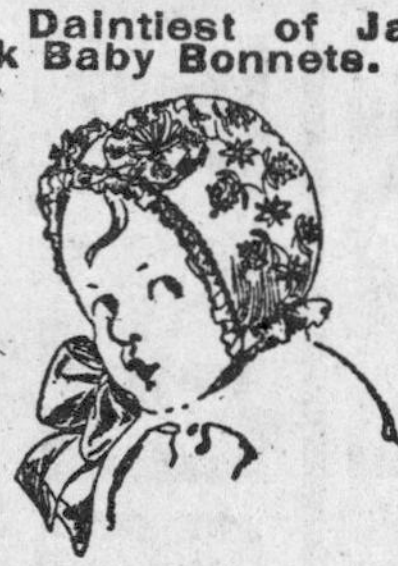

Color, cream only.
No. 38K8746 Price............98c
If by mail, postage extra, 6 cents.

42c Infants' Hand Crocheted Hoods.

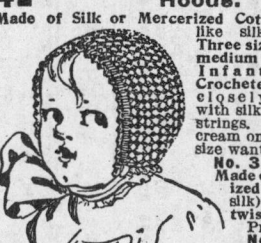

Made of Silk or Mercerized Cotton (looks like silk) Twist. Three sizes, small, medium and large.

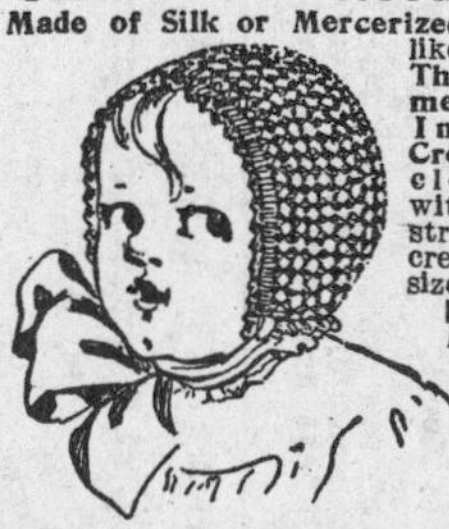

Infants' Hand Crocheted Hoods, closely stitched, with silk ribbon tie strings. Color, cream only. State size wanted.

No. 36K8750
Made of mercerized (looks like silk) cotton twist.
Price 25c
No. 38K8752
Made of silk twist.
Price.................................42c
If by mail, postage extra, each, 6 cents.

23c Neat Embroidered Bonnet.

This Infants' Bonnet is made of embroidered lawn, crown embroidered to match front. Double ruching around face with ribbon bow on either side. Single ruching around neck. Has wide ties strings. White only.

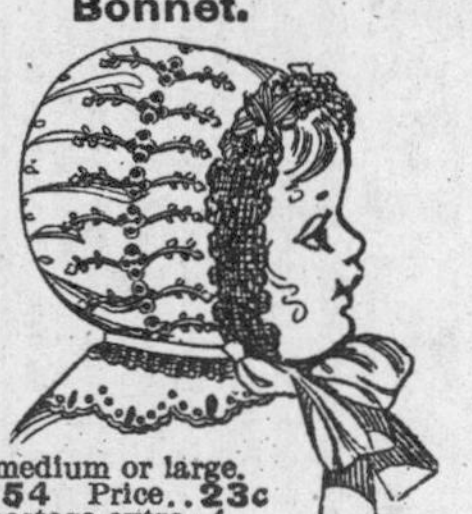

Sizes, small, medium or large.
No. 38K8754 Price..23c
If by mail, postage extra, 4 cents.

46c Elaborately Trimmed with Insertion and Lace.

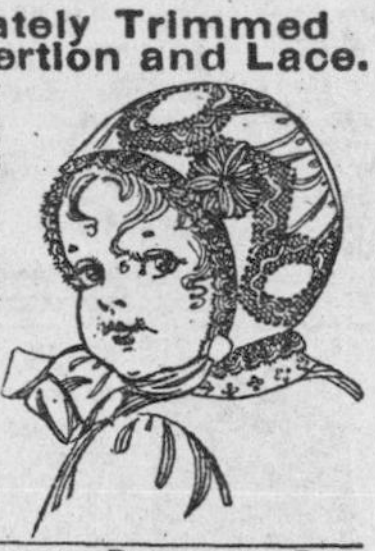

Artistically applied insertion elaborates this neat white lawn bonnet as illustrated. One row of insertion in crown. Finished around face and neck with lace edge. Ribbon pompon on each side of front. Wide lawn string ties. Sizes, small, medium or large. State size.

No. 38K8758
Price 46c
If by mail, postage extra, 5 cents.

Here is something new, Panamette Bonnets for the baby (looks like Panama Straw). A novelty. Light in weight, and the most stylish bonnet on the market.

48c A Little Beauty Made of Panamette Straw.

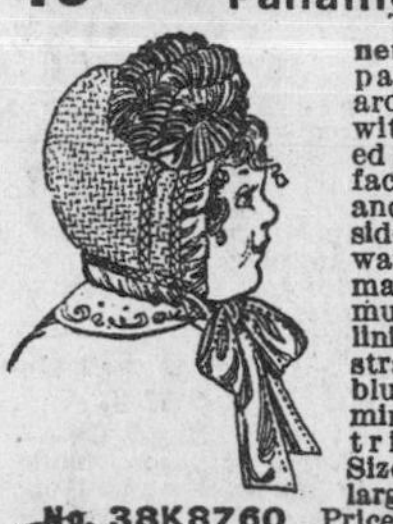

This handsome Bonnet is made of fine panamette, finished around front and neck with straw braid. Fluted mull ruching around face and back of neck and trimmed on either side with two large wavy pompons to match. Extra wide mull ties. Nice lawn lining. Colors, natural straw color with pink, blue or white trimmings. State color of trimming preferred. Sizes small, medium or large. State size.

No. 38K8760 Price 48c
If by mail, postage extra, 7 cents.

75c A New Creation in Babies' Bonnets.

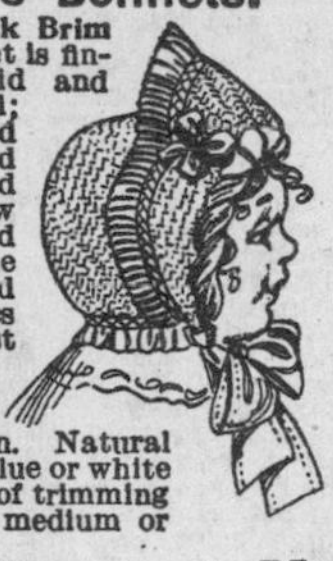

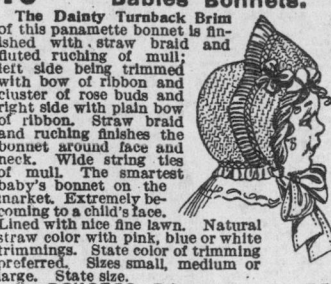

The Dainty Turnback Brim of this panamette bonnet is finished with straw braid and fluted ruching of mull; left side being trimmed with bow of ribbon and cluster of rose buds and right side with plain bow of ribbon. Straw braid and ruching finishes the bonnet around face and neck. Wide string ties of mull. The smartest baby's bonnet on the market. Extremely becoming to a child's face. Lined with nice fine lawn. Natural straw color with pink, blue or white trimmings. State color of trimming preferred. Sizes small, medium or large. State size.

No. 38K8762 Price 75c
If by mail, postage extra, 7 cents.

Poke Bonnets, 42 Cents.
For Children Ages 1 to 5 Years.

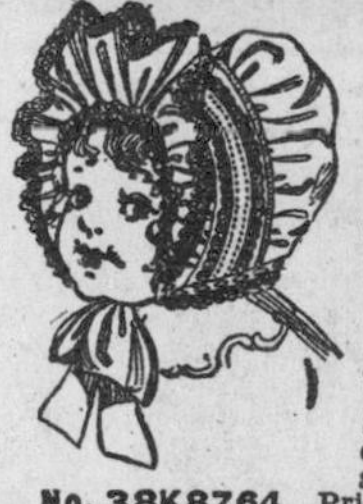

Sheer Lawn Poke Bonnet, daintily trimmed on front and back of crown with hemstitched tucks, edged with narrow valenciennes ruffle. Double valenciennes ruching around face and graduated double ruffle finished with narrow lace. Lace edge with beading at neck. Wide lawn ties. An exquisite bonnet. Color, white, blue or pink. Sizes, small, medium or large. State size and color wanted.

No. 38K8764 Price 42c
If by mail, postage extra, 6 cents.

75c Poke Bonnet, Made of Embroidered Swiss.

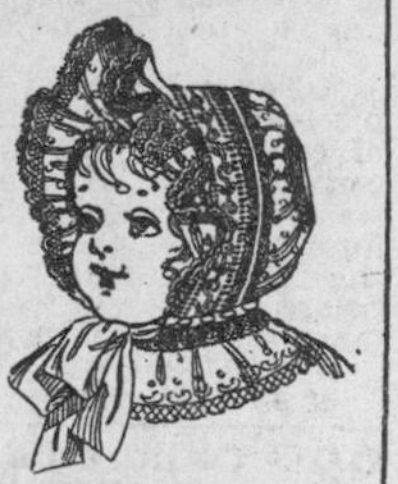

Trimmed around front with band of embroidery insertion and two narrow valenciennes lace ruffles. Ruffles to match around crown. Valenciennes ruching around neck. Double ruching to match around face and two widegraduated ruffles edged with lace. Wide plain lawn ties. Color, white. Sizes, small, medium or large. State size.

No. 38K8766
Price........75c
If by mail, postage extra, 6 cents.

CHILDREN'S NIGHT GOWNS.

AGES 2 TO 14 YEARS.

Girls' Serviceable Gown.

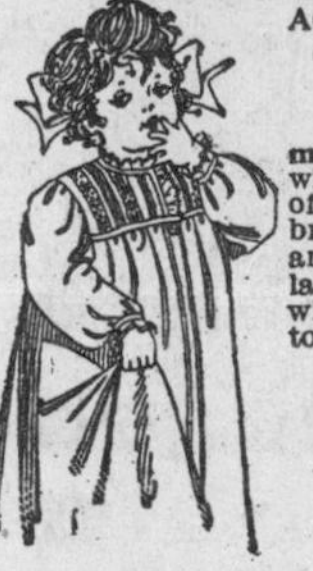

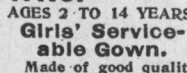

Made of good quality muslin, yoke trimmed with alternating clusters of tucks and rows of embroidery insertion. Neck and sleeves finished with lawn ruffle. Nice width with good hem. Be sure to order by age.

No. 38K8780
Ages, 2 to 8 years.
Price 43c
No. 38K8781
Ages, 10 to 14 years.
Price 50c
If by mail, postage extra, 8 cents.

Good Muslin Gown.

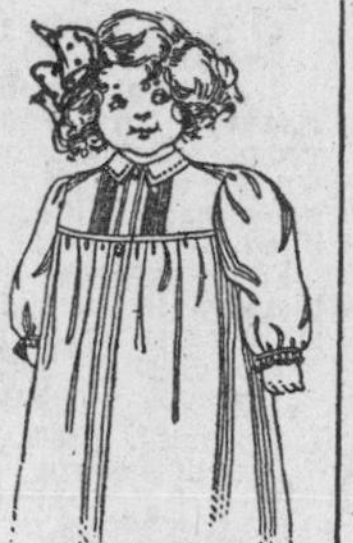

This girls' gown is made with plain yoke in front and back, front with wide cluster of tucks on either side. Neck is finished with plain hemstitched turnover collar; sleeves with lawn ruffle, made nice and wide and well finished. State age.

No. 38K8784
Ages, 2 to 8 years.
Price 63c
No. 38K8785
Ages, 10 to 14 years.
Price 70c
If by mail, postage extra, each, 8c.

Girls' Outing Flannel Gown.

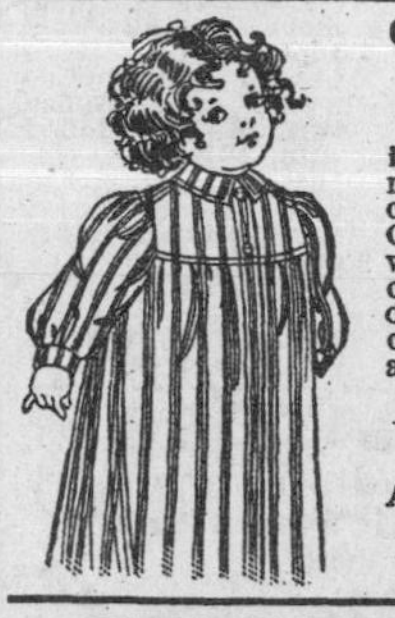

Good quality outing flannel gown, made with turnover collar and plain cuffs. Gown is nice and full with good hem. It comes in either pink, or blue stripe. State color preference and age when ordering.

No. 38K8788
Ages, 2 to 8 years.
Price............39c
No. 38K8789
Ages, 10 to 14 years.
Price............47c
If by mail, postage extra, each, 9c.

GIRLS' DRAWERS.

AGES 2 TO 14 YEARS.

14c Muslin Drawers. 18c

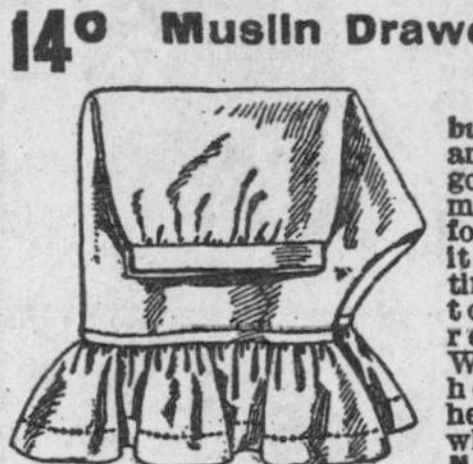

You could not buy the material and make these good quality muslin drawers for the price and it is economy of time and money to buy them ready made. Wide ruffle with hemstitched hem. Give age when ordering.

No. 38K8800
Ages, 2 to 8 years. Price............14c
No. 38K8801 Ages 10 to 14 years.
Price............18c
If by mail, postage extra, each, 4 cents.

21c Trimmed with Neat Embroidery Edge Ruffle. 26c

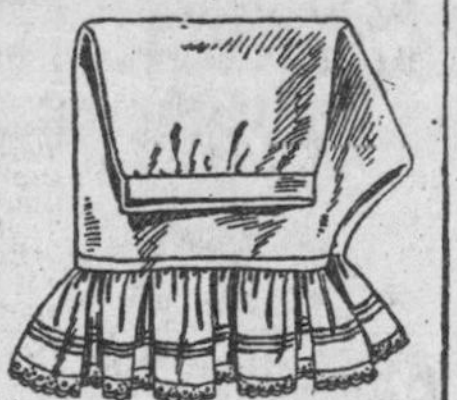

These girls' drawers are excellent value. They are made of good quality muslin and trimmed with cambric ruffle with cluster of small tucks and narrow embroidery edge. State age when ordering.

No. 38K8804
Ages 2 to 8 years. Price............21c
No. 38K8805 Ages, 10 to 14 years.
Price............26c
If by mail, postage extra, each, 4 cents.

29c Dainty Lace Trimmed Drawers. 34c

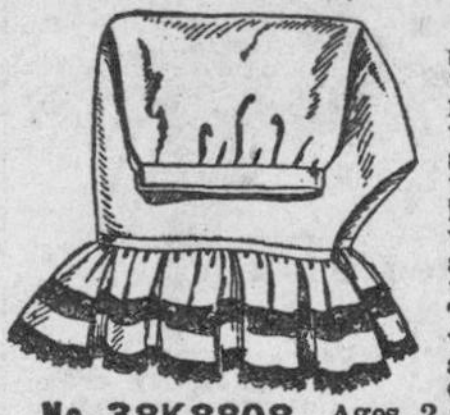

Good quality muslin drawers, trimmed with neat lawn ruffle with row of insertion and lace to match. This is an excellent wearing garment and is just the thing for best. They are very well made and are a rare value. Give age of child.

No. 38K8808 Ages, 2 to 8 years.
Price............29c
No. 38K8809 Ages, 10 to 14 years.
Price............34c
If by mail, postage extra, each, 5 cents.

19c Neatly Trimmed Cambric Drawers. 24c

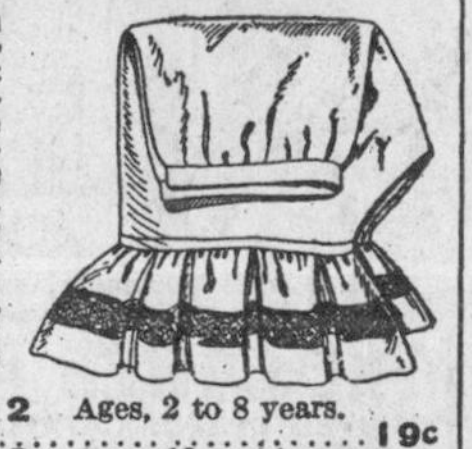

The Ruffle on these good quality cambric drawers is trimmed with wide hem and lace insertion. Ruffle is nice and full and the drawers are very pretty and will wear well. You could not make them at our price. State age when ordering.

No. 38K8812 Ages, 2 to 8 years.
Price............19c
No. 38K8813 Ages, 10 to 14 years.
Price............24c
If by mail, postage extra, each, 5 cents.

29c Trimmed with Tucks all Embroidery. 35c

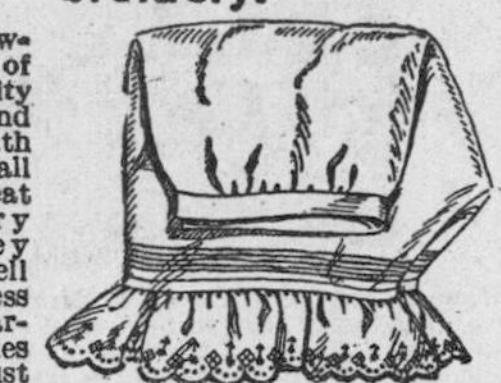

Girls' drawers made of good quality nainsook, and trimmed with cluster of small tucks and neat embroidery ruffle. They are very well made, possess excellent wearing qualities and are just the thing for best. You couldn't buy them elsewhere at our price. Age, please?

No. 38K8816 Ages, 2 to 8 years.
Price............29c
No. 38K8817 Ages, 10 to 14 years.
Price............35c
If by mail, postage extra, each, 5 cents.

GIRLS' SKIRTS.

AGES 4 TO 14 YEARS.

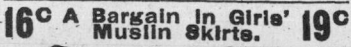

16c A Bargain in Girls' Muslin Skirts. 19c

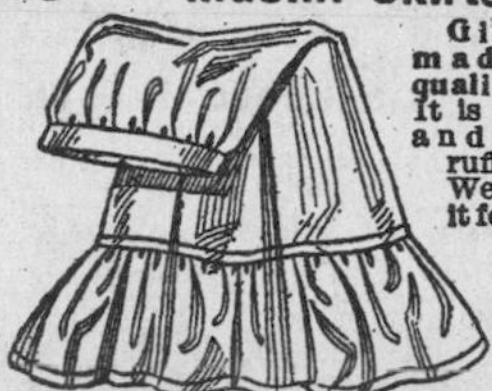

Girls' skirt made of good quality muslin. It is nice and full and has wide ruffle at bottom. We recommend it for its wearing qualities. Just the thing for everyday wear. Of course it is plain and untrimmed, but think of the price! Give age.

No. 38K8850 Ages, 4 to 8 years.
Price............16c
No. 38K8851 Ages, 10 to 14 years.
Price............19c
If by mail, postage extra, each, 5 cents.

29c Made of Good Grade Cambric. 35c

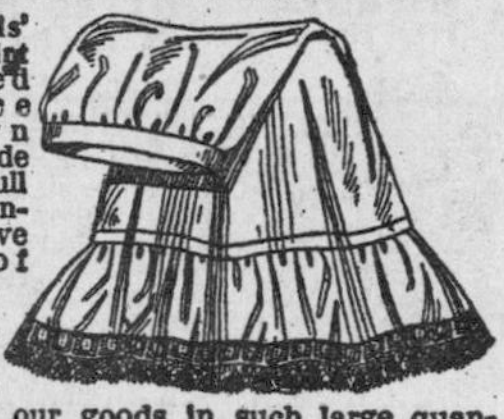

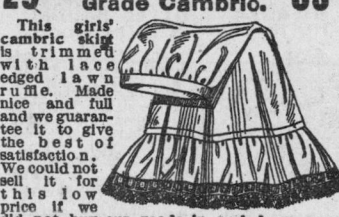

This girls' cambric skirt is trimmed with lace edged lawn ruffle. Made nice and full and we guarantee it to give the best of satisfaction. We could not sell it for this low price if we did not buy our goods in such large quantities. Order by age.

No. 38K8854 Ages, 4 to 8 years.
Price............29c
No. 38K8855 Ages, 10 to 14 years.
Price............35c
If by mail, postage extra, each, 6 cents.

42c Nicely Trimmed Cambric Skirt. 47c

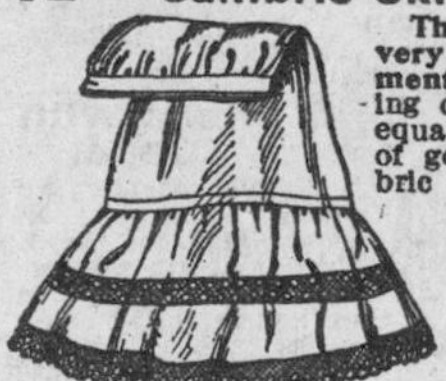

This is not only a very pretty garment, but its wearing qualities are unequaled. It is made of good grade cambric with wide ruffle of same material trimmed with row of insertion and lace to match. Skirt is extra wide. You'll like it. Don't forget to give age.

No. 38K8858 Ages, 4 to 8 years.
Price............42c
No. 38K8859 Ages, 10 to 14 years.
Price............47c
If by mail, postage extra, each, 6 cents.

39c A Nice Skirt at a Pleasing Price. 45c

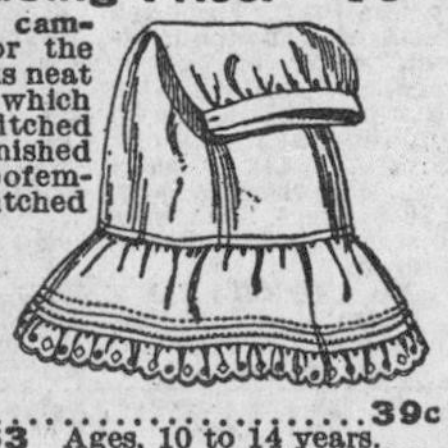

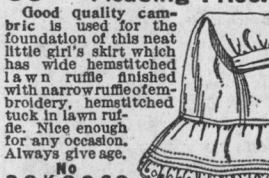

Good quality cambric is used for the foundation of this neat little girl's skirt which has wide hemstitched lawn ruffle finished with narrow ruffle of embroidery, hemstitched tuck in lawn ruffle. Nice enough for any occasion. Always give age.

No. 38K8862 Ages, 4 to 8 years. Price............39c
No. 38K8863 Ages, 10 to 14 years.
Price............45c
If by mail, postage extra, each, 7 cents.

23c Fancy All Wool Zephyr Bootees.

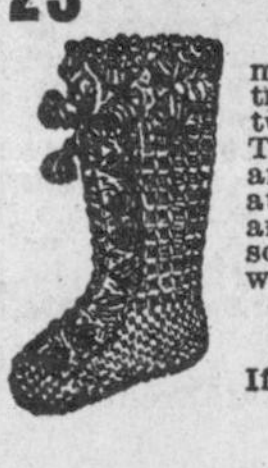

Infant's pretty bootees made of all wool zephyr, and trimmed with mercerized twist which looks like silk. They are very closely knit and have yarn draw strings at top. The colors are white and blue, white and pink, or solid white. State color wanted.

No. 38K9008
Price, per pair.......23c
If by mail, postage extra, per pair, 2 cents.

CHILDREN'S ROMPERS.

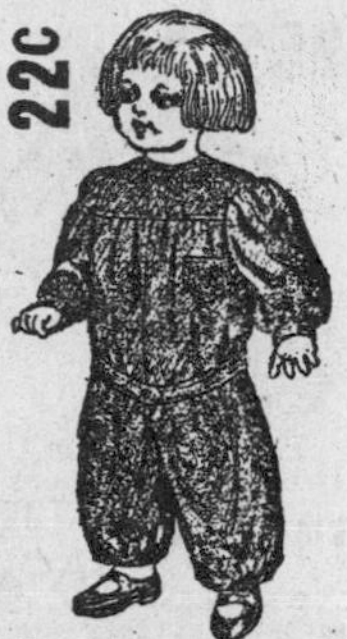

Every child should wear these rompers especially when at play, as they give them freedom of movement. They save clothes. They come in two qualities as described below.

A Romper Only 22 Cents.

Child's rompers made of fancy gingham, has pocket, belt buttoned in back. This is a very desirable garment for little girls or boys; when at play they will save clothes.

A supply of three or four of these rompers will be quite a saving. Ages, 2 to 5 years. Colors, blue or pink. State color and size.

No. 38K8910
Price, ea. 22c; 4 for 85c
If by mail, postage extra, each, 6 cents.

Children's Rompers or Play Suits. 43c

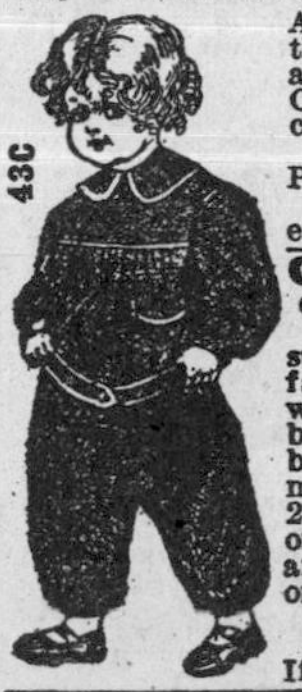

Child's romper or play suit, made of good quality fancy washable gingham, with a yoke to button in back. Has pocket and a belt. A serviceable garment for children, ages 2 to 8 years. Colors, blue or red. Always state color and age wanted when ordering.

No. 38K8914
Price............43c
If by mail, postage extra, 8c.

CHILDREN'S APRONS.

EXCELLENT PROTECTION FOR CHILDREN'S DRESSES.

24c Gingham Apron.

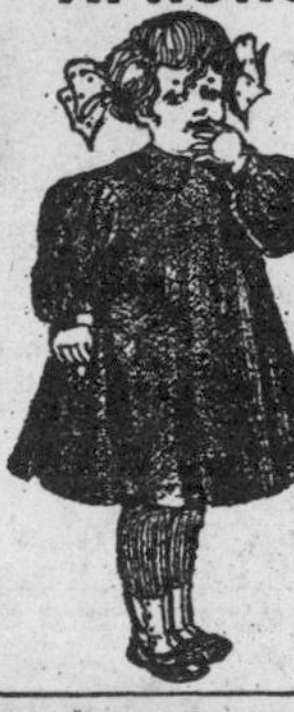

Girls' Allover Apron, made of fancy gingham with slashed collar and belt in back. This apron buttons in the back, made with a pocket. For children, ages 2 to 6 years. Color, blue and brown. Be sure to state color and age when ordering.

No. 38K8916
Price............24c
If by mail, postage extra, 8 cents.

43c Made of Extra Good Quality Gingham

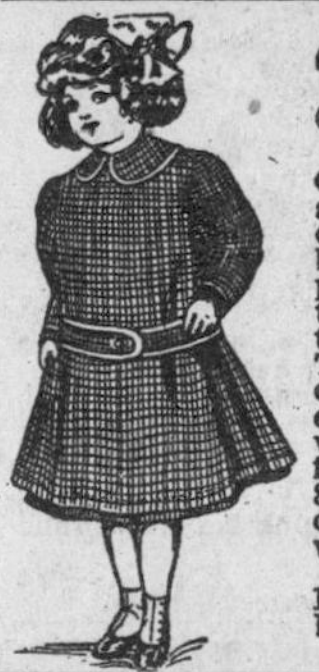

This Fancy Check Gingham Apron is bound around slash turnover collar, turn back cuffs, belt and pocket flap with plain white. Belt extends all around and buttons in front and back. These aprons form an excellent protection to the dress. Colors, blue and white, or red and white, fancy checks. Ages 2 to 8 years. State age of child and color desired when ordering.

No. 38K8918
Price............43c
If by mail, postage extra, 10 cents.

INFANTS' KNIT BOOTEES.

All hand crocheted and seamless. We do not handle machine made bootees, as they are made with raw seams.

10c It Doesn't Pay to Make Them, Does It?

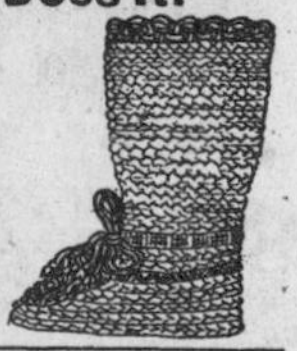

Infants' Pretty Bootees, made of all wool Shetland yarn. They are very closely hand knitted with draw string at ankle of yarn with tassels. Colors, white and pink, white and blue or solid white. Give color desired.

No. 38K9000
Price, per pair.......10c
If by mail, postage extra, per pair, 2 cents.

Nice Mercerized Bootees, 19c.

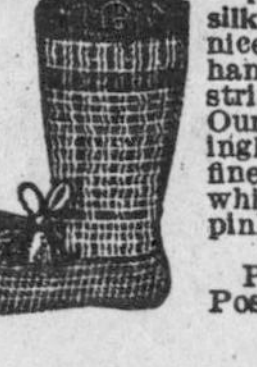

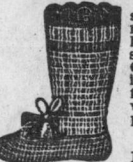

They look, exactly like silk yet they are made of nice mercerized and are hand knitted with draw string and tassel at ankle. Our price on them is exceedingly low considering the fine quality. Colors, solid white, or white with blue or pink. State color desired.

No. 38K9004
Price, per pair...19c
Postage extra, per pair, 2c.

25c Knitted Moccasins.

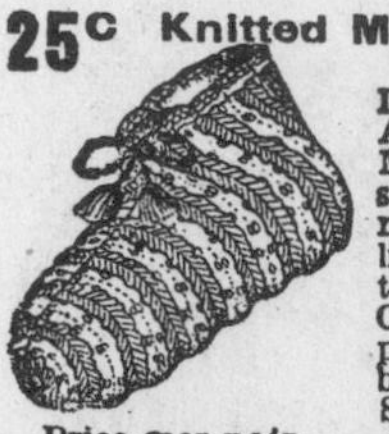

No. 38K2526 Infants' Knitted All Wool Zephyr Moccasins, stitched with mercerized (looks like silk) twist. Has tie strings to match. Colors, white and pink, white and blue or solid white. State color wanted.
Price, per pair 25c
If by mail, postage extra, per pair, 4c.

INFANTS' HAND KNITTED SACQUES.

We quote only the hand made knitted sacques, as they are made seamless—neater and finer than machine made sacques, which are made very coarse and with raw seams.

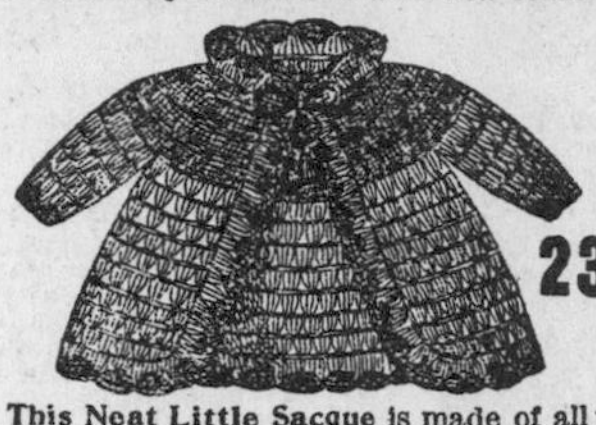

23c

This Neat Little Sacque is made of all wool Shetland yarn with shell border. Crocheted cord with tassels for draw strings at neck. Comes in solid cream, pink and cream and light blue and cream. State color preferred.
No. 38K9050 Price............23c
If by mail, postage extra, 3 cents.

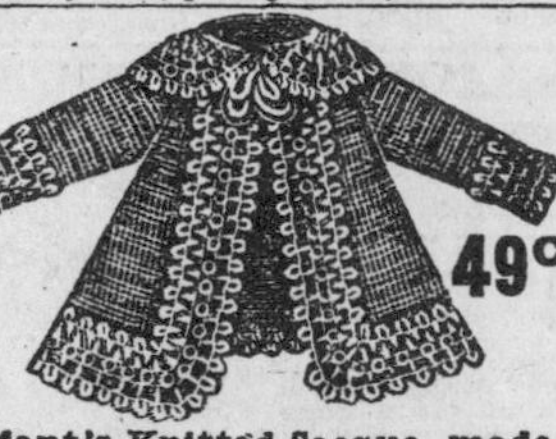

49c

Infant's Knitted Sacque, made of all wool Shetland yarn. Has a fancy border and sleeves to match. Wool tie strings with tassels. Colors, pink or blue with white border, or solid white. Give color wanted.
No. 38K9054 Price........49c
If by mail, postage extra, 8 cents.

Extra Fine Sacque, 87c

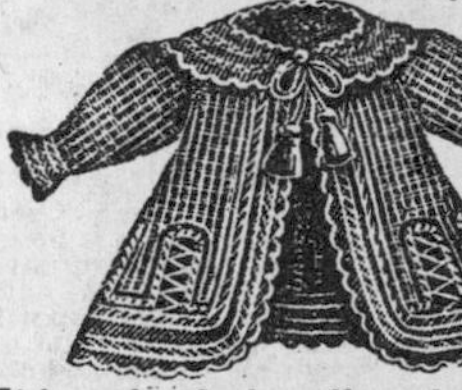

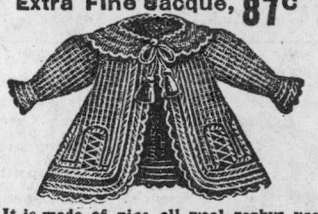

It is made of nice all wool zephyr yarn and is knitted in very neat design with circular shoulder cape. Crocheted beading with cord draw string and tassels at neck. Pretty shaped sleeves with a neat scalloped edge. Very pretty crocheted border with intermingled threads of mercerized twist. Colors, white with either blue or pink border, or solid white. Give color desired.
No. 38K9058 Price............87c
If by mail, postage extra, 8 cents.

Infants' and Children's Knitted Sweaters and Jackets.

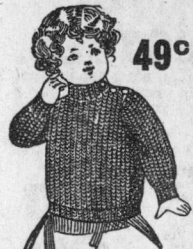

Sizes for Infants, also 1, 2 and 3-year old children.

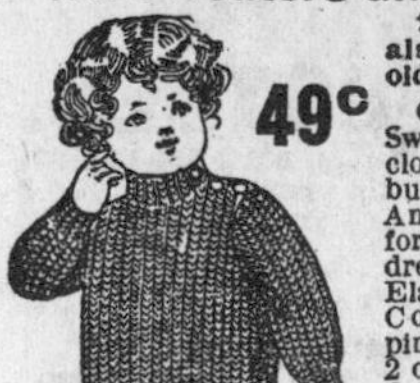

49c

Child's Knitted Sweater. Double closely knitted collar, buttons on shoulder. An excellent garment for infants and children for service. Elastic ribbed cuffs. Colors, pale blue, pink or white, also 1, 2 or 3-year old children. Be sure to give size and color desired.
No. 38K9080
Price..........49c
If by mail, postage extra, 9 cents.

48c Child's Wool Knitted Jacket.

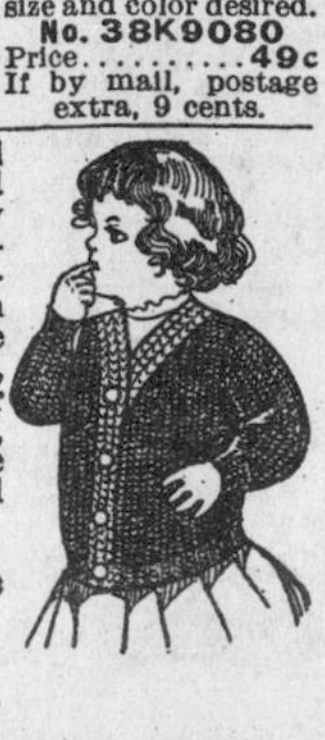

Very closely knitted collar, and facing in contrasting colors. Buttoned with pearl buttons. A nice garment for infants, also 1, 2 and 3-year old children. Colors, pale blue or pink. Be sure to give age and color.
No. 38K9084
Price..........48c
If by mail, postage extra, 9 cents.

87c Baby Carriage or Go-Cart Blankets.

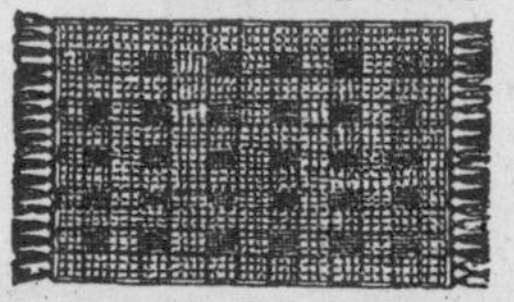

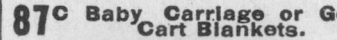

Baby Carriage or Go-Cart Blankets. Knitted of all worsted Shetland wool yarns. Fancy knotted fringe. Can also be used as a wrap for baby. Colors are white and pink or baby blue designs in the form of squares. Size, 32x28 inches. State color desired.
No. 38K2107 Price............87c
If by mail, postage, extra, 8 cents.

21c Infants' and Children's Combination Knitted Legging Drawers.

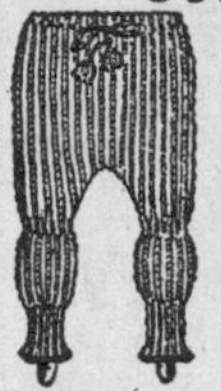

Combination Knitted Legging Drawers. Has wool draw string and tassel at waist. Closely knitted. For 6 months, 1, 2 and 3-year old children. Colors white or black. Be sure to give age and color.
No. 38K9090 Price, per pair..................21c
If by mail, postage extra, per pair, 7 cents.

42c Made of Nice Soft Yarn.

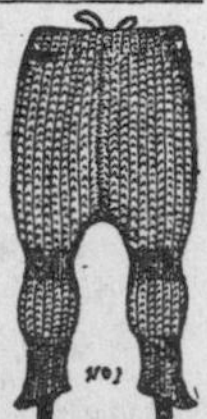

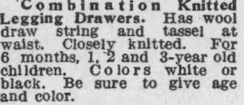

Knitted Legging Drawers, knitted of soft yarns. Very closely knitted. Exceptionally fine and warm legging drawers for children, ages, 6 months, 1, 2 or 3 years. Colors, white or black. Be sure to give age and color.
No. 38K9092 Price, per pair..................42c
If by mail, postage extra, per pair, 9 cents.

INFANTS' KNITTED HOODS. Our 15-Cent Knitted Hood.

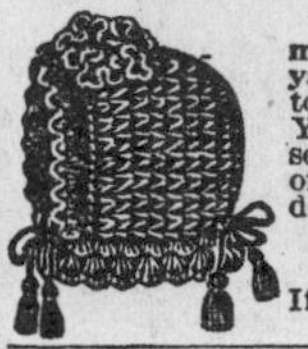

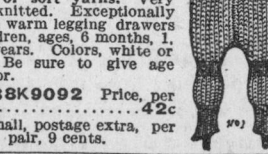

Infant's Knitted Hood, made of all wool zephyr yarn. Ruffled yarn on top, flounced at the neck. Yarn tie strings with tassels. Colors, white, pink or pale blue. State color desired.
No. 38K9100
Price..............15c
If by mail, postage extra, 4 cents.

23c All Wool Knitted Hood.

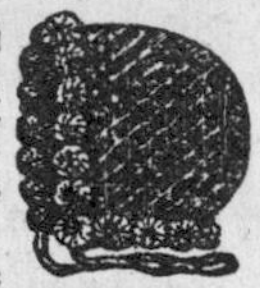

Infant's Knitted Hood, made of all wool Shetland yarn, trimmed with mercerized twist. Trimmed around face and neck with pompons made of Shetland floss. All wool tie strings at neck. Colors, cream, sky blue or pink. State color desired.
No. 38K9104
Price..............23c
If by mail, postage extra, 5c.

39c Hood with Cape.

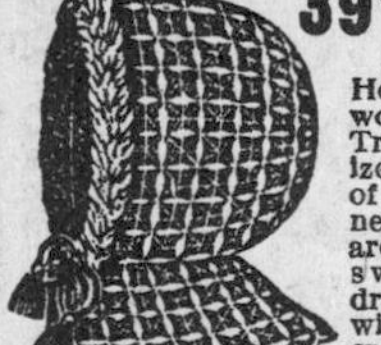

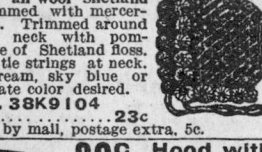

Child's Knitted Hood, made of all wool Shetland yarn. Trimmed with mercerized twist in the form of squares. Has wide neck cape. Trimmed around face with white swansdown. Wool draw strings at neck, with tassels. Colors, cream or sky blue. State color desired.
No. 38K9110 Price..............39c
If by mail, postage extra, 6 cents.

63c A Novelty, Toque Style.

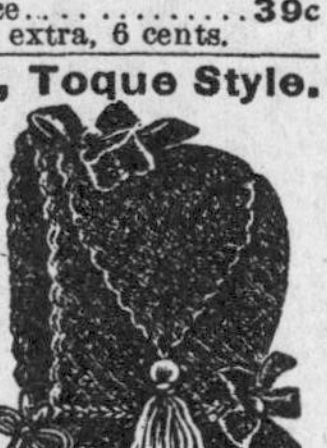

A Very Pretty Designed Hood with the toque effect, made of zephyr yarn, and knitted with twist, has ribbon bow on top and back. Colors, cardinal, pink or navy blue. For children, ages 2 to 6 years. Be sure to state color and size desired.
No. 38K9122
Price.........63c
If by mail, postage extra, 6 cents.

GIRLS' HOODS.
Suitable for Girls 6 to 12 Years.

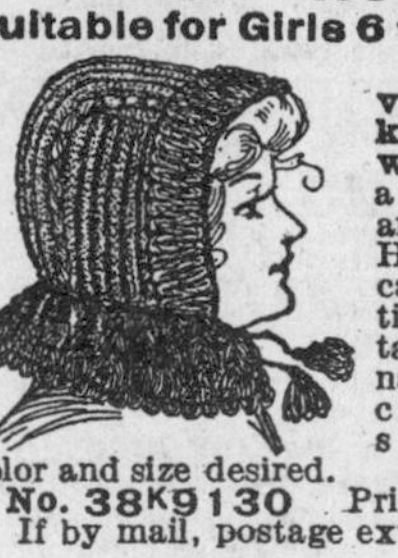

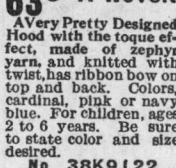

Girl's Hood, very closely knitted of all wool yarn. Has a ruffle of wool around the front. Has a wide neck cape and wool tie string with tassels. Colors, navy blue or cardinal. Be sure to state color and size desired.
No. 38K9130 Price.......39c
If by mail, postage extra, 7 cents.

LADIES' HOODS.

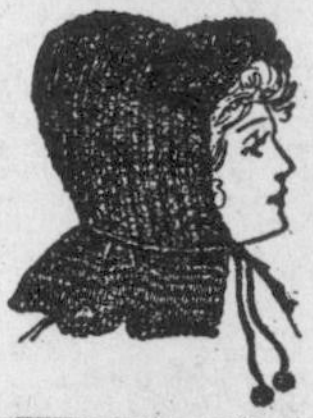

Ladies' Hood, knitted of wool yarn. Ruffled top and has a wide neck cape. Fleece lined. Colors, navy blue, cardinal or black. Be sure to state color desired.
No. 38K9134
Price.......48c
If by mail, postage extra, 9 cents.

$1.23 Zephyr Yarn.

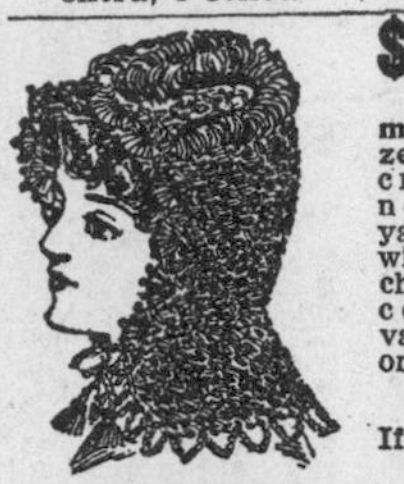

Ladies' Hood, made of all wool zephyr yarn. Hand crocheted. Wide neck cape, ruffled yarn on top. Lined with closely crocheted yarn. Exceptionally good value. Color, black only.
No. 38K9136
Price......$1.23
If by mail, postage extra, 9 cents.

FASCINATORS.

These Fascinators are very useful in all seasons of the year.

23c

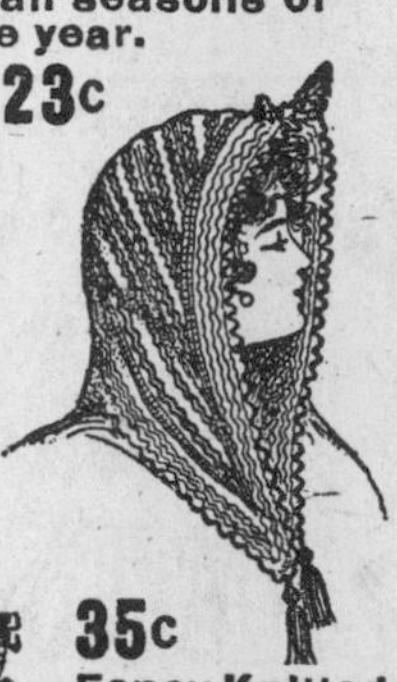

Fancy Knitted Fascinator with ruffled yarn on top, fleece lined. Wool tassel at each end. Colors, cream with blue, pink or black. State color desired.
No. 38K9210
Price .23c
If by mail, postage extra, 9 cents.

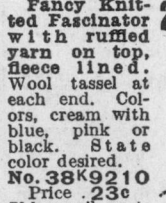

35c Fancy Knitted Fascinator.

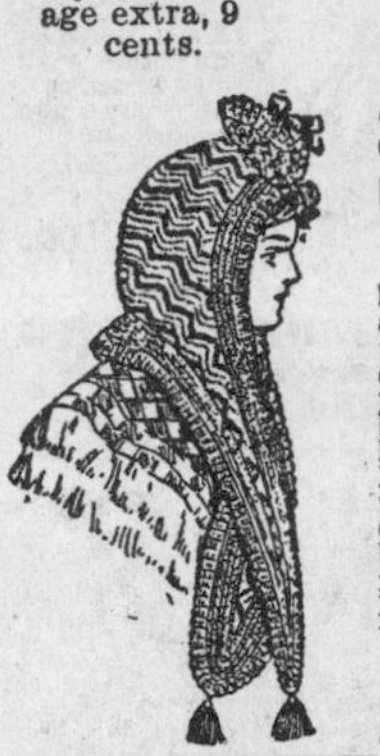

Ladies' Fascinator, knitted with worsted and mercerized cotton yarns in zigzag designs. Fancy pompon on top with ribbon rosette. A fancy lace effect border. Fleece lined. Has a tassel at each end. Colors, white with black, pink or blue mercerized stitching. Don't forget to mention color.
No. 38K9212
Price........35c
If by mail, postage extra, 9 cents.

68c Imported Ice Wool Fascinator.

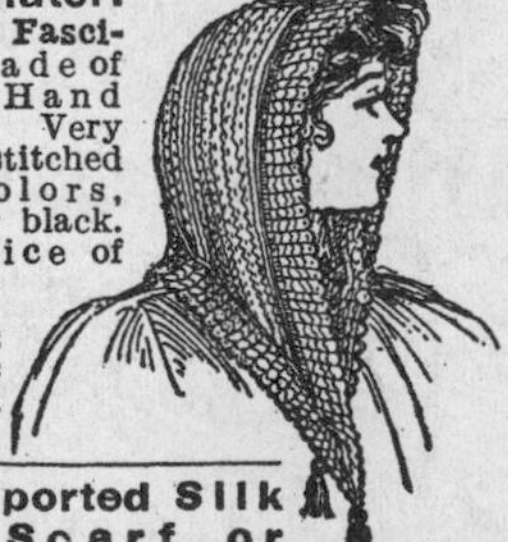

Ladies' Fascinator. Made of ice wool. Hand crocheted. Very neatly stitched border. Colors, cream or black. Your choice of color.
No. 38K9218
Price, 68c
Postage extra, 10c.

Fine Imported Silk Head Scarf or Shoulder Shawl.

79c

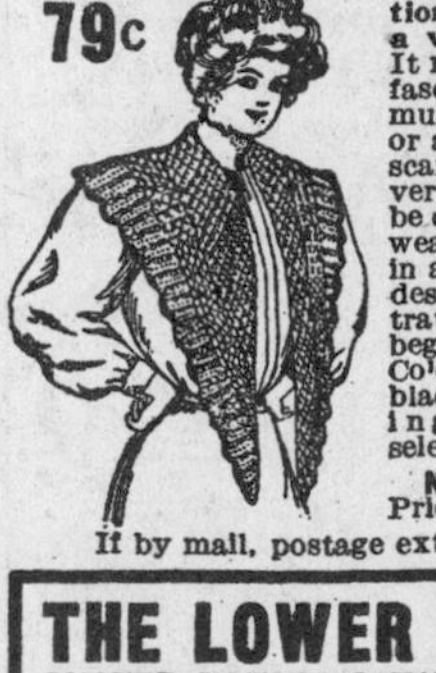

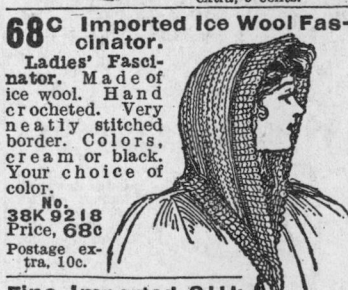

This dainty creation may be worn in a variety of ways. It may be worn as a fascinator, as a neck muffler inside of coat, or as a light shoulder scarf. It is not only very stylish but very becoming to the wearer. It is knitted in a beautiful raised design and the illustration does not begin to do it justice. Colors, cream or black. When ordering give color selection.
No. 38K9220
Price..........79c
If by mail, postage extra, 8 cents.

THE LOWER PRICES
QUOTED IN THIS CATALOGUE will be more interesting to you than the prices quoted by any other firm or individual.

21c Infant's Knitted Toque.

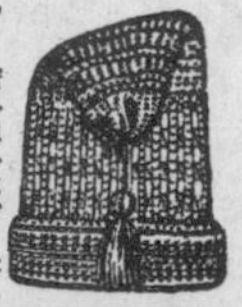

Infants' Toques, made of all wool. Nice wide turnover which can be pulled over the ears. All wool tassel. Colors are blue, pink or red stripes. State color desired.
No. 38K9650 Price, 21c
If by mail, postage extra, 4c.

22c Children's Toque.

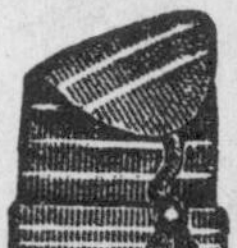

Wool Toque with fancy stripe. Has a fancy tassel to match. Length of toque, 15 inches. Colors, cardinal, white or navy blue with stripes in contrasting colors. State color desired.
No. 38K9658 Price, 22c
If by mail, postage extra, 7c.

39c Children's Toques.

Be sure to state color when ordering.

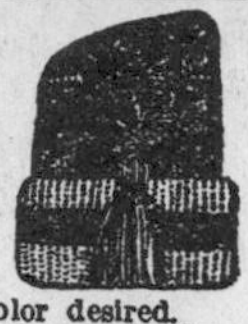

A very fine Double Toque, made of soft wool yarn, with wool tassel to match. Length of toque, 17 inches. Colors, navy blue, red or white, with stripes in contrasting colors. State color desired.
No. 38K9662 Price..........39c
If by mail, postage extra, 8 cents.

59c Ladies' Hand Crocheted Slippers.

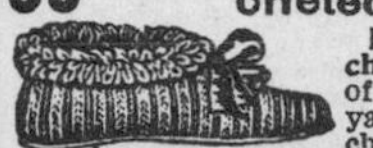

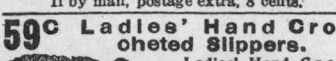

Ladies' Hand Crocheted Slippers, made of fine all wool knitting yarn, with fancy crocheted top and satin ribbon bows. This slipper is made with the genuine peerless lamb's wool soles. Colors, cardinal, blue or black. Sizes, 2 to 7. State color and size desired. Exceptionally good value.
No. 38K9680 Price, per pair....59c
If by mail, postage extra, per pair, 12 cents.

Knitted Underskirt, 98c

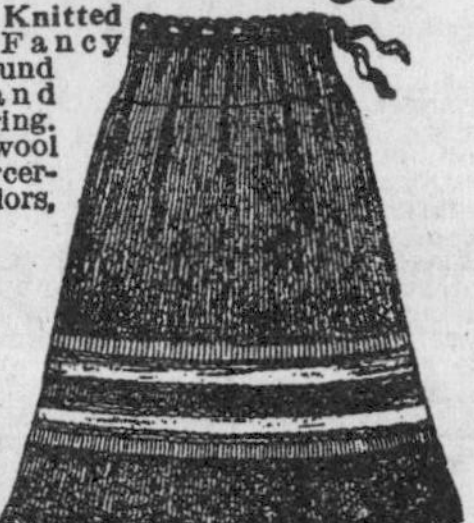

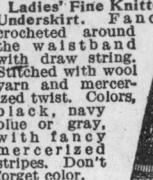

Ladies' Fine Knitted Underskirt. Fancy crocheted around the waistband with draw string. Stitched with wool yarn and mercerized twist. Colors, black, navy blue or gray, with fancy mercerized stripes. Don't forget color.
No. 38K9690
Price....98c
If by mail, postage extra, 15 cents.

Knitted Underskirt 87c

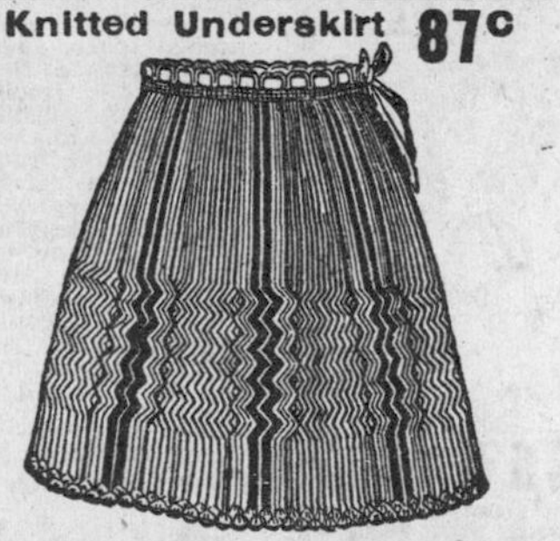

A Fancy Knitted Underskirt. Very nicely designed in stripes. Combination of colors in zigzag pattern with mercerized yarn. Has a fancy crocheted waistband with an insertion of tape forming draw string. Crocheted around the bottom with mercerized twist. Colors, gray with either blue or red fancy stripes. Always state color.
No. 38K9692 Price......87c
If by mail, postage extra, 16 cents.

32c Children's Knitted Underskirts.

Ages, 2, 3 and 4 years.

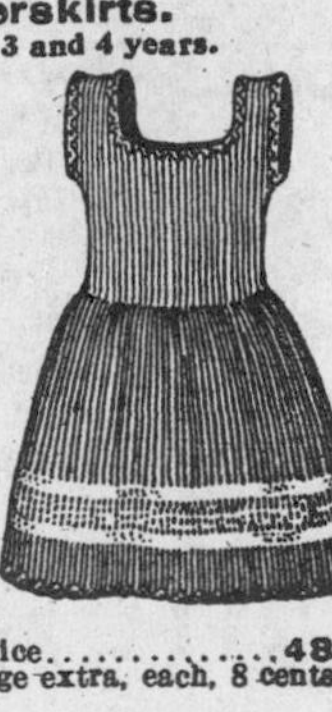

Children's Knit Underskirt, made of good quality wool yarn. Has fitted bodice and shoulder straps. Stitched with mercerized twist. Colors are gray with red stripes around bottom, or sky blue with pink stripes. Be sure to give color when ordering.
No. 38K9696
Age 2 years.
Price......32c
No. 38K9697
Age 3 years.
Price......39c
No. 38K9698
Age 4 years. Price..................48c
If by mail, postage extra, each, 8 cents.

YOUR MONEY WILL BE IMMEDIATELY RETURNED TO YOU FOR ANY GOODS NOT PERFECTLY SATISFACTORY.

691

STRICTLY NEW STYLES OF WAISTS AND SKIRTS, JUST OUT

SIZES: Bust measure, 32 to 42 inches; waist measure, 22 to 30 inches; front length of skirt, 37 to 44 inches.

WAIST 27K6695
SKIRT 27K3435

WAIST 27K6690
SKIRT 27K3445

WAIST 27K6680
SKIRT 27K3455

WAIST 27K6700
SKIRT 27K3300

WAIST 27K6685
SKIRT 27K3465

$4.95 A BEAUTIFUL LACE WAIST ELABORATELY TRIMMED WITH CLUNY LACE. Valenciennes lace and blas folds of liberty silk as shown in illustration; allover lace medallion on front of waist at neck. The medallion is made of silk lace edged with cluny lace and fold of silk extend over shoulders and to waist line in back. Kimono sleeve, under sleeve is elbow length. Waist is lined with Jap silk and buttons in back. Very dressy. Be sure to give bust measure when ordering. Price
No. 27K6695 Color, ecru......$4.95
No. 27K6696 Color, white......4.95
If by mail, postage extra, 18 cents.

$4.75 A VERY NOBBY SKIRT MADE OF PANAMA CLOTH IN THE PLAITED STYLE HERE ILLUSTRATED, and trimmed on bias taffeta bands. It has plain gores with self material, and self colored bands. It is a five-gored model, which flares gracefully about the hips, and is finished with heart bottom. All seams are bound. Don't forget to give waist measure and front length of skirt when ordering. Price
No. 27K3435 Color, black......$4.75
No. 27K3436 Color, blue......4.75
No. 27K3437 Color, brown......4.75
If by mail, postage extra, 28 cents.

$3.98 AN EXQUISITELY DAINTY WAIST MADE OF FINE JAP SILK IN SURPLICE EFFECT and handsomely trimmed with wide insertion and valenciennes insertion and lace. Elbow sleeves with lapers, made of Jap silk and back of waist are made exactly alike. Collar and cuffs are trimmed with frill of narrow valenciennes lace to match insertion. Buttons in back. Jap silk is very fashionable this season. Don't fail to give bust measure when ordering. Price
No. 27K6690 Color, white......$3.98
No. 27K6691 Color, ecru......3.98
If by mail, postage extra, 16 cents.

$4.95 A VERY ATTRACTIVE STYLE IS BROUGHT OUT IN THIS GOOD GRADE PANAMA SKIRT. Front gore is ornamented with six self covered buttons. Two wide bias folds of self material extend from either side of front gore around to back; folds being trimmed with two narrow bias bands of self colored taffeta. The waist is excellently tailored, with hem at bottom, and has band at waistband. Give waist measure and front length when ordering. Price
No. 27K3445 Color, black......$4.95
No. 27K3446 Color, navy blue......4.95
No. 27K3447 Color, brown......4.95
If by mail, postage extra, 30 cents.

$3.50 ANOTHER LACE WAIST THAT WILL PLEASE YOU. It is the acme of elegant simplicity. It is made of fine, soft net, the only trimming being the wide bands of lace up the front with fine shoulder sleeves on three-quarter sleeve. Waist is tucked in front and back to yoke depth between bands of insertion. Two bands of insertion in back. The Japanese sleeve is finished with wide fold of silk; undersleeve is elbow length and has cuff to match collar. Lined with Jap silk. Buttons in back. Mention size.
No. 27K6680 Color, white......$3.50
No. 27K6681 Color, ecru......3.50
If by mail, postage extra, 15 cents.

$5.75 FOR DRESSY OCCASIONS THIS LACE WAIST HAS NO EQUAL. It is made of a beautiful, fine net, tucked on sleeves and body of waist as shown in illustration, and elaborately trimmed with wide lace and insertion. Collar and cuffs on three-quarter sleeves are trimmed with lace. This waist is patterned after one of the latest models, finished with shoulder effect. Buttons in back. Lined with Jap silk. Be sure to give bust measure when ordering. Price
No. 27K6700 Color, ecru......$5.75
No. 27K6701 Color, white......5.75
If by mail, postage extra, 16 cents.

$3.75 AN UNUSUALLY PRETTY STYLE IS THIS SURPLICE EFFECT LACE WAIST. Surplice effect and Japanese sleeve is formed by frill of cluny and valenciennes lace. Frill of valenciennes lace on three-quarter sleeve. Yoke, shoulder tabs, collar and cuffs are of the net tucked in squares, finished with heavy beading and valenciennes lace. Lace medallion on front of yoke. Lined with Jap silk. Buttons in back. Give bust measure.
No. 27K6685 Color, white......$3.75
No. 27K6686 Color, ecru......3.75
If by mail, postage extra, 19 cents.

$5.75 THIS HANDSOME CHIFFON PANAMA SKIRT IS AN EXCELLENT VALUE. The illustration gives you an exact idea of the style, but cannot do justice to the quality of material. It is a chiffon panama in the full plaited model, and is trimmed in an extremely pretty plaited model, and is trimmed with six narrow bias bands of self colored taffeta. The tailoring is perfect, skirt being hemmed at bottom, and having finished seams. Give waist measure and front length of skirt when ordering. Price
No. 27K3465 Color, black......$5.75
No. 27K3466 Color, navy blue......5.75
No. 27K3467 Color, brown......5.75
If by mail, postage extra, 28 cents.

$4.50 ONE OF THE NOBBIEST SKIRTS SHOWN THIS SEASON. It is made of fine quality chiffon panama in the full plaited style illustrated, and is handsomely trimmed with one wide and two narrower bias folds of taffeta silk. It flares gracefully at bottom and fits perfectly at hips. Well tailored, with finished seams and hem at bottom. Give waist measure and front length of skirt when ordering. Price
No. 27K3300 Color, black......$4.50
No. 27K3301 Color, navy blue......4.50
No. 27K3302 Color, brown......4.50
If by mail, postage extra, 45 cents.

JUMPER SUITS, SHIRTWAIST SUITS AND THREE SPECIAL SKIRT BARGAINS

INFORMATION ON SIZES CAN BE HAD ON REGULAR PAGES.

$4.55 THERE IS NOTHING MORE STYLISH THAN ONE OF THESE PLAITED PANAMA SKIRTS. The material is of an extra good quality, and the style is one that is becoming to all figures. The plaits which extend all the way around to back are very deep. It is making the garment nice and full, around giving a graceful flare so desirable. It is trimmed around bottom with three bias bands of taffeta to match the skirt in color. Skirt is well made, and it is finished at bottom with deep hem. It will wear like iron, and we guarantee it to give satisfaction. Average sweep is 3½ yards. Don't fail to give waist measure and front length of skirt, when ordering.

No. 27K3401 Color, navy blue.
Price **$4.55**
No. 27K3402 Color, brown. Price **$4.55**
No. 27K3403 Color, gray. Price **$4.55**
If by mail, postage extra, 35 cents.

$5.75 THE BLACK TAFFETA FOLDS ON THIS FINE QUALITY VOILE SKIRT give it an air of elegance, and they are applied in the very latest style. The plain front panel gives the desirable long lines to the figure, and makes it equally suitable for stout or slender women. Wide fold is ornamented on front with two silk covered buttons. The tailoring on this garment is perfect, all the seams being neatly bound, and skirt being hemmed at bottom. We know that you will like it and you will vote it one of the best values you ever purchased. Average sweep, 3½ yards. When ordering give waist measure and length of skirt in front.

No. 27K3700 Color, black. Price **$5.75**
No. 27K3701 Color, navy blue. Price **5.75**
No. 27K3702 Color, brown. Price **5.75**
(Postage extra, 32c.).

$3.35 THIS NOBBY SKIRT IS MADE OF A HIGH GRADE SICILIAN in a five-gored style, with plain front panel and two folds around each side extending all the way around to back. The deep side plaits at seams give the garment plenty of fullness and make it flare prettily. The tailoring on this garment is perfect, all the seams being bound and bottom hemmed. We know that you will like it and you will vote it one of the best values you ever purchased. Average sweep, 3½ yards. When ordering give waist measure and length of skirt in front.

No. 27K3230 Color, black. **$3.35**
No. 27K3231 Color, navy blue.
Price **3.35**
No. 27K3232 Color, brown. **3.35**
No. 27K3233 Color, gray. **3.35**
No. 27K3234 Color, white. **3.35**
If by mail, postage extra, 30 cents.

$2.98 VERY DAINTY SHIRTWAIST SUIT made of fine white lawn and elaborately trimmed with embroidery and valenciennes insertion as shown in illustration; waist is tucked in front and back to yoke depth; tucked stock collar edged with valenciennes lace; three-quarter or full length sleeve. Sleeve has tucked cuff finished with insertion and lace; waist buttons in back. Skirt is shirred at waist and has deep tucked flounce headed by insertion. Flounce is made with finished seams and hemmed at bottom; flounce has 4-yard sweep; detached belt. When ordering don't fail to mention waist and bust measure and skirt length.

No. 27K1940 Color, white with ¾ sleeves. Price **2.98**
No. 27K1941 Color, white, with full length sleeves. Price **2.98**
If by mail, postage extra, 25 cents.

$2.75 A VERY NOBBY JUMPER SUIT OF POLKA DOT CHALLY, a beautiful soft finished washable material, and neatly trimmed with fancy border of self material as shown in illustration. The jumper is made in surplice effect and trimmed with fancy braid. This suit does not include waist. Skirt measures 3½ yards. Don't fail to state waist and bust measure and length of skirt in front when ordering.

No. 27K1850 Color, navy blue with white dots.
Price **$2.75**
No. 27K1851 Color, white with navy blue dots.
Price **2.75**
If by mail, postage extra, 25 cents.

$2.75 DAINTY CHECKED GINGHAM JUMPER SUIT trimmed around V neck and on Japanese sleeve with band of white embroidery, front of jumper is tucked to yoke depth; the three tucks on either side. Seven-gored skirt has side plaits at every seam and is trimmed around bottom with 2-inch self fold; has width with deep hem and measures 4 yards around. Waist is trimmed with lace as shown in illustration and buttons in back. Always give bust and waist measure and skirt length when ordering. Suit does not include shirtwaist.

No. 27K1830 Color, blue and white checks. Price, **$2.75**
No. 27K1831 Color, pink and white checks. Price, **2.75**
If by mail, postage extra, 25 cents.

$3.95 NEAT SURPLICE JUMPER SUIT of polka dot fast colored lawn or percale. It is finished on kimono sleeve, around neck and front with embroidered scallops. It buttons in front. The nine-gored skirt is made as illustrated, with seam and is finished with inverted plaits in back; is finished around. Suit is trimmed with buttons as shown in illustration and buttons in back. Be sure to state bust and waist measure and front skirt length when ordering.

No. 27K2020 Color, white with black dots. Price, **$3.95**
No. 27K2021 Color, white with red dots. Price, **3.95**
If by mail, postage extra, 30 cents.

YOUR MONEY WILL BE IMMEDIATELY RETURNED TO YOU FOR ANY GOODS NOT PERFECTLY SATISFACTORY.

693

HERE IS A PAGE OF SPLENDID JACKETS QUOTED AT ASTONISHINGLY LOW PRICES

SIZES, 32 to 42 inches bust measure. Larger sizes can be made to order for 20 per cent above the regular catalogue price.

No. 17K2080

$8.75 THIS JAUNTY JACKET IS MADE OF GOOD QUALITY ALL WOOL COVERT with fitted back; half fitted fly front. It is neatly trimmed with self strapping and buttons as shown in illustration; coat shaped collar and lapels; plain coat sleeves trimmed in cuff effect with self strapping and buttons; lined throughout with good grade satin. Length, 24 inches. Be sure to state bust measure.

No. 17K2080 Color, castor. **$8.75**
Price.....
If by mail, postage extra, 48 cents.

No. 17K2070

$7.50 NOBBY ALL WOOL BROADCLOTH JACKET made with half fitted back and fly front; plain sleeves, stitched on cuffs; coat shaped collar and lapels and two slash pockets with pointed tabs; trimmed with silk braid as shown in illustration. It is lined throughout with satin. Length, 21 inches. An excellent value. Give bust measure, please.

No. 17K2070 Color, black. **$7.50**
Price.....
If by mail, postage extra, 43 cents.

No. 17K2010

$4.75 NEAT COAT MADE OF LIGHT WEIGHT CHEVIOT with coat shaped collar and lapels, and plain coat sleeves; half fitted back with short vents at side seams; two slash pockets with flaps and is trimmed with silk braid as illustrated. Length, 23 inches. An excellent value.

No. 17K2010 Color, black. **$4.75**
Price.....
No. 17K2011 Color, brown. **$4.75**
Price.....
If by mail, postage extra, 43 cents.

No. 17K2030

$4.98 CHIC HALF FITTED JACKET of good grade covert cloth with stitched down collar and lapels, collar being trimmed with three rows of silk soutache; cuff effect on plain coat sleeves is finished with two buttons; fitted back trimmed with pointed tabs and buttons; fly front; jacket is lined with satin. Length, 22 inches. Always give bust measure when ordering.

No. 17K2030 Color, castor. **$4.98**
Price.....
If by mail, postage extra, 42 cents.

No. 17K2040

$5.95 BOX COATS ARE VERY POPULAR THIS SEASON and this one made of good quality covert is neatly trimmed with self strapping. It is made with coat shaped collar and lapels; stitched down with turn back cuffs; fly front. Unlined. Length, 26 inches. A very comfortable garment. You'll like it. Be sure to state bust measure when ordering.

No. 17K2040 Color, castor. **$5.95**
Price.....
If by mail, postage extra, 44 cents.

No. 17K2060

$6.75 ANOTHER STYLISH COVERT COAT MADE WITH FITTED BACK and trimmed with self strapping and buttons; half fitted front; coat shaped collar and lapels; stitched down cuff effect finished with buttons on plain sleeves. Coat is lined throughout with satin. Length, 21 inches. Always remember to give bust-measure.

No. 17K2060 Color, castor. **$6.75**
Price.....
If by mail, postage extra, 43 cents.

No. 17K2000

$3.75 STYLISH BOX COAT MADE OF COVERT CLOTH with inlaid velvet collar trimmed with self strapping and coat shaped lapels; turn-back cuffs; two patch pockets with three narrow straps of self material; new shaped sleeves; unlined. Length, 27 inches. Don't forget to give bust measure when ordering.

No. 17K2000 Color, castor. **$3.75**
Price.....
If by mail, postage extra, 40 cents.

No. 17K2090

$8.50 SWAGGER COAT MADE OF GOOD QUALITY BROADCLOTH. It is double breasted and made with half fitted back; has deep vent at center back seam; half military collar of inlaid taffeta trimmed with three rows of soutache; one breast pocket; plain sleeves with fancy turnback cuffs; cuffs trimmed with silk braid and two rows of soutache braid as illustrated; satin lined. Length, 24 inches. Bust measure, please?

No. 17K2090 Color, black. **$8.50**
Price.....
If by mail, postage extra, 44 cents.

No. 17K2050

$5.95 THIS SMART COAT IS MADE OF ALL WOOL FANCY MIXTURE. It is artistically trimmed with self strapping and fancy buttons; inlaid velvet collar; coat shaped lapels; half fitted back with vent at center seam; fly front with two slash pockets finished with flap; turn-back cuffs trimmed with button. Coat is unlined, and measures 25 inches. Don't fail to state bust measure when ordering.

No. 17K2050 Color, gray plaid mixture. **$5.95**
Price.....
If by mail, postage extra, 42 cents.

No. 17K2020

$4.75 JAUNTY COVERT CLOTH COAT is made with half-fitted back with deep vents at side seams and trimmed with self strapping as shown in illustration; coat is made with four pockets finished with tabs which button. Coat shaped collar and lapels; fly front; plain coat sleeves; lined throughout with Romaine silk. Length, 24 inches. Don't fail to state bust measure when ordering.

No. 17K2020 Color, castor. **$4.75**
Price.....
If by mail, postage extra, 45 cents.

OUR LINE OF LONG COATS SHOWS A WONDERFUL VARIETY IN STYLE, FINISH AND MATERIAL

SIZES, 32 to 42 inches bust measure. Larger sizes will be made to order for 20 per cent more than regular price.

OUR TREMENDOUS SALES OF WEARING APPAREL ENABLE US TO NAME THE WONDERFULLY LOW PRICES QUOTED ON EVERY PAGE OF THIS WEARING APPAREL SECTION OF OUR CATALOGUE.

Sizes, 32 to 42 inches bust measure.

No. 17K2600 $6.75   No. 17K2370 $5.75   No. 17K2650 $12.00   No. 17K2450 $7.75 $6.50

No. 17K2600   No. 17K2601   No. 17K2370   No. 17K2500   No. 17K2330   No. 17K2550   No. 17K2650   No. 17K2450   No. 17K2400

$6.75 THIS HANDSOME COAT, made of broadcloth, is elaborately embroidered with silk cord. It is double breasted loose style. The stitched shawl collar is in the popular loose style; has laid with velvet trimmed with silk braid and rows of silk soutache braid. The straps of self material which extend over the shoulders are finished with velvet and soutache to match collar; turn back cuff effect; two patch pockets with stitch down tabs; side vents. Length, 45 inches. Coat is unlined. When ordering be sure to give bust measure.

No. 17K2600. Color, black. Price.. **$6.75**
No. 17K2601. Color, brown. Price.. **6.75**
Postage on brown coat, 52c. Black, not mailable.

$5.75 A VERY SERVICEABLE COAT is made of wool covert cloth in double breasted loose style. The shawl collar is trimmed on collar effect with inlaid velvet, silk braid and rows of silk soutache; fullness in sleeves is laid and sleeves in three box plaits, sleeves trimmed with silk braid and soutache; cloth colored buttons, unlined. Length, 45 inches. When ordering to give bust measure.

No. 17K2370. Color, castor. Price.. **$5.75**
If by mail, postage extra, 50c.

$7.50 THIS STYLISH COAT IS MADE OF BROADCLOTH WEIGHT FANCY PLAID MIXTURE COAT is a very stylish garment and is especially adapted for spring and fall wear. It is made in the loose style, here illustrated, with deep side vents, velvet collar and lapels of self material; exceptionally big value for the money, of good material and real style. Length, 48 inches. Remember, when ordering to give bust measure.

No. 17K2500. Color, black. Price.. **$7.50**
No. 17K2550. Color, gray mixture. Price.. **5.75**
If by mail, postage extra, 45 cents.

$4.75 THIS MEDIUM HEAVY WEIGHT FANCY PLAID MIXTURE COAT is a very stylish garment and is especially adapted for spring and fall wear. It is made in the loose style, here illustrated, with deep side vents with turnback cuffs trimmed with silk braid and soutache; cloth colored buttons, unlined. Length, 48 inches. Coat is unlined. When ordering to give bust measure.

No. 17K2330. Color, gray mixture. Price.. **$4.75**
Not mailable.

$12.00 THIS ELEGANT BROADCLOTH COAT will please the fastidious dresser. It is made with loose front and back, it is double breasted and has wide silk braid and narrow soutache braid, as shown in illustration. Coat is made loose in front with turnback cuffs trimmed with pointed cuffs, tabs on vertical silar; pockets coat is lined throughout with satin and is finished around neck and front with narrow fancy braid. Length, 48 inches. Bust measure, please.

No. 17K2650. Color, black with black satin lining. Price.. **$12.00**
No. 17K2651. Color, black, with gray satin lining. Price.. **$12.00**

$7.75 A NOBBY COATMADE OF ALL WOOL FANCY STRIPED MIXTURE. Elaborately trimmed with wide silk braid and silk soutache and silk inlaid velvet trimmed with silk braid and soutache. Plain coat sleeves and collarless; plain sleeves with turnback cuffs in braid and soutache in collar effect and cuffs, on effect coat sleeves, and flaps on patched pockets and trimmed with braid to match. This coat is unlined has deep side vents, and is 48 inches long. A nice weight garment for spring and fall. Give bust measure when ordering.

No. 17K2450. Color, gray mixture. Price.. **$7.75**
No. 17K2451. Color, tan mixture. Price.. **7.15**
If by mail, postage extra, 55c.

$6.50 THIS NOBBY COAT IS MADE OF MEDIUM WEIGHT BROADCLOTH, in double breasted style, with seam down center of back, which gives it a very graceful flare. It is trimmed at neck with velvet, wide silk braid and soutache in collar effect and soutache in front. Length, 45 inches. Be sure to state bust measure.

No. 17K2400. Color, black. If by mail, postage extra, 55c. **$6.50**

YOUR MONEY WILL BE IMMEDIATELY RETURNED TO YOU FOR ANY GOODS NOT PERFECTLY SATISFACTORY.

695

SUPERB MATERIALS AND HIGH CLASS TAILORING CHARACTERIZE EVERY GARMENT ON THIS PAGE

SIZES, 32 TO 38 INCHES BUST MEASURE. LARGER SIZES WILL BE MADE TO ORDER FOR 20 PER CENT ABOVE REGULAR PRICE.

No. 17G3755

No. 17K3750

No. 17K3760

No. 17K3765

No. 17K3770

No. 17K3785

No. 17K3775

No. 17K3795

No. 17G3755 $3.75 A SWAGGER LITTLE COAT made of fancy striped all wool mixture in double breasted style with half fitted back, small side plaits at side back seams, velvet collar, three pockets with flaps, turn-back cuff effect on plain sleeves, trimmed with tiny buttons to match those on front. Coat is unlined and is 23 inches long. Bust measure, please?

No. 17K3755. Color, gray mixture. $3.75
Price.......................$3.75
If by mail, postage extra, 31 cents.

No. 17K3750 $2.98 THIS STYLISH MISSES' COAT is made of a fancy plaid mixture in a loose box style with side vents trimmed with buttons, inlaid velvet collar and coat shaped lapels, two side pockets with flaps, plain coat sleeve finished with buttons. Coat is unlined and is 26 inches long. Don't fail to state bust measure when ordering.

No. 17K3750. Color, gray mixture. $2.98
Price.......................$2.98
If by mail, postage extra, 40 cents.

No. 17K3760 $3.65 STYLISH DOUBLE BREASTED BOX COAT made of all wool broadcloth with velvet collar and coat shaped lapels; style with small plaits at side back seams and fly front; coat shaped collar and lapels; one breast pocket and two side pockets with pointed tabs and trimmed with self strapping; fancy with flaps; plain sleeves with turn-back cuffs. Coat is unlined and is 25 inches long. Always state bust measure when ordering.

No. 17K3760. Color, navy blue. $3.65
Price.......................$3.65
No. 17K3761. Color, brown. Price.. $3.65
No. 17K3762. Color, red. Price.. $3.65
If by mail, postage extra, 34c.

No. 17K3765 $3.98 THIS NEAT COAT is made of COAT. Made of all wool covert cloth in half fitted style with side vents. The breast, pocket, and cloth buttons are inlaid with velvet; fancy turnback cuffs on plain coat sleeves. It is one of the prettiest misses' jackets that we are showing and will give the wearer an air of style. Coat is unlined and is 42 inches long. Mention bust measure when ordering.

No. 17K3765. Color, castor. $3.98
Price.......................$3.98
If by mail, postage extra, 40 cents.

No. 17K3770 $4.75 AN EXTREMELY SMART SINGLE BREASTED LOOSE COAT is made of a fancy plaid mixture with stitched down shawl collar of red velvet trimmed with wide braid and soutache; flapson patch pockets to match; plain coat sleeves with turn-back cuffs, piped with velvet and ornamented with button; deep side vents; two side pockets with flaps. Coat is unlined and is especially adapted for spring and fall wear. Length, 42 inches. Don't fail to mention bust measure when ordering.

No. 17K3770. Color, gray plaid mixture with velvet trimming. $5.75
Price.......................$5.75
No. 17K3771. Color, gray plaid mixture with black velvet trimming. Price..$5.75

No. 17K3775 $5.98 THIS NOBBY SERVICEABLE COAT is made of a medium weight mixture in a pretty assortment of fancy plaids. It is made in the double breasted style with inlaid velvet collar trimmed with fancy braid and buttons. Full coat sleeves with turn-back cuffs, sleeves being made with tab, piped with velvet and ornamented with button; two side pockets with button; deep side pockets with flaps. Coat is unlined and is 42 inches long. Please give bust measure when ordering.

No. 17K3775
Color, gray mixture. Price....$3.75
If by mail, postage extra, 52 cents.

No. 17K3795 $5.98 ALL WOOL FANCY STRIPED MIXTURE is the material used in this stylish misses' coat which is trimmed on body, turn-back cuffs and pocket flaps with wide pull braid and narrow soutache as illustrated. Coat is made loose and is a most desirable garment. It is well made, is unlined and is 42 inches long.

No. 17K3795
Color, gray mixture. Price....$5.98
If by mail, postage extra, 52 cents.
Not mailable.

No. 17K3785 Color, gray mixture.
Price......$4.75
If by mail, postage extra, 52c.

THESE STYLES IN GIRLS' COATS HAVE A DISTINCTIVENESS

YOU WILL NOT FIND IN THE OFFERINGS OF OTHERS, EVEN AT DOUBLE OUR PRICES

SIZES, 6 TO 14 YEAR OLD CHILDREN. STATE AGE AND BUST MEASURE WHEN ORDERING.

NO EXTRA SIZES.

No. 17K4000 — $1.89

A VERY STYLISH LITTLE CHILD'S JACKET, made of fancy striped mixture with repellant cloth; trimmed on collar and cuffs with shade with contrasting metal buttons; double breasted front trimmed with large buttons to match; two patch pockets. Sizes, 6 to 14 years. Coat is 20 inches long. State age and bust measure when ordering.

No. 17K4000 Color, blue with red trimming. Price....$1.89
No. 17K4001 Color, brown with castor trimming. Price....$1.89
If by mail, postage extra, 25 cents.

No. 17K4010 — $1.75

A NOBBY LITTLE COAT of good grade striped mixture with stitched down shawl collar effect, trimmed with fancy braid and piped with fancy cord. It is made loose with double breasted front finished with fancy metal buttons; two patch pockets; unlined; length, 20 inches. Sizes, 6 to 14 years. Always give age and age of child.

No. 17K4010 Color, gray mixture. Price....$1.75
If by mail, postage extra, 25 cents.

No. 17K4015 — $2.37

HANDSOME LITTLE CHILD'S COAT made of medium weight all wool repellant cloth, trimmed on collar and cuffs with inlaid silk poplin, gilt soutache and silk braid; flaps on patch pockets are also piped with silk; fancy metal buttons on double breasted front. Coat is unlined and is 20 inches long. Size, 6 to 14 years. Always give age and bust measure when ordering.

No. 17K4015 Color, blue with light blue trimming. Price....$2.37
No. 17K4016 Color, brown with tan trimming. Price....$2.37
If by mail, postage extra, 26 cents.

No. 17K4020 — $2.55

A VERY HANDSOME CHILD'S COAT made of fine Venetian or covert cloth with stylish inlaid collar of fancy blue gross grain silk, artistically trimmed with soutache and tiny fancy tache. It is made loose and cloth out in artistic fashion and finished with fancy braid and buttons; two metal buttons; plain coat sleeves with turn back cuffs. Coat is unlined and is 22 inches long. Sizes, 6 to 14 years. Be sure to mention age and bust measure when ordering.

No. 17K4020 Color, castor. Price....$2.55
If by mail, postage extra, 27 cents.

No. 17K4040 — $2.75

STRIKINGLY HANDSOME CHILD'S COAT with all wool covert cloth with shawl collar, turn back cuffs and tabs on pockets of light blue gross grain silk, inlaid with dark blue broadcloth, three rows of soutache braid. Large buttons trimmed front with six fancy metal buttons; two patch pockets with flaps; plain coat front to match; two metal buttons; plain coat sleeves. A nice weight garment for spring and fall. Unlined and is 26 inches long. Sizes, 6 to 14 years, member to give age and bust measure when ordering.

No. 17K4040 Color, light blue with light blue trimming. Price....$2.75
No. 17K4041 Color, tan with light blue trimming. Price....$2.75
If by mail, postage extra, 28 cents.

No. 17K4050 — $2.75

THIS THREE-QUARTER CHILD'S COAT, made of fancy gray mixture, is a bargain at our price. The collar and turn back cuffs are inlaid with fancy white panne velvet with lapels of self material; plain sleeves with silk emblem on and turn back cuff effect; two patch pockets with flaps; cloth buttons trimmed with buttons to match. Coat is made loose with side pockets with metal rims. A nice weight garment for fall and spring. Unlined. Sizes, 6 to 14 years. When ordering, don't fail to give age and bust measure.

No. 17K4050 Color, gray mixture. Price....$2.75
If by mail, postage extra, 30 cents.

No. 17K4060 — $3.55

ANOTHER NOBBY WINTER CHILD'S COAT, made of some fancy stripe mixture in the double breasted loose style which is so popular. The collar is of and turnback cuffs which are ornamented with fancy white braid, which forms a pleasing contrast to the material, as do also the large white cloth centers on front. Coat is lined throughout with light blue mercerized sateen and is 26 inches long. Sizes, 6 to 14 years. Mention age and bust measure when ordering.

No. 17K4060 Color, gray mixture. Price....$3.55
No. 17K4061 Color, black. Price....$3.55
Postage extra, 24c.

No. 17K4080 — $3.98

VERY DRESSY CHILD'S COAT, made of black peau de soie silk, trimmed on wide shawl collar and loose style which is so wide broadcloth cuffs, which are inlaid with fancy white velvet with lapels of self material; turn back cuff of the mixture and fancy buckle. Two side pockets with flaps. Six gilt rim buttons on front. Coat is unlined. Length, 30 inches. Sizes, 6 to 14 years. Don't fail to give age and bust measure when ordering.

No. 17K4080 Color, black. Price....$3.98
Postage extra, 24c.

No. 17K4090 — $3.95

THIS SMART LITTLE CHILD'S COAT will please you. It is made of all wool fancy striped mixture with velvet collar with red velvet collar, the turnback cuffs and piped with velvet to match. Six large pockets being laid in box plait. Six double breasted front. Coat is lined throughout with mercerized. Two inverted plaits down center of back. Sizes, 6 to 14 years. Give age and bust measure when ordering.

No. 17K4090 Color, tan stripe mixture. Price....$3.95
No. 17K4091 Color, gray stripe mixture. Price....$3.95
Postage extra, 24c.

No. 17K4100 — $4.75

ONE OF THE DRESSIEST CHILD'S COATS ON THE MARKET and we know that you will be delighted with it. It is made of fine all wool serge with red velvet collar, the turnback cuffs and flaps or side pockets being piped with velvet to match. Two side pockets with flaps. Fullness in sleeves at wrist. Six large pockets laid in box plait. Six double breasted front. Coat is lined throughout with mercerized sateen.

No. 17K4100 Color, white with red velvet trim. Price....$4.75
No. 17K4101 Color, navy blue with red velvet. Price....$4.75
Postage extra, 24 cents.

HIGH GRADE MATERIALS, NEWNESS OF STYLE, PERFECTION OF FIT AND EXCELLENT WORKMANSHIP

Are the features that we emphasize on every one of these nobby suits. Sizes, 32 to 42 inches bust measure; 22 to 28 inches waist measure; 37 to 44 inches long. Don't fail to state size when ordering if you would avoid delay. Samples of material will be sent free on request.

No. 27K200

No. 27K210

No. 27K220

No. 27K230

No. 27K240

No. 27K250

$16.75 A VERY NATTY TWO-PIECE SUIT made of invisible all wool striped serge, the stripe being effected by the weave. The jacket is very smart style, is strictly tailored with inlaid velvet collar, turned back cuffs, two side pockets and one breast pocket, with flaps. Vents at back seams; side back seams being ornamented with four fancy buttons. Coat is lined with satin, and is 24 inches long. Seven-gored skirt, with two side plaits at each seam, and trimmed with bias straps of self material. Seams are bound, and skirt is hemmed at bottom, and has an average sweep of 125 to 135 inches. When ordering state waist measure, bust measure, and front length of skirt.

No. 27K200 Color, black. **$16.75**
Price.......
No. 27K201 Color, navy **16.75**
blue. Price.......
No. 27K202 Color, brown. **16.75**
Price.......
Unmailable.

$13.75 THE STYLISH PRINCE CHAP SUIT HERE SHOWN is made of fine all wool cloth, the grade jacket being panama suiting. Jacket is very smart style, is semi-fitting, with vents at side back seams; has two side pockets with flaps also outlined with braid; breast pocket, trimmed with braid. Collar and cuffs are of taffeta silk and finished with braid. The jacket has center back seam, is lined with satin and is 25 inches long. The fifteen-gored skirt has deep plaits at seams and is trimmed with wide fold of self material finished with braid to match that on self jacket. All seams are bound, and skirt is hemmed at bottom, and has an average sweep of 125 to 135 inches. When ordering state waist measure, bust measure, and front length of skirt.

No. 27K210 Color, black. **$13.75**
Price.......
No. 27K211 Color, blue. **13.75**
Price.......
No. 27K212 Color brown. **13.75**
Price.......
Unmailable.

$11.50 TAILORED SIMPLICITY CHARACTERIZES THIS CHIC MODEL, which is made of all wool suiting. Jacket is semi-fitting, with vents at side back seams; has two side pockets with flaps and one breast pocket; turned back cuffs on plain coat sleeves. Jacket is lined with fine satin finished venetian, and is 24 inches long. The fifteen-gored skirt fits beautifully at hips, has deep side plaits and is trimmed at bottom, nicely bound and it is hemmed at bottom. Average sweep, 125 to 135 inches. When ordering be sure to state waist measure, bust measure, and front length of skirt.

No. 27K220 Color, light **$11.50**
gray. Price.......
No. 27K221 Color, black. **11.50**
Price.......
No. 27K222 Color, medium **11.50**
dark gray. Price.......
Unmailable.

$11.50 ONE OF THE NOBBIEST SUITS THAT WE ARE SHOWING. It is made of good quality chiffon Panama in the popular, half fitted single breasted style. Velvet collar, and coat shaped lapels of self materials. Artistically applied self straping and silk buttons form the only trimming on this pretty suit. Jacket is lined with fine satin finished venetian, has center back seam and is 23 inches long. The eleven-gored skirt has deep side plaits and is trimmed at bottom. Bound seams; hemmed at bottom. Average sweep, 125 to 135 inches. When ordering be sure to state bust measure, and front length of skirt.

No. 27K230 Color, black. **$11.50**
Price.......
No. 27K231 Color, navy **11.50**
blue. Price.......
No. 27K232 Color, brown. **11.50**
Price.......
Unmailable.

$9.98 THIS FASHIONABLE SUIT is made of good grade broadcloth in the half fitted style here shown with stitched down inlaid velvet collar; turned back velvet cuffs, and inserts of velvet on front and back of jacket, at termination of braid trimming. The collar and cuffs are outlined with silk braid, and trimmed with soutache, velvet inserts also trimmed with soutache. Jacket is lined with good grade venetian, and is 22 inches long. Skirt is made with slashed side gores, with velvet and soutache-run trimmed in picture. Side plaits at seams, inverted plaits in back. Bound seams; hemmed at bottom. Average sweep, 125 to 135 inches. When ordering be sure to state waist measure, bust measure, and front length of skirt.

No. 27K240 Color, black. **$9.98**
Price.......
No. 27K241 Color blue. **9.98**
Price.......
No. 27K242 Color, brown. **9.98**
Price.......
Unmailable.

$9.98 A VERY SMART SUIT made of fancy shadow stripe mixture suiting stripe broadcloth with wide braid and artistically trimmed with wide braid as shown in illustration. Coat shaped collar and lapels; plain coat sleeve ornamented with buttons to match those on front. The jacket is half fitted; it is lined with a good grade venetian cloth, and is 23 inches long. The skirt is a thirteen-gored model which flares prettily at bottom, and has inverted plaits at back. It is made with finished seams, and has an average sweep of 125 to 135 inches.

No. 27K250 Color, black. **$9.98**
Price.......
No. 27K251 Color, blue. **9.98**
Price.......
No. 27K252 Color, brown. **9.98**
Price.......
Unmailable.

NO RETAIL DEALER CAN BEGIN TO OFFER YOU SUCH VALUES AS ARE QUOTED ON THIS PAGE

SIZES: 32 to 42 inches bust measure, and 38 to 44 inches long skirts. Larger sizes must be made to order for 20 per cent above regular catalogue price.

No. 27K1250

$8.75   AN EXTREMELY PRETTY MISSES' SHIRT WAIST

SUIT, made of checked taffeta silk. Trimmed on kimono sleeves. Most of them are like the illustration, but we have a few that are different in style, in fact quite a number of them are prettier. We are closing out these small lots at a sacrifice, and give our customers one of the greatest values ever offered in a silk shirt waist suit. The skirts are made full, and they are up to date skirt, averages 4¼ yards around bottom. Don't delay ordering. Send in your order and get the best suit for the money.

No. 27K1250   Color, black and white check.   Price.... **$8.75**

No. 27K1251   Color, blue and white check.   Price.... **8.75**

No. 27K1252   Color, brown and white check.   Price.... **8.75**

If by mail, postage extra, 25 cents.

No. 27K1220

$8.35   THIS LOT CONSISTS OF SHORT SLEEVED,

fine chiffon taffeta silk waist suits. Most of them under are described under this number are not all like the illustration, and most of them are far prettier. There are some suits in this lot that sold for $3.00, $4.00 and $5.00 more, and they are all exceptionally good values. The lots are not big enough to be listed separately, and thus we are forced to put them under a general description. If it isn't the greatest value you ever received for the money, return it at our expense, and we will refund your money.

No. 27K1220   Color, black.   Price.... **$8.35**

No. 27K1221   Color, royal blue.   Price.... **8.35**

No. 27K1222   Color, brown.   Price.... **8.35**

No. 27K1225   Color, navy.   Price.... **8.35**

If by mail, postage extra, 26 cents.

No. 27K1200

$7.75   EXTREMELY POPULAR SILK SHIRT WAIST

SUIT. Waist made with long sleeves, a full skirt. The garments trimmed with pin tucking and entire tucking with tucks on small yoke meeting in points at center; yoke is crossed by self bands of the cream valenciennes lace; kimono sleeve effect; trimmed on shoulders and front with straps of self material and finished with large silk covered buttons; tucks to yoke depth in front and back; waist buttons in back with yoke depth on either side; long sleeves. Nine-gored skirt with side plaits at seams, giving a wide box plait effect with alternating gores tucked at hips; hemmed at bottom; 3½ yards sweep. Don't fail to give bust measure, waist measure and length of skirt when ordering.

No. 27K1200   Color, black.   Price.... **$7.75**

No. 27K1201   Color, navy.   Price.... **7.75**

No. 27K1202   Color, brown.   Price.... **7.75**

No. 27K1204   Color, wine.   Price.... **7.75**

No. 27K1205   Color, allce blue.   Price.... **7.75**

If by mail, postage extra, 28c.

No. 27K1290

$11.75   NOBBY SILK SHIRT WAIST SUIT.

The collar, cuffs and entire front are trimmed in front with heavy cream allover lace; collar and yoke ornamented with the cream valenciennes lace; no sleeve effect; collar is made with tab button; long sleeves with tab trimmed cuffs which fasten at side; waist closes invisibly in front; tucked in back. The seven-gored skirt is made with clusters of two tucks and is trimmed on each front with two stitched tabs of self material; all seams are bound; skirt is finished with hem and measures 3¼ yards sweep. Neat crushed belt with tab ends. Remember to mention bust measure, waist measure and length of skirt when ordering.

No. 27K1290   Color, black.   Price.... **$11.75**

No. 27K1291   Color, navy blue.   Price.... **11.75**

No. 27K1292   Color, brown.   Price.... **11.75**

If by mail, postage extra, 28 cents.

No. 27K1300

$12.50   AN EXTREMELY STYLISH SHIRT WAIST

SUIT OF CHIFFON TAFFETA SILK, trimmed in front with self tabs ornamented with buttons which hold in place the long ends of the which is attached to collar; collar is made with pin tucking and sleeves with trimmed with tab trimmed cuffs and front is further trimmed with large self material and finished with large silk covered buttons; tucks to yoke depth in front and back; tucked in back. The seven-gored skirt is made with inverted plaits on front and sides and is trimmed with wide bias fold of material; all seams are bound; hemmed at bottom; 3½ yards sweep. Neat crushed belt with tab ends. Remember to mention bust measure, waist measure and skirt length when ordering.

No. 27K1300   Color, black.   Price.... **$12.50**

No. 27K1301   Color, navy blue.   Price.... **12.50**

No. 27K1302   Color, brown.   Price.... **12.50**

If by mail, postage extra, 28 cents.

No. 27K1270

$10.75   CHIC SHIRT WAIST SUIT OF CHIFFON

TAFFETA SILK. Waist is tucked to yoke depth in front and is trimmed in center with self strapping, self tabs ornamented with buttons which hold in place the long ends of tie which is attached to collar; three-quarter length sleeves with deep tucked cuffs. The seven-gored skirt, has panel front of two close set box plaits and side plaits at seams, inverted plaits in back; trimmed around bottom with bias fold; excellently made and measures 3½ yards sweep. Be sure to give bust and waist measure and skirt length when ordering.

No. 27K1270   Color, black.   Price.... **$10.75**

No. 27K1271   Color, navy blue.   Price.... **10.75**

No. 27K1272   Color, brown.   Price.... **10.75**

If by mail, postage extra, 26 cents.

No. 27K1240

$9.98   A VERY PRETTY SHIRT WAIST SUIT of taffeta

silk trimmed on front with pin tucking, self strapping and fancy ornaments; tucks at shoulders in front and back; pin tucked yoke; long sleeves; three-quarter tucked collar; three-quarter sleeves with deep tucked cuffs; waist stitched belt. The seven-gored skirt trimmed around bottom in back; trimmed around bottom with bias fold; excellently made and measures 3½ yards fold with deep hem. Be sure to give bust and waist measure and skirt length when ordering.

No. 27K1240   Color, black.   Price.... **$9.98**

No. 27K1241   Color, navy blue.   Price.... **9.98**

No. 27K1242   Color, brown.   Price.... **9.98**

If by mail, postage extra, 28 cents.

THESE UNUSUALLY ARTISTIC SUITS ARE REALLY WORTH DOUBLE OUR PRICES

SIZES: 32 to 42 inches bust measure. 22 to 28 inches waist measure and 38 to 44 inches long skirt. Larger sizes will be made to order for 20 per cent above the regular price.

**No. 27K1380   AN UNUSU- $12.75
ALLY PRETTY
JUMPER SUIT**
is made of soft striped taffeta silk and trimmed as shown with plain taffeta and small fancy buttons; fitted belt of plain taffeta; jumper buttons in back and has short sleeves. The nine-gored skirt is tucked at hips and is trimmed with two wide bias bands of plain taffeta. Skirt is made with finished seams and hem and has 3½ yards sweep. Don't fail to state waist and bust measure and length of skirt in front when ordering. Suit consists of jumper and skirt only.

No. 27K1380   Color, gray and white with black trim- $12.75
ming.   Price....
No. 27K1381   Color, brown
and white with brown $12.75
trimming.   Price....
If by mail, postage extra, 25 cents.

**No. 27K1320   THIS BEAUTI- $12.75
FUL JUMP-
ER SUIT** is
made of chiffon taffeta silk and is elaborately embroidered with silk in conventional design as shown in illustration; tucked at shoulders in front and back. Six-gored skirt is made with clusters of double tucks extending all the way around to back; is hemmed at bottom and has 3½ yards sweep. This suit does not include waist but it may be worn with any fancy waist and makes an elegant party dress. Always mention waist and bust measure and length of skirt when ordering.

No. 27K1320   Color, blue
with green piping. $12.50
Price....
No. 27K1321   Color, brown
with tan piping. $12.50
Price....
If by mail, postage extra, 25 cents.

**No. 27K1340   THIS NOVEL $12.50
JUMPER SUIT**
is made of fine chiffon taffeta silk with bias straps of same material in front and over shoulder, trimmed with small buttons in front. The skirt is a six-gored model and has panel front of two close set box plaits with two side plaits on either side. Waist is trimmed in front and back and is trimmed with bias fold of self material; skirt is finished with hem and has 3½ yards sweep; crushed belt. When ordering please state waist measure, bust measure and length of skirt.

No. 27K1340   Color, blue
and white polka dots. $13.75
Price.
No. 27K1341   Color, brown
and white polka dots. $13.75
Price.
If by mail, postage extra, 25 cents.

**No. 27K1360   SWAGGER $13.75
JUMPER SUIT**
of dark blue polka dot satin foulard. The jumper is made in surplice effect and is trimmed around kimono sleeves and opening in front and back with band of plain taffeta, the latter being piped with silk; jumper has wide tucks over shoulders. Closes in back and is trimmed in front with fancy buttons. The skirt is a six-gored model and is made with wide band of tan contrasting color. The nine-gored skirt is trimmed with two side plaits in front with wide fold of self material and pointed tabs of same material, both being piped to match sleeve; crushed belt. Skirt is finished with hem, and measures 3½ yards around bottom. Don't fail to give bust and waist measure and length of skirt in front when ordering.

No. 27K1360   Color, navy blue
and white polka dots. $13.75
Price.
No. 27K1361   Color, brown
and white polka dots. $13.75
Price.
If by mail, postage extra, 25 cents.

**No. 27K1400   DRESSY $13.75
GOWN,** made
of black taffeta silk with front, stock and sleeves of white net; collar and center of front is pin tucked; front being also trimmed with lace over folds of pale blue silk; collar is finished with fold of blue silk, as are also the black sleeve bands; foundation of sleeve is of net and the sleeves are finished with deep accordion plaited net ruffles are finished with valenciennes lace. Waist is tucked around sides and back in front and back with self strappings, silk buttons and tiny silk ornaments; two shoulder tabs are fastened to yoke with folds of silk. Waist buttons in back. New style skirt is finished with deep hem; neat crushed belt; 3½ yards sweep. Be sure to give bust measure and length of skirt when ordering.

No. 27K1400   Color, black
with white net waist. $13.75
Price.
If by mail, postage extra, 25 cents.

**No. 27K1420   NOBBY SHIRT $13.75
WAIST SUIT**
of fine quality chiffon taffeta silk. It is neatly trimmed as shown in illustration with fancy braid also cuffs, collar and front, collar being trimmed with French knots and front with three rows of French knots and silk cord applique; box plaits in front and back to yoke depth in front and back; sleeve is tucked in front and back and is trimmed with bias fold of self silk tucked at bottom; has 3½ yards sweep; fitted waist buttons in back. Be sure to state waist and bust measure and length of skirt in front when ordering.

No. 27K1420
Color, black.   Price..... $13.75
No. 27K1421
Color, navy.   Price.....   13.75
No. 27K1422   Color, brown.
Price.   13.75
If by mail, postage extra, 25 cents.

**No. 27K1430   PRETTY SHIRT $13.75
WAIST SUIT**
of best quality chiffon taffeta silk. Round yoke of bias bands tagored together with folds of light colored taffeta. Yoke is finished with self strapping cut in neat design and trimmed with French knots; collar and cuffs on three-quarter sleeves to match yoke. Waist is tucked in front and back to pointed yoke depth. Six-gored skirt with two double box plaits in front and clusters of two single plaits extending around to back; hemmed at bottom; 3½ yards sweep. Mention bust and waist measure and skirt length.

No. 27K1430
Color, black.   Price.... $13.75
No. 27K1431
Color, navy blue with light
bias bands.   Price.   13.75
No. 27K1432
Color, brown with tan
trimmings.   Price.   13.75
If by mail, postage extra, 25 cents.

ATTRACTIVE STYLES AT ATTRACTIVE LOW PRICES.

SIZES: 32 TO 42 INCHES BUST MEASURE. 22 TO 28 INCHES WAIST MEASURE. 38 TO 44 INCHES LONG SKIRT.

WE CANNOT FURNISH LARGER SIZES IN THESE STYLES

No. 27K1760

No. 27K1750

No. 27K1770

No. 27K1780

No. 27K1790

No. 27K1800

No. 27K1810

No. 27K1820

$2.55 PRETTY SHIRT WAIST SUIT is here shown made of fine white lawn. Waist is trimmed with five rows of cluny lace on either side on front, and one row down back, and trimmed with four sleeves; collar and cuffs are also made of cluny; half-inch tucks alternate with rows of insertion on front of waist; three-quarter sleeves' waist buttons in back. The seven-gored skirt has side plaits at each seam and includes only seven gores. This suit includes only jumper and skirt. Skirt is well made and finished around bottom with bias fold, 3½ yards sweep. When ordering give bust and waist measure and skirt length.

No. 27K1760   Color, white.
Price.......... **$2.55**
If by mail, postage extra, 28 cents.

$1.98 THIS BLACK AND WHITE PLAID JUMPER SUIT is made of fine percale. The plaid is an unusually pretty pattern; faced around square neck with bias fold piped with black, and piped with black, also piped with black; attached belt, made with Nice full skirt, made with has side plaits at each seam and is finished around bottom with row of cluny insertion and wide bias fold, 3½ yards sweep. When ordering give bust and waist measure and skirt length.

No. 27K1750   Color, black and white.
Price.......... **$1.98**
If by mail, postage extra, 30c.

$2.18 STYLISH AND SERVICEABLE SHIRT WAIST SUIT of blue German linen. The waist buttons in front with half-inch tucks on either side; long sleeves with button cuffs; plain back; attached tucked stock. The seven-gored skirt is made to button on either side of front panel with fancy pearl buttons, giving an unusually attractive appearance to the skirt, with inverted plaits in the back; stitched belt is attached across center of back; 3½ yards sweep. Give waist and bust measure and skirt length when ordering.

No. 27K1770   Color, light blue.
Price.......... **$2.18**
No. 27K1771   Color, white.
Price.......... **$2.18**
If by mail, postage extra, 34 cents.

$2.39 NOBBY SHIRT WAIST SUIT of blue gingham trimmed with fancy embroidered braid and piped with white as shown in illustration. Waist closes invisibly at left of tucked panel with button tucked stock. The front, and fullness is laid in two tucks to yoke depth; tucks in back; long sleeves with button cuffs; detached stock collar. Five-gored skirt with side plaits at seams; box plait down center front; white; skirt is trimmed to match waist; 3½ yards sweep. When ordering give waist and bust measure and skirt length.

No. 27K1780   Color, light blue.
Price.......... **$2.39**
No. 27K1781   Color, tan.
Price.......... **$2.39**
If by mail, postage extra, 32c.

$2.65 ONE OF THE DAINTIEST WAIST DRESSES made of good quality white lawn; the front of waist and body of skirt are beautifully embroidered in artistic design and deep flounce at bottom of skirt is set on with band of embroidery. Three-quarter sleeves with tucked cuff, edged with valenciennes lace, stock to match; waist buttons invisibly in back. The deep flounce on skirt is gathered very full, is hemmed at bottom and measures 3¾ yards around. When ordering give waist and bust measure and front length of skirt.

No. 27K1790   Color, light blue.
Price.......... **$2.39**
No. 27K1791   Color, white.
Price.......... **$2.39**
If by mail, postage extra, 28 cents.

$2.46 STYLISH SUSPENDER SUIT made of light blue German linen and finished on straps with tiny pearl buttons; waist between clusters of tucks; buttons in front under tucked box plait; two wide tucks in back, which button; detached tucked stock collar. The five-gored skirt is trimmed with two bands of self material and finished with wide hem; 3¼ yards deep hem and 3¾ yards sweep. Always state waist and bust measure and skirt length when ordering.

No. 27K1800   Color, light blue.
Price.......... **$2.65**
If by mail, postage extra, 40 cents.

$2.48 BLACK LAWN OR MOURNING SHIRT WAIST SUIT neatly embroidered on front of shirt waist; detached dickey; tucks; two wide plaits at every seam, and is trimmed around bottom with deep plait on either side of front gore and is trimmed around bottom with wide fancy border to match that on waist. The garment is well made, has with wide hem; 3¼ yards deep hem and 3¾ yards sweep. Always state bust and skirt length.

No. 27K1810   Color, black only.
Price.......... **$2.46**
If by mail, postage extra, 24 cents.

$2.35 NEAT SHIRT WAIST SUIT of striped soft finish percale, made with wide sailor collar and trimmed with fancy border. The cuffs on full length sleeves and four-in-hand are also trimmed to match. Waist is made with a plain back and buttons invisibly in front. Five-gored skirt is made with deep plait on either side of front gore and side plaits around bottom. When ordering state bust and skirt length.

No. 27K1820   Color, blue and white stripes. Price.......... **$2.35**
No. 27K1821   Color, pink and white stripes. Price.......... **$2.35**
If by mail, postage extra, 28c.

THESE PRETTY LOW PRICED SHIRT WAIST SUITS WILL DELIGHT ANY WOMAN

SIZES! 32 to 42 inches bust measure, 22 to 28 inches waist measure, and 38 to 44 inches long skirts. We cannot make larger sizes in these styles.

No. 27K1920
No. 27K1860
No. 27K1840
No. 27K1880
No. 27K1890
No. 27K1900
No. 27K1910
No. 27K1870

$2.98 PRETTY SHIRT WAIST SUIT is made of lingerie with square yoke of good quality gingham. It is trimmed on panel of allover embroidery and fancy pearl buttons and piped with white tucked front trimmed with fancy insertion; three-quarter sleeves with tucked cuffs trimmed with insertion and lace; tucked collar also piped with white and tucked collar to match; buttons in front, cluster of tucks on either side. Seven-gored skirt with deep flounce set on with insertion; deep hem. Flounce has 4 yards sweep. When ordering don't fail to mention bust and waist measure and skirt length.

No. 27K1920 Color, white.
Price............ **$2.98**
If by mail, postage extra, 26 cents.

$2.75 THIS CHIC SHIRT WAIST SUIT is made of good quality gingham. It is trimmed on panel front with white tucked quarter sleeves with buttoned cuffs also piped with white and lace; waist buttons in back of waist has one wide tuck on either side, and two narrow tucks on each side; wide tuck also piped with white. Nine-gored skirt with wide plaits at seams and trimmed around bottom with bias fold piped with white; deep hem; 3½ yards sweep; plain stitched belt. Be sure to give bust and waist measure and skirt length.

No. 27K1860 Color, blue. Price.. **2.75**
No. 27K1861 Color, gray. Price.. **2.75**
If by mail, postage extra, 34c.

$2.48 THIS UNUSUALLY PRETTY SHIRT WAIST SUIT is made of dainty check lawn. The waist is made in surplice effect and is trimmed with, valenciennes insertion and bias folds of plain color to match color in illustration; long sleeves with buttoned the stock and cuffs on three-quarter sleeves are made of band of the plain color between rows of insertion and edged with lace to match; two tucks on either side of front to yoke depth and three in back; waist buttons in back. Full seven-gored skirt fitted at hips by inverted box plait, bottom with two graduated bias folds of plain lawn; 4 yards sweep; detached belt. Don't fail to state bust measure, waist inch tucks. Flounce has 3½ yards sweep. Don't fail to give and skirt length.

No. 27K1840 Color, light blue. Price **$2.48**
No. 27K1841 Color, pink. Price.. **2.48**
If by mail, postage extra, 28c.

$2.98 DRESSY SHIRT WAIST SUIT made of German linen and trimmed with heavy insertion as shown in illustration; front is made with three box plaits and row of valenciennes lace; two side plaits; back with two wide bias folds of self material; has two clusters of narrow tucks in center of front and one wide tuck at shoulder seam; eleven-gored skirt is cut in two parts, the upper part being trimmed to match the lower part with alternating panels made in two parts, lower part being made with three wide plaits; plain panels are finished at bottom with bias fold around bottom. Remember Skirt measures 3½ yards around bottom. Remember wide plaits; plain panels are finished at bottom with bias fold and bias sweep. Mention waist measure, bust measure and skirt length when ordering.

No. 27K1890 Color, cadet, blue.
Price............. **$2.98**
No. 27K1891 Color, Brown. Price... **2.98**
If by mail, postage extra, 26c.

$2.75 VERY STYLISH SHIRT WAIST SUIT made of black and white check percale. It is made with tucked front seam and down front tab with white, unique on front of waist and front tab being trimmed with three-quarter sleeves; long sleeves bias folds of self material, wide plait at shoulder seam; The finished with velvet plait at shoulder seam; Buttons invisibly in back; long sleeves with pointed cuffs. skirt with side plaits at seams; detached belt; skirt has 3½ yards sweep. This suit does not include waist. Be sure to give bust and waist measure and skirt length when ordering.

No. 27K1900 Color, black and white check.
Price............. **$2.75**
If by mail, postage extra, 32c.

$2.95 NATTY STYLISH SHIRT WAIST SUIT of light blue sheplinen. Piped around neck, broidered around V shaped neck, on kimono sleeves and made with tucked yoke of white lawn and is front tab with white, mercerized with thread; tucks on either side small pearl buttons; wide of waist in front; it buttons in back. Seven-gored skirt with side plaits dainty guimpe of sheer tucked lawn, with three-quarter sleeves and tucked cuffs. Nine-gored five-gored skirt trimmed at outside of waist; fullness laid at hip in quarter-inch tucks. body of skirt and deep flounce are finished with three one-half yards sweep. Mention bust measure and skirt length when ordering.

No. 27K1910 Color, light blue.
Price............. **$2.95**
No. 27K1911 Color, tan.
Price............. **2.95**
If by mail, postage extra, 30 cents.

$2.95 BLUE GINGHAM JUMPER SUIT, embroidered around neck, shoulder, neck, on kimono sleeves and skirt seam and on front of waist and skirt yoke; cuffs also buttoned with three tab at shoulder. velvet baby ribbon; alternating guimpe of sheer lawn, with buttons which buttons with bias cuffs which buttons and is trimmed with four rows of ribbon. skirt with alternating panels.

No. 27K1870 Color, blue.
Price........ **$2.95**
No. 27K1871 Color, tan.
Price........ **2.95**
If by mail, postage extra, 34 cents.

WE INVITE COMPARISON OF THE STYLES SHOWN IN THIS CATALOGUE

WITH THOSE SHOWN BY ANY OTHER FIRM OR INDIVIDUAL AT HOME OR ELSEWHERE.

IN STYLE, DRESSMAKING, MATERIALS AND PRICE, WE OFFER OUR CUSTOMERS THE GREATEST POSSIBLE VALUE.

SIZES: 32 to 42 inches bust measure; 22 to 28 inches waist measure; and 38 to 44 inches skirt length. Larger sizes can be made to order for 20 per cent above regular price.

No. 27K2140 $7.50

No. 27K2080 $4.75

No. 27K2110

No. 27K2100

No. 27K2090

No. 27K2120 $5.75

No. 27K2130 $10.50

No. 27K2130 $10.50 VALENCIENNES INSERTION AND WIDE EMBROIDERY are employed in this charming two-piece dress made of sheer white lingerie. Wide tucks and pin tucks are also used with artistic effect. The picture gives a perfect idea of the style but cannot do justice to the beauty of the garment. Cuffs on three-quarter sleeves and collar are edged with lace. The dress fits beautifully at waist and around the hips and is a style that is becoming to all figures. Be sure to mention bust and waist measure and length of skirt in front when ordering.
No. 27K2130 Color, white. Price....$10.50
If by mail, postage extra, 25 cents.

No. 27K2120 $5.75 THERE IS AN AIR OF ELEGANCE ABOUT THIS FINE SOFT FINISHED WASHABLE VOILE JUMPER SUIT, and no matter how careful a dresser you may be we know that it will please you. The illustration gives an exact representation on waist style and it is trimmed on waist and kimono sleeves with contrasting color in same material. Front trimmed with four cloth covered buttons; sleeves also trimmed with lace insertion. Skirt is made up of plaits at each seam around bottom with wide bias fold to match trimming on waist, and has shaped attached belt of same material. Deep hem at bottom and averages four yards sweep. Be sure to give bust measure, waist measure and front of skirt length.
No. 27K2120 Color, white with light blue trimming. Price....$5.75
No. 27K2121 Color, light blue with white trimming. Price....$5.75
If by mail, postage extra, 28 cents.

No. 27K2090 $5.75 BEAUTIFUL TWO-PIECE LINGERIE DRESS with fancy pin tucked yoke artistically trimmed with valenciennes insertion; front is trimmed with alternating rows of embroidery and tucks; it buttons in back with wide cluster of tucks on either side; three-quarter sleeves with cuffs of pin tucking, insertion and lace to match collar. The skirt is tucked in clusters to yoke depth and is made with alternating panels of tucks, embroidery and lace insertion, and plain panels. Deep flounce has fullness laid in tucks with clusters of wide tucks and insertion at bottom. Deep hem; four yards average sweep. Remember to state waist and bust measure and skirt length when ordering.
No. 27K2090 Color, white only. Price....$5.75
If by mail, postage extra, 28 cents.

No. 27K2100 $5.75 ONE OF THE DAINTIEST AND MOST STYLISH SHIRT WAIST SUITS SHOWN THIS SEASON, made of good quality lawn in the pretty surplice style here shown. The front of waist, belt and cuffs on three-quarter sleeves are made with alternating folds of plain white lawn. Front gives a very dainty effect to the garment; waist fastens in front. The skirt is plaited very full and is trimmed around bottom with bias band of self material; finished with deep hem. Suit does not include dickey. Remember to give bust and waist measure and length of skirt in front when ordering.
No. 27K2100 Color, light blue, with white folds. Price....$5.75
No. 27K2101 Color, lavender, with white folds. Price....$5.75
If by mail, postage extra, 28 cents.

No. 27K2080 $4.75 CHARMING DRESS of fine lingerie elaborately trimmed with tucks, insertion and lace, as shown in illustration; center square in front has beautiful solid floral design. This dress fits beautifully about the waist, hips, blouses slightly in front, buttons invisibly in back. Skirt hangs perfectly. The three wide tucks on flounce and upper part of skirt add a great deal to its attractiveness; three-quarter length sleeves trimmed as shown with cuffs of tucking, insertion and lace to match collar. Flounce averages 3⅜ yards around bottom. Don't forget to state bust and waist measure and skirt length when ordering.
No. 27K2080 Color, white. Price....$4.75
No. 27K2081 Color, pink. Price....$4.75
No. 27K2082 Color, light blue. Price....$4.75
If by mail, postage extra, 25 cents.

No. 27K2110 $4.95 ONE OF THE PRETTIEST WASH JUMPER SUITS THAT WE ARE SHOWING. It is made of blue and white checked gingham in style exactly as shown in illustration; center square extending over shoulders and tucked front. Neck and sleeves are finished with bias folds of self material, and the self strapping on shoulders and sleeves finished with pearl buttons make it a very fine garment. The elevengored skirt is made with single box plait down front, and side plaits all the way around to back. Well made and finished with finest of tailored straps and stitches with deep hem; averages 4½ yards. Be sure to mention waist and bust measure and skirt length when ordering.
No. 27K2110 Color, blue and white check. Price....$4.95
No. 27K2111 Color, blue and white check. Price....$4.95
If by mail, postage extra, 32 cents.

No. 27K2140 $7.50 THIS BEAUTIFUL TWO-PIECE DRESS is made of fine soft finished voile and is daintily trimmed with pin tucking, wide tucks, valenciennes lace and insertion, and small embroidered squares, as shown in illustration. It is one of the prettiest styles that we are showing and we know that you cannot fail to like it. It is made with three-quarter sleeves, and buttons invisibly in back; skirt averages 4½ yards around bottom. When ordering always state bust and waist measure and skirt length.
No. 27K2140 Color, pink and white check. Price....$7.50
No. 27K2141 Color, white. Price....7.50
If by mail, postage extra, 30 cents.

THE MOST EXCLUSIVE DESIGNS IN FASHIONABLE WEARING APPAREL

AT THE PRICES QUOTED FOR THESE BEAUTIFUL GOWNS, YOU COULD NOT PURCHASE THE MATERIALS ALONE IN THE AVERAGE RETAIL STORE.

REGULAR SIZES ARE 32 TO 42 INCHES BUST, 22 TO 28 INCHES WAIST AND 38 TO 44 INCHES LENGTH. LARGER SIZES WILL BE MADE TO ORDER FOR 20 PER CENT ABOVE REGULAR PRICE.

No. 27K2170.
$10.75 THIS EXQUISITE NET GOWN is elaborately trimmed with allover lace on yoke and has entire front of frills of valenciennes lace crossed by three vertical rows of heavy lace beading, lace and insertion to match. The three-quarter sleeves are made with three tucks trimmed with lace; cuffs made of pin tucked net bordered in back as illustrated and buttoned in back. Skirt is made with lace edged with valenciennes silk ruffle in flounce also edged with lace. Lined throughout with lingerie; ruffle on drop skirt is edged with lace; crushed belt. Skirt averages 5 yards sweep. State bust and waist measure, length of skirt in front when ordering.
No. 27K2170 Color, white. Price.... $10.75
If by mail, postage extra, 38 cents.

No. 27K2160.
$8.75 HANDSOME PARTY DRESS made of fine silk mull with yoke and stock collar of heavy allover lace and trimmed in bolero effect with lace frills; cuffs are of valenciennes lace and insertion also with tucks; three-quarter sleeves trimmed with lace to match, plain cuffs trimmed with lace and insertion; waist fastens in back. The skirt is made with plain front panel having fullness at sides and then laid in narrow tucks; skirt trimmed with two rows of insertion and bias fold of material; has attached belt covered with insertion; deep hem; 3½ yards average sweep. Always mention waist and bust measure and skirt length when ordering.
No. 27K2160 Color, light blue. Price.. $8.75
No. 27K2161 Color, white. Price.... 8.75
If by mail, postage extra, 22 cents.

No. 27K2210
$17.50 THE EMBROIDERED NET DRESS is trimmed on front with two rows of wide allover lace Gibson shoulder pieces which give the popular broad effect; tapering panel front has three clusters of shirring at neck. The cuffs on lar skirt has two graduated ruffles of embroidered net and has fullness laid in tiny tucks at hips. Lined throughout with fine lingerie, and drop skirt also of lingerie is trimmed at bottom with two double ruffles. Boned, crushed belt is made of Jap silk. This gown will be made to your special measure for our regular price.
No. 27K2210 Color, white lace over pink. Price.... $17.50
No. 27K2211 Color, white lace over blue. Price.... $17.50
No. 27K2212 Color, white lace over pink. Price.... 17.50
If by mail, postage extra, 48 cents.

No. 27K2180
$11.75 THE ATTRACTIVE FEATURE of this net dress is the wide allover lace frills; cuffs are of insertion and lace; collar also edged with lace; collar also trimmed with insertion and lace. The circular skirt has two graduated ruffles with insertion and lace. The three-quarter sleeves, and collar are finished with insertion and lace; waist buttons in back. The four-gored skirt has fullness shirred at waist; is finished with attached belt covered with two flounces of self material; has fullness around bottom.
No. 27K2180 Col-$11.75 or light blue. Price....
No. 27K2181 Col-11.75 or white. Price....
If by mail, postage extra, 24 cents.

No. 27K2220
$18.75 A HANDSOME LACE GOWN of elaborately embroidered net. Waist is made with elbow sleeves, being of valenciennes insertion and lace and heavy wide insertion applied as shown in illustration. Waist has elbow sleeves and it fastens in back. The skirt is shirred at waist and has wide cluster of tucks with flounce at bottom finished with three ruffles to match trimming on waist. Waist is lined with lingerie and skirt has drop of same material with lace edged ruffles; dress has boned, crushed girdle of soft silk. Skirt averages 5 yards around bottom. State waist and bust measure and skirt length when ordering.
No. 27K2220 Color, white lace over white. Price.... $18.75
No. 27K2221 Color, white lace over blue. Price.... $18.75
No. 27K2222 Color, white lace over pink. Price.... $18.75
If by mail, postage extra, 32 cents.

No. 27K2200
$12.50 ELABORATELY TRIMMED NET GOWN, best describes this imported model. It is made of embroidered net in style exactly as illustrated. The Waist is made with fine lingerie and fastens invisibly at left side. Waist has elbow sleeves invisibly at left side. The skirt is made in circular style and has drop lining of lingerie, two double ruffles; waist is made with crushed girdle of soft silk. This really is a very dainty gown and an extraordinary value at our price. Be sure to state bust and waist measure and length of skirt in front when ordering.
No. 27K2200 Color, blue. Price.... $12.50
No. 27K2201 Color, pink. Price.... $12.50
No. 27K2202 Color, white. Price.... $12.50
If by mail, postage extra, 34c.

No. 27K2190

No. 27K2150
$16.75 SIMPLE ELEGANCE best describes this imported gown. Is made of embroidered net, trimmed being of valenciennes insertion and lace and heavy wide insertion applied as shown in illustration. Waist has elbow sleeves invisibly at left side. The skirt is made in circular style and fastens invisibly at left side. The skirt is made with two double ruffles and it requires from 10 to 14 days to make.

No. 27K2150.
$9.65 A VERY HANDSOME DRESS made of fine silk mull with valenciennes lace yoke and trimmed as shown with black velvet ribbon in Greek border design, three-quarter length sleeves with cuffs edged with lace. Waist is shirred in. Waist buttons invisibly in back. Skirt is shirred in and trimmed with clusters of wide tucks, yoke being trimmed to match with two rows of black velvet ribbon. Skirt measures 4 yards around bottom. Please give bust and waist measure when ordering and length of skirt in front.

GIVE BUST AND WAIST MEASURE AND SKIRT LENGTH.

No. 27K2150 Color, blue. Price.... $9.65
No. 27K2151 Color, pink. Price.... $9.65
No. 27K2152 Color, white on pink. Price.... $9.65
If by mail, postage extra, 34c.

THE NEWEST AND PRETTIEST MODELS IN LADIES' WASH SKIRTS.

SIZES: 22 TO 30 INCHES WAIST MEASURE AND 37 TO 44 INCHES IN LENGTH. NO EXTRA SIZES.

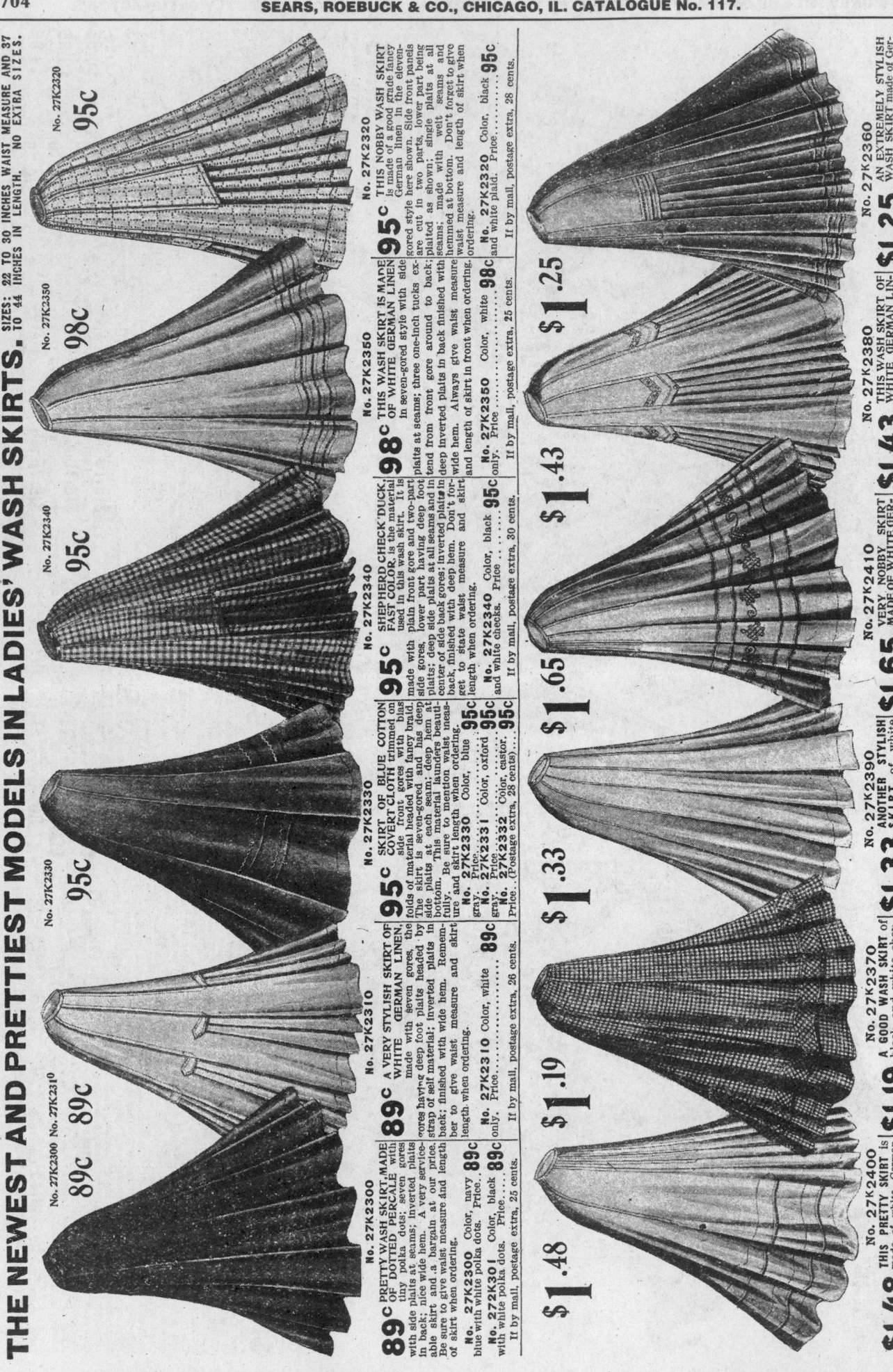

No. 27K2300 89c   THIS PRETTY WASH SKIRT is made of DOTTED PERCALE with tiny polka dots; seven gores with side plaits at seams; inverted plaits in back; nice wide hem. A very serviceable skirt and a bargain at our price. Be sure to give waist measure and length of skirt when ordering.
No. 27K2300 Color, navy blue with white polka dots. Price.... 89c
No. 27K2301 Color, black with white polka dots. Price........ 89c
If by mail, postage extra, 25 cents.

No. 27K2310 89c   A VERY STYLISH SKIRT OF WHITE GERMAN LINEN, made with seven gores, the gores having deep foot plaits headed by strap of self material; inverted plaits in back; finished with wide hem. Remember to give waist measure and skirt length when ordering.
No. 27K2310 Color, white only. Price................ 89c
If by mail, postage extra, 26 cents.

No. 27K2330 95c   SKIRT OF BLUE COTTON COVERT CLOTH trimmed on side with bias folds of material headed with fancy braid. The skirt is seven-gored and has deep side plaits at each seam; deep hem at bottom. This material launders beautifully. Be sure to mention waist measure and skirt length when ordering.
No. 27K2330 Color, blue gray. Price................ 95c
No. 27K2331 Color, oxford gray. Price............. 95c
No. 27K2332 Color, castor. Price. (Postage extra, 28 cents)..... 95c

No. 27K2340 95c   SHEPHERD CHECK DUCK, FAST COLOR, is the material used in this wash skirt. It is made with plain front gore and two-part side gores, lower part having deep foot plaits; deep side plaits at all seams and in back, finished with deep hem. Don't forget to state waist measure and skirt length when ordering.
No. 27K2340 Color, black and white checks. Price...... 95c
If by mail, postage extra, 30 cents.

No. 27K2350 98c   THIS WASH SKIRT IS MADE OF WHITE GERMAN LINEN in seven-gored style with side plaits at seams; three one-inch tucks extend from front gore around to back; plaited as shown; single plaits at all seams; made with welt seams and deep inverted plaits in back finished with wide hem. Always give waist measure and length of skirt in front when ordering.
No. 27K2350 Color, white only. Price........ 98c
If by mail, postage extra, 25 cents.

No. 27K2320 95c   THIS NOBBY WASH SKIRT is made of a good grade fancy German linen in the eleven-gored style here shown. Side front panels are cut in two parts, single plaits at all seams; made with welt seams and hemmed at bottom. Don't forget to give waist measure and length of skirt when ordering.
No. 27K2320 Color, black and white plaid. Price.... 95c
If by mail, postage extra, 28 cents.

No. 27K2360 $1.25   AN EXTREMELY STYLISH WASH SKIRT made of German linen with front and side gores of two close set box plaits; side front gores are made in two parts, upper part with embroidery and pearl button; lower part finished with three tucks, lower part being made with deep foot plaits; inverted plaits in back. Skirt is finished by two tucks and deep hem. Please state waist measure and length of skirt when ordering.
No. 27K2360 Color, light blue. $1.25
No. 27K2361 Color, tan. Price. (Postage extra, 30c.)...... 1.25

No. 27K2380 $1.43   THIS WASH SKIRT OF WHITE GERMAN LINEN is made with alternating plain and two-piece gores. The two-piece gores are trimmed on upper part with inverted plaits. Finished with hem at bottom. Don't fail to mention waist measure and skirt length when ordering.
No. 27K2380 Color, white only. Price.......... $1.43
If by mail, postage extra, 30 cents.

No. 27K2410 $1.65   VERY NOBBY SKIRT MADE OF WHITE GERMAN LINEN with two wide box plaits in front and single plaits extending around to back. Skirt is trimmed with two bias folds of self material and is finished with and cord embroidery applied in conventional design. Hemmed at bottom. Always fail to mention waist measure and skirt length when ordering.
No. 27K2410 Color, white only. Price............ $1.65
If by mail, postage extra, 30 cents.

No. 27K2390 $1.33   ANOTHER STYLISH SKIRT of white German linen with deep center box plait and single plaits extending around to back. It is trimmed with deep center box plait and single plaits well made and is finished with deep hem at bottom. Don't mention waist measure and skirt length when ordering.
No. 27K2390 Color, black white only. Price........ $1.33
If by mail, postage extra, 30 cents.

No. 27K2370 $1.19   A GOOD WASH SKIRT of black and white check made shepherd check duck made in seven-gored style with deep side plaits at seams and trimmed at bottom with wide bias band of self material, inverted plaits in back; deep hem at bottom. Always mention waist measure and skirt length when ordering.
No. 27K2370 Color, black and white checks only. Price..... $1.19
If by mail, postage extra, 30 cents.

No. 27K2400 $1.48   THIS PRETTY SKIRT is made of white German linen with panel front of forward turning plaits, and simple plaits at seams, it is trimmed from front of gore all around with fold of self material. Deep hem at bottom. Very nobby skirt. Don't forget to state waist measure and length of skirt when ordering.
No. 27K2400 Color, white only. Price............. $1.48
If by mail, postage extra, 30 cents.

OUR LINE OF NOBBY WASH SKIRTS FOR LADIES AND MISSES CANNOT BE EQUALED ELSEWHERE

COMPARE OUR PRICES WITH THOSE ASKED BY OTHERS FOR EQUAL STYLE AND QUALITY. NO EXTRA SIZES.

MISSES' SIZES: 22 TO 26 INCHES WAIST MEASURE, 26 TO 38 INCHES LENGTH. LADIES' SIZES: 22 TO 30 INCHES WAIST MEASURE, AND 37 TO 44 INCHES IN LENGTH.

LADIES' SKIRTS

No. 27K2470 $2.75 — **No. 27K2460 $1.98** — **No. 27K2450 $1.75** — **No. 27K2440 $1.48** — **No. 27K2430 $1.75** — **No. 27K2420 $1.75**

No. 27K2420 $1.75 STRICTLY TAILORED WASH SKIRT of white German linen with narrow box plait in front, and side plaits with clusters of four side plaits extending all the way around to back; finished with deep hem. Exceptionally full and well made. When ordering be sure to mention waist measure and length of skirt in front. No. 27K2420 Color, white only. Price.......$1.75. If by mail, postage extra, 25 cents.

No. 27K2430 $1.75 THIS WASH SKIRT of pink linen with light blue polka dots is made with two box plaits in front, and single plaits extending all around to back; trimmed with three graduated bands of self material; well made with deep hem; very pretty. Be sure to mention waist measure and length of skirt in front when ordering. No. 27K2430 Color, tan, with light blue dots. Price.......$1.75. If by mail, postage extra, 25 cents.

No. 27K2440 $1.48 WASH SKIRT made of white German linen, panel front having two side plaits at seams; side gores are elaborately embroidered in a pretty design; inverted plaits made with French seams and hemmed with white; finished with hem. Please give waist measure and skirt length when ordering. No. 27K2440 Color, white with light blue and white embroidery. Price.......$1.48. If by mail, postage extra, 25 cents.

No. 27K2450 $1.75 ONE OF THE PRETTIEST WASH SKIRTS, made of light blue German linen in unique style here shown; trimmed all around with two soft folds of material piped on either side with white; upper part of cut panel also piped with white; finished with hem. Be sure to mention waist measure and length of skirt in front when ordering. No. 27K2450 Color, light blue with white piping. Price.......$1.75. If by mail, postage extra, 25 cents.

No. 27K2460 $1.98 NOBBY WHITE PIQUE SKIRT made with alternating box plaited panels and plain panels, trimmed with self strappings as shown on illustration; gores are plaited as shown and stitched with French depth. Skirt is excellently made with French seams and deep hem. Thoroughly tailored. Always mention waist measure and skirt length. No. 27K2460 Color, white only. Price.......$1.98. If by mail, postage extra, 25 cents.

No. 27K2470 $2.75 VERY STYLISH SKIRT made of white German linen; lower part of alternating gores are plaited as shown and stitched with self strapping down depth; also piped with French embroidery. Inverted plaits in back. Skirt is hemmed at bottom. Mention waist measure and skirt length when ordering. No. 27K2470 Color, white only. Price.......$2.75. If by mail, postage extra, 25 cents.

No. 27K2600 77c — **No. 27K2650 $1.33** — **No. 27K2640 98c** — **No. 27K2630 93c** — **No. 27K2620 79c** — **No. 27K2610 89c**

89c SERVICEABLE WASH SKIRT of white German linen. It is made with two close set box plaits in front, and, side plaits all around to back. Trimmed around bottom with 2-inch fold of self material; finished with hem. Don't forget to mention skirt length and waist measure when ordering. No. 27K2610 Color, white only. Price.......89c. If by mail, postage extra, 20 cents.

79c NEAT WASH SKIRT OF BLACK AND WHITE SHEPHERD CHECK PERCALE trimmed with two bias folds of self material piped by bias band of plain black, plain black band between folds. Skirt is five gored. Hemmed at bottom. Remember to give waist measure and skirt length in front when ordering. No. 27K2620 Color, black and white checks only. Price.......79c. If by mail, postage extra, 20 cents.

93c VERY SERVICEABLE MISSES' SKIRT made of Covert cloth and trimmed with two pointed self straps on upper portion of side gores, lower part being trimmed with two straight bands; single plait at bottom. Always give waist measure and skirt length in front when ordering. No. 27K2630 Color, blue gray. Price.......93c. No. 27K2631 Color, oxford gray. Price.......93c. If by mail, postage extra, 20 cents.

98c VERY NEAT WASH SKIRT OF WHITE GERMAN LINEN, made with single box plait in front and side plaits extending around to back. Finished at bottom with deep hem; well material and finished with deep hem. Don't fail to state waist measure and skirt length. Always give waist measure and skirt length in front. No. 27K2640 Color, white only. Price.......98c. If by mail, postage extra, 20 cents.

$1.33 PRETTY WHITE WASH SKIRT MADE OF GERMAN LINEN. The skirt is made with single box plait in front, trimmed with two graduated folds of self material and finished with deep hem; well material and made with French seams. When ordering be sure to state waist measure and length of skirt in front. No. 27K2650 Color, white only. Price.......$1.33. If by mail, postage extra, 20 cents.

77c NEAT SKIRT OF DOTTED PERCALE trimmed on side gores with fancy braid, single plaits at side back seams; inverted plaits in back. When ordering be sure to state waist measure and length of skirt in front. No. 27K2600 Color, black, 77c. No. 27K2601 Color, navy, 77c, blue, white polka dots. If by mail, postage extra, 20 cents.

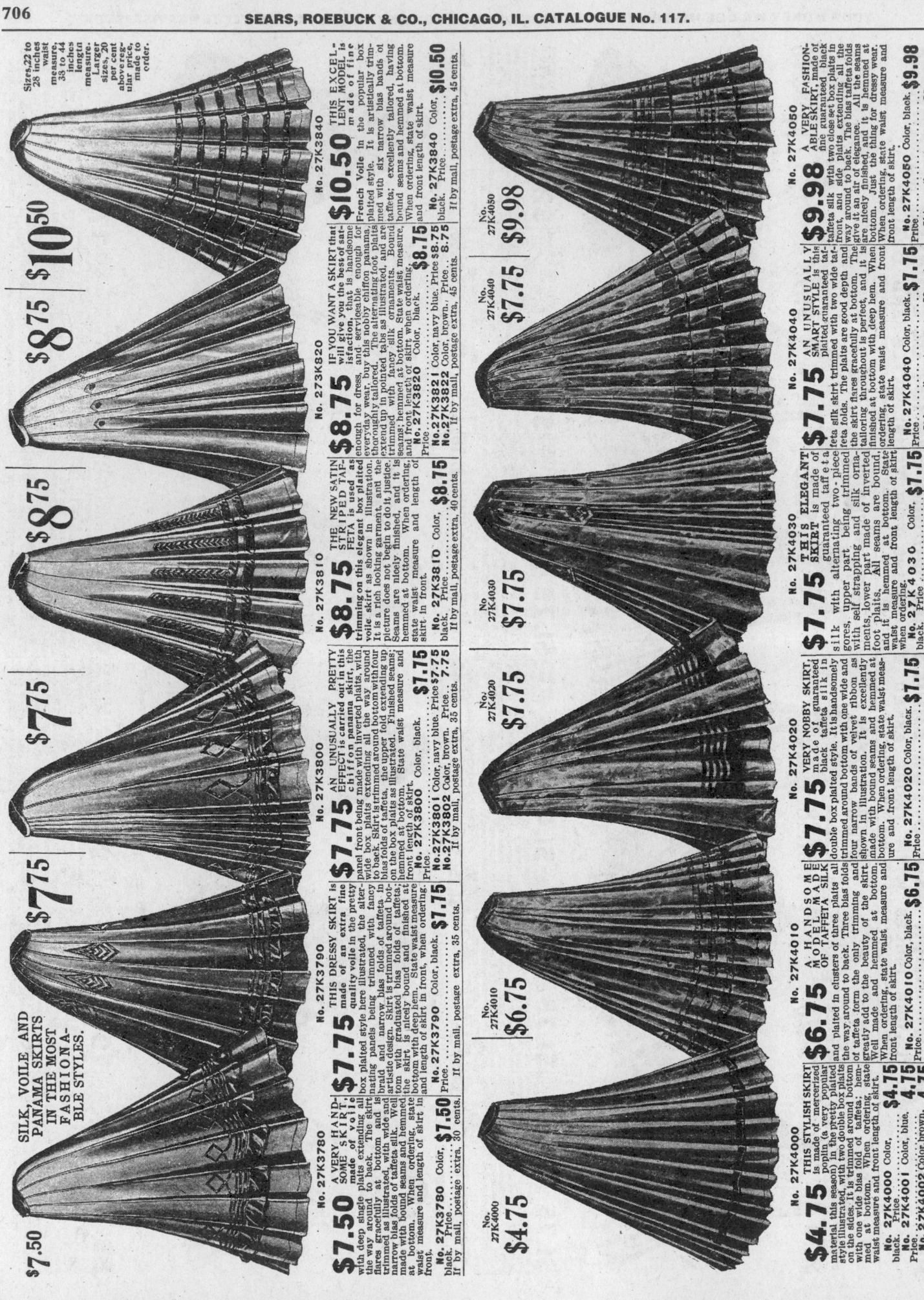

SILK, VOILE AND PANAMA SKIRTS IN THE MOST FASHIONABLE STYLES.

$7.50 $7.75 $8.75 $8.75 $10.50

Sizes 22 to 28 inches waist measure, 38 to 44 inches length measure. Larger sizes, 20 per cent above regular price, made to order.

No. 27K3780

$7.50 A VERY HANDSOME SKIRT is made of mercerized poplin (a very popular material this season) in the pretty plaited style illustrated, with two double box plaits on the sides. Three bias folds of taffeta form the only trimming, and four narrow bands of velvet ribbon greatly add to the beauty of the skirt. Well made and hemmed at bottom. When ordering, state waist measure and front length of skirt.

No. 27K3780   Color, black.
Price.................. **$7.50**
No. 27K3781   Color, blue.
Price.................. 7.50
If by mail, postage extra, 30 cents.

No. 27K3790

$7.75 THIS DRESSY SKIRT is made of an extra fine quality voile in the pretty box plaited style here illustrated, the alternating panels being trimmed with fancy braid and narrow bias folds of taffeta in artistic design. Skirt is trimmed around bottom with graduated bias folds of taffeta; the skirt is nicely bound and finished at bottom with deep hem. State waist measure and length of skirt in front, when ordering. Price.

No. 27K3790   Color, black.
Price.................. **$7.75**
If by mail, postage extra, 35 cents.

No. 27K3800

$7.75 AN UNUSUALLY PRETTY EFFECT is carried out in this chiffon panama skirt, the panel front being made with illuminating panels extending all the way around to back. The skirt flares gracefully at bottom and is trimmed with wide and narrow bias folds of taffeta, the upper fold extending up on the box plaits as illustrated. Finished seams; hemmed at bottom. When ordering, state front length of skirt.

No. 27K3800   Color, black.   **$7.75**
No. 27K3801 Color, navy blue. Price $7.75
No. 27K3802 Color, brown. Price. 7.75
If by mail, postage extra, 35 cents.

No. 27K3810

$8.75 THE NEW SATIN STRIPED TAFFETA is used as enough for dress, everyday wear, buy this nobby voile skirt as shown in illustration. It is a rich looking garment, and the picture does not begin to do it justice. Seams are nicely finished, and it is hemmed at bottom. When ordering, state waist measure and length of skirt in front.

No. 27K3810   Color, **$8.75**
black. Price.................. 8.75
If by mail, postage extra, 40 cents.

No. 273K820

$8.75 IF YOU WANT A SKIRT that will give you the best of satisfaction, this is handsome trimming on this elegant box plaited French Voile in the popular box plaited style. The alternating foot plaits extend up in pointed tabs as illustrated, and are trimmed with fancy silk ornaments. Bound seams are hemmed at bottom. State waist measure, and front length of skirt, when ordering.

No. 27K3820 Color, black.   **$8.75**
Price.
No. 27K3821 Color, navy blue. Price $8.75
No. 27K3822 Color, brown. Price. 8.75
If by mail, postage extra, 45 cents.

No. 27K3840

$10.50 THIS EXCELLENT MODEL is made of fine French Voile in the handsome panel front with peachiffon panama, thoroughly tailored, having excellently tailored, having bound seams and hemmed at bottom. When ordering, state waist measure and front length of skirt.

No. 27K3840 Color, black. **$10.50**
Price.................. If by mail, postage extra, 45 cents.

No. 27K4000

$4.75

$4.75 THIS STYLISH SKIRT is made of mercerized poplin in the pretty plaited and plaited in clusters of three plaits in style illustrated, with two double box plaits the way around to back. Three bias folds of taffeta form the only trimming, and it is excellently made and hemmed at bottom. When ordering, state waist measure and front length of skirt.

No. 27K4000   Color, black.   **$4.75**
Price.................. 4.75
No. 27K4001 Color, blue.
Price.................. 4.75
No. 27K4002 Color, brown. 4.75
Price.................. (Postage extra, 30c)

No. 27K4010

$6.75

$6.75 A HANDSOME MODEL MADE OF TAFFETA SILK double box plaited style. It is handsomely trimmed around bottom with one wide and four narrow bands of velvet ribbon as shown in illustration. It is excellently made with bound seams and hemmed at bottom. When ordering, state waist measure and front length of skirt.

No. 27K4010 Color, black. **$6.75**
Price.

No. 27K4020

$7.75

$7.75 VERY NOBBY SKIRT, made of guaranteed black taffeta silk in double box plaited style. It is trimmed around bottom with two wide and three bias folds trimmed with silk ornaments, lower part made of inverted foot plaits. All seams are bound, and it is hemmed at bottom. State waist measure and front length of skirt, when ordering.

No. 27K4020 Color, black. **$7.75**
Price.

No. 27K4030

$7.75

$7.75 THIS ELEGANT SKIRT is made of guaranteed taffeta silk with alternating two-piece gores, upper part being trimmed with self strapping and silk ornaments, lower part made of inverted foot plaits. All seams are bound, and it is hemmed at bottom. State waist measure and front length of skirt, when ordering.

No. 27K4030   Color, black. **$7.75**
Price.
If by mail, postage extra, 30 cents.

No. 27K4040

$7.75

$7.75 AN UNUSUALLY SMART STYLE is the plaited guaranteed taffeta silk skirt trimmed with two close set box plaits in front, and side plaits extending all the way around to back. The bias taffeta folds give an air of elegance. All the seams are nicely finished, and it is finished at bottom with deep hem. When ordering, state waist measure and front length of skirt.

No. 27K4040 Color, black. **$7.75**
Price.
If by mail, postage extra, 30 cents.

No. 27K4050

$9.98

$9.98 A VERY FASHIONABLE SKIRT, made of fine guaranteed black taffeta silk with two close set box plaits in front, and side plaits extending all the way around to back. The bias taffeta folds give an air of elegance. All the seams are nicely finished, and it is hemmed at bottom. State waist measure and front length of skirt.

No. 27K4050 Color, black. **$9.98**
Price.
If by mail, postage extra, 35 cents.

A PAGE OF DAINTY WAISTS IN THE NEWEST SPRING STYLES

SUCH VALUES AS THESE CANNOT BE FOUND IN ANY RETAIL ESTABLISHMENT ANYWHERE

Sizes, 32 to 42 inches bust measure. No extra sizes.

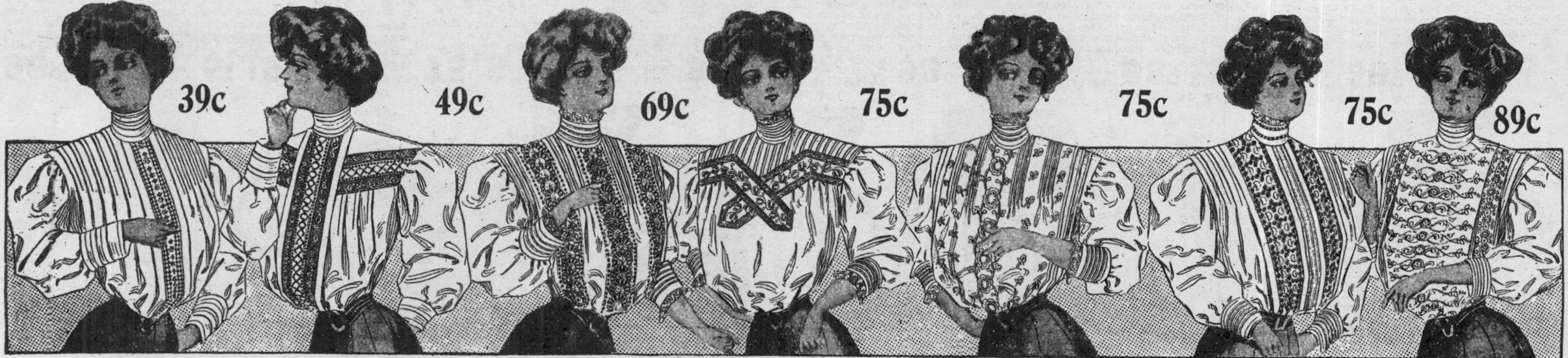

No. 27K5000

39c WHITE LAWN WAIST TRIMMED WITH EMBROIDERY INSERTION DOWN CENTER OF FRONT, wide tuck on either side; front is tucked to graduated yoke depth. Two tucks in back. Long sleeves with tucked cuffs. Detachable tucked stock. Waist buttons in front. A good value. Be sure to give bust measure when ordering.

No. 27K5000 Price.............. 39c

If by mail, postage extra, 12 cents.

No. 27K5005

49c THIS PRETTY WHITE WAIST IS MADE OF LAWN AND IS TRIMMED ACROSS YOKE AND DOWN FRONT WITH EMBROIDERY INSERTION between rows of lace; wide tuck on either side of front panel; front tucked as shown; two tucks in back; long sleeves with tucked cuffs; detachable tucked collar. Waist buttons in front. Don't forget to give bust measure.

No. 27K5005 Price.............. 49c

If by mail, postage extra, 12 cents.

No. 27K5010

69c A NICE, SERVICEABLE WHITE LAWN WAIST TRIMMED DOWN FRONT WITH THREE EMBROIDERY PANELS, alternating with clusters of narrow tucks; three-quarter length sleeves with narrow tucked cuffs edged with valenciennes lace; attached tucked collar also edged with lace to match cuffs. Waist buttons in back. Clusters of three tucks on either side of back. State bust measure when ordering.

No. 27K5010 Price.... 69c

If by mail, postage extra, 12 cents.

No. 27K5015

75c A VERY PRETTY DESIGN IS BROUGHT OUT IN THIS WHITE LAWN WAIST, which has a tucked pointed yoke, finished with insertions of dainty embroidery and valenciennes lace, which cross at center front. Three-quarter sleeves with tucked cuffs edged with valenciennes lace; tucked stock to match. Waist buttons in back with two clusters of tucks stitched to yoke depth on either side. Size, please?

No. 27K5015 Price.... 75c

If by mail, postage extra, 12 cents.

No. 27K5020

75c HERE IS AN EXTREMELY PRETTY WAIST AT A REASONABLE FIGURE. It is made of white lawn with allover embroidery front, and trimmed with four clusters of narrow tucks and two clusters of wider tucks. Three-quarter length sleeves with tucked cuffs edged with lace, attached stock to match. Waist buttons in back, with two clusters of tiny tucks on either side. Size, please?

No. 27K5020 Price.... 75c

If by mail, postage extra, 13 cents.

No. 27K5025

75c GOOD QUALITY WHITE LAWN WAIST WITH FRONT TUCKED AS SHOWN IN ILLUSTRATION and trimmed with two embroidery panels. Waist buttons under plait in front. Long sleeves with tucked cuffs. Detached collar finished with two rows of hemstitching and valenciennes lace. Neat and stylish. What size, please?

No. 27K5025 Price.............. 75c

If by mail, postage extra, 13 cents.

No. 27K5030

89c DAINTY WAIST MADE OF SHEER WHITE LAWN WITH ALLOVER EMBROIDERY FRONT, fullness being laid in four narrow tucks on either side. Waist closes in back with cluster of tucks on each side extending to waist line. Three-quarter sleeves finished with narrow tucked cuffs, attached to match. Always mention bust measure.

No. 27K5030 Price.............. 89c

If by mail, postage extra, 13 cents.

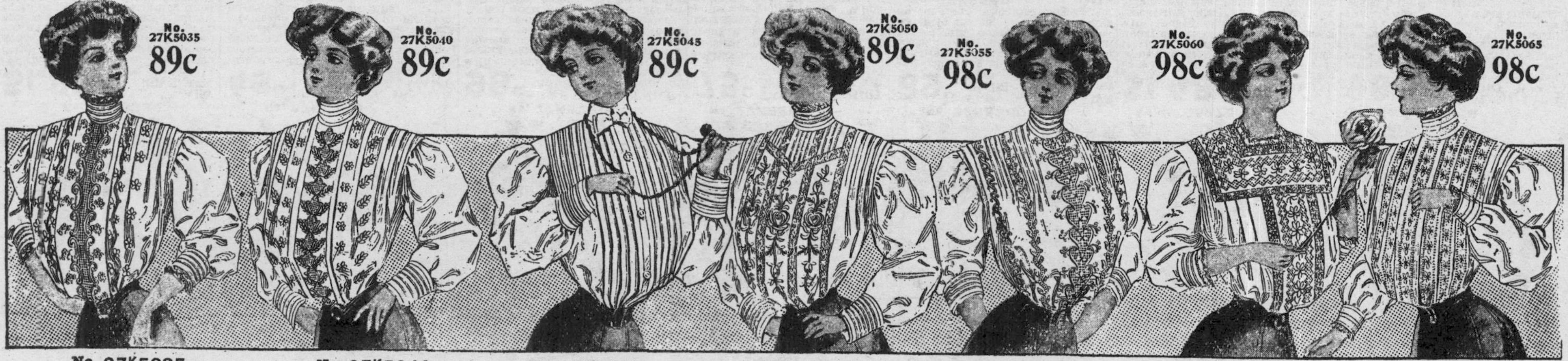

No. 27K5035

89c A VERY ATTRACTIVE WAIST made of white lawn and handsomely embroidered on front as shown in illustration; five wide tucks at shoulders; waist buttons in back with two wide tucks on either side; attached tucked collar edged with lace, cuffs on three-quarter sleeves to match. Don't fail to mention bust measure when ordering.

No. 27K5035 Price.............. 89c

If by mail, postage extra, 14 cents.

No. 27K5040

89c AN UNUSUALLY ATTRACTIVE WAIST, made of sheer white lawn with allover embroidered front and five wide tucks on either side. Waist buttons at side of front panel; two tucks extending from shoulder seams in back on either side. Full length sleeves with deep tucked cuffs; attached tucked stock. One of the best values ever offered. Do not fail to state size when ordering.

No. 27K5040 Price.............. 89c

If by mail, postage extra, 13 cents.

No. 27K5045

89c FASHIONABLE TAILOR MADE WAIST of sheer white lawn. Front has four half-inch tucks on either side of center box plait extending to waist line; quarter-inch tucks on either side stitched to yoke depth. Laundered turnover collar furnished with waist. Tie not furnished. Waist buttons in front. Back of waist has two half-inch tucks extending from shoulder seams to waist line. Long plain shirt sleeves with tucked cuff. Size?

No. 27K5045 Price.... 89c

If by mail, postage extra, 14 cents.

No. 27K5050

89c WHITE LAWN WAIST trimmed in front as shown in illustration with valenciennes insertion, embroidery panels and tucks. Full length sleeves with tucked cuffs; attached tucked collar edged with valenciennes lace; waist buttons in back with two wide tucks on either side. Very pretty waist and a good value. Always give size when ordering.

No. 27K5050 Price.............. 89c

If by mail, postage extra, 13 cents.

No. 27K5055

98c THE FRONT OF THIS NEAT WHITE LAWN WAIST is prettily embroidered as shown in illustration having cluster of narrow tucks stitched to yoke depth alternating with embroidery; two wide tucks near shoulder seam. Waist buttons in back; four small tucks on either side; elbow sleeves with narrow tucked cuffs; attached stock collar to match. Size, please?

No. 27K5055 Price.............. 98c

If by mail, postage extra, 14 cents.

No. 27K5060

98c THIS DAINTY LAWN WAIST is made with Dutch neck and is trimmed with wide embroidery, valenciennes lace and insertion as shown in illustration. Fullness is laid in tucks at bottom of square yoke; three-quarter sleeves with tucked cuffs edged with lace. Waist buttons in back with two tucks on either side. Be sure to state size wanted when ordering.

No. 27K5060 Price.............. 98c

If by mail, postage extra, 13 cents.

No. 27K5065

98c A VERY HANDSOME WAIST of fine lawn with allover embroidered front in a very pretty pattern, the embroidery alternating with narrow tucks as illustrated. Waist buttons under box plait in front. Back of waist is made with cluster of three tucks on either side; long sleeves with tucked cuffs edged with valenciennes lace. Attached stock collar to match. Be sure to mention size wanted when ordering.

No. 27K5065 Price.... 98c

If by mail, postage extra, 14 cents.

STYLES FROM THE FASHION CENTERS OF THE WORLD

ARE SHOWN ON THESE PAGES, IN DESIGN, IN FABRIC, IN WORKMANSHIP THESE WAISTS ARE GUARANTEED TO PLEASE.

Sizes, 32 to 42 Inches Bust Measure.

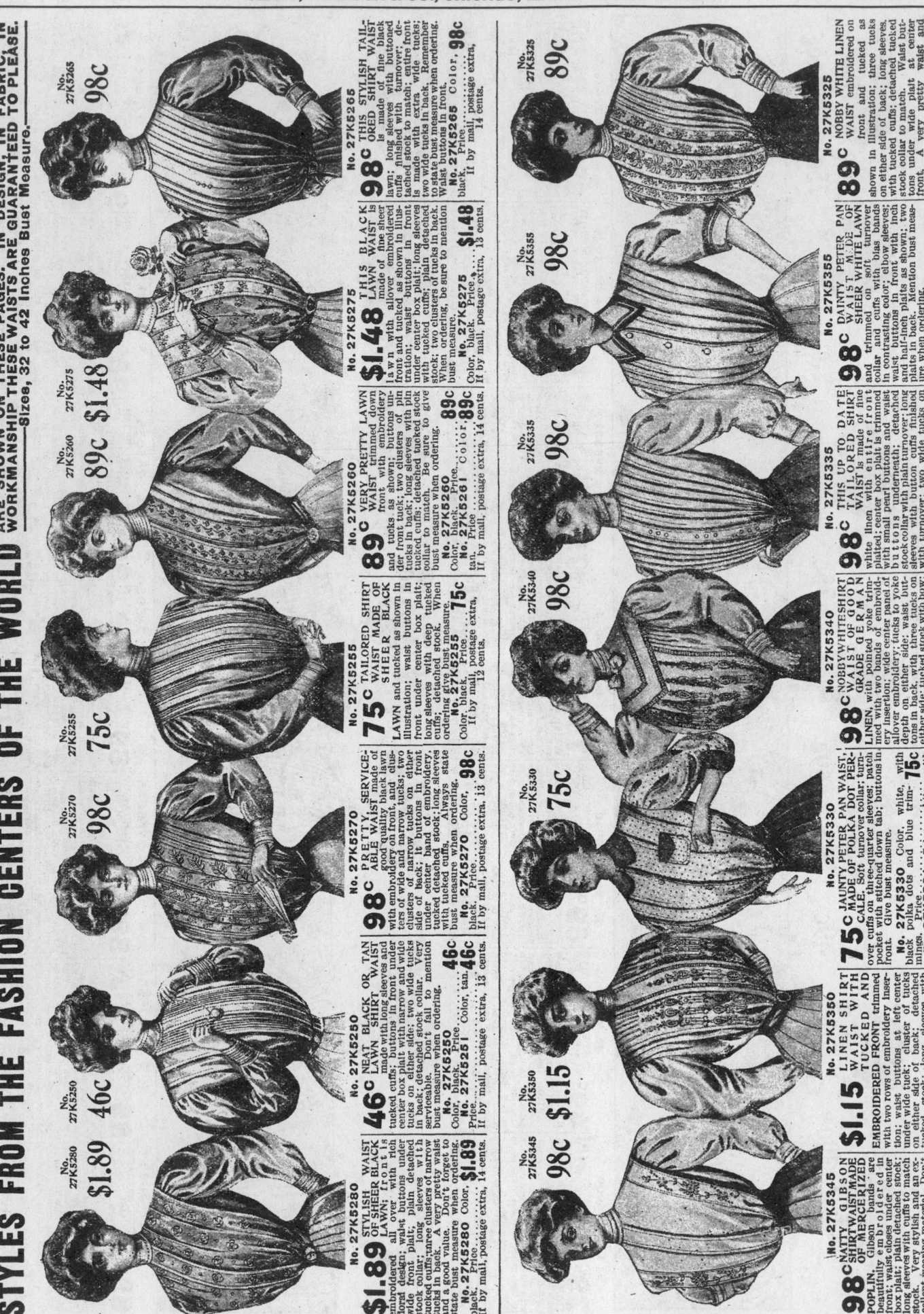

No. 27K5280
$1.89

No. 27K5250
46c

No. 27K5255
75c

No. 27K5260
98c

No. 27K5270
98c

No. 27K5265
98c

No. 27K5275
$1.48

No. 27K5325
89c

No. 27K5355
98c

No. 27K5335
98c

No. 27K5340
98c

No. 27K5330
75c

No. 27K5350
$1.15

No. 27K5345
98c

No. 27K5280 STYLISH WAIST OF SHEER BLACK LAWN; front is embroidered all over with rich floral design; waist buttons under stock front plait; plain detached back; long sleeves with cuffs to match; three clusters of narrow tucked in back. A very pretty waist and a good value. Don't forget to state bust measure when ordering. No. 27K5280 Color, black. Price... $1.89 If by mail, postage extra, 14 cents.

No. 27K5250 NEAT BLACK OR TAN LAWN SHIRT WAIST made with long sleeves and tucked cuffs; buttons in front under center box plait with narrow and wide tucks on either side; two narrow tucks on each side of back. It buttons in front under center band of embroidery, tucked detached stock; long sleeves with tucked cuffs. Always state bust measure when ordering. No. 27K5250 Color, black. Price... 46c No. 27K5251 Color, tan. 46c Price... If by mail, postage extra, 13 cents.

No. 27K5255 TAILORED SHIRT WAIST MADE OF SHEER BLACK LAWN and tucked as shown in illustration; waist buttons in front under center box plait; long sleeves with deep tucked cuffs; detached stock. When ordering give bust measure. No. 27K5255 Color, black. Price... 75c If by mail, postage extra, 12 cents.

No. 27K5260 VERY PRETTY LAWN WAIST trimmed down front with embroidery and tucks as shown; buttons under front tuck; two clusters of pin tucks in back; long sleeves with pin tucked cuffs; detached tucked stock collar to match. Be sure to give bust measure when ordering. No. 27K5260 Color, black. Price... 89c No. 27K5261 Color, tan. 89c Price... If by mail, postage extra, 14 cents.

No. 27K5270 PRETTY, SERVICEABLE WAIST made of good quality black lawn with embroidery on front, and clusters of wide and narrow tucks; two rows of embroidery insertion on back. It buttons in front under center band of embroidery, detached stock; long sleeves with tucked cuffs. Remember to mention bust measure when ordering. No. 27K5270 Color, black. Price... 98c If by mail, postage extra, 13 cents.

No. 27K5265 THIS STYLISH TAILORED SHIRT WAIST is made of fine black lawn; long sleeves with buttoned cuffs; finished with turnover collar; entire front is made with extra wide tucks; two wide tucks in back. Remember to state bust measure when ordering. Waist buttons in front. No. 27K5265 Color, black. Price... 98c If by mail, postage extra, 14 cents.

No. 27K5275 THIS BLACK LAWN WAIST is made of fine sheer lawn, with allover embroidered front and tucked as shown in illustration; waist buttons in front under center box plait; long sleeves with tucked cuffs; plain detached stock; two clusters of tucks in back. When ordering, be sure to mention bust measure. No. 27K5275 Color, black. Price... $1.48 If by mail, postage extra, 13 cents.

No. 27K5325 NOBBY WHITE LINEN WAIST embroidered on front and tucked as shown in illustration; three tucks on either side of back; long sleeves with tucked cuffs; detached stock collar to match. Waist buttons under wide plait at center front. A very pretty waist, and made of excellent material. Always state bust measure when ordering. No. 27K5325 Color, white. Price... 89c If by mail, postage extra, 16 cents.

No. 27K5355 DAINTY PETER PAN WAIST MADE OF SHEER WHITE LAWN and trimmed on soft turnover collar and cuffs with blue ribbons in contrasting color; long sleeves with elbow sleeves; detached depth in front, with inch plaits in back. Mention bust measure when ordering. No. 27K5355 Color, white with blue trimming. Price... 98c No. 27K5356 Color, white with pink trimming. Price... 98c If by mail, postage extra, 16 cents.

No. 27K5335 THIS UP TO DATE TAILORED SHIRT WAIST is made of fine white linen with entire front plaited; center box plait is trimmed with small pearl buttons and waist closes underneath; detached stock collar with button finished with turnover; two wide tucks on either side of back. Don't fail to give bust measure when ordering. No. 27K5335 Color, white. Price... 98c If by mail, postage extra, 16c.

No. 27K5340 NOBBY WHITE SHIRT WAIST MADE OF GOOD GRADE GERMAN LINEN, with pointed yoke trimmed with two bands of embroidery insertion; wide center panel of allover embroidery; tucks to yoke depth in back, with three tucks on either side; tucked stock with bow; wide tucked cuffs on long sleeves. Bust measure, please. No. 27K5340 Color, white. Price... 98c If by mail, postage extra, 16c.

No. 27K5330 JAUNTY PETER PAN WAIST MADE OF POLKA DOT PERCALE. Soft turnover collar; turnover cuffs on three-quarter sleeves; breast pocket with stitched down tab; buttons in front. Give bust measure. No. 27K5330 Color, white, with black polka dots and blue trimmings. Price... 75c No. 27K5331 Color, white, with blue polka dots and blue trimmings. Price... 75c No. 27K5332 Color, white, with red polka dots and blue trimmings. Price... 75c

No. 27K5350 LINEN SHIRT WAIST WITH TUCKED AND EMBROIDERED FRONT trimmed with two rows of embroidery insertion; waist buttons at left center under wide tuck; cluster of tucks on either side of back; detached tucked stock; long sleeves with tucked cuffs. Remember to state bust measure when ordering. No. 27K5350 Color, white. Price... $1.15 If by mail, postage extra, 16c.

No. 27K5345 NATTY GIBSON SHIRTWAIST MADE OF MERCERIZED POPLIN. Gibson bands are beautifully embroidered in front; waist closes under center box plait; plain detached stock. Very stylish and an excellent wearing material. Don't fail to mention bust measure when ordering. No. 27K5345 Color, white. Price... 98c If by mail, postage extra, 18c.

SUCH VARIETY IN STYLE AND PRICE MAKE SELECTION EASY

Even Our Lowest Priced Waists Have a Distinctiveness of Style Which Makes Them Unusually Attractive.

Sizes, 32 to 42 inches bust measure.

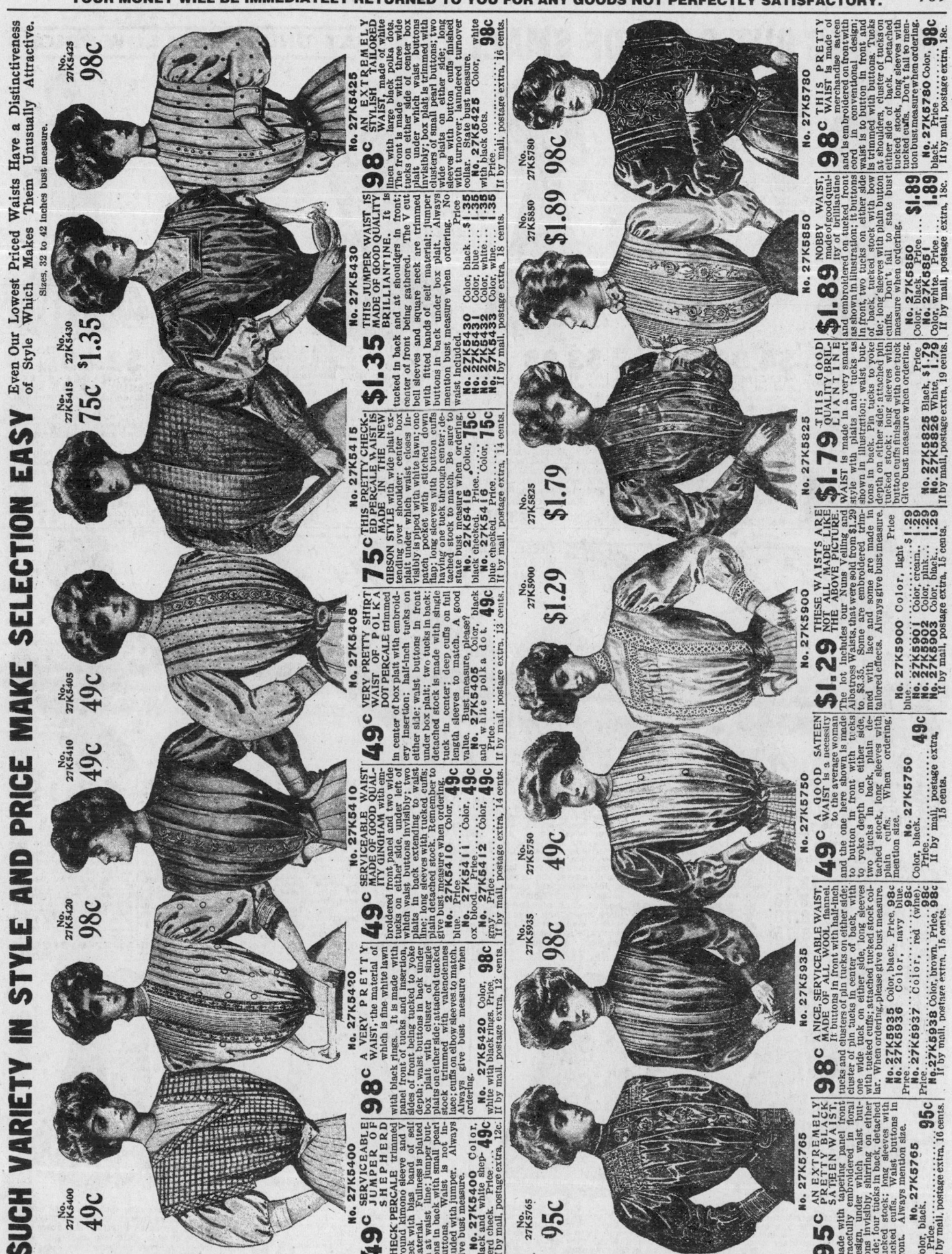

No. 27K5400

49c SERVICEABLE JUMPER OF SHEPHERD CHECK PERCALE trimmed around kimono sleeve and waist with plaited band of material. Fullness is plaited in at waist line; jumper buttons in back with small pearl buttons. Waist is not included with jumper. Always give bust measure.

No. 27K5400 Color, black and white shepherd check. Price....49c
If by mail, postage extra, 12c.

No. 27K5410

49c A VERY PRETTY WAIST, the material of which is the white lawn with black rings. It is made with tucks and insertion, which waist buttons invisibly; two plaits in back extending to yoke depth; waist buttons in front under box plait with cluster of single plaits on either side; attached tucked stock trimmed with valenciennes lace; cuffs on elbow sleeves to match. Always give bust measure when ordering.

No. 27K5410 Color, blue. Price....49c
No. 27K5411 Color, pink. Price....49c
No. 27K5412 Color, white. Price....49c
If by mail, postage extra, 14 cents.

No. 27K5420

98c SERVICEABLE WAIST MADE OF GOOD QUALITY GINGHAM with embroidered front panel and two wide tucks on either side, under left of which waist buttons invisibly; shirring on either side; four tucks in back, detached stock; long sleeves with tucked cuffs; long sleeves with tucked stock to match. Always give bust measure when ordering.

No. 27K5420 Color, white with black rings. Price....98c
If by mail, postage extra, 16 cents.

No. 27K5405

49c VERY PRETTY SHIRT WAIST OF POLKA DOT PERCALE trimmed in center of box plait with embroidery insertion; half-inch tucks on either side; waist closes in visibly with white lawn; one patch pocket with stitched down flap; long sleeves with button cuffs having one tuck through center; detached stock is made with single tuck in center; deep cuffs on full length sleeves to match. A good value. Bust measure, please state bust measure when ordering.

No. 27K5405 Color, black check. Price....49c
No. 27K5406 Color, black and white polka dot. Price....49c
If by mail, postage extra, 13 cents.

No. 27K5415

75c THIS PRETTY CHECKED PERCALE WAIST IS MADE IN THE NEW GIBSON STYLE with wide plait extending over which waist, center box plait under which waist closes invisibly; box plait is trimmed with clusters of small pearl buttons; two buttons in back under box plait. Always mention bust measure when ordering.

No. 27K5415 Color, blue check. Price....75c
No. 27K5416 Color, black and white polka dot. Price....75c
If by mail, postage extra, 14 cents.

No. 27K5425

98c AN EXTREMELY STYLISH TAILORED WAIST, made of white linen with large black polka dots. The front is made with three wide tucks on either side of center box plait under which waist buttons invisibly; box plait is trimmed with clusters of small pearl buttons; two wide plaits in back finished sleeves with button cuffs finished with turnover; laundered turnover collar. State bust measure.

No. 27K5425 Color, white with black dots. Price....98c
If by mail, postage extra, 16 cents.

No. 27K5430

$1.35 THIS JUMPER WAIST IS MADE OF GOOD QUALITY BRILLIANTINE. It is tucked in back and at shoulders in front; center of front being gathered. The V cut bell sleeves and square neck are trimmed with fitted bands of self material. Jumper buttons in back under box plait. Always mention bust measure when ordering. No waist included. Price

No. 27K5430 Color, black....$1.35
No. 27K5431 Color, blue....1.35
No. 27K5433 Color, white....1.35
If by mail, postage extra, 18 cents.

No. 27K5765

95c AN EXTREMELY PRETTY BLACK SATEEN WAIST, made with tapering panel front gracefully embroidered in floral design, under which waist buttons invisibly, shirring on either side; four tucks in back, detached stock; long sleeves with tucked cuffs. Always mention size.

No. 27K5765 Color, black. Price....95c
If by mail, postage extra, 16 cents.

No. 27K5750

49c A GOOD SATEEN WAIST is a necessity to the average woman and the one here shown is made to button in front with tucks to yoke depth on either side; long sleeves with plain detached stock, long sleeves with tailored effects. Always give bust measure.

No. 27K5750 Color, black. Price....49c
If by mail, postage extra, 15 cents.

No. 27K5935

98c A NICE, SERVICEABLE WAIST, MADE OF ALL WOOL flannel. It buttons in front with half-inch tucks and clusters of pin tucks on either side; one wide tuck on either side, long sleeves with tucked cuffs; attached tucked collar. When ordering, please give bust measure.

No. 27K5935 Color, black. Price....98c
No. 27K5936 Color, navy blue. Price....98c
No. 27K5937 Color, red (wine). Price....98c
No. 27K5938 Color, brown. Price, 98c
If by mail, postage extra, 15 cents.

No. 27K5900

$1.29 THESE WAISTS ARE NOT ALL MADE LIKE THE ABOVE PICTURE. The lot includes our Nuns Veiling and Albatross Waists, that were sold from $1.29 to $3.35. Some are embroidered and trimmed with lace and some are made in tailored effects. Always give bust measure.

No. 27K5900 Color, light blue....$1.29
No. 27K5901 Color, cream....1.29
No. 27K5902 Color, pink....1.29
No. 27K5903 Color, black....1.29
If by mail, postage extra, 19 cents.

No. 27K5825

$1.79 THIS GOOD QUALITY BRILLIANTINE WAIST is made in a very smart style with plaits and tucks as shown in illustration; it buttons in front, two tucks on either side to button in front; waist buttons to yoke depth in back. Pin tucks form depth on either side; attached pin tucked stock; long sleeves with cuffs. Don't fail to state bust button cuffs finished with one tuck Give bust measure when ordering.

No. 27K5825 Black, Price....$1.79
No. 27K5826 White, $1.79
If by mail, postage extra, 19 cents.

No. 27K5850

$1.89 NOBBY WAIST, made of good quality of brilliantine. It is embroidered on tucked front as shown in illustration; waist buttons to yoke of back, tucked stock with bow is trimmed with button; long sleeves with plain button in tie; tucked stock; long sleeves with cuffs. Don't fail to state bust measure.

No. 27K5850 Color, black. Price....$1.89
No. 27K5851 Color, white. $1.89
If by mail, postage extra, 18c.

No. 27K5780

98c THIS PRETTY STYLISH WAIST is made of merchandise sateen and is embroidered on front with cord in conventional design; it is to button in front and is trimmed with buttons. Tucks at shoulders, cluster of tucks on either side of back. Detached tucked stock. Don't fail to mention bust measure when ordering.

No. 27K5780 Color, black. Price....98c
If by mail, postage extra, 18c.

CLOSING OUT SALE OF SMALL LOTS AT UNUSUALLY LOW PRICES

BE SURE TO SNAP UP SOME OF THESE WONDER VALUES.

BE SURE TO STATE YOUR SIZES.

$3.89 SHIRT-WAIST SUITS. Made of good quality fancy flannel, not too heavy, in fact, it is just the proper thing for spring and early fall. We will sell them at the price you would have to pay for the skirt alone. The skirt itself can be worn without the shirt waist and with any other style of waist you may have, and a woman always looks neat in a plain shirt-waist suit. Colors, black, blue and wine. State size and color wanted. All regular sizes. No. 27K9100 Price.........**$3.89**

$4.95 IN THIS LOT WE PUT OUR ENTIRE STOCK OF LADIES' VELVETEEN SHIRT WAIST SUITS. Most of them are like illustration above, and quite a number of them are much neater. Some are made with open backs; others open fronts; a few with short sleeves, and some with long sleeves. When you order state your preference, with the privilege that we may give you what we have in case we are sold out of your first choice. At this price these suits will not last long. Colors, black, navy blue, green, wine and brown. State size and color wanted. All regular sizes. No. 27K9101 Price.. **$4.95**

$3.98 IN THIS LOT WE HAVE INCLUDED our entire stock of sicilian and brilliantine shirt waist suits. Material is that light weight nice luster cloth that is so well liked by the ladies at present. The skirt is full, nicely paited, and well tailored. Colors, black, navy blue and green. All regular sizes. State size and color wanted. No. 27K9102 Price.........**$3.98**

98c WASHABLE SHIRT WAIST SUITS MADE OF PERCALE. Most of them are like illustration. Our intention is to clean up our stock of all small lots of suits that sold as high as $2.00 and $2.50. We have them in the following colors; Black and white checks, blue with wine polka dots, brown and blue, brown and tan, white with fancy flower designs, all black and navy blue. Please remember that these suits are sold at cut prices, the prices are below the original cost, and it may happen that a skirt will be an inch or two longer than your order calls for, in which case it will not be much trouble to you to make this alteration,. No. 27K9103 Price.........**98c**

$1.89 THIS ELEGANT MISSES' SAILOR SUIT IS MADE OF GOOD WASH MATERIALS. Consists of very nice sailor blouse, beautifully trimmed. Inlaid dickey. All suits in this lot are not like illustration but are very similar. Don't miss this great bargain. Colors, tan or blue. Sizes, 32 to 38 bust, 22 to 28 waist and 36 to 40 inches length skirt. Always state size and color when ordering. No. 27K9104 Price.........**$1.89**

$2.89 THIS ENTIRE LOT OF WASHABLE SERGE SHIRT WAIST SUITS, made just like illustration. They are very pretty in style and neat in design; well made in every respect. They are worth a great deal more than we ask and we are satisfied they will give the best of satisfaction. State size and color wanted. All regular sizes. No. 27K9105 Color, black with white hairline stripes. Price.........**$2.89**

THESE GOODS ARE WORTH FROM TWO TO THREE TIMES OUR PRICE.

$3.75 UNDER THIS ILLUSTRATION WE SHOW OUR ENTIRE STOCK OF LAST YEAR'S SAILOR BLOUSE SUITS made of mohairs. They are just the thing for at home or for the school. They are very handy and are always stylish. We can furnish them in the following colors. All regular sizes. Be sure to state size wanted.

No. 27K9107	Color, black. Price....	$3.75
No. 27K9108	Color, blue. Price....	3.75
No. 27K9109	Color, brown. Price....	3.75
No. 27K9110	Color, cream. Price....	3.75
No. 27K9111	Color, wine. Price....	3.75

98c MOST OF THE WAISTS IN THIS LOT are very similar to illustration; quite a number of them are far prettier and much better. Materials used are good sicilians with a nice luster. They are all nicely tailored, made very full with long sleeves. All regular sizes. Be sure to state size and color wanted. No. 27K9117 Color, black. Price... **98c** No. 27K9118 Color, blue. Price... **98c** No. 27K9119 Color, brown. Price **98c**

68c THIS LOT INCLUDES OUR ENTIRE LINE OF JUMPERS made of flannelette and flannel fancy plaid materials that are especially adapted for early spring, and can be worn with almost any waist. This particular style is a great favorite in the large cities. At the price we sell them they should not last very long, and we would advise you to send in your order stating the choice of your color. Colors, black and white checks, dark blue and red plaids, dark green and blue plaids, all black and white plaids, and blue and red plaids. State size wanted. All regular sizes. No. 27K9114 Price.........**68c**

69c IN THIS LOT YOU WILL FIND our entire line of last fall's flannelette ladies' waists, all nicely tailored; made similar to illustration, and in a beautiful assortment of patterns. A waist of this kind is always handy, as on cool mornings there is nothing so serviceable as a flannelette or flannel shirt waist and, considering the low price, you should not hesitate to order at once. Colors, blue plaid, red and green plaid, light blue stripe, red with stripes, dark blue with stripes, black and white checks, white with black checks, white with blue checks, gray plaid, green plaid, and tan plaid. State size wanted. All regular sizes. No. 27K9115 Price.........**69c**

$1.89 GUARANTEED TAFFETA SILK JUMPER, for $1.89. The jumper is not only dressy, but it will cover the greater part of the white waist which you will wear with this jumper. It is nicely tailored, made of good materials, and we consider it a great bargain at our price. We have them in all sizes. Color, black only. State size wanted. No. 27K9120 Price.........**$1.89**

$2.19 TAFFETA SILK JUMPERS in black and white, blue and green plaids. We have but a few of them left and while they last we will sell them at a sacrifice price of $2.19. This jumper is a great bargain at our price, and we know you will be greatly pleased when you receive this handsome garment. Sizes, 32 to 42 bust measure. State size and color wanted. No. 27K9121 Price.........**$2.19**

$3.98 TAFFETA SILK SKIRTS MADE IN THE NEWEST PLAITED STYLES, measuring over three yards in sweep; well made in every respect for the cost of the material. We have a few hundred of these in black, navy blue and brown colors, and will sell them while they last at the ridiculously low price of $3.98. Please remember that this skirt is sold to you with the understanding that if it is not satisfactory in every respect, you have the privilege of returning it to us. We have them in 38 to 43 inches length and 22 to 28 inches waist; no other sizes. Give measurements. No. 27K9122 Price.........**$3.98**

$2.39 EVERY SKIRT IN THIS LOT is MADE OF ALL WOOL FANCY MIXTURE. Nicely tailored, plaited and self strapping. Former price, $3.35. We have about 187 of these in stock and we will sell them at a sacrifice. Colors, black mixture, blue mixture and brown mixture. Sizes, 22 to 28 inches waist measure, and 38 to 42 inches in length; no other sizes. While they last. Give measurements and color wanted. No. 27K9123 Price.........**$2.39**

$2.98 YOU COULD NOT DO BETTER THAN TO ORDER ONE OF THESE STYLISH TAILORED SKIRTS made in a fancy plaid material. Every skirt in this lot is made just like the illustration, with plaits and self  strapping. The shadow plaids have been and still are very popular. Color, light or dark gray plaids only. We have these skirts in dark and medium gray colors, in following sizes: 24 to 28 inches waist measure and 38 to 44 inches in length; no other sizes Give size and color wanted. No. 27K9124 Price.........**$2.98**

$1.98 THIS LOT CONSISTS OF ALL SMALL LOTS IN SKIRTS MADE OF FANCY MIXTURE MATERIALS. Most of them are similar to illustration. We have cut up all the odd pieces we had in the factory—this is what you might call a cleaning up sale—and some of the skirts in this lot are worth a great deal more than we ask for them. We have these in fancy blue mixtures, brown mixtures, gray mixtures and green mixtures. Be sure to state size and color when you order. All regular sizes. No. 27K9125 Price.........**$1.98**

OUR BARGAIN COUNTER GOODS SOLD AT LESS THAN COST OF MATERIAL

DON'T FAIL TO GET ONE OR MORE OF THESE BARGAINS.

$1.89 HERE IS AN EXCEPTIONALLY GOOD VALUE FOR THE MONEY. Made in good quality melton in black, brown and dark gray colors. Can you imagine a skirt made up in this neat style of good material for anything like our price? Sizes, 22 to 28 inches waist measure, and from 40 to 45 inches in length; no other sizes. State size and color wanted.
No. 27K9112
Price............$1.89

$1.68 EVEN IF YOU ARE NOT IN NEED OF A SKIRT DON'T OVERLOOK THIS OPPORTUNITY to get a good quality melton skirt made in the style like illustration. If for no other reason than to save your good skirt, this to be worn in bad weather only. It will pay you to send for it today providing you are lucky enough to wear the sizes we have them in. All regular sizes. Do not ask for any other sizes because we cannot make them for this price.
No. 27K9113
Color, black only. Price..$1.68

$2.98 THIS NOBBY SKIRT is made of a good quality broadcloth measuring 110 to 115 inches in sweep. Plaits all around as shown in illustration. Trimmed with small buttons. There is nothing wrong with this skirt; it is perfectly up to date. We have them in the following colors: Black, navy blue and brown. Sizes, 22 to 26 inches waist measure, and 37 to 43 inches in length. No other sizes. State size and color wanted.
Price............$2.98

$1.89 MISSES' WASHCOATS. They are all very similar to the illustration; well made, neat in style, and in good condition. We have them in the following colors: Tan, white and alice blue. When ordering be sure to state the color and size you desire. Sizes, from 32 to 38 inches bust measure.
No. 17K9011
Price............$1.89

$1.98 SHORT JACKETS, 24 to 27 inches long, made of beaver, melton, kersey and cheviot cloths. Most of them are neatly made and very similar to illustration. Colors, black, blue, brown or castor. All regular sizes. State size and color when ordering.
No. 17K9002
Price............$1.98

GET A COAT AT THESE PRICES WHILE THEY LAST.

DON'T FORGET TO STATE SIZE AND COLOR WANTED.

$2.95 FANCY GRAY MIXTURES. 42 inches long. They are all similar to illustration and are good values. You will be surprised at the low price when you see the garment that we offer you. Colors, gray mixtures. Just the right weight for spring and fall. All regular sizes. State bust measure.
No. 17K9003
Price............$2.95

$3.39 AN EXTREMELY CHEAP LOT OF LADIES' COATS. Made of medium weight diagonal material; 42 to 45 inches long; coat shaped collar and lapels; wide facing of same material. On account of its medium weight this coat is well adapted for spring and early fall. All regular sizes. State length wanted.
No. 17K9005
Color, navy blue. Price....$3.39
No. 17K9006
Color, oxford gray. Price..3.39

$2.98 EXCEPTIONALLY GOOD VALUES OFFERED IN THIS LOT OF LADIES' COATS. Made of fine wool mixture material; collarless effect, neatly trimmed; wide facing of same material; loose back and front; 42 to 45 inches long. Give length.
No. 17K9009 Color, fancy brown mixture. Price....$2.98
No. 17K9010 Color, fancy gray mixture. Price............$2.98

$2.98 THIS LOT CONSISTS OF 42-INCH LONG COATS. Made of melton, and a few kerseys; they are all similar to illustration, with loose back and front. This lot consists of several small lots, but every one of them is as nice if not nicer than the illustration. Have them in all sizes. Colors, black, blue, castor or brown. State size and color wanted.
No. 17K9008
Price............$2.98

$3.75 THIS LOT CONSISTS OF FULL LENGTH COATS. Made of gray melton or black or brown cheviot. The coats are all very similar to illustration; they are very nice and comfortable, cover the entire body; the proper thing for traveling, and are very neat for street wear. All regular sizes. Give a second choice in color when ordering. Colors, black, navy blue or gray. State size and color when ordering.
No. 17K9018 Price..$3.75

INCLUDE SOME OF THESE WONDER VALUES WITH YOUR ORDER.

TAKE ADVANTAGE OF THESE ASTONISHING VALUES AT ONCE.

$1.89 IN THIS LOT WE SHOW MISSES' JACKETS made of good quality medium weight materials, such as meltons, cheviots, and other neat styles. We have them in blue and castor colors. Sizes, 32, 34 and 36 only. No others. We have but a few left, and while they last we will sell them at this low price. State size and color wanted.
No. 17K9012
Price............$1.89

98c OUR ENTIRE STOCK OF WASHABLE CHILDREN'S REEFERS AND THREE-QUARTER COATS. The styles are very neat, up to date wash coats, and are very dressy and serviceable, as they can be kept clean, and it is no trouble to wash them. Colors, white with black trimming, blue with white trimming and tan. When ordering be sure to state the color you desire, and give a second choice. Sizes for 6 to 14-year old children.
No. 17K9037
Price............98c

98c A SPLENDID LOT OF CHILDREN'S SHORT REEFER JACKETS. Some with shoulder capes, and a few in the collarless effect, made of melton and cheviot in blue, brown or red colors. Sizes, for 6 to 14-year old girls. State size and color wanted.
No. 17K9038
Price............98c

$1.78 THIS LOT CONSISTS OF FANCY MIXTURES in the collarless style, or coat shaped effect, made of fancy gray mixture cloakings. Fancy mixtures for children are especially serviceable, as the spots won't show on this cloth. The material not being too heavy makes the coat very proper for spring and early fall. All sizes, for 6 to 14-year old girls. Colors, fancy gray mixtures. Don't forget to state size and style wanted.
No. 17K9036
Price............$1.78

$1.89 IN THIS LOT WE HAVE OUR ENTIRE STOCK OF SPRING CAPES that range from 20 to 25 inches in length. Color, black; some are trimmed and others are plain. We have them in the following sizes, 32 to 38 inches bust measure only. State size.
No. 17K9045
Price............$1.89

YOUR CHOICE OF ANY ARTICLE ON THESE

2 cents each

BY SELLING THE ARTICLES SHOWN ON THESE TWO PAGES (the articles commonly used in every home) at the exact cost to us plus only our one small percentage of profit, the same way as all our other goods are priced, reduces the selling price on them to 2 cents each, a price so low that economy compels us to make the condition that you order not less than twelve articles, and to make up a list of twelve articles you may select some from these pages at 2 cents each and some from our 4-cent pages, some from our 6-cent pages and some from our 8-cent pages, but any that you order from these two pages here will be 2 cents each. Every housewife knows the usual selling price of these eight pages, but any that you order from these two pages here will be 2 cents each. Every housewife knows the usual selling price of these articles and can readily compare our prices with those asked by dealers everywhere. These pages form a good basis for comparison on the question of value and show clearly what big savings you can make by buying all your items of merchandise from us. Please include other goods with your order for these articles for the freight on 50 to 100 pounds of merchandise will not cost you any more than the freight or express charges on an order for these goods alone. Therefore, we urge you, in your own interest, to include the articles from these special pages always with an order for other goods that you may be needing.

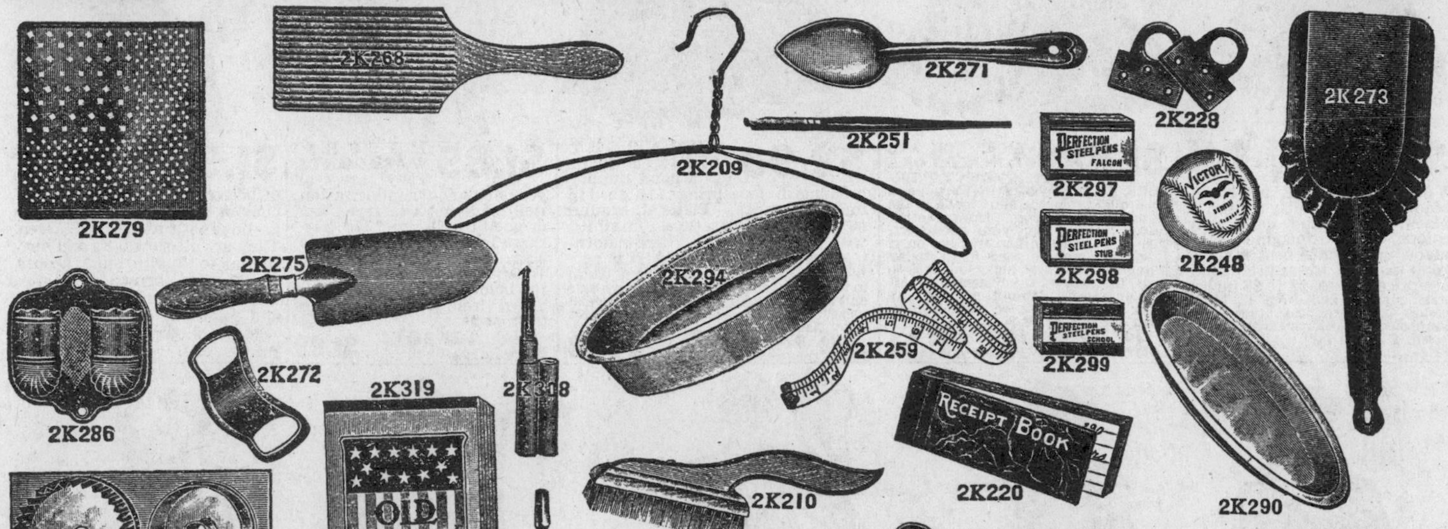

DESCRIPTIONS OF ARTICLES.

No. 2K201 Asbestos Stove Mat, 8½-inch, metal bound.
No. 2K202 Wrought 10-inch Hasp, with hook and staples.
No. 2K203 Cold Handle Stove Lid Lifter.
No. 2K204 Steel Shelf Bracket, size, 4x5 inches, one only.
No. 2K205 Tack Puller, steel, enameled wood handle.
No. 2K206 Full Size Nickel Plated Nut Cracker.
No. 2K207 Screw Pulley, iron wheel, size, 1½ inches.
No. 2K208 Horse Shoe Magnet, 2 inches.
No. 2K209 Rustproof Coat Hanger, made of heavy wire.
No. 2K210 Handy House Brush, with handle.
No. 2K211 Large Size Hinged Tea Ball, tinned wire.
No. 2K212 Iron Quilt Frame Clamp, opens 2½ inches.
No. 2K213 Iron Door Bolt, full length, 4 inches.
No. 2K214 Iron Clothes Line Hook, japanned, full size.
No. 2K215 One Dozen High Grade Blotters, 4x9 inches.
No. 2K216 Black Writing Ink, 2-ounce bottle.
No. 2K218 Child's Bib, lace trimmed.
No. 2K219 1 Box of about 1,000 Hardwood Tooth Picks.
No. 2K220 Receipt Book, pocket size, 50 receipts.
No. 2K221 Hardwood Mixing or Kitchen Spoon.
No. 2K222 Door Spring, steel, full length 16 inches.
No. 2K223 Metal Door Pull, plated, old copper finish.
No. 2K224 Cast Door Hinges, one pair, size, 2½ inches.
No. 2K225 1 Card of 4 Enameled Cover Knobs.
No. 2K226 Spring Hinge for Screen Doors, one only.
No. 2K227 Japanned Cupboard Catch, length, 2½ inches.
No. 2K228 1 Pair Iron Padlock Eyes, japanned.
No. 2K229 Hinge Hasp and Staple, length, 8 inches.
No. 2K230 Galvanized Awning Pulley, ¾-inch iron wheel.
No. 2K231 Steel Gimlet Bit, full size, fits any brace.
No. 2K232 Picket Rope Swivel, full length, 3½ inches.
No. 2K233 1 Box of 100 Coppered Iron Clinch Rivets.
No. 2K234 Handled Wire Tea Strainer, full size, tinned.
No. 2K235 Galvanized Steel Hose Band, to fit ¾-inch hose.
No. 2K236 Heavy Iron Door Pull, length, 6 inches.
No. 2K237 Hickory Framing Chisel Handle, with iron ring.
No. 2K238 Hanging Bill or Memorandum File, tinned.
No. 2K239 1 Package, about 300 Steel Carpet Tacks.
No. 2K240 Flat Bristle Brush, 1 inch.
No. 2K241 Tinned Iron Meat Hook, to fit 2-inch bar.
No. 2K242 Fancy Brass Box Hinge, full length, open, 3 inches, one only.
No. 2K243 Full Size Chisel Handle, hickory, with brass ferrule for tanged chisel.
No. 2K244 Full Size Iron Sash Lock, lacquered finish.
No. 2K245 Wrought Steel T Hinge, size, 4 inches, one only.
No. 2K246 Brass Box Corners, full size, one only.
No. 2K247 Brass Furniture Handle, full size, one only.
No. 2K248 Boys' Baseball, leather covered, well sewed.
No. 2K249 Extra Quality, Full Size Cotton Chalk Line.
No. 2K250 Suit Case Catch or Fastener, stamped steel, brass plated, full size, one only.
No. 2K251 High Grade Full Size Pen Holder, metal tip.
No. 2K252 Iron Hose Mender, fits ¾-inch hose, one only.
No. 2K253 Famous "Devil" Mouse Trap.
No. 2K254 Brass Ox Ball for End of Horn, one only.
No. 2K255 Iron Chest Handle, full size, one only.
No. 2K256 Combination Pencil and Ink Eraser.
No. 2K257 Fish Line, furnished with bob, sinker, line and hook on winder.

TWO PAGES FOR ONLY 2 CENTS EACH

2 cents each

THIS LOW PRICE IS MADE ON CONDITION that you send us an order for twelve or more articles selected from any of these eight pages, from page 1176 to page 1183, inclusive. You may select them all from one page, or some from one page and some from another, just as you choose, so long as you order twelve at least. Allow the prices according to prices on the pages from which you select them.

OUR MARK OF QUALITY as spoken of on the last page of our Big Catalogue applies just as much to the articles we offer on these eight pages at 2 cents, 4 cents, 6 cents and 8 cents each as it does to any of the larger items we offer elsewhere in our Big Catalogue, for example, a suit of clothes or a stove or a vehicle. No retail store in any part of the country offers any such articles as we offer on these two pages at 2 cents each for less than 5 to 10 cents each; those on our 4-cent pages are good retail value at 10 to 25 cents, those on our 6-cent pages are worth from 15 cents to over 25 cents at retail, and those on our 8-cent pages are worth all the way from 20 cents to 50 cents. If you wish you can select some from these two pages at 2 cents each, some from the following two pages at 4 cents each, some from the next two pages at 6 cents each and some from the next two pages for 8 cents each, so long as you make up an order of twelve or more. Don't forget to give the catalogue number of each article you select in your order. Always make up an order for all the goods you need, selected from our various departments, at the same time that you order goods from these special pages. The freight charges will not be increased and your saving on these goods will be all the greater by reason of reducing the transportation charges on each article to the minimum. Be sure to read the last paragraph on page 1184.

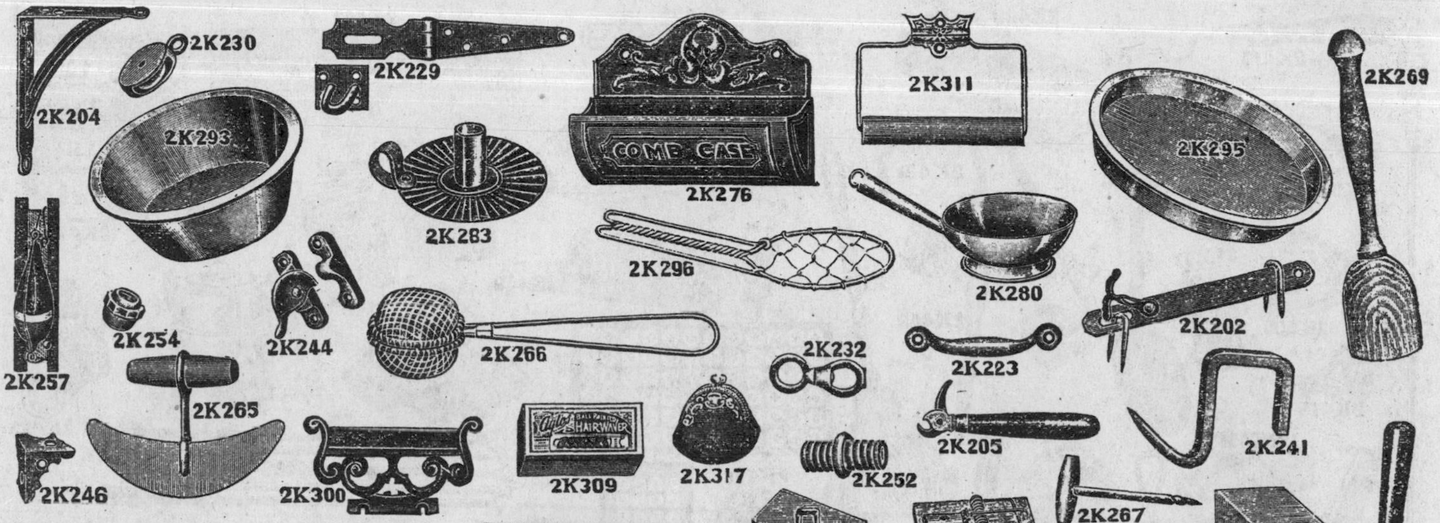

DESCRIPTIONS OF ARTICLES.

No. 2K258 Collar or Flange to fit 6-inch stove pipe, bronzed finish.
No. 2K259 Double Stitched Metal End Tape Measure, 60 inches.
No. 2K260 Kitchen Paring Knife, 3-inch blade, regular 10-cent value.
No. 2K261 1 Package about 100 Double Pointed Steel Tacks.
No. 2K263 Steel Cake Turner, full size.
No. 2K264 Tin Table Spoon, extra heavy, full size.
No. 2K265 Mincing Knife, steel blade, full size.
No. 2K266 Soap Saver, tinned wire, full size.
No. 2K267 Household Steel Gimlet, metal head, full size.
No. 2K268 Hardwood Butter Ladle, full length, 11 inches.
No. 2K269 Hardwood Potato Masher, full size.
No. 2K270 1 Pair Cloth Covered Elastic Sleeve Holders.
No. 2K271 Tinned Iron Kitchen Spoon, length, 10 inches.
No. 2K272 Heavy Iron Breast Strap Slide, 10-cent value.
No. 2K273 One-Piece Short Handled Stove Shovel.
No. 2K274 Adjustable Flue Stop, fancy bronzed finish.
No. 2K275 Steel Garden Trowel, full size.
No. 2K276 Tin Comb Case, nicely finished.
No. 2K277 Hatchet Handle, hickory, full length, 14 inches.
No. 2K278 Hammer Handle, hickory, full length, 14 inches.
No. 2K279 Extra Large Turkey Red Handkerchief.
No. 2K280 Tin Gravy Strainer, full size, well made.
No. 2K281 Handy Apple Corer, tin, full size.
No. 2K282 Milk Skimmer, tin, full size.
No. 2K283 Candlestick, tin, nicely finished.
No. 2K284 Tin Cup, size, 1 pint, well made.
No. 2K285 Tin Nutmeg Grater, full length, 5 inches.
No. 2K286 Tin Double Match Safe, nicely finished.
No. 2K287 Tin Fruit Jar Filler, well made.
No. 2K288 Tin Kitchen Grater, full length, 9 inches.
No. 2K290 Tin Pie Plate, diameter, 9 inches, full depth.
No. 2K291 Tin Pastry and Doughnut Cutters, full size, one each.
No. 2K292 1 Set of Six Tin Tart or Patty Pans, assorted.
No. 2K293 Tin Pudding Pan, size, 1½ quarts.
No. 2K294 Tin Dairy or Milk Pan, size, 2 quarts.
No. 2K295 Tin Layer Cake Pan, diameter, 9 inches.
No. 2K296 Wire Egg Beater, well made, tinned wire.
No. 2K297 1 Dozen Falcon Pens, usually sold two for 5c.
No. 2K298 1 Dozen Stub Pens, regular two for 5c value.
No. 2K299 1 Dozen Fine Point School Pens, regular two for 5c value.
No. 2K300 Iron Foot Scraper, full size.
No. 2K301 Large Package Fine Toilet Paper.
No. 2K302 Pocket Cork Screw, with wooden cover.
No. 2K303 Fruit Jar Cover to fit Mason jar, one only.
No. 2K304 Fruit Jar Rubbers to fit Mason jar, one dozen.
No. 2K305 1 Pair Steel Pants Guards.
No. 2K306 Fine Japanese Fan, opens 17 inches.
No. 2K307 Stocking Darner, 6 inches long, polished.
No. 2K308 Three-Piece Crochet Set, in wooden box.
No. 2K309 Ball Pointed Hair Wavers, set of four.
No. 2K310 Steel Key Chain, with ring.
No. 2K311 Holder for Roll Toilet Paper, full size.
No. 2K312 Wire Teapot Stand, tinned wire, full size.
No. 2K313 Wire Fly Killer, full size, well made.
No. 2K314 Child's Fancy Border Handkerchief.
No. 2K315 Iron End Clevis, full length 3, inches.
No. 2K316 Steel Tracing Wheel, full length, 6 inches.
No. 2K317 Leather Coin Purse.
No. 2K318 Memorandum Book, 4x7 inches, 144 pages.
No. 2K319 Old Glory Ink Tablet, note size, 44 sheets, ruled white paper.
No. 2K320 Pencil Tablet, large size, 75 sheets, ruled.
No. 2K321 Tin Funnel, diameter of top, 5½ inches.

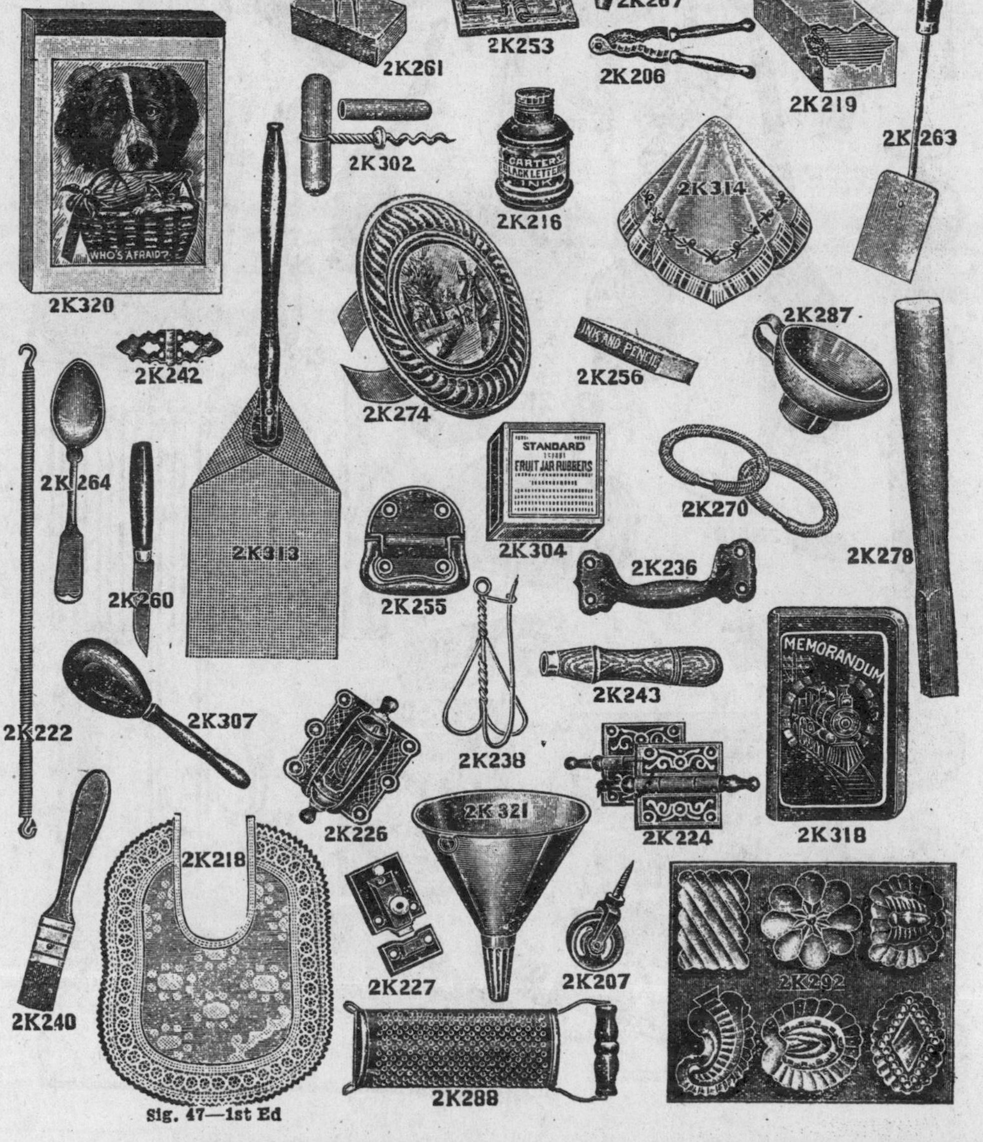

2K204
2K230
2K229
2K293
2K311
2K269
2K295
2K283
2K276
2K296
2K280
2K202
2K257
2K254
2K244
2K266
2K232
2K223
2K241
2K265
2K205
2K267
2K246
2K300
2K309
2K317
2K252
2K206
2K219
2K261
2K253
2K263
2K302
2K216
2K314
2K320
2K287
2K256
2K242
2K274
2K264
2K304
2K270
2K260
2K313
2K255
2K236
2K278
2K222
2K307
2K243
2K238
2K226
2K321
2K224
2K318
2K218
2K227
2K207
2K292
2K240
2K288

Sig. 47—1st Ed

4 cents each FOR ANY ARTICLE ON THESE TWO

SELECT TWELVE OR MORE ARTICLES from any of these eight pages, from page 1176 to page 1183 inclusive. Your order must be for twelve articles at least and as many more as you like and you may choose them all from these two pages at 4 cents each, or part of them from any of the other six pages at 2 cents, 6 cents or 8 cents each, according to the prices on the pages from which you select them. The smallness of the items makes it necessary to ask that your order be for at least twelve articles. Most anybody can find twelve articles on these eight pages that they really need at once or will soon need and if it should happen that you think you can't find use for twelve, surely your neighbor would willingly order enough to make up twelve, seeing that the values are so great as compared with what is charged at retail for similar goods, for the articles on these two pages at 4 cents each are generally retailed at 10 to 25 cents. Don't order these goods alone if you can possibly help it, but always include them with an order for other goods that you can use. Shipped with other goods the freight charges on each item will be reduced to the very smallest amount; in fact, the total freight charges on a shipment of 50 to 100 pounds will not be more than for these goods alone.

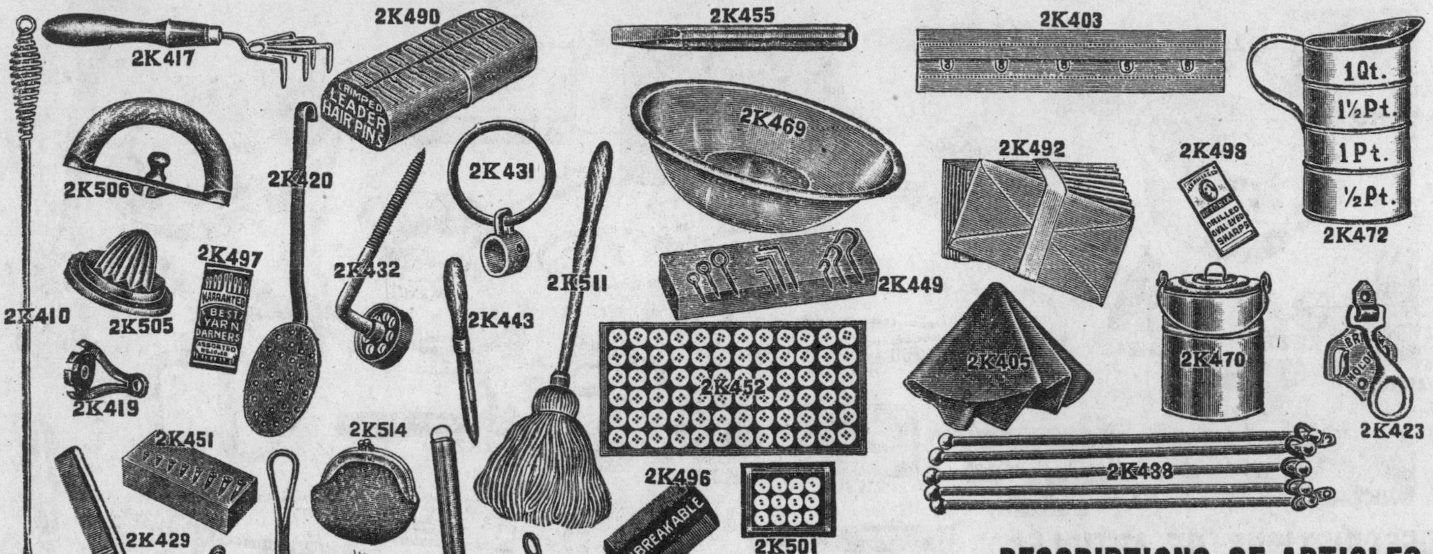

DESCRIPTIONS OF ARTICLES.

No. 2K401   1 Pair Men's Elastic Hose Supporters.
No. 2K402   1 Package, 3 Dozen Assorted Nickel Plated Safety Pins.
No. 2K403   1 Pair 5-Hook Cloth Covered Steel Corset Stays.
No. 2K404   Baby's Lace Trimmed Bib, with rubber back.
No. 2K405   Chamois Skin, 6x8 inches.
No. 2K406   Iron Bird Cage Hook, full size, lacquered finish.
No. 2K407   Putty Knife, steel blade, 1¼ inches wide.
No. 2K408   Fiber Lunch Box, with wire handle.
No. 2K409   Steel Blade Screwdriver, full length, 7 inches.
No. 2K410   Cold Handle Straight Stove Poker, full length, 20 inches.
No. 2K411   Cold Handle Bent Stove Poker, full length, 20 inches.
No. 2K412   Best Quality Steel Nail Set, full length, 4 inches.
No. 2K413   1 Pair Misses' Elastic Side Garters.
No. 2K414   1 Dozen Braided Whip Snappers, length, 7 inches.
No. 2K415   1 Box of 100 Hill's Hog Rings, full size.
No. 2K416   Hill's Hog Ringer, iron, full length, 7 inches.
No. 2K417   Tinned Weeding Hook, full length, 10 inches.
No. 2K418   Handy Can Opener, full length, 9 inches.
No. 2K419   Handy Knife Sharpener.
No. 2K420   Tinned Kitchen Skimmer, full length, 13 inches.
No. 2K421   Harmonica, loud and clear.
No. 2K422   Full Coil (about 20 washers) Adjustable Leather Axle Washers.
No. 2K423   Iron Broom and Dust Pan Holder, nicely finished.
No. 2K424   Extra Quality Tack Puller, full length, 6½ inches.
No. 2K425   Black Enamel Whip Socket, full size.
No. 2K426   1 Full Box of 144 Small Size Pants Buttons.
No. 2K427   Heavy Braided Fish Line, 84 feet long.
No. 2K428   Tinned Cattle Tie Iron and Snap.
No. 2K429   Metallic Back 7-inch Comb.
No. 2K430   Crayola Crayon Set, pocket size, 14 colors.
No. 2K431   Iron Neck Yoke Ferrule, with 3½-inch ring.
No. 2K432   Wrought Barn Door Roller, with 3½-inch screw.
No. 2K433   1 Set of Four Furniture Casters, 1-inch iron wheels.
No. 2K434   1 Pair Steel Anti-Rattlers for Buggy Shafts.
No. 2K435   Dover Pattern Revolving Egg Beater.
No. 2K436   1 Only Fancy Wrought Box Hinge, old copper finish, full length 3 inches.
No. 2K437   Slim Taper Saw File, full length 8 inches.
No. 2K438   Wooden Towel Rack, with five arms, full size.
No. 2K439   Steel Stove Shovel, extra size, length, 20 inches.
No. 2K440   D Head for Fork or Shovel Handle.
No. 2K441   1 Package, about 25 Yards Tinned Picture Wire, braided.
No. 2K442   Potato Masher, heavily tinned wire.
No. 2K443   Safety Vegetable Parer, tempered steel blade.
No. 2K444   Iron Cattle Leader, full length, 5 inches, extra quality.
No. 2K445   Steel Paring Knife, 3½-inch blade.
No. 2K446   Steel Ring Pot Scraper.
No. 2K447   Fruit Jar Cover Wrench, full size.
No. 2K448   Combination Glass Cutter, Cork Screw and Can Opener.
No. 2K449   1 Package, 2 Dozen Assorted Iron Screw Hooks and Eyes.
No. 2K450   1 Package, 4 Dozen Assorted Flat Head Iron Screws.
No. 2K451   1 Package, 2 Dozen Assorted Flat Head Brass Screws.
No. 2K452   1 Card of 6 Dozen Agate Buttons, size ¾ inch.
No. 2K453   1 Dozen Imitation Shell Hair Pins.
No. 2K454   Fine Tooth Brush, full size.
No. 2K455   Cold Chisel, extra quality, ½-inch cut.
No. 2K459   1 Only Adjustable Cross Cut Saw Handle.

PAGES IN LOTS OF TWELVE OR MORE

4 cents each

WE INVITE YOU TO MAKE A CAREFUL STUDY AND COMPARISON of our prices with the prices of others on such goods as we show on these two pages, on the two preceding pages and on the four following pages, just for the purpose of illustrating the relative big values and the relative average big difference between our prices and the prices charged by others for similar goods, for these eight pages may be called an A B C lesson, or object lesson, of what it means in money saving to you to send us your orders for everything you need, thus buying your goods at prices that mean but one small profit added to the actual cost of the goods to us and that the lowest cost (always for the best standard quality) for which such articles can be bought because we buy them in such vast quantities. Remember these are not the articles commonly offered on 5 and 10-cent counters. They are a very much higher standard and better quality throughout. Select twelve or more from this page or from any of these eight pages at 2 cents, 4 cents, 6 cents and 8 cents each. We do not accept orders for less than twelve of these articles. Don't fail to make up a complete order for all the goods you are needing at the same time that you order goods from these pages. You will not be increasing your freight charges; in fact you will reduce the cost of transportation on each item by sending us a miscellaneous order, and in this way you can make the greatest possible saving.

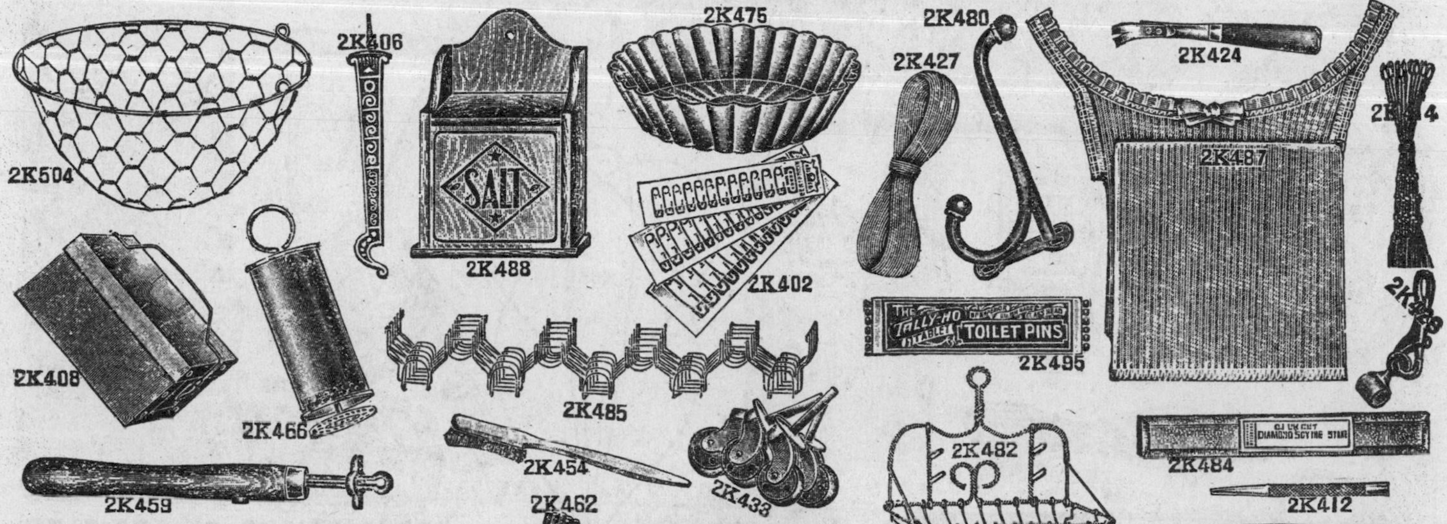

DESCRIPTIONS OF ARTICLES.

No. 2K460 Iron Flower Pot Bracket for pots up to 4-inch.
No. 2K461 1 Pair Men's Rockford Socks, 10-cent value.
No. 2K462 One Dozen Cedar Lead Pencils.
No. 2K463 Trouser Hanger and Stretcher, steel japanned.
No. 2K464 Tin Cake Pan, diameter at top, 8 inches.
No. 2K465 Tin Water Dipper, size, 1 quart.
No. 2K466 Tin Cream Whip or Egg Churn.
No. 2K467 Tin Cake or Baking Pan, length, 11 inches.
No. 2K469 Tin Wash Basin, top diameter, 11½ inches.
No. 2K470 Covered Tin Pail, size, 1 quart.
No. 2K471 Tin Milk or Dairy Pan, size, 3 quarts.
No. 2K472 Graduated Tin Measure, capacity, 1 quart.
No. 2K473 Shallow Tin Baking Pan, length, 11½ inches.
No. 2K474 Family Size Tinned Scoop, extra quality.
No. 2K475 Tin Cake Pan, diameter at top, 9½ inches.
No. 2K476 Tinned Soup Ladle, full length, 10 inches.
No. 2K477 Tin Dust Pan, full size, nicely finished.
No. 2K478 Tin Dinner Horn, good quality.
No. 2K479 Spring Bottom Machine Oiler, tin, full height, 8 inches.
No. 2K480 Heavy Iron Harness Hook, 8 inches.
No. 2K481 Cupboard or Wardrobe Lock with Key, length, 3 inches.
No. 2K482 Full Size Comb and Brush Holder, tinned wire.
No. 2K483 Tinned Safety Gate Hook with Staples, length, 6 inches.
No. 2K484 Quick Cut Scythe Stone, extra quality, full size.
No. 2K485 Tinned Wire Folding Card or Photograph Holder, capacity, 28 pictures.
No. 2K486 Tinned Wire Broiler, size, 9x10 inches.
No. 2K487 Ladies' Ribbed Cotton Vest.
No. 2K488 Wooden Salt Box, full size.
No. 2K489 Men's Hemstitched White Handkerchief.
No. 2K490 1 Package, 128 Hair Pins. Full size.
No. 2K491 1 Dozen Aluminum Thimbles, assorted sizes.
No. 2K492 1 Package of 100 Manila Envelopes, size 6.
No. 2K493 Ruled Pencil Composition Book, 172 pages, 86 leaves.
No. 2K494 Ruled Ink Composition Book, 96 pages, 48 leaves.
No. 2K495 1 Dozen Steel Hat Pins.
No. 2K496 Fine Tooth Comb. Regular 10-cent value.
No. 2K497 1 Package of 30 Darning Needles, assorted sizes.
No. 2K498 1 Package of 75 Sewing Needles, assorted sizes, 3 to 10.
No. 2K499 1 Bundle of 12 yards of ½-inch Torchon Lace.
No. 2K500 1 Dozen Bone Collar Buttons.
No. 2K501 1 Dozen Pearl Buttons, ½ inch.
No. 2K502 Gold Plated Separable Collar Button, celluloid back.
No. 2K503 Iron Baking or Drip Pan, size, 6x9 inches.
No. 2K504 Wire Hen's Nest, size, 13 inches.
No. 2K505 Lemon Juice Extractor, glass, full size.
No. 2K506 Mrs. Potts' Iron Handle, full size, extra quality.
No. 2K507 Ladies' Hemstitched Fancy Handkerchief.
No. 2K508 Ladies' Lace Trimmed White Handkerchief.
No. 2K509 1 Dozen Wire Moulding or Picture Hooks.
No. 2K510 Flat Tin Grater.
No. 2K511 Cotton Dish Mop, full size, extra quality.
No. 2K512 Silver Plated Teaspoon, beaded pattern.
No. 2K513 Curling Iron, full size.
No. 2K514 Leather Coin Purse, two compartments.
No. 2K515 Box of Ruled Ink Writing Paper and Envelopes.
No. 2K516 Tin Pudding Pan, 3-quart size.

YOUR CHOICE OF ANY ARTICLE ON THESE

6 cents each

THE ARTICLES WE OFFER on these two pages at 6 cents each, on condition that you order twelve articles or more from this page or from any of the eight pages, pages 1176 to 1183 inclusive, are everywhere retailed at 15 cents to 50 cents each. Remember they represent high standard makes, and are not by any means the common varieties retailed as 10-cent articles in many stores. You will note their better quality at once on seeing the articles. To give you the exact same relative value on all these small articles that we give on everything in this big book, to sell these little everyday useful things on our one small profit plan, as everything in this Big Catalogue is priced and sold, it brings the price to you on each article to such a few cents (often one-fifth or one-quarter the usual retail price) that we must, as a necessary economy, make it a condition that you order twelve or more articles from these eight pages, from page 1176 to page 1183 inclusive. Select any article, one or more of a kind or number from any of these eight pages, give the number of each article and allow the price according to the page from which you select, but be sure your order is for twelve or more. **Don't fail to read the last paragraph on page 1184.**

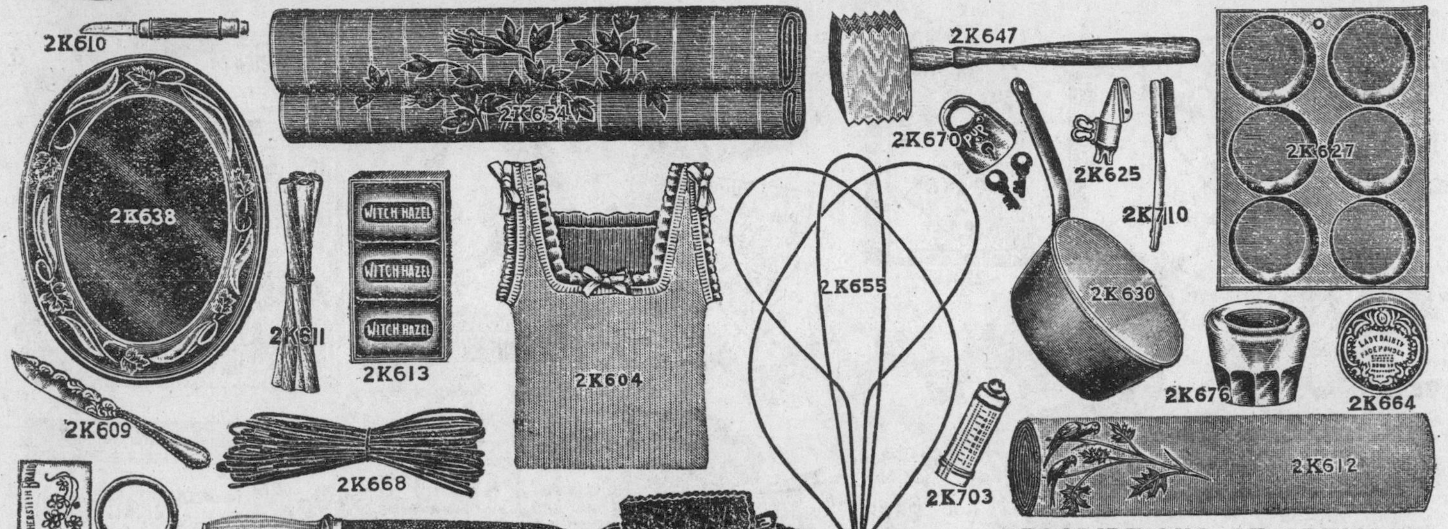

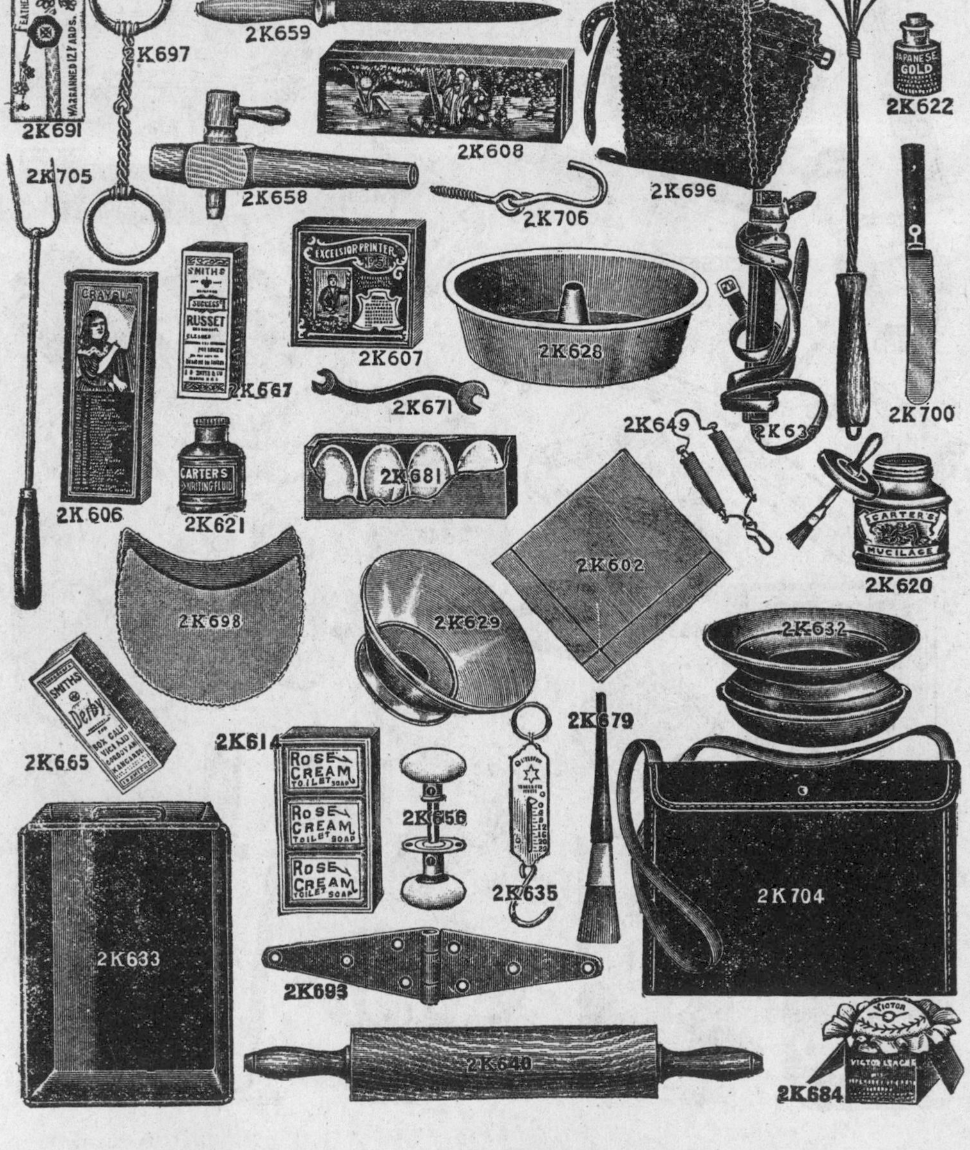

DESCRIPTIONS OF ARTICLES.

No. 2K601   Men's Fancy Border Handkerchief.
No. 2K602   Men's Plain White Hemstitched Handkerchief.
No. 2K603   Ladies' Japanese Silk Embroidered Handkerchief, extraordinary value.
No. 2K604   Misses' Ribbed Cotton Vest.
No. 2K605   Fancy Autograph Album, 6x9 inches.
No. 2K606   Crayola Crayon Outfit, assorted, 28 colors.
No. 2K607   Rubber Type Printing Outfit.
No. 2K608   Ebonized Japanese Pencil Box, fancy top with lock and key.
No. 2K609   Butter Knife, silver plated.
No. 2K610   Automatic Pen Knife.
No. 2K611   1 Bundle of Four Carpenter's Lead Pencils.
No. 2K612   1 Bundle of 100 Japanese Crepe Paper Napkins.
No. 2K613   1 Box, Three bars Witch Hazel Soap.
No. 2K614   1 Box, Three bars Rose Cream Soap.
No. 2K615   1 Box, Three bars Transparent Glycerine Soap.
No. 2K620   Carter's fine Mucilage, regular 10-cent bottle.
No. 2K621   Carter's Writing Fluid, regular 10-cent bottle.
No. 2K622   Japanese Gold Ink, for correspondence, etc.
No. 2K623   Brass Pen Rack.
No. 2K624   Ideal Sanitary Bread Pan. The best made.
No. 2K625   Pencil Sharpener, thoroughly practical.
No. 2K626   Extra Quality Tin Sanitary Sink Strainer.
No. 2K627   Extra Quality 6-cup Tin Muffin Pan.
No. 2K628   Full Size 9-inch Tin Cake Pan.
No. 2K629   Full Size Tin Milk Strainer.
No. 2K630   Lipped Tin Sauce Pan, 2-quart size.
No. 2K631   Tin Flour Sifter with Crank, size, 1 quart.
No. 2K632   Full Size Japanned Tin Cuspidor.
No. 2K633   Sheet Steel Drip or Baking Pan, 8x12 inches.
No. 2K634   1-Quart Size Wire Corn Popper, with handle.
No. 2K635   Extra Quality Spring Balance, capacity, 24 pounds.
No. 2K636   Good Quality Steel Blade Grass Shears, full size.
No. 2K637   Leather Shawl or Book Strap, very durable.
No. 2K638   Extra Quality Japanned Oval Tray, full length, 12 inches.
No. 2K639   Full Size Milk Bottle Brush, extra quality bristles.
No. 2K640   Hardwood Rolling Pin, full size, extra quality.
No. 2K641   Extra Quality Cotton Clothes Line, length, 50 feet.
No. 2K642   Full Size Extra Quality Handled Stove Brush.
No. 2K643   Heavy Fiber Scrub Brush, full size, very durable.
No. 2K644   All Iron Steak Beater, best quality.
No. 2K645   Tinned Heavy Steel Mixing Spoon, best quality.
No. 2K646   Patent Sliding Nutmeg Grater, the best made.
No. 2K647   Hardwood Steak Beater, extra quality.
No. 2K648   Iron Thumb or Door Latch Set, complete.
No. 2K649   Brass Double Spring Bird Cage Hanger.
No. 2K650   Mounted Quick Cutting Kitchen Sandstone.
No. 2K651   All Metal Nickel Plated 3-Bar Towel Rack.
No. 2K652   1 Package of 100 Brass Head Upholstery Tacks.
No. 2K653   Double Steel Bladed Mincing Knife.
No. 2K654   Fancy Wood Splint Decorated Splasher Mat.
No. 2K655   Extra Quality Full Size Wire Carpet Beater.
No. 2K656   One Pair White Door Knobs, complete with spindle as shown, standard quality.

TWO PAGES FOR ONLY 6 CENTS EACH

THE PRICES ON THESE ARTICLES of everyday use in and about the home, by our method of selling them in lots of twelve or more, as explained on these pages, are brought so low, as compared with the prices on similar articles offered in retail stores, that anyone can plainly see a wonderful saving in buying all such supplies from us, and when you understand that all the merchandise in this Big Catalogue is priced on the same basis the saving you will make by buying all your goods from us will amount to hundreds of dollars year after year. Understand, to make up an order of twelve or more articles, to get the benefit of this 6 cent price on these two pages, you may select some of the items from these pages at 6 cents and some from the other pages at 2 cents, 4 cents and 8 cents each, just so long as we get an order for twelve of these articles from you. **When ordering** be sure to give the catalogue number of each article you select. The number of each article is given under the illustration and the description corresponding with the article is found in the middle part of these pages. **Don't forget to give the numbers of articles. Don't fail to read the last paragraph on page 1184.**

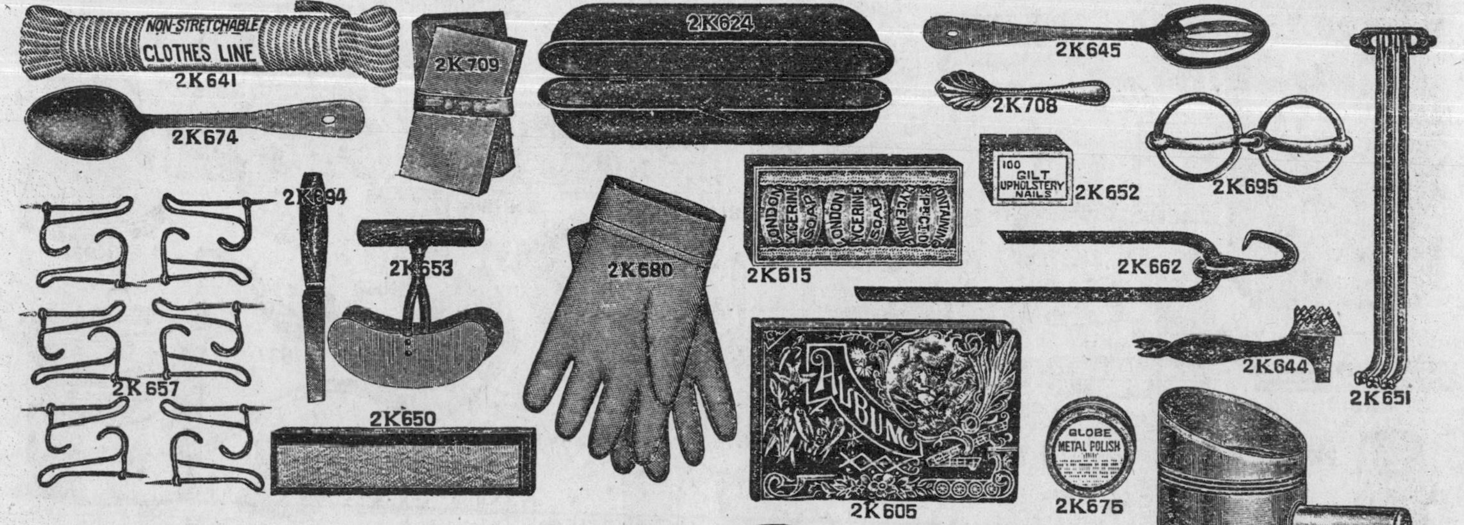

DESCRIPTIONS OF ARTICLES.

No. 2K657 One Dozen Full Size Wire Coat or Closet Hooks.
No. 2K658 Extra Quality full size lined Wood Faucet.
No. 2K659 Emery Knife Sharpener, 12-inch.
No. 2K660 Double End Taper Saw File, extra quality, full length, 10 inches, complete with handle.
No. 2K661 Extra Quality Flat Mill File, full length, 10 inches.
No. 2K662 Heavy Wrought Singletree Strap and Hook.
No. 2K663 Forged Steel Alligator Jaw Wrench, full length, 5¼ inches.
No. 2K664 Face Powder. Regular 25-cent box.
No. 2K665 Shoe Polish, liquid and paste, black.
No. 2K666 Lily White Polish, for canvas shoes.
No. 2K667 Shoe Polish, liquid and paste, tan or russet.
No. 2K668 One Dozen Men's Shoe Laces.
No. 2K669 Nickel Plated Bicycle or Adjustable Wrench, 5 inches long.
No. 2K670 Brass Plated Wrought Padlock, two keys.
No. 2K671 Forged Steel S Wrench for ⅜ and ½-inch nuts.
No. 2K672 Malleable Iron Clevis, size, 2x4 inches.
No. 2K673 Wrought Steel Clevis, size, 2x4 inches.
No. 2K674 Heavy Tinned Stamped Kitchen Spoon, full length, 12 inches.
No. 2K675 Globe Metal Polish, large box.
No. 2K676 Glass Non-Spilling Ink Well.
No. 2K677 Fine Tooth Powder, 2-ounce box.
No. 2K678 One Set of Six Heavy Tin Teaspoons.
No. 2K679 1-Inch Sash Tool (paint brush.)
No. 2K680 One Pair Heavy Canvas Gloves.
No. 2K681 One Set of Four China Nest Eggs.
No. 2K682 Shaving Brush, with fine bristles.
No. 2K683 One Full Box of 144 Metal Suspender or Pantaloon Buttons.
No. 2K684 Genuine "Little Victor" Baseball.
No. 2K685 Horse Brush, 7 inches.
No. 2K686 One Card of Six Steel Harness Snaps 1-inch.
No. 2K687 Canvas Catching Mitt, full padded.
No. 2K688 1-Inch Camel's Hair Brush.
No. 2K689 Horse Tail Strap, nickel plated.
No. 2K690 Boys' Elastic Suspenders.
No. 2K691 One Bundle 12 yards of Featherstitched Braid, ¼ inch wide.
No. 2K692 Jackknife, two blades, 15-cent value.
No. 2K693 One Pair wrought steel heavy Strap Hinges, full length open, 12 inches.
No. 2K694 Leather Knife, 7½ inches.
No. 2K695 Jointed Horse Bit, heavy tinned.
No. 2K696 Heavy Felt Sweat Pad, 4x14 inches.
No. 2K697 Jointed Horse Bit, heavy, single twist, tinned.
No. 2K698 One Pair Good Quality Dress Shields.
No. 2K699 Child's Knife and Fork, polished steel.
No. 2K700 Steel Table Knife, 9-inch, finely polished.
No. 2K701 Talcum Powder, fine grade, large can.
No. 2K702 Leather Coin Purse, two compartments.
No. 2K703 Automatic Dime Savings Bank, nickel plated.
No. 2K704 Waterproof School Bag, with leather carrying strap.
No. 2K705 Extra Size Heavily Tinned Kitchen Fork.
No. 2K706 One Pair Heavy Wrought Tinned Hammock Hooks.
No. 2K707 Wood Chopping or Mixing Bowl, top diameter, 11 inches.
No. 2K708 Sugar Shell, silver plated.
No. 2K709 One Package 100 White Wove Envelopes, No. 5.
No. 2K710 Tooth Brush, usually retails at 25 cents.

8 cents each FOR ANY ARTICLE ON THESE TWO

THE GREAT VALUE WE ARE OFFERING from these two pages will be fully appreciated by you when you receive any of these goods, as there are articles on this page that would retail at 50 cents or upward and scarcely any article that a storekeeper would sell for less than 25 cents. By making it a condition that you order twelve or more articles at a time, which twelve articles you may select from the eight pages, from page 1176 to 1183, inclusive, according to the prices quoted on the pages from which you select, we can thus figure and price these little things (the same as everything else we handle) on our one small profit above actual cost. Please look at the retail price of every article shown on these eight pages which we offer at 2 cents, 4 cents, 6 cents and 8 cents each, far most everyone knows the commonly asked price of many of these things and can at once closely estimate how much money they can save on anything in this Big Book, for everything from cover to cover is priced alike on our one small profit above actual cost to us. Most anybody will find need for twelve of these articles but if you think you could not use twelve at this time you would have no trouble in getting a neighbor to take enough to make up twelve with your order. Be sure to give the catalogue number of each article you select. Don't fail to read the last paragraph on page 1184.

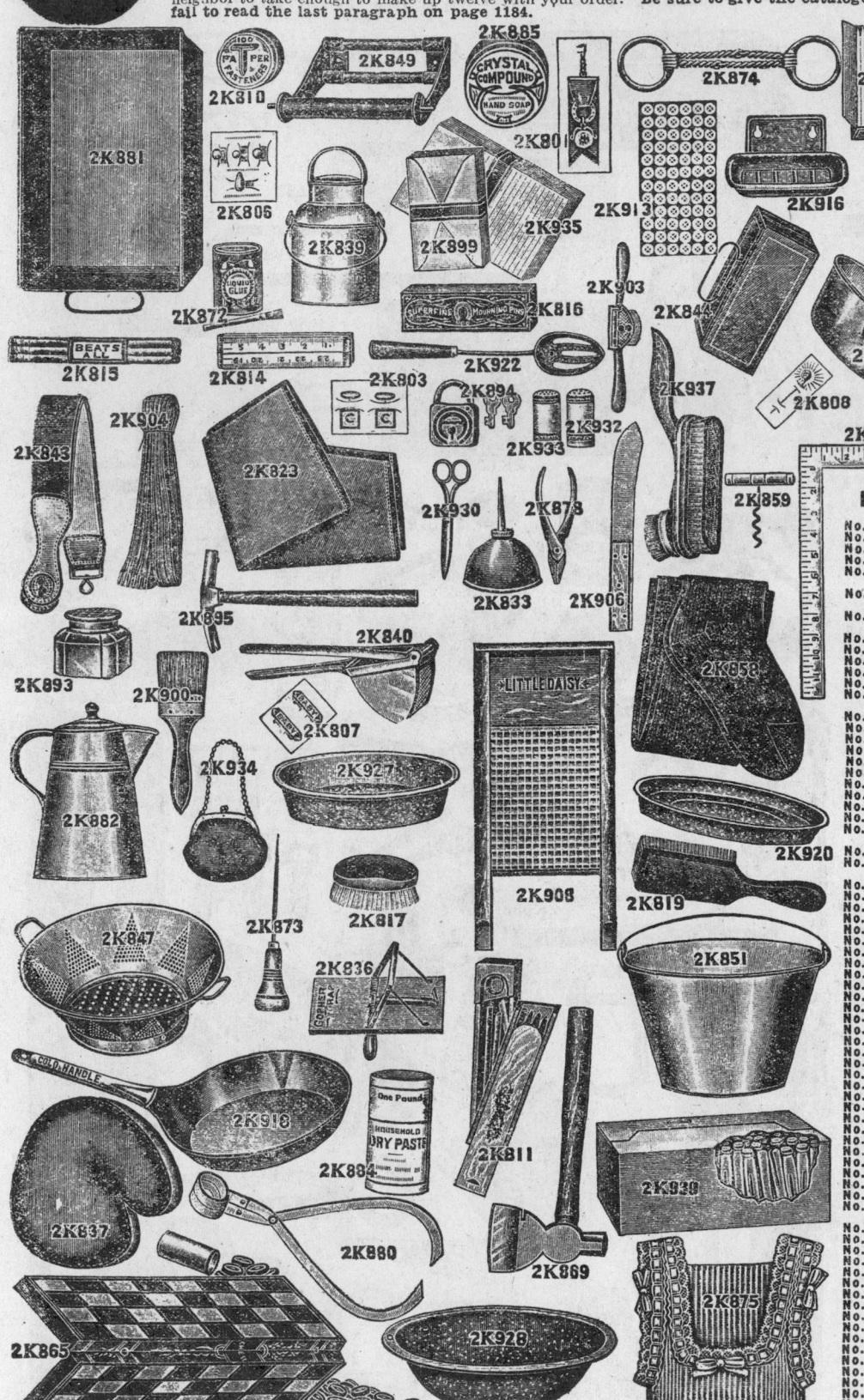

DESCRIPTIONS OF ARTICLES.

No.	
2K801	Handsome Ribbon Fob, with gold plated charm.
2K802	One Pair Gold Plated Stone Set Cuff Buttons.
2K803	One Pair Gold Plated Stone Set Cuff Buttons.
2K804	One Set of Three Dress Pins, gold plated.
2K805	One Set Gold Plated Cuff and Collar Buttons, celluloid back, six pieces.
2K806	One Set Gold Plated Collar Buttons, aluminum back.
2K807	One Set of Two Baby Pins, Gold Plated and Enameled.
2K808	Scarf Pin, gold plated.
2K809	Scarf Pin, pearl horseshoe setting.
2K810	One Box of 100 Brass Paper Fasteners.
2K811	Swivel Pencil Box, six compartments.
2K812	Metal Fob Chain. Very attractive.
2K813	One Pair Baby's Leather Moccasins, 20-cent value.
2K814	Brass Joint Carpenters' Two-Foot Rule.
2K815	One Bundle (6) Lead Pencils, with erasers.
2K816	One Box 500 Assorted Mourning Pins.
2K817	Ebony Finished White Bristle Military Brush.
2K818	Black Bristle Hair Brush, great value.
2K819	Wire Hair Brush, 10-row, 25-cent value.
2K820	One Package of Pins containing 12 papers.
2K821	Solid Back Black Bristle Clothes Brush.
2K822	One Imitation Tortoise Shell Comb Set, 3 pieces.
2K823	One Pair Heavy Black Oversleeves.
2K824	One Pair Men's Heavy 3-pound Rockford Socks. Regular 20-cent value.
2K825	Men's Elastic Suspenders, strong and durable.
2K826	One Dozen 50-yard Spools Black Mending Thread.
2K827	Men's Curved Stem Pipe, 20-cent value.
2K828	Men's Straight Stem Pipe, 20-cent value.
2K829	One Box Three Large Cakes of Castile Soap.
2K830	One Box Metal Polish, ½ pint.
2K831	Practical Fountain Pen.
2K832	Pressed Steel Curry and Mane Comb.
2K833	Fine Copper Plated Large Size Oiler.
2K834	Cast Hammer for Home Use, hardwood handle.
2K835	Famous O. K. Gopher Trap.
2K836	Catching Mit, leather faced and canvas back.
2K837	High Grade 2-Inch Metal Bound Varnish Brush.
2K838	One-Quart Size Tin Milk Kettle, with cover.
2K839	Standard Quality Tin Oil Can, one-gallon size.
2K840	Extra Quality Tinned Fruit or Vegetable Press.
2K841	Ladies' Belt Hose Supporter, great value.
2K842	Fine Double Leather and Canvas Razor Strop.
2K843	Japanned Tin Folding Lunch Box, regular size.
2K844	One Box of 100 Smooth, Round Slate Pencils.
2K845	1 Dozen Porcelain Head Picture Nails.
2K846	Tin Kitchen Colander, 10-inch top diameter.
2K847	Full Size Hardwood Towel Roller, extra quality.
2K848	Plated Wrought Steel Toilet Paper Holder.
2K849	Tin Baking or Drip Pan, full length, 12 inches.
2K850	Flaring Open Top Tin Milk Pail, 6-quart size.
2K851	Wrought Steel Trunk Lock with key.
2K852	Standard Full Size Pruning Shears, steel blade.
2K853	Tin Pail or Bucket, with cover, 4-quart size.
2K854	Sheepskin Polishing Mit, with dauber.
2K855	One Pair Men's Black Cotton Socks.
2K857	One Pair Ladies' Long Black Hose, double heel and toe.
2K858	
2K859	Nickel Plated Extra Quality Pocket Corkscrew.
2K860	Electric Fabric Cleanser, 1-pound can.
2K861	Steel Blade Ice Shave, with hardwood handle.
2K862	Wall Paper Cleaner, 1-pint can.
2K863	Fine Chamois Skin, 8x10 inches.
2K864	Child's Knit Waist, size, 6 years and younger.
2K865	Checker Board and Set of Checkers.
2K866	Steel Blade Hardwood Handle Try Square.
2K867	Household Machine Oil Can, half-pint.
2K868	Polished Spirit Level, 12-inch size.
2K869	Cast Hatchet, for home use, hardwood handle.
2K870	Copper Plated Wrought Steel Cow Bell.
2K871	Polished Wrought Household Square.
2K872	Best Made Liquid Glue, ¼-pint can, with brush.
2K873	Steel Ice Pick, hardwood handle, metal head.
2K874	Double Twist Jointed Driving Bit, tinned.
2K875	Ladies' Fancy Ribbed Cotton Vest.
2K876	Hardwood Vegetable Slicer, with adjustable blade, full length, 16 inches, extra quality.

PAGES IN LOTS OF TWELVE OR MORE

8 cents each

THESE ARE NOT THE ORDINARY GRADE OF ARTICLES found on 10-cent counters in department stores in the towns or in the retail stores throughout the country. Please don't confuse them with the common grades of 10-cent articles. Our policy on the question of quality, as explained on the last page of this Big Catalogue coupled with our immense sales at just cost and one small profit, enables us to offer you such articles as you see offered on these two pages for 8 cents each while the retail value of them ranges from 25 to 50 cents apiece. In order that we may be able to sell such small goods as these on our usual one small profit plan above actual cost, considering the cost of the transaction in writing up the order, selecting them from our stock, packing and shipping, etc., we must necessarily ask that your orders be for twelve or more articles selected from these eight pages from page 1176 to page 1183, inclusive. You can select one or more articles of the same kind or all different, just as you choose. You can pick some from one page, some from another or some from all eight pages, or select the entire twelve from one page, just as you choose, allowing the price of each article according to the price on the page from which you select it, and **always give the catalogue number of each article. Don't** fail to read the last paragraph on page 1184.

DESCRIPTIONS OF ARTICLES.

No. 2K877 Full Size Household Pincers or Nippers.
No. 2K878 Full Size Wrought Steel Household Plier.
No. 2K879 Extra Quality Lever Saw Set, hardwood handle.
No. 2K880 Household Ice Tongs, 50 pounds capacity.
No. 2K881 Iron Drip or Baking Pan, full length, 14 inches.
No. 2K882 Tin Flat Bottom Coffee Pot, size, 1½ quarts.
No. 2K883 Tin Flat Bottom Teapot, size, 1½ quarts.
No. 2K884 1-Pound Package Household Paste.
No. 2K885 1 Can, ½-Pound Crystal Soap Compound.
No. 2K886 1 Can, ½-Pint Egyptian Stove Pipe Enamel.
No. 2K887 1 Dozen Rubber Tipped Lead Pencils.
No. 2K888 Boys' Baseball Fielding Glove.
No. 2K889 Full Size Iron Twine Holder, to hang.
No. 2K890 Fine Quality Black Enameled Handle Tea Bell.
No. 2K891 Full Size Nickel Plated Tap or Call Bell.
No. 2K892 Full Size Cast Rim Door Lock, with key.
No. 2K893 Pressed Cut Glass Ink Well, with cover.
No. 2K894 Extra Size Two-Keyed Brass Plated Padlock.
No. 2K895 Hardwood Handle Tack Hammer.
No. 2K896 Forged Steel S Wrench, for ½ and ⅜-inch nuts.
No. 2K897 Wooden Dry Measure, iron bound ½-peck size.
No. 2K898 Round Handle 8-Inch Tin Soup Strainer.
No. 2K899 1 Bundle of 100 No. 6 White Wove Envelopes.
No. 2K900 Varnish Brush, 2½-inch.
No. 2K901 Cast Ribbed Pattern Lemon Squeezer.
No. 2K902 Pocket Level, standard quality, full size.
No. 2K903 Draw or Spoke Shave, 1¾-inch steel blade.
No. 2K904 One Dozen Ladies' Shoe Strings.
No. 2K905 Steel Blade Household Hand Saw.
No. 2K906 Steel Blade Hardwood Handle Butcher Knife.
No. 2K907 Gray Enameled Full Size Household Dipper.
No. 2K908 Pail Size "Little Daisy" Zinc Washboard.
No. 2K909 Champion Pattern Hardwood Handle Steel Blade Screwdriver, full length, 10½ inches, extra value.
No. 2K910 Cast Vise with Screw, 1½-inch jaws.
No. 2K911 Bit Brace, hardwood head and handle.
No. 2K912 Sanitary Sink Cleaner, good quality.
No. 2K913 1 Card, ½-Gross Fancy Agate Buttons, ⅝-inch size.
No. 2K914 Wood Butter Mould, fancy pattern, 1-lb. size.
No. 2K915 Rubber Window Cleaner, extra quality.
No. 2K916 Gray Enameled Full Size Soap Dish.
No. 2K917 Good Quality Tin Sprinkler, 2-quart size.
No. 2K918 Cold Handle Wrought Steel Frying Pan, 10-inch top diameter, extra quality.
No. 2K919 Gray Enameled Long Handled Skimmer.
No. 2K920 Full Size 9-inch Gray Enameled Cake Pan.
No. 2K921 Gray Enameled 2-Quart Size Milk Pan.
No. 2K922 Gray Enameled Kitchen Spoon, length, 12 inches.
No. 2K923 Lipped Tin Sauce Pan, 3-quart, extra value.
No. 2K924 Lipped Tin Preserving Kettle, 4-quart size.
No. 2K925 Gray Enameled 9-Inch Pie Pan, good value.
No. 2K927 Gray Enameled Pudding Pan, 1½-quart size.
No. 2K928 Gray Enameled Wash Basin, 10½-inch top diameter, extra quality.
No. 2K929 Gray Enameled 2-Quart Lipped Sauce Pan.
No. 2K930 Steel Scissors, 8-inch. Good value.
No. 2K931 Wood Base Standard Pattern Wire Fly Trap.
No. 2K932 Silver Plated Salt Shaker.
No. 2K933 Silver Plated Pepper Shaker.
No. 2K934 All Leather Chatelaine Bag.
No. 2K935 1-Pound Package Superfine White Ruled Paper, note size.
No. 2K936 Handy Cleaver, 7-inch blade, 35-cent value.
No. 2K937 One Full Size Shoe Brush with Dauber.
No. 2K938 Tin Dish Pan, 8-quart size, extra value.
No. 2K939 1 box, 8 dozen, Standard Hardwood Clothes Pins.

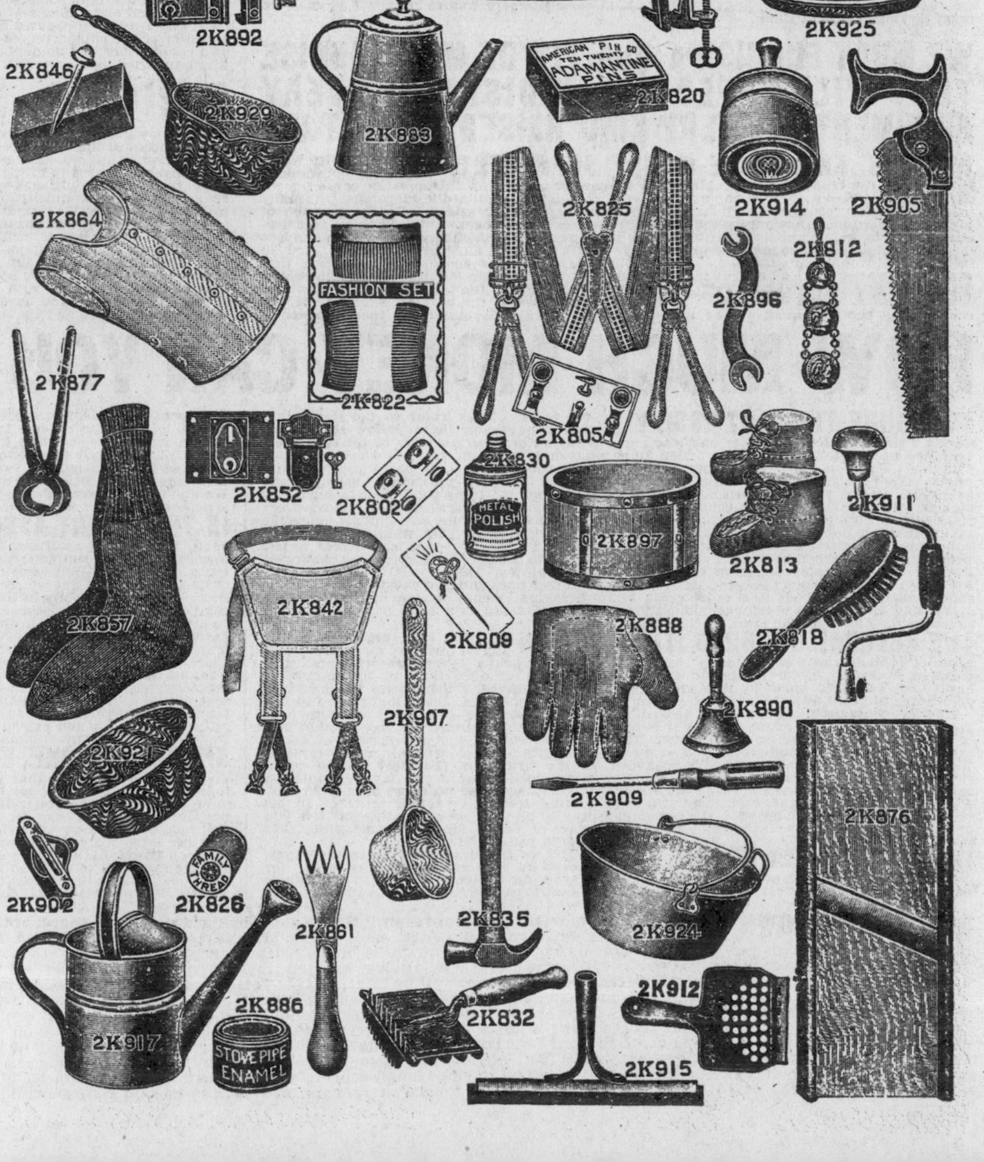

PRICE AND QUALITY

WE WANT TO DIRECT YOUR ATTENTION especially to the several hundred everyday useful household articles shown on the eight preceding pages, and especially do we wish to ask you to carefully compare the prices at which we offer these goods as against the prices the same goods are sold at in retail stores generally.

WE ASK YOU TO GIVE SPECIAL ATTENTION to the several hundred articles which we sell at 2 CENTS, 4 CENTS, 6 CENTS and 8 CENTS EACH. Look them over carefully, if you will, for you will find yourself familiar with most of these everyday household necessities and acquainted with the average retail selling price of the same. We ask you to look them over carefully for the reason that among the items we offer for 2 cents each are many that retail at 10 cents to 25 cents each, and we believe none that ever retail at less than 5 cents, while among those we offer at 4 cents, 6 cents and 8 cents each, are many that retail at from 25 cents to 50 cents.

IF YOU WILL LOOK the first eight preceding pages over carefully, making a careful study of the values we give, comparing our prices with the prices at which similar goods are retailed generally, you will get a pretty thorough index into the money saving possibilities shown on every page in this catalogue, for the eight pages referred to are what might be called the A B C lesson or illustration of what it means in money saving to you to send your orders to us for everything you need, and buy your goods at prices that mean but one small profit above our actual cost.

IN INVITING YOU TO A CAREFUL STUDY and comparison of our prices with others, of the goods shown on the first eight preceding pages, for the purpose of illustrating the relatively big values, the relative average big difference between our prices and the prices charged by others for similar goods, we wish at the same time to take advantage of the opportunity of plainly stating our position on the great PRICE AND QUALITY QUESTION.

OUR POSITION ON THE QUESTION OF PRICE AND QUALITY—QUALITY AND PRICE

QUALITY WITH US is always the first consideration. Price cannot be determined until quality has been fully established, for the very good reason that quality is in itself the first great measure of value, therefore, measures the meaning of price.

QUALITY WITH US, by the very nature of our business, means more than with any retail dealer, manufacturer or wholesaler in the world and, mark you, this assertion is not made with the intention of the slightest reflection on any maker or seller of merchandise, but the assertion is made more for defending our position, so peculiar to itself, so entirely unique as to make the great question of quality vastly more important to us than it is to any other retailer, wholesaler or manufacturer.

QUALITY WITH US is the measure of success or failure, profit or loss, decline or perpetuity. Every dealer in every commodity in every town is disposed to attack us on the question of quality, being unable to meet our very low prices. Often failing to understand how thoroughly reliable goods of a high standard of quality can be sold at such very low prices, he often takes for granted that the low price must be at the expense of quality; or the wholesale dealer, the traveling salesman, or the manufacturer from whom the retail dealer buys, being unable to furnish the retailer goods at prices that will enable him to meet our low selling prices, will either take for granted or assume, for the purpose of justifying their price, that our goods are probably of a lower quality.

WHEREAS, WE ARE BEING ATTACKED by the hundreds of thousands of retail dealers, wholesale dealers, manufacturers, salesmen, etc., in all lines of merchandise in all parts of the United States on this one great question of quality, and realizing too that we are not on the ground to refute and, with the goods to lay side by side to compare, prove that our goods are of the highest standard of quality, there is but one thing left for us to do. It is imperative that we do this one thing. If we don't do it we fail to hold our customers, and to get new customers we must do this one great thing.

WE MUST FURNISH A QUALITY OF MERCHANDISE THAT WILL EFFECTIVELY DISPROVE EVERY ARGUMENT OF EVERY KIND RAISED AGAINST US.

WITH US, FAIR GRADE IS NOT SUFFICIENT, ordinary quality won't do. What is commonly known to the trade as acceptable goods we cannot use, for in this question of quality we dare take no chance. To us one mark short of the highest standard is dangerous. As many marks above the recognized high standard as we can get is our safety. On the question of high quality we must not only stand erect but must even lean backward. With us commercially all wool, commercially pure, what may be known as commercially a yard wide or a foot long or a pound dare not measure our quality. With us a foot must be 12 inches, a yard 36 inches. All wool means the plain English all wool. It means no cotton. It means that which grows on a sheep's back. It means that a pound is 16 ounces (avoirdupois) on the scales.

THE VERY NATURE OF OUR BUSINESS, the life of our institution, the burning necessity of our combatting the argument raised against us, the X-ray searchlight of the commercial world that is focused on us, compels, even though our dispositions were different, compels us as a matter of policy, that on this great question of quality we should stand so that every one of the hundreds of thousands of articles that go out of our institution every day will be an actual example of our policy, an everlasting demonstration of the error or misrepresentation of any one who tries to attack us on the quality question.

OUR BUYERS ARE INSTRUCTED AND REINSTRUCTED in private audience repeatedly and gathered in assembly are instructed to buy nothing, accept nothing, contract for nothing that will not pass the most rigid inspection, coming up at least to a plane of the highest standard of quality, and where possible to be made better to so be made, lest we fall in some instance to refute the quality argument that is being thrown at us.

A DEPARTMENT OF INSPECTION such as we doubt exists in any other institution in the country is maintained by us for the most exacting scrutiny of all goods made or purchased, to make sure that they come up to the required high standard of quality, and nothing is permitted to go into our stock and nothing is shipped to a customer in any line that does not pass this careful criticising quality sentinel.

MILLIONS OF DOLLARS HAVE BEEN EXPENDED BY US in the development of sources of supply, that we might so thoroughly control the quality of raw materials used, the iron, the steel, the lumber, the hides, the leather, the wool, the cloth, the metals, the various parts that go into the construction and even the manufacturing itself, so that we may not only meet any competition on the question of quality, but on a vast portion of the goods we handle we might establish, as we have, a much higher standard of quality than is found in the goods that are sold by dealers generally throughout the land, and whether or not we have succeeded in placing a vast variety of merchandise on a much higher plane of quality than goods sold by others generally, and whether everything offered in our catalogue and everything sent out to our millions of customers successfully refutes any argument that may be introduced by any one in competition, we are glad to leave the answer to the upwards of six million people who have sent us their orders, received the goods, made their own comparisons and no doubt have in their minds made the decision, and with these people who have tried us we are glad to rest our case.

PRICES. FIRST, HAVING FOUND AN ARTICLE of a satisfactory high standard of quality, with us the question of price is easy. It's only the calculation of the cost of the goods to us to which we add our one small percentage of profit. As we sell far more goods to the consumer than any other concern in the world, we feel it only reasonable that we should be able to buy our goods lower on the whole, than any other concern in the world. Especially is this true when you consider that many of the goods sold by us are made in factories we either own outright or control, and many, if not most of our contracts for merchandise with other manufacturers are the largest in quantity placed in this country, and incidentally such contracts are surrounded by high quality conditions, such as are not common to any of the goods made to be sold through the regular channels of trade. This being the fact it is not unreasonable for us to believe and to ask you to believe that we own our goods, quality for quality, lower than any other house. Doing vastly more business direct with the user than any other institution, it is only fair for us to believe and ask you to believe that we can do the business cheaper and at a lower cost than any other house. It is only fair for us to believe and to ask you to believe that we can be satisfied with a much smaller profit than any other house. Accepting these claims as facts, you have the simple problem of addition, our cost plus our one small percentage of profit, and that's the price to you.

HOW MUCH MONEY CAN YOU SAVE BY SENDING YOUR ORDERS TO US?

TO FIGURE THIS OUT EASILY we ask you to please refer to the first eight preceding pages on these yellow sheets, for here's a simple calculation, for on these eight pages we picture hundreds of the commonly everyday used household articles. You know what most of them are, you know what you paid for them, you know what your dealer asks for them. On these pages you have our prices. They range 2 cents, 4 cents, 6 cents and 8 cents each for your choice among many hundreds. Make your comparisons here as a starting point. It's a good place to start only because there's a great many small, useful, everyday household articles that almost every housewife is familiar with and knows the average cost of, therefore can quickly figure the saving that our one small profit makes. Leaving these eight pages with whatever conclusion you may have arrived at by comparison of our 2-cent, 4-cent, 6-cent and 8-cent prices with the prices charged by dealers generally, we ask you to go carefully through the catalogue, through the big staple departments of Hardware, Clothing, Dry Goods, Shoes, Jewelry, Furniture, Cloaks, Carpets, Sewing Machines and all other lines and you will find by the same careful comparison about the same great relative saving, money saving opportunities on everything in this great catalogue, almost everything you would ever have occasion to buy, to use in the home, on the farm, in the shop or elsewhere.

THE SEVERAL HUNDRED ITEMS SHOWN on the first eight preceding pages, which we offer at 2 cents, 4 cents, 6 cents and 8 cents each, your choice in the several assortments, each common, everyday, useful household articles which, when we offer them on the exact same basis that all other goods in this great catalogue are offered, which means but one small percentage of profit above the actual cost to us, it brings many of these items down to but very few cents each. Many items figured at our cost plus our one small percentage of profit, figures 2 cents, 4 cents, 6 cents or 8 cents, although the same articles may retail at two to five times the price we ask. However, figuring these small items the same as all goods throughout this great book are figured, it makes the price on each article so very, very low that we feel compelled, as a matter of economy, in the writing of the order and the selection from our stock, in the packing and shipping of the goods, that if you favor us with an order for any of the goods shown on the first eight preceding pages which we offer at 2 cents, 4 cents, 6 cents and 8 cents each, that you do not order less than a dozen articles. In this way the handling of the order is done economically by us, and we can in this way sell you these small useful things on the same small percentage of profit, the exact same policy that make all the goods in this great catalogue so very low in price to you.

IN ORDERING ANY OF THE ARTICLES on the first eight preceding pages, be sure to send us an order for twelve or more. You may, if you wish, make the order for twelve or more articles, selecting part from the 2-cent assortment, part from the 4-cent, part from the 6-cent and part from the 8-cent assortment. Select any and as many and from whatever priced assortment you like, so long as your order is for twelve or more items. For example, if you will select twelve articles from those shown in the 2-cent assortment, making your order amount to 24 cents or more, this is entirely satisfactory, or you may select two or three items at 2 cents each and from the 4-cent assortment two or three items at 4 cents each, and from the 6-cent assortment you may select several items at 6 cents each and then a few from the 8-cent assortment. We don't care how you select them or what articles you take so long as the total number of articles selected is twelve or more in number.

IN THE 8-CENT ASSORTMENT we might point out certain special articles that retail generally at 25 cents to 50 cents each, in the 6-cent assortment we could point out articles that retail at 25 cents each and upwards, in the 4-cent assortment we could point out articles that retail at 15 cents to 25 cents, and in the 2-cent assortment we could point out many articles that retail generally at 10 cents and upwards, but we prefer to leave to you the selection, the comparison of prices; in short, we wish especially in these eight pages to let you be the judge in comparing values, in comparing prices, and decide for yourself how much money we can save you, what we ask for goods compared with what others ask for the same or similar goods; but in making your comparison in this great eight-page assortment of 2-cent, 4-cent, 6-cent and 8-cent articles, don't forget that this same low price policy follows through everything in our catalogue, and as a guarantee that you will find this great difference in money saving on anything you may buy from us, we will gladly accept your order for any of the articles shown on the first eight preceding pages or any article shown on any page in this entire catalogue, the goods to be sent to you with the understanding and agreement that they must be found perfectly satisfactory and, further, that you must see a great saving in cost to you; otherwise you can return the goods at our expense, and we will cheerfully return your money, together with any transportation charges you may have paid.

SHOULD ANYONE EVER RAISE THE QUESTION as to the low prices of Sears, Roebuck & Co., we especially urge that you make your price comparison on any goods in this catalogue, that you can compare intelligently, being reasonably sure you are comparing the exact same goods, and then you will see a vast difference in price in our favor, and more for the purpose of making it easy for you to make this comparison, and to remove so far as possible every chance for doubt or error, for this reason more than anything else have we thrown together these 400 to 500 items, offering them at 2 cents, 4 cents, 6 cents and 8 cents each, common goods that everyone knows and are generally familiar with the retail selling prices and are thus able to make an accurate price and value comparison; but if you will study this book through, from page to page, we assure you that you will find correspondingly low prices, the same relative big money saving opportunities.

☛ **IN YOUR OWN INTEREST** we wish to recommend that in ordering twelve or more articles which you may select at 2 cents, 4 cents, 6 cents and 8 cents each from the variety shown on the first eight preceding pages, that you at the same time order other goods, including the dozen or more of these items with a general order, so that the goods may all be packed together and go in one shipment, thus making the freight charges on these twelve selected articles next to nothing; in other words, **the saving of money to you on these hundreds of small articles shown in the eight preceding pages will be enormous if you will order these goods with other goods,** that they may be shipped together, thus making an economical freight shipment and reducing the freight charges on each item in the entire order to next to nothing; whereas, if an order for an assortment of twelve of these items were sent to us to be shipped alone in one shipment only, by freight or express, it would not be an economical shipment for you, as the freight charges on from one to ten pounds, representing a dozen of these articles assorted, would be as much as on 50 to 100 pounds of miscellaneous merchandise that you might select from this Big Catalogue, **so in your own interest in ordering these goods, we advise that you order them together with other goods and ship all together in one shipment.** For example, if you are sending us a general order for miscellaneous merchandise as taken from the great catalogue, goods that represent the same money saving to you that is shown in these small articles, you can then add to your order for other goods one dozen or more of these 2-cent, 4-cent, 6-cent and 8-cent items and it will not add 2 cents to the freight charges you will have to pay on your general order.